Content

Preface

For over 50 years, *The College Handbook* has provided generations of college-bound students and their advisers with the authoritative and up-to-date information needed to make informed college decisions. With the cooperation of the educational community and the advice of students and parents, the *Handbook* is revised yearly to meet the information needs of new groups of college-bound students.

Developments in technology are changing the college-going process in profound and exciting ways. How students get information, and how they and their counselors communicate with colleges, are likely to be very different in the next few years. Increasingly, institutions will be linked electronically: students will be able to get information about colleges, describe themselves to colleges, and even apply to colleges through interactive software. The College Board is currently pilot-testing *ExPAN*, the *Explorer Plus Application Network*, in Washington State. This electronic application system enables students to apply to participating colleges without using paper or pencil! The network will be expanded during the coming year, and eventually students throughout the country may be able to use *ExPAN* to manage many aspects of the college choice and application process.

There will always be a place, of course, for directories of college information. The 1994 edition of *The College Handbook* presents millions of facts about the nation's colleges. The descriptions are preceded by an extensive guidance section that provides step-by-step advice on choosing a college. This section was prepared in collaboration with students, admissions officers, and guidance counselors.

There are 3,136 colleges described in the *Handbook*. The information was supplied in the winter and spring of 1993 by the institutions themselves via the College Board's Annual Survey of Colleges. It was verified with the colleges by a staff of editors to ensure that the descriptions are as complete and accurate as possible. However, college information changes, and students are urged to confirm facts with the colleges themselves.

To be eligible for inclusion in the *Handbook*, an institution must be accredited by a national accrediting association. In addition, the college must offer some undergraduate degree programs. Six institutions in foreign countries are included in the *Handbook* on the basis of their membership in the College Board.

The enormous task of data collection, management, and verification was directed by Nica Ganley, Director of Guidance Publishing Information Services, Dorothy Siegfried, Data Supervisor, and Janet Hobbins, Information Services Associate.

We thank our readers—you and the millions of students, parents, and counselors who have provided comments and suggestions over the years that have made the *Handbook* the most widely used college directory in the nation. We welcome your suggestions on how the *Handbook* can continue to improve and meet the ever-changing needs of future generations of college-bound students.

Renée Gernand
Senior Editor
Guidance Publishing

Mission Statement

The College Board champions educational excellence for all students through the ongoing collaboration of member schools, colleges, universities, educational systems, and organizations. It promotes—by means of responsive forums, research, programs, and policy development—universal access to high standards of learning, equity of opportunity, and sufficient financial support so that every student is prepared for success in college and work.

The College Board

Educational Excellence for *All* Students

College decisions

Choosing a college

More than 2.5 million students start college each fall. For most of them, the first day on campus marks the end of a year or more of anxious planning, difficult choices, and plain hard work. If you are just beginning the college selection process, the planning, choices, and hard work are still ahead of you.

Chances are that you are both excited and bewildered by the prospect of choosing one college from close to 3,200 accredited colleges in the United States. Maybe you are confused by the amount of information (and misinformation) that is available and by contradictory advice about "good" and "bad" colleges. Or maybe you do not have enough information about colleges and are not sure how to get the facts you need. If you are like many college-bound students, you are worried about grades and test scores and whether you will be accepted by any of the colleges you think would be right for you.

Relax. Choosing a college is an important and sometimes difficult task, but if you plan now and take it step by step, chances are you will make a decision that is good for you. Before you begin, take a look at some of the myths that complicate the college decision-making process.

Myth	Fact
"There's one college that's exactly right for me."	Chances are that you won't find a college that is perfect in every way—the one and only choice for you—but you probably will find many colleges that meet some of your most important needs and objectives, and where you would be happy.
"All colleges are alike, so why waste time choosing?"	No two colleges are exactly alike and, in fact, some are very different. To make sure that you make the best possible choice, the selection process should be a careful one.
"The cost of a college education (or *that* college) is beyond my reach."	Millions of college students qualify for financial aid to cover the difference between what a college costs and what they can afford to pay. *Don't rule out any college because of its cost until you find out whether you are eligible for financial aid.*
"That college is too selective. I'll probably be rejected, so why apply?"	Don't second-guess college admissions officers. If you think you qualify for a college you would like to attend, you should apply. You may not be accepted (depending on the number of applicants and the qualifications of the *other* applicants), but you will never know if you don't try.
"If I can't go to my first-choice college (or don't like it when I get there), I'll be unhappy for the next four years."	Believe it or not, most students end up loving their second- or third- or fourth-choice college. The trick is to apply to several colleges where you think you would be happy. If it turns out to be a mistake, your decision is not irreversible. Thousands of students transfer to other colleges every year.

Why college?

If you are like many college-bound students, you probably made the decision to continue your education fairly early, even before you started high school. Looking back, you may find your reasons for making that decision are no longer clear to you, or the reasons may have changed, just as you have changed in the past few years. Whether you have always known you were going to college, or whether you are considering it now for the first time, take this opportunity to think about your reasons. If you can state your objectives clearly at the start, your college search will be much easier.

"I've always known that I was going to go to college." (High school senior, Ohio)

Make a list of your reasons for going to college, putting your most important at the top of your list.

1. ______
2. ______
3. ______
4. ______
5. ______

The chart above gives you space to list your objectives. Discuss your reasons for going to college with your parents, counselors, friends, and anyone else who can help you focus on your long-term goals. Don't worry if your reasons are not the same as those of your friends or advisers; you are an individual and your reasons have to make sense to *you*.

Ask yourself if the best way to achieve your objectives is by going to college. If you think it is, then you are off to a good start.

"Learning about colleges, selecting the ones I liked, and then deciding where to apply . . . those were the first really adult actions of my life. And it felt good." (High school senior, California)

What are you like?

The picture you have of yourself—of your abilities, interests, attitudes, and personality—plays an important role in the college decision-making process. What you know about yourself will help you define what you are looking for in a college. Try to get a clear picture of your strengths and weaknesses, your likes and dislikes.

The following questions may help you begin.

Academic. Are you a good student, average, below average? Does your school record reflect your capabilities? What kinds of courses have you taken in high school? Do you excel, or are you weak, in any area? Do you learn best in a competitive or relaxed academic climate?

Extracurricular. Do you participate in school activities or in community or local affairs? What clubs, sports, cultural groups do you belong to? Have you traveled a lot or not at all? What are your interests and hobbies?

Personal attitudes and values. Do you prefer a familiar environment or are you ready for a change? Do you work best independently or with others? Do you want to go out on your own or stay near family or friends?

Do you think others—your parents or a friend or a counselor—would agree with your self-description? How does your picture of yourself relate to your reasons for going to college? Are your objectives realistic based on what you know about your interests and abilities?

"College is a . . . place in which one hopes to be able to be what one is, a place in which one hopes to be able to become what one is capable of becoming."
(Donald E. Super, Preparing School Counselors in Education Guidance)

College characteristics

"My brother's room was wall-to-wall catalogs, but he never got around to reading half of them. I'm going to be more systematic when I start looking at colleges." (High school junior, Pennsylvania)

After you have explored your reasons for going to college and considered your own interests and abilities, it's time to investigate the kinds of higher education available to you.

Over 3,100 colleges, universities, technical institutes, junior colleges, seminaries, and other institutions of higher education are listed in *The College Handbook, 1994*. Almost all of them have programs for students entering college for the first time. You cannot learn about all these colleges in a few short months, so even before you start gathering information about individual colleges, you need to reduce the alternatives to a reasonable number without eliminating desirable choices.

Consider your list of objectives one at a time. Ask yourself what you need to know about a college in order to determine if you will be able to meet each of your objectives there.

Besides those college characteristics that are necessary for your educational objectives, there may be others that interest you for personal reasons. You may want to be sure there is a church or synagogue nearby. A certain climate may be important for your health or for the opportunity to participate in your favorite sport during the school year. If you plan on frequent visits home, you will want to know about available transportation, travel time, and cost. Make a list of your personal requirements and refer to it as you search for colleges that would be appropriate for you.

The following worksheet lists some college characteristics mentioned frequently by students as important in the selection process. Not all of them will matter to you, and some will seem more important than others. You can duplicate this checklist or use it as a model for creating your own characteristics' list. Check only those characteristics that are important to *you*. To the right of each characteristic, indicate your specific requirement. Don't put down anything you are not sure about or try to limit your options too early in the college selection process. At this stage your aim should be to find out about *many* colleges that meet your most important requirements. You can always come back and add to the list as your needs and interests become clearer to you.

To see how quickly your list of characteristics will help you narrow your choices of colleges, consider the sample worksheet completed by Emma Juarez. Emma will graduate from a high school in Washington, D.C., next June. She plans to study for a

Characteristics	*Specific preference*
☑ Location (state, city, region)	D.C., Maryland, New York
☑ Type (2-year community college, 4-year university, etc.)	4 year college
☑ Enrollment by sex (men, women, coed)	coed
☑ Religious affiliation, if any	none
☑ Size of college (undergraduate enrollment)	small to medium
❑ Academic calendar	
❑ Campus environment	
☑ Majors or course offerings	computer sciences
☑ On-campus housing	
❑ Special academic programs	
☑ Cost	about $7,000
☑ Financial aid	
❑ Student activities	
☑ Athletics	track
❑ Academic caliber of students	
❑ Student body characteristics	
☑ Social life	fraternities and sororities
❑ Competitive atmosphere of college	
☑ Credit by Examination	AP English and Math
❑	
❑	

Characteristics	Specific preference
❑ Location (state, city, region)	
❑ Type (2-year community college, 4-year university, etc.)	
❑ Enrollment by sex (men, women, coed)	
❑ Religious affiliation, if any	
❑ Size of college (undergraduate enrollment)	
❑ Academic calendar	
❑ Campus environment	
❑ Majors or course offerings	
❑ On-campus housing	
❑ Special academic programs	
❑ *Cost	
❑ Financial aid	
❑ Student activities	
❑ Athletics	
❑ Academic caliber of students	
❑ Student body characteristics	
❑ Social life	
❑ Competitive atmosphere of college	
❑	
❑	
❑	

* Don't eliminate any college because of cost until you find out whether or not you qualify for financial aid.

bachelor's degree in computer science and hopes to get a job that will offer her a good salary and the opportunity for career advancement. She is looking forward to living on campus but wants to be able to go home on some weekends to visit her family and friends. She would like to go to a coed college small enough that she won't feel "lost" but large enough to attract a diverse student body and offer a wide variety of campus social activities, including fraternities and sororities. She is a good runner and would like to compete in track meets at college.

How do Emma's requirements affect her alternatives? The *Handbook* lists 175 undergraduate institutions in the District of Columbia, Maryland, and New York that grant bachelor's degrees. Of these, 116 offer a major in computer and information sciences. By applying some of her requirements in turn, Emma developed a list of 7 colleges.

175	grant bachelor's degrees
116	offer a major in computer and information sciences
89	have no religious affiliation
84	are coed colleges
47	have college housing for women
24	offer intercollegiate track and field for women
24	have sororities
7	enroll more than 750 but less than 4,000 undergraduates

Emma used most of her important requirements in finding these seven colleges. She followed her counselor's advice not to eliminate colleges on the basis of cost until she finds out whether she is eligible for financial aid at the colleges that meet all her other requirements. Emma's list would have looked very different if she had included cost as a factor. Only two of the seven colleges that meet her needs report annual costs under $7,000, and that is the student budget for state residents only; out-of-state students pay a higher tuition cost. Emma could choose to expand her list by considering colleges in other nearby states or colleges with larger enrollments. You may find you want to change or modify your requirements as you search for colleges. By all means, stick to your educational objectives, but don't limit your other options until you are certain that a particular characteristic is essential to your college experience. Even then, it is possible that no college will meet all your needs. If this happens, you may have to decide which characteristics are most important to you.

Narrowing your list of colleges

At this point, your goal is to have a list of some 10 or 20 colleges to explore in more depth. This book and the *Index of Majors and Graduate Degrees*, as well as the College Board's *College Explorer* and *College Cost Explorer FUND FINDER* software programs have been designed to help you with this task.

If you know the state or states where you want to attend college, turn to them in *The College Handbook*. The first seven characteristics on the worksheet you completed will be found in the opening paragraph of each college description. If the college meets these basic requirements, read on. If you are looking for specific types of colleges, check the college indexes where colleges are listed by various features.

If you know what you want to study, but not where, consult the *Index of Majors and Graduate Degrees*. The *Index* lists nearly 600 major fields of study and the colleges, state by state, that offer them. It also lists colleges with special academic programs. If you don't know *what* you want to study, consult the new *College Board Guide to 150 Popular College Majors*, an in-depth look at what you will learn in a variety of widely available majors.

The microcomputer is a powerful tool to help you in the college selection process. For example, *College Explorer* software lets you choose the college features most important to you and then searches through the colleges described in the *Handbook* to give you information on those that match your requirements. *FUND FINDER* software not only provides detailed information about costs, but shows what share of college costs students and their families will be expected to bear, estimates eligibility for financial aid at each college, and enables students to search a data base of private and public scholarships for ones they're eligible for. Check to see whether your guidance office or library has a copy of *College Explorer* or *College Cost Explorer FUND FINDER* for you to use.

Once you know the names of the colleges that meet one or more of your important requirements, turn to their descriptions in the *Handbook*. When you have complet-

"Reading the student newspaper from a college on the West Coast gave me a real feeling for the social and academic life the college could offer. I don't think I would have been interested in that college if I hadn't read the newspaper." (High school senior, New Jersey)

ed your initial search and identified colleges you want to explore in more depth, you are ready for the next step.

Learning more about colleges

The more information you can gather on the colleges that interest you, the better your chance of making a good decision. Start a file folder for each college you are interested in. Use it to keep copies of any correspondence you have with the institution as well as application forms and financial aid information.

Make a record of any college interview or conversation you have while your impressions are still fresh. Jot down the names of people you meet while on campus or the names of recent alumni who might serve as sources of additional information. (*College Planner* software and the *College Admissions Organizer* are handy means of keeping track of the vast—and detailed—information you'll soon have about the colleges that interest you. With *College Planner*, you enter and update college information, interview dates, and application deadlines on a planning calendar on your computer; the *Organizer* enables you to keep all this information in one handy binder, which comes with planning charts, a planning calendar, and other useful features.)

College information

Your first contact with a college will probably be a letter expressing your interest in the institution and requesting additional information. Be specific about what you want to know, and tell the college something about yourself. Check the letter for spelling and grammar. Whether or not you keep a file on the college, the college will certainly keep a file on you.

College catalogs and descriptive materials. The catalog is a basic source of information about a college. Although catalogs vary widely, most contain detailed information on admissions, student life, academic offerings, degree requirements, costs, and financial aid. Often the catalog will come to you with inserts indicating tuition and fee changes, adjustments to the academic program, or revised deadlines. College catalogs sometimes are available in your school library or guidance office, or may be obtained by writing directly to the college. Keep the catalog on file.

In addition to the catalog, many colleges provide descriptive materials that highlight important features of the institution. These include pictures of the campus and of student life that can help give you a feel for the college. Don't rely on pictures, however, or on an enthusiastic writer's description of the college in making a final decision. Read the college's materials carefully and critically, keeping your own objectives and needs clearly in mind.

College newspapers. If you are looking for current and candid information about day-to-day student life, try to obtain a copy of the student newspaper. Its news coverage, editorials, and listings of campus events could tell you a lot about college issues, student concerns, and campus activities.

College representatives. To learn more about a college that interests you, meet with a college representative. Someone with firsthand knowledge of the institution, who is qualified to answer your questions, can help you focus on what the college can do for you. Check with your school guidance office to see whether a recruitment or admissions officer from the college is scheduled to visit your high school. If not, write to the college requesting an appointment with a college representative in your area. Find out in advance whether a college you are considering will participate in a nearby college fair. Before you meet with a representative, draw up a list of questions about the college. Be prepared to explain what features of the college interest you most. The impression you make through an early contact with the college might be important if you decide to apply.

College visits. Probably the best way to learn more about a college is to visit the campus. If possible, plan to visit a college during the academic year, when students are in residence and classes are in session. Many colleges schedule regular campus tours conducted by student representatives and will arrange for you to spend the night in student housing if you write in advance.

During your visit, walk around the campus until you have a feeling for its size and atmosphere. Find out about the things that are important to you. You might be interested in how old or new the buildings and facilities are, how crowded the classrooms are, how large the dormitory space is, or what the recreational facilities are like.

Plan to visit the student center, the cafeteria, and the library. Talk to students wherever you go. Ask about the social life on campus, student lifestyles, and anything else that might help you decide if you would be comfortable at the college. Check bulletin boards to find out about student activities and cultural events. Try to attend some classes and meet with students and faculty in the academic area that interests you.

If you plan to combine your campus visit with an admissions interview, be sure to write the admissions office and set up an appointment before you arrive. *Campus Visits and College Interviews* (Zola Dincin Schneider, College Board, 1987) thoroughly covers this important part of the college exploration process. The book includes lists of questions you might want to ask when face-to-face with a college interviewer.

College students or recent alumni. If you are considering a college far from home, it may be impossible for you to visit the campus. Ask the college for names of recent graduates or current students who live in your area. If you plan in advance, you may be able to meet with students who are home on vacation. Often college alumni will be happy to talk to you about their alma mater. Impressions and opinions about current student life and campus activities can be useful to you.

High school guidance counselor and teachers

Your high school guidance counselor and teachers can be invaluable sources of information about colleges. Don't miss out on their expertise. Your guidance counselor is a trained professional who can not only help you make realistic decisions about college applications but also help you predict what the outcome of your decision will be. Consult your adviser as early as possible in the college selection process; discuss your goals and objectives and get advice on which colleges might best help you accomplish your objectives. If you already have some colleges in mind, your counselor may be able to give you some facts about the number of students in your high school or region who applied and were accepted in previous years and what their college experience has been. Frequently your adviser has the most objective view of your school record and can give you sound advice on your chances of being accepted—or of being comfortable—at one or more of the colleges you are considering.

Parents and friends

According to a group of recent college-bound students, family and friends are among the best sources of information about colleges. Like admissions counselors, your parents and close friends can help not only in giving you information about colleges but also in evaluating the information in terms of your own objectives and needs. Discuss the colleges you are considering with your parents. Can they recommend alternatives? Do they think you should be considering other types of colleges? Why? Do you agree or disagree with their advice? Why? Go over your checklist of college characteristics. Based on your discussions, is there anything you would like to change?

Your friends, too, can be a good source of information and advice. Find out what colleges they are considering and why. Are any of your friends or classmates considering applying to the same colleges you are? Pool your resources and exchange information. Share the college selection process with them. Talk to recent graduates from your high school and ask them about their experiences at college. Even though the final decision is yours, it often helps to talk it over with people whose opinions you trust and can rely on.

"My parents helped me evaluate all the college information. They listened and sometimes gave advice but never tried to make up my mind for me." (High school senior, Texas)

Deciding where to apply

"You can play games with yourself. You can say it's not important or that you don't care. But deep down, you spend half your time worrying." (High school senior, Illinois)

You will probably find that the most difficult part of the college selection process is trying to predict what will happen as a result of your decision. Will you be accepted by a college if you apply? Will you be happy at the "college of your choice?" Unfortunately, even good decisions cannot guarantee successful results. By its nature, decision making involves risks. You will be in a better position, however, to judge the degree of risk and uncertainty if you do a thorough job of collecting and evaluating information.

College admissions: Predicting your chances

What are your chances of being accepted at the college or colleges you prefer? According to a survey conducted by the American Council on Education and the University of California at Los Angeles, 92 percent of freshmen entering college in 1991 got into their first- or second-choice college. Your chances of being admitted to a particular college, however, depend on the type of institution you are considering.

Most colleges fall into one of three categories of accessibility:

Open admissions colleges. These accept virtually all interested students who have a high school degree or its equivalent, and even that requirement is sometimes waived for applicants above a certain age. Some open admissions institutions have selective requirements for specific programs, such as nursing.

Selective colleges. These colleges offer admission to all or most applicants who meet their explicit requirements. The requirements may vary widely from college to college and may be extremely rigorous, but you can be fairly sure of admission if you meet their specifications. The vast majority of four-year colleges in this country classify themselves as "selective."

Competitive colleges. Like selective institutions, competitive colleges have explicit admissions requirements, but more applicants meet those requirements than they are willing or able to accommodate. You cannot be sure of admission to a competitive college, even though you satisfy its entrance requirements, because you will be competing with other equally qualified applicants. On the average, competitive colleges offer admission to about 56 percent of their applicants. In the face of such odds, you would be wise to apply to more than one college.

To find out whether a college you are considering has a competitive or selective admissions policy, read the College ABCs at the beginning of the descriptions of most colleges. The percentage of accepted applicants appears, followed by the bases for selection, listed in order of importance, used by the college in making admissions decisions. In addition, most colleges list the number of students who applied, were accepted, and enrolled, and the academic background of the freshman class under the "Freshman Class Profile" section within the descriptions. This information helps you estimate your chance of admission at a particular college.

Carefully read through the admissions section in the description where the college states its admissions criteria and requirements. Unless you find that you are clearly not qualified, you should probably continue to consider a college rather than assume that you would not be admitted. Leave that decision to the college.

Factors mentioned most frequently by colleges as playing an important role in their admissions decisions are academic performance in high school (as indicated by school grade average or class rank), test scores, pattern of high school subjects completed, recommendations, and personal qualifications, such as motivation, special skills or abilities, leadership capabilities, community or church involvement, and good moral character. Compare your own achievements in these areas with the colleges' stated requirements. Note that the more competitive the college, the more likely it is to consider personal qualifications in admissions decisions. The contact you have with an admissions officer through your interview, essay, and recommendations can increase your chances of being admitted to an institution.

Number of colleges to apply to

There is no ideal number of applications for every student. A good rule of thumb is to file as many applications as you need—but not more than you need—to ensure that you will be accepted by a college you prefer. That may be one application or several, depending on your own requirements and on the admissions and financial aid procedures of the colleges you choose.

You have to make the final decision yourself on how many colleges you apply to, but most educators would advise you to limit the number of applications. Your high school guidance counselor may make a strong recommendation on the total number of applications you should file. Don't apply indiscriminately. Think about your reasons for multiple applications.

If you are applying for financial aid and are not certain of receiving the aid you need, you may want to increase the number of applications you file. If you are considering several competitive colleges and cannot be certain that you will be admitted to any of them, you may want to apply to all of them. If you cannot choose between two colleges and believe that extra time will help you make a final decision, then apply to both. You should certainly apply to at least one college that meets all your requirements (including costs) and where you are quite certain of being admitted. Don't apply to colleges that you don't want to attend simply to satisfy someone else or to prove that you can get in.

Early decision plans

If you are sure of the college you want to attend and think you are likely to be accepted, consider applying for an early decision. Under early decision or early action plans, you complete your application for admission (and financial aid, if appropriate) early in the fall of your senior year; the college will notify you of its admissions and financial aid decisions earlier than usual—generally by December 15. Under some plans, you apply only to the college from which you want an early decision; under others, you can apply to other colleges but agree to attend your first-choice college if you're accepted.

Be sure you understand the exact terms of and your responsibilities under the plan or plans at the colleges to which you are applying. The college descriptions in this book indicate which colleges subscribe to one of the most common plans, the Early Decision Plan Agreement (see "How to Use *The College Handbook*" for a description). An index lists the participating colleges.

Applying to college

The procedures of applying for admission vary from one college to another, but usually the first step is to get an application form and instructions from the college. (If you requested an application when you first wrote to the institution, it should be in your college file). Follow the college's instructions carefully. Make sure you know *what* you must supply and *when* it must reach the college.

What colleges require

Application fee. Most colleges charge an application fee, usually not refundable even if your application is rejected. Many colleges will waive this fee for applicants from low-income families, such as those who are eligible for public assistance. If you think you qualify for a fee waiver, ask your counselor about the procedures to follow.

Application form. Almost all colleges require that you submit an official application form providing information about your background, previous education, and college plans. At many institutions the form is brief and uncomplicated and can be completed very quickly. At other colleges, particularly

"Perhaps the most valuable result of all education is the ability to make yourself do the thing you have to do, when it ought to be done, whether you like it or not." (Thomas Huxley, Technical Education)

"I was positive that my school record wasn't good enough for certain colleges,but my guidance counselor persuaded me to apply, and I was accepted by two out of three colleges I didn't think I'd get into." (College freshman, Colorado)

competitive institutions, you will be asked to provide detailed information about your academic record, extracurricular activities, work experience, interests, talents, and achievements. Be prepared to give the time and thought needed to provide a complete picture of yourself for the college to consider.

If you are applying to more than one college within a system, such as part of a state university system, check to see whether you need to file more than one application. Many systems have standard applications that can be used for more than one college within the system. Some groups of colleges or consortiums may also share application forms. The most widely used standard application form is the Common Application distributed by the National Association of Secondary School Principals. Colleges that accept the Common Application are listed in the "College Indexes" section. You may be able to reduce the number of individual applications you need to complete if the colleges that interest you accept a standard form like the Common Application.

Secondary school or college transfer record. You may receive a form for an official of your high school or college to complete with a transcript of your courses and final marks, test scores, and teacher and counselor recommendations. If this is included in your admissions materials, take it to your guidance office as soon as you have completed your part of the application. Some colleges send this form directly to the school or college after receiving your application.

Admissions test scores. Many colleges require that you take one or more standardized admissions tests. The most common tests used are the College Board's SAT and Achievement Tests (ACH) and the American College Testing Program Assessment (ACT). Plan to take the tests at least six weeks before the college's application deadline to allow enough time for the score report to reach the college. Use the Schedule of 1993-94 Test Registration and Administration Dates on page 16 for planning purposes.

IMPORTANT—In March 1994 a new SAT will be introduced, called SAT I: Reasoning Test. In addition, the Achievement Test offerings will be revised and renamed SAT II: Subject Tests. Be sure to read the next section, "The New SAT and PSAT/NMSQT," for information about the new tests.

If you have already taken the SAT, ACH, or ACT and want your scores sent to a college not listed on your original application, allow at least four weeks for the score report to reach the college. If less time is available, rush reporting can be ordered by telephone.

If you take the SAT or the Achievement Tests, your scores will be sent to you along with information that can help you and your parents and counselors in the college planning process. The report you will receive displays your scores in a way that indicates the range of your abilities and helps you estimate what your scores might be if you took the test again. It also reports the personal information that you provided on the registration form (educational background, type of college you wish to attend), lists the colleges that you requested receive your scores, and provides admissions and financial aid information for those colleges.

Letter of recommendation. Some colleges, especially private institutions, require that you submit one or more letters of recommendation from a teacher, counselor, clergyman, alumnus, or adult member of the community. As a courtesy, you should give people ample time to complete the recommendations and meet the college deadline.

Essay. A personal essay or autobiographical statement is required by some institutions, particularly four-year private colleges. The essay can be especially important if you are not able to have an interview. Whether the college requests a general autobiographical statement or an essay on a specific theme, you should take the opportunity to express your individuality in a way that will set you apart from other applicants.

Interview. Many colleges require or recommend an interview of all or some of their applicants. Whether required or not, it is to your benefit to set up an interview—this is your chance to express personally your background, your interests and goals, and why you are interested in the college. An interview can be very important at institutions that have many applicants competing for admission. The interview also is your opportunity to assess the college. For this reason, an on-campus interview is best, but most colleges will arrange for you to be interviewed near your home if you live far from the college. Be prepared with your own questions. You can use this opportunity to get the information you need about a college to make your decision.

Audition/portfolio. If you are applying for admission to a particular program at the college, such as music, art, or design, you may have to demonstrate or document prior work. Be sure to check each college's requirements in the *Handbook* descriptions.

When to apply

You should begin the application process as soon as you have identified the college or colleges where you wish to apply. This should be as early as possible in your senior year or at the end of your junior year if you are seeking early admission.

Colleges may state a closing date or deadline for applying, but this is often no more than a guideline. A college may cut off applications earlier than its final date if it fills its class before then, or it may continue to accept applications beyond that date if it still has room for more students. If you decide you want to apply to a college whose application deadline has passed, telephone or write the admissions office to find out if applications are still being accepted. As a general rule, be aware of college deadlines, but set your own deadlines for completion of your part of the process. Make a checklist to help you outline the admissions requirements and deadlines for each college. If you are applying for aid, include financial aid deadlines so that you have a central list of the college's requirements.

Your College Application (Gelband, Kubale, and Schorr, College Board, 1991) provides step-by-step advice on putting your best self forward on your applications.

When you hear from colleges

Even after you have had a response to your applications, you still may face some difficult decisions. One of your responsibilities in this process is to respond to all offers of admission by the indicated deadline. Though you may not have to respond to colleges until May 1, you may in fact have to respond to some offers of admission before you have heard from all the colleges you've applied to. Strategies for handling those situations fairly and responsibly are described below.

If you are accepted by more than one college

If you applied and were admitted to several colleges, you have to decide which to attend. You may already know your order of preference, but if you are still unsure, you may have to go through the decision-making process again, clarifying your objectives, getting additional information, and talking to your parents and counselors. Don't be surprised if all your efforts at deciding still leave you with two or more colleges that seem to offer equal prospects. It probably means that you have done such a good job of selecting that you will be happy with whichever college you attend.

If you hear from your second-choice college first

Your final decision can be complicated if you have to respond to your second- or third-choice college before having heard from your first choice. Often that response includes a substantial first payment of a tuition fee or dormitory charge. Some students make the required first payment to the college they hear from first and then change their mind when another acceptance arrives. Rather than do that, ask your counselor for help in deciding on a course of action. You may be able to get an extension on making the deposit, or you may be able to get a preliminary, if unofficial, decision from your first-choice college by calling or writing the admissions office. If you deposit money at a college that you later decide not to attend, advise the college immediately—thereby enabling the college to offer admission to another student. You are obliged to notify every college or university that accepts you regardless of whether you are accepting or rejecting their offer.

If you are not accepted at a college you want to attend . . . or at any college

Your world won't suddenly end if you are not accepted at the college you dreamed of, or at any of the colleges to which you applied. First, give yourself a day to feel dejected, but only one, since you still have options open to you, and probably not much time in which to pursue them. Next, talk to your parents and guidance counselor to get their advice about colleges you may not have considered seriously during your first round of applications. Your counselor is the best source of information about colleges that may still be accepting applications. Some colleges with closing dates may still accept applications after that date if they have places open in their freshman classes. You may also want to check the index in this book for colleges with no closing dates or late closing dates. And remember, it is possible to enroll in one college for a year or two and then apply and be accepted for transfer to a college that originally did not accept you.

If you are not offered the financial aid you need
You may have to choose between different aid packages offered by different institutions. Your first-choice college, for example, may offer less aid in relation to costs than your second or third choices. Try to determine if there are other resources that you can tap for additional financial support. Only you can decide if your preference is so strong that it justifies the additional financial burden.

Looking ahead

If you follow the steps described in this section, you will probably find the colleges that offer you the best chance of getting the most from your college experience. There is no guarantee, of course, that things will turn out just as you had hoped. In fact, you can be sure that they won't, because you will change during your college years, the college will change, and, most of all, the world will change in ways that can't be foreseen. But you will also be developing your ability to adapt to change and to meet new situations, so there is an excellent chance that the differences you will encounter will add up to an even better college experience than you had expected.

Schedule of 1993-94 test registration and administration dates

1993-94 ACT test dates*

Test date	*Registration date*	*Late registration*
October 23, 1993	September 24, 1993	October 8, 1993
December 11, 1993	November 12, 1993	November 29, 1993
February 5, 1994	January 7, 1994	January 24, 1994
April 9, 1994	March 11, 1994	March 28, 1994
June 11, 1994	May 13, 1994	May 27, 1994

*There is no February test administration in New York State.

Note: The 1993-94 academic year is one of transition in which the current SAT will be given and, starting in March 1994, the new SAT I: Reasoning Test will be given. For more information on the new SAT, see the next section.

1993-94 SAT and SAT I: Reasoning Test dates
First administration of SAT I: Reasoning Test is March 19, 1994

1993-94 SAT test dates*

Test date	*Registration date*	*Late registration*
October 9, 1993**	September 10, 1993	September 17, 1993
November 6, 1993	October 1, 1993	October 13, 1993
December 4, 1993***	October 29, 1993	November 10, 1993
January 22, 1994	December 16, 1993	December 30, 1993
March 19, 1994 (SAT I)	February 11, 1994	February 23, 1994
May 7, 1994 (SAT I)	April 1, 1994	April 13, 1994
June 4, 1994 (SAT I)***	April 29, 1994	May 11, 1994

*Sunday administrations will be held following each Saturday date.

**Offered only in California, Florida, Georgia, Hawaii, Illinois, New Jersey, North Carolina, Pennsylvania, South Carolina, Texas, and Virginia.

***The New York State Standardized Testing Law is currently being challenged in court. Depending upon the developments in that case, the SAT/SAT I might not be offered in New York State in December or June.

1993-94 Achievement Tests and SAT II: Subject Tests dates*
First administration of SAT II: Subject Tests is May 7, 1994

Test date	*Registration date*	*Late registration*
November 6, 1993	October 1, 1993	October 13, 1993
December 4, 1993	October 29, 1993	November 10, 1993
January 22, 1994	December 16, 1993	December 30, 1993
May 7, 1994 (SAT II)	April 1, 1994	April 13, 1994
June 4, 1994 (SAT II)	April 29, 1994	May 11, 1994

*Sunday administrations will be held following each Saturday date.

The New SAT and PSAT/NMSQT

The 1993-94 testing year will be one of transition for the College Board's SAT Program. In October 1993 a new PSAT/NMSQT (Preliminary SAT/National Merit Scholarship Qualifying Test) will be administered for the first time. The first administration of the new SAT I: Reasoning Test will be March 1994; this test replaces the former SAT. Achievement Tests will also be revised and renamed SAT II: Subject Tests and introduced in May 1994.

This section answers some of the questions most often asked by juniors and seniors preparing to take these tests.

1. What are the new tests?

There will be two types: SAT I: Reasoning Test (replacing the SAT) and SAT II: Subject Tests (replacing the Achievement Tests).

SAT I consists of revised and expanded versions of the current SAT verbal and mathematical tests. The new test will include:

- Longer reading passages with questions that measure critical reading skills and knowledge of vocabulary in context;
- Sentence completions and analogies, but not antonyms;
- Math questions requiring students to produce their own responses and to enter them on grids, as well as multiple-choice and quantitative comparison questions;
- An opportunity to use calculators on the math test (though using them is not required).

The Subject Tests consist of a major new test in writing, additional subject-matter tests (see the list of all subject tests in Question 10), and revisions to current Achievement Tests (a listening component has been added in foreign language exams).

The 200-800 scale for scores will still be used.

The dates on which the new SAT I and Subject Tests will first be given appear on the chart on the previous page.

2. How has the PSAT/NMSQT changed?

The PSAT/NMSQT given in October 1993 will be a shorter version of the new SAT I. The new test will reflect the changes in SAT I. There will be increased emphasis on critical reading in the verbal section. In the math section, there will be some questions that require student-generated answers, and calculator use will be recommended.

Taking the new PSAT/NMSQT will provide excellent practice for the new SAT. Juniors should be sure to register for the October administration at their high school.

After taking the new PSAT/NMSQT, you'll get back your test book along with a report showing how you did on each qeustion, so that you can apply the experience when you take the SAT I: Reasoning Test in spring 1994.

3. Why have the SAT and Achievement Tests been changed?

The SAT has been changed because education has changed. In general, the changes were made so that the test better reflects the type of work you will do when you get to college. High school and college teachers from around the country suggested that the new SAT emphasize thinking and reasoning: that is, emphasize the ability to use information, knowledge, and skills. The changes in the tests reflect this advice.

4. What will be on the SAT I: Reasoning Test?

SAT I will have a verbal section and a math section. It will take three hours, just like the current SAT.

5. What will the verbal sections be like?

Verbal sections consist of: analogies, sentence completion questions, and other multiple-choice questions based on reading passages.

The new test will place more emphasis on questions that measure your ability to do the kinds of reading that you do in college—reading that requires you to make inferences and to follow the logic of an argument. Each SAT I will contain four reading passages, with 5 to 13 questions based on each. The passages will be selected from the areas of humanities, natural sciences, and social sciences.

6. What will the math sections be like?

Math sections will have three question formats: multiple choice, quantitative comparisons, and a new type which requires students to do the computation and fill in the answer on a grid rather than selecting from multiple choices.

7. How many questions will be "grid ins"?

Of approximately 50 math questions on the PSAT/NMSQT and 60 math questions on SAT I, about 10 will be "grid ins."

8. Is it true that you'll have to "show your work" on the math section of the new SAT I?

No. As in the SAT, there is space for math scratchwork in the test book, and you're encouraged to use that space, but *only* the answer that you "bubble in" on the special grid will be scored.

9. Will I be allowed to use a calculator?

Yes. In fact, it's recommended that you bring one with you to both the PSAT/NMSQT and SAT I. Any four-function, scientific, or graphing calculator will be allowed. You should bring one that you're familiar with and have used. However, if you are not accustomed to using a calculator, do not buy one just to take this test. Remember, no question requires the use of a calculator and all can be solved without one.

10. What are the SAT II: Subject Tests?

These are one-hour subject-specific exams designed to find out how well you have mastered a variety of high school subjects. The tests do not depend on any particular curriculum but reflect the expected outcome of a typical high school course. There are Subject Tests in these areas:

English
Writing (replaces English Composition)
Literature

History
American History and Social Studies
World History (replaces European History and World Cultures)

Foreign Language
Chinese
French
German
Modern Hebrew
Italian
Japanese
Latin
Spanish

Mathematics
Mathematics Level I
Mathematics Level IIC

Science
Biology
Chemistry
Physics

Many colleges that require SAT I will also require SAT II: Subject Tests for admission or placement. But you don't have to wait until your senior year to take them. In fact, you may want to take them as soon as you finish a course in that subject, while the material is still fresh in your mind. These tests (except for Writing and Chinese) are offered until spring 1994 under the name Achievement Tests.

11. How can I prepare for the new SAT I and Subject Tests?

The same way you prepare for college—by building a strong educational foundation. Take the most challenging academic courses for which you're prepared; work hard in school; participate in class discussions; and read for pleasure—regularly!

You should familiarize yourself ahead of time with what's in the tests so that you'll be comfortable with the format. When you register to take the PSAT/NMSQT, the SAT I, or the SAT II, you will be given materials that describe the question types on the tests. A full-length practice test will be available as well (see Question 14).

A new book, *Introducing the New SAT* (College Entrance Examination Board, 1993, $12) provides sample questions, a full SAT I: Reasoning Test, and information and practice materials for the new test. The book is available in book stores, local libraries and high school guidance offices.

12. Is the new test harder?

The new test is different. There are fewer questions that ask, "Do you know this?" and more that ask, "Based on this, what do you think, or what else can you figure out?" But it is not harder.

13. How do I know what tests the colleges I'm applying to will require?

You will have to ask the colleges to which you are applying what tests they require. In most cases, colleges that now require the SAT will require SAT I, and colleges that require Achievement Tests will require SAT II tests. College policies in this book apply to 1994-95 freshman applicants. If you are a junior, you should check with the colleges to which you are applying to determine additional SAT Program requirements for fall 1995-96.

14. Where can I get more information about the new tests?

When you register to take the tests, you will find information about the tests on the Registration Form. You will also receive a brochure with sample questions and explanation of the types/formats of the test questions. Copies of these free publications, *Taking the SAT I: Reasoning Test* and *Taking the SAT II: Subject Tests*, should be available in your guidance office.

Your high school guidance counselor can request additional practice materials for you as well.

Paying for college

The *Handbook* descriptions include a section on annual expenses in which the typical expenses for undergraduate students living on campus are shown for a nine-month academic year. Keep in mind that college costs, like most other costs, are rising. All expenses are likely to be somewhat higher by the time you enter college, and they will continue to rise while you attend. Be sure to verify current costs with the institution. Use the worksheet below to compare college costs.

The cost of going to college is something that you and your parents should think about early in the college selection process. You must have a clear idea of the costs at an institution in order to know whether you will need financial assistance to pay the bill.

Costs differ from one college to another, so you should make an estimate for each college you are considering. There are two categories of college expenses to think about—direct educational costs and living costs. (See the figure on the next page.)

Financial aid

Millions of students receive financial aid to help them continue their education. You do not have to be poor to qualify for financial aid, because aid is based on what you and your family are able to pay. Even students from families with high incomes are often eligible for aid, especially at higher cost colleges.

Student expense budget	College 1	College 2	College 3	College 4
(Write in college name)				
Tuition and fees				
Room/board*				
Books and supplies				
Other expenses				
Transportation**				
Other (such as cost of child care, expenses because of disability)				
Total budget				

*You should consider these as expenses to your family if you live at home.

**You should add your own estimate of the round trips you will make to your home. Students living at home should figure the costs of daily transportation to the college. College estimates of transportation costs are listed in *The College Costs and Financial Aid Handbook, 1994*.

Direct educational costs		*Living costs*		*Total costs*
Tuition and fees Books and supplies	+	Room and board Personal expenses (clothing, laundry, entertainment) Transportation	=	

Demonstrated need

Colleges, state scholarship programs, and other organizations award financial aid on the basis of demonstrated need. They believe that you and your parents have a responsibility to pay as much as you can toward your educational costs. Demonstrated need is the difference between what it costs to attend a college and how much your family can reasonably be expected to contribute.

Total college expense	–	**Family contribution**	=	**Demonstrated need**

Usually you are eligible for financial aid equal to the amount of your demonstrated financial need. A set need analysis formula has been established that will be used by all colleges in determining your eligibility for federal student aid programs. Since what you can afford to pay for education will be the same at all colleges whether college costs are high or low, your eligibility for federal aid will be different at different institutions. It will be likely, particularly at high cost schools, that a different formula will be used in determining your need for nonfederal funds. The important thing is that you don't rule out any college that interests you on the basis of its costs alone.

Types of aid available

Grants or scholarships. These are types of aid that do not have to be repaid (sometimes called gift aid).

Loans. These usually have low interest rates and must be repaid, but generally only after you have graduated or left college.

Student employment. This can be a job that the college finds for you or work you find on your own that is funded through a financial aid program.

Sources of financial aid

Financial aid can come from several different sources: the federal government, state government, colleges themselves, and a wide variety of private organizations and scholarship programs. The major financial aid programs are described here:

Institutional funds. Most colleges have their own scholarships or grants as well as loan and work programs funded from endowments and operational budgets.

Federal programs. *Campus-based aid.* There are three major federal programs that are campus-based—that is, directly administered by colleges. Most colleges participate in these programs.

The Federal Supplemental Educational Opportunity Grant Program (FSEOG) provides grants of up to $4,000 for students with financial need.

The Federal Perkins Loan Program, formerly the National Direct Student Loan Program, provides loans for students with demonstrated need. No interest is paid while you are enrolled in college. When you leave college, you must repay the loan with 5 percent interest.

The Federal Work-Study Program (FWSP) provides jobs for students with demonstrated need.

Colleges may also administer other federal programs, including ones to assist students who enter nursing and other health programs.

Federal Pell Grants. The federal government also sponsors the Federal Pell Grant program. The grants are based on your family's financial circumstances and may be used at the college of your choice.

Federal Stafford Loan. The federally sponsored Stafford Loan Program is an important source of loan funds. These loans are made primarily by banks, savings and loan associations, and credit unions, but some colleges are also lenders.

The federal government pays the full interest on loans while you are enrolled in college if your loan was made on the basis of demonstrated need. For students who have not demonstrated need, unsubsidized Federal Stafford Loans are available. For unsubsidized loans, students will usually be asked to make interest payments while enrolled in school. Following a grace period, all students borrowing in the Federal Stafford Loan Program must begin repaying principal and interest after graduating or leaving school. Federal Stafford Loans have a variable interest rate set at 3.1 percent above the federal 91-day treasury-bill.

Federal Supplemental Loan for Students. Self-supporting undergraduate students and graduate students are eligible to apply for these loans in addition to the Federal Stafford Loan.

Federal Parent Loan for Undergraduate Students. The federally sponsored FPLUS loan program permits parents of undergraduate students to borrow up to the full cost of education less any other financial aid the student may have received. The interest rate is variable, set at 3.1 percent above the one-year treasury bill, capped at 10 percent.

State funds. All states have scholarship or grant programs to help you attend the college of your choice. The regulations and application procedures for these programs vary from state to state. Ask your guidance counselor for information about your state's program or write to the state department of higher education in your state capital.

Community funds and other sources. Financial aid is also provided by community agencies, foundations, corporations, unions, religious organizations, clubs, and civic, cultural, and fraternal groups. Need is usually considered, but other factors may be taken into account in determining eligibility. Check with your counselor for information on local aid sources.

Comparing financial aid

You should compare the types of aid offered by the colleges you are considering. Remember that the percentages listed under grants, loans, and jobs in the *Handbook* are for the total financial aid dollars distributed by each college in the 1992-93 academic year (or the most recent year for which information was available). If you are eligible for financial aid, you probably will get a combination of gift aid and self-help aid (loans and jobs). This combination is called a *financial aid package*.

Financial aid checklist

If you think you need aid to continue your education, your chances of getting it are best if you apply in the right way at the right time.

Begin at least a year before you expect to enter college.

❑ **Ask for information about financial aid opportunities and application procedures** when writing to the admissions office of each college on your list.

❑ **Search for special sources of aid.** Your guidance counselor, high school library, and public library will often have this type of information. Your guidance counselor, high school library, and public library will often have this type of information. In addition to publications, they may have *College Cost Explorer FUND FINDER* software, which can speed your search for appropriate scholarships. You build a personal profile which is then used to search a data base of private and public scholarships for ones you are eligible for.

You may qualify for a private scholarship, grant, or loan program based on academic achievement, religious affiliation, ethnic or racial heritage, community activities, hobbies or special interests, organizational membership, artistic talents, athletic abilities, other special skills, career plans, or proposed field of study. Since many private grant and scholarship programs have earlier deadlines than most colleges and government programs, start this search early.

❑ **Ask for information on federal student aid programs** from your high school counselor.

❑ **Ask about student aid available to residents of your state** and how to apply for it.

❑ **Make a financial aid calendar for yourself.** Include (1) the name of each program for which you may be eligible, (2) the deadline for applying to the program, and (3) an earlier deadline *for yourself*—a date by which you must have received and completed the application form and any other requirements in time to file your application by the program deadline.

❑ **Make certain you know what need analysis form to file.** All students must file the federally sponsored Free Application for Federal Student Aid (FAFSA) to apply for the federal financial aid programs. For many colleges, this may be the only need analysis form you will need to file. The FAFSA is filed after January 1 for the academic year that begins the following fall. For other schools, particularly private colleges, the Financial Aid Form (FAF) may also be required. For many Pennsylvania colleges, the PHEAA Aid Information Request (PAIR) form may be required. For colleges requiring the FAF or the PAIR, these forms must be submitted in addition to the the FAFSA. Need analysis forms are generally available prior to January 1 from your high school guidance office or from the financial aid office at the colleges you are interested in.

❑ **Plan a time when you can spend several hours on your applications.** If you are a dependent of your parents, you should plan the time when they can work with you. Your parent(s) should have a draft or complete version of their federal income tax return for the year immediately preceding your enrollment (e.g., 1993 tax return if you will start college in fall 1994). Your parents need not actually have *filed* their return, but they should at least have worked through it because questions on the need analysis form are cross-referenced to questions on the tax form.

❑ **Carefully follow the instructions** for filling out your need analysis form. Make sure your answers are complete, correct, and legible.

❑ **Apply for a state scholarship or grant.** In many states your need analysis form can also be used to apply for state aid. Your guidance counselor should know whether you must fill out additional application forms for state aid.

❑ **Mail your completed need analysis form** as early as possible. File the FAFSA as soon as possible after January 1. For other forms, follow the instructions that come with the application to determine when you should file. In general, send the form for processing at least four weeks before the earliest financial aid deadline set by the colleges, state scholarship programs, or other grant programs for which you may be eligible (but not before January 1).

❑ **Review the Student Aid Report (SAR) and any other acknowledgment you receive** after submitting your need analysis form. Respond promptly to any request for additional information.

❑ **Check to see if other financial aid applications are required** by the colleges to which you are applying. Complete and return the forms as early as possible.

❑ **If you think you may be eligible for aid** through the Veterans Administration or a vocational rehabilitation or other social service agency, contact the nearest office for information.

❑ **Determine how payments from each aid source will be made to you.** Generally, payment of financial aid is made at the time you enroll. Find out if there are additional procedures or forms to file in order to receive the aid.

❑ **Pay close attention to award letters.** Notify the college whose offer you are accepting, and inform the other colleges of your decision so that the financial aid reserved for you can be freed for other applicants. If you also receive aid notices from the state or federal programs, read them carefully and be sure to follow any directions they contain so that you can be certain of getting your aid.

❑ **Explore alternatives.** If the college of your choice cannot provide you with enough aid to meet your full financial need or if your family cannot contribute what is expected, you may want to consider borrowing. Learn about loans—the interest rates, repayment schedules, and other terms and conditions—*before* you apply. Government-sponsored loans, such as the Federal Stafford Loan Program, usually have the lowest interest rates and the most flexible repayment arrangements. If you do apply for a Federal Stafford Loan, submit it to the financial aid office as early as possible.

Glossary

Definitions of commonly used terms vary from college to college. Consult specific college catalogs for more detailed information.

Accelerated study. A college program of study completed in less time than is usually required, most often by attending classes in summer or by taking extra courses during the regular academic terms. Completion of a bachelor's degree program in three years is an example of acceleration.

Accreditation. Recognition by an accrediting organization or agency that a college meets certain acceptable standards in its education programs, services, and facilities. Regional accreditation applies to a college as a whole and not to any particular programs or courses of study. Specialized accreditation of specific types of schools, such as Bible colleges or trade and technical schools, may also be determined by a national organization. Institutional accreditation by regional accrediting associations and by national accrediting organizations is included in the *Handbook*'s description of colleges. Information about the accreditation of specialized programs within a college by organizations such as American Chemical Society, American Dietetic Association, etc., is given in *Accredited Institutions of Postsecondary Education* published for the Council on Postsecondary Accreditation by the American Council on Education.

Accrediting associations

Regional accreditation

Middle States Association of Colleges and Schools
3624 Market Street
Philadelphia, Pennsylvania 19104-2680

Delaware, District of Columbia, Maryland, New Jersey, New York, Pennsylvania, Puerto Rico, Virgin Islands

New England Association of Schools and Colleges
The Sanborn House
15 High Street
Winchester, Massachusetts 01890

Connecticut, Maine, Massachusetts, New Hampshire, Rhode Island, Vermont

North Central Association of Colleges and Schools
159 North Dearborn Street
Chicago, Illinois 60601

Arizona, Arkansas, Colorado, Illinois, Indiana, Iowa, Kansas, Michigan, Minnesota, Missouri, Nebraska, New Mexico, North Dakota, Ohio, Oklahoma, South Dakota, West Virginia, Wisconsin, Wyoming

Northwest Association of Schools and Colleges
3700-B University Way, N.E.
Seattle, Washington 98105

Alaska, Idaho, Montana, Nevada, Oregon, Utah, Washington

Southern Association of Colleges and Schools
1866 Southern Lane
Decatur, Georgia 30033-4097

Alabama, Florida, Georgia, Kentucky, Louisiana, Mississippi, North Carolina, South Carolina, Tennessee, Texas, Virginia

Western Association of Schools and Colleges
Accrediting Commission for Senior Colleges and Universities
c/o Mills College, Box 9990
Oakland, California 94613

Accrediting Commission for Community and Junior Colleges
3060 Valencia Avenue
Aptos, California 95003

American Samoa, California, Guam, Hawaii, Trust Territory of the Pacific

Other institutional accreditation

American Association of Bible Colleges (AABC)
P.O. Box 1523
130-F North College Avenue
Fayetteville, Arkansas 72702

Association of Advanced Rabbinical and Talmudic Schools (AARTS)
175 Fifth Avenue, Room 711
New York, New York 10010

Association of Theological Schools in the United States and Canada (ATS)
10 Summit Park Drive
Pittsburgh, Pennsylvania 15275-1103

Career College Association (CCA)
750 First Street, NE, Suite 900
Washington, D.C. 20002

National Home Study Council (NHSC)
1601 18th Street NW
Washington, D.C. 20009

New York Board of Regents
State Education Department
Washington Avenue
Albany, New York 12234

Achievement Tests (ACH). College Board tests in specific secondary school subjects, given at test centers in the United States and other countries on specified dates throughout the year. Used by colleges not only to help with decisions about admissions but also in course placement and exemption of enrolled freshmen. In March 1994, the Achievement Tests will be revised and expanded. The new tests will be called SAT II: Subject Tests. Students will be allowed to select which SAT II test scores they want released to colleges. See also *SAT*.

Advanced placement. Admission or assignment of a freshman to an advanced course in a certain subject on the basis of evidence that the student has already completed the equivalent of the college's freshman course in that subject.

Advanced Placement (AP) Program. A service of the College Board that provides high schools with course descriptions in college subjects and Advanced Placement Examinations in those subjects. High schools implement the courses and administer the examinations to interested students, who are then eligible for advanced placement, college credit, or both, on the basis of satisfactory grades.

American College Testing Program Assessment (ACT). Test battery of the American College Testing Program, given at test centers in the United States and other countries on specified dates throughout the year. It includes tests in English, mathematics, reading, and science reasoning. The ACT composite score referred to in some colleges' descriptions is the average of students' scores on these four tests.

Associate degree. A degree granted by a college or university after the satisfactory completion of a two-year full-time program of study or its part-time equivalent. In general, the associate of arts (AA) or associate of science (AS) degree is granted after students complete a program of study similar to the first two years of a four-year college curriculum. The associate in applied science (AAS) is awarded by many colleges upon completion of technological or vocational programs of study.

Bachelor's, or baccalaureate, degree. A degree received after the satisfactory completion of a four- or five-year, full-time program of study (or its part-time equivalent) at a college or university. The bachelor of arts (BA) and bachelor of science (BS) are the most common baccalaureates. There is no absolute difference between the degrees, and policies concerning their award vary from college to college.

Calendar. The system by which an institution divides its year into shorter periods for instruction and awarding credit. The most common calendars are those based on the semester, trimester, quarter, and 4-1-4.

Candidates Reply Date Agreement (CRDA). A college subscribing to this agreement will not require any applicants offered admission as freshmen to notify the college of their decision to attend (or to accept an offer of financial aid) before May 1 of the year the applicant applies. The purpose of the agreement is to give applicants time to hear from all the colleges to which they have applied before having to make a commitment to any of them.

College-Level Examination Program (CLEP). A program of examinations in undergraduate college courses that provides students and adults the opportunity to demonstrate college-level achievement. The examinations are used by colleges to award credit to entering freshmen and adults completing their education. They are also used by business, industry, government, and professional groups to satisfy educational requirements for advancement, licensing, and admission to training programs.

College-preparatory subjects. A term used to describe subjects required for admission to, or recommended as preparation for, college. It is usually understood to mean subjects from the fields of English, history and social studies, foreign languages, mathematics, science, and the arts.

College Scholarship Service (CSS). A service of the College Board that assists postsecondary institutions, state scholarship programs, and other organizations in the equitable distribution of student financial aid funds by measuring a family's financial strength and analyzing its ability to contribute to college costs. CSS provides the Financial Aid Form (FAF) with which students may apply for nonfederal aid at some colleges.

Combined bachelor's/graduate degree. A program to which students are accepted for study at both the undergraduate and graduate levels. The program usually can be completed in less time than two individual programs.

Cooperative education. A college program in which a student alternates between periods of full-time study and full-time employment in a related field. Students are paid for their work at the prevailing rate. Typically, five years are required to complete a bachelor's degree under the cooperative plan, but graduates have the advantage of about a year's practical work experience in addition to their studies.

Some colleges refer to this sort of program as work-study, but it should not be confused with the federally sponsored Federal Work-Study Program.

Cross-registration. The practice, through agreements between colleges, of permitting students enrolled at one college or university to enroll in courses at another institution without formally applying for admission to the second institution.

Deferred admission. The practice of permitting students to postpone enrollment for one year after acceptance to the college.

Double major. Any program of study in which a student completes the requirements of two majors concurrently.

Dual enrollment. The practice of colleges of allowing high school seniors to enroll in certain courses while completing their senior year. These students are not considered full-time college students.

Early admission. The practice of some colleges of admitting certain students who have not completed high school—usually students of exceptional ability who have complete their junior year. These students are enrolled full-time in college.

Early decision. Early decision plans are offered to applicants who are sure of the college they want to attend and are likely to be accepted by that college. An early decision application is initiated by the student, who is then notified of the college's decision earlier than usual—generally by December 15 of the senior year.

Early Decision Plan (EDP-F, EDP-S). Colleges that subscribe to this plan agree to follow a common schedule for early decision applicants. Colleges may offer either of two plans. A student applying under the first-choice plan (EDP-F) must withdraw applications from all other colleges as soon as he or she is notified of acceptance by the first-choice college. A student applying under the single-choice plan (EDP-S) may not apply to any colleges other than his or her first choice unless rejected by that institution. If a college follows either type of plan, applications (including financial aid applications) must be received by a specified date no later than November 15, and the college agrees to notify the applicant by a specified date not later than December 15.

External degree program. A system of study whereby a student earns credit toward a degree through independent study, college courses, proficiency examinations, and personal experience. External degree colleges generally have no campus or classroom facilities.

Federal Pell Grant Program. A federally sponsored and administered program that provides grants based on need to undergraduate students. Congress annually sets the dollar range. Currently a Pell Grant cannot exceed $2,400 per year.

Federal Perkins Loan Program. (Formerly called the National Direct Student Loan Program or NDSL.) A federally funded program based on need, administered by colleges, that provides low-interest loans of up to $3,000 per year during undergraduate study and up to $15,000 for the total undergraduate program. The combined cumulative total of loan funds available to an individual for undergraduate and graduate education is $30,000. Repayment need not begin until completion of the student's education or after limited periods of service in the military, Peace Corps, or approved comparable organizations.

Federal Stafford Loan. This is a federal program based on need that allows students to borrow money for educational expenses directly from banks and other lending institutions (sometimes from the colleges themselves). The amounts that may be borrowed depend on the student's year in school. The undergraduate loan limits are as follows: first year, $2,625; second year, $3,500; third and fourth years, $5,500; to a total amount as an undergraduate of $23,000. Graduate students may borrow $8,500 per year to an aggregate limit, including undergraduate borrowing, of $65,000. Loan limits are the same for borrowers of unsubsidized Federal Stafford Loans, or for borrowers of a combination subsidized/unsubsidized loan.

Federal Supplemental Educational Opportunity Grant Program (FSEOG). A federal program administered by colleges that provides grants of up to $4,000 a year for undergraduate students on the basis of need.

Federal Work-Study Program. An arrangement by which a student combines employment and college study. The employment may be an integral part of the academic program (as in cooperative education or internships) or simply a means of paying for college.

Financial Aid Form (FAF). *See* Need analysis forms.

4-4-1. A variation of the semester calendar program, the 4-4-1 calendar consists of two terms of about 16 weeks each, followed by a one-month term used for intensive short courses, independent study, off-campus work, or other types of instruction.

4-1-4. A variation of the semester calendar system, the 4-1-4 calendar consists of two terms of about 16 weeks each, separated by a one-month intersession used for intensive short courses, independent study, off-campus work, or other types of instruction.

Free Application for Federal Student Aid (FAFSA). *See* Need analysis form.

General Educational Development (GED). A series of five tests that adults who did not complete high school may take through their state education system to qualify for a high school equivalency certificate. These tests are also administered at centers outside the United States and to members of the armed services through the United States Armed Forces Institute. The tests cover correctness and effectiveness of expression, interpretation of reading materials in the natural sciences, interpretation of literary materials, and general mathematics ability. Many colleges accept satisfactory GED test results in lieu of high school graduation.

Grade-point average or ratio (GPA). A system used by many schools for evaluating the overall scholastic performance of students. It is found by first determining the number of grade points a student has earned in each course completed and then dividing the sum of all grade points by the number of hours of course work carried. Grade points are found by multiplying the number of hours given for a course by the student's grade in the course. The most common system of numerical values for grades is A = 4, B = 3, C = 2, D = 1, and E or F = 0. Also called quality-point average ratio.

Honors program. Any special program for very able students that offers the opportunity for educational enrichment, independent study, acceleration, or some combination of these.

Independent study. An arrangement that allows students to complete some of their college program by studying independently instead of attending scheduled classes and completing group assignments. Typically, students plan programs of study in consultation with a faculty adviser or committee, to whom they may report periodically and submit a final report for evaluation.

Interdisciplinary. Refers to programs or courses that use the knowledge from a number of academic disciplines, such as a combination of biology and physical science or of engineering and business.

International Baccalaureate (IB). A comprehensive and rigorous two-year curriculum (usually taken in the final two years of high school) that is similar to the final year of secondary school in Europe. More than 100 high schools in the United States have an IB program. Some colleges award credit or advanced placement to students who have completed an IB program.

Internships. Short-term, supervised work experiences, usually related to a student's major field, for which the student earns academic credit. The work can be full- or part-time, on or off campus, paid or unpaid. Student teaching and apprenticeships are examples.

Liberal arts and career combination. A program in which a student completes two or three years of study in the liberal arts field followed by two or three years of professional/technical study (for example, engineering or forestry), at the end of which the student is awarded the bachelor of arts and bachelor of science degrees. Often referred to as 2-3 or 3-2 programs.

Need analysis form. The starting point in applying for financial aid. All students must file the federally sponsored Free Application for Federal Student Aid (FAFSA) to apply for the federal financial aid programs. For many colleges, this may be the only need analysis form students will need to file. For other schools, particularly private colleges, the Financial Aid Form (FAF) may also be required. To apply for state financial aid programs, the FAFSA may be all that is needed, but you should check with the state agency to learn if any other application forms need to be submitted. The forms that will be most commonly required are the following:

- Free Application for Federal Student Aid (FAFSA) of the U.S. Department of Education
- Financial Aid Form (FAF) of the College Scholarship Service
- PHEAA Aid Information Request (PAIR) of the Pennsylvania Higher Education Assistance Agency (Pennsylvania applicants only).

Open admissions. The college admissions policy of admitting high school graduates and other adults generally without regard to conventional academic qualifications, such as high school subjects, high school grades, and admissions test scores. Virtually all applicants with high school diplomas or their equivalent are accepted.

PHEAA Aid Information Request (PAIR). *See* Need analysis form.

Prueba de Aptitude Academica (PAA). Spanish-language college aptitude test developed by the College Board. The PAA is similar in structure to the SAT. Many colleges in Puerto Rico require the

PAA of some or all applicants.

PSAT/NMSQT (Preliminary SAT/National Merit Scholarship Qualifying Test). A shorter version of the SAT administered by high schools each year in October. The PSAT/NMSQT aids high schools in the early guidance of students planning for college and serves as the qualifying test for scholarship awarded by the National Merit Scholarship Corporation and the National Hispanic Scholar Awards Program. In October 1993 the new PSAT/NMSQT will be administered. See "The New SAT and PSAT/NMSQT" for more information.

Quarter. An academic calendar period of about 11 weeks. Four quarters make up an academic year, but at colleges using the quarter system, students make normal academic progress by attending three quarters each year. In some colleges, students can accelerate their programs by attending all four quarters in one or more years.

Reserve Officers' Training Corps (ROTC). Programs conducted by certain colleges in cooperation with the United States Air Force, Army, and Navy. Local recruiting offices of the services themselves can supply detailed information about these programs, as can participating colleges.

Residency requirements. Most colleges and universities require that a student spend a minimum number of terms taking courses on campus (as opposed to independent study or transfer credits from other colleges) to be eligible for graduation. Also, residency requirements can refer to the minimum amount of time a student is required to have lived in a state in order to be eligible for in-state tuition at a public (state-controlled) college or university.

Rolling admissions. An admissions procedure by which the college considers each student's application as soon as all the required credentials, such as school record and test scores, have been received. The college usually notifies applicants of its decision without delay.

SAT. The College Board's test of developed verbal and mathematical reasoning abilities, given on specified dates throughout the year at test centers in the United States and other countries. The SAT is required by many colleges and sponsors of financial aid programs. In March 1994, a new SAT program will be introduced. The new SAT I: Reasoning Test will take the place of the SAT. The Achievement Tests will be expanded and called SAT II: Subject Tests.

SAT Program. A program of the College Board that provides college entrance tests and services for students planning to go to college. Included are the SAT, Achievement Tests, and the Student Descriptive Questionnaire. In March 1994, new SAT and Achievement Tests will be introduced. The new SAT will be known as SAT I: Reasoning Test and the Achievement Tests will be called SAT II: Subject Tests. See the section "The New SAT and PSAT/NMSQT" for more information.

Semester. A period of about 17 or 18 weeks that makes up half of the usual academic year in colleges using this kind of calendar.

Semester at sea. A program for credit, usually for students with majors in oceanography or marine-related fields, in which students live for part of a semester on a ship, frequently a research vessel. Academic courses are generally taken in conjunction with the sea experience or at separate times during the semester.

Student Descriptive Questionnaire (SDQ). A questionnaire that can be completed by students when they register for the SAT/SAT I: Reasoning Test or Achievement Tests/SAT II: Subject Tests. It gives the student an opportunity to provide information about academic experience in high school, educational objectives, extracurricular activities, and areas in which counseling or assistance may be needed. The responses are sent, along with test scores, to the student's high school and designated colleges and scholarship sponsors. For those students who give their permission, selected information from the SDQ is also used by the Student Search Service.

Student-designed major. An academic program that allows a student to construct a major field of study not formally offered by the college. Often nontraditional and interdisciplinary in nature, the major is developed by the student with the approval of a designated college officer or committee.

Student Search Service. A College Board program designed to help colleges identify potential applicants with the particular academic or personal characteristics they are seeking. The service also provides students with an opportunity to learn about colleges with programs and characteristics they want. Information is gathered about students who wish to participate through the Student Descriptive Questionnaire of the SAT Program and the biographical section of the PSAT/NMSQT answer sheet. The College Board then supplies each participating college with the names and addresses of students who have the particular characteristics they specify. The service is free to students. Colleges can also identify students who participated in the Advanced Placement Program through the Advanced Placement Program Search.

Study abroad. Any arrangement by which a student completes part of the college program—typically the junior year but sometimes only a semester or a summer—studying in another country. A college may operate a campus abroad, or it may have a cooperative agreement with some other U.S. college or an institution of the other country.

Teacher preparation. A college program designed to prepare students to meet the requirements for certification as teachers in elementary and secondary school.

Telecourses. Televised courses, taken for credit, that are broadcast on public or cable stations and that may be viewed in the home or on campus.

Terminal program. An education program designed to prepare students for immediate employment. These programs usually can be completed in less than four years beyond high school and are available in many junior colleges, community colleges, and vocational-technical institutes.

Transfer program. An education program in a two-year college (or a four-year college that offers associate degrees) primarily for students who plan to continue their studies in a four-year college or university.

Transfer student. A student who has attended another college for any period, which may be defined by various colleges as any time from a single term up to three years. A transfer student may receive credit for all or some of the courses successfully completed before the transfer. (*The College Handbook for Transfer Students*, updated annually, contains current transfer admissions policies at 2,700 colleges, and thorough guidance information for students planning transfer.)

Trimester. An academic calendar period of about 15 weeks. Three trimesters make up one year. Students normally progress by attending two of the trimesters each year and in some colleges can accelerate their programs by attending all three trimesters in one or more years.

Two-year upper-division college. A college offering bachelor's degree programs that begin with the junior year. Entering students must have completed the freshman and sophomore years at other colleges.

2-3 programs. *See* Liberal arts and career combination.

United Nations semester. A program in which students generally take courses at a college in the New York City metropolitan area while participating in an internship program at the United Nations.

Upper division. The junior and senior years of study. Some colleges offer only upper-division study—students must have completed the freshman and sophomore years (lower division) at other institutions before entering the upper-division institution to earn their bachelor's degree.

Visiting/exchange student program. Any arrangement between a student and a college that permits study for a semester or more at another college without extending the amount of time required for a degree.

Washington semester. A program in which students participate in an internship program with a government agency or department in the Washington, D.C., metropolitan area. Students earn field service credit for their work and frequently take courses at area colleges.

Weekend college. A program that allows students to take a complete course of study and attend classes only on weekends. These programs are generally restricted to a few areas of study at a college and require more than the traditional number of years to complete.

Work-study. An arrangement by which a student combines employment and college study. The employment may be an integral part of the academic program (as in cooperative education and internships) or simply a means of paying for college (as in the Federal Work-Study Program).

How to use *The College Handbook*

The college indexes

Once you have examined your reasons for going to college and have completed the checklist of college characteristics, you should have a fairly good idea of what you want to look for in a college description in the *Handbook*. You can use the College Indexes that appear before the college descriptions to help locate colleges that may interest you.

In addition to using the indexes to look for *types* of colleges, such as community colleges, business colleges, or predominantly black institutions, you can look for policies that may ease the application process (the Common Application list) or for programs of potential interest (ROTC availability). The list of colleges requiring the Achievement Tests will help you plan which tests to take and when to take them if you find that you might attend a college that requires Achievements.

In the indexes, colleges are listed alphabetically by state because for many students geographic location is a primary requirement. Institutions that are part of a system are listed alphabetically under the system name.

The following discussion of index terms may help you to decide if a certain type of institution or a special program or policy interests you.

Types of colleges

Four-year colleges. These colleges award the bachelor's degree at the completion of four years of full-time college study. Some four-year colleges also offer two-year programs from which students can transfer into bachelor's degree programs. Many four-year colleges also offer graduate study. Frequently, faculty who teach graduate courses also teach undergraduate courses.

Liberal arts colleges. These undergraduate colleges are sometimes known as colleges of arts and sciences. The study of liberal arts is intended to develop general knowledge and reasoning ability as opposed to specific preparation for a career. Students at colleges of arts and sciences usually study letters/literature, philosophy, history, foreign languages, social sciences, and natural sciences. Most liberal arts colleges are privately controlled. They generally do not offer as many majors in the technical or scientific disciplines as comprehensive colleges or universities.

University. A university generally offers a broad range of both undergraduate and graduate degree programs. Universities, however, can vary considerably in size and in the diversity of the programs that they offer. There are more than 500 universities, but only about 320 of them offer doctoral degrees. Universities are generally larger than other types of colleges. They typically offer more majors and have more research facilities than do other colleges.

Upper-division colleges. These colleges offer the last two years of undergraduate study, usually in specialized programs leading to the bachelor's degree. Students generally transfer to upper-division colleges after completing an associate degree or after finishing their second year of study at a four-year college. Students usually need at least 60 semester hours of college credit to be eligible for admission.

Community/junior colleges. The majority of these two-year institutions are public, though some are private (nonprofit) or proprietary (profit making). These colleges award associate degrees at the completion of two years of full-time study. They frequently offer technical programs of study that prepare students for immediate entry into the job market and are said to result in "terminal" degrees. In addition, many of these colleges offer general education programs that are the equivalent of the first two years of a bachelor's degree program. These are called "transfer" or "university parallel" programs; on completion, students may enter bachelor's degree programs at the third-year level. The majority of two-year public colleges have open admissions policies, although some individual programs, like nursing, may be selective. Private or proprietary junior colleges may have admissions requirements.

Single-sex colleges. There are nearly 140 colleges in the United States that enroll either men only or women only. Some of these colleges may enroll a few men or women, but their student bodies are predominantly of one sex. If you are interested in reading about colleges that are for men only or women only, you should use this index.

Specialized colleges. Colleges that concentrate their offerings in one or two specific areas are classified as specialized colleges. They include colleges offering the following types of study: agricultural/technical, art/music, Bible, business, engineering, health sciences, military, seminary/rabbinical, and teacher preparation. Some are two-year colleges; others offer four years of study. Of course, universities, liberal arts, upper-division, and community/junior colleges also offer study in these areas. Students who enroll at specialized colleges generally have a specific idea of what they want to study. Few institutions identify themselves as specialized colleges.

Campus environment

Both the size and location of a college help determine its environment. It is often difficult to imagine what a place is like—and whether you will be comfortable there—until you actually visit it. For example, it is hard to imagine how large New York City is, or how hot Fort Worth can get, or how windy Chicago can be. It is equally hard to know from pictures in catalogs just what a college campus is like. You can't be sure if there are enough trees on campus or too many to suit your taste. Grouping colleges by their campus environment, however, can give you a clue.

These groupings are based on two facts: total undergraduate enrollment and the colleges's description of its campus setting—urban, suburban, or rural.

Small colleges. These colleges enroll fewer than 1,000 students. They are frequently specialized colleges with highly focused curriculum offerings, or they may offer liberal arts curriculums with some technical and science majors. They generally do not offer graduate study. If you like knowing nearly everyone you go to school with, this size college may interest you.

Medium-sized colleges. These colleges have between 1,000 and 3,000 undergraduates. Most offer both liberal arts and technical degree programs. Many offer some graduate programs. If you like a variety of social groups from which to choose, but are concerned about being overwhelmed by too many choices, this size college may be of interest to you.

Large colleges. These colleges enroll between 3,000 and 7,500 undergraduates. They have a larger range of curriculum offerings than smaller colleges, and many offer graduate and doctoral degree programs of study. Some of these colleges actually qualify as universities. If you like a broad range of groups and activities from which to choose, and enjoy developing a small circle of friends within a large community, this size college may be of interest to you.

Very large colleges. These colleges enroll more than 7,500 undergraduates. The majority of these colleges are either two-year community colleges or universities. They offer a large variety of majors and generally have a greater array of facilities than other institutions. If you like to be challenged by a wide range of choices, and enjoy developing a small circle of friends within a large community, this size college may interest you.

Urban campuses. Urban campuses are generally located in densely populated urban areas. The campuses themselves can be as different as the cities in which they are located They include some of the nation's oldest colleges, with historic buildings and parklike quadrangles, as well as colleges located in a single high-rise building with no traditional campus at all. What most urban campuses share is ready access to the extended cultural life of the city itself—museums, theaters, professional sports, concerts, etc.

Suburban campuses. Suburban campuses can be quite varied. They can range from converted shopping malls to traditional, ivy-covered buildings. They are usually in less populated areas than urban campuses and generally cover a larger geographic area. Suburban campuses are by definition located near cities; students who have transportation into the city can take advantage of a diversity of cultural events.

Rural campuses. Rural campuses are generally some distance from metropolitan areas and students must rely almost entirely on the social and cultural events offered on campus. Rural campuses may provide greater opportunities for outdoor activities, as well as educational opportunities, because of nearby mountains, wilderness areas, etc. Some rural campuses may have farms, arboretums, and nature preserves. The "sense of community" may be increased because the college is more self-contained than in larger communities.

Colleges with religious affiliation

Colleges are asked to list their religious affiliation, if any. Student life at some colleges is greatly influenced by the religious affiliation of the institution. At other colleges, a religious affiliation may be historic only, having no direct or indirect influence on college life. If you are interested in attending a college with a specific religious affiliation, remember that this index lists each institution under the official name of the denomination with which it is affiliated.

Historically black colleges

This list identifies historically or predominantly black colleges that are committed to educating black students. The information was obtained from the National Association for Equal Opportunity in Higher Education and the U.S. Government. Within this list you will find research universities, liberal arts colleges, church-affiliated institutions, and more.

Hispanic-serving institutions

Colleges in this list are members of the Hispanic Association of Colleges and Universities. At least 25 percent of the students at these colleges—which are both public and private, large and small, specialized and general—are Hispanic. If you are interested in attending an institution with a commitment to educating Hispanic students, consult this list.

Colleges with services for the learning disabled

Colleges were asked to indicate whether they offer any services or facilities for students with learning disabilities, such as dyslexia. The type and extent of these offerings will vary from college to college. If you have an interest in such services, first consult this list and then contact the institution directly to learn more about their specific services.

Colleges that offer ROTC

The United States armed forces offer Reserve Officers' Training Corps programs that prepare candidates for commissions in the Air Force, Army, and Navy. These programs are offered either at the colleges listed in the index or at cooperating institutions. ROTC programs may take either two or four years to complete. Use this index, organized by the individual branch of the service, to find those colleges that offer the ROTC program of interest to you.

Open admissions colleges

Both two- and four-year colleges may have open admissions policies. Open admissions institutions admit virtually all applicants regardless of academic qualifications. Many public institutions offer open admissions to state residents but have selective admissions requirements for out-of-state students. Be sure to check a college's description to determine whether its open admissions policy applies to you. Most open admissions colleges require that applicants have a high school diploma (or its GED equivalent) or that they are at least 18 years of age. If you are interested in open admissions institutions, you should consult these indexes.

Colleges that require Achievement Tests

This list shows colleges that require all or some applicants to take one or more Achievement Tests for either admissions or placement. The college descriptions provide more detailed information, such as whether tests in certain subjects are required.

This list is intended to help you plan: use it to determine which tests you need or want to take, when you should take them, and even (if you are planning early) which high school courses you should take to be well-prepared for the Achievement Tests you need.

As of spring 1994, the Achievement Tests will be called SAT II: Subject Tests, and some new tests will be available. See "The New SAT and PSAT/NMSQT" earlier in this book for information on the new tests.

Fall-term application indexes

Colleges that accept the Common Application. More than 600 colleges now accept the Common Application distributed by the National Association of Secondary School Principals. Those that are Common Application members have been noted with an asterisk on this list. Check this index to see whether the institutions that interest you have indicated that they accept the Common Application form. The application deadlines and fees vary with each college, but you only need to complete the form once and submit copies to each college.

Candidates Reply Date Agreement (CRDA). Colleges on this list will not require any applicant offered admission as a freshman to notify them of a decision to attend (or accept a financial aid offer) before May 1 of the year in which the applicant applies.

Early Decision Plan (EDP). These colleges agree to follow a common schedule for early decision applicants. They may subscribe to either of two plans. A student applying under the first-choice plan (EDP-F) must withdraw applications from all other colleges as soon as he or she is notified of acceptance by the first-choice college. A student applying under the single-choice plan (EDP-S) may not apply to any colleges other than his or her first choice unless rejected by that institution. Be sure that you understand the exact terms of the plan offered at the college to which you are applying, and your responsibilities and options under the plan.

You can cut down on the number of applications you file without reducing your chances of admission or financial aid at any participating college by applying under the Early Decision Plan. If you are sure of the college you want to attend and think you are likely to be accepted, consider applying for early decision under the single- or first-choice plan. Both plans require that

- *you* (not the college) initiate the application;
- you complete your application for admission (and financial aid, if appropriate) early in the fall of your senior year and no later than November 15;
- you take all required tests before the fall of your senior year.

The college will notify you of its admissions and financial aid decisions by December 15. If you are not accepted under early decision, your application is reconsidered without bias under the college's regular admissions plan.

Application filing dates. There are two dates that colleges may list that are of concern to prospective applicants: priority date and closing date. Some colleges review applications as they arrive but withhold their final decisions until a specific date. Other colleges process applications on a first-come, first-served basis. If your application is received after all freshman class places have been filled, you will not even be considered for admission. For some very popular colleges, this can happen even before the college's priority date.

When a college indicates that it has a priority date, you should consider that date as your application deadline. Do not give up on a college, however, if you do not file your application before its priority date; get your application in before the final deadline.

Some colleges indicate their willingness to accept applications until registration, and in some rare instances, into the beginning of the academic year. These are usually open admissions institutions that, if you have a high school diploma or its equivalent, permit you to enter their general degree programs. In some cases, colleges with closing dates will continue to accept applications if they have not yet filled their freshman classes.

You should check with your guidance counselor regarding the significance of the priority and closing dates listed in each college's description.

Colleges that offer NCAA sports

Nearly 900 colleges and universities are members of the National Collegiate Athletic Association. The NCAA is the best known athletic association because it includes all of the best-known sports. You may want to attend a college where you can watch NCAA sports. Colleges must offer at least four sports and have at least one in each season (fall, winter, and spring), in order to be an NCAA member, so there's a lot of high-level athletic competition to watch throughout the academic year.

Or, you may want to play NCAA-level sports. Whether you want to watch, play, or do both, use the list in *The College Handbook* to find the sport you want to play, the colleges that offer it, the division level of play available, and whether the sport is offered to men, women, or both.

The rules of eligibility for NCAA play are strict and are designed to encourage high levels of amateur sportsmanship; the association arose out of the need to monitor the once-brutal sport of college football. If you want to play an NCAA sport, discuss your goals with your coach, the school athletic director, or your high school counselor. Find out what the requirements are. The NCAA calls participants "student-athletes," and you must meet certain academic requirements in order to play NCAA sports. A level of academic achievement must be maintained while in college, as well as standards of good conduct on the playing field.

Colleges determine which of the three divisions is most appropriate for their program. Division I and II colleges have different academic and eligibility requirements than Division III institutions. Division I members may award grants based on athletic ability. Division II colleges may award grants as well, but generally not as many as Division I colleges. Division III institutions do not award athletic grants. Division I-A members must meet minimum paid football attendance criteria. These are just a few of the distinctions; if you are an athlete hoping to play NCAA college sports, talk to your coach about the division level that is appropriate for you.

Information in this list was supplied by the colleges and, where necessary, was supplemented by information in the 1992-93 NCAA Directory.

College descriptions

College descriptions follow a common outline to make it easy to find a particular item of information in any description and to compare one college with another. Most descriptions begin with the College ABCs—capsule information on freshman admissions acceptance rates, basis for selection, and completion rates of enrolled students. The main part of each college statement begins with general information about the college, followed by separate paragraphs on degrees awarded, majors offered, academic programs, academic requirements, freshman admissions, freshman class profile, fall-term applications, student life, athletics, student services, annual expenses, financial aid, and where to write or call for more information.

Colleges are listed by their full names, which are not always the ones in popular use. If a college is part of a complex system, it usually appears under the system name. College Board membership is indicated by an oak leaf symbol following the college's name. The city and state appear below the name along with the College Board (CB) code number.

The following guide to reading college descriptions shows you exactly where to find information in each description. Consult the Glossary for complete explanations of terms used in descriptions.

College ABCs

Admissions. The percentage of applicants admitted to the 1992 freshman class is given for colleges with selective admissions policies.

Basis for selection. Some of the factors colleges use when making admissions decisions are listed here. Colleges were asked to rank five selection criteria as most important (designated by •••), important (••), or considered (•). The factors are: school and community activities, essay, interview, recommendations, high school achievement record, special talents, religious affiliation and/or commitment, and test scores.

Completion. The information here can help you determine what happens to students who enroll at a college. You will see the percentage of freshmen who complete the freshman year in good academic standing; the percentage who graduate with a bachelor's degree within five years or with an associate degree within three years of entrance as a freshman; the percentage of two-year program graduates who enter four-year programs; and the percentage of four-year graduates who enter graduate programs within one year of graduation.

General information

The general information makes it possible to classify colleges quickly according to certain basic facts: *number of years* of undergraduate education available; *type of institution* (college of arts and sciences, university, etc.); *public, private, or proprietary* control; *men only, women only*, or *coed* student body; *religious affiliation*, if any; college's *founding date*. Other major characteristics presented here are:

Accreditation. All institutions in the *Handbook* are accredited by a national accrediting association. Regional accreditation means the institution is accredited by one of six regional associations which cover the entire United States. Institutions may also be accredited by specialized bodies that accredit specific types of schools, such as rabbinical or technical schools. If a college has regional accreditation, only that is noted, even if the institution is accredited by other national accrediting organizations. Accreditation information was taken from the current rosters of the individual accrediting associations and is the only information in the descriptions that does not come from the colleges themselves. See the Glossary for additional information on accreditation and the accrediting associations.

Undergraduate and graduate enrollment. Use this information to determine the size of the college and the ratio of men to women and undergraduate to graduate students. Full-time and part-time enrollment for men and women enrolled in degree-granting programs are listed. If you need to gauge whether certain enrollments are big or small look up the statistics for some colleges in your community in order to develop a point of comparison.

Faculty. The total number of faculty, the number who are full time, and the number who hold doctoral degrees are given here.

Location. This information gives you a picture of the campus environment and the size of the city in which the college is located. The campus environment may be urban, suburban, or rural. Community sizes are: rural communities, fewer than 2,500 residents; small towns, 2,500 to 9,999; large towns, 10,000 to 49,999; small cities, 50,000 to 249,999; large cities, 250,000 to 499,999; very large cities, more than 500,000. In addition, the college's distance from the nearest large city may be reported. If possible, try to visit the college to get your own impression.

Calendar. Most colleges use the semester, quarter, trimester, or 4-1-4 systems described in the Glossary. Unusual calendar systems are also listed here, as well as the availability of summer sessions, Saturday classes, and early morning/evening classes. The calendar system used can affect jobs you may take when not in college, vacation periods, and the length of time it takes to complete a degree.

Microcomputers. This information indicates whether microcomputers are generally available for student use, the number, where they are located (in dormitories, libraries, classrooms, or computer centers), and whether there is a campus-wide network.

Special facilities. Some colleges have unique facilities on campus that can be accessible to students, faculty, and sometimes the surrounding community. Examples are a nature preserve, nuclear reactor, or planetarium.

Additional facts. Some colleges have unique characteristics that are of interest to applicants. These features can include special programs or unusual campus locations.

Degrees offered 1992

This shows what degrees a college awards, the number of degrees awarded in academic year 1991-92, and the percentage of degrees awarded by general category.

Use this information to determine whether a college offers the undergraduate degree level you seek, and to determine the scope of a college's graduate programs. Though many colleges offer even more degrees than are represented in their description in this book, the level of study offered is more significant to your choice of a college than knowing the exact degree you're going to pursue.

The breakdown of degrees awarded in general categories may indicate something about the nature of the college—whether it is oriented toward study of the liberal arts or sciences, or toward technical fields for example—as well as how many students major in areas of interest to you. Only those categories that represent at least 5 percent of the degrees awarded in 1992 are listed.

You can discover how many different graduate and professional degrees a college may offer. Professional programs require at least two academic years of previous college work for entrance and a total of at least six years of college work for completion.

Undergraduate and graduate degrees listed and their abbreviations are:

AA	Associate of Arts
AS	Associate of Science
AAS	Associate of Applied Science
B	Bachelor's
BA	Bachelor of Arts
BS	Bachelor of Sciences
BFA	Bachelor of Fine Arts
BArch	Bachelor of Architecture
M	Master's
MA	Master of Arts
MS	Master of Science
MBA	Master of Business Administration
MFA	Master of Fine Arts
MEd	Master of Education
MSW	Master of Social Work
D	Doctoral
EdD	Doctor of Education
PhD	Doctor of Philosophy

The professional degrees and their abbreviations are:

DC	Chiropractic
DDS or DMD	Dentistry
JD	Law
MD	Medicine
OD	Optometry
DO	Osteopathic medicine
BPharm, PharmD	Pharmacy
DPM	Podiatry
BDiv, MDiv, Rab, Talm	Theological professions
DVM	Veterinary medicine

Majors

Undergraduate majors offered by the college are listed alphabetically in this section. Colleges reported their major programs by checking a standard list based on the 1985 Classification of Instructional Programs (CIP) taxonomy of the U.S. Department of Education. However, colleges could and often did add the names of other majors that they felt did not conform closely enough to any title on the list. These additional fields of study are also listed. In the following section of this introduction, "Major fields of study by discipline," specific majors are grouped into general categories corresponding to the CIP taxonomy. If you know the broad discipline in which you are interested but seek information about what specific majors are offered within the discipline, you should look here.

Academic programs

Many colleges offer special programs that provide enhanced opportunities for advanced study, offer education through travel or other unusual experiences, or offer special programs that can lead to a degree in less than the traditional number of years.

A college may indicate that it offers special academic programs, such as accelerated program, cooperative education, double major, honors program, independent study, internships, external degree, exchange student program, study abroad, teacher preparation, liberal arts/career combination, cross-registration, weekend college, New York semester, Washington semester, United Nations semester, semester at sea, combined bachelor's/graduate degree programs, as well as other special programs. Some colleges that award associate degrees offer transfer programs for students who plan to continue their studies at a four-year institution. See the Glossary for brief descriptions of many of these academic programs.

Remedial services. Services are available at many colleges to help you improve or enhance your basic academic skills and provide you with remedial instruction, counseling, and support services. These include: special counselors, learning centers, preadmission summer programs, tutoring, remedial instruction, and reduced course load.

ROTC. Air Force, Army, or Naval ROTC can prepare you for service as an officer in the armed forces after graduation. These programs can also provide financial aid toward your educational expenses in exchange for longer periods of military service.

Placement/credit examinations. Receiving college credit for what you already know, or being placed in an advanced-level course, can save you time and money in earning a college degree. College policies covering some commonly used tests are listed here, including the maximum number of credit hours through examination that may be counted toward a degree. More information about the Advanced Placement (AP) Program, the International Baccalaureate (IB), and the College-Level Examination Program (CLEP) is given in the Glossary.

Academic requirements

At many colleges, freshmen must meet certain academic requirements to continue in good academic standing. Those requirements are given here.

Graduation requirements. The number of credit hours required for the associate and bachelor's degrees is given here, as well as the number of credit hours of study that you will be required to complete in your major field of study. Colleges may also indicate at what point students must declare their majors. Most colleges permit students to change their majors, however, without affecting the graduation date—as long as requirements have been met for the new major.

Many colleges require that all or most students complete some form of general education requirement. Areas of study that are required of all or most students are listed here.

Postgraduate studies. The percentage of students who continue their education within one year of completing their undergraduate degrees is listed.

Admissions

Selection criteria. Admissions criteria used by the college in its selection process are listed here. Some colleges indicate which criteria are most important, or even the level of grade-point average or test score considered acceptable. SAT-V is used within the descriptions for SAT-verbal score and SAT-M is used for SAT-mathematical score. Special consideration given to particular groups of applicants is also listed if applicable. Colleges may also indicate whether applicants to specific programs have to meet special requirements.

High school preparation. Almost all colleges listed in the *Handbook* require a high school diploma or its equivalent. Some colleges have very specific requirements in terms of educational background and high school courses taken. The required and recommended number of course units that applicants should have taken in high school is listed here. Where a range is given, the lower number represents the required units; the higher number is a recommendation.

Test requirements. Look here to see the national standardized admissions tests (SAT, ACT, PAA, or ACH—see the Glossary for definitions) that a college requires of its applicants. At many colleges, your test scores will be used for counseling and placement purposes as well as in the admissions process. In some cases the tests required are used for counseling or placement only.

If you do not meet all the requirements of a college in which you are interested, do not assume that the college will not accept you. Write to the college about your strengths as well as those areas where you may not meet published requirements, giving evidence of any other qualifications that you can offer.

In 1993-94 a new SAT will first be administered. See "The New SAT and PSAT/NMSQT" for information on how this may affect you.

1992 Freshman class profile

To help you measure the chances that you or any other applicant will be admitted to a college, institutions were asked to report the number of students who applied, were accepted, and enrolled in their fall 1992 freshman class.

Academic background. Colleges were asked to provide the percentages of freshmen with grade-point averages above 3.0 and between 2.0 and 2.99. Some colleges also indicate what percentage of the freshmen were in the top tenth or top quarter of their graduating class. They may also give the SAT and ACT score ranges of the middle 50 percent of enrolled freshmen along with the percentages of freshmen who submitted SAT and ACT scores. This information will give you an indication of how you might fit into a college's student body.

Characteristics. Information provided here includes percentages of freshmen who are state residents, who live in college housing, who commute from home or private housing, who have minority backgrounds (American Indian, Asian American, black, Mexican American, Puerto Rican), who are foreign students studying on student visas, and who join fraternities or sororities. The average age of entering freshmen is also included.

Fall-term applications

Pay careful attention to any application deadline or priority date listed by a college. The date on which colleges begin notifying applicants of their admissions decisions can also be important in your college planning. Information about required or recommended interviews, portfolios, auditions, and essays is also included here. Special admissions policies and procedures, such as the Early Decision Plan (EDP), Candidates Reply Date Agreement (CRDA), deferred admission, and early admission, are listed here and described in the Glossary.

Student life

Housing. The availability of college-affiliated housing and the types of accommodation offered are indicated if applicable. These include dormitories for men and women, apartments, fraternity and sorority housing, and cooperative housing.

Activities. A broad range of activities available through each college is listed, including: student government, newspaper, yearbook, radio station, drama groups, choral groups, dance, orchestra, band, political groups, religious organizations, fraternities, and sororities.

Athletics

The intercollegiate and intramural sports that are sponsored by each college are listed here. Whether a sport is offered for men (M) or women (W) only is indicated. (If an M or W does not appear after the sport, it is available to both men and women.) The sports that colleges were asked about are: archery, badminton, baseball, basketball, bowling, boxing, cross-country, diving, fencing, field hockey, football, golf, gymnastics, handball, horseback riding, ice hockey, lacrosse, racquetball, rifle, rowing (crew), rugby, sailing, skiing, skin diving, soccer, softball, squash, swimming, table tennis, tennis, track and field, volleyball, water polo, and wrestling. Some colleges list club sports, too.

The college's membership in an athletic association is listed here as well. Consult the college catalog to check on the availability of additional sports and the most current listing of all athletics.

If you are interested in NCAA division offerings, consult the index of NCAA sports in the College Indexes section; it shows the division level of play a college offers in a sport-by-sport index.

Student services

Most colleges offer some counseling, health, or advising services to their students. Colleges were asked to indicate whether they offer any of the following services: personal counseling, career counseling, aptitude testing, health services, employment service for undergraduates, placement service for graduates, special advisers for adults or veterans, on-campus day care, veterans counselor, and services or facilities for handicapped students.

Annual expenses

Tuition and fees. Unless otherwise noted, costs are for the 1993-94 academic year and are based on full-time enrollment (approximately 30 semester hours or 45 quarter hours). When tuition and fees are higher for out-of-state or out-of-district students, the *additional* amount is also reported. If 1993-94 tuition and fees were not available by time of publication, but the college could provide a reliable forecast of 1993-94 expenses, these projected costs are indicated. When no 1993-94 figures were available, the 1992-93 tuition and fees supplied by the college are indicated. If the college combines tuition, fees, and room and board expenses, the single figure is called a comprehensive fee.

Room and board. The costs are for the 1993-94 academic year and represent the cost for a full-time dependent student living in a double room in college housing with the meal plan offering the maximum number of meals. If single rooms or rooms for three or more students are available, and you are interested in these living arrangements, your cost could be substantially more or less than the figure reported here. Also, colleges often offer meal plans for fewer meals per week, and this, too, may change the amount you spend for your meals.

Books and supplies. These estimated costs may vary considerably depending on the specific program in which you enroll. Some fields, such as art or architecture, may require more expensive supplies than average. Some colleges offer a book rental program, which can cut your costs.

Other expenses. The estimated miscellaneous expenses for full-time dependent students living in college-affiliated housing include items such as clothing, laundry, entertainment, medical insurance (if not a required fee), and furnishings. Transportation costs are not included. If a college has no housing, the estimated miscellaneous expenses for commuters are given.

Financial aid

The percentage of freshmen and continuing students who received some form of financial aid during academic year 1992-93 is listed.

The percentages of need-based financial aid dollars distributed by an institution in the form of grants, loans, and jobs are given. Colleges were asked to include all undergraduate aid that is college-funded, as well as certain federal programs for which colleges determine the recipients according to federal guidelines, or that are processed by the institution. (See the Glossary for brief descriptions of some of these programs—Federal Work-Study Program, Federal Pell Grant, Federal Stafford Loan, and Federal Perkins Loan.) For additional information on financial aid, see "Paying for college."

To help you measure your chances of receiving aid from a college, institutions were asked to report the number of enrolled freshmen who were judged to have need and the number of those who were offered aid. Remember that many of the students awarded aid do not receive the full amount of their need.

Some colleges offer scholarships based solely on criteria other than need. Colleges indicated whether scholarships are available based on: academics; music/drama, art, athletic abilities; state residency; leadership; alumni affiliation; job skills; religious affiliation; and minority status.

Financial aid applications. Priority dates, closing dates, notification dates, and reply dates are listed here for fall term financial aid applications. All colleges that offer Federal financial aid require applicants or their parents to fill out the FAFSA; some colleges may require additional forms as well. (See "Need analysis form" in the Glossary for further information about these forms.) Remember that some colleges also require students to complete a separate institutional need analysis document. Ask the colleges you apply to which forms you should file and verify the deadlines for applying for aid.

Address/telephone

The last item in each description lists the mailing address and telephone number of the college office you should contact for further information and applications. Toll-free numbers for those calling from outside the state and fax numbers are also indicated.

Major fields of study by discipline

Agribusiness and agricultural production

Agribusiness
Agricultural business and management
Agricultural economics
Agricultural mechanics
Agricultural production
Agricultural products and processing
Equestrian science
Horticulture
International agriculture

Agricultural sciences

Agricultural sciences
Agronomy
Animal sciences
Dairy
Food sciences
Horticultural science
Ornamental horticulture
Plant protection (pest management)
Soil sciences

Allied health services

Allied health
Community health work
Dental laboratory technology
Geriatric aide
Medical assistant
Medical illustrating
Medical records technology
Mental health/human services
Ophthalmic services
Physician's assistant
Practical nursing
Rehabilitation counseling/services
Veterinarian's assistant

Architecture

Architecture

Area studies

African studies
American studies
Asian studies
Canadian studies
Caribbean studies
East Asian studies
Eastern European studies
European studies
Latin American studies
Middle Eastern studies
Pacific area studies
Russian and Slavic studies
Scandinavian studies
South Asian studies
Southeast Asian studies
Western European studies

Biology

Biochemistry
Biology
Biophysics
Biotechnology
Cell biology
Microbiology
Molecular biology

Botany

Bacteriology
Botany
Mycology
Plant genetics
Plant pharmacology
Plant physiology

Business and management

Accounting
Aviation management
Business administration and management
Business economics
Business and management
Business statistics
Contract management and procurement/purchasing
Engineering management
Finance
Food management
Hotel/motel and restaurant management
Human resources development
Institutional management
Insurance and risk management
International business management
Investments and securities
Labor/industrial relations
Management information systems
Management science
Marketing management
Marketing research
Music business management
Operations research (quantitative methods)
Organizational behavior
Personnel management
Real estate
Small business management and ownership
Sports management
Taxation
Trade and industrial supervision and management
Transportation management

Business and office

Business computer, console, and peripheral equipment operation

Business data entry equipment operation

Business data processing and related programs
Business data programming
Business and office
Business systems analysis
Court reporting
Legal secretary
Medical secretary
Office supervision and management
Secretarial and related programs
Word processing

Chemistry

Analytical chemistry
Chemistry
Inorganic chemistry
Organic chemistry
Pharmaceutical chemistry
Physical chemistry

Civil technologies

Civil technology
Drafting and design technology
Survey and mapping technology
Urban planning technology

Communications

Advertising
Communications
Communications research
Journalism (mass communication)
Public relations
Radio/television (includes news broadcast)
Telecommunications

Communication technologies

Educational media technology
Interpreter for the deaf
Motion picture technology
Photographic technology
Radio/television technology

Computer and information sciences

Computer graphics
Computer and information sciences
Computer mathematics
Computer programming
Data processing
Information sciences and systems
Microcomputer software
Robotics
Systems analysis

Construction trades

Carpentry
Construction
Electrical installation
Masonry, tile setting
Plumbing/pipefitting/steamfitting

Crafts and design

Ceramics
Crafts
Enameling
Fiber/textiles/weaving
Glass
Graphic arts technology
Graphic design
Illustration design
Industrial design
Metal/jewelry
Printmaking
Theater design

Diagnostic and treatment services

Electrodiagnostic technologies
Emergency medical technologies (including ambulance and paramedic)
Medical radiation dosimetry
Nuclear medical technology
Radiograph medical technology
Respiratory therapy technology
Surgical technology
Ultrasound therapy

Education administration

Administration of special education

Adult and continuing education administration
Community college education administration
Education administration
Educational supervision
Higher education administration

Education, general

Adult and continuing education research
Curriculum and instruction
Education
Educational statistics and research
Educational testing/evaluation/measurement
Higher education research
International and comparative education
School psychology
Social foundations
Student counseling and personnel services

Engineering

Aerospace, aeronautical, and astronautical engineering
Agricultural engineering
Architectural engineering
Bioengineering and biomedical engineering
Ceramic engineering
Chemical engineering
Civil engineering
Computer engineering
Electrical, electronics, and communications engineering
Engineering
Engineering mechanics
Engineering physics
Engineering science
Environmental health engineering
Geological engineering
Geophysical engineering
Industrial engineering
Materials engineering
Mechanical engineering
Metallurgical engineering
Mining and mineral engineering
Naval architecture and marine engineering
Nuclear engineering
Ocean engineering
Paper engineering
Petroleum engineering
Preengineering
Surveying and mapping sciences
Systems engineering
Textile engineering

Engineering technologies

Architectural technologies
Computer technology
Electrical technology
Electronic technology
Engineering and engineering related technologies
Laser electro-optic technology
Mining and petroleum technologies
Occupational safety and health technology
Quality control technology

Environmental control technologies

Air conditioning/heating/refrigeration technology
Air pollution control technology
Energy conservation and use technology
Sanitation technology
Solar heating and cooling technology
Water and wastewater technology

Environmental design

City/community/regional planning
Environmental design
Historic preservation
Interior design
Landscape architecture
Urban design

Ethnic studies

Afro-American (black) studies
American Indian studies
Hispanic American studies
Islamic studies
Jewish studies
Mexican American studies

Fine arts

Art conservation
Art history
Arts management
Drawing
Fine arts
Painting
Sculpture
Studio art

Geological sciences

Geochemistry
Geology
Geophysics and seismology
Paleontology

Health science

Basic clinical health sciences
Chiropractic (includes all work except D.C. or D.C.M. degree)
Clinical laboratory science
Dental specialties (includes work beyond first professional degree only)
Emergency/disaster science
Gerontology
Health care administration
Health sciences
Medical records administration
Medical specialties (includes work beyond first professional degree only)
Nurse anesthetist
Nursing
Optometry (includes all work except O.D. degree)
Pharmacy (includes all work except Pharm. D. degree)
Population and family planning
Predentistry
Premedicine
Prepharmacy
Preveterinary
Public health laboratory science (includes epidemiology)
Speech pathology/audiology
Sports medicine

Home economics

Business home economics
Family and community services
Family/consumer resource management
Fashion design
Food science and nutrition
Geriatric services
Home economics
Human environment and housing
Individual and family development
International/comparative home economics
Marriage and family counseling
Textiles and clothing

Industrial production

Chemical manufacturing technology
Industrial technology
Manufacturing technology
Optical technology
Plastic technology
Textile technology
Welding technology

Languages

African languages (non-Semitic)
Arabic
Chinese
Foreign languages (multiple emphasis)
French
German
Greek (classical)
Greek (modern)
Hebrew
Indic languages (including Hindi and Sanskrit)
Iranian languages
Italian
Japanese
Korean
Latin
Native American languages
Portuguese
Russian
Scandinavian languages
Slavic languages (other than Russian)
Spanish
Yiddish

Law

Law (includes all work except J.D. degree)
Legal assistant/paralegal
Prelaw

Letters/literature

American literature
Classics
Comparative literature
Creative writing
English
English literature
Folklore and mythology
Language interpretation and translation
Linguistics (includes phonetics, semantics, and philology)
Medieval studies
Rhetoric
Speech, debate, and forensics
Technical and business writing

Library and archival sciences

Archival science

Library assistant

Library science
Museum studies

Life sciences, specialized areas

Anatomy
Biomedical science
Biometrics and biostatistics
Ecology
Embryology
Environmental science

Histology
Marine biology
Neurosciences
Nutritional sciences
Parasitology
Radiobiology
Toxicology

Marketing and distribution

Apparel and accessories marketing
Fashion merchandising
Hospitality and recreation marketing
Insurance marketing
Marketing and distribution
Personal services
Retailing
Tourism
Transportation and travel marketing

Mathematics

Actuarial sciences
Applied mathematics
Mathematics
Pure mathematics
Statistics

Mechanical and electromechanical technologies

Aeronautical technology
Automotive technology
Biomedical equipment technology
Computer servicing technology
Electromechanical technology
Instrumentation technology
Mechanical design technology

Mechanics and repairers

Air conditioning/heating/refrigeration mechanics
Aircraft mechanics
Automotive mechanics
Diesel engine mechanics
Electrical and electronics equipment repair
Industrial equipment maintenance and repair
Power plant operation and maintenance (stationary energy sources)

Medical laboratory technologies

Cytotechnology
Medical laboratory science

Military sciences

Aerospace science (Air Force)
Coast Guard science
Merchant Marine
Military science (Army)
Naval science (Navy, Marines)

Multi/interdisciplinary studies

Biological and physical sciences
Clinical pastoral care
Engineering and other disciplines
Humanities
Humanities and social sciences
International studies
Liberal/general studies
Peace studies
Women's studies

Music

Music
Music history and appreciation
Music performance
Music theory and composition

Parks and recreation

Parks and recreation management
Recreation and community services technologies
Water resources

Philosophy

Philosophy

Physical sciences

Astronomy
Astrophysics
Atmospheric sciences and meteorology
Earth sciences
Metallurgy
Oceanography
Physical sciences
Planetary science

Physics

Atomic/molecular physics
Electron physics
Elementary particle physics
Fluids and plasmas
Nuclear physics
Optics
Physics
Solid state physics

Precision production

Commercial art
Drafting
Graphic and printing production
Machine tool operation/machine shop
Precision metal work
Woodworking

Protective services

Criminal justice studies
Criminal justice technology
Fire control and safety technology (includes firefighting)
Fire protection
Forensic studies
Law enforcement and corrections
Law enforcement and corrections technologies
Protective services

Psychology

Clinical psychology
Cognitive psychology
Community psychology
Comparative psychology
Counseling psychology
Developmental psychology
Experimental psychology
Industrial and organizational psychology
Personality psychology
Psychology
Physiological psychology
Psycholinguistics
Psychometrics
Quantitative psychology
Social psychology

Public affairs

Community services
Funeral services/mortuary science
International public service
Medical social work
Public administration
Public affairs
Public policy studies
Public utilities
Social work

Rehabilitation services

Art therapy
Dance therapy
Music therapy
Occupational therapy
Occupational therapy assistant
Physical therapy
Physical therapy assistant
Recreation therapy
Respiratory therapy

Religion

Religion

Renewable natural resources

Conservation and regulation
Fishing and fisheries
Forest products processing technology
Forestry and related sciences
Forestry production and processing
Renewable natural resources
Wildlife management

Science technologies
Biological laboratory technology
Nuclear technologies
Oceanographic technologies
Science technologies

Social sciences

Anthropology
Archaeology
Behavioral sciences
Criminology
Demography
Economics
Geography
History
International development
International relations
Political science and government
Rural sociology
Social sciences
Sociology
Urban studies

Special education

Bilingual/bicultural education
Education of the culturally disadvantaged
Education of the deaf and hearing impaired
Education of the emotionally handicapped
Education of exceptional children, not otherwise classified
Education of the gifted and talented
Education of the mentally handicapped
Education of the physically handicapped
Education of the visually handicapped
Remedial education
Special education
Specific learning disabilities
Speech correction
Teaching English as a second language/foreign language

Teacher education, general

Early childhood education
Elementary education
Junior high education
Secondary education
Teacher's aide

Teacher education, specific subjects

Agricultural education
Art education

Business education
Driver and safety education
English education
Foreign languages education
Health education
Home economics education
Industrial arts education
Marketing and distributive education
Mathematics education
Music education
Nursing education
Nutritional education
Physical education
Reading education
Science education
Social science education
Social studies education
Speech/communication/theater education
Technical education
Trade and industrial education

Theology

Bible studies
Biblical languages
Missionary studies
Religious education
Religious music
Theological studies

Transportation

Airline piloting and navigation
Air traffic control
Aviation computer technology
Flight attendant
Marine maintenance
Vehicle and equipment operation

Visual and performing arts

Cinematography/film
Dance
Dramatic arts
Film animation
Film arts
Jazz
Musical theater
Photography
Video
Visual and performing arts

Vocational home economics

Child development, care, and guidance
Clothing and textiles management, production, and services
Dietetic aid/assistant
Food production, management, and services
Home furnishings and equipment management, production, and services
Institutional/home management, and supporting programs

Zoology

Entomology
Genetics, human and animal
Pathology, human and animal
Pharmacology, human and animal
Physiology, human and animal
Zoology

First professional degrees

Chiropractic (D.C. degree)
Dentistry (D.D.S. or D.M.D. degrees)
Law (J.D. degree)
Medicine (M.D. degree)
Optometry (O.D. degree)
Osteopathic medicine (D.O. degree)
Pharmacy (Pharm. D. degree)
Podiatry (D.P.M. degree, includes chiropody)
Theological professions (B. Div., M. Div., Rabbinical, or Talmudical)
Veterinary medicine (D.V.M. degree)

College indexes

The College ABC's

Admissions	Percentage of applicants accepted
Based on:	••• Most important selection criteria
	•• Important selection criteria
	• Considered selection criteria
Completion:	Percentage of freshmen ending year in good standing
	Percentage who graduate; percentage who enter graduate programs

Abbreviations used in the college descriptions

CB . . . . College Board code
ACH . . . . Achievement Tests
ACT . . . . American College Testing Program
AP . . . . Advanced Placement
CLEP . . . . College-Level Examination Program
CRDA . . . . Candidates Reply Date Agreement
EDP-F . . . . Early Decision Plan-first choice
EDP-S . . . . Early Decision Plan-single choice
FAFSA . . . . Free Application for Federal Student Aid
IB . . . . International Baccalaureate
ROTC . . . . Reserve Officers' Training Corps
SAT . . . . Scholastic Assessment Tests (previously, Scholastic Aptitude Test)
[oak leaf symbol] . . . . College Board membership

National accrediting associations

AABC . . . . American Association of Bible Colleges
AARTS. . . . . Association of Advanced Rabbinical and Talmudic Schools
ATS . . . . Association of Theological Schools in the United States and Canada
CCA. . . . . Career College Association
NHSC. . . . . National Home Study Council

Collegiate athletic associations

NAIA . . . . National Association of Intercollegiate Athletics
NCAA . . . . National Collegiate Athletic Association
NCCAA . . . . National Christian College Athletic Association
NJCAA. . . . . National Junior College Athletic Association
NSCAA . . . . National Small College Athletic Association

General colleges

4-year liberal arts colleges

Alabama
Athens State College
Birmingham-Southern College
Faulkner University
Huntingdon College
Judson College
Miles College
Oakwood College
Spring Hill College
Stillman College
Talladega College
University of Mobile
University of Montevallo

Alaska
Sheldon Jackson College

Arizona
Grand Canyon University
Prescott College
Western International University

Arkansas
Arkansas Baptist College
Arkansas College
Hendrix College
John Brown University
Philander Smith College
Williams Baptist College

California
American Armenian International College
Antioch Southern California at Los Angeles
California Baptist College
California State University
San Bernardino
Stanislaus
Chapman University
Christian Heritage College
Claremont McKenna College
College of Notre Dame
Concordia University
Dominican College of San Rafael
Fresno Pacific College
Holy Names College
John F. Kennedy University
Lincoln University
Master's College
Menlo College
Mills College
Monterey Institute of International Studies
Mount St. Mary's College
New College of California
Occidental College
Pacific Union College
Pitzer College
Point Loma Nazarene College
Pomona College
St. Mary's College of California
San Jose State University
Scripps College
Simpson College
Southern California College
Thomas Aquinas College
University of Judaism
University of La Verne
University of Redlands
Westmont College
Whittier College

Colorado
Adams State College
Colorado Christian University
Colorado College
Fort Lewis College
Naropa Institute
Regis University
Western State College of Colorado

Connecticut
Albertus Magnus College
Connecticut College
St. Joseph College
Trinity College
Wesleyan University

Delaware
Delaware State College
Wesley College
Wilmington College

District of Columbia
Mount Vernon College
Trinity College

Florida
Bethune-Cookman College
Clearwater Christian College
Eckerd College
Edward Waters College
Flagler College
Florida Memorial College
Florida Southern College
Lynn University
New College of the University of South Florida
Palm Beach Atlantic College
Rollins College
St. Leo College
Trinity College at Miami
University of Tampa
Warner Southern College

Georgia
Agnes Scott College
Albany State College
Armstrong State College
Augusta College
Brewton-Parker College
Clayton State College
Columbus College
Covenant College
Emmanuel College
Fort Valley State College
Georgia Southern University
Georgia Southwestern College
LaGrange College
Morehouse College
Morris Brown College
North Georgia College
Oglethorpe University
Paine College
Piedmont College
Savannah State College
Shorter College
Spelman College
Thomas College
Toccoa Falls College
Valdosta State College
Wesleyan College
West Georgia College

Hawaii
Brigham Young University-Hawaii
Hawaii Pacific University
University of Hawaii: West Oahu

Idaho
Albertson College
Lewis Clark State College
Northwest Nazarene College

Illinois
Augustana College
Barat College
Blackburn College
College of St. Francis
Columbia College
Concordia University
Elmhurst College
Eureka College
Greenville College
Illinois Benedictine College
Illinois College
Judson College
Kendall College
Knox College
Lake Forest College
MacMurray College
McKendree College
Monmouth College
North Central College
North Park College
Olivet Nazarene University
Principia College
Rockford College
Rosary College
Shimer College
Trinity Christian College
Trinity College
University of Chicago
Wheaton College

Indiana
Anderson University
Bethel College
Calumet College of St. Joseph
Earlham College
Franklin College
Goshen College
Grace College
Hanover College
Huntington College
Indiana University East
Indiana Wesleyan University
Manchester College
Marian College
Oakland City College
St. Francis College
St. Joseph's College
St. Mary-of-the-Woods College
St. Mary's College
St. Meinrad College
Taylor University
University of Southern Indiana
Wabash College

Iowa
Briar Cliff College
Buena Vista College
Central College
Clarke College
Coe College
Cornell College
Divine Word College
Dordt College
Graceland College
Grand View College
Grinnell College
Iowa Wesleyan College
Loras College
Luther College
Morningside College
Mount Mercy College
Mount St. Clare College
Northwestern College
St. Ambrose University
Simpson College
Teikyo Westmar University
University of Dubuque
Upper Iowa University
Wartburg College
William Penn College

Kansas
Baker University
Benedictine College
Bethany College
Bethel College
Friends University
Kansas Newman College
Kansas Wesleyan University
McPherson College
MidAmerica Nazarene College
Ottawa University
St. Mary College
Southwestern College
Sterling College
Tabor College
Wichita State University

Kentucky
Alice Lloyd College
Asbury College
Bellarmine College
Berea College
Brescia College
Campbellsville College
Centre College
Cumberland College
Georgetown College
Kentucky Wesleyan College
Lindsey Wilson College
Midway College
Pikeville College
Thomas More College
Transylvania University
Union College

Louisiana
Centenary College of Louisiana
Dillard University
Louisiana College
Loyola University
Our Lady of Holy Cross College
St. Joseph Seminary College

Maine
Bates College
Bowdoin College
Colby College
St. Joseph's College
Unity College
University of Maine at Farmington
University of New England
Westbrook College

Maryland
College of Notre Dame of Maryland
Columbia Union College
Coppin State College

Frostburg State University
Goucher College
Hood College
Loyola College in Maryland
Morgan State University
Mount St. Mary's College
St. John's College
St. Mary's College of Maryland
Salisbury State University
Sojourner-Douglass College
Villa Julie College
Washington College
Western Maryland College

Massachusetts

American International College
Amherst College
Anna Maria College for Men and Women
Assumption College
Atlantic Union College
Bradford College
Bridgewater State College
College of the Holy Cross
Curry College
Eastern Nazarene College
Elms College
Emmanuel College
Fitchburg State College
Framingham State College
Gordon College
Hampshire College
Harvard and Radcliffe Colleges
Hebrew College
Hellenic College
Lasell College
Merrimack College
Mount Holyoke College
Mount Ida College
Nichols College
North Adams State College
Pine Manor College
Regis College
St. Hyacinth College and Seminary
St. John's Seminary College
Simmons College
Simon's Rock College of Bard
Smith College
Springfield College
Stonehill College
Wellesley College
Western New England College
Westfield State College
Wheaton College
Wheelock College
Williams College
Worcester Polytechnic Institute
Worcester State College

Michigan

Adrian College
Albion College
Alma College
Aquinas College
Calvin College
Concordia College
Ferris State University
Grand Rapids Baptist College and Seminary
Hillsdale College
Hope College
Kalamazoo College
Kendall College of Art and Design
Madonna University
Marygrove College
Michigan Christian College
Olivet College
Saginaw Valley State University
St. Mary's College
Siena Heights College
Spring Arbor College
William Tyndale College

Minnesota

Augsburg College
Carleton College
College of St. Benedict
College of St. Catherine: St. Catherine Campus
College of St. Scholastica
Concordia College: Moorhead
Concordia College: St. Paul
Gustavus Adolphus College
Macalester College
North Central Bible College
Northwestern College
St. John's University
St. Mary's College of Minnesota
St. Olaf College
Southwest State University
University of Minnesota: Morris
University of St. Thomas
Winona State University

Mississippi

Belhaven College
Millsaps College
Mississippi College
Rust College
Tougaloo College
William Carey College

Missouri

Avila College
Central Methodist College
College of the Ozarks
Culver-Stockton College
Drury College
Evangel College
Fontbonne College
Hannibal-LaGrange College
Lincoln University
Lindenwood College
Maryville University
Missouri Baptist College
Missouri Valley College
Missouri Western State College
Park College
Rockhurst College
Southwest Baptist University
Stephens College
Westminster College
William Jewell College
William Woods College

Montana

Carroll College
College of Great Falls
Eastern Montana College
Northern Montana College
Rocky Mountain College

Nebraska

Bellevue College
Chadron State College
College of St. Mary
Concordia College
Dana College
Doane College
Midland Lutheran College
Nebraska Wesleyan University
Peru State College
Union College
Wayne State College

Nevada

Sierra Nevada College

New Hampshire

Colby-Sawyer College
Dartmouth College
Franklin Pierce College
Keene State College
New England College
New Hampshire College
Notre Dame College
Plymouth State College of the University System of New Hampshire
Rivier College
St. Anselm College
University of New Hampshire at Manchester

New Jersey

Bloomfield College
Caldwell College
Centenary College
College of St. Elizabeth
Felician College
Georgian Court College
Jersey City State College
Kean College of New Jersey
Ramapo College of New Jersey
Rider College
Rowan College of New Jersey
Rutgers—The State University of New Jersey
- Camden College of Arts and Sciences
- Douglass College
- Livingston College
- Newark College of Arts and Sciences
- Rutgers College
- University College Camden
- University College New Brunswick
- University College Newark

St. Peter's College
Stockton State College
Thomas Edison State College
Trenton State College
Upsala College
William Paterson College of New Jersey

New Mexico

College of Santa Fe
College of the Southwest
St. John's College

New York

Bard College
Barnard College
Boricua College
Canisius College
City University of New York
- Baruch College
- Brooklyn College
- College of Staten Island
- Hunter College
- John Jay College of Criminal Justice
- Lehman College
- Medgar Evers College
- Queens College
- York College

Colgate University
College of Mount St. Vincent
College of New Rochelle
- New Rochelle
- School of New Resources

College of St. Rose
Columbia University
- Columbia College
- School of General Studies

Concordia College
Daemen College
Dominican College of Blauvelt
Dowling College
D'Youville College
Elmira College
Eugene Lang College/New School for Social Research
Five Towns College
Hamilton College
Hartwick College
Hilbert College
Hobart College
Houghton College
Iona College
Ithaca College
Keuka College
King's College
Le Moyne College
Long Island University: Southampton Campus
Manhattan College
Manhattanville College
Marymount College
Marymount Manhattan College
Medaille College
Mercy College
Molloy College
Mount St. Mary College
Nazareth College of Rochester
New York Institute of Technology
Nyack College
Roberts Wesleyan College
Russell Sage College
St. Francis College
St. John Fisher College
St. Joseph's College
- Brooklyn
- Suffolk Campus

St. Lawrence University
St. Thomas Aquinas College
Sarah Lawrence College
Siena College
Skidmore College
State University of New York
- Purchase
- College at Brockport
- College at Buffalo
- College at Cortland
- College at Fredonia
- College at Geneseo
- College at New Paltz
- College at Old Westbury
- College at Oneonta
- College at Plattsburgh
- College at Potsdam
- Empire State College
- Oswego

Touro College
Union College
United States Military Academy
University of the State of New York: Regents College
Utica College of Syracuse University
Vassar College
Wadhams Hall Seminary-College
Wagner College
Wells College
William Smith College

North Carolina

Barber-Scotia College
Barton College
Belmont Abbey College
Bennett College
Catawba College
Chowan College
Davidson College
Elizabeth City State University
Elon College
Gardner-Webb University
Greensboro College
Guilford College
High Point University
Johnson C. Smith University
Lees-McRae College
Lenoir-Rhyne College
Livingstone College
Mars Hill College
Meredith College
Methodist College
Montreat-Anderson College
Mount Olive College
North Carolina Agricultural and Technical State University
North Carolina Wesleyan College

Pembroke State University
Pfeiffer College
Queens College
St. Andrews Presbyterian College
St. Augustine's College
Salem College
Shaw University
University of North Carolina at Asheville
Warren Wilson College
Wingate College

North Dakota

Jamestown College
Mayville State University
Minot State University
University of Mary

Ohio

Antioch College
Antioch School for Adult and Experiential Learning
Baldwin-Wallace College
Bluffton College
Capital University
Cedarville College
Central State University
Cleveland College of Jewish Studies
College of Mount St. Joseph
College of Wooster
Defiance College
Denison University
Heidelberg College
Hiram College
Kenyon College
Lake Erie College
Lourdes College
Malone College
Marietta College
Mount Union College
Muskingum College
Notre Dame College of Ohio
Oberlin College
Ohio Dominican College
Ohio Wesleyan University
Otterbein College
Pontifical College Josephinum
University of Rio Grande
Urbana University
Ursuline College
Wilberforce University
Wilmington College
Wittenberg University

Oklahoma

Bartlesville Wesleyan College
Cameron University
Langston University
Oklahoma Baptist University
Oklahoma Christian University of Science and Arts
Oklahoma Panhandle State University
Oral Roberts University
Phillips University
Southern Nazarene University
University of Science and Arts of Oklahoma

Oregon

Concordia College
Eastern Oregon State College
George Fox College
Lewis and Clark College
Linfield College
Marylhurst College
Northwest Christian College
Reed College
Southern Oregon State College
Warner Pacific College
Western Baptist College
Western Oregon State College
Willamette University

Pennsylvania

Academy of the New Church
Albright College
Allegheny College
Allentown College of St. Francis de Sales
Alvernia College
Beaver College
Bryn Mawr College
Cabrini College
Carlow College
Cedar Crest College
Chatham College
Chestnut Hill College
Cheyney University of Pennsylvania
College Misericordia
Dickinson College
Eastern College
Elizabethtown College
Franklin and Marshall College
Gannon University
Geneva College
Gettysburg College
Gratz College
Grove City College
Gwynedd-Mercy College
Haverford College
Holy Family College
Immaculata College
Juniata College
King's College
La Roche College
La Salle University
Lafayette College
Lebanon Valley College of Pennsylvania
Lincoln University
Lycoming College
Marywood College
Mercyhurst College
Messiah College
Moravian College
Muhlenberg College
Neumann College
Rosemont College
St. Francis College
St. Vincent College
Seton Hill College
Shippensburg University of Pennsylvania
Swarthmore College
Thiel College
University of Pittsburgh
  Bradford
  Johnstown
Ursinus College
Washington and Jefferson College
Waynesburg College
Westminster College
Wilson College
York College of Pennsylvania

Puerto Rico

Caribbean University
Colegio Universitario del Este
Inter American University of Puerto Rico
  Aguadilla Campus
  Arecibo Campus
Universidad Adventista de las Antillas
Universidad Metropolitana
University of Puerto Rico: Cayey University College

Rhode Island

Providence College
Salve Regina University

South Carolina

Allen University
Anderson College
Benedict College
Central Wesleyan College
Charleston Southern University
The Citadel
Claflin College
Coker College
College of Charleston
Columbia College
Converse College
Erskine College
Francis Marion University
Furman University
Lander University
Limestone College
Morris College
Newberry College
Presbyterian College
South Carolina State University
University of South Carolina
  Aiken
  Coastal Carolina College
Voorhees College
Wofford College

South Dakota

Augustana College
Black Hills State University
Dakota Wesleyan University
Huron University
Mount Marty College
Northern State University
Oglala Lakota College
Sinte Gleska University
Sioux Falls College

Tennessee

Bethel College
Carson-Newman College
Christian Brothers University
Crichton College
Cumberland University
David Lipscomb University
Fisk University
Freed-Hardeman University
King College
Knoxville College
Lambuth University
Lane College
Lee College
LeMoyne-Owen College
Lincoln Memorial University
Maryville College
Milligan College
Rhodes College
Southern College of Seventh-day Adventists
Tennessee Temple University
Tennessee Wesleyan College
Trevecca Nazarene College
Tusculum College
Union University
William Jennings Bryan College

Texas

Abilene Christian University
Austin College
Concordia Lutheran College
East Texas Baptist University
Houston Baptist University
Howard Payne University
Huston-Tillotson College
Incarnate Word College
Jarvis Christian College
Lubbock Christian University
McMurry University
Midwestern State University
Paul Quinn College
St. Edward's University
Schreiner College
Southwestern Adventist College
Southwestern Christian College
Southwestern University
Texas College
Texas Lutheran College
Trinity University
University of Dallas
University of Texas: Pan American
Wayland Baptist University
Wiley College

Utah

Westminster College of Salt Lake City

Vermont

Bennington College
Burlington College
Castleton State College
College of St. Joseph in Vermont
Goddard College
Green Mountain College
Johnson State College
Lyndon State College
Marlboro College
Middlebury College
St. Michael's College
Trinity College of Vermont

Virginia

Averett College
Bluefield College
Bridgewater College
Christendom College
Clinch Valley College of the University of Virginia
Eastern Mennonite College
Emory and Henry College
Ferrum College
Hampden-Sydney College
Hampton University
Hollins College
Lynchburg College
Mary Baldwin College
Mary Washington College
Randolph-Macon College
Randolph-Macon Woman's College
Roanoke College
St. Paul's College
Sweet Briar College
University of Richmond
Virginia Intermont College
Virginia Military Institute
Virginia Wesleyan College
Washington and Lee University

Washington

Antioch University Seattle
Evergreen State College
Heritage College
Northwest College of the Assemblies of God
St. Martin's College
University of Puget Sound
Walla Walla College
Whitman College
Whitworth College

West Virginia

Alderson-Broaddus College
Bethany College
Bluefield State College
College of West Virginia
Concord College
Davis and Elkins College
Fairmont State College
Glenville State College
Ohio Valley College
Shepherd College
West Liberty State College
West Virginia State College
West Virginia Wesleyan College
Wheeling Jesuit College

Wisconsin

Alverno College
Beloit College
Cardinal Stritch College
Carroll College
Carthage College
Edgewood College

Lakeland College
Lawrence University
Marian College of Fond du Lac
Mount Mary College
Mount Senario College
Northland College
Northwestern College
Ripon College
St. Norbert College
Silver Lake College
Viterbo College
Wisconsin Lutheran College

American Samoa, Caroline Islands, Guam, Marianas, Virgin Islands

University of the Virgin Islands

France

American University of Paris

Switzerland

American College of Switzerland
Franklin College: Switzerland

Universities

Alabama

Alabama Agricultural and Mechanical University
Alabama State University
Auburn University
  Auburn
  Montgomery
Jacksonville State University
Livingston University
Samford University
Selma University
Troy State University
  Dothan
  Montgomery
  Troy
Tuskegee University
University of Alabama
  Birmingham
  Huntsville
  Tuscaloosa
University of North Alabama
University of South Alabama

Alaska

Alaska Pacific University
University of Alaska
  Anchorage
  Fairbanks
  Southeast

Arizona

Arizona State University
Embry-Riddle Aeronautical University: Prescott Campus
Northern Arizona University
University of Arizona
University of Phoenix

Arkansas

Arkansas State University
Arkansas Tech University
Harding University
Henderson State University
Ouachita Baptist University
Southern Arkansas University
University of Arkansas
University of Arkansas
  Little Rock
  Medical Sciences
  Monticello
  Pine Bluff
University of Central Arkansas
University of the Ozarks

California

Azusa Pacific University
Biola University
California Institute of Technology
California Lutheran University
California Polytechnic State University: San Luis Obispo
California State Polytechnic University: Pomona
California State University
  Bakersfield
  Chico
  Dominguez Hills
  Fresno
  Fullerton
  Hayward
  Long Beach
  Los Angeles
  Northridge
  Sacramento
  San Marcos
Charles R. Drew University: College of Allied Health
Golden Gate University
Humboldt State University
La Sierra University
Loyola Marymount University
National University
Pepperdine University
San Diego State University
San Francisco State University
Santa Clara University
Sonoma State University
Stanford University
United States International University
University of California
  Berkeley
  Davis
  Irvine
  Los Angeles
  Riverside
  San Diego
  San Francisco
  Santa Barbara
  Santa Cruz
University of the Pacific
University of San Diego
University of San Francisco
University of Southern California
West Coast University
Woodbury University

Colorado

Colorado State University
University of Colorado
  Boulder
  Colorado Springs
  Denver
University of Denver
University of Northern Colorado
University of Southern Colorado

Connecticut

Central Connecticut State University
Eastern Connecticut State University
Fairfield University
Sacred Heart University
Southern Connecticut State University
Teikyo-Post University
University of Bridgeport
University of Connecticut
University of Hartford
University of New Haven
Western Connecticut State University
Yale University

Delaware

University of Delaware

District of Columbia

American University
Catholic University of America
George Washington University
Georgetown University
Howard University
Southeastern University
University of the District of Columbia

Florida

Barry University
Caribbean Center for Advanced Studies: Miami Institute of Psychology
Embry-Riddle Aeronautical University
Florida Agricultural and Mechanical University
Florida Atlantic University
Florida Institute of Technology
Florida International University
Florida State University
Jacksonville University
Nova University
St. Thomas University
Schiller International University
Stetson University
University of Central Florida
University of Florida
University of Miami
University of North Florida
University of South Florida
University of West Florida

Georgia

Brenau University
Clark Atlanta University
Emory University
Georgia Institute of Technology
Georgia State University
Mercer University
University of Georgia

Hawaii

University of Hawaii
  Hilo
  Manoa

Idaho

Boise State University
Idaho State University
University of Idaho

Illinois

Aurora University
Bradley University
Chicago State University
De Paul University
Eastern Illinois University
East-West University
Governors State University
Illinois Institute of Technology
Illinois State University
Illinois Wesleyan University
Lewis University
Loyola University of Chicago
Millikin University
National-Louis University
Northeastern Illinois University
Northern Illinois University
Northwestern University
Quincy University
Roosevelt University
St. Xavier University
Sangamon State University
Southern Illinois University
  Carbondale
  Edwardsville
University of Illinois
  Chicago
  Urbana-Champaign
Western Illinois University

Indiana

Ball State University
Butler University
DePauw University
Indiana State University
Indiana University
  Bloomington
  Northwest
  South Bend
Indiana University—Purdue University
  Fort Wayne
  Indianapolis
Martin University
Purdue University
  Calumet
  West Lafayette
Tri-State University
University of Evansville
University of Indianapolis
University of Notre Dame
Valparaiso University

Iowa

Drake University
Iowa State University
Maharishi International University
Teikyo Marycrest University
University of Iowa
University of Northern Iowa

Kansas

Emporia State University
Fort Hays State University
Kansas State University
Pittsburg State University
University of Kansas
  Lawrence
  Medical Center
Washburn University of Topeka

Kentucky

Eastern Kentucky University
Kentucky State University
Morehead State University
Murray State University
Northern Kentucky University
Spalding University
University of Kentucky
University of Louisville
Western Kentucky University

Louisiana

Grambling State University
Louisiana State University
  Agricultural and Mechanical College
  Shreveport
Louisiana Tech University
McNeese State University
Nicholls State University
Northeast Louisiana University
Northwestern State University
Southeastern Louisiana University
Southern University at New Orleans
Southern University and Agricultural and Mechanical College
Tulane University
University of New Orleans
University of Southwestern Louisiana
Xavier University of Louisiana

Maine

University of Maine
  Fort Kent
  Machias
  Orono
  Presque Isle
University of Southern Maine

Maryland

Bowie State University

Johns Hopkins University
Towson State University
University of Baltimore
University of Maryland
- Baltimore County
- College Park
- Eastern Shore
- University College

Massachusetts

Boston College
Boston University
Brandeis University
Clark University
Massachusetts Institute of Technology
Northeastern University
Salem State College
Suffolk University
Tufts University
University of Massachusetts
- Amherst
- Boston
- Dartmouth
- Lowell

Michigan

Andrews University
Central Michigan University
Eastern Michigan University
Grand Valley State University
Lawrence Technological University
Michigan State University
Michigan Technological University
Northern Michigan University
Oakland University
University of Detroit Mercy
University of Michigan
- Ann Arbor
- Dearborn
- Flint

Wayne State University
Western Michigan University

Minnesota

Bemidji State University
Hamline University
Mankato State University
Metropolitan State University
Moorhead State University
St. Cloud State University
University of Minnesota
- Duluth
- Twin Cities

Mississippi

Alcorn State University
Delta State University
Jackson State University
Mississippi State University
Mississippi University for Women
Mississippi Valley State University
University of Mississippi
University of Southern Mississippi

Missouri

Central Missouri State University
Northwest Missouri State University
St. Louis University
Southeast Missouri State University
Southwest Missouri State University
University of Missouri
- Columbia
- Kansas City
- Rolla
- St. Louis

Washington University
Webster University

Montana

Montana State University
University of Montana

Nebraska

Creighton University
University of Nebraska
- Medical Center
- Kearney
- Lincoln
- Omaha

Nevada

University of Nevada
- Las Vegas
- Reno

New Hampshire

University of New Hampshire

New Jersey

Drew University
Fairleigh Dickinson University
New Jersey Institute of Technology
Princeton University
Rutgers—The State University of New Jersey Camden: School of Law
Seton Hall University
Stevens Institute of Technology

New Mexico

Eastern New Mexico University
New Mexico Highlands University
New Mexico Institute of Mining and Technology
New Mexico State University
University of New Mexico
Western New Mexico University

New York

Adelphi University
Alfred University
City University of New York: City College
Clarkson University
Cornell University
Fordham University
Hofstra University
Jewish Theological Seminary of America
Long Island University
- Brooklyn Campus
- C. W. Post Campus

New York University
Niagara University
Pace University
- College of White Plains
- New York
- Pleasantville/Briarcliff

Polytechnic University
- Brooklyn
- Long Island Campus

Rensselaer Polytechnic Institute
Rochester Institute of Technology
St. Bonaventure University
St. John's University
State University of New York
- Albany
- Binghamton
- Buffalo
- Stony Brook
- Health Sciences Center at Stony Brook

Syracuse University
University of Rochester
Yeshiva University

North Carolina

Appalachian State University
Campbell University
Duke University
East Carolina University
Fayetteville State University
North Carolina Central University
North Carolina State University
University of North Carolina
- Chapel Hill
- Charlotte
- Greensboro
- Wilmington

Wake Forest University
Western Carolina University
Winston-Salem State University

North Dakota

Dickinson State University
North Dakota State University
University of North Dakota

Ohio

Ashland University
Bowling Green State University
Case Western Reserve University
Cleveland State University
Franciscan University of Steubenville
Franklin University
John Carroll University
Kent State University
Miami University: Oxford Campus
Ohio Northern University
Ohio State University: Columbus Campus
Ohio University
University of Akron
University of Cincinnati
University of Dayton
University of Findlay
University of Toledo
Walsh University
Wright State University
Xavier University
Youngstown State University

Oklahoma

East Central University
Northeastern State University
Northwestern Oklahoma State University
Oklahoma City University
Oklahoma State University
Southeastern Oklahoma State University
Southwestern Oklahoma State University
University of Central Oklahoma
University of Oklahoma
University of Tulsa

Oregon

Oregon Health Sciences University
Oregon State University
Pacific University
Portland State University
University of Oregon
- Eugene
- Robert Donald Clark Honors College

University of Portland

Pennsylvania

Bloomsburg University of Pennsylvania
Bucknell University
California University of Pennsylvania
Carnegie Mellon University
Clarion University of Pennsylvania
Drexel University
Duquesne University
East Stroudsburg University of Pennsylvania
Edinboro University of Pennsylvania
Indiana University of Pennsylvania
Kutztown University of Pennsylvania
Lehigh University
Lock Haven University of Pennsylvania
Mansfield University of Pennsylvania
Millersville University of Pennsylvania
Penn State University Park Campus
St. Joseph's University
Slippery Rock University of Pennsylvania
Temple University
University of Pennsylvania
University of Pittsburgh
University of Scranton
Villanova University
West Chester University of Pennsylvania
Widener University
Wilkes University

Puerto Rico

Bayamon Central University
Inter American University of Puerto Rico
- Metropolitan Campus
- San German Campus

Pontifical Catholic University of Puerto Rico
Turabo University
University of Puerto Rico
- Mayaguez Campus
- Medical Sciences Campus
- Rio Piedras Campus

University of the Sacred Heart

Rhode Island

Brown University
Johnson & Wales University
Roger Williams University
University of Rhode Island

South Carolina

Clemson University
Medical University of South Carolina
University of South Carolina
- Columbia
- Spartanburg

Winthrop University

South Dakota

Dakota State University
South Dakota School of Mines and Technology
South Dakota State University
University of South Dakota

Tennessee

Austin Peay State University
Belmont University
East Tennessee State University
Memphis State University
Middle Tennessee State University
Tennessee State University
Tennessee Technological University
University of the South
University of Tennessee
- Chattanooga
- Knoxville
- Martin

Vanderbilt University

Texas

Amber University
Angelo State University
Baylor University
Corpus Christi State University
Dallas Baptist University
East Texas State University
- Commerce
- Texarkana

Hardin-Simmons University
Lamar University—Beaumont
Laredo State University

LeTourneau University
Northwood University: Texas Campus
Our Lady of the Lake University of San Antonio
Prairie View A&M University
Rice University
St. Mary's University
Sam Houston State University
Southern Methodist University
Southwest Texas State University
Stephen F. Austin State University
Sul Ross State University
Tarleton State University
Texas A&I University
Texas A&M University
  College Station
  Galveston
Texas Christian University
Texas Southern University
Texas Tech University
Texas Wesleyan University
Texas Woman's University
University of Houston
  Clear Lake
  Downtown
  Houston
  Victoria
University of Mary Hardin-Baylor
University of North Texas
University of St. Thomas
University of Texas
  Arlington
  Austin
  Dallas
  El Paso
  Health Science Center at Houston
  Health Science Center at San Antonio
  Permian Basin
  San Antonio
  Tyler
West Texas A & M University

Utah
Brigham Young University
Southern Utah University
University of Utah
Utah State University
Weber State University

Vermont
Norwich University
University of Vermont

Virginia
Christopher Newport University
College of William and Mary
George Mason University
James Madison University
Liberty University
Marymount University
Norfolk State University
Old Dominion University
Radford University
Shenandoah University
University of Virginia
Virginia Commonwealth University
Virginia Polytechnic Institute and State University
Virginia State University
Virginia Union University

Washington
Central Washington University
City University
Eastern Washington University
Gonzaga University
Pacific Lutheran University
Seattle Pacific University
Seattle University
University of Washington
Washington State University
Western Washington University

West Virginia
Marshall University
Salem-Teikyo University
University of Charleston
West Virginia University

Wisconsin
Concordia University Wisconsin
Marquette University
University of Wisconsin
  Eau Claire
  Green Bay
  La Crosse
  Madison
  Oshkosh
  Parkside
  Platteville
  River Falls
  Stevens Point
  Stout
  Superior
  Whitewater

Wyoming
University of Wyoming

Arab Republic of Egypt
American University in Cairo

Canada
McGill University

Mexico
Sistema Instituto Tecnologico y de Estudios Superiores de Monterrey

2-year upper-division colleges

Alabama
Athens State College
Southern Christian University

Arizona
University of Phoenix

California
Antioch Southern California at Los Angeles
California State University: San Marcos
Dominican School of Philosophy and Theology
Hebrew Union College: Jewish Institute of Religion
Monterey Institute of International Studies
Pacific Oaks College
University of California: San Francisco
University of West Los Angeles

Colorado
University of Colorado Health Sciences Center

District of Columbia
Oblate College

Florida
Caribbean Center for Advanced Studies: Miami Institute of Psychology

Georgia
Medical College of Georgia
Mercer University Atlanta

Hawaii
University of Hawaii: West Oahu

Illinois
Governors State University
Mennonite College of Nursing
National College of Chiropractic
Rush University
St. Francis Medical Center College of Nursing
St. Joseph College of Nursing
Sangamon State University

Iowa
University of Osteopathic Medicine and Health Sciences

Kansas
University of Kansas Medical Center

Louisiana
Louisiana State University Medical Center

Maryland
University of Baltimore
University of Maryland: Baltimore

Michigan
Walsh College of Accountancy and Business Administration

Minnesota
Metropolitan State University

Mississippi
University of Mississippi Medical Center

New York
Columbia University: School of Nursing
State University of New York
  Health Science Center at Brooklyn
  Health Sciences Center at Stony Brook
  Institute of Technology at Utica/Rome

North Dakota
Medcenter One College of Nursing

Oklahoma
University of Oklahoma Health Sciences Center

Pennsylvania
Penn State Harrisburg Capital College
Thomas Jefferson University: College of Allied Health Sciences

South Carolina
Medical University of South Carolina

Tennessee
University of Tennessee: Memphis

Texas
Amber University
Baylor College of Dentistry
Corpus Christi State University
East Texas State University at Texarkana
Institute for Christian Studies
Laredo State University
University of Houston
  Clear Lake
  Victoria
University of Texas
  Brownsville
  Health Science Center at Houston
  Health Science Center at San Antonio
  Medical Branch at Galveston
  Southwestern Medical Center at Dallas Southwestern Allied Health Sciences School
  Tyler

Vermont
School for International Training

Washington
Antioch University Seattle
Bastyr College
City University

Community/junior colleges

Alabama
Alabama Southern Community College
Bevill State Community College
Bishop State Community College
Central Alabama Community College: Alexander City Campus
Chattahoochee Valley Community College
Community College of the Air Force
Concordia College
Draughons Junior College
Enterprise State Junior College
Gadsden State Community College
George C. Wallace State Community College
  Dothan
  Selma
James H. Faulkner State Community College
Jefferson Davis State Junior College
Jefferson State Community College
John C. Calhoun State Community College
Lawson State Community College
Lurleen B. Wallace State Junior College
Marion Military Institute
Northeast Alabama Community College
Northwest Alabama Community College
Phillips Junior College: Birmingham
Shelton State Community College
Shoals Community College
Snead State Community College
Southern Union State Junior College
Wallace State Community College at Hanceville

Alaska
Prince William Sound Community College

Arizona
Arizona Western College
Central Arizona College
Cochise College
Eastern Arizona College
Gateway Community College
Glendale Community College
Mesa Community College
Mohave Community College
Navajo Community College
Northland Pioneer College

Paradise Valley Community College
Phoenix College
Pima Community College
Rio Salado Community College
Scottsdale Community College
South Mountain Community College
Yavapai College

Arkansas

Arkansas State University: Beebe Branch
Capital City Junior College
East Arkansas Community College
Garland County Community College
Mississippi County Community College
North Arkansas Community/Technical College
Phillips County Community College
Rich Mountain Community College
Shorter College
South Arkansas Community College
Southern Arkansas University: Technical Branch
Westark Community College

California

Allan Hancock College
Antelope Valley College
Bakersfield College
Barstow College
Canada College
Cerritos Community College
Cerro Coso Community College
Chabot College
Chaffey Community College
Citrus College
City College of San Francisco
Coastline Community College
College of the Canyons
College of Marin: Kentfield
College of the Redwoods
College of San Mateo
College of the Sequoias
College of the Siskiyous
Columbia College
Compton Community College
Contra Costa College
Cosumnes River College
Crafton Hills College
Cuesta College
Cuyamaca College
Cypress College
Diablo Valley College
D-Q University
Evergreen Valley College
Fashion Institute of Design and Merchandising
- Los Angeles
- San Francisco

Feather River College
Foothill College
Fresno City College
Fullerton College
Glendale Community College
Golden West College
Grossmont Community College
Heald Business College: San Jose
Kelsey-Jenney College
Lake Tahoe Community College
Laney College
Lassen College
Long Beach City College
Los Angeles City College
Los Angeles Harbor College
Los Angeles Mission College
Los Angeles Pierce College
Los Angeles Trade and Technical College
Los Angeles Valley College
Los Medanos College
Marymount College
Mendocino College
Merced College
Merritt College
MiraCosta College
Mission College
Modesto Junior College
Monterey Peninsula College
Moorpark College
Mount San Antonio College
Mount San Jacinto College
Napa Valley College
Palomar College
Pasadena City College
Phillips Junior College
- Condie Campus
- Fresno Campus

Porterville College
Rio Hondo College
Sacramento City College
Saddleback College
San Diego City College
San Diego Mesa College
San Diego Miramar College
San Joaquin Delta College
San Jose City College
Santa Barbara City College
Santa Monica College
Santa Rosa Junior College
Shasta College
Sierra College
Skyline College
Solano Community College
Southwestern College
Taft College
Ventura College
Victor Valley College
West Hills Community College
West Valley College
Yuba College

Colorado

Aims Community College
Arapahoe Community College
Colorado Mountain College
- Alpine Campus
- Spring Valley Campus
- Timberline Campus

Colorado Northwestern Community College
Community College of Aurora
Community College of Denver
Front Range Community College
Lamar Community College
Mesa State College
Morgan Community College
Northeastern Junior College
Otero Junior College
Parks Junior College
Pikes Peak Community College
Pueblo Community College
Red Rocks Community College
Trinidad State Junior College

Connecticut

Asnuntuck Community-Technical College
Briarwood College
Capital Community-Technical College
Gateway Community-Technical College
Housatonic Community-Technical College
Middlesex Community-Technical College
Mitchell College
Northwestern Connecticut Community-Technical College
Norwalk Community-Technical College
Quinebaug Valley Community-Technical College
Three Rivers Community-Technical College
Tunxis Community-Technical College

Delaware

Delaware Technical and Community College
- Southern Campus
- Terry Campus

Florida

Brevard Community College
Broward Community College
Central Florida Community College
Chipola Junior College
Daytona Beach Community College
Edison Community College
Florida College
Florida Community College at Jacksonville
Gulf Coast Community College
Hillsborough Community College
Indian River Community College
Keiser College of Technology
Lake City Community College
Lake-Sumter Community College
Manatee Community College
Miami-Dade Community College
North Florida Junior College
Okaloosa-Walton Community College
Palm Beach Community College
Pasco-Hernando Community College
Pensacola Junior College
Phillips Junior College: Melbourne
Polk Community College
St. Johns River Community College
St. Petersburg Junior College
Santa Fe Community College
Seminole Community College
South College: Palm Beach Campus
South Florida Community College
Southern College
Tallahassee Community College
Valencia Community College

Georgia

Abraham Baldwin Agricultural College
Andrew College
Atlanta Metropolitan College
Bainbridge College
Brunswick College
Dalton College
Darton College
DeKalb College
East Georgia College
Floyd College
Gainesville College
Georgia Military College
Gordon College
Kennesaw State College
Macon College
Meadows College of Business
Middle Georgia College
Reinhardt College
South College
South Georgia College
Waycross College
Young Harris College

Hawaii

University of Hawaii
- Hawaii Community College
- Honolulu Community College
- Kapiolani Community College
- Kauai Community College
- Windward Community College

Idaho

College of Southern Idaho
North Idaho College
Ricks College

Illinois

Belleville Area College
Black Hawk College
- East Campus
- Moline

Carl Sandburg College
City Colleges of Chicago
- Harold Washington College
- Kennedy-King College
- Malcolm X College
- Olive-Harvey College

College of DuPage
College of Lake County
Danville Area Community College
Elgin Community College
Highland Community College
Illinois Central College
Illinois Eastern Community Colleges
- Frontier Community College
- Lincoln Trail College
- Olney Central College
- Wabash Valley College

Illinois Valley Community College
John A. Logan College
Joliet Junior College
Kankakee Community College
Kaskaskia College
Kishwaukee College
Lake Land College
Lewis and Clark Community College
Lexington Institute of Hospitality Careers
Lincoln College
Lincoln Land Community College
MacCormac Junior College
McHenry County College
Montay College
Moraine Valley Community College
Morton College
Oakton Community College
Richland Community College
Robert Morris College: Chicago
Rock Valley College
St. Augustine College
Sauk Valley Community College
Shawnee Community College
Southeastern Illinois College
Spoon River College
Springfield College in Illinois
State Community College
Triton College
William Rainey Harper College

Indiana

Ancilla College
Holy Cross College
Purdue University: North Central Campus
Vincennes University

Iowa

American Institute of Business
American Institute of Commerce
Clinton Community College
Des Moines Area Community College
Ellsworth Community College
Hawkeye Community College
Indian Hills Community College
Iowa Central Community College
Iowa Lakes Community College
Iowa Western Community College
Kirkwood Community College
Marshalltown Community College
Muscatine Community College
North Iowa Area Community College
Northeast Iowa Community College
Northwest Iowa Community College
Scott Community College

Southeastern Community College
North Campus
South Campus
Southwestern Community College
Waldorf College
Western Iowa Tech Community College

Kansas
Allen County Community College
Barton County Community College
Brown Mackie College
Butler County Community College
Central College
Coffeyville Community College
Colby Community College
Dodge City Community College
Donnelly College
Fort Scott Community College
Garden City Community College
Haskell Indian Junior College
Hesston College
Highland Community College
Hutchinson Community College
Independence Community College
Johnson County Community College
Kansas City Kansas Community College
Labette Community College
Neosho County Community College
Pratt Community College
Seward County Community College

Kentucky
Ashland Community College
Elizabethtown Community College
Henderson Community College
Hopkinsville Community College
Jefferson Community College
Lexington Community College
Madisonville Community College
Maysville Community College
Owensboro Junior College of Business
Paducah Community College
Prestonburg Community College
Southeast Community College
Sue Bennett College

Louisiana
Bossier Parish Community College
Louisiana State University at Eunice
Nunez Community College
Phillips Junior College: New Orleans
Southern University in Shreveport

Maine
Andover College
Beal College
Casco Bay College
University of Maine at Augusta

Maryland
Allegany Community College
Anne Arundel Community College
Baltimore City Community College
Catonsville Community College
Cecil Community College
Charles County Community College
Chesapeake College
Dundalk Community College
Essex Community College
Frederick Community College
Hagerstown Business College
Hagerstown Junior College
Harford Community College
Howard Community College
Montgomery College
Germantown Campus
Rockville Campus
Takoma Park Campus
Prince George's Community College
Wor-Wic Community College

Massachusetts
Aquinas College at Milton
Aquinas College at Newton
Bay Path College
Bay State College
Becker College
Leicester Campus
Worcester Campus
Bristol Community College
Bunker Hill Community College
Cape Cod Community College
Dean Junior College
Endicott College
Fisher College
Greenfield Community College
Holyoke Community College
Katharine Gibbs School
Marian Court Junior College
Massachusetts Bay Community College
Massasoit Community College
Middlesex Community College
Mount Wachusett Community College
Newbury College
North Shore Community College
Northern Essex Community College
Quincy College
Quinsigamond Community College
Roxbury Community College
Springfield Technical Community College

Michigan
Alpena Community College
Bay de Noc Community College
Charles Stewart Mott Community College
Delta College
Glen Oaks Community College
Gogebic Community College
Grand Rapids Community College
Great Lakes Junior College of Business
Henry Ford Community College
Highland Park Community College
Jackson Community College
Jordan College
Kalamazoo Valley Community College
Kellogg Community College
Kirtland Community College
Lake Michigan College
Lansing Community College
Lewis College of Business
Macomb Community College
Mid Michigan Community College
Monroe County Community College
Montcalm Community College
Muskegon Community College
Northwestern Michigan College
Oakland Community College
St. Clair County Community College
Schoolcraft College
Southwestern Michigan College
Suomi College
Washtenaw Community College
Wayne County Community College
West Shore Community College

Minnesota
Anoka-Ramsey Community College
Austin Community College
Bethany Lutheran College
Brainerd Community College
Fergus Falls Community College
Hibbing Community College
Inver Hills Community College
Itasca Community College: Arrowhead Region
Lakewood Community College
Mesabi Community College: Arrowhead Region
Minneapolis Community College
NEI College of Technology
Normandale Community College
North Hennepin Community College
Rainy River Community College
Rochester Community College
Vermilion Community College
Willmar Community College
Worthington Community College

Mississippi
Copiah-Lincoln Community College
East Central Community College
East Mississippi Community College
Hinds Community College
Holmes Community College
Meridian Community College
Mississippi Delta Community College
Mississippi Gulf Coast Community College
Jackson County Campus
Jefferson Davis Campus
Perkinston
Northwest Mississippi Community College
Pearl River Community College
Southwest Mississippi Community College
Wood Junior College

Missouri
Cottey College
Crowder College
East Central College
Jefferson College
Kemper Military School and College
Longview Community College
Maple Woods Community College
Mineral Area College
Moberly Area Community College
Northwest Missouri Community College
Penn Valley Community College
Phillips Junior College
St. Charles County Community College
St. Louis Community College
Florissant Valley
Forest Park
Meramec
State Fair Community College
Three Rivers Community College

Montana
Blackfeet Community College
Dawson Community College
Dull Knife Memorial College
Flathead Valley Community College
Fort Belknap College
Fort Peck Community College
Little Big Horn College
Miles Community College
Salish Kootenai College
Stone Child College

Nebraska
Central Community College
Lincoln School of Commerce
McCook Community College
Metropolitan Community College
Mid Plains Community College
Nebraska Indian Community College
Northeast Community College
Southeast Community College
Beatrice Campus
Lincoln Campus
Milford Campus
Western Nebraska Community College: Scottsbluff Campus

Nevada
Northern Nevada Community College
Truckee Meadows Community College
Western Nevada Community College

New Hampshire
Castle College
Hesser College
White Pines College

New Jersey
Atlantic Community College
Bergen Community College
Berkeley College of Business
Brookdale Community College
Burlington County College
Camden County College
County College of Morris
Cumberland County College
Essex County College
Fairleigh Dickinson University: Edward Williams College
Gloucester County College
Hudson County Community College
Katharine Gibbs School
Mercer County Community College
Ocean County College
Passaic County Community College
Raritan Valley Community College
Salem Community College
Sussex County Community College
Union County College
Warren County Community College

New Mexico
Albuquerque Technical-Vocational Institute
Clovis Community College
Dona Ana Branch Community College of New Mexico State University
Eastern New Mexico University: Roswell Campus
Institute of American Indian Arts
New Mexico Junior College
New Mexico State University at Carlsbad
Northern New Mexico Community College
Parks College
San Juan College
Santa Fe Community College

New York
Adirondack Community College
Berkeley College
Berkeley School: New York City
Bramson ORT Technical Institute
Broome Community College
Cayuga County Community College
Cazenovia College
City University of New York
Borough of Manhattan Community College
Bronx Community College
Hostos Community College
Kingsborough Community College
La Guardia Community College
Queensborough Community College
Clinton Community College
Columbia-Greene Community College
Corning Community College
Dutchess Community College

Erie Community College
City Campus
North Campus
South Campus
Finger Lakes Community College
Fulton-Montgomery Community College
Genesee Community College
Herkimer County Community College
Hudson Valley Community College
Institute of Design and Construction
Jamestown Community College
Jefferson Community College
Katharine Gibbs School: Melville
Maria College
Mater Dei College
Mohawk Valley Community College
Monroe College
Monroe Community College
Nassau Community College
North Country Community College
Onondaga Community College
Orange County Community College
Paul Smith's College
Rockland Community College
Sage Junior College of Albany
Schenectady County Community College
Suffolk County Community College
Eastern Campus
Selden
Western Campus
Sullivan County Community College
Tompkins-Cortland Community College
Trocaire College
Ulster County Community College
Villa Maria College of Buffalo
Westchester Community College

North Carolina

Alamance Community College
Anson Community College
Asheville Buncombe Technical Community College
Beaufort County Community College
Bladen Community College
Blue Ridge Community College
Brevard College
Brunswick Community College
Caldwell Community College and Technical Institute
Cape Fear Community College
Carteret Community College
Catawba Valley Community College
Central Carolina Community College
Central Piedmont Community College
Cleveland Community College
Coastal Carolina Community College
College of the Albemarle
Craven Community College
Davidson County Community College
Durham Technical Community College
Edgecombe Community College
Fayetteville Technical Community College
Gaston College
Halifax Community College
Haywood Community College
Isothermal Community College
James Sprunt Community College
Lenoir Community College
Louisburg College
Martin Community College
Mayland Community College
McDowell Technical Community College
Mitchell Community College
Montgomery Community College
Nash Community College
Pamlico Community College
Peace College
Piedmont Community College
Pitt Community College
Richmond Community College
Roanoke-Chowan Community College
Robeson Community College
Rockingham Community College
Rowan-Cabarrus Community College
St. Mary's College
Sampson Community College
Sandhills Community College
Southeastern Community College
Southwestern Community College
Stanly Community College
Surry Community College
Tri-County Community College
Vance-Granville Community College
Wake Technical Community College
Wayne Community College
Western Piedmont Community College
Wilkes Community College

North Dakota

Bismarck State College
Little Hoop Community College
North Dakota State College of Science
North Dakota State University: Bottineau
Standing Rock College
Turtle Mountain Community College
University of North Dakota
Lake Region
Williston

Ohio

Clark State Community College
Columbus State Community College
Cuyahoga Community College
Eastern Campus
Metropolitan Campus
Western Campus
Davis Junior College of Business
Edison State Community College
Lakeland Community College
Lorain County Community College
Miami-Jacobs College
Sinclair Community College
Southern Ohio College
Southern State Community College
University of Akron: Wayne College
University of Cincinnati
Access Colleges
Clermont College

Oklahoma

Bacone College
Carl Albert State College
Connors State College
Eastern Oklahoma State College
Northeastern Oklahoma Agricultural and Mechanical College
Oklahoma City Community College
Oklahoma State University: Oklahoma City
Redlands Community College
Rogers State College
Rose State College
Seminole Junior College
Tulsa Junior College
Western Oklahoma State College

Oregon

Blue Mountain Community College
Central Oregon Community College
Chemeketa Community College
Clackamas Community College
Clatsop Community College
Lane Community College
Linn-Benton Community College
Mount Hood Community College
Portland Community College
Rogue Community College
Treasure Valley Community College
Umpqua Community College

Pennsylvania

Bucks County Community College
Butler County Community College
Community College of Allegheny County
Allegheny Campus
Boyce Campus
North Campus
South Campus
Community College of Beaver County
Community College of Philadelphia
Delaware County Community College
Harcum Junior College
Harrisburg Area Community College
Keystone Junior College
Lackawanna Junior College
Lehigh County Community College
Luzerne County Community College
Manor Junior College
Montgomery County Community College
Northampton County Area Community College
Reading Area Community College
Valley Forge Military College
Westmoreland County Community College

Puerto Rico

Huertas Junior College
University of Puerto Rico: Carolina Regional College

Rhode Island

Community College of Rhode Island

South Carolina

Aiken Technical College
Columbia Junior College of Business
Greenville Technical College
Midlands Technical College
North Greenville College
Spartanburg Methodist College
Technical College of the Lowcountry
Tri-County Technical College
Trident Technical College
Williamsburg Technical College

South Dakota

Kilian Community College
Sisseton-Wahpeton Community College

Tennessee

Aquinas Junior College
Chattanooga State Technical Community College
Cleveland State Community College
Columbia State Community College
Draughons Junior College of Business: Nashville
Dyersburg State Community College
Hiwassee College
Knoxville Business College
Motlow State Community College
Northeast State Technical Community College
Pellissippi State Technical Community College
Roane State Community College
Shelby State Community College
Volunteer State Community College
Walters State Community College

Texas

Alvin Community College
Amarillo College
Angelina College
Austin Community College
Bee County College
Blinn College
Brazosport College
Brookhaven College
Cedar Valley College
Central Texas College
Cisco Junior College
Clarendon College
College of the Mainland
Collin County Community College District
Cooke County College
Del Mar College
Eastfield College
El Centro College
El Paso Community College
Frank Phillips College
Galveston College
Grayson County College
Hill College
Houston Community College
Howard College
Kilgore College
Laredo Junior College
Lee College
Lon Morris College
Midland College
Miss Wade's Fashion Merchandising College
Mountain View College
Navarro College
North Harris Montgomery Community College District
North Lake College
Northeast Texas Community College
Odessa College
Palo Alto College
Panola College
Paris Junior College
Ranger Junior College
Richland College
St. Philip's College
San Antonio College
San Jacinto College: North
South Plains College
Southwest Texas Junior College
Tarrant County Junior College
Temple Junior College
Texarkana College
Trinity Valley Community College
Tyler Junior College
Vernon Regional Junior College
Victoria College
Weatherford College
Wharton County Junior College

Utah

College of Eastern Utah
Dixie College
LDS Business College
Phillips Junior College: Salt Lake City Campus
Salt Lake Community College
Snow College
Utah Valley Community College

Vermont
Champlain College
Community College of Vermont
Sterling College

Virginia
Blue Ridge Community College
Central Virginia Community College
Dabney S. Lancaster Community College
Danville Community College
Eastern Shore Community College
J. Sargeant Reynolds Community College
John Tyler Community College
Lord Fairfax Community College
Mountain Empire Community College
National Business College
New River Community College
Northern Virginia Community College
Patrick Henry Community College
Paul D. Camp Community College
Piedmont Virginia Community College
Rappahannock Community College
Richard Bland College
Southside Virginia Community College
Southwest Virginia Community College
Tidewater Community College
Virginia Western Community College
Wytheville Community College

Washington
Bellevue Community College
Big Bend Community College
Centralia College
Clark College
Columbia Basin College
Edmonds Community College
Everett Community College
Grays Harbor College
Green River Community College
Highline Community College
Lower Columbia College
North Seattle Community College
Olympic College
Peninsula College
Pierce College
Seattle Central Community College
Shoreline Community College
Skagit Valley College
South Puget Sound Community College
South Seattle Community College
Spokane Community College
Spokane Falls Community College
Tacoma Community College
Walla Walla Community College
Wenatchee Valley College
Whatcom Community College
Yakima Valley Community College

West Virginia
Potomac State College of West Virginia University
Southern West Virginia Community College
West Virginia Northern Community College
West Virginia University at Parkersburg

Wisconsin
Madison Area Technical College
Madison Junior College of Business
Nicolet Area Technical College
Stratton College
University of Wisconsin Center
- Barron County
- Marshfield/Wood County
- Sheboygan County
- Waukesha

Wyoming
Casper College
Central Wyoming College
Eastern Wyoming College
Laramie County Community College
Northwest College
Sheridan College
Western Wyoming Community College

American Samoa, Caroline Islands, Guam, Marianas, Virgin Islands
College of Micronesia-FSM
Guam Community College

Colleges for men only

Colorado
Yeshiva Toras Chaim Talmudical Seminary

Florida
St. John Vianney College Seminary
Talmudic College of Florida

Georgia
Morehouse College

Indiana
Rose-Hulman Institute of Technology
St. Meinrad College
Wabash College

Iowa
Divine Word College

Louisiana
St. Joseph Seminary College

Maryland
Ner Israel Rabbinical College

Massachusetts
St. Hyacinth College and Seminary
St. John's Seminary College

Minnesota
St. John's University

Missouri
Conception Seminary College

Nevada
Deep Springs College

New York
Beth Hamedrash Shaarei Yosher Institute
Beth Hatalmud Rabbinical College
Central Yeshiva Tomchei Tmimim Lubavitz
Darkei No'Am Rabbinical College
Hobart College
Kehilath Yakov Rabbinical Seminary
Kol Yaakov Torah Center
Machzikei Hadath Rabbinical College
Mesivta Tifereth Jerusalem of America
Mesivta Torah Vodaath Seminary
Mirrer Yeshiva Central Institute
Ohr Hameir Theological Seminary
Ohr Somayach Tanenbaum Education Center
Rabbinical College Ch'san Sofer of New York
Rabbinical College of Long Island
Rabbinical Seminary Adas Yereim
Rabbinical Seminary of America
Rabbinical Seminary M'Kor Chaim
Talmudical Institute of Upstate New York
Talmudical Seminary Oholei Torah
United Talmudical Academy
Yeshiva Derech Chaim
Yeshiva Gedolah Zichron Moshe
Yeshiva Karlin Stolin Beth Aron Y'Israel Rabbinical Institute
Yeshiva of Nitra Rabbinical College
Yeshiva Shaar Hatorah
Yeshivat Mikdash Melech

Ohio
Pontifical College Josephinum

Pennsylvania
St. Charles Borromeo Seminary
Talmudical Yeshiva of Philadelphia
Valley Forge Military College
Williamson Free School of Mechanical Trades

South Carolina
The Citadel

Virginia
Hampden-Sydney College
Virginia Military Institute

Wisconsin
Northwestern College

Colleges for women only

Alabama
Judson College

California
Mills College
Mount St. Mary's College
Scripps College

Connecticut
St. Joseph College

District of Columbia
Mount Vernon College
Trinity College

Georgia
Agnes Scott College
Brenau University
Spelman College
Wesleyan College

Illinois
Lexington Institute of Hospitality Careers

Indiana
St. Mary-of-the-Woods College
St. Mary's College

Kentucky
Midway College

Maryland
College of Notre Dame of Maryland
Hood College

Massachusetts
Aquinas College at Milton
Aquinas College at Newton
Bay Path College
Elms College
Emmanuel College
Endicott College
Fisher College
Lasell College
Lesley College
Mount Holyoke College
Pine Manor College
Regis College
Simmons College
Smith College
Wellesley College

Minnesota
College of St. Benedict
College of St. Catherine: St. Catherine Campus

Missouri
Cottey College
Stephens College
William Woods College

Nebraska
College of St. Mary

New Jersey
Assumption College for Sisters
College of St. Elizabeth
Georgian Court College
Rutgers—The State University of New Jersey: Douglass College

New York
Barnard College
College of New Rochelle
Russell Sage College
Wells College
William Smith College

North Carolina
Bennett College
Meredith College
Peace College
St. Mary's College
Salem College

Ohio
Notre Dame College of Ohio
Ursuline College

Pennsylvania
Bryn Mawr College
Carlow College
Cedar Crest College
Chatham College
Chestnut Hill College
Harcum Junior College
Immaculata College
Moore College of Art and Design
Rosemont College
Seton Hill College
Wilson College

South Carolina
Columbia College
Converse College

Vermont
Trinity College of Vermont

Virginia
Hollins College
Mary Baldwin College
Randolph-Macon Woman's College
Southern Virginia College for Women
Sweet Briar College

Wisconsin

Alverno College
Mount Mary College

Specialized colleges

Agricultural and technical colleges

Alabama
Alabama Aviation and Technical College
Auburn University
Bessemer State Technical College
Bevill State Community College
Bishop State Community College
Central Alabama Community College: Childersburg Campus
Douglas MacArthur State Technical College
Harry M. Ayers State Technical College
J. F. Drake State Technical College
John M. Patterson State Technical College
Reid State Technical College
Shoals Community College
Sparks State Technical College
Trenholm State Technical College
Virginia College

Arizona
DeVry Institute of Technology: Phoenix
Gateway Community College
ITT Technical Institute
- Phoenix
- Tucson

Arkansas
North Arkansas Community/Technical College
Southern Arkansas University: Technical Branch

California
Brooks College
Cosumnes River College
DeVry Institute of Technology: City of Industry
ITT Technical Institute: Sacramento
Los Angeles Trade and Technical College
Phillips Junior College: Condie Campus
San Francisco College of Mortuary Science

Colorado
Colorado Technical College
Denver Institute of Technology
Denver Technical College
ITT Technical Institute: Aurora

Connecticut
Capital Community-Technical College
Norwalk Community-Technical College

Delaware
Delaware Technical and Community College
- Southern Campus
- Stanton/Wilmington Campus
- Terry Campus

Florida
Art Institute of Fort Lauderdale
Daytona Beach Community College
Flagler Career Institute
Keiser College of Technology
National Education Center: Tampa Technical Institute Campus
New England Institute of Technology
South Florida Community College

Georgia
Abraham Baldwin Agricultural College
Art Institute of Atlanta
Athens Area Technical Institute
Chattahoochee Technical Institute
DeKalb Technical Institute
DeVry Institute of Technology: Atlanta
Georgia Institute of Technology
Gupton Jones College of Funeral Service
Gwinnett Technical Institute
Savannah Technical Institute
Southern College of Technology

Idaho
ITT Technical Institute: Boise

Illinois
DeVry Institute of Technology
- Addison
- Chicago

Gem City College
ITT Technical Institute: Hoffman Estates
Morrison Institute of Technology
Parks College of St. Louis University

Indiana
Indiana Vocational Technical College
- Central Indiana
- Columbus
- Eastcentral
- Kokomo
- Lafayette
- Northcentral
- Northeast
- Northwest
- Southcentral
- Southeast
- Southwest
- Wabash Valley
- Whitewater

ITT Technical Institute
- Evansville
- Fort Wayne
- Indianapolis

Iowa
American Institute of Business
Hamilton Technical College
Iowa Lakes Community College

Kansas
Dodge City Community College
Kansas State University

Kentucky
Institute of Electronic Technology
Lexington Community College
Louisville Technical Institute
RETS Electronic Institute
Sullivan College

Louisiana
Louisiana State University and Agricultural and Mechanical College

Maine
Central Maine Technical College
Eastern Maine Technical College
Maine Maritime Academy
Northern Maine Technical College
Southern Maine Technical College

Maryland
Capitol College

Massachusetts
Essex Agricultural and Technical Institute
Franklin Institute of Boston
Springfield Technical Community College
Wentworth Institute of Technology

Michigan
Baker College
- Cadillac
- Flint
- Mount Clemens
- Owosso

Jordan College

Minnesota
Alexandria Technical College
NEI College of Technology
Northwest Technical Institute
St. Paul Technical College
Saint Cloud Technical College
Southwest State University
University of Minnesota: Crookston
Willmar Technical College

Missouri
DeVry Institute of Technology: Kansas City
ITT Technical Institute: St. Louis
Lincoln University
Northwest Missouri Community College
Ranken Technical College

Montana
Billings Vocational-Technical Center
Butte Vocational-Technical Center
Helena Vocational-Technical Center
Missoula Vocational-Technical Center
Northern Montana College

Nebraska
Central Community College
Metropolitan Community College
Nebraska College of Technical Agriculture
Southeast Community College: Milford Campus

New Hampshire
New Hampshire Technical College
- Berlin
- Claremont
- Laconia
- Manchester
- Nashua
- Stratham

New Hampshire Technical Institute

New Jersey
New Jersey Institute of Technology

New Mexico
Albuquerque Technical-Vocational Institute
New Mexico Junior College

New York
Bramson ORT Technical Institute
City University of New York: New York City Technical College
College of Aeronautics
Culinary Institute of America
Institute of Design and Construction
State University of New York
- College of Agriculture and Technology at Cobleskill
- College of Agriculture and Technology at Morrisville
- College of Technology at Alfred
- College of Technology at Canton
- College of Technology at Delhi
- College of Technology at Farmingdale
- Institute of Technology at Utica/Rome

Taylor Business Institute
Technical Career Institutes

North Carolina
Asheville Buncombe Technical Community College
Caldwell Community College and Technical Institute
Fayetteville Technical Community College
Johnston Community College
McDowell Technical Community College
North Carolina Agricultural and Technical State University
Randolph Community College
Robeson Community College
Rowan-Cabarrus Community College
Wilson Technical Community College

North Dakota
North Dakota State College of Science
North Dakota State University: Bottineau
United Tribes Technical College

Ohio
Antonelli Institute of Art and Photography
Belmont Technical College
Central Ohio Technical College
Cleveland Institute of Electronics

DeVry Institute of Technology: Columbus
Hocking Technical College
ITT Technical Institute
Dayton
Youngstown
Jefferson Technical College
Lima Technical College
Marion Technical College
North Central Technical College
Northwest Technical College
Northwestern College
Ohio Institute of Photography and Technology
Ohio State University Agricultural Technical Institute
Owens Technical College
Findlay Campus
Toledo
Stark Technical College
Terra Technical College
University of Akron: Wayne College
University of Rio Grande

Oklahoma
Connors State College
Oklahoma Panhandle State University
Oklahoma State University
Oklahoma City
Technical Branch: Okmulgee

Oregon
ITT Technical Institute: Portland
Oregon Polytechnic Institute

Pennsylvania
Antonelli Institute of Art and Photography
Dean Institute of Technology
Delaware Valley College
Electronic Institutes
Middletown
Pittsburgh
ICS Center for Degree Studies
Johnson Technical Institute
Lincoln Technical Institute
McCarrie Schools of Health Sciences and Technology
National Education Center: Vale Tech Campus
Pennsylvania College of Technology
Pennsylvania Institute of Technology
Pittsburgh Institute of Mortuary Science
Pittsburgh Technical Institute
Triangle Tech
Erie School
Greensburg School
Pittsburgh Campus
Williamson Free School of Mechanical Trades

Puerto Rico
Technological College of the Municipality of San Juan
University of Puerto Rico
Aguadilla
Bayamon Technological University College
La Montana Regional College
Ponce Technological University College

Rhode Island
New England Institute of Technology

South Carolina
Aiken Technical College
Central Carolina Technical College
Chesterfield-Marlboro Technical College
Denmark Technical College
Florence-Darlington Technical College
Greenville Technical College
Horry-Georgetown Technical College
Midlands Technical College
Spartanburg Technical College
Technical College of the Lowcountry
Tri-County Technical College
Trident Technical College
Williamsburg Technical College
York Technical College

South Dakota
Lake Area Vocational Technical Institute
Mitchell Vocational Technical Institute
National College
Western Dakota Vocational Technical Institute

Tennessee
Chattanooga State Technical Community College
ITT Technical Institute: Nashville
Nashville State Technical Institute
Northeast State Technical Community College
Pellissippi State Technical Community College
State Technical Institute at Memphis

Texas
Central Texas College
DeVry Institute of Technology: Irving
Texas State Technical College
Amarillo
Harlingen
Sweetwater
Waco

Utah
ITT Technical Institute: Salt Lake City
Salt Lake Community College

Vermont
Vermont Technical College

Washington
Art Institute of Seattle
ITT Technical Institute: Spokane
Renton Technical College

West Virginia
Fairmont State College
West Virginia Institute of Technology

Wisconsin
Blackhawk Technical College
Chippewa Valley Technical College
Fox Valley Technical College
Gateway Technical College
Lakeshore Technical College
Mid-State Technical College
Moraine Park Technical College
Nicolet Area Technical College
Northcentral Technical College
Northeast Wisconsin Technical College
Southwest Wisconsin Technical College
Stratton College
Waukesha County Technical College
Western Wisconsin Technical College
Wisconsin Indianhead Technical College

Bible colleges

Alabama
International Bible College
Southeastern Bible College

Alaska
Alaska Bible College

Arizona
American Indian Bible College
Arizona College of the Bible
Southwestern College

Arkansas
Central Baptist College

California
Bethany College
LIFE Bible College
Pacific Christian College
Patten College
San Jose Christian College

Colorado
Colorado Christian University
Nazarene Bible College

Florida
Florida Baptist Theological College
Florida Bible College
Florida Christian College
Hobe Sound Bible College
Southeastern College of the Assemblies of God

Georgia
Atlanta Christian College
Toccoa Falls College

Idaho
Boise Bible College

Illinois
Lincoln Christian College and Seminary
Moody Bible Institute

Iowa
Emmaus Bible College
Faith Baptist Bible College and Theological Seminary
Vennard College

Kansas
Barclay College
Manhattan Christian College

Kentucky
Mid-Continent Baptist Bible College

Maryland
Washington Bible College

Michigan
Grace Bible College
Great Lakes Christian College
Reformed Bible College
William Tyndale College

Minnesota
Crown College
Minnesota Bible College
North Central Bible College
Northwestern College
Oak Hills Bible College
Pillsbury Baptist Bible College

Mississippi
Magnolia Bible College
Southeastern Baptist College

Missouri
Berean College
Calvary Bible College
Central Christian College of the Bible
Ozark Christian College
St. Louis Christian College

Nebraska
Grace College of the Bible
Nebraska Christian College
York College

North Carolina
East Coast Bible College
John Wesley College
Piedmont Bible College
Roanoke Bible College

North Dakota
Trinity Bible College

Ohio
Cincinnati Bible College and Seminary
Circleville Bible College
God's Bible School and College

Oklahoma
Mid-America Bible College
Southwestern College of Christian Ministries

Oregon
Eugene Bible College
Multnomah School of the Bible
Northwest Christian College
Western Baptist College

Pennsylvania
Baptist Bible College of Pennsylvania
Lancaster Bible College
Philadelphia College of Bible
Valley Forge Christian College

South Carolina
Columbia Bible College and Seminary

Tennessee
American Baptist College of ABT Seminary
Free Will Baptist Bible College
Johnson Bible College
Tennessee Temple University

Texas
Arlington Baptist College
Baptist Missionary Association Theological Seminary
Criswell College
Dallas Christian College
Institute for Christian Studies
Southwestern Assemblies of God College
Southwestern Christian College

Washington
Lutheran Bible Institute of Seattle
Northwest College of the Assemblies of God
Puget Sound Christian College

West Virginia
Appalachian Bible College

Wisconsin
Maranatha Baptist Bible College

Art/music colleges

California

Academy of Art College
American College for the Applied Arts: Los Angeles
Art Center College of Design
Art Institute of Southern California
California College of Arts and Crafts
Fashion Institute of Design and Merchandising
  Los Angeles
  San Francisco
Otis School of Art and Design
San Francisco Art Institute
San Francisco Conservatory of Music

Colorado

Rocky Mountain College of Art & Design

Connecticut

Paier College of Art

District of Columbia

Corcoran School of Art

Florida

Art Institute of Fort Lauderdale
Ringling School of Art and Design

Georgia

American College for the Applied Arts
Savannah College of Art and Design
Toccoa Falls College
Valdosta State College

Illinois

American Academy of Art
American Conservatory of Music
Ray College of Design
School of the Art Institute of Chicago
VanderCook College of Music

Kansas

Wichita State University

Louisiana

Loyola University

Maine

Maine College of Art

Maryland

Johns Hopkins University: Peabody Conservatory of Music
Maryland Institute College of Art

Massachusetts

Berklee College of Music
Massachusetts College of Art
Montserrat College of Art
New England Conservatory of Music
School of the Museum of Fine Arts

Michigan

Center for Creative Studies: College of Art and Design
Kendall College of Art and Design

Minnesota

College of Associated Arts
Minneapolis College of Art and Design

Missouri

Kansas City Art Institute

New Jersey

Westminster Choir College School of Music of Rider College

New Mexico

Institute of American Indian Arts

New York

Eastman School of Music of the University of Rochester
Five Towns College
Manhattan School of Music
Mannes College of Music
Parsons School of Design
School of Visual Arts

Ohio

Art Academy of Cincinnati
Capital University
Cleveland Institute of Art
Cleveland Institute of Music
Columbus College of Art and Design
Oberlin College
Virginia Marti College of Fashion and Art

Oregon

Pacific Northwest College of Art

Pennsylvania

Art Institute of Pittsburgh
Moore College of Art and Design

Puerto Rico

Escuela de Artes Plasticas de Puerto Rico

Rhode Island

Rhode Island School of Design

South Carolina

Converse College

Tennessee

Memphis College of Art

Texas

Miss Wade's Fashion Merchandising College

Washington

Art Institute of Seattle

Wisconsin

Lawrence University
Milwaukee Institute of Art & Design

Business colleges

Alabama

Draughons Junior College
University of Montevallo

Arizona

DeVry Institute of Technology: Phoenix
Western International University

California

American College for the Applied Arts: Los Angeles
Armstrong University
California State University: Stanislaus
Central California Commercial College
DeVry Institute of Technology: City of Industry
Heald Business College
  Concord
  San Jose
Kelsey-Jenney College
Lincoln University
Menlo College
Phillips Junior College: Condie Campus

Connecticut

Quinnipiac College

Delaware

Goldey-Beacom College

District of Columbia

Southeastern University
Strayer College

Florida

Art Institute of Fort Lauderdale
Fort Lauderdale College
Jones College
Lynn University
Tampa College
Webber College

Georgia

American College for the Applied Arts
Clayton State College
DeVry Institute of Technology: Atlanta
Mercer University Atlanta
Savannah State College
Valdosta State College

Hawaii

Hawaii Pacific University

Idaho

Lewis Clark State College

Illinois

DeVry Institute of Technology
  Addison
  Chicago
Gem City College
Robert Morris College: Chicago

Iowa

American Institute of Commerce

Kansas

Brown Mackie College
Friends University
Wichita State University

Kentucky

Campbellsville College
Owensboro Junior College of Business
Sullivan College

Louisiana

Loyola University

Maine

Andover College
Beal College
Casco Bay College
Husson College
Thomas College

Maryland

Hagerstown Business College
Morgan State University

Massachusetts

American International College
Aquinas College at Milton
Babson College
Bay Path College
Bentley College
Katharine Gibbs School
Lasell College
New England Banking Institute
Nichols College
North Adams State College
Western New England College

Michigan

Baker College
  Auburn Hills
  Cadillac
  Flint
  Mount Clemens
  Muskegon
  Owosso
  Port Huron
Cleary College
Davenport College of Business
Detroit College of Business
Ferris State University
GMI Engineering & Management Institute
Great Lakes Junior College of Business
Lawrence Technological University
Lewis College of Business
Northwood University
Saginaw Valley State University
Walsh College of Accountancy and Business Administration

Missouri

DeVry Institute of Technology: Kansas City
Lincoln University
Missouri Southern State College
Missouri Western State College
National College
Rockhurst College

Montana

Eastern Montana College
Northern Montana College

Nebraska

Bellevue College

Nevada

Sierra Nevada College

New Hampshire

Castle College
Franklin Pierce College
Hesser College
McIntosh College
New England College
New Hampshire College
Plymouth State College of the University System of New Hampshire

New Jersey

Berkeley College of Business
Katharine Gibbs School
Rider College
Thomas Edison State College

New Mexico

College of the Southwest
National College

New York

Berkeley College
Berkeley School: New York City
Bryant & Stratton Business Institute
  Albany
  Syracuse
Central City Business Institute
City University of New York: Baruch College
College of Insurance
Dowling College

Jamestown Business College
Katharine Gibbs School: New York
Monroe College
Olean Business Institute
St. John Fisher College
Taylor Business Institute
Utica School of Commerce
Westchester Business Institute

North Dakota
North Dakota State University: Bottineau

Ohio
Bliss College
Bradford School
Central State University
DeVry Institute of Technology: Columbus
Dyke College
Northwestern College
Ohio Valley Business College
Tiffin University
University of Rio Grande
Virginia Marti College of Fashion and Art

Pennsylvania
Central Pennsylvania Business School
Churchman Business School
Delaware Valley College
DuBois Business College
ICS Center for Degree Studies
Robert Morris College
Shippensburg University of Pennsylvania

Puerto Rico
American University of Puerto Rico
Caribbean University
Colegio Universitario del Este

Rhode Island
Bryant College

South Carolina
Columbia Junior College of Business

South Dakota
Huron University
National College
Northern State University

Tennessee
Bristol University
Christian Brothers University
Draughons Junior College of Business: Nashville

Texas
DeVry Institute of Technology: Irving
Miss Wade's Fashion Merchandising College
Northwood University: Texas Campus
University of Dallas

Utah
LDS Business College
Phillips Junior College: Salt Lake City Campus
Stevens-Henager College of Business

Vermont
Champlain College
College of St. Joseph in Vermont

Virginia
National Business College

West Virginia
Fairmont State College

Wisconsin
Milwaukee College of Business
Milwaukee School of Engineering
Stratton College

Engineering colleges

California
Cogswell Polytechnical College
Harvey Mudd College

Colorado
Colorado School of Mines
Colorado Technical College
National College

Connecticut
Bridgeport Engineering Institute
United States Coast Guard Academy

Illinois
Illinois Institute of Technology
Parks College of St. Louis University

Indiana
Rose-Hulman Institute of Technology

Kansas
Wichita State University

Louisiana
Grantham College of Engineering

Maine
Maine Maritime Academy

Maryland
Capitol College
Morgan State University

Massachusetts
Franklin Institute of Boston
Massachusetts Institute of Technology
Worcester Polytechnic Institute

Michigan
GMI Engineering & Management Institute
Lake Superior State University
Saginaw Valley State University

Missouri
University of Missouri: Rolla

Montana
Montana College of Mineral Science and Technology

New Jersey
Rutgers—The State University of New Jersey: College of Engineering
Stevens Institute of Technology

New Mexico
New Mexico Institute of Mining and Technology

New York
Columbia University: School of Engineering and Applied Science
Manhattan College
Union College
United States Merchant Marine Academy

Oklahoma
Oklahoma Christian University of Science and Arts

Pennsylvania
Lafayette College
University of Pittsburgh at Johnstown

Puerto Rico
Universidad Politecnica de Puerto Rico

South Dakota
South Dakota School of Mines and Technology

Tennessee
Christian Brothers University
Tennessee Technological University

Washington
Cogswell College North

West Virginia
West Virginia Institute of Technology

Wisconsin
Milwaukee School of Engineering

Colleges of health science

Alabama
Draughons Junior College

Arkansas
University of Arkansas for Medical Sciences

California
California College for Health Sciences
Samuel Merritt College

Colorado
University of Colorado Health Sciences Center

Connecticut
Quinnipiac College

Georgia
Valdosta State College

Idaho
Lewis Clark State College

Illinois
Blessing-Reiman College of Nursing
Concordia University
Lakeview College of Nursing
Mennonite College of Nursing
National College of Chiropractic
St. Francis Medical Center College of Nursing
St. Joseph College of Nursing
Trinity Christian College
West Suburban College of Nursing

Indiana
Lutheran College of Health Professions

Iowa
Iowa Lakes Community College

Kansas
University of Kansas Medical Center
Wichita State University

Kentucky
Lees College

Maine
Central Maine Medical Center School of Nursing
Husson College

Maryland
Coppin State College

Massachusetts
Forsyth School for Dental Hygienists
Massachusetts College of Pharmacy and Allied Health Sciences

Michigan
Baker College of Port Huron
Ferris State University
Lake Superior State University
Saginaw Valley State University

Minnesota
St. Mary's Campus of the College of St. Catherine

Mississippi
University of Mississippi Medical Center

Missouri
Deaconess College of Nursing
Research College of Nursing
Rockhurst College
St. Louis College of Pharmacy

Montana
Northern Montana College

Nebraska
Clarkson College
Nebraska Methodist College of Nursing and Allied Health
University of Nebraska Medical Center

New Jersey
Rutgers—The State University of New Jersey
  College of Nursing
  College of Pharmacy
University of Medicine and Dentistry of New Jersey: School of Health Related Professions
University of Medicine and Dentistry of New Jersey: School of Nursing

New York
Albany College of Pharmacy
Catholic Medical Center of Brooklyn and Queens School of Nursing
City University of New York: Hunter College
Cochran School of Nursing-St. John's Riverside Hospital
College of New Rochelle
Columbia University: School of Nursing
Helene Fuld School of Nursing
Ithaca College
Long Island College Hospital School of Nursing
Phillips Beth Israel School of Nursing
St. Joseph's School of Nursing

State University of New York
Health Science Center at Brooklyn
Health Science Center at Syracuse

North Dakota
Medcenter One College of Nursing

Ohio
Capital University
Kettering College of Medical Arts
University of Rio Grande

Oklahoma
University of Oklahoma Health Sciences Center

Pennsylvania
Hahnemann University School of Health Sciences and Humanities
McCarrie Schools of Health Sciences and Technology
Philadelphia College of Pharmacy and Science

Puerto Rico
Technological College of the Municipality of San Juan

South Carolina
Medical University of South Carolina

South Dakota
Huron University
Presentation College

Tennessee
University of Tennessee: Memphis

Texas
University of Texas
Health Science Center at Houston
Medical Branch at Galveston
Southwestern Medical Center at Dallas Southwestern Allied Health Sciences School

Virginia
College of Health Sciences

Washington
Bastyr College

Wisconsin
Bellin College of Nursing
Columbia College of Nursing

Military colleges

Alabama
Marion Military Institute

Colorado
United States Air Force Academy

Connecticut
United States Coast Guard Academy

Georgia
Georgia Military College
North Georgia College

Maryland
United States Naval Academy

Missouri
Kemper Military School and College

New Mexico
New Mexico Military Institute

New York
United States Merchant Marine Academy
United States Military Academy

Pennsylvania
Valley Forge Military College

South Carolina
The Citadel

Vermont
Norwich University

Virginia
Virginia Military Institute

Seminary/rabbinical colleges

Alabama
Southern Christian University

California
Dominican School of Philosophy and Theology
Hebrew Union College: Jewish Institute of Religion
Queen of the Holy Rosary College
University of Judaism

District of Columbia
Oblate College

Florida
St. John Vianney College Seminary
Talmudic College of Florida

Georgia
Toccoa Falls College

Illinois
Lincoln Christian College and Seminary

Indiana
St. Meinrad College

Iowa
Divine Word College
Faith Baptist Bible College and Theological Seminary
University of Dubuque

Louisiana
St. Joseph Seminary College

Maryland
Ner Israel Rabbinical College
Washington Bible College

Massachusetts
Hellenic College
St. Hyacinth College and Seminary
St. John's Seminary College

Michigan
Sacred Heart Major Seminary
Yeshiva Beth Yehuda-Yeshiva Gedolah of Greater Detroit

Minnesota
St. John's University

Missouri
Conception Seminary College

New York
Beth Hamedrash Shaarei Yosher Institute
Beth Hatalmud Rabbinical College
Central Yeshiva Tomchei Tmimim Lubavitz
Darkei No'Am Rabbinical College
Kehilath Yakov Rabbinical Seminary
Kol Yaakov Torah Center
Machzikei Hadath Rabbinical College
Mesivta Tifereth Jerusalem of America
Mesivta Torah Vodaath Seminary
Mirrer Yeshiva Central Institute
Ohr Hameir Theological Seminary
Ohr Somayach Tanenbaum Education Center
Rabbinical College Bobover Yeshiva B'nei Zion
Rabbinical College Ch'san Sofer of New York
Rabbinical College of Long Island
Rabbinical Seminary Adas Yereim
Rabbinical Seminary of America
Rabbinical Seminary M'Kor Chaim
Talmudical Institute of Upstate New York
Talmudical Seminary Oholei Torah
United Talmudical Academy
Wadhams Hall Seminary-College
Yeshiva Derech Chaim
Yeshiva Karlin Stolin Beth Aron Y'Israel Rabbinical Institute
Yeshiva of Nitra Rabbinical College
Yeshiva Shaar Hatorah
Yeshivat Mikdash Melech

North Carolina
Southeastern Baptist Theological Seminary

Ohio
Pontifical College Josephinum

Oregon
Multnomah School of the Bible

Pennsylvania
Talmudical Yeshiva of Philadelphia

Tennessee
University of the South

Texas
Baptist Missionary Association Theological Seminary
Criswell College

Virginia
Eastern Mennonite College
Liberty University

Wisconsin
Northwestern College

Teachers' colleges

Alabama
University of Montevallo

California
Hebrew Union College: Jewish Institute of Religion
Pacific Oaks College

Florida
Southeastern College of the Assemblies of God

Georgia
Valdosta State College

Idaho
Lewis Clark State College

Illinois
Concordia University
Eastern Illinois University
National-Louis University
Trinity Christian College

Kansas
Wichita State University

Kentucky
Campbellsville College

Maine
University of Maine at Farmington

Maryland
Coppin State College
Morgan State University
Ner Israel Rabbinical College

Massachusetts
Hebrew College
Wheelock College

Michigan
Saginaw Valley State University

Minnesota
Concordia College: St. Paul
Dr. Martin Luther College

Missouri
Harris Stowe State College
Missouri Southern State College

Montana
Eastern Montana College
Northern Montana College
Western Montana College of the University of Montana

Nebraska
Chadron State College
Concordia College
Peru State College
Wayne State College

New Hampshire
Plymouth State College of the University System of New Hampshire

New Mexico
College of the Southwest

New York
Rabbinical College of Long Island
State University of New York College at Plattsburgh

North Dakota
Mayville State University
Valley City State University

Ohio
Central State University
Circleville Bible College
Cleveland College of Jewish Studies
University of Rio Grande

Oklahoma
Langston University
Oklahoma Christian University of Science and Arts

Oklahoma Panhandle State University
Oral Roberts University

Oregon

Southern Oregon State College

Pennsylvania

Cheyney University of Pennsylvania
Shippensburg University of Pennsylvania

Puerto Rico

American University of Puerto Rico

South Dakota

Black Hills State University
Huron University
Northern State University

West Virginia

Fairmont State College
Glenville State College

Campus environment—2-year colleges

Small colleges with urban campuses

Alabama
Concordia College
Harry M. Ayers State Technical College
J. F. Drake State Technical College
John M. Patterson State Technical College
Phillips Junior College: Birmingham
Trenholm State Technical College
Virginia College

Arizona
ITT Technical Institute: Phoenix

Arkansas
Capital City Junior College
Shorter College

California
College of Oceaneering
Fashion Institute of Design and Merchandising: San Francisco
Kelsey-Jenney College
Phillips Junior College: Condie Campus
San Francisco College of Mortuary Science

Colorado
ITT Technical Institute: Aurora

Florida
Flagler Career Institute
Keiser College of Technology
New England Institute of Technology
South College: Palm Beach Campus
Southern College

Georgia
Meadows College of Business

Illinois
American Academy of Art
Lexington Institute of Hospitality Careers
Montay College
Springfield College in Illinois

Iowa
American Institute of Business

Kansas
Brown Mackie College
Coffeyville Community College
Donnelly College

Kentucky
Owensboro Junior College of Business

Louisiana
Phillips Junior College: New Orleans

Maine
Andover College
Beal College
Casco Bay College
Central Maine Medical Center School of Nursing
Northern Maine Technical College

Maryland
Baltimore International Culinary College

Massachusetts
Bay State College
Becker College: Worcester Campus
Fisher College
Franklin Institute of Boston
Katharine Gibbs School

Michigan
Lewis College of Business

Minnesota
Bethany Lutheran College

Missouri
Phillips Junior College

Nebraska
Lincoln School of Commerce

New Hampshire
McIntosh College

New Mexico
Santa Fe Community College

New York
American Academy of Dramatic Arts
American Academy McAllister Institute of Funeral Service
Berkeley School: New York City
Bryant & Stratton Business Institute
- Albany
- Rochester
- Syracuse

Catholic Medical Center of Brooklyn and Queens School of Nursing
Central City Business Institute
Cochran School of Nursing-St. John's Riverside Hospital
Helene Fuld School of Nursing
Institute of Design and Construction
Katharine Gibbs School: New York
Long Island College Hospital School of Nursing
Maria College
Phillips Beth Israel School of Nursing
Sage Junior College of Albany
St. Joseph's School of Nursing
Taylor Business Institute
Utica School of Commerce
Wood Tobe-Coburn School

North Carolina
Peace College
St. Mary's College

Ohio
Antonelli Institute of Art and Photography
Bliss College
Davis Junior College of Business
ITT Technical Institute: Youngstown
Kent State University: East Liverpool Regional Campus
Miami University: Hamilton Campus
Miami-Jacobs College
Ohio Valley Business College
Southern Ohio College
Virginia Marti College of Fashion and Art

Oregon
Oregon Polytechnic Institute

Pennsylvania
American Institute of Design
Churchman Business School
Dean Institute of Technology
Electronic Institutes: Pittsburgh
Lackawanna Junior College
McCarrie Schools of Health Sciences and Technology
Penn Technical Institute
Pittsburgh Institute of Mortuary Science
Pittsburgh Technical Institute
Thaddeus Stevens State School of Technology
Triangle Tech
- Erie School
- Pittsburgh Campus

South Dakota
Kilian Community College

Tennessee
Aquinas Junior College
Draughons Junior College of Business: Nashville
ITT Technical Institute: Nashville
Knoxville Business College

Texas
Commonwealth Institute of Funeral Service
Dallas Institute of Funeral Service
Miss Wade's Fashion Merchandising College

Utah
ITT Technical Institute: Salt Lake City
LDS Business College
Stevens-Henager College of Business

Virginia
College of Health Sciences

Washington
ITT Technical Institute: Seattle

Wisconsin
Milwaukee College of Business
Stratton College
University of Wisconsin Center: Manitowoc County

Small colleges with suburban campuses

Alabama
Draughons Junior College
Walker College

Arizona
ITT Technical Institute: Tucson

California
American Academy of Dramatic Arts: West
Brooks College
Central California Commercial College
Heald Business College
- Concord
- San Jose

ITT Technical Institute: Sacramento
Phillips Junior College: Fresno Campus
Queen of the Holy Rosary College

Colorado
Bel-Rea Institute of Animal Technology
Denver Institute of Technology
Parks Junior College

Connecticut
Briarwood College
Mitchell College

Florida
Florida College
ITT Technical Institute: Tampa
Phillips Junior College: Melbourne

Georgia
Art Institute of Atlanta
Bauder College
Gupton Jones College of Funeral Service
Oxford College of Emory University
South College

Idaho
ITT Technical Institute: Boise

Illinois
ITT Technical Institute: Hoffman Estates
MacCormac Junior College

Indiana
Holy Cross College
Indiana Vocational Technical College: Southeast
ITT Technical Institute: Evansville
Mid-America College of Funeral Service

Iowa
American Institute of Commerce

Kansas
Central College
Haskell Indian Junior College

Kentucky
Institute of Electronic Technology
Louisville Technical Institute

RETS Electronic Institute

Maryland

Hagerstown Business College

Massachusetts

Aquinas College at Milton
Aquinas College at Newton
Becker College: Leicester Campus
Essex Agricultural and Technical Institute
Marian Court Junior College

Michigan

Baker College of Auburn Hills

Minnesota

NEI College of Technology
Northwest Technical Institute

Missouri

ITT Technical Institute: St. Louis
Northwest Missouri Community College

Montana

Billings Vocational-Technical Center
Butte Vocational-Technical Center
Helena Vocational-Technical Center
Missoula Vocational-Technical Center

New Hampshire

New Hampshire Technical College
 Berlin
 Laconia

New Jersey

Katharine Gibbs School

New Mexico

Institute of American Indian Arts
New Mexico Military Institute
Parks College

New York

Berkeley College
Jamestown Business College
Katharine Gibbs School: Melville
Olean Business Institute
Villa Maria College of Buffalo

North Carolina

Brevard College

North Dakota

United Tribes Technical College
University of North Dakota: Williston

Ohio

Bradford School
ITT Technical Institute: Dayton
Kettering College of Medical Arts
Ohio Institute of Photography and Technology

Oklahoma

Bacone College

Pennsylvania

Antonelli Institute of Art and Photography
Central Pennsylvania Business School
CHI Institute
DuBois Business College
Electronic Institutes: Middletown
Harcum Junior College
Johnson Technical Institute
Lincoln Technical Institute
Manor Junior College
Pennsylvania Institute of Technology
University of Pittsburgh at Titusville
Valley Forge Military College

South Carolina

Columbia Junior College of Business
Spartanburg Methodist College

Texas

Bauder Fashion College
ITT Technical Institute: Houston
Jacksonville College
Lon Morris College
Texas State Technical College: Amarillo

Utah

Phillips Junior College: Salt Lake City Campus

Washington

ITT Technical Institute: Spokane

Wisconsin

Madison Junior College of Business
University of Wisconsin Center
 Marshfield/Wood County
 Rock County
 Sheboygan County
 Washington County

American Samoa, Caroline Islands, Guam, Marianas, Virgin Islands

Micronesian Occupational College

Small colleges with rural campuses

Alabama

Alabama Aviation and Technical College
Central Alabama Community College: Childersburg Campus
Douglas MacArthur State Technical College
Marion Military Institute
Reid State Technical College
Sparks State Technical College

Alaska

Prince William Sound Community College

Arkansas

Rich Mountain Community College

California

D-Q University

Colorado

Colorado Mountain College
 Alpine Campus
 Spring Valley Campus
 Timberline Campus
Lamar Community College
Morgan Community College
Otero Junior College

Georgia

Andrew College
East Georgia College
Reinhardt College
Waycross College
Young Harris College

Illinois

Black Hawk College: East Campus
Gem City College
Morrison Institute of Technology

Indiana

Ancilla College

Iowa

Ellsworth Community College
Northwest Iowa Community College
Southeastern Community College: South Campus
Waldorf College

Kansas

Hesston College

Kentucky

Lees College

Michigan

Suomi College

Minnesota

Rainy River Community College
Vermilion Community College
Worthington Community College

Mississippi

Wood Junior College

Missouri

Cottey College
Kemper Military School and College

Montana

Blackfeet Community College
Dawson Community College
Dull Knife Memorial College
Fort Belknap College
Fort Peck Community College
Little Big Horn College
Miles Community College
Salish Kootenai College
Stone Child College

Nebraska

Nebraska College of Technical Agriculture
Nebraska Indian Community College
Southeast Community College
 Beatrice Campus
 Milford Campus
York College

Nevada

Deep Springs College

New Hampshire

Castle College
New Hampshire Technical College
 Claremont
 Stratham
White Pines College

New Jersey

Assumption College for Sisters
Warren County Community College

New York

Mater Dei College
Paul Smith's College

North Carolina

Anson Community College
Bladen Community College
Brunswick Community College
Louisburg College
Martin Community College
Mayland Community College
McDowell Technical Community College
Montgomery Community College
Pamlico Community College
Roanoke-Chowan Community College
Southeastern Baptist Theological Seminary
Tri-County Community College

North Dakota

Little Hoop Community College
North Dakota State University: Bottineau
Standing Rock College
Turtle Mountain Community College
University of North Dakota: Lake Region

Ohio

Chatfield College
Ohio State University Agricultural Technical Institute
Ohio University: Eastern Campus
Wright State University: Lake Campus

Oklahoma

St. Gregory's College

Pennsylvania

National Education Center: Vale Tech Campus
Triangle Tech: Greensburg School

Puerto Rico

University of Puerto Rico: La Montana Regional College

South Carolina

Chesterfield-Marlboro Technical College
Denmark Technical College
North Greenville College
University of South Carolina at Union
Williamsburg Technical College

South Dakota

Mitchell Vocational Technical Institute
Sisseton-Wahpeton Community College
Western Dakota Vocational Technical Institute

Tennessee

Hiwassee College

Texas

Clarendon College
Frank Phillips College
Ranger Junior College
Texas State Technical College: Sweetwater

Vermont

Landmark College
New England Culinary Institute
Sterling College
Vermont Technical College

Virginia

Eastern Shore Community College
Southern Virginia College for Women

Wisconsin

University of Wisconsin Center
 Baraboo/Sauk County
 Barron County
 Marinette County
 Richland

American Samoa, Caroline Islands, Guam, Marianas, Virgin Islands

College of Micronesia-FSM

Medium-sized colleges with urban campuses

Arizona

South Mountain Community College

California

Fashion Institute of Design and Merchandising

Colorado

Colorado Institute of Art
Pueblo Community College

Connecticut

Housatonic Community-Technical College

Florida

Art Institute of Fort Lauderdale

Georgia

Atlanta Metropolitan College
Darton College
Savannah Technical Institute

Illinois

City Colleges of Chicago
- Kennedy-King College
- Malcolm X College

St. Augustine College
State Community College

Indiana

Indiana Vocational Technical College
- Columbus
- Northcentral
- Northwest
- Southwest
- Wabash Valley

Iowa

Iowa Lakes Community College

Kansas

Independence Community College

Maine

Eastern Maine Technical College

Massachusetts

New England Banking Institute
Roxbury Community College

Michigan

Great Lakes Junior College of Business
Highland Park Community College

Minnesota

St. Mary's Campus of the College of St. Catherine
Saint Cloud Technical College

Missouri

Ranken Technical College

Montana

Flathead Valley Community College

New Mexico

New Mexico State University at Alamogordo

New York

Bramson ORT Technical Institute
Monroe College
Trocaire College

Ohio

Northwestern College
Owens Technical College: Findlay Campus

Oklahoma

Northeastern Oklahoma Agricultural and Mechanical College

Pennsylvania

Art Institute of Pittsburgh

Puerto Rico

Huertas Junior College
Technological College of the Municipality of San Juan
University of Puerto Rico: Carolina Regional College

South Carolina

University of South Carolina
- Beaufort
- Sumter

Texas

Galveston College
Temple Junior College

Washington

Art Institute of Seattle

West Virginia

West Virginia Northern Community College

Wisconsin

University of Wisconsin Center
- Fox Valley
- Marathon County

Medium-sized colleges with suburban campuses

Alabama

Bessemer State Technical College
Chattahoochee Valley Community College
Jefferson Davis State Junior College
Lawson State Community College
Shoals Community College

Arkansas

Arkansas State University: Beebe Branch
Garland County Community College
North Arkansas Community/Technical College
Phillips County Community College

California

Marymount College

Connecticut

Asnuntuck Community-Technical College

Delaware

Delaware Technical and Community College: Terry Campus

Georgia

Athens Area Technical Institute
Brunswick College
Chattahoochee Technical Institute
Dalton College
DeKalb Technical Institute
Gainesville College
Georgia Military College

Hawaii

University of Hawaii: Windward Community College

Indiana

Indiana Vocational Technical College
- Eastcentral
- Kokomo
- Lafayette
- Southcentral
- Whitewater

Iowa

Clinton Community College
Marshalltown Community College
Southeastern Community College: North Campus
Western Iowa Tech Community College

Louisiana

Nunez Community College
Southern University in Shreveport

Maine

Central Maine Technical College
Southern Maine Technical College

Maryland

Allegany Community College
Wor-Wic Community College

Massachusetts

Dean Junior College
Quincy College

Michigan

Alpena Community College

Minnesota

Austin Community College

Nebraska

Mid Plains Community College

New Hampshire

New Hampshire Technical College
- Manchester
- Nashua

New Hampshire Technical Institute

New Jersey

Berkeley College of Business
Fairleigh Dickinson University: Edward Williams College
Sussex County Community College

New Mexico

Eastern New Mexico University: Roswell Campus

New York

Culinary Institute of America
Jefferson Community College
Westchester Business Institute

North Carolina

Cleveland Community College
Mitchell Community College
Rowan-Cabarrus Community College
Wayne Community College

Ohio

Central Ohio Technical College
Jefferson Technical College
Kent State University
- Ashtabula Regional Campus
- Stark Campus
- Trumbull Regional Campus

Lima Technical College
Marion Technical College
Miami University: Middletown Campus
North Central Technical College
Ohio State University
- Lima Campus
- Mansfield Campus
- Newark Campus

Ohio University: Lancaster Campus
University of Cincinnati: Clermont College

Pennsylvania

Community College of Beaver County

Puerto Rico

University of Puerto Rico: Aguadilla

Rhode Island

New England Institute of Technology

South Carolina

Central Carolina Technical College
Florence-Darlington Technical College
Spartanburg Technical College

Texas

Weatherford College

Vermont

Champlain College

Virginia

Richard Bland College

Wisconsin

University of Wisconsin Center: Waukesha

Wyoming

Western Wyoming Community College

American Samoa, Caroline Islands, Guam, Marianas, Virgin Islands

Guam Community College

Medium-sized colleges with rural campuses

Alabama

Alabama Southern Community College
Bevill State Community College
Enterprise State Junior College
George C. Wallace State Community College at Selma
Lurleen B. Wallace State Junior College
Northeast Alabama Community College
Northwest Alabama Community College
Snead State Community College

Arizona

Navajo Community College

Arkansas

East Arkansas Community College
Mississippi County Community College

South Arkansas Community College
Southern Arkansas University: Technical Branch

California
College of the Siskiyous
Feather River College
Lassen College
Porterville College
Taft College

Colorado
Colorado Northwestern Community College
Trinidad State Junior College

Connecticut
Northwestern Connecticut Community-Technical College
Quinebaug Valley Community-Technical College

Florida
Chipola Junior College
Lake City Community College
Lake-Sumter Community College
North Florida Junior College
South Florida Community College

Georgia
Abraham Baldwin Agricultural College
Bainbridge College
Floyd College
Gordon College
Middle Georgia College
South Georgia College
Truett-McConnell College

Hawaii
University of Hawaii
Hawaii Community College
Kauai Community College

Illinois
Illinois Eastern Community Colleges
Frontier Community College
Lincoln Trail College
Olney Central College
Wabash Valley College
Lincoln College
Sauk Valley Community College
Shawnee Community College
Spoon River College

Iowa
Hawkeye Community College
Iowa Central Community College
Muscatine Community College
Northeast Iowa Community College
Southwestern Community College

Kansas
Allen County Community College
Colby Community College
Dodge City Community College
Fort Scott Community College
Garden City Community College
Highland Community College
Labette Community College
Neosho County Community College
Pratt Community College
Seward County Community College

Kentucky
Henderson Community College
Madisonville Community College
Maysville Community College
Prestonburg Community College
Southeast Community College

Louisiana
Louisiana State University
Alexandria
Eunice

Maryland
Cecil Community College
Chesapeake College

Massachusetts
Cape Cod Community College
Greenfield Community College
Mount Wachusett Community College

Michigan
Glen Oaks Community College
Gogebic Community College
Kirtland Community College
Mid Michigan Community College
Montcalm Community College
Southwestern Michigan College
West Shore Community College

Minnesota
Alexandria Technical College
Brainerd Community College
Fergus Falls Community College
Hibbing Community College
Itasca Community College: Arrowhead Region
Mesabi Community College: Arrowhead Region
University of Minnesota: Crookston
Willmar Community College
Willmar Technical College

Mississippi
Copiah-Lincoln Community College
East Central Community College
East Mississippi Community College
Holmes Community College
Mississippi Delta Community College
Pearl River Community College
Southwest Mississippi Community College

Missouri
Crowder College
Moberly Area Community College
State Fair Community College

Nebraska
McCook Community College
Western Nebraska Community College: Scottsbluff Campus

Nevada
Northern Nevada Community College

New Jersey
Cumberland County College
Salem Community College

New Mexico
New Mexico Junior College
New Mexico State University at Carlsbad
Northern New Mexico Community College

New York
Cayuga County Community College
Clinton Community College
Columbia-Greene Community College
Fulton-Montgomery Community College
Herkimer County Community College
North Country Community College
State University of New York
College of Agriculture and Technology at Cobleskill
College of Technology at Canton
College of Technology at Delhi
Suffolk County Community College: Eastern Campus
Sullivan County Community College
Tompkins-Cortland Community College
Ulster County Community College

North Carolina
Beaufort County Community College
Blue Ridge Community College
Caldwell Community College and Technical Institute
Carteret Community College
College of the Albemarle
Craven Community College
Davidson County Community College
Edgecombe Community College
Halifax Community College
Haywood Community College
Isothermal Community College
James Sprunt Community College
Johnston Community College
Lenoir Community College
Nash Community College
Piedmont Community College
Randolph Community College
Richmond Community College
Robeson Community College
Rockingham Community College
Sampson Community College
Sandhills Community College
Southeastern Community College
Southwestern Community College
Stanly Community College
Vance-Granville Community College
Western Piedmont Community College
Wilkes Community College
Wilson Technical Community College

North Dakota
Bismarck State College
North Dakota State College of Science

Ohio
Belmont Technical College
Bowling Green State University: Firelands College
Kent State University
Salem Regional Campus
Tuscarawas Campus
Northwest Technical College
Ohio University: Chillicothe Campus
Southern State Community College
Terra Technical College
University of Akron: Wayne College

Oklahoma
Carl Albert State College
Connors State College
Eastern Oklahoma State College
Oklahoma State University Technical Branch: Okmulgee
Redlands Community College
Seminole Junior College
Western Oklahoma State College

Oregon
Clatsop Community College
Rogue Community College
Umpqua Community College

Pennsylvania
Keystone Junior College

South Carolina
Aiken Technical College
Horry-Georgetown Technical College
Technical College of the Lowcountry
University of South Carolina: Salkehatchie Regional Campus

South Dakota
Lake Area Vocational Technical Institute

Tennessee
Dyersburg State Community College

Texas
Bee County College
Cisco Junior College
Hill College
Howard College
Northeast Texas Community College
Panola College
Paris Junior College
Southwest Texas Junior College
Vernon Regional Junior College

Utah
College of Eastern Utah
Dixie College
Snow College

Virginia
Blue Ridge Community College
Dabney S. Lancaster Community College
Mountain Empire Community College
Patrick Henry Community College
Paul D. Camp Community College
Rappahannock Community College
Wytheville Community College

Washington
Big Bend Community College
Peninsula College
Wenatchee Valley College

West Virginia
Potomac State College of West Virginia University

Wisconsin
Blackhawk Technical College
Lakeshore Technical College
Mid-State Technical College
Nicolet Area Technical College
Southwest Wisconsin Technical College

Wyoming
Central Wyoming College
Eastern Wyoming College
Northwest College
Sheridan College

Large colleges with urban campuses

Alabama
Bishop State Community College
Gadsden State Community College

California
Compton Community College
Merritt College

Colorado
Community College of Aurora
Community College of Denver

Connecticut
Capital Community-Technical College
Gateway Community-Technical College
Norwalk Community-Technical College

Hawaii
University of Hawaii
Honolulu Community College
Kapiolani Community College

Idaho
North Idaho College

Illinois
Black Hawk College
City Colleges of Chicago: Olive-Harvey College
Danville Area Community College
Richland Community College
Robert Morris College: Chicago

Indiana
Indiana Vocational Technical College
Central Indiana
Northeast

Kansas
Hutchinson Community College

Maryland
Baltimore City Community College
Dundalk Community College
Montgomery College: Takoma Park Campus

Massachusetts
Bristol Community College
Bunker Hill Community College
Massasoit Community College
Quinsigamond Community College
Springfield Technical Community College

Michigan
Muskegon Community College
St. Clair County Community College

Minnesota
Minneapolis Community College
Rochester Community College
St. Paul Technical College

Mississippi
Meridian Community College

Missouri
Penn Valley Community College

New Hampshire
Hesser College

New Jersey
Hudson County Community College
Passaic County Community College

New York
City University of New York: Hostos Community College
Erie Community College: City Campus
Mohawk Valley Community College
Schenectady County Community College
Technical Career Institutes

North Carolina
Asheville Buncombe Technical Community College
Cape Fear Community College
Durham Technical Community College

Ohio
Cuyahoga Community College: Metropolitan Campus

Oklahoma
Oklahoma State University: Oklahoma City

Pennsylvania
Reading Area Community College

Tennessee
Shelby State Community College

Texas
Amarillo College
El Centro College
Laredo Junior College
Lee College
Odessa College
Palo Alto College
St. Philip's College
Texarkana College
Victoria College

Virginia
Virginia Western Community College

Washington
South Seattle Community College
Spokane Community College
Tacoma Community College

Wisconsin
Chippewa Valley Technical College
Moraine Park Technical College
Western Wisconsin Technical College

Wyoming
Casper College

Large colleges with suburban campuses

Alabama
Jefferson State Community College
Shelton State Community College

Arizona
Paradise Valley Community College

Arkansas
Westark Community College

California
Canada College
College of the Canyons
Cuyamaca College
Mission College
Napa Valley College
San Diego Miramar College

Colorado
Northeastern Junior College
Pikes Peak Community College
Red Rocks Community College

Connecticut
Middlesex Community-Technical College
Three Rivers Community-Technical College
Tunxis Community-Technical College

Delaware
Delaware Technical and Community College: Stanton/Wilmington Campus

Florida
Central Florida Community College
Gulf Coast Community College
Polk Community College

Georgia
Gwinnett Technical Institute
Macon College

Idaho
College of Southern Idaho

Illinois
Lewis and Clark Community College
Morton College

Iowa
Iowa Western Community College
North Iowa Area Community College
Scott Community College

Kansas
Kansas City Kansas Community College

Kentucky
Ashland Community College
Elizabethtown Community College
Hopkinsville Community College
Lexington Community College
Paducah Community College

Louisiana
Bossier Parish Community College

Maryland
Frederick Community College
Hagerstown Junior College
Harford Community College
Howard Community College
Montgomery College: Germantown Campus

Massachusetts
Holyoke Community College
Massachusetts Bay Community College
Middlesex Community College
Newbury College
North Shore Community College
Northern Essex Community College

Michigan
Northwestern Michigan College

Minnesota
Anoka-Ramsey Community College
Inver Hills Community College
Lakewood Community College
North Hennepin Community College

Mississippi
Mississippi Gulf Coast Community College
Jackson County Campus
Jefferson Davis Campus
Northwest Mississippi Community College

Missouri
Maple Woods Community College
St. Charles County Community College

Nebraska
Southeast Community College: Lincoln Campus

Nevada
Western Nevada Community College

New Jersey
Mercer County Community College

New Mexico
Dona Ana Branch Community College of New Mexico State University

New York
Broome Community College
Erie Community College
North Campus
South Campus
Orange County Community College
Suffolk County Community College: Western Campus

North Carolina
Catawba Valley Community College
Coastal Carolina Community College
Fayetteville Technical Community College
Gaston College
Wake Technical Community College

Ohio
Clark State Community College
Cuyahoga Community College: Eastern Campus
Stark Technical College
University of Cincinnati: Raymond Walters College

Oklahoma
Rogers State College

Oregon
Clackamas Community College

Pennsylvania
Butler County Community College
Community College of Allegheny County
Boyce Campus
North Campus
South Campus
ICS Center for Degree Studies
Luzerne County Community College
Northampton County Area Community College

South Carolina
York Technical College

Tennessee
Cleveland State Community College
Nashville State Technical Institute
Northeast State Technical Community College
Volunteer State Community College
Walters State Community College

Texas
Alvin Community College
Angelina College
Brazosport College
Cedar Valley College
Central Texas College
College of the Mainland
Midland College
Mountain View College
North Lake College
San Jacinto College: North

South Plains College
Texas State Technical College
Harlingen
Waco

Virginia

Central Virginia Community College
Danville Community College
John Tyler Community College
Piedmont Virginia Community College

Washington

Centralia College
Columbia Basin College
Everett Community College
Grays Harbor College
Highline Community College
Lower Columbia College
Olympic College
Renton Technical College
South Puget Sound Community College
Spokane Falls Community College
Walla Walla Community College

West Virginia

West Virginia University at Parkersburg

Wisconsin

Northcentral Technical College
Waukesha County Technical College

Large colleges with rural campuses

Alabama

Central Alabama Community College: Alexander City Campus
George C. Wallace State Community College at Dothan
James H. Faulkner State Community College
Southern Union State Junior College
Wallace State Community College at Hanceville

Arizona

Arizona Western College
Central Arizona College
Cochise College
Eastern Arizona College
Mohave Community College
Northland Pioneer College
Yavapai College

California

Barstow College
Cerro Coso Community College
College of the Redwoods
Columbia College
Crafton Hills College
Lake Tahoe Community College
Mendocino College
Mount San Jacinto College
West Hills Community College

Delaware

Delaware Technical and Community College: Southern Campus

Florida

Okaloosa-Walton Community College
Pasco-Hernando Community College
St. Johns River Community College

Illinois

Carl Sandburg College
Highland Community College
Illinois Valley Community College
John A. Logan College
Kankakee Community College
Kaskaskia College
Kishwaukee College
Lake Land College
McHenry County College
Southeastern Illinois College

Iowa

Indian Hills Community College

Kansas

Barton County Community College
Butler County Community College

Maryland

Charles County Community College

Michigan

Bay de Noc Community College
Lake Michigan College
Monroe County Community College

Missouri

East Central College
Jefferson College
Mineral Area College
Three Rivers Community College

Nebraska

Northeast Community College

New Jersey

Atlantic Community College
Burlington County College
Gloucester County College
Raritan Valley Community College

New Mexico

Clovis Community College
San Juan College

New York

Adirondack Community College
Corning Community College
Finger Lakes Community College
Genesee Community College
Jamestown Community College
Niagara County Community College
State University of New York
College of Agriculture and Technology at Morrisville
College of Technology at Alfred

North Carolina

Alamance Community College
Central Carolina Community College
Pitt Community College
Surry Community College

Ohio

Edison State Community College
Hocking Technical College

Oregon

Blue Mountain Community College
Central Oregon Community College
Linn-Benton Community College
Treasure Valley Community College

Pennsylvania

Lehigh County Community College
Westmoreland County Community College

South Carolina

Tri-County Technical College

Tennessee

Columbia State Community College
Motlow State Community College
Roane State Community College

Texas

Cooke County College
Grayson County College
Kilgore College
Navarro College
Trinity Valley Community College
Wharton County Junior College

Vermont

Community College of Vermont

Virginia

Lord Fairfax Community College
New River Community College
Southside Virginia Community College
Southwest Virginia Community College

Washington

Green River Community College
Skagit Valley College
Whatcom Community College
Yakima Valley Community College

West Virginia

Southern West Virginia Community College

Wisconsin

Wisconsin Indianhead Technical College

Wyoming

Laramie County Community College

Very large colleges with urban campuses

Arizona

Gateway Community College
Glendale Community College
Mesa Community College
Phoenix College
Pima Community College
Rio Salado Community College

California

Chabot College
City College of San Francisco
Coastline Community College
Contra Costa College
Cypress College
Fresno City College
Glendale Community College
Laney College
Long Beach City College
Los Angeles City College
Los Angeles Trade and Technical College
Pasadena City College
Sacramento City College
San Diego City College
San Diego Mesa College
San Joaquin Delta College
San Jose City College
Santa Monica College
Santa Rosa Junior College
Southwestern College

Colorado

Aims Community College

Florida

Broward Community College
Hillsborough Community College
Miami-Dade Community College
Pensacola Junior College

Georgia

DeKalb College

Illinois

City Colleges of Chicago: Harold Washington College

Kentucky

Jefferson Community College

Michigan

Charles Stewart Mott Community College
Grand Rapids Community College
Lansing Community College
Wayne County Community College

Missouri

St. Louis Community College at Forest Park

Nebraska

Metropolitan Community College

New Jersey

Essex County College

New Mexico

Albuquerque Technical-Vocational Institute

New York

City University of New York
Borough of Manhattan Community College
Bronx Community College
Kingsborough Community College
La Guardia Community College

North Carolina

Central Piedmont Community College

Ohio

Cleveland Institute of Electronics
Columbus State Community College
Sinclair Community College
University of Cincinnati: Access Colleges

Oklahoma

Oklahoma City Community College
Rose State College
Tulsa Junior College

Oregon

Portland Community College

Pennsylvania

Community College of Allegheny County: Allegheny Campus
Community College of Philadelphia
Harrisburg Area Community College

South Carolina

Midlands Technical College
Trident Technical College

Texas

Austin Community College
Del Mar College
El Paso Community College

Houston Community College
San Antonio College
Tarrant County Junior College
Tyler Junior College

Utah
Salt Lake Community College

Washington
Clark College
North Seattle Community College
Seattle Central Community College

Wisconsin
Gateway Technical College
Madison Area Technical College

Very large colleges with suburban campuses

Alabama
Community College of the Air Force
John C. Calhoun State Community College

Arizona
Scottsdale Community College

California
Allan Hancock College
Antelope Valley College
Bakersfield College
Cerritos Community College
Chaffey Community College
Citrus College
College of Marin: Kentfield
College of San Mateo
College of the Sequoias
Cosumnes River College
Diablo Valley College
Evergreen Valley College
Foothill College
Fullerton College
Golden West College
Grossmont Community College
Los Angeles Harbor College
Los Angeles Mission College
Los Angeles Pierce College
Los Angeles Valley College
Los Medanos College
MiraCosta College
Modesto Junior College
Monterey Peninsula College
Moorpark College
Mount San Antonio College
Palomar College
Rio Hondo College
Saddleback College
Santa Barbara City College
Sierra College
Skyline College
Solano Community College
Ventura College
West Valley College

Colorado
Arapahoe Community College
Front Range Community College

Florida
Brevard Community College
Daytona Beach Community College
Edison Community College
Florida Community College at Jacksonville
Indian River Community College
Manatee Community College
Palm Beach Community College
St. Petersburg Junior College
Santa Fe Community College
Seminole Community College
Tallahassee Community College
Valencia Community College

Illinois
Belleville Area College
College of DuPage
College of Lake County
Elgin Community College
Illinois Central College
Joliet Junior College
Lincoln Land Community College
Moraine Valley Community College
Oakton Community College
Rock Valley College
Triton College
William Rainey Harper College

Indiana
Vincennes University

Iowa
Des Moines Area Community College
Kirkwood Community College

Kansas
Johnson County Community College

Maryland
Anne Arundel Community College
Catonsville Community College
Essex Community College
Montgomery College: Rockville Campus
Prince George's Community College

Michigan
Delta College
Henry Ford Community College
Jackson Community College
Kalamazoo Valley Community College
Kellogg Community College
Macomb Community College
Oakland Community College
Schoolcraft College
Washtenaw Community College

Minnesota
Normandale Community College

Mississippi
Hinds Community College

Missouri
Longview Community College
St. Louis Community College
Florissant Valley
Meramec

Nevada
Truckee Meadows Community College

New Jersey
Bergen Community College
Brookdale Community College
Camden County College
County College of Morris
Ocean County College
Union County College

New York
City University of New York: Queensborough Community College
Dutchess Community College
Hudson Valley Community College
Monroe Community College
Nassau Community College
Onondaga Community College
Rockland Community College
State University of New York College of Technology at Farmingdale
Suffolk County Community College
Westchester Community College

Ohio
Cuyahoga Community College: Western Campus
Lakeland Community College
Lorain County Community College
Owens Technical College: Toledo

Oregon
Chemeketa Community College
Lane Community College
Mount Hood Community College

Pennsylvania
Bucks County Community College
Delaware County Community College
Montgomery County Community College

Rhode Island
Community College of Rhode Island

South Carolina
Greenville Technical College

Tennessee
Chattanooga State Technical Community College
Pellissippi State Technical Community College
State Technical Institute at Memphis

Texas
Brookhaven College
Collin County Community College District
Eastfield College
North Harris Montgomery Community College District
Richland College

Utah
Utah Valley Community College

Virginia
J. Sargeant Reynolds Community College
Northern Virginia Community College
Tidewater Community College

Washington
Bellevue Community College
Edmonds Community College
Pierce College
Shoreline Community College

Wisconsin
Fox Valley Technical College
Northeast Wisconsin Technical College

Very large colleges with rural campuses

California
Cuesta College
Merced College
Shasta College
Victor Valley College
Yuba College

Idaho
Ricks College

Mississippi
Mississippi Gulf Coast Community College: Perkinston

Nebraska
Central Community College

Texas
Blinn College

Campus environment—4-year colleges

Small colleges with urban campuses

Alabama
Miles College
Selma University

Arizona
American Indian Bible College
Southwestern College

Arkansas
Arkansas Baptist College
Central Baptist College
Philander Smith College
University of Arkansas for Medical Sciences

California
American College for the Applied Arts: Los Angeles
Antioch Southern California at Los Angeles
Armstrong University
Brooks Institute of Photography
Charles R. Drew University: College of Allied Health
Coleman College
Columbia College: Hollywood
Dominican School of Philosophy and Theology
Hebrew Union College: Jewish Institute of Religion
Holy Names College
Lincoln University
Louise Salinger Academy of Fashion
Mills College
New College of California
Otis School of Art and Design
Pacific Oaks College
Patten College
Samuel Merritt College
San Francisco Art Institute
San Francisco Conservatory of Music
San Jose Christian College
Southern California Institute of Architecture
University of California: San Francisco
University of West Los Angeles
West Coast University

Colorado
Beth-El College of Nursing
Naropa Institute
National College
Nazarene Bible College
Rocky Mountain College of Art & Design
University of Colorado Health Sciences Center
Yeshiva Toras Chaim Talmudical Seminary

Connecticut
Albertus Magnus College
Paier College of Art
United States Coast Guard Academy
University of Bridgeport

District of Columbia
Corcoran School of Art
Mount Vernon College
Oblate College
Southeastern University
Trinity College

Florida
Caribbean Center for Advanced Studies: Miami Institute of Psychology
Edward Waters College
National Education Center
Bauder Campus
Tampa Technical Institute Campus
Talmudic College of Florida
Trinity College at Miami

Georgia
Agnes Scott College
American College for the Applied Arts
Medical College of Georgia
Paine College
Shorter College

Illinois
American Conservatory of Music
Blessing-Reiman College of Nursing
East-West University
Harrington Institute of Interior Design
International Academy of Merchandising and Design
Lakeview College of Nursing
Mennonite College of Nursing
North Park College
Ray College of Design
Rush University
St. Francis Medical Center College of Nursing
VanderCook College of Music

Indiana
Lutheran College of Health Professions
Martin University

Iowa
Clarke College
Emmaus Bible College
Mount St. Clare College
University of Osteopathic Medicine and Health Sciences

Kansas
Ottawa University
University of Kansas Medical Center

Kentucky
Brescia College
Spalding University
Transylvania University

Maine
Maine College of Art
Westbrook College

Maryland
Baltimore Hebrew University
Johns Hopkins University: Peabody Conservatory of Music
Maryland Institute College of Art
Ner Israel Rabbinical College
St. John's College
Sojourner-Douglass College
University of Maryland: Baltimore

Massachusetts
Boston Architectural Center
Boston Conservatory
Forsyth School for Dental Hygienists
Lesley College
New England Conservatory of Music
St. John's Seminary College
School of the Museum of Fine Arts
Wheelock College

Michigan
Baker College of Port Huron
Center for Creative Studies: College of Art and Design
Cleary College
Kendall College of Art and Design
Sacred Heart Major Seminary

Minnesota
College of Associated Arts
Minneapolis College of Art and Design

Mississippi
University of Mississippi Medical Center

Missouri
Berean College
Deaconess College of Nursing
Kansas City Art Institute
National College
Ozark Christian College
Research College of Nursing
St. Louis College of Pharmacy
Stephens College

Nebraska
Clarkson College
Grace College of the Bible

New Hampshire
University of New Hampshire at Manchester

New Jersey
Rutgers—The State University of New Jersey
College of Nursing
University College Camden
University of Medicine and Dentistry of New Jersey: School of Health Related Professions
University of Medicine and Dentistry of New Jersey: School of Nursing

New Mexico
National College

New York
Albany College of Pharmacy
Audrey Cohen College
Beth Hamedrash Shaarei Yosher Institute
Beth Hatalmud Rabbinical College
Central Yeshiva Tomchei Tmimim Lubavitz
College of Insurance
Columbia University: School of Nursing
Cooper Union
Darkei No'Am Rabbinical College
Eastman School of Music of the University of Rochester
Eugene Lang College/New School for Social Research
Jewish Theological Seminary of America
Juilliard School
Kehilath Yakov Rabbinical Seminary
Machzikei Hadath Rabbinical College
Manhattan School of Music
Mannes College of Music
Mesivta Tifereth Jerusalem of America
Mesivta Torah Vodaath Seminary
Mirrer Yeshiva Central Institute
New York School of Interior Design
Rabbinical College Bobover Yeshiva B'nei Zion
Rabbinical College Ch'san Sofer of New York
Rabbinical Seminary Adas Yereim
Rabbinical Seminary of America
Rabbinical Seminary M'Kor Chaim
St. Joseph's College
State University of New York
Health Science Center at Brooklyn
Health Science Center at Syracuse
Talmudical Institute of Upstate New York
Talmudical Seminary Oholei Torah
United Talmudical Academy
Yeshiva Karlin Stolin Beth Aron Y'Israel Rabbinical Institute
Yeshiva Shaar Hatorah
Yeshivat Mikdash Melech

North Carolina
Barber-Scotia College
Bennett College
East Coast Bible College
John Wesley College
Livingstone College
North Carolina School of the Arts
Piedmont Bible College
Salem College

North Dakota
Medcenter One College of Nursing

Ohio
Art Academy of Cincinnati
Cincinnati Bible College and Seminary
Cincinnati College of Mortuary Science
Cleveland Institute of Art
Cleveland Institute of Music
God's Bible School and College
Lake Erie College
Union Institute

Oregon
Bassist College
Eugene Bible College
Multnomah School of the Bible

Northwest Christian College
Oregon Health Sciences University
Pacific Northwest College of Art
University of Oregon: Robert Donald Clark Honors College
Warner Pacific College

Pennsylvania

Chatham College
Curtis Institute of Music
Hahnemann University School of Health Sciences and Humanities
Moore College of Art and Design

Puerto Rico

Escuela de Artes Plasticas de Puerto Rico

South Carolina

Allen University
Claflin College
Converse College
Medical University of South Carolina
Morris College

Tennessee

American Baptist College of ABT Seminary
Bristol University
Cumberland University
Fisk University
Knoxville College
Memphis College of Art
Tennessee Temple University
Tennessee Wesleyan College
University of Tennessee: Memphis

Texas

Arlington Baptist College
Baylor College of Dentistry
Concordia Lutheran College
Criswell College
Huston-Tillotson College
Institute for Christian Studies
Laredo State University
Paul Quinn College
Texas College
University of Houston: Victoria
University of Texas
- Health Science Center at Houston
- Health Science Center at San Antonio
- Southwestern Medical Center at Dallas Southwestern Allied Health Sciences School

Wayland Baptist University
Wiley College

Vermont

Burlington College
Trinity College of Vermont

Virginia

Virginia Intermont College

Washington

Bastyr College
Cornish College of the Arts

Wisconsin

Bellin College of Nursing
Columbia College of Nursing
Maranatha Baptist Bible College
Milwaukee Institute of Art & Design

Small colleges with suburban campuses

Alabama

Huntingdon College
International Bible College
Southeastern Bible College
Southern Christian University
Stillman College

Alaska

Alaska Pacific University
Sheldon Jackson College

Arizona

Arizona College of the Bible
Prescott College

California

American Armenian International College
Art Institute of Southern California
Bethany College
California Baptist College
California Institute of the Arts
California Institute of Technology
California Maritime Academy
Christian Heritage College
Claremont McKenna College
Cogswell Polytechnical College
College of Notre Dame
Concordia University
Dominican College of San Rafael
Fresno Pacific College
Harvey Mudd College
Humphreys College
ITT Technical Institute: West Covina
John F. Kennedy University
LIFE Bible College
Master's College
Menlo College
Monterey Institute of International Studies
Pacific Christian College
Pitzer College
Scripps College
Southern California College
United States International University
University of Judaism
Woodbury University

Colorado

Colorado Christian University

Connecticut

Bridgeport Engineering Institute

Florida

Clearwater Christian College
Florida Bible College
Florida Christian College
Hobe Sound Bible College
Jones College
New College of the University of South Florida
Ringling School of Art and Design
St. John Vianney College Seminary

Georgia

Atlanta Christian College
Covenant College
LaGrange College
Mercer University Atlanta
Wesleyan College

Hawaii

University of Hawaii: West Oahu

Idaho

Boise Bible College

Illinois

Barat College
Judson College
Kendall College
Lake Forest College
Lincoln Christian College and Seminary
National College of Chiropractic
Rosary College
St. Joseph College of Nursing
Shimer College
Trinity Christian College
Trinity College
West Suburban College of Nursing

Indiana

Bethel College
St. Francis College

Iowa

Briar Cliff College
Faith Baptist Bible College and Theological Seminary
Hamilton Technical College
University of Dubuque

Kansas

Bethel College
Kansas Wesleyan University
Manhattan Christian College
McPherson College
MidAmerica Nazarene College
Southwestern College

Kentucky

Kentucky Wesleyan College

Louisiana

Centenary College of Louisiana

Maryland

Capitol College
Goucher College
Washington Bible College

Massachusetts

Anna Maria College for Men and Women
Bay Path College
Bradford College
Eastern Nazarene College
Endicott College
Hebrew College
Hellenic College
Lasell College
Montserrat College of Art
Pine Manor College
St. Hyacinth College and Seminary

Michigan

Concordia College
Grace Bible College
Grand Rapids Baptist College and Seminary
Great Lakes Christian College
Michigan Christian College
Reformed Bible College
St. Mary's College
William Tyndale College
Yeshiva Beth Yehuda-Yeshiva Gedolah of Greater Detroit

Minnesota

Crown College
Minnesota Bible College
Pillsbury Baptist Bible College

Mississippi

Magnolia Bible College
Southeastern Baptist College

Missouri

Calvary Bible College
Central Christian College of the Bible
Fontbonne College
Hannibal-LaGrange College
Park College
St. Louis Christian College

Montana

Rocky Mountain College

Nebraska

Midland Lutheran College
Nebraska Christian College
Nebraska Methodist College of Nursing and Allied Health
Union College

New Hampshire

Daniel Webster College
Notre Dame College
Rivier College

New Jersey

Centenary College
Felician College
Rutgers—The State University of New Jersey
- College of Pharmacy
- Mason Gross School of the Arts

Westminster Choir College School of Music of Rider College

New Mexico

College of the Southwest

New York

College of New Rochelle
Concordia College
Five Towns College
Hilbert College
King's College
Ohr Hameir Theological Seminary
Ohr Somayach Tanenbaum Education Center
Pace University: College of White Plains
Polytechnic University: Long Island Campus
Rabbinical College of Long Island
Roberts Wesleyan College
State University of New York
- Health Sciences Center at Stony Brook
- Maritime College

Webb Institute of Naval Architecture
Yeshiva of Nitra Rabbinical College

North Carolina

Catawba College
North Carolina Wesleyan College
Roanoke Bible College
St. Andrews Presbyterian College

Ohio

Antioch College
Antioch School for Adult and Experiential Learning
Cleveland College of Jewish Studies
Notre Dame College of Ohio
Pontifical College Josephinum

Oklahoma

Bartlesville Wesleyan College
Mid-America Bible College
Phillips University
Southwestern College of Christian Ministries

Oregon
ITT Technical Institute: Portland
Pacific University
Western Baptist College

Pennsylvania
Academy of the New Church
Baptist Bible College of Pennsylvania
Chestnut Hill College
Gratz College
Lancaster Bible College
Philadelphia College of Bible
Rosemont College
St. Charles Borromeo Seminary
Seton Hill College
Talmudical Yeshiva of Philadelphia
Williamson Free School of Mechanical Trades

Puerto Rico
Universidad Adventista de las Antillas

South Carolina
Coker College
Columbia Bible College and Seminary
Newberry College

South Dakota
National College
Sioux Falls College

Tennessee
Crichton College
Free Will Baptist Bible College
King College
Lane College
Maryville College
Milligan College

Texas
Amber University
Dallas Christian College
East Texas State University at Texarkana
Southwestern Assemblies of God College
University of Texas Medical Branch at Galveston

Virginia
Hollins College
Randolph-Macon Woman's College

Washington
Antioch University Seattle
Cogswell College North
Lutheran Bible Institute of Seattle
Northwest College of the Assemblies of God
Puget Sound Christian College
St. Martin's College

West Virginia
Ohio Valley College

Wisconsin
Wisconsin Lutheran College

Switzerland
Franklin College: Switzerland

Small colleges with rural campuses

Alabama
Judson College
Talladega College

Alaska
Alaska Bible College

Arkansas
Arkansas College
University of the Ozarks
Williams Baptist College

California
Simpson College
Thomas Aquinas College

Florida
Florida Baptist Theological College
St. Leo College
Warner Southern College
Webber College

Georgia
Emmanuel College
Piedmont College
Thomas College
Toccoa Falls College

Idaho
Albertson College

Illinois
Blackburn College
Eureka College
Greenville College
Illinois College
Knox College
MacMurray College
Monmouth College
Principia College

Indiana
Franklin College
Grace College
Huntington College
Oakland City College
St. Meinrad College
Wabash College

Iowa
Buena Vista College
Divine Word College
Iowa Wesleyan College
Maharishi International University
Teikyo Westmar University
Vennard College
William Penn College

Kansas
Barclay College
Bethany College
Sterling College
Tabor College

Kentucky
Alice Lloyd College
Centre College
Mid-Continent Baptist Bible College
Midway College
Pikeville College
Sue Bennett College
Union College

Louisiana
St. Joseph Seminary College

Maine
College of the Atlantic
Maine Maritime Academy
St. Joseph's College
Thomas College
Unity College
University of Maine
  Fort Kent
  Machias
University of New England

Maryland
Washington College

Massachusetts
Massachusetts Maritime Academy
Simon's Rock College of Bard

Michigan
Baker College of Cadillac
Olivet College
Siena Heights College
Spring Arbor College

Minnesota
Dr. Martin Luther College
Oak Hills Bible College

Missouri
Central Methodist College
Conception Seminary College
Westminster College
William Woods College

Nebraska
Concordia College
Dana College

Nevada
Sierra Nevada College

New Hampshire
Colby-Sawyer College

New Mexico
St. John's College

New York
Keuka College
Wadhams Hall Seminary-College
Wells College
William Smith College
Yeshiva Gedolah Zichron Moshe

North Carolina
Chowan College
Lees-McRae College
Montreat-Anderson College
Mount Olive College
Pfeiffer College
Warren Wilson College

North Dakota
Mayville State University
Trinity Bible College

Ohio
Bluffton College
Circleville Bible College
Defiance College
Hiram College
Tiffin University
Urbana University
Wilberforce University
Wilmington College

Pennsylvania
Thiel College
University of Pittsburgh at Bradford
Valley Forge Christian College
Wilson College

South Carolina
Erskine College
Voorhees College

South Dakota
Dakota Wesleyan University
Huron University
Presentation College
Sinte Gleska University

Tennessee
Bethel College
Johnson Bible College
Tusculum College
William Jennings Bryan College

Texas
Baptist Missionary Association Theological Seminary
Jarvis Christian College
Northwood University: Texas Campus
Schreiner College
Southwestern Adventist College
Southwestern Christian College

Vermont
Bennington College
College of St. Joseph in Vermont
Goddard College
Green Mountain College
Marlboro College
School for International Training
Southern Vermont College

Virginia
Bluefield College
Bridgewater College
Christendom College
Eastern Mennonite College
Emory and Henry College
Hampden-Sydney College
St. Paul's College
Sweet Briar College

Washington
Heritage College

West Virginia
Alderson-Broaddus College
Appalachian Bible College
Bethany College
Davis and Elkins College
Salem-Teikyo University

Wisconsin
Mount Senario College
Northland College
Northwestern College
Ripon College
Silver Lake College

Switzerland
American College of Switzerland

Medium-sized colleges with urban campuses

Alabama
Birmingham-Southern College
Troy State University
  Dothan
  Montgomery

Arizona
Grand Canyon University

California
Academy of Art College
California College of Arts and Crafts
DeVry Institute of Technology: City of Industry
Golden Gate University
Occidental College
Point Loma Nazarene College

Colorado
Colorado College
Denver Technical College

Connecticut
Trinity College

District of Columbia
Catholic University of America
Gallaudet University

Florida
Bethune-Cookman College
Palm Beach Atlantic College
Tampa College
University of Tampa

Georgia
Albany State College
Morehouse College
Morris Brown College
Savannah College of Art and Design
Savannah State College
Spelman College

Illinois
Augustana College
Illinois Institute of Technology
Illinois Wesleyan University
Moody Bible Institute
St. Xavier University
School of the Art Institute of Chicago

Indiana
Anderson University
ITT Technical Institute: Fort Wayne
Marian College

Iowa
Coe College
Grand View College
Loras College
Mount Mercy College
St. Ambrose University

Kansas
Friends University
Kansas Newman College

Kentucky
Kentucky State University

Louisiana
Dillard University
Louisiana State University Medical Center

Maryland
Coppin State College

Massachusetts
American International College
Berklee College of Music
Clark University
Emerson College
Emmanuel College
Massachusetts College of Art
Massachusetts College of Pharmacy and Allied Health Sciences
Simmons College
Wentworth Institute of Technology

Michigan
Baker College of Muskegon
Marygrove College

Minnesota
Augsburg College
Concordia College: St. Paul
Hamline University
Macalester College
North Central Bible College

Mississippi
Belhaven College
Millsaps College

Missouri
Drury College
Evangel College
Harris Stowe State College
Rockhurst College

Montana
College of Great Falls
Montana College of Mineral Science and Technology

Nebraska
University of Nebraska Medical Center

New Jersey
Rutgers—The State University of New Jersey
Camden College of Arts and Sciences
University College Newark
Stevens Institute of Technology
Upsala College

New Mexico
College of Santa Fe

New York
Barnard College
Boricua College
College of St. Rose
Columbia University
School of Engineering and Applied Science
School of General Studies
D'Youville College
Manhattan College
Marymount Manhattan College
Medaille College
Parsons School of Design
Polytechnic University
Pratt Institute
Russell Sage College
St. Francis College
State University of New York College of Environmental Science and Forestry
Yeshiva University

North Carolina
Johnson C. Smith University
Meredith College
St. Augustine's College
Shaw University
Winston-Salem State University

Ohio
Columbus College of Art and Design
Dyke College
Franciscan University of Steubenville

Oklahoma
Oklahoma City University
University of Oklahoma Health Sciences Center

Oregon
University of Portland

Pennsylvania
Carlow College
King's College
Philadelphia College of Pharmacy and Science
Point Park College
Thomas Jefferson University: College of Allied Health Sciences
University of the Arts
Wilkes University

Puerto Rico
Inter American University of Puerto Rico: Guayama Campus
University of Puerto Rico
Medical Sciences Campus
Ponce Technological University College

Rhode Island
Rhode Island School of Design

South Carolina
Benedict College
The Citadel
Columbia College
Lander University
Wofford College

South Dakota
Northern State University
South Dakota School of Mines and Technology

Tennessee
Belmont University
Christian Brothers University
Lambuth University
Lee College
LeMoyne-Owen College

Texas
Hardin-Simmons University
Incarnate Word College
Our Lady of the Lake University of San Antonio
Rice University
St. Edward's University
Texas Wesleyan University
Trinity University
University of St. Thomas
University of Texas
Permian Basin
Tyler

Virginia
Virginia Union University

Washington
City University
Gonzaga University
Seattle Pacific University
Seattle University

West Virginia
University of Charleston

Wisconsin
Beloit College
Edgewood College
Lawrence University
Milwaukee School of Engineering
University of Wisconsin: Superior
Viterbo College

France
American University of Paris

Medium-sized colleges with suburban campuses

Alabama
Athens State College
Faulkner University
Oakwood College
Spring Hill College
University of Mobile
University of Montevallo

Arizona
DeVry Institute of Technology: Phoenix
Western International University

Arkansas
Hendrix College

California
Art Center College of Design
Azusa Pacific University
Biola University
California Lutheran University
California State University: San Marcos
Chapman University
La Sierra University
Mount St. Mary's College
Pepperdine University
Pomona College
St. Mary's College of California
University of Redlands
Westmont College
Whittier College

Colorado
Colorado School of Mines
Colorado Technical College
Regis University

Connecticut
Charter Oak State College
Connecticut College
St. Joseph College
Teikyo-Post University
Wesleyan University

Delaware
Delaware State College
Goldey-Beacom College
Wesley College
Wilmington College

Florida
Eckerd College
Flagler College
Florida Institute of Technology
Florida Memorial College
Florida Southern College
Fort Lauderdale College
Jacksonville University
Lynn University
Rollins College
St. Thomas University
Southeastern College of the Assemblies of God
Stetson University

Georgia
Brenau University
DeVry Institute of Technology: Atlanta
Georgia Southwestern College
Oglethorpe University

Idaho
Northwest Nazarene College

Illinois
Aurora University
College of St. Francis
Concordia University
DeVry Institute of Technology: Addison
Elmhurst College
Governors State University
Illinois Benedictine College
Millikin University
North Central College
Olivet Nazarene University
Parks College of St. Louis University
Quincy University
Rockford College
Sangamon State University
Wheaton College

Indiana
Butler University
Calumet College of St. Joseph
Earlham College
Indiana Wesleyan University
ITT Technical Institute: Indianapolis
St. Mary-of-the-Woods College
St. Mary's College
University of Evansville
University of Indianapolis
Valparaiso University

Iowa
Morningside College
Simpson College
Teikyo Marycrest University

Kansas
St. Mary College

Kentucky
Bellarmine College
Georgetown College
Sullivan College
Thomas More College

Louisiana
Grantham College of Engineering
Louisiana College
Our Lady of Holy Cross College

Maine
Bates College
Bowdoin College
Husson College
University of Maine at Augusta

Maryland
College of Notre Dame of Maryland
Columbia Union College
Hood College
Villa Julie College

Massachusetts
Amherst College
Assumption College
Babson College
Brandeis University
College of the Holy Cross
Curry College
Elms College
Gordon College
Merrimack College
Mount Holyoke College
Mount Ida College
Regis College
Smith College
Springfield College
Wellesley College
Western New England College
Worcester Polytechnic Institute

Michigan
Adrian College
Aquinas College
GMI Engineering & Management Institute
Hillsdale College
Hope College
Kalamazoo College
Northwood University
Walsh College of Accountancy and Business Administration

Minnesota
College of St. Catherine: St. Catherine Campus
College of St. Scholastica
Concordia College: Moorhead
Gustavus Adolphus College
Northwestern College

Mississippi
Mississippi College
Mississippi University for Women
Tougaloo College
William Carey College

Missouri
Avila College
DeVry Institute of Technology: Kansas City
Lindenwood College
Missouri Baptist College
William Jewell College

Montana
Carroll College

Nebraska
Bellevue College
College of St. Mary
Nebraska Wesleyan University

New Hampshire
New Hampshire College
St. Anselm College
School for Lifelong Learning

New Jersey
Bloomfield College
Caldwell College
College of St. Elizabeth
Drew University
Georgian Court College
Monmouth College
Rutgers—The State University of New Jersey
College of Engineering
Cook College

New Mexico
New Mexico Institute of Mining and Technology

New York
Cazenovia College
College of Aeronautics
College of Mount St. Vincent
Daemen College
Dominican College of Blauvelt
Elmira College
Le Moyne College
Manhattanville College
Marymount College
Molloy College
Mount St. Mary College
Nazareth College of Rochester
Niagara University
Nyack College
St. Bonaventure University
St. John Fisher College
St. Joseph's College: Suffolk Campus
St. Thomas Aquinas College
Sarah Lawrence College
Skidmore College
State University of New York
Purchase
Institute of Technology at Utica/Rome
Union College
United States Merchant Marine Academy
Utica College of Syracuse University
Vassar College
Wagner College

North Carolina
Barton College
Belmont Abbey College
Davidson College
Greensboro College
Guilford College
High Point University
Lenoir-Rhyne College
Methodist College
Queens College
Wingate College

Ohio
Capital University
College of Mount St. Joseph
DeVry Institute of Technology: Columbus
Heidelberg College
Lourdes College
Malone College
Marietta College
Mount Union College
Ohio Dominican College
Ohio State University: Marion Campus
Ohio Wesleyan University
Otterbein College
Ursuline College
Walsh University
Wittenberg University

Oklahoma
Oklahoma Baptist University
Oklahoma Christian University of Science and Arts
Oral Roberts University
Southern Nazarene University

Oregon
Concordia College
George Fox College
Lewis and Clark College
Linfield College
Marylhurst College
Oregon Institute of Technology
Reed College
Willamette University

Pennsylvania
Albright College
Alvernia College
Beaver College
Bryn Mawr College
Cabrini College
Cedar Crest College
College Misericordia
Delaware Valley College
Dickinson College
Eastern College
Elizabethtown College
Franklin and Marshall College
Geneva College
Gettysburg College
Gwynedd-Mercy College
Haverford College
Holy Family College
Immaculata College
La Roche College
Lafayette College
Lycoming College
Marywood College
Mercyhurst College
Messiah College
Moravian College
Muhlenberg College
Neumann College
Penn State
Erie Behrend College
Harrisburg Capital College
Philadelphia College of Textiles and Science
Swarthmore College
University of Pittsburgh at Greensburg
Ursinus College
Washington and Jefferson College
Widener University

Puerto Rico
Bayamon Central University

Rhode Island
Salve Regina University

South Carolina
Anderson College
Charleston Southern University
Limestone College
Presbyterian College

South Dakota
Augustana College

Tennessee
David Lipscomb University
Rhodes College
Trevecca Nazarene College
Union University

Texas
Austin College
Dallas Baptist University
DeVry Institute of Technology: Irving
East Texas Baptist University
Houston Baptist University
LeTourneau University
Lubbock Christian University
McMurry University
St. Mary's University
Southwestern University
Texas A&M University at Galveston
Texas Lutheran College
University of Dallas
University of Mary Hardin-Baylor

Utah
Westminster College of Salt Lake City

Vermont
St. Michael's College

Virginia
Averett College
Longwood College
Lynchburg College
Mary Baldwin College
Marymount University
National Business College
Randolph-Macon College
Roanoke College
Shenandoah University
Virginia Wesleyan College

Washington
Pacific Lutheran University
University of Puget Sound
Whitworth College

West Virginia
Bluefield State College
College of West Virginia
Wheeling Jesuit College

Wisconsin
Alverno College
Cardinal Stritch College
Carroll College
Carthage College
Concordia University Wisconsin
Mount Mary College
St. Norbert College

American Samoa, Caroline Islands, Guam, Marianas, Virgin Islands
University of the Virgin Islands

Medium-sized colleges with rural campuses

Alabama
Livingston University

Arizona
Embry-Riddle Aeronautical University: Prescott Campus

Arkansas
John Brown University
Ouachita Baptist University
Southern Arkansas University
University of Arkansas at Monticello

California
Pacific Union College

Colorado
Adams State College
Western State College of Colorado

Georgia
Brewton-Parker College
Fort Valley State College
North Georgia College

Hawaii
Brigham Young University-Hawaii
University of Hawaii at Hilo

Illinois
McKendree College

Indiana
DePauw University
Goshen College
Hanover College
Indiana University East
Manchester College
Rose-Hulman Institute of Technology
St. Joseph's College
Taylor University
Tri-State University

Iowa
Central College
Cornell College
Dordt College
Graceland College
Grinnell College
Luther College
Northwestern College
Upper Iowa University
Wartburg College

Kansas
Baker University
Benedictine College

Kentucky
Asbury College
Berea College
Campbellsville College
Cumberland College
Lindsey Wilson College

Maine
Colby College
University of Maine
  Farmington
  Presque Isle

Maryland
Mount St. Mary's College
St. Mary's College of Maryland
University of Maryland: Eastern Shore
Western Maryland College

Massachusetts
Atlantic Union College
Hampshire College
Nichols College
North Adams State College
Wheaton College
Williams College

Michigan
Albion College
Alma College
Andrews University
Baker College of Owosso
Jordan College

Minnesota
Carleton College
College of St. Benedict
St. John's University
St. Mary's College of Minnesota
Southwest State University
University of Minnesota: Morris

Mississippi
Alcorn State University
Mississippi Valley State University
Rust College

Missouri
College of the Ozarks
Culver-Stockton College
Missouri Valley College

Montana
Northern Montana College
Western Montana College of the University of Montana

Nebraska
Chadron State College
Doane College
Peru State College

New Hampshire
Franklin Pierce College
New England College

New Mexico
New Mexico Highlands University
Western New Mexico University

New York
Alfred University
Bard College
Clarkson University
Colgate University
Hamilton College
Hartwick College
Hobart College
Houghton College
Long Island University: Southampton Campus
St. Lawrence University

North Carolina
Elizabeth City State University
Gardner-Webb University
Mars Hill College
Pembroke State University

North Dakota
Dickinson State University
Jamestown College
University of Mary
Valley City State University

Ohio
Ashland University
Cedarville College
College of Wooster
Denison University
Kenyon College
Muskingum College
Oberlin College
Ohio Northern University
Ohio University
  Southern Campus at Ironton
  Zanesville Campus
University of Rio Grande

Oklahoma
Northwestern Oklahoma State University
Oklahoma Panhandle State University
University of Science and Arts of Oklahoma

Oregon
Eastern Oregon State College

Pennsylvania
Allegheny College
Allentown College of St. Francis de Sales
Cheyney University of Pennsylvania
Grove City College
Juniata College
Lebanon Valley College of Pennsylvania
Lincoln University
Mansfield University of Pennsylvania
Mount Aloysius College
St. Francis College
St. Vincent College
Susquehanna University
Waynesburg College
Westminster College

South Carolina
Central Wesleyan College

South Dakota
Black Hills State University
Dakota State University
Mount Marty College
Oglala Lakota College

Tennessee
Carson-Newman College
Freed-Hardeman University
Lincoln Memorial University
Southern College of Seventh-day Adventists
University of the South

Texas
Howard Payne University
Sul Ross State University

Vermont
Castleton State College
Johnson State College
Lyndon State College
Middlebury College
Norwich University

Virginia
Clinch Valley College of the University of Virginia
Ferrum College
Virginia Military Institute
Washington and Lee University

Washington
Walla Walla College
Whitman College

West Virginia
Concord College
Glenville State College
West Liberty State College
West Virginia Wesleyan College

Wisconsin
Lakeland College
Marian College of Fond du Lac

Large colleges with urban campuses

Alabama
Alabama State University
University of North Alabama

Arizona
University of Phoenix

Arkansas
Harding University
University of Arkansas at Pine Bluff

California
National University
University of San Diego
University of San Francisco

Colorado
University of Colorado at Denver

Connecticut
Western Connecticut State University
Yale University

District of Columbia
George Washington University
Georgetown University
Strayer College

Florida
Embry-Riddle Aeronautical University
University of North Florida

Georgia
Augusta College
Clark Atlanta University

Hawaii
Hawaii Pacific University

Idaho
Lewis Clark State College

Illinois
Bradley University
Chicago State University
Columbia College
DeVry Institute of Technology: Chicago
Roosevelt University
University of Chicago

Indiana
Indiana University
  Northwest
  South Bend

Iowa
Drake University

Kansas
Washburn University of Topeka

Louisiana
Louisiana State University in Shreveport
Loyola University
Southern University at New Orleans
Tulane University
Xavier University of Louisiana

Maryland
Johns Hopkins University
Loyola College in Maryland
Morgan State University
University of Baltimore

Massachusetts
Fitchburg State College
Harvard and Radcliffe Colleges
Massachusetts Institute of Technology
Suffolk University
University of Massachusetts at Lowell
Worcester State College

Michigan
Baker College: Flint
Davenport College of Business
University of Detroit Mercy
University of Michigan: Flint

Minnesota
Metropolitan State University
University of St. Thomas

Mississippi
Jackson State University

Missouri
St. Louis University
University of Missouri: Kansas City

Montana
Eastern Montana College

Nebraska
Creighton University

New Jersey
Jersey City State College
New Jersey Institute of Technology
Rutgers—The State University of New Jersey: Newark College of Arts and Sciences
St. Peter's College

New York
Canisius College
City University of New York
Medgar Evers College
York College
Columbia University: Columbia College
Fordham University
Long Island University: Brooklyn Campus
Pace University
School of Visual Arts

North Carolina
Fayetteville State University
North Carolina Agricultural and Technical State University
North Carolina Central University
University of North Carolina at Asheville

Ohio
Case Western Reserve University
Franklin University
University of Findlay

Oklahoma
Cameron University
East Central University
University of Tulsa

Pennsylvania
Carnegie Mellon University
Duquesne University
Gannon University
La Salle University
Pennsylvania College of Technology
University of Scranton

Puerto Rico
American University of Puerto Rico
Colegio Universitario del Este
Inter American University of Puerto Rico: Arecibo Campus
Turabo University
Universidad Metropolitana
Universidad Politecnica de Puerto Rico
University of Puerto Rico: Cayey University College
University of the Sacred Heart

Rhode Island
Brown University
Johnson & Wales University

South Carolina
South Carolina State University
Winthrop University

Tennessee
Austin Peay State University
Tennessee State University
University of Tennessee: Chattanooga
Vanderbilt University

Texas
University of Houston: Downtown

Virginia
Hampton University

Arab Republic of Egypt
American University in Cairo

Large colleges with suburban campuses

Alabama
Alabama Agricultural and Mechanical University
Auburn University at Montgomery
Samford University
University of Alabama in Huntsville

Alaska
University of Alaska Fairbanks

California
California State University
Bakersfield
Dominguez Hills
Loyola Marymount University
Santa Clara University
Sonoma State University
Stanford University
University of California: Riverside
University of La Verne
University of the Pacific

Colorado
Mesa State College
United States Air Force Academy
University of Colorado at Colorado Springs
University of Denver
University of Southern Colorado

Connecticut
Eastern Connecticut State University
Fairfield University
Quinnipiac College
Sacred Heart University
University of Hartford
University of New Haven

District of Columbia
American University

Florida
Barry University
Nova University
University of West Florida

Georgia
Armstrong State College
Clayton State College
Columbus College
Emory University
Georgia College
Mercer University
Southern College of Technology
Valdosta State College
West Georgia College

Illinois
National-Louis University
Northwestern University

Indiana
University of Southern Indiana

Louisiana
McNeese State University
Nicholls State University

Maryland
Bowie State University
Salisbury State University
United States Naval Academy

Massachusetts
Bentley College
Bridgewater State College
Framingham State College
Stonehill College
Tufts University
University of Massachusetts at Dartmouth
Westfield State College

Michigan
Calvin College
Detroit College of Business
Lake Superior State University
Lawrence Technological University
Madonna University
Saginaw Valley State University
University of Michigan: Dearborn

Minnesota
University of Minnesota: Duluth

Missouri
Lincoln University
Maryville University
Missouri Western State College
Washington University
Webster University

New Hampshire
Keene State College
Plymouth State College of the University System of New Hampshire

New Jersey
Fairleigh Dickinson University
Princeton University
Ramapo College of New Jersey
Rider College
Rutgers—The State University of New Jersey
Douglass College
Livingston College
University College New Brunswick
Seton Hall University
Stockton State College
Trenton State College

New York
Adelphi University
College of New Rochelle: School of New Resources
Dowling College
Iona College
Ithaca College
Long Island University: C. W. Post Campus
Marist College
Mercy College
New York Institute of Technology
Pace University: Pleasantville/Briarcliff
Rensselaer Polytechnic Institute
Siena College
State University of New York
College at Cortland
College at Old Westbury
Oswego
University of Rochester

North Carolina
Duke University
Elon College
University of North Carolina at Wilmington
Wake Forest University

North Dakota
Minot State University

Ohio
Baldwin-Wallace College
John Carroll University
University of Dayton
Xavier University

Oregon
Southern Oregon State College

Pennsylvania
Lehigh University
Millersville University of Pennsylvania
Robert Morris College
St. Joseph's University
University of Pittsburgh at Johnstown
York College of Pennsylvania

Puerto Rico
Caribbean University
Inter American University of Puerto Rico: San German Campus
University of Puerto Rico
Bayamon Technological University College
Humacao University College

Rhode Island
Bryant College
Providence College
Roger Williams University

South Carolina
Furman University
University of South Carolina
Aiken
Coastal Carolina College
Spartanburg

Texas
Abilene Christian University
Angelo State University
Corpus Christi State University
Midwestern State University
Southern Methodist University
Texas Christian University
Texas Woman's University
University of Houston: Clear Lake
University of Texas at Dallas
West Texas A & M University

Virginia
Christopher Newport University
Liberty University
Mary Washington College
University of Richmond
Virginia State University

West Virginia
Fairmont State College
West Virginia State College

Wisconsin
University of Wisconsin
  Parkside
  River Falls

Nebraska
University of Nebraska—Kearney
Wayne State College

New Hampshire
Dartmouth College

New Mexico
Eastern New Mexico University

New York
State University of New York
  College at Brockport
  College at Fredonia
  College at Geneseo
  College at New Paltz
  College at Oneonta
  College at Plattsburgh
  College at Potsdam
United States Military Academy

Washington
Central Washington University
Evergreen State College

West Virginia
Shepherd College
West Virginia Institute of Technology

Wisconsin
University of Wisconsin
  Green Bay
  Platteville
  Stout

Large colleges with rural campuses

Alabama
Jacksonville State University
Troy State University
Tuskegee University

Alaska
University of Alaska Southeast

Arkansas
Arkansas Tech University
Henderson State University

California
California State University: Stanislaus
Humboldt State University

Colorado
Fort Lewis College

Illinois
Lewis University

Indiana
Purdue University: North Central Campus

Kansas
Emporia State University
Fort Hays State University
Pittsburg State University

Kentucky
Murray State University

Louisiana
Grambling State University

Maryland
Frostburg State University

Michigan
Michigan Technological University

Minnesota
Bemidji State University
St. Olaf College
Winona State University

Mississippi
Delta State University

Missouri
Missouri Southern State College
Northeast Missouri State University
Northwest Missouri State University
Southwest Baptist University
University of Missouri: Rolla

North Carolina
Campbell University
Western Carolina University

Ohio
Central State University

Oklahoma
Langston University
Southeastern Oklahoma State University
Southwestern Oklahoma State University

Oregon
Western Oregon State College

Pennsylvania
Bloomsburg University of Pennsylvania
Bucknell University
California University of Pennsylvania
Clarion University of Pennsylvania
East Stroudsburg University of Pennsylvania
Kutztown University of Pennsylvania
Lock Haven University of Pennsylvania
Shippensburg University of Pennsylvania
Slippery Rock University of Pennsylvania

Puerto Rico
Inter American University of Puerto Rico: Aguadilla Campus

South Carolina
Francis Marion University

South Dakota
University of South Dakota

Tennessee
Tennessee Technological University
University of Tennessee: Martin

Texas
East Texas State University
Prairie View A&M University
Tarleton State University
Texas A&I University

Utah
Southern Utah University

Virginia
College of William and Mary

Very large colleges with urban campuses

Alabama
University of Alabama in Birmingham

Alaska
University of Alaska Anchorage

Arizona
University of Arizona

Arkansas
University of Arkansas
University of Arkansas at Little Rock

California
California College for Health Sciences
California State University
  Fresno
  Los Angeles
  Sacramento
San Francisco State University
San Jose State University
University of California
  Berkeley
  Los Angeles
University of Southern California

Colorado
Metropolitan State College of Denver

Connecticut
Southern Connecticut State University

District of Columbia
Howard University
University of the District of Columbia

Florida
Florida Agricultural and Mechanical University
Florida International University

Georgia
Georgia Institute of Technology
Georgia State University

Hawaii
University of Hawaii at Manoa

Idaho
Boise State University
Idaho State University

Illinois
De Paul University
Loyola University of Chicago
Northeastern Illinois University
Northern Illinois University
University of Illinois
  Chicago
  Urbana-Champaign

Indiana
Indiana State University
Indiana University Bloomington
Indiana University—Purdue University at Indianapolis
Purdue University: Calumet

Iowa
University of Iowa

Kansas
Wichita State University

Kentucky
University of Kentucky
University of Louisville

Louisiana
Louisiana State University and Agricultural and Mechanical College
Northeast Louisiana University
University of New Orleans
University of Southwestern Louisiana

Maine
University of Southern Maine

Massachusetts
Boston University
Northeastern University
University of Massachusetts at Boston

Michigan
Northern Michigan University
Wayne State University
Western Michigan University

Minnesota
Moorhead State University
St. Cloud State University
University of Minnesota: Twin Cities

Mississippi
University of Southern Mississippi

Missouri
Southwest Missouri State University
University of Missouri: St. Louis

Nebraska
University of Nebraska
  Lincoln
  Omaha

Nevada
University of Nevada
  Las Vegas
  Reno

New Jersey
Thomas Edison State College

New Mexico
University of New Mexico

New York
City University of New York
- Baruch College
- Brooklyn College
- City College
- College of Staten Island
- Hunter College
- John Jay College of Criminal Justice
- Lehman College
- New York City Technical College
- Queens College

Fashion Institute of Technology
New York University
St. John's University
State University of New York College at Buffalo
Syracuse University
Touro College
University of the State of New York: Regents College

North Carolina
University of North Carolina
- Charlotte
- Greensboro

North Dakota
North Dakota State University
University of North Dakota

Ohio
Cleveland State University
Ohio State University: Columbus Campus
University of Akron
University of Cincinnati
Youngstown State University

Oregon
Portland State University
University of Oregon

Pennsylvania
Drexel University
Temple University
University of Pennsylvania
University of Pittsburgh

Puerto Rico
Inter American University of Puerto Rico: Metropolitan Campus
Pontifical Catholic University of Puerto Rico
University of Puerto Rico
- Mayaguez Campus
- Rio Piedras Campus

South Carolina
College of Charleston
University of South Carolina

Tennessee
Memphis State University
University of Tennessee: Knoxville

Texas
Baylor University
Lamar University—Beaumont
Texas Southern University
Texas Tech University
University of Houston
University of Texas
- Austin
- El Paso

Utah
University of Utah
Weber State University

Virginia
Norfolk State University
Virginia Commonwealth University

Washington
University of Washington

West Virginia
Marshall University

Wisconsin
Marquette University
University of Wisconsin
- La Crosse
- Madison

Canada
McGill University

Mexico
Sistema Instituto Tecnologico y de Estudios Superiores de Monterrey

Very large colleges with suburban campuses

Alabama
University of Alabama
University of South Alabama

Arizona
Arizona State University

Arkansas
Arkansas State University
University of Central Arkansas

California
California State Polytechnic University: Pomona
California State University
- Fullerton
- Hayward
- Long Beach
- Northridge
- San Bernardino

San Diego State University
University of California
- Davis
- Irvine
- San Diego
- Santa Barbara
- Santa Cruz

Colorado
Colorado State University
University of Colorado at Boulder

Connecticut
Central Connecticut State University

Delaware
University of Delaware

Florida
Florida Atlantic University
Florida State University
University of Central Florida
University of Florida
University of Miami
University of South Florida

Georgia
Georgia Southern University
Kennesaw State College
University of Georgia

Illinois
Illinois State University
Southern Illinois University at Edwardsville

Indiana
Ball State University
Indiana University—Purdue University at Fort Wayne
Purdue University
University of Notre Dame

Iowa
Iowa State University
University of Northern Iowa

Kansas
Kansas State University
University of Kansas

Kentucky
Northern Kentucky University
Western Kentucky University

Louisiana
Northwestern State University
Southeastern Louisiana University
Southern University and Agricultural and Mechanical College

Maryland
Towson State University
University of Maryland
- Baltimore County
- College Park
- University College

Massachusetts
Boston College
Salem State College

Michigan
Eastern Michigan University
Grand Valley State University
Michigan State University
Oakland University
University of Michigan

Missouri
Central Missouri State University

Montana
University of Montana

New Jersey
Kean College of New Jersey
Montclair State College
Rutgers—The State University of New Jersey: Rutgers College
William Paterson College of New Jersey

New Mexico
New Mexico State University

New York
Hofstra University
Rochester Institute of Technology
State University of New York
- Albany
- Binghamton
- Buffalo
- Stony Brook

North Carolina
East Carolina University
North Carolina State University
University of North Carolina at Chapel Hill

Ohio
Kent State University
University of Toledo
Wright State University

Oklahoma
University of Central Oklahoma
University of Oklahoma

Oregon
Oregon State University

Pennsylvania
Penn State University Park Campus
Villanova University
West Chester University of Pennsylvania

Rhode Island
Rhode Island College

South Carolina
Clemson University

Tennessee
East Tennessee State University
Middle Tennessee State University

Texas
Sam Houston State University
Southwest Texas State University
Texas A&M University
University of North Texas
University of Texas
- Arlington
- San Antonio

Utah
Brigham Young University

Vermont
University of Vermont

Virginia
George Mason University
Old Dominion University
University of Virginia

Washington
Western Washington University

West Virginia
West Virginia University

Wisconsin
University of Wisconsin
- Oshkosh
- Whitewater

Very large colleges with rural campuses

Alabama
Auburn University

Arizona
Northern Arizona University

California
California Polytechnic State University: San Luis Obispo
California State University: Chico

Colorado
University of Northern Colorado

Connecticut
University of Connecticut

Idaho
University of Idaho

Illinois
Eastern Illinois University
Southern Illinois University at Carbondale
Western Illinois University

Kentucky
Eastern Kentucky University
Morehead State University

Louisiana
Louisiana Tech University

Maine
University of Maine

Massachusetts
University of Massachusetts at Amherst

Michigan
Central Michigan University
Ferris State University

Minnesota
Mankato State University

Mississippi
Mississippi State University
University of Mississippi

Missouri
Southeast Missouri State University
University of Missouri: Columbia

Montana
Montana State University

New Hampshire
University of New Hampshire

New Jersey
Rowan College of New Jersey

New York
Cornell University

North Carolina
Appalachian State University

Ohio
Bowling Green State University
Miami University: Oxford Campus
Ohio University

Oklahoma
Northeastern State University
Oklahoma State University

Pennsylvania
Edinboro University of Pennsylvania
Indiana University of Pennsylvania

Rhode Island
University of Rhode Island

South Dakota
South Dakota State University

Texas
Stephen F. Austin State University
University of Texas: Pan American

Utah
Utah State University

Virginia
James Madison University
Radford University
Virginia Polytechnic Institute and State University

Washington
Eastern Washington University
Washington State University

Wisconsin
University of Wisconsin
Eau Claire
Stevens Point

Wyoming
University of Wyoming

Colleges with religious affiliations

African Methodist Episcopal Church

Arkansas
Shorter College

Florida
Edward Waters College

Georgia
Morris Brown College

Ohio
Wilberforce University

South Carolina
Allen University

Texas
Paul Quinn College

African Methodist Episcopal Zion Church

North Carolina
Livingstone College

American Baptist Churches in the USA

Arkansas
Arkansas Baptist College

Illinois
Judson College

Indiana
Franklin College

Kansas
Ottawa University

Michigan
Kalamazoo College

New York
Keuka College

Oklahoma
Bacone College

Oregon
Linfield College

Pennsylvania
Eastern College

South Carolina
Benedict College

South Dakota
Sioux Falls College

Virginia
Virginia Union University

West Virginia
Alderson-Broaddus College

Assemblies of God

Arizona
American Indian Bible College

California
Bethany College
Southern California College

Florida
Southeastern College of the Assemblies of God

Minnesota
North Central Bible College

Missouri
Berean College
Evangel College

North Dakota
Trinity Bible College

Pennsylvania
Valley Forge Christian College

Texas
Southwestern Assemblies of God College

Washington
Northwest College of the Assemblies of God

Baptist General Conference

Texas
Baylor University

Brethren Church

Indiana
Grace College

Ohio
Ashland University

Brethren in Christ Church

Pennsylvania
Messiah College

Christian Church

Kansas
Manhattan Christian College

Minnesota
Minnesota Bible College

Missouri
Central Christian College of the Bible

Tennessee
Johnson Bible College

Washington
Puget Sound Christian College

Christian Church (Disciples of Christ)

California
Chapman University

Illinois
Eureka College

Kentucky
Midway College
Transylvania University

Missouri
Culver-Stockton College

North Carolina
Barton College

Ohio
Hiram College

Oklahoma
Phillips University

Texas
Jarvis Christian College
Texas Christian University

Virginia
Lynchburg College

West Virginia
Bethany College

Christian Methodist Episcopal Church

Alabama
Miles College

Tennessee
Lane College

Texas
Texas College

Christian and Missionary Alliance

California
Simpson College

Minnesota
Crown College

New York
Nyack College

Christian Reformed Church

Iowa
Dordt College

Michigan
Calvin College

Church of Christ

Alabama
Faulkner University
International Bible College
Southern Christian University

Arkansas
Harding University

California
Pepperdine University

Illinois
Lincoln Christian College and Seminary

Michigan
Michigan Christian College

Mississippi
Magnolia Bible College

Nebraska
York College

North Carolina
Roanoke Bible College

Oklahoma
Oklahoma Christian University of Science and Arts

Tennessee
David Lipscomb University
Freed-Hardeman University

Texas
Abilene Christian University
Institute for Christian Studies
Lubbock Christian University
Southwestern Christian College

West Virginia
Ohio Valley College

Church of God

Indiana
Anderson University

North Carolina
East Coast Bible College

Oklahoma
Mid-America Bible College

Oregon
Warner Pacific College

Tennessee
Lee College

Church of the Brethren

California
University of La Verne

Indiana
Manchester College

Kansas
McPherson College

Pennsylvania
Elizabethtown College

Virginia
Bridgewater College

Church of Jesus Christ of Latter-day Saints

Hawaii
Brigham Young University-Hawaii

Idaho
Ricks College

Utah
Brigham Young University
LDS Business College

Church of the Nazarene

California
Point Loma Nazarene College

Colorado
Nazarene Bible College

Idaho
Northwest Nazarene College

Illinois
Olivet Nazarene University

Kansas
MidAmerica Nazarene College

Massachusetts
Eastern Nazarene College

Oklahoma
Southern Nazarene University

Tennessee
Trevecca Nazarene College

Cumberland Presbyterian Church

Tennessee
Bethel College

Episcopal Church

Illinois
St. Augustine College

Nebraska
Clarkson College

New York
Bard College
Hobart College

North Carolina
St. Augustine's College
St. Mary's College

Ohio
Kenyon College

South Carolina
Voorhees College

Tennessee
University of the South

Virginia
St. Paul's College

Evangelical Covenant Church of America

Illinois
North Park College

Evangelical Free Church of America

Florida
Trinity College at Miami

Illinois
Trinity College

Evangelical Lutheran Church in America

California
California Lutheran University

Illinois
Augustana College

Iowa
Grand View College
Luther College
Waldorf College
Wartburg College

Kansas
Bethany College

Michigan
Suomi College

Minnesota
Augsburg College
Concordia College: Moorhead
Gustavus Adolphus College
St. Olaf College

Nebraska
Dana College
Midland Lutheran College

New Jersey
Upsala College

Ohio
Capital University
Wittenberg University

Pennsylvania
Thiel College

South Carolina
Newberry College

South Dakota
Augustana College

Texas
Texas Lutheran College

Virginia
Roanoke College

Washington
Pacific Lutheran University

Wisconsin
Carthage College

Evangelical Lutheran Synod

Minnesota
Bethany Lutheran College

Free Methodist Church of North America

Illinois
Greenville College

Kansas
Central College

Michigan
Spring Arbor College

New York
Roberts Wesleyan College

Washington
Seattle Pacific University

Free Will Baptists

North Carolina
Mount Olive College

Tennessee
Free Will Baptist Bible College

Friends United Meeting

Iowa
William Penn College

General Association of Regular Baptist Churches

Iowa
Faith Baptist Bible College and Theological Seminary

Michigan
Grand Rapids Baptist College and Seminary

Ohio
Cedarville College

Pennsylvania
Baptist Bible College of Pennsylvania

General Conference, Mennonite Church

Kansas
Bethel College

Ohio
Bluffton College

Greek Orthodox Archdiocese of North and South America

Massachusetts
Hellenic College

Interdenominational

Alaska
Alaska Bible College

Arkansas
John Brown University

California
Azusa Pacific University
Biola University
Patten College
San Jose Christian College

Colorado
Colorado Christian University

Florida
Hobe Sound Bible College

Georgia
Toccoa Falls College

Indiana
Taylor University

Iowa
Vennard College

Kentucky
Asbury College

Minnesota
Northwestern College
Oak Hills Bible College

Nebraska
Grace College of the Bible

North Carolina
John Wesley College

Ohio
God's Bible School and College

Oklahoma
Oral Roberts University

Oregon
Multnomah School of the Bible

Tennessee
Crichton College
William Jennings Bryan College

Washington
Heritage College

Jewish faith

California
Hebrew Union College: Jewish Institute of Religion
University of Judaism

Colorado
Yeshiva Toras Chaim Talmudical Seminary

Florida
Talmudic College of Florida

Maryland
Ner Israel Rabbinical College

Massachusetts
Hebrew College

Michigan
Yeshiva Beth Yehuda-Yeshiva Gedolah of Greater Detroit

New York
Beth Hamedrash Shaarei Yosher Institute
Beth Hatalmud Rabbinical College
Bramson ORT Technical Institute
Darkei No'Am Rabbinical College
Jewish Theological Seminary of America
Machzikei Hadath Rabbinical College
Mesivta Torah Vodaath Seminary
Mirrer Yeshiva Central Institute
Ohr Hameir Theological Seminary
Ohr Somayach Tanenbaum Education Center
Rabbinical College Ch'san Sofer of New York
Rabbinical College of Long Island
Rabbinical Seminary Adas Yereim
Rabbinical Seminary of America
Rabbinical Seminary M'Kor Chaim
Talmudical Institute of Upstate New York
Talmudical Seminary Oholei Torah
United Talmudical Academy
Yeshiva Gedolah Zichron Moshe
Yeshiva Karlin Stolin Beth Aron Y'Israel Rabbinical Institute
Yeshiva of Nitra Rabbinical College
Yeshiva Shaar Hatorah
Yeshivat Mikdash Melech

Ohio
Cleveland College of Jewish Studies

Pennsylvania
Gratz College
Talmudical Yeshiva of Philadelphia

Lutheran Church in America

North Carolina
Lenoir-Rhyne College

Lutheran Church — Missouri Synod

Alabama
Concordia College

California
Concordia University

Illinois
Concordia University

Indiana
Lutheran College of Health Professions
Valparaiso University

Michigan
Concordia College

Minnesota
Concordia College: St. Paul

Nebraska
Concordia College

New York
Concordia College

Oregon
Concordia College

Texas
Concordia Lutheran College

Wisconsin
Concordia University Wisconsin

Mennonite Brethren Church

California
Fresno Pacific College

Kansas
Tabor College

Mennonite Church

Indiana
Goshen College

Kansas
Hesston College

Virginia
Eastern Mennonite College

Missionary Church

Indiana
Bethel College

Moravian Church in America

North Carolina
Salem College

Pennsylvania
Moravian College

Nondenominational

Alabama
Southeastern Bible College

Arizona
Arizona College of the Bible

California
Christian Heritage College
Master's College

Florida
Clearwater Christian College
Florida Bible College

Georgia
Atlanta Christian College

Idaho
Boise Bible College

Iowa
Emmaus Bible College

Kentucky
Berea College

Maryland
Washington Bible College

New York
Iona College
King's College

Pennsylvania
Lancaster Bible College
Philadelphia College of Bible
Valley Forge Military College
Williamson Free School of Mechanical Trades

Texas
Amber University
LeTourneau University

West Virginia
Appalachian Bible College

Pentecostal Holiness Church

Georgia
Emmanuel College

Oklahoma
Southwestern College of Christian Ministries

Presbyterian Church (USA)

Alabama
Stillman College

Alaska
Sheldon Jackson College

Arkansas
Arkansas College
University of the Ozarks

Florida
Eckerd College

Georgia
Agnes Scott College

Illinois
Blackburn College
Lake Forest College
Millikin University
Monmouth College

Indiana
Hanover College

Iowa
Buena Vista College
Coe College
University of Dubuque

Kansas
Sterling College

Kentucky
Centre College
Lees College
Pikeville College

Michigan
Alma College

Minnesota
Macalester College

Mississippi
Belhaven College

Missouri
College of the Ozarks
Lindenwood College
Missouri Valley College
Westminster College

New Jersey
Bloomfield College

North Carolina
Barber-Scotia College
Davidson College
Lees-McRae College
Montreat-Anderson College
Peace College
Queens College
St. Andrews Presbyterian College
Warren Wilson College

North Dakota
Jamestown College

Ohio
College of Wooster
Muskingum College

Oklahoma
University of Tulsa

Oregon
Lewis and Clark College

Pennsylvania
Beaver College
Grove City College
Lafayette College
Waynesburg College
Westminster College
Wilson College

South Carolina
Presbyterian College

Tennessee
King College
Knoxville College
Maryville College
Rhodes College
Tusculum College

Texas
Austin College
Schreiner College
Trinity University

Virginia
Hampden-Sydney College
Mary Baldwin College

Washington
Whitworth College

West Virginia
Davis and Elkins College

Wisconsin
Carroll College

Reformed Church in America

Iowa
Central College
Northwestern College

Michigan
Hope College

Reformed Presbyterian Church of North America

Pennsylvania
Geneva College

Reorganized Church of Jesus Christ of Latter-day Saints

Iowa
Graceland College

Missouri
Park College

Roman Catholic Church

Alabama
Spring Hill College

California
College of Notre Dame
Dominican College of San Rafael
Dominican School of Philosophy and Theology
Holy Names College
Loyola Marymount University
Marymount College
Mount St. Mary's College
Queen of the Holy Rosary College
St. Mary's College of California
Santa Clara University
Thomas Aquinas College
University of San Diego
University of San Francisco

Colorado
Regis University

Connecticut
Albertus Magnus College
Fairfield University
Sacred Heart University
St. Joseph College

District of Columbia
Catholic University of America
Georgetown University
Oblate College
Trinity College

Florida
Barry University
St. John Vianney College Seminary
St. Leo College
St. Thomas University

Illinois
Barat College
College of St. Francis
De Paul University
Illinois Benedictine College
Lewis University
Loyola University of Chicago
Montay College
Parks College of St. Louis University
Quincy University
Rosary College
St. Francis Medical Center College of Nursing
St. Joseph College of Nursing
St. Xavier University
Springfield College in Illinois

Indiana
Ancilla College
Calumet College of St. Joseph
Holy Cross College
Marian College
St. Francis College
St. Joseph's College
St. Mary-of-the-Woods College
St. Mary's College
St. Meinrad College
University of Notre Dame

Iowa
Briar Cliff College
Clarke College
Divine Word College
Loras College
Mount Mercy College
Mount St. Clare College
St. Ambrose University

Kansas
Benedictine College
Donnelly College
Kansas Newman College
St. Mary College

Kentucky
Bellarmine College
Brescia College
Spalding University
Thomas More College

Louisiana
Loyola University
Our Lady of Holy Cross College
St. Joseph Seminary College
Xavier University of Louisiana

Maine
St. Joseph's College

Maryland
College of Notre Dame of Maryland
Loyola College in Maryland
Mount St. Mary's College

Massachusetts
Anna Maria College for Men and Women
Aquinas College at Milton
Aquinas College at Newton
Assumption College
Boston College
College of the Holy Cross
Elms College
Emmanuel College
Marian Court Junior College
Merrimack College
Regis College
St. Hyacinth College and Seminary
St. John's Seminary College
Stonehill College

Michigan
Aquinas College
Madonna University
Marygrove College
Sacred Heart Major Seminary
St. Mary's College
Siena Heights College
University of Detroit Mercy

Minnesota
College of St. Benedict
College of St. Catherine: St. Catherine Campus
College of St. Scholastica
St. John's University
St. Mary's Campus of the College of St. Catherine
St. Mary's College of Minnesota
University of St. Thomas

Missouri
Avila College
Conception Seminary College
Fontbonne College
Rockhurst College
St. Louis University

Montana
Carroll College
College of Great Falls

Nebraska
College of St. Mary
Creighton University

New Hampshire
Castle College
Notre Dame College
Rivier College
St. Anselm College

New Jersey
Assumption College for Sisters
Caldwell College
College of St. Elizabeth
Felician College
Georgian Court College
St. Peter's College
Seton Hall University

New Mexico
College of Santa Fe

New York
Canisius College
Catholic Medical Center of Brooklyn and Queens School of Nursing
College of Mount St. Vincent
College of New Rochelle
College of St. Rose
Dominican College of Blauvelt
Fordham University
Le Moyne College
Mater Dei College
Molloy College
St. Bonaventure University
St. John Fisher College
St. John's University
St. Joseph's School of Nursing
Villa Maria College of Buffalo
Wadhams Hall Seminary-College

North Carolina
Belmont Abbey College

North Dakota
University of Mary

Ohio
Chatfield College
College of Mount St. Joseph
Franciscan University of Steubenville
John Carroll University
Lourdes College
Notre Dame College of Ohio
Ohio Dominican College
Pontifical College Josephinum
University of Dayton
Ursuline College
Walsh University
Xavier University

Oklahoma
St. Gregory's College

Oregon
Marylhurst College
University of Portland

Pennsylvania
Allentown College of St. Francis de Sales
Alvernia College
Cabrini College
Carlow College
Chestnut Hill College
College Misericordia
Duquesne University
Gannon University
Gwynedd-Mercy College
Holy Family College
Immaculata College
King's College
La Roche College
La Salle University
Marywood College
Mercyhurst College
Neumann College
Rosemont College
St. Charles Borromeo Seminary
St. Francis College
St. Joseph's University
St. Vincent College
Seton Hill College
University of Scranton
Villanova University

Puerto Rico
Bayamon Central University
Pontifical Catholic University of Puerto Rico
University of the Sacred Heart

Rhode Island
Providence College
Salve Regina University

South Dakota
Mount Marty College
Presentation College

Tennessee
Aquinas Junior College
Christian Brothers University

Texas
Incarnate Word College
Our Lady of the Lake University of San Antonio
St. Edward's University
St. Mary's University
University of Dallas
University of St. Thomas

Vermont
College of St. Joseph in Vermont
St. Michael's College
Trinity College of Vermont

Virginia
Christendom College
Marymount University

Washington
Gonzaga University
St. Martin's College
Seattle University

West Virginia
Wheeling Jesuit College

Wisconsin
Alverno College
Cardinal Stritch College
Edgewood College
Marian College of Fond du Lac
Marquette University
Mount Mary College
St. Norbert College
Silver Lake College
Viterbo College

Seventh-day Adventists

Alabama
Oakwood College

California
La Sierra University
Pacific Union College

Maryland
Columbia Union College

Massachusetts
Atlantic Union College

Michigan
Andrews University

Nebraska
Union College

Ohio
Kettering College of Medical Arts

Puerto Rico
Universidad Adventista de las Antillas

Tennessee
Southern College of Seventh-day Adventists

Texas
Southwestern Adventist College

Washington
Walla Walla College

Southern Baptist Convention

Alabama
Judson College
Samford University
University of Mobile

Arizona
Grand Canyon University

Arkansas
Ouachita Baptist University
Williams Baptist College

California
California Baptist College

Florida
Florida Baptist Theological College
Palm Beach Atlantic College

Georgia
Brewton-Parker College
Mercer University
- Atlanta
- Macon

Shorter College
Truett-McConnell College

Kentucky
Cumberland College
Georgetown College
Mid-Continent Baptist Bible College

Louisiana
Louisiana College

Mississippi
Mississippi College
William Carey College

Missouri
Hannibal-LaGrange College
Missouri Baptist College
Southwest Baptist University

North Carolina
Campbell University
Chowan College
Gardner-Webb University
Mars Hill College
Meredith College
Southeastern Baptist Theological Seminary
Wingate College

Oklahoma
Oklahoma Baptist University

South Carolina
Anderson College
Charleston Southern University
Morris College
North Greenville College

Tennessee
American Baptist College of ABT Seminary
Belmont University
Carson-Newman College
Union University

Texas
Criswell College
Dallas Baptist University
East Texas Baptist University
Howard Payne University
University of Mary Hardin-Baylor
Wayland Baptist University

Virginia
Averett College
Bluefield College

Ukrainian Catholic Church

Pennsylvania
Manor Junior College

United Brethren in Christ

Indiana
Huntington College

United Church of Christ

Illinois
Elmhurst College

Maryland
Hood College

Missouri
Deaconess College of Nursing

Nebraska
Doane College

North Carolina
Catawba College
Elon College

Ohio
Defiance College
Heidelberg College

Oregon
Pacific University

Pennsylvania
Cedar Crest College
Ursinus College

Tennessee
Fisk University

Wisconsin
Lakeland College
Northland College

United Methodist Church

Alabama
Birmingham-Southern College
Huntingdon College

Alaska
Alaska Pacific University

Arkansas
Hendrix College
Philander Smith College

Colorado
University of Denver

Delaware
Wesley College

District of Columbia
American University

Florida
Bethune-Cookman College
Florida Southern College

Georgia
Andrew College
Clark Atlanta University
Emory University
LaGrange College
Oxford College of Emory University
Reinhardt College
Wesleyan College
Young Harris College

Illinois
Illinois Wesleyan University
Kendall College
MacMurray College
McKendree College
North Central College

Indiana
DePauw University
University of Evansville
University of Indianapolis

Iowa
Cornell College
Iowa Wesleyan College
Morningside College
Simpson College

Kansas
Baker University
Kansas Wesleyan University
Southwestern College

Kentucky
Kentucky Wesleyan College
Lindsey Wilson College
Sue Bennett College
Union College

Louisiana
Centenary College of Louisiana

Michigan
Adrian College
Albion College

Minnesota
Hamline University

Mississippi
Millsaps College
Rust College
Wood Junior College

Missouri
Central Methodist College

Nebraska
Nebraska Methodist College of Nursing and Allied Health
Nebraska Wesleyan University

New Jersey
Centenary College
Drew University

North Carolina
Bennett College
Brevard College
Duke University
Greensboro College
High Point University
Louisburg College
Methodist College
North Carolina Wesleyan College
Pfeiffer College

Ohio
Baldwin-Wallace College
Mount Union College
Ohio Northern University
Ohio Wesleyan University
Otterbein College

Oklahoma
Oklahoma City University

Oregon
Willamette University

Pennsylvania
Albright College
Allegheny College
Lebanon Valley College of Pennsylvania
Lycoming College

South Carolina
Claflin College
Columbia College
Spartanburg Methodist College
Wofford College

South Dakota
Dakota Wesleyan University

Tennessee
Hiwassee College
Lambuth University
Tennessee Wesleyan College

Texas
Lon Morris College
McMurry University
Southern Methodist University
Southwestern University
Texas Wesleyan University
Wiley College

Virginia
Emory and Henry College
Ferrum College
Randolph-Macon College
Randolph-Macon Woman's College
Shenandoah University
Virginia Wesleyan College

Washington
University of Puget Sound

West Virginia
West Virginia Wesleyan College

Wesleyan Church

Indiana
Indiana Wesleyan University

New York
Houghton College

Oklahoma
Bartlesville Wesleyan College

South Carolina
Central Wesleyan College

Wisconsin Evangelical Lutheran Synod

Minnesota
Dr. Martin Luther College

Wisconsin
Northwestern College
Wisconsin Lutheran College

Other religious affiliations

Alabama
Selma University
Talladega College

Arizona
Southwestern College

Arkansas
Central Baptist College

California
LIFE Bible College
Pacific Christian College
Pacific Oaks College
University of the Pacific
University of Redlands
Westmont College

Florida
Florida Christian College
Florida Memorial College
Stetson University
Warner Southern College

Georgia
Covenant College
Paine College
Piedmont College

Illinois
Illinois College
Moody Bible Institute
Trinity Christian College
Wheaton College

Indiana
Earlham College
Oakland City College

Iowa
Teikyo Marycrest University

Kansas
Barclay College
Friends University

Kentucky
Campbellsville College

Louisiana
Dillard University

Massachusetts
Gordon College

Michigan
Grace Bible College
Great Lakes Christian College
Olivet College
Reformed Bible College
William Tyndale College

Minnesota
Pillsbury Baptist Bible College

Mississippi
Southeastern Baptist College
Tougaloo College

Missouri
Calvary Bible College
Drury College
Ozark Christian College
Research College of Nursing
St. Louis Christian College
William Jewell College
William Woods College

Montana
Rocky Mountain College

Nebraska
Nebraska Christian College

New York
Manhattan College
Marist College
Siena College
Wagner College

North Carolina
Guilford College
Piedmont Bible College
Shaw University

Ohio
Cincinnati Bible College and Seminary
Circleville Bible College
Malone College
University of Findlay
Urbana University
Wilmington College

Oregon
Eugene Bible College
George Fox College
Northwest Christian College
Western Baptist College

Pennsylvania
Academy of the New Church
Franklin and Marshall College
Gettysburg College
Juniata College
Mount Aloysius College
Muhlenberg College
Susquehanna University

South Carolina
Columbia Bible College and Seminary
Erskine College
Furman University

Tennessee
LeMoyne-Owen College
Milligan College
Tennessee Temple University

Texas
Arlington Baptist College
Baptist Missionary Association Theological Seminary
Dallas Christian College
Hardin-Simmons University
Houston Baptist University
Huston-Tillotson College
Jacksonville College

Utah
Westminster College of Salt Lake City

Virginia

Liberty University
University of Richmond
Virginia Intermont College

Washington

Lutheran Bible Institute of Seattle

Wisconsin

Maranatha Baptist Bible College
Ripon College

Historically black colleges

Alabama

Alabama A&M University
Alabama State University
Bishop State Junior College
Carver State Technical College
Concordia College
J.F. Drake State Technical College
Lawson State Community College
Miles College
Oakwood College
Selma University
Stillman College
Talladega College
Trenholm State Technical College
Tuskegee University

Arkansas

Arkansas Baptist College
Philander Smith College
Shorter College
University of Arkansas at Pine Bluff

Delaware

Delaware State College

District of Columbia

Howard University
University of the District of Columbia

Florida

Bethune Cookman College
Edward Waters College
Florida A&M University
Florida Memorial College

Georgia

Albany State College
Clark Atlanta University
Fort Valley State College
Morehouse College
Morris Brown College
Paine College
Savannah State College
Spelman College

Kentucky

Kentucky State University

Louisiana

Dillard University
Grambling State University
Southern University A&M College
Southern University/New Orleans
Southern University/ Shreveport
Xavier University

Maryland

Bowie State University
Coppin State College
Morgan State University
University of Maryland Eastern Shore

Michigan

Lewis College of Business

Mississippi

Alcorn State University
Tougaloo College
Jackson State University
Mary Holmes College
Mississippi Valley State University
Coahoma Community College
Rust College
Hinds Community College

Missouri

Harris Stowe State College
Lincoln University

North Carolina

Barber-Scotia College
Bennett College
Elizabeth City State University
Fayetteville State University
Johnson C. Smith University
Livingstone College
North Carolina Agricultural and Technical State University
North Carolina Central University
St. Augustine's College
Shaw University
Winston-Salem State University

Ohio

Central State University
Wilberforce University

Oklahoma

Langston University

Pennsylvania

Cheyney University of Pennsylvania
Lincoln University

South Carolina

Allen University
Benedict College
Claflin College
Clinton Junior College
Denmark Technical College
Morris College
South Carolina State University
Voorhees College

Tennessee

Fisk University
Knoxville College
Lane College
Lemoyne-Owen College
Tennessee State University

Texas

Huston-Tillotston College
Jarvis Christian College
Paul Quinn College/Dallas
Paul Quinn College/Waco
Prairie View A&M University
St. Philip's College
Southwestern Christian College
Texas College
Texas Southern University
Wiley College

U.S. Virgin Islands

University of the Virgin Islands

Virginia

Hampton University
Norfolk State University
Virginia State University
St. Paul's College
Virginia Union University

West Virginia

West Virginia State College
Bluefield State College

Hispanic-serving institutions

Arizona

Arizona Western College
South Mountain Community College

California

California State University, Los Angeles
Cerritos Community College
College of the Sequoias
Compton Community College
Don Bosco Technical Institute
East Los Angeles College
Gavilan Community College
Hartnell College
Imperial Valley College
Kings River Community College
Los Angeles City College
Los Angeles Harbor College
Los Angeles Mission College
Los Angeles Trade and Technical College
Mount Saint Mary's College
Mount San Antonio College
Oxnard College
Palo Verde College
Rio Hondo College
St. John's Seminary College
San Diego State University
Southwestern College
West Coast Christian College
West Hills Community College

Colorado

Pueblo Community College
Trinidad State Junior College

Florida

Barry University
Florida International University
Miami-Dade Community College
St. John Vianney College Seminary
St. Thomas University

Illinois

City College of Chicago: Harry S. Truman College
MacCormac Junior College
St. Augustine College

New Jersey

Hudson County Community College
Passaic County Community College

New Mexico

Albuquerque Technical-Vocational Institute
College of Santa Fe
Dona Ana Branch Community College of New Mexico State University
Eastern New Mexico University: Roswell Campus
New Mexico Highlands University
New Mexico State University
New Mexico State University at Grants
Northern New Mexico Community College
Santa Fe Community College
University of New Mexico
Western New Mexico University

New York

Boricua College
City University of New York: Borough of Manhattan Community College
City University of New York: Bronx Community College
City University of New York: City College
City University of New York: Hostos Community College
City University of New York: John Jay College of Criminal Justice
City University of New York: LaGuardia Community College
City University of New York: Lehman College
College of Aeronautics
Mercy College

Puerto Rico

American University of Puerto Rico
Bayamon Central University
Caribbean University College
Catholic University of Puerto Rico
Colegio Universitario del Este
Conservatory of Music of Puerto Rico
Inter-American University of Puerto Rico: Aguadilla Campus
Inter-American University of Puerto Rico: Arecibo Campus
Inter-American University of Puerto Rico: Barranquitas Campus
Inter-American University of Puerto Rico: Bayamon Campus
Inter-American University of Puerto Rico: Fajardo Campus
Inter-American University of Puerto Rico: Guayama Campus
Inter-American University of Puerto Rico: Metropolitan Campus
Inter-American University of Puerto Rico: Ponce Campus
Inter-American University of Puerto Rico: San German Campus
Technological College of the Municipality of San Juan
Turabo University
Universidad Metropolitana
Universidad Politecnica de Puerto Rico
University of Puerto Rico at Aguadilla
University of Puerto Rico: Arecibo Campus
University of Puerto Rico: Bayamon Technological University College
University of Puerto Rico: Carolina Regional College
University of Puerto Rico: Cayey University College
University of Puerto Rico: Hamacao University College
University of Puerto Rico: La Montana Regional College
University of Puerto Rico: Mayaguez Campus
University of Puerto Rico: Medical Sciences Campus
University of Puerto Rico: Ponce Technological University College
University of Puerto Rico: Rio Piedras Campus
University of the Sacred Heart

Texas

Bee County College
Corpus Christi State University
Del Mar College
El Paso Community College
Incarnate Word College
Laredo Junior College
Laredo State University
Our Lady of the Lake University at San Antonio
Palo Alto College
St. Edwards University
St. Mary's University
St. Philip's College
San Antonio College
Southwest Texas Junior College
Sul Ross State University
Texas A&I University
Texas Southmost College
Texas State Technical Institute: Harlingen
University of Houston, Downtown
University of Texas at Brownsville
University of Texas at El Paso
University of Texas at San Antonio
University of Texas: Pan American

Colleges with learning disabled services

Alabama

Alabama Agricultural and Mechanical University
Auburn University
  Auburn
  Montgomery
Bevill State Community College
Bishop State Community College
Concordia College
Gadsden State Community College
George C. Wallace State Community College at Selma
Harry M. Ayers State Technical College
J. F. Drake State Technical College
Jacksonville State University
James H. Faulkner State Community College
John C. Calhoun State Community College
Northeast Alabama Community College
Northwest Alabama Community College
Reid State Technical College
Spring Hill College
Troy State University in Montgomery
University of Alabama
  Birmingham
  Huntsville
  Tuscaloosa
University of Montevallo

Alaska

Sheldon Jackson College
University of Alaska Anchorage

Arizona

Arizona State University
Arizona Western College
Embry-Riddle Aeronautical University: Prescott Campus
Gateway Community College
Glendale Community College
Mesa Community College
Northern Arizona University
Northland Pioneer College
Paradise Valley Community College
Phoenix College
Pima Community College
Rio Salado Community College
Scottsdale Community College
University of Arizona
Yavapai College

Arkansas

Arkansas State University
Arkansas Tech University
East Arkansas Community College
Henderson State University
Mississippi County Community College
Ouachita Baptist University
Rich Mountain Community College
Southern Arkansas University
University of Arkansas
University of Arkansas at Little Rock
University of the Ozarks
Westark Community College

California

Allan Hancock College
Antelope Valley College
Azusa Pacific University
Barstow College
California Polytechnic State University: San Luis Obispo
California State Polytechnic University: Pomona
California State University
  Bakersfield
  Chico
  Dominguez Hills
  Fresno
  Fullerton
  Hayward
  Long Beach
  Los Angeles
  Northridge
  Sacramento
  San Bernardino
  San Marcos
  Stanislaus
Canada College
Cerritos Community College
Cerro Coso Community College
Chabot College
Chaffey Community College
Citrus College
City College of San Francisco
Coastline Community College
College of the Canyons
College of the Redwoods
College of San Mateo
College of the Sequoias
College of the Siskiyous
Columbia College
Compton Community College
Contra Costa College
Cosumnes River College
Crafton Hills College
Cuesta College
Cuyamaca College
Cypress College
Diablo Valley College
Evergreen Valley College
Fashion Institute of Design and Merchandising
Feather River College
Foothill College
Fresno City College
Fullerton College
Glendale Community College
Golden West College
Grossmont Community College
Holy Names College
Humboldt State University
Lake Tahoe Community College
Laney College
Lassen College
Long Beach City College
Los Angeles City College
Los Angeles Harbor College
Los Angeles Mission College
Los Angeles Pierce College
Los Angeles Valley College
Los Medanos College
Marymount College
Mendocino College
Menlo College
Merced College
Merritt College
Mills College
MiraCosta College
Mission College
Modesto Junior College
Monterey Peninsula College
Moorpark College
Mount San Antonio College
Mount San Jacinto College
Napa Valley College
Occidental College
Pacific Union College
Palomar College
Pepperdine University
Point Loma Nazarene College
Porterville College
Rio Hondo College
Sacramento City College
Saddleback College
Samuel Merritt College
San Diego City College
San Diego Mesa College
San Francisco Art Institute
San Francisco State University
San Joaquin Delta College
San Jose City College
San Jose State University
Santa Barbara City College
Santa Monica College
Santa Rosa Junior College
Shasta College
Sierra College
Skyline College
Solano Community College
Sonoma State University
Southwestern College
Stanford University
Taft College
University of California
  Berkeley
  Davis
  Irvine
  Los Angeles
  Riverside
  San Diego
  San Francisco
  Santa Barbara
  Santa Cruz
University of the Pacific
University of Redlands
University of San Diego
University of San Francisco
University of Southern California
Ventura College
Victor Valley College
West Hills Community College
West Valley College
Yuba College

Colorado

Aims Community College
Arapahoe Community College
Colorado Northwestern Community College
Colorado State University
Community College of Aurora
Community College of Denver
Fort Lewis College
Front Range Community College
Lamar Community College
Mesa State College
Metropolitan State College of Denver
Otero Junior College
Pikes Peak Community College
Pueblo Community College
Red Rocks Community College
Regis University
University of Colorado
  Boulder
  Colorado Springs
University of Denver
University of Northern Colorado
University of Southern Colorado
Western State College of Colorado

Connecticut

Asnuntuck Community-Technical College
Briarwood College
Capital Community-Technical College
Central Connecticut State University
Connecticut College
Gateway Community-Technical College
Housatonic Community-Technical College
Mitchell College
Norwalk Community-Technical College
Quinnipiac College
Sacred Heart University
St. Joseph College
Southern Connecticut State University
Three Rivers Community-Technical College
University of Bridgeport
University of Connecticut
University of New Haven
Western Connecticut State University
Yale University

Delaware

Delaware Technical and Community College: Stanton/Wilmington Campus
Goldey-Beacom College
University of Delaware
Wesley College

District of Columbia

American University
Catholic University of America
George Washington University
Georgetown University
Howard University
University of the District of Columbia

Florida

Brevard Community College
Broward Community College
Central Florida Community College
Daytona Beach Community College
Edison Community College
Embry-Riddle Aeronautical University
Florida Agricultural and Mechanical University
Florida Atlantic University
Florida Community College at Jacksonville
Florida International University
Florida State University
Gulf Coast Community College
Hillsborough Community College
Indian River Community College
Lake City Community College
Lake-Sumter Community College
Manatee Community College
Miami-Dade Community College
New College of the University of South Florida

Okaloosa-Walton Community College
Pasco-Hernando Community College
Pensacola Junior College
Polk Community College
Rollins College
St. Petersburg Junior College
St. Thomas University
Santa Fe Community College
Seminole Community College
South Florida Community College
Tallahassee Community College
University of Central Florida
University of Florida
University of North Florida
University of South Florida
Valencia Community College
Webber College

Georgia

Abraham Baldwin Agricultural College
Athens Area Technical Institute
Atlanta Metropolitan College
Bainbridge College
Brenau University
Chattahoochee Technical Institute
Clayton State College
Columbus College
DeKalb College
Emory University
Fort Valley State College
Georgia College
Georgia Institute of Technology
Georgia Southern University
Georgia Southwestern College
Georgia State University
Kennesaw State College
Morehouse College
Reinhardt College
Southern College of Technology
University of Georgia
Valdosta State College
West Georgia College

Hawaii

University of Hawaii
  Hawaii Community College
  Hilo
  Honolulu Community College
  Kapiolani Community College
  Manoa
  Windward Community College

Idaho

Albertson College
Lewis Clark State College
North Idaho College
Ricks College
University of Idaho

Illinois

Barat College
Belleville Area College
Black Hawk College
  East Campus
  Moline
Bradley University
City Colleges of Chicago: Malcolm X College
College of DuPage
College of Lake County
De Paul University
Eastern Illinois University
Elgin Community College
Governors State University
Illinois Benedictine College
Illinois Central College
Illinois Eastern Community Colleges
  Frontier Community College
  Lincoln Trail College
  Olney Central College
  Wabash Valley College
Illinois Institute of Technology
Illinois State University
Illinois Valley Community College
Illinois Wesleyan University
John A. Logan College
Joliet Junior College
Kaskaskia College
Kishwaukee College
Knox College
Lake Land College
Lewis and Clark Community College
Lewis University
Lincoln Christian College and Seminary
McHenry County College
Moraine Valley Community College
Morton College
National-Louis University
Northeastern Illinois University
Northern Illinois University
Oakton Community College
Richland Community College
Roosevelt University
St. Xavier University
School of the Art Institute of Chicago
Shawnee Community College
Southeastern Illinois College
Southern Illinois University
  Carbondale
  Edwardsville
State Community College
Triton College
University of Illinois
  Chicago
  Urbana-Champaign
Western Illinois University
Wheaton College
William Rainey Harper College

Indiana

Anderson University
Ball State University
Bethel College
Earlham College
Goshen College
Indiana State University
Indiana University
  Bloomington
  East
  Northwest
Indiana University—Purdue University
  Fort Wayne
  Indianapolis
Indiana Vocational Technical College
  Central Indiana
  Columbus
  Kokomo
  Northcentral
  Whitewater
Indiana Wesleyan University
Manchester College
Martin University
Purdue University
  Calumet
  North Central Campus
  West Lafayette
St. Francis College
University of Evansville
University of Indianapolis
University of Southern Indiana
Vincennes University
Wabash College

Iowa

Briar Cliff College
Cornell College
Ellsworth Community College
Graceland College
Hawkeye Community College
Indian Hills Community College
Iowa Central Community College
Iowa Lakes Community College
Iowa State University
Iowa Western Community College
Kirkwood Community College
Loras College
North Iowa Area Community College
Northeast Iowa Community College
Northwest Iowa Community College
St. Ambrose University
Scott Community College
Southeastern Community College: North Campus
University of Iowa
University of Northern Iowa
Upper Iowa University

Kansas

Baker University
Butler County Community College
Colby Community College
Donnelly College
Emporia State University
Fort Hays State University
Hesston College
Hutchinson Community College
Independence Community College
Johnson County Community College
Kansas City Kansas Community College
Kansas State University
MidAmerica Nazarene College
Pittsburg State University
Pratt Community College
University of Kansas

Kentucky

Asbury College
Ashland Community College
Centre College
Eastern Kentucky University
Jefferson Community College
Lexington Community College
Madisonville Community College
Morehead State University
Murray State University
Northern Kentucky University
Paducah Community College
Spalding University
Thomas More College
University of Louisville
Western Kentucky University

Louisiana

Louisiana State University
  Agricultural and Mechanical College
  Medical Center
Loyola University
McNeese State University
Nicholls State University
Northeast Louisiana University
University of New Orleans
University of Southwestern Louisiana

Maine

Bates College
Bowdoin College
Central Maine Technical College
Colby College
Husson College
Southern Maine Technical College
Unity College
University of Maine
  Augusta
  Farmington
  Fort Kent
  Orono
  Presque Isle
University of New England
University of Southern Maine

Maryland

Allegany Community College
Anne Arundel Community College
Bowie State University
Catonsville Community College
Charles County Community College
Chesapeake College
Dundalk Community College
Essex Community College
Frederick Community College
Frostburg State University
Goucher College
Hagerstown Junior College
Harford Community College
Howard Community College
Johns Hopkins University
Johns Hopkins University: Peabody Conservatory of Music
Montgomery College
  Germantown Campus
  Rockville Campus
  Takoma Park Campus
Morgan State University
Prince George's Community College
St. Mary's College of Maryland
Salisbury State University
Towson State University
University of Maryland
  Baltimore County
  College Park
  Eastern Shore
Villa Julie College
Western Maryland College
Wor-Wic Community College

Massachusetts

American International College
Anna Maria College for Men and Women
Aquinas College at Newton
Babson College
Bentley College
Boston College
Boston University
Bradford College
Brandeis University
Bridgewater State College
Bunker Hill Community College
Cape Cod Community College
Clark University
Curry College
Dean Junior College
Eastern Nazarene College
Emerson College
Emmanuel College
Endicott College
Essex Agricultural and Technical Institute
Fitchburg State College
Greenfield Community College
Holyoke Community College
Lasell College
Lesley College
Massachusetts Bay Community College
Massasoit Community College
Middlesex Community College
Mount Holyoke College
Mount Ida College
Mount Wachusett Community College
Newbury College
North Adams State College
Northeastern University
Northern Essex Community College

Pine Manor College
Quinsigamond Community College
St. John's Seminary College
Simmons College
Smith College
Stonehill College
Suffolk University
Tufts University
University of Massachusetts
  Amherst
  Boston
  Lowell
Wellesley College
Wentworth Institute of Technology
Westfield State College
Worcester Polytechnic Institute

Michigan

Adrian College
Andrews University
Aquinas College
Calvin College
Center for Creative Studies: College of Art and Design
Charles Stewart Mott Community College
Davenport College of Business
Delta College
Eastern Michigan University
Ferris State University
Glen Oaks Community College
Grand Rapids Community College
Grand Valley State University
Henry Ford Community College
Highland Park Community College
Jackson Community College
Kalamazoo Valley Community College
Kellogg Community College
Kirtland Community College
Lake Michigan College
Lansing Community College
Macomb Community College
Madonna University
Marygrove College
Michigan State University
Mid Michigan Community College
Monroe County Community College
Muskegon Community College
Northern Michigan University
Northwestern Michigan College
Oakland Community College
Saginaw Valley State University
St. Clair County Community College
St. Mary's College
Schoolcraft College
Southwestern Michigan College
Spring Arbor College
Suomi College
University of Michigan
  Ann Arbor
  Dearborn
Wayne State University
West Shore Community College
Western Michigan University

Minnesota

Alexandria Technical College
Anoka-Ramsey Community College
Augsburg College
Austin Community College
Bemidji State University
College of Associated Arts
College of St. Benedict
College of St. Catherine: St. Catherine Campus
College of St. Scholastica
Concordia College: Moorhead
Concordia College: St. Paul
Hibbing Community College
Inver Hills Community College
Itasca Community College: Arrowhead Region
Lakewood Community College
Mankato State University
Mesabi Community College: Arrowhead Region
Minneapolis Community College
Moorhead State University
Normandale Community College
North Hennepin Community College
Rainy River Community College
Rochester Community College
St. Cloud State University
St. John's University
St. Mary's Campus of the College of St. Catherine
St. Mary's College of Minnesota
St. Olaf College
St. Paul Technical College
Saint Cloud Technical College
Southwest State University
University of Minnesota
  Crookston
  Duluth
  Twin Cities
University of St. Thomas
Willmar Community College
Worthington Community College

Mississippi

East Mississippi Community College
Hinds Community College
Jackson State University
Mississippi State University
Northwest Mississippi Community College
University of Mississippi
  Medical Center
  University

Missouri

Central Missouri State University
Hannibal-LaGrange College
Lincoln University
Longview Community College
Maple Woods Community College
Mineral Area College
Moberly Area Community College
Northwest Missouri State University
Park College
Penn Valley Community College
Ranken Technical College
Rockhurst College
St. Charles County Community College
St. Louis Community College
  Florissant Valley
  Meramec
Southwest Missouri State University
Stephens College
University of Missouri
  Columbia
  Kansas City
  St. Louis
Washington University
Webster University
Westminster College
William Jewell College
William Woods College

Montana

Dawson Community College
Eastern Montana College
Helena Vocational-Technical Center
Montana State University
Northern Montana College
Rocky Mountain College
University of Montana

Nebraska

Chadron State College
Concordia College
Creighton University
Dana College
Metropolitan Community College
Northeast Community College
Peru State College
Southeast Community College
  Lincoln Campus
  Milford Campus
University of Nebraska
  Lincoln
  Omaha
Wayne State College
Western Nebraska Community College: Scottsbluff Campus

Nevada

Truckee Meadows Community College
University of Nevada
  Las Vegas
  Reno
Western Nevada Community College

New Hampshire

Dartmouth College
Franklin Pierce College
Keene State College
New England College
New Hampshire College
New Hampshire Technical College
  Berlin
  Laconia
New Hampshire Technical Institute
Notre Dame College
Plymouth State College of the University System of New Hampshire
University of New Hampshire
  Durham
  Manchester
White Pines College

New Jersey

Atlantic Community College
Bergen Community College
Brookdale Community College
Burlington County College
Centenary College
County College of Morris
Cumberland County College
Drew University
Essex County College
Fairleigh Dickinson University
  Edward Williams College
  Madison
Georgian Court College
Gloucester County College
Hudson County Community College
Jersey City State College
Mercer County Community College
Monmouth College
New Jersey Institute of Technology
Ocean County College
Princeton University
Ramapo College of New Jersey
Raritan Valley Community College
Rider College
Rutgers—The State University of New Jersey
  Camden College of Arts and Sciences
  College of Engineering
  College of Pharmacy
  Cook College
  Douglass College
  Livingston College
  Mason Gross School of the Arts
  Newark College of Arts and Sciences
  Rutgers College
  University College New Brunswick
  University College Newark
Seton Hall University
Stockton State College
Sussex County Community College
Trenton State College
Union County College
University of Medicine and Dentistry of New Jersey: School of Nursing
William Paterson College of New Jersey

New Mexico

Albuquerque Technical-Vocational Institute
Clovis Community College
College of Santa Fe
Dona Ana Branch Community College of New Mexico State University
Eastern New Mexico University
  Portales
  Roswell Campus
New Mexico Junior College
New Mexico State University
  Alamogordo
  Carlsbad
  Las Cruces
Northern New Mexico Community College
San Juan College
Santa Fe Community College
University of New Mexico
Western New Mexico University

New York

Adelphi University
Adirondack Community College
Alfred University
Barnard College
Bramson ORT Technical Institute
Broome Community College
Canisius College
Cayuga County Community College
Cazenovia College
Central City Business Institute
City University of New York
  Baruch College
  Bronx Community College
  Brooklyn College
  College of Staten Island
  Hunter College
  John Jay College of Criminal Justice
  Kingsborough Community College
  La Guardia Community College
  New York City Technical College
  Queens College
  Queensborough Community College
  York College
Clarkson University
Clinton Community College
College of Mount St. Vincent
College of St. Rose

Columbia University: Columbia College
Columbia-Greene Community College
Cornell University
Corning Community College
Culinary Institute of America
Dowling College
Dutchess Community College
D'Youville College
Eastman School of Music of the University of Rochester
Erie Community College
- City Campus
- North Campus
- South Campus

Fashion Institute of Technology
Finger Lakes Community College
Fulton-Montgomery Community College
Genesee Community College
Herkimer County Community College
Hofstra University
Hudson Valley Community College
Iona College
Jamestown Community College
Jefferson Community College
King's College
Long Island University: Brooklyn Campus
Manhattan College
Manhattanville College
Marist College
Marymount College
Marymount Manhattan College
Medaille College
Mercy College
Mohawk Valley Community College
Molloy College
Mount St. Mary College
Nassau Community College
New York Institute of Technology
New York University
Niagara County Community College
Niagara University
North Country Community College
Onondaga Community College
Paul Smith's College
Phillips Beth Israel School of Nursing
Pratt Institute
Rensselaer Polytechnic Institute
Rochester Institute of Technology
Rockland Community College
St. Bonaventure University
St. Francis College
St. John Fisher College
St. John's University
St. Joseph's College: Suffolk Campus
St. Lawrence University
St. Thomas Aquinas College
Schenectady County Community College
State University of New York
- Albany
- Binghamton
- Buffalo
- Stony Brook
- College of Agriculture and Technology at Cobleskill
- College at Brockport
- College at Buffalo
- College of Environmental Science and Forestry
- College at New Paltz
- College at Old Westbury
- College at Oneonta
- College at Plattsburgh
- College at Potsdam
- College of Technology at Alfred
- College of Technology at Canton
- College of Technology at Farmingdale
- Health Sciences Center at Stony Brook
- Institute of Technology at Utica/Rome
- Oswego

Suffolk County Community College
- Eastern Campus
- Selden
- Western Campus

Syracuse University
Tompkins-Cortland Community College
Ulster County Community College
University of Rochester
Utica College of Syracuse University
Wagner College
Westchester Community College

North Carolina

Appalachian State University
Asheville Buncombe Technical Community College
Beaufort County Community College
Blue Ridge Community College
Brunswick Community College
Caldwell Community College and Technical Institute
Cape Fear Community College
Carteret Community College
Catawba Valley Community College
Central Piedmont Community College
Chowan College
Cleveland Community College
Craven Community College
Duke University
Durham Technical Community College
East Carolina University
Edgecombe Community College
Elizabeth City State University
Elon College
Gaston College
Guilford College
Haywood Community College
Mars Hill College
Mayland Community College
McDowell Technical Community College
Mitchell Community College
Nash Community College
North Carolina Agricultural and Technical State University
North Carolina State University
Peace College
Piedmont Community College
Pitt Community College
Randolph Community College
Roanoke-Chowan Community College
Robeson Community College
Sampson Community College
Sandhills Community College
Southeastern Community College
Southwestern Community College
University of North Carolina
- Asheville
- Chapel Hill
- Charlotte
- Greensboro
- Wilmington

Wake Forest University
Wake Technical Community College
Wayne Community College
Western Carolina University
Western Piedmont Community College
Wilkes Community College
Wingate College

North Dakota

Bismarck State College
Dickinson State University
Little Hoop Community College
North Dakota State College of Science
North Dakota State University
University of North Dakota
- Grand Forks
- Williston

Ohio

Baldwin-Wallace College
Bowling Green State University
Case Western Reserve University
Cedarville College
Central Ohio Technical College
Chatfield College
Cincinnati College of Mortuary Science
Cleveland Institute of Art
College of Mount St. Joseph
College of Wooster
Columbus State Community College
Cuyahoga Community College
- Metropolitan Campus
- Western Campus

Edison State Community College
Franklin University
Jefferson Technical College
Kent State University
- Kent
- Trumbull Regional Campus

Lakeland Community College
Lima Technical College
Lorain County Community College
Malone College
Marion Technical College
Miami University
- Hamilton Campus
- Middletown Campus
- Oxford Campus

Muskingum College
North Central Technical College
Oberlin College
Ohio State University
- Agricultural Technical Institute
- Columbus Campus
- Lima Campus
- Mansfield Campus
- Marion Campus
- Newark Campus

Ohio University
- Athens
- Lancaster Campus

Ohio Wesleyan University
Otterbein College
Owens Technical College
- Findlay Campus
- Toledo

Sinclair Community College
Terra Technical College
Tiffin University
University of Akron
University of Cincinnati
- Clermont College
- Raymond Walters College

University of Dayton
University of Findlay
University of Rio Grande
University of Toledo
Urbana University
Virginia Marti College of Fashion and Art
Wilmington College
Wright State University
- Dayton
- Lake Campus

Xavier University
Youngstown State University

Oklahoma

Bartlesville Wesleyan College
Cameron University
Carl Albert State College
East Central University
Northeastern State University
Northwestern Oklahoma State University
Oklahoma City University
Oklahoma State University
- Stillwater
- Technical Branch: Okmulgee

Oral Roberts University
Tulsa Junior College
University of Oklahoma

Oregon

Bassist College
Blue Mountain Community College
Central Oregon Community College
Chemeketa Community College
Clackamas Community College
Eastern Oregon State College
George Fox College
Lane Community College
Linn-Benton Community College
Mount Hood Community College
Oregon Institute of Technology
Oregon State University
Pacific University
Portland Community College
Portland State University
Rogue Community College
Treasure Valley Community College
University of Oregon
- Eugene
- Robert Donald Clark Honors College

Warner Pacific College
Willamette University

Pennsylvania

Albright College
Allegheny College
Bloomsburg University of Pennsylvania
Bucks County Community College
Cabrini College
California University of Pennsylvania
Carlow College
Carnegie Mellon University
Cheyney University of Pennsylvania
Clarion University of Pennsylvania
College Misericordia
Community College of Allegheny County
- Allegheny Campus
- Boyce Campus
- North Campus
- South Campus

Community College of Beaver County
Community College of Philadelphia
Delaware County Community College

Dickinson College
Drexel University
Duquesne University
East Stroudsburg University of Pennsylvania
Edinboro University of Pennsylvania
Gannon University
Harcum Junior College
Haverford College
Immaculata College
Indiana University of Pennsylvania
Kutztown University of Pennsylvania
Lackawanna Junior College
Lafayette College
Lebanon Valley College of Pennsylvania
Lehigh County Community College
Lock Haven University of Pennsylvania
Luzerne County Community College
Lycoming College
Marywood College
Mercyhurst College
Millersville University of Pennsylvania
Muhlenberg College
Northampton County Area Community College
Penn State
- Erie Behrend College
- University Park Campus

Pennsylvania College of Technology
Pennsylvania Institute of Technology
Pittsburgh Technical Institute
Point Park College
Reading Area Community College
Robert Morris College
Shippensburg University of Pennsylvania
Slippery Rock University of Pennsylvania
Temple University
Thomas Jefferson University: College of Allied Health Sciences
University of the Arts
University of Pennsylvania
University of Pittsburgh
- Bradford
- Pittsburgh

West Chester University of Pennsylvania
Westmoreland County Community College

Puerto Rico

Inter American University of Puerto Rico: Guayama Campus
University of the Sacred Heart

Rhode Island

Brown University
Community College of Rhode Island
Johnson & Wales University
New England Institute of Technology
Providence College
Rhode Island College
Rhode Island School of Design
University of Rhode Island

South Carolina

Aiken Technical College
Anderson College
Central Carolina Technical College
Central Wesleyan College
The Citadel
Clemson University
College of Charleston
Converse College
Florence-Darlington Technical College
Francis Marion University
Trident Technical College
University of South Carolina
- Columbia
- Sumter

York Technical College

South Dakota

Black Hills State University
Dakota State University
Dakota Wesleyan University
Lake Area Vocational Technical Institute
Mitchell Vocational Technical Institute
Mount Marty College
Northern State University
South Dakota State University
University of South Dakota
Western Dakota Vocational Technical Institute

Tennessee

Chattanooga State Technical Community College
Cleveland State Community College
East Tennessee State University
Lambuth University
Lee College
Maryville College
Memphis State University
Middle Tennessee State University
Nashville State Technical Institute
Pellissippi State Technical Community College
Roane State Community College
Tennessee Technological University
Tusculum College
University of Tennessee
- Chattanooga
- Knoxville
- Martin
- Memphis

Vanderbilt University

Texas

Abilene Christian University
Alvin Community College
Amarillo College
Angelina College
Angelo State University
Austin Community College
Brookhaven College
Cedar Valley College
Central Texas College
Collin County Community College District
Del Mar College
Eastfield College
El Centro College
El Paso Community College
Galveston College
Houston Community College
Howard College
Jarvis Christian College
Lamar University—Beaumont
Laredo Junior College
Lubbock Christian University
Midwestern State University
Mountain View College
North Harris Montgomery Community College District
Richland College
St. Mary's University
St. Philip's College
San Antonio College
San Jacinto College: North
Schreiner College
Southern Methodist University
Southwest Texas State University
Southwestern Assemblies of God College
Tarleton State University
Tarrant County Junior College
Texas A&M University
Texas Christian University
Texas State Technical College: Waco
Texas Tech University
Texas Woman's University
Trinity Valley Community College
Tyler Junior College
University of Houston
University of North Texas
University of Texas
- Arlington
- Austin
- Dallas
- El Paso
- Permian Basin
- Tyler

West Texas A & M University
Wiley College

Utah

Brigham Young University
Dixie College
Salt Lake Community College
Snow College
University of Utah
Weber State University
Westminster College of Salt Lake City

Vermont

Burlington College
Champlain College
College of St. Joseph in Vermont
Community College of Vermont
Johnson State College
Landmark College
Lyndon State College
Norwich University
St. Michael's College
Southern Vermont College
University of Vermont
Vermont Technical College

Virginia

Blue Ridge Community College
Bluefield College
Central Virginia Community College
College of William and Mary
Dabney S. Lancaster Community College
Eastern Shore Community College
George Mason University
Hampden-Sydney College
Hollins College
J. Sargeant Reynolds Community College
James Madison University
Longwood College
Lord Fairfax Community College
Mary Baldwin College
Marymount University
New River Community College
Northern Virginia Community College
Old Dominion University
Patrick Henry Community College
Radford University
Randolph-Macon College
Randolph-Macon Woman's College
Roanoke College
Southern Virginia College for Women
Tidewater Community College
University of Virginia
Virginia Commonwealth University
Virginia Intermont College
Virginia Polytechnic Institute and State University
Virginia Wesleyan College
Virginia Western Community College
Wytheville Community College

Washington

Bellevue Community College
Big Bend Community College
Central Washington University
Centralia College
Clark College
Columbia Basin College
Cornish College of the Arts
Eastern Washington University
Edmonds Community College
Everett Community College
Evergreen State College
Highline Community College
Olympic College
Pacific Lutheran University
Peninsula College
Pierce College
Seattle Central Community College
Seattle Pacific University
Seattle University
Shoreline Community College
Skagit Valley College
South Puget Sound Community College
South Seattle Community College
Tacoma Community College
University of Washington
Washington State University
Wenatchee Valley College
Western Washington University
Whatcom Community College
Whitworth College
Yakima Valley Community College

West Virginia

Bethany College
Davis and Elkins College
Marshall University
Potomac State College of West Virginia University
Salem-Teikyo University
Southern West Virginia Community College
West Virginia Institute of Technology
West Virginia University
West Virginia Wesleyan College

Wisconsin

Blackhawk Technical College
Carroll College
Chippewa Valley Technical College
Edgewood College
Fox Valley Technical College
Gateway Technical College
Lakeshore Technical College
Madison Area Technical College
Marian College of Fond du Lac
Mid-State Technical College
Milwaukee School of Engineering
Moraine Park Technical College
Nicolet Area Technical College
Northeast Wisconsin Technical College
Ripon College
St. Norbert College
Silver Lake College
Southwest Wisconsin Technical College
University of Wisconsin
- Eau Claire
- La Crosse
- Madison
- Oshkosh
- Parkside
- River Falls
- Stevens Point
- Stout
- Whitewater

University of Wisconsin Center
- Baraboo/Sauk County
- Fox Valley
- Marinette County
- Richland
- Rock County
- Waukesha

Waukesha County Technical College
Wisconsin Indianhead Technical College

Wyoming

Casper College
Laramie County Community College
Northwest College
Sheridan College
University of Wyoming
Western Wyoming Community College

American Samoa, Caroline Islands, Guam, Marianas, Virgin Islands

Guam Community College

Canada

McGill University

Colleges that offer ROTC

Air Force ROTC

Alabama
Alabama State University
Auburn University
    Auburn
    Montgomery
Birmingham-Southern College
Jefferson State Community College
Samford University
Spring Hill College
Stillman College
Troy State University
    Montgomery
    Troy
Tuskegee University
University of Alabama
    Birmingham
    Huntsville
    Tuscaloosa
University of Mobile
University of Montevallo
University of South Alabama

Arizona
Arizona State University
Embry-Riddle Aeronautical University: Prescott Campus
Glendale Community College
Grand Canyon University
Northern Arizona University
Phoenix College
Pima Community College
South Mountain Community College
University of Arizona
Yavapai College

Arkansas
University of Arkansas

California
Antelope Valley College
Biola University
California Institute of Technology
California Lutheran University
California State University
    Dominguez Hills
    Fresno
    Hayward
    Long Beach
    Los Angeles
    Northridge
    Sacramento
Chabot College
Chapman University
Claremont McKenna College
College of Notre Dame
College of the Sequoias
Contra Costa College
Cuyamaca College
Dominican College of San Rafael
Evergreen Valley College
Foothill College
Fresno City College
Golden West College
Harvey Mudd College
Holy Names College
John F. Kennedy University
Los Angeles City College
Los Angeles Mission College
Loyola Marymount University
Marymount College
Mission College
Mount St. Mary's College
National University
Occidental College
Pepperdine University
Point Loma Nazarene College
Pomona College
San Diego State University
San Francisco State University
San Jose City College
San Jose State University
Santa Clara University
Scripps College
Stanford University
University of California
    Berkeley
    Irvine
    Los Angeles
    Riverside
University of the Pacific
University of San Diego
University of San Francisco
University of Southern California
West Valley College

Colorado
Aims Community College
Arapahoe Community College
Metropolitan State College of Denver
Regis University
University of Colorado
    Boulder
    Denver
University of Denver
University of Northern Colorado

Connecticut
Central Connecticut State University
Eastern Connecticut State University
Quinnipiac College
Southern Connecticut State University
University of Connecticut
University of Hartford
Western Connecticut State University
Yale University

Delaware
Delaware State College
University of Delaware
Wilmington College

District of Columbia
American University
Catholic University of America
Georgetown University
Howard University
Trinity College
University of the District of Columbia

Florida
Barry University
Bethune-Cookman College
Brevard Community College
Daytona Beach Community College
Eckerd College
Embry-Riddle Aeronautical University
Florida Agricultural and Mechanical University
Florida Atlantic University
Florida International University
Florida Southern College
Florida State University
Miami-Dade Community College
New College of the University of South Florida
St. Leo College
St. Petersburg Junior College
St. Thomas University
Santa Fe Community College
Tallahassee Community College
University of Central Florida
University of Florida
University of Miami
University of South Florida
University of Tampa

Georgia
Agnes Scott College
Clark Atlanta University
Georgia Institute of Technology
Morehouse College
Oglethorpe University
Spelman College
University of Georgia
Valdosta State College

Hawaii
Hawaii Pacific University
University of Hawaii
    Manoa
    Windward Community College

Idaho
University of Idaho

Illinois
Belleville Area College
Chicago State University
City Colleges of Chicago
    Harold Washington College
    Olive-Harvey College
Elmhurst College
Governors State University
Illinois Institute of Technology
John A. Logan College
Lewis and Clark Community College
Lewis University
McKendree College
North Central College
Northeastern Illinois University
Northwestern University
Parks College of St. Louis University
St. Xavier University
Southern Illinois University
    Carbondale
    Edwardsville
University of Illinois
    Chicago
    Urbana-Champaign

Indiana
Butler University
DePauw University
Holy Cross College
Indiana State University
Indiana University
    Bloomington
    South Bend
Purdue University
Rose-Hulman Institute of Technology
St. Mary's College
University of Notre Dame

Iowa
Drake University
Iowa State University
Iowa Western Community College
University of Iowa

Kansas
Baker University
Kansas State University
MidAmerica Nazarene College
University of Kansas
Washburn University of Topeka

Kentucky
Bellarmine College
Centre College
Eastern Kentucky University
Georgetown College
Kentucky State University
Lexington Community College
Thomas More College
Transylvania University
University of Kentucky
University of Louisville
Western Kentucky University

Louisiana
Dillard University
Grambling State University
Louisiana State University and Agricultural and Mechanical College
Louisiana Tech University
Our Lady of Holy Cross College
Southern University at New Orleans
Tulane University
University of New Orleans
Xavier University of Louisiana

Maine
Husson College
University of Maine

Maryland
Bowie State University
Johns Hopkins University
Towson State University
University of Maryland
    Baltimore County
    College Park

Massachusetts
American International College
Anna Maria College for Men and Women
Becker College: Worcester Campus
Bentley College
Boston College
Boston University
Bridgewater State College
Elms College
Gordon College
Harvard and Radcliffe Colleges
Massachusetts Institute of Technology
Middlesex Community College
Mount Holyoke College
Northeastern University
Northern Essex Community College
Smith College
Springfield College
Tufts University

University of Massachusetts
Amherst
Lowell
Wellesley College
Wentworth Institute of Technology
Western New England College
Worcester Polytechnic Institute
Worcester State College

Michigan

Eastern Michigan University
Lansing Community College
Lawrence Technological University
Michigan State University
Michigan Technological University
University of Michigan
Ann Arbor
Dearborn
Wayne State University

Minnesota

Augsburg College
College of St. Catherine: St. Catherine Campus
College of St. Scholastica
Concordia College: Moorhead
Concordia College: St. Paul
Hamline University
Macalester College
Moorhead State University
Normandale Community College
Northwestern College
University of Minnesota
Duluth
Twin Cities
University of St. Thomas

Mississippi

Delta State University
Mississippi State University
Mississippi University for Women
Mississippi Valley State University
Northwest Mississippi Community College
Rust College
University of Mississippi
University of Southern Mississippi
William Carey College

Missouri

Harris Stowe State College
St. Louis Community College at Florissant Valley
St. Louis University
Southeast Missouri State University
Stephens College
University of Missouri
Columbia
Rolla
St. Louis
Washington University
Westminster College

Montana

Montana State University

Nebraska

Bellevue College
College of St. Mary
Concordia College
Creighton University
Doane College
Nebraska Wesleyan University
University of Nebraska
Lincoln
Omaha

New Hampshire

Colby-Sawyer College
Daniel Webster College
Franklin Pierce College
Keene State College
New England College
New Hampshire College
Plymouth State College of the University System of New Hampshire
Rivier College
St. Anselm College
University of New Hampshire

New Jersey

Brookdale Community College
Fairleigh Dickinson University
Edward Williams College
Madison
Kean College of New Jersey
Mercer County Community College
Montclair State College
New Jersey Institute of Technology
Princeton University
Raritan Valley Community College
Rider College
Rutgers—The State University of New Jersey
Camden College of Arts and Sciences
College of Engineering
College of Nursing
College of Pharmacy
Cook College
Douglass College
Livingston College
Mason Gross School of the Arts
Newark College of Arts and Sciences
Rutgers College
University College Camden
University College New Brunswick
University College Newark
Seton Hall University
Stevens Institute of Technology
Trenton State College
Union County College
William Paterson College of New Jersey

New Mexico

Dona Ana Branch Community College of New Mexico State University
New Mexico State University
University of New Mexico

New York

Adelphi University
Clarkson University
College of Aeronautics
College of Mount St. Vincent
College of St. Rose
Cornell University
Dowling College
Elmira College
Fordham University
Fulton-Montgomery Community College
Iona College
Ithaca College
Le Moyne College
Long Island University: C. W. Post Campus
Manhattan College
Mercy College
Molloy College
Monroe Community College
New York Institute of Technology
New York University
Onondaga Community College
Pace University
College of White Plains
New York
Pleasantville/Briarcliff
Polytechnic University
Brooklyn
Long Island Campus
Rensselaer Polytechnic Institute
Roberts Wesleyan College
Rochester Institute of Technology
Russell Sage College
St. Francis College
St. John Fisher College
St. Joseph's College: Suffolk Campus
St. Lawrence University
St. Thomas Aquinas College
Siena College
Skidmore College
State University of New York
Albany
College at Cortland
College of Environmental Science and Forestry
College at Geneseo
College at Old Westbury
College at Potsdam
College of Technology at Canton
College of Technology at Farmingdale
Maritime College
Syracuse University
Union College
University of Rochester
Utica College of Syracuse University
Wagner College

North Carolina

Barber-Scotia College
Belmont Abbey College
Bennett College
Duke University
East Carolina University
Fayetteville State University
Greensboro College
Johnson C. Smith University
Meredith College
Methodist College
North Carolina Agricultural and Technical State University
North Carolina Central University
North Carolina State University
Pembroke State University
St. Augustine's College
University of North Carolina
Chapel Hill
Charlotte
Greensboro
Wingate College

North Dakota

North Dakota State University

Ohio

Ashland University
Baldwin-Wallace College
Bowling Green State University
Case Western Reserve University
Cedarville College
College of Mount St. Joseph
Cuyahoga Community College: Metropolitan Campus
DeVry Institute of Technology: Columbus
Franklin University
Kent State University
Kent
Salem Regional Campus
Miami University
Hamilton Campus
Middletown Campus
Oxford Campus
Mount Union College
Ohio Northern University
Ohio State University: Columbus Campus
Ohio University
Athens
Chillicothe Campus
Lancaster Campus
Ohio Wesleyan University
Otterbein College
University of Akron
University of Cincinnati
Access Colleges
Cincinnati
University of Dayton
University of Findlay
University of Toledo
Wilberforce University
Wittenberg University
Wright State University

Oklahoma

Oklahoma Christian University of Science and Arts
Oklahoma City University
Oklahoma State University
St. Gregory's College
University of Oklahoma

Oregon

Linfield College
Linn-Benton Community College
Oregon State University
Portland State University
University of Portland
Warner Pacific College
Western Oregon State College

Pennsylvania

Bloomsburg University of Pennsylvania
Bryn Mawr College
Carlow College
Carnegie Mellon University
Chatham College
College Misericordia
Community College of Allegheny County: Allegheny Campus
Drexel University
Duquesne University
East Stroudsburg University of Pennsylvania
Eastern College
Keystone Junior College
King's College
Kutztown University of Pennsylvania
La Roche College
La Salle University
Lehigh University
Lincoln University
Luzerne County Community College
Marywood College
Northampton County Area Community College
Penn State University Park Campus
Point Park College
Robert Morris College
St. Joseph's University
St. Vincent College
Thomas Jefferson University: College of Allied Health Sciences
University of Pennsylvania
University of Pittsburgh
University of Scranton
Valley Forge Military College
Villanova University
Widener University
Wilkes University

Puerto Rico

Bayamon Central University
Inter American University of Puerto Rico: San German Campus
Universidad Politecnica de Puerto Rico
University of Puerto Rico
Carolina Regional College
Mayaguez Campus
Rio Piedras Campus

South Carolina
Anderson College
Benedict College
Charleston Southern University
The Citadel
Claflin College
Clemson University
College of Charleston
South Carolina State University
Tri-County Technical College
University of South Carolina

South Dakota
South Dakota State University

Tennessee
Belmont University
Christian Brothers University
David Lipscomb University
Fisk University
Free Will Baptist Bible College
Knoxville College
LeMoyne-Owen College
Memphis State University
Rhodes College
Shelby State Community College
State Technical Institute at Memphis
Tennessee State University
Trevecca Nazarene College
University of Tennessee: Knoxville
Vanderbilt University

Texas
Angelo State University
Austin Community College
Baylor University
Concordia Lutheran College
Dallas Baptist University
Lubbock Christian University
Paul Quinn College
St. Edward's University
Southern Methodist University
Southwest Texas State University
Texas A&M University
Texas Christian University
Texas Tech University
Texas Wesleyan University
Texas Woman's University
University of Dallas
University of Mary Hardin-Baylor
University of North Texas
University of Texas
- Austin
- Dallas
- El Paso
- San Antonio

Weatherford College

Utah
Brigham Young University
Salt Lake Community College
University of Utah
Utah State University
Utah Valley Community College
Weber State University
Westminster College of Salt Lake City

Vermont
Champlain College
Lyndon State College
Norwich University
St. Michael's College
Trinity College of Vermont
University of Vermont

Virginia
George Mason University
Piedmont Virginia Community College
University of Virginia
Virginia Military Institute
Virginia Polytechnic Institute and State University

Washington
Central Washington University
Highline Community College
Seattle Pacific University
Seattle University
University of Washington
Washington State University

West Virginia
Salem-Teikyo University
Shepherd College
West Virginia University

Wisconsin
Marquette University
Milwaukee School of Engineering
University of Wisconsin
- Madison
- Superior

Wyoming
University of Wyoming

Army ROTC

Alabama
Alabama Agricultural and Mechanical University
Auburn University
- Auburn
- Montgomery

Birmingham-Southern College
Jacksonville State University
James H. Faulkner State Community College
Jefferson State Community College
John C. Calhoun State Community College
Judson College
Marion Military Institute
Spring Hill College
Stillman College
Talladega College
Troy State University in Montgomery
Tuskegee University
University of Alabama
- Birmingham
- Huntsville
- Tuscaloosa

University of Mobile
University of Montevallo
University of North Alabama
University of South Alabama

Alaska
University of Alaska Fairbanks

Arizona
Arizona State University
Embry-Riddle Aeronautical University: Prescott Campus
Glendale Community College
Grand Canyon University
Mesa Community College
Northern Arizona University
Phoenix College
Pima Community College
University of Arizona
Yavapai College

Arkansas
Arkansas State University
Central Baptist College
Harding University
Hendrix College
John Brown University
Philander Smith College
University of Arkansas
University of Arkansas
- Little Rock
- Medical Sciences
- Pine Bluff

University of Central Arkansas

California
Azusa Pacific University
Biola University
California Baptist College
California Institute of Technology
California Lutheran University
California Polytechnic State University: San Luis Obispo
California State Polytechnic University: Pomona
California State University
- Chico
- Dominguez Hills
- Fresno
- Fullerton
- Hayward
- Long Beach
- Los Angeles
- Northridge
- Sacramento
- San Bernardino

Chabot College
Chapman University
Christian Heritage College
Claremont McKenna College
College of Notre Dame
Cuyamaca College
Evergreen Valley College
Foothill College
Fresno City College
Harvey Mudd College
Holy Names College
Los Angeles City College
Los Angeles Mission College
Mission College
Mount St. Mary's College
National University
Occidental College
Pepperdine University
Point Loma Nazarene College
Pomona College
St. Mary's College of California
San Diego State University
San Francisco State University
San Jose City College
San Jose State University
Santa Clara University
Santa Rosa Junior College
Scripps College
Stanford University
United States International University
University of California
- Berkeley
- Davis
- Los Angeles
- Riverside
- Santa Barbara

University of San Diego
University of San Francisco
University of Southern California
West Valley College
Westmont College

Colorado
Arapahoe Community College
Colorado Christian University
Colorado College
Colorado School of Mines
Colorado State University
Colorado Technical College
Metropolitan State College of Denver
Pikes Peak Community College
Pueblo Community College
Regis University
University of Colorado
- Boulder
- Colorado Springs
- Denver

University of Denver
University of Northern Colorado

Connecticut
Central Connecticut State University
Eastern Connecticut State University
Sacred Heart University
Southern Connecticut State University
Teikyo-Post University
University of Bridgeport
University of Connecticut
University of Hartford
Western Connecticut State University
Yale University

Delaware
Delaware State College
University of Delaware
Wilmington College

District of Columbia
American University
Catholic University of America
Georgetown University
Howard University
Trinity College
University of the District of Columbia

Florida
Barry University
Bethune-Cookman College
Brevard Community College
Broward Community College
Daytona Beach Community College
Eckerd College
Edward Waters College
Embry-Riddle Aeronautical University
Florida Agricultural and Mechanical University
Florida Atlantic University
Florida Community College at Jacksonville
Florida Institute of Technology
Florida International University
Florida Southern College
Florida State University
Gulf Coast Community College
Jacksonville University
Miami-Dade Community College
New College of the University of South Florida
Pasco-Hernando Community College
Pensacola Junior College
Polk Community College
St. Leo College
St. Petersburg Junior College
Santa Fe Community College
Seminole Community College
Southeastern College of the Assemblies of God
Stetson University
Tallahassee Community College
University of Central Florida
University of Florida
University of Miami
University of North Florida
University of South Florida
University of Tampa
University of West Florida
Valencia Community College

Georgia
Albany State College
Armstrong State College
Augusta College
Brenau University
Clark Atlanta University
Columbus College
Covenant College
Fort Valley State College
Georgia College
Georgia Institute of Technology
Georgia Military College
Georgia Southern University
Georgia Southwestern College
Georgia State University
Kennesaw State College
Mercer University
Morehouse College
Morris Brown College
North Georgia College
Oglethorpe University
Paine College
Savannah State College
Spelman College
University of Georgia
West Georgia College

Hawaii
Hawaii Pacific University
University of Hawaii
  Manoa
  Windward Community College

Idaho
Boise State University
Lewis Clark State College
Northwest Nazarene College
Ricks College
University of Idaho

Illinois
Carl Sandburg College
Chicago State University
De Paul University
DeVry Institute of Technology: Addison
Eastern Illinois University
Elmhurst College
Governors State University
Illinois Institute of Technology
Illinois State University
Illinois Wesleyan University
John A. Logan College
Kishwaukee College
Lewis University
Monmouth College
North Central College
Northeastern Illinois University
Northern Illinois University
Northwestern University
Olivet Nazarene University
Parks College of St. Louis University
Rockford College
Southern Illinois University
  Carbondale
  Edwardsville
University of Illinois
  Chicago
  Urbana-Champaign
Western Illinois University
Wheaton College

Indiana
Ball State University
Butler University
DePauw University
Franklin College
Holy Cross College
Indiana State University
Indiana University
  Bloomington
  Northwest
  South Bend
Indiana University—Purdue University at Indianapolis
Marian College
Purdue University
Rose-Hulman Institute of Technology
St. Mary-of-the-Woods College
St. Mary's College
University of Indianapolis
University of Notre Dame

Iowa
Coe College
Drake University
Grand View College
Iowa State University
Iowa Western Community College
University of Iowa
University of Northern Iowa

Kansas
Baker University
Benedictine College
Emporia State University
Kansas State University
MidAmerica Nazarene College
Pittsburg State University
University of Kansas
Washburn University of Topeka

Kentucky
Bellarmine College
Centre College
Cumberland College
Eastern Kentucky University
Georgetown College
Kentucky State University
Lees College
Lexington Community College
Morehead State University
Murray State University
Northern Kentucky University
Spalding University
Thomas More College
Transylvania University
Union College
University of Kentucky
University of Louisville
Western Kentucky University

Louisiana
Centenary College of Louisiana
Dillard University
Grambling State University
Louisiana State University
  Agricultural and Mechanical College
  Shreveport
Loyola University
McNeese State University
Northeast Louisiana University
Northwestern State University
Our Lady of Holy Cross College
Southeastern Louisiana University
Southern University at New Orleans
Southern University and Agricultural and Mechanical College
Tulane University
University of New Orleans
University of Southwestern Louisiana
Xavier University of Louisiana

Maine
Colby College
Husson College
St. Joseph's College
Thomas College
Unity College
University of Maine

Maryland
Allegany Community College
Bowie State University
College of Notre Dame of Maryland
Coppin State College
Essex Community College
Frostburg State University
Goucher College
Johns Hopkins University
Loyola College in Maryland
Morgan State University
Mount St. Mary's College
Salisbury State University
Towson State University
University of Baltimore
University of Maryland
  Baltimore County
  Eastern Shore
Villa Julie College
Western Maryland College

Massachusetts
American International College
Anna Maria College for Men and Women
Assumption College
Bay Path College
Becker College: Worcester Campus
Bentley College
Boston College
Boston University
Bridgewater State College
Clark University
Curry College
Elms College
Emmanuel College
Fitchburg State College
Harvard and Radcliffe Colleges
Massachusetts College of Pharmacy and Allied Health Sciences
Massachusetts Institute of Technology
Mount Holyoke College
Mount Wachusett Community College
Nichols College
Northeastern University
Simmons College
Smith College
Springfield College
Stonehill College
Tufts University
University of Massachusetts
  Amherst
  Lowell
Wellesley College
Wentworth Institute of Technology
Western New England College
Westfield State College
Worcester Polytechnic Institute
Worcester State College

Michigan
Adrian College
Alma College
Central Michigan University
Eastern Michigan University
Ferris State University
Grand Rapids Baptist College and Seminary
Lansing Community College
Lawrence Technological University
Michigan State University
Michigan Technological University
Northern Michigan University
Northwood University
University of Michigan
  Ann Arbor
  Dearborn
Wayne State University
Western Michigan University

Minnesota
Bethany Lutheran College
College of St. Benedict
College of St. Scholastica
Concordia College: Moorhead
Concordia College: St. Paul
Gustavus Adolphus College
Mankato State University
Moorhead State University
Normandale Community College
St. Cloud State University
St. John's University
University of Minnesota
  Duluth
  Twin Cities

Mississippi
Alcorn State University
Delta State University
Hinds Community College
Jackson State University
Millsaps College
Mississippi College
Mississippi State University
Mississippi University for Women
Mississippi Valley State University
Rust College
Tougaloo College
University of Mississippi
University of Southern Mississippi
William Carey College

Missouri
Central Methodist College
Central Missouri State University
Evangel College
Fontbonne College
Harris Stowe State College
Kemper Military School and College
Lincoln University
Maryville University
Missouri Baptist College
Missouri Southern State College
Missouri Western State College
Northeast Missouri State University
Northwest Missouri State University
Park College
Research College of Nursing
St. Louis Community College at Florissant Valley
St. Louis University
Southeast Missouri State University
Southwest Baptist University
Southwest Missouri State University
Stephens College
University of Missouri
  Columbia
  Kansas City
  Rolla
  St. Louis
Washington University
Westminster College

Montana
Eastern Montana College
Montana State University
Rocky Mountain College
University of Montana

Nebraska
Bellevue College
Clarkson College
College of St. Mary
Concordia College
Creighton University
Dana College
Doane College
Midland Lutheran College
Nebraska Wesleyan University
Peru State College

University of Nebraska
- Kearney
- Lincoln
- Omaha

Nevada

Sierra Nevada College
University of Nevada: Reno

New Hampshire

Colby-Sawyer College
Daniel Webster College
Keene State College
New England College
New Hampshire College
Plymouth State College of the University System of New Hampshire
St. Anselm College
University of New Hampshire

New Jersey

Brookdale Community College
Caldwell College
Fairleigh Dickinson University
- Edward Williams College
- Madison

Kean College of New Jersey
Mercer County Community College
Montclair State College
Princeton University
Rider College
Rowan College of New Jersey
Rutgers—The State University of New Jersey
- Camden College of Arts and Sciences
- College of Engineering
- College of Nursing
- College of Pharmacy
- Cook College
- Douglass College
- Livingston College
- Mason Gross School of the Arts
- Newark College of Arts and Sciences
- Rutgers College
- University College Camden
- University College New Brunswick
- University College Newark

Seton Hall University
Stevens Institute of Technology
Trenton State College

New Mexico

Dona Ana Branch Community College of New Mexico State University
Eastern New Mexico University
New Mexico Military Institute
New Mexico State University
University of New Mexico

New York

Adelphi University
Alfred University
Canisius College
City University of New York
- John Jay College of Criminal Justice
- Lehman College

Clarkson University
College of St. Rose
Columbia University: School of Nursing
Cornell University
Daemen College
Dominican College of Blauvelt
D'Youville College
Elmira College
Erie Community College
- City Campus
- North Campus
- South Campus

Fordham University
Fulton-Montgomery Community College
Hofstra University
Houghton College
Hudson Valley Community College
Iona College
Ithaca College
Keuka College
Le Moyne College
Long Island University: C. W. Post Campus
Medaille College
Mercy College
Molloy College
Mount St. Mary College
Nassau Community College
New York University
Niagara University
Polytechnic University
- Brooklyn
- Long Island Campus

Rensselaer Polytechnic Institute
Roberts Wesleyan College
Rochester Institute of Technology
Russell Sage College
St. Bonaventure University
St. Francis College
St. John Fisher College
St. John's University
St. Joseph's College: Suffolk Campus
St. Lawrence University
Siena College
Skidmore College
State University of New York
- Albany
- College at Brockport
- College at Cortland
- College of Environmental Science and Forestry
- College at Geneseo
- College at Old Westbury
- College at Potsdam
- College of Technology at Canton
- College of Technology at Farmingdale
- Oswego

Syracuse University
Union College
University of Rochester
Utica College of Syracuse University
Wagner College

North Carolina

Appalachian State University
Barber-Scotia College
Belmont Abbey College
Bennett College
Campbell University
Catawba College
Davidson College
Duke University
East Carolina University
Elizabeth City State University
Elon College
Greensboro College
Johnson C. Smith University
Lenoir-Rhyne College
Livingstone College
Meredith College
Methodist College
North Carolina Agricultural and Technical State University
North Carolina Central University
North Carolina State University
Pembroke State University
Pfeiffer College
St. Augustine's College
Shaw University
University of North Carolina
- Chapel Hill
- Charlotte
- Greensboro

Wake Forest University
Western Carolina University
Wingate College
Winston-Salem State University

North Dakota

North Dakota State University
University of North Dakota

Ohio

Baldwin-Wallace College
Bowling Green State University
Capital University
Case Western Reserve University
Cedarville College
Central State University
Cleveland State University
College of Mount St. Joseph
Columbus State Community College
DeVry Institute of Technology: Columbus
Franklin University
Hocking Technical College
John Carroll University
Kent State University
- Kent
- Salem Regional Campus

Marietta College
Miami University: Middletown Campus
Mount Union College
Ohio Northern University
Ohio State University: Columbus Campus
Ohio University
- Athens
- Chillicothe Campus
- Lancaster Campus

Otterbein College
Sinclair Community College
University of Akron
University of Cincinnati
- Access Colleges
- Cincinnati

University of Dayton
University of Findlay
University of Rio Grande
University of Toledo
Wilberforce University
Wittenberg University
Wright State University
Xavier University
Youngstown State University

Oklahoma

Cameron University
East Central University
Northeastern State University
Oklahoma Christian University of Science and Arts
Oklahoma City University
Oklahoma State University
Oral Roberts University
Southern Nazarene University
University of Central Oklahoma
University of Oklahoma
University of Tulsa

Oregon

Linn-Benton Community College
Oregon State University
Pacific University
Portland State University
Reed College
University of Oregon
- Eugene
- Robert Donald Clark Honors College

University of Portland
Warner Pacific College
Western Baptist College
Western Oregon State College

Pennsylvania

Allegheny College
Allentown College of St. Francis de Sales
Baptist Bible College of Pennsylvania
Bloomsburg University of Pennsylvania
Bryn Mawr College
Bucknell University
Cabrini College
California University of Pennsylvania
Carlow College
Carnegie Mellon University
Cedar Crest College
Chatham College
Chestnut Hill College
Cheyney University of Pennsylvania
College Misericordia
Community College of Allegheny County: Allegheny Campus
Delaware Valley College
Dickinson College
Drexel University
Duquesne University
East Stroudsburg University of Pennsylvania
Eastern College
Edinboro University of Pennsylvania
Gannon University
Gwynedd-Mercy College
Harrisburg Area Community College
Indiana University of Pennsylvania
Keystone Junior College
King's College
Kutztown University of Pennsylvania
La Roche College
La Salle University
Lafayette College
Lebanon Valley College of Pennsylvania
Lehigh County Community College
Lehigh University
Lock Haven University of Pennsylvania
Lycoming College
Mansfield University of Pennsylvania
Marywood College
Mercyhurst College
Millersville University of Pennsylvania
Moravian College
Muhlenberg College
Northampton County Area Community College
Penn State
- Harrisburg Capital College
- University Park Campus

Philadelphia College of Pharmacy and Science
Point Park College
Robert Morris College
St. Francis College
Shippensburg University of Pennsylvania
Slippery Rock University of Pennsylvania
Susquehanna University
Temple University
University of Pennsylvania
University of Pittsburgh
- Bradford
- Pittsburgh

University of Scranton

Valley Forge Military College
Villanova University
Widener University
Wilkes University

Puerto Rico
American University of Puerto Rico
Bayamon Central University
Caribbean University
Inter American University of Puerto Rico
- Guayama Campus
- San German Campus

Pontifical Catholic University of Puerto Rico
Universidad Metropolitana
Universidad Politecnica de Puerto Rico
University of Puerto Rico
- Bayamon Technological University College
- Carolina Regional College
- Cayey University College
- Humacao University College
- Mayaguez Campus
- Ponce Technological University College
- Rio Piedras Campus

Rhode Island
Bryant College
Community College of Rhode Island
Johnson & Wales University
Providence College
Rhode Island College
Roger Williams University
Salve Regina University
University of Rhode Island

South Carolina
Allen University
Anderson College
Benedict College
Central Wesleyan College
The Citadel
Claflin College
Clemson University
Converse College
Denmark Technical College
Florence-Darlington Technical College
Francis Marion University
Furman University
Lander University
Morris College
Newberry College
Presbyterian College
South Carolina State University
Spartanburg Methodist College
Tri-County Technical College
University of South Carolina
- Aiken
- Columbia
- Spartanburg

Voorhees College
Wofford College

South Dakota
Black Hills State University
Mount Marty College
National College
South Dakota School of Mines and Technology
South Dakota State University
University of South Dakota

Tennessee
Austin Peay State University
Belmont University
Carson-Newman College
Chattanooga State Technical Community College
Christian Brothers University
East Tennessee State University
Fisk University
Free Will Baptist Bible College
King College
Knoxville College
LeMoyne-Owen College
Memphis State University
Middle Tennessee State University
Milligan College
Rhodes College
Shelby State Community College
State Technical Institute at Memphis
Tennessee Technological University
Tennessee Temple University
Trevecca Nazarene College
University of Tennessee
- Chattanooga
- Knoxville
- Martin

Vanderbilt University
Walters State Community College

Texas
Abilene Christian University
Austin Community College
Concordia Lutheran College
Corpus Christi State University
Dallas Baptist University
Del Mar College
Hardin-Simmons University
Houston Community College
Incarnate Word College
Lamar University—Beaumont
Lubbock Christian University
McMurry University
Our Lady of the Lake University of San Antonio
Prairie View A&M University
Rice University
St. Edward's University
St. Mary's University
St. Philip's College
Sam Houston State University
Southern Methodist University
Southwest Texas State University
Stephen F. Austin State University
Tarleton State University
Tarrant County Junior College
Texas A&I University
Texas A&M University
Texas Christian University
Texas Tech University
Texas Wesleyan University
Texas Woman's University
University of Dallas
University of Houston
- Clear Lake
- Downtown
- Houston

University of St. Thomas
University of Texas
- Arlington
- Austin
- Dallas
- El Paso
- Pan American
- San Antonio

Utah
Brigham Young University
Salt Lake Community College
University of Utah
Utah State University
Utah Valley Community College
Weber State University
Westminster College of Salt Lake City

Vermont
Champlain College
Norwich University
St. Michael's College
University of Vermont

Virginia
Christopher Newport University
College of William and Mary
George Mason University
Hampden-Sydney College
Hampton University
J. Sargeant Reynolds Community College
James Madison University
John Tyler Community College
Liberty University
Longwood College
Lynchburg College
Mary Baldwin College
Marymount University
Norfolk State University
Old Dominion University
Piedmont Virginia Community College
Radford University
Randolph-Macon College
Randolph-Macon Woman's College
Richard Bland College
St. Paul's College
Southside Virginia Community College
Tidewater Community College
University of Richmond
University of Virginia
Virginia Commonwealth University
Virginia Military Institute
Virginia Polytechnic Institute and State University
Virginia State University
Virginia Union University

Washington
Central Washington University
Eastern Washington University
Gonzaga University
Highline Community College
Pacific Lutheran University
Pierce College
St. Martin's College
Seattle Pacific University
Seattle University
Spokane Community College
Spokane Falls Community College
University of Washington
Washington State University
Whitworth College
Yakima Valley Community College

West Virginia
Fairmont State College
Marshall University
Ohio Valley College
University of Charleston
West Virginia Institute of Technology
West Virginia State College
West Virginia University

Wisconsin
Alverno College
Bellin College of Nursing
Marian College of Fond du Lac
Marquette University
Milwaukee School of Engineering
Ripon College
St. Norbert College
University of Wisconsin
- Green Bay
- La Crosse
- Madison
- Oshkosh
- Stevens Point
- Whitewater

Viterbo College

Wyoming
University of Wyoming

American Samoa, Caroline Islands, Guam, Marianas, Virgin Islands
Guam Community College

Naval ROTC

Alabama
Auburn University

Arizona
Pima Community College
University of Arizona

California
Biola University
California Institute of Technology
California Maritime Academy
California State University: Hayward
College of Notre Dame
Foothill College
Los Angeles City College
Mount St. Mary's College
Pepperdine University
Point Loma Nazarene College
St. Mary's College of California
San Diego State University
San Francisco State University
Santa Clara University
Stanford University
University of California
- Berkeley
- Irvine
- Los Angeles

University of San Diego
University of Southern California

Colorado
University of Colorado at Boulder

District of Columbia
American University
Catholic University of America
George Washington University
Georgetown University
University of the District of Columbia

Florida
Florida Agricultural and Mechanical University
Florida Community College at Jacksonville
Florida State University
Jacksonville University
Santa Fe Community College
Tallahassee Community College
University of Florida

Georgia
Agnes Scott College
Armstrong State College
Clark Atlanta University
Georgia Institute of Technology
Morehouse College
Morris Brown College
Savannah State College
Spelman College

Idaho
University of Idaho

Illinois
Illinois Institute of Technology
Lewis University
North Central College
Northwestern University
University of Illinois
- Chicago
- Urbana-Champaign

Indiana
Bethel College
Purdue University
St. Mary's College
University of Notre Dame

Iowa
Iowa State University

Kansas
MidAmerica Nazarene College
University of Kansas

Louisiana
Dillard University
Louisiana State University and Agricultural and Mechanical College
Southern University and Agricultural and Mechanical College
Tulane University
Xavier University of Louisiana

Maine
Husson College
Maine Maritime Academy
University of Maine

Massachusetts
Anna Maria College for Men and Women
Assumption College
Becker College: Worcester Campus
Boston College
Boston University
College of the Holy Cross
Harvard and Radcliffe Colleges
Massachusetts Institute of Technology
Northeastern University
Tufts University
Worcester Polytechnic Institute
Worcester State College

Michigan
Eastern Michigan University
University of Michigan
  Ann Arbor
  Dearborn

Minnesota
Augsburg College
Concordia College: St. Paul
Macalester College
Normandale Community College
University of Minnesota: Twin Cities

Mississippi
University of Mississippi

Missouri
Stephens College

Nebraska
Nebraska Wesleyan University
University of Nebraska—Lincoln

New Hampshire
Daniel Webster College

New Jersey
Rutgers—The State University of New Jersey
  Camden College of Arts and Sciences
  University College Camden

New York
College of St. Rose
Cornell University
Fordham University
Fulton-Montgomery Community College
Monroe Community College
Rensselaer Polytechnic Institute
Rochester Institute of Technology
Russell Sage College
State University of New York
  Albany
  Maritime College
Union College
University of Rochester

North Carolina
Duke University
North Carolina State University
University of North Carolina at Chapel Hill

Ohio
Miami University
  Hamilton Campus
  Middletown Campus
  Oxford Campus
Ohio State University: Columbus Campus
Ohio University: Lancaster Campus
Otterbein College

Oklahoma
University of Oklahoma

Oregon
Linn-Benton Community College
Oregon State University

Pennsylvania
Bryn Mawr College
Carlow College
Carnegie Mellon University
Chatham College
Drexel University
La Salle University
Penn State University Park Campus
University of Pennsylvania
University of Pittsburgh
Villanova University

Puerto Rico
Inter American University of Puerto Rico: San German Campus

South Carolina
The Citadel
University of South Carolina

Tennessee
Belmont University
Christian Brothers University
Fisk University
LeMoyne-Owen College
Memphis State University
Trevecca Nazarene College
Vanderbilt University

Texas
Concordia Lutheran College
Lubbock Christian University
Prairie View A&M University
Rice University
St. Edward's University
Texas A&M University
  College Station
  Galveston
Texas Tech University
University of Houston
  Downtown
  Houston
University of St. Thomas
University of Texas at Austin

Utah
University of Utah
Weber State University
Westminster College of Salt Lake City

Vermont
Champlain College
Norwich University

Virginia
Hampton University
Norfolk State University
Old Dominion University
University of Virginia
Virginia Military Institute
Virginia Polytechnic Institute and State University

Washington
Seattle Pacific University
Seattle University
University of Washington
Washington State University

Wisconsin
Marquette University
University of Wisconsin: Madison

Open admissions colleges

Open admissions 2-year colleges

Alabama

Alabama Aviation and Technical College
Alabama Southern Community College
Bevill State Community College
Bishop State Community College
Central Alabama Community College
  Alexander City Campus
  Childersburg Campus
Chattahoochee Valley Community College
Concordia College
Douglas MacArthur State Technical College
Enterprise State Junior College
Gadsden State Community College
George C. Wallace State Community College
  Dothan
  Selma
Harry M. Ayers State Technical College
J. F. Drake State Technical College
James H. Faulkner State Community College
Jefferson Davis State Junior College
Jefferson State Community College
John C. Calhoun State Community College
John M. Patterson State Technical College
Lawson State Community College
Lurleen B. Wallace State Junior College
Northeast Alabama Community College
Northwest Alabama Community College
Phillips Junior College: Birmingham
Reid State Technical College
Shelton State Community College
Shoals Community College
Snead State Community College
Southern Union State Junior College
Sparks State Technical College
Trenholm State Technical College
Virginia College
Walker College
Wallace State Community College at Hanceville

Alaska

Prince William Sound Community College

Arizona

Arizona Western College
Central Arizona College
Cochise College
Eastern Arizona College
Gateway Community College
Glendale Community College
Mesa Community College
Mohave Community College
Navajo Community College
Northland Pioneer College
Paradise Valley Community College
Phoenix College
Pima Community College
Rio Salado Community College
Scottsdale Community College
South Mountain Community College
Yavapai College

Arkansas

Arkansas State University: Beebe Branch
Capital City Junior College
East Arkansas Community College
Garland County Community College
Mississippi County Community College
North Arkansas Community/Technical College
Phillips County Community College
Rich Mountain Community College
South Arkansas Community College
Southern Arkansas University: Technical Branch
Westark Community College

California

Allan Hancock College
Antelope Valley College
Bakersfield College
Barstow College
Canada College
Cerritos Community College
Cerro Coso Community College
Chabot College
Chaffey Community College
Citrus College
City College of San Francisco
Coastline Community College
College of the Canyons
College of Marin: Kentfield
College of Oceaneering
College of the Redwoods
College of San Mateo
College of the Sequoias
College of the Siskiyous
Columbia College
Compton Community College
Contra Costa College
Cosumnes River College
Crafton Hills College
Cuesta College
Cuyamaca College
Cypress College
Diablo Valley College
D-Q University
Evergreen Valley College
Feather River College
Foothill College
Fresno City College
Fullerton College
Glendale Community College
Golden West College
Grossmont Community College
Lake Tahoe Community College
Laney College
Las Positas College
Lassen College
Long Beach City College
Los Angeles City College
Los Angeles Harbor College
Los Angeles Mission College
Los Angeles Pierce College
Los Angeles Trade and Technical College
Los Angeles Valley College
Los Medanos College
Mendocino College
Merced College
Merritt College
MiraCosta College
Mission College
Modesto Junior College
Monterey Peninsula College
Moorpark College
Mount San Antonio College
Mount San Jacinto College
Napa Valley College
Palomar College
Pasadena City College
Porterville College
Rio Hondo College
Sacramento City College
Saddleback College
San Diego City College
San Diego Mesa College
San Diego Miramar College
San Francisco College of Mortuary Science
San Joaquin Delta College
San Jose City College
Santa Barbara City College
Santa Monica College
Santa Rosa Junior College
Shasta College
Sierra College
Skyline College
Solano Community College
Southwestern College
Taft College
Ventura College
Victor Valley College
West Hills Community College
West Valley College
Yuba College

Colorado

Aims Community College
Arapahoe Community College
Colorado Institute of Art
Colorado Mountain College
  Alpine Campus
  Spring Valley Campus
  Timberline Campus
Colorado Northwestern Community College
Community College of Aurora
Community College of Denver
Front Range Community College
Lamar Community College
Morgan Community College
Northeastern Junior College
Otero Junior College
Pikes Peak Community College
Pueblo Community College
Red Rocks Community College
Trinidad State Junior College

Connecticut

Asnuntuck Community-Technical College
Briarwood College
Capital Community-Technical College
Gateway Community-Technical College
Housatonic Community-Technical College
Middlesex Community-Technical College
Northwestern Connecticut Community-Technical College
Norwalk Community-Technical College
Quinebaug Valley Community-Technical College
Three Rivers Community-Technical College
Tunxis Community-Technical College

Delaware

Delaware Technical and Community College
  Southern Campus
  Stanton/Wilmington Campus
  Terry Campus

Florida

Art Institute of Fort Lauderdale
Brevard Community College
Broward Community College
Central Florida Community College
Chipola Junior College
Daytona Beach Community College
Edison Community College
Florida Community College at Jacksonville
Gulf Coast Community College
Hillsborough Community College
Indian River Community College
Lake City Community College
Lake-Sumter Community College
Manatee Community College
Miami-Dade Community College
New England Institute of Technology
North Florida Junior College
Okaloosa-Walton Community College
Palm Beach Community College
Pasco-Hernando Community College
Pensacola Junior College
Phillips Junior College: Melbourne
Polk Community College
St. Johns River Community College
St. Petersburg Junior College
Santa Fe Community College
Seminole Community College
South Florida Community College
Southern College
Tallahassee Community College
Valencia Community College

Georgia

Athens Area Technical Institute
Georgia Military College
Gupton Jones College of Funeral Service
Meadows College of Business
Savannah Technical Institute

Hawaii

University of Hawaii
  Hawaii Community College
  Honolulu Community College
  Kapiolani Community College
  Kauai Community College
  Windward Community College

Idaho

College of Southern Idaho
North Idaho College

Illinois

Black Hawk College
- East Campus
- Moline

Carl Sandburg College
City Colleges of Chicago
- Harold Washington College
- Kennedy-King College
- Malcolm X College
- Olive-Harvey College

College of DuPage
Danville Area Community College
Elgin Community College
Gem City College
Highland Community College
Illinois Central College
Illinois Eastern Community Colleges
- Frontier Community College
- Lincoln Trail College
- Olney Central College
- Wabash Valley College

Illinois Valley Community College
John A. Logan College
Joliet Junior College
Kankakee Community College
Kaskaskia College
Kishwaukee College
Lake Land College
Lewis and Clark Community College
Lincoln Land Community College
McHenry County College
Moraine Valley Community College
Morrison Institute of Technology
Morton College
Oakton Community College
Richland Community College
Rock Valley College
St. Augustine College
Sauk Valley Community College
Shawnee Community College
Southeastern Illinois College
Spoon River College
State Community College
Triton College
William Rainey Harper College

Indiana

Indiana Vocational Technical College
- Central Indiana
- Columbus
- Eastcentral
- Kokomo
- Lafayette
- Northcentral
- Northeast
- Northwest
- Southcentral
- Southeast
- Southwest
- Wabash Valley
- Whitewater

Mid-America College of Funeral Service
Vincennes University

Iowa

American Institute of Commerce
Clinton Community College
Des Moines Area Community College
Ellsworth Community College
Hawkeye Community College
Indian Hills Community College
Iowa Central Community College
Iowa Lakes Community College
Iowa Western Community College
Kirkwood Community College
Marshalltown Community College
Muscatine Community College
North Iowa Area Community College
Northeast Iowa Community College
Northwest Iowa Community College
Scott Community College
Southeastern Community College
- North Campus
- South Campus

Southwestern Community College
Western Iowa Tech Community College

Kansas

Allen County Community College
Barton County Community College
Brown Mackie College
Butler County Community College
Coffeyville Community College
Colby Community College
Dodge City Community College
Donnelly College
Fort Scott Community College
Garden City Community College
Haskell Indian Junior College
Highland Community College
Hutchinson Community College
Independence Community College
Johnson County Community College
Kansas City Kansas Community College
Labette Community College
Neosho County Community College
Pratt Community College
Seward County Community College

Kentucky

Ashland Community College
Elizabethtown Community College
Henderson Community College
Hopkinsville Community College
Jefferson Community College
Lexington Community College
Madisonville Community College
Maysville Community College
Paducah Community College
Prestonburg Community College
RETS Electronic Institute
Southeast Community College

Louisiana

Bossier Parish Community College
Louisiana State University
- Alexandria
- Eunice

Nunez Community College
Southern University in Shreveport

Maine

Andover College
Beal College
Casco Bay College

Maryland

Allegany Community College
Anne Arundel Community College
Baltimore City Community College
Catonsville Community College
Cecil Community College
Charles County Community College
Chesapeake College
Dundalk Community College
Essex Community College
Frederick Community College
Hagerstown Business College
Hagerstown Junior College
Harford Community College
Howard Community College
Montgomery College
- Germantown Campus
- Rockville Campus
- Takoma Park Campus

Prince George's Community College
Wor-Wic Community College

Massachusetts

Bristol Community College
Bunker Hill Community College
Cape Cod Community College
Essex Agricultural and Technical Institute
Greenfield Community College
Holyoke Community College
Massachusetts Bay Community College
Massasoit Community College
Middlesex Community College
Mount Wachusett Community College
North Shore Community College
Quincy College
Roxbury Community College
Springfield Technical Community College

Michigan

Alpena Community College
Baker College
- Auburn Hills
- Mount Clemens

Bay de Noc Community College
Charles Stewart Mott Community College
Delta College
Glen Oaks Community College
Gogebic Community College
Grand Rapids Community College
Great Lakes Junior College of Business
Henry Ford Community College
Highland Park Community College
Jackson Community College
Kalamazoo Valley Community College
Kellogg Community College
Kirtland Community College
Lake Michigan College
Lansing Community College
Lewis College of Business
Macomb Community College
Mid Michigan Community College
Monroe County Community College
Montcalm Community College
Muskegon Community College
Northwestern Michigan College
Oakland Community College
St. Clair County Community College
Schoolcraft College
Southwestern Michigan College
Washtenaw Community College
Wayne County Community College
West Shore Community College

Minnesota

Alexandria Technical College
Anoka-Ramsey Community College
Austin Community College
Brainerd Community College
Fergus Falls Community College
Hibbing Community College
Inver Hills Community College
Itasca Community College: Arrowhead Region
Lakewood Community College
Mesabi Community College: Arrowhead Region
Minneapolis Community College
Normandale Community College
North Hennepin Community College
Rainy River Community College
St. Paul Technical College
Saint Cloud Technical College
University of Minnesota: Crookston
Vermilion Community College
Willmar Community College
Willmar Technical College
Worthington Community College

Mississippi

Copiah-Lincoln Community College
East Central Community College
East Mississippi Community College
Hinds Community College
Meridian Community College
Mississippi Gulf Coast Community College
- Jackson County Campus
- Jefferson Davis Campus
- Perkinston

Northwest Mississippi Community College
Pearl River Community College
Southwest Mississippi Community College

Missouri

Crowder College
East Central College
Jefferson College
Kemper Military School and College
Longview Community College
Maple Woods Community College
Mineral Area College
Moberly Area Community College
Penn Valley Community College
St. Charles County Community College
St. Louis Community College
- Florissant Valley
- Forest Park
- Meramec

State Fair Community College
Three Rivers Community College

Montana

Billings Vocational-Technical Center
Blackfeet Community College
Butte Vocational-Technical Center
Dawson Community College
Dull Knife Memorial College
Flathead Valley Community College
Fort Belknap College
Fort Peck Community College
Helena Vocational-Technical Center
Little Big Horn College
Miles Community College
Missoula Vocational-Technical Center
Salish Kootenai College
Stone Child College

Nebraska

Central Community College
McCook Community College
Metropolitan Community College
Mid Plains Community College
Nebraska College of Technical Agriculture
Nebraska Indian Community College
Northeast Community College
Southeast Community College
- Beatrice Campus
- Lincoln Campus
- Milford Campus

Western Nebraska Community College: Scottsbluff Campus

Nevada

Northern Nevada Community College
Truckee Meadows Community College
Western Nevada Community College

New Hampshire
McIntosh College
New Hampshire Technical College: Nashua

New Jersey
Atlantic Community College
Bergen Community College
Brookdale Community College
Burlington County College
Camden County College
County College of Morris
Cumberland County College
Essex County College
Gloucester County College
Hudson County Community College
Mercer County Community College
Ocean County College
Passaic County Community College
Raritan Valley Community College
Salem Community College
Sussex County Community College
Union County College
Warren County Community College

New Mexico
Clovis Community College
Dona Ana Branch Community College of New Mexico State University
Eastern New Mexico University: Roswell Campus
New Mexico Junior College
New Mexico State University
  Alamogordo
  Carlsbad
Northern New Mexico Community College
San Juan College
Santa Fe Community College

New York
Adirondack Community College
American Academy McAllister Institute of Funeral Service
Bramson ORT Technical Institute
Broome Community College
Cayuga County Community College
City University of New York
  Borough of Manhattan Community College
  Bronx Community College
  Hostos Community College
  Kingsborough Community College
  La Guardia Community College
  Queensborough Community College
Clinton Community College
Columbia-Greene Community College
Corning Community College
Dutchess Community College
Erie Community College
  City Campus
  North Campus
  South Campus
Finger Lakes Community College
Fulton-Montgomery Community College
Genesee Community College
Herkimer County Community College
Hudson Valley Community College
Institute of Design and Construction
Jamestown Community College
Jefferson Community College
Mohawk Valley Community College
Monroe Community College
Nassau Community College
Niagara County Community College
North Country Community College
Onondaga Community College
Orange County Community College
Rockland Community College
Schenectady County Community College
Suffolk County Community College
  Eastern Campus
  Selden
  Western Campus
Sullivan County Community College
Tompkins-Cortland Community College
Ulster County Community College
Westchester Community College

North Carolina
Alamance Community College
Anson Community College
Asheville Buncombe Technical Community College
Beaufort County Community College
Bladen Community College
Blue Ridge Community College
Brunswick Community College
Caldwell Community College and Technical Institute
Cape Fear Community College
Carteret Community College
Catawba Valley Community College
Central Carolina Community College
Central Piedmont Community College
Cleveland Community College
Coastal Carolina Community College
College of the Albemarle
Craven Community College
Davidson County Community College
Durham Technical Community College
Edgecombe Community College
Fayetteville Technical Community College
Gaston College
Halifax Community College
Haywood Community College
Isothermal Community College
James Sprunt Community College
Johnston Community College
Lenoir Community College
Martin Community College
Mayland Community College
McDowell Technical Community College
Mitchell Community College
Montgomery Community College
Nash Community College
Pamlico Community College
Piedmont Community College
Pitt Community College
Randolph Community College
Richmond Community College
Roanoke-Chowan Community College
Robeson Community College
Rockingham Community College
Rowan-Cabarrus Community College
Sampson Community College
Sandhills Community College
Southeastern Baptist Theological Seminary
Southeastern Community College
Southwestern Community College
Stanly Community College
Surry Community College
Tri-County Community College
Vance-Granville Community College
Wake Technical Community College
Wayne Community College
Western Piedmont Community College
Wilkes Community College
Wilson Technical Community College

North Dakota
Bismarck State College
Little Hoop Community College
North Dakota State College of Science
North Dakota State University: Bottineau
Standing Rock College
Turtle Mountain Community College
United Tribes Technical College
University of North Dakota
  Lake Region
  Williston

Ohio
Belmont Technical College
Bowling Green State University: Firelands College
Bradford School
Central Ohio Technical College
Chatfield College
Clark State Community College
Cleveland Institute of Electronics
Columbus State Community College
Cuyahoga Community College
  Eastern Campus
  Metropolitan Campus
Edison State Community College
Hocking Technical College
Jefferson Technical College
Kent State University
  Ashtabula Regional Campus
  East Liverpool Regional Campus
  Salem Regional Campus
  Stark Campus
  Trumbull Regional Campus
  Tuscarawas Campus
Lakeland Community College
Lima Technical College
Lorain County Community College
Marion Technical College
Miami University
  Hamilton Campus
  Middletown Campus
North Central Technical College
Northwest Technical College
Northwestern College
Ohio State University
  Agricultural Technical Institute
  Lima Campus
  Mansfield Campus
  Newark Campus
Ohio University
  Chillicothe Campus
  Eastern Campus
  Lancaster Campus
Owens Technical College
  Findlay Campus
  Toledo
Sinclair Community College
Southern State Community College
Stark Technical College
Terra Technical College
University of Akron: Wayne College
University of Cincinnati
  Access Colleges
  Clermont College
  Raymond Walters College
Wright State University: Lake Campus

Oklahoma
Bacone College
Carl Albert State College
Connors State College
Eastern Oklahoma State College
Northeastern Oklahoma Agricultural and Mechanical College
Oklahoma City Community College
Oklahoma State University
  Oklahoma City
  Technical Branch: Okmulgee
Redlands Community College
Rogers State College
Rose State College
Seminole Junior College
Tulsa Junior College
Western Oklahoma State College

Oregon
Blue Mountain Community College
Central Oregon Community College
Chemeketa Community College
Clackamas Community College
Clatsop Community College
Lane Community College
Linn-Benton Community College
Mount Hood Community College
Portland Community College
Rogue Community College
Treasure Valley Community College
Umpqua Community College

Pennsylvania
American Institute of Design
Art Institute of Pittsburgh
Bucks County Community College
Butler County Community College
Central Pennsylvania Business School
Community College of Allegheny County
  Allegheny Campus
  Boyce Campus
  North Campus
  South Campus
Community College of Beaver County
Community College of Philadelphia
Dean Institute of Technology
Delaware County Community College
DuBois Business College
Electronic Institutes: Pittsburgh
Harrisburg Area Community College
ICS Center for Degree Studies
Lackawanna Junior College
Lehigh County Community College
Lincoln Technical Institute
Luzerne County Community College
McCarrie Schools of Health Sciences and Technology
Montgomery County Community College
National Education Center: Vale Tech Campus
Northampton County Area Community College
Penn Technical Institute
Pennsylvania Institute of Technology
Pittsburgh Institute of Mortuary Science
Pittsburgh Technical Institute
Reading Area Community College
Triangle Tech
  Erie School
  Greensburg School
Westmoreland County Community College

Puerto Rico
Huertas Junior College

Rhode Island
Community College of Rhode Island
New England Institute of Technology

South Carolina
Aiken Technical College
Central Carolina Technical College
Chesterfield-Marlboro Technical College
Columbia Junior College of Business
Denmark Technical College
Florence-Darlington Technical College
Horry-Georgetown Technical College
Midlands Technical College
Spartanburg Technical College
Technical College of the Lowcountry
Tri-County Technical College
Trident Technical College
University of South Carolina: Salkehatchie Regional Campus
Williamsburg Technical College
York Technical College

South Dakota
Kilian Community College
Lake Area Vocational Technical Institute
Mitchell Vocational Technical Institute
Sisseton-Wahpeton Community College
Western Dakota Vocational Technical Institute

Tennessee
Chattanooga State Technical Community College
Cleveland State Community College
Columbia State Community College
Draughons Junior College of Business: Nashville
Dyersburg State Community College
Motlow State Community College
Nashville State Technical Institute
Northeast State Technical Community College
Pellissippi State Technical Community College
Roane State Community College
Shelby State Community College
State Technical Institute at Memphis
Volunteer State Community College
Walters State Community College

Texas
Alvin Community College
Amarillo College
Angelina College
Austin Community College
Bee County College
Blinn College
Brazosport College
Brookhaven College
Cedar Valley College
Central Texas College
Cisco Junior College
Clarendon College
College of the Mainland
Collin County Community College District
Commonwealth Institute of Funeral Service
Cooke County College
Dallas Institute of Funeral Service
Del Mar College
Eastfield College
El Centro College
El Paso Community College
Frank Phillips College
Galveston College
Grayson County College
Hill College
Houston Community College
Howard College
Jacksonville College
Kilgore College
Laredo Junior College
Lee College
Midland College
Mountain View College
Navarro College
North Harris Montgomery Community College District
North Lake College
Northeast Texas Community College
Odessa College
Palo Alto College
Panola College
Paris Junior College
Ranger Junior College
Richland College
St. Philip's College
San Antonio College
San Jacinto College: North
South Plains College
Southwest Texas Junior College
Tarrant County Junior College
Temple Junior College
Texarkana College
Texas State Technical College
- Amarillo
- Harlingen
- Sweetwater
- Waco

Trinity Valley Community College
Tyler Junior College
Vernon Regional Junior College
Victoria College
Weatherford College
Wharton County Junior College

Utah
College of Eastern Utah
Dixie College
LDS Business College
Salt Lake Community College
Snow College
Utah Valley Community College

Vermont
Community College of Vermont

Virginia
Blue Ridge Community College
Central Virginia Community College
Dabney S. Lancaster Community College
Danville Community College
Eastern Shore Community College
J. Sargeant Reynolds Community College
John Tyler Community College
Lord Fairfax Community College
Mountain Empire Community College
New River Community College
Northern Virginia Community College
Patrick Henry Community College
Paul D. Camp Community College
Piedmont Virginia Community College
Rappahannock Community College
Southside Virginia Community College
Southwest Virginia Community College
Tidewater Community College
Virginia Western Community College
Wytheville Community College

Washington
Art Institute of Seattle
Bellevue Community College
Big Bend Community College
Centralia College
Clark College
Columbia Basin College
Edmonds Community College
Everett Community College
Grays Harbor College
Green River Community College
Highline Community College
Lower Columbia College
North Seattle Community College
Olympic College
Peninsula College
Pierce College
Renton Technical College
Seattle Central Community College
Shoreline Community College
Skagit Valley College
South Puget Sound Community College
South Seattle Community College
Spokane Community College
Spokane Falls Community College
Tacoma Community College
Walla Walla Community College
Wenatchee Valley College
Whatcom Community College
Yakima Valley Community College

West Virginia
Potomac State College of West Virginia University
Southern West Virginia Community College
West Virginia Northern Community College
West Virginia University at Parkersburg

Wisconsin
Blackhawk Technical College
Chippewa Valley Technical College
Fox Valley Technical College
Gateway Technical College
Lakeshore Technical College
Madison Area Technical College
Madison Junior College of Business
Milwaukee College of Business
Moraine Park Technical College
Nicolet Area Technical College
Northcentral Technical College
Northeast Wisconsin Technical College
Southwest Wisconsin Technical College
Waukesha County Technical College
Western Wisconsin Technical College
Wisconsin Indianhead Technical College

Wyoming
Casper College
Central Wyoming College
Eastern Wyoming College
Laramie County Community College
Northwest College
Sheridan College
Western Wyoming Community College

American Samoa, Caroline Islands, Guam, Marianas, Virgin Islands
Guam Community College
Micronesian Occupational College

Open admissions 4-year colleges

Alabama
Alabama State University
Miles College
Selma University
Troy State University in Montgomery

Alaska
Sheldon Jackson College

Arizona
Arizona College of the Bible

Arkansas
Arkansas State University
Philander Smith College
Southern Arkansas University
University of Arkansas
- Little Rock
- Monticello
- Pine Bluff

California
Academy of Art College
American College for the Applied Arts: Los Angeles
Art Institute of Southern California
Humphreys College
National University
New College of California
West Coast University

Colorado
National College

Connecticut
Bridgeport Engineering Institute
Charter Oak State College

Delaware
Wilmington College

District of Columbia
University of the District of Columbia

Florida
Edward Waters College
Hobe Sound Bible College
National Education Center
- Bauder Campus
- Tampa Technical Institute Campus

Schiller International University

Georgia
American College for the Applied Arts
Brewton-Parker College
Clayton State College
Savannah State College

Illinois
Columbia College
East-West University

Indiana
Indiana University East
Martin University
University of Southern Indiana

Colleges that accept the Common Application

Alabama
Birmingham-Southern College
Huntingdon College
Miles College
Spring Hill College

Alaska
Alaska Pacific University
Prince William Sound Community College
University of Alaska Anchorage

Arizona
Cochise College
Grand Canyon University
ITT Technical Institute: Tucson
Rio Salado Community College
Western International University

Arkansas
Arkansas Baptist College
Arkansas College
Harding University
Hendrix College
Shorter College
Southern Arkansas University: Technical Branch
University of the Ozarks

California
Academy of Art College
American Armenian International College
California State Polytechnic University: Pomona
Charles R. Drew University: College of Allied Health
Claremont McKenna College*
College of Notre Dame
Dominican College of San Rafael
Marymount College
Mills College*
Mount St. Mary's College
Mount San Jacinto College
Occidental College*
Patten College
Phillips Junior College: Fresno Campus
Pitzer College*
Pomona College*
St. Mary's College of California
Santa Clara University
Scripps College*
United States International University
University of La Verne
University of the Pacific
University of Redlands*
Westmont College
Whittier College*
Woodbury University

Colorado
Colorado College*
ITT Technical Institute: Aurora
Regis University
Rocky Mountain College of Art & Design
University of Colorado
- Colorado Springs
- Denver

University of Denver*
Western State College of Colorado

Connecticut
Briarwood College
Connecticut College*
Eastern Connecticut State University
Fairfield University*
Mitchell College
Northwestern Connecticut Community-Technical College
Quinnipiac College
Sacred Heart University
Teikyo-Post University
Trinity College*
University of Bridgeport
University of Connecticut
University of New Haven
Wesleyan University*
Western Connecticut State University

Delaware
Goldey-Beacom College
Wesley College

District of Columbia
American University*
Catholic University of America
George Washington University*
Trinity College

Florida
Broward Community College
Eckerd College*
Florida Atlantic University
Florida Institute of Technology
Florida International University
Gulf Coast Community College
Jacksonville University
Lynn University
National Education Center: Bauder Campus
New England Institute of Technology
Palm Beach Atlantic College
Phillips Junior College: Melbourne
Rollins College*
St. Thomas University
Southern College
Stetson University*
University of Central Florida
Webber College

Georgia
Agnes Scott College
Andrew College
Brewton-Parker College
Chattahoochee Technical Institute
Clark Atlanta University
Emmanuel College
Emory University*
Georgia Southern University
Georgia State University
Morehouse College*
Oglethorpe University
Oxford College of Emory University
Paine College
Piedmont College
Savannah State College
South Georgia College
Spelman College*
Thomas College
Wesleyan College
Young Harris College

Hawaii
Hawaii Pacific University

Idaho
Albertson College

Illinois
Augustana College
Barat College
City Colleges of Chicago: Malcolm X College
College of Lake County
East-West University
Elmhurst College
Harrington Institute of Interior Design
Illinois Institute of Technology
Kendall College
Knox College*
Lake Forest College*
MacMurray College
McKendree College
Monmouth College
Montay College
Morrison Institute of Technology
North Central College
Rockford College
Shimer College
Southeastern Illinois College
Trinity Christian College

Indiana
Ancilla College
Butler University
DePauw University*
Earlham College*
Goshen College
Oakland City College
Purdue University: Calumet
St. Francis College
St. Joseph's College
University of Evansville
Valparaiso University*
Vincennes University
Wabash College

Iowa
Central College
Clarke College
Coe College*
Cornell College*
Drake University
Graceland College
Grinnell College*
Iowa Wesleyan College
Luther College
Mount Mercy College
Mount St. Clare College
Teikyo Marycrest University
Wartburg College

Kansas
Brown Mackie College
McPherson College
Tabor College

Kentucky
Bellarmine College
Brescia College
Centre College*
Cumberland College
Kentucky Wesleyan College
Lees College
Lindsey Wilson College
Pikeville College

Union College

Louisiana
Centenary College of Louisiana*
Loyola University
Tulane University*
University of Southwestern Louisiana
Xavier University of Louisiana

Maine
Bates College*
Bowdoin College*
Casco Bay College
Colby College*
Maine Maritime Academy
St. Joseph's College
Thomas College
Unity College
University of New England
Westbrook College

Maryland
College of Notre Dame of Maryland
Coppin State College
Goucher College*
Hagerstown Business College
Hood College*
Johns Hopkins University*
Maryland Institute College of Art
Mount St. Mary's College
University of Maryland
- College Park
- Eastern Shore
- University College

Villa Julie College
Washington College*
Western Maryland College*

Massachusetts
American International College
Anna Maria College for Men and Women
Aquinas College at Milton
Aquinas College at Newton
Babson College*
Bay Path College
Bay State College
Bentley College
Boston University*
Bradford College
Brandeis University*
Clark University*
Curry College
Dean Junior College
Eastern Nazarene College
Elms College
Emerson College
Emmanuel College
Fisher College
Fitchburg State College
Hampshire College*
Katharine Gibbs School
Marian Court Junior College
Massachusetts Bay Community College
Merrimack College
Mount Holyoke College*
Mount Ida College
Newbury College
Nichols College
North Adams State College
Northeastern University
Pine Manor College

*Common Application member

Regis College
St. Hyacinth College and Seminary
St. John's Seminary College
Simmons College*
Simon's Rock College of Bard
Smith College*
Suffolk University
Tufts University
Wellesley College*
Wentworth Institute of Technology
Wheaton College*
Williams College*
Worcester Polytechnic Institute*

Michigan

Adrian College
Baker College of Auburn Hills
Grand Valley State University
Henry Ford Community College
Highland Park Community College
Jordan College
Kalamazoo College*
Kendall College of Art and Design
Lansing Community College
Madonna University
Marygrove College
Northwestern Michigan College
Western Michigan University

Minnesota

Bemidji State University
Carleton College*
College of Associated Arts
College of St. Catherine: St. Catherine Campus
Concordia College: Moorhead
Concordia College: St. Paul
Gustavus Adolphus College*
Macalester College*
St. John's University
St. Olaf College*
Winona State University

Mississippi

Alcorn State University
Belhaven College
Millsaps College*
Mississippi Valley State University
Tougaloo College

Missouri

Central Methodist College
Cottey College
Culver-Stockton College
Drury College
Fontbonne College
Jefferson College
Lindenwood College
Northeast Missouri State University
Park College
Stephens College
Three Rivers Community College
University of Missouri: Kansas City
Webster University
William Jewell College

Montana

Montana State University

Nebraska

Dana College
Metropolitan Community College
Union College
Western Nebraska Community College: Scottsbluff Campus

Nevada

Sierra Nevada College

New Hampshire

Castle College
Colby-Sawyer College*
Daniel Webster College
Franklin Pierce College
Hesser College
New Hampshire College
Rivier College

New Jersey

Centenary College
College of St. Elizabeth
Drew University*
Fairleigh Dickinson University
  Edward Williams College
  Madison
Hudson County Community College
New Jersey Institute of Technology
St. Peter's College
Salem Community College
Seton Hall University
Stevens Institute of Technology
Sussex County Community College
Trenton State College
Union County College
University of Medicine and Dentistry of New Jersey: School of Health Related Professions
Upsala College

New Mexico

College of Santa Fe
College of the Southwest
Dona Ana Branch Community College of New Mexico State University
Eastern New Mexico University
New Mexico Highlands University

New York

Adirondack Community College
Alfred University*
American Academy of Dramatic Arts
Bard College*
Barnard College*
Bramson ORT Technical Institute
Canisius College
Cazenovia College
City University of New York: Hostos Community College
Cochran School of Nursing-St. John's Riverside Hospital
Colgate University*
College of Aeronautics
College of Insurance
College of New Rochelle
Daemen College
Dominican College of Blauvelt
Elmira College*
Eugene Lang College/New School for Social Research
Five Towns College
Fordham University*
Genesee Community College
Hamilton College*
Hartwick College*
Hobart College*
Keuka College
Le Moyne College
Long Island University: Southampton Campus
Manhattan College*
Manhattanville College*
Marist College
Mount St. Mary College
Nazareth College of Rochester
New York University*
Niagara County Community College
Onondaga Community College
Pace University
  College of White Plains
  New York
  Pleasantville/Briarcliff
Pratt Institute
Rensselaer Polytechnic Institute*
Rochester Institute of Technology*
Russell Sage College
Sage Junior College of Albany
St. Bonaventure University
St. John Fisher College
St. Joseph's College
St. Lawrence University*
Sarah Lawrence College*
Schenectady County Community College
School of Visual Arts
Skidmore College*
State University of New York
  College of Environmental Science and Forestry
  College at Plattsburgh
  Oswego
Union College*
University of Rochester*
Vassar College*
Villa Maria College of Buffalo
Wagner College
Wells College*
Westchester Business Institute
William Smith College*

North Carolina

Barber-Scotia College
Bennett College
Bladen Community College
Brevard College
Brunswick Community College
Catawba College
Davidson College
Duke University*
Elon College
Guilford College*
Johnson C. Smith University
Lenoir-Rhyne College
Montreat-Anderson College
North Carolina Wesleyan College
Peace College
Pfeiffer College
Queens College
Roanoke Bible College
Robeson Community College
Salem College*
University of North Carolina at Asheville
Wake Forest University*
Western Piedmont Community College

North Dakota

Jamestown College
North Dakota State College of Science
North Dakota State University
Turtle Mountain Community College
University of Mary

Ohio

Antioch College*
Art Academy of Cincinnati
Ashland University
Bliss College
Bradford School
Capital University
Case Western Reserve University*
Central Ohio Technical College
Clark State Community College
Cleveland Institute of Electronics
College of Mount St. Joseph
College of Wooster*
Defiance College
Denison University*
Franciscan University of Steubenville
Heidelberg College
Hiram College
Hocking Technical College
Kenyon College*
Lake Erie College
Lakeland Community College
Lourdes College
Malone College
Marietta College
Miami University: Middletown Campus
Miami-Jacobs College
Mount Union College
Muskingum College
Oberlin College*
Ohio State University: Marion Campus
Ohio Valley Business College
Ohio Wesleyan University*
Sinclair Community College
Southern Ohio College
Terra Technical College
Tiffin University
University of Cincinnati: Raymond Walters College
University of Rio Grande
Urbana University
Ursuline College
Wilberforce University
Wilmington College
Wittenberg University
Xavier University

Oklahoma

Bartlesville Wesleyan College
Oklahoma Panhandle State University
Phillips University
Redlands Community College
Southwestern College of Christian Ministries
Southwestern Oklahoma State University
University of Tulsa*
Western Oklahoma State College

Oregon

Bassist College
Central Oregon Community College
Lewis and Clark College*
Linfield College*
Mount Hood Community College
Reed College*
Willamette University*

Pennsylvania

Albright College
Allegheny College*
Allentown College of St. Francis de Sales
Beaver College
Bryn Mawr College*
Bucknell University*
Bucks County Community College
Butler County Community College
Cedar Crest College
Chatham College
Chestnut Hill College
College Misericordia
Dickinson College*
Elizabethtown College*
Franklin and Marshall College*
Gannon University
Geneva College
Gettysburg College*
Haverford College*
Holy Family College
Juniata College
Keystone Junior College
King's College
La Roche College
Lafayette College*
Lehigh University*
Lycoming College
Manor Junior College
Marywood College
McCarrie Schools of Health Sciences and Technology
Mercyhurst College
Moravian College
Muhlenberg College*
Neumann College

*Common Application member

Penn Technical Institute
Point Park College
Robert Morris College
St. Vincent College
Seton Hill College
Shippensburg University of Pennsylvania
Susquehanna University*
Swarthmore College*
University of the Arts
Ursinus College*
Valley Forge Military College
Villanova University
Washington and Jefferson College
Westmoreland County Community College
Widener University*
Wilkes University
Wilson College

Puerto Rico

Inter American University of Puerto Rico: San German Campus
Technological College of the Municipality of San Juan
University of Puerto Rico
  Aguadilla
  Carolina Regional College
  Cayey University College
University of the Sacred Heart

Rhode Island

Bryant College
Johnson & Wales University

South Carolina

Benedict College
Claflin College
Columbia College
Columbia Junior College of Business
Converse College
Florence-Darlington Technical College
North Greenville College
Presbyterian College
Spartanburg Methodist College
Williamsburg Technical College
Wofford College

South Dakota

Dakota Wesleyan University
Huron University
Kilian Community College
University of South Dakota

Tennessee

Carson-Newman College
Fisk University*
LeMoyne-Owen College
Lincoln Memorial University
Maryville College
Memphis College of Art
Northeast State Technical Community College
Rhodes College*
Tennessee State University
University of the South*
Vanderbilt University*

Texas

Abilene Christian University
Austin College
Cooke County College
Dallas Baptist University
East Texas Baptist University
East Texas State University
Houston Baptist University
Howard College
Huston-Tillotson College
Incarnate Word College
Jarvis Christian College
Lubbock Christian University
Midland College
Miss Wade's Fashion Merchandising College
Rice University*
Richland College
St. Edward's University
Schreiner College
Southern Methodist University*
Southwestern Christian College
Southwestern University*
Stephen F. Austin State University
Texas A&I University
Texas Christian University*
Texas College
Texas Lutheran College
Trinity University*
University of Houston: Downtown

Utah

Phillips Junior College: Salt Lake City Campus
Stevens-Henager College of Business

Vermont

Bennington College*
Castleton State College
Champlain College
Green Mountain College
Marlboro College
New England Culinary Institute
St. Michael's College
Sterling College

Virginia

Averett College
Central Virginia Community College
Clinch Valley College of the University of Virginia
Dabney S. Lancaster Community College
Emory and Henry College
Ferrum College
Hampden-Sydney College*
Hollins College*
Longwood College
Lynchburg College
Marymount University
Randolph-Macon College*
Randolph-Macon Woman's College*
Richard Bland College
Roanoke College
St. Paul's College
Shenandoah University
Southern Virginia College for Women
Sweet Briar College
University of Richmond*
Virginia Intermont College
Virginia Polytechnic Institute and State University
Virginia Union University
Virginia Wesleyan College
Washington and Lee University*

Washington

Big Bend Community College
Central Washington University
Columbia Basin College
Cornish College of the Arts
Everett Community College
Gonzaga University
Green River Community College
North Seattle Community College
Northwest College of the Assemblies of God
Pacific Lutheran University
Seattle Central Community College
Seattle Pacific University
Seattle University
Tacoma Community College
University of Puget Sound*
Whitman College*
Whitworth College
Yakima Valley Community College

West Virginia

Alderson-Broaddus College
Bethany College
Bluefield State College
Salem-Teikyo University
West Virginia Institute of Technology
West Virginia Northern Community College
West Virginia Wesleyan College
Wheeling Jesuit College

Wisconsin

Beloit College*
Cardinal Stritch College
Carroll College
Lakeland College
Lawrence University*
Marian College of Fond du Lac
Milwaukee College of Business
Mount Mary College
Mount Senario College
Northland College
Ripon College*
St. Norbert College
Stratton College
University of Wisconsin: Green Bay
University of Wisconsin Center: Marathon County

Wyoming

Eastern Wyoming College
Western Wyoming Community College

American Samoa, Caroline Islands, Guam, Marianas, Virgin Islands

Micronesian Occupational College

Switzerland

Franklin College: Switzerland

*Common Application member

Application priority and closing dates

November priority dates

California
California State Polytechnic University: Pomona
California State University
Bakersfield
Chico
Fullerton
Hayward
Long Beach
Sacramento
Stanislaus
Holy Names College
San Jose State University
Sonoma State University
University of California: Irvine

Illinois
De Paul University
University of Illinois at Urbana-Champaign

Maryland
College of Notre Dame of Maryland

Missouri
Lindenwood College
Northeast Missouri State University

New Jersey
Georgian Court College

New York
State University of New York
Albany
College of Technology at Alfred

North Carolina
North Carolina State University

Pennsylvania
Grove City College
Penn State
Erie Behrend College
University Park Campus

Puerto Rico
University of Puerto Rico: Aguadilla

Texas
Texas Christian University

Vermont
St. Michael's College
University of Vermont

November closing dates

California
California State University: Chico*
University of California: Irvine*

*College also has priority date

December priority dates

Alabama
Birmingham-Southern College
International Bible College

California
St. Mary's College of California

Connecticut
Quinnipiac College

Illinois
Monmouth College
Principia College

Indiana
DePauw University
Rose-Hulman Institute of Technology
University of Evansville
University of Notre Dame

Iowa
Coe College

Maryland
Goucher College
University of Maryland
Baltimore County
College Park

Massachusetts
Bentley College

Minnesota
University of Minnesota: Twin Cities

New York
New York University
St. Joseph's School of Nursing
State University of New York
College at Buffalo
College at Old Westbury
College at Potsdam
College of Technology at Canton

North Carolina
East Carolina University
Peace College
Western Carolina University

Ohio
Hocking Technical College

Pennsylvania
Bloomsburg University of Pennsylvania
Chatham College
Clarion University of Pennsylvania
Lock Haven University of Pennsylvania
Mansfield University of Pennsylvania

Puerto Rico
University of Puerto Rico: Bayamon Technological University College
University of the Sacred Heart

South Carolina
Wofford College

Tennessee
Carson-Newman College
Union University

Texas
University of Dallas

Vermont
Sterling College

Virginia
James Madison University

Wisconsin
Bellin College of Nursing
Blackhawk Technical College
University of Wisconsin
Eau Claire
Green Bay

January priority dates

California
California Lutheran University
Cogswell Polytechnical College
Cosumnes River College
Fresno Pacific College
University of Judaism

Connecticut
Western Connecticut State University

Delaware
University of Delaware

Florida
Florida International University

Georgia
Morehouse College

Illinois
MacMurray College

Iowa
Central College

Maine
Central Maine Medical Center School of Nursing

Maryland
Bowie State University
Johns Hopkins University: Peabody Conservatory of Music
St. Mary's College of Maryland
Salisbury State University

Massachusetts
Boston University
Fitchburg State College
Salem State College
Springfield Technical Community College

Michigan
Hillsdale College

Minnesota
University of St. Thomas

Missouri
College of the Ozarks
Fontbonne College
Ranken Technical College

New York
Albany College of Pharmacy
City University of New York
Bronx Community College
City College
College of Staten Island
Hunter College
La Guardia Community College
Lehman College
New York City Technical College
Queens College
Queensborough Community College
Daemen College
Manhattan College
Manhattan School of Music
State University of New York
Binghamton
Buffalo
College at Brockport
College at Fredonia
College at Geneseo
College at Oneonta
Maritime College
Oswego

North Carolina
Davidson College
Guilford College
Mount Olive College

Ohio
Denison University
Heidelberg College
Ohio University
Ursuline College

Pennsylvania
Duquesne University
East Stroudsburg University of Pennsylvania
Gwynedd-Mercy College
Kutztown University of Pennsylvania
Lehigh University
Moravian College

South Carolina
College of Charleston

South Dakota
South Dakota State University

Tennessee
Vanderbilt University

Texas
Southern Methodist University
Southwestern University
University of Texas at Dallas

Vermont
Marlboro College

Virginia
George Mason University
Roanoke College
Virginia Commonwealth University

Wisconsin
University of Wisconsin
La Crosse
River Falls
Stout
Whitewater

January closing dates

California
California Institute of Technology
Charles R. Drew University: College of Allied Health
Pomona College

Colorado
United States Air Force Academy

Connecticut
Connecticut College
Trinity College
Wesleyan University

District of Columbia
Georgetown University

Florida
University of Florida

Illinois
Northwestern University
University of Chicago
University of Illinois at Urbana-Champaign*

Indiana
University of Notre Dame*

Louisiana
Tulane University

Maine
Bowdoin College
Colby College

Maryland
Johns Hopkins University

Massachusetts
Amherst College
Boston College
Harvard and Radcliffe Colleges
Massachusetts Institute of Technology
New England Conservatory of Music
Smith College
Tufts University
Wellesley College
Williams College

Minnesota
Macalester College

Missouri
Washington University

New Hampshire
Dartmouth College

New Jersey
Princeton University
Rutgers—The State University of New Jersey
College of Engineering
College of Pharmacy
Cook College
Douglass College
Livingston College
Rutgers College

New York
Barnard College
City University of New York:
Baruch College
Colgate University
Columbia University
Columbia College
School of Engineering and Applied Science
Cornell University
Hamilton College
Juilliard School
Rensselaer Polytechnic Institute
University of Rochester
Vassar College

North Carolina
Duke University
University of North Carolina at Chapel Hill
Wake Forest University

Ohio
Cleveland Institute of Music
Miami University: Oxford Campus
Oberlin College

Pennsylvania
Bryn Mawr College
Bucknell University
Curtis Institute of Music
Haverford College
Lafayette College
University of Pennsylvania
Villanova University

Puerto Rico
University of Puerto Rico
Aguadilla*
Bayamon Technological University College*

Rhode Island
Brown University
Rhode Island School of Design

Texas
Rice University

Vermont
Bennington College
Middlebury College

Virginia
College of William and Mary
James Madison University*
University of Virginia
Washington and Lee University

Canada
McGill University

February priority dates

Alabama
Samford University

Arkansas
John Brown University
Ouachita Baptist University

California
Academy of Art College
Biola University
California Institute of the Arts
Harvey Mudd College
Loyola Marymount University
Mills College
Southern California Institute of Architecture
University of Southern California
Whittier College

Connecticut
Mitchell College
University of Hartford

District of Columbia
George Washington University

Florida
Flagler College

Georgia
Agnes Scott College
University of Georgia

Illinois
Knox College
Northern Illinois University
Trinity Christian College
University of Illinois at Chicago

Indiana
Hanover College
Taylor University
Wabash College

Iowa
Buena Vista College

Kentucky
Berea College
University of Kentucky

Louisiana
Centenary College of Louisiana

Maine
Eastern Maine Technical College
University of Maine
University of New England

Maryland
Villa Julie College

Massachusetts
Emerson College
Gordon College
Massachusetts College of Pharmacy and Allied Health Sciences
Northern Essex Community College

Michigan
Alma College
Aquinas College
Eastern Michigan University
GMI Engineering & Management Institute
Grand Valley State University
Kalamazoo College
Michigan Technological University
Northern Michigan University

Minnesota
College of St. Benedict
St. John's University
St. Olaf College
University of Minnesota: Duluth
Winona State University

Missouri
Kansas City Art Institute
Rockhurst College
Southwest Missouri State University
University of Missouri: Columbia

New York
City University of New York:
Borough of Manhattan Community College
Clarkson University
College of Mount St. Vincent
Eastman School of Music of the University of Rochester
Fordham University
Hofstra University
Le Moyne College
Nazareth College of Rochester
Pace University
College of White Plains
New York
Pleasantville/Briarcliff
Polytechnic University
Brooklyn
Long Island Campus
Pratt Institute
St. John Fisher College
State University of New York
College at Cortland
College of Environmental Science and Forestry
College at Plattsburgh
Wells College
Yeshiva University

North Carolina
Central Carolina Community College
Meredith College
St. Mary's College
University of North Carolina at Wilmington

Ohio
Bowling Green State University
Kettering College of Medical Arts
Ohio State University: Newark Campus

Oregon
Lewis and Clark College
Willamette University

Pennsylvania
Allentown College of St. Francis de Sales
St. Vincent College
Shippensburg University of Pennsylvania
University of Scranton
West Chester University of Pennsylvania
Widener University

South Carolina
Converse College
University of South Carolina

South Dakota
Augustana College

Tennessee
Maryville College
Rhodes College
University of Tennessee: Knoxville

Texas
Texas A&M University
Texas Woman's University
West Texas A & M University

Utah
Weber State University

Virginia
Hollins College
Longwood College

*College also has priority date

Washington
Eastern Washington University
Seattle Pacific University
Seattle University

West Virginia
Marshall University
West Virginia Wesleyan College

Wisconsin
University of Wisconsin: Platteville

February closing dates

California
Claremont McKenna College
Harvey Mudd College*
Occidental College
Pepperdine University
Pitzer College
Santa Clara University
Scripps College
University of San Diego

Colorado
Colorado College
University of Colorado at Boulder

District of Columbia
American University
Catholic University of America

Florida
Rollins College

Georgia
Emory University
Georgia Institute of Technology
Morehouse College*
Spelman College

Illinois
Wheaton College

Indiana
DePauw University*
Earlham College
Indiana University Bloomington
University of Evansville*

Iowa
Grinnell College

Kansas
University of Kansas

Maine
Bates College

Maryland
College of Notre Dame of Maryland*
Goucher College*
Loyola College in Maryland

Massachusetts
Babson College
Bentley College*
Clark University
College of the Holy Cross
Hampshire College
Mount Holyoke College
Simmons College
Stonehill College
University of Massachusetts at Amherst
Wheaton College
Wheelock College
Worcester Polytechnic Institute

*College also has priority date

Michigan
University of Michigan

Minnesota
Carleton College

New Hampshire
University of New Hampshire

New Jersey
Drew University

New York
Alfred University
Bard College
Eugene Lang College/New School for Social Research
Hartwick College
Hobart College
Jewish Theological Seminary of America
New York University*
St. Lawrence University
Sarah Lawrence College
Skidmore College
State University of New York
- Albany*
- College at Geneseo*

Syracuse University
Union College
Webb Institute of Naval Architecture
William Smith College

North Carolina
Davidson College*
Guilford College*
North Carolina State University*

Ohio
Antioch College
Case Western Reserve University
College of Wooster
Denison University*
Kenyon College
Ohio State University: Columbus Campus

Oregon
Reed College
University of Oregon: Robert Donald Clark Honors College

Pennsylvania
Albright College
Allegheny College
Carnegie Mellon University
Dickinson College
Franklin and Marshall College
Gettysburg College
Grove City College*
Lehigh University*
Muhlenberg College
Swarthmore College
Ursinus College

Puerto Rico
University of Puerto Rico
- Cayey University College
- Mayaguez Campus

Rhode Island
Providence College

South Carolina
Furman University
Wofford College*

Tennessee
University of the South

Texas
Southwestern University*
Texas Christian University*
Trinity University
University of Dallas*
University of Texas at Austin

Utah
Brigham Young University

Vermont
St. Michael's College*
University of Vermont*

Virginia
College of Health Sciences*
George Mason University*
Hollins College*
Mary Washington College
Sweet Briar College
University of Richmond
Virginia Commonwealth University*
Virginia Polytechnic Institute and State University

Washington
University of Washington
Whitman College

West Virginia
Shepherd College

Wisconsin
Lawrence University
University of Wisconsin
- Green Bay*
- Madison

March priority dates

Arizona
University of Arizona

Arkansas
Arkansas College
Harding University

California
Azusa Pacific University
California College of Arts and Crafts
Chapman University
College of Notre Dame
Mount St. Mary's College
New College of California
Otis School of Art and Design
Palomar College
Southern California College
University of La Verne
University of the Pacific
University of Redlands
University of San Francisco
Westmont College
Woodbury University

Colorado
Mesa State College
University of Denver

Connecticut
Eastern Connecticut State University
Sacred Heart University

District of Columbia
Corcoran School of Art

Florida
Eckerd College
Florida Atlantic University
Florida Institute of Technology
Ringling School of Art and Design
University of North Florida

Georgia
Covenant College
Oglethorpe University

Hawaii
University of Hawaii at Hilo

Idaho
Albertson College

Illinois
Bradley University
College of St. Francis
Illinois Wesleyan University
Lake Forest College
School of the Art Institute of Chicago
VanderCook College of Music

Indiana
Anderson University
Ball State University
Butler University
Holy Cross College
Lutheran College of Health Professions
St. Francis College
St. Mary's College
University of Indianapolis

Iowa
Cornell College
Drake University
Luther College
Wartburg College

Kansas
Manhattan Christian College
MidAmerica Nazarene College

Kentucky
Transylvania University

Maine
College of the Atlantic
Husson College
Maine College of Art
Unity College
University of Maine at Presque Isle
Westbrook College

Maryland
Maryland Institute College of Art
St. John's College
Washington College

Massachusetts
Berklee College of Music
Boston Conservatory
Eastern Nazarene College
Framingham State College
Holyoke Community College
Northeastern University
School of the Museum of Fine Arts
University of Massachusetts at Boston

Michigan
Calvin College
Center for Creative Studies: College of Art and Design
Central Michigan University
Sacred Heart Major Seminary
Spring Arbor College
University of Michigan: Dearborn

Minnesota
Gustavus Adolphus College
Hamline University
Minneapolis College of Art and Design

Missouri
Drury College

Montana
Carroll College

Nebraska
Clarkson College

New Hampshire
New Hampshire Technical College: Laconia
St. Anselm College

New Jersey
Caldwell College
Seton Hall University
Upsala College

New Mexico
New Mexico Institute of Mining and Technology
St. John's College

New York
Adelphi University
City University of New York: John Jay College of Criminal Justice
Houghton College
Iona College
Ithaca College
Marist College
Marymount Manhattan College
Mercy College
Molloy College
Monroe Community College
Rochester Institute of Technology
Russell Sage College
Sage Junior College of Albany
St. Bonaventure University
St. John's University
St. Joseph's College
State University of New York
College of Agriculture and Technology at Cobleskill
College at New Paltz
Utica College of Syracuse University
Wagner College

North Carolina
Greensboro College
High Point University
Lees-McRae College
North Carolina Wesleyan College
Pfeiffer College
St. Andrews Presbyterian College
Salem College
Warren Wilson College

North Dakota
University of North Dakota

Ohio
Art Academy of Cincinnati
Cleveland Institute of Art
Franciscan University of Steubenville
Ohio Wesleyan University

Oklahoma
Langston University

Oregon
Linfield College
Multnomah School of the Bible
Pacific University

Pennsylvania
Elizabethtown College
Hahnemann University School of Health Sciences and Humanities
Immaculata College
Messiah College
Northampton County Area Community College
St. Charles Borromeo Seminary
Susquehanna University
Thaddeus Stevens State School of Technology
University of Pittsburgh at Johnstown
Westminster College
Wilson College

Puerto Rico
Colegio Universitario del Este

Rhode Island
Rhode Island College

South Carolina
Anderson College
The Citadel
Coker College
Columbia College
Greenville Technical College
Limestone College
Presbyterian College

South Dakota
Mount Marty College

Tennessee
Fisk University
King College
Tennessee Temple University

Texas
Austin College
Concordia Lutheran College
Huston-Tillotson College
Lamar University—Beaumont
McMurry University
St. Mary's University
University of St. Thomas

Vermont
Johnson State College

Virginia
Old Dominion University
Randolph-Macon College
Randolph-Macon Woman's College
Shenandoah University
Virginia State University

Washington
Central Washington University
Cornish College of the Arts
Pacific Lutheran University
St. Martin's College
Whitworth College

West Virginia
West Virginia University

Wisconsin
Carroll College
Concordia University Wisconsin
Ripon College
St. Norbert College

Wyoming
University of Wyoming

March closing dates

Alabama
Birmingham-Southern College*

California
California Maritime Academy
St. Mary's College of California*

Connecticut
Fairfield University

Delaware
University of Delaware*

Florida
Flagler College*
Florida State University
Stetson University
University of Central Florida
University of Miami

Georgia
Clark Atlanta University
Wesleyan College

Hawaii
Brigham Young University-Hawaii

Idaho
Ricks College

Indiana
Hanover College*
Rose-Hulman Institute of Technology*

Iowa
University of Dubuque

Kentucky
Centre College

Louisiana
Xavier University of Louisiana

Maryland
Hood College
Mount St. Mary's College
St. Mary's College of Maryland*
Salisbury State University*
Towson State University
United States Naval Academy
Western Maryland College

Massachusetts
Assumption College
Bridgewater State College
Fitchburg State College*
Merrimack College
Salem State College*
Westfield State College

Minnesota
University of Minnesota: Morris

Missouri
Northeast Missouri State University*

New Jersey
Monmouth College
Montclair State College
Ramapo College of New Jersey
Rowan College of New Jersey
Rutgers—The State University of New Jersey: College of Nursing
Stevens Institute of Technology
Trenton State College

New York
Le Moyne College*
Long Island College Hospital School of Nursing
Manhattan College*
Manhattanville College
Siena College
State University of New York
College at Cortland*
College at Old Westbury*
United States Merchant Marine Academy
United States Military Academy
Wells College*

North Carolina
Appalachian State University
East Carolina University*

Ohio
Kent State University
Ohio University*
Wittenberg University

Oregon
Oregon State University
University of Oregon

Pennsylvania
Chatham College*
Drexel University
East Stroudsburg University of Pennsylvania*
Juniata College
Kutztown University of Pennsylvania*
Moravian College*
University of Scranton*
Washington and Jefferson College

Rhode Island
University of Rhode Island

Texas
Concordia Lutheran College*
Texas A&M University*

Virginia
Hampden-Sydney College
Mary Baldwin College
Roanoke College*
Virginia Military Institute
Virginia Wesleyan College

Washington
Evergreen State College
University of Puget Sound
Western Washington University

Switzerland
Franklin College: Switzerland

April priority dates

Alabama
Faulkner University
Judson College

Alaska
University of Alaska Anchorage

Arizona
Arizona State University
Northern Arizona University

Arkansas
Hendrix College

California
American Academy of Dramatic Arts: West
Chaffey Community College
Concordia University
Diablo Valley College
Fresno City College
Golden West College
San Francisco Art Institute
Santa Rosa Junior College

Colorado
Colorado Christian University
Colorado School of Mines
Northeastern Junior College
Western State College of Colorado

*College also has priority date

Connecticut
University of Bridgeport

Delaware
Wesley College

District of Columbia
Gallaudet University

Florida
Barry University
Florida Memorial College
Jacksonville University
Trinity College at Miami

Georgia
Savannah College of Art and Design

Illinois
American Conservatory of Music
Augustana College
Barat College

Indiana
Grace College
Huntington College
Oakland City College
St. Meinrad College
Valparaiso University

Iowa
Briar Cliff College
Mount Mercy College
Simpson College
Teikyo Marycrest University

Kansas
Tabor College

Kentucky
Georgetown College

Louisiana
Dillard University

Maine
St. Joseph's College
University of Maine at Machias
University of Southern Maine

Maryland
Capitol College
Frostburg State University
Morgan State University

Massachusetts
Elms College
Lesley College
Marian Court Junior College
North Adams State College
Pine Manor College
University of Massachusetts at Lowell

Michigan
Hope College
Northwood University
Oakland University

Minnesota
Hibbing Community College
Itasca Community College: Arrowhead Region
St. Mary's Campus of the College of St. Catherine
St. Mary's College of Minnesota

Mississippi
Millsaps College
University of Mississippi

*College also has priority date

Missouri
Culver-Stockton College
Park College
St. Louis College of Pharmacy
Webster University

New Hampshire
Colby-Sawyer College
Franklin Pierce College
New England College
New Hampshire Technical College: Stratham
University of New Hampshire at Manchester

New Jersey
Jersey City State College
New Jersey Institute of Technology
William Paterson College of New Jersey

New Mexico
College of the Southwest

New York
Adirondack Community College
College of New Rochelle
Elmira College
Marymount College
Parsons School of Design
Suffolk County Community College
Eastern Campus
Selden
Western Campus

Ohio
Baldwin-Wallace College
Ohio Dominican College
Ohio Valley Business College
Otterbein College
University of Findlay
Xavier University

Oklahoma
Oklahoma Baptist University
Oral Roberts University

Oregon
Bassist College
Northwest Christian College
Pacific Northwest College of Art

Pennsylvania
Lebanon Valley College of Pennsylvania
Lycoming College
Millersville University of Pennsylvania
Moore College of Art and Design
Slippery Rock University of Pennsylvania
University of the Arts
Williamson Free School of Mechanical Trades

Puerto Rico
Bayamon Central University
Technological College of the Municipality of San Juan

South Dakota
Dakota Wesleyan University

Tennessee
Bethel College
Christian Brothers University
Free Will Baptist Bible College
Milligan College

Texas
Incarnate Word College
Stephen F. Austin State University
Texas Wesleyan University
University of Houston

Vermont
Castleton State College
Green Mountain College

Virginia
Christendom College
Christopher Newport University
Dabney S. Lancaster Community College
Virginia Union University

West Virginia
Bethany College
Wheeling Jesuit College

Wisconsin
Cardinal Stritch College
Columbia College of Nursing
Marian College of Fond du Lac
Milwaukee Institute of Art & Design
University of Wisconsin: Superior
University of Wisconsin Center: Richland

Wyoming
Casper College

April closing dates

Arizona
University of Arizona*

California
San Francisco Conservatory of Music

Colorado
Beth-El College of Nursing

Connecticut
Sacred Heart University*
University of Connecticut
Western Connecticut State University*

District of Columbia
Howard University

Florida
Florida International University*

Illinois
Monmouth College*

Maryland
Baltimore Hebrew University
Bowie State University*
Johns Hopkins University: Peabody Conservatory of Music*
University of Maryland: College Park*

Massachusetts
Curry College
Gordon College*
Massachusetts College of Art
Springfield College

Minnesota
Gustavus Adolphus College*
University of St. Thomas*

New Hampshire
Keene State College
Plymouth State College of the University System of New Hampshire
St. Anselm College*

New Mexico
Institute of American Indian Arts

New York
Manhattan School of Music*
Nazareth College of Rochester*
Phillips Beth Israel School of Nursing
State University of New York
College at Fredonia*
College at Oneonta*
College at Potsdam*

North Carolina
University of North Carolina at Asheville*

Ohio
Hiram College

Oregon
Western Oregon State College

Pennsylvania
West Chester University of Pennsylvania*
Widener University*

South Carolina
Converse College*
Presbyterian College*

Tennessee
Carson-Newman College*

Texas
Southern Methodist University*

Virginia
Radford University

Washington
Gonzaga University

Wisconsin
Beloit College

American Samoa, Caroline Islands, Guam, Marianas, Virgin Islands
University of the Virgin Islands

May priority dates

Alabama
Alabama Agricultural and Mechanical University
Stillman College
Tuskegee University

Alaska
Alaska Pacific University

Arizona
Mohave Community College
Prescott College

Arkansas
Shorter College
Williams Baptist College

California
Patten College
Queen of the Holy Rosary College
Samuel Merritt College
Santa Barbara City College

Colorado
Metropolitan State College of Denver

Connecticut
Southern Connecticut State University
Teikyo-Post University

Delaware
Goldey-Beacom College

District of Columbia
University of the District of Columbia

Florida
Florida Agricultural and Mechanical University
Florida Bible College
St. Thomas University
University of Tampa

Georgia
Augusta College
DeKalb Technical Institute
Reinhardt College

Illinois
Eureka College
Illinois College
MacCormac Junior College
Parks College of St. Louis University
St. Xavier University
Trinity College

Indiana
Ancilla College
Goshen College
Indiana State University

Iowa
Ellsworth Community College

Kansas
Benedictine College
Kansas Newman College
Ottawa University
Sterling College

Kentucky
Bellarmine College
Northern Kentucky University
University of Louisville

Louisiana
Loyola University

Maine
Thomas College
University of Maine at Farmington

Maryland
Baltimore International Culinary College
University of Maryland: Eastern Shore

Massachusetts
Anna Maria College for Men and Women
Cape Cod Community College
Hellenic College
Montserrat College of Art
Newbury College
Quincy College
Suffolk University
Worcester State College

Michigan
Grand Rapids Baptist College and Seminary
Lansing Community College
Marygrove College
Monroe County Community College
Olivet College
Suomi College

Minnesota
Bemidji State University
College of Associated Arts
St. Cloud State University

Mississippi
Belhaven College
Delta State University
Pearl River Community College
Rust College
William Carey College

Missouri
Deaconess College of Nursing
Maryville University
Stephens College
University of Missouri: Kansas City

Nebraska
Chadron State College
Nebraska Wesleyan University

New Hampshire
New Hampshire Technical College
  Berlin
  Claremont
Notre Dame College

New Jersey
College of St. Elizabeth
Rutgers—The State University of New Jersey
  University College New Brunswick
  University College Newark
St. Peter's College
Westminster Choir College School of Music of Rider College

New Mexico
College of Santa Fe

New York
Audrey Cohen College
City University of New York: Brooklyn College
Finger Lakes Community College
Roberts Wesleyan College
St. Joseph's College: Suffolk Campus
Wadhams Hall Seminary-College

North Carolina
Barton College
Brevard College
Gardner-Webb University
Louisburg College
Mars Hill College
Montreat-Anderson College
Roanoke Bible College
Winston-Salem State University

Ohio
Capital University
Cedarville College
Defiance College
Muskingum College
University of Dayton
University of Rio Grande
Urbana University
Wright State University

Oklahoma
Southern Nazarene University

Oregon
Central Oregon Community College
George Fox College

Pennsylvania
Baptist Bible College of Pennsylvania
Butler County Community College
Cabrini College
California University of Pennsylvania
Eastern College
La Salle University
Mercyhurst College
Neumann College
University of Pittsburgh
  Bradford
  Titusville

Puerto Rico
Inter American University of Puerto Rico
  Arecibo Campus
  Guayama Campus

South Carolina
Columbia Bible College and Seminary
Columbia Junior College of Business

South Dakota
Presentation College

Tennessee
Belmont University
Lane College
LeMoyne-Owen College
William Jennings Bryan College

Texas
Houston Baptist University
Texas Lutheran College
University of Texas: Pan American

Utah
Snow College

Vermont
Lyndon State College
Norwich University

Virginia
Averett College
Ferrum College
Liberty University
Lynchburg College

Washington
Puget Sound Christian College
Washington State University

West Virginia
Davis and Elkins College
University of Charleston

Wisconsin
Edgewood College
Moraine Park Technical College
University of Wisconsin Center
  Baraboo/Sauk County
  Marinette County
  Waukesha
Wisconsin Lutheran College

France
American University of Paris

May closing dates

Alaska
University of Alaska Anchorage*

California
California State University
  Fresno
  Hayward*
  Long Beach*
Whittier College*

Connecticut
Central Connecticut State University*
Eastern Connecticut State University*
St. Joseph College

Hawaii
University of Hawaii at Manoa

Illinois
Moody Bible Institute

Indiana
Lutheran College of Health Professions*

Iowa
Buena Vista College*
University of Iowa

Louisiana
Dillard University*

Maryland
Maryland Institute College of Art*
University of Maryland: Baltimore County*

Massachusetts
Elms College*

Mississippi
Millsaps College*

Missouri
Ranken Technical College*
University of Missouri: Columbia*

New Jersey
Rutgers—The State University of New Jersey
  Camden College of Arts and Sciences
  Newark College of Arts and Sciences
  University College Camden
Stockton State College

New York
City University of New York
  Brooklyn College*
  Queens College*
College of Insurance
State University of New York
  Purchase
  College at Brockport*
  College at New Paltz*
  College at Plattsburgh*

North Carolina
University of North Carolina at Wilmington*
Western Carolina University*

Oregon
Pacific University*

Pennsylvania
Bucks County Community College
Clarion University of Pennsylvania*
Messiah College*
St. Vincent College*
Slippery Rock University of Pennsylvania*
Williamson Free School of Mechanical Trades*

Puerto Rico
Escuela de Artes Plasticas de Puerto Rico

*College also has priority date

Inter American University of Puerto Rico
- Arecibo Campus*
- Metropolitan Campus
- San German Campus

Rhode Island

Rhode Island College*

South Carolina

Winthrop University

Tennessee

David Lipscomb University

Vermont

Castleton State College*

Virginia

Longwood College*
Old Dominion University*
Virginia State University*

Washington

Pacific Lutheran University*

Arab Republic of Egypt

American University in Cairo

*College also has priority date

Colleges with late or no closing dates

Late closing dates

Alabama
Alabama State University
Auburn University
Draughons Junior College
International Bible College
Jacksonville State University
Judson College
Marion Military Institute
Miles College
Reid State Technical College
Snead State Community College
Southeastern Bible College
Stillman College
Tuskegee University
University of Alabama
Huntsville
Tuscaloosa
University of Mobile
University of Montevallo
University of North Alabama
University of South Alabama

Alaska
Alaska Bible College
Alaska Pacific University
University of Alaska Fairbanks

Arizona
American Indian Bible College
Embry-Riddle Aeronautical University: Prescott Campus
Paradise Valley Community College
Southwestern College

Arkansas
Arkansas Baptist College
Arkansas College
Central Baptist College
Harding University
John Brown University
Ouachita Baptist University
Southern Arkansas University
Magnolia
Technical Branch
University of Arkansas
University of Arkansas
Little Rock
Monticello
University of Central Arkansas

California
Allan Hancock College
American Academy of Dramatic Arts: West
American Armenian International College
Armstrong University
Bakersfield College
Barstow College
Bethany College
Biola University
California College for Health Sciences
California Lutheran University
California State University
Bakersfield
Stanislaus
Christian Heritage College
Coastline Community College
College of Notre Dame
College of the Sequoias
Concordia University
Cypress College
Diablo Valley College
Dominican College of San Rafael
Fresno City College
Fresno Pacific College
Holy Names College
Lassen College
LIFE Bible College
Los Angeles City College
Los Angeles Harbor College
Los Angeles Mission College
Los Angeles Pierce College
Marymount College
Master's College
Mills College
Mount San Jacinto College
New College of California
Pacific Christian College
Palomar College
Patten College
Queen of the Holy Rosary College
San Diego Mesa College
San Francisco Art Institute
San Joaquin Delta College
San Jose Christian College
San Jose State University
Santa Barbara City College
Sierra College
Skyline College
University of Redlands
Westmont College
Woodbury University

Colorado
Colorado School of Mines
Colorado State University
Fort Lewis College
ITT Technical Institute: Aurora
Mesa State College
Metropolitan State College of Denver
Nazarene Bible College
Northeastern Junior College
Otero Junior College
Pikes Peak Community College
Regis University
University of Colorado
Colorado Springs
Denver
University of Denver
University of Southern Colorado

Connecticut
Bridgeport Engineering Institute
Gateway Community-Technical College
Middlesex Community-Technical College
Southern Connecticut State University
University of Bridgeport
University of New Haven

Delaware
Delaware State College
Delaware Technical and Community College
Southern Campus
Stanton/Wilmington Campus
Terry Campus
Goldey-Beacom College
Wesley College

District of Columbia
University of the District of Columbia

Florida
Barry University
Bethune-Cookman College
Brevard Community College
Central Florida Community College
Chipola Junior College
Clearwater Christian College
Eckerd College
Edison Community College
Edward Waters College
Embry-Riddle Aeronautical University
Florida Agricultural and Mechanical University
Florida Atlantic University
Florida Baptist Theological College
Florida Bible College
Florida Christian College
Florida College
Florida Institute of Technology
Florida Memorial College
Florida Southern College
Jacksonville University
New College of the University of South Florida
St. John Vianney College Seminary
St. Leo College
St. Petersburg Junior College
Santa Fe Community College
Southern College
Tallahassee Community College
University of North Florida
University of South Florida
University of West Florida
Valencia Community College
Warner Southern College
Webber College

Georgia
Abraham Baldwin Agricultural College
Albany State College
Atlanta Christian College
Atlanta Metropolitan College
Augusta College
Bainbridge College
Brunswick College
Chattahoochee Technical Institute
Clayton State College
Columbus College
Dalton College
DeKalb College
DeKalb Technical Institute
East Georgia College
Fort Valley State College
Gainesville College
Georgia College
Georgia Military College
Georgia Southern University
Georgia Southwestern College
Georgia State University
Gordon College
Kennesaw State College
LaGrange College
Meadows College of Business
Middle Georgia College
North Georgia College
Oglethorpe University
Paine College
Piedmont College
Reinhardt College
Savannah State College
Southern College of Technology
Toccoa Falls College
Truett-McConnell College
University of Georgia
Valdosta State College
Waycross College
West Georgia College

Hawaii
University of Hawaii
Hilo
Kapiolani Community College
Kauai Community College
Windward Community College

Idaho
Boise Bible College
Boise State University
Idaho State University
University of Idaho

Illinois
American Academy of Art
Blackburn College
Bradley University
City Colleges of Chicago: Kennedy-King College
College of St. Francis
De Paul University
Elmhurst College
Greenville College
Illinois College
Judson College
Lakeview College of Nursing
Lexington Institute of Hospitality Careers
Lincoln College
Loyola University of Chicago
MacMurray College
Montay College
Morrison Institute of Technology
North Park College
Northeastern Illinois University
Northern Illinois University
Olivet Nazarene University
Parks College of St. Louis University
Principia College
St. Xavier University
Shimer College
Southeastern Illinois College
Southern Illinois University at Edwardsville
Trinity Christian College
University of Illinois at Chicago
VanderCook College of Music
West Suburban College of Nursing
Western Illinois University

Indiana
Anderson University
Bethel College
Butler University
Franklin College
Grace College
Holy Cross College
Huntington College
Indiana State University
Indiana University
East
South Bend

Indiana University—Purdue University
- Fort Wayne
- Indianapolis

Indiana Wesleyan University
Martin University
Oakland City College
St. Francis College
University of Indianapolis
Vincennes University
Wabash College

Iowa

Divine Word College
Dordt College
Ellsworth Community College
Faith Baptist Bible College and Theological Seminary
Grand View College
Iowa Wesleyan College
Loras College
Mount Mercy College
Mount St. Clare College
North Iowa Area Community College
Northwestern College
University of Northern Iowa
Upper Iowa University
Vennard College

Kansas

Allen County Community College
Benedictine College
Bethel College
Haskell Indian Junior College
Seward County Community College
Southwestern College
Washburn University of Topeka

Kentucky

Asbury College
Ashland Community College
Georgetown College
Kentucky Wesleyan College
Lexington Community College
Louisville Technical Institute
Murray State University
Northern Kentucky University
Owensboro Junior College of Business
Pikeville College
Spalding University
Sullivan College
Thomas More College
Transylvania University
Union College
University of Kentucky
Western Kentucky University

Louisiana

Centenary College of Louisiana
Grambling State University
Louisiana State University
- Agricultural and Mechanical College
- Shreveport

Louisiana Tech University
Loyola University
Nunez Community College
Our Lady of Holy Cross College
Southeastern Louisiana University
Southern University at New Orleans
Southern University and Agricultural and Mechanical College
University of New Orleans

Maine

Central Maine Medical Center School of Nursing
Eastern Maine Technical College
Husson College
Maine College of Art
Maine Maritime Academy
Southern Maine Technical College
University of Maine
- Fort Kent
- Presque Isle

University of Southern Maine
Westbrook College

Maryland

Baltimore City Community College
Baltimore International Culinary College
Columbia Union College
Coppin State College
Hagerstown Junior College
University of Maryland: Eastern Shore
Washington College

Massachusetts

Anna Maria College for Men and Women
Aquinas College at Newton
Bay State College
Cape Cod Community College
Framingham State College
Massachusetts College of Pharmacy and Allied Health Sciences
Mount Wachusett Community College
North Adams State College
Northern Essex Community College
Regis College
Roxbury Community College
St. John's Seminary College
Simon's Rock College of Bard
Suffolk University
University of Massachusetts at Boston
Wentworth Institute of Technology
Worcester State College

Michigan

Adrian College
Alma College
Aquinas College
Baker College: Flint
Center for Creative Studies: College of Art and Design
Charles Stewart Mott Community College
Detroit College of Business
Eastern Michigan University
Grace Bible College
Grand Rapids Baptist College and Seminary
Grand Rapids Community College
Grand Valley State University
Great Lakes Christian College
Hillsdale College
Lake Superior State University
Lansing Community College
Lawrence Technological University
Macomb Community College
Madonna University
Marygrove College
Michigan State University
Michigan Technological University
Northern Michigan University
Northwood University
Oakland University
Olivet College
St. Mary's College
Siena Heights College
Suomi College
University of Michigan
- Dearborn
- Flint

Washtenaw Community College
Wayne State University

Minnesota

Augsburg College
Bemidji State University
Bethany Lutheran College
Dr. Martin Luther College
Itasca Community College: Arrowhead Region
Minneapolis Community College
Minnesota Bible College
Moorhead State University
Normandale Community College
Rochester Community College
St. Cloud State University
St. Mary's College of Minnesota
University of Minnesota: Crookston
Willmar Community College
Willmar Technical College
Winona State University

Mississippi

Copiah-Lincoln Community College
Hinds Community College
Jackson State University
Mississippi College
Mississippi Delta Community College
Mississippi State University
Mississippi University for Women
Northwest Mississippi Community College
Rust College
Southeastern Baptist College
University of Mississippi
William Carey College

Missouri

Central Methodist College
Central Missouri State University
College of the Ozarks
Conception Seminary College
Cottey College
Culver-Stockton College
Deaconess College of Nursing
Drury College
Fontbonne College
Maple Woods Community College
Missouri Southern State College
Missouri Western State College
National College
Ozark Christian College
Research College of Nursing
Rockhurst College
St. Louis Christian College
St. Louis College of Pharmacy
Southwest Baptist University
Southwest Missouri State University
Stephens College
University of Missouri: Kansas City
Webster University

Montana

Carroll College
Fort Peck Community College
Rocky Mountain College
University of Montana

Nebraska

Concordia College
Creighton University
Dana College
Midland Lutheran College
Nebraska Christian College
Nebraska College of Technical Agriculture
Nebraska Wesleyan University
Union College
University of Nebraska
- Kearney
- Lincoln
- Omaha

Nevada

University of Nevada
- Las Vegas
- Reno

New Hampshire

New Hampshire Technical College
- Claremont
- Stratham

Notre Dame College
University of New Hampshire at Manchester

New Jersey

Atlantic Community College
Bergen Community College
Camden County College
College of St. Elizabeth
Georgian Court College
Hudson County Community College
Jersey City State College
Kean College of New Jersey
Rutgers—The State University of New Jersey
- University College New Brunswick
- University College Newark

Salem Community College
Upsala College
Westminster Choir College School of Music of Rider College
William Paterson College of New Jersey

New Mexico

Albuquerque Technical-Vocational Institute
College of the Southwest
Eastern New Mexico University
New Mexico Highlands University
New Mexico Institute of Mining and Technology
New Mexico State University at Carlsbad
San Juan College
University of New Mexico
Western New Mexico University

New York

Adirondack Community College
American Academy McAllister Institute of Funeral Service
Broome Community College
Cazenovia College
City University of New York
- Borough of Manhattan Community College
- Bronx Community College
- College of Staten Island
- Hostos Community College
- Kingsborough Community College
- Medgar Evers College

Cochran School of Nursing-St. John's Riverside Hospital
College of Mount St. Vincent
College of St. Rose
Columbia University: School of General Studies
Dominican College of Blauvelt
Elmira College
Erie Community College
- City Campus
- North Campus
- South Campus

Finger Lakes Community College
Genesee Community College
Hilbert College
Houghton College
Mannes College of Music
Maria College
Marymount College
Mater Dei College
Mount St. Mary College
Nassau Community College
Niagara County Community College
Niagara University
Nyack College
Onondaga Community College

Orange County Community College
Pace University
- College of White Plains
- New York
- Pleasantville/Briarcliff

Parsons School of Design
Rabbinical Seminary of America
Roberts Wesleyan College
Rochester Institute of Technology
Russell Sage College
Sage Junior College of Albany
St. Joseph's College
- Brooklyn
- Suffolk Campus

State University of New York at Stony Brook
Suffolk County Community College
- Eastern Campus
- Selden
- Western Campus

Talmudical Institute of Upstate New York
Technical Career Institutes
Villa Maria College of Buffalo
Wadhams Hall Seminary-College

North Carolina

Belmont Abbey College
Bennett College
Brevard College
Campbell University
Central Piedmont Community College
Durham Technical Community College
Fayetteville State University
Gardner-Webb University
John Wesley College
Livingstone College
Mars Hill College
Nash Community College
North Carolina Agricultural and Technical State University
North Carolina Central University
North Carolina Wesleyan College
Pembroke State University
Richmond Community College
Roanoke Bible College
Robeson Community College
St. Andrews Presbyterian College
St. Augustine's College
Shaw University
Southeastern Baptist Theological Seminary
University of North Carolina
- Charlotte
- Greensboro

Warren Wilson College
Wingate College

North Dakota

Bismarck State College
Little Hoop Community College
North Dakota State University
University of North Dakota

Ohio

Art Academy of Cincinnati
Ashland University
Bluffton College
Bowling Green State University: Firelands College
Capital University
Central Ohio Technical College
Central State University
Cincinnati Bible College and Seminary
Cleveland Institute of Art
College of Mount St. Joseph
Franciscan University of Steubenville
God's Bible School and College
Heidelberg College
Kent State University
- Trumbull Regional Campus
- Tuscarawas Campus

Kettering College of Medical Arts
Lake Erie College
Lorain County Community College
Lourdes College
Muskingum College
Ohio Northern University
Ohio State University
- Agricultural Technical Institute
- Lima Campus
- Mansfield Campus
- Marion Campus

Ohio University: Zanesville Campus
Ohio Valley Business College
Otterbein College
Owens Technical College
- Findlay Campus
- Toledo

Union Institute
University of Akron
University of Cincinnati: Clermont College
University of Rio Grande
University of Toledo
Wilberforce University
Wright State University
Xavier University
Youngstown State University

Oklahoma

Northeastern State University
Oklahoma Baptist University
Oklahoma State University
- Oklahoma City
- Technical Branch: Okmulgee

Oral Roberts University
Redlands Community College
Southern Nazarene University
Southwestern College of Christian Ministries
Southwestern Oklahoma State University
University of Science and Arts of Oklahoma

Oregon

Bassist College
Clackamas Community College
Concordia College
Eastern Oregon State College
Eugene Bible College
George Fox College
ITT Technical Institute: Portland
Multnomah School of the Bible
Northwest Christian College
Pacific Northwest College of Art
Portland State University
Umpqua Community College
Western Baptist College
Willamette University

Pennsylvania

Allentown College of St. Francis de Sales
Baptist Bible College of Pennsylvania
Butler County Community College
Cabrini College
California University of Pennsylvania
Central Pennsylvania Business School
Churchman Business School
Duquesne University
Holy Family College
Immaculata College
King's College
La Salle University
Luzerne County Community College
Manor Junior College
Mansfield University of Pennsylvania
Neumann College
Pittsburgh Institute of Mortuary Science
St. Francis College
Temple University
Thaddeus Stevens State School of Technology
University of Pittsburgh
- Bradford
- Greensburg

Valley Forge Christian College

Puerto Rico

American University of Puerto Rico
Bayamon Central University
Pontifical Catholic University of Puerto Rico
Technological College of the Municipality of San Juan
Universidad Adventista de las Antillas
Universidad Metropolitana
Universidad Politecnica de Puerto Rico
University of the Sacred Heart

Rhode Island

Community College of Rhode Island

South Carolina

Aiken Technical College
Anderson College
Central Wesleyan College
The Citadel
Coker College
College of Charleston
Columbia College
Erskine College
Florence-Darlington Technical College
Newberry College
North Greenville College
South Carolina State University
University of South Carolina
- Aiken
- Coastal Carolina College

South Dakota

Augustana College
Dakota Wesleyan University
Huron University
Mount Marty College
National College
Presentation College
Sisseton-Wahpeton Community College
South Dakota School of Mines and Technology
South Dakota State University

Tennessee

American Baptist College of ABT Seminary
Aquinas Junior College
Austin Peay State University
Belmont University
Bethel College
Chattanooga State Technical Community College
Christian Brothers University
Columbia State Community College
East Tennessee State University
Freed-Hardeman University
Hiwassee College
Johnson Bible College
King College
Lane College
LeMoyne-Owen College
Maryville College
Memphis State University
Middle Tennessee State University
Milligan College
Motlow State Community College
Northeast State Technical Community College
Roane State Community College
Southern College of Seventh-day Adventists
Tennessee State University
Tennessee Temple University
Union University
University of Tennessee
- Chattanooga
- Knoxville
- Martin

Volunteer State Community College
William Jennings Bryan College

Texas

Alvin Community College
Baptist Missionary Association Theological Seminary
Brazosport College
Criswell College
Dallas Christian College
East Texas State University
El Paso Community College
Grayson County College
Houston Baptist University
Howard College
Incarnate Word College
ITT Technical Institute: Houston
Lamar University—Beaumont
LeTourneau University
Lubbock Christian University
McMurry University
Midwestern State University
Palo Alto College
St. Edward's University
St. Mary's University
St. Philip's College
Schreiner College
Southwest Texas State University
Southwestern Christian College
Tarleton State University
Temple Junior College
Texas A&M University at Galveston
Texas College
Texas Lutheran College
Texas Southern University
Texas Tech University
Texas Wesleyan University
Texas Woman's University
University of Houston
- Downtown
- Houston

University of North Texas
University of St. Thomas
University of Texas
- Arlington
- El Paso
- Pan American
- San Antonio

Wayland Baptist University
Wharton County Junior College

Utah

Dixie College
Southern Utah University
University of Utah
Utah State University
Weber State University

Vermont

Burlington College

Virginia

Averett College
Bridgewater College
Christendom College
Christopher Newport University
Clinch Valley College of the University of Virginia
Eastern Mennonite College

Eastern Shore Community College
Ferrum College
Hampton University
Liberty University
Lord Fairfax Community College
Rappahannock Community College
Richard Bland College
Shenandoah University
Southern Virginia College for Women
Virginia Union University

Washington

Cornish College of the Arts
Eastern Washington University
Heritage College
Lutheran Bible Institute of Seattle
North Seattle Community College
Puget Sound Christian College
St. Martin's College
Seattle Pacific University
Seattle University
Yakima Valley Community College

West Virginia

Alderson-Broaddus College
Bethany College
College of West Virginia
Fairmont State College
Marshall University
Potomac State College of West Virginia University
West Virginia Institute of Technology
West Virginia Wesleyan College

Wisconsin

Alverno College
Carthage College
Chippewa Valley Technical College
Concordia University Wisconsin
Edgewood College
Lakeland College
Madison Area Technical College
Marian College of Fond du Lac
Mid-State Technical College
Milwaukee College of Business
Moraine Park Technical College
Mount Mary College
Mount Senario College
Northland College
Northwestern College
University of Wisconsin
  Parkside
  Superior
University of Wisconsin Center
  Fox Valley
  Marathon County
  Richland

Wyoming

Northwest College
University of Wyoming

American Samoa, Caroline Islands, Guam, Marianas, Virgin Islands

College of Micronesia-FSM
Guam Community College
Micronesian Occupational College

France

American University of Paris

Mexico

Sistema Instituto Tecnologico y de Estudios Superiores de Monterrey

No closing date

Alabama

Alabama Agricultural and Mechanical University
Alabama Aviation and Technical College
Alabama Southern Community College
Auburn University at Montgomery
Bessemer State Technical College
Bevill State Community College
Bishop State Community College
Central Alabama Community College
  Alexander City Campus
  Childersburg Campus
Chattahoochee Valley Community College
Community College of the Air Force
Concordia College
Douglas MacArthur State Technical College
Enterprise State Junior College
Faulkner University
Gadsden State Community College
George C. Wallace State Community College
  Dothan
  Selma
Harry M. Ayers State Technical College
J. F. Drake State Technical College
James H. Faulkner State Community College
Jefferson Davis State Junior College
Jefferson State Community College
John C. Calhoun State Community College
John M. Patterson State Technical College
Lawson State Community College
Livingston University
Lurleen B. Wallace State Junior College
Northeast Alabama Community College
Northwest Alabama Community College
Oakwood College
Phillips Junior College: Birmingham
Selma University
Shelton State Community College
Shoals Community College
Southern Union State Junior College
Spring Hill College
Talladega College
Trenholm State Technical College
Troy State University
  Dothan
  Montgomery
  Troy
University of Alabama in Birmingham
Virginia College
Walker College
Wallace State Community College at Hanceville

Alaska

Prince William Sound Community College
Sheldon Jackson College
University of Alaska Southeast

Arizona

Arizona College of the Bible
Arizona State University
Arizona Western College
Central Arizona College
Cochise College
Eastern Arizona College
Gateway Community College
Glendale Community College
Grand Canyon University
ITT Technical Institute
  Phoenix
  Tucson
Mesa Community College
Mohave Community College
Navajo Community College
Northland Pioneer College
Phoenix College
Pima Community College
Prescott College
Rio Salado Community College
Scottsdale Community College
South Mountain Community College
Western International University
Yavapai College

Arkansas

Arkansas State University
  Beebe Branch
  Jonesboro
Arkansas Tech University
Capital City Junior College
East Arkansas Community College
Garland County Community College
Henderson State University
Hendrix College
Mississippi County Community College
North Arkansas Community/Technical College
Philander Smith College
Phillips County Community College
Rich Mountain Community College
Shorter College
South Arkansas Community College
University of Arkansas at Pine Bluff
University of the Ozarks
Westark Community College
Williams Baptist College

California

Academy of Art College
American College for the Applied Arts: Los Angeles
Antelope Valley College
Art Center College of Design
Art Institute of Southern California
Azusa Pacific University
Brooks College
Brooks Institute of Photography
California Baptist College
California College of Arts and Crafts
California Institute of the Arts
California State Polytechnic University: Pomona
California State University
  Dominguez Hills
  Fullerton
  Los Angeles
  Sacramento
  San Bernardino
Canada College
Central California Commercial College
Cerritos Community College
Cerro Coso Community College
Chabot College
Chaffey Community College
Chapman University
Citrus College
City College of San Francisco
Cogswell Polytechnical College
Coleman College
College of the Canyons
College of Marin: Kentfield
College of Oceaneering
College of the Redwoods
College of San Mateo
College of the Siskiyous
Columbia College
Columbia College: Hollywood
Compton Community College
Contra Costa College
Cosumnes River College
Crafton Hills College
Cuesta College
Cuyamaca College
D-Q University
Evergreen Valley College
Fashion Institute of Design and Merchandising
  Los Angeles
  San Francisco
Feather River College
Foothill College
Fullerton College
Glendale Community College
Golden Gate University
Golden West College
Grossmont Community College
Heald Business College
  Concord
  San Jose
Humphreys College
ITT Technical Institute
  Sacramento
  West Covina
Kelsey-Jenney College
La Sierra University
Lake Tahoe Community College
Laney College
Las Positas College
Lincoln University
Long Beach City College
Los Angeles Trade and Technical College
Los Angeles Valley College
Los Medanos College
Louise Salinger Academy of Fashion
Loyola Marymount University
Mendocino College
Menlo College
Merced College
Merritt College
MiraCosta College
Mission College
Modesto Junior College
Monterey Peninsula College
Moorpark College
Mount St. Mary's College
Mount San Antonio College
Napa Valley College
National University
Otis School of Art and Design
Pacific Union College
Pasadena City College
Phillips Junior College
  Condie Campus
  Fresno Campus
Point Loma Nazarene College
Porterville College
Rio Hondo College
Sacramento City College
Saddleback College
Samuel Merritt College
San Diego City College
San Diego Miramar College
San Francisco College of Mortuary Science
San Jose City College
Santa Monica College
Santa Rosa Junior College
Shasta College
Simpson College
Solano Community College
Sonoma State University
Southern California College
Southern California Institute of Architecture

Southwestern College
Taft College
Thomas Aquinas College
United States International University
University of Judaism
University of La Verne
University of the Pacific
University of San Francisco
University of Southern California
Ventura College
Victor Valley College
West Coast University
West Hills Community College
West Valley College
Yuba College

Colorado

Adams State College
Aims Community College
Arapahoe Community College
Bel-Rea Institute of Animal Technology
Colorado Christian University
Colorado Institute of Art
Colorado Mountain College
- Alpine Campus
- Spring Valley Campus
- Timberline Campus

Colorado Northwestern Community College
Colorado Technical College
Community College of Aurora
Community College of Denver
Denver Institute of Technology
Denver Technical College
Front Range Community College
Lamar Community College
Morgan Community College
National College
Parks Junior College
Pueblo Community College
Red Rocks Community College
Rocky Mountain College of Art & Design
Trinidad State Junior College
University of Northern Colorado
Western State College of Colorado

Connecticut

Albertus Magnus College
Asnuntuck Community-Technical College
Briarwood College
Capital Community-Technical College
Charter Oak State College
Housatonic Community-Technical College
Mitchell College
Northwestern Connecticut Community-Technical College
Norwalk Community-Technical College
Paier College of Art
Quinebaug Valley Community-Technical College
Quinnipiac College
Teikyo-Post University
Three Rivers Community-Technical College
Tunxis Community-Technical College
University of Hartford

Delaware

Wilmington College

District of Columbia

Corcoran School of Art
Gallaudet University
George Washington University
Mount Vernon College
Southeastern University
Strayer College
Trinity College

Florida

Art Institute of Fort Lauderdale
Broward Community College
Daytona Beach Community College
Flagler Career Institute
Florida Community College at Jacksonville
Fort Lauderdale College
Gulf Coast Community College
Hillsborough Community College
Hobe Sound Bible College
Indian River Community College
ITT Technical Institute: Tampa
Jones College
Keiser College of Technology
Lake City Community College
Lake-Sumter Community College
Lynn University
Manatee Community College
Miami-Dade Community College
National Education Center
- Bauder Campus
- Tampa Technical Institute Campus

New England Institute of Technology
North Florida Junior College
Nova University
Okaloosa-Walton Community College
Palm Beach Atlantic College
Palm Beach Community College
Pasco-Hernando Community College
Pensacola Junior College
Phillips Junior College: Melbourne
Polk Community College
Ringling School of Art and Design
St. Johns River Community College
St. Thomas University
Schiller International University
Seminole Community College
South College: Palm Beach Campus
South Florida Community College
Southeastern College of the Assemblies of God
Tampa College
Trinity College at Miami
University of Tampa

Georgia

Agnes Scott College
American College for the Applied Arts
Andrew College
Art Institute of Atlanta
Athens Area Technical Institute
Bauder College
Brenau University
Brewton-Parker College
Covenant College
Darton College
Emmanuel College
Floyd College
Gwinnett Technical Institute
Macon College
Mercer University
Morris Brown College
Oxford College of Emory University
Savannah College of Art and Design
Savannah Technical Institute
Shorter College
South College
South Georgia College
Thomas College
Young Harris College

Hawaii

Hawaii Pacific University
University of Hawaii
- Hawaii Community College
- Honolulu Community College

Idaho

Albertson College
College of Southern Idaho
ITT Technical Institute: Boise
Lewis Clark State College
North Idaho College
Northwest Nazarene College

Illinois

American Conservatory of Music
Augustana College
Aurora University
Barat College
Belleville Area College
Black Hawk College
- East Campus
- Moline

Blessing-Reiman College of Nursing
Carl Sandburg College
Chicago State University
City Colleges of Chicago
- Harold Washington College
- Malcolm X College
- Olive-Harvey College

College of DuPage
College of Lake County
Columbia College
Concordia University
Danville Area Community College
Eastern Illinois University
East-West University
Elgin Community College
Eureka College
Gem City College
Harrington Institute of Interior Design
Highland Community College
Illinois Benedictine College
Illinois Central College
Illinois Eastern Community Colleges
- Frontier Community College
- Lincoln Trail College
- Olney Central College
- Wabash Valley College

Illinois State University
Illinois Valley Community College
Illinois Wesleyan University
International Academy of Merchandising and Design
ITT Technical Institute: Hoffman Estates
John A. Logan College
Joliet Junior College
Kankakee Community College
Kaskaskia College
Kendall College
Kishwaukee College
Knox College
Lake Forest College
Lake Land College
Lewis and Clark Community College
Lewis University
Lincoln Christian College and Seminary
Lincoln Land Community College
MacCormac Junior College
McHenry County College
McKendree College
Millikin University
Moraine Valley Community College
Morton College
National-Louis University
North Central College
Oakton Community College
Quincy University
Ray College of Design
Richland Community College
Robert Morris College: Chicago
Rock Valley College
Rockford College
Roosevelt University
Rosary College
St. Augustine College
Sauk Valley Community College
School of the Art Institute of Chicago
Shawnee Community College
Southern Illinois University at Carbondale
Spoon River College
Springfield College in Illinois
State Community College
Trinity College
Triton College
William Rainey Harper College

Indiana

Ancilla College
Ball State University
Calumet College of St. Joseph
Goshen College
Indiana University Northwest
Indiana Vocational Technical College
- Central Indiana
- Columbus
- Eastcentral
- Kokomo
- Lafayette
- Northcentral
- Northeast
- Northwest
- Southcentral
- Southeast
- Southwest
- Wabash Valley
- Whitewater

ITT Technical Institute
- Evansville
- Fort Wayne
- Indianapolis

Manchester College
Marian College
Mid-America College of Funeral Service
Purdue University
- Calumet
- North Central Campus
- West Lafayette

St. Joseph's College
St. Mary-of-the-Woods College
St. Mary's College
St. Meinrad College
Taylor University
Tri-State University
University of Southern Indiana
Valparaiso University

Iowa

American Institute of Business
American Institute of Commerce
Briar Cliff College
Central College
Clarke College
Clinton Community College
Coe College
Cornell College
Des Moines Area Community College
Emmaus Bible College
Graceland College
Hamilton Technical College
Hawkeye Community College
Indian Hills Community College
Iowa Central Community College
Iowa Lakes Community College
Iowa State University
Iowa Western Community College
Kirkwood Community College
Luther College

Maharishi International University
Marshalltown Community College
Morningside College
Muscatine Community College
Northeast Iowa Community College
Northwest Iowa Community College
St. Ambrose University
Scott Community College
Simpson College
Southeastern Community College
- North Campus
- South Campus

Southwestern Community College
Teikyo Marycrest University
Teikyo Westmar University
Waldorf College
Wartburg College
Western Iowa Tech Community College
William Penn College

Kansas

Baker University
Barclay College
Barton County Community College
Bethany College
Brown Mackie College
Butler County Community College
Central College
Coffeyville Community College
Colby Community College
Dodge City Community College
Donnelly College
Emporia State University
Fort Hays State University
Fort Scott Community College
Friends University
Garden City Community College
Hesston College
Highland Community College
Hutchinson Community College
Independence Community College
Johnson County Community College
Kansas City Kansas Community College
Kansas Newman College
Kansas State University
Kansas Wesleyan University
Labette Community College
Manhattan Christian College
McPherson College
MidAmerica Nazarene College
Neosho County Community College
Ottawa University
Pittsburg State University
Pratt Community College
St. Mary College
Sterling College
Tabor College
Wichita State University

Kentucky

Alice Lloyd College
Bellarmine College
Berea College
Brescia College
Campbellsville College
Cumberland College
Eastern Kentucky University
Elizabethtown Community College
Henderson Community College
Hopkinsville Community College
Institute of Electronic Technology
Jefferson Community College
Kentucky State University
Lees College
Lindsey Wilson College
Madisonville Community College
Maysville Community College
Mid-Continent Baptist Bible College
Midway College
Morehead State University
Paducah Community College
Prestonburg Community College
RETS Electronic Institute
Southeast Community College
Sue Bennett College
University of Louisville

Louisiana

Bossier Parish Community College
Grantham College of Engineering
Louisiana College
Louisiana State University
- Alexandria
- Eunice

McNeese State University
Nicholls State University
Northeast Louisiana University
Northwestern State University
Phillips Junior College: New Orleans
St. Joseph Seminary College
Southern University in Shreveport
University of Southwestern Louisiana

Maine

Andover College
Beal College
Casco Bay College
Central Maine Technical College
College of the Atlantic
Northern Maine Technical College
St. Joseph's College
Thomas College
Unity College
University of Maine
- Augusta
- Farmington
- Machias
- Orono

University of New England

Maryland

Allegany Community College
Anne Arundel Community College
Capitol College
Catonsville Community College
Cecil Community College
Charles County Community College
Chesapeake College
Dundalk Community College
Essex Community College
Frederick Community College
Frostburg State University
Hagerstown Business College
Harford Community College
Howard Community College
Montgomery College
- Germantown Campus
- Rockville Campus
- Takoma Park Campus

Morgan State University
Ner Israel Rabbinical College
Prince George's Community College
St. John's College
Sojourner-Douglass College
University of Maryland: University College
Villa Julie College
Wor-Wic Community College

Massachusetts

American International College
Aquinas College at Milton
Atlantic Union College
Bay Path College
Becker College
- Leicester Campus
- Worcester Campus

Berklee College of Music
Boston Architectural Center
Boston Conservatory
Boston University
Bradford College
Bristol Community College
Bunker Hill Community College
Dean Junior College
Eastern Nazarene College
Emerson College
Emmanuel College
Endicott College
Essex Agricultural and Technical Institute
Fisher College
Forsyth School for Dental Hygienists
Franklin Institute of Boston
Greenfield Community College
Hebrew College
Hellenic College
Holyoke Community College
Katharine Gibbs School
Lasell College
Lesley College
Marian Court Junior College
Massachusetts Bay Community College
Massachusetts Maritime Academy
Massasoit Community College
Middlesex Community College
Montserrat College of Art
Mount Ida College
New England Banking Institute
Newbury College
Nichols College
North Shore Community College
Northeastern University
Pine Manor College
Quincy College
Quinsigamond Community College
St. Hyacinth College and Seminary
School of the Museum of Fine Arts
Springfield Technical Community College
University of Massachusetts
- Dartmouth
- Lowell

Western New England College

Michigan

Albion College
Alpena Community College
Andrews University
Baker College
- Auburn Hills
- Cadillac
- Mount Clemens
- Muskegon
- Owosso
- Port Huron

Bay de Noc Community College
Calvin College
Central Michigan University
Cleary College
Concordia College
Davenport College of Business
Delta College
Ferris State University
Glen Oaks Community College
GMI Engineering & Management Institute
Gogebic Community College
Great Lakes Junior College of Business
Henry Ford Community College
Highland Park Community College
Hope College
Jackson Community College
Jordan College
Kalamazoo Valley Community College
Kellogg Community College
Kendall College of Art and Design
Kirtland Community College
Lake Michigan College
Lewis College of Business
Michigan Christian College
Mid Michigan Community College
Monroe County Community College
Montcalm Community College
Muskegon Community College
Northwestern Michigan College
Oakland Community College
Reformed Bible College
Sacred Heart Major Seminary
Saginaw Valley State University
St. Clair County Community College
Schoolcraft College
Southwestern Michigan College
Spring Arbor College
University of Detroit Mercy
Wayne County Community College
West Shore Community College
Western Michigan University
William Tyndale College

Minnesota

Alexandria Technical College
Anoka-Ramsey Community College
Austin Community College
Brainerd Community College
College of Associated Arts
College of St. Benedict
College of St. Catherine: St. Catherine Campus
College of St. Scholastica
Concordia College: Moorhead
Concordia College: St. Paul
Crown College
Fergus Falls Community College
Hamline University
Hibbing Community College
Inver Hills Community College
Lakewood Community College
Mankato State University
Mesabi Community College: Arrowhead Region
NEI College of Technology
North Central Bible College
North Hennepin Community College
Northwest Technical Institute
Northwestern College
Pillsbury Baptist Bible College
Rainy River Community College
St. John's University
St. Mary's Campus of the College of St. Catherine
St. Olaf College
St. Paul Technical College
Saint Cloud Technical College
Southwest State University
University of Minnesota
- Duluth
- Twin Cities

Vermilion Community College
Worthington Community College

Mississippi

Alcorn State University
Belhaven College
Delta State University
East Central Community College
East Mississippi Community College
Holmes Community College
Magnolia Bible College
Meridian Community College
Mississippi Gulf Coast Community College
- Jackson County Campus
- Jefferson Davis Campus
- Perkinston

Mississippi Valley State University
Pearl River Community College
Southwest Mississippi Community College
Tougaloo College
University of Southern Mississippi
Wood Junior College

Missouri
Avila College
Berean College
Calvary Bible College
Central Christian College of the Bible
Crowder College
East Central College
Evangel College
Hannibal-LaGrange College
Harris Stowe State College
ITT Technical Institute: St. Louis
Jefferson College
Kansas City Art Institute
Kemper Military School and College
Lincoln University
Lindenwood College
Longview Community College
Maryville University
Mineral Area College
Missouri Baptist College
Missouri Valley College
Moberly Area Community College
Northwest Missouri Community College
Northwest Missouri State University
Park College
Penn Valley Community College
Phillips Junior College
St. Charles County Community College
St. Louis Community College
- Florissant Valley
- Forest Park
- Meramec

St. Louis University
Southeast Missouri State University
State Fair Community College
Three Rivers Community College
University of Missouri
- Rolla
- St. Louis

Westminster College
William Jewell College
William Woods College

Montana
Billings Vocational-Technical Center
Blackfeet Community College
Butte Vocational-Technical Center
College of Great Falls
Dawson Community College
Dull Knife Memorial College
Eastern Montana College
Flathead Valley Community College
Fort Belknap College
Helena Vocational-Technical Center
Little Big Horn College
Miles Community College
Missoula Vocational-Technical Center
Montana College of Mineral Science and Technology
Montana State University
Northern Montana College
Salish Kootenai College
Stone Child College
Western Montana College of the University of Montana

Nebraska
Bellevue College
Central Community College
Chadron State College
Clarkson College
College of St. Mary
Doane College
Grace College of the Bible
Lincoln School of Commerce
McCook Community College
Metropolitan Community College
Mid Plains Community College
Nebraska Indian Community College
Northeast Community College
Peru State College
Southeast Community College
- Beatrice Campus
- Lincoln Campus
- Milford Campus

Wayne State College
Western Nebraska Community College: Scottsbluff Campus
York College

Nevada
Northern Nevada Community College
Sierra Nevada College
Truckee Meadows Community College
Western Nevada Community College

New Hampshire
Castle College
Colby-Sawyer College
Daniel Webster College
Franklin Pierce College
Hesser College
McIntosh College
New England College
New Hampshire College
New Hampshire Technical College
- Berlin
- Laconia
- Manchester
- Nashua

New Hampshire Technical Institute
Rivier College
School for Lifelong Learning
White Pines College

New Jersey
Assumption College for Sisters
Berkeley College of Business
Bloomfield College
Brookdale Community College
Burlington County College
Caldwell College
Centenary College
County College of Morris
Cumberland County College
Essex County College
Fairleigh Dickinson University
- Edward Williams College
- Madison

Felician College
Gloucester County College
Katharine Gibbs School
Mercer County Community College
New Jersey Institute of Technology
Ocean County College
Passaic County Community College
Raritan Valley Community College
Rider College
St. Peter's College
Seton Hall University
Sussex County Community College
Thomas Edison State College
Union County College
Warren County Community College

New Mexico
Clovis Community College
College of Santa Fe
Dona Ana Branch Community College of New Mexico State University
Eastern New Mexico University: Roswell Campus
National College
New Mexico Junior College
New Mexico Military Institute
New Mexico State University
- Alamogordo
- Las Cruces

Northern New Mexico Community College
Parks College
St. John's College

New York
Adelphi University
Albany College of Pharmacy
American Academy of Dramatic Arts
Audrey Cohen College
Berkeley College
Berkeley School: New York City
Boricua College
Bramson ORT Technical Institute
Bryant & Stratton Business Institute
- Albany
- Rochester
- Syracuse

Canisius College
Catholic Medical Center of Brooklyn and Queens School of Nursing
Cayuga County Community College
Central City Business Institute
City University of New York
- City College
- Hunter College
- John Jay College of Criminal Justice
- La Guardia Community College
- Lehman College
- New York City Technical College
- Queensborough Community College
- York College

Clarkson University
Clinton Community College
College of Aeronautics
College of New Rochelle
- New Rochelle
- School of New Resources

Columbia-Greene Community College
Concordia College
Corning Community College
Culinary Institute of America
Daemen College
Dowling College
Dutchess Community College
D'Youville College
Eastman School of Music of the University of Rochester
Fashion Institute of Technology
Five Towns College
Fordham University
Fulton-Montgomery Community College
Helene Fuld School of Nursing
Herkimer County Community College
Hofstra University
Hudson Valley Community College
Institute of Design and Construction
Iona College
Ithaca College
Jamestown Business College
Jamestown Community College
Jefferson Community College
Katharine Gibbs School
- Melville
- New York

Keuka College
King's College
Long Island University
- Brooklyn Campus
- C. W. Post Campus
- Southampton Campus

Marist College
Marymount Manhattan College
Medaille College
Mercy College
Mohawk Valley Community College
Molloy College
Monroe College
Monroe Community College
New York Institute of Technology
New York School of Interior Design
North Country Community College
Ohr Somayach Tanenbaum Education Center
Olean Business Institute
Paul Smith's College
Polytechnic University
- Brooklyn
- Long Island Campus

Pratt Institute
Rockland Community College
St. Bonaventure University
St. Francis College
St. John Fisher College
St. John's University
St. Joseph's School of Nursing
St. Thomas Aquinas College
Schenectady County Community College
School of Visual Arts
State University of New York
- Binghamton
- Buffalo
- College of Agriculture and Technology at Cobleskill
- College of Agriculture and Technology at Morrisville
- College at Buffalo
- College of Environmental Science and Forestry
- College of Technology at Alfred
- College of Technology at Canton
- College of Technology at Delhi
- College of Technology at Farmingdale
- Empire State College
- Health Science Center at Syracuse
- Maritime College
- Oswego

Sullivan County Community College
Talmudical Seminary Oholei Torah
Taylor Business Institute
Tompkins-Cortland Community College
Touro College
Trocaire College
Ulster County Community College
University of the State of New York: Regents College
Utica College of Syracuse University
Utica School of Commerce
Wagner College
Westchester Business Institute
Westchester Community College
Wood Tobe-Coburn School
Yeshiva Shaar Hatorah
Yeshiva University

North Carolina
Alamance Community College
Anson Community College
Asheville Buncombe Technical Community College
Barber-Scotia College
Barton College
Beaufort County Community College
Bladen Community College
Blue Ridge Community College

Brunswick Community College
Caldwell Community College and Technical Institute
Cape Fear Community College
Carteret Community College
Catawba College
Catawba Valley Community College
Central Carolina Community College
Chowan College
Cleveland Community College
Coastal Carolina Community College
College of the Albemarle
Craven Community College
Davidson County Community College
East Coast Bible College
Edgecombe Community College
Elizabeth City State University
Elon College
Fayetteville Technical Community College
Gaston College
Greensboro College
Halifax Community College
Haywood Community College
High Point University
Isothermal Community College
James Sprunt Community College
Johnson C. Smith University
Johnston Community College
Lees-McRae College
Lenoir Community College
Lenoir-Rhyne College
Louisburg College
Martin Community College
Mayland Community College
McDowell Technical Community College
Meredith College
Methodist College
Mitchell Community College
Montgomery Community College
Montreat-Anderson College
Mount Olive College
North Carolina School of the Arts
Pamlico Community College
Peace College
Pfeiffer College
Piedmont Bible College
Piedmont Community College
Pitt Community College
Queens College
Randolph Community College
Roanoke-Chowan Community College
Rockingham Community College
Rowan-Cabarrus Community College
St. Mary's College
Salem College
Sampson Community College
Sandhills Community College
Southeastern Community College
Southwestern Community College
Stanly Community College
Surry Community College
Tri-County Community College
Vance-Granville Community College
Wake Technical Community College
Wayne Community College
Western Piedmont Community College
Wilkes Community College
Wilson Technical Community College
Winston-Salem State University

North Dakota

Dickinson State University
Jamestown College
Mayville State University
Minot State University
North Dakota State College of Science
North Dakota State University: Bottineau
Standing Rock College
Trinity Bible College
Turtle Mountain Community College
United Tribes Technical College
University of Mary
University of North Dakota
- Lake Region
- Williston

Valley City State University

Ohio

Antonelli Institute of Art and Photography
Baldwin-Wallace College
Belmont Technical College
Bliss College
Bowling Green State University
Bradford School
Cedarville College
Chatfield College
Cincinnati College of Mortuary Science
Circleville Bible College
Clark State Community College
Cleveland College of Jewish Studies
Cleveland Institute of Electronics
Cleveland State University
Columbus College of Art and Design
Columbus State Community College
Cuyahoga Community College
- Eastern Campus
- Metropolitan Campus
- Western Campus

Davis Junior College of Business
Defiance College
DeVry Institute of Technology: Columbus
Dyke College
Edison State Community College
Franklin University
Hocking Technical College
ITT Technical Institute
- Dayton
- Youngstown

Jefferson Technical College
John Carroll University
Kent State University
- Ashtabula Regional Campus
- East Liverpool Regional Campus
- Salem Regional Campus
- Stark Campus

Lakeland Community College
Lima Technical College
Malone College
Marietta College
Marion Technical College
Miami University
- Hamilton Campus
- Middletown Campus

Miami-Jacobs College
Mount Union College
North Central Technical College
Northwest Technical College
Northwestern College
Notre Dame College of Ohio
Ohio Dominican College
Ohio Institute of Photography and Technology
Ohio University
- Chillicothe Campus
- Eastern Campus
- Lancaster Campus
- Southern Campus at Ironton

Ohio Wesleyan University
Pontifical College Josephinum
Sinclair Community College
Southern Ohio College
Southern State Community College
Stark Technical College
Terra Technical College
Tiffin University
University of Akron: Wayne College
University of Cincinnati
- Access Colleges
- Cincinnati
- Raymond Walters College

University of Dayton
University of Findlay
Urbana University
Ursuline College
Virginia Marti College of Fashion and Art
Walsh University
Wilmington College
Wright State University: Lake Campus

Oklahoma

Bacone College
Bartlesville Wesleyan College
Cameron University
Carl Albert State College
Connors State College
East Central University
Eastern Oklahoma State College
Langston University
Mid-America Bible College
Northeastern Oklahoma Agricultural and Mechanical College
Northwestern Oklahoma State University
Oklahoma Christian University of Science and Arts
Oklahoma City Community College
Oklahoma City University
Oklahoma Panhandle State University
Oklahoma State University
Phillips University
Rogers State College
Rose State College
St. Gregory's College
Seminole Junior College
Southeastern Oklahoma State University
Tulsa Junior College
University of Central Oklahoma
University of Oklahoma
University of Tulsa
Western Oklahoma State College

Oregon

Blue Mountain Community College
Central Oregon Community College
Chemeketa Community College
Clatsop Community College
Lane Community College
Linfield College
Linn-Benton Community College
Marylhurst College
Mount Hood Community College
Oregon Institute of Technology
Oregon Polytechnic Institute
Portland Community College
Rogue Community College
Southern Oregon State College
Treasure Valley Community College
University of Portland
Warner Pacific College

Pennsylvania

Academy of the New Church
Alvernia College
American Institute of Design
Antonelli Institute of Art and Photography
Art Institute of Pittsburgh
Beaver College
Bloomsburg University of Pennsylvania
Carlow College
Cedar Crest College
Chestnut Hill College
Cheyney University of Pennsylvania
CHI Institute
College Misericordia
Community College of Allegheny County
- Allegheny Campus
- Boyce Campus
- North Campus
- South Campus

Community College of Beaver County
Community College of Philadelphia
Dean Institute of Technology
Delaware County Community College
Delaware Valley College
DuBois Business College
Eastern College
Edinboro University of Pennsylvania
Electronic Institutes
- Middletown
- Pittsburgh

Gannon University
Geneva College
Gratz College
Gwynedd-Mercy College
Hahnemann University School of Health Sciences and Humanities
Harcum Junior College
Harrisburg Area Community College
ICS Center for Degree Studies
Indiana University of Pennsylvania
Johnson Technical Institute
Keystone Junior College
La Roche College
Lackawanna Junior College
Lancaster Bible College
Lebanon Valley College of Pennsylvania
Lehigh County Community College
Lincoln Technical Institute
Lincoln University
Lock Haven University of Pennsylvania
Lycoming College
Marywood College
McCarrie Schools of Health Sciences and Technology
Mercyhurst College
Millersville University of Pennsylvania
Montgomery County Community College
Moore College of Art and Design
Mount Aloysius College
National Education Center: Vale Tech Campus
Northampton County Area Community College
Penn State
- Erie Behrend College
- University Park Campus

Penn Technical Institute
Pennsylvania College of Technology
Pennsylvania Institute of Technology
Philadelphia College of Bible
Philadelphia College of Pharmacy and Science
Philadelphia College of Textiles and Science
Pittsburgh Technical Institute
Point Park College
Reading Area Community College
Robert Morris College
Rosemont College
St. Charles Borromeo Seminary

St. Joseph's University
Seton Hill College
Shippensburg University of Pennsylvania
Thiel College
Triangle Tech
- Erie School
- Greensburg School
- Pittsburgh Campus

University of the Arts
University of Pittsburgh
- Johnstown
- Pittsburgh
- Titusville

Valley Forge Military College
Waynesburg College
Westminster College
Westmoreland County Community College
Wilkes University
Wilson College
York College of Pennsylvania

Puerto Rico

Caribbean University
Colegio Universitario del Este
Huertas Junior College
Inter American University of Puerto Rico: Guayama Campus
Turabo University

Rhode Island

Bryant College
Johnson & Wales University
New England Institute of Technology
Roger Williams University
Salve Regina University

South Carolina

Allen University
Benedict College
Central Carolina Technical College
Charleston Southern University
Chesterfield-Marlboro Technical College
Claflin College
Clemson University
Columbia Bible College and Seminary
Columbia Junior College of Business
Denmark Technical College
Francis Marion University
Greenville Technical College
Horry-Georgetown Technical College
Lander University
Limestone College
Midlands Technical College
Morris College
Spartanburg Methodist College
Spartanburg Technical College
Technical College of the Lowcountry
Tri-County Technical College
Trident Technical College
University of South Carolina
- Beaufort
- Columbia
- Salkehatchie Regional Campus
- Spartanburg
- Sumter
- Union

Voorhees College
Williamsburg Technical College
York Technical College

South Dakota

Black Hills State University
Dakota State University
Kilian Community College
Lake Area Vocational Technical Institute
Mitchell Vocational Technical Institute
Northern State University
Oglala Lakota College
Sinte Gleska University
Sioux Falls College
University of South Dakota
Western Dakota Vocational Technical Institute

Tennessee

Bristol University
Cleveland State Community College
Cumberland University
Draughons Junior College of Business: Nashville
Dyersburg State Community College
Fisk University
Free Will Baptist Bible College
ITT Technical Institute: Nashville
Knoxville Business College
Knoxville College
Lambuth University
Lee College
Lincoln Memorial University
Memphis College of Art
Nashville State Technical Institute
Pellissippi State Technical Community College
Rhodes College
Shelby State Community College
State Technical Institute at Memphis
Tennessee Technological University
Tennessee Wesleyan College
Trevecca Nazarene College
Tusculum College
Vanderbilt University
Walters State Community College

Texas

Abilene Christian University
Amarillo College
Angelina College
Angelo State University
Arlington Baptist College
Austin College
Austin Community College
Bauder Fashion College
Baylor University
Bee County College
Blinn College
Brookhaven College
Cedar Valley College
Central Texas College
Cisco Junior College
Clarendon College
College of the Mainland
Collin County Community College District
Commonwealth Institute of Funeral Service
Cooke County College
Dallas Baptist University
Dallas Institute of Funeral Service
Del Mar College
East Texas Baptist University
Eastfield College
El Centro College
Frank Phillips College
Galveston College
Hardin-Simmons University
Hill College
Houston Community College
Howard Payne University
Huston-Tillotson College
Jacksonville College
Jarvis Christian College
Kilgore College
Laredo Junior College
Lee College
Lon Morris College
Midland College
Miss Wade's Fashion Merchandising College
Mountain View College
Navarro College
North Harris Montgomery Community College District
North Lake College
Northeast Texas Community College
Northwood University: Texas Campus
Odessa College
Our Lady of the Lake University of San Antonio
Panola College
Paris Junior College
Paul Quinn College
Prairie View A&M University
Ranger Junior College
Richland College
Sam Houston State University
San Antonio College
San Jacinto College: North
South Plains College
Southwest Texas Junior College
Southwestern Adventist College
Southwestern Assemblies of God College
Stephen F. Austin State University
Sul Ross State University
Tarrant County Junior College
Texarkana College
Texas A&I University
Texas State Technical College
- Amarillo
- Harlingen
- Sweetwater
- Waco

Trinity Valley Community College
Tyler Junior College
University of Mary Hardin-Baylor
University of Texas at Dallas
Vernon Regional Junior College
Victoria College
Weatherford College
West Texas A & M University
Wiley College

Utah

College of Eastern Utah
ITT Technical Institute: Salt Lake City
LDS Business College
Phillips Junior College: Salt Lake City Campus
Salt Lake Community College
Snow College
Stevens-Henager College of Business
Utah Valley Community College
Westminster College of Salt Lake City

Vermont

Champlain College
College of St. Joseph in Vermont
Community College of Vermont
Goddard College
Green Mountain College
Johnson State College
Landmark College
Lyndon State College
Marlboro College
New England Culinary Institute
Norwich University
Southern Vermont College
Sterling College
Trinity College of Vermont
Vermont Technical College

Virginia

Blue Ridge Community College
Bluefield College
Central Virginia Community College
Dabney S. Lancaster Community College
Danville Community College
Emory and Henry College
J. Sargeant Reynolds Community College
John Tyler Community College
Lynchburg College
Marymount University
Mountain Empire Community College
National Business College
New River Community College
Norfolk State University
Northern Virginia Community College
Patrick Henry Community College
Paul D. Camp Community College
Piedmont Virginia Community College
Randolph-Macon College
Randolph-Macon Woman's College
St. Paul's College
Southside Virginia Community College
Southwest Virginia Community College
Tidewater Community College
Virginia Intermont College
Virginia Western Community College
Wytheville Community College

Washington

Art Institute of Seattle
Bellevue Community College
Big Bend Community College
Central Washington University
Centralia College
Clark College
Cogswell College North
Columbia Basin College
Edmonds Community College
Everett Community College
Grays Harbor College
Green River Community College
Highline Community College
ITT Technical Institute
- Seattle
- Spokane

Lower Columbia College
Northwest College of the Assemblies of God
Olympic College
Peninsula College
Pierce College
Renton Technical College
Seattle Central Community College
Shoreline Community College
Skagit Valley College
South Puget Sound Community College
South Seattle Community College
Spokane Community College
Spokane Falls Community College
Tacoma Community College
Walla Walla College
Walla Walla Community College
Washington State University
Wenatchee Valley College
Whatcom Community College
Whitworth College

West Virginia

Appalachian Bible College
Bluefield State College
Concord College
Davis and Elkins College
Glenville State College
Ohio Valley College
Salem-Teikyo University
Southern West Virginia Community College
University of Charleston

West Liberty State College
West Virginia Northern Community College
West Virginia State College
West Virginia University
- Morgantown
- Parkersburg

Wheeling Jesuit College

Wisconsin

Bellin College of Nursing
Blackhawk Technical College
Cardinal Stritch College
Carroll College
Columbia College of Nursing
Fox Valley Technical College
Gateway Technical College
Lakeshore Technical College
Madison Junior College of Business
Maranatha Baptist Bible College
Marquette University
Milwaukee Institute of Art & Design
Milwaukee School of Engineering
Nicolet Area Technical College
Northcentral Technical College
Northeast Wisconsin Technical College
Ripon College
St. Norbert College
Silver Lake College
Southwest Wisconsin Technical College
Stratton College
University of Wisconsin
- Eau Claire
- La Crosse
- Oshkosh
- Platteville
- River Falls
- Stevens Point
- Stout
- Whitewater

University of Wisconsin Center
- Baraboo/Sauk County
- Barron County
- Manitowoc County
- Marinette County
- Marshfield/Wood County
- Rock County
- Sheboygan County
- Washington County
- Waukesha

Viterbo College
Waukesha County Technical College
Western Wisconsin Technical College
Wisconsin Indianhead Technical College
Wisconsin Lutheran College

Wyoming

Casper College
Central Wyoming College
Eastern Wyoming College
Laramie County Community College
Sheridan College
Western Wyoming Community College

Switzerland

American College of Switzerland

Colleges with special admissions programs

Candidates Reply Date Agreement

Alabama
Birmingham-Southern College
Faulkner University
Judson College
Marion Military Institute
Samford University
Southeastern Bible College
Spring Hill College
Tuskegee University

Alaska
University of Alaska Fairbanks

Arizona
University of Arizona

Arkansas
Arkansas College
Hendrix College
Williams Baptist College

California
Biola University
California College of Arts and Crafts
California Institute of Technology
California Lutheran University
California Maritime Academy
California State University
- Bakersfield
- Stanislaus

Claremont McKenna College
Cogswell Polytechnical College
College of Notre Dame
Cypress College
Fresno City College
Harvey Mudd College
Holy Names College
Loyola Marymount University
Menlo College
Mills College
Mount St. Mary's College
New College of California
Occidental College
Otis School of Art and Design
Pepperdine University
Pitzer College
Point Loma Nazarene College
Pomona College
St. Mary's College of California
San Francisco Art Institute
San Francisco Conservatory of Music
Santa Clara University
Scripps College
Southern California College
Southern California Institute of Architecture
Stanford University
United States International University
University of California
- Berkeley
- Davis
- Los Angeles
- Riverside
- Santa Barbara
- Santa Cruz

University of Judaism
University of La Verne
University of the Pacific
University of Redlands
University of San Diego
University of San Francisco
University of Southern California
Westmont College
Whittier College
Woodbury University

Colorado
Colorado College
Colorado School of Mines
Fort Lewis College
Regis University
United States Air Force Academy
University of Colorado at Boulder
University of Denver

Connecticut
Albertus Magnus College
Central Connecticut State University
Connecticut College
Eastern Connecticut State University
Fairfield University
Quinnipiac College
Sacred Heart University
St. Joseph College
Trinity College
United States Coast Guard Academy
University of Connecticut
University of Hartford
University of New Haven
Wesleyan University
Yale University

Delaware
Goldey-Beacom College
University of Delaware

District of Columbia
American University
Catholic University of America
Corcoran School of Art
George Washington University
Georgetown University
Mount Vernon College
Southeastern University
Trinity College

Florida
Barry University
Eckerd College
Florida Atlantic University
Florida Institute of Technology
Florida Southern College
Hobe Sound Bible College
Jacksonville University
New College of the University of South Florida
Nova University
Palm Beach Atlantic College
Ringling School of Art and Design
Rollins College
St. Thomas University
Stetson University
University of Miami
University of North Florida
University of Tampa
Webber College

Georgia
Agnes Scott College
Andrew College
Augusta College
Brenau University
Brewton-Parker College
Covenant College
East Georgia College
Emory University
Georgia College
Georgia Institute of Technology
Mercer University
Oglethorpe University
Oxford College of Emory University
Paine College
Piedmont College
Reinhardt College
South Georgia College
Spelman College
Thomas College
Truett-McConnell College
University of Georgia
Wesleyan College
Young Harris College

Idaho
Lewis Clark State College
University of Idaho

Illinois
Augustana College
Aurora University
Barat College
Bradley University
College of St. Francis
Concordia University
De Paul University
Elmhurst College
Greenville College
Illinois Benedictine College
Illinois Institute of Technology
Illinois Wesleyan University
Knox College
Lake Forest College
Loyola University of Chicago
MacMurray College
Monmouth College
National-Louis University
North Central College
Northwestern University
Roosevelt University
Rosary College
School of the Art Institute of Chicago
Shimer College
Trinity Christian College
Trinity College
University of Chicago
Wheaton College

Indiana
Ancilla College
Anderson University
Ball State University
Butler University
DePauw University
Earlham College
Franklin College
Goshen College
Grace College
Hanover College
Huntington College
Indiana University Bloomington
Indiana Vocational Technical College: Southwest
Indiana Wesleyan University
Marian College
Oakland City College
Purdue University
St. Francis College
St. Joseph's College
St. Mary-of-the-Woods College
St. Mary's College
Taylor University
Tri-State University
University of Indianapolis
University of Notre Dame
Valparaiso University
Wabash College

Iowa
Briar Cliff College
Buena Vista College
Central College
Clarke College
Coe College
Cornell College
Grinnell College
Loras College
Luther College
Mount Mercy College
Teikyo Marycrest University
University of Dubuque

Kansas
Benedictine College
Fort Scott Community College
Kansas Newman College
Seward County Community College
Southwestern College

Kentucky
Alice Lloyd College
Asbury College
Bellarmine College
Berea College
Campbellsville College
Centre College
Cumberland College
Georgetown College
Kentucky Wesleyan College
Midway College
Pikeville College
Spalding University
Thomas More College
Transylvania University
Union College
University of Kentucky

Louisiana
Centenary College of Louisiana
Loyola University
Tulane University
Xavier University of Louisiana

Maine
Bates College
Bowdoin College
Colby College
College of the Atlantic
Eastern Maine Technical College
Husson College
Maine College of Art
Maine Maritime Academy
St. Joseph's College
Thomas College
Unity College

University of Maine
- Augusta
- Fort Kent
- Orono
- Presque Isle

University of New England
Westbrook College

Maryland

Capitol College
College of Notre Dame of Maryland
Goucher College
Hood College
Johns Hopkins University
Maryland Institute College of Art
Morgan State University
Mount St. Mary's College
St. John's College
St. Mary's College of Maryland
Salisbury State University
Towson State University
United States Naval Academy
University of Maryland
- Baltimore County
- College Park

Villa Julie College
Washington College
Western Maryland College

Massachusetts

American International College
Amherst College
Anna Maria College for Men and Women
Aquinas College at Newton
Assumption College
Babson College
Bay Path College
Becker College
- Leicester Campus
- Worcester Campus

Bentley College
Boston College
Boston Conservatory
Boston University
Bradford College
Brandeis University
Bridgewater State College
Bristol Community College
Bunker Hill Community College
Cape Cod Community College
Clark University
College of the Holy Cross
Curry College
Eastern Nazarene College
Elms College
Emerson College
Emmanuel College
Endicott College
Fitchburg State College
Forsyth School for Dental Hygienists
Framingham State College
Franklin Institute of Boston
Gordon College
Greenfield Community College
Hampshire College
Harvard and Radcliffe Colleges
Lasell College
Lesley College
Marian Court Junior College
Massachusetts College of Art
Massachusetts College of Pharmacy and Allied Health Sciences
Massachusetts Institute of Technology
Massachusetts Maritime Academy
Merrimack College
Mount Holyoke College
Mount Wachusett Community College
New England Conservatory of Music
Nichols College
North Adams State College
Northeastern University
Northern Essex Community College
Pine Manor College
Quincy College
Quinsigamond Community College
Regis College
Salem State College
School of the Museum of Fine Arts
Simmons College
Smith College
Springfield College
Springfield Technical Community College
Stonehill College
Suffolk University
Tufts University
University of Massachusetts
- Amherst
- Boston
- Dartmouth

Wellesley College
Wentworth Institute of Technology
Western New England College
Westfield State College
Wheaton College
Wheelock College
Williams College
Worcester Polytechnic Institute
Worcester State College

Michigan

Adrian College
Alma College
Aquinas College
Calvin College
Center for Creative Studies: College of Art and Design
Concordia College
Eastern Michigan University
Grand Valley State University
Hillsdale College
Hope College
Kalamazoo College
Lawrence Technological University
Marygrove College
Michigan Christian College
Michigan Technological University
Montcalm Community College
Oakland University
Olivet College
Saginaw Valley State University
University of Detroit Mercy
University of Michigan
- Ann Arbor
- Dearborn
- Flint

West Shore Community College

Minnesota

Augsburg College
Austin Community College
Carleton College
College of Associated Arts
College of St. Catherine: St. Catherine Campus
Concordia College: Moorhead
Concordia College: St. Paul
Gustavus Adolphus College
Macalester College
Mankato State University
Minneapolis College of Art and Design
St. Mary's Campus of the College of St. Catherine
St. Mary's College of Minnesota
St. Olaf College
University of Minnesota
- Crookston
- Morris

University of St. Thomas

Mississippi

Millsaps College

Missouri

Central Methodist College
Conception Seminary College
Deaconess College of Nursing
Drury College
Evangel College
Fontbonne College
Harris Stowe State College
Kansas City Art Institute
Lindenwood College
Missouri Baptist College
Northeast Missouri State University
Northwest Missouri State University
Park College
Research College of Nursing
Rockhurst College
St. Louis College of Pharmacy
St. Louis University
Washington University
Webster University
Westminster College
William Jewell College

Montana

Carroll College
Rocky Mountain College
Western Montana College of the University of Montana

Nebraska

Bellevue College
Concordia College
Creighton University
Dana College
Doane College

Nevada

Deep Springs College
Sierra Nevada College

New Hampshire

Castle College
Colby-Sawyer College
Daniel Webster College
Dartmouth College
Franklin Pierce College
New England College
Notre Dame College
Plymouth State College of the University System of New Hampshire
Rivier College
St. Anselm College
University of New Hampshire
- Durham
- Manchester

New Jersey

Bloomfield College
Caldwell College
Centenary College
College of St. Elizabeth
Drew University
Fairleigh Dickinson University
Georgian Court College
Jersey City State College
Kean College of New Jersey
Monmouth College
Montclair State College
New Jersey Institute of Technology
Princeton University
Ramapo College of New Jersey
Rowan College of New Jersey
Rutgers—The State University of New Jersey
- Camden College of Arts and Sciences
- College of Engineering
- College of Nursing
- College of Pharmacy
- Cook College
- Douglass College
- Livingston College
- Mason Gross School of the Arts
- Newark College of Arts and Sciences
- Rutgers College

St. Peter's College
Seton Hall University
Stevens Institute of Technology
Stockton State College
Trenton State College
Union County College
Upsala College
Westminster Choir College School of Music of Rider College
William Paterson College of New Jersey

New Mexico

College of Santa Fe
Eastern New Mexico University
New Mexico Institute of Mining and Technology
St. John's College

New York

Adelphi University
Adirondack Community College
Alfred University
Bard College
Barnard College
Canisius College
Catholic Medical Center of Brooklyn and Queens School of Nursing
Cayuga County Community College
Clarkson University
Colgate University
College of Mount St. Vincent
College of New Rochelle
College of St. Rose
Columbia University
- Columbia College
- School of Engineering and Applied Science

Concordia College
Cooper Union
Cornell University
Dominican College of Blauvelt
D'Youville College
Elmira College
Eugene Lang College/New School for Social Research
Fashion Institute of Technology
Fordham University
Hamilton College
Hartwick College
Hobart College
Hofstra University
Houghton College
Iona College
Ithaca College
Jamestown Community College
Jewish Theological Seminary of America
Juilliard School
Keuka College
Le Moyne College
Long Island University
- Brooklyn Campus
- C. W. Post Campus
- Southampton Campus

Manhattan College
Manhattan School of Music
Manhattanville College

Maria College
Marist College
Marymount College
Marymount Manhattan College
Molloy College
Mount St. Mary College
Nazareth College of Rochester
New York University
Niagara University
Ohr Somayach Tanenbaum Education Center
Onondaga Community College
Pace University
- College of White Plains
- New York
- Pleasantville/Briarcliff

Parsons School of Design
Paul Smith's College
Polytechnic University
- Brooklyn
- Long Island Campus

Pratt Institute
Rensselaer Polytechnic Institute
Roberts Wesleyan College
Rochester Institute of Technology
Russell Sage College
Sage Junior College of Albany
St. Bonaventure University
St. John Fisher College
St. Joseph's College
- Brooklyn
- Suffolk Campus

St. Lawrence University
St. Thomas Aquinas College
Sarah Lawrence College
School of Visual Arts
Siena College
Skidmore College
State University of New York
- Albany
- Binghamton
- Buffalo
- Purchase
- College at Brockport
- College at Buffalo
- College at Cortland
- College of Environmental Science and Forestry
- College at Fredonia
- College at Geneseo
- College at New Paltz
- College at Plattsburgh
- College at Potsdam
- College of Technology at Farmingdale
- Health Science Center at Syracuse
- Maritime College
- Oswego

Suffolk County Community College
Syracuse University
Touro College
Union College
United States Merchant Marine Academy
University of Rochester
Utica College of Syracuse University
Vassar College
Villa Maria College of Buffalo
Wadhams Hall Seminary-College
Wagner College
Wells College
William Smith College
Yeshiva University

North Carolina

Barton College
Belmont Abbey College
Brevard College
Chowan College
Davidson College
Duke University
East Carolina University
Elon College
Greensboro College
Guilford College
Lenoir-Rhyne College
Louisburg College
Mars Hill College
Meredith College
Montreat-Anderson College
Nash Community College
North Carolina Agricultural and Technical State University
North Carolina State University
North Carolina Wesleyan College
Pfeiffer College
Queens College
St. Andrews Presbyterian College
Salem College
University of North Carolina
- Asheville
- Chapel Hill
- Greensboro

Wake Forest University
Warren Wilson College
Wingate College

North Dakota

Minot State University
University of Mary

Ohio

Antioch College
Ashland University
Baldwin-Wallace College
Bluffton College
Capital University
Case Western Reserve University
Cedarville College
Clark State Community College
Cleveland Institute of Art
Cleveland Institute of Music
College of Mount St. Joseph
College of Wooster
Defiance College
Denison University
Heidelberg College
Hiram College
John Carroll University
Kenyon College
Lourdes College
Malone College
Marietta College
Miami University
- Hamilton Campus
- Oxford Campus

Mount Union College
Muskingum College
Oberlin College
Ohio State University
- Agricultural Technical Institute
- Columbus Campus
- Lima Campus
- Mansfield Campus
- Marion Campus
- Newark Campus

Ohio University
Ohio Wesleyan University
Otterbein College
Pontifical College Josephinum
University of Cincinnati
University of Dayton
University of Findlay
Urbana University
Ursuline College
Walsh University
Wilmington College
Xavier University

Oklahoma

St. Gregory's College
Southeastern Oklahoma State University
University of Tulsa

Oregon

Central Oregon Community College
Clatsop Community College
George Fox College
Lane Community College
Lewis and Clark College
Linfield College
Oregon State University
Pacific Northwest College of Art
Pacific University
Portland State University
Reed College
Willamette University

Pennsylvania

Albright College
Allegheny College
Allentown College of St. Francis de Sales
Alvernia College
Beaver College
Bryn Mawr College
Bucknell University
Butler County Community College
Cabrini College
Carnegie Mellon University
Cedar Crest College
Chatham College
Chestnut Hill College
Clarion University of Pennsylvania
Dickinson College
Duquesne University
Elizabethtown College
Franklin and Marshall College
Gannon University
Gettysburg College
Haverford College
Immaculata College
Juniata College
King's College
Kutztown University of Pennsylvania
La Salle University
Lafayette College
Lebanon Valley College of Pennsylvania
Lehigh University
Lycoming College
Marywood College
Mercyhurst College
Messiah College
Moore College of Art and Design
Moravian College
Muhlenberg College
Neumann College
Point Park College
Robert Morris College
Rosemont College
St. Francis College
St. Joseph's University
St. Vincent College
Seton Hill College
Slippery Rock University of Pennsylvania
Susquehanna University
Swarthmore College
University of the Arts
University of Pennsylvania
University of Pittsburgh
- Bradford
- Greensburg
- Johnstown
- Pittsburgh
- Titusville

University of Scranton
Ursinus College
Valley Forge Christian College
Valley Forge Military College
Villanova University
Washington and Jefferson College
Westminster College
Widener University
Wilkes University
Wilson College

Rhode Island

Brown University
Bryant College
Providence College
Rhode Island College
Rhode Island School of Design
Roger Williams University
Salve Regina University
University of Rhode Island

South Carolina

Aiken Technical College
Anderson College
Clemson University
College of Charleston
Columbia College
Columbia Junior College of Business
Converse College
Erskine College
Furman University
Newberry College
North Greenville College
Presbyterian College
Tri-County Technical College
University of South Carolina
- Columbia
- Spartanburg

Winthrop University
Wofford College

South Dakota

Black Hills State University
Northern State University

Tennessee

Christian Brothers University
Lambuth University
Maryville College
Memphis College of Art
Rhodes College
Tennessee State University
University of the South
Vanderbilt University
William Jennings Bryan College

Texas

Austin College
Baylor University
Central Texas College
Cooke County College
Eastfield College
Frank Phillips College
LeTourneau University
Our Lady of the Lake University of San Antonio
Rice University
St. Edward's University
St. Mary's University
Schreiner College
Southern Methodist University
Southwest Texas State University
Southwestern Christian College
Southwestern University
Stephen F. Austin State University
Texas Christian University
Texas Lutheran College
Texas Wesleyan University
Trinity University
University of Dallas
University of Mary Hardin-Baylor
University of Texas at Austin

Utah

Utah State University
Westminster College of Salt Lake City

Vermont

Bennington College
Castleton State College
Champlain College
College of St. Joseph in Vermont
Goddard College
Green Mountain College

Johnson State College
Lyndon State College
Marlboro College
Middlebury College
Norwich University
St. Michael's College
Sterling College
Trinity College of Vermont
University of Vermont
Vermont Technical College

Virginia
Averett College
Christopher Newport University
College of William and Mary
Emory and Henry College
George Mason University
Hampden-Sydney College
Hollins College
James Madison University
Longwood College
Mary Baldwin College
Mary Washington College
Marymount University
Old Dominion University
Randolph-Macon College
Randolph-Macon Woman's College
Richard Bland College
Roanoke College
St. Paul's College
Shenandoah University
Southern Virginia College for Women
Sweet Briar College
University of Richmond
University of Virginia
Virginia Commonwealth University
Virginia Intermont College
Virginia Military Institute
Virginia Polytechnic Institute and State University
Virginia State University
Virginia Wesleyan College
Washington and Lee University

Washington
Central Washington University
Cornish College of the Arts
Eastern Washington University
Evergreen State College
Gonzaga University
Lutheran Bible Institute of Seattle
Pacific Lutheran University
St. Martin's College
Seattle Pacific University
Seattle University
Shoreline Community College
University of Puget Sound
University of Washington
Washington State University
Western Washington University
Whitman College
Whitworth College

West Virginia
Appalachian Bible College
Bethany College
Davis and Elkins College
Shepherd College
University of Charleston
West Virginia State College
Wheeling Jesuit College

Wisconsin
Alverno College
Beloit College
Cardinal Stritch College
Carthage College
Concordia University Wisconsin
Lawrence University
Marian College of Fond du Lac
Marquette University
Milwaukee Institute of Art & Design
Mount Mary College
Mount Senario College
Northland College
Ripon College
St. Norbert College
University of Wisconsin
Eau Claire
Green Bay
Madison
Platteville
Whitewater
University of Wisconsin Center
Fox Valley
Marathon County

Switzerland
Franklin College: Switzerland

Early Decision Plan Agreement

Alabama
Alabama Agricultural and Mechanical University *F*
Southeastern Bible College *F*
Talladega College *F*

California
Academy of Art College *F*
Brooks College *F*
California Institute of Technology *F*
California Lutheran University *F*
California State University
Fresno *S*
Stanislaus *F*
Chabot College *F*
Chapman University *F*
Claremont McKenna College *F*
Golden Gate University *F*
Harvey Mudd College *F*
Loyola Marymount University *F*
Menlo College *F*
Occidental College *F*
Otis School of Art and Design *S*
Point Loma Nazarene College *F*
Pomona College *F*
Samuel Merritt College *F*
Scripps College *F*
United States International University *S*
Whittier College *F*

Colorado
Colorado Technical College *F*

Connecticut
Connecticut College *F*
Fairfield University *F*
Sacred Heart University *F*
St. Joseph College *S*
Teikyo-Post University *F*
Wesleyan University *F*

Delaware
Wilmington College *F*

District of Columbia
American University *F*
George Washington University *F*
Mount Vernon College *F*
Trinity College *S*

Florida
Barry University *F*
Rollins College *F*
St. Thomas University *F*
Stetson University *F*
University of Florida *S*
University of Miami *F*

Georgia
Agnes Scott College *S*
Andrew College *F*
Armstrong State College *S*
Emory University *F*
Oglethorpe University *F*
Paine College *F*
Reinhardt College *F*
Spelman College *F*
Toccoa Falls College *F*
Wesleyan College *S*

Illinois
Lake Forest College *F*
Monmouth College *F*
Northwestern University *F*
Parks College of St. Louis University *S*
St. Xavier University *S*
Western Illinois University *S*

Indiana
Anderson University *F*
Earlham College *F*
Franklin College *F*
Grace College *F*
Oakland City College *F*
St. Mary's College *F*
Valparaiso University *F*

Iowa
Coe College *S*
Cornell College *F*
Grinnell College *F*
Morningside College *S*
William Penn College *F*

Kansas
Fort Scott Community College *F*
Kansas Newman College *F*

Kentucky
Asbury College *S*
Centre College *F*
Pikeville College *F*
Transylvania University *F*

Maine
Bates College *F*
Bowdoin College *F*
Colby College *F*
Husson College *F*
University of Maine
Augusta *S*
Fort Kent *F*
Presque Isle *F*
University of New England *F*

Maryland
Bowie State University *S*
Goucher College *F*
Johns Hopkins University *F*
Maryland Institute College of Art *F*
St. Mary's College of Maryland *F*
Washington College *F*
Western Maryland College *F*

Massachusetts
American International College *F*
Amherst College *F*
Assumption College *F*
Bay Path College *S*
Boston Conservatory *F*
Boston University *F*
Brandeis University *F*
Clark University *F*
College of the Holy Cross *F*
Curry College *F*
Emmanuel College *F*
Gordon College *F*
Hampshire College *F*
Lesley College *F*
Massachusetts College of Art *F*
Massachusetts College of Pharmacy and Allied Health Sciences *F*
Massachusetts Maritime Academy *F*
Merrimack College *F*
Mount Holyoke College *F*
Nichols College *F*
Northern Essex Community College *F*
Pine Manor College *F*
Simmons College *F*
Smith College *F*
Springfield College *F*
Tufts University *F*
University of Massachusetts at Dartmouth *F*
Wellesley College *S*
Wheelock College *F*
Williams College *F*
Worcester Polytechnic Institute *F*

Michigan
Alma College *F*
Olivet College *F*

Minnesota
Augsburg College *F*
Carleton College *F*
Gustavus Adolphus College *F*
Macalester College *S*
St. Olaf College *S*
University of Minnesota: Morris *S*

Mississippi
Jackson State University *F*
Rust College *S*

Missouri
Conception Seminary College *F*
Drury College *F*
Lindenwood College *F*
Maryville University *F*
Missouri Southern State College *F*
Washington University *F*

Montana
Carroll College *F*

Nebraska
Bellevue College *F*

New Hampshire
Dartmouth College *F*
Notre Dame College *F*
St. Anselm College *F*

New Jersey
Bloomfield College *F*
College of St. Elizabeth *F*
Drew University *F*
Fairleigh Dickinson University
Edward Williams College *F*
Madison *F*
Georgian Court College *F*
St. Peter's College *F*
Stevens Institute of Technology *S*
Trenton State College *S*
Union County College *F*
Upsala College *F*
Westminster Choir College School of Music of Rider College *F*

New York
Alfred University *F*
Bard College *F*
Barnard College *F*
Clarkson University *F*
Colgate University *F*
College of Insurance *S*
College of Mount St. Vincent *S*
College of New Rochelle *F*

Note: F—first-choice plan; S—single-choice plan

Columbia University
Columbia College *F*
School of Engineering and Applied Science *F*
Cooper Union *F*
Cornell University *F*
Dominican College of Blauvelt *F*
Eugene Lang College/New School for Social Research *F*
Fordham University *S*
Hamilton College *F*
Hartwick College *F*
Hobart College *F*
Hofstra University *S*
Iona College *F*
Ithaca College *F*
Jewish Theological Seminary of America *F*
Le Moyne College *F*
Long Island University: Brooklyn Campus *S*
Manhattan College *S*
Manhattanville College *F*
Molloy College *F*
Mount St. Mary College *F*
New York University *F*
Ohr Somayach Tanenbaum Education Center *F*
Pace University
College of White Plains *F*
New York *F*
Pleasantville/Briarcliff *F*
Polytechnic University
Brooklyn *F*
Long Island Campus *F*
Pratt Institute *F*
Rensselaer Polytechnic Institute *F*
Rochester Institute of Technology *F*
Russell Sage College *F*
St. John Fisher College *S*
St. Lawrence University *F*
Sarah Lawrence College *S*
Skidmore College *F*
State University of New York
Albany *F*
Binghamton *F*
College at Brockport *F*
College at Buffalo *F*
College at Cortland *F*
College of Environmental Science and Forestry *F*
College at Geneseo *F*
Maritime College *F*
Syracuse University *F*
Union College *F*
University of Rochester *F*
Utica College of Syracuse University *F*
Vassar College *F*
Wagner College *F*
Webb Institute of Naval Architecture *F*
Wells College *F*
Westchester Business Institute *F*
William Smith College *F*

North Carolina

Belmont Abbey College *S*
Davidson College *S*
Duke University *F*
Elon College *F*
Gardner-Webb University *F*
Greensboro College *F*
Lenoir-Rhyne College *F*
Meredith College *S*
University of North Carolina at Greensboro *S*
Wake Forest University *S*

Ohio

Case Western Reserve University *F*
Cleveland Institute of Art *F*
College of Wooster *F*
Denison University *F*
Heidelberg College *S*
Kenyon College *F*
Marietta College *F*
Miami University: Oxford Campus *F*
Oberlin College *F*
Pontifical College Josephinum *S*
University of Toledo *F*
Urbana University *F*
Walsh University *F*

Oklahoma

Northeastern State University *F*
Oral Roberts University *F*
St. Gregory's College *F*
Southeastern Oklahoma State University *F*

Oregon

Oregon State University *F*
Reed College *F*
Willamette University *S*

Pennsylvania

Albright College *F*
Allegheny College *F*
Beaver College *F*
Bryn Mawr College *F*
Bucknell University *F*
California University of Pennsylvania *F*
Carlow College *F*
Carnegie Mellon University *F*
Chatham College *F*
Cheyney University of Pennsylvania *S*
Dickinson College *F*
Drexel University *F*
Duquesne University *F*
Franklin and Marshall College *F*
Gettysburg College *F*
Grove City College *F*
Haverford College *F*
Indiana University of Pennsylvania *F*
Juniata College *F*
King's College *F*
Lafayette College *F*
Lincoln University *F*
Montgomery County Community College *F*
Moore College of Art and Design *F*
Moravian College *F*
Muhlenberg College *F*
Susquehanna University *F*
Swarthmore College *F*
University of Pennsylvania *F*
University of Pittsburgh at Bradford *F*
Ursinus College *F*
Valley Forge Christian College *F*
Washington and Jefferson College *F*

Rhode Island

Bryant College *F*
Salve Regina University *S*

South Carolina

Columbia Junior College of Business *F*
North Greenville College *F*

South Dakota

Mount Marty College *F*
Northern State University *F*
Presentation College *F*

Tennessee

Rhodes College *F*
University of the South *F*
Vanderbilt University *F*

Texas

Central Texas College *F*
Cooke County College *F*
Frank Phillips College *F*
Our Lady of the Lake University of San Antonio *F*
Paul Quinn College *F*
Rice University *S*
Southwestern Christian College *F*
Southwestern University *F*
Trinity University *S*
University of Mary Hardin-Baylor *F*

Utah

Westminster College of Salt Lake City *F*

Vermont

Bennington College *F*
Green Mountain College *F*
Marlboro College *S*
Middlebury College *F*
Norwich University *F*
University of Vermont *F*

Virginia

Christopher Newport University *F*
College of William and Mary *F*
Hampden-Sydney College *F*
Hollins College *F*
Mary Baldwin College *F*
Mary Washington College *F*
Randolph-Macon College *F*
Randolph-Macon Woman's College *F*
Roanoke College *F*
Shenandoah University *F*
Sweet Briar College *S*
University of Richmond *F*
University of Virginia *F*
Virginia Commonwealth University *F*
Virginia Wesleyan College *F*
Washington and Lee University *S*

Washington

Pacific Lutheran University *F*
Seattle Pacific University *F*
Seattle University *F*
University of Puget Sound *F*
Whitman College *F*
Whitworth College *F*

West Virginia

University of Charleston *F*

Wisconsin

Beloit College *F*
Northland College *F*
Ripon College *F*

Wyoming

Eastern Wyoming College *F*
Northwest College *F*

Switzerland

Franklin College: Switzerland *F*

Colleges that offer NCAA sports

Baseball — Division I

Alabama

Alabama State University *M*
Auburn University *M*
Samford University *M*
University of Alabama
Birmingham *M*
Tuscaloosa *M*
University of South Alabama *M*

Arizona

Arizona State University *M*
Grand Canyon University *M*
University of Arizona *M*

Arkansas

Arkansas State University *M*
University of Arkansas *M*
University of Arkansas at Little Rock *M*

California

California State University
Fresno *M*
Fullerton *M*
Long Beach *M*
Northridge *M*
Sacramento *M*
Chapman University *M*
Loyola Marymount University *M*
Pepperdine University *M*
St. Mary's College of California *M*
San Diego State University *M*
San Jose State University *M*
Santa Clara University *M*
Stanford University *M*
University of California
Berkeley *M*
Irvine *M*
Los Angeles *M*
Santa Barbara *M*
University of the Pacific *M*
University of San Diego *M*
University of San Francisco *M*
University of Southern California *M*

Colorado

United States Air Force Academy *M*

Connecticut

Central Connecticut State University *M*
Fairfield University *M*
University of Connecticut *M*
University of Hartford *M*
Yale University *M*

Delaware

Delaware State College *M*
University of Delaware *M*

District of Columbia

George Washington University *M*
Georgetown University *M*
Howard University *M*

Florida

Bethune-Cookman College *M*
Florida Agricultural and Mechanical University *M*
Florida International University *M*
Florida State University *M*
Jacksonville University *M*
Stetson University *M*
University of Central Florida *M*
University of Florida *M*
University of Miami *M*
University of South Florida *M*

Georgia

Augusta College *M*
Georgia Institute of Technology *M*
Georgia Southern University *M*
Georgia State University *M*
Mercer University *M*
University of Georgia *M*

Hawaii

University of Hawaii
Hilo *M*
Manoa *M*

Illinois

Bradley University *M*
Chicago State University *M*
Eastern Illinois University *M*
Illinois State University *M*
Northeastern Illinois University *M*
Northern Illinois University *M*
Northwestern University *M*
Southern Illinois University at Carbondale *M*
University of Illinois
Chicago *M*
Urbana-Champaign *M*
Western Illinois University *M*

Indiana

Ball State University *M*
Butler University *M*
Indiana State University *M*
Indiana University Bloomington *M*
Purdue University *M*
University of Evansville *M*
University of Notre Dame *M*
Valparaiso University *M*

Iowa

Iowa State University *M*
University of Iowa *M*
University of Northern Iowa *M*

Kansas

Kansas State University *M*
University of Kansas *M*
Wichita State University *M*

Kentucky

Eastern Kentucky University *M*
Morehead State University *M*
Murray State University *M*
University of Kentucky *M*
University of Louisville *M*
Western Kentucky University *M*

Louisiana

Centenary College of Louisiana *M*
Grambling State University *M*
Louisiana Tech University *M*
McNeese State University *M*
Nicholls State University *M*
Northeast Louisiana University *M*
Northwestern State University *M*
Southeastern Louisiana University *M*
Southern University and Agricultural and Mechanical College *M*
Tulane University *M*
University of New Orleans *M*
University of Southwestern Louisiana *M*

Maine

University of Maine *M*

Maryland

Coppin State College *M*
Mount St. Mary's College *M*
Towson State University *M*
United States Naval Academy *M*
University of Maryland
Baltimore County *M*
College Park *M*
Eastern Shore *M*

Massachusetts

Boston College *M*
Boston University *M*
College of the Holy Cross *M*
Harvard and Radcliffe Colleges *M*
Northeastern University *M*
University of Massachusetts at Amherst *M*

Michigan

Central Michigan University *M*
Eastern Michigan University *M*
Michigan State University *M*
University of Detroit Mercy *M*
University of Michigan *M*
Western Michigan University *M*

Minnesota

University of Minnesota: Twin Cities *M*

Mississippi

Alcorn State University *M*
Jackson State University *M*
Mississippi State University *M*
Mississippi Valley State University *M*
University of Mississippi *M*
University of Southern Mississippi *M*

Missouri

St. Louis University *M*
Southeast Missouri State University *M*
Southwest Missouri State University *M*
University of Missouri: Columbia *M*

Nebraska

Creighton University *M*
University of Nebraska—Lincoln *M*

Nevada

University of Nevada
Las Vegas *M*
Reno *M*

New Hampshire

Dartmouth College *M*
University of New Hampshire *M*

New Jersey

Fairleigh Dickinson University: Edward Williams College *M*
Monmouth College *M*
Princeton University *M*
Rider College *M*
Rutgers—The State University of New Jersey
College of Engineering *M*
Cook College *M*
Livingston College *M*
Mason Gross School of the Arts *M*
Rutgers College *M*
St. Peter's College *M*
Seton Hall University *M*

New Mexico

New Mexico State University *M*
University of New Mexico *M*

New York

Canisius College *M*
Colgate University *M*
Columbia University: Columbia College *M*
Cornell University *M*
Fordham University *M*
Hofstra University *M*
Iona College *M*
Le Moyne College *M*
Long Island University
Brooklyn Campus *M*
C. W. Post Campus *M*
Manhattan College *M*
Marist College *M*
New York Institute of Technology *M*
Niagara University *M*
Pace University
College of White Plains *M*
New York *M*
Pleasantville/Briarcliff *M*
St. Bonaventure University *M*
St. Francis College *M*
St. John's University *M*
Siena College *M*
United States Military Academy *M*
Wagner College *M*

North Carolina

Appalachian State University *M*
Campbell University *M*
Davidson College *M*
Duke University *M*
East Carolina University *M*
North Carolina Agricultural and Technical State University *M*
North Carolina State University *M*
University of North Carolina
Asheville *M*
Chapel Hill *M*
Charlotte *M*
Greensboro *M*
Wilmington *M*
Wake Forest University *M*
Western Carolina University *M*

Ohio

Bowling Green State University *M*
Cleveland State University *M*
Kent State University *M*
Miami University: Oxford Campus *M*

Ohio State University: Columbus Campus *M*
Ohio University *M*
University of Akron *M*
University of Cincinnati *M*
University of Dayton *M*
University of Toledo *M*
Wright State University *M*
Xavier University *M*
Youngstown State University *M*

Oklahoma

Oklahoma State University *M*
University of Oklahoma *M*

Oregon

Oregon State University *M*
Portland State University *M*
University of Portland *M*

Pennsylvania

Bucknell University *M*
Drexel University *M*
Duquesne University *M*
La Salle University *M*
Lafayette College *M*
Lehigh University *M*
Penn State University Park Campus *M*
St. Joseph's University *M*
Temple University *M*
University of Pennsylvania *M*
University of Pittsburgh *M*
Villanova University *M*
West Chester University of Pennsylvania *M*

Rhode Island

Brown University *M*
Providence College *M*
University of Rhode Island *M*

South Carolina

Charleston Southern University *M*
The Citadel *M*
Clemson University *M*
College of Charleston *M*
Furman University *M*
South Carolina State University *M*
University of South Carolina
  Coastal Carolina College *M*
  Columbia *M*
Winthrop University *M*

Tennessee

Austin Peay State University *M*
East Tennessee State University *M*
Memphis State University *M*
Middle Tennessee State University *M*
Tennessee State University *M*
Tennessee Technological University *M*
University of Tennessee
  Knoxville *M*
  Martin *M*
Vanderbilt University *M*

Texas

Baylor University *M*
Lamar University—Beaumont *M*
Prairie View A&M University *M*
Rice University *M*
Sam Houston State University *M*
Southwest Texas State University *M*
Stephen F. Austin State University *M*
Texas A&M University *M*
Texas Christian University *M*
Texas Southern University *M*
Texas Tech University *M*
University of Houston *M*
University of Texas
  Arlington *M*
  Austin *M*
  Pan American *M*
  San Antonio *M*

Utah

Brigham Young University *M*
Southern Utah University *M*
University of Utah *M*

Vermont

University of Vermont *M*

Virginia

College of William and Mary *M*
George Mason University *M*
James Madison University *M*
Liberty University *M*
Old Dominion University *M*
Radford University *M*
University of Richmond *M*
University of Virginia *M*
Virginia Commonwealth University *M*
Virginia Military Institute *M*
Virginia Polytechnic Institute and State University *M*

Washington

Gonzaga University *M*
University of Washington *M*
Washington State University *M*

West Virginia

Marshall University *M*
West Virginia University *M*

Wisconsin

University of Wisconsin: Madison *M*

Wyoming

University of Wyoming *M*

Baseball — Division II

Alabama

Alabama Agricultural and Mechanical University *M*
Jacksonville State University *M*
Livingston University *M*
Miles College *M*
Troy State University *M*
Tuskegee University *M*
University of North Alabama *M*

Arkansas

Henderson State University *M*
University of Central Arkansas *M*

California

California Polytechnic State University: San Luis Obispo *M*
California State Polytechnic University: Pomona *M*
California State University
  Chico *M*
  Dominguez Hills *M*
  Hayward *M*
  Los Angeles *M*
  San Bernardino *M*
  Stanislaus *M*
San Francisco State University *M*
Sonoma State University *M*
University of California
  Davis *M*
  Riverside *M*

Colorado

Colorado School of Mines *M*
Mesa State College *M*
Metropolitan State College of Denver *M*
Regis University *M*
University of Denver *M*
University of Northern Colorado *M*

Connecticut

Quinnipiac College *M*
Sacred Heart University *M*
Southern Connecticut State University *M*
University of Bridgeport *M*
University of New Haven *M*

Florida

Barry University *M*
Eckerd College *M*
Florida Atlantic University *M*
Florida Institute of Technology *M*
Florida Southern College *M*
Rollins College *M*
St. Leo College *M*
University of North Florida *M*
University of Tampa *M*

Georgia

Albany State College *M*
Armstrong State College *M*
Columbus College *M*
Georgia College *M*
Kennesaw State College *M*
Paine College *M*
Savannah State College *M*
Valdosta State College *M*
West Georgia College *M*

Illinois

College of St. Francis *M*
Lewis University *M*
Quincy University *M*
Southern Illinois University at Edwardsville *M*

Indiana

Indiana University—Purdue University at Fort Wayne *M*
Oakland City College *M*
St. Joseph's College *M*
University of Indianapolis *M*
University of Southern Indiana *M*

Iowa

Morningside College *M*

Kansas

Emporia State University *M*
Fort Hays State University *M*
Pittsburg State University *M*
Washburn University of Topeka *M*

Kentucky

Bellarmine College *M*
Kentucky State University *M*
Kentucky Wesleyan College *M*
Northern Kentucky University *M*

Maryland

Bowie State University *M*

Massachusetts

American International College *M*
Assumption College *M*
Bentley College *M*
Merrimack College *M*
Springfield College *M*
Stonehill College *M*
University of Massachusetts at Lowell *M*

Michigan

Ferris State University *M*
Grand Valley State University *M*
Hillsdale College *M*
Northwood University *M*
Oakland University *M*
Saginaw Valley State University *M*
Wayne State University *M*

Minnesota

Bemidji State University *M*
Mankato State University *M*
St. Cloud State University *M*
University of Minnesota: Duluth *M*
Winona State University *M*

Mississippi

Delta State University *M*
Mississippi College *M*

Missouri

Central Missouri State University *M*
Lincoln University *M*
Missouri Southern State College *M*
Missouri Western State College *M*
Northeast Missouri State University *M*
Northwest Missouri State University *M*
Southwest Baptist University *M*
University of Missouri
  Rolla *M*
  St. Louis *M*

Nebraska

University of Nebraska
  Kearney *M*
  Omaha *M*
Wayne State College *M*

New Hampshire

Franklin Pierce College *M*
Keene State College *M*
New Hampshire College *M*
St. Anselm College *M*

New Mexico

Eastern New Mexico University *M*
New Mexico Highlands University *M*

New York

Adelphi University *M*
City University of New York: Queens College *M*
College of St. Rose *M*
Concordia College *M*
Dowling College *M*
Mercy College *M*
Molloy College *M*

North Carolina

Catawba College *M*
Elizabeth City State University *M*
Elon College *M*
Gardner-Webb University *M*
High Point University *M*
Lenoir-Rhyne College *M*
Mars Hill College *M*
Mount Olive College *M*
Pembroke State University *M*
Pfeiffer College *M*
St. Augustine's College *M*
Shaw University *M*
Wingate College *M*

North Dakota

North Dakota State University *M*
University of North Dakota *M*

Ohio

Ashland University *M*

Oklahoma

Cameron University *M*

University of Central Oklahoma *M*

Pennsylvania

Bloomsburg University of Pennsylvania *M*
California University of Pennsylvania *M*
Clarion University of Pennsylvania *M*
East Stroudsburg University of Pennsylvania *M*
Edinboro University of Pennsylvania *M*
Gannon University *M*
Indiana University of Pennsylvania *M*
Kutztown University of Pennsylvania *M*
Lock Haven University of Pennsylvania *M*
Mansfield University of Pennsylvania *M*
Mercyhurst College *M*
Millersville University of Pennsylvania *M*
Philadelphia College of Textiles and Science *M*
Shippensburg University of Pennsylvania *M*
Slippery Rock University of Pennsylvania *M*
University of Pittsburgh at Johnstown *M*

Rhode Island

Bryant College *M*

South Carolina

Erskine College *M*
Francis Marion University *M*
Limestone College *M*
Newberry College *M*
Presbyterian College *M*
University of South Carolina
Aiken *M*
Spartanburg *M*
Wofford College *M*

South Dakota

Augustana College *M*
South Dakota State University *M*
University of South Dakota *M*

Tennessee

Carson-Newman College *M*
LeMoyne-Owen College *M*
Lincoln Memorial University *M*

Texas

Abilene Christian University *M*
Hardin-Simmons University *M*
Texas A&I University *M*

Vermont

St. Michael's College *M*

Virginia

Longwood College *M*
Norfolk State University *M*
St. Paul's College *M*
Virginia State University *M*

West Virginia

Alderson-Broaddus College *M*
Davis and Elkins College *M*
Shepherd College *M*
University of Charleston *M*
West Liberty State College *M*
West Virginia Wesleyan College *M*

Wisconsin

University of Wisconsin: Parkside *M*

Baseball — Division III

Alabama

Stillman College *M*

Arkansas

Hendrix College *M*

California

California Institute of Technology *M*
California Lutheran University *M*
Claremont McKenna College *M*
Harvey Mudd College *M*
Menlo College *M*
Occidental College *M*
Pomona College *M*
University of California: San Diego *M*
University of La Verne *M*
University of Redlands *M*
Whittier College *M*

Colorado

Colorado College *M*

Connecticut

Albertus Magnus College *M*
Eastern Connecticut State University *M*
Trinity College *M*
United States Coast Guard Academy *M*
Wesleyan University *M*
Western Connecticut State University *M*

Delaware

Wesley College *M*

District of Columbia

Catholic University of America *M*
Gallaudet University *M*

Georgia

Emory University *M*
Oglethorpe University *M*
Savannah College of Art and Design *M*

Illinois

Augustana College *M*
Aurora University *M*
Blackburn College *M*
Concordia University *M*
Elmhurst College *M*
Eureka College *M*
Illinois Benedictine College *M*
Illinois College *M*
Illinois Wesleyan University *M*
Knox College *M*
MacMurray College *M*
Millikin University *M*
Monmouth College *M*
North Central College *M*
North Park College *M*
Parks College of St. Louis University *M*
Principia College *M*
Rockford College *M*
University of Chicago *M*
Wheaton College *M*

Indiana

Anderson University *M*
DePauw University *M*
Earlham College *M*
Franklin College *M*
Hanover College *M*
Manchester College *M*
Rose-Hulman Institute of Technology *M*
Wabash College *M*

Iowa

Buena Vista College *M*
Central College *M*
Coe College *M*
Cornell College *M*
Grinnell College *M*
Loras College *M*
Luther College *M*
Simpson College *M*
University of Dubuque *M*
Upper Iowa University *M*
Wartburg College *M*
William Penn College *M*

Kentucky

Centre College *M*
Thomas More College *M*

Maine

Bates College *M*
Bowdoin College *M*
Colby College *M*
St. Joseph's College *M*
University of Southern Maine *M*

Maryland

Frostburg State University *M*
Johns Hopkins University *M*
St. Mary's College of Maryland *M*
Salisbury State University *M*
Washington College *M*
Western Maryland College *M*

Massachusetts

Amherst College *M*
Anna Maria College for Men and Women *M*
Babson College *M*
Brandeis University *M*
Bridgewater State College *M*
Clark University *M*
Curry College *M*
Eastern Nazarene College *M*
Emerson College *M*
Fitchburg State College *M*
Framingham State College *M*
Gordon College *M*
Massachusetts Institute of Technology *M*
Massachusetts Maritime Academy *M*
Nichols College *M*
North Adams State College *M*
Salem State College *M*
Suffolk University *M*
Tufts University *M*
University of Massachusetts
Boston *M*
Dartmouth *M*
Wentworth Institute of Technology *M*
Western New England College *M*
Westfield State College *M*
Williams College *M*
Worcester Polytechnic Institute *M*
Worcester State College *M*

Michigan

Adrian College *M*
Albion College *M*
Alma College *M*
Calvin College *M*
Hope College *M*
Kalamazoo College *M*
Olivet College *M*

Minnesota

Augsburg College *M*
Carleton College *M*
College of St. Scholastica *M*
Concordia College: Moorhead *M*
Gustavus Adolphus College *M*
Hamline University *M*
Macalester College *M*
St. John's University *M*
St. Mary's College of Minnesota *M*
St. Olaf College *M*
University of St. Thomas *M*

Mississippi

Millsaps College *M*
Rust College *M*

Missouri

Maryville University *M*
Washington University *M*
Webster University *M*
Westminster College *M*

Nebraska

Nebraska Wesleyan University *M*

New Hampshire

Daniel Webster College *M*
New England College *M*
Plymouth State College of the University System of New Hampshire *M*

New Jersey

Drew University *M*
Fairleigh Dickinson University *M*
Jersey City State College *M*
Kean College of New Jersey *M*
Montclair State College *M*
New Jersey Institute of Technology *M*
Ramapo College of New Jersey *M*
Rowan College of New Jersey *M*
Rutgers—The State University of New Jersey
Camden College of Arts and Sciences *M*
Newark College of Arts and Sciences *M*
Stevens Institute of Technology *M*
Trenton State College *M*
Upsala College *M*
William Paterson College of New Jersey *M*

New York

City University of New York
Baruch College *M*
City College *M*
College of Staten Island *M*
Hunter College *M*
John Jay College of Criminal Justice *M*
Lehman College *M*
York College *M*
Clarkson University *M*
Hamilton College *M*
Hartwick College *M*
Hilbert College *M*
Hobart College *M*
Ithaca College *M*
Manhattanville College *M*
Mount St. Mary College *M*
New York University *M*
Polytechnic University *M*
Rensselaer Polytechnic Institute *M*
Rochester Institute of Technology *M*
St. John Fisher College *M*
St. Lawrence University *M*
Skidmore College *M*

State University of New York
Albany *M*
Binghamton *M*
Stony Brook *M*
College at Brockport *M*
College at Cortland *M*
College at Fredonia *M*
College at New Paltz *M*
College at Old Westbury *M*
College at Oneonta *M*
Institute of Technology at Utica/Rome *M*
Maritime College *M*
Oswego *M*
Union College *M*
United States Merchant Marine Academy *M*
University of Rochester *M*
Utica College of Syracuse University *M*
Vassar College *M*

North Carolina
Greensboro College *M*
Guilford College *M*
Methodist College *M*
North Carolina Wesleyan College *M*

Ohio
Baldwin-Wallace College *M*
Bluffton College *M*
Capital University *M*
Case Western Reserve University *M*
College of Wooster *M*
Defiance College *M*
Denison University *M*
Heidelberg College *M*
Hiram College *M*
John Carroll University *M*
Kenyon College *M*
Marietta College *M*
Mount Union College *M*
Muskingum College *M*
Oberlin College *M*
Ohio Northern University *M*
Ohio Wesleyan University *M*
Otterbein College *M*
Wilmington College *M*
Wittenberg University *M*

Pennsylvania
Albright College *M*
Allegheny College *M*
Allentown College of St. Francis de Sales *M*
College Misericordia *M*
Delaware Valley College *M*
Dickinson College *M*
Elizabethtown College *M*
Franklin and Marshall College *M*
Gettysburg College *M*
Grove City College *M*
Haverford College *M*
Juniata College *M*
King's College *M*
Lebanon Valley College of Pennsylvania *M*
Lincoln University *M*
Messiah College *M*
Moravian College *M*
Muhlenberg College *M*
Penn State Erie Behrend College *M*
Susquehanna University *M*
Swarthmore College *M*
Thiel College *M*
University of Scranton *M*
Ursinus College *M*
Washington and Jefferson College *M*
Waynesburg College *M*
Widener University *M*
Wilkes University *M*
York College of Pennsylvania *M*

Rhode Island
Rhode Island College *M*
Roger Williams University *M*
Salve Regina University *M*

Tennessee
Fisk University *M*
Lane College *M*
Maryville College *M*
Rhodes College *M*
University of the South *M*

Texas
Southwestern University *M*
Trinity University *M*

Vermont
Johnson State College *M*
Middlebury College *M*
Norwich University *M*

Virginia
Bridgewater College *M*
Christopher Newport University *M*
Eastern Mennonite College *M*
Emory and Henry College *M*
Ferrum College *M*
Hampden-Sydney College *M*
Lynchburg College *M*
Mary Washington College *M*
Randolph-Macon College *M*
Shenandoah University *M*
Virginia Wesleyan College *M*
Washington and Lee University *M*

West Virginia
Bethany College *M*

Wisconsin
Beloit College *M*
Carroll College *M*
Carthage College *M*
Lawrence University *M*
Northwestern College *M*
Ripon College *M*
St. Norbert College *M*
University of Wisconsin
Eau Claire *M*
La Crosse *M*
Oshkosh *M*
Platteville *M*
River Falls *M*
Stevens Point *M*
Stout *M*
Superior *M*
Whitewater *M*

Basketball — Division I

Alabama
Alabama State University *M, W*
Auburn University *M, W*
Samford University *M*
University of Alabama
Birmingham *M, W*
Tuscaloosa *M, W*
University of South Alabama *M, W*

Arizona
Arizona State University *M, W*
Northern Arizona University *M, W*
University of Arizona *M, W*

Arkansas
Arkansas State University *M, W*
University of Arkansas *M, W*
University of Arkansas at Little Rock *M*

California
California State University
Fresno *M, W*
Fullerton *M, W*
Long Beach *M, W*
Northridge *M, W*
Sacramento *M, W*
Loyola Marymount University *M, W*
Pepperdine University *M, W*
St. Mary's College of California *M, W*
San Diego State University *M, W*
San Jose State University *M, W*
Santa Clara University *M, W*
Stanford University *M, W*
University of California
Berkeley *M, W*
Irvine *M, W*
Los Angeles *M, W*
Santa Barbara *M, W*
University of the Pacific *M, W*
University of San Diego *M, W*
University of San Francisco *M, W*
University of Southern California *M, W*

Colorado
Colorado State University *M, W*
United States Air Force Academy *M*
University of Colorado at Boulder *M, W*

Connecticut
Central Connecticut State University *M, W*
Fairfield University *M, W*
University of Connecticut *M, W*
University of Hartford *M, W*
Yale University *M, W*

Delaware
Delaware State College *M, W*
University of Delaware *M, W*

District of Columbia
American University *M, W*
George Washington University *M, W*
Georgetown University *M, W*
Howard University *M, W*

Florida
Bethune-Cookman College *M, W*
Florida Agricultural and Mechanical University *M, W*
Florida International University *M, W*
Florida State University *M, W*
Jacksonville University *M*
Stetson University *M, W*
University of Central Florida *M, W*
University of Florida *M, W*
University of Miami *M, W*
University of South Florida *M, W*

Georgia
Georgia Institute of Technology *M, W*
Georgia Southern University *M, W*
Georgia State University *M, W*
Mercer University *M, W*
University of Georgia *M, W*

Hawaii
University of Hawaii at Manoa *M, W*

Idaho
Boise State University *M, W*
Idaho State University *M, W*
University of Idaho *M, W*

Illinois
Bradley University *M, W*
Chicago State University *M, W*
De Paul University *M, W*
Eastern Illinois University *M, W*
Illinois State University *M, W*
Loyola University of Chicago *M, W*
Northeastern Illinois University *M, W*
Northern Illinois University *M, W*
Northwestern University *M, W*
Southern Illinois University at Carbondale *M, W*
University of Illinois
Chicago *M, W*
Urbana-Champaign *M, W*
Western Illinois University *M, W*

Indiana
Ball State University *M, W*
Butler University *M, W*
Indiana State University *M, W*
Indiana University Bloomington *M, W*
Purdue University *M, W*
University of Evansville *M, W*
University of Notre Dame *M, W*
Valparaiso University *M, W*

Iowa
Drake University *M, W*
Iowa State University *M, W*
University of Iowa *M, W*
University of Northern Iowa *M, W*

Kansas
Kansas State University *M, W*
University of Kansas *M, W*
Wichita State University *M, W*

Kentucky
Eastern Kentucky University *M, W*
Morehead State University *M, W*
Murray State University *M, W*
University of Kentucky *M, W*
University of Louisville *M, W*
Western Kentucky University *M, W*

Louisiana
Centenary College of Louisiana *M*
Grambling State University *M, W*
Louisiana State University and Agricultural and Mechanical College *M, W*
Louisiana Tech University *M, W*
McNeese State University *M, W*
Nicholls State University *M, W*
Northeast Louisiana University *M, W*
Northwestern State University *M, W*
Southeastern Louisiana University *M, W*
Southern University and Agricultural and Mechanical College *M, W*
Tulane University *M, W*
University of New Orleans *M, W*
University of Southwestern Louisiana *M, W*

Maine
University of Maine *M, W*

Maryland
Coppin State College *M, W*

Loyola College in Maryland *M, W*
Morgan State University *M, W*
Mount St. Mary's College *M, W*
Towson State University *M, W*
United States Naval Academy *M, W*
University of Maryland
Baltimore County *M, W*
College Park *M, W*
Eastern Shore *M, W*

Massachusetts

Boston College *M, W*
Boston University *M, W*
College of the Holy Cross *M, W*
Harvard and Radcliffe Colleges *M, W*
Northeastern University *M, W*
University of Massachusetts at Amherst *M, W*

Michigan

Central Michigan University *M, W*
Eastern Michigan University *M, W*
Michigan State University *M, W*
University of Detroit Mercy *M, W*
University of Michigan *M, W*
Western Michigan University *M, W*

Minnesota

University of Minnesota: Twin Cities *M, W*

Mississippi

Alcorn State University *M, W*
Jackson State University *M, W*
Mississippi State University *M, W*
Mississippi Valley State University *M, W*
University of Mississippi *M, W*
University of Southern Mississippi *M, W*

Missouri

St. Louis University *M, W*
Southeast Missouri State University *M, W*
Southwest Missouri State University *M, W*
University of Missouri
Columbia *M, W*
Kansas City *M, W*

Montana

Montana State University *M, W*
University of Montana *M, W*

Nebraska

Creighton University *M, W*
University of Nebraska—Lincoln *M, W*

Nevada

University of Nevada
Las Vegas *M, W*
Reno *M, W*

New Hampshire

Dartmouth College *M, W*
University of New Hampshire *M, W*

New Jersey

Fairleigh Dickinson University: Edward Williams College *M, W*
Monmouth College *M, W*
Princeton University *M, W*
Rider College *M, W*
Rutgers—The State University of New Jersey
College of Engineering *M, W*
Cook College *M, W*
Douglass College *W*
Livingston College *M, W*
Mason Gross School of the Arts *M, W*
Rutgers College *M, W*
St. Peter's College *M, W*
Seton Hall University *M, W*

New Mexico

New Mexico State University *M, W*
University of New Mexico *M, W*

New York

Barnard College *W*
Canisius College *M, W*
Colgate University *M, W*
Columbia University: Columbia College *M, W*
Cornell University *M, W*
Fordham University *M, W*
Hofstra University *M, W*
Iona College *M, W*
Long Island University: Brooklyn Campus *M, W*
Manhattan College *M, W*
Marist College *M, W*
Niagara University *M, W*
St. Bonaventure University *M, W*
St. Francis College *M, W*
St. John's University *M, W*
Siena College *M, W*
State University of New York at Buffalo *M, W*
Syracuse University *M, W*
United States Military Academy *M, W*
Wagner College *M, W*

North Carolina

Appalachian State University *M, W*
Campbell University *M, W*
Davidson College *M, W*
Duke University *M, W*
East Carolina University *M, W*
North Carolina Agricultural and Technical State University *M, W*
North Carolina State University *M, W*
University of North Carolina
Asheville *M, W*
Chapel Hill *M, W*
Charlotte *M, W*
Greensboro *M, W*
Wilmington *M, W*
Wake Forest University *M, W*
Western Carolina University *M, W*

Ohio

Bowling Green State University *M, W*
Cleveland State University *M, W*
Kent State University *M, W*
Miami University: Oxford Campus *M, W*
Ohio State University: Columbus Campus *M, W*
Ohio University *M, W*
University of Akron *M, W*
University of Cincinnati *M, W*
University of Dayton *M, W*
University of Toledo *M, W*
Wright State University *M, W*
Xavier University *M, W*
Youngstown State University *M, W*

Oklahoma

Oklahoma State University *M, W*
University of Oklahoma *M, W*
University of Tulsa *M*

Oregon

Oregon State University *M, W*
University of Oregon *M, W*
University of Portland *M, W*

Pennsylvania

Bucknell University *M, W*
Drexel University *M, W*
Duquesne University *M, W*
La Salle University *M, W*
Lafayette College *M, W*
Lehigh University *M, W*
Penn State University Park Campus *M, W*
Robert Morris College *M, W*
St. Francis College *M, W*
St. Joseph's University *M, W*
Temple University *M, W*
University of Pennsylvania *M, W*
University of Pittsburgh *M, W*
Villanova University *M, W*

Rhode Island

Brown University *M, W*
Providence College *M, W*
University of Rhode Island *M, W*

South Carolina

Charleston Southern University *M, W*
The Citadel *M*
Clemson University *M, W*
College of Charleston *M, W*
Furman University *M, W*
South Carolina State University *M, W*
University of South Carolina
Coastal Carolina College *M, W*
Columbia *M, W*
Winthrop University *M, W*

Tennessee

Austin Peay State University *M, W*
East Tennessee State University *M, W*
Memphis State University *M, W*
Middle Tennessee State University *M, W*
Tennessee State University *M, W*
Tennessee Technological University *M, W*
University of Tennessee
Chattanooga *M, W*
Knoxville *M, W*
Martin *M, W*
Vanderbilt University *M, W*

Texas

Baylor University *M, W*
Lamar University—Beaumont *M, W*
Prairie View A&M University *M, W*
Rice University *M, W*
Sam Houston State University *M, W*
Southern Methodist University *M, W*
Southwest Texas State University *M, W*
Stephen F. Austin State University *M, W*
Texas A&M University *M, W*
Texas Christian University *M, W*
Texas Southern University *M, W*
Texas Tech University *M, W*
University of Houston *M, W*
University of North Texas *M, W*
University of Texas
Arlington *M, W*
Austin *M, W*
El Paso *M, W*
Pan American *M, W*
San Antonio *M, W*

Utah

Brigham Young University *M, W*
Southern Utah University *M, W*
University of Utah *M, W*
Utah State University *M*
Weber State University *M, W*

Vermont

University of Vermont *M, W*

Virginia

College of William and Mary *M, W*
George Mason University *M, W*
James Madison University *M, W*
Liberty University *M, W*
Old Dominion University *M, W*
Radford University *M, W*
University of Richmond *M, W*
University of Virginia *M, W*
Virginia Commonwealth University *M, W*
Virginia Military Institute *M*
Virginia Polytechnic Institute and State University *M, W*

Washington

Eastern Washington University *M, W*
Gonzaga University *M, W*
University of Washington *M, W*
Washington State University *M, W*

West Virginia

Marshall University *M, W*
West Virginia University *M, W*

Wisconsin

Marquette University *M, W*
University of Wisconsin
Green Bay *M, W*
Madison *M, W*

Wyoming

University of Wyoming *M, W*

Basketball — Division II

Alabama

Alabama Agricultural and Mechanical University *M, W*
Jacksonville State University *M, W*
Livingston University *M, W*
Miles College *M, W*
Troy State University *M, W*
Tuskegee University *M, W*
University of Alabama in Huntsville *M, W*
University of North Alabama *M, W*

Alaska

University of Alaska
Anchorage *M, W*
Fairbanks *M, W*

Arizona

Grand Canyon University *M, W*

Arkansas

Henderson State University *M, W*
University of Central Arkansas *M, W*

California
California Polytechnic State University: San Luis Obispo *M, W*
California State Polytechnic University: Pomona *M, W*
California State University
Bakersfield *M*
Chico *M, W*
Dominguez Hills *M, W*
Hayward *M, W*
Los Angeles *M, W*
San Bernardino *M, W*
Stanislaus *M, W*
Chapman University *M, W*
College of Notre Dame *M, W*
Humboldt State University *M, W*
San Francisco State University *M, W*
Sonoma State University *M, W*
University of California
Davis *M, W*
Riverside *M, W*

Colorado
Adams State College *M, W*
Colorado Christian University *M, W*
Colorado School of Mines *M, W*
Fort Lewis College *M, W*
Mesa State College *M, W*
Metropolitan State College of Denver *M, W*
Regis University *M, W*
United States Air Force Academy *W*
University of Colorado at Colorado Springs *M, W*
University of Denver *M, W*
University of Northern Colorado *M, W*
University of Southern Colorado *M, W*
Western State College of Colorado *M, W*

Connecticut
Quinnipiac College *M, W*
Sacred Heart University *M, W*
Southern Connecticut State University *M, W*
University of Bridgeport *M, W*
University of New Haven *M, W*

District of Columbia
University of the District of Columbia *M, W*

Florida
Barry University *M, W*
Eckerd College *M, W*
Florida Atlantic University *M, W*
Florida Institute of Technology *M, W*
Florida Southern College *M, W*
Rollins College *M, W*
St. Leo College *M, W*
University of North Florida *M, W*
University of Tampa *M, W*

Georgia
Albany State College *M, W*
Armstrong State College *M, W*
Augusta College *M, W*
Clark Atlanta University *M, W*
Columbus College *M, W*
Fort Valley State College *M, W*
Georgia College *M, W*
Kennesaw State College *W*
Morehouse College *M*
Morris Brown College *M, W*
Paine College *M, W*
Savannah State College *M, W*
Valdosta State College *M, W*
West Georgia College *M, W*

Illinois
College of St. Francis *M, W*
Lewis University *M, W*
Quincy University *M, W*
Southern Illinois University at Edwardsville *M, W*

Indiana
Indiana University—Purdue University at Fort Wayne *M, W*
Oakland City College *M, W*
St. Joseph's College *M, W*
University of Indianapolis *M, W*
University of Southern Indiana *M, W*

Iowa
Morningside College *M, W*

Kansas
Emporia State University *M, W*
Fort Hays State University *M, W*
Pittsburg State University *M, W*
Washburn University of Topeka *M, W*

Kentucky
Bellarmine College *M, W*
Kentucky State University *M, W*
Kentucky Wesleyan College *M, W*
Northern Kentucky University *M, W*

Maryland
Bowie State University *M, W*

Massachusetts
American International College *M, W*
Assumption College *M, W*
Bentley College *M, W*
Merrimack College *M, W*
Springfield College *M, W*
Stonehill College *M, W*
University of Massachusetts at Lowell *M, W*

Michigan
Ferris State University *M, W*
Grand Valley State University *M, W*
Hillsdale College *M, W*
Lake Superior State University *M, W*
Michigan Technological University *M, W*
Northern Michigan University *M, W*
Northwood University *M, W*
Oakland University *M, W*
Saginaw Valley State University *M, W*
Wayne State University *M, W*

Minnesota
Bemidji State University *M, W*
Mankato State University *M, W*
Moorhead State University *W*
St. Cloud State University *M, W*
University of Minnesota: Duluth *M, W*
Winona State University *M, W*

Mississippi
Delta State University *M, W*
Mississippi College *M, W*
Mississippi University for Women *W*

Missouri
Central Missouri State University *M, W*
Drury College *M*
Lincoln University *M, W*
Missouri Southern State College *M, W*
Missouri Western State College *M, W*
Northeast Missouri State University *M, W*
Northwest Missouri State University *M, W*
Southwest Baptist University *M, W*
University of Missouri
Rolla *M, W*
St. Louis *M, W*

Montana
Eastern Montana College *M, W*

Nebraska
Chadron State College *M, W*
University of Nebraska
Kearney *M, W*
Omaha *M, W*
Wayne State College *M, W*

New Hampshire
Franklin Pierce College *M, W*
Keene State College *M, W*
New Hampshire College *M, W*
St. Anselm College *M, W*

New Mexico
Eastern New Mexico University *M, W*
New Mexico Highlands University *M, W*

New York
Adelphi University *M, W*
City University of New York: Queens College *M, W*
College of St. Rose *M, W*
Concordia College *M, W*
Dowling College *M, W*
Le Moyne College *M, W*
Long Island University
C. W. Post Campus *M, W*
Southampton Campus *M, W*
Mercy College *M, W*
Molloy College *M, W*
New York Institute of Technology *M*
Pace University
College of White Plains *M, W*
New York *M, W*
Pleasantville/Briarcliff *M, W*

North Carolina
Catawba College *M, W*
Elizabeth City State University *M, W*
Elon College *M, W*
Fayetteville State University *M, W*
Gardner-Webb University *M, W*
High Point University *W*
Johnson C. Smith University *M, W*
Lenoir-Rhyne College *M, W*
Livingstone College *W*
Mars Hill College *M, W*
Mount Olive College *W*
North Carolina Central University *M, W*
Pembroke State University *M, W*
Pfeiffer College *M, W*
Queens College *M, W*
St. Augustine's College *M, W*
Shaw University *M, W*
Wingate College *M, W*
Winston-Salem State University *M, W*

North Dakota
North Dakota State University *M, W*
University of North Dakota *M, W*

Ohio
Ashland University *M, W*

Oklahoma
Cameron University *M, W*
University of Central Oklahoma *M, W*

Oregon
Portland State University *W*

Pennsylvania
Bloomsburg University of Pennsylvania *M, W*
California University of Pennsylvania *M, W*
Cheyney University of Pennsylvania *M, W*
Clarion University of Pennsylvania *M, W*
East Stroudsburg University of Pennsylvania *M, W*
Edinboro University of Pennsylvania *M, W*
Gannon University *M, W*
Indiana University of Pennsylvania *M, W*
Kutztown University of Pennsylvania *M, W*
Lock Haven University of Pennsylvania *M, W*
Mansfield University of Pennsylvania *M, W*
Mercyhurst College *M, W*
Millersville University of Pennsylvania *M, W*
Philadelphia College of Textiles and Science *M, W*
Shippensburg University of Pennsylvania *M, W*
Slippery Rock University of Pennsylvania *M, W*
University of Pittsburgh at Johnstown *M, W*
West Chester University of Pennsylvania *M, W*

Rhode Island
Bryant College *M, W*

South Carolina
Erskine College *M, W*
Francis Marion University *M, W*
Lander University *M, W*
Limestone College *M, W*
Newberry College *M, W*
Presbyterian College *M, W*
University of South Carolina
Aiken *M, W*
Spartanburg *M, W*
Wofford College *M, W*

South Dakota
Augustana College *M, W*
South Dakota State University *M, W*
University of South Dakota *M, W*

Tennessee
Carson-Newman College *M, W*
LeMoyne-Owen College *M, W*
Lincoln Memorial University *M, W*

Texas
Abilene Christian University *M, W*
Angelo State University *M, W*
East Texas State University *M, W*
Hardin-Simmons University *M, W*

Texas A&I University *M, W*
Texas Woman's University *W*
West Texas A & M University *M, W*

Vermont

St. Michael's College *M, W*

Virginia

Hampton University *M, W*
Longwood College *M, W*
Norfolk State University *M, W*
St. Paul's College *M, W*
Virginia State University *M, W*
Virginia Union University *M, W*

Washington

Seattle Pacific University *M, W*

West Virginia

Alderson-Broaddus College *W*
Davis and Elkins College *M, W*
Shepherd College *M, W*
West Liberty State College *M, W*
West Virginia Wesleyan College *W*
Wheeling Jesuit College *M, W*

Wisconsin

University of Wisconsin: Parkside *M, W*

Basketball — Division III

Alabama

Stillman College *M, W*

Arkansas

Hendrix College *M, W*

California

California Institute of Technology *M*
California Lutheran University *M, W*
Claremont McKenna College *M, W*
Harvey Mudd College *M, W*
Menlo College *M*
Mills College *W*
Occidental College *M, W*
Pitzer College *M, W*
Pomona College *M, W*
Scripps College *W*
University of California
San Diego *M, W*
Santa Cruz *M, W*
University of La Verne *M, W*
University of Redlands *M, W*
Whittier College *M, W*

Colorado

Colorado College *M, W*

Connecticut

Albertus Magnus College *M, W*
Connecticut College *M, W*
Eastern Connecticut State University *M, W*
Trinity College *M, W*
United States Coast Guard Academy *M, W*
Wesleyan University *M, W*
Western Connecticut State University *M, W*

Delaware

Wesley College *M, W*

District of Columbia

Catholic University of America *M, W*
Gallaudet University *M, W*

Georgia

Emory University *M, W*
Oglethorpe University *M, W*
Savannah College of Art and Design *M, W*

Illinois

Augustana College *M, W*
Aurora University *M, W*
Blackburn College *M, W*
Concordia University *M, W*
Elmhurst College *M, W*
Eureka College *M, W*
Illinois Benedictine College *M, W*
Illinois College *M, W*
Illinois Wesleyan University *M, W*
Knox College *M, W*
Lake Forest College *M, W*
MacMurray College *M, W*
Millikin University *M, W*
Monmouth College *M, W*
North Central College *M, W*
North Park College *M, W*
Parks College of St. Louis University *M*
Principia College *M, W*
Rockford College *M, W*
University of Chicago *M, W*
Wheaton College *M, W*

Indiana

Anderson University *M, W*
DePauw University *M, W*
Earlham College *M, W*
Franklin College *M, W*
Hanover College *M, W*
Manchester College *M, W*
Rose-Hulman Institute of Technology *M*
St. Mary's College *W*
Wabash College *M*

Iowa

Buena Vista College *M, W*
Central College *M, W*
Coe College *M, W*
Cornell College *M, W*
Grinnell College *M, W*
Loras College *M, W*
Luther College *M, W*
Simpson College *M, W*
University of Dubuque *M, W*
Upper Iowa University *M, W*
Wartburg College *M, W*
William Penn College *M, W*

Kentucky

Asbury College *M, W*
Berea College *M, W*
Centre College *M, W*
Thomas More College *M, W*

Maine

Bates College *M, W*
Bowdoin College *M, W*
Colby College *M, W*
Maine Maritime Academy *M*
St. Joseph's College *M, W*
University of Southern Maine *M, W*

Maryland

College of Notre Dame of Maryland *W*
Frostburg State University *M, W*
Goucher College *M, W*
Johns Hopkins University *M, W*
St. Mary's College of Maryland *M, W*
Salisbury State University *M, W*
Washington College *M, W*
Western Maryland College *M, W*

Massachusetts

Amherst College *M, W*
Anna Maria College for Men and Women *M, W*
Babson College *M, W*
Brandeis University *M, W*
Bridgewater State College *M, W*
Clark University *M, W*
Curry College *M, W*
Eastern Nazarene College *M, W*
Elms College *W*
Emerson College *M, W*
Emmanuel College *W*
Fitchburg State College *M, W*
Framingham State College *M, W*
Gordon College *M, W*
Massachusetts Institute of Technology *M, W*
Mount Holyoke College *W*
Nichols College *M, W*
North Adams State College *M, W*
Pine Manor College *W*
Regis College *W*
Salem State College *M, W*
Simmons College *W*
Smith College *W*
Suffolk University *M, W*
Tufts University *M, W*
University of Massachusetts
Boston *M, W*
Dartmouth *M, W*
Wellesley College *W*
Wentworth Institute of Technology *M, W*
Western New England College *M, W*
Westfield State College *M, W*
Wheaton College *M, W*
Williams College *M, W*
Worcester Polytechnic Institute *M, W*
Worcester State College *M, W*

Michigan

Adrian College *M, W*
Albion College *M, W*
Alma College *M, W*
Calvin College *M, W*
Hope College *M, W*
Kalamazoo College *M, W*
Olivet College *M, W*

Minnesota

Augsburg College *M, W*
Carleton College *M, W*
College of St. Benedict *W*
College of St. Scholastica *M, W*
Concordia College: Moorhead *M, W*
Gustavus Adolphus College *M, W*
Hamline University *M, W*
Macalester College *M, W*
St. John's University *M*
St. Mary's College of Minnesota *M, W*
St. Olaf College *M, W*
University of St. Thomas *M, W*

Mississippi

Millsaps College *M, W*
Rust College *M, W*

Missouri

Fontbonne College *M, W*
Maryville University *M, W*
Washington University *M, W*
Webster University *M, W*
Westminster College *M, W*

Nebraska

Nebraska Wesleyan University *M, W*

New Hampshire

Colby-Sawyer College *M, W*
Daniel Webster College *M*
New England College *M, W*
Plymouth State College of the University System of New Hampshire *M, W*

New Jersey

College of St. Elizabeth *W*
Drew University *M, W*
Fairleigh Dickinson University *M, W*
Jersey City State College *M, W*
Kean College of New Jersey *M, W*
Montclair State College *M, W*
New Jersey Institute of Technology *M, W*
Ramapo College of New Jersey *M, W*
Rowan College of New Jersey *M, W*
Rutgers—The State University of New Jersey
Camden College of Arts and Sciences *M, W*
Newark College of Arts and Sciences *M, W*
Stevens Institute of Technology *M*
Stockton State College *M, W*
Trenton State College *M, W*
Upsala College *M, W*
William Paterson College of New Jersey *M, W*

New York

Alfred University *M, W*
Bard College *M*
City University of New York
Baruch College *M, W*
City College *M, W*
College of Staten Island *M, W*
Hunter College *M, W*
John Jay College of Criminal Justice *M, W*
Lehman College *M*
Medgar Evers College *M, W*
York College *M, W*
Clarkson University *M, W*
College of Mount St. Vincent *M, W*
College of New Rochelle *W*
Elmira College *M, W*
Hamilton College *M, W*
Hartwick College *M, W*
Hilbert College *M, W*
Hobart College *M, W*
Ithaca College *M, W*
Keuka College *M, W*
Manhattanville College *M, W*
Mount St. Mary College *M, W*
Nazareth College of Rochester *M, W*
New York University *M, W*
Polytechnic University
Brooklyn *M*
Long Island Campus *M*
Rensselaer Polytechnic Institute *M, W*
Rochester Institute of Technology *M, W*
Russell Sage College *W*
St. John Fisher College *M, W*
St. Lawrence University *M, W*
Skidmore College *M, W*

State University of New York
- Albany *M, W*
- Binghamton *M, W*
- Stony Brook *M, W*
- College at Brockport *M, W*
- College at Buffalo *M, W*
- College at Cortland *M, W*
- College at Fredonia *M, W*
- College at Geneseo *M, W*
- College at New Paltz *M, W*
- College at Old Westbury *M, W*
- College at Oneonta *M, W*
- College at Plattsburgh *M, W*
- College at Potsdam *M, W*
- Institute of Technology at Utica/Rome *M, W*
- Maritime College *M, W*
- Oswego *M, W*

Union College *M, W*
United States Merchant Marine Academy *M*
University of Rochester *M, W*
Utica College of Syracuse University *M, W*
Vassar College *M, W*
William Smith College *W*
Yeshiva University *M*

North Carolina

Bennett College *W*
Greensboro College *M, W*
Guilford College *M, W*
Meredith College *W*
Methodist College *M, W*
North Carolina Wesleyan College *M, W*

Ohio

Baldwin-Wallace College *M, W*
Bluffton College *M, W*
Capital University *M, W*
Case Western Reserve University *M, W*
College of Wooster *M, W*
Defiance College *M, W*
Denison University *M, W*
Heidelberg College *M, W*
Hiram College *M, W*
John Carroll University *M, W*
Kenyon College *M, W*
Marietta College *M, W*
Mount Union College *M, W*
Muskingum College *M, W*
Oberlin College *M, W*
Ohio Northern University *M, W*
Ohio Wesleyan University *M, W*
Otterbein College *M, W*
Wilmington College *W*
Wittenberg University *M, W*

Pennsylvania

Albright College *M, W*
Allegheny College *M, W*
Allentown College of St. Francis de Sales *M, W*
Bryn Mawr College *W*
Cabrini College *M, W*
Carnegie Mellon University *M, W*
Cedar Crest College *W*
College Misericordia *M, W*
Delaware Valley College *M, W*
Dickinson College *M, W*
Elizabethtown College *M, W*
Franklin and Marshall College *M, W*
Gettysburg College *M, W*
Grove City College *M, W*
Haverford College *M, W*
Immaculata College *W*
Juniata College *M, W*
King's College *M, W*
Lebanon Valley College of Pennsylvania *M, W*
Lincoln University *M, W*
Lycoming College *M, W*
Marywood College *W*
Messiah College *M, W*
Moravian College *M, W*
Muhlenberg College *M, W*
Penn State Erie Behrend College *M, W*
Rosemont College *W*
Susquehanna University *M, W*
Swarthmore College *W*
Thiel College *M, W*
University of Scranton *M, W*
Ursinus College *M, W*
Washington and Jefferson College *M, W*
Waynesburg College *M, W*
Widener University *M, W*
Wilkes University *M, W*
York College of Pennsylvania *M, W*

Puerto Rico

American University of Puerto Rico *M, W*

Rhode Island

Rhode Island College *M, W*
Roger Williams University *M, W*
Salve Regina University *M, W*

Tennessee

Fisk University *M, W*
Lane College *W*
Maryville College *M, W*
Rhodes College *M, W*
University of the South *M, W*

Texas

Jarvis Christian College *M, W*
Southwestern University *M, W*
Trinity University *M, W*
Wiley College *M, W*

Vermont

Castleton State College *M, W*
Johnson State College *M, W*
Middlebury College *M, W*
Norwich University *M, W*

Virginia

Averett College *M, W*
Bridgewater College *M, W*
Christopher Newport University *M, W*
Eastern Mennonite College *M, W*
Emory and Henry College *M, W*
Ferrum College *M, W*
Hampden-Sydney College *M*
Hollins College *W*
Lynchburg College *M, W*
Mary Baldwin College *W*
Mary Washington College *M, W*
Marymount University *M, W*
Randolph-Macon College *M, W*
Randolph-Macon Woman's College *W*
Roanoke College *M, W*
Shenandoah University *M, W*
Virginia Wesleyan College *M, W*
Washington and Lee University *M*

West Virginia

Bethany College *M, W*

Wisconsin

Beloit College *M, W*
Carroll College *M, W*
Carthage College *M, W*
Lawrence University *M, W*
Northwestern College *M*
Ripon College *M, W*
St. Norbert College *M, W*
University of Wisconsin
- Eau Claire *M, W*
- La Crosse *M, W*
- Oshkosh *M, W*
- Platteville *M, W*
- River Falls *M, W*
- Stevens Point *M, W*
- Stout *M, W*
- Superior *M, W*
- Whitewater *M, W*

Cross-country — Division I

Alabama

Alabama State University *M, W*
Auburn University *M, W*
Samford University *M, W*
University of Alabama
- Birmingham *M, W*
- Tuscaloosa *M, W*

University of South Alabama *M, W*

Arizona

Arizona State University *M, W*
Northern Arizona University *M, W*
University of Arizona *M, W*

Arkansas

Arkansas State University *M, W*
University of Arkansas *M, W*
University of Arkansas at Little Rock *M, W*

California

California State University
- Fresno *M, W*
- Fullerton *M, W, Mixed*
- Long Beach *M, W*
- Northridge *M, W*
- Sacramento *M, W*

Loyola Marymount University *M, W*
Pepperdine University *M, W*
St. Mary's College of California *M, W*
San Diego State University *M, W*
Santa Clara University *M, W*
Stanford University *M, W*
University of California
- Berkeley *M, W*
- Irvine *M, W*
- Los Angeles *M, W*
- Santa Barbara *M, W*

University of the Pacific *W*
University of San Diego *M, W*
University of San Francisco *M, W*
University of Southern California *M, W*

Colorado

Colorado State University *M, W*
United States Air Force Academy *M*
University of Colorado at Boulder *M, W*

Connecticut

Central Connecticut State University *M, W*
Fairfield University *M, W*
University of Connecticut *M, W*
University of Hartford *M, W*
Yale University *M, W*

Delaware

Delaware State College *M, W, Mixed*
University of Delaware *M, W*

District of Columbia

American University *M, W*
George Washington University *M, W*
Georgetown University *M, W*
Howard University *M, W*

Florida

Bethune-Cookman College *M, W*
Florida Agricultural and Mechanical University *M, W*
Florida International University *M, W*
Florida State University *M, W*
Jacksonville University *M, W*
Stetson University *M, W*
University of Central Florida *M, W*
University of Florida *M, W*
University of Miami *M, W*
University of South Florida *M, W*

Georgia

Georgia Institute of Technology *M, W*
Georgia Southern University *M, W*
Georgia State University *M, W, Mixed*
Mercer University *M, W*
University of Georgia *M, W*

Hawaii

University of Hawaii at Manoa *W*

Idaho

Boise State University *M, W*
Idaho State University *M, W*
University of Idaho *M, W*

Illinois

Bradley University *M, W*
Chicago State University *M, W*
De Paul University *M, W*
Eastern Illinois University *M, W*
Illinois State University *M, W*
Loyola University of Chicago *M, W*
Northeastern Illinois University *M, W*
Southern Illinois University at Carbondale *M, W*
University of Illinois
- Chicago *M, W*
- Urbana-Champaign *M, W*

Western Illinois University *M, W*

Indiana

Ball State University *M, W*
Butler University *M, W*
Indiana State University *M, W*
Indiana University Bloomington *M, W*
Purdue University *M, W*
University of Evansville *M, W*
University of Notre Dame *M, W*
Valparaiso University *M, W*

Iowa

Drake University *M, W*
Iowa State University *M, W*
University of Iowa *M, W*
University of Northern Iowa *M, W*

Kansas

Kansas State University *M, W*
University of Kansas *M, W*
Wichita State University *M, W*

Kentucky

Eastern Kentucky University *M, W*
Morehead State University *M, W*
Murray State University *M, W*
University of Kentucky *M, W*

University of Louisville *M, W*
Western Kentucky University *M, W*

Louisiana

Centenary College of Louisiana *M, W*
Grambling State University *M, W*
Louisiana State University and Agricultural and Mechanical College *M, W*
Louisiana Tech University *M, W*
McNeese State University *M, W*
Nicholls State University *M, W*
Northeast Louisiana University *M, W*
Northwestern State University *M, W*
Southeastern Louisiana University *M, W*
Southern University and Agricultural and Mechanical College *M, W*
Tulane University *M, W*
University of New Orleans *M, W*
University of Southwestern Louisiana *M, W*

Maine

University of Maine *M, W*

Maryland

Coppin State College *M, W*
Loyola College in Maryland *M, W*
Morgan State University *M, W*
Mount St. Mary's College *M, W*
Towson State University *M, W*
United States Naval Academy *M, W*
University of Maryland
  Baltimore County *M, W*
  College Park *M, W*
  Eastern Shore *M, W, Mixed*

Massachusetts

Boston College *M, W*
Boston University *M, W*
College of the Holy Cross *M, W*
Harvard and Radcliffe Colleges *M, W*
Northeastern University *M, W*
University of Massachusetts at Amherst *M, W*

Michigan

Central Michigan University *M, W*
Eastern Michigan University *M, W*
Michigan State University *M, W*
University of Detroit Mercy *M, W*
University of Michigan *M, W*
Western Michigan University *M, W*

Minnesota

University of Minnesota: Twin Cities *M, W*

Mississippi

Alcorn State University *M, W*
Jackson State University *M, W*
Mississippi State University *M, W*
Mississippi Valley State University *M, W*
University of Mississippi *M, W*
University of Southern Mississippi *M, W*

Missouri

St. Louis University *M, W*
Southeast Missouri State University *M, W, Mixed*
Southwest Missouri State University *M, W*
University of Missouri
  Columbia *M, W*
  Kansas City *M, W*

Montana

Montana State University *M, W*
University of Montana *M, W*

Nebraska

Creighton University *M, W*
University of Nebraska—Lincoln *M, W*

Nevada

University of Nevada
  Las Vegas *W*
  Reno *M, W*

New Hampshire

Dartmouth College *M, W*
University of New Hampshire *M, W*

New Jersey

Fairleigh Dickinson University
  Edward Williams College *M, W*
  Madison *M, W, Mixed*
Monmouth College *M, W*
Princeton University *M, W*
Rider College *M*
Rutgers—The State University of New Jersey
  College of Engineering *M, W*
  Cook College *M, W*
  Douglass College *W*
  Livingston College *M, W*
  Mason Gross School of the Arts *M, W*
  Rutgers College *M, W*
St. Peter's College *M, W*
Seton Hall University *M, W, Mixed*

New Mexico

New Mexico State University *M, W*
University of New Mexico *M, W*

New York

Barnard College *W*
Canisius College *M, W*
Colgate University *M, W*
Columbia University: Columbia College *M, W*
Cornell University *M, W*
Fordham University *M, W*
Hofstra University *M, W*
Iona College *M, W*
Long Island University: Brooklyn Campus *M, W*
Manhattan College *M, W*
Marist College *M, W*
Niagara University *M, W*
St. Bonaventure University *M, W, Mixed*
St. Francis College *M, W*
St. John's University *M, W*
Siena College *M, W*
State University of New York at Buffalo *M, W*
Syracuse University *M, W*
United States Military Academy *M, W*
Wagner College *M, W*

North Carolina

Appalachian State University *M, W*
Campbell University *M, W*
Davidson College *M, W*
Duke University *M, W*
East Carolina University *M, W*
North Carolina Agricultural and Technical State University *M, W*
North Carolina State University *M, W*
University of North Carolina
  Asheville *M, W*
  Chapel Hill *M, W*
  Charlotte *M, W*
  Greensboro *M, W*
  Wilmington *M, W*
Wake Forest University *M, W*
Western Carolina University *M, W*

Ohio

Bowling Green State University *M, W*
Cleveland State University *M, W*
Kent State University *M, W*
Miami University: Oxford Campus *M, W*
Ohio State University: Columbus Campus *M, W*
Ohio University *M, W*
University of Akron *M, W*
University of Cincinnati *M, W*
University of Dayton *M, W, Mixed*
University of Toledo *M, W*
Wright State University *M, W*
Xavier University *M, W*
Youngstown State University *M, W*

Oklahoma

Oklahoma State University *M, W*
Oral Roberts University *M, W*
University of Oklahoma *M, W*
University of Tulsa *M, W*

Oregon

University of Oregon *M, W*
University of Portland *M, W*

Pennsylvania

Bucknell University *M, W*
Drexel University *M*
Duquesne University *M, W*
La Salle University *M, W, Mixed*
Lafayette College *M, W, Mixed*
Lehigh University *M, W*
Penn State University Park Campus *M, W*
Robert Morris College *M, W*
St. Francis College *M, W*
St. Joseph's University *M, W*
University of Pennsylvania *M, W*
University of Pittsburgh *M, W*
Villanova University *M, W*

Rhode Island

Brown University *M, W*
Providence College *M, W*
University of Rhode Island *M, W*

South Carolina

Charleston Southern University *M, W*
The Citadel *M*
Clemson University *M, W*
College of Charleston *M, W*
Furman University *M, W*
South Carolina State University *M, W*
University of South Carolina
  Coastal Carolina College *M, W*
  Columbia *M, W*
Winthrop University *M, W*

Tennessee

Austin Peay State University *M, W*
East Tennessee State University *M, W*
Memphis State University *M, W*
Middle Tennessee State University *M, W*
Tennessee State University *M, W*
Tennessee Technological University *M, W*
University of Tennessee
  Chattanooga *M, W*
  Knoxville *M, W*
  Martin *M, W*
Vanderbilt University *M, W*

Texas

Baylor University *M, W*
Lamar University—Beaumont *M, W*
Prairie View A&M University *M, W*
Rice University *M, W*
Sam Houston State University *M, W*
Southern Methodist University *M, W*
Southwest Texas State University *M, W*
Stephen F. Austin State University *M, W*
Texas A&M University *M, W*
Texas Christian University *M, W*
Texas Southern University *M, W*
Texas Tech University *M, W*
University of Houston *M, W*
University of North Texas *M, W*
University of Texas
  Arlington *M, W*
  Austin *M, W*
  El Paso *M, W*
  Pan American *M, W*
  San Antonio *M, W*

Utah

Brigham Young University *M, W*
Southern Utah University *M, W*
University of Utah *M, W*
Utah State University *M, W*
Weber State University *M, W*

Vermont

University of Vermont *M, W*

Virginia

College of William and Mary *M, W*
George Mason University *M, W*
James Madison University *M, W*
Liberty University *M, W*
Old Dominion University *M, W*
Radford University *M, W*
University of Richmond *M, W*
University of Virginia *M, W*
Virginia Commonwealth University *M, W, Mixed*
Virginia Military Institute *M*
Virginia Polytechnic Institute and State University *M, W*

Washington

Eastern Washington University *M, W*
Gonzaga University *M, W*
University of Washington *M, W*
Washington State University *M, W*

West Virginia

Marshall University *M, W*
West Virginia University *M, W*

Wisconsin

Marquette University *M, W*
University of Wisconsin
  Green Bay *M, W*
  Madison *M, W*

Wyoming

University of Wyoming *M, W*

Cross-country — Division II

Alabama

Alabama Agricultural and Mechanical University *M, W*
Miles College *M, W*
Troy State University *M, W*
Tuskegee University *M, W*
University of Alabama in Huntsville *M, W*
University of North Alabama *M, W*

Alaska

University of Alaska
Anchorage *M*
Fairbanks *M, W*

Arizona

Grand Canyon University *M, W*

Arkansas

Henderson State University *M, W*
University of Central Arkansas *W*

California

California Polytechnic State University: San Luis Obispo *M, W*
California State Polytechnic University: Pomona *M, W*
California State University
Bakersfield *M, W*
Chico *M, W*
Los Angeles *M, W*
Stanislaus *M, W*
Chapman University *M*
College of Notre Dame *M, W*
Humboldt State University *M, W*
San Francisco State University *M, W*
University of California
Davis *M, W*
Riverside *M, W*

Colorado

Adams State College *M, W*
Colorado School of Mines *M, W, Mixed*
Fort Lewis College *M, W*
Mesa State College *W*
United States Air Force Academy *W*
University of Southern Colorado *M, W*
Western State College of Colorado *M, W*

Connecticut

Quinnipiac College *M, W*
Sacred Heart University *M, W*
Southern Connecticut State University *M, W*
University of Bridgeport *M*
University of New Haven *M*

District of Columbia

University of the District of Columbia *M, W*

Florida

Barry University *M, W*
Eckerd College *M, W*
Florida Atlantic University *M, W*
Florida Institute of Technology *M, W, Mixed*
Florida Southern College *M, W, Mixed*
Rollins College *M, W*
St. Leo College *M, W*
University of North Florida *M, W*
University of Tampa *M, W*

Georgia

Albany State College *M, W*
Armstrong State College *M, W*
Augusta College *M, W*
Columbus College *M, W*
Georgia College *M, W*
Kennesaw State College *M, W*
Morehouse College *M*
Morris Brown College *M, W*
Paine College *M, W*
Savannah State College *W*
Valdosta State College *M, W*
West Georgia College *M, W*

Hawaii

University of Hawaii at Hilo *M*

Illinois

Lewis University *M, W*
Southern Illinois University at Edwardsville *M, W*

Indiana

Indiana University—Purdue University at Fort Wayne *M, W*
Oakland City College *M, W*
St. Joseph's College *M, W*
University of Indianapolis *M, W*
University of Southern Indiana *M, W*

Iowa

Morningside College *M, W*

Kansas

Emporia State University *M, W*
Fort Hays State University *M, W*
Pittsburg State University *M, W*

Kentucky

Bellarmine College *M, W*
Kentucky State University *M, W*
Northern Kentucky University *M, W*

Maryland

Bowie State University *M, W*

Massachusetts

Assumption College *M, W*
Bentley College *M, W*
Merrimack College *M, W*
Springfield College *M, W*
Stonehill College *M, W*
University of Massachusetts at Lowell *M, W*

Michigan

Ferris State University *M, W*
Grand Valley State University *M, W*
Hillsdale College *M, W*
Lake Superior State University *M, W*
Michigan Technological University *M, W*
Northern Michigan University *M, W*
Northwood University *M, W, Mixed*
Oakland University *M*
Saginaw Valley State University *M, W*
Wayne State University *M*

Minnesota

Mankato State University *M, W*
Moorhead State University *M, W*
St. Cloud State University *M, W*
University of Minnesota: Duluth *M, W*
Winona State University *M, W*

Mississippi

Delta State University *W*
Mississippi College *M, W*

Missouri

Central Missouri State University *M, W*
Missouri Southern State College *M, W, Mixed*
Northeast Missouri State University *M, W*
Northwest Missouri State University *M, W*
Southwest Baptist University *M, W*
University of Missouri: Rolla *M, W*

Montana

Eastern Montana College *M, W, Mixed*

Nebraska

University of Nebraska
Kearney *M, W*
Omaha *W*
Wayne State College *M, W*

New Hampshire

Keene State College *M, W*
St. Anselm College *M, W*

New Jersey

Monmouth College *M*

New Mexico

New Mexico Highlands University *M, W*

New York

City University of New York: Queens College *M, W*
College of St. Rose *M, W*
Concordia College *M, W*
Le Moyne College *M, W*
Long Island University: C. W. Post Campus *M, W*
Mercy College *M, W*
Molloy College *M*
New York Institute of Technology *M, W*
Pace University
College of White Plains *M, W*
New York *M, W*
Pleasantville/Briarcliff *M, W*
State University of New York College at New Paltz *Mixed*

North Carolina

Catawba College *M, W*
Elizabeth City State University *M, W*
Fayetteville State University *M, W*
Gardner-Webb University *M, W*
High Point University *M, W*
Johnson C. Smith University *M, W*
Lenoir-Rhyne College *M, W*
Livingstone College *M, W*
Mars Hill College *M, W*
North Carolina Central University *M, W*
Pembroke State University *M, W*
Pfeiffer College *M, W*
St. Augustine's College *M, W*
Shaw University *M, W*
Winston-Salem State University *M, W*

North Dakota

North Dakota State University *M, W*
University of North Dakota *M, W*

Ohio

Ashland University *M, W*

Oklahoma

University of Central Oklahoma *M, W*

Oregon

Portland State University *M, W, Mixed*

Pennsylvania

Bloomsburg University of Pennsylvania *M, W*
California University of Pennsylvania *M, W*
Cheyney University of Pennsylvania *M, W*
Clarion University of Pennsylvania *M, W*
East Stroudsburg University of Pennsylvania *M, W*
Edinboro University of Pennsylvania *M, W*
Indiana University of Pennsylvania *M, W*
Kutztown University of Pennsylvania *M, W, Mixed*
Lock Haven University of Pennsylvania *M, W*
Mansfield University of Pennsylvania *M, W*
Mercyhurst College *M, W*
Millersville University of Pennsylvania *M, W*
Shippensburg University of Pennsylvania *M, W*
Slippery Rock University of Pennsylvania *M, W*
University of Pittsburgh *W*
West Chester University of Pennsylvania *M, W*

Rhode Island

Bryant College *M, W*

South Carolina

Erskine College *M*
Francis Marion University *M, W*
Lander University *M, W*
University of South Carolina
Aiken *M, W, Mixed*
Spartanburg *M*
Wofford College *M, W*

South Dakota

Augustana College *M, W*
South Dakota State University *M, W*
University of South Dakota *M, W*

Tennessee

Carson-Newman College *M, W*
LeMoyne-Owen College *M, W*
Lincoln Memorial University *M, W*

Texas

Abilene Christian University *M, W*
Angelo State University *M, W*
East Texas State University *M, W, Mixed*
Texas A&I University *M, W*

Vermont

St. Michael's College *M, W*

Virginia

Hampton University *M, W*

Norfolk State University *M, W*
St. Paul's College *M, W*
Virginia State University *M, W*
Virginia Union University *M, W*

Washington

Seattle Pacific University *M, W, Mixed*

West Virginia

Alderson-Broaddus College *W*
Davis and Elkins College *W*
Shepherd College *M, W*
West Liberty State College *M, W*
West Virginia Wesleyan College *M, W*
Wheeling Jesuit College *M, W, Mixed*

Wisconsin

University of Wisconsin: Parkside *M, W*

Cross-country — Division III

Alabama

Stillman College *M*

Arkansas

Hendrix College *M, W*

California

California Institute of Technology *M, W*
California Lutheran University *M, W*
Claremont McKenna College *M, W*
Harvey Mudd College *M, W*
Menlo College *M, W, Mixed*
Mills College *W*
Occidental College *M, W*
Pitzer College *M, W*
Pomona College *M, W*
Scripps College *W*
University of California: San Diego *M, W*
University of La Verne *M, W*
University of Redlands *M, W*
Whittier College *M, W*

Colorado

Colorado College *M, W*

Connecticut

Albertus Magnus College *M*
Connecticut College *M, W*
Eastern Connecticut State University *M, W*
Trinity College *M, W*
United States Coast Guard Academy *M, W*
Wesleyan University *M, W*

District of Columbia

Catholic University of America *M, W*
Gallaudet University *M, W*

Georgia

Emory University *M, W*
Oglethorpe University *M, W*

Illinois

Augustana College *M, W*
Blackburn College *M, Mixed*
Concordia University *M, W*
Elmhurst College *M, W*
Illinois Benedictine College *M, W*
Illinois College *M, W*
Illinois Wesleyan University *M, W*
Knox College *M, W*
Millikin University *M, W*
Monmouth College *M, W*
North Central College *M, W*
North Park College *M, W*
Principia College *M, W, Mixed*
University of Chicago *M, W*
Wheaton College *M, W*

Indiana

Anderson University *M, W*
DePauw University *M, W*
Earlham College *M, W*
Franklin College *M, W*
Hanover College *M, W*
Rose-Hulman Institute of Technology *M*
Wabash College *M*

Iowa

Buena Vista College *M, W*
Central College *M, W*
Coe College *M, W*
Cornell College *M, W*
Grinnell College *M, W*
Loras College *M, W*
Luther College *M, W*
Simpson College *M, W*
University of Dubuque *M, W*
Upper Iowa University *M*
Wartburg College *M, W*

Kentucky

Asbury College *M, W*
Berea College *M, W*
Centre College *M, W*

Maine

Bates College *M, W*
Bowdoin College *M, W*
Colby College *M, W*
Maine Maritime Academy *M*
St. Joseph's College *M, W*
University of Southern Maine *M, W*

Maryland

Frostburg State University *M, W*
Johns Hopkins University *M, W, Mixed*
Salisbury State University *M, W*
Western Maryland College *M, W*

Massachusetts

Amherst College *M, W*
Babson College *M, W, Mixed*
Brandeis University *M, W*
Bridgewater State College *M, W*
Clark University *M, W*
Eastern Nazarene College *M, W, Mixed*
Fitchburg State College *M, W*
Framingham State College *M, W, Mixed*
Gordon College *M, W*
Massachusetts Institute of Technology *M, W*
Massachusetts Maritime Academy *M, W*
Mount Holyoke College *W*
North Adams State College *M, W, Mixed*
Pine Manor College *W*
Regis College *W*
Salem State College *M, W*
Simmons College *W*
Smith College *W*
Suffolk University *M, W*
Tufts University *M, W*
University of Massachusetts
  Boston *M, W*
  Dartmouth *M, W*
Wellesley College *W*
Westfield State College *M, W*
Wheaton College *M, W*
Williams College *M, W*
Worcester Polytechnic Institute *M, W*
Worcester State College *M, W*

Michigan

Adrian College *M, W*
Albion College *M, W*
Alma College *M, W*
Calvin College *M, W*
Hope College *M, W*
Kalamazoo College *M, W*
Olivet College *M*

Minnesota

Augsburg College *M, W*
Carleton College *M, W*
College of St. Benedict *W*
College of St. Catherine: St. Catherine Campus *W*
College of St. Scholastica *M, W*
Concordia College: Moorhead *M, W*
Gustavus Adolphus College *M, W*
Hamline University *M, W*
Macalester College *M, W*
St. John's University *M*
St. Mary's College of Minnesota *M, W*
St. Olaf College *M, W*
University of St. Thomas *M, W*

Mississippi

Millsaps College *M, W*
Rust College *M, W*

Missouri

Fontbonne College *M, W*
Maryville University *M, W*
Webster University *W*
Westminster College *M, W*

Nebraska

Nebraska Wesleyan University *M, W*

New Jersey

Drew University *M, W, Mixed*
Jersey City State College *W*
Montclair State College *M, W*
New Jersey Institute of Technology *M, Mixed*
Ramapo College of New Jersey *M, W*
Rowan College of New Jersey *M, W*
Rutgers—The State University of New Jersey: Camden College of Arts and Sciences *M, W*
Stevens Institute of Technology *M, W*
Stockton State College *M, W*
Trenton State College *M, W*
Upsala College *W*
William Paterson College of New Jersey *M, W*

New York

Bard College *M, W*
City University of New York
  City College *M, W*
  Hunter College *M, W*
  John Jay College of Criminal Justice *M, W*
  Lehman College *M, W*
  Medgar Evers College *M, W*
  York College *M, W*
Clarkson University *M, W*
College of Mount St. Vincent *M, W*
Hamilton College *M, W*
Hartwick College *M, W*
Hilbert College *M*
Hobart College *M*
Ithaca College *M, W*
Keuka College *M, W, Mixed*
New York University *M, W*
Polytechnic University *M, W*
Rensselaer Polytechnic Institute *M, W*
Rochester Institute of Technology *M*
St. John Fisher College *Mixed*
St. Lawrence University *M, W*
State University of New York
  Albany *M, W*
  Binghamton *M, W*
  Stony Brook *M, W*
  College at Brockport *M, W, Mixed*
  College at Buffalo *M, W*
  College at Cortland *M, W*
  College at Fredonia *M, W*
  College at Geneseo *M, W*
  College at New Paltz *Mixed*
  College at Oneonta *M, W*
  College at Plattsburgh *M, W*
  College at Potsdam *M, W, Mixed*
  Maritime College *M, W*
  Oswego *M, W*
Union College *M, W*
United States Merchant Marine Academy *M, W*
University of Rochester *M, W*
Vassar College *M, W*
Yeshiva University *M*

North Carolina

Bennett College *W*
Methodist College *M, W*

Ohio

Baldwin-Wallace College *M, W*
Bluffton College *M*
Case Western Reserve University *M, W*
College of Wooster *M, W*
Defiance College *M, W*
Denison University *M, W*
Heidelberg College *M, W*
Hiram College *M, W*
John Carroll University *M, W*
Kenyon College *M, W*
Mount Union College *M, W*
Muskingum College *M, W, Mixed*
Oberlin College *M, W*
Ohio Northern University *M, W*
Ohio Wesleyan University *M, W*
Otterbein College *M, W*
Wilmington College *M, W*
Wittenberg University *M, W*

Pennsylvania

Albright College *M, W, Mixed*
Allegheny College *M, W*
Allentown College of St. Francis de Sales *M, W*
Bryn Mawr College *W*
Cabrini College *M, W*
Carnegie Mellon University *M, W*
Cedar Crest College *W*
Delaware Valley College *M, W*
Dickinson College *M, W*
Elizabethtown College *M, W, Mixed*
Franklin and Marshall College *M, W*
Gettysburg College *M, W*
Grove City College *M, W*
Haverford College *M, W*
Juniata College *M, W*
King's College *M, W*
Lebanon Valley College of Pennsylvania *M, W*
Lincoln University *M, W*

Lycoming College *M, W*
Messiah College *M, W*
Moravian College *M, W*
Muhlenberg College *M, W*
Susquehanna University *M, W*
Swarthmore College *M, W*
Thiel College *M, W*
University of Scranton *M, W*
Ursinus College *M, W, Mixed*
Washington and Jefferson College *M, W*
Widener University *M, W*
Wilkes University *M*
York College of Pennsylvania *M*

Puerto Rico

American University of Puerto Rico *M, W*

Rhode Island

Rhode Island College *M, W*
Roger Williams University *M, W, Mixed*
Salve Regina University *M, W*

Tennessee

Fisk University *M, W*
Rhodes College *M, W*
University of the South *M, W*

Texas

Jarvis Christian College *M*
Southwestern University *M, W*
Trinity University *M, W*
Wiley College *M*

Vermont

Castleton State College *M, W*
Johnson State College *M, W*
Middlebury College *M, W*
Norwich University *M, W*

Virginia

Bridgewater College *M, W, Mixed*
Christopher Newport University *M, W*
Eastern Mennonite College *M, W*
Emory and Henry College *W*
Hampden-Sydney College *M*
Lynchburg College *M, W*
Mary Washington College *M, W*
Randolph-Macon College *M, W*
Washington and Lee University *M, W*

West Virginia

Bethany College *M, W*

Wisconsin

Beloit College *M, W*
Carroll College *M, W*
Carthage College *M, W*
Lawrence University *M, W*
Northwestern College *M*
Ripon College *M, W*
St. Norbert College *M, W*
University of Wisconsin
- Eau Claire *M, W*
- La Crosse *M, W*
- Oshkosh *M, W*
- Platteville *M, W*
- River Falls *M, W*
- Stevens Point *M, W*
- Stout *M, W*
- Superior *M, W*
- Whitewater *M, W*

Fencing — Division I

California

California State University
- Fullerton *M, W*
- Long Beach *M, W*

Stanford University *M, W*

Connecticut

Yale University *M, W*

Illinois

Northwestern University *M, W*
University of Illinois at Urbana-Champaign *M*

Indiana

University of Notre Dame *M, W*

Maryland

United States Naval Academy *M, W*

Massachusetts

Boston College *M, W*
Harvard and Radcliffe Colleges *M, W*

Michigan

Michigan State University *M*
University of Detroit Mercy *M*

New Jersey

Fairleigh Dickinson University
- Edward Williams College *W*
- Madison *W*

Princeton University *M, W*
Rutgers—The State University of New Jersey
- College of Engineering *M, W*
- Cook College *M, W*
- Douglass College *W*
- Livingston College *M, W*
- Mason Gross School of the Arts *M, W*
- Rutgers College *M, W*

New York

Barnard College *W*
Columbia University: Columbia College *M, W*
Cornell University *M, W*
St. John's University *M, W*

North Carolina

Duke University *M, W*
University of North Carolina at Chapel Hill *M, W*

Ohio

Cleveland State University *M, W*
Ohio State University: Columbus Campus *M, W*

Pennsylvania

Lafayette College *Mixed*
Penn State University Park Campus *M, W*
Temple University *W*
University of Pennsylvania *M, W*

Rhode Island

Brown University *M, W*

Virginia

College of William and Mary *M*
James Madison University *W*

Fencing — Division II

Colorado

United States Air Force Academy *M, W*

Michigan

Wayne State University *M, W*

Fencing — Division III

California

California Institute of Technology *M, W*
University of California: San Diego *M, W*

Illinois

University of Chicago *M*

Maryland

Johns Hopkins University *M, W*

Massachusetts

Brandeis University *M, W*
Massachusetts Institute of Technology *M, W*
Wellesley College *W*

New Jersey

Drew University *M, Mixed*
New Jersey Institute of Technology *M*
Stevens Institute of Technology *M, W*

New York

Bard College *M, W*
City University of New York
- Baruch College *W*
- City College *W*
- Hunter College *W*

New York University *M, W*
Vassar College *M, W*
Yeshiva University *M*

Ohio

Case Western Reserve University *M, W*

Pennsylvania

Haverford College *M, W*

Virginia

Hollins College *W*

Wisconsin

Lawrence University *M, W*

Field hockey — Division I

California

Stanford University *W*
University of California: Berkeley *W*
University of the Pacific *W*

Connecticut

Fairfield University *W*
University of Connecticut *W*
Yale University *W*

Delaware

University of Delaware *W*

District of Columbia

American University *W*
Georgetown University *W*

Illinois

Northern Illinois University *W*
Northwestern University *W*

Indiana

Ball State University *W*

Iowa

University of Iowa *W*

Kentucky

University of Louisville *W*

Maine

University of Maine *W*

Maryland

Towson State University *W*
University of Maryland: College Park *W*

Massachusetts

Boston College *W*
Boston University *W*
College of the Holy Cross *W*
Harvard and Radcliffe Colleges *W*
Northeastern University *W*
Springfield College *W*
University of Massachusetts at Amherst *W*

Michigan

Central Michigan University *W*
Michigan State University *W*
University of Michigan *W*

Missouri

St. Louis University *W*
Southwest Missouri State University *W*

New Hampshire

Dartmouth College *W*
University of New Hampshire *W*

New Jersey

Princeton University *W*
Rider College *W*
Rutgers—The State University of New Jersey
- College of Engineering *W*
- Cook College *W*
- Douglass College *W*
- Livingston College *W*
- Mason Gross School of the Arts *W*
- Rutgers College *W*

New York

Colgate University *W*
Cornell University *W*
Hofstra University *W*
Siena College *W*
Syracuse University *W*

North Carolina

Appalachian State University *W*
Davidson College *W*
Duke University *W*
University of North Carolina at Chapel Hill *W*
Wake Forest University *W*

Ohio

Kent State University *W*
Miami University: Oxford Campus *W*
Ohio State University: Columbus Campus *W*
Ohio University *W*

Pennsylvania

Bucknell University *W*
Drexel University *W*
La Salle University *W*
Lafayette College *W*
Lehigh University *W*
Penn State University Park Campus *W*
St. Joseph's University *W*
Temple University *W*
University of Pennsylvania *W*
Ursinus College *W*
Villanova University *W*
West Chester University of Pennsylvania *W*

Rhode Island

Brown University *W*
Providence College *W*
University of Rhode Island *W*

Vermont

University of Vermont *W*

Virginia

College of William and Mary *W*
James Madison University *W*
Old Dominion University *W*
Radford University *W*
University of Richmond *W*
University of Virginia *W*
Virginia Commonwealth University *W*

West Virginia

Davis and Elkins College *W*

Field hockey — Division II

Connecticut

Southern Connecticut State University *W*

Kentucky

Bellarmine College *W*

Massachusetts

Assumption College *W*
Bentley College *W*
University of Massachusetts at Lowell *W*

New Hampshire

Keene State College *W*

New York

Long Island University: C. W. Post Campus *W*

North Carolina

Catawba College *W*
Pfeiffer College *W*

Pennsylvania

Bloomsburg University of Pennsylvania *W*
East Stroudsburg University of Pennsylvania *W*
Kutztown University of Pennsylvania *W*
Lock Haven University of Pennsylvania *W*
Mansfield University of Pennsylvania *W*
Millersville University of Pennsylvania *W*
Philadelphia College of Textiles and Science *W*
Shippensburg University of Pennsylvania *W*
Slippery Rock University of Pennsylvania *W*

Vermont

St. Michael's College *W*

Virginia

Longwood College *W*

Field hockey — Division III

Connecticut

Connecticut College *W*
Trinity College *W*
Wesleyan University *W*
Western Connecticut State University *W*

Delaware

Wesley College *W*

District of Columbia

Catholic University of America *W*

Indiana

DePauw University *W*
Earlham College *W*
Franklin College *W*
Hanover College *W*

Kentucky

Berea College *W*
Centre College *W*

Maine

Bates College *W*
Bowdoin College *W*
Colby College *W*
University of Southern Maine *W*

Maryland

College of Notre Dame of Maryland *W*
Frostburg State University *W*
Goucher College *W*
Hood College *W*
Johns Hopkins University *W*
Salisbury State University *W*
Washington College *W*
Western Maryland College *W*

Massachusetts

Amherst College *W*
Anna Maria College for Men and Women *W*
Babson College *W*
Bridgewater State College *W*
Clark University *W*
Elms College *W*
Fitchburg State College *W*
Framingham State College *W*
Gordon College *W*
Massachusetts Institute of Technology *W*
Mount Holyoke College *W*
Nichols College *W*
Pine Manor College *W*
Salem State College *W*
Simmons College *W*
Smith College *W*
Tufts University *W*
University of Massachusetts at Dartmouth *W*
Wellesley College *W*
Western New England College *W*
Westfield State College *W*
Wheaton College *W*
Williams College *W*
Worcester Polytechnic Institute *W*
Worcester State College *W*

New Hampshire

New England College *W*
Plymouth State College of the University System of New Hampshire *W*

New Jersey

Drew University *W*
Fairleigh Dickinson University *W*
Kean College of New Jersey *W*
Montclair State College *W*
Rowan College of New Jersey *W*
Trenton State College *W*
William Paterson College of New Jersey *W*

New York

Hamilton College *W*
Hartwick College *W*
Ithaca College *W*
Manhattanville College *W*
Rensselaer Polytechnic Institute *W*
St. Lawrence University *W*
Skidmore College *W*
State University of New York
College at Brockport *W*
College at Cortland *W*
College at Oneonta *W*
Oswego *W*
Union College *W*
University of Rochester *W*
Vassar College *W*
Wells College *W*
William Smith College *W*

Ohio

College of Wooster *W*
Denison University *W*
Kenyon College *W*
Oberlin College *W*
Ohio Wesleyan University *W*
Wittenberg University *W*

Pennsylvania

Albright College *W*
Bryn Mawr College *W*
Cabrini College *W*
Cedar Crest College *W*
College Misericordia *W*
Delaware Valley College *W*
Dickinson College *W*
Elizabethtown College *W*
Franklin and Marshall College *W*
Gettysburg College *W*
Haverford College *W*
Immaculata College *W*
Juniata College *W*
King's College *W*
Lebanon Valley College of Pennsylvania *W*
Lycoming College *W*
Marywood College *W*
Messiah College *W*
Moravian College *W*
Muhlenberg College *W*
Rosemont College *W*
Susquehanna University *W*
Swarthmore College *W*
University of Scranton *W*
Widener University *W*
Wilkes University *W*
York College of Pennsylvania *W*

Rhode Island

Salve Regina University *W*

Tennessee

University of the South *W*

Vermont

Middlebury College *W*

Virginia

Bridgewater College *W*
Eastern Mennonite College *W*
Hollins College *W*
Lynchburg College *W*
Mary Baldwin College *W*
Mary Washington College *W*
Randolph-Macon College *W*
Randolph-Macon Woman's College *W*
Roanoke College *W*
Sweet Briar College *W*
Virginia Wesleyan College *W*

Football — Division IA

Alabama

Auburn University
University of Alabama

Arizona

Arizona State University
University of Arizona

Arkansas

Arkansas State University
University of Arkansas

California

California State University
Fresno
Fullerton
Long Beach
San Diego State University
San Jose State University
Stanford University
University of California
Berkeley
Los Angeles
University of the Pacific
University of Southern California

Colorado

Colorado State University
United States Air Force Academy
University of Colorado at Boulder

Florida

Florida State University
University of Florida
University of Miami

Georgia

Georgia Institute of Technology
University of Georgia

Hawaii

University of Hawaii at Manoa

Illinois

Northern Illinois University
Northwestern University
University of Illinois at Urbana-Champaign

Indiana

Ball State University
Indiana University Bloomington
Purdue University
University of Notre Dame

Iowa

Iowa State University
University of Iowa

Kansas

Kansas State University
University of Kansas

Kentucky

University of Kentucky
University of Louisville

Louisiana
Louisiana State University and Agricultural and Mechanical College
Louisiana Tech University
Tulane University
University of Southwestern Louisiana

Maryland
United States Naval Academy
University of Maryland: College Park

Massachusetts
Boston College

Michigan
Central Michigan University
Eastern Michigan University
Michigan State University
University of Michigan
Western Michigan University

Minnesota
University of Minnesota: Twin Cities

Mississippi
Mississippi State University
University of Mississippi
University of Southern Mississippi

Missouri
University of Missouri: Columbia

Nebraska
University of Nebraska—Lincoln

Nevada
University of Nevada
Las Vegas
Reno

New Jersey
Rutgers—The State University of New Jersey
College of Engineering
Cook College
Livingston College
Mason Gross School of the Arts
Rutgers College

New Mexico
New Mexico State University
University of New Mexico

New York
Syracuse University
United States Military Academy

North Carolina
Duke University
East Carolina University
North Carolina State University
University of North Carolina at Chapel Hill
Wake Forest University

Ohio
Bowling Green State University
Kent State University
Miami University: Oxford Campus
Ohio State University: Columbus Campus
Ohio University
University of Akron
University of Cincinnati
University of Toledo

Oklahoma
Oklahoma State University
University of Oklahoma
University of Tulsa

Oregon
Oregon State University
University of Oregon

Pennsylvania
Penn State University Park Campus
Temple University
University of Pittsburgh

South Carolina
Clemson University
University of South Carolina

Tennessee
Memphis State University
University of Tennessee: Knoxville
Vanderbilt University

Texas
Baylor University
Rice University
Southern Methodist University
Texas A&M University
Texas Christian University
Texas Tech University
University of Houston
University of Texas
Austin
El Paso

Utah
Brigham Young University
University of Utah
Utah State University

Virginia
University of Virginia
Virginia Polytechnic Institute and State University

Washington
University of Washington
Washington State University

West Virginia
West Virginia University

Wisconsin
University of Wisconsin: Madison

Wyoming
University of Wyoming

Football — Division IAA

Alabama
Alabama State University
Samford University

Arizona
Northern Arizona University

Connecticut
University of Connecticut
Yale University

Delaware
Delaware State College
University of Delaware

District of Columbia
Howard University

Florida
Bethune-Cookman College
Florida Agricultural and Mechanical University
University of Central Florida

Georgia
Georgia Southern University

Idaho
Boise State University
Idaho State University
University of Idaho

Illinois
Eastern Illinois University
Illinois State University
Southern Illinois University at Carbondale
Western Illinois University

Indiana
Indiana State University

Iowa
University of Northern Iowa

Kentucky
Eastern Kentucky University
Morehead State University
Murray State University
Western Kentucky University

Louisiana
Grambling State University
McNeese State University
Nicholls State University
Northeast Louisiana University
Northwestern State University
Southern University and Agricultural and Mechanical College

Maine
University of Maine

Maryland
Morgan State University
Towson State University

Massachusetts
Boston University
College of the Holy Cross
Harvard and Radcliffe Colleges
Northeastern University
University of Massachusetts at Amherst

Mississippi
Alcorn State University
Jackson State University
Mississippi Valley State University

Missouri
Southeast Missouri State University
Southwest Missouri State University

Montana
Montana State University
University of Montana

New Hampshire
Dartmouth College
University of New Hampshire

New Jersey
Princeton University

New York
Colgate University
Columbia University: Columbia College
Cornell University
Fordham University

North Carolina
Appalachian State University
North Carolina Agricultural and Technical State University
Western Carolina University

Ohio
Youngstown State University

Pennsylvania
Bucknell University
Duquesne University
Lafayette College
Lehigh University
University of Pennsylvania
Villanova University

Rhode Island
Brown University
University of Rhode Island

South Carolina
The Citadel
Furman University
South Carolina State University

Tennessee
Austin Peay State University
East Tennessee State University
Middle Tennessee State University
Tennessee State University
Tennessee Technological University
University of Tennessee
Chattanooga
Martin

Texas
Prairie View A&M University
Sam Houston State University
Southwest Texas State University
Stephen F. Austin State University
Texas Southern University
University of North Texas

Utah
Weber State University

Virginia
College of William and Mary
James Madison University
Liberty University
University of Richmond
Virginia Military Institute

Washington
Eastern Washington University

West Virginia
Marshall University

Football — Division II

Alabama
Alabama Agricultural and Mechanical University
Jacksonville State University
Livingston University
Miles College
Troy State University
Tuskegee University
University of Alabama in Birmingham
University of North Alabama

Arkansas
Henderson State University
University of Central Arkansas

California
California Polytechnic State University: San Luis Obispo
California State University
Chico
Hayward
Northridge
Sacramento
Humboldt State University

St. Mary's College of California
San Francisco State University
Sonoma State University
University of California
Davis
Santa Barbara

Colorado

Adams State College
Colorado School of Mines
Fort Lewis College
Mesa State College
University of Northern Colorado
Western State College of Colorado

Connecticut

Central Connecticut State University
Sacred Heart University
Southern Connecticut State University
University of New Haven

District of Columbia

Georgetown University

Georgia

Albany State College
Clark Atlanta University
Fort Valley State College
Morehouse College
Morris Brown College
Savannah State College
Valdosta State College
West Georgia College

Illinois

Quincy University

Indiana

Butler University
St. Joseph's College
University of Evansville
University of Indianapolis

Iowa

Drake University
Morningside College

Kansas

Emporia State University
Fort Hays State University
Pittsburg State University
Washburn University of Topeka

Kentucky

Kentucky State University
Kentucky Wesleyan College

Maryland

Bowie State University

Massachusetts

American International College
Assumption College
Bentley College
Springfield College
Stonehill College
University of Massachusetts at Lowell

Michigan

Ferris State University
Grand Valley State University
Hillsdale College
Michigan Technological University
Northern Michigan University
Northwood University
Saginaw Valley State University
Wayne State University

Minnesota

Bemidji State University
Mankato State University
St. Cloud State University
University of Minnesota: Duluth
Winona State University

Mississippi

Delta State University
Mississippi College

Missouri

Central Missouri State University
Missouri Southern State College
Missouri Western State College
Northeast Missouri State University
Northwest Missouri State University
Southwest Baptist University
University of Missouri: Rolla

Nebraska

Chadron State College
University of Nebraska
Kearney
Omaha
Wayne State College

New Jersey

St. Peter's College

New Mexico

Eastern New Mexico University
New Mexico Highlands University

New York

Canisius College
Hofstra University
Iona College
Long Island University: C. W. Post Campus
Marist College
Pace University
College of White Plains
New York
Pleasantville/Briarcliff
St. John's University
State University of New York
Buffalo
College at Buffalo
Wagner College

North Carolina

Catawba College
Elizabeth City State University
Elon College
Fayetteville State University
Gardner-Webb University
Johnson C. Smith University
Lenoir-Rhyne College
Livingstone College
Mars Hill College
North Carolina Central University
Wingate College
Winston-Salem State University

North Dakota

North Dakota State University
University of North Dakota

Ohio

Ashland University

Oklahoma

Cameron University
University of Central Oklahoma

Oregon

Portland State University

Pennsylvania

Bloomsburg University of Pennsylvania
California University of Pennsylvania
Cheyney University of Pennsylvania
Clarion University of Pennsylvania
East Stroudsburg University of Pennsylvania
Edinboro University of Pennsylvania
Gannon University
Indiana University of Pennsylvania
Kutztown University of Pennsylvania
Lock Haven University of Pennsylvania
Mansfield University of Pennsylvania
Mercyhurst College
Millersville University of Pennsylvania
St. Francis College
Shippensburg University of Pennsylvania
Slippery Rock University of Pennsylvania
West Chester University of Pennsylvania

South Carolina

Charleston Southern University
Newberry College
Presbyterian College
Wofford College

South Dakota

Augustana College
South Dakota State University
University of South Dakota

Tennessee

Carson-Newman College

Texas

Abilene Christian University
Angelo State University
East Texas State University
Texas A&I University
West Texas A & M University

Utah

Southern Utah University

Virginia

Hampton University
Norfolk State University
Virginia State University
Virginia Union University

West Virginia

Shepherd College
West Liberty State College

Football — Division III

California

California Lutheran University
Claremont McKenna College
Harvey Mudd College
Menlo College
Occidental College
Pitzer College
Pomona College
University of La Verne
University of Redlands
University of San Diego
Whittier College

Colorado

Colorado College

Connecticut

Trinity College
United States Coast Guard Academy
Wesleyan University
Western Connecticut State University

Delaware

Wesley College

District of Columbia

Catholic University of America
Gallaudet University

Illinois

Augustana College
Aurora University
Blackburn College
Concordia University
Elmhurst College
Eureka College
Illinois Benedictine College
Illinois College
Illinois Wesleyan University
Knox College
Lake Forest College
MacMurray College
Millikin University
Monmouth College
North Central College
North Park College
Principia College
University of Chicago
Wheaton College

Indiana

Anderson University
DePauw University
Earlham College
Franklin College
Hanover College
Manchester College
Rose-Hulman Institute of Technology
Wabash College

Iowa

Buena Vista College
Central College
Coe College
Cornell College
Grinnell College
Loras College
Luther College
Simpson College
University of Dubuque
Upper Iowa University
Wartburg College
William Penn College

Kentucky

Centre College
Thomas More College

Maine

Bates College
Bowdoin College
Colby College
Maine Maritime Academy

Maryland

Frostburg State University
Johns Hopkins University
Salisbury State University
Western Maryland College

Massachusetts

Amherst College
Bridgewater State College
Curry College
Fitchburg State College
Framingham State College
Massachusetts Institute of Technology
Massachusetts Maritime Academy
Nichols College
Tufts University

University of Massachusetts
- Boston
- Dartmouth

Western New England College
Westfield State College
Williams College
Worcester Polytechnic Institute
Worcester State College

Michigan

Adrian College
Albion College
Alma College
Hope College
Kalamazoo College
Olivet College

Minnesota

Augsburg College
Carleton College
Concordia College: Moorhead
Gustavus Adolphus College
Hamline University
Macalester College
St. John's University
St. Olaf College
University of St. Thomas

Mississippi

Millsaps College

Missouri

Washington University

Nebraska

Nebraska Wesleyan University

New Hampshire

Plymouth State College of the University System of New Hampshire

New Jersey

Fairleigh Dickinson University
Jersey City State College
Kean College of New Jersey
Montclair State College
Ramapo College of New Jersey
Rowan College of New Jersey
Trenton State College
Upsala College
William Paterson College of New Jersey

New York

Alfred University
Hamilton College
Hartwick College
Hobart College
Ithaca College
Rensselaer Polytechnic Institute
St. John Fisher College
St. Lawrence University
State University of New York
- Albany
- Stony Brook
- College at Brockport
- College at Cortland

Union College
United States Merchant Marine Academy
University of Rochester

North Carolina

Davidson College
Guilford College
Methodist College

Ohio

Baldwin-Wallace College
Bluffton College
Capital University
Case Western Reserve University
College of Wooster
Defiance College
Denison University
Heidelberg College
Hiram College
John Carroll University
Kenyon College
Marietta College
Mount Union College
Muskingum College
Oberlin College
Ohio Northern University
Ohio Wesleyan University
Otterbein College
Wilmington College
Wittenberg University

Pennsylvania

Albright College
Allegheny College
Carnegie Mellon University
Delaware Valley College
Dickinson College
Franklin and Marshall College
Gettysburg College
Grove City College
Juniata College
Lebanon Valley College of Pennsylvania
Lycoming College
Moravian College
Muhlenberg College
Susquehanna University
Swarthmore College
Thiel College
Ursinus College
Washington and Jefferson College
Waynesburg College
Widener University
Wilkes University

Rhode Island

Salve Regina University

Tennessee

Maryville College
Rhodes College
University of the South

Texas

Hardin-Simmons University
Trinity University

Vermont

Middlebury College
Norwich University

Virginia

Bridgewater College
Emory and Henry College
Ferrum College
Hampden-Sydney College
Randolph-Macon College
Washington and Lee University

West Virginia

Bethany College

Wisconsin

Beloit College
Carroll College
Carthage College
Lawrence University
Northwestern College
Ripon College
St. Norbert College
University of Wisconsin
- Eau Claire
- La Crosse
- Oshkosh
- Platteville
- River Falls
- Stevens Point
- Stout
- Superior
- Whitewater

Golf — Division I

Alabama

Alabama State University *M, W*
Auburn University *M, W*
Samford University *M, W*
University of Alabama
- Birmingham *M, W*
- Tuscaloosa *M, W*

University of South Alabama *M, W*

Arizona

Arizona State University *M, W*
University of Arizona *M, W*

Arkansas

Arkansas State University *M, W*
University of Arkansas *M*
University of Arkansas at Little Rock *M, W*

California

California State University
- Fresno *M*
- Long Beach *M, W*
- Northridge *M*
- Sacramento *M*

Loyola Marymount University *M*
Pepperdine University *M, W*
St. Mary's College of California *M*
San Jose State University *M, W*
Santa Clara University *M, W*
Stanford University *M, W*
University of California
- Berkeley *M*
- Irvine *M*
- Los Angeles *M, W*
- Santa Barbara *M*

University of the Pacific *M*
University of San Diego *M*
University of San Francisco *M, W*
University of Southern California *M, W*

Colorado

Colorado State University *M, W*
United States Air Force Academy *M*
University of Colorado at Boulder *M*

Connecticut

Central Connecticut State University *M*
Fairfield University *M*
University of Connecticut *M*
University of Hartford *M, W*
Yale University *M, W*

Delaware

University of Delaware *M*

District of Columbia

American University *M*
George Washington University *M*
Georgetown University *M*

Florida

Florida Agricultural and Mechanical University *M*
Florida International University *M, W*
Florida State University *M, W*
Jacksonville University *M, W*
Stetson University *M, W*
University of Central Florida *M, W*
University of Florida *M, W*
University of Miami *W*
University of South Florida *M, W*

Georgia

Augusta College *M*
Georgia Institute of Technology *M*
Georgia Southern University *M*
Georgia State University *M, W, Mixed*
Mercer University *M*
University of Georgia *M, W*

Hawaii

University of Hawaii at Manoa *M, W*

Idaho

Boise State University *M, W*
University of Idaho *M, W*

Illinois

Bradley University *M, W*
De Paul University *M*
Eastern Illinois University *M*
Illinois State University *M, W*
Loyola University of Chicago *M*
Northeastern Illinois University *M*
Northern Illinois University *M, W*
Northwestern University *M, W*
Southern Illinois University at Carbondale *M, W*
University of Illinois at Urbana-Champaign *M, W*
Western Illinois University *M*

Indiana

Ball State University *M*
Butler University *M*
Indiana University Bloomington *M, W*
Purdue University *M, W*
University of Evansville *M*
University of Notre Dame *M, W*

Iowa

Drake University *M*
Iowa State University *M, W*
University of Iowa *M, W*
University of Northern Iowa *M, W*

Kansas

Kansas State University *M, W*
University of Kansas *M, W*
Wichita State University *M, W*

Kentucky

Eastern Kentucky University *M*
Morehead State University *M*
Murray State University *M*
University of Kentucky *M, W*
University of Louisville *M*
Western Kentucky University *M, W*

Louisiana

Centenary College of Louisiana *M*
Grambling State University *M, W*
Louisiana State University and Agricultural and Mechanical College *M, W*
Louisiana Tech University *M*
McNeese State University *M*
Nicholls State University *M*

Northeast Louisiana University *M*
Northwestern State University *M*
Southeastern Louisiana University *M*
Southern University and Agricultural and Mechanical College *M, W*
Tulane University *M*
University of New Orleans *M*
University of Southwestern Louisiana *M*

Maine

University of Maine *M*

Maryland

Loyola College in Maryland *M*
Mount St. Mary's College *M*
Towson State University *M*
United States Naval Academy *M*
University of Maryland
Baltimore County *M*
College Park *M*

Massachusetts

Boston College *M, W*
Boston University *M*
College of the Holy Cross *M*
Harvard and Radcliffe Colleges *M*
Northeastern University *M*

Michigan

Eastern Michigan University *M*
Michigan State University *M, W*
University of Detroit Mercy *M*
University of Michigan *M, W*

Minnesota

University of Minnesota: Twin Cities *M, W*

Mississippi

Alcorn State University *M*
Jackson State University *M*
Mississippi State University *M, W*
Mississippi Valley State University *M, W*
University of Mississippi *M, W*
University of Southern Mississippi *M, W*

Missouri

St. Louis University *M*
Southwest Missouri State University *M, W*
University of Missouri
Columbia *M, W*
Kansas City *M, W*

Nebraska

Creighton University *M, W*
University of Nebraska—Lincoln *M, W*

Nevada

University of Nevada
Las Vegas *M*
Reno *M*

New Hampshire

Dartmouth College *M, W*
University of New Hampshire *M*

New Jersey

Fairleigh Dickinson University: Edward Williams College *M*
Monmouth College *M*
Princeton University *M, W*
Rider College *M*
Rutgers—The State University of New Jersey
College of Engineering *M, W*
Cook College *M, W*
Douglass College *W*
Livingston College *M, W*
Mason Gross School of the Arts *M, W*
Rutgers College *M, W*
St. Peter's College *M*
Seton Hall University *M*

New Mexico

New Mexico State University *M, W*
University of New Mexico *M, W*

New York

Canisius College *M*
Colgate University *M*
Columbia University: Columbia College *M*
Cornell University *M*
Hofstra University *M, Mixed*
Iona College *M*
Long Island University: Brooklyn Campus *M*
Manhattan College *M*
Niagara University *M*
St. Bonaventure University *M*
St. John's University *M*
Siena College *M*
United States Military Academy *M*
Wagner College *M*

North Carolina

Appalachian State University *M, W*
Campbell University *M, W*
Davidson College *M*
Duke University *M, W*
East Carolina University *M*
North Carolina State University *M*
University of North Carolina
Asheville *M*
Chapel Hill *M, W*
Charlotte *M*
Greensboro *M, W*
Wilmington *M, W*
Wake Forest University *M, W*
Western Carolina University *M*

Ohio

Bowling Green State University *M, W*
Cleveland State University *M*
Kent State University *M*
Miami University: Oxford Campus *M*
Ohio State University: Columbus Campus *M, W*
Ohio University *M*
University of Akron *M*
University of Cincinnati *M, W*
University of Dayton *M, W*
University of Toledo *M*
Wright State University *M*
Xavier University *M, W*
Youngstown State University *M*

Oklahoma

Oklahoma State University *M, W*
University of Oklahoma *M, W*
University of Tulsa *M, W*

Oregon

Oregon State University *M, W*
University of Oregon *M, W*
University of Portland *M*

Pennsylvania

Bucknell University *M*
Drexel University *M*
Duquesne University *M*
La Salle University *M*
Lafayette College *M, Mixed*
Lehigh University *M*
Penn State University Park Campus *M, W*
Robert Morris College *M*
St. Francis College *M, W*
St. Joseph's University *M*
Temple University *M*
University of Pennsylvania *M*
Villanova University *M*

Rhode Island

Providence College *M*
University of Rhode Island *M*

South Carolina

Charleston Southern University *M, W*
The Citadel *M*
Clemson University *M*
College of Charleston *M, W*
Furman University *M, W*
South Carolina State University *M*
University of South Carolina
Coastal Carolina College *M, W*
Columbia *M, W*
Winthrop University *M, W*

Tennessee

Austin Peay State University *M*
East Tennessee State University *M*
Memphis State University *M, W*
Middle Tennessee State University *M*
Tennessee State University *M*
Tennessee Technological University *M, W*
University of Tennessee
Chattanooga *M, W*
Knoxville *M*
Martin *M*
Vanderbilt University *M, W*

Texas

Baylor University *M, W*
Lamar University—Beaumont *M, W*
Prairie View A&M University *M, W*
Rice University *M*
Sam Houston State University *M*
Southern Methodist University *M, W*
Southwest Texas State University *M*
Stephen F. Austin State University *M*
Texas A&M University *M, W*
Texas Christian University *M, W*
Texas Southern University *M, W*
Texas Tech University *M, W*
University of Houston *M*
University of North Texas *M, W*
University of Texas
Arlington *M*
Austin *M, W*
El Paso *M, W*
Pan American *M*
San Antonio *M, W*

Utah

Brigham Young University *M, W*
Southern Utah University *M*
University of Utah *M*
Utah State University *M*
Weber State University *M*

Vermont

University of Vermont *M*

Virginia

College of William and Mary *M, W*
George Mason University *M*
James Madison University *M, W*
Liberty University *M*
Old Dominion University *M*
Radford University *M, W*
University of Richmond *M*
University of Virginia *M*
Virginia Commonwealth University *M, Mixed*
Virginia Military Institute *M*
Virginia Polytechnic Institute and State University *M*

Washington

Eastern Washington University *M, W*
Gonzaga University *M*
University of Washington *M, W*
Washington State University *M, W*

West Virginia

Marshall University *M*

Wisconsin

Marquette University *M*
University of Wisconsin
Green Bay *M*
Madison *M, W*

Wyoming

University of Wyoming *M, W*

Golf — Division II

Alabama

Jacksonville State University *M*
Troy State University *M, W*
University of North Alabama *M*

Arizona

Grand Canyon University *M*

Arkansas

Henderson State University *M*
University of Central Arkansas *M*

California

California State University
Dominguez Hills *M*
San Bernardino *M*
Stanislaus *M*
University of California: Davis *M*

Colorado

Adams State College *M*
Colorado Christian University *M*
Colorado School of Mines *M, Mixed*
Fort Lewis College *M*
Regis University *M*
University of Colorado at Colorado Springs *M*
University of Denver *M*
University of Northern Colorado *M*
University of Southern Colorado *M*

Connecticut

Quinnipiac College *M*
Sacred Heart University *M, W*
Southern Connecticut State University *M*

Florida

Barry University *M*
Eckerd College *M*
Florida Atlantic University *M, W*

Florida Southern College *M*
Rollins College *M, W*
University of North Florida *M*
University of Tampa *M*

Georgia
Columbus College *M*
Georgia College *M*
Kennesaw State College *M*
Valdosta State College *M*
West Georgia College *M*

Illinois
Lewis University *M, W*
Southern Illinois University at Edwardsville *M*

Indiana
Indiana University—Purdue University at Fort Wayne *M*
Oakland City College *M, W*
St. Joseph's College *M, W*
University of Indianapolis *M, W*
University of Southern Indiana *M*

Kansas
Emporia State University *M*
Fort Hays State University *M*
Pittsburg State University *M*
Washburn University of Topeka *M*

Kentucky
Bellarmine College *M*
Kentucky State University *M*
Kentucky Wesleyan College *M*
Northern Kentucky University *M*

Massachusetts
American International College *M*
Assumption College *M*
Bentley College *M*
Merrimack College *M, Mixed*
Springfield College *M, W*
University of Massachusetts at Lowell *M*

Michigan
Ferris State University *M, W*
Hillsdale College *M*
Lake Superior State University *M*
Northern Michigan University *M*
Northwood University *M*
Oakland University *M*
Saginaw Valley State University *M*
Wayne State University *M*

Minnesota
Bemidji State University *M*
Mankato State University *M, W*
Moorhead State University *M*
St. Cloud State University *M, W*
Winona State University *M, W*

Mississippi
Delta State University *M*
Mississippi College *M*

Missouri
Central Missouri State University *M*
Drury College *M*
Lincoln University *M*
Missouri Southern State College *M*
Missouri Western State College *M*
Northeast Missouri State University *M, W*
Southwest Baptist University *M*
University of Missouri
Rolla *M*
St. Louis *M*

Nebraska
Chadron State College *W*
University of Nebraska—Kearney *M*
Wayne State College *M, W*

New Hampshire
Franklin Pierce College *M*
St. Anselm College *M*

New York
Adelphi University *M*
City University of New York: Queens College *M*
Dowling College *M*
Le Moyne College *M*
Mercy College *M, Mixed*
Molloy College *M*

North Carolina
Catawba College *M*
Elon College *M*
Fayetteville State University *M*
Gardner-Webb University *M*
Johnson C. Smith University *M*
Lenoir-Rhyne College *M*
Livingstone College *M*
Mars Hill College *M*
Mount Olive College *M*
Pembroke State University *M*
Pfeiffer College *M*
Queens College *M*
St. Augustine's College *M*
Wingate College *M*

North Dakota
North Dakota State University *M*
University of North Dakota *M*

Ohio
Ashland University *M*

Oklahoma
Cameron University *M*
University of Central Oklahoma *M*

Oregon
Portland State University *M*

Pennsylvania
Clarion University of Pennsylvania *M*
Edinboro University of Pennsylvania *M*
Gannon University *M*
Indiana University of Pennsylvania *M*
Lock Haven University of Pennsylvania *M*
Mercyhurst College *M*
Millersville University of Pennsylvania *M*
Philadelphia College of Textiles and Science *M*
Slippery Rock University of Pennsylvania *M*
West Chester University of Pennsylvania *M*

Rhode Island
Bryant College *M, Mixed*

South Carolina
Erskine College *M*
Francis Marion University *M*
Newberry College *M*
Presbyterian College *M*
University of South Carolina at Aiken *M*
Wofford College *M*

South Dakota
South Dakota State University *M, W*

Tennessee
Carson-Newman College *M*
Lincoln Memorial University *M*

Texas
Abilene Christian University *M*
East Texas State University *M*
Hardin-Simmons University *M, W*

Vermont
St. Michael's College *M*

Virginia
Hampton University *M*
Longwood College *M, W*
St. Paul's College *M*
Virginia Union University *M*

West Virginia
Davis and Elkins College *M*
Shepherd College *M*
West Liberty State College *M*
West Virginia Wesleyan College *M*
Wheeling Jesuit College *M, W, Mixed*

Wisconsin
University of Wisconsin: Parkside *M*

Golf — Division III

Arkansas
Hendrix College *M*

California
California Institute of Technology *M*
California Lutheran University *M, Mixed*
Menlo College *M*
Occidental College *Mixed*
Pitzer College *M*
Pomona College *M*
University of California: San Diego *M*
University of La Verne *M*
University of Redlands *M*
Whittier College *M*

Colorado
Colorado College *M*

Connecticut
Trinity College *M*
Wesleyan University *M*

Delaware
Wesley College *M*

Georgia
Emory University *M*
Oglethorpe University *M*
Savannah College of Art and Design *M, W*

Illinois
Augustana College *M*
Aurora University *M*
Blackburn College *M*
Elmhurst College *M*
Eureka College *Mixed*
Illinois Benedictine College *M, Mixed*
Illinois College *M*
Illinois Wesleyan University *M*
Knox College *M*
MacMurray College *M*
Millikin University *M*
North Central College *M*
Principia College *M*
Rockford College *M*
Wheaton College *M*

Indiana
Anderson University *M*
DePauw University *M, W*
Earlham College *M*
Franklin College *M, W*
Hanover College *M*
Manchester College *M*
Rose-Hulman Institute of Technology *M*
Wabash College *M*

Iowa
Buena Vista College *M, W*
Central College *M, W*
Coe College *M*
Cornell College *M*
Grinnell College *M*
Loras College *M, W*
Luther College *M, W*
Simpson College *M, W*
University of Dubuque *M, W*
Upper Iowa University *M, W*
Wartburg College *M, W*
William Penn College *M, W*

Kentucky
Berea College *M*
Centre College *M, Mixed*

Maine
Bates College *Mixed*
Bowdoin College *Mixed*

Maryland
Johns Hopkins University *M*

Massachusetts
Amherst College *M, W*
Anna Maria College for Men and Women *M*
Babson College *M, Mixed*
Brandeis University *M*
Clark University *M*
Emerson College *M*
Massachusetts Institute of Technology *M*
Mount Holyoke College *W*
Nichols College *M*
Salem State College *M*
Suffolk University *M, Mixed*
Tufts University *M*
University of Massachusetts at Dartmouth *M*
Western New England College *M*
Williams College *M*
Worcester Polytechnic Institute *M*
Worcester State College *M*

Michigan
Adrian College *M, W*
Albion College *M, W*
Alma College *M, W*
Calvin College *M, W*
Hope College *M, W*
Kalamazoo College *M, W*
Olivet College *M*

Minnesota
Augsburg College *M*
Carleton College *M, W*
College of St. Benedict *W*
College of St. Catherine: St. Catherine Campus *W*
College of St. Scholastica *M, W*
Concordia College: Moorhead *M, W*
Gustavus Adolphus College *M, W*
Hamline University *M*
Macalester College *M, W*
St. John's University *M*

St. Mary's College of Minnesota *M*
St. Olaf College *M, W*
University of St. Thomas *M, W*

Mississippi
Millsaps College *M*

Missouri
Fontbonne College *M, W*
Maryville University *M, W*
Westminster College *M, W*

Nebraska
Nebraska Wesleyan University *M, W*

New Jersey
Fairleigh Dickinson University *M*
Montclair State College *M*
New Jersey Institute of Technology *M, Mixed*
Ramapo College of New Jersey *M*
Rutgers—The State University of New Jersey: Camden College of Arts and Sciences *M*
Trenton State College *M*

New York
Alfred University *M, W*
Clarkson University *M*
Elmira College *M*
Hamilton College *M*
Hartwick College *M, Mixed*
Hobart College *M*
Ithaca College *M*
Nazareth College of Rochester *M*
New York University *M*
Rensselaer Polytechnic Institute *M*
St. John Fisher College *M, Mixed*
Skidmore College *M*
State University of New York
Binghamton *M*
College at New Paltz *M, Mixed*
Institute of Technology at Utica/Rome *M*
Oswego *M, Mixed*
Union College *M*
United States Merchant Marine Academy *M*
University of Rochester *M, Mixed*
Utica College of Syracuse University *M*
Yeshiva University *M*

North Carolina
Greensboro College *M*
Guilford College *M*
Meredith College *W*
Methodist College *M, W*
North Carolina Wesleyan College *M*

Ohio
Baldwin-Wallace College *M*
Bluffton College *M*
Capital University *M*
Case Western Reserve University *M*
College of Wooster *M*
Defiance College *M*
Denison University *M*
Heidelberg College *M*
Hiram College *M, Mixed*
John Carroll University *M*
Kenyon College *M*
Marietta College *M*
Mount Union College *M*
Muskingum College *M*
Ohio Northern University *M*
Ohio Wesleyan University *M*
Otterbein College *M*
Wilmington College *M*
Wittenberg University *M*

Pennsylvania
Albright College *M*
Allegheny College *M*
Allentown College of St. Francis de Sales *M*
Cabrini College *M*
Carnegie Mellon University *M*
College Misericordia *M*
Delaware Valley College *M*
Dickinson College *M*
Elizabethtown College *M*
Franklin and Marshall College *Mixed*
Gettysburg College *M*
Grove City College *M*
Juniata College *M*
King's College *M*
Lebanon Valley College of Pennsylvania *M*
Lycoming College *M*
Messiah College *M*
Moravian College *M*
Muhlenberg College *M*
Penn State Erie Behrend College *M*
Susquehanna University *M*
Swarthmore College *M*
Thiel College *M*
University of Scranton *M*
Ursinus College *M, Mixed*
Washington and Jefferson College *M*
Waynesburg College *M*
Widener University *M*
York College of Pennsylvania *M*

Rhode Island
Roger Williams University *M, Mixed*
Salve Regina University *Mixed*

Tennessee
Fisk University *M*
Rhodes College *M*
University of the South *M*

Texas
Southwestern University *M, W, Mixed*
Trinity University *M*

Vermont
Middlebury College *M*
Norwich University *M*

Virginia
Averett College *M*
Bridgewater College *M*
Christopher Newport University *M*
Emory and Henry College *M*
Ferrum College *M, Mixed*
Hampden-Sydney College *M*
Lynchburg College *M*
Marymount University *M*
Randolph-Macon College *M*
Roanoke College *M*
Shenandoah University *M*
Virginia Wesleyan College *M*
Washington and Lee University *M*

West Virginia
Bethany College *M, Mixed*

Wisconsin
Beloit College *M*
Carroll College *M*
Carthage College *M*
Lawrence University *M*
Northwestern College *M*
Ripon College *M*
St. Norbert College *Mixed*
University of Wisconsin
Eau Claire *M*
Platteville *M*
River Falls *M*
Stevens Point *M*
Whitewater *W*

Gymnastics — Division I

Alabama
Auburn University *W*
University of Alabama *M, W*

Arizona
Arizona State University *M, W*
University of Arizona *W*

California
California State University
Fullerton *W*
Sacramento *W*
San Jose State University *M, W*
Stanford University *M, W*
University of California
Berkeley *M, W*
Los Angeles *M, W*
Santa Barbara *M, W*

Colorado
United States Air Force Academy *M*
University of Denver *W*

Connecticut
Southern Connecticut State University *M*
Yale University *W*

District of Columbia
George Washington University *W*

Florida
University of Florida *W*

Georgia
University of Georgia *W*

Idaho
Boise State University *W*

Illinois
Illinois State University *W*
Northern Illinois University *W*
University of Illinois
Chicago *M, W*
Urbana-Champaign *M, W*

Indiana
Ball State University *W*

Iowa
Iowa State University *M, W*
University of Iowa *M, W*

Kentucky
University of Kentucky *W*

Louisiana
Centenary College of Louisiana *W*
Louisiana State University and Agricultural and Mechanical College *W*

Maryland
Towson State University *W*
United States Naval Academy *M, W*
University of Maryland: College Park *W*

Massachusetts
Northeastern University *W*
University of Massachusetts at Amherst *M, W*

Michigan
Central Michigan University *W*
Eastern Michigan University *W*
Michigan State University *M, W*
University of Michigan *M, W*
Western Michigan University *M, W*

Minnesota
University of Minnesota: Twin Cities *M, W*

Missouri
Southeast Missouri State University *W*
University of Missouri: Columbia *W*

Nebraska
University of Nebraska—Lincoln *M, W*

New Hampshire
Dartmouth College *M*
University of New Hampshire *W*

New Jersey
Rutgers—The State University of New Jersey
College of Engineering *W*
Cook College *W*
Douglass College *W*
Livingston College *W*
Mason Gross School of the Arts *W*
Rutgers College *W*

New Mexico
University of New Mexico *M*

New York
Cornell University *M, W*
Syracuse University *M*
United States Military Academy *M*

North Carolina
North Carolina State University *W*
University of North Carolina at Chapel Hill *W*

Ohio
Bowling Green State University *W*
Kent State University *M, W*
Ohio State University: Columbus Campus *M, W*

Oklahoma
University of Oklahoma *M, W*

Oregon
Oregon State University *W*

Pennsylvania
Penn State University Park Campus *M, W*
Temple University *M, W*
University of Pennsylvania *W*
University of Pittsburgh *M, W*

Rhode Island
Brown University *W*
University of Rhode Island *W*

Utah
Brigham Young University *M, W*
Southern Utah University *W*
University of Utah *W*
Utah State University *W*

Vermont
University of Vermont *M, W*

Virginia
College of William and Mary *M, W*
James Madison University *M, W*
Radford University *M, W*

Washington
University of Washington *W*

West Virginia
West Virginia University *W*

Gymnastics — Division II

Alaska
University of Alaska Anchorage *W*

California
University of California: Davis *W*

Colorado
United States Air Force Academy *W*

Connecticut
Southern Connecticut State University *W*

Massachusetts
Springfield College *M, W*

Minnesota
Winona State University *W*

Pennsylvania
Indiana University of Pennsylvania *W*
West Chester University of Pennsylvania *W*

Texas
Texas Woman's University *W*

Washington
Seattle Pacific University *W*

Gymnastics — Division III

Massachusetts
Massachusetts Institute of Technology *M, W*

Minnesota
Gustavus Adolphus College *W*
Hamline University *W*

New York
City University of New York: City College *M*
Ithaca College *W*
State University of New York
College at Brockport *W*
College at Cortland *M, W*

Pennsylvania
Ursinus College *W*

Rhode Island
Rhode Island College *W*

Wisconsin
University of Wisconsin
Eau Claire *W*
La Crosse *W*
Oshkosh *M, W*
River Falls *W*
Whitewater *W*

Ice hockey — Division I

Alaska
University of Alaska
Anchorage *M*
Fairbanks *M*

Colorado
Colorado College *M*
United States Air Force Academy *M*
University of Denver *M*

Connecticut
Fairfield University *M*
University of Connecticut *M*
Yale University *M*

Illinois
University of Illinois at Chicago *M*

Indiana
University of Notre Dame *M*

Maine
University of Maine *M*

Massachusetts
Boston College *M*
Boston University *M*
Harvard and Radcliffe Colleges *M*
Merrimack College *M*
Northeastern University *M*
University of Massachusetts at Lowell *M*

Michigan
Ferris State University *M*
Lake Superior State University *M*
Michigan State University *M*
Michigan Technological University *M*
Northern Michigan University *M*
University of Michigan *M*
Western Michigan University *M*

Minnesota
St. Cloud State University *M*
University of Minnesota
Duluth *M*
Twin Cities *M*

New Hampshire
Dartmouth College *M*
University of New Hampshire *M*

New Jersey
Princeton University *M*

New York
Canisius College *M*
Clarkson University *M*
Colgate University *M*
Cornell University *M*
Iona College *M*
Rensselaer Polytechnic Institute *M*
St. Bonaventure University *M*
St. Lawrence University *M*
Union College *M*
United States Military Academy *M*

North Dakota
University of North Dakota *M*

Ohio
Bowling Green State University *M*
Kent State University *M*
Miami University: Oxford Campus *M*
Ohio State University: Columbus Campus *M*

Pennsylvania
Villanova University *M*

Rhode Island
Brown University *M*
Providence College *M*

Vermont
University of Vermont *M*

Wisconsin
University of Wisconsin: Madison *M*

Ice hockey — Division II

Massachusetts
American International College *M*
Assumption College *M*
Bentley College *M*
Stonehill College *M*

Minnesota
Mankato State University *M*

New Hampshire
New Hampshire College *M*
St. Anselm College *M*

Vermont
St. Michael's College *M*

Ice hockey — Division III

Connecticut
Connecticut College *M*
Trinity College *M*
Wesleyan University *M*

Illinois
Lake Forest College *M*

Maine
Bowdoin College *M*
Colby College *M*
University of Southern Maine *M*

Massachusetts
Amherst College *M*
Babson College *M*
Curry College *M*
Emerson College *M*
Fitchburg State College *M*
Framingham State College *M*
Nichols College *M*
North Adams State College *M*
Salem State College *M*
Suffolk University *M*
Tufts University *M*
University of Massachusetts
Boston *M*
Dartmouth *M*
Wentworth Institute of Technology *M*
Western New England College *M*
Williams College *M*
Worcester State College *M*

Minnesota
Augsburg College *M*
College of St. Scholastica *M*
Concordia College: Moorhead *M*
Gustavus Adolphus College *M*
Hamline University *M*
St. John's University *M*
St. Mary's College of Minnesota *M*
St. Olaf College *M*
University of St. Thomas *M*

New Hampshire
New England College *M*
Plymouth State College of the University System of New Hampshire *M*

New York
Elmira College *M*
Hamilton College *M*
Hobart College *M*
Rochester Institute of Technology *M*
Skidmore College *M*
State University of New York
College at Brockport *M*
College at Cortland *M*
College at Fredonia *M*
College at Geneseo *M*
College at Plattsburgh *M*
College at Potsdam *M*
Oswego *M*

Pennsylvania
University of Scranton *M*

Rhode Island
Roger Williams University *M*

Vermont
Middlebury College *M*
Norwich University *M*

Wisconsin
Lawrence University *M*
St. Norbert College *M*
University of Wisconsin
Eau Claire *M*
River Falls *M*
Stevens Point *M*
Superior *M*

Lacrosse — Division I

California
Stanford University *M*

Colorado
United States Air Force Academy *M*

Connecticut
Fairfield University *M*
University of Hartford *M*
Yale University *M, W*

Delaware
University of Delaware *M, W*

District of Columbia
American University *W*
Georgetown University *M, W*

Indiana
Butler University *M**
University of Notre Dame *M*

Maryland
Loyola College in Maryland *M, W*
Mount St. Mary's College *M*
Towson State University *M, W*
United States Naval Academy *M*
University of Maryland
Baltimore County *M, W*
College Park *M, W*

Massachusetts
Boston College *M, W*
College of the Holy Cross *M, W*
Harvard and Radcliffe Colleges *M, W*
University of Massachusetts at Amherst *M, W*

Michigan
Michigan State University *M*

New Hampshire
Dartmouth College *M, W*
University of New Hampshire *M, W*

New Jersey
Princeton University *M, W*
Rutgers—The State University of New Jersey
College of Engineering *M, W*
Cook College *M, W*
Douglass College *W*
Livingston College *M, W*
Mason Gross School of the Arts *M, W*
Rutgers College *M, W*

New York
Canisius College *M*
Colgate University *M, W*
Cornell University *M, W*
Hofstra University *M, W*
Marist College *M*
St. Bonaventure University *M*
St. John's University *M*
Siena College *M*
State University of New York at Stony Brook *M*
Syracuse University *M*
United States Military Academy *M*

North Carolina
Duke University *M*
University of North Carolina at Chapel Hill *M*

Ohio
Bowling Green State University *M*
Ohio State University: Columbus Campus *M*

Pennsylvania
Bucknell University *M, W*
Drexel University *M, W*
Lafayette College *M, W*
Lehigh University *M, W*
Penn State University Park Campus *M, W*
St. Joseph's University *M, W*
Temple University *W*
University of Pennsylvania *M, W*
Villanova University *M, W*

Rhode Island
Brown University *M, W*
Providence College *M*

Vermont
University of Vermont *M, W*

Virginia
College of William and Mary *W*
James Madison University *W*
Old Dominion University *W*
Radford University *M*
University of Richmond *W*
University of Virginia *M, W*
Virginia Military Institute *M*

Lacrosse — Division II

Colorado
Colorado School of Mines *M*
University of Denver *M*

Connecticut
Quinnipiac College *M*
Sacred Heart University *M, W*
University of New Haven *M*

Massachusetts
American International College *M*
Assumption College *M*
Bentley College *M*
Merrimack College *M*
Springfield College *M, W*

New Hampshire
New Hampshire College *M*

New York
Adelphi University *M*
City University of New York: Queens College *M*
Dowling College *M*
Le Moyne College *M*
Long Island University
C. W. Post Campus *M*
Southampton Campus *M*
New York Institute of Technology *M*
Pace University
College of White Plains *M*
New York *M*
Pleasantville/Briarcliff *M*

North Carolina
Pfeiffer College *M*

Pennsylvania
Bloomsburg University of Pennsylvania *W*
East Stroudsburg University of Pennsylvania *W*
Lock Haven University of Pennsylvania *W*
Millersville University of Pennsylvania *W*
Philadelphia College of Textiles and Science *W*
Shippensburg University of Pennsylvania *W*
West Chester University of Pennsylvania *M, W*

South Carolina
Limestone College *M*

Vermont
St. Michael's College *M, W*

Virginia
Longwood College *W*

Lacrosse — Division III

California
Whittier College *M*

Colorado
Colorado College *M*

Connecticut
Connecticut College *M, W*
Trinity College *M, W*
Wesleyan University *M, W*

Delaware
Wesley College *M*

Illinois
Lake Forest College *M*

Indiana
Earlham College *W*

Maine
Bates College *M, W*
Bowdoin College *M, W*
Colby College *M, W*

Maryland
College of Notre Dame of Maryland *W*
Frostburg State University *W*
Goucher College *M, W*
Hood College *W*
Johns Hopkins University *W*
St. Mary's College of Maryland *M, W*
Salisbury State University *M, W*
Washington College *M, W*
Western Maryland College *M, W*

Massachusetts
Amherst College *M, W*
Babson College *M, W*
Bridgewater State College *W*
Clark University *M*
Curry College *M*
Elms College *W*
Massachusetts Institute of Technology *M, W*
Massachusetts Maritime Academy *M*
Mount Holyoke College *W*
Nichols College *M*
Pine Manor College *W*
Smith College *W*
Tufts University *M, W*
University of Massachusetts at Boston *M*
Wellesley College *W*
Western New England College *M*
Wheaton College *M, W*
Williams College *M, W*

New Hampshire
Colby-Sawyer College *W*
New England College *M*
Plymouth State College of the University System of New Hampshire *M, W*

New Jersey
Drew University *M, W*
Fairleigh Dickinson University *M*
Kean College of New Jersey *M*
Montclair State College *M*
Rowan College of New Jersey *W*
Stockton State College *M*
Trenton State College *W*
Upsala College *M*

New York
Alfred University *M*
City University of New York: City College *M*
Clarkson University *M, W*
Elmira College *M*
Hamilton College *M, W*
Hartwick College *M, W*
Hobart College *M*
Ithaca College *M, W*
Keuka College *M*
Manhattanville College *M*
Nazareth College of Rochester *M, W*
Polytechnic University
Brooklyn *M*
Long Island Campus *M*
Rensselaer Polytechnic Institute *M, W*
Rochester Institute of Technology *M*
St. Lawrence University *M, W*
Skidmore College *M, W*
State University of New York
Albany *M, W*
College at Cortland *M, W*
College at Geneseo *M*
College at Oneonta *M, W*
College at Potsdam *M*
Maritime College *M*
Oswego *M*
Union College *M, W*
United States Merchant Marine Academy *M*
Vassar College *M, W*
Wells College *W*
William Smith College *W*

North Carolina
Greensboro College *M, W*
Guilford College *M, W*

Ohio
College of Wooster *M, W*
Denison University *M, W*
Kenyon College *M, W*
Marietta College *M*
Oberlin College *M, W*
Ohio Wesleyan University *M, W*
Wittenberg University *M, W*

Pennsylvania
Bryn Mawr College *W*
Cedar Crest College *W*
Dickinson College *M, W*
Franklin and Marshall College *M, W*
Gettysburg College *W*
Haverford College *M, W*
Muhlenberg College *W*
Susquehanna University *W*
Swarthmore College *M, W*
University of Scranton *M*
Ursinus College *W*
Widener University *M, W*

Rhode Island
Roger Williams University *M*

Vermont
Castleton State College *M, W*
Middlebury College *M, W*
Norwich University *M*

Virginia
Bridgewater College *W*
Hampden-Sydney College *M*
Hollins College *W*
Lynchburg College *M, W*
Mary Baldwin College *W*
Mary Washington College *M, W*
Marymount University *M*
Randolph-Macon College *M, W*
Randolph-Macon Woman's College *W*
Roanoke College *M, W*
Shenandoah University *M*
Sweet Briar College *W*
Virginia Wesleyan College *M*
Washington and Lee University *M, W*

Rifle — Division I

Alabama
University of Alabama in Birmingham *Mixed*

California
University of San Francisco *W, Mixed*

Florida
Jacksonville University *M, W*

Illinois
De Paul University *W, Mixed*

Kentucky
Murray State University *W, Mixed*
University of Kentucky *W*

Louisiana
Centenary College of Louisiana *M, W*

Maryland
United States Naval Academy *M*

Missouri
Southwest Missouri State University *Mixed*
University of Missouri: Kansas City *Mixed*

New York
Canisius College *W, Mixed*
St. John's University *Mixed*
United States Military Academy *W, Mixed*

North Carolina
North Carolina State University *Mixed*

Ohio
Ohio State University: Columbus Campus *W*
University of Akron *W*
University of Cincinnati *Mixed*
Xavier University *Mixed*

Pennsylvania
Duquesne University *W, Mixed*

South Carolina
The Citadel *M, W*

Tennessee
Memphis State University *M*
Middle Tennessee State University *W*
Tennessee Technological University *W*
University of Tennessee: Martin *Mixed*

Texas
Texas A&M University *W*
Texas Christian University *W*
University of Texas at El Paso *W*

West Virginia
West Virginia University *Mixed*

Wisconsin
Marquette University *Mixed*

Rifle — Division II

Alaska
University of Alaska Fairbanks *W, Mixed*

Missouri
Northeast Missouri State University *Mixed*
University of Missouri: Rolla *M, W*

New Mexico
Eastern New Mexico University *M, W*

Texas
West Texas A & M University *M, W*

Rifle — Division III

Indiana
Rose-Hulman Institute of Technology *M*

Massachusetts
Wentworth Institute of Technology *M, W, Mixed*

Missouri
Westminster College *M, W*

New York
State University of New York Maritime College *M, W*
United States Merchant Marine Academy *M*

Pennsylvania
Carnegie Mellon University *M*

Vermont
Norwich University *M, Mixed*

Skiing — Division I

Colorado
University of Colorado at Boulder *M, W*

Massachusetts
Boston College *M, W*
Harvard and Radcliffe Colleges *M, W*
University of Massachusetts at Amherst *M, W*

New Hampshire
Dartmouth College *M, W*
University of New Hampshire *M, W*

New Mexico
University of New Mexico *M, W, Mixed*

Utah
University of Utah *M, W*

Vermont
University of Vermont *M, W*

Wisconsin
University of Wisconsin: Green Bay *M*

Skiing — Division II

Alaska
University of Alaska
Anchorage *M, W*
Fairbanks *M, W*

Colorado
University of Denver *M, W*
Western State College of Colorado *M, W*

Michigan
Michigan Technological University *Mixed*
Northern Michigan University *M, W*

New Hampshire
Franklin Pierce College *M, W*
Keene State College *M, W*
St. Anselm College *M, W*

Vermont
St. Michael's College *M, W*

Skiing — Division III

Maine
Bates College *M, W*
Bowdoin College *M, W*
Colby College *M, W*

Massachusetts
Massachusetts Institute of Technology *M, W*
Smith College *W*
Western New England College *M*
Williams College *M, W*

Minnesota
Carleton College *Mixed*
St. Mary's College of Minnesota *M, W*
St. Olaf College *M, W*

New Hampshire
Colby-Sawyer College *M, W*
New England College *M, W, Mixed*
Plymouth State College of the University System of New Hampshire *M, W*

New Jersey
New Jersey Institute of Technology *M, W*

New York
Alfred University *M, W*
St. Lawrence University *M*

Vermont
Johnson State College *M, W*
Middlebury College *M, W*
Norwich University *M*

Soccer — Division I

Alabama
Alabama Agricultural and Mechanical University *M*
University of Alabama in Birmingham *M*
University of South Alabama *M*

Arkansas
University of Arkansas *W*
University of Arkansas at Little Rock *M, W*

California
California State University
Fresno *M*
Fullerton *M*
Northridge *M*
Sacramento *M*
Loyola Marymount University *M*
St. Mary's College of California *M, W*
San Diego State University *M, W*
San Jose State University *M*
Santa Clara University *M, W*
Stanford University *M, W*
University of California
Berkeley *M, W*
Irvine *M, W*
Los Angeles *M*
Santa Barbara *M, W*
University of the Pacific *W*
University of San Diego *M, W*
University of San Francisco *M, W*

Colorado
Colorado College *W*
United States Air Force Academy *M*

Connecticut
Central Connecticut State University *M*
Fairfield University *M, W*
University of Connecticut *M, W*
University of Hartford *M, W*
Yale University *M, W*

Delaware
University of Delaware *M, W*

District of Columbia
American University *M, W*
George Washington University *M, W*
Georgetown University *M, W*
Howard University *M*

Florida
Florida International University *M, W*
Jacksonville University *M*
Stetson University *M*
University of Central Florida *M*
University of South Florida *M*

Georgia
Georgia Southern University *M*
Georgia State University *M, W*
Mercer University *M, W*

Illinois
Bradley University *M*
De Paul University *M*
Eastern Illinois University *M*
Illinois State University *M*
Loyola University of Chicago *M, W*
Northern Illinois University *M*
Northwestern University *M*
Quincy University *M*
Southern Illinois University at Edwardsville *M*
University of Illinois at Chicago *M*
Western Illinois University *M*

Indiana
Butler University *M, W*
Indiana University Bloomington *M*
University of Evansville *M*
University of Notre Dame *M, W*
University of Southern Indiana *M*

Valparaiso University *M*

Iowa
Drake University *M*

Kentucky
University of Kentucky *M, W*
University of Louisville *M, W*
Western Kentucky University *M*

Louisiana
Centenary College of Louisiana *M, W*

Maine
University of Maine *M, W*

Maryland
Loyola College in Maryland *M, W*
Mount St. Mary's College *M, W*
Towson State University *M, W*
United States Naval Academy *M*
University of Maryland
Baltimore County *M, W*
College Park *M, W*
Eastern Shore *M*

Massachusetts
Boston College *M, W*
Boston University *M*
College of the Holy Cross *M, W*
Harvard and Radcliffe Colleges *M, W*
Northeastern University *M*
University of Massachusetts at Amherst *M, W*

Michigan
Central Michigan University *M*
Eastern Michigan University *M*
Michigan State University *M, W*
University of Detroit Mercy *M*
Western Michigan University *M*

Missouri
St. Louis University *M*
Southwest Missouri State University *M*
University of Missouri: Kansas City *M*

Nebraska
Creighton University *M, W*

Nevada
University of Nevada: Las Vegas *M*

New Hampshire
Dartmouth College *M, W*
University of New Hampshire *M, W*

New Jersey
Fairleigh Dickinson University: Edward Williams College *M*
Monmouth College *M, W*
Princeton University *M, W*
Rider College *M*
Rutgers—The State University of New Jersey
College of Engineering *M, W*
Cook College *M, W*
Douglass College *W*
Livingston College *M, W*
Mason Gross School of the Arts *M, W*
Rutgers College *M, W*
St. Peter's College *M, W*
Seton Hall University *M*

New Mexico
University of New Mexico *M*

New York
Adelphi University *M*
Barnard College *W*
Canisius College *M, W*
Colgate University *M, W*
Columbia University: Columbia College *M, W*
Cornell University *M, W*
Fordham University *M*
Hartwick College *M*
Hofstra University *M*
Iona College *M, W*
Long Island University: Brooklyn Campus *M*
Manhattan College *M, W*
Marist College *M*
Niagara University *M, W*
St. Bonaventure University *M, W*
St. Francis College *M*
St. John's University *M, W*
Siena College *M, W*
State University of New York
Buffalo *M, W*
Stony Brook *W*
College at Oneonta *M*
Syracuse University *M*
United States Military Academy *M, W*

North Carolina
Appalachian State University *M*
Campbell University *M, W*
Davidson College *M, W*
Duke University *M, W*
East Carolina University *M*
North Carolina State University *M, W*
University of North Carolina
Asheville *M*
Chapel Hill *M, W*
Charlotte *M*
Greensboro *M, W*
Wilmington *M*
Wake Forest University *M*

Ohio
Bowling Green State University *M*
Cleveland State University *M*
Miami University: Oxford Campus *M*
Ohio State University: Columbus Campus *M*
University of Akron *M*
University of Cincinnati *M, W*
University of Dayton *M, W*
Wright State University *M, W*
Xavier University *M, W*

Oklahoma
University of Tulsa *M, W*

Oregon
Oregon State University *M, W*
University of Portland *M, W*

Pennsylvania
Bucknell University *M, W*
Drexel University *M*
La Salle University *M, W*
Lafayette College *M, W*
Lehigh University *M, W*
Penn State University Park Campus *M*
Philadelphia College of Textiles and Science *M*
Robert Morris College *M, W*
St. Francis College *M, W*
St. Joseph's University *M*
Temple University *M, W*
University of Pennsylvania *M, W*
University of Pittsburgh *M*
Villanova University *M, W*

Rhode Island
Brown University *M, W*
Providence College *M, W*
University of Rhode Island *M, W*

South Carolina
Charleston Southern University *M*
The Citadel *M*
Clemson University *M*
College of Charleston *M*
Furman University *M*
University of South Carolina
Coastal Carolina College *M*
Columbia *M*
Winthrop University *M*

Tennessee
Memphis State University *M*
Vanderbilt University *M, W*

Texas
Southern Methodist University *M, W*
Texas A&M University *W*
Texas Christian University *M, W*
University of North Texas *M*
University of Texas: Pan American *M*

Vermont
University of Vermont *M, W*

Virginia
College of William and Mary *M, W*
George Mason University *M, W*
James Madison University *M, W*
Liberty University *M, W*
Old Dominion University *M*
Radford University *M, W*
University of Richmond *M*
University of Virginia *M, W*
Virginia Commonwealth University *M*
Virginia Military Institute *M*
Virginia Polytechnic Institute and State University *M*

Washington
Gonzaga University *M, W*
University of Washington *M, W*
Washington State University *W*

West Virginia
Marshall University *M*

Wisconsin
Marquette University *M*
University of Wisconsin
Green Bay *M, W*
Madison *M, W*

Soccer — Division II

Alabama
University of Alabama in Huntsville *M*

Arizona
Grand Canyon University *M*

California
California Polytechnic State University: San Luis Obispo *M, W*
California State Polytechnic University: Pomona *M, W*
California State University
Bakersfield *M*
Chico *M, W*
Dominguez Hills *M, W*
Hayward *M, W*
Los Angeles *M*
San Bernardino *M, W*
Stanislaus *M*
Chapman University *M, W*
College of Notre Dame *M*
Humboldt State University *M*
San Francisco State University *M, W*
Sonoma State University *M, W*
University of California: Davis *M, W*

Colorado
Colorado Christian University *M, W*
Colorado School of Mines *M*
Fort Lewis College *M*
Metropolitan State College of Denver *M, W*
Regis University *M, W*
United States Air Force Academy *W*
University of Colorado at Colorado Springs *M*
University of Denver *M, W*
University of Northern Colorado *W*
University of Southern Colorado *M*

Connecticut
Quinnipiac College *M, W*
Sacred Heart University *M, W*
Southern Connecticut State University *M*
University of Bridgeport *W*
University of New Haven *M*

District of Columbia
University of the District of Columbia *M*

Florida
Barry University *M, W*
Eckerd College *M*
Florida Atlantic University *M, W*
Florida Institute of Technology *M*
Florida Southern College *M*
Rollins College *M*
St. Leo College *M*
University of North Florida *M*
University of Tampa *M*

Georgia
Augusta College *M*

Illinois
Lewis University *M, W*
Quincy University *W*
Southern Illinois University at Edwardsville *W*

Indiana
Indiana University—Purdue University at Fort Wayne *M*
St. Joseph's College *M, W*
University of Indianapolis *M*

Kentucky
Bellarmine College *M, W*
Kentucky Wesleyan College *M*
Northern Kentucky University *M*

Massachusetts
American International College *M, W*
Assumption College *M, W*
Bentley College *M, W*
Merrimack College *M, W*

Springfield College *M, W*
Stonehill College *M, W*
University of Massachusetts at Lowell *M*

Michigan

Oakland University *M*

Missouri

Drury College *M, W*
Lincoln University *M*
Missouri Southern State College *M*
Northeast Missouri State University *M, W*
University of Missouri
Rolla *M, W*
St. Louis *M, W*

New Hampshire

Franklin Pierce College *M, W*
Keene State College *M, W*
New Hampshire College *M, W*
St. Anselm College *M, W*

New York

Adelphi University *W*
City University of New York: Queens College *M*
College of St. Rose *M, W*
Concordia College *M, W*
Dowling College *M*
Le Moyne College *M, W*
Long Island University
C. W. Post Campus *M*
Southampton Campus *M, W*
Mercy College *M*
New York Institute of Technology *M, W*

North Carolina

Catawba College *M, W*
Elon College *M, W*
Gardner-Webb University *M, W*
High Point University *M, W*
Lenoir-Rhyne College *M, W*
Mars Hill College *M, W*
Mount Olive College *M*
Pembroke State University *M*
Pfeiffer College *M*
Queens College *M, W*
Wingate College *M, W*

Ohio

Ashland University *M*

Pennsylvania

Bloomsburg University of Pennsylvania *M, W*
California University of Pennsylvania *M, W*
East Stroudsburg University of Pennsylvania *M, W*
Gannon University *M, W*
Kutztown University of Pennsylvania *M, W*
Lock Haven University of Pennsylvania *M*
Mercyhurst College *M, W*
Millersville University of Pennsylvania *M*
Philadelphia College of Textiles and Science *W*
Shippensburg University of Pennsylvania *M*
Slippery Rock University of Pennsylvania *M*
University of Pittsburgh at Johnstown *M*
West Chester University of Pennsylvania *M, W*

Rhode Island

Bryant College *M, W*

South Carolina

Erskine College *M, W*
Francis Marion University *M*
Lander University *M*
Limestone College *M, W*
Presbyterian College *M, W*
University of South Carolina
Aiken *M*
Spartanburg *M*
Wofford College *M*

Tennessee

Carson-Newman College *M, W*
Lincoln Memorial University *M*

Texas

Hardin-Simmons University *M, W*
West Texas A & M University *M*

Vermont

St. Michael's College *M, W*

Virginia

Longwood College *M*

Washington

Seattle Pacific University *M*

West Virginia

Alderson-Broaddus College *M*
Davis and Elkins College *M*
Shepherd College *M*
University of Charleston *M*
West Virginia Wesleyan College *M, W*
Wheeling Jesuit College *M, W*

Wisconsin

University of Wisconsin: Parkside *M*

Soccer — Division III

Arkansas

Hendrix College *M, W*

California

California Institute of Technology *M*
California Lutheran University *M, W*
Claremont McKenna College *M, W*
Harvey Mudd College *M, W*
Menlo College *M*
Occidental College *M, W*
Pitzer College *M, W*
Pomona College *M, W*
Scripps College *W*
University of California
San Diego *M, W*
Santa Cruz *M, W*
University of La Verne *M, W*
University of Redlands *M, W*
Whittier College *M, W*

Colorado

Colorado College *M*

Connecticut

Albertus Magnus College *M*
Connecticut College *M, W*
Eastern Connecticut State University *M, W*
Trinity College *M, W*
United States Coast Guard Academy *M*
Wesleyan University *M, W*
Western Connecticut State University *M*

Delaware

Wesley College *M*

District of Columbia

Catholic University of America *M, W*
Gallaudet University *M*

Georgia

Emory University *M, W*
Oglethorpe University *M, W*
Savannah College of Art and Design *M, W*

Illinois

Augustana College *M*
Aurora University *M*
Blackburn College *M*
College of St. Francis *M*
Illinois Benedictine College *M*
Illinois College *M, W*
Illinois Wesleyan University *M*
Knox College *M, W*
Lake Forest College *M, W*
MacMurray College *M, W*
Millikin University *M*
Monmouth College *M*
North Central College *M*
North Park College *M*
Parks College of St. Louis University *M*
Principia College *M, W*
Rockford College *M, W*
University of Chicago *M, W*
Wheaton College *M, W*

Indiana

Anderson University *M*
DePauw University *M, W*
Earlham College *M, W*
Franklin College *M*
Hanover College *M*
Manchester College *M*
Rose-Hulman Institute of Technology *M*
St. Mary's College *W*
Wabash College *M*

Iowa

Coe College *M, W*
Cornell College *M, W*
Grinnell College *M, W*
Loras College *M*
Luther College *M, W*
Wartburg College *M, W*

Kentucky

Asbury College *M*
Berea College *M*
Centre College *M, W*
Thomas More College *M, W*

Maine

Bates College *M, W*
Bowdoin College *M, W*
Colby College *M, W*
Maine Maritime Academy *M*
St. Joseph's College *M, W*
University of Southern Maine *M, W*

Maryland

College of Notre Dame of Maryland *W*
Frostburg State University *M*
Goucher College *M, W*
Johns Hopkins University *M, W*
St. Mary's College of Maryland *M, W*
Salisbury State University *M*
Washington College *M*
Western Maryland College *M, W*

Massachusetts

Amherst College *M, W*
Anna Maria College for Men and Women *M, W*
Babson College *M, W*
Brandeis University *M, W*
Bridgewater State College *M, W*
Clark University *M, W*
Curry College *M, W*
Eastern Nazarene College *M*
Elms College *W*
Emerson College *M, W*
Fitchburg State College *M*
Framingham State College *M, W*
Gordon College *M*
Massachusetts Institute of Technology *M, W*
Massachusetts Maritime Academy *M*
Mount Holyoke College *W*
Nichols College *M, W*
North Adams State College *M, W*
Pine Manor College *W*
Regis College *W*
Salem State College *M, W*
Simmons College *W*
Smith College *W*
Suffolk University *M*
Tufts University *M, W*
University of Massachusetts
Boston *M*
Dartmouth *M, W*
Wellesley College *W*
Wentworth Institute of Technology *M*
Western New England College *M, W*
Westfield State College *M, W*
Wheaton College *M, W*
Williams College *M, W*
Worcester Polytechnic Institute *M*
Worcester State College *M, W*

Michigan

Adrian College *M, W*
Albion College *M, W*
Alma College *M, W*
Calvin College *M, W*
Hope College *M, W*
Kalamazoo College *M, W*
Olivet College *M, W*

Minnesota

Augsburg College *M, W*
Carleton College *M, W*
College of St. Benedict *W*
College of St. Scholastica *M, W*
Concordia College: Moorhead *M, W*
Gustavus Adolphus College *M, W*
Hamline University *M, W*
Macalester College *M, W*
St. John's University *M*
St. Mary's College of Minnesota *M, W*
St. Olaf College *M, W*
University of St. Thomas *M, W*

Mississippi

Millsaps College *M, W*

Missouri

Fontbonne College *M*
Maryville University *M, W*
Washington University *M, W*
Webster University *M*
Westminster College *M, W*

New Hampshire

Colby-Sawyer College *M, W*
Daniel Webster College *M*
New England College *M*

Plymouth State College of the University System of New Hampshire *M, W*

New Jersey

Drew University *M, W*
Fairleigh Dickinson University *M*
Jersey City State College *M*
Kean College of New Jersey *M, W*
Montclair State College *M, W*
New Jersey Institute of Technology *M*
Ramapo College of New Jersey *M*
Rowan College of New Jersey *M*
Rutgers—The State University of New Jersey
  Camden College of Arts and Sciences *M*
  Newark College of Arts and Sciences *M*
Stevens Institute of Technology *M, W*
Stockton State College *M, W*
Trenton State College *M, W*
Upsala College *M, W*
William Paterson College of New Jersey *M*

New York

Alfred University *M, W*
Bard College *M, W*
City University of New York
  Baruch College *M*
  City College *M*
  College of Staten Island *M*
  Hunter College *M*
  John Jay College of Criminal Justice *M*
  Lehman College *M*
  Medgar Evers College *M*
  York College *M*
Clarkson University *M, W*
College of Mount St. Vincent *W*
Elmira College *M, W*
Hamilton College *M, W*
Hartwick College *W*
Hilbert College *M, W*
Hobart College *M, W*
Ithaca College *M, W*
Keuka College *M, W*
Manhattanville College *M, W*
Mount St. Mary College *M, W*
Nazareth College of Rochester *M, W*
New York University *M*
Polytechnic University *M*
Rensselaer Polytechnic Institute *M, W*
Rochester Institute of Technology *M, W*
Russell Sage College *W*
St. John Fisher College *M, W*
St. Lawrence University *M, W*
Skidmore College *M, W*
State University of New York
  Albany *M, W*
  Binghamton *M, W*
  Stony Brook *M*
  College at Brockport *M, W*
  College at Buffalo *M, W*
  College at Cortland *M, W*
  College at Fredonia *M, W*
  College at Geneseo *M, W*
  College at New Paltz *M, W*
  College at Old Westbury *M*
  College at Oneonta *W*
  College at Plattsburgh *M, W*
  College at Potsdam *M, W*
  Institute of Technology at Utica/Rome *M, W*
  Maritime College *M*
  Oswego *M, W*
Union College *M, W*
United States Merchant Marine Academy *M*
University of Rochester *M, W*
Utica College of Syracuse University *M, W*
Vassar College *M, W*
Wells College *W*

North Carolina

Greensboro College *M, W*
Guilford College *M, W*
Methodist College *M, W*
North Carolina Wesleyan College *M, W*

Ohio

Baldwin-Wallace College *M, W*
Bluffton College *M, W*
Capital University *M, W*
Case Western Reserve University *M, W*
College of Wooster *M, W*
Defiance College *M*
Denison University *M, W*
Heidelberg College *M, W*
Hiram College *M, W*
John Carroll University *M, W*
Kenyon College *M, W*
Marietta College *M, W*
Mount Union College *M, W*
Muskingum College *M, W*
Oberlin College *M, W*
Ohio Northern University *M, W*
Ohio Wesleyan University *M, W*
Otterbein College *M, W*
Wilmington College *M, W*
Wittenberg University *M, W*

Pennsylvania

Albright College *M*
Allegheny College *M, W*
Allentown College of St. Francis de Sales *M*
Bryn Mawr College *W*
Cabrini College *M*
Carnegie Mellon University *M, W*
College Misericordia *M, W*
Delaware Valley College *M*
Dickinson College *M, W*
Elizabethtown College *M, W*
Franklin and Marshall College *M, W*
Gettysburg College *M, W*
Grove City College *M*
Haverford College *M, W*
Juniata College *M*
King's College *M*
Lebanon Valley College of Pennsylvania *M*
Lincoln University *M*
Lycoming College *M*
Messiah College *M, W*
Moravian College *M*
Muhlenberg College *M, W*
Penn State Erie Behrend College *M*
Susquehanna University *M*
Swarthmore College *M, W*
University of Scranton *M, W*
Ursinus College *M*
Washington and Jefferson College *M, W*
Waynesburg College *M, W*
Widener University *M*
Wilkes University *M, W*
York College of Pennsylvania *M*

Rhode Island

Rhode Island College *M*
Roger Williams University *M, W*
Salve Regina University *M, W*

Tennessee

Maryville College *M, W*
Rhodes College *M, W*
University of the South *M, W*

Texas

Trinity University *M, W*

Vermont

Castleton State College *M, W*
Johnson State College *M, W*
Middlebury College *M, W*
Norwich University *M, W*

Virginia

Averett College *M*
Bridgewater College *M*
Christopher Newport University *M*
Eastern Mennonite College *M*
Ferrum College *M, W*
Hampden-Sydney College *M*
Hollins College *W*
Lynchburg College *M, W*
Mary Washington College *M, W*
Marymount University *M, W*
Randolph-Macon College *M, W*
Randolph-Macon Woman's College *W*
Roanoke College *M, W*
Shenandoah University *M, W*
Sweet Briar College *W*
Virginia Wesleyan College *M, W*
Washington and Lee University *M, W*

West Virginia

Bethany College *M, W*

Wisconsin

Beloit College *M, W*
Carroll College *M, W*
Lawrence University *M, W*
Northwestern College *M*
Ripon College *M, W*
St. Norbert College *M, W*
University of Wisconsin
  Eau Claire *W*
  La Crosse *W*
  Oshkosh *M*
  Platteville *M, W*
  Stevens Point *W*
  Whitewater *M, W*

Softball — Division I

Alabama

Samford University *W*

Arizona

Arizona State University *W*
University of Arizona *W*

California

California State Polytechnic University: Pomona *W*
California State University
  Fresno *W*
  Fullerton *W*
  Long Beach *W*
  Northridge *W*
  Sacramento *W*
Loyola Marymount University *W*
St. Mary's College of California *W*
San Diego State University *W*
San Jose State University *W*
Santa Clara University *W*
Stanford University *W*
University of California
  Berkeley *W*
  Los Angeles *W*
University of the Pacific *W*
University of San Diego *W*

Connecticut

Central Connecticut State University *W*
Fairfield University *W*
University of Connecticut *W*
University of Hartford *W*
Yale University *W*

Delaware

Delaware State College *W*
University of Delaware *W*

Florida

Bethune-Cookman College *W*
Florida Agricultural and Mechanical University *W*
Florida State University *W*
Jacksonville University *W*
Stetson University *W*
University of South Florida *W*

Georgia

Georgia Institute of Technology *W*
Georgia Southern University *W*
Georgia State University *W*
Mercer University *W*

Hawaii

University of Hawaii at Manoa *W*

Illinois

Bradley University *W*
De Paul University *W*
Eastern Illinois University *W*
Illinois State University *W*
Loyola University of Chicago *W*
Northeastern Illinois University *W*
Northern Illinois University *W*
Northwestern University *W*
Southern Illinois University at Carbondale *W*
University of Illinois at Chicago *W*
Western Illinois University *W*

Indiana

Ball State University *W*
Butler University *W*
Indiana State University *W*
Indiana University Bloomington *W*
University of Evansville *W*
University of Notre Dame *W*
Valparaiso University *W*

Iowa

Drake University *W*
Iowa State University *W*
University of Iowa *W*
University of Northern Iowa *W*

Kansas

University of Kansas *W*
Wichita State University *W*

Kentucky

Eastern Kentucky University *W*
Morehead State University *W*

Louisiana

Centenary College of Louisiana *W*
Louisiana Tech University *W*
McNeese State University *W*
Nicholls State University *W*
Northeast Louisiana University *W*
Northwestern State University *W*
Southeastern Louisiana University *W*
University of Southwestern Louisiana *W*

Maine

University of Maine *W*

Maryland

Coppin State College *W*

Loyola College in Maryland *W*
Morgan State University *W*
Mount St. Mary's College *W*
Towson State University *W*
University of Maryland
Baltimore County *W*
Eastern Shore *W*

Massachusetts

Boston College *W*
Boston University *W*
College of the Holy Cross *W*
Harvard and Radcliffe Colleges *W*
University of Massachusetts at Amherst *W*

Michigan

Central Michigan University *W*
Eastern Michigan University *W*
Michigan State University *W*
University of Detroit Mercy *W*
University of Michigan *W*
Western Michigan University *W*

Minnesota

University of Minnesota: Twin Cities *W*

Missouri

St. Louis University *W*
Southeast Missouri State University *W*
Southwest Missouri State University *W*
University of Missouri
Columbia *W*
Kansas City *W*

Nebraska

Creighton University *W*
University of Nebraska—Lincoln *W*

Nevada

University of Nevada: Las Vegas *W*

New Jersey

Monmouth College *W*
Princeton University *W*
Rider College *W*
Rutgers—The State University of New Jersey
College of Engineering *W*
Cook College *W*
Douglass College *W*
Livingston College *W*
Mason Gross School of the Arts *W*
Rutgers College *W*
St. Peter's College *W*
Seton Hall University *W*

New Mexico

New Mexico State University *W*
University of New Mexico *W*

New York

Adelphi University *W*
Canisius College *W*
Colgate University *W*
Fordham University *W*
Hofstra University *W*
Iona College *W*
Long Island University: Brooklyn Campus *W*
Manhattan College *W*
Marist College *W*
Niagara University *W*
St. Bonaventure University *W*
St. Francis College *W*
St. John's University *W*
Siena College *W*
United States Military Academy *W*
Wagner College *W*

North Carolina

Campbell University *W*
East Carolina University *W*
North Carolina Agricultural and Technical State University *W*
University of North Carolina
Asheville *W*
Chapel Hill *W*
Charlotte *W*
Greensboro *W*
Wilmington *W*

Ohio

Bowling Green State University *W*
Cleveland State University *W*
Kent State University *W*
Miami University: Oxford Campus *W*
Ohio State University: Columbus Campus *W*
Ohio University *W*
University of Akron *W*
University of Dayton *W*
University of Toledo *W*
Wright State University *W*
Youngstown State University *W*

Oklahoma

Oklahoma State University *W*
University of Oklahoma *W*
University of Tulsa *W*

Oregon

Oregon State University *W*
University of Oregon *W*

Pennsylvania

Bucknell University *W*
Drexel University *W*
La Salle University *W*
Lafayette College *W*
Lehigh University *W*
Penn State University Park Campus *W*
Robert Morris College *W*
St. Francis College *W*
St. Joseph's University *W*
Temple University *W*
University of Pennsylvania *W*
Villanova University *W*

Rhode Island

Brown University *W*
Providence College *W*
University of Rhode Island *W*

South Carolina

Charleston Southern University *W*
College of Charleston *W*
Furman University *W*
University of South Carolina
Coastal Carolina College *W*
Columbia *W*
Winthrop University *W*

Tennessee

Austin Peay State University *W*
Middle Tennessee State University *W*
Tennessee Technological University *W*
University of Tennessee: Martin *W*

Texas

Sam Houston State University *W*
Southwest Texas State University *W*
Stephen F. Austin State University *W*
Texas A&M University *W*
University of Texas
Arlington *W*
San Antonio *W*

Utah

Southern Utah University *W*
University of Utah *W*
Utah State University *W*

Vermont

University of Vermont *W*

Virginia

George Mason University *W*
Radford University *W*
University of Virginia *W*

Washington

University of Washington *W*

Wisconsin

University of Wisconsin: Green Bay *W*

Softball — Division II

Alabama

Livingston University *W*
Troy State University *W*
University of North Alabama *W*

California

California Polytechnic State University: San Luis Obispo *W*
California State University
Bakersfield *W*
Chico *W*
Dominguez Hills *W*
Hayward *W*
San Bernardino *W*
Stanislaus *W*
Chapman University *W*
College of Notre Dame *W*
Humboldt State University *W*
San Francisco State University *W*
Sonoma State University *W*
University of California
Davis *W*
Riverside *W*

Colorado

Adams State College *W*
Colorado School of Mines *W*
Fort Lewis College *W*
Mesa State College *W*
Regis University *W*
University of Colorado at Colorado Springs *W*

Connecticut

Quinnipiac College *W*
Sacred Heart University *W*
Southern Connecticut State University *W*
University of Bridgeport *W*
University of New Haven *W*

Florida

Barry University *W*
Eckerd College *W*
Florida Institute of Technology *W*
Florida Southern College *W*
Rollins College *W*
St. Leo College *W*
University of North Florida *W*
University of Tampa *W*

Georgia

Augusta College *W*
Columbus College *W*
Georgia College *W*
Paine College *W*
Valdosta State College *W*
West Georgia College *W*

Illinois

College of St. Francis *W*
Lewis University *W*
Quincy University *W*
Southern Illinois University at Edwardsville *W*

Indiana

Oakland City College *W*
St. Joseph's College *W*
University of Indianapolis *W*
University of Southern Indiana *W*

Iowa

Morningside College *W*

Kansas

Emporia State University *W*
Pittsburg State University *W*
Washburn University of Topeka *W*

Kentucky

Bellarmine College *W*
Kentucky State University *W*
Kentucky Wesleyan College *W*
Northern Kentucky University *W*

Maryland

Bowie State University *W*

Massachusetts

American International College *W*
Assumption College *W*
Bentley College *W*
Merrimack College *W*
Springfield College *W*
Stonehill College *W*
University of Massachusetts at Lowell *W*

Michigan

Ferris State University *W*
Grand Valley State University *W*
Hillsdale College *W*
Lake Superior State University *W*
Northwood University *W*
Saginaw Valley State University *W*
Wayne State University *W*

Minnesota

Bemidji State University *W*
Mankato State University *W*
Moorhead State University *W*
St. Cloud State University *W*
University of Minnesota: Duluth *W*
Winona State University *W*

Mississippi

Delta State University *W*
Mississippi College *W*
Mississippi University for Women *W*

Missouri

Central Missouri State University *W*
Lincoln University *W*
Missouri Southern State College *W*
Missouri Western State College *W*
Northeast Missouri State University *W*
Northwest Missouri State University *W*
Southwest Baptist University *W*
University of Missouri
Rolla *W*
St. Louis *W*

Nebraska
University of Nebraska
Kearney *W*
Omaha *W*
Wayne State College *W*

New Hampshire
Franklin Pierce College *W*
Keene State College *W*
New Hampshire College *W*
St. Anselm College *W*

New Mexico
New Mexico Highlands University *W*

New York
City University of New York:
Queens College *W*
College of St. Rose *W*
Concordia College *W*
Dowling College *W*
Le Moyne College *W*
Long Island University
C. W. Post Campus *W*
Southampton Campus *W*
Mercy College *W*
Molloy College *W*
New York Institute of Technology *W*
Pace University
College of White Plains *W*
New York *W*
Pleasantville/Briarcliff *W*

North Carolina
Catawba College *W*
Elizabeth City State University *W*
Elon College *W*
Fayetteville State University *W*
Gardner-Webb University *W*
Johnson C. Smith University *W*
Lenoir-Rhyne College *W*
Livingstone College *W*
Mars Hill College *W*
Mount Olive College *W*
North Carolina Central University *W*
Pembroke State University *W*
Pfeiffer College *W*
Queens College *W*
St. Augustine's College *W*
Shaw University *W*
Wingate College *W*
Winston-Salem State University *W*

North Dakota
North Dakota State University *W*
University of North Dakota *W*

Ohio
Ashland University *W*

Oklahoma
Cameron University *W*
University of Central Oklahoma *W*

Oregon
Portland State University *W*

Pennsylvania
Bloomsburg University of Pennsylvania *W*
California University of Pennsylvania *W*
Clarion University of Pennsylvania *W*
East Stroudsburg University of Pennsylvania *W*
Edinboro University of Pennsylvania *W*
Gannon University *W*
Indiana University of Pennsylvania *W*
Kutztown University of Pennsylvania *W*
Lock Haven University of Pennsylvania *W*
Mansfield University of Pennsylvania *W*
Mercyhurst College *W*
Millersville University of Pennsylvania *W*
Philadelphia College of Textiles and Science *W*
Shippensburg University of Pennsylvania *W*
Slippery Rock University of Pennsylvania *W*
West Chester University of Pennsylvania *W*

Rhode Island
Bryant College *W*

South Carolina
Erskine College *W*
Francis Marion University *W*
Lander University *W*
Limestone College *W*
Newberry College *W*
University of South Carolina
Aiken *W*
Spartanburg *W*

South Dakota
Augustana College *W*
South Dakota State University *W*
University of South Dakota *W*

Tennessee
Carson-Newman College *W*
Lincoln Memorial University *W*

Vermont
St. Michael's College *W*

Virginia
Hampton University *W*
Longwood College *W*
Norfolk State University *W*
St. Paul's College *W*
Virginia Union University *W*

West Virginia
Davis and Elkins College *W*
Shepherd College *W*
University of Charleston *W*
West Liberty State College *W*
West Virginia Wesleyan College *W*

Wisconsin
University of Wisconsin: Parkside *W*

Softball — Division III

California
California Lutheran University *W*
Claremont McKenna College *W*
Harvey Mudd College *W*
Menlo College *W*
Occidental College *W*
Pomona College *W*
Scripps College *W*
University of California: San Diego *W*
University of La Verne *W*
University of Redlands *W*
Whittier College *W*

Connecticut
Albertus Magnus College *W*
Eastern Connecticut State University *W*
Trinity College *W*
United States Coast Guard Academy *W*
Wesleyan University *W*
Western Connecticut State University *W*

Delaware
Wesley College *W*

District of Columbia
Catholic University of America *W*
Gallaudet University *W*

Illinois
Augustana College *W*
Aurora University *W*
Blackburn College *W*
Concordia University *W*
Elmhurst College *W*
Eureka College *W*
Illinois Benedictine College *W*
Illinois College *W*
Illinois Wesleyan University *W*
Knox College *W*
Lake Forest College *W*
MacMurray College *W*
Millikin University *W*
Monmouth College *W*
North Central College *W*
North Park College *W*
Principia College *W*
Rockford College *W*
University of Chicago *W*
Wheaton College *W*

Indiana
Anderson University *W*
Earlham College *W*
Franklin College *W*
Hanover College *W*
Manchester College *W*
St. Mary's College *W*

Iowa
Buena Vista College *W*
Central College *W*
Coe College *W*
Cornell College *W*
Grinnell College *W*
Loras College *W*
Luther College *W*
Simpson College *W*
University of Dubuque *W*
Upper Iowa University *W*
Wartburg College *W*
William Penn College *W*

Kentucky
Thomas More College *W*

Maine
Bates College *W*
Bowdoin College *W*
Colby College *W*
St. Joseph's College *W*
University of Southern Maine *W*

Maryland
Salisbury State University *W*
Washington College *W*
Western Maryland College *W*

Massachusetts
Anna Maria College for Men and Women *W*
Babson College *W*
Brandeis University *W*
Bridgewater State College *W*
Clark University *W*
Curry College *W*
Eastern Nazarene College *W*
Elms College *W*
Emerson College *W*
Emmanuel College *W*
Fitchburg State College *W*
Framingham State College *W*
Gordon College *W*
Massachusetts Institute of Technology *W*
Massachusetts Maritime Academy *W*
Mount Holyoke College *W*
Nichols College *W*
North Adams State College *W*
Pine Manor College *W*
Regis College *W*
Salem State College *W*
Smith College *W*
Suffolk University *W*
Tufts University *W*
University of Massachusetts
Boston *W*
Dartmouth *W*
Wentworth Institute of Technology *W*
Western New England College *W*
Westfield State College *W*
Wheaton College *W*
Williams College *W*
Worcester Polytechnic Institute *W*
Worcester State College *W*

Michigan
Adrian College *W*
Albion College *W*
Alma College *W*
Calvin College *W*
Hope College *W*
Kalamazoo College *W*
Olivet College *W*

Minnesota
Augsburg College *W*
Carleton College *W*
College of St. Benedict *W*
College of St. Catherine: St. Catherine Campus *W*
College of St. Scholastica *W*
Concordia College: Moorhead *W*
Gustavus Adolphus College *W*
Hamline University *W*
Macalester College *W*
St. Mary's College of Minnesota *W*
St. Olaf College *W*
University of St. Thomas *W*

Missouri
Maryville University *W*
Westminster College *W*

Nebraska
Nebraska Wesleyan University *W*

New Hampshire
Daniel Webster College *W*
New England College *W*
Plymouth State College of the University System of New Hampshire *W*

New Jersey
Drew University *W*
Fairleigh Dickinson University *W*
Jersey City State College *W*
Kean College of New Jersey *W*
Montclair State College *W*
New Jersey Institute of Technology *W*
Ramapo College of New Jersey *W*
Rowan College of New Jersey *W*
Rutgers—The State University of New Jersey
Camden College of Arts and Sciences *W*
Newark College of Arts and Sciences *W*

Stockton State College *W*
Trenton State College *W*
Upsala College *W*
William Paterson College of New Jersey *W*

New York
City University of New York
College of Staten Island *W*
Hunter College *W*
John Jay College of Criminal Justice *W*
Lehman College *W*
Medgar Evers College *W*
College of Mount St. Vincent *W*
College of New Rochelle *W*
Elmira College *W*
Hamilton College *W*
Hartwick College *W*
Hilbert College *W*
Ithaca College *W*
Keuka College *W*
Manhattanville College *W*
Mount St. Mary College *W*
Rensselaer Polytechnic Institute *W*
Rochester Institute of Technology *W*
Russell Sage College *W*
St. John Fisher College *W*
Skidmore College *W*
State University of New York
Albany *W*
Binghamton *W*
Stony Brook *W*
College at Brockport *W*
College at Buffalo *W*
College at Cortland *W*
College at Geneseo *W*
College at New Paltz *W*
College at Old Westbury *W*
College at Oneonta *W*
Institute of Technology at Utica/Rome *W*
Maritime College *W*
Oswego *W*
Union College *W*
Utica College of Syracuse University *W*

North Carolina
Bennett College *W*
Meredith College *W*
Methodist College *W*
North Carolina Wesleyan College *W*

Ohio
Baldwin-Wallace College *W*
Bluffton College *W*
Capital University *W*
Defiance College *W*
Heidelberg College *W*
Hiram College *W*
John Carroll University *W*
Marietta College *W*
Mount Union College *W*
Muskingum College *W*
Ohio Northern University *W*
Otterbein College *W*
Wilmington College *W*
Wittenberg University *W*

Pennsylvania
Albright College *W*
Allegheny College *W*
Cabrini College *W*
College Misericordia *W*
Delaware Valley College *W*
Dickinson College *W*
Elizabethtown College *W*
Franklin and Marshall College *W*
Gettysburg College *W*
Grove City College *W*
Immaculata College *W*
Juniata College *W*
King's College *W*
Lebanon Valley College of Pennsylvania *W*
Lycoming College *W*
Messiah College *W*
Moravian College *W*
Muhlenberg College *W*
Penn State Erie Behrend College *W*
Rosemont College *W*
Susquehanna University *W*
Swarthmore College *W*
Thiel College *W*
University of Scranton *W*
Ursinus College *W*
Washington and Jefferson College *W*
Waynesburg College *W*
Widener University *W*
Wilkes University *W*
York College of Pennsylvania *W*

Puerto Rico
American University of Puerto Rico *W*

Rhode Island
Rhode Island College *W*
Roger Williams University *W*
Salve Regina University *W*

Tennessee
Maryville College *W*

Texas
Trinity University *W*
Wiley College *W*

Vermont
Castleton State College *W*
Johnson State College *W*
Norwich University *W*

Virginia
Averett College *W*
Bridgewater College *W*
Christopher Newport University *W*
Eastern Mennonite College *W*
Ferrum College *W*
Lynchburg College *W*
Mary Washington College *W*
Shenandoah University *W*
Virginia Wesleyan College *W*

West Virginia
Bethany College *W*

Wisconsin
Beloit College *W*
Carroll College *W*
Carthage College *W*
Lawrence University *W*
Ripon College *W*
St. Norbert College *W*
University of Wisconsin
Eau Claire *W*
La Crosse *W*
Oshkosh *W*
Platteville *W*
River Falls *W*
Stevens Point *W*
Stout *W*
Superior *W*
Whitewater *W*

Swimming and Diving — Division I

Alabama
Auburn University *M, W*
University of Alabama *M, W*

Arizona
Arizona State University *M, W*
Northern Arizona University *M, W*
University of Arizona *M, W*

Arkansas
University of Arkansas *M, W*
University of Arkansas at Little Rock *M, W*

California
California State University
Fresno *M, W*
Northridge *M, W*
Sacramento *M, W*
Loyola Marymount University *W*
Pepperdine University *W*
San Jose State University *W*
Stanford University *M, W*
University of California
Berkeley *M, W*
Irvine *M, W*
Los Angeles *M, W*
Santa Barbara *M, W*
University of the Pacific *M, W*
University of San Diego *W*
University of Southern California *M, W*

Colorado
Colorado State University *W*
United States Air Force Academy *M*

Connecticut
Central Connecticut State University *M, W*
Fairfield University *M, W*
University of Connecticut *M, W*
Yale University *M, W*

Delaware
University of Delaware *M, W*

District of Columbia
American University *M, W*
George Washington University *M, W*
Georgetown University *M, W*
Howard University *M, W*

Florida
Florida Agricultural and Mechanical University *M, W*
Florida State University *M, W*
University of Florida *M, W*
University of Miami *M, W*

Georgia
Georgia Institute of Technology *M*
Georgia Southern University *M, W*
University of Georgia *M, W*

Hawaii
University of Hawaii at Manoa *M, W*

Illinois
Bradley University *M*
Eastern Illinois University *M, W*
Illinois State University *W*
Loyola University of Chicago *M*
Northeastern Illinois University *M, W*
Northern Illinois University *M, W*
Northwestern University *M, W*
Southern Illinois University at Carbondale *M, W*
University of Illinois
Chicago *M, W*
Urbana-Champaign *M, W*
Western Illinois University *M, W*

Indiana
Ball State University *M, W*
Butler University *M, W*
Indiana University Bloomington *M, W*
Purdue University *M, W*
University of Evansville *M, W*
University of Notre Dame *M, W*
Valparaiso University *M, W*

Iowa
Iowa State University *M, W*
University of Iowa *M, W*
University of Northern Iowa *M, W*

Kansas
University of Kansas *M, W*

Kentucky
Morehead State University *M, W*
University of Kentucky *M, W*
University of Louisville *M, W*
Western Kentucky University *M*

Louisiana
Louisiana State University and Agricultural and Mechanical College *M, W*
Northeast Louisiana University *M, W*
University of New Orleans *M, W*

Maine
University of Maine *M, W*

Maryland
Coppin State College *Mixed*
Loyola College in Maryland *M, W*
Towson State University *M, W*
United States Naval Academy *M, W*
University of Maryland
Baltimore County *M, W*
College Park *M, W*

Massachusetts
Boston College *M, W*
Boston University *M, W*
College of the Holy Cross *M, W*
Harvard and Radcliffe Colleges *M, W*
Northeastern University *M, W*
University of Massachusetts at Amherst *M, W*

Michigan
Eastern Michigan University *M, W*
Michigan State University *M, W*
University of Michigan *M, W*

Minnesota
University of Minnesota: Twin Cities *M, W*

Missouri
St. Louis University *M, W*
Southwest Missouri State University *Mixed*
University of Missouri: Columbia *M, W*

Nebraska
University of Nebraska—Lincoln *M, W*

Nevada
University of Nevada
Las Vegas *M, W*
Reno *W*

New Hampshire
Dartmouth College *M, W*

University of New Hampshire *M, W*

New Jersey

Princeton University *M, W*
Rider College *M, W*
Rutgers—The State University of New Jersey
  College of Engineering *M, W*
  Cook College *M, W*
  Douglass College *W*
  Livingston College *M, W*
  Mason Gross School of the Arts *M, W*
  Rutgers College *M, W*
St. Peter's College *M, W*
Seton Hall University *M, W*

New Mexico

New Mexico State University *M, W*
University of New Mexico *M, W*

New York

Barnard College *W*
Canisius College *M, W*
Colgate University *M, W*
Columbia University: Columbia College *M, W*
Cornell University *M, W*
Fordham University *M, W*
Iona College *M, W*
Manhattan College *W*
Marist College *M, W*
Niagara University *M, W*
St. Bonaventure University *M, W*
St. Francis College *M, W*
St. John's University *M, W*
State University of New York at Buffalo *M, W*
Syracuse University *M, W*
United States Military Academy *M, W*

North Carolina

Davidson College *M, W*
Duke University *M, W*
East Carolina University *M, W*
North Carolina State University *M, W*
University of North Carolina
  Chapel Hill *M, W*
  Wilmington *M, W*

Ohio

Bowling Green State University *M, W*
Cleveland State University *M, W*
Miami University: Oxford Campus *M, W*
Ohio State University: Columbus Campus *M, W*
Ohio University *M, W*
University of Cincinnati *M, W*
University of Toledo *M, W*
Wright State University *M, W*
Xavier University *M, W*

Oklahoma

Oral Roberts University *M*

Oregon

Oregon State University *W*

Pennsylvania

Bucknell University *M, W*
Drexel University *M, W*
Duquesne University *M, W*
La Salle University *M, W*
Lafayette College *M, W*
Lehigh University *M, W*
Penn State University Park Campus *M, W*
University of Pennsylvania *M, W*
University of Pittsburgh *M, W*
Villanova University *M, W*

Rhode Island

Brown University *M, W*
Providence College *M, W*
University of Rhode Island *M, W*

South Carolina

Clemson University *M, W*
College of Charleston *M, W*
University of South Carolina *M, W*

Tennessee

University of Tennessee: Knoxville *M, W*

Texas

Rice University *M, W*
Southern Methodist University *M, W*
Texas A&M University *M, W*
Texas Christian University *M, W*
University of Houston *W*
University of Texas at Austin *M, W*

Utah

Brigham Young University *M, W*
University of Utah *M, W*

Vermont

University of Vermont *M, W*

Virginia

College of William and Mary *M, W*
James Madison University *M, W*
Old Dominion University *M, W*
University of Richmond *M, W*
University of Virginia *M, W*
Virginia Military Institute *M*
Virginia Polytechnic Institute and State University *M, W*

Washington

University of Washington *M, W*
Washington State University *W*

West Virginia

West Virginia University *M, W*

Wisconsin

University of Wisconsin
  Green Bay *W*
  Madison *M, W*

Wyoming

University of Wyoming *M, W*

Swimming and Diving — Division II

Alaska

University of Alaska Anchorage *M*

Arkansas

Henderson State University *M, W*

California

California Polytechnic State University: San Luis Obispo *M, W*
California State University: Bakersfield *M, W*
San Francisco State University *M, W*
University of California
  Berkeley *M*
  Davis *M, W*

Colorado

Colorado School of Mines *M, W*
Metropolitan State College of Denver *M, W.*
United States Air Force Academy *W*
University of Denver *M, W*
University of Northern Colorado *W*

Connecticut

Southern Connecticut State University *M, W*

Florida

Florida Atlantic University *M, W*
University of Tampa *M, W*

Georgia

Kennesaw State College *W*
Morehouse College *M*

Indiana

University of Indianapolis *M, W*

Massachusetts

Springfield College *M, W*
University of Massachusetts at Lowell *M*

Michigan

Ferris State University *M, W*
Grand Valley State University *M, W*
Hillsdale College *W*
Northern Michigan University *W*
Oakland University *M, W*
Wayne State University *Mixed*

Minnesota

Mankato State University *M, W*
St. Cloud State University *M, W*

Mississippi

Delta State University *M, W*

Missouri

Drury College *M, W*
Northeast Missouri State University *M, W*
University of Missouri
  Rolla *M*
  St. Louis *M, Mixed*

Nebraska

University of Nebraska—Kearney *W*

New Hampshire

Keene State College *M, W*

New York

Adelphi University *Mixed*
City University of New York: Queens College *M, W*
College of St. Rose *M, W*
Le Moyne College *M, W*

North Carolina

Pfeiffer College *W*

North Dakota

University of North Dakota *M, W*

Ohio

Ashland University *M, W*

Pennsylvania

Bloomsburg University of Pennsylvania *M, W*
Clarion University of Pennsylvania *M, W*
Edinboro University of Pennsylvania *M, W*
Gannon University *M, W*
Indiana University of Pennsylvania *M, W*
Kutztown University of Pennsylvania *M, W*
Lock Haven University of Pennsylvania *W*
Mansfield University of Pennsylvania *W*
Millersville University of Pennsylvania *W*
Shippensburg University of Pennsylvania *M, W*
Slippery Rock University of Pennsylvania *M, W*
West Chester University of Pennsylvania *M, W*

South Dakota

South Dakota State University *M, W*
University of South Dakota *M, W*

Vermont

St. Michael's College *M, W*

West Virginia

West Virginia Wesleyan College *M, W*

Swimming and Diving — Division III

Arkansas

Hendrix College *M, W*

California

California Institute of Technology *M, W*
Claremont McKenna College *M, W*
Harvey Mudd College *M, W*
Occidental College *M, W*
Pitzer College *W*
Pomona College *M, W*
Scripps College *W*
University of California
  San Diego *M, W*
  Santa Cruz *M, W, Mixed*
University of Redlands *M, W*
Whittier College *M, W*

Colorado

Colorado College *M, W*

Connecticut

Connecticut College *M, W*
Trinity College *M, W*
United States Coast Guard Academy *M*
Wesleyan University *M, W*

District of Columbia

Catholic University of America *M, W*
Gallaudet University *W*

Georgia

Emory University *M, W*

Illinois

Augustana College *M, W*
Eureka College *M, W*
Illinois Benedictine College *M, W*
Illinois Wesleyan University *M, W*
Knox College *M, W*
Lake Forest College *M, W*
Millikin University *M, W*
North Central College *M, W*
Principia College *M, W*
Rockford College *Mixed*

University of Chicago *M, W*
Wheaton College *M, W*

Indiana
DePauw University *M, W*
Rose-Hulman Institute of Technology *M*
St. Mary's College *W*
Wabash College *M*

Iowa
Buena Vista College *Mixed*
Coe College *M, W*
Cornell College *M, W*
Grinnell College *M, W*
Loras College *M, W*
Luther College *M, W*

Kentucky
Asbury College *M, W*
Berea College *Mixed*
Centre College *M, W*

Maine
Bates College *M, W*
Bowdoin College *M, W*
Colby College *M, W*

Maryland
College of Notre Dame of Maryland *W*
Frostburg State University *M, W*
Goucher College *M, W*
Hood College *W*
Johns Hopkins University *M, W*
St. Mary's College of Maryland *M, W*
Salisbury State University *W*
Washington College *M, W*
Western Maryland College *M, W*

Massachusetts
Amherst College *M, W*
Babson College *M, W*
Brandeis University *M, W*
Bridgewater State College *M, W*
Clark University *M, W*
Massachusetts Institute of Technology *M, W*
Mount Holyoke College *W*
Pine Manor College *W*
Regis College *W*
Salem State College *M, W*
Simmons College *W*
Smith College *W*
Tufts University *M, W*
University of Massachusetts
Boston *M, W*
Dartmouth *M, W*
Wellesley College *W*
Westfield State College *W*
Wheaton College *M, W*
Williams College *M, W*
Worcester Polytechnic Institute *M, W*

Michigan
Adrian College *M, W*
Albion College *M, W*
Alma College *M, W*
Calvin College *M, W*
Hope College *M, W*
Kalamazoo College *M, W*
Olivet College *W*

Minnesota
Carleton College *M, W*
College of St. Benedict *W*
College of St. Catherine: St. Catherine Campus *W*
Gustavus Adolphus College *M, W*
Hamline University *M, W*
Macalester College *M, W*
St. John's University *M*
St. Olaf College *M, W*
University of St. Thomas *M, W*

Missouri
Washington University *M, W*

New Hampshire
Plymouth State College of the University System of New Hampshire *W*

New Jersey
College of St. Elizabeth *W*
Kean College of New Jersey *W*
Montclair State College *M, W*
Rowan College of New Jersey *M, W*
Rutgers—The State University of New Jersey: Camden College of Arts and Sciences *M, W*
Trenton State College *M, W*
William Paterson College of New Jersey *M, W*

New York
Alfred University *M, W*
City University of New York
City College *M*
Hunter College *W*
Lehman College *M*
Clarkson University *M, W*
College of New Rochelle *W*
Hamilton College *M, W*
Hartwick College *M, W*
Hobart College *M*
Ithaca College *M, W*
Manhattanville College *W*
Nazareth College of Rochester *M, W*
New York University *M, W*
Rensselaer Polytechnic Institute *M, W*
Rochester Institute of Technology *M, W*
St. Lawrence University *M, W*
Skidmore College *W*
State University of New York
Albany *M, W*
Binghamton *M, W*
Stony Brook *M, W*
College at Brockport *M, W*
College at Buffalo *M, W*
College at Cortland *M, W*
College at Geneseo *M, W*
College at New Paltz *M, W*
College at Oneonta *W*
College at Plattsburgh *M, W*
College at Potsdam *M, W*
Maritime College *Mixed*
Oswego *M, W*
Union College *M, W*
United States Merchant Marine Academy *M, W*
University of Rochester *M, W*
Utica College of Syracuse University *M, W*
Vassar College *M, W*
Wells College *W*
William Smith College *W*

Ohio
Baldwin-Wallace College *M, W*
Case Western Reserve University *M, W*
College of Wooster *M, W*
Denison University *M, W*
Hiram College *M, W*
John Carroll University *M, W*
Kenyon College *M, W*
Mount Union College *M, W*
Oberlin College *M, W*
Ohio Northern University *M, W*
Ohio Wesleyan University *M, W*
Wittenberg University *M, W*

Pennsylvania
Albright College *M, W*
Allegheny College *M, W*
Bryn Mawr College *W*
Carnegie Mellon University *M, W*
Dickinson College *M, W*
Elizabethtown College *M, W*
Franklin and Marshall College *M, W*
Gettysburg College *M, W*
Grove City College *M, W*
Juniata College *M, W*
King's College *M, W*
Lebanon Valley College of Pennsylvania *M, W*
Lycoming College *M, W*
Susquehanna University *M, W*
Swarthmore College *M, W*
University of Scranton *M, W*
Ursinus College *M, W*
Washington and Jefferson College *M, Mixed*
Widener University *M, W*
York College of Pennsylvania *M, W*

Puerto Rico
American University of Puerto Rico *M, W*

Tennessee
University of the South *M, W*

Texas
Trinity University *M, W*

Vermont
Middlebury College *M, W*
Norwich University *M, W*

Virginia
Hollins College *W*
Mary Baldwin College *W*
Mary Washington College *M, W*
Marymount University *M, W*
Randolph-Macon Woman's College *W*
Sweet Briar College *W*
Washington and Lee University *M, W*

West Virginia
Bethany College *M, W, Mixed*

Wisconsin
Beloit College *M, W*
Carroll College *M, W*
Carthage College *M, W*
Lawrence University *M, W*
Ripon College *M, W*
University of Wisconsin
Eau Claire *M, W*
La Crosse *M, W, Mixed*
Oshkosh *M, W*
River Falls *M, W*
Stevens Point *M, W*
Whitewater *M, W*

Tennis — Division I

Alabama
Alabama State University *M, W*
Auburn University *M, W*
Samford University *M, W*
University of Alabama
Birmingham *M, W*
Tuscaloosa *M, W*
University of South Alabama *M, W*

Arizona
Arizona State University *M, W*
Northern Arizona University *M, W*
University of Arizona *M, W*

Arkansas
Arkansas State University *W*
University of Arkansas *M, W*
University of Arkansas at Little Rock *M, W*

California
California State University
Fresno *M, W*
Fullerton *W*
Long Beach *W*
Northridge *W*
Sacramento *M, W*
Loyola Marymount University *M, W*
Pepperdine University *M, W*
St. Mary's College of California *M, W*
San Diego State University *M, W*
San Jose State University *M, W*
Santa Clara University *M, W*
Stanford University *M, W*
University of California
Berkeley *M, W*
Irvine *M, W*
Los Angeles *M, W*
Santa Barbara *M, W*
University of the Pacific *M, W*
University of San Diego *M, W*
University of San Francisco *M, W*
University of Southern California *M, W*

Colorado
Colorado State University *M, W*
United States Air Force Academy *M*
University of Colorado at Boulder *M, W*

Connecticut
Central Connecticut State University *M, W*
Fairfield University *M, W*
University of Connecticut *M, W*
University of Hartford *M, W*
Yale University *M, W*

Delaware
Delaware State College *M, W, Mixed*
University of Delaware *M, W*

District of Columbia
American University *M, W*
George Washington University *M, W*
Georgetown University *M, W*
Howard University *M, W*

Florida
Bethune-Cookman College *M, W*
Florida Agricultural and Mechanical University *M, W*
Florida International University *M, W*
Florida State University *M, W*
Jacksonville University *M, W*
Rollins College *W*
Stetson University *M, W*
University of Central Florida *M, W*
University of Florida *M, W*
University of Miami *M, W*
University of South Florida *M, W*

Georgia
Georgia Institute of Technology *M, W*
Georgia Southern University *M, W*
Georgia State University *M, W*
Mercer University *M, W*
University of Georgia *M, W*

Hawaii
University of Hawaii at Manoa *M, W*

Idaho
Boise State University *M, W*
Idaho State University *M, W*
University of Idaho *M, W*

Illinois
Bradley University *M, W*
Chicago State University *M, W*
De Paul University *M, W*
Eastern Illinois University *M, W*
Illinois State University *M, W*
Northeastern Illinois University *M, W*
Northern Illinois University *M, W*
Northwestern University *M, W*
Southern Illinois University at Carbondale *M, W*
University of Illinois
Chicago *M, W*
Urbana-Champaign *M, W*
Western Illinois University *M, W*

Indiana
Ball State University *M, W*
Butler University *M, W*
Indiana State University *M, W*
Indiana University Bloomington *M, W*
Purdue University *M, W*
University of Evansville *M, W*
University of Notre Dame *M, W*
Valparaiso University *M, W*

Iowa
Drake University *M, W*
Iowa State University *M, W*
University of Iowa *M, W*
University of Northern Iowa *M, W*

Kansas
Kansas State University *W*
University of Kansas *M, W*
Wichita State University *M, W*

Kentucky
Eastern Kentucky University *M, W*
Morehead State University *M, W*
Murray State University *M, W*
University of Kentucky *M, W*
University of Louisville *M, W*
Western Kentucky University *M, W*

Louisiana
Centenary College of Louisiana *M, W*
Grambling State University *M, W*
Louisiana State University and Agricultural and Mechanical College *M, W*
Louisiana Tech University *W*
Nicholls State University *W*
Northeast Louisiana University *M, W*
Northwestern State University *W*
Southeastern Louisiana University *M, W*
Southern University and Agricultural and Mechanical College *M, W*
Tulane University *M, W*
University of New Orleans *W*
University of Southwestern Louisiana *M, W*

Maine
University of Maine *W*

Maryland
Coppin State College *M, W*
Loyola College in Maryland *M, W*
Morgan State University *M, W*
Mount St. Mary's College *M, W*
Towson State University *M, W*
United States Naval Academy *M*
University of Maryland
Baltimore County *M, W*
College Park *M, W*
Eastern Shore *M, W, Mixed*

Massachusetts
Boston College *M, W*
Boston University *M, W*
College of the Holy Cross *M, W*
Harvard and Radcliffe Colleges *M, W*
Northeastern University *M*
University of Massachusetts at Amherst *W*

Michigan
Eastern Michigan University *M, W*
Michigan State University *M, W*
University of Detroit Mercy *M, W*
University of Michigan *M, W*
Western Michigan University *M, W*

Minnesota
University of Minnesota: Twin Cities *M, W*

Mississippi
Alcorn State University *M, W, Mixed*
Jackson State University *M, W*
Mississippi State University *M, W*
Mississippi Valley State University *M, W*
University of Mississippi *M, W*
University of Southern Mississippi *M, W*

Missouri
St. Louis University *M, W*
Southeast Missouri State University *Mixed*
Southwest Missouri State University *M, W*
University of Missouri
Columbia *M, W*
Kansas City *M, W*

Montana
Montana State University *M, W*
University of Montana *M, W*

Nebraska
Creighton University *M, W*
University of Nebraska—Lincoln *M, W*

Nevada
University of Nevada
Las Vegas *M, W*
Reno *M, W*

New Hampshire
Dartmouth College *M, W*
University of New Hampshire *M, W*

New Jersey
Fairleigh Dickinson University: Edward Williams College *M, W*
Monmouth College *M, W*
Princeton University *M, W*
Rider College *M, W*
Rutgers—The State University of New Jersey
College of Engineering *M, W*
Cook College *M, W*
Douglass College *W*
Livingston College *M, W*
Mason Gross School of the Arts *M, W*
Rutgers College *M, W*
St. Peter's College *M, W*
Seton Hall University *M, W*

New Mexico
New Mexico State University *M, W*
University of New Mexico *M, W*

New York
Barnard College *W*
Canisius College *M, W*
Colgate University *M, W*
Columbia University: Columbia College *M, W*
Cornell University *M, W*
Fordham University *M, W*
Hofstra University *M, W*
Iona College *M, W*
Long Island University: Brooklyn Campus *W*
Manhattan College *M, W*
Marist College *M, W*
Niagara University *M, W*
St. Bonaventure University *M, W*
St. Francis College *M, W*
St. John's University *M, W*
Siena College *M, W*
State University of New York at Buffalo *M, W*
Syracuse University *W*
United States Military Academy *M, W*
Wagner College *M, W*

North Carolina
Appalachian State University *M, W*
Campbell University *M, W*
Davidson College *M, W*
Duke University *M, W*
East Carolina University *M, W*
North Carolina Agricultural and Technical State University *M, W*
North Carolina State University *M, W*
University of North Carolina
Asheville *M, W*
Chapel Hill *M, W*
Charlotte *M, W*
Greensboro *M, W*
Wilmington *M, W*
Wake Forest University *M, W*
Western Carolina University *M, W*

Ohio
Bowling Green State University *M, W*
Cleveland State University *W*
Miami University: Oxford Campus *M, W*
Ohio State University: Columbus Campus *M, W*
University of Akron *M, W*
University of Cincinnati *M, W*
University of Dayton *M, W*
University of Toledo *M, W*
Wright State University *M, W*
Xavier University *M, W*
Youngstown State University *M, W*

Oklahoma
Oklahoma State University *M, W*
University of Oklahoma *M, W*
University of Tulsa *M, W*

Oregon
University of Oregon *M, W*
University of Portland *M, W*

Pennsylvania
Bucknell University *M, W*
Drexel University *M, W*
Duquesne University *M, W*
La Salle University *M, W*
Lafayette College *M, W, Mixed*
Lehigh University *M, W*
Penn State University Park Campus *M, W*
Robert Morris College *M, W*
St. Francis College *M, W*
St. Joseph's University *M, W*
Temple University *M, W*
University of Pennsylvania *M, W*
University of Pittsburgh *M, W*
Villanova University *M, W*

Rhode Island
Brown University *M, W*
Providence College *M, W*
University of Rhode Island *M, W*

South Carolina
Charleston Southern University *M, W*
The Citadel *M*
Clemson University *M, W*
College of Charleston *M, W*
Furman University *M, W*
South Carolina State University *M, W*
University of South Carolina
Coastal Carolina College *M, W*
Columbia *M, W*
Winthrop University *M, W*

Tennessee
Austin Peay State University *M, W*
East Tennessee State University *M, W*
Memphis State University *M, W*
Middle Tennessee State University *M, W*
Tennessee State University *M, W*
Tennessee Technological University *M, W*
University of Tennessee
Chattanooga *M, W*
Knoxville *M, W*
Martin *M, W, Mixed*
Vanderbilt University *M, W*

Texas
Baylor University *M, W*
Lamar University—Beaumont *M, W*
Prairie View A&M University *M, W*
Rice University *M, W*
Sam Houston State University *W*
Southern Methodist University *M, W*
Southwest Texas State University *M, W*
Texas A&M University *M, W*
Texas Christian University *M, W*
Texas Southern University *M, W*
Texas Tech University *M, W*
University of Houston *W*
University of North Texas *M, W*

University of Texas
- Arlington *M, W*
- Austin *M, W*
- El Paso *M, W*
- Pan American *M, W*
- San Antonio *M, W*

Utah

Brigham Young University *M, W*
University of Utah *M, W*
Utah State University *M, W*
Weber State University *M, W*

Vermont

University of Vermont *M, W*

Virginia

College of William and Mary *M, W*
George Mason University *M, W*
James Madison University *M, W*
Liberty University *M*
Old Dominion University *M, W*
Radford University *M, W*
University of Richmond *M, W*
University of Virginia *M, W*
Virginia Commonwealth University *M, W, Mixed*
Virginia Military Institute *M*
Virginia Polytechnic Institute and State University *M, W*

Washington

Eastern Washington University *M, W*
Gonzaga University *M, W*
University of Washington *M, W*
Washington State University *M, W*

West Virginia

Marshall University *W*
West Virginia University *M, W*

Wisconsin

Marquette University *M, W*
University of Wisconsin
- Green Bay *M, W*
- Madison *M, W*

Tennis — Division II

Alabama

Alabama Agricultural and Mechanical University *M*
Jacksonville State University *M, W*
Livingston University *M, W*
Miles College *W*
Troy State University *M, W*
Tuskegee University *M, W*
University of Alabama in Huntsville *M, W*
University of North Alabama *M, W*

Arizona

Grand Canyon University *W*

Arkansas

Henderson State University *M, W*
University of Central Arkansas *W*

California

California Polytechnic State University: San Luis Obispo *M, W*
California State Polytechnic University: Pomona *M, W*
California State University
- Bakersfield *M, W*
- Los Angeles *M, W*

Chapman University *M*
College of Notre Dame *M, W*
University of California
- Davis *M, W*
- Riverside *M, W*

Colorado

Colorado Christian University *M, W*
Colorado School of Mines *M, Mixed*
Mesa State College *M, W, Mixed*
Metropolitan State College of Denver *M, W*
Regis University *M, W*
United States Air Force Academy *W*
University of Colorado at Colorado Springs *M, W*
University of Denver *M, W*
University of Northern Colorado *M, W*
University of Southern Colorado *M, W*

Connecticut

Quinnipiac College *M, W*
Southern Connecticut State University *M, W*
University of Bridgeport *M, W*
University of New Haven *W*

District of Columbia

University of the District of Columbia *M, W*

Florida

Barry University *M, W*
Eckerd College *M, W*
Florida Atlantic University *M, W*
Florida Institute of Technology *M*
Florida Southern College *W*
Rollins College *M*
St. Leo College *M, W*
University of North Florida *M, W*
University of Tampa *M, W*

Georgia

Armstrong State College *M, W*
Augusta College *M, W*
Clark Atlanta University *M, W*
Columbus College *M, W*
Fort Valley State College *M, W*
Georgia College *M, W*
Morehouse College *M*
Morris Brown College *M, W*
Savannah State College *W*
Valdosta State College *M, W*
West Georgia College *M, W*

Illinois

College of St. Francis *W*
Lewis University *M, W*
Quincy University *M, W*
Southern Illinois University at Edwardsville *M, W*

Indiana

Indiana University—Purdue University at Fort Wayne *M, W*
St. Joseph's College *M, W*
University of Indianapolis *W*
University of Southern Indiana *M, W*

Kansas

Emporia State University *M, W*
Fort Hays State University *W*
Washburn University of Topeka *M, W*

Kentucky

Bellarmine College *M, W*
Kentucky State University *M, W*
Kentucky Wesleyan College *W*
Northern Kentucky University *M, W*

Massachusetts

American International College *M, W*
Assumption College *M, W*
Bentley College *M, W*
Merrimack College *M, W*
Springfield College *M, W*
Stonehill College *M, W*
University of Massachusetts at Lowell *M, W*

Michigan

Ferris State University *M, W*
Grand Valley State University *M, W*
Hillsdale College *M, W*
Lake Superior State University *M, W*
Michigan Technological University *M, W*
Northern Michigan University *W*
Northwood University *M, W, Mixed*
Oakland University *M, W*
Saginaw Valley State University *W*
Wayne State University *M, W*

Minnesota

Bemidji State University *W*
Mankato State University *M, W*
St. Cloud State University *M, W*
University of Minnesota: Duluth *M, W*
Winona State University *M, W*

Mississippi

Delta State University *M, W*
Mississippi College *W*
Mississippi University for Women *W*

Missouri

Drury College *M, W*
Lincoln University *W*
Missouri Southern State College *W*
Missouri Western State College *W*
Northeast Missouri State University *M, W*
Northwest Missouri State University *M, W*
Southwest Baptist University *M, W*
University of Missouri
- Rolla *M*
- St. Louis *M, W*

Montana

Eastern Montana College *M, W*

Nebraska

University of Nebraska—Kearney *M, W*

New Hampshire

Franklin Pierce College *M, W*
St. Anselm College *M, W*

New Mexico

Eastern New Mexico University *W*

New York

Adelphi University *M, W*
City University of New York: Queens College *M, W*
College of St. Rose *M, W*
Concordia College *M, W*
Dowling College *M, W*
Le Moyne College *M*
Long Island University: C. W. Post Campus *W*
Mercy College *M, Mixed*
Molloy College *W*
Pace University
- College of White Plains *M*
- New York *M, W*
- Pleasantville/Briarcliff *M*

North Carolina

Catawba College *M, W*
Elon College *M, W*
Gardner-Webb University *M, W*
Johnson C. Smith University *M*
Lenoir-Rhyne College *M, W*
Livingstone College *M*
Mars Hill College *M, W*
Mount Olive College *W*
North Carolina Central University *M, Mixed*
Pfeiffer College *M, W*
Queens College *M, W*
St. Augustine's College *M*
Wingate College *M, W*
Winston-Salem State University *M*

Ohio

Ashland University *M, W*

Oklahoma

Cameron University *W*
University of Central Oklahoma *M, W*

Oregon

Portland State University *W*

Pennsylvania

Bloomsburg University of Pennsylvania *M, W*
California University of Pennsylvania *W*
Cheyney University of Pennsylvania *M, W*
Clarion University of Pennsylvania *W*
East Stroudsburg University of Pennsylvania *M, W*
Edinboro University of Pennsylvania *M, W*
Gannon University *M, W*
Indiana University of Pennsylvania *W*
Kutztown University of Pennsylvania *M, W*
Lock Haven University of Pennsylvania *M, W*
Mercyhurst College *M, W*
Millersville University of Pennsylvania *M, W*
Philadelphia College of Textiles and Science *M, W*
Shippensburg University of Pennsylvania *W*
Slippery Rock University of Pennsylvania *M, W*
West Chester University of Pennsylvania *M, W*

Rhode Island

Bryant College *M, W*

South Carolina

Erskine College *M, W*
Francis Marion University *M, W*
Lander University *M, W*
Newberry College *M, W*
Presbyterian College *M, W*
University of South Carolina
- Aiken *M*
- Spartanburg *M, W*

Wofford College *M, W*

South Dakota

Augustana College *M, W*
South Dakota State University *M, W*

University of South Dakota *M, W*

Tennessee

Carson-Newman College *M, W*
Lincoln Memorial University *M, W*

Texas

Abilene Christian University *M, W*
Hardin-Simmons University *M, W*
Texas Woman's University *W*
West Texas A & M University *M, W*

Vermont

St. Michael's College *M, W*

Virginia

Hampton University *M*
Longwood College *M, W*
St. Paul's College *M*
Virginia State University *M*
Virginia Union University *M*

West Virginia

Davis and Elkins College *M, W*
Shepherd College *M, W*
University of Charleston *M, W*
West Liberty State College *M, W*
West Virginia Wesleyan College *W*

Tennis — Division III

Alabama

Stillman College *M, W*

Arkansas

Hendrix College *M, W*

California

California Institute of Technology *M, W*
California Lutheran University *M, W*
Claremont McKenna College *M, W*
Harvey Mudd College *M, W*
Menlo College *M, W, Mixed*
Mills College *W*
Occidental College *M, W*
Pitzer College *M*
Pomona College *M, W*
Scripps College *W*
University of California
San Diego *M, W*
Santa Cruz *M, W*
University of La Verne *M, W*
University of Redlands *M, W*
Whittier College *M, W*

Colorado

Colorado College *M, W*

Connecticut

Albertus Magnus College *M, W*
Connecticut College *M, W*
Trinity College *M, W*
United States Coast Guard Academy *M*
Wesleyan University *M, W*
Western Connecticut State University *M, W*

Delaware

Wesley College *M, W*

District of Columbia

Catholic University of America *M, W*
Gallaudet University *M, W*

Georgia

Emory University *M, W*
Oglethorpe University *M, W*
Savannah College of Art and Design *M, W*

Illinois

Augustana College *M, W*
Aurora University *M, W*
Blackburn College *W*
Concordia University *M, W*
Elmhurst College *M, W*
Eureka College *M, W*
Illinois Benedictine College *M, W*
Illinois College *M, W*
Illinois Wesleyan University *M, W*
Knox College *M, W*
Lake Forest College *M, W*
MacMurray College *M, W*
Millikin University *M, W*
North Central College *M, W*
North Park College *M, W*
Parks College of St. Louis University *M*
Principia College *M, W*
Rockford College *M, W*
University of Chicago *M, W*
Wheaton College *M, W*

Indiana

Anderson University *M, W*
DePauw University *M, W*
Earlham College *M, W*
Franklin College *M, W*
Hanover College *M, W*
Manchester College *M, W*
Rose-Hulman Institute of Technology *M*
St. Mary's College *M, W*
Wabash College *M*

Iowa

Buena Vista College *M, W*
Central College *M, W*
Coe College *M, W*
Cornell College *M, W*
Grinnell College *M, W*
Loras College *M, W*
Luther College *M, W*
Simpson College *M, W*
University of Dubuque *M, W*
Upper Iowa University *M, W*
Wartburg College *M, W*
William Penn College *M, W*

Kentucky

Asbury College *M, W*
Berea College *M, W*
Centre College *M, W*
Thomas More College *M, W*

Maine

Bates College *M, W*
Bowdoin College *M, W*
Colby College *M, W*
University of Southern Maine *Mixed*

Maryland

College of Notre Dame of Maryland *W*
Frostburg State University *M, W*
Goucher College *M, W*
Hood College *W*
Johns Hopkins University *M, W*
St. Mary's College of Maryland *M, W*
Salisbury State University *M, W*
Washington College *M, W*
Western Maryland College *M, W*

Massachusetts

Amherst College *M, W*
Babson College *M, W*
Brandeis University *M, W*
Bridgewater State College *M, W*
Clark University *M, W*
Curry College *M, W*
Eastern Nazarene College *M, W*
Emerson College *M, W*
Emmanuel College *W*
Gordon College *M, W*
Massachusetts Institute of Technology *M, W*
Mount Holyoke College *W*
Nichols College *M, W*
North Adams State College *M, W*
Pine Manor College *W*
Regis College *W*
Salem State College *M, W*
Simmons College *W*
Smith College *W*
Suffolk University *M, W*
Tufts University *M, W*
University of Massachusetts
Boston *M*
Dartmouth *M, W*
Wellesley College *W*
Wentworth Institute of Technology *M, W*
Western New England College *M*
Wheaton College *M, W*
Williams College *M, W*
Worcester Polytechnic Institute *M, W*
Worcester State College *M, W*

Michigan

Adrian College *M, W*
Albion College *M, W*
Alma College *M, W*
Calvin College *M, W*
Hope College *M, W*
Kalamazoo College *M, W*
Olivet College *M, W*

Minnesota

Augsburg College *M, W*
Carleton College *M, W*
College of St. Benedict *W*
College of St. Catherine: St. Catherine Campus *W*
College of St. Scholastica *M, W*
Concordia College: Moorhead *M, W*
Gustavus Adolphus College *M, W*
Hamline University *M, W*
Macalester College *M, W*
St. John's University *M*
St. Mary's College of Minnesota *M, W*
St. Olaf College *M, W*
University of St. Thomas *M, W*

Mississippi

Millsaps College *M, W*
Rust College *M, W*

Missouri

Maryville University *M, W*
Washington University *M, W*
Webster University *M, W*
Westminster College *M, W*

Nebraska

Nebraska Wesleyan University *M, W*

New Hampshire

Colby-Sawyer College *M, W*
Plymouth State College of the University System of New Hampshire *M, W*

New Jersey

College of St. Elizabeth *W*
Drew University *M, W*
Fairleigh Dickinson University *M, W*
Jersey City State College *M*
Montclair State College *M, W*
New Jersey Institute of Technology *M, W*
Ramapo College of New Jersey *M, W*
Rowan College of New Jersey *M, W*
Rutgers—The State University of New Jersey
Camden College of Arts and Sciences *M, W*
Newark College of Arts and Sciences *M, W*
Stevens Institute of Technology *M, W*
Trenton State College *M, W*
Upsala College *M, W*

New York

Alfred University *M, W*
Bard College *M, W*
City University of New York
Baruch College *M, W*
City College *M, W*
College of Staten Island *M, W*
Hunter College *M, W*
John Jay College of Criminal Justice *M*
Lehman College *M, W*
York College *M*
Clarkson University *M, W*
College of Mount St. Vincent *M, W*
College of New Rochelle *W*
Elmira College *M, W*
Hamilton College *M, W*
Hartwick College *M, W*
Hobart College *M, W*
Ithaca College *M, W*
Manhattanville College *M, W*
Mount St. Mary College *M, W*
Nazareth College of Rochester *M, W*
New York University *M, W*
Polytechnic University *M, W*
Rensselaer Polytechnic Institute *M, W*
Rochester Institute of Technology *M, W*
Russell Sage College *W*
St. John Fisher College *M, W*
St. Lawrence University *M, W*
Skidmore College *M, W*
State University of New York
Albany *M, W*
Binghamton *M, W*
Stony Brook *M, W*
College at Brockport *W*
College at Buffalo *M, W*
College at Cortland *W*
College at Fredonia *M, W*
College at New Paltz *M, W*
College at Old Westbury *M, W*
College at Oneonta *M, W*
College at Plattsburgh *W*
College at Potsdam *W*
Maritime College *M, Mixed*
Oswego *M, W*
Union College *M, W*
United States Merchant Marine Academy *M*
University of Rochester *M, W*
Utica College of Syracuse University *M, W*
Vassar College *M, W*
Wells College *W*
William Smith College *W*
Yeshiva University *M*

North Carolina
Bennett College *W*
Greensboro College *M, W*
Guilford College *M, W*
Meredith College *W*
Methodist College *M, W*

Ohio
Baldwin-Wallace College *M, W*
Bluffton College *M, W*
Capital University *M, W*
Case Western Reserve University *M, W*
College of Wooster *M, W*
Defiance College *M, W*
Denison University *M, W*
Heidelberg College *M, W*
Hiram College *M, W*
John Carroll University *M, W*
Kenyon College *M, W*
Marietta College *M, W*
Mount Union College *M, W*
Muskingum College *M, W*
Oberlin College *M, W*
Ohio Northern University *M, W*
Ohio Wesleyan University *M, W*
Otterbein College *M, W*
Wilmington College *M, W*
Wittenberg University *M, W*

Pennsylvania
Albright College *M, W, Mixed*
Allegheny College *M, W*
Allentown College of St. Francis de Sales *M, W*
Bryn Mawr College *W*
Cabrini College *M, W*
Carnegie Mellon University *M, W*
Cedar Crest College *W*
Dickinson College *M, W*
Elizabethtown College *M, W, Mixed*
Franklin and Marshall College *M, W*
Gettysburg College *M, W*
Grove City College *M, W*
Haverford College *M, W*
Immaculata College *W*
Juniata College *M, W*
King's College *M, W*
Lebanon Valley College of Pennsylvania *M*
Lincoln University *M, Mixed*
Lycoming College *M, W*
Marywood College *W*
Messiah College *M, W*
Moravian College *M, W*
Muhlenberg College *M, W*
Penn State Erie Behrend College *M, W*
Rosemont College *W*
Susquehanna University *M, W*
Swarthmore College *M, W*
Thiel College *M, W*
University of Scranton *M, W*
Ursinus College *M, W, Mixed*
Washington and Jefferson College *M, W*
Waynesburg College *M, W*
Widener University *M, W*
Wilkes University *M, W*
York College of Pennsylvania *M, W*

Puerto Rico
American University of Puerto Rico *M*

Rhode Island
Rhode Island College *M, W*
Roger Williams University *M, W*
Salve Regina University *M, W*

Tennessee
Fisk University *M, W*
Rhodes College *M, W*
University of the South *M, W*

Texas
Southwestern University *M, W*
Trinity University *M, W*

Vermont
Castleton State College *M, W*
Johnson State College *M, W*
Middlebury College *M, W*
Norwich University *M*

Virginia
Averett College *M, W*
Bridgewater College *M, W*
Christopher Newport University *M, W*
Eastern Mennonite College *M*
Emory and Henry College *M, W*
Ferrum College *W*
Hampden-Sydney College *M*
Hollins College *W*
Lynchburg College *M, W*
Mary Baldwin College *W*
Mary Washington College *M, W*
Marymount University *M, W*
Randolph-Macon College *M, W*
Randolph-Macon Woman's College *W*
Roanoke College *M, W*
Shenandoah University *M, W*
Sweet Briar College *W*
Virginia Wesleyan College *M, W*
Washington and Lee University *M, W*

Wisconsin
Beloit College *M, W*
Carroll College *M, W*
Carthage College *M, W*
Lawrence University *M, W*
Northwestern College *M*
Ripon College *M, W*
St. Norbert College *M, W*
University of Wisconsin
  Eau Claire *M, W*
  La Crosse *M, W*
  Oshkosh *M, W*
  Platteville *M, W*
  River Falls *M, W*
  Stevens Point *W*
  Stout *M, W*
  Whitewater *M, W*

Track, indoor — Division I

Alabama
Alabama State University *W*
Auburn University *M, W*
Samford University *M, W*
University of Alabama
  Birmingham *W*
  Tuscaloosa *M, W*
University of South Alabama *M, W*

Arizona
Arizona State University *M, W*
Northern Arizona University *M, W*
University of Arizona *W*

Arkansas
Arkansas State University *M*
University of Arkansas *M, W*
University of Arkansas at Little Rock *M, W*

California
California State University
  Fresno *M, W*
  Long Beach *M*
  Northridge *M, W*
San Diego State University *M, W*
Stanford University *M, W*
University of California
  Berkeley *M, W*
  Los Angeles *M, W*

Colorado
Colorado State University *M, W*
United States Air Force Academy *M*
University of Colorado at Boulder *M, W*

Connecticut
Central Connecticut State University *M, W*
University of Connecticut *M, W*
University of Hartford *W*
Yale University *M, W*

Delaware
Delaware State College *M, W, Mixed*
University of Delaware *M, W*

District of Columbia
Georgetown University *M, W*
Howard University *M, W*

Florida
Florida Agricultural and Mechanical University *M, W*
Florida International University *M, W*
Florida State University *M, W*
University of Central Florida *M, W*
University of Florida *M, W*
University of Miami *M, W*
University of South Florida *M, W*

Georgia
Georgia Institute of Technology *M, W*
Georgia State University *Mixed*
University of Georgia *M, W*

Idaho
Boise State University *M, W*
Idaho State University *M, W*
University of Idaho *M, W*

Illinois
Bradley University *M, W*
Chicago State University *M, W*
De Paul University *M, W*
Eastern Illinois University *M, W*
Illinois State University *M, W*
Loyola University of Chicago *M, W*
Southern Illinois University at Carbondale *M, W*
University of Illinois at Urbana-Champaign *M, W*
Western Illinois University *M, W*

Indiana
Ball State University *M, W*
Butler University *M, W*
Indiana State University *M, W*
Indiana University Bloomington *M, W*
Purdue University *M, W*
University of Notre Dame *M, W*
Valparaiso University *M, W*

Iowa
Drake University *M, W*
Iowa State University *M, W*
University of Iowa *M, W*
University of Northern Iowa *M, W*

Kansas
Kansas State University *M, W*
University of Kansas *M, W*
Wichita State University *M, W*

Kentucky
Eastern Kentucky University *M, W*
Morehead State University *M, W*
Murray State University *M, W*
University of Kentucky *M, W*
University of Louisville *M, W*
Western Kentucky University *M, W*

Louisiana
Grambling State University *M, W*
Louisiana State University and Agricultural and Mechanical College *M, W*
Louisiana Tech University *M, W*
McNeese State University *M, W*
Nicholls State University *M, W*
Northeast Louisiana University *M, W*
Northwestern State University *M, W*
Southeastern Louisiana University *M, W*
Southern University and Agricultural and Mechanical College *M, W*
Tulane University *M, W*
University of New Orleans *M, W*
University of Southwestern Louisiana *M, W*

Maine
University of Maine *M, W*

Maryland
Coppin State College *M, W*
Morgan State University *M, W*
Mount St. Mary's College *M, W*
United States Naval Academy *M, W*
University of Maryland
  Baltimore County *M, W*
  College Park *M, W*
  Eastern Shore *M, W, Mixed*

Massachusetts
Boston College *M, W*
Boston University *M, W*
College of the Holy Cross *M, W*
Harvard and Radcliffe Colleges *M, W*
Northeastern University *M, W*
University of Massachusetts at Amherst *M, W*

Michigan
Central Michigan University *M, W*
Eastern Michigan University *M, W*
Michigan State University *M, W*
University of Detroit Mercy *M, W*
University of Michigan *M, W*
Western Michigan University *M, W*

Minnesota
University of Minnesota: Twin Cities *M, W*

Mississippi
Alcorn State University *W*
Jackson State University *M, W*
Mississippi State University *M, W*
Mississippi Valley State University *M, W*
University of Mississippi *M, W*

University of Southern Mississippi *M, W*

Missouri
Southeast Missouri State University *M, W, Mixed*
Southwest Missouri State University *M, W*
University of Missouri: Columbia *M, W*

Montana
Montana State University *M, W*
University of Montana *M, W*

Nebraska
University of Nebraska—Lincoln *M, W*

Nevada
University of Nevada: Reno *M, W*

New Hampshire
Dartmouth College *M, W*
University of New Hampshire *M, W*

New Jersey
Fairleigh Dickinson University
Edward Williams College *M, W*
Madison *Mixed*
Monmouth College *M, W*
Princeton University *M, W*
Rider College *M*
Rutgers—The State University of New Jersey
College of Engineering *M, W*
Cook College *M, W*
Douglass College *W*
Livingston College *M, W*
Mason Gross School of the Arts *M, W*
Rutgers College *M, W*
St. Peter's College *M, W*
Seton Hall University *M, W*

New Mexico
University of New Mexico *M, W*

New York
Barnard College *W*
Canisius College *M, W*
Colgate University *M, W*
Columbia University: Columbia College *M, W*
Cornell University *M, W*
Fordham University *M, W*
Iona College *M*
Long Island University: Brooklyn Campus *M, W*
Manhattan College *M, W*
Marist College *M, W*
St. Francis College *M, W*
St. John's University *M, W*
Siena College *M, W*
State University of New York at Buffalo *M, W*
Syracuse University *M, W*
United States Military Academy *M, W*
Wagner College *M, W*

North Carolina
Appalachian State University *M, W*
Davidson College *M, W*
Duke University *M, W*
East Carolina University *M, W*
North Carolina Agricultural and Technical State University *M, W*
North Carolina State University *M, W*
University of North Carolina at Chapel Hill *M, W*
Wake Forest University *M, W*
Western Carolina University *M, W*

Ohio
Bowling Green State University *M, W*
Cleveland State University *M, W*
Kent State University *M, W*
Miami University: Oxford Campus *M, W*
Ohio State University: Columbus Campus *M, W*
Ohio University *M, W*
University of Akron *M, W*
University of Cincinnati *M*
University of Toledo *M, W*
Youngstown State University *M, W*

Oklahoma
Oklahoma State University *M, W*
University of Oklahoma *M, W*
University of Tulsa *M, W*

Oregon
University of Oregon *M, W*
University of Portland *M, W*

Pennsylvania
Bucknell University *M, W*
Drexel University *M*
Duquesne University *W*
La Salle University *M, W*
Lafayette College *M, W, Mixed*
Lehigh University *M, W*
Penn State University Park Campus *M, W*
Robert Morris College *M, W*
St. Francis College *W*
St. Joseph's University *M, W*
Temple University *M, W*
University of Pennsylvania *M, W*
University of Pittsburgh *M, W*
Villanova University *M, W*

Rhode Island
Brown University *M, W*
Providence College *M, W*
University of Rhode Island *M, W*

South Carolina
The Citadel *M*
Clemson University *M, W*
Furman University *W*
South Carolina State University *M, W*
University of South Carolina *M, W*

Tennessee
Austin Peay State University *W*
East Tennessee State University *M, W*
Memphis State University *M, W*
Middle Tennessee State University *M, W*
Tennessee State University *W*
Tennessee Technological University *M, W*
University of Tennessee
Chattanooga *M, W*
Knoxville *M, W*
Martin *W, Mixed*
Vanderbilt University *W*

Texas
Baylor University *M, W*
Lamar University—Beaumont *M, W*
Prairie View A&M University *M, W*
Rice University *M, W*
Sam Houston State University *M, W*
Southern Methodist University *M, W*
Southwest Texas State University *M*
Stephen F. Austin State University *M, W*
Texas A&M University *M, W*
Texas Christian University *M, W*
Texas Southern University *M*
Texas Tech University *M*
University of Houston *M, W*
University of North Texas *M, W*
University of Texas
Arlington *M*
Austin *M, W*
El Paso *M, W*
Pan American *M*
San Antonio *M, W*

Utah
Brigham Young University *M, W*
Southern Utah University *M, W*
University of Utah *W*
Utah State University *M*
Weber State University *M, W*

Vermont
University of Vermont *M, W*

Virginia
College of William and Mary *M, W*
George Mason University *M, W*
James Madison University *M, W*
Liberty University *M, W*
Old Dominion University *M, W*
University of Richmond *M, W*
University of Virginia *M, W*
Virginia Commonwealth University *M, W, Mixed*
Virginia Military Institute *M*
Virginia Polytechnic Institute and State University *M, W*

Washington
Eastern Washington University *M, W*
University of Washington *M, W*
Washington State University *M, W*

West Virginia
Marshall University *M, W*
West Virginia University *M*

Wisconsin
Marquette University *M, W*
University of Wisconsin: Madison *M, W*

Wyoming
University of Wyoming *M, W*

Track, indoor — Division II

Alabama
Alabama Agricultural and Mechanical University *M, W*
Troy State University *M, W*

Arkansas
Henderson State University *M*

California
California Polytechnic State University: San Luis Obispo *M*
California State University
Bakersfield *M, W*
Los Angeles *M, W*
University of California
Davis *M, W*
Riverside *M, W*

Colorado
Adams State College *M, W*
Colorado School of Mines *M, W, Mixed*
United States Air Force Academy *W*
University of Northern Colorado *M, W*
University of Southern Colorado *M, W*
Western State College of Colorado *M, W*

Connecticut
Southern Connecticut State University *M, W*
University of New Haven *M*

District of Columbia
University of the District of Columbia *M, W*

Georgia
Kennesaw State College *W*

Illinois
Lewis University *M, W*
Southern Illinois University at Edwardsville *M, W*

Indiana
St. Joseph's College *M, W*
University of Indianapolis *M, W*
University of Southern Indiana *M*

Iowa
Morningside College *M, W*

Kansas
Emporia State University *M, W*
Fort Hays State University *M, W*
Pittsburg State University *M, W*

Kentucky
Bellarmine College *M, W*
Kentucky State University *M, W*

Maryland
Bowie State University *M, W*

Massachusetts
Bentley College *M, W*
Springfield College *M, W*
Stonehill College *M*
University of Massachusetts at Lowell *M, W*

Michigan
Ferris State University *M, W*
Grand Valley State University *M, W*
Hillsdale College *M, W*
Lake Superior State University *M, W*
Northern Michigan University *W*
Northwood University *M, W, Mixed*
Saginaw Valley State University *M, W*

Minnesota
Bemidji State University *M, W*
Mankato State University *M, W*
Moorhead State University *M, W*
St. Cloud State University *M, W*
University of Minnesota: Duluth *M, W*
Winona State University *M, W*

Mississippi

Mississippi College *M, W*

Missouri

Central Missouri State University *M, W*
Lincoln University *M, W*
Missouri Southern State College *M, W, Mixed*
Northeast Missouri State University *M, W*
Northwest Missouri State University *W*
Southwest Baptist University *M, W*
University of Missouri: Rolla *M, W*

Nebraska

Chadron State College *M, W*
University of Nebraska
Kearney *M, W*
Omaha *W*
Wayne State College *M, W*

New Hampshire

Keene State College *M, W*

New York

City University of New York: Queens College *M, W*
Long Island University: C. W. Post Campus *M, W*
New York Institute of Technology *M, W*
Pace University
New York *M*
Pleasantville/Briarcliff *W*

North Carolina

Elizabeth City State University *M, W*
Johnson C. Smith University *M*
North Carolina Central University *W*
Pembroke State University *M*
St. Augustine's College *M, W*
Shaw University *M, W*

North Dakota

North Dakota State University *M, W*
University of North Dakota *M, W*

Ohio

Ashland University *M, W*

Oklahoma

University of Central Oklahoma *M, W*

Oregon

Portland State University *M, W*

Pennsylvania

California University of Pennsylvania *M, W*
Cheyney University of Pennsylvania *M, W*
Clarion University of Pennsylvania *M, W*
East Stroudsburg University of Pennsylvania *M, W*
Edinboro University of Pennsylvania *M, W*
Indiana University of Pennsylvania *M, W*
Kutztown University of Pennsylvania *M, W*
Lock Haven University of Pennsylvania *M, W*
Mansfield University of Pennsylvania *M, W*
Millersville University of Pennsylvania *M, W*
Shippensburg University of Pennsylvania *M, W*
Slippery Rock University of Pennsylvania *M, W*
University of Pittsburgh at Johnstown *W*
West Chester University of Pennsylvania *M, W*

South Dakota

Augustana College *M, W*
South Dakota State University *M, W*
University of South Dakota *M, W*

Tennessee

Carson-Newman College *M, W*

Texas

Abilene Christian University *M, W*
Texas A&I University *M, W*

Virginia

Hampton University *M, W*
Norfolk State University *M, W*
St. Paul's College *M, W*
Virginia State University *M, W*

Washington

Seattle Pacific University *M, W, Mixed*

West Virginia

Wheeling Jesuit College *M*

Wisconsin

University of Wisconsin: Parkside *M, W*

Track, indoor — Division III

California

Menlo College *Mixed*

Colorado

Colorado College *M, W*

Connecticut

Connecticut College *M, W*
Eastern Connecticut State University *M, W*
Trinity College *M, W*
United States Coast Guard Academy *M, W*
Wesleyan University *M, W*

District of Columbia

Catholic University of America *M, W*
Gallaudet University *M, W*

Georgia

Emory University *M, W*

Illinois

Augustana College *M, W*
Concordia University *M, W*
Elmhurst College *M, W*
Eureka College *M, W*
Illinois Benedictine College *M, W*
Illinois College *M, W*
Illinois Wesleyan University *M*
Knox College *M, W*
Millikin University *M*
Monmouth College *M, W*
North Central College *M, W*
North Park College *M, W*
Principia College *Mixed*
University of Chicago *M, W*
Wheaton College *W*

Indiana

Anderson University *M, W*
DePauw University *M, W*
Earlham College *M, W*
Franklin College *M, W*
Manchester College *M, W*
Rose-Hulman Institute of Technology *M*
St. Mary's College *W*
Wabash College *M*

Iowa

Buena Vista College *M, W*
Central College *M, W*
Coe College *M, W*
Cornell College *M, W*
Grinnell College *M, W*
Loras College *M, W*
Luther College *M, W*
Simpson College *M, W*
Upper Iowa University *M*
Wartburg College *M, W*

Maine

Bates College *M, W*
Bowdoin College *M, W*
Colby College *M, W*
University of Southern Maine *W*

Maryland

Frostburg State University *M, W*
Johns Hopkins University *M, W*

Massachusetts

Amherst College *M, W*
Brandeis University *M, W*
Fitchburg State College *M, W*
Massachusetts Institute of Technology *M*
Mount Holyoke College *W*
Smith College *W*
Tufts University *M, W*
University of Massachusetts at Dartmouth *M, W*
Wellesley College *W*
Westfield State College *M, W*
Wheaton College *M*
Williams College *M, W*
Worcester Polytechnic Institute *M, W*
Worcester State College *M, W*

Minnesota

Augsburg College *M, W*
Carleton College *M, W*
College of St. Benedict *W*
Concordia College: Moorhead *M, W*
Gustavus Adolphus College *M, W*
Hamline University *M, W*
Macalester College *M, W*
St. John's University *M*
St. Mary's College of Minnesota *M, W*
St. Olaf College *M, W*
University of St. Thomas *M, W*

Missouri

Washington University *M, W*

Nebraska

Nebraska Wesleyan University *M, W*

New Jersey

Montclair State College *M, W*
Stockton State College *M, W*
Trenton State College *M, W*

New York

Alfred University *M*
City University of New York
City College *M, W*
Hunter College *M, W*
Lehman College *M, W*
Medgar Evers College *M, W*
York College *M, W*
Hamilton College *M, W*
Hartwick College *M, W*
Ithaca College *M, W*
New York University *M, W*
Rensselaer Polytechnic Institute *M, W*
Rochester Institute of Technology *M, W*
St. Lawrence University *M, W*
State University of New York
Albany *M, W*
Binghamton *M, W*
Stony Brook *M, W*
College at Brockport *M, W, Mixed*
College at Buffalo *M, W*
College at Cortland *M, W*
College at Fredonia *M, W*
College at Geneseo *M, W*
College at Plattsburgh *M, W*
Union College *M, W*
United States Merchant Marine Academy *M, W*
University of Rochester *M, W*

North Carolina

Bennett College *W*
Methodist College *M, W*

Ohio

Baldwin-Wallace College *M, W*
Bluffton College *M, W*
Case Western Reserve University *M, W*
College of Wooster *M, W*
Defiance College *M, W*
Denison University *M, W*
Heidelberg College *M, W*
Hiram College *M, W*
John Carroll University *M, W*
Kenyon College *M, W*
Mount Union College *M, W*
Muskingum College *M, W*
Oberlin College *M, W*
Ohio Northern University *M, W, Mixed*
Ohio Wesleyan University *M, W*
Otterbein College *M, W*
Wilmington College *M, W*
Wittenberg University *M, W*

Pennsylvania

Albright College *M, W, Mixed*
Allegheny College *M, W*
Carnegie Mellon University *M, W*
Delaware Valley College *M, W*
Dickinson College *M, W*
Franklin and Marshall College *M, W*
Gettysburg College *M, W*
Haverford College *M, W*
Lebanon Valley College of Pennsylvania *M, W*
Lincoln University *M, W*
Lycoming College *M, W*
Moravian College *M, W*
Muhlenberg College *M, W*
Susquehanna University *M, W*
Swarthmore College *M, W*
Thiel College *M, W*
Ursinus College *M, W, Mixed*
Widener University *M, W*

Rhode Island

Salve Regina University *M, W*

Tennessee

Rhodes College *M, W*

Vermont
Middlebury College *M, W*
Norwich University *M, W, Mixed*

Virginia
Bridgewater College *M*
Christopher Newport University *M, W*
Eastern Mennonite College *M, W*
Lynchburg College *M, W*
Mary Washington College *M, W*
Roanoke College *Mixed*
Washington and Lee University *M, W*

Wisconsin
Beloit College *M, W*
Carroll College *M, W*
Carthage College *M, W*
Lawrence University *M, W*
Northwestern College *M*
Ripon College *M, W*
St. Norbert College *M, W*
University of Wisconsin
Eau Claire *M, W*
La Crosse *M, W*
Oshkosh *M, W*
Platteville *M, W*
River Falls *M, W*
Stevens Point *M, W*
Stout *M, W*
Whitewater *M, W*

Track, outdoor — Division I

Alabama
Alabama State University *M, W*
Auburn University *M, W*
Samford University *M, W*
University of Alabama
Birmingham *M, W*
Tuscaloosa *M, W*
University of South Alabama *M, W*

Arizona
Arizona State University *M, W*
Northern Arizona University *M, W*
University of Arizona *M, W*

Arkansas
Arkansas State University *M, W*
University of Arkansas *M, W*
University of Arkansas at Little Rock *M, W*

California
California State University
Fresno *M, W*
Fullerton *M, W*
Long Beach *M, W*
Northridge *M, W*
Sacramento *M, W*
San Diego State University *W*
Stanford University *M, W*
University of California
Berkeley *M, W*
Irvine *M, W*
Los Angeles *M, W*
Santa Barbara *M, W*
University of Southern California *M, W*

Colorado
Colorado State University *M, W*
United States Air Force Academy *M*

Connecticut
Central Connecticut State University *M, W*
University of Connecticut *M, W*
University of Hartford *M, W*
Yale University *M, W*

Delaware
Delaware State College *M, W*
University of Delaware *M, W*

District of Columbia
Georgetown University *M, W*
Howard University *M, W*

Florida
Bethune-Cookman College *M, W*
Florida Agricultural and Mechanical University *M, W*
Florida International University *M, W*
Florida State University *M, W*
Jacksonville University *W*
University of Central Florida *M, W*
University of Florida *M, W*
University of Miami *M, W*
University of South Florida *M, W*

Georgia
Georgia Institute of Technology *M, W*
University of Georgia *M, W*

Idaho
Boise State University *M, W*
Idaho State University *M, W*
University of Idaho *M, W*

Illinois
Bradley University *M, W*
Chicago State University *M, W*
De Paul University *M, W*
Eastern Illinois University *M, W*
Illinois State University *M, W*
Loyola University of Chicago *M, W*
Southern Illinois University at Carbondale *M, W*
University of Illinois at Urbana-Champaign *M, W*
Western Illinois University *M, W*

Indiana
Ball State University *M, W*
Butler University *M, W*
Indiana State University *M, W*
Indiana University Bloomington *M, W*
Purdue University *M, W*
University of Notre Dame *M, W*
Valparaiso University *M, W*

Iowa
Drake University *M, W*
Iowa State University *M, W*
University of Iowa *M, W*
University of Northern Iowa *M, W*

Kansas
Kansas State University *M, W*
University of Kansas *M, W*
Wichita State University *M, W*

Kentucky
Eastern Kentucky University *M, W*
Morehead State University *M, W*
Murray State University *M, W*
University of Kentucky *M, W*
University of Louisville *M, W*
Western Kentucky University *M, W*

Louisiana
Grambling State University *M, W*
Louisiana State University and Agricultural and Mechanical College *M, W*
Louisiana Tech University *M, W*
McNeese State University *M, W*
Nicholls State University *M, W*
Northeast Louisiana University *M, W*
Northwestern State University *M, W*
Southeastern Louisiana University *M, W*
Southern University and Agricultural and Mechanical College *M, W*
Tulane University *M, W*
University of New Orleans *M, W*
University of Southwestern Louisiana *M, W*

Maine
University of Maine *M, W*

Maryland
Coppin State College *M, W*
Morgan State University *M, W*
Mount St. Mary's College *M, W*
Towson State University *M, W*
United States Naval Academy *M, W*
University of Maryland
Baltimore County *M, W*
College Park *M, W*
Eastern Shore *M, W*

Massachusetts
Boston College *M, W*
Boston University *M, W*
College of the Holy Cross *M, W*
Harvard and Radcliffe Colleges *M, W*
Northeastern University *M, W*
University of Massachusetts at Amherst *M, W*

Michigan
Central Michigan University *M, W*
Eastern Michigan University *M, W*
Michigan State University *M, W*
University of Detroit Mercy *M, W*
University of Michigan *M, W*
Western Michigan University *M, W*

Minnesota
University of Minnesota: Twin Cities *M, W*

Mississippi
Alcorn State University *M, W*
Jackson State University *M, W*
Mississippi State University *M, W*
Mississippi Valley State University *M, W*
University of Mississippi *M*
University of Southern Mississippi *M, W*

Missouri
Southeast Missouri State University *M, W*
Southwest Missouri State University *M, W*
University of Missouri: Columbia *M, W*

Montana
Montana State University *M, W*
University of Montana *M, W*

Nebraska
University of Nebraska—Lincoln *M, W*

Nevada
University of Nevada
Las Vegas *W*
Reno *M, W*

New Hampshire
Dartmouth College *M, W*
University of New Hampshire *M, W*

New Jersey
Fairleigh Dickinson University: Edward Williams College *M, W*
Monmouth College *M, W*
Princeton University *M, W*
Rider College *M*
Rutgers—The State University of New Jersey
College of Engineering *M, W*
Cook College *M, W*
Douglass College *W*
Livingston College *M, W*
Mason Gross School of the Arts *M, W*
Rutgers College *M, W*
St. Peter's College *M, W*
Seton Hall University *M, W*

New Mexico
New Mexico State University *M, W*
University of New Mexico *M, W*

New York
Barnard College *W*
Colgate University *M, W*
Columbia University: Columbia College *M, W*
Cornell University *M, W*
Fordham University *M, W*
Iona College *M*
Long Island University: Brooklyn Campus *M, W*
Manhattan College *M, W*
Marist College *M, W*
St. Francis College *M, W*
St. John's University *M, W*
State University of New York at Buffalo *M, W*
Syracuse University *M, W*
United States Military Academy *M, W*
Wagner College *M, W*

North Carolina
Appalachian State University *M, W*
Campbell University *M, W*
Davidson College *M, W*
Duke University *M, W*
East Carolina University *M, W*
North Carolina Agricultural and Technical State University *M, W*
North Carolina State University *M, W*
University of North Carolina
Asheville *W*
Chapel Hill *M, W*
Charlotte *M, W*
Wilmington *M, W*
Wake Forest University *M, W*
Western Carolina University *M, W*

Ohio
Bowling Green State University *M, W*
Cleveland State University *M, W*
Kent State University *M, W*

Miami University: Oxford Campus M, W
Ohio State University: Columbus Campus M, W
Ohio University M, W
University of Akron M, W
University of Cincinnati M
University of Toledo M, W
Youngstown State University M, W

Oklahoma

Oklahoma State University M, W
Oral Roberts University M, W
University of Oklahoma M, W
University of Tulsa M, W

Oregon

University of Oregon M, W
University of Portland M, W

Pennsylvania

Bucknell University M, W
Drexel University M
Duquesne University W
La Salle University M, W
Lafayette College M, W
Lehigh University M, W
Penn State University Park Campus M, W
Robert Morris College M, W
St. Francis College M, W
St. Joseph's University M, W
Temple University M, W
University of Pennsylvania M, W
University of Pittsburgh M, W
Villanova University M, W

Rhode Island

Brown University M, W
Providence College M, W
University of Rhode Island M, W

South Carolina

Charleston Southern University M, W
The Citadel M
Clemson University M, W
Furman University M, W
South Carolina State University M, W
University of South Carolina M, W

Tennessee

Austin Peay State University W
East Tennessee State University M, W
Memphis State University M, W
Middle Tennessee State University M, W
Tennessee State University W
Tennessee Technological University M, W
University of Tennessee
- Chattanooga M, W
- Knoxville M, W
- Martin W

Vanderbilt University W

Texas

Baylor University M, W
Lamar University—Beaumont M, W
Prairie View A&M University M, W
Rice University M, W
Sam Houston State University M, W
Southern Methodist University M, W
Southwest Texas State University W
Stephen F. Austin State University M, W
Texas A&M University M, W
Texas Christian University M, W
Texas Southern University M, W
Texas Tech University M, W
University of Houston M, W
University of North Texas M, W
University of Texas
- Arlington M, W
- Austin M, W
- El Paso M, W
- Pan American M, W
- San Antonio M, W

Utah

Brigham Young University M, W
Southern Utah University M, W
University of Utah M, W
Utah State University M, W
Weber State University M, W

Vermont

University of Vermont M, W

Virginia

College of William and Mary M, W
George Mason University M, W
James Madison University M, W
Liberty University M, W
Old Dominion University M, W
University of Richmond M, W
University of Virginia M, W
Virginia Commonwealth University M, W
Virginia Military Institute M
Virginia Polytechnic Institute and State University M, W

Washington

Eastern Washington University M, W
University of Washington M, W
Washington State University M, W

West Virginia

Marshall University M, W
West Virginia University M, W

Wisconsin

Marquette University M, W
University of Wisconsin: Madison M, W

Wyoming

University of Wyoming M, W

Track, outdoor — Division II

Alabama

Alabama Agricultural and Mechanical University M, W
Miles College M, W
Troy State University M, W
Tuskegee University M, W

Arizona

Grand Canyon University M, W

Arkansas

Henderson State University M
University of Central Arkansas W

California

California Polytechnic State University: San Luis Obispo M, W
California State Polytechnic University: Pomona M, W
California State University
- Bakersfield M, W
- Chico M, W
- Hayward M
- Los Angeles M, W
- Stanislaus M, W

College of Notre Dame Mixed
Humboldt State University M, W
San Francisco State University M, W
University of California
- Davis M, W
- Riverside M, W

Colorado

Adams State College M, W
Colorado School of Mines M, W
United States Air Force Academy W
University of Northern Colorado M, W
University of Southern Colorado M, W
Western State College of Colorado M, W

Connecticut

Southern Connecticut State University M, W
University of New Haven M

District of Columbia

University of the District of Columbia M, W

Georgia

Albany State College M, W
Clark Atlanta University M, W
Fort Valley State College M, W
Morehouse College M
Morris Brown College M, W
Paine College M, W
Savannah State College M

Illinois

Lewis University M, W
Southern Illinois University at Edwardsville M, W

Indiana

St. Joseph's College M, W
University of Indianapolis M, W
University of Southern Indiana M, W

Iowa

Morningside College M, W

Kansas

Emporia State University M, W
Fort Hays State University M, W
Pittsburg State University M, W

Kentucky

Bellarmine College M, W
Kentucky State University M, W

Maryland

Bowie State University M, W

Massachusetts

Bentley College M, W
Springfield College M, W
Stonehill College M
University of Massachusetts at Lowell M, W

Michigan

Ferris State University M, W
Grand Valley State University M, W
Hillsdale College M, W
Lake Superior State University M, W
Michigan Technological University M, W
Northwood University W
Saginaw Valley State University M, W

Minnesota

Bemidji State University M, W
Mankato State University M, W
Moorhead State University M, W
St. Cloud State University M, W
University of Minnesota: Duluth M, W
Winona State University M, W

Mississippi

Mississippi College M, W

Missouri

Central Missouri State University M, W
Lincoln University M, W
Missouri Southern State College M, W
Northeast Missouri State University M, W
Northwest Missouri State University M, W
Southwest Baptist University M, W
University of Missouri: Rolla M, W

Nebraska

Chadron State College M, W
University of Nebraska
- Kearney M, W
- Omaha W

Wayne State College M, W

New Hampshire

Keene State College M, W

New York

City University of New York: Queens College M, W
Long Island University: C. W. Post Campus M, W
New York Institute of Technology M, W
Pace University M, W

North Carolina

Elizabeth City State University M, W, Mixed
Elon College M
High Point University M
Johnson C. Smith University M, W
Livingstone College M, W
North Carolina Central University M, W
Pembroke State University M
St. Augustine's College M, W
Shaw University M, W
Winston-Salem State University M

North Dakota

North Dakota State University M, W
University of North Dakota M, W

Ohio

Ashland University M, W

Oklahoma

University of Central Oklahoma M, W

Oregon

Portland State University M, W

Pennsylvania

Bloomsburg University of Pennsylvania M, W

California University of Pennsylvania *M, W*
Cheyney University of Pennsylvania *M, W*
Clarion University of Pennsylvania *M, W*
East Stroudsburg University of Pennsylvania *M, W*
Edinboro University of Pennsylvania *M, W*
Indiana University of Pennsylvania *M, W*
Kutztown University of Pennsylvania *M, W*
Lock Haven University of Pennsylvania *M, W*
Mansfield University of Pennsylvania *M, W*
Millersville University of Pennsylvania *M, W*
Shippensburg University of Pennsylvania *M, W*
Slippery Rock University of Pennsylvania *M, W*
University of Pittsburgh at Johnstown *W*
West Chester University of Pennsylvania *M, W*

Rhode Island
Bryant College *M, W*

South Carolina
Francis Marion University *M*
Presbyterian College *M*

South Dakota
Augustana College *M, W*
South Dakota State University *M, W*
University of South Dakota *M, W*

Tennessee
Carson-Newman College *M, W*
LeMoyne-Owen College *M, W*

Texas
Abilene Christian University *M, W*
Angelo State University *M, W*
East Texas State University *M, W*
Texas A&I University *M, W*

Virginia
Hampton University *M, W*
Norfolk State University *M, W*
St. Paul's College *M, W*
Virginia State University *M, W*
Virginia Union University *M, W*

Washington
Seattle Pacific University *M, W*

West Virginia
West Virginia Wesleyan College *M, W*
Wheeling Jesuit College *M, W*

Wisconsin
University of Wisconsin: Parkside *M, W*

Track, outdoor — Division III

Alabama
Stillman College *M, W*

Arkansas
Hendrix College *M, W*

California
California Institute of Technology *M, W*
California Lutheran University *M, W*
Claremont McKenna College *M, W*
Harvey Mudd College *M, W*
Menlo College *W*
Occidental College *M, W*
Pomona College *M, W*
Scripps College *W*
University of California: San Diego *M, W*
University of La Verne *M, W*
University of Redlands *M, W*
Whittier College *M, W*

Colorado
Colorado College *M, W*

Connecticut
Connecticut College *M, W*
Eastern Connecticut State University *M, W*
Trinity College *M, W*
United States Coast Guard Academy *M*
Wesleyan University *M, W*

District of Columbia
Catholic University of America *M, W*
Gallaudet University *M, W*

Georgia
Emory University *M, W*
Oglethorpe University *M, W*

Illinois
Augustana College *M, W*
Concordia University *M, W*
Elmhurst College *M, W*
Eureka College *M, W*
Illinois Benedictine College *M, W*
Illinois College *M, W*
Illinois Wesleyan University *M, W*
Knox College *M, W*
Millikin University *M, W*
Monmouth College *M, W*
North Central College *M, W*
North Park College *M, W*
Principia College *M, W*
University of Chicago *M, W*
Wheaton College *M, W*

Indiana
Anderson University *M, W*
DePauw University *M, W*
Earlham College *M, W*
Franklin College *M, W*
Hanover College *M, W*
Manchester College *M, W, Mixed*
Rose-Hulman Institute of Technology *M*
St. Mary's College *W*
Wabash College *M*

Iowa
Buena Vista College *M, W*
Central College *M, W*
Coe College *M, W*
Cornell College *M, W*
Grinnell College *M, W*
Loras College *M, W*
Luther College *M, W*
Simpson College *M, W*
University of Dubuque *M, W*
Upper Iowa University *M*
Wartburg College *M, W*
William Penn College *M, W*

Kentucky
Berea College *M, W*
Centre College *M, W*

Maine
Bates College *M, W*
Bowdoin College *M, W*
Colby College *M, W*
University of Southern Maine *W*

Maryland
Frostburg State University *M, W*
Johns Hopkins University *M, W*
Salisbury State University *M, W*
Western Maryland College *M, W*

Massachusetts
Amherst College *M, W*
Brandeis University *M, W*
Bridgewater State College *M, W*
Clark University *M, W*
Fitchburg State College *M, W*
Massachusetts Institute of Technology *M, W*
Mount Holyoke College *W*
Nichols College *M, W*
Salem State College *M, W*
Simmons College *W*
Smith College *W*
Tufts University *M, W*
University of Massachusetts at Dartmouth *M, W*
Wellesley College *W*
Westfield State College *M, W*
Wheaton College *M, W*
Williams College *M, W*
Worcester Polytechnic Institute *M, W*
Worcester State College *M, W*

Michigan
Adrian College *M, W*
Albion College *M, W*
Alma College *M, W*
Calvin College *M, W*
Hope College *M, W*
Olivet College *M*

Minnesota
Augsburg College *M, W*
Carleton College *M, W*
College of St. Benedict *W*
College of St. Catherine: St. Catherine Campus *W*
Concordia College: Moorhead *M, W*
Gustavus Adolphus College *M, W*
Hamline University *M, W*
Macalester College *M, W*
St. John's University *M*
St. Mary's College of Minnesota *M, W*
St. Olaf College *M, W*
University of St. Thomas *M, W*

Mississippi
Rust College *M, W*

Missouri
Fontbonne College *M, W*
Washington University *M, W*

Nebraska
Nebraska Wesleyan University *M, W*

New Jersey
Montclair State College *M, W*
Ramapo College of New Jersey *M, W*
Rowan College of New Jersey *M, W*
Rutgers—The State University of New Jersey: Camden College of Arts and Sciences *M, W*
Stockton State College *M, W*
William Paterson College of New Jersey *M, W*

New York
Alfred University *M*
City University of New York
  City College *M, W*
  Hunter College *M, W*
  Lehman College *M, W*
  Medgar Evers College *M, W*
  York College *M, W*
College of Mount St. Vincent *W*
Hamilton College *M, W*
Hartwick College *M, W*
Ithaca College *M, W*
New York University *M, W*
Rensselaer Polytechnic Institute *M, W*
Rochester Institute of Technology *M, W*
St. Lawrence University *M, W*
State University of New York
  Albany *M, W*
  Binghamton *M, W*
  Stony Brook *M, W*
  College at Brockport *M, W*
  College at Buffalo *M, W*
  College at Cortland *M, W*
  College at Fredonia *M, W*
  College at Geneseo *M, W*
  College at Plattsburgh *M, W*
Union College *M, W*
United States Merchant Marine Academy *M, W*
University of Rochester *M, W*

North Carolina
Bennett College *W*
Methodist College *M, W*

Ohio
Baldwin-Wallace College *M, W*
Bluffton College *M, W*
Case Western Reserve University *M, W*
College of Wooster *M, W*
Defiance College *M, W*
Denison University *M, W*
Heidelberg College *M, W*
Hiram College *M, W*
John Carroll University *M, W*
Kenyon College *M, W*
Mount Union College *M, W*
Muskingum College *M, W, Mixed*
Oberlin College *M, W*
Ohio Northern University *W*
Ohio Wesleyan University *M, W*
Otterbein College *M, W*
Wilmington College *M, W*
Wittenberg University *M, W*

Pennsylvania
Albright College *M, W*
Allegheny College *M, W*
Cabrini College *Mixed*
Carnegie Mellon University *M, W*
Delaware Valley College *M, W*
Dickinson College *M, W*
Franklin and Marshall College *M, W*
Gettysburg College *M, W*
Grove City College *M, W*
Haverford College *M, W*
Juniata College *M, W*
Lebanon Valley College of Pennsylvania *M, W*
Lincoln University *M, W*
Lycoming College *M, W*
Messiah College *M, W*
Moravian College *M, W*
Muhlenberg College *M, W*
Susquehanna University *M, W*
Swarthmore College *M, W*
Thiel College *M, W*

Ursinus College *M, W*
Washington and Jefferson College *M*
Widener University *M, W*
York College of Pennsylvania *M*

Puerto Rico
American University of Puerto Rico *M, W*

Rhode Island
Rhode Island College *M, W*
Salve Regina University *M, W*

Tennessee
Fisk University *M, W*
Rhodes College *M, W*
University of the South *M, W*

Texas
Jarvis Christian College *M, W*
Trinity University *M, W*
Wiley College *M, W*

Vermont
Middlebury College *M, W*
Norwich University *M, W*

Virginia
Bridgewater College *M*
Christopher Newport University *M, W*
Eastern Mennonite College *M, W*
Lynchburg College *M, W*
Mary Washington College *M, W*
Roanoke College *Mixed*
Washington and Lee University *M, W*

West Virginia
Bethany College *M, W*

Wisconsin
Beloit College *M, W*
Carroll College *M, W*
Carthage College *M, W*
Lawrence University *M, W*
Northwestern College *M*
Ripon College *M, W*
St. Norbert College *M, W*
University of Wisconsin
Eau Claire *M, W*
La Crosse *W*
Oshkosh *M, W*
Platteville *M, W*
River Falls *M, W*
Stevens Point *M, W*
Stout *M, W*
Whitewater *M, W*

Volleyball — Division I

Alabama
Alabama State University *W*
Auburn University *W*
Samford University *W*
University of Alabama
Birmingham *W*
Tuscaloosa *W*
University of South Alabama *W*

Arizona
Arizona State University *W*
Northern Arizona University *W*
University of Arizona *W*

Arkansas
Arkansas State University *W*
University of Arkansas *W*

California
California Polytechnic State University: San Luis Obispo *W*
California State University
Fresno *W*
Fullerton *W*
Long Beach *M, W*
Northridge *M, W*
Sacramento *W*
Loyola Marymount University *M, W*
Pepperdine University *M, W*
St. Mary's College of California *W*
San Diego State University *M*
San Jose State University *W*
Santa Clara University *W*
Stanford University *M, W*
University of California
Berkeley *W*
Irvine *M, W*
Los Angeles *M, W*
Santa Barbara *M, W*
University of the Pacific *M, W*
University of San Diego *W*
University of San Francisco *W*
University of Southern California *M, W*

Colorado
Colorado State University *W*
University of Colorado at Boulder *W*

Connecticut
Central Connecticut State University *W*
Fairfield University *W*
University of Connecticut *W*
University of Hartford *W*
Yale University *W*

Delaware
Delaware State College *W*
University of Delaware *W*

District of Columbia
American University *W*
George Washington University *W*
Georgetown University *W*
Howard University *W*

Florida
Bethune-Cookman College *W*
Florida Agricultural and Mechanical University *W*
Florida International University *W*
Florida State University *W*
Jacksonville University *W*
Stetson University *W*
University of Central Florida *W*
University of Florida *W*
University of South Florida *W*

Georgia
Georgia Institute of Technology *W*
Georgia Southern University *W*
Georgia State University *W*
Mercer University *W*
University of Georgia *W*

Hawaii
University of Hawaii
Honolulu Community College *M*
Manoa *M, W*

Idaho
Boise State University *W*
Idaho State University *W*
University of Idaho *W*

Illinois
Bradley University *W*
Chicago State University *W*
De Paul University *W*
Eastern Illinois University *W*
Illinois State University *W*
Loyola University of Chicago *W*
Northeastern Illinois University *W*
Northern Illinois University *W*
Northwestern University *W*
Southern Illinois University at Carbondale *W*
University of Illinois
Chicago *W*
Urbana-Champaign *W*
Western Illinois University *W*

Indiana
Ball State University *M, W*
Butler University *W*
Indiana State University *W*
Indiana University Bloomington *W*
Purdue University *W*
University of Evansville *W*
University of Notre Dame *W*
Valparaiso University *W*

Iowa
Drake University *W*
Iowa State University *W*
University of Iowa *W*
University of Northern Iowa *W*

Kansas
Kansas State University *W*
University of Kansas *W*
Wichita State University *W*

Kentucky
Eastern Kentucky University *W*
Morehead State University *W*
Murray State University *W*
University of Kentucky *W*
University of Louisville *W*
Western Kentucky University *W*

Louisiana
Centenary College of Louisiana *W*
Grambling State University *W*
Louisiana State University and Agricultural and Mechanical College *W*
Louisiana Tech University *W*
McNeese State University *W*
Nicholls State University *W*
Northeast Louisiana University *W*
Northwestern State University *W*
Southeastern Louisiana University *W*
Southern University and Agricultural and Mechanical College *W*
Tulane University *W*
University of New Orleans *W*
University of Southwestern Louisiana *W*

Maryland
Coppin State College *W*
Loyola College in Maryland *W*
Morgan State University *W*
Towson State University *W*
United States Naval Academy *M, W*
University of Maryland
Baltimore County *W*
College Park *W*
Eastern Shore *W*

Massachusetts
Boston College *W*
College of the Holy Cross *W*
Harvard and Radcliffe Colleges *M, W*
Northeastern University *W*

Michigan
Central Michigan University *W*
Eastern Michigan University *W*
Michigan State University *W*
University of Michigan *W*
Western Michigan University *W*

Minnesota
University of Minnesota: Twin Cities *W*

Mississippi
Alcorn State University *W*
Jackson State University *W*
Mississippi State University *W*
Mississippi Valley State University *W*
University of Mississippi *W*
University of Southern Mississippi *W*

Missouri
St. Louis University *W*
Southeast Missouri State University *W*
Southwest Missouri State University *W*
University of Missouri
Columbia *W*
Kansas City *W*

Montana
Montana State University *W*
University of Montana *W*

Nebraska
University of Nebraska—Lincoln *W*

Nevada
University of Nevada: Reno *W*

New Hampshire
Dartmouth College *M, W*

New Jersey
Fairleigh Dickinson University
Edward Williams College *W*
Madison *W*
Princeton University *M, W*
Rider College *W*
Rutgers—The State University of New Jersey
College of Engineering *W*
Cook College *W*
Douglass College *W*
Livingston College *W*
Mason Gross School of the Arts *W*
Newark College of Arts and Sciences *M*
Rutgers College *W*
University College New Brunswick *W*
St. Peter's College *W*
Seton Hall University *W*

New Mexico
New Mexico State University *W*
University of New Mexico *W*

New York
Barnard College *W*
Canisius College *W*
Colgate University *W*
Cornell University *W*
Fordham University *W*
Hofstra University *W*
Iona College *W*
Manhattan College *W*
Marist College *W*
Niagara University *W*
St. Bonaventure University *W*
St. Francis College *W*

Siena College *W*
State University of New York at Buffalo *W*
Syracuse University *W*
United States Military Academy *W*
Wagner College *W*

North Carolina
Appalachian State University *W*
Campbell University *W*
Davidson College *W*
Duke University *W*
East Carolina University *W*
North Carolina Agricultural and Technical State University *W*
North Carolina State University *W*
University of North Carolina
Asheville *W*
Chapel Hill *W*
Charlotte *W*
Greensboro *W*
Wilmington *W*
Western Carolina University *W*

Ohio
Bowling Green State University *W*
Cleveland State University *W*
Kent State University *W*
Miami University: Oxford Campus *W*
Ohio State University: Columbus Campus *M, W*
Ohio University *W*
University of Akron *W*
University of Cincinnati *W*
University of Dayton *W*
University of Toledo *W*
Wright State University *W*
Xavier University *W*
Youngstown State University *W*

Oklahoma
University of Oklahoma *W*
University of Tulsa *W*

Oregon
Oregon State University *W*
University of Oregon *W*
University of Portland *W*

Pennsylvania
Bucknell University *W*
Drexel University *W*
Duquesne University *W*
La Salle University *W*
Lafayette College *W*
Lehigh University *W*
Penn State University Park Campus *M, W*
Robert Morris College *W*
St. Francis College *M, W*
Temple University *W*
University of Pennsylvania *W*
University of Pittsburgh *W*
Villanova University *W*

Rhode Island
Brown University *W*
Providence College *W*
University of Rhode Island *W*

South Carolina
Charleston Southern University *W*
Clemson University *W*
College of Charleston *W*
Furman University *W*
South Carolina State University *W*
University of South Carolina
Coastal Carolina College *W*
Columbia *W*
Winthrop University *W*

Tennessee
Austin Peay State University *W*
East Tennessee State University *W*
Memphis State University *W*
Middle Tennessee State University *W*
Tennessee State University *W*
Tennessee Technological University *W*
University of Tennessee
Chattanooga *W*
Knoxville *W*
Martin *W*

Texas
Baylor University *W*
Lamar University—Beaumont *W*
Prairie View A&M University *W*
Rice University *W*
Sam Houston State University *W*
Southwest Texas State University *W*
Stephen F. Austin State University *W*
Texas A&M University *W*
Texas Southern University *W*
Texas Tech University *W*
University of Houston *W*
University of North Texas *W*
University of Texas
Arlington *W*
Austin *W*
El Paso *W*
Pan American *W*
San Antonio *W*

Utah
Brigham Young University *M, W*
University of Utah *W*
Utah State University *W*
Weber State University *W*

Vermont
University of Vermont *W*

Virginia
College of William and Mary *W*
George Mason University *M*
James Madison University *W*
Liberty University *W*
Radford University *W*
University of Virginia *W*
Virginia Commonwealth University *W*
Virginia Polytechnic Institute and State University *W*

Washington
Eastern Washington University *W*
Gonzaga University *W*
University of Washington *W*
Washington State University *W*

West Virginia
Marshall University *W*
West Virginia University *W*

Wisconsin
Marquette University *W*
University of Wisconsin
Green Bay *W*
Madison *M, W*

Wyoming
University of Wyoming *W*

Volleyball — Division II

Alabama
Alabama Agricultural and Mechanical University *W*
Jacksonville State University *W*
Livingston University *W*
Miles College *W*
Troy State University *W*
Tuskegee University *W*
University of Alabama in Huntsville *W*
University of North Alabama *W*

Alaska
University of Alaska
Anchorage *W*
Fairbanks *W*

Arizona
Grand Canyon University *W*

Arkansas
Henderson State University *W*
University of Central Arkansas *W*

California
California State Polytechnic University: Pomona *W*
California State University
Bakersfield *W*
Chico *W*
Dominguez Hills *W*
Hayward *W*
Los Angeles *W*
San Bernardino *W*
Stanislaus *W*
Chapman University *W*
College of Notre Dame *W*
Humboldt State University *W*
San Francisco State University *W*
Sonoma State University *W*
University of California
Davis *W*
Riverside *W*

Colorado
Adams State College *W*
Colorado Christian University *W*
Colorado School of Mines *W*
Fort Lewis College *W*
Mesa State College *W*
Metropolitan State College of Denver *W*
Regis University *W*
United States Air Force Academy *W*
University of Colorado at Colorado Springs *W*
University of Denver *W*
University of Northern Colorado *W*
University of Southern Colorado *W*
Western State College of Colorado *W*

Connecticut
Quinnipiac College *W*
Sacred Heart University *M, W*
Southern Connecticut State University *W*
University of Bridgeport *M*
University of New Haven *W*

District of Columbia
University of the District of Columbia *W*

Florida
Barry University *W*
Eckerd College *W*
Florida Atlantic University *W*
Florida Institute of Technology *W*
Florida Southern College *W*
Rollins College *W*
St. Leo College *W*
University of North Florida *W*
University of Tampa *W*

Georgia
Albany State College *W*
Armstrong State College *W*
Augusta College *W*
Clark Atlanta University *W*
Fort Valley State College *W*
Morris Brown College *W*
Paine College *W*
Savannah State College *W*
West Georgia College *W*

Illinois
College of St. Francis *W*
Lewis University *W*
Quincy University *M, W*

Indiana
Indiana University—Purdue University at Fort Wayne *M, W*
Oakland City College *W*
St. Joseph's College *W*
University of Indianapolis *W*
University of Southern Indiana *W*

Iowa
Morningside College *W*

Kansas
Emporia State University *W*
Fort Hays State University *W*
Pittsburg State University *W*
Washburn University of Topeka *W*

Kentucky
Bellarmine College *W*
Kentucky State University *W*
Kentucky Wesleyan College *W*
Northern Kentucky University *W*

Maryland
Bowie State University *W*

Massachusetts
American International College *W*
Assumption College *W*
Bentley College *W*
Merrimack College *W*
Springfield College *M, W*
Stonehill College *W*
University of Massachusetts at Lowell *W*

Michigan
Ferris State University *W*
Grand Valley State University *W*
Hillsdale College *W*
Lake Superior State University *W*
Michigan Technological University *W*
Northern Michigan University *W*
Northwood University *W*
Oakland University *W*
Saginaw Valley State University *W*
Wayne State University *W*

Minnesota
Bemidji State University *M*
Mankato State University *W*
Moorhead State University *W*
St. Cloud State University *W*
University of Minnesota: Duluth *W*
Winona State University *W*

Mississippi
Mississippi College *W*
Mississippi University for Women *W*

Missouri
Central Missouri State University *W*
Missouri Southern State College *W*
Missouri Western State College *W*

Northeast Missouri State University *W*
Northwest Missouri State University *W*
Southwest Baptist University *W*
University of Missouri: St. Louis *W*

Montana
Eastern Montana College *M, W*

Nebraska
Chadron State College *W*
University of Nebraska
Kearney *W*
Omaha *W*
Wayne State College *W*

New Hampshire
Franklin Pierce College *W*
Keene State College *W*
New Hampshire College *W*

New Mexico
Eastern New Mexico University *W*
New Mexico Highlands University *W*

New York
Adelphi University *W*
City University of New York: Queens College *M, W*
College of St. Rose *W*
Concordia College *M, W*
Dowling College *W*
Le Moyne College *W*
Long Island University
C. W. Post Campus *W*
Southampton Campus *M, W*
Mercy College *W*
Molloy College *W*
New York Institute of Technology *W*
Pace University
New York *W*
Pleasantville/Briarcliff *W*

North Carolina
Catawba College *W*
Elizabeth City State University *W*
Elon College *W*
Fayetteville State University *W*
Gardner-Webb University *W*
High Point University *W*
Johnson C. Smith University *W*
Lenoir-Rhyne College *W*
Livingstone College *W*
Mars Hill College *W*
Mount Olive College *W*
North Carolina Central University *W*
Pembroke State University *W*
Pfeiffer College *W*
Queens College *W*
St. Augustine's College *W*
Shaw University *W*
Wingate College *W*
Winston-Salem State University *W*

North Dakota
North Dakota State University *W*
University of North Dakota *W*

Ohio
Ashland University *W*

Oklahoma
Cameron University *W*
University of Central Oklahoma *W*

Oregon
Portland State University *W*

Pennsylvania
California University of Pennsylvania *W*
Cheyney University of Pennsylvania *W*
Clarion University of Pennsylvania *W*
East Stroudsburg University of Pennsylvania *M, W*
Edinboro University of Pennsylvania *W*
Gannon University *W*
Indiana University of Pennsylvania *W*
Kutztown University of Pennsylvania *W*
Lock Haven University of Pennsylvania *W*
Mercyhurst College *W*
Millersville University of Pennsylvania *W*
Shippensburg University of Pennsylvania *W*
Slippery Rock University of Pennsylvania *W*
University of Pittsburgh at Johnstown *W*
West Chester University of Pennsylvania *W*

Rhode Island
Bryant College *W*

South Carolina
Erskine College *W*
Francis Marion University *W*
Limestone College *W*
Newberry College *W*
Presbyterian College *W*
University of South Carolina
Aiken *W*
Spartanburg *W*
Wofford College *W*

South Dakota
Augustana College *W*
South Dakota State University *W*
University of South Dakota *W*

Tennessee
Carson-Newman College *W*
LeMoyne-Owen College *W*
Lincoln Memorial University *W*

Texas
Abilene Christian University *W*
Angelo State University *W*
East Texas State University *W*
Hardin-Simmons University *W*
Texas A&I University *W*
Texas Woman's University *W*
West Texas A & M University *W*

Vermont
St. Michael's College *W*

Virginia
Hampton University *W*
Norfolk State University *W*
St. Paul's College *W*
Virginia State University *W*
Virginia Union University *W*

Washington
Seattle Pacific University *W*

West Virginia
West Virginia Wesleyan College *W*
Wheeling Jesuit College *W*

Wisconsin
University of Wisconsin: Parkside *W*

Volleyball — Division III

Alabama
Stillman College *W*

Arkansas
Hendrix College *W*

California
California Lutheran University *W*
Claremont McKenna College *W*
Harvey Mudd College *W*
Menlo College *M, W*
Mills College *W*
Occidental College *W*
Pitzer College *W*
Pomona College *W*
Scripps College *W*
University of California
San Diego *M, W*
Santa Cruz *M, W*
University of La Verne *M, W*
University of Redlands *W*
Whittier College *W*

Colorado
Colorado College *W*

Connecticut
Albertus Magnus College *W*
Connecticut College *W*
Eastern Connecticut State University *W*
Trinity College *W*
United States Coast Guard Academy *W*
Wesleyan University *W*
Western Connecticut State University *W*

District of Columbia
Catholic University of America *W*
Gallaudet University *W*

Georgia
Emory University *W*
Oglethorpe University *W*
Savannah College of Art and Design *W*

Illinois
Augustana College *W*
Aurora University *W*
Blackburn College *W*
Concordia University *W*
Elmhurst College *W*
Eureka College *W*
Illinois Benedictine College *W*
Illinois College *W*
Illinois Wesleyan University *W*
Knox College *W*
Lake Forest College *W*
MacMurray College *W*
Millikin University *W*
Monmouth College *W*
North Central College *W*
North Park College *W*
Principia College *W*
Rockford College *W*
University of Chicago *W*
Wheaton College *W*

Indiana
Anderson University *W*
DePauw University *W*
Earlham College *W*
Franklin College *W*
Hanover College *W*
Manchester College *W*
St. Mary's College *W*

Iowa
Buena Vista College *W*
Central College *W*
Coe College *W*
Cornell College *W*
Grinnell College *W*
Loras College *W*
Luther College *W*
Simpson College *W*
University of Dubuque *W*
Upper Iowa University *W*
Wartburg College *W*
William Penn College *W*

Kentucky
Asbury College *W*
Berea College *W*
Centre College *W*
Thomas More College *W*

Maine
Bates College *W*
Bowdoin College *W*
St. Joseph's College *W*

Maryland
College of Notre Dame of Maryland *W*
Goucher College *W*
Hood College *W*
Johns Hopkins University *W*
St. Mary's College of Maryland *W*
Salisbury State University *W*
Washington College *W*
Western Maryland College *W*

Massachusetts
Amherst College *W*
Anna Maria College for Men and Women *W*
Babson College *W*
Brandeis University *W*
Bridgewater State College *W*
Clark University *W*
Eastern Nazarene College *W*
Emmanuel College *W*
Fitchburg State College *W*
Framingham State College *W*
Gordon College *W*
Massachusetts Institute of Technology *M, W*
Massachusetts Maritime Academy *W*
Mount Holyoke College *W*
North Adams State College *W*
Regis College *W*
Salem State College *W*
Simmons College *W*
Smith College *W*
Tufts University *W*
University of Massachusetts
Boston *W*
Dartmouth *W*
Wellesley College *W*
Wentworth Institute of Technology *M, W*
Wheaton College *W*
Williams College *W*
Worcester Polytechnic Institute *W*
Worcester State College *W*

Michigan
Adrian College *W*
Albion College *W*
Alma College *W*
Calvin College *W*
Hope College *W*
Kalamazoo College *W*
Olivet College *W*

Minnesota
Augsburg College *W*
Carleton College *W*
College of St. Benedict *W*

College of St. Catherine: St. Catherine Campus *W*
College of St. Scholastica *W*
Concordia College: Moorhead *W*
Gustavus Adolphus College *W*
Hamline University *W*
Macalester College *W*
St. Mary's College of Minnesota *W*
St. Olaf College *W*
University of St. Thomas *W*

Mississippi

Millsaps College *W*

Missouri

Fontbonne College *W*
Maryville University *W*
Washington University *W*
Webster University *W*
Westminster College *W*

Nebraska

Nebraska Wesleyan University *W*

New Hampshire

Colby-Sawyer College *W*
Daniel Webster College *W*

New Jersey

College of St. Elizabeth *W*
Fairleigh Dickinson University *W*
Jersey City State College *M, W*
Kean College of New Jersey *W*
Montclair State College *W*
New Jersey Institute of Technology *M, W*
Ramapo College of New Jersey *M, W*
Rutgers—The State University of New Jersey: Newark College of Arts and Sciences *W*
Stevens Institute of Technology *M, W*
Stockton State College *W*
Upsala College *W*
William Paterson College of New Jersey *W*

New York

Alfred University *W*
Bard College *M, W*
City University of New York
- Baruch College *M, W*
- City College *M, W*
- College of Staten Island *W*
- Hunter College *M, W*
- John Jay College of Criminal Justice *W*
- Lehman College *M, W*
- Medgar Evers College *W*
- York College *M, W*

Clarkson University *W*
College of Mount St. Vincent *M, W*
College of New Rochelle *W*
Elmira College *W*
Hamilton College *W*
Hartwick College *W*
Hilbert College *W*
Ithaca College *W*
Keuka College *W*
Manhattanville College *W*
Mount St. Mary College *W*
Nazareth College of Rochester *W*
New York University *M, W*
Polytechnic University
- Brooklyn *W*
- Long Island Campus *W*

Rochester Institute of Technology *W*
Russell Sage College *W*
St. John Fisher College *W*
St. Lawrence University *W*
Skidmore College *W*
State University of New York
- Albany *W*
- Binghamton *W*
- Stony Brook *W*
- College at Brockport *W*
- College at Buffalo *W*
- College at Cortland *W*
- College at Fredonia *W*
- College at Geneseo *W*
- College at New Paltz *M, W*
- College at Old Westbury *W*
- College at Oneonta *W*
- College at Plattsburgh *W*
- College at Potsdam *W*
- Institute of Technology at Utica/Rome *W*
- Oswego *W*

Union College *W*
United States Merchant Marine Academy *W*
University of Rochester *W*
Vassar College *M, W*
Yeshiva University *M, W*

North Carolina

Bennett College *W*
Greensboro College *W*
Guilford College *W*
Meredith College *W*
Methodist College *W*
North Carolina Wesleyan College *W*

Ohio

Baldwin-Wallace College *W*
Bluffton College *W*
Capital University *W*
Case Western Reserve University *W*
College of Wooster *W*
Defiance College *W*
Denison University *W*
Heidelberg College *W*
Hiram College *W*
John Carroll University *W*
Kenyon College *W*
Marietta College *W*
Mount Union College *W*
Muskingum College *W*
Oberlin College *W*
Ohio Northern University *W*
Ohio Wesleyan University *W*
Otterbein College *W*
Wilmington College *W*
Wittenberg University *W*

Pennsylvania

Albright College *W*
Allegheny College *W*
Allentown College of St. Francis de Sales *W*
Bryn Mawr College *W*
Cabrini College *W*
Carnegie Mellon University *W*
Cedar Crest College *W*
College Misericordia *W*
Delaware Valley College *W*
Dickinson College *W*
Elizabethtown College *W*
Franklin and Marshall College *W*
Gettysburg College *W*
Grove City College *W*
Haverford College *W*
Immaculata College *W*
Juniata College *M, W*
King's College *W*
Lebanon Valley College of Pennsylvania *W*
Lincoln University *W*
Lycoming College *W*
Marywood College *W*
Messiah College *W*
Moravian College *W*
Muhlenberg College *W*
Penn State Erie Behrend College *W*
Rosemont College *W*
Susquehanna University *W*
Swarthmore College *W*
Thiel College *W*
University of Scranton *W*
Ursinus College *W*
Washington and Jefferson College *W*
Waynesburg College *W*
Widener University *W*
Wilkes University *W*
York College of Pennsylvania *W*

Puerto Rico

American University of Puerto Rico *M, W*

Rhode Island

Rhode Island College *W*
Roger Williams University *M, W*

Tennessee

Fisk University *W*
Maryville College *W*
Rhodes College *W*
University of the South *W*

Texas

Jarvis Christian College *W*
Southwestern University *W*
Trinity University *W*
Wiley College *W*

Virginia

Averett College *W*
Bridgewater College *W*
Christopher Newport University *W*
Eastern Mennonite College *M, W*
Emory and Henry College *W*
Ferrum College *W*
Hollins College *W*
Lynchburg College *W*
Mary Baldwin College *W*
Mary Washington College *W*
Marymount University *W*
Randolph-Macon Woman's College *W*
Roanoke College *W*
Shenandoah University *W*
Sweet Briar College *W*
Washington and Lee University *W*

West Virginia

Bethany College *W*

Wisconsin

Beloit College *W*
Carroll College *W*
Carthage College *W*
Lawrence University *W*
Ripon College *W*
St. Norbert College *W*
University of Wisconsin
- Eau Claire *W*
- La Crosse *W*
- Oshkosh *W*
- Platteville *W*
- River Falls *W*
- Stevens Point *W*
- Stout *W*
- Superior *W*
- Whitewater *W*

Water polo — Division I

Arkansas

University of Arkansas at Little Rock *M*

California

California State University
- Fresno *M*
- Long Beach *M*

Loyola Marymount University *M*
Pepperdine University *M*
Santa Clara University *M*
Stanford University *M*
University of California
- Berkeley *M*
- Irvine *M*
- Los Angeles *M*
- Santa Barbara *M*

University of the Pacific *M*
University of Southern California *M*

Colorado

United States Air Force Academy *M*

District of Columbia

George Washington University *M*

Maryland

United States Naval Academy *M*

Massachusetts

Boston College *M*
Harvard and Radcliffe Colleges *M*
University of Massachusetts at Amherst *M*

New Jersey

Princeton University *M*
St. Peter's College *M*

New York

Fordham University *M*
Iona College *M*
St. Francis College *M*
United States Military Academy *M*

Ohio

University of Dayton *M*

Pennsylvania

Bucknell University *M*
Villanova University *M*

Rhode Island

Brown University *M*

Virginia

University of Richmond *M*

Water polo — Division II

California

Chapman University *M*
University of California
- Davis *M*
- Riverside *M*

New York

City University of New York: Queens College *M*

Pennsylvania

Slippery Rock University of Pennsylvania *M*

Water polo — Division III

California
California Institute of Technology *M*
Claremont McKenna College *M*
Harvey Mudd College *M*
Occidental College *M*
Pitzer College *M*
Pomona College *M*
University of California: San Diego *M*
University of Redlands *M*
Whittier College *M*

Massachusetts
Massachusetts Institute of Technology *M*

New York
United States Merchant Marine Academy *M*

Virginia
Hampden-Sydney College *M*
Washington and Lee University *M*

Wrestling — Division I

Arizona
Arizona State University *M*

California
California Polytechnic State University: San Luis Obispo *M*
California State University
Bakersfield *M*
Fresno *M*
Fullerton *M*
Stanford University *M*
University of California: Davis *M*

Colorado
United States Air Force Academy *M*

Connecticut
Central Connecticut State University *M*

Delaware
Delaware State College *M*

District of Columbia
American University *M*
Howard University *M*

Georgia
Georgia State University *M*

Idaho
Boise State University *M*

Illinois
Chicago State University *M*
Eastern Illinois University *M*
Illinois State University *M*
Northern Illinois University *M*
Northwestern University *M*
University of Illinois at Urbana-Champaign *M*

Indiana
Indiana University Bloomington *M*
Purdue University *M*
Valparaiso University *M*

Iowa
Drake University *M*
Iowa State University *M*
University of Iowa *M*
University of Northern Iowa *M*

Maryland
Coppin State College *M*
Morgan State University *M*
United States Naval Academy *M*
University of Maryland: College Park *M*

Massachusetts
Boston College *M*
Boston University *M*
Harvard and Radcliffe Colleges *M*

Michigan
Central Michigan University *M*
Eastern Michigan University *M*
Michigan State University *M*
University of Michigan *M*

Minnesota
University of Minnesota: Twin Cities *M*

Missouri
Southwest Missouri State University *M*
University of Missouri: Columbia *M*

Nebraska
University of Nebraska—Lincoln *M*

New Jersey
Princeton University *M*
Rider College *M*
Rutgers—The State University of New Jersey
College of Engineering *M*
Cook College *M*
Livingston College *M*
Mason Gross School of the Arts *M*
Rutgers College *M*
Seton Hall University *M*

New Mexico
University of New Mexico *M*

New York
Columbia University: Columbia College *M*
Cornell University *M*
Hofstra University *M*
Manhattan College *M*
State University of New York at Buffalo *M*
Syracuse University *M*
United States Military Academy *M*
Wagner College *M*

North Carolina
Appalachian State University *M*
Campbell University *M*
Davidson College *M*
Duke University *M*
North Carolina State University *M*
University of North Carolina at Chapel Hill *M*

Ohio
Cleveland State University *M*
Kent State University *M*
Miami University: Oxford Campus *M*
Ohio State University: Columbus Campus *M*
Ohio University *M*
University of Dayton *M*
University of Toledo *M*

Oklahoma
Oklahoma State University *M*
University of Oklahoma *M*

Oregon
Oregon State University *M*
University of Oregon *M*

Pennsylvania
Bloomsburg University of Pennsylvania *M*
Bucknell University *M*
California University of Pennsylvania *M*
Clarion University of Pennsylvania *M*
Drexel University *M*
Duquesne University *M*
East Stroudsburg University of Pennsylvania *M*
Edinboro University of Pennsylvania *M*
Franklin and Marshall College *M*
La Salle University *M*
Lehigh University *M*
Lock Haven University of Pennsylvania *M*
Millersville University of Pennsylvania *M*
Penn State University Park Campus *M*
Shippensburg University of Pennsylvania *M*
Slippery Rock University of Pennsylvania *M*
University of Pennsylvania *M*
University of Pittsburgh *M*
Wilkes University *M*

Rhode Island
Brown University *M*

South Carolina
The Citadel *M*
Clemson University *M*

Tennessee
University of Tennessee: Chattanooga *M*

Utah
Brigham Young University *M*

Virginia
College of William and Mary *M*
George Mason University *M*
James Madison University *M*
Liberty University *M*
Old Dominion University *M*
University of Virginia *M*
Virginia Military Institute *M*
Virginia Polytechnic Institute and State University *M*

West Virginia
West Virginia University *M*

Wisconsin
Marquette University *M*
University of Wisconsin: Madison *M*

Wyoming
University of Wyoming *M*

Wrestling — Division II

California
San Francisco State University *M*

Colorado
Adams State College *M*
Colorado School of Mines *M*
Fort Lewis College *M*
University of Northern Colorado *M*
University of Southern Colorado *M*
Western State College of Colorado *M*

Connecticut
Southern Connecticut State University *M*

Illinois
Southern Illinois University at Edwardsville *M*

Indiana
University of Indianapolis *M*

Kansas
Fort Hays State University *M*

Massachusetts
American International College *M*
Springfield College *M*
University of Massachusetts at Lowell *M*

Michigan
Ferris State University *M*
Grand Valley State University *M*
Lake Superior State University *M*

Minnesota
Mankato State University *M*
St. Cloud State University *M*
University of Minnesota: Duluth *M*

Missouri
Central Missouri State University *M*
Northeast Missouri State University *M*

Nebraska
Chadron State College *M*
University of Nebraska
Kearney *M*
Omaha *M*

North Carolina
Gardner-Webb University *M*
Pembroke State University *M*

North Dakota
North Dakota State University *M*
University of North Dakota *M*

Ohio
Ashland University *M*

Oklahoma
University of Central Oklahoma *M*

Oregon
Portland State University *M*

Pennsylvania
Cheyney University of Pennsylvania *M*
Gannon University *M*
Kutztown University of Pennsylvania *M*

Mansfield University of Pennsylvania *M*
University of Pittsburgh at Johnstown *M*

South Dakota
Augustana College *M*
South Dakota State University *M*

Tennessee
Carson-Newman College *M*

Virginia
Longwood College *M*
Norfolk State University *M*

West Virginia
West Liberty State College *M*

Wisconsin
University of Wisconsin: Parkside *M*

Wrestling — Division III

Connecticut
Trinity College *M*
United States Coast Guard Academy *M*
Wesleyan University *M*

District of Columbia
Gallaudet University *M*

Illinois
Augustana College *M*
Concordia University *M*
Elmhurst College *M*
Illinois College *M*
Knox College *M*
MacMurray College *M*
Millikin University *M*
Monmouth College *M*
North Central College *M*
University of Chicago *M*
Wheaton College *M*

Indiana
Manchester College *M*
Rose-Hulman Institute of Technology *M*
Wabash College *M*

Iowa
Buena Vista College *M*
Central College *M*
Coe College *M*
Cornell College *M*
Loras College *M*
Luther College *M*
Simpson College *M*
University of Dubuque *M*
Upper Iowa University *M*
Wartburg College *M*
William Penn College *M*

Maryland
Johns Hopkins University *M*
Western Maryland College *M*

Massachusetts
Bridgewater State College *M*
Massachusetts Institute of Technology *M*
University of Massachusetts at Boston *M*
Wentworth Institute of Technology *M*
Western New England College *M*
Williams College *M*
Worcester Polytechnic Institute *M*

Michigan
Olivet College *M*

Minnesota
Augsburg College *M*
Carleton College *M*
Concordia College: Moorhead *M*
St. John's University *M*
St. Olaf College *M*
University of St. Thomas *M*

New Hampshire
Plymouth State College of the University System of New Hampshire *M*

New Jersey
Kean College of New Jersey *M*
Montclair State College *M*
Rutgers—The State University of New Jersey
- Camden College of Arts and Sciences *M*
- Newark College of Arts and Sciences *M*

Trenton State College *M*
Upsala College *M*

New York
City University of New York
- Hunter College *M*
- John Jay College of Criminal Justice *M*

Ithaca College *M*
New York University *M*
Rochester Institute of Technology *M*
St. Lawrence University *M*
State University of New York
- Albany *M*
- Binghamton *M*
- College at Brockport *M*
- College at Cortland *M*
- College at Oneonta *M*
- Oswego *M*

United States Merchant Marine Academy *M*
Yeshiva University *M*

Ohio
Baldwin-Wallace College *M*
Capital University *M*
Case Western Reserve University *M*
Heidelberg College *M*
John Carroll University *M*
Mount Union College *M*
Muskingum College *M*
Ohio Northern University *M*
Wilmington College *M*

Pennsylvania
Albright College *M*
Allegheny College *M*
Delaware Valley College *M*
Elizabethtown College *M*
Gettysburg College *M*
Juniata College *M*
King's College *M*
Lebanon Valley College of Pennsylvania *M*
Lycoming College *M*
Messiah College *M*
Moravian College *M*
Muhlenberg College *M*
Susquehanna University *M*
Swarthmore College *M*
Thiel College *M*
University of Scranton *M*
Ursinus College *M*
Washington and Jefferson College *M*
Waynesburg College *M*
York College of Pennsylvania *M*

Puerto Rico
American University of Puerto Rico *M*

Rhode Island
Rhode Island College *M*
Roger Williams University *M*

Vermont
Norwich University *M*

Virginia
Washington and Lee University *M*

Wisconsin
Carroll College *M*
Carthage College *M*
Lawrence University *M*
Northwestern College *M*
Ripon College *M*
University of Wisconsin
- Eau Claire *M*
- La Crosse *M*
- Oshkosh *M*
- Platteville *M*
- River Falls *M*
- Stevens Point *M*
- Stout *M*
- Whitewater *M*

College descriptions

Alabama

Alabama Agricultural and Mechanical University
Normal, Alabama CB code: 1003

Admissions: 83% of applicants accepted
Based on: ••• School record, test scores
• Essay, special talents
Completion: 85% of freshmen end year in good standing
36% graduate, 65% of these enter graduate study

4-year public university, coed. Founded in 1875. **Accreditation:** Regional. **Undergraduate enrollment:** 1,680 men, 1,853 women full time; 151 men, 230 women part time. **Graduate enrollment:** 157 men, 123 women full time; 299 men, 576 women part time. **Faculty:** 357 total (281 full time), 169 with doctorates or other terminal degrees. **Location:** Suburban campus in small city; 2 miles from downtown Huntsville, 95 miles from Birmingham. **Calendar:** Semester, extensive summer session. **Microcomputers:** Located in libraries, classrooms, computer centers. **Special facilities:** State Black Archives, art gallery. **Additional facts:** Bachelor of technical studies available to adult learners in nontraditional fields.

DEGREES OFFERED. AA, AS, BA, BS, MS, MBA, MEd, MSW, PhD. 1 associate degree awarded in 1992. 380 bachelor's degrees awarded. 30% in business and management, 5% communications, 8% computer sciences, 15% teacher education, 11% engineering technologies. Graduate degrees offered in 29 major fields of study.

UNDERGRADUATE MAJORS. Associate: Civil technology, drafting, electromechanical technology, engineering and engineering-related technologies, graphic and printing production, mechanical design technology, medical laboratory technologies. **Bachelor's:** Accounting, agribusiness, agricultural business and management, agricultural economics, animal sciences, art education, biology, business administration and management, business and management, business economics, chemistry, city/community/regional planning, civil engineering, civil technology, commercial art, computer and information sciences, counseling psychology, crop science, developmental psychology, drafting, early childhood education, electromechanical technology, elementary education, engineering and engineering-related technologies, English, environmental science, fashion merchandising, finance, food science and nutrition, food sciences, forestry production and processing, French, graphic and printing production, history, horticulture, industrial arts education, industrial technology, junior high education, marketing management, mathematics, mechanical design technology, music education, office supervision and management, physical education, physics, political science and government, preveterinary, psychology, secondary education, social work, sociology, soil sciences, special education, speech correction, speech pathology/audiology, telecommunications, textiles and clothing, trade and industrial education, urban studies.

ACADEMIC PROGRAMS. Accelerated program, cooperative education, double major, dual enrollment of high school students, education specialist degree, honors program, internships, study abroad, cross-registration, technical studies program; liberal arts/career combination in engineering, health sciences. **Remedial services:** Learning center, reduced course load, remedial instruction, special counselor, tutoring. **ROTC:** Army. **Placement/credit:** AP, CLEP General and Subject, institutional tests; 3 credit hours maximum for bachelor's degree. Scores from DANTES, CLEP, ACE, and similar tests, and work experiences considered for credit toward degree.

ACADEMIC REQUIREMENTS. Freshmen must earn minimum GPA of 1.6 to continue in good standing. 67% of freshmen return for sophomore year. Students must declare major by end of second year. **Graduation requirements:** 74 hours for associate, 132 hours for bachelor's (36 in major). Most students required to take courses in arts/fine arts, computer science, English, history, humanities, mathematics, philosophy/religion, biological/physical sciences, social sciences. **Postgraduate studies:** 15% enter law school, 10% enter medical school, 35% enter MBA programs, 5% enter other graduate study.

FRESHMAN ADMISSIONS. Selection criteria: High school diploma or GED, 2.0 GPA required. Test scores important, but may be waived dependent upon evaluation of GPA and other achievements. **High school preparation:** 22 units required. Required units include English 4, mathematics 2, social science 3 and science 2. College-preparatory curriculum desirable. 11 units of electives in academic subjects required. **Test requirements:** SAT or ACT (ACT preferred); score report by July 1.

1992 FRESHMAN CLASS PROFILE. 1,792 men and women applied, 1,480 accepted; 498 men enrolled, 494 women enrolled. **Characteristics:** 55% from in state, 66% commute, 92% have minority backgrounds, 4% are foreign students. Average age is 18.

FALL-TERM APPLICATIONS. $10 fee. No closing date; priority given to applications received by May 1; applicants notified on a rolling basis; must reply within 4 weeks. Essay recommended. Deferred and early admission available. EDP-F.

STUDENT LIFE. Housing: Dormitories (men, women). **Activities:** Student government, film, student newspaper, yearbook, choral groups, concert band, dance, drama, jazz band, marching band, music ensembles, pep band, fraternities, sororities, YWCA, YMCA, honor society, service clubs, NAACP, African-American political club, Baptist Student Union, Islamic Association, Caribbean Students Association.

ATHLETICS. NCAA. **Intercollegiate:** Basketball, cross-country, football M, soccer M, tennis, track and field, volleyball W. **Intramural:** Badminton, basketball, cross-country, football M, gymnastics, soccer M, softball, swimming, table tennis, tennis, volleyball W.

STUDENT SERVICES. Career counseling, employment service for undergraduates, freshman orientation, health services, on-campus day care, personal counseling, placement service for graduates, special adviser for adult students, veterans counselor, services/facilities for handicapped.

ANNUAL EXPENSES. Tuition and fees: $1,550, $1,600 additional for out-of-state students. **Room and board:** $2,675. **Books and supplies:** $500. **Other expenses:** $835.

FINANCIAL AID. 88% of freshmen, 75% of continuing students receive some form of aid. 71% of grants, 82% of loans, 41% of jobs based on need. 872 enrolled freshmen were judged to have need, all were offered aid. Academic, music/drama, athletic, leadership scholarships available. **Aid applications:** Closing date June 1; priority given to applications received by April 1; applicants notified on a rolling basis beginning on or about April 16; must reply within 10 days.

ADDRESS/TELEPHONE. James O. Heyward, Director of Admissions, Alabama Agricultural and Mechanical University, PO Box 908, Normal, AL 35762. (205) 851-5245. (800) 533-0816. Fax: (205) 851-9747.

Alabama Aviation and Technical College
Ozark, Alabama CB code: 0177

2-year public technical college, coed. Founded in 1960. **Accreditation:** Regional. **Undergraduate enrollment:** 345 men, 13 women full time; 95 men, 27 women part time. **Faculty:** 33 total (22 full time). **Location:** Rural campus in large town; 17 miles from Dothan. **Calendar:** Quarter. Saturday and extensive evening/early morning classes. **Microcomputers:** 9 located in libraries, computer centers. **Special facilities:** College-operated fleet of 14 fixed-wing aircraft and training on Pt-6 engines, and navigational and communication systems. **Additional facts:** Federal Aviation Administration (FAA) Education Resource Center.

DEGREES OFFERED. AAS. 107 associate degrees awarded in 1992. 100% in trade and industry.

UNDERGRADUATE MAJORS. Aerospace/aeronautical/astronautical engineering, aircraft mechanics, airline piloting and navigation, electrical and electronics equipment repair, flight technology.

ACADEMIC PROGRAMS. Dual enrollment of high school students, internships. **Remedial services:** Learning center, remedial instruction, special counselor, tutoring. **Placement/credit:** AP, CLEP General and Subject, institutional tests.

ACADEMIC REQUIREMENTS. Freshmen must earn minimum GPA of 1.75 to continue in good standing. 70% of freshmen return for sophomore year. Students must declare major on enrollment. **Graduation requirements:** 114 hours for associate (63 in major). Most students required to take courses in arts/fine arts, computer science, English, mathematics, philosophy/religion, biological/physical sciences.

FRESHMAN ADMISSIONS. Selection criteria: Open admissions. **Test requirements:** ACT for placement and counseling only.

1992 FRESHMAN CLASS PROFILE. 63 men enrolled. **Characteristics:** 72% from in state, 80% commute, 25% have minority backgrounds. Average age is 21.

FALL-TERM APPLICATIONS. No fee. No closing date; applicants notified on a rolling basis. Deferred admission available.

STUDENT LIFE. Housing: Dormitories (coed). **Activities:** Student government, National Vocational-Technical Honor Society, Professional Aircraft Maintenance Association, flying club.

STUDENT SERVICES. Aptitude testing, career counseling, employment service for undergraduates, freshman orientation, personal counseling, placement service for graduates, veterans counselor, services/facilities for handicapped.

ANNUAL EXPENSES. Tuition and fees (1992-93): $855, $608 additional for out-of-state students. **Room and board:** $855 room only. **Books and supplies:** $1,625. **Other expenses:** $1,300.

FINANCIAL AID. 85% of grants, 69% of loans, all jobs based on need. Academic, leadership scholarships available. **Aid applications:** No closing date; applicants notified on a rolling basis.

ADDRESS/TELEPHONE. Robert J. Miller, Jr, Director of Admissions and Registrar, Alabama Aviation and Technical College, Box 1209, Highway 231, Ozark, AL 36361-1209. (205) 774-5113. (800) 624-3468. Fax: (205) 774-5113.

Alabama Southern Community College
Monroeville, Alabama CB code: 1644

2-year public community, junior college, coed. Founded in 1965. **Accreditation:** Regional. **Undergraduate enrollment:** 272 men, 301 women full time; 149 men, 350 women part time. **Faculty:** 46 total (25 full time), 4 with doctorates or other terminal degrees. **Location:** Rural campus in small town; 85 miles from Mobile. **Calendar:** Quarter, extensive summer session. **Microcomputers:** Located in libraries, classrooms, computer centers. **Special facilities:** Nature trail. **Additional facts:** Institution has 3 campuses and 3 centers.

DEGREES OFFERED. AA, AS, AAS. 78 associate degrees awarded in 1992. 25% in business and management, 10% business/office and marketing/distribution, 10% teacher education, 10% engineering, 22% allied health, 5% law, 5% life sciences.

UNDERGRADUATE MAJORS. Agricultural sciences, allied health, art education, biology, business administration and management, business computer/console/peripheral equipment operation, business data entry equipment operation, business data processing and related programs, business data programming, business education, chemistry, clinical laboratory science, computer and information sciences, early childhood education, education, elementary education, emergency medical technologies, engineering, English, fine arts, forestry production and processing, history, home economics, humanities, liberal/general studies, mathematics, medical assistant, medical laboratory technologies, medical records administration, medical records technology, music, music education, nursing, occupational therapy assistant, physical education, physical therapy assistant, physics, predentistry, prelaw, premedicine, prepharmacy, preveterinary, psychology, radiograph medical technology, respiratory therapy technology, science technologies, secondary education, secretarial and related programs.

ACADEMIC PROGRAMS. 2-year transfer program, accelerated program, dual enrollment of high school students, honors program, independent study, degrees in allied health available through University of Alabama at Birmingham, registered nurse program through Jefferson Davis State Junior College. **Remedial services:** Learning center, preadmission summer program, reduced course load, remedial instruction, special counselor, tutoring. **Placement/credit:** AP, CLEP General and Subject, institutional tests; 30 credit hours maximum for associate degree.

ACADEMIC REQUIREMENTS. Freshmen must earn minimum GPA of 1.5 to continue in good standing. 56% of freshmen return for sophomore year. Students must declare major on enrollment. **Graduation requirements:** 96 hours for associate. Most students required to take courses in arts/fine arts, English, history, mathematics, biological/physical sciences, social sciences.

FRESHMAN ADMISSIONS. Selection criteria: Open admissions.

1992 FRESHMAN CLASS PROFILE. 173 men, 232 women enrolled. **Characteristics:** 98% from in state, 100% commute. Average age is 18.

FALL-TERM APPLICATIONS. No closing date; applicants notified on a rolling basis. Early admission available.

STUDENT LIFE. Activities: Student government, choral groups, concert band, dance, drama, jazz band, Baptist Student Union, Circle K.

ATHLETICS. NJCAA. **Intercollegiate:** Baseball M, basketball M. **Intramural:** Basketball M, softball, table tennis, tennis, volleyball.

STUDENT SERVICES. Career counseling, freshman orientation, personal counseling, placement service for graduates, special adviser for adult students, veterans counselor, student support services, services/facilities for handicapped.

ANNUAL EXPENSES. Tuition and fees (1992-93): $1,035, $608 additional for out-of-state students. **Books and supplies:** $600. **Other expenses:** $400.

FINANCIAL AID. 76% of grants, 86% of jobs based on need. Academic, music/drama, art, athletic, leadership scholarships available. **Aid applications:** No closing date; priority given to applications received by July 15; applicants notified on a rolling basis; must reply within 4 weeks.

ADDRESS/TELEPHONE. Lynda Malone, Dean of Students/Director of Student Development, Alabama Southern Community College, P.O. Box 2000, Monroeville, AL 36461-2000. (205) 575-3156 ext. 270. Fax: (205) 575-3156.

Alabama State University
Montgomery, Alabama CB code: 1006

4-year public university, coed. Founded in 1874. **Accreditation:** Regional. **Undergraduate enrollment:** 2,125 men, 2,572 women full time; 199 men, 219 women part time. **Graduate enrollment:** 23 men, 63 women full time; 77 men, 210 women part time. **Faculty:** 309 total (219 full time), 140 with doctorates or other terminal degrees. **Location:** Urban campus in small city; 91 miles from Birmingham. **Calendar:** Semester, limited summer session. **Microcomputers:** 259 located in classrooms, computer centers. **Special facilities:** Black history collection, E. D. Nixon papers from civil rights movement of 1960s.

DEGREES OFFERED. AA, AS, BA, BS, MA, MS, MEd. 4 associate degrees awarded in 1992. 25% in business and management, 25% computer sciences, 50% home economics. 242 bachelor's degrees awarded. 22% in business and management, 6% business/office and marketing/distribution, 8% communications, 8% computer sciences, 12% teacher education, 6% life sciences, 5% mathematics, 13% parks/recreation, protective services, public affairs. Graduate degrees offered in 23 major fields of study.

UNDERGRADUATE MAJORS. Associate: Business and management, business and office, business data processing and related programs, child development/care/guidance, community services, liberal/general studies, parks and recreation management, secretarial and related programs, sociology, teacher aide. **Bachelor's:** Accounting, art education, biology, business administration and management, business and management, business economics, business education, chemistry, communications, community services, computer and information sciences, criminal justice studies, dramatic arts, driver and safety education, early childhood education, economics, education of the mentally handicapped, elementary education, engineering, English, English education, finance, fine arts, foreign languages education, French, history, journalism, liberal/general studies, marine biology, marketing management, mathematics, mathematics education, medical laboratory technologies, music, music education, music history and appreciation, office supervision and management, parks and recreation management, physical education, political science and government, psychology, public relations, radio/television broadcasting, science education, secondary education, secretarial and related programs, social science education, social work, sociology, Spanish, special education, specific learning disabilities, speech, visual and performing arts.

ACADEMIC PROGRAMS. 2-year transfer program, cooperative education, double major, education specialist degree, honors program, internships, teacher preparation, visiting/exchange student program, weekend college, cross-registration; liberal arts/career combination in engineering. **Remedial services:** Learning center, remedial instruction, special counselor, tutoring. **ROTC:** Air Force. **Placement/credit:** AP, CLEP General and Subject, institutional tests; 45 credit hours maximum for bachelor's degree.

ACADEMIC REQUIREMENTS. Freshmen must earn minimum GPA of 1.6 to continue in good standing. 60% of freshmen return for sophomore year. Students must declare major by end of first year. **Graduation requirements:** 62 hours for associate (24 in major), 128 hours for bachelor's (59 in major). Most students required to take courses in computer science, English, history, humanities, mathematics, philosophy/religion, biological/physical sciences, social sciences.

FRESHMAN ADMISSIONS. Selection criteria: Open admissions. Out-of-state 2.0 minimum. Minimum ACT of 15 desired. Exceptions for children of alumni and minorities. **High school preparation:** 12 units recommended. Recommended units include English 4, foreign language 2, mathematics 2, social science 2 and science 2. **Test requirements:** SAT or ACT (ACT preferred) for placement and counseling only; score report by August 1.

1992 FRESHMAN CLASS PROFILE. 729 men, 783 women enrolled. 15% had high school GPA of 3.0 or higher, 80% between 2.0 and 2.99. **Academic background:** Mid 50% of enrolled freshmen had SAT-V between 270-360, SAT-M between 300-410; ACT composite between 14-18. 27% submitted SAT scores, 83% submitted ACT scores. **Characteristics:** 55% from in state, 100% commute, 99% have minority backgrounds. Average age is 18.

FALL-TERM APPLICATIONS. No fee. Closing date August 1; priority given to applications received by July 1; applicants notified on a rolling basis. Audition required for music applicants. Interview recommended. Portfolio recommended for art applicants. Essay recommended. Deferred and early admission available.

STUDENT LIFE. Housing: Dormitories (men, women); apartment housing available. **Activities:** Student government, radio, student newspaper, yearbook, choral groups, concert band, drama, jazz band, marching band, music ensembles, musical theater, opera, symphony orchestra, fraternities, sororities, Student Christian Association.

ATHLETICS. NCAA. **Intercollegiate:** Baseball M, basketball, cross-country, football M, golf M, tennis, track and field, volleyball W. **Intramural:** Baseball M, basketball, tennis, track and field, volleyball W.

STUDENT SERVICES. Aptitude testing, career counseling, freshman orientation, health services, personal counseling, placement service for graduates, special adviser for adult students, veterans counselor, services/facilities for handicapped.

ANNUAL EXPENSES. Tuition and fees (1992-93): $1,608, $1,500 additional for out-of-state students. **Room and board:** $2,110. **Books and supplies:** $600. **Other expenses:** $1,500.

FINANCIAL AID. 90% of freshmen, 75% of continuing students receive some form of aid. 99% of grants, all loans, all jobs based on need. Academic, music/drama, art, athletic, state/district residency, leadership, alumni affiliation, religious affiliation, minority scholarships available. **Aid applications:** No closing date; priority given to applications received by April 1; applicants notified on a rolling basis beginning on or about May 15; must reply within 2 weeks.

ADDRESS/TELEPHONE. Debbie Moore, Staff Associate, Enrollment Management, Alabama State University, 915 Jackson Street, Montgomery, AL 36101-0271. (205) 293-4291. (800) 354-8865. Fax: (205) 834-6861.

Athens State College
Athens, Alabama CB code: 0706

2-year upper-division public college of arts and sciences, coed. Founded in 1822. **Accreditation:** Regional. **Undergraduate enrollment:** 460 men, 1,045 women full time; 788 men, 460 women part time. **Faculty:** 172 total (68 full time), 58 with doctorates or other terminal degrees. **Location:** Suburban campus in large town; 14 miles from Decatur, 24 miles from Huntsville. **Calendar:** Quarter, extensive summer session. **Microcomputers:** Located in classrooms, computer centers. **Additional facts:** State's only 2-year senior college serving transfers from junior, community, technical colleges and other 4-year accredited institutions.

DEGREES OFFERED. BA, BS. 929 bachelor's degrees awarded in 1992. 39% in business and management, 6% computer sciences, 32% teacher education, 5% mathematics, 6% psychology.

UNDERGRADUATE MAJORS. Accounting, behavioral sciences, biological and physical sciences, biology, business administration and management, business and management, business and office, chemistry, computer and information sciences, contract management and procurement/purchasing, criminal justice studies, education, electronic technology, elementary education, English, fire control and safety technology, health sciences, history, humanities and social sciences, junior high education, liberal/general studies, mathematics, office supervision and management, philosophy, physics, political science and government, psychology, recreational physical education, religion, secondary education, social sciences, sociology, special education, specific learning disabilities, trade and industrial education.

ACADEMIC PROGRAMS. Cooperative education, double major, internships, weekend college, cross-registration. **Remedial services:** Learning center, reduced course load, tutoring. **Placement/credit:** CLEP General and Subject; 45 credit hours maximum for bachelor's degree.

ACADEMIC REQUIREMENTS. Students must declare major on enrollment. **Graduation requirements:** 192 hours for bachelor's (127 in major). Most students required to take courses in arts/fine arts, computer science, English, history, humanities, mathematics, philosophy/religion, biological/physical sciences, social sciences.

ADMISSIONS. Transfers from junior college must have associate degree or equivalent hours; transfers from technical college must have degree, diploma, or certificate; transfers from four-year college must have 96 credit hours. SAT or ACT required for education majors.

FALL-TERM APPLICATIONS. $30 fee. Deferred admission available.

STUDENT LIFE. Housing: Dormitories (men, women, coed). **Activities:** Student government, student newspaper, television, choral groups, drama, musical theater, fraternities, sororities, Baptist Student Union, psychology club, religious society, service organization, physical education club, ministerial association, biology club, Bear Paw Spirit Club, honor societies.

ATHLETICS. NAIA. **Intercollegiate:** Basketball M, softball W. **Intramural:** Archery, badminton, basketball, bowling, soccer, softball, swimming, table tennis, tennis, volleyball.

STUDENT SERVICES. Career counseling, employment service for undergraduates, personal counseling, placement service for graduates, veterans counselor, services/facilities for handicapped.

ANNUAL EXPENSES. Tuition and fees (projected): $1,590, $1,440 additional for out-of-state students. **Room and board:** $825 room only. **Books and supplies:** $450. **Other expenses:** $971.

FINANCIAL AID. 60% of continuing students receive some form of aid. 69% of grants, all loans, 33% of jobs based on need. Academic, music/drama, art, athletic, leadership, religious affiliation scholarships available. **Aid applications:** No closing date; priority given to applications received by June 1; applicants notified on a rolling basis beginning on or about June 10; must reply within 2 weeks. **Additional information:** Scholarship awarded annually by Alumni Office to child of graduate.

ADDRESS/TELEPHONE. John W. King, Director of Admissions/Registrar, Athens State College, Beaty Street, Athens, AL 35611. (205) 233-8164. Fax: (205) 233-8164.

Auburn University
Auburn, Alabama CB code: 1005

Admissions: 89% of applicants accepted
Based on: ••• School record, test scores
• Special talents
Completion: 90% of freshmen end year in good standing
57% graduate, 38% of these enter graduate study

4-year public university and agricultural and technical college, coed. Founded in 1856. **Accreditation:** Regional. **Undergraduate enrollment:** 8,977 men, 7,641 women full time; 1,116 men, 584 women part time. **Graduate enrollment:** 1,063 men, 759 women full time; 807 men, 604 women part time. **Faculty:** 1,181 total (1,098 full time), 1,007 with doctorates or other terminal degrees. **Location:** Rural campus in large town; 55 miles from Montgomery, 110 miles from Atlanta, Georgia. **Calendar:** Quarter, extensive summer session. **Microcomputers:** 600 located in dormitories, libraries, classrooms, computer centers. **Special facilities:** Space power institute, electron microscopes, rhizotron, nuclear science center, arboretum, government documents repository, torsatron, center for arts and humanities.

DEGREES OFFERED. BA, BS, BFA, BArch, MA, MS, MBA, MFA, MEd, PhD, EdD, B. Pharm, Pharm D, DVM. 4,176 bachelor's degrees awarded in 1992. 5% in agriculture, 26% business and management, 6% teacher education, 19% engineering, 5% health sciences, 6% social sciences. Graduate degrees offered in 113 major fields of study.

UNDERGRADUATE MAJORS. Accounting, adult and continuing education research, adult and vocational education, aerospace/aeronautical/astronautical engineering, agribusiness, agricultural economics, agricultural education, agricultural engineering, agricultural journalism, agricultural sciences, agronomy, animal sciences, anthropology, applied discrete mathematics, applied mathematics, applied physics, architecture, aviation management, biochemistry, biological laboratory technology, biology, botany, building science, business administration and management, business economics, business education, chemical engineering, chemistry, civil engineering, clinical laboratory science, computer and information sciences, computer engineering, criminal justice studies, criminology, dramatic arts, early childhood education, earth sciences, economics, education of the emotionally handicapped, education of the mentally handicapped, education of the physically handicapped, electrical/electronics/communications engineering, elementary education, English, English education, entomology, environmental design, environmental science, fashion merchandising, finance, fine arts, fishing and fisheries, food science and nutrition, food sciences, foreign language/international trade, foreign languages education, forest engineering, forestry and related sciences, forestry production and processing, French, geography, geological engineering, geology, German, graphic design, health care administration, health education, history, home economics education, horticultural science, hotel/motel and restaurant management, human environment and housing, human resources development, individual and family development, industrial arts education, industrial design, industrial engineering, interior design, international business management, journalism, junior high education, landscape architecture, law enforcement and corrections, management information systems, marine biology, marketing and distributive education, marketing management, materials engineering, mathematics, mathematics education, mechanical engineering, medical laboratory technologies, microbiology, molecular biology, music, music education, nursing, operations management, ornamental horticulture, parks and recreation management, pharmacy, philosophy, physical education, physics, plant protection, political science and government, poultry, predentistry, premedicine, preveterinary, psychology, public administration, public relations, radio/television broadcasting, reading education, rehabilitation counseling/services, religion, rural sociology, Russian and Slavic studies, science education, secondary education, social science education, social work, sociology, soil sciences, Spanish, speech, speech correction, speech pathology/audiology, textile chemistry, textile engineering, textile technology, textiles and clothing, trade and industrial education, transportation management, visual and performing arts, wildlife management, zoology.

ACADEMIC PROGRAMS. Accelerated program, cooperative education, double major, dual enrollment of high school students, education specialist degree, honors program, independent study, internships, study abroad, teacher preparation, dual doctor of veterinary medicine (DVM) and master's in a veterinary specialty; dual option program in education/subject areas; liberal arts/career combination in engineering. **Remedial services:** Learning center, reduced course load, special counselor, tutoring, English composition laboratory. **ROTC:** Air Force, Army, Naval. **Placement/credit:** AP, CLEP General and Subject, institutional tests.

ACADEMIC REQUIREMENTS. Freshmen must earn minimum GPA of 2.2 to continue in good standing. 84% of freshmen return for sophomore year. **Graduation requirements:** 210 hours for bachelor's (75 in major). Most students required to take courses in arts/fine arts, English, history, humanities, mathematics, philosophy/religion, biological/physical sciences, social sciences. **Postgraduate studies:** 2% enter law school, 1% enter medical school, 10% enter MBA programs, 25% enter other graduate study.

FRESHMAN ADMISSIONS. Selection criteria: High school GPA and test scores considered equally. Preference to state residents and alumni children. **High school preparation:** 12 units required; 15 recommended. Required and recommended units include biological science 1, English 4, mathematics 3, physical science 1 and social science 3-4. Foreign language 1 and science 1 recommended. Mathematics must include Algebra I, Algebra II, and either geometry, trigonometry, calculus or analysis. **Test requirements:** SAT or ACT; score report by September 1.

1992 FRESHMAN CLASS PROFILE. 4,384 men applied, 3,777 accepted, 1,514 enrolled; 4,277 women applied, 3,893 accepted, 1,615 enrolled. 65% had high school GPA of 3.0 or higher, 35% between 2.0 and 2.99. 19% were in top tenth and 54% were in top quarter of graduating class. **Academic background:** Mid 50% of enrolled freshmen had SAT-V between 450-550, SAT-M between 530-630; ACT composite between 20-26. 33% submitted SAT scores, 79% submitted ACT scores. **Characteristics:** 58% from in state, 70% commute, 8% have minority backgrounds, 1% are foreign students, 28% join fraternities/sororities. Average age is 18.

FALL-TERM APPLICATIONS. $25 fee. Closing date September 1; applicants notified on a rolling basis. Deferred and early admission available. Students should apply for fall quarter admission well in advance of September 1 deadline; admission for out-of-state applicants may close months earlier.

STUDENT LIFE. Housing: Dormitories (men, women); apartment, fraternity, sorority, handicapped housing available. Many dorms recently renovated. **Activities:** Student government, film, magazine, radio, student newspaper, television, yearbook, choral groups, concert band, dance, drama, jazz band, marching band, music ensembles, musical theater, opera, pep band, symphony orchestra, readers' theater, gospel choir, fraternities, sororities, over 300 religious, political, ethnic, and social service organizations. **Additional information:** Excellent recreational facilities available: lighted intramural fields, new tennis complex, student activity center, racquetball courts, and swim complex.

ATHLETICS. NCAA. **Intercollegiate:** Baseball M, basketball, cross-country, diving, football M, golf, gymnastics W, swimming, tennis, track and field, volleyball W. **Intramural:** Badminton, basketball, bowling, golf, racquetball, softball, swimming, table tennis, tennis, track and field, volleyball, wrestling M. **Clubs:** Many sports available through sports clubs.

STUDENT SERVICES. Aptitude testing, career counseling, employment service for undergraduates, freshman orientation, health services, personal counseling, placement service for graduates, special adviser for adult students, veterans counselor, on-campus speech and hearing clinic, services/facilities for handicapped.

ANNUAL EXPENSES. Tuition and fees: $1,950, $3,900 additional for out-of-state students. **Room and board:** $3,873. **Books and supplies:** $600. **Other expenses:** $1,275.

FINANCIAL AID. 55% of freshmen, 45% of continuing students receive some form of aid. 69% of grants, 96% of loans, 34% of jobs based on need. 1,389 enrolled freshmen were judged to have need, all were offered aid. Academic, music/drama, art, athletic, state/district residency, leadership, minority scholarships available. **Aid applications:** No closing date; priority given to applications received by April 15; applicants notified on a rolling basis beginning on or about June 1; must reply within 2 weeks. **Additional information:** State of Alabama has Pre-paid College Tuition Plan for residents.

ADDRESS/TELEPHONE. Dr. Charles F. Reeder, Director of Admissions, Auburn University, 202 Mary Martin Hall, Auburn, AL 36849-5145. (205) 844-4080.

Auburn University at Montgomery
Montgomery, Alabama CB code: 1036

4-year public university, coed. Founded in 1967. **Accreditation:** Regional. **Undergraduate enrollment:** 1,379 men, 2,121 women full time; 743 men, 997 women part time. **Graduate enrollment:** 166 men, 230 women full time; 175 men, 264 women part time. **Faculty:** 335 total (205 full time), 145 with doctorates or other terminal degrees. **Location:** Suburban campus in small city; 6 miles from downtown. **Calendar:** Quarter. Saturday and extensive evening/early morning classes. **Microcomputers:** 80 located in libraries, computer centers.

DEGREES OFFERED. BA, BS, MA, MS, MBA, MEd. 700 bachelor's degrees awarded in 1992. 35% in business and management, 6% communications, 20% teacher education, 7% health sciences, 6% multi/interdisciplinary studies, 5% parks/recreation, protective services, public affairs, 5% social sciences. Graduate degrees offered in 24 major fields of study.

UNDERGRADUATE MAJORS. Accounting, anthropology, art education, biological and physical sciences, biological laboratory technology, biology, business and management, business economics, chemistry, clinical laboratory science, communications, criminal justice studies, dramatic arts, early childhood education, education, education of the mentally handicapped, elementary education, English, English education, environmental science, finance, fine arts, history, information sciences and systems, international studies, junior high education, law enforcement and corrections, legal assistant/paralegal, liberal/general studies, management information systems, marine biology, marketing management, mathematics, mathematics education, medical laboratory technologies, nursing, operations research, personnel management, physical education, physical sciences, prelaw, psychology, science education, secondary education, social science education, social studies education, sociology, special education, speech, speech pathology/audiology, speech/communication/theater education, urban studies.

ACADEMIC PROGRAMS. Accelerated program, cooperative education, double major, dual enrollment of high school students, education specialist degree, honors program, independent study, internships, student-designed major, study abroad, teacher preparation, visiting/exchange student program, weekend college, cross-registration, cooperative PhD in public administration with Auburn University; EdD in cooperation with Auburn University. **Remedial services:** Learning center, reduced course load, remedial instruction, special counselor, tutoring. **ROTC:** Air Force, Army. **Placement/credit:** AP, CLEP Subject, institutional tests; 90 credit hours maximum for bachelor's degree.

ACADEMIC REQUIREMENTS. Freshmen must earn minimum GPA of 2.0 to continue in good standing. Students must declare major by end of second year. **Graduation requirements:** 200 hours for bachelor's. Most students required to take courses in English, history, mathematics, biological/physical sciences.

FRESHMAN ADMISSIONS. Selection criteria: Decision based on GPA in 5 areas (English, social studies, mathematics, foreign language, science) and SAT or ACT scores. Recommended units include biological science 2, English 4, foreign language 2, mathematics 3, physical science 2 and social science 3. **Test requirements:** SAT or ACT (ACT preferred); score report by September 1.

1992 FRESHMAN CLASS PROFILE. 337 men, 496 women enrolled. **Characteristics:** 99% from in state, 06% live in college housing, 22% have minority backgrounds, 1% are foreign students, 10% join fraternities/sororities. Average age is 20.

FALL-TERM APPLICATIONS. $15 fee. No closing date; priority given to applications received by September 1; applicants notified on a rolling basis. Interview recommended. Deferred and early admission available.

STUDENT LIFE. Housing: Apartment, handicapped housing available. **Activities:** Student government, magazine, student newspaper, choral groups, drama, pep band, fraternities, sororities, Students in Action (minority students), International Student Association, Baptist Campus Ministry, Omicron Delta Kappa.

ATHLETICS. NAIA. **Intercollegiate:** Baseball M, basketball, soccer M, tennis. **Intramural:** Archery, badminton, basketball, bowling, softball, table tennis, tennis, volleyball.

STUDENT SERVICES. Aptitude testing, career counseling, employment service for undergraduates, freshman orientation, health services, on-campus day care, personal counseling, placement service for graduates, special adviser for adult students, veterans counselor, services/facilities for handicapped.

ANNUAL EXPENSES. Tuition and fees: $1,800, $3,600 additional for out-of-state students. **Room and board:** $1,600 room only. **Books and supplies:** $600. **Other expenses:** $1,260.

FINANCIAL AID. 40% of freshmen, 40% of continuing students receive some form of aid. 89% of grants, 87% of loans, all jobs based on need. Academic, music/drama, athletic, state/district residency, leadership scholarships available. **Aid applications:** No closing date; priority given to applications received by April 15; applicants notified on a rolling basis beginning on or about July 15; must reply by registration.

ADDRESS/TELEPHONE. Lee Davis, Director of Admissions, Auburn University at Montgomery, 7300 University Drive, Montgomery, AL 36117-3596. (205) 244-3611. Fax: (205) 244-3762.

Bessemer State Technical College
Bessemer, Alabama CB code: 0179

Admissions:	65% of applicants accepted
Based on:	••• Test scores
	• Interview, school record
Completion:	95% of freshmen end year in good standing
	50% graduate, 2% of these enter 4-year programs

2-year public technical college, coed. Founded in 1964. **Accreditation:** Regional. **Undergraduate enrollment:** 601 men, 394 women full time; 626 men, 409 women part time. **Faculty:** 106 total (56 full time). **Location:** Suburban campus in large town; 17 miles from Birmingham. **Calendar:** Quarter. Saturday and extensive evening/early morning classes.

DEGREES OFFERED. AAS. 125 associate degrees awarded in 1992. 14% in business and management, 13% business/office and marketing/distribution, 10% computer sciences, 57% engineering technologies.

UNDERGRADUATE MAJORS. Accounting, automotive technology, construction, data processing, drafting, drafting and design technology, electronic technology, machine tool operation/machine shop, ornamental horticulture, retailing, secretarial and related programs.

ACADEMIC PROGRAMS. Cooperative education, dual enrollment of high school students, internships, weekend college. **Remedial services:** Learning center, reduced course load, remedial instruction, special counselor, tutoring. **Placement/credit:** Institutional tests.

ACADEMIC REQUIREMENTS. Freshmen must earn minimum GPA of 2.0 to continue in good standing. 50% of freshmen return for sophomore year. Students must declare major on application. **Graduation requirements:** 120 hours for associate (110 in major). Most students required to take courses in English, mathematics.

FRESHMAN ADMISSIONS. Selection criteria: ASSET test scores and school achievement considered. LPN applicants also take a pre-nursing test. **Test requirements:** ACT/ASSET required for admissions, placement, and counseling.

1992 FRESHMAN CLASS PROFILE. Characteristics: 100% from in state, 100% commute, 30% have minority backgrounds. Average age is 26.

FALL-TERM APPLICATIONS. No fee. No closing date; applicants notified on a rolling basis. Interview required for dental assistant applicants.

STUDENT LIFE. Activities: Student government, Phi Beta Lambda, Collegiate Secretaries International, Vocational Industrial Clubs of America, Society of Manufacturing Engineers.

STUDENT SERVICES. Career counseling, employment service for

undergraduates, freshman orientation, personal counseling, placement service for graduates, veterans counselor, Student Support Services, services/facilities for handicapped.

ANNUAL EXPENSES. Tuition and fees (projected): $858, $608 additional for out-of-state students. **Books and supplies:** $618. **Other expenses:** $800.

FINANCIAL AID. 65% of freshmen, 65% of continuing students receive some form of aid. 92% of grants, all loans, 82% of jobs based on need. 500 enrolled freshmen were judged to have need, 480 were offered aid. Academic, leadership scholarships available. **Aid applications:** No closing date; priority given to applications received by September 1; applicants notified on a rolling basis; must reply within 10 days. **Additional information:** Also offers veterans benefits, two large job Training Partnership Act programs, displaced homemaker funding, and a student employment center.

ADDRESS/TELEPHONE. Jim Natale, Coordinator of Admissions, Bessemer State Technical College, PO Box 308, Bessemer, AL 35021. (205) 428-6391. Fax: (205) 424-5119.

Bevill State Community College

Sumiton, Alabama CB code: 0723

2-year public junior, technical college, coed. Founded in 1969. **Accreditation:** Regional. **Undergraduate enrollment:** 622 men, 1,002 women full time; 430 men, 912 women part time. **Faculty:** 129 total (58 full time), 13 with doctorates or other terminal degrees. **Location:** Rural campus in small town; Brewer campus 41 miles from Tuscaloosa, Walker campus 25 miles from Birmingham. **Calendar:** Quarter, limited summer session. Saturday and extensive evening/early morning classes. **Microcomputers:** 105 located in libraries, classrooms, computer centers. **Special facilities:** Observatory, simulated underground mine. **Additional facts:** Two main campuses Brewer State Junior College and Walker State Technical College, merged May 1992. Off-campus centers in Jasper, Vernon, Carrallton.

DEGREES OFFERED. AA, AS, AAS. 129 associate degrees awarded in 1992. 6% in business and management, 34% business/office and marketing/distribution, 10% computer sciences, 10% allied health, 12% letters/literature, 28% trade and industry.

UNDERGRADUATE MAJORS. Agribusiness, agricultural education, agricultural sciences, air conditioning/heating/refrigeration mechanics, air conditioning/heating/refrigeration technology, allied health, automotive mechanics, biological and physical sciences, biology, biomedical equipment technology, botany, business and management, business and office, business computer/console/peripheral equipment operation, business data processing and related programs, business data programming, chemistry, computer and information sciences, computer technology, criminal justice studies, data processing, diesel engine mechanics, drafting, drafting and design technology, early childhood education, education, electrical and electronics equipment repair, electrical technology, electronic technology, elementary education, emergency medical technologies, engineering, engineering and engineering-related technologies, English, fine arts, forestry and related sciences, health sciences, home economics, humanities, humanities and social sciences, junior high education, liberal/general studies, machine tool operation/machine shop, management science, marketing and distribution, mathematics, medical assistant, medical laboratory technologies, medical records technology, music, nursing, office supervision and management, physical sciences, physical therapy assistant, physics, prelaw, psychology, radiograph medical technology, respiratory therapy, respiratory therapy technology, secondary education, secretarial and related programs, small business management and ownership, social sciences, technical drafting and design, visual and performing arts, water and wastewater technology, welding technology, zoology.

ACADEMIC PROGRAMS. 2-year transfer program, accelerated program, cooperative education, dual enrollment of high school students, honors program, telecourses, weekend college, 2-year degree programs in allied health available requiring 1 year study at University of Alabama at Birmingham. **Remedial services:** Learning center, reduced course load, remedial instruction, special counselor, tutoring. **Placement/credit:** AP, CLEP General and Subject, institutional tests; 30 credit hours maximum for associate degree.

ACADEMIC REQUIREMENTS. Freshmen must earn minimum GPA of 2.0 to continue in good standing. 55% of freshmen return for sophomore year. **Graduation requirements:** 96 hours for associate. Most students required to take courses in arts/fine arts, computer science, English, history, humanities, mathematics, biological/physical sciences, social sciences.

FRESHMAN ADMISSIONS. Selection criteria: Open admissions. Admission to nursing programs competitive and limited. High school diploma not required in some technical programs. **Additional information:** ACT ASSET examination administered twice weekly, required of all applicants.

1992 FRESHMAN CLASS PROFILE. 279 men, 402 women enrolled. **Characteristics:** 100% commute, 9% have minority backgrounds. Average age is 22.

FALL-TERM APPLICATIONS. No fee. No closing date; applicants notified on a rolling basis beginning on or about July 15. Deferred and early admission available. Institution administers ACT ASSET examination if student scores less than 16 or has not taken ACT ASSET.

STUDENT LIFE. Housing: Apartment housing available. Housing for student athletes. **Activities:** Student government, choral groups, concert band, dance, drama, jazz band, music ensembles, pep band, Inter-Varsity Christian Fellowship, Black Student Union, Circle-K.

ATHLETICS. NJCAA. **Intercollegiate:** Baseball M, basketball, softball W, volleyball W. **Intramural:** Basketball, softball, table tennis, volleyball.

STUDENT SERVICES. Aptitude testing, career counseling, employment service for undergraduates, freshman orientation, health services, personal counseling, placement service for graduates, special adviser for adult students, veterans counselor, night program coordinator, off-campus program coordinator, free bus transportation, services/facilities for handicapped.

ANNUAL EXPENSES. Tuition and fees (1992-93): $936, $668 additional for out-of-state students. **Books and supplies:** $450. **Other expenses:** $800.

FINANCIAL AID. 43% of freshmen, 46% of continuing students receive some form of aid. Grants, jobs available. Academic, music/drama, athletic, leadership scholarships available. **Aid applications:** No closing date; priority given to applications received by August 1; applicants notified on a rolling basis beginning on or about August 1; must reply within 10 days.

ADDRESS/TELEPHONE. Nelda L. Oswalt, Director of Admissions and Records, Bevill State Community College, PO Box 800, Sumiton, AL 35148. (205) 648-3271. (800) 526-5755. Fax: (205) 648-3311.

Birmingham-Southern College

Birmingham, Alabama CB code: 1064

Admissions: 73% of applicants accepted
Based on: ••• Essay, recommendations, school record, test scores
•• Activities, interview, special talents
Completion: 98% of freshmen end year in good standing
73% graduate, 38% of these enter graduate study

4-year private liberal arts college, coed, affiliated with United Methodist Church. Founded in 1856. **Accreditation:** Regional. **Undergraduate enrollment:** 651 men, 793 women full time; 60 men, 165 women part time. **Graduate enrollment:** 28 men, 24 women full time; 24 men, 18 women part time. **Faculty:** 141 total (99 full time), 78 with doctorates or other terminal degrees. **Location:** Urban campus in large city; 3 miles from downtown. **Calendar:** 4-1-4, limited summer session. Saturday and extensive evening/early morning classes. **Microcomputers:** 111 located in dormitories, libraries, classrooms, computer centers, campus-wide network. **Special facilities:** Planetarium, Kennedy Art Gallery, Olin Mathematics and Computer Center, College Theater, Charles Andrew Rush Learning Center, Stephens Science Laboratory Center.

DEGREES OFFERED. BA, BS, BFA, MA. 430 bachelor's degrees awarded in 1992. 33% in business and management, 5% teacher education, 8% health sciences, 7% letters/literature, 10% life sciences, 6% mathematics, 5% physical sciences, 5% psychology, 7% social sciences, 8% visual and performing arts. Graduate degrees offered in 2 major fields of study.

UNDERGRADUATE MAJORS. Accounting, art education, art history, biological and physical sciences, biology, business administration and management, business and management, chemistry, computer mathematics, dance, dramatic arts, early childhood education, economics, education, elementary education, English, English education, foreign languages (multiple emphasis), foreign languages education, French, German, history, human resources development, humanities and social sciences, international business management, liberal/general studies, mathematics, mathematics education, music, music education, music history and appreciation, nursing, philosophy, physics, political science and government, premedicine, psychology, religion, science education, secondary education, social science education, sociology, Spanish.

ACADEMIC PROGRAMS. Accelerated program, double major, dual enrollment of high school students, honors program, independent study, internships, semester at sea, student-designed major, study abroad, teacher preparation, visiting/exchange student program, weekend college, cross-registration; liberal arts/career combination in engineering, health sciences. **Remedial services:** Preadmission summer program, reduced course load, special counselor, tutoring. **ROTC:** Air Force, Army. **Placement/credit:** AP, CLEP General and Subject, IB, institutional tests; 64 credit hours maximum for bachelor's degree.

ACADEMIC REQUIREMENTS. Freshmen must earn minimum GPA of 1.5 to continue in good standing. 92% of freshmen return for sophomore year. Students must declare major by end of second year. **Graduation requirements:** 144 hours for bachelor's (46 in major). Most students required to take courses in arts/fine arts, computer science, English, foreign languages, history, humanities, mathematics, philosophy/religion, biological/physical sciences, social sciences. **Postgraduate studies:** 6% enter law school, 6% enter medical school, 2% enter MBA programs, 24% enter other graduate study.

FRESHMAN ADMISSIONS. Selection criteria: High school record most important, followed by test scores, recommendations, and 1 required essay. No fixed test scores or GPA; each applicant reviewed individually. **High school preparation:** 12 units required. Required and recommended units include English 4, mathematics 2, social science 2 and science 2. Foreign language 2 recommended. **Test requirements:** SAT or ACT; score report by February 15.

1992 FRESHMAN CLASS PROFILE. 421 men applied, 304 accepted, 160 enrolled; 380 women applied, 284 accepted, 161 enrolled. 85% had high school GPA of 3.0 or higher, 15% between 2.0 and 2.99. 60% were in top tenth and 70% were in top quarter of graduating class. **Academic background:** Mid 50% of enrolled freshmen had SAT-V between 450-660, SAT-M between 460-670; ACT composite between 23-29. 62% submitted SAT scores, 93% submitted ACT scores. **Characteristics:** 64% from in state, 89% live in college housing, 7% have minority backgrounds, 1% are foreign students, 65% join fraternities/sororities. Average age is 18.

FALL-TERM APPLICATIONS. $25 fee, may be waived for applicants with need. Closing date March 1; priority given to applications received by December 15; applicants notified on a rolling basis; must reply by May 1. Essay required. Interview recommended for borderline applicants. Audition recommended for music, theater, dance applicants. CRDA. Deferred and early admission available. Institutional early decision plan. 3 notification dates: December 15, January 15, March 1.

STUDENT LIFE. Housing: Dormitories (men, women); apartment, fraternity, sorority housing available. Handicapped students accommodated on individual basis. **Activities:** Student government, magazine, student newspaper, yearbook, choral groups, concert band, dance, drama, jazz band, music ensembles, musical theater, opera, pep band, fraternities, sororities, Black Student Union, Art Students League, Circle-K, International Student Association. Fellowship of Christian Athletes.

ATHLETICS. NAIA. **Intercollegiate:** Baseball M, basketball M, soccer M, tennis. **Intramural:** Basketball, racquetball, softball, table tennis, volleyball.

STUDENT SERVICES. Aptitude testing, career counseling, employment service for undergraduates, freshman orientation, health services, personal counseling, placement service for graduates, special adviser for adult students, veterans counselor, services/facilities for handicapped.

ANNUAL EXPENSES. Tuition and fees (1992-93): $10,306. **Room and board:** $4,090. **Books and supplies:** $400. **Other expenses:** $900.

FINANCIAL AID. 83% of freshmen, 86% of continuing students receive some form of aid. 30% of grants, 98% of loans, 89% of jobs based on need. 130 enrolled freshmen were judged to have need, all were offered aid. Academic, music/drama, art, athletic, state/district residency, leadership, religious affiliation scholarships available. **Aid applications:** No closing date; priority given to applications received by March 31; applicants notified on a rolling basis beginning on or about April 1; must reply within 10 days. **Additional information:** Auditions required for music, theater, dance applicants seeking scholarships. Portfolios required for art applicants seeking scholarships, and essays recommended for all applicants seeking scholarships.

ADDRESS/TELEPHONE. Robert D. Dortch, Vice President of Admissions Services, Birmingham-Southern College, 900 Arkadelphia Road, Birmingham, AL 35254. (205) 226-4686. (800) 523-5793. Fax: (205) 226-4931.

Bishop State Community College
Mobile, Alabama — CB code: 1517

2-year public community, technical college, coed. Founded in 1963. **Accreditation:** Regional. **Undergraduate enrollment:** 856 men, 1,454 women full time; 667 men, 1,217 women part time. **Faculty:** 307 total (121 full time), 4 with doctorates or other terminal degrees. **Location:** Urban campus in small city; 1.5 miles from downtown. **Calendar:** Quarter, limited summer session. Saturday and extensive evening/early morning classes. **Microcomputers:** Located in libraries, classrooms, computer centers. **Additional facts:** Carver campus 2 miles from downtown; southwest campus 3 miles from downtown.

DEGREES OFFERED. AA, AS, AAS. 237 associate degrees awarded in 1992. 6% in business/office and marketing/distribution, 6% computer sciences, 32% education, 35% health sciences, 7% allied health, 10% social sciences.

UNDERGRADUATE MAJORS. Accounting, aerospace science (Air Force), allied health, biology, business administration and management, business and management, chemical technology, chemistry, civil engineering, civil technology, computer and information sciences, criminal justice technology, drafting, elementary education, emergency medical technologies, engineering, fine arts, fire protection, forestry and related sciences, funeral services/mortuary science, history, library assistant, marketing management, mathematics, medical assistant, medical laboratory technologies, medical records administration, medical records technology, mental health/human services, metal/jewelry, music, nursing, occupational therapy assistant, office supervision and management, physical therapy assistant, political science and government, practical nursing, predentistry, prelaw, premedicine, prepharmacy, respiratory therapy technology, secretarial and related programs, sociology, water and wastewater technology.

ACADEMIC PROGRAMS. 2-year transfer program, accelerated program, cooperative education, dual enrollment of high school students, honors program, internships, weekend college, cross-registration, degree programs available in allied health through University of Alabama at Birmingham. **Remedial services:** Learning center, preadmission summer program, reduced course load, remedial instruction, special counselor, tutoring. **Placement/credit:** Institutional tests.

ACADEMIC REQUIREMENTS. Freshmen must earn minimum GPA of 1.5 to continue in good standing. Students must declare major on enrollment. **Graduation requirements:** 96 hours for associate. Most students required to take courses in English, history, humanities, mathematics, biological/physical sciences, social sciences. **Additional information:** Students must complete 112 credit hours for graduation from technical programs.

FRESHMAN ADMISSIONS. Selection criteria: Open admissions.

1992 FRESHMAN CLASS PROFILE. 374 men, 1,586 women enrolled. **Characteristics:** 98% from in state, 100% commute, 41% have minority backgrounds, 1% are foreign students. Average age is 22.

FALL-TERM APPLICATIONS. No closing date; priority given to applications received by August 15; applicants notified on a rolling basis beginning on or about August 15. Deferred and early admission available.

STUDENT LIFE. Activities: Student government, magazine, radio, student newspaper, television, yearbook, choral groups, concert band, dance, jazz band, music ensembles, social service organization, Baptist Student Union.

ATHLETICS. NJCAA. **Intercollegiate:** Baseball M, basketball.

STUDENT SERVICES. Aptitude testing, career counseling, employment service for undergraduates, freshman orientation, health services, on-campus day care, personal counseling, placement service for graduates, special adviser for adult students, veterans counselor, services/facilities for handicapped.

ANNUAL EXPENSES. Tuition and fees (1992-93): $1,026, $668 additional for out-of-state students. **Books and supplies:** $400. **Other expenses:** $738.

FINANCIAL AID. 40% of freshmen, 43% of continuing students receive some form of aid. All grants, all jobs based on need. Academic, music/drama, athletic, leadership scholarships available. **Aid applications:** No closing date; priority given to applications received by June 15; applicants notified on a rolling basis beginning on or about July 20; must reply within 1 week.

ADDRESS/TELEPHONE. Terry Hazzard, Dean of Student Personnel, Bishop State Community College, 351 North Broad Street, Mobile, AL 36603-5898. (205) 690-6801. (800) 523-7235. Fax: (205) 438-9523.

Central Alabama Community College: Alexander City Campus
Alexander City, Alabama — CB code: 0715

2-year public community college, coed. Founded in 1965. **Accreditation:** Regional. **Undergraduate enrollment:** 3,300 men and women. **Faculty:** 96 total (33 full time), 6 with doctorates or other terminal degrees. **Location:** Rural campus in large town; 50 miles from Montgomery. **Calendar:** Quarter, extensive summer session. **Microcomputers:** 45 located in classrooms, computer centers. **Special facilities:** Wildlife museum, wellness center.

DEGREES OFFERED. AA, AS, AAS. 180 associate degrees awarded in 1992.

UNDERGRADUATE MAJORS. Agribusiness, agricultural production, agricultural sciences, architecture, business administration and management, business and management, business and office, business data processing and related programs, business data programming, computer and information sciences, criminal justice technology, drafting and design technology, education, electrodiagnostic technologies, electronic technology, emergency medical technologies, engineering, finance, fire control and safety technology, institutional/home management/supporting programs, law enforcement and corrections, law enforcement and corrections technologies, liberal/general studies, medical assistant, medical laboratory technologies, medical records technology, mental health/human services, nursing, occupational therapy assistant, physical therapy assistant, physician's assistant, public affairs, radiograph medical technology, respiratory therapy, respiratory therapy technology, secretarial and related programs, textile technology.

ACADEMIC PROGRAMS. 2-year transfer program, cooperative education, dual enrollment of high school students, independent study. **Remedial services:** Learning center, remedial instruction, special counselor, tutoring. **Placement/credit:** AP, CLEP General and Subject, institutional tests; 48 credit hours maximum for associate degree.

ACADEMIC REQUIREMENTS. Freshmen must earn minimum GPA of 2.0 to continue in good standing. 65% of freshmen return for sophomore year. Students must declare major on application. **Graduation requirements:** 96 hours for associate. Most students required to take courses in English, history, humanities, mathematics, biological/physical sciences, social sciences.

FRESHMAN ADMISSIONS. Selection criteria: Open admissions.

1992 FRESHMAN CLASS PROFILE. 1,250 men and women enrolled.

Characteristics: 99% from in state, 100% commute, 15% have minority backgrounds, 1% are foreign students. Average age is 19.

FALL-TERM APPLICATIONS. $10 fee. No closing date; applicants notified on a rolling basis. Early admission available.

STUDENT LIFE. Activities: Student government, radio, choral groups, dance, drama, jazz band.

ATHLETICS. NJCAA. **Intercollegiate:** Baseball M, golf M, volleyball W.

STUDENT SERVICES. Aptitude testing, career counseling, freshman orientation, personal counseling, veterans counselor, services/facilities for handicapped.

ANNUAL EXPENSES. Tuition and fees (1992-93): $1,116, $668 additional for out-of-state students. **Books and supplies:** $300. **Other expenses:** $500.

FINANCIAL AID. 64% of grants, all jobs based on need. Academic, music/drama, art, athletic, leadership scholarships available. **Aid applications:** No closing date; priority given to applications received by July 15; applicants notified on a rolling basis; must reply within 10 days.

ADDRESS/TELEPHONE. Robert Saxon, Dean of Student Services, Central Alabama Community College: Alexander City Campus, PO Box 699, Alexander City, AL 35010. (205) 234-6346.

Central Alabama Community College: Childersburg Campus
Childersburg, Alabama — CB code: 0189

2-year public technical college, coed. Founded in 1965. **Accreditation:** Regional. **Undergraduate enrollment:** 700 men and women. **Faculty:** 65 total (47 full time), 2 with doctorates or other terminal degrees. **Location:** Rural campus in small town; 40 miles from Birmingham. **Calendar:** Quarter. **Microcomputers:** Located in classrooms.

DEGREES OFFERED. AAS. 50 associate degrees awarded in 1992. 35% in architecture and environmental design, 35% computer sciences, 30% engineering technologies.

UNDERGRADUATE MAJORS. Computer and information sciences, computer graphics, drafting and design technology, electrical installation, electrical/electronics/communications engineering.

ACADEMIC PROGRAMS. Accelerated program, cooperative education, dual enrollment of high school students. **Remedial services:** Remedial instruction, special counselor, tutoring.

ACADEMIC REQUIREMENTS. Freshmen must earn minimum GPA of 1.0 to continue in good standing. 65% of freshmen return for sophomore year. Students must declare major on application. **Graduation requirements:** 96 hours for associate (55 in major). Most students required to take courses in computer science.

FRESHMAN ADMISSIONS. Selection criteria: Open admissions.

1992 FRESHMAN CLASS PROFILE. 480 men and women enrolled. 10% had high school GPA of 3.0 or higher, 45% between 2.0 and 2.99. **Characteristics:** 100% commute, 40% have minority backgrounds. Average age is 29.

FALL-TERM APPLICATIONS. $8 fee. No closing date; applicants notified on a rolling basis beginning on or about August 15; must reply by registration.

STUDENT LIFE. Activities: Student government.

STUDENT SERVICES. Aptitude testing, career counseling, freshman orientation, personal counseling, placement service for graduates, veterans counselor, services/facilities for handicapped.

ANNUAL EXPENSES. Tuition and fees (1992-93): $1,116, $668 additional for out-of-state students. **Books and supplies:** $450. **Other expenses:** $675.

FINANCIAL AID. 77% of continuing students receive some form of aid. Grants, jobs available. **Aid applications:** No closing date; applicants notified on a rolling basis; must reply within 2 weeks.

ADDRESS/TELEPHONE. Erskine R. Penton, Dean of Students, Central Alabama Community College: Childersburg Campus, PO Box 389, Childersburg, AL 35044. (205) 378-5576.

Chattahoochee Valley Community College
Phenix City, Alabama — CB code: 1187

2-year public community college, coed. Founded in 1974. **Accreditation:** Regional. **Undergraduate enrollment:** 357 men, 493 women full time; 367 men, 546 women part time. **Faculty:** 77 total (42 full time), 11 with doctorates or other terminal degrees. **Location:** Suburban campus in large town; 4 miles from Columbus, Georgia. **Calendar:** Quarter, extensive summer session. **Microcomputers:** 47 located in libraries, classrooms, computer centers.

DEGREES OFFERED. AA, AS, AAS. 190 associate degrees awarded in 1992. 9% in business and management, 8% business/office and marketing/distribution, 5% computer sciences, 7% teacher education, 6% life sciences, 45% multi/interdisciplinary studies, 18% parks/recreation, protective services, public affairs.

UNDERGRADUATE MAJORS. Accounting, agribusiness, agricultural economics, agricultural sciences, allied health, art history, biology, business administration and management, business and office, business education, chemistry, communications, computer and information sciences, criminal justice studies, data processing, elementary education, emergency medical technologies, engineering, finance, fire control and safety technology, forestry and related sciences, graphic arts technology, insurance marketing, law enforcement and corrections technologies, liberal/general studies, mathematics, medical assistant, medical laboratory technologies, medical records technology, music, nursing, occupational therapy assistant, physical education, physical therapy assistant, physics, prelaw, radio/television technology, radiograph medical technology, real estate, respiratory therapy technology, science technologies, secondary education, secretarial and related programs, small business management and ownership, visual and performing arts.

ACADEMIC PROGRAMS. 2-year transfer program, accelerated program, cooperative education, dual enrollment of high school students, honors program, independent study, 2-year degree programs in allied health available requiring 1 year study at University of Alabama at Birmingham. **Remedial services:** Learning center, reduced course load, remedial instruction, special counselor. **Placement/credit:** CLEP Subject, institutional tests; 48 credit hours maximum for associate degree.

ACADEMIC REQUIREMENTS. Freshmen must earn minimum GPA of 2.0 to continue in good standing. 60% of freshmen return for sophomore year. Students must declare major by end of first year. **Graduation requirements:** 96 hours for associate. Most students required to take courses in arts/fine arts, computer science, English, history, humanities, mathematics, biological/physical sciences, social sciences.

FRESHMAN ADMISSIONS. Selection criteria: Open admissions. Selective admissions to health occupation programs.

1992 FRESHMAN CLASS PROFILE. 845 men and women applied, 845 accepted; 574 enrolled. **Characteristics:** 75% from in state, 100% commute. Average age is 18.

FALL-TERM APPLICATIONS. No fee. No closing date; applicants notified on a rolling basis.

STUDENT LIFE. Activities: Student government, magazine, choral groups, drama, music ensembles, musical theater.

ATHLETICS. NJCAA. **Intercollegiate:** Baseball M, basketball, softball W.

STUDENT SERVICES. Career counseling, freshman orientation, personal counseling, placement service for graduates, veterans counselor, services/facilities for handicapped.

ANNUAL EXPENSES. Tuition and fees (1992-93): $1,135, $668 additional for out-of-state students. **Books and supplies:** $500. **Other expenses:** $500.

FINANCIAL AID. 41% of freshmen, 41% of continuing students receive some form of aid. All grants, all jobs based on need. 320 enrolled freshmen were judged to have need, all were offered aid. Academic, music/drama, art, athletic scholarships available. **Aid applications:** No closing date; priority given to applications received by July 15; applicants notified on a rolling basis; must reply within 1 week.

ADDRESS/TELEPHONE. Patricia Weeks, Director of Admissions, Chattahoochee Valley Community College, 2602 College Drive, Phenix City, AL 36869. (205) 297-4941. (800) 842-2822. Fax: (205) 291-4980.

Community College of the Air Force
Maxwell AFB, Alabama — CB code: 1175

2-year public community college, coed. Founded in 1972. **Accreditation:** Regional. **Undergraduate enrollment:** 50,300 men, 8,891 women full time; 118,248 men, 20,900 women part time. **Location:** Suburban campus in small city. **Calendar:** Continuous entry. Extensive evening/early morning classes. **Microcomputers:** Located in classrooms, computer centers. **Additional facts:** Multicampus, worldwide, for United States Air Force enlisted personnel. Administrative offices at Maxwell Air Force Base. Primary campuses are technical training centers located at 6 Air Force bases in 4 states. Other campuses include USAF PME Centers, USAF Command Sponsored Schools, and Field Training Detachments.

DEGREES OFFERED. AAS. 12,646 associate degrees awarded in 1992. 13% in business and management, 7% business/office and marketing/distribution, 12% teacher education, 15% engineering technologies, 8% parks/recreation, protective services, public affairs, 25% trade and industry.

UNDERGRADUATE MAJORS. Aeronautical technology, air conditioning/heating/refrigeration mechanics, air conditioning/heating/refrigeration technology, air traffic control, aircraft mechanics, allied health, archival science, atmospheric sciences and meteorology, automotive mechanics, automotive technology, bioengineering and biomedical engineering, biomedical equipment technology, business and office, business data processing and related programs, clinical laboratory science, clothing and textiles management/production/services, communications, computer and information sciences, construction, contract management and procurement/purchasing, criminal justice studies, cytotechnology, data processing, dental assistant, dental hygiene, dental laboratory technology, education administration, educational media technology, electrical and electronics equipment repair, electrical technology, electrical/electronics/communications engineering, electromechanical technology, electronic technology, emergency/disaster science, engineering and engineering-related technologies, engineering science, environmental health engineering, financial management, fire control and safety technology, food management, food production/management/services, graphic and printing production, graphic arts technology, health care administration, health sciences, histology, history, hospitality and recreation marketing, hotel/motel and restaurant management, industrial equipment maintenance and repair, industrial technology, institutional management, instrumentation technology, intelligence, law enforcement and corrections technologies, legal assistant/paralegal, management information systems, marketing and distribution, marketing management, mechanical design technology, medical assistant, medical laboratory technologies, music, nuclear medical technology, nuclear technologies, nutritional sciences, occupational safety and health technology, office supervision and management, ophthalmic services, personnel management, pharmacy, photographic technology, physical therapy assistant, power plant operation and maintenance, precision metal work, protective services, public affairs, radio/television technology, radiograph medical technology, recreation and community services technologies, secretarial and related programs, social work, surgical technology, survey and mapping technology, telecommunications, trade and industrial education, transportation management, vehicle and equipment operation, veterinarian's assistant.

ACADEMIC PROGRAMS. Accelerated program, computer delivered (on-line) credit-bearing course offerings, independent study, internships. **Remedial services:** Remedial instruction, tutoring. **Placement/credit:** AP, CLEP General and Subject; 30 credit hours maximum for associate degree.

ACADEMIC REQUIREMENTS. Minimum of 15 semester hours must be earned in general education. 40% of freshmen return for sophomore year. Students must declare major on application. **Graduation requirements:** 64 hours for associate (24 in major). Most students required to take courses in English, humanities, mathematics, biological/physical sciences, social sciences.

FRESHMAN ADMISSIONS. Selection criteria: Open admissions for Air Force enlisted personnel, enlisted members of Selected Reserve in Air National Guard, Air Force Reserve units, or mobilization augmentees who have completed basic training. **Test requirements:** Armed Services Vocational Aptitude Battery (ASVAB). **Additional information:** All USAF enlisted personnel automatically registered.

FALL-TERM APPLICATIONS. No fee. No closing date; applicants notified on a rolling basis.

STUDENT LIFE. Housing: Dormitories (men, women, coed); apartment housing available. **Additional information:** Air Force bases provide housing, student services, activities, and athletics.

ATHLETICS. Intramural: Badminton, baseball M, basketball, bowling, boxing M, cross-country, golf, handball, racquetball, soccer M, softball, squash, swimming, table tennis, tennis, track and field, volleyball.

STUDENT SERVICES. Aptitude testing, career counseling, health services, on-campus day care, personal counseling, special adviser for adult students, veterans counselor.

ANNUAL EXPENSES. Tuition and fees (1992-93): $0. No fee for Air Force technical courses.

FINANCIAL AID. 100% of freshmen, 100% of continuing students receive some form of aid. Jobs available. **Aid applications:** No closing date; applicants notified on a rolling basis. **Additional information:** Air Force tuition assistance available for general and technical education courses taken at civilian colleges and universities. Pays 75% of tuition costs.

ADDRESS/TELEPHONE. CMSgt. Lloyd L. Wilson, Director of Enrollment Management/Registrar Division, Community College of the Air Force, 130 West Maxwell Boulevard, Maxwell AFB, AL 36112-6613. (205) 953-6436. Fax: (205) 953-5231.

Concordia College
Selma, Alabama — CB code: 1989

2-year private junior, liberal arts college, coed, affiliated with Lutheran Church—Missouri Synod. Founded in 1922. **Accreditation:** Regional. **Undergraduate enrollment:** 354 men and women. **Faculty:** 17 total (13 full time), 5 with doctorates or other terminal degrees. **Location:** Urban campus in large town; 50 miles from Montgomery. **Calendar:** Semester, limited summer session. **Microcomputers:** 30 located in classrooms, computer centers.

DEGREES OFFERED. AA. 74 associate degrees awarded in 1992. 100% in multi/interdisciplinary studies.

UNDERGRADUATE MAJORS. Liberal/general studies.

ACADEMIC PROGRAMS. 2-year transfer program, independent study. **Remedial services:** Learning center, preadmission summer program, reduced course load, remedial instruction, special counselor, tutoring. **Placement/credit:** Institutional tests.

ACADEMIC REQUIREMENTS. Freshmen must earn minimum GPA of 2.0 to continue in good standing. 90% of freshmen return for sophomore year. Students must declare major by end of second year. **Graduation requirements:** 64 hours for associate. Most students required to take courses in English, history, humanities, mathematics, philosophy/religion, biological/physical sciences, social sciences.

FRESHMAN ADMISSIONS. Selection criteria: Open admissions. **High school preparation:** 20 units recommended. Recommended units include biological science 2, English 4, foreign language 1, mathematics 2 and social science 3. **Test requirements:** SAT or ACT (ACT preferred) for placement and counseling only; score report by August 15.

1992 FRESHMAN CLASS PROFILE. 143 men and women enrolled. 1% had high school GPA of 3.0 or higher, 2% between 2.0 and 2.99. **Characteristics:** 80% from in state, 60% live in college housing, 100% have minority backgrounds, 10% are foreign students. Average age is 18.

FALL-TERM APPLICATIONS. $15 fee, may be waived for applicants with need. No closing date; applicants notified on a rolling basis beginning on or about August 15. Deferred admission available.

STUDENT LIFE. Housing: Dormitories (men, women). **Activities:** Student government, student newspaper, yearbook, choral groups, concert band, dance, drama, jazz band, music ensembles, pep band, Phi Theta Kappa, Gentlemen Care Group Club, Ambassador's Club, American Red Cross Club.

ATHLETICS. Intercollegiate: Basketball. **Intramural:** Baseball, softball, table tennis, tennis, volleyball.

STUDENT SERVICES. Career counseling, employment service for undergraduates, freshman orientation, health services, personal counseling, special adviser for adult students, veterans counselor, services/facilities for handicapped.

ANNUAL EXPENSES. Tuition and fees: $4,186. **Room and board:** $2,600. **Books and supplies:** $550. **Other expenses:** $3,375.

FINANCIAL AID. 98% of freshmen, 98% of continuing students receive some form of aid. 58% of grants, all jobs based on need. **Aid applications:** No closing date; applicants notified on a rolling basis beginning on or about June 15; must reply within 2 weeks.

ADDRESS/TELEPHONE. Shelia Lewis, Director of Enrollment Management, Concordia College, 1804 Green Street, Selma, AL 36701. (205) 874-5700.

Douglas MacArthur State Technical College
Opp, Alabama — CB code: 0198

2-year public technical college, coed. Founded in 1965. **Accreditation:** Regional. **Undergraduate enrollment:** 211 men, 303 women full time; 11 men, 24 women part time. **Faculty:** 29 total (25 full time). **Location:** Rural campus in small town; 85 miles from Montgomery. **Calendar:** Quarter, extensive summer session. **Microcomputers:** 85 located in classrooms, computer centers.

DEGREES OFFERED. 40 associate degrees awarded in 1992. 32% in business/office and marketing/distribution, 25% computer sciences, 43% trade and industry.

UNDERGRADUATE MAJORS. Accounting, business data programming, data processing, drafting, electrical and electronics equipment repair, radio/television technology.

ACADEMIC PROGRAMS. Cooperative education. **Remedial services:** Learning center, remedial instruction, special counselor.

ACADEMIC REQUIREMENTS. Freshmen must earn minimum GPA of 2.0 to continue in good standing. 60% of freshmen return for sophomore year. Students must declare major on enrollment. **Graduation requirements:** 96 hours for associate. Most students required to take courses in computer science, English, humanities, mathematics.

FRESHMAN ADMISSIONS. Selection criteria: Open admissions.

1992 FRESHMAN CLASS PROFILE. 14 men, 33 women enrolled. **Characteristics:** 89% from in state, 100% commute, 13% have minority backgrounds. Average age is 30.

FALL-TERM APPLICATIONS. No fee. No closing date; applicants notified on a rolling basis. for licensed practical nurse applicants.

STUDENT LIFE. Activities: Student government.

STUDENT SERVICES. Aptitude testing, career counseling, employment service for undergraduates, freshman orientation, health services, personal counseling, placement service for graduates, veterans counselor, services/facilities for handicapped.

ANNUAL EXPENSES. Tuition and fees (1992-93): $855, $608 additional for out-of-state students. **Books and supplies:** $400. **Other expenses:** $668.

FINANCIAL AID. 90% of freshmen, 90% of continuing students receive some form of aid. 96% of grants, all loans based on need. Academic, leadership scholarships available. **Aid applications:** No closing date; priority given to applications received by June 1; applicants notified on a rolling basis.

ADDRESS/TELEPHONE. Wayne Bennett, Director, Student Personnel Services, Douglas MacArthur State Technical College, PO Box 649, Opp, AL 36467. (205) 493-3573. Fax: (205) 493-7003.

Draughons Junior College
Montgomery, Alabama CB code: 3947

2-year proprietary business, health science, junior college, coed. Founded in 1887. **Undergraduate enrollment:** 23 men, 127 women full time; 16 men, 101 women part time. **Faculty:** 23 total (8 full time), 1 with doctorate or other terminal degree. **Location:** Suburban campus in small city. **Calendar:** Quarter. **Microcomputers:** 25 located in computer centers.

DEGREES OFFERED. AS. 27 associate degrees awarded in 1992. 45% in business and management, 22% business/office and marketing/distribution, 22% computer sciences, 11% allied health.

UNDERGRADUATE MAJORS. Accounting, business administration and management, business and office, computer and information sciences, law , medical assistant.

ACADEMIC PROGRAMS. Double major, internships. **Remedial services:** Remedial instruction. **Placement/credit:** CLEP Subject, institutional tests; 20 credit hours maximum for associate degree.

ACADEMIC REQUIREMENTS. Freshmen must earn minimum GPA of 2.0 to continue in good standing. Students must declare major on enrollment. **Graduation requirements:** 102 hours for associate (35 in major). Most students required to take courses in computer science, English, humanities, mathematics, social sciences.

FRESHMAN ADMISSIONS. Selection criteria: Entrance test most important. **Test requirements:** Career Programs Assessment Test (CPAT) required for admission.

1992 FRESHMAN CLASS PROFILE. 7 men, 45 women enrolled. **Characteristics:** 100% commute. Average age is 24.

FALL-TERM APPLICATIONS. $25 fee. Closing date October 1; applicants notified on a rolling basis. Interview recommended. Deferred admission available. ACT or SAT recommended.

STUDENT SERVICES. Personal counseling, placement service for graduates, services/facilities for handicapped.

ANNUAL EXPENSES. Tuition and fees (1992-93): $4,525. **Books and supplies:** $400.

FINANCIAL AID. Aid applications: Closing date September 26; applicants notified on a rolling basis.

ADDRESS/TELEPHONE. Sonya Blackwell, Director, Office of Admissions, Draughons Junior College, 122 Commerce Street, Montgomery, AL 36104. (205) 263-1013.

Enterprise State Junior College
Enterprise, Alabama CB code: 1213

2-year public junior college, coed. Founded in 1963. **Accreditation:** Regional. **Undergraduate enrollment:** 541 men, 733 women full time; 428 men, 583 women part time. **Faculty:** 121 total (53 full time), 15 with doctorates or other terminal degrees. **Location:** Rural campus in large town; 85 miles from Montgomery, 30 miles from Dothan. **Calendar:** Quarter, limited summer session. **Microcomputers:** 125 located in classrooms, computer centers. **Additional facts:** Courses offered at Ft. Rucker.

DEGREES OFFERED. AA, AS, AAS. 289 associate degrees awarded in 1992.

UNDERGRADUATE MAJORS. Agricultural business and management, automotive mechanics, business administration and management, business and management, business computer/console/peripheral equipment operation, business data processing and related programs, business data programming, communications, computer and information sciences, emergency medical technologies, engineering and engineering-related technologies, finance, food production/management/services, insurance marketing, law enforcement and corrections technologies, legal assistant/paralegal, liberal/general studies, marketing and distribution, medical assistant, medical laboratory technologies, medical records technology, occupational therapy assistant, office supervision and management, physical therapy assistant, prelaw, real estate, recreation and community services technologies, respiratory therapy, respiratory therapy technology, secretarial and related programs.

ACADEMIC PROGRAMS. 2-year transfer program, dual enrollment of high school students, honors program, internships, 2-year degree programs in allied health available requiring 1 year at University of Alabama at Birmingham and in aviation technology through Alabama Aviation and Technical College in Ozark. **Remedial services:** Learning center, preadmission summer program, remedial instruction, special counselor, tutoring. **Placement/credit:** AP, CLEP General and Subject, institutional tests; 45 credit hours maximum for associate degree.

ACADEMIC REQUIREMENTS. Freshmen must earn minimum GPA of 1.5 to continue in good standing. 27% of freshmen return for sophomore year. Students must declare major by end of first year. **Graduation requirements:** 96 hours for associate. Most students required to take courses in English, history, humanities, mathematics, biological/physical sciences, social sciences.

FRESHMAN ADMISSIONS. Selection criteria: Open admissions.

1992 FRESHMAN CLASS PROFILE. 422 men, 600 women enrolled. **Characteristics:** 100% from in state, 100% commute, 17% have minority backgrounds. Average age is 19.

FALL-TERM APPLICATIONS. No fee. No closing date; applicants notified on a rolling basis. Deferred and early admission available.

STUDENT LIFE. Activities: Student government, student newspaper, choral groups, concert band, dance, drama, music ensembles, musical theater, scholastic honorary fraternity.

ATHLETICS. NJCAA. **Intercollegiate:** Baseball M, basketball M, softball W, tennis. **Intramural:** Volleyball.

STUDENT SERVICES. Aptitude testing, career counseling, employment service for undergraduates, freshman orientation, on-campus day care, personal counseling, placement service for graduates, special adviser for adult students, veterans counselor, displaced homemaker program, women's center, services/facilities for handicapped.

ANNUAL EXPENSES. Tuition and fees (1992-93): $1,035, $675 additional for out-of-state students. **Books and supplies:** $345. **Other expenses:** $550.

FINANCIAL AID. 50% of continuing students receive some form of aid. 78% of grants, all loans, all jobs based on need. Academic, music/drama, art, athletic scholarships available. **Aid applications:** No closing date; priority given to applications received by April 1; applicants notified on a rolling basis beginning on or about July 15; must reply within 2 weeks.

ADDRESS/TELEPHONE. Robin Wyatt, Director of Admissions, Enterprise State Junior College, PO Box 1300, Enterprise, AL 36331. (205) 347-2623 ext. 233. Fax: (205) 347-2623 ext. 306.

Faulkner University
Montgomery, Alabama CB code: 1034

4-year private university and liberal arts college, coed, affiliated with Church of Christ. Founded in 1942. **Accreditation:** Regional. **Undergraduate enrollment:** 718 men, 690 women full time; 219 men, 320 women part time. **Graduate enrollment:** 214 men, 113 women full time. **Faculty:** 101 total (38 full time), 26 with doctorates or other terminal degrees. **Location:** Suburban campus in small city; 5 miles from downtown. **Calendar:** Semester, limited summer session. **Microcomputers:** Located in computer centers. **Additional facts:** Extension centers in Birmingham, Florence, Huntsville, and Mobile offer associate degrees.

DEGREES OFFERED. AA, BA, BS. 138 associate degrees awarded in 1992. 298 bachelor's degrees awarded. Graduate degrees offered in 1 major field of study.

UNDERGRADUATE MAJORS. Associate: Allied health, business administration and management, business and office, computer and information sciences, drafting, emergency medical technologies, legal assistant/paralegal, liberal/general studies, medical assistant, medical laboratory technologies, medical records technology, multiple competency clinical technician, occupational therapy assistant, physical therapy assistant, radiograph medical technology, respiratory therapy, respiratory therapy technology, secretarial and related programs. **Bachelor's:** Accounting, American studies, Bible studies, biological and physical sciences, biology, business administration and management, business and management, education, elementary education, English, English education, finance, human resources development, humanities and social sciences, information sciences and systems, junior high education, liberal/general studies, marketing management, mathematics education, office supervision and management, physical education, prelaw, psychology, religion, religious education, secondary education, social studies education, sports management, theological studies, visual and performing arts.

ACADEMIC PROGRAMS. 2-year transfer program, cooperative education, double major, independent study, internships, teacher preparation, cross-registration; liberal arts/career combination in health sciences; combined bachelor's/graduate program in law. **Remedial services:** Learning center, reduced course load, remedial instruction, special counselor, tutoring, study skills program. **Placement/credit:** AP, CLEP General and Subject, institutional tests; 16 credit hours maximum for associate degree; 32 credit hours maximum for bachelor's degree.

ACADEMIC REQUIREMENTS. Freshmen must earn minimum GPA of 1.5 to continue in good standing. 65% of freshmen return for sophomore year. Students must declare major by end of first year. **Graduation requirements:** 64 hours for associate, 128 hours for bachelor's. Most students required to take courses in arts/fine arts, computer science, English, history, mathematics, philosophy/religion, biological/physical sciences, social sciences. **Additional information:** Full-time students required to take 1 Bible course per semester.

FRESHMAN ADMISSIONS. Selection criteria: Academic record, test scores, and personal or career goals most important. **High school preparation:** 15 units required. Required units include English 3. Also 9 units from among social sciences, foreign language, mathematics, and science required. **Test requirements:** SAT or ACT (ACT preferred); score report by July 1.

1992 FRESHMAN CLASS PROFILE. 380 men, 549 women enrolled. **Characteristics:** 53% from in state, 53% live in college housing, 22% have minority backgrounds. Average age is 19.

FALL-TERM APPLICATIONS. $10 fee. No closing date; priority given to applications received by April 1; applicants notified on a rolling basis. Interview recommended. CRDA. Deferred and early admission available.

STUDENT LIFE. Housing: Dormitories (men, women). **Activities:** Student government, student newspaper, yearbook, choral groups, drama, music ensembles, musical theater, fraternities, sororities, minister's club, service organization, religious organization, Young Republicans. **Additional information:** Religious observance required.

ATHLETICS. NAIA. **Intercollegiate:** Baseball M, basketball M. **Intramural:** Badminton, basketball, softball, table tennis, tennis, track and field, volleyball.

STUDENT SERVICES. Aptitude testing, career counseling, employment service for undergraduates, health services, personal counseling, placement service for graduates, special adviser for adult students, veterans counselor, special program designed to orient first-generation, handicapped, or disabled students to college life, services/facilities for handicapped.

ANNUAL EXPENSES. Tuition and fees: $5,250. **Room and board:** $3,050. **Books and supplies:** $600. **Other expenses:** $1,000.

FINANCIAL AID. 90% of freshmen, 98% of continuing students receive some form of aid. Grants, loans, jobs available. Academic, athletic, state/district residency, leadership, religious affiliation, minority scholarships available. **Aid applications:** No closing date; priority given to applications received by May 1; applicants notified on a rolling basis beginning on or about June 1; must reply within 3 weeks.

ADDRESS/TELEPHONE. Joey Wiginton, Director of Admissions, Faulkner University, 5345 Atlanta Highway, Montgomery, AL 36109-3398. (205) 272-5820.

Gadsden State Community College
Gadsden, Alabama CB code: 1262

2-year public community college, coed. Founded in 1985. **Accreditation:** Regional. **Undergraduate enrollment:** 1,614 men, 1,813 women full time; 1,324 men, 1,459 women part time. **Faculty:** 303 total (158 full time), 21 with doctorates or other terminal degrees. **Location:** Urban campus in large town; 60 miles from Birmingham. **Calendar:** Quarter, extensive summer session. Extensive evening/early morning classes. **Microcomputers:** 200 located in computer centers. **Special facilities:** Bevill Center for Advanced Technology and Job Corps. **Additional facts:** Off-campus sites Ft. McCleham and St. Clair Correctional Facility.

DEGREES OFFERED. AA, AS, AAS. 519 associate degrees awarded in 1992.

UNDERGRADUATE MAJORS. Agribusiness, air conditioning/heating/refrigeration mechanics, air conditioning/heating/refrigeration technology, art education, biology, biomedical equipment technology, business and management, business and office, business economics, business education, chemical engineering, chemistry, civil engineering, civil technology, clinical laboratory science, computer and information sciences, computer mathematics, computer servicing technology, court reporting, criminal justice studies, criminal justice technology, drafting and design technology, education, electrical and electronics equipment repair, electrical installation, electrical technology, electronic technology, elementary education, emergency medical technologies, engineering, English education, finance, fire control and safety technology, health sciences, history, home economics, home economics education, industrial equipment maintenance and repair, industrial technology, instrumentation technology, legal assistant/paralegal, liberal/general studies, machine tool operation/machine shop, manufacturing technology, marketing and distribution, marketing research, mathematics, mathematics education, medical assistant, medical laboratory technologies, medical records administration, medical records technology, medical secretary, mental health/human services, music education, nursing, occupational therapy assistant, physical education, physical therapy assistant, physician's assistant, physics, political science and government, predentistry, prelaw, premedicine, prepharmacy, preveterinary, psychology, radio/television broadcasting, radiograph medical technology, religion, respiratory therapy, respiratory therapy technology, retailing, science education, secretarial and related programs, social sciences, social work, sociology, telecommunications, veterinarian's assistant, water and wastewater technology.

ACADEMIC PROGRAMS. 2-year transfer program, cooperative education, dual enrollment of high school students, teacher preparation, telecourses, weekend college, 2-year degree programs in allied health available requiring 1 year study at University of Alabama at Birmingham. 2-year degree program in veterinary technology available through Snead State Junior College. **Remedial services:** Remedial instruction, tutoring. **Placement/credit:** AP, CLEP General; 30 credit hours maximum for associate degree.

ACADEMIC REQUIREMENTS. Freshmen must earn minimum GPA of 1.5 to continue in good standing. 50% of freshmen return for sophomore year. Students must declare major on application. **Graduation requirements:** 96 hours for associate. Most students required to take courses in English, mathematics, biological/physical sciences, social sciences.

FRESHMAN ADMISSIONS. Selection criteria: Open admissions. Selective admissions for some programs. **Test requirements:** ACT/ASSET, Career Program Assessment Test required for some programs.

1992 FRESHMAN CLASS PROFILE. 1,373 men, 1,513 women enrolled. **Characteristics:** 95% from in state, 95% commute, 1% are foreign students. Average age is 20.

FALL-TERM APPLICATIONS. No fee. No closing date; applicants notified on a rolling basis. Interview recommended for nursing, medical laboratory technology, radiologic technology, computer technology, court reporting applicants. Deferred and early admission available.

STUDENT LIFE. Housing: Dormitories (coed). **Activities:** Student government, radio, student newspaper, choral groups, concert band, dance, drama, jazz band, pep band, Circle-K, International Club, Baptist Student Union, Phi Beta Lambda (business service organization).

ATHLETICS. NJCAA. **Intercollegiate:** Baseball M, basketball, cross-country, softball W, volleyball W.

STUDENT SERVICES. Career counseling, employment service for undergraduates, freshman orientation, health services, personal counseling, placement service for graduates, veterans counselor, success center, services/facilities for handicapped.

ANNUAL EXPENSES. Tuition and fees (projected): $1,125, $743 additional for out-of-state students. **Room and board:** $2,025. **Books and supplies:** $525. **Other expenses:** $525.

FINANCIAL AID. 36% of freshmen, 32% of continuing students receive some form of aid. 78% of grants, all loans, all jobs based on need. 900 enrolled freshmen were judged to have need, all were offered aid. Academic, music/drama, athletic, leadership, alumni affiliation scholarships available. **Aid applications:** No closing date; priority given to applications received by April 1; applicants notified on a rolling basis beginning on or about May 2; must reply within 2 weeks.

ADDRESS/TELEPHONE. Dr. Marie Luttrell, Director of Admissions, Gadsden State Community College, PO Box 227, Gadsden, AL 35902-0227. (205) 549-8201.

George C. Wallace State Community College at Dothan
Dothan, Alabama CB code: 1264

2-year public community college, coed. Founded in 1949. **Accreditation:** Regional. **Undergraduate enrollment:** 4,060 men and women. **Faculty:** 163 total (94 full time), 6 with doctorates or other terminal degrees. **Location:** Rural campus in small city; 6 miles from downtown. **Calendar:** Quarter, extensive summer session. Extensive evening/early morning classes. **Microcomputers:** Located in classrooms, computer centers.

DEGREES OFFERED. AA, AS, AAS. 255 associate degrees awarded in 1992.

UNDERGRADUATE MAJORS. Accounting, agricultural production, air conditioning/heating/refrigeration mechanics, air conditioning/heating/refrigeration technology, automotive mechanics, automotive technology, biology, biomedical equipment technology, business administration and management, business and management, business and office, business data entry equipment operation, business data processing and related programs, business data programming, carpentry, computer and information sciences, computer programming, dance, data processing, drafting, drafting and design technology, dramatic arts, education, electrical and electronics equipment repair, electrical installation, electronic technology, emergency medical technologies, English, fine arts, French, graphic and printing production, graphic arts technology, history, industrial technology, law enforcement and corrections, law enforcement and corrections technologies, liberal/general studies, machine tool operation/machine shop, masonry/tile setting, mathematics, medical assistant, medical laboratory technologies, medical records technology, music, nursing, occupational therapy, office supervision and management, optical technology, physical therapy, precision metal work, psychology, radiograph medical technology, respiratory therapy, respiratory therapy technology, secretarial and related programs, sociology, Spanish, speech, vehicle and equipment operation, welding technology.

ACADEMIC PROGRAMS. Accelerated program, cooperative education, dual enrollment of high school students, honors program, cross-registration. **Remedial services:** Learning center, preadmission summer program, remedial instruction, tutoring. **Placement/credit:** AP, CLEP General and Subject, institutional tests; 48 credit hours maximum for associate degree.

ACADEMIC REQUIREMENTS. Freshmen must earn minimum GPA of 1.5 to continue in good standing. Students must declare major on application. **Graduation requirements:** 96 hours for associate. Most students required to take courses in English, history, mathematics, biological/physical sciences, social sciences.

FRESHMAN ADMISSIONS. Selection criteria: Open admissions. Selective admission to allied health, nursing programs. **Test requirements:** National League for Nursing examination required for nursing applicants.

1992 FRESHMAN CLASS PROFILE. 900 men and women enrolled. **Characteristics:** 99% from in state, 100% commute, 23% have minority backgrounds. Average age is 19.

FALL-TERM APPLICATIONS. No fee. No closing date; applicants notified on a rolling basis. Interview required for nursing applicants. Early admission available.

STUDENT LIFE. Activities: Student government, student newspaper, choral groups, dance, drama, jazz band, music ensembles, pep band, Fellowship of Christian Athletes, Circle-K, Afro-American organization, service organizations, Vocational Industrial Clubs of America, Women's Network, Diplomats (official student hosts and hostesses), Adult Student Association, Young Republicans.

ATHLETICS. NJCAA. **Intercollegiate:** Baseball M, basketball, golf M, softball W, tennis. **Intramural:** Basketball M.

STUDENT SERVICES. Aptitude testing, career counseling, employment service for undergraduates, freshman orientation, personal counseling, veterans counselor, services/facilities for handicapped.

ANNUAL EXPENSES. Tuition and fees (1992-93): $1,125, $743 additional for out-of-state students. **Books and supplies:** $300. **Other expenses:** $300.

FINANCIAL AID. 65% of freshmen, 65% of continuing students receive some form of aid. Grants, loans, jobs available. Academic, music/drama, athletic, leadership scholarships available. **Aid applications:** No closing date; applicants notified on a rolling basis.

ADDRESS/TELEPHONE. Mrs. Brenda Barnes, Admissions Coordinator, George C. Wallace State Community College at Dothan, Route 6, Box 62, Dothan, AL 36303-9234. (205) 983-3521. Fax: (205) 983-4255.

George C. Wallace State Community College at Selma
Selma, Alabama CB code: 3146

2-year public community college, coed. Founded in 1963. **Accreditation:** Regional. **Undergraduate enrollment:** 479 men, 705 women full time; 235 men, 397 women part time. **Faculty:** 61 total (45 full time), 4 with doctorates or other terminal degrees. **Location:** Rural campus in large town. **Calendar:** Quarter, extensive summer session. **Microcomputers:** Located in classrooms, computer centers.

DEGREES OFFERED. AA, AS, AAS. 154 associate degrees awarded in 1992. 15% in business and management, 15% computer sciences, 50% health sciences, 20% trade and industry.

UNDERGRADUATE MAJORS. Air conditioning/heating/refrigeration mechanics, business and management, business data processing and related programs, computer and information sciences, drafting, electrical and electronics equipment repair, electrical installation, emergency medical technologies, fine arts, fire control and safety technology, liberal/general studies, machine tool operation/machine shop, medical assistant, medical records technology, nursing, occupational therapy assistant, physical therapy assistant, protective services, radiograph medical technology, respiratory therapy, secretarial and related programs.

ACADEMIC PROGRAMS. 2-year transfer program, accelerated program, double major, dual enrollment of high school students. **Remedial services:** Learning center, reduced course load, remedial instruction, special counselor, tutoring. **Placement/credit:** AP, CLEP Subject, institutional tests; 30 credit hours maximum for associate degree.

ACADEMIC REQUIREMENTS. Freshmen must earn minimum GPA of 1.5 to continue in good standing. 50% of freshmen return for sophomore year. Students must declare major by end of first year. **Graduation requirements:** 98 hours for associate (30 in major). Most students required to take courses in computer science, English, history, humanities, mathematics, biological/physical sciences, social sciences.

FRESHMAN ADMISSIONS. Selection criteria: Open admissions. Selective admission to health occupation programs. Nursing candidates need minimum ACT composite score of 18, or 50th percentile ranking in National League of Nursing Examination. **Test requirements:** ACT required for nursing applicants. National League of Nursing examination may be substituted for ACT.

1992 FRESHMAN CLASS PROFILE. 417 men, 582 women enrolled. **Characteristics:** 100% from in state, 100% commute, 38% have minority backgrounds, 1% join fraternities/sororities. Average age is 20.

FALL-TERM APPLICATIONS. No fee. No closing date; priority given to applications received by September 3; applicants notified on a rolling basis.

STUDENT LIFE. Activities: Student government, choral groups, drama, jazz band, music ensembles, sororities, Baptist Student Union, Phi Beta Kappa.

ATHLETICS. NJCAA. **Intercollegiate:** Baseball M, basketball M, softball W, tennis. **Intramural:** Badminton, baseball, basketball, tennis, volleyball.

STUDENT SERVICES. Aptitude testing, career counseling, employment service for undergraduates, freshman orientation, personal counseling, placement service for graduates, veterans counselor, services/facilities for handicapped.

ANNUAL EXPENSES. Tuition and fees (projected): $1,035, $608 additional for out-of-state students. **Books and supplies:** $600. **Other expenses:** $962.

FINANCIAL AID. 60% of freshmen, 60% of continuing students receive some form of aid. 73% of grants, all jobs based on need. Academic, music/drama, athletic, leadership scholarships available. **Aid applications:** No closing date; priority given to applications received by June 1; applicants notified on a rolling basis beginning on or about June 15; must reply by deadline in award letter.

ADDRESS/TELEPHONE. W. D. Beaty, Dean of Students, George C. Wallace State Community College at Selma, PO Drawer 1049, Selma, AL 36701-1049. (205) 875-2634. Fax: (205) 874-7116.

Harry M. Ayers State Technical College
Anniston, Alabama CB code: 1828

2-year public technical college, coed. Founded in 1965. **Accreditation:** Regional. **Undergraduate enrollment:** 277 men, 176 women full time; 92 men, 61 women part time. **Faculty:** 38 total (23 full time). **Location:** Urban campus in large town; 60 miles from Birmingham, 100 miles from Atlanta, Georgia. **Calendar:** Quarter. Extensive evening/early morning classes. **Microcomputers:** 51 located in libraries, classrooms, computer centers, campus-wide network.

DEGREES OFFERED. 75 associate degrees awarded in 1992.

UNDERGRADUATE MAJORS. Accounting, air conditioning/heating/refrigeration mechanics, air conditioning/heating/refrigeration technology, computer and information sciences, drafting, drafting and design technology, electronic technology, machine tool operation/machine shop, patternmaking, water and wastewater technology, welding technology. industrial electricity/electronics.

ACADEMIC PROGRAMS. Dual enrollment of high school students. **Remedial services:** Learning center, special counselor, tutoring. **Placement/credit:** CLEP General, institutional tests; 20 credit hours maximum for associate degree.

ACADEMIC REQUIREMENTS. Freshmen must earn minimum GPA of 2.0 to continue in good standing. Students must declare major on application. **Graduation requirements:** Most students required to take courses in computer science, English, mathematics.

FRESHMAN ADMISSIONS. Selection criteria: Open admissions. Practical nursing requires pre-entrance testing prior to acceptance.

1992 FRESHMAN CLASS PROFILE. 121 men, 98 women enrolled. **Characteristics:** 100% commute, 20% have minority backgrounds. Average age is 29.

FALL-TERM APPLICATIONS. No fee. No closing date. Interview recommended. Deferred admission available.

STUDENT LIFE. Activities: Student government.

STUDENT SERVICES. Aptitude testing, career counseling, personal counseling, placement service for graduates, veterans counselor, services/facilities for handicapped.

ANNUAL EXPENSES. Tuition and fees (1992-93): $903, $576 additional for out-of-state students. Georgia residents pay in-state tuition. **Books and supplies:** $400.

FINANCIAL AID. 65% of continuing students receive some form of aid. Grants available. **Aid applications:** No closing date; applicants notified on a rolling basis.

ADDRESS/TELEPHONE. T. David Cunningham, Coordinator of Student Services, Harry M. Ayers State Technical College, PO Box 1647, Anniston, AL 36202. (205) 835-5400 ext. 5410.

Huntingdon College ⇆
Montgomery, Alabama CB code: 1303

Admissions:	89% of applicants accepted
Based on:	••• School record, test scores
	•• Activities, interview, recommendations
	• Essay, special talents
Completion:	85% of freshmen end year in good standing
	46% enter graduate study

4-year private liberal arts college, coed, affiliated with United Methodist Church. Founded in 1854. **Accreditation:** Regional. **Undergraduate enrollment:** 294 men, 318 women full time; 35 men, 113 women part time. **Faculty:** 65 total (43 full time), 33 with doctorates or other terminal degrees. **Location:** Suburban campus in small city; 180 miles from Atlanta, Georgia, 90 miles from Birmingham. **Calendar:** Semester (2 week winter term). **Microcomputers:** 30 located in computer centers. **Special facilities:** Art gallery, church archives, recital hall with individual practice studios.

DEGREES OFFERED. AA, BA. 3 associate degrees awarded in 1992. 134 bachelor's degrees awarded. 31% in business and management, 7% teacher education, 10% letters/literature, 5% life sciences, 7% physical sciences, 5% psychology, 18% social sciences, 5% visual and performing arts.

UNDERGRADUATE MAJORS. Associate: Liberal/general studies. **Bachelor's:** Accounting, art education, biology, business administration and management, business and management, business economics, chemistry, computer and information sciences, computer programming, dance, dramatic arts, early childhood education, elementary education, English, English education, finance, fine arts, history, junior high education, liberal/general studies, marketing management, mathematics, mathematics education, music, music education, music performance, music theory and composition, musical theater, philosophy, physical education, predentistry, prelaw, premedicine, prepharmacy, preveterinary, psychology, religion, religious education, religious music, science education, secondary education, social science education, social studies education, visual and performing arts.

ACADEMIC PROGRAMS. Cooperative education, double major, dual enrollment of high school students, honors program, independent study, internships, student-designed major, study abroad, teacher preparation, cross-registration; liberal arts/career combination in engineering. **Remedial services:** Reduced course load, special counselor, tutoring, mentor program for freshmen, reading and writing laboratory. **Placement/credit:** AP, CLEP General and Subject, IB; 30 credit hours maximum for bachelor's degree.

ACADEMIC REQUIREMENTS. Freshmen must earn minimum GPA of 1.5 to continue in good standing. 60% of freshmen return for sophomore year. Students must declare major by end of second year. **Graduation requirements:** 64 hours for associate (18 in major), 124 hours for bachelor's (30 in major). Most students required to take courses in arts/fine arts, English, history, mathematics, philosophy/religion, biological/physical sciences. **Postgraduate studies:** 10% enter law school, 8% enter medical school, 8% enter MBA programs, 20% enter other graduate study. **Additional information:** Off-campus study and nontraditional courses available in January term.

FRESHMAN ADMISSIONS. Selection criteria: GPA and test scores important. 3 letters of recommendation and interview strongly suggested in marginal cases. **High school preparation:** 12 units recommended. Recommended units include English 4, mathematics 3, social science 2 and science 2. **Test requirements:** SAT or ACT; score report by August 1.

1992 FRESHMAN CLASS PROFILE. 217 men applied, 184 accepted, 79 enrolled; 273 women applied, 254 accepted, 90 enrolled. 55% had high school GPA of 3.0 or higher, 39% between 2.0 and 2.99. **Academic background:** Mid 50% of enrolled freshmen had SAT-V between 410-520, SAT-M between 440-570; ACT composite between 21-27. 40% submitted SAT scores, 84% submitted ACT scores. **Characteristics:** 60% from in state, 76% live in college housing, 10% have minority backgrounds, 2% are foreign students, 33% join fraternities/sororities. Average age is 18.

FALL-TERM APPLICATIONS. $25 fee, may be waived for applicants with need. No closing date; priority given to applications received by August 1; applicants notified on a rolling basis; must reply within 30 days. Audition required for music, drama applicants. Portfolio required for art applicants. Interview recommended for academically marginal applicants. Essay recommended. Deferred and early admission available.

STUDENT LIFE. Housing: Dormitories (men, women). **Activities:** Student government, magazine, student newspaper, yearbook, choral groups, concert band, dance, drama, music ensembles, musical theater, opera, fraternities, sororities, Campus Ministries Organization, Young Republicans, Circle-K, Black Student Union, International Student Organization, Enviromental Awareness, and Action Club.

ATHLETICS. NAIA. **Intercollegiate:** Baseball M, golf M, soccer, softball W, tennis, volleyball W. **Intramural:** Basketball, fencing, football, softball, swimming, volleyball.

STUDENT SERVICES. Aptitude testing, career counseling, employment service for undergraduates, freshman orientation, health services, personal counseling, placement service for graduates, special adviser for adult students.

ANNUAL EXPENSES. Tuition and fees: $7,640. **Room and board:** $3,760. **Books and supplies:** $500. **Other expenses:** $600.

FINANCIAL AID. 92% of freshmen, 90% of continuing students receive some form of aid. Grants, loans, jobs available. 96 enrolled freshmen were judged to have need, all were offered aid. Academic, music/drama, art, athletic, leadership, religious affiliation scholarships available. **Aid applications:** No closing date; priority given to applications received by June 1; applicants notified on a rolling basis beginning on or about January 15; must reply within 2 weeks.

ADDRESS/TELEPHONE. Paul J. Mittelhammer, Dean of Enrollment Management, Huntingdon College, 1500 East Fairview Avenue, Montgomery, AL 36106-2148. (205) 834-3300. (800) 763-0313. Fax: (205) 264-2951.

International Bible College
Florence, Alabama — CB code: 0805

4-year private Bible college, coed, affiliated with Church of Christ. Founded in 1971. **Undergraduate enrollment:** 15 men, 2 women full time; 15 men, 23 women part time. **Faculty:** 19 total (9 full time), 4 with doctorates or other terminal degrees. **Location:** Suburban campus in large town; 125 miles northwest of Birmingham, 115 miles south of Nashville, Tennessee. **Calendar:** Semester, limited summer session. **Additional facts:** Founded to recruit, train, and motivate faithful men and women for evangelistic ministry as servants and leaders in the Churches of Christ. Special emphasis placed on preparing church leadership with international perspective.

DEGREES OFFERED. AA, BA. 2 associate degrees awarded in 1992. 24 bachelor's degrees awarded.

UNDERGRADUATE MAJORS. Associate: Bible studies. **Bachelor's:** Bible studies.

ACADEMIC PROGRAMS. Independent study, internships. **Remedial services:** Review of English fundamentals. **Placement/credit:** Institutional tests.

ACADEMIC REQUIREMENTS. Freshmen must earn minimum GPA of 2.0 to continue in good standing. Students must declare major on application. **Graduation requirements:** 65 hours for associate, 128 hours for bachelor's. Most students required to take courses in English, foreign languages, history, philosophy/religion.

FRESHMAN ADMISSIONS. Selection criteria: Religious affiliation, recommendations, and school achievement considered.

1992 FRESHMAN CLASS PROFILE. 25 men and women enrolled. **Characteristics:** 100% live in college housing. Average age is 23.

FALL-TERM APPLICATIONS. No fee. Closing date July 15; priority given to applications received by December 1; applicants notified on a rolling basis beginning on or about July 27. Interview recommended.

STUDENT LIFE. Housing: Dormitories (men, women). **Activities:** Student government, film, radio, television, Christian service program, mission club. **Additional information:** Programs designed to encourage and cultivate spiritual life.

STUDENT SERVICES. Career counseling, employment service for undergraduates, on-campus day care, personal counseling, placement service for graduates, veterans counselor, services/facilities for handicapped.

ANNUAL EXPENSES. Tuition and fees: $3,370. **Room and board:** $1,200 room only. **Books and supplies:** $400. **Other expenses:** $1,500.

FINANCIAL AID. 100% of freshmen, 62% of continuing students receive some form of aid. Grants, loans, jobs available. **Aid applications:** No closing date; applicants notified on a rolling basis beginning on or about August 1; must reply within 2 weeks.

ADDRESS/TELEPHONE. Charles Payne, Director of Enrollment Services, International Bible College, PO Box IBC, Florence, AL 35630. (205) 766-6610 ext. 23.

J. F. Drake State Technical College
Huntsville, Alabama — CB code: 2108

2-year public technical college, coed. Founded in 1961. **Accreditation:** Regional. **Undergraduate enrollment:** 197 men, 246 women full time; 270 men, 157 women part time. **Faculty:** 45 total (24 full time), 1 with doctorate or other terminal degree. **Location:** Urban campus in small city; 100 miles from Birmingham, 100 miles from Nashville, Tennessee, 200 miles from Atlanta, Georgia. **Calendar:** Quarter. **Microcomputers:** 50 located in libraries, classrooms, computer centers.

DEGREES OFFERED. AAS. 62 associate degrees awarded in 1992.

UNDERGRADUATE MAJORS. Accounting, computer and information sciences, drafting, electronic technology, graphic and printing production, machine tool operation/machine shop, secretarial and related programs.

ACADEMIC PROGRAMS. 2-year transfer program, cooperative education. **Remedial services:** Learning center, remedial instruction. **Placement/credit:** Institutional tests.

ACADEMIC REQUIREMENTS. Freshmen must earn minimum GPA of 2.0 to continue in good standing. 60% of freshmen return for sophomore year. Students must declare major on enrollment. **Graduation requirements:** 96 hours for associate (61 in major). Most students required to take courses in English, mathematics.

FRESHMAN ADMISSIONS. Selection criteria: Open admissions. Nursing applicants must pass pre-entrance examination.

1992 FRESHMAN CLASS PROFILE. 76 men, 65 women enrolled. **Characteristics:** 97% from in state, 100% commute, 56% have minority backgrounds, 1% are foreign students. Average age is 21.

FALL-TERM APPLICATIONS. No fee. No closing date; applicants notified on a rolling basis.

STUDENT LIFE. Activities: Student government, student newspaper, Phi Beta Lambda, VICA, national vocational technical honor society.

STUDENT SERVICES. Aptitude testing, career counseling, employment service for undergraduates, freshman orientation, personal counseling, placement service for graduates, veterans counselor, Peer Counseling, services/facilities for handicapped.

ANNUAL EXPENSES. Tuition and fees (1992-93): $900, $608 additional for out-of-state students. **Books and supplies:** $500.

FINANCIAL AID. 75% of freshmen, 75% of continuing students receive some form of aid. All grants, all jobs based on need. **Aid applications:** No closing date; applicants notified on a rolling basis.

ADDRESS/TELEPHONE. Johnny L. Harris, Coordinator, Title III, J. F. Drake State Technical College, 3421 Meridian Street, North, Huntsville, AL 35811-3421. (205) 539-8161. Fax: (205) 539-6439.

Jacksonville State University
Jacksonville, Alabama CB code: 1736

Admissions: 91% of applicants accepted
Based on: ••• Test scores
•• School record
Completion: 85% of freshmen end year in good standing
20% enter graduate study

4-year public university, coed. Founded in 1883. **Accreditation:** Regional. **Undergraduate enrollment:** 2,665 men, 3,132 women full time; 660 men, 649 women part time. **Graduate enrollment:** 96 men, 116 women full time; 245 men, 459 women part time. **Faculty:** 359 total (274 full time), 233 with doctorates or other terminal degrees. **Location:** Rural campus in small town; 75 miles from Birmingham: 100 miles from Atlanta, GA. **Calendar:** 4-4-1-1-1. **Microcomputers:** 300 located in classrooms, computer centers. **Special facilities:** Stellar observatory.

DEGREES OFFERED. BA, BS, BFA, MA, MS, MBA, MEd. 1,116 bachelor's degrees awarded in 1992. 15% in business and management, 6% business/office and marketing/distribution, 38% education, 5% health sciences, 7% parks/recreation, protective services, public affairs, 5% social sciences. Graduate degrees offered in 29 major fields of study.

UNDERGRADUATE MAJORS. Accounting, biology, business administration and management, business and management, chemistry, communications, computer and information sciences, criminal justice studies, dramatic arts, early childhood education, economics, education of the deaf and hearing impaired, education of the emotionally handicapped, education of the mentally handicapped, elementary education, engineering and engineering-related technologies, English, English education, fashion merchandising, finance, fine arts, food management, food science and nutrition, French, geography, German, health education, history, home economics, home economics education, information sciences and systems, institutional/home management/supporting programs, liberal/general studies, marketing and distribution, mathematics, mathematics education, music, music education, music performance, nursing, parks and recreation management, physical education, physics, political science and government, psychology, science education, secondary education, social science education, social studies education, social work, sociology, Spanish, special education, speech/communication/theater education, textiles and clothing.

ACADEMIC PROGRAMS. Accelerated program, cooperative education, double major, dual enrollment of high school students, education specialist degree, honors program, independent study, internships, teacher preparation. **Remedial services:** Learning center, preadmission summer program, reduced course load, remedial instruction, special counselor, tutoring. **ROTC:** Army. **Placement/credit:** AP, CLEP General and Subject, institutional tests; 46 credit hours maximum for bachelor's degree.

ACADEMIC REQUIREMENTS. No policy requiring minimum GPA; records of students having academic difficulty are reviewed individually. Students must pass 60% of courses to remain in good academic standing. 65% of freshmen return for sophomore year. Students must declare major by end of second year. **Graduation requirements:** 128 hours for bachelor's (30 in major). Most students required to take courses in arts/fine arts, computer science, English, history, mathematics, biological/physical sciences, social sciences.

FRESHMAN ADMISSIONS. Test requirements: SAT or ACT (ACT preferred); score report by September 1.

1992 FRESHMAN CLASS PROFILE. 1,867 men and women applied, 1,691 accepted; 496 men enrolled, 606 women enrolled. **Academic background:** Mid 50% of enrolled freshmen had ACT composite between 13-20. 70% submitted ACT scores. **Characteristics:** 81% from in state, 67% live in college housing. Average age is 19.

FALL-TERM APPLICATIONS. $20 fee. Closing date September 1; applicants notified on a rolling basis. Deferred and early admission available.

STUDENT LIFE. Housing: Dormitories (men, women, coed); apartment, fraternity housing available. **Activities:** Student government, film, radio, student newspaper, yearbook, choral groups, concert band, dance, drama, jazz band, marching band, music ensembles, musical theater, fraternities, sororities.

ATHLETICS. NCAA. **Intercollegiate:** Baseball M, basketball, football M, golf M, rifle, softball W, tennis, volleyball W. **Intramural:** Baseball M, basketball, soccer M, softball, tennis M, volleyball.

STUDENT SERVICES. Career counseling, employment service for undergraduates, freshman orientation, health services, on-campus day care, personal counseling, placement service for graduates, veterans counselor, services/facilities for handicapped.

ANNUAL EXPENSES. Tuition and fees (projected): $1,680, $1,680 additional for out-of-state students. Students residing in Georgia counties bordering upon Alabama not charged out-of-state tuition. Fees varying from $3 to $25 required for some programs. **Room and board:** $2,600. **Books and supplies:** $600. **Other expenses:** $1,200.

FINANCIAL AID. 45% of freshmen, 50% of continuing students receive some form of aid. 68% of grants, 93% of loans, 50% of jobs based on need. 500 enrolled freshmen were judged to have need, all were offered aid. Academic, music/drama, art, athletic, leadership scholarships available. **Aid applications:** No closing date; priority given to applications received by April 1; applicants notified on a rolling basis beginning on or about May 15; must reply within 2 weeks.

ADDRESS/TELEPHONE. Jerry D. Smith, EdD, Dean of Admissions and Records, Jacksonville State University, 700 Pelham Road North, Jacksonville, AL 36265-9982. (205) 782-5400. Fax: (205) 782-5291. (800) 231-5291 ext. 5400.

James H. Faulkner State Community College
Bay Minette, Alabama CB code: 1939

2-year public community college, coed. Founded in 1965. **Accreditation:** Regional. **Undergraduate enrollment:** 979 men, 1,188 women full time; 465 men, 864 women part time. **Faculty:** 205 total (43 full time), 12 with doctorates or other terminal degrees. **Location:** Rural campus in small town; 35 miles from Mobile. **Calendar:** Quarter, extensive summer session. Saturday and extensive evening/early morning classes. **Microcomputers:** 148 located in libraries, classrooms, computer centers. **Additional facts:** Three off-campus sites in Fairhope, South Baldwin (Foley), and Gulf Shores.

DEGREES OFFERED. AA, AS, AAS. 212 associate degrees awarded in 1992. 36% in business and management, 9% computer sciences, 13% teacher education, 5% health sciences, 5% law, 12% letters/literature, 5% parks/recreation, protective services, public affairs.

UNDERGRADUATE MAJORS. Agricultural business and management, agricultural sciences, biology, business and management, business and office, business data programming, business education, commercial art, communications, computer and information sciences, court reporting, dental assistant, elementary education, emergency medical technologies, English, fashion merchandising, finance, fine arts, fire control and safety technology, forestry and related sciences, home economics, hotel/motel and restaurant management, journalism, law enforcement and corrections, legal assistant/paralegal, legal secretary, liberal/general studies, marketing and distribution, marketing management, mathematics, medical assistant, medical laboratory technologies, medical records technology, medical secretary, music, nursing, occupational therapy assistant, office supervision and management, physical education, physical therapy assistant, prechiropractic, predentistry, preengineering, prelaw, premedicine, prepharmacy, preveterinary, radiograph medical technology, respiratory therapy technology, secondary education, secretarial and related programs, social sciences, water and wastewater technology, word processing.

ACADEMIC PROGRAMS. 2-year transfer program, accelerated program, cooperative education, double major, honors program, independent study, internships. **Remedial services:** Learning center, remedial instruction, special counselor, tutoring. **ROTC:** Army. **Placement/credit:** AP, CLEP General; 30 credit hours maximum for associate degree.

ACADEMIC REQUIREMENTS. Freshmen must earn minimum GPA of 1.5 to continue in good standing. 62% of freshmen return for sophomore year. Students must declare major on enrollment. **Graduation requirements:** 96 hours for associate. Most students required to take courses in arts/fine arts, English, history, humanities, mathematics, biological/physical sciences, social sciences.

FRESHMAN ADMISSIONS. Selection criteria: Open admissions.

1992 FRESHMAN CLASS PROFILE. 1,058 men, 1,456 women enrolled. 12% had high school GPA of 3.0 or higher, 36% between 2.0 and 2.99. **Characteristics:** 96% from in state, 89% commute, 15% have minority backgrounds. Average age is 20.

FALL-TERM APPLICATIONS. No fee. No closing date; applicants notified on a rolling basis. Audition recommended for music applicants. Portfolio recommended for art applicants.

STUDENT LIFE. Housing: Dormitories (men, women). **Activities:** Student government, film, magazine, radio, student newspaper, television, choral groups, dance, drama, jazz band, music ensembles, pep band, Baptist Student Union, Pow-wow leadership, Phi Beta Lambda.

ATHLETICS. NJCAA. **Intercollegiate:** Baseball M, basketball, golf, softball W. **Intramural:** Basketball M, racquetball, softball, volleyball.

STUDENT SERVICES. Career counseling, employment service for undergraduates, freshman orientation, health services, personal counseling, veterans counselor, services/facilities for handicapped.

ANNUAL EXPENSES. Tuition and fees (projected): $1,125, $743 additional for out-of-state students. **Room and board:** $2,025. **Books and supplies:** $450. **Other expenses:** $800.

FINANCIAL AID. 63% of freshmen, 63% of continuing students receive some form of aid. 84% of grants based on need. Academic, music/drama, art, athletic, leadership scholarships available. **Aid applications:** Closing date August 1; priority given to applications received by July 1; applicants notified on a rolling basis beginning on or about August 1; must reply within 10 days.

ADDRESS/TELEPHONE. Linda Brown, Director of Admissions, James H. Faulkner State Community College, Hammond Circle, Bay Minette, AL 36507. (205) 937-9581. Fax: (205) 937-3404.

Jefferson Davis State Junior College
Brewton, Alabama CB code: 1355

2-year public junior college, coed. Founded in 1965. **Accreditation:** Regional. **Undergraduate enrollment:** 1,161 men and women. **Faculty:** 55 total (24 full time), 2 with doctorates or other terminal degrees. **Location:** Suburban campus in small town; 60 miles from Pensacola, Florida. **Calendar:** Quarter, limited summer session. **Microcomputers:** Located in classrooms. **Special facilities:** Museum, golf course, college park.

DEGREES OFFERED. AA, AS, AAS. 161 associate degrees awarded in 1992.

UNDERGRADUATE MAJORS. Allied health, Bible studies, business and office, business data processing and related programs, drafting and design technology, education, engineering, fine arts, home economics, law enforcement and corrections technologies, liberal/general studies, mathematics, medical assistant, medical records technology, music, nursing, physical therapy assistant, psychology, radiograph medical technology, recreation and community services technologies, respiratory therapy technology, secretarial and related programs, social sciences.

ACADEMIC PROGRAMS. 2-year transfer program. **Remedial services:** Remedial instruction, tutoring.

ACADEMIC REQUIREMENTS. Freshmen must earn minimum GPA of 1.5 to continue in good standing. 40% of freshmen return for sophomore year. **Graduation requirements:** 96 hours for associate.

FRESHMAN ADMISSIONS. Selection criteria: Open admissions. Selective admission to health occupation programs.

1992 FRESHMAN CLASS PROFILE. 310 men and women enrolled. **Characteristics:** 90% from in state, 100% commute. Average age is 18.

FALL-TERM APPLICATIONS. $5 fee. No closing date; applicants notified on a rolling basis.

STUDENT LIFE. Activities: Student government, magazine, choral groups, dance, drama, jazz band, music ensembles, musical theater, Baptist Student Union, Phi Theta Kappa, Collegians, college host group.

ATHLETICS. NJCAA. **Intercollegiate:** Baseball M, basketball M, tennis.

STUDENT SERVICES. Career counseling, freshman orientation, special adviser for adult students, veterans counselor, services/facilities for handicapped.

ANNUAL EXPENSES. Tuition and fees (1992-93): $900, $608 additional for out-of-state students. **Books and supplies:** $525. **Other expenses:** $600.

FINANCIAL AID. 69% of grants, 71% of loans, all jobs based on need. Academic, music/drama, art, athletic, leadership scholarships available. **Aid applications:** No closing date; applicants notified on a rolling basis.

ADDRESS/TELEPHONE. Cynthia Moore, Registrar, Jefferson Davis State Junior College, 220 Alco Drive, Brewton, AL 36426. (205) 867-4832.

Jefferson State Community College
Birmingham, Alabama CB code: 1352

2-year public community college, coed. Founded in 1963. **Accreditation:** Regional. **Undergraduate enrollment:** 1,242 men, 1,628 women full time; 1,309 men, 2,477 women part time. **Faculty:** 312 total (156 full time), 46 with doctorates or other terminal degrees. **Location:** Suburban campus in large city. **Calendar:** Quarter, extensive summer session. Saturday and extensive evening/early morning classes. **Microcomputers:** 255 located in libraries. **Special facilities:** Museum of natural history.

DEGREES OFFERED. AA, AS, AAS. 401 associate degrees awarded in 1992. 10% in business and management, 5% business/office and marketing/distribution, 22% health sciences, 13% allied health, 27% multi/interdisciplinary studies, 12% parks/recreation, protective services, public affairs.

UNDERGRADUATE MAJORS. Accounting, agricultural business and management, allied health, architectural technologies, biomedical equipment technology, business administration and management, business and management, child development/care/guidance, civil technology, computer and information sciences, computer programming, construction, drafting and design technology, electromechanical technology, electronic technology, emergency medical technologies, finance, fire control and safety technology, food production/management/services, funeral services/mortuary science, home furnishings and equipment management/production/services, hotel/motel and restaurant management, institutional management, insurance marketing, law enforcement and corrections technologies, liberal/general studies, marketing and distribution, mechanical design technology, medical assistant, medical laboratory technologies, medical records technology, music performance, nursing, occupational therapy assistant, parks and recreation management, physical therapy assistant, radiograph medical technology, real estate, respiratory therapy technology, retailing, secretarial and related programs, trade and industrial supervision and management, water and wastewater technology.

ACADEMIC PROGRAMS. 2-year transfer program, dual enrollment of high school students, honors program, internships, study abroad, telecourses, weekend college. **Remedial services:** Learning center, reduced course load, remedial instruction, tutoring. **ROTC:** Air Force, Army. **Placement/credit:** AP, CLEP Subject, institutional tests; 20 credit hours maximum for associate degree.

ACADEMIC REQUIREMENTS. Freshmen must earn minimum GPA of 2.0 to continue in good standing. **Graduation requirements:** 96 hours for associate (25 in major). Most students required to take courses in English, humanities, mathematics, biological/physical sciences, social sciences. **Additional information:** Some degree programs in allied health available through University of Alabama at Birmingham.

FRESHMAN ADMISSIONS. Selection criteria: Open admissions. Special admissions requirements for nursing and X-ray programs. Recommended units include English 4, foreign language 2, mathematics 4, social science 2 and science 3.

1992 FRESHMAN CLASS PROFILE. 417 men, 708 women enrolled. **Characteristics:** 99% from in state, 100% commute, 11% have minority backgrounds, 1% are foreign students.

FALL-TERM APPLICATIONS. No fee. No closing date; applicants notified on a rolling basis. Deferred admission available.

STUDENT LIFE. Activities: Student government, magazine, radio, student newspaper, choral groups, concert band, dance, drama, music ensembles, musical theater, Baptist campus ministries, Afro-American Society, Senior Adult Student Club.

ATHLETICS. NJCAA. **Intercollegiate:** Baseball M, tennis. **Intramural:** Badminton, basketball, bowling, soccer, softball, tennis, volleyball.

STUDENT SERVICES. Career counseling, employment service for undergraduates, freshman orientation, personal counseling, placement service for graduates, special adviser for adult students, veterans counselor, services/facilities for handicapped.

ANNUAL EXPENSES. Tuition and fees (1992-93): $1,215, $743 additional for out-of-state students. **Books and supplies:** $450. **Other expenses:** $525.

FINANCIAL AID. 40% of freshmen, 32% of continuing students receive some form of aid. 92% of grants, 98% of loans, all jobs based on need. Academic, music/drama, athletic, leadership scholarships available. **Aid applications:** No closing date; priority given to applications received by May 1; applicants notified on a rolling basis beginning on or about May 1; must reply within 10 days. **Additional information:** Approximately 15% of students receive employee tuition assistance and other agency-assisted tuition payment. Any Alabama resident over age 60 may attend classes tuition free.

ADDRESS/TELEPHONE. Jim Blackburn, Director of Admissions, Jefferson State Community College, 2601 Carson Road, Birmingham, AL 35215-3098. (205) 853-1200 ext. 1281. Fax: (205) 853-0340.

John C. Calhoun State Community College
Decatur, Alabama CB code: 1356

2-year public community college, coed. Founded in 1963. **Accreditation:** Regional. **Undergraduate enrollment:** 1,591 men, 1,725 women full time; 2,085 men, 2,659 women part time. **Faculty:** 404 total (144 full time), 68 with doctorates or other terminal degrees. **Location:** Suburban campus in large town; 75 miles from Birmingham, 100 miles from Nashville, Tennessee. **Calendar:** Quarter, limited summer session. Saturday and extensive evening/early morning classes. **Microcomputers:** 120 located in libraries, classrooms, computer centers. **Special facilities:** Art gallery, recording studio. **Additional facts:** Two off-campus sites in Huntsville offer evening classes.

DEGREES OFFERED. AA, AS, AAS. 634 associate degrees awarded in 1992. 12% in business and management, 30% education, 5% teacher education, 12% engineering technologies, 15% health sciences, 9% trade and industry.

UNDERGRADUATE MAJORS. Accounting, agricultural sciences, air conditioning/heating/refrigeration mechanics, air conditioning/heating/refrigeration technology, art education, automotive technology, biology, biomedical equipment technology, business administration and management, business and office, chemistry, clinical laboratory science, computer and information sciences, computer programming, criminal justice studies, criminal justice technology, dental assistant, drafting, drafting and design technology, education, electrical and electronics equipment repair, electrical technology, electrodiagnostic technologies, electronic technology, elementary education, engineering and engineering-related technologies, English, English education, film arts, finance, fire control and safety technology, graphic arts technology, health education, information sciences and systems, law enforcement and corrections technologies, legal assistant/paralegal, liberal/general studies, machine tool operation/machine shop, management science, marketing and distribution, mathematics, mechanical design technology, medical assistant, medical laboratory technologies, medical records technology, music, music education, nursing, occupational therapy assistant, office supervision and management, photographic technology, photography, physical education, physical therapy assistant, physician's assistant, practical nursing, predentistry, preengineering, prelaw, premedicine, prepharmacy, preveterinary, radiograph medical technology, real estate, recreation and community services technologies, respiratory therapy, respiratory therapy technology, retailing, secondary education, secretarial and related programs, transportation management, water and wastewater technology, welding technology.

ACADEMIC PROGRAMS. 2-year transfer program, accelerated program, cooperative education, double major, dual enrollment of high school students, honors program, internships, telecourses, weekend college, 2-year degree programs in allied health requiring 1 year at University of Alabama at Birmingham. **Remedial services:** Learning center, preadmission summer program, reduced course load, remedial instruction, special counselor, tutoring. **ROTC:** Army. **Placement/credit:** AP, CLEP General and Subject, institutional tests; 45 credit hours maximum for associate degree.

ACADEMIC REQUIREMENTS. Freshmen must earn minimum GPA of 1.0 to continue in good standing. 40% of freshmen return for sophomore year. Students must declare major on enrollment. **Graduation requirements:** 96 hours for associate (37 in major). Most students required to take courses in computer science, English, mathematics, biological/physical sciences, social sciences.

FRESHMAN ADMISSIONS. Selection criteria: Open admissions. Selective admissions for foreign students. **High school preparation:** 24 units recommended. Recommended units include biological science 1, English 4, foreign language 2, mathematics 2, physical science 1 and social science 4. In-state high school graduates must pass state high school competency examination.

1992 FRESHMAN CLASS PROFILE. 2,600 men applied, 2,600 accepted, 2,370 enrolled; 3,000 women applied, 3,000 accepted, 2,853 enrolled. **Characteristics:** 98% from in state, 100% commute, 10% have minority backgrounds, 1% are foreign students. Average age is 24.

FALL-TERM APPLICATIONS. No fee. No closing date; applicants notified on a rolling basis. Portfolio recommended for art applicants. Deferred admission available.

STUDENT LIFE. Housing: Housing available for athletes on full scholarship. **Activities:** Student government, radio, student newspaper, choral groups, drama, jazz band, music ensembles, Baptist Student Union, National Organization of Human Services, Students for Black Progress, Circle-K.

ATHLETICS. NJCAA. **Intercollegiate:** Baseball M, basketball, softball W. **Intramural:** Baseball M, basketball, softball, volleyball.

STUDENT SERVICES. Aptitude testing, career counseling, employment service for undergraduates, freshman orientation, health services, on-campus day care, personal counseling, placement service for graduates, services/facilities for handicapped.

ANNUAL EXPENSES. Tuition and fees (1992-93): $1,035, $608 additional for out-of-state students. **Books and supplies:** $500. **Other expenses:** $774.

FINANCIAL AID. 21% of freshmen, 7% of continuing students receive some form of aid. 92% of grants, 88% of loans, all jobs based on need. Academic, music/drama, art, athletic, state/district residency, leadership, minority scholarships available. **Aid applications:** No closing date; priority given to applications received by May 1; applicants notified on a rolling basis beginning on or about July 1; must reply within 2 weeks.

ADDRESS/TELEPHONE. M. Wayne Tosh, Director of Admissions and Registrar, John C. Calhoun State Community College, PO Box 2216, Decatur, AL 35609-2216. (205) 353-3102 ext. 321.

John M. Patterson State Technical College
Montgomery, Alabama — CB code: 0187

2-year public technical college, coed. Founded in 1962. **Accreditation:** Regional. **Undergraduate enrollment:** 943 men and women. **Faculty:** 49 total (30 full time). **Location:** Urban campus in large city. **Calendar:** Quarter. **Microcomputers:** Located in classrooms, computer centers. **Additional facts:** Short courses available at off-campus sites when needed.

DEGREES OFFERED. 60 associate degrees awarded in 1992. 33% in computer sciences, 67% engineering technologies.

UNDERGRADUATE MAJORS. Air conditioning/heating/refrigeration technology, data processing, drafting, drafting and design technology, electrical and electronics equipment repair, electronic technology, industrial equipment maintenance and repair, instrumentation technology.

ACADEMIC PROGRAMS. Dual enrollment of high school students, independent study, student-designed major, teacher preparation. **Remedial services:** Learning center, remedial instruction, tutoring. **Placement/credit:** CLEP General.

ACADEMIC REQUIREMENTS. Freshmen must earn minimum GPA of 1.5 to continue in good standing. 65% of freshmen return for sophomore year. Students must declare major on enrollment. **Graduation requirements:** 90 hours for associate (70 in major). Most students required to take courses in English, humanities, mathematics, philosophy/religion.

FRESHMAN ADMISSIONS. Selection criteria: Open admissions. High school diploma or GED equivalent and ACT/ASSET test scores required for some programs.

1992 FRESHMAN CLASS PROFILE. 175 men and women enrolled. **Characteristics:** 95% from in state, 100% commute, 33% have minority backgrounds, 2% are foreign students. Average age is 20.

FALL-TERM APPLICATIONS. No fee. No closing date; applicants notified on a rolling basis beginning on or about August 15.

STUDENT LIFE. Activities: Student government, student newspaper, college bowl.

STUDENT SERVICES. Aptitude testing, career counseling, employment service for undergraduates, personal counseling, services/facilities for handicapped.

ANNUAL EXPENSES. Tuition and fees (1992-93): $1,125, $743 additional for out-of-state students. **Books and supplies:** $400. **Other expenses:** $200.

FINANCIAL AID. 50% of freshmen, 50% of continuing students receive some form of aid. Grants, jobs available. Academic, leadership scholarships available. **Aid applications:** No closing date.

ADDRESS/TELEPHONE. Admissions Office, John M. Patterson State Technical College, 3920 Troy Highway, Montgomery, AL 36116. (205) 284-9356. Fax: (205) 284-9357.

Judson College
Marion, Alabama — CB code: 1349

Admissions: 38% of applicants accepted
Based on:
- ••• Recommendations, school record, test scores
- •• Activities, interview
- • Essay, special talents

Completion: 94% of freshmen end year in good standing
61% graduate, 59% of these enter graduate study

4-year private liberal arts college, women only, affiliated with Southern Baptist Convention. Founded in 1838. **Accreditation:** Regional. **Undergraduate enrollment:** 280 women full time; 9 men, 38 women part time. **Faculty:** 38 total (28 full time), 15 with doctorates or other terminal degrees. **Location:** Rural campus in small town; 75 miles from Birmingham. **Calendar:** 2 terms of about 16 weeks each with one 8-week end session. **Microcomputers:** 26 located in classrooms, computer centers. **Special facilities:** College archives, Alabama Women's Hall of Fame, Baptist missionary memorabilia, equestrian facilities. **Additional facts:** Office of External Degree Program enrollment and advising located in Huntsville. Men are accepted for nondegree programs.

DEGREES OFFERED. BA, BS, B.Div. 63 bachelor's degrees awarded in 1992. 11% in business and management, 14% teacher education, 7% home economics, 9% letters/literature, 15% life sciences, 25% psychology, 6% social sciences. Graduate degrees offered in 1 major field of study.

UNDERGRADUATE MAJORS. Air traffic control, biology, business and management, chemistry, clinical laboratory science, computer and information sciences, criminal justice studies, elementary education, English, English education, fashion design, fine arts, foreign languages (multiple emphasis), history, humanities, humanities and social sciences, interior design, junior high education, mathematics, mathematics education, music, music education, music performance, nursing, physical sciences, predentistry, preengineering, prelaw, premedicine, prepharmacy, preveterinary, psychology, religion, science education, secondary education, social science education, social sciences, social work, sociology, Spanish, studio art, technical and business writing, telecommunications, textiles and clothing.

ACADEMIC PROGRAMS. Cooperative education, double major, dual enrollment of high school students, external degree, honors program, independent study, internships, study abroad, teacher preparation, cross-registration, Air Traffic Control Cooperative Program with Federal Aviation Administration. Affiliations with nursing schools in various parts of state; liberal arts/career combination in business. **Remedial services:** Reduced course load, remedial instruction, special counselor, tutoring. **ROTC:** Army. **Placement/credit:** AP, CLEP General and Subject; 30 credit hours maximum for bachelor's degree.

ACADEMIC REQUIREMENTS. Freshmen must earn minimum GPA of 2.0 to continue in good standing. 85% of freshmen return for sophomore year. Students must declare major on enrollment. **Graduation requirements:** 128 hours for bachelor's (30 in major). Most students required to take courses in arts/fine arts, computer science, English, history, humanities, mathematics, philosophy/religion, biological/physical sciences, social sciences. **Postgraduate studies:** 2% enter law school, 4% enter medical school, 2% enter MBA programs, 51% enter other graduate study.

FRESHMAN ADMISSIONS. Selection criteria: Academic record, recommendations, test scores reviewed. **High school preparation:** 15 units required. Required and recommended units include English 4. Mathematics 2, social science 2 and science 2 recommended. 8 units among social studies, science, mathematics and/or foreign languages also required. **Test requirements:** SAT or ACT (ACT preferred); score report by August 25.

1992 FRESHMAN CLASS PROFILE. 326 women applied, 124 accepted, 109 enrolled. 61% had high school GPA of 3.0 or higher, 39% between 2.0 and 2.99. **Academic background:** Mid 50% of enrolled freshmen had ACT composite between 19-25. 100% submitted ACT scores. **Characteristics:** 62% from in state, 99% live in college housing, 8% have minority backgrounds. Average age is 18.

FALL-TERM APPLICATIONS. $20 fee, may be waived for applicants

with need. Closing date August 25; priority given to applications received by April 15; applicants notified on a rolling basis; must reply by May 12. Audition required for music applicants. Portfolio required for art, clothing and textiles, interior design applicants. Interview recommended. Essay recommended. CRDA. Deferred and early admission available.

STUDENT LIFE. Housing: Dormitories (women). **Activities:** Student government, student newspaper, yearbook, choral groups, dance, drama, music ensembles, campus ministries, Students in Free Enterprise. **Additional information:** Religious observance required.

ATHLETICS. NAIA. **Intercollegiate:** Basketball, golf, tennis. **Intramural:** Basketball, field hockey, horseback riding, softball, volleyball.

STUDENT SERVICES. Career counseling, employment service for undergraduates, freshman orientation, health services, personal counseling, placement service for graduates, special adviser for adult students.

ANNUAL EXPENSES. Tuition and fees (projected): $5,450. **Room and board:** $3,275. **Books and supplies:** $650. **Other expenses:** $1,520.

FINANCIAL AID. 94% of freshmen, 95% of continuing students receive some form of aid. 27% of grants, 91% of loans, 86% of jobs based on need. 70 enrolled freshmen were judged to have need, all were offered aid. Academic, music/drama, art, athletic, state/district residency, leadership, religious affiliation scholarships available. **Aid applications:** No closing date; priority given to applications received by April 1; applicants notified on a rolling basis beginning on or about April 1; must reply within 2 weeks.

ADDRESS/TELEPHONE. Ginger Bagby, Director of Admissions, Judson College, PO Box 120, Marion, AL 36756. (205) 683-6161 ext. 834. Fax: (205) 683-6675.

Lawson State Community College

Birmingham, Alabama — CB code: 1933

2-year public community college, coed. Founded in 1965. **Accreditation:** Regional. **Undergraduate enrollment:** 646 men, 964 women full time; 116 men, 315 women part time. **Faculty:** 89 total (51 full time), 3 with doctorates or other terminal degrees. **Location:** Suburban campus in large city; 10 miles from Birmingham. **Calendar:** Quarter, limited summer session. Saturday and extensive evening/early morning classes. **Microcomputers:** 44 located in libraries, classrooms, computer centers.

DEGREES OFFERED. AA, AS, AAS. 86 associate degrees awarded in 1992. 17% in business and management, 9% business/office and marketing/distribution, 9% computer sciences, 17% health sciences, 8% allied health, 10% social sciences, 24% trade and industry.

UNDERGRADUATE MAJORS. Accounting, allied health, business administration and management, business and office, business data processing and related programs, business education, criminal justice studies, data processing, drafting, education, electrical and electronics equipment repair, electrical installation, electrodiagnostic technologies, engineering and engineering-related technologies, English, English education, food production/management/services, history, industrial equipment maintenance and repair, law enforcement and corrections technologies, legal secretary, liberal/general studies, library assistant, mathematics, mathematics education, medical assistant, medical laboratory technologies, medical records technology, medical secretary, microcomputer software, music education, nursing, occupational therapy assistant, physical education, physical therapy assistant, predentistry, prelaw, premedicine, prepharmacy, psychology, radiograph medical technology, recreation and community services technologies, respiratory therapy technology, science education, science technologies, secretarial and related programs, social sciences, sociology, teacher aide.

ACADEMIC PROGRAMS. 2-year transfer program, accelerated program, double major, internships, student-designed major, 2-year degree programs in allied health available requiring 1 year study at University of Alabama at Birmingham. **Remedial services:** Learning center, reduced course load, remedial instruction, special counselor, tutoring. **Placement/credit:** Institutional tests.

ACADEMIC REQUIREMENTS. Freshmen must earn minimum GPA of 1.5 to continue in good standing. 25% of freshmen return for sophomore year. Students must declare major on application. **Graduation requirements:** 96 hours for associate (72 in major). Most students required to take courses in English, mathematics.

FRESHMAN ADMISSIONS. Selection criteria: Open admissions. Advanced placement option for licensed practical nurses (LPN) and nursing education. **Test requirements:** ASSET required for placement.

1992 FRESHMAN CLASS PROFILE. 325 men, 548 women enrolled. **Characteristics:** 99% from in state, 80% commute, 95% have minority backgrounds. Average age is 23.

FALL-TERM APPLICATIONS. No fee. No closing date; applicants notified on a rolling basis. Deferred and early admission available.

STUDENT LIFE. Activities: Student government, student newspaper, television, yearbook, choral groups, dance, drama, music ensembles, fraternities, Scholars Bowl Team, Sophist Club.

ATHLETICS. NJCAA. **Intercollegiate:** Basketball, track and field, volleyball. **Intramural:** Baseball, tennis.

STUDENT SERVICES. Career counseling, employment service for undergraduates, health services, personal counseling, placement service for graduates, veterans counselor, services/facilities for handicapped.

ANNUAL EXPENSES. Tuition and fees: $1,134, $720 additional for out-of-district students, $1,557 additional for out-of-state students. **Books and supplies:** $400. **Other expenses:** $700.

FINANCIAL AID. 85% of freshmen, 85% of continuing students receive some form of aid. 88% of grants, all jobs based on need. Athletic scholarships available. **Aid applications:** No closing date; priority given to applications received by June 1; applicants notified on a rolling basis beginning on or about August 1; must reply within 2 weeks.

ADDRESS/TELEPHONE. Myra P. Davis, Coordinator of Admissions and Records, Lawson State Community College, 3060 Wilson Road Southwest, Birmingham, AL 35221-1717. (205) 925-2515 ext. 309. Fax: (205) 929-6316.

Livingston University

Livingston, Alabama — CB code: 1737

Admissions:	76% of applicants accepted
Based on:	••• School record, test scores
Completion:	75% of freshmen end year in good standing
	15% enter graduate study

4-year public university, coed. Founded in 1835. **Accreditation:** Regional. **Undergraduate enrollment:** 743 men, 903 women full time; 63 men, 77 women part time. **Graduate enrollment:** 24 men, 47 women full time; 30 men, 90 women part time. **Faculty:** 105 total (90 full time), 47 with doctorates or other terminal degrees. **Location:** Rural campus in small town; 60 miles from Tuscaloosa. **Calendar:** Quarter, limited summer session. **Microcomputers:** 80 located in computer centers.

DEGREES OFFERED. AS, BA, BS, MA, MEd. 48 associate degrees awarded in 1992. 6% in engineering technologies, 89% health sciences. 240 bachelor's degrees awarded. 20% in business and management, 8% computer sciences, 40% teacher education, 13% social sciences. Graduate degrees offered in 14 major fields of study.

UNDERGRADUATE MAJORS. Associate: Accounting, computer and information sciences, emergency medical technologies, industrial equipment maintenance and repair, industrial maintenance, medical assistant, medical laboratory technologies, medical records technology, nursing, occupational therapy assistant, physical therapy assistant, radiograph medical technology, respiratory therapy technology, secretarial and related programs. **Bachelor's:** Accounting, biology, business administration and management, business and management, business education, chemistry, clinical laboratory science, computer and information sciences, early childhood education, elementary education, English, English education, environmental science, health education, history, industrial arts education, marine biology, mathematics, mathematics education, music, music education, physical education, physical sciences, science education, secondary education, social science education, social sciences, social studies education, sociology, sports medicine, technical education.

ACADEMIC PROGRAMS. Accelerated program; liberal arts/career combination in engineering, health sciences. **Remedial services:** Learning center, reduced course load, remedial instruction, special counselor, tutoring. **Placement/credit:** AP, CLEP General and Subject, institutional tests; 48 credit hours maximum for bachelor's degree.

ACADEMIC REQUIREMENTS. No policy requiring minimum GPA; records of students having academic difficulty are reviewed individually. 61% of freshmen return for sophomore year. Students must declare major by end of first year. **Graduation requirements:** 96 hours for associate (40 in major), 192 hours for bachelor's (60 in major). Most students required to take courses in arts/fine arts, English, history, humanities, mathematics, biological/physical sciences, social sciences. **Postgraduate studies:** 10% from 2-year programs enter 4-year programs. 1% enter law school, 1% enter medical school, 1% enter MBA programs, 12% enter other graduate study.

FRESHMAN ADMISSIONS. Selection criteria: School achievement record and test scores most important. **High school preparation:** 15 units required. Required units include biological science 2, English 4, mathematics 2 and social science 2. **Test requirements:** SAT or ACT (ACT preferred); score report by September 12.

1992 FRESHMAN CLASS PROFILE. 515 men applied, 371 accepted, 174 enrolled; 675 women applied, 531 accepted, 226 enrolled. **Academic background:** Mid 50% of enrolled freshmen had ACT composite between 16-21. 98% submitted ACT scores. **Characteristics:** 66% from in state, 80% live in college housing, 39% have minority backgrounds, 1% are foreign students, 25% join fraternities/sororities. Average age is 18.

FALL-TERM APPLICATIONS. $15 fee. No closing date; applicants notified on a rolling basis. Deferred and early admission available.

STUDENT LIFE. Housing: Dormitories (men, women, coed); apartment, fraternity housing available. **Activities:** Student government, student newspaper, yearbook, choral groups, concert band, drama, marching band, fraternities, sororities.

ATHLETICS. NCAA. **Intercollegiate:** Baseball M, basketball, football

M, softball W, tennis, volleyball W. **Intramural:** Basketball, golf, softball, table tennis, tennis, volleyball.

STUDENT SERVICES. Aptitude testing, career counseling, employment service for undergraduates, freshman orientation, health services, personal counseling, placement service for graduates, veterans counselor, services/facilities for handicapped.

ANNUAL EXPENSES. Tuition and fees (projected): $1,827. Foreign students required to pay $1,500 deposit upon entering. **Room and board:** $2,340. **Books and supplies:** $570. **Other expenses:** $1,200.

FINANCIAL AID. 65% of freshmen, 80% of continuing students receive some form of aid. 63% of grants, 94% of loans, all jobs based on need. Academic, music/drama, art, athletic, state/district residency, leadership, alumni affiliation scholarships available. **Aid applications:** No closing date; priority given to applications received by April 20; applicants notified on a rolling basis beginning on or about May 1; must reply within 2 weeks.

ADDRESS/TELEPHONE. Ervin L. Wood, Vice President of Student Services, Livingston University, Station 4, Livingston, AL 35470. (205) 652-9661. (800) 621-8044.

Lurleen B. Wallace State Junior College
Andalusia, Alabama CB code: 1429

2-year public junior college, coed. Founded in 1969. **Accreditation:** Regional. **Undergraduate enrollment:** 384 men, 499 women full time; 128 men, 252 women part time. **Faculty:** 44 total (27 full time), 4 with doctorates or other terminal degrees. **Location:** Rural campus in small town; 90 miles from Montgomery. **Calendar:** Quarter, limited summer session. Extensive evening/early morning classes. **Microcomputers:** 20 located in computer centers. **Special facilities:** Art gallery, nature trail. **Additional facts:** Off-campus sites in Greenville and Luverne.

DEGREES OFFERED. AA, AS, AAS. 160 associate degrees awarded in 1992. 90% in multi/interdisciplinary studies.

UNDERGRADUATE MAJORS. Allied health, business and management, computer and information sciences, finance, fire protection, forestry production and processing, liberal/general studies, marketing management, medical assistant, medical laboratory technologies, medical records administration, medical records technology, occupational therapy assistant, physical therapy assistant, radio/television broadcasting, radiograph medical technology, respiratory therapy technology, secretarial and related programs.

ACADEMIC PROGRAMS. 2-year transfer program, accelerated program, cooperative education, dual enrollment of high school students, honors program, 2-year degree programs in allied health available requiring 1 year study at University of Alabama at Birmingham. **Remedial services:** Learning center, remedial instruction, special counselor, tutoring. **Placement/credit:** AP, CLEP General and Subject, institutional tests; 45 credit hours maximum for associate degree.

ACADEMIC REQUIREMENTS. Freshmen must earn minimum GPA of 1.75 to continue in good standing. 50% of freshmen return for sophomore year. Students must declare major on enrollment. **Graduation requirements:** 96 hours for associate. Most students required to take courses in arts/fine arts, English, history, mathematics, biological/physical sciences, social sciences.

FRESHMAN ADMISSIONS. Selection criteria: Open admissions. **Additional information:** Prospective students must be immunized against measles.

1992 FRESHMAN CLASS PROFILE. 282 men, 396 women enrolled. **Characteristics:** 99% from in state, 100% commute.

FALL-TERM APPLICATIONS. No fee. No closing date; applicants notified on a rolling basis beginning on or about June 1.

STUDENT LIFE. Activities: Student government, choral groups, drama, jazz band, music ensembles, musical theater, Collegiate Civitan Club, Compass Club, Circle-K, Christian Student Union, adult re-entry club, international club.

ATHLETICS. NJCAA. **Intercollegiate:** Baseball M, basketball, softball W, tennis M. **Intramural:** Basketball M, volleyball M.

STUDENT SERVICES. Career counseling, employment service for undergraduates, freshman orientation, personal counseling, placement service for graduates, veterans counselor, services/facilities for handicapped.

ANNUAL EXPENSES. Tuition and fees (projected): $1,145, $742 additional for out-of-state students. **Books and supplies:** $375. **Other expenses:** $600.

FINANCIAL AID. 70% of freshmen, 70% of continuing students receive some form of aid. Grants, jobs available. Academic, music/drama, art, athletic scholarships available. **Aid applications:** No closing date; priority given to applications received by June 1; applicants notified on a rolling basis beginning on or about July 1; must reply within 2 weeks.

ADDRESS/TELEPHONE. Judy Hall, Director of Admissions and Financial Aid, Lurleen B. Wallace State Junior College, PO Box 1418, Andalusia, AL 36420-1418. (205) 222-6591 ext. 273. Fax: (205) 222-6567.

Marion Military Institute
Marion, Alabama CB code: 1447

2-year private junior, military college, coed. Founded in 1842. **Accreditation:** Regional. **Undergraduate enrollment:** 76 men, 10 women full time. **Faculty:** 36 total (32 full time), 1 with doctorate or other terminal degree. **Location:** Rural campus in small town; 70 miles from Birmingham. **Calendar:** Semester, limited summer session. **Microcomputers:** Located in libraries, computer centers. **Special facilities:** Alabama Military Hall of Honor.

DEGREES OFFERED. AA, AS. 55 associate degrees awarded in 1992.

UNDERGRADUATE MAJORS. Aerospace science (Air Force), African languages, biology, business and office, computer and information sciences, engineering, health sciences, law , law enforcement and corrections technologies, liberal/general studies, mathematics, psychology, social sciences.

ACADEMIC PROGRAMS. 2-year transfer program, dual enrollment of high school students, cross-registration. **Remedial services:** Preadmission summer program, reduced course load, remedial instruction, special counselor, tutoring. **ROTC:** Army.

ACADEMIC REQUIREMENTS. 71% of freshmen return for sophomore year. **Graduation requirements:** 64 hours for associate. Most students required to take courses in English, history, humanities, mathematics, biological/physical sciences, social sciences. **Additional information:** Special preparation for national service academies offered.

FRESHMAN ADMISSIONS. Selection criteria: Test scores and academic record most important. Recommendations and interview also considered. **High school preparation:** 12 units required; 15 recommended. Required and recommended units include biological science 1, English 4, mathematics 3, physical science 1-2 and social science 3. Foreign language 2 recommended. **Test requirements:** SAT or ACT; score report by August 25.

1992 FRESHMAN CLASS PROFILE. 12% had high school GPA of 3.0 or higher, 60% between 2.0 and 2.99. **Characteristics:** 35% from in state, 100% live in college housing, 15% have minority backgrounds. Average age is 18.

FALL-TERM APPLICATIONS. $100 fee. Closing date August 25; applicants notified on a rolling basis. Interview recommended. CRDA. Deferred and early admission available.

STUDENT LIFE. Housing: Dormitories (men, women). All students required to live on campus. **Activities:** Student government, magazine, student newspaper, yearbook, choral groups, concert band, drama, marching band, Fellowship of Christian Athletes, Jefferson Society, student campus service organizations: Dolphins, Morgan's Raiders. **Additional information:** Students participate in precision drill team, orienteering team, and United States Army Ranger-type training.

ATHLETICS. NJCAA. **Intercollegiate:** Rifle. **Intramural:** Baseball M, basketball M, cross-country, diving, golf, gymnastics, handball, rifle, soccer M, softball, swimming, tennis, track and field M, volleyball, water polo M.

STUDENT SERVICES. Aptitude testing, career counseling, freshman orientation, health services, personal counseling.

ANNUAL EXPENSES. Tuition and fees: $5,926. **Room and board:** $3,790. **Books and supplies:** $644. **Other expenses:** $1,822.

FINANCIAL AID. 60% of freshmen, 45% of continuing students receive some form of aid. 22% of grants, 95% of loans, all jobs based on need. Academic, music/drama, athletic, state/district residency, leadership scholarships available. **Aid applications:** No closing date; priority given to applications received by June 15; applicants notified on a rolling basis beginning on or about June 15; must reply within 2 weeks. **Additional information:** Eligible students may reduce cost by enrolling in advanced ROTC program.

ADDRESS/TELEPHONE. Lt. Col. C. J. Makee, Director of Admissions, Director of Financial Aid, Marion Military Institute, Washington Street, Marion, AL 36756-0420. (205) 683-2304. Fax: (205) 683-2380.

Miles College
Fairfield, Alabama CB code: 1468

4-year private liberal arts college, coed, affiliated with Christian Methodist Episcopal Church. Founded in 1905. **Accreditation:** Regional. **Undergraduate enrollment:** 720 men and women. **Faculty:** 49 total (41 full time), 18 with doctorates or other terminal degrees. **Location:** Urban campus in large town; 6 miles from downtown Birmingham. **Calendar:** Semester, limited summer session. **Microcomputers:** Located in computer centers. **Special facilities:** Afro-American materials center, media center.

DEGREES OFFERED. BA, BS. 92 bachelor's degrees awarded in 1992. 53% in business and management, 14% communications, 6% education, 8% mathematics, 17% social sciences.

UNDERGRADUATE MAJORS. Accounting, biology, business administration and management, chemistry, communications, education, elementary education, English, mathematics, music performance, secondary education, social science education, social sciences, sociology.

ACADEMIC PROGRAMS. Cooperative education, double major, dual enrollment of high school students, honors program, independent study, internships, visiting/exchange student program, cross-registration; liberal arts/career combination in health sciences. **Remedial services:** Reduced course load, remedial instruction, special counselor, tutoring, reading and writing laboratories. **Placement/credit:** Institutional tests.

ACADEMIC REQUIREMENTS. Freshmen must earn minimum GPA of 2.0 to continue in good standing. 65% of freshmen return for sophomore year. Students must declare major by end of first year. **Graduation requirements:** 127 hours for bachelor's (72 in major). Most students required to take courses in arts/fine arts, computer science, English, history, humanities, mathematics, philosophy/religion, biological/physical sciences, social sciences. **Postgraduate studies:** 1% enter law school, 33% enter other graduate study.

FRESHMAN ADMISSIONS. Selection criteria: Open admissions. Selective admission to education program based on 2.0 high school GPA, ACT composite score of 16 and recommendations. 3 letters of recommendation required of all. 4 units mathematics and science required of natural science applicants. **Test requirements:** ACT for placement and counseling only; score report by July 31.

1992 FRESHMAN CLASS PROFILE. 398 men and women enrolled. **Characteristics:** 21% from in state, 52% live in college housing, 98% have minority backgrounds, 1% are foreign students, 15% join fraternities/sororities. Average age is 18.

FALL-TERM APPLICATIONS. $25 fee, may be waived for applicants with need. Closing date July 15; applicants notified on a rolling basis; must reply by August 1.

STUDENT LIFE. Housing: Dormitories (men, women); apartment housing available. **Activities:** Student government, radio, student newspaper, television, yearbook, choral groups, drama, marching band, fraternities, sororities, Interdenominational Ministerial Association, International Intercultural Association.

ATHLETICS. NCAA. **Intercollegiate:** Baseball M, basketball, cross-country, football M, track and field. **Intramural:** Badminton, basketball, softball, tennis, volleyball.

STUDENT SERVICES. Aptitude testing, career counseling, employment service for undergraduates, health services, personal counseling, placement service for graduates, services/facilities for handicapped.

ANNUAL EXPENSES. Tuition and fees: $4,150. **Room and board:** $2,400. **Books and supplies:** $400. **Other expenses:** $1,000.

FINANCIAL AID. 84% of freshmen, 80% of continuing students receive some form of aid. 84% of grants, 98% of loans, all jobs based on need. Academic scholarships available. **Aid applications:** No closing date; priority given to applications received by April 15; applicants notified on a rolling basis beginning on or about July 15; must reply within 2 weeks.

ADDRESS/TELEPHONE. Gloria Ann W. Beverly, Director of Admissions, Miles College, 5500 Myron-Massey Boulevard, Fairfield, AL 35064. (205) 923-2771. Fax: (205) 923-9292.

Northeast Alabama Community College
Rainsville, Alabama CB code: 1576

2-year public community, liberal arts college, coed. Founded in 1963. **Accreditation:** Regional. **Undergraduate enrollment:** 353 men, 634 women full time; 285 men, 516 women part time. **Faculty:** 55 total (36 full time), 8 with doctorates or other terminal degrees. **Location:** Rural campus in small town; 55 miles from Huntsville, 100 miles from Birmingham. **Calendar:** Quarter. Extensive evening/early morning classes. **Microcomputers:** 30 located in libraries, computer centers.

DEGREES OFFERED. AA, AS, AAS. 150 associate degrees awarded in 1992.

UNDERGRADUATE MAJORS. Accounting, business and management, business and office, business data entry equipment operation, business data processing and related programs, business data programming, computer and information sciences, education, electrodiagnostic technologies, emergency medical technologies, engineering, finance, law enforcement and corrections technologies, legal secretary, liberal/general studies, medical assistant, medical laboratory technologies, medical records technology, medical secretary, nursing, occupational therapy assistant, physical therapy assistant, radiograph medical technology, real estate, respiratory therapy technology, secretarial and related programs.

ACADEMIC PROGRAMS. 2-year transfer program, accelerated program, double major, dual enrollment of high school students, honors program, independent study, study abroad, 2-year degree programs in allied health available requiring 1 year study at University of Alabama at Birmingham. **Remedial services:** Learning center, preadmission summer program, reduced course load, remedial instruction, tutoring. **Placement/credit:** AP, CLEP General and Subject, institutional tests; 30 credit hours maximum for associate degree.

ACADEMIC REQUIREMENTS. Freshmen must earn minimum GPA of 1.5 to continue in good standing. 60% of freshmen return for sophomore year. Students must declare major by end of first year. **Graduation requirements:** 96 hours for associate. Most students required to take courses in arts/fine arts, computer science, English, humanities, mathematics, biological/physical sciences, social sciences.

FRESHMAN ADMISSIONS. Selection criteria: Open admissions. Selective admission to nursing program. **Additional information:** All first-time college students must take ASSET for placement purposes.

1992 FRESHMAN CLASS PROFILE. 434 men, 767 women enrolled. **Characteristics:** 95% from in state, 100% commute, 1% have minority backgrounds, 1% are foreign students. Average age is 26.

FALL-TERM APPLICATIONS. No fee. No closing date; applicants notified on a rolling basis. Deferred and early admission available.

STUDENT LIFE. Activities: Student government, yearbook, choral groups, concert band, drama, jazz band, music ensembles, Baptist campus ministries.

STUDENT SERVICES. Career counseling, employment service for undergraduates, freshman orientation, personal counseling, placement service for graduates, special adviser for adult students, veterans counselor, services/facilities for handicapped.

ANNUAL EXPENSES. Tuition and fees (projected): $909, $547 additional for out-of-state students. **Books and supplies:** $400. **Other expenses:** $1,500.

FINANCIAL AID. 45% of freshmen, 35% of continuing students receive some form of aid. 77% of grants, all jobs based on need. Academic, music/drama, art, leadership scholarships available. **Aid applications:** Closing date May 1; applicants notified on or about August 15.

ADDRESS/TELEPHONE. Dr. Joe Burke, Director of Admissions, Northeast Alabama Community College, PO Box 159, Highway 35 West, Rainsville, AL 35986. (205) 638-4418. Fax: (205) 228-6558.

Northwest Alabama Community College
Phil Campbell, Alabama CB code: 0729

2-year public community college, coed. Founded in 1961. **Accreditation:** Regional. **Undergraduate enrollment:** 2,211 men and women. **Faculty:** 98 total (66 full time), 6 with doctorates or other terminal degrees. **Location:** Rural campus in rural community; 100 miles from Birmingham. **Calendar:** Quarter, limited summer session. **Microcomputers:** Located in computer centers.

DEGREES OFFERED. AA, AS. 178 associate degrees awarded in 1992.

UNDERGRADUATE MAJORS. Business and management, data processing, dental hygiene, fine arts, general science, information sciences and systems, medical assistant, medical laboratory technologies, medical records technology, music, nursing, predentistry, premedicine, preveterinary, respiratory therapy technology, secretarial and related programs.

ACADEMIC PROGRAMS. Accelerated program, cooperative education, dual enrollment of high school students, telecourses. **Remedial services:** Learning center, preadmission summer program, reduced course load, remedial instruction, special counselor, tutoring. **Placement/credit:** CLEP General and Subject, institutional tests.

ACADEMIC REQUIREMENTS. Freshmen must earn minimum GPA of 1.5 to continue in good standing. 35% of freshmen return for sophomore year. Students must declare major on application. **Graduation requirements:** 96 hours for associate. Most students required to take courses in arts/fine arts, English, history, mathematics, philosophy/religion, biological/physical sciences, social sciences.

FRESHMAN ADMISSIONS. Selection criteria: Open admissions. Selective admission to health occupation programs. **Test requirements:** ACT required of nursing applicants.

1992 FRESHMAN CLASS PROFILE. 1,032 men and women enrolled. **Characteristics:** 99% from in state, 99% commute.

FALL-TERM APPLICATIONS. No fee. No closing date; applicants notified on a rolling basis. Deferred and early admission available.

STUDENT LIFE. Housing: Dormitories (coed). **Activities:** Student government, student newspaper, yearbook, choral groups, jazz band, Phi Theta Kappa.

ATHLETICS. NJCAA. **Intercollegiate:** Baseball M, basketball, cross-country M, golf M, softball W, track and field M, volleyball W. **Intramural:** Basketball, volleyball.

STUDENT SERVICES. Aptitude testing, career counseling, personal counseling, services/facilities for handicapped.

ANNUAL EXPENSES. Tuition and fees (1992-93): $1,035, $608 additional for out-of-state students. **Books and supplies:** $400.

FINANCIAL AID. Grants, loans, jobs available. **Aid applications:** No closing date; applicants notified on a rolling basis beginning on or about August 15; must reply within 2 weeks. **Additional information:** Auditions required of music scholarship candidates.

ADDRESS/TELEPHONE. Charles T. Taylor, Sr, Director of Admissions/Registrar, Northwest Alabama Community College, PO Route 3, Box 77, Phil Campbell, AL 35581. (205) 993-5331. (800) 645-8967.

Oakwood College

Huntsville, Alabama CB code: 1586

Admissions: 64% of applicants accepted
Based on: ••• Recommendations, school record, test scores
•• Essay
• Special talents
Completion: 87% of freshmen end year in good standing

4-year private liberal arts college, coed, affiliated with Seventh-day Adventists. Founded in 1896. **Accreditation:** Regional. **Undergraduate enrollment:** 498 men, 727 women full time; 48 men, 61 women part time. **Faculty:** 134 total (79 full time), 55 with doctorates or other terminal degrees. **Location:** Suburban campus in small city; 5 miles from downtown. **Calendar:** Quarter, limited summer session. **Microcomputers:** 138 located in libraries, classrooms.

DEGREES OFFERED. AA, AS, BA, BS. 16 associate degrees awarded in 1992. 6% in business and management, 13% communications, 75% health sciences, 6% visual and performing arts. 148 bachelor's degrees awarded. 13% in business and management, 5% communications, 8% teacher education, 5% home economics, 18% life sciences, 11% parks/recreation, protective services, public affairs, 16% philosophy, religion, theology, 6% social sciences.

UNDERGRADUATE MAJORS. Associate: Accounting, Bible studies, communications, computer and information sciences, graphic design, illustration design, journalism, nursing, office supervision and management. **Bachelor's:** Accounting, biochemistry, biological and physical sciences, biology, business administration and management, business and management, business economics, business education, chemistry, communications, computer and information sciences, early childhood education, elementary education, English, English education, food science and nutrition, history, home economics, home economics education, individual and family development, information sciences and systems, language arts education, liberal/general studies, management information systems, mathematics, mathematics and computer science, mathematics education, music, music education, music performance, nursing, physical education, psychology, religion, religious education, science education, secondary education, social science education, social sciences, social work, theological studies.

ACADEMIC PROGRAMS. Cooperative education, double major, honors program, study abroad. **Remedial services:** Learning center, reduced course load, remedial instruction, special counselor, tutoring. **Placement/credit:** AP, CLEP Subject, institutional tests.

ACADEMIC REQUIREMENTS. Freshmen must earn minimum GPA of 2.0 to continue in good standing. 65% of freshmen return for sophomore year. Students must declare major by end of first year. **Graduation requirements:** 96 hours for associate (59 in major), 192 hours for bachelor's (60 in major). Most students required to take courses in arts/fine arts, computer science, English, foreign languages, history, humanities, mathematics, philosophy/religion, biological/physical sciences, social sciences.

FRESHMAN ADMISSIONS. Selection criteria: Applicants with GPA between 1.5 and 2.0 considered for acceptance. Special consideration for exceptional applicants. **High school preparation:** 18 units required. Required units include English 4, foreign language 2, mathematics 2, social science 2 and science 2. 1 typing recommended. **Test requirements:** SAT or ACT for placement and counseling only; score report by August 15.

1992 FRESHMAN CLASS PROFILE. 382 men applied, 227 accepted, 138 enrolled; 500 women applied, 337 accepted, 214 enrolled. 32% had high school GPA of 3.0 or higher, 50% between 2.0 and 2.99. **Characteristics:** 9% from in state, 92% live in college housing, 84% have minority backgrounds, 15% are foreign students. Average age is 19.

FALL-TERM APPLICATIONS. $15 fee, may be waived for applicants with need. No closing date; applicants notified on a rolling basis. Essay recommended. Deferred admission available.

STUDENT LIFE. Housing: Dormitories (men, women); apartment housing available. **Activities:** Student government, radio, student newspaper, yearbook, choral groups, college band, Outreach, NAACP. **Additional information:** Students sit on most faculty and administrative committees. Religious observance required.

ATHLETICS. Intramural: Baseball, basketball, golf, gymnastics, soccer, softball, tennis, volleyball.

STUDENT SERVICES. Aptitude testing, career counseling, employment service for undergraduates, health services, on-campus day care, personal counseling, placement service for graduates, special adviser for adult students, veterans counselor.

ANNUAL EXPENSES. Tuition and fees (1992-93): $6,216. **Room and board:** $3,663. **Books and supplies:** $600. **Other expenses:** $1,500.

FINANCIAL AID. 90% of freshmen, 90% of continuing students receive some form of aid. Grants, loans, jobs available. **Aid applications:** Closing date September 11; priority given to applications received by April 15; must reply within 15 days. **Additional information:** Deadline for Winter, January 15, 1994; Spring, April 2, 1994.

ADDRESS/TELEPHONE. Lovey Verdun, Director of Admissions and Records, Oakwood College, Oakwood Road, Huntsville, AL 35896. (205) 726-7000 ext. 7939. (800) 824-5312. Fax: (205) 726-7409.

Opelika State Technical College

Opelika, Alabama CB code: 0086

2-year public institution, coed. Founded in 1963. **Accreditation:** Regional. **Undergraduate enrollment:** 706 men and women. **Calendar:** Quarter.

ANNUAL EXPENSES. Tuition and fees (1992-93):

ADDRESS/TELEPHONE. Opelika State Technical College, 1701 La Fayette Parkway, Opelika, AL.

Phillips Junior College: Birmingham

Birmingham, Alabama CB code: 1614

2-year proprietary junior college, coed. Founded in 1938. **Accreditation:** Regional. **Undergraduate enrollment:** 900 men and women. **Location:** Urban campus in large city. **Calendar:** Quarter. **Microcomputers:** 100 located in classrooms, computer centers.

DEGREES OFFERED. AAS. 231 associate degrees awarded in 1992.

UNDERGRADUATE MAJORS. Business administration and management, business data processing and related programs, electronic technology, fashion merchandising, medical secretary, secretarial and related programs.

ACADEMIC PROGRAMS. 2-year transfer program. **Remedial services:** Remedial instruction.

ACADEMIC REQUIREMENTS. Freshmen must earn minimum GPA of 2.0 to continue in good standing.

FRESHMAN ADMISSIONS. Selection criteria: Open admissions. **Additional information:** Entrance examination required of all first-time students, except those with bachelor's degree.

1992 FRESHMAN CLASS PROFILE. Characteristics: 99% from in state, 100% commute, 99% have minority backgrounds. Average age is 19.

FALL-TERM APPLICATIONS. $75 fee. No closing date; applicants notified on a rolling basis. Interview required. Deferred admission available.

STUDENT LIFE. Activities: Student government, student newspaper, newspaper for clubs, choral groups, Phi Theta Kappa, Honorary Scholastic Fraternity, Medical Assisting Student Association, Interior Design Organization.

ATHLETICS. NJCAA.

STUDENT SERVICES. Aptitude testing, career counseling, employment service for undergraduates, freshman orientation, personal counseling, placement service for graduates, veterans counselor, services/facilities for handicapped.

ANNUAL EXPENSES. Tuition and fees: $10,425. **Books and supplies:** $325.

FINANCIAL AID. 90% of freshmen, 90% of continuing students receive some form of aid. All aid based on need. **Aid applications:** No closing date; applicants notified on a rolling basis.

ADDRESS/TELEPHONE. Teresa Murton, Director of Admissions, Phillips Junior College: Birmingham, 115 Office Park Drive, Birmingham, AL 35223. (205) 251-2821.

Reid State Technical College

Evergreen, Alabama CB code: 0193

2-year public technical college, coed. Founded in 1966. **Accreditation:** Regional. **Undergraduate enrollment:** 132 men, 323 women full time; 62 men, 100 women part time. **Faculty:** 45 total (32 full time). **Location:** Rural campus in small town; 75 miles from Montgomery , 100 miles from Mobile. **Calendar:** Quarter. Saturday and extensive evening/early morning classes. **Microcomputers:** 35 located in classrooms, computer centers. **Additional facts:** Off-site campus in Atmore, Alabama, primarily for practical nursing program. Free transportation from 5 surrounding counties to main campus.

DEGREES OFFERED. AAS. 30 associate degrees awarded in 1992. 100% in engineering technologies.

UNDERGRADUATE MAJORS. Electrical technology, electronic technology, forestry production and processing.

ACADEMIC PROGRAMS. Dual enrollment of high school students. **Remedial services:** Learning center, preadmission summer program, reduced course load, remedial instruction, special counselor, tutoring. **Placement/credit:** Institutional tests.

ACADEMIC REQUIREMENTS. Freshmen must earn minimum GPA of 1.5 to continue in good standing. 75% of freshmen return for sophomore year. Students must declare major on enrollment. **Graduation requirements:** 53 hours for associate (43 in major). Most students required to take courses in English, mathematics.

FRESHMAN ADMISSIONS. Selection criteria: Open admissions. High school diploma required for some programs.Ability to benefit must be proven for non-high school graduates. **Test requirements:** ACT ASSET required for placement and counseling.

1992 FRESHMAN CLASS PROFILE. 107 men, 187 women enrolled. **Characteristics:** 95% from in state, 100% commute, 41% have minority backgrounds. Average age is 24.

FALL-TERM APPLICATIONS. No fee. Closing date September 20; priority given to applications received by August 1; applicants notified on a rolling basis beginning on or about August 1; must reply by registration. Interview required for practical nursing applicants. Deferred admission available.

STUDENT LIFE. Activities: Student government, student newspaper, pep band.

STUDENT SERVICES. Aptitude testing, career counseling, employment service for undergraduates, freshman orientation, personal counseling, placement service for graduates, veterans counselor, services/facilities for handicapped.

ANNUAL EXPENSES. Tuition and fees (1992-93): $990, $675 additional for out-of-state students. **Books and supplies:** $400.

FINANCIAL AID. 80% of freshmen, 83% of continuing students receive some form of aid. Grants, jobs available. **Aid applications:** No closing date; applicants notified on a rolling basis.

ADDRESS/TELEPHONE. Alesia Stuart, Admissions Office / Public Relations, Reid State Technical College, PO Box 588, Evergreen, AL 36401. (205) 578-1313. Fax: (205) 578-5355 ext. 123.

Samford University

Birmingham, Alabama — CB code: 1302

Admissions: 82% of applicants accepted
Based on:
••• School record, test scores
•• Essay, recommendations
• Activities, interview, religious affiliation/commitment, special talents
Completion: 85% of freshmen end year in good standing
65% graduate, 37% of these enter graduate study

4-year private university, coed, affiliated with Southern Baptist Convention. Founded in 1841. **Accreditation:** Regional. **Undergraduate enrollment:** 1,175 men, 1,664 women full time; 141 men, 322 women part time. **Graduate enrollment:** 483 men, 314 women full time; 153 men, 109 women part time. **Faculty:** 540 total (377 full time), 184 with doctorates or other terminal degrees. **Location:** Suburban campus in large city; 6 miles from downtown. **Calendar:** 4-1-4, extensive summer session. Extensive evening/early morning classes. **Microcomputers:** 250 located in libraries, classrooms, computer centers. **Special facilities:** Computer-assisted laboratory for journalism, observatory.

DEGREES OFFERED. AS, BA, BS, MBA, MEd, B. Pharm, M.Div. 50 associate degrees awarded in 1992. 38% in health sciences, 27% law, 35% social sciences. 550 bachelor's degrees awarded. 24% in business and management, 10% teacher education, 22% health sciences, 7% philosophy, religion, theology, 9% social sciences, 5% visual and performing arts. Graduate degrees offered in 21 major fields of study.

UNDERGRADUATE MAJORS. Associate: Bible studies, humanities and social sciences, legal assistant/paralegal, liberal/general studies, nursing, social sciences. **Bachelor's:** Accounting, art education, athletic training, Bible studies, biology, business administration and management, business and management, business and office, business economics, chemistry, church recreation, clinical laboratory science, commercial art, communications, computer and information sciences, cytotechnology, dramatic arts, early childhood education, economics, education, elementary education, engineering physics, English, English education, English literature, environmental science, fashion design, finance, fine arts, food science and nutrition, foreign languages education, French, German, graphic design, health education, history, home economics, home economics education, human resources development, humanities and social sciences, insurance and risk management, interior design, international business management, international relations, journalism, junior high education, law enforcement and corrections, legal assistant/paralegal, liberal/general studies, management information systems, marine biology, marketing and distribution, marketing management, mathematics, mathematics education, medical records administration, music, music education, music performance, music theory and composition, nuclear medical technology, nursing, occupational therapy, ophthalmic services, pharmacy, physical education, physics, psychology, public administration, radiograph medical technology, real estate, religion, religious education, religious music, science education, secondary education, social science education, social sciences, social studies education, sociology, Spanish, speech, textiles and clothing, theological studies.

ACADEMIC PROGRAMS. Accelerated program, cooperative education, double major, dual enrollment of high school students, education specialist degree, honors program, independent study, internships, student-designed major, study abroad, teacher preparation, cross-registration; liberal arts/career combination in engineering, forestry, health sciences. **Remedial services:** Reduced course load, remedial instruction, tutoring. **ROTC:** Air Force. **Placement/credit:** AP, CLEP General and Subject, institutional tests; 32 credit hours maximum for bachelor's degree.

ACADEMIC REQUIREMENTS. Freshmen must earn minimum GPA of 2.0 to continue in good standing. Students must declare major by end of second year. **Graduation requirements:** 64 hours for associate, 128 hours for bachelor's (30 in major). Most students required to take courses in arts/fine arts, English, history, mathematics, philosophy/religion, biological/physical sciences, social sciences. **Postgraduate studies:** 75% from 2-year programs enter 4-year programs. 2% enter law school, 3% enter medical school, 4% enter MBA programs, 28% enter other graduate study.

FRESHMAN ADMISSIONS. Selection criteria: High school GPA, test scores, recommendations, essay, academic content and trend of high school grades considered. **High school preparation:** 18 units required. Required and recommended units include English 4. Biological science 1, foreign language 2, mathematics 2, physical science 1 and social science 2 recommended. **Test requirements:** SAT or ACT (SAT preferred); score report by May 1.

1992 FRESHMAN CLASS PROFILE. 645 men applied, 527 accepted, 275 enrolled; 968 women applied, 791 accepted, 412 enrolled. 90% had high school GPA of 3.0 or higher, 10% between 2.0 and 2.99. 34% were in top tenth and 65% were in top quarter of graduating class. **Academic background:** Mid 50% of enrolled freshmen had SAT-V between 410-550, SAT-M between 420-580; ACT composite between 22-28. 35% submitted SAT scores, 65% submitted ACT scores. **Characteristics:** 45% from in state, 75% live in college housing, 6% have minority backgrounds, 1% are foreign students, 25% join fraternities/sororities. Average age is 18.

FALL-TERM APPLICATIONS. $25 fee, may be waived for applicants with need. No closing date; priority given to applications received by February 1; applicants notified on a rolling basis; must reply by May 1. Audition required for music applicants. Essay required. Interview recommended. Portfolio recommended. CRDA. Deferred and early admission available. Institutional early decision plan.

STUDENT LIFE. Housing: Dormitories (men, women); apartment, fraternity, sorority, handicapped housing available. Applicants requiring campus housing should apply for admission prior to April 1 to insure availability. Furnished suites with living area, kitchenette and private bath available on campus for upperclassmen. **Activities:** Student government, magazine, radio, student newspaper, television, yearbook, choral groups, concert band, drama, jazz band, marching band, music ensembles, musical theater, opera, pep band, fraternities, sororities, campus ministries, Rio Grande River Ministry, summer ministries, Black Student Organization, Alpha Phi Omega. **Additional information:** Chapel convocation required.

ATHLETICS. NCAA. **Intercollegiate:** Baseball M, basketball M, cross-country, football M, golf, softball W, tennis, track and field, volleyball W. **Intramural:** Badminton, basketball, bowling, golf, racquetball, soccer, softball, table tennis, tennis, track and field, volleyball, water polo. **Clubs:** Soccer club.

STUDENT SERVICES. Aptitude testing, career counseling, employment service for undergraduates, freshman orientation, health services, personal counseling, placement service for graduates, special adviser for adult students, veterans counselor, services/facilities for handicapped.

ANNUAL EXPENSES. Tuition and fees: $7,770. **Room and board:** $3,838. **Books and supplies:** $524. **Other expenses:** $1,650.

FINANCIAL AID. 70% of freshmen, 79% of continuing students receive some form of aid. 33% of grants, 80% of loans, 29% of jobs based on need. 423 enrolled freshmen were judged to have need, all were offered aid. Academic, music/drama, art, athletic, state/district residency, leadership, religious affiliation scholarships available. **Aid applications:** No closing date; priority given to applications received by March 1; applicants notified on a rolling basis beginning on or about April 1; must reply within 21 days.

ADDRESS/TELEPHONE. Dr. Don Belcher, Dean of Admissions and Financial Aid, Samford University, 800 Lakeshore Drive, Birmingham, AL 35229-0000. (205) 870-2901. (800) 888-7218. Fax: (205) 870-2171.

Selma University

Selma, Alabama — CB code: 1792

4-year private university, coed, affiliated with Alabama Baptist State Convention. Founded in 1878. **Accreditation:** Regional candidate. **Undergraduate enrollment:** 264 men and women. **Faculty:** 29 total (23 full time), 4 with doctorates or other terminal degrees. **Location:** Urban campus in large town; 50 miles from Montgomery. **Calendar:** Semester, limited summer session.

DEGREES OFFERED. AA, AS, AAS, BA, BS. 4 associate degrees awarded in 1992. 13 bachelor's degrees awarded.

UNDERGRADUATE MAJORS. Associate: Accounting, Bible studies, biochemistry, biology, botany, business administration and management, business and management, business and office, business data processing and related programs, business economics, communications, computer and information sciences, computer programming, data processing, health sciences, liberal/general studies, marketing management, mathematics, microcomputer software, nursing, premedicine, psychology, secretarial and related programs, social sciences, word processing. **Bachelor's:** Religious education, theological studies.

ACADEMIC PROGRAMS. Remedial services: Reduced course load, remedial instruction, special counselor, tutoring. **Placement/credit:** Institutional tests.

ACADEMIC REQUIREMENTS. Freshmen must earn minimum GPA of 2.0 to continue in good standing. 54% of freshmen return for sophomore year. **Graduation requirements:** 66 hours for associate, 126 hours for bachelor's. Most students required to take courses in arts/fine arts, English, history, humanities, mathematics, philosophy/religion, biological/physical sciences, social sciences. **Postgraduate studies:** 50% from 2-year programs enter 4-year programs.

FRESHMAN ADMISSIONS. Selection criteria: Open admissions. **Test requirements:** SAT or ACT (ACT preferred) for placement and counseling only. Stanford Test of Academic Skills required. **Additional information:** Students with deficient high school record or low test scores must take remedial courses.

1992 FRESHMAN CLASS PROFILE. 125 men and women enrolled. **Characteristics:** 97% from in state, 90% live in college housing, 94% have minority backgrounds, 6% are foreign students, 10% join fraternities/sororities. Average age is 21.

FALL-TERM APPLICATIONS. $10 fee. No closing date; applicants notified on a rolling basis beginning on or about August 1.

STUDENT LIFE. Housing: Dormitories (men, women). **Activities:** Student government, student newspaper, yearbook, choral groups, drama, music ensembles, fraternities, sororities, Baptist Student Union.

ATHLETICS. NJCAA. **Intercollegiate:** Baseball M, basketball, volleyball M. **Intramural:** Basketball, softball, table tennis, volleyball.

STUDENT SERVICES. Aptitude testing, career counseling, personal counseling.

ANNUAL EXPENSES. Tuition and fees: $4,200. **Room and board:** $3,700. **Books and supplies:** $200. **Other expenses:** $600.

FINANCIAL AID. 95% of freshmen, 95% of continuing students receive some form of aid. All jobs based on need. **Aid applications:** No closing date; priority given to applications received by September 15; applicants notified on a rolling basis beginning on or about August 23; must reply within 2 weeks.

ADDRESS/TELEPHONE. Raymond Brown, Director of Admissions and Records, Selma University, 1501 Lapsley Street, Selma, AL 36701. (205) 872-2533.

Shelton State Community College
Tuscaloosa, Alabama — CB code: 3338

2-year public community college, coed. Founded in 1963. **Accreditation:** Regional. **Undergraduate enrollment:** 4,845 men and women. **Faculty:** 125 total (70 full time), 15 with doctorates or other terminal degrees. **Location:** Suburban campus in small city; 60 miles from Birmingham. **Calendar:** Semester, extensive summer session. **Microcomputers:** 27 located in computer centers. **Additional facts:** Fredd State Technical is a branch campus of Sheldon State Community College.

DEGREES OFFERED. AA, AS, AAS. 100 associate degrees awarded in 1992. 30% in business and management, 5% business/office and marketing/distribution, 12% education, 8% health sciences, 39% multi/interdisciplinary studies.

UNDERGRADUATE MAJORS. Air conditioning/heating/refrigeration technology, allied health, automotive mechanics, biology, biomedical equipment technology, business administration and management, business and management, business and office, business data entry equipment operation, business data processing and related programs, business data programming, clinical laboratory science, computer and information sciences, cytotechnology, data processing, diesel engine mechanics, drafting, drafting and design technology, education, electrical installation, electrical technology, electronic technology, elementary education, engineering, finance, fine arts, fire control and safety technology, health sciences, home economics, liberal/general studies, mathematics, medical assistant, medical laboratory technologies, medical records administration, medical records technology, music, nursing, occupational therapy assistant, personal services, physical therapy assistant, precision metal work, predentistry, prelaw, premedicine, prepharmacy, preveterinary, quality control technology, radiograph medical technology, respiratory therapy, respiratory therapy technology, secretarial and related programs, social sciences, ultrasound technology, visual and performing arts, water and wastewater technology.

ACADEMIC PROGRAMS. 2-year transfer program, accelerated program, double major, dual enrollment of high school students, honors program, weekend college, 2-year degree programs in allied health available requiring 1-year study at University of Alabama at Birmingham. **Remedial services:** Learning center, reduced course load, remedial instruction, special counselor, tutoring. **Placement/credit:** AP, institutional tests.

ACADEMIC REQUIREMENTS. Freshmen must earn minimum GPA of 1.5 to continue in good standing. 48% of freshmen return for sophomore year. Students must declare major on enrollment. **Graduation requirements:** 65 hours for associate (27 in major). Most students required to take courses in computer science, English, humanities, mathematics, biological/physical sciences, social sciences.

FRESHMAN ADMISSIONS. Selection criteria: Open admissions. **Test requirements:** ASSET test required of all first-time freshmen, used for placement.

1992 FRESHMAN CLASS PROFILE. 3,386 men and women enrolled. **Characteristics:** 99% from in state, 100% commute, 37% have minority backgrounds, 1% are foreign students. Average age is 18.

FALL-TERM APPLICATIONS. No fee. No closing date; applicants notified on a rolling basis.

STUDENT LIFE. Activities: Student government, student newspaper, choral groups, dance, drama, jazz band, music ensembles, musical theater, Phi Theta Kappa.

ATHLETICS. NJCAA. **Intercollegiate:** Baseball M, basketball, fencing M, golf M, softball W.

STUDENT SERVICES. Aptitude testing, career counseling, freshman orientation, on-campus day care, personal counseling, veterans counselor, services/facilities for handicapped.

ANNUAL EXPENSES. Tuition and fees (projected): $1,095, $675 additional for out-of-state students. **Books and supplies:** $450. **Other expenses:** $200.

FINANCIAL AID. 30% of freshmen, 42% of continuing students receive some form of aid. All grants, 62% of jobs based on need. 875 enrolled freshmen were judged to have need, 869 were offered aid. Academic, music/drama, art, athletic, leadership, minority scholarships available. **Aid applications:** No closing date; priority given to applications received by June 30; applicants notified on a rolling basis beginning on or about July 30.

ADDRESS/TELEPHONE. Joan C. Kempster, Assistant Dean of Student Services, Shelton State Community College, 202 Skyland Boulevard, Tuscaloosa, AL 35405. (205) 759-1541. Fax: (205) 759-2495.

Shoals Community College
Muscle Shoals, Alabama — CB code: 0188

2-year public community, technical college, coed. Founded in 1966. **Accreditation:** Regional candidate. **Undergraduate enrollment:** 2,669 men and women. **Faculty:** 89 total (50 full time), 6 with doctorates or other terminal degrees. **Location:** Suburban campus in large town; 120 miles from Birmingham, 134 miles from Memphis, Tennessee. **Calendar:** Quarter. **Microcomputers:** Located in libraries, computer centers.

DEGREES OFFERED. AA, AS, AAS. 78 associate degrees awarded in 1992. 5% in business and management, 10% business/office and marketing/distribution, 18% computer sciences, 12% education, 13% teacher education, 20% engineering technologies, 12% allied health, 10% multi/interdisciplinary studies.

UNDERGRADUATE MAJORS. Agricultural sciences, biomedical equipment technology, business administration and management, chemical manufacturing technology, clinical laboratory science, computer and information sciences, computer programming, criminal justice studies, criminal justice technology, data processing, drafting and design technology, early childhood education, education, electronic technology, emergency medical technologies, engineering, fire control and safety technology, forestry and related sciences, laser electro-optic technology, liberal/general studies, medical assistant, medical laboratory technologies, medical records technology, mental health/human services, music, occupational therapy assistant, office supervision and management, physical therapy assistant, physician's assistant, predentistry, prelaw, premedicine, prepharmacy, presecondary education, preveterinary, radiograph medical technology, respiratory therapy, respiratory therapy technology, secretarial and related programs, ultrasound technology, water and wastewater technology.

ACADEMIC PROGRAMS. 2-year transfer program, cooperative education, dual enrollment of high school students, internships, weekend college, cross-registration. **Remedial services:** Learning center, preadmission summer program, remedial instruction, tutoring. **Placement/credit:** AP, CLEP General and Subject, institutional tests.

ACADEMIC REQUIREMENTS. Freshmen must earn minimum GPA of 2.0 to continue in good standing. Students must declare major on application. **Graduation requirements:** 96 hours for associate (60 in major). Most students required to take courses in arts/fine arts, English, humanities, mathematics, biological/physical sciences, social sciences.

FRESHMAN ADMISSIONS. Selection criteria: Open admissions. **High school preparation:** 22 units recommended. Recommended units include biological science 1, English 4, mathematics 2, physical science 1, social science 3 and science 2. High school diploma or GED required for all associate degree programs.

1992 FRESHMAN CLASS PROFILE. 1,036 men and women enrolled. **Characteristics:** 99% from in state, 100% commute.

FALL-TERM APPLICATIONS. $10 fee. No closing date; applicants notified on a rolling basis. Early admission available.

STUDENT LIFE. Activities: Student government, student newspaper, yearbook, music ensembles, Rotaract, Leaders of the Future, Phi Theta Kappa.

ATHLETICS. NJCAA. **Intercollegiate:** Basketball.

STUDENT SERVICES. Aptitude testing, career counseling, employment service for undergraduates, freshman orientation, on-campus day care, personal counseling, placement service for graduates, veterans counselor, services/facilities for handicapped.

ANNUAL EXPENSES. Tuition and fees (1992-93): $1,116, $668 additional for out-of-state students. **Books and supplies:** $405. **Other expenses:** $900.

FINANCIAL AID. 40% of freshmen, 45% of continuing students re-

ceive some form of aid. 83% of grants, all loans, all jobs based on need. 350 enrolled freshmen were judged to have need, all were offered aid. Academic, music/drama, athletic, state/district residency, leadership scholarships available. **Aid applications:** No closing date; priority given to applications received by June 1; applicants notified on a rolling basis beginning on or about August 1.

ADDRESS/TELEPHONE. Jean Love, Director of Admissions and Records, Shoals Community College, PO Box 2545, Muscle Shoals, AL 35662. (205) 381-2813. Fax: (205) 381-2813 ext. 341.

Snead State Community College
Boaz, Alabama CB code: 1721

2-year public community college, coed. Founded in 1898. **Accreditation:** Regional. **Undergraduate enrollment:** 536 men, 620 women full time; 198 men, 361 women part time. **Faculty:** 72 total (35 full time), 10 with doctorates or other terminal degrees. **Location:** Rural campus in small town; 65 miles from Birmingham, 60 miles from Huntsville. **Calendar:** Quarter, limited summer session. Saturday classes. **Microcomputers:** Located in classrooms, computer centers.

DEGREES OFFERED. AA, AS, AAS. 180 associate degrees awarded in 1992. 18% in business and management, 7% business/office and marketing/distribution, 11% computer sciences, 56% education, 7% health sciences.

UNDERGRADUATE MAJORS. Agribusiness, agricultural business and management, agricultural education, agricultural sciences, allied health, art education, biology, business administration and management, business and management, business and office, business data processing and related programs, chemistry, computer and information sciences, criminal justice studies, data processing, early childhood education, education, electronic technology, elementary education, engineering, engineering and engineering-related technologies, finance, fine arts, fire control and safety technology, forestry and related sciences, law enforcement and corrections technologies, liberal/general studies, mathematics, music, music performance, office supervision and management, physical education, physics, predentistry, prelaw, premedicine, prenursing, real estate, secondary education, secretarial and related programs, special education, veterinarian's assistant.

ACADEMIC PROGRAMS. 2-year transfer program, accelerated program, dual enrollment of high school students, internships, telecourses, 2-year degree programs in allied health available requiring 1 year study at University of Alabama in Birmingham. **Remedial services:** Remedial instruction. **Placement/credit:** AP, CLEP Subject, institutional tests; 30 credit hours maximum for associate degree.

ACADEMIC REQUIREMENTS. Freshmen must earn minimum GPA of 1.75 to continue in good standing. 50% of freshmen return for sophomore year. Students must declare major on enrollment. **Graduation requirements:** 96 hours for associate. Most students required to take courses in English, history, humanities, mathematics, biological/physical sciences, social sciences.

FRESHMAN ADMISSIONS. Selection criteria: Open admissions. Veterinary technician applicants must pass personal interview for admission.

1992 FRESHMAN CLASS PROFILE. 325 men applied, 325 accepted, 215 enrolled; 366 women applied, 366 accepted, 211 enrolled. **Characteristics:** 99% from in state, 95% commute, 1% have minority backgrounds.

FALL-TERM APPLICATIONS. No fee. Closing date September 10; applicants notified on a rolling basis. Deferred admission available. No international students are admitted.

STUDENT LIFE. Housing: Dormitories (men, women). **Activities:** Student government, student newspaper, choral groups, concert band, jazz band, music ensembles, Action Group for Christ, New Beginnings Club, Canterbury Club.

ATHLETICS. NJCAA. **Intercollegiate:** Baseball M, basketball, golf M, softball W, tennis, volleyball W. **Intramural:** Basketball M.

STUDENT SERVICES. Aptitude testing, career counseling, freshman orientation, personal counseling, veterans counselor, services/facilities for handicapped.

ANNUAL EXPENSES. Tuition and fees (projected): $1,101, $720 additional for out-of-state students. **Room and board:** $1,643. **Books and supplies:** $450. **Other expenses:** $700.

FINANCIAL AID. 65% of freshmen, 30% of continuing students receive some form of aid. All grants, all jobs based on need. Academic, music/drama, art, athletic scholarships available. **Aid applications:** No closing date; priority given to applications received by April 15; applicants notified on a rolling basis beginning on or about August 15; must reply within 10 days.

ADDRESS/TELEPHONE. Joan R. Osborn, Director of Admissions and Records, Snead State Community College, PO Drawer D, 220 Walnut Street West, Boaz, AL 35957. (205) 593-5120 ext. 209. Fax: (205) 593-7180.

Southeastern Bible College
Birmingham, Alabama CB code: 1723

4-year private Bible college, coed, nondenominational. Founded in 1935. **Undergraduate enrollment:** 61 men, 48 women full time; 15 men, 14 women part time. **Faculty:** 21 total (13 full time), 9 with doctorates or other terminal degrees. **Location:** Suburban campus in large city; 120 miles from Hunstville, 55 miles from Tuscalossa. **Calendar:** Semester, limited summer session. **Microcomputers:** 10 located in libraries. **Special facilities:** Homiletics (preaching) video laboratory.

DEGREES OFFERED. AA, BA, BS, MA. 3 associate degrees awarded in 1992. 100% in philosophy, religion, theology. 12 bachelor's degrees awarded. 30% in teacher education, 70% philosophy, religion, theology. Graduate degrees offered in 2 major fields of study.

UNDERGRADUATE MAJORS. Associate: Bible studies, liberal/general studies. **Bachelor's:** Bible studies, elementary education, missionary studies, physical education, religious education, religious music, secondary education, theological studies.

ACADEMIC PROGRAMS. Double major, external degree, independent study, teacher preparation. **Remedial services:** Reduced course load, remedial instruction, tutoring. **Placement/credit:** AP, CLEP General, institutional tests; 15 credit hours maximum for associate degree; 30 credit hours maximum for bachelor's degree.

ACADEMIC REQUIREMENTS. Freshmen must earn minimum GPA of 2.0 to continue in good standing. 65% of freshmen return for sophomore year. Students must declare major by end of first year. **Graduation requirements:** 64 hours for associate (20 in major), 128 hours for bachelor's (30 in major). Most students required to take courses in English, history, humanities, philosophy/religion, biological/physical sciences, social sciences. **Postgraduate studies:** 50% from 2-year programs enter 4-year programs. 25% enter other graduate study.

FRESHMAN ADMISSIONS. Selection criteria: Minimum 2.0 GPA required. Serious commitment to Christian life and service, 3 recommendations important. **High school preparation:** 16 units recommended. Recommended units include biological science 1, English 4, foreign language 2, mathematics 1, physical science 1 and social science 1. **Test requirements:** SAT or ACT (ACT preferred); score report by August 20.

1992 FRESHMAN CLASS PROFILE. 16 men, 7 women enrolled. 15% had high school GPA of 3.0 or higher, 60% between 2.0 and 2.99. **Academic background:** Mid 50% of enrolled freshmen had ACT composite between 19-28. 80% submitted ACT scores. **Characteristics:** 50% from in state, 50% commute, 10% have minority backgrounds, 5% are foreign students. Average age is 23.

FALL-TERM APPLICATIONS. $20 fee. Closing date August 15; applicants notified on a rolling basis; must reply by May 1 or within 2 weeks if notified thereafter. Essay required. Interview recommended. CRDA. Deferred admission available. EDP-F.

STUDENT LIFE. Housing: Dormitories (men, women); apartment housing available. **Activities:** Student government, yearbook, choral groups, music ensembles, Student Missions Fellowship. **Additional information:** Religious observance required.

ATHLETICS. Intercollegiate: Basketball. **Intramural:** Baseball, basketball, softball, volleyball.

STUDENT SERVICES. Career counseling, employment service for undergraduates, freshman orientation, health services, personal counseling, placement service for graduates, services/facilities for handicapped.

ANNUAL EXPENSES. Tuition and fees: $4,050. **Room and board:** $2,700. **Books and supplies:** $300. **Other expenses:** $1,500.

FINANCIAL AID. 81% of freshmen, 65% of continuing students receive some form of aid. Grants, loans, jobs available. Academic, music/drama, state/district residency, leadership scholarships available. **Aid applications:** Closing date September 8; priority given to applications received by May 30; applicants notified on a rolling basis; must reply by May 1 or within 2 weeks if notified thereafter.

ADDRESS/TELEPHONE. Leon W. Gillaspie, Dean of Admissions and Records, Southeastern Bible College, 3001 Highway 280 East, Birmingham, AL 35243-4181. (205) 969-0880. (800) 749-8878. Fax: (205) 969-0880 ext. 207.

Southern Christian University
Montgomery, Alabama CB code: 7001

2-year upper-division private seminary college, coed, affiliated with Church of Christ. **Accreditation:** Regional. **Undergraduate enrollment:** 8 men, 2 women full time; 40 men, 9 women part time. **Graduate enrollment:** 13 men, 1 woman full time; 27 men, 6 women part time. **Faculty:** 34 total (11 full time), 13 with doctorates or other terminal degrees. **Location:** Suburban campus in small city; 100 miles from Birmingham, 150 miles from Atlanta, Georgia. **Calendar:** Quarter. **Microcomputers:** Located in libraries. **Special facilities:** Archelogy laboratory.

DEGREES OFFERED. BA, BS, MA, MS, M.Div. 10 bachelor's degrees awarded in 1992. 100% in philosophy, religion, theology. Graduate degrees offered in 2 major fields of study.

UNDERGRADUATE MAJORS. Religion.

ACADEMIC PROGRAMS. Independent study, internships.

ACADEMIC REQUIREMENTS. Graduation requirements: 192 hours for bachelor's. Most students required to take courses in computer science, English, history, humanities, mathematics, philosophy/religion, biological/physical sciences, social sciences. **Postgraduate studies:** 50% enter other graduate study.

STUDENT LIFE. 1992 freshman class profile: 100% commute. **Activities:** Student government, Christian Student Center. **Additional information:** Religious observance required.

STUDENT SERVICES. Aptitude testing, career counseling, health services, personal counseling, placement service for graduates, veterans counselor.

ANNUAL EXPENSES. Tuition and fees: $5,420. **Books and supplies:** $633. **Other expenses:** $3,602.

FINANCIAL AID. 90% of freshmen, 98% of continuing students receive some form of aid. 73% of grants, 98% of loans, all jobs based on need. 7 enrolled freshmen were judged to have need, all were offered aid. Academic scholarships available. **Aid applications:** Closing date July 30; priority given to applications received by May 30; applicants notified on or about September 1. **Additional information:** Scholarships based on need and grades.

ADDRESS/TELEPHONE. Mac Adkins, Director of Student Services, Southern Christian University, 1200 Taylor Road, Montgomery, AL 36117-3553. (205) 277-2277. (800) 351-4040. Fax: (205) 271-0002.

Southern Union State Junior College
Wadley, Alabama CB code: 1728

2-year public junior college, coed. Founded in 1922. **Accreditation:** Regional. **Undergraduate enrollment:** 3,334 men and women. **Faculty:** 167 total (52 full time), 13 with doctorates or other terminal degrees. **Location:** Rural campus in rural community; 100 miles from Birmingham and Atlanta, Georgia. **Calendar:** Quarter, extensive summer session. **Microcomputers:** Located in classrooms, computer centers.

DEGREES OFFERED. AA, AS, AAS. 285 associate degrees awarded in 1992.

UNDERGRADUATE MAJORS. Business and management, data processing, education, emergency medical technologies, finance, fine arts, legal secretary, liberal/general studies, medical assistant, medical records technology, medical secretary, nursing, occupational therapy assistant, office supervision and management, physical therapy assistant, respiratory therapy technology, secretarial and related programs, word processing.

ACADEMIC PROGRAMS. 2-year transfer program, dual enrollment of high school students. **Remedial services:** Learning center, remedial instruction, tutoring. **Placement/credit:** AP, CLEP General and Subject, institutional tests.

ACADEMIC REQUIREMENTS. Freshmen must earn minimum GPA of 1.5 to continue in good standing. Students must declare major by end of first year. **Graduation requirements:** 96 hours for associate. Most students required to take courses in arts/fine arts, English, history, mathematics, biological/physical sciences, social sciences.

FRESHMAN ADMISSIONS. Selection criteria: Open admissions. Selective admissions to nursing program. **Test requirements:** ACT required of nursing applicants.

1992 FRESHMAN CLASS PROFILE. 418 men, 547 women enrolled. **Characteristics:** 98% from in state, 92% commute, 17% have minority backgrounds.

FALL-TERM APPLICATIONS. No fee. No closing date; applicants notified on a rolling basis. Deferred admission available.

STUDENT LIFE. Housing: Dormitories (men, women). **Activities:** Student government, student newspaper, choral groups, dance, drama, jazz band, music ensembles, musical theater, opera.

ATHLETICS. NJCAA. **Intercollegiate:** Baseball M, basketball, cross-country, softball W, volleyball W. **Intramural:** Archery, basketball, softball, swimming, tennis, volleyball.

STUDENT SERVICES. Career counseling, freshman orientation, health services, personal counseling, veterans counselor, services/facilities for handicapped.

ANNUAL EXPENSES. Tuition and fees (projected): $1,116, $693 additional for out-of-state students. Out-of-state tuition waiver available to Georgia residents residing in Harris, Troup, Heard, Muscogee and Carroll counties. **Room and board:** $1,950. **Books and supplies:** $435. **Other expenses:** $1,100.

FINANCIAL AID. 49% of freshmen, 17% of continuing students receive some form of aid. 76% of grants, 63% of loans, 51% of jobs based on need. **Aid applications:** No closing date; priority given to applications received by April 1; applicants notified on a rolling basis beginning on or about June 1; must reply within 2 weeks.

ADDRESS/TELEPHONE. Susan Elliott-Salatto, Director of Enrollment Services, Southern Union State Junior College, Roberts Street, Wadley, AL 36276. (205) 395-2211 ext. 120. Fax: (205) 395-2215.

Sparks State Technical College
Eufaula, Alabama CB code: 0103

2-year public technical college, coed. Founded in 1966. **Accreditation:** Regional. **Undergraduate enrollment:** 510 men and women full time; 110 men and women part time. **Faculty:** 32 total (24 full time). **Location:** Rural campus in small town; located in Eufaula, Alabama. **Calendar:** Quarter.

DEGREES OFFERED. 30 associate degrees awarded in 1992. 14% in architecture and environmental design, 43% business and management, 25% computer sciences, 18% engineering technologies.

UNDERGRADUATE MAJORS. Accounting, drafting, drafting and design technology, electrical technology, electronic technology.

ACADEMIC PROGRAMS. Cooperative education. **Remedial services:** Remedial instruction, tutoring.

ACADEMIC REQUIREMENTS. Students must declare major on enrollment.

FRESHMAN ADMISSIONS. Selection criteria: Open admissions. Practical nursing applicants must pass entrance examination.

STUDENT LIFE. Activities: Student government.

STUDENT SERVICES. Career counseling, freshman orientation, on-campus day care, personal counseling, services/facilities for handicapped.

ANNUAL EXPENSES. Tuition and fees (1992-93): $1,056. **Books and supplies:** $790.

ADDRESS/TELEPHONE. Director of Student Services, SparksState Technical College, P.O. Drawer 580, Eufaula, AL 36072-0580. (205) 687-3543 ext.228. Fax: (205) 687-0255.

Spring Hill College
Mobile, Alabama CB code: 1733

Admissions: 83% of applicants accepted
Based on: ••• School record
•• Recommendations, test scores
• Activities, essay, interview, special talents
Completion: 89% of freshmen end year in good standing
55% graduate, 35% of these enter graduate study

4-year private liberal arts college, coed, affiliated with Roman Catholic Church. Founded in 1830. **Accreditation:** Regional. **Undergraduate enrollment:** 427 men, 522 women full time; 64 men, 134 women part time. **Graduate enrollment:** 3 men, 7 women full time; 54 men, 122 women part time. **Faculty:** 84 total (60 full time), 62 with doctorates or other terminal degrees. **Location:** Suburban campus in small city; 140 miles from New Orleans, Louisiana, 60 miles from Pensacola, Florida. **Calendar:** Semester, limited summer session. **Microcomputers:** 90 located in libraries, classrooms, computer centers. **Special facilities:** 18-hole golf course, national historical buildings. **Additional facts:** Institution in the Jesuit tradition. First institution of higher education in Alabama.

DEGREES OFFERED. AS, BA, BS, MA, MS, MBA, MEd. 197 bachelor's degrees awarded. 20% in business and management, 16% communications, 8% letters/literature, 6% life sciences, 13% multi/interdisciplinary studies, 9% psychology, 14% social sciences, 5% visual and performing arts. Graduate degrees offered in 5 major fields of study.

UNDERGRADUATE MAJORS. Associate: Legal assistant/paralegal. **Bachelor's:** Accounting, advertising, art therapy, arts management, biology, business administration and management, business chemistry, business economics, chemistry, communications, creative writing, early childhood education, elementary education, English, English education, finance, fine arts, foreign languages education, history, humanities, humanities and social sciences, information sciences and systems, international business management, international relations, international studies, journalism, junior high education, liberal/general studies, management information systems, marine biology, marketing management, mathematics, mathematics education, philosophy, political science and government, predentistry, preengineering, prelaw, premedicine, psychology, public relations, radio/television broadcasting, science education, secondary education, social science education, sociology, studio art, theological studies.

ACADEMIC PROGRAMS. Accelerated program, double major, dual enrollment of high school students, honors program, independent study, internships, student-designed major, study abroad, teacher preparation, United Nations semester, Washington semester, Human Relations Institute programs in management and race relations; marine biology majors take credit courses at Dauphin Island Sea Laboratory of the Marine Environmental Sciences Consortium; liberal arts/career combination in engineering; combined bachelor's/graduate program in business administration. **Remedial services:** Learning center, preadmission summer program, reduced course load, special counselor, tutoring, 6-week summer development session. **ROTC:** Air Force, Army. **Placement/credit:** AP, CLEP General and Subject, institutional tests; 30 credit hours maximum for bachelor's degree.

ACADEMIC REQUIREMENTS. Freshmen must earn minimum GPA of 2.0 to continue in good standing. 76% of freshmen return for sophomore year. Students must declare major by end of second year. **Graduation requirements:** 68 hours for associate (34 in major), 128 hours for bachelor's

(40 in major). Most students required to take courses in arts/fine arts, computer science, English, foreign languages, history, humanities, mathematics, philosophy/religion, biological/physical sciences, social sciences. **Postgraduate studies:** 8% enter law school, 7% enter medical school, 5% enter MBA programs, 15% enter other graduate study. **Additional information:** Office of Career Services offers extensive internship programs for students in most majors.

FRESHMAN ADMISSIONS. Selection criteria: High school record most important. Test scores, guidance counselor recommendation, essay, and interview considered. **High school preparation:** 16 units required. Required and recommended units include English 4, mathematics 2-3, social science 2 and science 2-3. Foreign language 2 recommended. **Test requirements:** SAT or ACT; score report by August 15.

1992 FRESHMAN CLASS PROFILE. 380 men applied, 312 accepted, 128 enrolled; 520 women applied, 438 accepted, 172 enrolled. 38% had high school GPA of 3.0 or higher, 57% between 2.0 and 2.99. 57% were in top quarter of graduating class. **Academic background:** Mid 50% of enrolled freshmen had SAT-V between 400-540, SAT-M between 420-560; ACT composite between 21-25. 33% submitted SAT scores, 67% submitted ACT scores. **Characteristics:** 35% from in state, 95% live in college housing, 15% have minority backgrounds, 1% are foreign students, 30% join fraternities/sororities. Average age is 18.

FALL-TERM APPLICATIONS. $30 fee, may be waived for applicants with need. No closing date; applicants notified on a rolling basis; must reply by May 1 or within 2 weeks if notified thereafter. Interview recommended. Portfolio recommended for art applicants. Essay recommended. CRDA. Deferred and early admission available.

STUDENT LIFE. Housing: Dormitories (men, women, coed); apartment housing available. All undergraduate students (except seniors) required to live on campus unless living with relatives or approved by Dean of Students. **Activities:** Student government, film, magazine, radio, student newspaper, television, yearbook, choral groups, dance, drama, music ensembles, musical theater, fraternities, sororities, Society for the Advancement of Management, Spring Hill Ocean Research and Exploration Society, Spring Hill Awakening Program, Christian Life Community, College Republicans, Interhall Council.

ATHLETICS. NAIA. **Intercollegiate:** Baseball M, basketball, cross-country, golf, tennis. **Intramural:** Baseball M, basketball, bowling, field hockey M, football M, golf, rugby M, sailing, soccer, softball, swimming, tennis, volleyball. **Clubs:** Sailing club.

STUDENT SERVICES. Aptitude testing, career counseling, employment service for undergraduates, freshman orientation, health services, personal counseling, placement service for graduates, special adviser for adult students, services/facilities for handicapped.

ANNUAL EXPENSES. Tuition and fees: $11,425. All tuition on per hour basis. **Room and board:** $4,590. **Books and supplies:** $550. **Other expenses:** $900.

FINANCIAL AID. 76% of freshmen, 68% of continuing students receive some form of aid. 52% of grants, 68% of loans, all jobs based on need. 177 enrolled freshmen were judged to have need, all were offered aid. Academic, athletic, state/district residency, alumni affiliation, minority scholarships available. **Aid applications:** No closing date; priority given to applications received by March 1; applicants notified on a rolling basis beginning on or about March 1; must reply by May 1 or within 2 weeks if notified thereafter. **Additional information:** PLUS loans and other long-term low-interest loans available to parents.

ADDRESS/TELEPHONE. Tim Williams, Director of Admissions, Spring Hill College, 4000 Dauphin Street, Mobile, AL 36608. (205) 460-2130. Fax: (205) 460-2095.

Stillman College

Tuscaloosa, Alabama — CB code: 1739

4-year private liberal arts college, coed, affiliated with Presbyterian Church (USA). Founded in 1876. **Accreditation:** Regional. **Undergraduate enrollment:** 260 men, 606 women full time; 11 men, 11 women part time. **Faculty:** 73 total (53 full time), 36 with doctorates or other terminal degrees. **Location:** Suburban campus in small city; 60 miles from Birmingham. **Calendar:** Semester, limited summer session. **Microcomputers:** 70 located in libraries, computer centers. **Special facilities:** Art gallery, learning centers in dormitories, learning resources center, telecommunications center.

DEGREES OFFERED. BA, BS. 114 bachelor's degrees awarded in 1992. 32% in business and management, 14% communications, 6% computer sciences, 11% teacher education, 6% letters/literature, 8% life sciences, 16% social sciences.

UNDERGRADUATE MAJORS. Biology, business and management, chemistry, communications, computer and information sciences, elementary education, English, history, international studies, mathematics, music, parks and recreation management, physics, religion, sociology, Spanish.

ACADEMIC PROGRAMS. Cooperative education, double major, honors program, independent study, internships, teacher preparation, cross-registration, cooperative programs with Indiana University, University of Alabama, and University of Alabama at Birmingham; liberal arts/career combination in engineering, health sciences. **Remedial services:** Learning center, reduced course load, remedial instruction, special counselor, tutoring. **ROTC:** Air Force, Army. **Placement/credit:** AP, CLEP General and Subject, institutional tests; 30 credit hours maximum for bachelor's degree.

ACADEMIC REQUIREMENTS. Freshmen must earn minimum GPA of 1.6 to continue in good standing. 62% of freshmen return for sophomore year. Students must declare major by end of second year. **Graduation requirements:** 124 hours for bachelor's (30 in major). Most students required to take courses in computer science, English, history, humanities, mathematics, philosophy/religion, biological/physical sciences, social sciences.

FRESHMAN ADMISSIONS. Selection criteria: School achievement record important. **High school preparation:** 15 units required. Required units include English 4, mathematics 1, social science 1 and science 1. **Test requirements:** SAT or ACT (ACT preferred) for placement.

1992 FRESHMAN CLASS PROFILE. 76 men, 177 women enrolled. 16% had high school GPA of 3.0 or higher, 44% between 2.0 and 2.99. **Characteristics:** 75% from in state, 95% live in college housing, 99% have minority backgrounds. Average age is 18.

FALL-TERM APPLICATIONS. $10 fee, may be waived for applicants with need. Closing date August 1; priority given to applications received by May 1; applicants notified on a rolling basis. Early admission available.

STUDENT LIFE. Housing: Dormitories (men, women). **Activities:** Student government, radio, student newspaper, yearbook, choral groups, concert band, drama, music ensembles, fraternities, sororities, Christian Student Association, Chancellorettes, Chancellors.

ATHLETICS. NCAA. **Intercollegiate:** Baseball M, basketball, cross-country M, tennis. **Intramural:** Bowling, softball, volleyball.

STUDENT SERVICES. Career counseling, employment service for undergraduates, freshman orientation, health services, personal counseling, placement service for graduates, veterans counselor.

ANNUAL EXPENSES. Tuition and fees: $4,460. **Room and board:** $2,629. **Books and supplies:** $500. **Other expenses:** $1,000.

FINANCIAL AID. 90% of freshmen, 90% of continuing students receive some form of aid. 82% of grants, 94% of loans, all jobs based on need. Academic, music/drama, state/district residency, leadership, religious affiliation scholarships available. **Aid applications:** No closing date; priority given to applications received by June 15; applicants notified on a rolling basis; must reply within 2 weeks.

ADDRESS/TELEPHONE. Barbara K. Smith, Director of Admissions/Registrar, Stillman College, PO Box 1430, 3600 Stillman Boulevard, Tuscaloosa, AL 35403. (205) 349-4240 ext. 346/347. (800) 841-5722 ext. 346/347. Fax: (205) 758-0821.

Talladega College

Talladega, Alabama — CB code: 1800

4-year private liberal arts college, coed, affiliated with the United Church of Christ. Founded in 1867. **Accreditation:** Regional. **Undergraduate enrollment:** 309 men, 524 women full time; 73 men, 12 women part time. **Faculty:** 65 total (49 full time), 31 with doctorates or other terminal degrees. **Location:** Rural campus in large town; 55 miles from Birmingham, 120 miles from Atlanta, Georgia. **Calendar:** Semester. **Microcomputers:** 45 located in libraries, computer centers. **Special facilities:** Campus is national historic district. **Additional facts:** Credit-bearing satellite program at Federal Correctional Institution.

DEGREES OFFERED. BA. 95 bachelor's degrees awarded in 1992. 26% in business and management, 13% education, 10% letters/literature, 14% life sciences, 8% mathematics, 12% physical sciences, 13% social sciences.

UNDERGRADUATE MAJORS. Biological and physical sciences, biology, business administration and management, business and management, business economics, chemistry, communications, computer and information sciences, economics, education of the deaf and hearing impaired, education of the physically handicapped, education of the visually handicapped, English, finance, history, humanities and social sciences, journalism, mathematics, mathematics education, music, music education, music performance, physics, psychology, public administration, science education, secondary education, social work, sociology.

ACADEMIC PROGRAMS. Cooperative education, independent study, internships, study abroad; liberal arts/career combination in engineering, health sciences. **Remedial services:** Learning center, reduced course load, remedial instruction, special counselor, tutoring. **ROTC:** Army. **Placement/credit:** CLEP General, institutional tests; 12 credit hours maximum for bachelor's degree.

ACADEMIC REQUIREMENTS. Freshmen must earn minimum GPA of 2.25 to continue in good standing. 75% of freshmen return for sophomore year. Students must declare major by end of second year. **Graduation requirements:** 124 hours for bachelor's (30 in major). Most students required to take courses in English, humanities, mathematics, biological/physical sciences, social sciences. **Postgraduate studies:** 2% enter law school, 4% enter medical school, 3% enter MBA programs, 18% enter other graduate study.

FRESHMAN ADMISSIONS. Selection criteria: Rank in top half of graduating class and minimum ACT composite score of 13 or SAT combined score of 700 or 2.35 GPA required. **High school preparation:** 16 units required. Required and recommended units include biological science 3, English 4, mathematics 3-4, physical science 2 and social science 3-4. Science 4 recommended. **Test requirements:** SAT or ACT (ACT preferred); score report by March 1.

1992 FRESHMAN CLASS PROFILE. 120 men, 224 women enrolled. 30% had high school GPA of 3.0 or higher, 55% between 2.0 and 2.99. **Academic background:** Mid 50% of enrolled freshmen had ACT composite between 12-17. 100% submitted ACT scores. **Characteristics:** 61% from in state, 90% live in college housing, 98% have minority backgrounds. Average age is 18.

FALL-TERM APPLICATIONS. $10 fee. No closing date; priority given to applications received by August 1; applicants notified on a rolling basis; must reply within 4 weeks. Audition required for music applicants. Early admission available. EDP-F.

STUDENT LIFE. Housing: Dormitories (men, women). **Activities:** Student government, student newspaper, yearbook, choral groups, concert band, dance, drama, jazz band, music ensembles, fraternities, sororities.

ATHLETICS. NAIA. **Intercollegiate:** Baseball M, basketball, golf M, tennis, track and field. **Intramural:** Baseball, softball, swimming, tennis, volleyball.

STUDENT SERVICES. Career counseling, employment service for undergraduates, health services, personal counseling, placement service for graduates.

ANNUAL EXPENSES. Tuition and fees: $5,584. **Room and board:** $2,664. **Books and supplies:** $600. **Other expenses:** $500.

FINANCIAL AID. 82% of freshmen, 72% of continuing students receive some form of aid. 99% of grants, all loans, all jobs based on need. Academic, athletic scholarships available. **Aid applications:** Closing date June 10; priority given to applications received by April 1; applicants notified on or about July 1; must reply within 2 weeks.

ADDRESS/TELEPHONE. Mr. Monroe Thornton, Director of Admissions, Talladega College, 627 West Battle Street, Talladega, AL 35160. (205) 362-0206. (800) 633-2440. Fax: (205) 362-2268.

Trenholm State Technical College
Montgomery, Alabama — CB code: 0207

2-year public technical college, coed. Founded in 1966. **Accreditation:** Regional. **Undergraduate enrollment:** 962 men and women. **Faculty:** 54 total (43 full time), 4 with doctorates or other terminal degrees. **Location:** Urban campus in small city. **Calendar:** Quarter. **Microcomputers:** Located in classrooms, computer centers.

DEGREES OFFERED. AA. 51 associate degrees awarded in 1992. 21% in business/office and marketing/distribution, 47% allied health, 32% trade and industry.

UNDERGRADUATE MAJORS. Accounting, business and office, electrical and electronics equipment repair, electrical technology, food production/management/services, food sciences, legal secretary, medical records administration, medical records technology, medical secretary, word processing.

ACADEMIC PROGRAMS. Cooperative education, internships, weekend college. **Remedial services:** Learning center, reduced course load, remedial instruction, special counselor, tutoring. **Placement/credit:** CLEP General and Subject, institutional tests.

ACADEMIC REQUIREMENTS. Freshmen must earn minimum GPA of 2.0 to continue in good standing. 85% of freshmen return for sophomore year. Students must declare major on application. **Graduation requirements:** 73 hours for associate (73 in major).

FRESHMAN ADMISSIONS. Selection criteria: Open admissions. Applicants for Health Services Technologies Division may submit ACT of 16 or better in lieu of failed ASSET examination (required of all applicants). Minimum scores of 16 in mathematics and 20 in reading required. **Test requirements:** SAT or ACT required for allied health students for admissions, placement, and counseling.

1992 FRESHMAN CLASS PROFILE. 595 men and women enrolled. **Characteristics:** 100% from in state, 100% commute, 85% have minority backgrounds. Average age is 27.

FALL-TERM APPLICATIONS. No fee. No closing date; applicants notified on a rolling basis beginning on or about July 31. Essay recommended for health services applicants. Interview required for dental assistant applicants, recommended for practical nursing applicants. ASSET recommended.

STUDENT LIFE. Activities: Student government, radio, student newspaper.

ATHLETICS. Intramural: Basketball, softball, volleyball.

STUDENT SERVICES. Aptitude testing, career counseling, on-campus day care, personal counseling, special adviser for adult students, veterans counselor, services/facilities for handicapped.

ANNUAL EXPENSES. Tuition and fees (projected): $1,125, $675 additional for out-of-state students. **Books and supplies:** $575. **Other expenses:** $350.

FINANCIAL AID. 20% of freshmen, 60% of continuing students receive some form of aid. Grants available. **Aid applications:** No closing date; priority given to applications received by August 18; applicants notified on a rolling basis.

ADDRESS/TELEPHONE. Admissions Office, Trenholm State Technical College, 1225 Air Base Boulevard, Montgomery, AL 36108. (205) 832-9000. Fax: (205) 832-9777.

Troy State University
Troy, Alabama — CB code: 1738

Admissions: 81% of applicants accepted
Based on: ••• School record, test scores
• Activities, recommendations
Completion: 50% of freshmen end year in good standing
5% enter graduate study

4-year public university, coed. Founded in 1887. **Accreditation:** Regional. **Graduate enrollment:** 27 men, 69 women full time; 42 men, 156 women part time. **Faculty:** 196 total (171 full time). **Location:** Rural campus in large town; 50 miles from Montgomery. **Calendar:** Quarter, extensive summer session. **Microcomputers:** 120 located in classrooms, computer centers. **Additional facts:** Dedicated to providing life-long learning opportunities for adult students. Off-campus evening programs at 62 Armed Service bases in United States, Europe, Cuba, and Pacific.

DEGREES OFFERED. AA, AS, BS, MBA, MEd. 271 associate degrees awarded in 1992. 99% in health sciences. 1,410 bachelor's degrees awarded. 44% in business and management, 17% teacher education, 10% parks/recreation, protective services, public affairs, 6% social sciences. Graduate degrees offered in 12 major fields of study.

UNDERGRADUATE MAJORS. Associate: Business and office, business data processing and related programs, business data programming, law enforcement and corrections technologies, liberal/general studies, nursing, secretarial and related programs. **Bachelor's:** Accounting, art history, biology, business administration and management, business and management, business economics, chemistry, clinical laboratory science, computer and information sciences, creative writing, data processing, dramatic arts, early childhood education, earth sciences, economics, education of the emotionally handicapped, education of the mentally handicapped, elementary education, English, environmental science, finance, history, journalism, junior high education, law enforcement and corrections, marine biology, mathematics, nursing, physical sciences, political science and government, psychology, radio/television broadcasting, school psychology, secondary education, secretarial and related programs, social sciences, social work, sociology, special education, speech.

ACADEMIC PROGRAMS. Accelerated program, double major, education specialist degree, honors program, independent study, student-designed major. **Remedial services:** Learning center, preadmission summer program, reduced course load, remedial instruction, special counselor, tutoring. **ROTC:** Air Force. **Placement/credit:** CLEP General and Subject, institutional tests.

ACADEMIC REQUIREMENTS. Freshmen must earn minimum GPA of 2.0 to continue in good standing. 60% of freshmen return for sophomore year. Students must declare major by end of first year. **Graduation requirements:** 92 hours for associate (50 in major), 180 hours for bachelor's (85 in major). Most students required to take courses in English, history, mathematics, biological/physical sciences.

FRESHMAN ADMISSIONS. Selection criteria: Minimum high school GPA of 2.0 and test scores important. **High school preparation:** 11 units required. Required units include English 3. **Test requirements:** SAT or ACT; score report by September 6.

1992 FRESHMAN CLASS PROFILE. Characteristics: 82% from in state, 58% commute, 14% have minority backgrounds, 1% are foreign students, 8% join fraternities/sororities. Average age is 19.

FALL-TERM APPLICATIONS. $15 fee. No closing date; applicants notified on a rolling basis. Audition required for music education applicants. Deferred and early admission available.

STUDENT LIFE. Housing: Dormitories (men, women, coed); apartment, fraternity, sorority housing available. **Activities:** Student government, film, magazine, radio, student newspaper, television, yearbook, choral groups, concert band, dance, drama, jazz band, marching band, music ensembles, musical theater, opera, pep band, fraternities, sororities, several religious and service organizations, international student organization.

ATHLETICS. NCAA. **Intercollegiate:** Baseball M, basketball, cross-country, football M, golf, softball W, tennis M, track and field, volleyball W. **Intramural:** Basketball, cross-country, diving, field hockey W, golf, handball M, softball, swimming, tennis, track and field, volleyball W.

STUDENT SERVICES. Aptitude testing, career counseling, employment service for undergraduates, health services, on-campus day care, personal counseling, placement service for graduates, veterans counselor, services/facilities for handicapped.

ANNUAL EXPENSES. Tuition and fees (1992-93): $1,620, $1,125 additional for out-of-state students. **Room and board:** $3,021. **Books and supplies:** $500. **Other expenses:** $600.

FINANCIAL AID. 50% of freshmen, 50% of continuing students receive some form of aid. All jobs based on need. **Aid applications:** No closing date; priority given to applications received by May 1; applicants notified on a rolling basis beginning on or about May 1; must reply within 2 weeks.

ADDRESS/TELEPHONE. Jim Hutto, Dean of Enrollment Services, Troy State University, University Avenue, Troy, AL 36082. (205) 670-3179. (800) 551-9716. Fax: (205) 670-3774.

Troy State University at Dothan

Dothan, Alabama — CB code: 0346

Admissions: 90% of applicants accepted
Based on: ••• Test scores
•• School record
Completion: 91% of freshmen end year in good standing
35% enter graduate study

4-year public university, coed. Founded in 1966. **Accreditation:** Regional. **Undergraduate enrollment:** 299 men, 515 women full time; 387 men, 539 women part time. **Graduate enrollment:** 98 men, 129 women full time; 124 men, 228 women part time. **Faculty:** 118 total (54 full time), 55 with doctorates or other terminal degrees. **Location:** Urban campus in small city; 100 miles from Montgomery, 75 miles from Tallahassee, Florida. **Calendar:** Quarter, extensive summer session. Saturday and extensive evening/early morning classes. **Microcomputers:** 44 located in computer centers.

DEGREES OFFERED. AS, AAS, BA, BS, MS, MBA, MEd. 21 associate degrees awarded in 1992. 10% in business and management, 90% multi/interdisciplinary studies. 320 bachelor's degrees awarded. 45% in business and management, 27% teacher education, 7% parks/recreation, protective services, public affairs, 6% psychology, 6% social sciences. Graduate degrees offered in 14 major fields of study.

UNDERGRADUATE MAJORS. Associate: Liberal/general studies. **Bachelor's:** Biology, business administration and management, computer and information sciences, criminal justice studies, early childhood education, elementary education, English, English education, history, junior high education, mathematics, mathematics education, physical sciences, psychology, science education, secondary education, social science education, social sciences, sociology.

ACADEMIC PROGRAMS. Double major, education specialist degree, independent study, internships, teacher preparation, telecourses, weekend college. **Remedial services:** Learning center, reduced course load, remedial instruction, special counselor, tutoring. **Placement/credit:** AP, CLEP General and Subject, institutional tests; 90 credit hours maximum for bachelor's degree.

ACADEMIC REQUIREMENTS. Freshmen must earn minimum GPA of 2.0 to continue in good standing. Students must declare major by end of first year. **Graduation requirements:** 180 hours for bachelor's (90 in major). Most students required to take courses in arts/fine arts, computer science, English, history, humanities, mathematics, philosophy/religion, biological/physical sciences, social sciences.

FRESHMAN ADMISSIONS. Selection criteria: SAT combined score of 740 or ACT composite score of 16 or enhanced ACT score of 17 and high school GPA of 2.0 ensures unconditional admission. First-time freshmen are admitted at Fort Rucker branch only. Applicants over 21 years of age need only submit high school diploma or GED. **High school preparation:** 15 units required. Required units include English 3. **Test requirements:** SAT or ACT (ACT preferred); score report by September 1.

1992 FRESHMAN CLASS PROFILE. 6 men applied, 5 accepted, 2 enrolled; 4 women applied, 4 accepted, 2 enrolled. **Characteristics:** 92% from in state, 100% commute.

FALL-TERM APPLICATIONS. $15 fee. No closing date; applicants notified on a rolling basis. Deferred and early admission available.

STUDENT LIFE. Activities: Student government.

STUDENT SERVICES. Career counseling, employment service for undergraduates, freshman orientation, personal counseling, placement service for graduates, veterans counselor, services/facilities for handicapped.

ANNUAL EXPENSES. Tuition and fees: $1,697, $1,187 additional for out-of-state students. **Books and supplies:** $600. **Other expenses:** $1,380.

FINANCIAL AID. 15% of freshmen, 17% of continuing students receive some form of aid. All aid based on need. Academic, leadership scholarships available. **Aid applications:** Closing date August 1; priority given to applications received by May 1; applicants notified on a rolling basis; must reply within 2 weeks.

ADDRESS/TELEPHONE. Reta Cordell, Director of Admissions, Troy State University at Dothan, PO Box 8368, Dothan, AL 36304-0368. (205) 983-6556. Fax: (205) 983-6322.

Troy State University in Montgomery

Montgomery, Alabama — CB code: 1798

4-year public university, coed. Founded in 1965. **Accreditation:** Regional. **Undergraduate enrollment:** 251 men, 355 women full time; 928 men, 1,304 women part time. **Graduate enrollment:** 100 men, 77 women full time; 154 men, 162 women part time. **Faculty:** 168 total (28 full time). **Location:** Urban campus in small city. **Calendar:** Quarter, extensive summer session. Saturday and extensive evening/early morning classes. **Microcomputers:** 113 located in libraries, classrooms, computer centers. **Special facilities:** College-operated planetarium. **Additional facts:** Primarily an evening and weekend institution.

DEGREES OFFERED. AS, BA, BS, MA, MS, MBA. 60 associate degrees awarded in 1992. 28% in business and management, 11% computer sciences, 61% multi/interdisciplinary studies. 160 bachelor's degrees awarded. 60% in business and management, 11% computer sciences, 6% multi/interdisciplinary studies, 11% psychology, 9% social sciences. Graduate degrees offered in 11 major fields of study.

UNDERGRADUATE MAJORS. Associate: Business administration and management, computer and information sciences, finance, law enforcement and corrections technologies, liberal/general studies. **Bachelor's:** Accounting, business administration and management, business and management, computer and information sciences, English, finance, history, law enforcement and corrections, mathematics, political science and government, psychology, social sciences.

ACADEMIC PROGRAMS. Double major, education specialist degree, external degree, honors program, independent study, teacher preparation, telecourses, cross-registration. **Remedial services:** Learning center, reduced course load, remedial instruction, special counselor, tutoring. **ROTC:** Air Force, Army. **Placement/credit:** CLEP General and Subject.

ACADEMIC REQUIREMENTS. Freshmen must earn minimum GPA of 2.5 to continue in good standing. 65% of freshmen return for sophomore year. Students must declare major on enrollment. **Graduation requirements:** 95 hours for associate (30 in major), 185 hours for bachelor's (70 in major). Most students required to take courses in computer science, English, history, humanities, mathematics, biological/physical sciences, social sciences.

FRESHMAN ADMISSIONS. Selection criteria: Open admissions. **High school preparation:** 11 units required; 15 recommended. Required units include English 3. **Test requirements:** SAT or ACT (ACT preferred) for placement and counseling only; score report by September 1.

1992 FRESHMAN CLASS PROFILE. 22 men, 81 women enrolled. **Characteristics:** 100% from in state, 100% commute, 24% have minority backgrounds. Average age is 26.

FALL-TERM APPLICATIONS. $10 fee. No closing date; applicants notified on a rolling basis. Deferred admission available.

STUDENT SERVICES. Aptitude testing, career counseling, employment service for undergraduates, freshman orientation, personal counseling, placement service for graduates, special adviser for adult students, veterans counselor, services/facilities for handicapped.

ANNUAL EXPENSES. Tuition and fees (1992-93): $1,485, $1,485 additional for out-of-state students. **Books and supplies:** $625.

FINANCIAL AID. Aid applications: No closing date; applicants notified on a rolling basis.

ADDRESS/TELEPHONE. Kay Webb, Director of Admissions, Troy State University in Montgomery, PO Drawer 4419, Montgomery, AL 36103-4419. (205) 241-9508. Fax: (205) 241-9505.

Tuskegee University

Tuskegee, Alabama — CB code: 1813

Admissions: 71% of applicants accepted
Based on: ••• Essay, school record
• Activities, recommendations, test scores
Completion: 85% of freshmen end year in good standing
35% graduate, 13% of these enter graduate study

4-year private university, coed. Founded in 1881. **Accreditation:** Regional. **Undergraduate enrollment:** 1,441 men, 1,605 women full time; 76 men, 69 women part time. **Graduate enrollment:** 107 men, 156 women full time; 79 men, 65 women part time. **Faculty:** 328 total (318 full time), 219 with doctorates or other terminal degrees. **Location:** Rural campus in large town; 40 miles from Montgomery, 45 miles from Columbus, GA. **Calendar:** Semester, limited summer session. **Microcomputers:** 135 located in dormitories, libraries, classrooms, computer centers. **Special facilities:** Carver Museum, Job Corps training center, General Daniel (Chappie) James Center for Aerospace Science and Health Education. **Additional facts:** Campus is National Historic Site.

DEGREES OFFERED. BA, BS, BArch, MS, MEd, DVM. 413 bachelor's degrees awarded in 1992. 7% in agriculture, 19% business and management, 27% engineering, 6% health sciences, 7% life sciences, 5% psychology, 12% social sciences. Graduate degrees offered in 15 major fields of study.

UNDERGRADUATE MAJORS. Accounting, aerospace/aeronautical/astronautical engineering, agribusiness, animal sciences, architectural technologies, architecture, biology, biology education, business administration and management, chemical engineering, chemistry, clinical laboratory science, computer and information sciences, construction management, early childhood education, economics, education of the mentally handicapped, electrical/electronics/communications engineering, elementary education, English, finance, food science and nutrition, history, hospitality management, language arts education, management science, marketing management, mathematics, mathematics education, mechanical engineering, nursing, occupational therapy, physical education, physics, plant sciences, political science and government, poultry, psychology, science education, social work, sociology, soil sciences, technical education, textiles and clothing.

ACADEMIC PROGRAMS. Cooperative education, double major, honors program, independent study, internships, teacher preparation, engineering program with 2-year colleges; liberal arts/career combination in engineering. **Remedial services:** Learning center, preadmission summer program, reduced course load, remedial instruction, tutoring. **ROTC:** Air Force, Army. **Placement/credit:** AP, CLEP General and Subject.

ACADEMIC REQUIREMENTS. Freshmen must earn minimum GPA of 2.0 to continue in good standing. 65% of freshmen return for sophomore year. Students must declare major by end of first year. **Graduation requirements:** 124 hours for bachelor's (33 in major). Most students required to take courses in computer science, English, history, mathematics, biological/physical sciences, social sciences. **Postgraduate studies:** 1% enter law school, 2% enter medical school, 3% enter MBA programs, 7% enter other graduate study.

FRESHMAN ADMISSIONS. Selection criteria: School achievement record and test scores reviewed. Minimum SAT combined score of 800 or equivalent ACT required for engineering and nursing applicants. **High school preparation:** 16 units required. Required units include biological science 1, English 4, mathematics 3, physical science 1 and social science 3. 4 elective courses recommended. **Test requirements:** SAT or ACT (SAT preferred); score report by June 15. National League for Nursing Guidance Examination required of nursing applicants.

1992 FRESHMAN CLASS PROFILE. 3,591 men and women applied, 2,558 accepted; 361 men enrolled, 373 women enrolled. 65% had high school GPA of 3.0 or higher, 35% between 2.0 and 2.99. **Characteristics:** 25% from in state, 90% live in college housing, 88% have minority backgrounds, 8% are foreign students. Average age is 18.

FALL-TERM APPLICATIONS. $25 fee, may be waived for applicants with need. Closing date July 15; priority given to applications received by May 15; applicants notified on a rolling basis beginning on or about March 1; must reply by May 1 or within 2 weeks if notified thereafter. Essay required. Interview recommended for veterinary medicine applicants. CRDA. Deferred and early admission available.

STUDENT LIFE. Housing: Dormitories (men, women); apartment housing available. Honors dormitories available. Freshmen and sophomores not living with parents or guardians required to reside on campus. **Activities:** Student government, film, radio, student newspaper, yearbook, choral groups, concert band, dance, drama, jazz band, marching band, fraternities, sororities.

ATHLETICS. NCAA. **Intercollegiate:** Baseball M, basketball, football M, tennis, track and field, volleyball W. **Intramural:** Basketball M, rifle.

STUDENT SERVICES. Aptitude testing, career counseling, freshman orientation, health services, on-campus day care, personal counseling, placement service for graduates, veterans counselor, services/facilities for handicapped.

ANNUAL EXPENSES. Tuition and fees: $6,735. **Room and board:** $3,395. **Books and supplies:** $600. **Other expenses:** $1,125.

FINANCIAL AID. 90% of freshmen, 87% of continuing students receive some form of aid. All grants, 92% of loans, all jobs based on need. 111 enrolled freshmen were judged to have need, all were offered aid. Academic, music/drama, athletic scholarships available. **Aid applications:** Closing date March 31; priority given to applications received by March 15; applicants notified on a rolling basis beginning on or about May 15; must reply within 2 weeks.

ADDRESS/TELEPHONE. Lee Young, Admissions Officer, Tuskegee University, Tuskegee, AL 36088. (205) 727-8500. Fax: (205)727-8451.

University of Alabama
Tuscaloosa, Alabama

CB code: 1830

Admissions: 76% of applicants accepted
Based on: ••• School record, test scores
•• Interview, recommendations
Completion: 85% of freshmen end year in good standing
47% graduate

4-year public university, coed. Founded in 1831. **Accreditation:** Regional. **Undergraduate enrollment:** 6,920 men, 6,969 women full time; 722 men, 749 women part time. **Graduate enrollment:** 1,355 men, 1,538 women full time; 175 men, 356 women part time. **Faculty:** 995 total (890 full time), 792 with doctorates or other terminal degrees. **Location:** Suburban campus in small city; 55 miles from Birmingham. **Calendar:** Semester, extensive summer session. **Microcomputers:** 4,000 located in dormitories, libraries, classrooms, computer centers. **Special facilities:** Alabama Museum of Natural History, art gallery, arboretum, marine science laboratory, Mound State Monument, special collections, observatory, access to CRAY X-UP/24 supercomputer in Huntsville, simulated coal mine setting. **Additional facts:** Provides weekend college, college for continuing studies, and Gadsden Education and Research Center for graduates only

DEGREES OFFERED. BA, BS, BFA, MA, MS, MBA, MFA, MSW, PhD, EdD, MD. 2,404 bachelor's degrees awarded in 1992. 20% in business and management, 9% business/office and marketing/distribution, 12% communications, 9% teacher education, 9% engineering, 9% social sciences. Graduate degrees offered in 114 major fields of study.

UNDERGRADUATE MAJORS. Accounting, advertising, aerospace/aeronautical/astronautical engineering, American studies, anthropology, applied mathematics, archeology, art education, art history, biology, botany, business and management, business economics, business statistics, chemical engineering, chemistry, civil engineering, classics, computer and information sciences, computer engineering, criminal justice studies, dance, early childhood education, Eastern European studies, economics, education of the deaf and hearing impaired, education of the emotionally handicapped, education of the gifted and talented, education of the mentally handicapped, education of the multiple handicapped, education of the physically handicapped, electrical/electronics/communications engineering, elementary education, English, English education, English literature, family/consumer resource management, fashion design, fashion merchandising, finance, food science and nutrition, foreign languages education, French, geography, geology, German, Greek (classical), Greek (modern), health care administration, health education, history, home economics, home economics education, home furnishings and equipment management/production/services, hospitality and recreation marketing, hotel/motel and restaurant management, individual and family development, industrial engineering, institutional/home management/supporting programs, insurance and risk management, interior design, international business management, international relations, international studies, investments and securities, journalism, labor/industrial relations, Latin, Latin American studies, library science, management information systems, management science, marine biology, marketing management, marketing research, mathematics, mathematics education, mechanical engineering, medical laboratory technologies, metallurgical engineering, microbiology, mining and mineral engineering, music, music education, music performance, music theory and composition, music therapy, nursing, operations research, personnel management, petroleum engineering, philosophy, physical education, physics, political science and government, predentistry, prelaw, premedicine, prepharmacy, psychology, public relations, radio/television broadcasting, real estate, religion, retailing, Russian, Russian and Slavic studies, science education, secondary education, small business management and ownership, social science education, social work, sociology, Spanish, special education, speech, speech correction, speech pathology/audiology, speech/communication/theater education, sports management, sports medicine, statistics, studio art, telecommunications, textiles and clothing, zoology.

ACADEMIC PROGRAMS. Accelerated program, cooperative education, double major, dual enrollment of high school students, education specialist degree, external degree, honors program, independent study, internships, student-designed major, study abroad, telecourses, visiting/exchange student program, weekend college, Washington semester, cross-registration, combined graduate degree MBA/JD; combined bachelor's/graduate program in business administration. **Remedial services:** Learning center, preadmission summer program, remedial instruction, special counselor, tutoring. **ROTC:** Air Force, Army. **Placement/credit:** AP, CLEP General and Subject, institutional tests; 45 credit hours maximum for bachelor's degree.

ACADEMIC REQUIREMENTS. Freshmen must earn minimum GPA of 2.0 to continue in good standing. 80% of freshmen return for sophomore year. Students must declare major by end of second year. **Graduation requirements:** 128 hours for bachelor's. Most students required to take courses in arts/fine arts, computer science, English, foreign languages, history, humanities, mathematics, biological/physical sciences, social sciences. **Additional information:** Tradition of excellence demonstrated by personalized attention to student needs. Large number of out-of-state students enrolled.

FRESHMAN ADMISSIONS. Selection criteria: Probability table based on SAT or ACT score and high school GPA in academic subjects. **High school preparation:** 12 units required; 22 recommended. Required and recommended units include English 4, mathematics 2-4 and social science 1-4. Biological science 2, foreign language 2 and physical science 1 recommended. Specific subjects required for admission to some divisions. **Test requirements:** SAT or ACT; score report by August 1.

1992 FRESHMAN CLASS PROFILE. 3,545 men applied, 2,680 accepted, 1,130 enrolled; 3,819 women applied, 2,887 accepted, 1,331 enrolled. 63% had high school GPA of 3.0 or higher, 34% between 2.0 and 2.99. 21% were in top tenth and 49% were in top quarter of graduating class. **Academic background:** Mid 50% of enrolled freshmen had SAT-V between 380-500, SAT-M between 420-570; ACT composite between 20-25. 15% submitted SAT scores, 85% submitted ACT scores. **Characteristics:** 60% from in state, 72% live in college housing, 10% have minority backgrounds, 1% are foreign students, 33% join fraternities/sororities. Average age is 18.

FALL-TERM APPLICATIONS. $20 fee. Closing date August 1; applicants notified on a rolling basis. Interview required for marginal applicants. Early admission available. SAT or ACT required, PSAT recommended for freshmen applicants.

STUDENT LIFE. Housing: Dormitories (men, women); apartment, fraternity, sorority, handicapped housing available. Foreign language housing available. **Activities:** Student government, film, magazine, radio, student newspaper, television, yearbook, choral groups, concert band, dance, drama, jazz band, marching band, music ensembles, musical theater, opera, pep band, symphony orchestra, fraternities, sororities, Campus Crusade for Christ, College Democrats, College Republicans, Afro-American Association.

ATHLETICS. NCAA. **Intercollegiate:** Basketball, cross-country, diving, football M, golf, swimming, tennis, track and field, volleyball W. **Intramural:** Badminton, basketball, bowling, diving, football, golf, lacrosse, racquetball, rowing (crew), rugby M, soccer, softball, swimming, table tennis, tennis, track and field, volleyball, water polo, wrestling M.

STUDENT SERVICES. Aptitude testing, career counseling, employment service for undergraduates, freshman orientation, health services, on-campus day care, personal counseling, placement service for graduates, special adviser for adult students, veterans counselor, services/facilities for handicapped.

ANNUAL EXPENSES. Tuition and fees (1992-93): $2,008, $3,008 additional for out-of-state students. **Room and board:** $3,288. **Books and supplies:** $501. **Other expenses:** $1,323.

FINANCIAL AID. 35% of freshmen, 35% of continuing students receive some form of aid. 51% of grants, 92% of loans, 32% of jobs based on need. 576 enrolled freshmen were judged to have need, 536 were offered aid. Academic, music/drama, art, athletic, state/district residency, leadership, minority scholarships available. **Aid applications:** No closing date; priority given to applications received by March 15; applicants notified on a rolling basis beginning on or about May 15; must reply within 3 weeks.

ADDRESS/TELEPHONE. Roy C. Smith, Director of Admission Services, University of Alabama, PO Box 870132, Tuscaloosa, AL 35487-0132. (205) 348-5666. (800) 933-BAMA. Fax: (205) 348-9046.

University of Alabama in Birmingham
Birmingham, Alabama — CB code: 1856

4-year public university, coed. Founded in 1969. **Accreditation:** Regional. **Undergraduate enrollment:** 3,036 men, 3,809 women full time; 2,191 men, 2,640 women part time. **Graduate enrollment:** 1,382 men, 1,282 women full time; 508 men, 894 women part time. **Faculty:** 1,830 total (1,683 full time). **Location:** Urban campus in large city; in downtown area of Birmingham. **Calendar:** Quarter, extensive summer session. Saturday and extensive evening/early morning classes. **Microcomputers:** Located in libraries. **Special facilities:** Reynolds Historical Library, Alabama Museum of Health Sciences, visual arts gallery.

DEGREES OFFERED. BA, BS, BFA, MA, MS, MBA, MEd, PhD, EdD, DMD, MD, OD. 1,487 bachelor's degrees awarded in 1992. 24% in business and management, 17% teacher education, 7% engineering, 13% health sciences, 5% allied health, 5% life sciences, 6% parks/recreation, protective services, public affairs, 5% social sciences. Graduate degrees offered in 59 major fields of study.

UNDERGRADUATE MAJORS. Accounting, allied health, anthropology, art education, art history, biological and physical sciences, biology, business and management, business economics, chemistry, civil engineering, communications, computer and information sciences, criminal justice studies, cytotechnology, dance, dental hygiene, dramatic arts, early childhood education, economics, electrical/electronics/communications engineering, elementary education, English, finance, French, geology, German, health education, history, international studies, linguistics, marketing management, materials engineering, mathematics, mechanical engineering, medical laboratory technologies, medical records administration, music, music education, nuclear medical technology, nursing, occupational therapy, optometry, philosophy, physical education, physician's assistant, physics, political science and government, psychology, radiograph medical technology, secondary education, social work, sociology, Spanish, special education, studio art, visual and performing arts.

ACADEMIC PROGRAMS. Cooperative education, double major, dual enrollment of high school students, education specialist degree, honors program, independent study, internships, student-designed major, study abroad, teacher preparation, visiting/exchange student program, weekend college, cross-registration; liberal arts/career combination in health sciences. **Remedial services:** Reduced course load, remedial instruction, special counselor, tutoring, academic support services for culturally disadvantaged students. **ROTC:** Air Force, Army. **Placement/credit:** AP, CLEP General and Subject, institutional tests; 64 credit hours maximum for bachelor's degree.

ACADEMIC REQUIREMENTS. Freshmen must earn minimum GPA of 1.75 to continue in good standing. 72% of freshmen return for sophomore year. Students must declare major by end of second year. **Graduation requirements:** 128 hours for bachelor's. Most students required to take courses in arts/fine arts, computer science, English, foreign languages, history, humanities, mathematics, philosophy/religion, biological/physical sciences, social sciences. **Postgraduate studies:** 20% enter other graduate study.

FRESHMAN ADMISSIONS. Selection criteria: Admissions based on test scores and high school record. **High school preparation:** 12 units required. Required units include English 4, mathematics 2, social science 2 and science 2. **Test requirements:** SAT or ACT (ACT preferred); score report by September 1.

1992 FRESHMAN CLASS PROFILE. 560 men, 574 women enrolled. **Academic background:** Mid 50% of enrolled freshmen had ACT composite between 18-23. 91% submitted ACT scores. **Characteristics:** 96% from in state, 76% commute, 30% have minority backgrounds, 5% join fraternities/sororities. Average age is 20.

FALL-TERM APPLICATIONS. $20 fee. No closing date; applicants notified on a rolling basis. Deferred and early admission available.

STUDENT LIFE. Housing: Dormitories (women); apartment housing available. **Activities:** Student government, magazine, student newspaper, yearbook, choral groups, dance, drama, jazz band, musical theater, pep band, fraternities, sororities, College Democrats, College Republicans, campus civitan club, veterans student organization, Catholic student association, United Methodist campus ministry, Baptist campus ministry, Muslim student association, Chinese student association, African student association.

ATHLETICS. NCAA. **Intercollegiate:** Baseball M, basketball, cross-country W, football M, golf, soccer M, tennis, track and field, volleyball W. **Intramural:** Badminton, basketball, bowling, golf, racquetball, soccer, softball, squash, swimming, table tennis, tennis, track and field, volleyball, wrestling M.

STUDENT SERVICES. Career counseling, employment service for undergraduates, freshman orientation, health services, personal counseling, placement service for graduates, veterans counselor, services/facilities for handicapped.

ANNUAL EXPENSES. Tuition and fees (projected): $2,238, $2,010 additional for out-of-state students. **Room and board:** $4,380. **Books and supplies:** $720. **Other expenses:** $1,200.

FINANCIAL AID. 50% of freshmen, 32% of continuing students receive some form of aid. 72% of grants, 82% of loans, all jobs based on need. 450 enrolled freshmen were judged to have need, all were offered aid. Academic, music/drama, art, athletic, leadership, minority scholarships available. **Aid applications:** No closing date; applicants notified on a rolling basis beginning on or about May 1; must reply within 3 weeks.

ADDRESS/TELEPHONE. Michael Bridges, Director of Admissions, University of Alabama in Birmingham, UAB Station, Birmingham, AL 35294-1150. (205) 934-8221. (800) 421-8743.

University of Alabama in Huntsville
Huntsville, Alabama — CB code: 1854

4-year public university, coed. Founded in 1950. **Accreditation:** Regional. **Undergraduate enrollment:** 1,411 men, 1,263 women full time; 1,766 men, 1,673 women part time. **Graduate enrollment:** 419 men, 202 women full time; 757 men, 535 women part time. **Faculty:** 507 total (348 full time), 310 with doctorates or other terminal degrees. **Location:** Suburban campus in small city; 100 miles from Birmingham, 100 miles from Nashville, Tennessee. **Calendar:** 4 terms per year with semester hour credit given. Extensive evening/early morning classes. **Microcomputers:** 238 located in libraries, classrooms, computer centers. **Special facilities:** University art gallery. **Additional facts:** Strong work study program due to presence of Marshall Space Flight Center, US Army Missile Command, and other companies in area.

DEGREES OFFERED. BA, BS, MA, MS, PhD. 607 bachelor's degrees awarded in 1992. 29% in business and management, 33% engineering, 12% health sciences, 5% life sciences. Graduate degrees offered in 20 major fields of study.

UNDERGRADUATE MAJORS. Accounting, art history, biology, business administration and management, business economics, chemical engineering, chemistry, civil engineering, communications, computer and information sciences, computer engineering, contract management and procurement/purchasing, education, electrical/electronics/communications engineering, elementary education, engineering, English, finance, French, German, history, industrial engineering, international trade/foreign language, management information systems, marketing management, mathematics, mathematics education, mechanical engineering, music, music education, nursing, optics, philosophy, physics, political science and government, premedicine, psychology, Russian and Slavic studies, sociology, Spanish, studio art, systems engineering.

ACADEMIC PROGRAMS. Cooperative education, double major, dual enrollment of high school students, honors program, independent study, internships, teacher preparation, cross-registration. **Remedial services:** Reduced course load, remedial instruction, special counselor, tutoring, studies skills classes. **ROTC:** Air Force, Army. **Placement/credit:** AP, CLEP General and Subject, institutional tests; 32 credit hours maximum for bachelor's degree.

ACADEMIC REQUIREMENTS. Freshmen must earn minimum 1.0 GPA in first term, 2.0 in next. 65% of freshmen return for sophomore year. Students must declare major by end of second year. **Graduation requirements:** 128 hours for bachelor's (30 in major). Most students required to take courses in English, history, mathematics, biological/physical sciences, social sciences.

FRESHMAN ADMISSIONS. Selection criteria: School achievement record and test scores most important. Special admission for applicants lacking usual requisites. Applicants must have minimum ACT composite score of 17 and GPA of 3.25 or ACT composite score of 24 and minimum GPA of 1.15. Engineering applicants must have minimum ACT composite score of 21 or minimum combined SAT score of 900. **High school preparation:** 20 units required. Required units include biological science 1, English 4, mathematics 3, physical science 1 and social science 3. 8 electives required. **Test requirements:** SAT or ACT (ACT preferred); score report by August 13.

1992 FRESHMAN CLASS PROFILE. 331 men, 267 women enrolled. **Academic background:** Mid 50% of enrolled freshmen had SAT-V between 370-530, SAT-M between 430-610; ACT composite between 20-26. 15% submitted SAT scores, 85% submitted ACT scores. **Characteristics:** 84% from in state, 21% have minority backgrounds, 3% are foreign students. Average age is 22.

FALL-TERM APPLICATIONS. $20 fee. Closing date August 13; applicants notified on a rolling basis. Interview recommended for special admission applicants. Deferred and early admission available.

STUDENT LIFE. Housing: Dormitories (coed); apartment housing available. **Activities:** Student government, magazine, student newspaper, choral groups, concert band, drama, jazz band, music ensembles, musical theater, pep band, symphony orchestra, fraternities, sororities, religious groups, campus hosts, Young Democrats, Young Republicans, Circle-K.

ATHLETICS. NCAA. **Intercollegiate:** Basketball, cross-country, ice hockey M, rowing (crew), soccer M, tennis, volleyball W. **Intramural:** Basketball, bowling, golf, racquetball, rowing (crew), softball, swimming, table tennis, tennis, volleyball.

STUDENT SERVICES. Aptitude testing, career counseling, employment service for undergraduates, freshman orientation, health services, personal counseling, placement service for graduates, services/facilities for handicapped.

ANNUAL EXPENSES. Tuition and fees (projected): $2,400, $2,400 additional for out-of-state students. **Room and board:** $4,200. **Books and supplies:** $600. **Other expenses:** $1,200.

FINANCIAL AID. 31% of freshmen, 35% of continuing students receive some form of aid. 45% of grants, 84% of loans, 2% of jobs based on need. Academic, music/drama, art, athletic, state/district residency, leadership, alumni affiliation, minority scholarships available. **Aid applications:** No closing date; priority given to applications received by April 1; applicants notified on a rolling basis beginning on or about May 1; must reply within 2 weeks.

ADDRESS/TELEPHONE. Dr. Ron R. Koger, Assistant Vice President of Enrollment Services, University of Alabama in Huntsville, University Center, Room 124, Huntsville, AL 35899. (205) 895-6070. (800) 824-2255. Fax: (205) 895-6073.

University of Mobile
Mobile, Alabama CB code: 1515

4-year private liberal arts college, coed, affiliated with Southern Baptist Convention. Founded in 1961. **Accreditation:** Regional. **Undergraduate enrollment:** 506 men, 770 women full time; 81 men, 187 women part time. **Graduate enrollment:** 17 men, 31 women full time; 40 men, 71 women part time. **Faculty:** 103 total (67 full time), 46 with doctorates or other terminal degrees. **Location:** Suburban campus in small city; 12 miles from downtown. **Calendar:** Semester, limited summer session. **Microcomputers:** 47 located in libraries, computer centers. **Special facilities:** Donald Art Gallery, Albert S. Dix Mineral Museum, forest resource center. **Additional facts:** Latin American branch campus in San Marcos, Nicaragua, 26 miles from Managua. Courses taught in English by U.S. faculty.

DEGREES OFFERED. AA, AS, BA, MA, MS, MBA. 51 associate degrees awarded in 1992. 100% in health sciences. 163 bachelor's degrees awarded. 14% in business and management, 5% communications, 5% computer sciences, 24% teacher education, 25% allied health, 7% philosophy, religion, theology, 6% psychology. Graduate degrees offered in 7 major fields of study.

UNDERGRADUATE MAJORS. Associate: Liberal/general studies, nursing. **Bachelor's:** Accounting, art history, behavioral sciences, biology, business administration and management, business and management, business economics, chemistry, communications, computer and information sciences, cytotechnology, early childhood education, elementary education, English, English education, finance, foreign languages education, French, German, history, liberal/general studies, marketing management, mathematics, mathematics education, music, nuclear medical technology, nursing, physical education, political science and government, predentistry, prelaw, preveterinary, psychology, religion, religious education, science education, science technologies, social studies education, sociology, Spanish, speech/theater.

ACADEMIC PROGRAMS. Accelerated program, double major, dual enrollment of high school students, honors program, independent study, internships, study abroad, teacher preparation, visiting/exchange student program, Washington semester, cross-registration; liberal arts/career combination in engineering, health sciences. **Remedial services:** Learning center, preadmission summer program, reduced course load, remedial instruction, tutoring. **ROTC:** Air Force, Army. **Placement/credit:** AP, CLEP General and Subject, institutional tests; 30 credit hours maximum for bachelor's degree.

ACADEMIC REQUIREMENTS. Freshmen must earn minimum GPA of 2.0 to continue in good standing. 55% of freshmen return for sophomore year. Students must declare major by end of second year. **Graduation requirements:** 70 hours for associate (39 in major), 128 hours for bachelor's (36 in major). Most students required to take courses in arts/fine arts, computer science, English, history, humanities, mathematics, philosophy/religion, biological/physical sciences, social sciences. **Postgraduate studies:** 2% enter law school, 3% enter medical school, 4% enter MBA programs, 14% enter other graduate study.

FRESHMAN ADMISSIONS. Selection criteria: Admissions based on test scores, high school record, and personal recommendations. Recommended units include English 4, foreign language 2, mathematics 3 and social science 3. **Test requirements:** SAT or ACT (ACT preferred); score report by July 1.

1992 FRESHMAN CLASS PROFILE. 84 men, 158 women enrolled. 35% had high school GPA of 3.0 or higher, 62% between 2.0 and 2.99. 17% were in top tenth and 37% were in top quarter of graduating class. **Academic background:** Mid 50% of enrolled freshmen had ACT composite between 18-24. 95% submitted ACT scores. **Characteristics:** 90% from in state, 80% commute, 1% have minority backgrounds, 2% are foreign students. Average age is 19.

FALL-TERM APPLICATIONS. $30 fee. Closing date August 1; priority given to applications received by June 1; applicants notified on or about July 30. Interview recommended for nursing applicants. Audition recommended for music applicants. Portfolio recommended for art applicants. Deferred and early admission available.

STUDENT LIFE. Housing: Dormitories (men, women). **Activities:** Student government, student newspaper, video yearbook, choral groups, concert band, drama, music ensembles, musical theater, pep band, symphony orchestra, Ministerial Association, Baptist Student Union, honor societies, academic organizations, Fellowship of Christian Athletes, Sigma Tau Delta, Kappa Delta Epsilon, Psi Chi, Phi Alpha Theta, Alpha Chi.

ATHLETICS. NAIA. **Intercollegiate:** Baseball M, basketball, cross-country, golf M, soccer M, softball W, tennis. **Intramural:** Basketball, bowling, softball, swimming, table tennis, tennis, volleyball.

STUDENT SERVICES. Aptitude testing, career counseling, employment service for undergraduates, freshman orientation, health services, on-campus day care, personal counseling, placement service for graduates, veterans counselor, services/facilities for handicapped.

ANNUAL EXPENSES. Tuition and fees (1992-93): $5,090. **Room and board:** $3,180. **Books and supplies:** $500. **Other expenses:** $1,000.

FINANCIAL AID. 96% of freshmen, 85% of continuing students receive some form of aid. 26% of grants, 91% of loans, 58% of jobs based on need. Academic, music/drama, art, athletic, state/district residency, leadership, religious affiliation scholarships available. **Aid applications:** No closing date; priority given to applications received by March 31; applicants notified on a rolling basis beginning on or about April 15.

ADDRESS/TELEPHONE. Herman R. Shoemaker, Vice President for Student Services, University of Mobile, PO Box 13220, Mobile, AL 36663-0220. (205) 675-5990 ext. 220. Fax: (205) 675-5446.

University of Montevallo
Montevallo, Alabama CB code: 1004

4-year public university and college of arts and sciences and business, liberal arts, teachers college, coed. Founded in 1896. **Accreditation:** Regional. **Undergraduate enrollment:** 2,746 men and women. **Graduate enrollment:** 508 men and women part time. **Faculty:** 167 total (134 full time), 100 with doctorates or other terminal degrees. **Location:** Suburban campus in small town; 30 miles from Birmingham. **Calendar:** Semester, extensive summer session. **Microcomputers:** 100 located in dormitories, classrooms, computer centers. **Special facilities:** Residential speech and hearing center, traffic safety center, art gallery, state-of-the-art foreign language laboratory, lake, golf course, child development center, mass communications center. **Additional facts:** A National Historic District.

DEGREES OFFERED. BA, BS, BFA, MA, MS, MEd. 417 bachelor's degrees awarded in 1992. 19% in business and management, 5% communications, 25% education, 10% letters/literature, 11% social sciences, 11% visual and performing arts. Graduate degrees offered in 26 major fields of study.

UNDERGRADUATE MAJORS. Accounting, art education, biological and physical sciences, biology, business administration and management, business and management, ceramics, chemistry, communications, dramatic arts, drawing, driver and safety education, early childhood education, education, education of the deaf and hearing impaired, elementary education, English, English education, finance, foreign languages education, French, graphic design, health education, history, home economics, home economics education, international studies, journalism, junior high education, marketing management, mathematics, mathematics education, merchandising, music education, music performance, music theory and composition, musical theater, painting, photography, physical education, piano pedagogy, political science and government, printmaking, psychology, science education, sculpture, secondary education, social science education, social sciences, social work, sociology, Spanish, speech, speech correction, speech pathology/audiology, speech/communication/theater education, student counseling and personnel services, studio art, theater design, visual and performing arts, vocational home economics.

ACADEMIC PROGRAMS. Accelerated program, cooperative education, double major, dual enrollment of high school students, education specialist degree, honors program, independent study, internships, study abroad, teacher preparation, visiting/exchange student program, weekend college, cross-registration. **Remedial services:** Learning center, preadmission summer program, reduced course load, remedial instruction, special counselor, tutoring. **ROTC:** Air Force, Army. **Placement/credit:** AP, CLEP Subject; 45 credit hours maximum for bachelor's degree.

ACADEMIC REQUIREMENTS. Freshmen must earn minimum GPA of 1.5 to continue in good standing. 70% of freshmen return for sophomore year. Students must declare major by end of second year. **Graduation requirements:** 130 hours for bachelor's (36 in major). Most students required to take courses in arts/fine arts, computer science, English, history, humanities, mathematics, biological/physical sciences, social sciences. **Additional information:** Academic support programs available to all first generation college students from low income families and students with disabilities. Writing laboratory open to all students.

FRESHMAN ADMISSIONS. Selection criteria: High school record and test scores essential factors in evaluation. Each application evaluated on individual basis regarding information pertinent to academic success in university curriculum. **High school preparation:** 15 units required. Required units include biological science 1, English 4, mathematics 2, physical science 1 and social science 4. **Test requirements:** SAT or ACT (ACT preferred); score report by August 1.

1992 FRESHMAN CLASS PROFILE. 522 men and women enrolled. 65% had high school GPA of 3.0 or higher, 35% between 2.0 and 2.99. **Academic background:** Mid 50% of enrolled freshmen had ACT composite between 18-23. 95% submitted ACT scores. **Characteristics:** 91% from in state, 66% live in college housing, 9% have minority backgrounds. Average age is 18.

FALL-TERM APPLICATIONS. $15 fee, may be waived for applicants with need. Closing date August 1; applicants notified on a rolling basis. Audition required for music applicants. Portfolio required for art applicants. Interview recommended. Essay recommended. Deferred and early admission available.

STUDENT LIFE. Housing: Dormitories (men, women); apartment, fraternity housing available. Several rooms are handicapped accessible. **Activities:** Student government, film, magazine, student newspaper, television, yearbook, choral groups, concert band, dance, drama, jazz band, music ensembles, musical theater, opera, debate, fraternities, sororities, Afro-American Society, Circle-K, Association of International Students, Young Republicans, Young Democrats.

ATHLETICS. NAIA. **Intercollegiate:** Baseball M, basketball, golf M, volleyball W. **Intramural:** Basketball, bowling, golf M, racquetball, softball, table tennis W, tennis, volleyball.

STUDENT SERVICES. Aptitude testing, career counseling, employment service for undergraduates, freshman orientation, health services, personal counseling, placement service for graduates, special adviser for adult students, veterans counselor, student support services, writing center, equal opportunity office, services/facilities for handicapped.

ANNUAL EXPENSES. Tuition and fees (1992-93): $2,164, $2,040 additional for out-of-state students. **Room and board:** $2,986. **Books and supplies:** $500. **Other expenses:** $1,500.

FINANCIAL AID. 57% of freshmen, 62% of continuing students receive some form of aid. 45% of grants, 98% of loans, 32% of jobs based on need. Academic, music/drama, athletic, state/district residency, leadership, alumni affiliation, minority scholarships available. **Aid applications:** No closing date; priority given to applications received by April 15; applicants notified on a rolling basis beginning on or about June 1; must reply within 2 weeks. **Additional information:** Financial needs of all low-income applicants eligible for admission met.

ADDRESS/TELEPHONE. Robert A. Doyle, Director of Admissions, University of Montevallo, Station 6030, Montevallo, AL 35115-6030. (205) 665-6030. (800) 292-4349.

University of North Alabama
Florence, Alabama — CB code: 1735

4-year public university, coed. Founded in 1872. **Accreditation:** Regional. **Undergraduate enrollment:** 1,663 men, 2,268 women full time; 433 men, 601 women part time. **Graduate enrollment:** 18 men, 41 women full time; 152 men, 374 women part time. **Faculty:** 246 total (196 full time), 115 with doctorates or other terminal degrees. **Location:** Urban campus in large town; 116 miles from Birmingham. **Calendar:** Semester, extensive summer session. **Microcomputers:** 120 located in libraries, classrooms, computer centers. **Special facilities:** Planetarium-observatory, Kilby laboratory school.

DEGREES OFFERED. BA, BS, BFA, MA, MBA. 720 bachelor's degrees awarded in 1992. 32% in business and management, 22% teacher education, 6% health sciences, 10% parks/recreation, protective services, public affairs. Graduate degrees offered in 16 major fields of study.

UNDERGRADUATE MAJORS. Accounting, art education, biology, business economics, business education, chemistry, commercial French, commercial German, commercial music, commercial Spanish, computer and information sciences, criminal justice studies, dramatic arts, early childhood education, earth and space science education, elementary education, English, English education, environmental science, fashion merchandising, finance, fine arts, foreign languages education, French, geography, German, health education, history, home economics, home economics education, industrial hygiene, interior design, journalism, language arts education, liberal/general studies, management information systems, management science, marine biology, marketing management, mathematics, mathematics and computer science education, mathematics education, music education, music performance, nursing, office supervision and management, parks and recreation management, physical education, physics, political science and government, professional writing, psychology, psychology education, public relations, radio/television broadcasting, science education, secondary education, social science education, social studies education, social work, sociology, Spanish, special education, speech, speech/communication/theater education.

ACADEMIC PROGRAMS. Cooperative education, double major, dual enrollment of high school students, independent study, teacher preparation. **Remedial services:** Learning center, reduced course load, remedial instruction, tutoring. **ROTC:** Army. **Placement/credit:** AP, CLEP Subject, institutional tests; 34 credit hours maximum for bachelor's degree.

ACADEMIC REQUIREMENTS. Freshmen must earn minimum GPA of 1.6 to continue in good standing. 65% of freshmen return for sophomore year. Students must declare major by end of second year. **Graduation requirements:** 128 hours for bachelor's (30 in major). Most students required to take courses in arts/fine arts, English, history, mathematics, biological/physical sciences, social sciences.

FRESHMAN ADMISSIONS. Selection criteria: Must score 18 or higher on ACT or 700 or higher on SAT, or rank in upper 50% of high school class, or score at least 35 on each section of the GED, or score average of 45 on all GED test sections. **High school preparation:** 13 units required. Required units include biological science 1, English 4, foreign language 2, mathematics 2, physical science 1 and social science 3. **Test requirements:** SAT or ACT; score report by July 1.

1992 FRESHMAN CLASS PROFILE. 368 men, 387 women enrolled. **Characteristics:** 81% from in state, 50% commute, 12% have minority backgrounds, 1% are foreign students, 12% join fraternities/sororities. Average age is 18.

FALL-TERM APPLICATIONS. $17 fee. Closing date July 1; applicants notified on a rolling basis. Audition required for music applicants. Interview recommended for education, nursing, social work, preprofessional program applicants. Portfolio recommended for art applicants. Deferred admission available.

STUDENT LIFE. Housing: Dormitories (men, women); apartment, fraternity, sorority housing available. **Activities:** Student government, student newspaper, yearbook, annual prose-poetry publication, choral groups, concert band, drama, jazz band, marching band, musical theater, opera, fraternities, sororities, Young Democrats, Young Republicans, Circle-K, Gold Triangle (honorary service organization), Black Student Alliance.

ATHLETICS. NCAA. **Intercollegiate:** Baseball M, basketball, cross-country, football M, golf M, rifle M, softball W, tennis, volleyball W. **Intramural:** Badminton M, baseball, basketball, bowling, cross-country, football M, golf M, racquetball, softball W, swimming, table tennis, tennis, volleyball.

STUDENT SERVICES. Career counseling, employment service for undergraduates, freshman orientation, health services, on-campus day care, personal counseling, placement service for graduates, special adviser for adult students, veterans counselor, services/facilities for handicapped.

ANNUAL EXPENSES. Tuition and fees (1992-93): $1,368, $600 additional for out-of-state students. **Room and board:** $2,580. **Books and supplies:** $550. **Other expenses:** $2,000.

FINANCIAL AID. 44% of freshmen, 44% of continuing students receive some form of aid. 75% of grants, 94% of loans, 44% of jobs based on need. 270 enrolled freshmen were judged to have need, all were offered aid. Academic, music/drama, art, athletic, state/district residency, leadership scholarships available. **Aid applications:** No closing date; priority given to applications received by April 1; applicants notified on a rolling basis; must reply within 2 weeks. **Additional information:** Student work opportunities in community are healthy.

ADDRESS/TELEPHONE. Dr. Fred J. Alexander, Dean of Enrollment Management, University of North Alabama, Florence, AL 35632-0001. (205) 760-4318. Fax: (205) 760-4644.

University of South Alabama
Mobile, Alabama CB code: 1880

Admissions: 92% of applicants accepted
Based on: ••• School record, test scores
Completion: 62% of freshmen end year in good standing
35% graduate, 18% of these enter graduate study

4-year public university, coed. Founded in 1963. **Accreditation:** Regional. **Undergraduate enrollment:** 3,412 men, 4,146 women full time; 1,225 men, 1,059 women part time. **Graduate enrollment:** 463 men, 536 women full time; 255 men, 523 women part time. **Faculty:** 823 total (668 full time), 587 with doctorates or other terminal degrees. **Location:** Suburban campus in small city; 10 miles from downtown. **Calendar:** Quarter, extensive summer session. Saturday and extensive evening/early morning classes. **Microcomputers:** 249 located in dormitories, classrooms, computer centers. **Special facilities:** Art gallery; Dauphin Island Sea Laboratory.

DEGREES OFFERED. BA, BS, BFA, MA, MS, MBA, MEd, PhD, EdD, MD. 1,277 bachelor's degrees awarded in 1992. 22% in business and management, 20% teacher education, 7% engineering, 12% health sciences, 6% allied health, 7% social sciences. Graduate degrees offered in 27 major fields of study.

UNDERGRADUATE MAJORS. Accounting, anthropology, art history, biology, biomedical science, business administration and management, business and management, business economics, chemical engineering, chemistry, civil engineering, communications, computer and information sciences, criminal justice studies, dramatic arts, early childhood education, economics, electrical/electronics/communications engineering, elementary education, English, finance, fine arts, French, geography, geology, German, health sciences, history, international studies, junior high education, liberal/general studies, marketing management, mathematics, mechanical engineering, medical laboratory technologies, music, music education, music performance, music theory and composition, nursing, philosophy, physical education, physical therapy, physics, political science and government, psychology, respiratory therapy technology, Russian, secondary education, sociology, Spanish, special education, speech pathology/audiology, statistics.

ACADEMIC PROGRAMS. Accelerated program, cooperative education, double major, dual enrollment of high school students, education specialist degree, independent study, internships, student-designed major, study abroad, teacher preparation, weekend college, cooperative EdD program with Auburn University; combined bachelor's/graduate program in business administration, medicine. **Remedial services:** Remedial instruction, special counselor, tutoring, Developmental Studies. **ROTC:** Air Force, Army. **Placement/credit:** AP, CLEP General and Subject, institutional tests; 48 credit hours maximum for bachelor's degree.

ACADEMIC REQUIREMENTS. Freshmen must earn minimum GPA of 2.0 to continue in good standing. 68% of freshmen return for sophomore year. Students must declare major by end of second year. **Graduation requirements:** 192 hours for bachelor's (40 in major). Most students required to take courses in English, humanities, mathematics, biological/physical sciences, social sciences. **Postgraduate studies:** 1% enter law school, 1% enter medical school, 3% enter MBA programs, 13% enter other graduate study.

FRESHMAN ADMISSIONS. Selection criteria: School achievement record and test scores important. **High school preparation:** 16 units recommended. Recommended units include English 4, mathematics 3, social science 2 and science 2. **Test requirements:** SAT or ACT (ACT preferred); score report by September 10. ACT used for counseling and advanced placement in 3-year degree program.

1992 FRESHMAN CLASS PROFILE. 1,038 men applied, 938 accepted, 542 enrolled; 1,234 women applied, 1,143 accepted, 698 enrolled. 56% had high school GPA of 3.0 or higher, 41% between 2.0 and 2.99. **Academic background:** Mid 50% of enrolled freshmen had ACT composite between 17-22. 85% submitted ACT scores. **Characteristics:** 64% from in state, 64% commute, 15% have minority backgrounds, 5% are foreign students, 10% join fraternities/sororities. Average age is 19.

FALL-TERM APPLICATIONS. $20 fee. Closing date September 10; applicants notified on a rolling basis. Audition required for music applicants. Deferred and early admission available.

STUDENT LIFE. Housing: Dormitories (men, women, coed); apartment, fraternity housing available. University-owned subdivision housing. Single homes available for married students, and qualified single undergraduates. **Activities:** Student government, student newspaper, yearbook, choral groups, concert band, dance, drama, jazz band, music ensembles, musical theater, pep band, symphony orchestra, fraternities, sororities.

ATHLETICS. NCAA. **Intercollegiate:** Baseball M, basketball, cross-country, golf, soccer M, tennis, track and field, volleyball W. **Intramural:** Basketball, bowling, gymnastics, handball, soccer, softball, table tennis, tennis, volleyball, water polo.

STUDENT SERVICES. Aptitude testing, career counseling, employment service for undergraduates, freshman orientation, health services, personal counseling, placement service for graduates, special adviser for adult students, veterans counselor, Handicapped student counselor, minority student advisor, services/facilities for handicapped.

ANNUAL EXPENSES. Tuition and fees (projected): $2,349, $900 additional for out-of-state students. **Room and board:** $3,378. **Books and supplies:** $470. **Other expenses:** $1,023.

FINANCIAL AID. 35% of freshmen, 44% of continuing students receive some form of aid. 85% of grants, 87% of loans, 55% of jobs based on need. Academic, music/drama, athletic scholarships available. **Aid applications:** No closing date; priority given to applications received by April 1; applicants notified on a rolling basis beginning on or about July 1; must reply within 2 weeks.

ADDRESS/TELEPHONE. Catherine King, Director of Admissions, University of South Alabama, AD 170, Mobile, AL 36688. (205) 460-6141. Fax: (205) 460-7023. (800) 872-5247 for FL, GA, KY, LA, MS, SC, TN only.

Virginia College
Birmingham, Alabama

2-year proprietary technical college, coed. Founded in 1975. **Undergraduate enrollment:** 350 men and women. **Faculty:** 16 total (15 full time). **Location:** Urban campus in large city. **Calendar:** Semester, extensive summer session. Extensive evening/early morning classes. **Microcomputers:** 16 located in classrooms.

DEGREES OFFERED. 60 associate degrees awarded in 1992. 100% in engineering technologies.

UNDERGRADUATE MAJORS. Electronic technology.

ACADEMIC PROGRAMS. Internships. **Remedial services:** Remedial instruction, tutoring. **Placement/credit:** Institutional tests; 45 credit hours maximum for associate degree.

ACADEMIC REQUIREMENTS. Freshmen must earn minimum GPA of 1.25 to continue in good standing. 65% of freshmen return for sophomore year. Students must declare major on application. **Graduation requirements:** 90 hours for associate.

FRESHMAN ADMISSIONS. Selection criteria: Open admissions.

1992 FRESHMAN CLASS PROFILE. 100 men and women enrolled. **Characteristics:** 80% from in state, 100% commute, 20% have minority backgrounds. Average age is 19.

FALL-TERM APPLICATIONS. $50 fee. No closing date; applicants notified on a rolling basis; must reply within 1 week.

STUDENT SERVICES. Career counseling, employment service for undergraduates, freshman orientation, personal counseling, placement service for graduates, veterans counselor, services/facilities for handicapped.

ANNUAL EXPENSES. Tuition and fees (1992-93): $5,460. **Books and supplies:** $300. **Other expenses:** $100.

FINANCIAL AID. 75% of freshmen, 75% of continuing students receive some form of aid. **Aid applications:** Closing date June 15; applicants notified on or about June 22.

ADDRESS/TELEPHONE. Mike Herrington, Admissions Coordinator, Virginia College, 1900 28th Avenue, South, Birmingham, AL 35234. (205) 251-7962. (800) 327-7962.

Walker College
Jasper, Alabama CB code: 0720

2-year private liberal arts college, coed. Founded in 1938. **Accreditation:** Regional. **Undergraduate enrollment:** 199 men, 347 women full time; 88 men, 259 women part time. **Faculty:** 54 total (30 full time), 9 with doctorates or other terminal degrees. **Location:** Suburban campus in large town; 40 miles from Birmingham, 50 miles from Tuscaloosa. **Calendar:** Semester, extensive summer session. **Microcomputers:** 24 located in computer centers.

DEGREES OFFERED. AA, AS, AAS. 153 associate degrees awarded in 1992.

UNDERGRADUATE MAJORS. Allied health, communications, emergency medical technologies, engineering, journalism, liberal/general studies, medical assistant, medical laboratory technologies, medical records technology, nursing, occupational therapy assistant, physical therapy assistant, radio/television broadcasting, radiograph medical technology, respiratory therapy technology.

ACADEMIC PROGRAMS. 2-year transfer program, dual enrollment of high school students, honors program, cross-registration. **Remedial services:** Reduced course load, remedial instruction. **Placement/credit:** AP, CLEP General and Subject; 24 credit hours maximum for associate degree.

ACADEMIC REQUIREMENTS. Freshmen must earn minimum GPA of 1.0 to continue in good standing. 76% of freshmen return for sophomore year. Students must declare major by end of first year. **Graduation requirements:** 60 hours for associate. Most students required to take courses in computer science, English, history, humanities, mathematics, biological/physical sciences, social sciences.

FRESHMAN ADMISSIONS. Selection criteria: Open admissions. Minimum ACT composite score of 18 required for applicants to nursing program. **High school preparation:** 22 units required. Required units include English 4, mathematics 2, social science 3 and science 2. **Test requirements:** ACT for placement and counseling only; score report by September 1.

1992 FRESHMAN CLASS PROFILE. 119 men, 238 women enrolled. **Characteristics:** 98% from in state, 88% commute, 3% have minority backgrounds. Average age is 18.

FALL-TERM APPLICATIONS. $10 fee. No closing date; applicants notified on a rolling basis. Deferred and early admission available.

STUDENT LIFE. Housing: Dormitories (men, women). **Activities:** Student government, student newspaper, yearbook, choral groups, drama, jazz band, music ensembles, musical theater, pep band, Circle-K, Christian youth organization, service organizations.

ATHLETICS. NJCAA. **Intercollegiate:** Basketball M, golf M. **Intramural:** Basketball, softball.

STUDENT SERVICES. Aptitude testing, career counseling, employment service for undergraduates, freshman orientation, on-campus day care, personal counseling, veterans counselor, services/facilities for handicapped.

ANNUAL EXPENSES. Tuition and fees (projected): $2,354. **Room and board:** $1,988. **Books and supplies:** $354. **Other expenses:** $4,040.

FINANCIAL AID. 61% of freshmen, 67% of continuing students receive some form of aid. 76% of grants, 95% of loans, 80% of jobs based on need. 230 enrolled freshmen were judged to have need, all were offered aid. Academic, art, athletic, state/district residency scholarships available. **Aid applications:** No closing date; priority given to applications received by July 1; applicants notified on a rolling basis beginning on or about July 20; must reply within 2 weeks.

ADDRESS/TELEPHONE. James E. West, Dean of Admissions and Academic Affairs, Walker College, 1411 Indiana Avenue, Jasper, AL 35501. (205) 387-0511. (800) 777-0372. Fax: (205) 387-5117.

Wallace State Community College at Hanceville

Hanceville, Alabama CB code: 0528

2-year public community college, coed. Founded in 1966. **Accreditation:** Regional. **Undergraduate enrollment:** 1,085 men, 1,771 women full time; 734 men, 1,220 women part time. **Faculty:** 222 total (102 full time), 9 with doctorates or other terminal degrees. **Location:** Rural campus in rural community; 35 miles from Birmingham, 50 miles from Huntsville. **Calendar:** Quarter, limited summer session. Saturday and extensive evening/early morning classes. **Microcomputers:** 65 located in classrooms, computer centers. **Special facilities:** Extensive microfiche collection on census, military, social security, death, and land records.

DEGREES OFFERED. AA, AS, AAS. 432 associate degrees awarded in 1992. 11% in business and management, 37% allied health, 28% multi/interdisciplinary studies, 10% parks/recreation, protective services, public affairs, 7% trade and industry.

UNDERGRADUATE MAJORS. Accounting, aeronautical technology, airline piloting and navigation, business administration and management, business and management, business data programming, computer programming, criminal justice technology, dental assistant, drafting, drafting and design technology, education, electrical technology, electrical/electronics/communications engineering, electronic technology, emergency medical technologies, engineering, fashion merchandising, finance, fire control and safety technology, food production/management/services, interior design, laser electro-optic technology, law enforcement and corrections technologies, legal assistant/paralegal, legal secretary, liberal/general studies, machine tool operation/machine shop, marketing and distribution, medical assistant, medical laboratory technologies, medical records technology, medical secretary, mental health/human services, music education, nursing, occupational safety and health technology, occupational therapy assistant, office supervision and management, personnel management, physical therapy assistant, physician's assistant, practical nursing, predentistry, prelaw, premedicine, prepharmacy, preveterinary, radiograph medical technology, real estate, religion, respiratory therapy, respiratory therapy technology, secretarial and related programs, small business management and ownership, ultrasound technology.

ACADEMIC PROGRAMS. 2-year transfer program, accelerated program, cooperative education, double major, dual enrollment of high school students, internships, 2-year degree programs in allied health available requiring 1 year study at University of Alabama at Birmingham. **Remedial services:** Learning center, reduced course load, remedial instruction, tutoring. **Placement/credit:** AP, CLEP General and Subject, institutional tests; 40 credit hours maximum for associate degree.

ACADEMIC REQUIREMENTS. Freshmen must earn minimum GPA of 1.5 to continue in good standing. 80% of freshmen return for sophomore year. Students must declare major by end of first year. **Graduation requirements:** 96 hours for associate (50 in major). Most students required to take courses in English, history, humanities, mathematics, biological/physical sciences, social sciences.

FRESHMAN ADMISSIONS. Selection criteria: Open admissions. Selective admission to nursing and allied health programs. **Test requirements:** ACT required of applicants to certain allied health programs. National League for Nursing, Pre-Nursing and Guidance Examination required for nursing applicants.

1992 FRESHMAN CLASS PROFILE. 545 men, 801 women enrolled. **Characteristics:** 99% from in state, 99% commute, 3% have minority backgrounds. Average age is 24.

FALL-TERM APPLICATIONS. No fee. No closing date; applicants notified on a rolling basis beginning on or about August 15. Interview recommended for health program applicants. Audition recommended for music education applicants. Deferred admission available.

STUDENT LIFE. Housing: Dormitories (men, women). **Activities:** Student government, student newspaper, yearbook, choral groups, concert band, jazz band, music ensembles, pep band, Baptist Campus Ministry.

ATHLETICS. NJCAA. **Intercollegiate:** Baseball M, basketball, cross-country, golf, softball W, volleyball. **Intramural:** Badminton, basketball, softball, tennis, track and field, volleyball.

STUDENT SERVICES. Aptitude testing, career counseling, employment service for undergraduates, freshman orientation, health services, personal counseling, placement service for graduates, services/facilities for handicapped.

ANNUAL EXPENSES. Tuition and fees (projected): $900, $608 additional for out-of-state students. **Room and board:** $1,050 room only. **Books and supplies:** $450. **Other expenses:** $2,650.

FINANCIAL AID. 50% of freshmen, 50% of continuing students receive some form of aid. 81% of grants, 92% of jobs based on need. Academic, music/drama, art, athletic, leadership scholarships available. **Aid applications:** No closing date; applicants notified on a rolling basis beginning on or about August 15; must reply within 2 weeks.

ADDRESS/TELEPHONE. Diane Harris, Director of Admissions/Registrar, Wallace State Community College at Hanceville, Box 2000, Hanceville, AL 35077-2000. (205) 352-6403.

Alaska

Alaska Bible College
Glennallen, Alaska CB code: 1237

Admissions: 61% of applicants accepted
Based on: ••• Essay, recommendations, religious affiliation/commitment
•• School record
• Activities, test scores
Completion: 90% of freshmen end year in good standing

4-year private Bible college, coed, interdenominational. Founded in 1966. **Undergraduate enrollment:** 18 men, 14 women full time; 3 men, 10 women part time. **Faculty:** 10 total (5 full time), 1 with doctorate or other terminal degree. **Location:** Rural campus in rural community; 187 miles from Anchorage. **Calendar:** Semester. **Microcomputers:** 4 located in libraries. **Special facilities:** Largest theological library collection in Alaska. **Additional facts:** Extension classes offered in Anchorage and Juneau each semester.

DEGREES OFFERED. AA, BA. 1 associate degree awarded in 1992. 100% in philosophy, religion, theology. 3 bachelor's degrees awarded. 100% in philosophy, religion, theology.

UNDERGRADUATE MAJORS. Associate: Bible studies. **Bachelor's:** Bible studies, pastoral studies.

ACADEMIC PROGRAMS. Internships, 1-year in-service Bible camp training program. **Remedial services:** Remedial instruction. **Placement/credit:** AP, CLEP General and Subject, institutional tests.

ACADEMIC REQUIREMENTS. Freshmen must earn minimum GPA of 2.0 to continue in good standing. Students must declare major by end of second year. **Graduation requirements:** 65 hours for associate (28 in major), 130 hours for bachelor's (40 in major). Most students required to take courses in English, history, mathematics, philosophy/religion, biological/physical sciences, social sciences.

FRESHMAN ADMISSIONS. Selection criteria: References and indications of religious commitment most important, followed by school grade record. Test scores and extracurricular activities also considered. **Test requirements:** SAT or ACT; score report by August 1.

1992 FRESHMAN CLASS PROFILE. Characteristics: 44% from in state, 93% live in college housing, 7% have minority backgrounds, 21% are foreign students. Average age is 24.

FALL-TERM APPLICATIONS. $25 fee. Closing date August 1; priority given to applications received by June 30; applicants notified on a rolling basis; must reply by August 15. Essay required. Deferred admission available.

STUDENT LIFE. Housing: Dormitories (men, women); apartment housing available. **Activities:** Student government, music ensembles. **Additional information:** Religious observance required.

ATHLETICS. Intramural: Basketball, volleyball.

STUDENT SERVICES. Freshman orientation, personal counseling.

ANNUAL EXPENSES. Tuition and fees: $2,670. **Room and board:** $3,200. **Books and supplies:** $250. **Other expenses:** $400.

FINANCIAL AID. 67% of freshmen, 90% of continuing students receive some form of aid. 78% of grants, all loans, all jobs based on need. 9 enrolled freshmen were judged to have need, all were offered aid. Academic, music/drama, leadership scholarships available. **Aid applications:** Closing date August 5; priority given to applications received by May 31; applicants notified on a rolling basis. **Additional information:** All full-time faculty and staff are missionaries and salaries are not charged to students.

ADDRESS/TELEPHONE. Sherry Nace, Director of Admissions, Alaska Bible College, PO Box 289, Glennallen, AK 99588. (907) 822-3201.

Alaska Pacific University
Anchorage, Alaska CB code: 4201

Admissions: 54% of applicants accepted
Based on: ••• School record, test scores
•• Interview
• Activities, recommendations
Completion: 60% of freshmen end year in good standing
18% graduate

4-year private university, coed, affiliated with United Methodist Church. Founded in 1957. **Accreditation:** Regional. **Undergraduate enrollment:** 80 men, 186 women full time; 77 men, 101 women part time. **Graduate enrollment:** 27 men, 73 women full time; 63 men, 84 women part time. **Faculty:** 102 total (28 full time), 32 with doctorates or other terminal degrees. **Location:** Suburban campus in small city; 8 miles from downtown. **Calendar:** Semester, limited summer session. **Microcomputers:** 26 located in libraries, computer centers. **Special facilities:** Share library with University of Alaska Anchorage.

DEGREES OFFERED. AA, BA, MA, MS, MBA. 3 associate degrees awarded in 1992. 66% in business and management, 34% social sciences. 82 bachelor's degrees awarded. 66% in business and management, 6% education, 7% teacher education, 5% letters/literature, 7% psychology. Graduate degrees offered in 9 major fields of study.

UNDERGRADUATE MAJORS. Associate: Business administration and management, business and management, environmental science, history, intercultural communications, Pacific area studies, philosophy/religion, social sciences, tourism. **Bachelor's:** Accounting, business administration and management, business and management, communications, comparative literature, dramatic arts, elementary education, environmental science, fine arts, history, human resources education, intercultural communications, international business management, marketing management, music, organizational administration, outdoor studies, Pacific area studies, philosophy/religion, precounseling, prelaw, psychology, renewable natural resources, social sciences, tourism.

ACADEMIC PROGRAMS. Accelerated program, double major, dual enrollment of high school students, independent study, internships, study abroad, teacher preparation, visiting/exchange student program, weekend college. **Remedial services:** Learning center, remedial instruction, special counselor, tutoring. **Placement/credit:** AP, CLEP General and Subject, institutional tests; 15 credit hours maximum for associate degree; 45 credit hours maximum for bachelor's degree.

ACADEMIC REQUIREMENTS. Freshmen must earn minimum GPA of 1.75 to continue in good standing. 33% of freshmen return for sophomore year. Students must declare major by end of second year. **Graduation requirements:** 64 hours for associate (24 in major), 128 hours for bachelor's (50 in major). Most students required to take courses in English, foreign languages, history, humanities, mathematics, biological/physical sciences, social sciences.

FRESHMAN ADMISSIONS. Selection criteria: High school record and test scores most important. **High school preparation:** 12 units recommended. Recommended units include biological science 1, English 3, mathematics 3, physical science 2 and social science 3. **Test requirements:** SAT or ACT; score report by August 15.

1992 FRESHMAN CLASS PROFILE. 245 men and women applied, 132 accepted; 19 men enrolled, 39 women enrolled. 45% had high school GPA of 3.0 or higher, 50% between 2.0 and 2.99. 31% were in top tenth and 38% were in top quarter of graduating class. **Academic background:** Mid 50% of enrolled freshmen had SAT-V between 360-500, SAT-M between 390-550; ACT composite between 18-26. 63% submitted SAT scores, 55% submitted ACT scores. **Characteristics:** 80% from in state, 90% commute, 28% have minority backgrounds. Average age is 21.

FALL-TERM APPLICATIONS. $25 fee. Closing date August 15; priority given to applications received by May 15; applicants notified on a rolling basis. Interview required. Deferred admission available.

STUDENT LIFE. Housing: Dormitories (coed); apartment housing available. **Activities:** Student government, magazine, student newspaper, yearbook, choral groups, dance, drama, music ensembles, Native Youth Games, International Student Association, Student Organization of Native Americans. **Additional information:** Student representation on faculty committees and councils stressed.

ATHLETICS. Intramural: Basketball, cross-country, skiing, soccer, table tennis, volleyball.

STUDENT SERVICES. Career counseling, employment service for undergraduates, freshman orientation, health services, personal counseling, placement service for graduates, 010, services/facilities for handicapped.

ANNUAL EXPENSES. Tuition and fees (1992-93): $6,930. **Room and board:** $4,050. **Books and supplies:** $600. **Other expenses:** $1,200.

FINANCIAL AID. 69% of freshmen, 50% of continuing students receive some form of aid. 97% of grants, 12% of loans, all jobs based on need. Academic, religious affiliation scholarships available. **Aid applications:** No closing date; priority given to applications received by March 15; applicants notified on a rolling basis beginning on or about March 15; must reply within 4 weeks.

ADDRESS/TELEPHONE. Curt Luttrell, Director of Admissions, Alaska Pacific University, 4101 University Drive, Anchorage, AK 99508-4672. (907) 564-8248. (800) 252-7528. Fax: (907) 562-4276.

Prince William Sound Community College
Valdez, Alaska CB code: 4636

2-year public community college, coed. Founded in 1978. **Accreditation:** Regional. **Undergraduate enrollment:** 22 men, 37 women full time; 326 men, 231 women part time. **Faculty:** 47 total (9 full time), 1 with doctorate or other terminal degree. **Location:** Rural campus in small town; 300 miles from Anchorage. **Calendar:** Semester, limited summer session. Extensive evening/early morning classes. **Microcomputers:** Located in computer centers.

DEGREES OFFERED. AA, AAS. 11 associate degrees awarded in 1992. 100% in multi/interdisciplinary studies.

UNDERGRADUATE MAJORS. Fishing and fisheries, liberal/general studies, radio/television broadcasting, secretarial and related programs, special education.

ACADEMIC PROGRAMS. 2-year transfer program, dual enrollment of high school students, independent study, internships, teacher preparation. **Remedial services:** Learning center, reduced course load, remedial instruction. **Placement/credit:** CLEP General and Subject, institutional tests.

ACADEMIC REQUIREMENTS. No policy requiring minimum GPA; records of students having academic difficulty are reviewed individually. Students must declare major on application. **Graduation requirements:** 60 hours for associate (30 in major). Most students required to take courses in English, humanities, mathematics, biological/physical sciences, social sciences.

FRESHMAN ADMISSIONS. Selection criteria: Open admissions.

1992 FRESHMAN CLASS PROFILE. 8 men, 16 women enrolled. **Characteristics:** 95% from in state, 90% commute, 25% have minority backgrounds. Average age is 26.

FALL-TERM APPLICATIONS. $10 fee. No closing date; applicants notified on a rolling basis. Early admission available.

STUDENT LIFE. Housing: Apartment housing available. **Activities:** Student government, film, radio, student newspaper, drama.

STUDENT SERVICES. Aptitude testing, career counseling, freshman orientation, services/facilities for handicapped.

ANNUAL EXPENSES. Tuition and fees: $1,172, $3,024 additional for out-of-state students. **Room and board:** $1,600 room only. **Books and supplies:** $500. **Other expenses:** $1,125.

FINANCIAL AID. 55% of freshmen, 35% of continuing students receive some form of aid. Grants, loans, jobs available. Academic, state/district residency, leadership, minority scholarships available. **Aid applications:** No closing date; applicants notified on a rolling basis. **Additional information:** Tuition waivers available to local residents and room scholarships available to Alaska residents.

ADDRESS/TELEPHONE. Dr. Dan Goehring, Dean of Instruction, Prince William Sound Community College, PO Box 97, Valdez, AK 99686. (907) 835-2678.

Sheldon Jackson College
Sitka, Alaska — CB code: 4742

4-year private liberal arts college, coed, affiliated with Presbyterian Church (USA). Founded in 1878. **Accreditation:** Regional. **Undergraduate enrollment:** 147 men, 152 women full time; 27 men, 26 women part time. **Faculty:** 34 total (26 full time), 12 with doctorates or other terminal degrees. **Location:** Suburban campus in small town; 882 air miles from Seattle, Washington, 90 miles from Juneau. **Calendar:** 4-1-4, limited summer session. **Microcomputers:** 20 located in libraries, classrooms, computer centers. **Special facilities:** Salmon hatchery, motor vessel for research and recreation, sea kayaks, wilderness center.

DEGREES OFFERED. AA, AS, BA, BS. 10 associate degrees awarded in 1992. 10% in agriculture, 30% business and management, 30% education, 30% multi/interdisciplinary studies. 21 bachelor's degrees awarded. 24% in agriculture, 12% business and management, 40% teacher education, 24% multi/interdisciplinary studies.

UNDERGRADUATE MAJORS. Associate: Aquaculture, business administration and management, business and management, education, fishing and fisheries, forestry and related sciences, history, humanities, humanities and social sciences, liberal/general studies, renewable natural resources, science technologies. **Bachelor's:** Aquaculture, business administration and management, business and management, education, elementary education, fishing and fisheries, humanities, humanities and social sciences, language arts, liberal/general studies, math/science education, parks and recreation management, renewable natural resources, secondary education, social science education, social sciences.

ACADEMIC PROGRAMS. 2-year transfer program, cooperative education, double major, dual enrollment of high school students, independent study, internships, teacher preparation, cross-registration; liberal arts/career combination in forestry. **Remedial services:** Learning center, remedial instruction, special counselor, tutoring. **Placement/credit:** AP, CLEP General and Subject, institutional tests; 40 credit hours maximum for associate degree; 100 credit hours maximum for bachelor's degree.

ACADEMIC REQUIREMENTS. Freshmen must earn minimum GPA of 1.5 to continue in good standing. 55% of freshmen return for sophomore year. Students must declare major by end of second year. **Graduation requirements:** 64 hours for associate (12 in major), 130 hours for bachelor's (30 in major). Most students required to take courses in arts/fine arts, computer science, English, humanities, mathematics, philosophy/religion, biological/physical sciences, social sciences. **Postgraduate studies:** 65% from 2-year programs enter 4-year programs. **Additional information:** Consortium course with Alaska Public Safety Academy offered.

FRESHMAN ADMISSIONS. Selection criteria: Open admissions. Recommended units include English 4, mathematics 2, social science 4 and science 2.

1992 FRESHMAN CLASS PROFILE. 39 men, 45 women enrolled. **Characteristics:** 59% from in state, 87% live in college housing, 36% have minority backgrounds.

FALL-TERM APPLICATIONS. $30 fee. No closing date; priority given to applications received by August 1; applicants notified on a rolling basis. Interview recommended. Deferred admission available.

STUDENT LIFE. Housing: Dormitories (men, women, coed); apartment housing available. Married student apartments very limited. **Activities:** Student government, yearbook, choral groups, drama, musical theater, religious student group, drama club, rod and gun club, Ten Ten Club(Bible study). **Additional information:** Hiking, fishing, hunting, sea kayaking, sailing, and several other outdoor activities available. Most students leave campus only at Christmas and at end of spring semester.

ATHLETICS. NAIA. **Intercollegiate:** Basketball. **Intramural:** Badminton, basketball, handball, racquetball, soccer, swimming, table tennis, volleyball, water polo, wrestling M.

STUDENT SERVICES. Career counseling, freshman orientation, on-campus day care, personal counseling, veterans counselor, services/facilities for handicapped.

ANNUAL EXPENSES. Tuition and fees: $9,116. **Room and board:** $4,800. **Books and supplies:** $500. **Other expenses:** $1,000.

FINANCIAL AID. 91% of freshmen, 91% of continuing students receive some form of aid. 76% of grants, 95% of loans, 94% of jobs based on need. Academic, music/drama, athletic, leadership, minority scholarships available. **Aid applications:** No closing date; priority given to applications received by April 1; applicants notified on a rolling basis beginning on or about March 15; must reply within 4 weeks. **Additional information:** Financial aid available from Bureau of Indian Affairs and Alaska State Loan Program.

ADDRESS/TELEPHONE. Dennis Trotter, Director of Admissions, Sheldon Jackson College, 801 Lincoln Street, Sitka, AK 99835. (907) 747-5221. (800) 544-2231. Fax: (907) 747-5212. (800) 478-5220 (within Alaska).

University of Alaska Anchorage
Anchorage, Alaska — CB code: 4896

4-year public university, coed. Founded in 1976. **Accreditation:** Regional. **Undergraduate enrollment:** 2,684 men, 3,448 women full time; 4,028 men, 6,522 women part time. **Graduate enrollment:** 74 men, 99 women full time; 148 men, 201 women part time. **Faculty:** 1,180 total (405 full time), 189 with doctorates or other terminal degrees. **Location:** Urban campus in small city; 7 miles from downtown. **Calendar:** Semester, limited summer session. Extensive evening/early morning classes. **Microcomputers:** Located in computer centers. **Special facilities:** Arctic Environment Information Data Center, film library, Alaska Center for International Business, Center for Alcohol and Addiction Studies, Center for High Latitude Health Research, Institute for Circumpolar Health, Institute for Social and Economic Research.

DEGREES OFFERED. AA, AAS, BA, BS, MA, MS, MBA, MFA, MEd. 475 associate degrees awarded in 1992. 11% in business and management, 5% engineering technologies, 12% allied health, 44% multi/interdisciplinary studies, 18% trade and industry. 524 bachelor's degrees awarded. 25% in business and management, 5% communications, 19% teacher education, 12% health sciences, 6% psychology, 15% social sciences. Graduate degrees offered in 23 major fields of study.

UNDERGRADUATE MAJORS. Associate: Accounting, air traffic control, aircraft mechanics, airline piloting and navigation, architectural technologies, automotive mechanics, automotive technology, aviation management, business administration and management, business and management, business and office, business computer/console/peripheral equipment operation, business data processing and related programs, business data programming, clinical laboratory science, computer programming, data processing, dental assistant, dental hygiene, diesel engine mechanics, drafting, electrical and electronics equipment repair, electronic technology, fire control and safety technology, food management, food production/management/services, home economics, industrial technology, instrumentation technology, interior design, liberal/general studies, medical assistant, medical laboratory technologies, medical records administration, mental health/human services, mining and petroleum technologies, nursing, office supervision and management, secretarial and related programs, survey and mapping technology, welding technology. **Bachelor's:** Accounting, advertising, anthropology, biological and physical sciences, biology, business administration and management, business and management, chemistry, civil engineering, computer and information sciences, criminal justice studies, dramatic arts, economics, elementary education, English, finance, fine arts, health sciences, history, journalism, liberal/general studies, management information systems, marketing management, marketing research, mathematics, music, music education, music performance, nursing, physical education, political science and government, psychology, public relations, radio/television technology, secondary education, social work, sociology, studio art, survey and mapping technology, surveying and mapping sciences.

ACADEMIC PROGRAMS. 2-year transfer program, cooperative education, double major, dual enrollment of high school students, independent study, internships, student-designed major, study abroad, teacher preparation, visiting/exchange student program; liberal arts/career combination in health sciences. **Remedial services:** Learning center, remedial instruction, special counselor, tutoring, adult basic education. **Placement/credit:** AP, CLEP General, institutional tests; 21 credit hours maximum for bachelor's degree.

ACADEMIC REQUIREMENTS. Freshmen must earn minimum GPA of 2.0 to continue in good standing. Students must declare major by end of second year. **Graduation requirements:** 60 hours for associate (20 in major), 120 hours for bachelor's (35 in major). Most students required to take courses in arts/fine arts, English, history, mathematics, biological/physical sciences, social sciences.

FRESHMAN ADMISSIONS. Selection criteria: 2.5 high school GPA required. Recommended units include English 3, foreign language 1, mathematics 2, social science 1 and science 1. One-2 additional units in computer science and 1-2 art also recommended. Specific recommendations vary by program. **Test requirements:** SAT or ACT; score report by August 1.

1992 FRESHMAN CLASS PROFILE. 617 men, 682 women enrolled. **Characteristics:** 90% from in state, 91% commute, 23% have minority backgrounds, 2% are foreign students.

FALL-TERM APPLICATIONS. $35 fee. Closing date May 1; priority given to applications received by April 1; applicants notified on a rolling basis. Interview required for nursing applicants. Portfolio required for art applicants. Deferred and early admission available.

STUDENT LIFE. Housing: Apartment housing available. **Activities:** Student government, radio, student newspaper, choral groups, concert band, drama, music ensembles, musical theater, pep band, university community ministry, Alaska Native Student Organization, African-American Association, Bahai' Club, College Republicans, Korean Campus Crusade for Christ, Intervarsity Christian Fellowship, La Tertulia (Spanish club), Korean-American Association.

ATHLETICS. NCAA. **Intercollegiate:** Basketball, cross-country M, diving M, gymnastics W, ice hockey M, skiing, swimming M, volleyball W. **Intramural:** Basketball, ice hockey, racquetball, skiing, softball, volleyball, water polo.

STUDENT SERVICES. Career counseling, employment service for undergraduates, freshman orientation, health services, on-campus day care, personal counseling, placement service for graduates, veterans counselor, services/facilities for handicapped.

ANNUAL EXPENSES. Tuition and fees: $1,788, $3,328 additional for out-of-state students. **Room and board:** $2,300 room only. **Books and supplies:** $490. **Other expenses:** $1,180.

FINANCIAL AID. 34% of freshmen, 70% of continuing students receive some form of aid. 90% of grants, 13% of loans, 69% of jobs based on need. Academic, music/drama, art, athletic, leadership scholarships available. **Aid applications:** No closing date; priority given to applications received by May 15; applicants notified on a rolling basis beginning on or about June 1; must reply within 3 weeks.

ADDRESS/TELEPHONE. Linda Berg Smith, Associate Vice Chancellor of Enrollment Services, University of Alaska Anchorage, 3211 Providence Drive, Anchorage, AK 99508-4675. (907) 786-1525. Fax: (907) 786-4888.

University of Alaska Fairbanks
Fairbanks, Alaska — CB code: 4866

Admissions:	76% of applicants accepted
Based on:	••• School record
	• Test scores
Completion:	85% of freshmen end year in good standing
	20% enter graduate study

4-year public university, coed. Founded in 1917. **Accreditation:** Regional. **Undergraduate enrollment:** 1,783 men, 1,659 women full time; 306 men, 594 women part time. **Graduate enrollment:** 246 men, 150 women full time; 183 men, 151 women part time. **Faculty:** 717 total (524 full time), 365 with doctorates or other terminal degrees. **Location:** Suburban campus in large town; 4 miles from downtown. **Calendar:** Semester, limited summer session. **Microcomputers:** Located in dormitories, libraries, classrooms, computer centers. **Special facilities:** Art and natural history museum, geophysical institute, wildlife and arctic biology library.

DEGREES OFFERED. AA, AAS, BA, BS, BFA, MA, MS, MBA, MFA, MEd, PhD. 103 associate degrees awarded in 1992. 17% in business and management, 8% allied health, 7% home economics, 45% multi/interdisciplinary studies, 9% parks/recreation, protective services, public affairs, 14% trade and industry. 437 bachelor's degrees awarded. 17% in business and management, 16% teacher education, 10% engineering, 6% letters/literature, 10% parks/recreation, protective services, public affairs, 5% psychology, 8% social sciences. Graduate degrees offered in 42 major fields of study.

UNDERGRADUATE MAJORS. Associate: Accounting, aircraft mechanics, airline piloting and navigation, business and management, business and office, child development/care/guidance, community health work, finance, fire control and safety technology, food production/management/services, legal assistant/paralegal, liberal/general studies, mental health/human services, secretarial and related programs. **Bachelor's:** Accounting, American Indian studies, anthropology, biological and physical sciences, biology, business administration and management, business and management, chemistry, civil engineering, computer and information sciences, criminal justice studies, dramatic arts, early childhood education, earth sciences, economics, education, electrical/electronics/communications engineering, elementary education, English, finance, fine arts, fishing and fisheries, foreign languages (multiple emphasis), geography, geological engineering, geology, history, humanities, humanities and social sciences, journalism, linguistics, mathematics, mechanical engineering, mining and mineral engineering, music, Native American languages, northern studies, petroleum engineering, philosophy, physical education, physics, political science and government, psychology, renewable natural resources, rural development, Russian and Slavic studies, secondary education, social work, sociology, speech, statistics, wildlife management.

ACADEMIC PROGRAMS. 2-year transfer program, double major, dual enrollment of high school students, education specialist degree, honors program, independent study, internships, student-designed major, study abroad, teacher preparation, telecourses, visiting/exchange student program. **Remedial services:** Remedial instruction, special counselor, tutoring. **ROTC:** Army. **Placement/credit:** AP, CLEP General and Subject, institutional tests.

ACADEMIC REQUIREMENTS. Freshmen must earn minimum GPA of 2.0 to continue in good standing. 55% of freshmen return for sophomore year. Students must declare major by end of second year. **Graduation requirements:** 60 hours for associate, 120 hours for bachelor's (30 in major). Most students required to take courses in English, humanities, mathematics, biological/physical sciences, social sciences. **Postgraduate studies:** 1% enter law school, 2% enter medical school, 5% enter MBA programs, 12% enter other graduate study.

FRESHMAN ADMISSIONS. Selection criteria: Minimum high school GPA of 2.0. SAT and ACT scores considered. **High school preparation:** 16 units required. Required units include English 4, mathematics 3, social science 3 and science 3. Mathematics should include: algebra, geometry and trigonometry. **Test requirements:** SAT or ACT (ACT preferred); score report by September 1.

1992 FRESHMAN CLASS PROFILE. 1,744 men and women applied, 1,326 accepted; 441 men enrolled, 466 women enrolled. 1% were in top tenth and 7% were in top quarter of graduating class. **Academic background:** Mid 50% of enrolled freshmen had SAT-V between 380-540, SAT-M between 410-590; ACT composite between 17-25. 54% submitted SAT scores, 59% submitted ACT scores. **Characteristics:** 82% from in state, 75% live in college housing, 23% have minority backgrounds, 1% are foreign students. Average age is 22.

FALL-TERM APPLICATIONS. $30 fee. Closing date August 1; applicants notified on a rolling basis. CRDA. Deferred admission available.

STUDENT LIFE. Housing: Dormitories (men, women, coed); apartment, handicapped housing available. Housing applicants advised to complete admissions process no later than July 1. **Activities:** Student government, magazine, radio, student newspaper, television, choral groups, concert band, dance, drama, jazz band, music ensembles, musical theater, pep band, symphony orchestra, fraternities, sororities, United Campus Ministry, Black Awareness, Young Republicans, Young Democrats, Alaska Native Student Organization, Disabled Students Association, North Star Chinese Association, Recreational Hockey Association, Alaska Alpine Club, Snowboarding Association. **Additional information:** Interactive environment that combines educational opportunity and outdoor recreational facilities.

ATHLETICS. NCAA. **Intercollegiate:** Basketball, cross-country, ice hockey M, rifle, skiing, volleyball W. **Intramural:** Badminton, basketball, bowling, cross-country, fencing, gymnastics, handball, ice hockey, racquetball, rifle, skiing, soccer, softball, swimming, table tennis, tennis, volleyball, water polo, wrestling.

STUDENT SERVICES. Career counseling, employment service for undergraduates, freshman orientation, health services, personal counseling, placement service for graduates, veterans counselor, adult re-entry services, rural student services, services/facilities for handicapped.

ANNUAL EXPENSES. Tuition and fees: $2,214, $3,328 additional for out-of-state students. **Room and board:** $3,220. **Books and supplies:** $550. **Other expenses:** $1,980.

FINANCIAL AID. 70% of continuing students receive some form of aid. 70% of grants, 98% of loans, 5% of jobs based on need. Music/drama, art, athletic, state/district residency scholarships available. **Aid applications:** No closing date; priority given to applications received by May 15; applicants notified on a rolling basis beginning on or about July 1; must reply within 2 weeks.

ADDRESS/TELEPHONE. Ann Tremarello, Director of Admissions and Records, University of Alaska Fairbanks, Fairbanks, AK 99775-0060. (907) 474-7821.

University of Alaska Southeast
Juneau, Alaska — CB code: 4897

4-year public university, coed. Founded in 1972. **Accreditation:** Regional. **Undergraduate enrollment:** 226 men, 388 women full time; 899 men, 1,561 women part time. **Graduate enrollment:** 2 men, 3 women full time; 16 men,

32 women part time. **Faculty:** 211 total (77 full time), 22 with doctorates or other terminal degrees. **Location:** Rural campus in large town; 900 miles from Seattle, Washington, and 700 miles from Anchorage. **Calendar:** Semester, limited summer session. Saturday and extensive evening/early morning classes. **Microcomputers:** 50 located in dormitories, classrooms, computer centers. **Additional facts:** All campuses accessible only by ferry or air.

DEGREES OFFERED. AA, AAS, BA, BS, MA, MBA, MEd. 80 associate degrees awarded in 1992. 8% in law, 79% multi/interdisciplinary studies, 7% trade and industry. 39 bachelor's degrees awarded. 33% in business and management, 31% teacher education, 10% life sciences, 23% multi/interdisciplinary studies. Graduate degrees offered in 3 major fields of study.

UNDERGRADUATE MAJORS. Associate: Automotive mechanics, business administration and management, construction, diesel engine mechanics, early childhood education, legal assistant/paralegal, liberal/general studies, marine maintenance, office supervision and management, secretarial and related programs, tourism, vehicle and mobile equipment mechanics. **Bachelor's:** Biology, business administration and management, early childhood education, elementary education, liberal/general studies, political science and government, secondary education.

ACADEMIC PROGRAMS. 2-year transfer program, computer delivered (on-line) credit-bearing course offerings, cooperative education, double major, dual enrollment of high school students, independent study, internships, student-designed major, teacher preparation, telecourses, cross-registration. **Remedial services:** Learning center, preadmission summer program, remedial instruction, tutoring. **Placement/credit:** AP, CLEP General and Subject, institutional tests; 30 credit hours maximum for bachelor's degree.

ACADEMIC REQUIREMENTS. Freshmen must earn minimum GPA of 2.0 to continue in good standing. Students must declare major on application. **Graduation requirements:** 60 hours for associate, 120 hours for bachelor's. Most students required to take courses in arts/fine arts, English, humanities, mathematics, biological/physical sciences, social sciences.

FRESHMAN ADMISSIONS. Selection criteria: High school record and test scores most important. Students not meeting BA requirements counseled to AA or certificate program with possibility of later transfer to BA program. Some BA programs admit students as pre-majors and upon satisfying prerequisites admitted to the major. **High school preparation:** 11 units recommended. Recommended units include English 4, mathematics 2, social science 3 and science 2. **Test requirements:** SAT or ACT; score report by September 1.

1992 FRESHMAN CLASS PROFILE. 42 men, 83 women enrolled. 22% had high school GPA of 3.0 or higher, 75% between 2.0 and 2.99. **Characteristics:** 93% from in state, 90% commute, 30% have minority backgrounds. Average age is 22.

FALL-TERM APPLICATIONS. $20 fee. No closing date; priority given to applications received by July 15; applicants notified on a rolling basis. Deferred admission available.

STUDENT LIFE. Housing: Apartment, handicapped housing available. Substance-free units for students under 21-years. **Activities:** Student government, student newspaper, choral groups, concert band, music ensembles, symphony orchestra.

ATHLETICS. NAIA. **Intramural:** Badminton, basketball, bowling, rifle, soccer, volleyball.

STUDENT SERVICES. Career counseling, freshman orientation, health services, on-campus day care, personal counseling, veterans counselor, services/facilities for handicapped.

ANNUAL EXPENSES. Tuition and fees: $1,698, $3,328 additional for out-of-state students. **Room and board:** $2,200 room only. **Books and supplies:** $500. **Other expenses:** $1,000.

FINANCIAL AID. 75% of freshmen, 75% of continuing students receive some form of aid. 68% of grants, 6% of loans, all jobs based on need. 45 enrolled freshmen were judged to have need, all were offered aid. Academic, music/drama, art, state/district residency, leadership scholarships available. **Aid applications:** No closing date; priority given to applications received by June 1; applicants notified on a rolling basis beginning on or about July 1; must reply within 2 weeks. **Additional information:** Foundation scholarships deadline February 15, freshman scholarship deadline March 31, continuing and transfer scholarship deadline May 15.

ADDRESS/TELEPHONE. Greg Wagner, Coordinator Recruitment/Placement, University of Alaska Southeast, 11120 Glacier Highway, Juneau, AK 99801. (907) 789-4458.

Arizona

American Indian Bible College
Phoenix, Arizona

4-year private Bible college, coed, affiliated with Assemblies of God. Founded in 1957. **Accreditation:** Regional. **Undergraduate enrollment:** 65 men, 59 women full time; 1 man, 2 women part time. **Faculty:** 12 total (9 full time), 3 with doctorates or other terminal degrees. **Location:** Urban campus in very large city. **Calendar:** Semester. **Microcomputers:** 5 located in computer centers.

DEGREES OFFERED. AA, BA. 1 associate degree awarded in 1992. 100% in business/office and marketing/distribution. 6 bachelor's degrees awarded. 30% in education, 70% philosophy, religion, theology.

UNDERGRADUATE MAJORS. Associate: Business and office. **Bachelor's:** Elementary education, ministerial studies, religious education.

ACADEMIC PROGRAMS. Double major, independent study, internships, student-designed major. **Remedial services:** Reduced course load, remedial instruction, special counselor, tutoring. **Placement/credit:** Institutional tests.

ACADEMIC REQUIREMENTS. Freshmen must earn minimum GPA of 1.5 to continue in good standing. Students must declare major by end of first year. **Graduation requirements:** 73 hours for associate (24 in major), 128 hours for bachelor's (42 in major). Most students required to take courses in English, history, mathematics, philosophy/religion, biological/physical sciences, social sciences. **Postgraduate studies:** 21% from 2-year programs enter 4-year programs.

FRESHMAN ADMISSIONS. Selection criteria: Applicants must show Christian commitment, willingness to abide by Student Handbook, and favorable reference from home pastor.

1992 FRESHMAN CLASS PROFILE. 17 men, 10 women enrolled. **Characteristics:** 51% from in state, 95% live in college housing, 82% have minority backgrounds. Average age is 21.

FALL-TERM APPLICATIONS. No fee. Closing date August 15; applicants notified on a rolling basis beginning on or about January 1; must reply by registration. Interview recommended.

STUDENT LIFE. Housing: Dormitories (men, women). **Activities:** Student government, yearbook, choral groups, music ensembles. **Additional information:** Religious observance required.

ATHLETICS. Intercollegiate: Basketball M, volleyball. **Intramural:** Basketball, bowling.

STUDENT SERVICES. Aptitude testing, career counseling, employment service for undergraduates, freshman orientation, personal counseling, placement service for graduates, special adviser for adult students, services/facilities for handicapped.

ANNUAL EXPENSES. Tuition and fees: $3,012. **Room and board:** $2,800. **Books and supplies:** $450. **Other expenses:** $1,400.

FINANCIAL AID. 100% of freshmen, 99% of continuing students receive some form of aid. 99% of grants, 82% of loans, all jobs based on need. Academic, leadership scholarships available. **Aid applications:** Closing date August 23; priority given to applications received by April 1; applicants notified on a rolling basis beginning on or about July 15; must reply by registration.

ADDRESS/TELEPHONE. Pete Cordona, Director of Admissions, 10020 North 15th Avenue, Phoenix, AZ 85021-2199. (602) 944-3335. (800) 933-3828. Fax: (602) 943-8299.

Arizona College of the Bible
Phoenix, Arizona — CB code: 1244

4-year private Bible college, coed, nondenominational. Founded in 1971. **Accreditation:** Regional candidate. **Undergraduate enrollment:** 45 men, 29 women full time; 16 men, 4 women part time. **Faculty:** 24 total (9 full time), 6 with doctorates or other terminal degrees. **Location:** Suburban campus in very large city. **Calendar:** Semester, limited summer session. **Microcomputers:** 6 located in libraries, computer centers.

DEGREES OFFERED. AA, BA. 100% in philosophy, religion, theology. 18 bachelor's degrees awarded. 22% in teacher education, 78% philosophy, religion, theology.

UNDERGRADUATE MAJORS. Associate: Religious education. **Bachelor's:** Bible studies, elementary education, missionary studies, pastoral studies, religious education, religious music, specialized religious studies, theological studies.

ACADEMIC PROGRAMS. Double major, dual enrollment of high school students, independent study, internships, teacher preparation, summer study trip to Jordan, Egypt, and the Holy Land in alternate years. **Remedial services:** Remedial instruction. **Placement/credit:** CLEP General and Subject.

ACADEMIC REQUIREMENTS. Freshmen must earn minimum GPA of 2.0 to continue in good standing. 50% of freshmen return for sophomore year. Students must declare major by end of second year. **Graduation requirements:** 64 hours for associate (24 in major), 130 hours for bachelor's (45 in major). Most students required to take courses in English, history, humanities, mathematics, philosophy/religion, biological/physical sciences, social sciences. **Postgraduate studies:** 33% from 2-year programs enter 4-year programs.

FRESHMAN ADMISSIONS. Selection criteria: Open admissions. Religious affiliation or commitment, essay, and recommendations are considered. **Test requirements:** SAT or ACT for placement.

1992 FRESHMAN CLASS PROFILE. 21 men, 9 women enrolled. 50% had high school GPA of 3.0 or higher, 45% between 2.0 and 2.99. 8% were in top tenth and 67% were in top quarter of graduating class. **Characteristics:** 90% from in state, 64% commute, 30% have minority backgrounds, 1% are foreign students. Average age is 20.

FALL-TERM APPLICATIONS. $20 fee. No closing date; applicants notified on a rolling basis beginning on or about August 15; must reply by registration. Audition required for religious music applicants. Essay required. Interview recommended. Deferred and early admission available.

STUDENT LIFE. Housing: Dormitories (men, women). **Activities:** Student government, yearbook, choral groups, music ensembles, musical theater, missionary prayer fellowship. **Additional information:** Religious observance required.

ATHLETICS. NSCAA. **Intercollegiate:** Basketball M, volleyball W. **Intramural:** Soccer M.

STUDENT SERVICES. Career counseling, freshman orientation, personal counseling, veterans counselor, services/facilities for handicapped.

ANNUAL EXPENSES. Tuition and fees: $4,830. **Room and board:** $1,420 room only. **Books and supplies:** $450. **Other expenses:** $1,400.

FINANCIAL AID. 44% of freshmen, 81% of continuing students receive some form of aid. 85% of grants, 54% of loans, all jobs based on need. 16 enrolled freshmen were judged to have need, all were offered aid. Academic, music/drama, leadership, alumni affiliation scholarships available. **Aid applications:** Closing date September 15; priority given to applications received by April 15; applicants notified on a rolling basis beginning on or about July 1; must reply within 2 weeks.

ADDRESS/TELEPHONE. B. Frances Scoggin, Director of Admissions, Arizona College of the Bible, 2045 West Northern Avenue, Phoenix, AZ 85021-5197. (602) 995-2670 ext.26. (800) 847-2138.

Arizona State University
Tempe, Arizona — CB code: 4007

Admissions:	82% of applicants accepted
Based on:	••• School record, test scores
	• Activities, essay, recommendations
Completion:	38% graduate

4-year public university, coed. Founded in 1885. **Accreditation:** Regional. **Undergraduate enrollment:** 12,061 men, 11,689 women full time; 4,107 men, 4,049 women part time. **Graduate enrollment:** 2,762 men, 2,321 women full time; 3,013 men, 3,643 women part time. **Faculty:** 1,822 total (1,774 full time), 1,475 with doctorates or other terminal degrees. **Location:** Suburban campus in small city; 10 miles from downtown Phoenix. **Calendar:** Semester, extensive summer session. **Microcomputers:** 1,250 located in dormitories, libraries, classrooms, computer centers. **Special facilities:** Center for meteorite studies, solar energy research laboratory, center for solid state science, university art collections, Northlight Gallery, herbarium.

DEGREES OFFERED. BA, BS, BFA, MA, MS, MBA, MFA, MEd, MSW, PhD, EdD, JD. 6,012 bachelor's degrees awarded in 1992. 26% in business and management, 9% communications, 8% education, 7% engineering, 8% parks/recreation, protective services, public affairs, 5% psychology, 11% social sciences. Graduate degrees offered in 79 major fields of study.

UNDERGRADUATE MAJORS. Accounting, aeronautical technology, aerospace/aeronautical/astronautical engineering, agribusiness, American studies, anthropology, architecture, art education, basic clinical health sciences, bilingual/bicultural education, bioengineering and biomedical engineering, biology, botany, business and management, business education, chemical engineering, chemistry, Chinese, city/community/regional planning, civil engineering, civil technology, communications, computer and information sciences, computer engineering, contract management and procurement/purchasing, crafts, criminal justice studies, dance, dramatic arts, early childhood education, economics, electrical/electronics/communications engineering, electronic technology, elementary education, engineering and other disciplines, English, English education, finance, fine arts, foreign languages education, French, geography, geology, German, history, home economics, home economics education, humanities, humanities and social sciences, industrial design, industrial engineering, industrial technology, information sciences and systems, institutional management, interior design, Italian, Japanese, journalism, landscape architecture, liberal/general studies, manufacturing technology, marketing management, materials engineering, mathematics, mathematics education, mechanical engineering, microbiology, music, music education, music performance, music theory and composition, music therapy, nursing, parks and recreation management, philosophy, physical education, physics, political science and government, psychology, radio/television broadcasting, real estate, religion, renewable natural resources, Russian, science education, secondary education, social studies education, social work, sociology, Spanish, special education, speech pathology/audiology, speech/communication/theater education, tourism, wildlife biology, women's studies, zoology.

ACADEMIC PROGRAMS. Accelerated program, cooperative education, double major, dual enrollment of high school students, education specialist degree, honors program, independent study, internships, student-designed major, study abroad, teacher preparation, telecourses, visiting/exchange student program, Washington semester, cross-registration; liberal arts/career combination in engineering; combined bachelor's/graduate program in business administration. **Remedial services:** Learning center, reduced course load, remedial instruction, special counselor, tutoring. **ROTC:** Air Force, Army. **Placement/credit:** AP, CLEP General and Subject, institutional tests; 60 credit hours maximum for bachelor's degree.

ACADEMIC REQUIREMENTS. Freshmen must earn minimum GPA of 1.6 to continue in good standing. 73% of freshmen return for sophomore year. Students must declare major by end of second year. **Graduation requirements:** 126 hours for bachelor's (30 in major). Most students required to take courses in arts/fine arts, computer science, English, foreign languages, history, humanities, mathematics, biological/physical sciences, social sciences. **Additional information:** University Honors College offers small classes, priority registration, special advising, scholars residence hall with classrooms and computer facilities and dual enrollment in college of student's disciplinary major.

FRESHMAN ADMISSIONS. Selection criteria: In-state applicants should graduate in top 25% of class or have GPA of 3.0 or minimum ACT composite scores of 22 or SAT combined scores of 930. Out-of-state applicants need ACT composite scores of 24 or SAT combined scores of 1010. Additional requirements for some programs. **High school preparation:** 11 units required. Required units include English 4, mathematics 3, social science 2 and science 2. 2 years laboratory science and 2 years social science including American history recommended. College of Liberal Arts and Sciences recommends 2 foreign languages. Nursing requires 1 each physics and chemistry. Engineering recommends 3.5 mathematics, including calculus. **Test requirements:** SAT or ACT; score report by August 1.

1992 FRESHMAN CLASS PROFILE. 5,109 men applied, 4,244 accepted, 1,657 enrolled; 5,308 women applied, 4,254 accepted, 1,700 enrolled. 51% had high school GPA of 3.0 or higher, 47% between 2.0 and 2.99. 23% were in top tenth of graduating class. **Academic background:** Mid 50% of enrolled freshmen had SAT-V between 390-500, SAT-M between 450-590; ACT composite between 20-25. 67% submitted SAT scores, 52% submitted ACT scores. **Characteristics:** 57% from in state, 59% live in college housing, 20% have minority backgrounds, 4% are foreign students, 16% join fraternities/sororities. Average age is 19.

FALL-TERM APPLICATIONS. No fee. $35 fee for out-of-state applicants. No closing date; priority given to applications received by April 15; applicants notified on a rolling basis; must reply 30 days before the first day of classes. Audition required for music, dance, theater applicants. Portfolio required for graphic design, post baccalaureate certification in art education, architecture and environmental design applicants. Early admission available.

STUDENT LIFE. Housing: Dormitories (men, women, coed); apartment, fraternity, sorority, handicapped housing available. Spaces reserved at least 6 months before semester begins. Application for residence hall may be submitted prior to admission. **Activities:** Student government, magazine, radio, student newspaper, television, yearbook, choral groups, concert band, dance, drama, jazz band, marching band, music ensembles, musical theater, opera, pep band, symphony orchestra, fraternities, sororities, over 300 organizations, including academic, social service, and honorary societies. **Additional information:** Student Recreation Complex offers variety of programming including sports fitness, intramurals, and adaptive recreation.

ATHLETICS. NCAA. **Intercollegiate:** Archery, badminton, baseball M, basketball, cross-country, diving, football M, golf, gymnastics, softball W, swimming, tennis, track and field, volleyball W, wrestling M. **Intramural:** Badminton, basketball, bowling, cross-country, diving, field hockey, golf, racquetball, rugby M, skiing, softball, swimming, tennis, track and field, volleyball, water polo, wrestling M.

STUDENT SERVICES. Aptitude testing, career counseling, employment service for undergraduates, freshman orientation, health services, on-campus day care, personal counseling, placement service for graduates, special adviser for adult students, veterans counselor, services/facilities for handicapped.

ANNUAL EXPENSES. Tuition and fees: $1,844, $5,506 additional for out-of-state students. Law school students pay additional $1000 per year. **Room and board:** $4,850. **Books and supplies:** $700.

FINANCIAL AID. 65% of freshmen, 60% of continuing students receive some form of aid. Academic, music/drama, art, athletic, state/district residency, leadership, alumni affiliation, minority scholarships available. **Aid applications:** No closing date; priority given to applications received by March 1; applicants notified on a rolling basis; must reply within 30 days.

ADDRESS/TELEPHONE. Susan Clouse, Director of Undergraduate Admissions, Arizona State University, Tempe, AZ 85287-0112. (602) 965-7788. (800) 252-ASU1.

Arizona Western College
Yuma, Arizona — CB code: 4013

2-year public community college, coed. Founded in 1963. **Accreditation:** Regional. **Undergraduate enrollment:** 663 men, 833 women full time; 1,647 men, 2,248 women part time. **Faculty:** 334 total (81 full time), 18 with doctorates or other terminal degrees. **Location:** Rural campus in small city; 7 miles from downtown. **Calendar:** Semester, limited summer session. **Microcomputers:** 30 located in libraries, classrooms, computer centers.

DEGREES OFFERED. AA, AAS. 212 associate degrees awarded in 1992. 32% in business and management, 5% business/office and marketing/distribution, 13% health sciences, 21% multi/interdisciplinary studies, 7% parks/recreation, protective services, public affairs.

UNDERGRADUATE MAJORS. Agribusiness, agricultural business and management, agricultural sciences, air conditioning/heating/refrigeration mechanics, air conditioning/heating/refrigeration technology, animal sciences, automotive technology, biological and physical sciences, biology, business administration and management, business and management, business and office, chemistry, child development/care/guidance, computer and information sciences, criminal justice studies, drafting, drafting and design technology, dramatic arts, education, electrical technology, engineering, engineering and engineering-related technologies, English, English literature, environmental science, finance, fine arts, geology, home economics, humanities and social sciences, individual and family development, law enforcement and corrections, liberal/general studies, manufacturing technology, marketing and distribution, marketing management, mathematics, music, nursing, oceanography, physical education, physical sciences, physics, plant sciences, predentistry, premedicine, prepharmacy, preveterinary, radio/television broadcasting, secretarial and related programs, social sciences, Spanish, speech, trade and industrial education, visual and performing arts, welding technology, zoology.

ACADEMIC PROGRAMS. 2-year transfer program, cooperative education, dual enrollment of high school students, honors program, independent study, telecourses. **Remedial services:** Learning center, reduced course load, remedial instruction, special counselor, tutoring. **Placement/credit:** AP, CLEP General and Subject, institutional tests; 45 credit hours maximum for associate degree.

ACADEMIC REQUIREMENTS. Freshmen must earn minimum GPA of 2.0 to continue in good standing. 65% of freshmen return for sophomore year. **Graduation requirements:** 64 hours for associate (22 in major). Most students required to take courses in English, humanities, mathematics, biological/physical sciences, social sciences.

FRESHMAN ADMISSIONS. Selection criteria: Open admissions. Out-of-state applicants screened for social or disciplinary problems. Selective admission for nursing program.

1992 FRESHMAN CLASS PROFILE. 929 men, 1,098 women enrolled. **Characteristics:** 92% from in state, 92% commute, 53% have minority backgrounds, 1% are foreign students. Average age is 27.

FALL-TERM APPLICATIONS. No fee. No closing date; applicants notified on a rolling basis; must reply by registration. Deferred admission available.

STUDENT LIFE. Housing: Dormitories (men, women); apartment housing available. **Activities:** Student government, radio, student newspaper, choral groups, concert band, drama, music ensembles, pep band, Maya Club, Newman Club, MECHA, Phi Theta Kappa.

ATHLETICS. NJCAA. **Intercollegiate:** Baseball M, basketball M, football M, soccer M, softball W, volleyball W. **Intramural:** Badminton, basketball, bowling, football M, soccer M, softball, swimming, table tennis, volleyball.

STUDENT SERVICES. Career counseling, employment service for undergraduates, health services, on-campus day care, personal counseling, placement service for graduates, veterans counselor, services/facilities for handicapped.

ANNUAL EXPENSES. Tuition and fees (1992-93): $720, $4,230 additional for out-of-state students. **Room and board:** $2,590. **Books and supplies:** $350. **Other expenses:** $952.

FINANCIAL AID. 70% of freshmen, 70% of continuing students receive some form of aid. Grants, loans, jobs available. Academic, music/drama, art scholarships available. **Aid applications:** No closing date; priority given to applications received by March 15; applicants notified on a rolling basis beginning on or about May 15; must reply within 2 weeks.

ADDRESS/TELEPHONE. Richard Lott, Director of Admissions/Registrar, Arizona Western College, PO Box 929, Yuma, AZ 85366-0929. (602) 726-1050. Fax: (602)344-7730.

Central Arizona College
Coolidge, Arizona — CB code: 4122

2-year public community college, coed. Founded in 1962. **Accreditation:** Regional. **Undergraduate enrollment:** 6,646 men and women. **Faculty:** 364 total (93 full time), 14 with doctorates or other terminal degrees. **Location:** Rural campus in small town; 45 miles south of Phoenix. **Calendar:** Semester.

Microcomputers: Located in libraries, computer centers. **Special facilities:** Observatory, art gallery, theater.

DEGREES OFFERED. AA, AAS. 200 associate degrees awarded in 1992.

UNDERGRADUATE MAJORS. Accounting, agricultural sciences, automotive mechanics, automotive technology, biological and physical sciences, business administration and management, business and office, business data processing and related programs, business data programming, civil engineering, computer and information sciences, construction, criminal justice studies, criminology, data processing, diesel engine mechanics, dietetic aide/assistant, early childhood education, electronic technology, emergency medical technologies, engineering, engineering and engineering-related technologies, engineering mechanics, hotel/motel and restaurant management, humanities and social sciences, industrial equipment maintenance and repair, industrial technology, law enforcement and corrections technologies, legal secretary, liberal/general studies, manufacturing engineering, manufacturing technology, marketing management, mechanical engineering, medical secretary, mining and mineral engineering, mining and petroleum technologies, nursing, office supervision and management, preconstruction, secretarial and related programs, special education, trade and industrial supervision and management, vehicle and equipment operation, word processing.

ACADEMIC PROGRAMS. 2-year transfer program, dual enrollment of high school students, honors program, independent study, internships, student-designed major. **Remedial services:** Learning center, preadmission summer program, reduced course load, remedial instruction, special counselor, tutoring. **Placement/credit:** AP, CLEP General, institutional tests; 30 credit hours maximum for associate degree.

ACADEMIC REQUIREMENTS. Freshmen must earn minimum GPA of 1.5 to continue in good standing. **Graduation requirements:** 62 hours for associate. Most students required to take courses in English, mathematics, biological/physical sciences, social sciences.

FRESHMAN ADMISSIONS. Selection criteria: Open admissions. Selective admission to nursing programs.

1992 FRESHMAN CLASS PROFILE. 2,100 men and women enrolled. **Characteristics:** 97% from in state, 97% commute, 33% have minority backgrounds. Average age is 19.

FALL-TERM APPLICATIONS. No fee. No closing date; applicants notified on a rolling basis. Interview required for nursing applicants. Deferred admission available.

STUDENT LIFE. Housing: Dormitories (men, women). **Activities:** Student government, student newspaper, choral groups, drama, jazz band, music ensembles, musical theater, pep band, Native American club, Movmiento Estudiante Chicano de Aztlan, religious groups, Phi Theta Kappa.

ATHLETICS. NJCAA. **Intercollegiate:** Baseball M, basketball, cross-country M, softball W, track and field M, volleyball W. **Intramural:** Basketball, swimming, tennis. **Clubs:** Rodeo.

STUDENT SERVICES. Aptitude testing, career counseling, employment service for undergraduates, freshman orientation, on-campus day care, personal counseling, placement service for graduates, special adviser for adult students, tutoring, services/facilities for handicapped.

ANNUAL EXPENSES. Tuition and fees (1992-93): $594, $4,230 additional for out-of-state students. **Room and board:** $2,690. **Books and supplies:** $400. **Other expenses:** $1,500.

FINANCIAL AID. 60% of freshmen, 60% of continuing students receive some form of aid. 87% of grants, 97% of loans, 29% of jobs based on need. 375 enrolled freshmen were judged to have need, all were offered aid. Academic, music/drama, art, athletic, state/district residency scholarships available. **Aid applications:** No closing date; priority given to applications received by April 15; applicants notified on a rolling basis beginning on or about June 1; must reply within 3 weeks.

ADDRESS/TELEPHONE. Cherie McGlynn, College Registrar and District Director of Student Records, Central Arizona College, 8470 North Overfield Road, Coolidge, AZ 85228. (602) 426-4265.

Cochise College
Douglas, Arizona — CB code: 4097

2-year public community college, coed. Founded in 1962. **Accreditation:** Regional. **Undergraduate enrollment:** 1,523 men and women full time; 3,415 men and women part time. **Faculty:** 341 total (109 full time), 20 with doctorates or other terminal degrees. **Location:** Rural campus in large town; 120 miles from Tucson. **Calendar:** Semester, limited summer session. **Microcomputers:** 100 located in libraries, classrooms, computer centers. **Special facilities:** Hansen Oriental Art Collection. **Additional facts:** Courses offered at 9 locations throughout county.

DEGREES OFFERED. AA, AS, AAS. 280 associate degrees awarded in 1992. 10% in business and management, 5% computer sciences, 10% health sciences, 57% multi/interdisciplinary studies, 11% trade and industry.

UNDERGRADUATE MAJORS. Accounting, agricultural sciences, aircraft mechanics, airline piloting and navigation, anthropology, art education, biological and physical sciences, biology, business administration and management, business and management, business and office, business data processing and related programs, business data programming, chemistry, communications, computer and information sciences, drafting, early childhood education, electronic technology, English, finance, fine arts, fire control and safety technology, history, hotel/motel and restaurant management, information sciences and systems, international public service, journalism, law enforcement and corrections technologies, legal secretary, liberal/general studies, management information systems, manufacturing technology, mathematics, medical secretary, nursing, office supervision and management, physical education, political science and government, precision metal work, preengineering, prelaw, psychology, public administration, secretarial and related programs, social work, Spanish, welding technology.

ACADEMIC PROGRAMS. 2-year transfer program, cooperative education, double major, dual enrollment of high school students, independent study, internships, student-designed major, telecourses, weekend college, cross-registration. **Remedial services:** Learning center, preadmission summer program, reduced course load, remedial instruction, tutoring. **Placement/credit:** CLEP General and Subject, institutional tests; 30 credit hours maximum for associate degree.

ACADEMIC REQUIREMENTS. Freshmen must earn minimum GPA of 2.0 to continue in good standing. 31% of freshmen return for sophomore year. Students must declare major on enrollment. **Graduation requirements:** 60 hours for associate (30 in major). Most students required to take courses in English, humanities, mathematics, biological/physical sciences, social sciences. **Additional information:** Freshman/sophomore courses offered for 4-year transfer programs in premedicine, predentistry, prepharmacy, preveterinary, and prelaw. Cross-registration with University of Arizona and Northern Arizona University; transfer program with New Mexico State University (NM).

FRESHMAN ADMISSIONS. Selection criteria: Open admissions. Selective admissions for professional pilot, aviation maintenance, and nursing programs. **Additional information:** Walk-in admission available. Early admission only for high school seniors planning to attend full time.

1992 FRESHMAN CLASS PROFILE. 713 men and women enrolled. **Characteristics:** 93% from in state, 90% commute, 50% have minority backgrounds, 4% are foreign students. Average age is 26.

FALL-TERM APPLICATIONS. No fee. $5 fee for out-of-state applicants. No closing date; applicants notified on a rolling basis; must reply by registration. Interview required for professional pilot, aviation maintenance, and nursing applicants. Deferred and early admission available.

STUDENT LIFE. Housing: Dormitories (men, women); apartment housing available. **Activities:** Student government, magazine, student newspaper, yearbook, choral groups, concert band, drama, music ensembles, International Students Club, scholastic honor society, Host Organization, Newman Club. **Additional information:** Intercollegiate rodeo available.

ATHLETICS. NJCAA. **Intercollegiate:** Baseball M, basketball. **Intramural:** Basketball, softball, tennis, volleyball.

STUDENT SERVICES. Aptitude testing, career counseling, employment service for undergraduates, freshman orientation, health services, personal counseling, placement service for graduates, veterans counselor, services/facilities for handicapped.

ANNUAL EXPENSES. Tuition and fees: $750, $3,810 additional for out-of-state students. **Room and board:** $2,950. **Books and supplies:** $600. **Other expenses:** $1,125.

FINANCIAL AID. 45% of freshmen, 52% of continuing students receive some form of aid. 94% of grants, 87% of loans, all jobs based on need. Academic, athletic scholarships available. **Aid applications:** Closing date April 15; priority given to applications received by March 15; applicants notified on or about June 15; must reply within 2 weeks.

ADDRESS/TELEPHONE. Ronald M. Slominski, Director of Admissions/Records, Cochise College, Route 1, Box 100, Douglas, AZ 85607. (602) 364-7943 ext. 336.

DeVry Institute of Technology: Phoenix
Phoenix, Arizona — CB code: 4277

Admissions: 93% of applicants accepted
Based on: ••• Test scores; • Interview
Completion: 47% graduate

4-year proprietary business, technical college, coed. Founded in 1967. **Accreditation:** Regional. **Undergraduate enrollment:** 1,703 men, 358 women full time; 407 men, 95 women part time. **Faculty:** 86 total (59 full time). **Location:** Suburban campus in very large city; 10 miles from downtown Phoenix. **Calendar:** Three continuous calendar terms. Extensive evening/early morning classes. **Microcomputers:** 185 located in computer centers.

DEGREES OFFERED. AAS, BS. 227 associate degrees awarded in 1992. 100% in engineering technologies. 410 bachelor's degrees awarded. 32% in business and management, 30% computer sciences, 38% engineering technologies.

UNDERGRADUATE MAJORS. Associate: Electronic technology. **Bachelor's:** Accounting, business administration and management, electronic technology, information sciences and systems.

ACADEMIC PROGRAMS. Accelerated program. **Remedial services:**

Learning center, reduced course load, special counselor, tutoring, developmental coursework. **Placement/credit:** Institutional tests; 30 credit hours maximum for associate degree. 47 to 55 hours of credit by examination may be counted toward bachelor's degree.

ACADEMIC REQUIREMENTS. Freshmen must earn minimum GPA of 2.0 to continue in good standing. 46% of freshmen return for sophomore year. Students must declare major on enrollment. **Graduation requirements:** 87 hours for associate, 134 hours for bachelor's. Most students required to take courses in computer science, English, history, humanities, mathematics, social sciences.

FRESHMAN ADMISSIONS. Selection criteria: Applicants must have high school diploma or equivalent, pass institutional entrance examination or submit acceptable SAT, ACT, or WPCT scores, and be 17 years of age. **Test requirements:** SAT or ACT. **Additional information:** New students may enter beginning of any semester.

1992 FRESHMAN CLASS PROFILE. 1,459 men and women applied, 1,364 accepted; 563 men enrolled, 100 women enrolled. **Characteristics:** 41% from in state, 100% commute, 27% have minority backgrounds.

FALL-TERM APPLICATIONS. $25 fee. Closing date November 4; applicants notified on a rolling basis; must reply within 4 weeks. Interview required. Deferred admission available.

STUDENT LIFE. Activities: Student government, student newspaper, Institute of Electrical and Electronic Engineers (IEEE), Data Processing Management Association (DPMA).

ATHLETICS. Intramural: Basketball, football, racquetball, soccer, softball, volleyball.

STUDENT SERVICES. Career counseling, employment service for undergraduates, freshman orientation, placement service for graduates, veterans counselor, services/facilities for handicapped.

ANNUAL EXPENSES. Tuition and fees: $5,580. **Books and supplies:** $525. **Other expenses:** $1,928.

FINANCIAL AID. 77% of freshmen, 81% of continuing students receive some form of aid. All grants, 71% of loans, all jobs based on need. Academic scholarships available. **Aid applications:** No closing date; applicants notified on a rolling basis beginning on or about July 1; must reply immediately. **Additional information:** Approximately 80% of students work part-time at jobs found through Institute.

ADDRESS/TELEPHONE. K. Joseph Galetti, Director of Admissions, DeVry Institute of Technology: Phoenix, 2149 West Dunlap, Phoenix, AZ 85021-2995. (602) 870-9201. (800) 528-0250. Fax: (602) 870-1209.

Eastern Arizona College

Thatcher, Arizona

CB code: 4297

2-year public community college, coed. Founded in 1888. **Accreditation:** Regional. **Undergraduate enrollment:** 786 men, 610 women full time; 1,315 men, 2,232 women part time. **Faculty:** 269 total (66 full time), 269 with doctorates or other terminal degrees. **Location:** Rural campus in small town; 160 miles from Phoenix, 130 miles from Tucson. **Calendar:** Semester, limited summer session. **Microcomputers:** 122 located in libraries, classrooms. **Special facilities:** Museum of anthropology. **Additional facts:** Near archaeological sites. Several continuing education centers within 165 miles of campus.

DEGREES OFFERED. AA, AAS. 153 associate degrees awarded in 1992. 7% in business and management, 20% business/office and marketing/distribution, 16% education, 29% multi/interdisciplinary studies, 5% parks/recreation, protective services, public affairs, 13% trade and industry.

UNDERGRADUATE MAJORS. Agribusiness, agricultural sciences, anthropology, art education, automotive mechanics, automotive technology, biology, business and management, business and office, business education, business home economics, chemistry, child development/care/guidance, commercial art, computer and information sciences, drafting, drafting and design technology, education, electrical and electronics equipment repair, electronic technology, elementary education, engineering, English, English education, finance, foreign languages education, forestry and related sciences, French, geology, history, home economics, home economics education, information sciences and systems, law enforcement and corrections technologies, liberal/general studies, library science, machine tool operation/machine shop, management science, marketing and distribution, mathematics, mathematics education, music, music education, nursing, office supervision and management, physical education, physics, political science and government, prechiropractic, predentistry, prelaw, premedicine, prepharmacy, preveterinary, psychology, science education, secondary education, small business management and ownership, social science education, social sciences, social studies education, Spanish, visual and performing arts, welding technology.

ACADEMIC PROGRAMS. 2-year transfer program, cooperative education, dual enrollment of high school students. **Remedial services:** Learning center, reduced course load, remedial instruction, tutoring. **Placement/credit:** AP, CLEP General and Subject, institutional tests.

ACADEMIC REQUIREMENTS. Freshmen must earn minimum GPA of 2.0 to continue in good standing. 44% of freshmen return for sophomore year. Students must declare major on enrollment. **Graduation requirements:** 64 hours for associate (42 in major). Most students required to take courses in English, humanities, mathematics, biological/physical sciences, social sciences.

FRESHMAN ADMISSIONS. Selection criteria: Open admissions. Applicants without high school diploma or GED and who are 18 or older must pass ability-to-benefit test. **Additional information:** High school diploma or GED required of applicants 18 or younger.

1992 FRESHMAN CLASS PROFILE. 303 men, 236 women enrolled. 13% were in top tenth and 37% were in top quarter of graduating class.

FALL-TERM APPLICATIONS. No fee. $5 for out-of-state applicants. No closing date; priority given to applications received by August 15; applicants notified on a rolling basis; must reply by registration. Early admission available.

STUDENT LIFE. Housing: Dormitories (men, women). **Activities:** Student government, student newspaper, yearbook, choral groups, concert band, dance, drama, jazz band, marching band, music ensembles, musical theater, pep band, symphony orchestra.

ATHLETICS. NJCAA. **Intercollegiate:** Basketball, football M, softball W, volleyball W. **Intramural:** Basketball, football M, racquetball, softball, swimming, table tennis, tennis, volleyball, water polo.

STUDENT SERVICES. Aptitude testing, career counseling, employment service for undergraduates, freshman orientation, personal counseling, placement service for graduates, veterans counselor.

ANNUAL EXPENSES. Tuition and fees: $628, $3,252 additional for out-of-state students. **Room and board:** $2,748. **Books and supplies:** $400. **Other expenses:** $900.

FINANCIAL AID. 74% of freshmen, 28% of continuing students receive some form of aid. 73% of grants, 77% of jobs based on need. All loans based on criteria other than need. Academic, music/drama, art, athletic, state/district residency, leadership scholarships available. **Aid applications:** No closing date; priority given to applications received by April 15; applicants notified on a rolling basis beginning on or about June 1; must reply within 2 weeks.

ADDRESS/TELEPHONE. Jesse U. DeVaney, Dean of Admissions, Research and Development, Eastern Arizona College, Church Street, Thatcher, AZ 85552-0769. (602) 428-8244. Fax: (602) 428-8462.

Embry-Riddle Aeronautical University: Prescott Campus

Prescott, Arizona

CB code: 4305

4-year private university, coed. Founded in 1978. **Accreditation:** Regional. **Undergraduate enrollment:** 1,085 men, 272 women full time; 122 men, 30 women part time. **Faculty:** 86 total (66 full time), 30 with doctorates or other terminal degrees. **Location:** Rural campus in large town; 90 miles from Phoenix. **Calendar:** Semester, extensive summer session. **Microcomputers:** 60 located in computer centers. **Special facilities:** Wind tunnel, fleet of aircraft. **Additional facts:** Eastern residential campus in Daytona Beach, Florida. More than 100 continuing education centers located throughout the U.S. and Europe.

DEGREES OFFERED. AS, BS. 10 associate degrees awarded in 1992. 70% in business and management, 30% trade and industry. 330 bachelor's degrees awarded. 11% in business and management, 19% engineering, 67% trade and industry.

UNDERGRADUATE MAJORS. Associate: Airline piloting and navigation, aviation management, business administration and management. **Bachelor's:** Aeronautical technology, aerospace/aeronautical/astronautical engineering, airline piloting and navigation, aviation computer technology, aviation management, business administration and management, computer and information sciences, electrical/electronics/communications engineering.

ACADEMIC PROGRAMS. Accelerated program, cooperative education, independent study, internships. **Remedial services:** Learning center, reduced course load, remedial instruction, tutoring. **ROTC:** Air Force, Army. **Placement/credit:** AP, CLEP General and Subject, institutional tests.

ACADEMIC REQUIREMENTS. Freshmen must earn minimum GPA of 2.0 to continue in good standing. 72% of freshmen return for sophomore year. Students must declare major on application. **Graduation requirements:** 72 hours for associate (60 in major), 126 hours for bachelor's (90 in major). Most students required to take courses in computer science, English, history, humanities, mathematics, biological/physical sciences, social sciences.

FRESHMAN ADMISSIONS. Selection criteria: High school GPA, rank in class, and SAT or ACT scores considered. Specific requirements vary by degree programs. Recommended units include English 4, mathematics 3, physical science 3 and social science 3. **Test requirements:** SAT or ACT; score report by August 15. Flight program applicants must be able to pass medical examination for Class I or II Federal Aviation Administration Medical Certificate.

1992 FRESHMAN CLASS PROFILE. 1,015 men and women applied, 800 accepted; 247 men enrolled, 49 women enrolled. **Academic background:** Mid 50% of enrolled freshmen had SAT-V between 420-550, SAT-M between 510-630; ACT composite between 21-27. 76% submitted SAT scores, 49% submitted ACT scores. **Characteristics:** 5% from in state, 93% commute, 9% have minority backgrounds, 1% are foreign students. Average age is 19.

FALL-TERM APPLICATIONS. $30 fee, may be waived for applicants with need. Closing date July 15; applicants notified on a rolling basis; must reply within 4 weeks. Essay required. Interview recommended. Deferred admission available. Early application encouraged, available facilities limit enrollment in some programs.

STUDENT LIFE. Housing: Dormitories (coed); apartment housing available. Dormitories for freshmen only. **Activities:** Student government, radio, student newspaper, yearbook, drama, fraternities, sororities, American Institute of Aeronautics and Astronautics.

ATHLETICS. NAIA. **Intercollegiate:** Wrestling M. **Intramural:** Badminton, baseball, basketball, bowling, golf, lacrosse, racquetball, rugby, skiing, skin diving, soccer, softball, swimming, table tennis, tennis, track and field, volleyball.

STUDENT SERVICES. Career counseling, employment service for undergraduates, freshman orientation, health services, personal counseling, placement service for graduates, veterans counselor, services/facilities for handicapped.

ANNUAL EXPENSES. Tuition and fees (1992-93): $6,790. **Room and board:** $3,196. **Books and supplies:** $490. **Other expenses:** $1,120.

FINANCIAL AID. 54% of freshmen, 66% of continuing students receive some form of aid. 70% of grants, 73% of loans, 17% of jobs based on need. Academic, state/district residency scholarships available. **Aid applications:** No closing date; priority given to applications received by April 15; applicants notified on a rolling basis beginning on or about April 1; must reply within 3 weeks.

ADDRESS/TELEPHONE. Darryl W. Niemeyer, Director of Admissions, Embry-Riddle Aeronautical University: Prescott Campus, 600 South Clyde Morris Boulevard, Daytona Beach, FL 32114-3900. (602) 776-3728. (800) 442-3728. Fax: (904) 226-7070.

Gateway Community College
Phoenix, Arizona — CB code: 0455

2-year public community, technical college, coed. Founded in 1968. **Accreditation:** Regional. **Undergraduate enrollment:** 8,000 men and women. **Faculty:** 287 total (60 full time), 12 with doctorates or other terminal degrees. **Location:** Urban campus in very large city. **Calendar:** Semester, limited summer session. Saturday classes. **Microcomputers:** Located in libraries, classrooms, computer centers, campus-wide network. **Special facilities:** Fitness/wellness centers.

DEGREES OFFERED. AA, AAS. 160 associate degrees awarded in 1992. 10% in business/office and marketing/distribution, 8% computer sciences, 13% engineering technologies, 35% health sciences, 34% allied health.

UNDERGRADUATE MAJORS. Accounting, advertising, air conditioning/heating/refrigeration mechanics, air conditioning/heating/refrigeration technology, automotive mechanics, automotive technology, business and management, business and office, commercial art, construction, court reporting, electrical installation, electromechanical technology, finance, health care administration, health services management, liberal/general studies, nuclear medical technology, nursing, office supervision and management, plumbing/pipefitting/steamfitting, precision metal work, radiograph medical technology, respiratory therapy, respiratory therapy technology, secretarial and related programs, ultrasound technology, water and wastewater technology.

ACADEMIC PROGRAMS. 2-year transfer program, computer delivered (on-line) credit-bearing course offerings, cooperative education, dual enrollment of high school students, honors program, independent study, internships, telecourses. **Remedial services:** Learning center, remedial instruction, tutoring, 5-week college readiness program for special groups such as the handicapped, those on welfare, and those who speak limited English. **Placement/credit:** AP, CLEP General and Subject, institutional tests; 30 credit hours maximum for associate degree.

ACADEMIC REQUIREMENTS. Freshmen must earn minimum GPA of 2.0 to continue in good standing. 21% of freshmen return for sophomore year. Students must declare major on application. **Graduation requirements:** 64 hours for associate (44 in major). Most students required to take courses in arts/fine arts, computer science, English, foreign languages, history, humanities, mathematics, philosophy/religion, biological/physical sciences, social sciences.

FRESHMAN ADMISSIONS. Selection criteria: Open admissions. Nursing and some allied health programs have selective admission criteria. **Test requirements:** General Aptitude Test Battery required of nursing and health science applicants. ASSET test recommended.

1992 FRESHMAN CLASS PROFILE. 7,000 men and women enrolled. **Characteristics:** 98% from in state, 100% commute, 22% have minority backgrounds. Average age is 31.

FALL-TERM APPLICATIONS. No fee. No closing date; applicants notified on a rolling basis. Interview required for health science applicants.

STUDENT LIFE. Activities: Student government, film, student newspaper, Newman Club, Mecha, Indian Tribal Club, Single Parents Association. **Additional information:** Students may participate in sports through other Maricopa county community colleges.

STUDENT SERVICES. Aptitude testing, career counseling, employment service for undergraduates, freshman orientation, on-campus day care, personal counseling, placement service for graduates, veterans counselor, academic assessment, services/facilities for handicapped.

ANNUAL EXPENSES. Tuition and fees (1992-93): $870, $3,750 additional for out-of-state students. **Books and supplies:** $400. **Other expenses:** $3,228.

FINANCIAL AID. 96% of grants, all loans, 22% of jobs based on need. Academic scholarships available. **Aid applications:** No closing date; priority given to applications received by April 15; applicants notified on a rolling basis beginning on or about July 1; must reply within 2 weeks.

ADDRESS/TELEPHONE. Madge Valladares, Associate Dean of Student Services, Gateway Community College, 108 North 40th Street, Phoenix, AZ 85034. (602) 275-8500. Fax: (602) 392-5329.

Glendale Community College
Glendale, Arizona — CB code: 4338

2-year public community college, coed. Founded in 1965. **Accreditation:** Regional. **Undergraduate enrollment:** 1,886 men, 1,980 women full time; 5,561 men, 7,944 women part time. **Faculty:** 663 total (223 full time), 92 with doctorates or other terminal degrees. **Location:** Urban campus in small city; 17 miles from downtown Phoenix. **Calendar:** Semester, limited summer session. **Microcomputers:** 600 located in libraries, classrooms, computer centers. **Special facilities:** Performing arts center, high-technology centers, international studies institute. **Additional facts:** Extension site at Estrella Mountain Community College Center in Avondale.

DEGREES OFFERED. AA, AAS. 574 associate degrees awarded in 1992. 17% in business and management, 8% business/office and marketing/distribution, 5% computer sciences, 8% teacher education, 6% engineering technologies, 8% health sciences, 17% multi/interdisciplinary studies, 5% parks/recreation, protective services, public affairs, 7% trade and industry.

UNDERGRADUATE MAJORS. Accounting, agribusiness, air traffic control, automotive mechanics, biology, biomedical equipment technology, business administration and management, business and management, business data processing and related programs, chemistry, child development/care/guidance, commercial art, computer technology, drafting, early childhood education, economics, education, electronic technology, engineering, engineering and engineering-related technologies, English, finance, fine arts, fire control and safety technology, French, geology, German, graphic design, history, horticulture, institutional/home management/supporting programs, international relations, international studies, Italian, Japanese, journalism, law enforcement and corrections technologies, liberal/general studies, management science, mathematics, mental health/human services, music, nursing, office supervision and management, philosophy, physical education, physical sciences, physical therapy, physics, political science and government, predentistry, prelaw, premedicine, prepharmacy, psychology, public relations, quality control technology, radio/television technology, real estate, retailing, Russian, secretarial and related programs, social sciences, social work, sociology, Spanish, speech, visual and performing arts.

ACADEMIC PROGRAMS. 2-year transfer program, computer delivered (on-line) credit-bearing course offerings, cooperative education, dual enrollment of high school students, honors program, independent study, internships, study abroad, telecourses, visiting/exchange student program, weekend college. **Remedial services:** Learning center, reduced course load, remedial instruction, special counselor, tutoring, literacy center, adult reentry center, writing center, English as a second language. **ROTC:** Air Force, Army. **Placement/credit:** AP, CLEP General and Subject, institutional tests; 30 credit hours maximum for associate degree.

ACADEMIC REQUIREMENTS. Freshmen must earn minimum GPA of 1.6 to continue in good standing. Students must declare major on application. **Graduation requirements:** 64 hours for associate (12 in major). Most students required to take courses in computer science, English, humanities, mathematics, biological/physical sciences, social sciences. **Additional information:** Students may begin open entry/open exit courses year round and compete at their own pace.

FRESHMAN ADMISSIONS. Selection criteria: Open admissions. Special requirements for nursing, basic emergency medical technology, General Motors and Ford automotive programs.

1992 FRESHMAN CLASS PROFILE. 2,125 men, 2,481 women enrolled. **Characteristics:** 98% from in state, 100% commute, 19% have minority backgrounds. Average age is 28.

FALL-TERM APPLICATIONS. No fee. No closing date; applicants notified on a rolling basis; must reply by registration.

STUDENT LIFE. Activities: Student government, student newspaper, television, choral groups, concert band, dance, drama, jazz band, marching band, musical theater, symphony orchestra, Baptist Student Union, LDS Institute of Religion, Inter-Varsity Christian Fellowship, Newman Club, Movemiento Estudiante de Aztlan, Black Student Union, International Club, Native American Club, Multicultural Students Association, Chi Alpha.

ATHLETICS. NJCAA. **Intercollegiate:** Archery W, baseball M, basketball, cross-country, football M, golf M, soccer M, softball W, tennis, track and field, volleyball W. **Intramural:** Basketball, bowling, golf, racquetball, softball, table tennis, tennis, volleyball.

STUDENT SERVICES. Aptitude testing, career counseling, employment service for undergraduates, on-campus day care, personal counseling, placement service for graduates, special adviser for adult students, veterans counselor, minority counselors, disabled student counselor, adult reentry program, services/facilities for handicapped.

ANNUAL EXPENSES. Tuition and fees (1992-93): $870, $3,750 additional for out-of-state students. **Books and supplies:** $500.

FINANCIAL AID. 25% of freshmen, 25% of continuing students receive some form of aid. 84% of grants, 99% of loans, 54% of jobs based on need. Academic, music/drama, art, athletic scholarships available. **Aid applications:** No closing date; priority given to applications received by April 15; applicants notified on a rolling basis beginning on or about June 1; must reply within 2 weeks. **Additional information:** President's scholarships available to Arizona high school graduates. Honor student scholarships available.

ADDRESS/TELEPHONE. Mary Lou Bayless, Associate Dean of Student Services, Glendale Community College, 6000 West Olive Avenue, Glendale, AZ 85302-3090. (602) 435-3300. Fax: (602) 435-3329.

Grand Canyon University

Phoenix, Arizona CB code: 4331

Admissions: 79% of applicants accepted
Based on: ••• School record, test scores
• Activities, essay, interview, recommendations
Completion: 62% graduate

4-year private liberal arts college, coed, affiliated with Southern Baptist Convention. Founded in 1949. **Accreditation:** Regional. **Undergraduate enrollment:** 472 men, 789 women full time; 125 men, 233 women part time. **Graduate enrollment:** 6 men, 18 women full time; 44 men, 60 women part time. **Faculty:** 164 total (75 full time), 43 with doctorates or other terminal degrees. **Location:** Urban campus in very large city. **Calendar:** Semester, limited summer session. **Microcomputers:** 65 located in computer centers. **Special facilities:** Art gallery, cadavers for laboratory study. **Additional facts:** Center for International Awareness has agreements for study with universities in China, Kazakhstan (CIS), Japan, United Kingdom, France, Germany, Hungary.

DEGREES OFFERED. BA, BS, MA, MBA, MEd. 326 bachelor's degrees awarded in 1992. 18% in business and management, 30% teacher education, 11% health sciences, 6% parks/recreation, protective services, public affairs, 6% psychology, 6% social sciences. Graduate degrees offered in 6 major fields of study.

UNDERGRADUATE MAJORS. Accounting, art education, Bible studies, biology, biology education, business education, chemistry, communications, computer and information sciences, computer science education, creative writing, criminal justice studies, dramatic arts, education of the emotionally handicapped, elementary education, English, English education, English literature, environmental science, finance, graphic design, history, human resources development, international business management, journalism, liberal/general studies, marketing and distribution, mathematics, mathematics education, music, music education, music performance, nursing, physical education, predentistry, prelaw, premedicine, prepharmacy, preveterinary, psychology, public relations, radio/television broadcasting, religion, religious music, science education, secondary education, social sciences, sociology, special education, specific learning disabilities, speech, speech/communication/theater education, studio art, theological studies, visual and performing arts.

ACADEMIC PROGRAMS. Double major, dual enrollment of high school students, honors program, independent study, internships, study abroad, visiting/exchange student program, Washington semester, cross-registration; liberal arts/career combination in engineering. **Remedial services:** Reduced course load, remedial instruction, tutoring. **ROTC:** Air Force, Army. **Placement/credit:** AP, CLEP General and Subject, institutional tests; 30 credit hours maximum for bachelor's degree.

ACADEMIC REQUIREMENTS. Freshmen must earn minimum GPA of 2.0 to continue in good standing. 85% of freshmen return for sophomore year. Students must declare major by end of second year. **Graduation requirements:** 128 hours for bachelor's (30 in major). Most students required to take courses in arts/fine arts, English, history, humanities, mathematics, philosophy/religion, biological/physical sciences, social sciences. **Additional information:** Old Testament and New Testament history courses required.

FRESHMAN ADMISSIONS. Selection criteria: High school students in top 25% of class with at least 3.0 GPA. ACT score above 22 or combined SAT score above 930 admitted without condition. Others may be admitted on probation. Recommended units include English 4, mathematics 3, social science 2 and science 2. Specifically recommended units include algebra and American history. **Test requirements:** SAT or ACT.

1992 FRESHMAN CLASS PROFILE. 189 men applied, 139 accepted, 52 enrolled; 308 women applied, 254 accepted, 121 enrolled. **Academic background:** Mid 50% of enrolled freshmen had SAT-V between 370-510, SAT-M between 400-530; ACT composite between 17-24. 49% submitted SAT scores, 67% submitted ACT scores. **Characteristics:** 66% commute. Average age is 19.

FALL-TERM APPLICATIONS. $25 fee. No closing date; priority given to applications received by August 1; applicants notified on a rolling basis; must reply by registration. Essay required. Interview recommended for academically weak applicants. Audition recommended for music, drama, speech applicants. Portfolio recommended for art applicants. Deferred admission available. Prefer applicants to file all required documents by August 1, but no penalty for late applications.

STUDENT LIFE. Housing: Dormitories (men, women); apartment housing available. **Activities:** Student government, student newspaper, yearbook, choral groups, concert band, drama, jazz band, music ensembles, musical theater, opera, pep band, symphony orchestra, Baptist Student Union, Fellowship of Christian Athletes, international student organizations, honors organizations, AWARE, Committee on World Awareness, professional clubs. **Additional information:** No smoking, alcohol, or dancing allowed. All students carrying 9 or more credit hours required to attend chapel services 15 times per semester. Religious observance required.

ATHLETICS. NCAA. **Intercollegiate:** Baseball M, basketball, cross-country, golf M, soccer M, tennis W, volleyball W. **Intramural:** Basketball, soccer, softball, swimming, table tennis, volleyball.

STUDENT SERVICES. Career counseling, employment service for undergraduates, freshman orientation, health services, personal counseling, placement service for graduates, veterans counselor, services/facilities for handicapped.

ANNUAL EXPENSES. Tuition and fees: $6,730. **Room and board:** $2,950. **Books and supplies:** $600. **Other expenses:** $1,125.

FINANCIAL AID. 85% of freshmen, 85% of continuing students receive some form of aid. 59% of grants, 88% of loans, 77% of jobs based on need. Academic, music/drama, art, athletic scholarships available. **Aid applications:** No closing date; priority given to applications received by March 15; applicants notified on a rolling basis beginning on or about April 15; must reply within 2 weeks.

ADDRESS/TELEPHONE. Sherri Willborn, Director of Admisssions and Enrollment Planning, Grand Canyon University, PO Box 11097, 3300 West Camelback Road, Phoenix, AZ 85061-1097. (602) 589-2855. (800) 800-9776.

ITT Technical Institute: Phoenix

Phoenix, Arizona CB code: 1112

2-year proprietary technical college, coed. Founded in 1963. **Undergraduate enrollment:** 233 men, 83 women full time. **Faculty:** 21 total (19 full time). **Location:** Urban campus in very large city; 5 miles from downtown. **Calendar:** Quarter. **Microcomputers:** 110 located in classrooms, computer centers.

DEGREES OFFERED. AAS. 240 associate degrees awarded in 1992.

UNDERGRADUATE MAJORS. Computer and information sciences, drafting, drafting and design technology, drafting/computer aided design, electrical and electronics equipment repair, electronic technology.

ACADEMIC PROGRAMS. Accelerated program. **Remedial services:** Tutoring. **Placement/credit:** Institutional tests.

ACADEMIC REQUIREMENTS. Freshmen must earn minimum GPA of 2.0 to continue in good standing. 95% of freshmen return for sophomore year. Students must declare major on enrollment. **Graduation requirements:** Most students required to take courses in mathematics. **Additional information:** Computer business applications associate degree offered in 12 months by taking 60 semester hours over 4 3-month quarters. Electronics is two year 8 quarter program. Computer aided drafting is 18 month 6 quarter program.

FRESHMAN ADMISSIONS. Selection criteria: Satisfactory scores on on-site test in English and mathematics required.

1992 FRESHMAN CLASS PROFILE. 223 men, 56 women enrolled. **Characteristics:** 100% commute, 30% have minority backgrounds.

FALL-TERM APPLICATIONS. $100 fee, may be waived for applicants with need. Application fee refunded if student not accepted. No closing date; applicants notified on a rolling basis. Interview required.

ATHLETICS. Intramural: Softball, volleyball.

STUDENT SERVICES. Aptitude testing, career counseling, employment service for undergraduates, freshman orientation, placement service for graduates, services/facilities for handicapped.

ANNUAL EXPENSES. Tuition and fees (1992-93): $11,768. **Books and supplies:** $1,100. **Other expenses:** $1,308.

FINANCIAL AID. 97% of freshmen, 97% of continuing students receive some form of aid. Grants, loans, jobs available. **Aid applications:** Closing date September 20; applicants notified on a rolling basis.

ADDRESS/TELEPHONE. Cliff Kline, Director of Recruitment, ITT Technical Institute: Phoenix, 4837 East McDowell Road, Phoenix, AZ 85008. (602) 252-2331. (800) 879-4881.

ITT Technical Institute: Tucson

Tucson, Arizona CB code: 3598

1-year proprietary technical college, coed. Founded in 1984. **Undergraduate enrollment:** 165 men, 20 women full time. **Faculty:** 14 total (11 full time). **Location:** Suburban campus in large city; within Tucson city limits. **Calendar:** Quarter. **Microcomputers:** 70 located in libraries, classrooms. **Additional facts:** Classes begin in March, June, September and December.

DEGREES OFFERED. AAS. 200 associate degrees awarded in 1992. 30% in computer sciences, 70% engineering technologies.

UNDERGRADUATE MAJORS. Business computer/console/peripheral equipment operation, business data processing and related programs, computer and information sciences, computer-aided drafting technology, drafting, drafting and design technology, electrical and electronics equipment repair, electrical/electronics/communications engineering, electronic technology.

ACADEMIC PROGRAMS. Honors program, internships. **Remedial services:** Learning center, remedial instruction, tutoring.

ACADEMIC REQUIREMENTS. Freshmen must earn minimum GPA of 1.5 to continue in good standing. 98% of freshmen return for sophomore year. Students must declare major on application. **Graduation requirements:** 60 hours for associate (60 in major). Most students required to take courses in computer science, mathematics, biological/physical sciences.

FRESHMAN ADMISSIONS. Recommended units include mathematics 2. **Test requirements:** Reading and mathematics entrance examinations required. Space relations examination required for some programs.

1992 FRESHMAN CLASS PROFILE. 165 men, 20 women enrolled. 10% had high school GPA of 3.0 or higher, 60% between 2.0 and 2.99. **Characteristics:** 90% from in state, 100% commute, 51% have minority backgrounds. Average age is 23.

FALL-TERM APPLICATIONS. $100 fee. No closing date; applicants notified on a rolling basis; must reply within 10 days. Interview required. Essay recommended. Deferred admission available.

STUDENT LIFE. Housing: Reduced rents at local apartments. **Activities:** Student newspaper. **Additional information:** School activities include picnics, cook-outs, specialty days.

STUDENT SERVICES. Aptitude testing, career counseling, employment service for undergraduates, freshman orientation, on-campus day care, personal counseling, placement service for graduates, veterans counselor, services/facilities for handicapped.

ANNUAL EXPENSES. Tuition and fees: Tuition for first calendar year ranges from $7500 to $9600 depending on program of study. **Books and supplies:** $1,400.

FINANCIAL AID. 90% of freshmen receive some form of aid. 99% of grants, 42% of loans, all jobs based on need. **Aid applications:** Closing date May 1; applicants notified on or about May 8; must reply within 1 week.

ADDRESS/TELEPHONE. Marianne Rittner, Director of Education, ITT Technical Institute: Tucson, 1840 East Benson Highway, Tucson, AZ 85714-1770. (602) 294-2944. Fax: (602) 889-9528.

Lamson Junior College

Phoenix, Arizona CB code: 5841

2-year proprietary business, junior college, coed. Founded in 1889. **Undergraduate enrollment:** 121 men, 521 women full time. **Location:** Urban campus in very large city. **Calendar:** Quarter. **Additional facts:** Additional campus located in Mesa.

FRESHMAN ADMISSIONS. Selection criteria: Open admissions. Career Program Assessment Test used for admission to degree-seeking programs.

ADDRESS/TELEPHONE. Admissions Office, Lamson Junior College, 2701 West Bethany Home Road, Phoenix, AZ 85017. (602) 433-2000. Fax: (602) 246-9746. Mesa campus: Admissions Office Lamson Junior College: Mesa 1980 West Main Mesa, AZ 85201 (602) 898-7000.

Mesa Community College

Mesa, Arizona CB code: 4513

2-year public community college, coed. Founded in 1965. **Accreditation:** Regional. **Undergraduate enrollment:** 5,846 men and women full time; 15,285 men and women part time. **Faculty:** 760 total (249 full time). **Location:** Urban campus in very large city; 5 miles from Phoenix. **Calendar:** Semester. **Microcomputers:** 600 located in libraries, classrooms, computer centers. **Special facilities:** High technology laboratory. **Additional facts:** Motorola University business and industry training for Motorola Corporation employees.

DEGREES OFFERED. AA, AAS. 803 associate degrees awarded in 1992.

UNDERGRADUATE MAJORS. Accounting, agricultural sciences, automotive technology, bilingual/bicultural education, business administration and management, business and management, business and office, business data processing and related programs, business data programming, carpentry, child development/care/guidance, civil technology, commercial art, computer and information sciences, computer programming, criminal justice studies, diesel engine mechanics, drafting and design technology, electrical technology, electronic technology, engineering science, fashion merchandising, finance, fine arts, fire control and safety technology, general life science, home economics, horticultural science, horticulture, industrial technology, journalism, management information systems, marketing management, mathematics, music, nursing, office supervision and management, practical nursing, psychology, public relations, secretarial and related programs, theater design, visual and performing arts.

ACADEMIC PROGRAMS. 2-year transfer program, computer delivered (on-line) credit-bearing course offerings, cooperative education, dual enrollment of high school students, honors program, independent study, internships, weekend college, cross-registration. **Remedial services:** Learning center, remedial instruction, special counselor, tutoring. **ROTC:** Army. **Placement/credit:** AP, CLEP General and Subject, institutional tests; 30 credit hours maximum for associate degree.

ACADEMIC REQUIREMENTS. Freshmen must earn minimum GPA of 1.75 to continue in good standing. 60% of freshmen return for sophomore year. Students must declare major on application. **Graduation requirements:** 64 hours for associate (28 in major). Most students required to take courses in arts/fine arts, computer science, English, history, humanities, mathematics, biological/physical sciences, social sciences. **Additional information:** Associate of General Studies degree offered that allows student to take half of credits in require courses and dictate own program of electives.

FRESHMAN ADMISSIONS. Selection criteria: Open admissions. **Test requirements:** Students enrolling must complete ACT/ASSET placement test.

1992 FRESHMAN CLASS PROFILE. 13,863 men and women enrolled. **Characteristics:** 100% commute. Average age is 26.

FALL-TERM APPLICATIONS. No fee. No closing date; applicants notified on a rolling basis. Early admission available. Diploma or GED required if applicant is under 18.

STUDENT LIFE. Activities: Student government, student newspaper, dance, drama, jazz band, marching band, music ensembles, musical theater, fraternities, sororities. **Additional information:** Computer facilities capable of serving 4,000 students each semester.

ATHLETICS. NJCAA. **Intercollegiate:** Baseball M, basketball, cross-country, football M, golf, gymnastics W, soccer M, softball W, swimming M, track and field, volleyball W, wrestling M. **Intramural:** Basketball, bowling, cross-country, football M, softball, track and field, volleyball.

STUDENT SERVICES. Aptitude testing, career counseling, employment service for undergraduates, freshman orientation, on-campus day care, personal counseling, placement service for graduates, special adviser for adult students, veterans counselor, transfer and advisement centers, services/facilities for handicapped.

ANNUAL EXPENSES. Tuition and fees (1992-93): $870, $3,750 additional for out-of-state students. **Books and supplies:** $400.

FINANCIAL AID. 15% of freshmen receive some form of aid. Grants, loans, jobs available. 4,831 enrolled freshmen were judged to have need, all were offered aid. Academic, athletic scholarships available. **Aid applications:** No closing date; priority given to applications received by May 15; applicants notified on a rolling basis. **Additional information:** Talent awards (such as for athletics, music, etc.) for Maricopa County residents only.

ADDRESS/TELEPHONE. Brian K. Johnson, Coordinator of Admissions and Recruitment, Mesa Community College, 1833 West Southern Avenue, Mesa, AZ 85202. (602) 461-7000. Fax: (602) 461-7804.

Mohave Community College

Kingman, Arizona CB code: 0443

2-year public community college, coed. Founded in 1971. **Accreditation:** Regional. **Undergraduate enrollment:** 213 men, 370 women full time; 1,737 men, 3,009 women part time. **Faculty:** 198 total (41 full time), 4 with doctorates or other terminal degrees. **Location:** Rural campus in large town; 100 miles from Las Vegas, Nevada. **Calendar:** Semester, limited summer session. **Microcomputers:** Located in libraries, classrooms, computer centers. **Additional facts:** 2-way audio-visual microwave system linking instructors with classrooms on all 3 campuses.

DEGREES OFFERED. AA, AS, AAS. 84 associate degrees awarded in 1992. 15% in business and management, 15% health sciences, 40% letters/literature, 7% mathematics, 5% psychology, 9% trade and industry, 7% visual and performing arts.

UNDERGRADUATE MAJORS. Accounting, automotive mechanics, automotive technology, biology, business administration and management, business and management, business and office, child development/care/guidance, computer and information sciences, electrical and electronics equipment repair, English, finance, fine arts, fire control and safety technology, law enforcement and corrections technologies, liberal/general studies, marketing and distribution, mathematics, metal/jewelry, music, nursing, practical nursing, psychology, secretarial and related programs, sociology.

ACADEMIC PROGRAMS. 2-year transfer program, dual enrollment of high school students, independent study, telecourses. **Remedial services:**

Learning center, reduced course load, remedial instruction, tutoring. **Placement/credit:** CLEP General and Subject, institutional tests; 20 credit hours maximum for associate degree.

ACADEMIC REQUIREMENTS. Freshmen must earn minimum GPA of 2.0 to continue in good standing. 30% of freshmen return for sophomore year. Students must declare major by end of first year. **Graduation requirements:** 64 hours for associate. Most students required to take courses in computer science, English, humanities, mathematics, biological/physical sciences, social sciences.

FRESHMAN ADMISSIONS. Selection criteria: Open admissions. Selective admissions to nursing and EMT/paramedic programs.

1992 FRESHMAN CLASS PROFILE. 2,952 men and women enrolled. **Characteristics:** 99% from in state, 100% commute, 5% have minority backgrounds. Average age is 38.

FALL-TERM APPLICATIONS. $5 fee. No closing date; priority given to applications received by May 1; applicants notified on a rolling basis; must reply by registration. Interview required for nursing, EMT/paramedic applicants. Deferred and early admission available.

STUDENT LIFE. Activities: Student government, choral groups, drama.

STUDENT SERVICES. Aptitude testing, career counseling, employment service for undergraduates, personal counseling, veterans counselor, services/facilities for handicapped.

ANNUAL EXPENSES. Tuition and fees: $520, $2,930 additional for out-of-state students. **Books and supplies:** $600. **Other expenses:** $900.

FINANCIAL AID. 30% of freshmen, 31% of continuing students receive some form of aid. 86% of grants, 94% of loans, 7% of jobs based on need. Academic, music/drama, state/district residency scholarships available. **Aid applications:** No closing date; priority given to applications received by March 1; applicants notified on a rolling basis beginning on or about May 1; must reply within 2 weeks.

ADDRESS/TELEPHONE. Roger L. Johnson, Director of Admissions and Records, Mohave Community College, 1971 Jagerson Avenue, Kingman, AZ 86401. (602) 757-0828. Fax: (602) 757-0836.

National Education Center: Arizona Automotive Institute

Glendale, Arizona CB code: 2127

2-year proprietary technical college, coed. Founded in 1967. **Undergraduate enrollment:** 650 men and women full time; 650 men part time. **Location:** Suburban campus in small city; adjacent to Phoenix. **Calendar:** Quarter. **Additional facts:** West Coast training institution of Chrysler Corporation.

FRESHMAN ADMISSIONS. Selection criteria: Interview, mechanical aptitude test considered.

ANNUAL EXPENSES. Tuition and fees (1992-93): Tuition includes most books, supplies, and tools. 18-month drafting program is $11,000, 12-month automotive and diesel programs are $7,845, 6-month diesel and CAD programs are $4,190. 2-year advertising design associate degree is $11,100; 18-month automotive and diesel degree is $11,160.

ADDRESS/TELEPHONE. Suzanne Harris, Director of Admissions, National Education Center: Arizona Automotive Institute, 6829 North 46th Avenue, Glendale, AZ 85301. (602) 934-7273. (800) 528-0717. Fax: (602) 930-9606.

Navajo Community College

Tsaile, Arizona CB code: 4550

2-year public community college, coed. Founded in 1968. **Accreditation:** Regional. **Undergraduate enrollment:** 278 men, 454 women full time; 266 men, 806 women part time. **Faculty:** 136 total (45 full time), 5 with doctorates or other terminal degrees. **Location:** Rural campus in rural community; 55 miles from Window Rock. **Calendar:** Semester, limited summer session. **Microcomputers:** 26 located in libraries, classrooms, computer centers. **Special facilities:** Museum, galleries.

DEGREES OFFERED. AA, AS, AAS. 227 associate degrees awarded in 1992. 21% in business and management, 27% education, 30% teacher education, 18% social sciences.

UNDERGRADUATE MAJORS. American Indian studies, business administration and management, business and management, business and office, computer and information sciences, education, elementary education, environmental science, fine arts, liberal/general studies, Native American languages, preengineering, psychology, renewable natural resources, secretarial and related programs, social sciences.

ACADEMIC PROGRAMS. 2-year transfer program, cooperative education, double major, independent study, internships. **Remedial services:** Learning center, preadmission summer program, remedial instruction, tutoring. **Placement/credit:** Institutional tests; 12 credit hours maximum for associate degree.

ACADEMIC REQUIREMENTS. Freshmen must earn minimum GPA of 2.0 to continue in good standing. 75% of freshmen return for sophomore year. Students must declare major by end of first year. **Graduation requirements:** 64 hours for associate. Most students required to take courses in English, mathematics.

FRESHMAN ADMISSIONS. Selection criteria: Open admissions.

1992 FRESHMAN CLASS PROFILE. 118 men, 192 women enrolled. **Characteristics:** 85% from in state, 80% commute, 96% have minority backgrounds. Average age is 18.

FALL-TERM APPLICATIONS. No fee. No closing date; applicants notified on a rolling basis. Deferred and early admission available.

STUDENT LIFE. Housing: Dormitories (men, women, coed). **Activities:** Student government, student newspaper, Red Dawn Indian Club.

ATHLETICS. NJCAA, NSCAA. **Intercollegiate:** Archery, cross-country. **Intramural:** Archery, badminton, basketball, bowling, cross-country, table tennis, tennis, volleyball.

STUDENT SERVICES. Career counseling, freshman orientation, personal counseling, veterans counselor.

ANNUAL EXPENSES. Tuition and fees: $620. **Room and board:** $2,740. **Books and supplies:** $450.

FINANCIAL AID. 75% of freshmen, 70% of continuing students receive some form of aid. 96% of grants, 78% of jobs based on need. Academic, athletic scholarships available. **Aid applications:** No closing date; priority given to applications received by April 15; applicants notified on a rolling basis beginning on or about May 1; must reply within 15 days.

ADDRESS/TELEPHONE. Louise Litzin, Registrar, Navajo Community College, Box 67, Tsaile, AZ 86556. (602) 724-3311 ext. 110. Fax: (602) 724-3327.

Northern Arizona University

Flagstaff, Arizona CB code: 4006

Admissions:	86% of applicants accepted
Based on:	••• School record, test scores
	• Activities, essay, interview, recommendations
Completion:	40% graduate

4-year public university, coed. Founded in 1899. **Accreditation:** Regional. **Undergraduate enrollment:** 5,335 men, 6,134 women full time; 1,147 men, 1,440 women part time. **Graduate enrollment:** 516 men, 743 women full time; 907 men, 2,269 women part time. **Faculty:** 970 total (607 full time), 540 with doctorates or other terminal degrees. **Location:** Rural campus in large town; 140 miles from Phoenix. **Calendar:** Semester, extensive summer session. Extensive evening/early morning classes. **Microcomputers:** 500 located in dormitories, libraries, classrooms, computer centers. **Special facilities:** Creative arts center, 400 acre forest, observatory, multidisciplinary research center, art gallery. **Additional facts:** 9 campus buildings are on the National Register of Historic Places.

DEGREES OFFERED. BA, BS, BFA, MA, MS, MBA, MFA, MEd, PhD, EdD. 2,322 bachelor's degrees awarded in 1992. 17% in business and management, 6% communications, 16% teacher education, 5% allied health, 5% life sciences, 9% multi/interdisciplinary studies, 5% parks/recreation, protective services, public affairs, 12% social sciences. Graduate degrees offered in 45 major fields of study.

UNDERGRADUATE MAJORS. Accounting, actuarial sciences, advertising, anthropology, applied mathematics, art education, arts management, astronomy, atmospheric sciences and meteorology, biology, botany, business administration and management, business economics, ceramics, chemistry, city/community/regional planning, civil engineering, communications, computer and information sciences, computer engineering, criminal justice studies, dental hygiene, dramatic arts, early childhood education, earth sciences, economics, electrical/electronics/communications engineering, elementary education, English, English education, environmental chemistry, environmental science, fashion merchandising, fiber/textiles/weaving, finance, fine arts, food science and nutrition, foreign languages education, forestry and related sciences, French, geochemistry, geography, geology, health education, history, hotel/motel and restaurant management, humanities, information sciences and systems, interior design, international relations, journalism, law enforcement and corrections, liberal/general studies, marketing management, mathematics, mathematics education, mechanical engineering, metal/jewelry, microbiology, music, music education, music performance, nursing, painting, parks and recreation management, philosophy, photography, physical education, physical sciences, physics, political science and government, predentistry, prelaw, premedicine, prepharmacy, preveterinary, printmaking, psychology, public administration, public relations, radio/television broadcasting, religion, science education, sculpture, secondary education, social science education, social sciences, social work, sociology, Spanish, special education, speech, speech pathology/audiology, speech/communication/theater education, sports medicine, statistics, trade and industrial education, trade and industrial supervision and management, zoology.

ACADEMIC PROGRAMS. Cooperative education, double major, dual enrollment of high school students, honors program, independent study, internships, study abroad, teacher preparation, telecourses, visiting/exchange student program; liberal arts/career combination in engineering, forestry, health sciences. **Remedial services:** Learning center, preadmission summer program, reduced course load, remedial instruction, special counselor, tutoring, Upward Bound, Talent Search. **ROTC:** Air Force, Army. **Placement/credit:** AP, CLEP General and Subject, institutional tests; 30 credit hours maximum for bachelor's degree.

ACADEMIC REQUIREMENTS. Freshmen must earn minimum GPA of 1.4 to continue in good standing. 67% of freshmen return for sophomore year. Students must declare major by end of second year. **Graduation requirements:** 125 hours for bachelor's (40 in major). Most students required to take courses in arts/fine arts, English, humanities, mathematics, biological/physical sciences, social sciences.

FRESHMAN ADMISSIONS. Selection criteria: Unconditional admission if cumulative high school GPA is 3.0, class rank is in upper quarter, or ACT composite score is 22 (24 for out-of-state applicants) or SAT combined score is 930 (1010 for non-resident applicants). Conditional admission if cumulative high school GPA is 2.5 to 2.99, class rank is in upper half to upper quarter, and test scores are lower than those for unconditional admission. **High school preparation:** 11 units required. Required and recommended units include English 4, mathematics 3, social science 2 and science 2. Foreign language 2 recommended. Mathematics must include 2 units algebra, 1 unit geometry. Science must be 2 units laboratory science (physics, biology, chemistry, earth science). One unit of social science must be U.S. history. Some programs have additional, more stringent requirements. **Test requirements:** SAT or ACT (ACT preferred); score report by July 15.

1992 FRESHMAN CLASS PROFILE. 5,660 men and women applied, 4,868 accepted; 2,156 enrolled. 60% had high school GPA of 3.0 or higher, 40% between 2.0 and 2.99. 24% were in top tenth and 51% were in top quarter of graduating class. **Academic background:** Mid 50% of enrolled freshmen had SAT-V between 360-550, SAT-M between 410-590; ACT composite between 16-24. 35% submitted SAT scores, 60% submitted ACT scores. **Characteristics:** 76% from in state, 86% live in college housing, 21% have minority backgrounds, 3% are foreign students, 5% join fraternities/sororities. Average age is 19.

FALL-TERM APPLICATIONS. No fee. $35 fee for out-of-state applicants only. No closing date; priority given to applications received by April 1; applicants notified on a rolling basis; must reply by registration. Audition required for music, music education applicants. Interview recommended for borderline applicants. Essay recommended for borderline applicants. Applicants encouraged to apply early. Admissions may close before start of fall semester.

STUDENT LIFE. Housing: Dormitories (men, women, coed); apartment, fraternity, sorority housing available. Honor halls, floors for students 21 years of age and older, coed floor for students 25 years of age and older. **Activities:** Student government, film, magazine, radio, student newspaper, television, choral groups, concert band, dance, drama, jazz band, marching band, music ensembles, musical theater, opera, pep band, symphony orchestra, fraternities, sororities, 155 student organizations.

ATHLETICS. NCAA. **Intercollegiate:** Basketball, cross-country, diving, football M, swimming, tennis, track and field, volleyball W. **Intramural:** Archery, badminton, baseball, basketball, bowling, cross-country, ice hockey M, lacrosse M, racquetball, rugby M, skiing, soccer, softball, swimming, table tennis, track and field, volleyball, water polo.

STUDENT SERVICES. Aptitude testing, career counseling, employment service for undergraduates, freshman orientation, health services, personal counseling, placement service for graduates, veterans counselor, counselor for handicapped students provided through Office of Disabled Student Services, services/facilities for handicapped.

ANNUAL EXPENSES. Tuition and fees: $1,844, $4,752 additional for out-of-state students. **Room and board:** $3,300. **Books and supplies:** $690. **Other expenses:** $1,350.

FINANCIAL AID. 65% of freshmen, 60% of continuing students receive some form of aid. 69% of grants, 93% of loans, 16% of jobs based on need. Academic, music/drama, art, athletic, state/district residency, leadership, minority scholarships available. **Aid applications:** No closing date; priority given to applications received by April 15; applicants notified on a rolling basis beginning on or about May 1; must reply within 4 weeks. **Additional information:** Nonresident and single-parent tuition waivers available.

ADDRESS/TELEPHONE. Molly S. Carder, Director of Admissions, Northern Arizona University, PO Box 4084, Flagstaff, AZ 86011-4084. (602) 523-2491.

Northland Pioneer College

Holbrook, Arizona CB code: 0325

2-year public community college, coed. Founded in 1973. **Accreditation:** Regional. **Undergraduate enrollment:** 323 men, 453 women full time; 1,293 men, 2,281 women part time. **Faculty:** 283 total (51 full time), 12 with doctorates or other terminal degrees. **Location:** Rural campus in small town; 200 miles from Phoenix. **Calendar:** Semester. **Microcomputers:** Located in libraries, classrooms, computer centers. **Additional facts:** 9 locations in Navajo County.

DEGREES OFFERED. AA, AAS. 99 associate degrees awarded in 1992. 18% in business/office and marketing/distribution, 5% computer sciences, 15% teacher education, 39% multi/interdisciplinary studies, 10% parks/recreation, protective services, public affairs, 12% trade and industry.

UNDERGRADUATE MAJORS. Automotive mechanics, automotive technology, business and management, carpentry, computer and information sciences, construction, early childhood education, electronic technology, fire control and safety technology, journalism, law enforcement and corrections technologies, liberal/general studies, library assistant, photographic technology, power plant operation and maintenance, recreation and community services technologies, secretarial and related programs, social work, teacher aide, welding technology.

ACADEMIC PROGRAMS. 2-year transfer program, cooperative education, dual enrollment of high school students, independent study. **Remedial services:** Learning center, remedial instruction, tutoring, reading and mathematics laboratories. **Placement/credit:** AP, CLEP General and Subject, institutional tests; 52 credit hours maximum for associate degree.

ACADEMIC REQUIREMENTS. Freshmen must earn minimum GPA of 2.0 to continue in good standing. 50% of freshmen return for sophomore year. Students must declare major by end of first year. **Graduation requirements:** 64 hours for associate (22 in major). Most students required to take courses in English, history, humanities, mathematics, biological/physical sciences, social sciences.

FRESHMAN ADMISSIONS. Selection criteria: Open admissions.

1992 FRESHMAN CLASS PROFILE. 2,500 men and women enrolled. **Characteristics:** 98% from in state, 99% commute, 40% have minority backgrounds. Average age is 33.

FALL-TERM APPLICATIONS. No fee for district residents, $10 for all other applicants. No closing date; applicants notified on a rolling basis; must reply by registration. Early admission available.

STUDENT LIFE. Housing: Dormitories (coed). **Activities:** Student government, student newspaper, choral groups, jazz band, musical theater, pep band, national honor society, Phi Theta Kappa.

ATHLETICS. NJCAA. **Intercollegiate:** Basketball.

STUDENT SERVICES. Aptitude testing, career counseling, employment service for undergraduates, personal counseling, placement service for graduates, veterans counselor, services/facilities for handicapped.

ANNUAL EXPENSES. Tuition and fees: $600, $1,650 additional for out-of-state students. **Room and board:** $1,400 room only. **Books and supplies:** $500. **Other expenses:** $1,120.

FINANCIAL AID. 10% of freshmen, 10% of continuing students receive some form of aid. 94% of grants, all loans, 95% of jobs based on need. 1,000 enrolled freshmen were judged to have need, 950 were offered aid. Academic, music/drama, art, athletic, leadership scholarships available. **Aid applications:** No closing date; priority given to applications received by June 1; applicants notified on a rolling basis beginning on or about May 15; must reply within 2 weeks.

ADDRESS/TELEPHONE. A. Daniel Simper, Dean of Admissions and Records, Northland Pioneer College, PO Box 610, Holbrook, AZ 86025. (602) 524-1993. Fax: (602) 524-1997.

Paradise Valley Community College

Phoenix, Arizona CB code: 2179

2-year public community college, coed. Founded in 1985. **Accreditation:** Regional. **Undergraduate enrollment:** 438 men, 520 women full time; 1,458 men, 2,845 women part time. **Faculty:** 217 total (54 full time), 23 with doctorates or other terminal degrees. **Location:** Suburban campus in very large city. **Calendar:** Semester, limited summer session. **Microcomputers:** 300 located in libraries, classrooms, computer centers.

DEGREES OFFERED. AA, AS, AAS. 150 associate degrees awarded in 1992.

UNDERGRADUATE MAJORS. Accounting, business and management, business and office, investments and securities, labor/industrial relations, management information systems, transportation and travel marketing.

ACADEMIC PROGRAMS. 2-year transfer program, cooperative education, dual enrollment of high school students, honors program, internships. **Remedial services:** Learning center, remedial instruction, tutoring. **Placement/credit:** AP, CLEP General and Subject, institutional tests; 30 credit hours maximum for associate degree.

ACADEMIC REQUIREMENTS. Freshmen must earn minimum GPA of 1.6 to continue in good standing. 79% of freshmen return for sophomore year. Students must declare major on application. **Graduation requirements:** 64 hours for associate (45 in major). Most students required to take courses in computer science, English, humanities, mathematics, biological/physical sciences, social sciences.

FRESHMAN ADMISSIONS. Selection criteria: Open admissions.

1992 FRESHMAN CLASS PROFILE. 881 men, 1,389 women enrolled. **Characteristics:** 98% from in state, 100% commute, 10% have minority backgrounds. Average age is 19.

FALL-TERM APPLICATIONS. No fee. Closing date August 28; must reply by registration.

STUDENT LIFE. Activities: Student government, magazine, student newspaper, Phi Theta Kappa, student Christian association, human service club, Returning Adults to Education, ECO Watch (environmental club), Latter Day Saints student association.

STUDENT SERVICES. Aptitude testing, career counseling, em-

ployment service for undergraduates, freshman orientation, on-campus day care, personal counseling, special adviser for adult students, veterans counselor, services/facilities for handicapped.

ANNUAL EXPENSES. Tuition and fees (1992-93): $885, $2,670 additional for out-of-district students, $3,750 additional for out-of-state students. **Books and supplies:** $400.

FINANCIAL AID. All aid based on need. Academic, state/district residency, leadership scholarships available. **Aid applications:** No closing date; applicants notified on a rolling basis beginning on or about June 1.

ADDRESS/TELEPHONE. Dr. Shirley Green, Director of Admissions and Records, Paradise Valley Community College, 18401 North 32nd Street, Phoenix, AZ 85032. (602) 493-2610. Fax: (602) 493-2978.

Phoenix College
Phoenix, Arizona — CB code: 4606

2-year public community college, coed. Founded in 1920. **Accreditation:** Regional. **Undergraduate enrollment:** 1,484 men, 1,919 women full time; 3,647 men, 6,213 women part time. **Faculty:** 532 total (150 full time), 40 with doctorates or other terminal degrees. **Location:** Urban campus in very large city. **Calendar:** Semester, limited summer session. **Microcomputers:** Located in classrooms, computer centers.

DEGREES OFFERED. AA, AAS. 500 associate degrees awarded in 1992.

UNDERGRADUATE MAJORS. Accounting, business administration and management, business and management, business and office, business data processing and related programs, chemical manufacturing technology, child development/care/guidance, civil technology, clothing and textiles management/production/services, computer and information sciences, dental assistant, dental hygiene, drafting, drafting and design technology, education, electrodiagnostic technologies, emergency medical technologies, engineering and engineering-related technologies, fashion design, fashion merchandising, finance, fire control and safety technology, food production/management/services, graphic arts technology, home economics, interior design, interpreter for the deaf, law enforcement and corrections, law enforcement and corrections technologies, legal assistant/paralegal, legal secretary, liberal/general studies, marketing and distribution, medical assistant, medical laboratory technologies, medical records technology, medical secretary, nursing, real estate, rehabilitation counseling/services, secretarial and related programs, transportation and travel marketing, word processing.

ACADEMIC PROGRAMS. 2-year transfer program, computer delivered (on-line) credit-bearing course offerings, cooperative education, dual enrollment of high school students, honors program, independent study, internships, study abroad, cross-registration. **Remedial services:** Learning center, reduced course load, remedial instruction, special counselor, tutoring. **ROTC:** Air Force, Army. **Placement/credit:** AP, CLEP General and Subject, institutional tests; 30 credit hours maximum for associate degree.

ACADEMIC REQUIREMENTS. Freshmen must earn minimum GPA of 1.6 to continue in good standing. Students must declare major on application. **Graduation requirements:** 64 hours for associate. Most students required to take courses in arts/fine arts, computer science, English, foreign languages, history, humanities, mathematics, philosophy/religion, biological/physical sciences, social sciences.

FRESHMAN ADMISSIONS. Selection criteria: Open admissions.

1992 FRESHMAN CLASS PROFILE. 4,911 men, 7,965 women enrolled. **Characteristics:** 98% from in state, 100% commute, 20% have minority backgrounds. Average age is 22.

FALL-TERM APPLICATIONS. No fee. No closing date; applicants notified on a rolling basis.

STUDENT LIFE. Activities: Student newspaper, television, choral groups, concert band, dance, drama, jazz band, marching band, music ensembles, musical theater, opera, symphony orchestra.

ATHLETICS. NJCAA. **Intercollegiate:** Archery, baseball M, basketball, cross-country, football M, golf M, softball W, tennis, track and field, volleyball W, wrestling M.

STUDENT SERVICES. Aptitude testing, career counseling, employment service for undergraduates, freshman orientation, on-campus day care, personal counseling, placement service for graduates, special adviser for adult students, veterans counselor, services/facilities for handicapped.

ANNUAL EXPENSES. Tuition and fees (1992-93): $870, $3,750 additional for out-of-state students. **Books and supplies:** $400. **Other expenses:** $2,016.

FINANCIAL AID. 30% of continuing students receive some form of aid. 87% of grants, 93% of loans, 55% of jobs based on need. Academic, music/drama, art, athletic, state/district residency, leadership, minority scholarships available. **Aid applications:** No closing date; priority given to applications received by April 15; applicants notified on a rolling basis beginning on or about May 15.

ADDRESS/TELEPHONE. Sherri Hancock, Associate Dean of Student Services, Phoenix College, 1202 West Thomas Road, Phoenix, AZ 85013. (602) 285-7500. Fax: (602) 285-7700.

Pima Community College
Tucson, Arizona — CB code: 4623

2-year public community college, coed. Founded in 1966. **Accreditation:** Regional. **Undergraduate enrollment:** 3,748 men, 3,945 women full time; 9,874 men, 12,608 women part time. **Faculty:** 1,632 total (312 full time), 191 with doctorates or other terminal degrees. **Location:** Urban campus in large city. **Calendar:** Semester, limited summer session. Saturday and extensive evening/early morning classes. **Microcomputers:** 1,500 located in libraries, classrooms, computer centers, campus-wide network. **Additional facts:** 4 campuses serve Tucson metropolitan area.

DEGREES OFFERED. AA, AS, AAS. 1,162 associate degrees awarded in 1992. 12% in business and management, 6% engineering technologies, 14% health sciences, 5% law, 42% multi/interdisciplinary studies, 7% parks/recreation, protective services, public affairs.

UNDERGRADUATE MAJORS. Accounting, agricultural sciences, air conditioning/heating/refrigeration mechanics, American Indian studies, anthropology, archeology, Asian studies, automotive technology, aviation structural repair, biology, business administration and management, business computer/console/peripheral equipment operation, business data programming, carpentry, chemistry, child development/care/guidance, clothing and textiles management/production/services, commercial art, communications, computer graphics, computer programming, construction, criminal justice technology, data processing, dental hygiene, dental laboratory technology, drafting, drafting and design technology, dramatic arts, early childhood education, education, electromechanical technology, electronic technology, elementary education, engineering, engineering and engineering-related technologies, fashion design, finance, fine arts, fire control and safety technology, food management, food production/management/services, food science and nutrition, geology, graphic and printing production, graphic arts technology, home economics, hotel/motel and restaurant management, individual and family development, interior design, international business management, interpreter for the deaf, landscape architecture, law enforcement and corrections technologies, legal assistant/paralegal, legal secretary, liberal/general studies, machine tool operation/machine shop, manufacturing technology, mathematics, mechanical design technology, medical records administration, medical records technology, medical secretary, microbiology, music, nursing, pharmacy, physical education, physics, predentistry, premedicine, prepharmacy, preveterinary, public administration, quality control technology, radiograph medical technology, real estate, respiratory therapy technology, secondary education, secretarial and related programs, social work, special education, speech, telecommunications, transportation management, water and wastewater technology, welding technology.

ACADEMIC PROGRAMS. 2-year transfer program, accelerated program, computer delivered (on-line) credit-bearing course offerings, cooperative education, double major, dual enrollment of high school students, honors program, independent study, student-designed major, weekend college. **Remedial services:** Learning center, remedial instruction, special counselor, tutoring. **ROTC:** Air Force, Army, Naval. **Placement/credit:** CLEP General and Subject, institutional tests; 30 credit hours maximum for associate degree.

ACADEMIC REQUIREMENTS. Freshmen must earn minimum GPA of 1.5 to continue in good standing. 40% of freshmen return for sophomore year. Students must declare major on application. **Graduation requirements:** 60 hours for associate. Most students required to take courses in English, mathematics.

FRESHMAN ADMISSIONS. Selection criteria: Open admissions.

1992 FRESHMAN CLASS PROFILE. 2,525 men, 2,602 women enrolled. **Characteristics:** 90% from in state, 100% commute, 42% have minority backgrounds, 5% are foreign students.

FALL-TERM APPLICATIONS. No fee. $10 fee for out-of-state applicants. No closing date; applicants notified on a rolling basis; must reply by registration.

STUDENT LIFE. Activities: Student government, magazine, radio, student newspaper, television, choral groups, concert band, dance, drama, jazz band, music ensembles, pep band, forensics activities, rodeo, speech communication program.

ATHLETICS. NJCAA. **Intercollegiate:** Baseball M, basketball, cross-country, golf M, soccer M, softball W, tennis, track and field, volleyball W. **Intramural:** Badminton, baseball M, basketball, cross-country, golf, handball, ice hockey M, racquetball, tennis, track and field, volleyball.

STUDENT SERVICES. Aptitude testing, career counseling, employment service for undergraduates, freshman orientation, personal counseling, placement service for graduates, veterans counselor, services/facilities for handicapped.

ANNUAL EXPENSES. Tuition and fees: $700, $3,630 additional for out-of-state students. **Books and supplies:** $450. **Other expenses:** $638.

FINANCIAL AID. 20% of freshmen, 20% of continuing students receive some form of aid. 99% of grants, 83% of loans, 55% of jobs based on need. Athletic, leadership, minority scholarships available. **Aid applications:** No closing date; priority given to applications received by April 1; applicants notified on a rolling basis beginning on or about May 15; must reply within 2 weeks.

ADDRESS/TELEPHONE. Denis F. Viri, District Director of Admissions and Records, Pima Community College, 2202 West Anklam Road, Tucson, AZ 85709-3010. (602) 884-6640. Fax: (602) 884-6728.

Prescott College
Prescott, Arizona CB code: 0484

4-year private liberal arts college, coed. Founded in 1966. **Accreditation:** Regional. **Undergraduate enrollment:** 197 men, 143 women full time; 13 men, 2 women part time. **Graduate enrollment:** 48 men and women. **Faculty:** 79 total (39 full time), 17 with doctorates or other terminal degrees. **Location:** Suburban campus in large town; 100 miles from Phoenix. **Calendar:** Two 10-week terms alternating with three 4-week practical sessions. **Microcomputers:** 16 located in libraries, computer centers. **Special facilities:** Kino Bay, Mexico, facility. **Additional facts:** Adult Degree Program is designed for working adults to obtain a degree on a year round, part-time basis. The Center for Indian Bilingual Teacher Education specializes in teacher certification for Native Americans.

DEGREES OFFERED. BA, MA. 69 bachelor's degrees awarded in 1992. Graduate degrees offered in 3 major fields of study.

UNDERGRADUATE MAJORS. Adult and continuing education research, American Indian studies, American literature, American studies, anthropology, archeology, behavioral sciences, bilingual/bicultural education, biological and physical sciences, biology, botany, business and management, city/community/regional planning, clinical psychology, community psychology, community services, comparative literature, comparative psychology, conservation and regulation, counseling psychology, crafts, creative writing, cultural and regional studies, developmental psychology, early childhood education, earth sciences, ecology, education, education of the culturally disadvantaged, education of the emotionally handicapped, education of the mentally handicapped, education of the physically handicapped, elementary education, English, English literature, environmental design, environmental science, fine arts, folklore and mythology, geography, geology, history, humanities, humanities and social sciences, individual and family development, international studies, junior high education, Latin American studies, liberal/general studies, marriage and family counseling, Mexican American studies, parks and recreation management, peace studies, philosophy, photography, physical sciences, political science and government, psychology, recreation and community services technologies, religion, renewable natural resources, school psychology, secondary education, small business management and ownership, social psychology, social sciences, social work, sociology, Spanish, special education, specific learning disabilities, student counseling and personnel services, teaching English as a second language/foreign language, visual and performing arts, wildlife management, women's studies.

ACADEMIC PROGRAMS. Accelerated program, double major, external degree, independent study, internships, student-designed major, study abroad, teacher preparation. **Remedial services:** Learning center, reduced course load, tutoring. **Placement/credit:** Institutional tests.

ACADEMIC REQUIREMENTS. No policy requiring minimum GPA; records of students having academic difficulty are reviewed individually. Successful completion of 75% of course load constitutes good academic standing. 80% of freshmen return for sophomore year. Students must declare major by end of second year. **Graduation requirements:** Most students required to take courses in English, mathematics.

FRESHMAN ADMISSIONS. Selection criteria: Each applicant considered on individual basis. Essay and GPA most important. Letters of recommendation, any personal additions important. Visit to the college recommended. **Test requirements:** SAT or ACT preferred, but not required, for admissions. **Additional information:** Developed writing style and reading comprehension recommended.

1992 FRESHMAN CLASS PROFILE. 50 men and women enrolled.

FALL-TERM APPLICATIONS. $25 fee. No closing date; priority given to applications received by May 1; applicants notified on a rolling basis; enrollment is on a first come, first served basis until class fills up. Essay required. Interview recommended. Deferred admission available. Applicants encouraged to apply early.

STUDENT LIFE. Activities: Student government, student newspaper, dance, drama, Student Environmental Network.

ATHLETICS. Intramural: Basketball, soccer, volleyball.

STUDENT SERVICES. Career counseling, freshman orientation, personal counseling, placement service for graduates, special adviser for adult students, veterans counselor.

ANNUAL EXPENSES. Tuition and fees: $9,545. **Books and supplies:** $353. **Other expenses:** $807.

FINANCIAL AID. 75% of freshmen, 66% of continuing students receive some form of aid. 98% of grants, 68% of loans, all jobs based on need. Academic, leadership scholarships available. **Aid applications:** No closing date; priority given to applications received by April 15; applicants notified on a rolling basis beginning on or about July 1; must reply within 3 weeks.

ADDRESS/TELEPHONE. Derk Janssen, Director of Admissions, Prescott College, 220-M Grove Avenue, Prescott, AZ 86301. (602) 776-5180. Fax: (602) 776-5137.

Rio Salado Community College
Phoenix, Arizona CB code: 0997

2-year public community college, coed. Founded in 1978. **Accreditation:** Regional. **Undergraduate enrollment:** 123 men, 115 women full time; 3,511 men, 5,180 women part time. **Faculty:** 488 total (9 full time), 2 with doctorates or other terminal degrees. **Location:** Urban campus in very large city. **Calendar:** Semester, extensive summer session. Saturday and extensive evening/early morning classes. **Microcomputers:** 300 located in classrooms, computer centers. **Special facilities:** KJZZ public radio station, sun sounds readings for the blind. **Additional facts:** College without walls at 257 countywide sites. Access to libraries at Arizona State University and 7 Maricopa County community colleges.

DEGREES OFFERED. AA, AS, AAS. 80 associate degrees awarded in 1992. 10% in business and management, 20% allied health, 55% multi/interdisciplinary studies, 11% trade and industry.

UNDERGRADUATE MAJORS. Accounting, air conditioning/heating/refrigeration mechanics, air conditioning/heating/refrigeration technology, business and management, carpentry, diesel engine mechanics, electrical and electronics equipment repair, electrical installation, electrical technology, electromechanical technology, electronic technology, finance, fire control and safety technology, flight attendants, liberal/general studies, masonry/tile setting, mental health/human services, microcomputer software, office supervision and management, photographic technology, plumbing/pipefitting/steamfitting, power plant operation and maintenance, precision metal work, public administration, quality control technology, radio/television technology, real estate, roofing, secretarial and related programs, trade and industrial supervision and management, vehicle and equipment operation, water and wastewater technology.

ACADEMIC PROGRAMS. 2-year transfer program, accelerated program, computer delivered (on-line) credit-bearing course offerings, cooperative education, dual enrollment of high school students, honors program, independent study, internships, telecourses, weekend college, cross-registration. **Remedial services:** Learning center, remedial instruction, tutoring. **Placement/credit:** AP, CLEP General and Subject, institutional tests; 30 credit hours maximum for associate degree.

ACADEMIC REQUIREMENTS. Freshmen must earn minimum GPA of 1.6 to continue in good standing. 30% of freshmen return for sophomore year. Students must declare major by end of first year. **Graduation requirements:** 64 hours for associate. Most students required to take courses in computer science, English, humanities, mathematics, biological/physical sciences, social sciences.

FRESHMAN ADMISSIONS. Selection criteria: Open admissions.

1992 FRESHMAN CLASS PROFILE. 3,185 men, 4,667 women enrolled. **Characteristics:** 99% from in state, 100% commute, 2% are foreign students. Average age is 32.

FALL-TERM APPLICATIONS. $5 fee. No closing date; applicants notified on a rolling basis; must reply by registration. Early admission available.

STUDENT LIFE. Activities: Student newspaper, Phi Theta Kappa.

STUDENT SERVICES. Aptitude testing, career counseling, personal counseling, special adviser for adult students, veterans counselor, services/facilities for handicapped.

ANNUAL EXPENSES. Tuition and fees (1992-93): $870, $2,820 additional for out-of-district students, $3,750 additional for out-of-state students. **Books and supplies:** $400. **Other expenses:** $800.

FINANCIAL AID. 2% of freshmen, 12% of continuing students receive some form of aid. 96% of grants, all loans based on need. **Aid applications:** No closing date; priority given to applications received by April 15; applicants notified on a rolling basis beginning on or about July 1.

ADDRESS/TELEPHONE. Patricia Cardenas Adame, Director of Admissions and Records, Rio Salado Community College, 640 North First Avenue, Phoenix, AZ 85003. (602) 223-4001. Fax: (602) 223-4329.

Scottsdale Community College
Scottsdale, Arizona CB code: 4755

2-year public community college, coed. Founded in 1969. **Accreditation:** Regional. **Undergraduate enrollment:** 1,292 men, 1,126 women full time; 2,934 men, 4,373 women part time. **Faculty:** 392 total (139 full time), 58 with doctorates or other terminal degrees. **Location:** Suburban campus in small city; near Phoenix, Arizona. **Calendar:** Semester. Saturday and extensive evening/early morning classes. **Microcomputers:** 600 located in libraries, classrooms, computer centers, campus-wide network.

DEGREES OFFERED. AA, AAS. 425 associate degrees awarded in 1992.

UNDERGRADUATE MAJORS. Accounting, business and management, business and office, business data entry equipment operation, business data processing and related programs, business data programming, child development/care/guidance, computer and information sciences, construction, criminal justice studies, early childhood education, electronic technology, electronic/microprocessor technology, equestrian science, finance, fire control and safety technology, food production/management/services, hospitality and recreation marketing, hotel/motel and restaurant management, law enforcement and corrections technologies, liberal/general studies, motion picture technology, nursing, nursing assistant, practical nursing, public administration, public relations, real estate, secretarial and related programs, teacher aide, tribal management, word processing.

ACADEMIC PROGRAMS. 2-year transfer program, cooperative education, dual enrollment of high school students, honors program, internships, study abroad, telecourses, cross-registration. **Remedial services:** Learning center, remedial instruction, tutoring. **Placement/credit:** CLEP General and Subject, institutional tests; 52 credit hours maximum for associate degree.

ACADEMIC REQUIREMENTS. Freshmen must earn minimum GPA of 1.6 to continue in good standing. **Graduation requirements:** 64 hours for associate. Most students required to take courses in computer science, English, humanities, mathematics, biological/physical sciences, social sciences.

FRESHMAN ADMISSIONS. Selection criteria: Open admissions. **Test requirements:** SAT or ACT (ACT preferred) for placement and counseling only; score report by August 15. **Additional information:** High school diploma required of applicants under 18 years of age.

1992 FRESHMAN CLASS PROFILE. 1,405 men, 1,641 women enrolled. **Characteristics:** 91% from in state, 100% commute, 5% have minority backgrounds. Average age is 23.

FALL-TERM APPLICATIONS. No fee. No closing date; applicants notified on a rolling basis; must reply by registration.

STUDENT LIFE. Activities: Student government, student newspaper, television, choral groups, concert band, dance, drama, jazz band, music ensembles, symphony orchestra. **Additional information:** Intercollegiate rodeo offered.

ATHLETICS. NAIA, NCAA, NJCAA. **Intercollegiate:** Baseball M, basketball, cross-country, football M, golf M, soccer M, softball W, tennis, track and field, volleyball W. **Intramural:** Baseball M.

STUDENT SERVICES. Aptitude testing, career counseling, employment service for undergraduates, freshman orientation, on-campus day care, personal counseling, placement service for graduates, special adviser for adult students, veterans counselor, women's reentry center, senior adult program, services/facilities for handicapped.

ANNUAL EXPENSES. Tuition and fees (1992-93): $870, $3,750 additional for out-of-state students. **Books and supplies:** $400.

FINANCIAL AID. 20% of freshmen, 16% of continuing students receive some form of aid. Grants, loans, jobs available. **Aid applications:** No closing date; priority given to applications received by April 15; applicants notified on a rolling basis. **Additional information:** Athletic scholarships offered in rodeo. All athletic scholarships limited to county residents.

ADDRESS/TELEPHONE. John M. Silvester, Associate Dean of Student Services, Scottsdale Community College, 9000 East Chaparral Road, Scottsdale, AZ 85250-2699. (602) 423-6000. Fax: (602) 423-6200.

South Mountain Community College
Phoenix, Arizona — CB code: 4734

2-year public community college, coed. Founded in 1979. **Accreditation:** Regional. **Undergraduate enrollment:** 287 men, 388 women full time; 976 men, 1,315 women part time. **Faculty:** 176 total (41 full time), 7 with doctorates or other terminal degrees. **Location:** Urban campus in very large city; 8 miles from downtown Phoenix. **Calendar:** Semester, limited summer session. **Microcomputers:** Located in libraries, classrooms, computer centers. **Additional facts:** Learning Center in Guadalupe, AZ.

DEGREES OFFERED. AA, AS, AAS. 69 associate degrees awarded in 1992.

UNDERGRADUATE MAJORS. Business and management, computer and information sciences, information sciences and systems, liberal/general studies, word processing.

ACADEMIC PROGRAMS. 2-year transfer program, cooperative education, dual enrollment of high school students, honors program, independent study, cross-registration. **Remedial services:** Learning center, remedial instruction, tutoring. **ROTC:** Air Force. **Placement/credit:** AP, CLEP General, institutional tests; 30 credit hours maximum for associate degree.

ACADEMIC REQUIREMENTS. Freshmen must earn minimum GPA of 1.6 to continue in good standing. Students must declare major on application. **Graduation requirements:** 64 hours for associate (45 in major). Most students required to take courses in computer science, English, humanities, mathematics, biological/physical sciences, social sciences.

FRESHMAN ADMISSIONS. Selection criteria: Open admissions.

1992 FRESHMAN CLASS PROFILE. 2,934 men and women enrolled. **Characteristics:** 52% have minority backgrounds.

FALL-TERM APPLICATIONS. No fee. No closing date; applicants notified on a rolling basis; must reply by registration. Deferred admission available.

STUDENT LIFE. Activities: Student government, student newspaper, yearbook, choral groups, concert band, dance, jazz band.

ATHLETICS. NJCAA. **Intercollegiate:** Baseball M, basketball, cross-country, soccer M, softball W, tennis, track and field, volleyball W.

STUDENT SERVICES. Aptitude testing, career counseling, on-campus day care, personal counseling, veterans counselor, services/facilities for handicapped.

ANNUAL EXPENSES. Tuition and fees: $960, $3,750 additional for out-of-state students. **Books and supplies:** $700.

FINANCIAL AID. 50% of freshmen, 50% of continuing students receive some form of aid. 99% of grants, 82% of loans, 46% of jobs based on need. Academic, music/drama, art, athletic, minority scholarships available. **Aid applications:** No closing date; priority given to applications received by May 1; applicants notified on a rolling basis beginning on or about May 15; must reply within 2 weeks.

ADDRESS/TELEPHONE. Tony Bracamonte, Associate Dean of Student Services, South Mountain Community College, 7050 South 24th Street, Phoenix, AZ 85040. (602) 243-8123. Fax: (602) 243-8FAX.

Southwestern College
Phoenix, Arizona — CB code: 4736

Admissions: 66% of applicants accepted
Based on: ••• Essay, recommendations, religious affiliation/commitment
•• School record, test scores
• Special talents
Completion: 80% of freshmen end year in good standing
32% graduate

4-year private Bible college, coed, affiliated with Conservative Baptist Association. Founded in 1960. **Accreditation:** Regional candidate. **Undergraduate enrollment:** 74 men, 68 women full time; 7 men, 11 women part time. **Faculty:** 21 total (9 full time), 5 with doctorates or other terminal degrees. **Location:** Urban campus in very large city. **Calendar:** 4-4-1. **Microcomputers:** Located in libraries.

DEGREES OFFERED. AA, BA, BS. 2 associate degrees awarded in 1992. 100% in philosophy, religion, theology. 31 bachelor's degrees awarded. 42% in teacher education, 58% philosophy, religion, theology.

UNDERGRADUATE MAJORS. Associate: Bible studies, liberal/general studies, missionary studies, religious education, religious music, theological studies. **Bachelor's:** Bible studies, elementary education, missionary studies, religious education, religious music, theological studies.

ACADEMIC PROGRAMS. Honors program, internships, teacher preparation. **Remedial services:** Reduced course load, remedial instruction. **Placement/credit:** AP, CLEP General and Subject; 30 credit hours maximum for bachelor's degree.

ACADEMIC REQUIREMENTS. Freshmen must earn minimum GPA of 1.5 to continue in good standing. 55% of freshmen return for sophomore year. Students must declare major by end of second year. **Graduation requirements:** 65 hours for associate (18 in major), 128 hours for bachelor's (36 in major). Most students required to take courses in English, history, humanities, mathematics, philosophy/religion, biological/physical sciences, social sciences. **Postgraduate studies:** 20% from 2-year programs enter 4-year programs. **Additional information:** Off-campus, noncredit Christian internship work required during each semester.

FRESHMAN ADMISSIONS. Selection criteria: School achievement record and recommendations very important. Written testimony of conversion experience required for admission. Recommended units include English 4, foreign language 2, mathematics 3, social science 3 and science 2. **Test requirements:** SAT or ACT (ACT preferred); score report by August 29.

1992 FRESHMAN CLASS PROFILE. 42 men applied, 29 accepted, 18 enrolled; 38 women applied, 24 accepted, 18 enrolled. 39% had high school GPA of 3.0 or higher, 46% between 2.0 and 2.99. 19% were in top tenth and 29% were in top quarter of graduating class. **Characteristics:** 69% from in state, 83% live in college housing, 11% have minority backgrounds. Average age is 19.

FALL-TERM APPLICATIONS. $25 fee. Closing date August 15; applicants notified on a rolling basis; must reply by registration. Audition required for music applicants. Essay required. Deferred admission available.

STUDENT LIFE. Housing: Dormitories (men, women); apartment housing available. **Activities:** Student government, student newspaper, yearbook, choral groups, drama, music ensembles, Chenaniah Singers, mixed softball team. **Additional information:** Religious observance required.

ATHLETICS. NSCAA. **Intercollegiate:** Basketball. **Intramural:** Football, soccer, table tennis, tennis, volleyball. **Clubs:** Softball.

STUDENT SERVICES. Aptitude testing, career counseling, employment service for undergraduates, health services, personal counseling, services/facilities for handicapped.

ANNUAL EXPENSES. Tuition and fees: $5,220. **Room and board:** $2,350. **Books and supplies:** $400. **Other expenses:** $2,200.

FINANCIAL AID. 89% of freshmen, 79% of continuing students receive some form of aid. 62% of grants, 82% of loans, 42% of jobs based on need. 29 enrolled freshmen were judged to have need, all were offered aid. Minority scholarships available. **Aid applications:** Closing date July 15; priority given to applications received by April 15; applicants notified on or about August 1.

ADDRESS/TELEPHONE. James A. Lanning, Dean of Admission, Southwestern College, 2625 East Cactus Road, Phoenix, AZ 85032-7042. (602) 992-6101. (800) 247-2697.

University of Arizona
Tucson, Arizona CB code: 4832

Admissions: 86% of applicants accepted
Based on: ••• School record, test scores
•• Recommendations
• Activities, essay, interview, special talents
Completion: 88% of freshmen end year in good standing
44% graduate, 35% of these enter graduate study

4-year public university, coed. Founded in 1885. **Accreditation:** Regional. **Undergraduate enrollment:** 11,156 men, 10,294 women full time; 2,387 men, 2,515 women part time. **Graduate enrollment:** 3,035 men, 2,288 women full time; 1,502 men, 1,952 women part time. **Faculty:** 1,728 total (1,652 full time). **Location:** Urban campus in large city; 120 miles from Phoenix. **Calendar:** Semester, extensive summer session. **Microcomputers:** 1,700 located in dormitories, classrooms, computer centers, campus-wide network. **Special facilities:** Geological museum, state anthropological museum, planetarium, observatory, art museum, center for creative photography. **Additional facts:** Sierra Vista offers credit-bearing classes in general studies and education.

DEGREES OFFERED. BA, BS, BFA, BArch, MA, MS, MBA, MFA, MEd, PhD, EdD, MD, Pharm D, JD. 4,587 bachelor's degrees awarded in 1992. 5% in area and ethnic studies, 19% business and management, 9% communications, 5% computer sciences, 7% teacher education, 11% engineering, 6% psychology, 14% social sciences, 5% visual and performing arts. Graduate degrees offered in 117 major fields of study.

UNDERGRADUATE MAJORS. Accounting, aerospace/aeronautical/astronautical engineering, agricultural economics, agricultural education, agricultural engineering, agricultural sciences, agricultural/biosystems engineering, animal sciences, anthropology, architecture, art education, art history, astronomy, atmospheric sciences and meteorology, biochemistry, biology, botany, business administration and management, business and management, business economics, chemical engineering, chemistry, civil engineering, classics, communications, computer and information sciences, computer engineering, creative writing, criminal justice studies, dance, dramatic arts, early childhood education, earth sciences, East Asian studies, ecology and evolutionary biology, economics, electrical/electronics/communications engineering, elementary education, engineering mathematics, engineering physics, English, English education, environmental science, family/consumer resource management, fashion merchandising, finance, fine arts, food science and nutrition, foreign languages education, French, geography, geological engineering, geology, German, Greek (classical), Greek (modern), health and human services administration, health care administration, health education, history, home economics, home economics education, industrial engineering, Italian, jazz, Jewish studies, journalism, landscape architecture, Latin, Latin American studies, liberal/general studies, linguistics, management information systems, marketing management, materials engineering, mathematics, mathematics education, mechanical engineering, media arts, medical laboratory technologies, Mexican American studies, microbiology, mining and mineral engineering, molecular biology, music, music education, music performance, musical theater, nuclear engineering, nursing, nutritional sciences, occupational safety and health technology, operations research, optics, personnel management, pharmacy, philosophy, photography, physical education, physics, plant sciences, political science and government, Portuguese, psychology, public administration, range management, real estate, recreation and community services technologies, religion, Russian, Russian and Slavic studies, secondary education, small business management and ownership, social sciences, social studies education, sociology, soil sciences, Spanish, speech, speech correction, speech pathology/audiology, speech/communication/theater education, studio art, systems engineering, veterinary science, visual and performing arts, wildlife management, women's studies.

ACADEMIC PROGRAMS. Accelerated program, cooperative education, double major, dual enrollment of high school students, education specialist degree, honors program, independent study, internships, semester at sea, student-designed major, study abroad, teacher preparation, telecourses, visiting/exchange student program; combined bachelor's/graduate program in business administration. **Remedial services:** Learning center, preadmission summer program, reduced course load, special counselor, tutoring. **ROTC:** Air Force, Army, Naval. **Placement/credit:** AP, CLEP General and Subject, IB, institutional tests; 60 credit hours maximum for bachelor's degree.

ACADEMIC REQUIREMENTS. Freshmen must earn minimum GPA of 2.0 to continue in good standing. 76% of freshmen return for sophomore year. Students must declare major by end of second year. **Graduation requirements:** 125 hours for bachelor's (30 in major). Most students required to take courses in arts/fine arts, English, foreign languages, history, humanities, mathematics, philosophy/religion, biological/physical sciences, social sciences.

FRESHMAN ADMISSIONS. Selection criteria: In and out-of-state applicants: top 25% of class or 3.0 cumulative GPA, SAT combined score of 1010 (930 in-state) or ACT composite score of 24 (22 in-state). Conditional admission may be offered to in-state applicants who meet one or more of the following: top half of class, cumulative GPA of 2.5, SAT combined score of 930, or ACT composite score of 22. **High school preparation:** 11 units required; 16 recommended. Required and recommended units include English 4-4, mathematics 3-4, social science 2-3 and science 2-3. Foreign language 2 recommended. Social sciences must include 1 unit American history. Engineering, architecture, mining, and pharmacy programs require additional courses. **Test requirements:** SAT or ACT; score report by August 1.

1992 FRESHMAN CLASS PROFILE. 6,659 men applied, 5,645 accepted, 1,995 enrolled; 6,662 women applied, 5,777 accepted, 2,031 enrolled. 72% had high school GPA of 3.0 or higher, 28% between 2.0 and 2.99. 30% were in top tenth and 57% were in top quarter of graduating class. **Academic background:** Mid 50% of enrolled freshmen had SAT-V between 400-520, SAT-M between 460-590; ACT composite between 20-26. 78% submitted SAT scores, 52% submitted ACT scores. **Characteristics:** 65% from in state, 71% live in college housing, 25% have minority backgrounds, 7% are foreign students, 14% join fraternities/sororities. Average age is 18.

FALL-TERM APPLICATIONS. $35 fee, may be waived for applicants with need. Closing date April 1; priority given to applications received by March 1; applicants notified on a rolling basis; must reply by May 1 or within 4 weeks if notified thereafter. Audition required for applied music applicants. Portfolio recommended for studio art applicants. Essay recommended. CRDA. Deferred and early admission available. Institutional early decision plan.

STUDENT LIFE. Housing: Dormitories (men, women, coed); apartment, fraternity, sorority, cooperative housing available. Temporary off-campus housing available. **Activities:** Student government, film, magazine, radio, student newspaper, television, yearbook, choral groups, concert band, dance, drama, jazz band, marching band, music ensembles, musical theater, opera, pep band, symphony orchestra, fraternities, sororities.

ATHLETICS. NCAA. **Intercollegiate:** Baseball M, basketball, cross-country, diving, football M, golf, gymnastics W, ice hockey M, lacrosse M, rugby M, softball W, swimming, tennis, track and field, volleyball W. **Intramural:** Badminton, basketball, bowling, cross-country, diving, golf, racquetball, soccer, softball, swimming, table tennis, tennis, track and field, volleyball, water polo, wrestling M. **Clubs:** Ice hockey, lacrosse, soccer.

STUDENT SERVICES. Aptitude testing, career counseling, employment service for undergraduates, freshman orientation, health services, personal counseling, placement service for graduates, special adviser for adult students, veterans counselor, minority student counseling, services/facilities for handicapped.

ANNUAL EXPENSES. Tuition and fees: $1,854, $5,506 additional for out-of-state students. Law school students pay additional $1000 per year. **Room and board:** $3,820. **Books and supplies:** $620. **Other expenses:** $1,750.

FINANCIAL AID. 24% of freshmen, 48% of continuing students receive some form of aid. 69% of grants, 89% of loans, 7% of jobs based on need. 1,207 enrolled freshmen were judged to have need, 1,151 were offered aid. Academic, music/drama, art, athletic, state/district residency, leadership, alumni affiliation, minority scholarships available. **Aid applications:** No closing date; priority given to applications received by March 1; applicants notified on a rolling basis beginning on or about May 1; must reply within 3 weeks.

ADDRESS/TELEPHONE. Loyd V. Bell, Director of Admissions and New Student Enrollment, University of Arizona, Robert L. Nugent Building, Tucson, AZ 85721. (602) 621-3237. Fax: (602) 621-9799.

University of Phoenix
Phoenix, Arizona CB code: 1024

2-year upper-division proprietary university, coed. Founded in 1976. **Accreditation:** Regional. **Undergraduate enrollment:** 7,379 men and women. **Graduate enrollment:** 5,547 men and women. **Faculty:** 1,800 total. **Location:** Urban campus in very large city. **Calendar:** Consecutive 5-week courses for 12 to 13 months. Students may enroll at beginning of designated courses. **Microcomputers:** Located in computer centers. **Additional facts:** Degree completion programs designed to meet needs of working adults. Regional offices in California, Utah, Colorado, New Mexico, Hawaii, and Puerto Rico.

DEGREES OFFERED. BA, BS, MA, MBA, MEd. 1,846 bachelor's degrees awarded in 1992. 88% in business and management, 12% health sciences. Graduate degrees offered in 9 major fields of study.

UNDERGRADUATE MAJORS. Business administration and management, nursing.

ACADEMIC PROGRAMS. Accelerated program, double major, external degree, independent study. **Remedial services:** Remedial instruction, special counselor. **Placement/credit:** CLEP General and Subject.

ACADEMIC REQUIREMENTS. Students must declare major on enrollment. **Graduation requirements:** 120 hours for bachelor's (41 in major).

Most students required to take courses in English, humanities, mathematics, biological/physical sciences, social sciences.

STUDENT SERVICES. Personal counseling, services/facilities for handicapped.

ANNUAL EXPENSES. Tuition and fees (1992-93): $5,478. **Books and supplies:** $500. **Other expenses:** $200.

FINANCIAL AID. 60% of continuing students receive some form of aid. All grants, 13% of loans based on need. **Aid applications:** No closing date; applicants notified on a rolling basis; must reply immediately.

ADDRESS/TELEPHONE. Vicki J. Peters, Director of Admissions, University of Phoenix, 4615 East Elwood Street, Phoenix, AZ 85072-2069. (602) 966-9577 ext. 1084. Fax: (602) 894-1758.

Western International University
Phoenix, Arizona CB code: 1316

4-year private university and college of arts and sciences and business college, coed. Founded in 1978. **Accreditation:** Regional. **Undergraduate enrollment:** 601 men, 432 women full time; 307 men, 193 women part time. **Graduate enrollment:** 215 men, 136 women full time; 72 men, 46 women part time. **Faculty:** 88 total, 43 with doctorates or other terminal degrees. **Location:** Suburban campus in very large city; 7 miles from downtown Phoenix. **Calendar:** Semester. **Microcomputers:** 45 located in libraries, computer centers. **Special facilities:** On-line career service data base. **Additional facts:** Adult student body. Intensive 2-month day or evening courses offered year round.

DEGREES OFFERED. AA, BA, BS, MS, MBA. 46 associate degrees awarded in 1992. 100% in multi/interdisciplinary studies. 256 bachelor's degrees awarded. 52% in business and management, 25% computer sciences, 23% multi/interdisciplinary studies. Graduate degrees offered in 6 major fields of study.

UNDERGRADUATE MAJORS. Associate: Computer and information sciences, liberal/general studies. **Bachelor's:** Accounting, business administration and management, computer and information sciences, finance, hotel/motel and restaurant management, international business management, law enforcement and corrections, liberal/general studies, marketing management.

ACADEMIC PROGRAMS. Accelerated program, double major, dual enrollment of high school students, independent study, internships, student-designed major, study abroad, visiting/exchange student program. **Remedial services:** Special counselor, tutoring. **Placement/credit:** CLEP General and Subject, institutional tests; 45 credit hours maximum for associate degree; 102 credit hours maximum for bachelor's degree. Maximum of 90 credits by examination and assessment may be counted toward degree; 36 hour residency requirement.

ACADEMIC REQUIREMENTS. Freshmen must earn minimum GPA of 2.0 to continue in good standing. Students must declare major by end of second year. **Graduation requirements:** 63 hours for associate, 126 hours for bachelor's (33 in major). Most students required to take courses in computer science, English, foreign languages, history, humanities, mathematics, philosophy/religion, biological/physical sciences, social sciences.

FRESHMAN ADMISSIONS. Selection criteria: Accomplishments in working world most important. Academic achievement, cumulative GPA, personal interview, recommendation considered. Recommended units include English 4, mathematics 3 and social science 1.

1992 FRESHMAN CLASS PROFILE. 35 men and women applied, 24 accepted; 18 enrolled. **Characteristics:** 75% from in state, 100% commute. Average age is 34.

FALL-TERM APPLICATIONS. $50 fee. No closing date; applicants notified on a rolling basis; must reply by registration. Interview required for all applicants for admission applicants. Essay recommended. Deferred and early admission available.

STUDENT LIFE. Activities: Student government, student newspaper, International Students Association. **Additional information:** Cultural activities and special seminars/workshops available.

STUDENT SERVICES. Career counseling, freshman orientation, personal counseling, special adviser for adult students, veterans counselor, services/facilities for handicapped.

ANNUAL EXPENSES. Tuition and fees: $6,120. **Books and supplies:** $720. **Other expenses:** $500.

FINANCIAL AID. 56% of freshmen, 44% of continuing students receive some form of aid. 96% of grants, 86% of loans, all jobs based on need. **Aid applications:** No closing date; applicants notified on a rolling basis.

ADDRESS/TELEPHONE. Kathie Westerfield, Director of Admissions, Western International University, 9215 North Black Canyon Highway, Phoenix, AZ 85021. (602) 943-2311. Fax: (602) 371-8637.

Yavapai College
Prescott, Arizona CB code: 4996

2-year public community college, coed. Founded in 1966. **Accreditation:** Regional. **Undergraduate enrollment:** 631 men, 673 women full time; 1,544 men, 2,887 women part time. **Faculty:** 364 total (82 full time), 23 with doctorates or other terminal degrees. **Location:** Rural campus in large town; 100 miles from Phoenix. **Calendar:** Semester, limited summer session. Saturday and extensive evening/early morning classes. **Microcomputers:** Located in libraries, classrooms, computer centers. **Special facilities:** Art gallery, solar laboratory, solar greenhouse. **Additional facts:** Classes offered at branch campus in Clarkdale and several locations in Yavapai County.

DEGREES OFFERED. AA, AAS. 197 associate degrees awarded in 1992.

UNDERGRADUATE MAJORS. Accounting, anthropology, architectural technologies, architecture, automotive mechanics, automotive technology, biology, business administration and management, business and office, business data processing and related programs, chemistry, communications, computer and information sciences, construction, drafting, drafting and design technology, elementary education, engineering, engineering and engineering-related technologies, English, fine arts, fire control and safety technology, forestry and related sciences, French, geography, graphic design, history, home economics, hotel/motel and restaurant management, humanities, industrial technology, law enforcement and corrections, liberal/general studies, manufacturing technology, mathematics, music, music education, nursing, office supervision and management, physical education, physical sciences, physics, precision metal work, psychology, secondary education, social work, sociology, Spanish, zoology.

ACADEMIC PROGRAMS. 2-year transfer program, accelerated program, dual enrollment of high school students, honors program, independent study, teacher preparation, telecourses, weekend college, 2 and 2 program with Northern Arizona University. **Remedial services:** Learning center, preadmission summer program, reduced course load, remedial instruction, special counselor, tutoring. **ROTC:** Air Force, Army. **Placement/credit:** AP, CLEP General and Subject, institutional tests; 30 credit hours maximum for associate degree.

ACADEMIC REQUIREMENTS. Freshmen must earn minimum GPA of 2.0 to continue in good standing. Students must declare major on enrollment. **Graduation requirements:** 64 hours for associate. Most students required to take courses in arts/fine arts, English, history, humanities, mathematics, philosophy/religion, biological/physical sciences, social sciences.

FRESHMAN ADMISSIONS. Selection criteria: Open admissions. Special admissions required of students entering registered nursing and gunsmithing programs.

1992 FRESHMAN CLASS PROFILE. 753 men, 1,008 women enrolled. **Characteristics:** 94% from in state, 72% commute, 12% have minority backgrounds. Average age is 19.

FALL-TERM APPLICATIONS. $10 fee for out-of-state applicants. No closing date; applicants notified on a rolling basis; must reply by registration. Interview required for nursing applicants.

STUDENT LIFE. Housing: Dormitories (men, women, coed). **Activities:** Student government, magazine, student newspaper, choral groups, dance, drama, jazz band, music ensembles, musical theater, pep band, Nursing Association, Native American Club, International Student Club.

ATHLETICS. NJCAA. **Intercollegiate:** Baseball M, basketball, cross-country, soccer M, volleyball W. **Intramural:** Badminton, basketball, softball, table tennis, tennis, volleyball, water polo.

STUDENT SERVICES. Aptitude testing, career counseling, employment service for undergraduates, freshman orientation, personal counseling, placement service for graduates, special adviser for adult students, veterans counselor, services/facilities for handicapped.

ANNUAL EXPENSES. Tuition and fees: $666, $4,450 additional for out-of-state students. **Room and board:** $2,720. **Books and supplies:** $500. **Other expenses:** $1,050.

FINANCIAL AID. 44% of freshmen, 42% of continuing students receive some form of aid. 80% of grants, 95% of loans, 22% of jobs based on need. 720 enrolled freshmen were judged to have need, 648 were offered aid. Academic, music/drama, art, athletic, state/district residency scholarships available. **Aid applications:** No closing date; priority given to applications received by April 15; applicants notified on a rolling basis; must reply within 20 days.

ADDRESS/TELEPHONE. Dr. Richard M. Boone, Registrar/Director of Admissions, Yavapai College, 1100 East Sheldon Street, Prescott, AZ 86301. (602) 445-7300 ext. 2147. Fax: (602) 776-2193.

Arkansas

Arkansas Baptist College
Little Rock, Arkansas CB code: 7301

4-year private liberal arts college, coed, affiliated with American Baptist Churches in the USA. Founded in 1884. **Accreditation:** Regional. **Undergraduate enrollment:** 411 men and women. **Faculty:** 47 total (28 full time), 8 with doctorates or other terminal degrees. **Location:** Urban campus in small city. **Calendar:** Semester, extensive summer session. **Microcomputers:** Located in computer centers.

DEGREES OFFERED. AA, BA, BS. 40 bachelor's degrees awarded. 34% in business and management, 6% education, 36% teacher education, 8% philosophy, religion, theology, 16% social sciences.

UNDERGRADUATE MAJORS. Associate: Business and management, business and office, liberal/general studies, secretarial and related programs. **Bachelor's:** Business and management, computer and information sciences, elementary education, religion, secondary education, social sciences.

ACADEMIC PROGRAMS. 2-year transfer program, double major, independent study. **Remedial services:** Tutoring, developmental classes in English and mathematics. **Placement/credit:** Institutional tests.

ACADEMIC REQUIREMENTS. Freshmen must earn minimum GPA of 2.0 to continue in good standing. 75% of freshmen return for sophomore year. Students must declare major by end of first year. **Graduation requirements:** 64 hours for associate (60 in major), 124 hours for bachelor's (72 in major). Most students required to take courses in English, history, mathematics, philosophy/religion, biological/physical sciences, social sciences. **Postgraduate studies:** 25% from 2-year programs enter 4-year programs.

FRESHMAN ADMISSIONS. Selection criteria: School achievement record, recommendations most important. Interview, special talents, alumni relations important. **High school preparation:** 18 units recommended. Recommended units include biological science 1, English 4, mathematics 4, physical science 1 and social science 1. Vocational and agriculture courses also recommended. **Additional information:** Academically borderline applicants may be admitted provisionally but must earn 2.0 GPA by end of first semester to continue in good academic standing.

1992 FRESHMAN CLASS PROFILE. 47 men and women enrolled. **Characteristics:** 95% from in state, 98% commute, 98% have minority backgrounds. Average age is 19.

FALL-TERM APPLICATIONS. $10 fee. Closing date September 30; applicants notified on a rolling basis beginning on or about June 30. Interview recommended. Deferred admission available.

STUDENT LIFE. Housing: Dormitories (men, women). **Activities:** Student government, choral groups, Baptist Student Union, student teacher organization. **Additional information:** Religious observance required.

ATHLETICS. NJCAA. **Intercollegiate:** Basketball, softball.

STUDENT SERVICES. Aptitude testing, career counseling, employment service for undergraduates, freshman orientation, health services, on-campus day care, personal counseling, placement service for graduates, veterans counselor.

ANNUAL EXPENSES. Tuition and fees (1992-93): $1,670. **Room and board:** $2,200. **Books and supplies:** $600. **Other expenses:** $850.

FINANCIAL AID. 43% of freshmen, 94% of continuing students receive some form of aid. Grants, loans, jobs available. Academic, athletic scholarships available. **Aid applications:** Closing date May 1; applicants notified on or about August 15; must reply by August 20.

ADDRESS/TELEPHONE. Annie A. Hightower, Registrar/Director of Admissions, Arkansas Baptist College, 1600 Bishop Street, Little Rock, AR 72202. (501) 374-7856.

Arkansas College
Batesville, Arkansas CB code: 6009

Admissions:	65% of applicants accepted
Based on:	••• School record, test scores
	•• Activities, interview, recommendations
	• Essay, religious affiliation/commitment, special talents
Completion:	68% of freshmen end year in good standing
	57% graduate, 23% of these enter graduate study

4-year private college of arts and sciences and liberal arts college, coed, affiliated with Presbyterian Church (USA). Founded in 1872. **Accreditation:** Regional. **Undergraduate enrollment:** 191 men, 307 women full time; 74 men, 129 women part time. **Faculty:** 73 total (44 full time), 33 with doctorates or other terminal degrees. **Location:** Rural campus in small town; 90 miles from Little Rock, 110 miles from Memphis, Tennessee. **Calendar:** 4-1-4, limited summer session. Extensive evening/early morning classes. **Microcomputers:** 48 located in libraries, computer centers. **Special facilities:** Kresge Gallery, Ozark Region Studies Collection, experimental theater. **Additional facts:** Endowed travel program allows students in good standing to travel abroad. Student-faculty research program and The Outdoor Experience available.

DEGREES OFFERED. BA, BS. 115 bachelor's degrees awarded in 1992. 31% in business and management, 26% teacher education, 6% letters/literature, 7% life sciences, 5% mathematics, 5% psychology, 7% social sciences.

UNDERGRADUATE MAJORS. Accounting, applied mathematics, biology, business and management, business economics, chemistry, communications, dramatic arts, elementary education, English, English education, history, mathematics, mathematics education, music, music education, philosophy, physical education, psychology, religion, science education, social studies education, social work, studio art.

ACADEMIC PROGRAMS. Cooperative education, double major, dual enrollment of high school students, honors program, independent study, internships, student-designed major, study abroad, teacher preparation. **Remedial services:** Learning center, reduced course load. **Placement/credit:** AP, CLEP General and Subject, institutional tests; 33 credit hours maximum for bachelor's degree.

ACADEMIC REQUIREMENTS. Freshmen must earn minimum GPA of 1.75 to continue in good standing. 68% of freshmen return for sophomore year. Students must declare major by end of second year. **Graduation requirements:** 128 hours for bachelor's. Most students required to take courses in arts/fine arts, English, history, humanities, mathematics, philosophy/religion, biological/physical sciences, social sciences. **Postgraduate studies:** 4% enter law school, 3% enter medical school, 2% enter MBA programs, 14% enter other graduate study. **Additional information:** Arkansas College students commit themselves to the highest standards of personal integrity through the Arkansas College Honor System, a system incorporating an honor pledge, a code of honorable conduct, and a series procedures carried out by an Honor Council chosen by the student body.

FRESHMAN ADMISSIONS. Selection criteria: Solid academic record, recommendations, extracurricular activities, personal interview all important. SAT or ACT scores considered. **High school preparation:** 15 units required; 18 recommended. Required and recommended units include English 4-4, mathematics 3-3, social science 3-3 and science 3-3. Foreign language 2 recommended. **Test requirements:** SAT or ACT; score report by August 15.

1992 FRESHMAN CLASS PROFILE. 207 men applied, 129 accepted, 90 enrolled; 215 women applied, 144 accepted, 121 enrolled. 75% had high school GPA of 3.0 or higher, 25% between 2.0 and 2.99. 40% were in top tenth and 67% were in top quarter of graduating class. **Academic background:** Mid 50% of enrolled freshmen had ACT composite between 21-27. 90% submitted ACT scores. **Characteristics:** 73% from in state, 79% live in college housing, 16% have minority backgrounds. Average age is 19.

FALL-TERM APPLICATIONS. $15 fee, may be waived for applicants with need. Closing date August 1; priority given to applications received by March 1; applicants notified on a rolling basis; must reply by May 1 or within 2 weeks if notified thereafter. Interview recommended. Audition recommended for choir, band, theater applicants. Portfolio recommended for art applicants. Essay recommended. CRDA. Deferred and early admission available.

STUDENT LIFE. Housing: Dormitories (men, women); apartment housing available. **Activities:** Student government, student newspaper, yearbook, choral groups, drama, music ensembles, pep band, bagpiping, fraternities, sororities, campus ministry board, black student association, Circle-K, social services club, Amnesty International, Harlequin Theater, Scottish Arts Company, residence hall association, Fellowship of Christian Athletes, Model United Nations.

ATHLETICS. NAIA. **Intercollegiate:** Baseball M, basketball, cross-country, golf M, tennis, track and field. **Intramural:** Badminton, basketball, golf, racquetball, soccer, softball, swimming, table tennis, tennis, volleyball.

STUDENT SERVICES. Career counseling, employment service for undergraduates, freshman orientation, health services, personal counseling, placement service for graduates, special adviser for adult students, services/facilities for handicapped.

ANNUAL EXPENSES. Tuition and fees (1992-93): $7,603. **Room and board:** $2,810. **Books and supplies:** $500. **Other expenses:** $500.

FINANCIAL AID. 94% of freshmen, 94% of continuing students receive some form of aid. 58% of grants, 83% of loans, all jobs based on need. 120 enrolled freshmen were judged to have need, all were offered aid. Academic, music/drama, art, athletic, leadership, alumni affiliation, religious affiliation, minority scholarships available. **Aid applications:** No closing date; priority given to applications received by April 1; applicants notified on a rolling basis beginning on or about January 1; must reply by May 1 or within 2 weeks if notified thereafter. **Additional information:** College meets 100% of demonstrated financial need for those who submit all forms on time.

ADDRESS/TELEPHONE. Mr. Jonathan Stroud, Dean of Admissions and Financial Aid, Arkansas College, PO Box 2317, 2300 Highland, Batesville, AR 72503-2317. (501) 698-4250. (800) 423-2542. Fax: (501) 698-4622.

Arkansas State University
Jonesboro, Arkansas CB code: 6011

4-year public university, coed. Founded in 1909. **Accreditation:** Regional. **Undergraduate enrollment:** 3,498 men, 4,091 women full time; 618 men, 1,007 women part time. **Graduate enrollment:** 167 men, 161 women full time; 181 men, 454 women part time. **Faculty:** 410 total, 286 with doctorates or other terminal degrees. **Location:** Suburban campus in large town; 75 miles from Memphis, Tennessee. **Calendar:** Semester, extensive summer session. **Microcomputers:** 200 located in classrooms, computer centers. **Special facilities:** Museum, computerized English writing laboratories.

DEGREES OFFERED. AS, AAS, BA, BS, BFA, MA, MS, MBA, EdD. 117 associate degrees awarded in 1992. 14% in business/office and marketing/distribution, 66% health sciences, 16% allied health. 1,075 bachelor's degrees awarded. 23% in business and management, 9% communications, 25% education, 7% teacher education. Graduate degrees offered in 39 major fields of study.

UNDERGRADUATE MAJORS. Associate: Information sciences and systems, law enforcement and corrections technologies, liberal/general studies, medical laboratory technologies, nursing, office supervision and management, practical nursing, radiograph medical technology, secretarial and related programs, trade and industrial education, vocational education. **Bachelor's:** Accounting, advertising, agribusiness, agricultural economics, agricultural education, agricultural engineering, agricultural sciences, animal sciences, art education, biology, botany, business administration and management, business and management, business economics, business education, chemistry, clinical laboratory science, computer and information sciences, computer applications, criminology, dramatic arts, early childhood education, economics, elementary education, engineering, English, English education, finance, fine arts, foreign languages education, French, geography, graphic and printing production, graphic design, health care administration, history, information sciences and systems, international business management, journalism, liberal/general studies, management science, manufacturing technology, marketing and distribution, marketing management, mathematics, mathematics education, medical laboratory technologies, music, music education, music performance, nursing, office supervision and management, philosophy, photography, photojournalism, physical education, physical sciences, physics, plant sciences, political science and government, practical nursing, prelaw, printing education, psychology, public relations, radio/television broadcasting, radio/television technology, real estate, real estate and insurance, religious music, science education, secretarial and related programs, social science education, social sciences, social work, sociology, Spanish, special education, speech, speech correction, speech pathology/audiology, speech/communication/theater education, sports management, transportation management, urban studies, vocal music, wildlife management, zoology.

ACADEMIC PROGRAMS. 2-year transfer program, accelerated program, double major, dual enrollment of high school students, education specialist degree, honors program, independent study, internships, study abroad, teacher preparation, visiting/exchange student program. **Remedial services:** Learning center, reduced course load, remedial instruction, special counselor, tutoring, Program for Academic Skills and Services (PASS). **ROTC:** Army. **Placement/credit:** AP, CLEP General and Subject, institutional tests; 30 credit hours maximum for bachelor's degree.

ACADEMIC REQUIREMENTS. Freshmen must earn minimum GPA of 2.0 to continue in good standing. 68% of freshmen return for sophomore year. Students must declare major by end of second year. **Graduation requirements:** 62 hours for associate (29 in major), 124 hours for bachelor's (60 in major). Most students required to take courses in arts/fine arts, English, history, humanities, mathematics, philosophy/religion, biological/physical sciences, social sciences. **Additional information:** Students allowed to repeat courses with final grade of less than C. No more than 18 semester hours of course work may be repeated.

FRESHMAN ADMISSIONS. Selection criteria: Open admissions. Selective admissions to nursing program. **High school preparation:** 12 units required. Required units include English 4, mathematics 2, social science 3 and science 2. **Test requirements:** SAT or ACT (ACT preferred) for placement and counseling only; score report by August 1. **Additional information:** High school course work and ACT scores used to determine admission status as either conditional or unconditional.

1992 FRESHMAN CLASS PROFILE. 1,455 men applied, 1,434 accepted, 792 enrolled; 1,598 women applied, 1,592 accepted, 920 enrolled. **Academic background:** Mid 50% of enrolled freshmen had ACT composite between 17-23. 97% submitted ACT scores. **Characteristics:** 83% from in state, 58% commute, 21% have minority backgrounds, 2% are foreign students. Average age is 19.

FALL-TERM APPLICATIONS. No fee. No closing date; applicants notified on a rolling basis beginning on or about June 1. Audition recommended for music, drama applicants. Portfolio recommended for fine arts applicants. Deferred and early admission available.

STUDENT LIFE. Housing: Dormitories (men, women); apartment, fraternity, sorority housing available. **Activities:** Student government, film, radio, student newspaper, television, yearbook, choral groups, concert band, dance, drama, jazz band, marching band, music ensembles, musical theater, pep band, symphony orchestra, theater, fraternities, sororities, over 100 organizations and clubs including religious organizations.

ATHLETICS. NCAA. **Intercollegiate:** Baseball M, basketball, cross-country, football M, golf M, rifle, tennis, track and field, volleyball W. **Intramural:** Archery, badminton, basketball, bowling, racquetball, soccer M, softball, swimming, table tennis, tennis, track and field, volleyball, wrestling M.

STUDENT SERVICES. Aptitude testing, career counseling, employment service for undergraduates, freshman orientation, health services, personal counseling, placement service for graduates, veterans counselor, international students office, services/facilities for handicapped.

ANNUAL EXPENSES. Tuition and fees (1992-93): $1,920, $1,830 additional for out-of-state students. **Room and board:** $2,420. **Books and supplies:** $500. **Other expenses:** $630.

FINANCIAL AID. 60% of freshmen, 65% of continuing students receive some form of aid. 76% of grants, 79% of loans, 52% of jobs based on need. Academic, music/drama, art, athletic, alumni affiliation scholarships available. **Aid applications:** No closing date; priority given to applications received by May 1; applicants notified on a rolling basis; must reply within 2 weeks.

ADDRESS/TELEPHONE. Leonard McDaniel, Director of Admissions and Records, Arkansas State University, PO Box 1630, State University, AR 72467-1630. (800) 382-3030. (800) 643-0080. Fax: (501) 972-3843.

Arkansas State University: Beebe Branch
Beebe, Arkansas CB code: 0782

2-year public branch campus, community college, coed. Founded in 1927. **Accreditation:** Regional. **Undergraduate enrollment:** 505 men, 645 women full time; 253 men, 469 women part time. **Faculty:** 78 total (49 full time), 10 with doctorates or other terminal degrees. **Location:** Suburban campus in small town; 35 miles from Little Rock. **Calendar:** Semester, extensive summer session. **Microcomputers:** Located in computer centers. **Additional facts:** Approved as Serviceman's Opportunity College.

DEGREES OFFERED. AA, AAS. 248 associate degrees awarded in 1992.

UNDERGRADUATE MAJORS. Agribusiness, agricultural sciences, animal sciences, biology, botany, business and management, business and office, business data programming, computer and information sciences, drafting and design technology, education, electronic technology, English, history, liberal/general studies, manufacturing technology, mathematics, medical laboratory technologies, nursing, office supervision and management, physical sciences, quality control technology, secretarial and related programs, social sciences, sociology, speech, zoology.

ACADEMIC PROGRAMS. 2-year transfer program, accelerated program, double major, dual enrollment of high school students, honors program, independent study. **Remedial services:** Learning center, reduced course load, remedial instruction, tutoring. **Placement/credit:** CLEP General and Subject; 30 credit hours maximum for associate degree.

ACADEMIC REQUIREMENTS. Freshmen must earn minimum GPA of 2.0 to continue in good standing. 75% of freshmen return for sophomore year. **Graduation requirements:** 60 hours for associate. Most students required to take courses in computer science, English, history, mathematics, biological/physical sciences, social sciences.

FRESHMAN ADMISSIONS. Selection criteria: Open admissions. **High school preparation:** 15 units recommended. Recommended units include biological science 1, English 3, mathematics 1, physical science 1 and social science 2. **Test requirements:** ACT for placement and counseling only; score report by August 1.

1992 FRESHMAN CLASS PROFILE. 537 men, 806 women enrolled. **Characteristics:** 97% from in state, 80% commute, 7% have minority backgrounds.

FALL-TERM APPLICATIONS. No fee. No closing date; applicants notified on a rolling basis beginning on or about August 1. Interview recommended. Early admission available.

STUDENT LIFE. Housing: Dormitories (men, women). **Activities:** Student government, student newspaper, choral groups, drama, Gamma Beta Phi.

ATHLETICS. NJCAA. **Intramural:** Archery, basketball, bowling, softball, table tennis, tennis, track and field, volleyball.

STUDENT SERVICES. Career counseling, freshman orientation, personal counseling, veterans counselor, services/facilities for handicapped.

ANNUAL EXPENSES. Tuition and fees (1992-93): $984, $660 additional for out-of-state students. **Room and board:** $1,780. **Books and supplies:** $500. **Other expenses:** $500.

FINANCIAL AID. 60% of freshmen, 70% of continuing students receive some form of aid. 93% of grants, 96% of loans, all jobs based on need. 365 enrolled freshmen were judged to have need, 350 were offered aid. Academic, music/drama, athletic, leadership scholarships available. **Aid applications:** No closing date; priority given to applications received by May 1; applicants notified on a rolling basis beginning on or about June 1; must reply within 2 weeks.

ADDRESS/TELEPHONE. James Washburn, Registrar/Director of Admissions, Arkansas State University: Beebe Branch, PO Drawer H, Beebe, AR 72012-1008. (501) 882-6452. Fax: (501) 882-6552 ext. 370.

Arkansas Tech University
Russellville, Arkansas CB code: 6010

4-year public university, coed. Founded in 1909. **Accreditation:** Regional. **Undergraduate enrollment:** 1,596 men, 1,814 women full time; 281 men, 468 women part time. **Graduate enrollment:** 196 men and women. **Faculty:** 230 total (180 full time), 104 with doctorates or other terminal degrees. **Location:** Rural campus in large town; 75 miles from Little Rock, 80 miles from Fort Smith. **Calendar:** Semester, extensive summer session. **Microcomputers:** 345 located in computer centers.

DEGREES OFFERED. AA, AS, BA, BS, BFA, MEd. 20 associate degrees awarded in 1992. 490 bachelor's degrees awarded. Graduate degrees offered in 10 major fields of study.

UNDERGRADUATE MAJORS. Associate: Liberal/general studies, medical assistant, secretarial and related programs. **Bachelor's:** Accounting, agribusiness, agricultural sciences, art education, biology, business administration and management, business and management, business economics, business education, chemistry, clinical laboratory science, commercial art, computer and information sciences, creative writing, economics, elementary education, engineering, English, French, geology, German, history, hotel/motel and restaurant management, journalism, mathematics, medical records administration, music, music education, nursing, parks and recreation management, physical education, physical sciences, physics, political science and government, psychology, secondary education, sociology, Spanish, speech, wildlife management.

ACADEMIC PROGRAMS. 2-year transfer program, double major, dual enrollment of high school students, honors program, teacher preparation, cross-registration, academic exchange program with Komazawa University (Japan). **Remedial services:** Remedial instruction, voluntary study skills program. **Placement/credit:** AP, CLEP General and Subject, institutional tests; 30 credit hours maximum for bachelor's degree.

ACADEMIC REQUIREMENTS. Freshmen must earn minimum GPA of 1.50 to continue in good standing. 59% of freshmen return for sophomore year. **Graduation requirements:** 62 hours for associate, 124 hours for bachelor's. Most students required to take courses in arts/fine arts, English, history, humanities, mathematics, biological/physical sciences, social sciences.

FRESHMAN ADMISSIONS. Selection criteria: Student needs 2.5 GPA or must have minimum ACT/SAT scores or must complete 6 semester hours in university summer school with 2.0 GPA. Applicants who do not meet requirements may be considered. **High school preparation:** 20 units recommended. Recommended units include English 4, mathematics 2, social science 2 and science 2. One additional mathematics or science, 1 additional social studies or practical arts recommended. **Test requirements:** SAT or ACT (ACT preferred); score report by August 20.

1992 FRESHMAN CLASS PROFILE. 748 men, 950 women enrolled. 39% were in top quarter of graduating class. **Characteristics:** 95% from in state, 50% commute. Average age is 18.

FALL-TERM APPLICATIONS. No fee. No closing date; applicants notified on a rolling basis beginning on or about January 15. Deferred and early admission available.

STUDENT LIFE. Housing: Dormitories (men, women); apartment housing available. **Activities:** Student government, radio, student newspaper, television, yearbook, choral groups, concert band, drama, jazz band, marching band, music ensembles, musical theater, pep band, symphony orchestra, fraternities, sororities.

ATHLETICS. NAIA. **Intercollegiate:** Baseball M, basketball, football M, golf M, tennis, volleyball W. **Intramural:** Basketball, softball, volleyball.

STUDENT SERVICES. Aptitude testing, career counseling, employment service for undergraduates, freshman orientation, health services, on-campus day care, personal counseling, placement service for graduates, services/facilities for handicapped.

ANNUAL EXPENSES. Tuition and fees (1992-93): $1,560, $1,500 additional for out-of-state students. **Room and board:** $2,410. **Books and supplies:** $450. **Other expenses:** $875.

FINANCIAL AID. 51% of freshmen, 47% of continuing students receive some form of aid. 79% of grants, 95% of loans, 63% of jobs based on need. Academic, music/drama, athletic, leadership scholarships available. **Aid applications:** No closing date; applicants notified on a rolling basis beginning on or about May 15; must reply within 2 weeks.

ADDRESS/TELEPHONE. Harold Cornett, Director of Admissions, Arkansas Tech University, Russellville, AR 72801-2222. (501) 968-0343. Fax: (501) 964-0839.

Capital City Junior College
Little Rock, Arkansas CB code: 1026

2-year proprietary junior college, coed. Founded in 1927. **Accreditation:** Regional. **Undergraduate enrollment:** 350 men and women. **Location:** Urban campus in small city. **Calendar:** Quarter, extensive summer session. Extensive evening/early morning classes.

DEGREES OFFERED. AAS. 150 associate degrees awarded in 1992.

UNDERGRADUATE MAJORS. Accounting, business administration and management, business and office, business data programming, child development/care/guidance, computer programming, marketing and distribution, medical assistant, medical laboratory technologies, radio/television broadcasting, secretarial and related programs.

ACADEMIC PROGRAMS. Double major, internships. **Remedial services:** Tutoring. **Placement/credit:** Institutional tests.

ACADEMIC REQUIREMENTS. Freshmen must earn minimum GPA of 1.5 to continue in good standing. Students must declare major on enrollment. **Graduation requirements:** 64 hours for associate. Most students required to take courses in English, mathematics.

FRESHMAN ADMISSIONS. Selection criteria: Open admissions. **Test requirements:** Institutional test required if applicant does not have high school diploma or equivalent.

1992 FRESHMAN CLASS PROFILE. 139 men and women enrolled. **Characteristics:** 99% from in state, 100% commute, 60% have minority backgrounds, 1% are foreign students.

FALL-TERM APPLICATIONS. $100 fee. No closing date; applicants notified on a rolling basis. Interview required. Deferred admission available.

STUDENT LIFE. Activities: Student government, radio, student newspaper, television.

STUDENT SERVICES. Career counseling, employment service for undergraduates, freshman orientation, on-campus day care, personal counseling, placement service for graduates.

ANNUAL EXPENSES. Tuition and fees (1992-93): $5,520.

FINANCIAL AID. 64% of freshmen, 68% of continuing students receive some form of aid. Grants, loans, jobs available. **Aid applications:** No closing date; applicants notified on a rolling basis.

ADDRESS/TELEPHONE. Fran Walker, Director of Admissions, Capital City Junior College, 7723 Asher Avenue, Little Rock, AR 72204. (501) 562-0700. Fax: (501) 565-7591.

Central Baptist College
Conway, Arkansas CB code: 0788

4-year private Bible college, coed, affiliated with Baptist Missionary Association of America. Founded in 1952. **Accreditation:** Regional candidate. **Undergraduate enrollment:** 126 men, 102 women full time; 14 men, 15 women part time. **Faculty:** 19 total (14 full time), 3 with doctorates or other terminal degrees. **Location:** Urban campus in large town; 30 miles from Little Rock. **Calendar:** Semester, limited summer session. **Microcomputers:** Located in computer centers.

DEGREES OFFERED. AA, BA, BS. 25 associate degrees awarded in 1992. 7 bachelor's degrees awarded.

UNDERGRADUATE MAJORS. Associate: Accounting, business and management, business and office, education, liberal/general studies, music, secretarial and related programs. **Bachelor's:** Bible studies, elementary education, missionary studies, religious education, religious music, theological studies.

ACADEMIC PROGRAMS. 2-year transfer program, internships, teacher preparation. **Remedial services:** Learning center, preadmission summer program, reduced course load, special counselor, tutoring. **ROTC:** Army. **Placement/credit:** AP, CLEP General and Subject; 27 credit hours maximum for bachelor's degree.

ACADEMIC REQUIREMENTS. Freshmen must earn minimum GPA of 1.25 to continue in good standing. 71% of freshmen return for sophomore year. **Graduation requirements:** 64 hours for associate (16 in major), 130 hours for bachelor's (30 in major). Most students required to take courses in arts/fine arts, English, foreign languages, history, mathematics, philosophy/religion, biological/physical sciences, social sciences. **Postgraduate studies:** 75% from 2-year programs enter 4-year programs.

FRESHMAN ADMISSIONS. Selection criteria: Religious commitment most important followed by school achievement record. **High school preparation:** 15 units recommended. Recommended units include English 3, mathematics 1, social science 2 and science 1. **Test requirements:** ACT; score report by August 15.

1992 FRESHMAN CLASS PROFILE. 61 men, 42 women enrolled. 56% had high school GPA of 3.0 or higher, 38% between 2.0 and 2.99. 21% were in top tenth and 42% were in top quarter of graduating class. **Characteristics:** 80% from in state, 80% live in college housing, 6% have minority backgrounds. Average age is 20.

FALL-TERM APPLICATIONS. $25 fee. Closing date August 15; applicants notified on a rolling basis. Interview recommended. Early admission available.

STUDENT LIFE. Housing: Dormitories (men, women); apartment housing available. **Activities:** Student government, student newspaper, yearbook, choral groups, music ensembles, Association of Baptist Students, College Republicans. **Additional information:** Religious observance required.

ATHLETICS. NJCAA. **Intercollegiate:** Basketball M. **Intramural:** Badminton, basketball, softball, table tennis, volleyball.

STUDENT SERVICES. Career counseling, freshman orientation, personal counseling, veterans counselor.

ANNUAL EXPENSES. Tuition and fees: $2,610. **Room and board:** $2,152. **Books and supplies:** $500. **Other expenses:** $800.

FINANCIAL AID. 56% of freshmen, 51% of continuing students receive some form of aid. 44% of grants, 96% of loans, 84% of jobs based on need. 71 enrolled freshmen were judged to have need, all were offered aid. Academic, music/drama, athletic, alumni affiliation, religious affiliation scholarships available. **Aid applications:** No closing date; applicants notified on a rolling basis beginning on or about July 1; work-study recipients must reply within 10 days.

ADDRESS/TELEPHONE. Gary McAllister, Registrar/Admissions Officer, Central Baptist College, CBC Station, Conway, AR 72032. (501) 329-6872 ext. 113.

East Arkansas Community College

Forrest City, Arkansas CB code: 0847

2-year public community college, coed. Founded in 1973. **Accreditation:** Regional. **Undergraduate enrollment:** 1,352 men and women. **Faculty:** 88 total (34 full time), 11 with doctorates or other terminal degrees. **Location:** Rural campus in large town; 40 miles from Memphis, Tennessee. **Calendar:** Semester, limited summer session. **Microcomputers:** 35 located in libraries, computer centers.

DEGREES OFFERED. AA, AS, AAS. 119 associate degrees awarded in 1992. 7% in business/office and marketing/distribution, 31% allied health, 46% multi/interdisciplinary studies, 7% social sciences. 119 bachelor's degrees awarded.

UNDERGRADUATE MAJORS. Agricultural sciences, automotive technology, business and management, business and office, business data processing and related programs, business data programming, criminal justice technology, drafting, electrical/electronics/communications engineering, engineering and engineering-related technologies, finance, industrial technology, law enforcement and corrections technologies, liberal/general studies, marketing and distribution, medical laboratory technologies, nursing, real estate, secretarial and related programs.

ACADEMIC PROGRAMS. 2-year transfer program, cooperative education, dual enrollment of high school students, honors program, weekend college. **Remedial services:** Learning center, remedial instruction, special counselor, tutoring. **Placement/credit:** AP, CLEP General and Subject, institutional tests; 30 credit hours maximum for associate degree.

ACADEMIC REQUIREMENTS. Freshmen must earn minimum GPA of 1.7 to continue in good standing. 54% of freshmen return for sophomore year. Students must declare major by end of first year. **Graduation requirements:** 64 hours for associate (32 in major). Most students required to take courses in English, history, mathematics, biological/physical sciences, social sciences.

FRESHMAN ADMISSIONS. Selection criteria: Open admissions. **Test requirements:** SAT or ACT (ACT preferred) for placement.

1992 FRESHMAN CLASS PROFILE. 431 men and women enrolled. **Characteristics:** 99% from in state, 100% commute, 30% have minority backgrounds. Average age is 26.

FALL-TERM APPLICATIONS. No fee. No closing date; applicants notified on a rolling basis. Interview required for nursing, emergency medical technology applicants. Early admission available.

STUDENT LIFE. Activities: Student government, student newspaper, yearbook, choral groups.

ATHLETICS. Intramural: Archery, badminton, basketball, bowling, racquetball, softball, tennis, volleyball.

STUDENT SERVICES. Aptitude testing, career counseling, employment service for undergraduates, health services, personal counseling, placement service for graduates, veterans counselor, services/facilities for handicapped.

ANNUAL EXPENSES. Tuition and fees (1992-93): $552, $168 additional for out-of-district students, $372 additional for out-of-state students. **Books and supplies:** $200. **Other expenses:** $400.

FINANCIAL AID. 50% of freshmen, 75% of continuing students receive some form of aid. Grants, loans, jobs available. **Aid applications:** No closing date; priority given to applications received by April 15; applicants notified on a rolling basis beginning on or about May 15; must reply within 2 weeks.

ADDRESS/TELEPHONE. Janice Hurd, Director of Admissions, East Arkansas Community College, Forrest City, AR 72335-9598. (501) 633-4480.

Garland County Community College

Hot Springs, Arkansas CB code: 6243

2-year public community college, coed. Founded in 1973. **Accreditation:** Regional. **Undergraduate enrollment:** 2,192 men and women. **Faculty:** 128 total (43 full time), 7 with doctorates or other terminal degrees. **Location:** Suburban campus in large town; 53 miles from Little Rock. **Calendar:** Semester, limited summer session. **Microcomputers:** Located in libraries, computer centers.

DEGREES OFFERED. AA, AS, AAS. 157 associate degrees awarded in 1992. 10% in business and management, 28% education, 45% health sciences, 16% letters/literature.

UNDERGRADUATE MAJORS. Accounting, business and management, business and office, business data processing and related programs, business data programming, clinical laboratory science, data processing, education, electronic technology, emergency medical technologies, finance, fire control and safety technology, graphic arts technology, law enforcement and corrections technologies, liberal/general studies, medical assistant, medical laboratory technologies, medical records technology, nursing, radiograph medical technology, real estate, secretarial and related programs, word processing.

ACADEMIC PROGRAMS. 2-year transfer program, dual enrollment of high school students, independent study, internships, student-designed major, telecourses, cross-registration. **Remedial services:** Learning center, preadmission summer program, reduced course load, remedial instruction, special counselor, tutoring. **Placement/credit:** CLEP Subject, institutional tests; 30 credit hours maximum for associate degree.

ACADEMIC REQUIREMENTS. Freshmen must earn minimum GPA of 2.0 to continue in good standing. 40% of freshmen return for sophomore year. Students must declare major by end of first year. **Graduation requirements:** 64 hours for associate (50 in major). Most students required to take courses in computer science, English, history, mathematics, social sciences.

FRESHMAN ADMISSIONS. Selection criteria: Open admissions. Selective admissions to allied health programs. **Test requirements:** ACT for placement and counseling only. ACT required of nursing applicants. ASSET may be submitted in place of ACT.

1992 FRESHMAN CLASS PROFILE. 2,192 men and women enrolled. **Characteristics:** 99% from in state, 100% commute, 8% have minority backgrounds. Average age is 30.

FALL-TERM APPLICATIONS. No fee. No closing date. Interview required for nursing, radiologic technology, paramedic technology, health informationtcehnology, medical laboratory technology. applicants. Early admission available.

STUDENT LIFE. Activities: Student government, student newspaper, choral groups, drama, music ensembles, musical theater, Baptist Student Union, Black Awareness,Association for Barrier Awareness.

ATHLETICS. NJCAA. **Intramural:** Softball, table tennis.

STUDENT SERVICES. Aptitude testing, career counseling, employment service for undergraduates, freshman orientation, personal counseling, placement service for graduates, veterans counselor, services/facilities for handicapped.

ANNUAL EXPENSES. Tuition and fees: $792, $216 additional for out-of-district students, $1,128 additional for out-of-state students. **Books and supplies:** $450. **Other expenses:** $795.

FINANCIAL AID. 68% of freshmen, 68% of continuing students receive some form of aid. All aid based on need. Academic, music/drama, art, athletic, state/district residency scholarships available. **Aid applications:** No closing date; priority given to applications received by April 1; applicants notified on a rolling basis beginning on or about May 1; must reply within 2 weeks.

ADDRESS/TELEPHONE. Ronald Garner, Dean of Student Services, Garland County Community College, 100 College Drive, Hot Springs, AR 71913-9120. (501) 767-9371. Fax: (501) 767-6896.

Harding University

Searcy, Arkansas CB code: 6267

Admissions:	69% of applicants accepted
Based on:	••• School record, special talents, test scores
	•• Interview, recommendations
	• Activities, essay
Completion:	70% of freshmen end year in good standing
	60% graduate, 35% of these enter graduate study

4-year private university, coed, affiliated with Church of Christ. Founded in 1924. **Accreditation:** Regional. **Undergraduate enrollment:** 1,425 men, 1,671 women full time; 115 men, 140 women part time. **Graduate enrollment:** 30 men, 21 women full time; 17 men, 22 women part time. **Faculty:** 186 total (162 full time), 122 with doctorates or other terminal degrees. **Location:** Urban campus in large town; 45 miles from Little Rock. **Calendar:** Semester, extensive summer session. **Microcomputers:** 230 located in libraries, classrooms, computer centers. **Special facilities:** Art gallery, electrical cogeneration facility, 1400-acre camp in the Ozarks, campus in Florence, Italy.

DEGREES OFFERED. AA, BA, BS, BFA, MA, MS, PhD. 2 associate degrees awarded in 1992. 100% in business/office and marketing/distribution. 491 bachelor's degrees awarded. 30% in business and management, 5% communications, 10% education, 5% health sciences, 7% letters/literature, 6% life sciences, 7% philosophy, religion, theology, 8% physical sciences, 5% social sciences. Graduate degrees offered in 17 major fields of study.

UNDERGRADUATE MAJORS. Associate: Office supervision and

management, secretarial and related programs. **Bachelor's:** Accounting, advertising, American studies, art education, biblical languages, biological and physical sciences, biology, business administration and management, business and management, business economics, business education, chemistry, clinical laboratory science, communications, computer and information sciences, computer programming, data processing, early childhood education, economics, education, education of the mentally handicapped, elementary education, English, English education, fine arts, food science and nutrition, foreign languages education, French, history, home economics, home economics education, human resources development, humanities and social sciences, institutional/home management/supporting programs, international studies, journalism, junior high education, marketing management, mathematics, mathematics education, music, music education, nursing, office supervision and management, physical education, physics, political science and government, prelaw, psychology, radio/television broadcasting, radio/television technology, reading education, religion, religious education, religious music, science education, secondary education, secretarial and related programs, social science education, social sciences, social studies education, social work, sociology, Spanish, special education, specific learning disabilities, speech, speech correction, speech pathology/audiology, speech/communication/theater education, systems analysis, textiles and clothing, theological studies.

ACADEMIC PROGRAMS. 2-year transfer program, cooperative education, double major, dual enrollment of high school students, honors program, independent study, internships, student-designed major, study abroad, teacher preparation. **Remedial services:** Learning center, preadmission summer program, reduced course load, remedial instruction, special counselor, tutoring, PASS program helps students whose academic test scores and high school record are below admission standards. **ROTC:** Army. **Placement/credit:** AP, CLEP General and Subject, institutional tests; 32 credit hours maximum for bachelor's degree.

ACADEMIC REQUIREMENTS. Freshmen must earn minimum GPA of 1.5 to continue in good standing. 77% of freshmen return for sophomore year. Students must declare major by end of second year. **Graduation requirements:** 64 hours for associate (28 in major), 128 hours for bachelor's (72 in major). Most students required to take courses in arts/fine arts, computer science, English, history, humanities, mathematics, philosophy/religion, biological/physical sciences, social sciences. **Postgraduate studies:** 5% enter law school, 5% enter medical school, 5% enter MBA programs, 20% enter other graduate study.

FRESHMAN ADMISSIONS. Selection criteria: Test scores, academic record, references, interview important. Selective admissions with limited openings, students must apply early. **High school preparation:** 17 units recommended. Recommended units include biological science 1, English 4, foreign language 2, mathematics 4, physical science 2 and social science 4. **Test requirements:** SAT or ACT; score report by June 1.

1992 FRESHMAN CLASS PROFILE. 568 men applied, 392 accepted, 392 enrolled; 653 women applied, 455 accepted, 455 enrolled. 80% had high school GPA of 3.0 or higher, 20% between 2.0 and 2.99. 30% were in top tenth and 85% were in top quarter of graduating class. **Academic background:** Mid 50% of enrolled freshmen had ACT composite between 21-28. 85% submitted ACT scores. **Characteristics:** 28% from in state, 85% live in college housing, 8% have minority backgrounds, 7% are foreign students, 85% join fraternities/sororities. Average age is 18.

FALL-TERM APPLICATIONS. $25 fee. Closing date June 1; priority given to applications received by March 1; applicants notified on a rolling basis. Interview required for all applicants. Audition recommended for music applicants. Portfolio recommended for art applicants. Essay recommended. Deferred and early admission available. Early application encouraged.

STUDENT LIFE. Housing: Dormitories (men, women); apartment housing available. Apartments available for single women. **Activities:** Student government, radio, student newspaper, television, yearbook, choral groups, concert band, drama, jazz band, marching band, music ensembles, musical theater, opera, pep band, symphony orchestra, fraternities, sororities, spiritual and religious clubs, campus ministry team, College Republicans, College Democrats, national honor societies. **Additional information:** Students expected to abide by code of conduct.

ATHLETICS. NAIA. **Intercollegiate:** Baseball M, basketball, cross-country, football M, golf M, softball W, tennis, track and field M, volleyball W. **Intramural:** Basketball, bowling, football, gymnastics, racquetball, skin diving, softball, swimming, table tennis, tennis, track and field, volleyball.

STUDENT SERVICES. Aptitude testing, career counseling, employment service for undergraduates, freshman orientation, health services, on-campus day care, personal counseling, placement service for graduates, special adviser for adult students, veterans counselor, services/facilities for handicapped.

ANNUAL EXPENSES. Tuition and fees (projected): $5,790. **Room and board:** $3,380. **Books and supplies:** $600. **Other expenses:** $930.

FINANCIAL AID. 85% of freshmen, 82% of continuing students receive some form of aid. 32% of grants, 84% of loans, 75% of jobs based on need. Academic, music/drama, art, athletic, leadership, religious affiliation, minority scholarships available. **Aid applications:** No closing date; priority given to applications received by April 1; applicants notified on a rolling basis beginning on or about April 15; must reply within 4 weeks. **Additional information:** Music scholarships available, audition recommended.

ADDRESS/TELEPHONE. Mike Williams, Director of Admissions, Harding University, 900 East Center Box 762, Searcy, AR 72143. (800) 477-4407. (800) 477-4407. Fax: (501) 279-4865.

Henderson State University
Arkadelphia, Arkansas CB code: 6272

4-year public university, coed. Founded in 1890. **Accreditation:** Regional. **Undergraduate enrollment:** 1,366 men, 1,629 women full time; 146 men, 295 women part time. **Graduate enrollment:** 16 men, 18 women full time; 73 men, 200 women part time. **Faculty:** 173 total (150 full time), 75 with doctorates or other terminal degrees. **Location:** Rural campus in large town; 67 miles from Little Rock. **Calendar:** Semester, limited summer session. **Microcomputers:** 44 located in libraries, computer centers. **Special facilities:** Natural history museum.

DEGREES OFFERED. AA, BA, BS, BFA, MA, MS, MBA. 12 associate degrees awarded in 1992. 431 bachelor's degrees awarded. Graduate degrees offered in 27 major fields of study.

UNDERGRADUATE MAJORS. Associate: Airline piloting and navigation, business and office, food production/management/services, office supervision and management, secretarial and related programs. **Bachelor's:** Accounting, art education, biological and physical sciences, biology, business administration and management, business and management, business data processing and related programs, business education, chemistry, communications, computer and information sciences, early childhood education, elementary education, English, English education, foreign languages education, history, home economics, home economics education, illustration design, journalism, mathematics, mathematics education, medical laboratory technologies, music, music education, music performance, music theory and composition, nursing, parks and recreation management, physical education, physical sciences, physics, political science and government, psychology, public administration, radio/television technology, science education, secondary education, secretarial and related programs, social science education, social sciences, social work, sociology, Spanish, speech, speech correction, speech pathology/audiology, speech/communication/theater education, studio art, transportation and travel marketing, visual and performing arts.

ACADEMIC PROGRAMS. Double major, honors program, independent study, teacher preparation, cross-registration. **Remedial services:** Learning center, reduced course load, tutoring. **Placement/credit:** AP, CLEP General and Subject, institutional tests; 30 credit hours maximum for bachelor's degree.

ACADEMIC REQUIREMENTS. Freshmen must earn minimum GPA of 1.25 to continue in good standing. 50% of freshmen return for sophomore year. Students must declare major by end of second year. **Graduation requirements:** 60 hours for associate (30 in major), 124 hours for bachelor's (30 in major). Most students required to take courses in English, history, humanities, mathematics, philosophy/religion, biological/physical sciences, social sciences.

FRESHMAN ADMISSIONS. Selection criteria: Applicants must have ACT composite of 19 and minimum 2.5 GPA for unconditional admission. Those not meeting GPA requirement admitted conditionally. **High school preparation:** 15 units recommended. Recommended units include biological science 1, English 4, mathematics 2, physical science 1 and social science 3. **Test requirements:** SAT or ACT (ACT preferred).

1992 FRESHMAN CLASS PROFILE. 362 men, 363 women enrolled. **Academic background:** Mid 50% of enrolled freshmen had ACT composite between 14-22. 100% submitted ACT scores. **Characteristics:** 90% from in state, 60% live in college housing, 20% have minority backgrounds, 1% are foreign students. Average age is 18.

FALL-TERM APPLICATIONS. No fee. No closing date; applicants notified on a rolling basis. Audition recommended for music applicants. Deferred admission available.

STUDENT LIFE. Housing: Dormitories (men, women); apartment, fraternity, sorority housing available. **Activities:** Student government, radio, student newspaper, yearbook, choral groups, concert band, dance, drama, jazz band, marching band, music ensembles, musical theater, opera, pep band, symphony orchestra, fraternities, sororities, Baptist student center, Methodist student center.

ATHLETICS. NAIA. **Intercollegiate:** Baseball M, basketball, cross-country M, diving, football M, golf M, swimming, tennis, track and field M, volleyball W. **Intramural:** Basketball, football, softball, swimming, volleyball.

STUDENT SERVICES. Aptitude testing, career counseling, employment service for undergraduates, freshman orientation, health services, on-campus day care, personal counseling, placement service for graduates, veterans counselor, services/facilities for handicapped.

ANNUAL EXPENSES. Tuition and fees: $1,660, $1,560 additional for out-of-state students. **Room and board:** $2,490. **Books and supplies:** $600. **Other expenses:** $1,800.

FINANCIAL AID. 55% of freshmen, 60% of continuing students receive some form of aid. 82% of grants, 90% of loans, 85% of jobs based on need. Academic, music/drama, art, athletic scholarships available. **Aid applications:** No closing date; priority given to applications received by April 15;

applicants notified on a rolling basis beginning on or about May 15; must reply within 2 weeks.

ADDRESS/TELEPHONE. Tom Gattin, Director of Admissions/Registrar, Henderson State University, PO Box 7534, Arkadelphia, AR 71923. (501) 246-5511.

Hendrix College

Conway, Arkansas CB code: 6273

Admissions: 91% of applicants accepted
Based on: ••• Essay, school record
•• Activities, interview, special talents, test scores
• Recommendations
Completion: 90% of freshmen end year in good standing
42% enter graduate study

4-year private liberal arts college, coed, affiliated with United Methodist Church. Founded in 1876. **Accreditation:** Regional. **Undergraduate enrollment:** 444 men, 542 women full time; 3 men, 61 women part time. **Faculty:** 86 total (74 full time), 60 with doctorates or other terminal degrees. **Location:** Suburban campus in large town; 30 miles from Little Rock. **Calendar:** 3 terms of 12 weeks each. **Microcomputers:** 45 located in libraries, classrooms, computer centers. **Special facilities:** Teaching theater, psychology labs, Arkansas state daffodil collection.

DEGREES OFFERED. BA. 217 bachelor's degrees awarded in 1992. 20% in business and management, 8% letters/literature, 17% life sciences, 12% physical sciences, 9% psychology, 18% social sciences.

UNDERGRADUATE MAJORS. Accounting, American studies, art history, Asian studies, biology, business economics, chemistry, communications, computer mathematics, dramatic arts, economics, elementary education, English, French, German, history, humanities, humanities and social sciences, international relations, journalism, liberal/general studies, mathematics, music, philosophy, physics, political science and government, predentistry, prelaw, premedicine, prepharmacy, preveterinary, psychology, religion, secondary education, sociology, Spanish.

ACADEMIC PROGRAMS. Double major, honors program, independent study, internships, student-designed major, study abroad, teacher preparation, visiting/exchange student program, Washington semester, Hendrix-in-Oxford, Hendrix-in-London, programs with Austria and Japan; liberal arts/career combination in engineering. **ROTC:** Army. **Placement/credit:** AP, CLEP General and Subject, institutional tests; 20 credit hours maximum for bachelor's degree.

ACADEMIC REQUIREMENTS. Freshmen must earn minimum GPA of 1.5 to continue in good standing. 84% of freshmen return for sophomore year. Students must declare major by end of second year. **Graduation requirements:** 120 hours for bachelor's. Most students required to take courses in English, foreign languages, history, humanities, mathematics, philosophy/religion, biological/physical sciences, social sciences. **Postgraduate studies:** 7% enter law school, 8% enter medical school, 3% enter MBA programs, 24% enter other graduate study.

FRESHMAN ADMISSIONS. Selection criteria: Academic competence, scholastic potential, motivation, character, and high school leadership considered. **High school preparation:** 15 units recommended. Recommended units include English 4, foreign language 3, mathematics 3, social science 3 and science 2. **Test requirements:** SAT or ACT; score report by August 1.

1992 FRESHMAN CLASS PROFILE. 357 men applied, 322 accepted, 156 enrolled; 460 women applied, 421 accepted, 190 enrolled. 77% had high school GPA of 3.0 or higher, 23% between 2.0 and 2.99. 51% were in top tenth and 85% were in top quarter of graduating class. **Academic background:** Mid 50% of enrolled freshmen had SAT-V between 460-580, SAT-M between 490-620; ACT composite between 23-28. 42% submitted SAT scores, 92% submitted ACT scores. **Characteristics:** 74% from in state, 100% live in college housing, 5% have minority backgrounds, 1% are foreign students. Average age is 19.

FALL-TERM APPLICATIONS. $15 fee, may be waived for applicants with need. No closing date; priority given to applications received by April 1; applicants notified on a rolling basis; must reply by May 1 or within 4 weeks if notified thereafter. Essay required. Interview may be required by request of committee. CRDA. Deferred and early admission available.

STUDENT LIFE. Housing: Dormitories (men, women, coed); apartment housing available. Coeducational foreign language houses (Spanish, French or German) available. **Activities:** Student government, magazine, radio, student newspaper, yearbook, choral groups, concert band, drama, jazz band, music ensembles, musical theater, opera, pep band, symphony orchestra, Hendrix Christian Movement, Students for Black Culture, Young Republicans, Young Democrats, S.A.V.E., Amnesty International, BACCHUS, Hendrix Peace Links. **Additional information:** Private lessons in voice, piano, organ, wind and string instruments available at no additional charge. Open auditions for 3 major theater productions each year. College-sponsored backpacking, canoeing, horseback riding, windsurfing, rock climbing and rappelling, jet skiing and skeet shooting.

ATHLETICS. NCAA. **Intercollegiate:** Basketball M, cross-country, diving, golf, rugby M, skin diving W, soccer, swimming, tennis, track and field, volleyball W. **Intramural:** Basketball, football, golf M, racquetball, softball, swimming, table tennis, tennis, track and field, volleyball.

STUDENT SERVICES. Career counseling, employment service for undergraduates, freshman orientation, personal counseling, placement service for graduates, services/facilities for handicapped.

ANNUAL EXPENSES. Tuition and fees (projected): $8,610. **Room and board:** $3,060. **Books and supplies:** $400. **Other expenses:** $625.

FINANCIAL AID. 78% of freshmen, 75% of continuing students receive some form of aid. 54% of grants, 97% of loans, 71% of jobs based on need. 184 enrolled freshmen were judged to have need, all were offered aid. Academic, music/drama, art, athletic, leadership, minority scholarships available. **Aid applications:** No closing date; priority given to applications received by April 1; applicants notified on a rolling basis beginning on or about April 1; must reply by May 1 or within 2 weeks if notified thereafter.

ADDRESS/TELEPHONE. Rudy R. Pollan, Vice President of Enrollment, Hendrix College, 1601 Harkrider Street, Conway, AR 72032-3080. (501) 329-6811 ext. 1362. Fax: (501) 450-1200.

John Brown University

Siloam Springs, Arkansas CB code: 6321

Admissions: 79% of applicants accepted
Based on: ••• School record, test scores
•• Interview, recommendations, religious affiliation/commitment, special talents
• Activities, essay
Completion: 85% of freshmen end year in good standing
45% graduate, 22% of these enter graduate study

4-year private liberal arts college, coed, interdenominational. Founded in 1919. **Accreditation:** Regional. **Undergraduate enrollment:** 463 men, 444 women full time; 45 men, 66 women part time. **Faculty:** 88 total (63 full time), 50 with doctorates or other terminal degrees. **Location:** Rural campus in small town; 30 miles from University of Arkansas at Fayetteville. **Calendar:** Semester, limited summer session. **Microcomputers:** 110 located in libraries, classrooms, computer centers. **Special facilities:** Fitness trail, lifetime health complex.

DEGREES OFFERED. AA, AS, BA, BS. 10 associate degrees awarded in 1992. 30% in business/office and marketing/distribution, 20% communications, 20% letters/literature, 20% multi/interdisciplinary studies, 10% philosophy, religion, theology. 168 bachelor's degrees awarded. 25% in business and management, 13% communications, 17% teacher education, 9% engineering, 8% letters/literature, 6% life sciences, 17% social sciences.

UNDERGRADUATE MAJORS. Associate: Bible studies, construction, engineering and engineering-related technologies, journalism, liberal/general studies, music, public relations, radio/television broadcasting, radio/television technology, science technologies, secretarial and related programs, teacher aide. **Bachelor's:** Accounting, Bible studies, biochemistry, biological and physical sciences, biology, business administration and management, business and management, business education, chemistry, civil engineering, clinical laboratory science, community health work, computer engineering, construction, early childhood education, electrical/electronics/communications engineering, elementary education, engineering, English, English education, graphic design, health education, history, international studies, journalism, junior high education, liberal/general studies, mathematics, mathematics education, mechanical engineering, missionary studies, music, music education, physical education, psychology, public relations, radio/television broadcasting, radio/television technology, recreation and community services technologies, recreation therapy, religion, religious education, religious music, science education, secondary education, secretarial and related programs, social sciences, social studies education, special education, sports medicine, theological studies.

ACADEMIC PROGRAMS. 2-year transfer program, double major, dual enrollment of high school students, honors program, independent study, internships, student-designed major, study abroad, Washington semester; liberal arts/career combination in engineering. **Remedial services:** Learning center, reduced course load, remedial instruction, special counselor, tutoring. **ROTC:** Army. **Placement/credit:** AP, CLEP General and Subject; 15 credit hours maximum for associate degree; 24 credit hours maximum for bachelor's degree.

ACADEMIC REQUIREMENTS. Freshmen must earn minimum GPA of 1.75 to continue in good standing. 75% of freshmen return for sophomore year. Students must declare major by end of second year. **Graduation requirements:** 60 hours for associate (40 in major), 124 hours for bachelor's (77 in major). Most students required to take courses in arts/fine arts, computer science, English, history, humanities, mathematics, philosophy/religion, biological/physical sciences, social sciences. **Postgraduate studies:** 25% from 2-year programs enter 4-year programs. 2% enter law school, 2% enter medical school, 8% enter MBA programs, 10% enter other graduate study.

FRESHMAN ADMISSIONS. Selection criteria: Top half of class and GPA of at least 2.5. Special talents, interview, essay, recommendations considered. Combined SAT score of 900; ACT score of 19 or above. **High**

school preparation: 16 units recommended. Recommended units include biological science 2, English 4, foreign language 2, mathematics 4, physical science 2 and social science 2. 4 units of mathematics required for engineering majors. **Test requirements:** SAT or ACT (ACT preferred); score report by July 1. **Additional information:** All applicants required to sign statement of life-style expectation compliance prior to admission.

1992 FRESHMAN CLASS PROFILE. 272 men applied, 215 accepted, 124 enrolled; 242 women applied, 191 accepted, 114 enrolled. 59% had high school GPA of 3.0 or higher, 38% between 2.0 and 2.99. 22% were in top tenth and 47% were in top quarter of graduating class. **Academic background:** Mid 50% of enrolled freshmen had SAT-V between 420-540, SAT-M between 460-570; ACT composite between 20-26. 56% submitted SAT scores, 64% submitted ACT scores. **Characteristics:** 32% from in state, 85% live in college housing, 4% have minority backgrounds, 10% are foreign students. Average age is 18.

FALL-TERM APPLICATIONS. $25 fee, may be waived for applicants with need. Closing date July 15; priority given to applications received by February 15; applicants notified on a rolling basis; must reply within 30 days. Audition required for music applicants. Essay required. Interview recommended for all applicants applicants. Deferred and early admission available.

STUDENT LIFE. Housing: Dormitories (men, women, coed); apartment housing available. **Activities:** Student government, magazine, radio, student newspaper, television, yearbook, choral groups, concert band, drama, music ensembles, musical theater, pep band, Council to Assist in the Unity of Student Evangelism, student ministries. **Additional information:** No alcohol, drugs, tobacco, or dancing allowed on campus. Religious observance required.

ATHLETICS. NAIA. **Intercollegiate:** Basketball, rugby M, soccer M, swimming, tennis, volleyball W. **Intramural:** Basketball, football, racquetball, soccer, softball, volleyball.

STUDENT SERVICES. Aptitude testing, career counseling, employment service for undergraduates, freshman orientation, health services, personal counseling, placement service for graduates, services/facilities for handicapped.

ANNUAL EXPENSES. Tuition and fees: $6,520. **Room and board:** $3,360. **Books and supplies:** $500. **Other expenses:** $1,400.

FINANCIAL AID. 83% of freshmen, 81% of continuing students receive some form of aid. 60% of grants, 87% of loans, 41% of jobs based on need. 142 enrolled freshmen were judged to have need, 140 were offered aid. Academic, music/drama, art, athletic, leadership scholarships available. **Aid applications:** No closing date; priority given to applications received by April 1; applicants notified on a rolling basis beginning on or about March 1; must reply within 30 days.

ADDRESS/TELEPHONE. Don Crandall, Director of Enrollment Management, John Brown University, 2000 West University Street, Siloam Springs, AR 72761. (800) 634-6969. (800) 634-6969. Fax: (501) 524-4196.

Mississippi County Community College
Blytheville, Arkansas — CB code: 1267

2-year public community college, coed. Founded in 1974. **Accreditation:** Regional. **Undergraduate enrollment:** 1,985 men and women. **Faculty:** 113 total (43 full time), 113 with doctorates or other terminal degrees. **Location:** Rural campus in large town; 65 miles from Memphis, Tennessee. **Calendar:** Semester, limited summer session. **Microcomputers:** 75 located in classrooms, computer centers.

DEGREES OFFERED. AA, AS, AAS. 154 associate degrees awarded in 1992. 12% in business and management, 6% computer sciences, 5% engineering technologies, 16% health sciences, 53% letters/literature.

UNDERGRADUATE MAJORS. Agribusiness, agricultural sciences, biological and physical sciences, biology, business administration and management, business and management, business and office, business data processing and related programs, data processing, education, engineering and engineering-related technologies, English, horticulture, humanities and social sciences, industrial technology, law enforcement and corrections technologies, liberal/general studies, marketing and distribution, mathematics, music, nursing, physical sciences, protective services, psychology, secretarial and related programs, visual and performing arts.

ACADEMIC PROGRAMS. 2-year transfer program, cooperative education, dual enrollment of high school students, independent study, weekend college. **Remedial services:** Learning center, reduced course load, remedial instruction, tutoring. **Placement/credit:** AP, CLEP General and Subject, institutional tests; 30 credit hours maximum for associate degree.

ACADEMIC REQUIREMENTS. Freshmen must earn minimum GPA of 1.5 to continue in good standing. 26% of freshmen return for sophomore year. Students must declare major on enrollment. **Graduation requirements:** 62 hours for associate (24 in major). Most students required to take courses in arts/fine arts, English, history, humanities, mathematics, biological/physical sciences, social sciences.

FRESHMAN ADMISSIONS. Selection criteria: Open admissions. **Test requirements:** ACT for placement.

1992 FRESHMAN CLASS PROFILE. 502 men and women enrolled. **Characteristics:** 81% from in state, 100% commute, 28% have minority backgrounds. Average age is 27.

FALL-TERM APPLICATIONS. No fee. No closing date; applicants notified on a rolling basis beginning on or about June 1. Interview recommended for nursing, industrial technology applicants. Deferred and early admission available.

STUDENT LIFE. Activities: Student newspaper, choral groups, drama, music ensembles, Black Cultural Society.

ATHLETICS. NJCAA. **Intercollegiate:** Basketball. **Intramural:** Basketball.

STUDENT SERVICES. Aptitude testing, career counseling, employment service for undergraduates, personal counseling, veterans counselor, services/facilities for handicapped.

ANNUAL EXPENSES. Tuition and fees (1992-93): $720, $144 additional for out-of-district students, $1,200 additional for out-of-state students. **Books and supplies:** $250. **Other expenses:** $2,416.

FINANCIAL AID. 78% of continuing students receive some form of aid. 80% of grants, all loans, all jobs based on need. 400 enrolled freshmen were judged to have need, all were offered aid. Academic, music/drama, art, athletic, state/district residency, leadership scholarships available. **Aid applications:** No closing date; priority given to applications received by April 15; applicants notified on a rolling basis beginning on or about May 1; must reply within 2 weeks.

ADDRESS/TELEPHONE. June Walters, Registrar, Mississippi County Community College, PO Box 1109, Blytheville, AR 72316-1109. (501) 762-1020. Fax: (501) 763-0948.

National Education Center: Arkansas College of Technology
Little Rock, Arkansas — CB code: 0378

2-year proprietary technical college, coed. Founded in 1969. **Undergraduate enrollment:** 441 men and women. **Location:** Suburban campus in small city; 15 miles from downtown Little Rock. **Calendar:** 4 terms of 12 weeks each; students attend 3 quarters to complete one full academic year.

FRESHMAN ADMISSIONS. Selection criteria: Open admissions.

ANNUAL EXPENSES. Tuition and fees (1992-93): $5,335. **Books and supplies:** $100. **Other expenses:** $1,152.

ADDRESS/TELEPHONE. Byron Thompson, School Director, National Education Center: Arkansas College of Technology, 9720 Rodney Parham, Little Rock, AR 72207-9979. (501) 224-8200. (800) 727-4344. Fax: (501) 227-9217.

North Arkansas Community/Technical College
Harrison, Arkansas — CB code: 1423

2-year public community, technical college, coed. Founded in 1974. **Accreditation:** Regional. **Undergraduate enrollment:** 318 men, 524 women full time; 152 men, 421 women part time. **Faculty:** 124 total (37 full time), 9 with doctorates or other terminal degrees. **Location:** Suburban campus in large town; 75 miles from Fayetteville. **Calendar:** Semester, limited summer session. Saturday and extensive evening/early morning classes. **Microcomputers:** 68 located in libraries, classrooms, computer centers. **Additional facts:** Campuses located in Harrison and Batesville.

DEGREES OFFERED. AA, AS, AAS. 226 associate degrees awarded in 1992. 9% in business/office and marketing/distribution, 20% health sciences, 66% multi/interdisciplinary studies.

UNDERGRADUATE MAJORS. Agribusiness, automotive mechanics, biomedical equipment technology, business administration and management, business and office, business data processing and related programs, criminal justice technology, electromechanical technology, emergency medical technologies, hotel/motel and restaurant management, industrial technology, liberal/general studies, machine tool operation/machine shop, marketing and distribution, nursing, secretarial and related programs.

ACADEMIC PROGRAMS. 2-year transfer program, computer delivered (on-line) credit-bearing course offerings, dual enrollment of high school students, honors program, independent study, telecourses, weekend college, cross-registration. **Remedial services:** Learning center, remedial instruction, tutoring. **Placement/credit:** CLEP General and Subject, institutional tests; 20 credit hours maximum for associate degree.

ACADEMIC REQUIREMENTS. Freshmen must earn minimum GPA of 1.4 to continue in good standing. 45% of freshmen return for sophomore year. **Graduation requirements:** 62 hours for associate. Most students required to take courses in computer science, English, history, humanities, mathematics, biological/physical sciences, social sciences.

FRESHMAN ADMISSIONS. Selection criteria: Open admissions. **Test requirements:** ACT for placement.

1992 FRESHMAN CLASS PROFILE. Characteristics: 95% from in state, 100% commute.

FALL-TERM APPLICATIONS. No fee. No closing date; applicants notified on a rolling basis. Early admission available.

STUDENT LIFE. Activities: Student government, dance, drama, Baptist Student Union.

ATHLETICS. NJCAA. **Intercollegiate:** Baseball M, basketball. **Intramural:** Basketball, football M, racquetball, softball, table tennis, volleyball.

STUDENT SERVICES. Aptitude testing, career counseling, employment service for undergraduates, freshman orientation, personal counseling, special adviser for adult students, veterans counselor, services/facilities for handicapped.

ANNUAL EXPENSES. Tuition and fees: $792, $216 additional for out-of-district students, $1,128 additional for out-of-state students. **Books and supplies:** $300. **Other expenses:** $3,958.

FINANCIAL AID. 65% of freshmen, 72% of continuing students receive some form of aid. 87% of grants, 88% of loans, all jobs based on need. Academic, music/drama, art, athletic, leadership scholarships available. **Aid applications:** No closing date; priority given to applications received by May 1; applicants notified on a rolling basis beginning on or about June 1; must reply within 4 weeks.

ADDRESS/TELEPHONE. Dr. Jerry Cash, Vice President of Student Services, North Arkansas Community/Technical College, Pioneer Ridge, Harrison, AR 72601. (501) 743-3000. Fax: (501) 743-3577.

Ouachita Baptist University
Arkadelphia, Arkansas — CB code: 6549

Admissions: 85% of applicants accepted
Based on: ••• School record, test scores
• Activities, interview, recommendations
Completion: 90% of freshmen end year in good standing
54% graduate, 50% of these enter graduate study

4-year private university, coed, affiliated with Southern Baptist Convention. Founded in 1886. **Accreditation:** Regional. **Undergraduate enrollment:** 600 men, 626 women full time; 35 men, 37 women part time. **Faculty:** 121 total (101 full time), 59 with doctorates or other terminal degrees. **Location:** Rural campus in large town; 65 miles from Little Rock. **Calendar:** Semester, limited summer session. **Microcomputers:** 130 located in libraries, classrooms, computer centers. **Special facilities:** Arboretum, biblical studies computer laboratory.

DEGREES OFFERED. BA, BS. 224 bachelor's degrees awarded in 1992. 20% in business and management, 7% communications, 18% education, 5% life sciences, 9% philosophy, religion, theology, 15% social sciences, 8% visual and performing arts.

UNDERGRADUATE MAJORS. Accounting, art education, Bible studies, biblical languages, biology, business administration and management, business and management, business economics, business education, chemistry, Christian counseling, communications, computer and information sciences, dramatic arts, early childhood education, economics, education, elementary education, engineering physics, English, English education, English literature, finance, food science and nutrition, foreign languages education, French, health education, history, home economics, home economics education, junior high education, liberal/general studies, marketing and distribution, marketing management, mathematics, mathematics education, missionary studies, music, music education, music history and appreciation, music performance, music theory and composition, musical theater, nutritional sciences, philosophy, physical education, physical sciences, physics, political science and government, predentistry, prelaw, premedicine, prepharmacy, preveterinary, psychology, public relations, pure mathematics, radio/television broadcasting, religion, religious education, religious music, science education, secondary education, social science education, social sciences, social studies education, sociology, Spanish, speech, speech pathology/audiology, speech/communication/theater education, studio art, technical education, textiles and clothing, theological studies, visual and performing arts.

ACADEMIC PROGRAMS. Accelerated program, cooperative education, double major, dual enrollment of high school students, honors program, independent study, internships, study abroad, teacher preparation, visiting/exchange student program, cross-registration; liberal arts/career combination in engineering, health sciences. **Remedial services:** Learning center, reduced course load, remedial instruction, special counselor, tutoring. **Placement/credit:** AP, CLEP Subject, institutional tests; 32 credit hours maximum for bachelor's degree.

ACADEMIC REQUIREMENTS. Freshmen must earn minimum GPA of 1.5 to continue in good standing. 74% of freshmen return for sophomore year. Students must declare major by end of second year. **Graduation requirements:** 128 hours for bachelor's (24 in major). Most students required to take courses in arts/fine arts, English, foreign languages, history, humanities, mathematics, philosophy/religion, biological/physical sciences, social sciences. **Additional information:** Classes in Arkansas Folkways taught at Old Washington State Park. International exchange programs in Japan, Kazakhstan, Uzbekistan, Europe, China.

FRESHMAN ADMISSIONS. Selection criteria: Test scores and school achievement record most important. High school GPA of 2.5 required, 16 or higher on ACT. SAT also accepted. **High school preparation:** 15 units required. Required units include English 4, foreign language 2, mathematics 2, social science 3 and science 2. **Test requirements:** SAT or ACT (ACT preferred); score report by August 15.

1992 FRESHMAN CLASS PROFILE. 307 men applied, 261 accepted, 150 enrolled; 327 women applied, 278 accepted, 152 enrolled. 66% had high school GPA of 3.0 or higher, 34% between 2.0 and 2.99. 21% were in top tenth and 38% were in top quarter of graduating class. **Academic background:** Mid 50% of enrolled freshmen had ACT composite between 21-26. 20% submitted ACT scores. **Characteristics:** 78% from in state, 92% live in college housing, 6% have minority backgrounds, 2% are foreign students, 33% join fraternities/sororities. Average age is 18.

FALL-TERM APPLICATIONS. $25 fee. Closing date August 15; priority given to applications received by February 15; applicants notified on a rolling basis. Interview recommended. Portfolio recommended for studio art, music applicants. Deferred admission available.

STUDENT LIFE. Housing: Dormitories (men, women); apartment housing available. **Activities:** Student government, magazine, student newspaper, television, yearbook, choral groups, concert band, drama, jazz band, marching band, music ensembles, musical theater, opera, pep band, fraternities, sororities, Baptist Student Union, International Student Fellowship, Black American Student Society, Young Republicans, Young Democrats. **Additional information:** Religious observance required.

ATHLETICS. NAIA. **Intercollegiate:** Baseball M, basketball, cross-country M, diving, football M, golf M, soccer M, swimming, tennis, track and field M, volleyball W. **Intramural:** Baseball M, basketball, bowling, cross-country, diving, football M, golf, handball, skin diving, softball, swimming, table tennis, tennis, track and field, volleyball.

STUDENT SERVICES. Aptitude testing, career counseling, employment service for undergraduates, freshman orientation, health services, personal counseling, placement service for graduates, veterans counselor, services/facilities for handicapped.

ANNUAL EXPENSES. Tuition and fees: $6,230. **Room and board:** $2,760. **Books and supplies:** $400. **Other expenses:** $900.

FINANCIAL AID. 90% of freshmen, 90% of continuing students receive some form of aid. 23% of grants, 96% of loans, 54% of jobs based on need. 250 enrolled freshmen were judged to have need, 230 were offered aid. Academic, music/drama, athletic, leadership, religious affiliation scholarships available. **Aid applications:** No closing date; priority given to applications received by May 1; applicants notified on a rolling basis beginning on or about May 1; must reply within 2 weeks.

ADDRESS/TELEPHONE. Michael L. Kolb, Director of Admissions/Registrar, Ouachita Baptist University, OBU Box 3776, Arkadelphia, AR 71998-0001. (501) 245-5000. (800) 342-5628. Fax: (501) 245-5500.

Philander Smith College
Little Rock, Arkansas — CB code: 6578

4-year private liberal arts college, coed, affiliated with United Methodist Church. Founded in 1877. **Accreditation:** Regional. **Undergraduate enrollment:** 280 men, 421 women full time; 102 men, 137 women part time. **Faculty:** 70 total (31 full time). **Location:** Urban campus in small city; in downtown area. **Calendar:** Semester, limited summer session. **Microcomputers:** Located in libraries, classrooms, computer centers.

DEGREES OFFERED. BA, BS. 68 bachelor's degrees awarded in 1992. 43% in business and management, 12% education, 7% physical sciences, 7% psychology, 16% social sciences, 6% visual and performing arts.

UNDERGRADUATE MAJORS. Biology, business administration and management, chemistry, computer and information sciences, elementary education, English, foreign languages (multiple emphasis), home economics, mathematics, music, philosophy, psychology, radio/television broadcasting, religion, secretarial and related programs, social work, sociology, special education.

ACADEMIC PROGRAMS. Cooperative education. **Remedial services:** Reduced course load, special counselor, tutoring. **ROTC:** Army. **Placement/credit:** 30 credit hours maximum for bachelor's degree.

ACADEMIC REQUIREMENTS. Freshmen must earn minimum GPA of 2.0 to continue in good standing. 79% of freshmen return for sophomore year. Students must declare major on enrollment. **Graduation requirements:** 124 hours for bachelor's. Most students required to take courses in English, foreign languages, humanities, mathematics, philosophy/religion, biological/physical sciences, social sciences.

FRESHMAN ADMISSIONS. Selection criteria: Open admissions. **Test requirements:** SAT or ACT (SAT preferred) for placement and counseling only.

1992 FRESHMAN CLASS PROFILE. 169 men, 265 women enrolled. **Characteristics:** 90% from in state, 50% commute, 90% have minority backgrounds, 15% are foreign students. Average age is 19.

FALL-TERM APPLICATIONS. $5 fee, may be waived for applicants with need. No closing date; applicants notified on a rolling basis. Deferred admission available.

STUDENT LIFE. Housing: Dormitories (men, women). **Activities:** Student government, radio, student newspaper, yearbook, choral groups, drama, music ensembles, fraternities, sororities, Alpha Phi Omega, Phi Beta Sigma,

Alpha Phi Alpha, Sigma Gamma Rho, Delta Sigma Theta, Zeta Phi Beta, Kappa Alpha Psi, Alpha Kappa Alpha.

ATHLETICS. NAIA. **Intercollegiate:** Baseball M, basketball, softball M, volleyball. **Intramural:** Badminton, basketball, soccer M, swimming, table tennis, tennis.

STUDENT SERVICES. Aptitude testing, career counseling, employment service for undergraduates, freshman orientation, health services, personal counseling, veterans counselor, services/facilities for handicapped.

ANNUAL EXPENSES. Tuition and fees (1992-93): $2,620. **Room and board:** $2,415. **Books and supplies:** $400. **Other expenses:** $750.

FINANCIAL AID. 90% of freshmen, 90% of continuing students receive some form of aid. Grants, loans, jobs available. **Aid applications:** No closing date; priority given to applications received by May 1; applicants notified on a rolling basis; must reply within 2 weeks.

ADDRESS/TELEPHONE. Picola Smith, Director of Admissions and Records, Philander Smith College, 812 West 13th Street, Little Rock, AR 72202. (501) 375-9845. Fax: (501) 370-5278.

Phillips County Community College
Helena, Arkansas — CB code: 6583

2-year public community college, coed. Founded in 1965. **Accreditation:** Regional. **Undergraduate enrollment:** 248 men, 592 women full time; 245 men, 596 women part time. **Faculty:** 118 total (61 full time), 3 with doctorates or other terminal degrees. **Location:** Suburban campus in large town; 65 miles from Memphis, Tennessee. **Calendar:** Semester, limited summer session. Extensive evening/early morning classes. **Microcomputers:** Located in libraries, computer centers.

DEGREES OFFERED. AA, AAS. 115 associate degrees awarded in 1992. 5% in business and management, 19% business/office and marketing/distribution, 5% computer sciences, 30% health sciences, 8% social sciences, 25% trade and industry.

UNDERGRADUATE MAJORS. Agribusiness, air conditioning/heating/refrigeration mechanics, automotive mechanics, automotive technology, biology, business administration and management, business and office, business computer/console/peripheral equipment operation, business data entry equipment operation, business data processing and related programs, business data programming, chemistry, data processing, drafting, education, engineering and engineering-related technologies, graphic and printing production, industrial equipment maintenance and repair, industrial technology, instrumentation technology, liberal/general studies, marketing and distribution, mathematics, medical laboratory technologies, medical records technology, nursing, personal services, precision metal work, printmaking, radiograph medical technology, secretarial and related programs, social sciences, welding technology.

ACADEMIC PROGRAMS. 2-year transfer program, dual enrollment of high school students, honors program, independent study. **Remedial services:** Learning center, remedial instruction, special counselor, tutoring. **Placement/credit:** AP, CLEP General and Subject, institutional tests; 49 credit hours maximum for associate degree.

ACADEMIC REQUIREMENTS. Freshmen must earn minimum GPA of 1.5 to continue in good standing. 62% of freshmen return for sophomore year. Students must declare major on enrollment. **Graduation requirements:** 64 hours for associate (44 in major). Most students required to take courses in English, history, mathematics, biological/physical sciences, social sciences.

FRESHMAN ADMISSIONS. Selection criteria: Open admissions. **Test requirements:** SAT or ACT (ACT preferred) for placement and counseling only; score report by August 21.

1992 FRESHMAN CLASS PROFILE. 160 men, 240 women enrolled. **Characteristics:** 89% from in state, 100% commute, 47% have minority backgrounds. Average age is 19.

FALL-TERM APPLICATIONS. No fee. No closing date; applicants notified on a rolling basis. Interview required for applicants with no high school transcript or test scores. Deferred and early admission available.

STUDENT LIFE. Activities: Student newspaper, choral groups, dance, drama, Baptist Student Union.

ATHLETICS. NJCAA. **Intercollegiate:** Basketball. **Intramural:** Archery, badminton, basketball, softball, table tennis, tennis, volleyball.

STUDENT SERVICES. Aptitude testing, career counseling, freshman orientation, personal counseling, placement service for graduates, veterans counselor.

ANNUAL EXPENSES. Tuition and fees (1992-93): $696, $192 additional for out-of-district students, $552 additional for out-of-state students. **Books and supplies:** $450. **Other expenses:** $1,925.

FINANCIAL AID. 70% of continuing students receive some form of aid. Grants, loans, jobs available. Academic, music/drama, athletic, leadership scholarships available. **Aid applications:** Closing date May 1; priority given to applications received by April 1; applicants notified on a rolling basis beginning on or about April 1; must reply within 2 weeks.

ADDRESS/TELEPHONE. James R. Brasel, Dean of Admissions, Phillips County Community College, Campus Drive, PO Box 785, Helena, AR 72342. (501) 338-6474. Fax: (501) 338-7542.

Rich Mountain Community College
Mena, Arkansas — CB code: 0226

2-year public community college, coed. Founded in 1983. **Accreditation:** Regional. **Undergraduate enrollment:** 697 men and women. **Faculty:** 36 total (17 full time). **Location:** Rural campus in small town; 85 miles from Fort Smith. **Calendar:** Semester, limited summer session. **Microcomputers:** Located in libraries, classrooms.

DEGREES OFFERED. AA, AS, AAS. 32 associate degrees awarded in 1992.

UNDERGRADUATE MAJORS. Automotive mechanics, business and management, business data processing and related programs, carpentry, diesel engine mechanics, education, precision metal work, secretarial and related programs.

ACADEMIC PROGRAMS. 2-year transfer program, dual enrollment of high school students, telecourses. **Remedial services:** Remedial instruction, tutoring. **Placement/credit:** CLEP General and Subject, institutional tests; 12 credit hours maximum for associate degree.

ACADEMIC REQUIREMENTS. Freshmen must earn minimum GPA of 1.6 to continue in good standing. Students must declare major on enrollment. **Graduation requirements:** 60 hours for associate. Most students required to take courses in computer science, English, history, mathematics, biological/physical sciences, social sciences.

FRESHMAN ADMISSIONS. Selection criteria: Open admissions. **Test requirements:** ACT for placement.

1992 FRESHMAN CLASS PROFILE. 227 men and women enrolled. **Characteristics:** 96% from in state, 100% commute, 3% have minority backgrounds. Average age is 26.

FALL-TERM APPLICATIONS. No fee. No closing date; applicants notified on a rolling basis.

STUDENT LIFE. Activities: Student government, student newspaper.

ATHLETICS. Intramural: Baseball, volleyball.

STUDENT SERVICES. Aptitude testing, career counseling, employment service for undergraduates, freshman orientation, personal counseling, special adviser for adult students, services/facilities for handicapped.

ANNUAL EXPENSES. Tuition and fees (1992-93): $580, $160 additional for out-of-district students, $1,242 additional for out-of-state students. **Books and supplies:** $300. **Other expenses:** $470.

FINANCIAL AID. 46% of freshmen, 65% of continuing students receive some form of aid. Grants, loans, jobs available. Academic, state/district residency scholarships available. **Aid applications:** No closing date; priority given to applications received by July 1; applicants notified on a rolling basis; must reply within 2 weeks.

ADDRESS/TELEPHONE. Dr. Robert Goldman, Dean of Instruction, Rich Mountain Community College, 601 Bush Street, Mena, AR 71953. (501) 394-5012. Fax: (501) 394-2828.

Shorter College
North Little Rock, Arkansas — CB code: 6649

Admissions:	55% of applicants accepted
Based on:	••• Recommendations
	•• Interview, religious affiliation/commitment
	• School record
Completion:	78% of freshmen end year in good standing
	48% graduate, 50% of these enter 4-year programs

2-year private junior, liberal arts college, coed, affiliated with African Methodist Episcopal Church. Founded in 1886. **Accreditation:** Regional. **Undergraduate enrollment:** 45 men, 60 women full time; 27 men, 40 women part time. **Faculty:** 24 total (10 full time), 2 with doctorates or other terminal degrees. **Location:** Urban campus in small city; 1.5 miles from Little Rock. **Calendar:** Semester. **Microcomputers:** 10 located in computer centers. **Additional facts:** Specifically caters to students inadequately prepared for 4-year schools.

DEGREES OFFERED. AA, AS, AAS. 16 associate degrees awarded in 1992. 20% in business and management, 10% teacher education, 70% allied health.

UNDERGRADUATE MAJORS. Accounting, allied health, business administration and management, business and management, business and office, computer and information sciences, education, elementary education, health sciences, humanities and social sciences, liberal/general studies, medical secretary, practical nursing, secretarial and related programs, social sciences.

ACADEMIC PROGRAMS. 2-year transfer program, double major, external degree, independent study, internships, weekend college, cross-registration. **Remedial services:** Preadmission summer program, reduced course load, remedial instruction, special counselor, tutoring, adult education program. **Placement/credit:** Institutional tests.

ACADEMIC REQUIREMENTS. Freshmen must earn minimum GPA of 1.5 to continue in good standing. 65% of freshmen return for sophomore year. Students must declare major by end of first year. **Graduation requirements:** 64 hours for associate (48 in major). Most students required to take courses in arts/fine arts, computer science, English, history, humanities, mathematics, philosophy/religion, biological/physical sciences, social sciences.

FRESHMAN ADMISSIONS. Selection criteria: Prospective students' interest in better education and willingness to apply themselves in a higher education setting most important.

1992 FRESHMAN CLASS PROFILE. 60 men applied, 32 accepted, 32 enrolled; 70 women applied, 40 accepted, 40 enrolled. **Characteristics:** 96% from in state, 77% commute, 95% have minority backgrounds, 3% are foreign students. Average age is 20.

FALL-TERM APPLICATIONS. $5 fee. No closing date; priority given to applications received by May 12; applicants notified on a rolling basis; must reply within 1 week. Deferred and early admission available. Applicants notified of fall term admissions decisions on or about day after taking entrance examination.

STUDENT LIFE. Housing: Dormitories (men, women). **Activities:** Student government, magazine, radio, television, yearbook, dance, campus ministry, Nigerian Students Association. **Additional information:** Religious observance required.

ATHLETICS. NJCAA. **Intercollegiate:** Basketball M. **Intramural:** Basketball.

STUDENT SERVICES. Aptitude testing, career counseling, employment service for undergraduates, freshman orientation, personal counseling, veterans counselor, services/facilities for handicapped.

ANNUAL EXPENSES. Tuition and fees (1992-93): $2,456. **Room and board:** $2,400. **Books and supplies:** $300. **Other expenses:** $200.

FINANCIAL AID. 33% of freshmen, 34% of continuing students receive some form of aid. All aid based on need. 19 enrolled freshmen were judged to have need, all were offered aid. Athletic, alumni affiliation scholarships available. **Aid applications:** No closing date; priority given to applications received by May 1; applicants notified on a rolling basis.

ADDRESS/TELEPHONE. DeLores Voliber, Director of Admissions, Shorter College, 604 Locust Street, North Little Rock, AR 72114. (501) 374-6305.

South Arkansas Community College
El Dorado, Arkansas CB code: 1550

2-year public community, junior college, coed. Founded in 1975. **Accreditation:** Regional. **Undergraduate enrollment:** 216 men, 345 women full time; 257 men, 382 women part time. **Faculty:** 67 total (38 full time), 8 with doctorates or other terminal degrees. **Location:** Rural campus in large town; 115 miles from Little Rock. **Calendar:** Semester, limited summer session. Extensive evening/early morning classes. **Microcomputers:** 42 located in libraries, computer centers.

DEGREES OFFERED. AA, AAS. 67 associate degrees awarded in 1992. 11% in business/office and marketing/distribution, 16% allied health, 70% multi/interdisciplinary studies.

UNDERGRADUATE MAJORS. Accounting, business administration and management, business and office, business data processing and related programs, chemical manufacturing technology, computer and information sciences, criminal justice technology, emergency medical technologies, liberal/general studies, medical laboratory technologies, radiograph medical technology, secretarial and related programs.

ACADEMIC PROGRAMS. 2-year transfer program, dual enrollment of high school students. **Remedial services:** Learning center, reduced course load, remedial instruction, special counselor, tutoring. **Placement/credit:** CLEP Subject, institutional tests; 30 credit hours maximum for associate degree.

ACADEMIC REQUIREMENTS. No policy requiring minimum GPA; records of students having academic difficulty are reviewed individually. **Graduation requirements:** 60 hours for associate. Most students required to take courses in English, history, humanities, mathematics, biological/physical sciences, social sciences.

FRESHMAN ADMISSIONS. Selection criteria: Open admissions. **Test requirements:** SAT or ACT (ACT preferred) for placement.

1992 FRESHMAN CLASS PROFILE. 288 men applied, 288 accepted, 278 enrolled; 402 women applied, 402 accepted, 402 enrolled. **Characteristics:** 95% from in state, 100% commute, 17% have minority backgrounds.

FALL-TERM APPLICATIONS. No fee. No closing date; applicants notified on a rolling basis. Early admission available.

STUDENT LIFE. Activities: Student newspaper, choral groups, Baptist Student Association, Phi Beta Lambda, Phi Theta Kappa, student leadership group.

ATHLETICS. Intramural: Tennis, volleyball.

STUDENT SERVICES. Aptitude testing, career counseling, employment service for undergraduates, personal counseling, veterans counselor, services/facilities for handicapped.

ANNUAL EXPENSES. Tuition and fees: $744, $144 additional for out-of-district students, $504 additional for out-of-state students. **Books and supplies:** $450. **Other expenses:** $450.

FINANCIAL AID. 54% of freshmen, 48% of continuing students receive some form of aid. 93% of grants, 99% of loans, 65% of jobs based on need. Academic, music/drama, athletic, leadership scholarships available. **Aid applications:** No closing date; priority given to applications received by July 1; applicants notified on a rolling basis beginning on or about July 1; must reply within 2 weeks.

ADDRESS/TELEPHONE. Elizabeth Dugal, Counselor, South Arkansas Community College, PO Box 7010, El Dorado, AR 71731-7010. (501) 862-8131. Fax: (561) 862-6412.

Southern Arkansas University
Magnolia, Arkansas CB code: 6661

4-year public university, coed. Founded in 1909. **Accreditation:** Regional. **Undergraduate enrollment:** 1,028 men, 1,287 women full time; 128 men, 359 women part time. **Graduate enrollment:** 7 men, 11 women full time; 14 men, 58 women part time. **Faculty:** 172 total (139 full time), 62 with doctorates or other terminal degrees. **Location:** Rural campus in large town; 53 miles from Texarkana and 70 miles from Shreveport, Louisiana. **Calendar:** Semester, extensive summer session. **Microcomputers:** 60 located in classrooms, computer centers.

DEGREES OFFERED. AA, AS, BA, BS, MEd. 112 associate degrees awarded in 1992. 99% in health sciences. 267 bachelor's degrees awarded. 43% in business and management, 23% teacher education, 23% physical sciences, 10% visual and performing arts. Graduate degrees offered in 3 major fields of study.

UNDERGRADUATE MAJORS. Associate: Business and office, business data programming, graphic arts technology, industrial technology, medical laboratory technologies, nursing, recreation and community services technologies, secretarial and related programs. **Bachelor's:** Accounting, agribusiness, agricultural education, agricultural sciences, art education, biology, business administration and management, business and management, business economics, business education, chemistry, clinical laboratory science, communications, computer programming, dramatic arts, early childhood education, elementary education, engineering physics, English, English education, finance, foreign languages (multiple emphasis), foreign languages education, French, history, industrial technology, international business management, marketing and distribution, mathematics, mathematics education, music, physical education, political science and government, psychology, radio/television broadcasting, radio/television technology, science education, secondary education, secretarial and related programs, social studies education, sociology, Spanish, special education, speech.

ACADEMIC PROGRAMS. 2-year transfer program, internships, teacher preparation, 4-year combined program in business and computer science. **Remedial services:** Learning center, reduced course load, special counselor, tutoring. **Placement/credit:** AP, CLEP Subject; 30 credit hours maximum for bachelor's degree.

ACADEMIC REQUIREMENTS. Freshmen must earn minimum GPA of 1.5 to continue in good standing. 74% of freshmen return for sophomore year. Students must declare major by end of second year. **Graduation requirements:** 71 hours for associate, 124 hours for bachelor's. Most students required to take courses in arts/fine arts, English, foreign languages, history, humanities, mathematics, biological/physical sciences, social sciences. **Postgraduate studies:** 15% from 2-year programs enter 4-year programs. 1% enter law school, 1% enter medical school, 3% enter MBA programs, 10% enter other graduate study.

FRESHMAN ADMISSIONS. Selection criteria: Open admissions. Selective admissions for out-of-state applicants (except those from bordering states) based on rank in top half of class. Recommended units include biological science 1, English 4, foreign language 1, mathematics 2, physical science 1 and social science 3. .5 unit computer science also recommended. **Test requirements:** ACT for placement and counseling only; score report by August 15.

1992 FRESHMAN CLASS PROFILE. 238 men, 296 women enrolled. 52% had high school GPA of 3.0 or higher, 48% between 2.0 and 2.99. 19% were in top tenth and 29% were in top quarter of graduating class. **Academic background:** Mid 50% of enrolled freshmen had ACT composite between 15-23. 100% submitted ACT scores. **Characteristics:** 83% from in state, 60% live in college housing, 26% have minority backgrounds, 1% are foreign students. Average age is 18.

FALL-TERM APPLICATIONS. No fee. Closing date August 15; applicants notified on a rolling basis beginning on or about January 1. Interview required for nursing applicants. Deferred and early admission available.

STUDENT LIFE. Housing: Dormitories (men, women); apartment housing available. **Activities:** Student government, radio, student newspaper, television, yearbook, choral groups, concert band, drama, jazz band, marching band, musical theater, pep band, symphony orchestra, fraternities, sororities.

ATHLETICS. NAIA. **Intercollegiate:** Baseball M, basketball, football M, golf M, tennis, track and field M, volleyball W. **Intramural:** Badminton, basketball, gymnastics, softball, tennis, volleyball.

STUDENT SERVICES. Career counseling, employment service for undergraduates, freshman orientation, health services, personal counseling, placement service for graduates, veterans counselor, services/facilities for handicapped.

ANNUAL EXPENSES. Tuition and fees (1992-93): $1,380, $770 additional for out-of-state students. **Room and board:** $2,200. **Books and supplies:** $350. **Other expenses:** $600.

FINANCIAL AID. 70% of freshmen, 75% of continuing students receive some form of aid. 75% of grants, 97% of loans, 73% of jobs based on need. 370 enrolled freshmen were judged to have need, all were offered aid. Academic, music/drama, athletic, leadership scholarships available. **Aid applications:** No closing date; priority given to applications received by June 1; applicants notified on a rolling basis beginning on or about June 1; must reply within 2 weeks.

ADDRESS/TELEPHONE. Sonny Whittington, Director of Admissions, Southern Arkansas University, SAU Box 1382, Magnolia, AR 71753-5000. (501) 235-4040. Fax: (501) 235-5005.

Southern Arkansas University: Technical Branch
Camden, Arkansas CB code: 6704

2-year public junior, technical college, coed. Founded in 1967. **Accreditation:** Regional. **Undergraduate enrollment:** 180 men, 207 women full time; 377 men, 433 women part time. **Faculty:** 44 total (29 full time), 4 with doctorates or other terminal degrees. **Location:** Rural campus in large town; 90 miles from Little Rock. **Calendar:** Semester, limited summer session. **Microcomputers:** Located in libraries, classrooms, computer centers.

DEGREES OFFERED. AA, AS, AAS. 65 associate degrees awarded in 1992. 29% in business and management, 22% business/office and marketing/distribution, 26% engineering technologies, 8% letters/literature, 10% trade and industry, 5% visual and performing arts.

UNDERGRADUATE MAJORS. Aircraft mechanics, business administration and management, business data programming, computer programming, computer servicing technology, drafting and design technology, education, electromechanical technology, electronic technology, graphic arts technology, hotel/motel and restaurant management, industrial technology, liberal/general studies, manufacturing technology, secretarial and related programs.

ACADEMIC PROGRAMS. 2-year transfer program, dual enrollment of high school students, telecourses, cross-registration. **Remedial services:** Learning center, preadmission summer program, remedial instruction, tutoring. **Placement/credit:** CLEP General and Subject, institutional tests; 12 credit hours maximum for associate degree.

ACADEMIC REQUIREMENTS. Freshmen must earn minimum GPA of 2.0 to continue in good standing. 50% of freshmen return for sophomore year. Students must declare major on enrollment. **Graduation requirements:** 64 hours for associate (48 in major). Most students required to take courses in computer science, English, history, mathematics, biological/physical sciences, social sciences.

FRESHMAN ADMISSIONS. Selection criteria: Open admissions. **High school preparation:** 18 units recommended. Recommended units include biological science 1, English 4, foreign language 1, mathematics 2, physical science 1, social science 1 and science 3. **Test requirements:** SAT or ACT for placement and counseling only; score report by August 15.

1992 FRESHMAN CLASS PROFILE. 102 men applied, 102 accepted, 66 enrolled; 129 women applied, 129 accepted, 87 enrolled. 15% had high school GPA of 3.0 or higher, 70% between 2.0 and 2.99. **Characteristics:** 95% from in state, 85% commute, 20% have minority backgrounds. Average age is 26.

FALL-TERM APPLICATIONS. No fee. Closing date August 15; applicants notified on a rolling basis beginning on or about August 15; must reply by August 31. Interview recommended. Portfolio recommended for graphic arts technology applicants. Deferred and early admission available.

STUDENT LIFE. Housing: Apartment housing available. **Activities:** Student government, choral groups, drama, Christian Student Union, Afro-American Club.

ATHLETICS. Intramural: Archery, basketball, golf, softball, table tennis, tennis, volleyball.

STUDENT SERVICES. Freshman orientation, personal counseling, placement service for graduates, veterans counselor, services/facilities for handicapped.

ANNUAL EXPENSES. Tuition and fees (1992-93): $840, $420 additional for out-of-state students. **Room and board:** $1,800 room only. **Books and supplies:** $400. **Other expenses:** $900.

FINANCIAL AID. 81% of grants, all loans, 58% of jobs based on need. Academic, music/drama, art, minority scholarships available. **Aid applications:** No closing date; priority given to applications received by July 15; applicants notified on a rolling basis beginning on or about July 1; must reply within 10 days.

ADDRESS/TELEPHONE. Charlotte Gilmore, Associate Dean of Enrollment Management, Southern Arkansas University: Technical Branch, SAU Tech Station, Camden, AR 71701. (501) 574-4504. Fax: (501) 574-4520.

University of Arkansas
Fayetteville, Arkansas CB code: 6866

Admissions: 90% of applicants accepted
Based on: ••• School record
Completion: 61% of freshmen end year in good standing
35% graduate

4-year public university, coed. Founded in 1871. **Accreditation:** Regional. **Undergraduate enrollment:** 11,767 men and women. **Graduate enrollment:** 2,368 men and women. **Faculty:** 955 total (862 full time), 771 with doctorates or other terminal degrees. **Location:** Urban campus in large town; 192 miles from Little Rock, 120 miles from Tulsa, Oklahoma. **Calendar:** Semester, extensive summer session. **Microcomputers:** 800 located in dormitories, libraries, classrooms, computer centers. **Special facilities:** Walton Arts Center, university museum, fitness and recreation center complex.

DEGREES OFFERED. AA, BA, BS, BFA, BArch, MA, MS, MBA, MFA, MEd, PhD, EdD, JD. 86 associate degrees awarded in 1992. 12% in business/office and marketing/distribution, 88% health sciences. 1,865 bachelor's degrees awarded. 28% in business and management, 7% communications, 16% education, 17% engineering, 6% social sciences. Graduate degrees offered in 71 major fields of study.

UNDERGRADUATE MAJORS. Associate: Nursing, secretarial and related programs. **Bachelor's:** Accounting, agribusiness, agricultural economics, agricultural education, agricultural engineering, agricultural mechanics, agricultural sciences, agronomy, animal sciences, anthropology, architecture, art education, botany, business administration and management, business and management, business economics, business education, chemical engineering, chemistry, civil engineering, classics, computer and information sciences, computer engineering, dairy, dance, dramatic arts, earth sciences, economics, education of exceptional children, electrical/electronics/communications engineering, elementary education, engineering science, English, English education, environmental science, fashion design, fashion merchandising, finance, food science and nutrition, food sciences, foreign languages education, French, geography, geology, German, health education, history, home economics, home economics education, horticulture, human environment and housing, individual and family development, industrial arts education, industrial engineering, insurance and risk management, interior design, international agricultural marketing, international agriculture, journalism, landscape architecture, law , law enforcement and corrections, marketing and distribution, mathematics, mathematics education, mechanical engineering, microbiology, music, music education, music performance, personnel management, philosophy, physical education, physics, plant protection, political science and government, poultry, psychology, public administration, real estate, recreation and community services technologies, science education, secondary education, secretarial and related programs, social studies education, social work, sociology, soil sciences, Spanish, special education, speech, speech correction, speech pathology/audiology, speech/communication/theater education, studio art, technical education, textiles and clothing, transportation management, zoology.

ACADEMIC PROGRAMS. 2-year transfer program, accelerated program, cooperative education, double major, dual enrollment of high school students, education specialist degree, honors program, independent study, internships, study abroad, teacher preparation, visiting/exchange student program; liberal arts/career combination in engineering; combined bachelor's/graduate program in law. **Remedial services:** Learning center, preadmission summer program, reduced course load, remedial instruction, special counselor, tutoring, College Mentor Program, transition status. **ROTC:** Air Force, Army. **Placement/credit:** AP, CLEP General and Subject, institutional tests; 24 credit hours maximum for bachelor's degree.

ACADEMIC REQUIREMENTS. Freshmen must earn minimum GPA of 2.0 to continue in good standing. 77% of freshmen return for sophomore year. Students must declare major by end of second year. **Graduation requirements:** 124 hours for bachelor's. Most students required to take courses in English, foreign languages, history, mathematics, biological/physical sciences, social sciences.

FRESHMAN ADMISSIONS. Selection criteria: For unconditional admission students must have 2.75 GPA and specified high school courses. Students may be admitted conditionally with 2.25 to 2.74 GPA. **High school preparation:** 16 units required. Required and recommended units include English 4, mathematics 3, social science 3 and science 3. Foreign language 2 recommended. Mathematics must include 1 algebra, and 2 units chosen from algebra, geometry, calculus/trigonometry. Science must include 2 laboratory sciences. 2 foreign language required for College of Arts and Sciences applicants, plus 3 additional units in mathematics, science, or foreign language communication. **Test requirements:** SAT or ACT for placement and counseling only; score report by August 23. **Additional information:** Students may be admitted with course deficiencies if they meet requirements for unconditional or conditional admission.

1992 FRESHMAN CLASS PROFILE. 2,002 men applied, 1,801 accepted, 1,289 enrolled; 1,996 women applied, 1,795 accepted, 1,093 enrolled. 60% had high school GPA of 3.0 or higher, 40% between 2.0 and 2.99. **Academic background:** Mid 50% of enrolled freshmen had ACT composite between 18-26. 90% submitted ACT scores. **Characteristics:** 86%

from in state, 55% live in college housing, 9% have minority backgrounds, 4% are foreign students, 20% join fraternities/sororities. Average age is 19.

FALL-TERM APPLICATIONS. $15 fee. Closing date August 15; applicants notified on a rolling basis. Early admission available.

STUDENT LIFE. Housing: Dormitories (men, women, coed); apartment, fraternity, sorority housing available. Honors Hall residence hall specifically for honors program students. **Activities:** Student government, radio, student newspaper, yearbook, choral groups, concert band, dance, drama, jazz band, marching band, music ensembles, musical theater, opera, pep band, symphony orchestra, fraternities, sororities, 55 academic interest/professional society groups; 15 cultural/social organizations; 7 entertainment/communication organizations; 19 honor societies; 15 religious organizations; 7 service organizations; 16 special interest organizations.

ATHLETICS. NCAA. **Intercollegiate:** Baseball M, basketball, cross-country, diving, football M, golf M, soccer W, swimming, tennis, track and field. **Intramural:** Badminton, basketball, bowling, cross-country, diving, golf, handball, racquetball, rugby, sailing, skiing, skin diving, soccer, softball, swimming, table tennis, tennis, track and field, volleyball, water polo.

STUDENT SERVICES. Aptitude testing, career counseling, employment service for undergraduates, freshman orientation, health services, personal counseling, placement service for graduates, special adviser for adult students, veterans counselor, services/facilities for handicapped.

ANNUAL EXPENSES. Tuition and fees: $1,838, $4,608 additional for out-of-state students. Members of Native American tribes that formerly resided in Arkansas (Caddo, Cherokee, Choctaw, Osage and Quapaw) are classified as in-state students for tuition and fee purposes. **Room and board:** $3,300. **Books and supplies:** $650. **Other expenses:** $950.

FINANCIAL AID. 66% of freshmen, 60% of continuing students receive some form of aid. 88% of grants, 76% of loans, 96% of jobs based on need. 1,200 enrolled freshmen were judged to have need, all were offered aid. Academic, music/drama, art, athletic, state/district residency, minority scholarships available. **Aid applications:** No closing date; priority given to applications received by April 1; applicants notified on a rolling basis beginning on or about April 15; must reply within 2 weeks.

ADDRESS/TELEPHONE. Maribeth Lynes/Linda Stafstrom, Co-Directors of Admissions, University of Arkansas, 200 Silas Hunt Hall, Fayetteville, AR 72701. (501) 575-5346. (800) 575-5346. Fax: (501) 575-7575.

University of Arkansas at Little Rock
Little Rock, Arkansas CB code: 6368

4-year public university, coed. Founded in 1927. **Accreditation:** Regional. **Undergraduate enrollment:** 2,722 men, 3,247 women full time; 1,884 men, 2,716 women part time. **Graduate enrollment:** 331 men, 496 women full time; 333 men, 690 women part time. **Faculty:** 786 total (482 full time), 370 with doctorates or other terminal degrees. **Location:** Urban campus in small city; in downtown Little Rock. **Calendar:** Semester, limited summer session. **Microcomputers:** 420 located in libraries, classrooms, computer centers. **Special facilities:** Planetarium, observatory, art gallery.

DEGREES OFFERED. AA, AS, AAS, BA, BS, MA, MS, MBA, MEd, MSW, PhD, EdD, MD, JD. 140 associate degrees awarded in 1992. 9% in engineering technologies, 57% health sciences, 26% multi/interdisciplinary studies, 6% parks/recreation, protective services, public affairs. 762 bachelor's degrees awarded. 25% in business and management, 90% communications, 6% teacher education, 5% letters/literature, 7% multi/interdisciplinary studies, 8% psychology, 15% social sciences. Graduate degrees offered in 29 major fields of study.

UNDERGRADUATE MAJORS. Associate: Architectural technologies, computer programming, construction, education of the deaf and hearing impaired, electronic technology, interpreter for the deaf, law enforcement and corrections technologies, liberal/general studies, manufacturing technology, mechanical design technology, nursing. **Bachelor's:** Accounting, advertising, biology, business administration and management, business and management, business data processing and related programs, business economics, chemistry, communications, computer and information sciences, computer technology, construction, criminal justice studies, dramatic arts, education of the deaf and hearing impaired, electronic technology, elementary education, English, environmental science, finance, fine arts, French, health education, health professions, health sciences, history, information sciences and systems, international studies, journalism, liberal/general studies, manufacturing technology, marketing management, mathematics, mechanical design technology, music, music performance, office supervision and management, philosophy, physics, political science and government, psychology, radio/television broadcasting, secretarial and related programs, sociology, Spanish, speech pathology/audiology, survey and mapping technology, technical and business writing, trade and industrial supervision and management.

ACADEMIC PROGRAMS. 2-year transfer program, accelerated program, double major, dual enrollment of high school students, education specialist degree, honors program, independent study, internships, student-designed major, study abroad, teacher preparation, telecourses, visiting/exchange student program, weekend college; combined bachelor's/graduate program in business administration. **Remedial services:** Learning center, reduced course load, remedial instruction, special counselor, tutoring. **ROTC:** Army. **Placement/credit:** AP, CLEP Subject, IB, institutional tests; 30 credit hours maximum for bachelor's degree.

ACADEMIC REQUIREMENTS. Freshmen must earn minimum GPA of 2.0 to continue in good standing. Students must declare major by end of second year. **Graduation requirements:** 64 hours for associate (30 in major), 124 hours for bachelor's (30 in major). Most students required to take courses in arts/fine arts, English, history, mathematics, biological/physical sciences, social sciences.

FRESHMAN ADMISSIONS. Selection criteria: Open admissions. Unconditional admission based on minimum ACT score of 21 enhanced or combined verbal/mathematics SAT score of 800, high school 2.5 GPA or above, and completion of college preparatory curriculum. **High school preparation:** 15 units required. **Test requirements:** SAT or ACT (ACT preferred); score report by August 1.

1992 FRESHMAN CLASS PROFILE. 793 men applied, 653 accepted, 607 enrolled; 1,013 women applied, 807 accepted, 732 enrolled. **Academic background:** Mid 50% of enrolled freshmen had ACT composite between 13-21. 99% submitted ACT scores. **Characteristics:** 93% from in state, 83% commute, 26% have minority backgrounds, 3% are foreign students, 1% join fraternities/sororities. Average age is 23.

FALL-TERM APPLICATIONS. $15 fee. Closing date August 1; applicants notified on a rolling basis. Interview recommended for academically weak applicants. Deferred and early admission available.

STUDENT LIFE. Housing: Dormitories (coed). **Activities:** Student government, magazine, radio, student newspaper, television, choral groups, concert band, dance, drama, jazz band, music ensembles, musical theater, opera, pep band, fraternities, sororities, Baptist Student Union, University Republicans, Methodist Student Club, Muslim Students Association, Young Democrats, Association for Minority Students Education Needs & Development (AMEND), Advocates for People with Disabilities.

ATHLETICS. NAIA, NCAA. **Intercollegiate:** Baseball M, basketball M, cross-country, golf, soccer, swimming, tennis, track and field W, volleyball W, water polo M. **Intramural:** Badminton, basketball, bowling, football, golf, softball, swimming, tennis, volleyball.

STUDENT SERVICES. Aptitude testing, career counseling, employment service for undergraduates, freshman orientation, health services, on-campus day care, personal counseling, placement service for graduates, veterans counselor, services/facilities for handicapped.

ANNUAL EXPENSES. Tuition and fees: $2,075, $4,921 additional for out-of-state students. **Books and supplies:** $500. **Other expenses:** $800.

FINANCIAL AID. 60% of freshmen, 40% of continuing students receive some form of aid. Grants, loans, jobs available. Academic, music/drama, art, athletic, leadership, minority scholarships available. **Aid applications:** No closing date; priority given to applications received by May 1; applicants notified on a rolling basis beginning on or about May 1; must reply within 15 days.

ADDRESS/TELEPHONE. Sue Pine, Director of Admissions, University of Arkansas at Little Rock, 2801 South University, Little Rock, AR 72204. (501) 569-3127.

University of Arkansas for Medical Sciences
Little Rock, Arkansas CB code: 0424

4-year public university and health science, nursing, pharmacy college, coed. Founded in 1876. **Accreditation:** Regional. **Undergraduate enrollment:** 120 men, 318 women full time; 27 men, 72 women part time. **Graduate enrollment:** 504 men, 473 women full time; 30 men, 190 women part time. **Faculty:** 987 total (824 full time). **Location:** Urban campus in small city; 1 mile from downtown. **Calendar:** Semester, limited summer session. **Microcomputers:** Located in libraries, computer centers. **Additional facts:** University has 5 colleges: medicine, nursing, pharmacy, health-related professions, and graduate.

DEGREES OFFERED. AS, BS, MS, PhD, MD, Pharm D. 30 associate degrees awarded in 1992. 100% in allied health. 161 bachelor's degrees awarded. 66% in health sciences, 34% allied health. Graduate degrees offered in 15 major fields of study.

UNDERGRADUATE MAJORS. Associate: Biomedical science, dental hygiene, emergency medical technologies, medical radiation dosimetry, respiratory therapy technology, surgical technology. **Bachelor's:** Clinical laboratory science, cytotechnology, dental hygiene, medical laboratory technologies, medical radiation dosimetry, nuclear medical technology, nursing.

ACADEMIC PROGRAMS. Independent study. **ROTC:** Army.

ACADEMIC REQUIREMENTS. Policy determining good academic standing varies with each program. **Graduation requirements:** 64 hours for associate, 162 hours for bachelor's.

FRESHMAN ADMISSIONS. Selection criteria: Criteria for admission vary with each college. **Additional information:** Most incoming students must have prior college credit.

1992 FRESHMAN CLASS PROFILE. 13 men, 11 women enrolled. **Characteristics:** 87% from in state, 75% commute. Average age is 21.

FALL-TERM APPLICATIONS. No fee. Must reply within 2 weeks. Application closing dates vary with program.

STUDENT LIFE. Housing: Dormitories (coed); apartment housing available. **Activities:** Student government, student newspaper, yearbook.

STUDENT SERVICES. Health services, on-campus day care.

ANNUAL EXPENSES. Tuition and fees: $1,812, $4,530 additional for out-of-state students. **Books and supplies:** $470. **Other expenses:** $1,600.

FINANCIAL AID. Grants, loans, jobs available. **Aid applications:** No closing date; applicants notified on a rolling basis beginning on or about May 1; must reply within 2 weeks.

ADDRESS/TELEPHONE. David Heron, Vice Chancellor of Admissions, University of Arkansas for Medical Sciences, 4301 West Markham, Little Rock, AR 72205-7199. (501) 686-5000. Fax: (501) 686-5905.

University of Arkansas at Monticello
Monticello, Arkansas CB code: 6007

4-year public university, coed. Founded in 1909. **Accreditation:** Regional. **Undergraduate enrollment:** 2,161 men and women full time; 287 men and women part time. **Graduate enrollment:** 72 men and women. **Faculty:** 126 total (106 full time), 58 with doctorates or other terminal degrees. **Location:** Rural campus in small town; 100 miles from Little Rock, 50 miles from Pine Bluff. **Calendar:** Semester, extensive summer session. **Microcomputers:** Located in classrooms, computer centers. **Special facilities:** Museum of natural history, extensive research forest, Pomery Planetarium, University Farm.

DEGREES OFFERED. AA, AS, BA, BS. 32 associate degrees awarded in 1992. 98% in health sciences. 213 bachelor's degrees awarded.

UNDERGRADUATE MAJORS. Associate: Data processing, nursing, secretarial and related programs. **Bachelor's:** Accounting, agricultural sciences, art education, biology, business administration and management, business and management, business education, chemistry, computer and information sciences, elementary education, English, English education, fine arts, forestry and related sciences, geology, history, marketing management, mathematics, mathematics education, music, music education, nursing, physical education, physical sciences, physics, political science and government, psychology, science education, secondary education, secretarial and related programs, social sciences, social studies education, speech, speech/communication/theater education, wildlife management.

ACADEMIC PROGRAMS. Double major, dual enrollment of high school students, internships, teacher preparation, cross-registration; liberal arts/career combination in forestry. **Remedial services:** Learning center, reduced course load, remedial instruction, special counselor, tutoring. **Placement/credit:** AP, CLEP General and Subject, institutional tests; 9 credit hours maximum for bachelor's degree.

ACADEMIC REQUIREMENTS. Freshmen must earn minimum GPA of 1.5 to continue in good standing. 54% of freshmen return for sophomore year. Students must declare major by end of first year. **Graduation requirements:** 64 hours for associate (30 in major), 124 hours for bachelor's (30 in major). Most students required to take courses in arts/fine arts, English, foreign languages, history, humanities, mathematics, biological/physical sciences, social sciences.

FRESHMAN ADMISSIONS. Selection criteria: Open admissions. **High school preparation:** 20 units required. Required units include English 3 and mathematics 2. **Test requirements:** ACT for placement and counseling only; score report by August 1.

1992 FRESHMAN CLASS PROFILE. 603 men and women enrolled. **Academic background:** Mid 50% of enrolled freshmen had ACT composite between 12-19. 99% submitted ACT scores. **Characteristics:** 91% from in state, 76% commute, 19% have minority backgrounds, 5% join fraternities/sororities. Average age is 21.

FALL-TERM APPLICATIONS. No fee. Closing date August 15; applicants notified on a rolling basis. Deferred and early admission available.

STUDENT LIFE. Housing: Dormitories (men, women); apartment housing available. **Activities:** Student government, yearbook, choral groups, concert band, jazz band, marching band, music ensembles, musical theater, pep band, fraternities, sororities.

ATHLETICS. NAIA. **Intercollegiate:** Baseball M, basketball, cross-country, football M, track and field. **Intramural:** Basketball, cross-country, racquetball, soccer, softball, table tennis, tennis, track and field, volleyball.

STUDENT SERVICES. Aptitude testing, career counseling, employment service for undergraduates, freshman orientation, health services, personal counseling, placement service for graduates, services/facilities for handicapped.

ANNUAL EXPENSES. Tuition and fees: $1,838, $4,608 additional for out-of-state students. **Room and board:** $2,200. **Books and supplies:** $450. **Other expenses:** $850.

FINANCIAL AID. 78% of freshmen, 66% of continuing students receive some form of aid. 67% of grants, 95% of loans, 49% of jobs based on need. Academic, music/drama, athletic, leadership scholarships available. **Aid applications:** No closing date; applicants notified on a rolling basis beginning on or about May 1; must reply within 2 weeks.

ADDRESS/TELEPHONE. Dr. H. Jack Lassiter, Vice Chancellor of University Relations and Student Affairs, University of Arkansas at Monticello, Monticello, AR 71655. (501) 460-1033.

University of Arkansas at Pine Bluff
Pine Bluff, Arkansas CB code: 6004

4-year public university, coed. Founded in 1873. **Accreditation:** Regional. **Undergraduate enrollment:** 1,118 men, 1,730 women full time; 362 men, 446 women part time. **Graduate enrollment:** 1 man, 2 women full time; 10 men, 40 women part time. **Faculty:** 205 total (179 full time), 98 with doctorates or other terminal degrees. **Location:** Urban campus in small city; 42 miles from Little Rock. **Calendar:** Semester, limited summer session. **Microcomputers:** 400 located in libraries, classrooms, computer centers. **Special facilities:** 220-acre farm.

DEGREES OFFERED. AA, AS, AAS, BA, BS, MEd. 321 bachelor's degrees awarded. 25% in business and management, 17% education, 5% health sciences, 5% home economics, 6% letters/literature, 15% parks/recreation, protective services, public affairs, 5% psychology, 6% social sciences. Graduate degrees offered in 6 major fields of study.

UNDERGRADUATE MAJORS. Associate: Criminal justice technology, industrial technology, law enforcement and corrections technologies. **Bachelor's:** Accounting, agricultural economics, agricultural education, agronomy, animal sciences, art education, automotive technology management, biology, business administration and management, business education, chemistry, child development/care/guidance, computer and information sciences, criminal justice studies, curriculum and instruction, dramatic arts, early childhood education, economics, elementary education, English, English education, fashion design, fishing and fisheries, gerontology, history, home economics education, hospitality and food service management, individual and family development, industrial arts education, industrial technology, journalism, liberal/general studies, mathematics, mathematics education, music, music education, nursing, parks and recreation management, physical education, physics, political science and government, psychology, regulatory science, science education, secondary education, social science education, social work, sociology, special education, speech, trade and industrial education.

ACADEMIC PROGRAMS. 2-year transfer program, cooperative education, double major, honors program, internships, teacher preparation. **Remedial services:** Learning center, reduced course load, remedial instruction, special counselor, tutoring. **ROTC:** Army. **Placement/credit:** CLEP General; 25 credit hours maximum for bachelor's degree.

ACADEMIC REQUIREMENTS. Freshmen must earn minimum GPA of 2.0 to continue in good standing. 74% of freshmen return for sophomore year. Students must declare major by end of second year. **Graduation requirements:** 60 hours for associate, 124 hours for bachelor's. Most students required to take courses in arts/fine arts, English, foreign languages, history, mathematics, biological/physical sciences.

FRESHMAN ADMISSIONS. Selection criteria: Open admissions. **High school preparation:** 15 units recommended. Recommended units include English 4, foreign language 1, mathematics 3, social science 3 and science 2. **Test requirements:** SAT or ACT (ACT preferred) for placement and counseling only; score report by August 20.

1992 FRESHMAN CLASS PROFILE. 344 men, 374 women enrolled. **Characteristics:** 82% from in state, 69% commute, 85% have minority backgrounds. Average age is 18.

FALL-TERM APPLICATIONS. No fee. No closing date; priority given to applications received by August 1; applicants notified on a rolling basis; must reply by registration. Deferred and early admission available.

STUDENT LIFE. Housing: Dormitories (men, women). **Activities:** Student government, student newspaper, television, yearbook, choral groups, concert band, drama, jazz band, marching band, fraternities, sororities, Baptist Student Union.

ATHLETICS. NAIA. **Intercollegiate:** Basketball, football M, track and field. **Intramural:** Baseball, basketball, cross-country M, football M, handball, racquetball, softball, swimming.

STUDENT SERVICES. Aptitude testing, career counseling, employment service for undergraduates, health services, personal counseling, placement service for graduates, services/facilities for handicapped.

ANNUAL EXPENSES. Tuition and fees: $1,838, $4,608 additional for out-of-state students. **Room and board:** $2,194. **Books and supplies:** $500. **Other expenses:** $800.

FINANCIAL AID. 88% of freshmen, 92% of continuing students receive some form of aid. Grants, loans, jobs available. **Aid applications:** No closing date; priority given to applications received by April 15; applicants notified on a rolling basis beginning on or about February 1; must reply within 2 weeks.

ADDRESS/TELEPHONE. Katherine King, Director of Admissions/Assistant Registrar, University of Arkansas at Pine Bluff, 1200 North University Drive, Pine Bluff, AR 71601. (501) 543-8485. (800) 264-8272. Fax: (501) 543-8001.

University of Central Arkansas
Conway, Arkansas CB code: 6012

Admissions: 86% of applicants accepted
Based on: ••• School record, test scores
• Activities, recommendations, special talents
Completion: 60% of freshmen end year in good standing
30% graduate

4-year public university, coed. Founded in 1907. **Accreditation:** Regional. **Undergraduate enrollment:** 2,982 men, 4,393 women full time; 117 men, 651 women part time. **Graduate enrollment:** 132 men, 252 women full time; 154 men, 473 women part time. **Faculty:** 523 total (360 full time), 290 with doctorates or other terminal degrees. **Location:** Suburban campus in large town; 30 miles from Little Rock. **Calendar:** Semester, extensive summer session. **Microcomputers:** 250 located in dormitories, libraries, computer centers. **Special facilities:** Observatory, greenhouse, student art gallery, honors center, visual arts center.

DEGREES OFFERED. AA, AAS, BA, BS, BFA, MA, MS, MBA, MFA. 34 associate degrees awarded in 1992. 20% in business/office and marketing/distribution, 80% allied health. 847 bachelor's degrees awarded. 21% in business and management, 31% teacher education, 9% health sciences, 9% allied health, 7% letters/literature, 8% social sciences. Graduate degrees offered in 49 major fields of study.

UNDERGRADUATE MAJORS. Associate: Child development/care/guidance, industrial arts education, marketing and distribution, physical therapy assistant, secretarial and related programs. **Bachelor's:** Accounting, administration of special education, applied mathematics, art education, biology, business administration and management, business and management, business and office, business economics, business education, chemistry, child development/care/guidance, clinical laboratory science, communications, computer and information sciences, computer programming, counseling psychology, data processing, dietetics, dramatic arts, early childhood education, economics, education, education administration, education of the emotionally handicapped, education of the gifted and talented, education of the mentally handicapped, education of the physically handicapped, educational statistics and research, educational supervision, educational testing, evaluation, and measurement, elementary education, English, English education, fashion merchandising, finance, fine arts, food science and nutrition, foreign languages education, French, geography, health education, history, home economics, home economics education, human resources development, industrial arts education, information sciences and systems, international business management, journalism, junior high education, manual arts therapy, marketing and distribution, marketing and distributive education, marketing management, mathematics, mathematics education, medical laboratory technologies, medical radiation dosimetry, medical records technology, military science (Army), music, music education, nuclear medical technology, nursing, occupational therapy, office supervision and management, operations research, personnel management, philosophy, physical education, physical sciences, physical therapy, physics, political science and government, predentistry, prelaw, premedicine, prepharmacy, preveterinary, psychology, public administration, radio/television broadcasting, radiograph medical technology, respiratory therapy, respiratory therapy technology, school psychology, science education, secondary education, secretarial and related programs, small business management and ownership, social psychology, social science education, social sciences, social studies education, sociology, Spanish, special education, specific learning disabilities, speech, speech correction, speech pathology/audiology, speech/communication/theater education, student counseling and personnel services, trade and industrial education.

ACADEMIC PROGRAMS. 2-year transfer program, accelerated program, cooperative education, double major, dual enrollment of high school students, education specialist degree, honors program, independent study, internships, study abroad, teacher preparation; liberal arts/career combination in health sciences. **Remedial services:** Learning center, preadmission summer program, remedial instruction, special counselor, tutoring. **ROTC:** Army. **Placement/credit:** AP, CLEP General and Subject, institutional tests; 30 credit hours maximum for bachelor's degree.

ACADEMIC REQUIREMENTS. Freshmen must earn minimum GPA of 2.0 to continue in good standing. 60% of freshmen return for sophomore year. Students must declare major by end of second year. **Graduation requirements:** 64 hours for associate, 124 hours for bachelor's. Most students required to take courses in arts/fine arts, English, history, humanities, mathematics, biological/physical sciences, social sciences. **Postgraduate studies:** 80% from 2-year programs enter 4-year programs. **Additional information:** 5-year professional programs in physical therapy and occupational therapy and 2-year physical therapy assistant program available.

FRESHMAN ADMISSIONS. Selection criteria: SAT or ACT scores, class rank, GPA, special talents considered. University seeks diverse student body. **Test requirements:** SAT or ACT; score report by August 15.

1992 FRESHMAN CLASS PROFILE. 1,344 men applied, 1,135 accepted, 812 enrolled; 1,787 women applied, 1,548 accepted, 1,219 enrolled. **Academic background:** Mid 50% of enrolled freshmen had ACT composite between 14-21. 97% submitted ACT scores. **Characteristics:** 99% from in state, 60% live in college housing, 16% have minority backgrounds, 5% are foreign students, 20% join fraternities/sororities. Average age is 18.

FALL-TERM APPLICATIONS. No fee. Closing date August 19; applicants notified on a rolling basis beginning on or about May 1. Deferred and early admission available.

STUDENT LIFE. Housing: Dormitories (men, women); fraternity, handicapped housing available. 12 month International Hall open through all breaks. **Activities:** Student government, magazine, radio, student newspaper, television, yearbook, choral groups, concert band, dance, drama, jazz band, marching band, music ensembles, musical theater, symphony orchestra, fraternities, sororities, Baptist Student Union, Methodist Student Union, Newman Club, Fellowship of Christian Athletes, Campus Crusade for Christ, Young Democrats, College Republicans, International Student Association, Students for Propagation of Black Culture.

ATHLETICS. NCAA. **Intercollegiate:** Baseball M, basketball, cross-country, football M, golf M, rifle, tennis, track and field M, volleyball W. **Intramural:** Archery, badminton, basketball, cross-country, golf, handball, racquetball, rifle, softball, swimming, table tennis, tennis, track and field, volleyball.

STUDENT SERVICES. Aptitude testing, career counseling, employment service for undergraduates, freshman orientation, health services, on-campus day care, personal counseling, placement service for graduates, veterans counselor, freshmen peer advisers, services/facilities for handicapped.

ANNUAL EXPENSES. Tuition and fees (1992-93): $1,546, $1,420 additional for out-of-state students. **Room and board:** $2,420. **Books and supplies:** $500. **Other expenses:** $1,000.

FINANCIAL AID. 58% of freshmen, 60% of continuing students receive some form of aid. 65% of grants, 93% of loans, 61% of jobs based on need. 1,080 enrolled freshmen were judged to have need, all were offered aid. Music/drama, art, athletic, state/district residency, alumni affiliation scholarships available. **Aid applications:** Closing date August 1; priority given to applications received by April 15; applicants notified on a rolling basis beginning on or about May 1; must reply within 2 weeks. **Additional information:** All tuition and fees due at time of enrollment. Room and board may be paid monthly.

ADDRESS/TELEPHONE. Joe F. Darling, Director of Admissions, University of Central Arkansas, 201 Donaghey Street, Conway, AR 72035-0001. (501) 450-3128. Fax: (501) 450-5168.

University of the Ozarks
Clarksville, Arkansas CB code: 6111

4-year private university, coed, affiliated with Presbyterian Church (USA). Founded in 1834. **Accreditation:** Regional. **Undergraduate enrollment:** 252 men, 313 women full time; 30 men, 61 women part time. **Graduate enrollment:** 2 men, 4 women full time; 2 men, 4 women part time. **Faculty:** 53 total (40 full time), 17 with doctorates or other terminal degrees. **Location:** Rural campus in small town; 100 miles from Little Rock, 65 miles from Fort Smith. **Calendar:** 4-4-1-1. **Microcomputers:** 9 located on campus. **Special facilities:** Jones Learning Center, Walton Fine Arts Center.

DEGREES OFFERED. AA, BA, BS, MEd. 133 bachelor's degrees awarded. Graduate degrees offered in 1 major field of study.

UNDERGRADUATE MAJORS. Associate: Institutional management, secretarial and related programs. **Bachelor's:** Accounting, art education, biological and physical sciences, biology, business administration and management, business and management, business education, chemistry, communications, dramatic arts, education, elementary education, English, English education, entrepreneurship, environmental science, fine arts, history, journalism, junior high education, liberal/general studies, marine biology, marketing and distribution, marketing management, mathematics, mathematics education, medical laboratory technologies, music, music business management, music education, philosophy, physical education, physical sciences, political science and government, predentistry, preengineering, prelaw, premedicine, prepharmacy, preveterinary, psychology, public administration, radiograph medical technology, religion, religious education, respiratory therapy technology, science education, secondary education, social sciences, social studies education, sociology, special education.

ACADEMIC PROGRAMS. 2-year transfer program, cooperative education, double major, dual enrollment of high school students, independent study, internships, student-designed major, teacher preparation; liberal arts/career combination in engineering. **Remedial services:** Learning center, remedial instruction, special counselor, tutoring. **Placement/credit:** AP, CLEP General and Subject, institutional tests; 30 credit hours maximum for bachelor's degree.

ACADEMIC REQUIREMENTS. Freshmen must earn minimum GPA of 2.0 to continue in good standing. 67% of freshmen return for sophomore year. Students must declare major by end of second year. **Graduation requirements:** 60 hours for associate, 128 hours for bachelor's (42 in major). Most students required to take courses in arts/fine arts, computer science, English, history, humanities, mathematics, philosophy/religion, biological/physical sciences, social sciences. **Postgraduate studies:** 3% enter law school, 1% enter medical school, 13% enter MBA programs, 2% enter other graduate study. **Additional information:** Candidates for Bachelor's degree required to complete some course work in foreign language.

FRESHMAN ADMISSIONS. Selection criteria: School achievement record and test scores. **High school preparation:** 15 units required. Required units include English 3, mathematics 2, social science 1 and science 1. **Test requirements:** SAT or ACT; score report by August 15.

1992 FRESHMAN CLASS PROFILE. 100 men, 110 women enrolled. 45% had high school GPA of 3.0 or higher, 52% between 2.0 and 2.99. 5% were in top tenth and 31% were in top quarter of graduating class. **Academic background:** Mid 50% of enrolled freshmen had ACT composite between 17-24. 85% submitted ACT scores. **Characteristics:** 60% from in state, 58% live in college housing, 21% are foreign students.

FALL-TERM APPLICATIONS. No fee. No closing date; applicants notified on a rolling basis. Audition required for music applicants. Interview recommended. Interview required of those with marginal grades. Deferred and early admission available.

STUDENT LIFE. Housing: Dormitories (men, women); apartment housing available. **Activities:** Student government, magazine, radio, student newspaper, television, yearbook, choral groups, concert band, dance, drama, jazz band, music ensembles, musical theater, Ozarks Area Mission, other religious, ethnic, and social service organizations.

ATHLETICS. NAIA. **Intercollegiate:** Basketball, cross-country, golf M, soccer M, tennis, track and field M. **Intramural:** Badminton, basketball, football M, racquetball, softball, tennis, track and field, volleyball.

STUDENT SERVICES. Aptitude testing, career counseling, employment service for undergraduates, freshman orientation, health services, personal counseling, placement service for graduates, veterans counselor, services/facilities for handicapped.

ANNUAL EXPENSES. Tuition and fees: $4,920. **Room and board:** $2,850. **Books and supplies:** $600. **Other expenses:** $2,700.

FINANCIAL AID. 65% of freshmen, 63% of continuing students receive some form of aid. 72% of grants, 97% of loans, 40% of jobs based on need. 66 enrolled freshmen were judged to have need, all were offered aid. Academic, music/drama, athletic scholarships available. **Aid applications:** No closing date; priority given to applications received by May 1; applicants notified on a rolling basis beginning on or about June 1; must reply within 3 weeks.

ADDRESS/TELEPHONE. Dr. Tim McElroy, Director of Admissions, University of the Ozarks, 415 College Avenue, Clarksville, AR 72830. (501) 754-3839 ext. 227. Fax: (501) 754-3839 ext. 355.

Westark Community College
Fort Smith, Arkansas — CB code: 6220

2-year public community college, coed. Founded in 1928. **Accreditation:** Regional. **Undergraduate enrollment:** 1,004 men, 1,368 women full time; 1,240 men, 1,860 women part time. **Faculty:** 234 total (114 full time), 18 with doctorates or other terminal degrees. **Location:** Suburban campus in small city; 150 miles from Little Rock. **Calendar:** Semester, extensive summer session. Saturday and extensive evening/early morning classes. **Microcomputers:** 140 located in libraries, classrooms, computer centers, campus-wide network.

DEGREES OFFERED. AA, AAS. 574 associate degrees awarded in 1992. 16% in business and management, 5% business/office and marketing/distribution, 5% computer sciences, 11% teacher education, 16% allied health, 9% multi/interdisciplinary studies, 29% trade and industry.

UNDERGRADUATE MAJORS. Accounting, aerospace/aeronautical/astronautical engineering, agribusiness, agricultural economics, agricultural engineering, agronomy, animal sciences, architectural engineering, architecture, art education, automotive mechanics, automotive technology, bioengineering and biomedical engineering, biology, business administration and management, business and office, business data processing and related programs, business education, chemical engineering, chemical manufacturing technology, chemistry, civil engineering, computer and information sciences, computer engineering, computer servicing technology, criminal justice studies, drafting, drafting and design technology, education, electrical and electronics equipment repair, electronic technology, elementary education, emergency medical technologies, engineering, engineering science, English, English education, fashion merchandising, finance, fine arts, food sciences, foreign languages education, French, geography, history, home economics, home economics education, hotel/motel and restaurant management, industrial engineering, journalism, legal assistant/paralegal, liberal/general studies, machine tool operation/machine shop, manufacturing technology, marketing management, mathematics, mathematics education, mechanical design technology, mechanical engineering, medical laboratory technologies, music, music education, nursing, physical education, physics, political science and government, predentistry, prelaw, premedicine, prepharmacy, preveterinary, psychology, quality control technology, radiograph medical technology, respiratory therapy, science education, science technologies, secondary education, secretarial and related programs, social work, sociology, Spanish, speech, speech/communication/theater education, surgical technology, teacher aide, welding technology, word processing.

ACADEMIC PROGRAMS. 2-year transfer program, computer delivered (on-line) credit-bearing course offerings, cooperative education, dual enrollment of high school students, honors program, internships, telecourses, cross-registration. **Remedial services:** Learning center, reduced course load, remedial instruction, tutoring. **Placement/credit:** AP, CLEP General and Subject, institutional tests; 30 credit hours maximum for associate degree.

ACADEMIC REQUIREMENTS. Freshmen must earn minimum GPA of 1.5 for up to 15 hours of study and 1.75 for 16-29 hours. 51% of freshmen return for sophomore year. Students must declare major by end of first year. **Graduation requirements:** 60 hours for associate (26 in major). Most students required to take courses in computer science, English, history, humanities, mathematics, biological/physical sciences, social sciences.

FRESHMAN ADMISSIONS. Selection criteria: Open admissions. Computer science also recommended. **Test requirements:** SAT or ACT for placement and counseling only; score report by August 1. ACT/ASSET required for placement.

1992 FRESHMAN CLASS PROFILE. 238 men, 253 women enrolled. **Characteristics:** 90% from in state, 100% commute, 5% have minority backgrounds, 1% are foreign students. Average age is 25.

FALL-TERM APPLICATIONS. No fee. No closing date; applicants notified on a rolling basis. Interview required for nursing applicants. Deferred and early admission available. Early applications advised for admission and financial aid. Scholarship deadline March 15, ACT scores recommended.

STUDENT LIFE. Activities: Student government, student newspaper, yearbook, choral groups, concert band, jazz band, music ensembles, pep band, symphony orchestra.

ATHLETICS. NJCAA. **Intercollegiate:** Baseball M, basketball. **Intramural:** Basketball, bowling, soccer M, softball, table tennis, tennis, volleyball.

STUDENT SERVICES. Aptitude testing, career counseling, employment service for undergraduates, freshman orientation, on-campus day care, personal counseling, placement service for graduates, veterans counselor, services/facilities for handicapped.

ANNUAL EXPENSES. Tuition and fees (1992-93): $778, $240 additional for out-of-district students, $1,032 additional for out-of-state students. **Books and supplies:** $400. **Other expenses:** $450.

FINANCIAL AID. 85% of grants, 51% of loans, 54% of jobs based on need. Academic scholarships available. **Aid applications:** No closing date; priority given to applications received by June 1; applicants notified on a rolling basis beginning on or about July 1; must reply within 2 weeks.

ADDRESS/TELEPHONE. Robert C. Cullins, Jr, Director of Admissions and Records, Westark Community College, PO Box 3649, Fort Smith, AR 72913-3649. (501) 785-7015. Fax: (501) 785-7015.

Williams Baptist College
Walnut Ridge, Arkansas — CB code: 6658

Admissions:	81% of applicants accepted
Based on:	•• Recommendations, test scores
	• Interview, religious affiliation/commitment, school record, special talents
Completion:	85% of freshmen end year in good standing

4-year private liberal arts college, coed, affiliated with Southern Baptist Convention. Founded in 1941. **Accreditation:** Regional. **Undergraduate enrollment:** 201 men, 309 women full time; 26 men, 76 women part time. **Faculty:** 27 total (18 full time), 6 with doctorates or other terminal degrees. **Location:** Rural campus in small town; 30 miles from Jonesboro. **Calendar:** Semester, limited summer session. **Microcomputers:** 15 located in computer centers.

DEGREES OFFERED. AA, AS, BA, BS. 18 associate degrees awarded in 1992. 28 bachelor's degrees awarded. 18% in business and management, 64% teacher education, 18% philosophy, religion, theology.

UNDERGRADUATE MAJORS. Associate: Bible studies, business and management, Christian ministries, liberal/general studies, music, secretarial and related programs. **Bachelor's:** Art education, business and management, Christian ministries, early childhood education, education, elementary education, music education, psychology, religious education, religious music, theological studies.

ACADEMIC PROGRAMS. 2-year transfer program, dual enrollment of high school students, independent study, internships. **Remedial services:** Learning center, remedial instruction, tutoring. **Placement/credit:** CLEP General, institutional tests; 30 credit hours maximum for bachelor's degree.

ACADEMIC REQUIREMENTS. Freshmen must earn minimum GPA of 1.5 to continue in good standing. 65% of freshmen return for sophomore year. Students must declare major by end of second year. **Graduation requirements:** 60 hours for associate, 128 hours for bachelor's. Most students required to take courses in arts/fine arts, English, history, humanities, mathematics, philosophy/religion, biological/physical sciences, social sciences. **Postgraduate studies:** 86% from 2-year programs enter 4-year programs.

FRESHMAN ADMISSIONS. Selection criteria: ACT scores most important. Recommendations required. **High school preparation:** 16 units required. Required units include English 4, mathematics 4, social science 4 and science 4. **Test requirements:** SAT or ACT (ACT preferred); score report by August 1.

1992 FRESHMAN CLASS PROFILE. 307 men and women applied, 250 accepted; 76 men enrolled, 137 women enrolled. 50% had high school GPA of 3.0 or higher, 45% between 2.0 and 2.99. 12% were in top tenth and 34% were in top quarter of graduating class. **Academic background:** Mid 50% of enrolled freshmen had ACT composite between 17-21. 92% submitted ACT scores. **Characteristics:** 83% from in state, 58% commute, 3% have minority backgrounds, 3% are foreign students. Average age is 18.

FALL-TERM APPLICATIONS. $15 fee. No closing date; priority given to applications received by May 1; applicants notified on a rolling basis; must reply by May 1 or within 3 weeks if notified thereafter. Interview recommended. Audition recommended for music, art applicants. CRDA. Deferred and early admission available.

STUDENT LIFE. Housing: Dormitories (men, women); apartment housing available. All students under 21 and full-time required to live in college housing, unless students is commuter. **Activities:** Student government, student newspaper, yearbook, choral groups, drama, music ensembles, Ministerial Association, Baptist Student Union, Black Renaissance Organization, Circle-K, Young Democrats, Young Republicans, international students organization, social clubs.

ATHLETICS. NAIA. **Intercollegiate:** Baseball M, basketball, volleyball W. **Intramural:** Archery, baseball, basketball, softball, table tennis, tennis.

STUDENT SERVICES. Aptitude testing, career counseling, freshman orientation, on-campus day care, personal counseling, placement service for graduates, veterans counselor, services/facilities for handicapped.

ANNUAL EXPENSES. Tuition and fees (1992-93): $3,262. **Room and board:** $2,332. **Books and supplies:** $500. **Other expenses:** $600.

FINANCIAL AID. 82% of freshmen, 97% of continuing students receive some form of aid. Grants, loans, jobs available. **Aid applications:** No closing date; priority given to applications received by June 1; applicants notified on a rolling basis beginning on or about July 1; must reply within 2 weeks.

ADDRESS/TELEPHONE. Jeff Main, Director of Admissions, Williams Baptist College, PO Box 3665, Walnut Ridge, AR 72476. (501) 886-6741.

California

Academy of Art College
San Francisco, California CB code: 1981

4-year proprietary art college, coed. Founded in 1929. **Undergraduate enrollment:** 1,932 men and women. **Graduate enrollment:** 270 men and women. **Faculty:** 182 total (40 full time), 57 with doctorates or other terminal degrees. **Location:** Urban campus in very large city. **Calendar:** Semester. **Microcomputers:** 60 located in computer centers. **Special facilities:** 3 galleries, photography dark rooms, computer graphics, desk-top publishing, in-house advertising agency, interior design resource room, foundry. **Additional facts:** Equal emphasis on both fine and applied arts. Accredited by the National Association of Schools of Art and Design.

DEGREES OFFERED. BFA, MFA. 270 bachelor's degrees awarded in 1992. 100% in visual and performing arts. Graduate degrees offered in 15 major fields of study.

UNDERGRADUATE MAJORS. Advertising, art education, drawing, fashion design, fine arts, graphic design, illustration design, industrial design, interior design, painting, photographic technology, photography, printmaking, sculpture.

ACADEMIC PROGRAMS. Double major, dual enrollment of high school students, honors program, independent study, student-designed major, teacher preparation, cross-registration. **Remedial services:** Preadmission summer program, reduced course load, remedial instruction, tutoring. **Placement/credit:** AP, institutional tests; 64 credit hours maximum for bachelor's degree.

ACADEMIC REQUIREMENTS. Freshmen must earn minimum GPA of 2.0 to continue in good standing. 50% of freshmen return for sophomore year. Students must declare major by end of second year. **Graduation requirements:** 129 hours for bachelor's (60 in major). Most students required to take courses in arts/fine arts, computer science, English, history, humanities, mathematics, philosophy/religion, biological/physical sciences, social sciences. **Postgraduate studies:** 5% enter other graduate study. **Additional information:** English as a Second Language(ESL) classes for International Students (English for Art purposes).

FRESHMAN ADMISSIONS. Selection criteria: Open admissions. **Additional information:** Continuing education program offered.

1992 FRESHMAN CLASS PROFILE. 541 men and women enrolled. 5% had high school GPA of 3.0 or higher, 95% between 2.0 and 2.99. **Characteristics:** 39% from in state, 7% have minority backgrounds, 10% are foreign students. Average age is 23.

FALL-TERM APPLICATIONS. $25 fee. No closing date; priority given to applications received by February 1; applicants notified on a rolling basis. Interview recommended. Portfolio recommended for bachelor of fine arts applicants. Essay recommended. Deferred and early admission available. EDP-F.

STUDENT LIFE. Housing: Dormitories (coed). **Activities:** Student government, student newspaper, Chinese Society, Circle of Nations, International Student Organization.

STUDENT SERVICES. Career counseling, employment service for undergraduates, freshman orientation, health services, personal counseling, placement service for graduates, veterans counselor, services/facilities for handicapped.

ANNUAL EXPENSES. Tuition and fees: $9,060. **Room and board:** $4,750 room only. **Books and supplies:** $700. **Other expenses:** $4,905.

FINANCIAL AID. 88% of grants, 86% of loans, all jobs based on need. Academic, art scholarships available. **Aid applications:** No closing date; applicants notified on a rolling basis beginning on or about June 1. **Additional information:** Grant-in-aid programs, yearly scholarships, presidential scholarships, and numerous summer grant programs available.

ADDRESS/TELEPHONE. Ann Marie Stillion, Director of Admissions, Academy of Art College, 79 New Montgomeny, San Francisco, CA 94115. (415) 274-4200. (800) 544-ARTS.

Allan Hancock College
Santa Maria, California CB code: 4002

2-year public community college, coed. Founded in 1920. **Accreditation:** Regional. **Undergraduate enrollment:** 1,952 men and women full time; 6,269 men and women part time. **Faculty:** 357 total (140 full time), 28 with doctorates or other terminal degrees. **Location:** Suburban campus in small city; 175 miles from Los Angeles. **Calendar:** Semester, extensive summer session. Saturday and extensive evening/early morning classes. **Microcomputers:** Located in libraries, classrooms, computer centers. **Special facilities:** Satellite dish.

DEGREES OFFERED. AA, AS. 478 associate degrees awarded in 1992. 15% in business and management, 55% multi/interdisciplinary studies, 6% parks/recreation, protective services, public affairs, 12% visual and performing arts.

UNDERGRADUATE MAJORS. Accounting, architecture, biology, business administration and management, business and management, business and office, computer and information sciences, computer technology, dance, dental assistant, diesel engine mechanics, education, electrical and electronics equipment repair, engineering, engineering and engineering-related technologies, fashion design, film arts, fine arts, fire control and safety technology, graphic and printing production, graphic design, information sciences and systems, international studies, law enforcement and corrections technologies, liberal/general studies, machine tool operation/machine shop, management science, medical assistant, mental health/human services, music, nursing, practical nursing, quality control technology, real estate, recreation and community services technologies, secretarial and related programs, social sciences, word processing.

ACADEMIC PROGRAMS. 2-year transfer program, accelerated program, cooperative education, double major, dual enrollment of high school students, independent study, internships, study abroad, telecourses, weekend college, cross-registration. **Remedial services:** Learning center, preadmission summer program, reduced course load, remedial instruction, special counselor, tutoring. **Placement/credit:** AP, CLEP General and Subject, institutional tests; 48 credit hours maximum for associate degree.

ACADEMIC REQUIREMENTS. Freshmen must earn minimum GPA of 2.0 to continue in good standing. Must complete minimum of 50% of all semester hours attempted. 60% of freshmen return for sophomore year. Students must declare major on enrollment. **Graduation requirements:** 60 hours for associate (25 in major). Most students required to take courses in arts/fine arts, English, history, humanities, mathematics, biological/physical sciences, social sciences.

FRESHMAN ADMISSIONS. Selection criteria: Open admissions. Selective admissions to allied health and drama programs. **Test requirements:** School and College Ability Test required for placement.

1992 FRESHMAN CLASS PROFILE. Characteristics: 99% from in state, 100% commute, 1% are foreign students. Average age is 19.

FALL-TERM APPLICATIONS. No fee. Closing date August 24; applicants notified on a rolling basis. Interview required for allied health applicants. Audition required for dance, drama applicants.

STUDENT LIFE. Activities: Student government, film, student newspaper, choral groups, concert band, dance, drama, jazz band, music ensembles, symphony orchestra, cheerleaders, religious, cultural, and special interest groups.

ATHLETICS. Intercollegiate: Baseball M, basketball, cross-country, football M, golf, soccer M, tennis, track and field, volleyball W.

STUDENT SERVICES. Aptitude testing, career counseling, employment service for undergraduates, health services, on-campus day care, personal counseling, placement service for graduates, special adviser for adult students, veterans counselor, services/facilities for handicapped.

ANNUAL EXPENSES. Tuition and fees (projected): $300, $3,120 additional for out-of-state students. **Books and supplies:** $612. **Other expenses:** $950.

FINANCIAL AID. 17% of freshmen, 17% of continuing students receive some form of aid. 63% of grants, 99% of loans, 17% of jobs based on need. Academic, music/drama, art, athletic, state/district residency, leadership, alumni affiliation scholarships available. **Aid applications:** Closing date May 1; applicants notified on a rolling basis; must reply immediately.

ADDRESS/TELEPHONE. Norma Razo, Registrar, Allan Hancock College, 800 South College Drive, Santa Maria, CA 93454. (805) 922-6966 ext. 3272. Fax: (805) 928-7905.

American Academy of Dramatic Arts: West
Pasadena, California CB code: 7024

2-year private school of dramatic arts, coed. Founded in 1974. **Accreditation:** Regional. **Undergraduate enrollment:** 132 men, 117 women full time. **Faculty:** 25 total (15 full time), 6 with doctorates or other terminal degrees. **Location:** Suburban campus in small city; 17 miles from Los Angeles. **Calendar:** 28-week, full-time program. **Special facilities:** 2 theaters. **Additional facts:** Only conservatory offering professional actor training in both of America's major centers of theatrical activity; America's first school for actor training

DEGREES OFFERED. AAS. 10 associate degrees awarded in 1992. 100% in visual and performing arts.

UNDERGRADUATE MAJORS. Dramatic arts.

ACADEMIC PROGRAMS. 2-year transfer program, cross-registration. **Placement/credit:** CLEP General.

ACADEMIC REQUIREMENTS. Freshmen must earn minimum GPA of 2.0 to continue in good standing. Freshmen invited back for second year after review based on academic record, attitude, and ability as demonstrated in classes and in one-act plays rehearsed and performed during 6-week examination-play period following second semester. 40% of freshmen return for sophomore year. **Graduation requirements:** 56 hours for associate. Most students required to take courses in English, biological/physical sciences, social sciences. **Additional information:** Select group of students invited to return for additional year of study and performance after graduation in repertory situation.

FRESHMAN ADMISSIONS. Selection criteria: Student attitude, seriousness of intent, and potential as professional actor as indicated by written recommendations, interview, and most important, audition. All applicants should have full command of English language.

1992 FRESHMAN CLASS PROFILE. 71 men and women enrolled. **Characteristics:** 45% from in state, 100% commute, 14% have minority backgrounds, 8% are foreign students. Average age is 19.

FALL-TERM APPLICATIONS. $35 fee. Closing date August 10; priority given to applications received by April 1; applicants notified on a rolling basis beginning on or about April 1; must reply within 4 weeks. Interview required. Audition required. Essay recommended. Deferred admission available. SAT or ACT recommended for admissions. Score report by April 1.

STUDENT LIFE. Activities: Student government.

STUDENT SERVICES. Personal counseling.

ANNUAL EXPENSES. Tuition and fees: $7,975. **Books and supplies:** $460. **Other expenses:** $1,204.

FINANCIAL AID. 63% of freshmen, 56% of continuing students receive some form of aid. All grants, 69% of loans, 47% of jobs based on need. **Aid applications:** No closing date; priority given to applications received by July 1; applicants notified on a rolling basis beginning on or about June 1; must reply within 3 weeks.

ADDRESS/TELEPHONE. James Wickline, Director of Admissions, American Academy of Dramatic Arts: West, 2550 Paloma Street, Pasadena, CA 91107. (818) 798-0777.

American Armenian International College
LaVerne, California CB code: 4987

Admissions:	88% of applicants accepted
Based on:	••• School record
	•• Test scores
	• Activities, essay, interview, recommendations
Completion:	90% of freshmen end year in good standing
	10% graduate, 31% of these enter graduate study

4-year private college of arts and sciences, coed. Founded in 1976. **Accreditation:** Regional candidate. **Undergraduate enrollment:** 32 men, 16 women full time; 52 men, 30 women part time. **Faculty:** 14 total (3 full time), 6 with doctorates or other terminal degrees. **Location:** Suburban campus in large town; 25 miles from Los Angeles. **Calendar:** 4-1-4, limited summer session. **Microcomputers:** 15 located in libraries, classrooms, computer centers. **Special facilities:** Unique Armenian book and periodical collection. **Additional facts:** Affiliated with University of LaVerne. Mission is to provide higher education in Armenian environment.

DEGREES OFFERED. BA, BS. 30 bachelor's degrees awarded in 1992. 7% in area and ethnic studies, 7% business and management, 73% engineering, 6% health sciences, 7% social sciences.

UNDERGRADUATE MAJORS. Armenian, business administration and management, business and management, computer engineering, computer technology, electrical/electronics/communications engineering, electronic technology, laser electro-optic technology, Middle Eastern studies, optics, religion.

ACADEMIC PROGRAMS. Double major, honors program, independent study, internships, study abroad, teacher preparation, cross-registration; liberal arts/career combination in engineering; combined bachelor's/graduate program in law. **Remedial services:** Learning center, tutoring. **Placement/credit:** AP, CLEP General and Subject, institutional tests; 8 credit hours maximum for bachelor's degree.

ACADEMIC REQUIREMENTS. Freshmen must earn minimum GPA of 2.0 to continue in good standing. 65% of freshmen return for sophomore year. Students must declare major by end of second year. **Graduation requirements:** 128 hours for bachelor's (32 in major). Most students required to take courses in arts/fine arts, computer science, English, foreign languages, history, humanities, mathematics, philosophy/religion, biological/physical sciences, social sciences. **Postgraduate studies:** 1% enter law school, 2% enter medical school, 8% enter MBA programs, 20% enter other graduate study. **Additional information:** Only college on West Coast to offer BS degree in optical engineering and BA degree in Armenian Studies.

FRESHMAN ADMISSIONS. Selection criteria: High school grades, test scores, interviews, school and community activities considered. **Test requirements:** SAT or ACT; score report by September 1.

1992 FRESHMAN CLASS PROFILE. 65 men applied, 55 accepted, 17 enrolled; 15 women applied, 15 accepted, 17 enrolled. 30% had high school GPA of 3.0 or higher, 68% between 2.0 and 2.99. **Characteristics:** 35% from in state, 60% live in college housing, 10% have minority backgrounds, 18% are foreign students. Average age is 18.

FALL-TERM APPLICATIONS. $25 fee. Closing date August 15; priority given to applications received by June 30; applicants notified on a rolling basis beginning on or about February 1; must reply by July 30. Interview recommended. Essay recommended. Deferred admission available.

STUDENT LIFE. Activities: Student government, film, magazine, radio, student newspaper, television, yearbook, choral groups, concert band, dance, drama, jazz band, music ensembles, musical theater, fraternities, sororities.

ATHLETICS. Intercollegiate: Badminton, baseball M, basketball, cross-country, football M, golf, soccer, softball W, tennis, track and field, volleyball, wrestling M. **Intramural:** Basketball M.

STUDENT SERVICES. Aptitude testing, career counseling, employment service for undergraduates, freshman orientation, health services, on-campus day care, personal counseling, placement service for graduates, services/facilities for handicapped.

ANNUAL EXPENSES. Tuition and fees (1992-93): $11,935. **Room and board:** $5,520. **Books and supplies:** $400.

FINANCIAL AID. 72% of freshmen, 63% of continuing students receive some form of aid. All grants, 76% of loans, all jobs based on need. 20 enrolled freshmen were judged to have need, 14 were offered aid. Academic, leadership scholarships available. **Aid applications:** Closing date May 31; priority given to applications received by March 2; applicants notified on or about July 30; must reply by August 1. **Additional information:** Students of Armenian descent have special financial grants available to them.

ADDRESS/TELEPHONE. John Khanjian, Academic Dean, American Armenian International College, 1950 Third Street, LaVerne, CA 91750. (714) 593-3511 ext. 4802. Fax: (714) 593-0879.

American College for the Applied Arts: Los Angeles
Los Angeles, California CB code: 3906

4-year proprietary art, business college, coed. Founded in 1982. **Accreditation:** Regional. **Undergraduate enrollment:** 127 men, 294 women full time; 16 men, 70 women part time. **Faculty:** 59 total (4 full time), 7 with doctorates or other terminal degrees. **Location:** Urban campus in very large city. **Calendar:** Quarter, extensive summer session. **Microcomputers:** Located in computer centers. **Special facilities:** Art gallery, photography laboratory, fashion photography archives.

DEGREES OFFERED. AA, BA. 13 associate degrees awarded in 1992. 117 bachelor's degrees awarded.

UNDERGRADUATE MAJORS. Associate: Business and management, clothing and textiles management/production/services, fashion design, graphic design, interior design. **Bachelor's:** Business and management, clothing and textiles management/production/services, fashion design, graphic design, hotel/motel and restaurant management, interior design.

ACADEMIC PROGRAMS. 2-year transfer program, double major, internships, study abroad. **Remedial services:** English as a second language.

ACADEMIC REQUIREMENTS. No policy requiring minimum GPA; records of students having academic difficulty are reviewed individually. 75% of freshmen return for sophomore year. Students must declare major on application. **Graduation requirements:** 120 hours for associate (85 in major), 190 hours for bachelor's (125 in major). Most students required to take courses in English, humanities, mathematics, social sciences.

FRESHMAN ADMISSIONS. Selection criteria: Open admissions.

1992 FRESHMAN CLASS PROFILE. 46 men, 94 women enrolled. **Characteristics:** 85% from in state, 85% commute, 18% have minority backgrounds, 44% are foreign students. Average age is 19.

FALL-TERM APPLICATIONS. $35 fee. No closing date; applicants notified on a rolling basis; must reply within 30 days. Essay required. Interview recommended. Deferred and early admission available.

STUDENT LIFE. Housing: Dormitories (coed); apartment housing available. **Activities:** Student government, student newspaper, Delta Epsilon Chi, Student Chapter of ASID, Dressers Club, Comma Club (commercial art).

STUDENT SERVICES. Career counseling, employment service for undergraduates, freshman orientation, personal counseling, placement service for graduates.

ANNUAL EXPENSES. Tuition and fees: $9,090. **Room and board:** $3,825 room only. **Books and supplies:** $750. **Other expenses:** $4,042.

FINANCIAL AID. 22% of freshmen, 49% of continuing students receive some form of aid. All grants, 47% of loans, all jobs based on need. **Aid applications:** No closing date; priority given to applications received by March 2; applicants notified on a rolling basis beginning on or about July 1; must reply within 15 days.

ADDRESS/TELEPHONE. Kevin L. Martin, Director of Admissions, American College for the Applied Arts: Los Angeles, 1651 Westward Boulevard, Los Angeles, CA 90024-5603. (310) 470-2000 ext. 32. (800) 333-2652. Fax: (310) 477-8640.

American River College
Sacramento, California CB code: 4004

2-year public community college, coed. Founded in 1955. **Accreditation:** Regional. **Undergraduate enrollment:** 20,910 men and women. **Location:** Suburban campus in large city; 10 miles from downtown. **Calendar:** Semester.

FRESHMAN ADMISSIONS. Selection criteria: Open admissions.

ANNUAL EXPENSES. Tuition and fees (projected): $900, $3,420 additional for out-of-state students. **Books and supplies:** $500. **Other expenses:** $880.

ADDRESS/TELEPHONE. Robert Allegre, Associate Dean of Admissions and Administration, American River College, 4700 College Oak Drive, Sacramento, CA 95841. (916) 484-8261.

Antelope Valley College
Lancaster, California CB code: 4005

2-year public community college, coed. Founded in 1929. **Accreditation:** Regional. **Undergraduate enrollment:** 10,751 men and women. **Faculty:** 371 total (101 full time), 15 with doctorates or other terminal degrees. **Location:** Suburban campus in small city; 50 miles from Los Angeles. **Calendar:** Semester, limited summer session. Saturday and extensive evening/early morning classes. **Microcomputers:** 90 located in classrooms, computer centers.

DEGREES OFFERED. AA, AS. 636 associate degrees awarded in 1992. 19% in business and management, 5% computer sciences, 5% engineering, 8% health sciences, 41% multi/interdisciplinary studies, 5% physical sciences, 15% trade and industry.

UNDERGRADUATE MAJORS. Agricultural sciences, air conditioning/heating/refrigeration mechanics, air conditioning/heating/refrigeration technology, automotive mechanics, automotive technology, biological and physical sciences, business administration and management, business and management, business and office, business computer/console/peripheral equipment operation, business data entry equipment operation, business data processing and related programs, business data programming, chemical manufacturing technology, child development/care/guidance, computer and information sciences, computer graphics, data processing, drafting, engineering, engineering and engineering-related technologies, food production/management/services, forestry and related sciences, graphic arts technology, home economics, law enforcement and corrections technologies, liberal/general studies, marketing and distribution, mathematics, medical assistant, music, nursing, office supervision and management, photographic technology, photography, practical nursing, precision metal work, protective services, public affairs, radiograph medical technology, real estate, recreation and community services technologies, renewable natural resources, science technologies, secretarial and related programs, teacher aide, trade and industrial supervision and management.

ACADEMIC PROGRAMS. 2-year transfer program, cooperative education, dual enrollment of high school students, honors program, independent study, study abroad, weekend college. **Remedial services:** Learning center, reduced course load, remedial instruction, special counselor, tutoring. **ROTC:** Air Force. **Placement/credit:** AP, CLEP General and Subject; 30 credit hours maximum for associate degree.

ACADEMIC REQUIREMENTS. Freshmen must earn minimum GPA of 2.0 to continue in good standing. 55% of freshmen return for sophomore year. Students must declare major on enrollment. **Graduation requirements:** 60 hours for associate (18 in major). Most students required to take courses in arts/fine arts, English, humanities, mathematics, biological/physical sciences, social sciences.

FRESHMAN ADMISSIONS. Selection criteria: Open admissions.

1992 FRESHMAN CLASS PROFILE. 2,122 men and women enrolled. **Characteristics:** 98% from in state, 100% commute, 31% have minority backgrounds, 1% are foreign students. Average age is 22.

FALL-TERM APPLICATIONS. No fee. No closing date; applicants notified on a rolling basis.

STUDENT LIFE. Activities: Student government, student newspaper, choral groups, concert band, dance, drama, jazz band, music ensembles, musical theater, pep band, symphony orchestra.

ATHLETICS. Intercollegiate: Baseball M, basketball, cross-country, football M, golf, softball W, tennis, track and field, volleyball W. **Intramural:** Badminton, basketball, volleyball W.

STUDENT SERVICES. Aptitude testing, career counseling, employment service for undergraduates, freshman orientation, health services, personal counseling, special adviser for adult students, veterans counselor, services/facilities for handicapped.

ANNUAL EXPENSES. Tuition and fees (1992-93): $120, $3,120 additional for out-of-state students. **Books and supplies:** $384. **Other expenses:** $1,340.

FINANCIAL AID. 20% of freshmen, 25% of continuing students receive some form of aid. 99% of grants, all loans, 29% of jobs based on need. 850 enrolled freshmen were judged to have need, all were offered aid. Academic, music/drama, art, leadership, minority scholarships available. **Aid applications:** No closing date; priority given to applications received by March 2; applicants notified on a rolling basis beginning on or about July 15; must reply within 2 weeks.

ADDRESS/TELEPHONE. James F. McDonald, Jr, Dean of Admissions and Records, Antelope Valley College, 3041 West Avenue K, Lancaster, CA 93536-5426. (805) 943-9241 ext. 229. Fax: (805) 943-5573.

Antioch Southern California at Los Angeles
Marina Del Rey, California CB code: 1862

2-year upper-division private liberal arts college, coed. Founded in 1972. **Accreditation:** Regional. **Undergraduate enrollment:** 17 men, 54 women full time; 26 men, 129 women part time. **Graduate enrollment:** 41 men, 144 women full time; 57 men, 142 women part time. **Faculty:** 105 total (13 full time), 60 with doctorates or other terminal degrees. **Location:** Urban campus in large town; in suburb of Los Angeles. **Calendar:** Quarter, extensive summer session. Saturday and extensive evening/early morning classes. **Microcomputers:** 8 located in computer centers.

DEGREES OFFERED. BA, MA. 68 bachelor's degrees awarded in 1992. 100% in multi/interdisciplinary studies. Graduate degrees offered in 3 major fields of study.

UNDERGRADUATE MAJORS. Liberal/general studies.

ACADEMIC PROGRAMS. Double major, independent study, student-designed major, study abroad, cross-registration. **Remedial services:** Learning center, remedial instruction. **Placement/credit:** AP, CLEP General and Subject.

ACADEMIC REQUIREMENTS. Students must declare major on enrollment. **Graduation requirements:** 180 hours for bachelor's (40 in major). Most students required to take courses in arts/fine arts, English, humanities, mathematics, biological/physical sciences, social sciences.

STUDENT LIFE. Activities: Student government.

STUDENT SERVICES. Career counseling, personal counseling, special adviser for adult students, veterans counselor, services/facilities for handicapped.

ANNUAL EXPENSES. Tuition and fees: $8,100. **Books and supplies:** $300.

FINANCIAL AID. 58% of continuing students receive some form of aid. All grants, 78% of loans, all jobs based on need. **Aid applications:** No closing date; applicants notified on a rolling basis; must reply within 4 weeks.

ADDRESS/TELEPHONE. Craig Taylor, Dean of Advancement, Antioch Southern California at Los Angeles, 13274 Fiji Way, Marina Del Rey, CA 90292-7090. (310) 578-1080. (800) 726-8624. Fax: (310) 822-4824.

Antioch Southern California at Santa Barbara
Santa Barbara, California CB code: 3071

2-year upper-division private liberal arts college, coed. Founded in 1852. **Accreditation:** Regional. **Undergraduate enrollment:** 10 men, 30 women full time; 15 men, 39 women part time. **Graduate enrollment:** 10 men, 66 women full time; 11 men, 68 women part time. **Location:** Urban campus in small city; in downtown area. **Calendar:** Quarter.

ANNUAL EXPENSES. Tuition and fees (1992-93): $7,200. **Books and supplies:** $350.

ADDRESS/TELEPHONE. Carmela Chaney, Admissions Coordinator, Antioch Southern California at Santa Barbara, 801 Garden Street, Santa Barbara, CA 93101. (805) 962-8179.

Armstrong University
Berkeley, California CB code: 4008

Admissions:	99% of applicants accepted
Based on:	•• School record
	• Activities, essay, interview, recommendations, test scores
Completion:	80% of freshmen end year in good standing
	40% enter graduate study

4-year proprietary business college, coed. Founded in 1918. **Undergraduate enrollment:** 34 men, 26 women full time. **Graduate enrollment:** 58 men, 32 women full time. **Faculty:** 20 total (11 full time), 4 with doctorates or other terminal degrees. **Location:** Urban campus in small city; 15 miles from San Francisco, adjacent to Oakland. **Calendar:** Quarter, extensive summer session. **Microcomputers:** 16 located in libraries, computer centers.

DEGREES OFFERED. AA, B, MBA. 3 associate degrees awarded in 1992. 7 bachelor's degrees awarded. 100% in business and management. Graduate degrees offered in 7 major fields of study.

UNDERGRADUATE MAJORS. Accounting, business administration and management, business and management, business and office, computer and information sciences, finance, international business management, liberal/general studies, management science, marketing and distribution, marketing management. accounting, business administration and management, business and management, computer and information sciences, finance, international business management, management science, marketing management.

ACADEMIC PROGRAMS. 2-year transfer program, accelerated program, double major, independent study, internships, student-designed major.

Remedial services: Reduced course load, tutoring. **Placement/credit:** CLEP General and Subject, institutional tests.

ACADEMIC REQUIREMENTS. Freshmen must earn minimum GPA of 2.0 to continue in good standing. 70% of freshmen return for sophomore year. Students must declare major on application. **Graduation requirements:** 93 hours for associate (21 in major), 186 hours for bachelor's (21 in major). Most students required to take courses in English, history, mathematics, biological/physical sciences, social sciences. **Postgraduate studies:** 70% from 2-year programs enter 4-year programs. 40% enter MBA programs. **Additional information:** Extensive English language program for foreign students and people in business.

FRESHMAN ADMISSIONS. Selection criteria: 2.0 high school GPA. College-preparatory program recommended.

1992 FRESHMAN CLASS PROFILE. 54 men applied, 53 accepted, 11 enrolled; 31 women applied, 31 accepted, 9 enrolled. 40% had high school GPA of 3.0 or higher, 60% between 2.0 and 2.99. **Characteristics:** 100% commute, 90% are foreign students. Average age is 19.

FALL-TERM APPLICATIONS. $35 fee. Closing date September 1; applicants notified on a rolling basis. Interview recommended. Essay recommended. Deferred admission available.

STUDENT LIFE. Activities: Student government, student newspaper.

ATHLETICS. Intramural: Bowling, soccer M, table tennis.

STUDENT SERVICES. Career counseling, employment service for undergraduates, freshman orientation, personal counseling, placement service for graduates, veterans counselor, services/facilities for handicapped.

ANNUAL EXPENSES. Tuition and fees: $7,470. **Books and supplies:** $450. **Other expenses:** $1,200.

ADDRESS/TELEPHONE. Rowena Ricafrente, Director of Admissions, Armstrong University, 2222 Harold Way, Berkeley, CA 94704. (510) 848-2500. Fax: (510) 848-9438.

Art Center College of Design

Pasadena, California — CB code: 4009

4-year private art college, coed. Founded in 1930. **Accreditation:** Regional. **Undergraduate enrollment:** 816 men, 459 women full time. **Graduate enrollment:** 27 men, 27 women full time. **Faculty:** 310 total (56 full time). **Location:** Suburban campus in small city; 15 miles from Los Angeles. **Calendar:** Trimester, extensive summer session. Extensive evening/early morning classes. **Microcomputers:** 81 located in libraries, computer centers. **Special facilities:** Two art galleries.

DEGREES OFFERED. BS, BFA, MS, MFA. 341 bachelor's degrees awarded in 1992. 5% in architecture and environmental design, 95% visual and performing arts. Graduate degrees offered in 9 major fields of study.

UNDERGRADUATE MAJORS. Advertising, cinematography/film, environmental design, fine arts, graphic design, illustration design, industrial design, painting, photography.

ACADEMIC PROGRAMS. Study abroad, cross-registration, concurrent program with Westlawn School of Yacht Design. **Placement/credit:** AP; 42 credit hours maximum for bachelor's degree.

ACADEMIC REQUIREMENTS. Freshmen must earn minimum GPA of 2.5 to continue in good standing. 75% of freshmen return for sophomore year. Students must declare major on application. **Graduation requirements:** 155 hours for bachelor's (115 in major). Most students required to take courses in English, humanities, biological/physical sciences, social sciences. **Additional information:** 42 academic units through transfer credit or simultaneous enrollment required for degree.

FRESHMAN ADMISSIONS. Selection criteria: Portfolio and high school academic record most important. Evidence of past creative work essential. Art classes and college-preparatory program recommended. **Test requirements:** SAT or ACT; score report by August 1.

1992 FRESHMAN CLASS PROFILE. 223 men and women enrolled. **Characteristics:** 100% commute, 24% have minority backgrounds. Average age is 24.

FALL-TERM APPLICATIONS. $35 fee, may be waived for applicants with need. No closing date; applicants notified on a rolling basis; must reply by May 1 or within 4 weeks if notified thereafter. Portfolio required. Interview recommended for local applicants. Essay recommended. Application 4 to 6 months before fall term recommended.

STUDENT LIFE. Activities: Student government.

STUDENT SERVICES. Career counseling, employment service for undergraduates, freshman orientation, personal counseling, placement service for graduates, services/facilities for handicapped.

ANNUAL EXPENSES. Tuition and fees: $13,430. **Books and supplies:** $3,312. **Other expenses:** $1,696.

FINANCIAL AID. 61% of freshmen, 60% of continuing students receive some form of aid. All grants, 58% of loans, all jobs based on need. 187 enrolled freshmen were judged to have need, all were offered aid. **Aid applications:** No closing date; priority given to applications received by March 1; applicants notified on a rolling basis beginning on or about May 15; must reply within 10 days.

ADDRESS/TELEPHONE. Gregory L. Price, Director of Admissions, Art Center College of Design, 1700 Lida Street, Pasadena, CA 91103. (818) 584-5035. Fax: (818) 405-9104.

Art Institute of Southern California

Laguna Beach, California — CB code: 7248

4-year private art college, coed. **Accreditation:** Regional candidate. **Undergraduate enrollment:** 65 men, 57 women full time; 7 men, 20 women part time. **Faculty:** 23 total (8 full time), 17 with doctorates or other terminal degrees. **Location:** Suburban campus in small town; 50 miles from Los Angeles, 75 miles from San Diego. **Microcomputers:** 15 located in classrooms, computer centers. **Special facilities:** 2 art galleries, library collection of over 25,000 slides. **Additional facts:** Accredited by National Association of Schools of Art and Design.

DEGREES OFFERED. BFA. 19 bachelor's degrees awarded in 1992. 100% in visual and performing arts.

UNDERGRADUATE MAJORS. Drawing, graphic design, illustration design, painting.

ACADEMIC PROGRAMS. Independent study, internships. **Placement/credit:** AP.

ACADEMIC REQUIREMENTS. Freshmen must earn minimum GPA of 2.0 to continue in good standing. 90% of freshmen return for sophomore year. Students must declare major by end of second year. **Graduation requirements:** 123 hours for bachelor's (45 in major). Most students required to take courses in arts/fine arts, computer science, English, history, humanities, mathematics, philosophy/religion, biological/physical sciences, social sciences.

FRESHMAN ADMISSIONS. Selection criteria: Open admissions.

1992 FRESHMAN CLASS PROFILE. 12 men, 10 women enrolled. 75% had high school GPA of 3.0 or higher, 25% between 2.0 and 2.99. **Characteristics:** 100% commute, 9% have minority backgrounds.

FALL-TERM APPLICATIONS. $35 fee. No closing date; applicants notified on a rolling basis. Essay required. Interview recommended. Portfolio recommended. Deferred admission available.

STUDENT LIFE. Activities: Student government, student newspaper.

STUDENT SERVICES. Career counseling, freshman orientation.

ANNUAL EXPENSES. Tuition and fees: $8,850. Tuition includes books. **Books and supplies:** $1,185. **Other expenses:** $2,263.

FINANCIAL AID. 47% of freshmen, 75% of continuing students receive some form of aid. 98% of grants, 57% of loans, all jobs based on need. 13 enrolled freshmen were judged to have need, all were offered aid. Academic, art scholarships available. **Aid applications:** No closing date; priority given to applications received by April 20; applicants notified on a rolling basis beginning on or about July 1; must reply within 2 weeks. **Additional information:** Need and Merit Based Scholarship deadline April 20.

ADDRESS/TELEPHONE. John Walker, Director of Admission, Art Institute of Southern California, 2222 Laguna Canyon Road, Laguna Beach, CA 92651. (714) 497-3309. (800) 255-0762. Fax: (714) 497-4399.

Azusa Pacific University

Azusa, California — CB code: 4596

Admissions:	59% of applicants accepted
Based on:	••• Essay, recommendations, school record, test scores
	•• Religious affiliation/commitment
	• Activities, interview, special talents
Completion:	85% of freshmen end year in good standing
	28% graduate

4-year private university, coed, interdenominational. Founded in 1899. **Accreditation:** Regional. **Undergraduate enrollment:** 771 men, 1,087 women full time; 34 men, 83 women part time. **Graduate enrollment:** 182 men, 176 women full time; 498 men, 820 women part time. **Faculty:** 319 total (143 full time), 103 with doctorates or other terminal degrees. **Location:** Suburban campus in large town; 30 miles from Los Angeles. **Calendar:** 4-4-1, limited summer session. **Microcomputers:** 100 located in computer centers. **Special facilities:** Special collections library with 15,000 volumes on history and culture of American west, western movement, California. **Additional facts:** Living-learning community stressing spiritual development.

DEGREES OFFERED. BA, BS, MA, MBA, MEd, EdD, M.Div. 266 bachelor's degrees awarded in 1992. 12% in business and management, 11% communications, 6% teacher education, 8% health sciences, 5% letters/literature, 16% multi/interdisciplinary studies, 9% philosophy, religion, theology, 9% psychology, 8% social sciences, 6% visual and performing arts. Graduate degrees offered in 19 major fields of study.

UNDERGRADUATE MAJORS. Accounting, art education, biochemistry, biology, business administration and management, business and management, business education, chemistry, communications, computer and information sciences, education, elementary education, English, English education, fine arts, foreign languages education, history, information sciences and systems, international studies, journalism, junior high education, liberal/general studies, management information systems, marketing and distribution, marketing management, mathematics, mathematics education, music, music education, music performance, music theory and composition, nursing, nursing education, philosophy, physical education, physics, political science and government, predentistry, prelaw, premedicine, psychology, religion, religious education, religious music, secondary education, social science education, social sciences, social studies education, social work, sociology, theological studies.

ACADEMIC PROGRAMS. Accelerated program, cooperative education, double major, honors program, independent study, internships, study abroad, teacher preparation, visiting/exchange student program, Washington semester, cross-registration; liberal arts/career combination in engineering. **Remedial services:** Learning center, reduced course load, remedial instruction, special counselor, tutoring. **ROTC:** Army. **Placement/credit:** AP, CLEP General and Subject, institutional tests; 15 credit hours maximum for bachelor's degree.

ACADEMIC REQUIREMENTS. Freshmen must earn minimum GPA of 2.0 to continue in good standing. 84% of freshmen return for sophomore year. Students must declare major by end of second year. **Graduation requirements:** 126 hours for bachelor's. Most students required to take courses in arts/fine arts, English, foreign languages, history, mathematics, philosophy/religion, biological/physical sciences, social sciences.

FRESHMAN ADMISSIONS. Selection criteria: GPA, SAT or ACT scores, references, application/essay considered. **High school preparation:** 16 units recommended. Recommended units include biological science 2, English 4, foreign language 2, mathematics 2, physical science 1, social science 4 and science 1. One fine arts. **Test requirements:** SAT or ACT (SAT preferred); score report by September 1.

1992 FRESHMAN CLASS PROFILE. 378 men applied, 215 accepted, 207 enrolled; 539 women applied, 325 accepted, 268 enrolled. **Academic background:** Mid 50% of enrolled freshmen had SAT-V between 370-460, SAT-M between 380-530; ACT composite between 15-23. 71% submitted SAT scores, 13% submitted ACT scores. **Characteristics:** 82% from in state, 98% live in college housing, 19% have minority backgrounds, 10% are foreign students. Average age is 18.

FALL-TERM APPLICATIONS. $40 fee, may be waived for applicants with need. No closing date; priority given to applications received by March 1; applicants notified on a rolling basis beginning on or about November 1; must reply by May 1 or within 2 weeks if notified thereafter. Audition required for music applicants. Essay required. Interview recommended for borderline applicants. Deferred and early admission available.

STUDENT LIFE. Housing: Dormitories (men, women); apartment, cooperative housing available. **Activities:** Student government, student newspaper, yearbook, choral groups, concert band, drama, jazz band, music ensembles, musical theater, pep band, symphony orchestra, International Students Association, Minority Student Association. **Additional information:** Religious observance required.

ATHLETICS. NAIA. **Intercollegiate:** Baseball M, basketball, cross-country, football M, soccer, softball W, tennis M, track and field, volleyball W. **Intramural:** Basketball, football M, skiing, volleyball.

STUDENT SERVICES. Aptitude testing, career counseling, employment service for undergraduates, freshman orientation, health services, personal counseling, placement service for graduates, veterans counselor, services/facilities for handicapped.

ANNUAL EXPENSES. Tuition and fees (1992-93): $10,292. **Room and board:** $3,700. **Books and supplies:** $600. **Other expenses:** $1,250.

FINANCIAL AID. 80% of freshmen, 85% of continuing students receive some form of aid. 44% of grants, 87% of loans based on need. Academic, music/drama, athletic, leadership scholarships available. **Aid applications:** No closing date; priority given to applications received by March 1; applicants notified on a rolling basis beginning on or about May 15; must reply by June 15 or within 2 weeks if notified thereafter.

ADDRESS/TELEPHONE. Mrs. Karen Sauve, Dean of Enrollment Management, Azusa Pacific University, P.O. Box 7000, 901 East Alosta Avenue, Azusa, CA 91702-7000. (818) 812-3016. (800) TALK-APU. Fax: (818) 969-7180.

Bakersfield College
Bakersfield, California

CB code: 4015

2-year public community college, coed. Founded in 1913. **Accreditation:** Regional. **Undergraduate enrollment:** 1,407 men, 1,791 women full time; 3,990 men, 5,079 women part time. **Faculty:** 448 total (248 full time), 26 with doctorates or other terminal degrees. **Location:** Suburban campus in small city; 114 miles from Los Angeles. **Calendar:** Semester, limited summer session. **Microcomputers:** Located in computer centers.

DEGREES OFFERED. AA, AS. 450 associate degrees awarded in 1992. 5% in agriculture, 15% business and management, 5% computer sciences, 13% allied health, 10% home economics, 5% letters/literature, 5% life sciences, 5% mathematics, 7% multi/interdisciplinary studies, 5% physical sciences, 7% social sciences, 5% trade and industry.

UNDERGRADUATE MAJORS. Accounting, aeronautical technology, agricultural business and management, agricultural mechanics, animal sciences, anthropology, architecture, automotive technology, bacteriology, biology, business administration and management, business and office, business data processing and related programs, business data programming, carpentry, chemistry, criminology, data processing, dental assistant, dietetic aide/assistant, drafting, economics, electrical installation, emergency medical technologies, engineering and engineering-related technologies, English, finance, fire control and safety technology, food management, food production/management/services, forestry and related sciences, geography, geology, German, graphic arts technology, history, home economics, horticulture, industrial technology, institutional/home management/supporting programs, interior design, journalism, law enforcement and corrections technologies, liberal/general studies, masonry/tile setting, mathematics, microbiology, music, nursing, ornamental horticulture, philosophy, photographic technology, photography, physics, plumbing/pipefitting/steamfitting, political science and government, practical nursing, precision metal work, predentistry, prelaw, premedicine, prepharmacy, preveterinary, protective services, psychology, radio/television broadcasting, radiograph medical technology, real estate, recreation and community services technologies, science technologies, secretarial and related programs, sociology, Spanish, woodworking, word processing.

ACADEMIC PROGRAMS. 2-year transfer program, double major, dual enrollment of high school students. **Remedial services:** Learning center, preadmission summer program, reduced course load, remedial instruction, special counselor, tutoring. **Placement/credit:** Institutional tests; 12 credit hours maximum for associate degree.

ACADEMIC REQUIREMENTS. Freshmen must earn minimum GPA of 2.0 to continue in good standing. Students must declare major on enrollment. **Graduation requirements:** 60 hours for associate (18 in major). Most students required to take courses in English, humanities, mathematics, social sciences.

FRESHMAN ADMISSIONS. Selection criteria: Open admissions.

1992 FRESHMAN CLASS PROFILE. 3,275 men and women enrolled.

FALL-TERM APPLICATIONS. No fee. Closing date August 15; applicants notified on a rolling basis.

STUDENT LIFE. Housing: Dormitories (men, women). **Activities:** Student government, magazine, radio, student newspaper, choral groups, drama, jazz band, marching band.

ATHLETICS. Intercollegiate: Baseball M, basketball, cross-country, diving, football M, golf M, softball W, swimming, tennis, track and field, volleyball W, wrestling M.

STUDENT SERVICES. Career counseling, employment service for undergraduates, health services, on-campus day care, services/facilities for handicapped.

ANNUAL EXPENSES. Tuition and fees (1992-93): $145, $3,120 additional for out-of-state students. **Room and board:** $3,636. **Books and supplies:** $500. **Other expenses:** $900.

FINANCIAL AID. 19% of freshmen, 21% of continuing students receive some form of aid. 96% of grants, 88% of loans, 32% of jobs based on need. 1,513 enrolled freshmen were judged to have need, 952 were offered aid. Academic, state/district residency, leadership scholarships available. **Aid applications:** No closing date; priority given to applications received by May 1; applicants notified on a rolling basis beginning on or about June 1; must reply within 2 weeks.

ADDRESS/TELEPHONE. Archie Sherman, Director of Admission, Bakersfield College, 1801 Panorama Drive, Bakersfield, CA 93305. (805) 395-4301.

Barstow College
Barstow, California

CB code: 4020

2-year public community college, coed. Founded in 1959. **Accreditation:** Regional. **Undergraduate enrollment:** 3,700 men and women. **Faculty:** 72 total (32 full time), 3 with doctorates or other terminal degrees. **Location:** Rural campus in large town; 70 miles from San Bernardino. **Calendar:** Semester, limited summer session. **Microcomputers:** 40 located in libraries, classrooms, computer centers.

DEGREES OFFERED. AA, AS. 100 associate degrees awarded in 1992.

UNDERGRADUATE MAJORS. Accounting, allied health, automotive mechanics, automotive technology, biological and physical sciences, biology, business administration and management, business and management, business and office, business computer/console/peripheral equipment operation, business data entry equipment operation, business data processing and related programs, business data programming, business economics, business systems analysis, child development/care/guidance, communications, computer and information sciences, computer programming, creative writing, curriculum and instruction, diesel engine mechanics, dramatic arts, education, education administration, elementary education, engineering and engineering-related technologies, English, fine arts, fire control and safety technology, health sciences, humanities, humanities and social sciences, law enforcement and corrections technologies, liberal/general studies, marketing and distribution, mathematics, music, nursing, office supervision and management, physical sciences, practical nursing, psychology, real estate, science technologies, secretarial and related programs, social sciences, student counseling and personnel services, teacher aide, welding technology, word processing.

ACADEMIC PROGRAMS. 2-year transfer program, accelerated program, cooperative education, dual enrollment of high school students, honors program, independent study, internships, telecourses, weekend college. **Remedial services:** Learning center, preadmission summer program, reduced course load, remedial instruction, special counselor, tutoring. **Placement/credit:** CLEP General and Subject, institutional tests; 30 credit hours maximum for associate degree.

ACADEMIC REQUIREMENTS. Freshmen must earn minimum GPA of 2.0 to continue in good standing. 60% of freshmen return for sophomore year. Students must declare major on application. **Graduation requirements:** 60 hours for associate (30 in major). Most students required to take courses in arts/fine arts, English, history, humanities, mathematics, biological/physical sciences, social sciences.

FRESHMAN ADMISSIONS. Selection criteria: Open admissions.

1992 FRESHMAN CLASS PROFILE. 750 men and women enrolled. **Characteristics:** 97% from in state, 100% commute, 34% have minority backgrounds, 1% are foreign students. Average age is 24.

FALL-TERM APPLICATIONS. No fee. Closing date August 1; priority given to applications received by July 1; applicants notified on a rolling basis. Interview required for full-time applicants. Deferred and early admission available.

STUDENT LIFE. Activities: Student government, student newspaper, choral groups, concert band, dance, drama, jazz band, music ensembles, musical theater, Circle-K, Christian club, Alpha Gamma Sigma.

ATHLETICS. NJCAA. **Intercollegiate:** Baseball M, basketball M, cross-country, golf, soccer, tennis, volleyball W. **Intramural:** Badminton, baseball, basketball, bowling, soccer, softball, swimming, tennis, volleyball.

STUDENT SERVICES. Aptitude testing, career counseling, employment service for undergraduates, freshman orientation, personal counseling, placement service for graduates, special adviser for adult students, veterans counselor, services/facilities for handicapped.

ANNUAL EXPENSES. Tuition and fees (1992-93): $120, $3,120 additional for out-of-state students. **Books and supplies:** $600. **Other expenses:** $1,250.

FINANCIAL AID. 80% of freshmen, 20% of continuing students receive some form of aid. 99% of grants, all loans, 85% of jobs based on need. 208 enrolled freshmen were judged to have need, all were offered aid. Academic, state/district residency, leadership, alumni affiliation, minority scholarships available. **Aid applications:** Closing date May 1; applicants notified on a rolling basis.

ADDRESS/TELEPHONE. Sharon Henthorne, Registrar, Barstow College, 2700 Barstow Road, Barstow, CA 92311-9984. (619) 252-2411. Fax: (619) 252-1875.

Bethany College
Scotts Valley, California — CB code: 4021

4-year private Bible college, coed, affiliated with Assemblies of God. Founded in 1919. **Accreditation:** Regional. **Undergraduate enrollment:** 200 men, 256 women full time; 53 men, 82 women part time. **Faculty:** 57 total (35 full time), 19 with doctorates or other terminal degrees. **Location:** Suburban campus in small town; 25 miles from San Jose. **Calendar:** 4-4-1, limited summer session. Saturday classes. **Microcomputers:** 15 located in libraries, classrooms, computer centers.

DEGREES OFFERED. AA, BA. 4 associate degrees awarded in 1992. 100% in business and management. 83 bachelor's degrees awarded. 7% in communications, 8% teacher education, 7% letters/literature, 52% philosophy, religion, theology, 10% psychology, 9% social sciences, 7% visual and performing arts.

UNDERGRADUATE MAJORS. Bachelor's: Addiction studies/counseling, Bible studies, business and management, business and office, communications, elementary education, English, English education, intercultural relations, liberal/general studies, ministry, missionary studies, music, music education, music performance, music theory and composition, psychology, religious education, social science education, social sciences, theological studies.

ACADEMIC PROGRAMS. Double major, external degree, independent study, internships, teacher preparation. **Remedial services:** Learning center, reduced course load, remedial instruction. **Placement/credit:** AP, CLEP General and Subject; 18 credit hours maximum for bachelor's degree.

ACADEMIC REQUIREMENTS. Freshmen must earn minimum GPA of 2.0 to continue in good standing. 85% of freshmen return for sophomore year. Students must declare major by end of second year. **Graduation requirements:** 66 hours for associate (24 in major), 124 hours for bachelor's (36 in major). Most students required to take courses in arts/fine arts, computer science, English, history, humanities, mathematics, philosophy/religion, biological/physical sciences, social sciences.

FRESHMAN ADMISSIONS. Selection criteria: Recommendations and religious affiliation/commitment very important. Test scores important. **Test requirements:** SAT or ACT; score report by August 1.

1992 FRESHMAN CLASS PROFILE. 91 men, 115 women enrolled. **Academic background:** Mid 50% of enrolled freshmen had ACT composite between 16-23. 75% submitted ACT scores. **Characteristics:** 75% from in state, 75% live in college housing, 11% have minority backgrounds, 2% are foreign students. Average age is 18.

FALL-TERM APPLICATIONS. $35 fee. Closing date July 1; applicants notified on a rolling basis; must reply by August 1. Audition recommended for music applicants. Essay recommended. Deferred admission available.

STUDENT LIFE. Housing: Dormitories (men, women). **Activities:** Student government, student newspaper, yearbook, choral groups, concert band, drama, music ensembles, musical theater, international students association. **Additional information:** Religious observance required.

ATHLETICS. NAIA. **Intercollegiate:** Baseball M, basketball M, volleyball W. **Intramural:** Basketball M, volleyball W.

STUDENT SERVICES. Career counseling, employment service for undergraduates, freshman orientation, health services, on-campus day care, personal counseling, placement service for graduates, veterans counselor.

ANNUAL EXPENSES. Tuition and fees (1992-93): $6,520. **Room and board:** $3,120. **Books and supplies:** $700. **Other expenses:** $2,000.

FINANCIAL AID. 82% of freshmen, 75% of continuing students receive some form of aid. Grants, loans, jobs available. Academic, leadership scholarships available. **Aid applications:** No closing date; priority given to applications received by June 1; applicants notified on a rolling basis beginning on or about July 1; must reply within 2 weeks.

ADDRESS/TELEPHONE. David Albanese, Director, Admissions and Records, Bethany College, 800 Bethany Drive, Scotts Valley, CA 95066-2898. (408) 438-3800 ext. 1401. (800) 843-9410.

Biola University
La Mirada, California — CB code: 4017

Admissions:	82% of applicants accepted
Based on:	••• Essay, recommendations, religious affiliation/commitment, school record
	•• Activities, interview, special talents, test scores
Completion:	92% of freshmen end year in good standing
	77% graduate

4-year private university, coed, interdenominational. Founded in 1908. **Accreditation:** Regional. **Undergraduate enrollment:** 817 men, 1,153 women full time; 49 men, 46 women part time. **Graduate enrollment:** 274 men, 166 women full time; 259 men, 119 women part time. **Faculty:** 216 total (132 full time). **Location:** Suburban campus in large town; 22 miles from downtown Los Angeles. **Calendar:** 4-1-4, extensive summer session. **Microcomputers:** Located in computer centers. **Special facilities:** Concert hall with pipe organ, art gallery.

DEGREES OFFERED. BA, BS, MA, MS, EdD, M.Div. 347 bachelor's degrees awarded in 1992. 15% in business and management, 12% communications, 10% education, 10% teacher education, 5% health sciences, 16% philosophy, religion, theology, 9% psychology, 9% social sciences, 6% visual and performing arts. Graduate degrees offered in 7 major fields of study.

UNDERGRADUATE MAJORS. Accounting, applied mathematics, art education, Bible studies, biochemistry, biology, business administration and management, business and management, business economics, chemistry, communications, computer and information sciences, education, elementary education, English, English education, fine arts, graphic design, history, humanities and social sciences, information sciences and systems, intercultural studies, junior high education, liberal/general studies, management information systems, marketing management, mathematics, mathematics education, motion picture technology, music, music education, music performance, music theory and composition, nursing, physical education, physical sciences, physical sciences/engineering, psychology, radio/television technology, religion, religious education, secondary education, social sciences, social work, sociology, studio art, theological studies.

ACADEMIC PROGRAMS. Double major, honors program, internships, study abroad, teacher preparation, Washington semester; liberal arts/career combination in engineering. **Remedial services:** Learning center, reduced course load, remedial instruction, special counselor, tutoring. **ROTC:** Air Force, Army, Naval. **Placement/credit:** AP, CLEP General and Subject; 30 credit hours maximum for bachelor's degree.

ACADEMIC REQUIREMENTS. Freshmen must earn minimum GPA of 2.0 to continue in good standing. 81% of freshmen return for sophomore year. Students must declare major by end of second year. **Graduation requirements:** 130 hours for bachelor's (30 in major). Most students required to take courses in arts/fine arts, English, foreign languages, history, mathematics, philosophy/religion, biological/physical sciences, social sciences.

FRESHMAN ADMISSIONS. Selection criteria: Christian commitment most important, then academic record, personal references, test scores. School, community, church activities helpful. Out-of-state and ethnic stu-

ferred admission available. SAT or ACT recommended for counseling and placement purposes.

STUDENT LIFE. Housing: Dormitories (coed); apartment housing available. Dormitory priority assigned to first-year undergraduate students outside commuting distance. **Activities:** Student government, film, student newspaper, drama, student gallery.

STUDENT SERVICES. Career counseling, employment service for undergraduates, freshman orientation, personal counseling, placement service for graduates, veterans counselor, services/facilities for handicapped.

ANNUAL EXPENSES. Tuition and fees: $13,080. **Room and board:** $5,526. **Books and supplies:** $600. **Other expenses:** $1,728.

FINANCIAL AID. 42% of freshmen, 60% of continuing students receive some form of aid. 40% of grants, 73% of loans, 45% of jobs based on need. 47 enrolled freshmen were judged to have need, all were offered aid. Academic, art, leadership scholarships available. **Aid applications:** No closing date; priority given to applications received by March 2; applicants notified on a rolling basis beginning on or about May 1; must reply within 2 weeks.

ADDRESS/TELEPHONE. Sheri Sivin McKenzie, Director of Enrollment Services, California College of Arts and Crafts, 5275 Broadway at College, Oakland, CA 94618-1487. (510) 653-8118. (800) 447-1-ART. Fax: (510) 655-3541.

California College for Health Sciences
National City, California CB code: 3354

4-year proprietary health science college, coed. Founded in 1975. **Undergraduate enrollment:** 11,326 men and women. **Graduate enrollment:** 500 men and women part time. **Faculty:** 18 total (11 full time). **Location:** Urban campus in small city; 7 miles from downtown San Diego. **Calendar:** Semester. **Microcomputers:** 1 located in libraries. **Additional facts:** Serves home study students primarily. Accredited by National Home Study Council for associate's, bachelor's, and master's degree.

DEGREES OFFERED. AAS, BS, MS. Graduate degrees offered in 1 major field of study.

UNDERGRADUATE MAJORS. Associate: Allied health, medical transcription, respiratory therapy technology. **Bachelor's:** Health care administration, science and health services management.

ACADEMIC PROGRAMS. 2-year transfer program, independent study. **Remedial services:** Tutoring. **Placement/credit:** AP, CLEP General and Subject; 60 credit hours maximum for bachelor's degree.

ACADEMIC REQUIREMENTS. Freshmen must earn minimum GPA of 2.0 to continue in good standing. Students must declare major on application. **Graduation requirements:** 62 hours for associate (45 in major), 120 hours for bachelor's (39 in major). Most students required to take courses in English, humanities, biological/physical sciences, social sciences.

FRESHMAN ADMISSIONS. Selection criteria: School achievement record, test scores, interview, essays, recommendations considered.

1992 FRESHMAN CLASS PROFILE. Characteristics: Average age is 24.

FALL-TERM APPLICATIONS. $35 fee. Closing date August 31; applicants notified on or about September 1. Interview required. Essay required.

STUDENT LIFE. Activities: Student newspaper.

STUDENT SERVICES. Services/facilities for handicapped.

ANNUAL EXPENSES. Tuition and fees (projected): Students pursuing associate degree pay $75 per credit hour. Students pursuing bachelor's or master's degrees pay $110 per credit hour. **Books and supplies:** $525.

ADDRESS/TELEPHONE. Gina Echito, Director of Admissions, California College for Health Sciences, 222 West 24th Street, National City, CA 91950. (619) 477-4800. (800) 221-7374. Fax: (619) 477-4360.

California Institute of the Arts
Valencia, California CB code: 4049

4-year private college of visual and performing arts, coed. Founded in 1964. **Accreditation:** Regional. **Undergraduate enrollment:** 390 men, 260 women full time; 4 men, 2 women part time. **Graduate enrollment:** 194 men, 125 women full time; 1 man, 1 woman part time. **Faculty:** 232 total (95 full time). **Location:** Suburban campus in small city; 30 miles from Los Angeles. **Calendar:** Semester. Extensive evening/early morning classes. **Microcomputers:** 30 located in libraries, classrooms, computer centers.

DEGREES OFFERED. BFA, MFA. 125 bachelor's degrees awarded in 1992. 100% in visual and performing arts. Graduate degrees offered in 19 major fields of study.

UNDERGRADUATE MAJORS. Cinematography/film, computer graphics, dance, dramatic arts, drawing, film animation, fine arts, graphic design, jazz, music, music performance, music theory and composition, painting, photography, printmaking, sculpture, studio art, theater design, video, visual and performing arts.

ACADEMIC PROGRAMS. Accelerated program, double major, independent study, student-designed major, study abroad. **Placement/credit:** AP, institutional tests; 24 credit hours maximum for bachelor's degree.

ACADEMIC REQUIREMENTS. No policy requiring minimum GPA; records of students having academic difficulty are reviewed individually. 90% of freshmen return for sophomore year. Students must declare major on application. **Graduation requirements:** 120 hours for bachelor's (72 in major). Most students required to take courses in arts/fine arts, English, history, humanities, mathematics, philosophy/religion, biological/physical sciences, social sciences.

FRESHMAN ADMISSIONS. Selection criteria: Talent, portfolio review, audition, most important. **Additional information:** Students encouraged to have applications in by February 1 because some programs close after that date.

1992 FRESHMAN CLASS PROFILE. 68 men and women enrolled. **Characteristics:** 34% from in state, 65% live in college housing, 36% have minority backgrounds, 8% are foreign students.

FALL-TERM APPLICATIONS. $50 fee, may be waived for applicants with need. No closing date; priority given to applications received by February 1; applicants notified on a rolling basis beginning on or about February 15; must reply within 30 days. Audition required for acting, dance, music applicants. Portfolio required for art/design, film/video, music composition applicants. Essay required. Interview recommended for directing/performance/production studies applicants. Music applicants may submit audio tape recordings in lieu of live audition. Deferred admission available. Early audition recommended for dance and acting applicants. Application deadline for Live Action Film Program February 1.

STUDENT LIFE. Housing: Dormitories (coed); apartment, handicapped housing available. **Activities:** Student government, radio, student newspaper, television, visual art exhibitions, dance, drama, jazz band, music ensembles, African, Indian, and Indonesian music, chamber orchestra.

STUDENT SERVICES. Career counseling, employment service for undergraduates, health services, personal counseling, placement service for graduates, veterans counselor, services/facilities for handicapped.

ANNUAL EXPENSES. Tuition and fees: $13,910. **Room and board:** $5,966. **Books and supplies:** $1,000. **Other expenses:** $1,680.

FINANCIAL AID. Grants, loans, jobs available. Music/drama, art, minority scholarships available. **Aid applications:** No closing date; priority given to applications received by March 2; applicants notified on a rolling basis beginning on or about April 15; must reply within 3 weeks.

ADDRESS/TELEPHONE. Kenneth Young, Director of Admissions, California Institute of the Arts, 24700 McBean Parkway, Valencia, CA 91355. (805) 255-1050. (800) 545-2787. Fax: (805) 254-8352.

California Institute of Technology
Pasadena, California CB code: 4034

4-year private university, coed. Founded in 1891. **Accreditation:** Regional. **Undergraduate enrollment:** 670 men, 242 women full time. **Graduate enrollment:** 858 men, 239 women full time. **Faculty:** 697 total (677 full time), 664 with doctorates or other terminal degrees. **Location:** Suburban campus in small city; 10 miles from Los Angeles. **Calendar:** Quarter. **Microcomputers:** Located in dormitories, libraries, classrooms, computer centers. **Special facilities:** Jet Propulsion Laboratories, Palomar Observatory, wind and water tunnels, Keck Observatory.

DEGREES OFFERED. BA, BS, MS, PhD. 190 bachelor's degrees awarded in 1992. 64% in engineering, 9% life sciences, 5% mathematics, 19% physical sciences. Graduate degrees offered in 22 major fields of study.

UNDERGRADUATE MAJORS. Aerospace/aeronautical/astronautical engineering, applied mathematics, astronomy, biology, chemical engineering, chemistry, civil engineering, computer and information sciences, computer engineering, economics, electrical/electronics/communications engineering, engineering, English literature, geochemistry, geology, geophysics and seismology, history, materials engineering, mechanical engineering, physics, planetary science, premedicine, pure mathematics, social sciences.

ACADEMIC PROGRAMS. Double major, independent study, internships, student-designed major, cross-registration, 3-2 engineering with Bowdoin, Bryn Mawr, Grinnell, Occidental, Pomona, Reed, Wesleyan University, Whitman, Ohio Wesleyan; liberal arts/career combination in engineering. **Remedial services:** Preadmission summer program, reduced course load, special counselor, tutoring. **ROTC:** Air Force, Army, Naval. **Placement/credit:** Institutional tests.

ACADEMIC REQUIREMENTS. No policy requiring minimum GPA; records of students having academic difficulty are reviewed individually. All freshman courses are pass/fail. 95% of freshmen return for sophomore year. Students must declare major by end of first year. **Graduation requirements:** 117 hours for bachelor's (64 in major). Most students required to take courses in computer science, English, humanities, mathematics, biological/physical sciences, social sciences. **Postgraduate studies:** 2% enter medical school, 50% enter other graduate study.

FRESHMAN ADMISSIONS. Selection criteria: Test scores, high school record (particularly in mathematics and science), extracurricular activities (science and nonscience-related), counselors' and teachers' recommendations are the chief considerations. **High school preparation:** 15 units required. Required and recommended units include English 3-4, mathematics 4 and physical science 2. One physics, 1 chemistry, and 1 US history and government also required. **Test requirements:** SAT; score report by March 1. 3 ACH required including Mathematics Level II, English Composition, and science (Chemistry, Biology, or Physics). Score report by March 1.

1992 FRESHMAN CLASS PROFILE. 232 men and women enrolled. 100% had high school GPA of 3.0 or higher. **Academic background:** Mid 50% of enrolled freshmen had SAT-V between 600-710, SAT-M between 720-780. 100% submitted SAT scores. **Characteristics:** 31% from in state, 100% live in college housing, 40% have minority backgrounds, 1% are foreign students. Average age is 17.

FALL-TERM APPLICATIONS. $40 fee, may be waived for applicants with need. Closing date January 1; applicants notified on or about March 15; must reply by May 1. Essay required. CRDA. Deferred and early admission available. EDP-F.

STUDENT LIFE. Housing: Dormitories (coed); cooperative housing available. Housing guaranteed for all students. **Activities:** Student government, student newspaper, yearbook, choral groups, concert band, dance, drama, jazz band, music ensembles, musical theater, symphony orchestra, YMCA, Christian Fellowship, Newman Club, Hillel.

ATHLETICS. NCAA. **Intercollegiate:** Baseball M, basketball M, cross-country, fencing, golf M, ice hockey M, swimming, tennis, track and field, water polo M, wrestling M. **Intramural:** Football M, ice hockey M, sailing, skin diving, soccer, volleyball W.

STUDENT SERVICES. Career counseling, employment service for undergraduates, freshman orientation, health services, on-campus day care, personal counseling, placement service for graduates, services/facilities for handicapped.

ANNUAL EXPENSES. Tuition and fees: $16,110. **Room and board:** $6,117. **Books and supplies:** $700. **Other expenses:** $2,670.

FINANCIAL AID. 70% of freshmen, 70% of continuing students receive some form of aid. 93% of grants, 92% of loans, 82% of jobs based on need. 180 enrolled freshmen were judged to have need, all were offered aid. Academic scholarships available. **Aid applications:** No closing date; priority given to applications received by February 1; applicants notified on a rolling basis beginning on or about April 1; must reply by May 1 or within 2 weeks if notified thereafter. **Additional information:** Students whose family cannot afford full cost of education will have demonstrated financial need met.

ADDRESS/TELEPHONE. Carole Snow, Director of Admissions, California Institute of Technology, 1201 East California Blvd, Pasadena, CA 91125. (818) 356-6341.

California Lutheran University
Thousand Oaks, California — CB code: 4088

Admissions: 86% of applicants accepted
Based on: ••• Essay, school record, test scores
•• Interview, recommendations
• Activities, special talents
Completion: 93% of freshmen end year in good standing
48% graduate, 33% of these enter graduate study

4-year private university, coed, affiliated with Evangelical Lutheran Church in America. Founded in 1959. **Accreditation:** Regional. **Undergraduate enrollment:** 644 men, 748 women full time; 218 men, 224 women part time. **Graduate enrollment:** 33 men, 81 women full time; 342 men, 447 women part time. **Faculty:** 250 total (110 full time), 150 with doctorates or other terminal degrees. **Location:** Suburban campus in small city; 45 miles from Los Angeles. **Calendar:** Semester, limited summer session. Extensive evening/early morning classes. **Microcomputers:** 72 located in dormitories, libraries, classrooms, computer centers. **Special facilities:** Science facility housing state-of-the-art electronic blackboard, hyper-media computer laboratory.

DEGREES OFFERED. BA, BS, MA, MS, MBA. 361 bachelor's degrees awarded in 1992. 29% in business and management, 7% business/office and marketing/distribution, 6% communications, 6% computer sciences, 13% teacher education, 7% psychology, 8% social sciences, 5% visual and performing arts. Graduate degrees offered in 21 major fields of study.

UNDERGRADUATE MAJORS. Accounting, advertising, art education, biochemistry, biological and physical sciences, biology, business administration and management, business and management, business economics, chemistry, communications, computer and information sciences, computer programming, criminal justice studies, criminology, dramatic arts, early childhood education, economics, education, elementary education, English, English education, fine arts, foreign languages education, French, geology, German, history, humanities and social sciences, information sciences and systems, international studies, junior high education, law enforcement and corrections, liberal/general studies, marketing and advertising, marketing management, mathematics, mathematics education, molecular biology, music, music education, philosophy, physical education, physics, political science and government, predentistry, prelaw, premedicine, psychology, reading education, religion, religious education, science education, secondary education, social science education, social studies education, sociology, Spanish, special education, speech, speech/communication/theater education, sports medicine, theological studies.

ACADEMIC PROGRAMS. Accelerated program, cooperative education, double major, honors program, independent study, internships, semester at sea, student-designed major, study abroad, teacher preparation, visiting/exchange student program; liberal arts/career combination in engineering; combined bachelor's/graduate program in business administration. **Remedial services:** Learning center, reduced course load, remedial instruction, special counselor, tutoring, Writing Center. **ROTC:** Air Force, Army. **Placement/credit:** AP, CLEP Subject, institutional tests; 30 credit hours maximum for bachelor's degree.

ACADEMIC REQUIREMENTS. Freshmen must earn minimum GPA of 2.5 to continue in good standing. 80% of freshmen return for sophomore year. Students must declare major by end of second year. **Graduation requirements:** 124 hours for bachelor's (36 in major). Most students required to take courses in arts/fine arts, English, foreign languages, history, humanities, mathematics, philosophy/religion, biological/physical sciences, social sciences. **Postgraduate studies:** 4% enter law school, 4% enter medical school, 10% enter MBA programs, 15% enter other graduate study.

FRESHMAN ADMISSIONS. Selection criteria: School achievement record, rank in top half of class, test scores, essay, letters of recommendation and school, church, community activities important. **High school preparation:** 12 units required; 20 recommended. Required and recommended units include biological science 1, English 4, foreign language 2-4, mathematics 2-4, physical science 1-3 and social science 2-3. **Test requirements:** SAT or ACT; score report by May 1.

1992 FRESHMAN CLASS PROFILE. 303 men applied, 250 accepted, 193 enrolled; 364 women applied, 322 accepted, 231 enrolled. 72% had high school GPA of 3.0 or higher, 28% between 2.0 and 2.99. **Academic background:** Mid 50% of enrolled freshmen had SAT-V between 380-490, SAT-M between 430-560. 90% submitted SAT scores. **Characteristics:** 76% from in state, 80% live in college housing, 19% have minority backgrounds, 5% are foreign students. Average age is 19.

FALL-TERM APPLICATIONS. $35 fee, may be waived for applicants with need. Closing date June 1; priority given to applications received by January 1; applicants notified on a rolling basis beginning on or about December 1; must reply by May 1 or within 4 weeks if notified thereafter. Essay required. Interview recommended. Audition recommended for music, drama applicants. CRDA. Deferred admission available. EDP-F.

STUDENT LIFE. Housing: Dormitories (coed). **Activities:** Student government, magazine, radio, student newspaper, television, yearbook, choral groups, concert band, dance, drama, jazz band, music ensembles, musical theater, pep band, symphony orchestra, Lutheran Church congregation, Circle-K, African American Student Association, Rotoract, United Students of the World, Latino Student Union, Habitat for Humanity, Asian American Club.

ATHLETICS. NCAA. **Intercollegiate:** Baseball M, basketball, cross-country, football M, golf M, soccer, softball W, tennis, track and field, volleyball W. **Intramural:** Archery, badminton, horseback riding, rugby M, skiing, softball, swimming, tennis, volleyball.

STUDENT SERVICES. Aptitude testing, career counseling, employment service for undergraduates, freshman orientation, health services, personal counseling, placement service for graduates, special adviser for adult students, veterans counselor, services/facilities for handicapped.

ANNUAL EXPENSES. Tuition and fees: $12,040. **Room and board:** $5,200. **Books and supplies:** $612. **Other expenses:** $1,548.

FINANCIAL AID. 85% of freshmen, 94% of continuing students receive some form of aid. 56% of grants, 77% of loans, 28% of jobs based on need. 200 enrolled freshmen were judged to have need, all were offered aid. Academic, music/drama, art, leadership, alumni affiliation, religious affiliation, minority scholarships available. **Aid applications:** No closing date; priority given to applications received by March 2; applicants notified on a rolling basis beginning on or about April 1; must reply by May 1 or within 2 weeks if notified thereafter. **Additional information:** Minority students advised on special funding.

ADDRESS/TELEPHONE. Ernie Sandlin, Dean of Admission, California Lutheran University, 60 West Olsen Road, Thousand Oaks, CA 91360-2787. (805) 493-3135. (800) 252-5884. Fax: (805) 493-3114.

California Maritime Academy
Vallejo, California — CB code: 4035

Admissions: 65% of applicants accepted
Based on: ••• School record
•• Activities, essay, test scores
• Interview, recommendations
Completion: 75% of freshmen end year in good standing
74% graduate, 2% of these enter graduate study

4-year public maritime academy, coed. Founded in 1929. **Accreditation:** Regional. **Undergraduate enrollment:** 422 men, 74 women full time. **Faculty:** 39 total (29 full time), 10 with doctorates or other terminal degrees.

Location: Suburban campus in small city; 30 miles from San Francisco. **Calendar:** Required 16-week fall, 16-week spring semester. **Microcomputers:** 28 located in dormitories, libraries, computer centers. **Special facilities:** 8,000-ton training ship and diesel tanker, computer-aided radar simulators. **Additional facts:** Annual 8-week spring sea training aboard academy ship for freshmen, sophomores, and juniors.

DEGREES OFFERED. BS. 84 bachelor's degrees awarded in 1992. 10% in business and management, 47% engineering, 43% military sciences.

UNDERGRADUATE MAJORS. Business administration and management, marine transportation, mechanical engineering, Merchant Marine, naval architecture and marine engineering.

ACADEMIC PROGRAMS. Double major, internships. **Remedial services:** Learning center, remedial instruction, tutoring. **ROTC:** Naval. **Placement/credit:** AP, CLEP Subject.

ACADEMIC REQUIREMENTS. 85% of freshmen return for sophomore year. Students must declare major on enrollment. **Graduation requirements:** 157 hours for bachelor's (60 in major). Most students required to take courses in computer science, English, history, humanities, mathematics, biological/physical sciences, social sciences. **Postgraduate studies:** 1% enter MBA programs, 1% enter other graduate study.

FRESHMAN ADMISSIONS. Selection criteria: Mathematics and science background, essay, test scores, extracurricular participation, and class rank considered. Minority applicants given special consideration. Recommended units include English 4, mathematics 3 and science 2. 3 mathematics and 1 laboratory science or 1 additional mathematics course required for mechanical engineering applicants. **Test requirements:** SAT or ACT (SAT preferred); score report by February 15.

1992 FRESHMAN CLASS PROFILE. 316 men applied, 195 accepted, 127 enrolled; 52 women applied, 45 accepted, 30 enrolled. 60% had high school GPA of 3.0 or higher, 40% between 2.0 and 2.99. 13% were in top tenth and 35% were in top quarter of graduating class. **Academic background:** Mid 50% of enrolled freshmen had SAT-V between 410-490, SAT-M between 430-510. 82% submitted SAT scores. **Characteristics:** 88% from in state, 100% live in college housing, 30% have minority backgrounds, 1% are foreign students. Average age is 21.

FALL-TERM APPLICATIONS. $40 fee, may be waived for applicants with need. Closing date March 15; applicants notified on a rolling basis beginning on or about November 1; must reply by May 1 or within 2 weeks if notified thereafter. Essay required. Interview recommended. CRDA.

STUDENT LIFE. Housing: Dormitories (coed). **Activities:** Student government, student newspaper, yearbook, drill team, color guard, Bible club.

ATHLETICS. Intercollegiate: Baseball, basketball, rowing (crew), sailing, soccer, volleyball, water polo M. **Intramural:** Badminton, basketball, boxing M, golf, racquetball, rowing (crew), rugby M, sailing, softball, tennis, volleyball, water polo.

STUDENT SERVICES. Career counseling, employment service for undergraduates, freshman orientation, health services, personal counseling, placement service for graduates, veterans counselor, services/facilities for handicapped.

ANNUAL EXPENSES. Tuition and fees (1992-93): $2,006, $4,590 additional for out-of-state students. **Room and board:** $4,770. **Books and supplies:** $550. **Other expenses:** $1,900.

FINANCIAL AID. 38% of freshmen, 47% of continuing students receive some form of aid. 97% of grants, 77% of loans, 36% of jobs based on need. 55 enrolled freshmen were judged to have need, 50 were offered aid. Academic, leadership scholarships available. **Aid applications:** No closing date; priority given to applications received by March 2; applicants notified on a rolling basis beginning on or about May 1; must reply by May 1 or within 3 weeks if notified thereafter. **Additional information:** US Maritime Administration provides annual incentive payment of $1,200 per student, with certain conditions. Tuition waiver for children of deceased or disabled California veterans.

ADDRESS/TELEPHONE. Albert T. Perkins, Director of Admissions, California Maritime Academy, PO Box 1392, Vallejo, CA 94590-0644. (707) 648-4222. Fax: (707) 648-4204.

California Polytechnic State University: San Luis Obispo

San Luis Obispo, California CB code: 4038

4-year public university, coed. Founded in 1901. **Accreditation:** Regional. **Undergraduate enrollment:** 8,204 men, 5,844 women full time; 1,287 men, 1,042 women part time. **Graduate enrollment:** 233 men, 251 women full time; 333 men, 392 women part time. **Faculty:** 1,069 total (760 full time), 569 with doctorates or other terminal degrees. **Location:** Rural campus in large town; 200 miles from Los Angeles, 250 miles from San Francisco. **Calendar:** Quarter, extensive summer session. **Microcomputers:** Located in libraries, classrooms, computer centers. **Special facilities:** Printing press museum, university farm.

DEGREES OFFERED. BA, BS, BArch, MA, MS, MBA, MEd. 3,407 bachelor's degrees awarded in 1992. 15% in agriculture, 10% architecture and environmental design, 14% business and management, 6% teacher education, 17% engineering, 6% home economics, 5% social sciences, 6% visual and performing arts. Graduate degrees offered in 21 major fields of study.

UNDERGRADUATE MAJORS. Aerospace/aeronautical/astronautical engineering, agribusiness, agricultural education, agricultural engineering, agricultural mechanics, animal sciences, applied art and design, architectural engineering, architecture, biochemistry, biology, business administration and management, business economics, chemistry, city/community/regional planning, civil engineering, computer and information sciences, computer engineering, construction, dairy, ecology, economics, electrical/electronics/communications engineering, elementary education, engineering and engineering-related technologies, engineering science, English, English education, environmental health engineering, food science and nutrition, food sciences, graphic and printing production, graphic design, history, home economics, horticulture, individual and family development, industrial engineering, industrial technology, journalism, landscape architecture, liberal/general studies, materials engineering, mathematics, mechanical engineering, metallurgical engineering, microbiology, ornamental horticulture, parks and recreation management, physical sciences, physics, plant sciences, political science and government, poultry, renewable natural resources, social science education, social sciences, soil sciences, speech, statistics.

ACADEMIC PROGRAMS. Cooperative education, double major, dual enrollment of high school students, education specialist degree, external degree, internships, study abroad, teacher preparation, visiting/exchange student program, cross-registration. **Remedial services:** Learning center, remedial instruction, tutoring. **ROTC:** Army. **Placement/credit:** AP, CLEP General and Subject, institutional tests; 45 credit hours maximum for bachelor's degree.

ACADEMIC REQUIREMENTS. Freshmen must earn minimum GPA of 2.0 to continue in good standing. 80% of freshmen return for sophomore year. Students must declare major on application. **Graduation requirements:** 186 hours for bachelor's (60 in major). Most students required to take courses in arts/fine arts, computer science, English, foreign languages, history, humanities, mathematics, philosophy/religion, biological/physical sciences, social sciences.

FRESHMAN ADMISSIONS. Selection criteria: Course work, high school GPA, test scores, extracurricular activities most important. **High school preparation:** 15 units required. Required units include English 4, foreign language 2, mathematics 3 and science 1. One visual and performing arts, and 1 US history/government also required. **Test requirements:** SAT or ACT (SAT preferred); score report by January 15.

1992 FRESHMAN CLASS PROFILE. 1,331 men and women enrolled. **Characteristics:** 99% from in state, 80% live in college housing, 44% have minority backgrounds, 1% are foreign students. Average age is 18.

FALL-TERM APPLICATIONS. $55 fee, may be waived for applicants with need. Closing date November 30; applicants notified on or about February 15. Portfolio required for art, design applicants.

STUDENT LIFE. Housing: Dormitories (men, women, coed); fraternity, sorority housing available. **Activities:** Student government, radio, student newspaper, yearbook, choral groups, concert band, dance, drama, jazz band, marching band, music ensembles, musical theater, pep band, symphony orchestra, fraternities, sororities, MECHA, Society of Black Engineers and Scientists, Minority Engineering Program.

ATHLETICS. NCAA. **Intercollegiate:** Baseball M, basketball, cross-country, football M, gymnastics W, soccer M, softball W, swimming, tennis, track and field, volleyball W, wrestling M. **Intramural:** Racquetball, rowing (crew), rugby M, sailing, softball, volleyball, water polo M.

STUDENT SERVICES. Aptitude testing, career counseling, employment service for undergraduates, freshman orientation, health services, on-campus day care, personal counseling, placement service for graduates, special adviser for adult students, veterans counselor, services/facilities for handicapped.

ANNUAL EXPENSES. Tuition and fees (1992-93): $1,553, $7,380 additional for out-of-state students. **Room and board:** $4,416. **Books and supplies:** $576. **Other expenses:** $1,119.

FINANCIAL AID. 15% of freshmen, 35% of continuing students receive some form of aid. Grants, loans, jobs available. Academic, art, athletic, state/district residency, leadership, minority scholarships available. **Aid applications:** Closing date March 1; applicants notified on or about May 30; must reply within 3 weeks.

ADDRESS/TELEPHONE. James Maraviglia, Admissions Officer, California Polytechnic State University: San Luis Obispo, San Luis Obispo, CA 93407. (805) 756-2311.

California State Polytechnic University: Pomona

Pomona, California CB code: 4082

Admissions: 62% of applicants accepted
Based on: ••• School record, test scores
Completion: 75% of freshmen end year in good standing
24% graduate, 13% of these enter graduate study

4-year public university, coed. Founded in 1938. **Accreditation:** Regional. **Undergraduate enrollment:** 7,053 men, 4,767 women full time; 2,847 men,

1,858 women part time. **Graduate enrollment:** 124 men, 143 women full time; 639 men, 866 women part time. **Faculty:** 904 total (603 full time), 510 with doctorates or other terminal degrees. **Location:** Suburban campus in small city; 30 miles from downtown Los Angeles. **Calendar:** Quarter, extensive summer session. Extensive evening/early morning classes. **Microcomputers:** 1,306 located in libraries, classrooms, computer centers, campus-wide network. **Special facilities:** Electron microscope center, international center, small ruminant center, Arabian horse center, equine research center, art gallery, land laboratory, Voorhis Ecological Reserve.

DEGREES OFFERED. BA, BS, BArch, MA, MS, MBA. 2,860 bachelor's degrees awarded in 1992. 6% in architecture and environmental design, 31% business and management, 9% computer sciences, 16% engineering, 5% engineering technologies, 6% multi/interdisciplinary studies, 7% social sciences. Graduate degrees offered in 18 major fields of study.

UNDERGRADUATE MAJORS. Accounting, aerospace/aeronautical/astronautical engineering, agribusiness, agricultural business and management, agricultural economics, agricultural engineering, agricultural products and processing, agricultural sciences, agronomy, American studies, animal sciences, anthropology, architecture, behavioral sciences, biology, biotechnology, botany, business administration and management, chemical engineering, chemistry, city/community/regional planning, civil engineering, communications, computer and information sciences, dramatic arts, earth sciences, economics, electrical/electronics/communications engineering, engineering and engineering-related technologies, English, finance, fine arts, food science and nutrition, geography, geology, history, home economics, horticultural science, hotel/motel and restaurant management, human resources development, humanities, industrial engineering, information sciences and systems, international agriculture, international business management, landscape architecture, landscape irrigation science, liberal/general studies, manufacturing engineering, marketing management, mathematics, mechanical engineering, microbiology, music, operations research, ornamental horticulture, parks and recreation management, philosophy, physical education, physics, plant protection, plant sciences, political science and government, psychology, recreation and community services technologies, social sciences, social work, sociology, soil sciences, zoology.

ACADEMIC PROGRAMS. Computer delivered (on-line) credit-bearing course offerings, cooperative education, double major, dual enrollment of high school students, external degree, honors program, internships, study abroad, teacher preparation, telecourses, visiting/exchange student program, cross-registration, ocean studies and desert studies consortium; combined bachelor's/graduate program in business administration. **Remedial services:** Learning center, preadmission summer program, remedial instruction, special counselor, tutoring. **ROTC:** Army. **Placement/credit:** AP, CLEP Subject, institutional tests; 36 credit hours maximum for bachelor's degree.

ACADEMIC REQUIREMENTS. Freshmen must earn minimum GPA of 2.0 to continue in good standing. 72% of freshmen return for sophomore year. Students must declare major on application. **Graduation requirements:** 198 hours for bachelor's (54 in major). Most students required to take courses in arts/fine arts, English, history, humanities, mathematics, philosophy/religion, biological/physical sciences, social sciences.

FRESHMAN ADMISSIONS. Selection criteria: High school GPA, courses, and test scores important. **High school preparation:** 15 units required. Required units include English 4, foreign language 2, mathematics 3 and science 1. One visual and performing arts, 1 US history/government, and 3 electives also required. **Test requirements:** SAT or ACT; score report by June 15.

1992 FRESHMAN CLASS PROFILE. 3,632 men applied, 2,192 accepted, 942 enrolled; 2,775 women applied, 1,764 accepted, 600 enrolled. 76% had high school GPA of 3.0 or higher, 24% between 2.0 and 2.99. **Academic background:** Mid 50% of enrolled freshmen had SAT-V between 320-460, SAT-M between 420-570; ACT composite between 17-24. 91% submitted SAT scores, 10% submitted ACT scores. **Characteristics:** 62% have minority backgrounds.

FALL-TERM APPLICATIONS. $55 fee, may be waived for applicants with need. No closing date; priority given to applications received by November 30; applicants notified on a rolling basis beginning on or about February 1. Early admission available. Application deadline for impacted programs (architecture and civil engineering) November 30.

STUDENT LIFE. Housing: Dormitories (coed); apartment, handicapped housing available. **Activities:** Student government, magazine, radio, student newspaper, television, yearbook, choral groups, concert band, dance, drama, jazz band, marching band, music ensembles, musical theater, pep band, symphony orchestra, fraternities, sororities.

ATHLETICS. NCAA. **Intercollegiate:** Baseball M, basketball, cross-country, soccer, softball W, tennis, track and field, volleyball W. **Intramural:** Badminton, basketball, golf, racquetball, soccer, softball, tennis, volleyball.

STUDENT SERVICES. Aptitude testing, career counseling, employment service for undergraduates, freshman orientation, health services, on-campus day care, personal counseling, placement service for graduates, veterans counselor, women's reentry resource centers, services/facilities for handicapped.

ANNUAL EXPENSES. Tuition and fees (projected): $1,523, $7,380 additional for out-of-state students. Parking fee $36 per quarter. **Room and board:** $5,526. **Books and supplies:** $612. **Other expenses:** $1,728.

FINANCIAL AID. 47% of freshmen, 46% of continuing students receive some form of aid. 96% of grants, 93% of loans, all jobs based on need. Academic, athletic, alumni affiliation, minority scholarships available. **Aid applications:** No closing date; priority given to applications received by March 2; applicants notified on a rolling basis beginning on or about May 15; must reply within 3 weeks.

ADDRESS/TELEPHONE. Joseph Marshall, Admissions Officer, California State Polytechnic University: Pomona, 3801 West Temple Avenue, Pomona, CA 91768-4019. (909) 869-2000.

California State University: Bakersfield

Bakersfield, California — CB code: 4110

Admissions:	67% of applicants accepted
Based on:	••• School record, test scores
Completion:	93% of freshmen end year in good standing 10% enter graduate study

4-year public university, coed. Founded in 1965. **Accreditation:** Regional. **Undergraduate enrollment:** 1,023 men, 1,557 women full time; 483 men, 751 women part time. **Graduate enrollment:** 218 men, 341 women full time; 342 men, 668 women part time. **Faculty:** 349 total (235 full time), 223 with doctorates or other terminal degrees. **Location:** Suburban campus in small city; 112 miles from Los Angeles. **Calendar:** Quarter, limited summer session. **Microcomputers:** Located in libraries, classrooms. **Special facilities:** 40-acre facility for wild animal care, archaeological information center, center for business and economic research, center for economic education, well-sample repository, Madigan Art Gallery, center for physiological research.

DEGREES OFFERED. BA, BS, MA, MS, MBA. 716 bachelor's degrees awarded in 1992. 29% in business and management, 22% education, 14% allied health, 9% letters/literature, 6% psychology. Graduate degrees offered in 26 major fields of study.

UNDERGRADUATE MAJORS. Accounting, American literature, anthropology, art education, basic clinical health sciences, biochemistry, biology, business administration and management, business and management, business education, chemistry, child development/care/guidance, clinical laboratory science, communications, community health work, computer and information sciences, criminal justice studies, criminology, developmental psychology, dramatic arts, early childhood education, economics, education, elementary education, English, English education, English literature, finance, fine arts, foreign languages education, geology, health sciences, history, information sciences and systems, international relations, junior high education, liberal/general studies, linguistics, management information systems, marketing and distribution, marketing management, marketing research, mathematics, mathematics education, medical laboratory technologies, microcomputer software, music, music education, nursing, petroleum engineering, petroleum land studies, philosophy, physical education, physics, political science and government, practical nursing, prelaw, psychology, public administration, radio/television broadcasting, religion, science education, secondary education, social science education, sociology, Spanish, speech/communication/theater education, visual and performing arts.

ACADEMIC PROGRAMS. Accelerated program, cooperative education, double major, dual enrollment of high school students, education specialist degree, external degree, honors program, independent study, internships, student-designed major, study abroad, teacher preparation, telecourses, visiting/exchange student program, cross-registration, 2 plus 2 at specified locations for liberal studies (teaching) majors; liberal arts/career combination in health sciences. **Remedial services:** Learning center, reduced course load, remedial instruction, special counselor, tutoring, preadmission assistance for Educational Opportunity Program students, Summer Bridge program for EOP students admitted to the university. **Placement/credit:** AP, CLEP General and Subject. Unlimited number of hours of credit by examination may be counted toward degree.

ACADEMIC REQUIREMENTS. Freshmen must earn minimum GPA of 2.0 to continue in good standing. 75% of freshmen return for sophomore year. Students must declare major by end of second year. **Graduation requirements:** 186 hours for bachelor's. Most students required to take courses in arts/fine arts, computer science, English, history, humanities, mathematics, philosophy/religion, biological/physical sciences, social sciences. **Additional information:** Most courses are 5 quarter units. Students enrolled in 3 courses are carrying full unit load.

FRESHMAN ADMISSIONS. Selection criteria: GPA, SAT or ACT scores, and certain honors courses must place applicant in upper third of California high school graduates (upper sixth for out-of-state applicants) using eligibility index table. Minimum SAT/ACT scores slightly higher for out-of-state students. **High school preparation:** 15 units required. Required units include English 4, foreign language 2, mathematics 3 and science 1. One visual and performing arts, 1 US history/government and 3 years of electives required. Agriculture course may be used. **Test requirements:** SAT or ACT; score report by September 20. SAT or ACT not required if GPA is above 3.0 (3.6 if ou.

1992 FRESHMAN CLASS PROFILE. 431 men applied, 293 accepted, 192 enrolled; 529 women applied, 352 accepted, 237 enrolled. **Characteris-**

tics: 95% from in state, 88% commute, 51% have minority backgrounds, 4% are foreign students. Average age is 19.

FALL-TERM APPLICATIONS. $55 fee, may be waived for applicants with need. Closing date September 23; priority given to applications received by November 30; applicants notified on a rolling basis beginning on or about July 1. CRDA. Deferred and early admission available.

STUDENT LIFE. Housing: Dormitories (women, coed). **Activities:** Student government, magazine, student newspaper, yearbook, choral groups, dance, drama, jazz band, music ensembles, musical theater, pep band, fraternities, sororities, Black Student Union, Movimiento Estudiantil Chicano de Aztlan, Christian Union, Student Nursing Association, Circle-K.

ATHLETICS. NCAA. **Intercollegiate:** Basketball M, cross-country, soccer M, softball W, swimming, tennis, track and field, volleyball W, wrestling M. **Intramural:** Badminton, basketball, handball, racquetball, softball, tennis, volleyball.

STUDENT SERVICES. Aptitude testing, career counseling, employment service for undergraduates, freshman orientation, health services, on-campus day care, personal counseling, placement service for graduates, special adviser for adult students, veterans counselor, services/facilities for handicapped.

ANNUAL EXPENSES. Tuition and fees (1992-93): $1,439, $7,380 additional for out-of-state students. **Room and board:** $3,635. **Books and supplies:** $576. **Other expenses:** $1,242.

FINANCIAL AID. 63% of freshmen, 37% of continuing students receive some form of aid. 88% of grants, 91% of loans, 11% of jobs based on need. Academic, music/drama, art, athletic, state/district residency, leadership, minority scholarships available. **Aid applications:** No closing date; priority given to applications received by March 2; applicants notified on a rolling basis beginning on or about August 1; must reply within 2 weeks.

ADDRESS/TELEPHONE. Dr. Homer S. Montalvo, Associate Dean of Admissions and Records, California State University: Bakersfield, 9001 Stockdale Highway, Bakersfield, CA 93311-1099. (805) 664-2011.

California State University: Chico

Chico, California — CB code: 4048

Admissions:	78% of applicants accepted
Based on:	••• School record, test scores
	• Special talents
Completion:	77% of freshmen end year in good standing
	39% graduate

4-year public university, coed. Founded in 1887. **Accreditation:** Regional. **Undergraduate enrollment:** 6,092 men, 5,974 women full time; 707 men, 685 women part time. **Graduate enrollment:** 231 men, 387 women full time; 482 men, 614 women part time. **Faculty:** 874 total (693 full time), 588 with doctorates or other terminal degrees. **Location:** Rural campus in small city; 90 miles from Sacramento, 175 miles from San Francisco. **Calendar:** Semester, limited summer session. **Microcomputers:** 1,000 located in dormitories, libraries, computer centers, campus-wide network. **Special facilities:** 800-acre farm, 2 museums, art galleries, planetarium, 10-meter satellite dish, Eagle Lake.

DEGREES OFFERED. BA, BS, BFA, MA, MS, MBA. 3,036 bachelor's degrees awarded in 1992. 20% in business and management, 11% communications, 5% health sciences, 5% home economics, 9% multi/interdisciplinary studies, 5% parks/recreation, protective services, public affairs, 7% psychology, 13% social sciences. Graduate degrees offered in 28 major fields of study.

UNDERGRADUATE MAJORS. Agribusiness, agricultural business and management, agricultural engineering, agricultural mechanics, agricultural sciences, allied health, American studies, animal sciences, anthropology, applied mathematics, art history, biology, business administration and management, chemistry, child development/care/guidance, cinematography/film, civil engineering, communications, community health work, computer and information sciences, computer engineering, computer mathematics, construction management, criminal justice studies, crop science, dramatic arts, earth sciences, economics, electrical/electronics/communications engineering, English, environmental science, ethnic and women's studies, film arts, finance, fine arts, food science and nutrition, French, geography, geology, German, health sciences, history, human resources development, humanities, industrial arts, industrial technology, interior design, international business management, international relations, journalism, Latin American studies, liberal studies education, liberal/general studies, management information systems, management science, marketing management, mathematics, mechanical engineering, microbiology, museum studies, music, music education, nursing, ornamental horticulture, parks and recreation management, philosophy, physical education, physical sciences, physics, political science and government, psychology, public administration, public relations, range management, religion, social sciences, social work, sociology, Spanish, special education, speech pathology/audiology, statistics, trade and industrial education, visual and performing arts.

ACADEMIC PROGRAMS. Cooperative education, double major, dual enrollment of high school students, education specialist degree, external degree, honors program, independent study, internships, student-designed major, study abroad, teacher preparation, telecourses, visiting/exchange student program, cross-registration, library media credential program; combined bachelor's/graduate program in business administration. **Remedial services:** Learning center, preadmission summer program, reduced course load, remedial instruction, tutoring. **ROTC:** Army. **Placement/credit:** AP, CLEP General and Subject, IB; 30 credit hours maximum for bachelor's degree.

ACADEMIC REQUIREMENTS. Freshmen must earn minimum GPA of 2.0 to continue in good standing. Basic literacy and quantitative skills must be demonstrated before admission to required English and mathematics courses. 80% of freshmen return for sophomore year. **Graduation requirements:** 124 hours for bachelor's. Most students required to take courses in arts/fine arts, computer science, English, history, mathematics, philosophy/religion, biological/physical sciences, social sciences.

FRESHMAN ADMISSIONS. Selection criteria: Eligibility index derived from high school GPA and SAT or ACT test scores. **High school preparation:** 15 units required. Required and recommended units include English 4, foreign language 2, mathematics 3 and science 1. Biological science 1, physical science 1 and social science 2 recommended. One visual and performing arts, and 1 US history/government also required. **Test requirements:** SAT or ACT; score report by July 30.

1992 FRESHMAN CLASS PROFILE. 2,085 men applied, 1,555 accepted, 586 enrolled; 2,750 women applied, 2,193 accepted, 778 enrolled. **Academic background:** Mid 50% of enrolled freshmen had SAT-V between 370-470, SAT-M between 420-540; ACT composite between 18-23. 82% submitted SAT scores, 11% submitted ACT scores. **Characteristics:** 99% from in state, 80% live in college housing, 19% have minority backgrounds. Average age is 18.

FALL-TERM APPLICATIONS. $55 fee. Fee may be waived for California resident applicants with financial need. Closing date November 30; priority given to applications received by November 1; applicants notified on a rolling basis beginning on or about March 15; no response date; registration forms due July 30. Portfolio required for art, communications applicants. Interview recommended for special action admission applicants. Audition recommended for music, drama applicants. Deferred and early admission available. Nursing program open only to state residents, and application must be made during priority periods of November and August.

STUDENT LIFE. Housing: Dormitories (coed); apartment, fraternity, sorority, handicapped housing available. Thematic housing for honors, international, language, minorities in engineering. **Activities:** Student government, film, magazine, radio, student newspaper, television, yearbook, choral groups, concert band, drama, jazz band, marching band, music ensembles, musical theater, opera, pep band, symphony orchestra, fraternities, sororities, 110 organizations, including community volunteer action groups.

ATHLETICS. NCAA. **Intercollegiate:** Baseball M, basketball, cross-country, football M, soccer, softball W, track and field, volleyball W. **Intramural:** Badminton, basketball, bowling, fencing, golf, lacrosse, racquetball, rugby, skiing, soccer, softball, swimming, tennis, volleyball.

STUDENT SERVICES. Aptitude testing, career counseling, employment service for undergraduates, freshman orientation, health services, on-campus day care, personal counseling, placement service for graduates, special adviser for adult students, veterans counselor, re-entry program, services/facilities for handicapped.

ANNUAL EXPENSES. Tuition and fees (1992-93): $1,468, $7,380 additional for out-of-state students. **Room and board:** $4,008. **Books and supplies:** $576. **Other expenses:** $1,368.

FINANCIAL AID. 24% of freshmen, 45% of continuing students receive some form of aid. 99% of grants, 91% of loans, 41% of jobs based on need. Academic, leadership scholarships available. **Aid applications:** No closing date; priority given to applications received by March 1; applicants notified on a rolling basis beginning on or about April 1.

ADDRESS/TELEPHONE. Caroline Aldrich-Langen, Associate Director of Admissions and Records, California State University: Chico, Chico, CA 95929-0720. (916) 898-6321. Fax: (916) 898-6824.

California State University: Dominguez Hills

Carson, California — CB code: 4098

Admissions:	61% of applicants accepted
Based on:	••• School record, test scores
Completion:	52% of freshmen end year in good standing
	21% graduate, 25% of these enter graduate study

4-year public university, coed. Founded in 1960. **Accreditation:** Regional. **Undergraduate enrollment:** 1,667 men, 2,725 women full time; 1,009 men, 1,799 women part time. **Graduate enrollment:** 434 men, 769 women full time; 695 men, 1,276 women part time. **Faculty:** 820 total (333 full time), 348 with doctorates or other terminal degrees. **Location:** Suburban campus in small city; 10 miles from Los Angeles. **Calendar:** Semester, extensive summer session. Saturday and extensive evening/early morning classes. **Microcomputers:** 210 located in libraries, classrooms, computer centers. **Special facilities:** Art gallery, nature preserve, greenhouse, observatory, social systems research center, Olympic cycling velodrome.

DEGREES OFFERED. BA, BS, MA, MS, MBA. 1,218 bachelor's degrees awarded in 1992. 30% in business and management, 8% education, 10% multi/interdisciplinary studies, 12% social sciences. Graduate degrees offered in 27 major fields of study.

UNDERGRADUATE MAJORS. Accounting, Afro-American (black) studies, anthropology, art history, basic clinical health sciences, behavioral sciences, biology, business administration and management, business and management, chemistry, clinical laboratory science, communications, community health work, community services, computer and information sciences, dental assistant, dramatic arts, earth sciences, economics, electronic music synthesis, English, English literature, finance, French, geography, geology, gerontology, health care administration, health sciences, history, human resources development, human services, international business management, journalism, labor/industrial relations, liberal/general studies, linguistics, management information systems, management science, marketing management, mathematics, Mexican American studies, microbiology, music, music performance, music theory and composition, nuclear medical technology, nursing, orthotics and prosthetics, parks and recreation management, personnel management, philosophy, physician's assistant, physics, political science and government, prelaw, psychology, public administration, public relations, real estate, recreation and community services technologies, small business management and ownership, sociology, Spanish.

ACADEMIC PROGRAMS. Accelerated program, cooperative education, double major, dual enrollment of high school students, external degree, honors program, independent study, internships, student-designed major, study abroad, teacher preparation, telecourses, visiting/exchange student program, weekend college, cross-registration; liberal arts/career combination in health sciences. **Remedial services:** Learning center, preadmission summer program, reduced course load, remedial instruction, special counselor, tutoring. **ROTC:** Air Force, Army. **Placement/credit:** AP, CLEP General and Subject, institutional tests; 30 credit hours maximum for bachelor's degree.

ACADEMIC REQUIREMENTS. Freshmen must earn minimum GPA of 2.0 to continue in good standing. 70% of freshmen return for sophomore year. Students must declare major by end of second year. **Graduation requirements:** 124 hours for bachelor's. Most students required to take courses in arts/fine arts, English, history, humanities, mathematics, biological/physical sciences, social sciences. **Additional information:** Interdisciplinary studies offered in experimental college within the university.

FRESHMAN ADMISSIONS. Selection criteria: Test scores and high school GPA. In-state applicants must rank in top third of class, out-of-state in top sixth. **High school preparation:** 15 units required. Required units include English 4, foreign language 2, mathematics 3 and science 1. One visual and performing arts, 1 US history or government also required. **Test requirements:** SAT or ACT; score report by June 1. SAT/ACT required of applicants who do not meet minimum requirement based on admissions eligibility index.

1992 FRESHMAN CLASS PROFILE. 617 men applied, 367 accepted, 163 enrolled; 1,260 women applied, 779 accepted, 355 enrolled. **Characteristics:** 95% commute, 78% have minority backgrounds. Average age is 20.

FALL-TERM APPLICATIONS. $55 fee, may be waived for applicants with need. No closing date; priority given to applications received by June 1; applicants notified on a rolling basis. Interview required for Educational Opportunity Program applicants. Early admission available. Institutional early decision plan.

STUDENT LIFE. Housing: Apartment housing available. On-campus 1- and 2-bedroom furnished apartments available on a year-round basis. **Activities:** Student government, magazine, student newspaper, television, yearbook, choral groups, concert band, dance, drama, jazz band, music ensembles, musical theater, symphony orchestra, fraternities, sororities, accounting society, African-American Business Student Association, dance club, literary club, Phi Alpha Delta, political science club, science society, Hispanic Association of Natural and Social Science, Campus Crusade for Christ, Hillel.

ATHLETICS. NCAA. **Intercollegiate:** Baseball M, basketball, golf M, soccer, softball W, volleyball W.

STUDENT SERVICES. Aptitude testing, career counseling, employment service for undergraduates, freshman orientation, health services, on-campus day care, personal counseling, placement service for graduates, special adviser for adult students, veterans counselor, women's center, older-adult center, services/facilities for handicapped.

ANNUAL EXPENSES. Tuition and fees (projected): $1,959, $7,380 additional for out-of-state students. **Room and board:** $2,610 room only. **Books and supplies:** $612. **Other expenses:** $1,464.

FINANCIAL AID. 70% of freshmen, 28% of continuing students receive some form of aid. Grants, loans, jobs available. Academic, music/drama, art, athletic, leadership, minority scholarships available. **Aid applications:** No closing date; priority given to applications received by April 15; applicants notified on a rolling basis beginning on or about May 1; must reply within 15 days.

ADDRESS/TELEPHONE. Anita Gash, Director of Admissions, California State University: Dominguez Hills, 1000 East Victoria Street, Carson, CA 90747-9960. (310) 516-3696. Fax: (310) 516-3449.

California State University: Fresno

Fresno, California — CB code: 4312

Admissions: 79% of applicants accepted
Based on: ••• School record, test scores
Completion: 81% of freshmen end year in good standing
52% graduate, 18% of these enter graduate study

4-year public university, coed. Founded in 1911. **Accreditation:** Regional. **Undergraduate enrollment:** 6,654 men, 7,403 women full time; 554 men, 668 women part time. **Graduate enrollment:** 709 men, 1,146 women full time; 683 men, 1,085 women part time. **Faculty:** 1,220 total (850 full time), 636 with doctorates or other terminal degrees. **Location:** Urban campus in large city; 217 miles from Los Angeles, 172 miles from Sacramento. **Calendar:** Semester, extensive summer session. Saturday and extensive evening/early morning classes. **Microcomputers:** 605 located in dormitories, libraries, classrooms, computer centers. **Special facilities:** 1,190-acre university farm, baseball stadium. **Additional facts:** Designated as an arboretum in 1978.

DEGREES OFFERED. BA, BS, MA, MS, MBA, EdD. 3,083 bachelor's degrees awarded in 1992. 5% in agriculture, 22% business and management, 20% teacher education, 5% engineering, 12% health sciences, 10% letters/literature, 9% social sciences. Graduate degrees offered in 59 major fields of study.

UNDERGRADUATE MAJORS. Accounting, advertising, agribusiness, agricultural business and management, agricultural economics, agricultural education, agricultural mechanics, agricultural sciences, agronomy, animal sciences, anthropology, applied mathematics, art education, art history, bacteriology, bilingual/bicultural education, biochemistry, biology, botany, business administration and management, business and management, business economics, business education, cell biology, chemistry, child development/care/guidance, civil engineering, clinical laboratory science, computer and information sciences, computer engineering, computer programming, criminology, dairy, dance, data processing, dramatic arts, driver and safety education, early childhood education, economics, education of the deaf and hearing impaired, electrical/electronics/communications engineering, elementary education, engineering, engineering mechanics, English, English education, English literature, entomology, environmental science, family/consumer resource management, finance, food science and nutrition, food sciences, foreign languages education, French, genetics, human and animal, geography, geology, German, health care administration, health education, health sciences, history, home economics, home economics education, horticultural science, human environment and housing, individual and family development, industrial arts education, industrial engineering, information sciences and systems, inorganic chemistry, institutional/home management/supporting programs, insurance and risk management, interior design, international business management, investments and securities, journalism, labor/industrial relations, law enforcement and corrections, linguistics, marine biology, marketing management, mathematics, mathematics education, mechanical engineering, medical social work, microbiology, molecular biology, music, music education, music history and appreciation, nursing, organic chemistry, ornamental horticulture, parks and recreation management, personnel management, philosophy, physical chemistry, physical education, physical sciences, physical therapy, physics, physiology, human and animal, political science and government, poultry, psychology, public administration, range management, real estate, recreation therapy, religion, Russian, science education, secondary education, social sciences, social studies education, social work, sociology, soil sciences, Spanish, specific learning disabilities, speech, speech correction, speech pathology/audiology, surveying and mapping sciences, systems analysis, telecommunications, textiles and clothing, trade and industrial education, transportation management, zoology.

ACADEMIC PROGRAMS. Accelerated program, computer delivered (on-line) credit-bearing course offerings, cooperative education, double major, dual enrollment of high school students, education specialist degree, independent study, internships, student-designed major, study abroad, teacher preparation, telecourses, visiting/exchange student program, marine science program at Moss Landing Marine Laboratory on Monterey Bay. **Remedial services:** Learning center, preadmission summer program, reduced course load, remedial instruction, special counselor, tutoring. **ROTC:** Air Force, Army. **Placement/credit:** AP, CLEP General and Subject, institutional tests; 30 credit hours maximum for bachelor's degree.

ACADEMIC REQUIREMENTS. Freshmen must earn minimum GPA of 2.0 to continue in good standing. 80% of freshmen return for sophomore year. Students must declare major by end of second year. **Graduation requirements:** 124 hours for bachelor's (30 in major). Most students required to take courses in English, history, mathematics, biological/physical sciences.

FRESHMAN ADMISSIONS. Selection criteria: Upper third of California high school graduates based on eligibility index and required college preparatory subjects. **High school preparation:** 15 units required. Required units include English 4, foreign language 2, mathematics 3 and science 1. One visual and performing arts, and 1 US history/government also required. Three of college approved electives. **Test requirements:** SAT or ACT; score report by August 9.

1992 FRESHMAN CLASS PROFILE. 4,874 men and women applied,

3,839 accepted; 707 men enrolled, 873 women enrolled. **Academic background:** Mid 50% of enrolled freshmen had SAT-V between 370-520, SAT-M between 390-560. 77% submitted SAT scores. **Characteristics:** 89% from in state, 80% commute, 48% have minority backgrounds, 7% are foreign students, 7% join fraternities/sororities. Average age is 19.

FALL-TERM APPLICATIONS. $55 fee, may be waived for applicants with need. Closing date May 15; applicants notified on a rolling basis beginning on or about March 1. EDP-S.

STUDENT LIFE. Housing: Dormitories (men, women, coed); apartment, fraternity, sorority housing available. **Activities:** Student government, magazine, radio, student newspaper, television, yearbook, choral groups, concert band, dance, drama, jazz band, marching band, music ensembles, musical theater, pep band, symphony orchestra, fraternities, sororities, over 225 student organizations including religious and ethnic organizations.

ATHLETICS. NCAA. **Intercollegiate:** Baseball M, basketball, cross-country, diving W, football M, golf M, soccer M, softball W, swimming, tennis, track and field, volleyball W, water polo M, wrestling M. **Intramural:** Archery, badminton, baseball, basketball, bowling, cross-country, fencing, golf, gymnastics, handball, horseback riding, racquetball, skiing, swimming, tennis, volleyball, water polo M, wrestling M.

STUDENT SERVICES. Aptitude testing, career counseling, employment service for undergraduates, freshman orientation, health services, on-campus day care, personal counseling, placement service for graduates, special adviser for adult students, veterans counselor, services/facilities for handicapped.

ANNUAL EXPENSES. Tuition and fees (projected): $1,446, $7,380 additional for out-of-state students. **Room and board:** $4,287. **Books and supplies:** $612. **Other expenses:** $1,242.

FINANCIAL AID. 33% of freshmen, 35% of continuing students receive some form of aid. 95% of grants, 91% of loans, all jobs based on need. Academic, music/drama, art, athletic, leadership, alumni affiliation, minority scholarships available. **Aid applications:** No closing date; priority given to applications received by March 2; applicants notified on a rolling basis beginning on or about June 7; must reply within 2 weeks.

ADDRESS/TELEPHONE. Richard Backer, Director of Admissions and Records, California State University: Fresno, 5150 N. Maple Avenue, Fresno, CA 93740-0057. (209) 278-2191.

California State University: Fullerton
Fullerton, California CB code: 4589

Admissions: 80% of applicants accepted
Based on: ••• School record, test scores
Completion: 74% of freshmen end year in good standing
28% graduate

4-year public university, coed. Founded in 1957. **Accreditation:** Regional. **Undergraduate enrollment:** 5,733 men, 7,239 women full time; 3,265 men, 4,004 women part time. **Graduate enrollment:** 213 men, 431 women full time; 1,495 men, 2,031 women part time. **Faculty:** 1,262 total (755 full time), 643 with doctorates or other terminal degrees. **Location:** Suburban campus in small city; 30 miles from Los Angeles. **Calendar:** Semester, limited summer session. Extensive evening/early morning classes. **Microcomputers:** 700 located in computer centers. **Special facilities:** California Desert Studies Center, wildlife sanctuary, arboretum, art galleries.

DEGREES OFFERED. BA, BS, BFA, MA, MS, MBA, MFA. 4,188 bachelor's degrees awarded in 1992. 32% in business and management, 12% communications, 8% home economics, 5% letters/literature, 6% psychology, 12% social sciences, 5% visual and performing arts. Graduate degrees offered in 83 major fields of study.

UNDERGRADUATE MAJORS. Accounting, advertising, Afro-American (black) studies, American studies, anthropology, applied mathematics, art education, art history, biochemistry, biology, botany, business administration and management, business economics, cell biology, ceramics, chemistry, chemistry/biochemistry, child development/care/guidance, city/community/regional planning, civil engineering, commercial music, communicative disorders, comparative literature, computer and information sciences, crafts, criminal justice studies, dance, dramatic arts, drawing, ecology, economics, electrical/electronics/communications engineering, engineering science, English, environmental design, finance, French, genetics, human and animal, geography, geology, German, graphic design, history, illustration design, international business management, journalism, Latin American studies, liberal/general studies, linguistics, management information systems, management science, marine biology, marketing management, mathematics, mathematics education, mechanical engineering, mental health/human services, Mexican American studies, microbiology, molecular biology, music, music education, music history and appreciation, music performance, music theory and composition, musical theater, nursing, painting, philosophy, photographic technology, photography, physical education, physics, political science and government, printmaking, psychology, public administration, public relations, radio/television broadcasting, religion, Russian and Slavic studies, sculpture, sociology, Spanish, speech, speech/communication/theater education, statistics, theater arts-history and theory, theater arts/directing, theater arts/playwriting, theater arts/television, theater design, visual and performing arts, zoology.

ACADEMIC PROGRAMS. Accelerated program, cooperative education, double major, honors program, independent study, internships, student-designed major, study abroad, teacher preparation, cross-registration. **Remedial services:** Learning center, preadmission summer program, reduced course load, remedial instruction, special counselor, tutoring, Educational Opportunity Program. **ROTC:** Army. **Placement/credit:** AP, CLEP General and Subject, institutional tests; 30 credit hours maximum for bachelor's degree.

ACADEMIC REQUIREMENTS. Freshmen must earn minimum GPA of 2.0 to continue in good standing. 73% of freshmen return for sophomore year. Students must declare major by end of second year. **Graduation requirements:** 124 hours for bachelor's (48 in major). Most students required to take courses in arts/fine arts, English, history, humanities, mathematics, biological/physical sciences, social sciences.

FRESHMAN ADMISSIONS. Selection criteria: Eligibility index consisting of combination of high school GPA and SAT or ACT score. **High school preparation:** 15 units required. Required units include English 4, foreign language 2, mathematics 3 and science 1. Science unit should include laboratory science. One visual and performing arts, and 1 US history/government also required. **Test requirements:** SAT or ACT; score report by August 1.

1992 FRESHMAN CLASS PROFILE. 2,775 men applied, 2,146 accepted, 873 enrolled; 3,596 women applied, 2,935 accepted, 1,197 enrolled. **Academic background:** Mid 50% of enrolled freshmen had SAT-V between 320-450, SAT-M between 390-550; ACT composite between 17-22. 92% submitted SAT scores, 8% submitted ACT scores. **Characteristics:** 97% from in state, 93% commute, 52% have minority backgrounds, 3% are foreign students. Average age is 19.

FALL-TERM APPLICATIONS. $55 fee, may be waived for applicants with need. No closing date; priority given to applications received by November 1; applicants notified on a rolling basis beginning on or about January 1. Audition required for music applicants. Early admission available.

STUDENT LIFE. Housing: Apartment, fraternity, sorority housing available. **Activities:** Student government, film, magazine, student newspaper, television, choral groups, concert band, dance, drama, jazz band, music ensembles, musical theater, opera, pep band, symphony orchestra, debate, fraternities, sororities.

ATHLETICS. NCAA. **Intercollegiate:** Baseball M, basketball, cross-country, fencing, gymnastics W, soccer, softball W, tennis W, track and field, volleyball W, wrestling M. **Intramural:** Badminton, basketball, bowling, fencing, gymnastics, handball M, racquetball, rugby M, skiing, soccer M, softball, swimming, tennis, volleyball, wrestling M.

STUDENT SERVICES. Aptitude testing, career counseling, employment service for undergraduates, freshman orientation, health services, on-campus day care, personal counseling, placement service for graduates, special adviser for adult students, veterans counselor, services/facilities for handicapped.

ANNUAL EXPENSES. Tuition and fees (1992-93): $1,480, $7,380 additional for out-of-state students. **Room and board:** $3,476 room only. **Books and supplies:** $574. **Other expenses:** $1,728.

FINANCIAL AID. 17% of freshmen, 25% of continuing students receive some form of aid. 90% of grants, 92% of loans, 21% of jobs based on need. 1,099 enrolled freshmen were judged to have need, 1,022 were offered aid. Academic, music/drama, art, athletic, state/district residency, leadership scholarships available. **Aid applications:** No closing date; priority given to applications received by March 2; applicants notified on a rolling basis beginning on or about June 15; must reply within 2 weeks. **Additional information:** Fee waiver for children of veterans killed in action or with service-connected disability whose annual income is $5,000 or less.

ADDRESS/TELEPHONE. James C. Blackburn, Director of Admissions and Records, California State University: Fullerton, Fullerton, CA 92634. (714) 773-2370.

California State University: Hayward
Hayward, California CB code: 4011

4-year public university, coed. Founded in 1957. **Accreditation:** Regional. **Undergraduate enrollment:** 2,671 men, 4,281 women full time; 1,182 men, 1,754 women part time. **Graduate enrollment:** 301 men, 604 women full time; 888 men, 1,305 women part time. **Faculty:** 546 total (406 full time). **Location:** Suburban campus in small city; 30 miles from San Francisco, 30 miles from San Jose. **Calendar:** Quarter, limited summer session. Saturday and extensive evening/early morning classes. **Microcomputers:** 500 located in libraries, classrooms, computer centers. **Special facilities:** Ecological field station, art galleries, museum of anthropology, marine laboratory, geology summer field camp. **Additional facts:** Branch campus (Conta Costa Campus) located in Concord.

DEGREES OFFERED. BA, BS, MA, MS, MBA. 1,960 bachelor's degrees awarded in 1992. 38% in business and management, 6% computer sciences, 12% multi/interdisciplinary studies, 5% parks/recreation, protective services, public affairs, 9% psychology, 5% social sciences. Graduate degrees offered in 48 major fields of study.

UNDERGRADUATE MAJORS. Accounting, advertising, Afro-American (black) studies, American Indian studies, anthropology, biochemistry, biology, business administration and management, business and management, business economics, chemistry, communications, computer and information sciences, contract management and procurement/purchasing, criminal justice studies, dance, dramatic arts, economics, English, environmental science, finance, fine arts, French, geography, geology, German, health sciences, history, human resources development, industrial and organizational psychology, information sciences and systems, investments and securities, labor/industrial relations, Latin American studies, liberal/general studies, management information systems, management science, marketing management, mathematics, Mexican American studies, music, nursing, organizational behavior, parks and recreation management, personnel management, philosophy, physical sciences, physics, political science and government, psychology, real estate, small business management and ownership, social work, sociology, Spanish, speech, speech pathology/audiology, statistics.

ACADEMIC PROGRAMS. Cooperative education, double major, dual enrollment of high school students, independent study, internships, student-designed major, study abroad, teacher preparation, visiting/exchange student program, cross-registration, master's degree program in marine sciences at Moss Landing Marine Laboratory. **Remedial services:** Learning center, preadmission summer program, reduced course load, remedial instruction, special counselor, tutoring. **ROTC:** Air Force, Army, Naval. **Placement/credit:** AP, CLEP General and Subject, institutional tests; 45 credit hours maximum for bachelor's degree.

ACADEMIC REQUIREMENTS. Freshmen must earn minimum GPA of 2.0 to continue in good standing. 83% of freshmen return for sophomore year. Students must declare major by end of second year. **Graduation requirements:** 186 hours for bachelor's (40 in major). Most students required to take courses in arts/fine arts, English, history, humanities, mathematics, biological/physical sciences, social sciences.

FRESHMAN ADMISSIONS. Selection criteria: Eligibility index based on GPA and test results. Out-of-state applicants should be in top sixth of high school class. **High school preparation:** 15 units required. Required units include English 4, foreign language 2, mathematics 3, social science 1 and science 1. One visual and performing arts, 3 electives also required. **Test requirements:** SAT or ACT; score report by August 1.

1992 FRESHMAN CLASS PROFILE. 2,345 men and women applied, 1,156 accepted; 188 men enrolled, 419 women enrolled. **Characteristics:** 94% from in state, 97% commute, 68% have minority backgrounds, 3% are foreign students. Average age is 19.

FALL-TERM APPLICATIONS. $55 fee, may be waived for applicants with need. Closing date May 15; priority given to applications received by November 30; applicants notified on a rolling basis. Deferred admission available.

STUDENT LIFE. Housing: Apartment housing available. Private coeducational dormitory immediately adjacent to campus. **Activities:** Student government, film, magazine, radio, student newspaper, television, yearbook, choral groups, concert band, dance, drama, jazz band, music ensembles, musical theater, opera, pep band, symphony orchestra, fraternities, sororities, 60 campus organizations. **Additional information:** Community and campus-based volunteer programs available.

ATHLETICS. NCAA. **Intercollegiate:** Baseball M, basketball, football M, soccer, softball W, volleyball W. **Intramural:** Badminton, basketball, golf, racquetball, soccer, softball, swimming, tennis, volleyball.

STUDENT SERVICES. Aptitude testing, career counseling, employment service for undergraduates, freshman orientation, health services, placement service for graduates, veterans counselor, independent travel service, daycare near campus, services/facilities for handicapped.

ANNUAL EXPENSES. Tuition and fees (1992-93): $1,423, $7,380 additional for out-of-state students. **Room and board:** $2,745 room only. **Books and supplies:** $612. **Other expenses:** $1,401.

FINANCIAL AID. 27% of freshmen, 21% of continuing students receive some form of aid. All grants, 89% of loans, all jobs based on need. Academic, minority scholarships available. **Aid applications:** No closing date; priority given to applications received by March 2; applicants notified on a rolling basis beginning on or about June 1; must reply within 2 weeks.

ADDRESS/TELEPHONE. Maria DeAnda-Ramos, Director of Admissions/Outreach, California State University: Hayward, 35200 Carlos Bee Boulevard, Hayward, CA 94542-3035. (510) 881-3817. Fax: (510) 881-3808.

California State University: Long Beach

Long Beach, California — CB code: 4389

Admissions:	75% of applicants accepted
Based on:	••• School record, test scores
	•• Special talents
	• Recommendations
Completion:	75% of freshmen end year in good standing
	22% graduate

4-year public university, coed. Founded in 1949. **Accreditation:** Regional. **Undergraduate enrollment:** 7,230 men, 8,570 women full time; 3,821 men, 3,963 women part time. **Graduate enrollment:** 442 men, 731 women full time; 2,409 men, 2,905 women part time. **Faculty:** 1,441 total (933 full time). **Location:** Suburban campus in large city; 25 miles from Los Angeles. **Calendar:** Semester, extensive summer session. Extensive evening/early morning classes. **Microcomputers:** 901 located in libraries, classrooms, computer centers. **Special facilities:** Art museum, galleries, Japanese garden.

DEGREES OFFERED. BA, BS, BFA, MA, MS, MBA, MFA, MSW, PhD. 4,674 bachelor's degrees awarded in 1992. 19% in business and management, 7% communications, 9% engineering, 11% multi/interdisciplinary studies, 7% psychology, 9% social sciences, 7% visual and performing arts. Graduate degrees offered in 81 major fields of study.

UNDERGRADUATE MAJORS. Accounting, Afro-American (black) studies, American studies, anthropology, applied mathematics, art education, art history, Asian studies, biochemistry, bioengineering and biomedical engineering, biology, botany, business administration and management, business and management, business statistics, cell biology, ceramics, chemical engineering, chemistry, cinematography/film, civil engineering, comparative literature, computer and information sciences, computer engineering, computer mathematics, construction management, creative writing, criminal justice studies, criminology, dance, dramatic arts, drawing, earth sciences, economics, electrical/electronics/communications engineering, electronic technology, engineering, English, English literature, family/consumer resource management, fiber/textiles/weaving, finance, fine arts, food science and nutrition, French, geography, geology, German, graphic design, health care administration, health education, health sciences, history, home economics, home economics education, human environment and housing, human resources development, illustration design, individual and family development, industrial arts education, industrial design, industrial engineering, information sciences and systems, interior design, international business management, international studies, jazz, journalism, law enforcement and corrections, liberal/general studies, management information systems, manufacturing technology, marine biology, marketing management, materials engineering, mathematics, mechanical engineering, metal/jewelry, Mexican American studies, microbiology, molecular biology, music, music education, music history and appreciation, music performance, music theory and composition, nursing, operations research, painting, parks and recreation management, philosophy, photography, physical education, physical therapy, physics, physiology, human and animal, political science and government, printmaking, psychology, quality control technology, quantitative psychology, radiation therapy, radio/television broadcasting, recreation and community services technologies, religion, rhetoric, sculpture, social work, sociology, Spanish, speech, speech correction, speech pathology/audiology, statistics, studio art, textiles and clothing, theater design, trade and industrial education, video, zoology.

ACADEMIC PROGRAMS. Cooperative education, double major, honors program, independent study, internships, student-designed major, study abroad, teacher preparation, visiting/exchange student program, Washington semester, cross-registration; liberal arts/career combination in engineering. **Remedial services:** Learning center, preadmission summer program, reduced course load, remedial instruction, special counselor, tutoring. **ROTC:** Air Force, Army. **Placement/credit:** AP, CLEP General and Subject, institutional tests.

ACADEMIC REQUIREMENTS. Freshmen must earn minimum GPA of 2.0 to continue in good standing. 70% of freshmen return for sophomore year. Students must declare major by end of second year. **Graduation requirements:** 124 hours for bachelor's (45 in major). Most students required to take courses in arts/fine arts, English, foreign languages, history, humanities, mathematics, biological/physical sciences, social sciences.

FRESHMAN ADMISSIONS. Selection criteria: In-state applicants with high school GPA 3.0 who have completed required pattern of 15 units of college-preparatory study. Out-of-state applicants with high school GPA of 3.75 and required preparatory course work. Other applicants are considered on the basis of index that combines high school GPA and SAT or ACT scores. **High school preparation:** 15 units required. Required units include English 4, foreign language 2, mathematics 3 and science 1. One visual and performing arts and 1 US history/government also required. **Test requirements:** SAT or ACT; score report by March 15.

1992 FRESHMAN CLASS PROFILE. 3,728 men applied, 2,658 accepted, 710 enrolled; 5,290 women applied, 4,092 accepted, 1,080 enrolled. 67% had high school GPA of 3.0 or higher, 33% between 2.0 and 2.99. **Academic background:** Mid 50% of enrolled freshmen had SAT-V between 280-440, SAT-M between 330-520. 91% submitted SAT scores. **Characteris-**

tics: 78% from in state, 50% commute, 61% have minority backgrounds, 2% are foreign students. Average age is 19.

FALL-TERM APPLICATIONS. $55 fee, may be waived for applicants with need. Closing date May 31; priority given to applications received by November 30; applicants notified on a rolling basis beginning on or about November 30. Audition required for dance, music applicants. Portfolio required for art, design applicants. Deferred admission available.

STUDENT LIFE. Housing: Dormitories (coed); fraternity, sorority housing available. **Activities:** Student government, magazine, radio, student newspaper, yearbook, choral groups, concert band, dance, drama, jazz band, music ensembles, musical theater, opera, pep band, symphony orchestra, fraternities, sororities, more than 150 political, ethnic, and social service organizations.

ATHLETICS. NCAA. **Intercollegiate:** Baseball M, basketball, cross-country, fencing, golf, softball W, tennis W, track and field, volleyball, water polo M. **Intramural:** Archery, badminton, basketball, bowling, diving, gymnastics, handball, racquetball, rowing (crew), rugby M, sailing, skiing, soccer, softball, swimming, table tennis, tennis, track and field, volleyball, water polo W.

STUDENT SERVICES. Aptitude testing, career counseling, employment service for undergraduates, freshman orientation, health services, on-campus day care, personal counseling, placement service for graduates, veterans counselor, services/facilities for handicapped.

ANNUAL EXPENSES. Tuition and fees (1992-93): $1,423, $7,380 additional for out-of-state students. **Room and board:** $4,800. **Books and supplies:** $576. **Other expenses:** $1,728.

FINANCIAL AID. 33% of freshmen, 33% of continuing students receive some form of aid. 85% of grants, 88% of loans, 24% of jobs based on need. 1,051 enrolled freshmen were judged to have need, 926 were offered aid. Academic, music/drama, art, athletic, state/district residency, leadership, minority scholarships available. **Aid applications:** No closing date; priority given to applications received by March 2; applicants notified on a rolling basis beginning on or about July 15; must reply within 3 weeks.

ADDRESS/TELEPHONE. Gloria Kapp, Director of Admissions and Records, California State University: Long Beach, 1250 Bellflower Boulevard, Long Beach, CA 90840-0108. (310) 985-5471.

California State University: Los Angeles
Los Angeles, California CB code: 4399

4-year public university, coed. Founded in 1947. **Accreditation:** Regional. **Undergraduate enrollment:** 4,042 men, 5,316 women full time; 2,237 men, 2,985 women part time. **Graduate enrollment:** 366 men, 639 women full time; 1,557 men, 2,261 women part time. **Faculty:** 991 total (578 full time). **Location:** Urban campus in very large city; 3 miles from downtown. **Calendar:** Quarter, extensive summer session. Extensive evening/early morning classes. **Microcomputers:** 767 located in classrooms, computer centers. **Special facilities:** Schlicker Baroque pipe organ, 4 megavolt Van de Graaff accelerator.

DEGREES OFFERED. BA, BS, MA, MS, MBA, MFA, PhD. 1,985 bachelor's degrees awarded in 1992. 30% in business and management, 5% business/office and marketing/distribution, 7% engineering, 6% health sciences, 9% home economics, 5% parks/recreation, protective services, public affairs, 6% social sciences. Graduate degrees offered in 102 major fields of study.

UNDERGRADUATE MAJORS. Accounting, advertising, Afro-American (black) studies, allied health, anthropology, applied mathematics, art education, art history, aviation management, biochemistry, biology, biophysics, business administration and management, business and management, business and office, business economics, business education, ceramics, chemistry, child development/care/guidance, civil engineering, clothing and textiles management/production/services, community health work, computer and information sciences, criminal justice studies, dance, dramatic arts, drawing, earth sciences, economics, electrical/electronics/communications engineering, enameling, engineering, English, English education, family and community services, fashion design, fiber/textiles/weaving, finance, fine arts, fire control and safety technology, fire protection, food science and nutrition, foreign languages education, French, geography, geology, graphic and printing production, graphic design, health education, health sciences, history, home economics, home economics education, home furnishings and equipment management/production/services, human environment and housing, human resources development, illustration design, individual and family development, industrial arts education, industrial design, industrial technology, information sciences and systems, interior design, international business management, investments and securities, Japanese, jazz, journalism, labor/industrial relations, Latin American studies, law enforcement and corrections, liberal/general studies, management information systems, marketing and distribution, marketing management, marketing research, mathematics, mathematics education, mechanical engineering, medical laboratory technologies, metal/jewelry, Mexican American studies, microbiology, music, music education, music history and appreciation, music performance, music theory and composition, nursing, office supervision and management, operations research, painting, personnel management, philosophy, physical education, physical sciences, physics, political science and government, prelaw, production technology, psychology, public administration, public relations, pure mathematics, radio/television broadcasting, radio/television technology, real estate, rehabilitation counseling/services, retailing, sculpture, small business management and ownership, social science education, social sciences, social work, sociology, Spanish, speech, speech pathology/audiology, studio art, telecommunications, textiles and clothing, trade and industrial education, transportation management, vocational education.

ACADEMIC PROGRAMS. Accelerated program, cooperative education, double major, dual enrollment of high school students, education specialist degree, honors program, independent study, internships, student-designed major, study abroad, teacher preparation, telecourses, visiting/exchange student program, cross-registration. **Remedial services:** Learning center, preadmission summer program, reduced course load, remedial instruction, special counselor, tutoring. **ROTC:** Air Force, Army. **Placement/credit:** AP, CLEP General and Subject, institutional tests.

ACADEMIC REQUIREMENTS. Freshmen must earn minimum GPA of 2.0 to continue in good standing. 75% of freshmen return for sophomore year. Students must declare major by end of second year. **Graduation requirements:** 186 hours for bachelor's. Most students required to take courses in arts/fine arts, English, foreign languages, history, humanities, mathematics, philosophy/religion, biological/physical sciences, social sciences.

FRESHMAN ADMISSIONS. Selection criteria: School GPA and test scores. **High school preparation:** 15 units required. Required units include English 4, foreign language 2, mathematics 3 and science 1. One visual and performing arts, 1 US history/government and 3 electives also required. **Test requirements:** SAT or ACT; score report by August 15.

1992 FRESHMAN CLASS PROFILE. 5,609 men and women applied, 2,756 accepted; 494 men enrolled, 774 women enrolled. **Characteristics:** 98% from in state, 91% commute, 86% have minority backgrounds, 7% are foreign students, 3% join fraternities/sororities. Average age is 18.

FALL-TERM APPLICATIONS. $55 fee, may be waived for applicants with need. No closing date; priority given to applications received by July 1; applicants notified on a rolling basis beginning on or about March 1. Early admission available.

STUDENT LIFE. Housing: Apartment, fraternity, sorority housing available. International house-area emphasizes the multicultural diversity. **Activities:** Student government, magazine, student newspaper, television, choral groups, concert band, dance, drama, jazz band, music ensembles, musical theater, opera, symphony orchestra, fraternities, sororities, Chicanos for Creative Medicine, Hispanic Business Society, Society of Women Engineers, Movimiento Estudiantil Chicanos de Aetlar (MECHA), Asian Student Union, Black Students Association, Sisters of the African Star, Vietnamese Student Association, Latin American Society, Chinese American Service Club.

ATHLETICS. NCAA. **Intercollegiate:** Baseball M, basketball, cross-country, soccer M, tennis, track and field, volleyball W. **Intramural:** Baseball M, basketball, football M, skiing, soccer M, softball W, tennis, volleyball.

STUDENT SERVICES. Aptitude testing, career counseling, employment service for undergraduates, freshman orientation, health services, on-campus day care, personal counseling, placement service for graduates, veterans counselor, services/facilities for handicapped.

ANNUAL EXPENSES. Tuition and fees (projected): $1,428, $5,904 additional for out-of-state students. **Room and board:** $2,805 room only. **Books and supplies:** $612. **Other expenses:** $1,728.

FINANCIAL AID. 48% of freshmen, 46% of continuing students receive some form of aid. 98% of grants, 81% of loans, all jobs based on need. Academic, music/drama, art, athletic, state/district residency, leadership, alumni affiliation, minority scholarships available. **Aid applications:** No closing date; priority given to applications received by March 1; applicants notified on a rolling basis beginning on or about May 1; must reply within 3 weeks.

ADDRESS/TELEPHONE. Kevin M. Browne, Director of Admissions/University Outreach, California State University: Los Angeles, 5151 State University Drive SA101, Los Angeles, CA 90032-8530. (213) 343-2752. Fax: (213) 343-3888.

California State University: Northridge
Northridge, California CB code: 4707

4-year public university, coed. Founded in 1958. **Accreditation:** Regional. **Undergraduate enrollment:** 6,887 men, 8,670 women full time; 3,310 men, 4,226 women part time. **Graduate enrollment:** 267 men, 725 women full time; 1,911 men, 3,088 women part time. **Faculty:** 1,280 total (840 full time), 672 with doctorates or other terminal degrees. **Location:** Suburban campus in very large city; 25 miles from Los Angeles Civic Center. **Calendar:** Semester, limited summer session. **Microcomputers:** 1,700 located in libraries, classrooms, computer centers. **Special facilities:** Anthropology museum, art galleries, botanical gardens, urban archives center, radio and TV station, observatory, map library, center for the study of cancer and development biology, National Center on Deafness, planetarium. **Additional facts:** University Center in Ventura.

DEGREES OFFERED. BA, BS, MA, MS, MBA. 4,047 bachelor's degrees awarded in 1992. 24% in business and management, 12% communications, 5% engineering, 7% health sciences, 10% multi/interdisciplinary studies, 8% psychology, 10% social sciences, 6% visual and performing arts. Graduate degrees offered in 92 major fields of study.

UNDERGRADUATE MAJORS. Aerospace/aeronautical/astronautical engineering, Afro-American (black) studies, anthropology, applied mathematics, art education, art history, biochemistry, biology, business administration and management, business economics, business education, business home economics, business systems analysis, cell biology, ceramics, chemical engineering, chemistry, child development/care/guidance, civil engineering, comparative literature, computer and information sciences, computer engineering, creative writing, dance, dramatic arts, drawing, earth sciences, economics, electrical/electronics/communications engineering, engineering, engineering mechanics, English, English education, English literature, family/consumer resource management, finance, fine arts, food science and nutrition, foreign languages education, French, geography, geology, geophysics and seismology, German, glass, graphic design, health education, health sciences, history, home economics, home economics education, human environment and housing, humanities, humanities and social sciences, individual and family development, industrial engineering, international business management, journalism, liberal/general studies, linguistics, management information systems, management science, marketing and distribution, marketing research, materials engineering, mathematics, mathematics education, mechanical engineering, metal/jewelry, Mexican American studies, microbiology, molecular biology, music, music education, music history and appreciation, music performance, music theory and composition, nursing, operations research, painting, personnel management, philosophy, physical education, physical sciences, physical therapy, physics, political science and government, printmaking, psychology, pure mathematics, radio/television broadcasting, real estate, recreation and community services technologies, religion, sculpture, social science education, social studies education, sociology, Spanish, speech, speech correction, speech pathology/audiology, speech/communication/theater education, statistics, textiles and clothing, urban studies.

ACADEMIC PROGRAMS. Double major, dual enrollment of high school students, honors program, independent study, internships, student-designed major, study abroad, teacher preparation, telecourses, visiting/exchange student program. **Remedial services:** Learning center, preadmission summer program, remedial instruction, special counselor, tutoring. **ROTC:** Air Force, Army. **Placement/credit:** AP, CLEP General and Subject, institutional tests.

ACADEMIC REQUIREMENTS. Freshmen must earn minimum GPA of 2.0 to continue in good standing. 70% of freshmen return for sophomore year. **Graduation requirements:** 124 hours for bachelor's (40 in major). Most students required to take courses in arts/fine arts, English, foreign languages, history, humanities, mathematics, philosophy/religion, biological/physical sciences, social sciences. **Additional information:** Army and Air Force ROTC available at cooperating institution.

FRESHMAN ADMISSIONS. Selection criteria: Index using high school GPA and SAT or ACT scores, and completion of subject requirements. In-state applicants should rank in top third of class; out-of-state in the top sixth. **High school preparation:** 15 units required. Required units include English 4, foreign language 2, mathematics 3, social science 1 and science 1. Science unit should include laboratory science. One visual and performing arts, 1 US history/government and 3 approved electives also required. **Test requirements:** SAT or ACT; score report by March 1. **Additional information:** Business administration, economics, engineering, computer science, and physical therapy open to residents of California only.

1992 FRESHMAN CLASS PROFILE. 909 men, 1,248 women enrolled. **Academic background:** Mid 50% of enrolled freshmen had SAT-V between 350-500, SAT-M between 350-550. 90% submitted SAT scores. **Characteristics:** 62% have minority backgrounds. Average age is 18.

FALL-TERM APPLICATIONS. $55 fee, may be waived for applicants with need. Closing date November 30; applicants notified on a rolling basis beginning on or about November 15. Audition required for music applicants. Early admission available. Institutional early decision plan. Applications must be completed by November 30 for business administration, economics and physical therapy programs.

STUDENT LIFE. Housing: Dormitories (coed); apartment, fraternity, sorority housing available. **Activities:** Student government, magazine, radio, student newspaper, television, yearbook, choral groups, concert band, dance, drama, jazz band, marching band, music ensembles, musical theater, opera, pep band, symphony orchestra, fraternities, sororities, women's center, communities, clubs and organizations representing varied interests.

ATHLETICS. NCAA. **Intercollegiate:** Baseball M, basketball, cross-country, diving, football M, golf M, soccer M, softball W, swimming, tennis W, track and field, volleyball. **Intramural:** Badminton, baseball, basketball, bowling, cross-country, diving, handball, ice hockey M, racquetball, rugby, sailing, skiing, soccer, softball, swimming, table tennis, tennis, track and field, volleyball.

STUDENT SERVICES. Aptitude testing, career counseling, employment service for undergraduates, freshman orientation, health services, on-campus day care, personal counseling, placement service for graduates, special adviser for adult students, veterans counselor, services/facilities for handicapped.

ANNUAL EXPENSES. Tuition and fees (projected): $2,002, $7,380 additional for out-of-state students. **Room and board:** $5,340. **Books and supplies:** $612. **Other expenses:** $1,384.

FINANCIAL AID. 25% of continuing students receive some form of aid. 98% of grants, 79% of loans, all jobs based on need. Academic, music/drama, art, athletic, state/district residency, leadership, minority scholarships available. **Aid applications:** No closing date; priority given to applications received by March 2; applicants notified on a rolling basis beginning on or about April 1.

ADDRESS/TELEPHONE. Lorraine Newlon, Director of Admissions and Records, California State University: Northridge, P.O. Box 1286, Northridge, CA 91328-1286. (818) 885-3700. Fax: (818) 885-3766.

California State University: Sacramento
Sacramento, California CB code: 4671

4-year public university, coed. Founded in 1947. **Accreditation:** Regional. **Undergraduate enrollment:** 6,628 men, 7,454 women full time; 2,347 men, 2,977 women part time. **Graduate enrollment:** 415 men, 967 women full time; 1,477 men, 2,203 women part time. **Faculty:** 1,776 total (1,214 full time), 757 with doctorates or other terminal degrees. **Location:** Urban campus in large city; 90 miles from San Francisco. **Calendar:** Semester, extensive summer session. Saturday and extensive evening/early morning classes. **Microcomputers:** 400 located in libraries, classrooms, computer centers. **Special facilities:** Aquatic center, 30 miles of bicycle trails along American River. **Additional facts:** Campus served by Sacramento light rail and transit systems.

DEGREES OFFERED. BA, BS, MA, MS, MBA. 3,700 bachelor's degrees awarded in 1992. 33% in business and management, 7% communications, 9% teacher education, 8% engineering, 5% health sciences, 9% parks/recreation, protective services, public affairs, 5% psychology, 7% social sciences. Graduate degrees offered in 44 major fields of study.

UNDERGRADUATE MAJORS. Accounting, Afro-American (black) studies, agricultural education, American Indian studies, anatomy, anthropology, applied mathematics, bilingual/bicultural education, biology, business administration and management, business education, chemistry, civil engineering, clinical laboratory science, communications, computer and information sciences, computer engineering, construction management, criminal justice studies, dramatic arts, early childhood education, economics, education, electrical/electronics/communications engineering, elementary education, engineering, English, English education, environmental science, ethnic studies/Asian American, finance, foreign languages education, French, geography, geology, German, health education, health sciences, history, home economics, home economics education, human resources development, humanities and social sciences, insurance and risk management, interior design, international business management, journalism, liberal/general studies, management information systems, management science, marketing management, mathematics, mathematics education, mechanical engineering, mechanical engineering technology, Mexican American studies, microbiology, molecular biology, music, music education, nursing, operations research, parks and recreation management, personnel management, philosophy, physical education, physical sciences, physics, physiology, human and animal, plant physiology, political science and government, psychology, public administration, real estate, secondary education, social science education, social sciences, social work, sociology, Spanish, speech pathology/audiology.

ACADEMIC PROGRAMS. Cooperative education, double major, dual enrollment of high school students, independent study, internships, student-designed major, study abroad, teacher preparation, visiting/exchange student program, cross-registration. **Remedial services:** Learning center, preadmission summer program, reduced course load, remedial instruction, tutoring, "summer bridge" program for economically disadvantaged students. **ROTC:** Air Force, Army. **Placement/credit:** AP, CLEP General and Subject, institutional tests; 30 credit hours maximum for bachelor's degree.

ACADEMIC REQUIREMENTS. Freshmen must earn minimum GPA of 2.0 to continue in good standing. 75% of freshmen return for sophomore year. Students must declare major by end of second year. **Graduation requirements:** 124 hours for bachelor's (31 in major). Most students required to take courses in English, history, humanities, mathematics, biological/physical sciences, social sciences.

FRESHMAN ADMISSIONS. Selection criteria: School achievement record, test scores, GPA weighted 5 times more than test scores; in-state applicants for regular admission normally in top third of class. **High school preparation:** 15 units required. Required units include English 4, foreign language 2, mathematics 3 and science 1. One visual and performing arts, 1 US history/ government and 3 elective from required units. **Test requirements:** SAT or ACT; score report by June 1. **Additional information:** Closing dates not applicable for special programs such as athletics and minority support programs; communications studies, criminal justice, environmental studies, interior design, liberal studies, psychology programs usually close on November 30, other programs have state-mandated application deadlines.

1992 FRESHMAN CLASS PROFILE. 1,451 men and women enrolled.

66% had high school GPA of 3.0 or higher, 34% between 2.0 and 2.99. **Academic background:** Mid 50% of enrolled freshmen had SAT-V between 380-540, SAT-M between 410-580; ACT composite between 16-24. 90% submitted SAT scores, 10% submitted ACT scores. **Characteristics:** 96% from in state, 50% commute, 28% have minority backgrounds, 2% are foreign students. Average age is 19.

FALL-TERM APPLICATIONS. $55 fee, may be waived for applicants with need. No closing date; priority given to applications received by November 1; applicants notified on a rolling basis beginning on or about December 1. Early admission available. Applicants for nursing and mechanical engineering should file by November 30.

STUDENT LIFE. Housing: Dormitories (men, women, coed). Half of all students live within 5 miles of campus. Off-campus apartments numerous and within bicycling distance. Shuttle service and light rail station on campus. **Activities:** Student government, film, radio, student newspaper, television, yearbook, debate, choral groups, concert band, dance, drama, jazz band, marching band, music ensembles, musical theater, opera, pep band, symphony orchestra, fraternities, sororities, more than 150 clubs, organizations, and special interest groups. **Additional information:** 70% of students employed, 87% of working students work off-campus (many jobs available in local area).

ATHLETICS. NCAA. **Intercollegiate:** Baseball M, basketball, cross-country, football M, golf M, gymnastics W, soccer M, softball W, swimming, tennis, track and field, volleyball W. **Intramural:** Badminton, basketball, bowling, cross-country, handball, racquetball, rowing (crew), soccer, softball, swimming, table tennis, tennis, volleyball.

STUDENT SERVICES. Aptitude testing, career counseling, employment service for undergraduates, freshman orientation, health services, on-campus day care, personal counseling, placement service for graduates, special adviser for adult students, veterans counselor, services/facilities for handicapped.

ANNUAL EXPENSES. Tuition and fees (1992-93): $1,420, $7,380 additional for out-of-state students. **Room and board:** $4,618. **Books and supplies:** $576. **Other expenses:** $1,251.

FINANCIAL AID. 28% of freshmen, 28% of continuing students receive some form of aid. All jobs based on need. **Aid applications:** No closing date; priority given to applications received by March 2; applicants notified on a rolling basis beginning on or about May 1; must reply within 2 weeks.

ADDRESS/TELEPHONE. Larry Glasmire, Director of Admissions/Records, California State University: Sacramento, 6000 J Street, Sacramento, CA 95819-6048. (916) 278-3901. Fax: (916) 278-5603.

California State University: San Bernardino
San Bernardino, California — CB code: 4099

4-year public university and liberal arts college, coed. Founded in 1962. **Accreditation:** Regional. **Undergraduate enrollment:** 2,797 men, 4,129 women full time; 883 men, 1,383 women part time. **Graduate enrollment:** 316 men, 558 women full time; 912 men, 1,505 women part time. **Faculty:** 604 total (429 full time), 376 with doctorates or other terminal degrees. **Location:** Suburban campus in small city; 60 miles east of Los Angeles. **Calendar:** Quarter, limited summer session. **Microcomputers:** 180 located in libraries, classrooms, computer centers. **Special facilities:** Art gallery, off-campus courses (satellite campuses), animal house, greenhouse, Desert Studies Center. **Additional facts:** School of Social and Behavioral Sciences offers masters in National Security Studies. Coachelle Valley Center, satellite campus in Palm Desert, offers day and evening courses in degree and credential programs.

DEGREES OFFERED. BA, BS, MA, MS, MBA, MSW. 1,481 bachelor's degrees awarded in 1992. Graduate degrees offered in 17 major fields of study.

UNDERGRADUATE MAJORS. American studies, anthropology, art history, biology, business and management, chemistry, communications, computer and information sciences, criminal justice studies, dramatic arts, economics, English, environmental science, food science and nutrition, French, geography, geology, health sciences, history, human development, humanities and social sciences, industrial technology, liberal/general studies, mathematics, music, nursing, philosophy, physical education, physics, political science and government, psychology, social sciences, sociology, Spanish, trade and industrial education.

ACADEMIC PROGRAMS. Double major, dual enrollment of high school students, independent study, internships, student-designed major, study abroad; combined bachelor's/graduate program in business administration. **Remedial services:** Learning center, preadmission summer program, remedial instruction, special counselor, tutoring. **ROTC:** Army. **Placement/credit:** AP, CLEP General and Subject, institutional tests.

ACADEMIC REQUIREMENTS. Freshmen must earn minimum GPA of 2.0 to continue in good standing. 65% of freshmen return for sophomore year. Students must declare major on enrollment. **Graduation requirements:** 186 hours for bachelor's (60 in major). Most students required to take courses in arts/fine arts, English, foreign languages, history, humanities, mathematics, philosophy/religion, biological/physical sciences, social sciences. **Postgraduate studies:** 4% enter law school, 1% enter medical school, 7% enter MBA programs.

FRESHMAN ADMISSIONS. Selection criteria: High school GPA and test scores. **High school preparation:** 15 units required. Required units include English 4, foreign language 2, mathematics 3 and science 1. One visual and performing arts, 1 US history/government, and 3 electives also required. Students with disabilities may substitute alternate courses for specific subject requirements. **Test requirements:** SAT or ACT; score report by September 19.

1992 FRESHMAN CLASS PROFILE. 333 men, 499 women enrolled. **Academic background:** Mid 50% of enrolled freshmen had SAT-V between 400-500, SAT-M between 300-500; ACT composite between 18-23. 95% submitted SAT scores, 5% submitted ACT scores. **Characteristics:** 98% from in state, 93% commute, 30% have minority backgrounds, 1% are foreign students. Average age is 19.

FALL-TERM APPLICATIONS. $55 fee, may be waived for applicants with need. No closing date; applicants notified on a rolling basis. Interview required for Educational Opportunity Program applicants. Early admission available.

STUDENT LIFE. Housing: Dormitories (men, women, coed). **Activities:** Student government, magazine, radio, student newspaper, choral groups, concert band, drama, jazz band, music ensembles, symphony orchestra, fraternities, sororities, more than 50 clubs and organizations.

ATHLETICS. NCAA. **Intercollegiate:** Baseball M, basketball, golf M, soccer, softball W, swimming, volleyball W. **Intramural:** Basketball, field hockey, soccer, softball M, volleyball.

STUDENT SERVICES. Aptitude testing, career counseling, employment service for undergraduates, freshman orientation, health services, on-campus day care, personal counseling, placement service for graduates, special adviser for adult students, veterans counselor, transfer student orientation, services/facilities for handicapped.

ANNUAL EXPENSES. Tuition and fees (1992-93): $1,440, $7,380 additional for out-of-state students. **Room and board:** $4,266. **Books and supplies:** $612. **Other expenses:** $1,728.

FINANCIAL AID. 30% of freshmen, 30% of continuing students receive some form of aid. 96% of grants, 84% of loans, all jobs based on need. Academic, leadership scholarships available. **Aid applications:** No closing date; priority given to applications received by March 2; applicants notified on a rolling basis beginning on or about May 1; must reply within 4 weeks.

ADDRESS/TELEPHONE. Cheryl Smith, Associate Vice President, Enrollment Services, California State University, San Bernardino, 5500 University Parkway, San Bernardino, CA 92407-2397. (909) 880-5200.

California State University: San Marcos
San Marcos, California — CB code: 5677

2-year upper-division public university, coed. Founded in 1989. **Accreditation:** Regional candidate. **Undergraduate enrollment:** 264 men, 617 women full time; 235 men, 549 women part time. **Graduate enrollment:** 23 men, 104 women full time; 20 men, 92 women part time. **Faculty:** 140 total (91 full time), 116 with doctorates or other terminal degrees. **Location:** Suburban campus in large town; 35 miles from San Diego. **Calendar:** Semester. Saturday and extensive evening/early morning classes. **Microcomputers:** 100 located on campus.

DEGREES OFFERED. BA, BS, MA. 89 bachelor's degrees awarded in 1992.

UNDERGRADUATE MAJORS. Accounting, biology, business and management, computer and information sciences, economics, English, history, liberal/general studies, management information systems, management science, mathematics, political science and government, psychology, social sciences, sociology.

ACADEMIC PROGRAMS. Double major, honors program, internships, student-designed major, study abroad, teacher preparation, visiting/exchange student program. **Remedial services:** Preadmission summer program, special counselor, tutoring. **Placement/credit:** AP, CLEP General, institutional tests; 30 credit hours maximum for bachelor's degree.

ACADEMIC REQUIREMENTS. Students must declare major on application. **Graduation requirements:** 124 hours for bachelor's (54 in major). Most students required to take courses in computer science, English, foreign languages, history, humanities, mathematics, biological/physical sciences, social sciences.

STUDENT LIFE. Activities: Student government, student newspaper, yearbook, music ensembles.

STUDENT SERVICES. Career counseling, employment service for undergraduates, health services, personal counseling, placement service for graduates, special adviser for adult students, veterans counselor, services/facilities for handicapped.

ANNUAL EXPENSES. Tuition and fees (1992-93): $1,354, $7,380 additional for out-of-state students. **Books and supplies:** $576. **Other expenses:** $1,406.

FINANCIAL AID. 25% of continuing students receive some form of aid. 97% of grants, 91% of loans, 83% of jobs based on need. Academic, minority scholarships available. **Aid applications:** No closing date; priority given to applications received by March 2; applicants notified on a rolling basis.

ADDRESS/TELEPHONE. Betty J. Huff, Director Enrollment Services, California State University: San Marcos, San Marcos, CA 92096-0001. (619) 752-4800. Fax: (619) 752-4030.

California State University: Stanislaus
Turlock, California CB code: 4713

Admissions: 81% of applicants accepted
Based on: ••• School record
•• Test scores
• Activities, essay, interview, recommendations, special talents
Completion: 93% of freshmen end year in good standing
39% enter graduate study

4-year public college of arts and sciences and business college, coed. Founded in 1957. **Accreditation:** Regional. **Undergraduate enrollment:** 1,262 men, 1,922 women full time; 459 men, 813 women part time. **Graduate enrollment:** 89 men, 249 women full time; 382 men, 731 women part time. **Faculty:** 335 total (247 full time), 204 with doctorates or other terminal degrees. **Location:** Rural campus in large town; 100 miles from San Francisco, 82 miles from Sacramento. **Calendar:** 4-1-4, extensive summer session. **Microcomputers:** 107 located in dormitories, libraries, classrooms, computer centers. **Special facilities:** Observatory, electron microscope, interactive television classrooms, laser laboratory, art gallery.

DEGREES OFFERED. BA, BS, MA, MS, MBA. 930 bachelor's degrees awarded in 1992. 21% in business and management, 14% computer sciences, 16% teacher education, 9% letters/literature, 8% life sciences, 9% mathematics, 10% psychology, 5% social sciences. Graduate degrees offered in 15 major fields of study.

UNDERGRADUATE MAJORS. Accounting, anthropology, applied mathematics, art history, bilingual/bicultural education, biology, botany, business administration and management, business and management, chemistry, cognitive studies, communications, computer and information sciences, criminology, developmental psychology, dramatic arts, early childhood education, earth sciences, economics, education of the deaf and hearing impaired, English, entomology, environmental science, experimental psychology, finance, French, geography, geology, gerontology, history, information sciences and systems, international relations, law enforcement and corrections, liberal/general studies, management information systems, marine biology, marketing management, mathematics, music, music performance, nursing, operations research, organizational communication, personnel management, philosophy, physical sciences, physics, political science and government, predentistry, prelaw, premedicine, prepharmacy, preveterinary, printmaking, psychology, public administration, social sciences, sociology, Spanish, speech pathology/audiology, statistics, studio art, urban studies, women's studies, zoology.

ACADEMIC PROGRAMS. Accelerated program, cooperative education, double major, dual enrollment of high school students, honors program, independent study, internships, student-designed major, study abroad, teacher preparation, visiting/exchange student program, cross-registration. **Remedial services:** Learning center, preadmission summer program, reduced course load, remedial instruction, special counselor, tutoring. **Placement/credit:** AP, CLEP General and Subject, IB, institutional tests; 24 credit hours maximum for bachelor's degree. Credit by examination does not count toward residency requirement.

ACADEMIC REQUIREMENTS. Freshmen must earn minimum GPA of 2.0 to continue in good standing. 77% of freshmen return for sophomore year. Students must declare major by end of first year. **Graduation requirements:** 124 hours for bachelor's (30 in major). Most students required to take courses in arts/fine arts, English, history, humanities, mathematics, biological/physical sciences, social sciences. **Postgraduate studies:** 3% enter law school, 1% enter medical school, 12% enter MBA programs, 23% enter other graduate study.

FRESHMAN ADMISSIONS. Selection criteria: High school GPA, courses taken, and test scores. Special consideration for veterans, low-income, and minority applicants. **High school preparation:** 15 units required. Required units include biological science 1, English 4, foreign language 2, mathematics 3 and science 1. One visual and performing arts, 1 US history/government also required. **Test requirements:** SAT or ACT; score report by August 15.

1992 FRESHMAN CLASS PROFILE. 863 men and women applied, 698 accepted; 348 enrolled. 68% had high school GPA of 3.0 or higher, 31% between 2.0 and 2.99. 35% were in top tenth and 65% were in top quarter of graduating class. **Academic background:** Mid 50% of enrolled freshmen had SAT-V between 380-520, SAT-M between 410-540; ACT composite between 18-24. 70% submitted SAT scores, 4% submitted ACT scores. **Characteristics:** 17% have minority backgrounds, 4% are foreign students. Average age is 19.

FALL-TERM APPLICATIONS. $55 fee, may be waived for applicants with need. Closing date August 1; priority given to applications received by November 1; applicants notified on a rolling basis beginning on or about March 1. Interview recommended for drama, music, physical education applicants. Audition recommended for music applicants. Portfolio recommended for art applicants. CRDA. Deferred admission available. EDP-F.

STUDENT LIFE. Housing: Dormitories (coed); apartment housing available. **Activities:** Student government, radio, student newspaper, literary magazine, choral groups, concert band, drama, jazz band, music ensembles, musical theater, pep band, symphony orchestra, various religious, political, ethnic, and social service organizations.

ATHLETICS. NCAA. **Intercollegiate:** Baseball M, basketball, cross-country, golf M, soccer M, softball W, tennis, track and field, volleyball W. **Intramural:** Badminton, basketball, bowling, cross-country, football M, soccer M, softball W, swimming, table tennis, tennis, volleyball.

STUDENT SERVICES. Aptitude testing, career counseling, employment service for undergraduates, freshman orientation, health services, on-campus day care, personal counseling, placement service for graduates, special adviser for adult students, veterans counselor, reentry counseling, services/facilities for handicapped.

ANNUAL EXPENSES. Tuition and fees (1992-93): $1,434, $7,380 additional for out-of-state students. **Room and board:** $4,119. **Books and supplies:** $576. **Other expenses:** $1,170.

FINANCIAL AID. 25% of freshmen, 49% of continuing students receive some form of aid. 88% of grants, all jobs based on need. Academic, music/drama, art, state/district residency, leadership, alumni affiliation, minority scholarships available. **Aid applications:** No closing date; priority given to applications received by March 2; applicants notified on a rolling basis beginning on or about June 1; must reply within 3 weeks.

ADDRESS/TELEPHONE. Edward J. Aubert, Director of Admissions, California State University: Stanislaus, 801 West Monte Vista Avenue, Turlock, CA 95380-0283. (209) 667-3248. Fax: (209) 667-3333.

Canada College
Redwood City, California CB code: 4109

2-year public community college, coed. Founded in 1968. **Accreditation:** Regional. **Undergraduate enrollment:** 641 men, 840 women full time; 1,683 men, 3,772 women part time. **Faculty:** 212 total (96 full time), 16 with doctorates or other terminal degrees. **Location:** Suburban campus in small city; 20 miles from San Francisco. **Calendar:** Semester, limited summer session. **Microcomputers:** 300 located in libraries, classrooms, computer centers. **Additional facts:** Limited number of courses held off campus at business and industrial sites and at senior centers.

DEGREES OFFERED. AA, AS. 243 associate degrees awarded in 1992. 9% in architecture and environmental design, 25% business and management, 6% teacher education, 8% allied health, 31% multi/interdisciplinary studies.

UNDERGRADUATE MAJORS. Accounting, anthropology, architecture, biology, business administration and management, business and management, business and office, business computer/console/peripheral equipment operation, business data processing and related programs, business data programming, chemistry, child development/care/guidance, computer and information sciences, computer programming, computer servicing technology, dramatic arts, early childhood education, engineering, English, fashion merchandising, finance, fine arts, French, geography, history, home economics, interior design, journalism, legal assistant/paralegal, liberal/general studies, management information systems, management science, mathematics, music, ophthalmic services, philosophy, physical sciences, physics, political science and government, psychology, radiograph medical technology, secretarial and related programs, social sciences, Spanish, tourism, word processing.

ACADEMIC PROGRAMS. 2-year transfer program, cooperative education, double major, dual enrollment of high school students, independent study, internships, study abroad, telecourses, cross-registration. **Remedial services:** Learning center, reduced course load, remedial instruction, special counselor, tutoring, full program of ESL for transition or occupational studies. **Placement/credit:** AP, institutional tests; 12 credit hours maximum for associate degree.

ACADEMIC REQUIREMENTS. Freshmen must earn minimum GPA of 2.0 to continue in good standing. 73% of freshmen return for sophomore year. Students must declare major on enrollment. **Graduation requirements:** 60 hours for associate (21 in major). Most students required to take courses in arts/fine arts, computer science, English, history, humanities, mathematics, biological/physical sciences, social sciences.

FRESHMAN ADMISSIONS. Selection criteria: Open admissions. Special admissions for ophthalmic dispensing and radiologic technology programs.

1992 FRESHMAN CLASS PROFILE. 644 men and women enrolled. **Characteristics:** 98% from in state, 100% commute, 29% have minority backgrounds, 2% are foreign students. Average age is 21.

FALL-TERM APPLICATIONS. No fee. No closing date; priority given to applications received by August 30; applicants notified on a rolling basis. Early admission available. English and mathematics placement tests recommended.

STUDENT LIFE. Activities: Student government, student newspaper, choral groups, concert band, dance, drama, music ensembles, symphony orchestra, Latin American club, Rotarians, international student club, black student union.

ATHLETICS. NJCAA. **Intercollegiate:** Baseball M, basketball M, golf M, soccer W, tennis M.

STUDENT SERVICES. Career counseling, freshman orientation, health services, personal counseling, special adviser for adult students, veterans counselor, day and evening special counseling for EI (English Institute), services/facilities for handicapped.

ANNUAL EXPENSES. Tuition and fees (1992-93): $135, $3,390 additional for out-of-state students. **Books and supplies:** $500. **Other expenses:** $1,450.

FINANCIAL AID. 10% of continuing students receive some form of aid. Grants, loans, jobs available. **Aid applications:** No closing date; priority given to applications received by May 8; applicants notified on a rolling basis beginning on or about July 15; must reply within 2 weeks.

ADDRESS/TELEPHONE. Scott Thomas, Dean of Admissions and Records, Canada College, 4200 Farm Hill Boulevard, Redwood City, CA 94061. (415) 306-3226.

Central California Commercial College
Fresno, California CB code: 2119

2-year private business college, coed. Founded in 1863. **Accreditation:** Regional. **Undergraduate enrollment:** 292 men and women. **Faculty:** 19 total (16 full time). **Location:** Suburban campus in large city; 200 miles from San Francisco. **Calendar:** Quarter. Extensive evening/early morning classes. **Microcomputers:** Located in classrooms.

DEGREES OFFERED. AAS. 180 associate degrees awarded in 1992. 40% in business and management, 30% business/office and marketing/distribution, 30% computer sciences.

UNDERGRADUATE MAJORS. Accounting, business and management, business and office, business data entry equipment operation, business data processing and related programs, data processing, engineering and engineering-related technologies, information sciences and systems, legal assistant/paralegal, legal secretary, medical secretary, secretarial and related programs, word processing.

ACADEMIC PROGRAMS. Remedial services: Tutoring.

ACADEMIC REQUIREMENTS. Freshmen must earn minimum GPA of 2.0 to continue in good standing. Students must declare major on application. **Graduation requirements:** 140 hours for associate. Most students required to take courses in English, mathematics, biological/physical sciences, social sciences.

FRESHMAN ADMISSIONS. Selection criteria: Institutional admissions test, interview important.

1992 FRESHMAN CLASS PROFILE. 105 men and women enrolled. **Characteristics:** 100% from in state, 100% commute, 57% have minority backgrounds, 1% are foreign students.

FALL-TERM APPLICATIONS. $25 fee. No closing date; applicants notified on a rolling basis. Interview required.

STUDENT SERVICES. Career counseling, employment service for undergraduates, freshman orientation, placement service for graduates, special adviser for adult students, services/facilities for handicapped.

ANNUAL EXPENSES. Tuition and fees (1992-93): $6,600. Tuition and fees for 4 quarters (12 months) **Books and supplies:** $600.

FINANCIAL AID. Aid applications: No closing date; applicants notified on a rolling basis.

ADDRESS/TELEPHONE. Vera Lord, Director of Admissions, Central California Commercial College, 255 West Bullard, Fresno, CA 93704-1706. (209) 438-4222. Fax: (209) 438-6368.

Cerritos Community College
Norwalk, California CB code: 4083

2-year public community college, coed. Founded in 1955. **Accreditation:** Regional. **Undergraduate enrollment:** 1,264 men, 1,548 women full time; 7,945 men, 10,276 women part time. **Faculty:** 683 total (255 full time), 41 with doctorates or other terminal degrees. **Location:** Suburban campus in small city; 15 miles from Los Angeles. **Calendar:** Semester, limited summer session. Saturday and extensive evening/early morning classes. **Microcomputers:** 100 located in computer centers. **Special facilities:** Art gallery.

DEGREES OFFERED. AA. 793 associate degrees awarded in 1992.

UNDERGRADUATE MAJORS. Accounting, agricultural sciences, anthropology, architecture, automotive mechanics, automotive technology, bilingual/bicultural education, biology, biomedical equipment technology, botany, business administration and management, business and management, business and office, business computer/console/peripheral equipment operation, business data entry equipment operation, business data processing and related programs, business data programming, business systems analysis, chemical manufacturing technology, chemistry, clothing and textiles management/production/services, computer and information sciences, computer programming, computer technology, court reporting, data processing, dental assistant, dental hygiene, drafting, dramatic arts, early childhood education, earth sciences, economics, electrical and electronics equipment repair, electrical technology, engineering and engineering-related technologies, English, finance, fine arts, food production/management/services, French, geography, geology, German, Hispanic American studies, history, home economics, humanities, interior design, journalism, law enforcement and corrections technologies, legal assistant/paralegal, liberal/general studies, logistics, manufacturing technology, marketing and distribution, marketing management, mathematics, medical assistant, medical records technology, microbiology, music, nursing, office supervision and management, ornamental horticulture, personnel management, philosophy, photography, physical therapy assistant, physics, plastic technology, political science and government, practical nursing, precision metal work, predentistry, premedicine, prepharmacy, preveterinary, psychology, real estate, recreation and community services technologies, robotics, secretarial and related programs, sociology, Spanish, special education, speech, systems analysis, teacher aide, wildlife management, word processing, zoology.

ACADEMIC PROGRAMS. 2-year transfer program, computer delivered (on-line) credit-bearing course offerings, cooperative education, dual enrollment of high school students, telecourses. **Remedial services:** Learning center, remedial instruction, tutoring. **Placement/credit:** Institutional tests; 12 credit hours maximum for associate degree.

ACADEMIC REQUIREMENTS. Freshmen must earn minimum GPA of 2.0 to continue in good standing. 60% of freshmen return for sophomore year. **Graduation requirements:** 64 hours for associate (18 in major). Most students required to take courses in arts/fine arts, English, history, humanities, mathematics, biological/physical sciences, social sciences.

FRESHMAN ADMISSIONS. Selection criteria: Open admissions.

1992 FRESHMAN CLASS PROFILE. 1,949 men, 2,170 women enrolled. **Characteristics:** 98% from in state, 100% commute, 73% have minority backgrounds, 1% are foreign students.

FALL-TERM APPLICATIONS. No fee. No closing date; applicants notified on a rolling basis.

STUDENT LIFE. Activities: Student government, film, magazine, radio, student newspaper, choral groups, concert band, dance, drama, jazz band, music ensembles, musical theater, pep band, symphony orchestra, fraternities, sororities, Mecha, Ahora, Indian Club, Vietnamese Club, Black-Student Union.

ATHLETICS. NJCAA. **Intercollegiate:** Baseball M, basketball, cross-country, diving, football M, golf M, soccer M, softball W, swimming, tennis, track and field, volleyball W, water polo M, wrestling M.

STUDENT SERVICES. Aptitude testing, career counseling, freshman orientation, health services, on-campus day care, personal counseling, veterans counselor, women's program, services/facilities for handicapped.

ANNUAL EXPENSES. Tuition and fees (projected): $240, $2,808 additional for out-of-state students. **Books and supplies:** $612. **Other expenses:** $1,000.

FINANCIAL AID. 10% of freshmen, 12% of continuing students receive some form of aid. Grants, loans, jobs available. Academic, state/district residency, minority scholarships available. **Aid applications:** No closing date; priority given to applications received by May 10; applicants notified on a rolling basis; must reply within 2 weeks.

ADDRESS/TELEPHONE. Viet Be, Director of Admissions and Records, Cerritos Community College, 11110 Alondra Boulevard, Norwalk, CA 90650. (310) 860-2451. Fax: (310) 860-9680.

Cerro Coso Community College
Ridgecrest, California CB code: 4027

2-year public community college, coed. Founded in 1973. **Accreditation:** Regional. **Undergraduate enrollment:** 613 men and women full time; 4,172 men and women part time. **Faculty:** 291 total (37 full time). **Location:** Rural campus in large town; 120 miles from Bakersfield. **Calendar:** Semester, limited summer session. **Microcomputers:** Located in libraries, computer centers. **Special facilities:** Art gallery, nature preserve.

DEGREES OFFERED. AA, AS. 160 associate degrees awarded in 1992.

UNDERGRADUATE MAJORS. Air conditioning/heating/refrigeration mechanics, biological and physical sciences, business administration and management, business and office, child development/care/guidance, computer and information sciences, drafting, electronic technology, engineering and engineering-related technologies, fine arts, humanities, law enforcement and corrections technologies, liberal/general studies, machine tool operation/machine shop, office supervision and management, physical sciences, practical nursing, quality control technology, secretarial and related programs, social sciences, word processing.

ACADEMIC PROGRAMS. 2-year transfer program, cooperative education, double major, dual enrollment of high school students, honors program, independent study, internships, study abroad. **Remedial services:** Learning center, remedial instruction, special counselor, tutoring. **Placement/credit:** AP, CLEP General and Subject; 30 credit hours maximum for associate degree.

ACADEMIC REQUIREMENTS. Freshmen must earn minimum GPA of 2.0 to continue in good standing. Must complete at least half of units attempted. Students must declare major on application. **Graduation requirements:** 60 hours for associate. Most students required to take courses in English, humanities, mathematics, biological/physical sciences, social sciences.

FRESHMAN ADMISSIONS. Selection criteria: Open admissions.

1992 FRESHMAN CLASS PROFILE. 1,192 men and women enrolled. **Characteristics:** 94% from in state, 100% commute, 18% have minority backgrounds.

FALL-TERM APPLICATIONS. No fee. No closing date; applicants notified on a rolling basis. Interview required for nursing applicants.

STUDENT LIFE. Activities: Student government, student newspaper, choral groups, symphony orchestra.

ATHLETICS. Intercollegiate: Basketball M, cross-country, golf M.

STUDENT SERVICES. Aptitude testing, career counseling, employment service for undergraduates, freshman orientation, on-campus day care, personal counseling, placement service for graduates, veterans counselor, services/facilities for handicapped.

ANNUAL EXPENSES. Tuition and fees (1992-93): $120, $3,120 additional for out-of-state students. **Books and supplies:** $480. **Other expenses:** $765.

FINANCIAL AID. 6% of freshmen, 5% of continuing students receive some form of aid. 98% of grants, 99% of loans, 42% of jobs based on need. Academic, music/drama, art, state/district residency, leadership, alumni affiliation scholarships available. **Aid applications:** No closing date; priority given to applications received by May 1; applicants notified on a rolling basis beginning on or about June 1; must reply within 2 weeks.

ADDRESS/TELEPHONE. Dottie Cowan, Registrar, Cerro Coso Community College, 3000 College Heights Boulevard, Ridgecrest, CA 93555-7777. (619) 375-5001 ext. 357. Fax: (619) 375-5001 ext. 252.

Chabot College
Hayward, California — CB code: 4725

2-year public community college, coed. Founded in 1961. **Accreditation:** Regional. **Undergraduate enrollment:** 2,018 men, 2,275 women full time; 4,893 men, 5,518 women part time. **Faculty:** 781 total (254 full time), 228 with doctorates or other terminal degrees. **Location:** Urban campus in small city; 30 miles from San Francisco. **Calendar:** Quarter, extensive summer session. Saturday and extensive evening/early morning classes. **Microcomputers:** Located in libraries, classrooms, computer centers. **Special facilities:** Planetarium, disabled resource center, art gallery, theater, sports complex.

DEGREES OFFERED. AA. 900 associate degrees awarded in 1992. 16% in business and management, 12% business/office and marketing/distribution, 5% communications, 13% computer sciences, 7% engineering technologies, 5% psychology, 15% trade and industry, 5% visual and performing arts.

UNDERGRADUATE MAJORS. Accounting, allied health, anatomy, apparel and accessories marketing, architectural technologies, architecture, astronomy, automotive mechanics, automotive technology, biology, botany, business and management, business and office, business computer/console/peripheral equipment operation, business data entry equipment operation, business data processing and related programs, business data programming, ceramics, chemistry, child development/care/guidance, city/community/regional planning, civil technology, clothing and textiles management/production/services, commercial art, computer and information sciences, computer programming, computer servicing technology, computer technology, construction, court reporting, criminology, dance, data processing, dental assistant, dental hygiene, drafting, drafting and design technology, drawing, ecology, education, electrical and electronics equipment repair, electrical installation, electrical technology, electromechanical technology, electronic technology, engineering, engineering and engineering-related technologies, English, English literature, fashion merchandising, finance, fine arts, fire control and safety technology, fire protection, flight attendants, French, geography, geology, German, graphic arts technology, history, horticultural science, horticulture, information sciences and systems, institutional/home management/supporting programs, instrumentation technology, investments and securities, Italian, law enforcement and corrections technologies, legal secretary, liberal/general studies, library assistant, management science, marketing and distribution, marketing management, mathematics, mechanical design technology, medical assistant, medical laboratory technologies, medical records administration, medical records technology, microcomputer software, music, music performance, nursing, occupational therapy assistant, office supervision and management, ornamental horticulture, painting, personal services, pharmacy, photographic technology, photography, physical sciences, physics, physiology, human and animal, political science and government, Portuguese, precision metal work, predentistry, prelaw, premedicine, prepharmacy, preveterinary, protective services, psychology, public affairs, radio/television broadcasting, radio/television technology, real estate, recreation and community services technologies, retailing, Russian, science technologies, sculpture, secretarial and related programs, social sciences, sociology, Spanish, speech, speech pathology/audiology, statistics, studio art, survey and mapping technology, teacher aide, technical and business writing, telecommunications, theater design, transportation and travel marketing, transportation management, welding technology, word processing, zoology.

ACADEMIC PROGRAMS. 2-year transfer program, cooperative education, double major, dual enrollment of high school students, independent study, internships, student-designed major, study abroad, telecourses, weekend college, cross-registration. **Remedial services:** Learning center, preadmission summer program, reduced course load, remedial instruction, special counselor, tutoring, learning disabled laboratory, physically handicapped laboratory. **ROTC:** Air Force, Army. **Placement/credit:** AP, institutional tests; 15 credit hours maximum for associate degree.

ACADEMIC REQUIREMENTS. Freshmen must earn minimum GPA of 2.0 to continue in good standing. 52% of freshmen return for sophomore year. Students must declare major on enrollment. **Graduation requirements:** 90 hours for associate (30 in major). Most students required to take courses in English, history, mathematics, biological/physical sciences, social sciences. **Additional information:** New district office in a modern industrial park has courses in computer science technologies.

FRESHMAN ADMISSIONS. Selection criteria: Open admissions. All applicants must be 18 years of age and/or a high school graduate. Selective admissions to nursing, dental hygiene, hospital pharmacy technician, and paramedic programs. **Test requirements:** Toledo Chemistry Placement Examination required for chemistry applicants; mathematics and English test required for placement.

1992 FRESHMAN CLASS PROFILE. 10% had high school GPA of 3.0 or higher, 50% between 2.0 and 2.99. **Characteristics:** 99% from in state, 100% commute, 44% have minority backgrounds, 1% are foreign students. Average age is 20.

FALL-TERM APPLICATIONS. No fee. $25 fee for foreign students. No closing date; priority given to applications received by July 15; applicants notified on a rolling basis. Early admission available. EDP-F.

STUDENT LIFE. Activities: Student government, film, radio, student newspaper, television, choral groups, concert band, drama, jazz band, musical theater, pep band, various religious, political, ethnic, and social service organizations.

ATHLETICS. NJCAA. **Intercollegiate:** Baseball M, basketball, cross-country, diving, football M, golf, soccer M, softball W, swimming, tennis, track and field, volleyball W, wrestling M. **Intramural:** Archery, badminton, basketball, bowling, gymnastics, handball, racquetball, soccer, softball, table tennis, tennis, volleyball.

STUDENT SERVICES. Aptitude testing, career counseling, employment service for undergraduates, freshman orientation, personal counseling, placement service for graduates, veterans counselor, career counseling and services for veterans, services/facilities for handicapped.

ANNUAL EXPENSES. Tuition and fees (1992-93): $123, $3,150 additional for out-of-state students. **Books and supplies:** $750. **Other expenses:** $500.

FINANCIAL AID. 25% of freshmen, 25% of continuing students receive some form of aid. 98% of grants, all loans, all jobs based on need. Academic, state/district residency, leadership, alumni affiliation, minority scholarships available. **Aid applications:** No closing date; priority given to applications received by August 1; applicants notified on a rolling basis; must reply immediately.

ADDRESS/TELEPHONE. Carlo Vecchiarelli, Director of Admissions and Records, Chabot College, 25555 Hesperian Boulevard, Hayward, CA 94545. (510) 786-6714.

Chaffey Community College
Rancho Cucamonga, California — CB code: 4046

2-year public community college, coed. Founded in 1883. **Accreditation:** Regional. **Undergraduate enrollment:** 4,304 men and women full time; 11,193 men and women part time. **Faculty:** 432 total (188 full time). **Location:** Suburban campus in small city; 50 miles from Los Angeles. **Calendar:** Quarter, limited summer session. **Microcomputers:** 175 located in computer centers. **Special facilities:** 25-acre nature preserve, art museum/gallery, natural history collection, planetarium.

DEGREES OFFERED. AA, AS. 744 associate degrees awarded in 1992.

UNDERGRADUATE MAJORS. Accounting, aeronautical technology, aircraft mechanics, anthropology, architectural technologies, automotive mechanics, automotive technology, biology, business administration and management, business and management, business and office, business computer/console/peripheral equipment operation, business data processing and related programs, business data programming, ceramics, chemistry, child development/care/guidance, commercial art, communications, computer and information sciences, computer graphics, criminal justice technology, dental assistant, dietetic aide/assistant, drafting, drawing, earth sciences, economics, education, electrical and electronics equipment repair, electrical technology, electronic technology, engineering, engineering and engineering-related technologies, English, fashion design, fashion merchandising, finance, fine arts, food management, food production/management/services, food science and nutrition, French, geography, geology, German, graphic and printing production, graphic arts technology, history, home economics, hotel/motel and restaurant management, humanities, humanities and social sciences, industrial design, industrial equipment maintenance and repair, interior design, legal secretary, liberal/general studies, mathematics, mechanical design technology, medical secretary, music, nursing, painting, philosophy, photographic technology, photography, physical sciences, physics, political science and government, practical nursing, psychology, quality control technology, radio/television broadcasting, radiograph medical technology, real estate, religion, science technologies, secretarial and related programs, small business management and ownership, social sciences, sociology, Spanish, speech, teacher aide, textiles and clothing, transportation management.

ACADEMIC PROGRAMS. 2-year transfer program, accelerated program, dual enrollment of high school students, honors program, independent study, study abroad. **Remedial services:** Learning center, remedial instruction, special counselor, tutoring. **Placement/credit:** AP, CLEP General and Subject, institutional tests.

ACADEMIC REQUIREMENTS. Freshmen must earn minimum GPA of 2.0 to continue in good standing. Students must declare major on application. **Graduation requirements:** 90 hours for associate (27 in major). Most students required to take courses in English, humanities, mathematics, biological/physical sciences, social sciences.

FRESHMAN ADMISSIONS. Selection criteria: Open admissions.

1992 FRESHMAN CLASS PROFILE. Characteristics: 95% from in state, 100% commute.

FALL-TERM APPLICATIONS. No fee. No closing date; priority given to applications received by April 20; applicants notified on a rolling basis.

STUDENT LIFE. Activities: Student government, film, student newspaper, television, choral groups, concert band, dance, drama, music ensembles, musical theater, pep band, children's theater, International club, Latter-Day Saints, Model United Nations, Newman Club, Vietnamese Club. **Additional information:** Inter-Club Council oversees activities of all clubs and organizations.

ATHLETICS. Intercollegiate: Baseball M, basketball, cross-country, diving, football M, golf W, softball W, swimming, tennis, track and field, volleyball W, water polo M.

STUDENT SERVICES. Aptitude testing, career counseling, employment service for undergraduates, freshman orientation, health services, on-campus day care, personal counseling, placement service for graduates, special adviser for adult students, veterans counselor, ride sharing information, services/facilities for handicapped.

ANNUAL EXPENSES. Tuition and fees (1992-93): $135, $3,150 additional for out-of-state students. **Books and supplies:** $576. **Other expenses:** $1,000.

FINANCIAL AID. 3% of freshmen, 3% of continuing students receive some form of aid. All aid based on need. **Aid applications:** No closing date; priority given to applications received by May 1; applicants notified on a rolling basis beginning on or about July 1.

ADDRESS/TELEPHONE. Jo Edmison, Director of Admissions and Records, Chaffey Community College, 5885 Haven Avenue, Rancho Cucamonga, CA 91701-3002. (714) 987-1737. Fax: (714) 941-2783.

Chapman University
Orange, California — CB code: 4047

Admissions: 83% of applicants accepted
Based on: ••• School record
•• Interview, test scores
• Activities, essay, recommendations, special talents
Completion: 37% graduate

4-year private liberal arts college, coed, affiliated with Christian Church (Disciples of Christ). Founded in 1861. **Accreditation:** Regional. **Undergraduate enrollment:** 641 men, 821 women full time; 103 men, 93 women part time. **Graduate enrollment:** 81 men, 204 women full time; 226 men, 399 women part time. **Faculty:** 205 total (104 full time), 75 with doctorates or other terminal degrees. **Location:** Suburban campus in small city; 35 miles from Los Angeles, 60 miles from San Diego. **Calendar:** 4-1-4, limited summer session. Extensive evening/early morning classes. **Microcomputers:** 130 located in libraries, classrooms, computer centers. **Special facilities:** Albert Schweitzer collection of photographs, artifacts, and memorabilia; Center for Economic Research, human performance laboratory; food science laboratory; Guggenheim Gallery.

DEGREES OFFERED. BA, BS, BFA, MA, MS, MBA, MFA. 315 bachelor's degrees awarded in 1992. 30% in business and management, 17% communications, 7% letters/literature, 8% life sciences, 14% multi/interdisciplinary studies, 10% psychology, 6% social sciences. Graduate degrees offered in 23 major fields of study.

UNDERGRADUATE MAJORS. Accounting, advertising, American studies, applied mathematics, art education, art history, biological and physical sciences, biology, business administration and management, business economics, chemistry, cinematography/film, communications, comparative literature, computer and information sciences, creative writing, criminal justice studies, dance, dramatic arts, economics, English, fine arts, food sciences, French, graphic design, health sciences, history, humanities and social sciences, information sciences and systems, interior design, international business management, journalism, liberal/general studies, marketing management, music, music education, music performance, music theory and composition, nutritional sciences, peace studies, philosophy, photography, physical education, physical sciences, political science and government, predentistry, prelaw, premedicine, preveterinary, psychology, public relations, radio/television broadcasting, religion, social sciences, sociology, Spanish, studio art, telecommunications, visual and performing arts.

ACADEMIC PROGRAMS. Accelerated program, cooperative education, double major, honors program, independent study, internships, study abroad, teacher preparation, visiting/exchange student program, Washington semester; combined bachelor's/graduate program in business administration. **Remedial services:** Learning center, preadmission summer program, reduced course load, remedial instruction, special counselor, tutoring. **ROTC:** Air Force, Army. **Placement/credit:** AP, CLEP General and Subject, institutional tests; 32 credit hours maximum for bachelor's degree.

ACADEMIC REQUIREMENTS. Freshmen must earn minimum GPA of 2.0 to continue in good standing. 69% of freshmen return for sophomore year. Students must declare major by end of second year. **Graduation requirements:** 124 hours for bachelor's (36 in major). Most students required to take courses in arts/fine arts, computer science, English, foreign languages, history, humanities, mathematics, philosophy/religion, biological/physical sciences, social sciences.

FRESHMAN ADMISSIONS. Selection criteria: Academic course work plus GPA. Test scores and recommendations secondary. **High school preparation:** 11 units required. Required units include English 2, foreign language 2, mathematics 2, social science 3 and science 2. Mathematics recommendation includes 1 algebra, 1 geometry. **Test requirements:** SAT or ACT; score report by March 1.

1992 FRESHMAN CLASS PROFILE. 821 men and women applied, 678 accepted; 148 men enrolled, 182 women enrolled. 47% had high school GPA of 3.0 or higher, 51% between 2.0 and 2.99. 17% were in top tenth and 34% were in top quarter of graduating class. **Academic background:** Mid 50% of enrolled freshmen had SAT-V between 360-490, SAT-M between 400-560; ACT composite between 18-23. 81% submitted SAT scores, 23% submitted ACT scores. **Characteristics:** 65% from in state, 63% live in college housing, 28% have minority backgrounds, 8% are foreign students, 24% join fraternities/sororities. Average age is 20.

FALL-TERM APPLICATIONS. $30 fee, may be waived for applicants with need. No closing date; priority given to applications received by March 1; applicants notified on a rolling basis beginning on or about January 1; must reply by June 1 or within 2 weeks if notified thereafter. Interview recommended. Audition recommended for music applicants. Portfolio recommended for art applicants. Essay recommended. Early admission available. EDP-F.

STUDENT LIFE. Housing: Dormitories (coed); apartment, handicapped housing available. **Activities:** Student government, film, magazine, radio, student newspaper, television, yearbook, choral groups, concert band, dance, drama, music ensembles, musical theater, opera, symphony orchestra, fraternities, sororities, Macondo, Hillel, Black Student Union, Peace Club, Amnesty International, Model UN, Habitat for Humanity, Gay and Lesbian Student Association.

ATHLETICS. NCAA. **Intercollegiate:** Baseball M, basketball, cross-country M, soccer, softball W, tennis M, volleyball W, water polo M. **Intramural:** Badminton, basketball, bowling, golf, soccer, softball, table tennis, tennis, volleyball.

STUDENT SERVICES. Aptitude testing, career counseling, employment service for undergraduates, freshman orientation, health services, on-campus day care, personal counseling, placement service for graduates, special adviser for adult students, veterans counselor, wellness center.

ANNUAL EXPENSES. Tuition and fees: $16,328. Graduate tuition varies from $275 to $375 per credit hour. **Room and board:** $5,780. **Books and supplies:** $600. **Other expenses:** $1,300.

FINANCIAL AID. 48% of freshmen, 62% of continuing students receive some form of aid. 75% of grants, 69% of loans, all jobs based on need. 187 enrolled freshmen were judged to have need, all were offered aid. Academic, music/drama, art, religious affiliation scholarships available. **Aid applications:** No closing date; priority given to applications received by March 2; applicants notified on a rolling basis beginning on or about March 15; must reply within 2 weeks.

ADDRESS/TELEPHONE. Michael Drummy, Director of Admissions, Chapman University, 333 North Glassell Street, Orange, CA 92666. (714) 997-6711. Fax: (714) 997-6685.

Charles R. Drew University: College of Allied Health
Los Angeles, California — CB code: 4982

4-year private university, coed. **Accreditation:** Regional candidate. **Undergraduate enrollment:** 200 men and women. **Faculty:** 68 total (29 full time), 18 with doctorates or other terminal degrees. **Location:** Urban campus in very large city; 50 miles from San Diego. **Calendar:** Semester. Extensive evening/early morning classes. **Microcomputers:** 15 located in libraries, classrooms. **Special facilities:** Students rotate through Dr. Martin Luther King, Jr. General Hospital trauma unit.

DEGREES OFFERED. AS, BS. 100% in allied health. 24 bachelor's degrees awarded. 100% in allied health.

UNDERGRADUATE MAJORS. Associate: Medical records technology, radiograph medical technology. **Bachelor's:** Physician's assistant.

ACADEMIC PROGRAMS. Independent study, internships, visiting/exchange student program, cross-registration; combined bachelor's/graduate program in medicine. **Remedial services:** Learning center, preadmission summer program, reduced course load, remedial instruction, special counselor, tutoring, Computer Laboratory, study rooms, assessment services. Skills development services. **Placement/credit:** AP.

ACADEMIC REQUIREMENTS. Freshmen must earn minimum GPA of 2.3 to continue in good standing. 100% of freshmen return for sophomore year. Students must declare major on application. **Graduation requirements:** 78 hours for associate (42 in major), 164 hours for bachelor's (98 in major). Most students required to take courses in arts/fine arts, computer science, English, foreign languages, history, humanities, mathematics, philosophy/religion, biological/physical sciences, social sciences. **Postgraduate studies:** 2% from 2-year programs enter 4-year programs. 1% enter medical school, 1% enter other graduate study.

FRESHMAN ADMISSIONS. Selection criteria: School achievement record and interview most important. Recommendations and essay also important. Recommended units include biological science 8, mathematics 4, physical science 4 and social science 12. Botany, chemistry, physics, anatomy required for some programs. **Test requirements:** SAT or ACT; score report by July 30. **Additional information:** Students required to take a physical examination with selected laboratory tests before matriculation, and present proof of current health insurance during orientation.

1992 FRESHMAN CLASS PROFILE. 92 men and women enrolled. 20% had high school GPA of 3.0 or higher, 80% between 2.0 and 2.99. **Characteristics:** 2% from in state, 97% commute, 83% have minority backgrounds, 3% are foreign students. Average age is 22.

FALL-TERM APPLICATIONS. $20 fee. Closing date January 30; applicants notified on or about April 30; must reply by May 15. Interview required. Essay required. Deferred admission available. Programs other than physician's assistant have closing date of February 28.

STUDENT LIFE. Housing: Apartment, handicapped housing available. On-campus housing available. Housing provided for those in the community and Medical Center College/University. Student housing provided on first-come, first-served basis. **Activities:** Student government, students have a page in college newsletter, yearly Christmas program (drama, music).

STUDENT SERVICES. Aptitude testing, career counseling, freshman orientation, health services, on-campus day care, personal counseling, veterans counselor, services/facilities for handicapped.

ANNUAL EXPENSES. Tuition and fees (1992-93): $2,500. **Books and supplies:** $2,268. **Other expenses:** $2,832.

FINANCIAL AID. 99% of freshmen, 30% of continuing students receive some form of aid. 83% of grants, 79% of loans, all jobs based on need. 18 enrolled freshmen were judged to have need, all were offered aid. Academic scholarships available. **Aid applications:** Closing date February 28; applicants notified on or about June 1. **Additional information:** Students are encouraged to apply for aid even if they feel they will not qualify due to income.

ADDRESS/TELEPHONE. Robert H. Irvin, Director of Student Services, Charles R. Drew University: College of Allied Health, 1621 East 120th Street, KB112, Los Angeles, CA 90059. (213) 563-4950. Fax: (213) 563-4923.

Christian Heritage College
El Cajon, California — CB code: 4150

Admissions: 79% of applicants accepted
Based on:
- ••• Recommendations, religious affiliation/commitment, school record
- •• Essay, test scores
- • Activities, interview

Completion: 85% of freshmen end year in good standing
25% graduate, 25% of these enter graduate study

4-year private liberal arts college, coed, nondenominational. Founded in 1970. **Accreditation:** Regional. **Undergraduate enrollment:** 128 men, 136 women full time; 22 men, 14 women part time. **Faculty:** 46 total (26 full time), 16 with doctorates or other terminal degrees. **Location:** Suburban campus in small city; 15 miles from San Diego. **Calendar:** Semester, limited summer session. **Microcomputers:** Located in libraries, computer centers. **Special facilities:** Museum supporting creationist view.

DEGREES OFFERED. BA, BS. 70 bachelor's degrees awarded in 1992. 15% in business and management, 25% teacher education, 10% home economics, 21% philosophy, religion, theology, 25% psychology.

UNDERGRADUATE MAJORS. Bible studies, business administration and management, business and office, business home economics, child development/care/guidance, counseling psychology, education, elementary education, English, English education, history, home economics, home economics education, information sciences and systems, international business management, marriage and family counseling, missionary studies, music, music education, physical education, religious music, secondary education, social science education, social sciences, theological studies.

ACADEMIC PROGRAMS. Accelerated program, double major, external degree, independent study, internships, teacher preparation. **Remedial services:** Learning center, preadmission summer program, reduced course load, remedial instruction, tutoring. **ROTC:** Army. **Placement/credit:** AP, CLEP General and Subject, institutional tests; 15 credit hours maximum for bachelor's degree.

ACADEMIC REQUIREMENTS. Freshmen must earn minimum GPA of 2.0 to continue in good standing. 65% of freshmen return for sophomore year. Students must declare major by end of second year. **Graduation requirements:** 130 hours for bachelor's. Most students required to take courses in arts/fine arts, computer science, English, history, humanities, mathematics, philosophy/religion, biological/physical sciences, social sciences.

FRESHMAN ADMISSIONS. Selection criteria: Academic abilities as indicated by school achievement record and test scores. Personal and spiritual qualities as indicated by autobiography, recommendations, and interview. **High school preparation:** 15 units recommended. Recommended units include English 4, foreign language 2, mathematics 3, social science 3 and science 3. **Test requirements:** SAT or ACT (SAT preferred); score report by August 15.

1992 FRESHMAN CLASS PROFILE. 108 men applied, 85 accepted, 38 enrolled; 115 women applied, 91 accepted, 42 enrolled. 65% had high school GPA of 3.0 or higher, 33% between 2.0 and 2.99. **Academic background:** Mid 50% of enrolled freshmen had SAT-V between 400-550, SAT-M between 400-550. 90% submitted SAT scores. **Characteristics:** 75% from in state, 60% live in college housing, 26% have minority backgrounds, 3% are foreign students. Average age is 19.

FALL-TERM APPLICATIONS. $25 fee, may be waived for applicants with need. Closing date August 26; priority given to applications received by June 1; applicants notified on a rolling basis. Essay required. Interview recommended. Audition recommended. Deferred admission available.

STUDENT LIFE. Housing: Dormitories (men, women). **Activities:** Student government, student newspaper, yearbook, choral groups, drama, music ensembles, pep band, recitals, missions club, art club. **Additional information:** Religious observance required.

ATHLETICS. NAIA. **Intercollegiate:** Basketball M, cross-country, soccer M, volleyball W. **Intramural:** Baseball, basketball, soccer, softball, tennis, volleyball.

STUDENT SERVICES. Aptitude testing, career counseling, employment service for undergraduates, freshman orientation, health services, personal counseling, placement service for graduates, services/facilities for handicapped.

ANNUAL EXPENSES. Tuition and fees (projected): $7,900. **Room and board:** $3,900. **Books and supplies:** $576. **Other expenses:** $1,638.

FINANCIAL AID. 85% of freshmen, 90% of continuing students receive some form of aid. 54% of grants, all jobs based on need. Academic, music/drama, athletic, leadership, religious affiliation scholarships available. **Aid applications:** No closing date; priority given to applications received by June 1; applicants notified on a rolling basis beginning on or about May 1; must reply within 3 weeks.

ADDRESS/TELEPHONE. Pam Daly, Director of Admissions, Christian Heritage College, 2100 Greenfield Drive, El Cajon, CA 92019. (619)441-2200. (800)676-2242. Fax: (619) 440-0209.

Citrus College
Glendora, California — CB code: 4051

2-year public community college, coed. Founded in 1915. **Accreditation:** Regional. **Undergraduate enrollment:** 1,491 men, 1,503 women full time; 3,298 men, 4,412 women part time. **Faculty:** 539 total (130 full time). **Location:** Suburban campus in large town; 30 miles from Los Angeles. **Calendar:** Semester, limited summer session. Extensive evening/early morning classes. **Microcomputers:** 225 located in libraries, classrooms, computer centers.

DEGREES OFFERED. AA, AS. 402 associate degrees awarded in 1992.

UNDERGRADUATE MAJORS. Air conditioning/heating/refrigeration mechanics, allied health, anatomy, automotive mechanics, automotive technology, biology, botany, business and management, business and office, business data processing and related programs, chemistry, communications, computer and information sciences, criminal justice studies, dental assistant, diesel engine mechanics, drafting, drafting and design technology, engineering, engineering and engineering-related technologies, English, fine arts, French, German, health sciences, liberal/general studies, library assistant, library science, machine tool operation/machine shop, mathematics, medical assistant, music, nursing, physical sciences, physics, practical nursing, protective services, psychology, public affairs, social sciences, Spanish, zoology.

ACADEMIC PROGRAMS. 2-year transfer program, cooperative educa-

tion, dual enrollment of high school students, study abroad, telecourses. **Remedial services:** Learning center, remedial instruction, special counselor, tutoring. **Placement/credit:** AP, CLEP General and Subject; 30 credit hours maximum for associate degree.

ACADEMIC REQUIREMENTS. Freshmen must earn minimum GPA of 2.0 to continue in good standing. **Graduation requirements:** 60 hours for associate (18 in major). Most students required to take courses in English, mathematics, biological/physical sciences, social sciences.

FRESHMAN ADMISSIONS. Selection criteria: Open admissions.

1992 FRESHMAN CLASS PROFILE. 2,173 men and women enrolled. **Characteristics:** 97% from in state, 100% commute, 50% have minority backgrounds, 3% are foreign students. Average age is 18.

FALL-TERM APPLICATIONS. No fee. No closing date; applicants notified on a rolling basis.

STUDENT LIFE. Activities: Student government, student newspaper, choral groups, concert band, drama, jazz band, music ensembles, musical theater, symphony orchestra.

ATHLETICS. Intercollegiate: Baseball M, basketball, cross-country, football M, golf M, softball W, swimming, tennis, track and field, volleyball W, water polo M.

STUDENT SERVICES. Aptitude testing, career counseling, employment service for undergraduates, freshman orientation, health services, on-campus day care, personal counseling, placement service for graduates, veterans counselor, services/facilities for handicapped.

ANNUAL EXPENSES. Tuition and fees (1992-93): $167, $3,120 additional for out-of-state students. **Books and supplies:** $450. **Other expenses:** $1,000.

FINANCIAL AID. 97% of grants, all loans, 19% of jobs based on need. Academic, music/drama, art, athletic, leadership, minority scholarships available. **Aid applications:** No closing date; priority given to applications received by May 1; applicants notified on a rolling basis; must reply within 2 weeks.

ADDRESS/TELEPHONE. Melanie Cox, Dean of Admissions and Financial Aid, Citrus College, 1000 West Foothill Boulevard, Glendora, CA 91740-1899. (818) 914-8511. Fax: (818) 335-3159.

City College of San Francisco
San Francisco, California — CB code: 4052

2-year public community college, coed. Founded in 1935. **Accreditation:** Regional. **Undergraduate enrollment:** 33,000 men and women. **Faculty:** 1,035 total (459 full time), 52 with doctorates or other terminal degrees. **Location:** Urban campus in very large city; in downtown area. **Calendar:** Semester, extensive summer session. Saturday and extensive evening/early morning classes. **Microcomputers:** 256 located in computer centers. **Special facilities:** Art gallery.

DEGREES OFFERED. AA, AS. 999 associate degrees awarded in 1992. 30% in business and management, 7% engineering technologies, 7% health sciences, 39% multi/interdisciplinary studies.

UNDERGRADUATE MAJORS. Accounting, aeronautical technology, Afro-American (black) studies, aircraft mechanics, architectural technologies, architecture, biology, business administration and management, business and office, business data processing and related programs, business data programming, chemical manufacturing technology, chemistry, Chinese studies, cinematography/film, civil engineering, civil technology, clinical laboratory science, computer and information sciences, computer programming, construction, construction management, court reporting, criminal justice technology, dental assistant, dental laboratory technology, dietetic aide/assistant, drafting, electrical technology, electrical/electronics/communications engineering, electromechanical technology, electronic technology, engineering, engineering and engineering-related technologies, engineering mechanics, environmental design, fashion merchandising, finance, fine arts, fire control and safety technology, food science and nutrition, gay and lesbian studies, graphic and printing production, graphic arts technology, graphic design, Hispanic American studies, home economics, hospitality and recreation marketing, hotel/motel and restaurant management, illustration design, industrial engineering, industrial technology, insurance marketing, interior design, journalism, labor/industrial relations, landscape architecture, law enforcement and corrections technologies, legal assistant/paralegal, legal secretary, liberal/general studies, library assistant, library science, marketing and distribution, marketing management, mechanical design technology, mechanical engineering, medical assistant, medical laboratory technologies, medical records administration, medical records technology, medical secretary, nursing, ornamental horticulture, personnel management, Philippine studies, photographic technology, photography, physician's assistant, predentistry, preengineering, premedicine, prepharmacy, printmaking, radio/television broadcasting, radiograph medical technology, real estate, secretarial and related programs, teacher aide, transportation and travel marketing, transportation management, word processing.

ACADEMIC PROGRAMS. 2-year transfer program, accelerated program, dual enrollment of high school students, independent study, internships, study abroad, telecourses, weekend college. **Remedial services:** Learning center, remedial instruction, special counselor, tutoring. **Placement/credit:** AP, CLEP General, institutional tests; 45 credit hours maximum for associate degree.

ACADEMIC REQUIREMENTS. Freshmen must earn minimum GPA of 2.0 to continue in good standing. 70% of freshmen return for sophomore year. **Graduation requirements:** 60 hours for associate (18 in major). Most students required to take courses in English, history, humanities, mathematics, biological/physical sciences, social sciences.

FRESHMAN ADMISSIONS. Selection criteria: Open admissions.

1992 FRESHMAN CLASS PROFILE. 1,662 men, 1,794 women enrolled. **Characteristics:** 98% from in state, 100% commute, 74% have minority backgrounds. Average age is 19.

FALL-TERM APPLICATIONS. No fee. No closing date; priority given to applications received by July 19; applicants notified on a rolling basis beginning on or about April 1. Early admission available.

STUDENT LIFE. Activities: Student government, film, radio, student newspaper, television, choral groups, dance, drama, music ensembles, musical theater, opera, Intervarsity Christian Fellowship, Newman Center, Baptist Campus Ministry, Black Students' Union, La Raza Unida, Chinese Culture Club, UPASA Filipino Club, Gay and Lesbian Alliance, campus police service organization.

ATHLETICS. Intercollegiate: Baseball M, basketball, cross-country, football M, soccer M, softball W, swimming, tennis, track and field, volleyball W. **Intramural:** Fencing W.

STUDENT SERVICES. Career counseling, employment service for undergraduates, freshman orientation, health services, on-campus day care, personal counseling, placement service for graduates, veterans counselor, women's reentry program, services/facilities for handicapped.

ANNUAL EXPENSES. Tuition and fees (projected): $300, $3,420 additional for out-of-state students. **Books and supplies:** $600. **Other expenses:** $3,880.

FINANCIAL AID. 6% of continuing students receive some form of aid. 98% of grants, all loans, all jobs based on need. Academic scholarships available. **Aid applications:** Closing date May 21; priority given to applications received by March 2; applicants notified on or about July 1.

ADDRESS/TELEPHONE. Robert Balestreri, Dean of Admissions and Records, City College of San Francisco, 50 Phelan Avenue, San Francisco, CA 94112. (415) 239-3835. Fax: (415) 239-3936.

Claremont McKenna College
Claremont, California — CB code: 4054

Admissions:	38% of applicants accepted
Based on:	••• School record, test scores
	•• Activities, essay, recommendations
	• Interview, special talents
Completion:	95% of freshmen end year in good standing
	84% graduate, 52% of these enter graduate study

4-year private liberal arts college, coed. Founded in 1946. **Accreditation:** Regional. **Undergraduate enrollment:** 515 men, 330 women full time; 2 men, 1 woman part time. **Faculty:** 97 total (80 full time), 83 with doctorates or other terminal degrees. **Location:** Suburban campus in large town; 35 miles from Los Angeles. **Calendar:** Semester. **Microcomputers:** 75 located in classrooms, computer centers. **Special facilities:** 7 research institutes, Marian Miner Cook Athenaeum (center of intellectual, cultural, and social activities), Keck Science Center, Weingart Leadership Laboratory. **Additional facts:** Shared facilities of Claremont Colleges cluster include libraries, Bridges Auditorium and Garrison Theater. Cross-enrollment available at any of the colleges.

DEGREES OFFERED. BA. 207 bachelor's degrees awarded in 1992. 5% in engineering, 8% letters/literature, 10% multi/interdisciplinary studies, 9% psychology, 52% social sciences.

UNDERGRADUATE MAJORS. Accounting, Afro-American (black) studies, American literature, American studies, Asian studies, biological and physical sciences, biology, chemistry, classics, computer and information sciences, dramatic arts, economics, economics and accounting, engineering and other disciplines, English, English literature, European studies, film arts, French, German, history, humanities and social sciences, international business management, international relations, international studies, Latin American studies, management engineering, mathematics, Mexican American studies, music, philosophy, physics, political science and government, preengineering, prelaw, premedicine, psychobiology, psychology, public affairs, religion, Spanish, women's studies.

ACADEMIC PROGRAMS. Accelerated program, double major, honors program, independent study, internships, student-designed major, study abroad, visiting/exchange student program, Washington semester, cross-registration; liberal arts/career combination in engineering; combined bachelor's/graduate program in business administration, law. **Remedial services:** Tutoring. **ROTC:** Air Force, Army. **Placement/credit:** AP, institutional tests; 64 credit hours maximum for bachelor's degree.

ACADEMIC REQUIREMENTS. Freshmen must earn minimum GPA of 2.0 to continue in good standing. 95% of freshmen return for sophomore year. Students must declare major by end of second year. **Graduation re-**

quirements: 128 hours for bachelor's (40 in major). Most students required to take courses in English, foreign languages, history, humanities, mathematics, philosophy/religion, biological/physical sciences, social sciences. **Postgraduate studies:** 15% enter law school, 7% enter medical school, 15% enter MBA programs, 15% enter other graduate study. **Additional information:** Politics, philosophy, and economics (PPE) major offered. Program patterned after PPE major at Oxford University and limited to 12-15 new students each year. Students accepted spring of sophomore year (includes semester in England). Environment, economics, and politics (EEP) major also offered.

FRESHMAN ADMISSIONS. Selection criteria: School achievement record most important. Extracurricular activities, test scores, recommendations, essays, and interview given careful consideration. **High school preparation:** 16 units required. Required and recommended units include English 4, foreign language 2-3, mathematics 3-4, social science 1 and science 2-3. Management-Engineering candidates and science majors should have had both physics and chemistry. Four years of mathematics is preferable for all candidates. **Test requirements:** SAT or ACT; score report by February 1. Three ACH tests recommended for all applicants, including one English Composition.

1992 FRESHMAN CLASS PROFILE. 935 men applied, 366 accepted, 118 enrolled; 801 women applied, 302 accepted, 89 enrolled. 100% had high school GPA of 3.0 or higher. 71% were in top tenth and 95% were in top quarter of graduating class. **Academic background:** Mid 50% of enrolled freshmen had SAT-V between 560-650, SAT-M between 610-710; ACT composite between 27-31. 99% submitted SAT scores, 26% submitted ACT scores. **Characteristics:** 62% from in state, 100% live in college housing, 37% have minority backgrounds, 5% are foreign students. Average age is 18.

FALL-TERM APPLICATIONS. $40 fee, may be waived for applicants with need. Closing date February 1; applicants notified on or about April 1; must reply by May 1. Essay required. Interview recommended. CRDA. Deferred and early admission available. EDP-F. Early Decision application deadline is December 1; students are notified by January 10 and must reply by February 1.

STUDENT LIFE. Housing: Dormitories (coed); apartment housing available. On-campus housing guaranteed for all students. **Activities:** Student government, film, magazine, radio, student newspaper, yearbook, choral groups, dance, drama, jazz band, music ensembles, musical theater, pep band, symphony orchestra, student-organized improvisational groups, debate/forensics, volunteer service, Young Republicans, Young Democrats, Pan-African Students Association, MEChA, Asian American Student Alliance, religious activities center, intramural/club sports. **Additional information:** Full-time rabbi, priest, and protestant minister on campus. Also services for Mormon, Islamic, Christian Science, Quaker and B'hai faiths.

ATHLETICS. NCAA. **Intercollegiate:** Baseball M, basketball, cross-country, diving, football M, golf, lacrosse, soccer, softball W, swimming, tennis, track and field, volleyball W, water polo M. **Intramural:** Badminton, basketball, bowling, fencing, racquetball, rugby, sailing, skiing, soccer, softball, squash, swimming, tennis, volleyball, water polo. **Clubs:** Lacrosse, water polo W, volleyball M.

STUDENT SERVICES. Aptitude testing, career counseling, employment service for undergraduates, freshman orientation, health services, personal counseling, placement service for graduates, services/facilities for handicapped.

ANNUAL EXPENSES. Tuition and fees: $16,400. **Room and board:** $5,750. **Books and supplies:** $600. **Other expenses:** $850.

FINANCIAL AID. 73% of freshmen, 73% of continuing students receive some form of aid. 72% of grants, 69% of loans, 33% of jobs based on need. 114 enrolled freshmen were judged to have need, all were offered aid. Academic, leadership scholarships available. **Aid applications:** Closing date February 1; applicants notified on or about April 1; must reply by May 1.

ADDRESS/TELEPHONE. Richard C. Vos, Dean of Admissions and Financial Aid, Claremont McKenna College, 890 Columbia Avenue, Claremont, CA 91711-6420. (909) 621-8088.

Coastline Community College
Fountain Valley, California — CB code: 0933

2-year public community college, coed. Founded in 1976. **Accreditation:** Regional. **Undergraduate enrollment:** 16,170 men and women. **Faculty:** 495 total (45 full time), 19 with doctorates or other terminal degrees. **Location:** Urban campus in small city; 30 miles from Los Angeles. **Calendar:** Semester, limited summer session. Saturday and extensive evening/early morning classes. **Microcomputers:** 100 located in classrooms, computer centers. **Special facilities:** Resource center.

DEGREES OFFERED. AA. 170 associate degrees awarded in 1992. 44% in business and management, 20% engineering technologies, 35% multi/interdisciplinary studies.

UNDERGRADUATE MAJORS. Accounting, business administration and management, business and management, business and office, business data entry equipment operation, computer servicing technology, contract management and procurement/purchasing, court reporting, electrical and electronics equipment repair, electrical installation, energy conservation and use technology, finance, insurance and risk management, insurance marketing, international business management, legal assistant/paralegal, legal secretary, liberal/general studies, management science, marketing and distribution, marketing management, personal services, personnel management, petroleum engineering, quality control technology, real estate, robotics, secretarial and related programs, small business management and ownership, telecommunications, tourism, trade and industrial supervision and management, transportation and travel marketing, word processing.

ACADEMIC PROGRAMS. 2-year transfer program, accelerated program, cooperative education, dual enrollment of high school students, independent study, telecourses, weekend college. **Remedial services:** Reduced course load, remedial instruction, special counselor, tutoring. **Placement/credit:** AP, CLEP General and Subject; 48 credit hours maximum for associate degree.

ACADEMIC REQUIREMENTS. Freshmen must earn minimum GPA of 2.0 to continue in good standing. Must complete more than 50% of course work attempted. Students must declare major on enrollment. **Graduation requirements:** 60 hours for associate (18 in major). Most students required to take courses in English, history, humanities, mathematics, philosophy/religion, biological/physical sciences, social sciences.

FRESHMAN ADMISSIONS. Selection criteria: Open admissions.

1992 FRESHMAN CLASS PROFILE. 2,419 men and women enrolled. **Characteristics:** 99% from in state, 100% commute, 10% have minority backgrounds.

FALL-TERM APPLICATIONS. No fee. Closing date September 6; applicants notified on a rolling basis. SAT or ACT used for placement and counseling when submitted.

STUDENT LIFE. Activities: Student government, choral groups, dance, drama.

STUDENT SERVICES. Aptitude testing, career counseling, health services, personal counseling, veterans counselor, services/facilities for handicapped.

ANNUAL EXPENSES. Tuition and fees (1992-93): $136, $3,060 additional for out-of-state students. **Books and supplies:** $432. **Other expenses:** $1,386.

FINANCIAL AID. 10% of freshmen, 5% of continuing students receive some form of aid. All aid based on need. 90 enrolled freshmen were judged to have need, all were offered aid. **Aid applications:** No closing date; applicants notified on a rolling basis beginning on or about July 1; must reply within 2 weeks.

ADDRESS/TELEPHONE. James E. Garmon, Vice President of Student Services, Coastline Community College, 11460 Warner Avenue, Fountain Valley, CA 92708. (714) 546-7600. Fax: (714) 241-6248.

Cogswell Polytechnical College
Cupertino, California — CB code: 4057

4-year private engineering college, coed. Founded in 1887. **Accreditation:** Regional. **Undergraduate enrollment:** 85 men, 15 women full time; 227 men, 21 women part time. **Faculty:** 48 total (12 full time), 8 with doctorates or other terminal degrees. **Location:** Suburban campus in large town; 45 miles from San Francisco, 4 miles from San Jose. **Calendar:** Trimester, extensive summer session. Extensive evening/early morning classes. **Microcomputers:** 25 located in libraries, classrooms. **Special facilities:** Electronic music laboratories, sound/recording studio, video studio, computer imaging laboratories.

DEGREES OFFERED. AS, BS. 8 associate degrees awarded in 1992. 10% in engineering, 90% engineering technologies. 45 bachelor's degrees awarded. 12% in engineering, 88% engineering technologies.

UNDERGRADUATE MAJORS. Associate: Computer and information sciences, computer and video imaging, electronic technology, engineering and engineering-related technologies, mechanical design technology, music technology, software engineering. **Bachelor's:** Computer and information sciences, computer and video imaging, computer graphics, computer technology, electrical/electronics/communications engineering, electronic technology, engineering and engineering-related technologies, fire control and safety technology, fire protection, mechanical design technology, music technology, software engineering, video.

ACADEMIC PROGRAMS. 2-year transfer program, double major, independent study, cross-registration. **Remedial services:** Learning center, preadmission summer program, reduced course load, remedial instruction, special counselor, tutoring, pretechnology program with San Francisco School District. **Placement/credit:** AP, CLEP General and Subject, institutional tests; 12 credit hours maximum for bachelor's degree.

ACADEMIC REQUIREMENTS. Freshmen must earn minimum GPA of 2.0 to continue in good standing. 80% of freshmen return for sophomore year. Students must declare major on enrollment. **Graduation requirements:** 65 hours for associate, 130 hours for bachelor's. Most students required to take courses in arts/fine arts, English, history, humanities, mathematics, philosophy/religion, biological/physical sciences, social sciences. **Postgraduate studies:** 90% from 2-year programs enter 4-year programs. 12% enter MBA programs, 10% enter other graduate study.

FRESHMAN ADMISSIONS. Selection criteria: Motivation, 2.5 GPA in academic subjects, and SAT scores. Recommendations, mathematics and science background also considered. **High school preparation:** 9 units required. Required units include English 3. One chemistry, 1 physics, 2 algebra, 1 geometry, 1 trigonometry required. **Test requirements:** SAT or ACT; score report by July 31.

1992 FRESHMAN CLASS PROFILE. 45 men, 11 women enrolled. 50% had high school GPA of 3.0 or higher, 50% between 2.0 and 2.99. **Academic background:** Mid 50% of enrolled freshmen had SAT-V between 450-500, SAT-M between 500-550. 40% submitted SAT scores. **Characteristics:** 80% from in state, 100% commute, 32% have minority backgrounds, 1% are foreign students. Average age is 21.

FALL-TERM APPLICATIONS. $30 fee, may be waived for applicants with need. No closing date; priority given to applications received by January 1; applicants notified on a rolling basis beginning on or about June 1; must reply within 2 weeks. Essay required. Interview recommended. CRDA. Deferred and early admission available.

STUDENT LIFE. Housing: Arrangement with local private college for dormitory housing. **Activities:** Student government, student chapters Institute of Electrical and Electronic Engineers (IEEE), American Society of Mechanical Engneers (ASME), Audio Engineering Society, Society of Motion Picture and Television Engineers, Music and Entertainment Industry Education Association (MEIEA).

ATHLETICS. Intramural: Skiing, table tennis.

STUDENT SERVICES. Career counseling, employment service for undergraduates, freshman orientation, personal counseling, placement service for graduates, veterans counselor, services/facilities for handicapped.

ANNUAL EXPENSES. Tuition and fees (1992-93): $6,640. **Books and supplies:** $600. **Other expenses:** $1,232.

FINANCIAL AID. 29% of freshmen, 18% of continuing students receive some form of aid. All grants, 64% of loans, all jobs based on need. Academic scholarships available. **Aid applications:** No closing date; priority given to applications received by May 1; applicants notified on a rolling basis beginning on or about June 1; must reply within 2 weeks.

ADDRESS/TELEPHONE. Paul A. Schreivogel, Dean of Student Services, Cogswell Polytechnical College, 10420 Bubb Road, Cupertino, CA 95014. (408) 252-5550. Fax: (408) 253-2413.

Coleman College
La Mesa, California CB code: 0955

4-year private college of information science and technology, coed. Founded in 1963. **Undergraduate enrollment:** 650 men and women. **Graduate enrollment:** 23 men and women. **Faculty:** 105 total (63 full time), 8 with doctorates or other terminal degrees. **Location:** Urban campus in small city; borders on San Diego. **Calendar:** Quarter. Saturday and extensive evening/early morning classes. **Microcomputers:** 420 located in libraries, computer centers. **Additional facts:** College uses inverted curriculum with major taken before general curriculum. Vast majority of students are transfers.

DEGREES OFFERED. AS, BS, MS, MBA. 120 associate degrees awarded in 1992. 130 bachelor's degrees awarded. Graduate degrees offered in 2 major fields of study.

UNDERGRADUATE MAJORS. Associate: Computer and information sciences, computer servicing technology, computer technology, office automation systems. **Bachelor's:** Business administration and management, computer and information sciences, computer industry technology, computer servicing technology, computer technology, office automation systems.

ACADEMIC PROGRAMS. 2-year transfer program, accelerated program, double major, independent study. **Remedial services:** Learning center, preadmission summer program, reduced course load, remedial instruction, special counselor, tutoring. **Placement/credit:** CLEP General and Subject, institutional tests; 26 credit hours maximum for associate degree; 36 credit hours maximum for bachelor's degree.

ACADEMIC REQUIREMENTS. Freshmen must earn minimum GPA of 2.0 to continue in good standing. Students must declare major on enrollment. **Graduation requirements:** 108 hours for associate (72 in major), 180 hours for bachelor's (80 in major). Most students required to take courses in English, history, humanities, mathematics, social sciences.

FRESHMAN ADMISSIONS. Selection criteria: Test score and interview considered. In special cases school record, special talents, recommendations will be taken into account. **Test requirements:** Institutionally administered aptitude test required of all applicants.

1992 FRESHMAN CLASS PROFILE. 125 men and women enrolled. **Characteristics:** 90% from in state, 100% commute, 17% have minority backgrounds. Average age is 24.

FALL-TERM APPLICATIONS. No fee. No closing date; applicants notified on a rolling basis. Interview required. Early admission available. SAT/ACT recommended for placement and credit.

STUDENT LIFE. Activities: Bulletin, student activities committee, international student association.

STUDENT SERVICES. Aptitude testing, career counseling, personal counseling, placement service for graduates, veterans counselor, services/facilities for handicapped.

ANNUAL EXPENSES. Tuition and fees: $6,403. Students attend classes for 5 10-week sessions (12 months). **Books and supplies:** $425. **Other expenses:** $1,000.

FINANCIAL AID. 87% of freshmen receive some form of aid. Grants, loans, jobs available. Academic scholarships available. **Aid applications:** No closing date; applicants notified on a rolling basis.

ADDRESS/TELEPHONE. Office of Admissions, Coleman College, 7380 Parkway Drive, La Mesa, CA 92042-1532. (619) 465-3990. Fax: (619) 463-0162.

College of Alameda
Alameda, California CB code: 4118

2-year public community college, coed. Founded in 1970. **Accreditation:** Regional. **Undergraduate enrollment:** 5,600 men and women. **Location:** Urban campus in small city; adjacent to Oakland. **Calendar:** Quarter. Saturday and extensive evening/early morning classes.

FRESHMAN ADMISSIONS. Selection criteria: Open admissions.

ANNUAL EXPENSES. Tuition and fees (1992-93): $124, $3,105 additional for out-of-state students. **Books and supplies:** $400.

ADDRESS/TELEPHONE. Henry Fort, District Dean of Admissions and Records, College of Alameda, 555 Atlantic Avenue, Alameda, CA 94501. (510) 522-7221.

College of the Canyons
Valencia, California CB code: 4117

2-year public community college, coed. Founded in 1967. **Accreditation:** Regional. **Undergraduate enrollment:** 929 men, 962 women full time; 1,830 men, 2,641 women part time. **Faculty:** 217 total (70 full time), 30 with doctorates or other terminal degrees. **Location:** Suburban campus in small city; 40 miles from Los Angeles. **Calendar:** 4-1-4, limited summer session. Extensive evening/early morning classes. **Microcomputers:** Located in computer centers. **Special facilities:** Child development center.

DEGREES OFFERED. AA, AS. 531 associate degrees awarded in 1992.

UNDERGRADUATE MAJORS. Accounting, biological and physical sciences, biology, business and management, business and office, business data processing and related programs, child development/care/guidance, computer and information sciences, computer technology, criminal justice studies, drafting, drafting and design technology, early childhood education, education, electronic technology, engineering and engineering-related technologies, English, fine arts, French, geology, German, health sciences, history, hotel/motel and restaurant management, humanities, humanities and social sciences, industrial technology, journalism, law enforcement and corrections technologies, liberal/general studies, mathematics, mechanical design technology, music, nursing, physical education, physical sciences, practical nursing, preengineering, quality control technology, radio/television technology, real estate, science technologies, secretarial and related programs, social sciences, Spanish, water and wastewater technology, water resources, welding technology.

ACADEMIC PROGRAMS. 2-year transfer program, cooperative education, dual enrollment of high school students, honors program, independent study, study abroad, telecourses. **Remedial services:** Learning center, remedial instruction, special counselor, tutoring. **Placement/credit:** AP, CLEP Subject, institutional tests; 18 credit hours maximum for associate degree.

ACADEMIC REQUIREMENTS. Freshmen must earn minimum GPA of 2.0 to continue in good standing. **Graduation requirements:** 60 hours for associate (18 in major). Most students required to take courses in English, history, humanities, mathematics, biological/physical sciences, social sciences.

FRESHMAN ADMISSIONS. Selection criteria: Open admissions. **Additional information:** Applicants must take institutional English and mathematics placement tests and attend new student orientation.

1992 FRESHMAN CLASS PROFILE. 596 men, 615 women enrolled. **Characteristics:** 98% from in state, 100% commute, 25% have minority backgrounds. Average age is 19.

FALL-TERM APPLICATIONS. No fee. No closing date; applicants notified on a rolling basis.

STUDENT LIFE. Activities: Student government, magazine, student newspaper, choral groups, dance, drama, jazz band, symphony orchestra.

ATHLETICS. NJCAA. **Intercollegiate:** Baseball M, basketball, cross-country, golf, softball W, swimming, track and field, volleyball W.

STUDENT SERVICES. Aptitude testing, career counseling, employment service for undergraduates, freshman orientation, health services, on-campus day care, personal counseling, placement service for graduates, veterans counselor, career center, services/facilities for handicapped.

ANNUAL EXPENSES. Tuition and fees: $295, $3,120 additional for out-of-state students. **Books and supplies:** $612. **Other expenses:** $1,551.

FINANCIAL AID. 16% of continuing students receive some form of aid. All grants, 92% of loans, all jobs based on need. Academic, athletic, state/district residency, leadership, alumni affiliation, minority scholarships available. **Aid applications:** No closing date; priority given to applications received by June 15; applicants notified on a rolling basis beginning on or about August 1.

ADDRESS/TELEPHONE. Dr. Glenn Hisayasu, Dean of Student Services, College of the Canyons, 26455 North Rockwell Canyon Road, Valencia, CA 91355. (805) 259-7800. Fax: (805) 259-8302.

College of the Desert
Palm Desert, California CB code: 4085

2-year public community college, coed. Founded in 1958. **Accreditation:** Regional. **Undergraduate enrollment:** 10,975 men and women. **Location:** Urban campus in large town; 10 miles from Palm Springs. **Calendar:** Semester. Extensive evening/early morning classes.

FRESHMAN ADMISSIONS. Selection criteria: Open admissions. Separate applications and deadlines for nursing, golf management, and foreign students.

ANNUAL EXPENSES. Tuition and fees (projected): $300, $3,180 additional for out-of-state students. **Books and supplies:** $612. **Other expenses:** $1,548.

ADDRESS/TELEPHONE. Gopal Raman, Director of Admissions, Records, and Financial Aid, College of the Desert, 43-500 Monterey Avenue, Palm Desert, CA 92260. (619) 346-8041.

College of Marin: Kentfield
Kentfield, California CB code: 4061

2-year public community college, coed. Founded in 1926. **Accreditation:** Regional. **Undergraduate enrollment:** 9,604 men and women. **Faculty:** 308 total (171 full time). **Location:** Suburban campus in small town; 25 miles from San Francisco. **Calendar:** Semester. Extensive evening/early morning classes. **Additional facts:** Additional campus at Indian Valley.

DEGREES OFFERED. AA, AS. 190 associate degrees awarded in 1992.

UNDERGRADUATE MAJORS. Accounting, architecture, business and management, communications, computer and information sciences, computer programming, engineering and engineering-related technologies, fine arts, liberal/general studies, mathematics, music, personnel management, public relations, radio/television broadcasting, real estate, small business management and ownership, systems analysis.

ACADEMIC PROGRAMS. 2-year transfer program. **Placement/credit:** Institutional tests.

ACADEMIC REQUIREMENTS. Students must declare major on application. **Graduation requirements:** 60 hours for associate (18 in major). Most students required to take courses in English, history, humanities, mathematics, biological/physical sciences, social sciences.

FRESHMAN ADMISSIONS. Selection criteria: Open admissions.

1992 FRESHMAN CLASS PROFILE. 2,961 men and women enrolled. **Characteristics:** 100% commute.

FALL-TERM APPLICATIONS. No fee. No closing date; applicants notified on a rolling basis.

STUDENT LIFE. Activities: Student government, student newspaper.

ATHLETICS. Intercollegiate: Baseball, basketball, cross-country, diving, football, soccer, softball, squash, tennis, track and field. **Intramural:** Cross-country, softball, swimming.

ANNUAL EXPENSES. Tuition and fees (projected): $320, $3,690 additional for out-of-state students. **Books and supplies:** $500. **Other expenses:** $1,710.

FINANCIAL AID. 10% of freshmen, 10% of continuing students receive some form of aid. All grants, 86% of loans, all jobs based on need. **Aid applications:** No closing date; priority given to applications received by March 1; applicants notified on a rolling basis beginning on or about May 15; must reply within 15 days.

ADDRESS/TELEPHONE. Pamela Mize, Director of Admissions and Records, College of Marin: Kentfield, 835 College Avenue, Kentfield, CA 94904. (415) 485-9411.

College of Notre Dame
Belmont, California CB code: 4063

Admissions:	75% of applicants accepted
Based on:	••• School record
	•• Essay, special talents, test scores
	• Activities, interview, recommendations
Completion:	79% of freshmen end year in good standing
	53% graduate, 11% of these enter graduate study

4-year private liberal arts college, coed, affiliated with Roman Catholic Church. Founded in 1868. **Accreditation:** Regional. **Undergraduate enrollment:** 172 men, 266 women full time; 62 men, 252 women part time. **Graduate enrollment:** 56 men, 211 women full time; 117 men, 361 women part time. **Faculty:** 147 total (60 full time), 72 with doctorates or other terminal degrees. **Location:** Suburban campus in large town; 25 miles from San Francisco. **Calendar:** Semester, limited summer session. **Microcomputers:** 50 located in computer centers. **Special facilities:** Professional art gallery, theater, recreation center.

DEGREES OFFERED. BA, BS, BFA, MA, MS, MBA, MFA, MEd. 140 bachelor's degrees awarded in 1992. 40% in business and management, 5% life sciences, 9% multi/interdisciplinary studies, 11% psychology, 17% social sciences, 8% visual and performing arts. Graduate degrees offered in 21 major fields of study.

UNDERGRADUATE MAJORS. Accounting, behavioral sciences, biochemistry, biology, business administration and management, business and management, business economics, communications, computer and information sciences, dramatic arts, English, environmental science, finance, fine arts, French, graphic design, history, humanities, industrial and organizational psychology, interior design, international business management, Latin American studies, liberal/general studies, marketing and distribution, music, music performance, philosophy, physical sciences, political science and government, predentistry, prelaw, premedicine, prepharmacy, preveterinary, psychology, religion, religious education, social sciences, sociology, studio art.

ACADEMIC PROGRAMS. Accelerated program, double major, dual enrollment of high school students, independent study, internships, student-designed major, study abroad, teacher preparation, visiting/exchange student program. **Remedial services:** Learning center, reduced course load, special counselor, tutoring. **ROTC:** Air Force, Army, Naval. **Placement/credit:** AP, CLEP General and Subject, IB, institutional tests; 30 credit hours maximum for bachelor's degree.

ACADEMIC REQUIREMENTS. Freshmen must earn minimum GPA of 2.0 to continue in good standing. Freshmen allowed 2 semesters to attain 2.0 GPA. 75% of freshmen return for sophomore year. Students must declare major by end of second year. **Graduation requirements:** 124 hours for bachelor's (30 in major). Most students required to take courses in arts/fine arts, English, foreign languages, history, mathematics, philosophy/religion, biological/physical sciences, social sciences. **Postgraduate studies:** 1% enter law school, 1% enter medical school, 4% enter MBA programs, 5% enter other graduate study.

FRESHMAN ADMISSIONS. Selection criteria: High school record and GPA most important; test scores also important. Essay, recommendation, and school and community activities considered. **High school preparation:** 13 units required. Required and recommended units include English 4, foreign language 2-3, mathematics 2-3, social science 2 and science 1-2. 2 additional units from fine arts, advanced laboratory science, advanced mathematics, or advanced foreign language also required. **Test requirements:** SAT or ACT (SAT preferred); score report by March 2.

1992 FRESHMAN CLASS PROFILE. 126 men applied, 87 accepted, 32 enrolled; 253 women applied, 196 accepted, 56 enrolled. 58% had high school GPA of 3.0 or higher, 42% between 2.0 and 2.99. 9% were in top tenth and 45% were in top quarter of graduating class. **Academic background:** Mid 50% of enrolled freshmen had SAT-V between 360-470, SAT-M between 390-510; ACT composite between 18-23. 83% submitted SAT scores, 22% submitted ACT scores. **Characteristics:** 80% from in state, 69% live in college housing, 52% have minority backgrounds, 11% are foreign students. Average age is 18.

FALL-TERM APPLICATIONS. $35 fee, may be waived for applicants with need. Closing date June 1; priority given to applications received by March 2; applicants notified on a rolling basis; must reply by May 1 or within 3 weeks if notified thereafter. Audition required for music applicants. Essay required. Interview recommended for academically weak applicants. Portfolio recommended for art applicants. CRDA. Deferred admission available.

STUDENT LIFE. Housing: Dormitories (coed); apartment housing available. Ample off-campus housing available near campus. **Activities:** Student government, magazine, student newspaper, choral groups, drama, music ensembles, musical theater, opera, symphony orchestra, campus ministry, Hawaiian club, international club, Rotoract, ski, Filipino club, Alianza Latina, Black Student Union, mathematics and science club.

ATHLETICS. NCAA. **Intercollegiate:** Basketball, cross-country, soccer M, softball W, tennis, track and field, volleyball W. **Intramural:** Softball, table tennis, tennis, volleyball. **Clubs:** Skiing.

STUDENT SERVICES. Career counseling, employment service for undergraduates, freshman orientation, health services, personal counseling, placement service for graduates, special adviser for adult students, career development, services/facilities for handicapped.

ANNUAL EXPENSES. Tuition and fees: $11,750. Additional $500 one-time fee for foreign students. **Room and board:** $5,832. **Books and supplies:** $612. **Other expenses:** $1,350.

FINANCIAL AID. 85% of freshmen, 67% of continuing students receive some form of aid. 95% of grants, 70% of loans, 52% of jobs based on need. Academic, music/drama, art, athletic, state/district residency, leadership, alumni affiliation, religious affiliation scholarships available. **Aid applications:** No closing date; priority given to applications received by March 2; applicants notified on a rolling basis beginning on or about May 1; must reply by May 1 or within 2 weeks if notified thereafter.

ADDRESS/TELEPHONE. Gregory Smith, Director of Admission, College of Notre Dame, 1500 Ralston Avenue, Belmont, CA 94002-1997. (415) 508-3607. Fax: (415) 637-0493.

College of Oceaneering
Wilmington, California CB code: 1243

2-year proprietary marine technologies college, coed. Founded in 1969. **Accreditation:** Regional. **Undergraduate enrollment:** 254 men, 7 women full time. **Faculty:** 24 total. **Location:** Urban campus in small city; 30 miles from Los Angeles, 5 miles from Long Beach. **Calendar:** Year-round. **Special facilities:** Bell saturation barge, welding pier, hemidome. **Additional facts:** Provides unique underwater training for the offshore oil industry and coastal and inland water and harbors.

DEGREES OFFERED. AS. 23 associate degrees awarded in 1992. 100% in trade and industry.

UNDERGRADUATE MAJORS. Marine maintenance, science technologies.

ACADEMIC PROGRAMS. Remedial services: Remedial instruction, special counselor, tutoring, twilight college. **Placement/credit:** Institutional tests.

ACADEMIC REQUIREMENTS. No policy requiring minimum GPA; records of students having academic difficulty are reviewed individually. 80% of freshmen return for sophomore year. Students must declare major by end of first year. **Graduation requirements:** 47 hours for associate (40 in major). Most students required to take courses in English, mathematics, biological/physical sciences, social sciences. **Additional information:** Special programs prepare students for work as underwater welders, diver medical technicians, and topside/underwater nondestructive testing/inspection personnel.

FRESHMAN ADMISSIONS. Selection criteria: Open admissions. Must be medically approved to dive and have high school diploma, GED or prove ability to benefit from program. Students accepted for second year must have maintained satisfactory progress. **Additional information:** Students expected to have mechanical aptitude and, if possible, experience in construction-related field.

1992 FRESHMAN CLASS PROFILE. 230 men, 7 women enrolled. **Characteristics:** 75% from in state, 100% commute, 14% have minority backgrounds, 12% are foreign students. Average age is 24.

FALL-TERM APPLICATIONS. $200 fee. No closing date; applicants notified on a rolling basis. Interview recommended. Deferred admission available.

STUDENT LIFE. Activities: Film, student newspaper. **Additional information:** All classes near or on water. Multi-faceted recreational facilities for water sports and all types of recreation/entertainment nearby.

STUDENT SERVICES. Aptitude testing, career counseling, employment service for undergraduates, freshman orientation, personal counseling, placement service for graduates, veterans counselor, financial aid counseling.

ANNUAL EXPENSES. Tuition and fees: $13,550. Tuition, fees, books, and some supplies for 34-week program $13,550. Additional tuition for advanced studies. **Other expenses:** $750.

FINANCIAL AID. 80% of freshmen, 90% of continuing students receive some form of aid. All grants, 52% of loans based on need. **Aid applications:** No closing date; applicants notified on a rolling basis.

ADDRESS/TELEPHONE. Tamera Mendoza, Admittance Manager, College of Oceaneering, 272 South Fries Avenue, Wilmington, CA 90744. (310) 834-2501. (800) 324-9027. Fax: (310) 834-7132.

College of the Redwoods
Eureka, California CB code: 4100

2-year public community college, coed. Founded in 1964. **Accreditation:** Regional. **Undergraduate enrollment:** 1,118 men, 1,210 women full time; 1,783 men, 2,797 women part time. **Faculty:** 443 total (118 full time), 11 with doctorates or other terminal degrees. **Location:** Rural campus in large town; 275 miles from San Francisco. **Calendar:** Semester, limited summer session. Saturday and extensive evening/early morning classes. **Microcomputers:** Located in dormitories, libraries, classrooms, computer centers. **Special facilities:** Observatories, art gallery. **Additional facts:** Centers at Fort Bragg and Crescent City.

DEGREES OFFERED. AA, AS. 414 associate degrees awarded in 1992.

UNDERGRADUATE MAJORS. Agricultural business and management, animal sciences, automotive technology, business and management, child development/care/guidance, construction, diesel engine mechanics, drafting and design technology, electronic technology, fishing and fisheries, food management, food production/management/services, forestry and related sciences, graphic arts technology, information sciences and systems, law enforcement and corrections technologies, legal assistant/paralegal, legal secretary, machine tool operation/machine shop, nursing, plant sciences, precision metal work, real estate, secretarial and related programs, small business management and ownership, welding technology, word processing.

ACADEMIC PROGRAMS. 2-year transfer program, cooperative education, double major, honors program, independent study, cross-registration. **Remedial services:** Learning center, preadmission summer program, remedial instruction, special counselor, tutoring. **Placement/credit:** AP, institutional tests.

ACADEMIC REQUIREMENTS. Freshmen must earn minimum GPA of 2.0 to continue in good standing. 60% of freshmen return for sophomore year. Students must declare major on enrollment. **Graduation requirements:** 60 hours for associate. Most students required to take courses in English, humanities, mathematics, biological/physical sciences, social sciences.

FRESHMAN ADMISSIONS. Selection criteria: Open admissions. Selective admissions for nursing applicants, based on school record and test scores.

1992 FRESHMAN CLASS PROFILE. 1,289 men and women enrolled. **Characteristics:** 95% from in state, 99% commute, 9% have minority backgrounds, 1% are foreign students.

FALL-TERM APPLICATIONS. No fee. No closing date; priority given to applications received by August 15; applicants notified on a rolling basis.

STUDENT LIFE. Housing: Dormitories (coed). Limited housing also available for police academy students. **Activities:** Student government, magazine, radio, student newspaper, television, choral groups, concert band, dance, drama, jazz band, pep band, symphony orchestra, Native American Club, African American Club, International Student Club.

ATHLETICS. Intercollegiate: Baseball M, basketball, cross-country, football M, golf M, softball W, tennis, track and field, volleyball W. **Intramural:** Badminton, bowling, diving, golf, gymnastics, volleyball, water polo.

STUDENT SERVICES. Aptitude testing, career counseling, employment service for undergraduates, freshman orientation, health services, on-campus day care, personal counseling, placement service for graduates, veterans counselor, services/facilities for handicapped.

ANNUAL EXPENSES. Tuition and fees (projected): $280, $3,510 additional for out-of-state students. **Room and board:** $4,001. **Books and supplies:** $612. **Other expenses:** $1,724.

FINANCIAL AID. 50% of freshmen, 30% of continuing students receive some form of aid. 98% of grants, all loans, 49% of jobs based on need. Academic, art scholarships available. **Aid applications:** No closing date; priority given to applications received by April 15; applicants notified on a rolling basis beginning on or about May 1; must reply within 2 weeks.

ADDRESS/TELEPHONE. Paul Mendoza, Vice President for Student Services, College of the Redwoods, 7351 Tompkins Hill Road, Eureka, CA 95501-9302. (707) 445-6720. (800) 458-5300. Fax: (707) 445-6990.

College of San Mateo
San Mateo, California CB code: 4070

2-year public community college, coed. Founded in 1922. **Accreditation:** Regional. **Undergraduate enrollment:** 14,962 men and women. **Faculty:** 485 total (174 full time). **Location:** Suburban campus in small city; 15 miles from San Francisco. **Calendar:** Semester, limited summer session. **Microcomputers:** 150 located in classrooms, computer centers. **Special facilities:** Planetarium.

DEGREES OFFERED. AA, AS. 417 associate degrees awarded in 1992. 18% in business and management, 6% engineering technologies, 8% health sciences, 34% multi/interdisciplinary studies, 8% parks/recreation, protective services, public affairs, 7% trade and industry.

UNDERGRADUATE MAJORS. Accounting, aeronautical technology, aircraft mechanics, airline piloting and navigation, architecture, biology, biomedical science, business and management, business and office, business computer/console/peripheral equipment operation, business data processing and related programs, chemistry, cinematography/film, commercial art, computer and information sciences, criminal justice studies, dental assistant, drafting, electronic technology, engineering, engineering and engineering-related technologies, English, environmental design, ethnic studies, fashion merchandising, fine arts, fire control and safety technology, foreign languages (multiple emphasis), French, geology, German, graphic arts technology, horticulture, humanities, interior design, journalism, legal secretary, liberal/general studies, machine tool operation/machine shop, marketing and distribution, marketing management, mathematics, medical assistant, music, nursing, ornamental horticulture, painting, personal services, photographic technology, physical sciences, physics, plumbing/pipefitting/steamfitting, radio/television broadcasting, radio/television technology, real estate, small business management and ownership, social sciences, Spanish, speech, transportation management, welding technology.

ACADEMIC PROGRAMS. Dual enrollment of high school students, honors program, independent study, study abroad. **Remedial services:** Learning center, remedial instruction, tutoring. **Placement/credit:** AP, institutional tests.

ACADEMIC REQUIREMENTS. Freshmen must earn minimum GPA of 2.0 to continue in good standing. **Graduation requirements:** 60 hours for associate (18 in major). Most students required to take courses in English, history, humanities, mathematics, biological/physical sciences, social sciences.

FRESHMAN ADMISSIONS. Selection criteria: Open admissions.

1992 FRESHMAN CLASS PROFILE. 2,008 men and women enrolled. **Characteristics:** 98% from in state, 100% commute, 1% are foreign students.

FALL-TERM APPLICATIONS. No fee. No closing date; priority given to applications received by July 1; applicants notified on a rolling basis. Completion of CSM Placement tests for English, reading and mathematics recommmended prior to counseling session.

STUDENT LIFE. Activities: Student government, radio, student newspaper, television available to students enrolled in select courses, choral groups, concert band, dance, jazz band, symphony orchestra, Asian Student Union, Beyond War, Christian Fellowship, Ethnic Awareness, Hillel, International Students Union, Just Sistas, Latin American Student Organization, Red Ribbon Committee, Worldwide Students Association.

ATHLETICS. Intercollegiate: Baseball M, basketball W, cross-country, football M, softball W, tennis W, track and field.

STUDENT SERVICES. Aptitude testing, career counseling, employment service for undergraduates, freshman orientation, health services, on-campus day care, personal counseling, special adviser for adult students, services/facilities for handicapped.

ANNUAL EXPENSES. Tuition and fees (1992-93): $135, $3,390 additional for out-of-state students. **Books and supplies:** $576. **Other expenses:** $1,000.

FINANCIAL AID. 38% of freshmen, 62% of continuing students receive some form of aid. All grants, 78% of loans, 26% of jobs based on need. 200 enrolled freshmen were judged to have need, all were offered aid. **Aid applications:** No closing date; priority given to applications received by May 10; applicants notified on a rolling basis beginning on or about July 30; must reply by September 1.

ADDRESS/TELEPHONE. John F. Mullen, Director of Admissions and Records, College of San Mateo, 1700 West Hillsdale Boulevard, San Mateo, CA 94402. (415) 574-6165. Fax: (415) 573-7027.

College of the Sequoias
Visalia, California — CB code: 4071

2-year public community college, coed. Founded in 1925. **Accreditation:** Regional. **Undergraduate enrollment:** 1,616 men, 2,097 women full time; 2,518 men, 3,268 women part time. **Faculty:** 376 total (175 full time), 19 with doctorates or other terminal degrees. **Location:** Suburban campus in small city; 40 miles from Fresno, 70 miles from Bakersfield. **Calendar:** Semester, limited summer session. **Microcomputers:** 150 located in classrooms. **Special facilities:** 160-acre self-sufficient farm.

DEGREES OFFERED. AA, AS. 643 associate degrees awarded in 1992. 11% in business and management, 12% allied health, 57% multi/interdisciplinary studies.

UNDERGRADUATE MAJORS. Agricultural sciences, air conditioning/heating/refrigeration mechanics, air conditioning/heating/refrigeration technology, architecture, automotive mechanics, automotive technology, biological and physical sciences, business and management, business and office, business data processing and related programs, chemistry, child development/care/guidance, communications, construction, criminal justice studies, drafting, drafting and design technology, electronic technology, engineering, engineering and engineering-related technologies, English, fine arts, fire control and safety technology, foreign languages (multiple emphasis), home economics, humanities and social sciences, industrial technology, interpreter for the deaf, journalism, law enforcement and corrections technologies, legal assistant/paralegal, liberal/general studies, mathematics, mechanical design technology, music, nursing, ornamental horticulture, physical sciences, practical nursing, precision metal work, public affairs, science technologies, secretarial and related programs, social sciences, sociology, Spanish, visual and performing arts, welding technology, word processing.

ACADEMIC PROGRAMS. 2-year transfer program, double major, dual enrollment of high school students, independent study, internships, student-designed major, study abroad. **Remedial services:** Learning center, preadmission summer program, reduced course load, remedial instruction, special counselor, tutoring. **ROTC:** Air Force. **Placement/credit:** AP, CLEP General, institutional tests; 12 credit hours maximum for associate degree.

ACADEMIC REQUIREMENTS. Freshmen must earn minimum GPA of 2.0 to continue in good standing. 35% of freshmen return for sophomore year. **Graduation requirements:** 60 hours for associate. Most students required to take courses in English, history, humanities, mathematics, biological/physical sciences, social sciences.

FRESHMAN ADMISSIONS. Selection criteria: Open admissions. **Test requirements:** SAT, ACT, or institutional test required for placement and counseling only. Score report by May 10.

1992 FRESHMAN CLASS PROFILE. 1,170 men, 1,230 women enrolled. **Characteristics:** 95% from in state, 100% commute, 35% have minority backgrounds, 1% are foreign students. Average age is 19.

FALL-TERM APPLICATIONS. No fee. Closing date August 14; applicants notified on a rolling basis beginning on or about June 9. Interview required for work program, word processing, nursing applicants. Audition required for music applicants. Early admission available.

STUDENT LIFE. Activities: Student government, student newspaper, television, yearbook, choral groups, concert band, dance, drama, jazz band, marching band, music ensembles, musical theater, pep band, symphony orchestra.

ATHLETICS. Intercollegiate: Baseball M, basketball, cross-country, diving, football M, golf, softball W, swimming, tennis, track and field, volleyball W, water polo M, wrestling M.

STUDENT SERVICES. Aptitude testing, career counseling, employment service for undergraduates, freshman orientation, health services, on-campus day care, personal counseling, special adviser for adult students, veterans counselor, women's reentry adviser, services/facilities for handicapped.

ANNUAL EXPENSES. Tuition and fees (projected): $620, $3,480 additional for out-of-state students. **Books and supplies:** $612. **Other expenses:** $900.

FINANCIAL AID. 31% of freshmen, 34% of continuing students receive some form of aid. 94% of grants, all loans, 26% of jobs based on need. 1,825 enrolled freshmen were judged to have need, all were offered aid. Academic, alumni affiliation scholarships available. **Aid applications:** No closing date; priority given to applications received by March 2; applicants notified on a rolling basis beginning on or about June 1; must reply within 2 weeks.

ADDRESS/TELEPHONE. Robert G. Heath, Dean of Admissions and Records, College of the Sequoias, 915 South Mooney Boulevard, Visalia, CA 93277. (209) 730-3727. Fax: (209) 730-3894.

College of the Siskiyous
Weed, California — CB code: 4087

2-year public community college, coed. Founded in 1957. **Accreditation:** Regional. **Undergraduate enrollment:** 461 men, 425 women full time; 562 men, 1,194 women part time. **Faculty:** 152 total (51 full time), 5 with doctorates or other terminal degrees. **Location:** Rural campus in small town; 270 miles from Sacramento. **Calendar:** Semester, limited summer session. **Microcomputers:** Located in classrooms, computer centers. **Additional facts:** Campus in Yreka.

DEGREES OFFERED. AA, AS. 146 associate degrees awarded in 1992.

UNDERGRADUATE MAJORS. Accounting, animal sciences, automotive mechanics, automotive technology, biological and physical sciences, biology, business and management, business and office, business data processing and related programs, business data programming, chemistry, child development/care/guidance, communications, computer and information sciences, crafts, criminal justice studies, data processing, dramatic arts, education, engineering, engineering and engineering-related technologies, engineering and other disciplines, English, family/consumer resource management, fine arts, fire control and safety technology, forestry and related sciences, French, geology, home economics, humanities, humanities and social sciences, law enforcement and corrections technologies, liberal/general studies, mathematics, music, photography, physical sciences, physics, plant sciences, practical nursing, precision metal work, predentistry, preengineering, prelaw, premedicine, prepharmacy, preveterinary, psychology, real estate, science technologies, secretarial and related programs, social sciences, Spanish.

ACADEMIC PROGRAMS. 2-year transfer program, cooperative education, dual enrollment of high school students, independent study, student-designed major, telecourses. **Remedial services:** Learning center, preadmission summer program, reduced course load, remedial instruction, special counselor, tutoring. **Placement/credit:** AP, CLEP General, institutional tests; 12 credit hours maximum for associate degree.

ACADEMIC REQUIREMENTS. Freshmen must earn minimum GPA of 2.0 to continue in good standing. 50% of freshmen return for sophomore year. **Graduation requirements:** 60 hours for associate (20 in major). Most students required to take courses in English, humanities, mathematics, biological/physical sciences, social sciences.

FRESHMAN ADMISSIONS. Selection criteria: Open admissions.

1992 FRESHMAN CLASS PROFILE. 235 men, 200 women enrolled. **Characteristics:** 95% from in state, 85% commute, 18% have minority backgrounds, 1% are foreign students.

FALL-TERM APPLICATIONS. No fee. No closing date; applicants notified on a rolling basis. Deferred and early admission available.

STUDENT LIFE. Housing: Dormitories (men, women, coed). **Activities:** Student government, student newspaper, television, yearbook, choral groups, concert band, dance, drama, jazz band, music ensembles, musical theater, pep band, symphony orchestra.

ATHLETICS. Intercollegiate: Baseball M, basketball, cross-country, football M, softball W, track and field, volleyball W.

STUDENT SERVICES. Aptitude testing, career counseling, freshman orientation, personal counseling, special adviser for adult students, veterans counselor, services/facilities for handicapped.

ANNUAL EXPENSES. Tuition and fees: $320, $3,120 additional for

out-of-state students. **Room and board:** $3,660. **Books and supplies:** $612. **Other expenses:** $1,548.

FINANCIAL AID. 25% of freshmen, 25% of continuing students receive some form of aid. 94% of grants, 94% of loans, 28% of jobs based on need. Academic, state/district residency, leadership scholarships available. **Aid applications:** No closing date; priority given to applications received by May 2; applicants notified on a rolling basis beginning on or about June 1; must reply within 2 weeks.

ADDRESS/TELEPHONE. James N. Arack, PhD, Vice President of Student Services, College of the Siskiyous, 800 College Avenue, Weed, CA 96094. (916) 938-4461.

Columbia College
Columbia, California CB code: 4108

2-year public community college, coed. Founded in 1968. **Accreditation:** Regional. **Undergraduate enrollment:** 1,030 men, 1,488 women full time; 221 men, 739 women part time. **Faculty:** 119 total (44 full time), 7 with doctorates or other terminal degrees. **Location:** Rural campus in small town; 250 miles from Sacramento. **Calendar:** Semester, limited summer session. **Microcomputers:** 60 located in computer centers. **Special facilities:** Wooded parcourse (jogging/fitness trail), arboretum, astronomy dome, seismograph, athletic/multipurpose facility. **Additional facts:** Located on more than 200 acres of forest land adjacent to Columbia State Historic Park.

DEGREES OFFERED. AA, AS. 120 associate degrees awarded in 1992. 23% in business and management, 6% computer sciences, 30% education, 15% health sciences, 6% psychology, 6% visual and performing arts.

UNDERGRADUATE MAJORS. Anthropology, automotive mechanics, automotive technology, biology, business administration and management, business and management, business and office, chemistry, computer and information sciences, computer programming, dance, earth sciences, English, fine arts, fire control and safety technology, food management, forestry and related sciences, history, hotel/motel and restaurant management, liberal/general studies, mathematics, music, photography, physics, psychology, renewable natural resources, secretarial and related programs, social sciences.

ACADEMIC PROGRAMS. 2-year transfer program, cooperative education, independent study, internships. **Remedial services:** Learning center, remedial instruction, tutoring, skills development classes. **Placement/credit:** AP, institutional tests; 20 credit hours maximum for associate degree.

ACADEMIC REQUIREMENTS. Freshmen must earn minimum GPA of 2.0 to continue in good standing. 35% of freshmen return for sophomore year. Students must declare major by end of first year. **Graduation requirements:** 60 hours for associate. Most students required to take courses in English, history, mathematics, philosophy/religion, biological/physical sciences, social sciences.

FRESHMAN ADMISSIONS. Selection criteria: Open admissions.

1992 FRESHMAN CLASS PROFILE. 919 men, 1,624 women enrolled. **Characteristics:** 81% from in state, 96% commute, 9% have minority backgrounds. Average age is 37.

FALL-TERM APPLICATIONS. No fee. No closing date; applicants notified on a rolling basis. Deferred and early admission available. Matriculation procedures required before new or returning students may register. Early application assures accommodation to new student priority registration periods.

STUDENT LIFE. Housing: Dormitories (coed); apartment, handicapped housing available. Privately owned apartments on campus available to single students. **Activities:** Student government, choral groups, concert band, dance, drama, music ensembles, musical theater, symphony orchestra, jazz choir.

ATHLETICS. Intercollegiate: Basketball M, volleyball W. **Intramural:** Tennis.

STUDENT SERVICES. Aptitude testing, career counseling, employment service for undergraduates, freshman orientation, health services, on-campus day care, personal counseling, placement service for graduates, veterans counselor, adult reentry, services/facilities for handicapped.

ANNUAL EXPENSES. Tuition and fees: $374, $3,300 additional for out-of-state students. **Room and board:** $2,100 room only. **Books and supplies:** $650. **Other expenses:** $1,200.

FINANCIAL AID. 13% of freshmen, 13% of continuing students receive some form of aid. 95% of grants, all loans, all jobs based on need. 161 enrolled freshmen were judged to have need, 144 were offered aid. Academic, music/drama, art, state/district residency, leadership scholarships available. **Aid applications:** No closing date; priority given to applications received by March 2; applicants notified on a rolling basis beginning on or about June 15; must reply within 2 weeks.

ADDRESS/TELEPHONE. Kathy Smith, Admission and Records Coordinator, Columbia College, PO Box 1849, Columbia, CA 95310. (209) 533-5106. Fax: (209) 533-5104.

Columbia College: Hollywood
Los Angeles, California CB code: 1247

4-year private college of motion picture and television arts and sciences, coed. Founded in 1952. **Undergraduate enrollment:** 236 men and women. **Faculty:** 37 total, 3 with doctorates or other terminal degrees. **Location:** Urban campus in very large city; 10 miles from downtown Los Angeles. **Calendar:** Quarter, limited summer session. **Special facilities:** Fully equipped facilities for television and motion picture production.

DEGREES OFFERED. AA, BA. 8 associate degrees awarded in 1992. 100% in communications. 67 bachelor's degrees awarded. 30% in communications, 70% visual and performing arts.

UNDERGRADUATE MAJORS. Associate: Radio/television broadcasting, radio/television technology, telecommunications, video. **Bachelor's:** Cinematography/film, film arts, motion picture technology, radio/television broadcasting, radio/television technology, telecommunications, video.

ACADEMIC PROGRAMS. Accelerated program, internships. **Placement/credit:** AP, CLEP Subject.

ACADEMIC REQUIREMENTS. Freshmen must earn minimum GPA of 2.0 to continue in good standing. 80% of freshmen return for sophomore year. Students must declare major by end of first year. **Graduation requirements:** 96 hours for associate (48 in major), 192 hours for bachelor's (96 in major). Most students required to take courses in English, history, humanities, philosophy/religion, biological/physical sciences, social sciences. **Postgraduate studies:** 80% from 2-year programs enter 4-year programs.

FRESHMAN ADMISSIONS. Selection criteria: References and demonstrated interest in communications most important. Children of alumni, minority applicants, and foreign applicants given special consideration. Applicants must be 18 or older.

1992 FRESHMAN CLASS PROFILE. 92 men and women enrolled. 45% had high school GPA of 3.0 or higher, 55% between 2.0 and 2.99. **Characteristics:** 20% from in state, 100% commute, 29% have minority backgrounds. Average age is 23.

FALL-TERM APPLICATIONS. $50 fee. No closing date; applicants notified on a rolling basis; must reply within 4 weeks. Essay required. Deferred admission available.

STUDENT LIFE. Activities: Film, student newspaper, television.

STUDENT SERVICES. Career counseling, personal counseling, placement service for graduates, special adviser for adult students, veterans counselor.

ANNUAL EXPENSES. Tuition and fees (1992-93): $5,490. **Books and supplies:** $550. **Other expenses:** $1,800.

FINANCIAL AID. 35% of freshmen, 38% of continuing students receive some form of aid. All grants, 95% of loans, all jobs based on need. **Aid applications:** No closing date; priority given to applications received by April 15; applicants notified on a rolling basis beginning on or about July 15; must reply within 3 weeks.

ADDRESS/TELEPHONE. Kurt Wolfe, Director of Admissions, Columbia College: Hollywood, 925 North La Brea Avenue, Los Angeles, CA 90038. (213) 851-0550. Fax: (213) 851-6401.

Compton Community College
Compton, California CB code: 4078

2-year public community college, coed. Founded in 1927. **Accreditation:** Regional. **Undergraduate enrollment:** 5,294 men and women. **Faculty:** 210 total (80 full time), 27 with doctorates or other terminal degrees. **Location:** Urban campus in small city; 25 miles from Los Angeles. **Calendar:** Semester, limited summer session. Saturday and extensive evening/early morning classes. **Microcomputers:** 35 located in computer centers.

DEGREES OFFERED. AA, AS. 200 associate degrees awarded in 1992.

UNDERGRADUATE MAJORS. Accounting, automotive technology, business and office, business computer/console/peripheral equipment operation, business data entry equipment operation, business data processing and related programs, business data programming, drafting, engineering and engineering-related technologies, finance, graphic and printing production, graphic arts technology, law enforcement and corrections technologies, liberal/general studies, marketing and distribution, medical assistant, nursing, personal services, photographic technology, practical nursing, precision metal work, protective services, public affairs, radiograph medical technology, real estate, recreation and community services technologies, respiratory therapy technology, science technologies, secretarial and related programs, teacher aide.

ACADEMIC PROGRAMS. 2-year transfer program, accelerated program, cooperative education, honors program, cross-registration. **Remedial services:** Learning center, reduced course load, remedial instruction, special counselor, tutoring. **Placement/credit:** Institutional tests; 12 credit hours maximum for associate degree.

ACADEMIC REQUIREMENTS. Freshmen must earn minimum GPA of 2.0 to continue in good standing. 50% of freshmen return for sophomore year. Students must declare major by end of first year. **Graduation requirements:** 64 hours for associate (18 in major). Most students required to take courses in computer science, English, humanities, mathematics, biological/physical sciences, social sciences.

FRESHMAN ADMISSIONS. Selection criteria: Open admissions. If under 18, applicant must have graduated from high school and passed the California High School Certificate of Proficiency test.

1992 FRESHMAN CLASS PROFILE. 1,515 men and women enrolled. **Characteristics:** 90% from in state, 100% commute, 98% have minority backgrounds, 2% are foreign students.

FALL-TERM APPLICATIONS. No fee. No closing date; applicants notified on a rolling basis. Deferred and early admission available.

STUDENT LIFE. Activities: Student government, student newspaper, television, yearbook, choral groups, dance, drama, jazz band, marching band, music ensembles, musical theater, pep band, Christian club, Moslem student association.

ATHLETICS. Intercollegiate: Baseball, basketball, cross-country, football M, tennis, track and field. **Intramural:** Basketball, tennis.

STUDENT SERVICES. Career counseling, employment service for undergraduates, freshman orientation, on-campus day care, personal counseling, placement service for graduates, veterans counselor, services/facilities for handicapped.

ANNUAL EXPENSES. Tuition and fees (1992-93): $120, $3,060 additional for out-of-state students. **Books and supplies:** $410.

FINANCIAL AID. 75% of freshmen, 70% of continuing students receive some form of aid. All grants, 96% of loans, all jobs based on need. Academic, music/drama, art, athletic, state/district residency, leadership, alumni affiliation, religious affiliation, minority scholarships available. **Aid applications:** Closing date May 15; applicants notified on or about August 1.

ADDRESS/TELEPHONE. Dr. Essie French-Preston, Associate Dean of Enrollment Services, Compton Community College, 1111 East Artesia Boulevard, Compton, CA 90221. (310) 637-2660 ext. 2026. Fax: (310) 639-8260.

Concordia University
Irvine, California — CB code: 4069

Admissions: 78% of applicants accepted
Based on:
- ••• School record
- •• Activities, recommendations, religious affiliation/commitment, test scores
- • Interview, special talents

Completion: 88% of freshmen end year in good standing
45% graduate, 33% of these enter graduate study

4-year private liberal arts college, coed, affiliated with Lutheran Church—Missouri Synod. Founded in 1972. **Accreditation:** Regional. **Undergraduate enrollment:** 224 men, 341 women full time; 13 men, 47 women part time. **Graduate enrollment:** 4 men, 2 women full time; 5 men, 15 women part time. **Faculty:** 69 total (39 full time), 34 with doctorates or other terminal degrees. **Location:** Suburban campus in small city; 40 miles from Los Angeles, 80 miles from San Diego. **Calendar:** Quarter, limited summer session. Extensive evening/early morning classes. **Microcomputers:** 38 located in computer centers.

DEGREES OFFERED. BA, MA. 5 associate degrees awarded in 1992. 130 bachelor's degrees awarded in 1992. 15% in business and management, 35% education, 10% letters/literature, 10% life sciences, 10% multi/interdisciplinary studies, 8% philosophy, religion, theology, 10% psychology, 5% social sciences, 5% visual and performing arts. Graduate degrees offered in 3 major fields of study.

UNDERGRADUATE MAJORS. Accounting, anthropology, art education, behavioral sciences, biblical languages, biological and physical sciences, biology, business administration and management, comparative cultures, dramatic arts, early childhood education, education, elementary education, English, English education, English literature, environmental science, fine arts, humanities and social sciences, junior high education, liberal/general studies, mathematics, mathematics education, music, music education, physical education, predentistry, prelaw, premedicine, prepharmacy, preveterinary, psychology, religion, religious education, religious music, science education, secondary education, social science education, social sciences, sociology, speech/communication/theater education, theological studies.

ACADEMIC PROGRAMS. Cooperative education, double major, independent study, internships, student-designed major, study abroad, teacher preparation. **Remedial services:** Learning center, reduced course load, special counselor, tutoring, mathematics and English remedial courses. **Placement/credit:** AP, CLEP Subject, institutional tests.

ACADEMIC REQUIREMENTS. Freshmen must earn minimum GPA of 2.0 to continue in good standing. 81% of freshmen return for sophomore year. Students must declare major by end of second year. **Graduation requirements:** 192 hours for bachelor's (48 in major). Most students required to take courses in arts/fine arts, computer science, English, foreign languages, history, humanities, mathematics, philosophy/religion, biological/physical sciences, social sciences. **Additional information:** Associate degree available only to International students.

FRESHMAN ADMISSIONS. Selection criteria: Evidence of Christian character, high school record, test scores, recommendation, extracurricular activities important. Special consideration given to minority and foreign applicants. **High school preparation:** 14 units required. Required and recommended units include English 4, mathematics 3, social science 2 and science 3. Biological science 1, foreign language 2 and physical science 1 recommended. Biology, chemistry, algebra I and II, geometry, 2 history, American history specifically recommended. Must complete 2 years of foreign language in high school or 1 year in college for graduation. **Test requirements:** SAT or ACT (SAT preferred); score report by July 1.

1992 FRESHMAN CLASS PROFILE. 512 men and women applied, 400 accepted; 38 men enrolled, 76 women enrolled. 55% had high school GPA of 3.0 or higher, 45% between 2.0 and 2.99. 25% were in top tenth and 50% were in top quarter of graduating class. **Academic background:** Mid 50% of enrolled freshmen had SAT-V between 330-490, SAT-M between 330-510; ACT composite between 15-25. 85% submitted SAT scores, 15% submitted ACT scores. **Characteristics:** 80% from in state, 85% live in college housing, 22% have minority backgrounds, 9% are foreign students. Average age is 19.

FALL-TERM APPLICATIONS. $25 fee. Closing date July 1; priority given to applications received by April 15; applicants notified on a rolling basis; must reply by May 1 or within 3 weeks if notified thereafter. Audition required for music applicants. Interview recommended. Deferred admission available.

STUDENT LIFE. Housing: Dormitories (men, women); apartment housing available. Student living quarters are apartments with kitchen facilities. **Activities:** Student government, student newspaper, yearbook, choral groups, drama, music ensembles, pep band, Students in Action for the Vision of Evangelism, Spiritual Life Inreach, Spiritual Life Outreach, Interac Center, art club, business club.

ATHLETICS. NAIA. **Intercollegiate:** Baseball M, basketball, cross-country, soccer M, softball W, track and field, volleyball W. **Intramural:** Baseball M, basketball, bowling, football M, handball, soccer, table tennis, tennis, volleyball.

STUDENT SERVICES. Aptitude testing, career counseling, freshman orientation, health services, personal counseling, placement service for graduates, services/facilities for handicapped.

ANNUAL EXPENSES. Tuition and fees (1992-93): $9,315. **Room and board:** $4,230. **Books and supplies:** $540. **Other expenses:** $900.

FINANCIAL AID. 84% of freshmen, 76% of continuing students receive some form of aid. All jobs based on need. Academic, music/drama, athletic, state/district residency, leadership, minority scholarships available. **Aid applications:** Closing date June 30; priority given to applications received by April 30; applicants notified on a rolling basis beginning on or about April 30; must reply within 3 weeks.

ADDRESS/TELEPHONE. W. Stan Meyer, Vice President for Enrollment Services, Concordia University, 1530 Concordia, Irvine, CA 92715-3299. (714) 854-8002 ext. 106. (800) 229-1200. Fax: (714) 854-6854.

Contra Costa College
San Pablo, California — CB code: 4943

2-year public community college, coed. Founded in 1948. **Accreditation:** Regional. **Undergraduate enrollment:** 8,991 men and women. **Faculty:** 288 total (137 full time), 9 with doctorates or other terminal degrees. **Location:** Urban campus in large town; 20 miles from San Francisco. **Calendar:** Semester, limited summer session. **Microcomputers:** Located in classrooms, computer centers.

DEGREES OFFERED. AA, AS. 274 associate degrees awarded in 1992.

UNDERGRADUATE MAJORS. Afro-American (black) studies, architectural technologies, automotive mechanics, automotive technology, bilingual/bicultural education, biology, business and office, business computer/console/peripheral equipment operation, business data programming, chemistry, computer and information sciences, cosmetology, dental assistant, drafting, drafting and design technology, dramatic arts, engineering, engineering and engineering-related technologies, English, food management, food production/management/services, geography, Hispanic American studies, history, interior design, law enforcement and corrections technologies, liberal/general studies, mathematics, medical assistant, music, nursing, physics, psychology, real estate, secretarial and related programs, sociology, teacher aide, trade and industrial supervision and management.

ACADEMIC PROGRAMS. 2-year transfer program, dual enrollment of high school students, honors program, independent study, cross-registration. **Remedial services:** Learning center, remedial instruction, tutoring. **ROTC:** Air Force. **Placement/credit:** AP, institutional tests; 12 credit hours maximum for associate degree.

ACADEMIC REQUIREMENTS. Freshmen must earn minimum GPA of 2.0 to continue in good standing. Students must declare major on enrollment. **Graduation requirements:** Most students required to take courses in English, history, humanities, mathematics, biological/physical sciences, social sciences.

FRESHMAN ADMISSIONS. Selection criteria: Open admissions.

1992 FRESHMAN CLASS PROFILE. 2,625 men and women enrolled. **Characteristics:** 99% from in state, 100% commute, 60% have minority backgrounds, 1% are foreign students.

FALL-TERM APPLICATIONS. No fee. No closing date; priority given to applications received by August 20.

STUDENT LIFE. Activities: Student government, student newspaper, choral groups, concert band, dance, drama, jazz band, music ensembles, musical theater, symphony orchestra.

ATHLETICS. Intercollegiate: Baseball M, basketball, football M, tennis, track and field.

STUDENT SERVICES. Aptitude testing, career counseling, employment service for undergraduates, health services, personal counseling, services/facilities for handicapped.

ANNUAL EXPENSES. Tuition and fees (projected): $302, $3,420 additional for out-of-state students. **Books and supplies:** $612. **Other expenses:** $1,548.

FINANCIAL AID. 37% of freshmen, 25% of continuing students receive some form of aid. All aid based on need. 1,011 enrolled freshmen were judged to have need, 749 were offered aid. **Aid applications:** No closing date; priority given to applications received by March 2; applicants notified on a rolling basis beginning on or about August 24; must reply within 2 weeks.

ADDRESS/TELEPHONE. Dean Eaton, Director of Admissions and Records, Contra Costa College, 2600 Mission Bell Drive, San Pablo, CA 94806. (510) 235-7800. Fax: (510) 263-6768.

Cosumnes River College
Sacramento, California — CB code: 4121

2-year public community, junior, technical college, coed. Founded in 1970. **Accreditation:** Regional. **Undergraduate enrollment:** 1,739 men, 2,054 women full time; 2,655 men, 4,524 women part time. **Faculty:** 398 total (119 full time), 25 with doctorates or other terminal degrees. **Location:** Suburban campus in large city. **Calendar:** Semester, limited summer session. Extensive evening/early morning classes. **Microcomputers:** Located in libraries, computer centers. **Special facilities:** Art gallery. **Additional facts:** Classes offered at Placerville Center, Folsom Prison and locations along highway 50 corridor going east to Lake Tahoe.

DEGREES OFFERED. AA, AS. 308 associate degrees awarded in 1992.

UNDERGRADUATE MAJORS. Accounting, advertising, agribusiness, agricultural business and management, agricultural sciences, American studies, animal sciences, architecture, art history, automotive mechanics, automotive technology, business administration and management, business and management, business and office, city/community/regional planning, communications, computer and information sciences, computer programming, construction, data processing, drafting, drafting and design technology, dramatic arts, education, electrical/electronics/communications engineering, electronic technology, environmental design, equestrian science, family/consumer resource management, finance, fine arts, fire control and safety technology, food management, food science and nutrition, health sciences, horticultural science, horticulture, humanities and social sciences, industrial technology, information sciences and systems, interior design, journalism, landscape architecture, law enforcement and corrections, liberal/general studies, management science, marketing management, mathematics, medical assistant, medical records administration, medical records technology, photographic technology, photography, plant sciences, public relations, radio/television broadcasting, radio/television technology, robotics, secretarial and related programs, social sciences, veterinarian's assistant, visual and performing arts, women's studies.

ACADEMIC PROGRAMS. 2-year transfer program, cooperative education, double major, dual enrollment of high school students, honors program, independent study, study abroad, telecourses. **Remedial services:** Learning center, reduced course load, remedial instruction, tutoring, English as second language. **Placement/credit:** AP, CLEP General; 15 credit hours maximum for associate degree.

ACADEMIC REQUIREMENTS. Freshmen must earn minimum GPA of 2.0 to continue in good standing. 55% of freshmen return for sophomore year. Students must declare major by end of first year. **Graduation requirements:** 60 hours for associate. Most students required to take courses in English, history, humanities, mathematics, biological/physical sciences, social sciences.

FRESHMAN ADMISSIONS. Selection criteria: Open admissions.

1992 FRESHMAN CLASS PROFILE. 1,363 men and women enrolled. **Characteristics:** 99% from in state, 100% commute, 32% have minority backgrounds, 1% are foreign students. Average age is 27.

FALL-TERM APPLICATIONS. No fee. No closing date; priority given to applications received by January 17; applicants notified on a rolling basis beginning on or about March 1. Deferred admission available. First-time students encouraged to participate in orientation and matriculation sessions.

STUDENT LIFE. Activities: Student government, radio, student newspaper, television, choral groups, concert band, drama, jazz band, African-American Students Association, Hispanic/Latino scholars, Asian American Club, Christian Club, Earth Club.

ATHLETICS. Intercollegiate: Baseball M, basketball, cross-country, soccer, softball W, tennis, track and field, volleyball W. **Intramural:** Badminton, bowling, fencing, golf, racquetball, skiing, swimming, tennis, track and field, volleyball.

STUDENT SERVICES. Aptitude testing, career counseling, employment service for undergraduates, freshman orientation, health services, on-campus day care, personal counseling, placement service for graduates, special adviser for adult students, veterans counselor, special services for students transferring to 4-year university, services/facilities for handicapped.

ANNUAL EXPENSES. Tuition and fees (1992-93): $120, $3,210 additional for out-of-state students. **Books and supplies:** $500. **Other expenses:** $3,000.

FINANCIAL AID. 3% of continuing students receive some form of aid. All grants, 90% of loans, all jobs based on need. **Aid applications:** No closing date; priority given to applications received by May 15; applicants notified on a rolling basis; must reply within 4 weeks.

ADDRESS/TELEPHONE. Howard L. Harris, Dean of Admission and Records, Cosumnes River College, 8401 Center Parkway, Sacramento, CA 95823-5799. (916) 688-7410.

Crafton Hills College
Yucaipa, California — CB code: 4126

2-year public community college, coed. Founded in 1972. **Accreditation:** Regional. **Undergraduate enrollment:** 589 men, 711 women full time; 1,556 men, 2,181 women part time. **Faculty:** 190 total (63 full time), 16 with doctorates or other terminal degrees. **Location:** Rural campus in large town; 16 miles from San Bernardino. **Calendar:** Semester, limited summer session. **Microcomputers:** Located in libraries, computer centers.

DEGREES OFFERED. AA, AS. 250 associate degrees awarded in 1992. 17% in business and management, 9% health sciences, 27% multi/interdisciplinary studies, 15% parks/recreation, protective services, public affairs, 6% visual and performing arts.

UNDERGRADUATE MAJORS. Accounting, allied health, anatomy, anthropology, biology, business administration and management, business and management, business and office, chemistry, child development/care/guidance, communications, computer and information sciences, economics, education, elementary education, emergency medical technologies, emergency/disaster science, English, fine arts, French, geography, history, law enforcement and corrections technologies, liberal/general studies, marketing and distribution, mathematics, medical secretary, microbiology, music, physics, political science and government, protective services, psychology, radiograph medical technology, respiratory therapy technology, science technologies, secondary education, secretarial and related programs, social sciences, sociology, Spanish, speech, visual and performing arts.

ACADEMIC PROGRAMS. 2-year transfer program, cooperative education, dual enrollment of high school students, independent study, teacher preparation, telecourses, weekend college, cross-registration. **Remedial services:** Learning center, preadmission summer program, remedial instruction, tutoring. **Placement/credit:** AP, CLEP Subject, institutional tests; 36 credit hours maximum for associate degree.

ACADEMIC REQUIREMENTS. Freshmen must earn minimum GPA of 2.0 to continue in good standing. 32% of freshmen return for sophomore year. Students must declare major on application. **Graduation requirements:** 60 hours for associate (18 in major). Most students required to take courses in English, humanities, mathematics, biological/physical sciences, social sciences.

FRESHMAN ADMISSIONS. Selection criteria: Open admissions.

1992 FRESHMAN CLASS PROFILE. 861 men and women enrolled. **Characteristics:** 99% from in state, 100% commute, 20% have minority backgrounds. Average age is 28.

FALL-TERM APPLICATIONS. No fee. No closing date; applicants notified on a rolling basis. Deferred and early admission available. Students under 18 admitted with special permission.

STUDENT LIFE. Activities: Student government, bimonthly student bulletin, choral groups, dance, drama, jazz band, music ensembles, musical theater.

STUDENT SERVICES. Aptitude testing, career counseling, employment service for undergraduates, freshman orientation, health services, personal counseling, placement service for graduates, veterans counselor, services/facilities for handicapped.

ANNUAL EXPENSES. Tuition and fees (1992-93): $135, $3,120 additional for out-of-state students. **Books and supplies:** $550. **Other expenses:** $550.

FINANCIAL AID. 17% of continuing students receive some form of aid. 97% of grants, 89% of loans, 65% of jobs based on need. Academic, leadership scholarships available. **Aid applications:** No closing date; priority given to applications received by May 1; applicants notified on a rolling basis beginning on or about July 31; must reply within 2 weeks.

ADDRESS/TELEPHONE. Dr. James Bisi, Dean of Student Services, Crafton Hills College, 11711 Sand Canyon Road, Yucaipa, CA 92399-1799. (909) 794-2161 ext. 350. Fax: (909) 389-9141.

Cuesta College
San Luis Obispo, California CB code: 4101

2-year public community college, coed. Founded in 1964. **Accreditation:** Regional. **Undergraduate enrollment:** 8,004 men and women. **Faculty:** 314 total (129 full time), 20 with doctorates or other terminal degrees. **Location:** Rural campus in large town; 200 miles from Los Angeles, 6 miles from San Luis Obispo. **Calendar:** Semester, limited summer session. Extensive evening/early morning classes. **Microcomputers:** 100 located in libraries, classrooms, computer centers. **Special facilities:** Art gallery, Hollister Adobe Museum (Chumash Indian).

DEGREES OFFERED. AA, AS. 533 associate degrees awarded in 1992.

UNDERGRADUATE MAJORS. Allied health, automotive technology, business administration and management, business and management, business and office, business computer/console/peripheral equipment operation, chemistry, engineering and engineering-related technologies, fashion merchandising, human resources development, industrial technology, liberal/general studies, marketing and distribution, mental health/human services, nursing, precision metal work, real estate, recreation and community services technologies, secretarial and related programs, teacher aide, telecommunications.

ACADEMIC PROGRAMS. 2-year transfer program, honors program, independent study, student-designed major, study abroad, teacher preparation. **Remedial services:** Learning center, remedial instruction, special counselor, tutoring. **Placement/credit:** AP, CLEP Subject, institutional tests; 12 credit hours maximum for associate degree.

ACADEMIC REQUIREMENTS. Freshmen must earn minimum GPA of 2.0 to continue in good standing. 38% of freshmen return for sophomore year. **Graduation requirements:** 60 hours for associate. Most students required to take courses in arts/fine arts, English, history, humanities, mathematics, philosophy/religion, biological/physical sciences, social sciences.

FRESHMAN ADMISSIONS. Selection criteria: Open admissions.

1992 FRESHMAN CLASS PROFILE. 1,605 men and women enrolled. **Characteristics:** 98% from in state, 100% commute, 20% have minority backgrounds, 1% are foreign students. Average age is 18.

FALL-TERM APPLICATIONS. No fee. No closing date; applicants notified on a rolling basis. Interview required for nursing applicants. Early admission available.

STUDENT LIFE. Activities: Student government, radio, student newspaper, television, choral groups, dance, drama, jazz band, music ensembles, musical theater, Alpha Gamma Sigma.

ATHLETICS. Intercollegiate: Baseball M, basketball, cross-country, diving, golf, softball W, swimming, tennis, track and field, volleyball W, water polo M, wrestling M.

STUDENT SERVICES. Aptitude testing, career counseling, employment service for undergraduates, freshman orientation, health services, on-campus day care, personal counseling, special adviser for adult students, veterans counselor, services/facilities for handicapped.

ANNUAL EXPENSES. Tuition and fees (projected): $350, $3,120 additional for out-of-state students. **Books and supplies:** $612. **Other expenses:** $1,548.

FINANCIAL AID. 15% of continuing students receive some form of aid. 97% of grants, all loans, all jobs based on need. Academic scholarships available. **Aid applications:** No closing date; priority given to applications received by February 19; applicants notified on a rolling basis beginning on or about April 15.

ADDRESS/TELEPHONE. Frank S. Gonzales, Dean of Student Services, Cuesta College, PO 8106, San Luis Obispo, CA 93403-8106. (805) 546-3100. Fax: (805) 546-3904. (800) 877-3140 California only toll-free number.

Cuyamaca College
El Cajon, California CB code: 4252

2-year public community college, coed. Founded in 1978. **Accreditation:** Regional. **Undergraduate enrollment:** 4,891 men and women. **Faculty:** 132 total (48 full time), 12 with doctorates or other terminal degrees. **Location:** Suburban campus in small city; 18 miles from San Diego. **Calendar:** Semester, limited summer session. Saturday and extensive evening/early morning classes. **Microcomputers:** Located in classrooms.

DEGREES OFFERED. AA, AS. 114 associate degrees awarded in 1992.

UNDERGRADUATE MAJORS. Accounting, air traffic control, architectural graphics, architecture, automotive technology, business administration and management, child development/care/guidance, computer technology, drafting, electronic technology, engineering and engineering-related technologies, graphic and printing production, graphic arts technology, interior design, liberal/general studies, ornamental horticulture, real estate, small business management and ownership, surveying and mapping sciences, trade and industrial supervision and management.

ACADEMIC PROGRAMS. 2-year transfer program, double major, dual enrollment of high school students, independent study, internships, student-designed major, weekend college, cross-registration. **Remedial services:** Remedial instruction, special counselor, tutoring. **ROTC:** Air Force, Army. **Placement/credit:** AP, institutional tests.

ACADEMIC REQUIREMENTS. Freshmen must earn minimum GPA of 2.0 to continue in good standing. Students must declare major on application. **Graduation requirements:** 60 hours for associate (18 in major). Most students required to take courses in arts/fine arts, English, humanities, mathematics, biological/physical sciences, social sciences.

FRESHMAN ADMISSIONS. Selection criteria: Open admissions.

1992 FRESHMAN CLASS PROFILE. 846 men and women enrolled. **Characteristics:** 100% commute.

FALL-TERM APPLICATIONS. No fee. No closing date; applicants notified on a rolling basis.

STUDENT LIFE. Activities: Student government, student newspaper.

ATHLETICS. Intercollegiate: Soccer M.

STUDENT SERVICES. Aptitude testing, career counseling, employment service for undergraduates, health services, personal counseling, veterans counselor, services/facilities for handicapped.

ANNUAL EXPENSES. Tuition and fees (1992-93): $145, $3,120 additional for out-of-state students. **Books and supplies:** $450. **Other expenses:** $700.

FINANCIAL AID. 8% of freshmen, 9% of continuing students receive some form of aid. Grants, loans, jobs available. **Aid applications:** No closing date; priority given to applications received by July 28; applicants notified on a rolling basis; must reply within 2 weeks.

ADDRESS/TELEPHONE. Jeanne M. Hyde, Director of Admissions and Records, Cuyamaca College, 2950 Jamacha Road, El Cajon, CA 92019-4304. (619) 670-1980. Fax: (619) 670-7204.

Cypress College
Cypress, California CB code: 4104

2-year public community college, coed. Founded in 1966. **Accreditation:** Regional. **Undergraduate enrollment:** 2,230 men, 2,706 women full time; 3,888 men, 5,778 women part time. **Faculty:** 430 total (210 full time), 23 with doctorates or other terminal degrees. **Location:** Urban campus in small city; 30 miles from Los Angeles. **Calendar:** Semester, limited summer session. Extensive evening/early morning classes. **Microcomputers:** 800 located in libraries, computer centers.

DEGREES OFFERED. AA, AS. 900 associate degrees awarded in 1992.

UNDERGRADUATE MAJORS. Accounting, aeronautical technology, air conditioning/heating/refrigeration mechanics, airline piloting and navigation, anthropology, Asian studies, automotive mechanics, automotive technology, aviation management, biology, business administration and management, business and management, business and office, business data processing and related programs, chemistry, computer and information sciences, court reporting, dance, data processing, dental assistant, dental hygiene, dental laboratory technology, dramatic arts, economics, education, electrical and electronics equipment repair, elementary education, engineering, engineering and engineering-related technologies, English, fine arts, flight attendants, food management, food production/management/services, forestry and related sciences, French, funeral services/mortuary science, geography, geology, German, history, hospitality and recreation marketing, hotel/motel and restaurant management, illustration design, industrial arts education, journalism, Latin American studies, legal secretary, liberal/general studies, management science, marketing and distribution, marketing management, mathematics, medical assistant, medical records administration, medical records technology, mental health/human services, music, music performance, nursing, philosophy, photographic technology, physical education, physical therapy, physics, political science and government, predentistry, prelaw, premedicine, prepharmacy, preveterinary, psychology, radiograph medical technology, recreation and community services technologies, secondary education, secretarial and related programs, sociology, Spanish, speech, theater design, tourism, visual and performing arts, word processing.

ACADEMIC PROGRAMS. 2-year transfer program, dual enrollment of high school students, independent study, internships, study abroad, telecourses. **Remedial services:** Learning center, reduced course load, remedial instruction, special counselor, tutoring. **Placement/credit:** AP, institutional tests; 12 credit hours maximum for associate degree.

ACADEMIC REQUIREMENTS. Freshmen must earn minimum GPA of 2.0 to continue in good standing. Students must declare major on application. **Graduation requirements:** 60 hours for associate. Most students required to take courses in English, humanities, mathematics, biological/physical sciences, social sciences.

FRESHMAN ADMISSIONS. Selection criteria: Open admissions. **Test requirements:** College Ability Tests may be substituted for SAT or ACT.

1992 FRESHMAN CLASS PROFILE. 1,064 men, 1,348 women enrolled. **Characteristics:** 95% from in state, 100% commute, 29% have minority backgrounds, 1% are foreign students.

FALL-TERM APPLICATIONS. No fee. Closing date August 12; applicants notified on a rolling basis beginning on or about August 1. CRDA.

STUDENT LIFE. Activities: Student government, magazine, student newspaper, choral groups, concert band, dance, drama, jazz band, music ensembles, musical theater.

ATHLETICS. NJCAA. **Intercollegiate:** Baseball M, basketball, diving, golf M, soccer, softball W, swimming, tennis, volleyball W, water polo M, wrestling M. **Intramural:** Badminton, baseball M, basketball, softball, volleyball.

STUDENT SERVICES. Aptitude testing, career counseling, employment service for undergraduates, freshman orientation, health services, on-campus day care, personal counseling, veterans counselor, services/facilities for handicapped.

ANNUAL EXPENSES. Tuition and fees (1992-93): $150, $3,300 additional for out-of-state students. **Books and supplies:** $500. **Other expenses:** $750.

FINANCIAL AID. 15% of freshmen, 20% of continuing students receive some form of aid. Grants, loans, jobs available. Music/drama, leadership scholarships available. **Aid applications:** No closing date; priority given to applications received by May 31; applicants notified on a rolling basis beginning on or about August 1; must reply within 2 weeks.

ADDRESS/TELEPHONE. Dr. Alexander McLeod, Dean of Admissions and Records, Cypress College, 9200 Valley View Street, Cypress, CA 90630. (714) 826-9999. Fax: (714) 527-8238.

De Anza College
Cupertino, California CB code: 4286

2-year public community college, coed. Founded in 1967. **Accreditation:** Regional. **Undergraduate enrollment:** 25,146 men and women. **Location:** Suburban campus in large town; 5 miles from San Jose, 40 miles from San Francisco. **Calendar:** Quarter.

FRESHMAN ADMISSIONS. Selection criteria: Open admissions. Exception to open admissions-Nursing and physical therapist assistant students.

ANNUAL EXPENSES. Tuition and fees (projected): $350, $3,465 additional for out-of-state students. **Books and supplies:** $612. **Other expenses:** $1,156.

ADDRESS/TELEPHONE. Lewis H. Ham, Jr, Director of Admissions and Records, De Anza College, 21250 Stevens Creek Boulevard, Cupertino, CA 95014. (408) 864-5300. Fax: (408) 864-8329.

DeVry Institute of Technology: City of Industry
City of Industry, California CB code: 4214

Admissions:	93% of applicants accepted
Based on:	••• Test scores
	• Interview
Completion:	34% graduate

4-year proprietary business, technical college, coed. Founded in 1983. **Accreditation:** Regional. **Undergraduate enrollment:** 1,339 men, 373 women full time; 324 men, 76 women part time. **Faculty:** 71 total (50 full time). **Location:** Urban campus in very large city; 13 miles from Los Angeles. **Calendar:** Three continuous calendar terms. Extensive evening/early morning classes. **Microcomputers:** 134 located in computer centers.

DEGREES OFFERED. AAS, BS. 128 associate degrees awarded in 1992. 100% in engineering technologies. 293 bachelor's degrees awarded. 25% in business and management, 22% communications, 30% computer sciences, 23% engineering technologies.

UNDERGRADUATE MAJORS. Associate: Electronic technology. **Bachelor's:** Accounting, business administration and management, electronic technology, information sciences and systems, telecommunications.

ACADEMIC PROGRAMS. Accelerated program. **Remedial services:** Learning center, reduced course load, special counselor, tutoring, developmental coursework. **Placement/credit:** Institutional tests; 43 credit hours maximum for associate degree; 69 credit hours maximum for bachelor's degree.

ACADEMIC REQUIREMENTS. Freshmen must earn minimum GPA of 2.0 to continue in good standing. 48% of freshmen return for sophomore year. Students must declare major on enrollment. **Graduation requirements:** 87 hours for associate, 134 hours for bachelor's. Most students required to take courses in computer science, English, history, humanities, mathematics, social sciences.

FRESHMAN ADMISSIONS. Selection criteria: Applicants must have high school diploma or equivalant, pass institutional entrance examination or submit acceptable ACT/SAT/WPCT scores, and be 17 years of age. **Test requirements:** SAT or ACT. **Additional information:** New students may enter at beginning of any semester.

1992 FRESHMAN CLASS PROFILE. 1,056 men and women applied, 980 accepted; 460 men enrolled, 114 women enrolled. **Characteristics:** 98% from in state, 100% commute, 66% have minority backgrounds, 11% are foreign students.

FALL-TERM APPLICATIONS. $25 fee. Closing date November 4; applicants notified on a rolling basis; must reply within 4 weeks. Interview required. Deferred admission available.

STUDENT LIFE. Housing: School-contracted furnished apartments available for single students. **Activities:** Student government, student newspaper, Alpha Omega Christian Club, Institute of Electrical and Electronic Engineers (IEEE).

ATHLETICS. Intramural: Basketball, football, soccer, softball, volleyball.

STUDENT SERVICES. Career counseling, employment service for undergraduates, freshman orientation, placement service for graduates, veterans counselor, services/facilities for handicapped.

ANNUAL EXPENSES. Tuition and fees: $5,580. **Books and supplies:** $500. **Other expenses:** $1,911.

FINANCIAL AID. 78% of freshmen, 80% of continuing students receive some form of aid. All grants, 75% of loans, all jobs based on need. Academic scholarships available. **Aid applications:** No closing date; applicants notified on a rolling basis; must reply immediately. **Additional information:** Approximately 80% of students work part-time at jobs found through Institute.

ADDRESS/TELEPHONE. Keith Paridy, Director of Admissions, DeVry Institute of Technology: City of Industry, 12801 Crossroads Parkway South, City of Industry, CA 91746-3495. (310) 692-0551. Fax: (310) 692-6272.

Diablo Valley College
Pleasant Hill, California CB code: 4295

2-year public community college, coed. Founded in 1948. **Accreditation:** Regional. **Undergraduate enrollment:** 22,875 men and women. **Faculty:** 703 total (282 full time), 35 with doctorates or other terminal degrees. **Location:** Suburban campus in large town; 25 miles from San Francisco. **Calendar:** Semester, limited summer session. **Microcomputers:** Located in libraries, classrooms, computer centers. **Special facilities:** Science museum, art gallery, planetarium, observatory.

DEGREES OFFERED. AA. 730 associate degrees awarded in 1992.

UNDERGRADUATE MAJORS. Accounting, architecture, business computer/console/peripheral equipment operation, business data entry equipment operation, business data processing and related programs, business data programming, dental assistant, dental hygiene, dental laboratory technology, drafting, engineering, engineering and engineering-related technologies, fashion design, finance, food management, hotel/motel and restaurant management, journalism, law enforcement and corrections technologies, liberal/general studies, precision metal work, real estate, secretarial and related programs.

ACADEMIC PROGRAMS. 2-year transfer program, cooperative education, dual enrollment of high school students, honors program, independent study, internships, study abroad, weekend college. **Remedial services:** Learning center, remedial instruction, special counselor, tutoring. **Placement/credit:** AP, CLEP General, institutional tests.

ACADEMIC REQUIREMENTS. Freshmen must earn minimum GPA of 2.0 to continue in good standing. Students must declare major by end of first year. **Graduation requirements:** 60 hours for associate (30 in major). Most students required to take courses in English, history, mathematics, biological/physical sciences, social sciences.

FRESHMAN ADMISSIONS. Selection criteria: Open admissions.

1992 FRESHMAN CLASS PROFILE. 5,811 men, 6,421 women enrolled. **Characteristics:** 99% from in state, 100% commute, 1% are foreign students. Average age is 22.

FALL-TERM APPLICATIONS. No fee. Closing date August 15; priority given to applications received by April 1; applicants notified on a rolling basis beginning on or about June 1. Deferred admission available.

STUDENT LIFE. Activities: Student government, film, magazine, student newspaper, television, choral groups, concert band, dance, drama, jazz band, music ensembles, musical theater, symphony orchestra.

ATHLETICS. Intercollegiate: Baseball M, basketball, cross-country, diving, football M, softball W, swimming, tennis, track and field M, volleyball W, water polo M, wrestling M.

STUDENT SERVICES. Aptitude testing, career counseling, employment service for undergraduates, freshman orientation, on-campus day care, personal counseling, placement service for graduates, services/facilities for handicapped.

ANNUAL EXPENSES. Tuition and fees (projected): $332, $3,300 additional for out-of-state students. **Books and supplies:** $612. **Other expenses:** $1,548.

FINANCIAL AID. 10% of freshmen, 12% of continuing students receive some form of aid. 80% of grants, 58% of loans, 97% of jobs based on need. Academic, state/district residency, minority scholarships available. **Aid applications:** No closing date; priority given to applications received by

March 2; applicants notified on a rolling basis beginning on or about June 1; must reply within 2 weeks.

ADDRESS/TELEPHONE. John Dravland, Director of Admissions and Records, Diablo Valley College, 321 Golf Club Road, Pleasant Hill, CA 94523. (510) 685-1230.

Dominican College of San Rafael

San Rafael, California — CB code: 4284

Admissions: 72% of applicants accepted
Based on: ••• Essay, recommendations, school record, test scores
•• Interview, special talents
• Activities
Completion: 83% of freshmen end year in good standing
40% graduate, 7% of these enter graduate study

4-year private liberal arts college, coed, affiliated with Roman Catholic Church. Founded in 1890. **Accreditation:** Regional. **Undergraduate enrollment:** 121 men, 406 women full time; 14 men, 108 women part time. **Graduate enrollment:** 70 men, 151 women full time; 15 men, 67 women part time. **Faculty:** 124 total (43 full time), 48 with doctorates or other terminal degrees. **Location:** Suburban campus in large town; 17 miles from San Francisco. **Calendar:** Semester, limited summer session. Extensive evening/early morning classes. **Microcomputers:** 20 located in computer centers. **Special facilities:** Art gallery, natural history museum. **Additional facts:** Semester off-campus available at Aquinas College (MI), St. Thomas Aguinas College (NY), Barry University (FL).

DEGREES OFFERED. BA, BS, BFA, MA, MS, MBA. 97 bachelor's degrees awarded in 1992. 9% in business and management, 32% health sciences, 5% mathematics, 12% multi/interdisciplinary studies, 18% psychology, 8% social sciences, 7% visual and performing arts. Graduate degrees offered in 7 major fields of study.

UNDERGRADUATE MAJORS. Accounting, art history, biology, business administration and management, creative writing, English literature, fine arts, history, humanities, international business management, international relations, international studies, liberal/general studies, marketing management, mathematics, music, music history and appreciation, music performance, music theory and composition, nursing, political science and government, predentistry, premedicine, preveterinary, psychology, religion.

ACADEMIC PROGRAMS. Double major, honors program, independent study, internships, student-designed major, study abroad, teacher preparation, visiting/exchange student program, cross-registration. **Remedial services:** Learning center, reduced course load, remedial instruction, tutoring. **ROTC:** Air Force. **Placement/credit:** AP, CLEP Subject, institutional tests; 12 credit hours maximum for bachelor's degree.

ACADEMIC REQUIREMENTS. Freshmen must earn minimum GPA of 2.0 to continue in good standing. 77% of freshmen return for sophomore year. Students must declare major by end of second year. **Graduation requirements:** 124 hours for bachelor's (24 in major). Most students required to take courses in arts/fine arts, English, history, humanities, mathematics, philosophy/religion, biological/physical sciences, social sciences. **Postgraduate studies:** 1% enter law school, 6% enter MBA programs. **Additional information:** Strong emphasis on interdisciplinary teaching in humanities and on global perspective in academic offering.

FRESHMAN ADMISSIONS. Selection criteria: In order of importance: school achievement record (2.5 high school GPA), recommendations, test scores, interview, extracurricular activities, work experience. **High school preparation:** 15 units required. Required and recommended units include English 4, foreign language 2, mathematics 2-4, social science 1-2 and science 1-2. Social science units should include 1 history, science units should include 1 laboratory science. **Test requirements:** SAT or ACT (SAT preferred); score report by August 15.

1992 FRESHMAN CLASS PROFILE. 192 men and women applied, 139 accepted; 18 men enrolled, 50 women enrolled. 60% had high school GPA of 3.0 or higher, 40% between 2.0 and 2.99. **Academic background:** Mid 50% of enrolled freshmen had SAT-V between 380-500, SAT-M between 420-520. 91% submitted SAT scores. **Characteristics:** 82% from in state, 83% live in college housing, 28% have minority backgrounds, 3% are foreign students. Average age is 18.

FALL-TERM APPLICATIONS. $35 fee, may be waived for applicants with need. Closing date August 15; applicants notified on a rolling basis beginning on or about October 15. Essay required. Interview recommended for borderline applicants. Audition recommended for music applicants. Portfolio recommended for art applicants. Deferred and early admission available.

STUDENT LIFE. Housing: Dormitories (coed). **Activities:** Student government, magazine, radio, student newspaper, choral groups, dance, drama, music ensembles, symphony orchestra, campus ministry, volunteer work with various community agencies, Amnesty International.

ATHLETICS. NAIA. **Intercollegiate:** Basketball, cross-country, tennis, volleyball W.

STUDENT SERVICES. Career counseling, employment service for undergraduates, freshman orientation, health services, personal counseling, placement service for graduates, peer tutoring support.

ANNUAL EXPENSES. Tuition and fees: $12,180. **Room and board:** $5,680. **Books and supplies:** $612. **Other expenses:** $1,350.

FINANCIAL AID. 76% of freshmen, 76% of continuing students receive some form of aid. 84% of grants, 91% of loans, 95% of jobs based on need. Academic, music/drama, athletic, leadership, alumni affiliation, religious affiliation scholarships available. **Aid applications:** No closing date; priority given to applications received by February 1; must reply by May 1 or within 3 weeks if notified thereafter.

ADDRESS/TELEPHONE. Gabe Del Real, Director of Enrollment Management Services, Dominican College of San Rafael, 50 Acacia Avenue, San Rafael, CA 94901-8008. (415) 485-3204. (800) 788-3522. Fax: (415) 485-3205.

Dominican School of Philosophy and Theology

Berkeley, California — CB code: 0877

2-year upper-division private seminary college, coed, affiliated with Roman Catholic Church. Founded in 1932. **Accreditation:** Regional. **Undergraduate enrollment:** 6 men full time; 2 women part time. **Graduate enrollment:** 82 men and women. **Faculty:** 30 total (11 full time), 21 with doctorates or other terminal degrees. **Location:** Urban campus in small city; 5 miles from San Francisco. **Calendar:** Semester. **Microcomputers:** 2 located in computer centers.

DEGREES OFFERED. BA, M, M.Div. 2 bachelor's degrees awarded in 1992. 100% in philosophy, religion, theology. Graduate degrees offered in 3 major fields of study.

UNDERGRADUATE MAJORS. Philosophy.

ACADEMIC PROGRAMS. Cross-registration. **Remedial services:** Reduced course load.

ACADEMIC REQUIREMENTS. Students must declare major on application. **Graduation requirements:** 120 hours for bachelor's (39 in major). Most students required to take courses in computer science, English, history, humanities, mathematics, philosophy/religion, biological/physical sciences, social sciences.

STUDENT LIFE. Housing: Apartment housing available. **Activities:** Student government.

STUDENT SERVICES. Career counseling, personal counseling, placement service for graduates, services/facilities for handicapped.

ANNUAL EXPENSES. Tuition and fees (1992-93): $5,065. **Books and supplies:** $522. **Other expenses:** $1,872.

FINANCIAL AID. Loans available. **Aid applications:** No closing date; applicants notified on a rolling basis. **Additional information:** Limited financial aid. Support available from religious orders.

ADDRESS/TELEPHONE. Inrid Honore', CSJ, Registrar, Dominican School of Philosophy and Theology, 2401 Ridge Road, Berkeley, CA 94709. (510) 849-2030. Fax: (510) 849-1372.

Don Bosco Technical Institute

Rosemead, California — CB code: 4279

2-year private junior, technical college, men only, affiliated with Roman Catholic Church. Founded in 1955. **Accreditation:** Regional. **Undergraduate enrollment:** 197 men full time. **Location:** Suburban campus in large town; 15 miles from Los Angeles. **Calendar:** Semester. **Additional facts:** High school completion and associate degree offered in 5-year program, beginning with grade 9.

FRESHMAN ADMISSIONS. Selection criteria: Students must complete 3-year high school program at this institute with 2.0 GPA.

ANNUAL EXPENSES. Tuition and fees: $4,510. **Books and supplies:** $400. **Other expenses:** $400.

ADDRESS/TELEPHONE. Margie McInteer, Director of Admissions, Don Bosco Technical Institute, 1151 San Gabriel Boulevard, Rosemead, CA 91770-4299. (818) 307-6500.

D-Q University

Davis, California — CB code: 1285

2-year private junior college, coed. Founded in 1971. **Accreditation:** Regional. **Undergraduate enrollment:** 350 men and women. **Faculty:** 25 total (1 full time). **Location:** Rural campus in large town; 7 miles from Davis, 30 miles from Sacramento. **Calendar:** Semester. Extensive evening/early morning classes. **Microcomputers:** Located in computer centers. **Special facilities:** Native American cultural resources. **Additional facts:** Controlled by Native Americans.

DEGREES OFFERED. AA, AS. 3 associate degrees awarded in 1992.

UNDERGRADUATE MAJORS. Agricultural sciences, American Indian studies, business and management, computer and information sciences, education, fine arts, graphic arts technology, liberal/general studies, protective services, social sciences.

ACADEMIC PROGRAMS. Independent study, internships. **Remedial services:** Learning center, remedial instruction, tutoring. **Placement/credit:** Institutional tests.

ACADEMIC REQUIREMENTS. No policy requiring minimum GPA; records of students having academic difficulty are reviewed individually. To continue in good academic standing, freshmen must successfully complete minimum 8 units per semester. **Graduation requirements:** 60 hours for associate (18 in major). Most students required to take courses in English, history, humanities, mathematics, philosophy/religion, biological/physical sciences, social sciences. **Additional information:** Native American studies offered.

FRESHMAN ADMISSIONS. Selection criteria: Open admissions.

1992 FRESHMAN CLASS PROFILE. 103 men and women enrolled. **Characteristics:** 95% from in state, 50% commute, 70% have minority backgrounds.

FALL-TERM APPLICATIONS. No fee. No closing date; applicants notified on a rolling basis. Essay required. Deferred admission available.

STUDENT LIFE. Housing: Dormitories (coed). **Activities:** Student government.

ATHLETICS. Intramural: Basketball.

STUDENT SERVICES. Freshman orientation, personal counseling, services/facilities for handicapped.

ANNUAL EXPENSES. Tuition and fees: $3,800. **Room and board:** $4,352. **Books and supplies:** $500. **Other expenses:** $1,622.

FINANCIAL AID. 70% of freshmen, 60% of continuing students receive some form of aid. All grants, all jobs based on need. **Aid applications:** No closing date; applicants notified on a rolling basis.

ADDRESS/TELEPHONE. Annzell Loufas, Vice President, D-Q University, PO Box 409, Davis, CA 95617. (916) 758-0470 ext. 9. Fax: (916) 758-2518.

East Los Angeles College
Monterey Park, California — CB code: 4296

2-year public community college, coed. Founded in 1945. **Accreditation:** Regional. **Undergraduate enrollment:** 15,494 men and women. **Location:** Suburban campus in small city; 5 miles from Los Angeles. **Calendar:** Semester. Saturday and extensive evening/early morning classes.

FRESHMAN ADMISSIONS. Selection criteria: Open admissions.

ANNUAL EXPENSES. Tuition and fees (1992-93): $170, $3,360 additional for out-of-state students. **Books and supplies:** $550. **Other expenses:** $1,300.

ADDRESS/TELEPHONE. Rudy Valles, Associate Dean of Admissions, East Los Angeles College, 1301 Brooklyn Avenue, Monterey Park, CA 91754. (213) 265-8650. Fax: (213) 265-8688.

El Camino College
Torrance, California — CB code: 4302

2-year public community college, coed. Founded in 1947. **Accreditation:** Regional. **Undergraduate enrollment:** 25,360 men and women. **Location:** Suburban campus in very large city; 15 miles from Los Angeles. **Calendar:** Semester.

FRESHMAN ADMISSIONS. Selection criteria: Open admissions.

ANNUAL EXPENSES. Tuition and fees (1992-93): $135, $3,600 additional for out-of-state students. **Books and supplies:** $612. **Other expenses:** $1,728.

ADDRESS/TELEPHONE. William Robinson, Director of Admissions and Records, El Camino College, 16007 Crenshaw Boulevard, Torrance, CA 90506. (310) 532-3670. Fax: (310) 715-7798.

Evergreen Valley College
San Jose, California — CB code: 4273

2-year public community college, coed. Founded in 1975. **Accreditation:** Regional. **Undergraduate enrollment:** 875 men, 985 women full time; 4,282 men, 5,113 women part time. **Faculty:** 264 total (104 full time), 36 with doctorates or other terminal degrees. **Location:** Suburban campus in very large city; 7 miles from downtown. **Calendar:** Semester, limited summer session. **Microcomputers:** 125 located in classrooms.

DEGREES OFFERED. AA, AS. 617 associate degrees awarded in 1992.

UNDERGRADUATE MAJORS. Automotive technology, business and office, business computer/console/peripheral equipment operation, business data processing and related programs, business data programming, computer and information sciences, drafting, engineering and engineering-related technologies, fashion merchandising, graphic arts technology, law enforcement and corrections technologies, liberal/general studies, nursing, precision metal work, secretarial and related programs.

ACADEMIC PROGRAMS. 2-year transfer program, accelerated program, double major, dual enrollment of high school students, honors program, independent study, internships, cross-registration. **Remedial services:** Learning center, reduced course load, remedial instruction, special counselor, tutoring, program for students with learning disabilities. **ROTC:** Air Force, Army. **Placement/credit:** AP, CLEP General and Subject, institutional tests; 12 credit hours maximum for associate degree.

ACADEMIC REQUIREMENTS. Freshmen must earn minimum GPA of 2.0 to continue in good standing. 52% of freshmen return for sophomore year. Students must declare major on application. **Graduation requirements:** 60 hours for associate (18 in major). Most students required to take courses in English, history, humanities, mathematics, philosophy/religion, biological/physical sciences, social sciences.

FRESHMAN ADMISSIONS. Selection criteria: Open admissions.

1992 FRESHMAN CLASS PROFILE. 3,385 men and women enrolled. **Characteristics:** 99% from in state, 100% commute, 31% have minority backgrounds, 1% are foreign students. Average age is 26.

FALL-TERM APPLICATIONS. No fee. No closing date; applicants notified on a rolling basis.

STUDENT LIFE. Activities: Student government, student newspaper, choral groups, dance, drama, Black Students Union.

ATHLETICS. Intercollegiate: Baseball M, basketball M, football M, golf M, soccer W, softball W, track and field, volleyball W, wrestling M. **Intramural:** Basketball M.

STUDENT SERVICES. Aptitude testing, career counseling, employment service for undergraduates, freshman orientation, health services, on-campus day care, personal counseling, career center, services/facilities for handicapped.

ANNUAL EXPENSES. Tuition and fees (projected): $300, $2,640 additional for out-of-state students. **Books and supplies:** $612. **Other expenses:** $1,548.

FINANCIAL AID. 16% of continuing students receive some form of aid. All aid based on need. Academic, music/drama, art, athletic, leadership, minority scholarships available. **Aid applications:** No closing date; priority given to applications received by May 31; applicants notified on or about August 16; must reply within 10 days.

ADDRESS/TELEPHONE. Robert L. Brown, District Director of Admissions and Records, Evergreen Valley College, 3095 Yerba Buena Road, San Jose, CA 95135. (408) 274-7900 ext. 6441. Fax: (408) 223-9351.

Fashion Institute of Design and Merchandising
Los Angeles, California — CB code: 4457

2-year proprietary art, junior college, coed. Founded in 1969. **Accreditation:** Regional. **Undergraduate enrollment:** 247 men, 1,590 women full time; 26 men, 183 women part time. **Faculty:** 167 total (49 full time). **Location:** Urban campus in very large city; in downtown area. **Calendar:** Quarter, extensive summer session. **Microcomputers:** 60 located in classrooms, computer centers. **Special facilities:** Historical costume museum, international fashion video library. **Additional facts:** Branch campuses in Costa Mesa, San Francisco, and San Diego. Students have convenient access to garment, retail and cultural centers.

DEGREES OFFERED. AA. 517 associate degrees awarded in 1992.

UNDERGRADUATE MAJORS. Apparel and accessories marketing, clothing and textiles management/production/services, communications, cosmetics and fragrance marketing, fashion design, fashion merchandising, graphic arts technology, graphic design, interior design, manufacturing technology, marketing and distribution, marketing management, retailing, textile technology, theater costume, trade and industrial supervision and management.

ACADEMIC PROGRAMS. Independent study, internships, study abroad, visiting/exchange student program. **Remedial services:** Learning center, preadmission summer program, reduced course load, remedial instruction, special counselor, tutoring. **Placement/credit:** AP, CLEP General and Subject, institutional tests; 15 credit hours maximum for associate degree.

ACADEMIC REQUIREMENTS. Freshmen must earn minimum GPA of 2.0 to continue in good standing. 53% of freshmen return for sophomore year. Students must declare major on enrollment. **Graduation requirements:** 90 hours for associate (66 in major). Most students required to take courses in arts/fine arts, English, history, humanities, mathematics, biological/physical sciences, social sciences. **Additional information:** Faculty and staff come from related industries. Project-oriented courses give students hands-on experience.

FRESHMAN ADMISSIONS. Selection criteria: High school record, institutional test scores, references, and evidence of interest in major area through work experience, high school preparation, or extracurricular activities.

1992 FRESHMAN CLASS PROFILE. 675 men and women enrolled. **Characteristics:** 100% commute. Average age is 20.

FALL-TERM APPLICATIONS. $125 fee. No closing date; applicants notified on a rolling basis. Interview required for in-state applicants. Portfolio required for fashion design, interior design applicants. Essay required. Deferred and early admission available.

STUDENT LIFE. Activities: Student government, honor society, International Club, Association of Manufacturing Students, ASIC Student Chapter.

STUDENT SERVICES. Career counseling, employment service for undergraduates, freshman orientation, personal counseling, placement service for graduates, special adviser for adult students, services/facilities for handicapped.

ANNUAL EXPENSES. Tuition and fees (1992-93): $9,545, $150 additional for out-of-state students. Tuition may vary up to $400 depending on program. **Books and supplies:** $1,050.

FINANCIAL AID. 74% of freshmen, 74% of continuing students receive some form of aid. 99% of grants, 48% of loans, 69% of jobs based on need. **Aid applications:** No closing date; priority given to applications received by March 2; applicants notified on a rolling basis beginning on or about March 15; must reply within 3 weeks. **Additional information:** Tuition/fee expenses may be reduced by applying for admission by December 31 of year before student plans to attend.

ADDRESS/TELEPHONE. Vivian Lowy, Vice President of Planning, Fashion Institute of Design and Merchandising, 919 South Grand Avenue, Los Angeles, CA 90015. (213) 624-1200. (800) 421-0127. Fax: (213) 622-9643.

Fashion Institute of Design and Merchandising: San Francisco
San Francisco, California CB code: 4988

2-year proprietary art, junior college, coed. Founded in 1969. **Accreditation:** Regional. **Undergraduate enrollment:** 300 men and women full time. **Faculty:** 46 total (9 full time). **Location:** Urban campus in very large city. **Calendar:** Quarter. **Microcomputers:** 40 located in classrooms, computer centers. **Special facilities:** Historical costume museum, specialized library. **Additional facts:** Part of 4-campus system in California specializing in fashion and interior design education.

DEGREES OFFERED. AA. 76 associate degrees awarded in 1992.

UNDERGRADUATE MAJORS. Apparel and accessories marketing, clothing and textiles management/production/services, cosmetics and fragrance merchandising, fashion design, fashion merchandising, graphic design, interior design, marketing management.

ACADEMIC PROGRAMS. Internships, study abroad, visiting/exchange student program. **Remedial services:** Learning center, reduced course load, tutoring. **Placement/credit:** CLEP Subject, institutional tests; 15 credit hours maximum for associate degree.

ACADEMIC REQUIREMENTS. Freshmen must earn minimum GPA of 2.0 to continue in good standing. Students must declare major on enrollment. **Graduation requirements:** 90 hours for associate (66 in major). Most students required to take courses in arts/fine arts, English, history, humanities, mathematics. **Additional information:** Industry-experienced faculty work with international advisory board to bring current information into classrooms. San Francisco students offered study tours to fashion centers in Europe, Asia, and United States.

FRESHMAN ADMISSIONS. Selection criteria: High school diploma, portfolio, recommendations, essay, and personal interview most important.

1992 FRESHMAN CLASS PROFILE. 45 men and women enrolled. **Characteristics:** 100% commute.

FALL-TERM APPLICATIONS. $25 fee. No closing date; applicants notified on a rolling basis. Interview required. Portfolio required for fashion design, interior design, design and visual presentation applicants. Essay required. Out-of-state applicants interviewed by telephone. Deferred admission available.

STUDENT LIFE. Activities: Honor Society, International Club, Association of Manufacturing Students, Alumni Association, DEX ASID Student chapter, and Student Activites Committee.

STUDENT SERVICES. Career counseling, employment service for undergraduates, freshman orientation, personal counseling, placement service for graduates, special adviser for adult students, services/facilities for handicapped.

ANNUAL EXPENSES. Tuition and fees (1992-93): $9,545, $150 additional for out-of-state students. **Books and supplies:** $975. **Other expenses:** $1,512.

FINANCIAL AID. All grants, 48% of loans based on need. **Aid applications:** No closing date; priority given to applications received by March 2; applicants notified on a rolling basis.

ADDRESS/TELEPHONE. Jane DeMordaunt, Director of Admissions, Fashion Institute of Design and Merchandising: San Francisco, 55 Stockton Street, San Francisco, CA 94108-5805. (415) 433-6691. (800) 227-3070. Fax: (415) 394-9700.

Feather River College
Quincy, California CB code: 4318

2-year public community, junior college, coed. Founded in 1968. **Accreditation:** Regional. **Undergraduate enrollment:** 210 men, 220 women full time; 450 men, 630 women part time. **Faculty:** 92 total (22 full time), 67 with doctorates or other terminal degrees. **Location:** Rural campus in small town; 150 miles from Sacramento, 80 miles from Reno, Nevada. **Calendar:** Semester, limited summer session. Extensive evening/early morning classes. **Microcomputers:** 60 located in classrooms, computer centers. **Special facilities:** Fish hatchery, horse boarding facility, observatory, state wildlife preserve.

DEGREES OFFERED. AA, AS. 63 associate degrees awarded in 1992. 20% in agriculture, 5% business and management, 5% business/office and marketing/distribution, 30% life sciences, 10% physical sciences, 30% social sciences.

UNDERGRADUATE MAJORS. Accounting, biological and physical sciences, biology, business administration and management, business and management, chemistry, child development/care/guidance, criminal justice studies, education, English, equestrian science, fishing and fisheries, forestry and related sciences, geology, history, humanities and social sciences, industrial technology, liberal/general studies, mathematics, physical sciences, political science and government, recreation and community services technologies, renewable natural resources, secretarial and related programs, social sciences, wildlife management.

ACADEMIC PROGRAMS. 2-year transfer program, accelerated program, cooperative education, double major, dual enrollment of high school students, honors program, independent study, telecourses, cross-registration, horse pack station and stable management program. **Remedial services:** Learning center, remedial instruction, special counselor, tutoring, Enabler Program for disabled students. **Placement/credit:** AP, CLEP General and Subject, IB, institutional tests; 12 credit hours maximum for associate degree.

ACADEMIC REQUIREMENTS. Freshmen must earn minimum GPA of 2.0 to continue in good standing. 45% of freshmen return for sophomore year. Students must declare major by end of first year. **Graduation requirements:** 60 hours for associate (23 in major). Most students required to take courses in computer science, English, history, humanities, mathematics, biological/physical sciences, social sciences. **Additional information:** General education/core courses are offered that transfer to California State University, University of California and University of Nevada system.

FRESHMAN ADMISSIONS. Selection criteria: Open admissions.

1992 FRESHMAN CLASS PROFILE. 190 men, 280 women enrolled. 10% had high school GPA of 3.0 or higher, 75% between 2.0 and 2.99. **Characteristics:** 97% from in state, 100% commute, 9% have minority backgrounds, 5% are foreign students.

FALL-TERM APPLICATIONS. No fee. No closing date; applicants notified on a rolling basis beginning on or about March 15; must reply by registration. Deferred and early admission available.

STUDENT LIFE. Activities: Student government, film, student newspaper, yearbook, choral groups, dance, drama, musical theater.

ATHLETICS. NJCAA. **Intercollegiate:** Basketball, golf, volleyball W. **Intramural:** Basketball, field hockey, horseback riding, rugby M, skiing, softball, volleyball.

STUDENT SERVICES. Aptitude testing, career counseling, employment service for undergraduates, freshman orientation, health services, on-campus day care, personal counseling, placement service for graduates, special adviser for adult students, veterans counselor, services/facilities for handicapped.

ANNUAL EXPENSES. Tuition and fees (projected): $279, $2,640 additional for out-of-state students. **Books and supplies:** $550. **Other expenses:** $1,638.

FINANCIAL AID. 25% of freshmen, 20% of continuing students receive some form of aid. 99% of grants, 99% of loans, 42% of jobs based on need. 100 enrolled freshmen were judged to have need, 90 were offered aid. Academic, leadership, minority scholarships available. **Aid applications:** No closing date; priority given to applications received by March 2; applicants notified on a rolling basis beginning on or about July 30; must reply within 3 weeks.

ADDRESS/TELEPHONE. Michelle Kozlowski, Admissions and Records Supervisor, Feather River College, PO Box 11110, Quincy, CA 95971. (916) 283-0202. (800) 442-9799. Fax: (916) 283-3757.

Foothill College
Los Altos Hills, California CB code: 4315

2-year public community college, coed. Founded in 1958. **Accreditation:** Regional. **Undergraduate enrollment:** 17,162 men and women. **Faculty:** 816 total (238 full time). **Location:** Suburban campus in small city; 15 miles from San Jose. **Calendar:** Quarter, limited summer session. Saturday and extensive evening/early morning classes. **Microcomputers:** 200 located in computer centers. **Special facilities:** Observatory, Japanese cultural center.

DEGREES OFFERED. AA, AS. 329 associate degrees awarded in 1992.

UNDERGRADUATE MAJORS. Accounting, airline piloting and navigation, American studies, anthropology, biology, business administration and management, business and office, business data processing and related programs, chemistry, classics, communications, computer and information sciences, computer graphics, computer servicing technology, creative writing, dental assistant, dental hygiene, drafting and design technology, dramatic arts, economics, electronic technology, engineering, engineering and engineering-related technologies, English, fine arts, French, geography, geology, German, graphic arts technology, history, humanities, international business management, Japanese, journalism, liberal/general studies, library assistant, linguistics, mathematics, multicultural studies, music, ornamental horticulture, philosophy, photography, physical education, physician's assistant, physics, political science and government, predentistry, prelaw, premedicine, prepharmacy, preveterinary, psychology, radio/television broadcasting, radiograph medical technology, real estate, respiratory therapy technology, secretarial and related programs, social sciences, sociology, Spanish, speech, tourism, trade and industrial supervision and management, veterinarian's assistant.

ACADEMIC PROGRAMS. 2-year transfer program, cooperative education, honors program, independent study, study abroad, visiting/exchange student program, weekend college, cross-registration. **Remedial services:** Learning center, remedial instruction, special counselor, tutoring. **ROTC:** Air Force, Army, Naval. **Placement/credit:** AP, CLEP General, institutional tests; 20 credit hours maximum for associate degree.

ACADEMIC REQUIREMENTS. Freshmen must earn minimum GPA of 2.0 to continue in good standing. 30% of freshmen return for sophomore year. **Graduation requirements:** 90 hours for associate (30 in major). Most students required to take courses in computer science, English, history, humanities, mathematics, biological/physical sciences, social sciences.

FRESHMAN ADMISSIONS. Selection criteria: Open admissions. Allied health programs are limited enrollment and each program has application deadline and prerequisites. Interviews required.

1992 FRESHMAN CLASS PROFILE. 3,100 men and women enrolled. **Characteristics:** 92% from in state, 100% commute, 23% have minority backgrounds, 1% are foreign students.

FALL-TERM APPLICATIONS. No fee. No closing date; applicants notified on a rolling basis.

STUDENT LIFE. Activities: Student government, film, radio, student newspaper, television, choral groups, concert band, dance, drama, jazz band, music ensembles, musical theater, symphony orchestra.

ATHLETICS. Intercollegiate: Baseball M, basketball, cross-country, football M, golf M, soccer, softball W, swimming M, tennis, track and field, volleyball W, water polo M. **Intramural:** Archery, baseball, golf, tennis, track and field.

STUDENT SERVICES. Aptitude testing, career counseling, employment service for undergraduates, freshman orientation, health services, on-campus day care, personal counseling, placement service for graduates, special adviser for adult students, veterans counselor, services/facilities for handicapped.

ANNUAL EXPENSES. Tuition and fees (projected): $315, $3,060 additional for out-of-state students. **Books and supplies:** $750. **Other expenses:** $1,000.

FINANCIAL AID. 11% of freshmen, 8% of continuing students receive some form of aid. Grants, loans, jobs available. 280 enrolled freshmen were judged to have need, all were offered aid. Academic, music/drama, art, athletic, state/district residency, leadership, alumni affiliation, religious affiliation, minority scholarships available. **Aid applications:** No closing date; priority given to applications received by April 30; applicants notified on a rolling basis beginning on or about August 15; must reply within 2 weeks.

ADDRESS/TELEPHONE. Carol George, Dean of Student Services, Foothill College, 12345 El Monte Road, Los Altos Hills, CA 94022-4599. (415) 949-7325. Fax: (415) 949-7375.

Fresno City College
Fresno, California — CB code: 4311

2-year public community college, coed. Founded in 1910. **Accreditation:** Regional. **Undergraduate enrollment:** 19,000 men and women. **Faculty:** 852 total (272 full time), 27 with doctorates or other terminal degrees. **Location:** Urban campus in large city; 185 miles from San Francisco. **Calendar:** Semester, extensive summer session. **Microcomputers:** 400 located in libraries, classrooms. **Special facilities:** Anthropology museum, art gallery, high-tech laboratory for disabled students.

DEGREES OFFERED. AA, AS. 1,020 associate degrees awarded in 1992. 9% in business and management, 7% business/office and marketing/distribution, 7% teacher education, 11% health sciences, 50% multi/interdisciplinary studies, 8% trade and industry.

UNDERGRADUATE MAJORS. Accounting, Afro-American (black) studies, agribusiness, air conditioning/heating/refrigeration mechanics, air conditioning/heating/refrigeration technology, American Indian studies, anthropology, architecture, automotive mechanics, automotive technology, bilingual/bicultural education, biological and physical sciences, biology, business administration and management, business and management, business and office, business data processing and related programs, child development/care/guidance, community services, computer and information sciences, computer technology, construction, criminal justice studies, criminal justice technology, dance, dental hygiene, dietetic aide/assistant, drafting, drafting and design technology, dramatic arts, electrical technology, electrical/electronics/communications engineering, electronic technology, engineering, engineering and engineering-related technologies, fashion merchandising, finance, fine arts, fire control and safety technology, food management, food production/management/services, foreign languages (multiple emphasis), graphic and printing production, graphic arts technology, Hispanic American studies, home economics, human environment and housing, humanities, industrial technology, insurance and risk management, insurance marketing, journalism, law enforcement and corrections, law enforcement and corrections technologies, legal assistant/paralegal, legal secretary, liberal/general studies, manufacturing technology, marketing and distribution, mathematics, mechanical design technology, medical assistant, medical records administration, medical records technology, medical secretary, mental health/human services, Mexican American studies, music, nursing, photographic technology, photography, physical sciences, political science and government, practical nursing, precision metal work, psychology, public administration, radiograph medical technology, real estate, recreation and community services technologies, respiratory therapy technology, science technologies, secretarial and related programs, social sciences, Spanish, teacher aide, water and wastewater technology, women's studies, word processing.

ACADEMIC PROGRAMS. 2-year transfer program, accelerated program, double major, dual enrollment of high school students, honors program, independent study, internships, study abroad, weekend college, cross-registration. **Remedial services:** Learning center, preadmission summer program, reduced course load, remedial instruction, special counselor, tutoring. **ROTC:** Air Force, Army. **Placement/credit:** AP, CLEP General and Subject, institutional tests; 48 credit hours maximum for associate degree.

ACADEMIC REQUIREMENTS. Freshmen must earn minimum GPA of 2.0 to continue in good standing. 73% of freshmen return for sophomore year. Students must declare major on application. **Graduation requirements:** 60 hours for associate (20 in major). Most students required to take courses in arts/fine arts, English, history, humanities, mathematics, biological/physical sciences, social sciences.

FRESHMAN ADMISSIONS. Selection criteria: Open admissions. Selective admissions to allied health programs.

1992 FRESHMAN CLASS PROFILE. 4,000 men and women enrolled. **Characteristics:** 98% from in state, 100% commute, 40% have minority backgrounds, 1% are foreign students. Average age is 21.

FALL-TERM APPLICATIONS. No fee. Closing date August 31; priority given to applications received by April 1; applicants notified on a rolling basis beginning on or about May 1. CRDA. Deferred and early admission available. Institutional early decision plan.

STUDENT LIFE. Activities: Student government, film, magazine, student newspaper, television, choral groups, concert band, dance, drama, jazz band, marching band, music ensembles, musical theater, pep band, symphony orchestra, Christian Athletes in Acting, MECHA, Pan American Association, Alpha Gamma Sigma, International Club, Phi Theta Kappa.

ATHLETICS. NJCAA. **Intercollegiate:** Baseball M, basketball, cross-country, football M, golf M, soccer, softball W, tennis, track and field, volleyball W, wrestling M.

STUDENT SERVICES. Aptitude testing, career counseling, employment service for undergraduates, freshman orientation, health services, on-campus day care, personal counseling, placement service for graduates, special adviser for adult students, veterans counselor, computer center for handicapped students, services/facilities for handicapped.

ANNUAL EXPENSES. Tuition and fees: $295, $3,459 additional for out-of-state students. **Books and supplies:** $612. **Other expenses:** $1,449.

FINANCIAL AID. 11% of freshmen, 66% of continuing students receive some form of aid. 99% of grants, all loans, all jobs based on need. Academic, music/drama, art, leadership, minority scholarships available. **Aid applications:** No closing date; priority given to applications received by April 15; applicants notified on a rolling basis beginning on or about April 1; must reply within 2 weeks. **Additional information:** Board of Governors Grant Program to offset enrollment fees based on untaxed income, low income, or calculated need. These students also automatically exempt from health fees.

ADDRESS/TELEPHONE. Joaquin Jimenez, Associate Dean of Students, Admissions, and Records, Fresno City College, 1101 East University Avenue, Fresno, CA 93741. (209) 442-8240. Fax: (209) 485-7304.

Fresno Pacific College
Fresno, California — CB code: 4616

4-year private liberal arts college, coed, affiliated with Mennonite Brethren Church. Founded in 1944. **Accreditation:** Regional. **Undergraduate enrollment:** 216 men, 313 women full time; 23 men, 29 women part time. **Graduate enrollment:** 8 men, 20 women full time; 170 men, 510 women part time. **Faculty:** 179 total (77 full time), 57 with doctorates or other terminal degrees. **Location:** Suburban campus in large city; midway between Los Angeles and San Francisco. **Calendar:** Semester, limited summer session. **Microcomputers:** 66 located in libraries, computer centers.

DEGREES OFFERED. AA, BA, MA. 1 associate degree awarded in 1992. 120 bachelor's degrees awarded. 12% in business and management,

62% teacher education, 6% philosophy, religion, theology, 7% social sciences. Graduate degrees offered in 10 major fields of study.

UNDERGRADUATE MAJORS. Associate: Accounting, business and office, liberal/general studies, science technologies. **Bachelor's:** Accounting, Bible studies, bilingual/bicultural education, biological and physical sciences, biology, business administration and management, business and management, business education, communications, computer and information sciences, education, elementary education, English, English education, English literature, history, humanities and social sciences, liberal/general studies, mathematics, mathematics education, missionary studies, music, music education, music performance, physical education, physical sciences, premedicine, psychology, religion, religious education, religious music, science education, secondary education, social science education, social sciences, social work, sports medicine.

ACADEMIC PROGRAMS. 2-year transfer program, double major, independent study, internships, student-designed major, study abroad, teacher preparation, Washington semester, cross-registration. **Remedial services:** Learning center, special counselor, tutoring. **Placement/credit:** AP, CLEP General.

ACADEMIC REQUIREMENTS. Freshmen must earn minimum GPA of 2.0 to continue in good standing. 73% of freshmen return for sophomore year. Students must declare major by end of second year. **Graduation requirements:** 60 hours for associate, 124 hours for bachelor's. Most students required to take courses in computer science, English, history, humanities, mathematics, philosophy/religion, biological/physical sciences, social sciences.

FRESHMAN ADMISSIONS. Selection criteria: School achievement record very important, minimum 3.1 high school GPA. Test scores, recommendations, autobiography also considered. **High school preparation:** 13 units required. Required units include biological science 1, English 14, foreign language 2, mathematics 3, physical science 1 and social science 2. **Test requirements:** SAT or ACT (ACT preferred); score report by July 31.

1992 FRESHMAN CLASS PROFILE. 84 men, 86 women enrolled. 88% had high school GPA of 3.0 or higher, 12% between 2.0 and 2.99. 50% were in top tenth and 82% were in top quarter of graduating class. **Academic background:** Mid 50% of enrolled freshmen had SAT-V between 420-530, SAT-M between 460-580. 88% submitted SAT scores. **Characteristics:** 85% from in state, 52% commute, 12% have minority backgrounds, 9% are foreign students. Average age is 18.

FALL-TERM APPLICATIONS. $30 fee, may be waived for applicants with need. Closing date July 31; priority given to applications received by January 31; applicants notified on a rolling basis beginning on or about December 1; must reply within 4 weeks. Essay required. Interview recommended for academically weak applicants. Audition recommended for music, English (with drama emphasis) applicants. Deferred and early admission available.

STUDENT LIFE. Housing: Dormitories (men, women); apartment housing available. **Activities:** Student government, student newspaper, yearbook, choral groups, drama, jazz band, music ensembles, musical theater, pep band, community service ministry group, Mexican-American student group (Amigos Unidos), Living Color (students of color).

ATHLETICS. NAIA. **Intercollegiate:** Basketball, cross-country, soccer M, track and field, volleyball W. **Intramural:** Archery, baseball M, bowling, cross-country M, golf, racquetball, skiing, softball M, swimming, table tennis, tennis, track and field M.

STUDENT SERVICES. Career counseling, employment service for undergraduates, personal counseling, placement service for graduates, teacher placement service, services/facilities for handicapped.

ANNUAL EXPENSES. Tuition and fees: $9,462. **Room and board:** $3,510. **Books and supplies:** $612. **Other expenses:** $1,350.

FINANCIAL AID. 90% of freshmen, 90% of continuing students receive some form of aid. 53% of grants, 77% of loans, 31% of jobs based on need. 93 enrolled freshmen were judged to have need, all were offered aid. Academic, music/drama, art, athletic, state/district residency, leadership, religious affiliation, minority scholarships available. **Aid applications:** No closing date; priority given to applications received by January 31; applicants notified on a rolling basis beginning on or about April 1; must reply within 3 weeks.

ADDRESS/TELEPHONE. Cary W. Templeton, Director of Admissions, Fresno Pacific College, 1717 South Chestnut Avenue, Fresno, CA 93702. (209) 453-2039.

Fullerton College
Fullerton, California — CB code: 4314

2-year public community college, coed. Founded in 1913. **Accreditation:** Regional. **Undergraduate enrollment:** 21,211 men and women. **Faculty:** 675 total (271 full time). **Location:** Suburban campus in small city; 35 miles from Los Angeles. **Calendar:** Semester, extensive summer session. Saturday and extensive evening/early morning classes. **Microcomputers:** Located in classrooms, computer centers.

DEGREES OFFERED. AA. 1,180 associate degrees awarded in 1992.

UNDERGRADUATE MAJORS. Accounting, anthropology, apparel and accessories marketing, architecture, astronomy, automotive mechanics, automotive technology, biological laboratory technology, biology, business administration and management, business and office, business data entry equipment operation, business data processing and related programs, business data programming, chemistry, child development/care/guidance, clothing and textiles management/production/services, commercial music, communications, computer and information sciences, construction, dance, data processing, drafting, dramatic arts, economics, electronic technology, engineering, engineering and engineering-related technologies, English, environmental science, fashion design, fashion merchandising, finance, fine arts, foreign languages (multiple emphasis), geography, geology, graphic and printing production, graphic arts technology, graphic design, history, home economics, home furnishings and equipment management/production/services, horticulture, industrial arts education, industrial technology, interior design, international business management, journalism, Latin American studies, law enforcement and corrections technologies, legal assistant/paralegal, legal secretary, liberal/general studies, library assistant, manufacturing technology, marketing and distribution, mathematics, mechanical design technology, microbiology, music, music performance, musical theater, oceanographic technologies, ornamental horticulture, personal services, philosophy, photographic technology, physical sciences, physics, plant sciences, political science and government, precision metal work, predentistry, prelaw, premedicine, prepharmacy, preveterinary, psychology, radio/television broadcasting, radio/television technology, real estate, recreation and community services technologies, secretarial and related programs, small business management and ownership, sociology, speech, teacher aide, tourism, visual and performing arts, welding technology, word processing.

ACADEMIC PROGRAMS. 2-year transfer program, dual enrollment of high school students, independent study, internships, study abroad. **Remedial services:** Learning center, remedial instruction, special counselor, tutoring. **Placement/credit:** AP, CLEP General and Subject, institutional tests; 15 credit hours maximum for associate degree.

ACADEMIC REQUIREMENTS. Freshmen must earn minimum GPA of 2.0 to continue in good standing. 24% of freshmen return for sophomore year. **Graduation requirements:** 60 hours for associate (18 in major). Most students required to take courses in arts/fine arts, English, history, humanities, mathematics, biological/physical sciences, social sciences.

FRESHMAN ADMISSIONS. Selection criteria: Open admissions.

1992 FRESHMAN CLASS PROFILE. 3,056 men and women enrolled. **Characteristics:** 95% from in state, 100% commute, 20% have minority backgrounds.

FALL-TERM APPLICATIONS. No fee. No closing date; applicants notified on a rolling basis. SAT or ACT scores used for placement in English composition and mathematics if submitted.

STUDENT LIFE. Housing: Student housing referral by student affairs office. **Activities:** Student government, film, magazine, radio, student newspaper, television, choral groups, concert band, dance, drama, jazz band, marching band, music ensembles, musical theater, symphony orchestra, volunteer bureau, Movimiento Estudiantil Chicano de Aztlan.

ATHLETICS. Intercollegiate: Badminton, baseball M, basketball, cross-country, diving, football M, golf, gymnastics, soccer M, softball W, swimming, tennis, track and field, volleyball, water polo M.

STUDENT SERVICES. Aptitude testing, career counseling, employment service for undergraduates, freshman orientation, health services, on-campus day care, personal counseling, placement service for graduates, special adviser for adult students, veterans counselor, services/facilities for handicapped.

ANNUAL EXPENSES. Tuition and fees (1992-93): $135, $3,300 additional for out-of-state students. **Books and supplies:** $550.

FINANCIAL AID. 3% of freshmen, 5% of continuing students receive some form of aid. Grants, loans, jobs available. Academic, music/drama, art, athletic, state/district residency, minority scholarships available. **Aid applications:** No closing date; priority given to applications received by May 1; applicants notified on a rolling basis. **Additional information:** Basic tuition may be waived by showing financial need.

ADDRESS/TELEPHONE. Carlene A. Gibson, Dean of Admissions and Records, Fullerton College, 321 East Chapman Avenue, Fullerton, CA 92634. (714) 992-7568.

Gavilan Community College
Gilroy, California — CB code: 4678

2-year public community college, coed. Founded in 1919. **Accreditation:** Regional. **Undergraduate enrollment:** 4,244 men and women. **Location:** Rural campus in large town; 40 miles from San Jose. **Calendar:** Semester.

FRESHMAN ADMISSIONS. Selection criteria: Open admissions.

ANNUAL EXPENSES. Tuition and fees (projected): $164, $3,540 additional for out-of-state students. **Books and supplies:** $576. **Other expenses:** $1,748.

ADDRESS/TELEPHONE. Joy Parker, Director of Admissions and Records, Gavilan Community College, 5055 Santa Teresa Boulevard, Gilroy, CA 95020. (408) 847-1400. Fax: (408) 848-4801.

Glendale Community College
Glendale, California — CB code: 4327

2-year public community college, coed. Founded in 1927. **Accreditation:** Regional. **Undergraduate enrollment:** 4,136 men and women full time; 11,188 men and women part time. **Faculty:** 661 total (211 full time). **Location:** Urban campus in small city; 10 miles from downtown Los Angeles. **Calendar:** Semester, limited summer session. **Microcomputers:** Located in classrooms, computer centers. **Special facilities:** Baja California (Mexico) Field Station.

DEGREES OFFERED. AA, AS. 532 associate degrees awarded in 1992.

UNDERGRADUATE MAJORS. Accounting, aeronautical technology, American studies, biological and physical sciences, biology, business data entry equipment operation, business data processing and related programs, business data programming, drafting, drafting and design technology, English, fashion merchandising, finance, fire control and safety technology, food production/management/services, foreign languages (multiple emphasis), graphic arts technology, hospitality and recreation marketing, humanities, humanities and social sciences, law enforcement and corrections technologies, liberal/general studies, marketing and distribution, mathematics, medical assistant, nursing, photographic technology, physical sciences, practical nursing, real estate, recreation and community services technologies, secretarial and related programs, social sciences, Spanish, speech.

ACADEMIC PROGRAMS. 2-year transfer program, computer delivered (on-line) credit-bearing course offerings, cooperative education, dual enrollment of high school students, honors program, independent study, internships, study abroad, telecourses. **Remedial services:** Learning center, remedial instruction, special counselor, tutoring. **Placement/credit:** Institutional tests; 12 credit hours maximum for associate degree.

ACADEMIC REQUIREMENTS. Freshmen must earn minimum GPA of 2.0 to continue in good standing. **Graduation requirements:** 60 hours for associate (18 in major). Most students required to take courses in arts/fine arts, computer science, English, foreign languages, history, humanities, mathematics, philosophy/religion, biological/physical sciences, social sciences.

FRESHMAN ADMISSIONS. Selection criteria: Open admissions.

1992 FRESHMAN CLASS PROFILE. 630 men, 723 women enrolled. **Characteristics:** 95% from in state, 100% commute, 56% have minority backgrounds, 3% are foreign students. Average age is 18.

FALL-TERM APPLICATIONS. No fee. No closing date; applicants notified on a rolling basis. Deferred admission available.

STUDENT LIFE. Activities: Student government, student newspaper, choral groups, concert band, dance, drama, music ensembles, musical theater, pep band, symphony orchestra.

ATHLETICS. Intercollegiate: Baseball M, basketball, cross-country, football M, soccer M, tennis, track and field, volleyball W.

STUDENT SERVICES. Aptitude testing, career counseling, employment service for undergraduates, freshman orientation, health services, on-campus day care, personal counseling, placement service for graduates, special adviser for adult students, veterans counselor, special services for economically disadvantaged, services/facilities for handicapped.

ANNUAL EXPENSES. Tuition and fees (1992-93): $185, $3,120 additional for out-of-state students.

FINANCIAL AID. 20% of freshmen, 15% of continuing students receive some form of aid. All jobs based on need. **Aid applications:** No closing date; priority given to applications received by July 1; applicants notified on a rolling basis beginning on or about July 15; must reply within 2 weeks.

ADDRESS/TELEPHONE. Dr. Gary Parker, Dean of Admissions and Records, Glendale Community College, 1500 North Verdugo Road, Glendale, CA 91208. (818) 240-1000 ext. 5901. Fax: (818) 549-9436.

Golden Gate University
San Francisco, California — CB code: 4329

4-year private university, coed. Founded in 1901. **Accreditation:** Regional. **Undergraduate enrollment:** 235 men, 318 women full time; 648 men, 826 women part time. **Graduate enrollment:** 351 men, 264 women full time; 2,153 men, 1,805 women part time. **Faculty:** 763 total (63 full time), 356 with doctorates or other terminal degrees. **Location:** Urban campus in very large city; in downtown area. **Calendar:** Trimester, extensive summer session. Saturday and extensive evening/early morning classes. **Microcomputers:** 50 located in libraries, classrooms, computer centers. **Additional facts:** Degree programs (evening classes) also available in San Jose, Los Altos, Walnut Creek, Sacramento, Monterey, Los Angeles, Orange County, and Seattle, Washington. Degree programs also available at selected military installations in California.

DEGREES OFFERED. AA, BA, BS, MA, MS, MBA, D. 1 associate degree awarded in 1992. 100% in business and management. 260 bachelor's degrees awarded. 86% in business and management. Graduate degrees offered in 22 major fields of study.

UNDERGRADUATE MAJORS. Associate: Business administration and management, business and management. **Bachelor's:** Accounting, aviation management, business administration and management, business and humanities, business and management, business economics, finance, health care administration, hotel/motel and restaurant management, human resources development, information sciences and systems, institutional management, international business management, management information systems, marketing and distribution, marketing management, political science and government, prelaw, security management, taxation, telecommunications, transportation management.

ACADEMIC PROGRAMS. 2-year transfer program, accelerated program, cooperative education, internships, weekend college, cross-registration. **Remedial services:** Learning center, reduced course load, remedial instruction, tutoring, English Language Skills Center. **Placement/credit:** AP, CLEP General and Subject, institutional tests; 30 credit hours maximum for associate degree; 45 credit hours maximum for bachelor's degree.

ACADEMIC REQUIREMENTS. Freshmen must earn minimum GPA of 2.0 to continue in good standing. 85% of freshmen return for sophomore year. Students must declare major on application. **Graduation requirements:** 60 hours for associate (15 in major), 123 hours for bachelor's (30 in major). Most students required to take courses in computer science, English, history, humanities, mathematics, social sciences. **Postgraduate studies:** 75% from 2-year programs enter 4-year programs.

FRESHMAN ADMISSIONS. Selection criteria: School achievement record most important. **High school preparation:** 16 units required. Required units include English 3, mathematics 2 and social science 1. **Test requirements:** SAT, ACT or School and College Ability Tests required of applicants with less than 3.0 GPA in 14 academic subjects; test scores considered for all applicants when available, but not required.

1992 FRESHMAN CLASS PROFILE. 76 men and women enrolled. 80% had high school GPA of 3.0 or higher, 20% between 2.0 and 2.99. **Characteristics:** 70% from in state, 100% commute, 42% have minority backgrounds, 50% are foreign students. Average age is 21.

FALL-TERM APPLICATIONS. $35 fee. No closing date; priority given to applications received by July 1; applicants notified on a rolling basis. Interview recommended for undecided major applicants. Deferred admission available. EDP-F.

STUDENT LIFE. Activities: Student government, magazine, student newspaper, Phi Alpha Delta, Chi Pi Alpha, Indonesian Students Organization, Malayan Students Association, Chinese Students Club.

STUDENT SERVICES. Career counseling, employment service for undergraduates, freshman orientation, personal counseling, placement service for graduates, special adviser for adult students, veterans counselor, services/facilities for handicapped.

ANNUAL EXPENSES. Tuition and fees: $7,010. **Books and supplies:** $504.

FINANCIAL AID. 33% of freshmen, 15% of continuing students receive some form of aid. 54% of grants, 69% of loans, all jobs based on need. Academic, leadership, minority scholarships available. **Aid applications:** No closing date; priority given to applications received by March 1; applicants notified on a rolling basis beginning on or about July 1; must reply within 2 weeks.

ADDRESS/TELEPHONE. Archie Porter, Registrar/Director of Admissions, Golden Gate University, 536 Mission Street, San Francisco, CA 94105-2968. (415) 442-7800. Fax: (415) 495-2671.

Golden West College
Huntington Beach, California — CB code: 4339

2-year public community college, coed. Founded in 1966. **Accreditation:** Regional. **Undergraduate enrollment:** 2,116 men, 2,007 women full time; 5,071 men, 5,961 women part time. **Faculty:** 457 total (230 full time), 40 with doctorates or other terminal degrees. **Location:** Suburban campus in small city; 40 miles from Los Angeles. **Calendar:** Semester, extensive summer session. Saturday and extensive evening/early morning classes. **Microcomputers:** Located in libraries, classrooms, computer centers. **Special facilities:** Natural history museum, art gallery.

DEGREES OFFERED. AA. 676 associate degrees awarded in 1992.

UNDERGRADUATE MAJORS. Accounting, architectural technologies, architecture, automotive mechanics, automotive technology, biological and physical sciences, business and management, business and office, business data processing and related programs, communications, computer and information sciences, criminal justice studies, diesel engine mechanics, drafting, drafting and design technology, engineering and engineering-related technologies, fine arts, graphic and printing production, graphic arts technology, graphic design, horticultural science, horticulture, humanities, interpreter for the deaf, journalism, law enforcement and corrections technologies, legal secretary, liberal/general studies, marketing management, music performance, music theory and composition, nursing, office supervision and management, physical sciences, public relations, radio/television technology, real estate, retailing, secretarial and related programs, small business management and ownership, social sciences, telecommunications.

ACADEMIC PROGRAMS. 2-year transfer program, cooperative education, double major, dual enrollment of high school students, honors program, independent study, study abroad. **Remedial services:** Learning center, preadmission summer program, remedial instruction, special counselor, tutoring. **ROTC:** Air Force. **Placement/credit:** AP, CLEP General and Subject, institutional tests; 6 credit hours maximum for associate degree.

ACADEMIC REQUIREMENTS. Freshmen must earn minimum GPA of 2.0 to continue in good standing. 60% of freshmen return for sophomore year. Students must declare major by end of first year. **Graduation requirements:** 60 hours for associate (18 in major). Most students required to take courses in English, humanities, mathematics, biological/physical sciences, social sciences.

FRESHMAN ADMISSIONS. Selection criteria: Open admissions. Any student at least 18 years of age is eligible for admission. Nursing applicants accepted on basis of prerequisite courses completed and GPA. **Additional information:** All new students expected to participate in program of orientation, assessment, and advisement prior to enrollment.

1992 FRESHMAN CLASS PROFILE. 2,670 men and women enrolled. **Characteristics:** 99% from in state, 100% commute, 17% have minority backgrounds.

FALL-TERM APPLICATIONS. No fee. No closing date; priority given to applications received by April 30; applicants notified on a rolling basis. SAT or ACT tests can be used for counseling and placement in lieu of college placement test.

STUDENT LIFE. Activities: Student government, film, magazine, radio, student newspaper, television, choral groups, concert band, dance, drama, jazz band, music ensembles, musical theater, pep band, symphony orchestra, MECHA (Latino club), Newman Club, Latter-Day-Saints Club.

ATHLETICS. NJCAA. **Intercollegiate:** Baseball M, basketball, cross-country, football M, golf M, soccer, softball W, swimming, tennis, track and field, volleyball, water polo M, wrestling M.

STUDENT SERVICES. Career counseling, employment service for undergraduates, freshman orientation, health services, on-campus day care, personal counseling, placement service for graduates, veterans counselor, services/facilities for handicapped.

ANNUAL EXPENSES. Tuition and fees (projected): $320, $2,568 additional for out-of-state students. **Books and supplies:** $612. **Other expenses:** $1,548.

FINANCIAL AID. 20% of freshmen, 10% of continuing students receive some form of aid. 97% of grants, 98% of loans, all jobs based on need. Academic, art, leadership scholarships available. **Aid applications:** No closing date; priority given to applications received by June 30; applicants notified on a rolling basis beginning on or about July 1; must reply within 3 weeks.

ADDRESS/TELEPHONE. John M. Breihan, Administrative Dean of Admissions and Records, Golden West College, 15744 Golden West Street,P-1092, Huntington Beach, CA 92647-0592. (714) 892-7711 ext. 8306.

Grossmont Community College
El Cajon, California — CB code: 4334

2-year public community college, coed. Founded in 1961. **Accreditation:** Regional. **Undergraduate enrollment:** 2,772 men, 2,989 women full time; 4,327 men, 6,572 women part time. **Faculty:** 572 total (204 full time), 39 with doctorates or other terminal degrees. **Location:** Suburban campus in small city; 25 miles from San Diego. **Calendar:** Semester, extensive summer session. Extensive evening/early morning classes. **Microcomputers:** 300 located in libraries, computer centers.

DEGREES OFFERED. AA, AS. 827 associate degrees awarded in 1992.

UNDERGRADUATE MAJORS. Accounting, art history, biology, business administration and management, business and office, business computer/console/peripheral equipment operation, ceramics, chemistry, child development/care/guidance, computer and information sciences, computer programming, creative writing, criminal justice technology, dance, drawing, economics, English, family/consumer resource management, fashion merchandising, finance, food production/management/services, food science and nutrition, French, geography, geology, German, history, international business management, law enforcement and corrections technologies, legal assistant/paralegal, liberal/general studies, management science, marketing and distribution, marketing management, mathematics, medical records administration, medical records technology, microcomputer software, music, nursing, painting, philosophy, photography, physics, political science and government, radio/television technology, recreation and community services technologies, respiratory therapy technology, retailing, sculpture, secretarial and related programs, Spanish, speech, taxation, telecommunications, visual and performing arts, word processing.

ACADEMIC PROGRAMS. 2-year transfer program, double major, dual enrollment of high school students, independent study, internships, student-designed major, study abroad, cross-registration. **Remedial services:** Learning center, reduced course load, remedial instruction, special counselor, tutoring. **Placement/credit:** AP.

ACADEMIC REQUIREMENTS. Freshmen must earn minimum GPA of 2.0 to continue in good standing. **Graduation requirements:** 60 hours for associate (18 in major). Most students required to take courses in English, mathematics, biological/physical sciences.

FRESHMAN ADMISSIONS. Selection criteria: Open admissions.

1992 FRESHMAN CLASS PROFILE. 5,111 men and women enrolled. **Characteristics:** 97% from in state, 100% commute, 20% have minority backgrounds, 1% are foreign students.

FALL-TERM APPLICATIONS. No fee. No closing date; priority given to applications received by August 2; applicants notified on a rolling basis. Interview required for health professions applicants. Early admission available.

STUDENT LIFE. Activities: Student government, film, radio, student newspaper, television, choral groups, concert band, dance, drama, jazz band, music ensembles, musical theater, pep band, symphony orchestra.

ATHLETICS. Intercollegiate: Baseball M, basketball, cross-country M, diving, football M, softball W, swimming, tennis, track and field M, volleyball W, water polo M.

STUDENT SERVICES. Aptitude testing, career counseling, employment service for undergraduates, freshman orientation, health services, on-campus day care, personal counseling, placement service for graduates, special adviser for adult students, services/facilities for handicapped.

ANNUAL EXPENSES. Tuition and fees (projected): $360, $3,120 additional for out-of-state students. **Books and supplies:** $600. **Other expenses:** $1,200.

FINANCIAL AID. 10% of freshmen, 7% of continuing students receive some form of aid. 97% of grants, all loans, all jobs based on need. Academic, music/drama, art, athletic, state/district residency, leadership, minority scholarships available. **Aid applications:** No closing date; priority given to applications received by April 1; applicants notified on a rolling basis beginning on or about July 15; must reply within 2 weeks.

ADDRESS/TELEPHONE. Brad Tiffany, Director of Admissions and Records, Grossmont Community College, 8800 Grossmont College Drive, El Cajon, CA 92020. (619) 465-1700 ext. 208.

Hartnell College
Salinas, California — CB code: 4340

2-year public community college, coed. Founded in 1920. **Accreditation:** Regional. **Undergraduate enrollment:** 2,045 men and women full time; 7,772 men and women part time. **Location:** Suburban campus in small city; 110 miles from San Francisco, 65 miles from San Jose. **Calendar:** Semester.

FRESHMAN ADMISSIONS. Selection criteria: Open admissions.

ANNUAL EXPENSES. Tuition and fees (projected): $250, $3,300 additional for out-of-state students. **Books and supplies:** $590. **Other expenses:** $1,380.

ADDRESS/TELEPHONE. Cheri Bishop, Director of Admissions and Records, Hartnell College, 156 Homestead Avenue, Salinas, CA 93901. (408) 755-6700.

Harvey Mudd College
Claremont, California — CB code: 4341

Admissions:	38% of applicants accepted
Based on:	••• Recommendations, school record, test scores
	•• Activities, essay, interview, special talents
Completion:	90% of freshmen end year in good standing
	79% graduate, 50% of these enter graduate study

4-year private engineering college, coed. Founded in 1955. **Accreditation:** Regional. **Undergraduate enrollment:** 485 men, 131 women full time. **Graduate enrollment:** 11 men, 2 women full time. **Faculty:** 79 total (70 full time), 78 with doctorates or other terminal degrees. **Location:** Suburban campus in large town; 35 miles east of Los Angeles. **Calendar:** Semester. **Microcomputers:** 100 located in dormitories, libraries, classrooms, computer centers. **Special facilities:** Observatory, biological field stations. **Additional facts:** One of 5 Claremont colleges sharing common facilities. Masters degree in engineering available to Harvey Mudd College graduates.

DEGREES OFFERED. BS. 134 bachelor's degrees awarded in 1992. 41% in engineering, 16% mathematics, 42% physical sciences.

UNDERGRADUATE MAJORS. Applied mathematics, biological and physical sciences, biology, chemistry, computer and information sciences, engineering, engineering and other disciplines, mathematics, physics.

ACADEMIC PROGRAMS. Double major, independent study, student-designed major, study abroad, visiting/exchange student program, cross-registration, applied engineering and mathematics clinics; liberal arts/career combination in business. **Remedial services:** Reduced course load, tutoring. **ROTC:** Air Force, Army. **Placement/credit:** AP, IB, institutional tests.

ACADEMIC REQUIREMENTS. High pass/pass/no credit grading system first semester. 90% of freshmen return for sophomore year. Students must declare major by end of second year. **Graduation requirements:** 128 hours for bachelor's (42 in major). Most students required to take courses in computer science, English, history, humanities, mathematics, philosophy/religion, biological/physical sciences, social sciences. **Postgraduate studies:**

50% enter other graduate study. **Additional information:** Course work divided equally between technical core, major, and humanities and social sciences.

FRESHMAN ADMISSIONS. Selection criteria: School achievement record, especially in mathematics and science, test scores, recommendations, school and community activities, interviews highly recommended. **High school preparation:** 15 units required. Required and recommended units include biological science 1, English 4, mathematics 4 and physical science 2. Foreign language 2 and social science 2 recommended. Calculus required. **Test requirements:** SAT; score report by February 1. 3 ACH required: Mathematics Level II, English Composition with or without essay, one of student's choice. Score report by February 1.

1992 FRESHMAN CLASS PROFILE. 1,071 men applied, 382 accepted, 138 enrolled; 259 women applied, 129 accepted, 33 enrolled. 100% had high school GPA of 3.0 or higher. **Academic background:** Mid 50% of enrolled freshmen had SAT-V between 580-690, SAT-M between 710-770. 100% submitted SAT scores. **Characteristics:** 50% from in state, 100% live in college housing, 27% have minority backgrounds, 1% are foreign students. Average age is 17.

FALL-TERM APPLICATIONS. $40 fee, may be waived for applicants with need. Closing date February 15; priority given to applications received by February 1; applicants notified on or about April 1; must reply by May 1. Essay required. Interview recommended. CRDA. Deferred and early admission available. EDP-F. Institutional early decision plan closing date December 1.

STUDENT LIFE. Housing: Dormitories (coed). **Activities:** Student government, film, radio, student newspaper, television, yearbook, ham radio, choral groups, concert band, dance, drama, jazz band, music ensembles, musical theater, pep band, symphony orchestra, forensics, volunteer service, Young Republicans, Young Democrats, religious center, Chicano studies center, Black student affairs, Asian Student Association, Hillel. **Additional information:** Student-directed honor code governs academic and nonacademic life on campus.

ATHLETICS. NCAA. **Intercollegiate:** Baseball M, basketball, cross-country, diving, field hockey W, football M, golf M, lacrosse M, soccer, softball W, swimming, tennis, track and field, volleyball W, water polo M. **Intramural:** Basketball, field hockey, lacrosse, racquetball, rugby M, sailing, soccer, softball, volleyball, water polo.

STUDENT SERVICES. Aptitude testing, career counseling, employment service for undergraduates, freshman orientation, health services, personal counseling, placement service for graduates, services/facilities for handicapped.

ANNUAL EXPENSES. Tuition and fees: $16,410. **Room and board:** $6,440. **Books and supplies:** $600. **Other expenses:** $900.

FINANCIAL AID. 78% of freshmen, 73% of continuing students receive some form of aid. Grants, loans, jobs available. Academic, leadership scholarships available. **Aid applications:** No closing date; priority given to applications received by February 15; applicants notified on or about February 1; must reply by May 1.

ADDRESS/TELEPHONE. Patrica A. Coleman, Dean of Admissions, Harvey Mudd College, Kingston Hall, 301 East 12th Street, Claremont, CA 91711-5990. (909) 621-8011. Fax: (909) 621-8360.

Heald Business College: Concord

Concord, California CB code: 0235

2-year private business college, coed. Founded in 1863. **Accreditation:** Regional. **Undergraduate enrollment:** 75 men, 125 women full time; 30 men, 30 women part time. **Faculty:** 12 total, 2 with doctorates or other terminal degrees. **Location:** Suburban campus in small city; 25 miles from San Francisco. **Calendar:** Quarter. Extensive evening/early morning classes. **Microcomputers:** 60 located in classrooms, computer centers.

DEGREES OFFERED. AAS. 55 associate degrees awarded in 1992. 100% in business and management.

UNDERGRADUATE MAJORS. Accounting, data processing, legal assistant/paralegal, secretarial and related programs.

ACADEMIC REQUIREMENTS. Freshmen must earn minimum GPA of 2.0 to continue in good standing. Students must declare major on enrollment. **Graduation requirements:** 108 hours for associate. Most students required to take courses in English, mathematics, social sciences.

FRESHMAN ADMISSIONS. Selection criteria: Institutional admissions examination and personal interview. **Test requirements:** Institutionally designed test used for admissions.

1992 FRESHMAN CLASS PROFILE. 90 men applied, 75 accepted, 30 enrolled; 145 women applied, 125 accepted, 60 enrolled. **Characteristics:** 100% from in state, 100% commute, 50% have minority backgrounds, 1% are foreign students. Average age is 19.

FALL-TERM APPLICATIONS. $25 fee. No closing date; applicants notified on a rolling basis. Interview required. Early admission available.

STUDENT SERVICES. Placement service for graduates, veterans counselor, services/facilities for handicapped.

ANNUAL EXPENSES. Tuition and fees (1992-93): $6,300. Books and supplies costs are included in tuition and fees.

FINANCIAL AID. Aid applications: No closing date; priority given to applications received by March 2; applicants notified on a rolling basis.

ADDRESS/TELEPHONE. Nancy Pargett, Director of Admissions, Heald Business College: Concord, 2150 John Glenn Drive, Suite 100, Concord, CA 94520. (510) 827-1300. Fax: (510) 827-1486.

Heald Business College: San Jose

San Jose, California CB code: 0405

2-year private business, junior college, coed. Founded in 1863. **Accreditation:** Regional. **Undergraduate enrollment:** 200 men and women. **Faculty:** 12 total (7 full time). **Location:** Suburban campus in very large city; 45 miles from San Francisco. **Calendar:** Quarter. Extensive evening/early morning classes. **Microcomputers:** Located in classrooms.

DEGREES OFFERED. AAS. 30 associate degrees awarded in 1992.

UNDERGRADUATE MAJORS. Accounting, computer and information sciences, microcomputer software, secretarial and related programs.

ACADEMIC PROGRAMS. Remedial services: Tutoring. **Placement/credit:** CLEP General and Subject, institutional tests; 45 credit hours maximum for associate degree.

ACADEMIC REQUIREMENTS. Freshmen must earn minimum GPA of 2.0 to continue in good standing. 78% of freshmen return for sophomore year. Students must declare major on enrollment. **Graduation requirements:** 96 hours for associate. Most students required to take courses in computer science, English, humanities, mathematics, social sciences.

FRESHMAN ADMISSIONS. Selection criteria: Institutional admissions test and personal interview most important.

1992 FRESHMAN CLASS PROFILE. 50 men and women enrolled. 20% had high school GPA of 3.0 or higher, 80% between 2.0 and 2.99. **Characteristics:** 90% from in state, 100% commute, 55% have minority backgrounds, 1% are foreign students. Average age is 21.

FALL-TERM APPLICATIONS. $25 fee. No closing date; applicants notified on a rolling basis. Interview required.

STUDENT SERVICES. Career counseling, employment service for undergraduates, freshman orientation, personal counseling, placement service for graduates, services/facilities for handicapped.

ANNUAL EXPENSES. Tuition and fees (1992-93): $5,850. **Books and supplies:** $450.

FINANCIAL AID. 80% of freshmen, 80% of continuing students receive some form of aid. All grants, 79% of loans based on need. **Aid applications:** No closing date; priority given to applications received by June 1; applicants notified on a rolling basis beginning on or about June 15; must reply within 2 weeks.

ADDRESS/TELEPHONE. D. Chris Tilley, Admissions Director, Heald Business College: San Jose, 684 El Paseo de Saratoga, San Jose, CA 95130. (408) 370-2400. Fax: (408) 374-3224.

Heald College: Sacramento

Rancho Cordova, California CB code: 0232

2-year private business college, coed. Founded in 1863. **Accreditation:** Regional. **Undergraduate enrollment:** 550 men and women. **Location:** Urban campus in very large city; 8 miles from downtown Sacramento. **Calendar:** Quarter.

FRESHMAN ADMISSIONS. Selection criteria: Institutional admissions test, interview.

ANNUAL EXPENSES. Tuition and fees: $5,940. **Books and supplies:** $450.

ADDRESS/TELEPHONE. Andrew Tannis, Admissions Director, Heald College: Sacramento, 2910 Prospect Park Drive, Rancho Cordova, CA 95670. (916) 638-1616. (800) 499-4333. Fax: (916) 638-1580.

Heald College: Santa Rosa

Santa Rosa, California CB code: 2141

2-year private business college, coed. Founded in 1863. **Accreditation:** Regional. **Undergraduate enrollment:** 150 men and women full time; 48 men and women part time. **Location:** Suburban campus in small city; 40 miles from San Francisco. **Calendar:** Quarter. Extensive evening/early morning classes.

FRESHMAN ADMISSIONS. Selection criteria: Institutional entrance examination, interview.

ANNUAL EXPENSES. Tuition and fees (1992-93): $5,400. **Books and supplies:** $450.

ADDRESS/TELEPHONE. Stan Decker, Dean of Admissions, Heald College: Santa Rosa, 24254 Mendocino Avenue, Rohnert Park, CA 95403. (707) 525-1300.

Heald Institute of Technology
Martinez, California CB code: 2148

2-year private technical college, coed. Founded in 1981. **Accreditation:** Regional. **Undergraduate enrollment:** 284 men and women. **Location:** Suburban campus in small city. **Calendar:** Quarter.

FRESHMAN ADMISSIONS. Selection criteria: Institutional admissions examination.

ANNUAL EXPENSES. Tuition and fees (projected): $7,585. Tuition and fees are for 4 quarters (12 months). **Books and supplies:** $1,000.

ADDRESS/TELEPHONE. Myron Brignoli, Director, Heald Institute of Technology, 2860 Howe Road, Martinez, CA 94553-4000. (510) 228-9000. Fax: (510) 229-3792.

Hebrew Union College: Jewish Institute of Religion
Los Angeles, California CB code: 1344

2-year upper-division private branch campus, rabbinical, teachers college, coed, affiliated with Jewish faith. Founded in 1954. **Accreditation:** Regional. **Undergraduate enrollment:** 24 men, 62 women full time. **Graduate enrollment:** 24 men, 62 women full time. **Faculty:** 41 total (24 full time), 20 with doctorates or other terminal degrees. **Location:** Urban campus in very large city; in downtown area. **Calendar:** Semester. **Microcomputers:** Located in computer centers. **Special facilities:** Judaic history and art museum. **Additional facts:** Primarily a graduate school, preparing students for careers in Jewish education, the rabbinate, and Jewish communal service. Serves as Judaic Studies and Hebrew Studies departments for University of Southern California.

DEGREES OFFERED. BA, MA, PhD, Rab. Graduate degrees offered in 5 major fields of study.

UNDERGRADUATE MAJORS. Jewish studies, religion.

ACADEMIC PROGRAMS. Internships, cross-registration. **Remedial services:** Learning center.

ACADEMIC REQUIREMENTS. Graduation requirements: 120 hours for bachelor's. Most students required to take courses in foreign languages, history, philosophy/religion.

STUDENT SERVICES. Services/facilities for handicapped.

ANNUAL EXPENSES. Tuition and fees (1992-93): $6,000. **Books and supplies:** $750.

FINANCIAL AID. Aid applications: No closing date; applicants notified on a rolling basis beginning on or about September 30. **Additional information:** Limited financial aid available through college funds includes scholarships, interest free loans, and paid internship opportunities.

ADDRESS/TELEPHONE. Rabbi Lee Bycel, Dean, Hebrew Union College: Jewish Institute of Religion, 3077 University Avenue, Los Angeles, CA 90007. (213) 749-3424. Fax: (213) 749-6128.

Holy Names College
Oakland, California CB code: 4059

Admissions: 70% of applicants accepted
Based on: ••• School record
•• Activities, essay, recommendations, special talents, test scores
• Interview
Completion: 95% of freshmen end year in good standing

4-year private liberal arts college, coed, affiliated with Roman Catholic Church. Founded in 1868. **Accreditation:** Regional. **Undergraduate enrollment:** 120 men, 183 women full time; 43 men, 281 women part time. **Graduate enrollment:** 36 men, 114 women full time; 69 men, 126 women part time. **Faculty:** 115 total (48 full time), 36 with doctorates or other terminal degrees. **Location:** Urban campus in large city; 14 miles from San Francisco. **Calendar:** Semester, limited summer session. Saturday classes. **Microcomputers:** 73 located in dormitories, libraries, computer centers. **Special facilities:** Folk music collection, Raskob Learning Institute (for learning disabled).

DEGREES OFFERED. BA, BS, MA, MBA, MEd. 137 bachelor's degrees awarded in 1992. 26% in business and management, 9% health sciences, 9% letters/literature, 19% multi/interdisciplinary studies, 7% philosophy, religion, theology, 11% psychology, 8% visual and performing arts. Graduate degrees offered in 8 major fields of study.

UNDERGRADUATE MAJORS. Applied mathematics, biology, business administration and management, communications, English, history, humanities, international relations, liberal/general studies, mathematics, music, music performance, nursing, philosophy, psychology, religion, social sciences, sociology, Spanish.

ACADEMIC PROGRAMS. Double major, honors program, independent study, internships, student-designed major, study abroad, teacher preparation, visiting/exchange student program, weekend college, cross-registration; liberal arts/career combination in engineering. **Remedial services:** Learning center, reduced course load, remedial instruction, tutoring, Raskob Institute provides diagnosis and remediation for learning-handicapped students. **ROTC:** Air Force, Army. **Placement/credit:** AP, CLEP General and Subject, institutional tests; 6 credit hours maximum for bachelor's degree.

ACADEMIC REQUIREMENTS. Freshmen must earn minimum GPA of 2.0 to continue in good standing. 78% of freshmen return for sophomore year. Students must declare major by end of second year. **Graduation requirements:** 120 hours for bachelor's (24 in major). Most students required to take courses in arts/fine arts, computer science, English, foreign languages, history, humanities, mathematics, philosophy/religion, biological/physical sciences, social sciences.

FRESHMAN ADMISSIONS. Selection criteria: Evidence of ability, academic accomplishment, and incentive; 2.8 GPA; 2 letters of recommendation and personal statement of academic goals; SAT or ACT scores. **High school preparation:** 15 units required. Required and recommended units include English 4-4, foreign language 2-3, mathematics 3-3, social science 1-3 and science 1. Biological science 1 and physical science 2 recommended. US history or government required, plus 1 additional year of mathematics, laboratory science, or foreign language. **Test requirements:** SAT or ACT; score report by August 1.

1992 FRESHMAN CLASS PROFILE. 320 men and women applied, 224 accepted; 68 enrolled. 46% had high school GPA of 3.0 or higher, 54% between 2.0 and 2.99. **Academic background:** Mid 50% of enrolled freshmen had SAT-V between 400-600, SAT-M between 400-600. 78% submitted SAT scores. **Characteristics:** 71% from in state, 53% live in college housing. Average age is 19.

FALL-TERM APPLICATIONS. $30 fee, may be waived for applicants with need. Closing date August 1; priority given to applications received by November 30; applicants notified on a rolling basis; must reply within 4 weeks. Essay required. Interview recommended. Audition recommended for music applicants. CRDA. Deferred admission available.

STUDENT LIFE. Housing: Dormitories (coed). **Activities:** Student government, student newspaper, choral groups, dance, drama, music ensembles, symphony orchestra, campus ministry, international club, Black African Student Alliance, pep club, ski club, psychology club, Latino club, human corps, Amnesty International, environmental club.

ATHLETICS. Intercollegiate: Basketball, volleyball. **Intramural:** Badminton, basketball, bowling, soccer M, softball, swimming, table tennis, tennis, volleyball, water polo.

STUDENT SERVICES. Aptitude testing, career counseling, employment service for undergraduates, freshman orientation, health services, on-campus day care, personal counseling, placement service for graduates, special adviser for adult students, services/facilities for handicapped.

ANNUAL EXPENSES. Tuition and fees: $10,834. **Room and board:** $4,876. **Books and supplies:** $612. **Other expenses:** $1,350.

FINANCIAL AID. 75% of freshmen, 75% of continuing students receive some form of aid. 66% of grants, 77% of loans, all jobs based on need. 35 enrolled freshmen were judged to have need, all were offered aid. Academic, music/drama, art, leadership, alumni affiliation scholarships available. **Aid applications:** No closing date; priority given to applications received by March 2; applicants notified on a rolling basis beginning on or about April 1; must reply within 2 weeks.

ADDRESS/TELEPHONE. Carol Sellman, Enrollment Manager, Holy Names College, 3500 Mountain Boulevard, Oakland, CA 94619-1699. (510) 436-1321. Fax: (510) 436-1199.

Humboldt State University
Arcata, California CB code: 4345

Admissions: 83% of applicants accepted
Based on: ••• School record, test scores
• Activities, essay, special talents
Completion: 90% of freshmen end year in good standing
19% enter graduate study

4-year public university, coed. Founded in 1913. **Accreditation:** Regional. **Undergraduate enrollment:** 3,256 men, 2,919 women full time; 337 men, 360 women part time. **Graduate enrollment:** 287 men, 352 women full time; 161 men, 179 women part time. **Faculty:** 594 total (315 full time), 257 with doctorates or other terminal degrees. **Location:** Rural campus in large town; 275 miles from San Francisco. **Calendar:** Semester. **Microcomputers:** 270 located in libraries, classrooms, computer centers. **Special facilities:** Marine research laboratory and vessel, fresh water fish hatchery, small animal game pen, fungal genetic stock center, 360-acre experimental forest, 280-acre dune preserve, natural history museum, Arcata Marsh and Wildlife Sanctuary, 170,000 specimen herbarium.

DEGREES OFFERED. BA, BS, MA, MS, MBA, MFA. 1,128 bachelor's degrees awarded in 1992. 8% in business and management, 14% teacher education, 10% letters/literature, 25% life sciences, 7% psychology, 15% social sciences, 7% visual and performing arts. Graduate degrees offered in 21 major fields of study.

UNDERGRADUATE MAJORS. Anthropology, art history, biology, botany, business administration and management, chemistry, child development/care/guidance, clinical laboratory science, communications, computer and information sciences, dramatic arts, drawing, economics, English, environmental health engineering, fishing and fisheries, forestry and related sciences, forestry production and processing, French, geography, geology, German, history, industrial arts education, industrial technology, information sciences and systems, journalism, mathematics, mathematics education, metal/jewelry, music, music education, music theory and composition, nursing, oceanography, painting, parks and recreation management, philosophy, physical education, physical sciences, physics, political science and government, predentistry, prelaw, premedicine, preveterinary, psychology, range management, religion, renewable natural resources, sculpture, social science education, social sciences, social studies education, social work, sociology, Spanish, speech, studio art, theater design, wildlife management, zoology.

ACADEMIC PROGRAMS. Cooperative education, double major, dual enrollment of high school students, independent study, internships, student-designed major, study abroad, teacher preparation, visiting/exchange student program, cross-registration. **Remedial services:** Learning center, remedial instruction, special counselor, tutoring, Educational Opportunity Program, special remedial programs for veterans. **Placement/credit:** AP, CLEP Subject, IB, institutional tests; 24 credit hours maximum for bachelor's degree.

ACADEMIC REQUIREMENTS. Freshmen must earn minimum GPA of 2.0 to continue in good standing. 80% of freshmen return for sophomore year. **Graduation requirements:** 124 hours for bachelor's (40 in major). Most students required to take courses in arts/fine arts, English, foreign languages, history, humanities, mathematics, philosophy/religion, biological/physical sciences, social sciences. **Additional information:** Native American Teacher Education project, Native American Career Education program in natural resources offered. Bilingual program for Native Americans.

FRESHMAN ADMISSIONS. Selection criteria: High school GPA grades 10-12 and test scores most important. **High school preparation:** 15 units required. Required units include English 4, foreign language 2, mathematics 3, social science 1 and science 1. One visual and performing arts and 3 electives also required. **Test requirements:** SAT or ACT; score report by June 15.

1992 FRESHMAN CLASS PROFILE. 3,143 men and women applied, 2,620 accepted; 363 men enrolled, 433 women enrolled. 60% had high school GPA of 3.0 or higher, 40% between 2.0 and 2.99. **Characteristics:** 97% from in state, 77% live in college housing, 11% have minority backgrounds, 1% are foreign students, 2% join fraternities/sororities. Average age is 18.

FALL-TERM APPLICATIONS. $55 fee, may be waived for applicants with need. Closing date November 30; applicants notified on a rolling basis beginning on or about December 1. Essay recommended for academically weak, special consideration applicants. Early admission available.

STUDENT LIFE. Housing: Dormitories (coed); apartment housing available. **Activities:** Student government, film, magazine, radio, student newspaper, choral groups, concert band, dance, drama, jazz band, marching band, music ensembles, musical theater, opera, pep band, symphony orchestra, fraternities, sororities, Newman Club, Campus Crusade for Christ, Youth Educational Services, Black Students Union, MECHA, Rowing Association, Native American Club, Jewish Student Union, Women's Association, Veterans Organization. **Additional information:** Special effort is made to address multi-cultural nature of our campus through social and educational events.

ATHLETICS. NCAA. **Intercollegiate:** Basketball, cross-country, football M, soccer M, softball W, track and field, volleyball W. **Intramural:** Archery, badminton, basketball, fencing, field hockey, golf, gymnastics, handball, lacrosse, racquetball, rowing (crew), rugby M, sailing, skiing, skin diving, soccer, softball, swimming W, volleyball, water polo.

STUDENT SERVICES. Aptitude testing, career counseling, employment service for undergraduates, freshman orientation, health services, on-campus day care, personal counseling, placement service for graduates, special adviser for adult students, veterans counselor, services/facilities for handicapped.

ANNUAL EXPENSES. Tuition and fees (1992-93): $1,468, $7,380 additional for out-of-state students. **Room and board:** $4,201. **Books and supplies:** $576. **Other expenses:** $1,277.

FINANCIAL AID. 44% of freshmen, 44% of continuing students receive some form of aid. 96% of loans, all jobs based on need. Academic, music/drama, art, state/district residency, leadership scholarships available. **Aid applications:** No closing date; priority given to applications received by March 2; applicants notified on a rolling basis beginning on or about March 1; must reply within 3 weeks.

ADDRESS/TELEPHONE. Robert L. Hannigan, Dean of Admissions and Records, Humboldt State University, Arcata, CA 95521. (707) 826-4402. Fax: (707) 826-6194.

Humphreys College
Stockton, California — CB code: 4346

4-year private college of business administration and law school, coed. Founded in 1896. **Accreditation:** Regional. **Undergraduate enrollment:** 45 men, 308 women full time; 39 men, 260 women part time. **Graduate enrollment:** 45 men, 48 women full time. **Faculty:** 61 total (27 full time), 14 with doctorates or other terminal degrees. **Location:** Suburban campus in large city; 80 miles from San Francisco. **Calendar:** Quarter, extensive summer session. Saturday and extensive evening/early morning classes. **Microcomputers:** 25 located in computer centers.

DEGREES OFFERED. AA, AS, BS, JD. 34 associate degrees awarded in 1992. 10 bachelor's degrees awarded. 62% in business and management, 15% computer sciences, 23% law. Graduate degrees offered in 1 major field of study.

UNDERGRADUATE MAJORS. Associate: Accounting, business and office, business computer/console/peripheral equipment operation, business data entry equipment operation, business data processing and related programs, business data programming, computer and information sciences, court reporting, education, humanities and social sciences, liberal/general studies, marketing and distribution, medical assistant, real estate, secretarial and related programs. **Bachelor's:** Accounting, business administration and management, computer and information sciences, legal assistant/paralegal.

ACADEMIC PROGRAMS. 2-year transfer program, honors program, independent study. **Remedial services:** Preadmission summer program, reduced course load, remedial instruction, special counselor, tutoring. **Placement/credit:** AP, CLEP General, institutional tests; 45 credit hours maximum for bachelor's degree.

ACADEMIC REQUIREMENTS. Freshmen must earn minimum GPA of 2.0 to continue in good standing. 80% of freshmen return for sophomore year. Students must declare major by end of first year. **Graduation requirements:** 90 hours for associate (30 in major), 180 hours for bachelor's (56 in major). Most students required to take courses in English, history, humanities, mathematics, biological/physical sciences, social sciences. **Postgraduate studies:** 33% from 2-year programs enter 4-year programs.

FRESHMAN ADMISSIONS. Selection criteria: Open admissions.

1992 FRESHMAN CLASS PROFILE. 73 men and women enrolled. **Characteristics:** 90% from in state, 85% commute, 23% have minority backgrounds. Average age is 29.

FALL-TERM APPLICATIONS. $20 fee. No closing date; applicants notified on a rolling basis. Interview recommended. Deferred and early admission available.

STUDENT LIFE. Housing: Dormitories (men, women); apartment housing available. **Activities:** Student government, student newspaper, sororities.

STUDENT SERVICES. Career counseling, employment service for undergraduates, personal counseling, placement service for graduates, veterans counselor, services/facilities for handicapped.

ANNUAL EXPENSES. Tuition and fees: $4,724. **Room and board:** $1,575 room only. **Books and supplies:** $812. **Other expenses:** $1,920.

FINANCIAL AID. 60% of freshmen, 60% of continuing students receive some form of aid. All grants, 66% of loans, all jobs based on need. 67 enrolled freshmen were judged to have need, all were offered aid. **Aid applications:** Closing date April 4; applicants notified on a rolling basis; must reply within 2 weeks.

ADDRESS/TELEPHONE. Pamela Knapp, Admissions Counselor, Humphreys College, 6650 Inglewood Avenue, Stockton, CA 95207-3896. (209) 478-0800. Fax: (209) 478-8721.

Imperial Valley College
Imperial, California — CB code: 4358

2-year public community college, coed. Founded in 1922. **Accreditation:** Regional. **Undergraduate enrollment:** 5,434 men and women. **Location:** Rural campus in small city; 6 miles from El Centro. **Calendar:** Semester.

FRESHMAN ADMISSIONS. Selection criteria: Open admissions.

ANNUAL EXPENSES. Tuition and fees (1992-93): $120, $3,120 additional for out-of-state students. **Books and supplies:** $600. **Other expenses:** $1,638.

ADDRESS/TELEPHONE. Sandra Standiford, Dean of Admissions and Student Activities, Imperial Valley College, PO Box 158, P.O. 158, Imperial, CA 92251-0158. (619) 352-8320.

Irvine Valley College
Irvine, California — CB code: 3356

2-year public community college, coed. **Accreditation:** Regional. **Undergraduate enrollment:** 10,059 men and women. **Location:** Suburban campus in small city; 50 miles from Los Angeles. **Calendar:** Semester.

FRESHMAN ADMISSIONS. Selection criteria: Open admissions.

ANNUAL EXPENSES. Tuition and fees (projected): $260, $2,520 additional for out-of-state students. **Books and supplies:** $612. **Other expenses:** $1,800.

ADDRESS/TELEPHONE. Jess Craig, Dean of Admissions and Enrollment Services, Irvine Valley College, 5500 Irvine Center Drive, Irvine, CA 92720. (714) 559-9300. Fax: (714) 559-3270.

ITT Technical Institute: Buena Park
Buena Park, California CB code: 3570

2-year proprietary technical college, coed. **Undergraduate enrollment:** 629 men and women. **Location:** Suburban campus in small city; 15 miles from Los Angeles. **Calendar:** Quarter. Extensive evening/early morning classes. **Additional facts:** Bachelor's degree available in electronics. Bachelor's program open to applicant's with associate from ITT or any 2-year community/junior college.

FRESHMAN ADMISSIONS. Selection criteria: Must score above certain levels on institution's entrance examinations in reading, and mathematics.

ANNUAL EXPENSES. Tuition and fees (1992-93): Tuition for 18-month computer-aided drafting program $12,817; books supplies, and tools, $1,300. Tuition for 2-year electronics program $14,405; books and supplies, $1,600. Bachelor's program is an additional 4 quarters at $7,253; books and supplies $850. Laboratory fees, $50 per quarter. **Books and supplies:** $800.

ADDRESS/TELEPHONE. Sanjay Advani, Director, ITT Technical Institute: Buena Park, 7100 Knott Avenue, Suite 100, Buena Park, CA 90620-1374. (714) 523-9080. Fax: (714) 670-1738.

ITT Technical Institute: Sacramento
Sacramento, California CB code: 3597

2-year proprietary technical college, coed. Founded in 1954. **Undergraduate enrollment:** 296 men, 57 women full time. **Faculty:** 17 total. **Location:** Suburban campus in very large city; 7 miles from downtown. **Calendar:** Quarter. **Microcomputers:** 32 located in libraries, classrooms, computer centers.

DEGREES OFFERED. AAS. 135 associate degrees awarded in 1992. 100% in engineering technologies.

UNDERGRADUATE MAJORS. Drafting and design technology, electronic technology.

ACADEMIC PROGRAMS. Honors program. **Remedial services:** Learning center, tutoring.

ACADEMIC REQUIREMENTS. Freshmen must earn minimum GPA of 1.5 to continue in good standing. 90% of freshmen return for sophomore year. Students must declare major on enrollment. **Graduation requirements:** 91 hours for associate (66 in major). Most students required to take courses in computer science, English, mathematics, biological/physical sciences.

FRESHMAN ADMISSIONS. Selection criteria: High school record important. Applicants must pass CPAT admissions test. **Test requirements:** SAT or ACT (ACT preferred).

1992 FRESHMAN CLASS PROFILE. 164 men, 26 women enrolled. 7% had high school GPA of 3.0 or higher, 60% between 2.0 and 2.99. **Characteristics:** 100% commute, 31% have minority backgrounds. Average age is 22.

FALL-TERM APPLICATIONS. $100 fee. Application fee refunded if student not accepted. No closing date; applicants notified on a rolling basis. Interview required.

STUDENT LIFE. Activities: Student government, film, magazine, student newspaper, television.

ATHLETICS. Intramural: Softball, volleyball.

STUDENT SERVICES. Employment service for undergraduates, freshman orientation, personal counseling, placement service for graduates, veterans counselor, services/facilities for handicapped.

ANNUAL EXPENSES. Tuition and fees (1992-93): $7,400. Tuition for 18-month computer-aided drafting program $12,817; books, supplies, and tools, $1,300. Tuition for 2-year electronics program $14,405; books and supplies, $1,750. Laboratory fees, $50 per quarter. **Books and supplies:** $750. **Other expenses:** $1,143.

FINANCIAL AID. All grants, 63% of loans, all jobs based on need. **Aid applications:** No closing date; applicants notified on a rolling basis; must reply by registration.

ADDRESS/TELEPHONE. Robert Johanneson, Director of Education, ITT Technical Institute: Sacramento, 9700 Goethe Road, Sacramento, CA 95827. (916) 366-3900. Fax: (916) 366-9225.

ITT Technical Institute: San Diego
San Diego, California CB code: 0206

2-year proprietary technical college, coed. Founded in 1981. **Undergraduate enrollment:** 597 men and women. **Location:** Suburban campus in very large city. **Calendar:** Quarter.

FRESHMAN ADMISSIONS. Selection criteria: Specialized on-site test results considered for certain courses.

ANNUAL EXPENSES. Tuition and fees (1992-93): Tuition for 18-month computer-aided drafting program $12,817; books, supplies, and tools, $1,100. Tuition for 2-year electronics program $14,405; books and supplies, $1,300. Laboratory fees, $50 per quarter. **Books and supplies:** $1,450. **Other expenses:** $900.

ADDRESS/TELEPHONE. Nayna Patel, Executive Secretary, ITT Technical Institute: San Diego, 9680 Granite Ridge Drive, San Diego, CA 92123. (619) 571-8500.

ITT Technical Institute: Van Nuys
Van Nuys, California CB code: 3571

2-year proprietary technical college, coed. Founded in 1982. **Undergraduate enrollment:** 441 men and women. **Location:** Urban campus in very large city; within Los Angeles County. **Calendar:** Quarter. Extensive evening/early morning classes.

FRESHMAN ADMISSIONS. Selection criteria: Institutional reading, mathematics, entrance examinations for EET programs. Reading, mathematics, and spatial relations examinations for CAD programs.

ANNUAL EXPENSES. Tuition and fees (1992-93): Tuition for 18-month computer-aided drafting program $12,817; books, supplies, and tools, $1,500. Tuition for 2-year electronics program $14,405; books and supplies, $1,600. Laboratory fees, $50 per quarter.

ADDRESS/TELEPHONE. Reza Shabestari, Director or Education, ITT Technical Institute: Van Nuys, 6723 Van Nuys Boulevard, Van Nuys, CA 91405. (818) 989-1177.

ITT Technical Institute: West Covina
West Covina, California CB code: 0216

4-year proprietary technical/career training institute, coed. Founded in 1982. **Undergraduate enrollment:** 710 men and women full time. **Faculty:** 28 total (21 full time), 1 with doctorate or other terminal degree. **Location:** Suburban campus in small city; 20 miles from Los Angeles. **Calendar:** Quarter. **Microcomputers:** 84 located in libraries, classrooms, computer centers.

DEGREES OFFERED. AAS, B. 244 associate degrees awarded in 1992. 100% in engineering technologies. 110 bachelor's degrees awarded. 100% in engineering technologies.

UNDERGRADUATE MAJORS. Electronic technology. drafting and design technology, manufacturing technology.

ACADEMIC PROGRAMS. Remedial services: Remedial instruction, tutoring. **Placement/credit:** Institutional tests.

ACADEMIC REQUIREMENTS. Freshmen must earn minimum GPA of 1.5 to continue in good standing. Students must declare major on application. **Graduation requirements:** 124 hours for associate, 198 hours for bachelor's. Most students required to take courses in mathematics. **Postgraduate studies:** 45% from 2-year programs enter 4-year programs. 1% enter other graduate study.

FRESHMAN ADMISSIONS. Selection criteria: Specialized on-site admissions test results considered for certain programs. **Test requirements:** CPAT Career Program Assessment Test required.

1992 FRESHMAN CLASS PROFILE. 245 men, 18 women enrolled. **Characteristics:** 98% from in state, 100% commute, 60% have minority backgrounds. Average age is 20.

FALL-TERM APPLICATIONS. $100 fee. Application fee refunded if student not accepted. No closing date; applicants notified on a rolling basis. Interview required. Class size limited.

STUDENT LIFE. Activities: Society of Manufacturing Engineers (student chapter).

STUDENT SERVICES. Career counseling, employment service for undergraduates, placement service for graduates, services/facilities for handicapped.

ANNUAL EXPENSES. Tuition and fees (1992-93): Tuition for 18-month computer-aided drafting program $12,817; books, supplies, and tools, $1,100. Tuition for 2-year electronics program $14,405; books and supplies, $1,600; automated manufacturing technology $6,877; books, supplies, $175. Laboratory fees, $50 per quarter.

FINANCIAL AID. Aid applications: No closing date; applicants notified on a rolling basis.

ADDRESS/TELEPHONE. Steve Douglas, District Manager, ITT Technical Institute: West Covina, 1530 West Cameron Avenue, West Covina, CA 91790. (818) 960-8681. Fax: (818) 960-4299.

John F. Kennedy University
Orinda, California CB code: 1362

4-year private liberal arts college, coed. Founded in 1964. **Accreditation:** Regional. **Undergraduate enrollment:** 10 men, 45 women full time; 76 men, 233 women part time. **Graduate enrollment:** 191 men, 396 women full time; 210 men, 592 women part time. **Faculty:** 264 total (16 full time), 77 with doctorates or other terminal degrees. **Location:** Suburban campus in large town; 5 miles from Berkeley. **Calendar:** Quarter, limited summer session. Saturday and extensive evening/early morning classes. **Microcomputers:** Located in libraries, computer centers. **Additional facts:** Institution serves educational needs of working adults; majority of courses held evenings and weekends.

DEGREES OFFERED. BA, BS, MA, MBA, JD. 60 bachelor's degrees awarded in 1992. 12% in business and management, 88% letters/literature. Graduate degrees offered in 14 major fields of study.

UNDERGRADUATE MAJORS. Accounting, business administration and management, business and management, food management, humanities and social sciences, liberal/general studies, religion.

ACADEMIC PROGRAMS. Accelerated program, double major, independent study, internships, student-designed major, teacher preparation, weekend college, cross-registration; combined bachelor's/graduate program in business administration, law. **ROTC:** Air Force. **Placement/credit:** AP, CLEP General and Subject, institutional tests.

ACADEMIC REQUIREMENTS. Students must declare major on enrollment. **Graduation requirements:** 180 hours for bachelor's (30 in major). Most students required to take courses in English, humanities, mathematics, philosophy/religion, biological/physical sciences, social sciences.

FALL-TERM APPLICATIONS. $50 fee.

STUDENT LIFE. Activities: Student government, student newspaper, student newsletter. **Additional information:** 95% of students are self-supporting.

STUDENT SERVICES. Career counseling, employment service for undergraduates, veterans counselor, services/facilities for handicapped.

ANNUAL EXPENSES. Tuition and fees (1992-93): $6,948. **Books and supplies:** $504.

FINANCIAL AID. 50% of freshmen, 50% of continuing students receive some form of aid. All grants, 75% of loans, all jobs based on need. Academic scholarships available. **Aid applications:** No closing date; priority given to applications received by April 1; applicants notified on a rolling basis beginning on or about June 13; must reply within 4 weeks.

ADDRESS/TELEPHONE. Ellena Bloedorn, Director of Admissions and Records, John F. Kennedy University, 12 Altarinda Road, Orinda, CA 94563. (510) 254-6964.

Kelsey-Jenney College
San Diego, California CB code: 4986

2-year private business, junior college, coed. Founded in 1887. **Accreditation:** Regional. **Undergraduate enrollment:** 330 men, 668 women full time. **Faculty:** 71 total (21 full time), 4 with doctorates or other terminal degrees. **Location:** Urban campus in very large city. **Calendar:** Quarter, extensive summer session. Saturday and extensive evening/early morning classes. **Microcomputers:** 150 located in libraries, classrooms, computer centers. **Additional facts:** Branch campus in San Diego.

DEGREES OFFERED. AAS. 80 associate degrees awarded in 1992.

UNDERGRADUATE MAJORS. Accounting, business administration and management, business and management, business data processing and related programs, court reporting, data processing, legal assistant/paralegal, legal secretary, medical assistant, medical secretary, microcomputer software, secretarial and related programs, word processing.

ACADEMIC PROGRAMS. Internships. **Remedial services:** Tutoring. **Placement/credit:** Institutional tests.

ACADEMIC REQUIREMENTS. Freshmen must earn minimum GPA of 2.0 to continue in good standing. Students must declare major on application. **Graduation requirements:** 120 hours for associate (85 in major). Most students required to take courses in arts/fine arts, computer science, English, humanities, mathematics, social sciences. **Additional information:** Students are trained for employment and not necessarily for transfer to 4-year institutions.

FRESHMAN ADMISSIONS. Selection criteria: Interview, test scores on institutional examination, high school diploma or equivalent.

1992 FRESHMAN CLASS PROFILE. 161 men and women enrolled. **Characteristics:** 98% from in state, 100% commute, 68% have minority backgrounds, 2% are foreign students. Average age is 19.

FALL-TERM APPLICATIONS. $25 fee, may be waived for applicants with need. No closing date; applicants notified on a rolling basis. Interview required.

STUDENT LIFE. Activities: Student newspaper.

STUDENT SERVICES. Career counseling, employment service for undergraduates, freshman orientation, placement service for graduates, veterans counselor, services/facilities for handicapped.

ANNUAL EXPENSES. Tuition and fees: $8,088. **Books and supplies:** $612. **Other expenses:** $1,548.

FINANCIAL AID. 85% of freshmen, 85% of continuing students receive some form of aid. All grants, 72% of jobs based on need. Academic, state/district residency scholarships available. **Aid applications:** No closing date; applicants notified on a rolling basis beginning on or about July 1; must reply within 30 days.

ADDRESS/TELEPHONE. Deberah Glenn, Director of Admissions, Kelsey-Jenney College, 201 A Street, San Diego, CA 92101. (619) 233-7418. Fax: (619) 549-2886.

Kings River Community College
Reedley, California CB code: 4655

2-year public community college, coed. Founded in 1926. **Accreditation:** Regional. **Undergraduate enrollment:** 1,953 men and women full time; 3,520 men and women part time. **Location:** Rural campus in large town; 30 miles from Fresno. **Calendar:** Semester. **Additional facts:** Courses also offered at community campus sites in Madera, Clovis, Sanger, Selma, Kerman, and Oakhurst.

FRESHMAN ADMISSIONS. Selection criteria: Open admissions.

ANNUAL EXPENSES. Tuition and fees: $295, $3,390 additional for out-of-state students. **Room and board:** $3,922. **Books and supplies:** $612. **Other expenses:** $1,200.

ADDRESS/TELEPHONE. Moire C. Charters, Associate Dean of Student Personnel, Admissions, and Records, Kings River Community College, 995 North Reed, Reedley, CA 93654. (209) 638-3641. Fax: (209) 638-5040.

La Sierra University
Riverside, California CB code: 4380

Admissions: 80% of applicants accepted
Based on:
•• Recommendations, religious affiliation/commitment, school record
• Activities, interview, test scores
Completion: 90% of freshmen end year in good standing
46% graduate

4-year private university, coed, affiliated with Seventh-day Adventists. Founded in 1922. **Accreditation:** Regional. **Undergraduate enrollment:** 538 men, 580 women full time; 63 men, 61 women part time. **Graduate enrollment:** 29 men, 19 women full time; 113 men, 121 women part time. **Faculty:** 108 total (97 full time), 72 with doctorates or other terminal degrees. **Location:** Suburban campus in small city; 65 miles from Los Angeles. **Calendar:** Quarter, limited summer session. **Microcomputers:** 500 located in computer centers. **Special facilities:** Museum of natural history with large freeze-dried collection of reptiles, mammals, and birds.

DEGREES OFFERED. AA, AS, BA, BS, BFA, MA, MS, MBA, EdD, DDS, MD, B.Div. 7 associate degrees awarded in 1992. 228 bachelor's degrees awarded. 20% in business and management, 5% communications, 10% education, 6% teacher education, 20% life sciences, 5% philosophy, religion, theology, 6% physical sciences, 13% psychology. Graduate degrees offered in 17 major fields of study.

UNDERGRADUATE MAJORS. Associate: Bible studies, business and office, child development/care/guidance, engineering physics, medical secretary, office supervision and management, secretarial and related programs, word processing. **Bachelor's:** Accounting, anthropology, behavioral sciences, biochemistry, biology, business administration and management, business and management, business economics, chemistry, child development/care/guidance, communications, computer and information sciences, criminal justice studies, education, elementary education, English, fine arts, history, human resources development, industrial and organizational psychology, liberal/general studies, marketing research, mathematics, music, music performance, physics, political science and government, prelaw, psychobiology, psychology, radio/television technology, religion, religious education, religious music, secretarial and related programs, sociology, Spanish, teaching English as a second language/foreign language, theological studies.

ACADEMIC PROGRAMS. 2-year transfer program, double major, dual enrollment of high school students, education specialist degree, external degree, honors program, internships, study abroad, teacher preparation, cross-registration. **Remedial services:** Learning center, preadmission summer program, reduced course load, remedial instruction, special counselor, tutoring. **Placement/credit:** AP, institutional tests.

ACADEMIC REQUIREMENTS. Freshmen must earn minimum GPA of 2.0 to continue in good standing. 68% of freshmen return for sophomore year. Students must declare major by end of second year. **Graduation requirements:** 96 hours for associate, 192 hours for bachelor's. Most students required to take courses in arts/fine arts, English, history, humanities, mathematics, philosophy/religion, biological/physical sciences, social sciences.

FRESHMAN ADMISSIONS. Selection criteria: School achievement record, recommendations, and religious affiliation or commitment important. **High school preparation:** 16 units required. Required units include English 3, foreign language 2, mathematics 2, social science 1 and science 2. **Test requirements:** SAT or ACT (ACT preferred) for placement and counseling only; score report by October 1.

1992 FRESHMAN CLASS PROFILE. 56% had high school GPA of 3.0 or higher, 40% between 2.0 and 2.99. **Characteristics:** 60% from in state, 75% commute, 60% have minority backgrounds, 20% are foreign students. Average age is 19.

FALL-TERM APPLICATIONS. $30 fee. No closing date; priority given to applications received by September 15; applicants notified on a rolling basis; must reply within 4 weeks. Interview required for non-Seventh-day Adventist applicants. Early admission available.

STUDENT LIFE. Housing: Dormitories (men, women); apartment housing available. **Activities:** Student government, student newspaper, yearbook, choral groups, concert band, drama, music ensembles, symphony orchestra, ethnic and international student organizations. **Additional information:** Religious observance required.

ATHLETICS. Intercollegiate: Basketball, tennis, volleyball. **Intramural:** Badminton, baseball, basketball, gymnastics, soccer, softball, swimming, tennis, volleyball.

STUDENT SERVICES. Aptitude testing, career counseling, employment service for undergraduates, freshman orientation, health services, on-campus day care, personal counseling, placement service for graduates, special adviser for adult students, services/facilities for handicapped.

ANNUAL EXPENSES. Tuition and fees (1992-93): $10,830. **Room and board:** $3,585. **Books and supplies:** $450. **Other expenses:** $1,314.

FINANCIAL AID. 65% of freshmen, 60% of continuing students receive some form of aid. 87% of grants, 97% of loans, 29% of jobs based on need. Academic, music/drama, art, athletic, leadership, religious affiliation scholarships available. **Aid applications:** No closing date; priority given to applications received by May 1; applicants notified on a rolling basis beginning on or about July 15; must reply within 2 weeks.

ADDRESS/TELEPHONE. Myrna Costa, Director of Admissions, La Sierra University, 4700 Pierce Street, Riverside, CA 92515-8247. (714) 785-2118. (800) 874-5587. Fax: (714) 785-2901.

Lake Tahoe Community College
South Lake Tahoe, California CB code: 4420

2-year public community college, coed. Founded in 1975. **Accreditation:** Regional. **Undergraduate enrollment:** 3,000 men and women. **Faculty:** 101 total (26 full time), 3 with doctorates or other terminal degrees. **Location:** Rural campus in large town; 55 miles from Reno, Nevada, 110 miles from Sacramento. **Calendar:** Quarter, limited summer session. **Microcomputers:** 50 located in classrooms.

DEGREES OFFERED. AA. 40 associate degrees awarded in 1992. 8% in business and management, 8% business/office and marketing/distribution, 34% multi/interdisciplinary studies, 12% parks/recreation, protective services, public affairs, 38% social sciences.

UNDERGRADUATE MAJORS. Accounting, biology, business administration and management, business and management, business and office, computer and information sciences, criminal justice studies, early childhood education, finance, fine arts, fire control and safety technology, health sciences, hospitality and recreation marketing, hotel/motel and restaurant management, humanities, law enforcement and corrections technologies, legal secretary, liberal/general studies, marketing and distribution, mathematics, mathematics and natural science studies, medical secretary, real estate, science technologies, secretarial and related programs, small business management and ownership, social sciences, Spanish.

ACADEMIC PROGRAMS. 2-year transfer program, double major, dual enrollment of high school students. **Remedial services:** Learning center, remedial instruction, tutoring. **Placement/credit:** Institutional tests.

ACADEMIC REQUIREMENTS. Freshmen must earn minimum GPA of 2.0 to continue in good standing. 37% of freshmen return for sophomore year. **Graduation requirements:** 90 hours for associate (30 in major). Most students required to take courses in arts/fine arts, computer science, English, history, humanities, mathematics, philosophy/religion, biological/physical sciences, social sciences.

FRESHMAN ADMISSIONS. Selection criteria: Open admissions.

1992 FRESHMAN CLASS PROFILE. 670 men and women enrolled. **Characteristics:** 97% from in state, 100% commute, 9% have minority backgrounds.

FALL-TERM APPLICATIONS. No fee. No closing date; applicants notified on a rolling basis. Early admission available.

STUDENT LIFE. Activities: Student government, magazine, student newspaper, choral groups, dance, drama, music ensembles, musical theater.

ATHLETICS. Intramural: Volleyball.

STUDENT SERVICES. Aptitude testing, career counseling, employment service for undergraduates, freshman orientation, personal counseling, placement service for graduates, veterans counselor, services/facilities for handicapped.

ANNUAL EXPENSES. Tuition and fees (projected): $321, $3,510 additional for out-of-state students. **Books and supplies:** $612. **Other expenses:** $1,386.

FINANCIAL AID. 10% of continuing students receive some form of aid. All aid based on need. Academic, music/drama, art, leadership scholarships available. **Aid applications:** No closing date; priority given to applications received by May 1; applicants notified on a rolling basis beginning on or about August 15; must reply within 2 weeks.

ADDRESS/TELEPHONE. Linda M. Stevenson, Director of Admissions and Records, Lake Tahoe Community College, PO Box 14445, One College Drive, South Lake Tahoe, CA 96151. (916) 541-4660 ext. 273.

Laney College
Oakland, California CB code: 4406

2-year public community college, coed. Founded in 1953. **Accreditation:** Regional. **Undergraduate enrollment:** 11,472 men and women. **Faculty:** 337 total (154 full time). **Location:** Urban campus in large city. **Calendar:** Semester. Saturday and extensive evening/early morning classes.

DEGREES OFFERED. AA, AS. 200 associate degrees awarded in 1992.

UNDERGRADUATE MAJORS. Accounting, Afro-American (black) studies, air conditioning/heating/refrigeration mechanics, architectural engineering, architectural technologies, architecture, Asian studies, biological and physical sciences, business and office, business data processing and related programs, carpentry, ceramics, computer and information sciences, construction, curriculum and instruction, dance, education, English, finance, fine arts, graphic and printing production, humanities and social sciences, information sciences and systems, interior design, journalism, Latin American studies, liberal/general studies, machine tool operation/machine shop, mathematics, music, photography, precision metal work, radio/television broadcasting, radio/television technology, secretarial and related programs, social sciences, telecommunications, trade and industrial supervision and management, woodworking, word processing.

ACADEMIC PROGRAMS. Remedial services: Learning center, remedial instruction, special counselor, tutoring.

ACADEMIC REQUIREMENTS. Graduation requirements: 60 hours for associate (20 in major). Most students required to take courses in computer science, English, humanities, mathematics, biological/physical sciences, social sciences.

FRESHMAN ADMISSIONS. Selection criteria: Open admissions.

1992 FRESHMAN CLASS PROFILE. 2,418 men and women enrolled. **Characteristics:** 100% from in state, 100% commute.

FALL-TERM APPLICATIONS. No fee. No closing date; applicants notified on a rolling basis.

STUDENT LIFE. Activities: Student government, student newspaper, television.

ATHLETICS. Intercollegiate: Baseball M, basketball M, football M, softball W, swimming.

STUDENT SERVICES. Services/facilities for handicapped.

ANNUAL EXPENSES. Tuition and fees (projected): $304, $2,808 additional for out-of-state students. **Books and supplies:** $612. **Other expenses:** $1,548.

FINANCIAL AID. 35% of continuing students receive some form of aid. All grants based on need. **Aid applications:** No closing date; priority given to applications received by April 15; applicants notified on a rolling basis.

ADDRESS/TELEPHONE. Howard Perdue, Director of Admissions and Records, Laney College, 900 Fallon Street, Oakland, CA 94607. (510) 464-3121.

Las Positas College
Livermore, California CB code: 6507

2-year public institution. **Accreditation:** Regional. **Undergraduate enrollment:** 6,000 men and women. **Faculty:** 67 total. **Location:** Small city.

DEGREES OFFERED. AA. 253 associate degrees awarded in 1992.

UNDERGRADUATE MAJORS. Accounting, business administration and management, commercial art, computer and information sciences, computer mathematics, drafting, drafting and design technology, electronic technology, engineering, fashion merchandising, fire control and safety technology, graphic design, horticulture, humanities, industrial technology, information sciences and systems, interior design, international studies, painting, radiograph medical technology, real estate, retailing, secretarial and related programs, social sciences, vacuum technology, welding technology.

FRESHMAN ADMISSIONS. Selection criteria: Open admissions. **Additional information:** High school diploma or GED required for student under 18 years.

1992 FRESHMAN CLASS PROFILE. Characteristics: 100% commute.

FALL-TERM APPLICATIONS. No fee. No closing date.

ANNUAL EXPENSES. Tuition and fees (1992-93):

ADDRESS/TELEPHONE. Carlo Vecchiarelli, Director of Admissions/Records, Las Positas Community College, 3033 Collier Canyon Road, Livermore, CA 94550. (510) 373-5800. Fax: (510) 443-0742.

Lassen College
Susanville, California CB code: 4383

2-year public community college, coed. Founded in 1925. **Accreditation:** Regional. **Undergraduate enrollment:** 811 men and women full time; 2,011 men and women part time. **Faculty:** 172 total (52 full time), 3 with doctorates or other terminal degrees. **Location:** Rural campus in small town; 100 miles from Chico, 84 miles from Reno, Nevada. **Calendar:** Semester, limited summer session. **Microcomputers:** 40 located in classrooms, computer centers.

DEGREES OFFERED. AA, AS. 180 associate degrees awarded in 1992. 8% in education, 6% allied health, 12% letters/literature, 12% mathematics, 5% parks/recreation, protective services, public affairs, 40% social sciences, 8% trade and industry.

UNDERGRADUATE MAJORS. Accounting, agricultural sciences, automotive mechanics, automotive technology, biological and physical sciences, business administration and management, business and office, business data processing and related programs, business data programming, computer and information sciences, construction, education, fine arts, humanities and social sciences, law enforcement and corrections technologies, liberal/general studies, mathematics, mathematics and science, physical sciences, power plant operation and maintenance, practical nursing, real estate, secretarial and related programs, social sciences, welding technology, word processing.

ACADEMIC PROGRAMS. 2-year transfer program, cooperative education, dual enrollment of high school students, honors program, independent study, internships, telecourses. **Remedial services:** Learning center, preadmission summer program, reduced course load, remedial instruction, special counselor, tutoring, developmental studies. **Placement/credit:** AP, institutional tests; 15 credit hours maximum for associate degree.

ACADEMIC REQUIREMENTS. Freshmen must earn minimum GPA of 2.0 to continue in good standing. 35% of freshmen return for sophomore year. Students must declare major by end of first year. **Graduation requirements:** 60 hours for associate (24 in major). Most students required to take courses in arts/fine arts, English, history, humanities, mathematics, philosophy/religion, biological/physical sciences, social sciences. **Additional information:** Gunsmithing and summer NRA programs offered.

FRESHMAN ADMISSIONS. Selection criteria: Open admissions.

1992 FRESHMAN CLASS PROFILE. 874 men and women enrolled. **Characteristics:** 80% from in state, 96% commute, 13% have minority backgrounds, 4% are foreign students. Average age is 19.

FALL-TERM APPLICATIONS. No fee. Closing date August 23; applicants notified on a rolling basis. Lassen College Placement Examinations recommended.

STUDENT LIFE. Housing: Dormitories (coed). **Activities:** Student government, film, student newspaper, choral groups, drama, over 20 student organizations and clubs.

ATHLETICS. NJCAA. **Intercollegiate:** Baseball M, basketball, cross-country, golf, rifle, softball W, track and field, volleyball W, wrestling M. **Intramural:** Skiing.

STUDENT SERVICES. Aptitude testing, career counseling, freshman orientation, health services, on-campus day care, personal counseling, veterans counselor, Native American counselor, Micronesian adviser, services/facilities for handicapped.

ANNUAL EXPENSES. Tuition and fees (projected): $295, $2,912 additional for out-of-state students. **Room and board:** $3,290. **Books and supplies:** $612. **Other expenses:** $1,350.

FINANCIAL AID. 85% of freshmen, 85% of continuing students receive some form of aid. 99% of grants, all loans, all jobs based on need. State/district residency scholarships available. **Aid applications:** No closing date; priority given to applications received by July 1; applicants notified on a rolling basis beginning on or about July 1; must reply within 2 weeks. **Additional information:** Board of Governors Grant: low-income California residents can have registration fees waived.

ADDRESS/TELEPHONE. Chris Alberico, Registrar and Admissions Director, Lassen College, PO Box 3000, Susanville, CA 96130. (916) 257-6181.

LIFE Bible College
San Dimas, California — CB code: 4264

4-year private Bible college, coed, affiliated with International Church of the Foursquare Gospel. Founded in 1925. **Undergraduate enrollment:** 148 men, 90 women full time; 90 men, 36 women part time. **Faculty:** 31 total (13 full time), 3 with doctorates or other terminal degrees. **Location:** Suburban campus in large town; 22 miles from Los Angeles. **Calendar:** Semester. Extensive evening/early morning classes. **Microcomputers:** Located in libraries.

DEGREES OFFERED. AA, BA. 5 associate degrees awarded in 1992. 100% in philosophy, religion, theology. 42 bachelor's degrees awarded. 100% in philosophy, religion, theology.

UNDERGRADUATE MAJORS. Associate: Bible studies. **Bachelor's:** Bible studies, biblical languages, Christian school teacher, missionary studies, religious education, theological studies.

ACADEMIC PROGRAMS. Internships, teacher preparation. **Placement/credit:** AP, CLEP General and Subject, institutional tests; 16 credit hours maximum for associate degree; 16 credit hours maximum for bachelor's degree.

ACADEMIC REQUIREMENTS. Freshmen must earn minimum GPA of 2.0 to continue in good standing. 59% of freshmen return for sophomore year. Students must declare major by end of second year. **Graduation requirements:** 64 hours for associate, 128 hours for bachelor's. Most students required to take courses in English, foreign languages, history, humanities, philosophy/religion, biological/physical sciences, social sciences. **Postgraduate studies:** 10% enter other graduate study.

FRESHMAN ADMISSIONS. Selection criteria: Christian character, motivation, and ability to accord with college's program. **Test requirements:** SAT or ACT; score report by July 25.

1992 FRESHMAN CLASS PROFILE. 25 men, 23 women enrolled. **Characteristics:** 53% from in state, 58% commute, 15% have minority backgrounds, 5% are foreign students. Average age is 19.

FALL-TERM APPLICATIONS. $35 fee. Closing date July 15; applicants notified on a rolling basis beginning on or about January 10. Essay required. Interview recommended. Deferred admission available.

STUDENT LIFE. Housing: Dormitories (men, women). **Activities:** Student government, yearbook, choral groups, drama, music ensembles. **Additional information:** Religious observance required.

ATHLETICS. Intercollegiate: Basketball M, volleyball W. **Intramural:** Basketball, cross-country M, football M, soccer, softball, volleyball.

STUDENT SERVICES. Career counseling, employment service for undergraduates, freshman orientation, personal counseling, placement service for graduates, services/facilities for handicapped.

ANNUAL EXPENSES. Tuition and fees: $4,450. **Room and board:** $2,900. **Books and supplies:** $375. **Other expenses:** $450.

FINANCIAL AID. 25% of freshmen, 40% of continuing students receive some form of aid. 93% of grants, all jobs based on need. 14 enrolled freshmen were judged to have need, all were offered aid. Academic, leadership, alumni affiliation, religious affiliation scholarships available. **Aid applications:** No closing date; priority given to applications received by June 1; applicants notified on a rolling basis; must reply within 10 days.

ADDRESS/TELEPHONE. Lyn Cruz, Admissions Director, LIFE Bible College, 1100 Covina Boulevard, San Dimas, CA 91773-3298. (714) 599-5433 ext. 217. (800) 356-0001. Fax: (714) 599-6690.

Lincoln University
San Francisco, California — CB code: 4386

4-year private university and business, liberal arts college, coed. Founded in 1919. **Undergraduate enrollment:** 212 men and women. **Graduate enrollment:** 128 men and women. **Faculty:** 35 total (8 full time), 17 with doctorates or other terminal degrees. **Location:** Urban campus in very large city. **Calendar:** Semester, limited summer session. **Microcomputers:** 30 located in computer centers. **Special facilities:** Language laboratory, media center.

DEGREES OFFERED. BA, BS, MBA, JD. 30 bachelor's degrees awarded in 1992. 83% in business and management, 17% computer sciences. Graduate degrees offered in 5 major fields of study.

UNDERGRADUATE MAJORS. Accounting, business administration and management, business and management, business economics, computer and information sciences, international business management, management information systems, management science.

ACADEMIC PROGRAMS. Cross-registration. **Remedial services:** Tutoring.

ACADEMIC REQUIREMENTS. Freshmen must earn minimum GPA of 2.0 to continue in good standing. Students must declare major by end of second year. **Graduation requirements:** 124 hours for bachelor's. Most students required to take courses in arts/fine arts, computer science, English, history, humanities, mathematics, philosophy/religion, social sciences.

FRESHMAN ADMISSIONS. Selection criteria: High school achievement record, institutional test scores most important.

1992 FRESHMAN CLASS PROFILE. 87 men and women enrolled. **Characteristics:** 100% commute.

FALL-TERM APPLICATIONS. $50 fee. No closing date; applicants notified on a rolling basis. Interview recommended.

STUDENT LIFE. Activities: Student government, student newspaper.

STUDENT SERVICES. Career counseling, employment service for undergraduates, freshman orientation, personal counseling, placement service for graduates, services/facilities for handicapped.

ANNUAL EXPENSES. Tuition and fees (1992-93): $5,250. **Books and supplies:** $400.

FINANCIAL AID. Aid applications: No closing date; applicants notified on a rolling basis.

ADDRESS/TELEPHONE. Dr. Pete Bogue, Director of Admission/Registrar, Lincoln University, 281 Masonic Avenue, San Francisco, CA 94118. (415) 221-1212. Fax: (415) 387-9730.

Long Beach City College
Long Beach, California — CB code: 4388

2-year public community college, coed. Founded in 1927. **Accreditation:** Regional. **Undergraduate enrollment:** 4,239 men and women full time; 19,560 men and women part time. **Faculty:** 832 total (322 full time), 146 with doctorates or other terminal degrees. **Location:** Urban campus in large city; 20 miles from downtown Los Angeles. **Calendar:** Semester, limited summer session. Saturday and extensive evening/early morning classes. **Microcomputers:** 150 located in libraries, computer centers.

DEGREES OFFERED. AA, AS. 854 associate degrees awarded in 1992.

UNDERGRADUATE MAJORS. Accounting, advertising, air conditioning/heating/refrigeration mechanics, air conditioning/heating/refrigeration technology, aircraft mechanics, airline piloting and navigation, applied art, architecture, art history, automotive mechanics, automotive technology, aviation management, biology, business administration and management, business and management, business and office, business data entry equipment operation, business data processing and related programs, business data programming, carpentry, child development/care/guidance, commercial art, commercial music, computer graphics, computer programming, creative writing, dance, data processing, diesel engine mechanics, dietetic aide/assistant, drafting, drafting and design technology, drawing, electrical and electronics equipment repair, electromechanical technology, electronic technology, engineering, English, English literature, fashion design, fashion merchandising, film arts, finance, fine arts, fire control and safety technology, food management, food production/management/services, food science and nutrition, foreign languages (multiple emphasis), French, German, home economics, home furnishings and equipment management/production/services, horticultural science, horticulture, hotel/motel and restaurant management, illustration design, insurance marketing, interior design, international business management, journalism, labor/industrial relations, language/literature, laser electro-optic technology, law enforcement and corrections technologies, legal secretary, liberal/general studies, machine tool operation/machine shop, management information systems, marketing and distribution, marketing management, mathematics, medical assistant, medical secretary, music, nursing, painting, parent education, photographic technology, photography, physical sciences, practical nursing, precision metal work, printmaking, public relations, radio/television broadcasting, radiograph medical technology, real estate, respiratory therapy technology, sculpture, secretarial and related programs, social sciences, Spanish, special education, speech, telecommunications, textiles and clothing, tourism, upholstery, welding technology, woodworking, word processing.

ACADEMIC PROGRAMS. 2-year transfer program, accelerated program, cooperative education, honors program, independent study, study abroad, telecourses, weekend college. **Remedial services:** Learning center, preadmission summer program, remedial instruction, special counselor, tutoring. **Placement/credit:** AP, institutional tests; 40 credit hours maximum for associate degree.

ACADEMIC REQUIREMENTS. Freshmen must earn minimum GPA of 2.0 to continue in good standing. **Graduation requirements:** 60 hours for associate (18 in major). Most students required to take courses in arts/fine arts, computer science, English, history, humanities, mathematics, biological/physical sciences, social sciences.

FRESHMAN ADMISSIONS. Selection criteria: Open admissions.

1992 FRESHMAN CLASS PROFILE. 4,998 men and women enrolled. **Characteristics:** 90% from in state, 100% commute, 35% have minority backgrounds, 1% are foreign students, 2% join fraternities/sororities.

FALL-TERM APPLICATIONS. No fee. No closing date; applicants notified on a rolling basis. Deferred and early admission available.

STUDENT LIFE. Activities: Student government, student newspaper, television, choral groups, concert band, dance, drama, jazz band, music ensembles, musical theater, pep band, symphony orchestra, fraternities, sororities.

ATHLETICS. NJCAA. **Intercollegiate:** Baseball M, basketball, cross-country, diving, football M, golf M, soccer M, softball W, swimming, tennis, track and field, volleyball, water polo M. **Intramural:** Archery, badminton, basketball M, bowling, golf, racquetball, soccer, softball, swimming M, table tennis, tennis, track and field, volleyball, wrestling M.

STUDENT SERVICES. Aptitude testing, career counseling, employment service for undergraduates, freshman orientation, health services, on-campus day care, personal counseling, veterans counselor, services/facilities for handicapped.

ANNUAL EXPENSES. Tuition and fees (projected): $312, $2,736 additional for out-of-state students. **Books and supplies:** $684. **Other expenses:** $1,535.

FINANCIAL AID. 20% of freshmen, 20% of continuing students receive some form of aid. All grants, 98% of loans, all jobs based on need. 3,400 enrolled freshmen were judged to have need, all were offered aid. Academic, music/drama, art, state/district residency, leadership, alumni affiliation, minority scholarships available. **Aid applications:** No closing date; priority given to applications received by May 1; applicants notified on a rolling basis beginning on or about May 19; must reply within 2 weeks.

ADDRESS/TELEPHONE. Richard Dawdy, Dean of Admissions and Records, Long Beach City College, 4901 East Carson Street, Long Beach, CA 90808. (310) 420-4206. Fax: (310) 420-4118.

Los Angeles City College
Los Angeles, California — CB code: 4391

2-year public community college, coed. Founded in 1929. **Accreditation:** Regional. **Undergraduate enrollment:** 14,579 men and women. **Faculty:** 10,620 total (10,500 full time), 63 with doctorates or other terminal degrees. **Location:** Urban campus in very large city; 5 miles from downtown. **Calendar:** Semester, limited summer session. Saturday classes. **Microcomputers:** 200 located in computer centers.

DEGREES OFFERED. AA, AS. 460 associate degrees awarded in 1992. 11% in business and management, 22% business/office and marketing/distribution, 5% communications, 8% engineering technologies, 5% health sciences, 20% allied health, 6% home economics, 13% multi/interdisciplinary studies.

UNDERGRADUATE MAJORS. Accounting, advertising, Afro-American (black) studies, architecture, Asian-American studies, biology, biomedical equipment technology, business administration and management, business and office, business computer/console/peripheral equipment operation, business data processing and related programs, business data programming, chemistry, child development/care/guidance, Chinese, cinematography/film, commercial art, computer and information sciences, computer servicing technology, computer technology, criminal justice studies, dental laboratory technology, dietetic aide/assistant, drafting, dramatic arts, electrical and electronics equipment repair, electronic technology, engineering, engineering and engineering-related technologies, engineering and other disciplines, English, film arts, finance, fine arts, French, German, home economics, humanities and social sciences, Italian, Japanese, journalism, law enforcement and corrections technologies, legal assistant/paralegal, legal secretary, liberal/general studies, marketing management, mathematics, medical records technology, medical secretary, mental health/human services, Mexican American studies, microcomputer software, music, photographic technology, photography, physics, psychology, public relations, radio/television broadcasting, radio/television technology, radiograph medical technology, real estate, secretarial and related programs, small business management and ownership, Spanish, tourism, transportation and travel marketing, word processing.

ACADEMIC PROGRAMS. 2-year transfer program, dual enrollment of high school students, honors program, independent study, study abroad, weekend college, cross-registration. **Remedial services:** Learning center, remedial instruction, special counselor, tutoring. **ROTC:** Air Force, Army, Naval. **Placement/credit:** AP, CLEP Subject, institutional tests; 15 credit hours maximum for associate degree.

ACADEMIC REQUIREMENTS. Freshmen must earn minimum GPA of 2.0 to continue in good standing. 50% of freshmen return for sophomore year. Students must declare major by end of first year. **Graduation requirements:** 60 hours for associate (18 in major). Most students required to take courses in English, history, humanities, mathematics, biological/physical sciences, social sciences.

FRESHMAN ADMISSIONS. Selection criteria: Open admissions.

1992 FRESHMAN CLASS PROFILE. 3,884 men and women enrolled. **Characteristics:** 90% from in state, 100% commute, 80% have minority backgrounds, 4% are foreign students. Average age is 23.

FALL-TERM APPLICATIONS. No fee. Closing date September 1; applicants notified on a rolling basis; must reply by registration. Audition required for theater academy, music applicants.

STUDENT LIFE. Activities: Student government, film, magazine, radio, student newspaper, television, choral groups, concert band, dance, drama, jazz band, music ensembles, musical theater, international folk dance, religious, political, ethnic, and foreign student clubs.

ATHLETICS. NJCAA. **Intercollegiate:** Baseball M, basketball M, cross-country, track and field.

STUDENT SERVICES. Aptitude testing, career counseling, employment service for undergraduates, freshman orientation, health services, on-campus day care, personal counseling, veterans counselor, services/facilities for handicapped.

ANNUAL EXPENSES. Tuition and fees (1992-93): $120, $3,690 additional for out-of-state students. **Books and supplies:** $576. **Other expenses:** $1,728.

FINANCIAL AID. 20% of freshmen, 20% of continuing students receive some form of aid. All grants, 89% of loans, all jobs based on need. **Aid applications:** Closing date June 26; applicants notified on a rolling basis; must reply within 2 weeks. **Additional information:** Fee waivers are available for public assistance, Social Security insurance recipients; fee credits available for low income families.

ADDRESS/TELEPHONE. Myra Siegel, Assistant Dean of Admissions and Records, Los Angeles City College, 855 North Vermont Avenue, Los Angeles, CA 90029-3589. (213) 953-4381. Fax: (213) 666-4294.

Los Angeles Harbor College
Wilmington, California — CB code: 4395

2-year public community college, coed. Founded in 1949. **Accreditation:** Regional. **Undergraduate enrollment:** 1,096 men, 1,577 women full time; 2,683 men, 3,861 women part time. **Faculty:** 335 total (135 full time). **Location:** Suburban campus in small city; 15 miles from downtown Los Angeles. **Calendar:** Semester, limited summer session. **Microcomputers:** Located in libraries, classrooms, computer centers. **Special facilities:** Art gallery, observatory, nature museum.

DEGREES OFFERED. AA, AS. 298 associate degrees awarded in 1992. 15% in health sciences, 69% multi/interdisciplinary studies.

UNDERGRADUATE MAJORS. Accounting, architectural technologies, architecture, automotive technology, business administration and management, business and management, business and office, business data processing and related programs, business data programming, child development/care/guidance, computer and information sciences, drafting, drafting and design technology, electrical and electronics equipment repair, electrical/electronics/communications engineering, electromechanical technology, engineering and engineering-related technologies, fire control and safety technology, humanities, interior design, law enforcement and corrections technologies, legal secretary, liberal/general studies, medical secretary, nursing, office supervision and management, real estate, science technologies, secretarial and related programs, word processing.

ACADEMIC PROGRAMS. 2-year transfer program, accelerated program, cooperative education, dual enrollment of high school students, honors program, study abroad, telecourses, weekend college, cross-registration, Project for Adult College Education (PACE), condensed program of study. **Remedial services:** Learning center, remedial instruction, special counselor, tutoring. **Placement/credit:** AP, CLEP General and Subject; 15 credit hours maximum for associate degree.

ACADEMIC REQUIREMENTS. Freshmen must earn minimum GPA of 2.0 to continue in good standing. Students must declare major by end of first year. **Graduation requirements:** 60 hours for associate (30 in major). Most students required to take courses in English, humanities, mathematics, biological/physical sciences, social sciences. **Additional information:** Transfer-Alliance Honors Program with UCLA.

FRESHMAN ADMISSIONS. Selection criteria: Open admissions. Recommended units include biological science 3, foreign language 2, mathematics 2, social science 2 and science 2. Nursing program requires high school diploma and high school chemistry and algebra.

1992 FRESHMAN CLASS PROFILE. 2,392 men and women enrolled. **Characteristics:** 95% from in state, 100% commute, 70% have minority backgrounds, 1% are foreign students.

FALL-TERM APPLICATIONS. No fee. Closing date August 30; priority given to applications received by June 30; applicants notified on a rolling basis. Early admission available. High school students accepted on part-time basis.

STUDENT LIFE. Activities: Student government, magazine, radio, student newspaper, choral groups, concert band, dance, drama, jazz band, music ensembles, musical theater, Bible study group, Equal Opportunity Program Student Association, New Life Club.

ATHLETICS. NJCAA. **Intercollegiate:** Baseball M, basketball M, football M, soccer. **Intramural:** Golf, softball.

STUDENT SERVICES. Aptitude testing, career counseling, freshman orientation, on-campus day care, personal counseling, veterans counselor, legal clinic, services/facilities for handicapped.

ANNUAL EXPENSES. Tuition and fees (1992-93): $120, $3,690 additional for out-of-state students. **Books and supplies:** $558.

FINANCIAL AID. 14% of freshmen, 14% of continuing students receive some form of aid. All grants, all loans, 59% of jobs based on need. 186 enrolled freshmen were judged to have need, all were offered aid. Academic, state/district residency scholarships available. **Aid applications:** No closing date; priority given to applications received by March 14; applicants notified on a rolling basis; must reply within 2 weeks.

ADDRESS/TELEPHONE. Luis M. Rosas, Assistant Dean of Admissions and Records, Los Angeles Harbor College, 1111 Figueroa Place, Wilmington, CA 90744. (310) 522-8214.

Los Angeles Mission College
Sylmar, California CB code: 4404

2-year public community college, coed. Founded in 1974. **Accreditation:** Regional. **Undergraduate enrollment:** 413 men, 837 women full time; 2,391 men, 3,901 women part time. **Faculty:** 90 total (55 full time), 5 with doctorates or other terminal degrees. **Location:** Suburban campus in large town; 20 miles from Los Angeles. **Calendar:** Semester, limited summer session. Saturday classes. **Microcomputers:** 10 located in libraries. **Additional facts:** College serves nontraditional student body.

DEGREES OFFERED. AA, AS. 231 associate degrees awarded in 1992.

UNDERGRADUATE MAJORS. Accounting, American studies, biological and physical sciences, biology, business administration and management, business and management, business and office, business data processing and related programs, chemistry, clothing and textiles management/production/services, computer and information sciences, dramatic arts, electrical and electronics equipment repair, electromechanical technology, English, environmental design, family/consumer resource management, finance, French, history, home economics, humanities and social sciences, individual and family development, journalism, legal assistant/paralegal, liberal/general studies, mathematics, music, physical sciences, psychology, real estate, secretarial and related programs, social sciences, Spanish, speech, teacher aide.

ACADEMIC PROGRAMS. 2-year transfer program, accelerated program, cooperative education, dual enrollment of high school students, independent study. **Remedial services:** Learning center, remedial instruction, tutoring, bilingual teacher aide. **ROTC:** Air Force, Army. **Placement/credit:** AP, CLEP General and Subject, institutional tests; 15 credit hours maximum for associate degree.

ACADEMIC REQUIREMENTS. Freshmen must earn minimum GPA of 2.0 to continue in good standing. 57% of freshmen return for sophomore year. Students must declare major on application. **Graduation requirements:** 60 hours for associate (18 in major). Most students required to take courses in English, history, humanities, mathematics, biological/physical sciences, social sciences. **Additional information:** Bilingual instruction available.

FRESHMAN ADMISSIONS. Selection criteria: Open admissions. First priority to district residents, second to in-state residents, third to out-of-state applicants.

1992 FRESHMAN CLASS PROFILE. 3,642 men and women enrolled. **Characteristics:** 98% from in state, 100% commute, 50% have minority backgrounds, 1% are foreign students. Average age is 25.

FALL-TERM APPLICATIONS. No fee. Closing date September 5; priority given to applications received by June 3; applicants notified on a rolling basis. Early admission available.

STUDENT LIFE. Activities: Student government, choral groups, drama.

ATHLETICS. Intercollegiate: Baseball M, cross-country, golf M, soccer M.

STUDENT SERVICES. Aptitude testing, career counseling, on-campus day care, personal counseling, placement service for graduates, veterans services, limited learning disability program, services/facilities for handicapped.

ANNUAL EXPENSES. Tuition and fees (1992-93): $120, $3,510 additional for out-of-state students. **Books and supplies:** $612. **Other expenses:** $1,548.

FINANCIAL AID. 5% of continuing students receive some form of aid. 99% of grants, all loans, all jobs based on need. Academic, leadership scholarships available. **Aid applications:** No closing date; priority given to applications received by August 1; applicants notified on a rolling basis beginning on or about August 15; must reply within 2 weeks. **Additional information:** Board of Governors Grant is available to those in receipt of AFDC, SSI, General Relief. If not in receipt of program, may qualify based on income.

ADDRESS/TELEPHONE. Adrienne Foster, Assoc Dean of Student Services, Los Angeles Mission College, 13356 Eldridge Avenue, Sylmar, CA 91342. (818) 364-7658. Fax: (818) 364-7826.

Los Angeles Pierce College
Woodland Hills, California CB code: 4398

2-year public community college, coed. Founded in 1947. **Accreditation:** Regional. **Undergraduate enrollment:** 2,712 men, 2,780 women full time; 5,656 men, 7,166 women part time. **Faculty:** 519 total (288 full time), 51 with doctorates or other terminal degrees. **Location:** Suburban campus in very large city; 27 miles from downtown Los Angeles. **Calendar:** Semester, limited summer session. Saturday and extensive evening/early morning classes. **Microcomputers:** Located in classrooms, computer centers, campus-wide network. **Special facilities:** Braille nature trail, life science museum, nature center, weather station, working farm, art gallery, stadium.

DEGREES OFFERED. AA, AS. 797 associate degrees awarded in 1992. 9% in allied health, 78% multi/interdisciplinary studies.

UNDERGRADUATE MAJORS. Accounting, accounting management, agribusiness, agricultural sciences, animal sciences, architectural technologies, automotive mechanics, automotive technology, business administration and management, business and office, business data processing and related programs, computer and information sciences, computer programming, computer technology, construction, drafting, dramatic arts, electronic technology, equestrian science, fine arts, graphic design, greenhouse and nursery management, horticultural science, horticulture, illustration design, industrial technology, interpreter for the deaf, journalism, legal secretary, liberal/general studies, machine tool operation/machine shop, management science, marketing and distribution, marketing management, music, nursing, office supervision and management, photography, photojournalism, preengineering, quality control technology, real estate, religion, renewable natural resources, secretarial and related programs, tooling technology, turf irrigation and management, veterinarian's assistant, welding technology, word processing.

ACADEMIC PROGRAMS. 2-year transfer program, cooperative education, dual enrollment of high school students, honors program, student-designed major, study abroad, telecourses. **Remedial services:** Learning center, remedial instruction, tutoring. **Placement/credit:** AP, CLEP General, institutional tests; 15 credit hours maximum for associate degree.

ACADEMIC REQUIREMENTS. Freshmen must earn minimum GPA of 2.0 to continue in good standing. **Graduation requirements:** 60 hours for associate. Most students required to take courses in English, history, humanities, mathematics, biological/physical sciences, social sciences.

FRESHMAN ADMISSIONS. Selection criteria: Open admissions. Special admissions to nursing and animal health technology programs.

1992 FRESHMAN CLASS PROFILE. 2,308 men and women enrolled. **Characteristics:** 99% from in state, 100% commute.

FALL-TERM APPLICATIONS. No fee. Closing date August 21; applicants notified on a rolling basis.

STUDENT LIFE. Activities: Student government, magazine, student newspaper, literary magazine, choral groups, concert band, dance, drama, jazz band, marching band, music ensembles, symphony orchestra, International Students Association, Bible Fellowship, Alpha Gamma Sigma Honor Society, Phi Theta Kappa Honor Society, Phi Beta Lambda Business Association, Hillel, Union of African American Students, Muslim Students Association.

ATHLETICS. NJCAA. **Intercollegiate:** Baseball M, basketball W, diving, football M, softball W, swimming, tennis, volleyball, water polo M.

STUDENT SERVICES. Aptitude testing, career counseling, employment service for undergraduates, freshman orientation, health services, on-campus day care, personal counseling, placement service for graduates, special adviser for adult students, veterans counselor, services/facilities for handicapped.

ANNUAL EXPENSES. Tuition and fees (1992-93): $120, $3,690 additional for out-of-state students. **Books and supplies:** $576. **Other expenses:** $1,728.

FINANCIAL AID. 1% of freshmen, 2% of continuing students receive some form of aid. All grants, 98% of loans, all jobs based on need. Academic, state/district residency scholarships available. **Aid applications:** No closing date; priority given to applications received by July 7; applicants notified on a rolling basis beginning on or about August 1.

ADDRESS/TELEPHONE. Shelley Gerstl, Coordinator of Admissions and Records, Los Angeles Pierce College, 6201 Winnetka Avenue, Woodland Hills, CA 91371. (818) 719-6404. Fax: (818) 710-9844.

Los Angeles Southwest College

Los Angeles, California — CB code: 4409

2-year public community college, coed. Founded in 1967. **Accreditation:** Regional. **Undergraduate enrollment:** 6,000 men and women. **Location:** Urban campus in very large city; 15 miles from Civic Center. **Calendar:** Semester.

FRESHMAN ADMISSIONS. Selection criteria: Open admissions.

ANNUAL EXPENSES. Tuition and fees (1992-93): $120, $3,690 additional for out-of-state students. **Books and supplies:** $576. **Other expenses:** $1,728.

ADDRESS/TELEPHONE. Jess Craig, Assistant Dean of Admissions, Los Angeles Southwest College, 1600 West Imperial Highway, Los Angeles, CA 90047. (213) 241-5225.

Los Angeles Trade and Technical College

Los Angeles, California — CB code: 4400

2-year public community, technical college, coed. Founded in 1925. **Accreditation:** Regional. **Undergraduate enrollment:** 2,005 men, 1,576 women full time; 5,492 men, 4,815 women part time. **Faculty:** 550 total (250 full time). **Location:** Urban campus in very large city. **Calendar:** Semester, limited summer session. **Microcomputers:** Located in libraries, classrooms, computer centers.

DEGREES OFFERED. AA, AS. 756 associate degrees awarded in 1992.

UNDERGRADUATE MAJORS. Accounting, air conditioning/heating/refrigeration mechanics, air conditioning/heating/refrigeration technology, architectural technologies, architecture, automotive mechanics, automotive technology, business administration and management, business and management, business and office, business computer/console/peripheral equipment operation, business data processing and related programs, business data programming, carpentry, chemical manufacturing technology, clothing and textiles management/production/services, commercial art, computer and information sciences, computer servicing technology, diesel engine mechanics, drafting, drafting and design technology, electrical and electronics equipment repair, electrical technology, electromechanical technology, electronic technology, fashion design, fashion merchandising, food production/management/services, graphic and printing production, graphic arts technology, hospitality and recreation marketing, hotel/motel and restaurant management, journalism, labor/industrial relations, liberal/general studies, library assistant, machine tool operation/machine shop, marketing and distribution, marketing research, mechanical design technology, mental health/human services, nursing, photographic technology, photography, plastic technology, plumbing/pipefitting/steamfitting, practical nursing, precision metal work, radio/television technology, real estate, secretarial and related programs, small business management and ownership, water and wastewater technology, welding technology.

ACADEMIC PROGRAMS. 2-year transfer program, cooperative education, dual enrollment of high school students, independent study, study abroad. **Remedial services:** Learning center, preadmission summer program, reduced course load, remedial instruction, special counselor, tutoring. **Placement/credit:** AP, institutional tests; 15 credit hours maximum for associate degree.

ACADEMIC REQUIREMENTS. Freshmen must earn minimum GPA of 2.0 to continue in good standing. 23% of freshmen return for sophomore year. Students must declare major on enrollment. **Graduation requirements:** 60 hours for associate. Most students required to take courses in English, mathematics.

FRESHMAN ADMISSIONS. Selection criteria: Open admissions.

1992 FRESHMAN CLASS PROFILE. 4,003 men, 3,855 women enrolled. **Characteristics:** 95% from in state, 100% commute, 89% have minority backgrounds, 1% are foreign students. Average age is 19.

FALL-TERM APPLICATIONS. No fee. No closing date; applicants notified on a rolling basis beginning on or about August 1. Interview required. Portfolio recommended for commercial art applicants. Deferred and early admission available.

STUDENT LIFE. Activities: Student government, student newspaper, dance, political organizations.

ATHLETICS. Intercollegiate: Basketball, cross-country, track and field. **Intramural:** Golf, swimming.

STUDENT SERVICES. Aptitude testing, career counseling, employment service for undergraduates, freshman orientation, on-campus day care, personal counseling, placement service for graduates, veterans counselor, services/facilities for handicapped.

ANNUAL EXPENSES. Tuition and fees (1992-93): $120, $3,510 additional for out-of-state students. **Books and supplies:** $504. **Other expenses:** $1,548.

FINANCIAL AID. 20% of continuing students receive some form of aid. All aid based on need. 2,250 enrolled freshmen were judged to have need, 1,500 were offered aid. **Aid applications:** No closing date; priority given to applications received by July 7; applicants notified on a rolling basis; must reply within 3 weeks.

ADDRESS/TELEPHONE. Dr. Robert K. Richards, Assistant Dean of Admissions and Records, Los Angeles Trade and Technical College, 400 West Washington Boulevard, Los Angeles, CA 90015-4181. (213) 744-9058. Fax: (213) 748-7334.

Los Angeles Valley College

Van Nuys, California — CB code: 4401

2-year public community college, coed. Founded in 1949. **Accreditation:** Regional. **Undergraduate enrollment:** 2,678 men and women full time; 13,693 men and women part time. **Faculty:** 351 total (192 full time). **Location:** Suburban campus in very large city; 15 miles from downtown Los Angeles. **Calendar:** Semester, limited summer session. Extensive evening/early morning classes. **Microcomputers:** 45 located in computer centers. **Special facilities:** Art gallery, planetarium.

DEGREES OFFERED. AA, AS. 586 associate degrees awarded in 1992.

UNDERGRADUATE MAJORS. American studies, art history, biology, business and management, business and office, business computer/console/peripheral equipment operation, business data entry equipment operation, business data processing and related programs, business data programming, chemistry, child development/care/guidance, data processing, earth sciences, economics, electronic technology, engineering and engineering-related technologies, English, ethnic studies, fashion merchandising, fine arts, French, geography, geology, German, graphic design, history, home economics, hospitality and recreation marketing, Italian, journalism, law enforcement and corrections technologies, liberal/general studies, marketing and distribution, mathematics, music, nursing, philosophy, physics, political science and government, psychology, radio/television broadcasting, recreation and community services technologies, respiratory therapy, respiratory therapy technology, secretarial and related programs, sociology, Spanish, word processing.

ACADEMIC PROGRAMS. 2-year transfer program, cooperative education, dual enrollment of high school students, honors program, independent study. **Remedial services:** Learning center, remedial instruction, special counselor, tutoring. **Placement/credit:** AP, CLEP General, institutional tests; 15 credit hours maximum for associate degree.

ACADEMIC REQUIREMENTS. Freshmen must earn minimum GPA of 2.0 to continue in good standing. 60% of freshmen return for sophomore year. **Graduation requirements:** 60 hours for associate. Most students required to take courses in English, history, humanities, mathematics, biological/physical sciences, social sciences.

FRESHMAN ADMISSIONS. Selection criteria: Open admissions. Registered nursing program has competitive admission based on points accumulated for prerequisite courses, grades, and placement test scores.

1992 FRESHMAN CLASS PROFILE. 3,107 men and women enrolled. **Characteristics:** 95% from in state, 100% commute, 40% have minority backgrounds, 1% are foreign students. Average age is 28.

FALL-TERM APPLICATIONS. No fee. No closing date; applicants notified on a rolling basis beginning on or about April 15. Early admission available.

STUDENT LIFE. Activities: Student government, film, magazine, radio, student newspaper, choral groups, concert band, dance, drama, jazz band, marching band, musical theater, pep band, symphony orchestra.

ATHLETICS. Intercollegiate: Baseball M, basketball, cross-country, diving, football M, softball M, swimming, track and field, water polo M.

STUDENT SERVICES. Aptitude testing, career counseling, employment service for undergraduates, freshman orientation, health services, on-campus day care, personal counseling, placement service for graduates, veterans counselor, special counseling for handicapped, services/facilities for handicapped.

ANNUAL EXPENSES. Tuition and fees (1992-93): $120, $3,540 additional for out-of-state students. **Books and supplies:** $450. **Other expenses:** $1,500.

FINANCIAL AID. 5% of freshmen, 15% of continuing students receive some form of aid. All grants, 88% of loans, all jobs based on need. **Aid applications:** No closing date; priority given to applications received by June 12; applicants notified on a rolling basis.

ADDRESS/TELEPHONE. Marilyn Moy, Assistant Dean of Admissions, Los Angeles Valley College, 5800 Fulton Avenue, Van Nuys, CA 91401-4096. (818) 781-1200. Fax: (818) 785-4672.

Los Medanos College
Pittsburg, California CB code: 4396

2-year public community college, coed. Founded in 1973. **Accreditation:** Regional. **Undergraduate enrollment:** 669 men, 756 women full time; 2,418 men, 3,770 women part time. **Faculty:** 227 total (99 full time). **Location:** Suburban campus in small city; 45 miles from San Franciso. **Calendar:** Semester. Saturday and extensive evening/early morning classes. **Microcomputers:** 150 located in classrooms, computer centers.

DEGREES OFFERED. AA, AS. 178 associate degrees awarded in 1992. 7% in business/office and marketing/distribution, 16% health sciences, 51% multi/interdisciplinary studies, 7% trade and industry.

UNDERGRADUATE MAJORS. Accounting, air conditioning/heating/refrigeration mechanics, anthropology, automotive mechanics, behavioral sciences, biological and physical sciences, biology, business and management, business and office, chemistry, child development/care/guidance, computer and information sciences, drafting and design technology, fine arts, fire control and safety technology, graphic arts technology, journalism, liberal/general studies, mathematics, music, nursing, office supervision and management, psychology, real estate, secretarial and related programs, small business management and ownership, social sciences, sociology, transportation and travel marketing, word processing.

ACADEMIC PROGRAMS. Cooperative education, independent study, study abroad, cross-registration. **Remedial services:** Remedial instruction, tutoring. **Placement/credit:** Institutional tests; 20 credit hours maximum for associate degree.

ACADEMIC REQUIREMENTS. Freshmen must earn minimum GPA of 2.0 to continue in good standing. Students must declare major on application. **Graduation requirements:** 60 hours for associate (18 in major). Most students required to take courses in arts/fine arts, computer science, English, history, humanities, mathematics, philosophy/religion, biological/physical sciences, social sciences.

FRESHMAN ADMISSIONS. Selection criteria: Open admissions.

1992 FRESHMAN CLASS PROFILE. 2,316 men and women enrolled. **Characteristics:** 98% from in state, 100% commute.

FALL-TERM APPLICATIONS. No fee. No closing date; applicants notified on a rolling basis.

STUDENT LIFE. Activities: Student government, student newspaper, choral groups, concert band, drama, jazz band, music ensembles.

ATHLETICS. Intercollegiate: Baseball M, basketball, football M, soccer M, softball W, volleyball W. **Intramural:** Basketball, softball, tennis.

STUDENT SERVICES. Career counseling, employment service for undergraduates, freshman orientation, on-campus day care, personal counseling, placement service for graduates, services/facilities for handicapped.

ANNUAL EXPENSES. Tuition and fees (projected): $152, $3,150 additional for out-of-state students. **Books and supplies:** $520. **Other expenses:** $2,000.

FINANCIAL AID. 13% of freshmen, 17% of continuing students receive some form of aid. 98% of grants, 26% of jobs based on need. Academic scholarships available. **Aid applications:** Closing date August 1; priority given to applications received by March 2; applicants notified on or about August 1; must reply by September 1.

ADDRESS/TELEPHONE. Gail Newman, Director, Los Medanos College, 2700 East Leland Road, Pittsburg, CA 94565. (510) 439-2188.

Louise Salinger Academy of Fashion
San Francisco, California CB code: 4421

4-year private college of fashion, coed. Founded in 1939. **Undergraduate enrollment:** 98 men and women. **Faculty:** 16 total (11 full time). **Location:** Urban campus in very large city. **Calendar:** Quarter. **Microcomputers:** 2 located in classrooms. **Special facilities:** Bound magazine collection from 1936, computer-aided fashion design and illustration system.

DEGREES OFFERED. AA, BA, BFA. 4 associate degrees awarded in 1992. 100% in home economics. 10 bachelor's degrees awarded. 100% in home economics.

UNDERGRADUATE MAJORS. Associate: Fashion design, fashion merchandising. **Bachelor's:** Fashion design, fashion merchandising.

ACADEMIC PROGRAMS. Double major, dual enrollment of high school students, internships. **Remedial services:** Tutoring.

ACADEMIC REQUIREMENTS. Freshmen must earn minimum GPA of 2.0 to continue in good standing. Students must declare major on enrollment. **Graduation requirements:** 120 hours for associate, 180 hours for bachelor's. Most students required to take courses in arts/fine arts, English, humanities, mathematics.

FRESHMAN ADMISSIONS. Selection criteria: Entrance evaluation test, recommendations, essay, portfolio. Recommended units include English 1 and mathematics 1. One art and 1 sewing class recommended. **Test requirements:** Institutional entrance evaluation test required.

1992 FRESHMAN CLASS PROFILE. 21 men and women enrolled. **Characteristics:** 100% commute. Average age is 22.

FALL-TERM APPLICATIONS. $150 fee. No closing date; applicants notified on a rolling basis. Portfolio required. Essay required. Interview recommended.

STUDENT SERVICES. Career counseling, employment service for undergraduates, freshman orientation, placement service for graduates, services/facilities for handicapped.

ANNUAL EXPENSES. Tuition and fees (1992-93): $12,180. **Books and supplies:** $1,000.

FINANCIAL AID. 60% of freshmen, 70% of continuing students receive some form of aid. **Aid applications:** No closing date; applicants notified on a rolling basis.

ADDRESS/TELEPHONE. Joe Herschelle, Director of Admissions, Louise Salinger Academy of Fashion, 101 Jessie Street, San Francisco, CA 94105. (415) 974-6666.

Loyola Marymount University
Los Angeles, California CB code: 4403

Admissions: 63% of applicants accepted
Based on:
••• School record
•• Activities, essay, religious affiliation/commitment, test scores
• Interview, recommendations, special talents
Completion: 94% of freshmen end year in good standing
66% graduate

4-year private university, coed, affiliated with Roman Catholic Church. Founded in 1911. **Accreditation:** Regional. **Undergraduate enrollment:** 1,625 men, 1,984 women full time; 143 men, 204 women part time. **Graduate enrollment:** 903 men, 857 women full time; 358 men, 325 women part time. **Faculty:** 496 total (301 full time), 265 with doctorates or other terminal degrees. **Location:** Suburban campus in very large city; 15 miles from downtown. **Calendar:** Semester, limited summer session. **Microcomputers:** 200 located in libraries, classrooms, computer centers, campus-wide network. **Special facilities:** Fine arts complex including recital hall, recording arts facilities, art gallery, Baja, California marine station.

DEGREES OFFERED. BA, BS, MA, MS, MBA, MEd, JD. 930 bachelor's degrees awarded in 1992. 35% in business and management, 12% communications, 5% engineering, 10% letters/literature, 5% multi/interdisciplinary studies, 9% psychology, 11% social sciences. Graduate degrees offered in 23 major fields of study.

UNDERGRADUATE MAJORS. Accounting, Afro-American (black) studies, art history, biochemistry, biology, business administration and management, chemistry, civil engineering, classics, communications, computer and information sciences, dance, dramatic arts, economics, electrical/electronics/communications engineering, English, English literature, environmental science, European studies, French, geochemistry, German, Greek (classical), history, humanities, Latin, liberal/general studies, management information systems, mathematics, mechanical engineering, Mexican American studies, music, philosophy, physics, political science and government, psychology, sociology, Spanish, speech, studio art, theological studies, urban studies.

ACADEMIC PROGRAMS. Double major, dual enrollment of high school students, honors program, independent study, internships, student-designed major, study abroad, teacher preparation, Washington semester, cross-registration, Encore Program for mature individuals 30 or older. **Remedial services:** Learning center, reduced course load, tutoring. **ROTC:** Air Force. **Placement/credit:** AP, institutional tests.

ACADEMIC REQUIREMENTS. Freshmen must earn minimum GPA of 2.0 to continue in good standing. 87% of freshmen return for sophomore year. Students must declare major by end of second year. **Graduation requirements:** 120 hours for bachelor's (27 in major). Most students required

to take courses in arts/fine arts, English, history, mathematics, philosophy/religion, biological/physical sciences, social sciences.

FRESHMAN ADMISSIONS. Selection criteria: High school GPA, curriculum, test scores, recommendations, activities. Consideration to children of alumni. **High school preparation:** 16 units required. Required units include English 4, foreign language 3, mathematics 3, social science 3 and science 2. 4 units of mathematics required of engineering, mathematics, and science majors; physics and chemistry required of engineering and science majors; biology and chemistry required (physics recommended) of biology majors. **Test requirements:** SAT or ACT; score report by February 1.

1992 FRESHMAN CLASS PROFILE. 3,737 men and women applied, 2,372 accepted; 304 men enrolled, 370 women enrolled. 70% had high school GPA of 3.0 or higher, 30% between 2.0 and 2.99. **Academic background:** Mid 50% of enrolled freshmen had SAT-V between 420-520, SAT-M between 480-600. 97% submitted SAT scores. **Characteristics:** 78% from in state, 86% live in college housing, 47% have minority backgrounds, 2% are foreign students. Average age is 18.

FALL-TERM APPLICATIONS. $35 fee, may be waived for applicants with need. No closing date; priority given to applications received by February 1; applicants notified on a rolling basis beginning on or about January 1; must reply by May 1 or within 2 weeks if notified thereafter. Essay required. Interview recommended for early admission, handicapped, academically weak applicants. CRDA. Deferred and early admission available. EDP-F. Applicants who desire housing or financial aid should apply by Feb.1.

STUDENT LIFE. Housing: Dormitories (men, women, coed); apartment housing available. Housing guaranteed on-campus for incoming freshmen submitting commitment deposits by May 1. **Activities:** Student government, film, radio, student newspaper, yearbook, choral groups, dance, drama, musical theater, fraternities, sororities, wide variety of religious, political, ethnic, social service organizations.

ATHLETICS. NCAA. **Intercollegiate:** Baseball M, basketball, cross-country, golf M, lacrosse M, rowing (crew), rugby M, soccer, softball W, swimming W, tennis, volleyball, water polo M. **Intramural:** Badminton, basketball, football, handball, lacrosse M, racquetball, sailing, soccer, softball, swimming, tennis, volleyball.

STUDENT SERVICES. Aptitude testing, career counseling, employment service for undergraduates, freshman orientation, health services, personal counseling, placement service for graduates, special adviser for adult students, veterans counselor, services/facilities for handicapped.

ANNUAL EXPENSES. Tuition and fees: $13,060. **Room and board:** $6,093. **Books and supplies:** $530. **Other expenses:** $1,350.

FINANCIAL AID. 63% of freshmen, 58% of continuing students receive some form of aid. 84% of grants, 73% of loans, 72% of jobs based on need. Academic, music/drama, athletic, leadership, alumni affiliation scholarships available. **Aid applications:** No closing date; priority given to applications received by February 15; applicants notified on a rolling basis beginning on or about April 10; must reply within 4 weeks.

ADDRESS/TELEPHONE. Matthew Fissinger, Director of Admissions, Loyola Marymount University, Loyola Boulevard at West 80th Street, Los Angeles, CA 90045-2699. (310) 338-2750.

Marymount College
Rancho Palos Verdes, California — CB code: 4515

Admissions: 94% of applicants accepted
Based on:
•• Interview, school record
• Activities, essay, recommendations, special talents, test scores
Completion: 85% of freshmen end year in good standing
60% graduate, 95% of these enter 4-year programs

2-year private junior, liberal arts college, coed, affiliated with Roman Catholic Church. Founded in 1933. **Accreditation:** Regional. **Undergraduate enrollment:** 336 men, 378 women full time; 89 men, 271 women part time. **Faculty:** 91 total (46 full time), 27 with doctorates or other terminal degrees. **Location:** Suburban campus in large town; 30 miles from Los Angeles. **Calendar:** Semester, limited summer session. Saturday classes. **Microcomputers:** 30 located in libraries, computer centers. **Additional facts:** Only 2-year private college in the 5 Pacific states specializing in the liberal arts and transfer to 4-year institutions.

DEGREES OFFERED. AA. 220 associate degrees awarded in 1992.

UNDERGRADUATE MAJORS. Accounting, behavioral sciences, biology, business and management, communications, early childhood education, economics, English, fashion merchandising, fine arts, history, humanities and social sciences, interior design, liberal/general studies, mathematics, music, philosophy, physical sciences, predentistry, prelaw, premedicine, prepharmacy, preveterinary, psychology, religion, social sciences, sociology, visual and performing arts.

ACADEMIC PROGRAMS. 2-year transfer program, dual enrollment of high school students, honors program, independent study, internships, study abroad, weekend college. **Remedial services:** Learning center, reduced course load, remedial instruction, special counselor, tutoring. **ROTC:** Air Force. **Placement/credit:** AP, CLEP General and Subject, institutional tests; 12 credit hours maximum for associate degree.

ACADEMIC REQUIREMENTS. Freshmen must earn minimum GPA of 2.0 to continue in good standing. 60% of freshmen return for sophomore year. **Graduation requirements:** 60 hours for associate. Most students required to take courses in arts/fine arts, English, history, mathematics, philosophy/religion, biological/physical sciences, social sciences.

FRESHMAN ADMISSIONS. Selection criteria: High school record, quality of academic preparation, and student's personal statement all considered.

1992 FRESHMAN CLASS PROFILE. 350 men applied, 322 accepted, 158 enrolled; 548 women applied, 521 accepted, 218 enrolled. 14% had high school GPA of 3.0 or higher, 72% between 2.0 and 2.99. **Academic background:** Mid 50% of enrolled freshmen had SAT-V between 330-450, SAT-M between 350-490. 50% submitted SAT scores. **Characteristics:** 60% from in state, 70% live in college housing, 24% have minority backgrounds, 22% are foreign students. Average age is 18.

FALL-TERM APPLICATIONS. $25 fee, may be waived for applicants with need. Closing date August 15; applicants notified on a rolling basis; must reply within 3 weeks. Interview recommended for borderline applicants. Essay recommended. Deferred and early admission available. SAT or ACT recommended for placement and counseling.

STUDENT LIFE. Housing: Apartment housing available. **Activities:** Student government, film, magazine, student newspaper, television, yearbook, choral groups, dance, drama, jazz band, music ensembles, musical theater, campus ministry, MOVE (Marymount Opportunities for Volunteer Experience), global awareness program.

ATHLETICS. Intercollegiate: Soccer, tennis. **Intramural:** Baseball, basketball, diving, skiing, soccer, softball, swimming, table tennis, tennis, volleyball, water polo.

STUDENT SERVICES. Aptitude testing, career counseling, employment service for undergraduates, freshman orientation, health services, personal counseling, special adviser for adult students, services/facilities for handicapped.

ANNUAL EXPENSES. Tuition and fees: $11,714. **Room and board:** $5,940. **Books and supplies:** $612. **Other expenses:** $1,350.

FINANCIAL AID. 40% of freshmen, 40% of continuing students receive some form of aid. 93% of grants, 78% of loans, 70% of jobs based on need. 227 enrolled freshmen were judged to have need, 214 were offered aid. Academic scholarships available. **Aid applications:** Closing date March 2; applicants notified on or about April 30; must reply within 2 weeks.

ADDRESS/TELEPHONE. Kenneth B. Mayer, Director of Admissions and School Relations, Marymount College, 30800 Palos Verdes Drive East, Rancho Palos Verdes, CA 90274-6299. (310) 377-5501. Fax: (310) 377-6223.

Master's College
Santa Clarita, California — CB code: 4411

Admissions: 86% of applicants accepted
Based on:
••• Essay, recommendations, religious affiliation/commitment, school record, test scores
•• Interview
• Activities, special talents
Completion: 80% of freshmen end year in good standing
32% graduate, 15% of these enter graduate study

4-year private liberal arts college, coed, nondenominational. Founded in 1927. **Accreditation:** Regional. **Undergraduate enrollment:** 367 men, 386 women full time; 34 men, 32 women part time. **Faculty:** 85 total (44 full time), 23 with doctorates or other terminal degrees. **Location:** Suburban campus in small city; 35 miles from downtown Los Angeles. **Calendar:** Semester, limited summer session. Extensive evening/early morning classes. **Microcomputers:** 20 located in libraries, computer centers. **Special facilities:** State-of-the-art mathematics computer laboratory, fully-equipped home economics center, Institute of Holy Land Studies.

DEGREES OFFERED. BA, BS. 176 bachelor's degrees awarded in 1992. 9% in business and management, 6% communications, 24% teacher education, 6% letters/literature, 27% philosophy, religion, theology, 5% physical sciences, 11% psychology, 10% social sciences.

UNDERGRADUATE MAJORS. Bible studies, biological and physical sciences, biology, business administration and management, communications, education, elementary education, English, history, home economics, liberal/general studies, mathematics, music, physical education, physical sciences, political science and government, psychology, religion, secondary education, special education, sports ministries.

ACADEMIC PROGRAMS. Cooperative education, double major, independent study, internships, study abroad, teacher preparation, Washington semester, cross-registration. **Remedial services:** Learning center, reduced course load, remedial instruction, tutoring. **Placement/credit:** AP, CLEP General; 30 credit hours maximum for bachelor's degree.

ACADEMIC REQUIREMENTS. Freshmen must earn minimum GPA of 2.0 to continue in good standing. 50% of freshmen return for sophomore

year. Students must declare major by end of second year. **Graduation requirements:** 122 hours for bachelor's (45 in major). Most students required to take courses in arts/fine arts, English, foreign languages, history, humanities, mathematics, philosophy/religion, biological/physical sciences, social sciences. **Postgraduate studies:** 1% enter law school, 2% enter MBA programs, 12% enter other graduate study. **Additional information:** Students who attend 4 years receive minor in Biblical Studies upon graduation.

FRESHMAN ADMISSIONS. Selection criteria: School achievement record, references, and religious commitment most important. **High school preparation:** 15 units required. Required units include English 3, foreign language 2, mathematics 3, social science 2 and science 2. **Test requirements:** SAT or ACT; score report by August 15. **Additional information:** Applications from all individuals who have placed their faith in Jesus Christ as Lord and Savior welcome.

1992 FRESHMAN CLASS PROFILE. 73% had high school GPA of 3.0 or higher, 26% between 2.0 and 2.99. 27% were in top tenth and 53% were in top quarter of graduating class. **Characteristics:** 67% from in state, 90% live in college housing, 10% have minority backgrounds, 4% are foreign students. Average age is 18.

FALL-TERM APPLICATIONS. $25 fee. Closing date August 15; priority given to applications received by June 1; applicants notified on a rolling basis beginning on or about January 1; must reply by June 15 or within 2 weeks if notified thereafter. Interview required for music applicants. Audition required for music applicants. Essay required. Portfolio recommended. Deferred admission available.

STUDENT LIFE. Housing: Dormitories (men, women); apartment housing available. **Activities:** Student government, radio, choral groups, concert band, drama, music ensembles, pep band. **Additional information:** Emphasis on Godly lifestyle in and out of classroom. Religious observance required.

ATHLETICS. NAIA. **Intercollegiate:** Baseball M, basketball, cross-country, soccer, track and field, volleyball W. **Intramural:** Basketball, softball, volleyball.

STUDENT SERVICES. Aptitude testing, career counseling, employment service for undergraduates, freshman orientation, health services, personal counseling, placement service for graduates, veterans counselor, services/facilities for handicapped.

ANNUAL EXPENSES. Tuition and fees: $8,394. **Room and board:** $4,472. **Books and supplies:** $612. **Other expenses:** $1,350.

FINANCIAL AID. 90% of freshmen, 75% of continuing students receive some form of aid. 47% of grants, 85% of loans, 40% of jobs based on need. 162 enrolled freshmen were judged to have need, 155 were offered aid. Academic, music/drama, athletic, leadership, alumni affiliation, minority scholarships available. **Aid applications:** Closing date July 31; priority given to applications received by March 31; applicants notified on a rolling basis beginning on or about April 15; must reply within 2 weeks.

ADDRESS/TELEPHONE. Donald Gilmore, Director of Admissions, Master's College, PO Box 878, Santa Clarita, CA 91322-0878. (805) 259-3540 ext. 347. (800)568-6248. Fax: (805) 254-1998.

Mendocino College
Ukiah, California — CB code: 4517

2-year public community college, coed. Founded in 1973. **Accreditation:** Regional. **Undergraduate enrollment:** 270 men, 560 women full time; 1,170 men, 2,240 women part time. **Faculty:** 327 total (57 full time), 21 with doctorates or other terminal degrees. **Location:** Rural campus in large town; 60 miles from Santa Rosa, 110 miles from San Francisco. **Calendar:** Semester, limited summer session. Saturday and extensive evening/early morning classes. **Microcomputers:** 40 located in libraries, classrooms, computer centers. **Special facilities:** Fine arts facility with exhibition arena.

DEGREES OFFERED. AA, AS. 134 associate degrees awarded in 1992. 16% in business and management, 6% home economics, 60% multi/interdisciplinary studies.

UNDERGRADUATE MAJORS. Accounting, art history, automotive mechanics, biology, business administration and management, business and management, computer and information sciences, criminal justice studies, dramatic arts, electrical and electronics equipment repair, English, French, health sciences, humanities and social sciences, liberal/general studies, mathematics, music, physical sciences, plant sciences, precision metal work, psychology, real estate, renewable natural resources, secretarial and related programs, small business management and ownership, social sciences, Spanish, speech, sports/physical education.

ACADEMIC PROGRAMS. 2-year transfer program, accelerated program, cooperative education, double major, dual enrollment of high school students, independent study, student-designed major, telecourses. **Remedial services:** Learning center, remedial instruction, special counselor, tutoring. **Placement/credit:** Institutional tests; 12 credit hours maximum for associate degree.

ACADEMIC REQUIREMENTS. Freshmen must earn minimum GPA of 2.0 to continue in good standing. 60% of freshmen return for sophomore year. Students must declare major by end of first year. **Graduation requirements:** 60 hours for associate (18 in major). Most students required to take courses in arts/fine arts, English, history, humanities, mathematics, biological/physical sciences, social sciences.

FRESHMAN ADMISSIONS. Selection criteria: Open admissions.

1992 FRESHMAN CLASS PROFILE. 1,013 men and women enrolled. **Characteristics:** 99% from in state, 100% commute, 13% have minority backgrounds, 1% are foreign students. Average age is 25.

FALL-TERM APPLICATIONS. No fee. No closing date; priority given to applications received by July 1; applicants notified on a rolling basis beginning on or about July 1. Early admission available. SAT or ACT recommended for counseling and placement.

STUDENT LIFE. Activities: Student government, student newspaper, choral groups, concert band, dance, drama, jazz band, music ensembles, musical theater, symphony orchestra.

ATHLETICS. NJCAA. **Intercollegiate:** Baseball M, basketball, football M, softball W, volleyball W. **Intramural:** Basketball, softball, volleyball.

STUDENT SERVICES. Aptitude testing, career counseling, employment service for undergraduates, freshman orientation, on-campus day care, personal counseling, placement service for graduates, veterans counselor, services/facilities for handicapped.

ANNUAL EXPENSES. Tuition and fees (projected): $300, $3,096 additional for out-of-district students, $3,096 additional for out-of-state students. **Books and supplies:** $612. **Other expenses:** $1,548.

FINANCIAL AID. 8% of continuing students receive some form of aid. 98% of grants, all loans, 48% of jobs based on need. 184 enrolled freshmen were judged to have need, 83 were offered aid. **Aid applications:** Closing date November 15; priority given to applications received by May 31; applicants notified on a rolling basis beginning on or about July 1; must reply within 2 weeks.

ADDRESS/TELEPHONE. Kristie A. Taylor, Registrar, Mendocino College, PO Box 3000, 1000 Hensley Creek, Ukiah, CA 95482. (707) 468-3100. Fax: (707) 468-3120.

Menlo College
Atherton, California — CB code: 4483

4-year private business, liberal arts college, coed. Founded in 1927. **Accreditation:** Regional. **Undergraduate enrollment:** 371 men, 159 women full time. **Faculty:** 75 total (41 full time), 21 with doctorates or other terminal degrees. **Location:** Suburban campus in small town; 30 miles from San Francisco. **Calendar:** Semester, limited summer session. **Microcomputers:** 72 located in classrooms, computer centers. **Special facilities:** Psychology laboratory. **Additional facts:** College devoted to preparing students for leadership in modern organizations.

DEGREES OFFERED. AA, BA, BS. 87 bachelor's degrees awarded. 49% in business and management, 30% communications, 10% computer sciences, 5% multi/interdisciplinary studies.

UNDERGRADUATE MAJORS. Associate: Liberal/general studies. **Bachelor's:** Biotechnology, business administration and management, communications, computer and information sciences, humanities and social sciences, information sciences and systems, psychology.

ACADEMIC PROGRAMS. Accelerated program, double major, dual enrollment of high school students, independent study, internships, study abroad. **Remedial services:** Learning center, reduced course load, special counselor, tutoring, course for students with specific language disabilities. **Placement/credit:** AP, institutional tests; 30 credit hours maximum for bachelor's degree.

ACADEMIC REQUIREMENTS. Freshmen must earn minimum GPA of 2.0 to continue in good standing. 65% of freshmen return for sophomore year. Students must declare major by end of second year. **Graduation requirements:** 62 hours for associate, 124 hours for bachelor's. Most students required to take courses in arts/fine arts, computer science, English, history, humanities, mathematics, philosophy/religion, biological/physical sciences, social sciences.

FRESHMAN ADMISSIONS. Selection criteria: High school record (minimum 2.0 GPA), test scores, recommendations, essay, depth of achievement in cocurricular activities. **High school preparation:** 12 units required; 24 recommended. Recommended units include English 4, foreign language 2, mathematics 4, social science 3 and science 2. **Test requirements:** SAT or ACT; score report by September 6.

1992 FRESHMAN CLASS PROFILE. 137 men and women enrolled. 19% had high school GPA of 3.0 or higher, 65% between 2.0 and 2.99. **Academic background:** Mid 50% of enrolled freshmen had SAT-V between 320-440, SAT-M between 370-510. 81% submitted SAT scores. **Characteristics:** 61% from in state, 80% live in college housing, 12% are foreign students. Average age is 18.

FALL-TERM APPLICATIONS. $40 fee, may be waived for applicants with need. No closing date; applicants notified on a rolling basis beginning on or about December 1; must reply by May 1 or within 2 weeks if notified thereafter. Essay required. Interview recommended. CRDA. Deferred and early admission available. EDP-F.

STUDENT LIFE. Housing: Dormitories (men, women, coed); apartment housing available. All students must reside on campus unless living at home, 21 years old or seniors. **Activities:** Student government, radio, student newspaper, television, yearbook, drama, fraternities, sororities, service organizations, international students club.

ATHLETICS. NCAA. **Intercollegiate:** Baseball M, basketball M, cross-country, football M, golf M, soccer M, softball W, tennis, track and field, volleyball. **Intramural:** Softball.

STUDENT SERVICES. Aptitude testing, career counseling, employment service for undergraduates, freshman orientation, health services, personal counseling, placement service for graduates, services/facilities for handicapped.

ANNUAL EXPENSES. Tuition and fees: $14,175. **Room and board:** $6,200. **Books and supplies:** $600. **Other expenses:** $1,625.

FINANCIAL AID. 53% of freshmen, 40% of continuing students receive some form of aid. All grants, 91% of loans, 17% of jobs based on need. 73 enrolled freshmen were judged to have need, all were offered aid. Academic, leadership scholarships available. **Aid applications:** No closing date; priority given to applications received by March 2; applicants notified on a rolling basis beginning on or about March 15; must reply within 2 weeks.

ADDRESS/TELEPHONE. James Whitaker, Dean Enrollment Management, Menlo College, 1000 El Camino Real, Atherton, CA 94027-4301. (415) 688-3753. (800) 55-MENLO. Fax: (415) 324-2347.

Merced College
Merced, California — CB code: 4500

2-year public community college, coed. Founded in 1962. **Accreditation:** Regional. **Undergraduate enrollment:** 7,803 men and women. **Faculty:** 425 total (125 full time), 9 with doctorates or other terminal degrees. **Location:** Rural campus in large town; 50 miles from Fresno. **Calendar:** Semester, limited summer session. **Microcomputers:** 80 located in classrooms, computer centers. **Additional facts:** Off-campus centers at Los Banos and Castle Air Force Base.

DEGREES OFFERED. AA, AS. 450 associate degrees awarded in 1992. 8% in agriculture, 15% business and management, 8% business/office and marketing/distribution, 34% education, 18% allied health.

UNDERGRADUATE MAJORS. Accounting, aeronautical technology, aerospace/aeronautical/astronautical engineering, agribusiness, agricultural mechanics, agricultural sciences, agronomy, aircraft mechanics, animal sciences, anthropology, archeology, automotive mechanics, automotive technology, biology, business administration and management, business and management, business and office, business data processing and related programs, business data programming, chemistry, clothing and textiles management/production/services, commercial art, communications, computer and information sciences, computer mathematics, computer programming, dental assistant, dental laboratory technology, diesel engine mechanics, drafting, drafting and design technology, dramatic arts, early childhood education, earth sciences, economics, education, electrical/electronics/communications engineering, engineering, engineering and engineering-related technologies, English, equestrian science, finance, fine arts, fire control and safety technology, food production/management/services, French, geography, German, graphic arts technology, history, home economics, horticulture, individual and family development, industrial equipment maintenance and repair, industrial technology, information sciences and systems, insurance and risk management, journalism, law enforcement and corrections technologies, legal secretary, liberal/general studies, library assistant, library science, marketing and distribution, marketing management, mathematics, mechanical engineering, medical assistant, medical secretary, music, nursing, office supervision and management, ornamental horticulture, personal services, philosophy, photography, physical sciences, physics, political science and government, practical nursing, precision metal work, psychology, radiograph medical technology, real estate, recreation and community services technologies, science technologies, secretarial and related programs, small business management and ownership, social sciences, social work, sociology, soil sciences, Spanish, speech, visual and performing arts, welding technology, woodworking.

ACADEMIC PROGRAMS. 2-year transfer program, dual enrollment of high school students, honors program, internships, study abroad. **Remedial services:** Learning center, preadmission summer program, remedial instruction, special counselor, tutoring. **Placement/credit:** AP, CLEP General, institutional tests; 12 credit hours maximum for associate degree.

ACADEMIC REQUIREMENTS. Freshmen must earn minimum GPA of 2.0 to continue in good standing. 60% of freshmen return for sophomore year. Students must declare major on enrollment. **Graduation requirements:** 60 hours for associate (18 in major). Most students required to take courses in English, history, biological/physical sciences.

FRESHMAN ADMISSIONS. Selection criteria: Open admissions. **Additional information:** Outreach program to local high school offers institutional placement tests at high school sites.

1992 FRESHMAN CLASS PROFILE. 2,101 men and women enrolled. **Characteristics:** 92% from in state, 100% commute, 43% have minority backgrounds, 1% are foreign students. Average age is 25.

FALL-TERM APPLICATIONS. No fee. No closing date; applicants notified on a rolling basis. Early admission available.

STUDENT LIFE. Activities: Student government, student newspaper, choral groups, concert band, dance, drama, jazz band, music ensembles, musical theater, pep band, symphony orchestra, Black Student Union, Movimiento Estudiantil Chicano de Aztlan, Intervarsity Christian group, Rotaract, Alpha Gamma Sigma.

ATHLETICS. NJCAA. **Intercollegiate:** Baseball, basketball, cross-country, diving, football M, golf, soccer M, softball W, swimming, tennis, track and field, volleyball W, water polo M.

STUDENT SERVICES. Aptitude testing, career counseling, employment service for undergraduates, freshman orientation, health services, on-campus day care, personal counseling, placement service for graduates, veterans counselor, re-entry center, services/facilities for handicapped.

ANNUAL EXPENSES. Tuition and fees (projected): $240, $3,120 additional for out-of-state students. **Books and supplies:** $612. **Other expenses:** $1,548.

FINANCIAL AID. 35% of freshmen, 40% of continuing students receive some form of aid. 96% of grants, all loans, all jobs based on need. Academic, state/district residency, leadership scholarships available. **Aid applications:** No closing date; priority given to applications received by June 1; applicants notified on a rolling basis beginning on or about January 2; must reply within 3 weeks.

ADDRESS/TELEPHONE. Stan Mattoon, Dean of Admissions and Records, Merced College, 3600 M Street, Merced, CA 95348-2898. (209) 384-6195. Fax: (209) 384-6339.

Merritt College
Oakland, California — CB code: 4502

2-year public community college, coed. Founded in 1953. **Accreditation:** Regional. **Undergraduate enrollment:** 6,700 men and women. **Faculty:** 239 total (109 full time), 15 with doctorates or other terminal degrees. **Location:** Urban campus in large city; 15 miles from San Francisco. **Calendar:** Semester, extensive summer session. Saturday and extensive evening/early morning classes. **Microcomputers:** 170 located in classrooms, computer centers. **Special facilities:** Merrit Anthropology Museum, landscape horticulture complex.

DEGREES OFFERED. AA, AS. 243 associate degrees awarded in 1992.

UNDERGRADUATE MAJORS. Afro-American (black) studies, allied health, Asian studies, behavioral sciences, biological and physical sciences, biology, business and management, child development/care/guidance, community services, computer and information sciences, data processing, economics, education, electronic technology, English, family and community services, health sciences, Hispanic American studies, humanities and social sciences, labor/industrial relations, law enforcement and corrections technologies, legal assistant/paralegal, liberal/general studies, mathematics, nursing, ornamental horticulture, practical nursing, radiograph medical technology, real estate, recreation and community services technologies, social sciences, teacher aide, textiles and clothing, trade and industrial supervision and management.

ACADEMIC PROGRAMS. Cooperative education, dual enrollment of high school students, honors program, independent study, cross-registration. **Remedial services:** Learning center, preadmission summer program, reduced course load, remedial instruction, special counselor, tutoring. **Placement/credit:** Institutional tests; 15 credit hours maximum for associate degree.

ACADEMIC REQUIREMENTS. Freshmen must earn minimum GPA of 2.0 to continue in good standing. **Graduation requirements:** 60 hours for associate (18 in major). Most students required to take courses in computer science, English, humanities, mathematics, biological/physical sciences, social sciences.

FRESHMAN ADMISSIONS. Selection criteria: Open admissions. **Test requirements:** SAT or ACT for placement. ACH required.

1992 FRESHMAN CLASS PROFILE. 1,297 men and women enrolled. **Characteristics:** 95% from in state, 100% commute, 60% have minority backgrounds, 5% are foreign students. Average age is 21.

FALL-TERM APPLICATIONS. No fee. No closing date; applicants notified on a rolling basis. Deferred and early admission available.

STUDENT LIFE. Activities: Student government, student newspaper, choral groups, dance, sororities, Merritt Christian Fellowship, LaRaza Student Union, Native American Association, Black Student Union, Asian Student Union, Ecology Action Club, Disabled Students Coalition.

ATHLETICS. Intercollegiate: Basketball, cross-country, track and field. **Intramural:** Badminton, golf, tennis, volleyball.

STUDENT SERVICES. Aptitude testing, career counseling, employment service for undergraduates, freshman orientation, health services, on-campus day care, personal counseling, placement service for graduates, special adviser for adult students, veterans counselor, services/facilities for handicapped.

ANNUAL EXPENSES. Tuition and fees (1992-93): $120, $3,510 additional for out-of-state students. **Books and supplies:** $450. **Other expenses:** $2,000.

FINANCIAL AID. 28% of freshmen, 33% of continuing students receive some form of aid. All grants, all jobs based on need. **Aid applications:** No closing date; priority given to applications received by April 1; applicants notified on a rolling basis beginning on or about June 1; must reply within 3 weeks.

ADDRESS/TELEPHONE. Howard Perdue, Dean of Admissions and Records, Merritt College, 12500 Campus Drive, Oakland, CA 94619. (510) 436-2487. Fax: (510) 436-2405.

Mills College
Oakland, California

CB code: 4485

Admissions: 86% of applicants accepted
Based on:
••• School record
•• Essay, recommendations, special talents, test scores
• Activities, interview
Completion: 93% of freshmen end year in good standing
62% graduate, 20% of these enter graduate study

4-year private liberal arts college, women only. Founded in 1852. **Accreditation:** Regional. **Undergraduate enrollment:** 747 women full time; 27 women part time. **Graduate enrollment:** 51 men, 210 women full time; 6 men, 42 women part time. **Faculty:** 144 total (71 full time), 54 with doctorates or other terminal degrees. **Location:** Urban campus in large city; 18 miles from San Francisco, 8 miles from Berkeley. **Calendar:** Semester. Saturday and extensive evening/early morning classes. **Microcomputers:** 117 located in dormitories, libraries, classrooms, computer centers. **Special facilities:** 2 art galleries, electronic writing laboratory, electronic music studio, on-campus elementary school for student teachers, botanical gardens, computer learning studio. **Additional facts:** Men accepted in graduate school.

DEGREES OFFERED. BA, MA, MFA. 225 bachelor's degrees awarded in 1992. 10% in communications, 5% education, 5% languages, 14% letters/literature, 9% life sciences, 10% multi/interdisciplinary studies, 7% psychology, 18% social sciences, 14% visual and performing arts. Graduate degrees offered in 15 major fields of study.

UNDERGRADUATE MAJORS. Afro-American (black) studies, American studies, anthropology, art history, biochemistry, biology, business economics, chemistry, communications, comparative literature, computer and information sciences, dance, developmental psychology, dramatic arts, economics, education, English, environmental science, environmental studies, ethnic studies, French, German, Hispanic American studies, history, international relations, international studies, liberal/general studies, mathematics, music, philosophy, political science and government, political, legal & economic analysis, psychology, sociology, sociology & anthropology, Spanish, studio art, women's studies.

ACADEMIC PROGRAMS. Double major, education specialist degree, honors program, independent study, internships, student-designed major, study abroad, teacher preparation, visiting/exchange student program, Washington semester, cross-registration; liberal arts/career combination in engineering. **Remedial services:** Preadmission summer program, tutoring. **Placement/credit:** AP, CLEP General and Subject, institutional tests; 7 credit hours maximum for bachelor's degree.

ACADEMIC REQUIREMENTS. Freshmen must earn minimum GPA of 2.0 to continue in good standing. 68% of freshmen return for sophomore year. Students must declare major by end of second year. **Graduation requirements:** 120 hours for bachelor's (40 in major). Most students required to take courses in arts/fine arts, English, humanities, mathematics, biological/physical sciences, social sciences. **Postgraduate studies:** 3% enter law school, 3% enter medical school, 14% enter other graduate study.

FRESHMAN ADMISSIONS. Selection criteria: School achievement record (3.0 minimum GPA required) most important; all credentials considered. **High school preparation:** 16 units recommended. Recommended units include English 4, foreign language 2, mathematics 3, social science 2 and science 2. **Test requirements:** SAT or ACT; score report by April 1.

1992 FRESHMAN CLASS PROFILE. 480 women applied, 415 accepted, 149 enrolled. 70% had high school GPA of 3.0 or higher, 30% between 2.0 and 2.99. 30% were in top tenth and 64% were in top quarter of graduating class. **Academic background:** Mid 50% of enrolled freshmen had SAT-V between 470-580, SAT-M between 470-590. 96% submitted SAT scores. **Characteristics:** 55% from in state, 96% live in college housing, 29% have minority backgrounds, 5% are foreign students. Average age is 19.

FALL-TERM APPLICATIONS. $35 fee, may be waived for applicants with need. Closing date July 15; priority given to applications received by February 1; applicants notified on a rolling basis beginning on or about April 1; must reply by May 1 or within 2 weeks if notified thereafter. Essay required. Interview recommended. CRDA. Deferred and early admission available. 3 ACH including English Composition recommended for placement and counseling. Score report by Februry 1.

STUDENT LIFE. Housing: Dormitories (women); apartment, cooperative housing available. French, Spanish, and German language houses. Apartments for single parents. Two-thirds of rooms are singles. Married student housing open to partners of lesbian and gay students. **Activities:** Student government, film, magazine, student newspaper, yearbook, choral groups, dance, drama, music ensembles, ethnic, political, social service, career-oriented, and feminist student organizations, religious groups, lesbian/bisexual student union, international student association.

ATHLETICS. NCAA. **Intercollegiate:** Basketball, cross-country, rowing (crew), tennis, volleyball. **Intramural:** Badminton, basketball, cross-country, fencing, gymnastics, horseback riding, sailing, skiing, soccer, softball, swimming, table tennis, tennis, volleyball, water polo.

STUDENT SERVICES. Aptitude testing, career counseling, employment service for undergraduates, freshman orientation, health services, on-campus day care, personal counseling, placement service for graduates, special adviser for adult students, services/facilities for handicapped.

ANNUAL EXPENSES. Tuition and fees (1992-93): $14,100. $300 major medicl insurance charge wavied with proof of comparable coverage; basic medical fee of $235 mandatory. **Room and board:** $6,000. **Books and supplies:** $420. **Other expenses:** $1,275.

FINANCIAL AID. 67% of freshmen, 70% of continuing students receive some form of aid. All grants, 84% of loans, all jobs based on need. 109 enrolled freshmen were judged to have need, all were offered aid. Academic, music/drama, art, state/district residency, leadership scholarships available. **Aid applications:** Closing date February 15; applicants notified on or about April 1; must reply by May 1.

ADDRESS/TELEPHONE. Genevieve Flaherty, Dean of Admissions and Financial Aid, Mills College, 5000 MacArthur Boulevard, Oakland, CA 94613. (510) 430-2135. (800) 87-MILLS. Fax: (510) 430-3314.

MiraCosta College
Oceanside, California

CB code: 4582

2-year public community college, coed. Founded in 1934. **Accreditation:** Regional. **Undergraduate enrollment:** 710 men, 940 women full time; 2,593 men, 4,092 women part time. **Faculty:** 505 total (115 full time), 23 with doctorates or other terminal degrees. **Location:** Suburban campus in small city; 35 miles from San Diego. **Calendar:** Semester, extensive summer session. Saturday and extensive evening/early morning classes. **Microcomputers:** 121 located in libraries, classrooms. **Special facilities:** Art gallery. **Additional facts:** Branch campus in Cardiff, adjacent to San Elijo Lagoon.

DEGREES OFFERED. AA. 219 associate degrees awarded in 1992. 12% in business and management, 63% multi/interdisciplinary studies.

UNDERGRADUATE MAJORS. Accounting, agricultural business and management, agricultural production, architectural technologies, automotive mechanics, automotive technology, behavioral sciences, biology, biotechnology, business administration and management, business data processing and related programs, chemistry, child development/care/guidance, drafting and design technology, dramatic arts, early childhood education, English, fine arts, foreign languages (multiple emphasis), French, German, history, horticulture, hotel/motel and restaurant management, journalism, law enforcement and corrections, liberal/general studies, life sciences, machine tool operation/machine shop, mathematics, multicultural studies, music, office supervision and management, philosophy, physical sciences, physics, practical nursing, prelaw, psychology, real estate, retailing, secretarial and related programs, social sciences, sociology, Spanish, speech, word processing.

ACADEMIC PROGRAMS. 2-year transfer program, cooperative education, double major, dual enrollment of high school students, honors program, independent study, study abroad, telecourses, weekend college. **Remedial services:** Learning center, preadmission summer program, reduced course load, remedial instruction, special counselor, tutoring. **Placement/credit:** AP, CLEP General and Subject, institutional tests; 15 credit hours maximum for associate degree.

ACADEMIC REQUIREMENTS. Freshmen must earn minimum GPA of 2.0 to continue in good standing. 52% of freshmen return for sophomore year. Students must declare major on application. **Graduation requirements:** 60 hours for associate. Most students required to take courses in English, history, humanities, mathematics, biological/physical sciences, social sciences.

FRESHMAN ADMISSIONS. Selection criteria: Open admissions. Licensed vocational nursing applicants must qualify for enrollment and must apply 5 months in advance.

1992 FRESHMAN CLASS PROFILE. 2,814 men, 3,710 women enrolled. **Characteristics:** 95% from in state, 100% commute, 28% have minority backgrounds, 1% are foreign students.

FALL-TERM APPLICATIONS. No fee. No closing date; applicants notified on a rolling basis. Deferred admission available.

STUDENT LIFE. Activities: Student government, film, magazine, student newspaper, television, student handbook, veterans newsletter, handicapped newsletter, and equal educational opportunity newsletter, choral groups, concert band, dance, drama, jazz band, music ensembles, musical theater, symphony orchestra, MECHA/Latina organization, Students for Christ, African American Students Alliance, Progressive Student network, women's issues & studies group, Asian American Student Group.

ATHLETICS. NJCAA. **Intercollegiate:** Basketball M, cross-country W, tennis W, track and field W. **Intramural:** Badminton, basketball, bowling, cross-country, golf, gymnastics, racquetball, skiing, softball, tennis, track and field, volleyball.

STUDENT SERVICES. Aptitude testing, career counseling, em-

ployment service for undergraduates, health services, on-campus day care, personal counseling, placement service for graduates, veterans counselor, services/facilities for handicapped.

ANNUAL EXPENSES. Tuition and fees: $333, $3,060 additional for out-of-state students. **Books and supplies:** $576. **Other expenses:** $1,080.

FINANCIAL AID. 10% of freshmen, 10% of continuing students receive some form of aid. 98% of grants, 91% of loans, 45% of jobs based on need. 500 enrolled freshmen were judged to have need, all were offered aid. Academic, music/drama, art, state/district residency, leadership, alumni affiliation scholarships available. **Aid applications:** No closing date; priority given to applications received by May 28; applicants notified on a rolling basis beginning on or about June 15.

ADDRESS/TELEPHONE. Norma Cooper, Admissions Officer, MiraCosta College, One Barnard Drive, Oceanside, CA 92056-3899. (619) 757-2121.

Mission College
Santa Clara, California — CB code: 7587

2-year public community college, coed. Founded in 1975. **Accreditation:** Regional. **Undergraduate enrollment:** 690 men, 667 women full time; 2,357 men, 2,188 women part time. **Faculty:** 400 total (130 full time). **Location:** Suburban campus in small city; 8 miles from San Jose. **Calendar:** Semester, limited summer session. Saturday and extensive evening/early morning classes. **Microcomputers:** Located in libraries, classrooms, computer centers.

DEGREES OFFERED. AA, AS. 222 associate degrees awarded in 1992. 13% in business and management, 14% engineering technologies, 39% multi/interdisciplinary studies, 13% parks/recreation, protective services, public affairs.

UNDERGRADUATE MAJORS. Accounting, allied health, biology, business administration and management, business and management, business and office, business computer/console/peripheral equipment operation, business data programming, chemistry, commercial art, computer and information sciences, computer mathematics, drafting, engineering, engineering and engineering-related technologies, finance, fine arts, fire control and safety technology, food management, food sciences, graphic and printing production, graphic arts technology, hotel/motel and restaurant management, information sciences and systems, institutional/home management/supporting programs, liberal/general studies, management information systems, management science, marketing and distribution, marketing management, mathematics, mental health/human services, nursing, office supervision and management, practical nursing, real estate, secretarial and related programs, social sciences.

ACADEMIC PROGRAMS. 2-year transfer program, cooperative education, dual enrollment of high school students, honors program, independent study, weekend college. **Remedial services:** Learning center, remedial instruction, special counselor, tutoring. **ROTC:** Air Force, Army. **Placement/credit:** Institutional tests; 12 credit hours maximum for associate degree.

ACADEMIC REQUIREMENTS. Freshmen must earn minimum GPA of 2.0 to continue in good standing. Students must declare major on application. **Graduation requirements:** 60 hours for associate (30 in major). Most students required to take courses in English, history, mathematics, philosophy/religion, biological/physical sciences, social sciences.

FRESHMAN ADMISSIONS. Selection criteria: Open admissions.

1992 FRESHMAN CLASS PROFILE. 879 men, 882 women enrolled. **Characteristics:** 99% from in state, 100% commute, 65% have minority backgrounds, 1% are foreign students. Average age is 26.

FALL-TERM APPLICATIONS. No fee. No closing date; applicants notified on a rolling basis. Interview required for nursing, psychiatric technician applicants. Early admission available.

STUDENT LIFE. Activities: Student government, television, choral groups, dance.

ATHLETICS. Intercollegiate: Baseball M, soccer M, softball W, tennis.

STUDENT SERVICES. Aptitude testing, career counseling, employment service for undergraduates, freshman orientation, health services, on-campus day care, personal counseling, placement service for graduates, special adviser for adult students, veterans counselor, services/facilities for handicapped.

ANNUAL EXPENSES. Tuition and fees (projected): $305, $3,300 additional for out-of-state students. **Books and supplies:** $612. **Other expenses:** $1,548.

FINANCIAL AID. 11% of continuing students receive some form of aid. 98% of grants, all loans, all jobs based on need. 800 enrolled freshmen were judged to have need, 700 were offered aid. Academic, state/district residency, leadership scholarships available. **Aid applications:** No closing date; priority given to applications received by May 1; applicants notified on a rolling basis beginning on or about August 1; must reply within 2 weeks.

ADDRESS/TELEPHONE. Jesse Guerrero, Assistant Dean of Student Services, Mission College, 3000 Mission College Boulevard, Santa Clara, CA 95054-1897. (408) 748-2700. Fax: (408) 496-0462.

Modesto Junior College
Modesto, California — CB code: 4486

2-year public junior college, coed. Founded in 1921. **Accreditation:** Regional. **Undergraduate enrollment:** 1,384 men, 1,561 women full time; 2,738 men, 3,775 women part time. **Faculty:** 692 total (216 full time), 20 with doctorates or other terminal degrees. **Location:** Suburban campus in small city; 90 miles from San Francisco. **Calendar:** Semester, limited summer session. Saturday and extensive evening/early morning classes. **Special facilities:** Art gallery, natural history museum.

DEGREES OFFERED. AA, AS. 800 associate degrees awarded in 1992.

UNDERGRADUATE MAJORS. Accounting, agribusiness, agricultural mechanics, agricultural sciences, agronomy, air conditioning/heating/refrigeration mechanics, animal sciences, anthropology, architectural engineering, architecture, astronomy, automotive mechanics, automotive technology, bilingual/bicultural education, biological and physical sciences, biology, botany, business administration and management, business and office, business computer/console/peripheral equipment operation, business data entry equipment operation, business data processing and related programs, business data programming, carpentry, chemistry, city/community/regional planning, civil engineering, clinical laboratory science, computer and information sciences, computer programming, dairy, dental assistant, drafting, earth sciences, electrical and electronics equipment repair, engineering, engineering and engineering-related technologies, engineering and other disciplines, English literature, fashion design, fashion merchandising, finance, fine arts, fire control and safety technology, food production/management/services, food science and nutrition, food sciences, forestry and related sciences, French, geography, geology, graphic and printing production, graphic arts technology, history, home economics, horticultural science, horticulture, humanities and social sciences, industrial equipment maintenance and repair, industrial technology, interpreter for the deaf, Italian, journalism, landscape architecture, law enforcement and corrections technologies, liberal/general studies, marine biology, marketing and distribution, marketing management, mathematics, mechanical design technology, medical assistant, microbiology, music, nursing, ornamental horticulture, photographic technology, photography, physical sciences, physics, physiology, human and animal, plant sciences, plumbing/pipefitting/steamfitting, poultry, practical nursing, precision metal work, prelaw, printmaking, protective services, psychology, public affairs, radio/television broadcasting, real estate, recreation and community services technologies, respiratory therapy technology, robotics, science technologies, secretarial and related programs, social sciences, sociology, soil sciences, Spanish, textiles and clothing, urban design, word processing, zoology.

ACADEMIC PROGRAMS. 2-year transfer program, cooperative education, double major, dual enrollment of high school students, independent study, internships, study abroad. **Remedial services:** Learning center, preadmission summer program, reduced course load, remedial instruction, special counselor, tutoring. **Placement/credit:** Institutional tests; 30 credit hours maximum for associate degree.

ACADEMIC REQUIREMENTS. Freshmen must earn minimum GPA of 2.0 to continue in good standing. **Graduation requirements:** 63 hours for associate (30 in major). Most students required to take courses in English, mathematics.

FRESHMAN ADMISSIONS. Selection criteria: Open admissions. Certain programs require specific courses.

1992 FRESHMAN CLASS PROFILE. 1,985 men and women enrolled. **Characteristics:** 90% from in state, 100% commute.

FALL-TERM APPLICATIONS. No fee. No closing date; applicants notified on a rolling basis beginning on or about April 1. Deferred and early admission available.

STUDENT LIFE. Activities: Student government, film, radio, student newspaper, television, choral groups, concert band, dance, drama, jazz band, music ensembles, opera, Christian Collegiate Fellowship, Able-Disabled Association, special interest and concern groups, foreign, ethnic, and minority student clubs.

ATHLETICS. Intercollegiate: Baseball M, basketball, cross-country, diving, football M, golf M, soccer M, softball W, swimming, tennis, track and field, volleyball W, water polo M, wrestling M. **Intramural:** Basketball, softball, table tennis, tennis.

STUDENT SERVICES. Aptitude testing, career counseling, employment service for undergraduates, freshman orientation, health services, on-campus day care, personal counseling, placement service for graduates, special adviser for adult students, veterans counselor, special physical education facilities and counseling, barrier-free campus, counseling programs for minority and educationally disadvantaged students, services/facilities for handicapped.

ANNUAL EXPENSES. Tuition and fees (projected): $830, $3,300 additional for out-of-state students. **Books and supplies:** $612. **Other expenses:** $1,548.

FINANCIAL AID. 30% of freshmen, 30% of continuing students receive some form of aid. 93% of grants, all loans, 76% of jobs based on need. Academic, music/drama, art scholarships available. **Aid applications:** No closing date; priority given to applications received by March 2; applicants notified on a rolling basis beginning on or about July 16; must reply within 2 weeks.

ADDRESS/TELEPHONE. Julius C. Manrique, Associate Dean of Student Services, Modesto Junior College, 435 College Avenue, Modesto, CA 95350. (209) 575-6060.

Monterey Institute of International Studies
Monterey, California CB code: 4507

2-year upper-division private liberal arts college, coed. Founded in 1955. **Accreditation:** Regional. **Undergraduate enrollment:** 24 men, 45 women full time; 2 women part time. **Graduate enrollment:** 218 men, 341 women full time; 37 men, 73 women part time. **Faculty:** 97 total (49 full time), 57 with doctorates or other terminal degrees. **Location:** Suburban campus in small city; 130 miles from San Francisco. **Calendar:** Semester, extensive summer session. **Microcomputers:** 35 located in computer centers. **Additional facts:** Intensive study of foreign cultures and native instruction in foreign languages.

DEGREES OFFERED. BA, MA, MBA. 36 bachelor's degrees awarded in 1992. 35% in languages, 65% social sciences. Graduate degrees offered in 14 major fields of study.

UNDERGRADUATE MAJORS. Computer languages, international relations, North American studies.

ACADEMIC PROGRAMS. Double major, honors program, independent study, internships, study abroad; combined bachelor's/graduate program in business administration. **Remedial services:** Preadmission summer program. **Placement/credit:** CLEP General and Subject, institutional tests.

ACADEMIC REQUIREMENTS. Students must declare major on application. **Graduation requirements:** 120 hours for bachelor's (48 in major). Most students required to take courses in English, foreign languages, history, humanities, mathematics, biological/physical sciences, social sciences. **Additional information:** Foreign language and related area studies required in all programs.

ADMISSIONS. Academic achievement and recommendations considered. Intensive English program or 12 semester hours of lower-division foreign language or attendance at intensive summer foreign language program required.

FALL-TERM APPLICATIONS. $50 fee.

STUDENT LIFE. Activities: Student government, magazine, student newspaper, Amnesty International. **Additional information:** Informal campus.

ATHLETICS. Intramural: Soccer, softball.

STUDENT SERVICES. Career counseling, employment service for undergraduates, personal counseling, placement service for graduates, foreign student advising, services/facilities for handicapped.

ANNUAL EXPENSES. Tuition and fees: $13,245. **Books and supplies:** $500. **Other expenses:** $1,400.

FINANCIAL AID. 70% of continuing students receive some form of aid. 65% of grants, 98% of loans, all jobs based on need. Academic, minority scholarships available. **Aid applications:** No closing date; priority given to applications received by March 1; applicants notified on or about May 15; must reply by September 1. **Additional information:** Wide variety of scholarships based on merit offered.

ADDRESS/TELEPHONE. Jane Roberts, Director of Admissions, Monterey Institute of International Studies, 425 Van Buren Street, Monterey, CA 93940. (408) 647-4123. (800) 824-7235. Fax: (408) 647-4199.

Monterey Peninsula College
Monterey, California CB code: 4490

2-year public community college, coed. Founded in 1947. **Accreditation:** Regional. **Undergraduate enrollment:** 11,789 men and women. **Faculty:** 340 total (100 full time), 25 with doctorates or other terminal degrees. **Location:** Suburban campus in large town; 120 miles from San Francisco. **Calendar:** Semester, limited summer session. Saturday and extensive evening/early morning classes. **Microcomputers:** Located in computer centers.

DEGREES OFFERED. AA, AS. 350 associate degrees awarded in 1992.

UNDERGRADUATE MAJORS. Accounting, art history, automotive technology, business and management, business and office, business data processing and related programs, business data programming, ceramics, dance, data processing, dental assistant, drafting, dramatic arts, finance, fire control and safety technology, graphic design, home economics, hotel/motel and restaurant management, interior design, law enforcement and corrections technologies, liberal/general studies, medical assistant, medical secretary, metal/jewelry, music, nursing, office supervision and management, ornamental horticulture, photography, real estate, secretarial and related programs, social work, studio art, visual and performing arts, word processing.

ACADEMIC PROGRAMS. 2-year transfer program, independent study. **Remedial services:** Learning center, remedial instruction, tutoring. **Placement/credit:** AP, CLEP General, institutional tests; 30 credit hours maximum for associate degree.

ACADEMIC REQUIREMENTS. Freshmen must earn minimum GPA of 2.0 to continue in good standing. **Graduation requirements:** 60 hours for associate. Most students required to take courses in English, humanities, mathematics, biological/physical sciences, social sciences.

FRESHMAN ADMISSIONS. Selection criteria: Open admissions.

1992 FRESHMAN CLASS PROFILE. Characteristics: 96% from in state, 100% commute, 13% have minority backgrounds, 3% are foreign students.

FALL-TERM APPLICATIONS. No fee. No closing date; applicants notified on a rolling basis. Interview required for dental assistant, nursing applicants.

STUDENT LIFE. Activities: Student government, choral groups, concert band, dance, drama, jazz band, musical theater, opera.

ATHLETICS. NJCAA. **Intercollegiate:** Baseball M, basketball, cross-country, football M, golf, softball W, swimming, tennis, track and field, volleyball W.

STUDENT SERVICES. Aptitude testing, career counseling, employment service for undergraduates, freshman orientation, health services, on-campus day care, personal counseling, services/facilities for handicapped.

ANNUAL EXPENSES. Tuition and fees (1992-93): $155, $3,240 additional for out-of-state students. **Books and supplies:** $576. **Other expenses:** $1,728.

FINANCIAL AID. 40% of freshmen, 15% of continuing students receive some form of aid. All grants, 80% of loans, all jobs based on need. Academic, music/drama, art, athletic, state/district residency, leadership scholarships available. **Aid applications:** No closing date; priority given to applications received by March 2; applicants notified on a rolling basis beginning on or about May 31; must reply within 30 days.

ADDRESS/TELEPHONE. Deborah H. Carroll, Director of Admissions and Records, Monterey Peninsula College, 980 Fremont Street, Monterey, CA 93940. (408) 646-4002. Fax: (408) 655-2627.

Moorpark College
Moorpark, California CB code: 4512

2-year public community college, coed. Founded in 1963. **Accreditation:** Regional. **Undergraduate enrollment:** 12,120 men and women. **Faculty:** 350 total (125 full time), 22 with doctorates or other terminal degrees. **Location:** Suburban campus in large town; 50 miles from Los Angeles. **Calendar:** Semester, limited summer session. **Microcomputers:** Located in classrooms. **Special facilities:** Exotic animal compound and teaching zoo, Charles Temple Observatory.

DEGREES OFFERED. AA, AS. 769 associate degrees awarded in 1992.

UNDERGRADUATE MAJORS. Accounting, animal sciences, biology, business administration and management, business data processing and related programs, business data programming, chemistry, child development/care/guidance, cinematography/film, computer and information sciences, conservation and regulation, dramatic arts, electromechanical technology, electronic technology, equestrian science, finance, fine arts, geology, graphic and printing production, graphic arts technology, graphic design, home economics, individual and family development, information sciences and systems, laser electro-optic technology, law enforcement and corrections technologies, liberal/general studies, marketing and distribution, mathematics, music, nursing, office supervision and management, ornamental horticulture, photographic technology, photography, physics, public affairs, radio/television broadcasting, radio/television technology, real estate, secretarial and related programs, social sciences, telecommunications, visual and performing arts.

ACADEMIC PROGRAMS. 2-year transfer program, independent study, internships, study abroad. **Remedial services:** Learning center, remedial instruction, tutoring. **Placement/credit:** AP; 12 credit hours maximum for associate degree.

ACADEMIC REQUIREMENTS. Freshmen must earn minimum GPA of 2.0 to continue in good standing. Students must declare major on enrollment. **Graduation requirements:** 60 hours for associate (24 in major). Most students required to take courses in arts/fine arts, English, history, humanities, mathematics, biological/physical sciences, social sciences.

FRESHMAN ADMISSIONS. Selection criteria: Open admissions.

1992 FRESHMAN CLASS PROFILE. 1,197 men, 1,334 women enrolled. **Characteristics:** 99% from in state, 100% commute, 15% have minority backgrounds, 1% are foreign students. Average age is 18.

FALL-TERM APPLICATIONS. No fee. No closing date; applicants notified on a rolling basis.

STUDENT LIFE. Activities: Student government, film, radio, student newspaper, television, choral groups, concert band, dance, drama, Mexican-American Club, Black Student Union.

ATHLETICS. Intercollegiate: Baseball M, basketball, cross-country, football M, golf M, softball W, tennis W, track and field, volleyball W, wrestling M.

STUDENT SERVICES. Aptitude testing, career counseling, employment service for undergraduates, freshman orientation, health services,

on-campus day care, personal counseling, veterans counselor, services/facilities for handicapped.

ANNUAL EXPENSES. Tuition and fees (1992-93): $135, $3,300 additional for out-of-state students. **Books and supplies:** $576. **Other expenses:** $1,000.

FINANCIAL AID. 5% of freshmen, 5% of continuing students receive some form of aid. Grants, loans, jobs available. **Aid applications:** No closing date; priority given to applications received by May 16; applicants notified on a rolling basis beginning on or about June 15; must reply within 2 weeks.

ADDRESS/TELEPHONE. Dr. William Bendat, Dean Student Services, Moorpark College, 7075 Campus Road, Moorpark, CA 93021. (805) 378-1400. Fax: (805) 378-1499.

Mount St. Mary's College

Los Angeles, California — CB code: 4493

Admissions: 78% of applicants accepted
Based on:
••• School record, test scores
•• Essay, interview
• Activities, recommendations, special talents
Completion: 95% of freshmen end year in good standing
61% graduate, 37% of these enter graduate study

4-year private liberal arts college, women only, affiliated with Roman Catholic Church. Founded in 1925. **Accreditation:** Regional. **Undergraduate enrollment:** 18 men, 940 women full time; 22 men, 176 women part time. **Graduate enrollment:** 36 men, 100 women full time; 66 men, 133 women part time. **Faculty:** 133 total (58 full time), 80 with doctorates or other terminal degrees. **Location:** Suburban campus in very large city. **Calendar:** Semester, limited summer session. **Microcomputers:** 71 located in libraries, computer centers. **Special facilities:** Art gallery.

DEGREES OFFERED. AA, BA, BS, MA, MS. 96 associate degrees awarded in 1992. 13% in business and management, 18% education, 45% health sciences, 8% allied health, 24% multi/interdisciplinary studies. 182 bachelor's degrees awarded. 15% in business and management, 5% teacher education, 35% health sciences, 6% letters/literature, 6% life sciences, 17% psychology, 6% social sciences. Graduate degrees offered in 9 major fields of study.

UNDERGRADUATE MAJORS. Associate: Accounting, business and office, early childhood education, health sciences, liberal/general studies, nursing, occupational therapy assistant, physical therapy assistant, teacher aide, tourism. **Bachelor's:** Accounting, American studies, applied mathematics, art education, biochemistry, biology, business administration and management, business and management, business education, chemistry, clinical laboratory science, elementary education, English, English and business administration, English education, fine arts, foreign languages education, French, health care administration, health sciences, history, international business management, junior high education, marketing management, mathematics, mathematics education, music, music education, music performance, music theory and composition, nursing, philosophy, physical science education, political science and government, predentistry, prelaw, premedicine, preveterinary, psychology, religion, religious music, science education, secondary education, social science education, social sciences, social studies education, sociology, Spanish.

ACADEMIC PROGRAMS. 2-year transfer program, double major, dual enrollment of high school students, honors program, independent study, internships, student-designed major, study abroad, teacher preparation, visiting/exchange student program, United Nations semester, Washington semester, cross-registration. **Remedial services:** Learning center, preadmission summer program, reduced course load, remedial instruction, tutoring. **ROTC:** Air Force, Army, Naval. **Placement/credit:** AP, CLEP Subject, institutional tests; 30 credit hours maximum for associate degree; 30 credit hours maximum for bachelor's degree.

ACADEMIC REQUIREMENTS. Freshmen must earn minimum GPA of 2.0 to continue in good standing. 82% of freshmen return for sophomore year. Students must declare major by end of second year. **Graduation requirements:** 60 hours for associate (30 in major), 124 hours for bachelor's (72 in major). Most students required to take courses in arts/fine arts, English, foreign languages, history, mathematics, philosophy/religion, biological/physical sciences, social sciences. **Postgraduate studies:** 60% from 2-year programs enter 4-year programs. 10% enter law school, 12% enter medical school, 10% enter MBA programs, 5% enter other graduate study.

FRESHMAN ADMISSIONS. Selection criteria: Primary emphasis on school academic record, then test scores, essay, and letters of recommendation. School and community activities also considered. Interview important. **High school preparation:** 15 units required; 16 recommended. Required and recommended units include English 4, foreign language 2, mathematics 3-4, social science 3 and science 2-3. For associate degree applicants, required courses include algebra, geometry, American history/government, laboratory science, and 3 units English. 2 foreign language and additional units of mathematics, laboratory science, or foreign language recommended. **Test requirements:** SAT or ACT (SAT preferred); score report by July 1. **Additional information:** Admission requirements considered very competitive in Baccalaureate Program.

1992 FRESHMAN CLASS PROFILE. 85% had high school GPA of 3.0 or higher, 15% between 2.0 and 2.99. **Academic background:** Mid 50% of enrolled freshmen had SAT-V between 380-490, SAT-M between 390-540; ACT composite between 17-26. 90% submitted SAT scores, 22% submitted ACT scores. **Characteristics:** 97% from in state, 51% live in college housing, 80% have minority backgrounds, 2% are foreign students. Average age is 19.

FALL-TERM APPLICATIONS. $30 fee, may be waived for applicants with need. No closing date; priority given to applications received by March 1; applicants notified on a rolling basis; must reply by May 1 or within 3 weeks if notified thereafter. Essay required. Interview recommended. Audition recommended for music applicants. Portfolio recommended for art applicants. CRDA. Deferred admission available.

STUDENT LIFE. Housing: Dormitories (women). **Activities:** Student government, student newspaper, yearbook, choral groups, dance, symphony orchestra, sororities, campus ministry, volunteer service.

ATHLETICS. NAIA. **Intercollegiate:** Cross-country, tennis, volleyball. **Intramural:** Basketball, cross-country, softball, swimming, tennis, track and field, volleyball.

STUDENT SERVICES. Career counseling, employment service for undergraduates, freshman orientation, health services, personal counseling, placement service for graduates, special adviser for adult students.

ANNUAL EXPENSES. Tuition and fees (1992-93): $10,800. **Room and board:** $4,700. **Books and supplies:** $558. **Other expenses:** $1,638.

FINANCIAL AID. 75% of freshmen, 77% of continuing students receive some form of aid. 87% of grants, 75% of loans, 93% of jobs based on need. 142 enrolled freshmen were judged to have need, 140 were offered aid. Academic, state/district residency, alumni affiliation scholarships available. **Aid applications:** No closing date; priority given to applications received by March 1; applicants notified on a rolling basis beginning on or about February 1; must reply by May 1 or within 2 weeks if notified thereafter.

ADDRESS/TELEPHONE. Katy Murphy, Director of Admissions, Mount St. Mary's College, 12001 Chalon Road, Los Angeles, CA 90049-1597. (310) 471-9557. (800) 999-9893. Fax: (310) 476-9296.

Mount San Antonio College

Walnut, California — CB code: 4494

2-year public community college, coed. Founded in 1946. **Accreditation:** Regional. **Undergraduate enrollment:** 2,804 men, 2,925 women full time; 4,939 men, 6,109 women part time. **Faculty:** 821 total (300 full time). **Location:** Suburban campus in large town; 25 miles from Los Angeles. **Calendar:** Semester, limited summer session. **Microcomputers:** Located in computer centers. **Special facilities:** Art gallery, planetarium, wildlife sanctuary.

DEGREES OFFERED. AA, AS. 1,014 associate degrees awarded in 1992.

UNDERGRADUATE MAJORS. Accounting, advertising, aeronautical technology, agribusiness, agricultural mechanics, air conditioning/heating/refrigeration mechanics, air conditioning/heating/refrigeration technology, air traffic control, airline piloting and navigation, animal sciences, apparel and accessories marketing, architectural technologies, biology, business administration and management, business and management, business and office, child development/care/guidance, computer servicing technology, data processing, drafting, drafting and design technology, electrical and electronics equipment repair, electronic technology, emergency medical technologies, engineering, engineering and engineering-related technologies, fashion merchandising, finance, fire control and safety technology, flight attendants, food management, forestry and related sciences, home economics, horticultural science, industrial technology, interior design, interpreter for the deaf, journalism, law enforcement and corrections technologies, legal assistant/paralegal, liberal/general studies, machine tool operation/machine shop, manufacturing technology, marketing management, mechanical design technology, medical secretary, mental health/human services, nursing, parks and recreation management, photographic technology, photography, physical sciences, quality control technology, radio/television broadcasting, radiograph medical technology, real estate, recreation and community services technologies, respiratory therapy technology, science technologies, secretarial and related programs, small business management and ownership, surveying and mapping sciences, water and wastewater technology, welding technology.

ACADEMIC PROGRAMS. 2-year transfer program, double major, dual enrollment of high school students, honors program, study abroad, telecourses. **Remedial services:** Learning center, remedial instruction, special counselor, tutoring, American Language and ESL classes. **Placement/credit:** 12 credit hours maximum for associate degree.

ACADEMIC REQUIREMENTS. Freshmen must earn minimum GPA of 2.0 to continue in good standing. 81% of freshmen return for sophomore year. Students must declare major on application. **Graduation requirements:** 60 hours for associate (20 in major). Most students required to take courses in English, mathematics, biological/physical sciences.

FRESHMAN ADMISSIONS. Selection criteria: Open admissions.

1992 FRESHMAN CLASS PROFILE. 1,584 men, 1,763 women enrolled. **Characteristics:** 98% from in state, 100% commute, 54% have minority backgrounds, 3% are foreign students. Average age is 25.

FALL-TERM APPLICATIONS. No fee. No closing date; applicants notified on a rolling basis. Early admission available.

STUDENT LIFE. Activities: Student government, radio, student newspaper, television, choral groups, concert band, dance, drama, jazz band, music ensembles, musical theater, pep band, Newman Club, Campus Crusade for Christ, Asian Student Association, Chinese Club, Black Student Alliance, Indo-Pak Club, Democratic Club, College Republican Club, Sign Language Club, MECHA.

ATHLETICS. Intercollegiate: Baseball M, basketball, cross-country, diving, football M, golf M, soccer, softball W, swimming, tennis, track and field, volleyball, water polo M, wrestling M.

STUDENT SERVICES. Aptitude testing, career counseling, employment service for undergraduates, freshman orientation, health services, on-campus day care, personal counseling, placement service for graduates, veterans counselor, services/facilities for handicapped.

ANNUAL EXPENSES. Tuition and fees (1992-93): $153, $3,150 additional for out-of-state students. **Books and supplies:** $576. **Other expenses:** $1,728.

FINANCIAL AID. 10% of continuing students receive some form of aid. 29% of jobs based on need. Academic, athletic, leadership, minority scholarships available. **Aid applications:** No closing date; priority given to applications received by May 22; applicants notified on a rolling basis beginning on or about June 29; must reply within 4 weeks.

ADDRESS/TELEPHONE. Lynn A. Hanks, Director of Admissions and Records, Mount San Antonio College, 1100 North Grand Avenue, Walnut, CA 91789. (909) 594-5611.

Mount San Jacinto College
San Jacinto, California CB code: 4501

2-year public community college, coed. Founded in 1962. **Accreditation:** Regional. **Undergraduate enrollment:** 699 men, 955 women full time; 1,888 men, 3,468 women part time. **Faculty:** 230 total (55 full time), 6 with doctorates or other terminal degrees. **Location:** Rural campus in large town; 35 miles from Riverside, 45 miles from Palm Springs. **Calendar:** Semester, limited summer session. **Microcomputers:** 45 located in classrooms, computer centers.

DEGREES OFFERED. AA, AS. 220 associate degrees awarded in 1992.

UNDERGRADUATE MAJORS. Automotive mechanics, automotive technology, behavioral sciences, biological and physical sciences, business administration and management, business and management, business and office, business computer/console/peripheral equipment operation, business data processing and related programs, business data programming, child development/care/guidance, computer and information sciences, dramatic arts, early childhood education, electrical/electronics/communications engineering, engineering, engineering and engineering-related technologies, engineering and other disciplines, fine arts, health sciences, humanities, humanities and social sciences, law enforcement and corrections technologies, liberal/general studies, mathematics, music, nursing, office supervision and management, photographic technology, photography, practical nursing, real estate, science technologies, secretarial and related programs, social sciences, teacher aide.

ACADEMIC PROGRAMS. 2-year transfer program, cooperative education, dual enrollment of high school students, independent study, internships. **Remedial services:** Learning center, remedial instruction, special counselor, tutoring. **Placement/credit:** AP, CLEP General and Subject, institutional tests; 12 credit hours maximum for associate degree.

ACADEMIC REQUIREMENTS. Freshmen must earn minimum GPA of 2.0 to continue in good standing. 20% of freshmen return for sophomore year. Students must declare major on application. **Graduation requirements:** 60 hours for associate (18 in major). Most students required to take courses in arts/fine arts, English, history, humanities, mathematics, biological/physical sciences, social sciences.

FRESHMAN ADMISSIONS. Selection criteria: Open admissions.

1992 FRESHMAN CLASS PROFILE. 5,843 men and women enrolled. **Characteristics:** 99% from in state, 100% commute, 18% have minority backgrounds, 1% are foreign students.

FALL-TERM APPLICATIONS. No fee. Closing date August 25; applicants notified on a rolling basis beginning on or about August 1. Interview required for nursing applicants. Audition required for performing arts applicants. Early admission available. SAT or ACT recommended for placement and counseling.

STUDENT LIFE. Activities: Student government, student newspaper, choral groups, concert band, dance, drama, jazz band, musical theater, opera.

ATHLETICS. Intercollegiate: Baseball M, basketball, football M, golf M, tennis, volleyball W. **Intramural:** Volleyball W.

STUDENT SERVICES. Aptitude testing, career counseling, employment service for undergraduates, freshman orientation, on-campus day care, personal counseling, special adviser for adult students, veterans counselor, services/facilities for handicapped.

ANNUAL EXPENSES. Tuition and fees (1992-93): $120, $3,690 additional for out-of-state students. **Books and supplies:** $576. **Other expenses:** $1,198.

FINANCIAL AID. 40% of freshmen, 32% of continuing students receive some form of aid. 97% of grants, 94% of loans, 53% of jobs based on need. 507 enrolled freshmen were judged to have need, 410 were offered aid. Academic, music/drama, art, athletic, state/district residency, leadership, alumni affiliation, minority scholarships available. **Aid applications:** No closing date; applicants notified on a rolling basis beginning on or about August 1; must reply within 3 weeks. **Additional information:** Board of Governors Grant Program available to low-income California residents to defray cost of enrollment fee.

ADDRESS/TELEPHONE. Elida Gonzales, Director of Admissions and Records, Mount San Jacinto College, 1499 North State Street, San Jacinto, CA 92583-2399. (714) 654-8011 ext.1410. Fax: (714) 487-9240.

Napa Valley College
Napa, California CB code: 4530

2-year public community college, coed. Founded in 1940. **Accreditation:** Regional. **Undergraduate enrollment:** 1,799 men and women full time; 5,303 men and women part time. **Faculty:** 297 total (97 full time), 10 with doctorates or other terminal degrees. **Location:** Suburban campus in small city; 60 miles from San Francisco. **Calendar:** Semester, limited summer session. Extensive evening/early morning classes. **Microcomputers:** Located in libraries, classrooms. **Special facilities:** Nature preserve, working vineyard, telecommunications laboratory, art gallery.

DEGREES OFFERED. AA, AS. 200 associate degrees awarded in 1992. 8% in business and management, 13% education, 19% health sciences, 11% allied health, 8% letters/literature, 10% physical sciences, 13% social sciences.

UNDERGRADUATE MAJORS. Accounting, agricultural sciences, aircraft mechanics, anthropology, astronomy, automotive technology, bioengineering and biomedical engineering, biology, botany, business and management, chemistry, computer and information sciences, criminal justice studies, drafting, dramatic arts, early childhood education, economics, education, electrical/electronics/communications engineering, engineering, engineering and other disciplines, English, finance, fine arts, fire control and safety technology, French, geography, geology, German, history, home economics, humanities and social sciences, law enforcement and corrections technologies, legal secretary, liberal/general studies, marketing and distribution, mathematics, medical secretary, mental health/human services, music, nursing, office supervision and management, ornamental horticulture, philosophy, photographic technology, photography, physical sciences, physics, plant sciences, political science and government, practical nursing, precision metal work, protective services, psychology, real estate, respiratory therapy, respiratory therapy technology, science technologies, secretarial and related programs, small business management and ownership, social sciences, sociology, telecommunications, welding technology, wildlife management, word processing.

ACADEMIC PROGRAMS. 2-year transfer program, dual enrollment of high school students, independent study, internships, study abroad, exchange program with Tafe College, Tasmania. **Remedial services:** Learning center, remedial instruction, tutoring, counselor for disabled. **Placement/credit:** Institutional tests; 12 credit hours maximum for associate degree.

ACADEMIC REQUIREMENTS. Freshmen must earn minimum GPA of 2.0 to continue in good standing. Students must declare major on enrollment. **Graduation requirements:** 60 hours for associate (18 in major). Most students required to take courses in arts/fine arts, English, history, humanities, mathematics, biological/physical sciences, social sciences.

FRESHMAN ADMISSIONS. Selection criteria: Open admissions. Special admission requirements for health occupations programs. **Additional information:** High school transcript required for health occupations program and athletic program applicants.

1992 FRESHMAN CLASS PROFILE. 4,450 men and women enrolled. **Characteristics:** 98% from in state, 100% commute.

FALL-TERM APPLICATIONS. No fee. No closing date; applicants notified on a rolling basis. Deferred and early admission available. College placement tests recommended for students enrolling in English or mathematics.

STUDENT LIFE. Activities: Student government, student newspaper, choral groups, concert band, dance, drama, jazz band, music ensembles, musical theater, symphony orchestra, various religious, ethnic, social service, and special interest organizations, International Student Club.

ATHLETICS. NJCAA. **Intercollegiate:** Baseball M, basketball, golf, gymnastics, softball W, swimming, tennis. **Intramural:** Volleyball.

STUDENT SERVICES. Aptitude testing, career counseling, employment service for undergraduates, freshman orientation, on-campus day care, personal counseling, special adviser for adult students, veterans counselor, services/facilities for handicapped.

ANNUAL EXPENSES. Tuition and fees (1992-93): $122, $3,390 additional for out-of-state students. **Books and supplies:** $576. **Other expenses:** $1,500.

FINANCIAL AID. 99% of grants, 90% of loans, 62% of jobs based on need. Academic, music/drama, art, athletic, state/district residency, leadership scholarships available. **Aid applications:** No closing date; priority given to applications received by May 5; applicants notified on a rolling basis beginning on or about June 1; must reply within 3 weeks.

ADDRESS/TELEPHONE. Delores E. Smith, Assistant Dean, Admissions of Records, Napa Valley College, 2277 Napa-Vallejo Highway, Napa, CA 94558. (707) 253-3000. Fax: (707) 253-3064.

National University
San Diego, California CB code: 0470

4-year private university, coed. Founded in 1971. **Accreditation:** Regional. **Undergraduate enrollment:** 913 men, 848 women full time; 1,175 men, 1,030 women part time. **Graduate enrollment:** 1,779 men, 1,950 women full time; 571 men, 700 women part time. **Faculty:** 1,766 total (68 full time), 603 with doctorates or other terminal degrees. **Location:** Urban campus in very large city; 3 miles from downtown San Diego. **Calendar:** Continuous academic calendar. Classes begin monthly. **Microcomputers:** Located in libraries, classrooms, computer centers. **Special facilities:** On-line library card catalog accessible from more than 40 locations. **Additional facts:** Most students are employed adults with prior credit who have had 5 or more years of work experience. Continuous 12-month class schedule for degree programs. Learning centers in Orange County, San Jose, Los Angeles, Sacramento, Fresno, Stockton, and Vista.

DEGREES OFFERED. AA, AS, BA, BS, MA, MS, MBA, JD. 230 associate degrees awarded in 1992. 1,590 bachelor's degrees awarded. 52% in business and management, 15% computer sciences, 5% education, 6% teacher education, 9% psychology. Graduate degrees offered in 25 major fields of study.

UNDERGRADUATE MAJORS. Associate: Liberal/general studies. **Bachelor's:** Accounting, aviation management, behavioral sciences, business administration and management, business and management, communications, computer and information sciences, computer programming, criminal justice studies, education, finance, human resources development, information sciences and systems, law , liberal/general studies, logistics, manufacturing technology, marketing management, mathematics, mathematics education, occupational safety and health technology, personnel management, psychology, technical education.

ACADEMIC PROGRAMS. 2-year transfer program, accelerated program, independent study, teacher preparation, cross-registration; combined bachelor's/graduate program in law. **Remedial services:** Learning center, remedial instruction, tutoring. **ROTC:** Air Force, Army. **Placement/credit:** AP, CLEP General and Subject, institutional tests; 25 credit hours maximum for bachelor's degree.

ACADEMIC REQUIREMENTS. Freshmen must earn minimum GPA of 2.0 to continue in good standing. Students must declare major on application. **Graduation requirements:** 90 hours for associate (30 in major), 180 hours for bachelor's (45 in major). Most students required to take courses in computer science, English, history, humanities, mathematics, biological/physical sciences, social sciences. **Postgraduate studies:** 61% from 2-year programs enter 4-year programs. 1% enter law school, 30% enter MBA programs, 15% enter other graduate study.

FRESHMAN ADMISSIONS. Selection criteria: Open admissions. Interview, previous business and work experience, academic record considered. **Test requirements:** IBM aptitude test from IBM for computer studies applicants, placement tests for English and mathematics.

1992 FRESHMAN CLASS PROFILE. 342 men and women enrolled. **Characteristics:** 100% commute, 29% have minority backgrounds, 1% are foreign students. Average age is 29.

FALL-TERM APPLICATIONS. $60 fee. No closing date; applicants notified on a rolling basis; must reply within 2 weeks. Interview required. Deferred admission available. Enrollment may occur throughout year.

STUDENT LIFE. 92% of undergraduate students are in upper division; most have active roles in community.

STUDENT SERVICES. Aptitude testing, career counseling, employment service for undergraduates, freshman orientation, personal counseling, special adviser for adult students, veterans counselor, services/facilities for handicapped.

ANNUAL EXPENSES. Tuition and fees (1992-93): $5,985. **Books and supplies:** $500.

FINANCIAL AID. 80% of freshmen, 80% of continuing students receive some form of aid. 64% of grants, 55% of loans, 11% of jobs based on need. Leadership, minority scholarships available. **Aid applications:** No closing date; priority given to applications received by March 2; applicants notified on a rolling basis; must reply within 4 weeks.

ADDRESS/TELEPHONE. Peter Casey, Interim VP Student/Public Services, National University, 4025 Camino del Rio South, San Diego, CA 92108-4107. (619) 563-7100. (800) 628-8648. Fax: (619) 563-7496.

New College of California
San Francisco, California CB code: 4555

4-year private liberal arts college, coed. Founded in 1971. **Accreditation:** Regional. **Undergraduate enrollment:** 126 men, 185 women full time; 177 men, 122 women part time. **Graduate enrollment:** 67 men, 121 women full time; 27 men, 53 women part time. **Faculty:** 70 total (30 full time), 34 with doctorates or other terminal degrees. **Location:** Urban campus in very large city; Located in San Francisco's Mission District. **Calendar:** Semester, limited summer session. Saturday and extensive evening/early morning classes. **Microcomputers:** 16 located in libraries, computer centers. **Special facilities:** 2 theaters, visual arts studio, print shop, video editing laboratory, desktop publishing laboratory, music laboratory. **Additional facts:** Alternative humanities college: Students choose from 12 emphasis areas or create their own emphasis.

DEGREES OFFERED. AA, BA, MA, MFA, JD. 1 associate degree awarded in 1992. 100% in multi/interdisciplinary studies. 104 bachelor's degrees awarded. 100% in multi/interdisciplinary studies. Graduate degrees offered in 5 major fields of study.

UNDERGRADUATE MAJORS. Associate: Humanities. **Bachelor's:** Humanities.

ACADEMIC PROGRAMS. 2-year transfer program, accelerated program, double major, independent study, internships, student-designed major, study abroad, teacher preparation, weekend college. **Remedial services:** Learning center, remedial instruction, special counselor, tutoring. **Placement/credit:** AP, CLEP General and Subject; 30 credit hours maximum for bachelor's degree.

ACADEMIC REQUIREMENTS. No policy requiring minimum GPA; records of students having academic difficulty are reviewed individually. **Graduation requirements:** 60 hours for associate, 120 hours for bachelor's. Most students required to take courses in arts/fine arts, English, history, humanities, mathematics, philosophy/religion, biological/physical sciences, social sciences. **Postgraduate studies:** 50% from 2-year programs enter 4-year programs. **Additional information:** Students required to complete at least 24 units in emphasis area.

FRESHMAN ADMISSIONS. Selection criteria: Open admissions. Applicants required to submit a 2-4 page personal statement. Interview with admissions counselor strongely recommended. **Additional information:** Applicants required to complete series of essay questions. Essay questions used to evaluate writing skills and select an appropriate faculty adviser.

1992 FRESHMAN CLASS PROFILE. 22 men, 14 women enrolled. **Characteristics:** 90% from in state, 100% commute, 11% have minority backgrounds, 3% are foreign students. Average age is 27.

FALL-TERM APPLICATIONS. $25 fee, may be waived for applicants with need. Closing date September 1; priority given to applications received by March 1; applicants notified on a rolling basis beginning on or about November 1; must reply by registration. Essay required. Interview recommended. CRDA. Deferred admission available.

STUDENT LIFE. Activities: Student government, student newspaper, television, student literature publication, choral groups, dance, drama, jazz band, music ensembles, student association. **Additional information:** Extensive interaction with San Francisco community.

ATHLETICS. Intercollegiate: Basketball M.

STUDENT SERVICES. Career counseling, personal counseling, services/facilities for handicapped.

ANNUAL EXPENSES. Tuition and fees (1992-93): $6,500. **Books and supplies:** $600. **Other expenses:** $2,268.

FINANCIAL AID. 85% of freshmen, 85% of continuing students receive some form of aid. All grants, 70% of loans, all jobs based on need. **Aid applications:** No closing date; priority given to applications received by March 1; applicants notified on a rolling basis beginning on or about May 15; must reply within 3 weeks.

ADDRESS/TELEPHONE. Katrina Fullman, Admissions Coordinator, New College of California, 766 Valencia Street, San Francisco, CA 94110. (415) 626-0884.

Occidental College
Los Angeles, California CB code: 4581

4-year private liberal arts college, coed. Founded in 1887. **Accreditation:** Regional. **Undergraduate enrollment:** 767 men, 838 women full time; 9 men, 9 women part time. **Graduate enrollment:** 9 men, 12 women full time; 5 men, 3 women part time. **Faculty:** 184 total (134 full time), 158 with doctorates or other terminal degrees. **Location:** Urban campus in very large city; 6 miles from Civic Center. **Calendar:** Trimester, limited summer session. **Microcomputers:** 200 located in dormitories, libraries, classrooms. **Special facilities:** 85-foot research vessel for marine biology program, small nuclear reactor, electronic music studio, nuclear magnetic resonator, zoology laboratory with collection of neo-tropical birds and mammals (70,000 specimens). **Additional facts:** Commitment to diversity and multiculturalism in curriculum, faculty, and student body.

DEGREES OFFERED. BA, MA. 426 bachelor's degrees awarded in 1992. 12% in letters/literature, 10% life sciences, 5% mathematics, 5% philosophy, religion, theology, 6% physical sciences, 8% psychology, 39% social sciences, 8% visual and performing arts. Graduate degrees offered in 11 major fields of study.

UNDERGRADUATE MAJORS. American studies, anthropology, art history, Asian studies, biochemistry, biology, chemistry, cognitive science, comparative literature, dramatic arts, economics, English, exercise science, film arts, foreign languages (multiple emphasis), French, geochemistry, geology, geophysics and seismology, German, history, international relations, international studies, liberal/general studies, mathematics, music, philosophy, physical sciences, physics, political science and government, psychobiology, psychology, public policy studies, religion, sociology, Spanish, sports medicine, studio art, urban studies, visual and performing arts, women's studies.

ACADEMIC PROGRAMS. Accelerated program, double major, honors program, independent study, internships, student-designed major, study abroad, teacher preparation, visiting/exchange student program, United Nations semester, Washington semester, cross-registration; liberal arts/career combination in engineering; combined bachelor's/graduate program in law. **Remedial services:** Learning center. **ROTC:** Air Force, Army. **Placement/credit:** AP, institutional tests. Unlimited number of hours of credit by examination may be counted toward degree.

ACADEMIC REQUIREMENTS. Freshmen must earn minimum GPA of 2.0 to continue in good standing. 91% of freshmen return for sophomore year. Students must declare major by end of second year. **Graduation requirements:** 140 hours for bachelor's (36 in major). Most students required to take courses in arts/fine arts, English, foreign languages, history, humanities, mathematics, philosophy/religion, biological/physical sciences, social sciences. **Postgraduate studies:** 19% enter law school, 12% enter medical school, 4% enter MBA programs, 30% enter other graduate study.

FRESHMAN ADMISSIONS. Selection criteria: Academic achievement most important, followed by school and teacher recommendations, SAT or ACT and ACH scores, writing ability, and involvement in curricular and cocurricular activities. **High school preparation:** 12 units required. Required units include biological science 1, English 4, mathematics 3, physical science 1 and social science 3. **Test requirements:** SAT or ACT (SAT preferred); score report by March 10. **Additional information:** Self-recommendation and copy of classroom writing assignment also required for freshman application.

1992 FRESHMAN CLASS PROFILE. 435 men and women enrolled. **Academic background:** Mid 50% of enrolled freshmen had SAT-V between 480-600, SAT-M between 530-650. 98% submitted SAT scores. **Characteristics:** 54% from in state, 100% live in college housing, 44% have minority backgrounds, 4% are foreign students, 20% join fraternities/sororities. Average age is 18.

FALL-TERM APPLICATIONS. $30 fee, may be waived for applicants with need. Closing date February 1; applicants notified on or about April 1; must reply by May 1. Essay required. Interview recommended. Audition recommended for music, drama applicants. Portfolio recommended for art applicants. CRDA. Deferred and early admission available. EDP-F. ACH recommended for admissions and placement; score report by March 10.

STUDENT LIFE. Housing: Dormitories (coed); fraternity, sorority housing available. Campus housing includes 11 residence halls, 4 fraternity houses, and 3 sorority houses. **Activities:** Student government, film, magazine, radio, student newspaper, yearbook, choral groups, dance, drama, jazz band, music ensembles, musical theater, pep band, symphony orchestra, chamber music group, gospel choir, fraternities, sororities, Movimiento Estudiantil Chicano de Aztlan (MECHA), Crossroads Africa, Asian Pacific Alliance, Model United Nations, Anti-Apartheid Coalition, Project Amigos, Black Students Alliance, Jewish Cultural Association, College Democrats, College Republicans, Volunteer Programs Center. **Additional information:** Students participate in college government, are active members of faculty, administrative and Board of Trustee committees, and have student government and residence hall responsibilities.

ATHLETICS. NCAA. **Intercollegiate:** Baseball M, basketball, cross-country, football M, golf, soccer, softball W, swimming, tennis, track and field, volleyball W, water polo M. **Intramural:** Badminton, baseball M, basketball, fencing, field hockey, golf, horseback riding, lacrosse, rugby M, skiing, soccer, softball, swimming, tennis, volleyball, water polo.

STUDENT SERVICES. Aptitude testing, career counseling, employment service for undergraduates, freshman orientation, health services, personal counseling, placement service for graduates, special adviser for adult students, leadership programs, peer mentor program, services/facilities for handicapped.

ANNUAL EXPENSES. Tuition and fees: $16,188. **Room and board:** $5,325. **Books and supplies:** $558. **Other expenses:** $1,152.

FINANCIAL AID. 55% of freshmen, 64% of continuing students receive some form of aid. 97% of grants, 66% of loans, all jobs based on need. Academic, music/drama, leadership scholarships available. **Aid applications:** Closing date February 1; applicants notified on or about April 1; must reply by May 1.

ADDRESS/TELEPHONE. Charlene Liebau, Dean of Admission, Occidental College, 1600 Campus Road, Los Angeles, CA 90041-3393. (213) 259-2700. (800) 825-5262. Fax: (213) 259-2958.

Ohlone College
Fremont, California — CB code: 4579

2-year public community college, coed. Founded in 1966. **Accreditation:** Regional. **Undergraduate enrollment:** 9,827 men and women. **Location:** Suburban campus in small city; 15 miles from San Jose. **Calendar:** Semester.

FRESHMAN ADMISSIONS. Selection criteria: Open admissions. Selected admissions for nursing and respiratory therapy programs.

ANNUAL EXPENSES. Tuition and fees (1992-93): $120, $3,240 additional for out-of-state students. **Books and supplies:** $520. **Other expenses:** $1,700.

ADDRESS/TELEPHONE. Ann Malveaux, Assistant Dean of Student Services, Ohlone College, 43600 Mission Boulevard, Fremont, CA 94539-0390. (510) 659-6100. Fax: (510) 659-6058.

Orange Coast College
Costa Mesa, California — CB code: 4584

2-year public community college, coed. Founded in 1947. **Accreditation:** Regional. **Undergraduate enrollment:** 26,927 men and women. **Location:** Urban campus in small city; 40 miles from Los Angeles. **Calendar:** Semester.

FRESHMAN ADMISSIONS. Selection criteria: Open admissions.

ANNUAL EXPENSES. Tuition and fees: $300, $3,120 additional for out-of-state students. **Books and supplies:** $612. **Other expenses:** $1,548.

ADDRESS/TELEPHONE. Susan Brown, Administrative Dean of Admissions and Records, Orange Coast College, 2701 Fairview Road, Costa Mesa, CA 92626-5005. (714) 432-5772. Fax: (714) 432-5609.

Otis School of Art and Design
Los Angeles, California — CB code: 4394

4-year private art college, coed. Founded in 1918. **Accreditation:** Regional. **Undergraduate enrollment:** 238 men, 402 women full time; 18 men, 64 women part time. **Graduate enrollment:** 4 men, 5 women full time. **Faculty:** 225 total (20 full time), 6 with doctorates or other terminal degrees. **Location:** Urban campus in very large city; one half mile west of downtown Los Angeles. **Calendar:** Semester, extensive summer session. **Microcomputers:** 20 located in dormitories, libraries, computer centers. **Special facilities:** Art gallery, rare art books collection, ceramics building with multi-kiln firing capabilities, full foundry and casting facilities, photographic darkroom, fully equiped printmaking studio, fine art book press room, woodworking and metal working shops.

DEGREES OFFERED. BFA, MFA. 2 associate degrees awarded in 1992. 100% in visual and performing arts. 90 bachelor's degrees awarded. 8% in architecture and environmental design, 92% visual and performing arts. Graduate degrees offered in 8 major fields of study.

UNDERGRADUATE MAJORS. Associate: Advertising, commercial art, environmental graphics, motion graphics and packaging design, fashion design, graphic and printing production, graphic arts technology, graphic design, photographic technology, photography. **Bachelor's:** Advertising, ceramics, commercial art, drawing, environmental design, fashion design, fiber/textiles/weaving, fine arts, graphic and printing production, graphic arts technology, graphic design, illustration design, metal/jewelry, painting, photographic technology, photography, printmaking, sculpture, studio art, visual and performing arts.

ACADEMIC PROGRAMS. 2-year transfer program, independent study, study abroad, visiting/exchange student program, New York semester, cross-registration. **Remedial services:** Remedial instruction, tutoring. **Placement/credit:** AP, institutional tests.

ACADEMIC REQUIREMENTS. Freshmen must earn minimum GPA of 2.0 to continue in good standing. 90% of freshmen return for sophomore year. Students must declare major by end of first year. **Graduation requirements:** 60 hours for associate (39 in major), 134 hours for bachelor's (72 in major). Most students required to take courses in arts/fine arts, English, history, humanities, philosophy/religion, biological/physical sciences, social sciences.

FRESHMAN ADMISSIONS. Selection criteria: Portfolio and home examination most important, followed by school achievement record and test scores. Activities, leadership, motivation also considered. As much art as possible recommended. **Test requirements:** SAT or ACT (SAT preferred); score report by July 1. Applicants required to complete home examination in 4 specific art and design problems as supplement to portfolio.

1992 FRESHMAN CLASS PROFILE. 64 men, 112 women enrolled. **Characteristics:** Average age is 20.

FALL-TERM APPLICATIONS. $40 fee, may be waived for applicants with need. No closing date; priority given to applications received by March 1; applicants notified on a rolling basis; must reply by May 1 or within 2 weeks if notified thereafter. Portfolio required. Essay required. Interview recommended. CRDA. Deferred and early admission available. EDP-S.

STUDENT LIFE. Housing: Dormitories (coed). **Activities:** Student government, film, magazine, student newspaper, yearbook, poetry and art publications, exhibition committee.

STUDENT SERVICES. Career counseling, employment service for undergraduates, freshman orientation, personal counseling, placement service for graduates, veterans counselor, minority student adviser, services/facilities for handicapped.

ANNUAL EXPENSES. Tuition and fees (1992-93): $11,990. **Room and board:** $2,650 room only. **Books and supplies:** $1,650. **Other expenses:** $1,375.

FINANCIAL AID. All grants, 63% of loans, all jobs based on need. **Aid applications:** No closing date; priority given to applications received by March 1; applicants notified on a rolling basis beginning on or about April 1; must reply within 3 weeks.

ADDRESS/TELEPHONE. Joseph Suszynski, Director of Admissions, Otis School of Art and Design, 2401 Wilshire Boulevard, Los Angeles, CA 90057. (213) 251-0505. (800) 527-6847. Fax: (213) 480-0059.

Oxnard College
Oxnard, California — CB code: 4591

2-year public community college, coed. Founded in 1975. **Accreditation:** Regional. **Undergraduate enrollment:** 6,420 men and women. **Location:** Urban campus in small city; 60 miles from Los Angeles. **Calendar:** Semester.

FRESHMAN ADMISSIONS. Selection criteria: Open admissions.

ANNUAL EXPENSES. Tuition and fees (1992-93): $135, $3,300 additional for out-of-state students. **Books and supplies:** $500. **Other expenses:** $1,000.

ADDRESS/TELEPHONE. Ronald Jackson, Vice President of Student Services, Oxnard College, 4000 South Rose Avenue, Oxnard, CA 93033. (805) 986-5810.

Pacific Christian College
Fullerton, California — CB code: 4614

4-year private Bible college, coed, affiliated with Christian Churches and Churches of Christ. Founded in 1928. **Accreditation:** Regional. **Undergraduate enrollment:** 180 men, 183 women full time; 20 men, 30 women part time. **Graduate enrollment:** 13 men, 19 women full time; 22 men, 10 women part time. **Faculty:** 46 total (19 full time), 18 with doctorates or other terminal degrees. **Location:** Suburban campus in small city; 45 miles from Los Angeles. **Calendar:** 4-1-4, limited summer session. **Microcomputers:** 10 located in libraries.

DEGREES OFFERED. AA, BA, MA. 17 associate degrees awarded in 1992. 35% in teacher education, 65% multi/interdisciplinary studies. 78 bachelor's degrees awarded. 21% in business and management, 22% teacher education, 25% philosophy, religion, theology, 10% psychology, 12% social sciences, 6% visual and performing arts. Graduate degrees offered in 5 major fields of study.

UNDERGRADUATE MAJORS. Associate: Early childhood education, liberal/general studies, missionary studies. **Bachelor's:** Bible studies, business administration and management, child development/care/guidance, communications, elementary education, English education, graphic design, missionary studies, music, music education, physical education, psychology, religion, religious education, religious music, secondary education, social science education, social sciences, social work, theological studies.

ACADEMIC PROGRAMS. 2-year transfer program, accelerated program, double major, dual enrollment of high school students, independent study, internships, student-designed major, teacher preparation, cross-registration. **Remedial services:** Learning center, reduced course load, remedial instruction, tutoring. **Placement/credit:** AP, CLEP General and Subject, institutional tests; 30 credit hours maximum for bachelor's degree.

ACADEMIC REQUIREMENTS. Freshmen must earn minimum GPA of 2.0 to continue in good standing. 75% of freshmen return for sophomore year. Students must declare major by end of second year. **Graduation requirements:** 63 hours for associate (20 in major), 124 hours for bachelor's (36 in major). Most students required to take courses in English, history, humanities, mathematics, philosophy/religion, biological/physical sciences, social sciences. **Postgraduate studies:** 50% from 2-year programs enter 4-year programs.

FRESHMAN ADMISSIONS. Selection criteria: All factors bearing on potential success considered. **High school preparation:** 14 units recommended. Recommended units include English 4, foreign language 1, mathematics 2, social science 1.5 and science 1. One visual or performing arts recommended, .5 speech and .5 computer science or literacy also recommended. **Test requirements:** SAT or ACT (SAT preferred); score report by August 31.

1992 FRESHMAN CLASS PROFILE. 47 men, 47 women enrolled. 57% had high school GPA of 3.0 or higher, 33% between 2.0 and 2.99. **Characteristics:** 49% from in state, 90% live in college housing, 13% have minority backgrounds, 1% are foreign students. Average age is 20.

FALL-TERM APPLICATIONS. $30 fee. Closing date July 1; applicants notified on a rolling basis. Essay required. Interview recommended for academically borderline applicants. Deferred admission available.

STUDENT LIFE. Housing: Dormitories (men, women); apartment housing available. Single students required to live on campus unless living at home or given special approval. **Activities:** Student government, magazine, student newspaper, yearbook, choral groups, concert band, drama, music ensembles, musical theater, International Students Club, AIM (active in missions). **Additional information:** Religious observance required.

ATHLETICS. Intercollegiate: Basketball, soccer M, softball W, volleyball. **Intramural:** Baseball, bowling, football, golf, skiing, soccer M, table tennis, tennis, volleyball.

STUDENT SERVICES. Aptitude testing, career counseling, employment service for undergraduates, freshman orientation, health services, on-campus day care, personal counseling, placement service for graduates, veterans counselor, services/facilities for handicapped.

ANNUAL EXPENSES. Tuition and fees: $6,710. **Room and board:** $4,584. **Books and supplies:** $612. **Other expenses:** $1,350.

FINANCIAL AID. 99% of freshmen, 94% of continuing students receive some form of aid. 57% of grants, 85% of loans, all jobs based on need. 72 enrolled freshmen were judged to have need, all were offered aid. Academic, music/drama, state/district residency, leadership, minority scholarships available. **Aid applications:** No closing date; priority given to applications received by March 2; applicants notified on a rolling basis beginning on or about April 1; must reply within 15 days. **Additional information:** Many part-time jobs available in local area.

ADDRESS/TELEPHONE. Diane LeJeune, Director of Admissions, Pacific Christian College, 2500 East Nutwood Avenue, Fullerton, CA 92631. (714) 879-3901 ext. 231. (800) 762-1294. Fax: (714) 526-0231.

Pacific Oaks College
Pasadena, California — CB code: 0482

2-year upper-division private teachers college, coed, historic affiliation with Quaker religion. Founded in 1951. **Accreditation:** Regional. **Undergraduate enrollment:** 38 men, 46 women full time; 6 men, 102 women part time. **Graduate enrollment:** 16 men, 64 women full time; 28 men, 322 women part time. **Faculty:** 73 total (23 full time), 24 with doctorates or other terminal degrees. **Location:** Urban campus in small city; 10 miles from downtown Los Angeles. **Calendar:** Semester, extensive summer session. Saturday and extensive evening/early morning classes. **Microcomputers:** 6 located in libraries, computer centers. **Special facilities:** Laboratory school for infants through grade 3. **Additional facts:** Outreach centers in Washington State, Oregon, San Diego, and San Francisco Bay area, and branch campus in Seattle for those who wish to earn Multiple Subject Teaching Credential at The Little School. College primarily serves part-time, adult students.

DEGREES OFFERED. BA, MA. 28 bachelor's degrees awarded in 1992. 20% in education, 80% teacher education. Graduate degrees offered in 16 major fields of study.

UNDERGRADUATE MAJORS. Child development/care/guidance, early childhood education, education, elementary education, human development/lactation consultant, individual and family development.

ACADEMIC PROGRAMS. Accelerated program, double major, independent study, internships, teacher preparation, weekend college. **Placement/credit:** CLEP General and Subject; 30 credit hours maximum for bachelor's degree.

ACADEMIC REQUIREMENTS. Students must declare major on application. **Graduation requirements:** 124 hours for bachelor's (30 in major). Most students required to take courses in English, humanities, mathematics, biological/physical sciences, social sciences. **Additional information:** Teacher education program prepares elementary and special education teachers.

STUDENT LIFE. Activities: Student government. **Additional information:** Most students work full time.

STUDENT SERVICES. Career counseling, special adviser for adult students, services/facilities for handicapped.

ANNUAL EXPENSES. Tuition and fees (1992-93): $10,400. **Books and supplies:** $450. **Other expenses:** $1,350.

FINANCIAL AID. 25% of continuing students receive some form of aid. All grants, 81% of loans, all jobs based on need. Academic, leadership scholarships available. **Aid applications:** No closing date; priority given to applications received by March 1; applicants notified on a rolling basis beginning on or about April 30; must reply within 4 weeks.

ADDRESS/TELEPHONE. Marsha A. Franker, Director of Admissions, Pacific Oaks College, 5 Westmoreland Place, Pasadena, CA 91103. (818) 397-1351. Fax: (818) 397-1356.

Pacific Union College
Angwin, California CB code: 4600

Admissions: 74% of applicants accepted
Based on: ••• Recommendations
•• Religious affiliation/commitment, school record
• Interview, test scores
Completion: 75% of freshmen end year in good standing

4-year private liberal arts college, coed, affiliated with Seventh-day Adventists. Founded in 1882. **Accreditation:** Regional. **Undergraduate enrollment:** 598 men, 724 women full time; 7 men, 116 women part time. **Graduate enrollment:** 2 women full time; 1 woman part time. **Faculty:** 128 total (109 full time), 49 with doctorates or other terminal degrees. **Location:** Rural campus in small town; 30 miles from Napa, 75 miles from San Francisco. **Calendar:** Quarter, limited summer session. **Microcomputers:** 100 located in libraries, classrooms, computer centers. **Special facilities:** Art gallery.

DEGREES OFFERED. AA, AS, BA, BS, MA. 67 associate degrees awarded in 1992. 251 bachelor's degrees awarded. Graduate degrees offered in 2 major fields of study.

UNDERGRADUATE MAJORS. Associate: Bible studies, business and office, business data processing and related programs, child development/care/guidance, dietetic aide/assistant, drafting, electronic technology, engineering and engineering-related technologies, family/consumer resource management, food production/management/services, graphic arts technology, industrial technology, information sciences and systems, interior design, laser electro-optic technology, legal secretary, liberal/general studies, manufacturing technology, medical secretary, nursing, photography, piano pedgogy, secretarial and related programs, textiles and clothing, word processing. **Bachelor's:** Accounting, applied mathematics, art history, behavioral sciences, biochemistry, biology, biophysics, business administration and management, business and management, chemistry, child development/care/guidance, clinical laboratory science, communications, computer and information sciences, data processing, drafting and design technology, electronic technology, elementary education, engineering and engineering-related technologies, English, fashion merchandising, fine arts, food science and nutrition, French, history, home economics, industrial equipment maintenance and repair, information sciences and systems, interior design, journalism, liberal/general studies, management information systems, manufacturing technology, marketing and distribution, marketing management, mathematics, medical laboratory technologies, music, music education, music performance, nursing, office supervision and management, parks and recreation management, physical education, physical sciences, physics, political science and government, predentistry, premedicine, preveterinary, psychology, public relations, recreation and community services technologies, religion, religious education, robotics, secretarial and related programs, social sciences, social work, Spanish, theological studies, visual and performing arts.

ACADEMIC PROGRAMS. 2-year transfer program, cooperative education, double major, honors program, independent study, internships, semester at sea, student-designed major, study abroad, teacher preparation; liberal arts/career combination in health sciences. **Remedial services:** Learning center, reduced course load, remedial instruction, tutoring. **Placement/credit:** AP, CLEP Subject, institutional tests; 24 credit hours maximum for associate degree; 45 credit hours maximum for bachelor's degree.

ACADEMIC REQUIREMENTS. Freshmen must earn minimum GPA of 2.0 to continue in good standing. **Graduation requirements:** 90 hours for associate, 192 hours for bachelor's (60 in major). Most students required to take courses in arts/fine arts, English, history, mathematics, philosophy/religion, biological/physical sciences, social sciences.

FRESHMAN ADMISSIONS. Selection criteria: Minimum GPA of 2.0 and acceptable recommendations. **High school preparation:** 16 units required. Required units include English 3, mathematics 2, physical science 1 and social science 1. **Test requirements:** ACT for placement and counseling only; score report by September 20.

1992 FRESHMAN CLASS PROFILE. 283 men applied, 215 accepted, 208 enrolled; 361 women applied, 260 accepted, 244 enrolled. **Academic background:** Mid 50% of enrolled freshmen had ACT composite between 18-24. 98% submitted ACT scores. **Characteristics:** 80% from in state, 92% live in college housing, 24% have minority backgrounds, 10% are foreign students. Average age is 19.

FALL-TERM APPLICATIONS. $30 fee. No closing date; applicants notified on a rolling basis beginning on or about December 15. Early admission available.

STUDENT LIFE. Housing: Dormitories (men, women); apartment housing available. **Activities:** Student government, radio, student newspaper, yearbook, choral groups, concert band, drama, music ensembles, symphony orchestra, chapel, assembly, clubs. **Additional information:** Religious observance required.

ATHLETICS. Intramural: Badminton, basketball, football M, golf, skiing, soccer, softball, swimming, table tennis, tennis, track and field, volleyball, water polo.

STUDENT SERVICES. Aptitude testing, career counseling, employment service for undergraduates, freshman orientation, health services, on-campus day care, personal counseling, placement service for graduates, special adviser for adult students, veterans counselor, services/facilities for handicapped.

ANNUAL EXPENSES. Tuition and fees: $11,400. **Room and board:** $3,675. **Books and supplies:** $612. **Other expenses:** $1,350.

FINANCIAL AID. 70% of freshmen, 70% of continuing students receive some form of aid. 87% of grants, 88% of loans, 5% of jobs based on need. 390 enrolled freshmen were judged to have need, all were offered aid. Academic, music/drama, state/district residency, leadership, minority scholarships available. **Aid applications:** No closing date; priority given to applications received by March 2; applicants notified on a rolling basis; must reply within 3 weeks.

ADDRESS/TELEPHONE. Gary Gifford, Director of Enrollment Services, Pacific Union College, Angwin, CA 94508. (707) 965-6673. (800) 862-7080.

Palo Verde College
Blythe, California CB code: 4603

2-year public community college, coed. Founded in 1947. **Accreditation:** Regional. **Undergraduate enrollment:** 1,412 men and women. **Location:** Rural campus in small town; 160 miles from Riverside. **Calendar:** Semester.

FRESHMAN ADMISSIONS. Selection criteria: Open admissions.

ANNUAL EXPENSES. Tuition and fees: $240, $2,400 additional for out-of-state students. **Books and supplies:** $600.

ADDRESS/TELEPHONE. Joyce Linares, Registrar, Palo Verde College, 811 West Chanslorway, Blythe, CA 92225. (619) 922-6168.

Palomar College
San Marcos, California CB code: 4602

2-year public community college, coed. Founded in 1946. **Accreditation:** Regional. **Undergraduate enrollment:** 24,335 men and women. **Faculty:** 802 total (274 full time), 37 with doctorates or other terminal degrees. **Location:** Suburban campus in large town; 40 miles from San Diego. **Calendar:** Semester, limited summer session. **Microcomputers:** 50 located in libraries, classrooms. **Special facilities:** Nature preserve, Palomar Observatory, Howard Brubeck Art Gallery.

DEGREES OFFERED. AA. 562 associate degrees awarded in 1992.

UNDERGRADUATE MAJORS. Accounting, aeronautical technology, airline piloting and navigation, archeology, astronomy, automotive mechanics, automotive technology, aviation management, biology, biomedical equipment technology, business and office, carpentry, ceramics, chemistry, computer and information sciences, construction, crafts, dance, dental assistant, diesel engine mechanics, drafting and design technology, electrical and electronics equipment repair, electrical installation, electronic technology, emergency medical technologies, engineering, fashion merchandising, finance, fire control and safety technology, food production/management/services, glass, graphic arts technology, graphic design, illustration design, institutional/home management/supporting programs, interior design, interpreter for the deaf, journalism, law enforcement and corrections technologies, legal assistant/paralegal, liberal/general studies, library assistant, mathematics, medical assistant, metal/jewelry, music, nursing, parks and recreation management, photographic technology, precision metal work, printmaking, psychology, public administration, quality control technology, radio/television broadcasting, real estate, recreation and community services technologies, sculpture, secretarial and related programs, speech, survey and mapping technology, teacher aide, tourism.

ACADEMIC PROGRAMS. 2-year transfer program, cooperative education, double major, dual enrollment of high school students, study abroad. **Remedial services:** Learning center, preadmission summer program, reduced course load, remedial instruction, tutoring. **Placement/credit:** AP, institutional tests; 15 credit hours maximum for associate degree.

ACADEMIC REQUIREMENTS. Freshmen must earn minimum GPA of 2.0 to continue in good standing. 16% of freshmen return for sophomore year. Students must declare major by end of first year. **Graduation requirements:** 60 hours for associate (24 in major). Most students required to take courses in English, history, humanities, mathematics, biological/physical sciences, social sciences.

FRESHMAN ADMISSIONS. Selection criteria: Open admissions. **Test requirements:** SAT or ACT for placement. ACH required of some applicants. **Additional information:** Nursing applicants required to take ASSET mathematics and English tests. Application deadlines for nursing program April 1 for fall semester, November 1 for spring semester.

1992 FRESHMAN CLASS PROFILE. 15,394 men and women enrolled. **Characteristics:** 98% from in state, 100% commute, 10% have minority backgrounds, 1% are foreign students. Average age is 19.

FALL-TERM APPLICATIONS. No fee. Closing date August 20; priority given to applications received by March 15; applicants notified on a rolling basis.

STUDENT LIFE. Activities: Student government, magazine, radio, student newspaper, television, choral groups, concert band, dance, drama, jazz band, music ensembles, musical theater, pep band, symphony orchestra.

ATHLETICS. NJCAA. **Intercollegiate:** Baseball M, basketball, football M, golf M, soccer, softball W, swimming, tennis, volleyball, water polo M, wrestling M. **Intramural:** Volleyball W.

STUDENT SERVICES. Aptitude testing, career counseling, employment service for undergraduates, freshman orientation, health services, on-campus day care, personal counseling, placement service for graduates, veterans counselor, services/facilities for handicapped.

ANNUAL EXPENSES. Tuition and fees (1992-93): $135, $3,240 additional for out-of-state students. **Books and supplies:** $560. **Other expenses:** $1,235.

FINANCIAL AID. 12% of freshmen, 6% of continuing students receive some form of aid. 84% of grants, 72% of loans, 14% of jobs based on need. 450 enrolled freshmen were judged to have need, all were offered aid. Academic, state/district residency scholarships available. **Aid applications:** No closing date; priority given to applications received by April 1; applicants notified on a rolling basis beginning on or about June 1.

ADDRESS/TELEPHONE. Herman C. Lee, Director of Enrollment Services, Palomar College, 1140 West Mission Road, San Marcos, CA 92069. (619) 744-1150. Fax: (619) 744-8123.

Pasadena City College

Pasadena, California CB code: 4604

2-year public community college, coed. Founded in 1924. **Accreditation:** Regional. **Undergraduate enrollment:** 2,899 men, 3,444 women full time; 8,165 men, 9,701 women part time. **Faculty:** 946 total (420 full time), 105 with doctorates or other terminal degrees. **Location:** Urban campus in small city; 10 miles from downtown Los Angeles. **Calendar:** Semester, limited summer session. Saturday and extensive evening/early morning classes. **Microcomputers:** 20 located in classrooms, computer centers. **Special facilities:** Art gallery, observatory.

DEGREES OFFERED. AA, AS. 850 associate degrees awarded in 1992.

UNDERGRADUATE MAJORS. Accounting, allied health, automotive mechanics, automotive technology, biology, business and management, business and office, business computer/console/peripheral equipment operation, business data processing and related programs, business data programming, carpentry, ceramics, chemistry, clinical laboratory science, commercial art, communications, computer programming, construction, crafts, data processing, dental assistant, dental hygiene, dental laboratory technology, drafting, drawing, early childhood education, engineering and engineering-related technologies, fashion merchandising, finance, fire control and safety technology, food management, graphic and printing production, graphic arts technology, graphic design, hospitality and recreation marketing, industrial technology, instrumentation technology, insurance marketing, journalism, law enforcement and corrections technologies, legal assistant/paralegal, legal secretary, liberal/general studies, library assistant, marketing and distribution, mechanical design technology, medical assistant, medical laboratory technologies, medical secretary, music, nursing, painting, personal services, photographic technology, practical nursing, precision metal work, printmaking, protective services, psychology, public affairs, radio/television broadcasting, radio/television technology, radiograph medical technology, real estate, recreation and community services technologies, retailing, science technologies, sculpture, secretarial and related programs, small business management and ownership, social sciences, speech, studio art, telecommunications, transportation and travel marketing.

ACADEMIC PROGRAMS. 2-year transfer program, accelerated program, dual enrollment of high school students, honors program, independent study, internships, study abroad, telecourses. **Remedial services:** Learning center, preadmission summer program, reduced course load, remedial instruction, special counselor, tutoring. **Placement/credit:** AP, CLEP General, institutional tests; 12 credit hours maximum for associate degree.

ACADEMIC REQUIREMENTS. Freshmen must earn minimum GPA of 2.0 to continue in good standing. 53% of freshmen return for sophomore year. Students must declare major by end of first year. **Graduation requirements:** 60 hours for associate (18 in major). Most students required to take courses in arts/fine arts, English, humanities, mathematics, biological/physical sciences, social sciences.

FRESHMAN ADMISSIONS. Selection criteria: Open admissions. Selective admissions to some programs based on test scores, interview, high school record, 2.0 high school GPA. **Test requirements:** School and College Ability Tests, SAT, ACT, or California Achievement tests used for admission to some programs.

1992 FRESHMAN CLASS PROFILE. 4,987 men and women enrolled. **Characteristics:** 97% from in state, 100% commute, 69% have minority backgrounds, 3% are foreign students.

FALL-TERM APPLICATIONS. No fee. No closing date; applicants notified on a rolling basis beginning on or about April 1. Interview required for dental hygiene applicants. Audition required for music applicants.

STUDENT LIFE. Activities: Student government, film, magazine, radio, student newspaper, television, choral groups, concert band, dance, drama, jazz band, marching band, music ensembles, musical theater, pep band, symphony orchestra, wide variety of religious, political, ethnic, and social service organizations.

ATHLETICS. NJCAA. **Intercollegiate:** Baseball M, basketball, cross-country, football M, golf, softball W, swimming, tennis, track and field, volleyball W, water polo M.

STUDENT SERVICES. Aptitude testing, career counseling, employment service for undergraduates, freshman orientation, health services, personal counseling, placement service for graduates, special adviser for adult students, services/facilities for handicapped.

ANNUAL EXPENSES. Tuition and fees (1992-93): $180, $4,200 additional for out-of-state students. **Books and supplies:** $450. **Other expenses:** $900.

FINANCIAL AID. 15% of freshmen, 14% of continuing students receive some form of aid. Grants, loans, jobs available. Academic, music/drama, art, athletic, state/district residency, leadership, minority scholarships available. **Aid applications:** No closing date; priority given to applications received by June 24; applicants notified on a rolling basis beginning on or about May 15; must reply within 2 weeks.

ADDRESS/TELEPHONE. Dr. Stuart A. Wilcox, Associate Dean of Admissions and Records, Pasadena City College, 1570 East Colorado Boulevard, Pasadena, CA 91106. (818) 578-7396. Fax: (818) 356-9826.

Patten College

Oakland, California CB code: 4620

Admissions:	86% of applicants accepted
Based on:	••• Essay, interview, recommendations, religious affiliation/commitment
	•• School record
	• Activities, test scores
Completion:	80% of freshmen end year in good standing
	45% graduate, 75% of these enter graduate study

4-year private Bible college, coed, interdenominational. Founded in 1945. **Accreditation:** Regional. **Undergraduate enrollment:** 50 men, 44 women full time; 57 men, 61 women part time. **Faculty:** 35 total (15 full time), 14 with doctorates or other terminal degrees. **Location:** Urban campus in large city; 18 miles from San Francisco. **Calendar:** Semester. Saturday and extensive evening/early morning classes. **Microcomputers:** 15 located in libraries, computer centers.

DEGREES OFFERED. AA, BA. 14 bachelor's degrees awarded.

UNDERGRADUATE MAJORS. Associate: Bible studies, liberal/general studies, religion. **Bachelor's:** Education, liberal/general studies, preseminary, religion, religious education, religious music, theological studies.

ACADEMIC PROGRAMS. 2-year transfer program, double major, dual enrollment of high school students, independent study, teacher preparation. **Remedial services:** Reduced course load, remedial instruction, special counselor, tutoring. **Placement/credit:** AP, CLEP General, institutional tests; 9 credit hours maximum for associate degree; 15 credit hours maximum for bachelor's degree.

ACADEMIC REQUIREMENTS. Freshmen must earn minimum GPA of 2.0 to continue in good standing. 70% of freshmen return for sophomore year. Students must declare major by end of second year. **Graduation requirements:** 63 hours for associate (23 in major), 130 hours for bachelor's (30 in major). Most students required to take courses in English, history, mathematics, philosophy/religion, biological/physical sciences, social sciences. **Postgraduate studies:** 35% from 2-year programs enter 4-year programs.

FRESHMAN ADMISSIONS. Selection criteria: High school record, interview, essay, recommendation important. Test scores also considered. **High school preparation:** 22 units required. Required units include biological science 1, English 4, foreign language 1, mathematics 2, physical science 1 and social science 4. **Test requirements:** SAT or ACT. Standardized placement tests in English, written expression, reading and mathematics. SAT or ACT recommended.

1992 FRESHMAN CLASS PROFILE. 45 men applied, 37 accepted, 33 enrolled; 40 women applied, 36 accepted, 28 enrolled. **Characteristics:** 95% from in state, 60% commute, 62% have minority backgrounds, 6% are foreign students. Average age is 24.

FALL-TERM APPLICATIONS. $3 fee, may be waived for applicants with need. Closing date July 15; priority given to applications received by May 15; applicants notified on a rolling basis beginning on or about April 20; must reply by August 15. Interview required. Essay required. Deferred admission available.

STUDENT LIFE. Housing: Dormitories (men, women, coed); apartment housing available. **Activities:** Student government, student newspaper, yearbook, choral groups, music ensembles, symphony orchestra, Christian service program, religious field work. **Additional information:** Christian Service Program designed to involve students in practical ministry. Religious observance required.

STUDENT SERVICES. Career counseling, employment service for

undergraduates, freshman orientation, personal counseling, placement service for graduates, veterans counselor, services/facilities for handicapped.

ANNUAL EXPENSES. Tuition and fees: $4,920. **Room and board:** $3,980. **Books and supplies:** $550. **Other expenses:** $1,100.

FINANCIAL AID. 80% of freshmen, 85% of continuing students receive some form of aid. 96% of grants, 84% of loans, all jobs based on need. 15 enrolled freshmen were judged to have need, all were offered aid. Academic, leadership, alumni affiliation, minority scholarships available. **Aid applications:** No closing date; priority given to applications received by March 2; applicants notified on a rolling basis beginning on or about July 1; must reply by May 1 or within 2 weeks if notified thereafter.

ADDRESS/TELEPHONE. Laura Dohrmann, Director of Admissions, Patten College, 2433 Coolidge Avenue, Oakland, CA 94601-2699. (510) 533-8306. Fax: (510) 534-8564.

Pepperdine University
Malibu, California — CB code: 4630

Admissions: 50% of applicants accepted
Based on:
••• School record, test scores
•• Essay, recommendations, special talents
• Activities, interview, religious affiliation/commitment
Completion: 92% of freshmen end year in good standing
70% graduate, 44% of these enter graduate study

4-year private university, coed, affiliated with Church of Christ. Founded in 1937. **Accreditation:** Regional. **Undergraduate enrollment:** 1,134 men, 1,511 women full time; 83 men, 78 women part time. **Graduate enrollment:** 1,448 men, 1,476 women full time; 701 men, 728 women part time. **Faculty:** 626 total (309 full time), 300 with doctorates or other terminal degrees. **Location:** Suburban campus in small city; 14 miles from Santa Monica, 30 miles from downtown Los Angeles. **Calendar:** Semester, limited summer session. **Microcomputers:** 180 located in dormitories, libraries, classrooms, computer centers. **Special facilities:** Frederick R. Weisman Art Gallery, marine biology laboratory, Japanese Tea Ceremony Rooms. **Additional facts:** Liberal arts college and law school in Malibu. Education, psychology, and business graduate colleges in Los Angeles. Educational centers in Irvine, Encino, and Long Beach. Three campuses in Europe, one in Asia, one in Australia.

DEGREES OFFERED. BA, BS, MA, MS, MBA, MEd, EdD, JD, M.Div. 745 bachelor's degrees awarded in 1992. 42% in business and management, 21% communications, 5% health sciences, 7% multi/interdisciplinary studies, 12% social sciences. Graduate degrees offered in 19 major fields of study.

UNDERGRADUATE MAJORS. Accounting, advertising, biochemistry, biology, business administration and management, chemistry, communications, computer and information sciences, computer mathematics, creative writing, economics, elementary education, English, fine arts, French, German, history, humanities, international relations, international studies, journalism, junior high education, liberal/general studies, mathematics, music, nutritional sciences, philosophy, physical education, political science and government, predentistry, prelaw, premedicine, psychology, public relations, religion, secondary education, sociology, Spanish, speech, sports medicine, telecommunications, theological studies, visual and performing arts.

ACADEMIC PROGRAMS. Accelerated program, double major, honors program, independent study, internships, student-designed major, study abroad, teacher preparation, Washington semester, 3-2 program in engineering with several 4-year universities; combined bachelor's/graduate program in business administration, law. **Remedial services:** Preadmission summer program, special counselor, tutoring. **ROTC:** Air Force, Army, Naval. **Placement/credit:** AP, CLEP General and Subject, IB, institutional tests; 32 credit hours maximum for bachelor's degree.

ACADEMIC REQUIREMENTS. Freshmen must earn minimum GPA of 2.0 to continue in good standing. 85% of freshmen return for sophomore year. Students must declare major by end of second year. **Graduation requirements:** 128 hours for bachelor's (40 in major). Most students required to take courses in arts/fine arts, computer science, English, foreign languages, history, humanities, mathematics, philosophy/religion, biological/physical sciences, social sciences. **Postgraduate studies:** 10% enter law school, 7% enter medical school, 12% enter MBA programs, 15% enter other graduate study. **Additional information:** Honors programs available. Great books colloquium. Freshman seminars and first year faculty mentor program for all students.

FRESHMAN ADMISSIONS. Selection criteria: School achievement record and test scores most important. Special talents, school and community activities, letters of recommendation, and personal qualities also considered. **High school preparation:** 15 units recommended. Recommended units include English 4, foreign language 2, mathematics 3, social science 2 and science 2. **Test requirements:** SAT or ACT; score report by February 1. ACH tests recommended. **Additional information:** Special admissions requirements for business program.

1992 FRESHMAN CLASS PROFILE. 1,339 men applied, 659 accepted, 292 enrolled; 2,145 women applied, 1,080 accepted, 302 enrolled. 79% had high school GPA of 3.0 or higher, 21% between 2.0 and 2.99. 85% were in top tenth and 95% were in top quarter of graduating class. **Academic background:** Mid 50% of enrolled freshmen had SAT-V between 440-540, SAT-M between 500-620; ACT composite between 22-28. 88% submitted SAT scores, 23% submitted ACT scores. **Characteristics:** 52% from in state, 96% live in college housing, 25% have minority backgrounds, 10% are foreign students, 15% join fraternities/sororities. Average age is 18.

FALL-TERM APPLICATIONS. $45 fee, may be waived for applicants with need. Closing date February 1; applicants notified on or about April 1; must reply by May 1. Essay required. Interview recommended. Audition recommended for music, theater applicants. Portfolio recommended for art applicants. CRDA. Institutional early decision plan. ACH strongly recommended. Early action is non-binding.

STUDENT LIFE. Housing: Dormitories (men, women); apartment, handicapped housing available. Freshmen and sophomores must live on campus or at home with parent or guardian. **Activities:** Student government, magazine, radio, student newspaper, television, yearbook, choral groups, concert band, dance, drama, jazz band, music ensembles, musical theater, opera, pep band, symphony orchestra, fraternities, sororities, Campus Crusade, College Republicans, Young Democrats, Volunteer Center, Black Student Union, Latin Student Association, Hawaiian Club, International Club, Korean Student Association, Japan Club. **Additional information:** Students required to attend a weekly assembly. Distinguished speakers address topics dealing with moral and ethical issues, environmental and sociological concerns, and world politics.

ATHLETICS. NCAA. **Intercollegiate:** Baseball M, basketball, cross-country, diving W, golf, soccer W, swimming W, tennis, volleyball, water polo M. **Intramural:** Badminton, baseball, basketball, golf, ice hockey, lacrosse M, rugby M, soccer, softball, swimming, table tennis, tennis, volleyball, water polo, wrestling M.

STUDENT SERVICES. Aptitude testing, career counseling, employment service for undergraduates, freshman orientation, health services, personal counseling, placement service for graduates, veterans counselor, services/facilities for handicapped.

ANNUAL EXPENSES. Tuition and fees: $17,260. **Room and board:** $6,530. **Books and supplies:** $800. **Other expenses:** $660.

FINANCIAL AID. 63% of freshmen, 59% of continuing students receive some form of aid. All grants, 82% of loans, all jobs based on need. Academic, music/drama, art, athletic, leadership scholarships available. **Aid applications:** Closing date March 1; priority given to applications received by February 15; applicants notified on or about April 15; must reply by May 1 or within 2 weeks if notified thereafter.

ADDRESS/TELEPHONE. Paul Long, Dean of Admission, Pepperdine University, 24255 Pacific Coast Highway, Malibu, CA 90263-4392. (310) 456-4392. Fax: (310) 456-4861.

Phillips Junior College: Condie Campus
Campbell, California — CB code: 0926

2-year proprietary business, junior, technical college, coed. Founded in 1968. **Accreditation:** Regional. **Undergraduate enrollment:** 300 men, 600 women full time. **Faculty:** 46 total (11 full time), 5 with doctorates or other terminal degrees. **Location:** Urban campus in large town; 5 miles from downtown San Jose. **Calendar:** Quarter. **Microcomputers:** 76 located in computer centers. **Additional facts:** Member of Phillips College System with 53 schools nationwide.

DEGREES OFFERED. AA, AS. 500 associate degrees awarded in 1992.

UNDERGRADUATE MAJORS. Business administration and management, business data processing and related programs, business data programming, computer and information sciences, computer programming, computer technology, computerized accounting, court reporting, data processing, electronic technology, legal assistant/paralegal, legal secretary, medical secretary, secretarial and related programs, transportation and travel marketing.

ACADEMIC PROGRAMS. 2-year transfer program, honors program, internships. **Remedial services:** Learning center, reduced course load, remedial instruction, tutoring. **Placement/credit:** Institutional tests.

ACADEMIC REQUIREMENTS. Freshmen must earn minimum GPA of 2.0 to continue in good standing. 70% of freshmen return for sophomore year. Students must declare major on enrollment. **Graduation requirements:** 66 hours for associate. Most students required to take courses in computer science, English, mathematics.

FRESHMAN ADMISSIONS. Selection criteria: Acceptable CPAT test score, interview, and school achievement record considered.

1992 FRESHMAN CLASS PROFILE. 214 men and women enrolled. **Characteristics:** 95% from in state, 100% commute, 35% have minority backgrounds.

FALL-TERM APPLICATIONS. $25 fee. No closing date; applicants notified on a rolling basis. Interview required. Deferred admission available. Applicants with high school diploma must score 115 on CPAT for diploma program and 118 for associate program. Non-diploma holders must score 120.

STUDENT LIFE. Activities: Student government, student newspaper, television, travel club, business club, electronics club, mathematics club, Data Processing Management Association.

STUDENT SERVICES. Aptitude testing, career counseling, employment service for undergraduates, freshman orientation, personal counseling, placement service for graduates, veterans counselor, services/facilities for handicapped.

ANNUAL EXPENSES. Tuition and fees (1992-93): Tuition and fees are $10,500 for complete associate program, and $4,400 for diploma program in court reporting. **Books and supplies:** $450. **Other expenses:** $1,458.

FINANCIAL AID. 80% of freshmen, 80% of continuing students receive some form of aid. 86% of loans, all jobs based on need. **Aid applications:** No closing date; applicants notified on a rolling basis.

ADDRESS/TELEPHONE. Marilyn McKnight, Director of Admissions, Phillips Junior College: Condie Campus, 1 West Campbell Avenue, Campbell, CA 95008. (408) 866-6666. Fax: (408) 866-5542.

Phillips Junior College: Fresno Campus
Fresno, California CB code: 5352

2-year proprietary junior college, coed. **Undergraduate enrollment:** 250 men, 250 women full time. **Faculty:** 14 total (10 full time). **Location:** Suburban campus in large city. **Calendar:** Quarter. Extensive evening/early morning classes. **Microcomputers:** 59 located in libraries, computer centers.

DEGREES OFFERED. AA, AS. 70 associate degrees awarded in 1992. 25% in business and management, 15% business/office and marketing/distribution, 30% computer sciences, 30% engineering technologies.

UNDERGRADUATE MAJORS. Accounting, apparel and accessories marketing, business administration and management, business and management, business and office, business computer/console/peripheral equipment operation, business data entry equipment operation, business data processing and related programs, business data programming, business systems analysis, computer and information sciences, computer programming, computer servicing technology, data processing, electrical/electronics/communications engineering, electronic technology, fashion merchandising, information sciences and systems, legal secretary, management information systems, medical secretary, microcomputer software, retailing, small business management and ownership, systems analysis, tourism.

ACADEMIC PROGRAMS. Accelerated program, double major, independent study, internships. **Remedial services:** Tutoring. **Placement/credit:** Institutional tests; 16 credit hours maximum for associate degree.

ACADEMIC REQUIREMENTS. Freshmen must earn minimum GPA of 2.0 to continue in good standing. 85% of freshmen return for sophomore year. Students must declare major on enrollment. **Graduation requirements:** 90 hours for associate (52 in major). Most students required to take courses in English, humanities, mathematics, biological/physical sciences, social sciences.

FRESHMAN ADMISSIONS. Selection criteria: A minimum of 120 on CPAT entrance test. CPAT may be replaced by comparable ACT or SAT scores. Interview also required.

1992 FRESHMAN CLASS PROFILE. 200 men and women enrolled. **Characteristics:** 99% from in state, 100% commute.

FALL-TERM APPLICATIONS. $25 fee. No closing date; applicants notified on a rolling basis. Interview required. Essay recommended. Deferred admission available.

STUDENT LIFE. Activities: Student government, student newspaper.

STUDENT SERVICES. Career counseling, employment service for undergraduates, freshman orientation, personal counseling, placement service for graduates, veterans counselor, services/facilities for handicapped.

ANNUAL EXPENSES. Tuition and fees: $4,644. Electronics majors pay $1400 laboratory fee. **Books and supplies:** $992. **Other expenses:** $1,638.

FINANCIAL AID. All aid based on need.

ADDRESS/TELEPHONE. Evonne Brown, Director of Admissions, Phillips Junior College: Fresno Campus, 2048 North Fine Avenue, Fresno, CA 93727. (209) 453-1000 ext. 261. Fax: (209) 453-1747.

Phillips Junior College: San Fernando Valley Campus
Northridge, California CB code: 4548

2-year proprietary business, junior, technical college, coed. Founded in 1945. **Undergraduate enrollment:** 250 men, 250 women full time. **Location:** Suburban campus in large town; 15 miles from Los Angeles. **Calendar:** Quarter.

FRESHMAN ADMISSIONS. Selection criteria: CPAT examination scores, interview, and personal statement most important.

ANNUAL EXPENSES. Tuition and fees (projected): $6,075. Tuition and fees are for 4 quarters(12 months). Book loan program available to students.

ADDRESS/TELEPHONE. Carolyn Greenleaf, Director of Admissions, Phillips Junior College: San Fernando Valley Campus, 8520 Balboa Boulevard, Northridge, CA 91325. (818) 895-2220. Fax: (818) 895-5282.

Pitzer College
Claremont, California CB code: 4619

Admissions: 55% of applicants accepted
Based on: ••• Essay, recommendations, school record
•• Activities, test scores
• Interview, special talents
Completion: 95% of freshmen end year in good standing
75% graduate, 37% of these enter graduate study

4-year private liberal arts college, coed. Founded in 1963. **Accreditation:** Regional. **Undergraduate enrollment:** 375 men, 425 women full time; 10 men, 22 women part time. **Faculty:** 72 total (62 full time), 70 with doctorates or other terminal degrees. **Location:** Suburban campus in large town; 35 miles from Los Angeles. **Calendar:** Semester. **Microcomputers:** Located in libraries, computer centers. **Special facilities:** Mission-style restored bungalow with poetry reading room and art gallery. **Additional facts:** One of 5 undergraduate Claremont colleges sharing common facilities.

DEGREES OFFERED. BA. 190 bachelor's degrees awarded in 1992. 5% in area and ethnic studies, 10% letters/literature, 16% multi/interdisciplinary studies, 6% physical sciences, 17% psychology, 20% social sciences, 12% visual and performing arts.

UNDERGRADUATE MAJORS. Afro-American (black) studies, American studies, anthropology, applied mathematics, art history, Asian studies, biochemistry, biology, biophysics, chemistry, cinematography/film, classics, dance, dramatic arts, economics, education, English, English literature, environmental science, European studies, folklore and mythology, French, German, history, international relations, Latin American studies, liberal/general studies, linguistics, mathematics, Mexican American studies, music, philosophy, physics, political science and government, psychobiology, psychology, sociology, Spanish, women's studies.

ACADEMIC PROGRAMS. Double major, honors program, independent study, internships, semester at sea, student-designed major, study abroad, visiting/exchange student program, Washington semester, cross-registration, New Resources (for students over age 25), 3-2 program in business administration at Claremont Graduate School; liberal arts/career combination in engineering; combined bachelor's/graduate program in business administration. **Remedial services:** Tutoring. **Placement/credit:** AP, institutional tests.

ACADEMIC REQUIREMENTS. Freshmen must earn minimum GPA of 2.0 to continue in good standing. 90% of freshmen return for sophomore year. Students must declare major by end of second year. **Graduation requirements:** 128 hours for bachelor's (48 in major). Most students required to take courses in English, humanities, mathematics, biological/physical sciences, social sciences. **Postgraduate studies:** 7% enter law school, 4% enter medical school, 6% enter MBA programs, 20% enter other graduate study. **Additional information:** Students may take up to one-third of their courses at other Claremont campuses.

FRESHMAN ADMISSIONS. Selection criteria: School record, essays (judged for writing ability, independence of thought and spirit), recommendations, and test scores considered. **High school preparation:** 16 units required; 17 recommended. Required and recommended units include English 4, foreign language 2-3, mathematics 3-4, social science 2-3 and science 2-3. **Test requirements:** SAT or ACT; score report by February 1.

1992 FRESHMAN CLASS PROFILE. 406 men applied, 255 accepted, 77 enrolled; 680 women applied, 340 accepted, 94 enrolled. 70% had high school GPA of 3.0 or higher, 30% between 2.0 and 2.99. 18% were in top tenth and 79% were in top quarter of graduating class. **Academic background:** Mid 50% of enrolled freshmen had SAT-V between 500-640, SAT-M between 530-660; ACT composite between 24-30. 92% submitted SAT scores, 8% submitted ACT scores. **Characteristics:** 42% from in state, 99% live in college housing, 36% have minority backgrounds, 7% are foreign students. Average age is 18.

FALL-TERM APPLICATIONS. $30 fee, may be waived for applicants with need. Closing date February 1; applicants notified on or about April 1; must reply by May 1. Essay required. Interview recommended. CRDA. Deferred and early admission available. Institutional early decision plan. ACH recommended for admissions and counseling. 2 letters of recommendation required. College's early action plan available to applicants whose file is complete by December 1, notification by January 1.

STUDENT LIFE. Housing: Dormitories (coed). Friendship suites and thematic corridors available. **Activities:** Student government, film, magazine, radio, student newspaper, television, yearbook, choral groups, concert band, dance, drama, jazz band, music ensembles, musical theater, pep band, symphony orchestra, Kabuki theater, Hillel, and other social service, religious, political, and ethnic organizations.

ATHLETICS. NAIA, NCAA. **Intercollegiate:** Badminton, baseball M, basketball, cross-country, diving, fencing, football M, golf M, rugby M, soccer, swimming, tennis, track and field, volleyball W, water polo M. **Intramural:** Archery, badminton, golf, lacrosse, sailing, skiing, soccer, softball W, tennis, water polo W.

STUDENT SERVICES. Career counseling, employment service for undergraduates, freshman orientation, health services, personal counseling, placement service for graduates, 3 full-time chaplains (minister, priest, rabbi), services/facilities for handicapped.

ANNUAL EXPENSES. Tuition and fees (1992-93): $17,158. **Room and board:** $5,264. **Books and supplies:** $650. **Other expenses:** $900.

FINANCIAL AID. 43% of freshmen, 42% of continuing students receive some form of aid. All aid based on need. 71 enrolled freshmen were judged to have need, all were offered aid. **Aid applications:** Closing date February 1; applicants notified on or about April 1; must reply by May 1.

ADDRESS/TELEPHONE. Paul B. Ranslow, Vice President of Admissions, Pitzer College, 1050 North Mills Avenue, Scott Hall, Claremont, CA 91711-6114. (909) 621-8129. Fax: (909) 621-8521.

Point Loma Nazarene College
San Diego, California CB code: 4605

Admissions: 81% of applicants accepted
Based on:
- ••• School record
- •• Essay, recommendations, religious affiliation/commitment, test scores
- • Activities, interview, special talents

Completion: 80% of freshmen end year in good standing
40% graduate

4-year private liberal arts college, coed, affiliated with Church of the Nazarene. Founded in 1902. **Accreditation:** Regional. **Undergraduate enrollment:** 738 men, 1,063 women full time; 86 men, 148 women part time. **Graduate enrollment:** 72 men, 198 women full time; 47 men, 98 women part time. **Faculty:** 138 total (114 full time), 71 with doctorates or other terminal degrees. **Location:** Urban campus in very large city; 5 miles from downtown. **Calendar:** Semester, extensive summer session. **Microcomputers:** 80 located in classrooms, computer centers.

DEGREES OFFERED. BA, BS, MA. 379 bachelor's degrees awarded in 1992. 21% in business and management, 7% communications, 8% health sciences, 6% letters/literature, 7% life sciences, 16% multi/interdisciplinary studies, 8% social sciences, 5% visual and performing arts. Graduate degrees offered in 11 major fields of study.

UNDERGRADUATE MAJORS. Accounting, applied communications, art education, athletic training, Bible studies, biochemistry, biology, business and management, business education, business home economics, chemistry, communications, computer and information sciences, dramatic arts, economics, engineering physics, English education, English literature, graphic arts technology, history, home economics, individual and family development, industrial and organizational psychology, information sciences and systems, journalism, liberal/general studies, management information systems, mathematics, music, music business management, music education, music performance, music theory and composition, nursing, office supervision and management, pastoral ministries, philosophy, physical education, physics, political science and government, psychology, religion, religious education, religious music, sociology, Spanish, speech, speech pathology/audiology, studio art, technical and business writing, theological studies.

ACADEMIC PROGRAMS. Education specialist degree, honors program, internships, study abroad, teacher preparation, Washington semester. **Remedial services:** Learning center, reduced course load, remedial instruction, special counselor, tutoring. **ROTC:** Air Force, Army, Naval. **Placement/credit:** AP, CLEP Subject, institutional tests; 32 credit hours maximum for bachelor's degree.

ACADEMIC REQUIREMENTS. Freshmen must earn minimum GPA of 1.6 to continue in good standing. 69% of freshmen return for sophomore year. Students must declare major by end of second year. **Graduation requirements:** 128 hours for bachelor's (48 in major). Most students required to take courses in arts/fine arts, English, foreign languages, history, humanities, mathematics, philosophy/religion, biological/physical sciences, social sciences.

FRESHMAN ADMISSIONS. Selection criteria: Moral character, maturity, intellectual ability, and academic achievement important considerations. Preference given to self-directed applicants who appear to share ideals and objectives of college. Recommended units include English 3, foreign language 2, mathematics 2, social science 1 and science 1. Recommended units should include 1 history, 1 algebra, 1 geometry. **Test requirements:** SAT or ACT (SAT preferred); score report by June 15.

1992 FRESHMAN CLASS PROFILE. 252 men applied, 252 accepted, 131 enrolled; 691 women applied, 511 accepted, 243 enrolled. 64% had high school GPA of 3.0 or higher, 35% between 2.0 and 2.99. 23% were in top tenth and 49% were in top quarter of graduating class. **Academic background:** Mid 50% of enrolled freshmen had SAT-V between 360-480, SAT-M between 390-540; ACT composite between 18-24. 84% submitted SAT scores, 21% submitted ACT scores. **Characteristics:** 80% from in state, 91% live in college housing, 12% have minority backgrounds, 1% are foreign students. Average age is 18.

FALL-TERM APPLICATIONS. $20 fee, may be waived for applicants with need. No closing date; applicants notified on a rolling basis. Interview recommended for marginal applicants. Audition recommended for music applicants. CRDA. Deferred and early admission available. EDP-F.

STUDENT LIFE. Housing: Dormitories (men, women); apartment housing available. **Activities:** Student government, student newspaper, yearbook, choral groups, concert band, drama, jazz band, music ensembles, opera, pep band, symphony orchestra, fraternities, sororities, urban ministries, habitat for humanity, Mexico outreach, elderly outreach, Project A.I.M. (Active in Ministries). **Additional information:** Religious observance required.

ATHLETICS. NAIA. **Intercollegiate:** Baseball M, basketball, cross-country, golf M, soccer M, softball W, tennis, track and field, volleyball W. **Intramural:** Badminton, basketball, bowling, cross-country, diving, football, golf, racquetball, sailing, softball, swimming, table tennis, tennis, track and field, volleyball, water polo.

STUDENT SERVICES. Career counseling, employment service for undergraduates, freshman orientation, health services, on-campus day care, personal counseling, placement service for graduates, veterans counselor, services/facilities for handicapped.

ANNUAL EXPENSES. Tuition and fees: $9,542. **Room and board:** $3,990. **Books and supplies:** $612. **Other expenses:** $1,350.

FINANCIAL AID. 72% of freshmen, 65% of continuing students receive some form of aid. 33% of grants, 84% of loans, all jobs based on need. Academic, athletic, religious affiliation scholarships available. **Aid applications:** No closing date; priority given to applications received by April 10; applicants notified on a rolling basis beginning on or about June 1; must reply by May 1 or within 3 weeks if notified thereafter.

ADDRESS/TELEPHONE. William J. Young, Jr, Executive Director of Enrollment Services, Point Loma Nazarene College, 3900 Lomaland Drive, San Diego, CA 92106-2899. (619) 221-2273. Fax: (619) 221-2579.

Pomona College
Claremont, California CB code: 4607

4-year private liberal arts college, coed. Founded in 1887. **Accreditation:** Regional. **Undergraduate enrollment:** 748 men, 639 women full time. **Faculty:** 162 total (153 full time), 153 with doctorates or other terminal degrees. **Location:** Suburban campus in large town; 35 miles from downtown Los Angeles. **Calendar:** Semester. **Microcomputers:** 65 located in dormitories, libraries, computer centers. **Special facilities:** Seaver Science Center, Oldenborg Center for Modern Language and International Relations, 2 art galleries, Brackett Observatory, Bernard Biological Field Station, Evey Canyon Ecological Preserve, Rancho Santa Ana Botanic Garden, Seaver Theatre, Rains Athletic Complex. **Additional facts:** One of 5 autonomous undergraduate Claremont colleges sharing common facilities. Extensive overseas studies. Pomona is the comprehensive liberal arts and sciences college of the Claremont colleges.

DEGREES OFFERED. BA. 360 bachelor's degrees awarded in 1992. 12% in letters/literature, 6% life sciences, 6% physical sciences, 11% psychology, 43% social sciences, 5% visual and performing arts.

UNDERGRADUATE MAJORS. Afro-American (black) studies, American literature, American studies, anthropology, art history, Asian studies, astronomy, biochemistry, biology, chemistry, Chinese, classics, comparative literature, computer and information sciences, dramatic arts, economics, English, English literature, foreign languages (multiple emphasis), French, geology, German, Greek (classical), Hebrew, Hispanic American studies, history, international relations, international studies, Japanese, Latin, liberal/general studies, linguistics, mathematics, Mexican American studies, molecular biology, music, philosophy, physics, policy analysis, political science and government, psychobiology, psychology, religion, Russian, science, technology and society, sociology, Spanish, studio art, women's studies.

ACADEMIC PROGRAMS. Double major, independent study, internships, student-designed major, study abroad, visiting/exchange student program, Washington semester, cross-registration, 3-2 program at California Institute of Technology or Washingtion University; liberal arts/career combination in engineering. **Remedial services:** Special counselor, tutoring. **ROTC:** Air Force, Army. **Placement/credit:** AP, CLEP General, institutional tests.

ACADEMIC REQUIREMENTS. No policy requiring minimum GPA; records of students having academic difficulty are reviewed individually. 99% of freshmen return for sophomore year. Students must declare major by end of second year. **Graduation requirements:** 128 hours for bachelor's. Most students required to take courses in arts/fine arts, English, foreign languages, humanities, mathematics, philosophy/religion, biological/physical sciences, social sciences.

FRESHMAN ADMISSIONS. Selection criteria: School achievement record, test scores, essays, recommendations most important. Special skills in music, art, drama, or athletics; leadership, motivation, and diversity of background also important. Some preference to children of alumni; special consideration for underrepresented ethnic groups. School, church, and community activities also considered. No specific GPA or ranking required. Recommended units include English 4, foreign language 3, mathematics 3, social science 2 and science 2. 3-4 years of laboratory science recommended for science applicants. Mathematics through trigonometry and precalculus recommended for all applicants. **Test requirements:** SAT or ACT; score report by February 1. **Additional information:** Applicants with musical talent encouraged to submit audition tape for faculty review. Videotapes may be submitted for dance and theater review, slides/other media for studio art.

1992 FRESHMAN CLASS PROFILE. 363 men and women enrolled. 98% had high school GPA of 3.0 or higher, 2% between 2.0 and 2.99. **Academic background:** Mid 50% of enrolled freshmen had SAT-V between 590-670, SAT-M between 640-740. 94% submitted SAT scores. **Characteristics:** 43% from in state, 100% live in college housing, 38% have minority backgrounds, 2% are foreign students. Average age is 18.

FALL-TERM APPLICATIONS. $45 fee, may be waived for applicants with need. Closing date January 15; applicants notified on or about April 10; must reply by May 1. Essay required. Interview recommended. Audition recommended. Portfolio recommended for studio art, music, dance, theatre applicants. Interview required for early admission applicants, and recommended for all applicants. 3 high school recommendations required. CRDA. Deferred and early admission available. EDP-F. 3 ACH recommended, particularly English Composition, scores reported by February 1. Early decision admission is binding: early decision candidates receive admit, defer, or deny decisions in December. Three years absence from any school necessary to quality for CLEP credit.

STUDENT LIFE. Housing: Dormitories (coed). Oldenborg Center is both dormitory for language study and home for international relations colloquia. Dining hall offering foreign language tables is open daily to all students. The center sponsors a nightly foreign language film. **Activities:** Student government, magazine, radio, student newspaper, television, yearbook, choral groups, concert band, dance, drama, jazz band, music ensembles, musical theater, pep band, symphony orchestra, mime, Kabuki, fraternities, McAlister Center for Religious Activities, Chicano Studies Center, Office of Black Student Affairs, International Place, Circle-K, Asian Students Association, Mortar Board (service organization), Women's Coalition, Gay and Lesbian Student Union.

ATHLETICS. NCAA. **Intercollegiate:** Baseball M, basketball, cross-country, diving, football M, golf M, soccer, softball W, swimming, tennis, track and field, volleyball W, water polo. **Intramural:** Badminton, basketball, fencing, field hockey W, golf, handball, horseback riding, lacrosse, racquetball, rugby, skiing, soccer, softball, squash, table tennis, track and field, volleyball, water polo.

STUDENT SERVICES. Aptitude testing, career counseling, employment service for undergraduates, freshman orientation, health services, personal counseling, placement service for graduates, services/facilities for handicapped.

ANNUAL EXPENSES. Tuition and fees (1992-93): $15,830. **Room and board:** $6,625. **Books and supplies:** $550. **Other expenses:** $850.

FINANCIAL AID. 52% of freshmen, 52% of continuing students receive some form of aid. All grants, 92% of loans, 90% of jobs based on need. 188 enrolled freshmen were judged to have need, all were offered aid. **Aid applications:** No closing date; priority given to applications received by February 11; applicants notified on a rolling basis beginning on or about April 10; must reply by May 1 or within 2 weeks if notified thereafter.

ADDRESS/TELEPHONE. Bruce J. Poch, Dean of Admissions, Pomona College, 333 North College Way, Claremont, CA 91711-6312. (714) 621-8134.

Porterville College
Porterville, California — CB code: 4608

2-year public community college, coed. Founded in 1927. **Accreditation:** Regional. **Undergraduate enrollment:** 384 men, 485 women full time; 813 men, 1,204 women part time. **Faculty:** 128 total (58 full time), 7 with doctorates or other terminal degrees. **Location:** Rural campus in large town; 75 miles from Fresno, 50 miles from Bakersfield. **Calendar:** Semester, limited summer session. **Microcomputers:** 25 located in libraries. **Additional facts:** Close to Sequoia, Kings Canyon, and Yosemite national parks.

DEGREES OFFERED. AA, AS. 103 associate degrees awarded in 1992.

UNDERGRADUATE MAJORS. Automotive mechanics, automotive technology, biological and physical sciences, biology, business administration and management, business and management, business and office, business data processing and related programs, carpentry, chemistry, child development/care/guidance, commercial art, computer and information sciences, criminology, drafting, drafting and design technology, education, English, finance, fine arts, law enforcement and corrections technologies, liberal/general studies, mathematics, music, physical sciences, practical nursing, real estate, secretarial and related programs, social sciences, studio art, visual and performing arts, welding technology.

ACADEMIC PROGRAMS. 2-year transfer program, double major, dual enrollment of high school students. **Remedial services:** Learning center, reduced course load, remedial instruction, special counselor, tutoring. **Placement/credit:** AP, CLEP General and Subject, institutional tests; 30 credit hours maximum for associate degree.

ACADEMIC REQUIREMENTS. Freshmen must earn minimum GPA of 2.0 to continue in good standing. 35% of freshmen return for sophomore year. Students must declare major by end of first year. **Graduation requirements:** 60 hours for associate (18 in major). Most students required to take courses in computer science, English, history, humanities, mathematics, biological/physical sciences, social sciences.

FRESHMAN ADMISSIONS. Selection criteria: Open admissions. **Test requirements:** ASSET scores required for first time college students.

1992 FRESHMAN CLASS PROFILE. 322 men, 354 women enrolled. **Characteristics:** 99% from in state, 100% commute.

FALL-TERM APPLICATIONS. No fee. No closing date; applicants notified on a rolling basis.

STUDENT LIFE. Activities: Student government, choral groups, drama, music ensembles, musical theater, Mexican-American Student Association.

ATHLETICS. NJCAA. **Intercollegiate:** Baseball M, basketball, cross-country, football M, soccer W, tennis, track and field M, volleyball W.

STUDENT SERVICES. Aptitude testing, career counseling, employment service for undergraduates, freshman orientation, health services, on-campus day care, personal counseling, placement service for graduates, veterans counselor, services/facilities for handicapped.

ANNUAL EXPENSES. Tuition and fees (1992-93): $140, $3,120 additional for out-of-state students. **Books and supplies:** $480. **Other expenses:** $630.

FINANCIAL AID. 50% of freshmen, 50% of continuing students receive some form of aid. All aid based on need. 400 enrolled freshmen were judged to have need, 208 were offered aid. Academic, state/district residency scholarships available. **Aid applications:** No closing date; priority given to applications received by June 1; applicants notified on a rolling basis beginning on or about June 1; must reply within 2 weeks.

ADDRESS/TELEPHONE. Norma Hodge, Director of Admissions and Records, Porterville College, 100 East College Avenue, Porterville, CA 93257. (209) 781-3130. Fax: (209) 784-4779.

Queen of the Holy Rosary College
Fremont, California — CB code: 0228

2-year private seminary college, coed, affiliated with Roman Catholic Church. Founded in 1930. **Accreditation:** Regional. **Undergraduate enrollment:** 9 women full time; 10 men, 253 women part time. **Faculty:** 21 total (6 full time), 2 with doctorates or other terminal degrees. **Location:** Suburban campus in small city; 40 miles from San Francisco, 22 miles from San Jose. **Calendar:** Semester, limited summer session. **Microcomputers:** 1 located in libraries. **Special facilities:** Curriculum teaching library. **Additional facts:** College dedicated to religious formation. Full-time students are members of the Dominican Order and are generally candidates for religious life.

DEGREES OFFERED. AA. 2 associate degrees awarded in 1992. 100% in philosophy, religion, theology.

UNDERGRADUATE MAJORS. Religion, theological studies.

ACADEMIC PROGRAMS. 2-year transfer program, external degree, independent study, internships, teacher preparation. **Remedial services:** Remedial instruction, tutoring. **Placement/credit:** Institutional tests.

ACADEMIC REQUIREMENTS. Freshmen must earn minimum GPA of 2.0 to continue in good standing. 75% of freshmen return for sophomore year. Students must declare major by end of first year. **Graduation requirements:** 70 hours for associate (30 in major). Most students required to take courses in arts/fine arts, computer science, English, foreign languages, history, humanities, mathematics, philosophy/religion, biological/physical sciences, social sciences. **Additional information:** Special emphasis on preparation of religious sisters for educational apostolate.

FRESHMAN ADMISSIONS. Selection criteria: Interview and religious commitment very important, following essay and recommendations. **High school preparation:** 20 units recommended. Recommended units include biological science 1, English 3, foreign language 2, mathematics 2, physical science 1 and social science 3. Religion courses desirable. Exceptions sometimes made to college-preparatory recommendations. **Test requirements:** SAT or ACT (SAT preferred) for counseling; score report by November 1.

1992 FRESHMAN CLASS PROFILE. 3 women applied, 3 accepted, 3 enrolled. **Characteristics:** 100% live in college housing.

FALL-TERM APPLICATIONS. $15 fee, may be waived for applicants with need. Closing date July 1; priority given to applications received by May 1; applicants notified on or about August 1. Interview required for full-time applicants. Essay required for full-time applicants.

STUDENT LIFE. Housing: Dormitories (women). Full-time students live at convent. **Activities:** Yearbook, choral groups. **Additional information:** Religious observance required.

STUDENT SERVICES. Aptitude testing, career counseling, freshman orientation, health services, personal counseling, placement service for graduates, services/facilities for handicapped.

ANNUAL EXPENSES. Tuition and fees: $2,500. **Books and supplies:** $100.

FINANCIAL AID. 100% of freshmen, 25% of continuing students receive some form of aid. Religious affiliation scholarships available. **Aid applications:** Closing date July 1; priority given to applications received by March 1; applicants notified on or about August 1. **Additional information:** Full-time students receive financial aid based on need.

ADDRESS/TELEPHONE. Sr. Mary Paul Mehegan, Dean, Queen of the Holy Rosary College, PO Box 3908, 43326 Mission Boulevard, Fremont, CA 94539. (510) 657-2468 ext. 322. Fax: (510) 657-1734.

Rancho Santiago Community College
Santa Ana, California CB code: 4689

2-year public community college, coed. Founded in 1915. **Accreditation:** Regional. **Undergraduate enrollment:** 21,506 men and women. **Location:** Urban campus in small city; 40 miles from Los Angeles. **Calendar:** Semester.

FRESHMAN ADMISSIONS. Selection criteria: Open admissions.

ANNUAL EXPENSES. Tuition and fees (projected): $180, $2,496 additional for out-of-state students. **Books and supplies:** $612. **Other expenses:** $1,728.

ADDRESS/TELEPHONE. Dr. Harold H. Bateman, Dean of Admissions and Enrollment Services, Rancho Santiago Community College, 17th at Bristol, Santa Ana, CA 92706. (714) 564-6000. Fax: (714) 564-6379.

Rio Hondo College
Whittier, California CB code: 4663

2-year public community college, coed. Founded in 1960. **Accreditation:** Regional. **Undergraduate enrollment:** 15,412 men and women. **Faculty:** 450 total (250 full time). **Location:** Suburban campus in small city; 16 miles from Los Angeles. **Calendar:** Semester, extensive summer session. **Special facilities:** Observatory, nature preserve.

DEGREES OFFERED. AA, AS. 350 associate degrees awarded in 1992.

UNDERGRADUATE MAJORS. Accounting, automotive technology, business and office, dental assistant, drafting, fire control and safety technology, graphic arts technology, law enforcement and corrections technologies, liberal/general studies, library assistant, mental health/human services, nursing, photographic technology, practical nursing, precision metal work, real estate, respiratory therapy technology, secretarial and related programs.

ACADEMIC PROGRAMS. 2-year transfer program, dual enrollment of high school students, honors program, independent study, study abroad, weekend college. **Remedial services:** Learning center, remedial instruction, special counselor, tutoring. **Placement/credit:** Institutional tests; 12 credit hours maximum for associate degree.

ACADEMIC REQUIREMENTS. Freshmen must earn minimum GPA of 2.0 to continue in good standing. Students must declare major on enrollment. **Graduation requirements:** 62 hours for associate. Most students required to take courses in arts/fine arts, English, history, humanities, mathematics, biological/physical sciences, social sciences.

FRESHMAN ADMISSIONS. Selection criteria: Open admissions.

1992 FRESHMAN CLASS PROFILE. 1,135 men and women enrolled. **Characteristics:** 96% from in state, 100% commute, 70% have minority backgrounds, 1% are foreign students.

FALL-TERM APPLICATIONS. No fee. No closing date; applicants notified on a rolling basis. Deferred admission available.

STUDENT LIFE. Activities: Film, magazine, radio, student newspaper, television, choral groups, dance, drama, jazz band, music ensembles, musical theater.

ATHLETICS. NJCAA. **Intercollegiate:** Baseball M, basketball M, cross-country, football M, golf, softball W, swimming, tennis, volleyball W, water polo, wrestling M.

STUDENT SERVICES. Aptitude testing, career counseling, employment service for undergraduates, health services, services/facilities for handicapped.

ANNUAL EXPENSES. Tuition and fees (1992-93): $135, $2,970 additional for out-of-state students. **Books and supplies:** $400.

FINANCIAL AID. 11% of freshmen, 11% of continuing students receive some form of aid. Grants, loans, jobs available. Academic, music/drama, art, athletic, leadership scholarships available. **Aid applications:** No closing date; priority given to applications received by July 15; applicants notified on a rolling basis; must reply within 20 days.

ADDRESS/TELEPHONE. Tom Huffman, Dean of Admissions and Records, Rio Hondo College, 3600 Workman Mill Road, Whittier, CA 90608. (310) 692-0921. Fax: (310) 699-7386.

Riverside Community College
Riverside, California CB code: 4658

2-year public community college, coed. Founded in 1916. **Accreditation:** Regional. **Undergraduate enrollment:** 22,002 men and women. **Location:** Urban campus in small city; 60 miles from Los Angeles. **Calendar:** Semester.

FRESHMAN ADMISSIONS. Selection criteria: Open admissions. Selective admissions to nursing programs.

ANNUAL EXPENSES. Tuition and fees (projected): $300, $3,360 additional for out-of-state students. **Books and supplies:** $470. **Other expenses:** $1,008.

ADDRESS/TELEPHONE. Margaret Ramey, Director of Admissions and Records, Riverside Community College, 4800 Magnolia Avenue, Riverside, CA 92506-1299. (714) 684-3240. Fax: (714) 275-0651.

Sacramento City College
Sacramento, California CB code: 4670

2-year public community college, coed. Founded in 1916. **Accreditation:** Regional. **Undergraduate enrollment:** 2,395 men, 2,380 women full time; 4,632 men, 6,996 women part time. **Faculty:** 523 total (314 full time), 75 with doctorates or other terminal degrees. **Location:** Urban campus in large city. **Calendar:** Semester, extensive summer session. Saturday and extensive evening/early morning classes. **Microcomputers:** 150 located in libraries, classrooms, computer centers. **Special facilities:** Art gallery, observatory, theater.

DEGREES OFFERED. AA, AS. 739 associate degrees awarded in 1992. 10% in business and management, 10% business/office and marketing/distribution, 18% allied health, 8% multi/interdisciplinary studies, 6% parks/recreation, protective services, public affairs, 5% physical sciences, 16% social sciences, 17% trade and industry.

UNDERGRADUATE MAJORS. Accounting, aeronautical technology, air conditioning/heating/refrigeration mechanics, air conditioning/heating/refrigeration technology, aircraft mechanics, biological and physical sciences, biology, business and management, business and office, business data processing and related programs, communications, computer and information sciences, criminal justice studies, criminology, data processing, dental assistant, dental hygiene, drafting, electrical and electronics equipment repair, electromechanical technology, engineering, engineering and engineering-related technologies, family/consumer resource management, fine arts, graphic and printing production, graphic arts technology, journalism, law enforcement and corrections technologies, legal secretary, liberal/general studies, library assistant, marketing and distribution, mathematics, medical secretary, music, nursing, office supervision and management, physical sciences, practical nursing, real estate, rehabilitation counseling/services, secretarial and related programs, social sciences, teacher aide, visual and performing arts, welding technology, word processing.

ACADEMIC PROGRAMS. 2-year transfer program, accelerated program, cooperative education, double major, dual enrollment of high school students, honors program, independent study, internships, study abroad, telecourses, weekend college, cross-registration. **Remedial services:** Learning center, remedial instruction, special counselor, tutoring. **Placement/credit:** AP, CLEP General, institutional tests; 15 credit hours maximum for associate degree.

ACADEMIC REQUIREMENTS. Freshmen must earn minimum GPA of 2.0 to continue in good standing. 50% of freshmen return for sophomore year. **Graduation requirements:** 60 hours for associate (18 in major). Most students required to take courses in English, history, humanities, mathematics, biological/physical sciences, social sciences.

FRESHMAN ADMISSIONS. Selection criteria: Open admissions.

1992 FRESHMAN CLASS PROFILE. 2,283 men and women enrolled. 15% had high school GPA of 3.0 or higher, 65% between 2.0 and 2.99. **Characteristics:** 95% from in state, 100% commute, 54% have minority backgrounds, 2% are foreign students. Average age is 20.

FALL-TERM APPLICATIONS. No fee. No closing date; priority given to applications received by July 29; applicants notified on a rolling basis; must reply by registration.

STUDENT LIFE. Activities: Student government, magazine, student newspaper, choral groups, concert band, dance, drama, jazz band, music ensembles, musical theater, pep band, symphony orchestra.

ATHLETICS. Intercollegiate: Baseball M, basketball, cross-country, football M, softball W, tennis, track and field, volleyball W, wrestling M. **Intramural:** Archery, badminton, baseball, basketball, bowling, boxing, fencing, football M, golf, gymnastics, handball, racquetball, skiing, softball, swimming, table tennis, tennis, volleyball.

STUDENT SERVICES. Aptitude testing, career counseling, employment service for undergraduates, freshman orientation, health services, on-campus day care, personal counseling, placement service for graduates, special adviser for adult students, veterans counselor, services/facilities for handicapped.

ANNUAL EXPENSES. Tuition and fees (1992-93): $120, $3,210 additional for out-of-state students. **Books and supplies:** $558. **Other expenses:** $1,206.

FINANCIAL AID. 35% of freshmen, 24% of continuing students receive some form of aid. 98% of grants, 91% of loans, all jobs based on need. **Aid applications:** No closing date; priority given to applications received by March 2; applicants notified on a rolling basis; must reply within 2 weeks.

ADDRESS/TELEPHONE. Sam T. Sandusky, Dean of Admissions, Sacramento City College, 3835 Freeport Boulevard, Sacramento, CA 95822. (916) 558-2351. Fax: (916) 441-4142.

Saddleback College
Mission Viejo, California

CB code: 4747

2-year public community college, coed. Founded in 1967. **Accreditation:** Regional. **Undergraduate enrollment:** 19,274 men and women. **Faculty:** 651 total (248 full time). **Location:** Suburban campus in small city; 55 miles from Los Angeles and San Diego. **Calendar:** Semester, limited summer session. Saturday and extensive evening/early morning classes. **Microcomputers:** 200 located in libraries, computer centers. **Special facilities:** Technology and applied sciences building.

DEGREES OFFERED. AA, AS. 900 associate degrees awarded in 1992. 20% in business and management, 9% business/office and marketing/distribution, 5% communications, 9% computer sciences, 14% health sciences, 11% letters/literature, 7% life sciences, 9% mathematics.

UNDERGRADUATE MAJORS. Accounting, advertising, American studies, anthropology, architecture, astronomy, automotive mechanics, automotive technology, biology, business administration and management, business and management, business and office, business computer/console/peripheral equipment operation, business data entry equipment operation, business data processing and related programs, business data programming, business systems analysis, chemistry, child development/care/guidance, cinematography/film, clinical laboratory science, clothing and textiles management/production/services, communications, computer and information sciences, computer programming, construction, drafting, drafting and design technology, dramatic arts, economics, educational media technology, electronic technology, emergency medical technologies, engineering, engineering and engineering-related technologies, English literature, fashion design, fashion merchandising, film arts, fine arts, flight attendants, food production/management/services, food science and nutrition, foreign languages (multiple emphasis), geography, geology, gerontology, graphic and printing production, graphic arts technology, graphic design, history, home economics, home furnishings and equipment management/production/services, human environment and housing, humanities, information sciences and systems, interior design, interpreter for the deaf, journalism, legal assistant/paralegal, legal secretary, liberal/general studies, marketing and distribution, mathematics, medical assistant, mental health/human services, microcomputer software, music, music performance, nursing, oceanographic technologies, office supervision and management, ornamental horticulture, philosophy, photographic technology, photography, physical sciences, physics, political science and government, practical nursing, printmaking, psychology, radio/television broadcasting, real estate, retailing, secretarial and related programs, small business management and ownership, social sciences, sociology, speech, survey and mapping technology, teacher aide, textiles and clothing, video, visual and performing arts, women's studies, woodworking, word processing.

ACADEMIC PROGRAMS. 2-year transfer program, double major, dual enrollment of high school students, honors program, independent study, internships, student-designed major, study abroad, telecourses, cross-registration. **Remedial services:** Learning center, reduced course load, remedial instruction, special counselor, tutoring, learning disabled program. **Placement/credit:** AP, CLEP General and Subject, institutional tests; 30 credit hours maximum for associate degree.

ACADEMIC REQUIREMENTS. Freshmen must earn minimum GPA of 2.0 to continue in good standing. 50% of freshmen return for sophomore year. Students must declare major on enrollment. **Graduation requirements:** 60 hours for associate (24 in major). Most students required to take courses in arts/fine arts, English, history, humanities, mathematics, biological/physical sciences, social sciences.

FRESHMAN ADMISSIONS. Selection criteria: Open admissions. Nursing candidates must complete core curriculum with 2.0 GPA or better before screening process. **High school preparation:** 10 units recommended. Recommended units include biological science 1, English 3, mathematics 2, physical science 1 and social science 3.

1992 FRESHMAN CLASS PROFILE. 3,855 men and women enrolled. **Characteristics:** 90% from in state, 100% commute, 12% have minority backgrounds.

FALL-TERM APPLICATIONS. No fee. No closing date; applicants notified on a rolling basis. Early admission available. SAT or ACT recommended for placement and counseling. Score report by July 11.

STUDENT LIFE. Activities: Student government, radio, student newspaper, television, choral groups, concert band, dance, drama, jazz band, music ensembles, musical theater, pep band, symphony orchestra, Democratic Club, Republican Club, Christian Club, Black Students, Christian Science Organization, EOPS Club, Japanese Club, Jewish Club.

ATHLETICS. Intercollegiate: Baseball M, basketball, cross-country, diving, football M, golf, soccer M, softball W, swimming, tennis, track and field, volleyball W, water polo M.

STUDENT SERVICES. Aptitude testing, career counseling, employment service for undergraduates, freshman orientation, health services, on-campus day care, personal counseling, special adviser for adult students, veterans counselor, services/facilities for handicapped.

ANNUAL EXPENSES. Tuition and fees (projected): $260, $2,520 additional for out-of-state students. **Books and supplies:** $612. **Other expenses:** $1,800.

FINANCIAL AID. 6% of freshmen, 11% of continuing students receive some form of aid. 82% of grants, 89% of loans, all jobs based on need. Academic, music/drama, art, state/district residency, leadership, minority scholarships available. **Aid applications:** Closing date May 2; priority given to applications received by March 2; applicants notified on a rolling basis beginning on or about August 15; must reply within 2 weeks.

ADDRESS/TELEPHONE. Gary S. Stakan, Dean of Admissions and Records, Saddleback College, 28000 Marguerite Parkway, Mission Viejo, CA 92692. (714) 582-4555.

St. John's Seminary College
Camarillo, California

CB code: 4673

4-year private liberal arts, seminary college, men only, affiliated with Roman Catholic Church. Founded in 1939. **Accreditation:** Regional. **Undergraduate enrollment:** 114 men full time. **Location:** Suburban campus in small city; 50 miles from Los Angeles. **Calendar:** Semester. **Additional facts:** Prepares young men for priesthood.

FRESHMAN ADMISSIONS. Selection criteria: Letter of recommendation from pastor, test scores, admissions testing, interview. Only those applicants interested in priesthood admitted.

ANNUAL EXPENSES. Tuition and fees (1992-93): Comprehensive fee: $5,500. **Books and supplies:** $612. **Other expenses:** $1,350.

ADDRESS/TELEPHONE. Rev. Gary Landry, CM, Director of Admissions, St. John's Seminary College, 5118 East Seminary Road, Camarillo, CA 93012-2599. (805) 482-2755. Fax: (805) 987-5097.

St. Mary's College of California
Moraga, California

CB code: 4675

Admissions:	64% of applicants accepted
Based on:	••• School record, test scores
	•• Essay, recommendations
	• Activities, interview, special talents
Completion:	91% of freshmen end year in good standing
	69% graduate, 46% of these enter graduate study

4-year private liberal arts college, coed, affiliated with Roman Catholic Church. Founded in 1863. **Accreditation:** Regional. **Undergraduate enrollment:** 1,113 men, 1,262 women full time; 51 men, 63 women part time. **Graduate enrollment:** 316 men, 447 women full time; 150 men, 331 women part time. **Faculty:** 190 total (139 full time), 176 with doctorates or other terminal degrees. **Location:** Suburban campus in large town; 25 miles from San Francisco. **Calendar:** 4-1-4. **Microcomputers:** Located in libraries, classrooms, computer centers. **Additional facts:** Shared library facilities with University of California: Berkeley.

DEGREES OFFERED. BA, BS, MA, MS, MBA, MEd. 809 bachelor's degrees awarded in 1992. 31% in business and management, 9% communications, 8% health sciences, 7% letters/literature, 10% multi/interdisciplinary studies, 7% psychology, 10% social sciences. Graduate degrees offered in 14 major fields of study.

UNDERGRADUATE MAJORS. Accounting, administration of special education, anthropology, art history, biology, business administration and management, business and management, business economics, chemistry, communications, dramatic arts, early childhood education, economics, education, education administration, education of the gifted and talented, elementary education, engineering, English, French, Greek (classical), health sciences, history, junior high education, Latin, liberal/general studies, mathematics, nursing, philosophy, physics, political science and government, predentistry, prelaw, premedicine, prepharmacy, preveterinary, psychology, religion, secondary education, sociology, Spanish, special education, specific learning disabilities, student counseling and personnel services.

ACADEMIC PROGRAMS. Double major, dual enrollment of high school students, education specialist degree, external degree, independent study, internships, student-designed major, study abroad, weekend college, Washington semester, cross-registration, 4-year interdisciplinary program with Great Books orientation; liberal arts/career combination in engineering. **Remedial services:** Learning center, tutoring. **ROTC:** Army, Naval. **Placement/credit:** AP, CLEP Subject; 30 credit hours maximum for bachelor's degree.

ACADEMIC REQUIREMENTS. Freshmen must earn minimum GPA of 2.0 to continue in good standing. 90% of freshmen return for sophomore year. Students must declare major by end of second year. **Graduation requirements:** 128 hours for bachelor's. Most students required to take courses in English, foreign languages, history, humanities, mathematics, philosophy/religion, biological/physical sciences, social sciences.

FRESHMAN ADMISSIONS. Selection criteria: School achievement record most important. **High school preparation:** 16 units required. Required and recommended units include biological science 1-1, English 4, mathematics 2-3, physical science 1 and social science 1. Foreign language 2 recommended. 2 laboratory sciences recommended. One unit each of chemistry, physics, advanced algebra, and trigonometry required for applicants to school of science. **Test requirements:** SAT or ACT; score report by March 15. ACH may be required of some applicants. Score report by March 15.

1992 FRESHMAN CLASS PROFILE. 1,116 men applied, 703 accepted, 210 enrolled; 1,392 women applied, 912 accepted, 277 enrolled. 86% had high school GPA of 3.0 or higher, 14% between 2.0 and 2.99. 15% were in top tenth and 46% were in top quarter of graduating class. **Academic background:** Mid 50% of enrolled freshmen had SAT-V between 450-560, SAT-M between 440-590. 82% submitted SAT scores. **Characteristics:** 68% from in state, 90% live in college housing, 30% have minority backgrounds, 3% are foreign students. Average age is 19.

FALL-TERM APPLICATIONS. $35 fee, may be waived for applicants with need. Closing date March 1; priority given to applications received by December 1; applicants notified on a rolling basis beginning on or about December 15; must reply by May 1 or within 2 weeks if notified thereafter. Essay required. CRDA. Deferred and early admission available. Institutional early decision plan.

STUDENT LIFE. Housing: Dormitories (men, women, coed); apartment housing available. **Activities:** Student government, film, magazine, radio, student newspaper, television, yearbook, choral groups, dance, drama, music ensembles, musical theater, pep band.

ATHLETICS. NCAA. **Intercollegiate:** Baseball M, basketball, cross-country, football M, golf M, lacrosse M, rowing (crew), rugby M, soccer, softball W, tennis, volleyball W. **Intramural:** Basketball, bowling, racquetball, softball, swimming, volleyball.

STUDENT SERVICES. Aptitude testing, career counseling, employment service for undergraduates, freshman orientation, health services, personal counseling, placement service for graduates, special adviser for adult students, veterans counselor, services/facilities for handicapped.

ANNUAL EXPENSES. Tuition and fees: $12,738. **Room and board:** $6,110. **Books and supplies:** $612. **Other expenses:** $1,350.

FINANCIAL AID. 46% of freshmen, 46% of continuing students receive some form of aid. 73% of grants, 79% of loans based on need. All jobs based on criteria other than need. Academic, athletic scholarships available. **Aid applications:** Closing date March 2; applicants notified on or about April 15; must reply by May 1 or within 2 weeks if notified thereafter.

ADDRESS/TELEPHONE. Michael Beseda, Director Admissions, St. Mary's College of California, PO Box 4800, Moraga, CA 94575-9988. (510) 631-4224. Fax: (510) 376-1847.

Samuel Merritt College
Oakland, California — CB code: 4750

Admissions:	44% of applicants accepted
Based on:	••• Essay, interview, recommendations, school record, test scores
	•• Activities
Completion:	90% of freshmen end year in good standing
	75% graduate

4-year private health science college, coed. Founded in 1909. **Accreditation:** Regional. **Undergraduate enrollment:** 19 men, 228 women full time; 1 man, 14 women part time. **Graduate enrollment:** 24 men, 69 women full time. **Faculty:** 48 total (30 full time), 13 with doctorates or other terminal degrees. **Location:** Urban campus in large city; in downtown area. **Calendar:** 4-1-4. **Microcomputers:** 9 located in libraries, computer centers. **Special facilities:** Nursing resource laboratory, health education center, largest private health science library in the East Bay, anatomy laboratory, therapeutic exercise laboratory. **Additional facts:** Part of Merritt Peralta Medical Center, a nonprofit, community based health care organization. Clinical opportunities at MPMC as well as many other health care agencies throughout the greater Bay Area. Nursing degree is intercollegiate with Saint Mary's College of California. Most students transfer in from other colleges.

DEGREES OFFERED. BS, M. 78 bachelor's degrees awarded in 1992. 100% in health sciences. Graduate degrees offered in 2 major fields of study.

UNDERGRADUATE MAJORS. Nursing.

ACADEMIC PROGRAMS. Accelerated program, double major, independent study, internships, study abroad, joint registration with St. Mary's College of California. **Remedial services:** Learning center, reduced course load, remedial instruction, special counselor, tutoring, study skills workshop and tutorial services offered on both campuses. **Placement/credit:** AP, CLEP General and Subject, institutional tests; 80 credit hours maximum for bachelor's degree.

ACADEMIC REQUIREMENTS. Freshmen must earn minimum GPA of 2.5 to continue in good standing. 90% of freshmen return for sophomore year. Students must declare major on application. **Graduation requirements:** 128 hours for bachelor's (69 in major). Most students required to take courses in English, history, humanities, mathematics, philosophy/religion, biological/physical sciences, social sciences. **Additional information:** Students take their first nursing course in the freshman year. Accelerated program for students who already have a bachelor degree. These students can get a BSN in 17 months of continuous study through our College Grad FasTrak option.

FRESHMAN ADMISSIONS. Selection criteria: School achievement record, test scores, interview, recommendations, and essay very important. **High school preparation:** 9 units required. Required units include English 3, mathematics 2, social science 2 and science 2. Mathematics requirement includes 1 algebra and 1 geometry. Science requirement includes 1 chemistry and 1 laboratory science. Unmet high school requirements may be completed in college. **Test requirements:** SAT or ACT (SAT preferred); score report by June 15.

1992 FRESHMAN CLASS PROFILE. 91 men and women applied, 40 accepted; 1 man enrolled, 12 women enrolled. 60% had high school GPA of 3.0 or higher, 40% between 2.0 and 2.99. **Academic background:** Mid 50% of enrolled freshmen had SAT-V between 390-420, SAT-M between 400-570. 100% submitted SAT scores. **Characteristics:** 100% from in state, 50% commute, 38% have minority backgrounds.

FALL-TERM APPLICATIONS. $35 fee, may be waived for applicants with need. No closing date; priority given to applications received by May 1; applicants notified on a rolling basis; must reply within 6 weeks. Interview required. Essay required. Deferred admission available. EDP-F.

STUDENT LIFE. Housing: Dormitories (coed). **Activities:** Student government, film, radio, student newspaper, television, yearbook, choral groups, dance, drama, Multi-cultural committee, American Physical Therapy Association, California Nursing Students Association, Christian Fellowship.

ATHLETICS. Intercollegiate: Baseball M, basketball, football M, skin diving, soccer, softball W, swimming, tennis, track and field, volleyball W, wrestling M. **Intramural:** Bowling, gymnastics, table tennis.

STUDENT SERVICES. Aptitude testing, career counseling, employment service for undergraduates, freshman orientation, health services, personal counseling, placement service for graduates, veterans counselor, services/facilities for handicapped.

ANNUAL EXPENSES. Tuition and fees: $11,890. Graduate program has a 12-month academic year. Figures quoted are for 9 months. **Room and board:** $5,520. **Books and supplies:** $865. **Other expenses:** $3,348.

FINANCIAL AID. 100% of freshmen, 87% of continuing students receive some form of aid. 52% of grants, 64% of loans, all jobs based on need. 6 enrolled freshmen were judged to have need, all were offered aid. Academic, state/district residency, minority scholarships available. **Aid applications:** No closing date; priority given to applications received by March 2; applicants notified on a rolling basis beginning on or about July 1. **Additional information:** Ongoing private scholarships available. Students eligible to work in Medical Center (associated with college).

ADDRESS/TELEPHONE. Charisse Hughen, Director of Admissions, Samuel Merritt College, 370 Hawthorne Avenue, Oakland, CA 94609-9954. (510) 420-6076. Fax: (510) 420-6025.

San Bernardino Valley College
San Bernardino, California — CB code: 4679

2-year public community college, coed. Founded in 1926. **Accreditation:** Regional. **Undergraduate enrollment:** 12,640 men and women. **Location:** Urban campus in small city; 60 miles from Los Angeles. **Calendar:** Semester.

FRESHMAN ADMISSIONS. Selection criteria: Open admissions. Special admission requirements for nursing program.

ANNUAL EXPENSES. Tuition and fees (projected): $382, $3,060 additional for out-of-state students. **Books and supplies:** $580. **Other expenses:** $1,580.

ADDRESS/TELEPHONE. Steven Smith, Dean of Student Services, San Bernardino Valley College, 701 South Mount Vernon Avenue, San Bernardino, CA 92410. (714) 888-6511 ext. 1141.

San Diego City College
San Diego, California — CB code: 4681

2-year public community college, coed. Founded in 1914. **Accreditation:** Regional. **Undergraduate enrollment:** 13,500 men and women. **Faculty:** 595 total (180 full time), 127 with doctorates or other terminal degrees. **Location:** Urban campus in very large city; in the heart of San Diego. **Calendar:** Semester, extensive summer session. Saturday and extensive evening/early morning classes. **Microcomputers:** Located in libraries, classrooms, computer centers. **Special facilities:** Computerized independent study and learning laboratories, tutoring laboratory, fitness center, vocational training centers. **Additional facts:** Complete evening program, short-term and weekend classes.

DEGREES OFFERED. AA, AS. 1,029 associate degrees awarded in 1992.

UNDERGRADUATE MAJORS. Accounting, African studies, Afro-American (black) studies, air conditioning/heating/refrigeration mechanics, air conditioning/heating/refrigeration technology, applied mathematics, art history, automotive mechanics, automotive technology, behavioral sciences, bilingual/bicultural education, biology, business administration and management, business and management, business and office, business data processing and related programs, business data programming, chemistry, child development/care/guidance, commercial art, computer and information sciences, contract management and procurement/purchasing, court reporting, data processing, drafting, drafting and design technology, dramatic arts, electrical installation, electrical technology, electronic technology, engineering, engineering and engineering-related technologies, English, environmental design, fine arts, foreign languages (multiple emphasis), French, German, Hispanic American studies, history, illustration design, information sciences and systems, institutional management, Italian, journalism, labor/industrial relations, laser electro-optic technology, Latin American studies, legal assistant/paralegal, liberal/general studies, management science, manufacturing technology, marketing and distribution, marketing management, mathematics, mechanical design technology, Mexican American studies, microcomputer software, music, nursing, occupational safety and health technology, philosophy, photographic technology, physical sciences, physics, plastic technology, plumbing/pipefitting/steamfitting, political science and government, practical nursing, precision metal work, prelaw, psychology, quality control technology, radio/television broadcasting, radio/television technology, real estate, robotics, Russian, secretarial and related programs, social sciences, solar heating and cooling technology, Spanish, speech, studio art, systems analysis, telecommunications, tourism, trade and industrial supervision and management, water and wastewater technology, word processing.

ACADEMIC PROGRAMS. 2-year transfer program, accelerated program, cooperative education, double major, dual enrollment of high school students, honors program, independent study, internships, student-designed major, study abroad, teacher preparation, weekend college, cross-registration. **Remedial services:** Learning center, preadmission summer program, reduced course load, remedial instruction, special counselor, tutoring. **Placement/credit:** AP, CLEP General and Subject, institutional tests; 15 credit hours maximum for associate degree.

ACADEMIC REQUIREMENTS. Freshmen must earn minimum GPA of 2.0 to continue in good standing. 63% of freshmen return for sophomore year. **Graduation requirements:** 60 hours for associate (18 in major). Most students required to take courses in English, history, humanities, mathematics, biological/physical sciences, social sciences.

FRESHMAN ADMISSIONS. Selection criteria: Open admissions. Placement test or verification of prerequisites may be required for some programs. High school diploma required of applicants under 18 years of age.

1992 FRESHMAN CLASS PROFILE. 2,345 men and women enrolled. **Characteristics:** 96% from in state, 100% commute, 51% have minority backgrounds, 1% are foreign students. Average age is 26.

FALL-TERM APPLICATIONS. No fee. No closing date; applicants notified on a rolling basis. Applications accepted on rolling basis but must be received 2 weeks prior to start of semester.

STUDENT LIFE. Activities: Student government, film, radio, student newspaper, television, choral groups, dance, drama, jazz band, musical theater, symphony orchestra.

ATHLETICS. NCAA. **Intercollegiate:** Baseball M, basketball M, cross-country, football M, golf M, soccer M, softball, swimming, tennis, track and field, volleyball W. **Intramural:** Basketball, bowling M, cross-country, racquetball, track and field.

STUDENT SERVICES. Aptitude testing, career counseling, employment service for undergraduates, freshman orientation, health services, on-campus day care, personal counseling, placement service for graduates, special adviser for adult students, veterans counselor, free tutoring, learning laboratory, services/facilities for handicapped.

ANNUAL EXPENSES. Tuition and fees (projected): $315, $3,150 additional for out-of-state students. **Books and supplies:** $612. **Other expenses:** $1,548.

FINANCIAL AID. 29% of continuing students receive some form of aid. All grants, 99% of loans, all jobs based on need. Academic, music/drama, art, athletic, state/district residency, leadership, alumni affiliation, minority scholarships available. **Aid applications:** No closing date; priority given to applications received by May 1; applicants notified on a rolling basis beginning on or about June 1.

ADDRESS/TELEPHONE. Frank G. Echevarria, Admissions and Records Officer, San Diego City College, 1313 12th Street, San Diego, CA 92101. (619) 230-2475. Fax: (619) 230-2135.

San Diego Mesa College
San Diego, California — CB code: 4735

2-year public community college, coed. Founded in 1962. **Accreditation:** Regional. **Undergraduate enrollment:** 25,906 men and women. **Faculty:** 782 total (289 full time). **Location:** Urban campus in very large city. **Calendar:** Semester, limited summer session. Saturday and extensive evening/early morning classes. **Special facilities:** Art gallery, anthropology museum.

DEGREES OFFERED. AA, AS. 771 associate degrees awarded in 1992.

UNDERGRADUATE MAJORS. Accounting, Afro-American (black) studies, air traffic control, architecture, biology, business administration and management, business and management, business and office, business data processing and related programs, chemistry, child development/care/guidance, computer programming, construction, data processing, dental assistant, dramatic arts, education of the deaf and hearing impaired, engineering, fashion merchandising, fine arts, flight attendants, food production/management/services, foreign languages (multiple emphasis), hospitality and recreation marketing, hotel/motel and restaurant management, interpreter for the deaf, liberal/general studies, marketing and distribution, marketing management, mathematics, medical assistant, medical records administration, medical records technology, music, physical sciences, physical therapy assistant, physics, psychology, radiograph medical technology, real estate, recreation and community services technologies, secretarial and related programs, social sciences, sociology, tourism, veterinarian's assistant, water and wastewater technology, word processing.

ACADEMIC PROGRAMS. 2-year transfer program, dual enrollment of high school students, honors program, study abroad. **Remedial services:** Learning center, reduced course load, remedial instruction, special counselor, tutoring. **Placement/credit:** CLEP General and Subject, institutional tests; 15 credit hours maximum for associate degree.

ACADEMIC REQUIREMENTS. Freshmen must earn minimum GPA of 2.0 to continue in good standing. Students must declare major on enrollment. **Graduation requirements:** 60 hours for associate. Most students required to take courses in English, history, humanities, mathematics, biological/physical sciences, social sciences.

FRESHMAN ADMISSIONS. Selection criteria: Open admissions.

1992 FRESHMAN CLASS PROFILE. Characteristics: 99% from in state, 100% commute, 1% are foreign students.

FALL-TERM APPLICATIONS. No fee. Closing date August 13; applicants notified on a rolling basis. Early admission available. Applications not accepted by mail.

STUDENT LIFE. Activities: Student government, student newspaper, choral groups, concert band, dance, drama, music ensembles.

ATHLETICS. Intercollegiate: Badminton, baseball M, basketball, cross-country, football M, gymnastics, swimming, track and field, volleyball, wrestling M. **Intramural:** Racquetball, softball W.

STUDENT SERVICES. Career counseling, freshman orientation, health services, on-campus day care, personal counseling, placement service for graduates, special adviser for adult students, veterans counselor, services/facilities for handicapped.

ANNUAL EXPENSES. Tuition and fees: $315, $3,150 additional for out-of-state students. **Books and supplies:** $450. **Other expenses:** $935.

FINANCIAL AID. 14% of continuing students receive some form of aid. All aid based on need. Academic scholarships available. **Aid applications:** No closing date; priority given to applications received by May 1; applicants notified on a rolling basis beginning on or about July 1; must reply within 3 weeks.

ADDRESS/TELEPHONE. Willetta Tomlinson, Admissions/Records Officer, San Diego Mesa College, 7250 Mesa College Drive, San Diego, CA 92111. (619) 627-2682.

San Diego Miramar College
San Diego, California — CB code: 4728

2-year public community college, coed. Founded in 1969. **Accreditation:** Regional. **Undergraduate enrollment:** 823 men, 730 women full time; 2,919 men, 2,589 women part time. **Faculty:** 205 total (69 full time), 12 with doctorates or other terminal degrees. **Location:** Suburban campus in very large city; 9 miles from downtown. **Calendar:** Semester, limited summer session. Saturday and extensive evening/early morning classes. **Microcomputers:** Located in libraries, classrooms.

DEGREES OFFERED. AA, AS. 280 associate degrees awarded in 1992.

UNDERGRADUATE MAJORS. Accounting, aeronautical technology, Afro-American (black) studies, biological and physical sciences, biology, business administration and management, business and management, business and office, business data processing and related programs, chemistry, child development/care/guidance, computer and information sciences, diesel engine mechanics, finance, fine arts, fire control and safety technology, foreign languages (multiple emphasis), human biology, humanities, instructional aide, journalism, law enforcement and corrections technologies, liberal/general studies, marketing and distribution, marketing management, mathematics, microcomputer software, personal services, physical sciences, psychology, real estate, science technologies, secretarial and related programs, social sciences, tourism.

ACADEMIC PROGRAMS. 2-year transfer program, accelerated program, dual enrollment of high school students, honors program, independent study, weekend college, cross-registration. **Remedial services:** Learning center, remedial instruction, special counselor, tutoring. **Placement/credit:** Institutional tests; 15 credit hours maximum for associate degree.

ACADEMIC REQUIREMENTS. Freshmen must earn minimum GPA of 2.0 to continue in good standing. 50% of freshmen return for sophomore year. Students must declare major on application. **Graduation requirements:** 60 hours for associate (18 in major). Most students required to take courses in English, mathematics, social sciences.

FRESHMAN ADMISSIONS. Selection criteria: Open admissions.

1992 FRESHMAN CLASS PROFILE. 2,048 men and women enrolled. **Characteristics:** 99% from in state, 100% commute, 30% have minority backgrounds. Average age is 24.

FALL-TERM APPLICATIONS. No fee. No closing date; applicants notified on a rolling basis. Institutional placement tests required.

STUDENT LIFE. Activities: Student government, student newspaper, International Club, Filipino-American Association.

STUDENT SERVICES. Career counseling, on-campus day care, personal counseling, veterans counselor, support services for disadvantaged students, services/facilities for handicapped.

ANNUAL EXPENSES. Tuition and fees (1992-93): $125, $3,180 additional for out-of-state students. **Books and supplies:** $576. **Other expenses:** $1,728.

FINANCIAL AID. 7% of freshmen, 7% of continuing students receive some form of aid. All aid based on need. 463 enrolled freshmen were judged to have need, all were offered aid. **Aid applications:** No closing date; priority given to applications received by May 1; applicants notified on a rolling basis beginning on or about July 30; must reply within 2 weeks.

ADDRESS/TELEPHONE. Barbara P. Penn, Executive Dean of Student Services, San Diego Miramar College, 10440 Black Mountain Road, San Diego, CA 92126-2999. (619) 536-7844.

San Diego State University

San Diego, California — CB code: 4682

4-year public university, coed. Founded in 1897. **Accreditation:** Regional. **Undergraduate enrollment:** 8,256 men, 8,902 women full time; 3,336 men, 3,668 women part time. **Graduate enrollment:** 519 men, 960 women full time; 2,089 men, 2,639 women part time. **Faculty:** 1,600 total (1,200 full time). **Location:** Suburban campus in very large city; 8 miles from downtown. **Microcomputers:** 250 located in computer centers. **Special facilities:** Art gallery. **Additional facts:** Upper-division branch campus located at Calexico in the Imperial Valley.

DEGREES OFFERED. BA, BS, MA, MS, MBA, MFA, PhD. 5,532 bachelor's degrees awarded in 1992. Graduate degrees offered in 56 major fields of study.

UNDERGRADUATE MAJORS. Accounting, aerospace/aeronautical/astronautical engineering, Afro-American (black) studies, American studies, anthropology, art history, Asian studies, astronomy, biology, botany, business administration and management, chemistry, civil engineering, classics, comparative literature, computer and information sciences, dramatic arts, economics, electrical/electronics/communications engineering, engineering, English, European studies, finance, food science and nutrition, French, geography, geology, German, history, home economics, individual and family development, information sciences and systems, insurance and risk management, journalism, Latin American studies, law enforcement and corrections, linguistics, mathematics, mechanical engineering, Mexican American studies, microbiology, music, nursing, philosophy, physical chemistry, physical sciences, physics, political science and government, psychology, public administration, radio/television broadcasting, real estate, religion, Russian, Russian and Slavic studies, social sciences, social work, sociology, Spanish, speech, speech pathology/audiology, zoology.

ACADEMIC PROGRAMS. Cooperative education, double major, external degree, honors program, independent study, internships, student-designed major, study abroad, teacher preparation, visiting/exchange student program. **Remedial services:** Learning center, reduced course load, remedial instruction, special counselor, tutoring, Educational Opportunity Program. **ROTC:** Air Force, Army, Naval. **Placement/credit:** AP, CLEP General and Subject; 30 credit hours maximum for bachelor's degree.

ACADEMIC REQUIREMENTS. Freshmen must earn minimum GPA of 2.0 to continue in good standing. 73% of freshmen return for sophomore year. Students must declare major on application. **Graduation requirements:** 124 hours for bachelor's (24 in major). Most students required to take courses in English, history, mathematics, philosophy/religion, biological/physical sciences, social sciences.

FRESHMAN ADMISSIONS. Selection criteria: High school GPA and test scores. **High school preparation:** 10 units required. Required units include biological science 1, English 4, foreign language 2 and mathematics 3. Also required: 1 unit U.S. History or U.S. History and Government, and 1 unit Visual and Performing Arts. **Test requirements:** SAT or ACT; score report by August 1.

1992 FRESHMAN CLASS PROFILE. 956 men, 1,238 women enrolled. **Academic background:** Mid 50% of enrolled freshmen had SAT-V between 350-460, SAT-M between 400-530; ACT composite between 16-23. 66% submitted SAT scores, 12% submitted ACT scores. **Characteristics:** 86% from in state, 74% commute, 42% have minority backgrounds, 1% are foreign students. Average age is 18.

FALL-TERM APPLICATIONS. $55 fee, may be waived for applicants with need. Closing date November 30; applicants notified on a rolling basis beginning on or about March 1. Early admission available.

STUDENT LIFE. Housing: Dormitories (men, women, coed); fraternity, sorority housing available. **Activities:** Student government, film, magazine, radio, student newspaper, television, yearbook, choral groups, concert band, dance, drama, jazz band, marching band, music ensembles, musical theater, pep band, symphony orchestra, fraternities, sororities, over 200 groups and organizations.

ATHLETICS. NCAA. **Intercollegiate:** Baseball M, basketball, cross-country, football M, golf, gymnastics W, soccer M, softball W, swimming, tennis, track and field, volleyball. **Intramural:** Bowling, fencing, lacrosse M, racquetball, sailing, soccer W, softball, water polo, wrestling M.

STUDENT SERVICES. Aptitude testing, career counseling, employment service for undergraduates, freshman orientation, health services, on-campus day care, personal counseling, placement service for graduates, veterans counselor, ombudsman, services/facilities for handicapped.

ANNUAL EXPENSES. Tuition and fees (1992-93): $1,490, $7,380 additional for out-of-state students. **Room and board:** $4,365. **Books and supplies:** $612. **Other expenses:** $1,728.

FINANCIAL AID. 49% of freshmen, 43% of continuing students receive some form of aid. 92% of grants, 90% of loans, 18% of jobs based on need. 965 enrolled freshmen were judged to have need, all were offered aid. Academic, music/drama, art, athletic, state/district residency, leadership, minority scholarships available. **Aid applications:** No closing date; priority given to applications received by March 2; applicants notified on a rolling basis beginning on or about June 1; must reply within 2 weeks.

ADDRESS/TELEPHONE. Nancy C. Sprotte, Director of Admissions and Records, San Diego State University, 5300 Campanile Drive, San Diego, CA 92182-0771. (619) 594-6871.

San Francisco Art Institute

San Francisco, California — CB code: 4036

Admissions:	75% of applicants accepted
Based on:	••• Essay, special talents
	•• Interview, school record, test scores
	• Recommendations
Completion:	87% of freshmen end year in good standing
	60% graduate, 35% of these enter graduate study

4-year private art college, coed. Founded in 1871. **Accreditation:** Regional. **Undergraduate enrollment:** 225 men, 240 women full time; 37 men, 80 women part time. **Graduate enrollment:** 60 men, 83 women full time. **Faculty:** 63 total (29 full time), 39 with doctorates or other terminal degrees. **Location:** Urban campus in very large city; in downtown area. **Calendar:** Semester, limited summer session. Extensive evening/early morning classes. **Special facilities:** Student gallery, Emmanual Walter/Athol McBean Gallery of Contemporary Art.

DEGREES OFFERED. BFA, MFA. 150 bachelor's degrees awarded in 1992. 100% in visual and performing arts. Graduate degrees offered in 8 major fields of study.

UNDERGRADUATE MAJORS. Cinematography/film, drawing, fine arts, painting, photography, sculpture, studio art, video.

ACADEMIC PROGRAMS. Double major, honors program, independent study, internships, study abroad, visiting/exchange student program, New York semester. **Remedial services:** Learning center, remedial instruction, tutoring, arts-oriented ESL. **Placement/credit:** AP, CLEP Subject, institutional tests; 20 credit hours maximum for bachelor's degree.

ACADEMIC REQUIREMENTS. Freshmen must earn minimum GPA of 2.0 to continue in good standing. 74% of freshmen return for sophomore year. Students must declare major by end of first year. **Graduation requirements:** 120 hours for bachelor's (36 in major). Most students required to take courses in arts/fine arts, English, history, humanities, philosophy/religion, biological/physical sciences, social sciences.

FRESHMAN ADMISSIONS. Selection criteria: Primarily portfolio, plus motivation and maturity as demonstrated by school achievement record and recommendations. Extensive high school and extracurricular art education recommended. **Test requirements:** SAT or ACT (SAT preferred); score report by August 1.

1992 FRESHMAN CLASS PROFILE. 100 men applied, 75 accepted, 46 enrolled; 98 women applied, 73 accepted, 47 enrolled. **Characteristics:** 42% from in state, 100% commute, 12% have minority backgrounds, 9% are foreign students. Average age is 19.

FALL-TERM APPLICATIONS. $50 fee, may be waived for applicants with need. Closing date August 1; priority given to applications received by April 1; applicants notified on a rolling basis beginning on or about December 1; must reply by May 1 or within 4 weeks if notified thereafter. Portfolio required. Essay required. Interview recommended. CRDA. Deferred admission available.

STUDENT LIFE. Activities: Student government, student newspaper, gallery shows.

STUDENT SERVICES. Career counseling, employment service for undergraduates, freshman orientation, health services, personal counseling, placement service for graduates, veterans counselor, services/facilities for handicapped.

ANNUAL EXPENSES. Tuition and fees: $12,900. **Books and supplies:** $1,100. **Other expenses:** $1,512.

FINANCIAL AID. 65% of freshmen, 69% of continuing students receive some form of aid. 86% of grants, all loans, all jobs based on need. Art scholarships available. **Aid applications:** No closing date; priority given to applications received by April 1; applicants notified on a rolling basis beginning on or about April 1; must reply within 30 days.

ADDRESS/TELEPHONE. Tim Robison, Director of Admissions, San Francisco Art Institute, 800 Chestnut Street, San Francisco, CA 94133-2299. (415) 749-4500. (800) 345-SFAI.

San Francisco College of Mortuary Science
San Francisco, California CB code: 3358

1-year private technical college, coed. **Accreditation:** Regional. **Undergraduate enrollment:** 51 men, 22 women full time. **Faculty:** 6 total (2 full time). **Location:** Urban campus in very large city. **Calendar:** Semester. **Microcomputers:** 1 located in libraries. **Special facilities:** Complete practical training facilities for embalming. **Additional facts:** One-year associate degree mortuary science program.

DEGREES OFFERED. AA. 12 associate degrees awarded in 1992.

UNDERGRADUATE MAJORS. Funeral services/mortuary science.

ACADEMIC PROGRAMS. Remedial services: Tutoring. **Placement/credit:** Institutional tests.

ACADEMIC REQUIREMENTS. Freshmen must earn minimum GPA of 2.0 to continue in good standing. 83% of freshmen return for sophomore year. Students must declare major on application. **Graduation requirements:** 69.5 hours for associate. Most students required to take courses in humanities, mathematics, biological/physical sciences, social sciences.

FRESHMAN ADMISSIONS. Selection criteria: Open admissions. Recommended units include biological science 3, English 3, mathematics 3, physical science 3 and social science 3.

1992 FRESHMAN CLASS PROFILE. 51 men, 22 women enrolled.

FALL-TERM APPLICATIONS. $25 fee. No closing date; applicants notified on a rolling basis; must reply within 30 days. Interview recommended.

STUDENT LIFE. Housing: The college assists students in arranging live-in housing in local funeral homes. **Activities:** Student government, student newspaper.

STUDENT SERVICES. Career counseling, employment service for undergraduates, freshman orientation, personal counseling, placement service for graduates.

ANNUAL EXPENSES. Tuition and fees (1992-93): $8,500. **Books and supplies:** $600. **Other expenses:** $1,200.

FINANCIAL AID. 85% of freshmen, 90% of continuing students receive some form of aid. Loans available. **Aid applications:** Closing date September 5; applicants notified on or about September 20; must reply by October 1.

ADDRESS/TELEPHONE. Admissions Office, San Francisco College of Mortuary Science, 1363 Divisadero Street, San Francisco, CA 94115-3912. (415) 567-0674.

San Francisco Conservatory of Music
San Francisco, California CB code: 4744

Admissions:	56% of applicants accepted
Based on:	••• Special talents
	•• Recommendations, school record, test scores
	• Activities, essay, interview
Completion:	90% of freshmen end year in good standing
	45% graduate, 55% of these enter graduate study

4-year private music college, coed. Founded in 1917. **Accreditation:** Regional. **Undergraduate enrollment:** 57 men, 85 women full time; 3 men, 2 women part time. **Graduate enrollment:** 40 men, 51 women full time; 3 men, 15 women part time. **Faculty:** 68 total (23 full time), 10 with doctorates or other terminal degrees. **Location:** Urban campus in very large city; 3 miles from downtown. **Calendar:** Semester. **Microcomputers:** 10 located in computer centers. **Special facilities:** Concert performance facility, library holdings include 10,000 records and tapes. **Additional facts:** All conservatory students receive extensive performance opportunities both on campus and in the San Francisco Bay Area.

DEGREES OFFERED. B, M. 43 bachelor's degrees awarded in 1992. 100% in visual and performing arts. Graduate degrees offered in 2 major fields of study.

UNDERGRADUATE MAJORS. Music performance, music theory and composition.

ACADEMIC PROGRAMS. Independent study. **Placement/credit:** AP, CLEP General, institutional tests.

ACADEMIC REQUIREMENTS. Freshmen must earn minimum GPA of 2.0 to continue in good standing. 85% of freshmen return for sophomore year. Students must declare major on application. **Graduation requirements:** 130 hours for bachelor's (100 in major). Most students required to take courses in English, history.

FRESHMAN ADMISSIONS. Selection criteria: Most important criterion is musical audition, followed by school achievement record, letters of recommendation, and test scores. Musical needs of institution also influence admissions decisions. **High school preparation:** 3 units required. Required and recommended units include English 3. Foreign language 3 recommended. **Test requirements:** SAT or ACT (SAT preferred); score report by July 1.

1992 FRESHMAN CLASS PROFILE. 68 men and women applied, 38 accepted; 4 men enrolled, 13 women enrolled. 50% had high school GPA of 3.0 or higher, 50% between 2.0 and 2.99. **Academic background:** Mid 50% of enrolled freshmen had SAT-V between 470-610, SAT-M between 500-630. 65% submitted SAT scores. **Characteristics:** 45% from in state, 100% commute, 17% have minority backgrounds, 41% are foreign students. Average age is 18.

FALL-TERM APPLICATIONS. $60 fee. Closing date April 1; applicants notified on a rolling basis beginning on or about March 1; must reply by June 1 or within 3 weeks if notified thereafter. Audition required. CRDA. Deferred and early admission available. Applicants urged to apply in February due to limitations in some majors.

STUDENT LIFE. Housing: Students can live in University of San Francisco dormitories. **Activities:** Student government, choral groups, drama, music ensembles, opera, symphony orchestra.

STUDENT SERVICES. Employment service for undergraduates, freshman orientation, health services, personal counseling, services/facilities for handicapped.

ANNUAL EXPENSES. Tuition and fees: $12,250. **Books and supplies:** $600. **Other expenses:** $1,800.

FINANCIAL AID. 63% of freshmen, 60% of continuing students receive some form of aid. All grants, 82% of loans, 65% of jobs based on need. 10 enrolled freshmen were judged to have need, all were offered aid. Music/drama scholarships available. **Aid applications:** No closing date; priority given to applications received by April 1; applicants notified on a rolling basis beginning on or about April 1; must reply by June 1 or as soon as possible if notified thereafter.

ADDRESS/TELEPHONE. Colleen Katzowitz, Director of Student Services, San Francisco Conservatory of Music, 1201 Ortega Street, San Francisco, CA 94122. (415) 759-3431. Fax: (415) 759-3499.

San Francisco State University
San Francisco, California CB code: 4684

4-year public university, coed. Founded in 1899. **Accreditation:** Regional. **Undergraduate enrollment:** 5,406 men, 7,454 women full time; 2,855 men, 3,620 women part time. **Graduate enrollment:** 585 men, 1,010 women full time; 2,190 men, 3,410 women part time. **Faculty:** 1,429 total (833 full time). **Location:** Urban campus in very large city; 10 miles from downtown San Francisco. **Calendar:** Semester, limited summer session. Extensive evening/early morning classes. **Microcomputers:** 500 located in libraries, computer centers, campus-wide network. **Special facilities:** Access to Moss Landing Marine Laboratories, Paul F. Romberg Tiburon Center for Environmental Studies, Sierra Nevada Field Campus, anthropology museum, facility for study of astronomy.

DEGREES OFFERED. BA, BS, BFA, MA, MS, MBA, MFA, MEd, MSW, PhD. 4,376 bachelor's degrees awarded in 1992. 34% in business and management, 6% education, 5% letters/literature, 8% multi/interdisciplinary studies, 9% psychology, 18% visual and performing arts. Graduate degrees offered in 100 major fields of study.

UNDERGRADUATE MAJORS. Accounting, Afro-American (black) studies, American literature, American studies, anthropology, applied mathematics, astronomy, astrophysics, atmospheric sciences and meteorology, biochemistry, biological laboratory technology, biology, botany, business administration and management, business and management, cell biology, chemistry, Chinese, cinematography/film, civil engineering, classics, clinical laboratory science, clinical psychology, clothing and textiles management/production/services, comparative literature, computer and information sciences, creative writing, dance, developmental psychology, dramatic arts, ecology, economics, electrical/electronics/communications engineering, English, English literature, film arts, finance, fine arts, food management, food science and nutrition, French, geography, geology, German, graphic design, health sciences, Hispanic American studies, history, home economics, home economics education, hospitality and recreation marketing, hotel/motel and restaurant management, humanities, industrial and organizational psychology, industrial arts education, industrial design, industrial technology, international business management, international relations, Italian, Japanese, journalism, labor/industrial relations, liberal/general studies, management information systems, management science, marine biology, marketing and distribution, marketing management, mathematics, mechanical engineering, Mexican American studies, microbiology, molecular biology, music, music history and appreciation, music performance, nursing, nursing education, nutritional sciences, operations research, parks and recreation management, personnel management, philosophy, physical education, physics, physiology, human and animal, political science and government, psychology, radio/television broadcasting, radio/television technology, real estate, religion, Russian, small business management and ownership, social science education, social sciences, social work, sociology, Spanish, speech, speech pathology/audiology, speech/communication/theater education, statistics, technical and business writing, trade and industrial education, transportation and travel marketing, transportation management, urban studies, women's studies, zoology.

ACADEMIC PROGRAMS. Double major, dual enrollment of high school students, honors program, independent study, student-designed major, study abroad, teacher preparation, cross-registration, joint doctorate in special education with University of California: Berkeley. **Remedial services:** Learning center, preadmission summer program, remedial instruction, special counselor, tutoring. **ROTC:** Air Force, Army, Naval. **Placement/credit:** AP, CLEP General and Subject, institutional tests; 30 credit hours maximum for bachelor's degree.

ACADEMIC REQUIREMENTS. Freshmen must earn minimum GPA of 2.0 to continue in good standing. Students must declare major on application. **Graduation requirements:** 124 hours for bachelor's. Most students required to take courses in arts/fine arts, English, history, humanities, mathematics, philosophy/religion, biological/physical sciences, social sciences. **Additional information:** ROTC through cross-registration with University of California at Berkley.

FRESHMAN ADMISSIONS. Selection criteria: School achievement record and score on SAT or ACT. **High school preparation:** 15 units required. Required units include English 4, foreign language 2, mathematics 3, social science 1 and science 1. One visual and performing arts and 1 US history/government also required. **Test requirements:** SAT or ACT. Last date for submitting SAT or ACT scores varies by program.

1992 FRESHMAN CLASS PROFILE. 1,279 men, 1,899 women enrolled. 51% had high school GPA of 3.0 or higher, 46% between 2.0 and 2.99. **Academic background:** Mid 50% of enrolled freshmen had SAT-V between 440-450, SAT-M between 510-520. 60% submitted SAT scores. **Characteristics:** 83% from in state, 94% commute, 49% have minority backgrounds, 4% are foreign students. Average age is 20.

FALL-TERM APPLICATIONS. $55 fee, may be waived for applicants with need. Closing date November 30; applicants notified on or about March 15. Early admission available.

STUDENT LIFE. Housing: Dormitories (coed); apartment housing available. **Activities:** Student government, film, magazine, radio, student newspaper, television, yearbook, choral groups, concert band, dance, drama, jazz band, music ensembles, musical theater, opera, pep band, symphony orchestra, fraternities, sororities.

ATHLETICS. NCAA. **Intercollegiate:** Basketball, cross-country, football M, soccer, softball W, swimming, track and field, volleyball W, wrestling M. **Intramural:** Basketball, wrestling M.

STUDENT SERVICES. Career counseling, employment service for undergraduates, freshman orientation, health services, on-campus day care, personal counseling, placement service for graduates, special adviser for adult students, veterans counselor, services/facilities for handicapped.

ANNUAL EXPENSES. Tuition and fees (1992-93): $1,424, $7,380 additional for out-of-state students. **Room and board:** $4,474. **Books and supplies:** $612. **Other expenses:** $1,728.

FINANCIAL AID. All grants, 98% of loans, all jobs based on need. Academic, music/drama, state/district residency, leadership, minority scholarships available. **Aid applications:** No closing date; priority given to applications received by March 1; applicants notified on a rolling basis beginning on or about June 15; must reply within 3 weeks.

ADDRESS/TELEPHONE. Patricia Wade, Director of Enrollment Services, San Francisco State University, 1600 Holloway Avenue, San Francisco, CA 94132. (415) 338-2411. Fax: (415) 338-2514.

San Joaquin Delta College
Stockton, California — CB code: 4706

2-year public community college, coed. Founded in 1935. **Accreditation:** Regional. **Undergraduate enrollment:** 5,239 men and women full time; 10,910 men and women part time. **Faculty:** 590 total (240 full time), 19 with doctorates or other terminal degrees. **Location:** Urban campus in large city; 75 miles from San Francisco. **Calendar:** Semester, extensive summer session. Saturday and extensive evening/early morning classes. **Microcomputers:** 200 located in classrooms, computer centers. **Special facilities:** Planetarium, electron microscopy laboratory. **Additional facts:** 14 off-campus sites located in the service district.

DEGREES OFFERED. AA. 1,139 associate degrees awarded in 1992.

UNDERGRADUATE MAJORS. Accounting, agribusiness, agricultural business and management, agricultural economics, agricultural mechanics, agricultural production, agricultural sciences, agronomy, air conditioning/heating/refrigeration mechanics, air conditioning/heating/refrigeration technology, allied health, American literature, anatomy, animal sciences, architectural engineering, architectural technologies, architecture, automotive mechanics, automotive technology, biology, botany, business administration and management, business and management, business and office, business data processing and related programs, business economics, carpentry, chemistry, child development/care/guidance, computer and information sciences, computer programming, conservation and regulation, construction, crafts, creative writing, criminal justice technology, data processing, diesel engine mechanics, drafting, drafting and design technology, electrical installation, electrical technology, electrodiagnostic technologies, emergency medical technologies, engineering, engineering and engineering-related technologies, English, fashion design, fashion merchandising, finance, fine arts, fire control and safety technology, food management, food production/management/services, food science and nutrition, food sciences, French, geology, German, graphic and printing production, graphic arts technology, health sciences, home economics, horticulture, interior design, journalism, landscape architecture, law enforcement and corrections technologies, liberal/general studies, machine tool operation/machine shop, mathematics, mechanical engineering, music, nursing, ornamental horticulture, photographic technology, physical sciences, physics, plant protection, plant sciences, practical nursing, precision metal work, prelaw, protective services, psychiatric technology, psychology, radio/television broadcasting, radiograph medical technology, real estate, science technologies, secretarial and related programs, social sciences, soil sciences, Spanish, speech, visual and performing arts, welding technology, wildlife management, woodworking, word processing, zoology.

ACADEMIC PROGRAMS. 2-year transfer program, cooperative education, dual enrollment of high school students, honors program, independent study, study abroad, telecourses. **Remedial services:** Learning center, preadmission summer program, reduced course load, remedial instruction, special counselor, tutoring. **Placement/credit:** AP, CLEP General and Subject, institutional tests; 15 credit hours maximum for associate degree. AP and CLEP credit granted after 12 semester hours in residence completed.

ACADEMIC REQUIREMENTS. Freshmen must earn minimum GPA of 2.0 to continue in good standing. Students must declare major on application. **Graduation requirements:** 60 hours for associate (18 in major). Most students required to take courses in English, history, humanities, mathematics, philosophy/religion, biological/physical sciences, social sciences.

FRESHMAN ADMISSIONS. Selection criteria: Open admissions. **Test requirements:** Comparative Guidance Placement Test required for placement.

1992 FRESHMAN CLASS PROFILE. 4,273 men and women enrolled. **Characteristics:** 100% commute. Average age is 19.

FALL-TERM APPLICATIONS. No fee. Closing date September 1; applicants notified on a rolling basis beginning on or about August 1. Early admission available.

STUDENT LIFE. Activities: Student government, magazine, radio, student newspaper, choral groups, concert band, dance, drama, musical theater, pep band, Black Student Union, Movimiento Estudiantil Chicano de Aztlan, Vietnamese and Asian student clubs, International Student Association.

ATHLETICS. NJCAA. **Intercollegiate:** Baseball M, basketball, cross-country M, diving, football M, golf, skiing, soccer, softball W, swimming, tennis, track and field, volleyball W, water polo, wrestling M.

STUDENT SERVICES. Aptitude testing, career counseling, employment service for undergraduates, freshman orientation, personal counseling, placement service for graduates, veterans counselor, services/facilities for handicapped.

ANNUAL EXPENSES. Tuition and fees (projected): $600, $3,210 additional for out-of-state students. **Books and supplies:** $612. **Other expenses:** $1,300.

FINANCIAL AID. 22% of freshmen, 22% of continuing students receive some form of aid. All loans, 71% of jobs based on need. 1,516 enrolled freshmen were judged to have need, 1,032 were offered aid. Academic, music/drama, art, leadership, minority scholarships available. **Aid applications:** No closing date; priority given to applications received by April 15; applicants notified on a rolling basis beginning on or about May 1; must reply within 3 weeks. **Additional information:** Enrollment fee waivers available for low-income Californiaresidents.

ADDRESS/TELEPHONE. Cheryl L. Clark, Registrar, San Joaquin Delta College, 5151 Pacific Avenue, Stockton, CA 95207. (209) 474-5625. Fax: (209) 474-5649.

San Jose Christian College
San Jose, California — CB code: 4756

4-year private Bible college, coed, interdenominational. Founded in 1939. **Undergraduate enrollment:** 84 men, 62 women full time; 98 men, 68 women part time. **Faculty:** 32 total (9 full time), 6 with doctorates or other terminal degrees. **Location:** Urban campus in very large city; 50 miles from San Francisco. **Calendar:** Quarter, limited summer session. **Additional facts:** Men and women prepared for Christian ministry.

DEGREES OFFERED. AA, BA, BS. 9 associate degrees awarded in 1992. 100% in philosophy, religion, theology. 53 bachelor's degrees awarded. 100% in philosophy, religion, theology.

UNDERGRADUATE MAJORS. Associate: Bible studies. **Bachelor's:** youth ministry, Bible studies, counseling psychology, missionary studies, pastoral studies, religious education, theological studies.

ACADEMIC PROGRAMS. 2-year transfer program, double major, honors program, independent study, internships. **Remedial services:** Special counselor, tutoring. **Placement/credit:** AP, CLEP Subject; 16 credit hours maximum for associate degree; 16 credit hours maximum for bachelor's degree.

ACADEMIC REQUIREMENTS. Freshmen must earn minimum GPA of 2.0 to continue in good standing. 60% of freshmen return for sophomore

year. Students must declare major by end of second year. **Graduation requirements:** 96 hours for associate (40 in major), 192 hours for bachelor's (64 in major). Most students required to take courses in English, foreign languages, history, humanities, philosophy/religion, biological/physical sciences, social sciences. **Postgraduate studies:** 50% from 2-year programs enter 4-year programs. **Additional information:** All degrees offer major in Bible and theology. Emphasis placed on pastoral training, missions, youth ministry, Christian education, and Christian counseling.

FRESHMAN ADMISSIONS. Selection criteria: Interest in Christian ministries, recommendation. Special consideration to spouses of students and children of ministers. **Test requirements:** SAT or ACT (ACT preferred) for placement and counseling only; score report by August 15.

1992 FRESHMAN CLASS PROFILE. 22 men and women enrolled. **Characteristics:** 83% from in state, 62% commute, 25% have minority backgrounds. Average age is 20.

FALL-TERM APPLICATIONS. $30 fee. Closing date August 1; applicants notified on a rolling basis. Interview recommended. Essay recommended. Deferred admission available.

STUDENT LIFE. Housing: Dormitories (men, women); apartment housing available. **Activities:** Student government, yearbook, choral groups, cross-cultural awareness team.

ATHLETICS. Intercollegiate: Basketball, volleyball W. **Intramural:** Softball, volleyball.

STUDENT SERVICES. Employment service for undergraduates, freshman orientation, personal counseling, placement service for graduates, veterans counselor.

ANNUAL EXPENSES. Tuition and fees (1992-93): $5,205. **Room and board:** $3,240. **Books and supplies:** $450. **Other expenses:** $1,314.

FINANCIAL AID. 80% of freshmen, 50% of continuing students receive some form of aid. 89% of grants, 50% of jobs based on need. Academic, music/drama, athletic, leadership scholarships available. **Aid applications:** No closing date; priority given to applications received by March 2; applicants notified on a rolling basis beginning on or about June 1; must reply within 3 weeks.

ADDRESS/TELEPHONE. Karen Spray, Director of Admissions, San Jose Christian College, 790 South 12th Street, San Jose, CA 95108-1090. (408) 293-9058. Fax: (408) 293-7352.

San Jose City College
San Jose, California — CB code: 4686

2-year public community college, coed. Founded in 1921. **Accreditation:** Regional. **Undergraduate enrollment:** 762 men, 858 women full time; 4,417 men, 4,819 women part time. **Faculty:** 357 total (157 full time), 17 with doctorates or other terminal degrees. **Location:** Urban campus in very large city; 55 miles from San Francisco. **Calendar:** Semester, limited summer session. **Microcomputers:** 250 located in computer centers.

DEGREES OFFERED. AA, AS. 364 associate degrees awarded in 1992. 19% in engineering technologies, 69% multi/interdisciplinary studies.

UNDERGRADUATE MAJORS. Accounting, air conditioning/heating/refrigeration mechanics, biology, business and office, business data processing and related programs, business data programming, ceramics, chemistry, computer and information sciences, construction, dental assistant, drafting, electrical and electronics equipment repair, electrical installation, engineering and engineering-related technologies, English, fashion merchandising, finance, fine arts, French, German, law enforcement and corrections technologies, liberal/general studies, machine tool operation/machine shop, marketing and distribution, masonry/tile setting, mathematics, mechanical design technology, microcomputer software, music, personal services, photographic technology, physical sciences, physics, plumbing/pipefitting/steamfitting, protective services, psychology, public affairs, radio/television technology, real estate, recreation and community services technologies, science technologies, secretarial and related programs, social sciences, Spanish, teacher aide, visual and performing arts.

ACADEMIC PROGRAMS. 2-year transfer program, accelerated program, cooperative education, dual enrollment of high school students, honors program, independent study, internships, weekend college, cross-registration. **Remedial services:** Learning center, preadmission summer program, reduced course load, remedial instruction, special counselor, tutoring. **ROTC:** Air Force, Army. **Placement/credit:** AP, CLEP General and Subject, institutional tests; 30 credit hours maximum for associate degree.

ACADEMIC REQUIREMENTS. Freshmen must earn minimum GPA of 2.0 to continue in good standing. Student will be placed on probation or dismissed if withdrawals exceed 50% of all units. 52% of freshmen return for sophomore year. **Graduation requirements:** 60 hours for associate (18 in major). Most students required to take courses in English, history, mathematics, biological/physical sciences, social sciences.

FRESHMAN ADMISSIONS. Selection criteria: Open admissions.

1992 FRESHMAN CLASS PROFILE. 3,291 men and women enrolled. **Characteristics:** 90% from in state, 100% commute, 51% have minority backgrounds, 2% are foreign students. Average age is 27.

FALL-TERM APPLICATIONS. No fee. No closing date; applicants notified on a rolling basis. Early admission available.

STUDENT LIFE. Activities: Student government, radio, student newspaper, choral groups, concert band, dance, drama, jazz band, music ensembles, musical theater, symphony orchestra.

ATHLETICS. Intercollegiate: Baseball M, basketball, cross-country, football M, golf M, softball W, track and field, volleyball W.

STUDENT SERVICES. Aptitude testing, career counseling, employment service for undergraduates, health services, on-campus day care, personal counseling, veterans counselor, services/facilities for handicapped.

ANNUAL EXPENSES. Tuition and fees: $310, $2,900 additional for out-of-state students. **Books and supplies:** $612.

FINANCIAL AID. 6% of freshmen, 8% of continuing students receive some form of aid. All aid based on need. **Aid applications:** No closing date; priority given to applications received by May 31; applicants notified on a rolling basis beginning on or about July 20; must reply within 4 weeks. **Additional information:** Board of Governors Grant (fee waivers) available to all qualified applicants.

ADDRESS/TELEPHONE. Robert L. Brown, District Director of Admissions and Records, San Jose City College, 2100 Moorpark Avenue, San Jose, CA 95128-2798. (408) 298-2181.

San Jose State University
San Jose, California — CB code: 4687

Admissions:	78% of applicants accepted
Based on:	••• School record
	•• Test scores
	• Special talents
Completion:	73% of freshmen end year in good standing
	24% graduate

4-year public university and liberal arts college, coed. Founded in 1857. **Accreditation:** Regional. **Undergraduate enrollment:** 7,769 men, 7,720 women full time; 3,934 men, 4,040 women part time. **Graduate enrollment:** 343 men, 851 women full time; 2,149 men, 2,820 women part time. **Faculty:** 1,522 total (857 full time). **Location:** Urban campus in very large city; 50 miles from San Francisco. **Calendar:** Semester, limited summer session. **Microcomputers:** 1,597 located in libraries, classrooms, computer centers. **Special facilities:** Moss Landing Marine Laboratory, Natural History Living Museum, Nuclear Science Lab, John Steinbeck Research Center, Ira Brilliant Center for Beethoven Studies, Chicano Resource Center, Art Metal Foundry, deep-sea research ship, electro-acoustic and recording studio.

DEGREES OFFERED. BA, BS, BFA, MA, MS, MBA, MFA, MSW. 4,012 bachelor's degrees awarded in 1992. 25% in business and management, 7% communications, 9% engineering, 7% health sciences, 5% psychology, 16% social sciences, 9% visual and performing arts. Graduate degrees offered in 90 major fields of study.

UNDERGRADUATE MAJORS. Accounting, advertising, aeronautical technology, aerospace/aeronautical/astronautical engineering, Afro-American (black) studies, American studies, analytical chemistry, anthropology, applied mathematics, art history, atmospheric sciences and meteorology, aviation management, behavioral sciences, biochemistry, biological and physical sciences, biology, botany, business administration and management, career writing, ceramics, chemical engineering, chemistry, child development/care/guidance, Chinese, civil engineering, clinical laboratory science, clinical psychology, cognitive psychology, community/occupational health education, computer and information sciences, computer engineering, computer technology, condensed matter physics, counseling psychology, crafts, criminal justice studies, dance, developmental psychology, dietetics, drafting and design technology, dramatic arts, drawing, economics, electrical/electronics/communications engineering, electronic technology, energy, power, control technology, engineering, English, entomology, environmental health, environmental science, European studies, film arts, finance, fine arts, food science and nutrition, French, general design studies, geography, geology, geophysics and seismology, German, graphic and printing production, graphic arts technology, graphic design, health care administration, health sciences, history, hospitality management, human resources development, humanities, improvised music studies, improvised music studies, industrial and organizational psychology, industrial arts education, industrial design, industrial engineering, industrial technology, instrumental music, interior design, international business management, Japanese, journalism, laser electro-optic technology, liberal/general studies, linguistics, management information systems, manufacturing management, manufacturing technology, marine biology, marketing management, materials engineering, mathematics, mechanical engineering, medical laboratory technologies, medical microbiology and immunology, microbiology, molecular biology, music, music history and appreciation, music performance, music theory and composition, nuclear and radiochemistry, nursing, nutritional sciences, occupational therapy, oceanography, optics, packaging technology, painting, parks and recreation management, personality psychology, pharmaceutical chemistry, philosophy, photography, photojournalism, physical education, physical sciences, physics, political science and government, printmaking, protective services, psychology, public administration, public health laboratory science, public policy studies, public relations, quality control technology, radio/television broadcasting, radio/television technology, recreation and community services technologies, recreation therapy, religion, sculpture, social psychology, social sciences, social work, sociology, Spanish, speech, speech pathology/audiology, statistics, studio art, systems physiology, therapeutic recreation, visual and performing arts, voice, wildlife ecology, zoology.

ACADEMIC PROGRAMS. Accelerated program, cooperative education, double major, dual enrollment of high school students, honors program, independent study, internships, student-designed major, study abroad, teacher preparation, telecourses, visiting/exchange student program, cross-registration. **Remedial services:** Learning center, preadmission summer program, reduced course load, remedial instruction, special counselor, tutoring, reading and writing laboratories. **ROTC:** Air Force, Army. **Placement/credit:** AP, CLEP General and Subject; 30 credit hours maximum for bachelor's degree.

ACADEMIC REQUIREMENTS. Freshmen must earn minimum GPA of 2.0 to continue in good standing. 77% of freshmen return for sophomore year. Students must declare major by end of second year. **Graduation requirements:** 124 hours for bachelor's (24 in major). Most students required to take courses in arts/fine arts, English, history, humanities, mathematics, biological/physical sciences, social sciences.

FRESHMAN ADMISSIONS. Selection criteria: GPA and test scores, plus completion of specified subjects. **High school preparation:** 15 units required. Required units include English 4, foreign language 2, mathematics 3 and science 1. One visual and performing arts, 1 US history/government and 3 electives required. **Test requirements:** SAT or ACT; score report by July 1.

1992 FRESHMAN CLASS PROFILE. 2,973 men applied, 2,283 accepted, 802 enrolled; 2,726 women applied, 2,140 accepted, 741 enrolled. 53% had high school GPA of 3.0 or higher, 45% between 2.0 and 2.99. **Academic background:** Mid 50% of enrolled freshmen had SAT-V between 310-450, SAT-M between 410-540; ACT composite between 16-21. 86% submitted SAT scores, 13% submitted ACT scores. **Characteristics:** 70% from in state, 65% have minority backgrounds, 1% are foreign students. Average age is 19.

FALL-TERM APPLICATIONS. $55 fee, may be waived for applicants with need. Closing date July 1; priority given to applications received by November 30; applicants notified on a rolling basis beginning on or about November 1. Audition required for music applicants. Portfolio required for graphic and interior design applicants. Interview recommended for nursing, occupational therapy, graphic and interior design applicants. Undergraduate engineering programs limited to state residents.

STUDENT LIFE. Housing: Dormitories (coed); apartment, fraternity, sorority, handicapped housing available. **Activities:** Student government, magazine, radio, student newspaper, television, yearbook, choral groups, concert band, dance, drama, jazz band, marching band, music ensembles, musical theater, opera, pep band, symphony orchestra, fraternities, sororities, over 250 professional, cultural, recreational, religious, social honorary, and service clubs. **Additional information:** Many academic programs offer internships in municipal government.

ATHLETICS. NCAA. **Intercollegiate:** Baseball M, basketball, football M, golf, gymnastics, soccer M, softball W, swimming W, tennis, volleyball W. **Intramural:** Badminton, basketball, bowling, racquetball, soccer, softball, swimming, tennis, volleyball, water polo. **Clubs:** Sports clubs.

STUDENT SERVICES. Aptitude testing, career counseling, employment service for undergraduates, freshman orientation, health services, on-campus day care, personal counseling, placement service for graduates, special adviser for adult students, veterans counselor, services/facilities for handicapped.

ANNUAL EXPENSES. Tuition and fees (1992-93): $1,502, $7,380 additional for out-of-state students. **Room and board:** $4,872. **Books and supplies:** $612. **Other expenses:** $1,548.

FINANCIAL AID. 30% of freshmen, 26% of continuing students receive some form of aid. 98% of grants, 99% of loans, 30% of jobs based on need. Athletic scholarships available. **Aid applications:** No closing date; priority given to applications received by March 1; applicants notified on a rolling basis beginning on or about May 15; must reply within 2 weeks.

ADDRESS/TELEPHONE. Edgar Chambers, Associate Executive Vice President: Admissions and Records, San Jose State University, One Washington Square, San Jose, CA 95192-0009. (408) 924-2009. Fax: (408) 924-2050.

Santa Barbara City College
Santa Barbara, California — CB code: 4690

2-year public community college, coed. Founded in 1908. **Accreditation:** Regional. **Undergraduate enrollment:** 2,400 men, 2,350 women full time; 4,016 men, 3,920 women part time. **Faculty:** 500 total (230 full time), 43 with doctorates or other terminal degrees. **Location:** Suburban campus in small city; 90 miles from Los Angeles. **Calendar:** Semester, limited summer session. Extensive evening/early morning classes. **Microcomputers:** 40 located in computer centers.

DEGREES OFFERED. AA, AS. 594 associate degrees awarded in 1992.

UNDERGRADUATE MAJORS. Afro-American (black) studies, American Indian studies, anthropology, art history, automotive mechanics, automotive technology, biology, business administration and management, business and management, business and office, chemistry, child development/care/guidance, communications, computer and information sciences, computer graphics, computer technology, criminal justice studies, drafting, drafting and design technology, dramatic arts, early childhood education, earth sciences, economics, electronic technology, engineering, engineering and engineering-related technologies, English, environmental science, escrow management, ethnic studies, finance, French, geography, geology, geoscience technology, German, graphic and printing production, graphic arts technology, history, hotel/motel and restaurant management, information sciences and systems, international studies, law , liberal/general studies, marketing and distribution, marketing management, mathematics, Mexican American studies, music, Natural history, nursing, office supervision and management, ornamental horticulture, philosophy, physics, political science and government, practical nursing, psychology, radiograph medical technology, real estate, recreation and community services technologies, sociology, Spanish, theater design.

ACADEMIC PROGRAMS. 2-year transfer program, cooperative education, honors program, independent study, internships, study abroad, cross-registration. **Remedial services:** Learning center, preadmission summer program, reduced course load, remedial instruction, special counselor, tutoring. **Placement/credit:** AP, institutional tests; 12 credit hours maximum for associate degree.

ACADEMIC REQUIREMENTS. Freshmen must earn minimum GPA of 2.0 to continue in good standing. 67% of freshmen return for sophomore year. Students must declare major on application. **Graduation requirements:** 60 hours for associate (18 in major). Most students required to take courses in English, history, humanities, mathematics, biological/physical sciences, social sciences.

FRESHMAN ADMISSIONS. Selection criteria: Open admissions. Must be 18 years of age or a high school graduate.

1992 FRESHMAN CLASS PROFILE. 1,079 men, 1,053 women enrolled. **Characteristics:** 96% from in state, 100% commute, 28% have minority backgrounds, 3% are foreign students. Average age is 20.

FALL-TERM APPLICATIONS. No fee. Closing date August 1; priority given to applications received by May 1; applicants notified on a rolling basis beginning on or about April 1. Interview required for nursing, hotel and restaurant management, marine technology applicants. Audition required for some music and theater applicants.

STUDENT LIFE. Activities: Student government, magazine, student newspaper, television, choral groups, concert band, dance, drama, jazz band, music ensembles, musical theater, symphony orchestra, Movimiento Estudiantil Chicano de Aztlan, EOPS, Young Republicans, history club, international students association, honors fellowship, hotel restaurant club, Society Latter-day Saints Club, philosophy club, student nurse association.

ATHLETICS. Intercollegiate: Baseball M, basketball, cross-country, football M, golf M, soccer, tennis, track and field, volleyball. **Clubs:** Skiing.

STUDENT SERVICES. Aptitude testing, career counseling, employment service for undergraduates, freshman orientation, health services, on-campus day care, personal counseling, placement service for graduates, special adviser for adult students, veterans counselor, services/facilities for handicapped.

ANNUAL EXPENSES. Tuition and fees (1992-93): $135, $3,120 additional for out-of-state students. **Books and supplies:** $558. **Other expenses:** $1,440.

FINANCIAL AID. 20% of freshmen, 31% of continuing students receive some form of aid. 94% of grants, 98% of loans, 86% of jobs based on need. Academic, leadership, minority scholarships available. **Aid applications:** No closing date; priority given to applications received by May 15; applicants notified on a rolling basis beginning on or about June 15; must reply within 2 weeks. **Additional information:** California residents may qualify for Board Financial Assistance Program which will allow institutions to waive enrollment fee.

ADDRESS/TELEPHONE. Jane Craven, Assistant Dean Admissions and Records, Santa Barbara City College, 721 Cliff Drive, Santa Barbara, CA 93109-2394. (805) 965-0581. Fax: (805) 963-SBCC.

Santa Clara University
Santa Clara, California — CB code: 4851

Admissions:	65% of applicants accepted
Based on:	••• School record
	•• Essay, test scores
	• Activities, interview, recommendations, special talents
Completion:	95% of freshmen end year in good standing
	75% graduate, 24% of these enter graduate study

4-year private university, coed, affiliated with Roman Catholic Church. Founded in 1851. **Accreditation:** Regional. **Undergraduate enrollment:** 2,010 men, 1,933 women full time; 66 men, 37 women part time. **Graduate enroll-**

ment: 746 men, 649 women full time; 1,402 men, 741 women part time. **Faculty:** 603 total (342 full time), 431 with doctorates or other terminal degrees. **Location:** Suburban campus in small city; 45 miles from San Francisco, 1 mile from San Jose. **Calendar:** Quarter, limited summer session. **Microcomputers:** 370 located in libraries, classrooms, computer centers. **Special facilities:** Historic mission church and art gallery with artifacts dating to California mission era, access to NASA Research Center.

DEGREES OFFERED. BA, BS, MA, MS, MBA, PhD, JD. 990 bachelor's degrees awarded in 1992. 27% in business and management, 5% communications, 11% engineering, 8% letters/literature, 5% multi/interdisciplinary studies, 7% psychology, 22% social sciences. Graduate degrees offered in 19 major fields of study.

UNDERGRADUATE MAJORS. Accounting, anthropology, art history, biological and physical sciences, biology, business administration and management, business economics, chemistry, civil engineering, classics, communications, computer and information sciences, computer engineering, decision and information sciences, dramatic arts, economics, electrical/electronics/communications engineering, engineering, engineering physics, English, finance, French, German, history, humanities and social sciences, international business management, Italian, liberal/general studies, marketing management, mathematics, mechanical engineering, music, music history and appreciation, operations research, philosophy, physics, political science and government, predentistry, prelaw, premedicine, preveterinary, psychology, religion, retailing, social and natural sciences, sociology, Spanish, studio art.

ACADEMIC PROGRAMS. Cooperative education, double major, honors program, independent study, internships, student-designed major, study abroad, teacher preparation, United Nations semester, Washington semester. **Remedial services:** Learning center, special counselor, tutoring, private tutoring and group sessions to improve English skills. **ROTC:** Air Force, Army, Naval. **Placement/credit:** AP; 40 credit hours maximum for bachelor's degree.

ACADEMIC REQUIREMENTS. Freshmen must earn minimum GPA of 1.6 to continue in good standing. 91% of freshmen return for sophomore year. Students must declare major by end of second year. **Graduation requirements:** 175 hours for bachelor's (60 in major). Most students required to take courses in English, foreign languages, mathematics, philosophy/religion, biological/physical sciences, social sciences. **Additional information:** Institutes with core of specially designed courses and speakers focusing on topics of current public debate, offered during most winter quarters.

FRESHMAN ADMISSIONS. Selection criteria: Rigor of high school curriculum and GPA most important, followed by SAT scores, teacher's recommendation, personal essay, and extracurricular acitivities. Ethnicity and alumni affiliations given special consideration. **High school preparation:** 16 units required. Required units include English 4, foreign language 3, mathematics 3, social science 1 and science 1. Additional mathematics and science courses recommended for applicants in business, engineering, mathematics, and science. **Test requirements:** SAT or ACT (SAT preferred); score report by February 15.

1992 FRESHMAN CLASS PROFILE. 1,878 men applied, 1,213 accepted, 442 enrolled; 2,061 women applied, 1,336 accepted, 457 enrolled. 88% had high school GPA of 3.0 or higher, 12% between 2.0 and 2.99. 40% were in top tenth and 73% were in top quarter of graduating class. **Academic background:** Mid 50% of enrolled freshmen had SAT-V between 450-550, SAT-M between 520-640. 99% submitted SAT scores. **Characteristics:** 69% from in state, 91% live in college housing, 33% have minority backgrounds, 7% are foreign students. Average age is 18.

FALL-TERM APPLICATIONS. $35 fee, may be waived for applicants with need. Closing date February 1; applicants notified on a rolling basis; must reply by May 1. Essay required. Audition recommended for music, theater arts applicants. CRDA.

STUDENT LIFE. Housing: Dormitories (coed); apartment, fraternity, sorority, handicapped housing available. Housing guaranteed to freshmen, sophomores and juniors. **Activities:** Student government, magazine, radio, student newspaper, television, yearbook, choral groups, dance, drama, jazz band, music ensembles, musical theater, pep band, symphony orchestra, fraternities, sororities, Black Student Union, Mecha El Frente Chicano Association, Volunteer Community Action Program, Varsity Christian Fellowship, Asian Pacific Student Union, Ka Mana o O'Hawaii, Multicultural Program Board.

ATHLETICS. NCAA. **Intercollegiate:** Baseball M, basketball, bowling, cross-country, football M, golf, lacrosse M, rowing (crew), rugby M, soccer, softball W, tennis, volleyball W, water polo M. **Intramural:** Badminton, basketball, boxing M, racquetball, rifle, skin diving, soccer, softball, swimming, tennis, volleyball.

STUDENT SERVICES. Aptitude testing, career counseling, employment service for undergraduates, freshman orientation, health services, on-campus day care, personal counseling, placement service for graduates, special adviser for adult students, counseling for Hispanic and black students, women's student resources, student resources for students with disabilities, international student resources, off campus student resources, campus ministry, tutorial & academic resource services, services/facilities for handicapped.

ANNUAL EXPENSES. Tuition and fees: $12,879. **Room and board:** $5,904. **Books and supplies:** $558. **Other expenses:** $1,638.

FINANCIAL AID. 53% of freshmen, 56% of continuing students receive some form of aid. 87% of grants, 96% of loans, all jobs based on need. Academic, music/drama, athletic, leadership, alumni affiliation, religious affiliation scholarships available. **Aid applications:** No closing date; priority given to applications received by February 1; applicants notified on a rolling basis beginning on or about March 15; must reply by May 1 or within 2 weeks if notified thereafter.

ADDRESS/TELEPHONE. Daniel Saracino, Dean of Admissions, Santa Clara University, 500 El Camino Real, Santa Clara, CA 95053. (408) 554-4700. Fax: (408) 554-2700.

Santa Monica College
Santa Monica, California — CB code: 4691

2-year public community college, coed. Founded in 1929. **Accreditation:** Regional. **Undergraduate enrollment:** 3,159 men, 3,189 women full time; 7,066 men, 9,789 women part time. **Faculty:** 700 total (250 full time), 86 with doctorates or other terminal degrees. **Location:** Urban campus in small city; 18 miles from downtown Los Angeles. **Calendar:** Semester, limited summer session. Saturday and extensive evening/early morning classes. **Microcomputers:** 30 located in libraries, computer centers. **Special facilities:** Art gallery, planetarium, photo gallery. **Additional facts:** Off campus program at Santa Monica College of Design, Humanities Center.

DEGREES OFFERED. AA. 893 associate degrees awarded in 1992. 40% in business and management, 7% business/office and marketing/distribution, 5% computer sciences, 15% health sciences, 7% allied health, 7% parks/recreation, protective services, public affairs, 10% visual and performing arts.

UNDERGRADUATE MAJORS. Accounting, architectural technologies, architecture, automotive mechanics, automotive technology, biological and physical sciences, biology, business administration and management, business and management, business and office, business data processing and related programs, chemistry, communications, computer programming, construction, criminal justice technology, dance, data processing, drafting, drafting and design technology, dramatic arts, electrical/electronics/communications engineering, electronic technology, English, fashion merchandising, finance, fine arts, fire control and safety technology, foreign languages (multiple emphasis), French, geology, German, graphic and printing production, graphic arts technology, graphic design, history, home economics, information sciences and systems, interior design, international relations, journalism, law enforcement and corrections technologies, liberal/general studies, management science, marketing and distribution, mathematics, Mexican American studies, music, nursing, office supervision and management, photographic technology, photography, physical sciences, physics, political science and government, precision metal work, radio/television broadcasting, real estate, recreation and community services technologies, respiratory therapy, respiratory therapy technology, secretarial and related programs, small business management and ownership, social sciences, Spanish.

ACADEMIC PROGRAMS. 2-year transfer program, accelerated program, cooperative education, dual enrollment of high school students, honors program, independent study, internships, study abroad. **Remedial services:** Learning center, preadmission summer program, remedial instruction, special counselor, tutoring. **Placement/credit:** AP, CLEP General and Subject, institutional tests; 30 credit hours maximum for associate degree.

ACADEMIC REQUIREMENTS. Freshmen must earn minimum GPA of 2.0 to continue in good standing. 60% of freshmen return for sophomore year. Students must declare major on application. **Graduation requirements:** 60 hours for associate (20 in major). Most students required to take courses in English, history, humanities, mathematics, philosophy/religion, biological/physical sciences, social sciences.

FRESHMAN ADMISSIONS. Selection criteria: Open admissions.

1992 FRESHMAN CLASS PROFILE. 1,860 men, 1,914 women enrolled. **Characteristics:** 100% commute, 48% have minority backgrounds, 5% are foreign students.

FALL-TERM APPLICATIONS. No fee. No closing date; applicants notified on a rolling basis. Audition required for music, theater arts applicants.

STUDENT LIFE. Activities: Student government, magazine, radio, student newspaper, choral groups, dance, drama, marching band, musical theater.

ATHLETICS. NJCAA. **Intercollegiate:** Baseball M, basketball, cross-country M, diving, football M, soccer M, softball W, swimming, tennis, track and field, volleyball, water polo M. **Intramural:** Badminton.

STUDENT SERVICES. Career counseling, employment service for undergraduates, freshman orientation, health services, on-campus day care, personal counseling, placement service for graduates, special adviser for adult students, veterans counselor, services/facilities for handicapped.

ANNUAL EXPENSES. Tuition and fees (1992-93): $155, $3,600 additional for out-of-state students. **Books and supplies:** $400.

FINANCIAL AID. 23% of freshmen, 27% of continuing students receive some form of aid. 93% of grants, 70% of loans, 54% of jobs based on need. Academic, music/drama, art, athletic, state/district residency, leadership, alumni affiliation, minority scholarships available. **Aid applications:** No closing date; priority given to applications received by May 15; applicants notified on a rolling basis beginning on or about July 1; must reply within 2 weeks.

ADDRESS/TELEPHONE. Gordon A. Newman, Dean of Admissions and Records, Santa Monica College, 1900 Pico Boulevard, Santa Monica, CA 90405-1628. (310) 452-9220. Fax: (310) 450-2387.

Santa Rosa Junior College
Santa Rosa, California — CB code: 4692

2-year public community, junior college, coed. Founded in 1918. **Accreditation:** Regional. **Undergraduate enrollment:** 3,147 men, 3,296 women full time; 7,382 men, 10,668 women part time. **Faculty:** 1,387 total (297 full time), 119 with doctorates or other terminal degrees. **Location:** Urban campus in small city; 55 miles from San Francisco. **Calendar:** Semester, extensive summer session. **Microcomputers:** Located in classrooms, computer centers. **Special facilities:** Native American art museum, farm, summer repertory theater, planetarium, art gallery.

DEGREES OFFERED. AA, AS. 1,055 associate degrees awarded in 1992. 5% in business and management, 63% education, 5% allied health.

UNDERGRADUATE MAJORS. Accounting, aeronautical technology, agribusiness, agricultural business and management, agricultural engineering, agricultural sciences, agronomy, allied health, animal sciences, anthropology, architectural technologies, automotive mechanics, automotive technology, biological and physical sciences, biology, biomedical equipment technology, business administration and management, business and management, business and office, business data processing and related programs, business data programming, carpentry, chemical engineering, chemistry, child development/care/guidance, civil engineering, civil technology, clothing and textiles management/production/services, communications, community services, computer and information sciences, computer programming, construction, criminal justice studies, dance, data processing, dental assistant, diesel engine mechanics, dramatic arts, early childhood education, economics, education, electrical installation, electrical/electronics/communications engineering, electronic technology, engineering, engineering and engineering-related technologies, English, environmental health engineering, ethnic studies, fashion merchandising, fine arts, fire control and safety technology, fishing and fisheries, food science and nutrition, food sciences, foreign languages (multiple emphasis), forest products processing technology, forestry and related sciences, French, geography, geology, German, graphic arts technology, health care administration, health sciences, history, home economics, horticultural science, humanities and social sciences, industrial arts education, journalism, landscape architecture, law enforcement and corrections, law enforcement and corrections technologies, legal secretary, liberal/general studies, library science, machine tool operation/machine shop, marketing and distribution, masonry/tile setting, mathematics, mechanical engineering, medical assistant, mental health/human services, music, nursing, occupational therapy, oceanography, ophthalmic services, ornamental horticulture, parks and recreation management, philosophy, photography, physical education, physical sciences, plumbing/pipefitting/steamfitting, political science and government, practical nursing, precision metal work, predentistry, prelaw, premedicine, prepharmacy, psychology, public administration, public affairs, public health laboratory science, radio/television broadcasting, radiograph medical technology, respiratory therapy technology, retailing, science technologies, secretarial and related programs, social sciences, social work, sociology, Spanish, special education, speech, teacher aide, visual and performing arts.

ACADEMIC PROGRAMS. 2-year transfer program, cooperative education, dual enrollment of high school students, independent study, internships, study abroad, telecourses. **Remedial services:** Learning center, preadmission summer program, reduced course load, remedial instruction, special counselor, tutoring, Extended Opportunity Program and services. **ROTC:** Army. **Placement/credit:** AP, institutional tests.

ACADEMIC REQUIREMENTS. Freshmen must earn minimum GPA of 2.0 to continue in good standing. Students must declare major on application. **Graduation requirements:** 60 hours for associate. Most students required to take courses in English, history, humanities, mathematics, biological/physical sciences, social sciences. **Additional information:** Army ROTC available through cross-registration.

FRESHMAN ADMISSIONS. Selection criteria: Open admissions.

1992 FRESHMAN CLASS PROFILE. 1,774 men, 1,867 women enrolled. **Characteristics:** 99% from in state, 99% commute, 19% have minority backgrounds. Average age is 19.

FALL-TERM APPLICATIONS. No fee. No closing date; priority given to applications received by April 15; applicants notified on a rolling basis beginning on or about April 15. Audition recommended for music performance, some physical education, some communications applicants. Early admission available. SAT or ACT recommended for counseling purposes, score report by August 17.

STUDENT LIFE. Housing: Dormitories (coed). **Activities:** Student government, film, radio, student newspaper, television, choral groups, concert band, dance, drama, jazz band, music ensembles, musical theater, symphony orchestra, various clubs and organizations.

ATHLETICS. Intercollegiate: Baseball M, basketball, cross-country, diving, football M, golf, soccer, softball W, swimming, tennis, track and field, volleyball W, water polo, wrestling M.

STUDENT SERVICES. Aptitude testing, career counseling, employment service for undergraduates, freshman orientation, health services, on-campus day care, personal counseling, placement service for graduates, special adviser for adult students, veterans counselor, services/facilities for handicapped.

ANNUAL EXPENSES. Tuition and fees (projected): $316, $3,510 additional for out-of-state students. **Room and board:** $1,600 room only. **Books and supplies:** $612. **Other expenses:** $1,548.

FINANCIAL AID. 22% of continuing students receive some form of aid. 70% of grants, 97% of loans, all jobs based on need. Academic, music/drama, art, athletic, state/district residency, leadership, minority scholarships available. **Aid applications:** No closing date; priority given to applications received by March 2; applicants notified on a rolling basis beginning on or about March 28; must reply within 30 days. **Additional information:** California's Board Fee Assistance Program (BFAP) provides fee waivers for $10 per unit enrollment fee for applicants with need, welfare recipients, and families with incomes under $17,000 per year. BFAP eligibles are exempt from health fees.

ADDRESS/TELEPHONE. Ricardo Navarrette, Dean of Admissions and Records, Santa Rosa Junior College, 1501 Mendocino Avenue, Santa Rosa, CA 95401. (707) 527-4799. Fax: (707) 527-4816.

Scripps College
Claremont, California — CB code: 4693

Admissions: 78% of applicants accepted
Based on: ••• School record, test scores
•• Essay, recommendations, special talents
• Activities, interview
Completion: 97% of freshmen end year in good standing
75% graduate, 52% of these enter graduate study

4-year private liberal arts college, women only. Founded in 1926. **Accreditation:** Regional. **Undergraduate enrollment:** 596 women full time; 10 women part time. **Faculty:** 86 total (58 full time), 79 with doctorates or other terminal degrees. **Location:** Suburban campus in large town; 35 miles from Los Angeles. **Calendar:** Semester. **Microcomputers:** 37 located in dormitories, computer centers. **Special facilities:** Art gallery, art slide library, biological field station, 2700-seat concert hall, humanities museum. **Additional facts:** One of 5 undergraduate Claremont colleges sharing common facilities.

DEGREES OFFERED. BA, BS. 158 bachelor's degrees awarded in 1992. 7% in business and management, 15% letters/literature, 5% life sciences, 14% psychology, 31% social sciences, 16% visual and performing arts.

UNDERGRADUATE MAJORS. Afro-American (black) studies, American studies, anthropology, art history, arts management, Asian studies, biochemistry, biological and physical sciences, biology, business economics, chemistry, Chinese, classics, communications, comparative literature, dance, dramatic arts, economics, English, English literature, European studies, foreign languages (multiple emphasis), French, German, Greek (classical), Hispanic American studies, history, humanities, humanities and social sciences, international business management, international relations, international studies, Italian, Japanese, Latin, Latin American studies, liberal/general studies, linguistics, mathematics, Mexican American studies, modern French civilization, music, music business management, music history and appreciation, music performance, organizational studies, philosophy, physics, political science and government, predentistry, prelaw, premedicine, preveterinary, psychobiology, psychology, religion, social sciences, sociology, Spanish, studio art, third world studies, visual and performing arts, women's studies.

ACADEMIC PROGRAMS. Accelerated program, double major, honors program, independent study, internships, student-designed major, study abroad, visiting/exchange student program, New York semester, United Nations semester, Washington semester, cross-registration, humanities internship program, corporate training for liberal arts women; liberal arts/career combination in engineering; combined bachelor's/graduate program in business administration. **Remedial services:** Reduced course load, tutoring. **ROTC:** Air Force, Army. **Placement/credit:** AP, IB, institutional tests; 16 credit hours maximum for bachelor's degree.

ACADEMIC REQUIREMENTS. Freshmen must earn minimum GPA of 2.0 to continue in good standing. 84% of freshmen return for sophomore year. Students must declare major by end of second year. **Graduation requirements:** 128 hours for bachelor's (36 in major). Most students required to take courses in arts/fine arts, English, foreign languages, history, humanities, mathematics, philosophy/religion, biological/physical sciences, social sciences. **Postgraduate studies:** 15% enter law school, 2% enter medical school, 35% enter other graduate study. **Additional information:** Almost half of junior class elects to study abroad for semester or year.

FRESHMAN ADMISSIONS. Selection criteria: Rigor of high school curriculum, GPA and rank, and aptitude as reflected in standardized testing performance weighted most heavily. Essays, recommendations, and required English paper significant factors along with extracurricular activities and talents. **High school preparation:** 17 units recommended. Recommended units include English 4, foreign language 3, mathematics 4, social science 3 and science 3. **Test requirements:** SAT or ACT; score report by February 1.

1992 FRESHMAN CLASS PROFILE. 780 women applied, 606 accepted, 165 enrolled. 88% had high school GPA of 3.0 or higher, 12% between 2.0 and 2.99. 50% were in top tenth and 75% were in top quarter of graduating class. **Academic background:** Mid 50% of enrolled freshmen had SAT-V between 520-620, SAT-M between 540-640. 96% submitted SAT scores. **Characteristics:** 57% from in state, 99% live in college housing, 21% have minority backgrounds, 2% are foreign students. Average age is 18.

FALL-TERM APPLICATIONS. $40 fee, may be waived for applicants with need. Closing date February 1; applicants notified on or about April 1; must reply by May 1. Essay required. Interview recommended. Audition recommended for music applicants. Portfolio recommended for art applicants. CRDA. Deferred and early admission available. EDP-F. Graded English paper required in addition to essay.

STUDENT LIFE. Housing: Dormitories (women); apartment housing available. Some sophomores and most juniors, and seniors have single rooms. **Activities:** Student government, radio, student newspaper, yearbook, choral groups, dance, drama, jazz band, music ensembles, musical theater, symphony orchestra, Student Investment Fund, Model United Nations, McAlister Center for Religious Activities, Pan African Student Association, Women in Leadership Programs, science club, MECHA, Association of Latinas, Women's Resource Center, Wanawak, Weusi, Community Service Program. **Additional information:** More than 200 clubs and organizations available through the Claremont Colleges consortium.

ATHLETICS. NCAA. **Intercollegiate:** Basketball, cross-country, diving, golf, soccer, softball, swimming, tennis, track and field, volleyball. **Intramural:** Badminton, basketball, bowling, lacrosse, skiing, soccer, softball, table tennis, tennis, volleyball, water polo.

STUDENT SERVICES. Career counseling, employment service for undergraduates, freshman orientation, health services, personal counseling, placement service for graduates, special adviser for adult students, services/facilities for handicapped.

ANNUAL EXPENSES. Tuition and fees (projected): $16,536. **Room and board:** $7,077. **Books and supplies:** $600. **Other expenses:** $800.

FINANCIAL AID. 48% of freshmen, 53% of continuing students receive some form of aid. 97% of grants, 95% of loans, all jobs based on need. Academic scholarships available. **Aid applications:** Closing date March 2; priority given to applications received by February 1; applicants notified on or about April 1; must reply by May 1 or within 2 weeks if notified thereafter.

ADDRESS/TELEPHONE. Leslie A. Miles, Dean of Admissions, Scripps College, 1030 North Columbia Avenue, Claremont, CA 91711-3948. (714) 621-8149. Fax: (714) 621-8323.

Shasta College
Redding, California — CB code: 4696

2-year public community college, coed. Founded in 1948. **Accreditation:** Regional. **Undergraduate enrollment:** 13,034 men and women. **Faculty:** 417 total (132 full time), 10 with doctorates or other terminal degrees. **Location:** Rural campus in small city; 160 miles from Sacramento. **Calendar:** Semester. **Microcomputers:** Located in classrooms, computer centers. **Special facilities:** Museum, art gallery, career center.

DEGREES OFFERED. AA. 509 associate degrees awarded in 1992.

UNDERGRADUATE MAJORS. Accounting, aeronautical technology, agribusiness, agricultural mechanics, agricultural production, agricultural sciences, aircraft mechanics, automotive mechanics, automotive technology, business and management, business and office, business computer/console/peripheral equipment operation, business data processing and related programs, business data programming, carpentry, child development/care/guidance, civil engineering, communications, computer and information sciences, diesel engine mechanics, drafting and design technology, electronic technology, engineering, engineering and engineering-related technologies, fashion merchandising, finance, fine arts, fire control and safety technology, food production/management/services, graphic design, home economics, journalism, law enforcement and corrections technologies, legal secretary, management information systems, marketing and distribution, medical assistant, music, nursing, office supervision and management, ornamental horticulture, precision metal work, real estate, renewable natural resources, retailing, secretarial and related programs, small business management and ownership.

ACADEMIC PROGRAMS. 2-year transfer program, cooperative education, double major, dual enrollment of high school students, independent study, internships. **Remedial services:** Learning center, reduced course load, remedial instruction, special counselor, tutoring. **Placement/credit:** AP; 12 credit hours maximum for associate degree.

ACADEMIC REQUIREMENTS. Freshmen must earn minimum GPA of 2.0 to continue in good standing. **Graduation requirements:** 60 hours for associate. Most students required to take courses in English, humanities, mathematics, biological/physical sciences, social sciences. **Additional information:** On-campus programs leading to bachelor's degree from California State University: Chico offered.

FRESHMAN ADMISSIONS. Selection criteria: Open admissions. Applicants to registered nursing program, must be high school graduate, take National League for Nursing examination, and complete series of courses outlined in college catalog. High School diploma only required of those under 18.

1992 FRESHMAN CLASS PROFILE. 2,997 men and women enrolled. **Characteristics:** 99% from in state, 99% commute, 5% have minority backgrounds, 1% are foreign students.

FALL-TERM APPLICATIONS. No fee. No closing date; applicants notified on a rolling basis.

STUDENT LIFE. Housing: Dormitories (men, women). **Activities:** Student government, magazine, student newspaper, choral groups, concert band, dance, drama, jazz band, marching band, music ensembles, musical theater, pep band, symphony orchestra.

ATHLETICS. Intercollegiate: Baseball M, basketball, cross-country, football M, golf M, softball W, tennis, track and field, volleyball W.

STUDENT SERVICES. Career counseling, employment service for undergraduates, freshman orientation, health services, on-campus day care, personal counseling, special adviser for adult students, veterans counselor, services/facilities for handicapped.

ANNUAL EXPENSES. Tuition and fees (1992-93): $126, $3,300 additional for out-of-state students. **Room and board:** $1,822 room only. **Books and supplies:** $434. **Other expenses:** $1,200.

FINANCIAL AID. 27% of freshmen, 15% of continuing students receive some form of aid. 98% of grants, 96% of loans, 20% of jobs based on need. Academic, music/drama, art, athletic, leadership scholarships available. **Aid applications:** No closing date; priority given to applications received by March 2; applicants notified on a rolling basis.

ADDRESS/TELEPHONE. Margaret Dominici, Vice President of Student Personnel Services, Shasta College, PO Box 496006, Redding, CA 96099. (916) 225-4600.

Sierra College
Rocklin, California — CB code: 4697

2-year public community college, coed. Founded in 1914. **Accreditation:** Regional. **Undergraduate enrollment:** 2,054 men, 2,058 women full time; 4,595 men, 6,296 women part time. **Faculty:** 531 total (147 full time), 10 with doctorates or other terminal degrees. **Location:** Suburban campus in large town; 25 miles from Sacramento. **Calendar:** Semester, limited summer session. Saturday and extensive evening/early morning classes. **Microcomputers:** Located in libraries, classrooms, computer centers. **Special facilities:** Nature trail, planetarium, science center displays.

DEGREES OFFERED. AA, AS. 708 associate degrees awarded in 1992. 17% in business and management, 58% multi/interdisciplinary studies.

UNDERGRADUATE MAJORS. Accounting, agricultural sciences, agronomy, animal sciences, automotive mechanics, automotive technology, biology, business and management, business and office, chemistry, child development/care/guidance, communications, computer and information sciences, computer programming, construction, data processing, drafting, drafting and design technology, electronic technology, finance, fine arts, fire control and safety technology, forestry and related sciences, geology, home economics, industrial technology, information sciences and systems, journalism, landscape architecture, law enforcement and corrections technologies, legal secretary, liberal/general studies, library assistant, marketing and distribution, medical secretary, nursing, ornamental horticulture, photography, practical nursing, precision metal work, real estate, secretarial and related programs, survey and mapping technology, surveying and mapping sciences, teacher aide, welding technology, wood/construction technology, word processing.

ACADEMIC PROGRAMS. 2-year transfer program, cooperative education, double major, dual enrollment of high school students, independent study, internships, study abroad, telecourses. **Remedial services:** Learning center, remedial instruction, special counselor, tutoring, learning disability program, special education program for developmentally disabled. **Placement/credit:** AP, CLEP General, institutional tests; 15 credit hours maximum for associate degree.

ACADEMIC REQUIREMENTS. Freshmen must earn minimum GPA of 2.0 to continue in good standing. Students must complete 50% of all courses attempted. 18% of freshmen return for sophomore year. Students must declare major by end of first year. **Graduation requirements:** 60 hours for associate (18 in major). Most students required to take courses in English, history, humanities, mathematics, biological/physical sciences, social sciences.

FRESHMAN ADMISSIONS. Selection criteria: Open admissions. **Test requirements:** Sierra College Assessment Program Test required for placement.

1992 FRESHMAN CLASS PROFILE. 1,145 men, 1,401 women enrolled. **Characteristics:** 99% from in state, 96% commute, 14% have minority backgrounds. Average age is 18.

FALL-TERM APPLICATIONS. No fee. Closing date August 12; priority given to applications received by July 5; applicants notified on a rolling basis beginning on or about July 1. Deferred admission available. ACT or SAT recommended for counseling, scores report by July 15.

STUDENT LIFE. Housing: Dormitories (coed). **Activities:** Student government, student newspaper, choral groups, concert band, drama, pep band.

ATHLETICS. Intercollegiate: Baseball M, basketball, cross-country, diving, football M, golf, skiing, softball W, swimming, tennis, track and field, volleyball W, water polo M, wrestling M. **Intramural:** Baseball M, basketball, football M, golf, softball, tennis, track and field, volleyball.

STUDENT SERVICES. Aptitude testing, career counseling, employment service for undergraduates, freshman orientation, health services, on-campus day care, personal counseling, placement service for graduates, veterans counselor, services/facilities for handicapped.

ANNUAL EXPENSES. Tuition and fees (projected): $315, $3,360 additional for out-of-state students. **Room and board:** $3,934. **Books and supplies:** $600. **Other expenses:** $1,500.

FINANCIAL AID. 5% of freshmen, 10% of continuing students receive some form of aid. 94% of grants, 96% of loans, 40% of jobs based on need. Academic, music/drama, art, athletic, state/district residency, leadership, alumni affiliation, religious affiliation, minority scholarships available. **Aid applications:** No closing date; priority given to applications received by June 15; applicants notified on a rolling basis beginning on or about July 1; must reply within 10 days.

ADDRESS/TELEPHONE. Mandy Davies, Asst Dean Admis/Records, Sierra College, 5000 Rocklin Road, Rocklin, CA 95677. (916) 624-3333.

Simpson College
Redding, California CB code: 4698

4-year private liberal arts college, coed, affiliated with Christian and Missionary Alliance. Founded in 1921. **Accreditation:** Regional. **Undergraduate enrollment:** 123 men, 233 women full time; 5 men, 9 women part time. **Graduate enrollment:** 15 men, 23 women full time; 13 men, 26 women part time. **Faculty:** 43 total (27 full time), 9 with doctorates or other terminal degrees. **Location:** Rural campus in small city; 170 miles from Sacramento. **Calendar:** 4-4-1, limited summer session. **Microcomputers:** 8 located in computer centers.

DEGREES OFFERED. AA, BA, MA. 98 bachelor's degrees awarded. 62% in business and management, 8% teacher education, 6% letters/literature, 18% philosophy, religion, theology, 6% psychology. Graduate degrees offered in 3 major fields of study.

UNDERGRADUATE MAJORS. Associate: Bible studies, lay counseling. **Bachelor's:** Bible studies, business administration and management, Christian education, elementary education, English, English education, history, human resources development, liberal/general studies, missionary studies, music, music education, music performance, psychology, religious education, religious music, secondary education, social science education, social sciences, theological studies.

ACADEMIC PROGRAMS. Double major, independent study, internships, student-designed major, study abroad, teacher preparation. **Remedial services:** Reduced course load, remedial instruction, special counselor, tutoring. **Placement/credit:** AP, CLEP General and Subject, institutional tests; 30 credit hours maximum for bachelor's degree.

ACADEMIC REQUIREMENTS. Freshmen must earn minimum GPA of 1.8 to continue in good standing. 62% of freshmen return for sophomore year. Students must declare major by end of first year. **Graduation requirements:** 124 hours for bachelor's (32 in major). Most students required to take courses in arts/fine arts, English, history, humanities, mathematics, philosophy/religion, biological/physical sciences, social sciences. **Additional information:** 32 semester hour Teacher Credentialing Program permits students to earn California Clear Credential for Grades K-8 (Elementary) or for Grades 7-12 (Secondary).

FRESHMAN ADMISSIONS. Selection criteria: Commitment to Jesus Christ as reflected in personal statement and required references, academic achievement, other recommendations, and standardized test scores considered. **High school preparation:** 20 units recommended. Recommended units include biological science 16, English 4, foreign language 2, mathematics 3, social science 3 and science 3. College-preparatory program highly recommended; GED required for graduates of nonapproved programs. **Test requirements:** SAT or ACT; score report by August 1.

1992 FRESHMAN CLASS PROFILE. 17 men, 26 women enrolled. **Characteristics:** Average age is 20.

FALL-TERM APPLICATIONS. $20 fee. No closing date; priority given to applications received by June 1; applicants notified on a rolling basis; must reply by May 1 or within 3 weeks if notified thereafter. Deferred admission available.

STUDENT LIFE. Housing: Dormitories (men, women); handicapped housing available. All single undergraduates under 25 required to live on-campus. Request for off-campus living must be approved by Dean of Student Development. **Activities:** Student government, yearbook, choral groups, drama, music ensembles, pep band, missionary service groups and prayer fellowships. **Additional information:** All students involved in family-like Christian atmosphere of college.

ATHLETICS. Intercollegiate: Basketball, soccer M, softball W, volleyball. **Intramural:** Basketball, football M, golf, soccer M, softball, swimming, table tennis, tennis, volleyball.

STUDENT SERVICES. Employment service for undergraduates, freshman orientation, personal counseling, placement service for graduates, veterans counselor, services/facilities for handicapped.

ANNUAL EXPENSES. Tuition and fees (1992-93): $6,738. **Room and board:** $3,570. **Books and supplies:** $576. **Other expenses:** $1,728.

FINANCIAL AID. 96% of freshmen, 80% of continuing students receive some form of aid. 82% of grants, 88% of loans, 49% of jobs based on need. Academic, music/drama, athletic, leadership, religious affiliation scholarships available. **Aid applications:** No closing date; priority given to applications received by March 31; applicants notified on a rolling basis beginning on or about April 30; must reply within 2 weeks.

ADDRESS/TELEPHONE. Marion Brown, Director of Admission and Records, Simpson College, 2211 College View Drive, Redding, CA 96003-8606. (916) 224-5600. (800) 598-2493. Fax: (916) 224-5608.

Skyline College
San Bruno, California CB code: 4746

2-year public community college, coed. Founded in 1969. **Accreditation:** Regional. **Undergraduate enrollment:** 1,121 men, 1,168 women full time; 2,761 men, 4,094 women part time. **Faculty:** 303 total (121 full time), 17 with doctorates or other terminal degrees. **Location:** Suburban campus in small city; 15 miles from San Francisco. **Calendar:** Semester, limited summer session. Saturday and extensive evening/early morning classes. **Microcomputers:** Located in libraries, classrooms.

DEGREES OFFERED. AA, AS. 633 associate degrees awarded in 1992.

UNDERGRADUATE MAJORS. Accounting, allied health, art history, automotive mechanics, biological and physical sciences, biology, business and office, computer and information sciences, computer programming, education, English, fashion merchandising, finance, home economics, humanities and social sciences, interior design, journalism, legal assistant/paralegal, legal secretary, liberal/general studies, marketing and distribution, mathematics, music, physical sciences, psychology, public administration, recreation and community services technologies, recreation therapy, science technologies, secretarial and related programs, social sciences, visual and performing arts, word processing.

ACADEMIC PROGRAMS. 2-year transfer program, cooperative education, dual enrollment of high school students, study abroad, cross-registration. **Remedial services:** Learning center, preadmission summer program, remedial instruction, special counselor, tutoring, Student Educational Assistance Program. **Placement/credit:** AP, CLEP General; 12 credit hours maximum for associate degree.

ACADEMIC REQUIREMENTS. Freshmen must earn minimum GPA of 2.0 to continue in good standing. **Graduation requirements:** 60 hours for associate (18 in major). Most students required to take courses in English, history, humanities, mathematics, biological/physical sciences, social sciences.

FRESHMAN ADMISSIONS. Selection criteria: Open admissions.

1992 FRESHMAN CLASS PROFILE. 2,737 men, 3,604 women enrolled. **Characteristics:** 98% from in state, 100% commute, 57% have minority backgrounds, 2% are foreign students. Average age is 22.

FALL-TERM APPLICATIONS. No fee. Closing date August 1; priority given to applications received by July 1; applicants notified on a rolling basis. Interview required for respiratory therapy applicants. SAT/ACT recommended for placement, counseling, and competency equivalency evaluation.

STUDENT LIFE. Activities: Student government, annual literary periodical, choral groups, concert band, dance, jazz band.

ATHLETICS. NJCAA. **Intercollegiate:** Baseball M, basketball M, cross-country, soccer M, softball W, track and field, volleyball W, wrestling M.

STUDENT SERVICES. Aptitude testing, career counseling, employment service for undergraduates, freshman orientation, health services, personal counseling, services/facilities for handicapped.

ANNUAL EXPENSES. Tuition and fees (1992-93): $135, $3,390 additional for out-of-state students. **Books and supplies:** $384. **Other expenses:** $1,332.

FINANCIAL AID. 8% of freshmen, 8% of continuing students receive some form of aid. All grants, 95% of loans, all jobs based on need. **Aid applications:** No closing date; priority given to applications received by May 13; applicants notified on a rolling basis beginning on or about July 1; must reply within 2 weeks.

ADDRESS/TELEPHONE. Dennis Arreola, Dean of Admissions and Records, Skyline College, 3300 College Drive, San Bruno, CA 94066-1698. (415) 738-4251.

Solano Community College
Suisun City, California CB code: 4930

2-year public community college, coed. Founded in 1945. **Accreditation:** Regional. **Undergraduate enrollment:** 2,742 men and women full time; 8,529 men and women part time. **Faculty:** 347 total (147 full time), 15 with doctorates or other terminal degrees. **Location:** Suburban campus in small city; 11 miles from Vallejo, 5 miles from Fairfield. **Calendar:** Semester, extensive summer session. Saturday and extensive evening/early morning classes. **Additional facts:** Classes offered in Vallejo, Vacaville, Dixon, and Benicia.

DEGREES OFFERED. AA, AS. 487 associate degrees awarded in 1992.

UNDERGRADUATE MAJORS. Accounting, aeronautical technology, Afro-American (black) studies, aircraft mechanics, auto body repair, automotive mechanics, automotive technology, biological and physical sciences, biology, business administration and management, business and management, business and office, business data programming, chemistry, clothing and textiles management/production/services, commercial art, computer and information sciences, computer programming, drafting, drafting and design technology, dramatic arts, drawing, early childhood education, electronic technology, engineering, English, fashion merchandising, finance, fine arts, fire control and safety technology, foreign languages (multiple emphasis), French, German, history, home economics, horticultural science, horticulture, industrial technology, interior design, interior design merchandising, journalism, law enforcement and corrections technologies, legal secretary, liberal/general studies, management science, marketing and distribution, marketing management, mathematics, Mexican American studies, music, nursing, ornamental horticulture, painting, photographic technology, photography, physics, psychology, public affairs, real estate, sculpture, secretarial and related programs, shipbuilding, small business management and ownership, social sciences, Spanish, teacher aide, telecommunications, television servicing, trade and industrial supervision and management, welding technology, word processing.

ACADEMIC PROGRAMS. 2-year transfer program, cooperative education, double major, dual enrollment of high school students, honors program, independent study, internships, telecourses, cross-registration. **Remedial services:** Learning center, reduced course load, remedial instruction, special counselor, tutoring. **Placement/credit:** AP, CLEP General and Subject, institutional tests; 15 credit hours maximum for associate degree.

ACADEMIC REQUIREMENTS. Freshmen must earn minimum GPA of 2.0 to continue in good standing. Students must declare major on application. **Graduation requirements:** 60 hours for associate (24 in major). Most students required to take courses in English, foreign languages, history, humanities, mathematics, philosophy/religion, biological/physical sciences, social sciences.

FRESHMAN ADMISSIONS. Selection criteria: Open admissions. Selective admissions to some programs. **Test requirements:** Institution's examinations required for admission to automotive body and fender, automotive technology, cosmetology, electronics technology, machine tool technology, nursing, welding technology, English, chemistry, and mathematics programs.

1992 FRESHMAN CLASS PROFILE. 2,300 men and women enrolled. **Characteristics:** 98% from in state, 100% commute, 30% have minority backgrounds.

FALL-TERM APPLICATIONS. No fee. No closing date; applicants notified on a rolling basis; must reply by September 8 or within 1 week if notified thereafter. Early admission available.

STUDENT LIFE. Activities: Student government, radio, student newspaper, choral groups, concert band, drama, jazz band, musical theater, symphony orchestra, Black Student Union, Women's Change, veterans organization, Sierra Club, Solano County student nurses, Filipino club, Democratic club.

ATHLETICS. NJCAA. **Intercollegiate:** Baseball M, basketball, cross-country, diving, football M, swimming, track and field, volleyball W, water polo M. **Intramural:** Table tennis, tennis.

STUDENT SERVICES. Aptitude testing, career counseling, employment service for undergraduates, freshman orientation, health services, personal counseling, placement service for graduates, veterans counselor, services/facilities for handicapped.

ANNUAL EXPENSES. Tuition and fees (1992-93): $131, $3,210 additional for out-of-state students. **Books and supplies:** $450. **Other expenses:** $1,386.

FINANCIAL AID. 10% of freshmen, 10% of continuing students receive some form of aid. All grants based on need. **Aid applications:** No closing date; priority given to applications received by June 1; applicants notified on a rolling basis beginning on or about July 5; must reply at award interview.

ADDRESS/TELEPHONE. Gerry Fisher, Assistant Dean of Admission and Records, Solano Community College, 4000 Suisun Valley Road, Suisun City, CA 94585. (707) 864-7112. Fax: (707) 864-7143.

Sonoma State University
Rohnert Park, California CB code: 4723

Admissions: 62% of applicants accepted
Based on: ••• School record, test scores
Completion: 95% of freshmen end year in good standing
29% enter graduate study

4-year public university, coed. Founded in 1960. **Accreditation:** Regional. **Undergraduate enrollment:** 1,788 men, 2,706 women full time; 589 men, 1,006 women part time. **Graduate enrollment:** 98 men, 208 women full time; 272 men, 738 women part time. **Faculty:** 422 total (261 full time), 198 with doctorates or other terminal degrees. **Location:** Suburban campus in large town; 50 miles from San Francisco, 10 miles from Santa Rosa. **Calendar:** Semester, extensive summer session. Extensive evening/early morning classes. **Microcomputers:** 40 located in libraries, classrooms, computer centers, campus-wide network. **Special facilities:** Art gallery, observatory, performing arts center.

DEGREES OFFERED. B, MA, MS, MBA. 1,230 bachelor's degrees awarded in 1992. 30% in business and management, 5% computer sciences, 5% health sciences, 10% life sciences, 10% multi/interdisciplinary studies, 5% physical sciences, 11% psychology, 10% social sciences, 6% visual and performing arts. Graduate degrees offered in 21 major fields of study.

UNDERGRADUATE MAJORS. Afro-American (black) studies, anthropology, art history, biology, business administration and management, chemistry, city/community/regional planning, communications, computer and information sciences, computer programming, criminology, dramatic arts, economics, English, environmental science, French, geography, geology, German, history, liberal/general studies, mathematics, Mexican American studies, music, nursing, philosophy, physics, political science and government, psychology, sociology, South Asian studies, Spanish, studio art.

ACADEMIC PROGRAMS. Double major, dual enrollment of high school students, education specialist degree, external degree, independent study, internships, student-designed major, study abroad, teacher preparation, visiting/exchange student program, cross-registration; combined bachelor's/graduate program in business administration. **Remedial services:** Learning center, preadmission summer program, reduced course load, remedial instruction, special counselor, tutoring, multicultural services program. **Placement/credit:** AP, CLEP General and Subject, institutional tests; 30 credit hours maximum for bachelor's degree.

ACADEMIC REQUIREMENTS. Freshmen must earn minimum GPA of 2.0 to continue in good standing. Students must declare major by end of second year. **Graduation requirements:** 124 hours for bachelor's (40 in major). Most students required to take courses in arts/fine arts, English, history, humanities, mathematics, philosophy/religion, biological/physical sciences, social sciences. **Postgraduate studies:** 2% enter law school, 2% enter medical school, 15% enter MBA programs, 10% enter other graduate study. **Additional information:** 2-year upper-division cluster schools within university in liberal arts and environmental studies.

FRESHMAN ADMISSIONS. Selection criteria: School GPA and test scores most important. **High school preparation:** 15 units required. Required units include English 4, foreign language 2, mathematics 3, social science 1 and science 1. One visual and performing arts, 1 US history/government, 1 science with laboratory also required. **Test requirements:** SAT or ACT; score report by August 30.

1992 FRESHMAN CLASS PROFILE. 2,865 men and women applied, 1,789 accepted; 215 men enrolled, 386 women enrolled. 55% had high school GPA of 3.0 or higher, 42% between 2.0 and 2.99. **Academic background:** Mid 50% of enrolled freshmen had SAT-V between 350-500, SAT-M between 430-500. 83% submitted SAT scores. **Characteristics:** 92% from in state, 92% commute, 18% have minority backgrounds, 8% are foreign students, 3% join fraternities/sororities. Average age is 19.

FALL-TERM APPLICATIONS. $55 fee, may be waived for applicants with need. No closing date; priority given to applications received by November 1; applicants notified on a rolling basis beginning on or about November 15. Early admission available.

STUDENT LIFE. Housing: Dormitories (coed); apartment housing available. **Activities:** Student government, magazine, radio, student newspaper, choral groups, dance, drama, jazz band, music ensembles, musical theater, opera, pep band, symphony orchestra, fraternities, sororities, Black Student Union, Newman Club, Intervarsity Christian Fellowship, Jewish Student Union, MECHA, Sonoma Earth Action, Reentry Students Association, Model United Nations.

ATHLETICS. NCAA. **Intercollegiate:** Baseball M, basketball, football M, soccer, softball W, volleyball W. **Intramural:** Badminton, basketball, golf, lacrosse M, softball, swimming, volleyball.

STUDENT SERVICES. Aptitude testing, career counseling, employment service for undergraduates, freshman orientation, health services, on-campus day care, personal counseling, placement service for graduates, special adviser for adult students, veterans counselor, services for reentering, disadvantaged, foreign, and ethnic students, services/facilities for handicapped.

ANNUAL EXPENSES. Tuition and fees (projected): $1,534, $5,904

additional for out-of-state students. **Room and board:** $5,062. **Books and supplies:** $612. **Other expenses:** $1,370.

FINANCIAL AID. 50% of freshmen, 55% of continuing students receive some form of aid. 95% of grants, 89% of loans, 29% of jobs based on need. 236 enrolled freshmen were judged to have need, 224 were offered aid. Academic, music/drama scholarships available. **Aid applications:** No closing date; priority given to applications received by March 2; applicants notified on a rolling basis beginning on or about April 1; must reply within 4 weeks.

ADDRESS/TELEPHONE. Dr. Frank Tansey, Dean of Admissions and Records, Sonoma State University, Rohnert Park, CA 94928. (707) 664-2778.

Southern California College
Costa Mesa, California CB code: 4701

Admissions: 86% of applicants accepted
Based on: ••• Essay, recommendations, religious affiliation/commitment, school record
• Activities, interview, special talents, test scores
Completion: 80% of freshmen end year in good standing
34% graduate

4-year private liberal arts college, coed, affiliated with Assemblies of God. Founded in 1920. **Accreditation:** Regional. **Undergraduate enrollment:** 338 men, 393 women full time; 50 men, 54 women part time. **Graduate enrollment:** 10 men full time; 51 men, 8 women part time. **Faculty:** 49 total (44 full time), 28 with doctorates or other terminal degrees. **Location:** Suburban campus in small city; 45 miles from Los Angeles, 70 miles from San Diego. **Calendar:** Semester, limited summer session. **Microcomputers:** 50 located in dormitories, libraries, computer centers. **Special facilities:** Archaeology laboratory.

DEGREES OFFERED. BA, MA. 168 bachelor's degrees awarded in 1992. 21% in business and management, 8% communications, 14% education, 14% philosophy, religion, theology, 7% physical sciences, 8% psychology, 18% social sciences. Graduate degrees offered in 3 major fields of study.

UNDERGRADUATE MAJORS. Accounting, anthropology, Bible studies, biological and physical sciences, biology, business administration and management, business and management, chemistry, counseling psychology, dramatic arts, education, elementary education, English, experimental psychology, finance, history, humanities and social sciences, marketing management, mathematics, missionary studies, music, music education, political science and government, predentistry, prelaw, premedicine, preveterinary, psychology, radio/television broadcasting, religion, religious education, secondary education, social sciences, sociology, speech, theological studies, video.

ACADEMIC PROGRAMS. Double major, independent study, internships, study abroad, teacher preparation, visiting/exchange student program, Washington semester. **Remedial services:** Learning center, reduced course load, remedial instruction, special counselor, tutoring. **Placement/credit:** AP, CLEP General and Subject; 24 credit hours maximum for bachelor's degree.

ACADEMIC REQUIREMENTS. Freshmen must earn minimum GPA of 2.5 to continue in good standing. 82% of freshmen return for sophomore year. Students must declare major by end of second year. **Graduation requirements:** 124 hours for bachelor's (38 in major). Most students required to take courses in arts/fine arts, English, history, humanities, mathematics, philosophy/religion, biological/physical sciences, social sciences.

FRESHMAN ADMISSIONS. Selection criteria: GPA of 2.5, Christian commitment essay, references from pastor and academic instructor, ACT or SAT, and interview in borderline cases. Recommended units include English 4, mathematics 2, social science 3 and science 2. **Test requirements:** SAT or ACT; score report by July 31. SAT or ACT used for admissions of borderline applicants.

1992 FRESHMAN CLASS PROFILE. 214 men applied, 184 accepted, 72 enrolled; 232 women applied, 200 accepted, 100 enrolled. 62% had high school GPA of 3.0 or higher, 37% between 2.0 and 2.99. 22% were in top tenth and 53% were in top quarter of graduating class. **Academic background:** Mid 50% of enrolled freshmen had SAT-V between 350-470, SAT-M between 390-540; ACT composite between 18-25. 59% submitted SAT scores, 11% submitted ACT scores. **Characteristics:** 71% from in state, 68% live in college housing, 26% have minority backgrounds, 5% are foreign students. Average age is 20.

FALL-TERM APPLICATIONS. $30 fee, may be waived for applicants with need. No closing date; priority given to applications received by March 2; applicants notified on a rolling basis; August 15. Essay required. Interview recommended for borderline applicants. Audition recommended for music applicants. CRDA. Deferred admission available.

STUDENT LIFE. Housing: Dormitories (men, women); apartment housing available. **Activities:** Student government, magazine, student newspaper, yearbook, choral groups, concert band, drama, music ensembles, musical theater, pep band, missionary assistance program, student ministries, College Republicans, Evangelicals for Social Action. **Additional information:** Religious observance required.

ATHLETICS. NAIA. **Intercollegiate:** Baseball M, basketball, cross-country, soccer M, softball W, tennis M, track and field, volleyball W. **Intramural:** Badminton, basketball, golf, racquetball, softball, table tennis, tennis, volleyball.

STUDENT SERVICES. Aptitude testing, career counseling, employment service for undergraduates, freshman orientation, health services, personal counseling, veterans counselor, services/facilities for handicapped.

ANNUAL EXPENSES. Tuition and fees: $8,836. **Room and board:** $3,820. **Books and supplies:** $612. **Other expenses:** $1,350.

FINANCIAL AID. 80% of freshmen, 80% of continuing students receive some form of aid. 91% of grants, 63% of loans, 6% of jobs based on need. 160 enrolled freshmen were judged to have need, all were offered aid. Academic, leadership, religious affiliation scholarships available. **Aid applications:** No closing date; priority given to applications received by March 2; applicants notified on a rolling basis beginning on or about May 1; must reply within 3 weeks.

ADDRESS/TELEPHONE. Richard Hardy, Assistant Dean for Enrollment Management, Southern California College, 55 Fair Drive, Costa Mesa, CA 92626-9601. (714) 556-3610. (800) 722-6279. Fax: (714) 957-9317.

Southern California Institute of Architecture
Los Angeles, California CB code: 1575

5-year private professional school of architectural design, coed. Founded in 1972. **Accreditation:** Regional candidate. **Undergraduate enrollment:** 138 men, 63 women full time. **Graduate enrollment:** 136 men, 83 women full time. **Faculty:** 79 total (40 full time), 2 with doctorates or other terminal degrees. **Location:** Urban campus in very large city; 10 miles from downtown Los Angeles. **Calendar:** Trimester, extensive summer session. Extensive evening/early morning classes. **Microcomputers:** 14 located in computer centers. **Special facilities:** Media center, architecture gallery, woodshop and modelmaking center, metal fabrication shop, graphics center, darkroom. **Additional facts:** Accredited by the National Architectural Accrediting Board (ARCH). School in Switzerland, exchange program in Japan.

DEGREES OFFERED. BArch, M. 60 bachelor's degrees awarded in 1992. 100% in architecture and environmental design. Graduate degrees offered in 1 major field of study.

UNDERGRADUATE MAJORS. Architecture.

ACADEMIC PROGRAMS. Independent study, internships, study abroad, visiting/exchange student program. **Remedial services:** Preadmission summer program, reduced course load, tutoring. **Placement/credit:** AP, CLEP Subject, institutional tests; 27 credit hours maximum for bachelor's degree.

ACADEMIC REQUIREMENTS. No policy requiring minimum GPA; records of students having academic difficulty are reviewed individually. 85% of freshmen return for sophomore year. Students must declare major on application. **Graduation requirements:** 150 hours for bachelor's. Most students required to take courses in arts/fine arts, English, history, humanities, mathematics, philosophy/religion, biological/physical sciences, social sciences. **Additional information:** Intensive summer session on introduction to architecture offered to graduates, and high school students.

FRESHMAN ADMISSIONS. Selection criteria: School achievement record, interview, portfolio, placement examination, recommendation, and statement of purpose. Recommended units include English 4, foreign language 2, mathematics 3, physical science 1 and social science 2. Art design and architecture courses recommended. **Test requirements:** SAT or ACT; score report by March 1. **Additional information:** One or 2 prior semesters of college recommended. Applicants should have started their general education requirement at another 2- or 4-year institution. General education requirements need to be completed prior to fourth year.

1992 FRESHMAN CLASS PROFILE. 47 men and women enrolled. 75% had high school GPA of 3.0 or higher, 25% between 2.0 and 2.99. **Characteristics:** 60% from in state, 100% commute, 25% have minority backgrounds, 25% are foreign students. Average age is 22.

FALL-TERM APPLICATIONS. $50 fee, may be waived for applicants with need. No closing date; priority given to applications received by February 15; applicants notified on a rolling basis beginning on or about April 1; must reply by May 1 or within 2 weeks if notified thereafter. Portfolio required. Essay required. Interview recommended. CRDA. Deferred admission available.

STUDENT LIFE. Activities: Student government, film, magazine, student newspaper, Architects, Designer, and Planners for Social Responibility, American Institute of Architects Student Affiliation, Women in Architecture. **Additional information:** Informal weekly gathering of entire school sponsored by student government.

ATHLETICS. Intramural: Soccer, softball, volleyball.

STUDENT SERVICES. Career counseling, freshman orientation, personal counseling, Foreign Student Advisor, services/facilities for handicapped.

ANNUAL EXPENSES. Tuition and fees (1992-93): $10,050. **Books and supplies:** $1,400.

FINANCIAL AID. 49% of freshmen, 33% of continuing students receive some form of aid. 95% of grants, 74% of loans, all jobs based on need. 24 enrolled freshmen were judged to have need, all were offered aid. Academic, art scholarships available. **Aid applications:** No closing date; priority given to applications received by March 2; applicants notified on a rolling basis beginning on or about May 1; within 2 weeks.

ADDRESS/TELEPHONE. Stephen Pile, Director of Admissions, Southern California Institute of Architecture, 5454 Beethoven Street, Los Angeles, CA 90066. (310) 574-3625.

Southwestern College
Chula Vista, California CB code: 4726

2-year public community college, coed. Founded in 1961. **Accreditation:** Regional. **Undergraduate enrollment:** 17,222 men and women. **Faculty:** 945 total (234 full time), 44 with doctorates or other terminal degrees. **Location:** Urban campus in small city; 10 miles south of San Diego. **Calendar:** Semester, extensive summer session. Saturday and extensive evening/early morning classes. **Microcomputers:** 600 located in classrooms, computer centers.

DEGREES OFFERED. AA, AS. 589 associate degrees awarded in 1992. 5% in business and management, 13% business/office and marketing/distribution, 8% health sciences, 58% multi/interdisciplinary studies.

UNDERGRADUATE MAJORS. Accounting, aeronautical technology, aerospace/aeronautical/astronautical engineering, African studies, Afro-American (black) studies, air traffic control, anthropology, architectural engineering, architectural technologies, architecture, astronomy, automotive mechanics, automotive technology, aviation computer technology, bilingual/bicultural education, biology, botany, business administration and management, business and management, business and office, business computer/console/peripheral equipment operation, business data entry equipment operation, business data processing and related programs, business data programming, business systems analysis, chemistry, comparative literature, computer and information sciences, computer graphics, computer mathematics, computer programming, computer servicing technology, computer technology, construction, criminal justice studies, criminology, dance, data processing, diesel engine mechanics, drafting, dramatic arts, early childhood education, earth sciences, ecology, economics, education, electrical and electronics equipment repair, electrical technology, electrical/electronics/communications engineering, electronic technology, emergency medical technologies, engineering, engineering and engineering-related technologies, English, environmental design, environmental science, finance, fine arts, fire control and safety technology, fishing and fisheries, food sciences, foreign languages (multiple emphasis), forestry and related sciences, French, geography, geology, graphic arts technology, graphic design, history, home economics, horticulture, industrial engineering, industrial technology, information sciences and systems, interior design, investments and securities, Italian, journalism, landscape architecture, law enforcement and corrections technologies, legal secretary, liberal/general studies, management science, manufacturing technology, marine biology, marketing and distribution, materials engineering, mathematics, mechanical design technology, medical records administration, medical records technology, metallurgical engineering, Mexican American studies, microbiology, microcomputer software, music, nursing, oceanography, office supervision and management, ornamental horticulture, philosophy, photographic technology, photography, physical sciences, physics, political science and government, practical nursing, prelaw, premedicine, preveterinary, psychology, public administration, public affairs, radio/television broadcasting, radio/television technology, range management, real estate, recreation and community services technologies, renewable natural resources, retailing, science technologies, secretarial and related programs, small business management and ownership, social sciences, social work, sociology, solar heating and cooling technology, Spanish, speech, speech pathology/audiology, systems analysis, teacher aide, telecommunications, tourism, transportation and travel marketing, wildlife management, word processing, zoology.

ACADEMIC PROGRAMS. 2-year transfer program, cooperative education, double major, dual enrollment of high school students, honors program, independent study, internships, study abroad, telecourses. **Remedial services:** Learning center, preadmission summer program, remedial instruction, special counselor, tutoring. **Placement/credit:** AP, CLEP General and Subject, institutional tests; 15 credit hours maximum for associate degree.

ACADEMIC REQUIREMENTS. Freshmen must earn minimum GPA of 2.0 to continue in good standing. **Graduation requirements:** 60 hours for associate. Most students required to take courses in computer science, English, foreign languages, history, mathematics, philosophy/religion, biological/physical sciences, social sciences.

FRESHMAN ADMISSIONS. Selection criteria: Open admissions. Student must be 18 years of age or have graduated from high school or have high school equivalent.

1992 FRESHMAN CLASS PROFILE. 4,133 men and women enrolled. **Characteristics:** 94% from in state, 100% commute, 74% have minority backgrounds, 1% are foreign students. Average age is 22.

FALL-TERM APPLICATIONS. No fee. No closing date; applicants notified on a rolling basis. Early admission available.

STUDENT LIFE. Activities: Student government, student newspaper, choral groups, dance, drama, jazz band, musical theater.

ATHLETICS. Intercollegiate: Baseball M, basketball, cross-country, football M, soccer M, softball W, tennis, track and field, volleyball W.

STUDENT SERVICES. Aptitude testing, career counseling, employment service for undergraduates, freshman orientation, health services, personal counseling, veterans counselor, services/facilities for handicapped.

ANNUAL EXPENSES. Tuition and fees: $180, $2,970 additional for out-of-state students. **Books and supplies:** $612. **Other expenses:** $1,728.

FINANCIAL AID. 29% of freshmen, 71% of continuing students receive some form of aid. All grants, all loans, 54% of jobs based on need. **Aid applications:** No closing date; priority given to applications received by March 2; applicants notified on a rolling basis beginning on or about July 1; must reply within 2 weeks.

ADDRESS/TELEPHONE. Georgia Copeland, Director of Admissions and Records, Southwestern College, 900 Otay Lakes Road, Chula Vista, CA 92010. (619) 421-6700. Fax: (619) 421-1189.

Stanford University
Stanford, California CB code: 4704

Admissions:	22% of applicants accepted
Based on:	••• Activities, recommendations, school record, test scores
	•• Special talents
	• Essay
Completion:	99% of freshmen end year in good standing
	88% graduate

4-year private university, coed. Founded in 1885. **Accreditation:** Regional. **Undergraduate enrollment:** 3,544 men, 3,020 women full time. **Graduate enrollment:** 4,555 men, 1,994 women full time; 506 men, 274 women part time. **Faculty:** 1,406 total, 1,378 with doctorates or other terminal degrees. **Location:** Suburban campus in large town; 29 miles from San Francisco, on outskirts of Palo Alto and Menlo Park. **Calendar:** Quarter, extensive summer session. **Microcomputers:** 600 located in dormitories, libraries, classrooms, computer centers. **Special facilities:** Observatory, linear accelerator, museum, art gallery, 75 libraries, nature preserve, marine station, instructional television.

DEGREES OFFERED. BA, BS, MA, MS, MBA, MFA, MEd, PhD, EdD, MD. 1,669 bachelor's degrees awarded in 1992. 17% in engineering, 7% letters/literature, 14% multi/interdisciplinary studies, 12% physical sciences, 33% social sciences. Graduate degrees offered in 75 major fields of study.

UNDERGRADUATE MAJORS. African studies, Afro-American (black) studies, American studies, anthropology, biology, chemical engineering, chemistry, Chinese, civil engineering, classics, communications, comparative literature, computer and information sciences, dramatic arts, earth sciences, East Asian studies, economics, electrical/electronics/communications engineering, engineering, English, English literature, fine arts, French, geology, geophysics and seismology, German, German studies, history, human biology, humanities, humanities and social sciences, industrial engineering, international relations, Italian, Japanese, language/literature/humanities, Latin American studies, liberal/general studies, linguistics, materials engineering, mathematical and computational sciences, mathematics, mechanical engineering, microbiology, music, petroleum engineering, philosophy, physics, political science and government, psychology, public policy studies, religion, Slavic languages, sociology, Spanish, statistics, symbolic systems, urban studies, values, technology, science and society, women's studies.

ACADEMIC PROGRAMS. Accelerated program, double major, honors program, independent study, internships, student-designed major, study abroad, visiting/exchange student program, Washington semester; liberal arts/career combination in engineering. **Remedial services:** Learning center, tutoring. **ROTC:** Air Force, Army, Naval. **Placement/credit:** AP, institutional tests; 45 credit hours maximum for bachelor's degree.

ACADEMIC REQUIREMENTS. No policy requiring minimum GPA; records of students having academic difficulty are reviewed individually. Freshmen must complete 36 quarter hours per year to continue in good academic standing. 98% of freshmen return for sophomore year. Students must declare major by end of second year. **Graduation requirements:** 180 hours for bachelor's. Most students required to take courses in arts/fine arts, English, humanities, mathematics, philosophy/religion, biological/physical sciences, social sciences.

FRESHMAN ADMISSIONS. Selection criteria: School achievement record, test scores, extracurricular activities, teacher and counselor evaluations, personal qualifications most important. Recommended units include biological science 1, English 4, foreign language 3, mathematics 3, physical science 2 and social science 2. **Test requirements:** SAT or ACT; score report by January 1.

1992 FRESHMAN CLASS PROFILE. 7,445 men applied, 1,518 accepted, 819 enrolled; 5,761 women applied, 1,334 accepted, 774 enrolled. 100% had high school GPA of 3.0 or higher. **Academic background:** Mid 50% of enrolled freshmen had SAT-V between 590-690, SAT-M between

660-750; ACT composite between 28-33. 96% submitted SAT scores, 18% submitted ACT scores. **Characteristics:** 32% from in state, 100% live in college housing, 43% have minority backgrounds, 3% are foreign students. Average age is 18.

FALL-TERM APPLICATIONS. $50 fee, may be waived for applicants with need. Closing date December 15; applicants notified on or about April 1; must reply by May 1. Essay required. CRDA. Deferred admission available. 3 ACH including English Composition strongly recommended. Score report by February 1.

STUDENT LIFE. Housing: Dormitories (coed); apartment, fraternity, cooperative housing available. **Activities:** Student government, film, magazine, radio, student newspaper, television, yearbook, choral groups, concert band, dance, drama, jazz band, marching band, music ensembles, musical theater, pep band, symphony orchestra, fraternities, sororities, volunteer service center, several ethnic organizations.

ATHLETICS. NCAA. **Intercollegiate:** Baseball M, basketball, cross-country, diving, fencing, field hockey W, football M, golf, gymnastics, rowing (crew), sailing, soccer, swimming, tennis, track and field, volleyball, water polo M, wrestling M. **Intramural:** Badminton, basketball, bowling, cross-country, diving, fencing W, field hockey M, football M, golf, gymnastics, handball, horseback riding, ice hockey M, lacrosse, racquetball, rugby, skiing, soccer, softball, squash, swimming, table tennis, tennis, track and field, volleyball, water polo, wrestling.

STUDENT SERVICES. Aptitude testing, career counseling, employment service for undergraduates, freshman orientation, health services, on-campus day care, personal counseling, placement service for graduates, services/facilities for handicapped.

ANNUAL EXPENSES. Tuition and fees: $17,775. **Room and board:** $6,535. **Books and supplies:** $815. **Other expenses:** $1,315.

FINANCIAL AID. 69% of freshmen, 61% of continuing students receive some form of aid. 81% of grants, 94% of loans, 84% of jobs based on need. Athletic scholarships available. **Aid applications:** Closing date February 1; applicants notified on or about April 1; must reply by May 1.

ADDRESS/TELEPHONE. James Montoya, Dean of Undergraduate Admissions, Stanford University, Old Union, Second Floor, Stanford, CA 94305. (415) 723-2091.

Taft College
Taft, California — CB code: 4820

2-year public community college, coed. Founded in 1922. **Accreditation:** Regional. **Undergraduate enrollment:** 231 men, 221 women full time; 202 men, 383 women part time. **Faculty:** 54 total (34 full time), 4 with doctorates or other terminal degrees. **Location:** Rural campus in large town; 40 miles from Bakersfield. **Calendar:** Semester, limited summer session. Saturday and extensive evening/early morning classes. **Microcomputers:** Located in computer centers.

DEGREES OFFERED. AA, AS. 90 associate degrees awarded in 1992.

UNDERGRADUATE MAJORS. Accounting, automotive mechanics, automotive technology, business and management, business and office, business data processing and related programs, computer and information sciences, criminal justice technology, data processing, drafting, drafting and design technology, early childhood education, electronic technology, engineering, engineering and engineering-related technologies, English, fine arts, industrial technology, journalism, liberal/general studies, life science, mathematics, mining and petroleum technologies, physical education, physical sciences, recreation and community services technologies, secretarial and related programs, social sciences.

ACADEMIC PROGRAMS. 2-year transfer program, dual enrollment of high school students, independent study. **Remedial services:** Learning center, preadmission summer program, reduced course load, remedial instruction, special counselor, tutoring, retention coordinator for probationary and provisional students. **Placement/credit:** AP, institutional tests; 12 credit hours maximum for associate degree.

ACADEMIC REQUIREMENTS. Freshmen must earn minimum GPA of 2.0 to continue in good standing. Students must declare major on enrollment. **Graduation requirements:** 60 hours for associate (18 in major). Most students required to take courses in English, history, humanities, mathematics, biological/physical sciences, social sciences.

FRESHMAN ADMISSIONS. Selection criteria: Open admissions.

1992 FRESHMAN CLASS PROFILE. 158 men, 142 women enrolled. **Characteristics:** 98% from in state, 76% commute, 26% have minority backgrounds, 4% are foreign students.

FALL-TERM APPLICATIONS. No fee. No closing date; priority given to applications received by June 1; applicants notified on a rolling basis beginning on or about May 1.

STUDENT LIFE. Housing: Dormitories (men, women). **Activities:** Student government, student newspaper, television, international club.

ATHLETICS. Intercollegiate: Baseball M, basketball W, cross-country, football M, golf M, softball W, track and field M, volleyball W.

STUDENT SERVICES. Career counseling, employment service for undergraduates, health services, personal counseling, special adviser for adult students, veterans counselor, off-campus daycare, services/facilities for handicapped.

ANNUAL EXPENSES. Tuition and fees: $365, $3,060 additional for out-of-state students. **Room and board:** $2,300. **Books and supplies:** $250. **Other expenses:** $1,548.

FINANCIAL AID. 35% of continuing students receive some form of aid. All grants, all jobs based on need. Academic, state/district residency scholarships available. **Aid applications:** No closing date; priority given to applications received by August 1; applicants notified on a rolling basis beginning on or about July 1; must reply within 4 weeks.

ADDRESS/TELEPHONE. Juanita Perry, Financial Aid/Admissions Officer, Taft College, 29 Emmons Park Drive, Taft, CA 93268. (805) 763-4282. Fax: (805) 763-1038.

Thomas Aquinas College
Santa Paula, California — CB code: 4828

Admissions:	57% of applicants accepted
Based on:	••• Essay, recommendations, school record, test scores
	•• Interview
	• Activities, religious affiliation/commitment, special talents
Completion:	85% of freshmen end year in good standing
	50% enter graduate study

4-year private liberal arts college, coed, affiliated with Roman Catholic Church. Founded in 1971. **Accreditation:** Regional. **Undergraduate enrollment:** 112 men, 91 women full time. **Faculty:** 22 total (21 full time), 12 with doctorates or other terminal degrees. **Location:** Rural campus in large town; 25 miles from Ventura, 75 miles from Los Angeles. **Calendar:** Semester. **Microcomputers:** 6 located in dormitories.

DEGREES OFFERED. BA. 38 bachelor's degrees awarded in 1992. 100% in multi/interdisciplinary studies.

UNDERGRADUATE MAJORS. Liberal/general studies.

ACADEMIC REQUIREMENTS. Freshmen must earn minimum GPA of 2.0 to continue in good standing. 80% of freshmen return for sophomore year. **Graduation requirements:** 146 hours for bachelor's. Most students required to take courses in English, foreign languages, history, humanities, mathematics, philosophy/religion, biological/physical sciences, social sciences. **Postgraduate studies:** 13% enter law school, 3% enter medical school, 1% enter MBA programs, 33% enter other graduate study. **Additional information:** Required study of logic, rhetoric, grammar, mathematics, experimental science, music, philosophy, theology, and humanities. Great Books of the Western World and disciplined round-table discussions used.

FRESHMAN ADMISSIONS. Selection criteria: Evidence of likely success in all parts of 4-year program. Required essays and 3 letters of reference supplement academic records and test scores. Interviews sometimes considered. **High school preparation:** 13 units required. Required and recommended units include English 4, foreign language 2, mathematics 2-3, social science 3 and science 2-3. **Test requirements:** SAT or ACT (SAT preferred); score report by September 1.

1992 FRESHMAN CLASS PROFILE. 77 men applied, 47 accepted, 40 enrolled; 58 women applied, 30 accepted, 28 enrolled. 71% had high school GPA of 3.0 or higher, 29% between 2.0 and 2.99. 28% were in top tenth and 59% were in top quarter of graduating class. **Academic background:** Mid 50% of enrolled freshmen had SAT-V between 500-630, SAT-M between 510-640; ACT composite between 24-30. 79% submitted SAT scores, 28% submitted ACT scores. **Characteristics:** 32% from in state, 99% live in college housing, 4% have minority backgrounds, 15% are foreign students. Average age is 20.

FALL-TERM APPLICATIONS. No fee. No closing date; applicants notified on a rolling basis; must reply within 4 weeks. Essay required. Interview recommended for early admissions applicants and for those whose academic preparation is uncertain. Deferred and early admission available.

STUDENT LIFE. Housing: Dormitories (men, women). All students must live on campus unless living with family. **Activities:** Choral groups, music ensembles, Legion of Mary Presidia.

ATHLETICS. Intramural: Baseball, basketball, football M, horseback riding, soccer M, softball, swimming, table tennis, tennis, volleyball.

STUDENT SERVICES. Health services, personal counseling, services/facilities for handicapped.

ANNUAL EXPENSES. Tuition and fees (projected): $12,480. **Room and board:** $5,410. **Books and supplies:** $275. **Other expenses:** $700.

FINANCIAL AID. 79% of freshmen, 80% of continuing students receive some form of aid. All grants, 96% of loans, all jobs based on need. 54 enrolled freshmen were judged to have need, all were offered aid. **Aid applications:** Closing date September 1; priority given to applications received by March 1; applicants notified on a rolling basis beginning on or about April 1; must reply within 3 weeks. **Additional information:** Attempts to meet demonstrated financial needs of every student accepted for admission.

ADDRESS/TELEPHONE. Thomas J. Susanka, Director of Admissions, Thomas Aquinas College, 10000 North Ojai Road, Santa Paula, CA 93060. (805) 525-4417. (800) 634-9797. Fax: (805) 525-0620.

United States International University
San Diego, California CB code: 4039

4-year private university, coed. Founded in 1952. **Accreditation:** Regional. **Undergraduate enrollment:** 170 men, 124 women full time; 33 men, 28 women part time. **Graduate enrollment:** 1,255 men and women. **Faculty:** 242 total (100 full time), 134 with doctorates or other terminal degrees. **Location:** Suburban campus in very large city; 16 miles from downtown. **Calendar:** Quarter, extensive summer session. **Microcomputers:** 69 located in libraries, classrooms, computer centers. **Special facilities:** Theater. **Additional facts:** Undergraduate programs also offered at associated campuses in Nairobi, Mexico City, and London.

DEGREES OFFERED. AA, BA, MA, MS, MBA, PhD, EdD. 240 bachelor's degrees awarded. 38% in business and management, 17% education, 12% engineering, 8% multi/interdisciplinary studies, 11% psychology, 14% visual and performing arts. Graduate degrees offered in 16 major fields of study.

UNDERGRADUATE MAJORS. Associate: Liberal/general studies. **Bachelor's:** Accounting, business administration and management, civil engineering, education, elementary education, engineering management, English, hospitality and recreation marketing, hotel/motel and restaurant management, international business management, international relations, liberal/general studies, management information systems, physical education, prelaw, psychology, secondary education, social sciences, tourism.

ACADEMIC PROGRAMS. 2-year transfer program, accelerated program, independent study, internships, study abroad, teacher preparation, visiting/exchange student program, weekend college. **Remedial services:** Learning center, reduced course load, remedial instruction, tutoring. **ROTC:** Army. **Placement/credit:** AP, CLEP General and Subject, IB, institutional tests; 45 credit hours maximum for associate degree; 45 credit hours maximum for bachelor's degree.

ACADEMIC REQUIREMENTS. Freshmen must earn minimum GPA of 2.0 to continue in good standing. 62% of freshmen return for sophomore year. Students must declare major by end of second year. **Graduation requirements:** 90 hours for associate, 180 hours for bachelor's (90 in major). Most students required to take courses in computer science, English, history, humanities, mathematics, biological/physical sciences, social sciences. **Postgraduate studies:** 90% from 2-year programs enter 4-year programs. 2% enter law school, 1% enter medical school, 15% enter MBA programs, 25% enter other graduate study.

FRESHMAN ADMISSIONS. Selection criteria: Academic achievement (minimum 2.5 high school GPA), test scores, extracurricular activities, personal recommendations, interviews, and enthusiasm for goals and philosophy of institution considered. **High school preparation:** 16 units required. Required units include biological science 1, English 4, foreign language 2, mathematics 3, physical science 1 and social science 3. 12 academic units in last 3 years of high school required. **Test requirements:** SAT or ACT; score report by August 15.

1992 FRESHMAN CLASS PROFILE. 16 men, 14 women enrolled. 60% had high school GPA of 3.0 or higher, 40% between 2.0 and 2.99. **Characteristics:** 31% from in state, 62% live in college housing, 37% have minority backgrounds, 45% are foreign students. Average age is 19.

FALL-TERM APPLICATIONS. $25 fee, may be waived for applicants with need. No closing date; priority given to applications received by June 1; applicants notified on a rolling basis beginning on or about February 1. CRDA. Deferred and early admission available. EDP-S.

STUDENT LIFE. Housing: Dormitories (men, women, coed). All dormitories are 2-bedroom suites with a central living room. **Activities:** Student government, magazine, student newspaper, yearbook, all major religious groups represented.

ATHLETICS. Intramural: Basketball, bowling, soccer M, softball, swimming, table tennis, tennis, volleyball.

STUDENT SERVICES. Aptitude testing, career counseling, employment service for undergraduates, freshman orientation, health services, personal counseling, placement service for graduates.

ANNUAL EXPENSES. Tuition and fees: $11,115. **Room and board:** $3,900. **Books and supplies:** $612. **Other expenses:** $1,773.

FINANCIAL AID. 57% of grants, 66% of loans, 75% of jobs based on need. Academic, leadership, religious affiliation, minority scholarships available. **Aid applications:** No closing date; priority given to applications received by April 15; applicants notified on a rolling basis beginning on or about May 15; must reply within 3 weeks.

ADDRESS/TELEPHONE. Darla J. Wilson, Director of Admissions, United States International University, 10455 Pomerado Road, San Diego, CA 92131-1799. (619) 693-4772. Fax: (619) 693-8562.

University of California: Berkeley
Berkeley, California CB code: 4833

Admissions:	43% of applicants accepted
Based on:	••• School record, test scores
	•• Activities, essay, special talents
Completion:	91% of freshmen end year in good standing
	70% graduate, 34% of these enter graduate study

4-year public university, coed. Founded in 1868. **Accreditation:** Regional. **Undergraduate enrollment:** 11,660 men, 10,181 women full time. **Graduate enrollment:** 5,164 men, 3,617 women full time. **Faculty:** 1,512 total. **Location:** Urban campus in small city; 10 miles from San Francisco. **Calendar:** Semester, extensive summer session. **Microcomputers:** 900 located in dormitories, libraries, classrooms, computer centers, campus-wide network. **Special facilities:** Museums of art, anthropology, archaeology and science, internationally known film archive, Leuscher Observatory (30-inch telescope), Lick Observatory (120-inch telescope), state-of-the-art recreational sports facility, Lawrence Hall of Science.

DEGREES OFFERED. BA, BS, MA, MS, MBA, MFA, MSW, PhD, EdD, OD, JD. 5,390 bachelor's degrees awarded in 1992. 5% in business and management, 5% computer sciences, 9% engineering, 17% letters/literature, 9% life sciences, 6% multi/interdisciplinary studies, 6% psychology, 29% social sciences. Graduate degrees offered in 112 major fields of study.

UNDERGRADUATE MAJORS. Afro-American (black) studies, American Indian studies, analytical chemistry, ancient Near Eastern archeology and art history, anthropology, applied mathematics, Arabic, architecture, art history, Asian studies, Asian-American studies, astrophysics, bioengineering and biomedical engineering, biology, bioresource science, botany, business administration and management, cell biology, chemical engineering, chemistry, Chinese, cinematography/film, civil engineering, classics, cognitive science, communications, comparative literature, computer and information sciences, conservation and regulation, dance, dramatic arts, Dutch studies, earth sciences, ecology, economics, electrical/electronics/communications engineering, engineering mathematics and statics, engineering physics, engineering science, English, English literature, entomology, environmental science, ethnic studies, fine arts, forest products processing technology, forestry and related sciences, French, genetics, human and animal, geography, geological engineering, geology, geophysics and seismology, German, Greek (classical), Hebrew, history, humanities, Indic languages, industrial engineering, inorganic chemistry, interdisciplinary studies, Italian, Japanese, landscape architecture, Latin, Latin American studies, legal studies, linguistics, materials engineering, mathematics, mechanical engineering, metallurgical engineering, metallurgy, Mexican American studies, microbiology, Middle Eastern studies, mining and mineral engineering, molecular biology, music, naval architecture and marine engineering, near East studies, neurosciences, nuclear engineering, nuclear physics, nutritional sciences, organic chemistry, paleontology, peace studies, petroleum engineering, philosophy, physical chemistry, physical education, physical sciences, physics, physiology, human and animal, political economy of industrial societies, political economy of natural resources, political science and government, psychology, religion, rhetoric, Russian, Russian and Slavic studies, Scandinavian languages, Slavic languages, social sciences, sociology, soil sciences, South Asian studies, Southeast Asian studies, Spanish, statistics, vision science, women's studies, zoology.

ACADEMIC PROGRAMS. Cooperative education, double major, dual enrollment of high school students, honors program, independent study, internships, student-designed major, study abroad, cross-registration. **Remedial services:** Learning center, preadmission summer program, reduced course load, remedial instruction, special counselor, tutoring. **ROTC:** Air Force, Army, Naval. **Placement/credit:** AP, institutional tests.

ACADEMIC REQUIREMENTS. Freshmen must earn minimum GPA of 2.0 to continue in good standing. 91% of freshmen return for sophomore year. Students must declare major by end of second year. **Graduation requirements:** 120 hours for bachelor's. Most students required to take courses in English, foreign languages, humanities, mathematics, biological/physical sciences, social sciences. **Additional information:** All students required to pass one American Cultures class in order to graduate.

FRESHMAN ADMISSIONS. Selection criteria: High school GPA and test scores important. Eligibility requirements identify top 12.5% of

California high school graduates. Rigor and diversity of academic curriculum and individual achievement also considered. **High school preparation:** 15 units required; 19 recommended. Required and recommended units include English 4, foreign language 2-3, mathematics 3-4, social science 2 and science 2-3. One American or US history, 2 additional units from the following areas : history, English, advanced mathematics, laboratory science, foreign language, social science and visual and performing arts required. **Test requirements:** SAT or ACT; score report by January 1. 3 ACH required (including English Composition, Mathematics Level I or II, and an additional test). Score report by January 1 Test scores used to develop a selection index to differentiate between students with similar credentials.

1992 FRESHMAN CLASS PROFILE. 10,797 men applied, 4,595 accepted, 1,863 enrolled; 9,484 women applied, 4,105 accepted, 1,557 enrolled. 97% had high school GPA of 3.0 or higher, 3% between 2.0 and 2.99. 95% were in top tenth of graduating class. **Academic background:** Mid 50% of enrolled freshmen had SAT-V between 500-640, SAT-M between 600-730. 99% submitted SAT scores. **Characteristics:** 82% from in state, 54% live in college housing, 61% have minority backgrounds, 3% are foreign students, 14% join fraternities/sororities. Average age is 19.

FALL-TERM APPLICATIONS. $40 fee. Fee may be waived for state resident applicants with financial need. Closing date November 30; applicants notified on or about March 15; must reply by May 1 or within 3 weeks if notified thereafter. Essay required. CRDA. Preadmission advising available.

STUDENT LIFE. Housing: Dormitories (men, women, coed); apartment, fraternity, sorority, cooperative housing available. Dormitory space guaranteed for new fall freshmen who submit housing applications before deadline. **Activities:** Student government, film, magazine, radio, student newspaper, yearbook, choral groups, concert band, dance, drama, jazz band, marching band, music ensembles, musical theater, pep band, symphony orchestra, fraternities, sororities, over 300 student organizations including political action groups, ethnic associations, sports clubs, religious clubs.

ATHLETICS. NCAA. **Intercollegiate:** Baseball M, basketball, cross-country, field hockey W, football M, golf M, gymnastics M, lacrosse M, rowing (crew), rugby M, skiing, soccer, softball W, squash, swimming, tennis, track and field, volleyball, water polo. **Intramural:** Archery, badminton, basketball, bowling, cross-country M, fencing, sailing, softball, volleyball.

STUDENT SERVICES. Career counseling, employment service for undergraduates, freshman orientation, health services, on-campus day care, personal counseling, placement service for graduates, special adviser for adult students, veterans counselor, disabled students programs, student life advising, women's resource center, services/facilities for handicapped.

ANNUAL EXPENSES. Tuition and fees (projected): $4,330, $7,699 additional for out-of-state students. **Room and board:** $5,992. **Books and supplies:** $600. **Other expenses:** $1,582.

FINANCIAL AID. 41% of freshmen, 50% of continuing students receive some form of aid. 95% of grants, 92% of loans, all jobs based on need. Academic, athletic, state/district residency, leadership, alumni affiliation, minority scholarships available. **Aid applications:** Closing date March 2; applicants notified on or about April 14; must reply within 3 weeks.

ADDRESS/TELEPHONE. Andre L. Bell, Director Undergraduate Admissions, University of California: Berkeley, 110 Sproul Hall, Berkeley, CA 94720. (510) 642-3175. Fax: (510) 642-7333.

University of California: Davis

Davis, California — CB code: 4834

Admissions:	64% of applicants accepted
Based on:	••• School record, test scores
	•• Activities, essay, special talents
	• Recommendations
Completion:	82% of freshmen end year in good standing
	73% graduate, 43% of these enter graduate study

4-year public university, coed. Founded in 1905. **Accreditation:** Regional. **Undergraduate enrollment:** 8,339 men, 8,698 women full time; 235 men, 236 women part time. **Graduate enrollment:** 3,004 men, 2,253 women full time; 82 men, 42 women part time. **Faculty:** 1,612 total (1,358 full time), 1,580 with doctorates or other terminal degrees. **Location:** Suburban campus in small city; 70 miles from San Francisco, 15 miles from Sacramento. **Calendar:** Quarter, extensive summer session. Saturday and extensive evening/early morning classes. **Microcomputers:** 400 located in dormitories, libraries, classrooms, computer centers, campus-wide network. **Special facilities:** Art galleries, museums, 150-acre arboretum, equestrian center, craft center, Bodega Marine Laboratory, Crocker Nuclear Labortary, Intercampus Institute for Research at Particle Accelerators, California Primate Research Center, Stebbins Cold Canyon Native Reserve.

DEGREES OFFERED. BA, BS, MA, MS, MBA, MFA, MEd, PhD, EdD, MD, DVM. 4,125 bachelor's degrees awarded in 1992. 11% in agriculture, 9% engineering, 8% letters/literature, 17% life sciences, 8% psychology, 26% social sciences. Graduate degrees offered in 82 major fields of study.

UNDERGRADUATE MAJORS. Aerospace/aeronautical/astronautical engineering, Afro-American (black) studies, agricultural business and management, agricultural education, agricultural engineering, agricultural sciences, American Indian studies, American studies, animal sciences, anthropology, art history, atmospheric sciences and meteorology, behavioral sciences, biochemistry, biology, botany, chemical engineering, chemistry, Chinese, civil engineering, classics, comparative literature, computer and information sciences, computer engineering, dramatic arts, East Asian studies, economics, electrical/electronics/communications engineering, English, entomology, environmental biology and management, environmental policy, planning and analysis, fermentation science, fiber and polymer science, food biochemistry, food science and nutrition, food sciences, French, genetics, human and animal, geography, geology, German, Greek (classical), history, individual and family development, international agriculture, international development, international relations, international studies, Italian, Japanese, landscape architecture, Latin, linguistics, materials engineering, mathematics, mechanical engineering, medieval studies, Mexican American studies, microbiology, music, nutritional sciences, philosophy, physical education, physics, physiology, human and animal, plant sciences, political science and government, poultry, psychology, range management, religion, renewable natural resources, rhetoric, Russian, sociology, sociology/organizational studies, soil sciences, Spanish, statistics, studio art, textiles and clothing, toxicology, wildlife management, women's studies, zoology.

ACADEMIC PROGRAMS. Double major, dual enrollment of high school students, education specialist degree, honors program, independent study, internships, student-designed major, study abroad, teacher preparation, Washington semester, cross-registration. **Remedial services:** Learning center, preadmission summer program, reduced course load, remedial instruction, special counselor, tutoring. **ROTC:** Army. **Placement/credit:** AP; 10 credit hours maximum for bachelor's degree.

ACADEMIC REQUIREMENTS. Freshmen must earn minimum GPA of 2.0 to continue in good standing. 93% of freshmen return for sophomore year. **Graduation requirements:** 180 hours for bachelor's. Most students required to take courses in English, history, humanities, biological/physical sciences, social sciences. **Postgraduate studies:** 4% enter law school, 5% enter medical school, 1% enter MBA programs, 33% enter other graduate study. **Additional information:** Extensive internship opportunites.

FRESHMAN ADMISSIONS. Selection criteria: Scholastic achievement most important, school and community activities, academic interests, and special achievements and awards. **High school preparation:** 15 units required. Required units include biological science 1, English 4, foreign language 2, mathematics 3, physical science 1 and social science 2. 2 electives which can include visual or performing arts, social science, foreign language, laboratory science, or advanced mathematics. **Test requirements:** SAT or ACT; score report by December 1. 3 ACH required (including English Composition and Mathematics Level I or II). Score report by January 1.

1992 FRESHMAN CLASS PROFILE. 16,179 men and women applied, 10,420 accepted; 1,427 men enrolled, 1,517 women enrolled. 95% had high school GPA of 3.0 or higher, 5% between 2.0 and 2.99. **Academic background:** Mid 50% of enrolled freshmen had SAT-V between 430-560, SAT-M between 530-650. 95% submitted SAT scores. **Characteristics:** 96% from in state, 90% live in college housing, 46% have minority backgrounds, 2% are foreign students, 3% join fraternities/sororities. Average age is 18.

FALL-TERM APPLICATIONS. $40 fee, may be waived for applicants with need. $40 fee for each additional application to other University of California campuses. Closing date November 30; applicants notified on a rolling basis beginning on or about March 1; must reply by May 1. Essay required. CRDA. Deferred admission available.

STUDENT LIFE. Housing: Dormitories (women, coed); apartment, fraternity, sorority, cooperative housing available. **Activities:** Student government, film, magazine, radio, student newspaper, choral groups, concert band, dance, drama, jazz band, marching band, music ensembles, musical theater, pep band, symphony orchestra, fraternities, sororities, over 250 student organizations including religious, political, ethnic, and social service organizations. **Additional information:** More than 36 miles of bicycle paths on campus and in town.

ATHLETICS. NCAA. **Intercollegiate:** Baseball M, basketball, cross-country, football M, golf M, gymnastics W, soccer, softball W, swimming, tennis, track and field, volleyball W, water polo M, wrestling M. **Intramural:** Badminton, basketball, bowling, golf, racquetball, soccer, softball, table tennis, tennis, volleyball, water polo. **Clubs:** 34 club sports.

STUDENT SERVICES. Aptitude testing, career counseling, employment service for undergraduates, freshman orientation, health services, on-campus day care, personal counseling, placement service for graduates, special adviser for adult students, veterans counselor, women's resources and research center, services/facilities for handicapped.

ANNUAL EXPENSES. Tuition and fees (projected): $3,975, $7,699 additional for out-of-state students. **Room and board:** $5,822. **Books and supplies:** $827. **Other expenses:** $1,507.

FINANCIAL AID. 61% of continuing students receive some form of aid. 84% of grants, 91% of loans, 85% of jobs based on need. 1,862 enrolled freshmen were judged to have need, all were offered aid. Academic, state/district residency, minority scholarships available. **Aid applications:** No closing date; priority given to applications received by March 2; applicants notified on a rolling basis beginning on or about April 1; must reply within 3 weeks. **Additional information:** Reduced fee for retired university employees.

ADDRESS/TELEPHONE. Gary Tudor, Director of Undergraduate Admissions, University of California: Davis, 175 Mrak Hall, Davis, CA 95616. (916) 752-2971. Fax: (916) 752-1280.

University of California: Irvine
Irvine, California — CB code: 4859

4-year public university, coed. Founded in 1964. **Accreditation:** Regional. **Undergraduate enrollment:** 13,888 men and women full time. **Graduate enrollment:** 2,126 men and women full time. **Faculty:** 811 total, 771 with doctorates or other terminal degrees. **Location:** Suburban campus in small city; 15 miles from Anaheim, 40 miles from Los Angeles. **Calendar:** Quarter, limited summer session. **Microcomputers:** 320 located in classrooms, computer centers. **Special facilities:** Outdoor laboratory, San Joaquin Freshwater Marsh Reserve, fine arts museum, nuclear reactor.

DEGREES OFFERED. BA, BS, BFA, MA, MS, MBA, MFA, PhD, MD. 2,900 bachelor's degrees awarded in 1992. 5% in computer sciences, 7% engineering, 9% letters/literature, 20% life sciences, 13% psychology, 35% social sciences, 5% visual and performing arts. Graduate degrees offered in 30 major fields of study.

UNDERGRADUATE MAJORS. Anthropology, applied ecology, art history, biology, chemistry, Chinese, civil engineering, classics, comparative culture, comparative literature, computer and information sciences, dance, dramatic arts, economics, electrical/electronics/communications engineering, engineering, English, film arts, fine arts, French, geography, German, history, humanities, Japanese, linguistics, mathematics, mechanical engineering, music, music performance, philosophy, physics, political science and government, psychology, Russian, social ecology, social sciences, sociology, Spanish, studio art, women's studies.

ACADEMIC PROGRAMS. Accelerated program, double major, dual enrollment of high school students, honors program, independent study, internships, study abroad, teacher preparation, Washington semester; combined bachelor's/graduate program in business administration. **Remedial services:** Learning center, preadmission summer program, reduced course load, remedial instruction, special counselor, tutoring. **ROTC:** Air Force, Naval. **Placement/credit:** AP, institutional tests.

ACADEMIC REQUIREMENTS. Freshmen must earn minimum GPA of 2.0 to continue in good standing. 91% of freshmen return for sophomore year. Students must declare major by end of second year. **Graduation requirements:** 180 hours for bachelor's (72 in major). Most students required to take courses in English, history, biological/physical sciences, social sciences.

FRESHMAN ADMISSIONS. Selection criteria: High school GPA and test scores most important. **High school preparation:** 15 units required. Required units include English 4, foreign language 2, mathematics 3, social science 1 and science 1. 4 additional units from at least 2 of the following: history, English, advanced mathematics, laboratory science, foreign language, social science, visual and performing arts. **Test requirements:** SAT or ACT; score report by June 30. 3 ACH required (including English Composition and Mathematics Level I or II) and additional test. Score report by June 30.

1992 FRESHMAN CLASS PROFILE. 2,946 men and women enrolled. **Characteristics:** 97% from in state, 63% live in college housing, 61% have minority backgrounds. Average age is 18.

FALL-TERM APPLICATIONS. $40 fee, may be waived for applicants with need. $40 fee for each additional application to other University of California campuses. Closing date November 30; priority given to applications received by November 1; applicants notified on a rolling basis beginning on or about February 1; must reply by May 1. Essay required. Deferred and early admission available.

STUDENT LIFE. Housing: Dormitories (women, coed); apartment, cooperative housing available. 80-space recreational vehicle park available. **Activities:** Student government, radio, student newspaper, yearbook, choral groups, dance, drama, jazz band, music ensembles, musical theater, pep band, symphony orchestra, fraternities, sororities, Black Student Union, Chinese Association, Kababayan, Movimiento Estudiantil Chicano de Aztlan, Women's Resource Center, religious groups, environmental groups, sports clubs, Third World groups, political groups.

ATHLETICS. NCAA. **Intercollegiate:** Baseball M, basketball, cross-country, diving, golf M, rowing (crew) M, sailing, soccer, swimming, tennis, track and field, volleyball W, water polo M. **Intramural:** Badminton, basketball, bowling, cross-country, diving, fencing, golf, ice hockey, lacrosse, racquetball, rowing (crew) W, rugby M, sailing, skiing, soccer, softball, swimming, table tennis, tennis, track and field, volleyball, water polo, wrestling M.

STUDENT SERVICES. Aptitude testing, career counseling, employment service for undergraduates, freshman orientation, health services, on-campus day care, personal counseling, placement service for graduates, special adviser for adult students, veterans counselor, cross-cultural center, tutorial assistance program (TAP), learning skills center, services/facilities for handicapped.

ANNUAL EXPENSES. Tuition and fees (1992-93): $3,074, $7,699 additional for out-of-state students. **Room and board:** $5,383. **Books and supplies:** $690. **Other expenses:** $1,728.

FINANCIAL AID. 33% of continuing students receive some form of aid. 93% of grants, 96% of loans, 14% of jobs based on need. Academic, music/drama, art, athletic, leadership, alumni affiliation scholarships available. **Aid applications:** Closing date May 1; priority given to applications received by March 2; applicants notified on a rolling basis beginning on or about April 1; must reply within 3 weeks.

ADDRESS/TELEPHONE. James E. Dunning, Director of Admissions, University of California: Irvine, 245 Administration Building, Irvine, CA 92717. (714) 856-6703.

University of California: Los Angeles
Los Angeles, California — CB code: 4837

Admissions:	42% of applicants accepted
Based on:	••• School record, test scores
	•• Essay
	• Activities, recommendations, special talents
Completion:	69% graduate, 60% of these enter graduate study

4-year public university, coed. Founded in 1919. **Accreditation:** Regional. **Undergraduate enrollment:** 11,854 men, 11,795 women full time. **Graduate enrollment:** 6,528 men, 5,162 women full time. **Faculty:** 1,626 total. **Location:** Urban campus in very large city. **Calendar:** Quarter, extensive summer session. **Microcomputers:** 1,000 located in computer centers.

DEGREES OFFERED. BA, BS, BFA, MA, MS, MBA, MFA, MEd, MSW, PhD, EdD, DDS, MD, JD. 5,673 bachelor's degrees awarded in 1992. 6% in engineering, 12% letters/literature, 8% life sciences, 12% psychology, 42% social sciences, 6% visual and performing arts. Graduate degrees offered in 88 major fields of study.

UNDERGRADUATE MAJORS. Aerospace/aeronautical/astronautical engineering, African languages, Afro-American (black) studies, anthropology, applied mathematics, Arabic, art history, astrophysics, atmospheric sciences and meteorology, biochemistry, biology, business economics, chemical engineering, chemistry, Chinese, cinematography/film, civil engineering, classics, cognitive psychology, cognitive science, communications, computer and information sciences, computer mathematics, computer science and engineering, cybernetics, dance, development studies, dramatic arts, earth sciences, East Asian studies, economics, electrical/electronics/communications engineering, engineering, English, ethnomusicology, French, geography, geography/environmental studies, geology, geophysics and seismology, German, Greek (classical), Hebrew, history, Italian, Japanese, Jewish studies, Latin, Latin American studies, linguistics, materials engineering, mathematics, mathematics of computation, mathematics/applied science, mechanical engineering, Mexican American studies, microbiology, music, musicology, Near Eastern studies, nuclear engineering, nursing, philosophy, physics, physiological science, political science and government, Portuguese, psychobiology, psychology, public health laboratory science, religion, Russian, Russian and Slavic studies, Scandinavian languages, Slavic languages, sociology, Spanish, statistics, world arts and cultures.

ACADEMIC PROGRAMS. Cooperative education, double major, dual enrollment of high school students, honors program, independent study, internships, student-designed major, study abroad, visiting/exchange student program. **Remedial services:** Learning center, remedial instruction, special counselor, tutoring, freshman and transfer summer programs. **ROTC:** Air Force, Army, Naval. **Placement/credit:** AP, institutional tests.

ACADEMIC REQUIREMENTS. Freshmen must earn minimum GPA of 2.0 to continue in good standing. 94% of freshmen return for sophomore year. Students must declare major by end of second year. **Graduation requirements:** 180 hours for bachelor's. Most students required to take courses in English, social sciences.

FRESHMAN ADMISSIONS. Selection criteria: Academic GPA, test scores, quality, level, and content of course work, number of and performance in honors and AP courses most important. Essay may play a role. Strong senior program important. **High school preparation:** 15 units required. Required and recommended units include English 4, foreign language 2-3, mathematics 3-4, social science 2 and science 2-3. Physical science 1 recommended. US history also required. 2 electives may include visual and performing arts. **Test requirements:** SAT or ACT; score report by January 1. 3 ACH required (including English Composition with or without essay, Mathematics Level I or II, and an additional test). Score report by January 1. **Additional information:** Admission is selective, based on performance in rigorous program.

1992 FRESHMAN CLASS PROFILE. 11,655 men applied, 5,167 accepted, 1,747 enrolled; 11,687 women applied, 4,660 accepted, 1,713 enrolled. 97% had high school GPA of 3.0 or higher, 3% between 2.0 and 2.99. **Academic background:** Mid 50% of enrolled freshmen had SAT-V between 460-600, SAT-M between 560-700. 98% submitted SAT scores. **Characteristics:** 94% from in state, 90% live in college housing, 64% have minority backgrounds, 2% are foreign students. Average age is 18.

FALL-TERM APPLICATIONS. $40 fee, may be waived for applicants

with need. $40 fee for each additional application to other University of California campuses. Closing date November 30; applicants notified on or about March 1; must reply by May 1. Audition required for music, dance, theater applicants. Portfolio required for art applicants. Essay required. CRDA.

STUDENT LIFE. Housing: Dormitories (coed); apartment, fraternity, sorority, cooperative housing available. **Activities:** Student government, film, magazine, radio, student newspaper, television, yearbook, choral groups, concert band, dance, drama, jazz band, marching band, music ensembles, musical theater, opera, symphony orchestra, fraternities, sororities.

ATHLETICS. NCAA. **Intercollegiate:** Baseball M, basketball, cross-country, diving, football M, golf, gymnastics, soccer M, softball W, swimming, tennis, track and field, volleyball, water polo M. **Intramural:** Badminton, basketball, bowling, cross-country, golf, handball, racquetball, rugby, soccer, softball, squash M, swimming, table tennis, tennis, track and field, volleyball, water polo M, wrestling M.

STUDENT SERVICES. Career counseling, employment service for undergraduates, health services, on-campus day care, personal counseling, placement service for graduates, veterans counselor, services/facilities for handicapped.

ANNUAL EXPENSES. Tuition and fees (projected): $3,899, $7,699 additional for out-of-state students. **Room and board:** $5,410. **Books and supplies:** $640. **Other expenses:** $135.

FINANCIAL AID. 52% of freshmen, 48% of continuing students receive some form of aid. 81% of grants, 90% of loans, 67% of jobs based on need. Academic, music/drama, art, athletic, state/district residency, alumni affiliation, minority scholarships available. **Aid applications:** Closing date March 2; applicants notified on a rolling basis beginning on or about May 15; must reply within 3 weeks.

ADDRESS/TELEPHONE. Rae Lee Siporin, Director of Undergraduate Admissions, University of California: Los Angeles, 405 Hilgard Avenue, Los Angeles, CA 90024. (310) 825-3101.

University of California: Riverside
Riverside, California — CB code: 4839

Admissions: 76% of applicants accepted
Based on:
••• School record, test scores
•• Essay
• Activities, recommendations, special talents
Completion: 88% of freshmen end year in good standing
58% graduate, 42% of these enter graduate study

4-year public university, coed. Founded in 1954. **Accreditation:** Regional. **Undergraduate enrollment:** 3,265 men, 3,656 women full time; 148 men, 148 women part time. **Graduate enrollment:** 727 men, 757 women full time; 38 men, 66 women part time. **Faculty:** 792 total (618 full time), 685 with doctorates or other terminal degrees. **Location:** Suburban campus in small city; 60 miles from Los Angeles. **Calendar:** Quarter, limited summer session. **Microcomputers:** 170 located in dormitories, libraries, classrooms, computer centers, campus-wide network. **Special facilities:** Botanical gardens, theater, art gallery, air pollution research center, California Museum of Photography, 7 nature preserves, citrus research center and agricultural experiment station, institute of geophysics and planetary physics, water resources center.

DEGREES OFFERED. BA, BS, MA, MS, MBA, PhD. 1,568 bachelor's degrees awarded in 1992. 20% in business and management, 13% letters/literature, 16% life sciences, 11% psychology, 25% social sciences. Graduate degrees offered in 48 major fields of study.

UNDERGRADUATE MAJORS. Anthropology, art history, Asian studies, biochemistry, biology, biomedical science, botany, business administration and management, business and management, business economics, chemical engineering, chemistry, classics, comparative literature, computer and information sciences, creative writing, dance, developmental psychology, dramatic arts, economics, electrical/electronics/communications engineering, English, English literature, entomology, environmental engineering, environmental science, ethnic studies, foreign languages (multiple emphasis), French, geography, geology, geophysics and seismology, German, history, humanities and social sciences, Latin American studies, liberal/general studies, linguistics, mathematics, music, philosophy, physical sciences, physics, political science and government, psychobiology, psychology, public administration, religion, Russian, Russian and Slavic studies, social relations, sociology, soil sciences, Spanish, statistics, studio art, women's studies.

ACADEMIC PROGRAMS. Accelerated program, cooperative education, double major, dual enrollment of high school students, education specialist degree, honors program, independent study, internships, student-designed major, study abroad, teacher preparation, visiting/exchange student program, Washington semester, Accelerated 7-year M.D. program in cooperation with UCLA School of Medicine; combined bachelor's/graduate program in medicine. **Remedial services:** Learning center, preadmission summer program, reduced course load, remedial instruction, special counselor, tutoring, study skills training. **ROTC:** Air Force, Army. **Placement/credit:** AP, IB, institutional tests.

ACADEMIC REQUIREMENTS. Freshmen must earn minimum GPA of 2.0 to continue in good standing. 90% of freshmen return for sophomore year. Students must declare major by end of second year. **Graduation requirements:** 180 hours for bachelor's. Most students required to take courses in English, foreign languages, humanities, mathematics, biological/physical sciences, social sciences. **Postgraduate studies:** 6% enter law school, 6% enter medical school, 5% enter MBA programs, 25% enter other graduate study.

FRESHMAN ADMISSIONS. Selection criteria: School achievement record and test scores most important. Special consideration given to ensure ethnic, geographic, and socioeconomic diversity. **High school preparation:** 15 units required. Required and recommended units include English 4, foreign language 2-3, mathematics 3-4, social science 1 and science 1-3. 4 additional units from at least 2 of the following: history, English, advanced mathematics, laboratory science, foreign language, social science, arts. Social science required unit must be U.S. History, or 1/2 History/1/2 Civics. **Test requirements:** SAT or ACT; score report by January 2. 3 ACH required (including English Composition, Mathematics Level I or II, and an additional test). Score report by January 2.

1992 FRESHMAN CLASS PROFILE. 4,865 men applied, 3,653 accepted, 605 enrolled; 5,411 women applied, 4,135 accepted, 698 enrolled. 91% had high school GPA of 3.0 or higher, 9% between 2.0 and 2.99. **Academic background:** Mid 50% of enrolled freshmen had SAT-V between 400-520, SAT-M between 480-610; ACT composite between 21-25. 98% submitted SAT scores, 18% submitted ACT scores. **Characteristics:** 96% from in state, 62% commute, 57% have minority backgrounds, 1% are foreign students, 16% join fraternities/sororities. Average age is 19.

FALL-TERM APPLICATIONS. $40 fee, may be waived for applicants with need. $40 fee for each additional application to other University of California campuses. Closing date November 30; applicants notified on a rolling basis beginning on or about February 1; must reply by May 1 or within 3 weeks if notified thereafter. Essay required. Interview recommended for Educational Opportunity Program applicants. CRDA. Early admission available. No closing date for underrepresented minority applicants.

STUDENT LIFE. Housing: Dormitories (coed); apartment, fraternity, sorority housing available. All new students guaranteed housing for 2 years. **Activities:** Student government, magazine, radio, student newspaper, yearbook, choral groups, concert band, dance, drama, jazz band, music ensembles, musical theater, symphony orchestra, fraternities, sororities, more than 130 academic, cultural, recreational, religious, political, ethnic, and community service organizations.

ATHLETICS. NCAA. **Intercollegiate:** Baseball M, basketball, cross-country, softball W, tennis, track and field, volleyball W, water polo M. **Intramural:** Basketball, bowling, golf, racquetball, soccer, softball, volleyball.

STUDENT SERVICES. Aptitude testing, career counseling, employment service for undergraduates, freshman orientation, health services, on-campus day care, personal counseling, placement service for graduates, special adviser for adult students, veterans counselor, tutoring, services/facilities for handicapped.

ANNUAL EXPENSES. Tuition and fees (1992-93): $2,923, $7,699 additional for out-of-state students. **Room and board:** $5,430. **Books and supplies:** $700. **Other expenses:** $1,100.

FINANCIAL AID. 50% of freshmen, 50% of continuing students receive some form of aid. 93% of grants, 98% of loans, 12% of jobs based on need. Academic, music/drama, art, athletic, leadership, alumni affiliation, minority scholarships available. **Aid applications:** No closing date; priority given to applications received by March 2; applicants notified on a rolling basis beginning on or about May 1; must reply within 5 weeks.

ADDRESS/TELEPHONE. Eric V. Gravenberg, Director of Undergraduate Admissions, University of California: Riverside, 1138 Hinderaker Hall, Riverside, CA 92521. (909) 787-3411.

University of California: San Diego
La Jolla, California — CB code: 4836

Admissions: 59% of applicants accepted
Based on:
••• School record
•• Test scores
• Activities, essay, special talents
Completion: 95% of freshmen end year in good standing
59% graduate, 43% of these enter graduate study

4-year public university, coed. Founded in 1959. **Accreditation:** Regional. **Undergraduate enrollment:** 7,611 men, 7,246 women full time. **Graduate enrollment:** 2,179 men, 1,205 women full time. **Faculty:** 1,384 total (1,175 full time), 1,140 with doctorates or other terminal degrees. **Location:** Suburban campus in large town; 12 miles from downtown San Diego. **Calendar:** Quarter, extensive summer session. **Microcomputers:** 300 located in libraries, classrooms, computer centers, campus-wide network. **Special facilities:** Stephen Birch Aquarium-Museum, performing arts center, art galleries, student-run co-ops, San Diego Supercomputer Center, nature preserves, electron beam lithography facility, Natatorium, Center for Music Experiment. **Additional facts:** Includes 5 small undergraduate cluster colleges, each with housing and different graduation requirements.

DEGREES OFFERED. BA, BS, MA, MS, MFA, PhD, MD. 2,890 bachelor's degrees awarded in 1992. Graduate degrees offered in 55 major fields of study.

UNDERGRADUATE MAJORS. American literature, anthropology, applied mathematics, applied physics, architecture, art history, biochemistry, bioengineering and biomedical engineering, biology, biophysics, cell biology, chemical engineering, chemical physics, chemistry, Chinese, Chinese studies, classics, cognitive psychology, communications, computer and information sciences, computer engineering, computer mathematics, creative writing, dramatic arts, earth sciences, ecology, economics, electrical/electronics/communications engineering, engineering, engineering mechanics, engineering physics, engineering science, English, English literature, ethnic studies, experimental psychology, film arts, French, German, German literature, history, information sciences and systems, Italian, Italian studies, Jewish studies, linguistics, materials engineering, mathematics, mechanical engineering, media arts, microbiology, molecular biology, music, music history and appreciation, music theory and composition, operations research, philosophy, photography, physics, physiology, human and animal, political science and government, premedicine, psychology, Russian, sociology, Spanish, studio art, systems analysis, systems engineering, theological studies, third world studies, urban studies, women's studies.

ACADEMIC PROGRAMS. Accelerated program, double major, dual enrollment of high school students, honors program, independent study, internships, semester at sea, student-designed major, study abroad, teacher preparation, visiting/exchange student program, Washington semester, cross-registration, exchange program with Dartmouth College, Morehouse College, Spelman College; cooperative program in public health with University of California, Los Angeles, and San Diego State University. **Remedial services:** Learning center, preadmission summer program, reduced course load, special counselor, tutoring, Summer Bridge program for select group of entering EOP and SAA students provides a bridge from high school to college for students who need additional support and encouragement. **Placement/credit:** AP, institutional tests.

ACADEMIC REQUIREMENTS. Freshmen must earn minimum GPA of 2.0 to continue in good standing. 91% of freshmen return for sophomore year. Students must declare major by end of second year. **Graduation requirements:** 180 hours for bachelor's (60 in major). Most students required to take courses in arts/fine arts, computer science, English, humanities, mathematics, biological/physical sciences, social sciences. **Postgraduate studies:** 14% enter law school, 17% enter medical school, 3% enter MBA programs, 9% enter other graduate study.

FRESHMAN ADMISSIONS. Selection criteria: High school course pattern, GPA, and test scores most important. Admission for out-of-state applicants more selective than for residents. **High school preparation:** 15 units required. Required and recommended units include English 4, foreign language 2-3, mathematics 3-4, social science 2 and science 2-3. 2 college-preparatory electives required. **Test requirements:** SAT or ACT; score report by January 15. 3 ACH required (including English Composition and Mathematics). Score report by January 15.

1992 FRESHMAN CLASS PROFILE. 9,231 men applied, 5,447 accepted, 1,309 enrolled; 9,886 women applied, 5,891 accepted, 1,341 enrolled. 100% had high school GPA of 3.0 or higher. 95% were in top tenth of graduating class. **Academic background:** Mid 50% of enrolled freshmen had SAT-V between 440-570, SAT-M between 530-660; ACT composite between 21-27. 95% submitted SAT scores, 5% submitted ACT scores. **Characteristics:** 94% from in state, 86% live in college housing, 41% have minority backgrounds, 1% are foreign students, 12% join fraternities/sororities. Average age is 18.

FALL-TERM APPLICATIONS. $40 fee, may be waived for applicants with need. Closing date November 30; applicants notified on a rolling basis beginning on or about March 1; must reply by May 1. Essay required. Interview recommended for music, visual arts, theater applicants. Audition recommended for music applicants. Portfolio recommended for art applicants. PSAT recommended.

STUDENT LIFE. Housing: Dormitories (coed); apartment, handicapped housing available. Language, cultural interest and international houses available. Guaranteed housing for new single freshmen and transfer students. Housing in residence halls or apartments depending on college choice and class level. **Activities:** Student government, film, magazine, radio, student newspaper, television, yearbook, choral groups, concert band, dance, drama, jazz band, music ensembles, musical theater, opera, pep band, symphony orchestra, fraternities, sororities, over 250 student organizations including MEChA, African-American Student Union, Lesbian, Gay and Bisexual Association, Student Advocates for Undergraduate Diversity, International Club, Phi Beta Kappa, Native-American Student Alliance.

ATHLETICS. NCAA. **Intercollegiate:** Baseball M, basketball, cross-country, diving, fencing, golf, rowing (crew), soccer, softball W, swimming, tennis, track and field, volleyball, water polo. **Intramural:** Badminton, baseball, basketball, bowling, cross-country, golf M, ice hockey M, lacrosse, sailing, skiing, soccer, softball, swimming, tennis, track and field, volleyball, water polo.

STUDENT SERVICES. Aptitude testing, career counseling, employment service for undergraduates, freshman orientation, health services, on-campus day care, personal counseling, placement service for graduates, special adviser for adult students, veterans counselor, Disabled Student Services, academic assistance/tutoring (OASIS), foreign student services, legal services, commuter services, student safety awareness, services/facilities for handicapped.

ANNUAL EXPENSES. Tuition and fees (projected): $4,008, $7,699 additional for out-of-state students. **Room and board:** $6,562. **Books and supplies:** $612. **Other expenses:** $1,598.

FINANCIAL AID. 40% of freshmen, 41% of continuing students receive some form of aid. 94% of grants, 91% of loans, all jobs based on need. 1,107 enrolled freshmen were judged to have need, all were offered aid. Academic scholarships available. **Aid applications:** Closing date May 3; priority given to applications received by March 2; applicants notified on a rolling basis beginning on or about May 15; must reply within 10 days.

ADDRESS/TELEPHONE. Ronald J. Bowker, Registrar and Admissions Officer, Univ. of California, San Diego, Student Center, Building B, 0337, La Jolla, CA 92093-0337. (619) 534-4831.

University of California: San Francisco
San Francisco, California — CB code: 0942

2-year upper-division public university, coed. Founded in 1864. **Accreditation:** Regional. **Undergraduate enrollment:** 6 men, 41 women full time. **Graduate enrollment:** 956 men, 1,574 women full time. **Faculty:** 1,659 total. **Location:** Urban campus in very large city. **Calendar:** Quarter. **Microcomputers:** Located in computer centers.

DEGREES OFFERED. BS, MA, MS, PhD, DMD, MD, B. Pharm. 117 bachelor's degrees awarded in 1992. 63% in health sciences, 37% allied health. Graduate degrees offered in 22 major fields of study.

UNDERGRADUATE MAJORS. Dental hygiene.

ACADEMIC PROGRAMS. Honors program, cross-registration. **Placement/credit:** AP, institutional tests.

ACADEMIC REQUIREMENTS. Students must declare major on application. **Graduation requirements:** 180 hours for bachelor's. Most students required to take courses in English, history. **Additional information:** All students enter professional or graduate schools. No general undergraduate or preprofessional programs offered.

STUDENT LIFE. Housing: Apartment, fraternity, handicapped housing available. **Activities:** Student government, film, student newspaper, choral groups, symphony orchestra, fraternities, Asian Health Caucus; Black Students Health Alliance; Chicanos in Health Education; Health Education and Mobilization for Filipinos; Native American Health Alliance; Lesbian, Gay and Bisexual Student Association.

ATHLETICS. Intramural: Badminton, basketball, cross-country, fencing, golf, horseback riding, racquetball, rowing (crew), sailing, skiing, skin diving, softball, squash, swimming, table tennis, tennis, volleyball.

STUDENT SERVICES. Career counseling, employment service for undergraduates, health services, on-campus day care, personal counseling, placement service for graduates, veterans counselor, services/facilities for handicapped.

ANNUAL EXPENSES. Tuition and fees (projected): $4,147, $7,699 additional for out-of-state students. **Room and board:** $7,470. **Books and supplies:** $3,187. **Other expenses:** $1,935.

FINANCIAL AID. 65% of continuing students receive some form of aid. 89% of grants, 85% of loans based on need. All jobs based on criteria other than need. Academic, leadership scholarships available. **Aid applications:** No closing date; priority given to applications received by July 1; applicants notified on a rolling basis beginning on or about June 1; must reply within 2 weeks.

ADDRESS/TELEPHONE. Clifford Attkisson, Associate Vice Chancellor for Student Academic Affairs, University of California: San Francisco, PO Box 0244, 500 Parnassus, San Francisco, CA 94143-0244. (415) 476-4986. Fax: (415) 476-9690.

University of California: Santa Barbara
Santa Barbara, California — CB code: 4835

Admissions:	80% of applicants accepted
Based on:	••• School record, special talents, test scores
	•• Essay
	• Activities
Completion:	90% of freshmen end year in good standing
	61% graduate

4-year public university, coed. Founded in 1898. **Accreditation:** Regional. **Undergraduate enrollment:** 7,602 men, 7,844 women full time; 455 men, 376 women part time. **Graduate enrollment:** 1,378 men, 876 women full time; 85 men, 48 women part time. **Faculty:** 853 total (720 full time). **Location:** Suburban campus in small city; 100 miles from Los Angeles. **Calendar:** Quarter, extensive summer session. Saturday and extensive evening/early morning classes. **Microcomputers:** Located in libraries, classrooms, computer centers. **Special facilities:** Art museum, several nature preserves with research facilities, seawater laboratories, Marine Science Institute, Institute for

Theoretical Physics, robotics laboratory, free electron laser laboratory, Institute for Polymers and Organic Solids, Social Process Research Institute, Quantum Institute, Intercampus Institute for Research of Particle Accelerators, National Center for Geographic Information and Analysis, Center for Quantized Electronic Structures.

DEGREES OFFERED. BA, BS, BFA, MA, MS, MFA, MEd, PhD. 3,832 bachelor's degrees awarded in 1992. 11% in business and management, 5% communications, 5% engineering, 10% letters/literature, 7% life sciences, 9% multi/interdisciplinary studies, 10% psychology, 30% social sciences, 5% visual and performing arts. Graduate degrees offered in 60 major fields of study.

UNDERGRADUATE MAJORS. Afro-American (black) studies, anthropology, archeology, art history, Asian studies, biochemistry, biological and physical sciences, biology, botany, business economics, cell biology, chemical engineering, chemistry, Chicano studies, Chinese, cinematography/film, classics, communications, comparative literature, computer and information sciences, computer engineering, criminal justice studies, dance, developmental psychology, dramatic arts, ecology, economics, electrical/electronics/communications engineering, English, environmental science, environmental studies, experimental psychology, film arts, French, geography, geology, geophysics and seismology, German, Greek (classical), history, international relations, Italian, Japanese, Latin, Latin American studies, liberal/general studies, linguistics, marine biology, mathematics, mechanical engineering, medieval studies, microbiology, molecular biology, music, nuclear engineering, personality psychology, pharmacology, human and animal, philosophy, physics, physiology, human and animal, political science and government, Portuguese, psychobiology, psychology, religion, Russian, Slavic languages, social sciences, sociology, Spanish, speech pathology/audiology, statistics, studio art, visual and performing arts, women's studies, zoology.

ACADEMIC PROGRAMS. Accelerated program, double major, dual enrollment of high school students, education specialist degree, honors program, independent study, internships, student-designed major, study abroad, teacher preparation, telecourses, visiting/exchange student program, Washington semester, cross-registration. **Remedial services:** Learning center, preadmission summer program, reduced course load, remedial instruction, special counselor, tutoring, reading clinic. **ROTC:** Army. **Placement/credit:** AP, institutional tests.

ACADEMIC REQUIREMENTS. Freshmen must earn minimum GPA of 2.0 to continue in good standing. 88% of freshmen return for sophomore year. Students must declare major by end of second year. **Graduation requirements:** 180 hours for bachelor's. Most students required to take courses in arts/fine arts, English, foreign languages, history, humanities, mathematics, philosophy/religion, biological/physical sciences, social sciences.

FRESHMAN ADMISSIONS. Selection criteria: Eligibility established by high school GPA, course requirement, and SAT scores. Special consideration for disadvantaged students. **High school preparation:** 14 units required. Required units include English 4, foreign language 2, mathematics 3, social science 1 and science 1. Social science unit should be US history, science unit should include laboratory. **Test requirements:** SAT or ACT (SAT preferred); score report by January 1. 3 ACH required (including English Composition and Mathematics Level I or II). Score report by January 1.

1992 FRESHMAN CLASS PROFILE. 7,989 men applied, 6,404 accepted, 1,477 enrolled; 9,412 women applied, 7,512 accepted, 1,741 enrolled. 95% had high school GPA of 3.0 or higher, 4% between 2.0 and 2.99. **Academic background:** Mid 50% of enrolled freshmen had SAT-V between 430-540, SAT-M between 510-620; ACT composite between 22-26. 99% submitted SAT scores, 20% submitted ACT scores. **Characteristics:** 93% from in state, 81% live in college housing, 30% have minority backgrounds, 1% are foreign students, 9% join fraternities/sororities. Average age is 18.

FALL-TERM APPLICATIONS. $40 fee, may be waived for applicants with need. $20 fee for each additional application to other University of California campuses. Closing date November 30; applicants notified on or about March 15; must reply by May 30. Audition required for music, dance, drama applicants. Portfolio required for art applicants. Essay required. CRDA. Early admission available.

STUDENT LIFE. Housing: Dormitories (coed); apartment, fraternity, sorority, cooperative housing available. **Activities:** Student government, film, magazine, radio, student newspaper, television, yearbook, choral groups, concert band, dance, drama, jazz band, music ensembles, musical theater, opera, pep band, symphony orchestra, fraternities, sororities, over 250 organizations representing range of interests.

ATHLETICS. NCAA. **Intercollegiate:** Basketball, cross-country, diving, golf M, gymnastics, rowing (crew) M, soccer, softball, swimming, tennis, track and field, volleyball, water polo M. **Intramural:** Badminton, basketball, bowling, fencing, field hockey, lacrosse, rugby, sailing, skiing, skin diving, soccer, softball M, tennis, volleyball, water polo M.

STUDENT SERVICES. Aptitude testing, career counseling, employment service for undergraduates, freshman orientation, health services, on-campus day care, personal counseling, placement service for graduates, special adviser for adult students, veterans counselor, services/facilities for handicapped.

ANNUAL EXPENSES. Tuition and fees (1992-93): $2,953, $7,699 additional for out-of-state students. **Room and board:** $5,780. **Books and supplies:** $576. **Other expenses:** $1,284.

FINANCIAL AID. 35% of freshmen, 34% of continuing students receive some form of aid. 95% of grants, 88% of loans, 30% of jobs based on need. 730 enrolled freshmen were judged to have need, all were offered aid. Academic, music/drama, art, athletic, state/district residency, alumni affiliation, minority scholarships available. **Aid applications:** No closing date; priority given to applications received by March 2; applicants notified on a rolling basis beginning on or about April 15; must reply within 2 weeks.

ADDRESS/TELEPHONE. William J. Villa, Director of Admissions and Relations with Schools, University of California: Santa Barbara, Santa Barbara, CA 93106. (805) 893-2485.

University of California: Santa Cruz ⇎
Santa Cruz, California — CB code: 4860

Admissions: 78% of applicants accepted
Based on: ••• Essay, school record, test scores
•• Activities, special talents
• Interview, recommendations
Completion: 57% graduate, 30% of these enter graduate study

4-year public university, coed. Founded in 1965. **Accreditation:** Regional. **Undergraduate enrollment:** 3,953 men, 5,311 women full time; 111 men, 185 women part time. **Graduate enrollment:** 534 men, 457 women full time; 16 men, 5 women part time. **Faculty:** 640 total (440 full time), 640 with doctorates or other terminal degrees. **Location:** Suburban campus in large town; 75 miles from San Francisco, 35 miles from San Jose. **Calendar:** Quarter, limited summer session. **Microcomputers:** 200 located in libraries, classrooms, computer centers. **Special facilities:** Lick Observatory/UC observatories, institute of marine sciences, institute of tectonics, arboretum, predatory bird research group, agroecology program farm, Santa Cruz Institute for particle physics, campus preserve, art galleries, center for nonlinear science.

DEGREES OFFERED. BA, BS, MA, MS, PhD. 2,268 bachelor's degrees awarded in 1992. 11% in letters/literature, 9% life sciences, 5% multi/interdisciplinary studies, 15% psychology, 35% social sciences, 11% visual and performing arts. Graduate degrees offered in 39 major fields of study.

UNDERGRADUATE MAJORS. American literature, American studies, anthropology, applied mathematics, art history, biology, business economics, cell biology, chemistry, cinematography/film, classics, clinical psychology, community studies, comparative literature, computational mathematics, computer and information sciences, computer engineering, creative writing, dance, developmental psychology, dramatic arts, earth sciences, East Asian studies, ecology, economics, environmental science, environmental studies, ethnic studies, experimental psychology, film arts, fine arts, French, French studies, geology, geophysics and seismology, German, German literature, Greek (classical), history, Italian, Japanese, Latin, Latin American studies, legal studies, linguistics, marine biology, mathematics, medieval studies, modern society/social thought, molecular biology, music, natural history and wildlife, painting, peace studies, personality psychology, philosophy, photography, physics, plant sciences, political science and government, printmaking, psychobiology, psychology, pure mathematics, religion, Russian, Russian and Slavic studies, sculpture, social psychology, sociology, South Asian studies, Southeast Asian studies, Spanish, Spanish for Spanish speakers, studio art, theater design, video, Western civilization, women's studies, world literature and culture.

ACADEMIC PROGRAMS. Double major, dual enrollment of high school students, independent study, internships, student-designed major, study abroad, teacher preparation, visiting/exchange student program, cross-registration; liberal arts/career combination in engineering. **Remedial services:** Learning center, special counselor, tutoring, SAA/EOP Summer Bridge Program. **Placement/credit:** AP, institutional tests.

ACADEMIC REQUIREMENTS. No policy requiring minimum GPA; records of students having academic difficulty are reviewed individually. Freshmen must pass at least 7 courses (35 units) to continue in good academic standing. 84% of freshmen return for sophomore year. Students must declare major by end of second year. **Graduation requirements:** 180 hours for bachelor's. Most students required to take courses in arts/fine arts, English, humanities, mathematics, biological/physical sciences, social sciences. **Postgraduate studies:** 30% enter other graduate study. **Additional information:** Student performance recorded by faculty in personalized narrative evaluation, part of every student's transcript. Traditional letter grades offered as option in all upper-division and many lower-division courses.

FRESHMAN ADMISSIONS. Selection criteria: Test scores, GPA in required subjects most important. Applicants must meet eligibility standards, but must be above minimum requirements to be admitted. Student affirmative action and academic re-entry programs. **High school preparation:** 15 units required. Required units include biological science 1, English 4, foreign language 2, mathematics 3 and social science 1. 4 electives from history, English, advanced mathematics, laboratory science, foreign language, social science, visual or performing arts. **Test requirements:** SAT or ACT; score report by January 1. 3 ACH required (including English Composition,

Mathematics Level I or II, and an additional test). Score report by January 1.

1992 FRESHMAN CLASS PROFILE. 4,412 men applied, 3,367 accepted, 687 enrolled; 6,305 women applied, 5,005 accepted, 1,123 enrolled. 85% had high school GPA of 3.0 or higher, 15% between 2.0 and 2.99. **Academic background:** Mid 50% of enrolled freshmen had SAT-V between 440-570, SAT-M between 490-620. 98% submitted SAT scores. **Characteristics:** 35% have minority backgrounds. Average age is 18.

FALL-TERM APPLICATIONS. $40 fee, may be waived for applicants with need. Closing date November 30; applicants notified on a rolling basis beginning on or about March 1; must reply by May 1. Audition required for music, theater arts applicants. Essay required. Interview recommended. Portfolio recommended for art applicants. CRDA.

STUDENT LIFE. Housing: Dormitories (men, women, coed); apartment housing available. Housing guaranteed to fall freshmen. **Activities:** Student government, film, radio, student newspaper, television, choral groups, dance, drama, jazz band, music ensembles, musical theater, opera, symphony orchestra, electronic music laboratory, over 100 student organizations.

ATHLETICS. NCAA. **Intercollegiate:** Basketball, diving, fencing, lacrosse, racquetball, rugby M, sailing, soccer, swimming, tennis, volleyball, water polo. **Intramural:** Basketball, soccer, softball, volleyball.

STUDENT SERVICES. Aptitude testing, career counseling, employment service for undergraduates, freshman orientation, health services, on-campus day care, personal counseling, special adviser for adult students, veterans counselor, minority and low-income student services, services/facilities for handicapped.

ANNUAL EXPENSES. Tuition and fees (1992-93): $3,023, $7,699 additional for out-of-state students. **Room and board:** $5,805. **Books and supplies:** $570. **Other expenses:** $1,509.

FINANCIAL AID. 33% of freshmen, 43% of continuing students receive some form of aid. 94% of grants, 98% of loans, 27% of jobs based on need. 740 enrolled freshmen were judged to have need, all were offered aid. Academic, music/drama, art, state/district residency, leadership scholarships available. **Aid applications:** No closing date; priority given to applications received by March 2; applicants notified on a rolling basis beginning on or about April 1; must reply within 3 weeks.

ADDRESS/TELEPHONE. Joseph P. Allen, Dean of Admissions, University of California: Santa Cruz, Cook House, Santa Cruz, CA 95064. (408) 459-4008.

University of Judaism
Los Angeles, California CB code: 4876

Admissions:	76% of applicants accepted
Based on:	••• Essay, school record
	•• Activities, recommendations, test scores
	• Interview, special talents
Completion:	90% of freshmen end year in good standing
	75% graduate, 90% of these enter graduate study

4-year private university and liberal arts, rabbinical college, coed, affiliated with Jewish faith. Founded in 1947. **Accreditation:** Regional. **Undergraduate enrollment:** 36 men, 48 women full time; 3 men, 3 women part time. **Graduate enrollment:** 40 men, 41 women full time; 6 men, 15 women part time. **Faculty:** 66 total (30 full time), 49 with doctorates or other terminal degrees. **Location:** Suburban campus in very large city. **Calendar:** Semester, limited summer session. **Microcomputers:** 20 located in computer centers. **Special facilities:** Art gallery, theater, Jewish community documentation center, educational resources center, computer center. **Additional facts:** Lee College, founded in 1982, is the liberal arts undergraduate school of the university.

DEGREES OFFERED. BA, MA, MBA, MEd, Talm. 14 bachelor's degrees awarded in 1992. 10% in architecture and environmental design, 8% business and management, 8% law, 25% letters/literature, 20% philosophy, religion, theology, 45% psychology. Graduate degrees offered in 5 major fields of study.

UNDERGRADUATE MAJORS. Bible studies, Bioethics, business and management, English, English literature, Jewish studies, liberal/general studies, political science and government, prelaw, psychology.

ACADEMIC PROGRAMS. Double major, dual enrollment of high school students, independent study, internships, student-designed major, study abroad, cross-registration; liberal arts/career combination in business; combined bachelor's/graduate program in business administration. **Remedial services:** Reduced course load, tutoring, untimed testing. **Placement/credit:** AP, institutional tests.

ACADEMIC REQUIREMENTS. Freshmen must earn minimum GPA of 2.0 to continue in good standing. 90% of freshmen return for sophomore year. Students must declare major by end of second year. **Graduation requirements:** 126 hours for bachelor's (36 in major). Most students required to take courses in arts/fine arts, computer science, English, foreign languages, history, humanities, mathematics, philosophy/religion, biological/physical sciences, social sciences. **Postgraduate studies:** 20% enter law school, 70% enter other graduate study. **Additional information:** In addition to majors and general education requirements, students take core curriculum of Jewish and Western Civilization classes.

FRESHMAN ADMISSIONS. Selection criteria: For Lee College, 3.2 GPA, SAT combined score of 1100, recommendations, school, and community activites important. **High school preparation:** 14 units recommended. Recommended units include English 4, foreign language 2, mathematics 2, social science 1 and science 1. **Test requirements:** SAT or ACT; score report by February 15. **Additional information:** Out-of-state students can call collect (310) 476-0236.

1992 FRESHMAN CLASS PROFILE. 21 men applied, 16 accepted, 10 enrolled; 38 women applied, 29 accepted, 9 enrolled. 90% had high school GPA of 3.0 or higher, 10% between 2.0 and 2.99. **Academic background:** Mid 50% of enrolled freshmen had SAT-V between 450-590, SAT-M between 500-600. 80% submitted SAT scores. **Characteristics:** 43% from in state, 85% live in college housing, 10% are foreign students. Average age is 19.

FALL-TERM APPLICATIONS. $25 fee, may be waived for applicants with need. No closing date; priority given to applications received by January 31; applicants notified on a rolling basis beginning on or about December 15; must reply by May 1 or within 2 weeks if notified thereafter. Essay required. Interview recommended. CRDA. Deferred admission available. Institutional early decision plan.

STUDENT LIFE. Housing: Dormitories (coed); apartment housing available. Kosher meals on campus. Students required to live on campus unless 21 or living with parents. **Activities:** Student government, magazine, radio, yearbook, choral groups, dance, drama, music ensembles, Hillel, Residence Life Council, Associated Students of Lee College, political sciences club. **Additional information:** Use of UCLA's athletic and recreational facilities.

ATHLETICS. Intramural: Baseball, basketball, cross-country, football, volleyball.

STUDENT SERVICES. Career counseling, employment service for undergraduates, freshman orientation, health services, personal counseling, placement service for graduates, health services in conjunction with Mount Saint Marys college, services/facilities for handicapped.

ANNUAL EXPENSES. Tuition and fees (1992-93): $8,950. **Room and board:** $5,850. **Books and supplies:** $700. **Other expenses:** $1,680.

FINANCIAL AID. 81% of freshmen, 66% of continuing students receive some form of aid. 50% of grants, 95% of loans, 61% of jobs based on need. 4 enrolled freshmen were judged to have need, all were offered aid. Academic, leadership scholarships available. **Aid applications:** No closing date; priority given to applications received by March 2; applicants notified on a rolling basis beginning on or about April 1; must reply by May 1 or within 2 weeks if notified thereafter.

ADDRESS/TELEPHONE. Tamara Greenebaum, Director of Admissions, University of Judaism, 15600 Mulholland Drive, Los Angeles, CA 90077. (310) 476-9777. Fax: (310) 471-1278.

University of La Verne
La Verne, California CB code: 4381

4-year private university and college of arts and sciences, coed, affiliated with Church of the Brethren. Founded in 1891. **Accreditation:** Regional. **Undergraduate enrollment:** 600 men, 733 women full time; 709 men, 1,088 women part time. **Graduate enrollment:** 437 men, 522 women full time; 858 men, 1,014 women part time. **Faculty:** 404 total (104 full time), 80 with doctorates or other terminal degrees. **Location:** Suburban campus in large town; 35 miles from Los Angeles. **Calendar:** 4-1-4, extensive summer session. **Microcomputers:** Located in libraries, computer centers. **Special facilities:** Jaeger Museum located in biology department.

DEGREES OFFERED. AA, AS, B, MEd, JD. 70 associate degrees awarded in 1992. 920 bachelor's degrees awarded. Graduate degrees offered in 17 major fields of study.

UNDERGRADUATE MAJORS. Business administration and management, information sciences and systems, legal assistant/paralegal. accounting, behavioral sciences, biology, business administration and management, business and management, business economics, chemistry, child development/care/guidance, communications, computer and information sciences, computer engineering, computer technology, criminal justice studies, criminology, dramatic arts, early childhood education, economics, education, electrical/electronics/communications engineering, electronic technology, elementary education, English, environmental science, fine arts, French, German, health care administration, history, humanities and social sciences, international business management, international relations, international studies, journalism, junior high education, laser electro-optic technology, legal assistant/paralegal, liberal/general studies, mathematics, music, philosophy, physical education, physical sciences, physics, political science and government, prelaw, psychology, public administration, radio/television broadcasting, radio/television technology, religion, secondary education, social sciences, sociology, Spanish, visual and performing arts.

ACADEMIC PROGRAMS. Accelerated program, double major, honors program, independent study, internships, student-designed major, study abroad, teacher preparation, weekend college; liberal arts/career combination in engineering, health sciences; combined bachelor's/graduate program in law. **Remedial services:** Learning center, reduced course load, special counselor, tutoring, writing center. **Placement/credit:** AP, CLEP General and Subject, institutional tests; 44 credit hours maximum for bachelor's degree.

ACADEMIC REQUIREMENTS. Freshmen must earn minimum GPA of 2.0 to continue in good standing. 65% of freshmen return for sophomore year. Students must declare major by end of second year. **Graduation requirements:** 60 hours for associate (18 in major), 128 hours for bachelor's (24 in major). Most students required to take courses in arts/fine arts, English, history, humanities, mathematics, philosophy/religion, biological/physical sciences, social sciences. **Additional information:** Accelerated program for adults in school of continuing education.

FRESHMAN ADMISSIONS. Selection criteria: High school record, test scores, school and community activities, student's written statement, and recommendations considered. Special consideration for alumni children. **High school preparation:** 14 units recommended. Recommended units include biological science 1, English 4, foreign language 2, mathematics 3, physical science 1 and social science 2. **Test requirements:** SAT or ACT (SAT preferred); score report by September 1.

1992 FRESHMAN CLASS PROFILE. 167 men, 138 women enrolled. 42% had high school GPA of 3.0 or higher, 56% between 2.0 and 2.99. **Characteristics:** 76% from in state, 70% live in college housing, 45% have minority backgrounds, 12% are foreign students, 21% join fraternities/sororities. Average age is 18.

FALL-TERM APPLICATIONS. $25 fee, may be waived for applicants with need. No closing date; priority given to applications received by March 1; applicants notified on a rolling basis beginning on or about December 15; must reply by May 1 or within 4 weeks if notified thereafter. Essay required. Interview recommended. CRDA. Deferred admission available.

STUDENT LIFE. Housing: Dormitories (men, women, coed); fraternity, sorority housing available. **Activities:** Student government, magazine, radio, student newspaper, television, yearbook, literary magazine, choral groups, dance, drama, jazz band, music ensembles, musical theater, fraternities, sororities, religious and academic societies, Black Students Union, Movimiento Estudiantil Chicano de Aztlan, Newman Club, Christian Union, Model UN. **Additional information:** Active participation in college community emphasized.

ATHLETICS. NCAA. **Intercollegiate:** Baseball M, basketball, cross-country, football M, golf M, soccer, softball W, tennis, track and field, volleyball. **Intramural:** Basketball, bowling, racquetball, skiing, softball, table tennis, tennis, volleyball.

STUDENT SERVICES. Aptitude testing, career counseling, employment service for undergraduates, freshman orientation, health services, on-campus day care, personal counseling, placement service for graduates, special adviser for adult students, veterans counselor, international student center, services/facilities for handicapped.

ANNUAL EXPENSES. Tuition and fees: $12,890. **Room and board:** $4,910. **Books and supplies:** $612. **Other expenses:** $1,584.

ADDRESS/TELEPHONE. Douglas Wible, Director of Admissions, University of La Verne, 1950 Third Street, La Verne, CA 91750-4443. (909) 593-3511. (800) 876-4858. Fax: (714) 593-0965.

University of the Pacific

Stockton, California — CB code: 4065

Admissions: 82% of applicants accepted
Based on:
••• School record
•• Recommendations, test scores
• Activities, essay, interview, special talents
Completion: 87% of freshmen end year in good standing
67% graduate, 30% of these enter graduate study

4-year private university, coed, Historic affiliation with the United Methodist Church. Founded in 1851. **Accreditation:** Regional. **Undergraduate enrollment:** 1,442 men, 1,801 women full time; 107 men, 141 women part time. **Graduate enrollment:** 77 men, 186 women full time; 72 men, 168 women part time. **Faculty:** 309 total (263 full time), 223 with doctorates or other terminal degrees. **Location:** Suburban campus in large city; 80 miles from San Francisco, 40 miles from Sacramento. **Calendar:** Semester, extensive summer session. **Microcomputers:** 110 located in dormitories, classrooms, computer centers. **Special facilities:** Recital facilities, Holt-Atherton Center for Western Studies housing the John Muir papers, art gallery, music conservatory. **Additional facts:** School of Dentistry in San Francisco. McGeorge School of Law in Sacramento.

DEGREES OFFERED. BA, BS, BFA, MA, MS, MBA, MEd, PhD, EdD, DDS, Pharm D, JD. 596 bachelor's degrees awarded in 1992. 19% in business and management, 10% communications, 14% engineering, 5% letters/literature, 11% social sciences, 7% visual and performing arts. Graduate degrees offered in 49 major fields of study.

UNDERGRADUATE MAJORS. Accounting, African studies, Afro-American (black) studies, American studies, anthropology, applied mathematics, art education, art history, arts management, Asian studies, bilingual/bicultural education, biochemistry, biological and physical sciences, biology, biotechnology, business administration and management, business and management, business economics, Caribbean studies, chemistry, civil engineering, classics, communications, computer and information sciences, computer engineering, dance, dramatic arts, East Asian studies, Eastern European studies, economics, education of the emotionally handicapped, electrical/electronics/communications engineering, elementary education, embryology, engineering, engineering and other disciplines, engineering management, engineering physics, English, English education, European studies, finance, fine arts, foreign languages (multiple emphasis), foreign languages education, French, geography, geology, geophysics and seismology, German, graphic design, Greek (classical), history, humanities, humanities and social sciences, information sciences and systems, international business management, international development, international public service, international relations, international studies, Japanese, journalism, junior high education, Latin, Latin American studies, liberal/general studies, linguistics, management engineering, marketing management, mathematics, mathematics education, mechanical engineering, Middle Eastern studies, music, music business management, music education, music history and appreciation, music performance, music theory and composition, music therapy, organizational behavior, Pacific area studies, philosophy, physical education, physical sciences, physical therapy, physics, political science and government, predentistry, prelaw, premedicine, prepharmacy, preveterinary, psychology, public administration, public relations, radio/television broadcasting, reading education, real estate, religion, remedial education, Russian and Slavic studies, Scandinavian studies, science education, secondary education, small business management and ownership, social science education, social sciences, social studies education, sociology, South Asian studies, Southeast Asian studies, Spanish, special education, specific learning disabilities, speech, speech pathology/audiology, speech/communication/theater education, sports management, sports medicine, studio art, teaching English as a second language/foreign language, urban studies, Western European studies, women's studies.

ACADEMIC PROGRAMS. Accelerated program, cooperative education, double major, education specialist degree, honors program, independent study, internships, student-designed major, study abroad, teacher preparation, United Nations semester, Washington semester; combined bachelor's/graduate program in business administration. **Remedial services:** Learning center, preadmission summer program, reduced course load, tutoring, English as a second language. **ROTC:** Air Force. **Placement/credit:** AP, CLEP General and Subject, IB, institutional tests; 20 credit hours maximum for bachelor's degree.

ACADEMIC REQUIREMENTS. Freshmen must earn minimum GPA of 2.0 to continue in good standing. 85% of freshmen return for sophomore year. Students must declare major by end of second year. **Graduation requirements:** 124 hours for bachelor's (36 in major). Most students required to take courses in arts/fine arts, English, history, humanities, mathematics, philosophy/religion, biological/physical sciences, social sciences. **Additional information:** Cooperative education/internship program available to all majors, required of engineering and pharmacy majors.

FRESHMAN ADMISSIONS. Selection criteria: School achievement record most important, followed by test scores and recommendations. Essay and extracurricular activities also considered. **High school preparation:** 16 units recommended. Recommended units include biological science 1, English 4, foreign language 2, mathematics 3, physical science 1 and social science 2. **Test requirements:** SAT or ACT.

1992 FRESHMAN CLASS PROFILE. 1,088 men applied, 859 accepted, 277 enrolled; 1,319 women applied, 1,124 accepted, 342 enrolled. 65% had high school GPA of 3.0 or higher, 35% between 2.0 and 2.99. **Academic background:** Mid 50% of enrolled freshmen had SAT-V between 430-540, SAT-M between 440-590. 97% submitted SAT scores. **Characteristics:** 79% from in state, 96% live in college housing, 30% have minority backgrounds, 6% are foreign students. Average age is 18.

FALL-TERM APPLICATIONS. $50 fee, may be waived for applicants with need. No closing date; priority given to applications received by March 1; applicants notified on a rolling basis beginning on or about January 15; must reply by May 1 or within 2 weeks if notified thereafter. Audition required for music/conservatory applicants. Essay required. Interview recommended. CRDA. Deferred and early admission available. Institutional early decision plan.

STUDENT LIFE. Housing: Dormitories (coed); apartment, fraternity, sorority housing available. Freshmen and sophomores required to live on campus unless living with family. **Activities:** Student government, magazine, radio, student newspaper, yearbook, debate team, choral groups, concert band, dance, drama, jazz band, music ensembles, musical theater, opera, pep band, symphony orchestra, fraternities, sororities, 75 student organizations.

ATHLETICS. NCAA. **Intercollegiate:** Baseball M, basketball, cross-country W, field hockey W, football M, golf M, soccer W, softball W, swimming, tennis, volleyball, water polo M. **Intramural:** Badminton, basketball, golf, ice hockey M, lacrosse, racquetball, rowing (crew), rugby M, soccer, softball, tennis, volleyball, water polo.

STUDENT SERVICES. Aptitude testing, career counseling, employment service for undergraduates, freshman orientation, health services, personal counseling, placement service for graduates, special adviser for adult students, veterans counselor, foreign student advising, services/facilities for handicapped.

ANNUAL EXPENSES. Tuition and fees: $15,800. **Room and board:** $5,300. **Books and supplies:** $565. **Other expenses:** $1,050.

FINANCIAL AID. 63% of freshmen, 64% of continuing students receive some form of aid. 87% of grants, 91% of loans, all jobs based on need. Music/drama, athletic scholarships available. **Aid applications:** No closing date; priority given to applications received by March 2; applicants notified on a rolling basis beginning on or about March 2; must reply by May 1 or within 2 weeks if notified thereafter.

ADDRESS/TELEPHONE. Edward L. Schoenberg, Dean of Admissions, University of the Pacific, 3601 Pacific Avenue, Stockton, CA 95211-0197. (209) 946-2211. (800) 959-2867. Fax: (209) 946-2689.

University of Redlands
Redlands, California CB code: 4848

4-year private liberal arts college, coed, historic affiliation with American Baptist Church. Founded in 1907. **Accreditation:** Regional. **Undergraduate enrollment:** 672 men, 718 women full time; 44 men, 31 women part time. **Graduate enrollment:** 11 men, 60 women full time; 6 men, 23 women part time. **Faculty:** 358 total (135 full time), 89 with doctorates or other terminal degrees. **Location:** Suburban campus in small city; 65 miles from Los Angeles, 40 miles from Palm Springs. **Calendar:** 4-1-4, limited summer session. **Microcomputers:** 131 located in libraries, classrooms, computer centers. **Special facilities:** Peppers Art Gallery, Farquhar Collection of the Native American Southwest, McNair Far East Collection.

DEGREES OFFERED. BA, BS, MA, MS, MBA. 346 bachelor's degrees awarded in 1992. 18% in business and management, 5% education, 10% health sciences, 11% letters/literature, 6% multi/interdisciplinary studies, 9% psychology, 16% social sciences, 11% visual and performing arts. Graduate degrees offered in 6 major fields of study.

UNDERGRADUATE MAJORS. Accounting, anthropology, art education, art history, Asian studies, biology, business administration and management, chemistry, computer and information sciences, creative writing, economics, electrical/electronics/communications engineering, elementary education, engineering, engineering science, English, English education, English literature, environmental science, ethnic studies, fine arts, foreign languages education, French, German, history, international relations, junior high education, liberal/general studies, mathematics, mathematics education, mechanical engineering, music, music education, music history and appreciation, music performance, music theory and composition, philosophy, physics, political science and government, prelaw, psychology, religion, science education, secondary education, social science education, sociology, Spanish, speech correction, speech pathology/audiology, technical and business writing.

ACADEMIC PROGRAMS. Accelerated program, double major, dual enrollment of high school students, honors program, independent study, internships, student-designed major, study abroad, teacher preparation, Washington semester; liberal arts/career combination in engineering. **Remedial services:** Learning center, reduced course load, remedial instruction, special counselor, tutoring. **Placement/credit:** AP, institutional tests; 15 credit hours maximum for bachelor's degree.

ACADEMIC REQUIREMENTS. Freshmen must earn minimum GPA of 2.0 to continue in good standing. 87% of freshmen return for sophomore year. Students must declare major by end of second year. **Graduation requirements:** 132 hours for bachelor's (36 in major). Most students required to take courses in arts/fine arts, English, foreign languages, history, humanities, mathematics, philosophy/religion, biological/physical sciences, social sciences. **Additional information:** Nontraditional study programs available through Johnston Center for Individualized Learning and Whitehead Center for Lifelong Learning. Credit for previous experience granted by Whitehead Center for Lifelong Learning.

FRESHMAN ADMISSIONS. Selection criteria: School achievement record, test scores, recommendations most important, then interview, extracurricular activities, leadership, motivation. **High school preparation:** 14 units required. Required and recommended units include English 4, mathematics 3, social science 2 and science 2. Foreign language 2 recommended. 3 history also recommended. **Test requirements:** SAT or ACT; score report by March 1.

1992 FRESHMAN CLASS PROFILE. 299 men and women enrolled. 70% had high school GPA of 3.0 or higher, 30% between 2.0 and 2.99. **Characteristics:** 55% from in state, 95% live in college housing, 23% have minority backgrounds, 8% join fraternities/sororities. Average age is 18.

FALL-TERM APPLICATIONS. $30 fee, may be waived for applicants with need. Closing date August 1; priority given to applications received by March 1; applicants notified on a rolling basis beginning on or about December 1; must reply by May 1. Audition required for music applicants. Essay required. Interview recommended. Portfolio recommended for art (slides only) applicants. Interview required of Johnston Center for Individualized Learning applicants; recommended for others. CRDA. Deferred and early admission available.

STUDENT LIFE. Housing: Dormitories (men, women, coed); apartment, fraternity, sorority, cooperative housing available. **Activities:** Student government, magazine, radio, student newspaper, yearbook, choral groups, concert band, dance, drama, jazz band, music ensembles, musical theater, opera, pep band, symphony orchestra, fraternities, sororities, Intervarsity Christian Fellowship, Amnesty International, Student Volunteers, Black Student Union, Hillel, Women's Center, international, political, feminist, and cultural groups.

ATHLETICS. NCAA. **Intercollegiate:** Baseball M, basketball, cross-country, football M, golf M, soccer, softball W, swimming, tennis, track and field, volleyball W, water polo M. **Intramural:** Basketball, racquetball, soccer, softball, swimming, table tennis, tennis, volleyball, water polo W.

STUDENT SERVICES. Aptitude testing, career counseling, employment service for undergraduates, freshman orientation, health services, personal counseling, placement service for graduates, special adviser for adult students, veterans counselor, chaplain, services/facilities for handicapped.

ANNUAL EXPENSES. Tuition and fees: $15,760. **Room and board:** $5,999. **Books and supplies:** $600.

FINANCIAL AID. 86% of freshmen, 76% of continuing students receive some form of aid. 86% of grants, 65% of loans, 70% of jobs based on need. Academic, music/drama, art, leadership, minority scholarships available. **Aid applications:** Closing date June 30; priority given to applications received by March 1; applicants notified on or about March 31; must reply within 15 days. **Additional information:** Parent Assistance Loan and Whitehead Loan programs.

ADDRESS/TELEPHONE. Paul M. Driscoll, Dean of Admissions, University of Redlands, PO Box 3080, 1200 E. Colton Avenue, Redlands, CA 92373-0999. (714) 793-2121 ext. 4074. Fax: (714) 793-2029.

University of San Diego
San Diego, California CB code: 4849

Admissions:	71% of applicants accepted
Based on:	••• School record, test scores
	•• Activities, essay, recommendations
	• Special talents
Completion:	95% of freshmen end year in good standing
	65% graduate, 45% of these enter graduate study

4-year private university, coed, affiliated with Roman Catholic Church. Founded in 1949. **Accreditation:** Regional. **Undergraduate enrollment:** 1,611 men, 2,094 women full time; 81 men, 128 women part time. **Graduate enrollment:** 584 men, 606 women full time; 429 men, 550 women part time. **Faculty:** 476 total (273 full time), 354 with doctorates or other terminal degrees. **Location:** Urban campus in very large city; 5 miles from downtown. **Calendar:** 4-1-4, extensive summer session. **Microcomputers:** 182 located in dormitories, libraries, classrooms, computer centers. **Special facilities:** Sea World/Hubbs Institute Research facilities available to marine studies students.

DEGREES OFFERED. BA, BS, MA, MS, MBA, MFA, MEd, EdD, JD. 944 bachelor's degrees awarded in 1992. 42% in business and management, 7% communications, 5% education, 6% letters/literature, 5% life sciences, 8% psychology, 16% social sciences. Graduate degrees offered in 23 major fields of study.

UNDERGRADUATE MAJORS. Accounting, anthropology, biology, business administration and management, business and management, business economics, chemistry, communications, computer and information sciences, economics, electrical/electronics/communications engineering, elementary education, English, fine arts, French, history, humanities, international relations, Latin American studies, marine biology, mathematics, music, nursing, oceanography, philosophy, physics, political science and government, psychology, religion, secondary education, sociology, Spanish.

ACADEMIC PROGRAMS. Double major, education specialist degree, honors program, independent study, internships, semester at sea, study abroad, teacher preparation, visiting/exchange student program, ocean studies and marine science with Hubbs Sea World; liberal arts/career combination in engineering; combined bachelor's/graduate program in business administration, law. **Remedial services:** Reduced course load, special counselor, tutoring, writing clinic, math clinic. **ROTC:** Air Force, Army, Naval. **Placement/credit:** AP, CLEP General and Subject, IB, institutional tests.

ACADEMIC REQUIREMENTS. Freshmen must earn minimum GPA of 2.0 to continue in good standing. 85% of freshmen return for sophomore year. Students must declare major by end of second year. **Graduation requirements:** 124 hours for bachelor's. Most students required to take courses in arts/fine arts, English, foreign languages, history, humanities, mathematics, philosophy/religion, biological/physical sciences, social sciences. **Postgraduate studies:** 7% enter law school, 3% enter medical school, 20% enter MBA programs, 15% enter other graduate study. **Additional information:** 2-year bachelor's nursing program available for registered nurses.

FRESHMAN ADMISSIONS. Selection criteria: School achievement record, test scores, recommendations, and extracurricular activities important. Out-of-state and international applicants encouraged. Special consideration given to underrepresented and economically disadvantaged students.

High school preparation: 16 units required; 20 recommended. Required and recommended units include English 4, foreign language 2-4, mathematics 3-4, social science 2-3 and science 3-4. **Test requirements:** SAT or ACT (SAT preferred); score report by March 1.

1992 FRESHMAN CLASS PROFILE. 1,571 men applied, 1,058 accepted, 405 enrolled; 2,015 women applied, 1,488 accepted, 525 enrolled. 72% had high school GPA of 3.0 or higher, 28% between 2.0 and 2.99. **Academic background:** Mid 50% of enrolled freshmen had SAT-V between 420-520, SAT-M between 490-590. 96% submitted SAT scores. **Characteristics:** 64% from in state, 85% live in college housing, 29% have minority backgrounds, 2% are foreign students, 15% join fraternities/sororities. Average age is 18.

FALL-TERM APPLICATIONS. $35 fee, may be waived for applicants with need. Closing date February 1; applicants notified on or about April 15; must reply by May 1. Essay required. CRDA. Institutional early decision plan.

STUDENT LIFE. Housing: Dormitories (men, women, coed); apartment, handicapped housing available. Freshman required to live on campus unless living with parents. **Activities:** Student government, magazine, student newspaper, yearbook, choral groups, dance, drama, jazz band, music ensembles, musical theater, opera, pep band, symphony orchestra, fraternities, sororities, campus ministry, international students association, Black Student Union, Asian Student Association, Young Democrats/Republicans, Hawaiian Club, Mecha.

ATHLETICS. NCAA. **Intercollegiate:** Baseball M, basketball, cross-country, diving W, football M, golf M, rowing (crew), soccer, softball W, swimming W, tennis, volleyball W. **Intramural:** Basketball, bowling, cross-country, fencing, golf, lacrosse M, rugby M, soccer, softball, swimming, tennis, volleyball, water polo.

STUDENT SERVICES. Aptitude testing, career counseling, employment service for undergraduates, freshman orientation, health services, on-campus day care, personal counseling, placement service for graduates, veterans counselor, services/facilities for handicapped.

ANNUAL EXPENSES. Tuition and fees: $12,990. **Room and board:** $6,400. **Books and supplies:** $550. **Other expenses:** $1,350.

FINANCIAL AID. 61% of freshmen, 52% of continuing students receive some form of aid. 95% of grants, 90% of loans, 63% of jobs based on need. 457 enrolled freshmen were judged to have need, all were offered aid. Academic, athletic, leadership scholarships available. **Aid applications:** No closing date; priority given to applications received by February 20; applicants notified on a rolling basis beginning on or about April 15; must reply by May 1 or within 2 weeks if notified thereafter.

ADDRESS/TELEPHONE. Warren W. Muller, Director of Admissions, University of San Diego, 5998 Alcala Park, San Diego, CA 92110. (619) 260-4506. (800) 248-4873. Fax: (619) 260-6836.

University of San Francisco

San Francisco, California — CB code: 4850

Admissions: 76% of applicants accepted
Based on: ••• Recommendations, school record, test scores
•• Essay
• Activities, interview, special talents
Completion: 90% of freshmen end year in good standing
60% graduate, 42% of these enter graduate study

4-year private university, coed, affiliated with Roman Catholic Church. Founded in 1855. **Accreditation:** Regional. **Undergraduate enrollment:** 1,436 men, 2,226 women full time; 87 men, 112 women part time. **Graduate enrollment:** 775 men, 1,021 women full time; 451 men, 497 women part time. **Faculty:** 713 total (249 full time), 214 with doctorates or other terminal degrees. **Location:** Urban campus in very large city; 3 miles from downtown. **Calendar:** 4-1-4, extensive summer session. Saturday and extensive evening/early morning classes. **Microcomputers:** 150 located in libraries, classrooms, computer centers. **Special facilities:** Rare book room, Institute for Chinese Western Cultural History, electron microscope, separate law library available to all students. **Additional facts:** Catholic Jesuit institution.

DEGREES OFFERED. BA, BS, BFA, MA, MS, MBA, EdD, JD. 1,186 bachelor's degrees awarded in 1992. 16% in business and management, 5% communications, 14% computer sciences, 8% health sciences, 30% multi/interdisciplinary studies, 9% social sciences. Graduate degrees offered in 43 major fields of study.

UNDERGRADUATE MAJORS. Accounting, advertising, applied science and business, art education, biology, biophysics, business administration and management, business and management, business education, chemistry, communications, community services, computer and information sciences, computer engineering, conservation and regulation, drawing, early childhood education, economics, electrical/electronics/communications engineering, elementary education, engineering physics, English, English education, environmental science, fashion design, finance, fine arts, foreign languages education, French, graphic design, history, hotel/motel and restaurant management, human resources development, illustration design, information sciences and systems, interior design, international business management, investments and securities, journalism, junior high education, labor/industrial relations, liberal/general studies, management information systems, marketing management, mathematics, mathematics education, nursing, operations research, organizational behavior, painting, personnel management, philosophy, photography, physical education, physics, political science and government, predentistry, premedicine, prepharmacy, preveterinary, psychology, public administration, radio/television broadcasting, religion, renewable natural resources, science education, sculpture, secondary education, social psychology, social science education, social sciences, sociology, Spanish, sports medicine, theological studies.

ACADEMIC PROGRAMS. Accelerated program, double major, dual enrollment of high school students, external degree, honors program, independent study, internships, student-designed major, study abroad, teacher preparation, visiting/exchange student program, New York semester, cross-registration; liberal arts/career combination in business; combined bachelor's/graduate program in business administration, law. **Remedial services:** Learning center, preadmission summer program, reduced course load, tutoring. **ROTC:** Air Force, Army. **Placement/credit:** AP, CLEP General and Subject, institutional tests; 9 credit hours maximum for bachelor's degree.

ACADEMIC REQUIREMENTS. Freshmen must earn minimum GPA of 2.0 to continue in good standing. 88% of freshmen return for sophomore year. Students must declare major by end of second year. **Graduation requirements:** 128 hours for bachelor's. Most students required to take courses in arts/fine arts, computer science, English, foreign languages, history, humanities, mathematics, philosophy/religion, biological/physical sciences, social sciences. **Postgraduate studies:** 5% enter law school, 6% enter medical school, 15% enter MBA programs, 16% enter other graduate study. **Additional information:** Rehabilitation administration program for government employees.

FRESHMAN ADMISSIONS. Selection criteria: School achievement record, test scores, class rank, school attended, recommendations, extracurricular activities, alumni relationship, personal essay. **High school preparation:** 20 units recommended. Recommended units include English 4, foreign language 2, mathematics 3, social science 3 and science 2. One chemistry and 1 biology or physics required of nursing and science applicants. **Test requirements:** SAT or ACT (SAT preferred); score report by July 1.

1992 FRESHMAN CLASS PROFILE. 748 men applied, 525 accepted, 174 enrolled; 1,259 women applied, 994 accepted, 325 enrolled. 76% had high school GPA of 3.0 or higher, 24% between 2.0 and 2.99. **Academic background:** Mid 50% of enrolled freshmen had SAT-V between 400-550, SAT-M between 450-560; ACT composite between 19-24. 92% submitted SAT scores, 14% submitted ACT scores. **Characteristics:** 50% from in state, 60% live in college housing, 44% have minority backgrounds, 11% are foreign students, 10% join fraternities/sororities. Average age is 18.

FALL-TERM APPLICATIONS. $35 fee, may be waived for applicants with need. No closing date; priority given to applications received by March 2; applicants notified on a rolling basis; must reply by May 1 or within 2 weeks if notified thereafter. Essay required. Interview recommended. CRDA. Deferred and early admission available.

STUDENT LIFE. Housing: Dormitories (women, coed). Freshman and sophomores under 21 required to live in residence halls; if they have permanent address within 20 mile radius of campus, eligible for exemption. **Activities:** Student government, magazine, radio, student newspaper, yearbook, choral groups, dance, drama, jazz band, musical theater, pep band, fraternities, sororities, St. Ignatius Institute, International Students Association, Greek Council, 13 ethnic clubs, People Advocating Cultural Endeavors.

ATHLETICS. NCAA. **Intercollegiate:** Baseball M, basketball, cross-country, golf, rifle, soccer, tennis, volleyball W. **Intramural:** Badminton, basketball, bowling, cross-country, fencing, field hockey, handball, lacrosse M, racquetball, rowing (crew) M, rugby M, sailing, skiing, soccer, softball, swimming, table tennis, tennis, track and field, volleyball.

STUDENT SERVICES. Aptitude testing, career counseling, employment service for undergraduates, freshman orientation, health services, personal counseling, placement service for graduates, services/facilities for handicapped.

ANNUAL EXPENSES. Tuition and fees: $12,578. **Room and board:** $6,174. **Books and supplies:** $725. **Other expenses:** $1,800.

FINANCIAL AID. 37% of freshmen, 49% of continuing students receive some form of aid. 75% of grants, 68% of loans, 36% of jobs based on need. 236 enrolled freshmen were judged to have need, 226 were offered aid. Academic, athletic, state/district residency, leadership scholarships available. **Aid applications:** No closing date; priority given to applications received by March 2; applicants notified on a rolling basis beginning on or about April 1; must reply by May 1 or within 2 weeks if notified thereafter. **Additional information:** 12-month budget plan and individualized installment plans available.

ADDRESS/TELEPHONE. William A. Henley, Director of Admissions, University of San Francisco, 2130 Fulton Street, San Francisco, CA 94117-1080. (415) 666-6563. (800) 225-5873. Fax: (415) 666-2217.

University of Southern California
Los Angeles, California CB code: 4852

Admissions: 68% of applicants accepted
Based on: ••• School record, test scores
•• Essay, interview
• Activities, recommendations, special talents
Completion: 60% graduate

4-year private university, coed. Founded in 1880. **Accreditation:** Regional. **Undergraduate enrollment:** 13,249 men and women full time; 1,459 men and women part time. **Graduate enrollment:** 6,516 men and women full time; 4,943 men and women part time. **Faculty:** 3,086 total (2,172 full time). **Location:** Urban campus in very large city; 3 miles from downtown. **Calendar:** Semester, extensive summer session. Saturday and extensive evening/early morning classes. **Microcomputers:** 600 located in dormitories, libraries, classrooms, computer centers. **Special facilities:** 4 art galleries, marine science center on Santa Catalina Island, permanent facilities for study in Sacramento and Washington, D.C., special collections library, the Gamble House designed by Greene and Greene, and Freeman House designed by Frank Lloyd Wright.

DEGREES OFFERED. BA, BS, BFA, BArch, MA, MS, MBA, MFA, MEd, MSW, PhD, EdD, DMD, MD, B. Pharm. 3,343 bachelor's degrees awarded in 1992. 32% in business and management, 13% communications, 11% engineering, 12% social sciences, 8% visual and performing arts. Graduate degrees offered in 128 major fields of study.

UNDERGRADUATE MAJORS. Accounting, aerospace/aeronautical/astronautical engineering, American literature, American studies, anthropology, architectural engineering, architecture, art history, astronomy, bioengineering and biomedical engineering, biology, biomedical/electrical engineering, biomedical/mechanical engineering, business administration and management, chemical engineering, chemistry, cinematography/film, city/community/regional planning, civil engineering, civil engineering construction, civil engineering structural, civil engineering-water resources, classics, communications, comparative literature, computer and information sciences, creative writing, dental hygiene, directing, dramatic arts, East Asian studies, economics, education, electrical/electronics/communications engineering, elementary education, engineering and other disciplines, engineering mechanics, English, English literature, environmental health engineering, Ethics, ethnic studies, Exercise science, film arts, fine arts, French, geography, geology, German, gerontology, Greek (classical), history, humanities and social sciences, industrial engineering, international relations, Italian, jazz, Jewish studies, journalism, Latin, linguistics, mathematics, mechanical engineering, music, music education, music performance, music recording, music theory and composition, nursing, occupational therapy, petroleum engineering, philosophy, photography, physical sciences, physics, political science and government, psychobiology, psycholinguistics, psychology, public administration, public relations, radio/television broadcasting, religion, Russian, Russian and Slavic studies, Safety, sociology, Spanish, stage management, studio art, theater design, urban studies, women's studies.

ACADEMIC PROGRAMS. Accelerated program, cooperative education, double major, dual enrollment of high school students, honors program, independent study, internships, student-designed major, study abroad, teacher preparation, visiting/exchange student program, Washington semester, cross-registration; liberal arts/career combination in engineering. **Remedial services:** Learning center, remedial instruction, special counselor, tutoring, American Language Institute. **ROTC:** Air Force, Army, Naval. **Placement/credit:** AP, IB, institutional tests; 32 credit hours maximum for bachelor's degree.

ACADEMIC REQUIREMENTS. Freshmen must earn minimum GPA of 2.0 to continue in good standing. 86% of freshmen return for sophomore year. Students must declare major by end of second year. **Graduation requirements:** 128 hours for bachelor's (32 in major). Most students required to take courses in arts/fine arts, English, foreign languages, history, humanities, philosophy/religion, biological/physical sciences, social sciences.

FRESHMAN ADMISSIONS. Selection criteria: Academic achievement, curriculum and test scores most important. Recommendations, activities, and class rank considered. **High school preparation:** 16 units recommended. Recommended units include English 4, foreign language 2, mathematics 3, social science 2 and science 2. 3 elective courses recommended. **Test requirements:** SAT or ACT (SAT preferred); score report by April 30.

1992 FRESHMAN CLASS PROFILE. 13,362 men and women applied, 9,088 accepted; 2,429 enrolled. 78% had high school GPA of 3.0 or higher, 22% between 2.0 and 2.99. 44% were in top tenth and 73% were in top quarter of graduating class. **Academic background:** Mid 50% of enrolled freshmen had SAT-V between 440-570, SAT-M between 530-660; ACT composite between 23-29. 95% submitted SAT scores, 27% submitted ACT scores. **Characteristics:** 57% from in state, 85% live in college housing, 37% have minority backgrounds, 5% are foreign students. Average age is 18.

FALL-TERM APPLICATIONS. $50 fee, may be waived for applicants with need. No closing date; priority given to applications received by February 1; applicants notified on a rolling basis. Audition required for music, drama applicants. Portfolio required for drama, fine arts applicants. Essay required. Interview recommended. CRDA. Deferred and early admission available. Recommend students take 3 achievement tests, including English Composition.

STUDENT LIFE. Housing: Dormitories (men, women, coed); apartment, fraternity, sorority housing available. Faculty-in-residence programs and residential college housing options offered. Honors housing opportunities available. **Activities:** Student government, film, magazine, radio, student newspaper, yearbook, choral groups, concert band, dance, drama, jazz band, marching band, music ensembles, musical theater, opera, symphony orchestra, fraternities, sororities, Academic Honors Assembly, Emerging Leaders Program, Minority Consortium, Religious Council, Residential Community Council, Student Program Board, Student Senate, Student Volunteers Center.

ATHLETICS. NCAA. **Intercollegiate:** Baseball M, basketball, cross-country, diving, football M, golf, rowing (crew), sailing M, swimming, tennis, track and field, volleyball, water polo M. **Intramural:** Badminton, basketball, bowling M, fencing, golf, gymnastics, horseback riding, ice hockey, lacrosse M, racquetball, rifle, rugby, sailing, skiing, soccer, softball, squash, swimming, table tennis, tennis, track and field, volleyball, wrestling.

STUDENT SERVICES. Aptitude testing, career counseling, employment service for undergraduates, freshman orientation, health services, on-campus day care, personal counseling, placement service for graduates, veterans counselor, services/facilities for handicapped.

ANNUAL EXPENSES. Tuition and fees: $16,810. **Room and board:** $6,244. **Books and supplies:** $600. **Other expenses:** $1,630.

FINANCIAL AID. 58% of freshmen, 53% of continuing students receive some form of aid. 88% of grants, 81% of loans, all jobs based on need. Academic, music/drama, art, athletic, leadership, alumni affiliation, minority scholarships available. **Aid applications:** Closing date August 15; priority given to applications received by February 15; applicants notified on a rolling basis beginning on or about April 1; must reply by May 1 or within 2 weeks if notified thereafter.

ADDRESS/TELEPHONE. Clifford F. Sjogren, Dean of Admissions and Financial Aid, University of Southern California, University Park, Los Angeles, CA 90089-0911. (213) 740-1111. Fax: (213) 740-6364.

University of West Los Angeles
Inglewood, California CB code: 0957

2-year upper-division private college of law and paralegal studies, coed. Founded in 1966. **Accreditation:** Regional. **Undergraduate enrollment:** 250 men and women. **Graduate enrollment:** 550 men and women. **Faculty:** 51 total (6 full time), 45 with doctorates or other terminal degrees. **Location:** Urban campus in very large city; 10 miles from downtown. **Calendar:** Trimester, limited summer session. Extensive evening/early morning classes. **Microcomputers:** 12 located in libraries, computer centers.

DEGREES OFFERED. BS. 33 bachelor's degrees awarded in 1992. 100% in law. Graduate degrees offered in 1 major field of study.

UNDERGRADUATE MAJORS. Legal assistant/paralegal.

ACADEMIC PROGRAMS. Accelerated program, internships. **Remedial services:** Learning center, reduced course load, remedial instruction, special counselor, tutoring. **Placement/credit:** CLEP General and Subject; 30 credit hours maximum for bachelor's degree.

ACADEMIC REQUIREMENTS. Students must declare major on application. **Graduation requirements:** 120 hours for bachelor's (45 in major). Most students required to take courses in arts/fine arts, English, foreign languages, history, humanities, mathematics, philosophy/religion, biological/physical sciences, social sciences. **Postgraduate studies:** 10% enter law school, 1% enter MBA programs, 5% enter other graduate study.

STUDENT LIFE. Activities: Student government, student newspaper, Hispanic Law Students Association, Black American Law Students Association, law fraternity. **Additional information:** 80% evening students.

STUDENT SERVICES. Career counseling, employment service for undergraduates, personal counseling, placement service for graduates, veterans counselor, services/facilities for handicapped.

ANNUAL EXPENSES. Tuition and fees (1992-93): $4,640. **Books and supplies:** $250. **Other expenses:** $1,500.

FINANCIAL AID. 30% of continuing students receive some form of aid. All grants, 96% of loans based on need. **Aid applications:** No closing date; priority given to applications received by June 1; applicants notified on a rolling basis beginning on or about June 1; must reply within 4 weeks.

ADDRESS/TELEPHONE. Scott Dicks, Director of Admisssions: School of Paralegal Studies, University of West Los Angeles, 1155 West Arbor Vitae Street, Inglewood, CA 90301. (310) 215-3339. Fax: (310) 670-9331.

Ventura College
Ventura, California CB code: 4931

2-year public community college, coed. Founded in 1925. **Accreditation:** Regional. **Undergraduate enrollment:** 12,200 men and women. **Faculty:** 575 total (175 full time), 65 with doctorates or other terminal degrees. **Location:** Suburban campus in small city; 60 miles from Los Angeles. **Calendar:** Semester, limited summer session. **Microcomputers:** Located in libraries, classrooms, computer centers. **Special facilities:** Theater, 2 art galleries.

DEGREES OFFERED. AA, AS. 884 associate degrees awarded in 1992. 9% in health sciences, 53% multi/interdisciplinary studies, 25% trade and industry.

UNDERGRADUATE MAJORS. Accounting, Afro-American (black) studies, agribusiness, agricultural sciences, agronomy, allied health, animal sciences, anthropology, architectural technologies, architecture, automotive mechanics, automotive technology, bilingual/bicultural education, biology, botany, business administration and management, business and management, business and office, business data processing and related programs, business data programming, business economics, ceramics, chemistry, child development/care/guidance, civil technology, communications, computer and information sciences, computer programming, criminal justice technology, data processing, dietetic aide/assistant, drafting and design technology, dramatic arts, economics, education, electronic technology, emergency medical technologies, engineering, engineering and engineering-related technologies, English, fashion design, fashion merchandising, finance, fine arts, French, geography, geology, German, graphic arts technology, health sciences, Hispanic American studies, history, home economics, horticulture, human resources development, industrial technology, information sciences and systems, interior design, journalism, law enforcement and corrections technologies, legal secretary, liberal/general studies, management information systems, management science, marketing and distribution, marketing management, masonry/tile setting, mathematics, mechanical design technology, medical records technology, medical secretary, mental health/human services, Mexican American studies, music, nursing, ornamental horticulture, personnel management, philosophy, photographic technology, physical sciences, physics, plant protection, plant sciences, plumbing/pipefitting/steamfitting, political science and government, practical nursing, precision metal work, predentistry, prelaw, premedicine, prepharmacy, preveterinary, psychology, public affairs, quality control technology, real estate, recreation and community services technologies, renewable natural resources, secretarial and related programs, social sciences, sociology, soil sciences, Spanish, speech, water and wastewater technology, welding technology, zoology.

ACADEMIC PROGRAMS. 2-year transfer program, dual enrollment of high school students, honors program, independent study, study abroad, cross-registration. **Remedial services:** Learning center, reduced course load, remedial instruction, special counselor, tutoring, diagnostic testing. **Placement/credit:** AP, institutional tests; 12 credit hours maximum for associate degree.

ACADEMIC REQUIREMENTS. Freshmen must earn minimum GPA of 2.0 to continue in good standing. 66% of freshmen return for sophomore year. Students must declare major by end of first year. **Graduation requirements:** 60 hours for associate (18 in major). Most students required to take courses in English, history, humanities, mathematics, biological/physical sciences, social sciences.

FRESHMAN ADMISSIONS. Selection criteria: Open admissions. Selective admissions to nursing program.

1992 FRESHMAN CLASS PROFILE. 12,200 men and women enrolled. **Characteristics:** 99% from in state, 100% commute, 27% have minority backgrounds. Average age is 21.

FALL-TERM APPLICATIONS. No fee. No closing date; applicants notified on a rolling basis. Deferred and early admission available.

STUDENT LIFE. Activities: Student government, magazine, student newspaper, choral groups, concert band, dance, drama, music ensembles, musical theater, symphony orchestra, religious, ethnic, political, and special interest organizations, Internation Student Club.

ATHLETICS. Intercollegiate: Baseball M, basketball, cross-country, diving, football M, golf M, rifle M, softball W, swimming, tennis, track and field, volleyball M, water polo M.

STUDENT SERVICES. Career counseling, employment service for undergraduates, health services, on-campus day care, personal counseling, placement service for graduates, special adviser for adult students, veterans counselor, services/facilities for handicapped.

ANNUAL EXPENSES. Tuition and fees (projected): $300, $3,300 additional for out-of-state students. **Books and supplies:** $600. **Other expenses:** $1,300.

FINANCIAL AID. 15% of freshmen, 20% of continuing students receive some form of aid. 91% of grants, 89% of loans, 48% of jobs based on need. Music/drama, art, leadership scholarships available. **Aid applications:** Closing date May 1; priority given to applications received by March 2; applicants notified on a rolling basis beginning on or about July 30.

ADDRESS/TELEPHONE. Joan Halk, Registrar, Ventura College, 4667 Telegraph Road, Ventura, CA 93003. (805) 642-3211. Fax: (805) 654-6466.

Victor Valley College
Victorville, California CB code: 4932

2-year public community college, coed. Founded in 1960. **Accreditation:** Regional. **Undergraduate enrollment:** 2,192 men and women full time; 5,552 men and women part time. **Faculty:** 373 total (88 full time), 12 with doctorates or other terminal degrees. **Location:** Rural campus in small city; 35 miles from San Bernardino. **Calendar:** Semester, limited summer session. Saturday and extensive evening/early morning classes. **Microcomputers:** 250 located in computer centers.

DEGREES OFFERED. AA, AS. 626 associate degrees awarded in 1992. 17% in business and management, 21% health sciences, 6% life sciences, 34% multi/interdisciplinary studies, 9% trade and industry.

UNDERGRADUATE MAJORS. Automotive mechanics, automotive technology, biology, business and management, business and office, business data entry equipment operation, business data processing and related programs, business data programming, child development/care/guidance, computer and information sciences, construction, electronic technology, fine arts, fire control and safety technology, law enforcement and corrections technologies, liberal/general studies, mathematics, nursing, ornamental horticulture, physical sciences, real estate, respiratory therapy technology, science technologies, secretarial and related programs, teacher aide.

ACADEMIC PROGRAMS. 2-year transfer program, cooperative education, double major, dual enrollment of high school students, honors program, independent study, study abroad, telecourses. **Remedial services:** Learning center, preadmission summer program, reduced course load, remedial instruction, special counselor, tutoring. **Placement/credit:** CLEP General and Subject, institutional tests; 32 credit hours maximum for associate degree.

ACADEMIC REQUIREMENTS. Freshmen must earn minimum GPA of 2.0 to continue in good standing. Students must declare major on application. **Graduation requirements:** 60 hours for associate (18 in major). Most students required to take courses in English, humanities, mathematics, biological/physical sciences, social sciences.

FRESHMAN ADMISSIONS. Selection criteria: Open admissions. Selective admissions to some programs. High school algebra, biology, chemistry required of nursing and health applicants.

1992 FRESHMAN CLASS PROFILE. 3,091 men and women enrolled. **Characteristics:** 91% from in state, 100% commute, 33% have minority backgrounds. Average age is 25.

FALL-TERM APPLICATIONS. No fee. No closing date; applicants notified on a rolling basis. Interview required for nursing, health applicants. Early admission available. Closing date for applications to health programs is March 1.

STUDENT LIFE. Activities: Student government, yearbook, choral groups, concert band, dance, drama, jazz band, music ensembles, musical theater, opera, symphony orchestra.

ATHLETICS. NJCAA. **Intercollegiate:** Baseball M, basketball, football M, golf, soccer M, softball W, tennis, volleyball W.

STUDENT SERVICES. Aptitude testing, career counseling, employment service for undergraduates, freshman orientation, on-campus day care, personal counseling, placement service for graduates, veterans counselor, services/facilities for handicapped.

ANNUAL EXPENSES. Tuition and fees (1992-93): $120, $2,910 additional for out-of-state students. **Books and supplies:** $576. **Other expenses:** $1,000.

FINANCIAL AID. 15% of continuing students receive some form of aid. All jobs based on need. 480 enrolled freshmen were judged to have need, all were offered aid. Academic scholarships available. **Aid applications:** No closing date; applicants notified on a rolling basis beginning on or about August 1; must reply within 2 weeks. **Additional information:** Board of Governors grant pays enrollment fee in full for low-income students.

ADDRESS/TELEPHONE. Laura White, Dean Student Services, Victor Valley College, 18422 Bear Valley Road, Victorville, CA 92392-9699. (619) 245-4271. Fax: (619) 245-9745.

Vista Community College
Berkeley, California CB code: 7711

2-year public community college, coed. Founded in 1974. **Accreditation:** Regional. **Undergraduate enrollment:** 4,022 men and women. **Location:** Urban campus in small city; 15 miles from San Francisco. **Calendar:** Semester. **Additional facts:** Noncampus college conducting approximately 200 classes each semester in 125 locations located in 6 cities adjacent to Berkeley. Access to other Peralta community college district libraries.

FRESHMAN ADMISSIONS. Selection criteria: Open admissions.

ANNUAL EXPENSES. Tuition and fees (1992-93): $120, $3,510 additional for out-of-state students. **Books and supplies:** $576.

ADDRESS/TELEPHONE. Howard Perdue, Dean of Admissions and Records, Vista Community College, 2020 Milvia Street, Berkeley, CA 94704. (510) 841-8431. Fax: (510) 841-7333.

West Coast University
Los Angeles, California CB code: 4966

4-year private university, coed. Founded in 1909. **Accreditation:** Regional. **Undergraduate enrollment:** 625 men, 150 women full time; 150 men, 50 women part time. **Graduate enrollment:** 425 men, 100 women full time; 150 men, 40 women part time. **Faculty:** 150 total, 75 with doctorates or other terminal degrees. **Location:** Urban campus in very large city. **Calendar:** Six

8-week terms (semisemesters). 4 terms equal conventional academic year. **Microcomputers:** Located in classrooms, computer centers. **Additional facts:** Evening only associate, bachelor's and master's programs offered in business and management, computer science, and engineering at five sites: Los Angeles, Vandenberg Air Force Base, Orange, San Diego and Camasillo.

DEGREES OFFERED. AS, BA, BS, MS, MBA. 10 associate degrees awarded in 1992. 33% in business and management, 34% computer sciences, 33% engineering. 90 bachelor's degrees awarded. 35% in business and management, 30% computer sciences, 35% engineering. Graduate degrees offered in 18 major fields of study.

UNDERGRADUATE MAJORS. Associate: Accounting, business and management, computer and information sciences, electrical/electronics/communications engineering, engineering and engineering-related technologies, health sciences, industrial engineering, industrial technology, information sciences and systems, management information systems, manufacturing technology, mechanical engineering. **Bachelor's:** Accounting, business administration and management, business and management, computer and information sciences, electrical/electronics/communications engineering, engineering and engineering-related technologies, industrial engineering, industrial technology, information sciences and systems, management information systems, manufacturing technology, mechanical engineering, robotics.

ACADEMIC PROGRAMS. 2-year transfer program, accelerated program, internships, cross-registration; combined bachelor's/graduate program in business administration. **Remedial services:** Reduced course load, tutoring. **Placement/credit:** AP, CLEP General and Subject, institutional tests; 12 credit hours maximum for associate degree; 12 credit hours maximum for bachelor's degree.

ACADEMIC REQUIREMENTS. Freshmen must earn minimum GPA of 2.0 to continue in good standing. Students must declare major on enrollment. **Graduation requirements:** 60 hours for associate (12 in major), 124 hours for bachelor's (40 in major). Most students required to take courses in arts/fine arts, English, history, humanities, mathematics, philosophy/religion, biological/physical sciences, social sciences. **Postgraduate studies:** 90% from 2-year programs enter 4-year programs. **Additional information:** In-plant certificate programs for business and industry also offered.

FRESHMAN ADMISSIONS. Selection criteria: Open admissions.

1992 FRESHMAN CLASS PROFILE. Characteristics: 85% from in state, 20% have minority backgrounds, 15% are foreign students. Average age is 23.

FALL-TERM APPLICATIONS. $35 fee. No closing date; applicants notified on a rolling basis. Deferred admission available. Foreign students must reply within 60 days.

STUDENT LIFE. Activities: Student newsletter.

STUDENT SERVICES. Academic counseling.

ANNUAL EXPENSES. Tuition and fees: $9,155. **Books and supplies:** $500.

FINANCIAL AID. 15% of continuing students receive some form of aid. All grants, 56% of loans, all jobs based on need. **Aid applications:** Closing date June 1; applicants notified on a rolling basis; must reply within 30 days.

ADDRESS/TELEPHONE. Roger A. Miller, Dean of Admissions and Registrar, West Coast University, 440 Shatto Place, Los Angeles, CA 90020-1765. (213) 487-4433. Fax: (213) 380-4362.

West Hills Community College
Coalinga, California — CB code: 4056

2-year public community college, coed. Founded in 1932. **Accreditation:** Regional. **Undergraduate enrollment:** 340 men, 364 women full time; 1,244 men, 1,233 women part time. **Faculty:** 113 total (44 full time), 8 with doctorates or other terminal degrees. **Location:** Rural campus in small town; 60 miles from Fresno. **Calendar:** Semester, limited summer session. **Microcomputers:** 10 located in libraries, classrooms.

DEGREES OFFERED. AA, AS. 127 associate degrees awarded in 1992. 6% in agriculture, 28% business and management, 40% multi/interdisciplinary studies, 6% parks/recreation, protective services, public affairs, 20% trade and industry.

UNDERGRADUATE MAJORS. Accounting, agribusiness, agricultural business and management, agricultural mechanics, agricultural sciences, agronomy, animal sciences, art history, automotive mechanics, automotive technology, biological and physical sciences, biology, botany, business administration and management, business and management, business and office, business computer/console/peripheral equipment operation, business data processing and related programs, business data programming, chemistry, commercial art, computer and information sciences, criminology, dairy, diesel engine mechanics, early childhood education, education, engineering, engineering and engineering-related technologies, engineering and other disciplines, entomology, geography, geology, graphic arts technology, horticultural science, humanities and social sciences, industrial technology, journalism, law enforcement and corrections, law enforcement and corrections technologies, liberal/general studies, marketing and distribution, mathematics, medical secretary, music, physical education, physical sciences, physics, precision metal work, predentistry, premedicine, prepharmacy, psychology, real estate, science technologies, secretarial and related programs, social sciences, soil sciences, studio art, welding technology, word processing.

ACADEMIC PROGRAMS. 2-year transfer program, cooperative education, dual enrollment of high school students, honors program, independent study. **Remedial services:** Learning center, reduced course load, remedial instruction, special counselor, tutoring. **Placement/credit:** CLEP General and Subject; 15 credit hours maximum for associate degree.

ACADEMIC REQUIREMENTS. Freshmen must earn minimum GPA of 2.0 to continue in good standing. 85% of freshmen return for sophomore year. Students must declare major on enrollment. **Graduation requirements:** 60 hours for associate. Most students required to take courses in arts/fine arts, English, humanities, mathematics, biological/physical sciences, social sciences.

FRESHMAN ADMISSIONS. Selection criteria: Open admissions.

1992 FRESHMAN CLASS PROFILE. 900 men and women enrolled. **Characteristics:** 85% from in state, 100% commute, 31% have minority backgrounds, 1% are foreign students.

FALL-TERM APPLICATIONS. No fee. No closing date; applicants notified on a rolling basis. Interview recommended. Early admission available.

STUDENT LIFE. Activities: Student government, student newspaper, choral groups, concert band, dance, jazz band, music ensembles, musical theater, opera, pep band.

ATHLETICS. NJCAA. **Intercollegiate:** Basketball M, football M, softball W.

STUDENT SERVICES. Career counseling, employment service for undergraduates, freshman orientation, on-campus day care, personal counseling, placement service for graduates, veterans counselor, re-entry coordinator, services/facilities for handicapped.

ANNUAL EXPENSES. Tuition and fees (projected): $268, $3,360 additional for out-of-state students. **Books and supplies:** $576. **Other expenses:** $1,728.

FINANCIAL AID. 68% of freshmen, 68% of continuing students receive some form of aid. 99% of grants, 90% of loans, 26% of jobs based on need. **Aid applications:** No closing date; priority given to applications received by March 2; applicants notified on a rolling basis beginning on or about April 30; must reply by registration.

ADDRESS/TELEPHONE. Office of Admissions, West Hills Community College, 300 Cherry Lane, Coalinga, CA 93210. (209) 935-0801 ext. 218.

West Los Angeles College
Culver City, California — CB code: 4964

2-year public community college, coed. Founded in 1968. **Accreditation:** Regional. **Undergraduate enrollment:** 9,000 men and women. **Location:** Urban campus in large town; 10 miles from Los Angeles Civic Center. **Calendar:** Semester.

FRESHMAN ADMISSIONS. Selection criteria: Open admissions.

ANNUAL EXPENSES. Tuition and fees (1992-93): $120, $3,690 additional for out-of-state students. **Books and supplies:** $576. **Other expenses:** $1,720.

ADDRESS/TELEPHONE. Office of Admissions, West Los Angeles College, 4800 Freshman Drive, Culver City, CA 90230. (310) 287-4373.

West Valley College
Saratoga, California — CB code: 4958

2-year public community college, coed. Founded in 1963. **Accreditation:** Regional. **Undergraduate enrollment:** 2,188 men, 1,892 women full time; 3,525 men, 5,472 women part time. **Faculty:** 560 total (210 full time). **Location:** Suburban campus in large town; 13 miles from San Jose. **Calendar:** Semester, limited summer session. Saturday and extensive evening/early morning classes. **Microcomputers:** 100 located in libraries, classrooms, computer centers. **Special facilities:** Planetarium.

DEGREES OFFERED. AA, AS. 597 associate degrees awarded in 1992. 8% in business and management, 9% business/office and marketing/distribution, 5% home economics, 53% multi/interdisciplinary studies.

UNDERGRADUATE MAJORS. Accounting, architecture, biology, business administration and management, business and management, business and office, chemistry, child development/care/guidance, computer and information sciences, computer programming, construction, court reporting, criminal justice studies, drafting, drafting and design technology, dramatic arts, early childhood education, engineering, English, fashion design, fashion merchandising, fine arts, foreign languages (multiple emphasis), geology, history, instrumentation technology, interior design, landscape architecture, legal assistant/paralegal, liberal/general studies, marketing and distribution, marketing management, mathematics, medical assistant, music, office supervision and management, parks and recreation management, physics, psychology, real estate, secretarial and related programs, social sciences, sociology, speech, women's studies, word processing.

ACADEMIC PROGRAMS. 2-year transfer program, double major, dual enrollment of high school students, honors program, independent study, teacher preparation. **Remedial services:** Learning center, preadmission summer program, remedial instruction, special counselor, tutoring. **ROTC:** Air Force, Army. **Placement/credit:** AP, CLEP General and Subject, institutional tests; 12 credit hours maximum for associate degree.

ACADEMIC REQUIREMENTS. Freshmen must earn minimum GPA of 2.0 to continue in good standing. 50% of freshmen return for sophomore year. **Graduation requirements:** 60 hours for associate (20 in major). Most students required to take courses in English, history, humanities, mathematics, biological/physical sciences, social sciences.

FRESHMAN ADMISSIONS. Selection criteria: Open admissions.

1992 FRESHMAN CLASS PROFILE. 2,434 men and women enrolled. **Characteristics:** 97% from in state, 100% commute, 18% have minority backgrounds, 1% are foreign students. Average age is 20.

FALL-TERM APPLICATIONS. No fee. No closing date; priority given to applications received by July 20; applicants notified on a rolling basis. Interview recommended for selected programs applicants.

STUDENT LIFE. Activities: Student government, student newspaper, television, choral groups, concert band, drama, jazz band, music ensembles, symphony orchestra, Vietnamese Student Association, Unlimited Horizons (handicapped), Descendants of Africa, Latin American Student Association, Alpha Gamma Sigma, Latter-Day Saints, Fashion Design, Puente, JC Ministries (Christian).

ATHLETICS. Intercollegiate: Baseball M, basketball, cross-country, field hockey W, football M, gymnastics W, soccer M, softball W, swimming, tennis, track and field, volleyball, water polo M, wrestling M. **Intramural:** Badminton, basketball, bowling, swimming, tennis, volleyball.

STUDENT SERVICES. Aptitude testing, career counseling, employment service for undergraduates, freshman orientation, health services, on-campus day care, personal counseling, special adviser for adult students, veterans counselor, services/facilities for handicapped.

ANNUAL EXPENSES. Tuition and fees (1992-93): $159, $3,120 additional for out-of-state students. **Books and supplies:** $504. **Other expenses:** $1,548.

FINANCIAL AID. 15% of freshmen, 10% of continuing students receive some form of aid. 94% of grants, 93% of loans, all jobs based on need. Academic, athletic, state/district residency, leadership, minority scholarships available. **Aid applications:** No closing date; priority given to applications received by May 31; applicants notified on a rolling basis beginning on or about July 16.

ADDRESS/TELEPHONE. Edward Myers, Dean of Student Services, West Valley College, 14000 Fruitvale Avenue, Saratoga, CA 95070-5698. (408) 741-2001. Fax: (408) 867-5033.

Western State University College of Law: Orange County

Fullerton, California — CB code: 1116

2-year upper-division proprietary college of law, coed. Founded in 1966. **Accreditation:** Regional. **Undergraduate enrollment:** 227 men and women. **Graduate enrollment:** 1,260 men and women. **Location:** Urban campus in small city; 30 miles from Los Angeles. **Calendar:** Semester. **Additional facts:** Undergraduate transfer students complete combined bachelor's/first professional degree program in law in 4 years. Branch campus located in Irvine.

ADMISSIONS. $35 application fee. Deferred admission available.

ANNUAL EXPENSES. Tuition and fees (1992-93): $10,960. **Books and supplies:** $576. **Other expenses:** $2,844.

ADDRESS/TELEPHONE. Joel Goodman, Vice President of Administration and Dean of Admissions, Western State University College of Law: Orange County, 1111 North State College Boulevard, Fullerton, CA 92631. (714) 738-1000. Fax: (714) 871-4806.

Westmont College

Santa Barbara, California — CB code: 4950

Admissions: 90% of applicants accepted
Based on: ••• Essay, religious affiliation/commitment, school record, test scores
•• Activities, interview, special talents
• Recommendations
Completion: 93% of freshmen end year in good standing
73% graduate, 53% of these enter graduate study

4-year private college of arts and sciences, coed, affiliated with interdenominational/evangelical. Founded in 1940. **Accreditation:** Regional. **Undergraduate enrollment:** 492 men, 821 women full time; 4 women part time. **Faculty:** 110 total (72 full time), 60 with doctorates or other terminal degrees. **Location:** Suburban campus in small city; 100 miles from Los Angeles. **Calendar:** Semester, limited summer session. **Microcomputers:** 30 located in libraries, classrooms, computer centers. **Special facilities:** Nuclear magnetic resonance spectroscope, observatory, art center with gallery, science center.

DEGREES OFFERED. BA, BS. 276 bachelor's degrees awarded in 1992. 16% in business and management, 10% communications, 12% teacher education, 12% letters/literature, 8% life sciences, 8% psychology, 20% social sciences.

UNDERGRADUATE MAJORS. Anthropology, art education, biology, business economics, chemistry, communications, computer and information sciences, dramatic arts, economics, elementary education, engineering physics, English, English education, English literature, fine arts, foreign languages (multiple emphasis), French, history, international relations, liberal/general studies, mathematics, mathematics education, music, music education, philosophy, physical education, physical sciences, physics, political science and government, predentistry, preengineering, prelaw, premedicine, prepharmacy, preveterinary, psychology, religion, religious education, science education, secondary education, social science education, social sciences, sociology, Spanish, visual and performing arts.

ACADEMIC PROGRAMS. Accelerated program, cooperative education, double major, honors program, independent study, internships, student-designed major, study abroad, teacher preparation, visiting/exchange student program, Washington semester, cross-cultural studies in Western and Eastern Europe, England, Africa, Costa Rica, and the Holy Lands; semester study available in San Francisco, Washington, D.C., and at one of the 12 other member colleges of the Christian College Consortium; liberal arts/career combination in engineering, health sciences. **Remedial services:** Learning center, special counselor, tutoring, writing center. **ROTC:** Army. **Placement/credit:** AP, CLEP General and Subject, IB, institutional tests; 20 credit hours maximum for bachelor's degree.

ACADEMIC REQUIREMENTS. Freshmen must earn minimum GPA of 2.0 to continue in good standing. 84% of freshmen return for sophomore year. Students must declare major by end of second year. **Graduation requirements:** 124 hours for bachelor's (36 in major). Most students required to take courses in arts/fine arts, English, foreign languages, history, humanities, mathematics, philosophy/religion, biological/physical sciences, social sciences. **Additional information:** Development of basic competencies and application of theory are priority concerns.

FRESHMAN ADMISSIONS. Selection criteria: Applicant's personal Christian statement, academic high school record, high school rank, and test scores. Personal interview and teacher, pastor, and other recommendations may enhance applicant's file. **High school preparation:** 16 units recommended. Recommended units include biological science 2, English 4, foreign language 2, mathematics 3 and social science 2. **Test requirements:** SAT or ACT; score report by March 1. **Additional information:** Applicants should demonstrate strong academic achievement and promising potential, have diverse interests and support values of college.

1992 FRESHMAN CLASS PROFILE. 297 men applied, 257 accepted, 123 enrolled; 615 women applied, 561 accepted, 288 enrolled. 81% had high school GPA of 3.0 or higher, 19% between 2.0 and 2.99. 28% were in top tenth and 57% were in top quarter of graduating class. **Academic background:** Mid 50% of enrolled freshmen had SAT-V between 420-530, SAT-M between 460-590; ACT composite between 21-26. 95% submitted SAT scores, 26% submitted ACT scores. **Characteristics:** 68% from in state, 100% live in college housing, 10% have minority backgrounds, 1% are foreign students. Average age is 18.

FALL-TERM APPLICATIONS. $30 fee, may be waived for applicants with need. Closing date June 1; priority given to applications received by March 1; applicants notified on a rolling basis beginning on or about January 1; must reply by May 1. Essay required. Interview recommended. CRDA. Deferred admission available. March 1 is a "preferential filing deadline" and may be extended as space remains available.

STUDENT LIFE. Housing: Dormitories (coed); apartment, handicapped housing available. Each residence hall has residence director and assistants who serve as facilitators in student development. **Activities:** Student government, magazine, radio, student newspaper, yearbook, choral groups, concert band, dance, drama, jazz band, music ensembles, musical theater, pep band, Christian Concerns, Student Missionary Fellowship, Commission on Diversity, Amnesty International, Habitat for Humanity, Potter's Clay, Barnabas, Musicians Fellowship, Weekend Warriors. **Additional information:** Students encouraged to pursue a balance of rigorous intellectual competence, healthy personal development, and strong Christian commitments. Religious observance required.

ATHLETICS. NAIA. **Intercollegiate:** Baseball M, basketball M, cross-country, soccer, tennis, track and field, volleyball W. **Intramural:** Badminton, basketball, cross-country, fencing, racquetball, softball, swimming, tennis, volleyball.

STUDENT SERVICES. Aptitude testing, career counseling, employment service for undergraduates, freshman orientation, health services, personal counseling, placement service for graduates, veterans counselor, individualized services for handicapped, services/facilities for handicapped.

ANNUAL EXPENSES. Tuition and fees: $13,660. **Room and board:** $5,072. **Books and supplies:** $480. **Other expenses:** $600.

FINANCIAL AID. 70% of freshmen, 70% of continuing students receive some form of aid. 85% of grants, 98% of loans, 24% of jobs based on need. 259 enrolled freshmen were judged to have need, all were offered aid. Academic, music/drama, art, athletic, leadership, minority scholarships available. **Aid applications:** No closing date; priority given to applications received by March 1; applicants notified on a rolling basis beginning on or about April 15; must reply by May 1 or within 2 weeks if notified thereafter.

ADDRESS/TELEPHONE. David A. Morley, Director of Admissions, Westmont College, 955 La Paz Road, Santa Barbara, CA 93108-1099. (805) 565-6200. (800) 777-9011. Fax: (805) 565-6234.

Whittier College
Whittier, California CB code: 4952

Admissions: 64% of applicants accepted
Based on: ••• Essay, school record
•• Interview, recommendations, test scores
• Activities, special talents
Completion: 85% of freshmen end year in good standing
52% graduate, 44% of these enter graduate study

4-year private liberal arts college, coed. Founded in 1887. **Accreditation:** Regional. **Undergraduate enrollment:** 545 men, 593 women full time; 14 men, 7 women part time. **Graduate enrollment:** 254 men, 204 women full time; 180 men, 147 women part time. **Faculty:** 101 total (78 full time), 93 with doctorates or other terminal degrees. **Location:** Suburban campus in small city; 18 miles from Los Angeles. **Calendar:** 4-1-4, limited summer session. **Microcomputers:** 75 located in dormitories, libraries, classrooms, computer centers, campus-wide network. **Special facilities:** Art gallery, collection of Quaker books and materials, John Greenleaf Whittier collection including manuscripts, letters and furniture, collection of Richard M. Nixon gifts, Keck Image Processing Laboratory.

DEGREES OFFERED. BA, MA, MS, JD. 173 bachelor's degrees awarded in 1992. 19% in business and management, 16% life sciences, 56% social sciences. Graduate degrees offered in 6 major fields of study.

UNDERGRADUATE MAJORS. Anthropology, applied arts, art history, biochemistry, biology, business administration and management, business and management, chemistry, Chinese, computer and information sciences, dramatic arts, economics, English, environmental science, fine arts, foreign languages (multiple emphasis), French, geology, history, international relations, Latin American studies, liberal/general studies, mathematics, music, philosophy, physics, political science and government, prelaw, psychology, religion, social sciences, social work, sociology, Spanish, speech correction, speech pathology/audiology, sports medicine, urban studies.

ACADEMIC PROGRAMS. Accelerated program, double major, independent study, internships, semester at sea, student-designed major, study abroad, teacher preparation, visiting/exchange student program, Washington semester; liberal arts/career combination in engineering. **Remedial services:** Tutoring. **Placement/credit:** AP, IB, institutional tests; 30 credit hours maximum for bachelor's degree.

ACADEMIC REQUIREMENTS. Freshmen must earn minimum GPA of 2.0 to continue in good standing. 82% of freshmen return for sophomore year. Students must declare major by end of second year. **Graduation requirements:** 120 hours for bachelor's (30 in major). Most students required to take courses in arts/fine arts, English, humanities, mathematics, biological/physical sciences, social sciences.

FRESHMAN ADMISSIONS. Selection criteria: GPA, course selection, and class rank most important followed by essays, references, interviews, test scores, activities, and geographic considerations. **High school preparation:** 11 units required. Required units include English 4, foreign language 2, mathematics 3, social science 1 and science 1. **Test requirements:** SAT or ACT; score report by May 1.

1992 FRESHMAN CLASS PROFILE. 667 men applied, 393 accepted, 150 enrolled; 788 women applied, 542 accepted, 188 enrolled. 63% had high school GPA of 3.0 or higher, 36% between 2.0 and 2.99. 36% were in top tenth and 62% were in top quarter of graduating class. **Academic background:** Mid 50% of enrolled freshmen had SAT-V between 390-510, SAT-M between 440-570. 99% submitted SAT scores. **Characteristics:** 60% from in state, 90% live in college housing, 40% have minority backgrounds, 4% are foreign students, 12% join fraternities/sororities. Average age is 18.

FALL-TERM APPLICATIONS. $35 fee, may be waived for applicants with need. Closing date May 1; priority given to applications received by February 15; applicants notified on a rolling basis beginning on or about March 1; must reply by May 1 or within 2 weeks if notified thereafter. Audition required. Portfolio required for Talent scholarship program applicants. Essay required. Interview recommended. CRDA. Deferred admission available. EDP-F.

STUDENT LIFE. Housing: Dormitories (coed). **Activities:** Student government, magazine, radio, student newspaper, yearbook, scholarly review, choral groups, concert band, dance, drama, jazz band, musical theater, symphony orchestra, fraternities, sororities, several ethnic, religious, and service groups, international student union, national honor societies.

ATHLETICS. NCAA. **Intercollegiate:** Baseball M, basketball, cross-country, diving, football M, golf, lacrosse M, soccer, softball W, swimming, tennis, track and field, volleyball W, water polo. **Intramural:** Basketball, handball, ice hockey M, lacrosse W, racquetball, softball, volleyball.

STUDENT SERVICES. Aptitude testing, career counseling, employment service for undergraduates, freshman orientation, health services, on-campus day care, personal counseling, placement service for graduates.

ANNUAL EXPENSES. Tuition and fees: $16,181. **Room and board:** $5,480. **Books and supplies:** $500. **Other expenses:** $1,450.

FINANCIAL AID. 83% of freshmen, 76% of continuing students receive some form of aid. 75% of grants, 94% of loans, 80% of jobs based on need. 238 enrolled freshmen were judged to have need, all were offered aid. Academic, music/drama, art, leadership, alumni affiliation scholarships available. **Aid applications:** No closing date; priority given to applications received by February 15; applicants notified on a rolling basis beginning on or about April 1; must reply by May 1 or within 2 weeks if notified thereafter. **Additional information:** Auditions required for talent scholarship applicants.

ADDRESS/TELEPHONE. Tom Enders, Associate Vice President of Enrollment, Whittier College, 13406 East Philadephia Street, Whittier, CA 90608-0634. (310) 907-4238. Fax: (310) 907-4870.

Woodbury University
Burbank, California CB code: 4955

Admissions: 76% of applicants accepted
Based on: ••• Essay, school record
•• Recommendations, special talents, test scores
• Activities, interview
Completion: 74% of freshmen end year in good standing

4-year private university, coed. Founded in 1884. **Accreditation:** Regional. **Undergraduate enrollment:** 345 men, 393 women full time; 79 men, 124 women part time. **Graduate enrollment:** 35 men, 38 women full time; 54 men, 38 women part time. **Faculty:** 123 total (23 full time), 27 with doctorates or other terminal degrees. **Location:** Suburban campus in small city; 15 miles from downtown Los Angeles. **Calendar:** Quarter, limited summer session. Saturday and extensive evening/early morning classes. **Microcomputers:** 75 located in classrooms, computer centers. **Special facilities:** Art gallery. **Additional facts:** The university combines professional programs in design, architecture, and business with liberal arts instruction.

DEGREES OFFERED. BS, BArch, MBA. 177 bachelor's degrees awarded in 1992. 26% in architecture and environmental design, 43% business and management, 11% business/office and marketing/distribution, 7% home economics, 11% visual and performing arts. Graduate degrees offered in 1 major field of study.

UNDERGRADUATE MAJORS. Accounting, architecture, business administration and management, business and management, computer and information sciences, fashion design, fashion merchandising, finance, graphic design, interior design, international business management, marketing and distribution, marketing management.

ACADEMIC PROGRAMS. Double major, independent study, internships, weekend college. **Remedial services:** Learning center, reduced course load, remedial instruction, tutoring. **Placement/credit:** AP, CLEP General and Subject, institutional tests.

ACADEMIC REQUIREMENTS. Freshmen must earn minimum GPA of 2.0 to continue in good standing. 70% of freshmen return for sophomore year. Students must declare major on application. **Graduation requirements:** 188 hours for bachelor's (72 in major). Most students required to take courses in arts/fine arts, computer science, English, history, humanities, mathematics, philosophy/religion, biological/physical sciences, social sciences.

FRESHMAN ADMISSIONS. Selection criteria: Official high school transcript, references, test scores, and essay important. **High school preparation:** 15 units recommended. Recommended units include English 4, foreign language 2, mathematics 3, social science 4 and science 2. Academic program emphasizing science, mathematics, social sciences, and foreign language recommended. **Test requirements:** SAT or ACT (SAT preferred); score report by September 1.

1992 FRESHMAN CLASS PROFILE. 157 men applied, 107 accepted, 47 enrolled; 284 women applied, 229 accepted, 87 enrolled. 50% had high school GPA of 3.0 or higher, 49% between 2.0 and 2.99. **Academic background:** Mid 50% of enrolled freshmen had SAT-V between 290-420, SAT-M between 380-500; ACT composite between 19-22. 93% submitted SAT scores, 7% submitted ACT scores. **Characteristics:** 88% from in state, 64% have minority backgrounds, 7% are foreign students. Average age is 19.

FALL-TERM APPLICATIONS. $30 fee, may be waived for applicants with need. Closing date September 1; priority given to applications received by March 1; applicants notified on a rolling basis beginning on or about March 1. Essay required. Interview recommended. CRDA. Deferred admission available.

STUDENT LIFE. Housing: Dormitories (coed); handicapped housing available. Housing applications received by May 1 receive first priority. **Activities:** Student government, student newspaper, yearbook, choral groups, drama, fraternities, sororities, Chinese Student Association, African American Student Union, Indonesian Student Association, International Connection, Latin Culture Club, Chinese Christian Fellowship, student curriculum committee, THINC (Together Helping in the Community), Woodbury

Christian Fellowship. **Additional information:** Many students work within their professional fields while studying at Woodbury.

ATHLETICS. Intramural: Basketball M, skiing, soccer M, table tennis, tennis, volleyball.

STUDENT SERVICES. Career counseling, employment service for undergraduates, freshman orientation, health services, personal counseling, placement service for graduates, special adviser for adult students, services/facilities for handicapped.

ANNUAL EXPENSES. Tuition and fees: $12,120. Bachelor of Architecture students pay tuition and fees of $12,570. **Room and board:** $5,490. **Books and supplies:** $612. **Other expenses:** $1,350.

FINANCIAL AID. 76% of freshmen, 71% of continuing students receive some form of aid. 96% of grants, 66% of loans, 75% of jobs based on need. 265 enrolled freshmen were judged to have need, 240 were offered aid. Academic scholarships available. **Aid applications:** No closing date; priority given to applications received by March 2; applicants notified on a rolling basis beginning on or about April 15; must reply by May 1 or within 3 weeks if notified thereafter.

ADDRESS/TELEPHONE. Patrick N. Contrades, Director of Admission, Woodbury University, 7500 Glenoaks Boulevard, Burbank, CA 91510-7846. (818) 767-0888 ext. 221. Fax: (818) 504-9320.

Yeshiva Ohr Elchonon Chabad/West Coast Talmudical Seminary
Los Angeles, California CB code: 1331

4-year private rabbinical college, men only, affiliated with Jewish faith. Founded in 1953. **Undergraduate enrollment:** 40 men full time. **Location:** Urban campus in very large city. **Calendar:** Semester. **Additional facts:** Ordination available.

FRESHMAN ADMISSIONS. Selection criteria: Interview, recommendations, religious affiliation or commitment, and test scores most important. Priority given to California residents.

ADDRESS/TELEPHONE. Rabbi Danny Yiftach, Director of Admissions, Yeshiva Ohr Elchonon Chabad, 7215 Waring Avenue, Los Angeles, CA 90046. (213) 937-3763.

Yuba College
Marysville, California CB code: 4994

2-year public community college, coed. Founded in 1927. **Accreditation:** Regional. **Undergraduate enrollment:** 12,373 men and women. **Faculty:** 228 total (138 full time), 8 with doctorates or other terminal degrees. **Location:** Rural campus in large town; 35 miles from Sacramento. **Calendar:** Semester, limited summer session. **Additional facts:** Program for students with learning disabilities offered.

DEGREES OFFERED. AA, AS. 570 associate degrees awarded in 1992. 8% in agriculture, 35% business and management, 20% business/office and marketing/distribution, 5% computer sciences, 7% allied health, 6% life sciences, 14% social sciences.

UNDERGRADUATE MAJORS. Accounting, agribusiness, agricultural business and management, automotive mechanics, automotive technology, biology, business administration and management, business and management, business and office, business computer/console/peripheral equipment operation, child development/care/guidance, communications, computer and information sciences, criminal justice studies, diesel engine mechanics, drafting and design technology, early childhood education, education, electrical and electronics equipment repair, electronic technology, engineering, fire control and safety technology, food management, food production/management/services, health sciences, home economics, industrial technology, instrumentation technology, law enforcement and corrections technologies, liberal/general studies, management science, manufacturing technology, marketing and distribution, marketing management, mental health/human services, music, nursing, personnel management, photographic technology, photography, practical nursing, precision metal work, radiograph medical technology, real estate, science technologies, secretarial and related programs, small business management and ownership, social sciences, social work, veterinarian's assistant, word processing.

ACADEMIC PROGRAMS. 2-year transfer program, dual enrollment of high school students, honors program, study abroad, telecourses. **Remedial services:** Learning center, remedial instruction, special counselor, tutoring. **Placement/credit:** AP, CLEP General and Subject, institutional tests.

ACADEMIC REQUIREMENTS. Freshmen must earn minimum GPA of 2.0 to continue in good standing. 50% of freshmen return for sophomore year. Students must declare major on enrollment. **Graduation requirements:** 62 hours for associate (18 in major). Most students required to take courses in arts/fine arts, English, mathematics, biological/physical sciences, social sciences.

FRESHMAN ADMISSIONS. Selection criteria: Open admissions. Selective admissions to allied health programs based on test scores and high school GPA.

1992 FRESHMAN CLASS PROFILE. 2,417 men and women enrolled. **Characteristics:** 97% from in state, 95% commute, 35% have minority backgrounds. Average age is 27.

FALL-TERM APPLICATIONS. No fee. No closing date; applicants notified on a rolling basis beginning on or about June 1. Early admission available. SAT or ACT tests recommended for counseling. Submit scores by August 15.

STUDENT LIFE. Housing: Dormitories (men, women, coed). **Activities:** Student government, newsletter, choral groups, drama, jazz band, music ensembles, musical theater.

ATHLETICS. Intercollegiate: Baseball M, basketball M, cross-country, football M, tennis, track and field, volleyball W. **Intramural:** Tennis.

STUDENT SERVICES. Aptitude testing, career counseling, employment service for undergraduates, freshman orientation, health services, on-campus day care, personal counseling, placement service for graduates, special adviser for adult students, veterans counselor, services/facilities for handicapped.

ANNUAL EXPENSES. Tuition and fees (projected): $340, $3,420 additional for out-of-state students. **Room and board:** $4,500. **Books and supplies:** $612. **Other expenses:** $5,588.

FINANCIAL AID. 12% of freshmen, 13% of continuing students receive some form of aid. 99% of grants, all loans, all jobs based on need. Academic, leadership, minority scholarships available. **Aid applications:** No closing date; priority given to applications received by March 2; applicants notified on a rolling basis beginning on or about July 1; must reply within 2 weeks. **Additional information:** Tuition fee waiver based on Board of Governors Grant (BOGG).

ADDRESS/TELEPHONE. Susan Singhas, Dean of Admissions, Counseling, and Records, Yuba College, 2088 North Beale Road, Marysville, CA 95901. (916) 741-6720. Fax: (916) 741-3541.

Colorado

Adams State College
Alamosa, Colorado CB code: 4001

4-year public liberal arts college, coed. Founded in 1921. **Accreditation:** Regional. **Undergraduate enrollment:** 906 men, 1,026 women full time; 68 men, 125 women part time. **Graduate enrollment:** 16 men, 18 women full time; 89 men, 234 women part time. **Faculty:** 120 total (104 full time), 70 with doctorates or other terminal degrees. **Location:** Rural campus in small town; 225 miles from Denver, 200 miles from Albuquerque, New Mexico. **Calendar:** Semester, limited summer session. **Microcomputers:** Located in libraries, classrooms, computer centers. **Special facilities:** Harry W. Zacheis Observatory and Planetarium, Luther Bean Art Museum.

DEGREES OFFERED. BA, BS, MA, MEd. 16 associate degrees awarded in 1992. 272 bachelor's degrees awarded. Graduate degrees offered in 9 major fields of study.

UNDERGRADUATE MAJORS. Associate: Industrial studies, liberal/general studies. **Bachelor's:** Accounting, advertising, biology, business administration and management, business data processing and related programs, business economics, chemistry, clinical laboratory science, computer and information sciences, crafts, dramatic arts, earth sciences, economics, education, elementary education, English, environmental science, finance, fine arts, geology, Hispanic American studies, history, industrial studies, industrial technology, journalism, management science, marketing management, mathematics, music, music performance, physical sciences, physics, political science and government, predentistry, prelaw, premedicine, prepharmacy, preveterinary, psychology, secondary education, secretarial and related programs, sociology, Spanish, speech.

ACADEMIC PROGRAMS. 2-year transfer program, accelerated program, double major, dual enrollment of high school students, independent study, internships, student-designed major, teacher preparation, cross-registration. **Remedial services:** Learning center, reduced course load, remedial instruction, special counselor, tutoring. **Placement/credit:** AP, CLEP General, institutional tests; 30 credit hours maximum for bachelor's degree.

ACADEMIC REQUIREMENTS. Freshmen must earn minimum GPA of 2.0 to continue in good standing. 63% of freshmen return for sophomore year. Students must declare major by end of second year. **Graduation requirements:** 62 hours for associate (24 in major), 124 hours for bachelor's (36 in major). Most students required to take courses in arts/fine arts, English, history, humanities, mathematics, biological/physical sciences, social sciences. **Postgraduate studies:** 30% from 2-year programs enter 4-year programs.

FRESHMAN ADMISSIONS. Selection criteria: Open admissions for associate degree programs only. Bachelor's degree candidates must have either 2.5 high school GPA, or rank in top two-thirds of class and have ACT composite score of 21 or SAT combined score of 850. **High school preparation:** 15 units required. 10 units from English, foreign language, mathematics, science, and social studies. **Test requirements:** SAT or ACT (ACT preferred); score report by August 1.

1992 FRESHMAN CLASS PROFILE. 277 men, 292 women enrolled. **Academic background:** Mid 50% of enrolled freshmen had ACT composite between 17-24. 88% submitted ACT scores. **Characteristics:** 78% from in state, 80% live in college housing, 38% have minority backgrounds, 1% are foreign students. Average age is 19.

FALL-TERM APPLICATIONS. $15 fee, may be waived for applicants with need. No closing date; priority given to applications received by August 1; applicants notified on a rolling basis; must reply by registration. Audition recommended for music applicants. Portfolio recommended for art applicants. Deferred and early admission available.

STUDENT LIFE. Housing: Dormitories (men, women, coed); apartment housing available. **Activities:** Student government, radio, student newspaper, choral groups, concert band, dance, drama, jazz band, marching band, music ensembles, pep band.

ATHLETICS. NCAA. **Intercollegiate:** Basketball, cross-country, football M, golf M, softball W, track and field, volleyball W, wrestling M. **Intramural:** Basketball, bowling, racquetball, skiing, soccer, softball, swimming, tennis, volleyball, water polo.

STUDENT SERVICES. Aptitude testing, career counseling, employment service for undergraduates, freshman orientation, on-campus day care, personal counseling, placement service for graduates, special adviser for adult students, veterans counselor, services/facilities for handicapped.

ANNUAL EXPENSES. Tuition and fees (1992-93): $1,649, $2,890 additional for out-of-state students. **Room and board:** $2,950. **Books and supplies:** $500. **Other expenses:** $1,200.

FINANCIAL AID. 84% of freshmen, 79% of continuing students receive some form of aid. 68% of grants, 89% of loans, 53% of jobs based on need. 496 enrolled freshmen were judged to have need, all were offered aid. Academic, music/drama, art, athletic, state/district residency scholarships available. **Aid applications:** No closing date; priority given to applications received by April 15; applicants notified on a rolling basis beginning on or about March 1; must reply within 4 weeks. **Additional information:** 50% tuition waiver scholarship offered to out-of-state students who live on-campus and are in top 30% of class.

ADDRESS/TELEPHONE. Cheryl Billingsley, Director for Admissions, Adams State College, Alamosa, CO 81102. (719) 589-7712. (800) 824-6494. Fax: (719) 589-7522.

Aims Community College
Greeley, Colorado CB code: 4204

2-year public community college, coed. Founded in 1967. **Accreditation:** Regional. **Undergraduate enrollment:** 1,091 men, 1,440 women full time; 2,537 men, 4,388 women part time. **Faculty:** 434 total (114 full time), 14 with doctorates or other terminal degrees. **Location:** Urban campus in small city; 55 miles from Denver. **Calendar:** Quarter, extensive summer session. Extensive evening/early morning classes. **Microcomputers:** 389 located in classrooms, computer centers.

DEGREES OFFERED. AA, AS, AAS. 418 associate degrees awarded in 1992. 12% in business and management, 6% business/office and marketing/distribution, 53% multi/interdisciplinary studies, 15% parks/recreation, protective services, public affairs, 5% trade and industry.

UNDERGRADUATE MAJORS. Accounting, agricultural business and management, airline piloting and navigation, auto body repair, automotive mechanics, business data processing and related programs, child development/care/guidance, criminal justice technology, drafting, electronic technology, engineering and engineering-related technologies, fire control and safety technology, graphic and printing production, liberal/general studies, marketing management, office supervision and management, precision metal work, radiograph medical technology.

ACADEMIC PROGRAMS. 2-year transfer program, cooperative education, double major, dual enrollment of high school students, independent study, internships, weekend college. **Remedial services:** Learning center, remedial instruction, special counselor, tutoring. **ROTC:** Air Force. **Placement/credit:** CLEP General and Subject, institutional tests; 72 credit hours maximum for associate degree.

ACADEMIC REQUIREMENTS. Freshmen must earn minimum GPA of 2.0 to continue in good standing. Students must declare major on enrollment. **Graduation requirements:** 96 hours for associate (60 in major). Most students required to take courses in English, mathematics, biological/physical sciences, social sciences.

FRESHMAN ADMISSIONS. Selection criteria: Open admissions. Selective admission to radiologic technology, police academy and biofeedback programs based on test scores.

1992 FRESHMAN CLASS PROFILE. 454 men, 426 women enrolled. **Academic background:** Mid 50% of enrolled freshmen had ACT composite between 13-19. 7% submitted ACT scores. **Characteristics:** 99% from in state, 100% commute, 19% have minority backgrounds. Average age is 19.

FALL-TERM APPLICATIONS. No fee. No closing date; applicants notified on a rolling basis. Interview required for radiologic technology, police academy, biofeedback applicants. Deferred and early admission available.

STUDENT LIFE. Activities: Student government, magazine, student newspaper, newsletter, concert band, dance, drama, musical theater.

ATHLETICS. Intramural: Baseball, basketball, golf, racquetball, softball, tennis, volleyball.

STUDENT SERVICES. Aptitude testing, career counseling, employment service for undergraduates, on-campus day care, placement service for graduates, veterans counselor, services/facilities for handicapped.

ANNUAL EXPENSES. Tuition and fees (1992-93): $753, $630 additional for out-of-district students, $3,582 additional for out-of-state students. **Books and supplies:** $290. **Other expenses:** $1,050.

FINANCIAL AID. 53% of continuing students receive some form of aid. 64% of grants, 84% of loans, 81% of jobs based on need. Academic, state/district residency, leadership scholarships available. **Aid applications:** No closing date; priority given to applications received by June 1; applicants notified on a rolling basis beginning on or about August 1; must reply within 2 weeks.

ADDRESS/TELEPHONE. William D. Green, Registrar, Aims Community College, PO Box 69, 5401 West 20th Street, Greeley, CO 80632. (303) 330-8008. Fax: (303) 330-5705.

Arapahoe Community College
Littleton, Colorado CB code: 4014

2-year public community college, coed. Founded in 1965. **Accreditation:** Regional. **Undergraduate enrollment:** 775 men, 1,212 women full time; 2,205 men, 3,450 women part time. **Faculty:** 898 total (98 full time), 6 with doctorates or other terminal degrees. **Location:** Suburban campus in small city; 10 miles from downtown Denver. **Calendar:** Semester, limited summer session. Saturday and extensive evening/early morning classes. **Microcomputers:** Located in libraries, classrooms, computer centers. **Special facilities:** Colorado Gallery of the Arts.

DEGREES OFFERED. AA, AS, AAS. 542 associate degrees awarded in 1992. 7% in architecture and environmental design, 7% business and management, 20% health sciences, 10% law, 12% physical sciences, 29% social sciences, 8% trade and industry.

UNDERGRADUATE MAJORS. Accounting, architectural technologies, automotive mechanics, automotive technology, business administration and management, business and management, business and office, commercial art, criminal justice technology, electronic technology, emergency medical technologies, fashion merchandising, finance, hotel/motel and restaurant management, information sciences and systems, interior design, international business management, law enforcement and corrections technologies, legal assistant/paralegal, legal secretary, liberal/general studies, management information systems, marketing and distribution, mechanical design technology, medical assistant, medical laboratory technologies, medical records technology, nursing, personnel management, physical sciences, physical therapy assistant, retailing, secretarial and related programs, small business management and ownership, social sciences, trade and industrial supervision and management, transportation and travel marketing, word processing.

ACADEMIC PROGRAMS. 2-year transfer program, cooperative education, dual enrollment of high school students, honors program, independent study, internships, study abroad, telecourses, weekend college, cross-registration. **Remedial services:** Learning center, remedial instruction, tutoring. **ROTC:** Air Force, Army. **Placement/credit:** AP, CLEP General and Subject, institutional tests; 30 credit hours maximum for associate degree.

ACADEMIC REQUIREMENTS. No policy requiring minimum GPA; records of students having academic difficulty are reviewed individually. 62% of freshmen return for sophomore year. Students must declare major by end of first year. **Graduation requirements:** 61 hours for associate. Most students required to take courses in arts/fine arts, English, humanities, mathematics, biological/physical sciences, social sciences.

FRESHMAN ADMISSIONS. Selection criteria: Open admissions. Selective admissions to allied health and legal assistant programs.

1992 FRESHMAN CLASS PROFILE. 1,064 men, 1,736 women enrolled. **Characteristics:** 96% from in state, 100% commute, 9% have minority backgrounds, 2% are foreign students. Average age is 27.

FALL-TERM APPLICATIONS. No fee. No closing date; applicants notified on a rolling basis. Interview required for allied health, legal assistant, automotive services applicants. Deferred admission available. Closing date for nursing applicants February 4.

STUDENT LIFE. Activities: Student government, magazine, student newspaper, choral groups, drama, musical theater, Phi Theta Kappa.

ATHLETICS. Intramural: Basketball, golf, skiing, soccer, softball, swimming, table tennis, tennis, volleyball.

STUDENT SERVICES. Aptitude testing, career counseling, employment service for undergraduates, freshman orientation, health services, on-campus day care, personal counseling, placement service for graduates, veterans counselor, services/facilities for handicapped.

ANNUAL EXPENSES. Tuition and fees (1992-93): $1,571, $4,320 additional for out-of-state students. **Books and supplies:** $450. **Other expenses:** $274.

FINANCIAL AID. 24% of freshmen, 24% of continuing students receive some form of aid. 90% of grants, 74% of loans, 83% of jobs based on need. Academic, state/district residency scholarships available. **Aid applications:** No closing date; priority given to applications received by March 15; applicants notified on a rolling basis beginning on or about June 15; must reply within 2 weeks.

ADDRESS/TELEPHONE. Dr. Don Carson, Director of Admissions, Arapahoe Community College, 2500 West College Drive PO Box 9002, Littleton, CO 80160-9002. (303) 794-1550.

Bel-Rea Institute of Animal Technology
Denver, Colorado CB code: 0928

Admissions:	55% of applicants accepted
Based on:	••• Interview, recommendations
	•• School record
Completion:	75% of freshmen end year in good standing
	9% enter 4-year programs

2-year proprietary veterinary technology college, coed. Founded in 1972. **Undergraduate enrollment:** 35 men, 180 women full time. **Faculty:** 16 total (5 full time), 8 with doctorates or other terminal degrees. **Location:** Suburban campus in very large city; 8 miles from downtown. **Calendar:** Program consists of 6 consecutive quarters (18 months). **Additional facts:** All students intern at college-affilated emergency veterinary hospital.

DEGREES OFFERED. AAS. 90 associate degrees awarded in 1992. 100% in allied health.

UNDERGRADUATE MAJORS. Veterinarian's assistant.

ACADEMIC PROGRAMS. Internships. **Remedial services:** Reduced course load, tutoring.

ACADEMIC REQUIREMENTS. Freshmen must earn minimum GPA of 2.0 to continue in good standing. 75% of freshmen return for sophomore year. Students must declare major on enrollment. **Graduation requirements:** 114 hours for associate. Most students required to take courses in English, humanities, mathematics, biological/physical sciences.

FRESHMAN ADMISSIONS. Selection criteria: Interview most important, followed by school achievement record. Recommendations considered. Minimum 2.0 school GPA required. As much science and mathematics as possible. Algebra and chemistry recommended.

1992 FRESHMAN CLASS PROFILE. 42 men applied, 18 accepted, 18 enrolled; 110 women applied, 65 accepted, 65 enrolled. 20% had high school GPA of 3.0 or higher, 80% between 2.0 and 2.99. **Academic background:** Mid 50% of enrolled freshmen had ACT composite between 13-18. 10% submitted ACT scores. **Characteristics:** 55% from in state, 100% commute, 10% have minority backgrounds, 3% are foreign students. Average age is 24.

FALL-TERM APPLICATIONS. No fee. No closing date; applicants notified on a rolling basis; must reply within 8 weeks of start date. Interview recommended.

STUDENT LIFE. Activities: Student government.

STUDENT SERVICES. Career counseling, employment service for undergraduates, personal counseling, placement service for graduates, veterans counselor, services/facilities for handicapped.

ANNUAL EXPENSES. Tuition and fees (1992-93): $4,550. **Books and supplies:** $800. **Other expenses:** $1,053.

FINANCIAL AID. 55% of freshmen, 84% of continuing students receive some form of aid. Grants, loans available. Academic, state/district residency scholarships available. **Aid applications:** No closing date; priority given to applications received by August 31; applicants notified on a rolling basis beginning on or about August 15; must reply by registration.

ADDRESS/TELEPHONE. Mindi Lorenz, Director of Admissions, Bel-Rea Institute of Animal Technology, 1681 South Dayton Street, Denver, CO 80231. (303) 751-8700. (800) 950-8001. Fax: (303) 751-9969.

Beth-El College of Nursing
Colorado Springs, Colorado CB code: 4022

4-year public institution, coed. **Accreditation:** Regional. **Undergraduate enrollment:** 346 men and women. **Location:** Urban campus in large city. **Calendar:** Semester.

DEGREES OFFERED. BS, M. 59 bachelor's degrees awarded in 1992. 100% in health sciences. Graduate degrees offered in 1 major field of study.

UNDERGRADUATE MAJORS. Nursing.

FRESHMAN ADMISSIONS. Selection criteria: Test scores, 2.5 GPA, essay and interview considered.

1992 FRESHMAN CLASS PROFILE. 30 men and women enrolled.

FALL-TERM APPLICATIONS. Closing date April 15; applicants notified on a rolling basis.

ANNUAL EXPENSES. Tuition and fees (1992-93): $4,435.

FINANCIAL AID. Aid applications: No closing date; applicants notified on a rolling basis.

ADDRESS/TELEPHONE. Marilyn Atwood, Dean of Student Affairs, Beth-El College of Nursing, 10 North Farragut Avenue, Colorado Springs, CO 80909. (719) 475-5170. Fax: (719) 475-5198.

Blair Junior College
Colorado Springs, Colorado CB code: 0934

2-year proprietary business, junior, technical college, coed. Founded in 1897. **Undergraduate enrollment:** 98 men, 477 women full time. **Location:** Urban campus in large city; 60 miles from Denver. **Calendar:** Quarter.

FRESHMAN ADMISSIONS. Selection criteria: Academic record, interview, CPAT Test most important.

ADDRESS/TELEPHONE. Dawn Collins, Director of Admissions, Blair Junior College, 828 Wooten Road, Colorado Springs, CO 80915. (719) 574-1082. Fax: (719) 574-4493.

Colorado Christian University
Denver, Colorado CB code: 4659

4-year private college of arts and sciences and Bible college, coed, interdenominational. Founded in 1914. **Accreditation:** Regional. **Undergraduate enrollment:** 676 men and women full time. **Graduate enrollment:** 85 men and women full time. **Faculty:** 81 total (41 full time), 25 with doctorates or other terminal degrees. **Location:** Suburban campus in very large city; 10 miles from downtown. **Calendar:** Semester, limited summer session. **Microcomputers:** 15 located in libraries, computer centers. **Special facilities:** Recording studios. **Additional facts:** Extension courses available at Colorado Springs and Grand Junction campuses.

DEGREES OFFERED. AA, BA, BS, MA. 1 associate degree awarded in 1992. 100% in multi/interdisciplinary studies. 253 bachelor's degrees awarded. 65% in business and management, 6% teacher education, 14% philosophy, religion, theology, 8% psychology, 6% visual and performing arts.

UNDERGRADUATE MAJORS. Associate: Computer and information sciences. **Bachelor's:** Accounting, art education, Bible studies, biology, business and management, chemistry, communications, computer and information sciences, contemporary Christian music, elementary education, English, fine arts, humanities and social sciences, liberal/general studies, missionary studies, music, music education, music performance, physical education, prelaw, premedicine, psychology, public relations, radio/television broadcasting, religious music, secondary education, social sciences, theological studies, visual and performing arts, youth ministries.

ACADEMIC PROGRAMS. 2-year transfer program, accelerated program, cooperative education, double major, dual enrollment of high school students, honors program, independent study, internships, student-designed major, teacher preparation, weekend college, cross-registration, programs in photography, interior design, fashion illustration, and commercial art with Colorado Institute of Art. **Remedial services:** Preadmission summer program. **ROTC:** Army. **Placement/credit:** AP, CLEP General and Subject, institutional tests; 30 credit hours maximum for bachelor's degree.

ACADEMIC REQUIREMENTS. Freshmen must earn minimum GPA of 2.0 to continue in good standing. 75% of freshmen return for sophomore year. Students must declare major by end of second year. **Graduation requirements:** 64 hours for associate (9 in major), 128 hours for bachelor's (39 in major). Most students required to take courses in arts/fine arts, English, history, humanities, mathematics, philosophy/religion, biological/physical sciences, social sciences. **Postgraduate studies:** 50% from 2-year programs enter 4-year programs.

FRESHMAN ADMISSIONS. Selection criteria: School achievement record, test scores, interview, motivation, ability to adopt institution's goals important. Applicants must show evidence of commitment to Christian faith through written statement. **High school preparation:** 15 units recommended. Recommended units include biological science 2, English 4, mathematics 2, physical science 1 and social science 3. **Test requirements:** SAT or ACT; score report by September 15.

1992 FRESHMAN CLASS PROFILE. 197 men and women enrolled. 47% had high school GPA of 3.0 or higher, 46% between 2.0 and 2.99. **Characteristics:** 70% from in state, 73% live in college housing, 2% have minority backgrounds, 1% are foreign students. Average age is 19.

FALL-TERM APPLICATIONS. $20 fee, may be waived for applicants with need. No closing date; priority given to applications received by April 1; applicants notified on a rolling basis; must reply within 4 weeks. Essay required. Interview recommended for academically weak applicants. Audition recommended for music applicants. Portfolio recommended for art applicants. Deferred admission available.

STUDENT LIFE. Housing: Apartment housing available. **Activities:** Student government, magazine, radio, student newspaper, television, yearbook, choral groups, drama, jazz band, music ensembles, musical theater, symphony orchestra, Cross-Cultural Concerns. **Additional information:** Use of alcoholic beverages, illegal drugs, and tobacco prohibited on campus and at college-sponsored activities. Religious observance required.

ATHLETICS. NCAA. **Intercollegiate:** Basketball, football M, golf, soccer, tennis, volleyball W. **Intramural:** Basketball, bowling, cross-country, skiing, softball, tennis, volleyball.

STUDENT SERVICES. Aptitude testing, career counseling, employment service for undergraduates, freshman orientation, personal counseling, placement service for graduates.

ANNUAL EXPENSES. Tuition and fees: $6,350. **Room and board:** $3,400. **Books and supplies:** $500. **Other expenses:** $2,070.

FINANCIAL AID. 80% of freshmen, 85% of continuing students receive some form of aid. 55% of grants, 64% of loans, all jobs based on need. 200 enrolled freshmen were judged to have need, all were offered aid. Academic, music/drama, athletic, leadership, alumni affiliation, religious affiliation, minority scholarships available. **Aid applications:** Closing date April 1; priority given to applications received by March 1; applicants notified on a rolling basis beginning on or about April 30; must reply within 2 weeks.

ADDRESS/TELEPHONE. Anna DiTorrice, Director of Admissions, Colorado Christian University, 180 South Garrison, Denver, CO 80226. (303) 238-5386 ext. 120. Fax: (303) 238-5386 ext. 123.

Colorado College
Colorado Springs, Colorado — CB code: 4072

Admissions: 50% of applicants accepted
Based on: ••• Essay, school record
•• Activities, recommendations, test scores
• Special talents
Completion: 99% of freshmen end year in good standing
78% graduate, 29% of these enter graduate study

4-year private liberal arts college, coed. Founded in 1874. **Accreditation:** Regional. **Undergraduate enrollment:** 915 men, 988 women full time; 6 men, 12 women part time. **Graduate enrollment:** 5 men, 19 women full time. **Faculty:** 199 total (150 full time), 142 with doctorates or other terminal degrees. **Location:** Urban campus in large city; 70 miles from Denver. **Calendar:** 8 blocks of 3.5 weeks each, with most students enrolling in 1 course per block (4 blocks in fall semester and 4 blocks in spring semester). **Microcomputers:** 190 located in dormitories, libraries, classrooms, computer centers. **Special facilities:** Electron microscope, electronic music studio, telescope dome, Coburn Art Gallery.

DEGREES OFFERED. BA, MA. 500 bachelor's degrees awarded in 1992. 16% in letters/literature, 10% life sciences, 6% multi/interdisciplinary studies, 6% physical sciences, 5% psychology, 41% social sciences, 9% visual and performing arts. Graduate degrees offered in 4 major fields of study.

UNDERGRADUATE MAJORS. Anthropology, art history, Asian studies, biology, chemistry, classics, clinical laboratory science, comparative literature, dance, dramatic arts, economics, English, foreign languages (multiple emphasis), French, geology, German, history, humanities and social sciences, liberal/general studies, mathematics, music, peace studies, philosophy, physics, political science and government, psychology, religion, Russian and Slavic studies, sociology, Southwest studies, Spanish, studio art, women's studies.

ACADEMIC PROGRAMS. Independent study, internships, student-designed major, study abroad, teacher preparation, Washington semester, Newberry library program, urban studies and urban education (Chicago), science semester (Oakridge, Tennessee), tropical field research (Costa Rica), wilderness field station (Minnesota), writing about drama program (London); liberal arts/career combination in engineering, forestry, health sciences; combined bachelor's/graduate program in business administration, law. **ROTC:** Army. **Placement/credit:** AP, IB, institutional tests.

ACADEMIC REQUIREMENTS. No policy requiring minimum GPA; records of students having academic difficulty are reviewed individually. Freshmen must pass minimum of 5 courses. 91% of freshmen return for sophomore year. Students must declare major by end of second year. **Graduation requirements:** Most students required to take courses in humanities, biological/physical sciences, social sciences. **Postgraduate studies:** 6% enter law school, 4% enter medical school, 3% enter MBA programs, 16% enter other graduate study. **Additional information:** 32 units required for graduation.

FRESHMAN ADMISSIONS. Selection criteria: Personal essays submitted with application, school achievement record, counselor and teacher recommendations, and test scores most important. Geographic, socioeconomic, and ethnic diversity considered. **High school preparation:** 16 units required; 18 recommended. **Test requirements:** SAT or ACT; score report by March 15.

1992 FRESHMAN CLASS PROFILE. 1,515 men applied, 700 accepted, 234 enrolled; 1,620 women applied, 882 accepted, 289 enrolled. 56% were in top tenth and 87% were in top quarter of graduating class. **Academic background:** Mid 50% of enrolled freshmen had SAT-V between 500-600, SAT-M between 550-660; ACT composite between 25-29. 88% submitted SAT scores, 60% submitted ACT scores. **Characteristics:** 29% from in state, 95% live in college housing, 11% have minority backgrounds, 2% are foreign students, 25% join fraternities/sororities. Average age is 18.

FALL-TERM APPLICATIONS. $30 fee, may be waived for applicants with need. Closing date February 1; applicants notified on or about April 1; must reply by May 1. Essay required. Campus visit recommended. CRDA. Deferred admission available. Institutional early decision plan. Early action and notification is available to applicants if requested in writing with reasons given; deadline is December 1.

STUDENT LIFE. Housing: Dormitories (men, women, coed); apartment, fraternity housing available. Theme and language houses available. Students required to live on campus first 3 years; housing available all 4 years. **Activities:** Student government, film, magazine, radio, student newspaper, yearbook, literary and artistic publications, choral groups, concert band, dance, drama, jazz band, music ensembles, musical theater, symphony orchestra, fraternities, sororities, broad range of political, religious, and ethnic organizations.

ATHLETICS. NCAA. **Intercollegiate:** Baseball M, basketball, cross-country, diving, field hockey W, football M, golf M, ice hockey M, lacrosse M, soccer, swimming, tennis, track and field, volleyball W. **Intramural:** Badminton, basketball, ice hockey, racquetball, soccer, softball, tennis, volleyball.

STUDENT SERVICES. Career counseling, employment service for undergraduates, freshman orientation, health services, on-campus day care, personal counseling, placement service for graduates, services/facilities for handicapped.

ANNUAL EXPENSES. Tuition and fees: $15,942. **Room and board:** $4,096. **Books and supplies:** $450. **Other expenses:** $900.

FINANCIAL AID. 50% of freshmen, 56% of continuing students receive some form of aid. 89% of grants, all loans, 73% of jobs based on need. 254 enrolled freshmen were judged to have need, all were offered aid. Academic, athletic scholarships available. **Aid applications:** No closing date; priority given to applications received by February 15; applicants notified on a rolling basis beginning on or about April 1.

ADDRESS/TELEPHONE. Terrance K. Swenson, Dean of Admissions/Financial Aid, Colorado College, 14 East Cache La Poudre, Colorado Springs, CO 80903. (719) 389-6344. (800) 542-7214. Fax: (719) 389-6816.

Colorado Institute of Art
Denver, Colorado CB code: 7150

2-year proprietary institute of visual and applied arts, coed. Founded in 1952. **Undergraduate enrollment:** 764 men, 545 women full time. **Faculty:** 77 total (47 full time). **Location:** Urban campus in very large city; near downtown area. **Calendar:** Quarter, extensive summer session. **Microcomputers:** 100 located in libraries, computer centers. **Special facilities:** Art gallery, audio laboratory, video studio, computer graphics laboratory, photography studios and laboratories, industrial design studios. **Additional facts:** Curriculum stresses career preparation in the visual and applied arts.

DEGREES OFFERED. AAS. 436 associate degrees awarded in 1992. 15% in business/office and marketing/distribution, 85% visual and performing arts.

UNDERGRADUATE MAJORS. Apparel and accessories marketing, commercial art, fashion design, fashion merchandising, graphic arts technology, graphic design, illustration design, industrial design, interior design, music business management, photographic technology, photography, radio/television technology, video.

ACADEMIC PROGRAMS. Remedial services: Learning center, remedial instruction.

ACADEMIC REQUIREMENTS. Freshmen must earn minimum GPA of 2.0 to continue in good standing. Students must declare major on enrollment. **Graduation requirements:** 120 hours for associate. Most students required to take courses in computer science, English, humanities, mathematics. **Additional information:** 17 credit hours minimum required in major. Total credit hours for graduation varies with field of study.

FRESHMAN ADMISSIONS. Selection criteria: Open admissions. Applicants with GED or high school GPA of less than 2.0 admitted provisionally. These applicants either must submit essay about career goals, or show evidence of 3 courses taken in major field, or have interview, or present portfolio.

1992 FRESHMAN CLASS PROFILE. 260 men, 215 women enrolled. **Characteristics:** 50% from in state, 95% commute, 20% have minority backgrounds. Average age is 20.

FALL-TERM APPLICATIONS. $50 fee. No closing date; applicants notified on a rolling basis; must reply within 2 weeks. Portfolio required for advanced standing applicants. Interview recommended. Deferred and early admission available.

STUDENT LIFE. Housing: Limited housing available at University of Denver campus. **Activities:** Student newspaper, fraternities.

STUDENT SERVICES. Employment service for undergraduates, freshman orientation, personal counseling, placement service for graduates, veterans counselor, services/facilities for handicapped.

ANNUAL EXPENSES. Tuition and fees (1992-93): $7,925. **Books and supplies:** $1,200. **Other expenses:** $1,250.

FINANCIAL AID. 80% of freshmen, 80% of continuing students receive some form of aid. 91% of grants, 53% of loans, 96% of jobs based on need. Academic, music/drama, art scholarships available. **Aid applications:** No closing date; applicants notified on a rolling basis; must reply within 2 weeks.

ADDRESS/TELEPHONE. Barbara Browning, Director of Admissions, Colorado Institute of Art, 200 East Ninth Avenue, Denver, CO 80203. (303) 837-0825. (800) 275-2420. Fax: (800) 275-2420 ext. 549.

Colorado Mountain College: Alpine Campus
Steamboat Springs, Colorado CB code: 4140

2-year public community college, coed. Founded in 1981. **Accreditation:** Regional. **Undergraduate enrollment:** 490 men and women. **Faculty:** 132 total (20 full time), 15 with doctorates or other terminal degrees. **Location:** Rural campus in small town; 190 miles from Denver. **Calendar:** Semester, limited summer session. Extensive evening/early morning classes. **Microcomputers:** 43 located in libraries, computer centers. **Additional facts:** Part of 3-residential campus system in the Colorado Rocky Mountains.

DEGREES OFFERED. AA, AS, AAS. 62 associate degrees awarded in 1992.

UNDERGRADUATE MAJORS. Accounting, biological and physical sciences, biology, business and management, business and office, hospitality and recreation marketing, hotel/motel and restaurant management, humanities and social sciences, liberal/general studies, marketing and distribution, marketing management, mathematics, microcomputer software, physical sciences, social sciences, sports medicine.

ACADEMIC PROGRAMS. 2-year transfer program, independent study, internships, telecourses. **Remedial services:** Learning center, reduced course load, remedial instruction, special counselor, tutoring. **Placement/credit:** AP, CLEP General and Subject, institutional tests; 30 credit hours maximum for associate degree.

ACADEMIC REQUIREMENTS. Freshmen must earn minimum GPA of 2.0 to continue in good standing. 58% of freshmen return for sophomore year. Students must declare major on application. **Graduation requirements:** 62 hours for associate. Most students required to take courses in computer science, English, humanities, mathematics, biological/physical sciences, social sciences. **Additional information:** Ski industry training programs available.

FRESHMAN ADMISSIONS. Selection criteria: Open admissions.

1992 FRESHMAN CLASS PROFILE. 130 men, 107 women enrolled. **Characteristics:** 40% from in state, 64% live in college housing, 13% have minority backgrounds, 2% are foreign students. Average age is 19.

FALL-TERM APPLICATIONS. No fee. No closing date; priority given to applications received by August 15; applicants notified on a rolling basis. Deferred and early admission available. SAT or ACT recommended for placement and counseling. Institutional test available in place of SAT or ACT.

STUDENT LIFE. Housing: Dormitories (coed). **Activities:** Student government, student newspaper, yearbook, international student club. **Additional information:** College takes advantage of outdoor recreational opportunities in the surrounding resort community.

ATHLETICS. Intercollegiate: Skiing. **Intramural:** Basketball, soccer, volleyball.

STUDENT SERVICES. Aptitude testing, career counseling, employment service for undergraduates, freshman orientation, personal counseling, placement service for graduates, special adviser for adult students, veterans counselor, services/facilities for handicapped.

ANNUAL EXPENSES. Tuition and fees: $1,030, $840 additional for out-of-district students, $4,500 additional for out-of-state students. **Room and board:** $3,600. **Books and supplies:** $700. **Other expenses:** $1,000.

FINANCIAL AID. 46% of freshmen, 51% of continuing students receive some form of aid. Grants, loans, jobs available. Academic, athletic, state/district residency, minority scholarships available. **Aid applications:** No closing date; priority given to applications received by March 31; applicants notified on a rolling basis beginning on or about May 15; must reply within 4 weeks.

ADDRESS/TELEPHONE. Barbara Edwards, Director of Pre-Enrollment Services, Collegewide, Colorado Mountain College: Alpine Campus, P.O. Box 775288, Dept. CB, Steamboat Springs, CO 80477. (303) 879-3288. (800) 621-8559. Fax: (303) 870-0485.

Colorado Mountain College: Spring Valley Campus
Glenwood Springs, Colorado CB code: 4112

2-year public community college, coed. Founded in 1965. **Accreditation:** Regional. **Undergraduate enrollment:** 495 men and women. **Faculty:** 60 total (24 full time), 10 with doctorates or other terminal degrees. **Location:** Rural campus in small town; 160 miles from Denver. **Calendar:** Semester, limited summer session. Extensive evening/early morning classes. **Microcomputers:** 25 located in libraries, classrooms. **Special facilities:** Outdoor education center, farm for veterinarian technician program. **Additional facts:** Part of 3-residential-campus system in the middle of the Colorado Rocky Mountains

DEGREES OFFERED. AA, AS, AAS. 129 associate degrees awarded in 1992.

UNDERGRADUATE MAJORS. Biological and physical sciences, biology, business and management, business and office, business data programming, criminal justice technology, criminology, dramatic arts, earth sciences, graphic arts technology, graphic design, humanities and social sciences, law enforcement and corrections technologies, liberal/general studies, mathematics, parks and recreation management, photographic technology, photography, physical sciences, psychology, recreation and community services technologies, social sciences, veterinarian's assistant, visual and performing arts.

ACADEMIC PROGRAMS. 2-year transfer program, independent study, internships, telecourses. **Remedial services:** Learning center, reduced course load, remedial instruction, special counselor, tutoring. **Placement/credit:** AP, CLEP General and Subject, institutional tests; 30 credit hours maximum for associate degree.

ACADEMIC REQUIREMENTS. Freshmen must earn minimum GPA of 2.0 to continue in good standing. 64% of freshmen return for sophomore year. Students must declare major on application. **Graduation requirements:** 62 hours for associate. Most students required to take courses in computer science, English, humanities, mathematics, biological/physical sciences, social sciences.

FRESHMAN ADMISSIONS. Selection criteria: Open admissions. Special requirements for veterinary technology and photography applicants.

1992 FRESHMAN CLASS PROFILE. 132 men, 136 women enrolled. **Academic background:** Mid 50% of enrolled freshmen had ACT composite between 14-21. 35% submitted ACT scores. **Characteristics:** 62% from in state, 58% commute, 14% have minority backgrounds, 1% are foreign students. Average age is 19.

FALL-TERM APPLICATIONS. No fee. No closing date; priority given to applications received by August 15; applicants notified on a rolling basis. Deferred and early admission available. SAT or ACT recommended for placement and counseling. College placement test may be given in place of SAT or ACT.

STUDENT LIFE. Housing: Dormitories (men, women). **Activities:** Student government, student newspaper, choral groups, dance, drama, jazz band, music ensembles, musical theater, World Awareness Society (WAS).

Additional information: College takes advantage of outdoor recreational opportunities in the surrounding resort community.

ATHLETICS. Intercollegiate: Skiing. **Intramural:** Basketball, skiing, soccer, softball, volleyball.

STUDENT SERVICES. Aptitude testing, career counseling, employment service for undergraduates, freshman orientation, personal counseling, placement service for graduates, special adviser for adult students, veterans counselor, services/facilities for handicapped.

ANNUAL EXPENSES. Tuition and fees: $1,030, $840 additional for out-of-district students, $4,500 additional for out-of-state students. **Room and board:** $3,600. **Books and supplies:** $700. **Other expenses:** $1,000.

FINANCIAL AID. 46% of freshmen, 51% of continuing students receive some form of aid. Grants, loans, jobs available. Academic, athletic, state/district residency, minority scholarships available. **Aid applications:** No closing date; priority given to applications received by March 31; applicants notified on a rolling basis beginning on or about May 15; must reply within 4 weeks.

ADDRESS/TELEPHONE. Barbara Edwards, Director of Pre-Enrollment Services, Collegewide, Colorado Mountain College: Spring Valley Campus, 3000 County Road 114, Dept. CB, Glenwood Springs, CO 81601. (303) 945-7481. (800) 621-8559. Fax: (303) 945-7279.

Colorado Mountain College: Timberline Campus

Leadville, Colorado CB code: 4113

2-year public community college, coed. Founded in 1965. **Accreditation:** Regional. **Undergraduate enrollment:** 425 men and women. **Faculty:** 42 total (14 full time), 6 with doctorates or other terminal degrees. **Location:** Rural campus in small town; 100 miles from Denver, 120 miles from Colorado Springs. **Calendar:** Semester, limited summer session. Extensive evening/early morning classes. **Microcomputers:** 20 located in libraries, classrooms. **Special facilities:** Community-owned recreational complex within walking distance. **Additional facts:** Part of 3-residential campus system in Colorado Rocky Mountains.

DEGREES OFFERED. AA, AAS. 44 associate degrees awarded in 1992.

UNDERGRADUATE MAJORS. Accounting, biological and physical sciences, biology, business and office, business data processing and related programs, energy conservation and use technology, environmental science, humanities and social sciences, liberal/general studies, secretarial and related programs, ski area operations, ski touring center operations, tourism, transportation and travel marketing, water and wastewater technology.

ACADEMIC PROGRAMS. 2-year transfer program, independent study, internships, telecourses. **Remedial services:** Learning center, reduced course load, remedial instruction, special counselor, tutoring. **Placement/credit:** AP, CLEP General and Subject, institutional tests; 30 credit hours maximum for associate degree.

ACADEMIC REQUIREMENTS. Freshmen must earn minimum GPA of 2.0 to continue in good standing. 61% of freshmen return for sophomore year. Students must declare major on application. **Graduation requirements:** 62 hours for associate. Most students required to take courses in computer science, English, humanities, mathematics, biological/physical sciences, social sciences. **Additional information:** Outdoor semester in the Rockies: academic liberal arts program balanced with outdoor learning experiences. Other environmental and ski industry programs available.

FRESHMAN ADMISSIONS. Selection criteria: Open admissions.

1992 FRESHMAN CLASS PROFILE. 88 men, 20 women enrolled. **Characteristics:** 55% from in state, 65% live in college housing, 26% have minority backgrounds, 1% are foreign students. Average age is 22.

FALL-TERM APPLICATIONS. No fee. No closing date; priority given to applications received by August 15; applicants notified on a rolling basis. Deferred and early admission available. Neither SAT or ACT is required but both are recommended for placement and counseling. Scores should be received by August 15.

STUDENT LIFE. Housing: Dormitories (coed); apartment housing available. **Activities:** Student government, student newspaper. **Additional information:** Many outdoor activities available: skiing, hiking, biking. Health club memberships also available at discount.

ATHLETICS. Intercollegiate: Skiing. **Intramural:** Basketball M, soccer M, volleyball.

STUDENT SERVICES. Aptitude testing, career counseling, employment service for undergraduates, freshman orientation, personal counseling, placement service for graduates, special adviser for adult students, veterans counselor, services/facilities for handicapped.

ANNUAL EXPENSES. Tuition and fees: $1,030, $840 additional for out-of-district students, $4,500 additional for out-of-state students. **Room and board:** $3,600. **Books and supplies:** $700. **Other expenses:** $1,000.

FINANCIAL AID. 46% of freshmen, 51% of continuing students receive some form of aid. Grants, loans, jobs available. Academic, athletic, state/district residency scholarships available. **Aid applications:** No closing date; priority given to applications received by March 31; applicants notified on a rolling basis beginning on or about May 15; must reply within 4 weeks.

ADDRESS/TELEPHONE. Barbara Edwards, Director of Pre-Enrollment Services, Collegewide, Colorado Mountain College: Timberline Campus, 901 South Highway 24, Dept. CB, Leadville, CO 80461. (719) 486-2015. (800) 621-8559. Fax: (719) 486-3212.

Colorado Northwestern Community College

Rangely, Colorado CB code: 4665

2-year public community college, coed. Founded in 1962. **Accreditation:** Regional. **Undergraduate enrollment:** 292 men, 220 women full time; 344 men, 722 women part time. **Faculty:** 197 total (41 full time), 2 with doctorates or other terminal degrees. **Location:** Rural campus in small town; 300 miles from Denver, 90 miles from Grand Junction. **Calendar:** Semester, limited summer session. Extensive evening/early morning classes. **Microcomputers:** 50 located in libraries, classrooms, computer centers. **Special facilities:** Flight simulator, firearms training simulator. **Additional facts:** Students can take courses at 4 off-campus sites located in Meeker, Craig, Hayden, and Oak Creek.

DEGREES OFFERED. AA, AS, AAS. 93 associate degrees awarded in 1992. 11% in business and management, 9% business/office and marketing/distribution, 5% teacher education, 15% allied health, 19% multi/interdisciplinary studies, 16% parks/recreation, protective services, public affairs, 22% trade and industry.

UNDERGRADUATE MAJORS. Aircraft mechanics, airline piloting and navigation, biological and physical sciences, business and management, business and office, business data processing and related programs, computer and information sciences, criminal justice studies, dental hygiene, instrumentation technology, law enforcement and corrections, legal secretary, liberal/general studies, medical secretary, physical education, physical sciences, secretarial and related programs, small business management and ownership, word processing.

ACADEMIC PROGRAMS. 2-year transfer program, dual enrollment of high school students, independent study, telecourses. **Remedial services:** Learning center, remedial instruction, special counselor, tutoring. **Placement/credit:** AP, CLEP Subject, institutional tests; 30 credit hours maximum for associate degree.

ACADEMIC REQUIREMENTS. Freshmen must earn minimum GPA of 1.75 to continue in good standing. 53% of freshmen return for sophomore year. Students must declare major on enrollment. **Graduation requirements:** 62 hours for associate (43 in major). Most students required to take courses in computer science, English, mathematics, biological/physical sciences, social sciences.

FRESHMAN ADMISSIONS. Selection criteria: Open admissions. Selective admissions to dental hygiene and aviation maintenance programs. Biological science and/or chemistry required for dental hygiene. Mathematics/science desirable for aviation technology and aviation maintenance.

1992 FRESHMAN CLASS PROFILE. 133 men, 55 women enrolled. 19% had high school GPA of 3.0 or higher, 56% between 2.0 and 2.99. **Characteristics:** 82% from in state, 85% live in college housing, 20% have minority backgrounds, 2% are foreign students. Average age is 21.

FALL-TERM APPLICATIONS. $10 fee, may be waived for applicants with need. No closing date; applicants notified on a rolling basis. Interview required for dental hygiene applicants. Deferred and early admission available. Application closing date for dental hygiene program is April 1.

STUDENT LIFE. Housing: Dormitories (men, women, coed); apartment housing available. **Activities:** Student government, newsletter, choral groups, concert band.

ATHLETICS. NJCAA, NSCAA. **Intercollegiate:** Baseball M, basketball, softball W, volleyball W, wrestling M. **Intramural:** Basketball, golf, racquetball, soccer, softball, table tennis, tennis, track and field, volleyball.

STUDENT SERVICES. Aptitude testing, career counseling, employment service for undergraduates, freshman orientation, personal counseling, placement service for graduates, special adviser for adult students, veterans counselor, services/facilities for handicapped.

ANNUAL EXPENSES. Tuition and fees (1992-93): $260, $770 additional for out-of-district students, $2,850 additional for out-of-state students. **Room and board:** $3,050. **Books and supplies:** $450. **Other expenses:** $2,250.

FINANCIAL AID. 95% of freshmen, 75% of continuing students receive some form of aid. 60% of grants, 72% of loans, 68% of jobs based on need. 103 enrolled freshmen were judged to have need, all were offered aid. Academic, athletic, state/district residency, minority scholarships available. **Aid applications:** No closing date; priority given to applications received by May 1; applicants notified on a rolling basis beginning on or about July 15; must reply within 4 weeks.

ADDRESS/TELEPHONE. Susan H. Shafer, Director of Admissions and Records, Colorado Northwestern Community College, 500 Kennedy Drive, Rangely, CO 81648-9988. (303) 675-3220. (800) 562-1105 ext. 220. Fax: (303) 675-3330.

Colorado School of Mines
Golden, Colorado CB code: 4073

Admissions: 48% of applicants accepted
Based on: ••• School record
•• Test scores
• Activities, essay, interview, recommendations, special talents
Completion: 90% of freshmen end year in good standing
65% graduate, 15% of these enter graduate study

4-year public engineering college, coed. Founded in 1874. **Accreditation:** Regional. **Undergraduate enrollment:** 1,490 men, 429 women full time; 56 men, 16 women part time. **Graduate enrollment:** 348 men, 96 women full time; 305 men, 76 women part time. **Faculty:** 250 total (175 full time), 179 with doctorates or other terminal degrees. **Location:** Suburban campus in large town; 15 miles from Denver. **Calendar:** Semester, limited summer session. **Microcomputers:** 200 located in dormitories, libraries, classrooms, computer centers, campus-wide network. **Special facilities:** Geology museum, geophysical observatory, Edgar experimental mine.

DEGREES OFFERED. BS, MS, PhD. 258 bachelor's degrees awarded in 1992. 85% in engineering, 7% mathematics, 8% physical sciences. Graduate degrees offered in 23 major fields of study.

UNDERGRADUATE MAJORS. Applied mathematics, chemical engineering, chemistry, computer and information sciences, engineering, engineering physics, geological engineering, geophysical engineering, materials engineering, metallurgical engineering, mining and mineral engineering, petroleum engineering, physics.

ACADEMIC PROGRAMS. Accelerated program, cooperative education, double major, dual enrollment of high school students, honors program, independent study. **Remedial services:** Preadmission summer program, reduced course load, remedial instruction, special counselor, tutoring. **ROTC:** Army. **Placement/credit:** AP, institutional tests.

ACADEMIC REQUIREMENTS. Freshmen must earn minimum GPA of 2.0 to continue in good standing. 85% of freshmen return for sophomore year. Students must declare major by end of second year. **Graduation requirements:** 144 hours for bachelor's (45 in major). Most students required to take courses in computer science, English, humanities, mathematics, biological/physical sciences, social sciences. **Postgraduate studies:** 1% enter law school, 1% enter medical school, 2% enter MBA programs, 11% enter other graduate study.

FRESHMAN ADMISSIONS. Selection criteria: Applicants should rank in top third of class, must complete 16 or more academic units, and submit aptitude test scores. Both scores and academic record considered with heavier weight given to academic record. **High school preparation:** 16 units required. Required and recommended units include English 4, mathematics 4, physical science 1, social science 2 and science 2. Foreign language 2 recommended. Mathematics units should include 2 algebra, 1 geometry, 1 trigonometry. Science units should include 1 unit of either chemistry or physics. **Test requirements:** SAT or ACT; score report by June 1.

1992 FRESHMAN CLASS PROFILE. 1,061 men applied, 378 accepted, 376 enrolled; 354 women applied, 307 accepted, 126 enrolled. 100% had high school GPA of 3.0 or higher. 56% were in top tenth and 90% were in top quarter of graduating class. **Academic background:** Mid 50% of enrolled freshmen had SAT-V between 470-600, SAT-M between 570-690; ACT composite between 24-28. 40% submitted SAT scores, 60% submitted ACT scores. **Characteristics:** 60% from in state, 80% live in college housing, 12% have minority backgrounds, 12% are foreign students, 10% join fraternities/sororities. Average age is 18.

FALL-TERM APPLICATIONS. $25 fee, may be waived for applicants with need. Closing date June 1; priority given to applications received by April 15; applicants notified on a rolling basis; must reply by May 1 or within 4 weeks if notified thereafter. Interview recommended. CRDA. Deferred and early admission available.

STUDENT LIFE. Housing: Dormitories (men, coed); apartment, fraternity, sorority housing available. **Activities:** Student government, magazine, student newspaper, yearbook, choral groups, concert band, drama, jazz band, marching band, music ensembles, symphony orchestra, fraternities, sororities, American Indian Science and Engineering Society, Asian Student Association, National Society of Black Engineers, Society of Hispanic Professional Engineers, various religious clubs.

ATHLETICS. NCAA. **Intercollegiate:** Baseball M, basketball, cross-country, football M, golf M, lacrosse M, skiing, soccer M, softball W, swimming, tennis M, track and field, volleyball W, wrestling M. **Intramural:** Badminton, basketball, cross-country, handball, racquetball, rugby M, softball, swimming, tennis, track and field, volleyball.

STUDENT SERVICES. Aptitude testing, career counseling, employment service for undergraduates, freshman orientation, health services, personal counseling, placement service for graduates, veterans counselor, services/facilities for handicapped.

ANNUAL EXPENSES. Tuition and fees (projected): $4,504, $7,260 additional for out-of-state students. **Room and board:** $4,050. **Books and supplies:** $700. **Other expenses:** $1,200.

FINANCIAL AID. 85% of freshmen, 85% of continuing students receive some form of aid. 95% of grants, 88% of loans, 81% of jobs based on need. 375 enrolled freshmen were judged to have need, all were offered aid. Academic, music/drama, athletic, state/district residency, leadership, alumni affiliation, minority scholarships available. **Aid applications:** No closing date; priority given to applications received by March 1; applicants notified on a rolling basis beginning on or about March 25; must reply by May 1 or within 2 weeks if notified thereafter. **Additional information:** Same room rate guaranteed to freshmen who want to live in college housing all 4 years.

ADDRESS/TELEPHONE. A. William Young, Director of Enrollment Management, Colorado School of Mines, Twin Towers-1811 Elm St, Golden, CO 80401-1873. (303) 273-3220. (800) 446-9488. Fax: (303) 273-3165.

Colorado State University
Fort Collins, Colorado CB code: 4075

Admissions: 68% of applicants accepted
Based on: ••• Essay, school record, test scores
• Activities, interview, recommendations, special talents
Completion: 49% graduate

4-year public university, coed. Founded in 1870. **Accreditation:** Regional. **Undergraduate enrollment:** 8,098 men, 7,550 women full time; 952 men, 972 women part time. **Graduate enrollment:** 1,408 men, 1,133 women full time; 597 men, 500 women part time. **Faculty:** 1,021 total, 896 with doctorates or other terminal degrees. **Location:** Suburban campus in small city; 60 miles from Denver. **Calendar:** Semester, extensive summer session. **Microcomputers:** Located in dormitories, libraries, classrooms, computer centers, campus-wide network. **Special facilities:** Student recreation center.

DEGREES OFFERED. BA, BS, BFA, MA, MS, MBA, MFA, MEd, MSW, PhD, DVM. 3,177 bachelor's degrees awarded in 1992. 9% in agriculture, 17% business and management, 7% engineering, 9% home economics, 7% life sciences, 6% multi/interdisciplinary studies, 12% social sciences. Graduate degrees offered in 79 major fields of study.

UNDERGRADUATE MAJORS. Accounting, agribusiness, agricultural business and management, agricultural economics, agricultural education, agricultural engineering, agricultural sciences, agricultural/natural resources journalism, agronomy, animal sciences, anthropology, art education, art history, biochemistry, biology, botany, business administration and management, ceramics, chemical engineering, chemistry, civil engineering, computer and information sciences, construction, creative writing, dance, dramatic arts, drawing, economics, electrical/electronics/communications engineering, engineering science, English, English education, environmental health, equestrian science, family/consumer resource management, fiber/textiles/weaving, finance, fine arts, food science and nutrition, food sciences, foreign languages education, forestry and related sciences, French, geology, German, graphic design, history, home economics, home economics education, horticulture, hotel/motel and restaurant management, humanities and social sciences, individual and family development, industrial arts education, industrial technology, interior design, journalism, landscape architecture, management information systems, management science, marketing management, mathematics, mathematics education, mechanical engineering, metal/jewelry, microbiology, music, music education, music performance, music therapy, occupational therapy, ornamental horticulture, painting, parks and recreation management, philosophy, photography, physical education, physical sciences, physics, political science and government, printmaking, psychology, range management, real estate, renewable natural resources, science education, sculpture, social sciences, social studies education, social work, sociology, Spanish, speech, speech/communication/theater education, sports medicine, statistics, studio art, technical education, textiles and clothing, trade and industrial education, watershed sciences, wildlife management, zoology.

ACADEMIC PROGRAMS. Cooperative education, double major, honors program, independent study, internships, study abroad, teacher preparation, telecourses, visiting/exchange student program; liberal arts/career combination in engineering. **Remedial services:** Special counselor, tutoring, intensive English program. **ROTC:** Army. **Placement/credit:** AP, CLEP General and Subject, institutional tests; 30 credit hours maximum for bachelor's degree.

ACADEMIC REQUIREMENTS. Freshmen must earn minimum GPA of 2.0 to continue in good standing. 83% of freshmen return for sophomore year. Students must declare major on application. **Graduation requirements:** 128 hours for bachelor's (27 in major). Most students required to take courses in English, humanities, mathematics, biological/physical sciences, social sciences.

FRESHMAN ADMISSIONS. Selection criteria: Admission based on numerical index in which cumulative GPA or class rank, whichever is higher, weighted along with highest set of ACT/SAT test scores received. Personal essay, achievement record, activities and recommendations considered. Minority status given added consideration. **High school preparation:** 15 units required. Required and recommended units include English 4, mathematics 3, social science 2 and science 2. Foreign language 2 recommended. Additional unit of either social science or natural science also required. .5

trigonometry, chemistry, 1 natural science (physics preferred) required for engineering major. **Test requirements:** SAT or ACT; score report by June 1.

1992 FRESHMAN CLASS PROFILE. 4,283 men applied, 2,798 accepted, 1,068 enrolled; 4,300 women applied, 3,001 accepted, 1,157 enrolled. 85% had high school GPA of 3.0 or higher, 15% between 2.0 and 2.99. **Academic background:** Mid 50% of enrolled freshmen had SAT-V between 410-530, SAT-M between 470-670; ACT composite between 21-26. 61% submitted SAT scores, 84% submitted ACT scores. **Characteristics:** 74% from in state, 95% live in college housing, 14% have minority backgrounds, 1% are foreign students. Average age is 18.

FALL-TERM APPLICATIONS. $30 fee, may be waived for applicants with need. Closing date July 1; applicants notified on a rolling basis. Essay required. Institutional early decision plan. Early application (once 6th semester transcript is available) is encouraged.

STUDENT LIFE. Housing: Dormitories (coed); apartment, fraternity, sorority housing available. Special dormitory floors for business, engineering, photography, preveterinary, performing and fine arts, and honors students. **Activities:** Student government, radio, student newspaper, yearbook, choral groups, concert band, dance, drama, jazz band, marching band, music ensembles, musical theater, opera, pep band, symphony orchestra, fraternities, sororities.

ATHLETICS. NCAA. **Intercollegiate:** Basketball, cross-country, football M, golf, swimming W, tennis, track and field, volleyball W. **Intramural:** Badminton, basketball, bowling, diving, fencing, golf, gymnastics, handball, horseback riding, ice hockey M, lacrosse, racquetball, rugby, skiing, soccer, softball, swimming, tennis, volleyball, water polo.

STUDENT SERVICES. Aptitude testing, career counseling, employment service for undergraduates, freshman orientation, health services, personal counseling, placement service for graduates, special adviser for adult students, veterans counselor, support offices for women and minorities, services/facilities for handicapped.

ANNUAL EXPENSES. Tuition and fees (1992-93): $2,510, $5,166 additional for out-of-state students. **Room and board:** $4,140. **Books and supplies:** $470. **Other expenses:** $1,500.

FINANCIAL AID. 92% of freshmen, 50% of continuing students receive some form of aid. 57% of grants, 82% of loans, 10% of jobs based on need. Academic, music/drama, art, athletic, minority scholarships available. **Aid applications:** No closing date; priority given to applications received by March 1; applicants notified on a rolling basis beginning on or about May 1; must reply within 3 weeks.

ADDRESS/TELEPHONE. Mary Ontiveros, Director of Admissions, Colorado State University, Administration Annex, Fort Collins, CO 80523-0015. (303) 491-6909. Fax: (303) 491-7799.

Colorado Technical College
Colorado Springs, Colorado — CB code: 4133

4-year proprietary engineering, technical college, coed. Founded in 1965. **Accreditation:** Regional. **Undergraduate enrollment:** 371 men, 71 women full time; 640 men, 142 women part time. **Graduate enrollment:** 212 men, 42 women full time. **Faculty:** 80 total (25 full time), 24 with doctorates or other terminal degrees. **Location:** Suburban campus in large city; 63 miles from Denver. **Calendar:** Quarter, extensive summer session. Saturday and extensive evening/early morning classes. **Microcomputers:** 123 located in libraries, computer centers. **Special facilities:** Extensive electronics laboratories and computer facilities.

DEGREES OFFERED. AS, BS, MS. 69 associate degrees awarded in 1992. 35% in computer sciences, 65% engineering technologies. 114 bachelor's degrees awarded. 29% in business and management, 21% computer sciences, 29% engineering, 21% engineering technologies. Graduate degrees offered in 3 major fields of study.

UNDERGRADUATE MAJORS. Associate: Electronic technology, engineering and engineering-related technologies. **Bachelor's:** Business and management, computer and information sciences, computer engineering, computer programming, contract management and procurement/purchasing, defense systems management, electrical/electronics/communications engineering, electronic technology, engineering and engineering-related technologies, logistics systems management.

ACADEMIC PROGRAMS. Accelerated program, cooperative education, double major, internships. **Remedial services:** Learning center, reduced course load, remedial instruction, tutoring. **ROTC:** Army. **Placement/credit:** AP, CLEP General and Subject, institutional tests; 15 credit hours maximum for associate degree; 30 credit hours maximum for bachelor's degree.

ACADEMIC REQUIREMENTS. Freshmen must earn minimum GPA of 2.0 to continue in good standing. 82% of freshmen return for sophomore year. Students must declare major on enrollment. **Graduation requirements:** 102 hours for associate, 199 hours for bachelor's. Most students required to take courses in arts/fine arts, computer science, English, history, humanities, mathematics, biological/physical sciences, social sciences. **Postgraduate studies:** 85% from 2-year programs enter 4-year programs. 3% enter MBA programs, 12% enter other graduate study.

FRESHMAN ADMISSIONS. Selection criteria: SAT or ACT scores are important. **Test requirements:** SAT or ACT; score report by September 30. Evaluation examination required of applicants with ACT composite score less than 24 or SAT combined score less than 1000.

1992 FRESHMAN CLASS PROFILE. 193 men, 32 women enrolled. **Characteristics:** 70% from in state, 100% commute, 16% have minority backgrounds, 5% are foreign students.

FALL-TERM APPLICATIONS. $50 fee, may be waived for applicants with need. No closing date; applicants notified on a rolling basis beginning on or about July 15. Interview recommended. Deferred admission available. EDP-F.

STUDENT LIFE. Activities: Student government, student newspaper.

ATHLETICS. Intramural: Basketball, skiing, soccer M, softball, volleyball.

STUDENT SERVICES. Career counseling, employment service for undergraduates, freshman orientation, personal counseling, placement service for graduates, veterans counselor, services/facilities for handicapped.

ANNUAL EXPENSES. Tuition and fees (1992-93): $6,240. **Books and supplies:** $700. **Other expenses:** $200.

FINANCIAL AID. 45% of freshmen, 37% of continuing students receive some form of aid. 73% of grants, 62% of loans, all jobs based on need. Academic scholarships available. **Aid applications:** No closing date; applicants notified on a rolling basis beginning on or about June 30.

ADDRESS/TELEPHONE. Director of Admissions, Colorado Technical College, 4435 Chestnut Street, Colorado Springs, CO 80907-3896. (719) 598-0200. Fax: (719) 598-3740.

Community College of Aurora
Aurora, Colorado — CB code: 0969

2-year public community college, coed. Founded in 1983. **Accreditation:** Regional. **Undergraduate enrollment:** 800 men and women full time; 4,200 men and women part time. **Faculty:** 232 total (12 full time). **Location:** Urban campus in small city. **Calendar:** Semester. Saturday and extensive evening/early morning classes.

DEGREES OFFERED. AA, AS, AAS. 270 associate degrees awarded in 1992.

UNDERGRADUATE MAJORS. Accounting, air conditioning/heating/refrigeration mechanics, automotive mechanics, business and management, carpentry, criminal justice technology, diesel engine mechanics, drafting, early childhood education, electrical installation, finance, food management, graphic and printing production, legal secretary, machine tool operation/machine shop, marketing management, medical secretary, secretarial and related programs, word processing.

ACADEMIC PROGRAMS. 2-year transfer program, internships, study abroad, weekend college. **Remedial services:** Learning center, remedial instruction, tutoring.

ACADEMIC REQUIREMENTS. Freshmen must earn minimum GPA of 2.0 to continue in good standing. Students must declare major on enrollment. **Graduation requirements:** 60 hours for associate. Most students required to take courses in English, humanities, mathematics, biological/physical sciences, social sciences.

FRESHMAN ADMISSIONS. Selection criteria: Open admissions.

1992 FRESHMAN CLASS PROFILE. 1,000 men and women enrolled. **Characteristics:** 97% from in state, 100% commute, 1% are foreign students.

FALL-TERM APPLICATIONS. No fee. No closing date; applicants notified on a rolling basis.

STUDENT LIFE. Activities: Student government, student newspaper.

ATHLETICS. Intramural: Basketball, softball, tennis, volleyball.

STUDENT SERVICES. Career counseling, employment service for undergraduates, veterans counselor, services/facilities for handicapped.

ANNUAL EXPENSES. Tuition and fees (1992-93): $1,510, $4,320 additional for out-of-state students. **Books and supplies:** $400.

FINANCIAL AID. 12% of freshmen, 12% of continuing students receive some form of aid. 84% of grants, all jobs based on need. Academic, minority scholarships available. **Aid applications:** No closing date; priority given to applications received by June 1; applicants notified on a rolling basis beginning on or about July 15.

ADDRESS/TELEPHONE. Jo Roth, Director of Admissions, Community College of Aurora, 1600 East CentreTech Parkway, Aurora, CO 80011. (303) 360-4700. Fax: (303) 360-4761.

Community College of Denver
Denver, Colorado — CB code: 4137

2-year public community college, coed. Founded in 1970. **Accreditation:** Regional. **Undergraduate enrollment:** 910 men, 1,370 women full time; 1,983 men, 2,712 women part time. **Faculty:** 281 total (110 full time), 57 with doctorates or other terminal degrees. **Location:** Urban campus in very large city. **Calendar:** Semester, limited summer session. Extensive evening/early morning classes. **Microcomputers:** Located in computer centers. **Additional facts:** Library, student center, and physical education facilities shared with Metropolitan State College and University of Colorado at Denver.

DEGREES OFFERED. AA, AS, AAS. 273 associate degrees awarded in 1992. 12% in business and management, 8% computer sciences, 10% engineering technologies, 17% health sciences, 16% allied health, 8% law, 5% social sciences, 15% trade and industry.

UNDERGRADUATE MAJORS. Accounting, air conditioning/heating/refrigeration mechanics, air conditioning/heating/refrigeration technology, aircraft mechanics, biology, biomedical equipment technology, business and management, business and office, business data processing and related programs, business data programming, business systems analysis, chemistry, child development/care/guidance, commercial art, computer and information sciences, computer programming, drafting, drafting and design technology, dramatic arts, electrical and electronics equipment repair, electronic technology, fine arts, graphic and printing production, graphic arts technology, hotel/motel and restaurant management, legal assistant/paralegal, legal secretary, liberal/general studies, marketing and distribution, marketing management, mathematics, medical radiation dosimetry, medical secretary, music, nuclear medical technology, nursing, photographic technology, physics, psychology, radiograph medical technology, respiratory therapy technology, secretarial and related programs, social sciences, social work, surgical technology, transportation management, word processing.

ACADEMIC PROGRAMS. 2-year transfer program, cooperative education, double major, dual enrollment of high school students, independent study, internships, study abroad, weekend college, cross-registration. **Remedial services:** Learning center, reduced course load, remedial instruction, tutoring. **Placement/credit:** AP, CLEP General and Subject, institutional tests; 45 credit hours maximum for associate degree.

ACADEMIC REQUIREMENTS. Freshmen must earn minimum GPA of 2.0 to continue in good standing. 30% of freshmen return for sophomore year. Students must declare major by end of first year. **Graduation requirements:** 60 hours for associate (48 in major). Most students required to take courses in English, history, mathematics, biological/physical sciences, social sciences.

FRESHMAN ADMISSIONS. Selection criteria: Open admissions. Selective admissions to health occupations programs.

1992 FRESHMAN CLASS PROFILE. 1,456 men, 1,677 women enrolled. **Characteristics:** 94% from in state, 100% commute, 42% have minority backgrounds, 6% are foreign students. Average age is 24.

FALL-TERM APPLICATIONS. No fee. No closing date; applicants notified on a rolling basis; must reply by registration. Interview recommended. Deferred and early admission available.

STUDENT LIFE. Housing: Dormitory housing sometimes available at University of Denver. **Activities:** Student government, student newspaper, Student Handbook, choral groups, drama, Mexican-American Student Organization, Black Student Organization, Amnesty International, Ad Hoc Nursing Club. **Additional information:** Many athletic activities available through Metropolitan State College. Computer facilities available for physically handicapped.

ATHLETICS. Intramural: Archery, badminton, baseball, basketball, bowling, cross-country, diving, fencing, field hockey, golf, gymnastics, handball, horseback riding, racquetball, rifle, rugby, skiing, soccer, softball, swimming, tennis, track and field, volleyball.

STUDENT SERVICES. Career counseling, employment service for undergraduates, freshman orientation, health services, on-campus day care, personal counseling, placement service for graduates, veterans counselor, women's center, legal services, services/facilities for handicapped.

ANNUAL EXPENSES. Tuition and fees (1992-93): $1,609, $4,320 additional for out-of-state students. **Books and supplies:** $415. **Other expenses:** $916.

FINANCIAL AID. 28% of freshmen, 36% of continuing students receive some form of aid. 86% of grants based on need. 1,056 enrolled freshmen were judged to have need, all were offered aid. Academic, music/drama, art, state/district residency, minority scholarships available. **Aid applications:** No closing date; priority given to applications received by June 1; applicants notified on a rolling basis beginning on or about June 1; must reply within 2 weeks.

ADDRESS/TELEPHONE. Michael Poindexter, Director of Registration and Records, Community College of Denver, P.O. Box 173363, Denver, CO 80217-3363. (303) 556-2600. Fax: (303) 556-8555.

Denver Institute of Technology
Denver, Colorado — CB code: 3948

2-year proprietary technical college, coed. Founded in 1953. **Undergraduate enrollment:** 750 men and women full time. **Faculty:** 50 total (38 full time). **Location:** Suburban campus in very large city; 10 miles from downtown. **Calendar:** Quarter, extensive summer session. Extensive evening/early morning classes. **Microcomputers:** Located in classrooms, computer centers.

DEGREES OFFERED. AAS. 400 associate degrees awarded in 1992. 39% in engineering technologies, 5% allied health, 56% trade and industry.

UNDERGRADUATE MAJORS. Architectural technologies, architecture, automotive mechanics, civil technology, drafting and design technology, electrical and electronics equipment repair, electronic technology, graphic and printing production, graphic design, laser electro-optic technology, mechanical design technology, medical assistant, occupational therapy assistant, recreation therapy, robotics, survey and mapping technology.

ACADEMIC PROGRAMS. Accelerated program, independent study. **Remedial services:** 6-week study skills and mathematics refresher courses. **Placement/credit:** AP, CLEP General and Subject, institutional tests; 45 credit hours maximum for associate degree.

ACADEMIC REQUIREMENTS. 70% of freshmen return for sophomore year. Students must declare major on enrollment. **Graduation requirements:** 100 hours for associate (72 in major). Most students required to take courses in English. **Additional information:** Heavy emphasis placed on laboratory work and practical application.

FRESHMAN ADMISSIONS. Selection criteria: Institutional test and interview most important. One unit minimum of algebra required for electronics, drafting, and surveying, programs. General mathematics required for all other programs. **Test requirements:** Science Research Associate Test of Mechanical Concepts and/or institutionally developed entrance examinations required for certain majors.

1992 FRESHMAN CLASS PROFILE. Characteristics: 80% from in state, 100% commute, 19% have minority backgrounds, 1% are foreign students.

FALL-TERM APPLICATIONS. $130 fee. No closing date; applicants notified on a rolling basis; must reply within 1 week. Interview required. On-campus interview required for in-state applicants, phone interview for out-of-state applicants.

STUDENT SERVICES. Employment service for undergraduates, on-campus day care, personal counseling, placement service for graduates, veterans counselor, services/facilities for handicapped.

ANNUAL EXPENSES. Tuition and fees (projected): Comprehensive charge for tuition, fees, books, and tools ranges from $7,695 to $15,445 for 12-, to 15-, 18-month programs. **Other expenses:** $150.

FINANCIAL AID. 94% of freshmen, 94% of continuing students receive some form of aid. 95% of grants, 59% of loans, all jobs based on need. Academic, state/district residency scholarships available. **Aid applications:** No closing date; applicants notified on a rolling basis; must reply immediately.

ADDRESS/TELEPHONE. Don Dunphy, Director of Admissions, Denver Institute of Technology, The Educational Plaza, 7350 North Broadway, Denver, CO 80221. (303) 650-5050. (800) 875-6050. Fax: (303) 426-4647.

Denver Technical College
Denver, Colorado — CB code: 1327

4-year proprietary technical college, coed. Founded in 1945. **Undergraduate enrollment:** 1,100 men and women. **Faculty:** 95 total (30 full time), 5 with doctorates or other terminal degrees. **Location:** Urban campus in very large city; 5 miles from downtown. **Calendar:** Quarter. Saturday and extensive evening/early morning classes. **Microcomputers:** 70 located in computer centers. **Special facilities:** Computerized resource center, branch of Aurora County public library.

DEGREES OFFERED. AS, BS. 220 associate degrees awarded in 1992. 50 bachelor's degrees awarded.

UNDERGRADUATE MAJORS. Associate: Accounting, architectural technologies, architecture, business and management, business data processing and related programs, business data programming, computer and information sciences, computer programming, drafting, drafting and design technology, electrical/electronics/communications engineering, electronic technology, information sciences and systems, medical assistant, medical records technology, physical therapy assistant, robotics, sports management, sports medicine, survey and mapping technology, word processing. **Bachelor's:** Business administration and management, business and management, electrical/electronics/communications engineering, health services management, small business management and ownership, technical management.

ACADEMIC PROGRAMS. Double major, internships, weekend college; liberal arts/career combination in health sciences. **Remedial services:** Learning center, reduced course load, remedial instruction, special counselor, tutoring. **Placement/credit:** Institutional tests; 32 credit hours maximum for associate degree; 32 credit hours maximum for bachelor's degree.

ACADEMIC REQUIREMENTS. Freshmen must earn minimum GPA of 1.5 to continue in good standing. 82% of freshmen return for sophomore year. Students must declare major by end of second year. **Graduation requirements:** 96 hours for associate, 192 hours for bachelor's. Most students required to take courses in computer science, English, history, mathematics, biological/physical sciences, social sciences. **Postgraduate studies:** 10% enter MBA programs. **Additional information:** Students must complete significant portion of freshman and sophomore years before being accepted into bachelor's degree program. Courses taught every quarter applicable to newly entering freshmen.

FRESHMAN ADMISSIONS. Selection criteria: Test scores, interview important. **Test requirements:** Wonderlic required for admission.

1992 FRESHMAN CLASS PROFILE. 350 men and women enrolled. **Characteristics:** 98% from in state, 100% commute, 35% have minority backgrounds.

FALL-TERM APPLICATIONS. $35 fee. No closing date; applicants notified on a rolling basis. Interview required. Deferred admission available.

STUDENT LIFE. Activities: Student government, student newspaper, student advisory committee.

ATHLETICS. Intramural: Basketball, bowling, softball.

STUDENT SERVICES. Aptitude testing, career counseling, employment service for undergraduates, freshman orientation, placement service for graduates, veterans counselor, services/facilities for handicapped.

ANNUAL EXPENSES. Tuition and fees (projected): $6,600. Tuition and fees includes books. **Other expenses:** $450.

FINANCIAL AID. 97% of freshmen, 94% of continuing students receive some form of aid. Grants, loans available. **Aid applications:** No closing date; applicants notified on a rolling basis.

ADDRESS/TELEPHONE. Raul Valdes-Pages, Chief Operating Officer, Denver Technical College, 925 South Niagara, Denver, CO 80222-1658. (303) 329-3000.

Fort Lewis College
Durango, Colorado CB code: 4310

Admissions:	87% of applicants accepted
Based on:	••• School record
	•• Test scores
	• Activities, essay, interview, recommendations
Completion:	75% of freshmen end year in good standing
	43% graduate, 32% of these enter graduate study

4-year public liberal arts college, coed. Founded in 1911. **Accreditation:** Regional. **Undergraduate enrollment:** 1,938 men, 1,700 women full time; 224 men, 234 women part time. **Faculty:** 221 total (183 full time), 160 with doctorates or other terminal degrees. **Location:** Rural campus in large town; 215 miles from Albuquerque, New Mexico, 330 miles from Denver. **Calendar:** Trimester, extensive summer session. Extensive evening/early morning classes. **Microcomputers:** 250 located in dormitories, libraries, classrooms, computer centers. **Special facilities:** Center for Southwest Studies, nuclear magnetic resonance spectrometer.

DEGREES OFFERED. AS, BA, BS. 5 associate degrees awarded in 1992. 100% in agriculture. 450 bachelor's degrees awarded. 27% in business and management, 20% communications, 10% teacher education, 5% multi/interdisciplinary studies, 10% physical sciences, 10% psychology, 11% social sciences.

UNDERGRADUATE MAJORS. Associate: Agricultural sciences. **Bachelor's:** Accounting, agribusiness, anthropology, bilingual/bicultural education, biochemistry, biological and physical sciences, biology, business administration and management, business and management, business economics, chemistry, communications, computer and information sciences, criminal justice studies, elementary education, engineering and other disciplines, engineering management, English, environmental science, finance, fine arts, geology, history, hotel/motel and restaurant management, humanities, humanities and social sciences, information sciences and systems, international business management, international studies, journalism, management information systems, management science, marketing and distribution, marketing research, mathematics, molecular biology, music, philosophy, physical sciences, physics, political science and government, predentistry, prelaw, premedicine, prepharmacy, preveterinary, psychology, secondary education, sociology, Spanish, statistics, teaching English as a second language/foreign language, visual and performing arts.

ACADEMIC PROGRAMS. Accelerated program, cooperative education, double major, dual enrollment of high school students, honors program, independent study, internships, student-designed major, study abroad, teacher preparation, visiting/exchange student program; liberal arts/career combination in engineering; combined bachelor's/graduate program in business administration. **Remedial services:** Learning center, remedial instruction, special counselor, tutoring. **Placement/credit:** AP, CLEP General and Subject, institutional tests; 28 credit hours maximum for bachelor's degree.

ACADEMIC REQUIREMENTS. Freshmen must earn minimum GPA of 2.0 to continue in good standing. 65% of freshmen return for sophomore year. Students must declare major by end of second year. **Graduation requirements:** 64 hours for associate (26 in major), 128 hours for bachelor's (45 in major). Most students required to take courses in arts/fine arts, English, biological/physical sciences, social sciences. **Postgraduate studies:** 75% from 2-year programs enter 4-year programs. 3% enter law school, 2% enter medical school, 12% enter MBA programs, 15% enter other graduate study. **Additional information:** Teacher certification available at elementary and secondary levels.

FRESHMAN ADMISSIONS. Selection criteria: Admission based on index system that uses GPA, rank, and ACT or SAT results. Students should have minimum 2.5 GPA and 810 SAT or 19 ACT. Stronger GPA can compensate for lower test scores and stronger test scores can compensate for lower GPA. **High school preparation:** 12 units required. Required and recommended units include biological science 1, English 3-4, mathematics 2-3, physical science 1-2, social science 2-3 and science 2-3. Foreign language 2 recommended. **Test requirements:** SAT or ACT (ACT preferred); score report by August 1.

1992 FRESHMAN CLASS PROFILE. 2,983 men and women applied, 2,587 accepted; 970 men enrolled, 735 women enrolled. 26% had high school GPA of 3.0 or higher, 70% between 2.0 and 2.99. 9% were in top tenth and 41% were in top quarter of graduating class. **Academic background:** Mid 50% of enrolled freshmen had ACT composite between 14-21. 70% submitted ACT scores. **Characteristics:** 75% from in state, 85% live in college housing, 19% have minority backgrounds, 1% are foreign students. Average age is 18.

FALL-TERM APPLICATIONS. $20 fee, may be waived for applicants with need. Closing date August 1; applicants notified on a rolling basis; must reply by May 1 or as soon as possible if notified thereafter. Interview recommended for academically weak or undecided applicants. Audition recommended. Portfolio recommended. Essay recommended. CRDA. Deferred and early admission available.

STUDENT LIFE. Housing: Dormitories (men, women, coed); apartment housing available. Early application for housing advised. First time students guaranteed on-campus housing until June 15. Freshmen required to live on campus. **Activities:** Student government, film, magazine, radio, student newspaper, yearbook, choral groups, concert band, drama, jazz band, marching band, music ensembles, musical theater, pep band, symphony orchestra, Newman Club, Raider Christian Fellowship, Windhover, Circle K International, United Coalition Against Prejudice, Black Student Organization.

ATHLETICS. NAIA, NCAA. **Intercollegiate:** Basketball, cross-country, football M, golf M, soccer M, softball W, volleyball W, wrestling M. **Intramural:** Basketball, fencing, soccer, softball, swimming, tennis, volleyball.

STUDENT SERVICES. Aptitude testing, career counseling, employment service for undergraduates, freshman orientation, health services, on-campus day care, personal counseling, placement service for graduates, special adviser for adult students, veterans counselor, services/facilities for handicapped.

ANNUAL EXPENSES. Tuition and fees (projected): $1,765, $4,750 additional for out-of-state students. **Room and board:** $3,540. **Books and supplies:** $500. **Other expenses:** $1,384.

FINANCIAL AID. 61% of freshmen, 59% of continuing students receive some form of aid. 86% of grants, 85% of loans, 63% of jobs based on need. 612 enrolled freshmen were judged to have need, all were offered aid. Academic, music/drama, art, athletic, state/district residency, leadership, alumni affiliation, religious affiliation, minority scholarships available. **Aid applications:** No closing date; priority given to applications received by April 15; applicants notified on a rolling basis beginning on or about May 1; must reply within 4 weeks. **Additional information:** Tuition waived for native Americans of federally recognized tribes; census number must accompany application.

ADDRESS/TELEPHONE. Sheri Rochford, Director of Admissions, Fort Lewis College, 1000 Rim Drive, Durango, CO 81301. (303) 247-7184. (800) 233-6731. Fax: (303) 247-7179.

Front Range Community College
Westminster, Colorado CB code: 4119

2-year public community college, coed. Founded in 1968. **Accreditation:** Regional. **Undergraduate enrollment:** 1,386 men, 1,936 women full time; 3,346 men, 4,676 women part time. **Faculty:** 488 total (138 full time), 15 with doctorates or other terminal degrees. **Location:** Suburban campus in small city; 10 miles from Denver. **Calendar:** Semester, limited summer session. Extensive evening/early morning classes. **Microcomputers:** 250 located in libraries, classrooms, computer centers. **Special facilities:** Basic literacy laboratory.

DEGREES OFFERED. AS, AAS. 693 associate degrees awarded in 1992.

UNDERGRADUATE MAJORS. Accounting, architectural technologies, architecture, automotive technology, business administration and management, business and management, business and office, business data programming, computer and information sciences, computer programming, dietetic aide/assistant, drafting, drafting and design technology, electronic technology, horticultural science, horticulture, interpreter for the deaf, legal secretary, liberal/general studies, marketing and distribution, marketing management, nursing, ornamental horticulture, practical nursing, precision metal work, respiratory therapy, respiratory therapy technology, science technologies, secretarial and related programs, technical and business writing, welding technology, word processing.

ACADEMIC PROGRAMS. 2-year transfer program, computer delivered (on-line) credit-bearing course offerings, cooperative education, double major, dual enrollment of high school students, honors program, independent study, internships, study abroad, telecourses, cross-registration. **Remedial services:** Learning center, remedial instruction, tutoring. **Placement/credit:** AP, CLEP General and Subject, institutional tests; 30 credit hours maximum for associate degree.

ACADEMIC REQUIREMENTS. Freshmen must earn minimum GPA of 2.0 to continue in good standing. 30% of freshmen return for sophomore

year. Students must declare major on application. **Graduation requirements:** 60 hours for associate. Most students required to take courses in English, humanities, mathematics, biological/physical sciences, social sciences.

FRESHMAN ADMISSIONS. Selection criteria: Open admissions. **Test requirements:** Institutional examination may be substituted for SAT or ACT.

1992 FRESHMAN CLASS PROFILE. 1,600 men and women enrolled. **Characteristics:** 98% from in state, 100% commute, 16% have minority backgrounds, 2% are foreign students. Average age is 27.

FALL-TERM APPLICATIONS. No fee. No closing date; applicants notified on a rolling basis; must reply by registration. Early admission available.

STUDENT LIFE. Activities: Student government, student newspaper, choral groups, fraternities, Phi Theta Kappa, Inter-varsity Christian Fellowship, Hispanic Club, Latter-Day Saints Student Organization, Student Ambassadors for Student Diversity, Philosophy Club, Business Club.

ATHLETICS. Intramural: Basketball, softball, volleyball.

STUDENT SERVICES. Aptitude testing, career counseling, employment service for undergraduates, freshman orientation, on-campus day care, personal counseling, placement service for graduates, veterans counselor, services/facilities for handicapped.

ANNUAL EXPENSES. Tuition and fees (1992-93): $1,572, $4,320 additional for out-of-state students. **Books and supplies:** $395. **Other expenses:** $675.

FINANCIAL AID. 36% of freshmen, 41% of continuing students receive some form of aid. 86% of grants, 82% of loans, 62% of jobs based on need. Academic, state/district residency scholarships available. **Aid applications:** No closing date; priority given to applications received by May 15; applicants notified on a rolling basis beginning on or about July 1; must reply within 2 weeks.

ADDRESS/TELEPHONE. Mark Boyko, Director of Admissions, Front Range Community College, 3645 West 112 Avenue, Westminster, CO 80030. (303) 466-8811. Fax: (303) 466-1623.

ITT Technical Institute: Aurora

Aurora, Colorado CB code: 3605

Admissions:	89% of applicants accepted
Based on:	••• Test scores
	•• Recommendations
	• Interview, school record
Completion:	65% of freshmen end year in good standing
	62% graduate, 35% of these enter 4-year programs

2-year proprietary technical college, coed. Founded in 1984. **Undergraduate enrollment:** 260 men, 23 women full time. **Faculty:** 14 total (9 full time), 3 with doctorates or other terminal degrees. **Location:** Urban campus in small city. **Calendar:** Quarter. Extensive evening/early morning classes. **Microcomputers:** 68 located in libraries, classrooms, computer centers. **Additional facts:** Bachelor of Applied Science in electronics engineering technology also offered.

DEGREES OFFERED. AAS. 77 associate degrees awarded in 1992. 100% in engineering technologies.

UNDERGRADUATE MAJORS. Computer-aided drafting, drafting, drafting and design technology, electrical and electronics equipment repair, electronic technology. electronic technology.

ACADEMIC PROGRAMS. Remedial services: Learning center, remedial instruction, tutoring. **Placement/credit:** Institutional tests; 60 credit hours maximum for associate degree.

ACADEMIC REQUIREMENTS. Freshmen must earn minimum GPA of 1.5 to continue in good standing. 63% of freshmen return for sophomore year. Students must declare major on application. **Graduation requirements:** 124 hours for associate. Most students required to take courses in mathematics.

FRESHMAN ADMISSIONS. Selection criteria: Satisfactory scores on English and/or mathematics and spatial relationships tests.

1992 FRESHMAN CLASS PROFILE. 240 men applied, 211 accepted, 137 enrolled; 16 women applied, 16 accepted, 14 enrolled. **Characteristics:** 92% from in state, 100% commute, 24% have minority backgrounds. Average age is 25.

FALL-TERM APPLICATIONS. $100 fee. Application fee refunded if student not accepted. Closing date September 1; applicants notified on a rolling basis. Interview required. Early admission available.

STUDENT LIFE. Activities: Student government, student newspaper.

ATHLETICS. Intercollegiate: Softball W. **Intramural:** Basketball, softball W.

STUDENT SERVICES. Career counseling, employment service for undergraduates, freshman orientation, personal counseling, placement service for graduates, services/facilities for handicapped.

ANNUAL EXPENSES. Tuition and fees (1992-93): Tuition for 2-year electronics program $14,405. Tuition for bachelor's program $5,439. Laboratory fees, $50 per quarter. **Books and supplies:** $1,450.

FINANCIAL AID. 80% of freshmen, 80% of continuing students receive some form of aid. 90% of grants, 66% of loans, all jobs based on need. Academic, leadership scholarships available. **Aid applications:** No closing date; applicants notified on a rolling basis.

ADDRESS/TELEPHONE. Fred Hansen, Director of Recruitment, ITT Technical Institute: Aurora, 2121 South Blackhawk Street, Aurora, CO 80014-1476. (303) 695-1913. (800) 395-4488. Fax: (303) 337-0683.

Lamar Community College

Lamar, Colorado CB code: 4382

2-year public community college, coed. **Accreditation:** Regional. **Undergraduate enrollment:** 253 men, 282 women full time; 113 men, 215 women part time. **Faculty:** 76 total (23 full time), 4 with doctorates or other terminal degrees. **Location:** Rural campus in large town; 117 miles from Pueblo. **Calendar:** Semester, limited summer session. Extensive evening/early morning classes. **Microcomputers:** 60 located in libraries, classrooms, computer centers.

DEGREES OFFERED. AA, AS, AAS. 80 associate degrees awarded in 1992. 43% in agriculture, 34% education, 14% trade and industry.

UNDERGRADUATE MAJORS. Accounting, agricultural business and management, agricultural sciences, agronomy, animal sciences, biological and physical sciences, biology, business administration and management, business and management, business and office, business data processing and related programs, communications, computer and information sciences, education, engineering, English, English literature, equestrian science, fine arts, history, humanities, humanities and social sciences, information sciences and systems, legal secretary, liberal/general studies, marketing management, mathematics, medical secretary, office supervision and management, physical sciences, predentistry, prepharmacy, preveterinary, psychology, quality control technology, range management, social sciences, social work, trade and industrial supervision and management.

ACADEMIC PROGRAMS. 2-year transfer program, cooperative education, dual enrollment of high school students, internships, student-designed major. **Remedial services:** Learning center, remedial instruction, special counselor, tutoring. **Placement/credit:** CLEP General and Subject, institutional tests; 16 credit hours maximum for associate degree.

ACADEMIC REQUIREMENTS. Freshmen must earn minimum GPA of 2.0 to continue in good standing. 76% of freshmen return for sophomore year. Students must declare major on application. **Graduation requirements:** 64 hours for associate (31 in major). Most students required to take courses in English, humanities, mathematics, biological/physical sciences, social sciences.

FRESHMAN ADMISSIONS. Selection criteria: Open admissions. Selective admission criteria for horse training management based on riding skills; admission to nursing based on test scores. **Additional information:** GED courses available at college.

1992 FRESHMAN CLASS PROFILE. 300 men and women enrolled. **Characteristics:** 80% from in state, 80% live in college housing, 9% have minority backgrounds, 1% are foreign students. Average age is 23.

FALL-TERM APPLICATIONS. $10 fee, may be waived for applicants with need. No closing date; applicants notified on a rolling basis; must reply by registration. Interview required for horse training and management applicants. Early admission available. Applicants to horse training and management and LPN nursing program encouraged to apply early.

STUDENT LIFE. Housing: Dormitories (men, women, coed). All single freshmen under age 21 not living with parent, guardian, or relatives must live in dormitory. **Activities:** Student government, student newspaper, television, yearbook, choral groups, dance, drama, Christian athletes, horse and rodeo club, Kosmetiques, LPN association, Phi Beta Lambda, nontraditional students club.

ATHLETICS. NJCAA, NSCAA. **Intercollegiate:** Baseball M, basketball M, volleyball W. **Intramural:** Bowling, golf, skiing, softball, tennis, volleyball. **Clubs:** Rodeo.

STUDENT SERVICES. Aptitude testing, career counseling, employment service for undergraduates, freshman orientation, personal counseling, veterans counselor, services/facilities for handicapped.

ANNUAL EXPENSES. Tuition and fees (1992-93): $1,720, $2,880 additional for out-of-state students. **Room and board:** $3,138. **Books and supplies:** $400. **Other expenses:** $400.

FINANCIAL AID. 80% of freshmen, 80% of continuing students receive some form of aid. 74% of grants, 93% of loans, 75% of jobs based on need. 190 enrolled freshmen were judged to have need, all were offered aid. Academic, art, athletic, leadership scholarships available. **Aid applications:** No closing date; priority given to applications received by May 1; applicants notified on a rolling basis beginning on or about July 7; must reply within 30 days.

ADDRESS/TELEPHONE. Beverly Carkhuff, Admissions Counselor, Lamar Community College, 2401 South Main Street, Lamar, CO 81052. (719) 336-2248 ext. 33. Fax: (719) 336-2448.

Mesa State College
Grand Junction, Colorado CB code: 4484

4-year public community, liberal arts college, coed. Founded in 1925. **Accreditation:** Regional. **Undergraduate enrollment:** 1,287 men, 1,600 women full time; 671 men, 1,061 women part time. **Faculty:** 212 total (163 full time), 81 with doctorates or other terminal degrees. **Location:** Suburban campus in large town; 250 miles from Denver, 300 miles from Salt Lake City, Utah. **Calendar:** Semester, limited summer session. Extensive evening/early morning classes. **Microcomputers:** 300 located in libraries, classrooms, computer centers. **Special facilities:** Agricultural farm, Johnson Art Gallery, electron microscope laboratory, plant herbarium, computer-aided drafting laboratory, technical training facility.

DEGREES OFFERED. AA, AS, AAS, BA, BS. 200 associate degrees awarded in 1992. 25% in business and management, 7% education, 24% health sciences, 11% parks/recreation, protective services, public affairs, 14% trade and industry. 402 bachelor's degrees awarded. 38% in business and management, 6% computer sciences, 8% health sciences, 16% letters/literature, 6% life sciences, 8% multi/interdisciplinary studies, 16% social sciences.

UNDERGRADUATE MAJORS. Associate: Accounting, agribusiness, agricultural sciences, anthropology, automotive mechanics, automotive technology, biology, business and management, business and office, business computer/console/peripheral equipment operation, business data entry equipment operation, business data processing and related programs, business data programming, chemistry, civil technology, commercial art, criminal justice studies, data processing, drafting, drafting and design technology, dramatic arts, early childhood education, electrical/electronics/communications engineering, electronic technology, engineering, engineering and engineering-related technologies, engineering science, English, fine arts, forestry and related sciences, geology, graphic and printing production, graphic arts technology, history, hospitality and recreation marketing, information sciences and systems, legal secretary, liberal/general studies, mathematics, medical secretary, music, nursing, office supervision and management, physics, political science and government, practical nursing, preengineering, premedicine, prepharmacy, preveterinary, printmaking, psychology, radiograph medical technology, science technologies, secretarial and related programs, transportation and travel marketing, visual and performing arts, welding technology. **Bachelor's:** Accounting, applied mathematics, behavioral sciences, biology, business administration and management, business and management, business and office, business computer/console/peripheral equipment operation, business economics, computer and information sciences, computer programming, counseling psychology, criminal justice studies, dramatic arts, economics, elementary education, English, English education, English literature, finance, fine arts, geology, health education, history, information sciences and systems, journalism, junior high education, liberal/general studies, management information systems, management science, marketing and distribution, marketing research, mathematics, mathematics education, music, music education, musical theater, nursing, outdoor recreation, parks and recreation management, personnel management, physical education, physics, political science and government, prelaw, psychology, public relations, radio/television broadcasting, secondary education, secretarial and related programs, small business management and ownership, social sciences, social work, sociology, speech/communication/theater education, visual and performing arts.

ACADEMIC PROGRAMS. 2-year transfer program, dual enrollment of high school students, independent study, internships, student-designed major, study abroad, teacher preparation. **Remedial services:** Learning center, reduced course load, remedial instruction, special counselor, tutoring. **Placement/credit:** AP, CLEP Subject, institutional tests; 12 credit hours maximum for associate degree; 20 credit hours maximum for bachelor's degree.

ACADEMIC REQUIREMENTS. Freshmen must earn minimum GPA of 2.0 to continue in good standing. 41% of freshmen return for sophomore year. Students must declare major by end of first year. **Graduation requirements:** 64 hours for associate, 124 hours for bachelor's (40 in major). Most students required to take courses in arts/fine arts, English, humanities, mathematics, biological/physical sciences, social sciences. **Additional information:** Students over age 25 not required to take physical education classes.

FRESHMAN ADMISSIONS. Selection criteria: Open admissions at associate level. Special requirements for admission to allied health programs. Applicants to bachelor's program must meet following criteria: if GPA 3.0, ACT composite score of 14 or SAT combined score of 600 required; if GPA 2.4, ACT composite score of 18 or SAT combined score of 750 required. If GPA 2.0, ACT composite score of 22 or SAT combined score of 910 required. College preparatory program preferred. **Test requirements:** SAT or ACT (ACT preferred); score report by August 1.

1992 FRESHMAN CLASS PROFILE. 920 men applied, 920 accepted, 466 enrolled; 955 women applied, 955 accepted, 524 enrolled. 32% had high school GPA of 3.0 or higher, 56% between 2.0 and 2.99. 5% were in top tenth and 19% were in top quarter of graduating class. **Academic background:** Mid 50% of enrolled freshmen had ACT composite between 16-22. 82% submitted ACT scores. **Characteristics:** 92% from in state, 62% commute, 8% have minority backgrounds, 2% are foreign students. Average age is 19.

FALL-TERM APPLICATIONS. $20 fee, may be waived for applicants with need. Closing date August 1; priority given to applications received by March 15; applicants notified on a rolling basis. Audition required. Interview recommended for nursing, allied health, teacher certification applicants. Deferred and early admission available.

STUDENT LIFE. Housing: Dormitories (coed); apartment housing available. **Activities:** Student government, magazine, radio, student newspaper, choral groups, concert band, dance, drama, jazz band, music ensembles, musical theater, pep band, Black Student Union, Hispanic Student Organization, Handicapped Student Organization, Newman Club (religious organization), Christian Fellowship, Outing Program, 10 Honor Societies, Latter Day Saints Student Association, Baptist Student Union, Circle K Club.

ATHLETICS. NCAA. **Intercollegiate:** Baseball M, basketball, cross-country W, football M, softball W, tennis, volleyball W. **Intramural:** Badminton, basketball, cross-country, golf, handball, racquetball, skiing, soccer, softball, swimming, tennis, track and field, volleyball, water polo.

STUDENT SERVICES. Aptitude testing, career counseling, employment service for undergraduates, freshman orientation, health services, on-campus day care, personal counseling, placement service for graduates, special adviser for adult students, veterans counselor, services/facilities for handicapped.

ANNUAL EXPENSES. Tuition and fees (1992-93): $1,684, $2,922 additional for out-of-state students. **Room and board:** $3,256. **Books and supplies:** $425. **Other expenses:** $800.

FINANCIAL AID. 70% of freshmen, 65% of continuing students receive some form of aid. 91% of grants, 93% of loans, 49% of jobs based on need. 630 enrolled freshmen were judged to have need, 600 were offered aid. Academic, music/drama, art, athletic, state/district residency, leadership, alumni affiliation, minority scholarships available. **Aid applications:** No closing date; priority given to applications received by March 1; applicants notified on a rolling basis beginning on or about May 1; must reply within 2 weeks. **Additional information:** Tuition Guarantee Scholarship available for qualified students.

ADDRESS/TELEPHONE. Sherri L. Pe'a, Director of Admissions, Mesa State College, PO Box 2647, Grand Junction, CO 81502. (303) 248-1376. Fax: (303) 248-1973.

Metropolitan State College of Denver
Denver, Colorado CB code: 4505

Admissions:	81% of applicants accepted
Based on:	••• School record, test scores
	• Activities, special talents
Completion:	60% of freshmen end year in good standing
	11% graduate

4-year public comprehensive college, coed. Founded in 1963. **Accreditation:** Regional. **Undergraduate enrollment:** 4,729 men, 4,959 women full time; 3,504 men, 4,372 women part time. **Faculty:** 908 total (376 full time). **Location:** Urban campus in very large city. **Calendar:** Semester, extensive summer session. Saturday and extensive evening/early morning classes. **Microcomputers:** 300 located in classrooms, computer centers, campus-wide network. **Special facilities:** Art galleries, indoor airport with flight simulators, CAD/CAM laboratory. **Additional facts:** Library, student center and physical education facilities shared with Community College of Denver and University of Colorado at Denver. Off-campus sites in suburb.

DEGREES OFFERED. BA, BS, BFA. 2,029 bachelor's degrees awarded in 1992. 24% in business and management, 8% computer sciences, 6% teacher education, 5% engineering technologies, 9% parks/recreation, protective services, public affairs, 5% psychology, 11% social sciences.

UNDERGRADUATE MAJORS. Accounting, Afro-American (black) studies, airline piloting and navigation, anthropology, art history, atmospheric sciences and meteorology, aviation management, behavioral sciences, biology, business administration and management, business economics, chemistry, civil technology, computer and information sciences, criminal justice studies, electronic technology, English, finance, fine arts, fire control and safety technology, foreign languages (multiple emphasis), geography, health care administration, history, hospitality, meeting, and travel administration, human services, industrial design, industrial technology, information sciences and systems, journalism, marketing management, mathematics, mechanical design technology, mental health/human services, Mexican American studies, music education, music performance, nursing, parks and recreation management, philosophy, physics, political science and government, psychology, recreation therapy, social work, sociology, Spanish, speech, sports communication, survey and mapping technology, technical communications, trade and industrial supervision and management, urban studies, visual and performing arts.

ACADEMIC PROGRAMS. Accelerated program, cooperative education, double major, dual enrollment of high school students, honors program, independent study, internships, student-designed major, study abroad, teacher preparation, telecourses, visiting/exchange student program, weekend college, cross-registration, study tours to Mexico and Africa, semester in

London. **ROTC:** Air Force, Army. **Placement/credit:** AP, CLEP General and Subject, institutional tests; 60 credit hours maximum for bachelor's degree.

ACADEMIC REQUIREMENTS. Freshmen must earn minimum GPA of 2.0 to continue in good standing. 59% of freshmen return for sophomore year. Students must declare major by end of second year. **Graduation requirements:** 120 hours for bachelor's (30 in major). Most students required to take courses in English, history, humanities, mathematics, biological/physical sciences, social sciences.

FRESHMAN ADMISSIONS. Selection criteria: Open admissions for applicants who are 20 years old or older. Selective admissions for applicants under 20. **Test requirements:** SAT or ACT (ACT preferred); score report by August 1.

1992 FRESHMAN CLASS PROFILE. 1,610 men applied, 1,286 accepted, 743 enrolled; 1,658 women applied, 1,348 accepted, 736 enrolled. 35% had high school GPA of 3.0 or higher, 61% between 2.0 and 2.99. 6% were in top tenth and 21% were in top quarter of graduating class. **Academic background:** Mid 50% of enrolled freshmen had SAT-V between 340-460, SAT-M between 390-520; ACT composite between 18-22. 19% submitted SAT scores, 70% submitted ACT scores. **Characteristics:** 97% from in state, 100% commute, 23% have minority backgrounds, 1% are foreign students. Average age is 23.

FALL-TERM APPLICATIONS. $10 fee, may be waived for applicants with need. Closing date August 1; priority given to applications received by May 2; applicants notified on a rolling basis. Audition required for music applicants. Deferred and early admission available.

STUDENT LIFE. Housing: Computerized rental and roommate listing, housing fairs on first day of classes. **Activities:** Student government, magazine, student newspaper, television, yearbook, choral groups, concert band, dance, drama, jazz band, music ensembles, musical theater, symphony orchestra, fraternities, Golden Key, Black Student Alliance, Hispanic Leadership Association, MEChA, Gay/Lesbian Alliance, College Republicans, Lutheran Students, Menorah Ministries, Psi Chi, Young Democrats.

ATHLETICS. NCAA. **Intercollegiate:** Baseball M, basketball, soccer, swimming, tennis, volleyball W. **Intramural:** Baseball, basketball, cross-country, diving, field hockey, golf, gymnastics, handball, lacrosse M, racquetball, rugby M, skiing, soccer, softball, swimming, tennis, volleyball.

STUDENT SERVICES. Aptitude testing, career counseling, employment service for undergraduates, freshman orientation, health services, on-campus day care, personal counseling, placement service for graduates, special adviser for adult students, veterans counselor, child care and child development centers, services/facilities for handicapped.

ANNUAL EXPENSES. Tuition and fees (1992-93): $1,595, $3,648 additional for out-of-state students. **Books and supplies:** $482. **Other expenses:** $1,096.

FINANCIAL AID. 67% of freshmen, 46% of continuing students receive some form of aid. Grants, loans, jobs available. 1,400 enrolled freshmen were judged to have need, 1,139 were offered aid. Academic, music/drama, athletic, state/district residency, leadership, minority scholarships available. **Aid applications:** No closing date; priority given to applications received by March 1; applicants notified on a rolling basis beginning on or about May 1; must reply within 2 weeks.

ADDRESS/TELEPHONE. Dr. Kenneth C. Curtis, Dean of Admissions and Records, Metropolitan State College of Denver, PO Box 173362, Denver, CO 80217-3362. (303) 556-3018. (800) 544-7899. Fax: (303) 556-3999.

Morgan Community College
Fort Morgan, Colorado CB code: 0444

2-year public community college, coed. Founded in 1967. **Accreditation:** Regional. **Undergraduate enrollment:** 130 men, 154 women full time; 241 men, 470 women part time. **Faculty:** 228 total (43 full time), 6 with doctorates or other terminal degrees. **Location:** Rural campus in large town; 81 miles from Denver. **Calendar:** Semester, limited summer session. Extensive evening/early morning classes. **Microcomputers:** Located in libraries, computer centers.

DEGREES OFFERED. AA, AS, AAS. 55 associate degrees awarded in 1992. 6% in business and management, 25% health sciences, 66% multi/interdisciplinary studies.

UNDERGRADUATE MAJORS. Accounting, agribusiness, automobile body repair, business administration and management, business and office, electronic technology, home economics, liberal/general studies, nursing, physical therapy assistant, secretarial and related programs.

ACADEMIC PROGRAMS. 2-year transfer program, double major, dual enrollment of high school students, independent study, student-designed major, teacher preparation. **Remedial services:** Learning center, remedial instruction. **Placement/credit:** AP, CLEP General and Subject, institutional tests; 31 credit hours maximum for associate degree.

ACADEMIC REQUIREMENTS. Freshmen must earn minimum GPA of 2.0 to continue in good standing. **Graduation requirements:** 62 hours for associate. Most students required to take courses in computer science, English, humanities, mathematics, biological/physical sciences, social sciences.

FRESHMAN ADMISSIONS. Selection criteria: Open admissions.

1992 FRESHMAN CLASS PROFILE. 265 men and women enrolled. **Characteristics:** 99% from in state, 100% commute.

FALL-TERM APPLICATIONS. No fee. No closing date; applicants notified on a rolling basis; must reply by registration.

STUDENT LIFE. Activities: Student government, student newspaper, yearbook.

STUDENT SERVICES. Aptitude testing, career counseling, services/facilities for handicapped.

ANNUAL EXPENSES. Tuition and fees (1992-93): $1,500, $4,320 additional for out-of-state students. **Books and supplies:** $475. **Other expenses:** $750.

FINANCIAL AID. 90% of freshmen, 70% of continuing students receive some form of aid. 58% of grants, 92% of loans, 84% of jobs based on need. Academic, state/district residency, leadership scholarships available. **Aid applications:** No closing date; priority given to applications received by March 1; applicants notified on a rolling basis beginning on or about July 1; must reply within 2 weeks.

ADDRESS/TELEPHONE. Beth Lebsock, Dean of Student Services, Morgan Community College, 17800 Road 20, Fort Morgan, CO 80701. (303) 867-3081 ext.110.

Naropa Institute
Boulder, Colorado CB code: 0908

3-year private liberal arts college, coed. Founded in 1974. **Accreditation:** Regional. **Undergraduate enrollment:** 47 men, 63 women full time; 8 men, 22 women part time. **Graduate enrollment:** 65 men, 152 women full time; 20 men, 71 women part time. **Faculty:** 150 total (30 full time), 23 with doctorates or other terminal degrees. **Location:** Urban campus in small city; 20 miles from Denver. **Calendar:** Semester, limited summer session. **Microcomputers:** 8 located in computer centers. **Special facilities:** Organic farm, meditation hall. **Additional facts:** No freshmen accepted. All students must transfer in with at least 30 credits.

DEGREES OFFERED. BA, MA, MFA. 40 bachelor's degrees awarded in 1992. 8% in health sciences, 36% allied health, 25% multi/interdisciplinary studies, 17% psychology, 8% visual and performing arts. Graduate degrees offered in 7 major fields of study.

UNDERGRADUATE MAJORS. Contemplative psychotherapy, creative writing, dance, dramatic arts, early childhood education, education, health sciences, liberal/general studies, music, psychology, religion.

ACADEMIC PROGRAMS. Double major, independent study, internships, student-designed major, study abroad. **Remedial services:** Reduced course load, remedial instruction, special counselor, tutoring, English as a second language. **Placement/credit:** AP, CLEP General and Subject; 30 credit hours maximum for bachelor's degree.

ACADEMIC REQUIREMENTS. Students must declare major on application. **Graduation requirements:** 60 hours for bachelor's (24 in major). Most students required to take courses in arts/fine arts, English, humanities, biological/physical sciences, social sciences. **Additional information:** Summer programs with intensive workshops and conferences in creative writing, dance, dance therapy, music, psychology, health, comparative religion.

STUDENT LIFE. Activities: Student government, student newspaper, poetry magazine, psychology journal, choral groups, dance, drama, jazz band, music ensembles, musical theater, poetry readings, choral ensemble.

ATHLETICS. Intramural: Archery, softball, volleyball.

STUDENT SERVICES. Career counseling, personal counseling, meditation adviser, services/facilities for handicapped.

ANNUAL EXPENSES. Tuition and fees: $8,100. **Books and supplies:** $450.

FINANCIAL AID. 79% of continuing students receive some form of aid. 98% of grants, 86% of loans, 78% of jobs based on need. Academic, leadership scholarships available. **Aid applications:** No closing date; priority given to applications received by March 31; applicants notified on a rolling basis beginning on or about May 1; must reply within 4 weeks.

ADDRESS/TELEPHONE. John Morecock, Admissions Director, Naropa Institute, 2130 Arapahoe Avenue, Boulder, CO 80302. (303) 444-0202 ext. 514. Fax: (303) 444-0410.

National College
Denver, Colorado CB code: 5354

4-year proprietary engineering college, coed. Founded in 1941. **Undergraduate enrollment:** 150 men and women full time; 100 men and women part time. **Faculty:** 35 total. **Location:** Urban campus in very large city. **Calendar:** Quarter. Saturday and extensive evening/early morning classes. **Microcomputers:** Located in libraries, computer centers.

DEGREES OFFERED. AAS, BS. 75 associate degrees awarded in 1992. 150 bachelor's degrees awarded. 50% in business and management, 30% business/office and marketing/distribution, 20% computer sciences.

UNDERGRADUATE MAJORS. Associate: Accounting, transportation and travel marketing. **Bachelor's:** Accounting, business administration and management, business and management, business and office, computer and information sciences.

ACADEMIC PROGRAMS. Accelerated program, computer delivered (on-line) credit-bearing course offerings, cooperative education, double major, external degree, independent study, internships, telecourses, weekend college. **Remedial services:** Remedial instruction. **Placement/credit:** Institutional tests; 48 credit hours maximum for bachelor's degree.

ACADEMIC REQUIREMENTS. Students must declare major on enrollment. **Graduation requirements:** 97 hours for associate, 173 hours for bachelor's. Most students required to take courses in arts/fine arts, computer science, English, humanities, mathematics, biological/physical sciences, social sciences.

FRESHMAN ADMISSIONS. Selection criteria: Open admissions.

1992 FRESHMAN CLASS PROFILE. 55 men and women enrolled. **Characteristics:** 95% from in state, 100% commute.

FALL-TERM APPLICATIONS. $25 fee. No closing date; applicants notified on a rolling basis.

STUDENT LIFE. Activities: Student government, Phi Beta Lamda (business club), Data Processing Management Association.

STUDENT SERVICES. Career counseling.

ANNUAL EXPENSES. Tuition and fees (1992-93): $4,765. **Books and supplies:** $300.

FINANCIAL AID. Academic scholarships available. **Aid applications:** No closing date; applicants notified on a rolling basis.

ADDRESS/TELEPHONE. Dr. Bill Heath, Director, National College, 1325 South Colorado Boulevard, Denver, CO 80222. (303) 758-6700. Fax: (303) 758-6810.

Nazarene Bible College
Colorado Springs, Colorado — CB code: 0476

4-year private Bible college, coed, affiliated with Church of the Nazarene. Founded in 1964. **Undergraduate enrollment:** 200 men, 49 women full time; 77 men, 110 women part time. **Faculty:** 29 total (14 full time), 29 with doctorates or other terminal degrees. **Location:** Urban campus in large city; 60 miles from Denver. **Calendar:** Quarter, limited summer session. Extensive evening/early morning classes. **Additional facts:** Full programs offered in evening classes. Caters to adult students.

DEGREES OFFERED. AA, BA. 52 associate degrees awarded in 1992. 100% in philosophy, religion, theology. 15 bachelor's degrees awarded. 100% in philosophy, religion, theology.

UNDERGRADUATE MAJORS. Associate: Bible studies, music, religious education, religious music. **Bachelor's:** Bible studies, religious education, religious music.

ACADEMIC PROGRAMS. 2-year transfer program, internships. **Remedial services:** Learning center, reduced course load, remedial instruction. **Placement/credit:** CLEP General, institutional tests.

ACADEMIC REQUIREMENTS. Freshmen must earn minimum GPA of 2.0 to continue in good standing. 80% of freshmen return for sophomore year. Students must declare major on application. **Graduation requirements:** 144 hours for associate (79 in major), 192 hours for bachelor's (94 in major). Most students required to take courses in English, philosophy/religion.

FRESHMAN ADMISSIONS. Selection criteria: Applicants must subscribe to Christian code of ethics. References must indicate applicant's ability to profit from program.

1992 FRESHMAN CLASS PROFILE. 45 men, 14 women enrolled. **Characteristics:** 4% from in state, 100% commute, 5% have minority backgrounds, 1% are foreign students. Average age is 32.

FALL-TERM APPLICATIONS. $10 fee. Closing date August 29; applicants notified on a rolling basis beginning on or about May 1; must reply by September 5. Essay required. Deferred admission available.

STUDENT LIFE. Activities: Student government, student newspaper, yearbook, choral groups, music ensembles, Missions in Action Club, Wesley Theological Society.

STUDENT SERVICES. Career counseling, employment service for undergraduates, freshman orientation, personal counseling, placement service for graduates.

ANNUAL EXPENSES. Tuition and fees (projected): $3,405. **Books and supplies:** $490. **Other expenses:** $500.

FINANCIAL AID. 95% of freshmen, 80% of continuing students receive some form of aid. All aid based on need. Academic, leadership, minority scholarships available. **Aid applications:** No closing date; priority given to applications received by June 1; applicants notified on a rolling basis beginning on or about June 15; Must reply by September 1 or within 2 weeks if notified thereafter. **Additional information:** Tuition waiver for students serving as student body officers.

ADDRESS/TELEPHONE. Phyllis H. Perkins, Director of Admissions, Nazarene Bible College, PO Box 15749, Colorado Springs, CO 80935. (719) 596-5110. (800) 873-3873. Fax: (719) 550-9437.

Northeastern Junior College
Sterling, Colorado — CB code: 4537

2-year public junior college, coed. Founded in 1941. **Accreditation:** Regional. **Undergraduate enrollment:** 450 men, 524 women full time; 1,455 men, 1,918 women part time. **Faculty:** 84 total (60 full time), 4 with doctorates or other terminal degrees. **Location:** Suburban campus in large town; 125 miles from Denver. **Calendar:** Semester, limited summer session. Extensive evening/early morning classes. **Microcomputers:** 80 located in dormitories, libraries, classrooms, computer centers.

DEGREES OFFERED. AA, AS, AAS. 189 associate degrees awarded in 1992.

UNDERGRADUATE MAJORS. Accounting, agribusiness, agricultural economics, agricultural sciences, animal sciences, automotive technology, biology, business and management, business and office, business data processing and related programs, communications, computer programming, diesel engine mechanics, dramatic arts, education, engineering, equestrian science, fashion merchandising, fine arts, legal secretary, liberal/general studies, marketing and distribution, mathematics, medical secretary, music, personal services, physical sciences, practical nursing, predentistry, prelaw, premedicine, prepharmacy, preveterinary, psychology, secretarial and related programs, small business management and ownership, social sciences, Spanish, visual and performing arts.

ACADEMIC PROGRAMS. 2-year transfer program, cooperative education, dual enrollment of high school students, independent study, telecourses. **Remedial services:** Tutoring, study skills center. **Placement/credit:** AP, institutional tests; 30 credit hours maximum for associate degree.

ACADEMIC REQUIREMENTS. Freshmen must earn minimum GPA of 2.0 to continue in good standing. 55% of freshmen return for sophomore year. Students must declare major on application. **Graduation requirements:** 62 hours for associate. Most students required to take courses in English, humanities, mathematics, biological/physical sciences, social sciences.

FRESHMAN ADMISSIONS. Selection criteria: Open admissions. **Test requirements:** SAT or ACT (ACT preferred) for placement and counseling only; score report by September 1. SAT or ACT required for some technical vocational programs. **Additional information:** Cooperative admissions program with Colorado State University.

1992 FRESHMAN CLASS PROFILE. 492 men, 541 women enrolled. 50% had high school GPA of 3.0 or higher, 45% between 2.0 and 2.99. **Characteristics:** 90% from in state, 70% commute, 10% have minority backgrounds, 1% are foreign students. Average age is 19.

FALL-TERM APPLICATIONS. $15 fee, may be waived for applicants with need. Closing date September 1; priority given to applications received by April 1; applicants notified on a rolling basis. Interview recommended for out-of-state, foreign, and borderline transfer applicants. Deferred and early admission available.

STUDENT LIFE. Housing: Dormitories (men, women, coed). **Activities:** Student government, magazine, student newspaper, yearbook, choral groups, concert band, dance, drama, jazz band, music ensembles, musical theater, pep band, Campus Christian Fellowship.

ATHLETICS. NJCAA. **Intercollegiate:** Basketball, cross-country M, softball W, tennis, track and field, volleyball W. **Intramural:** Archery, baseball, basketball W, field hockey, golf, handball, racquetball, soccer M, swimming, table tennis.

STUDENT SERVICES. Aptitude testing, career counseling, employment service for undergraduates, freshman orientation, health services, personal counseling, placement service for graduates, services/facilities for handicapped.

ANNUAL EXPENSES. Tuition and fees: $709, $859 additional for out-of-district students, $3,131 additional for out-of-state students. **Room and board:** $3,468. **Books and supplies:** $430. **Other expenses:** $800.

FINANCIAL AID. 35% of freshmen, 35% of continuing students receive some form of aid. Grants, loans, jobs available. Academic, music/drama, art, athletic, leadership, alumni affiliation, minority scholarships available. **Aid applications:** No closing date; priority given to applications received by April 1; applicants notified on a rolling basis beginning on or about April 15; must reply within 4 weeks. **Additional information:** Sophomore-year scholarships available.

ADDRESS/TELEPHONE. Garnie A. Johnson, Director of Enrollment Management, Northeastern Junior College, 100 College Drive, Sterling, CO 80751. (303) 522-6600 ext. 651.

Otero Junior College
La Junta, Colorado — CB code: 4588

2-year public community college, coed. Founded in 1941. **Accreditation:** Regional. **Undergraduate enrollment:** 270 men, 360 women full time; 138 men, 189 women part time. **Faculty:** 61 total (33 full time), 6 with doctorates or other terminal degrees. **Location:** Rural campus in small town; 60 miles from Pueblo. **Calendar:** Semester, limited summer session. Extensive evening/early morning classes. **Microcomputers:** Located in computer centers. **Special facilities:** Koshare Indian Kiva Museum.

DEGREES OFFERED. AA, AS, AAS. 140 associate degrees awarded in 1992.

UNDERGRADUATE MAJORS. Business and management, business and office, business data entry equipment operation, business data processing and related programs, drafting and design technology, engineering, liberal/general studies, nursing, secretarial and related programs, teacher aide.

ACADEMIC PROGRAMS. 2-year transfer program, dual enrollment of high school students. **Remedial services:** Learning center, remedial instruction. **Placement/credit:** AP, CLEP General, institutional tests; 33 credit hours maximum for associate degree.

ACADEMIC REQUIREMENTS. No policy requiring minimum GPA; records of students having academic difficulty are reviewed individually. 55% of freshmen return for sophomore year. Students must declare major on enrollment. **Graduation requirements:** 60 hours for associate. Most students required to take courses in English, humanities, mathematics, biological/physical sciences, social sciences.

FRESHMAN ADMISSIONS. Selection criteria: Open admissions. **Test requirements:** ACT for placement and counseling only; score report by August 1. ACT/ASSET may be substituted for ACT.

1992 FRESHMAN CLASS PROFILE. 170 men, 256 women enrolled. 23% had high school GPA of 3.0 or higher, 38% between 2.0 and 2.99. **Academic background:** Mid 50% of enrolled freshmen had ACT composite between 13-18. 78% submitted ACT scores. **Characteristics:** 92% from in state, 88% commute, 38% have minority backgrounds, 1% are foreign students. Average age is 26.

FALL-TERM APPLICATIONS. $10 fee, may be waived for applicants with need. Closing date August 15; applicants notified on a rolling basis beginning on or about February 1. Early admission available.

STUDENT LIFE. Housing: Dormitories (coed). **Activities:** Student government, student newspaper, choral groups, drama, jazz band.

ATHLETICS. NJCAA. **Intercollegiate:** Baseball M, basketball, golf, volleyball W. **Intramural:** Basketball, bowling, softball, table tennis, tennis, volleyball.

STUDENT SERVICES. Aptitude testing, career counseling, personal counseling, placement service for graduates, veterans counselor, services/facilities for handicapped.

ANNUAL EXPENSES. Tuition and fees (1992-93): $1,562, $2,880 additional for out-of-state students. **Room and board: $3,464. Books and supplies:** $400. **Other expenses:** $1,200.

FINANCIAL AID. 70% of freshmen, 80% of continuing students receive some form of aid. 85% of grants, 95% of loans, 81% of jobs based on need. Athletic scholarships available. **Aid applications:** No closing date; priority given to applications received by May 1; applicants notified on a rolling basis beginning on or about June 1; must reply within 2 weeks.

ADDRESS/TELEPHONE. Student Personnel Services, Otero Junior College, 1802 Colorado Avenue, La Junta, CO 81050. (719) 384-6831. Fax: (719) 384-6880.

Parks Junior College
Thornton, Colorado — CB code: 0349

2-year proprietary junior college, coed. Founded in 1895. **Undergraduate enrollment:** 600 men and women. **Faculty:** 58 total (18 full time). **Location:** Suburban campus in large town; 7 miles from downtown Denver. **Calendar:** Quarter, extensive summer session. Saturday and extensive evening/early morning classes. **Microcomputers:** Located in computer centers. **Additional facts:** Branch campus in Aurora.

DEGREES OFFERED. AS, AAS. 225 associate degrees awarded in 1992.

UNDERGRADUATE MAJORS. Accounting, business administration and management, computer and information sciences, fashion merchandising, international business management, legal assistant/paralegal, legal secretary, medical assistant, secretarial and related programs, tourism.

ACADEMIC PROGRAMS. Internships. **Remedial services:** Reduced course load, remedial instruction, tutoring. **Placement/credit:** Institutional tests.

ACADEMIC REQUIREMENTS. Freshmen must earn minimum GPA of 2.0 to continue in good standing. 70% of freshmen return for sophomore year. Students must declare major on enrollment. **Graduation requirements:** 96 hours for associate. Most students required to take courses in English, humanities.

FRESHMAN ADMISSIONS. Selection criteria: Score on institution's entrance examination, personal qualities, preliminary and qualifying interview reviewed. **Test requirements:** Institutional examinations required for admissions and placement.

1992 FRESHMAN CLASS PROFILE. 80 men and women enrolled. **Characteristics:** 75% from in state, 100% commute, 20% have minority backgrounds.

FALL-TERM APPLICATIONS. $25 fee, may be waived for applicants with need. No closing date; applicants notified on a rolling basis. Interview required.

STUDENT LIFE. Activities: Student government, student newspaper.

STUDENT SERVICES. Career counseling, employment service for undergraduates, placement service for graduates.

ANNUAL EXPENSES. Tuition and fees (projected): Comprehensive 2-year program tuition $10,080, including books. **Other expenses:** $650.

FINANCIAL AID. 95% of freshmen, 95% of continuing students receive some form of aid. 98% of grants, 67% of loans, 64% of jobs based on need. State/district residency scholarships available. **Aid applications:** No closing date; applicants notified on a rolling basis beginning on or about August 1.

ADDRESS/TELEPHONE. Joyce Ritthaler, Director of Admissions, Parks Junior College, 9065 Grant Street, Thornton, CO 80229. (303) 457-2757.

Pikes Peak Community College
Colorado Springs, Colorado — CB code: 4291

2-year public community college, coed. Founded in 1967. **Accreditation:** Regional. **Undergraduate enrollment:** 1,131 men, 1,529 women full time; 1,610 men, 2,507 women part time. **Faculty:** 358 total (128 full time), 26 with doctorates or other terminal degrees. **Location:** Suburban campus in large city; 60 miles from Denver. **Calendar:** Semester, extensive summer session. Extensive evening/early morning classes. **Microcomputers:** Located in libraries, classrooms.

DEGREES OFFERED. AA, AS, AAS. 604 associate degrees awarded in 1992. 7% in business and management, 8% engineering technologies, 12% health sciences, 51% multi/interdisciplinary studies, 5% parks/recreation, protective services, public affairs, 8% trade and industry.

UNDERGRADUATE MAJORS. Accounting, air conditioning/heating/refrigeration mechanics, allied health, anthropology, architectural technologies, automotive mechanics, automotive technology, aviation management, biology, business and management, chemistry, commercial art, communications, computer and information sciences, computer technology, construction, criminal justice studies, dental assistant, early childhood education, education, electrical and electronics equipment repair, electrical technology, electronic technology, engineering science, English, finance, fine arts, fire control and safety technology, food management, food production/management/services, foreign languages (multiple emphasis), geology, gerontology, graphic and printing production, graphic arts technology, history, humanities, insurance and risk management, journalism, legal assistant/paralegal, liberal/general studies, machine tool operation/machine shop, marketing management, mathematics, mathematics/science, mechanical design technology, nursing, office information technology, optical technology, physics, political science and government, premedicine, psychology, radio/television broadcasting, secretarial and related programs, social work, sociology, space science, supermarket management, systems engineering, visual and performing arts, welding technology.

ACADEMIC PROGRAMS. 2-year transfer program, accelerated program, dual enrollment of high school students, independent study, internships, telecourses. **Remedial services:** Learning center, remedial instruction, special counselor, tutoring, learning problems program. **ROTC:** Army. **Placement/credit:** CLEP General and Subject, institutional tests.

ACADEMIC REQUIREMENTS. Freshmen must earn minimum GPA of 2.0 to continue in good standing. Students must declare major on application. **Graduation requirements:** 60 hours for associate. Most students required to take courses in arts/fine arts, English, history, humanities, mathematics, philosophy/religion, biological/physical sciences, social sciences.

FRESHMAN ADMISSIONS. Selection criteria: Open admissions.

1992 FRESHMAN CLASS PROFILE. 1,879 men, 2,787 women enrolled. **Characteristics:** 98% from in state, 100% commute, 20% have minority backgrounds, 1% are foreign students.

FALL-TERM APPLICATIONS. No fee. Closing date August 26; applicants notified on a rolling basis; must reply by registration. Early admission available.

STUDENT LIFE. Activities: Student government, film, radio, student newspaper, television, dance, drama, cultural/artist series, Phi Theta Kappa. **Additional information:** Community service projects, wellness and lifestyle improvement workshops.

ATHLETICS. Intramural: Basketball M, golf, soccer M, volleyball.

STUDENT SERVICES. Aptitude testing, career counseling, employment service for undergraduates, health services, on-campus day care, personal counseling, placement service for graduates, special adviser for adult students, veterans counselor, services/facilities for handicapped.

ANNUAL EXPENSES. Tuition and fees (1992-93): $1,514, $4,320 additional for out-of-state students. **Books and supplies:** $400. **Other expenses:** $1,350.

FINANCIAL AID. 68% of continuing students receive some form of aid. 99% of grants, 90% of loans, 89% of jobs based on need. Academic, state/district residency scholarships available. **Aid applications:** No closing date; priority given to applications received by July 1; applicants notified on a rolling basis beginning on or about August 1; must reply within 2 weeks.

ADDRESS/TELEPHONE. Roberta Erickson, Director of Admissions, Pikes Peak Community College, 5675 South Academy Boulevard, Colorado Springs, CO 80906-5498. (719) 576-7711. (800) 456-6847. Fax: (719) 540-7016.

Pueblo Community College
Pueblo, Colorado CB code: 4634

2-year public community college, coed. Founded in 1979. **Accreditation:** Regional. **Undergraduate enrollment:** 602 men, 1,092 women full time; 228 men, 1,044 women part time. **Faculty:** 288 total (111 full time), 6 with doctorates or other terminal degrees. **Location:** Urban campus in small city; 50 miles from Colorado Springs, 100 miles from Denver. **Calendar:** Semester, limited summer session. Saturday and extensive evening/early morning classes. **Microcomputers:** 80 located in libraries, classrooms, computer centers.

DEGREES OFFERED. AA, AS, AAS. 276 associate degrees awarded in 1992. 7% in business and management, 24% business/office and marketing/distribution, 19% computer sciences, 27% allied health, 8% parks/recreation, protective services, public affairs, 15% trade and industry.

UNDERGRADUATE MAJORS. Accounting, air conditioning/heating/refrigeration mechanics, automotive technology, business and management, business and office, business data entry equipment operation, business data processing and related programs, business data programming, criminal justice studies, data processing, dental hygiene, drafting, drafting and design technology, electronic technology, food production/management/services, nursing, occupational therapy assistant, physical therapy assistant, precision metal work, radiograph medical technology, respiratory therapy technology, secretarial and related programs, small business management and ownership, welding technology.

ACADEMIC PROGRAMS. 2-year transfer program, accelerated program, computer delivered (on-line) credit-bearing course offerings, double major, dual enrollment of high school students, telecourses. **Remedial services:** Learning center, remedial instruction, special counselor, tutoring. **ROTC:** Army. **Placement/credit:** AP, CLEP General, institutional tests; 30 credit hours maximum for associate degree.

ACADEMIC REQUIREMENTS. Freshmen must earn minimum GPA of 1.6 to continue in good standing. 66% of freshmen return for sophomore year. Students must declare major on enrollment. **Graduation requirements:** 65 hours for associate (45 in major). Most students required to take courses in computer science, English, history, humanities, mathematics, biological/physical sciences, social sciences.

FRESHMAN ADMISSIONS. Selection criteria: Open admissions. Selective admission to health programs based on GPA, high school courses, and test scores. **Test requirements:** ACT required of allied health applicants; score report by May 1.

1992 FRESHMAN CLASS PROFILE. 1,293 men and women enrolled. **Characteristics:** 98% from in state, 100% commute, 36% have minority backgrounds, 1% are foreign students.

FALL-TERM APPLICATIONS. $10 fee, may be waived for applicants with need. No closing date; priority given to applications received by August 1; applicants notified on a rolling basis; must reply by registration. Interview required for allied health applicants. Deferred admission available. Foreign applicants must pay for 1 full academic year before acceptance. Application closing date for allied health programs, April 1.

STUDENT LIFE. Housing: Students may live in University of Southern Colorado dormitories. **Activities:** Student government, student newspaper, choral groups, Inter-Varsity Christian Fellowship.

STUDENT SERVICES. Aptitude testing, career counseling, employment service for undergraduates, freshman orientation, personal counseling, placement service for graduates, special adviser for adult students, veterans counselor, services/facilities for handicapped.

ANNUAL EXPENSES. Tuition and fees (1992-93): $1,666, $4,320 additional for out-of-state students. **Books and supplies:** $500.

FINANCIAL AID. 51% of freshmen, 63% of continuing students receive some form of aid. 96% of grants, 98% of loans, all jobs based on need. Academic, state/district residency scholarships available. **Aid applications:** Closing date May 1; priority given to applications received by March 15; applicants notified on or about June 1; must reply within 2 weeks.

ADDRESS/TELEPHONE. Debra Sagona, Director of Admissions and Records, Pueblo Community College, 900 West Orman Avenue, Pueblo, CO 81004. (719) 549-3311.

Red Rocks Community College
Lakewood, Colorado CB code: 4130

2-year public community college, coed. Founded in 1969. **Accreditation:** Regional. **Undergraduate enrollment:** 846 men, 759 women full time; 1,998 men, 3,181 women part time. **Faculty:** 280 total (67 full time), 14 with doctorates or other terminal degrees. **Location:** Suburban campus in small city; 10 miles from downtown Denver. **Calendar:** Semester, extensive summer session. Saturday and extensive evening/early morning classes. **Microcomputers:** 175 located in libraries, classrooms, computer centers.

DEGREES OFFERED. AA, AS, AAS. 330 associate degrees awarded in 1992. 5% in business and management, 8% business/office and marketing/distribution, 18% engineering technologies, 46% multi/interdisciplinary studies, 12% parks/recreation, protective services, public affairs, 8% trade and industry.

UNDERGRADUATE MAJORS. Accounting, automotive mechanics, business and office, business data programming, carpentry, computer and information sciences, computer technology, criminal justice studies, diesel engine mechanics, drafting, drafting and design technology, electrical and electronics equipment repair, electrical installation, electronic technology, fire control and safety technology, legal secretary, liberal/general studies, management science, marketing and distribution, marketing management, medical secretary, office supervision and management, preengineering, public administration, real estate, secretarial and related programs, solar heating and cooling technology, survey and mapping technology, water and wastewater technology, welding technology, word processing.

ACADEMIC PROGRAMS. 2-year transfer program, accelerated program, double major, dual enrollment of high school students, independent study, internships, study abroad, telecourses, weekend college, cross-registration. **Remedial services:** Learning center, reduced course load, remedial instruction, special counselor, tutoring. **Placement/credit:** AP, CLEP General and Subject, institutional tests; 45 credit hours maximum for associate degree.

ACADEMIC REQUIREMENTS. Freshmen must earn minimum GPA of 2.0 to continue in good standing. Students must declare major on application. **Graduation requirements:** 60 hours for associate (48 in major). Most students required to take courses in English, history, humanities, mathematics, biological/physical sciences, social sciences.

FRESHMAN ADMISSIONS. Selection criteria: Open admissions. **Additional information:** Basic skills assessment required for course level placement.

1992 FRESHMAN CLASS PROFILE. 2,250 men, 3,198 women enrolled. **Characteristics:** 96% from in state, 100% commute, 9% have minority backgrounds, 2% are foreign students.

FALL-TERM APPLICATIONS. No fee. No closing date; applicants notified on a rolling basis; must reply by registration. Early admission available.

STUDENT LIFE. Activities: Student government, student newspaper, drama, Phi Theta Kappa, environment club, international club.

ATHLETICS. NJCAA. **Intramural:** Softball, volleyball.

STUDENT SERVICES. Aptitude testing, career counseling, employment service for undergraduates, freshman orientation, health services, on-campus day care, personal counseling, placement service for graduates, special adviser for adult students, veterans counselor, services/facilities for handicapped.

ANNUAL EXPENSES. Tuition and fees (1992-93): $1,548, $4,320 additional for out-of-state students. **Books and supplies:** $450. **Other expenses:** $875.

FINANCIAL AID. 18% of freshmen, 18% of continuing students receive some form of aid. 88% of grants, 70% of loans, 60% of jobs based on need. Academic scholarships available. **Aid applications:** No closing date; priority given to applications received by June 1; applicants notified on a rolling basis beginning on or about August 1; must reply within 2 weeks.

ADDRESS/TELEPHONE. Robert Schantz, Director of Admissions, Red Rocks Community College, 13300 West Sixth Avenue, Lakewood, CO 80401. (303) 988-6160. Fax: (303) 969-8039.

Regis University ⇎
Denver, Colorado CB code: 4656

Admissions:	88% of applicants accepted
Based on:	••• Recommendations, school record, test scores
	•• Activities, essay, interview
	• Special talents
Completion:	88% of freshmen end year in good standing
	43% graduate, 13% of these enter graduate study

4-year private university and liberal arts college, coed, affiliated with Roman Catholic Church. Founded in 1877. **Accreditation:** Regional. **Undergraduate enrollment:** 489 men, 608 women full time; 18 men, 46 women part time. **Graduate enrollment:** 337 men, 347 women full time; 290 men, 306 women part time. **Faculty:** 87 total (62 full time), 57 with doctorates or other terminal degrees. **Location:** Suburban campus in very large city; 10 miles from downtown. **Calendar:** Semester, limited summer session. **Microcomputers:** 200 located in dormitories, libraries, computer centers. **Additional facts:** Institution in the Jesuit tradition.

DEGREES OFFERED. BA, BS, MA, MS, MBA. 237 bachelor's degrees awarded in 1992. 26% in business and management, 9% communications, 13% health sciences, 8% mathematics, 5% psychology, 19% social sciences. Graduate degrees offered in 2 major fields of study.

UNDERGRADUATE MAJORS. Accounting, biological and physical

sciences, biology, business administration and management, business economics, chemistry, communications, computer and information sciences, ecology, economics, education, elementary education, English, environmental science, finance, French, health care administration, history, humanities and social sciences, international business management, liberal/general studies, marketing management, mathematics, medical records administration, nursing, philosophy, political science and government, predentistry, prelaw, premedicine, psychology, religion, religious education, secondary education, sociology, Spanish.

ACADEMIC PROGRAMS. Double major, dual enrollment of high school students, honors program, independent study, internships, student-designed major, study abroad, teacher preparation, cross-registration, 3-2 engineering program with Washington University; liberal arts/career combination in engineering. **Remedial services:** Learning center, preadmission summer program, reduced course load, remedial instruction, special counselor, tutoring. **ROTC:** Air Force, Army. **Placement/credit:** AP, CLEP General and Subject, institutional tests; 30 credit hours maximum for bachelor's degree.

ACADEMIC REQUIREMENTS. Freshmen must earn minimum GPA of 2.0 to continue in good standing. 68% of freshmen return for sophomore year. Students must declare major by end of second year. **Graduation requirements:** 128 hours for bachelor's (30 in major). Most students required to take courses in arts/fine arts, English, foreign languages, history, humanities, mathematics, philosophy/religion, biological/physical sciences, social sciences. **Postgraduate studies:** 8% enter law school, 5% enter medical school.

FRESHMAN ADMISSIONS. Selection criteria: High school record, test scores, recommendations, school and community activities and interview are important. **High school preparation:** 15 units required. Required units include English 3. **Test requirements:** SAT or ACT; score report by August 15.

1992 FRESHMAN CLASS PROFILE. 488 men applied, 413 accepted, 146 enrolled; 563 women applied, 513 accepted, 163 enrolled. **Academic background:** Mid 50% of enrolled freshmen had SAT-V between 370-480, SAT-M between 380-550; ACT composite between 18-24. 60% submitted SAT scores, 77% submitted ACT scores. **Characteristics:** 48% from in state, 50% commute, 12% have minority backgrounds, 1% are foreign students. Average age is 18.

FALL-TERM APPLICATIONS. $35 fee, may be waived for applicants with need. Closing date August 1; applicants notified on a rolling basis; must reply by May 1 or within 2 weeks if notified thereafter. Interview recommended for academically weak applicants. Audition recommended for music, theater applicants. Essay recommended. CRDA. Deferred admission available.

STUDENT LIFE. Housing: Dormitories (coed); handicapped housing available. Freshmen and sophomores required to live on campus unless residing with parent, guardian or spouse in Denver metropolitan area. **Activities:** Student government, radio, student newspaper, yearbook, literary magazine, choral groups, dance, drama, jazz band, musical theater, multicultural achievement and awareness committee, Alpha Sigma Nu, Pi Kappa Delta, Polaris, honors organization, pre-law club/mock trial club, Middle Eastern Concerns Association, Christian Life Community, Circle K International.

ATHLETICS. NAIA, NCAA. **Intercollegiate:** Baseball M, basketball, golf M, soccer, softball W, tennis, volleyball W. **Intramural:** Basketball, golf M, racquetball, soccer, softball, tennis, volleyball.

STUDENT SERVICES. Career counseling, employment service for undergraduates, freshman orientation, health services, personal counseling, placement service for graduates, services/facilities for handicapped.

ANNUAL EXPENSES. Tuition and fees (1992-93): $11,520. **Room and board:** $5,300. **Books and supplies:** $500. **Other expenses:** $1,415.

FINANCIAL AID. 71% of freshmen, 79% of continuing students receive some form of aid. 65% of grants, 87% of loans, 54% of jobs based on need. 125 enrolled freshmen were judged to have need, all were offered aid. Academic, athletic, state/district residency, leadership, religious affiliation, minority scholarships available. **Aid applications:** No closing date; priority given to applications received by March 15; applicants notified on a rolling basis beginning on or about February 15; must reply within 30 days.

ADDRESS/TELEPHONE. Robert Blust, Director of Admissions, Regis University, 3333 Regis Boulevard, Denver, CO 80221-1099. (303) 458-4900. (800) 388-2366. Fax: (303) 458-4901.

Rocky Mountain College of Art & Design

Denver, Colorado — CB code: 1943

4-year proprietary art college, coed. Founded in 1963. **Undergraduate enrollment:** 91 men, 74 women full time; 37 men, 79 women part time. **Faculty:** 48 total (8 full time). **Location:** Urban campus in very large city; near downtown. **Calendar:** Trimester, extensive summer session. Saturday and extensive evening/early morning classes. **Microcomputers:** 25 located in computer centers. **Special facilities:** Philip J. Steele Gallery of Art.

DEGREES OFFERED. BA. 45 associate degrees awarded in 1992. 15% in architecture and environmental design, 85% visual and performing arts. 5 bachelor's degrees awarded. 15% in architecture and environmental design, 85% visual and performing arts.

UNDERGRADUATE MAJORS. Associate: Environmental design, graphic design, illustration design, interior design, painting, sculpture. **Bachelor's:** Environmental design, graphic design, illustration design, interior design, painting, sculpture.

ACADEMIC PROGRAMS. Double major, internships. **Remedial services:** Reduced course load, remedial instruction, tutoring. **Placement/credit:** AP, CLEP General and Subject, institutional tests.

ACADEMIC REQUIREMENTS. Freshmen must earn minimum GPA of 2.0 to continue in good standing. Students must declare major by end of second year. **Graduation requirements:** 96 hours for associate (87 in major), 128 hours for bachelor's (87 in major). Most students required to take courses in arts/fine arts, computer science, English, history, humanities, mathematics, philosophy/religion, biological/physical sciences, social sciences. **Postgraduate studies:** 10% from 2-year programs enter 4-year programs.

FRESHMAN ADMISSIONS. Selection criteria: Applicants must show desire to pursue art career. Portfolio of art work considered. SAT or ACT scores required for BA degree candidates. Interview recommended. High school art courses strongly recommended. **Test requirements:** SAT or ACT; score report by September 1.

1992 FRESHMAN CLASS PROFILE. 39 men, 20 women enrolled. **Characteristics:** 65% from in state, 100% commute, 22% have minority backgrounds. Average age is 20.

FALL-TERM APPLICATIONS. $25 fee. No closing date; applicants notified on a rolling basis. Portfolio recommended. Essay recommended. Portfolio and interview required of local applicants, recommended for others. Deferred admission available. Fall admission is first come, first served.

STUDENT LIFE. Housing: Majority of students live in apartments, many within walking distance. Roommate matching service available through admissions office. **Activities:** Student newspaper.

ATHLETICS. Intramural: Softball.

STUDENT SERVICES. Career counseling, employment service for undergraduates, freshman orientation, placement service for graduates, veterans counselor.

ANNUAL EXPENSES. Tuition and fees: $5,880. **Books and supplies:** $1,000. **Other expenses:** $1,067.

FINANCIAL AID. 80% of freshmen, 80% of continuing students receive some form of aid. 87% of grants, 69% of loans, 30% of jobs based on need. Academic, art scholarships available. **Aid applications:** No closing date; priority given to applications received by July 31; applicants notified on a rolling basis beginning on or about May 15; must reply within 2 weeks.

ADDRESS/TELEPHONE. Rex Whisman, Admissions Director, Rocky Mountain College of Art & Design, 6875 East Evans Avenue, Denver, CO 80224-2359. (303) 753-6046. (800) 888-ARTS. Fax: (303) 759-4970.

Trinidad State Junior College

Trinidad, Colorado — CB code: 4821

2-year public junior college, coed. Founded in 1925. **Accreditation:** Regional. **Undergraduate enrollment:** 410 men, 348 women full time; 567 men, 326 women part time. **Faculty:** 117 total (50 full time), 4 with doctorates or other terminal degrees. **Location:** Rural campus in small town; 90 miles from Pueblo. **Calendar:** Semester, limited summer session. Extensive evening/early morning classes. **Microcomputers:** 40 located in libraries, classrooms, computer centers. **Special facilities:** Museum of anthropology and geology, art exhibition room, gunsmithing laboratory.

DEGREES OFFERED. AA, AS, AAS. 163 associate degrees awarded in 1992.

UNDERGRADUATE MAJORS. Accounting, agricultural sciences, anthropology, architecture, automotive mechanics, automotive technology, biological and physical sciences, biology, business administration and management, business and management, business and office, business data processing and related programs, business data programming, chemistry, civil technology, computer and information sciences, computer servicing technology, criminal justice technology, data processing, drafting, drafting and design technology, dramatic arts, education, electrical and electronics equipment repair, electronic technology, engineering, fine arts, forestry and related sciences, geography, home economics, humanities and social sciences, journalism, liberal/general studies, mathematics, music, nursing, office supervision and management, physical sciences, practical nursing, precision metal work, predentistry, prelaw, premedicine, prepharmacy, preveterinary, psychology, renewable natural resources, secretarial and related programs, social sciences, survey and mapping technology, teacher aide.

ACADEMIC PROGRAMS. 2-year transfer program, cooperative education, dual enrollment of high school students, independent study. **Remedial services:** Learning center, preadmission summer program, reduced course load, remedial instruction, special counselor, tutoring. **Placement/credit:** CLEP General and Subject, institutional tests.

ACADEMIC REQUIREMENTS. No policy requiring minimum GPA; records of students having academic difficulty are reviewed individually. 73% of freshmen return for sophomore year. Students must declare major on enrollment. **Graduation requirements:** 68 hours for associate. Most students required to take courses in computer science, English, humanities, mathematics, biological/physical sciences, social sciences.

FRESHMAN ADMISSIONS. Selection criteria: Open admissions. Selective admission to nursing program. **Test requirements:** ACT for placement and counseling only; score report by August 1.

1992 FRESHMAN CLASS PROFILE. 526 men and women enrolled. **Characteristics:** 67% from in state, 73% commute, 47% have minority backgrounds.

FALL-TERM APPLICATIONS. $10 fee, may be waived for applicants with need. No closing date; priority given to applications received by August 10; applicants notified on a rolling basis beginning on or about January 15. Interview recommended for nursing applicants.

STUDENT LIFE. Housing: Dormitories (men, women); apartment housing available. **Activities:** Student government, student newspaper, choral groups, drama, jazz band.

ATHLETICS. NJCAA. **Intercollegiate:** Baseball M, basketball M, volleyball W. **Intramural:** Baseball, basketball, golf, handball, rifle, soccer, softball, tennis, volleyball.

STUDENT SERVICES. Aptitude testing, career counseling, employment service for undergraduates, freshman orientation, personal counseling, placement service for graduates, special adviser for adult students, veterans counselor.

ANNUAL EXPENSES. Tuition and fees (1992-93): $1,564, $2,880 additional for out-of-state students. **Room and board:** $3,598. **Books and supplies:** $470. **Other expenses:** $1,125.

FINANCIAL AID. 68% of freshmen, 81% of continuing students receive some form of aid. 95% of grants, 87% of loans, all jobs based on need. Academic, music/drama, art, athletic, state/district residency, leadership, alumni affiliation, minority scholarships available. **Aid applications:** No closing date; priority given to applications received by May 1; applicants notified on a rolling basis beginning on or about July 1; must reply within 2 weeks.

ADDRESS/TELEPHONE. John Giron, Dean of Student Services, Trinidad State Junior College, 600 Prospect Street, Trinidad, CO 81082. (719) 846-5621. (800) 621-8752.

United States Air Force Academy

Colorado Springs, Colorado — CB code: 4830

Admissions: 15% of applicants accepted
Based on:
••• Activities, interview, school record, test scores
•• Special talents
• Essay, recommendations
Completion: 82% of freshmen end year in good standing
72% graduate, 3% of these enter graduate study

4-year public military college, coed. Founded in 1954. **Accreditation:** Regional. **Undergraduate enrollment:** 3,833 men, 510 women full time. **Faculty:** 517 total, 207 with doctorates or other terminal degrees. **Location:** Suburban campus in large city; 10 miles from downtown, 60 miles from Denver. **Calendar:** Semester, limited summer session. **Microcomputers:** 4,600 located in dormitories, libraries, classrooms, computer centers. Lease or purchase required**Special facilities:** 2 airfields, planetarium, tri-sonic wind tunnel, observatory, art gallery; aeronautics, instrumentation, research, and radio-frequency systems laboratories.

DEGREES OFFERED. BS. 1,076 bachelor's degrees awarded in 1992. 9% in business and management, 24% engineering, 5% life sciences, 24% multi/interdisciplinary studies, 10% physical sciences, 8% psychology, 15% social sciences.

UNDERGRADUATE MAJORS. Aeronautical technology, aerospace science (Air Force), aerospace/aeronautical/astronautical engineering, behavioral sciences, biological and physical sciences, biological laboratory technology, biology, business administration and management, chemistry, civil engineering, computer and information sciences, computer technology, economics, electrical technology, electrical/electronics/communications engineering, engineering, engineering and engineering-related technologies, engineering management, engineering mechanics, engineering physics, engineering science, English, geography, history, humanities, humanities and social sciences, industrial and organizational psychology, international relations, international studies, liberal/general studies, mathematics, mechanical engineering, operations research, organizational behavior, physical sciences, physics, political science and government, prelaw, psychology, science technologies, social sciences.

ACADEMIC PROGRAMS. Double major, honors program, independent study, study abroad, visiting/exchange student program, exchange programs with Ecole de l'Air (French air force academy), U.S. Military, Naval, and Coast Guard Academies. **Remedial services:** Learning center, reduced course load, remedial instruction, special counselor, tutoring. **Placement/credit:** AP, institutional tests.

ACADEMIC REQUIREMENTS. Freshmen must earn minimum GPA of 2.0 to continue in good standing. 82% of freshmen return for sophomore year. Students must declare major by end of second year. **Graduation requirements:** 160 hours for bachelor's (47 in major). Most students required to take courses in computer science, English, foreign languages, history, humanities, mathematics, philosophy/religion, biological/physical sciences, social sciences. **Additional information:** All graduates, if U.S. citizens and physically qualified, commissioned as officers in U.S. Air Force. Must serve on active-duty for at least 6 years after graduation.

FRESHMAN ADMISSIONS. Selection criteria: Must be at least 17 and not yet 22 on July 1 of admission year, U.S. citizen, and unmarried with no dependents and be nominated by member of Congress or eligible in other competitive categories. Application interview and high school extracurricular activities are very important. Candidates must take Fitness Test and meet Air Force medical and weight standards. Applicants should rank in top 10% of class. Recommended units include English 4, foreign language 2, mathematics 4, social science 3 and science 4. High school graduation strongly recommended but not required. **Test requirements:** SAT or ACT; score report by March 31.

1992 FRESHMAN CLASS PROFILE. 8,996 men applied, 1,426 accepted, 1,064 enrolled; 1,999 women applied, 223 accepted, 154 enrolled. 97% had high school GPA of 3.0 or higher, 3% between 2.0 and 2.99. 73% were in top tenth and 95% were in top quarter of graduating class. **Academic background:** Mid 50% of enrolled freshmen had SAT-V between 520-610, SAT-M between 610-700; ACT composite between 27-31. 52% submitted SAT scores, 48% submitted ACT scores. **Characteristics:** 2% from in state, 100% live in college housing, 18% have minority backgrounds, 1% are foreign students. Average age is 18.

FALL-TERM APPLICATIONS. No fee. Closing date January 31; applicants notified on a rolling basis beginning on or about December 1; must reply by May 1. Interview required. Essay required. CRDA. Request for application should be made spring semester of junior year or fall semester of senior year.

STUDENT LIFE. Housing: Dormitories (coed). All students required to live in dormitories. **Activities:** Radio, student newspaper, television, yearbook, choral groups, drama, jazz band, marching band, musical theater. **Additional information:** Cadets are from all 50 states in proportion to number of Congressional representatives from each state.

ATHLETICS. NCAA. **Intercollegiate:** Baseball M, basketball, cross-country, diving, fencing, football M, golf, gymnastics, ice hockey M, lacrosse M, rifle M, rugby, skiing, soccer, softball W, swimming, tennis, track and field, volleyball W, water polo M, wrestling M. **Intramural:** Basketball, boxing M, cross-country, diving, football M, racquetball, soccer, softball, squash, swimming, table tennis, tennis, track and field, volleyball, water polo M, wrestling M.

STUDENT SERVICES. Aptitude testing, career counseling, employment service for undergraduates, freshman orientation, health services, personal counseling, placement service for graduates.

ANNUAL EXPENSES. Tuition and fees: $0. All cadets receive tuition, room and board, including medical and dental care at government expense. Monthly pay of $544 (year round) is deposited in cadet account, from which fees for books, uniforms, and supplies (including microcomputer) deducted. $1,500 fee required on admission to cover initial cost of uniforms and equipment.

ADDRESS/TELEPHONE. Robert Y. Foerster, Colonel, USAF, Director of Admissions, United States Air Force Academy, 2304 Cadet Drive, Suite 210, Colorado Springs, CO 80840-5025. (719) 472-2520. Fax: (719) 472-3647.

University of Colorado at Boulder

Boulder, Colorado — CB code: 4841

Admissions: 76% of applicants accepted
Based on:
••• School record, test scores
• Activities, essay, recommendations, special talents
Completion: 90% of freshmen end year in good standing
58% graduate, 60% of these enter graduate study

4-year public university, coed. Founded in 1877. **Accreditation:** Regional. **Undergraduate enrollment:** 9,904 men, 8,700 women full time; 719 men, 720 women part time. **Graduate enrollment:** 2,647 men, 1,762 women full time; 333 men, 304 women part time. **Faculty:** 1,193 total (961 full time). **Location:** Suburban campus in small city; 30 miles from Denver. **Calendar:** Semester, extensive summer session. Extensive evening/early morning classes. **Microcomputers:** 820 located in dormitories, libraries, classrooms, computer centers, campus-wide network. **Special facilities:** Museum, Sommers-Bausch Observatory, Fiske Planetarium and Science Center, electron microscope.

DEGREES OFFERED. BA, BS, BFA, MA, MS, MBA, MFA, PhD, EdD, B. Pharm. 4,218 bachelor's degrees awarded in 1992. 18% in business and management, 9% communications, 9% engineering, 6% letters/literature, 6% life sciences, 9% psychology, 24% social sciences, 5% visual and performing arts. Graduate degrees offered in 61 major fields of study.

UNDERGRADUATE MAJORS. Accounting, advertising, aerospace/

aeronautical/astronautical engineering, Afro-American (black) studies, American studies, anthropology, applied mathematics, architectural engineering, art education, art history, Asian studies, biological and physical sciences, biology, broadcast production management, business and management, cell biology, central and eastern European studies, chemical engineering, chemistry, Chinese, cinematography/film, civil engineering, classics, communications, communications and speech science, computer and information sciences, computer engineering, computer science applications, conservation and regulation, dance, dramatic arts, economics, electrical/electronics/communications engineering, elementary education, engineering and other disciplines, engineering physics, English, environmental design, environmental science, environmental, population, organismic biology, film arts, finance, French, geography, geology, German, Greek (classical), history, human resources development, humanities and social sciences, information sciences and systems, international business management, international relations, Italian, Japanese, journalism, junior high education, Latin, Latin American studies, liberal/general studies, linguistics, management information systems, marketing management, mathematics, mechanical engineering, molecular biology, music, music education, music history and appreciation, music performance, music theory and composition, operations research, organizational behavior, parks and recreation management, personnel management, pharmacy, philosophy, physics, political science and government, psychology, radio/television broadcasting, radio/television technology, real estate, religion, Russian, small business management and ownership, sociology, Spanish, speech pathology/audiology, studio art, transportation management, women's studies.

ACADEMIC PROGRAMS. Double major, dual enrollment of high school students, education specialist degree, honors program, independent study, internships, semester at sea, student-designed major, study abroad, teacher preparation, visiting/exchange student program, Washington semester, cross-registration, residential academic programs (small-college environment for freshmen, some sophomores); liberal arts/career combination in engineering, business. **Remedial services:** Learning center, reduced course load, special counselor, tutoring, upward bound program for minority students. **ROTC:** Air Force, Army, Naval. **Placement/credit:** AP, CLEP Subject, institutional tests; 30 credit hours maximum for bachelor's degree.

ACADEMIC REQUIREMENTS. Freshmen must earn minimum GPA of 2.0 to continue in good standing. 81% of freshmen return for sophomore year. Students must declare major by end of second year. **Graduation requirements:** 120 hours for bachelor's (30 in major). Most students required to take courses in English, foreign languages, history, humanities, mathematics, philosophy/religion, biological/physical sciences, social sciences. **Postgraduate studies:** 2% enter law school, 9% enter medical school, 3% enter MBA programs, 46% enter other graduate study. **Additional information:** Certificates available in conjunction with baccalaurate degree for education majors. Pre-professional programs available.

FRESHMAN ADMISSIONS. Selection criteria: Secondary school record (breadth and rigor of courses, grades, class rank) most important. **High school preparation:** 16 units required. Required units include English 4, foreign language 3, mathematics 3, social science 3 and science 3. Requirements vary for the 5 colleges. Science units must include 2 laboratory science. Engineering requires 4 mathematics, 1 physics, 1 chemistry. Business requires 4 mathematics. **Test requirements:** SAT or ACT; score report by February 15. **Additional information:** Admissions competitive. Insufficient space for all qualified applicants. Some preference for students of underrepresented ethnic groups or geographic regions, close relations of alumni, and students with special talents.

1992 FRESHMAN CLASS PROFILE. 13,761 men and women applied, 10,473 accepted; 1,884 men enrolled, 1,720 women enrolled. 82% had high school GPA of 3.0 or higher, 17% between 2.0 and 2.99. 25% were in top tenth and 66% were in top quarter of graduating class. **Academic background:** Mid 50% of enrolled freshmen had SAT-V between 450-550, SAT-M between 520-630; ACT composite between 23-28. 83% submitted SAT scores, 61% submitted ACT scores. **Characteristics:** 45% from in state, 95% live in college housing, 18% have minority backgrounds, 1% are foreign students. Average age is 19.

FALL-TERM APPLICATIONS. $40 fee, may be waived for applicants with need. Closing date February 15; applicants notified on a rolling basis; must reply by May 1. Audition required for music applicants. Essay recommended. CRDA. Fall and summer applications completed by February 15 and spring applications completed by November 1 assured equal consideration. After those dates, consideration given only if places still available in college to which student applies. Test scores must be received no later than February 15 to complete application.

STUDENT LIFE. Housing: Dormitories (men, women, coed); apartment, fraternity, sorority housing available. Free tutorial services offered in dormitories. Engineering dormitories and special residential academic programs available. Academic honors section of dormitory complex available. **Activities:** Student government, film, magazine, radio, student newspaper, television, yearbook, choral groups, concert band, dance, drama, jazz band, marching band, music ensembles, musical theater, opera, pep band, symphony orchestra, Colorado Shakespeare Festival, fraternities, sororities, more than 250 religious, political, ethnic, and social organizations.

ATHLETICS. NCAA. **Intercollegiate:** Basketball, cross-country, football M, golf M, skiing, tennis, track and field, volleyball W. **Intramural:** Badminton, basketball, handball, racquetball, softball, squash, swimming, table tennis, volleyball, water polo.

STUDENT SERVICES. Aptitude testing, career counseling, employment service for undergraduates, freshman orientation, health services, on-campus day care, personal counseling, placement service for graduates, special adviser for adult students, veterans counselor, services/facilities for handicapped.

ANNUAL EXPENSES. Tuition and fees (1992-93): $2,540, $8,792 additional for out-of-state students. **Room and board:** $3,664. **Books and supplies:** $520. **Other expenses:** $2,334.

FINANCIAL AID. 44% of continuing students receive some form of aid. 60% of loans, all jobs based on need. Academic, music/drama, art, athletic, state/district residency, leadership, minority scholarships available. **Aid applications:** No closing date; priority given to applications received by April 1; applicants notified on a rolling basis beginning on or about April 15; must reply within 3 weeks.

ADDRESS/TELEPHONE. Gary M. Kelsey, Director of Admissions, University of Colorado at Boulder, 125 Regent Administrative Center, Campus Box 30, Boulder, CO 80309-0030. (303) 492-6301.

University of Colorado at Colorado Springs

Colorado Springs, Colorado — CB code: 4874

Admissions:	73% of applicants accepted
Based on:	••• School record
	•• Test scores
	• Activities, essay, interview, recommendations, special talents
Completion:	85% of freshmen end year in good standing

4-year public university, coed. Founded in 1965. **Accreditation:** Regional. **Undergraduate enrollment:** 1,075 men, 1,375 women full time; 562 men, 809 women part time. **Graduate enrollment:** 412 men, 396 women full time; 554 men, 568 women part time. **Faculty:** 394 total (202 full time), 182 with doctorates or other terminal degrees. **Location:** Suburban campus in large city; 60 miles from Denver. **Calendar:** Semester, limited summer session. Extensive evening/early morning classes. **Microcomputers:** 250 located in libraries, classrooms, computer centers, campus-wide network. **Special facilities:** Gallery of contemporary arts.

DEGREES OFFERED. BA, BS, MA, MS, MBA, PhD. 555 bachelor's degrees awarded in 1992. 28% in business and management, 14% communications, 9% engineering, 12% psychology, 14% social sciences. Graduate degrees offered in 17 major fields of study.

UNDERGRADUATE MAJORS. Accounting, anthropology, applied mathematics, biology, business administration and management, business and management, chemistry, communications, computer and information sciences, economics, electrical/electronics/communications engineering, elementary education, English, English education, finance, fine arts, geography, history, human resources development, information sciences and systems, liberal/general studies, management information systems, marketing management, mathematics, mathematics education, operations research, organizational behavior, personnel management, philosophy, physics, political science and government, psychology, real estate, science education, secondary education, small business management and ownership, social science education, sociology, Spanish.

ACADEMIC PROGRAMS. Accelerated program, double major, dual enrollment of high school students, independent study, study abroad, teacher preparation, telecourses. **Remedial services:** Learning center, preadmission summer program, reduced course load, tutoring. **ROTC:** Army. **Placement/credit:** AP, CLEP Subject; 30 credit hours maximum for bachelor's degree.

ACADEMIC REQUIREMENTS. Freshmen must earn minimum GPA of 2.0 to continue in good standing. 62% of freshmen return for sophomore year. Students must declare major on enrollment. **Graduation requirements:** 124 hours for bachelor's (36 in major). Most students required to take courses in English, humanities, mathematics, biological/physical sciences, social sciences.

FRESHMAN ADMISSIONS. Selection criteria: Rank in top 40% of graduating class, minimum 2.8 GPA required. Additional requirements for engineering and business applicants. **High school preparation:** 15 units required. Required units include English 4, foreign language 2, mathematics 3, social science 2 and science 3. 4 mathematics, 1 each physics and chemistry required for engineering program. 4 mathematics required for business. **Test requirements:** SAT or ACT; score report by July 1. Test of Standard Written English required of liberal arts applicants.

1992 FRESHMAN CLASS PROFILE. 868 men and women applied, 636 accepted; 138 men enrolled, 193 women enrolled. 60% had high school GPA of 3.0 or higher, 40% between 2.0 and 2.99. 11% were in top tenth and 40% were in top quarter of graduating class. **Academic background:** Mid 50% of enrolled freshmen had SAT-V between 420-520, SAT-M between 450-570; ACT composite between 21-26. 32% submitted SAT scores, 68% submitted ACT scores. **Characteristics:** 88% from in state, 100% commute, 21% have minority backgrounds. Average age is 21.

FALL-TERM APPLICATIONS. $30 fee, may be waived for applicants with need. Closing date July 1; applicants notified on a rolling basis; must reply by registration. Deferred admission available.

STUDENT LIFE. Activities: Student government, film, student newspaper, literary magazine, choral groups, dance, drama, music ensembles, El Movimento Estudiantil Chicano De Aztlan (MECHA), Inter-Varsity Christian Fellowship, Black Student Union, Asian American Club, Campus Libertarians, Young Republicans, Baha'i Club, Baptish Student Union, Campus Advance, High Country College Ministry.

ATHLETICS. NCAA. **Intercollegiate:** Basketball, golf M, soccer M, softball W, tennis, volleyball W. **Intramural:** Badminton, basketball, bowling, cross-country, fencing, football M, racquetball, skiing, soccer, softball, table tennis, tennis, volleyball.

STUDENT SERVICES. Aptitude testing, career counseling, employment service for undergraduates, freshman orientation, on-campus day care, personal counseling, placement service for graduates, veterans counselor, services/facilities for handicapped.

ANNUAL EXPENSES. Tuition and fees (1992-93): $2,143, $4,678 additional for out-of-state students. **Books and supplies:** $454. **Other expenses:** $330.

FINANCIAL AID. 40% of freshmen, 42% of continuing students receive some form of aid. 92% of grants, 85% of loans, 49% of jobs based on need. 127 enrolled freshmen were judged to have need, 115 were offered aid. Academic, athletic, state/district residency, alumni affiliation, minority scholarships available. **Aid applications:** No closing date; priority given to applications received by April 1; applicants notified on a rolling basis beginning on or about May 15; must reply within 2 weeks.

ADDRESS/TELEPHONE. Randall E. Kouba, Director of Admissions/Records, University of Colorado at Colorado Springs, P.O. Box 7150, Colorado Springs, CO 80933-7150. (719) 593-3383.

University of Colorado at Denver
Denver, Colorado — CB code: 4875

4-year public university, coed. Founded in 1912. **Accreditation:** Regional. **Undergraduate enrollment:** 1,825 men, 1,981 women full time; 1,182 men, 1,167 women part time. **Graduate enrollment:** 615 men, 638 women full time; 1,637 men, 2,044 women part time. **Faculty:** 627 total (327 full time), 300 with doctorates or other terminal degrees. **Location:** Urban campus in very large city. **Calendar:** Semester, extensive summer session. Extensive evening/early morning classes. **Microcomputers:** 330 located in computer centers, campus-wide network. **Additional facts:** Library, student center, and classrooms shared with Metropolitan State College and Community College of Denver.

DEGREES OFFERED. BA, BS, BFA, MA, MS, MBA, MEd, PhD, EdD. 853 bachelor's degrees awarded in 1992. 30% in business and management, 7% communications, 15% engineering, 14% letters/literature, 6% mathematics, 5% physical sciences, 9% psychology, 5% visual and performing arts. Graduate degrees offered in 40 major fields of study.

UNDERGRADUATE MAJORS. Accounting, anthropology, applied mathematics, art history, biological and physical sciences, biology, business administration and management, business and management, business statistics, chemistry, civil engineering, communications, computer and information sciences, computer engineering, creative writing, dramatic arts, economics, electrical/electronics/communications engineering, English, English literature, finance, fine arts, foreign languages (multiple emphasis), French, geography, geology, German, history, human resources development, humanities and social sciences, international business management, international studies, liberal/general studies, management information systems, management science, marketing management, mathematics, mechanical engineering, music performance, music theory and composition, music, sound synthesis and recording, personnel management, philosophy, photography, physical sciences, physics, political science and government, psychology, real estate, social sciences, sociology, Spanish, speech, studio art, visual and performing arts.

ACADEMIC PROGRAMS. Cooperative education, double major, dual enrollment of high school students, honors program, independent study, internships, semester at sea, student-designed major, study abroad, cross-registration; liberal arts/career combination in engineering, business; combined bachelor's/graduate program in business administration. **Remedial services:** Reduced course load, special counselor, tutoring, study skills center. **ROTC:** Air Force, Army. **Placement/credit:** AP, CLEP Subject, institutional tests; 30 credit hours maximum for bachelor's degree.

ACADEMIC REQUIREMENTS. Freshmen must earn minimum GPA of 2.0 to continue in good standing. 62% of freshmen return for sophomore year. Students must declare major by end of second year. **Graduation requirements:** 120 hours for bachelor's (30 in major). Most students required to take courses in arts/fine arts, English, history, humanities, mathematics, biological/physical sciences, social sciences.

FRESHMAN ADMISSIONS. Selection criteria: Rank in top 30% of class with minimum ACT composite score of 25 or SAT combined score of 1050 required. **High school preparation:** 15 units required. Required units include English 4, foreign language 2, mathematics 3, social science 2 and science 3. 16 units including 4 mathematics required for engineering and business students. **Test requirements:** SAT or ACT; score report by July 22.

1992 FRESHMAN CLASS PROFILE. 107 men, 180 women enrolled. **Academic background:** Mid 50% of enrolled freshmen had SAT-V between 420-520, SAT-M between 460-570; ACT composite between 19-25. 40% submitted SAT scores, 79% submitted ACT scores. **Characteristics:** 96% from in state, 100% commute, 49% have minority backgrounds, 1% are foreign students. Average age is 24.

FALL-TERM APPLICATIONS. $30 fee, may be waived for applicants with need. Closing date July 22; applicants notified on a rolling basis. Audition required for music applicants. Deferred admission available.

STUDENT LIFE. Activities: Student government, student newspaper, choral groups, dance, drama, jazz band, music ensembles, Asian-American Student Alliance, Black Student Alliance, International Club, Native American Student Organization, United Mexican-American Students.

STUDENT SERVICES. Aptitude testing, career counseling, employment service for undergraduates, freshman orientation, health services, on-campus day care, personal counseling, placement service for graduates, veterans counselor, services/facilities for handicapped.

ANNUAL EXPENSES. Tuition and fees (1992-93): $1,917, $6,148 additional for out-of-state students. **Books and supplies:** $450. **Other expenses:** $830.

FINANCIAL AID. 30% of continuing students receive some form of aid. Grants, loans, jobs available. Academic, music/drama, art scholarships available. **Aid applications:** No closing date; priority given to applications received by March 30; applicants notified on a rolling basis; must reply within 3 weeks.

ADDRESS/TELEPHONE. Barbara Schneider, Executive Director Admissions and Records, University of Colorado at Denver, PO Box 173364, Campus Box 167, Denver, CO 80217-3364. (303) 556-2660. Fax: (303) 556-4822.

University of Colorado Health Sciences Center
Denver, Colorado — CB code: 0968

2-year upper-division public health science college, coed. Founded in 1924. **Accreditation:** Regional. **Undergraduate enrollment:** 158 men, 456 women full time; 8 men, 48 women part time. **Graduate enrollment:** 466 men, 647 women full time; 65 men, 179 women part time. **Faculty:** 2,651 total (1,144 full time), 1,444 with doctorates or other terminal degrees. **Location:** Urban campus in large city. **Calendar:** Both semester and quarter systems used, depending on program. **Microcomputers:** Located in libraries, computer centers. **Additional facts:** University includes 2 hospitals, schools of Nursing, medicine, dentistry, and pharmacy, graduate school, programs in allied health professions, and 8 affiliated institutes.

DEGREES OFFERED. BS, MS, PhD, DDS, MD, Pharm D. 275 bachelor's degrees awarded in 1992. 85% in health sciences, 15% allied health. Graduate degrees offered in 21 major fields of study.

UNDERGRADUATE MAJORS. Dental hygiene, medical laboratory technologies, nursing, pharmacy.

ACADEMIC PROGRAMS. Independent study, internships, cross-registration. **Placement/credit:** Institutional tests.

ACADEMIC REQUIREMENTS. Students must declare major on application. **Graduation requirements:** 124 hours for bachelor's.

STUDENT LIFE. Activities: Student government.

STUDENT SERVICES. Health services, personal counseling, veterans counselor, daycare referral service, services/facilities for handicapped.

ANNUAL EXPENSES. Tuition and fees (1992-93): $3,748, $7,166 additional for out-of-state students. **Books and supplies:** $865. **Other expenses:** $2,340.

FINANCIAL AID. 59% of continuing students receive some form of aid. 81% of loans based on need. Academic, state/district residency, leadership scholarships available. **Aid applications:** No closing date; priority given to applications received by March 15; applicants notified on a rolling basis.

ADDRESS/TELEPHONE. David P. Sorenson, Director of Admissions and Student Services, University of Colorado Health Sciences Center, 4200 East Ninth Avenue, Box A 054, Denver, CO 80262. (303) 270-7676. Fax: (303) 270-5969.

University of Denver
Denver, Colorado — CB code: 4842

Admissions:	67% of applicants accepted
Based on:	••• School record
	•• Activities, essay, interview, recommendations, test scores
	• Special talents
Completion:	85% of freshmen end year in good standing
	66% graduate, 26% of these enter graduate study

4-year private university, coed, affiliated with United Methodist Church. Founded in 1864. **Accreditation:** Regional. **Undergraduate enrollment:** 1,259 men, 1,347 women full time; 99 men, 454 women part time. **Graduate enrollment:** 1,339 men, 1,398 women full time; 1,140 men, 1,036 women part time. **Faculty:** 402 total (384 full time), 343 with doctorates or other terminal degrees. **Location:** Suburban campus in very large city; 8 miles from downtown. **Calendar:** Quarter, limited summer session. Saturday classes. **Microcomputers:** 384 located in dormitories, libraries, classrooms, computer centers. **Special facilities:** Chamberlain Observatory, high altitude research laboratory at Mount Evans, Rocky Mountain Regional Conservation Center, University Center for Gifted Children, electron microscope.

DEGREES OFFERED. BA, BS, BFA, MA, MS, MBA, MFA, MSW, PhD, JD. 717 bachelor's degrees awarded in 1992. 47% in business and management, 9% communications, 15% psychology, 6% social sciences, 6% visual and performing arts. Graduate degrees offered in 62 major fields of study.

UNDERGRADUATE MAJORS. Accounting, American studies, anthropology, art education, art history, biology, business administration and management, business and management, business economics, business statistics, chemistry, classics, communications, comparative literature, computer and information sciences, computer engineering, construction management, creative writing, economics, electrical/electronics/communications engineering, English, English literature, environmental science, film arts, finance, fine arts, foreign languages (multiple emphasis), French, geography, German, graphic design, history, hotel/motel and restaurant management, international business management, international studies, jazz, Jewish studies, journalism, Latin American studies, marketing management, mathematics, mechanical engineering, music, music education, music history and appreciation, music performance, music theory and composition, operations research, philosophy, physical sciences, physics, political science and government, predentistry, prelaw, premedicine, preveterinary, psychology, public affairs, real estate, religion, Russian, Russian and Slavic studies, social sciences, sociology, Spanish, statistics, studio art, systems analysis, women's studies.

ACADEMIC PROGRAMS. Accelerated program, cooperative education, double major, dual enrollment of high school students, honors program, independent study, internships, study abroad, teacher preparation, weekend college, joint PhD program in theological studies with Iliff School of Theology; combined bachelor's/graduate program in business administration. **Remedial services:** Special program for learning disabled students. **ROTC:** Air Force, Army. **Placement/credit:** AP, CLEP General and Subject, IB, institutional tests; 45 credit hours maximum for bachelor's degree.

ACADEMIC REQUIREMENTS. Freshmen must earn minimum GPA of 2.0 to continue in good standing. 81% of freshmen return for sophomore year. Students must declare major by end of second year. **Graduation requirements:** 183 hours for bachelor's (40 in major). Most students required to take courses in arts/fine arts, computer science, English, foreign languages, history, humanities, mathematics, philosophy/religion, biological/physical sciences, social sciences. **Additional information:** Special inter-term courses for focused concentration on 1 subject for 3 weeks. Minimum quarter hours required in major varies from 40 to 60 depending on field.

FRESHMAN ADMISSIONS. Selection criteria: High school GPA and curriculum most important, followed by test scores, class rank, recommendations from teacher and counselor, personal essay. Academic maturity, independence, contributions to school and community extracurricular activities, leadership also considered. Recommended units include English 4, foreign language 4, mathematics 4, social science 4 and science 4. 4 years of mathematics through calculus required for immediate admission to engineering program. **Test requirements:** SAT or ACT; score report by August 1.

1992 FRESHMAN CLASS PROFILE. 2,703 men and women applied, 1,807 accepted; 373 men enrolled, 378 women enrolled. 29% were in top tenth and 60% were in top quarter of graduating class. **Academic background:** Mid 50% of enrolled freshmen had SAT-V between 430-540, SAT-M between 470-490; ACT composite between 21-27. 73% submitted SAT scores, 65% submitted ACT scores. **Characteristics:** 38% from in state, 72% live in college housing, 16% have minority backgrounds, 8% are foreign students, 35% join fraternities/sororities. Average age is 18.

FALL-TERM APPLICATIONS. $30 fee, may be waived for applicants with need. Closing date August 1; priority given to applications received by March 1; applicants notified on a rolling basis beginning on or about January 1; must reply by May 1 or within 4 weeks if notified thereafter. Audition required for music applicants. Essay required. Interview recommended. Portfolio recommended for art applicants. CRDA. Deferred and early admission available. Institutional early decision plan. Deposit required within 30 days of acceptance, fully refundable if requested by May 1. Early action applicants must apply by December 20, notified by February 1.

STUDENT LIFE. Housing: Dormitories (coed); apartment, fraternity, sorority housing available. **Activities:** Student government, film, magazine, radio, student newspaper, yearbook, choral groups, concert band, drama, jazz band, music ensembles, musical theater, opera, pep band, symphony orchestra, fraternities, sororities, 15 active student religious organizations, Hispanic organizations, Black Student Alliance, numerous service and ethnic organizations.

ATHLETICS. NCAA. **Intercollegiate:** Baseball M, basketball, diving, golf M, gymnastics W, ice hockey M, lacrosse M, skiing, soccer, swimming, tennis, volleyball W. **Intramural:** Badminton, basketball, bowling, golf, ice hockey M, racquetball, rugby, skiing, soccer, softball, tennis, volleyball, wrestling M.

STUDENT SERVICES. Aptitude testing, career counseling, employment service for undergraduates, freshman orientation, health services, personal counseling, placement service for graduates, veterans counselor, services for learning disabled students, services/facilities for handicapped.

ANNUAL EXPENSES. Tuition and fees (1992-93): $13,572. **Room and board:** $4,302. **Books and supplies:** $400. **Other expenses:** $1,350.

FINANCIAL AID. 54% of freshmen, 49% of continuing students receive some form of aid. 54% of grants, all loans, 91% of jobs based on need. 275 enrolled freshmen were judged to have need, all were offered aid. Academic, music/drama, art, athletic, state/district residency, leadership, minority scholarships available. **Aid applications:** Closing date March 1; priority given to applications received by February 21; applicants notified on a rolling basis beginning on or about April 1; must reply by May 1 or within 3 weeks if notified thereafter.

ADDRESS/TELEPHONE. Roger Campbell, Dean of Admissions and Financial Aid, University of Denver, Mary Reed Building #107, Denver, CO 80208-0132. (303) 871-2036. (800) 525-9495. Fax: (303) 871-4000.

University of Northern Colorado
Greeley, Colorado — CB code: 4074

Admissions:	70% of applicants accepted
Based on:	••• School record, test scores
	•• Activities, essay, interview
	• Recommendations, special talents
Completion:	79% of freshmen end year in good standing
	30% graduate

4-year public university, coed. Founded in 1889. **Accreditation:** Regional. **Undergraduate enrollment:** 3,313 men, 4,588 women full time; 365 men, 415 women part time. **Graduate enrollment:** 405 men, 550 women full time; 223 men, 469 women part time. **Faculty:** 601 total (462 full time), 315 with doctorates or other terminal degrees. **Location:** Rural campus in small city; 50 miles from Denver, 50 miles from Cheyenne, Wyoming. **Calendar:** Semester, extensive summer session. Extensive evening/early morning classes. **Microcomputers:** 450 located in dormitories, libraries, classrooms, computer centers. **Special facilities:** Marcus Garvey cultural center, Hispanic Cultural Center, Marianni Art Gallery, laboratory school, additional 80-acre mountain campus near Estes Park.

DEGREES OFFERED. BA, BS, MA, MS, PhD, EdD. 1,465 bachelor's degrees awarded in 1992. 17% in business and management, 9% communications, 12% teacher education, 12% health sciences, 8% parks/recreation, protective services, public affairs, 6% psychology, 15% social sciences, 5% visual and performing arts. Graduate degrees offered in 46 major fields of study.

UNDERGRADUATE MAJORS. Accounting, actuarial sciences, advertising, Afro-American (black) studies, applied mathematics, art education, athletic training, atmospheric sciences and meteorology, bilingual/bicultural education, biology, business and management, cell biology, chemistry, communications, community health work, dance, dramatic arts, earth sciences, economics, English, English education, finance, fine arts, fitness and exercise, food science and nutrition, foreign languages education, French, geography, geology, German, gerontology, graphic arts technology, history, interdisciplinary studies, international studies, journalism, kinesiology, Latin American studies, management information systems, management science, marketing management, mathematics, mathematics education, medical laboratory technologies, Mexican American studies, music, music education, music performance, music theory and composition, musical theater, nursing, parks and recreation management, philosophy, physical sciences, physics, political science and government, psychology, public relations, recreation therapy, rehabilitation counseling/services, science education, social science education, social sciences, sociology, Spanish, speech pathology/audiology, speech/communication/theater education, statistics, telecommunications, theater design, visual and performing arts.

ACADEMIC PROGRAMS. Cooperative education, double major, dual enrollment of high school students, education specialist degree, external degree, honors program, independent study, internships, student-designed major, study abroad, teacher preparation, visiting/exchange student program, cross-registration. **Remedial services:** Learning center, reduced course load, remedial instruction, special counselor, tutoring. **ROTC:** Air Force, Army. **Placement/credit:** AP, CLEP General and Subject, institutional tests; 30 credit hours maximum for bachelor's degree.

ACADEMIC REQUIREMENTS. Freshmen must earn minimum GPA of 2.0 to continue in good standing. 64% of freshmen return for sophomore year. Students must declare major by end of second year. **Graduation requirements:** 120 hours for bachelor's (40 in major). Most students required to take courses in arts/fine arts, English, humanities, mathematics, biological/physical sciences, social sciences.

FRESHMAN ADMISSIONS. Selection criteria: Expected cumulative GPA of 2.8 or higher, and ACT composite score of 22 or combined SAT score of 890. Applicants evaluated individually; students with cumulative GPA above minimum or with higher class rank may be admitted with lower standardized test scores, students with higher standardized test scores may be admitted with cumulative GPA below minimum or with lower class rank. **High school preparation:** 15 units required. Required and recommended units include mathematics 2-3. English 4, social science 2 and science 2 recommended. Mathematics should include 2 algebra or 1 algebra, 1 geometry. **Test requirements:** SAT or ACT; score report by August 31.

1992 FRESHMAN CLASS PROFILE. 2,217 men applied, 1,436 accepted, 549 enrolled; 3,059 women applied, 2,264 accepted, 925 enrolled. 62% had high school GPA of 3.0 or higher, 37% between 2.0 and 2.99. 12% were in top tenth and 39% were in top quarter of graduating class. **Academic background:** Mid 50% of enrolled freshmen had SAT-V between 380-480, SAT-M between 410-540; ACT composite between 19-24. 41% submitted SAT scores, 90% submitted ACT scores. **Characteristics:** 86% from in state, 89% live in college housing, 19% have minority backgrounds, 1% are foreign students. Average age is 18.

FALL-TERM APPLICATIONS. $30 fee, may be waived for applicants with need. No closing date; applicants notified on a rolling basis beginning on or about October 1. Audition required for music applicants. Deferred and early admission available.

STUDENT LIFE. Housing: Dormitories (women, coed); apartment, fraternity, sorority housing available. **Activities:** Student government, magazine, radio, student newspaper, choral groups, concert band, dance, drama, jazz band, marching band, music ensembles, musical theater, opera, pep band, symphony orchestra, fraternities, sororities, Black Student Union, Organization of Hispanic Students, International Students Association.

ATHLETICS. NCAA. **Intercollegiate:** Baseball M, basketball, football M, golf M, soccer W, swimming W, tennis, track and field, volleyball W, wrestling M. **Intramural:** Badminton, basketball, racquetball, soccer, softball, tennis, volleyball, water polo.

STUDENT SERVICES. Aptitude testing, career counseling, employment service for undergraduates, freshman orientation, health services, on-campus day care, personal counseling, placement service for graduates, veterans counselor, services/facilities for handicapped.

ANNUAL EXPENSES. Tuition and fees (1992-93): $2,027, $4,861 additional for out-of-state students. **Room and board:** $3,814. **Books and supplies:** $500. **Other expenses:** $1,730.

FINANCIAL AID. 68% of freshmen, 69% of continuing students receive some form of aid. 57% of grants, 96% of loans, 42% of jobs based on need. 950 enrolled freshmen were judged to have need, 872 were offered aid. Academic, music/drama, art, athletic, state/district residency, leadership, alumni affiliation, minority scholarships available. **Aid applications:** No closing date; priority given to applications received by March 1; applicants notified on a rolling basis beginning on or about May 31; must reply within 2 weeks.

ADDRESS/TELEPHONE. Gary O. Gullickson, Director of Admissions, University of Northern Colorado, Greeley, CO 80639. (303) 351-2881.

University of Southern Colorado

Pueblo, Colorado — CB code: 4611

Admissions: 90% of applicants accepted
Based on: ••• School record, test scores
• Activities, essay, interview, recommendations, special talents
Completion: 70% of freshmen end year in good standing
26% graduate, 10% of these enter graduate study

4-year public university, coed. Founded in 1933. **Accreditation:** Regional. **Undergraduate enrollment:** 1,786 men, 1,912 women full time; 258 men, 347 women part time. **Graduate enrollment:** 13 men, 7 women full time; 85 men, 80 women part time. **Faculty:** 278 total (168 full time), 141 with doctorates or other terminal degrees. **Location:** Suburban campus in small city; 42 miles from Colorado Springs, 100 miles from Denver. **Calendar:** Semester, extensive summer session. **Microcomputers:** 60 located in dormitories, libraries, classrooms, computer centers. **Special facilities:** Recital hall, outdoor recreation facilities, electron microscope, golf course, art gallery. **Additional facts:** Curricular emphasis on applied, career-oriented programs, including nursing, business, engineering technologies.

DEGREES OFFERED. BA, BS, MS, MBA. 582 bachelor's degrees awarded in 1992. 27% in business and management, 6% communications, 14% engineering technologies, 5% health sciences, 5% letters/literature, 8% life sciences, 8% psychology, 16% social sciences. Graduate degrees offered in 3 major fields of study.

UNDERGRADUATE MAJORS. Accounting, advertising, automotive technology, biology, business administration and management, business economics, chemistry, civil technology, communications, computer and information sciences, electronic technology, elementary education, English, foreign languages (multiple emphasis), history, industrial engineering, industrial technology, journalism, Kinesiology, marketing management, mathematics, mechanical design technology, music, nursing, parks and recreation management, physical education, physics, political science and government, psychology, public relations, radio/television broadcasting, secondary education, social sciences, social work, sociology, Spanish, speech, sports medicine, telecommunications, visual and performing arts.

ACADEMIC PROGRAMS. Cooperative education, double major, dual enrollment of high school students, honors program, independent study, internships, study abroad, teacher preparation, telecourses, visiting/exchange student program, cross-registration. **Remedial services:** Learning center, special counselor, tutoring. **Placement/credit:** AP, CLEP General, institutional tests.

ACADEMIC REQUIREMENTS. Freshmen must earn minimum GPA of 2.0 to continue in good standing. 62% of freshmen return for sophomore year. Students must declare major by end of second year. **Graduation requirements:** 128 hours for bachelor's (40 in major). Most students required to take courses in computer science, English, history, humanities, mathematics, biological/physical sciences, social sciences. **Postgraduate studies:** 1% enter law school, 2% enter medical school, 2% enter MBA programs, 5% enter other graduate study.

FRESHMAN ADMISSIONS. Selection criteria: High school achievement record and test scores most important. Recommended units include English 4, foreign language 2, mathematics 3, physical science 2 and social science 2. **Test requirements:** SAT or ACT (ACT preferred); score report by July 21.

1992 FRESHMAN CLASS PROFILE. 673 men applied, 606 accepted, 330 enrolled; 729 women applied, 656 accepted, 365 enrolled. 45% had high school GPA of 3.0 or higher, 50% between 2.0 and 2.99. 6% were in top tenth and 24% were in top quarter of graduating class. **Academic background:** Mid 50% of enrolled freshmen had SAT-V between 330-460, SAT-M between 410-520; ACT composite between 19-24. 4% submitted SAT scores, 96% submitted ACT scores. **Characteristics:** 92% from in state, 74% commute, 31% have minority backgrounds, 2% are foreign students. Average age is 20.

FALL-TERM APPLICATIONS. $15 fee, may be waived for applicants with need. Closing date July 22; applicants notified on a rolling basis. Audition recommended for music applicants. Portfolio recommended for art applicants. Deferred admission available.

STUDENT LIFE. Housing: Dormitories (coed). **Activities:** Student government, radio, student newspaper, television, choral groups, concert band, drama, jazz band, music ensembles, musical theater, pep band, fraternities, several religious, ethnic, and professional service organizations.

ATHLETICS. NCAA. **Intercollegiate:** Baseball M, basketball, golf, soccer M, softball W, tennis, volleyball W, wrestling M. **Intramural:** Basketball, softball, volleyball.

STUDENT SERVICES. Aptitude testing, career counseling, employment service for undergraduates, freshman orientation, health services, personal counseling, placement service for graduates, veterans counselor, services/facilities for handicapped.

ANNUAL EXPENSES. Tuition and fees (1992-93): $1,834, $4,552 additional for out-of-state students. **Room and board:** $3,720. **Books and supplies:** $500. **Other expenses:** $1,200.

FINANCIAL AID. 58% of freshmen, 70% of continuing students receive some form of aid. 85% of grants, 89% of loans, 74% of jobs based on need. 470 enrolled freshmen were judged to have need, 393 were offered aid. Academic, music/drama, art, athletic, state/district residency, leadership, minority scholarships available. **Aid applications:** Closing date April 15; priority given to applications received by March 1; applicants notified on a rolling basis beginning on or about April 15; must reply within 2 weeks. **Additional information:** Tuition and fee waivers available for employees.

ADDRESS/TELEPHONE. Dr. Martha G. Wade, Dean of Admissions and Enrollment Services, University of Southern Colorado, 2200 Bonforte Boulevard, Pueblo, CO 81001-4901. (719) 549-2461. (800) 872-4769. Fax: (719) 549-2938.

Western State College of Colorado

Gunnison, Colorado — CB code: 4946

Admissions: 85% of applicants accepted
Based on: ••• School record, test scores
•• Essay, recommendations
• Activities, interview, special talents
Completion: 85% of freshmen end year in good standing
20% enter graduate study

4-year public liberal arts college, coed. Founded in 1911. **Accreditation:** Regional. **Undergraduate enrollment:** 1,494 men, 983 women full time; 102 men, 83 women part time. **Faculty:** 173 total (104 full time), 70 with doctorates or other terminal degrees. **Location:** Rural campus in small town; 200 miles from Denver. **Calendar:** Calendar year consists of 4 sessions, alternating 12 and 8 weeks in length. One 8-week session during summer. Extensive evening/early morning classes. **Microcomputers:** 88 located in dormitories, libraries, classrooms, computer centers. **Special facilities:** Thornton Botanical Gardens, art gallery.

DEGREES OFFERED. BA. 342 bachelor's degrees awarded in 1992. 32% in business and management, 8% communications, 9% languages, 10%

life sciences, 9% psychology, 12% social sciences, 6% visual and performing arts.

UNDERGRADUATE MAJORS. Accounting, American studies, art education, art history, biology, business administration and management, chemistry, clinical psychology, commercial art, communications, counseling psychology, dramatic arts, ecology, economics, elementary education, English, English education, environmental science, finance, fine arts, foreign languages education, French, geography, geology, geophysics and seismology, history, hotel/motel and restaurant management, industrial arts education, law enforcement and corrections, library science, library science/archival science/museum studies, management science, marketing management, mathematics, molecular biology, music, music education, parks and recreation management, personnel management, physical education, physics, political science and government, predentistry, preengineering, prelaw, premedicine, prepharmacy, preveterinary, psychobiology, psychology, public policy studies, radio/television broadcasting, religion, secondary education, ski resort management, small business management and ownership, social work, sociology, Spanish, speech/communication/theater education, sports management, studio art.

ACADEMIC PROGRAMS. Accelerated program, double major, dual enrollment of high school students, honors program, independent study, internships, student-designed major, study abroad, teacher preparation, visiting/exchange student program, cross-registration. **Remedial services:** Learning center, remedial instruction, special counselor, tutoring. **Placement/credit:** AP, CLEP General and Subject, institutional tests; 40 credit hours maximum for bachelor's degree.

ACADEMIC REQUIREMENTS. Freshmen must earn minimum GPA of 1.88 to continue in good standing. 63% of freshmen return for sophomore year. Students must declare major by end of second year. **Graduation requirements:** 120 hours for bachelor's (30 in major). Most students required to take courses in arts/fine arts, English, history, humanities, mathematics, biological/physical sciences, social sciences.

FRESHMAN ADMISSIONS. Selection criteria: School achievement record and test scores very important. Recommended units include English 3, foreign language 2, mathematics 3, social science 2 and science 3. **Test requirements:** SAT or ACT; score report by April 15.

1992 FRESHMAN CLASS PROFILE. 1,366 men applied, 1,173 accepted, 454 enrolled; 910 women applied, 764 accepted, 291 enrolled. 28% had high school GPA of 3.0 or higher, 69% between 2.0 and 2.99. 7% were in top tenth and 24% were in top quarter of graduating class. **Academic background:** Mid 50% of enrolled freshmen had SAT-V between 360-470, SAT-M between 400-520; ACT composite between 18-22. 31% submitted SAT scores, 70% submitted ACT scores. **Characteristics:** 65% from in state, 100% live in college housing, 10% have minority backgrounds, 1% are foreign students, 4% join fraternities/sororities. Average age is 18.

FALL-TERM APPLICATIONS. $25 fee, may be waived for applicants with need. No closing date; priority given to applications received by April 15; applicants notified on a rolling basis. Interview recommended for academically weak applicants. Essay recommended. Deferred admission available. Applications received after April 15 will be considered on a space available basis only.

STUDENT LIFE. Housing: Dormitories (men, women, coed); apartment, fraternity housing available. **Activities:** Student government, magazine, radio, student newspaper, television, yearbook, choral groups, concert band, dance, drama, jazz band, marching band, music ensembles, musical theater, symphony orchestra, fraternities, sororities, Newman, Baptist Student Union, Fellowship of Christain Athletes, NAACP, Omega Zi Phi, Kappa Delta Psi, Sigma Beta Phi, Bacchus, Aware.

ATHLETICS. NCAA. **Intercollegiate:** Basketball, cross-country, football M, skiing, track and field, volleyball W, wrestling M. **Intramural:** Basketball, bowling, boxing M, cross-country, golf, ice hockey, lacrosse M, racquetball, rugby M, skiing, soccer, softball, swimming, table tennis, tennis, track and field, volleyball, wrestling M.

STUDENT SERVICES. Aptitude testing, career counseling, employment service for undergraduates, freshman orientation, on-campus day care, personal counseling, placement service for graduates, special adviser for adult students, veterans counselor, services/facilities for handicapped.

ANNUAL EXPENSES. Tuition and fees (projected): $1,924, $3,556 additional for out-of-state students. **Room and board:** $3,744. **Books and supplies:** $500. **Other expenses:** $1,250.

FINANCIAL AID. 70% of freshmen, 70% of continuing students receive some form of aid. 85% of grants, 78% of loans, 53% of jobs based on need. 500 enrolled freshmen were judged to have need, 350 were offered aid. Academic, music/drama, art, athletic, leadership scholarships available. **Aid applications:** No closing date; priority given to applications received by April 1; applicants notified on a rolling basis beginning on or about April 15; must reply by May 1 or within 2 weeks if notified thereafter.

ADDRESS/TELEPHONE. Monica Bruning, Director of Admissions, Western State College of Colorado, College Heights, Gunnison, CO 81231. (303) 943-2119. (800) 876-5309. Fax: (303) 943-7069.

Yeshiva Toras Chaim Talmudical Seminary

Denver, Colorado — CB code: 7008

4-year private institution, men only, affiliated with Jewish faith. **Undergraduate enrollment:** 28 men. **Graduate enrollment:** 4 men full time. **Location:** Urban campus in very large city.

DEGREES OFFERED. BA, Talm, Rab. Graduate degrees offered in 1 major field of study.

FRESHMAN ADMISSIONS. Selection criteria: Interview, test scores considered.

1992 FRESHMAN CLASS PROFILE. 16 men and women enrolled.

ANNUAL EXPENSES. Tuition and fees (1992-93): $4,050. **Room and board:** $4,400.

ADDRESS/TELEPHONE. Yeshiva Toras Chaim Talmudical Seminary, 1400 Quitman Street, Denver, CO 80204. (303) 629-8200.

Connecticut

Albertus Magnus College
New Haven, Connecticut CB code: 3001

4-year private liberal arts college, coed, affiliated with Roman Catholic Church. Founded in 1925. **Accreditation:** Regional. **Undergraduate enrollment:** 155 men, 261 women full time; 44 men, 186 women part time. **Graduate enrollment:** 3 men, 6 women part time. **Faculty:** 62 total (30 full time), 28 with doctorates or other terminal degrees. **Location:** Urban campus in small city; 90 miles from New York City. **Calendar:** Semester, limited summer session. **Microcomputers:** 24 located in libraries, computer centers.

DEGREES OFFERED. AA, BA, BFA, MA. 25 associate degrees awarded in 1992. 100% in multi/interdisciplinary studies. 111 bachelor's degrees awarded. 32% in business and management, 14% communications, 9% letters/literature, 10% multi/interdisciplinary studies, 11% psychology, 12% social sciences, 6% visual and performing arts. Graduate degrees offered in 1 major field of study.

UNDERGRADUATE MAJORS. Associate: Liberal/general studies. **Bachelor's:** Accounting, art history, art therapy, biological and physical sciences, biology, business economics, classics, communications, community psychology, criminology, dramatic arts, economics, English, fine arts, French, history, humanities, humanities and social sciences, industrial and organizational psychology, Italian, liberal/general studies, mathematics, mental health/human services, philosophy, physical sciences, political science and government, predentistry, prelaw, premedicine, preveterinary, psychology, religion, romance languages, social sciences, sociology, Spanish, studio art, urban studies, visual and performing arts.

ACADEMIC PROGRAMS. Double major, dual enrollment of high school students, honors program, independent study, internships, study abroad, Washington semester, cross-registration. **Remedial services:** Learning center, reduced course load, tutoring. **Placement/credit:** AP, CLEP General and Subject, institutional tests; 21 credit hours maximum for associate degree; 45 credit hours maximum for bachelor's degree.

ACADEMIC REQUIREMENTS. Freshmen must earn minimum GPA of 1.7 to continue in good standing. 75% of freshmen return for sophomore year. Students must declare major by end of second year. **Graduation requirements:** 60 hours for associate (15 in major), 120 hours for bachelor's (30 in major). Most students required to take courses in arts/fine arts, English, foreign languages, history, humanities, mathematics, philosophy/religion, biological/physical sciences, social sciences. **Postgraduate studies:** 95% from 2-year programs enter 4-year programs. 8% enter law school, 2% enter medical school, 10% enter MBA programs, 20% enter other graduate study.

FRESHMAN ADMISSIONS. Selection criteria: School achievement record most important. Recommendations, then test scores, interview, school and community activities also considered. **High school preparation:** 16 units required. Required and recommended units include English 4. Foreign language 2, mathematics 3, social science 1 and science 1 recommended. **Test requirements:** SAT or ACT (SAT preferred); score report by August 25.

1992 FRESHMAN CLASS PROFILE. 34 men, 40 women enrolled. 18% had high school GPA of 3.0 or higher, 57% between 2.0 and 2.99. 5% were in top tenth and 10% were in top quarter of graduating class. **Characteristics:** 74% from in state, 60% live in college housing, 22% have minority backgrounds, 3% are foreign students. Average age is 18.

FALL-TERM APPLICATIONS. $30 fee, may be waived for applicants with need. No closing date; applicants notified on a rolling basis; must reply by May 1 or within 4 weeks if notified thereafter. Interview recommended. CRDA. Deferred and early admission available.

STUDENT LIFE. Housing: Dormitories (women, coed). **Activities:** Student government, magazine, student newspaper, yearbook, choral groups, dance, drama, musical theater, Student Minority Advisory Council.

ATHLETICS. NCAA. **Intercollegiate:** Baseball M, basketball, cross-country, soccer M, softball W, swimming, tennis, volleyball W. **Intramural:** Fencing, golf, racquetball, softball M, water polo.

STUDENT SERVICES. Career counseling, employment service for undergraduates, freshman orientation, health services, personal counseling, placement service for graduates, special adviser for adult students, veterans counselor, services/facilities for handicapped.

ANNUAL EXPENSES. Tuition and fees (projected): $11,420. Beginning in fall 1993 optional Tri-Session Plan will enable students to earn college degree in 3 years or less while saving a year's tuition. **Room and board:** $5,240. **Books and supplies:** $400. **Other expenses:** $847.

FINANCIAL AID. 74% of freshmen, 70% of continuing students receive some form of aid. 98% of grants, 84% of loans, all jobs based on need. 56 enrolled freshmen were judged to have need, all were offered aid. Academic, leadership, religious affiliation, minority scholarships available. **Aid applications:** No closing date; priority given to applications received by February 15; applicants notified on a rolling basis beginning on or about April 1; must reply by May 1 or within 2 weeks if notified thereafter.

ADDRESS/TELEPHONE. Richard LoLatte, Dean of Admissions and Enrollment Management, Albertus Magnus College, 700 Prospect Street, New Haven, CT 06511-1189. (203) 773-8501. Fax: (203) 773-9539.

Asnuntuck Community-Technical College
Enfield, Connecticut CB code: 3656

2-year public community college, coed. Founded in 1972. **Accreditation:** Regional. **Undergraduate enrollment:** 144 men, 138 women full time; 771 men, 1,069 women part time. **Faculty:** 70 total (23 full time), 5 with doctorates or other terminal degrees. **Location:** Suburban campus in large town; 15 miles from Hartford, 10 miles from Springfield, Massachusetts. **Calendar:** Semester, extensive summer session. **Microcomputers:** Located in libraries, classrooms, computer centers.

DEGREES OFFERED. AA, AS. 140 associate degrees awarded in 1992.

UNDERGRADUATE MAJORS. Accounting, business administration and management, business and office, communications, computer and information sciences, fine arts, liberal/general studies, rehabilitation counseling/services, secretarial and related programs.

ACADEMIC PROGRAMS. 2-year transfer program, internships, cross-registration. **Remedial services:** Learning center, remedial instruction, tutoring. **Placement/credit:** AP, CLEP General and Subject, institutional tests; 48 credit hours maximum for associate degree.

ACADEMIC REQUIREMENTS. Freshmen must earn minimum GPA of 1.5 to continue in good standing. **Graduation requirements:** 60 hours for associate (27 in major). Most students required to take courses in English, mathematics, biological/physical sciences, social sciences.

FRESHMAN ADMISSIONS. Selection criteria: Open admissions.

1992 FRESHMAN CLASS PROFILE. 295 men, 358 women enrolled. **Characteristics:** 96% from in state, 100% commute.

FALL-TERM APPLICATIONS. $10 fee, may be waived for applicants with need. No closing date; applicants notified on a rolling basis. Deferred and early admission available.

STUDENT LIFE. Activities: Student government, yearbook, drama, professional clubs.

STUDENT SERVICES. Aptitude testing, career counseling, employment service for undergraduates, freshman orientation, on-campus day care, personal counseling, placement service for graduates, veterans counselor, services/facilities for handicapped.

ANNUAL EXPENSES. Tuition and fees: $1,398, $2,808 additional for out-of-state students. **Books and supplies:** $600. **Other expenses:** $950.

FINANCIAL AID. 20% of freshmen, 20% of continuing students receive some form of aid. All grants, 86% of loans, 25% of jobs based on need. 250 enrolled freshmen were judged to have need, all were offered aid. **Aid applications:** No closing date; priority given to applications received by August 1; applicants notified on a rolling basis; must reply within 10 days.

ADDRESS/TELEPHONE. Vince Fulginiti, Director of Student Services and Admissions, Asnuntuck Community-Technical College, 170 Elm Street, Enfield, CT 06082. (203) 253-3010. Fax: (203) 253-3029.

Beth Benjamin Academy of Connecticut
Stamford, Connecticut CB code: 3359

5-year private rabbinical college, men only, affiliated with Jewish faith. **Undergraduate enrollment:** 15 men. **Location:** Suburban campus in small city. **Additional facts:** Ordination available.

FRESHMAN ADMISSIONS. Selection criteria: Interview most important.

ADDRESS/TELEPHONE. Office of Admissions, Beth Benjamin Academy of Connecticut, 132 Prospect Street, Stamford, CT 06901. (203) 325-4351.

Briarwood College
Southington, Connecticut CB code: 3121

2-year proprietary junior college, coed. Founded in 1966. **Accreditation:** Regional. **Undergraduate enrollment:** 54 men, 247 women full time; 15 men, 132 women part time. **Faculty:** 53 total (25 full time). **Location:** Suburban campus in large town; 19 miles from Hartford. **Calendar:** Semester, limited summer session. Saturday classes. **Microcomputers:** 30 located in libraries, classrooms. **Additional facts:** Medical terminology course offered at St. Raphael's Hospital, New Haven.

DEGREES OFFERED. AAS. 121 associate degrees awarded in 1992. 64% in business/office and marketing/distribution, 18% allied health, 17% home economics.

UNDERGRADUATE MAJORS. Accounting, business and management, business and office, child development/care/guidance, dental assistant, dietetic aide/assistant, fashion merchandising, hotel/motel and restaurant management, legal assistant/paralegal, legal secretary, medical assistant, medical records technology, medical secretary, office supervision and management, radio/television broadcasting, retailing, secretarial and related programs, tourism, word processing.

ACADEMIC PROGRAMS. Double major, independent study, internships. **Remedial services:** Learning center, preadmission summer program, reduced course load, remedial instruction, tutoring. **Placement/credit:** CLEP General and Subject, institutional tests; 15 credit hours maximum for associate degree.

ACADEMIC REQUIREMENTS. Freshmen must earn minimum GPA of 1.8 to continue in good standing. 88% of freshmen return for sophomore year. Students must declare major on application. **Graduation requirements:** 62 hours for associate (41 in major). Most students required to take courses in computer science, English, humanities, mathematics, social sciences.

FRESHMAN ADMISSIONS. Selection criteria: Open admissions.

1992 FRESHMAN CLASS PROFILE. 22 men, 113 women enrolled. **Characteristics:** 93% from in state, 63% commute, 30% have minority backgrounds. Average age is 18.

FALL-TERM APPLICATIONS. $25 fee, may be waived for applicants with need. No closing date; applicants notified on a rolling basis; must reply within 4 weeks. Interview recommended. Deferred admission available.

STUDENT LIFE. Housing: Dormitories (coed); apartment housing available. Townhouse apartments with kitchens available. **Activities:** Student government, film, magazine, radio, television, yearbook, choral groups, Phi Beta Lambda, Lending our Vital Efforts (LOVE), YMCA.

ATHLETICS. Intramural: Badminton, basketball, bowling, golf, racquetball, skiing, softball, swimming, table tennis, tennis, volleyball.

STUDENT SERVICES. Aptitude testing, career counseling, employment service for undergraduates, freshman orientation, health services, personal counseling, placement service for graduates, special adviser for adult students, services/facilities for handicapped.

ANNUAL EXPENSES. Tuition and fees: $8,847. **Room and board:** $2,296 room only. **Books and supplies:** $500. **Other expenses:** $1,400.

FINANCIAL AID. 70% of freshmen, 65% of continuing students receive some form of aid. 99% of grants, 98% of loans based on need. Academic scholarships available. **Aid applications:** No closing date; priority given to applications received by April 30; applicants notified on a rolling basis beginning on or about May 15; must reply within 2 weeks. **Additional information:** Presidential scholarships, competitive evaluation scholarships, and campus employment are available.

ADDRESS/TELEPHONE. Debra LaRoche, Director of Admissions, Briarwood College, 2279 Mount Vernon Road, Southington, CT 06489. (203) 628-4751. Fax: (203) 628-6444.

Bridgeport Engineering Institute
Fairfield, Connecticut — CB code: 3093

4-year private engineering college, coed. Founded in 1924. **Accreditation:** Regional. **Undergraduate enrollment:** 7 men full time; 356 men, 22 women part time. **Faculty:** 83 total, 17 with doctorates or other terminal degrees. **Location:** Suburban campus in small city; 60 miles from New York City, 60 miles from Hartford. **Calendar:** Semester, extensive summer session. **Microcomputers:** 45 located in libraries, computer centers. **Special facilities:** 3 engineering laboratories, robotics laboratory, 3 computer laboratories. **Additional facts:** All classes are evening classes. Evening division in Danbury in association with Western Connecticut State University. Upper-division undergraduate evening engineering courses at higher education center in Waterbury.

DEGREES OFFERED. AS, BS. 25 associate degrees awarded in 1992. 100% in engineering. 48 bachelor's degrees awarded. 100% in engineering.

UNDERGRADUATE MAJORS. Associate: Engineering, preengineering. **Bachelor's:** Electrical/electronics/communications engineering, information sciences and systems, manufacturing engineering, mechanical engineering.

ACADEMIC PROGRAMS. 2-year transfer program, double major. **Remedial services:** Remedial instruction, special counselor, tutoring. **Placement/credit:** AP, CLEP General and Subject, institutional tests.

ACADEMIC REQUIREMENTS. Freshmen must earn minimum GPA of 2.0 to continue in good standing. 60% of freshmen return for sophomore year. Students must declare major on enrollment. **Graduation requirements:** 70 hours for associate (16 in major), 139 hours for bachelor's (44 in major). Most students required to take courses in computer science, English, history, humanities, mathematics, biological/physical sciences, social sciences. **Postgraduate studies:** 90% from 2-year programs enter 4-year programs. 5% enter MBA programs, 5% enter other graduate study.

FRESHMAN ADMISSIONS. Selection criteria: Open admissions. Recommended units include English 4, mathematics 3 and physical science 2. 2 algebra recomended.

1992 FRESHMAN CLASS PROFILE. Characteristics: 90% from in state, 100% commute. Average age is 26.

FALL-TERM APPLICATIONS. $50 fee. Closing date September 4; applicants notified on a rolling basis. Interview recommended. Deferred and early admission available.

STUDENT LIFE. Activities: Student government, student newspaper.

STUDENT SERVICES. Career counseling, freshman orientation, personal counseling, services/facilities for handicapped.

ANNUAL EXPENSES. Tuition and fees: $5,780. **Books and supplies:** $400.

FINANCIAL AID. 18% of continuing students receive some form of aid. All grants, 59% of loans based on need. **Aid applications:** No closing date; applicants notified on a rolling basis beginning on or about September 30; must reply within 2 weeks.

ADDRESS/TELEPHONE. Anthony Guglielmo, Associate Dean of Students, Bridgeport Engineering Institute, 785 Unquowa Road, Fairfield, CT 06430. (203) 259-5717. (800) 582-5419. Fax: (203) 259-9372.

Capital Community-Technical College
Hartford, Connecticut — CB code: 3421

2-year public community, technical college, coed. Founded in 1946. **Accreditation:** Regional. **Undergraduate enrollment:** 424 men, 375 women full time; 1,134 men, 1,840 women part time. **Faculty:** 202 total (72 full time), 16 with doctorates or other terminal degrees. **Location:** Urban campus in small city; in city of Hartford. **Calendar:** Semester, limited summer session. Saturday and extensive evening/early morning classes. **Microcomputers:** 94 located in computer centers. **Special facilities:** Mathematics development center, computerized English as a second language laboratory, interactive videodisc instruction for nursing students. **Additional facts:** Comprehensive 2-year college serving the Hartford region, resulting from the merger in July 1992 of Greater Hartford Community College and Hartford State Technical College.

DEGREES OFFERED. AA, AS, AAS. 377 associate degrees awarded in 1992. 12% in business and management, 26% engineering technologies, 34% health sciences, 22% multi/interdisciplinary studies.

UNDERGRADUATE MAJORS. Accounting, architectural technologies, building facilities technology, business administration and management, business data processing and related programs, chemical and environmental technology, civil technology, computer technology, data processing, drug/alcohol rehabilitation counselor, early childhood education, electrical technology, emergency medical technologies, fire control and safety technology, labor/industrial relations, liberal/general studies, manufacturing technology, marketing management, mechanical design technology, nursing, office supervision and management, radiograph medical technology, secretarial and related programs, word processing.

ACADEMIC PROGRAMS. 2-year transfer program, accelerated program, double major, dual enrollment of high school students, independent study, internships, telecourses, weekend college, cross-registration, interdisciplinary summer program with Smith College. **Remedial services:** Learning center, remedial instruction, special counselor, tutoring, developmental ESL, mathematics development center. **Placement/credit:** CLEP General and Subject.

ACADEMIC REQUIREMENTS. Freshmen must earn minimum GPA of 1.6 to continue in good standing. **Graduation requirements:** 60 hours for associate. Most students required to take courses in computer science, English, mathematics, biological/physical sciences.

FRESHMAN ADMISSIONS. Selection criteria: Open admissions. SAT scores and school achievement record considered for nursing applicants. For nursing program, high school courses required include algebra, biology, and chemistry. **Test requirements:** SAT required for admissions to nursing program.

1992 FRESHMAN CLASS PROFILE. 612 men, 928 women enrolled. **Characteristics:** 99% from in state, 100% commute, 39% have minority backgrounds, 8% are foreign students. Average age is 28.

FALL-TERM APPLICATIONS. $10 fee, may be waived for applicants with need. No closing date. Deferred and early admission available.

STUDENT LIFE. Activities: Student government, film, magazine, television, choral groups, dance, drama, music ensembles.

STUDENT SERVICES. Aptitude testing, career counseling, employment service for undergraduates, freshman orientation, health services, on-campus day care, personal counseling, placement service for graduates, veterans counselor, services/facilities for handicapped.

ANNUAL EXPENSES. Tuition and fees: $1,398, $624 additional for out-of-district students, $2,808 additional for out-of-state students. **Books and supplies:** $400. **Other expenses:** $1,700.

FINANCIAL AID. 21% of freshmen, 15% of continuing students receive some form of aid. 99% of grants, all loans, 70% of jobs based on need. 360 enrolled freshmen were judged to have need, 320 were offered aid. Academic, leadership scholarships available. **Aid applications:** No closing date; priority given to applications received by July 1; applicants notified on a rolling basis beginning on or about August 1; must reply within 2 weeks.

ADDRESS/TELEPHONE. Judith C. Pierson, Enrollment Management, Capital Community-Technical College, 61 Woodland Street, Hartford, CT 06105-2354. (203) 520-7831.

Central Connecticut State University
New Britain, Connecticut CB code: 3898

Admissions: 59% of applicants accepted
Based on: ••• School record
•• Test scores
• Activities, essay, interview, recommendations, special talents
Completion: 80% of freshmen end year in good standing
40% graduate, 18% of these enter graduate study

4-year public university, coed. Founded in 1849. **Accreditation:** Regional. **Undergraduate enrollment:** 3,278 men, 3,461 women full time; 929 men, 1,337 women part time. **Graduate enrollment:** 125 men, 190 women full time; 350 men, 985 women part time. **Faculty:** 774 total (383 full time), 251 with doctorates or other terminal degrees. **Location:** Suburban campus in small city; 9 miles from Hartford. **Calendar:** Semester, extensive summer session. **Microcomputers:** 145 located in dormitories, libraries, classrooms, computer centers. **Special facilities:** Observatory, planetarium.

DEGREES OFFERED. BA, BS, BFA, MA, MS. 1,579 bachelor's degrees awarded in 1992. 30% in business and management, 8% business/office and marketing/distribution, 6% communications, 5% computer sciences, 16% teacher education, 10% engineering technologies, 5% psychology, 6% social sciences. Graduate degrees offered in 35 major fields of study.

UNDERGRADUATE MAJORS. Accounting, actuarial sciences, anthropology, art education, biology, business administration and management, business administrative science, business education, chemistry, communications, computer and information sciences, dramatic arts, early childhood education, earth sciences, East Asian studies, economics, elementary education, engineering and engineering-related technologies, English, finance, fine arts, French, geography, German, history, industrial arts education, industrial technology, international studies, Italian, liberal/general studies, management information systems, manufacturing technology, marketing and distribution, marketing and distributive education, marketing management, mathematics, music, music education, nursing, office supervision and management, philosophy, physical education, physical sciences, physics, political science and government, psychology, social sciences, social work, sociology, Spanish, special education, technical education, trade and industrial education.

ACADEMIC PROGRAMS. Cooperative education, double major, education specialist degree, honors program, independent study, internships, student-designed major, study abroad, teacher preparation, visiting/exchange student program, cross-registration. **Remedial services:** Preadmission summer program, reduced course load, remedial instruction, special counselor, tutoring, writing center, study skills, test taking. **ROTC:** Air Force, Army. **Placement/credit:** AP, CLEP Subject, institutional tests; 30 credit hours maximum for bachelor's degree.

ACADEMIC REQUIREMENTS. Freshmen must earn minimum GPA of 1.5 to continue in good standing. 74% of freshmen return for sophomore year. Students must declare major by end of second year. **Graduation requirements:** 122 hours for bachelor's (36 in major). Most students required to take courses in arts/fine arts, English, foreign languages, history, mathematics, philosophy/religion, biological/physical sciences, social sciences. **Postgraduate studies:** 5% enter MBA programs, 13% enter other graduate study.

FRESHMAN ADMISSIONS. Selection criteria: High school record, class rank, SAT scores considered. **High school preparation:** 13 units required. Required and recommended units include English 4, mathematics 3, social science 2 and science 2. Foreign language 3 recommended. One laboratory science required. Social science should include U.S. history; mathematics should include algebra I & II and geometry. **Test requirements:** SAT; score report by May 1.

1992 FRESHMAN CLASS PROFILE. 2,293 men applied, 1,241 accepted, 413 enrolled; 2,436 women applied, 1,543 accepted, 551 enrolled. **Academic background:** Mid 50% of enrolled freshmen had SAT-V between 360-460, SAT-M between 390-520. 97% submitted SAT scores. **Characteristics:** 91% from in state, 54% live in college housing, 14% have minority backgrounds, 3% are foreign students, 1% join fraternities/sororities. Average age is 18.

FALL-TERM APPLICATIONS. $20 fee, may be waived for applicants with need. Closing date May 1; priority given to applications received by October 1; applicants notified on a rolling basis beginning on or about December 1; must reply by May 1 or within 2 weeks if notified thereafter. Audition required for music education applicants. Portfolio required for art applicants. Interview optional but will be considered. CRDA. Deferred admission available.

STUDENT LIFE. Housing: Dormitories (men, women, coed). **Activities:** Student government, film, magazine, radio, student newspaper, television, yearbook, choral groups, concert band, dance, drama, musical theater, pep band, fraternities, sororities, Newman Club, Union of Jewish Students, Christian Fellowship, Christian Science Organization, Afro-American and African students, Latin American Student Association.

ATHLETICS. NCAA. **Intercollegiate:** Baseball M, basketball, cross-country, football M, golf M, soccer M, softball W, swimming, tennis, track and field, volleyball W, wrestling M. **Intramural:** Badminton, basketball, soccer, softball, tennis, volleyball, water polo M.

STUDENT SERVICES. Career counseling, employment service for undergraduates, freshman orientation, health services, on-campus day care, personal counseling, placement service for graduates, special adviser for adult students, veterans counselor, services/facilities for handicapped.

ANNUAL EXPENSES. Tuition and fees: $2,976, $3,924 additional for out-of-state students. **Room and board:** $4,324. **Books and supplies:** $500. **Other expenses:** $1,023.

FINANCIAL AID. 35% of freshmen, 28% of continuing students receive some form of aid. 70% of grants, 88% of loans, 31% of jobs based on need. Academic, athletic, state/district residency, leadership, minority scholarships available. **Aid applications:** No closing date; priority given to applications received by March 15; applicants notified on a rolling basis beginning on or about June 15; must reply within 2 weeks.

ADDRESS/TELEPHONE. Dr. Hakim Salahu-Din, Director of Admissions, Central Connecticut State University, 1615 Stanley Street, New Britain, CT 06050. (203) 827-7543. Fax: (203) 827-7200.

Charter Oak State College
Farmington, Connecticut

4-year public external degree college, coed. Founded in 1973. **Accreditation:** Regional. **Undergraduate enrollment:** 570 men, 575 women part time. **Faculty:** 56 total, 46 with doctorates or other terminal degrees. **Location:** Suburban campus in large town. **Calendar:** Students may enroll at any time. **Additional facts:** College offers no formalized instruction. Credit awarded on basis of standardized tests, evaluation of credits earned in accredited institutions and programs, and through assessment of college-level learning acquired outside a traditional classroom. Students from any state may enroll and complete degree while residing in states other than Connecticut. Academic counseling available.

DEGREES OFFERED. AA, AS, BA, BS. 76 associate degrees awarded in 1992. 100% in multi/interdisciplinary studies. 161 bachelor's degrees awarded. 100% in multi/interdisciplinary studies.

UNDERGRADUATE MAJORS. Associate: Liberal/general studies. **Bachelor's:** Liberal/general studies.

ACADEMIC PROGRAMS. 2-year transfer program, accelerated program, external degree, honors program, independent study. **Placement/credit:** AP, CLEP General and Subject, institutional tests. Unlimited number of hours of credit by examination may be counted toward degree.

ACADEMIC REQUIREMENTS. Graduation requirements: 60 hours for associate, 120 hours for bachelor's (36 in major). Most students required to take courses in English, history, humanities, mathematics, biological/physical sciences, social sciences. **Postgraduate studies:** 4% enter law school, 1% enter medical school, 20% enter MBA programs, 9% enter other graduate study.

FRESHMAN ADMISSIONS. Selection criteria: Open admissions.

FALL-TERM APPLICATIONS. $25 fee, may be waived for applicants with need. $285 enrollment fee for in-state, $410 for out-of-state applicants. No closing date; applicants notified on a rolling basis. Interview recommended.

STUDENT SERVICES. Services/facilities for handicapped.

ANNUAL EXPENSES. Tuition and fees: All students pay a one-time only enrollment fee of $314 for in-state residents and $451 for out-of-state residents. After an initial year of enrollment all students must pay a yearly Annual Advisement and Record Maintenance fee of $220 for in-state and $347 for out-of-state residents. All students pay a one-time baccalaureate program planning fee of $195.

ADDRESS/TELEPHONE. Ruth Budlong, Director Student Services, Charter Oak State College, The Exchange, Suite 171, 270 Farmington Avenue, Farmington, CT 06032-1934. (203) 677-0076. Fax: (203) 566-5147.

Connecticut College
New London, Connecticut CB code: 3284

Admissions: 48% of applicants accepted
Based on: ••• Recommendations, school record
•• Activities, essay, special talents, test scores
• Interview
Completion: 95% of freshmen end year in good standing
91% graduate, 31% of these enter graduate study

4-year private liberal arts college, coed. Founded in 1911. **Accreditation:** Regional. **Undergraduate enrollment:** 720 men, 899 women full time; 15 men, 60 women part time. **Graduate enrollment:** 7 men, 30 women full time; 5 men, 34 women part time. **Faculty:** 180 total (146 full time), 137 with doctorates or other terminal degrees. **Location:** Suburban campus in large town; 100 miles from New York City, 60 miles from Boston. **Calendar:** Semester, limited summer session. **Microcomputers:** 130 located in libraries, computer centers. **Special facilities:** 426-acre arboretum, Lyman Allyn Museum, greenhouse, ion accelerator, refracting telescope and observatory, environment control laboratories, preschool used by child development majors, art gallery, Center for Arts and Technology.

DEGREES OFFERED. BA, MA. 446 bachelor's degrees awarded in 1992. 8% in languages, 10% letters/literature, 6% life sciences, 5% psychology, 53% social sciences, 6% visual and performing arts. Graduate degrees offered in 9 major fields of study.

UNDERGRADUATE MAJORS. Anthropology, applied mathematics, art history, Asian studies, biochemistry, biology, botany, chemistry, child development/care/guidance, Chinese, classics, dance, dramatic arts, ecology, economics, English, European studies, French, German, German studies, Hispanic American studies, history, international relations, Italian, Italian and related studies, Japanese, mathematics, medieval studies, music, music history and appreciation, music performance, music theory and composition, philosophy, physics, political science and government, psychology, psychology-based human relations, religion, Russian, Russian and Slavic studies, sociology, Spanish, studio art, urban studies, zoology.

ACADEMIC PROGRAMS. Accelerated program, double major, honors program, independent study, internships, semester at sea, student-designed major, study abroad, teacher preparation, visiting/exchange student program, Washington semester, cross-registration, 12-college exchange, National Theater Institute, Mystic Seaport Program in American Maritime Studies, Institute for Architecture and Urban Studies, American Academy in Rome, Associated Kyoto Program; liberal arts/career combination in engineering. **Remedial services:** Tutoring, writing center. **Placement/credit:** AP, institutional tests.

ACADEMIC REQUIREMENTS. Freshmen must earn minimum GPA of 2.0 to continue in good standing. 91% of freshmen return for sophomore year. Students must declare major by end of second year. **Graduation requirements:** 128 hours for bachelor's (32 in major). Most students required to take courses in arts/fine arts, English, foreign languages, history, mathematics, philosophy/religion, biological/physical sciences, social sciences. **Postgraduate studies:** 5% enter law school, 2% enter medical school, 2% enter MBA programs, 22% enter other graduate study. **Additional information:** Concentration in international studies including paid internship abroad offered. College venture program, private service, finds jobs or interships in field of interest for students wanting semester off.

FRESHMAN ADMISSIONS. Selection criteria: School achievement record most important. Test scores, personal qualities, personal essay, special talents, extracurricular involvement also significant. **High school preparation:** 16 units required. Required and recommended units include English 4, mathematics 3-4, social science 3 and science 2-3. Social science units must include 1 history. **Test requirements:** SAT or ACT (SAT preferred); score report by March 1. 3 ACH required (including English Composition). Score report by March 1.

1992 FRESHMAN CLASS PROFILE. 1,099 men applied, 674 accepted, 210 enrolled; 2,040 women applied, 827 accepted, 233 enrolled. 52% were in top tenth and 66% were in top quarter of graduating class. **Academic background:** Mid 50% of enrolled freshmen had SAT-V between 550-640, SAT-M between 570-670. 96% submitted SAT scores. **Characteristics:** 18% from in state, 100% live in college housing, 12% have minority backgrounds, 6% are foreign students. Average age is 18.

FALL-TERM APPLICATIONS. $40 fee, may be waived for applicants with need. Closing date January 15; applicants notified on or about April 1; must reply by May 1. Essay required. Interview recommended. Audition recommended for dance, music applicants. Portfolio recommended for art applicants. CRDA. Deferred and early admission available. EDP-F. Early decision deadlines November 15, notification mid-December, and January 15, notification mid-Febuary.

STUDENT LIFE. Housing: Dormitories (coed); cooperative housing available. Coeducational dormitories, many with own dining rooms, all fully integrated by class, available. Undergraduate student housing guaranteed for 4 years. Single occupancy rooms guaranteed except for freshmen. Theme dormitories. **Activities:** Student government, film, magazine, radio, student newspaper, yearbook, choral groups, dance, drama, music ensembles, musical theater, symphony orchestra, Chapel Board, La Unidad, Umoja, Chavurah, Christian Fellowship, political clubs, community service programs, Students Organized.

ATHLETICS. NCAA. **Intercollegiate:** Basketball, cross-country, diving, field hockey W, golf, ice hockey M, lacrosse, rowing (crew), sailing, soccer, squash, swimming, tennis, track and field, volleyball W. **Intramural:** Badminton, basketball, football, horseback riding, ice hockey, racquetball, soccer, softball, squash, tennis, volleyball.

STUDENT SERVICES. Career counseling, employment service for undergraduates, freshman orientation, health services, personal counseling, placement service for graduates, special adviser for adult students, services/facilities for handicapped.

ANNUAL EXPENSES. Tuition and fees: $18,130. **Room and board:** $6,030. **Books and supplies:** $500. **Other expenses:** $500.

FINANCIAL AID. 43% of freshmen, 44% of continuing students receive some form of aid. All grants, 98% of loans, 53% of jobs based on need. 186 enrolled freshmen were judged to have need, all were offered aid. **Aid applications:** Closing date February 15; applicants notified on or about April 10; must reply by May 1. **Additional information:** School meets full demonstrated need and has a need-blind admissions policy.

ADDRESS/TELEPHONE. Claire K. Matthews, Dean of Admission and Planning, Connecticut College, 270 Mohegan Avenue, New London, CT 06320. (203) 439-2200. Fax: (203) 439-4301.

Eastern Connecticut State University
Willimantic, Connecticut

CB code: 3966

Admissions: 69% of applicants accepted
Based on: ••• School record, test scores
•• Recommendations
• Activities, essay, interview, special talents
Completion: 72% of freshmen end year in good standing
50% graduate, 17% of these enter graduate study

4-year public university, coed. Founded in 1889. **Accreditation:** Regional. **Undergraduate enrollment:** 1,233 men, 1,462 women full time; 505 men, 946 women part time. **Graduate enrollment:** 7 men, 14 women full time; 41 men, 247 women part time. **Faculty:** 195 total (124 full time), 99 with doctorates or other terminal degrees. **Location:** Suburban campus in large town; 29 miles from Hartford. **Calendar:** Semester, extensive summer session. Saturday classes. **Microcomputers:** 400 located in dormitories, libraries, classrooms, computer centers, campus-wide network. **Special facilities:** Planetarium, 2 electron microscopes, art gallery.

DEGREES OFFERED. AS, BA, BS, MS. 14 associate degrees awarded in 1992. 100% in multi/interdisciplinary studies. 673 bachelor's degrees awarded. 32% in business and management, 9% communications, 16% teacher education, 6% multi/interdisciplinary studies, 10% psychology, 12% social sciences. Graduate degrees offered in 7 major fields of study.

UNDERGRADUATE MAJORS. Associate: Liberal/general studies. **Bachelor's:** American studies, biological and physical sciences, biology, business and management, communications, computer and information sciences, early childhood education, earth sciences, economics, elementary education, English, environmental science, fine arts, history, humanities and social sciences, junior high education, liberal/general studies, mathematics, physical education, political science and government, predentistry, prelaw, premedicine, preveterinary, psychology, public administration, secondary education, social sciences, sociology, Spanish, telecommunications.

ACADEMIC PROGRAMS. 2-year transfer program, accelerated program, cooperative education, double major, dual enrollment of high school students, honors program, independent study, internships, student-designed major, study abroad, teacher preparation, visiting/exchange student program, weekend college, Washington semester, cross-registration. **Remedial services:** Learning center, preadmission summer program, reduced course load, remedial instruction, special counselor, tutoring. **ROTC:** Air Force, Army. **Placement/credit:** AP, CLEP General and Subject, institutional tests; 60 credit hours maximum for bachelor's degree.

ACADEMIC REQUIREMENTS. Freshmen must earn minimum GPA of 2.0 to continue in good standing. 78% of freshmen return for sophomore year. Students must declare major by end of second year. **Graduation requirements:** 60 hours for associate (15 in major), 120 hours for bachelor's (33 in major). Most students required to take courses in arts/fine arts, computer science, English, history, humanities, mathematics, biological/physical sciences, social sciences. **Postgraduate studies:** 2% enter law school, 2% enter medical school, 6% enter MBA programs, 7% enter other graduate study.

FRESHMAN ADMISSIONS. Selection criteria: Applicants should be in top half of high school class and recommended by high school. SAT score also important. Extracurricular activities considered. Quality of course work very important; minimum 2.5 GPA in college preparatory program. **High school preparation:** 16 units required. Required units include English 4, foreign language 2, mathematics 3, social science 2 and science 2. Students admitted without having met foreign language requirement must complete 1 year of foreign language at the University. **Test requirements:** SAT; score report by April 1.

1992 FRESHMAN CLASS PROFILE. 907 men applied, 611 accepted, 232 enrolled; 1,179 women applied, 834 accepted, 335 enrolled. 26% had high school GPA of 3.0 or higher, 70% between 2.0 and 2.99. **Academic background:** Mid 50% of enrolled freshmen had SAT-V between 430-470, SAT-M between 430-470. 98% submitted SAT scores. **Characteristics:** 90% from in state, 90% live in college housing, 18% have minority backgrounds, 2% are foreign students. Average age is 19.

FALL-TERM APPLICATIONS. $20 fee, may be waived for applicants with need. Closing date May 1; priority given to applications received by March 1; applicants notified on a rolling basis; must reply by May 1 or within 2 weeks if notified thereafter. Audition required for music applicants. Interview recommended for special admissions applicants. Portfolio recommended for art applicants. Essay optional but will be considered. CRDA. Deferred and early admission available.

STUDENT LIFE. Housing: Dormitories (women, coed); apartment housing available. **Activities:** Student government, film, magazine, radio, student newspaper, television, yearbook, choral groups, concert band, dance, drama, music ensembles, pep band, political, ethnic, social service, social organizations, national and university honor societies, campus ministry, women's center.

ATHLETICS. NCAA. **Intercollegiate:** Baseball M, basketball, cross-country, soccer, softball W, track and field, volleyball W. **Intramural:** Badminton, basketball, bowling, field hockey, football M, gymnastics, handball, racquetball, rugby M, skiing, soccer, softball, squash, swimming, tennis, track and field, volleyball, water polo.

STUDENT SERVICES. Aptitude testing, career counseling, employment service for undergraduates, freshman orientation, health services, on-campus day care, personal counseling, placement service for graduates, special adviser for adult students, veterans counselor, tutoring services, academic advisement center, job match program, substance abuse program, services/facilities for handicapped.

ANNUAL EXPENSES. Tuition and fees (1992-93): $2,764, $3,568 additional for out-of-state students. **Room and board:** $3,826. **Books and supplies:** $500. **Other expenses:** $1,100.

FINANCIAL AID. 50% of freshmen, 50% of continuing students receive some form of aid. 99% of grants, 63% of loans, 21% of jobs based on need. Academic, leadership scholarships available. **Aid applications:** Closing date March 15; applicants notified on a rolling basis beginning on or about April 1; must reply within 4 weeks. **Additional information:** Tuition waiver for veterans and members of National Guard. Time Payment plan through AMJ.

ADDRESS/TELEPHONE. Arthur C. Forst Jr. PhD, Director of Admissions and Enrollment Planning, Eastern Connecticut State University, Hurley Hall, Willimantic, CT 06226-2295. (203) 456-5286. Fax: (203) 456-5520.

Fairfield University

Fairfield, Connecticut CB code: 3390

Admissions: 71% of applicants accepted
Based on: ••• School record, test scores
•• Activities, recommendations
• Interview, special talents
Completion: 88% of freshmen end year in good standing
86% graduate, 19% of these enter graduate study

4-year private university, coed, affiliated with Roman Catholic Church. Founded in 1942. **Accreditation:** Regional. **Undergraduate enrollment:** 1,344 men, 1,728 women full time; 380 men, 757 women part time. **Graduate enrollment:** 16 men, 71 women full time; 129 men, 519 women part time. **Faculty:** 319 total (189 full time), 169 with doctorates or other terminal degrees. **Location:** Suburban campus in small city; 45 miles from New York City. **Calendar:** Semester, limited summer session. **Microcomputers:** 125 located in libraries, classrooms, computer centers. **Special facilities:** Fine arts center containing 2 theaters and art gallery, 200 acres of park-like grounds, Arupe Campus Ministry Center. **Additional facts:** Independent institution in the Jesuit tradition.

DEGREES OFFERED. BA, BS, MA, MS. 781 bachelor's degrees awarded in 1992. 28% in business and management, 6% health sciences, 12% letters/literature, 7% life sciences, 7% psychology, 23% social sciences. Graduate degrees offered in 15 major fields of study.

UNDERGRADUATE MAJORS. Accounting, American studies, art history, biology, business administration and management, chemistry, classics, communications, computer and information sciences, creative writing, dramatic arts, economics, engineering and other disciplines, English, English literature, finance, French, German, history, information sciences and systems, Latin American studies, management information systems, marketing management, mathematics, music, nursing, philosophy, physics, political science and government, preengineering, psychology, religion, secondary education, sociology, Spanish, visual and performing arts.

ACADEMIC PROGRAMS. Double major, honors program, independent study, internships, semester at sea, study abroad, teacher preparation, visiting/exchange student program, Washington semester, cross-registration, 3-2 Engineering Program with University of Connecticut, Rensselaer Polytechnic Institute (NY), Columbia University (NY); liberal arts/career combination in engineering. **Remedial services:** Special counselor, tutoring, minority counselor. **Placement/credit:** AP, CLEP General and Subject, institutional tests; 30 credit hours maximum for bachelor's degree.

ACADEMIC REQUIREMENTS. Freshmen must earn minimum GPA of 1.8 to continue in good standing. 90% of freshmen return for sophomore year. Students must declare major by end of second year. **Graduation requirements:** 120 hours for bachelor's (30 in major). Most students required to take courses in arts/fine arts, English, foreign languages, history, mathematics, philosophy/religion, biological/physical sciences, social sciences. **Postgraduate studies:** 5% enter law school, 4% enter medical school, 3% enter MBA programs, 7% enter other graduate study. **Additional information:** Writing center available to all students. Internships with Fortune 500 companies. Honors program begins in freshman year. Credit may be earned for work on school newspaper.

FRESHMAN ADMISSIONS. Selection criteria: School achievement record, test scores, recommendations, school activities important. Special consideration given to minority groups and relatives of alumni. **High school preparation:** 15 units required. Required units include English 4, foreign language 2, mathematics 3, social science 3 and science 2. 4 mathematics and 1 biological science required for science majors. **Test requirements:** SAT or ACT (SAT preferred); score report by March 1. ACH recommended for science and nursing applicants. Score report by May 15.

1992 FRESHMAN CLASS PROFILE. 1,950 men applied, 1,425 accepted, 362 enrolled; 2,855 women applied, 1,995 accepted, 508 enrolled. 32% were in top tenth and 60% were in top quarter of graduating class. **Academic background:** Mid 50% of enrolled freshmen had SAT-V between 460-540, SAT-M between 510-610. 100% submitted SAT scores. **Characteristics:** 30% from in state, 92% live in college housing, 10% have minority backgrounds, 1% are foreign students. Average age is 18.

FALL-TERM APPLICATIONS. $35 fee, may be waived for applicants with need. Closing date March 1; applicants notified on or about April 1; must reply by May 1. Interview recommended. CRDA. Deferred and early admission available. EDP-F. 3 ACH recommended for placement, including English composition, mathematics, and foreign language (French, German, Spanish), science for science majors, physics for engineering majors, chemistry or biology for nursing majors.

STUDENT LIFE. Housing: Dormitories (coed); apartment, handicapped housing available. Cars not allowed for freshman resident students. On-campus townhouses for juniors and seniors. Juniors and seniors may enter a lottery to move off-campus. **Activities:** Student government, film, magazine, radio, student newspaper, television, yearbook, choral groups, concert band, dance, drama, jazz band, music ensembles, musical theater, pep band, symphony orchestra, AHANA (Asian, Hispanic, Afro-American, Native American), Circle-K, University Service Council, Peer Counselors, Appalachian Volunteers, Campus Ministry, Young Democrats, College Republicans, International Relations Club. **Additional information:** Campus ministry sponsors activities that enable students to travel to other parts of country, Central America, and neighboring urban centers as community service volunteers.

ATHLETICS. NCAA. **Intercollegiate:** Baseball M, basketball, cross-country, diving, fencing M, field hockey W, golf M, ice hockey M, lacrosse M, rugby M, sailing, skiing, soccer, softball W, swimming, tennis, volleyball W. **Intramural:** Badminton, basketball, football M, racquetball, softball, table tennis, tennis, volleyball, water polo.

STUDENT SERVICES. Aptitude testing, career counseling, employment service for undergraduates, freshman orientation, health services, personal counseling, placement service for graduates, special adviser for adult students, veterans counselor, services/facilities for handicapped.

ANNUAL EXPENSES. Tuition and fees: $14,590. **Room and board:** $5,900. **Books and supplies:** $450. **Other expenses:** $900.

FINANCIAL AID. 65% of freshmen, 65% of continuing students receive some form of aid. All jobs based on need. 411 enrolled freshmen were judged to have need, all were offered aid. **Aid applications:** Closing date February 1; applicants notified on or about April 4; must reply by May 1. **Additional information:** Financial aid available to students with demonstrated need who have a retarded sibling.

ADDRESS/TELEPHONE. David M. Flynn, Dean of Undergraduate Admissions, Fairfield University, North Benson Road, Fairfield, CT 06430-7524. (203) 254-4100. Fax: (203) 254-4060.

Gateway Community-Technical College

New Haven, Connecticut CB code: 3425

2-year public community college, coed. Founded in 1968. **Accreditation:** Regional. **Undergraduate enrollment:** 665 men, 719 women full time; 1,372 men, 2,451 women part time. **Faculty:** 259 total (78 full time), 28 with doctorates or other terminal degrees. **Location:** Urban campus in small city; 75 miles from New York City, 130 miles from Boston. **Calendar:** Semester, limited summer session. **Microcomputers:** 100 located in classrooms, computer centers. **Special facilities:** Early childhood learning center. **Additional facts:** In July 1992, South Central Community College (New Haven) and Greater New Haven State Technical College (North Haven) merged to form Gateway Community Technical College. All programs offered at both colleges will continue.

DEGREES OFFERED. AA, AS, AAS. 360 associate degrees awarded in 1992. 20% in business/office and marketing/distribution, 6% education, 19% engineering technologies, 11% allied health, 8% home economics, 24% multi/interdisciplinary studies, 9% trade and industry.

UNDERGRADUATE MAJORS. Accounting, automotive mechanics, automotive technology, bilingual/bicultural education, biomedical equipment technology, business and management, business data processing and related programs, data processing, dietetic aide/assistant, drafting and design technology, early childhood education, fashion merchandising, food management, gerontology, graphic and printing production, graphic arts technology, hotel/motel and restaurant management, insurance and risk management, legal secretary, liberal/general studies, manufacturing technology, mechanical design technology, medical radiation dosimetry, medical secretary, mental health/human services, nuclear medical technology, office supervision and management, radiograph medical technology, rehabilitation counseling/services, retailing, word processing.

ACADEMIC PROGRAMS. 2-year transfer program, dual enrollment of

high school students, independent study, internships, telecourses, weekend college. **Remedial services:** Learning center, reduced course load, remedial instruction, special counselor, tutoring. **Placement/credit:** AP, CLEP General and Subject, institutional tests; 30 credit hours maximum for associate degree.

ACADEMIC REQUIREMENTS. Freshmen must earn minimum GPA of 1.7 to continue in good standing. Minimum 2.0 GPA required of students in technical programs. 60% of freshmen return for sophomore year. Students must declare major on enrollment. **Graduation requirements:** 60 hours for associate (39 in major). Most students required to take courses in computer science, English, humanities, mathematics, biological/physical sciences, social sciences. **Additional information:** Academic policies may vary for curricula offered at North Haven campus. Students advised to contact dean of students for information on particular programs.

FRESHMAN ADMISSIONS. Selection criteria: Open admissions. Selective admissions to radiology, human services, drug and alcohol rehabilitation counselor, and dietetic technician programs. Placement test and/or interview required.

1992 FRESHMAN CLASS PROFILE. 479 men, 610 women enrolled. **Characteristics:** 99% from in state, 100% commute, 31% have minority backgrounds, 1% are foreign students. Average age is 29.

FALL-TERM APPLICATIONS. $10 fee, may be waived for applicants with need. Closing date September 1; priority given to applications received by June 1; applicants notified on a rolling basis beginning on or about February 1; must reply within 4 weeks. Interview required for radiology, human services, dietetic technician, drug and alcohol rehabilitation counselor applicants. Deferred and early admission available. Application closing date for drug and alcohol rehabilitation counseling programs February 1. Early application recommended for radiologic technologies, business administration, data processing programs.

STUDENT LIFE. Activities: Student government, magazine, radio, student newspaper, yearbook, choral groups, drama, music ensembles, African-American Student Union, Spanish-American club, international students club.

ATHLETICS. NJCAA. **Intercollegiate:** Baseball M, basketball, golf, softball W, tennis.

STUDENT SERVICES. Aptitude testing, career counseling, employment service for undergraduates, freshman orientation, health services, on-campus day care, personal counseling, placement service for graduates, veterans counselor, women's center, services/facilities for handicapped.

ANNUAL EXPENSES. Tuition and fees (1992-93): $1,276, $564 additional for out-of-district students, $2,640 additional for out-of-state students. **Books and supplies:** $600. **Other expenses:** $1,800.

FINANCIAL AID. 19% of freshmen, 14% of continuing students receive some form of aid. All grants, 47% of jobs based on need. Academic scholarships available. **Aid applications:** No closing date; applicants notified on a rolling basis beginning on or about August 1; must reply within 2 weeks.

ADDRESS/TELEPHONE. Myrna E. Garcia-Bowen, Director of Admissions, Gateway Community-Technical College, 60 Sargent Drive, New Haven, CT 06511-5970. (203) 789-7043.

Holy Apostles College and Seminary
Cromwell, Connecticut — CB code: 0921

4-year private seminary college, coed, affiliated with Roman Catholic Church. Founded in 1956. **Accreditation:** Regional. **Undergraduate enrollment:** 15 men full time; 59 men, 28 women part time. **Graduate enrollment:** 81 men full time; 45 men, 14 women part time. **Location:** Rural campus in small town; 13 miles from Hartford. **Calendar:** Semester. **Additional facts:** Most students are seminarians preparing for priesthood or lay people preparing for or involved in religious education.

FRESHMAN ADMISSIONS. Selection criteria: Interview and recommendations most important.

ANNUAL EXPENSES. Tuition and fees (1992-93): $3,500. **Room and board:** $5,050. **Books and supplies:** $600. **Other expenses:** $700.

ADDRESS/TELEPHONE. Rev. Bradley W. Pierce, Director of Admissions and Vocations, Holy Apostles College and Seminary, 33 Prospect Hill Road, Cromwell, CT 06416. (203) 632-3000. Fax: (203) 632-3075.

Housatonic Community-Technical College
Bridgeport, Connecticut — CB code: 3446

2-year public community college, coed. Founded in 1966. **Accreditation:** Regional. **Undergraduate enrollment:** 178 men, 294 women full time; 661 men, 1,525 women part time. **Faculty:** 105 total (39 full time), 6 with doctorates or other terminal degrees. **Location:** Urban campus in small city; 60 miles from Hartford. 60 miles form New York City. **Calendar:** Semester. Extensive evening/early morning classes. **Microcomputers:** 100 located in libraries, classrooms, computer centers. **Special facilities:** Art museum.

DEGREES OFFERED. AA, AS. 142 associate degrees awarded in 1992. 10% in business and management, 5% teacher education, 12% allied health, 60% multi/interdisciplinary studies, 9% parks/recreation, protective services, public affairs.

UNDERGRADUATE MAJORS. Accounting, aeronautical technology, business administration and management, business and office, business data processing and related programs, child development/care/guidance, clinical laboratory science, communications, computer and information sciences, early childhood education, environmental science, fine arts, graphic design, humanities and social sciences, journalism, law enforcement and corrections technologies, liberal/general studies, medical laboratory technologies, nursing, physical therapy assistant, preengineering, public administration, rehabilitation counseling/services, secretarial and related programs, word processing.

ACADEMIC PROGRAMS. 2-year transfer program, cooperative education, double major, dual enrollment of high school students, honors program, independent study, internships, telecourses. **Remedial services:** Learning center, reduced course load, remedial instruction, special counselor, tutoring. **Placement/credit:** AP, CLEP General and Subject, institutional tests; 30 credit hours maximum for associate degree.

ACADEMIC REQUIREMENTS. Freshmen must earn minimum GPA of 1.75 to continue in good standing. Students must declare major on application. **Graduation requirements:** 60 hours for associate. Most students required to take courses in English, mathematics, biological/physical sciences, social sciences.

FRESHMAN ADMISSIONS. Selection criteria: Open admissions. Selective admissions to drug and alcohol rehabilitation counseling, medical laboratory technician, physical therapist assistant, and nursing programs. **Additional information:** New Jersey Basic Skills Placement Test required for advising and placement.

1992 FRESHMAN CLASS PROFILE. 863 men and women enrolled. **Characteristics:** 99% from in state, 100% commute.

FALL-TERM APPLICATIONS. $10 fee, may be waived for applicants with need. No closing date; applicants notified on a rolling basis. Interview required for drug and alcohol rehabilitation counselor, medical laboratory technician, physical therapist assistant, nursing, pre-allied health applicants. Early admission available.

STUDENT LIFE. Activities: Student government, student newspaper, yearbook.

ATHLETICS. NJCAA. **Intercollegiate:** Baseball M.

STUDENT SERVICES. Career counseling, freshman orientation, health services, on-campus day care, personal counseling, placement service for graduates, veterans counselor, services/facilities for handicapped.

ANNUAL EXPENSES. Tuition and fees (1992-93): $1,276, $564 additional for out-of-district students, $2,640 additional for out-of-state students. **Books and supplies:** $500. **Other expenses:** $960.

FINANCIAL AID. 25% of continuing students receive some form of aid. All grants, 60% of loans, all jobs based on need. 485 enrolled freshmen were judged to have need, all were offered aid. **Aid applications:** No closing date; priority given to applications received by July 1; applicants notified on a rolling basis.

ADDRESS/TELEPHONE. Deloris Y. Curtis, Director of Admissions, Housatonic Community-Technical College, 510 Barnum Avenue, Bridgeport, CT 06608. (203) 579-6475. Fax: (203) 579-6993.

Manchester Community-Technical College
Manchester, Connecticut — CB code: 3544

2-year public community college, coed. Founded in 1963. **Accreditation:** Regional. **Undergraduate enrollment:** 6,673 men and women. **Location:** Suburban campus in small city; 8 miles from Hartford. **Calendar:** Semester.

FRESHMAN ADMISSIONS. Selection criteria: Open admissions. 2.0 school GPA, minimum SAT combined score of 800, rank in top half of class considered for admission to allied health programs.

ANNUAL EXPENSES. Tuition and fees: $1,398, $2,808 additional for out-of-state students. **Books and supplies:** $600.

ADDRESS/TELEPHONE. Joseph Mesquita, Director of Admissions, Manchester Community-Technical College, PO Box 1046, Manchester, CT 06040. (203) 647-6140.

Middlesex Community-Technical College
Middletown, Connecticut — CB code: 3551

2-year public community college, coed. Founded in 1966. **Accreditation:** Regional. **Undergraduate enrollment:** 837 men and women full time; 2,416 men and women part time. **Faculty:** 130 total (50 full time), 5 with doctorates or other terminal degrees. **Location:** Suburban campus in large town; 20 miles from Hartford. **Calendar:** Semester, limited summer session. **Microcomputers:** Located in libraries, computer centers.

DEGREES OFFERED. AA, AS. 333 associate degrees awarded in 1992.

UNDERGRADUATE MAJORS. Accounting, business administration and management, business and management, business and office, business data programming, communications, computer programming, environmental science, fine arts, graphic arts technology, humanities, legal secretary, liberal/general studies, marketing and distribution, marketing management, medical secretary, mental health/human services, nuclear technologies, ophthalmic services, radio/television broadcasting, radiograph medical technology, secretarial and related programs.

ACADEMIC PROGRAMS. 2-year transfer program, dual enrollment of high school students, independent study, internships, student-designed major, cross-registration. **Remedial services:** Reduced course load, remedial instruction, tutoring, mathematics and reading laboratories. **Placement/credit:** AP, CLEP General and Subject, institutional tests; 48 credit hours maximum for associate degree.

ACADEMIC REQUIREMENTS. Freshmen must earn minimum GPA of 1.75 to continue in good standing. 60% of freshmen return for sophomore year. Students must declare major on application. **Graduation requirements:** 60 hours for associate. Most students required to take courses in English, humanities, mathematics, biological/physical sciences, social sciences.

FRESHMAN ADMISSIONS. Selection criteria: Open admissions. Selective admissions to mental health, information systems, ophthalmic design and dispensing, radiologic technology, nuclear medicine technology, and drug and alcohol rehabilitation programs.

1992 FRESHMAN CLASS PROFILE. 1,097 men and women enrolled. **Characteristics:** 99% from in state, 100% commute, 8% have minority backgrounds, 1% are foreign students. Average age is 27.

FALL-TERM APPLICATIONS. $10 fee, may be waived for applicants with need. Closing date August 1; applicants notified on a rolling basis beginning on or about January 1. Interview required for mental health, radiology, drug and alcohol counseling programs applicants. Deferred and early admission available.

STUDENT LIFE. Activities: Student government, magazine, radio, yearbook, drama, Black Student Alliance, national scholastic honor society.

STUDENT SERVICES. Aptitude testing, career counseling, employment service for undergraduates, freshman orientation, on-campus day care, personal counseling, placement service for graduates, services/facilities for handicapped.

ANNUAL EXPENSES. Tuition and fees (1992-93): $1,276, $564 additional for out-of-district students, $2,640 additional for out-of-state students. **Books and supplies:** $500. **Other expenses:** $650.

FINANCIAL AID. 25% of continuing students receive some form of aid. All aid based on need. **Aid applications:** No closing date; priority given to applications received by August 15; applicants notified on a rolling basis beginning on or about June 1; must reply within 2 weeks.

ADDRESS/TELEPHONE. Irod L. Lee, Director of Admissions, Middlesex Community-Technical College, 100 Training Hill Road, Middletown, CT 06457. (203) 343-5719.

Mitchell College
New London, Connecticut — CB code: 3528

2-year private junior college, coed. Founded in 1938. **Accreditation:** Regional. **Undergraduate enrollment:** 264 men, 224 women full time; 143 men, 265 women part time. **Faculty:** 52 total (25 full time), 3 with doctorates or other terminal degrees. **Location:** Suburban campus in large town; 100 miles from both New York City and Boston. **Calendar:** Semester, extensive summer session. Extensive evening/early morning classes. **Microcomputers:** 25 located in computer centers.

DEGREES OFFERED. AA, AS. 235 associate degrees awarded in 1992. 40% in business and management, 5% computer sciences, 10% education, 5% health sciences, 10% letters/literature, 10% parks/recreation, protective services, public affairs, 10% social sciences.

UNDERGRADUATE MAJORS. Accounting, biological and physical sciences, biology, business and management, business and office, community services, computer and information sciences, early childhood education, education, engineering, engineering and engineering-related technologies, engineering and other disciplines, English, gerontology, health fitness, humanities and social sciences, liberal/general studies, marine biology, marketing and distribution, mathematics, physical sciences, physics, political science and government, protective services, public affairs, recreation and community services technologies, recreation therapy, secretarial and related programs, social sciences, special education.

ACADEMIC PROGRAMS. 2-year transfer program, accelerated program, independent study, internships. **Remedial services:** Learning center, preadmission summer program, reduced course load, remedial instruction, special counselor, tutoring, reading specialist. **Placement/credit:** CLEP General and Subject, institutional tests; 30 credit hours maximum for associate degree.

ACADEMIC REQUIREMENTS. Freshmen must earn minimum GPA of 1.8 to continue in good standing. 68% of freshmen return for sophomore year. Students must declare major on application. **Graduation requirements:** 62 hours for associate (30 in major). Most students required to take courses in English, history, mathematics, social sciences.

FRESHMAN ADMISSIONS. Selection criteria: High school achievement, recommendations, interview very important. Subject requirements vary by program.

1992 FRESHMAN CLASS PROFILE. 164 men, 130 women enrolled. 5% had high school GPA of 3.0 or higher, 60% between 2.0 and 2.99. 1% were in top tenth and 10% were in top quarter of graduating class. **Characteristics:** 26% from in state, 90% live in college housing, 6% have minority backgrounds, 6% are foreign students. Average age is 18.

FALL-TERM APPLICATIONS. $30 fee, may be waived for applicants with need. No closing date; priority given to applications received by February 1; applicants notified on a rolling basis; must reply by April 1 or within 10 days if notified thereafter. Interview recommended. Essay recommended. Deferred and early admission available. SAT test scores recommended.

STUDENT LIFE. Housing: Dormitories (men, women). 4 residence halls are Victorian houses, 4 waterfront dormitories. **Activities:** Student government, radio, student newspaper, yearbook, choral groups, dance, drama.

ATHLETICS. NJCAA. **Intercollegiate:** Baseball M, basketball, field hockey W, soccer, softball W, tennis, volleyball W. **Intramural:** Basketball, sailing, soccer M, softball, tennis, volleyball.

STUDENT SERVICES. Aptitude testing, career counseling, employment service for undergraduates, freshman orientation, health services, on-campus day care, personal counseling, placement service for graduates, special adviser for adult students, services/facilities for handicapped.

ANNUAL EXPENSES. Tuition and fees (1992-93): $10,696. **Room and board:** $4,700. **Books and supplies:** $500. **Other expenses:** $500.

FINANCIAL AID. 58% of freshmen, 35% of continuing students receive some form of aid. All grants, all loans, 30% of jobs based on need. 200 enrolled freshmen were judged to have need, all were offered aid. **Aid applications:** Closing date July 15; priority given to applications received by March 1; applicants notified on a rolling basis beginning on or about February 15; must reply by May 1 or within 1 week if notified thereafter. **Additional information:** For full need to be met, applications should be received by May 1.

ADDRESS/TELEPHONE. Kathleen H. Crowley, Director of Admissions/Director of Financial Aid, Mitchell College, 437 Pequot Avenue, New London, CT 06320. (203) 443-2811. (800) 223-2769. Fax: (203) 437-0632.

Naugatuck Valley Community-Technical College
Waterbury, Connecticut — CB code: 3550

2-year public community, technical college, coed. Founded in 1967. **Accreditation:** Regional. **Undergraduate enrollment:** 5,571 men and women. **Location:** Urban campus in small city; 32 miles from Hartford. **Calendar:** Semester. **Additional facts:** Mattatuck Community College and Waterbury State Technical College merged in July 1992 and have formed Naugatuck Valley Community-Technical College, a comprehensive community and technical institution.

FRESHMAN ADMISSIONS. Selection criteria: Open admissions. Selective admissions to some programs based on school achievement, recommendations, test scores, maturity of student, and motivation.

ANNUAL EXPENSES. Tuition and fees (1992-93): $1,276, $564 additional for out-of-district students, $2,640 additional for out-of-state students. **Books and supplies:** $420. **Other expenses:** $500.

ADDRESS/TELEPHONE. Nancy Merritt, Director of Admissions, Naugatuck Valley Community-Technical College, 750 Chase Parkway, Waterbury, CT 06708. (203) 575-8151. Fax: (203) 575-8096.

Northwestern Connecticut Community-Technical College
Winsted, Connecticut — CB code: 3652

2-year public community college, coed. Founded in 1965. **Accreditation:** Regional. **Undergraduate enrollment:** 204 men, 325 women full time; 411 men, 1,112 women part time. **Faculty:** 87 total (35 full time), 15 with doctorates or other terminal degrees. **Location:** Rural campus in large town; 25 miles from Hartford and 25 miles from Waterbury. **Calendar:** Semester, limited summer session. **Microcomputers:** 80 located in libraries, classrooms, computer centers.

DEGREES OFFERED. AA, AS. 163 associate degrees awarded in 1992. 18% in business and management, 9% business/office and marketing/distribution, 5% education, 5% allied health, 25% multi/interdisciplinary studies, 10% parks/recreation, protective services, public affairs, 15% visual and performing arts.

UNDERGRADUATE MAJORS. Accounting, behavioral sciences, biology, business administration and management, business and management, business and office, child development/care/guidance, computer and information sciences, computer graphics, computer programming, criminal justice studies, criminal justice technology, early childhood education, education of the deaf and hearing impaired, English, fine arts, graphic arts technology, graphic design, interpreter for the deaf, law enforcement and corrections, law enforcement and corrections technologies, legal assistant/paralegal, liberal/general studies, marketing and distribution, mathematics, medical assistant, office supervision and management, parks and recreation management, photography, physical sciences, preengineering, recreation and community services technologies, recreation therapy, secretarial and related programs, social sciences, video.

ACADEMIC PROGRAMS. 2-year transfer program, dual enrollment of high school students, independent study, internships, cross-registration. **Remedial services:** Learning center, reduced course load, remedial instruction, special counselor, tutoring, developmental program. **Placement/credit:** AP, CLEP General and Subject, institutional tests; 48 credit hours maximum for associate degree.

ACADEMIC REQUIREMENTS. Freshmen must earn minimum GPA of 1.7 to continue in good standing. 60% of freshmen return for sophomore year. Students must declare major on enrollment. **Graduation requirements:** 60 hours for associate (24 in major). Most students required to take courses in arts/fine arts, computer science, English, history, mathematics, philosophy/religion, biological/physical sciences, social sciences. **Additional information:** Career education for the deaf program offers full range of services and participation in all majors by deaf and hearing impaired students. Interpreting major prepares hearing students for National Registry test for interpreters for the deaf.

FRESHMAN ADMISSIONS. Selection criteria: Open admissions. Selective admissions to some programs.

1992 FRESHMAN CLASS PROFILE. 614 men and women applied, 614 accepted; 455 enrolled. **Characteristics:** 95% from in state, 100% commute, 3% have minority backgrounds, 1% are foreign students. Average age is 25.

FALL-TERM APPLICATIONS. $10 fee, may be waived for applicants with need. No closing date; applicants notified on a rolling basis beginning on or about February 1. Portfolio required for art, graphic design, visual communication applicants. Deferred admission available.

STUDENT LIFE. Housing: Dormitory for hearing impaired and interpreting students available in Winsted sponsored by Community Associates of Connecticut Inc. **Activities:** Student government, magazine, sign and mime productions by deaf and interpreting students, Spectrum (minority), Community Service Club, Signs of our Times (Hearing Impaired and Interpretory Students).

STUDENT SERVICES. Aptitude testing, career counseling, employment service for undergraduates, freshman orientation, personal counseling, placement service for graduates, veterans counselor, services/facilities for handicapped.

ANNUAL EXPENSES. Tuition and fees: $1,398, $624 additional for out-of-district students, $2,808 additional for out-of-state students. **Books and supplies:** $500. **Other expenses:** $1,000.

FINANCIAL AID. 33% of freshmen, 25% of continuing students receive some form of aid. 99% of grants, 90% of loans, 43% of jobs based on need. 75 enrolled freshmen were judged to have need, all were offered aid. Academic, leadership scholarships available. **Aid applications:** No closing date; priority given to applications received by June 15; applicants notified on a rolling basis beginning on or about June 15.

ADDRESS/TELEPHONE. Richard G. Tracy, Director of Admissions, Northwestern Connecticut Community-Technical College, Park Place, Winsted, CT 06098. (203) 738-6329. Fax: (203) 379-4995.

Norwalk Community-Technical College
Norwalk, Connecticut — CB code: 3677

2-year public community, technical college, coed. Founded in 1961. **Accreditation:** Regional. **Undergraduate enrollment:** 864 men and women full time; 3,182 men and women part time. **Faculty:** 185 total (85 full time), 5 with doctorates or other terminal degrees. **Location:** Urban campus in small city; 50 miles from New York City. **Calendar:** Semester, limited summer session. Saturday and extensive evening/early morning classes. **Microcomputers:** 170 located in libraries, classrooms, computer centers. **Special facilities:** Theater, rotating art and cultural exhibits. **Additional facts:** Norwalk Community College and Norwalk State Technical College merged in July 1992. Students may cross-register in community college and technical divisions.

DEGREES OFFERED. AA, AS, AAS. 252 associate degrees awarded in 1992. 31% in business and management, 5% business/office and marketing/distribution, 7% education, 11% allied health, 6% law, 28% multi/interdisciplinary studies.

UNDERGRADUATE MAJORS. Accounting, architectural technologies, architecture, business administration and management, business and management, business and office, business computer/console/peripheral equipment operation, business data processing and related programs, business data programming, civil technology, communications, community services, computer and information sciences, computer technology, data processing, education, electrical technology, electromechanical technology, engineering and engineering-related technologies, fine arts, graphic design, hotel/motel and restaurant management, industrial technology, information sciences and systems, journalism, law enforcement and corrections technologies, legal assistant/paralegal, legal secretary, liberal/general studies, library assistant, library science, manufacturing technology, marketing and distribution, nursing, optical technology, parks and recreation management, recreation and community services technologies, respiratory therapy, respiratory therapy technology, science and mathematics, secretarial and related programs, social work.

ACADEMIC PROGRAMS. Double major, dual enrollment of high school students, honors program, independent study, internships, study abroad, weekend college, cross-registration. **Remedial services:** Learning center, preadmission summer program, reduced course load, remedial instruction, special counselor, tutoring. **Placement/credit:** AP, CLEP General and Subject, institutional tests; 45 credit hours maximum for associate degree.

ACADEMIC REQUIREMENTS. Freshmen must earn minimum GPA of 2.0 to continue in good standing. 50% of freshmen return for sophomore year. Students must declare major by end of first year. **Graduation requirements:** 60 hours for associate (15 in major). Most students required to take courses in arts/fine arts, computer science, English, foreign languages, history, humanities, mathematics, philosophy/religion, biological/physical sciences, social sciences.

FRESHMAN ADMISSIONS. Selection criteria: Open admissions. Chemistry, biology, and algebra required for nursing and respiratory therapy applicants. Nursing applicants must have taken chemistry within past 5 years.

1992 FRESHMAN CLASS PROFILE. 1,333 men and women enrolled. **Characteristics:** 98% from in state, 100% commute, 25% have minority backgrounds, 2% are foreign students. Average age is 23.

FALL-TERM APPLICATIONS. $10 fee, may be waived for applicants with need. No closing date; applicants notified on a rolling basis beginning on or about March 1. Deferred and early admission available. Applicants to nursing, respiratory therapy, legal assistant programs should apply by February 15. All entering freshmen must take the New Jersey College Placement Test, used for placement only.

STUDENT LIFE. Activities: Student government, radio, student newspaper, yearbook, choral groups, music ensembles, musical theater.

ATHLETICS. NJCAA. **Intercollegiate:** Basketball M, golf M, soccer M, tennis M. **Intramural:** Basketball M, golf M.

STUDENT SERVICES. Aptitude testing, career counseling, employment service for undergraduates, freshman orientation, on-campus day care, personal counseling, placement service for graduates, special adviser for adult students, veterans counselor, services/facilities for handicapped.

ANNUAL EXPENSES. Tuition and fees: $1,398, $624 additional for out-of-district students, $2,808 additional for out-of-state students. **Books and supplies:** $400. **Other expenses:** $1,600.

FINANCIAL AID. 25% of freshmen, 23% of continuing students receive some form of aid. All grants, 88% of loans, all jobs based on need. **Aid applications:** No closing date; priority given to applications received by April 15; applicants notified on a rolling basis beginning on or about July 1; must reply within 10 days.

ADDRESS/TELEPHONE. Barbara E. Drotman, Director of Enrollment Management, Norwalk Community-Technical College, 188 Richards Avenue, Norwalk, CT 06854. (203) 857-7060.

Paier College of Art
Hamden, Connecticut — CB code: 3699

4-year proprietary art college, coed. Founded in 1946. **Undergraduate enrollment:** 98 men, 85 women full time; 29 men, 80 women part time. **Faculty:** 46 total (12 full time), 3 with doctorates or other terminal degrees. **Location:** Urban campus in small city; 2 miles from New Haven. **Calendar:** Semester, limited summer session. **Special facilities:** Image picture file.

DEGREES OFFERED. BFA. 5 associate degrees awarded in 1992. 100% in visual and performing arts. 33 bachelor's degrees awarded. 98% in visual and performing arts.

UNDERGRADUATE MAJORS. Associate: Photography. **Bachelor's:** Fine arts, graphic design, illustration design, interior design, painting.

ACADEMIC PROGRAMS. Independent study. **Remedial services:** Reduced course load, remedial instruction, special counselor.

ACADEMIC REQUIREMENTS. Freshmen must earn minimum GPA of 2.0 to continue in good standing. 85% of freshmen return for sophomore year. Students must declare major on application. **Graduation requirements:** 64 hours for associate (43 in major), 130 hours for bachelor's (88 in major). Most students required to take courses in arts/fine arts, English, mathematics, philosophy/religion, biological/physical sciences, social sciences.

FRESHMAN ADMISSIONS. Selection criteria: Evidence of career interest in art as reflected in portfolio and interview very important. **Test requirements:** SAT or ACT (SAT preferred); score report by August 15.

1992 FRESHMAN CLASS PROFILE. 28 men, 27 women enrolled. **Academic background:** Mid 50% of enrolled freshmen had SAT-V between 330-470, SAT-M between 320-450. 100% submitted SAT scores. **Characteristics:** 98% from in state, 100% commute, 2% have minority backgrounds, 2% are foreign students. Average age is 18.

FALL-TERM APPLICATIONS. $25 fee. No closing date; applicants notified on a rolling basis beginning on or about February 15; must reply within 2 weeks. Interview required. Portfolio required.

STUDENT LIFE. Activities: Student government, yearbook.

STUDENT SERVICES. Career counseling, employment service for

undergraduates, freshman orientation, personal counseling, placement service for graduates, services/facilities for handicapped.

ANNUAL EXPENSES. Tuition and fees: $10,120. **Books and supplies:** $600. **Other expenses:** $1,200.

FINANCIAL AID. 39% of freshmen, 40% of continuing students receive some form of aid. All grants, 91% of loans based on need. **Aid applications:** No closing date; priority given to applications received by May 1; applicants notified on a rolling basis beginning on or about June 1; must reply within 2 weeks.

ADDRESS/TELEPHONE. Sante Graziani, Dean of the College, Paier College of Art, Six Prospect Court, Hamden, CT 06517-4025. (203) 777-3851. Fax: (203) 287-3021.

Quinebaug Valley Community-Technical College
Danielson, Connecticut CB code: 3716

2-year public community college, coed. Founded in 1971. **Accreditation:** Regional. **Undergraduate enrollment:** 89 men, 205 women full time; 203 men, 679 women part time. **Faculty:** 53 total (17 full time), 9 with doctorates or other terminal degrees. **Location:** Rural campus in small town; 50 miles from Hartford, 25 miles from Providence, Rhode Island. **Calendar:** Semester, limited summer session. **Microcomputers:** 50 located in computer centers.

DEGREES OFFERED. AA, AS. 91 associate degrees awarded in 1992.

UNDERGRADUATE MAJORS. Accounting, aircraft mechanics, business administration and management, fine arts, liberal/general studies, medical assistant, mental health/human services, office supervision and management, rehabilitation counseling/services, secretarial and related programs, social work.

ACADEMIC PROGRAMS. 2-year transfer program, accelerated program, double major, dual enrollment of high school students, honors program, independent study, internships, study abroad, cross-registration. **Remedial services:** Learning center, reduced course load, remedial instruction, tutoring. **Placement/credit:** CLEP General and Subject, institutional tests; 30 credit hours maximum for associate degree.

ACADEMIC REQUIREMENTS. Freshmen must earn minimum GPA of 2.0 to continue in good standing. Students must declare major by end of first year. **Graduation requirements:** 60 hours for associate (30 in major). Most students required to take courses in English, history, humanities, mathematics, biological/physical sciences, social sciences.

FRESHMAN ADMISSIONS. Selection criteria: Open admissions. Drug and Alcohol Counseling degree candidates must file special application after completing general education component.

1992 FRESHMAN CLASS PROFILE. 113 men, 243 women enrolled. **Characteristics:** 99% from in state, 100% commute.

FALL-TERM APPLICATIONS. $10 fee, may be waived for applicants with need. No closing date; priority given to applications received by August 1; applicants notified on a rolling basis. Interview recommended. Interview recommended for counseling purposes. Deferred admission available.

STUDENT LIFE. Activities: Student government, student newspaper, television.

ATHLETICS. Intramural: Basketball.

STUDENT SERVICES. Career counseling, freshman orientation, on-campus day care, personal counseling, placement service for graduates, veterans counselor, services/facilities for handicapped.

ANNUAL EXPENSES. Tuition and fees: $1,398, $624 additional for out-of-district students, $2,808 additional for out-of-state students. **Books and supplies:** $600. **Other expenses:** $1,000.

FINANCIAL AID. 18% of freshmen, 32% of continuing students receive some form of aid. 96% of grants, 38% of jobs based on need. 131 enrolled freshmen were judged to have need, all were offered aid. Academic, music/drama, state/district residency, leadership scholarships available. **Aid applications:** Closing date November 1; applicants notified on a rolling basis; must reply within 10 days.

ADDRESS/TELEPHONE. Antonio L. Veloso, Director of Admissions, Quinebaug Valley Community-Technical College, 742 Upper Maple Street, Danielson, CT 06239-1440. (203) 774-1130 ext. 320. Fax: (203) 774-7768.

Quinnipiac College ⇄
Hamden, Connecticut CB code: 3712

Admissions:	58% of applicants accepted
Based on:	••• School record
	•• Special talents, test scores
	• Activities, essay, interview, recommendations
Completion:	83% of freshmen end year in good standing
	66% graduate, 40% of these enter graduate study

4-year private business, health science college, coed. Founded in 1929. **Accreditation:** Regional. **Undergraduate enrollment:** 939 men, 1,743 women full time; 226 men, 536 women part time. **Graduate enrollment:** 150 men, 342 women full time; 409 men, 433 women part time. **Faculty:** 333 total (208 full time), 220 with doctorates or other terminal degrees. **Location:** Suburban campus in small city; 9 miles from New Haven, 35 miles from Hartford. **Calendar:** Semester, limited summer session. **Microcomputers:** 100 located in dormitories, libraries, classrooms, computer centers, campus-wide network.

DEGREES OFFERED. BA, BS, MS, MBA, JD. 56 associate degrees awarded in 1992. 426 bachelor's degrees awarded in 1992. 31% in business and management, 6% health sciences, 31% allied health, 7% psychology, 7% social sciences. Graduate degrees offered in 41 major fields of study.

UNDERGRADUATE MAJORS. Accounting, actuarial sciences, advertising, American studies, anthropology, biochemistry, biology, biotechnology, business administration and management, business and management, business economics, business systems analysis, chemistry, chiropractic, clinical chemistry, clinical laboratory science, clinical microbiology, clinical psychology, communications, communications research, computer and information sciences, computer mathematics, computer programming, developmental psychology, economics, English, environmental health, experimental psychology, finance, gerontology, health care administration, history, human resources development, humanities and social sciences, information sciences and systems, international business management, investments and securities, legal assistant/paralegal, liberal/general studies, management information systems, marketing and distribution, marketing management, marketing research, mathematics, medical laboratory technologies, microbiology, nursing, occupational therapy, operations research, organizational behavior, personnel management, physical therapy, physics, political science and government, predentistry, prelaw, premedicine, prepharmacy, preveterinary, psychobiology, psychology, public health laboratory science, public relations, radio/television broadcasting, radiograph medical technology, respiratory therapy, respiratory therapy technology, retailing, small business management and ownership, social psychology, social sciences, social work, sociology, statistics, systems analysis, taxation, trade and industrial supervision and management, urban studies, veterinarian's assistant, women's studies, zoology.

ACADEMIC PROGRAMS. Accelerated program, cooperative education, double major, dual enrollment of high school students, external degree, honors program, independent study, internships, student-designed major, study abroad, teacher preparation, telecourses, visiting/exchange student program, cross-registration; liberal arts/career combination in health sciences, business; combined bachelor's/graduate program in law. **Remedial services:** Learning center, reduced course load, remedial instruction, special counselor, tutoring, academic assistance program. **ROTC:** Air Force. **Placement/credit:** AP, CLEP General and Subject, IB, institutional tests; 32 credit hours maximum for bachelor's degree.

ACADEMIC REQUIREMENTS. Freshmen must earn minimum GPA of 1.7 to continue in good standing. 94% of freshmen return for sophomore year. Students must declare major by end of second year. **Graduation requirements:** 120 hours for bachelor's (30 in major). Most students required to take courses in arts/fine arts, computer science, English, foreign languages, history, humanities, mathematics, biological/physical sciences, social sciences.

FRESHMAN ADMISSIONS. Selection criteria: Primarily school achievement record, test scores, and class rank. Interview, special talents, and extracurricular activities also considered. Special consideration given to achieving diversity within the student body. **High school preparation:** 16 units required. Required and recommended units include biological science 2, English 4, mathematics 3, physical science 1 and social science 3. Foreign language 2 recommended. 2 laboratory sciences, 2 history required. 3 laboratory sciences required for some allied health programs. Biology, chemistry, physics required for physical therapy program, 2 algebra for nursing. **Test requirements:** SAT or ACT; score report by June 1.

1992 FRESHMAN CLASS PROFILE. 4,083 men and women applied, 2,363 accepted; 343 men enrolled, 636 women enrolled. 35% had high school GPA of 3.0 or higher, 65% between 2.0 and 2.99. 11% were in top tenth and 40% were in top quarter of graduating class. **Academic background:** Mid 50% of enrolled freshmen had SAT-V between 410-550, SAT-M between 440-570; ACT composite between 18-24. 99% submitted SAT scores, 1% submitted ACT scores. **Characteristics:** 50% from in state, 82% live in college housing, 8% have minority backgrounds, 3% are foreign students, 10% join fraternities/sororities. Average age is 19.

FALL-TERM APPLICATIONS. $40 fee, may be waived for applicants with need. No closing date; priority given to applications received by December 31; applicants notified on a rolling basis; must reply by May 1 or within 4 weeks if notified thereafter. Essay required. Interview recommended for all applicants. CRDA. Deferred admission available. Applicants to allied health programs (including physical therapy) advised to apply by December 31.

STUDENT LIFE. Housing: Dormitories (men, women, coed); apartment, handicapped housing available. Guaranteed housing for full-time undergraduates. **Activities:** Student government, film, magazine, radio, student newspaper, television, yearbook, choral groups, dance, drama, jazz band, musical theater, fraternities, sororities, Hillel, Catholic Community, Bible studies, Black Student Union, Greenpeace Club, Amnesty International, Special Olympics, SADD, Women's Center, Debate Club.

ATHLETICS. NCAA. **Intercollegiate:** Baseball M, basketball, cross-country, golf M, ice hockey M, lacrosse M, soccer, softball W, tennis, volleyball W. **Intramural:** Archery, badminton, basketball, bowling, field hockey, football M, soccer, softball, table tennis, tennis, volleyball.

STUDENT SERVICES. Aptitude testing, career counseling, employment service for undergraduates, freshman orientation, health services, on-campus day care, personal counseling, placement service for graduates, special adviser for adult students, services/facilities for handicapped.

ANNUAL EXPENSES. Tuition and fees: $11,810. **Room and board:** $6,077. **Books and supplies:** $500. **Other expenses:** $800.

FINANCIAL AID. 50% of freshmen, 61% of continuing students receive some form of aid. 76% of grants, 89% of loans, all jobs based on need. Academic, athletic, leadership, minority scholarships available. **Aid applications:** No closing date; priority given to applications received by March 1; applicants notified on a rolling basis beginning on or about April 1; must reply by May 1 or within 2 weeks if notified thereafter.

ADDRESS/TELEPHONE. David Tilley, VP/Dean of Admissions, Quinnipiac College, 275 Mount Carmel Avenue, Hamden, CT 06518-1908. (203) 281-8600. (800) 462-1944. Fax: (203) 248-4703.

Sacred Heart University
Fairfield, Connecticut

CB code: 3780

Admissions: 83% of applicants accepted
Based on:
••• School record
•• Interview, recommendations, test scores
• Activities, essay, special talents
Completion: 82% of freshmen end year in good standing
75% graduate, 14% of these enter graduate study

4-year private university, coed, affiliated with Roman Catholic Church. Founded in 1963. **Accreditation:** Regional. **Undergraduate enrollment:** 803 men, 794 women full time; 590 men, 1,473 women part time. **Graduate enrollment:** 547 men, 978 women part time. **Faculty:** 303 total (108 full time), 122 with doctorates or other terminal degrees. **Location:** Suburban campus in small city; 55 miles from New York City. **Calendar:** Semester, extensive summer session. Saturday and extensive evening/early morning classes. **Microcomputers:** 133 located in dormitories, libraries, classrooms, computer centers. **Special facilities:** Professional radio station, computer science wing, Contemporary Art Gallery, theater, University Learning Center, multipurpose communication studios, state-of-the art language laboratory.

DEGREES OFFERED. AA, AS, BA, BS, MA, MS, MBA. 118 associate degrees awarded in 1992. 39% in business and management, 22% business/office and marketing/distribution, 5% communications, 6% allied health, 23% law. 352 bachelor's degrees awarded. 55% in business and management, 7% computer sciences, 7% health sciences, 6% psychology, 5% social sciences, 5% visual and performing arts. Graduate degrees offered in 19 major fields of study.

UNDERGRADUATE MAJORS. Associate: Accounting, allied health, biology, business and management, business economics, chemistry, communications, data processing, economics, English, finance, fine arts, French, graphic design, history, illustration design, Italian, Japanese, Latin, legal assistant/paralegal, liberal/general studies, mathematics, music, painting, philosophy, political science and government, psychology, religion, respiratory therapy, respiratory therapy technology, sociology, Spanish. **Bachelor's:** Accounting, allied health, arts management, biochemistry, biological and physical sciences, biology, biomedical science, business administration and management, business and management, business economics, business education, chemistry, clinical laboratory science, communications, computer and information sciences, criminal justice studies, criminology, data processing, dental hygiene, dramatic arts, early childhood education, economics, education, elementary education, engineering, English, English education, film arts, finance, fine arts, foreign languages education, French, graphic design, health sciences, history, humanities and social sciences, illustration design, information sciences and systems, interior design, international business management, international development, international public service, international relations, international studies, Italian, journalism, junior high education, law enforcement and corrections, legal assistant/paralegal, liberal/general studies, management science, marketing and distributive education, marketing management, mathematics, mathematics education, medical laboratory technologies, medical social work, military science (Army), musical theater, nursing, occupational therapy, painting, philosophy, physical therapy, political science and government, predentistry, prelaw, premedicine, prepharmacy, preveterinary, psychology, radio/television broadcasting, religion, science education, secondary education, social sciences, social studies education, social work, sociology, Spanish, sports management, sports medicine, visual and performing arts.

ACADEMIC PROGRAMS. Accelerated program, cooperative education, double major, dual enrollment of high school students, honors program, independent study, internships, student-designed major, study abroad, teacher preparation, visiting/exchange student program, weekend college, Washington semester, cross-registration; combined bachelor's/graduate program in business administration. **Remedial services:** Learning center, reduced course load, remedial instruction, special counselor, tutoring, English as a second language. **ROTC:** Army. **Placement/credit:** AP, CLEP General and Subject, institutional tests; 30 credit hours maximum for bachelor's degree.

ACADEMIC REQUIREMENTS. Freshmen must earn minimum GPA of 1.5 to continue in good standing. 85% of freshmen return for sophomore year. Students must declare major by end of second year. **Graduation requirements:** 60 hours for associate (15 in major), 120 hours for bachelor's (45 in major). Most students required to take courses in arts/fine arts, computer science, English, foreign languages, history, humanities, mathematics, philosophy/religion, biological/physical sciences, social sciences. **Postgraduate studies:** 1% enter law school, 8% enter MBA programs, 5% enter other graduate study.

FRESHMAN ADMISSIONS. Selection criteria: High school achievement, class rank, college preparatory curriculum and SAT/ACT scores most important. **High school preparation:** 16 units required; 20 recommended. Required and recommended units include biological science 1, English 4, foreign language 2-3, mathematics 3-4, social science 2-3 and science 2-4. 4 mathematics recommended for accounting majors, 4 sciences recommended for nursing, premedical, physical therapy and occupational therapy majors. **Test requirements:** SAT or ACT; score report by April 15. Prueba de Aptitud Academica for Spanish speaking applicants.

1992 FRESHMAN CLASS PROFILE. 948 men applied, 736 accepted, 257 enrolled; 684 women applied, 622 accepted, 248 enrolled. 32% had high school GPA of 3.0 or higher, 67% between 2.0 and 2.99. 12% were in top tenth and 40% were in top quarter of graduating class. **Academic background:** Mid 50% of enrolled freshmen had SAT-V between 440-540, SAT-M between 470-560; ACT composite between 21-25. 95% submitted SAT scores, 5% submitted ACT scores. **Characteristics:** 60% from in state, 60% live in college housing, 28% have minority backgrounds, 3% are foreign students, 2% join fraternities/sororities. Average age is 18.

FALL-TERM APPLICATIONS. $30 fee, may be waived for applicants with need. Closing date April 15; priority given to applications received by March 1; applicants notified on a rolling basis; must reply by May 1. Essay required. Interview recommended. Portfolio recommended for art applicants. CRDA. Deferred and early admission available. EDP-F. ACH Mathematics Level I recommended for accounting applicants.

STUDENT LIFE. Housing: Dormitories (coed); apartment housing available. 3 condominium complexes available just off campus. On campus 4 new apartment styled residence halls opened in 1992. 2 additional residence halls will open in August 1993 and 1 in August 1994. **Activities:** Student government, magazine, radio, student newspaper, television, yearbook, choral groups, drama, jazz band, marching band, music ensembles, musical theater, pep band, symphony orchestra, gospel choir, fraternities, sororities, Young Democrats, Young Republicans, Campus Ministry, International Club, La Hispanidad, Jewish Friendship Organization, Irish Club, Italian Club, African American Student Organization.

ATHLETICS. NCAA. **Intercollegiate:** Baseball M, basketball, bowling, cross-country, field hockey W, football M, golf, ice hockey M, lacrosse, soccer, softball W, tennis, volleyball. **Intramural:** Badminton, basketball, bowling, football, golf, rugby, softball, table tennis, volleyball.

STUDENT SERVICES. Career counseling, employment service for undergraduates, freshman orientation, health services, personal counseling, placement service for graduates, special adviser for adult students, veterans counselor, services/facilities for handicapped.

ANNUAL EXPENSES. Tuition and fees (1992-93): $9,740. **Room and board:** $5,100. **Books and supplies:** $400.

FINANCIAL AID. 86% of freshmen, 75% of continuing students receive some form of aid. 76% of grants, 73% of loans, 64% of jobs based on need. Academic, art, athletic, leadership, religious affiliation, minority scholarships available. **Aid applications:** No closing date; priority given to applications received by March 1; applicants notified on a rolling basis beginning on or about April 1; must reply within 2 weeks.

ADDRESS/TELEPHONE. James M. Barquinero, VP of Enrollment Planning/Student Affairs, Sacred Heart University, 5151 Park Avenue, Fairfield, CT 06432-1000. (203) 371-7880. Fax: (203) 371-7889.

St. Joseph College
West Hartford, Connecticut

CB code: 3754

Admissions: 75% of applicants accepted
Based on:
••• School record
•• Interview, test scores
• Activities, recommendations, special talents
Completion: 90% of freshmen end year in good standing
70% graduate, 19% of these enter graduate study

4-year private liberal arts college, women only, affiliated with Roman Catholic Church. Founded in 1932. **Accreditation:** Regional. **Undergraduate enrollment:** 560 women full time; 66 men, 679 women part time. **Graduate enrollment:** 13 men, 66 women full time; 86 men, 555 women part time. **Faculty:** 155 total (75 full time), 69 with doctorates or other terminal degrees. **Location:** Suburban campus in small city; 3 miles from Hartford. **Calendar:** Semester, limited summer session. **Microcomputers:** 37 located in libraries, classrooms, computer centers. **Special facilities:** Art study gallery, 2 laboratory schools, nursing laboratory. **Additional facts:** Men admitted as part-time students for weekend college. Graduate school admits men as full-time and part-time students.

DEGREES OFFERED. BA, BS, MA, MS. 203 bachelor's degrees awarded in 1992. 6% in area and ethnic studies, 10% business and management, 22% teacher education, 19% health sciences, 6% home economics, 5% letters/literature, 7% psychology, 12% social sciences. Graduate degrees offered in 24 major fields of study.

UNDERGRADUATE MAJORS. Accounting, American studies, art education, art history, biochemistry, biological and physical sciences, biology, business administration and management, business administration/accounting, business administration/economics and finance, business economics, chemistry, early childhood education, economics, elementary education, English, English education, family/consumer resource management, food science and nutrition, foreign languages (multiple emphasis), foreign languages education, French, history, history/political science, home economics, home economics education, humanities, humanities and social sciences, junior high education, mathematics, mathematics education, mathematics/computer science, mathematics/economics, medical laboratory technologies, nursing, nutritional sciences, philosophy, physical sciences, political science and government, predentistry, prelaw, premedicine, psychology, religion, science education, secondary education, social science education, social science/history, social studies education, social work, sociology, Spanish, special education.

ACADEMIC PROGRAMS. Double major, dual enrollment of high school students, education specialist degree, honors program, independent study, internships, student-designed major, study abroad, teacher preparation, weekend college, cross-registration. **Remedial services:** Learning center, preadmission summer program, reduced course load, tutoring. **Placement/credit:** AP, CLEP General and Subject, institutional tests; 30 credit hours maximum for bachelor's degree.

ACADEMIC REQUIREMENTS. Freshmen must earn minimum GPA of 2.0 to continue in good standing. 88% of freshmen return for sophomore year. Students must declare major by end of second year. **Graduation requirements:** 120 hours for bachelor's (30 in major). Most students required to take courses in arts/fine arts, computer science, English, foreign languages, history, humanities, mathematics, philosophy/religion, biological/physical sciences, social sciences. **Postgraduate studies:** 1% enter law school, 1% enter medical school, 2% enter MBA programs, 15% enter other graduate study. **Additional information:** Seminar offered to introduce students to college experience and philosophy of education.

FRESHMAN ADMISSIONS. Selection criteria: School achievement record, test scores, recommendation of high school principal, teacher or counselor, personal interview, school and community activities considered. **High school preparation:** 16 units recommended. Recommended units include English 4, foreign language 3, mathematics 3, social science 3 and science 3. **Test requirements:** SAT or ACT; score report by May 1. ACH not required however, if submitted ACH results will be considered in admissions and placement.

1992 FRESHMAN CLASS PROFILE. 304 women applied, 229 accepted, 147 enrolled. **Academic background:** Mid 50% of enrolled freshmen had SAT-V between 400-480, SAT-M between 400-520. 98% submitted SAT scores. **Characteristics:** 88% from in state, 73% live in college housing, 16% have minority backgrounds, 1% are foreign students. Average age is 19.

FALL-TERM APPLICATIONS. $25 fee, may be waived for applicants with need. Closing date May 1; applicants notified on a rolling basis; must reply by May 1 or within 2 weeks if notified thereafter. Interview recommended. CRDA. Deferred and early admission available. EDP-S. Interviews strongly recommended.

STUDENT LIFE. Housing: Dormitories (women); handicapped housing available. Single rooms available for nontraditional students. Medical singles with private bathrooms available. **Activities:** Student government, magazine, student newspaper, yearbook, choral groups, dance, drama, music ensembles, musical theater, folk group, various religious, volunteer, and political organizations including Latino-American Club, Intercultural Student Association, Amnesty International, Justice Action Service Peace, AWARE (for adults returning to education). **Additional information:** Students are involved in a wide variety of activites throughout the year. Mixers, sporting events, and semi-formals are regularly scheduled along with lectures, plays, concert recitals, poetry readings, and trips to Boston and New York.

ATHLETICS. Intercollegiate: Basketball, softball, tennis, volleyball. **Intramural:** Badminton, softball, tennis, track and field, volleyball.

STUDENT SERVICES. Aptitude testing, career counseling, employment service for undergraduates, freshman orientation, health services, personal counseling, placement service for graduates, special adviser for adult students, campus ministry, services/facilities for handicapped.

ANNUAL EXPENSES. Tuition and fees: $11,600. **Room and board:** $4,625. **Books and supplies:** $550. **Other expenses:** $900.

FINANCIAL AID. 79% of freshmen, 69% of continuing students receive some form of aid. 92% of grants, 72% of loans, 38% of jobs based on need. 70 enrolled freshmen were judged to have need, all were offered aid. Academic scholarships available. **Aid applications:** Closing date March 1; applicants notified on a rolling basis beginning on or about March 1; must reply by May 1 or within 2 weeks if notified thereafter.

ADDRESS/TELEPHONE. Mary C. Demo, Director of Admissions, St. Joseph College, 1678 Asylum Avenue, West Hartford, CT 06117-2700. (203) 232-4571 ext. 216. Fax: (203) 233-5695.

Southern Connecticut State University
New Haven, Connecticut — CB code: 3662

Admissions:	62% of applicants accepted
Based on:	••• School record
	•• Activities, essay, recommendations, test scores
	• Special talents
Completion:	65% of freshmen end year in good standing
	33% enter graduate study

4-year public university, coed. Founded in 1893. **Accreditation:** Regional. **Undergraduate enrollment:** 2,740 men, 3,402 women full time; 1,251 men, 1,482 women part time. **Graduate enrollment:** 128 men, 393 women full time; 752 men, 2,272 women part time. **Faculty:** 747 total (368 full time), 241 with doctorates or other terminal degrees. **Location:** Urban campus in small city; 75 miles from New York City. **Calendar:** Semester, extensive summer session. **Microcomputers:** 400 located in dormitories, libraries, classrooms, computer centers. **Special facilities:** Art gallery, planetarium, photonics laboratory.

DEGREES OFFERED. AS, BA, BS, MA, MS, MSW. 1 associate degree awarded in 1992. 1,415 bachelor's degrees awarded. 23% in business and management, 12% communications, 21% teacher education, 9% health sciences, 5% psychology, 7% social sciences, 5% visual and performing arts. Graduate degrees offered in 54 major fields of study.

UNDERGRADUATE MAJORS. Associate: Liberal/general studies. **Bachelor's:** Accounting, applied mathematics, art education, art history, biochemistry, biology, botany, business administration and management, business and management, business economics, chemistry, communications, comparative literature, computer and information sciences, dramatic arts, early childhood education, earth sciences, economics, education, education of the culturally disadvantaged, education of the emotionally handicapped, education of the mentally handicapped, education of the multiple handicapped, education of the physically handicapped, elementary education, English, English education, English literature, finance, foreign languages education, French, geography, German, health education, health sciences, history, Italian, journalism, junior high education, liberal/general studies, library science, marketing management, mathematics, mathematics education, nursing, nursing education, philosophy, physical education, physics, political science and government, predentistry, psychology, public and community health, public health laboratory science, radio/television technology, recreation and community services technologies, science education, secondary education, social science education, social sciences, social studies education, social work, sociology, Spanish, special education, specific learning disabilities, speech, speech correction, speech pathology/audiology, sports medicine, studio art, zoology.

ACADEMIC PROGRAMS. 2-year transfer program, accelerated program, cooperative education, dual enrollment of high school students, honors program, independent study, internships, study abroad, teacher preparation, cross-registration. **Remedial services:** Learning center, reduced course load, remedial instruction, special counselor, tutoring, preadmission summer program for minority students. **ROTC:** Air Force, Army. **Placement/credit:** AP, CLEP General and Subject, institutional tests.

ACADEMIC REQUIREMENTS. Freshmen must earn minimum GPA of 1.5 to continue in good standing. 75% of freshmen return for sophomore year. Students must declare major by end of first year. **Graduation requirements:** 62 hours for associate (18 in major), 122 hours for bachelor's (30 in major). Most students required to take courses in arts/fine arts, English, foreign languages, history, mathematics, philosophy/religion, biological/physical sciences, social sciences.

FRESHMAN ADMISSIONS. Selection criteria: School achievement record, test scores. Special consideration to culturally disadvantaged. **High school preparation:** 16 units required. Required units include biological science 1, English 4, foreign language 2, mathematics 3, physical science 1 and social science 2. 2 art recommended for art applicants. **Test requirements:** SAT; score report by May 1.

1992 FRESHMAN CLASS PROFILE. 1,784 men applied, 1,056 accepted, 444 enrolled; 2,068 women applied, 1,322 accepted, 500 enrolled. **Academic background:** Mid 50% of enrolled freshmen had SAT-V between 370-470, SAT-M between 390-490. 95% submitted SAT scores. **Characteristics:** 81% from in state, 66% commute, 9% have minority backgrounds, 1% are foreign students. Average age is 19.

FALL-TERM APPLICATIONS. $20 fee, may be waived for applicants with need. Closing date July 1; priority given to applications received by May 1; applicants notified on a rolling basis beginning on or about December 1; must reply by May 1 or within 2 weeks if notified thereafter. Essay required. Deferred and early admission available.

STUDENT LIFE. Housing: Dormitories (coed); apartment, handicapped housing available. **Activities:** Student government, film, magazine, radio, student newspaper, yearbook, choral groups, concert band, dance, drama, marching band, music ensembles, symphony orchestra, fraternities, sororities, Christian Fellowship, Newman Club, United Ministries, Organization of Latin American Students, Black Student Union, People to People, Students for Disability Rights, veterans club.

ATHLETICS. NCAA. **Intercollegiate:** Baseball, basketball, cross-country, diving, field hockey W, football M, golf M, gymnastics, soccer M, softball W, swimming, tennis, track and field, volleyball W, wrestling M. **Intramural:** Archery, badminton, baseball, basketball, bowling, diving, fencing, field hockey, gymnastics, ice hockey M, lacrosse, rugby, skiing, skin diving, soccer, swimming, table tennis, tennis, track and field, volleyball, water polo, wrestling.

STUDENT SERVICES. Career counseling, employment service for undergraduates, freshman orientation, health services, on-campus day care, personal counseling, placement service for graduates, special adviser for adult students, veterans counselor, services/facilities for handicapped.

ANNUAL EXPENSES. Tuition and fees (1992-93): $2,646, $3,568 additional for out-of-state students. **Room and board:** $4,104. **Books and supplies:** $700. **Other expenses:** $976.

FINANCIAL AID. 33% of freshmen, 40% of continuing students receive some form of aid. 95% of grants, 61% of loans, all jobs based on need. Academic scholarships available. **Aid applications:** No closing date; priority given to applications received by March 16; applicants notified on a rolling basis beginning on or about June 15; must reply within 2 weeks.

ADDRESS/TELEPHONE. Sharon A. Brennan, Director of Admissions, Southern Connecticut State University, 501 Crescent Street, New Haven, CT 06515. (203) 397-4450.

Teikyo-Post University
Waterbury, Connecticut — CB code: 3698

Admissions: 94% of applicants accepted
Based on:
- ••• Essay, interview, recommendations, school record
- •• Activities, special talents
- • Test scores

Completion: 87% of freshmen end year in good standing
9% enter graduate study

4-year private university, coed. Founded in 1890. **Accreditation:** Regional. **Undergraduate enrollment:** 611 men and women full time; 1,353 men and women part time. **Faculty:** 166 total (28 full time), 9 with doctorates or other terminal degrees. **Location:** Suburban campus in small city; 32 miles from Hartford, 20 miles from New Haven. **Calendar:** Day division: semester; evening division: semester accelerated. **Microcomputers:** 88 located in dormitories, libraries, computer centers. **Special facilities:** Congressional Record depository with extensive collection of references on taxes. **Additional facts:** Cross-cultural education offered at multiple campuses, including campuses in The Netherlands, Germany, and Japan.

DEGREES OFFERED. AA, AS, BA, BS. 99 associate degrees awarded in 1992. 60% in business and management, 40% social sciences. 265 bachelor's degrees awarded. 80% in business and management, 18% social sciences.

UNDERGRADUATE MAJORS. Associate: Accounting, business administration and management, business and management, early childhood education, English, equestrian science, fashion merchandising, history, home furnishings and equipment management/production/services, humanities, humanities and social sciences, interior design, legal assistant/paralegal, liberal/general studies, marketing and distribution, marketing management, psychology, recreation therapy, sociology. **Bachelor's:** Accounting, apparel and accessories marketing, business administration and management, business and management, English, equestrian science, fashion merchandising, finance, history, home furnishings and equipment management/production/services, hotel/motel and restaurant management, humanities, humanities and social sciences, interior design, international business management, legal assistant/paralegal, liberal/general studies, marketing and distribution, marketing management, prelaw, psychology, sociology.

ACADEMIC PROGRAMS. 2-year transfer program, accelerated program, cooperative education, double major, dual enrollment of high school students, honors program, independent study, internships, student-designed major, study abroad, weekend college, cross-registration. **Remedial services:** Learning center, reduced course load, remedial instruction, tutoring. **ROTC:** Army. **Placement/credit:** AP, CLEP Subject, institutional tests; 15 credit hours maximum for bachelor's degree.

ACADEMIC REQUIREMENTS. Freshmen must earn minimum GPA of 2.0 to continue in good standing. Students must declare major by end of first year. **Graduation requirements:** 60 hours for associate, 120 hours for bachelor's (36 in major). Most students required to take courses in English, history, humanities, mathematics, biological/physical sciences, social sciences. **Postgraduate studies:** 15% from 2-year programs enter 4-year programs. **Additional information:** Support instruction and tutoring available in PALS laboratory to assist students in English and mathematics. ESL summer institute and courses.

FRESHMAN ADMISSIONS. Selection criteria: School achievement record, interview, and class rank in top 50% of graduating class most important. Counselor's recommendation also important. School and community activities considered. SAT/ACT scores reviewed and considered. **High school preparation:** 16 units recommended. **Test requirements:** SAT or ACT (SAT preferred); score report by September 1.

1992 FRESHMAN CLASS PROFILE. 367 men and women applied, 344 accepted; 104 men enrolled, 207 women enrolled. **Characteristics:** 57% from in state, 65% commute, 7% have minority backgrounds, 4% are foreign students. Average age is 18.

FALL-TERM APPLICATIONS. $40 fee, may be waived for applicants with need. No closing date; priority given to applications received by May 1; applicants notified on a rolling basis; must reply within 4 weeks. Essay required. Interview recommended. Deferred and early admission available. EDP-F.

STUDENT LIFE. Housing: Dormitories (men, women, coed). Residence hall for adults over 22 available. Off-campus apartment building used for student housing. **Activities:** Student government, student newspaper, yearbook, choral groups, drama, music ensembles, Phi Theta Kappa, black student organization, voluntary income tax assistance, ambassadors, peer guides, international club, global partnership.

ATHLETICS. NAIA. **Intercollegiate:** Basketball, horseback riding, soccer M, softball W. **Intramural:** Baseball M, basketball, bowling M, cross-country, diving, football M, handball, racquetball, softball, swimming, tennis, volleyball. **Clubs:** Skiing.

STUDENT SERVICES. Aptitude testing, career counseling, employment service for undergraduates, freshman orientation, health services, on-campus day care, personal counseling, placement service for graduates, special adviser for adult students, veterans counselor, services/facilities for handicapped.

ANNUAL EXPENSES. Tuition and fees: $11,110. **Room and board:** $5,450. **Books and supplies:** $600. **Other expenses:** $400.

FINANCIAL AID. 85% of freshmen, 80% of continuing students receive some form of aid. 86% of grants, 89% of loans, all jobs based on need. 210 enrolled freshmen were judged to have need, all were offered aid. Academic, athletic, state/district residency, leadership, alumni affiliation, minority scholarships available. **Aid applications:** No closing date; priority given to applications received by March 15; applicants notified on a rolling basis beginning on or about March 15; must reply within 10 days.

ADDRESS/TELEPHONE. Aline C. Rossiter, Director of Admissions, Teikyo-Post University, PO Box 2540, Waterbury, CT 06723-2540. (203) 596-4520. (800) 345-2562. Fax: (203) 756-5810.

Three Rivers Community-Technical College
Norwich, Connecticut — CB code: 3558

2-year public community college, coed. Founded in 1969. **Accreditation:** Regional. **Undergraduate enrollment:** 4,137 men and women. **Faculty:** 240 total (90 full time). **Location:** Suburban campus in large town; 45 miles from Hartford. **Calendar:** Semester, limited summer session. Saturday and extensive evening/early morning classes. **Microcomputers:** 125 located in libraries, classrooms, computer centers. **Additional facts:** Mohegan Community College and Thames Valley Technical College merged in July, 1992. All programs continue at the 2 campuses.

DEGREES OFFERED. AA, AS, AAS. 510 associate degrees awarded in 1992.

UNDERGRADUATE MAJORS. Accounting, aeronautical technology, business administration and management, business data processing and related programs, business data programming, chemical manufacturing technology, civil technology, computer and information sciences, computer programming, computer technology, criminal justice studies, data processing, drafting and design technology, early childhood special education, electrical technology, electromechanical technology, engineering and engineering-related technologies, engineering management, environmental engineering technology, fire control and safety technology, food management, industrial technology, information sciences and systems, law enforcement and corrections technologies, legal secretary, liberal/general studies, library assistant, manufacturing technology, marketing and distribution, marketing management, mechanical design technology, medical secretary, mental health/human services, nursing, public administration, public affairs, rehabilitation counseling/services, secretarial and related programs, trade and industrial supervision and management, word processing.

ACADEMIC PROGRAMS. 2-year transfer program, double major, dual enrollment of high school students, independent study, internships, study abroad, cross-registration. **Remedial services:** Remedial instruction, tutoring. **Placement/credit:** AP, CLEP General and Subject, institutional tests; 30 credit hours maximum for associate degree.

ACADEMIC REQUIREMENTS. Freshmen must earn minimum GPA of 1.7 to continue in good standing. 50% of freshmen return for sophomore year. **Graduation requirements:** Most students required to take courses in computer science, English, humanities, mathematics, biological/physical sciences, social sciences.

FRESHMAN ADMISSIONS. Selection criteria: Open admissions.

1992 FRESHMAN CLASS PROFILE. 1,103 men and women enrolled. **Characteristics:** 99% from in state, 100% commute, 9% have minority backgrounds.

FALL-TERM APPLICATIONS. $10 fee, may be waived for applicants with need. No closing date; applicants notified on a rolling basis beginning on or about March 30.

STUDENT LIFE. Activities: Student government, student newspaper, yearbook, drama, international club, minority organization, Spanish American Association, Afro-American Association.

ATHLETICS. Intercollegiate: Basketball M, golf M. **Intramural:** Basketball, golf, skiing, soccer, volleyball.

STUDENT SERVICES. Career counseling, employment service for undergraduates, freshman orientation, on-campus day care, personal counseling, placement service for graduates, special adviser for adult students, veterans counselor, women's center, services/facilities for handicapped.

ANNUAL EXPENSES. Tuition and fees: $1,398, $624 additional for out-of-district students, $2,808 additional for out-of-state students. **Books and supplies:** $450. **Other expenses:** $400.

FINANCIAL AID. 40% of freshmen, 40% of continuing students receive some form of aid. All grants, 96% of loans, all jobs based on need. **Aid applications:** No closing date; applicants notified on a rolling basis; must reply within 2 weeks.

ADDRESS/TELEPHONE. Barbara Segal, Director of Marketing and Recruitment, Three Rivers Community-Technical College, Mahan Drive, Norwich, CT 06360-2479. (203) 886-1931. Fax: (203) 886-0691.

Trinity College
Hartford, Connecticut — CB code: 3899

Admissions:	61% of applicants accepted
Based on:	••• School record
	•• Activities, essay, recommendations, special talents, test scores
	• Interview
Completion:	95% of freshmen end year in good standing
	88% graduate

4-year private liberal arts college, coed. Founded in 1823. **Accreditation:** Regional. **Undergraduate enrollment:** 912 men, 852 women full time; 88 men, 163 women part time. **Graduate enrollment:** 102 men, 103 women part time. **Faculty:** 214 total (152 full time), 186 with doctorates or other terminal degrees. **Location:** Urban campus in large city; 125 miles from New York City, 100 miles from Boston. **Calendar:** Semester, limited summer session. **Microcomputers:** 120 located in libraries, classrooms, computer centers, campus-wide network. **Special facilities:** Watkinson Library collections on Native Americans, maritime history, early American texts, and Mark Twain.

DEGREES OFFERED. BA, BS, MA, MS. 477 bachelor's degrees awarded in 1992. 9% in area and ethnic studies, 12% letters/literature, 5% life sciences, 5% multi/interdisciplinary studies, 5% philosophy, religion, theology, 5% psychology, 44% social sciences, 5% visual and performing arts. Graduate degrees offered in 7 major fields of study.

UNDERGRADUATE MAJORS. African studies, Afro-American (black) studies, American studies, art history, Asian studies, biochemistry, biological and physical sciences, biology, chemistry, classics, comparative literature, computer and information sciences, dance, dramatic arts, economics, engineering, English, English literature, environmental science, French, German, history, Italian, Jewish studies, Latin American studies, mathematics, music, neurosciences, philosophy, physical sciences, physics, political science and government, psychology, public policy studies, religion, Russian, Russian and Slavic studies, sociology, Spanish, studio art, urban studies, women's studies.

ACADEMIC PROGRAMS. Accelerated program, double major, independent study, internships, student-designed major, study abroad, visiting/exchange student program, New York semester, Washington semester, cross-registration. **Remedial services:** Reduced course load, special counselor, tutoring, writing and mathematics centers. **Placement/credit:** AP, institutional tests.

ACADEMIC REQUIREMENTS. Freshmen must earn minimum GPA of 1.7 to continue in good standing. 95% of freshmen return for sophomore year. Students must declare major by end of second year. **Graduation requirements:** Most students required to take courses in arts/fine arts, humanities, mathematics, biological/physical sciences, social sciences.

FRESHMAN ADMISSIONS. Selection criteria: School record and recommendations are most important. **High school preparation:** 16 units required. Required units include English 4, foreign language 2, mathematics 3 and science 1. One U.S. history also required. **Test requirements:** SAT or ACT; score report by February 1. ACH in English Composition required. Score report by February 1.

1992 FRESHMAN CLASS PROFILE. 1,512 men applied, 886 accepted, 233 enrolled; 1,339 women applied, 845 accepted, 242 enrolled. **Academic background:** Mid 50% of enrolled freshmen had SAT-V between 520-610, SAT-M between 560-660; ACT composite between 23-29. 91% submitted SAT scores, 9% submitted ACT scores. **Characteristics:** 19% from in state, 98% live in college housing, 16% have minority backgrounds, 2% are foreign students. Average age is 18.

FALL-TERM APPLICATIONS. $45 fee, may be waived for applicants with need. Closing date January 15; applicants notified on or about April 5; must reply by May 1. Essay required. Interview recommended. CRDA. Deferred and early admission available. Institutional early decision plan.

STUDENT LIFE. Housing: Dormitories (coed); fraternity, sorority housing available. **Activities:** Student government, magazine, radio, student newspaper, yearbook, choral groups, dance, drama, jazz band, music ensembles, musical theater, gospel choir, fraternities, sororities, Hillel, Newman Club, Christian Fellowship, Pan-African Alliance, La Voz Latina, Asian organization, community outreach.

ATHLETICS. NCAA. **Intercollegiate:** Baseball M, basketball, cross-country, diving, fencing, field hockey W, football M, golf M, horseback riding, ice hockey M, lacrosse, rowing (crew), rugby, skiing, soccer, softball W, squash, swimming, tennis, track and field, volleyball, water polo, wrestling M. **Intramural:** Badminton, basketball, field hockey W, lacrosse, soccer, softball, tennis, volleyball.

STUDENT SERVICES. Aptitude testing, career counseling, employment service for undergraduates, freshman orientation, health services, on-campus day care, personal counseling, placement service for graduates, special adviser for adult students, services/facilities for handicapped.

ANNUAL EXPENSES. Tuition and fees: $18,700. **Room and board:** $5,420. **Books and supplies:** $500. **Other expenses:** $680.

FINANCIAL AID. 46% of freshmen, 42% of continuing students receive some form of aid. All grants, 95% of loans, all jobs based on need. 231 enrolled freshmen were judged to have need, all were offered aid. **Aid applications:** Closing date February 1; applicants notified on or about April 1; must reply by May 1.

ADDRESS/TELEPHONE. David M. Borus, Dean of Admissions and Financial Aid, Trinity College, 300 Summit Street, Hartford, CT 06106. (203) 297-2180. Fax: (203) 297-2257.

Tunxis Community-Technical College
Farmington, Connecticut — CB code: 3897

2-year public community college, coed. Founded in 1970. **Accreditation:** Regional. **Undergraduate enrollment:** 373 men, 493 women full time; 891 men, 1,974 women part time. **Faculty:** 175 total (43 full time), 24 with doctorates or other terminal degrees. **Location:** Suburban campus in large town; 15 miles from Hartford. **Calendar:** Semester, limited summer session. **Microcomputers:** 95 located in computer centers.

DEGREES OFFERED. AA, AS. 248 associate degrees awarded in 1992. 32% in business and management, 20% business/office and marketing/distribution, 12% allied health, 22% multi/interdisciplinary studies, 7% parks/recreation, protective services, public affairs, 7% visual and performing arts.

UNDERGRADUATE MAJORS. Accounting, business administration and management, computer and information sciences, criminal justice studies, dental hygiene, family and community services, fashion merchandising, fine arts, graphic design, legal secretary, liberal/general studies, marketing and distribution, marketing management, medical secretary, rehabilitation counseling/services, secretarial and related programs.

ACADEMIC PROGRAMS. Double major, dual enrollment of high school students, internships, cross-registration. **Remedial services:** Learning center, preadmission summer program, reduced course load, remedial instruction, tutoring. **Placement/credit:** CLEP General and Subject, institutional tests; 45 credit hours maximum for associate degree.

ACADEMIC REQUIREMENTS. Freshmen must earn minimum GPA of 1.65 to continue in good standing. 50% of freshmen return for sophomore year. Students must declare major on application. **Graduation requirements:** 60 hours for associate. Most students required to take courses in English, mathematics, biological/physical sciences, social sciences.

FRESHMAN ADMISSIONS. Selection criteria: Open admissions. Selective admissions for dental hygiene program, based on mimimum 2.0 GPA in algebra, biology, and chemistry. **Test requirements:** Dental Hygiene Candidate Admissions Test required of dental hygiene applicants, score report by January 31.

1992 FRESHMAN CLASS PROFILE. 217 men, 310 women enrolled. **Characteristics:** 99% from in state, 100% commute, 8% have minority backgrounds, 1% are foreign students. Average age is 19.

FALL-TERM APPLICATIONS. $10 fee, may be waived for applicants with need. No closing date; applicants notified on a rolling basis. Interview required for dental hygiene, drug and alcohol rehabilitation counselor applicants. Deferred admission available. Dental hygiene program closing date January 1, notification by March 1. Drug and alcohol rehabilitation counselor program closing date February 1.

STUDENT LIFE. Activities: Student government, poetry review, Minority Student Alliance, International Partners, human services club, criminal justice club.

STUDENT SERVICES. Freshman orientation, on-campus day care, personal counseling, services/facilities for handicapped.

ANNUAL EXPENSES. Tuition and fees (1992-93): $1,276, $564 additional for out-of-district students, $2,640 additional for out-of-state students. **Books and supplies:** $420. **Other expenses:** $1,400.

FINANCIAL AID. 20% of freshmen, 25% of continuing students receive some form of aid. 98% of grants, all loans, 61% of jobs based on need. Academic, state/district residency scholarships available. **Aid applications:** No closing date; priority given to applications received by July 1; applicants notified on a rolling basis beginning on or about June 1; must reply within 2 weeks. **Additional information:** Financial aid available to all students showing need. Part-time students encouraged to apply.

ADDRESS/TELEPHONE. Barbara A. Boccaccio, Director of Admissions, Tunxis Community-Technical College, Routes 6 and 177, Farmington, CT 06032-9980. (203) 677-7701. Fax: (203) 676-8906.

United States Coast Guard Academy
New London, Connecticut CB code: 5807

Admissions: 8% of applicants accepted
Based on: ••• Activities, recommendations, school record, special talents, test scores
•• Essay
Completion: 87% of freshmen end year in good standing
65% graduate

4-year public engineering, military college, coed. Founded in 1876. **Accreditation:** Regional. **Undergraduate enrollment:** 790 men, 150 women full time. **Faculty:** 105 total, 29 with doctorates or other terminal degrees. **Location:** Urban campus in small city; 50 miles from Hartford. **Calendar:** Semester, limited summer session. **Microcomputers:** 130 located in dormitories, libraries, classrooms, computer centers, campus-wide network. Lease or purchase required**Special facilities:** Ship model towing tank, Coast Guard museum, ship's bridge simulator. **Additional facts:** Summer professional training aboard sailing ship Eagle and other Coast Guard cutters. Summer training also involves flight operations, damage control, weapons (rifle and pistol), and time spent at Coast Guard Groups/stations.

DEGREES OFFERED. BS. 190 bachelor's degrees awarded in 1992. 10% in business and management, 5% computer sciences, 60% engineering, 5% mathematics, 10% physical sciences, 10% social sciences.

UNDERGRADUATE MAJORS. Business administration and management, civil engineering, Coast Guard science, computer and information sciences, electrical/electronics/communications engineering, marine biology, mathematics, mechanical engineering, naval architecture and marine engineering, physical sciences, political science and government.

ACADEMIC PROGRAMS. Honors program, independent study, visiting/exchange student program, cross-registration. **Remedial services:** Learning center, reduced course load, remedial instruction, special counselor, tutoring. **Placement/credit:** AP, institutional tests.

ACADEMIC REQUIREMENTS. No policy requiring minimum GPA; records of students having academic difficulty are reviewed individually. 86% of freshmen return for sophomore year. Students must declare major on enrollment. **Graduation requirements:** 126 hours for bachelor's. Most students required to take courses in computer science, English, history, humanities, mathematics, biological/physical sciences, social sciences.

FRESHMAN ADMISSIONS. Selection criteria: Nationwide competition in which test scores, high school class rank, recommendations, essay, leadership potential as demonstrated by participation in extracurricular activities, athletics, community affairs, and part-time employment considered. **High school preparation:** 15 units required. Required and recommended units include English 4, mathematics 3-4 and science 2. Mathematics units should include algebra, quadratics, and plane or coordinate geometry or equivalent. **Test requirements:** SAT or ACT; score report by January 15. **Additional information:** 36 positions available at Naval Academy Preparatory School (NAPS) for minority students and Coast Guard (active or reserve) enlisted personnel.

1992 FRESHMAN CLASS PROFILE. 4,924 men applied, 396 accepted, 256 enrolled; 826 women applied, 88 accepted, 54 enrolled. 76% were in top tenth and 97% were in top quarter of graduating class. **Characteristics:** 10% from in state, 100% live in college housing, 20% have minority backgrounds, 2% are foreign students. Average age is 18.

FALL-TERM APPLICATIONS. No fee. Closing date December 15; applicants notified on a rolling basis; must reply by May 1. Essay required. CRDA. Application by November 1 recommended to allow time to complete essays and supplemental forms, obtain teacher recommendations, and schedule required physical.

STUDENT LIFE. Housing: Dormitories (coed). On-campus residence mandatory. **Activities:** Student government, magazine, student newspaper, yearbook, choral groups, concert band, dance, drama, jazz band, marching band, music ensembles, musical theater, pep band, Officers Christian Fellowship, Genesis, Fellowship of Christian Athletes, Big Brothers and Big Sisters, Boy Scouts.

ATHLETICS. NCAA. **Intercollegiate:** Baseball M, basketball, cross-country, diving, football M, rifle, rowing (crew), sailing, soccer M, softball W, swimming M, tennis M, track and field, volleyball W, wrestling M. **Intramural:** Basketball, bowling, football M, golf M, ice hockey M, lacrosse M, racquetball, soccer, softball, tennis, volleyball, water polo M, wrestling M. **Clubs:** Ice hockey(M), rugby(M), bowling(M).

STUDENT SERVICES. Aptitude testing, career counseling, health services, personal counseling, placement service for graduates.

ANNUAL EXPENSES. Tuition and fees (1992-93): $0. Cadets receive a stipend of approximately $6,500 a year plus daily food allowance. Allowance is not wage or salary, but money furnished by the government for uniforms, equipment, textbooks, and incidental expenses during training. Allowances cover all expenses and are disbursed as directed by superintendent. Any funds remaining in account are returned to cadet upon graduation. Enrollment deposit of $1,500 required of freshmen. Waivers available.

ADDRESS/TELEPHONE. Capt. R. W. Thorne, Director of Admissions, United States Coast Guard Academy, 15 Mohegan Avenue, New London, CT 06320-4195. (203) 444-8501. Fax: (203) 444-8289.

University of Bridgeport
Bridgeport, Connecticut CB code: 3914

Admissions: 61% of applicants accepted
Based on: ••• School record, test scores
•• Essay, recommendations
• Activities, interview, special talents
Completion: 71% of freshmen end year in good standing
50% graduate, 16% of these enter graduate study

4-year private university, coed. Founded in 1927. **Accreditation:** Regional. **Undergraduate enrollment:** 162 men, 254 women full time; 145 men, 170 women part time. **Graduate enrollment:** 165 men, 103 women full time; 166 men, 218 women part time. **Faculty:** 226 total (109 full time), 145 with doctorates or other terminal degrees. **Location:** Urban campus in small city; 60 miles from New York City. **Calendar:** Semester, extensive summer session. Extensive evening/early morning classes. **Microcomputers:** 200 located in libraries, classrooms, computer centers. **Special facilities:** Art gallery, theater, cinema studio, recital halls, studios, exhibit rooms. **Additional facts:** Off-campus facility in Stamford, Connecticut.

DEGREES OFFERED. AA, AS, BA, BS, BFA, MA, MS, MBA, EdD, DC. 111 associate degrees awarded in 1992. 22% in business/office and marketing/distribution, 40% allied health, 22% law, 12% social sciences. 407 bachelor's degrees awarded. 21% in business and management, 22% engineering, 24% multi/interdisciplinary studies, 10% visual and performing arts. Graduate degrees offered in 18 major fields of study.

UNDERGRADUATE MAJORS. Associate: Business administration and management, dental hygiene, fashion merchandising, legal assistant/paralegal, liberal/general studies, photographic technology, retailing, visual and performing arts. **Bachelor's:** Accounting, advertising, biology, business administration and management, business and management, business economics, chemistry, cinematography/film, communications, computer and information sciences, computer engineering, dental hygiene, electrical/electronics/communications engineering, English, fashion merchandising, finance, fine arts, graphic design, history, illustration design, industrial design, interior design, international business management, journalism, labor/industrial relations, liberal/general studies, manufacturing engineering, marketing management, mathematics, mechanical engineering, medical laboratory technologies, mental health/human services, motion picture technology, music, photographic technology, physics, political science and government, predentistry, prelaw, premedicine, preveterinary, psychology, respiratory therapy, retailing, visual and performing arts.

ACADEMIC PROGRAMS. Accelerated program, cooperative education, double major, dual enrollment of high school students, external degree, honors program, independent study, internships, student-designed major, study abroad, teacher preparation, visiting/exchange student program, weekend college, New York semester, Washington semester, cross-registration; liberal arts/career combination in engineering, health sciences; combined bachelor's/graduate program in business administration. **Remedial services:** Learning center, preadmission summer program, reduced course load, remedial instruction, special counselor, tutoring, basic studies program. **ROTC:** Army. **Placement/credit:** AP, CLEP Subject, institutional tests; 30 credit hours maximum for associate degree; 30 credit hours maximum for bachelor's degree.

ACADEMIC REQUIREMENTS. Freshmen must earn minimum GPA of 2.0 to continue in good standing. 60% of freshmen return for sophomore year. Students must declare major by end of second year. **Graduation requirements:** 60 hours for associate (30 in major), 120 hours for bachelor's (36 in major). Most students required to take courses in arts/fine arts, English, history, humanities, mathematics, biological/physical sciences, social sciences. **Postgraduate studies:** 65% from 2-year programs enter 4-year programs. 2% enter law school, 1% enter medical school, 5% enter MBA programs, 8% enter other graduate study.

FRESHMAN ADMISSIONS. Selection criteria: School achievement record, test scores, activities, trend of grades, and curriculum in high school. **High school preparation:** 16 units required. Required units include English 4, foreign language 2, mathematics 3, social science 1 and science 1. 4

mathematics and 2 laboratory sciences required for mathematics, science, computer science and engineering applicants. 3 mathematics required for business program. Chemistry required for dental hygiene, 2 social studies for dental hygiene and human services. **Test requirements:** SAT or ACT; score report by August 1. Prueba de Aptitud Academica for Spanish speaking applicants.

1992 FRESHMAN CLASS PROFILE. 209 men applied, 119 accepted, 37 enrolled; 201 women applied, 131 accepted, 35 enrolled. 27% had high school GPA of 3.0 or higher, 73% between 2.0 and 2.99. 13% were in top tenth and 27% were in top quarter of graduating class. **Academic background:** Mid 50% of enrolled freshmen had SAT-V between 350-480, SAT-M between 370-520. 97% submitted SAT scores. **Characteristics:** 50% from in state, 64% commute, 27% have minority backgrounds, 32% are foreign students, 3% join fraternities/sororities. Average age is 18.

FALL-TERM APPLICATIONS. $35 fee, may be waived for applicants with need. Closing date July 1; priority given to applications received by April 1; applicants notified on or about March 1; must reply by May 1 or within 2 weeks if notified thereafter. Audition required for music applicants. Portfolio required for fine arts applicants. Interview recommended for cinema, dental hygiene, basic studies applicants. Essay recommended. Deferred and early admission available.

STUDENT LIFE. Housing: Dormitories (men, women, coed). Dormitories have special facilities (e.g., dark rooms, exercise rooms) arranged by interested groups of students. **Activities:** Student government, film, magazine, radio, student newspaper, yearbook, choral groups, concert band, dance, drama, jazz band, music ensembles, musical theater, symphony orchestra, fraternities, sororities, Interfaith Center, Black Student Alliance, International Relations Club, social service sorority, Newman Center, Hillel, Protestant Fellowship, Women's Forum, Home Base Community Service Project. **Additional information:** Student and dormitory governments plan student life activities.

ATHLETICS. NCAA. **Intercollegiate:** Baseball M, basketball, golf M, gymnastics W, soccer, softball W, tennis, volleyball. **Intramural:** Basketball, ice hockey W, racquetball, soccer, softball, tennis, volleyball.

STUDENT SERVICES. Career counseling, employment service for undergraduates, freshman orientation, health services, personal counseling, placement service for graduates, special adviser for adult students, veterans counselor, minority students adviser, foreign students adviser, services/facilities for handicapped.

ANNUAL EXPENSES. Tuition and fees (1992-93): $12,375. **Room and board:** $6,150. **Books and supplies:** $550. **Other expenses:** $500.

FINANCIAL AID. 100% of freshmen, 71% of continuing students receive some form of aid. 85% of grants, 84% of loans, 36% of jobs based on need. Academic, athletic, leadership, minority scholarships available. **Aid applications:** No closing date; priority given to applications received by April 1; applicants notified on a rolling basis beginning on or about March 1; must reply within 4 weeks.

ADDRESS/TELEPHONE. Barbara L. Maryak, Exec Director of Admissions, University of Bridgeport, 126 Park Avenue/Wahlstrom Library, Bridgeport, CT 06601. (203) 576-4552. (800) 243-9496. Fax: (203) 576-4941.

University of Connecticut

Storrs, Connecticut CB code: 3915

Admissions: 70% of applicants accepted
Based on: ••• School record, test scores
•• Special talents
• Activities, essay, interview, recommendations
Completion: 90% of freshmen end year in good standing
63% graduate, 18% of these enter graduate study

4-year public university, coed. Founded in 1881. **Accreditation:** Regional. **Undergraduate enrollment:** 5,569 men, 5,697 women full time; 420 men, 373 women part time. **Graduate enrollment:** 1,758 men, 1,757 women full time; 1,366 men, 1,459 women part time. **Faculty:** 1,232 total (1,193 full time); 1,072 with doctorates or other terminal degrees. **Location:** Rural campus in large town; 26 miles from Hartford, 80 miles from Boston. **Calendar:** Semester, extensive summer session. **Microcomputers:** 1,800 located in dormitories, libraries, classrooms, computer centers. **Special facilities:** William Benton Museum, Museum of Natural History, Jorgensen Auditorium and Theater, Gampel Athletic Pavilion. **Additional facts:** Students may take freshman and sophomore courses at nonresidential campuses in Groton, Hartford, Stamford, Waterbury, and Torrington.

DEGREES OFFERED. BA, BS, BFA, MA, MS, MBA, MFA, MSW, PhD, DMD, MD, JD. 3,441 bachelor's degrees awarded in 1992. 14% in business and management, 6% communications, 7% engineering, 5% health sciences, 6% home economics, 8% letters/literature, 8% multi/interdisciplinary studies, 7% psychology, 21% social sciences. Graduate degrees offered in 77 major fields of study.

UNDERGRADUATE MAJORS. Accounting, actuarial sciences, agricultural economics, agricultural education, agricultural sciences, agronomy, animal sciences, anthropology, applied mathematics, applied music, art history, biology, biophysics, cell biology, ceramics, chemical engineering, chemistry, civil engineering, classics, computer engineering, cytotechnology, design and technical theatre, dramatic arts, Eastern European studies, economics, electrical/electronics/communications engineering, elementary education, English, family/consumer resource management, finance, food science and nutrition, French, geography, geology, geology and geophysics, German, graphic design, health care administration, history, horticulture, individual and family development, insurance and risk management, Italian, journalism, landscape architecture, Latin American studies, liberal/general studies, linguistics, linguistics and philosophy, management information systems, management science, marketing management, materials engineering, mathematics, mechanical engineering, medical cytogenetic technology, medical laboratory technologies, Middle Eastern studies, music, music education, nursing, nutritional sciences, painting, pathobiology, pharmacy, philosophy, photography, physical education, physical therapy, physics, physiology and neurobiology, physiology, human and animal, political science and government, Portuguese, printmaking, psychology, puppetry, real estate, renewable natural resources, Russian, Russian and Slavic studies, sculpture, secondary education, sociology, Spanish, special education, speech, sports, leisure and exercise science, statistics, theater design, urban studies, women's studies.

ACADEMIC PROGRAMS. Cooperative education, double major, honors program, independent study, internships, student-designed major, study abroad, teacher preparation, urban semester; combined bachelor's/graduate program in business administration. **Remedial services:** Learning center, preadmission summer program, reduced course load, special counselor, tutoring, reading improvement center, speech and hearing clinic. **ROTC:** Air Force, Army. **Placement/credit:** AP, CLEP Subject, IB, institutional tests; 30 credit hours maximum for bachelor's degree.

ACADEMIC REQUIREMENTS. Freshmen must earn minimum GPA of 1.6 first semester, 1.8 second semester. 87% of freshmen return for sophomore year. Students must declare major by end of second year. **Graduation requirements:** 120 hours for bachelor's (36 in major). Most students required to take courses in arts/fine arts, computer science, English, foreign languages, history, humanities, mathematics, philosophy/religion, biological/physical sciences, social sciences.

FRESHMAN ADMISSIONS. Selection criteria: Curriculum, grades, rank in class most important followed by test scores. Consideration given to disadvantaged or minority applicants. **High school preparation:** 16 units required. Required and recommended units include English 4, foreign language 2-3, mathematics 3-4, social science 2 and science 2. 2 other academic units. 2 science units must be laboratory science. Some programs may require units in addition to those listed. **Test requirements:** SAT; score report by April 1. **Additional information:** Out-of-state applicants encouraged.

1992 FRESHMAN CLASS PROFILE. 5,189 men applied, 3,461 accepted, 1,054 enrolled; 5,444 women applied, 3,981 accepted, 1,134 enrolled. **Academic background:** Mid 50% of enrolled freshmen had SAT-V between 430-530, SAT-M between 490-600. 100% submitted SAT scores. **Characteristics:** 75% from in state, 93% live in college housing, 14% have minority backgrounds, 1% are foreign students. Average age is 19.

FALL-TERM APPLICATIONS. $40 fee, may be waived for applicants with need. Closing date April 1; applicants notified on a rolling basis beginning on or about January 15; must reply by May 1. Audition required for music, acting applicants. Interview recommended. Essay recommended. CRDA. Deferred and early admission available.

STUDENT LIFE. Housing: Dormitories (men, women, coed); fraternity, sorority housing available. Foreign language house, Living Learning Center, laboratory science house, designated floors for older students and substance free floor available. **Activities:** Student government, magazine, radio, student newspaper, yearbook, drama, marching band, music ensembles, chamber music, recital series, fraternities, sororities, Young Democrats, Young Republicans, Hillel, Christian organizations, black, Asian, Puerto Rican, and Native American associations, Greek Club, service organizations, international organizations. **Additional information:** Over 200 organizations on campus available for student participation.

ATHLETICS. NCAA. **Intercollegiate:** Baseball M, basketball, cross-country, diving, field hockey W, football M, golf M, ice hockey M, soccer, softball W, swimming, tennis, track and field, volleyball W. **Intramural:** Badminton, baseball M, basketball, bowling, cross-country, diving W, fencing, football M, horseback riding, ice hockey, lacrosse, racquetball, rowing (crew), rugby, sailing, skiing, soccer, softball W, squash, swimming W, table tennis, tennis, track and field, volleyball M, water polo M.

STUDENT SERVICES. Aptitude testing, career counseling, employment service for undergraduates, freshman orientation, health services, on-campus day care, personal counseling, placement service for graduates, veterans counselor, services/facilities for handicapped.

ANNUAL EXPENSES. Tuition and fees (1992-93): $3,902, $6,472 additional for out-of-state students. **Room and board:** $4,878. **Books and supplies:** $570. **Other expenses:** $1,350.

FINANCIAL AID. 35% of freshmen, 50% of continuing students receive some form of aid. All grants, 63% of loans, 37% of jobs based on need. Academic, music/drama, athletic, alumni affiliation, minority scholarships available. **Aid applications:** Closing date May 1; priority given to applications received by February 15; applicants notified on a rolling basis beginning on or about April 1; must reply by May 1 or within 2 weeks if notified thereafter.

ADDRESS/TELEPHONE. Ann Huckenbeck, Director of Admissions, University of Connecticut, PO Box U-88, 28 North Eagleville Road, Storrs, CT 06269-3088. (203) 486-3137. Fax: (203) 486-1476.

University of Hartford
West Hartford, Connecticut — CB code: 3436

Admissions: 85% of applicants accepted
Based on:
••• School record
•• Test scores
• Activities, essay, interview, recommendations, special talents
Completion: 89% of freshmen end year in good standing
58% graduate

4-year private university, coed. Founded in 1877. **Accreditation:** Regional. **Undergraduate enrollment:** 1,920 men, 1,807 women full time; 687 men, 768 women part time. **Graduate enrollment:** 375 men, 333 women full time; 674 men, 776 women part time. **Faculty:** 730 total (354 full time), 256 with doctorates or other terminal degrees. **Location:** Suburban campus in small city; 4 miles from downtown Hartford, 100 miles from New York City and Boston. **Calendar:** Semester, extensive summer session. **Microcomputers:** 455 located in libraries, classrooms, computer centers. **Special facilities:** Talcott Mountain Science Center, Museum of American Poltical Life, engineering applications center, humanities center.

DEGREES OFFERED. AA, AS, AAS, BA, BS, BFA, MA, MS, MBA, MFA, MEd, D. 194 associate degrees awarded in 1992. 5% in engineering technologies, 95% multi/interdisciplinary studies. 1,113 bachelor's degrees awarded. 17% in business and management, 9% business/office and marketing/distribution, 14% communications, 13% engineering, 5% engineering technologies, 5% health sciences, 6% psychology, 5% social sciences, 15% visual and performing arts. Graduate degrees offered in 28 major fields of study.

UNDERGRADUATE MAJORS. Associate: Biology, communications, computer technology, electrical and electronics equipment repair, electronic technology, humanities, legal assistant/paralegal, liberal/general studies, physical sciences, social sciences. **Bachelor's:** Accounting, actuarial sciences, architectural technologies, art history, biology, biology education, business administration and management, business economics, ceramics, chemistry, chemistry education, civil engineering, communications, computer and information sciences, computer engineering, criminal justice studies, criminology, dramatic arts, drawing, early childhood education, economics, electrical/electronics/communications engineering, electronic technology, elementary education, engineering, engineering and other disciplines, English, English education, English literature, finance, foreign languages (multiple emphasis), foreign languages education, French, German, graphic design, health sciences, history, history education, human services, illustration design, information sciences and systems, insurance and risk management, Italian, jazz, Jewish studies, law enforcement and corrections, legal assistant/paralegal, linguistics, management information systems, marketing and distribution, marketing management, mathematics, mechanical engineering, medical laboratory technologies, music, music business management, music education, music history and appreciation, music performance, music theory and composition, musical theater, nursing, occupational therapy, painting, philosophy, photography, physics, physics education, political science and government, predentistry, prelaw, premedicine, printmaking, psychology, public administration, radiograph medical technology, respiratory therapy, science education, sculpture, secondary education, social studies education, sociology, Spanish, special education, studio art, video.

ACADEMIC PROGRAMS. 2-year transfer program, cooperative education, double major, dual enrollment of high school students, honors program, independent study, internships, student-designed major, study abroad, teacher preparation, visiting/exchange student program, Washington semester, cross-registration; liberal arts/career combination in engineering. **Remedial services:** Learning center, preadmission summer program, reduced course load, special counselor, tutoring. **ROTC:** Air Force, Army. **Placement/credit:** AP, CLEP General and Subject, institutional tests; 30 credit hours maximum for associate degree; 60 credit hours maximum for bachelor's degree.

ACADEMIC REQUIREMENTS. Freshmen must earn minimum GPA of 1.7 to continue in good standing. 75% of freshmen return for sophomore year. Students must declare major by end of second year. **Graduation requirements:** 60 hours for associate, 120 hours for bachelor's. Most students required to take courses in arts/fine arts, computer science, English, humanities, mathematics, biological/physical sciences, social sciences. **Postgraduate studies:** 85% from 2-year programs enter 4-year programs.

FRESHMAN ADMISSIONS. Selection criteria: Quality of academic program, school achievement record, class rank important. Test scores secondary. Employment, extracurricular activities, and community service considered. Writing samples and interview also considered. **High school preparation:** 16 units required. Required and recommended units include English 4, foreign language 2, mathematics 2-3, social science 2-3 and science 2. Biological science 1 and physical science 2 recommended. Physics, chemistry, and 3.5 mathematics (including trigonometry) recommended for engineering and science applicants. **Test requirements:** SAT or ACT; score report by March 1. **Additional information:** Admission committee can offer admission to alternative program.

1992 FRESHMAN CLASS PROFILE. 2,351 men applied, 2,002 accepted, 512 enrolled; 2,398 women applied, 2,016 accepted, 442 enrolled. **Academic background:** Mid 50% of enrolled freshmen had SAT-V between 400-500, SAT-M between 440-560. 95% submitted SAT scores. **Characteristics:** 29% from in state, 92% live in college housing, 15% have minority backgrounds, 4% are foreign students, 12% join fraternities/sororities. Average age is 18.

FALL-TERM APPLICATIONS. $35 fee, may be waived for applicants with need. No closing date; priority given to applications received by February 1; applicants notified on a rolling basis; must reply by May 1 or within 2 weeks if notified thereafter. Audition required for music applicants. Portfolio required for art applicants. Interview recommended. Essay recommended. CRDA. Deferred and early admission available. English Composition ACH recommended, especially if SAT verbal score is low.

STUDENT LIFE. Housing: Dormitories (men, women, coed); apartment, handicapped housing available. Special dormitories for students with resident faculty members; students selected on basis of academic achievement. New residence halls have suites and apartments, some with cooking facilities. **Activities:** Student government, film, magazine, radio, student newspaper, television, yearbook, art magazine, choral groups, concert band, dance, drama, jazz band, music ensembles, musical theater, opera, pep band, symphony orchestra, fraternities, sororities, Hillel Foundation, Protestant Student Organization, Newman Club, African-American Students Association, academic department clubs, prelaw and premedical societies.

ATHLETICS. NCAA. **Intercollegiate:** Baseball M, basketball, cross-country, golf, lacrosse M, soccer, softball W, tennis, volleyball W. **Intramural:** Basketball, racquetball, soccer, softball, tennis, volleyball, water polo.

STUDENT SERVICES. Aptitude testing, career counseling, employment service for undergraduates, freshman orientation, health services, personal counseling, placement service for graduates, veterans counselor, off-campus daycare, services/facilities for handicapped.

ANNUAL EXPENSES. Tuition and fees: $14,260. **Room and board:** $5,598. **Books and supplies:** $400. **Other expenses:** $424.

FINANCIAL AID. 54% of freshmen, 48% of continuing students receive some form of aid. 79% of grants, 96% of loans, 47% of jobs based on need. 730 enrolled freshmen were judged to have need, 680 were offered aid. Academic, music/drama, art, athletic, state/district residency scholarships available. **Aid applications:** No closing date; priority given to applications received by March 1; applicants notified on a rolling basis beginning on or about March 15; must reply by May 1 or within 2 weeks if notified thereafter.

ADDRESS/TELEPHONE. Richard A. Zeiser, Director of Admission, University of Hartford, Bates House, West Hartford, CT 06117-0395. (203) 768-4296. (800) 947-4303. Fax: (203) 768-4961.

University of New Haven
West Haven, Connecticut — CB code: 3663

Admissions: 84% of applicants accepted
Based on:
••• School record
•• Activities, recommendations, test scores
• Essay, interview, special talents
Completion: 85% of freshmen end year in good standing
50% graduate, 3% of these enter graduate study

4-year private university, coed. Founded in 1920. **Accreditation:** Regional. **Undergraduate enrollment:** 1,014 men, 412 women full time; 1,341 men, 637 women part time. **Graduate enrollment:** 265 men, 161 women full time; 1,326 men, 760 women part time. **Faculty:** 401 total (151 full time), 125 with doctorates or other terminal degrees. **Location:** Suburban campus in small city; 3 miles from center of New Haven. **Calendar:** 4-1-4, limited summer session. Extensive evening/early morning classes. **Microcomputers:** 140 located in libraries, classrooms, computer centers. **Special facilities:** Art gallery, theater. **Additional facts:** Branch campus in Groton serves approximately 1000 part-time undergraduate and graduate students. Graduate courses also offered at several off-campus sites.

DEGREES OFFERED. AS, BA, BS, MA, MS, MBA, D. 65 associate degrees awarded in 1992. 485 bachelor's degrees awarded. Graduate degrees offered in 32 major fields of study.

UNDERGRADUATE MAJORS. Associate: Airline piloting and navigation, biology, business administration and management, civil engineering, communications, computer and information sciences, criminal justice studies, electrical/electronics/communications engineering, environmental science, fire control and safety technology, graphic design, hotel/motel and restaurant management, industrial engineering, interior design, journalism, law enforcement and corrections, legal assistant/paralegal, liberal/general studies, materials technology, mechanical engineering, occupational safety and health technology, photography, tourism. **Bachelor's:** Accounting, air transportation management, applied mathematics, aviation management, biology, biomedical computing, business administration and management, business and management, business economics, chemical engineering, chemistry, civil engineering, clinical psychology, communications, computer and information sciences, computer programming, criminal justice studies, economics, electrical/electronics/communications engineering, English, English literature, environmental science, finance, fine arts, fire control and safety technology, fire protection, food science and nutrition, forensic studies, graphic design, health care administration, history, hotel/motel and restaurant management, human resources development, industrial and organizational psychology, industrial engineering, information sciences and systems, interior design, international business management, journalism, law enforcement and corrections, management information systems, marketing and distribution, marketing management, materials technology, mathematics, mechanical engineering, microbiology, music and sound recording, occupational safety and health technology, photography, political science and government, prearchitecture, predentistry, prelaw, premedicine, preveterinary, psychology, public administration, public relations, security management, social work, sociology, sports management, tourism, visual and performing arts.

ACADEMIC PROGRAMS. 2-year transfer program, accelerated program, cooperative education, double major, dual enrollment of high school students, honors program, independent study, internships, student-designed major, cross-registration. **Remedial services:** Learning center, preadmission summer program, reduced course load, remedial instruction, special counselor, tutoring. **Placement/credit:** AP, CLEP General and Subject, institutional tests.

ACADEMIC REQUIREMENTS. Freshmen must earn minimum GPA of 1.5 to continue in good standing. 74% of freshmen return for sophomore year. Students must declare major by end of second year. **Graduation requirements:** 60 hours for associate (12 in major), 120 hours for bachelor's (33 in major). Most students required to take courses in arts/fine arts, computer science, English, history, humanities, mathematics, philosophy/religion, biological/physical sciences, social sciences. **Postgraduate studies:** 70% from 2-year programs enter 4-year programs. **Additional information:** Unlimited number of hours of credit available by AP Examinations, military experience, and life experience provided 30 hours in residency is achieved.

FRESHMAN ADMISSIONS. Selection criteria: Academic record, recommendations, test scores, class rank, and extracurricular activities reviewed. **High school preparation:** 16 units recommended. Required and recommended units include English 4. Biological science 1, foreign language 2, mathematics 3, physical science 1 and social science 2 recommended. **Test requirements:** SAT or ACT (SAT preferred); score report by August 15.

1992 FRESHMAN CLASS PROFILE. 2,349 men and women applied, 1,976 accepted; 317 men enrolled, 107 women enrolled. **Characteristics:** 61% from in state, 55% live in college housing, 12% have minority backgrounds, 1% are foreign students, 5% join fraternities/sororities. Average age is 18.

FALL-TERM APPLICATIONS. $25 fee, may be waived for applicants with need. Closing date August 15; applicants notified on a rolling basis; must reply by May 1 or within 2 weeks if notified thereafter. Interview recommended. Portfolio recommended for art applicants. CRDA. Deferred admission available.

STUDENT LIFE. Housing: Dormitories (coed); apartment housing available. Freshman dormitory arranged in suites. Students in freshman dormitory must be on meal plan. **Activities:** Student government, magazine, radio, student newspaper, yearbook, drama, pep band, fraternities, sororities, black student union, pilots' association, international relations club, political science and prelaw club, international student association.

ATHLETICS. NCAA. **Intercollegiate:** Baseball M, basketball, cross-country M, football M, lacrosse M, soccer, softball W, tennis W, track and field, volleyball W. **Intramural:** Badminton, basketball, bowling, cross-country M, lacrosse M, racquetball, soccer, softball, table tennis, tennis, volleyball.

STUDENT SERVICES. Aptitude testing, career counseling, employment service for undergraduates, freshman orientation, health services, personal counseling, placement service for graduates, special adviser for adult students, veterans counselor, student affairs offices for minority, disabled students, and international students, services/facilities for handicapped.

ANNUAL EXPENSES. Tuition and fees: $10,180. **Room and board:** $4,990. **Books and supplies:** $500. **Other expenses:** $1,000.

FINANCIAL AID. 65% of freshmen, 65% of continuing students receive some form of aid. 75% of grants, 89% of loans, 90% of jobs based on need. Academic, athletic scholarships available. **Aid applications:** No closing date; priority given to applications received by March 15; applicants notified on a rolling basis beginning on or about April 1; must reply by May 1 or within 3 weeks if notified thereafter. **Additional information:** Tuition-free program for selected outstanding high school seniors.

ADDRESS/TELEPHONE. Steven Briggs, Dean of Undergraduate Admissions and Financial Aid, University of New Haven, 300 Orange Avenue, West Haven, CT 06516. (203) 932-7319. (800) DIAL-UNH.

Wesleyan University
Middletown, Connecticut

CB code: 3959

Admissions: 40% of applicants accepted
Based on:
- ••• School record
- •• Activities, essay, recommendations, special talents, test scores
- • Interview

Completion: 97% of freshmen end year in good standing
92% graduate, 27% of these enter graduate study

4-year private university and liberal arts college, coed. Founded in 1831. **Accreditation:** Regional. **Undergraduate enrollment:** 1,339 men, 1,356 women full time; 9 men, 20 women part time. **Graduate enrollment:** 104 men, 94 women full time; 151 men, 258 women part time. **Faculty:** 347 total (292 full time). **Location:** Suburban campus in large town; 15 miles from Hartford, 25 miles from New Haven. **Calendar:** Semester, limited summer session. **Microcomputers:** 300 located in libraries, classrooms, computer centers. **Special facilities:** 11-building arts center, Van Vleck observatory, science center with electron microscopes and nuclear magnetic resonance spectrometers, Freeman Athletic Center, film archives, Center for Humanities, East Asian Studies Center, Center for Afro-American Studies.

DEGREES OFFERED. BA, MA, PhD. 703 bachelor's degrees awarded in 1992. 16% in letters/literature, 8% life sciences, 5% multi/interdisciplinary studies, 6% philosophy, religion, theology, 5% physical sciences, 6% psychology, 31% social sciences, 12% visual and performing arts. Graduate degrees offered in 16 major fields of study.

UNDERGRADUATE MAJORS. African studies, Afro-American (black) studies, American literature, American studies, anthropology, archeology, architecture, art history, Asian studies, astronomy, astrophysics, behavioral sciences, biochemistry, biological and physical sciences, biology, biopsychology, cell biology, chemistry, Chinese, cinematography/film, classics, cognitive psychology, comparative literature, comparative psychology, computer and information sciences, creative writing, dance, developmental psychology, dramatic arts, earth sciences, East Asian studies, ecology, economics, engineering and other disciplines, English, English literature, environmental science, European studies, experimental psychology, fine arts, French, genetics, human and animal, geology, German, Greek (classical), Hebrew, history, humanities, humanities and social sciences, inorganic chemistry, international relations, Italian, Japanese, Jewish studies, Latin, Latin American studies, liberal/general studies, linguistics, mathematics, medieval studies, Middle Eastern studies, molecular biology, music, music history and appreciation, oceanography, organic chemistry, philosophy, photography, physical chemistry, physics, physiological psychology, political science and government, prelaw, premedicine, psychobiology, psycholinguistics, psychology, public policy studies, pure mathematics, religion, Russian, Russian and Slavic studies, social psychology, social sciences, sociology, Spanish, statistics, studio art, urban studies, visual and performing arts, women's studies.

ACADEMIC PROGRAMS. Accelerated program, double major, honors program, independent study, internships, semester at sea, student-designed major, study abroad, teacher preparation, visiting/exchange student program, Washington semester, cross-registration, 12-College Exchange; liberal arts/career combination in engineering, health sciences. **Remedial services:** Reduced course load, special counselor, tutoring, mathematics clinic, writing workshop, preadmission summer science enrichment program. **Placement/credit:** AP, institutional tests.

ACADEMIC REQUIREMENTS. No policy requiring minimum GPA; records of students having academic difficulty are reviewed individually. 98% of freshmen return for sophomore year. Students must declare major by end of second year. **Graduation requirements:** 120 hours for bachelor's (35 in major). **Postgraduate studies:** 7% enter law school, 5% enter medical school, 5% enter MBA programs, 10% enter other graduate study. **Additional information:** Students expected to complete 3 classes in each of following areas before graduation: natural sciences and mathematics, arts and humanities, social and behavioral sciences. Teacher certification available in many subject areas.

FRESHMAN ADMISSIONS. Selection criteria: High school transcript, class rank, test scores, extracurricular activities, teacher evaluations, 2 application essays, and other evidence of outstanding accomplishments considered. **High school preparation:** 16 units required; 20 recommended. Required and recommended units include English 4, foreign language 3-4, mathematics 3-4, social science 3-4 and science 3-4. **Test requirements:** SAT or ACT; score report by January 15. 3 ACH (including English Composition) required of applicants who do not submit ACT scores. Score report by January 15.

1992 FRESHMAN CLASS PROFILE. 2,156 men applied, 878 accepted, 345 enrolled; 2,641 women applied, 1,061 accepted, 361 enrolled. **Academic background:** Mid 50% of enrolled freshmen had SAT-V between 580-680, SAT-M between 630-730. 95% submitted SAT scores. **Characteristics:** 10% from in state, 100% live in college housing, 32% have minority backgrounds, 2% are foreign students. Average age is 18.

FALL-TERM APPLICATIONS. $50 fee, may be waived for applicants with need. Closing date January 15; applicants notified on or about April 15;

must reply by May 1. Essay required. Interview recommended. CRDA. Deferred and early admission available. EDP-F.

STUDENT LIFE. Housing: Dormitories (men, women, coed); apartment, fraternity, sorority, cooperative housing available. **Activities:** Student government, film, magazine, radio, student newspaper, yearbook, choral groups, concert band, dance, drama, jazz band, music ensembles, musical theater, pep band, symphony orchestra, gamelan, African music and dance ensemble, fraternities, sororities, more than 125 religious, political, ethnic, and social service organizations.

ATHLETICS. NCAA. **Intercollegiate:** Baseball M, basketball, cross-country, diving, field hockey W, football M, golf M, horseback riding, ice hockey, lacrosse, rowing (crew), rugby, soccer, softball W, squash, swimming, tennis, track and field, volleyball W, water polo, wrestling M. **Intramural:** Basketball, cross-country, fencing, handball, ice hockey, racquetball, sailing, skiing, soccer, softball, squash, swimming, table tennis, tennis, volleyball.

STUDENT SERVICES. Aptitude testing, career counseling, employment service for undergraduates, freshman orientation, health services, personal counseling, placement service for graduates, special adviser for adult students, services/facilities for handicapped.

ANNUAL EXPENSES. Tuition and fees: $18,780. **Room and board:** $5,390. **Books and supplies:** $500. **Other expenses:** $850.

FINANCIAL AID. 51% of freshmen, 45% of continuing students receive some form of aid. All grants, 99% of loans, all jobs based on need. 363 enrolled freshmen were judged to have need, all were offered aid. **Aid applications:** Closing date January 15; applicants notified on or about April 15; Must reply by May 1 or within 15 days if notified thereafter.

ADDRESS/TELEPHONE. Barbara-Jan Wilson, Dean of Admissions and Financial Aid, Wesleyan University, High Street and Wyllys Avenue, Middletown, CT 06457. (203) 344-7900.

Western Connecticut State University
Danbury, Connecticut

CB code: 3350

4-year public university, coed. Founded in 1903. **Accreditation:** Regional. **Undergraduate enrollment:** 4,669 men and women. **Graduate enrollment:** 1,061 men and women. **Faculty:** 326 total (176 full time), 111 with doctorates or other terminal degrees. **Location:** Urban campus in small city; 68 miles from New York City, 58 miles from Hartford. **Calendar:** Semester, extensive summer session. **Microcomputers:** Located in libraries, computer centers. **Special facilities:** Weather station, motorized astronomical observatory.

DEGREES OFFERED. AS, BA, BS, MA, MS, MBA. 371 bachelor's degrees awarded. Graduate degrees offered in 21 major fields of study.

UNDERGRADUATE MAJORS. Associate: Criminal justice studies, law enforcement and corrections, liberal/general studies, social sciences. **Bachelor's:** Accounting, American studies, anthropology, astronomy, atmospheric sciences and meteorology, biology, chemistry, clinical laboratory science, communications, computer and information sciences, criminal justice studies, dramatic arts, earth sciences, economics, elementary education, English, English education, environmental science, finance, fine arts, foreign languages education, graphic design, health education, history, law enforcement and corrections, liberal/general studies, library science, management information systems, marketing management, mathematics, mathematics education, medical laboratory technologies, music, music education, music theory and composition, nursing, political science and government, psychology, secondary education, social science education, social sciences, social studies education, social work, sociology, Spanish, speech correction.

ACADEMIC PROGRAMS. Accelerated program, cooperative education, double major, dual enrollment of high school students, honors program, independent study, internships, student-designed major, study abroad, teacher preparation, cross-registration; liberal arts/career combination in engineering. **Remedial services:** Learning center, preadmission summer program, reduced course load, remedial instruction, tutoring. **ROTC:** Air Force, Army. **Placement/credit:** AP, CLEP General and Subject, institutional tests; 30 credit hours maximum for associate degree; 60 credit hours maximum for bachelor's degree.

ACADEMIC REQUIREMENTS. Freshmen must earn minimum GPA of 2.0 to continue in good standing. 62% of freshmen return for sophomore year. Students must declare major by end of second year. **Graduation requirements:** 60 hours for associate (24 in major), 120 hours for bachelor's (30 in major). Most students required to take courses in arts/fine arts, computer science, English, foreign languages, history, humanities, mathematics, philosophy/religion, biological/physical sciences, social sciences. **Postgraduate studies:** 94% from 2-year programs enter 4-year programs. 2% enter law school, 1% enter medical school, 8% enter MBA programs, 8% enter other graduate study.

FRESHMAN ADMISSIONS. Selection criteria: Limited freshman class spaces given to students with strongest academic and extracurricular backgrounds, including SAT or ACT test results. Children of alumni, minority, and low-income applicants also given special consideration. **High school preparation:** 16 units required. Required and recommended units include biological science 1, English 4, foreign language 3-4, mathematics 3-4, physical science 1 and social science 3. Fine arts or computer science strongly recommended. **Test requirements:** SAT or ACT (SAT preferred); score report by March 1. **Additional information:** Freshman class will be filled on a "first-come" basis by major.

1992 FRESHMAN CLASS PROFILE. 384 men and women enrolled. 78% had high school GPA of 3.0 or higher, 22% between 2.0 and 2.99. **Characteristics:** 89% from in state, 51% live in college housing, 15% have minority backgrounds, 1% are foreign students, 3% join fraternities/sororities. Average age is 18.

FALL-TERM APPLICATIONS. $20 fee, may be waived for applicants with need. Closing date April 1; priority given to applications received by January 1; applicants notified on a rolling basis beginning on or about December 1; must reply by May 1 or within 2 weeks if notified thereafter. Audition required for music applicants. Portfolio recommended for graphic design applicants. Essay recommended. Deferred and early admission available. Institutional early decision plan.

STUDENT LIFE. Housing: Dormitories (women, coed); apartment, handicapped housing available. On campus housing is assigned on a first-come basis. **Activities:** Student government, film, magazine, radio, student newspaper, television, yearbook, choral groups, concert band, dance, drama, jazz band, marching band, music ensembles, musical theater, pep band, symphony orchestra, fraternities, sororities, Black Student Alliance, religious groups, nontraditional student and international student association.

ATHLETICS. NCAA. **Intercollegiate:** Baseball M, basketball, fencing, field hockey W, football M, golf M, soccer M, softball W, tennis, volleyball W. **Intramural:** Archery, badminton, basketball, bowling, cross-country, lacrosse M, rifle, skiing, softball, table tennis, tennis, volleyball.

STUDENT SERVICES. Aptitude testing, career counseling, employment service for undergraduates, freshman orientation, health services, personal counseling, placement service for graduates, special adviser for adult students, veterans counselor, services/facilities for handicapped.

ANNUAL EXPENSES. Tuition and fees: $2,887, $3,924 additional for out-of-state students. **Room and board:** $3,722. **Books and supplies:** $700. **Other expenses:** $1,149.

FINANCIAL AID. 65% of freshmen, 54% of continuing students receive some form of aid. 95% of grants, 99% of loans, 10% of jobs based on need. Academic scholarships available. **Aid applications:** Closing date March 15; applicants notified on a rolling basis; must reply by May 1 or within 2 weeks if notified thereafter.

ADDRESS/TELEPHONE. Delmore Kinney Jr, Director of Admissions, Western Connecticut State University, 181 White Street, Danbury, CT 06810. (203) 797-4298. Fax: (203) 731-2804.

Yale University
New Haven, Connecticut

CB code: 3987

Admissions:	22% of applicants accepted
Based on:	••• Activities, recommendations, school record, test scores
	•• Essay, special talents
	• Interview
Completion:	98% of freshmen end year in good standing
	93% graduate, 27% of these enter graduate study

4-year private university, coed. Founded in 1701. **Accreditation:** Regional. **Undergraduate enrollment:** 2,841 men, 2,353 women full time; 35 men, 58 women part time. **Graduate enrollment:** 3,035 men, 2,385 women full time; 84 men, 159 women part time. **Faculty:** 2,624 total (2,287 full time). **Location:** Urban campus in small city; 75 miles from New York City. **Calendar:** Semester, limited summer session. **Microcomputers:** Located in dormitories, libraries, classrooms, computer centers. **Special facilities:** Art galleries, museums, sailing center, observatory.

DEGREES OFFERED. BA, BS, MA, MS, PhD, MD, JD, M.Div. 1,305 bachelor's degrees awarded in 1992. 8% in area and ethnic studies, 13% letters/literature, 11% life sciences, 6% multi/interdisciplinary studies, 6% psychology, 32% social sciences, 5% visual and performing arts. Graduate degrees offered in 71 major fields of study.

UNDERGRADUATE MAJORS. African studies, Afro-American (black) studies, American studies, anthropology, applied mathematics, applied physics, archeology, architecture, art history, astronomy, biochemistry, biological and physical sciences, biology, biophysics, chemical engineering, chemistry, Chinese, classics, comparative literature, computer and information sciences, computer science/psychology, dramatic arts, East Asian studies, Eastern European studies, economics, economics/mathematics, economics/political science, electrical/electronics/communications engineering, engineering, engineering and other disciplines, engineering science, English literature, environmental studies, ethics politics/economics, film arts, fine arts, foreign languages (multiple emphasis), French, geology, geophysics and seismology, German, Germanic studies, Greek (classical), history, history of science/medicine, humanities, humanities and social sciences, international relations, Italian, Japanese, Jewish studies, Latin, Latin American studies, linguistics, mathematics, mathematics/computer science, mathematics/philosophy, mathematics/physics, mechanical engineering, molecular biology, music, organismal biology, philosophy, physics, physics/philosophy, political science and government, psychology, religion, renaissance studies, Russian, Russian and Slavic studies, sociology, Spanish, women's studies.

ACADEMIC PROGRAMS. Accelerated program, double major, honors program, independent study, student-designed major, study abroad, teacher preparation. **ROTC:** Air Force, Army. **Placement/credit:** AP, institutional tests.

ACADEMIC REQUIREMENTS. No policy requiring minimum GPA; records of students having academic difficulty are reviewed individually. Freshmen must pass 4 term courses during first semester and total of 8 term courses during academic year to continue in good academic standing. 98% of freshmen return for sophomore year. Students must declare major by end of second year. **Graduation requirements:** Most students required to take courses in foreign languages, humanities, biological/physical sciences, social sciences. **Postgraduate studies:** 5% enter law school, 8% enter medical school, 14% enter other graduate study.

FRESHMAN ADMISSIONS. Selection criteria: First criterion is evidence of ability to do successful academic work. Diversity of interests, background, and special talents also sought. Successful candidates usually have done honors work at the secondary level, have SAT verbal and mathematical scores in the 500-800 range, and present high degree of accomplishment in a nonacademic area. No prescribed high school program required, but students recommended to take richest possible mix of academic offerings. **Test requirements:** SAT or ACT; score report by March 1. 3 ACH required. Score report by March 1.

1992 FRESHMAN CLASS PROFILE. 5,924 men applied, 1,272 accepted, 686 enrolled; 5,130 women applied, 1,183 accepted, 641 enrolled. **Academic background:** Mid 50% of enrolled freshmen had SAT-V between 600-700, SAT-M between 650-740. 100% submitted SAT scores. **Characteristics:** 9% from in state, 100% live in college housing, 31% have minority backgrounds, 3% are foreign students. Average age is 18.

FALL-TERM APPLICATIONS. $60 fee, may be waived for applicants with need. Closing date December 31; applicants notified on or about April 15; must reply by May 1. Essay required. Interview recommended. CRDA. Deferred and early admission available. Nonbinding Early Action program available; closing date for Early Action applications November 1, notification in mid-December.

STUDENT LIFE. Housing: Dormitories (coed). **Activities:** Student government, film, magazine, radio, student newspaper, yearbook, choral groups, concert band, dance, drama, jazz band, marching band, music ensembles, musical theater, opera, pep band, symphony orchestra, Guild of Carilloneurs, fraternities, sororities, more than 21 religious organizations, 21 political organizations, 12 ethnic organizations, 16 social service organizations. **Additional information:** Undergraduates assigned to 1 of 12 residential colleges, each with full program of extracurricular activities.

ATHLETICS. NCAA. **Intercollegiate:** Baseball M, basketball, cross-country, diving, fencing, field hockey W, football M, golf, gymnastics W, ice hockey, lacrosse, rowing (crew), soccer, softball W, squash, swimming, tennis, track and field, volleyball W. **Intramural:** Baseball M, basketball, bowling, cross-country, field hockey, football M, golf, ice hockey, racquetball, rowing (crew), skiing M, soccer, softball, squash, swimming, table tennis, tennis, volleyball, water polo, wrestling M.

STUDENT SERVICES. Career counseling, employment service for undergraduates, freshman orientation, health services, personal counseling, placement service for graduates, services/facilities for handicapped.

ANNUAL EXPENSES. Tuition and fees: $18,630. **Room and board:** $6,480. **Books and supplies:** $620. **Other expenses:** $1,400.

FINANCIAL AID. 46% of freshmen, 44% of continuing students receive some form of aid. All grants, 99% of loans, 46% of jobs based on need. 639 enrolled freshmen were judged to have need, all were offered aid. **Aid applications:** Closing date February 1; applicants notified on or about April 1; must reply by May 1. **Additional information:** All financial aid is awarded based on demonstrated need, except for campus jobs which are available to all students.

ADDRESS/TELEPHONE. Richard H. Shaw, Jr, Dean of Undergraduate Admissions, Yale University, PO Box 1502A Yale Station, New Haven, CT 06520. (203) 432-1900.

Delaware

Delaware State College

Dover, Delaware CB code: 5153

Admissions: 74% of applicants accepted
Based on: ••• School record, test scores
•• Recommendations
• Activities, interview
Completion: 62% of freshmen end year in good standing
23% graduate, 15% of these enter graduate study

4-year public liberal arts college, coed. Founded in 1891. **Accreditation:** Regional. **Undergraduate enrollment:** 1,001 men, 1,198 women full time; 183 men, 313 women part time. **Graduate enrollment:** 17 men, 48 women full time; 59 men, 116 women part time. **Faculty:** 166 total (128 full time), 98 with doctorates or other terminal degrees. **Location:** Suburban campus in large town; 46 miles from Wilmington. **Calendar:** Semester, extensive summer session. **Microcomputers:** 150 located in libraries, classrooms, computer centers. **Special facilities:** Science center observatory, herbarium, art gallery.

DEGREES OFFERED. BA, BS, MA, MS, MBA, MSW. 260 bachelor's degrees awarded in 1992. 42% in business and management, 24% education, 9% social sciences. Graduate degrees offered in 8 major fields of study.

UNDERGRADUATE MAJORS. Accounting, aerospace/aeronautical/astronautical engineering, agribusiness, agricultural education, agricultural sciences, air traffic control, airline piloting and navigation, art education, arts management, aviation management, biology, biology education, business administration and management, business and management, business economics, business education, chemical engineering, chemical laboratory technology, chemistry, chemistry education, child development/care/guidance, civil engineering, clothing and textiles management/production/services, communications, community health work, computer and information sciences, computer technology, criminal justice studies, criminal justice technology, criminology, dramatic arts, driver and safety education, early childhood education, education of exceptional children, electrical/electronics/communications engineering, elementary education, engineering, engineering and engineering-related technologies, English, English education, environmental health, fine arts, fire protection, fishing and fisheries, food science and nutrition, foreign languages education, French, health education, history, home economics, home economics education, horticultural science, hotel/motel and restaurant management, journalism, junior high education, library science, marketing and distributive education, marketing management, mathematics, mathematics education, mathematics/computer science, mechanical engineering, music, music education, nursing, office supervision and management, parks and recreation management, physical education, physics, physics education, plant sciences, political science and government, preveterinary, psychology, public relations, radio/television broadcasting, recreation and community services technologies, renewable natural resources, science education, secretarial and related programs, social studies education, social work, sociology, soil sciences, Spanish, special education, speech/communication/theater education, textiles and clothing, trade and industrial education, vegetation management, wildlife management.

ACADEMIC PROGRAMS. Accelerated program, cooperative education, double major, dual enrollment of high school students, honors program, independent study, internships, student-designed major, teacher preparation, visiting/exchange student program, weekend college; liberal arts/career combination in engineering. **Remedial services:** Learning center, reduced course load, remedial instruction, special counselor, tutoring. **ROTC:** Air Force, Army. **Placement/credit:** AP, CLEP General and Subject; 30 credit hours maximum for bachelor's degree.

ACADEMIC REQUIREMENTS. Freshmen must earn minimum GPA of 1.7 to continue in good standing. 59% of freshmen return for sophomore year. Students must declare major by end of first year. **Graduation requirements:** 121 hours for bachelor's (30 in major). Most students required to take courses in English, humanities, mathematics, biological/physical sciences, social sciences. **Postgraduate studies:** 1% enter law school, 1% enter medical school, 3% enter MBA programs, 10% enter other graduate study.

FRESHMAN ADMISSIONS. Selection criteria: High school curriculum and GPA most important. Test scores only used in conjunction with GPA. Class rank considered. **High school preparation:** 15 units required. Required units include English 4, mathematics 2, physical science 2 and social science 2. **Test requirements:** SAT or ACT (SAT preferred); score report by August 15.

1992 FRESHMAN CLASS PROFILE. 963 men applied, 662 accepted, 274 enrolled; 1,035 women applied, 813 accepted, 306 enrolled. 11% had high school GPA of 3.0 or higher, 64% between 2.0 and 2.99. **Characteristics:** 51% from in state, 79% live in college housing, 76% have minority backgrounds, 2% are foreign students. Average age is 19.

FALL-TERM APPLICATIONS. $10 fee. Closing date July 30; priority given to applications received by June 1; applicants notified on a rolling basis; must reply by May 15. Interview recommended for nursing, some academically weak applicants applicants. Deferred and early admission available.

STUDENT LIFE. Housing: Dormitories (men, women). Apartment-style residence hall for senior women. **Activities:** Student government, radio, student newspaper, yearbook, choral groups, concert band, dance, drama, jazz band, marching band, music ensembles, fraternities, sororities, Wesley Foundation, United College Ministry.

ATHLETICS. NCAA. **Intercollegiate:** Baseball M, basketball, cross-country, football M, tennis, track and field, volleyball W, wrestling M. **Intramural:** Basketball, bowling, softball, table tennis, tennis, track and field, volleyball.

STUDENT SERVICES. Aptitude testing, career counseling, freshman orientation, health services, on-campus day care, personal counseling, placement service for graduates, special adviser for adult students, veterans counselor, services/facilities for handicapped.

ANNUAL EXPENSES. Tuition and fees (1992-93): $1,788, $880 additional for out-of-state students. **Room and board:** $3,454. **Books and supplies:** $400. **Other expenses:** $1,250.

FINANCIAL AID. 67% of continuing students receive some form of aid. 60% of grants, all loans, all jobs based on need. Academic, music/drama, athletic, state/district residency, leadership, alumni affiliation, minority scholarships available. **Aid applications:** No closing date; priority given to applications received by May 1; applicants notified on a rolling basis beginning on or about June 1; must reply within 2 weeks.

ADDRESS/TELEPHONE. Jethro C. Williams, Director of Admissions, Delaware State College, 1200 N. DuPont Highway, Dover, DE 19901. (302) 739-4917. Fax: (302)739-5309.

Delaware Technical and Community College: Southern Campus

Georgetown, Delaware CB code: 5169

2-year public community, technical college, coed. Founded in 1967. **Accreditation:** Regional. **Undergraduate enrollment:** 546 men, 948 women full time; 554 men, 999 women part time. **Faculty:** 160 total (71 full time). **Location:** Rural campus in rural community; 80 miles from Wilmington. **Calendar:** Quarter. **Microcomputers:** Located in computer centers.

DEGREES OFFERED. AAS. 305 associate degrees awarded in 1992. 17% in business and management, 6% business/office and marketing/distribution, 9% engineering technologies, 19% health sciences, 28% allied health, 11% parks/recreation, protective services, public affairs.

UNDERGRADUATE MAJORS. Accounting, agribusiness, air conditioning/heating/refrigeration mechanics, air conditioning/heating/refrigeration technology, allied health, architectural technologies, automotive mechanics, automotive technology, business and management, business and office, business data processing and related programs, chemical manufacturing technology, child development/care/guidance, civil technology, criminal justice technology, data processing, dental hygiene, diesel engine mechanics, drafting, drafting and design technology, electrical technology, electronic technology, food production/management/services, hospitality and recreation marketing, hotel/motel and restaurant management, journalism, law enforcement and corrections technologies, legal assistant/paralegal, liberal/general studies, marketing and distribution, marketing management, medical assistant, medical laboratory technologies, mental health/human services, nursing, poultry, practical nursing, radiograph medical technology, recreation and community services technologies, science technologies, secretarial and related programs, veterinarian's assistant, welding technology.

ACADEMIC PROGRAMS. Dual enrollment of high school students, internships. **Remedial services:** Learning center, preadmission summer program, reduced course load, remedial instruction, special counselor, tutoring.

ACADEMIC REQUIREMENTS. Freshmen must earn minimum GPA of 2.0 to continue in good standing. 45% of freshmen return for sophomore year. **Graduation requirements:** 97 hours for associate. Most students required to take courses in computer science.

FRESHMAN ADMISSIONS. Selection criteria: Open admissions. Restricted admission to health technology and nursing programs.

1992 FRESHMAN CLASS PROFILE. 238 men, 372 women enrolled. **Characteristics:** 98% from in state, 100% commute, 20% have minority backgrounds. Average age is 19.

FALL-TERM APPLICATIONS. $10 fee, may be waived for applicants with need. Closing date August 1; applicants notified on a rolling basis; must reply within 3 weeks. Interview required for health technology applicants. Deferred and early admission available.

STUDENT LIFE. Activities: Student government, radio, student newspaper.

STUDENT SERVICES. Employment service for undergraduates, personal counseling, placement service for graduates, services/facilities for handicapped.

ANNUAL EXPENSES. Tuition and fees (1992-93): $1,119, $1,566 additional for out-of-state students. **Books and supplies:** $450. **Other expenses:** $300.

FINANCIAL AID. 33% of freshmen, 34% of continuing students receive some form of aid. 99% of grants, 97% of loans, all jobs based on need.

Academic scholarships available. **Aid applications:** No closing date; applicants notified on a rolling basis.

ADDRESS/TELEPHONE. Admissions Office, Delaware Technical and Community College: Southern Campus, PO Box 610, Georgetown, DE 19947. (302) 856-5400.

Delaware Technical and Community College: Stanton/ Wilmington Campus

Wilmington, Delaware CB code: 5154

2-year public technical college, coed. Founded in 1967. **Accreditation:** Regional. **Undergraduate enrollment:** 1,017 men, 1,169 women full time; 1,616 men, 2,419 women part time. **Faculty:** 342 total (119 full time). **Location:** Suburban campus in small city. **Calendar:** Quarter, limited summer session. **Microcomputers:** Located in libraries, computer centers. **Additional facts:** Multilocation institution.

DEGREES OFFERED. AAS. 507 associate degrees awarded in 1992. 18% in business and management, 27% engineering technologies, 20% health sciences, 21% allied health, 8% parks/recreation, protective services, public affairs.

UNDERGRADUATE MAJORS. Accounting, architectural technologies, architecture, automotive technology, biomedical equipment technology, biomedical science, business and management, business and office, business computer/console/peripheral equipment operation, business data entry equipment operation, business data processing and related programs, chemical manufacturing technology, child development/care/guidance, civil technology, criminal justice technology, data processing, dental assistant, dental hygiene, drafting, drafting and design technology, electrical technology, electronic technology, engineering and engineering-related technologies, finance, fire control and safety technology, food production/management/services, hotel/motel and restaurant management, industrial technology, instrumentation technology, law enforcement and corrections technologies, mechanical design technology, medical assistant, medical secretary, mental health/human services, microcomputer software, nuclear medical technology, nursing, physical therapy assistant, plastic technology, radiograph medical technology, respiratory therapy, respiratory therapy technology, robotics, secretarial and related programs, trade and industrial supervision and management, transportation management.

ACADEMIC PROGRAMS. Cooperative education, double major, dual enrollment of high school students, independent study, internships. **Remedial services:** Learning center, reduced course load, remedial instruction, special counselor, tutoring. **Placement/credit:** CLEP General and Subject, institutional tests.

ACADEMIC REQUIREMENTS. Freshmen must earn minimum GPA of 2.0 to continue in good standing. 50% of freshmen return for sophomore year. **Graduation requirements:** 97 hours for associate. Most students required to take courses in computer science.

FRESHMAN ADMISSIONS. Selection criteria: Open admissions. Admission to health technologies program restricted to state residents. Restricted admission to dental hygiene and nursing programs.

1992 FRESHMAN CLASS PROFILE. 692 men, 821 women enrolled. **Characteristics:** 94% from in state, 100% commute, 22% have minority backgrounds, 1% are foreign students. Average age is 19.

FALL-TERM APPLICATIONS. $10 fee. Closing date August 1; applicants notified on a rolling basis; must reply within 3 weeks. Interview required for health technology applicants. Deferred and early admission available. Application closing date for registered nursing and inhalation therapy programs December 1.

STUDENT LIFE. Activities: Student government, student newspaper.

ATHLETICS. NJCAA. **Intercollegiate:** Baseball, basketball, soccer M. **Intramural:** Baseball, basketball, soccer, softball, tennis, volleyball.

STUDENT SERVICES. Aptitude testing, career counseling, employment service for undergraduates, health services, personal counseling, placement service for graduates, veterans counselor, services/facilities for handicapped.

ANNUAL EXPENSES. Tuition and fees (1992-93): $1,119, $1,566 additional for out-of-state students. **Books and supplies:** $450. **Other expenses:** $300.

FINANCIAL AID. 25% of freshmen, 24% of continuing students receive some form of aid. Grants, loans, jobs available. Academic, athletic scholarships available. **Aid applications:** No closing date; priority given to applications received by July 1; applicants notified on a rolling basis beginning on or about July 1; must reply within 2 weeks.

ADDRESS/TELEPHONE. Patty Nash, Admission Aide, Delaware Technical and Community College: Stanton/Wilmington Campus, PO Box 10290, Wilmington, DE 19850. (302) 571-5343. Fax: (302) 571-2548.

Delaware Technical and Community College: Terry Campus

Dover, Delaware CB code: 5201

2-year public branch campus, community, technical college, coed. Founded in 1972. **Accreditation:** Regional. **Undergraduate enrollment:** 230 men, 388 women full time; 529 men, 826 women part time. **Faculty:** 102 total (41 full time), 10 with doctorates or other terminal degrees. **Location:** Suburban campus in large town; 90 miles from Baltimore, 75 miles from Philadelphia. **Calendar:** Quarter, limited summer session. **Microcomputers:** 100 located in computer centers.

DEGREES OFFERED. AAS. 115 associate degrees awarded in 1992. 28% in business and management, 59% computer sciences, 11% engineering technologies, 12% health sciences, 24% allied health.

UNDERGRADUATE MAJORS. Accounting, aeronautical technology, airline piloting and navigation, architectural technologies, architecture, aviation management, biomedical equipment technology, business and management, business and office, business computer/console/peripheral equipment operation, business data processing and related programs, civil technology, computer technology, construction, criminal justice technology, data processing, dental hygiene, drafting, drafting and design technology, electrical and electronics equipment repair, electrical technology, electromechanical technology, electronic technology, engineering and engineering-related technologies, finance, law enforcement and corrections technologies, marketing and distribution, marketing management, mental health/human services, microcomputer software, nursing, secretarial and related programs, word processing.

ACADEMIC PROGRAMS. 2-year transfer program, cooperative education, double major, dual enrollment of high school students, internships, cross-registration, specialized occupations program. **Remedial services:** Reduced course load, remedial instruction, tutoring. **Placement/credit:** CLEP General and Subject, institutional tests.

ACADEMIC REQUIREMENTS. Freshmen must earn minimum GPA of 2.0 to continue in good standing. 45% of freshmen return for sophomore year. Students must declare major on enrollment. **Graduation requirements:** 90 hours for associate. Most students required to take courses in computer science, English, mathematics, social sciences.

FRESHMAN ADMISSIONS. Selection criteria: Open admissions.

1992 FRESHMAN CLASS PROFILE. 138 men, 238 women enrolled. **Characteristics:** 98% from in state, 100% commute, 27% have minority backgrounds. Average age is 19.

FALL-TERM APPLICATIONS. $10 fee, may be waived for applicants with need. Closing date August 1; applicants notified on a rolling basis. Interview required. Early admission available.

STUDENT LIFE. Activities: Student government.

ATHLETICS. Intercollegiate: Golf. **Intramural:** Racquetball, softball, tennis.

STUDENT SERVICES. Career counseling, employment service for undergraduates, freshman orientation, personal counseling, placement service for graduates, veterans counselor, services/facilities for handicapped.

ANNUAL EXPENSES. Tuition and fees (1992-93): $1,119, $1,566 additional for out-of-state students. **Books and supplies:** $450. **Other expenses:** $300.

FINANCIAL AID. 25% of freshmen, 25% of continuing students receive some form of aid. Grants, loans, jobs available. **Aid applications:** No closing date; priority given to applications received by May 30; applicants notified on a rolling basis.

ADDRESS/TELEPHONE. Kenneth L. Hogan, Registrar/Admissions Officer, Delaware Technical and Community College: Terry Campus, 1832 North Dupont Parkway, Dover, DE 19903. (302) 739-5412. Fax: (302) 735-6169.

Goldey-Beacom College

Wilmington, Delaware CB code: 5255

Admissions: 79% of applicants accepted
Based on: ••• School record, test scores
•• Recommendations
• Interview
Completion: 88% of freshmen end year in good standing
50% graduate, 2% of these enter graduate study

4-year private business college, coed. Founded in 1886. **Accreditation:** Regional. **Undergraduate enrollment:** 313 men, 539 women full time; 258 men, 647 women part time. **Faculty:** 70 total (23 full time), 8 with doctorates or other terminal degrees. **Location:** Suburban campus in small city; 15 miles from downtown. **Calendar:** 4-1-4, limited summer session. Saturday and extensive evening/early morning classes. **Microcomputers:** 200 located in libraries, classrooms, computer centers. **Additional facts:** Branch campus downtown.

DEGREES OFFERED. AS, BS, MBA. 139 associate degrees awarded in 1992. 60% in business and management, 33% business/office and marketing/distribution, 7% computer sciences. 167 bachelor's degrees awarded. 68% in business and management, 22% business/office and marketing/distribution, 10% computer sciences. Graduate degrees offered in 2 major fields of study.

UNDERGRADUATE MAJORS. Associate: Accounting, business administration and management, business and management, business and office, business data programming, computer and information sciences, office supervision and management, office technologies administration, word processing. **Bachelor's:** Accounting, business administration and management, business and management, communications, computer and information sciences, finance, information sciences and systems, international business management, management information systems, marketing management, office supervision and management, office technologies administration.

ACADEMIC PROGRAMS. Cooperative education, double major, dual enrollment of high school students, honors program, internships, cross-registration. **Remedial services:** Learning center, preadmission summer program, reduced course load, remedial instruction, special counselor, tutoring. **Placement/credit:** AP, CLEP General, institutional tests.

ACADEMIC REQUIREMENTS. Freshmen must earn minimum GPA of 2.0 to continue in good standing. 80% of freshmen return for sophomore year. Students must declare major on application. **Graduation requirements:** 66 hours for associate (30 in major), 126 hours for bachelor's (66 in major). Most students required to take courses in computer science, English, humanities, mathematics, philosophy/religion, social sciences. **Postgraduate studies:** 58% from 2-year programs enter 4-year programs. 2% enter MBA programs.

FRESHMAN ADMISSIONS. Selection criteria: School record most important. Test scores important for bachelor's degree applicants. Associate and certificate degree applicants may be required to take placement tests. 3 mathematics required for bachelor's degree applicants. **Test requirements:** SAT or ACT (SAT preferred); score report by August 31.

1992 FRESHMAN CLASS PROFILE. 224 men applied, 171 accepted, 121 enrolled; 345 women applied, 279 accepted, 196 enrolled. 29% had high school GPA of 3.0 or higher, 59% between 2.0 and 2.99. 7% were in top tenth and 20% were in top quarter of graduating class. **Academic background:** Mid 50% of enrolled freshmen had SAT-V between 350-450, SAT-M between 350-550. 79% submitted SAT scores. **Characteristics:** 45% from in state, 85% commute, 25% have minority backgrounds, 11% are foreign students, 2% join fraternities/sororities. Average age is 18.

FALL-TERM APPLICATIONS. $25 fee, may be waived for applicants with need. Closing date August 31; priority given to applications received by May 1; applicants notified on a rolling basis; must reply by August 31. Interview recommended. CRDA. Deferred admission available. Institutional early decision plan. SAT not required but recommended for associate degree applicants for placement and counseling.

STUDENT LIFE. Housing: Dormitories (coed); apartment, fraternity, sorority, handicapped housing available. Apartment-style residence halls. **Activities:** Student government, choral groups, fraternities, sororities, Christian Fellowship, Minority Student Union, Circle-K, International Student Association.

ATHLETICS. NAIA. **Intercollegiate:** Soccer M, softball W. **Intramural:** Basketball M, soccer M, softball, volleyball.

STUDENT SERVICES. Career counseling, employment service for undergraduates, freshman orientation, health services, personal counseling, placement service for graduates, services/facilities for handicapped.

ANNUAL EXPENSES. Tuition and fees (1992-93): $5,575. **Room and board:** $2,757 room only. **Books and supplies:** $485. **Other expenses:** $6,035.

FINANCIAL AID. 60% of freshmen, 59% of continuing students receive some form of aid. 68% of grants, 96% of loans, all jobs based on need. 233 enrolled freshmen were judged to have need, all were offered aid. Academic, athletic, state/district residency, leadership, alumni affiliation scholarships available. **Aid applications:** No closing date; priority given to applications received by April 1; applicants notified on a rolling basis beginning on or about February 15; No deadline. **Additional information:** Essays required for scholarship applicants.

ADDRESS/TELEPHONE. Gail H. Lear, Director of Admissions, Goldey-Beacom College, 4701 Limestone Road, Wilmington, DE 19808. (302) 998-8814. (800) 833-4877. Fax: (302) 998-3467.

University of Delaware
Newark, Delaware — CB code: 5811

Admissions: 70% of applicants accepted
Based on: ••• School record, test scores
• Activities, essay, recommendations, special talents
Completion: 68% graduate, 18% of these enter graduate study

4-year private university, coed. Founded in 1743. **Accreditation:** Regional. **Undergraduate enrollment:** 5,803 men, 7,595 women full time; 571 men, 676 women part time. **Graduate enrollment:** 913 men, 674 women full time; 619 men, 638 women part time. **Faculty:** 954 total (909 full time), 791 with doctorates or other terminal degrees. **Location:** Suburban campus in large town; 12 miles from Wilmington. **Calendar:** 4-1-4, limited summer session. **Microcomputers:** 605 located in dormitories, libraries, computer centers. **Special facilities:** Ice Skating Science Development Center and Human Performance Laboratory, 400-acre experimental farm, Center for Composites Manufacturing and Research, on-campus preschool laboratory.

DEGREES OFFERED. AA, AS, BA, BS, BFA, MA, MS, MBA, MFA, MEd, PhD, EdD. 11 associate degrees awarded in 1992. 3,237 bachelor's degrees awarded. Graduate degrees offered in 75 major fields of study.

UNDERGRADUATE MAJORS. Associate: Liberal/general studies. **Bachelor's:** Accounting, agricultural business and management, agricultural economics, agricultural education, agricultural engineering, agricultural sciences, agronomy, animal sciences, anthropology, art history, biochemistry, biology, biotechnology, business administration and management, chemical engineering, chemistry, civil engineering, classics education, clinical laboratory science, communications, community services, comparative literature, computer and information sciences, criminal justice studies, early childhood education, economics, education, education of exceptional children, electrical/electronics/communications engineering, elementary education, engineering and engineering-related technologies, English, English education, entomology, environmental science, family and community services, fashion design, fashion merchandising, finance, fine arts, food sciences, foreign languages (multiple emphasis), foreign languages education, French, geography, geology, geophysics and seismology, German, graphic design, health education, history, home economics, home economics education, hotel/motel and restaurant management, international relations, Italian, journalism, Latin, Latin American studies, liberal/general studies, marketing management, mathematics, mathematics education, mechanical engineering, medical laboratory technologies, music, music education, music performance, music theory and composition, nursing, nutritional sciences, ornamental horticulture, parks and recreation management, philosophy, physical education, physics, plant pathology, plant sciences, political science and government, predentistry, prelaw, premedicine, preveterinary, psychology, recreation and community services technologies, Russian, science education, secondary education, social science education, social studies education, sociology, soil sciences, Spanish, special education, statistics, technical and business writing, textiles and clothing, theater production.

ACADEMIC PROGRAMS. Accelerated program, double major, dual enrollment of high school students, honors program, independent study, internships, student-designed major, study abroad, teacher preparation, telecourses, visiting/exchange student program; liberal arts/career combination in engineering; combined bachelor's/graduate program in business administration. **Remedial services:** Reduced course load, remedial instruction, special counselor, tutoring, writing and mathematics centers. **ROTC:** Air Force, Army. **Placement/credit:** AP, IB, institutional tests.

ACADEMIC REQUIREMENTS. Freshmen must earn minimum GPA of 2.0 to continue in good standing. 84% of freshmen return for sophomore year. Students must declare major by end of second year. **Graduation requirements:** 60 hours for associate, 124 hours for bachelor's. Most students required to take courses in English, foreign languages, mathematics. **Postgraduate studies:** 4% enter law school, 1% enter medical school, 3% enter MBA programs, 10% enter other graduate study. **Additional information:** University Honors Program emphasizes small classes, undergraduate research program, honors housing, special scholarship opportunities; special application required. All graduates must complete 3 credits involving multicultural, ethnic, and/or gender-related content.

FRESHMAN ADMISSIONS. Selection criteria: High school record, program of study, SAT scores, references, extracurricular activities considered. Special consideration given to children and/or dependents of alumni and to minorities. **High school preparation:** 16 units required; 19 recommended. Required and recommended units include English 4-4, foreign language 2-4, mathematics 2-4, social science 3-4 and science 2-3. 3 units of academic electives. 4 mathematics strongly recommended for engineering, business, science or mathematics applicants. 4 laboratory science strongly recommended for science, nursing, and engineering applicants. **Test requirements:** SAT; score report by March 1. ACH recommended for honor program applications, score report by April 1.

1992 FRESHMAN CLASS PROFILE. 6,534 men applied, 4,293 accepted, 1,246 enrolled; 7,499 women applied, 5,460 accepted, 1,761 enrolled. 61% had high school GPA of 3.0 or higher, 39% between 2.0 and 2.99. 25% were in top tenth and 61% were in top quarter of graduating class. **Academic background:** Mid 50% of enrolled freshmen had SAT-V between 450-540, SAT-M between 520-620. 99% submitted SAT scores. **Characteristics:** 32% from in state, 93% live in college housing, 9% have minority backgrounds, 1% are foreign students. Average age is 18.

FALL-TERM APPLICATIONS. $40 fee, may be waived for applicants with need. Closing date March 1; priority given to applications received by January 1; applicants notified on or about April 15; must reply by May 1. CRDA. Deferred and early admission available. Clearly admissable or inadmissable candidates are notified immediately. Other applicants notified by April 15. Written request needed for deferred admission.

STUDENT LIFE. Housing: Dormitories (men, women, coed); apartment, fraternity, sorority housing available. Special interest housing including language houses, humanities house, honors hall, music house, international house, farmhouse, education house. **Activities:** Student government, magazine, radio, student newspaper, yearbook, choral groups, concert band, dance, drama, jazz band, marching band, music ensembles, musical theater, symphony orchestra, fraternities, sororities, more than 180 clubs and student organizations.

ATHLETICS. NCAA. **Intercollegiate:** Baseball M, basketball, cross-country, field hockey W, football M, golf M, lacrosse, soccer, softball W, swimming, tennis, track and field, volleyball W. **Intramural:** Badminton, basketball, bowling, cross-country, fencing, field hockey W, golf, gymnastics, horseback riding, ice hockey M, lacrosse, racquetball, rowing (crew), rugby, sailing, soccer, softball, squash, table tennis, tennis, track and field, volleyball, water polo M.

STUDENT SERVICES. Aptitude testing, career counseling, employment service for undergraduates, freshman orientation, health services, personal counseling, placement service for graduates, special adviser for adult students, veterans counselor, services/facilities for handicapped.

ANNUAL EXPENSES. Tuition and fees (1992-93): $3,721, $5,660 additional for out-of-state students. **Room and board:** $3,756. **Books and supplies:** $530. **Other expenses:** $1,300.

FINANCIAL AID. 63% of freshmen, 47% of continuing students receive some form of aid. 55% of grants, 72% of loans, 56% of jobs based on need. 1,259 enrolled freshmen were judged to have need, 1,238 were offered aid. Academic, music/drama, athletic, leadership, alumni affiliation, minority scholarships available. **Aid applications:** Closing date May 1; priority given to applications received by March 15; applicants notified on a rolling basis; must reply within 2 weeks. **Additional information:** January 1 application deadline to receive scholarship consideration. Sibling/parent tuition credit plan. Senior citizen tuition credit for state residents over 60.

ADDRESS/TELEPHONE. Dr. N. Bruce Walker, Associate Provost, Admissions and Financial Aid, University of Delaware, 116 Hullihen Hall, Newark, DE 19716. (302) 831-8123.

Wesley College
Dover, Delaware — CB code: 5894

Admissions: 80% of applicants accepted
Based on: ••• Essay, interview, school record
•• Recommendations, special talents, test scores
• Activities
Completion: 75% of freshmen end year in good standing
39% graduate

4-year private college of arts and sciences, coed, affiliated with United Methodist Church. Founded in 1873. **Accreditation:** Regional. **Undergraduate enrollment:** 424 men, 504 women full time; 203 men, 215 women part time. **Faculty:** 104 total (51 full time), 30 with doctorates or other terminal degrees. **Location:** Suburban campus in large town; 75 miles from Philadelphia, 90 miles from Washington, D.C. **Calendar:** Semester, limited summer session. Saturday and extensive evening/early morning classes. **Microcomputers:** 42 located in libraries, classrooms, computer centers.

DEGREES OFFERED. AA, AS, BA, BS. 65 associate degrees awarded in 1992. 15% in business and management, 11% business/office and marketing/distribution, 10% communications, 40% health sciences, 11% law. 135 bachelor's degrees awarded. 48% in business and management, 10% business/office and marketing/distribution, 10% communications, 5% computer sciences, 14% life sciences, 5% psychology.

UNDERGRADUATE MAJORS. Associate: Agricultural sciences, art history, business and management, communications, computer and information sciences, dramatic arts, engineering, fashion merchandising, French, legal assistant/paralegal, liberal/general studies, mathematics, nursing, physical sciences, science technologies, social sciences, Spanish. **Bachelor's:** Accounting, biology, business administration and management, business and management, business economics, communications, computer and information sciences, education, elementary education, environmental science, fashion merchandising, history, information sciences and systems, legal assistant/paralegal, liberal/general studies, marketing management, medical laboratory technologies, physical education, political science and government, prelaw, psychology, science education, secondary education, social science education.

ACADEMIC PROGRAMS. 2-year transfer program, dual enrollment of high school students, independent study, internships, study abroad, teacher preparation, visiting/exchange student program. **Remedial services:** Learning center, reduced course load, remedial instruction, special counselor, tutoring. **Placement/credit:** AP, CLEP General and Subject, institutional tests; 30 credit hours maximum for bachelor's degree.

ACADEMIC REQUIREMENTS. Freshmen must earn minimum GPA of 1.7 to continue in good standing. 62% of freshmen return for sophomore year. Students must declare major by end of second year. **Graduation requirements:** 64 hours for associate, 124 hours for bachelor's (30 in major). Most students required to take courses in arts/fine arts, English, history, mathematics, philosophy/religion, biological/physical sciences, social sciences.

FRESHMAN ADMISSIONS. Selection criteria: High school performance most important. Campus interview very important. **High school preparation:** 16 units required. Required and recommended units include biological science 2, English 4, mathematics 2 and social science 1. Foreign language 2 and physical science 1 recommended. **Test requirements:** SAT or ACT; score report by May 31. SAT required for bachelor's degree, paralegal, and nursing applicants; recommended for other applicants.

1992 FRESHMAN CLASS PROFILE. 1,024 men and women applied, 815 accepted; 306 enrolled. 24% had high school GPA of 3.0 or higher, 41% between 2.0 and 2.99. 5% were in top tenth and 10% were in top quarter of graduating class. **Academic background:** Mid 50% of enrolled freshmen had SAT-V between 330-410, SAT-M between 350-450. 85% submitted SAT scores. **Characteristics:** 28% from in state, 75% live in college housing, 14% have minority backgrounds, 1% are foreign students. Average age is 18.

FALL-TERM APPLICATIONS. $20 fee, may be waived for applicants with need. Closing date August 20; priority given to applications received by April 1; applicants notified on a rolling basis; must reply within 3 weeks. Essay required. Interview recommended. Deferred and early admission available.

STUDENT LIFE. Housing: Dormitories (men, women, coed); fraternity, sorority, handicapped housing available. **Activities:** Student government, radio, student newspaper, television, yearbook, choral groups, drama, jazz band, music ensembles, fraternities, sororities, community action, student Christian associations.

ATHLETICS. NCAA. **Intercollegiate:** Baseball M, basketball, field hockey W, football M, golf M, lacrosse M, soccer M, softball W, tennis. **Intramural:** Basketball, soccer M, volleyball.

STUDENT SERVICES. Career counseling, employment service for undergraduates, freshman orientation, health services, personal counseling, placement service for graduates, special adviser for adult students, veterans counselor, services/facilities for handicapped.

ANNUAL EXPENSES. Tuition and fees: $9,645. **Room and board:** $4,100. **Books and supplies:** $500. **Other expenses:** $695.

FINANCIAL AID. 70% of freshmen, 75% of continuing students receive some form of aid. 82% of grants, 87% of loans, all jobs based on need. 254 enrolled freshmen were judged to have need, all were offered aid. Academic, music/drama, leadership, religious affiliation scholarships available. **Aid applications:** No closing date; priority given to applications received by April 15; applicants notified on a rolling basis beginning on or about March 15; must reply within 2 weeks.

ADDRESS/TELEPHONE. Joseph R. Slights, Jr, Dean of Admissions, Wesley College, 120 North State Street, Dover, DE 19901-3875. (302) 736-2400. (800) WESLEYU. Fax: (302) 736-2301.

Wilmington College
New Castle, Delaware — CB code: 5925

4-year private liberal arts college, coed. Founded in 1967. **Accreditation:** Regional. **Undergraduate enrollment:** 191 men, 330 women full time; 407 men, 845 women part time. **Graduate enrollment:** 41 men, 53 women full time; 293 men, 422 women part time. **Faculty:** 245 total (28 full time), 84 with doctorates or other terminal degrees. **Location:** Suburban campus in large town; 7 miles from Wilmington. **Calendar:** Trimester, limited summer session. Saturday and extensive evening/early morning classes. **Microcomputers:** 50 located in libraries, classrooms, computer centers. **Additional facts:** Two 8-week modular sessions within each trimester in addition to regular trimester sessions and weekend modules.

DEGREES OFFERED. AA, AS, BA, BS, MS, MBA, MEd, EdD. 12 associate degrees awarded in 1992. 100% in social sciences. 293 bachelor's degrees awarded. 46% in business and management, 17% health sciences, 13% parks/recreation, protective services, public affairs, 23% social sciences. Graduate degrees offered in 5 major fields of study.

UNDERGRADUATE MAJORS. Associate: Early childhood education, liberal/general studies. **Bachelor's:** Accounting, aviation management, behavioral sciences, business administration and management, business and management, communications, criminal justice studies, elementary education, finance, human resources development, nursing.

ACADEMIC PROGRAMS. 2-year transfer program, accelerated program, double major, independent study, internships, teacher preparation, weekend college. **Remedial services:** Learning center, remedial instruction, special counselor, tutoring. **ROTC:** Air Force, Army. **Placement/credit:** AP, CLEP General and Subject, institutional tests; 30 credit hours maximum for associate degree; 75 credit hours maximum for bachelor's degree.

ACADEMIC REQUIREMENTS. Freshmen must earn minimum GPA of 1.6 to continue in good standing. 70% of freshmen return for sophomore year. Students must declare major by end of second year. **Graduation requirements:** 60 hours for associate (33 in major), 120 hours for bachelor's (54 in major). Most students required to take courses in arts/fine arts, computer science, English, history, humanities, mathematics, biological/physical sciences, social sciences. **Postgraduate studies:** 40% from 2-year programs enter 4-year programs.

FRESHMAN ADMISSIONS. Selection criteria: Open admissions. Grades, interviews, recommendations, community activities, school achievement. **Test requirements:** SAT or ACT for placement; score report by May 1.

1992 FRESHMAN CLASS PROFILE. 83 men, 116 women enrolled. 40% had high school GPA of 3.0 or higher, 60% between 2.0 and 2.99. **Characteristics:** 92% from in state, 100% commute, 15% have minority backgrounds, 1% are foreign students, 2% join fraternities/sororities. Average age is 21.

FALL-TERM APPLICATIONS. $25 fee. No closing date; priority given to applications received by August 1; applicants notified on a rolling basis; must reply within 4 weeks and no later than August 31. Interview required. Deferred and early admission available. EDP-F.

STUDENT LIFE. Activities: Student government, film, radio, student newspaper, yearbook, drama, fraternities, professional fraternities/organizations.

ATHLETICS. NAIA. **Intercollegiate:** Baseball M, basketball, softball W, volleyball W.

STUDENT SERVICES. Aptitude testing, career counseling, employment service for undergraduates, freshman orientation, personal counseling, placement service for graduates, veterans counselor, academic development center, services/facilities for handicapped.

ANNUAL EXPENSES. Tuition and fees (1992-93): $5,140. **Books and supplies:** $700. **Other expenses:** $1,500.

FINANCIAL AID. 47% of freshmen, 38% of continuing students receive some form of aid. 90% of grants, 80% of loans, all jobs based on need. 173 enrolled freshmen were judged to have need, all were offered aid. Academic, athletic, leadership scholarships available. **Aid applications:** No closing date; priority given to applications received by June 1; applicants notified on a rolling basis beginning on or about July 15; must reply within 4 weeks and no later than August 31.

ADDRESS/TELEPHONE. Michael Lee, Director of Admissions, Wilmington College, 320 Dupont Highway, New Castle, DE 19720. (302) 328-9401 ext. 102/104. Fax: (302) 328-9442.

District of Columbia

American University
Washington, D.C. CB code: 5007

Admissions: 81% of applicants accepted
Based on: ••• School record
•• Essay, recommendations, test scores
• Activities, special talents
Completion: 85% of freshmen end year in good standing
66% graduate

4-year private university, coed, affiliated with United Methodist Church. Founded in 1893. **Accreditation:** Regional. **Undergraduate enrollment:** 2,024 men, 2,952 women full time; 220 men, 302 women part time. **Graduate enrollment:** 1,145 men, 1,355 women full time; 1,081 men, 1,180 women part time. **Faculty:** 1,265 total (544 full time), 489 with doctorates or other terminal degrees. **Location:** Suburban campus in very large city; 2 miles from downtown. **Calendar:** Semester, extensive summer session. Saturday and extensive evening/early morning classes. **Microcomputers:** 358 located in dormitories, computer centers.

DEGREES OFFERED. AA, BA, BS, BFA, MA, MS, MBA, MFA, PhD, EdD, JD. 3 associate degrees awarded in 1992. 100% in multi/interdisciplinary studies. 1,478 bachelor's degrees awarded. 18% in business and management, 12% communications, 8% parks/recreation, protective services, public affairs, 40% social sciences. Graduate degrees offered in 66 major fields of study.

UNDERGRADUATE MAJORS. Associate: Liberal/general studies. **Bachelor's:** Accounting, American studies, anthropology, applied mathematics, art history, audio technology, biological and physical sciences, biology, chemistry, cinematography/film, communications, communications/legal studies, computer and information sciences, criminal justice studies, dramatic arts, economics, elementary education, English literature, environmental science, film arts, finance, fine arts, foreign language and communication media, French, German, graphic design, history, information sciences and systems, institutional/economics/government, international business management, international relations, Jewish studies, journalism, Latin American studies, law liberal/general studies, management information systems, marketing management, mathematics, music, music and technology, music history and appreciation, music performance, music theory and composition, personnel management, philosophy, physics, political science and government, predentistry, preengineering, prelaw, premedicine, preveterinary, psychology, public relations, radio/television broadcasting, real estate, religion, Russian, Russian and Slavic studies, sociology, Spanish, statistics, studio art, video, Western European studies.

ACADEMIC PROGRAMS. Cooperative education, double major, honors program, independent study, internships, student-designed major, study abroad, teacher preparation, Washington semester, cross-registration, combined program with Washington College of Law leading to JD, host institution of Washington Semester Program for students from other universities, combined JD/MBA, JD/MA (law and international affairs). **Remedial services:** Learning center, remedial instruction, special counselor, tutoring. **ROTC:** Air Force, Army, Naval. **Placement/credit:** AP, CLEP Subject; 30 credit hours maximum for bachelor's degree.

ACADEMIC REQUIREMENTS. Freshmen must earn minimum GPA of 2.0 to continue in good standing. 85% of freshmen return for sophomore year. Students must declare major by end of second year. **Graduation requirements:** 60 hours for associate, 120 hours for bachelor's (36 in major). Most students required to take courses in arts/fine arts, English, mathematics, biological/physical sciences, social sciences. **Additional information:** Study Abroad programs available in London, Rome, Brussels, Vienna, Copenhagen, Poznan (Poland), Beijing, Buenos Aires, Paris, Madrid, Moscow, Prague, Budapest, and Santiago.

FRESHMAN ADMISSIONS. Selection criteria: SAT or ACT scores, scholastic record, class rank, writing sample and recommendations are most important. High school record includes overall GPA, breadth and rigor of curriculum and 4-year trend (grade improvement over 4 years). **High school preparation:** 16 units required. Required units include English 4, foreign language 2, mathematics 3, social science 3 and science 2. **Test requirements:** SAT or ACT (SAT preferred); score report by March 1. Prueba de Aptitud Academica (PAA) required of Puerto Rican applicants.

1992 FRESHMAN CLASS PROFILE. 1,759 men applied, 1,352 accepted, 417 enrolled; 2,528 women applied, 2,108 accepted, 642 enrolled. 69% had high school GPA of 3.0 or higher, 31% between 2.0 and 2.99. 35% were in top tenth and 72% were in top quarter of graduating class. **Academic background:** Mid 50% of enrolled freshmen had SAT-V between 500-600, SAT-M between 530-630. 88% submitted SAT scores. **Characteristics:** 2% from in state, 97% live in college housing, 13% have minority backgrounds, 6% are foreign students, 20% join fraternities/sororities. Average age is 18.

FALL-TERM APPLICATIONS. $35 fee, may be waived for applicants with need. Closing date February 1; applicants notified on or about April 15; must reply by May 1 or within 4 weeks if notified thereafter. Audition required for music performance majors and provisional status performing arts applicants. Essay required. Interview recommended for fine arts applicants. Portfolio recommended for fine arts applicants. CRDA. Deferred and early admission available. EDP-F.

STUDENT LIFE. Housing: Dormitories (coed). Honors floors, intercultural/international hall available. Housing for handicapped students handled individually. **Activities:** Student government, magazine, radio, student newspaper, television, yearbook, choral groups, dance, drama, jazz band, music ensembles, musical theater, opera, pep band, symphony orchestra, fraternities, sororities, more than 120 clubs and organizations including Black Student Alliance, Kennedy Political Union (nonpartisan), College Democrats, College Republicans, Mortar Board, SAVE Volunteer Effort, Women's Confederation, American Students Against Poverty, International Student Association.

ATHLETICS. NCAA. **Intercollegiate:** Basketball, cross-country, diving, field hockey W, golf M, lacrosse W, soccer, swimming, tennis, volleyball W, wrestling M. **Intramural:** Badminton, basketball, racquetball, soccer, softball, squash, swimming, table tennis, tennis, volleyball, water polo.

STUDENT SERVICES. Career counseling, employment service for undergraduates, freshman orientation, health services, on-campus day care, personal counseling, placement service for graduates, special adviser for adult students, veterans counselor, services/facilities for handicapped.

ANNUAL EXPENSES. Tuition and fees: $15,386. **Room and board:** $6,154. **Books and supplies:** $450. **Other expenses:** $600.

FINANCIAL AID. 60% of freshmen, 60% of continuing students receive some form of aid. 69% of grants, 65% of loans, all jobs based on need. 530 enrolled freshmen were judged to have need, all were offered aid. Academic, athletic, religious affiliation scholarships available. **Aid applications:** No closing date; priority given to applications received by March 1; applicants notified on a rolling basis beginning on or about March 1; must reply by May 1 or within 3 weeks if notified thereafter.

ADDRESS/TELEPHONE. Joan Powers, Vice Provost for Admissions and Financial Aid, American University, 4400 Massachusetts Avenue Northwest, Washington, DC 20016-8001. (202) 885-6000. Fax: (202) 885-6014.

Catholic University of America
Washington, D.C. CB code: 5104

Admissions: 86% of applicants accepted
Based on: ••• School record, test scores
•• Activities, recommendations
• Essay, interview, religious affiliation/commitment, special talents
Completion: 93% of freshmen end year in good standing
68% graduate, 45% of these enter graduate study

4-year private university, coed, affiliated with Roman Catholic Church. Founded in 1887. **Accreditation:** Regional. **Undergraduate enrollment:** 1,062 men, 1,295 women full time; 79 men, 125 women part time. **Graduate enrollment:** 847 men, 784 women full time; 1,057 men, 1,215 women part time. **Faculty:** 733 total (411 full time), 386 with doctorates or other terminal degrees. **Location:** Urban campus in very large city; 4 miles from of US Capitol building. **Calendar:** Semester, limited summer session. **Microcomputers:** 100 located in dormitories, classrooms, computer centers. **Special facilities:** Oliveira Lima Library, Clementine Rare Book Collection.

DEGREES OFFERED. BA, BS, BArch, MA, MS, MFA, MSW, PhD, JD, M.Div. 825 bachelor's degrees awarded in 1992. 11% in architecture and environmental design, 11% business and management, 6% engineering, 10% health sciences, 10% letters/literature, 6% psychology, 25% social sciences, 7% visual and performing arts. Graduate degrees offered in 61 major fields of study.

UNDERGRADUATE MAJORS. Accounting, American studies, anthropology, applied mathematics, architecture, art history, biochemistry, bioengineering and biomedical engineering, biological and physical sciences, biology, business administration and management, business and management, business economics, chemistry, city/community/regional planning, civil engineering, classics, communications, computer and information sciences, data processing, dramatic arts, early childhood education, economics, education, electrical/electronics/communications engineering, elementary education, engineering, engineering and other disciplines, English, English literature, French, German, Greek (classical), history, humanities and social sciences, international public service, Latin, liberal/general studies, mathematics, mechanical engineering, medical laboratory technologies, medieval studies, music, music performance, music theory and composition, musical theater, nursing, peace studies, philosophy, physics, political science and government, psychology, religion, religious education, secondary education, social work, sociology, Spanish, special education, studio art.

ACADEMIC PROGRAMS. Accelerated program, double major, dual enrollment of high school students, honors program, independent study, internships, student-designed major, study abroad, teacher preparation, visiting/exchange student program, cross-registration; liberal arts/career combination in engineering; combined bachelor's/graduate program in law. **Remedial services:** Learning center, reduced course load, tutoring. **ROTC:** Air Force, Army, Naval. **Placement/credit:** AP, CLEP General and Subject, institutional tests.

ACADEMIC REQUIREMENTS. Freshmen must earn minimum GPA of 2.0 to continue in good standing. 81% of freshmen return for sophomore year. Students must declare major by end of second year. **Graduation requirements:** 120 hours for bachelor's (30 in major). Most students required to take courses in English, foreign languages, history, humanities, mathematics, philosophy/religion, biological/physical sciences, social sciences. **Postgraduate studies:** 12% enter law school, 4% enter medical school, 5% enter MBA programs, 24% enter other graduate study.

FRESHMAN ADMISSIONS. Selection criteria: School achievement record most important, followed by test scores and recommendations. Extracurricular activities and social action also considered. **High school preparation:** 17 units required. Required units include English 4, foreign language 2, mathematics 3, social science 4 and science 3. One fine arts or humanities. **Test requirements:** SAT or ACT (SAT preferred); score report by February 15. 3 ACH required. Score report by July 1 Prueba de Aptitud Academica for Spanish speaking applicants.

1992 FRESHMAN CLASS PROFILE. 797 men applied, 663 accepted, 233 enrolled; 1,011 women applied, 899 accepted, 266 enrolled. 66% had high school GPA of 3.0 or higher, 32% between 2.0 and 2.99. 27% were in top tenth and 52% were in top quarter of graduating class. **Academic background:** Mid 50% of enrolled freshmen had SAT-V between 440-560, SAT-M between 470-610; ACT composite between 23-27. 91% submitted SAT scores, 11% submitted ACT scores. **Characteristics:** 3% from in state, 84% live in college housing, 14% have minority backgrounds, 9% are foreign students, 1% join fraternities/sororities. Average age is 18.

FALL-TERM APPLICATIONS. $30 fee, may be waived for applicants with need. Closing date February 15; applicants notified on or about March 15; must reply by May 1. Audition required for music applicants. Essay required. Interview recommended. Portfolio recommended for art applicants. CRDA. Deferred and early admission available. Institutional early decision plan. Early Action applications must be submitted by November 15, notification by December 15. Students have until May 1 to reply.

STUDENT LIFE. Housing: Dormitories (men, women, coed). Honor student and social service housing available. **Activities:** Student government, film, magazine, radio, student newspaper, yearbook, choral groups, concert band, dance, drama, jazz band, music ensembles, musical theater, opera, pep band, symphony orchestra, fraternities, sororities, campus ministry, Community Action Network, Black Organization of Students, Best Buddies, Muslim Student Association, Hispanic Association, Young Republicans, Young Democrats. **Additional information:** Special Community outreach programs in Washington, D.C.

ATHLETICS. NCAA. **Intercollegiate:** Baseball M, basketball, cross-country, field hockey W, football M, soccer, softball W, swimming, tennis, track and field, volleyball W. **Intramural:** Baseball M, basketball, cross-country, racquetball, soccer, softball, swimming, table tennis, tennis, track and field, volleyball, water polo.

STUDENT SERVICES. Aptitude testing, career counseling, employment service for undergraduates, freshman orientation, health services, on-campus day care, personal counseling, placement service for graduates, special adviser for adult students, veterans counselor, international student services, services/facilities for handicapped.

ANNUAL EXPENSES. Tuition and fees: $13,644. **Room and board:** $6,220. **Books and supplies:** $480. **Other expenses:** $1,100.

FINANCIAL AID. 80% of freshmen, 80% of continuing students receive some form of aid. 55% of grants, 93% of loans, all jobs based on need. Academic, music/drama scholarships available. **Aid applications:** No closing date; priority given to applications received by February 15; applicants notified on a rolling basis beginning on or about April 1; must reply by May 1 or within 2 weeks if notified thereafter.

ADDRESS/TELEPHONE. David R. Gibson, Dean of Admissions and Financial Aid, Catholic University of America, 620 Michigan Avenue Northeast, Washington, DC 20064. (202) 319-5305. (800) 673-2772. Fax: (202) 319-5199.

Corcoran School of Art
Washington, D.C.

CB code: 5705

4-year private art college, coed. Founded in 1890. **Accreditation:** Regional. **Undergraduate enrollment:** 120 men, 160 women full time. **Faculty:** 81 total (45 full time). **Location:** Urban campus in very large city; one block from White House. **Calendar:** Semester, extensive summer session. **Microcomputers:** 12 located in computer centers. **Special facilities:** Corcoran Gallery of Art, student exhibition spaces.

DEGREES OFFERED. BFA. 80 bachelor's degrees awarded in 1992. 100% in visual and performing arts.

UNDERGRADUATE MAJORS. Fine arts, graphic design, photography.

ACADEMIC PROGRAMS. Internships, study abroad, visiting/exchange student program, New York semester, mobility programs with 11 member schools of Art College Exchange and 8 members of Independent Colleges of Art. **Remedial services:** Preadmission summer program. **Placement/credit:** AP, CLEP General and Subject; 15 credit hours maximum for bachelor's degree.

ACADEMIC REQUIREMENTS. Freshmen must earn minimum GPA of 2.0 to continue in good standing. 75% of freshmen return for sophomore year. Students must declare major by end of first year. **Graduation requirements:** 126 hours for bachelor's (55 in major). Most students required to take courses in arts/fine arts, English, humanities.

FRESHMAN ADMISSIONS. Selection criteria: Class rank, school achievement record, school and community activities, art teacher's recommendation, motivation, test scores, interview, and portfolio. Recommended units include English 4. Advanced art courses also recommended. **Test requirements:** SAT or ACT (SAT preferred).

1992 FRESHMAN CLASS PROFILE. 35 men, 40 women enrolled. 50% had high school GPA of 3.0 or higher, 50% between 2.0 and 2.99. **Academic background:** Mid 50% of enrolled freshmen had SAT-V between 440-530, SAT-M between 420-500. 97% submitted SAT scores. **Characteristics:** 36% from in state, 72% commute, 41% have minority backgrounds, 11% are foreign students. Average age is 19.

FALL-TERM APPLICATIONS. $30 fee, may be waived for applicants with need. No closing date; priority given to applications received by March 15; applicants notified on a rolling basis; must reply by May 1 or within 2 weeks if notified thereafter. Interview required for geographically close applicants. Portfolio required. Essay may replace interview, slides may replace original portfolio. CRDA. Deferred and early admission available.

STUDENT LIFE. Housing: Dormitories (coed). **Activities:** Student government, film, student newspaper, Senior Portfolio, gallery shows, student art openings.

STUDENT SERVICES. Career counseling, freshman orientation, personal counseling, placement service for graduates, veterans counselor, services/facilities for handicapped.

ANNUAL EXPENSES. Tuition and fees (1992-93): $9,980. **Room and board:** $2,940 room only. **Books and supplies:** $1,680. **Other expenses:** $1,785.

FINANCIAL AID. 64% of freshmen, 60% of continuing students receive some form of aid. 98% of grants, 76% of loans, all jobs based on need. Academic, art scholarships available. **Aid applications:** Closing date June 15; priority given to applications received by March 15; applicants notified on a rolling basis beginning on or about May 1; must reply within 2 weeks.

ADDRESS/TELEPHONE. Mark Sistek, Director of Admissions, Corcoran School of Art, 17th Street and New York Avenue, Northwest, Washington, DC 20006. (202) 628-9484. Fax: (202) 628-3186.

Gallaudet University
Washington, D.C.

CB code: 5240

Admissions:	76% of applicants accepted
Based on:	••• Essay, recommendations, test scores
	•• School record
	• Interview, special talents
Completion:	85% of freshmen end year in good standing
	75% graduate

4-year private liberal arts university for hearing impaired, coed. Founded in 1857. **Accreditation:** Regional. **Undergraduate enrollment:** 780 men, 888 women full time; 59 men, 60 women part time. **Graduate enrollment:** 50 men, 200 women full time; 31 men, 76 women part time. **Faculty:** 299 total (270 full time), 198 with doctorates or other terminal degrees. **Location:** Urban campus in very large city. **Calendar:** Semester, limited summer session. **Microcomputers:** 145 located in dormitories, libraries, classrooms, computer centers. **Special facilities:** National center for law and the deaf, information center on deafness, campus-wide facilities to assist the hearing impaired. **Additional facts:** Undergraduate program open only to hearing-impaired students; graduate program open to all. Interpreter training program open only to non-hearing-impaired students.

DEGREES OFFERED. AAS, BA, BS, MA, MS, MSW, PhD, EdD. 10 associate degrees awarded in 1992. 170 bachelor's degrees awarded. Graduate degrees offered in 17 major fields of study.

UNDERGRADUATE MAJORS. Associate: Business computer/console/peripheral equipment operation. **Bachelor's:** Accounting, advertising art, American studies, art education, art history, biology, business administration and management, business and management, chemistry, child development/care/guidance, civil engineering, commercial art, communications, computer and information sciences, computer engineering, computer technology, creative writing, dramatic arts, early childhood education, economics, education, education of the deaf and hearing impaired, education of the multiple handicapped, electrical technology, electrical/electronics/communications engineering, elementary education, engineering, English, English literature, food science and nutrition, French, German, history, home economics, home economics education, information sciences and systems, international studies, Latin American studies, leadership and programming, liberal/general studies, mathematics, mechanical engineering, museum studies, philosophy, physical education, physics, political science and government, psychology, recreation and community services technologies, recreation therapy, religion, Russian, school psychology, secondary education, small business management and ownership, social philosophy, social work, sociology, Spanish, studio art, television/film/photography, visual and performing arts, Western European studies.

ACADEMIC PROGRAMS. Accelerated program, cooperative education, double major, education specialist degree, honors program, independent study, internships, study abroad, teacher preparation, visiting/exchange student program, cross-registration, experiential programs off-campus (EPOC) including orientation program for employers of deaf students; liberal arts/career combination in engineering. **Remedial services:** Learning center, preadmission summer program, reduced course load, remedial instruction, special counselor, tutoring, writing center. **Placement/credit:** AP, CLEP General and Subject, institutional tests.

ACADEMIC REQUIREMENTS. Freshmen must earn minimum GPA of 1.5 to continue in good standing. 83% of freshmen return for sophomore year. Students must declare major by end of second year. **Graduation requirements:** 62 hours for associate, 124 hours for bachelor's. Most students required to take courses in English, foreign languages, humanities, biological/physical sciences, social sciences. **Postgraduate studies:** 50% from 2-year programs enter 4-year programs.

FRESHMAN ADMISSIONS. Selection criteria: Applicants with severe hearing losses who show evidence of academic ability and motivation considered. Test scores, grades, class rank, essay, and recommendation also considered. College-preparatory courses recommended, including algebra and geometry. **Test requirements:** Stanford achievement tests and audiogram required.

1992 FRESHMAN CLASS PROFILE. 694 men and women applied, 527 accepted; 366 enrolled. **Characteristics:** 90% live in college housing, 16% have minority backgrounds, 10% are foreign students. Average age is 20.

FALL-TERM APPLICATIONS. $35 fee. No closing date; priority given to applications received by April 15; applicants notified on a rolling basis; must reply by May 1 or within 4 weeks if notified thereafter. Essay required. Interview recommended. Deferred and early admission available.

STUDENT LIFE. Housing: Dormitories (coed). All dormitories equipped for hearing impaired. **Activities:** Student government, film, magazine, student newspaper, television, yearbook, dance, drama, music ensembles, fraternities, sororities, numerous academic, special interest, and religious organizations.

ATHLETICS. NCAA. **Intercollegiate:** Baseball M, basketball, cross-country, field hockey W, football M, soccer M, softball W, swimming, tennis, track and field, volleyball W, wrestling M. **Intramural:** Badminton, baseball M, basketball, bowling, cross-country, gymnastics, racquetball, soccer, softball, table tennis, tennis, track and field, volleyball.

STUDENT SERVICES. Aptitude testing, career counseling, employment service for undergraduates, freshman orientation, health services, on-campus day care, personal counseling, placement service for graduates, campus-wide communication facilities including telephone accessibility, alerting devices, audio loops, as well as interpreting and audiological services, services/facilities for handicapped.

ANNUAL EXPENSES. Tuition and fees: $4,570. **Room and board:** $5,110. **Books and supplies:** $630. **Other expenses:** $2,232.

FINANCIAL AID. 68% of freshmen receive some form of aid. All grants, 88% of loans, all jobs based on need. 253 enrolled freshmen were judged to have need, 251 were offered aid. State/district residency scholarships available. **Aid applications:** No closing date; priority given to applications received by April 15; applicants notified on a rolling basis beginning on or about May 15; must reply within 3 weeks. **Additional information:** Due to special nature of student body, institution receives substantial aid from state vocational rehabilitation agencies, supplemented by institutional grants when needed.

ADDRESS/TELEPHONE. Astrid Goodstein, Executive Director of Enrollment Services, Gallaudet University, 800 Florida Avenue, N.E, Washington, DC 20002. (202) 651-5114. Fax: (202) 651-5744.

George Washington University

Washington, D.C. CB code: 5246

Admissions: 79% of applicants accepted
Based on:
- ••• School record
- •• Essay, recommendations, special talents, test scores
- • Activities

Completion: 90% of freshmen end year in good standing
71% graduate

4-year private university, coed. Founded in 1821. **Accreditation:** Regional. **Undergraduate enrollment:** 2,549 men, 2,721 women full time; 546 men, 385 women part time. **Graduate enrollment:** 2,528 men, 1,942 women full time; 3,253 men, 2,368 women part time. **Faculty:** 2,088 total (1,397 full time), 1,653 with doctorates or other terminal degrees. **Location:** Urban campus in very large city. **Calendar:** Semester, extensive summer session. Extensive evening/early morning classes. **Microcomputers:** 550 located in dormitories, libraries, classrooms, computer centers. **Special facilities:** Dimock art gallery, rooftop open-air observatory.

DEGREES OFFERED. AS, BA, BS, BFA, MA, MS, MBA, MFA, MEd, PhD, EdD, MD, JD. 29 associate degrees awarded in 1992. 100% in allied health. 1,579 bachelor's degrees awarded. 22% in business and management, 7% engineering, 6% health sciences, 5% letters/literature, 8% psychology, 28% social sciences. Graduate degrees offered in 131 major fields of study.

UNDERGRADUATE MAJORS. Associate: Clinical laboratory science, nuclear medical technology, prehospital clinical medicine, radiation therapy technology. **Bachelor's:** Accounting, anthropology, applied mathematics, archeology, art history, biological and physical sciences, biology, business administration and management, business and management, business economics, chemistry, Chinese, civil engineering, classics, communications, computer and information sciences, computer engineering, criminal justice studies, dance, dramatic arts, dramatic literature, East Asian studies, economics, electrical/electronics/communications engineering, emergency medical technologies, emergency/disaster science, engineering, engineering and other disciplines, engineering mechanics, English, environmental science, European studies, finance, fine arts, French, geography, geology, German, history, human services, human services, humanities and social sciences, information sciences and systems, international business management, international relations, international studies, Jewish studies, journalism, Latin American studies, liberal/general studies, logistics/operations/materials management, marketing and distribution, mathematics, mechanical engineering, medical laboratory technologies, Middle Eastern studies, music, operations research, philosophy, physical education, physician's assistant, physics, political communication, political science and government, prelaw, premedicine, psychology, radio/television broadcasting, radiological sciences and administration, religion, Russian, sociology, Spanish, speech, speech pathology/audiology, statistics, visual and performing arts.

ACADEMIC PROGRAMS. Accelerated program, cooperative education, double major, dual enrollment of high school students, education specialist degree, honors program, independent study, internships, student-designed major, study abroad, teacher preparation, visiting/exchange student program, cross-registration, 7-year integrated BA/MA liberal arts program; liberal arts/career combination in engineering, business; combined bachelor's/graduate program in medicine. **Remedial services:** Reduced course load, special counselor, tutoring, speech and hearing clinic. **ROTC:** Naval. **Placement/credit:** AP, CLEP Subject, institutional tests; 30 credit hours maximum for bachelor's degree.

ACADEMIC REQUIREMENTS. Freshmen must earn minimum GPA of 2.0 to continue in good standing. 85% of freshmen return for sophomore year. Students must declare major by end of second year. **Graduation requirements:** 60 hours for associate, 120 hours for bachelor's (40 in major). Most students required to take courses in arts/fine arts, English, foreign languages, humanities, mathematics, biological/physical sciences, social sciences. **Additional information:** Students may earn credit through internships in the arts, business, communications, sciences, social sciences, humanities, government, and through cooperative education programs in engineering, education, business.

FRESHMAN ADMISSIONS. Selection criteria: Strong college-preparatory program, GPA of 3.0 and class rank in top third important. SAT or ACT required. Teacher and counselor recommendation and personal statement also required.Supplemental applications required for honors program and 7-year integrated liberal arts/MD program. **High school preparation:** 16 units required. Required units include English 4, foreign language 2, mathematics 3, social science 2 and science 2. One physics, 1 chemistry, and additional 1 unit in mathematics required for school of engineering and applied science. **Test requirements:** SAT or ACT; score report by February 1. ACH required of applicants to 7-year BA/MA liberal arts program. Score report by February 1. **Additional information:** Applications received after February 1 reviewed on space available basis.

1992 FRESHMAN CLASS PROFILE. 2,833 men applied, 2,226 accepted, 582 enrolled; 3,168 women applied, 2,526 accepted, 651 enrolled. 33% were in top tenth and 70% were in top quarter of graduating class. **Academic background:** Mid 50% of enrolled freshmen had SAT-V between 480-590, SAT-M between 530-640; ACT composite between 24-29. 93% submitted SAT scores, 13% submitted ACT scores. **Characteristics:** 6% from in state, 96% live in college housing, 25% have minority backgrounds, 7% are foreign students. Average age is 18.

FALL-TERM APPLICATIONS. $45 fee, may be waived for applicants with need. No closing date; priority given to applications received by February 1; applicants notified on a rolling basis beginning on or about March 15; must reply by May 1 or if notified thereafter letter will specify reply date. Interview required for early admission applicants. Audition required for bachelor of music applicants applicants. Essay required. CRDA. Deferred and early admission available. EDP-F. 2 ACH (English composition and mathematics) strongly preferred for all applicants.

STUDENT LIFE. Housing: Dormitories (women, coed); apartment, fraternity housing available. Residential programs available in politics and values, Roots: Western Civilization, and technology and society, multilingual floors, and creative and performing arts floors, substance-free living floors. **Activities:** Student government, magazine, radio, student newspaper, television, yearbook, choral groups, dance, drama, jazz band, music ensembles, musical theater, opera, pep band, symphony orchestra, fraternities, sororities, religious groups, national political party organizations, ethnic, social action, and public affairs groups.

ATHLETICS. NCAA. **Intercollegiate:** Baseball M, basketball, cross-country, diving, golf M, gymnastics W, rowing (crew), soccer, swimming, tennis, volleyball W, water polo M. **Intramural:** Badminton W, basketball, bowling, cross-country, golf, handball, racquetball, soccer, softball, squash, swimming, table tennis, tennis, volleyball, water polo.

STUDENT SERVICES. Aptitude testing, career counseling, employment service for undergraduates, freshman orientation, health services, personal counseling, placement service for graduates, veterans counselor, multi-cultural student center, services/facilities for handicapped.

ANNUAL EXPENSES. Tuition and fees (1992-93): $16,080. **Room and board:** $6,310. **Books and supplies:** $500. **Other expenses:** $950.

FINANCIAL AID. 80% of freshmen, 46% of continuing students receive some form of aid. 70% of grants, 70% of loans, all jobs based on need. 569 enrolled freshmen were judged to have need, 567 were offered aid. Academic, music/drama, athletic scholarships available. **Aid applications:** Closing date February 1; applicants notified on a rolling basis beginning on or about March 30; must reply by May 1. **Additional information:** Financially disadvantaged Washington, D.C. residents may apply for tuition remission grants. Auditions required for performing arts scholarships.

ADDRESS/TELEPHONE. George W. G. Stoner, Director of Admissions, George Washington University, 2121 I Street Northwest, Suite 201, Washington, DC 20052. (202) 994-6040. (800)447-3765. Fax: (202) 994-0458.

Georgetown University
Washington, D.C. CB code: 5244

Admissions: 29% of applicants accepted
Based on: ••• School record
•• Activities, essay, interview, recommendations, special talents, test scores
Completion: 96% of freshmen end year in good standing
90% graduate, 24% of these enter graduate study

4-year private university, coed, affiliated with Roman Catholic Church. Founded in 1789. **Accreditation:** Regional. **Undergraduate enrollment:** 2,838 men, 2,998 women full time; 128 men, 265 women part time. **Graduate enrollment:** 2,290 men, 1,758 women full time; 933 men, 874 women part time. **Faculty:** 698 total (500 full time), 548 with doctorates or other terminal degrees. **Location:** Urban campus in very large city; 1.5 miles from downtown Washington, DC. **Calendar:** Semester, extensive summer session. **Microcomputers:** 200 located in libraries, computer centers. **Special facilities:** Seismological observatory, fine arts gallery, satellite link for language.

DEGREES OFFERED. BA, BS, MA, MS, MBA, PhD, MD, JD. 1,468 bachelor's degrees awarded in 1992. 20% in business and management, 9% languages, 9% letters/literature, 5% psychology, 40% social sciences. Graduate degrees offered in 37 major fields of study.

UNDERGRADUATE MAJORS. Accounting, American studies, Arabic, Asian studies, biology, business administration and management, business and management, chemistry, Chinese, classics, computer and information sciences, Eastern European studies, economics, electrical/electronics/communications engineering, English, finance, fine arts, French, German, history, international business management, international relations, Italian, Japanese, Latin American studies, liberal/general studies, linguistics, marketing management, mathematics, mechanical engineering, nursing, philosophy, physics, political science and government, Portuguese, psychology, religion, Russian, sociology, Spanish, Western European studies.

ACADEMIC PROGRAMS. Double major, honors program, independent study, internships, student-designed major, study abroad, visiting/exchange student program, cross-registration; liberal arts/career combination in engineering; combined bachelor's/graduate program in business administration, medicine, law. **Remedial services:** Learning center, preadmission summer program, special counselor, tutoring. **ROTC:** Air Force, Army, Naval. **Placement/credit:** AP, institutional tests.

ACADEMIC REQUIREMENTS. Freshmen must earn minimum GPA of 2.0 to continue in good standing. 96% of freshmen return for sophomore year. Students must declare major by end of second year. **Graduation requirements:** 120 hours for bachelor's (30 in major). Most students required to take courses in English, foreign languages, history, humanities, philosophy/religion, biological/physical sciences, social sciences. **Postgraduate studies:** 8% enter law school, 4% enter medical school, 1% enter MBA programs, 11% enter other graduate study. **Additional information:** Early assurance program to university's medical and law schools.

FRESHMAN ADMISSIONS. Selection criteria: School academic record most important consideration in addition to test scores, essays, extracurricular activities, interview, and recommendations. Special consideration is given to qualified minorities, athletes, internationals, and alumni relatives. Recommended units include English 4, foreign language 4, mathematics 4, social science 2 and science 1. Additional units in science, mathematics, and foreign language recommended for some programs. **Test requirements:** SAT or ACT; score report by January 10. **Additional information:** Alumni interview in local area of applicant's residence will take place after application is submitted.

1992 FRESHMAN CLASS PROFILE. 4,773 men applied, 1,434 accepted, 655 enrolled; 5,343 women applied, 1,539 accepted, 736 enrolled. 84% had high school GPA of 3.0 or higher, 12% between 2.0 and 2.99. 69% were in top tenth and 92% were in top quarter of graduating class. **Academic background:** Mid 50% of enrolled freshmen had SAT-V between 540-650, SAT-M between 590-690; ACT composite between 26-31. 98% submitted SAT scores, 21% submitted ACT scores. **Characteristics:** 3% from in state, 98% live in college housing, 23% have minority backgrounds, 10% are foreign students. Average age is 18.

FALL-TERM APPLICATIONS. $45 fee, may be waived for applicants with need. Closing date January 10; applicants notified on or about April 1; must reply by May 1. Interview required. Essay required. Portfolio recommended for fine arts applicants. CRDA. Deferred admission available. Institutional early decision plan. Nonbinding Early Action plan deadline November 1, notification December 15. 3 ACH strongly recommended; score report by January 10.

STUDENT LIFE. Housing: Dormitories (coed); apartment, handicapped housing available. Students guaranteed on-campus housing for 3 of 4 years with option of living all 4 years on campus. Freshmen and sophomores required to live on campus. **Activities:** Student government, magazine, radio, student newspaper, yearbook, choral groups, concert band, dance, drama, jazz band, music ensembles, musical theater, pep band, symphony orchestra, Community Action Coalition, Campus Ministries, College Republicans, College Democrats, Black Student Alliance, Jewish Students Association, over 100 other clubs and organizations.

ATHLETICS. NCAA. **Intercollegiate:** Baseball M, basketball, cross-country, diving, field hockey W, football M, golf M, lacrosse, rowing (crew), sailing, soccer M, swimming, tennis, track and field, volleyball W. **Intramural:** Badminton, basketball, cross-country, diving, football M, golf, handball, ice hockey M, racquetball, skiing, soccer, softball, squash, swimming, table tennis, tennis, track and field, volleyball, water polo.

STUDENT SERVICES. Aptitude testing, career counseling, employment service for undergraduates, freshman orientation, health services, personal counseling, placement service for graduates, veterans counselor, services/facilities for handicapped.

ANNUAL EXPENSES. Tuition and fees: $17,586. **Room and board:** $6,824. **Books and supplies:** $630. **Other expenses:** $1,170.

FINANCIAL AID. 50% of freshmen, 52% of continuing students receive some form of aid. 80% of grants, 97% of loans, 38% of jobs based on need. 541 enrolled freshmen were judged to have need, all were offered aid. **Aid applications:** No closing date; priority given to applications received by February 1; applicants notified on a rolling basis; must reply by May 1 or within 4 weeks if notified thereafter.

ADDRESS/TELEPHONE. Charles A. Deacon, Dean of Undergraduate Admissions, Georgetown University, 37th and O Streets, Northwest, Washington, DC 20057. (202) 687-3600. Fax: (202) 687-5084.

Howard University
Washington, D.C. CB code: 5297

Admissions: 48% of applicants accepted
Based on: ••• School record, test scores
•• Recommendations
• Essay
Completion: 66% of freshmen end year in good standing
45% graduate, 66% of these enter graduate study

4-year private university, coed. Founded in 1867. **Accreditation:** Regional. **Undergraduate enrollment:** 2,659 men, 4,242 women full time; 455 men, 640 women part time. **Graduate enrollment:** 983 men, 1,183 women full time; 347 men, 454 women part time. **Faculty:** 1,995 total (1,232 full time), 1,550 with doctorates or other terminal degrees. **Location:** Urban campus in very large city; located in northwest section of city. **Calendar:** Semester, extensive summer session. **Microcomputers:** Located in dormitories, libraries, classrooms, computer centers. **Special facilities:** Hotel training facility, museum, 3 galleries. **Additional facts:** 4 campuses: Main, West, Divinity School, and Beltsville.

DEGREES OFFERED. BA, BS, BFA, BArch, MA, MS, MBA, MFA, MEd, MSW, PhD, EdD, DMD, MD, B. Pharm, M.Div. 1,484 bachelor's degrees awarded in 1992. 25% in business and management, 13% communications, 9% engineering, 6% health sciences, 9% life sciences, 5% psychology, 9% social sciences. Graduate degrees offered in 73 major fields of study.

UNDERGRADUATE MAJORS. Accounting, African languages, Afro-American (black) studies, anthropology, Arabic, architecture, art history, astronomy, botany, business administration and management, ceramics, chemical engineering, chemistry, civil engineering, classics, communications, computer and information sciences, computer programming, dance, dental hygiene, dramatic arts, economics, electrical/electronics/communications engineering, elementary education, English, finance, food science and nutrition, French, German, graphic arts technology, history, hotel/motel and restaurant management, human environment and housing, individual and family development, information sciences and systems, institutional/home management/supporting programs, insurance and risk management, interior design, international business management, jazz, journalism, marketing and distribution, marketing management, mathematics, mechanical engineering, medical dietetics, medical laboratory technologies, medical radiation dosimetry, microbiology, music, music history and appreciation, music theory and composition, nursing, occupational therapy, painting, pharmacy, philosophy, photography, physical education, physical therapy, physician's assistant, physics, political science and government, printmaking, psychology, public relations, radiation therapy technology, radio/television broadcasting, radio/television technology, recreation and community services technologies, Russian, sculpture, secondary education, sociology, Spanish, textiles and clothing, visual and performing arts, zoology.

ACADEMIC PROGRAMS. Accelerated program, cooperative education, double major, dual enrollment of high school students, honors program, independent study, internships, student-designed major, study abroad, teacher preparation, visiting/exchange student program, cross-registration; combined bachelor's/graduate program in medicine. **Remedial services:** Learning center, reduced course load, remedial instruction, special counselor, tutoring, Center for Academic Reinforcement. **ROTC:** Air Force, Army. **Placement/credit:** AP, CLEP General, institutional tests; 60 credit hours maximum for bachelor's degree.

ACADEMIC REQUIREMENTS. Freshmen must earn minimum GPA of 2.0 to continue in good standing. 65% of freshmen return for sophomore year. Students must declare major by end of second year. **Graduation requirements:** 127 hours for bachelor's. Most students required to take courses in English, foreign languages, mathematics, social sciences. **Postgraduate studies:** 6% enter law school, 3% enter medical school, 10% enter MBA programs, 47% enter other graduate study.

FRESHMAN ADMISSIONS. Selection criteria: School achievement record and SAT scores most important. Requirements vary from college to college. **High school preparation:** 16 units required. Required units include English 4, mathematics 2, social science 2 and science 2. **Test requirements:** SAT or ACT; score report by April 1. One ACH required of engineering applicants. Score report by April 1 Dental Hygiene Aptitude Test required of dental hygiene applicants.

1992 FRESHMAN CLASS PROFILE. 5,800 men and women applied, 2,800 accepted; 1,350 enrolled. **Academic background:** Mid 50% of enrolled freshmen had SAT-V between 370-470, SAT-M between 400-510; ACT composite between 18-22. 71% submitted SAT scores, 29% submitted ACT scores. **Characteristics:** 22% from in state, 80% live in college housing, 96% have minority backgrounds, 12% are foreign students. Average age is 18.

FALL-TERM APPLICATIONS. $25 fee. Closing date April 1; applicants notified on a rolling basis; must reply within 4 weeks. Audition required for music, drama applicants. Portfolio required for art applicants. Interview recommended for pharmacy and pharmacological sciences, college of fine arts applicants. Essay recommended. Deferred and early admission available.

STUDENT LIFE. Housing: Dormitories (men, women, coed); apartment housing available. Campus housing available on first-come, first-served basis. **Activities:** Student government, film, magazine, radio, student newspaper, television, yearbook, choral groups, concert band, dance, drama, jazz band, marching band, music ensembles, musical theater, fraternities, sororities, Absalom Jones Student Association, Adventist Committee, Baptist Student Union, Christian Science Organization, Christian Fellowship-Igbimo Otito, Lutheran Student Organization, Muslim Students, Wesley Foundation Methodist Fellowship, William J. Seymour Pentacostal Fellowship, academic honorary societies. **Additional information:** Campus life supplemented by political, cultural, scientific, educational, business, and recreational resources available in Washington, D.C.

ATHLETICS. NCAA. **Intercollegiate:** Baseball M, basketball, cross-country, diving, football M, gymnastics, soccer M, swimming, tennis, track and field, volleyball W, wrestling M. **Intramural:** Badminton W, basketball, bowling, soccer W, softball, table tennis.

STUDENT SERVICES. Aptitude testing, career counseling, employment service for undergraduates, freshman orientation, health services, on-campus day care, personal counseling, placement service for graduates, veterans counselor, services/facilities for handicapped.

ANNUAL EXPENSES. Tuition and fees (1992-93): $7,005. **Room and board:** $3,600. **Books and supplies:** $600. **Other expenses:** $2,250.

FINANCIAL AID. 48% of grants, 90% of loans, 33% of jobs based on need. Academic, music/drama, art, athletic scholarships available. **Aid applications:** Closing date April 1; priority given to applications received by March 1; applicants notified on or about May 1; must reply within 4 weeks.

ADDRESS/TELEPHONE. Emmett R. Griffin, Director of Admissions, Howard University, 2400 Sixth Street Northwest, Washington, DC 20059. (202) 806-2752. (800) 822-6363. Fax: (202) 806-5961.

Mount Vernon College
Washington, D.C.

CB code: 5422

4-year private liberal arts college, women only. Founded in 1875. **Accreditation:** Regional. **Undergraduate enrollment:** 273 women full time; 123 women part time. **Faculty:** 55 total (40 full time). **Location:** Urban campus in very large city. **Calendar:** Semester, limited summer session. **Microcomputers:** 50 located in libraries, computer centers. **Special facilities:** Gatehouse Gallery to display student artwork.

DEGREES OFFERED. AA, BA. 110 bachelor's degrees awarded.

UNDERGRADUATE MAJORS. Associate: Liberal/general studies. **Bachelor's:** Allied health, art conservation, business administration and management, business economics, communications, computer and information sciences, fine arts, health sciences, interior design, international relations, international studies, liberal/general studies, management science, marketing management, music history and appreciation, nursing, political science and government, psychology, urban studies, visual and performing arts.

ACADEMIC PROGRAMS. 2-year transfer program, double major, dual enrollment of high school students, honors program, independent study, internships, student-designed major, study abroad, weekend college, cross-registration. **Remedial services:** Learning center, reduced course load, tutoring. **Placement/credit:** AP, CLEP General, institutional tests; 30 credit hours maximum for bachelor's degree.

ACADEMIC REQUIREMENTS. Freshmen must earn minimum GPA of 2.0 to continue in good standing. 70% of freshmen return for sophomore year. Students must declare major by end of second year. **Graduation requirements:** 60 hours for associate (30 in major), 120 hours for bachelor's (40 in major). Most students required to take courses in arts/fine arts, English, history, humanities, mathematics, biological/physical sciences, social sciences. **Postgraduate studies:** 4% enter law school, 3% enter medical school, 2% enter MBA programs, 1% enter other graduate study.

FRESHMAN ADMISSIONS. Selection criteria: School achievement record most important, followed by test scores, recommendations, school and community activities, essay. **High school preparation:** 16 units recommended. Recommended units include English 4, foreign language 2, mathematics 2, social science 1 and science 2. **Test requirements:** SAT or ACT; score report by February 1.

1992 FRESHMAN CLASS PROFILE. 89 men and women enrolled. **Academic background:** Mid 50% of enrolled freshmen had SAT-V between 380-460, SAT-M between 350-440. 95% submitted SAT scores. **Characteristics:** 8% from in state, 84% live in college housing, 15% have minority backgrounds, 8% are foreign students. Average age is 18.

FALL-TERM APPLICATIONS. $25 fee, may be waived for applicants with need. No closing date; applicants notified on a rolling basis; must reply by May 1 or within 5 weeks if notified thereafter. Essay required. Interview recommended. Portfolio recommended for art, interior design applicants. CRDA. Deferred and early admission available. EDP-F.

STUDENT LIFE. Housing: Dormitories (women). **Activities:** Student government, magazine, student newspaper, yearbook, choral groups, dance, drama, music ensembles, Ambassador Club, Black Student Union, International Club.

ATHLETICS. Intercollegiate: Field hockey, lacrosse, tennis. **Intramural:** Basketball, golf, gymnastics, lacrosse, soccer, softball, tennis, volleyball.

STUDENT SERVICES. Career counseling, freshman orientation, health services, personal counseling, placement service for graduates, special adviser for adult students.

ANNUAL EXPENSES. Tuition and fees: $13,250. **Room and board:** $6,918. **Books and supplies:** $500. **Other expenses:** $600.

FINANCIAL AID. 60% of freshmen, 42% of continuing students receive some form of aid. 98% of grants, 53% of loans, 72% of jobs based on need. 30 enrolled freshmen were judged to have need, all were offered aid. Academic, music/drama, state/district residency, leadership, alumni affiliation scholarships available. **Aid applications:** No closing date; priority given to applications received by March 1; applicants notified on a rolling basis beginning on or about April 1; must reply by May 1 or within 2 weeks if notified thereafter.

ADDRESS/TELEPHONE. Meg Artley, Dean of Admissions, Mount Vernon College, 2100 Foxhall Road Northwest, Washington, DC 20007. (202) 625-4682. (800) 682-4636. Fax: (202) 337-0259.

Oblate College
Washington, D.C.

CB code: 5524

2-year upper-division private seminary college, coed, affiliated with Roman Catholic Church. Founded in 1916. **Accreditation:** Regional. **Undergraduate enrollment:** 7 men full time. **Graduate enrollment:** 13 men full time. **Faculty:** 9 total (6 full time), 7 with doctorates or other terminal degrees. **Location:** Urban campus in very large city. **Calendar:** Semester.

DEGREES OFFERED. BA, MA, M.Div. Graduate degrees offered in 2 major fields of study.

UNDERGRADUATE MAJORS. Philosophy.

ACADEMIC PROGRAMS. Independent study, cross-registration. **Placement/credit:** Institutional tests.

ACADEMIC REQUIREMENTS. Students must declare major by end of third year. **Graduation requirements:** 120 hours for bachelor's (25 in major). Most students required to take courses in English, history, mathematics, philosophy/religion, biological/physical sciences, social sciences.

STUDENT LIFE. Housing: Dormitories (men).

STUDENT SERVICES. Services/facilities for handicapped.

ANNUAL EXPENSES. Tuition and fees: $4,250. **Books and supplies:** $500.

FINANCIAL AID. Loans available. **Aid applications:** No closing date; applicants notified on a rolling basis.

ADDRESS/TELEPHONE. Rev. Don Dietz, Academic Dean/Dean of Admissions, Oblate College, 391 Michigan Avenue, Northeast, Washington, DC 20017-1587. (202) 529-6544.

Southeastern University
Washington, D.C. CB code: 5622

4-year private university and business college, coed. Founded in 1879. **Accreditation:** Regional. **Undergraduate enrollment:** 67 men, 44 women full time; 69 men, 113 women part time. **Graduate enrollment:** 88 men, 42 women full time; 55 men, 68 women part time. **Faculty:** 99 total (8 full time). **Location:** Urban campus in very large city. **Calendar:** Four 12-week terms per year. Saturday and extensive evening/early morning classes. **Microcomputers:** 100 located in libraries, classrooms, computer centers.

DEGREES OFFERED. AS, BS, MS, MBA. 20 associate degrees awarded in 1992. 80 bachelor's degrees awarded. Graduate degrees offered in 16 major fields of study.

UNDERGRADUATE MAJORS. Associate: Accounting, business and management, computer programming, finance, food management, management information systems, management science, marketing and distribution, marketing management, public affairs, small business management and ownership. **Bachelor's:** Accounting, business administration and management, business and management, business statistics, computer programming, contract management and procurement/purchasing, economics, finance, food management, human resources development, international business management, management information systems, management science, marketing management, marketing research, public administration, small business management and ownership.

ACADEMIC PROGRAMS. Accelerated program, dual enrollment of high school students, external degree, honors program, independent study, study abroad, weekend college, cross-registration; combined bachelor's/graduate program in business administration. **Remedial services:** Learning center, remedial instruction, tutoring. **Placement/credit:** Institutional tests.

ACADEMIC REQUIREMENTS. Freshmen must earn minimum GPA of 2.0 to continue in good standing. 75% of freshmen return for sophomore year. Students must declare major by end of first year. **Graduation requirements:** 60 hours for associate, 120 hours for bachelor's. Most students required to take courses in computer science, English, humanities, mathematics, biological/physical sciences, social sciences. **Postgraduate studies:** 70% from 2-year programs enter 4-year programs. **Additional information:** Weekend college degree programs available in accounting, taxation, business administration, public administration, computer information and finance.

FRESHMAN ADMISSIONS. Selection criteria: School achievement record most important. Special consideration given to veterans. **Test requirements:** SAT; score report by August 30.

1992 FRESHMAN CLASS PROFILE. 44 men, 68 women enrolled. **Characteristics:** 66% from in state, 100% commute, 60% have minority backgrounds, 30% are foreign students. Average age is 25.

FALL-TERM APPLICATIONS. $45 fee, may be waived for applicants with need. No closing date; applicants notified on a rolling basis. Interview recommended. CRDA. Deferred and early admission available.

STUDENT LIFE. Activities: Student government, yearbook, fraternities, sororities.

STUDENT SERVICES. Aptitude testing, career counseling, employment service for undergraduates, personal counseling, placement service for graduates.

ANNUAL EXPENSES. Tuition and fees (1992-93): $7,695. **Books and supplies:** $400. **Other expenses:** $850.

FINANCIAL AID. 45% of freshmen, 45% of continuing students receive some form of aid. Grants, loans, jobs available. Academic scholarships available. **Aid applications:** No closing date; priority given to applications received by June 1; applicants notified on a rolling basis; must reply within 2 weeks.

ADDRESS/TELEPHONE. Mahalia Rahman, Director of Marketing, Admissions, and Financial Aid, Southeastern University, 501 I Street Southwest, Washington, DC 20024. (202) 265-5343.

Strayer College
Washington, DC CB code: 5632

4-year proprietary business college, coed. Founded in 1892. **Accreditation:** Regional. **Undergraduate enrollment:** 1,169 men, 1,160 women full time; 1,016 men, 1,407 women part time. **Graduate enrollment:** 261 men, 190 women full time; 223 men, 140 women part time. **Faculty:** 166 total (48 full time), 43 with doctorates or other terminal degrees. **Location:** Urban campus in very large city; in downtown area. **Calendar:** Quarter, extensive summer session. Saturday and extensive evening/early morning classes. **Microcomputers:** 287 located in libraries, classrooms, computer centers. **Additional facts:** Branch campuses in Arlington, Alexandria, Ashburn, Fredericksburg, Manassas, and Woodbridge, Virginia

DEGREES OFFERED. AA, BS, MS. 117 associate degrees awarded in 1992. 50% in business and management, 50% computer sciences. 391 bachelor's degrees awarded. 59% in business and management, 41% computer sciences. Graduate degrees offered in 3 major fields of study.

UNDERGRADUATE MAJORS. Associate: Accounting, business administration and management, business and management, business economics, economics, information sciences and systems, liberal/general studies, marketing and distribution, social sciences. **Bachelor's:** Accounting, business administration and management, business and management, business economics, economics, information sciences and systems.

ACADEMIC PROGRAMS. Accelerated program, weekend college. **Remedial services:** Reduced course load, tutoring. **Placement/credit:** AP, CLEP General and Subject, institutional tests.

ACADEMIC REQUIREMENTS. Freshmen must earn minimum GPA of 2.0 to continue in good standing. 50% of freshmen return for sophomore year. Students must declare major on enrollment. **Graduation requirements:** 90 hours for associate (36 in major), 180 hours for bachelor's (54 in major). Most students required to take courses in arts/fine arts, computer science, English, humanities, mathematics, philosophy/religion, social sciences. **Postgraduate studies:** 71% from 2-year programs enter 4-year programs.

FRESHMAN ADMISSIONS. Selection criteria: Institutional placement tests required.

1992 FRESHMAN CLASS PROFILE. 380 men, 556 women enrolled. **Characteristics:** 52% from in state, 100% commute, 50% have minority backgrounds, 20% are foreign students. Average age is 20.

FALL-TERM APPLICATIONS. $25 fee. No closing date; applicants notified on a rolling basis. Interview recommended. Deferred and early admission available.

STUDENT LIFE. Activities: Accounting club, honor society, international club, Data Processing Management Association, business administration club, marketing club.

STUDENT SERVICES. Career counseling, employment service for undergraduates, placement service for graduates, veterans counselor, services/facilities for handicapped.

ANNUAL EXPENSES. Tuition and fees (1992-93): $4,860. **Books and supplies:** $450. **Other expenses:** $2,100.

FINANCIAL AID. 64% of freshmen, 42% of continuing students receive some form of aid. All grants, all loans based on need. Academic, leadership scholarships available. **Aid applications:** No closing date; priority given to applications received by July 1; applicants notified on a rolling basis beginning on or about August 1; must reply within 2 weeks. **Additional information:** April 15 closing date for academic scholarships.

ADDRESS/TELEPHONE. Admissions Office, Strayer College, 1025 15th Street, Northwest, Washington, DC 20005. (202) 408-2400. Fax: (202) 289-1831.

Trinity College
Washington, D.C. CB code: 5796

Admissions: 91% of applicants accepted
Based on:
••• School record
•• Activities, recommendations, test scores
• Essay, interview, special talents
Completion: 95% of freshmen end year in good standing
87% graduate, 50% of these enter graduate study

4-year private liberal arts college, women only, affiliated with Roman Catholic Church. Founded in 1897. **Accreditation:** Regional. **Undergraduate enrollment:** 378 women full time; 474 women part time. **Graduate enrollment:** 3 men, 30 women full time; 22 men, 257 women part time. **Faculty:** 110 total (48 full time), 46 with doctorates or other terminal degrees. **Location:** Urban campus in very large city. **Calendar:** Semester, extensive summer session. Saturday and extensive evening/early morning classes. **Microcomputers:** 40 located in dormitories, libraries, computer centers. **Special facilities:** Art gallery.

DEGREES OFFERED. BA, BS, MA, MS. 115 bachelor's degrees awarded in 1992. 26% in business and management, 5% communications, 7% teacher education, 8% letters/literature, 8% multi/interdisciplinary studies, 8% philosophy, religion, theology, 8% psychology, 27% social sciences. Graduate degrees offered in 13 major fields of study.

UNDERGRADUATE MAJORS. Advertising design, American studies, art history, biochemistry, biology, business administration and management, business economics, chemistry, communications, early childhood education, economics, education, education of the emotionally handicapped, education of the mentally handicapped, elementary education, English, English literature, French, graphic design, history, international relations, international studies, mathematics, music, political science and government, psychology, Spanish, special education.

ACADEMIC PROGRAMS. Accelerated program, double major, dual enrollment of high school students, education specialist degree, internships, student-designed major, study abroad, teacher preparation, visiting/exchange student program, weekend college, cross-registration; combined bachelor's/graduate program in law. **Remedial services:** Learning center, reduced course load, remedial instruction, tutoring. **ROTC:** Air Force, Army. **Placement/credit:** AP, institutional tests.

ACADEMIC REQUIREMENTS. Freshmen must earn minimum GPA of 2.0 to continue in good standing. 89% of freshmen return for sophomore year. Students must declare major by end of second year. **Graduation requirements:** 128 hours for bachelor's (32 in major). Most students required to take courses in arts/fine arts, English, foreign languages, history, mathematics, philosophy/religion, biological/physical sciences, social sciences. **Postgraduate studies:** 15% enter law school, 21% enter MBA programs, 14% enter other graduate study.

FRESHMAN ADMISSIONS. Selection criteria: School achievement record, test scores, recommendations, interview, school and community activities all considered. 3.0 GPA preferred. Special consideration given to children of alumnae. **High school preparation:** 16 units required; 19 recommended. Required and recommended units include English 4, foreign language 3, mathematics 4, social science 2-3 and science 3. Biological science 2 recommended. 3 history also recommended. **Test requirements:** SAT or ACT (SAT preferred); score report by May 15.

1992 FRESHMAN CLASS PROFILE. 227 women applied, 207 accepted, 89 enrolled. 52% had high school GPA of 3.0 or higher, 48% between 2.0 and 2.99. **Academic background:** Mid 50% of enrolled freshmen had SAT-V between 440-550, SAT-M between 460-560. 94% submitted SAT scores. **Characteristics:** 4% from in state, 95% live in college housing, 52% have minority backgrounds, 6% are foreign students. Average age is 18.

FALL-TERM APPLICATIONS. $35 fee, may be waived for applicants with need. No closing date; applicants notified on a rolling basis; must reply by May 1 or within 2 weeks if notified thereafter. Essay required. Interview recommended. CRDA. Deferred and early admission available. EDP-S.

STUDENT LIFE. Housing: Dormitories (women). **Activities:** Student government, film, magazine, student newspaper, yearbook, choral groups, dance, drama, music ensembles, Young Democrats, Young Republicans, Black Student Alliance, International Student Association, Inter-American Club, Peer Ministry. **Additional information:** Student life mostly self-governed. Honor code exists.

ATHLETICS. NCAA. **Intercollegiate:** Field hockey, lacrosse, rowing (crew), soccer, tennis. **Intramural:** Lacrosse, soccer, softball, tennis, volleyball.

STUDENT SERVICES. Aptitude testing, career counseling, employment service for undergraduates, freshman orientation, health services, personal counseling, special adviser for adult students, services/facilities for handicapped.

ANNUAL EXPENSES. Tuition and fees: $11,230. **Room and board:** $6,430. **Books and supplies:** $500. **Other expenses:** $800.

FINANCIAL AID. 81% of freshmen, 76% of continuing students receive some form of aid. 53% of jobs based on need. Academic scholarships available. **Aid applications:** No closing date; priority given to applications received by March 1; applicants notified on a rolling basis beginning on or about April 1; must reply by May 1 or within 2 weeks if notified thereafter.

ADDRESS/TELEPHONE. Mary-Agnes D. Evans, Director of Admissions, Trinity College, 125 Michigan Avenue, Northeast, Washington, DC 20017-1094. (202) 939-5040. (800) 492-6882. Fax: (202) 939-5314.

University of the District of Columbia
Washington, D.C. CB code: 5929

4-year public university, coed. Founded in 1975. **Accreditation:** Regional. **Undergraduate enrollment:** 1,779 men, 1,971 women full time; 3,004 men, 4,145 women part time. **Graduate enrollment:** 102 men, 129 women full time; 197 men, 251 women part time. **Faculty:** 623 total (414 full time), 211 with doctorates or other terminal degrees. **Location:** Urban campus in very large city. **Calendar:** Semester, limited summer session. Saturday and extensive evening/early morning classes. **Microcomputers:** Located in libraries, classrooms, computer centers.

DEGREES OFFERED. AA, AS, BA, BS, MA, MS, MBA. 225 associate degrees awarded in 1992. 24% in business and management, 8% computer sciences, 15% engineering technologies, 8% library science, 23% parks/recreation, protective services, public affairs, 15% visual and performing arts. 510 bachelor's degrees awarded. 10% in business and management, 10% business/office and marketing/distribution, 5% computer sciences, 8% education, 7% teacher education, 10% letters/literature, 10% mathematics, 13% parks/recreation, protective services, public affairs. Graduate degrees offered in 13 major fields of study.

UNDERGRADUATE MAJORS. Associate: Accounting, aeronautical technology, air pollution control technology, aircraft mechanics, architectural technologies, architecture, business administration and management, business and office, business computer/console/peripheral equipment operation, business data entry equipment operation, business data processing and related programs, business data programming, child development/care/guidance, civil technology, computer and information sciences, computer technology, criminal justice technology, criminology, electrical technology, electronic technology, engineering and engineering-related technologies, fashion merchandising, finance, fire control and safety technology, food production/management/services, French, funeral services/mortuary science, German, graphic and printing production, graphic arts technology, history, information sciences and systems, instrumentation technology, law enforcement and corrections technologies, legal assistant/paralegal, library science, marine biology, marketing and distribution, mechanical design technology, medical laboratory technologies, music, nursing, philosophy, physical sciences, public affairs, radiograph medical technology, respiratory therapy technology, secretarial and related programs, urban studies, water resources. **Bachelor's:** Accounting, animal sciences, anthropology, art education, biology, business administration and management, chemistry, city/community/regional planning, civil engineering, clothing and textiles management/production/services, communications, computer and information sciences, construction, construction management, criminal justice studies, dramatic arts, economics, electrical/electronics/communications engineering, elementary education, English, environmental science, film arts, finance, fire control and safety technology, food science and nutrition, food sciences, French, geography, German, graphic and printing production, health education, history, home economics, home economics education, individual and family development, industrial arts education, information sciences and systems, journalism, library science, mathematics, mechanical engineering, music, music education, nursing, ornamental horticulture, philosophy, physical education, physics, political science and government, psychology, public administration, radio/television broadcasting, reading education, secondary education, secretarial and related programs, social foundations, social work, sociology, Spanish, special education, speech correction, speech pathology/audiology, studio art, textiles and clothing, urban studies.

ACADEMIC PROGRAMS. 2-year transfer program, cooperative education, dual enrollment of high school students, honors program, independent study, internships, weekend college, cross-registration. **Remedial services:** Learning center, preadmission summer program, remedial instruction, tutoring. **ROTC:** Air Force, Army, Naval. **Placement/credit:** CLEP General and Subject, institutional tests.

ACADEMIC REQUIREMENTS. Freshmen must earn minimum GPA of 2.0 to continue in good standing. 20% of freshmen return for sophomore year. Students must declare major by end of first year. **Graduation requirements:** 65 hours for associate (53 in major), 120 hours for bachelor's (90 in major). Most students required to take courses in English, foreign languages, history, mathematics, philosophy/religion, biological/physical sciences, social sciences. **Postgraduate studies:** 10% from 2-year programs enter 4-year programs. 1% enter law school, 1% enter medical school, 20% enter MBA programs.

FRESHMAN ADMISSIONS. Selection criteria: Open admissions. Selective admissions to nursing, art, and music programs. **High school preparation:** 18 units recommended. Recommended units include biological science 1, English 4, mathematics 2, physical science 1 and social science 2.

1992 FRESHMAN CLASS PROFILE. 1,534 men and women enrolled. **Characteristics:** 95% from in state, 100% commute, 93% have minority backgrounds, 1% join fraternities/sororities. Average age is 21.

FALL-TERM APPLICATIONS. $20 fee. Closing date June 1; priority given to applications received by May 1; applicants notified on a rolling basis. Interview recommended for nursing applicants. Audition recommended for music applicants. Portfolio recommended for art applicants. Deferred admission available.

STUDENT LIFE. Activities: Student government, radio, student newspaper, television, yearbook, choral groups, concert band, dance, drama, jazz band, marching band, fraternities, sororities.

ATHLETICS. NCAA. **Intercollegiate:** Basketball, soccer M, tennis, track and field, volleyball W. **Intramural:** Basketball, softball, swimming, tennis, volleyball.

STUDENT SERVICES. Career counseling, employment service for undergraduates, health services, personal counseling, placement service for graduates, veterans counselor, services/facilities for handicapped.

ANNUAL EXPENSES. Tuition and fees (1992-93): $800, $2,880 additional for out-of-state students. **Books and supplies:** $600. **Other expenses:** $1,400.

FINANCIAL AID. 4% of freshmen, 11% of continuing students receive some form of aid. 83% of grants, 96% of loans, 43% of jobs based on need. 300 enrolled freshmen were judged to have need, 250 were offered aid. Academic, music/drama, athletic scholarships available. **Aid applications:** No closing date; priority given to applications received by March 15; applicants notified on a rolling basis beginning on or about June 1; must reply by July 1 or within 10 days if notified thereafter.

ADDRESS/TELEPHONE. Sandra Dolphin, Director of Admissions, Univ of the District of Columbia, 4200 Connecticut Ave NW, Washington, DC 20008. (202) 282-3200.

Florida

Art Institute of Fort Lauderdale
Fort Lauderdale, Florida CB code: 5040

2-year proprietary art, business, technical college, coed. Founded in 1968. **Undergraduate enrollment:** 930 men, 1,007 women full time; 68 men, 74 women part time. **Faculty:** 100 total (45 full time). **Location:** Urban campus in small city; 25 miles from Miami, 30 miles from West Palm Beach. **Calendar:** Quarter, extensive summer session. **Microcomputers:** Located in computer centers. **Special facilities:** Art gallery,photography laboratory, computer graphic studio, full video studio, audio/recording equipment studio.

DEGREES OFFERED. AS, BS. 833 associate degrees awarded in 1992. 10% in business/office and marketing/distribution, 90% visual and performing arts.

UNDERGRADUATE MAJORS. Associate: Advertising, apparel and accessories marketing, clothing and textiles management/production/services, commercial art, drawing, fashion design, fashion merchandising, graphic arts technology, graphic design, illustration design, interior design, marketing and distribution, music, music business management, painting, photography, psychology, retailing, tourism, transportation and travel marketing, video. **Bachelor's:** Business and management, interior design.

ACADEMIC PROGRAMS. Honors program, independent study, internships. **Remedial services:** Special counselor, learning laboratories.

ACADEMIC REQUIREMENTS. Freshmen must earn minimum GPA of 2.0 to continue in good standing. 60% of freshmen return for sophomore year. Students must declare major on enrollment. **Graduation requirements:** 120 hours for associate (120 in major). Most students required to take courses in arts/fine arts, English, humanities, mathematics, biological/physical sciences. **Additional information:** Academic program designed to simulate working environment, focusing coursework towards job-related skills. After completion of associate's degree students may continue to earn a bachelor of science in either interior design or business management.

FRESHMAN ADMISSIONS. Selection criteria: Open admissions. Students must show commitment to succeed in applied arts, fashion, music and video, or design fields. Interview important. Prefer students with background in chosen major.

1992 FRESHMAN CLASS PROFILE. 373 men, 405 women enrolled. 10% had high school GPA of 3.0 or higher, 80% between 2.0 and 2.99. **Characteristics:** 50% from in state, 85% commute, 8% have minority backgrounds, 6% are foreign students. Average age is 20.

FALL-TERM APPLICATIONS. $50 fee. No closing date; applicants notified on a rolling basis; must reply within 2 weeks. Interview recommended. Portfolio recommended. Deferred admission available.

STUDENT LIFE. Housing: Dormitories (coed). **Activities:** Radio, student newspaper, television, newsletter, student chapter of American Society of Interior Designers, photography club, fashion club, Distributive Education Club junior collegiate chapter, music and video club, Professional Photographers of America student chapter, International Student Organization. **Additional information:** Many student activities revolve around student major specializations such as art exhibits and fashion shows.

ATHLETICS. Intercollegiate: Basketball M.

STUDENT SERVICES. Career counseling, employment service for undergraduates, freshman orientation, personal counseling, placement service for graduates, veterans counselor, services/facilities for handicapped.

ANNUAL EXPENSES. Tuition and fees (1992-93): $8,014. **Room and board:** $3,300 room only. **Books and supplies:** $953. **Other expenses:** $750.

FINANCIAL AID. 51% of freshmen, 52% of continuing students receive some form of aid. Grants, loans, jobs available. **Aid applications:** No closing date; applicants notified on a rolling basis beginning on or about May 30; must reply within 2 weeks. **Additional information:** Internal scholarships available. Financial planning program allows personalized service to budget and meet college costs through individualized payment plans.

ADDRESS/TELEPHONE. Eileen L. Northrop, VP Director of Admissions, Art Institute of Fort Lauderdale, 1799 Southeast 17th Street, Fort Lauderdale, FL 33316-3000. (305) 463-3000. (800) 275-7603. Fax: (800) 275-7603 ext. 509.

Barry University
Miami Shores, Florida CB code: 5053

Admissions: 66% of applicants accepted
Based on:
••• School record
•• Activities, essay, recommendations, test scores
• Interview, special talents
Completion: 80% of freshmen end year in good standing
40% graduate, 40% of these enter graduate study

4-year private university, coed, affiliated with Roman Catholic Church. Founded in 1940. **Accreditation:** Regional. **Undergraduate enrollment:** 703 men, 1,159 women full time; 1,043 men, 1,778 women part time. **Graduate enrollment:** 248 men, 421 women full time; 348 men, 796 women part time. **Faculty:** 483 total (220 full time), 133 with doctorates or other terminal degrees. **Location:** Suburban campus in large town; within greater Miami area, 10 miles from Fort Lauderdale. **Calendar:** Semester, limited summer session. **Microcomputers:** Located in libraries, classrooms, computer centers. **Special facilities:** Satellite base.

DEGREES OFFERED. BA, BS, BFA, MA, MS, MBA, MSW, PhD. 945 bachelor's degrees awarded in 1992. 7% in business and management, 8% business/office and marketing/distribution, 14% health sciences, 55% multi/interdisciplinary studies. Graduate degrees offered in 22 major fields of study.

UNDERGRADUATE MAJORS. Accounting, allied health, arts management, athletic training, biology, business administration and management, business and management, business economics, chemistry, clinical laboratory science, communications, computer and information sciences, criminal justice studies, cytotechnology, dramatic arts, early childhood education, economics, economics/finance, education, electrodiagnostic technologies, elementary education, English, finance, fine arts, French, health sciences, history, international business management, international relations, international studies, journalism, liberal/general studies, management information systems, marine biology, marketing and distribution, mathematics, medical laboratory technologies, music education, nuclear medical technology, nursing, occupational therapy, office automation, philosophy, photography, physical therapy, political science and government, predentistry, prelaw, premedicine, prepharmacy, prepodiatry, preveterinary, psychology, public relations, sociology, Spanish, sports management, sports medicine, theater management, theological studies, ultrasound technology, visual and performing arts.

ACADEMIC PROGRAMS. Accelerated program, double major, dual enrollment of high school students, education specialist degree, honors program, independent study, internships, study abroad, teacher preparation, Washington semester; liberal arts/career combination in engineering. **Remedial services:** Learning center, preadmission summer program, reduced course load, remedial instruction, special counselor, tutoring. **ROTC:** Air Force, Army. **Placement/credit:** AP, CLEP General and Subject, institutional tests; 30 credit hours maximum for bachelor's degree.

ACADEMIC REQUIREMENTS. Freshmen must earn minimum GPA of 2.0 to continue in good standing. 75% of freshmen return for sophomore year. Students must declare major by end of second year. **Graduation requirements:** 120 hours for bachelor's (45 in major). Most students required to take courses in arts/fine arts, English, humanities, mathematics, philosophy/religion, biological/physical sciences, social sciences.

FRESHMAN ADMISSIONS. Selection criteria: Test scores, 2.5 GPA, counselor recommendation used. Extracurricular activities considered. **High school preparation:** 16 units required. Nursing majors need 1 chemistry, 1 biology, algebra. Biology and science majors need 1 biology, 1 chemistry, 3.5 mathematics. Mathematics majors need 3.5 mathematics (algebra, geometry, trigonometry). **Test requirements:** SAT or ACT; score report by August 1.

1992 FRESHMAN CLASS PROFILE. 1,754 men applied, 1,160 accepted, 409 enrolled; 2,630 women applied, 1,752 accepted, 756 enrolled. 45% had high school GPA of 3.0 or higher, 50% between 2.0 and 2.99. **Academic background:** Mid 50% of enrolled freshmen had SAT-V between 380-500, SAT-M between 410-540; ACT composite between 17-22. 82% submitted SAT scores, 53% submitted ACT scores. **Characteristics:** 62% from in state, 50% commute, 40% have minority backgrounds, 20% are foreign students, 2% join fraternities/sororities. Average age is 18.

FALL-TERM APPLICATIONS. $30 fee, may be waived for applicants with need. Closing date August 1; priority given to applications received by April 1. Essay required. Interview recommended. CRDA. Deferred and early admission available. EDP-F.

STUDENT LIFE. Housing: Dormitories (men, women, coed). **Activities:** Student government, student newspaper, television, yearbook, weekly publications, choral groups, dance, drama, jazz band, music ensembles, musical theater, mime and puppet theater, fraternities, sororities, campus ministry, departmental clubs, chapel services, Circle-K, International Students Organization.

ATHLETICS. NCAA. **Intercollegiate:** Baseball M, basketball, cross-country, golf M, soccer, softball W, tennis, volleyball W. **Intramural:**

Basketball, racquetball, rugby M, skin diving, soccer, softball, swimming, table tennis, tennis, volleyball.

STUDENT SERVICES. Aptitude testing, career counseling, employment service for undergraduates, freshman orientation, health services, personal counseling, placement service for graduates, special adviser for adult students, services/facilities for handicapped.

ANNUAL EXPENSES. Tuition and fees (1992-93): $10,270. **Room and board:** $5,600. **Books and supplies:** $500. **Other expenses:** $800.

FINANCIAL AID. 75% of freshmen, 71% of continuing students receive some form of aid. 68% of grants, 76% of loans, all jobs based on need. Academic, music/drama, athletic, state/district residency, alumni affiliation scholarships available. **Aid applications:** No closing date; priority given to applications received by April 1; applicants notified on a rolling basis beginning on or about July 1; must reply by May 1 or within 2 weeks if notified thereafter.

ADDRESS/TELEPHONE. Robin Ray Roberts, Dean of Admissions and Enrollment Planning, Barry University, 11300 Northeast Second Avenue, Miami Shores, FL 33161. (305) 899-3100. (800) 621-3388. Fax: (305) 899-3104.

Bethune-Cookman College

Daytona Beach, Florida — CB code: 5061

Admissions: 82% of applicants accepted
Based on:
- ••• Recommendations
- •• Essay
- • Activities, interview, school record, special talents

Completion: 86% of freshmen end year in good standing
42% graduate, 16% of these enter graduate study

4-year private liberal arts college, coed, affiliated with United Methodist Church. Founded in 1904. **Accreditation:** Regional. **Undergraduate enrollment:** 882 men, 1,356 women full time; 25 men, 38 women part time. **Faculty:** 205 total (129 full time), 76 with doctorates or other terminal degrees. **Location:** Urban campus in small city; 60 miles from Orlando. **Calendar:** Semester, limited summer session. Saturday classes. **Microcomputers:** 140 located in dormitories, libraries, computer centers. **Special facilities:** Founder Mary McLeod Bethune's home and grave site (national historic landmarks), archives.

DEGREES OFFERED. BA, BS. 253 bachelor's degrees awarded in 1992. 36% in business and management, 7% communications, 5% computer sciences, 11% teacher education, 13% parks/recreation, protective services, public affairs, 8% psychology, 8% social sciences.

UNDERGRADUATE MAJORS. Accounting, biology, business administration and management, business education, chemistry, computer and information sciences, criminal justice studies, education of exceptional children, elementary education, English, English education, foreign languages (multiple emphasis), foreign languages education, history, hotel/motel and restaurant management, information sciences and systems, liberal/general studies, materials engineering, mathematics, mathematics education, medical laboratory technologies, music, music education, nursing, physical education, political science and government, psychology, radio/television broadcasting, religion and philosophy, religious education, science education, social studies education, sociology.

ACADEMIC PROGRAMS. Accelerated program, cooperative education, double major, honors program, internships, study abroad, teacher preparation, weekend college; liberal arts/career combination in engineering. **Remedial services:** Learning center, preadmission summer program, reduced course load, remedial instruction, special counselor, tutoring. **ROTC:** Air Force, Army. **Placement/credit:** AP, CLEP General and Subject, institutional tests; 30 credit hours maximum for bachelor's degree.

ACADEMIC REQUIREMENTS. Freshmen must earn minimum GPA of 1.5 to continue in good standing. 81% of freshmen return for sophomore year. Students must declare major on application. **Graduation requirements:** 124 hours for bachelor's (36 in major). Most students required to take courses in English, foreign languages, history, humanities, mathematics, philosophy/religion, biological/physical sciences, social sciences. **Postgraduate studies:** 1% enter law school, 8% enter MBA programs, 7% enter other graduate study.

FRESHMAN ADMISSIONS. Selection criteria: Letters of recommendation most important. School achievement record considered. **High school preparation:** 24 units required. Required and recommended units include English 4, mathematics 3, social science 5 and science 3. Foreign language 2 recommended. **Test requirements:** Test scores encouraged but not required.

1992 FRESHMAN CLASS PROFILE. 695 men applied, 603 accepted, 275 enrolled; 1,041 women applied, 824 accepted, 328 enrolled. 25% had high school GPA of 3.0 or higher, 67% between 2.0 and 2.99. 15% were in top tenth and 30% were in top quarter of graduating class. **Characteristics:** 81% from in state, 75% live in college housing, 96% have minority backgrounds, 2% are foreign students. Average age is 18.

FALL-TERM APPLICATIONS. $25 fee. Closing date July 30; priority given to applications received by June 1; applicants notified on a rolling basis beginning on or about January 3; must reply by August 15 or within 2 weeks if notified thereafter. Interview required for music applicants. Essay required. Deferred and early admission available. SAT/ACT recommended.

STUDENT LIFE. Housing: Dormitories (men, women). Special wings in dormitories reserved for honor students and social organization members. **Activities:** Student government, radio, student newspaper, television, yearbook, choral groups, concert band, dance, drama, jazz band, marching band, music ensembles, fraternities, sororities, several honor, social, and political organizations.

ATHLETICS. NCAA. **Intercollegiate:** Baseball M, basketball, cross-country, football M, tennis, track and field, volleyball W. **Intramural:** Basketball, football M, racquetball, softball W, table tennis, tennis, volleyball.

STUDENT SERVICES. Aptitude testing, career counseling, employment service for undergraduates, freshman orientation, health services, personal counseling, placement service for graduates, special adviser for adult students, veterans counselor, financial aid counselor, services/facilities for handicapped.

ANNUAL EXPENSES. Tuition and fees: $5,165. **Room and board:** $3,396. **Books and supplies:** $500. **Other expenses:** $1,520.

FINANCIAL AID. 84% of freshmen, 94% of continuing students receive some form of aid. 78% of grants, 96% of loans, 89% of jobs based on need. 519 enrolled freshmen were judged to have need, 501 were offered aid. Academic, music/drama, athletic scholarships available. **Aid applications:** No closing date; priority given to applications received by March 1; applicants notified on a rolling basis beginning on or about May 1; must reply within 2 weeks.

ADDRESS/TELEPHONE. Dr. Roberto Barragan, Jr, Director of Admissions, Bethune-Cookman College, 640 Second Avenue, Daytona Beach, FL 32115. (904) 238-3803. (800) 448-0228. Fax: (904) 257-5338.

Brevard Community College

Cocoa, Florida — CB code: 5073

2-year public community college, coed. Founded in 1960. **Accreditation:** Regional. **Undergraduate enrollment:** 2,237 men, 2,489 women full time; 3,953 men, 5,404 women part time. **Faculty:** 1,072 total (233 full time), 80 with doctorates or other terminal degrees. **Location:** Suburban campus in large town; 50 miles from Orlando. **Calendar:** Semester, extensive summer session. Saturday and extensive evening/early morning classes. **Microcomputers:** 30 located in libraries. **Special facilities:** Planetarium, solar observatory. **Additional facts:** 4 campuses: Cocoa, Titusville, Melbourne, and Palm Bay

DEGREES OFFERED. AA, AS. 1,173 associate degrees awarded in 1992. 13% in business and management, 5% allied health, 49% multi/interdisciplinary studies, 5% physical sciences, 5% trade and industry.

UNDERGRADUATE MAJORS. Air conditioning/heating/refrigeration technology, allied health, biology, business administration and management, business and management, business and office, business data programming, clinical laboratory science, computer and information sciences, criminal justice studies, data processing, dental hygiene, drafting, drafting and design technology, education, engineering, engineering and engineering-related technologies, English, fashion merchandising, fine arts, fire control and safety technology, foreign languages (multiple emphasis), graphic design, hospitality and recreation marketing, industrial technology, instrumentation technology, international business management, legal assistant/paralegal, liberal/general studies, marketing and distribution, marketing management, mathematics, medical laboratory technologies, music, nursing, office supervision and management, photographic technology, physical sciences, physics, protective services, quality control technology, radiograph medical technology, respiratory therapy technology, science technologies, secretarial and related programs, social sciences, visual and performing arts.

ACADEMIC PROGRAMS. 2-year transfer program, accelerated program, cooperative education, double major, dual enrollment of high school students, honors program, independent study, internships, student-designed major, study abroad, telecourses. **Remedial services:** Learning center, reduced course load, remedial instruction, special counselor, tutoring, reading improvement classes. **ROTC:** Air Force, Army. **Placement/credit:** AP, CLEP General and Subject, institutional tests; 45 credit hours maximum for associate degree.

ACADEMIC REQUIREMENTS. Freshmen must earn minimum GPA of 2.0 to continue in good standing. Students must declare major on application. **Graduation requirements:** 64 hours for associate. Most students required to take courses in English, history, mathematics, biological/physical sciences, social sciences.

FRESHMAN ADMISSIONS. Selection criteria: Open admissions. Selective admissions to allied health, human services, law enforcement, and cosmetology programs. **Test requirements:** SAT or ACT for placement and counseling only; score report by August 1. MAPS or ASSET test may be submitted in place of SAT or ACT. California Achievement Tests and Stanford Test of Academic Skills required of applicants to health programs.

1992 FRESHMAN CLASS PROFILE. 1,030 men, 1,223 women enrolled. **Characteristics:** 93% from in state, 100% commute, 16% have minority backgrounds, 2% are foreign students. Average age is 23.

FALL-TERM APPLICATIONS. $20 fee, may be waived for applicants with need. Closing date August 31; applicants notified on a rolling basis. Interview required for allied health, cosmetology applicants. Audition required for music applicants. Deferred and early admission available.

STUDENT LIFE. Activities: Student government, magazine, student newspaper, television, student bulletin, choral groups, concert band, drama, music ensembles, musical theater, Circle-K, Distributive Education Clubs of America, international students club, Student Nurses Association of Florida, Joy Explosion, Black Student Union.

ATHLETICS. NJCAA. **Intercollegiate:** Baseball M, basketball, cross-country, diving, golf M, softball W, swimming, track and field, volleyball W. **Intramural:** Archery, bowling, fencing, racquetball, sailing, skiing, soccer M, tennis.

STUDENT SERVICES. Aptitude testing, career counseling, employment service for undergraduates, freshman orientation, health services, on-campus day care, personal counseling, placement service for graduates, veterans counselor, services/facilities for handicapped.

ANNUAL EXPENSES. Tuition and fees (1992-93): $990, $2,719 additional for out-of-state students. **Books and supplies:** $450. **Other expenses:** $600.

FINANCIAL AID. 27% of freshmen, 30% of continuing students receive some form of aid. 86% of grants, 79% of loans, 40% of jobs based on need. 1,470 enrolled freshmen were judged to have need, all were offered aid. Academic, music/drama, art, athletic, state/district residency, leadership, minority scholarships available. **Aid applications:** No closing date; priority given to applications received by May 8; applicants notified on a rolling basis beginning on or about June 12; must reply within 2 weeks. **Additional information:** Tuition assistance work programs.

ADDRESS/TELEPHONE. Robert A. Anderson, Dean of Collegewide Student Services, Chief Admissions Officer, Brevard Community College, 1519 Clearlake Road, Cocoa, FL 32922-9987. (407) 632-1111 ext. 2720. Fax: (407) 633-1013. Students can also write to Office of Admissions at 1111 North Washington Avenue, Titusville, FL 32780 or 3865 N. Wickham Rd., Melbourne, Fl 32935 and 250 Grassland St., Palm Bay, FL 32909.

Broward Community College
Fort Lauderdale, Florida CB code: 5074

2-year public community college, coed. Founded in 1959. **Accreditation:** Regional. **Undergraduate enrollment:** 3,585 men, 4,363 women full time; 6,603 men, 10,797 women part time. **Faculty:** 732 total (306 full time), 58 with doctorates or other terminal degrees. **Location:** Urban campus in small city; 20 miles from Miami. **Calendar:** Trimester, limited summer session. **Microcomputers:** Located in classrooms. **Special facilities:** Bailey Concert Hall, planetarium, Omni Auditorium, golf course. **Additional facts:** Multilocation institution. North campus located in Pompano Beach, central campus in Davie, south campus in Pembroke Pines. Credit courses also offered at corporate sites.

DEGREES OFFERED. AA, AS. 1,843 associate degrees awarded in 1992.

UNDERGRADUATE MAJORS. Accounting, aeronautical technology, airline piloting and navigation, architectural technologies, architecture, automotive technology, aviation management, business administration and management, business and management, business and office, business computer/console/peripheral equipment operation, business data processing and related programs, business data programming, civil technology, clinical laboratory science, computer and information sciences, court reporting, criminal justice technology, dental assistant, early childhood education, electrical technology, electromechanical technology, emergency medical technologies, engineering and engineering-related technologies, fashion merchandising, finance, fire control and safety technology, food production/management/services, food sciences, graphic arts technology, hospitality and recreation marketing, hotel/motel and restaurant management, insurance and risk management, insurance marketing, interior design, international business management, landscape architecture, law enforcement and corrections technologies, legal secretary, liberal/general studies, management information systems, marketing and distribution, marketing management, mechanical design technology, medical assistant, medical laboratory technologies, medical records technology, medical secretary, nursing, occupational therapy, ornamental horticulture, personal services, physical therapy assistant, plant protection, public affairs, radiograph medical technology, real estate, recreation and community services technologies, respiratory therapy technology, secretarial and related programs, tourism, transportation and travel marketing, ultrasound technology.

ACADEMIC PROGRAMS. 2-year transfer program, accelerated program, cooperative education, dual enrollment of high school students, honors program, independent study, internships, study abroad, telecourses, visiting/exchange student program, weekend college. **Remedial services:** Learning center, remedial instruction, tutoring. **ROTC:** Army. **Placement/credit:** AP, CLEP General and Subject, institutional tests; 30 credit hours maximum for associate degree.

ACADEMIC REQUIREMENTS. Freshmen must earn minimum GPA of 2.0 to continue in good standing. 60% of freshmen return for sophomore year. Students must declare major on enrollment. **Graduation requirements:** 62 hours for associate. Most students required to take courses in English, foreign languages, humanities, mathematics, biological/physical sciences, social sciences.

FRESHMAN ADMISSIONS. Selection criteria: Open admissions. **High school preparation:** 13 units required. Required units include English 4, foreign language 3, physical science 3 and science 3. **Test requirements:** SAT or ACT for placement.

1992 FRESHMAN CLASS PROFILE. 1,473 men, 1,899 women enrolled. **Characteristics:** 95% from in state, 100% commute, 35% have minority backgrounds, 1% are foreign students. Average age is 24.

FALL-TERM APPLICATIONS. $20 fee. No closing date; priority given to applications received by August 20; applicants notified on a rolling basis beginning on or about February 15. Deferred and early admission available.

STUDENT LIFE. Activities: Student government, magazine, student newspaper, choral groups, concert band, drama, jazz band, music ensembles, opera, symphony orchestra, fraternities, sororities, F-Troop (service), Circle-K, Distributive Education Clubs of America, Intervarsity Christian Fellowship, Hillel, Young Democrats, Young Republicans, Society for the Brotherhood Elite, Alpha Phi Omega, service fraternities.

ATHLETICS. NCAA, NJCAA. **Intercollegiate:** Baseball M, basketball, golf M, soccer M, softball W, swimming, tennis, volleyball W. **Intramural:** Basketball, bowling, cross-country, golf, handball, racquetball, sailing, soccer, softball, swimming, tennis, volleyball.

STUDENT SERVICES. Aptitude testing, career counseling, employment service for undergraduates, freshman orientation, personal counseling, placement service for graduates, special adviser for adult students, veterans counselor, services/facilities for handicapped.

ANNUAL EXPENSES. Tuition and fees (projected): $960, $2,778 additional for out-of-state students. **Books and supplies:** $640. **Other expenses:** $1,080.

FINANCIAL AID. 93% of grants based on need. Academic, music/drama, art, athletic, state/district residency, leadership, minority scholarships available. **Aid applications:** No closing date; priority given to applications received by April 15; applicants notified on a rolling basis beginning on or about July 15; must reply within 5 weeks.

ADDRESS/TELEPHONE. Dr. Theodore D. Taylor, Director of Admissions, Broward Community College, 225 East Las Olas Boulevard, Fort Lauderdale, FL 33301. (305) 475-6500.

Caribbean Center for Advanced Studies: Miami Institute of Psychology
Miami, Florida CB code: 2102

2-year upper-division private university and branch campus college. **Accreditation:** Regional. **Undergraduate enrollment:** 5 men, 14 women full time; 7 men, 9 women part time. **Graduate enrollment:** 98 men, 169 women full time; 11 men, 44 women part time. **Faculty:** 50 total (10 full time), 26 with doctorates or other terminal degrees. **Location:** Urban campus in very large city. **Microcomputers:** 3 located in computer centers.

DEGREES OFFERED. BS, MS, PhD. 4 bachelor's degrees awarded in 1992. 100% in psychology. Graduate degrees offered in 3 major fields of study.

UNDERGRADUATE MAJORS. Psychology.

ACADEMIC PROGRAMS. Placement/credit: 6 credit hours maximum for bachelor's degree.

ACADEMIC REQUIREMENTS. Graduation requirements: 120 hours for bachelor's (30 in major). Most students required to take courses in foreign languages. **Postgraduate studies:** 60% enter other graduate study.

STUDENT LIFE. Activities: Student government, student newspaper.

STUDENT SERVICES. Services/facilities for handicapped.

ANNUAL EXPENSES. Tuition and fees $5,600.

ADDRESS/TELEPHONE. Noemi Paravisini, Admissions Officer, Caribbean Center for Advanced Studies: Miami Institute of Psychology, 8180 NW 36th Street, 2nd Floor, Miami, FL 33166. (305) 593-1223. Fax: (305) 592-7930.

Central Florida Community College
Ocala, Florida CB code: 5127

2-year public community college, coed. Founded in 1957. **Accreditation:** Regional. **Undergraduate enrollment:** 2,314 men and women full time; 3,097 men and women part time. **Faculty:** 200 total (110 full time), 18 with doctorates or other terminal degrees. **Location:** Suburban campus in small city; 72 miles from Orlando. **Calendar:** Semester, extensive summer session. **Microcomputers:** Located in classrooms, computer centers. **Special facilities:** Appleton Art Museum, operated jointly with Florida State Universty; College Park Primary School, a cooperative facility for education interns.

DEGREES OFFERED. AA, AS. 641 associate degrees awarded in

1992. 17% in business and management, 5% communications, 9% education, 16% teacher education, 17% allied health.

UNDERGRADUATE MAJORS. Business administration and management, business and office, chemistry, child development/care/guidance, computer programming, criminal justice studies, criminal justice technology, criminology, drafting and design technology, economics, education, electrical and electronics equipment repair, electromechanical technology, electronic technology, elementary education, emergency medical technologies, emergency/disaster science, engineering, English, fine arts, fire control and safety technology, fire protection, horticulture, interior design, journalism, law enforcement and corrections technologies, legal assistant/paralegal, legal secretary, liberal/general studies, mathematics, medical secretary, nursing, physical sciences, physics, psychology, public relations, science technologies, secondary education, secretarial and related programs, social sciences, word processing.

ACADEMIC PROGRAMS. 2-year transfer program, cooperative education, dual enrollment of high school students, honors program, independent study, internships, study abroad. **Remedial services:** Learning center, reduced course load, remedial instruction, special counselor, tutoring. **Placement/credit:** AP, CLEP General and Subject, institutional tests; 45 credit hours maximum for associate degree.

ACADEMIC REQUIREMENTS. Freshmen must earn minimum GPA of 2.0 to continue in good standing. 60% of freshmen return for sophomore year. Students must declare major on application. **Graduation requirements:** 65 hours for associate. Most students required to take courses in computer science, English, humanities, mathematics, biological/physical sciences, social sciences.

FRESHMAN ADMISSIONS. Selection criteria: Open admissions. Recommended units include English 4, mathematics 3, social science 3 and science 3. **Test requirements:** SAT, ACT, or Florida CPT required of all applicants for placement. CPT preferred.

1992 FRESHMAN CLASS PROFILE. 791 men and women enrolled. **Characteristics:** 95% from in state, 100% commute, 10% have minority backgrounds, 1% are foreign students. Average age is 24.

FALL-TERM APPLICATIONS. $20 fee. Closing date July 1; applicants notified on a rolling basis. Deferred and early admission available.

STUDENT LIFE. Activities: Student government, student newspaper, choral groups, concert band, drama, jazz band, music ensembles, musical theater, pep band, symphony orchestra, Afro-Student Union, Hispanic Club, Phi Theta Kappa, Campus Diplomats, Community of Scholars, Brain Bowl, Phi Beta Lambda and Student Nurses in action.

ATHLETICS. NJCAA. **Intercollegiate:** Baseball M, basketball, softball W. **Intramural:** Bowling, diving, gymnastics, handball, racquetball, soccer M, softball, swimming, volleyball.

STUDENT SERVICES. Aptitude testing, career counseling, employment service for undergraduates, freshman orientation, health services, on-campus day care, personal counseling, placement service for graduates, special adviser for adult students, veterans counselor, services/facilities for handicapped.

ANNUAL EXPENSES. Tuition and fees (1992-93): $1,044, $2,870 additional for out-of-state students. **Books and supplies:** $540. **Other expenses:** $666.

FINANCIAL AID. 81% of grants, 84% of loans, 73% of jobs based on need. Academic, music/drama, athletic, leadership, minority scholarships available. **Aid applications:** No closing date; priority given to applications received by May 1; applicants notified on a rolling basis beginning on or about June 1; must reply within 2 weeks.

ADDRESS/TELEPHONE. Captoria Rawls, Director Admissions/Records, Central Florida Community College, PO Box 1388, 3001 SW College Road, Ocala, FL 34478. (904) 237-2111. Fax: (904) 237-3747.

Chipola Junior College
Marianna, Florida — CB code: 5106

2-year public community college, coed. Founded in 1947. **Accreditation:** Regional. **Undergraduate enrollment:** 522 men, 626 women full time; 990 men, 859 women part time. **Faculty:** 73 total (66 full time), 7 with doctorates or other terminal degrees. **Location:** Rural campus in small town; 70 miles from Tallahassee. **Calendar:** Semester, limited summer session. **Microcomputers:** 45 located in libraries, classrooms, computer centers.

DEGREES OFFERED. AA, AS. 285 associate degrees awarded in 1992.

UNDERGRADUATE MAJORS. Agricultural sciences, architecture, business and management, business and office, business data processing and related programs, communications, computer and information sciences, criminology, education, finance, law enforcement and corrections technologies, liberal/general studies, nursing, secretarial and related programs.

ACADEMIC PROGRAMS. 2-year transfer program, accelerated program, cooperative education, dual enrollment of high school students, independent study. **Remedial services:** Learning center, remedial instruction, tutoring. **Placement/credit:** AP, CLEP General and Subject; 42 credit hours maximum for associate degree.

ACADEMIC REQUIREMENTS. Freshmen must earn minimum GPA of 2.0 to continue in good standing. 70% of freshmen return for sophomore year. Students must declare major by end of first year. **Graduation requirements:** 64 hours for associate. Most students required to take courses in English, foreign languages, history, humanities, mathematics, biological/physical sciences, social sciences.

FRESHMAN ADMISSIONS. Selection criteria: Open admissions. **Test requirements:** SAT or ACT (ACT preferred) for placement and counseling only; score report by August 13.

1992 FRESHMAN CLASS PROFILE. 593 men, 764 women enrolled. **Characteristics:** 95% from in state, 90% commute, 18% have minority backgrounds.

FALL-TERM APPLICATIONS. No fee. Closing date August 1; applicants notified on a rolling basis. Early admission available.

STUDENT LIFE. Housing: Dormitories (men, women). **Activities:** Student government, student newspaper, choral groups, concert band, dance, drama, music ensembles, Baptist campus ministry.

ATHLETICS. NJCAA. **Intercollegiate:** Baseball M, basketball M, softball W. **Intramural:** Badminton, basketball, handball, racquetball, table tennis, volleyball.

STUDENT SERVICES. Aptitude testing, career counseling, personal counseling, veterans counselor, services/facilities for handicapped.

ANNUAL EXPENSES. Tuition and fees (1992-93): $893, $2,550 additional for out-of-state students. **Room and board:** $1,100 room only. **Books and supplies:** $375. **Other expenses:** $500.

FINANCIAL AID. 62% of freshmen, 56% of continuing students receive some form of aid. 71% of grants, 80% of loans, 88% of jobs based on need. 700 enrolled freshmen were judged to have need, all were offered aid. Academic, music/drama, art, athletic, leadership scholarships available. **Aid applications:** No closing date; priority given to applications received by June 15; applicants notified on a rolling basis beginning on or about July 15; must reply within 20 days.

ADDRESS/TELEPHONE. Annette Widner, Registration Specialist, Chipola Junior College, 3094 Indian Circle, Marianna, FL 32446. (904) 526-2761. Fax: (904) 526-4153.

Clearwater Christian College
Clearwater, Florida — CB code: 5142

4-year private liberal arts college, coed, nondenominational. Founded in 1966. **Accreditation:** Regional. **Undergraduate enrollment:** 455 men and women. **Faculty:** 36 total (22 full time). **Location:** Suburban campus in small city; 4 miles from city center. **Calendar:** Semester, limited summer session. **Additional facts:** Daily chapel service. Scripture integrated into various subject areas. Baptist theology.

DEGREES OFFERED. AA, AS, BA, BS. 1 associate degree awarded in 1992. 69 bachelor's degrees awarded.

UNDERGRADUATE MAJORS. Associate: Liberal/general studies, secretarial and related programs. **Bachelor's:** Accounting, Bible education, Bible studies, biology, business administration and management, elementary education, English education, English literature, history, history education, humanities, liberal/general studies, mathematics, music, office supervision and management, pastoral studies, physical education, prelaw, psychology, secondary education, social science education.

ACADEMIC PROGRAMS. Double major, internships, teacher preparation. **Remedial services:** Reduced course load. **Placement/credit:** AP, CLEP General and Subject, institutional tests; 12 credit hours maximum for bachelor's degree.

ACADEMIC REQUIREMENTS. Freshmen must earn minimum GPA of 2.0 to continue in good standing. Students must declare major on application. **Graduation requirements:** 64 hours for associate, 128 hours for bachelor's. Most students required to take courses in arts/fine arts, English, foreign languages, history, humanities, mathematics, biological/physical sciences, social sciences.

FRESHMAN ADMISSIONS. Selection criteria: Pastor's recommendation, 2.0 high school GPA, Christian testimony very important. **Test requirements:** SAT or ACT; score report by August 15.

1992 FRESHMAN CLASS PROFILE. 103 men and women enrolled. **Characteristics:** 51% live in college housing.

FALL-TERM APPLICATIONS. $20 fee. Closing date August 15; applicants notified on a rolling basis. Essay required. Interview recommended for nearby applicants.

STUDENT LIFE. Housing: Dormitories (men, women). **Activities:** Student government, yearbook, choral groups, drama, music ensembles, Christian service organizations, Student Missionary Fellowship. **Additional information:** Attendance at evening group devotions and prayer meetings is required of dormitory residents. Religious observance required.

ATHLETICS. Intercollegiate: Baseball M, basketball, soccer M, softball W, volleyball W. **Intramural:** Basketball M, volleyball M.

STUDENT SERVICES. Aptitude testing, career counseling, employment service for undergraduates, health services, personal counseling, placement service for graduates.

ANNUAL EXPENSES. Tuition and fees: $5,300. **Room and board:** $3,200. **Books and supplies:** $500. **Other expenses:** $800.

FINANCIAL AID. 51% of freshmen, 79% of continuing students receive some form of aid. 66% of grants, 88% of loans, all jobs based on need. Academic scholarships available. **Aid applications:** No closing date; priority given to applications received by May 1; applicants notified on a rolling basis; must reply within 2 weeks. **Additional information:** Special consideration for financial aid given children of Christian service workers.

ADDRESS/TELEPHONE. Benjamin J. Puckett, Director of Admissions, Clearwater Christian College, 3400 Gulf-to-Bay Boulevard, Clearwater, FL 34619-9997. (813) 726-1153.

Daytona Beach Community College

Daytona Beach, Florida CB code: 5159

2-year public community, technical college, coed. Founded in 1958. **Accreditation:** Regional. **Undergraduate enrollment:** 1,934 men, 2,653 women full time; 2,480 men, 4,227 women part time. **Faculty:** 809 total (209 full time), 100 with doctorates or other terminal degrees. **Location:** Suburban campus in small city; 90 miles from Jacksonville, 65 miles from Orlando. **Calendar:** Semester, limited summer session. Saturday and extensive evening/early morning classes. **Microcomputers:** 565 located in libraries, classrooms, computer centers. **Special facilities:** Southeast Museum of Photography, dance studio, experimental Goddard Theater, WCEU TV (PBS), interactive TV system.

DEGREES OFFERED. AA, AS. 1,163 associate degrees awarded in 1992. 21% in business and management, 5% business/office and marketing/distribution, 6% communications, 12% education, 5% engineering technologies, 16% health sciences, 6% allied health, 15% multi/interdisciplinary studies.

UNDERGRADUATE MAJORS. Accounting, air conditioning/heating/refrigeration technology, architectural technologies, automotive technology, business administration and management, business data processing and related programs, child development/care/guidance, civil technology, computer and information sciences, computer programming, computer servicing technology, computer technology, construction, court reporting, criminal justice studies, drafting, drafting and design technology, education, electronic technology, emergency medical technologies, engineering, engineering and engineering-related technologies, fashion design, finance, fire control and safety technology, graphic arts technology, graphic design, hotel/motel and restaurant management, information sciences and systems, interior design, law enforcement and corrections, legal assistant/paralegal, legal secretary, liberal/general studies, marketing management, medical records technology, medical secretary, mental health/human services, music, nursing, office supervision and management, photographic technology, photography, postal service management, prechiropractic, radiograph medical technology, respiratory therapy technology, tourism, trade and industrial supervision and management, word processing.

ACADEMIC PROGRAMS. 2-year transfer program, cooperative education, dual enrollment of high school students, honors program, independent study, internships, study abroad, telecourses, weekend college. **Remedial services:** Learning center, preadmission summer program, remedial instruction, special counselor, tutoring. **ROTC:** Air Force, Army. **Placement/credit:** AP, CLEP General and Subject, institutional tests; 45 credit hours maximum for associate degree.

ACADEMIC REQUIREMENTS. Freshmen must earn minimum GPA of 2.0 to continue in good standing. **Graduation requirements:** 62 hours for associate. Most students required to take courses in English, foreign languages, history, humanities, mathematics, biological/physical sciences, social sciences. **Additional information:** Students whose native language is not English offered instruction by the English Language Institute.

FRESHMAN ADMISSIONS. Selection criteria: Open admissions. Selective admissions for nursing, allied health, and public service programs. **Test requirements:** ASSET test required for placement and counseling.

1992 FRESHMAN CLASS PROFILE. 583 men, 747 women enrolled. **Academic background:** Mid 50% of enrolled freshmen had SAT-V between 350-460, SAT-M between 400-530; ACT composite between 18-22. 18% submitted SAT scores, 5% submitted ACT scores. **Characteristics:** 95% from in state, 100% commute, 11% have minority backgrounds, 3% are foreign students.

FALL-TERM APPLICATIONS. $25 fee. No closing date; applicants notified on a rolling basis. Deferred and early admission available. Application closing date is last day of registration.

STUDENT LIFE. Housing: Assistance in locating off-campus housing available to international students. **Activities:** Student government, student newspaper, television, literary magazine, choral groups, concert band, dance, drama, jazz band, music ensembles, musical theater, opera, pep band, symphony orchestra, Amnesty International, Baptist Campus Ministry, Human Services Paraprofessional Organization, African-American Student Union.

ATHLETICS. NJCAA. **Intercollegiate:** Basketball M, softball W. **Intramural:** Basketball, bowling, fencing, racquetball, soccer, table tennis, tennis, volleyball. **Clubs:** Billiards.

STUDENT SERVICES. Aptitude testing, career counseling, employment service for undergraduates, freshman orientation, on-campus day care, personal counseling, placement service for graduates, veterans counselor, international student services, Women's Center, services/facilities for handicapped.

ANNUAL EXPENSES. Tuition and fees (projected): $1,040, $2,868 additional for out-of-state students. **Books and supplies:** $464. **Other expenses:** $1,000.

FINANCIAL AID. 89% of grants, 72% of loans, 42% of jobs based on need. Academic, music/drama, art, athletic scholarships available. **Aid applications:** No closing date; applicants notified on a rolling basis beginning on or about June 15; must reply within 2 weeks.

ADDRESS/TELEPHONE. Office of Admissions, Daytona Beach Community College, PO Box 2811, Daytona Beach, FL 32120-2811. (904) 255-8131. Fax: (904) 254-3044.

Eckerd College

St. Petersburg, Florida CB code: 5223

Admissions:	74% of applicants accepted
Based on:	••• School record
	•• Activities, essay, interview, test scores
	• Recommendations, special talents
Completion:	90% of freshmen end year in good standing
	65% graduate, 52% of these enter graduate study

4-year private liberal arts college, coed, affiliated with Presbyterian Church (USA). Founded in 1958. **Accreditation:** Regional. **Undergraduate enrollment:** 662 men, 688 women full time; 9 men, 9 women part time. **Faculty:** 135 total (97 full time), 103 with doctorates or other terminal degrees. **Location:** Suburban campus in large city; 25 miles from Tampa. **Calendar:** 4-1-4, limited summer session. **Microcomputers:** 60 located in classrooms, computer centers. **Special facilities:** Art gallery, computer laboratory, marine science laboratory, necropsy laboratory.

DEGREES OFFERED. BA, BS. 321 bachelor's degrees awarded in 1992. 25% in business and management, 8% letters/literature, 11% life sciences, 14% multi/interdisciplinary studies, 8% psychology, 18% social sciences.

UNDERGRADUATE MAJORS. American literature, American studies, anthropology, art education, biology, business administration and management, chemistry, clinical laboratory science, comparative literature, computer and information sciences, creative writing, dramatic arts, economics, elementary education, English education, English literature, environmental science, fine arts, foreign languages (multiple emphasis), foreign languages education, French, German, history, human resources development, humanities, international and comparative education, international business management, international relations, international studies, marine biology, mathematics, music, music education, oceanography, philosophy, physics, political science and government, predentistry, prelaw, premedicine, preveterinary, psychology, religion, religious education, Russian, Russian and Slavic studies, science education, secondary education, social science education, social studies education, sociology, Spanish, women's studies.

ACADEMIC PROGRAMS. Accelerated program, double major, external degree, honors program, independent study, internships, semester at sea, student-designed major, study abroad, teacher preparation, visiting/exchange student program, cross-registration, winter term exchange with other 4-1-4 colleges, 3-2 engineering program; liberal arts/career combination in engineering. **Remedial services:** Reduced course load, tutoring. **ROTC:** Air Force, Army. **Placement/credit:** AP, CLEP Subject, IB, institutional tests; 63 credit hours maximum for bachelor's degree.

ACADEMIC REQUIREMENTS. No policy requiring minimum GPA; records of students having academic difficulty are reviewed individually. 80% of freshmen return for sophomore year. Students must declare major by end of second year. **Graduation requirements:** 126 hours for bachelor's (35 in major). Most students required to take courses in arts/fine arts, English, foreign languages, history, humanities, mathematics, philosophy/religion, biological/physical sciences, social sciences. **Postgraduate studies:** 8% enter law school, 6% enter medical school, 13% enter MBA programs, 25% enter other graduate study.

FRESHMAN ADMISSIONS. Selection criteria: School achievement record, school and community involvement most important. Test scores secondary. **High school preparation:** 15 units required; 18 recommended. Required and recommended units include biological science 1, English 4, foreign language 2-3, mathematics 3-4, physical science 2 and social science 3-4. **Test requirements:** SAT or ACT; score report by March 15. Prueba de Aptitud Academica for Spanish speaking applicants.

1992 FRESHMAN CLASS PROFILE. 702 men applied, 497 accepted, 164 enrolled; 805 women applied, 613 accepted, 185 enrolled. 80% had high school GPA of 3.0 or higher, 20% between 2.0 and 2.99. 32% were in top tenth and 61% were in top quarter of graduating class. **Academic background:** Mid 50% of enrolled freshmen had SAT-V between 440-550, SAT-M between 480-620; ACT composite between 21-28. 83% submitted SAT scores, 35% submitted ACT scores. **Characteristics:** 25% from in state, 95% live in college housing, 8% have minority backgrounds, 11% are foreign students. Average age is 18.

FALL-TERM APPLICATIONS. $25 fee, may be waived for applicants

with need. Closing date June 1; priority given to applications received by March 1; applicants notified on a rolling basis; must reply by May 1 or within 4 weeks if notified thereafter. Essay required. Interview recommended. Audition recommended for music applicants. Portfolio recommended for art applicants. CRDA. Deferred and early admission available.

STUDENT LIFE. Housing: Dormitories (men, women, coed). **Activities:** Student government, magazine, radio, student newspaper, television, yearbook, choral groups, dance, drama, music ensembles, musical theater, Afro-American Society, International Students Organization, water safety rescue team, student religious organizations, Circle-K, honor societies, Rotaract,Young Republicans, Young Democrats, Earth Society.

ATHLETICS. NCAA. **Intercollegiate:** Baseball M, basketball, cross-country, golf M, sailing, soccer M, softball W, tennis, volleyball W. **Intramural:** Baseball M, basketball, bowling, racquetball, sailing, soccer, softball, swimming, table tennis, tennis, volleyball. **Clubs:** Volleyball (m), soccer (w).

STUDENT SERVICES. Aptitude testing, career counseling, employment service for undergraduates, freshman orientation, health services, personal counseling, placement service for graduates, special adviser for adult students, veterans counselor, women's center, services/facilities for handicapped.

ANNUAL EXPENSES. Tuition and fees: $14,930. **Room and board:** $3,925. **Books and supplies:** $575. **Other expenses:** $590.

FINANCIAL AID. 79% of freshmen, 80% of continuing students receive some form of aid. 66% of grants, 89% of loans, 97% of jobs based on need. 197 enrolled freshmen were judged to have need, all were offered aid. Academic, music/drama, art, athletic, state/district residency, leadership, religious affiliation scholarships available. **Aid applications:** No closing date; priority given to applications received by April 1; applicants notified on a rolling basis beginning on or about March 15; must reply by May 1 or within 4 weeks if notified thereafter.

ADDRESS/TELEPHONE. Dr. Richard R. Hallin, Dean of Admissions and Records, Eckerd College, 4200 54th Avenue South, St. Petersburg, FL 33711. (813) 864-8331. (800) 456-9009. Fax: (813) 866-2304.

Edison Community College
Fort Myers, Florida — CB code: 5191

2-year public community college, coed. Founded in 1961. **Accreditation:** Regional. **Undergraduate enrollment:** 1,482 men, 1,749 women full time; 2,382 men, 4,202 women part time. **Faculty:** 357 total (108 full time), 30 with doctorates or other terminal degrees. **Location:** Suburban campus in small city; 150 miles from Tampa and Miami. **Calendar:** Semester, limited summer session. **Microcomputers:** 60 located in computer centers. **Special facilities:** Art gallery, Barbara B. Mann Performing Arts Hall. **Additional facts:** Satellite campuses in Port Charlotte and Naples.

DEGREES OFFERED. AA, AS. 908 associate degrees awarded in 1992. 15% in business and management, 5% computer sciences, 6% engineering technologies, 46% health sciences, 14% allied health, 11% parks/recreation, protective services, public affairs.

UNDERGRADUATE MAJORS. Accounting, astronomy, biology, business and management, cardiopulmonary technology, chemistry, computer and information sciences, criminal justice studies, dental assistant, education, electrical technology, emergency medical technologies, engineering and engineering-related technologies, English, finance, fine arts, fire control and safety technology, foreign languages (multiple emphasis), geology, horticultural science, horticulture, hotel/motel and restaurant management, legal assistant/paralegal, liberal/general studies, music, nursing, philosophy, physical sciences, physics, prelaw, psychology, radio/television broadcasting, real estate, respiratory therapy technology, secretarial and related programs, sociology, teacher aide, visual and performing arts.

ACADEMIC PROGRAMS. 2-year transfer program, accelerated program, cooperative education, double major, dual enrollment of high school students, honors program, independent study, study abroad, cross-registration. **Remedial services:** Learning center, preadmission summer program, reduced course load, remedial instruction, special counselor, tutoring. **Placement/credit:** AP, CLEP General and Subject; 45 credit hours maximum for associate degree.

ACADEMIC REQUIREMENTS. Freshmen must earn minimum GPA of 2.0 to continue in good standing. 75% of freshmen return for sophomore year. Students must declare major on enrollment. **Graduation requirements:** 64 hours for associate. Most students required to take courses in English, history, mathematics, biological/physical sciences, social sciences.

FRESHMAN ADMISSIONS. Selection criteria: Open admissions. Selective admissions to allied health programs. **High school preparation:** 13 units required. Required units include English 4, mathematics 3, social science 3 and science 3. **Test requirements:** SAT or ACT for placement; score report by August 12. No specific high school courses required for AS or certificate programs, MAPS, ASSET or CPT test accepted in place of SAT/ACT.

1992 FRESHMAN CLASS PROFILE. 781 men, 984 women enrolled. **Characteristics:** 85% from in state, 100% commute, 7% have minority backgrounds, 1% are foreign students. Average age is 27.

FALL-TERM APPLICATIONS. No fee. Closing date August 24; applicants notified on a rolling basis; must reply by August 23. Early admission available. Adults with no high school diploma/GED may take up to 15 credits.

STUDENT LIFE. Activities: Student government, radio, student newspaper, television, choral groups, concert band, drama, jazz band, music ensembles, symphony orchestra, fraternities, Black Student Union, honor societies, Intervarsity Christian Fellowship, Young Republicans, environmental club, Foreign Student Club, Young Democrats, Rotaract.

ATHLETICS. NJCAA. **Intercollegiate:** Baseball M, softball W, volleyball W.

STUDENT SERVICES. Aptitude testing, career counseling, employment service for undergraduates, health services, personal counseling, placement service for graduates, veterans counselor, services/facilities for handicapped.

ANNUAL EXPENSES. Tuition and fees (1992-93): $910, $2,355 additional for out-of-state students. **Books and supplies:** $450. **Other expenses:** $732.

FINANCIAL AID. 35% of freshmen, 35% of continuing students receive some form of aid. 64% of grants, 51% of loans, all jobs based on need. Academic, music/drama, art, athletic, leadership, minority scholarships available. **Aid applications:** No closing date; priority given to applications received by June 1; applicants notified on a rolling basis beginning on or about July 1; must reply within 2 weeks.

ADDRESS/TELEPHONE. Sandra Fahey, Director of Admission and Records, Edison Community College, PO Box 06210, Fort Myers, FL 33906-6210. (813) 489-9318. Fax: (813) 489-9399.

Edward Waters College
Jacksonville, Florida — CB code: 5182

4-year private liberal arts college, coed, affiliated with African Methodist Episcopal Church. Founded in 1866. **Accreditation:** Regional. **Undergraduate enrollment:** 587 men and women. **Location:** Urban campus in very large city; 150 miles from Orlando. **Calendar:** Semester, limited summer session.

DEGREES OFFERED. BA, BS. 80 bachelor's degrees awarded in 1992.

UNDERGRADUATE MAJORS. Biological and physical sciences, biology, business and management, criminal justice studies, elementary education, English, humanities and social sciences, liberal/general studies, mathematics, military science (Army), personnel management, philosophy, psychology, public administration, religion, religious education, social psychology, social work, sociology.

ACADEMIC PROGRAMS. Accelerated program, cooperative education, double major, independent study, internships, cross-registration. **Remedial services:** Learning center, preadmission summer program, reduced course load, remedial instruction, special counselor, tutoring. **ROTC:** Army.

ACADEMIC REQUIREMENTS. Freshmen must earn minimum GPA of 2.0 to continue in good standing.

FRESHMAN ADMISSIONS. Selection criteria: Open admissions.

1992 FRESHMAN CLASS PROFILE. 197 men and women enrolled. **Characteristics:** 83% from in state, 70% commute, 94% have minority backgrounds, 4% are foreign students.

FALL-TERM APPLICATIONS. $10 fee, may be waived for applicants with need. Closing date August 31; applicants notified on a rolling basis; must reply by registration. Deferred admission available.

STUDENT LIFE. Housing: Dormitories (coed). **Activities:** Student government, student newspaper, yearbook, choral groups, concert band, dance, drama, music ensembles, fraternities, sororities, NAACP, International Student Organization.

ATHLETICS. Intercollegiate: Baseball M, basketball, track and field M.

STUDENT SERVICES. Aptitude testing, career counseling, employment service for undergraduates, health services, personal counseling, placement service for graduates.

ANNUAL EXPENSES. Tuition and fees (1992-93): $3,930. **Room and board:** $3,400. **Books and supplies:** $400. **Other expenses:** $750.

FINANCIAL AID. 83% of freshmen, 90% of continuing students receive some form of aid. All jobs based on need. **Aid applications:** No closing date; applicants notified on a rolling basis.

ADDRESS/TELEPHONE. Mercedes Cullins, Director of Admissions, Edward Waters College, 1658 Kings Road, Jacksonville, FL 32209. (904) 366-2506.

Embry-Riddle Aeronautical University
Daytona Beach, Florida CB code: 5190

Admissions: 68% of applicants accepted
Based on: ••• School record
•• Test scores
• Activities, essay, interview, recommendations, special talents
Completion: 33% graduate

4-year private university, coed. Founded in 1926. **Accreditation:** Regional. **Undergraduate enrollment:** 4,341 men and women. **Graduate enrollment:** 167 men and women. **Faculty:** 261 total (219 full time), 147 with doctorates or other terminal degrees. **Location:** Urban campus in small city; 60 miles from Orlando. **Calendar:** Semester, extensive summer session. **Microcomputers:** 85 located in libraries, computer centers. **Special facilities:** Wind tunnel, fleet of aircraft, airway simulation laboratory. **Additional facts:** Only fully accredited aviation and aerospace-oriented private university in the world. Includes Western residential campus in Prescott, Arizona, and over 90 continuing education centers throughout United States and Europe.

DEGREES OFFERED. AS, BS, MS, MBA. 287 associate degrees awarded in 1992. 36% in business and management, 63% trade and industry. 904 bachelor's degrees awarded. 23% in business and management, 15% engineering, 57% trade and industry. Graduate degrees offered in 5 major fields of study.

UNDERGRADUATE MAJORS. Associate: Aeronautical technology, aircraft mechanics, airline piloting and navigation, aviation management, business administration and management, transportation management. **Bachelor's:** Aeronautical technology, aerospace studies, aerospace/aeronautical/astronautical engineering, air traffic control, aircraft mechanics, airline piloting and navigation, aviation computer technology, aviation management, business administration and management, computer and information sciences, engineering and engineering-related technologies, engineering physics, information sciences and systems, management information systems, transportation management.

ACADEMIC PROGRAMS. 2-year transfer program, accelerated program, cooperative education, independent study, internships, study abroad. **Remedial services:** Learning center, remedial instruction, tutoring. **ROTC:** Air Force, Army. **Placement/credit:** AP, CLEP General and Subject, institutional tests.

ACADEMIC REQUIREMENTS. Freshmen must earn minimum GPA of 2.0 to continue in good standing. 60% of freshmen return for sophomore year. Students must declare major on application. **Graduation requirements:** 72 hours for associate (60 in major), 126 hours for bachelor's (90 in major). Most students required to take courses in computer science, English, humanities, mathematics, biological/physical sciences, social sciences.

FRESHMAN ADMISSIONS. Selection criteria: High school GPA, rank in class, and SAT/ACT scores considered. Specific requirements vary by degree program. Recommended units include English 4, mathematics 3, physical science 3 and social science 3. **Test requirements:** SAT or ACT; score report by August 15.

1992 FRESHMAN CLASS PROFILE. 2,421 men and women applied, 1,637 accepted; 608 enrolled. **Academic background:** Mid 50% of enrolled freshmen had SAT-V between 420-520, SAT-M between 500-650; ACT composite between 21-27. 82% submitted SAT scores, 34% submitted ACT scores. **Characteristics:** 13% from in state, 14% have minority backgrounds, 6% are foreign students. Average age is 18.

FALL-TERM APPLICATIONS. $30 fee, may be waived for applicants with need. Closing date July 15; applicants notified on a rolling basis; must reply within 4 weeks. Interview recommended. Essay recommended. Deferred admission available. Early application encouraged since available facilities limit enrollment in some programs.

STUDENT LIFE. Housing: Dormitories (coed); apartment, fraternity housing available. **Activities:** Student government, student newspaper, yearbook, drama, fraternities, sororities, International Student Association, Veterans Association.

ATHLETICS. NAIA. **Intercollegiate:** Baseball M, basketball M, golf, soccer M, tennis. **Intramural:** Baseball M, bowling, golf, handball, lacrosse, racquetball, rugby, sailing, soccer, softball, swimming, table tennis, tennis, volleyball.

STUDENT SERVICES. Career counseling, employment service for undergraduates, freshman orientation, health services, personal counseling, placement service for graduates, veterans counselor, services/facilities for handicapped.

ANNUAL EXPENSES. Tuition and fees: $7,430. **Room and board:** $3,400. **Books and supplies:** $540. **Other expenses:** $1,200.

FINANCIAL AID. 75% of freshmen, 78% of continuing students receive some form of aid. 81% of grants, 71% of loans, 13% of jobs based on need. 430 enrolled freshmen were judged to have need, 427 were offered aid. Academic, athletic, state/district residency scholarships available. **Aid applications:** No closing date; priority given to applications received by April 15; applicants notified on a rolling basis beginning on or about April 1; must reply within 3 weeks.

ADDRESS/TELEPHONE. Darryl W. Neimeyer, Director of Admissions, Embry-Riddle Aeronautical University, 600 South Clyde Morris Boulevard, Daytona Beach, FL 32114-9970. (904) 226-6100. (800) 226-3728. Fax: (904) 226-6459.

Flagler Career Institute
Jacksonville, Florida CB code: 2136

2-year proprietary technical college, coed. Founded in 1979. **Undergraduate enrollment:** 210 men and women. **Faculty:** 17 total (12 full time). **Location:** Urban campus in very large city; 5 miles from downtown. **Calendar:** Semester. **Microcomputers:** Located in classrooms.

DEGREES OFFERED. AAS. 55 associate degrees awarded in 1992. 100% in allied health.

UNDERGRADUATE MAJORS. Nursing assistant, respiratory therapy.

ACADEMIC PROGRAMS. Remedial services: Remedial instruction, tutoring.

ACADEMIC REQUIREMENTS. Students must declare major on application. **Graduation requirements:** 76 hours for associate.

FRESHMAN ADMISSIONS. Selection criteria: Score on institutional admissions examination plus personal interview with admission staff and program directors. Science background recommended.

1992 FRESHMAN CLASS PROFILE. 140 men and women enrolled. **Characteristics:** 100% from in state, 100% commute, 35% have minority backgrounds.

FALL-TERM APPLICATIONS. $150 fee. No closing date; applicants notified on a rolling basis. Interview required.

STUDENT LIFE. Activities: Student newspaper.

STUDENT SERVICES. Career counseling, employment service for undergraduates, placement service for graduates.

ANNUAL EXPENSES. Tuition and fees (1992-93): Tuition and fees for 12-month period are $10,895.

FINANCIAL AID. 75% of continuing students receive some form of aid. **Aid applications:** No closing date; applicants notified on a rolling basis.

ADDRESS/TELEPHONE. Sandy Williams, Admissions Supervisor, Flagler Career Institute, 3225 University Boulevard South, Jacksonville, FL 32216. (904) 721-1622.

Flagler College
St. Augustine, Florida CB code: 5235

Admissions: 49% of applicants accepted
Based on: ••• School record
•• Interview, recommendations, test scores
• Activities, essay, special talents
Completion: 88% of freshmen end year in good standing
23% enter graduate study

4-year private liberal arts college, coed. Founded in 1968. **Accreditation:** Regional. **Undergraduate enrollment:** 536 men, 746 women full time; 11 men, 14 women part time. **Faculty:** 110 total (49 full time), 35 with doctorates or other terminal degrees. **Location:** Suburban campus in large town; 35 miles from Jacksonville. **Calendar:** Semester, limited summer session. **Microcomputers:** 96 located in libraries, computer centers. **Additional facts:** Center for Historic Research co-sponsored by Flagler College and St. Augustine Foundation on campus.

DEGREES OFFERED. BA. 264 bachelor's degrees awarded in 1992. 31% in business and management, 14% communications, 17% teacher education, 9% letters/literature, 6% social sciences, 12% visual and performing arts.

UNDERGRADUATE MAJORS. Accounting, art education, business administration and management, commercial art, communications, dramatic arts, education of exceptional children, education of the deaf and hearing impaired, elementary education, English, English education, fine arts, foreign languages education, graphic design, history, human services, Latin American studies, liberal/general studies, mathematics, mathematics education, parks and recreation management, philosophy, physical education, prelaw, psychology, religion, secondary education, social science education, social sciences, social studies education, Spanish, specific learning disabilities, visual and performing arts, youth ministries.

ACADEMIC PROGRAMS. Double major, independent study, internships, student-designed major, study abroad, teacher preparation, visiting/exchange student program. **Remedial services:** Reduced course load, remedial instruction. **Placement/credit:** AP, CLEP General, IB, institutional tests; 30 credit hours maximum for bachelor's degree.

ACADEMIC REQUIREMENTS. Freshmen must earn minimum GPA of 1.5 to continue in good standing. 78% of freshmen return for sophomore year. Students must declare major by end of second year. **Graduation requirements:** 120 hours for bachelor's (33 in major). Most students required to take courses in English, humanities, mathematics, social sciences. **Postgraduate studies:** 2% enter law school, 5% enter MBA programs, 16% enter other graduate study. **Additional information:** Students majoring in education of the deaf work with faculty and students at nearby Florida School for the Deaf. Freshman must earn at least 24 semester hours credit for good academic standing.

FRESHMAN ADMISSIONS. Selection criteria: Academic record, including pattern of courses and class rank, most important, followed by test scores. Extracurricular activities, recommendations, and intended major also considered. Applicants to education majors must score at or above 40th percentile on SAT or ACT. **High school preparation:** 16 units required. Required and recommended units include English 4, mathematics 2-3, social science 4 and science 2-3. Foreign language 2 recommended. **Test requirements:** SAT or ACT (SAT preferred); score report by March 29.

1992 FRESHMAN CLASS PROFILE. 627 men applied, 318 accepted, 129 enrolled; 778 women applied, 368 accepted, 171 enrolled. 34% had high school GPA of 3.0 or higher, 64% between 2.0 and 2.99. 19% were in top tenth and 54% were in top quarter of graduating class. **Academic background:** Mid 50% of enrolled freshmen had SAT-V between 430-510, SAT-M between 460-560; ACT composite between 20-24. 82% submitted SAT scores, 47% submitted ACT scores. **Characteristics:** 54% from in state, 87% live in college housing, 4% have minority backgrounds, 3% are foreign students. Average age is 18.

FALL-TERM APPLICATIONS. $20 fee, may be waived for applicants with need. Closing date March 1; priority given to applications received by February 15; applicants notified on a rolling basis beginning on or about January 1; must reply within 3 weeks. Interview required for early admission applicants. Audition recommended. Portfolio recommended. Essay recommended. Deferred and early admission available.

STUDENT LIFE. Housing: Dormitories (men, women). **Activities:** Student government, radio, student newspaper, yearbook, choral groups, drama, Circle-K, Rotaract, Intervarsity Christian Fellowship, Best Buddies, SADD/Bacchus, Chrysalis(environmental club). **Additional information:** Interdorm visitation not allowed in residence halls. Drinking prohibited on campus.

ATHLETICS. NAIA. **Intercollegiate:** Baseball M, basketball, cross-country, golf M, soccer M, tennis, volleyball W. **Intramural:** Basketball, soccer W, softball, tennis, volleyball. **Clubs:** (m) flag football.

STUDENT SERVICES. Aptitude testing, career counseling, employment service for undergraduates, freshman orientation, health services, personal counseling, placement service for graduates, veterans counselor, services/facilities for handicapped.

ANNUAL EXPENSES. Tuition and fees: $4,920. **Room and board:** $3,070. **Books and supplies:** $500. **Other expenses:** $1,360.

FINANCIAL AID. 75% of freshmen, 78% of continuing students receive some form of aid. 38% of grants, 93% of loans, 57% of jobs based on need. 150 enrolled freshmen were judged to have need, all were offered aid. Academic, music/drama, art, athletic, state/district residency, leadership scholarships available. **Aid applications:** Closing date April 1; priority given to applications received by March 15; applicants notified on a rolling basis beginning on or about March 1; must reply within 2 weeks.

ADDRESS/TELEPHONE. Marc G. Williar, Director of Admissions, Flagler College, King Street, St. Augustine, FL 32084. (904) 829-6481.

Florida Agricultural and Mechanical University
Tallahassee, Florida — CB code: 5215

Admissions: 51% of applicants accepted
Based on: ••• School record, test scores
• Essay, interview, recommendations, special talents
Completion: 90% of freshmen end year in good standing
30% enter graduate study

4-year public university, coed. Founded in 1887. **Accreditation:** Regional. **Undergraduate enrollment:** 3,199 men, 4,352 women full time; 584 men, 758 women part time. **Graduate enrollment:** 127 men, 206 women full time; 74 men, 187 women part time. **Faculty:** 586 total (457 full time), 238 with doctorates or other terminal degrees. **Location:** Urban campus in small city; 169 miles from Jacksonville. **Calendar:** Semester, extensive summer session. **Microcomputers:** Located in libraries, computer centers. **Special facilities:** Black archive, observatory.

DEGREES OFFERED. AA, BA, BS, BArch, MA, MS, MBA, MEd, PhD, Pharm D. 13 associate degrees awarded in 1992. 818 bachelor's degrees awarded. 20% in business and management, 5% communications, 6% computer sciences, 11% teacher education, 10% engineering technologies, 13% allied health, 15% social sciences. Graduate degrees offered in 37 major fields of study.

UNDERGRADUATE MAJORS. Associate: Liberal/general studies. **Bachelor's:** Accounting, actuarial sciences, Afro-American (black) studies, agribusiness, agricultural sciences, agronomy, animal sciences, architectural technologies, architecture, art education, biology, business administration and management, business education, chemical engineering, chemistry, civil engineering, civil technology, computer and information sciences, criminal justice studies, dramatic arts, economics, electrical/electronics/communications engineering, electronic technology, elementary education, English, English education, entomology, finance, fine arts, graphic arts technology, graphic design, health care administration, health information management, history, industrial arts education, industrial engineering, journalism, landscape architecture, mathematics, mathematics education, mechanical engineering, medical records administration, medical records technology, music, music education, music performance, nursing, occupational therapy, office supervision and management, ornamental horticulture, pharmacy, philosophy, physical education, physical therapy, physics, political science and government, predentistry, premedicine, psychology, religion, respiratory therapy, respiratory therapy technology, science education, social studies education, social work, sociology, trade and industrial education, visual and performing arts.

ACADEMIC PROGRAMS. Accelerated program, cooperative education, double major, dual enrollment of high school students, honors program, independent study, internships, teacher preparation, weekend college, cross-registration; liberal arts/career combination in engineering, health sciences; combined bachelor's/graduate program in business administration. **Remedial services:** Learning center, reduced course load, special counselor, tutoring. **ROTC:** Air Force, Army, Naval. **Placement/credit:** AP, CLEP General and Subject; 30 credit hours maximum for bachelor's degree.

ACADEMIC REQUIREMENTS. Freshmen must earn minimum GPA of 2.0 to continue in good standing. 80% of freshmen return for sophomore year. Students must declare major by end of second year. **Graduation requirements:** 60 hours for associate, 120 hours for bachelor's (30 in major). Most students required to take courses in English, foreign languages, history, humanities, mathematics, biological/physical sciences, social sciences. **Postgraduate studies:** 65% from 2-year programs enter 4-year programs.

FRESHMAN ADMISSIONS. Selection criteria: School achievement record and test scores; minimum 2.5 high school GPA required. Test scores important. **High school preparation:** 19 units required. Required units include English 4, foreign language 2, mathematics 3, social science 3 and science 3. **Test requirements:** SAT or ACT; score report by July 1.

1992 FRESHMAN CLASS PROFILE. 2,256 men applied, 1,057 accepted, 572 enrolled; 2,813 women applied, 1,552 accepted, 826 enrolled. 57% had high school GPA of 3.0 or higher, 42% between 2.0 and 2.99. **Characteristics:** 60% from in state, 72% commute, 99% have minority backgrounds, 4% are foreign students. Average age is 18.

FALL-TERM APPLICATIONS. $20 fee. Closing date July 15; priority given to applications received by May 1; applicants notified on a rolling basis. Audition required for music applicants. Portfolio required for architecture applicants. Essay required for borderline applicants. Interview recommended for nursing, physical therapy, architecture, pharmacy, engineering applicants. Deferred and early admission available.

STUDENT LIFE. Housing: Dormitories (men, women); apartment housing available. **Activities:** Student government, radio, student newspaper, television, yearbook, choral groups, concert band, dance, drama, jazz band, marching band, music ensembles, pep band, symphony orchestra, fraternities, sororities.

ATHLETICS. NCAA. **Intercollegiate:** Baseball M, basketball, cross-country, football M, golf, softball W, swimming, tennis, track and field, volleyball W. **Intramural:** Badminton, basketball, bowling, football M, gymnastics, soccer, softball, table tennis, tennis, track and field, volleyball.

STUDENT SERVICES. Aptitude testing, career counseling, employment service for undergraduates, freshman orientation, health services, on-campus day care, personal counseling, placement service for graduates, veterans counselor, services/facilities for handicapped.

ANNUAL EXPENSES. Tuition and fees (1992-93): $1,751, $4,759 additional for out-of-state students. **Room and board:** $2,770. **Books and supplies:** $315. **Other expenses:** $1,050.

FINANCIAL AID. Grants, loans, jobs available. Academic, music/drama, athletic scholarships available. **Aid applications:** No closing date; priority given to applications received by April 1; applicants notified on a rolling basis beginning on or about May 1; must reply within 2 weeks.

ADDRESS/TELEPHONE. Barbara Cox, Director of Admissions/Deputy Registrar, Florida Agricultural and Mechanical University, Tallahassee, FL 32307. (904) 599-3796. Fax: (904) 561-2428.

Florida Atlantic University
Boca Raton, Florida — CB code: 5229

Admissions: 69% of applicants accepted
Based on: ••• School record, test scores
• Activities, recommendations, special talents
Completion: 80% of freshmen end year in good standing
44% graduate

4-year public university, coed. Founded in 1961. **Accreditation:** Regional. **Undergraduate enrollment:** 2,672 men, 3,140 women full time; 2,144 men, 3,434 women part time. **Graduate enrollment:** 483 men, 320 women full time; 994 men, 1,612 women part time. **Faculty:** 560 total (547 full time), 486 with doctorates or other terminal degrees. **Location:** Suburban campus in small city; 15 miles from Fort Lauderdale and 25 miles from West Palm Beach. **Calendar:** Semester, limited summer session. **Microcomputers:** 262 located in libraries, classrooms, computer centers, campus-wide network.

Special facilities: Environmental center, native fish research center, art gallery, ocean engineering laboratory, marine research facility, robotics laboratory. **Additional facts:** Courses and degree programs offered at additional sites in Palm Beach, Broward, and Indian River Counties.

DEGREES OFFERED. AA, BA, BS, BFA, MA, MS, MBA, MFA, MEd, PhD, EdD. 1,825 bachelor's degrees awarded. 34% in business and management, 5% computer sciences, 11% education, 6% engineering, 14% social sciences. Graduate degrees offered in 65 major fields of study.

UNDERGRADUATE MAJORS. Bachelor's: Accounting, anthropology, art education, art history, biological and physical sciences, biology, botany, business administration and management, business and management, business economics, chemistry, clinical laboratory science, communications, comparative literature, computer and information sciences, criminal justice studies, dramatic arts, early childhood education, economics, education of the deaf and hearing impaired, education of the emotionally handicapped, education of the mentally handicapped, electrical/electronics/communications engineering, elementary education, English, English education, exercise/wellness, finance, fine arts, foreign languages education, French, geography, geology, German, health care administration, history, humanities and social sciences, information sciences and systems, international business management, jazz, Latin American studies, linguistics, management information systems, marine biology, marketing management, mathematics, mathematics education, mechanical engineering, medical laboratory technologies, microbiology, music, music education, music history and appreciation, music performance, nursing, ocean engineering, philosophy, physics, political science and government, predentistry, premedicine, prepharmacy, preveterinary, psychology, public administration, public affairs, real estate, science education, small business management and ownership, social psychology, social science education, social sciences, social studies education, social work, sociology, Spanish, special education, specific learning disabilities, theater design, urban studies, zoology.

ACADEMIC PROGRAMS. Accelerated program, cooperative education, dual enrollment of high school students, education specialist degree, honors program, independent study, internships, student-designed major, study abroad, teacher preparation, visiting/exchange student program, weekend college, cross-registration. **Remedial services:** Reduced course load, special counselor, tutoring, freshman early warning system. **ROTC:** Air Force, Army. **Placement/credit:** AP, CLEP General and Subject, IB; 45 credit hours maximum for bachelor's degree.

ACADEMIC REQUIREMENTS. Freshmen must earn minimum GPA of 2.0 to continue in good standing. 75% of freshmen return for sophomore year. Students must declare major by end of second year. **Graduation requirements:** 120 hours for bachelor's (30 in major). Most students required to take courses in English, foreign languages, history, humanities, mathematics, biological/physical sciences, social sciences.

FRESHMAN ADMISSIONS. Selection criteria: Admission competitive, based on profile including high school academic record and results of SAT or ACT. Special consideration may be given to minority applicants. **High school preparation:** 19 units required. Required units include English 4, foreign language 2, mathematics 3, social science 3 and science 3. 2 years each of algebra and foreign language, formal geometry and 4 academic electives required. 2 science units must be laboratory. **Test requirements:** SAT or ACT; score report by July 1.

1992 FRESHMAN CLASS PROFILE. 1,491 men applied, 1,019 accepted, 422 enrolled; 1,787 women applied, 1,236 accepted, 471 enrolled. 60% had high school GPA of 3.0 or higher, 40% between 2.0 and 2.99. **Academic background:** Mid 50% of enrolled freshmen had SAT-V between 440-550, SAT-M between 480-590; ACT composite between 18-27. 81% submitted SAT scores, 42% submitted ACT scores. **Characteristics:** 79% from in state, 52% commute, 18% have minority backgrounds, 5% are foreign students. Average age is 18.

FALL-TERM APPLICATIONS. $20 fee, may be waived for applicants with need. Closing date June 1; priority given to applications received by March 1; applicants notified on a rolling basis beginning on or about November 1; must reply by May 1. Audition recommended. Portfolio recommended. CRDA. Deferred and early admission available.

STUDENT LIFE. Housing: Dormitories (men, women, coed). **Activities:** Student government, magazine, student newspaper, television, choral groups, concert band, dance, drama, jazz band, music ensembles, opera, pep band, symphony orchestra, fraternities, sororities, Circle-K, College Democrats, Young Republicans, B'nai B'rith Hillel, Catholic Student Union, Pan-African Student Association, Amnesty International.

ATHLETICS. NCAA. **Intercollegiate:** Baseball M, basketball, cross-country, diving, golf, soccer M, swimming, tennis, volleyball W. **Intramural:** Badminton, basketball, fencing, ice hockey, rowing (crew), rugby, sailing, soccer, softball, table tennis, tennis, track and field, volleyball.

STUDENT SERVICES. Aptitude testing, career counseling, employment service for undergraduates, freshman orientation, health services, on-campus day care, personal counseling, placement service for graduates, special adviser for adult students, veterans counselor, United campus ministries, services/facilities for handicapped.

ANNUAL EXPENSES. Tuition and fees (projected): $1,550, $3,800 additional for out-of-state students. **Room and board:** $4,090. **Books and supplies:** $600. **Other expenses:** $1,120.

FINANCIAL AID. 50% of freshmen, 35% of continuing students receive some form of aid. 58% of grants, 81% of loans, 7% of jobs based on need. Academic, music/drama, athletic, state/district residency, leadership, minority scholarships available. **Aid applications:** No closing date; priority given to applications received by April 15; applicants notified on a rolling basis beginning on or about May 1; must reply within 2 weeks.

ADDRESS/TELEPHONE. Dr. Brian Levin-Stankevich, Director of Admissions and Enrollment Management, Florida Atlantic University, 500 Northwest 20th Street, Boca Raton, FL 33431-0991. (407) 367-3040. (800) 299-4FAU. Fax: (407) 367-2758.

Florida Baptist Theological College
Graceville, Florida — CB code: 7322

Admissions: 81% of applicants accepted
Based on:
- ••• Recommendations, religious affiliation/commitment
- •• Essay
- • Interview

Completion: 85% of freshmen end year in good standing; 24% enter graduate study

4-year private Bible college, coed, affiliated with Southern Baptist Convention. Founded in 1943. **Accreditation:** Regional. **Undergraduate enrollment:** 331 men, 89 women full time; 55 men, 23 women part time. **Faculty:** 22 total (13 full time), 14 with doctorates or other terminal degrees. **Location:** Rural campus in small town; 20 miles from Dothan, Alabama, 60 miles from Panama City. **Calendar:** 4-4-1-1. **Microcomputers:** 14 located in computer centers. **Additional facts:** Prepares students for service as pastors and staff members of churches affiliated with Southern Baptist Convention.

DEGREES OFFERED. B. 4 associate degrees awarded in 1992. 75% in philosophy, religion, theology, 25% visual and performing arts. 45 bachelor's degrees awarded. 90% in philosophy, religion, theology, 10% visual and performing arts.

UNDERGRADUATE MAJORS. Bible studies, religious education, religious music, theological studies. Bible studies, religious education, religious education/music, religious music, theological studies.

ACADEMIC PROGRAMS. Accelerated program, double major, internships. **Remedial services:** Learning center, reduced course load, remedial instruction. **Placement/credit:** CLEP Subject, institutional tests; 30 credit hours maximum for bachelor's degree.

ACADEMIC REQUIREMENTS. Freshmen must earn minimum GPA of 1.0 to continue in good standing. 86% of freshmen return for sophomore year. Students must declare major on enrollment. **Graduation requirements:** 66 hours for associate (16 in major), 130 hours for bachelor's (30 in major). Most students required to take courses in English, history, mathematics, philosophy/religion, biological/physical sciences, social sciences. **Postgraduate studies:** 24% enter other graduate study.

FRESHMAN ADMISSIONS. Selection criteria: Minimum age requirement 18 years; applicant must be member in good standing of church affiliated with Southern Baptist Convention or other evangelical body. Degree applicants must have high school diploma or equivalent. Special program for non-high school graduates. Approval by committee based on application, recommendations, and possible interview. **Additional information:** Special admissions procedures for married couples.

1992 FRESHMAN CLASS PROFILE. 41 men applied, 36 accepted, 36 enrolled; 22 women applied, 15 accepted, 15 enrolled. **Characteristics:** 55% from in state, 52% live in college housing, 10% have minority backgrounds. Average age is 27.

FALL-TERM APPLICATIONS. $20 fee. Closing date August 1; priority given to applications received by June 30; applicants notified on a rolling basis. Essay required. Interview recommended for borderline applicants. Audition recommended for church music applicants. Deferred admission available. Placement test given at beginning of fall and spring semesters.

STUDENT LIFE. Housing: Dormitories (men, women); apartment housing available. Mobile home living arrangements available. **Activities:** Student government, yearbook, choral groups, music ensembles, Theology Club, Religious Education Club, Music Guild, Christian Social Ministries Club, religious social organizations, Baptist Campus Young Women. **Additional information:** Religious observance required.

ATHLETICS. Intramural: Basketball, softball, table tennis, tennis, volleyball.

STUDENT SERVICES. Aptitude testing, career counseling, employment service for undergraduates, freshman orientation, on-campus day care, personal counseling, placement service for graduates, veterans counselor, services/facilities for handicapped.

ANNUAL EXPENSES. Tuition and fees (1992-93): $1,750. Tuition is double for members of non-Southern Baptist churches. **Room and board:** $1,350 room only. **Books and supplies:** $400. **Other expenses:** $600.

FINANCIAL AID. 85% of freshmen, 82% of continuing students receive some form of aid. 78% of grants, 90% of loans, 30% of jobs based on need. State/district residency, religious affiliation scholarships available. **Aid applications:** No closing date; priority given to applications received by May

1; applicants notified on a rolling basis beginning on or about June 15; must reply within 4 weeks.

ADDRESS/TELEPHONE. O. Lavan Wilson, Director of Student Affairs and Admissions, Florida Baptist Theological College, 5400 College Drive, Graceville, FL 32440-1830. (904) 263-3261 ext. 60. (800) 328-2660 ext. 60. Fax: (904) 263-7506.

Florida Bible College
Kissimmee, Florida CB code: 5202

Admissions: 99% of applicants accepted
Based on: ••• Essay, interview, religious affiliation/commitment, school record
•• Recommendations
• Activities, special talents, test scores
Completion: 90% of freshmen end year in good standing
20% graduate, 5% of these enter graduate study

4-year private Bible college, coed, nondenominational. Founded in 1962. **Undergraduate enrollment:** 49 men, 43 women full time; 13 men, 10 women part time. **Faculty:** 16 total (5 full time), 2 with doctorates or other terminal degrees. **Location:** Suburban campus in large town; 20 miles from Orlando. **Calendar:** Semester, limited summer session. **Microcomputers:** 4 located on campus.

DEGREES OFFERED. AA, BA. 10 associate degrees awarded in 1992. 20% in teacher education, 80% philosophy, religion, theology. 12 bachelor's degrees awarded. 16% in teacher education, 84% philosophy, religion, theology.

UNDERGRADUATE MAJORS. Associate: Bible studies, biblical counseling and psychology, elementary education, missionary studies, pastoral studies, religious education, theological studies. **Bachelor's:** Bible studies, elementary education, missionary studies, pastoral studies, religious education, secondary education, theological studies.

ACADEMIC PROGRAMS. Double major, dual enrollment of high school students, teacher preparation. **Remedial services:** Reduced course load. **Placement/credit:** AP, CLEP General and Subject; 15 credit hours maximum for associate degree; 15 credit hours maximum for bachelor's degree.

ACADEMIC REQUIREMENTS. Freshmen must earn minimum GPA of 2.0 to continue in good standing. 67% of freshmen return for sophomore year. Students must declare major by end of second year. **Graduation requirements:** 64 hours for associate (28 in major), 128 hours for bachelor's (56 in major). Most students required to take courses in English, history, mathematics, philosophy/religion, biological/physical sciences.

FRESHMAN ADMISSIONS. Selection criteria: High school achievement record, essay, religious commitment very important. Interview important. Other factors considered. College-preparatory program recommended. **Test requirements:** SAT or ACT (ACT preferred); score report by August 1.

1992 FRESHMAN CLASS PROFILE. 37 men applied, 36 accepted, 27 enrolled; 33 women applied, 33 accepted, 23 enrolled. **Characteristics:** 33% from in state, 75% live in college housing, 12% have minority backgrounds, 12% are foreign students. Average age is 22.

FALL-TERM APPLICATIONS. $25 fee. Closing date July 1; priority given to applications received by May 1; applicants notified on a rolling basis beginning on or about July 1; must reply within 4 weeks. Essay required. Interview recommended. Audition recommended for religious music applicants. Deferred admission available.

STUDENT LIFE. Housing: Dormitories (men, women); apartment housing available. Private bathroom for each dormitory room. **Activities:** Student government, yearbook, choral groups, music ensembles, outreach ministries. **Additional information:** Religious observance required.

ATHLETICS. Intercollegiate: Basketball M, soccer M, volleyball W. **Intramural:** Softball M, volleyball W.

STUDENT SERVICES. Career counseling, personal counseling, placement service for graduates, veterans counselor, services/facilities for handicapped.

ANNUAL EXPENSES. Tuition and fees: $4,090. **Room and board:** $2,050. **Books and supplies:** $350. **Other expenses:** $2,973.

FINANCIAL AID. 65% of freshmen, 65% of continuing students receive some form of aid. 65% of grants, 88% of loans, all jobs based on need. 10 enrolled freshmen were judged to have need, all were offered aid. Academic, music/drama, leadership, alumni affiliation scholarships available. **Aid applications:** No closing date; priority given to applications received by May 31; applicants notified on a rolling basis beginning on or about April 30.

ADDRESS/TELEPHONE. Marie Brady, Director of Admissions, Florida Bible College, 1701 Poinciana Boulevard, Kissimmee, FL 34758. (407) 933-4500. (800) 869-0258.

Florida Christian College
Kissimmee, Florida CB code: 2167

4-year private Bible college, coed, affiliated with Christian Church and Church of Christ. Founded in 1975. **Undergraduate enrollment:** 72 men, 32 women full time; 15 men, 20 women part time. **Faculty:** 14 total (10 full time), 3 with doctorates or other terminal degrees. **Location:** Suburban campus in large town; 20 miles from Orlando. **Calendar:** Quarter. **Microcomputers:** 2 located in libraries. **Additional facts:** Christian ministry emphasis.

DEGREES OFFERED. AA, BA, BS. 14 associate degrees awarded in 1992. 100% in philosophy, religion, theology. 15 bachelor's degrees awarded. 100% in philosophy, religion, theology.

UNDERGRADUATE MAJORS. Associate: Liberal/general studies. **Bachelor's:** Bible studies, biblical languages, elementary education, missionary studies, religion, religious education, religious music, theological studies.

ACADEMIC PROGRAMS. Double major, dual enrollment of high school students, internships, student-designed major, teacher preparation. **Remedial services:** Reduced course load. **Placement/credit:** AP, CLEP General and Subject, institutional tests.

ACADEMIC REQUIREMENTS. Freshmen must earn minimum GPA of 2.0 to continue in good standing. 59% of freshmen return for sophomore year. Students must declare major by end of second year. **Graduation requirements:** 101 hours for associate, 202 hours for bachelor's. Most students required to take courses in arts/fine arts, English, foreign languages, history, humanities, mathematics, philosophy/religion, biological/physical sciences, social sciences.

FRESHMAN ADMISSIONS. Selection criteria: Discipleship profile, personal recommendations, and church references required. **High school preparation:** 24 units recommended. Recommended units include biological science 1, English 4, foreign language 2, mathematics 3, physical science 2 and social science 3. **Test requirements:** ACT; score report by August 15. Taylor-Johnson Temperament Analysis required.

1992 FRESHMAN CLASS PROFILE. 54 men and women enrolled. **Characteristics:** 88% from in state, 87% live in college housing, 1% have minority backgrounds. Average age is 22.

FALL-TERM APPLICATIONS. $25 fee. Closing date July 15; priority given to applications received by July 1; applicants notified on a rolling basis; must reply within 10 days. Essay required. Interview recommended. Deferred and early admission available.

STUDENT LIFE. Housing: Apartment housing available. **Activities:** Student government, student newspaper, yearbook, choral groups, drama, music ensembles, Christian service activities, mission group. **Additional information:** Emphasis on developing mature Christian life style. Religious observance required.

ATHLETICS. Intercollegiate: Basketball M, softball W, volleyball W. **Intramural:** Softball, table tennis, volleyball.

STUDENT SERVICES. Freshman orientation, personal counseling, veterans counselor, services/facilities for handicapped.

ANNUAL EXPENSES. Tuition and fees: $3,695. **Room and board:** $1,620 room only. **Books and supplies:** $625. **Other expenses:** $1,440.

FINANCIAL AID. 87% of freshmen, 93% of continuing students receive some form of aid. 34% of grants, 80% of loans, all jobs based on need. 39 enrolled freshmen were judged to have need, all were offered aid. Academic, music/drama, state/district residency, leadership, religious affiliation scholarships available. **Aid applications:** Closing date July 15; priority given to applications received by April 15; applicants notified on a rolling basis beginning on or about June 15; must reply within 3 weeks.

ADDRESS/TELEPHONE. Tony Buchanan, Academic Dean/ Registrar, Florida Christian College, 1011 Bill Beck Boulevard, Kissimmee, FL 34744-4402. (407) 847-8966 ext. 311.

Florida College
Temple Terrace, Florida CB code: 5216

2-year private junior, liberal arts college, coed. Founded in 1944. **Accreditation:** Regional. **Undergraduate enrollment:** 186 men, 179 women full time; 9 men, 7 women part time. **Faculty:** 33 total (25 full time), 11 with doctorates or other terminal degrees. **Location:** Suburban campus in large town; 2 miles from Tampa. **Calendar:** Semester. **Microcomputers:** 12 located in libraries.

DEGREES OFFERED. AA. 105 associate degrees awarded in 1992. 100% in multi/interdisciplinary studies.

UNDERGRADUATE MAJORS. Liberal/general studies.

ACADEMIC PROGRAMS. 2-year transfer program, cross-registration. **Remedial services:** Reduced course load, remedial instruction, tutoring. **Placement/credit:** AP, CLEP General and Subject, institutional tests; 30 credit hours maximum for associate degree.

ACADEMIC REQUIREMENTS. Freshmen must earn minimum GPA of 1.6 to continue in good standing. **Graduation requirements:** 64 hours for associate. Most students required to take courses in arts/fine arts, English, history, humanities, mathematics, philosophy/religion, biological/physical sciences, social sciences.

FRESHMAN ADMISSIONS. Selection criteria: Student composition telling why he or she selected Florida College, 3 recommendations, school achievement record, ACT scores, moral character considered. **High school preparation:** 14 units required; 16 recommended. Required and recommended units include English 4, mathematics 2-3, social science 2-3 and science 2. Biological science 2 and foreign language 2 recommended. Science units must include laboratory work. **Test requirements:** ACT; score report by August 15.

1992 FRESHMAN CLASS PROFILE. 99 men, 97 women enrolled. **Academic background:** Mid 50% of enrolled freshmen had SAT-V between 380-540, SAT-M between 410-600; ACT composite between 18-24. 35% submitted SAT scores, 98% submitted ACT scores. **Characteristics:** 21% from in state, 95% live in college housing, 4% have minority backgrounds, 1% are foreign students. Average age is 18.

FALL-TERM APPLICATIONS. $25 fee. Closing date August 15; applicants notified on a rolling basis; must reply within 4 weeks. Essay required. Deferred admission available.

STUDENT LIFE. Housing: Dormitories (men, women). **Activities:** Student government, magazine, student newspaper, yearbook, forensics, choral groups, concert band, drama, jazz band, music ensembles, pep band, religious organizations, junior college honor society, social clubs.

ATHLETICS. NJCAA. **Intercollegiate:** Basketball M, golf M. **Intramural:** Basketball, soccer M, softball, volleyball.

STUDENT SERVICES. Freshman orientation, health services, personal counseling, veterans counselor.

ANNUAL EXPENSES. Tuition and fees: $4,350. **Room and board:** $3,100. **Books and supplies:** $800. **Other expenses:** $950.

FINANCIAL AID. 80% of freshmen, 78% of continuing students receive some form of aid. 55% of grants, 98% of loans, 71% of jobs based on need. 103 enrolled freshmen were judged to have need, all were offered aid. Academic, music/drama, athletic, state/district residency, alumni affiliation scholarships available. **Aid applications:** No closing date; priority given to applications received by June 1; applicants notified on a rolling basis beginning on or about April 1. **Additional information:** Music and forensic scholarships available. Audition required for music.

ADDRESS/TELEPHONE. Kenneth Moorer, Director of Enrollment Management, Florida College, 119 North Glen Arven Avenue, Temple Terrace, FL 33617. (813) 988-5131 ext. 225. Fax: (813) 985-9654.

Florida Community College at Jacksonville

Jacksonville, Florida — CB code: 5232

2-year public community college, coed. Founded in 1963. **Accreditation:** Regional. **Undergraduate enrollment:** 2,440 men, 3,252 women full time; 3,814 men, 6,234 women part time. **Faculty:** 1,503 total (401 full time), 77 with doctorates or other terminal degrees. **Location:** Suburban campus in very large city. **Calendar:** Semester, limited summer session. Saturday and extensive evening/early morning classes. **Microcomputers:** 801 located in libraries, classrooms, computer centers. **Special facilities:** Art galleries at 3 campuses. **Additional facts:** Multilocation institution Florida with four campus locations and open campus including cable television classes, on-site classes at 3 military bases and local businesses, and college centers.

DEGREES OFFERED. AA, AS. 1,730 associate degrees awarded in 1992.

UNDERGRADUATE MAJORS. Accounting, air conditioning/heating/refrigeration technology, airline piloting and navigation, architectural technologies, automotive technology, aviation management, biomedical equipment technology, business administration and management, child care center management, civil technology, computer programming, computer servicing technology, computer technology, construction, criminal justice technology, dental hygiene, dietetic aide/assistant, drafting and design technology, electronic technology, emergency medical technologies, fashion merchandising, fire control and safety technology, graphic arts technology, histology, hotel/motel and restaurant management, information sciences and systems, insurance and risk management, interior design, legal assistant/paralegal, marketing management, medical laboratory technologies, nursing, office supervision and management, postal service management, radio/television technology, radiograph medical technology, real estate, respiratory therapy technology, secretarial and related programs.

ACADEMIC PROGRAMS. 2-year transfer program, accelerated program, double major, dual enrollment of high school students, honors program, independent study, internships, study abroad, telecourses, weekend college, New York semester, Washington semester, cross-registration. **Remedial services:** Learning center, reduced course load, remedial instruction, special counselor, tutoring. **ROTC:** Army, Naval. **Placement/credit:** AP, CLEP General and Subject, institutional tests; 45 credit hours maximum for associate degree.

ACADEMIC REQUIREMENTS. Freshmen must earn minimum GPA of 1.0 to continue in good standing. 58% of freshmen return for sophomore year. Students must declare major on application. **Graduation requirements:** Most students required to take courses in English, humanities, mathematics, biological/physical sciences, social sciences. **Additional information:** Associate of Arts degree requires 62 credit hours for graduation, Associate of Science degree requires 60 to 102 credit hours.

FRESHMAN ADMISSIONS. Selection criteria: Open admissions. Selective admission to some Associate of Science degree programs. Some require specific application in addition to school application. **Test requirements:** MAPS test required for placement, unless SAT or ACT submitted.

1992 FRESHMAN CLASS PROFILE. 1,391 men, 1,787 women enrolled. **Characteristics:** 96% from in state, 100% commute, 22% have minority backgrounds.

FALL-TERM APPLICATIONS. $20 fee. No closing date; priority given to applications received by August 17; applicants notified on a rolling basis. Deferred and early admission available.

STUDENT LIFE. Housing: Housing assistance available to qualified Talent Grant students. **Activities:** Student government, magazine, student newspaper, television, Artist Series, choral groups, concert band, drama, jazz band, music ensembles, musical theater, Forensic Team, Brain Bowl Team, International Student Association, Phi Theta Kappa.

ATHLETICS. NJCAA. **Intercollegiate:** Baseball M, basketball, cross-country, golf M, softball W, tennis, track and field, volleyball W. **Intramural:** Badminton, basketball, bowling, golf, skin diving, soccer M, softball, table tennis, tennis, volleyball.

STUDENT SERVICES. Aptitude testing, career counseling, employment service for undergraduates, freshman orientation, on-campus day care, personal counseling, placement service for graduates, special adviser for adult students, veterans counselor, services/facilities for handicapped.

ANNUAL EXPENSES. Tuition and fees (projected): $990, $2,610 additional for out-of-state students. **Books and supplies:** $450. **Other expenses:** $1,149.

FINANCIAL AID. 54% of continuing students receive some form of aid. 86% of grants, 76% of loans, 61% of jobs based on need. Academic, music/drama, art, athletic, state/district residency, leadership, minority scholarships available. **Aid applications:** No closing date; priority given to applications received by March 1; applicants notified on a rolling basis beginning on or about April 1; must reply within 2 weeks.

ADDRESS/TELEPHONE. Sue Williams, Enrollment Services Officer, Florida Community College at Jacksonville, 501 West State Street, Jacksonville, FL 32202-4030. (904) 632-3388. Fax: (904) 632-3266.

Florida Institute of Technology

Melbourne, Florida — CB code: 5080

Admissions:	85% of applicants accepted
Based on:	••• School record
	•• Test scores
	• Activities, essay, interview, recommendations
Completion:	80% of freshmen end year in good standing
	60% graduate, 32% of these enter graduate study

4-year private university, coed. Founded in 1958. **Accreditation:** Regional. **Undergraduate enrollment:** 1,559 men, 551 women full time; 160 men, 72 women part time. **Graduate enrollment:** 499 men, 228 women full time; 1,593 men, 843 women part time. **Faculty:** 502 total (222 full time), 316 with doctorates or other terminal degrees. **Location:** Suburban campus in large town; 65 miles from of Orlando, 35 miles from Kennedy Space Center. **Calendar:** Semester, limited summer session. **Microcomputers:** 250 located in libraries, classrooms, computer centers. **Special facilities:** Observatory, botanical gardens.

DEGREES OFFERED. BS, MS, MBA, MEd, PhD. 573 bachelor's degrees awarded in 1992. 47% in business and management, 27% engineering, 10% life sciences, 9% physical sciences. Graduate degrees offered in 41 major fields of study.

UNDERGRADUATE MAJORS. Accounting, aerospace/aeronautical/astronautical engineering, airline piloting and navigation, applied mathematics, astronomy, aviation management, biochemistry, biology, business administration and management, business and management, business data processing and related programs, business economics, chemical engineering, chemistry, civil engineering, communications, computer and information sciences, computer engineering, contract management and procurement/purchasing, economics, electrical/electronics/communications engineering, environmental health engineering, environmental science, finance, humanities, management information systems, marine biology, marketing and distribution, marketing management, mathematics education, mechanical engineering, molecular biology, ocean engineering, oceanography, physics, planetary science, predentistry, prelaw, premedicine, preveterinary, psychology, science education, secondary education, technical and business writing.

ACADEMIC PROGRAMS. Cooperative education, dual enrollment of high school students, education specialist degree, independent study, internships, teacher preparation, cross-registration; liberal arts/career combination in engineering. **Remedial services:** Learning center, preadmission summer program, reduced course load, remedial instruction, tutoring. **ROTC:** Army. **Placement/credit:** AP, CLEP Subject, IB, institutional tests.

ACADEMIC REQUIREMENTS. Freshmen must earn minimum GPA of 1.5 to continue in good standing. 75% of freshmen return for sophomore year. Students must declare major on application. **Graduation requirements:** 192 hours for bachelor's. Most students required to take courses in computer science, English, history, humanities, mathematics, biological/physical sciences, social sciences. **Postgraduate studies:** 60% from 2-year programs enter 4-year programs. 1% enter law school, 1% enter medical school, 12% enter MBA programs, 18% enter other graduate study.

FRESHMAN ADMISSIONS. Selection criteria: GPA, test scores, class rank, specific course grades considered. Marginal applicants reviewed by academic departments. Minimum requirements vary depending on intended program. **High school preparation:** 12 units required. Required and recommended units include biological science 1, English 4, mathematics 4 and physical science 2-3. **Test requirements:** SAT or ACT (SAT preferred); score report by June 1. **Additional information:** Students in college-preparatory programs may be informed of admission after first semester grades in junior year.

1992 FRESHMAN CLASS PROFILE. 1,320 men applied, 1,112 accepted, 347 enrolled; 472 women applied, 413 accepted, 127 enrolled. 75% had high school GPA of 3.0 or higher, 25% between 2.0 and 2.99. 42% were in top tenth and 66% were in top quarter of graduating class. **Academic background:** Mid 50% of enrolled freshmen had SAT-V between 470-550, SAT-M between 550-620. 90% submitted SAT scores. **Characteristics:** 30% from in state, 95% live in college housing, 14% have minority backgrounds, 10% are foreign students, 6% join fraternities/sororities. Average age is 18.

FALL-TERM APPLICATIONS. $35 fee, may be waived for applicants with need. Closing date June 1; priority given to applications received by March 1; applicants notified on a rolling basis; must reply by May 1 or within 4 weeks if notified thereafter. Interview recommended. CRDA. Deferred and early admission available.

STUDENT LIFE. Housing: Dormitories (men, women, coed); apartment, fraternity housing available. **Activities:** Student government, radio, student newspaper, television, yearbook, drama, rock bands, fraternities, sororities, Newman Community; Intervarsity Christian Fellowship; Caribbean, Latin American, and Islantic Student Alliances; Habitat for Humanity; Alpha Phi Omega; Florida Tech Republians; Florida Tech Democrats.

ATHLETICS. NCAA. **Intercollegiate:** Baseball M, basketball, cross-country, fencing, rowing (crew), soccer, softball W, tennis M, volleyball W. **Intramural:** Baseball M, basketball, golf M, handball, ice hockey M, racquetball, rifle, rugby M, sailing M, soccer M, softball, tennis, volleyball, water polo M, wrestling M.

STUDENT SERVICES. Aptitude testing, career counseling, employment service for undergraduates, freshman orientation, health services, personal counseling, placement service for graduates, veterans counselor, services/facilities for handicapped.

ANNUAL EXPENSES. Tuition and fees (1992-93): $11,718. **Room and board:** $3,723. **Books and supplies:** $750. **Other expenses:** $1,452.

FINANCIAL AID. 70% of freshmen, 63% of continuing students receive some form of aid. 52% of grants, 60% of loans, 84% of jobs based on need. 412 enrolled freshmen were judged to have need, all were offered aid. Academic, athletic, state/district residency scholarships available. **Aid applications:** No closing date; priority given to applications received by February 1; applicants notified on a rolling basis beginning on or about April 15; must reply by May 1 or within 3 weeks if notified thereafter.

ADDRESS/TELEPHONE. Louis T. Levy, Director of Admissions, Florida Institute of Technology, 150 West University Boulevard, Melbourne, FL 32901-6988. (407) 768-8000 ext. 8030. (800) 888-4348. Fax: (407) 723-9468.

Florida International University

Miami, Florida — CB code: 5206

Admissions: 59% of applicants accepted
Based on:
••• School record, test scores
•• Special talents
• Activities, essay, interview, recommendations
Completion: 93% of freshmen end year in good standing
56% graduate, 34% of these enter graduate study

4-year public university, coed. Founded in 1965. **Accreditation:** Regional. **Undergraduate enrollment:** 4,088 men, 5,491 women full time; 4,004 men, 5,512 women part time. **Graduate enrollment:** 557 men, 671 women full time; 1,338 men, 2,130 women part time. **Faculty:** 1,310 total (951 full time), 914 with doctorates or other terminal degrees. **Location:** Urban campus in large city; 10 miles from downtown, 6 miles from Miami International Airport. **Calendar:** Semester, extensive summer session. **Microcomputers:** 1,500 located in libraries, classrooms, computer centers. **Special facilities:** Art galleries, nature preserve.

DEGREES OFFERED. BA, BS, BFA, MA, MS, MBA, MFA, MEd, MSW, PhD, EdD. 2,075 bachelor's degrees awarded in 1992. 30% in business and management, 5% communications, 5% computer sciences, 12% teacher education, 6% engineering, 7% health sciences, 6% parks/recreation, protective services, public affairs, 6% social sciences. Graduate degrees offered in 69 major fields of study.

UNDERGRADUATE MAJORS. Accounting, anthropology, apparel management, applied mathematics, art education, biology, business administration and management, chemistry, civil engineering, communications, computer and information sciences, computer engineering, construction, construction management, criminal justice studies, dance, dramatic arts, economics, education of the emotionally handicapped, education of the mentally handicapped, electrical/electronics/communications engineering, elementary education, English, English education, environmental and urban systems, environmental science, finance, fine arts, food science and nutrition, foreign languages education, French, French education, geology, German, health care administration, health education, health occupation education, history, home economics education, hotel/motel and restaurant management, humanities, industrial arts education, industrial engineering, information sciences and systems, insurance and risk management, interior design, international business management, international relations, Italian, liberal/general studies, management information systems, marketing management, mathematics, mathematics education, mechanical engineering, medical laboratory technologies, medical records administration, music, music education, nursing, occupational therapy, orthotics and prosthetics, parks and recreation management, personnel management, philosophy, physical education, physical therapy, physics, political science and government, Portuguese, predentistry, premedicine, preveterinary, psychology, public administration, real estate, religion, science education, social studies education, social work, sociology, Spanish, Spanish education, specific learning disabilities, statistics, technical education, trade and industrial education, transportation management, urban studies.

ACADEMIC PROGRAMS. Accelerated program, cooperative education, double major, dual enrollment of high school students, education specialist degree, honors program, independent study, internships, study abroad, teacher preparation, visiting/exchange student program, weekend college, cross-registration. **Remedial services:** Learning center, special counselor, tutoring. **ROTC:** Air Force, Army. **Placement/credit:** AP, CLEP General and Subject, institutional tests; 45 credit hours maximum for bachelor's degree.

ACADEMIC REQUIREMENTS. Freshmen must earn minimum GPA of 2.0 to continue in good standing. 86% of freshmen return for sophomore year. Students must declare major by end of second year. **Graduation requirements:** 120 hours for bachelor's (60 in major). Most students required to take courses in arts/fine arts, English, foreign languages, history, humanities, mathematics, philosophy/religion, biological/physical sciences, social sciences. **Postgraduate studies:** 1% enter law school, 1% enter medical school, 14% enter MBA programs, 18% enter other graduate study.

FRESHMAN ADMISSIONS. Selection criteria: Minimum high school GPA 3.0. Lower GPA considered with higher test score. Lower test score considered with higher GPA. **High school preparation:** 19 units required. Required units include English 4, foreign language 2, mathematics 3, social science 3 and science 3. **Test requirements:** SAT or ACT; score report by April 1.

1992 FRESHMAN CLASS PROFILE. 1,380 men applied, 775 accepted, 450 enrolled; 1,748 women applied, 1,060 accepted, 655 enrolled. 75% had high school GPA of 3.0 or higher, 25% between 2.0 and 2.99. **Academic background:** Mid 50% of enrolled freshmen had SAT-V between 470-520, SAT-M between 540-590; ACT composite between 23-25. 80% submitted SAT scores, 47% submitted ACT scores. **Characteristics:** 89% from in state, 01% live in college housing, 69% have minority backgrounds, 5% are foreign students, 4% join fraternities/sororities. Average age is 19.

FALL-TERM APPLICATIONS. $20 fee, may be waived for applicants with need. Closing date April 1; priority given to applications received by January 1; applicants notified on a rolling basis; must reply by May 1 or within 3 weeks if notified thereafter. Audition required for music performance, theatre, dance applicants. Portfolio required for art applicants. Interview recommended for academically marginal applicants. Essay recommended. Deferred and early admission available.

STUDENT LIFE. Housing: Apartment housing available. Student housing available on first-come, first-served basis. **Activities:** Student government, radio, student newspaper, yearbook, choral groups, concert band, dance, drama, jazz band, music ensembles, musical theater, pep band, symphony orchestra, fraternities, sororities, Hillel, Young Democrats, College Republicans, over 150 other clubs.

ATHLETICS. NCAA. **Intercollegiate:** Baseball M, basketball, cross-country, golf, soccer, tennis, track and field, volleyball W. **Intramural:** Basketball, bowling, cross-country, football, golf, lacrosse M, racquetball M, rugby M, sailing, skin diving, soccer, softball, swimming, tennis, volleyball, water polo M.

STUDENT SERVICES. Career counseling, employment service for undergraduates, freshman orientation, health services, on-campus day care, personal counseling, placement service for graduates, special adviser for adult students, veterans counselor, services/facilities for handicapped.

ANNUAL EXPENSES. Tuition and fees (projected): $1,870, $5,234 additional for out-of-state students. **Room and board:** $5,820. **Books and supplies:** $750. **Other expenses:** $1,708.

FINANCIAL AID. 40% of freshmen, 38% of continuing students receive some form of aid. 58% of grants, 90% of loans, all jobs based on need. Academic, music/drama, art, athletic, minority scholarships available. **Aid applications:** Closing date May 1; priority given to applications received by March 15; applicants notified on a rolling basis beginning on or about May 15; must reply within 4 weeks.

ADDRESS/TELEPHONE. Carmen Brown, Director of Admissions, Florida International University, University Park, Miami, FL 33199. (305) 348-2363. Fax: (305) 348-3648.

Florida Keys Community College
Key West, Florida CB code: 5236

2-year public community college, coed. Founded in 1965. **Accreditation:** Regional. **Undergraduate enrollment:** 2,224 men and women. **Location:** Suburban campus in large town; 154 miles from Miami. **Calendar:** Semester. **Additional facts:** 2-year transfer programs offered at main campus and Coral Shores and Marathon branch campuses.

FRESHMAN ADMISSIONS. Selection criteria: Open admissions. Placement examination, physical examination, and interview required for nursing technology applicants.

ANNUAL EXPENSES. Tuition and fees (projected): $960, $2,610 additional for out-of-state students. **Books and supplies:** $500. **Other expenses:** $1,000.

ADDRESS/TELEPHONE. Mitchell A. Grabois, Admissions Coordinator, Florida Keys Community College, 5901 W. Junior College Road, Key West, FL 33040. (305) 296-9081. Fax: (305) 292-5155.

Florida Memorial College
Miami, Florida CB code: 5217

Admissions:	75% of applicants accepted
Based on:	••• Essay, interview, school record, test scores
	•• Activities, recommendations, special talents
Completion:	80% of freshmen end year in good standing
	69% graduate, 17% of these enter graduate study

4-year private college of arts and sciences, coed, affiliated with American Baptist Churches in the USA, Progressive Missionary and Educational Baptist Convention, and Baptist General State Convention. Founded in 1879. **Accreditation:** Regional. **Undergraduate enrollment:** 1,489 men and women. **Faculty:** 139 total (69 full time), 63 with doctorates or other terminal degrees. **Location:** Suburban campus in large city; 15 miles from downtown Miami. **Calendar:** Semester, limited summer session. **Microcomputers:** 120 located in classrooms, computer centers. **Special facilities:** Black archives, airway science building with simulator and control tower. **Additional facts:** Christian principles emphasized. 4 branch campuses.

DEGREES OFFERED. BA, BS. 195 bachelor's degrees awarded in 1992. 50% in business and management, 8% computer sciences, 7% teacher education, 25% social sciences.

UNDERGRADUATE MAJORS. Accounting, air traffic control, airway science, aviation computer technology, aviation management, biology, business administration and management, computer and information sciences, criminal justice studies, data processing, elementary education, English, mathematics, medical laboratory technologies, medical social work, physical education, political science and government, psychology, public administration, religion, sociology.

ACADEMIC PROGRAMS. Cooperative education, double major, dual enrollment of high school students, honors program, internships, teacher preparation. **Remedial services:** Learning center, remedial instruction, special counselor, tutoring. **Placement/credit:** Institutional tests; 30 credit hours maximum for bachelor's degree.

ACADEMIC REQUIREMENTS. Freshmen must earn minimum GPA of 2.0 to continue in good standing. 80% of freshmen return for sophomore year. Students must declare major by end of second year. **Graduation requirements:** 124 hours for bachelor's (30 in major). Most students required to take courses in computer science, English, foreign languages, history, humanities, mathematics, philosophy/religion, biological/physical sciences, social sciences. **Postgraduate studies:** 2% enter law school, 1% enter medical school, 4% enter MBA programs, 10% enter other graduate study.

FRESHMAN ADMISSIONS. Selection criteria: High school GPA of 2.0 required. School achievement record, test scores, interview, recommendations, alumni affiliation considered. **High school preparation:** 15 units recommended. Recommended units include biological science 1, English 4, foreign language 2, mathematics 4, physical science 2 and social science 2. College-preparatory program strongly recommended. **Test requirements:** SAT or ACT for placement and counseling only; score report by July 1.

1992 FRESHMAN CLASS PROFILE. 2,400 men and women applied, 1,800 accepted; 557 enrolled. 7% had high school GPA of 3.0 or higher, 75% between 2.0 and 2.99. **Academic background:** Mid 50% of enrolled freshmen had ACT composite between 21-32. 30% submitted ACT scores. **Characteristics:** 80% from in state, 80% live in college housing, 90% have minority backgrounds, 5% are foreign students. Average age is 19.

FALL-TERM APPLICATIONS. $15 fee, may be waived for applicants with need. Closing date July 1; priority given to applications received by April 1; applicants notified on a rolling basis; must reply by August 1. Essay required. Interview recommended. Deferred admission available.

STUDENT LIFE. Housing: Dormitories (men, women). **Activities:** Student government, film, student newspaper, television, yearbook, choral groups, drama, jazz band, music ensembles, fraternities, sororities, Christian Student Union, international students, broadcasting club, Circle-K, Young Republicans, Junior NAACP, Toastmasters, Professional Women of Tomorrow.

ATHLETICS. NAIA. **Intercollegiate:** Baseball M, basketball, track and field, volleyball W. **Intramural:** Baseball M, basketball, soccer M, softball W, swimming, tennis, volleyball.

STUDENT SERVICES. Aptitude testing, career counseling, employment service for undergraduates, freshman orientation, health services, personal counseling, placement service for graduates, campus ministry.

ANNUAL EXPENSES. Tuition and fees (1992-93): $4,450. **Room and board:** $2,800. **Books and supplies:** $500. **Other expenses:** $810.

FINANCIAL AID. 95% of freshmen, 95% of continuing students receive some form of aid. All grants, 93% of loans, all jobs based on need. Academic, music/drama, minority scholarships available. **Aid applications:** No closing date; priority given to applications received by April 1; applicants notified on a rolling basis; must reply within 10 days.

ADDRESS/TELEPHONE. Mrs. Peggy Kelly, Director of Admissions, Florida Memorial College, 15800 Northwest 42 Avenue, Miami, FL 33054. (305) 626-3750. (800) 822-1362. Fax: (305) 626-3769.

Florida Southern College
Lakeland, Florida CB code: 5218

Admissions:	65% of applicants accepted
Based on:	••• School record
	•• Activities, essay, recommendations, test scores
	• Interview, special talents
Completion:	82% of freshmen end year in good standing
	70% graduate, 37% of these enter graduate study

4-year private liberal arts college, coed, affiliated with United Methodist Church. Founded in 1885. **Accreditation:** Regional. **Undergraduate enrollment:** 619 men, 855 women full time; 542 men, 588 women part time. **Graduate enrollment:** 50 men, 20 women part time. **Faculty:** 175 total (100 full time), 75 with doctorates or other terminal degrees. **Location:** Suburban campus in small city; 30 miles from Tampa, 50 miles from Orlando. **Calendar:** Semester, limited summer session. **Microcomputers:** 60 located in libraries, computer centers. **Special facilities:** Art gallery, planetarium. **Additional facts:** Campus includes world's largest collection of Frank Lloyd Wright architecture.

DEGREES OFFERED. BA, BS, MBA. 532 bachelor's degrees awarded in 1992. 38% in business and management, 12% communications, 9% teacher education, 6% health sciences, 5% mathematics, 6% psychology, 11% social sciences. Graduate degrees offered in 2 major fields of study.

UNDERGRADUATE MAJORS. Accounting, advertising, art education, biological and physical sciences, biology, business administration and management, chemistry, citrus science, communications, criminal justice studies, criminology, dramatic arts, early childhood education, economics, education of the emotionally handicapped, elementary education, English, finance, French, German, history, horticultural science, horticulture, humanities and social sciences, information sciences and systems, international business management, journalism, management information systems, marketing management, mathematics, medical laboratory technologies, music, music business management, music education, music performance, ornamental horticulture, parks and recreation management, personnel management, physical education, physics, political science and government, predentistry, prelaw, premedicine, preveterinary, psychology, public relations, radio/television broadcasting, religion, religious education, religious music, secondary education, social sciences, social work, sociology, Spanish, special education, specific learning disabilities, sports management, studio art, visual and performing arts.

ACADEMIC PROGRAMS. Double major, dual enrollment of high school students, independent study, internships, study abroad, teacher preparation, visiting/exchange student program, New York semester, United Nations semester, Washington semester; liberal arts/career combination in engineering, forestry. **Remedial services:** Preadmission summer program, tutoring. **ROTC:** Air Force, Army. **Placement/credit:** AP, CLEP General and Subject; 60 credit hours maximum for bachelor's degree.

ACADEMIC REQUIREMENTS. Freshmen must earn minimum GPA of 2.0 to continue in good standing. 65% of freshmen return for sophomore year. Students must declare major by end of second year. **Graduation requirements:** 124 hours for bachelor's (34 in major). Most students required to take courses in arts/fine arts, English, history, humanities, mathematics, philosophy/religion, biological/physical sciences, social sciences.

FRESHMAN ADMISSIONS. Selection criteria: School achievement record most important, followed by test scores and recommendations. Character and motivation and extracurricular activities considered. **High school preparation:** 17 units required. Required units include biological science 1, English 4, foreign language 2, mathematics 3, physical science 2 and social science 4. **Test requirements:** SAT or ACT; score report by July 15.

1992 FRESHMAN CLASS PROFILE. 30% had high school GPA of 3.0 or higher, 65% between 2.0 and 2.99. 10% were in top tenth and 30% were in top quarter of graduating class. **Academic background:** Mid 50% of enrolled freshmen had SAT-V between 420-540, SAT-M between 430-540; ACT composite between 19-23. 70% submitted SAT scores, 30% submitted

ACT scores. **Characteristics:** 60% from in state, 84% live in college housing, 4% have minority backgrounds, 2% are foreign students, 32% join fraternities/sororities. Average age is 18.

FALL-TERM APPLICATIONS. $30 fee, may be waived for applicants with need. Closing date August 1; applicants notified on a rolling basis; must reply by May 1 or within 2 weeks if notified thereafter. Essay required. Interview recommended for academically weak applicants. Audition recommended for music applicants. Portfolio recommended for art applicants. CRDA. Deferred and early admission available.

STUDENT LIFE. Housing: Dormitories (men, women); fraternity, sorority housing available. On-campus housing required unless married or living locally with parents or legal guardian. **Activities:** Student government, radio, student newspaper, television, yearbook, choral groups, concert band, drama, jazz band, music ensembles, musical theater, symphony orchestra, fraternities, sororities, Wesley Fellowship, International Club, tutorial service organizations for local community, Fellowship of Christian Athletes.

ATHLETICS. NCAA. **Intercollegiate:** Baseball M, basketball, cross-country, golf M, skiing, soccer M, softball W, tennis W, volleyball W. **Intramural:** Badminton, basketball, bowling, cross-country M, golf M, racquetball W, soccer W, softball, table tennis, tennis, volleyball.

STUDENT SERVICES. Aptitude testing, career counseling, employment service for undergraduates, freshman orientation, health services, personal counseling, placement service for graduates, veterans counselor, services/facilities for handicapped.

ANNUAL EXPENSES. Tuition and fees (1992-93): $6,800. **Room and board:** $4,400. **Books and supplies:** $300. **Other expenses:** $600.

FINANCIAL AID. 82% of freshmen, 85% of continuing students receive some form of aid. 29% of grants, 93% of loans, 47% of jobs based on need. 200 enrolled freshmen were judged to have need, 193 were offered aid. Academic, music/drama, art, athletic, state/district residency, religious affiliation scholarships available. **Aid applications:** No closing date; priority given to applications received by April 15; applicants notified on a rolling basis beginning on or about May 1; must reply within 2 weeks.

ADDRESS/TELEPHONE. Mr. William B. Stephens, Jr, Director of Admissions, Florida Southern College, 111 Lake Hollingsworth Drive, Lakeland, FL 33801-5698. (813) 680-4131. (800) 274-4131. Fax: (813) 680-4120.

Florida State University
Tallahassee, Florida CB code: 5219

Admissions: 72% of applicants accepted
Based on: ••• School record, test scores
•• Special talents
• Activities, recommendations
Completion: 90% of freshmen end year in good standing
47% graduate

4-year public university, coed. Founded in 1851. **Accreditation:** Regional. **Undergraduate enrollment:** 8,478 men, 10,124 women full time; 1,220 men, 1,294 women part time. **Graduate enrollment:** 1,891 men, 1,830 women full time; 886 men, 1,151 women part time. **Faculty:** 1,526 total (1,374 full time), 1,166 with doctorates or other terminal degrees. **Location:** Suburban campus in small city; 191 miles from Pensacola and 163 miles from Jacksonville. **Calendar:** Semester, extensive summer session. **Microcomputers:** Located in dormitories, libraries, classrooms, computer centers, campus-wide network. **Special facilities:** Marine laboratory, Geophysical Fluid Dynamics Institute, National High Magnetic Field Laboratory, Center for Music Research, art gallery, FSU Supercomputer, Computations Research Institute, Tandem Van de Graaff Accelaterator.

DEGREES OFFERED. AA, BA, BS, BFA, MA, MS, MBA, MFA, MEd, MSW, PhD, EdD, JD. 647 associate degrees awarded in 1992. 5,587 bachelor's degrees awarded. 24% in business and management, 6% communications, 11% teacher education, 6% parks/recreation, protective services, public affairs, 6% psychology, 19% social sciences. Graduate degrees offered in 123 major fields of study.

UNDERGRADUATE MAJORS. Associate: Liberal/general studies. **Bachelor's:** Accounting, advertising, American studies, analytical chemistry, anthropology, archeology, art education, art history, Asian studies, atmospheric sciences and meteorology, biochemistry, biology, botany, business administration and management, business and management, Caribbean studies, chemical engineering, chemistry, civil engineering, classics, clinical psychology, communications, communications research, computer and information sciences, computer engineering, contract management and procurement/purchasing, creative writing, criminology, dance, dramatic arts, early childhood education, Eastern European studies, ecology, economics, education of the emotionally handicapped, education of the mentally handicapped, education of the visually handicapped, electrical/electronics/communications engineering, elementary education, embryology, English, English education, environmental science, fashion design, fashion merchandising, finance, food science and nutrition, foreign languages education, French, genetics, human and animal, geography, geology, German, Greek (classical), health education, history, home economics, home economics education, hotel/motel and restaurant management, human environment and housing, human resources development, humanities, individual and family development, industrial engineering, inorganic chemistry, insurance and risk management, interior design, international business management, international relations, Italian, journalism, Latin, Latin American studies, leisure services and studies, management information systems, management science, marine biology, marketing management, marketing research, mathematics, mathematics education, mechanical engineering, motion picture technology, music, music education, music history and appreciation, music performance, music theory and composition, music therapy, musical theater, neurosciences, nursing, nutrition and fitness, nutritional sciences, organic chemistry, personnel management, philosophy, physical chemistry, physical education, physics, physiology, human and animal, plant genetics, plant physiology, political communication, political science and government, predentistry, prelaw, premedicine, prepharmacy, preveterinary, psychology, public relations, radio/television broadcasting, radio/television technology, real estate, rehabilitation counseling/services, religion, Russian, Russian and Slavic studies, science education, secondary science and mathematics teching, small business management and ownership, social science education, social sciences, social work, sociology, Spanish, specific learning disabilities, speech, speech pathology/audiology, statistics, studio art, systems engineering, textiles and clothing, zoology.

ACADEMIC PROGRAMS. Accelerated program, cooperative education, double major, dual enrollment of high school students, education specialist degree, honors program, independent study, internships, study abroad, teacher preparation, cooperative programs with Florida Agricultural and Mechanical University and Tallahassee Community College; study abroad programs in London and Florence. **Remedial services:** Learning center, reduced course load, special counselor, tutoring. **ROTC:** Air Force, Army, Naval. **Placement/credit:** AP, CLEP General and Subject, institutional tests; 60 credit hours maximum for bachelor's degree.

ACADEMIC REQUIREMENTS. Freshmen must earn minimum GPA of 2.0 to continue in good standing. 85% of freshmen return for sophomore year. Students must declare major by end of second year. **Graduation requirements:** 60 hours for associate, 120 hours for bachelor's. Most students required to take courses in arts/fine arts, English, history, humanities, mathematics, biological/physical sciences, social sciences. **Additional information:** Credit hours in major toward bachelor's varies according to program.

FRESHMAN ADMISSIONS. Selection criteria: Most Florida students accepted present at least a B average in all academic subjects (grades 9-12) and test scores of at least 25 composite on the Enhanced ACT or 1050 (verbal plus math SAT). Out-of-state applicants will ordinarily be held to higher standards. **High school preparation:** 19 units required. Required units include English 4, foreign language 2, mathematics 3, social science 3 and science 3. Mathematics courses must be algebra I and above; two units of same foreign language required. **Test requirements:** SAT or ACT; score report by March 1.

1992 FRESHMAN CLASS PROFILE. 5,964 men applied, 4,112 accepted, 1,218 enrolled; 6,802 women applied, 5,096 accepted, 1,723 enrolled. 87% had high school GPA of 3.0 or higher, 13% between 2.0 and 2.99. **Academic background:** Mid 50% of enrolled freshmen had SAT-V between 460-560, SAT-M between 520-630; ACT composite between 23-27. 80% submitted SAT scores, 65% submitted ACT scores. **Characteristics:** 91% from in state, 80% live in college housing, 17% have minority backgrounds, 1% are foreign students, 15% join fraternities/sororities. Average age is 18.

FALL-TERM APPLICATIONS. $20 fee, may be waived for applicants with need. Closing date March 1; applicants notified on a rolling basis. Audition required for music, dance, BFA theater applicants. Portfolio required for BFA art, interior design applicants. Early admission available.

STUDENT LIFE. Housing: Dormitories (men, women, coed); apartment, fraternity, sorority housing available. Southern Scholarship Foundation-Cooperative housing. **Activities:** Student government, film, magazine, radio, student newspaper, television, yearbook, choral groups, concert band, dance, drama, jazz band, marching band, music ensembles, musical theater, opera, pep band, symphony orchestra, circus, fraternities, sororities, campus ministries, Black Student Union, International Student House.

ATHLETICS. NCAA. **Intercollegiate:** Baseball M, basketball, cross-country, diving, football M, golf, softball W, swimming, tennis, track and field, volleyball W. **Intramural:** Badminton, basketball, bowling, cross-country, diving, fencing, golf, lacrosse M, racquetball, rugby, sailing, skiing, skin diving, soccer, softball, swimming, table tennis, tennis, track and field, volleyball, water polo, wrestling M.

STUDENT SERVICES. Aptitude testing, career counseling, employment service for undergraduates, freshman orientation, health services, on-campus day care, personal counseling, placement service for graduates, special adviser for adult students, veterans counselor, services/facilities for handicapped.

ANNUAL EXPENSES. Tuition and fees (1992-93): $1,745, $4,759 additional for out-of-state students. **Room and board:** $3,880. **Books and supplies:** $500. **Other expenses:** $850.

FINANCIAL AID. 52% of freshmen, 51% of continuing students receive some form of aid. 61% of grants, 83% of loans, 8% of jobs based on need. 1,033 enrolled freshmen were judged to have need, all were offered aid. Academic, music/drama, art, athletic, state/district residency, alumni affiliation, minority scholarships available. **Aid applications:** Closing date March 1; applicants notified on a rolling basis beginning on or about May 1; must reply within 3 weeks. **Additional information:** Out-of-state tuition costs sometimes waived for honors program, National Merit and National Achievement students, and some southwest Georgia residents.

ADDRESS/TELEPHONE. Dr. Peter F. Metarko, Director of Admissions, Florida State University, 216B WJB, Tallahassee, FL 32306-1009. (904) 644-6200.

Fort Lauderdale College
Fort Lauderdale, Florida CB code: 5171

4-year proprietary business college, coed. Founded in 1940. **Undergraduate enrollment:** 1,130 men and women. **Faculty:** 35 total (14 full time), 4 with doctorates or other terminal degrees. **Location:** Suburban campus in small city; 35 miles from Miami. **Calendar:** Quarter, extensive summer session. **Microcomputers:** Located in libraries, classrooms, computer centers.

DEGREES OFFERED. AS, BS, MBA. 176 associate degrees awarded in 1992. 99% in business and management. 24 bachelor's degrees awarded. 100% in business and management. Graduate degrees offered in 1 major field of study.

UNDERGRADUATE MAJORS. **Associate:** Accounting, business administration and management, business and management, hotel/motel and restaurant management, information sciences and systems, international business management, legal assistant/paralegal, management information systems, marketing management, video. **Bachelor's:** Accounting, business administration and management, business and management, hotel/motel and restaurant management, information sciences and systems, international business management, management information systems, marketing management.

ACADEMIC PROGRAMS. Accelerated program, cooperative education, double major, independent study, internships, student-designed major. **Remedial services:** Learning center, reduced course load, tutoring. **Placement/credit:** CLEP General and Subject, institutional tests; 24 credit hours maximum for associate degree; 48 credit hours maximum for bachelor's degree.

ACADEMIC REQUIREMENTS. Freshmen must earn minimum GPA of 1.75 to continue in good standing. 80% of freshmen return for sophomore year. Students must declare major on enrollment. **Graduation requirements:** 96 hours for associate (24 in major), 192 hours for bachelor's (48 in major). Most students required to take courses in computer science, English, mathematics, social sciences. **Postgraduate studies:** 85% from 2-year programs enter 4-year programs.

FRESHMAN ADMISSIONS. **Selection criteria:** School achievement record, interview considered.

1992 FRESHMAN CLASS PROFILE. 289 men and women enrolled. **Characteristics:** 22% from in state, 60% commute, 35% have minority backgrounds, 15% are foreign students. Average age is 22.

FALL-TERM APPLICATIONS. $25 fee. No closing date; applicants notified on a rolling basis; must reply as soon as possible. Interview required. Deferred and early admission available.

STUDENT LIFE. **Housing:** Apartment housing available. **Activities:** Student government, student newspaper.

ATHLETICS. **Intramural:** Basketball, soccer M, softball, volleyball.

STUDENT SERVICES. Career counseling, employment service for undergraduates, freshman orientation, personal counseling, placement service for graduates, veterans counselor, services/facilities for handicapped.

ANNUAL EXPENSES. **Tuition and fees (1992-93):** $4,511. Commercial art and video/film production currently $125 per-credit-hour. **Room and board:** $2,925 room only. **Books and supplies:** $150. **Other expenses:** $360.

FINANCIAL AID. 45% of freshmen, 40% of continuing students receive some form of aid. Grants, loans, jobs available. Academic scholarships available. **Aid applications:** No closing date; applicants notified on a rolling basis beginning on or about June 1.

ADDRESS/TELEPHONE. Wendy Hopkins, Director of Admissions, Fort Lauderdale College, 1040 Bayview Drive, Fort Lauderdale, FL 33304. (305) 568-1600. (800) 468-0168. Fax: (305) 568-2008.

Gulf Coast Community College
Panama City, Florida CB code: 5271

2-year public community college, coed. Founded in 1957. **Accreditation:** Regional. **Undergraduate enrollment:** 994 men, 1,242 women full time; 1,416 men, 2,281 women part time. **Faculty:** 338 total (93 full time), 47 with doctorates or other terminal degrees. **Location:** Suburban campus in small city; 100 miles from Tallahassee, 100 miles from Pensacola. **Calendar:** Semester, limited summer session. Saturday and extensive evening/early morning classes. **Microcomputers:** 600 located in libraries, classrooms, computer centers.

DEGREES OFFERED. AA, AS. 350 associate degrees awarded in 1992.

UNDERGRADUATE MAJORS. Accounting, advertising, aeronautical technology, airline piloting and navigation, anthropology, archeology, architecture, atmospheric sciences and meteorology, aviation management, biological and physical sciences, biology, business administration and management, business and management, business and office, business computer/console/peripheral equipment operation, business data entry equipment operation, business data processing and related programs, business data programming, business education, chemistry, child development/care/guidance, clothing and textiles management/production/services, communications, computer and information sciences, computer programming, construction, criminal justice technology, data processing, dental assistant, drafting, drafting and design technology, economics, education, electrical and electronics equipment repair, electromechanical technology, electronic technology, elementary education, emergency medical technologies, engineering, engineering and engineering-related technologies, engineering and other disciplines, English, English education, fashion merchandising, finance, fine arts, fire control and safety technology, food management, food production/management/services, foreign languages (multiple emphasis), forestry and related sciences, geology, graphic arts technology, health education, history, home economics, hospitality and recreation marketing, hotel/motel and restaurant management, humanities and social sciences, journalism, law enforcement and corrections technologies, liberal/general studies, library science, marketing and distribution, marketing and distributive education, marketing management, mathematics, mechanical design technology, medical records administration, medical records technology, mental health/human services, music, music performance, nursing, oceanography, philosophy, physical education, physical sciences, physical therapy, physician's assistant, physics, political science and government, practical nursing, predentistry, prelaw, premedicine, prepharmacy, preveterinary, psychology, public affairs, public relations, radio/television broadcasting, radio/television technology, radiograph medical technology, real estate, religion, respiratory therapy technology, science education, secondary education, secretarial and related programs, social sciences, social studies education, social work, special education, speech, systems analysis.

ACADEMIC PROGRAMS. 2-year transfer program, accelerated program, cooperative education, dual enrollment of high school students, honors program, independent study, internships, teacher preparation, telecourses, weekend college. **Remedial services:** Learning center, reduced course load, remedial instruction, special counselor, tutoring, writing center. **ROTC:** Army. **Placement/credit:** AP, CLEP General and Subject, institutional tests; 45 credit hours maximum for associate degree.

ACADEMIC REQUIREMENTS. Freshmen must earn minimum GPA of 2.0 to continue in good standing. 47% of freshmen return for sophomore year. Students must declare major by end of first year. **Graduation requirements:** 65 hours for associate (20 in major). Most students required to take courses in arts/fine arts, English, history, humanities, mathematics, philosophy/religion, biological/physical sciences, social sciences. **Additional information:** 2-year transfer program direct to Florida State University, Panama City Campus offered.

FRESHMAN ADMISSIONS. **Selection criteria:** Open admissions. Admission to health science programs determined through high school transcripts and arithmetic portion of school placement examination. Recommended units include English 4, mathematics 3, social science 3 and science 3. **Test requirements:** California Psychological Inventory required of human services and mental health technology applicants.

1992 FRESHMAN CLASS PROFILE. 966 men and women enrolled. **Characteristics:** 99% from in state, 100% commute, 8% have minority backgrounds, 1% are foreign students. Average age is 21.

FALL-TERM APPLICATIONS. No fee. No closing date; applicants notified on a rolling basis. Interview required for allied health applicants. Audition recommended for music applicants. Deferred and early admission available. Application deadline for nursing program February 15.

STUDENT LIFE. **Activities:** Student government, magazine, radio, student newspaper, choral groups, concert band, dance, drama, jazz band, music ensembles, musical theater, pep band, symphony orchestra, fraternities, sororities, Black Union, Baptist campus ministry.

ATHLETICS. NJCAA. **Intercollegiate:** Baseball M, basketball M, softball W. **Intramural:** Archery, badminton, basketball, bowling, softball.

STUDENT SERVICES. Aptitude testing, career counseling, employment service for undergraduates, freshman orientation, personal counseling, special adviser for adult students, veterans counselor, services/facilities for handicapped.

ANNUAL EXPENSES. **Tuition and fees (projected):** $910, $2,440 additional for out-of-state students. **Books and supplies:** $600. **Other expenses:** $900.

FINANCIAL AID. 59% of freshmen, 53% of continuing students receive some form of aid. 69% of grants, 70% of loans, 46% of jobs based on need. Academic, music/drama, art, athletic, state/district residency, leadership, minority scholarships available. **Aid applications:** No closing date; priority given to applications received by April 1; applicants notified on a rolling basis beginning on or about August 1; must reply within 2 weeks. **Additional information:** Extensive short-term emergency loans available.

ADDRESS/TELEPHONE. Roy W. Smith, Director of Admissions and Records, Gulf Coast Community College, 5230 West Highway 98, Panama City, FL 32401-1041. (904) 769-1551. Fax: (904) 872-3836.

Hillsborough Community College

Tampa, Florida — CB code: 5304

2-year public community college, coed. Founded in 1968. **Accreditation:** Regional. **Undergraduate enrollment:** 2,970 men, 3,138 women full time; 5,946 men, 8,784 women part time. **Faculty:** 343 total (247 full time), 61 with doctorates or other terminal degrees. **Location:** Urban campus in large city; 2 miles from downtown. **Calendar:** Semester, limited summer session. **Special facilities:** Cockroach Bay and Upper Tampa Bay Park environmental study centers, Florida Studies Center (site of International Wetlands Conference). **Additional facts:** 4 campuses in county.

DEGREES OFFERED. AA, AS. 1,872 associate degrees awarded in 1992.

UNDERGRADUATE MAJORS. Air conditioning/heating/refrigeration mechanics, air conditioning/heating/refrigeration technology, architecture, business administration and management, business and management, business and office, child care center management, computer and information sciences, computer engineering, computer technology, criminal justice technology, drafting, electrical/electronics/communications engineering, engineering, engineering and engineering-related technologies, finance, fire control and safety technology, horticultural science, horticulture, hotel/motel and restaurant management, information sciences and systems, interior design, interpreter for the deaf, law enforcement and corrections technologies, legal secretary, liberal/general studies, marketing and distribution, medical secretary, mental health/human services, music, nuclear medical technology, nursing, office supervision and management, practical nursing.

ACADEMIC PROGRAMS. 2-year transfer program, cooperative education, double major, dual enrollment of high school students, independent study, study abroad, telecourses, weekend college, cross-registration. **Remedial services:** Learning center, remedial instruction, tutoring. **Placement/credit:** AP, CLEP General and Subject, institutional tests.

ACADEMIC REQUIREMENTS. Freshmen must earn minimum GPA of 2.0 to continue in good standing. 66% of freshmen return for sophomore year. Students must declare major on application. **Graduation requirements:** 62 hours for associate (45 in major). Most students required to take courses in English, history, mathematics, biological/physical sciences, social sciences.

FRESHMAN ADMISSIONS. Selection criteria: Open admissions. **High school preparation:** 24 units recommended. Recommended units include English 4, foreign language 2, mathematics 3, social science 3 and science 3. One physical education and 6.5 electives, 1.5 each health, performing arts and practical arts, recommended.

1992 FRESHMAN CLASS PROFILE. 1,415 men, 1,595 women enrolled. **Characteristics:** 96% from in state, 100% commute, 30% have minority backgrounds, 1% are foreign students.

FALL-TERM APPLICATIONS. $15 fee. No closing date; applicants notified on a rolling basis. Deferred and early admission available.

STUDENT LIFE. Activities: Student government, magazine, student newspaper, yearbook, choral groups, concert band, drama, jazz band, music ensembles, fraternities.

ATHLETICS. NJCAA. **Intercollegiate:** Baseball M, basketball, softball W, tennis W, volleyball W. **Intramural:** Bowling, soccer M.

STUDENT SERVICES. Aptitude testing, career counseling, employment service for undergraduates, personal counseling, placement service for graduates, special adviser for adult students, veterans counselor, services/facilities for handicapped.

ANNUAL EXPENSES. Tuition and fees (projected): $848, $2,317 additional for out-of-state students. **Books and supplies:** $600. **Other expenses:** $2,000.

FINANCIAL AID. 25% of continuing students receive some form of aid. 90% of grants, 72% of loans, all jobs based on need. Academic, music/drama, art, athletic scholarships available. **Aid applications:** No closing date; priority given to applications received by April 15; applicants notified on a rolling basis beginning on or about July 1; must reply within 2 weeks.

ADDRESS/TELEPHONE. Philip T. Dreier, Registrar, Hillsborough Community College, PO Box 31127, Tampa, FL 33631-3127. (813) 253-7004. Fax: (813) 253-7136.

Hobe Sound Bible College

Hobe Sound, Florida — CB code: 5306

4-year private Bible college, coed, interdenominational. Founded in 1960. **Undergraduate enrollment:** 57 men, 77 women full time; 19 men, 35 women part time. **Faculty:** 28 total (16 full time), 4 with doctorates or other terminal degrees. **Location:** Suburban campus in small town; 25 miles from West Palm Beach. **Calendar:** 4-1-4, limited summer session. **Microcomputers:** 10 located in computer centers.

DEGREES OFFERED. AA, AS, BA. 8 associate degrees awarded in 1992. 100% in philosophy, religion, theology. 13 bachelor's degrees awarded. 46% in teacher education, 54% philosophy, religion, theology.

UNDERGRADUATE MAJORS. Associate: Bible studies, secretarial and related programs. **Bachelor's:** Elementary education, English education, mathematics education, missionary studies, music education, religion, religious music, theological studies.

ACADEMIC PROGRAMS. Double major, internships, teacher preparation. **Remedial services:** Reduced course load, remedial instruction. **Placement/credit:** AP, CLEP General and Subject, institutional tests.

ACADEMIC REQUIREMENTS. No policy requiring minimum GPA; records of students having academic difficulty are reviewed individually. 63% of freshmen return for sophomore year. Students must declare major by end of second year. **Graduation requirements:** 70 hours for associate (30 in major), 136 hours for bachelor's (30 in major). Most students required to take courses in arts/fine arts, computer science, English, history, humanities, mathematics, philosophy/religion, biological/physical sciences. **Additional information:** Double major required of all students in 4-year programs. All students complete major in Bible as well as major in Christian vocational field.

FRESHMAN ADMISSIONS. Selection criteria: Open admissions. Recommended units include biological science 1, English 4, mathematics 3, physical science 1 and social science 3.

1992 FRESHMAN CLASS PROFILE. 44 men and women enrolled. 18% were in top tenth and 41% were in top quarter of graduating class. **Characteristics:** 18% from in state, 91% live in college housing, 1% have minority backgrounds. Average age is 18.

FALL-TERM APPLICATIONS. $25 fee, may be waived for applicants with need. No closing date; applicants notified on a rolling basis beginning on or about March 1. Essay required. CRDA.

STUDENT LIFE. Housing: Dormitories (men, women); apartment housing available. Unmarried students under 25 required to live in campus dormitories or with parents. **Activities:** Student government, yearbook, choral groups, music ensembles, Christian service organizations. **Additional information:** Religious observance required.

ATHLETICS. Intramural: Basketball, football M, softball, volleyball.

STUDENT SERVICES. Career counseling, employment service for undergraduates, freshman orientation, health services, personal counseling, placement service for graduates.

ANNUAL EXPENSES. Tuition and fees: $4,000. **Room and board:** $2,475. **Books and supplies:** $400. **Other expenses:** $2,000.

FINANCIAL AID. 55% of freshmen, 60% of continuing students receive some form of aid. All grants, all loans based on need. 30 enrolled freshmen were judged to have need, all were offered aid. **Aid applications:** No closing date; applicants notified on a rolling basis.

ADDRESS/TELEPHONE. Ann French, Director of Admissions, Hobe Sound Bible College, PO Box 1065, Hobe Sound, FL 33475-1065. (407) 546-5534 ext. 248. (800) 881-5534. Fax: (407) 546-9379.

Indian River Community College

Fort Pierce, Florida — CB code: 5322

2-year public community college, coed. Founded in 1960. **Accreditation:** Regional. **Undergraduate enrollment:** 2,538 men and women full time; 11,923 men and women part time. **Faculty:** 821 total (153 full time), 63 with doctorates or other terminal degrees. **Location:** Suburban campus in small city; 65 miles from West Palm Beach. **Calendar:** Semester, extensive summer session. Saturday and extensive evening/early morning classes. **Microcomputers:** Located in classrooms. **Special facilities:** Olympic-size pool complex, fine arts center. **Additional facts:** Off-campus centers in Vero Beach, Stuart, Okeechobee, Port St. Lucie and Criminal Justice Academy and Marine Center, Fort Pierce.

DEGREES OFFERED. AA, AS. 696 associate degrees awarded in 1992.

UNDERGRADUATE MAJORS. Accounting, agricultural business and management, agricultural sciences, air conditioning/heating/refrigeration mechanics, air conditioning/heating/refrigeration technology, American literature, architecture, automotive mechanics, automotive technology, behavioral sciences, biology, business administration and management, business and management, business and office, business data processing and related programs, business data programming, chemistry, communications, computer and information sciences, computer graphics, computer programming, criminal justice studies, dental hygiene, dental laboratory technology, drafting, drafting and design technology, education, electrical/electronics/communications engineering, electronic technology, elementary education, emergency medical technologies, engineering, engineering and engineering-related technologies, English, English literature, fashion merchandising, finance, fine arts, fire control and safety technology, food production/management/services, history, home economics, interior design, junior high education, law enforcement and corrections technologies, legal secretary, liberal/general studies, library assistant, marketing and distribution, mathematics, medical laboratory technologies, medical records administration, medical records technology, medical secretary, mental health/human services, music, nursing, office supervision and management, physical sciences, physics, predentistry, preengineering, prelaw, premedicine, prepharmacy, preveterinary, psychology, radiograph medical technology, recreation and community services technologies, respiratory therapy, respiratory therapy technology, retailing, science technologies, secondary education, secretarial and related programs, social sciences, sociology, Spanish, teacher aide, visual and performing arts, word processing.

ACADEMIC PROGRAMS. 2-year transfer program, dual enrollment of high school students, independent study, weekend college. **Remedial services:** Learning center, preadmission summer program, reduced course load, remedial instruction, special counselor, tutoring. **Placement/credit:** AP, CLEP General and Subject, IB, institutional tests; 30 credit hours maximum for associate degree.

ACADEMIC REQUIREMENTS. Freshmen must earn minimum GPA of 1.5 to continue in good standing. 40% of freshmen return for sophomore year. Students must declare major by end of first year. **Graduation requirements:** 64 hours for associate. Most students required to take courses in English, history, humanities, mathematics, biological/physical sciences, social sciences.

FRESHMAN ADMISSIONS. Selection criteria: Open admissions. Testing, interview, and academic records determine admission to allied health programs. 4 English, 3 mathematics, 3 social studies, and 3 sciences required for associate of arts applicants. **Test requirements:** SAT or ACT (ACT preferred) for placement and counseling only; score report by August 20.

1992 FRESHMAN CLASS PROFILE. 4,816 men and women enrolled. **Characteristics:** 92% from in state, 100% commute, 9% have minority backgrounds. Average age is 22.

FALL-TERM APPLICATIONS. No fee. No closing date; applicants notified on a rolling basis. Interview required for allied health applicants. Deferred and early admission available.

STUDENT LIFE. Activities: Student government, film, magazine, radio, student newspaper, choral groups, concert band, dance, drama, jazz band, music ensembles, musical theater, symphony orchestra, Circle-K, Distributive Education Clubs of America, ethnic organizations.

ATHLETICS. NCAA, NJCAA. **Intercollegiate:** Baseball M, basketball, diving, golf M, swimming, tennis, volleyball W. **Intramural:** Basketball, handball, softball.

STUDENT SERVICES. Career counseling, employment service for undergraduates, freshman orientation, health services, on-campus day care, personal counseling, placement service for graduates, veterans counselor, disabled student coordinator, services/facilities for handicapped.

ANNUAL EXPENSES. Tuition and fees (1992-93): $900, $2,664 additional for out-of-state students. **Books and supplies:** $450. **Other expenses:** $400.

FINANCIAL AID. 80% of grants, 93% of loans, 88% of jobs based on need. 650 enrolled freshmen were judged to have need, 575 were offered aid. Academic, music/drama, art, athletic, minority scholarships available. **Aid applications:** No closing date; applicants notified on a rolling basis beginning on or about April 1; must reply within 10 days.

ADDRESS/TELEPHONE. Linda W. Hays, Assistant Dean of Educational Services, Indian River Community College, 3209 Virginia Avenue, Fort Pierce, FL 34981-5599. (407) 462-4740.

International Fine Arts College
Miami, Florida CB code: 5327

2-year proprietary art college, coed. Founded in 1965. **Accreditation:** Regional. **Undergraduate enrollment:** 658 men and women full time. **Location:** Urban campus in very large city. **Calendar:** Semester.

FRESHMAN ADMISSIONS. Selection criteria: Keen interest in fashion, merchandising, art, interior design, or related areas of fundamental importance.

ANNUAL EXPENSES. Tuition and fees: $8,630. **Room and board:** $2,640 room only. **Books and supplies:** $500. **Other expenses:** $1,900.

ADDRESS/TELEPHONE. Thea Lozada, Director of Admissions, International Fine Arts College, 1737 North Bayshore Drive, Miami, FL 33132. (305) 373-4684. (800) 255-9023. Fax: (305) 374-7946.

ITT Technical Institute: Tampa
Tampa, Florida CB code: 2145

2-year proprietary Technical/Career Education School, coed. Founded in 1981. **Undergraduate enrollment:** 650 men and women. **Faculty:** 49 total (47 full time). **Location:** Suburban campus in large city; 5 miles from downtown. **Calendar:** Quarter.

DEGREES OFFERED. AAS. 185 associate degrees awarded in 1992. 100% in engineering technologies.

UNDERGRADUATE MAJORS. Architectural technologies, computer-aided drafting, electronic technology.

ACADEMIC PROGRAMS. Remedial services: Remedial instruction.

ACADEMIC REQUIREMENTS. Freshmen must earn minimum GPA of 1.9 to continue in good standing. **Graduation requirements:** 124 hours for associate. Most students required to take courses in mathematics.

FRESHMAN ADMISSIONS. Selection criteria: Specialized on-site test results considered for certain programs.

1992 FRESHMAN CLASS PROFILE. 150 men and women enrolled. **Characteristics:** 99% from in state, 28% have minority backgrounds.

FALL-TERM APPLICATIONS. $100 fee. Application fee refunded if student not accepted. No closing date; applicants notified on a rolling basis. Interview required. Class size limited.

ATHLETICS. Intramural: Baseball M.

STUDENT SERVICES. Career counseling, employment service for undergraduates, placement service for graduates, services/facilities for handicapped.

ANNUAL EXPENSES. Tuition and fees (1992-93): Tuition for 12-month period $7,202 for electronics engineering technology and $8,544 for computer-aided drafting technology. Laboratory fees, $50 per quarter. **Books and supplies:** $800.

FINANCIAL AID. All grants, 73% of loans, all jobs based on need. **Aid applications:** No closing date; priority given to applications received by September 10; applicants notified on a rolling basis.

ADDRESS/TELEPHONE. Ray Sokohl, Director of Recruitment, ITT Technical Institute: Tampa, 5225 Memorial Highway, Tampa, FL 33634. (813) 885-2244.

Jacksonville University
Jacksonville, Florida CB code: 5331

Admissions:	83% of applicants accepted
Based on:	••• School record
	•• Interview, recommendations, test scores
	• Activities, essay, special talents
Completion:	88% of freshmen end year in good standing
	43% graduate, 35% of these enter graduate study

4-year private university, coed. Founded in 1934. **Accreditation:** Regional. **Undergraduate enrollment:** 982 men, 802 women full time; 190 men, 270 women part time. **Graduate enrollment:** 68 men, 29 women full time; 84 men, 142 women part time. **Faculty:** 240 total (125 full time), 68 with doctorates or other terminal degrees. **Location:** Suburban campus in very large city. **Calendar:** Semester, limited summer session. Saturday classes. **Microcomputers:** 180 located in computer centers. **Special facilities:** Art museum, marine science research vessels, Theodore Roosevelt Preserve, Brest Observatory.

DEGREES OFFERED. BA, BS, BFA, MBA. 388 bachelor's degrees awarded in 1992. 36% in business and management, 7% communications, 8% education, 8% life sciences, 5% psychology, 9% social sciences, 7% visual and performing arts. Graduate degrees offered in 17 major fields of study.

UNDERGRADUATE MAJORS. Accounting, art education, art history, aviation management, biology, business administration and management, business and management, business economics, chemistry, commercial art, communications, computer and information sciences, dance, dramatic arts, economics, education of the emotionally handicapped, elementary education, English, environmental science, finance, French, geography, German, history, humanities and social sciences, international business management, international relations, international studies, junior high education, liberal/general studies, management information systems, marine biology, marketing management, mathematics, medical laboratory technologies, music, music business management, music education, music history and appreciation, music performance, music theory and composition, musical theater, naval science (Navy, Marines), nursing, philosophy, physical education, physics, political science and government, predentistry, prelaw, premedicine, preveterinary, psychology, public administration, secondary education, sociology, Spanish, special education, specific learning disabilities, studio art.

ACADEMIC PROGRAMS. Accelerated program, cooperative education, double major, dual enrollment of high school students, honors program, independent study, internships, student-designed major, study abroad, teacher preparation, weekend college; liberal arts/career combination in engineering. **Remedial services:** Learning center, preadmission summer program, remedial instruction, special counselor, tutoring. **ROTC:** Army, Naval. **Placement/credit:** AP, CLEP General and Subject, institutional tests; 64 credit hours maximum for bachelor's degree.

ACADEMIC REQUIREMENTS. Freshmen must earn minimum GPA of 2.0 to continue in good standing. 70% of freshmen return for sophomore year. Students must declare major by end of second year. **Graduation requirements:** 128 hours for bachelor's. Most students required to take courses in arts/fine arts, computer science, English, history, humanities, mathematics, philosophy/religion, biological/physical sciences, social sciences.

FRESHMAN ADMISSIONS. Selection criteria: School achievement record most important, followed by counselors' recommendations, test scores, activities. **High school preparation:** 18 units required. Required units include biological science 1, English 4, foreign language 3, mathematics 3, physical science 2, social science 2 and science 2. **Test requirements:** SAT or ACT; score report by August 1.

1992 FRESHMAN CLASS PROFILE. 1,009 men applied, 909 accepted, 193 enrolled; 1,099 women applied, 846 accepted, 145 enrolled. 10% were in top tenth and 16% were in top quarter of graduating class. **Academic background:** Mid 50% of enrolled freshmen had ACT composite between 20-24. 28% submitted ACT scores. **Characteristics:** 84% commute, 20% have minority backgrounds, 4% are foreign students, 23% join fraternities/sororities. Average age is 19.

FALL-TERM APPLICATIONS. $25 fee, may be waived for applicants with need. Closing date August 1; priority given to applications received by April 1; applicants notified on a rolling basis. Audition required for music, dance applicants. Portfolio required for commercial and studio art applicants. Essay required. Interview recommended. CRDA. Deferred and early admission available.

STUDENT LIFE. Housing: Dormitories (men, women). **Activities:** Student government, magazine, radio, student newspaper, yearbook, choral groups, concert band, dance, drama, jazz band, music ensembles, musical theater, opera, pep band, symphony orchestra, fraternities, sororities, political science society, United Black Students, Baptist campus ministry, Hillel, Circle-K, Rotaract.

ATHLETICS. NCAA. **Intercollegiate:** Baseball M, basketball M, cross-country, golf M, rifle, rowing (crew), soccer M, softball W, tennis, volleyball W. **Intramural:** Archery, badminton, basketball, bowling, cross-country, handball, racquetball, soccer, softball, swimming, table tennis, tennis, volleyball.

STUDENT SERVICES. Career counseling, employment service for undergraduates, freshman orientation, health services, personal counseling, placement service for graduates, special adviser for adult students, veterans counselor, services/facilities for handicapped.

ANNUAL EXPENSES. Tuition and fees (1992-93): $9,320. **Room and board:** $4,070. **Books and supplies:** $700. **Other expenses:** $800.

FINANCIAL AID. 63% of freshmen, 73% of continuing students receive some form of aid. 16% of grants, 50% of loans, 34% of jobs based on need. 169 enrolled freshmen were judged to have need, all were offered aid. Academic, music/drama, art, athletic, state/district residency, leadership, alumni affiliation scholarships available. **Aid applications:** No closing date; priority given to applications received by March 15; applicants notified on a rolling basis beginning on or about April 15; must reply within 2 weeks.

ADDRESS/TELEPHONE. Robert Merritt, Director of Admissions, Jacksonville University, 2800 University Boulevard North, Jacksonville, FL 32211. (904) 744-3950.

Jones College
Jacksonville, Florida CB code: 5343

4-year private business college, coed. Founded in 1918. **Undergraduate enrollment:** 700 men and women. **Faculty:** 46 total (15 full time), 14 with doctorates or other terminal degrees. **Location:** Suburban campus in very large city. **Calendar:** Trimester, extensive summer session. **Microcomputers:** 80 located in classrooms, computer centers. **Special facilities:** 2 campus radio stations. **Additional facts:** Branch campus in Miami.

DEGREES OFFERED. AS, BS. 90 associate degrees awarded in 1992. 92% in business and management, 8% computer sciences. 120 bachelor's degrees awarded. 62% in business and management, 38% computer sciences.

UNDERGRADUATE MAJORS. Associate: Accounting, business administration and management, business and management, business and office, business data processing and related programs, business data programming, computer and information sciences, computer programming, court reporting, data processing, legal assistant/paralegal, legal secretary, marketing and distribution, marketing management, medical assistant, medical secretary, microcomputer software, office supervision and management, secretarial and related programs, word processing. **Bachelor's:** Accounting, business administration and management, business and management, business and office, business data processing and related programs, business data programming, computer and information sciences, computer programming, court reporting, data processing, marketing and distribution, marketing management, office supervision and management, secretarial and related programs.

ACADEMIC PROGRAMS. Accelerated program, double major, independent study, internships, student-designed major, weekend college. **Remedial services:** Reduced course load, remedial instruction, tutoring. **Placement/credit:** CLEP General and Subject, institutional tests; 15 credit hours maximum for associate degree; 30 credit hours maximum for bachelor's degree.

ACADEMIC REQUIREMENTS. Freshmen must earn minimum GPA of 2.0 to continue in good standing. 55% of freshmen return for sophomore year. Students must declare major on application. **Graduation requirements:** 60 hours for associate (24 in major), 120 hours for bachelor's (36 in major). Most students required to take courses in computer science, English, mathematics, social sciences. **Postgraduate studies:** 40% from 2-year programs enter 4-year programs.

FRESHMAN ADMISSIONS. Selection criteria: School achievement record and score on institutional test most important. Interview and recommendations considered.

1992 FRESHMAN CLASS PROFILE. 200 men and women enrolled. **Characteristics:** 92% from in state, 100% commute, 40% have minority backgrounds, 1% are foreign students, 3% join fraternities/sororities.

FALL-TERM APPLICATIONS. No fee. No closing date; applicants notified on a rolling basis; must reply as soon as possible. Interview required. Deferred admission available.

STUDENT LIFE. Activities: Radio, fraternities, sororities.

STUDENT SERVICES. Career counseling, employment service for undergraduates, freshman orientation, personal counseling, placement service for graduates, veterans counselor.

ANNUAL EXPENSES. Tuition and fees (1992-93): $3,600. **Books and supplies:** $750. **Other expenses:** $1,700.

FINANCIAL AID. 80% of freshmen, 80% of continuing students receive some form of aid. All grants, 94% of loans based on need. 457 enrolled freshmen were judged to have need, 365 were offered aid. **Aid applications:** No closing date; applicants notified on a rolling basis.

ADDRESS/TELEPHONE. Barry Durden, Director of Admissions, Jones College, 5353 Arlington Expressway, Jacksonville, FL 32211. (904) 743-1122 ext. 112.

Keiser College of Technology
Fort Lauderdale, Florida CB code: 7004

2-year proprietary junior, technical college, coed. Founded in 1977. **Accreditation:** Regional. **Undergraduate enrollment:** 220 men, 330 women full time. **Faculty:** 30 total (15 full time). **Location:** Urban campus in large city; 35 miles from Miami. **Calendar:** Semester, extensive summer session. **Microcomputers:** Located in libraries, classrooms.

DEGREES OFFERED. AA, AS. 21 associate degrees awarded in 1992.

UNDERGRADUATE MAJORS. Accounting, bioengineering and biomedical engineering, biomedical equipment technology, clinical laboratory science, computer and information sciences, computer engineering, computer programming, computer technology, drafting and design technology, legal assistant/paralegal, medical assistant, medical laboratory technologies.

ACADEMIC PROGRAMS. Accelerated program.

ACADEMIC REQUIREMENTS. Freshmen must earn minimum GPA of 2.0 to continue in good standing. Students must declare major on enrollment. **Graduation requirements:** 60 hours for associate (30 in major).

FRESHMAN ADMISSIONS. Test requirements: Institutional entrance examination or SAT or ACT test required.

1992 FRESHMAN CLASS PROFILE. 240 men, 180 women enrolled. **Characteristics:** 100% commute. Average age is 26.

FALL-TERM APPLICATIONS. $50 fee. No closing date; applicants notified on a rolling basis; must reply by registration. Interview required.

STUDENT LIFE. Activities: Student government, student newspaper. **Additional information:** Campus chaplain available to students.

ATHLETICS. Intercollegiate: Softball W, volleyball.

STUDENT SERVICES. Career counseling, employment service for undergraduates, freshman orientation, placement service for graduates, services/facilities for handicapped.

ANNUAL EXPENSES. Tuition and fees (1992-93): Tuition, fees, and supplies, including books, vary according to program, ranging from $4,080.00 for paralegal program to $10,720.00 for biomedical electronic technician program.

FINANCIAL AID. 80% of freshmen, 80% of continuing students receive some form of aid. All grants, 48% of loans based on need. 328 enrolled freshmen were judged to have need, all were offered aid. **Aid applications:** No closing date.

ADDRESS/TELEPHONE. Roberta Hubbard, Director of Admissions, Keiser College of Technology, 1401 West Cypress Creek Road, Fort Lauderdale, FL 33309. (800) 749-4456. Fax: (305) 772-5883.

Lake City Community College
Lake City, Florida CB code: 5377

2-year public community college, coed. Founded in 1947. **Accreditation:** Regional. **Undergraduate enrollment:** 642 men, 669 women full time; 372 men, 681 women part time. **Faculty:** 219 total (68 full time), 13 with doctorates or other terminal degrees. **Location:** Rural campus in large town; 60 miles from Jacksonville, 45 miles from Gainesville. **Calendar:** Semester, limited summer session. Saturday and extensive evening/early morning classes. **Microcomputers:** Located in libraries, computer centers. **Special facilities:** Performing arts center.

DEGREES OFFERED. AA, AS. 230 associate degrees awarded in 1992.

UNDERGRADUATE MAJORS. Allied health, business administration and management, business and office, computer programming, criminal justice technology, education, electronic technology, emergency medical technologies, engineering, forestry and related sciences, golf course operations, health sciences, landscape architecture, law enforcement and corrections, law enforcement and corrections technologies, liberal/general studies, marketing management, medical laboratory technologies, nursing, radio/television broadcasting, radio/television technology, secretarial and related programs, surgical technology.

ACADEMIC PROGRAMS. 2-year transfer program, cooperative education, dual enrollment of high school students, independent study, internships, study abroad, telecourses, visiting/exchange student program. **Remedial services:** Learning center, reduced course load, remedial instruction, special counselor, tutoring. **Placement/credit:** AP, CLEP General and Subject, institutional tests; 30 credit hours maximum for associate degree.

ACADEMIC REQUIREMENTS. Freshmen must earn minimum GPA of 2.0 to continue in good standing. 65% of freshmen return for sophomore year. Students must declare major on application. **Graduation requirements:** 64 hours for associate. Most students required to take courses in English, foreign languages, history, humanities, mathematics, philosophy/religion, biological/physical sciences, social sciences.

FRESHMAN ADMISSIONS. Selection criteria: Open admissions. Selective admissions to some technical programs. **High school preparation:** 13 units required. Required units include English 4, mathematics 3, social science 3 and science 3. Applicants to forestry programs should have good mathematics background. **Test requirements:** SAT or ACT (ACT preferred) for placement; score report by August 15.

1992 FRESHMAN CLASS PROFILE. 872 men and women enrolled. 10% had high school GPA of 3.0 or higher, 80% between 2.0 and 2.99. **Characteristics:** 95% from in state, 90% commute, 9% have minority backgrounds, 3% are foreign students. Average age is 19.

FALL-TERM APPLICATIONS. $15 fee. No closing date; priority given to applications received by August 1; applicants notified on a rolling basis. Interview recommended for forestry, nursing, golf course operations applicants. Deferred and early admission available. Some technical programs reach maximum enrollment and are closed prior to August 1.

STUDENT LIFE. Housing: Dormitories (coed). **Activities:** Student government, film, magazine, student newspaper, television, choral groups, concert band, drama, jazz band, music ensembles.

ATHLETICS. NJCAA. **Intercollegiate:** Baseball M, basketball M, softball W. **Intramural:** Basketball, golf, handball, racquetball, softball, table tennis, tennis, volleyball.

STUDENT SERVICES. Aptitude testing, career counseling, freshman orientation, health services, personal counseling, placement service for graduates, veterans counselor, services/facilities for handicapped.

ANNUAL EXPENSES. Tuition and fees (projected): $900, $2,460 additional for out-of-state students. **Room and board:** $2,774. **Books and supplies:** $350.

FINANCIAL AID. 12% of freshmen, 9% of continuing students receive some form of aid. Grants, loans, jobs available. Academic, athletic scholarships available. **Aid applications:** No closing date; priority given to applications received by June 1; applicants notified on a rolling basis beginning on or about July 14; must reply within 2 weeks.

ADDRESS/TELEPHONE. Rayanne Giddis, Director of Admissions, Lake City Community College, Route 3, Box 7, Lake City, FL 32055. (904) 752-1822 ext. 287. Fax: (904) 755-1521.

Lake-Sumter Community College

Leesburg, Florida — CB code: 5376

2-year public community college, coed. Founded in 1962. **Accreditation:** Regional. **Undergraduate enrollment:** 323 men, 471 women full time; 607 men, 1,202 women part time. **Faculty:** 119 total (40 full time), 8 with doctorates or other terminal degrees. **Location:** Rural campus in large town; 35 miles from Orlando. **Calendar:** Semester, extensive summer session. **Microcomputers:** 275 located in libraries, classrooms, computer centers. **Special facilities:** Fine arts auditorium, small-business center, nature trail, art gallery, museum and literacy center.

DEGREES OFFERED. AA, AS. 235 associate degrees awarded in 1992.

UNDERGRADUATE MAJORS. Business and management, computer and information sciences, criminal justice technology, emergency medical technologies, finance, fire control and safety technology, graphic design, hotel/motel and restaurant management, liberal/general studies, nursing, office supervision and management.

ACADEMIC PROGRAMS. 2-year transfer program, cooperative education, dual enrollment of high school students, independent study, internships, study abroad, telecourses, visiting/exchange student program, weekend college. **Remedial services:** Learning center, reduced course load, remedial instruction, special counselor, tutoring. **Placement/credit:** AP, CLEP Subject, institutional tests; 39 credit hours maximum for associate degree.

ACADEMIC REQUIREMENTS. No policy requiring minimum GPA; records of students having academic difficulty are reviewed individually. Students must declare major on application. **Graduation requirements:** 64 hours for associate. Most students required to take courses in computer science, English, humanities, mathematics, biological/physical sciences, social sciences.

FRESHMAN ADMISSIONS. Selection criteria: Open admissions.

1992 FRESHMAN CLASS PROFILE. 247 men, 380 women enrolled. **Characteristics:** 99% from in state, 100% commute, 7% have minority backgrounds.

FALL-TERM APPLICATIONS. $15 fee. No closing date; priority given to applications received by August 15; applicants notified on a rolling basis. Deferred and early admission available.

STUDENT LIFE. Housing: Private apartments within walking distance of campus. **Activities:** Student government, magazine, student newspaper, television, yearbook, choral groups, concert band, drama, jazz band, music ensembles, musical theater, Baptist Campus Ministry, Young Democrats,Young Republicans, Florida African American Student Association, Spanish Club, Accepting Challenges Together (ACT), Ecology Club, Blue Stocking Circle, Computer Club, LITE Center for the Blind.

ATHLETICS. NJCAA. **Intramural:** Badminton, basketball, bowling, racquetball, sailing, soccer, softball, table tennis, tennis, volleyball.

STUDENT SERVICES. Aptitude testing, career counseling, employment service for undergraduates, freshman orientation, health services, personal counseling, placement service for graduates, special adviser for adult students, veterans counselor, services/facilities for handicapped.

ANNUAL EXPENSES. Tuition and fees (1992-93): $1,043, $2,685 additional for out-of-state students. **Books and supplies:** $370. **Other expenses:** $500.

FINANCIAL AID. 24% of continuing students receive some form of aid. 87% of grants, all loans, all jobs based on need. Academic, music/drama, art, state/district residency, leadership, minority scholarships available. **Aid applications:** No closing date; priority given to applications received by May 1; applicants notified on a rolling basis beginning on or about June 15; must reply within 3 weeks.

ADDRESS/TELEPHONE. Earl Evans, Associate Dean of Students and Admissions, Lake-Sumter Community College, 9501 US Highway 441, Leesburg, FL 34788. (904) 365-3573. Fax: (904) 365-3501.

Lynn University

Boca Raton, Florida — CB code: 5437

Admissions:	75% of applicants accepted
Based on:	••• School record
	•• Activities, interview, recommendations, special talents
	• Essay, test scores
Completion:	85% of freshmen end year in good standing
	35% enter graduate study

4-year private college of arts and sciences and business college, coed. Founded in 1962. **Accreditation:** Regional. **Undergraduate enrollment:** 1,200 men and women. **Graduate enrollment:** 50 men and women. **Faculty:** 75 total (40 full time), 40 with doctorates or other terminal degrees. **Location:** Suburban campus in small city; 20 miles equidistant from Fort Lauderdale and Palm Beach. **Calendar:** Semester, extensive summer session. **Microcomputers:** 60 located in libraries, computer centers. **Special facilities:** Academic resource center, art gallery, university club (private dining room thath serves as laboratory for hotel and restaurant management students).

DEGREES OFFERED. AA, AS, BA, BS, M. 80 associate degrees awarded in 1992. 20% in architecture and environmental design, 70% business/office and marketing/distribution, 10% education. 190 bachelor's degrees awarded. 5% in architecture and environmental design, 50% business and management, 10% business/office and marketing/distribution, 5% communications, 5% education, 10% letters/literature, 15% social sciences. Graduate degrees offered in 4 major fields of study.

UNDERGRADUATE MAJORS. Associate: Drawing, early childhood education, education, fashion merchandising, fine arts, funeral services/mortuary science, liberal/general studies, painting. **Bachelor's:** Accounting, advertising, airline piloting and navigation, aviation management, behavioral sciences, business administration and management, business and office, communications, crafts, early childhood education, education, elementary education, fashion merchandising, general design, gerontology, graphic design, health care administration, health sciences, history, hotel/motel and restaurant management, humanities and social sciences, interior design, international business management, journalism, marketing and distribution, parks and recreation management, political science and government, prelaw, psychology, public relations, recreation and community services technologies, small business management and ownership, social sciences, sociology, sports management, tourism, transportation and travel marketing.

ACADEMIC PROGRAMS. 2-year transfer program, accelerated program, double major, dual enrollment of high school students, independent study, internships, student-designed major, study abroad, teacher preparation. **Remedial services:** Learning center, reduced course load, remedial instruction, special counselor, tutoring, learning disabled specialist on faculty. **Placement/credit:** AP, CLEP General and Subject, institutional tests; 30 credit hours maximum for associate degree; 30 credit hours maximum for bachelor's degree.

ACADEMIC REQUIREMENTS. Freshmen must earn minimum GPA of 1.8 to continue in good standing. 70% of freshmen return for sophomore year. Students must declare major by end of second year. **Graduation re-**

quirements: 62 hours for associate, 122 hours for bachelor's. Most students required to take courses in computer science, English, history, humanities, mathematics, biological/physical sciences, social sciences. **Postgraduate studies:** 80% from 2-year programs enter 4-year programs. 5% enter law school, 20% enter MBA programs, 10% enter other graduate study.

FRESHMAN ADMISSIONS. Selection criteria: School achievement record, high school counselor's recommendation, test scores, class rank, school and community activities. Special consideration given to foreign and minority applicants. **Test requirements:** SAT or ACT for placement and counseling only; score report by August 1.

1992 FRESHMAN CLASS PROFILE. 1,518 men and women applied, 1,140 accepted; 454 enrolled. **Characteristics:** 25% from in state, 70% live in college housing, 10% have minority backgrounds, 15% are foreign students. Average age is 18.

FALL-TERM APPLICATIONS. $25 fee, may be waived for applicants with need. No closing date; applicants notified on a rolling basis; must reply within 4 weeks. Interview recommended. Portfolio recommended. Essay recommended. Deferred and early admission available.

STUDENT LIFE. Housing: Dormitories (men, women). **Activities:** Student government, student newspaper, International Students Organization, Newman Club, Hillel, co-curricular organizations, academic fraternities, Knights of the Roundtable.

ATHLETICS. NAIA. **Intercollegiate:** Baseball M, basketball, golf, soccer, tennis. **Intramural:** Basketball M, bowling, golf, ice hockey, soccer, softball, swimming, tennis, volleyball.

STUDENT SERVICES. Aptitude testing, career counseling, employment service for undergraduates, freshman orientation, health services, personal counseling, placement service for graduates, special adviser for adult students, services/facilities for handicapped.

ANNUAL EXPENSES. Tuition and fees: $13,200. **Room and board:** $5,100. **Books and supplies:** $500. **Other expenses:** $1,100.

FINANCIAL AID. 51% of freshmen, 48% of continuing students receive some form of aid. 40% of grants, 79% of loans, all jobs based on need. 105 enrolled freshmen were judged to have need, 104 were offered aid. Academic, athletic, state/district residency, leadership, minority scholarships available. **Aid applications:** No closing date; priority given to applications received by February 15; applicants notified on a rolling basis beginning on or about March 15; must reply within 2 weeks. **Additional information:** Presidential scholarships available to new students; academic incentive scholarships available to new Florida students; part-time jobs available off-campus.

ADDRESS/TELEPHONE. Chuck Somma, Director of Admissions, Lynn University, 3601 North Military Trail, Boca Raton, FL 33431-5598. (407) 994-0770 ext. 157. (800) 544-8035. Fax: (407) 241-3552.

Manatee Community College
Bradenton, Florida — CB code: 5427

2-year public community college, coed. Founded in 1957. **Accreditation:** Regional. **Undergraduate enrollment:** 1,434 men, 1,820 women full time; 1,626 men, 2,950 women part time. **Faculty:** 314 total (142 full time), 41 with doctorates or other terminal degrees. **Location:** Suburban campus in large town; 40 miles from Tampa, 20 miles from St. Petersburg. **Calendar:** Semester, extensive summer session. Saturday and extensive evening/early morning classes. **Microcomputers:** Located in libraries, computer centers. **Special facilities:** Art gallery. **Additional facts:** Students may take courses at south campus in Venice.

DEGREES OFFERED. AA, AS. 800 associate degrees awarded in 1992.

UNDERGRADUATE MAJORS. Aeronautical technology, agricultural sciences, architecture, business administration and management, business and office, business data programming, civil engineering, communications, computer programming, computer technology, criminal justice technology, criminology, drafting, education, electrical technology, electrical/electronics/communications engineering, electromechanical technology, electronic technology, elementary education, engineering, engineering and engineering-related technologies, English, fashion merchandising, finance, fine arts, fire control and safety technology, food production/management/services, health sciences, home economics, home economics education, hospitality and recreation marketing, hotel/motel and restaurant management, industrial engineering, industrial technology, interior design, journalism, law enforcement and corrections, law enforcement and corrections technologies, legal assistant/paralegal, marketing and distribution, mathematics, mechanical engineering, music, music education, nursing, nutritional education, pharmacy, photographic technology, predentistry, preengineering, prelaw, premedicine, preveterinary, psychology, radiograph medical technology, respiratory therapy, respiratory therapy technology, secondary education, secretarial and related programs, social work, speech, speech/communication/theater education, systems analysis.

ACADEMIC PROGRAMS. 2-year transfer program, cooperative education, dual enrollment of high school students, honors program, independent study, telecourses. **Remedial services:** Remedial instruction, special counselor, tutoring. **Placement/credit:** AP, CLEP General and Subject; 30 credit hours maximum for associate degree.

ACADEMIC REQUIREMENTS. Freshmen must earn minimum GPA of 2.0 to continue in good standing. 50% of freshmen return for sophomore year. Students must declare major on enrollment. **Graduation requirements:** 68 hours for associate (21 in major). Most students required to take courses in English, history, humanities, mathematics, philosophy/religion, biological/physical sciences, social sciences.

FRESHMAN ADMISSIONS. Selection criteria: Open admissions. Limited enrollment programs in nursing, radiologic technology and respiratory therapy. Priority given to nursing applicants with most hours already completed and 2.25 GPA overall. Recommended units include biological science 3, English 4, foreign language 2, mathematics 3 and physical science 3. **Test requirements:** SAT or ACT for placement and counseling only; score report by August 24. SAT, ACT, or Florida MAPS required. MAPS preferred.

1992 FRESHMAN CLASS PROFILE. 1,220 men and women enrolled. **Characteristics:** 98% from in state, 100% commute, 5% have minority backgrounds. Average age is 19.

FALL-TERM APPLICATIONS. $15 fee. No closing date; applicants notified on a rolling basis. Interview recommended for nursing, radiologic technology, respiratory therapy applicants. Early admission available.

STUDENT LIFE. Activities: Student government, film, student newspaper, literary journal, choral groups, concert band, drama, jazz band, music ensembles, musical theater, opera, symphony orchestra, Baptist campus ministry, Circle-K, African-American Student Union, service organization.

ATHLETICS. NJCAA. **Intercollegiate:** Baseball M, basketball, golf M, volleyball W. **Intramural:** Archery, badminton, basketball, racquetball, tennis.

STUDENT SERVICES. Aptitude testing, career counseling, employment service for undergraduates, freshman orientation, health services, personal counseling, placement service for graduates, veterans counselor, services/facilities for handicapped.

ANNUAL EXPENSES. Tuition and fees (projected): $967, $2,296 additional for out-of-state students. **Books and supplies:** $535. **Other expenses:** $1,020.

FINANCIAL AID. 33% of freshmen, 33% of continuing students receive some form of aid. 72% of grants, 76% of loans, 38% of jobs based on need. Academic, music/drama, art, athletic, state/district residency scholarships available. **Aid applications:** Closing date July 1; priority given to applications received by June 1; applicants notified on a rolling basis beginning on or about July 1; must reply within 30 days. **Additional information:** Short term loans available for tuition and book costs for financial aid recipients.

ADDRESS/TELEPHONE. James C. Brown, Dean of Admissions and Records, Manatee Community College, PO Box 1849, Bradenton, FL 34206-1849. (813) 755-1511 ext. 4350. Fax: (813) 755-1511 ext. 4331.

Miami-Dade Community College
Miami, Florida — CB code: 5457

2-year public community college, coed. Founded in 1959. **Accreditation:** Regional. **Undergraduate enrollment:** 8,580 men, 11,272 women full time; 14,822 men, 21,794 women part time. **Faculty:** 2,163 total (923 full time), 392 with doctorates or other terminal degrees. **Location:** Urban campus in large city. **Calendar:** 2 major 16-week terms, 2 minor 6-week terms. **Microcomputers:** Located in classrooms, computer centers. **Special facilities:** 4 art galleries, environmental demonstration center, bilingual center, greenhouse, fire science laboratories and fire tower. **Additional facts:** Multilocation institution.

DEGREES OFFERED. AA, AS. 5,072 associate degrees awarded in 1992. 21% in business and management, 17% teacher education, 5% engineering, 9% health sciences, 5% allied health, 12% multi/interdisciplinary studies, 5% parks/recreation, protective services, public affairs, 5% psychology.

UNDERGRADUATE MAJORS. Accounting, aeronautical technology, agribusiness, air conditioning/heating/refrigeration mechanics, airline piloting and navigation, American literature, American studies, anthropology, apparel and accessories marketing, architectural engineering, architectural technologies, architecture, Asian studies, atmospheric sciences and meteorology, automotive technology, aviation management, biology, business administration and management, business and office, business data processing and related programs, business data programming, chemical engineering, chemistry, chiropractic, cinematography/film, civil engineering, civil technology, clinical laboratory science, commercial art, computer and information sciences, construction, court reporting, criminal justice studies, dance, dental hygiene, drafting and design technology, dramatic arts, economics, electrical/electronics/communications engineering, electrodiagnostic technologies, electromechanical technology, electronic technology, elementary education, emergency medical technologies, English, English literature, fashion design, fashion merchandising, fashion studies, finance, fine arts, fire control and safety technology, food production/management/services, food science and nutrition, foreign languages (multiple emphasis), forestry and related sciences, French, funeral services/mortuary science, geology, German, graphic and printing production, graphic arts technology, health care administration, history, horticulture, hospitality and recreation marketing, hotel/motel and restaurant management, human environment and housing, industrial arts education, industrial engineering, industrial technology, instrumentation technology, interior design, international public service, international relations, Italian, journalism, landscape architecture, Latin American studies, law enforcement and corrections, legal assistant/paralegal, legal secretary, liberal/general studies, management science, marketing and distribution, mathematics, mechanical engineering, medical laboratory technologies, medical records administration, medical records technology, medical secretary, music, nursing, occupational therapy, ocean engineering, ophthalmic services, optometry, philosophy, photographic technology, physical education, physical therapy, physical therapy assistant, physics, political science and government, Portuguese, postal management, power plant operation and maintenance, predentistry, prelaw, premedicine, prepharmacy, preveterinary, psychology, public affairs, radio/television broadcasting, radiograph medical technology, real estate, recreation and community services technologies, religion, respiratory therapy, respiratory therapy technology, Russian, secondary education, secretarial and related programs, sign language studies, social work, sociology, Spanish, speech, surveying and mapping sciences, tourism, transportation and travel marketing.

ACADEMIC PROGRAMS. 2-year transfer program, accelerated program, cooperative education, dual enrollment of high school students, honors program, independent study, internships, student-designed major, study abroad, weekend college, cross-registration. **Remedial services:** Learning center, reduced course load, remedial instruction, special counselor, tutoring. **ROTC:** Air Force, Army. **Placement/credit:** AP, CLEP General and Subject, institutional tests; 45 credit hours maximum for associate degree.

ACADEMIC REQUIREMENTS. Freshmen must earn minimum GPA of 1.5 to continue in good standing. 63% of freshmen return for sophomore year. Students must declare major on enrollment. **Graduation requirements:** 62 hours for associate. Most students required to take courses in English, history, humanities, mathematics, biological/physical sciences, social sciences.

FRESHMAN ADMISSIONS. Selection criteria: Open admissions. **Test requirements:** Florida MAPS required of all degree-seeking freshman applicants. SAT or ACT accepted for placement. MAPS preferred.

1992 FRESHMAN CLASS PROFILE. 3,667 men, 4,692 women enrolled. **Characteristics:** 88% from in state, 100% commute, 81% have minority backgrounds, 5% are foreign students. Average age is 23.

FALL-TERM APPLICATIONS. $15 fee. No closing date; applicants notified on a rolling basis. Audition required for performing arts applicants. Portfolio required for visual arts applicants. Deferred and early admission available.

STUDENT LIFE. Activities: Student government, film, radio, student newspaper, yearbook, choral groups, concert band, dance, drama, jazz band, music ensembles, musical theater, fraternities, sororities, Newman Club.

ATHLETICS. NCAA, NJCAA. **Intercollegiate:** Baseball M, basketball, diving, golf M, soccer M, softball W, swimming, tennis, volleyball. **Intramural:** Basketball, racquetball, table tennis.

STUDENT SERVICES. Aptitude testing, career counseling, employment service for undergraduates, freshman orientation, health services, personal counseling, placement service for graduates, special adviser for adult students, veterans counselor, corporate physical fitness testing, services/facilities for handicapped.

ANNUAL EXPENSES. Tuition and fees (1992-93): $996, $2,469 additional for out-of-state students. **Books and supplies:** $920. **Other expenses:** $2,726.

FINANCIAL AID. 47% of freshmen, 40% of continuing students receive some form of aid. 96% of grants, 86% of loans, 92% of jobs based on need. Academic, music/drama, art, athletic, state/district residency, leadership, alumni affiliation, minority scholarships available. **Aid applications:** No closing date; priority given to applications received by April 15; applicants notified on a rolling basis beginning on or about May 15; must reply within 2 weeks.

ADDRESS/TELEPHONE. Samuel LaRoue, District Director, Admissions and Registration Services, Miami-Dade Community College, 300 NE 2nd Ave, Miami, FL 33132-2297. (305) 347-7478. Students may also write to the following campuses' Admissions Offices for information: North Campus, 11380 Northwest 27th Avenue, Miami, FL 33167; Medical Center Campus, 950 Northwest 20th Street, Miami, FL 33127; South Campus, 11011 SW. 104 Street, Miami FL 33176; Wolfson Campus, 300 NE 2nd Avenue, Miami, FL 33132; Homestead Campus, 500 College Terrace, Homestead FL 33030.

National Education Center: Bauder Campus

Fort Lauderdale, Florida — CB code: 5712

3-year proprietary junior, career, and technical college, coed. Founded in 1964. **Undergraduate enrollment:** 321 men, 285 women full time. **Faculty:** 27 total (22 full time), 16 with doctorates or other terminal degrees. **Location:** Urban campus in small city. **Calendar:** Quarter, extensive summer session. **Microcomputers:** 20 located in classrooms.

DEGREES OFFERED. AS, AAS, B. 280 associate degrees awarded in 1992. 10% in architecture and environmental design, 35% business/office and marketing/distribution, 35% engineering technologies, 10% home economics, 10% trade and industry. 1 bachelor's degrees awarded.

UNDERGRADUATE MAJORS. Electronic technology, fashion merchandising, interior design, radio/television broadcasting, tourism. interior design, management science.

ACADEMIC PROGRAMS. Remedial services: Remedial instruction, tutoring. **Placement/credit:** AP, institutional tests; 15 credit hours maximum for associate degree.

ACADEMIC REQUIREMENTS. Freshmen must earn minimum GPA of 2.0 to continue in good standing. Students must declare major on enrollment. **Graduation requirements:** 90 hours for associate (65 in major). Most students required to take courses in English, humanities, social sciences. **Postgraduate studies:** 10% from 2-year programs enter 4-year programs. **Additional information:** Bachelor's degree program in interior design takes 36 months. Bachelor's degree program in management studies takes 18 months after awarded associates degree.

FRESHMAN ADMISSIONS. Selection criteria: Open admissions.

1992 FRESHMAN CLASS PROFILE. 76 men, 65 women enrolled. **Characteristics:** 60% from in state, 60% commute, 35% have minority backgrounds, 8% are foreign students, 2% join fraternities/sororities. Average age is 19.

FALL-TERM APPLICATIONS. No fee. No closing date; applicants notified on a rolling basis. Audition required for broadcasting applicants. Essay required. Interview recommended. Portfolio recommended for interior design applicants. Deferred admission available.

STUDENT LIFE. Housing: Apartment housing available. **Activities:** Student government, fraternities, sororities.

ATHLETICS. Intercollegiate: Basketball M, volleyball.

STUDENT SERVICES. Career counseling, employment service for undergraduates, freshman orientation, personal counseling, placement service for graduates, services/facilities for handicapped.

ANNUAL EXPENSES. Tuition and fees (1992-93): $5,717. **Room and board:** $1,908 room only. **Books and supplies:** $450. **Other expenses:** $1,206.

FINANCIAL AID. 85% of freshmen, 85% of continuing students receive some form of aid. All grants, 59% of loans based on need. State/district residency scholarships available. **Aid applications:** No closing date; applicants notified on a rolling basis.

ADDRESS/TELEPHONE. Glen Dorman, Director of Admissions, National Education Center: Bauder Campus, 4801 North Dixie Highway, Fort Lauderdale, FL 33334-3971. (305) 491-7171. (800) 327-2009. Fax: (305) 491-7227.

National Education Center: Tampa Technical Institute Campus

Tampa, Florida — CB code: 0123

3-year proprietary technical college, coed. Founded in 1948. **Undergraduate enrollment:** 890 men and women. **Location:** Urban campus in large city. **Calendar:** Quarter.

DEGREES OFFERED. AAS, BS. 300 associate degrees awarded in 1992. 50 bachelor's degrees awarded.

UNDERGRADUATE MAJORS. Associate: Engineering and engineering-related technologies, graphic arts technology. **Bachelor's:** Electrical/electronics/communications engineering.

ACADEMIC PROGRAMS. Accelerated program. **Remedial services:** Remedial instruction, tutoring.

ACADEMIC REQUIREMENTS. Freshmen must earn minimum GPA of 2.0 to continue in good standing. 95% of freshmen return for sophomore year. **Postgraduate studies:** 9% from 2-year programs enter 4-year programs.

FRESHMAN ADMISSIONS. Selection criteria: Open admissions. Interview, high school record, and recommendations considered. **Test requirements:** Flanagan Aptitude Classification Tests and Wonderlic Personnel Test.

1992 FRESHMAN CLASS PROFILE. 240 men and women enrolled. **Characteristics:** 30% from in state, 100% commute, 19% have minority backgrounds, 3% are foreign students, 10% join fraternities/sororities. Average age is 22.

FALL-TERM APPLICATIONS. $100 fee refundable if application rejected. No closing date; applicants notified on a rolling basis. Portfolio recommended for commercial art applicants. Deferred admission available.

STUDENT LIFE. Activities: Student newsletter, fraternities.

STUDENT SERVICES. Aptitude testing, career counseling, employment service for undergraduates, personal counseling, placement service for graduates.

ANNUAL EXPENSES. Tuition and fees (1992-93): For 18-month computer engineering program, tuition is $11,250; commercial art, $12,860; bachelor's program, $11,180. **Books and supplies:** $500. **Other expenses:** $1,116.

FINANCIAL AID. 51% of continuing students receive some form of aid.

ADDRESS/TELEPHONE. Kathy Miller, Director of Admissions, National Education Center: Tampa Technical Institute Campus, 2410 East Bush Boulevard, Tampa, FL 33612. (813) 935-5700. Fax: (813) 239-2163.

National School of Technology
North Miami Beach, Florida CB code: 3361

2-year proprietary technical college, coed. **Undergraduate enrollment:** 300 men and women. **Location:** Urban campus in large town. **Calendar:** Continuous classes. **Additional facts:** All programs also offered at Hialeah branch campus.

FRESHMAN ADMISSIONS. Selection criteria: Aptitude analysis test.

ANNUAL EXPENSES. Tuition and fees (1992-93): Costs, including tuition, fees, books and supplies, vary from $2,995 to $9,815 (for entire degree program).

ADDRESS/TELEPHONE. Celeste Budhoo, Director of Admissions, National School of Technology, 16150 Northeast 17th Avenue, North Miami Beach, FL 33162. (305) 949-9500.

New College of the University of South Florida
Sarasota, Florida CB code: 5506

Admissions: 28% of applicants accepted
Based on: ••• Essay, school record
•• Activities, interview, recommendations, test scores
• Special talents
Completion: 85% of freshmen end year in good standing
47% graduate, 49% of these enter graduate study

4-year public liberal arts college, coed. Founded in 1960. **Accreditation:** Regional. **Undergraduate enrollment:** 236 men, 268 women full time. **Faculty:** 54 total, 48 with doctorates or other terminal degrees. **Location:** Suburban campus in small city; 50 miles from Tampa. **Calendar:** 4-1-4. **Microcomputers:** 40 located in libraries, classrooms, computer centers. **Special facilities:** Fourier transform infrared spectrometer, vacuum atmosphere glove box, UV visible spectrophotometer, scanning electron microscopes, environmental studies laboratory, anthropology laboratory, psychology laboratory, language laboratory, media center and computer laboratory. **Additional facts:** Honors College of Florida state university system.

DEGREES OFFERED. BA. 107 bachelor's degrees awarded in 1992. 13% in letters/literature, 11% life sciences, 30% multi/interdisciplinary studies, 7% physical sciences, 12% psychology, 23% social sciences.

UNDERGRADUATE MAJORS. American literature, American studies, analytical chemistry, anthropology, art history, atomic/molecular physics, behavioral sciences, biological and physical sciences, biology, cell biology, ceramics, chemistry, classics, cognitive psychology, comparative literature, computer and information sciences, computer mathematics, counseling psychology, developmental psychology, drawing, Eastern European studies, ecology, economics, English, English literature, environmental science, European studies, experimental psychology, fine arts, folklore and mythology, foreign languages (multiple emphasis), French, genetics, human and animal, German, gerontology, Greek (classical), history, humanities, humanities and social sciences, industrial and organizational psychology, inorganic chemistry, international relations, international studies, Latin, liberal/general studies, marine biology, mathematics, medieval studies, molecular biology, music, music history and appreciation, music theory and composition, organic chemistry, painting, peace studies, philosophy, physical chemistry, physical sciences, physics, physiological psychology, physiology, human and animal, political science and government, prelaw, premedicine, psychobiology, psycholinguistics, psychology, public policy studies, quantitative psychology, religion, rural sociology, Russian, Russian and Slavic studies, sculpture, social psychology, social sciences, sociology, solid state physics, Spanish, studio art, Western European studies, women's studies.

ACADEMIC PROGRAMS. Accelerated program, double major, honors program, independent study, internships, semester at sea, student-designed major, study abroad, visiting/exchange student program, New York semester, United Nations semester, Washington semester. **ROTC:** Air Force, Army. **Placement/credit:** Institutional tests.

ACADEMIC REQUIREMENTS. No policy requiring minimum GPA; records of students having academic difficulty are reviewed individually. 80% of freshmen return for sophomore year. Students must declare major by end of second year. **Postgraduate studies:** 9% enter law school, 6% enter medical school, 34% enter other graduate study. **Additional information:** College operates under contract system. All students pursue self-designed programs within liberal arts and sciences. Individual programs include mix of traditional classroom study, independent study, one-to-one tutorials with faculty, and senior thesis with oral baccalaureate examination.

FRESHMAN ADMISSIONS. Selection criteria: Candidates must demonstrate high degree of motivation and self-discipline. Level of challenge in high school courses and writing ability are of primary importance. Essays, graded high school research papers or creative writing pieces, grades, test scores, class rank, recommendations, and interview considered. **High school preparation:** 19 units required. Required units include English 4, foreign language 2, mathematics 3, social science 3 and science 3. 4 additional academic courses required. Special attention to honors, advanced placement, accelerated courses, and independent work. **Test requirements:** SAT or ACT; score report by June 1. **Additional information:** Personal strengths, motivation, self-discipline, self-awareness, and understanding of the college's unique approach plays significant role in evaluation of candidates.

1992 FRESHMAN CLASS PROFILE. 344 men applied, 94 accepted, 42 enrolled; 519 women applied, 147 accepted, 69 enrolled. 89% had high school GPA of 3.0 or higher, 8% between 2.0 and 2.99. 43% were in top tenth and 85% were in top quarter of graduating class. **Academic background:** Mid 50% of enrolled freshmen had SAT-V between 580-680, SAT-M between 580-690; ACT composite between 27-31. 94% submitted SAT scores, 50% submitted ACT scores. **Characteristics:** 61% from in state, 95% live in college housing, 14% have minority backgrounds, 4% are foreign students. Average age is 18.

FALL-TERM APPLICATIONS. $20 fee, may be waived for applicants with need. Closing date June 1; applicants notified on a rolling basis; must reply by May 1 or within 2 weeks if notified thereafter. Essay required. Interview required of local applicants, recommended for all others. CRDA. Deferred and early admission available.

STUDENT LIFE. Housing: Dormitories (coed); cooperative housing available. **Activities:** Student government, film, magazine, student newspaper, dance, OJMELA (Organisacion Jose Marti de Estudios Latino Americanos), Amnesty International, international student association, visiting speakers committee, Womyn's Tea, multicultural society, film series, center for service learning. **Additional information:** Individual initiative and Socratic method emphasized.

ATHLETICS. Intramural: Basketball, handball, racquetball, skin diving, softball, swimming, tennis, volleyball.

STUDENT SERVICES. Career counseling, employment service for undergraduates, freshman orientation, health services, personal counseling, placement service for graduates, veterans counselor, services/facilities for handicapped.

ANNUAL EXPENSES. Tuition and fees (projected): $1,855, $5,705 additional for out-of-state students. **Room and board:** $3,612. **Books and supplies:** $600. **Other expenses:** $2,100.

FINANCIAL AID. 76% of freshmen, 83% of continuing students receive some form of aid. 31% of grants, 99% of loans, 42% of jobs based on need. 48 enrolled freshmen were judged to have need, 44 were offered aid. Academic, athletic, state/district residency, leadership, minority scholarships available. **Aid applications:** Closing date June 1; priority given to applications received by February 1; applicants notified on a rolling basis beginning on or about April 15; must reply within 3 weeks.

ADDRESS/TELEPHONE. David Anderson, Director of Admissions, New College of the University of South Florida, 5700 North Tamiami Trail, Sarasota, FL 34243-2197. (813) 359-4269.

New England Institute of Technology
West Palm Beach, Florida CB code: 0529

2-year proprietary technical college, coed. Founded in 1982. **Undergraduate enrollment:** 570 men, 385 women full time. **Faculty:** 49 total (48 full time). **Location:** Urban campus in small city; 60 miles from Miami. **Calendar:** Quarter. Extensive evening/early morning classes.

DEGREES OFFERED. AS. 400 associate degrees awarded in 1992. 8% in business/office and marketing/distribution, 14% computer sciences, 8% allied health, 70% trade and industry.

UNDERGRADUATE MAJORS. Air conditioning/heating/refrigeration mechanics, air conditioning/heating/refrigeration technology, architectural drafting, architectural technologies, architecture, automotive mechanics, automotive technology, computer programming, computer servicing technology, drafting and design technology, electrical and electronics equipment repair, electronic technology, food production/management/services, interior design, mechanical design technology, medical assistant, secretarial and related programs.

ACADEMIC PROGRAMS. Double major, internships. **Remedial services:** Remedial instruction, special counselor, tutoring. **Placement/credit:** Institutional tests; 30 credit hours maximum for associate degree.

ACADEMIC REQUIREMENTS. Freshmen must earn minimum GPA of 1.5 to continue in good standing. 85% of freshmen return for sophomore year. Students must declare major on application. **Graduation requirements:** 90 hours for associate.

FRESHMAN ADMISSIONS. Selection criteria: Open admissions.

1992 FRESHMAN CLASS PROFILE. 450 men and women enrolled. **Characteristics:** 90% from in state, 100% commute, 24% have minority backgrounds.

FALL-TERM APPLICATIONS. $150 fee. No closing date; priority given to applications received by October 4; applicants notified on a rolling basis. Interview required.

STUDENT SERVICES. Career counseling, employment service for undergraduates, personal counseling, placement service for graduates, special adviser for adult students, services/facilities for handicapped.

ANNUAL EXPENSES. Tuition and fees (1992-93): $6,300. **Books and supplies:** $265. **Other expenses:** $1,190.

FINANCIAL AID. 70% of freshmen, 70% of continuing students receive some form of aid. 95% of grants, 52% of loans, all jobs based on need. Academic scholarships available. **Aid applications:** No closing date; applicants notified on a rolling basis.

ADDRESS/TELEPHONE. Scott Spitolnick, Admissions Director, New England Institute of Technology, 1126 53rd Court, West Palm Beach, FL 33407. (407) 842-8324. (800) 826-9988.

North Florida Junior College
Madison, Florida — CB code: 5503

2-year public junior college, coed. Founded in 1958. **Accreditation:** Regional. **Undergraduate enrollment:** 218 men, 262 women full time; 182 men, 389 women part time. **Faculty:** 51 total (26 full time), 4 with doctorates or other terminal degrees. **Location:** Rural campus in small town; 56 miles from Tallahassee. **Calendar:** Semester, limited summer session. **Microcomputers:** Located in classrooms.

DEGREES OFFERED. AA. 115 associate degrees awarded in 1992. 100% in multi/interdisciplinary studies.

UNDERGRADUATE MAJORS. Education, liberal/general studies.

ACADEMIC PROGRAMS. 2-year transfer program, dual enrollment of high school students, honors program, independent study, weekend college. **Remedial services:** Remedial instruction, tutoring. **Placement/credit:** AP, CLEP General and Subject, institutional tests; 36 credit hours maximum for associate degree.

ACADEMIC REQUIREMENTS. Freshmen must earn minimum GPA of 2.0 to continue in good standing. 70% of freshmen return for sophomore year. **Graduation requirements:** 64 hours for associate. Most students required to take courses in English, history, humanities, mathematics, biological/physical sciences, social sciences.

FRESHMAN ADMISSIONS. Selection criteria: Open admissions. **High school preparation:** 13 units required. Required units include biological science 3, English 4, mathematics 3 and social science 3. **Test requirements:** SAT or ACT (ACT preferred) for placement; score report by August 23.

1992 FRESHMAN CLASS PROFILE. 165 men, 283 women enrolled. 16% had high school GPA of 3.0 or higher, 29% between 2.0 and 2.99. **Academic background:** Mid 50% of enrolled freshmen had SAT-V between 350-480, SAT-M between 320-460; ACT composite between 9-20. 5% submitted SAT scores, 95% submitted ACT scores. **Characteristics:** 95% from in state, 100% commute, 33% have minority backgrounds. Average age is 20.

FALL-TERM APPLICATIONS. $10 fee. No closing date; applicants notified on a rolling basis. Early admission available.

STUDENT LIFE. Activities: Student government, student newspaper, choral groups, drama, jazz band, music ensembles, musical theater.

ATHLETICS. NJCAA. **Intercollegiate:** Baseball M, basketball. **Intramural:** Baseball M, golf, racquetball, tennis, volleyball.

STUDENT SERVICES. Career counseling, employment service for undergraduates, freshman orientation, placement service for graduates, special adviser for adult students, veterans counselor, services/facilities for handicapped.

ANNUAL EXPENSES. Tuition and fees (projected): $773, $2,227 additional for out-of-state students. **Books and supplies:** $400. **Other expenses:** $475.

FINANCIAL AID. 25% of freshmen, 25% of continuing students receive some form of aid. 80% of grants, all loans, 74% of jobs based on need. 308 enrolled freshmen were judged to have need, all were offered aid. Academic, music/drama, art, athletic scholarships available. **Aid applications:** No closing date; priority given to applications received by July 1; applicants notified on a rolling basis beginning on or about June 10; must reply within 2 weeks.

ADDRESS/TELEPHONE. William O. Brazil, Dean of Students, Director of Admissions, Financial Aid Officer, Registrar, North Florida Junior College, 1000 Turner Davis Drive, Madison, FL 32340. (904) 973-2288. Fax: (904) 973-2288 ext. 104.

Nova University
Fort Lauderdale, Florida — CB code: 5514

Admissions:	75% of applicants accepted
Based on:	••• School record
	•• Essay, interview, test scores
	• Activities, recommendations, special talents
Completion:	90% of freshmen end year in good standing
	50% graduate

4-year private university, coed. Founded in 1964. **Accreditation:** Regional. **Undergraduate enrollment:** 725 men, 1,270 women full time; 533 men, 889 women part time. **Graduate enrollment:** 860 men, 1,196 women full time; 2,179 men, 2,839 women part time. **Faculty:** 435 total (174 full time), 148 with doctorates or other terminal degrees. **Location:** Suburban campus in small city; 10 miles from downtown. **Calendar:** Six 8-week terms. **Microcomputers:** 300 located in dormitories, libraries, computer centers, campus-wide network. **Special facilities:** Oceanographic center, law center, demonstration/model school, family center. **Additional facts:** 78 field-based programs in 29 cities in Florida and 73 such programs in 21 other states. Baccalaureate programs operated at 30 of these sites.

DEGREES OFFERED. BA, BS, MA, MS, MBA, MEd, PhD, EdD, JD. 922 bachelor's degrees awarded in 1992. 50% in business and management, 10% computer sciences, 20% education, 10% law, 10% psychology. Graduate degrees offered in 44 major fields of study.

UNDERGRADUATE MAJORS. Accounting, business administration and management, business and management, computer and information sciences, computer education, computer engineering, education of exceptional children, education of the mentally handicapped, elementary education, hotel/motel and restaurant management, information sciences and systems, international relations, international studies, legal studies, liberal/general studies, life sciences, general, marine biology, ocean studies, oceanographic technologies, predentistry, prelaw, premedicine, prepharmacy, preveterinary, psychology, secondary education, special education, specific learning disabilities, systems analysis.

ACADEMIC PROGRAMS. Accelerated program, computer delivered (on-line) credit-bearing course offerings, cooperative education, double major, dual enrollment of high school students, education specialist degree, external degree, independent study, internships, study abroad, teacher preparation, weekend college. **Remedial services:** Learning center, remedial instruction, writing and mathematics laboratories. **Placement/credit:** AP, CLEP General and Subject, IB, institutional tests; 90 credit hours maximum for bachelor's degree.

ACADEMIC REQUIREMENTS. Freshmen must earn minimum GPA of 1.5 to continue in good standing. 60% of freshmen return for sophomore year. Students must declare major by end of second year. **Graduation requirements:** 120 hours for bachelor's (30 in major). Most students required to take courses in English, history, humanities, mathematics, biological/physical sciences, social sciences. **Additional information:** Innovative undergraduate program focuses on concepts to encourage analytical and critical thinking.

FRESHMAN ADMISSIONS. Selection criteria: Test scores, high school GPA, and interview for day program. Career Development Program requires only high school diploma/GED. **High school preparation:** 10 units required. Required units include English 4, mathematics 2, social science 2 and science 2. **Test requirements:** SAT or ACT; score report by August 1.

1992 FRESHMAN CLASS PROFILE. 326 men applied, 245 accepted, 142 enrolled; 388 women applied, 291 accepted, 169 enrolled. 25% had high school GPA of 3.0 or higher, 74% between 2.0 and 2.99. **Academic background:** Mid 50% of enrolled freshmen had SAT-V between 390-490, SAT-M between 410-520. 90% submitted SAT scores. **Characteristics:** 77% from in state, 78% commute, 25% have minority backgrounds, 12% are foreign students. Average age is 32.

FALL-TERM APPLICATIONS. $40 fee, may be waived for applicants with need. No closing date; applicants notified on a rolling basis. Essay required. Interview recommended. CRDA. Deferred and early admission available. Institutional early decision plan.

STUDENT LIFE. Housing: Dormitories (coed); apartment housing available. Furnished apartments available, utilities included. **Activities:** Student government, radio, student newspaper, yearbook, literary publication, choral groups, black student association, international student association, psychology club, outdoor club, student government association, business club, Hillel.

ATHLETICS. NAIA, NSCAA. **Intercollegiate:** Baseball M, basketball M, cross-country M, golf M, soccer M, tennis W, volleyball W. **Intramural:** Softball M, swimming, table tennis, tennis.

STUDENT SERVICES. Aptitude testing, career counseling, employment service for undergraduates, freshman orientation, personal counseling, placement service for graduates, special adviser for adult students, veterans counselor, services/facilities for handicapped.

ANNUAL EXPENSES. Tuition and fees (projected): $8,320. **Room and board:** $4,600. **Books and supplies:** $700. **Other expenses:** $1,950.

FINANCIAL AID. 90% of freshmen, 75% of continuing students receive some form of aid. 87% of grants, 70% of loans, all jobs based on need.

100 enrolled freshmen were judged to have need, all were offered aid. Academic, athletic, minority scholarships available. **Aid applications:** No closing date; priority given to applications received by April 1; applicants notified on a rolling basis beginning on or about April 1; must reply within 4 weeks.

ADDRESS/TELEPHONE. Kenneth R. Dose, Director of Admissions, Nova University, 3301 College Avenue, Fort Lauderdale, FL 33314. (305) 475-7360. (800) 541-NOVA ext. 7360. Fax: (305) 476-1999.

Okaloosa-Walton Community College
Niceville, Florida CB code: 5526

2-year public community college, coed. Founded in 1963. **Accreditation:** Regional. **Undergraduate enrollment:** 700 men, 916 women full time; 1,817 men, 2,387 women part time. **Faculty:** 265 total (77 full time), 27 with doctorates or other terminal degrees. **Location:** Rural campus in large town; 55 miles from Pensacola. **Calendar:** Two 16-week semesters followed by one 12-week semester concurrent with two 6-week terms. Saturday and extensive evening/early morning classes. **Microcomputers:** 300 located in classrooms. **Special facilities:** Art gallery exhibiting local work. **Additional facts:** Additional teaching centers at Ft. Walton Beach, Eglin Air Force Base, Hurlburt Field, and DeFuniak Springs. Extensive evening and some weekend courses available.

DEGREES OFFERED. AA, AS. 512 associate degrees awarded in 1992. 13% in business and management, 6% teacher education, 52% multi/interdisciplinary studies, 5% social sciences.

UNDERGRADUATE MAJORS. Accounting, air conditioning/heating/refrigeration technology, allied health, automotive mechanics, automotive technology, biology, business administration and management, business and management, business and office, business education, chemistry, child development/care/guidance, computer and information sciences, computer programming, construction, criminal justice technology, drafting and design technology, early childhood education, education, electronic technology, elementary education, engineering, family/consumer resource management, fashion design, finance, fine arts, fire control and safety technology, French, German, graphic arts technology, graphic design, health sciences, home economics, hotel/motel and restaurant management, human resources development, humanities, industrial technology, information sciences and systems, legal assistant/paralegal, legal secretary, liberal/general studies, manufacturing technology, marketing management, mathematics, ministry, physics, predentistry, premedicine, prenursing, prepharmacy, preveterinary, protective services, real estate, recreation and community services technologies, secondary education, secretarial and related programs, social sciences, social work, solar heating and cooling technology, Spanish, welding technology.

ACADEMIC PROGRAMS. 2-year transfer program, dual enrollment of high school students, independent study, internships, student-designed major, cross-registration. **Remedial services:** Learning center, remedial instruction, special counselor, tutoring, college-preparatory English, mathematics, algebra, reading. **Placement/credit:** AP, CLEP General and Subject, institutional tests; 32 credit hours maximum for associate degree.

ACADEMIC REQUIREMENTS. Incremental GPA requirements, based on credits attempted, progressing to minimum GPA of 2.0. Students must declare major by end of first year. **Graduation requirements:** 64 hours for associate (22 in major). Most students required to take courses in English, humanities, mathematics, biological/physical sciences, social sciences.

FRESHMAN ADMISSIONS. Selection criteria: Open admissions. Applicants without high school diploma may be admitted to credit-bearing certificate and/or associate of science programs. Recommended units include English 4, mathematics 3, social science 3 and science 3. **Test requirements:** SAT or ACT for placement.

1992 FRESHMAN CLASS PROFILE. 567 men applied, 567 accepted, 382 enrolled; 751 women applied, 751 accepted, 497 enrolled. 6% were in top tenth and 16% were in top quarter of graduating class. **Characteristics:** 100% commute, 13% have minority backgrounds, 1% are foreign students. Average age is 28.

FALL-TERM APPLICATIONS. $15 fee. No closing date; applicants notified on a rolling basis; must reply by registration. Deferred and early admission available.

STUDENT LIFE. Activities: Student government, choral groups, concert band, dance, drama, jazz band, music ensembles, musical theater, symphony orchestra, show choir, Student Christian Fellowship, Baptist Campus Ministry, Black Student Union, Circle-K, College Republicans, Environmental Club.

ATHLETICS. NJCAA. **Intercollegiate:** Baseball M, basketball, softball W. **Intramural:** Archery, badminton, bowling, cross-country, football M, golf, handball, racquetball, soccer, softball, table tennis, tennis, volleyball.

STUDENT SERVICES. Aptitude testing, career counseling, employment service for undergraduates, freshman orientation, health services, on-campus day care, personal counseling, placement service for graduates, special adviser for adult students, veterans counselor, services/facilities for handicapped.

ANNUAL EXPENSES. Tuition and fees (projected): $966, $2,718 additional for out-of-state students. **Books and supplies:** $496. **Other expenses:** $900.

FINANCIAL AID. 40% of freshmen, 50% of continuing students receive some form of aid. 89% of grants, 67% of loans, 38% of jobs based on need. Academic, music/drama, art, athletic, state/district residency, leadership, minority scholarships available. **Aid applications:** No closing date; priority given to applications received by April 1; applicants notified on a rolling basis beginning on or about February 1; must reply within 2 weeks. **Additional information:** Students not qualifying for need-based aid can use OWCC General Student Loan Fund to assist with tuition and book costs.

ADDRESS/TELEPHONE. Eugene Benvenutti, Registrar/Director of Admissions, Okaloosa-Walton Community College, 100 College Boulevard, Niceville, FL 32578. (904) 678-5111. Fax: (904) 729-5215.

Orlando College
Orlando, Florida CB code: 0742

4-year proprietary business college, coed. Founded in 1918. **Undergraduate enrollment:** 2,355 men and women. **Graduate enrollment:** 90 men, 60 women full time. **Location:** Urban campus in large city; 2 miles from downtown. **Calendar:** Quarter. **Additional facts:** Additional campus downtown.

FRESHMAN ADMISSIONS. Selection criteria: Personal interview most important.

ANNUAL EXPENSES. Tuition and fees (1992-93): Tuition and fees, dependent on degree, range from $10,255 to $20,510. Books included in tuition; supplies $90 per academic year for undergraduate students. **Other expenses:** $200.

ADDRESS/TELEPHONE. Nancy Rogers, Director of Admissions, Orlando College, 5500 Diplomat Circle, Orlando, FL 32810. (407) 628-5870. Fax: (407) 628-1344.

Palm Beach Atlantic College
West Palm Beach, Florida CB code: 5553

Admissions:	79% of applicants accepted
Based on:	••• School record
	•• Recommendations, religious affiliation/commitment, special talents, test scores
	• Activities, essay, interview
Completion:	45% enter graduate study

4-year private liberal arts college, coed, affiliated with Southern Baptist Convention. Founded in 1968. **Accreditation:** Regional. **Undergraduate enrollment:** 594 men, 773 women full time; 97 men, 124 women part time. **Graduate enrollment:** 10 men, 5 women full time; 36 men, 29 women part time. **Faculty:** 121 total (66 full time), 71 with doctorates or other terminal degrees. **Location:** Urban campus in large city; 60 miles from Miami. **Calendar:** Semester, limited summer session. **Microcomputers:** 50 located in libraries, computer centers. **Special facilities:** Kravis Center for Performing Arts, Norton Gallery of Art.

DEGREES OFFERED. BA, BS, MBA. 282 bachelor's degrees awarded in 1992. 29% in business and management, 6% teacher education, 8% health sciences, 8% life sciences, 8% mathematics, 18% philosophy, religion, theology, 18% psychology. Graduate degrees offered in 1 major field of study.

UNDERGRADUATE MAJORS. Accounting, art education, biology, business administration and management, business and management, business economics, business education, communications, computer and information sciences, early childhood education, elementary education, English, English education, finance, health sciences, history, information sciences and systems, international business management, marketing management, mathematics, music, physical education, political science and government, psychology, religion, social science education, speech/communication/theater education, speech/communications/drama.

ACADEMIC PROGRAMS. Double major, dual enrollment of high school students, honors program, independent study, internships, study abroad, Washington semester. **Remedial services:** Learning center, preadmission summer program, reduced course load, remedial instruction, tutoring. **Placement/credit:** AP, CLEP Subject, institutional tests; 30 credit hours maximum for bachelor's degree.

ACADEMIC REQUIREMENTS. Freshmen must earn minimum GPA of 2.0 to continue in good standing. 62% of freshmen return for sophomore year. Students must declare major by end of second year. **Graduation requirements:** 128 hours for bachelor's (30 in major). Most students required to take courses in arts/fine arts, computer science, English, history, humanities, mathematics, philosophy/religion, biological/physical sciences, social sciences. **Postgraduate studies:** 20% enter MBA programs, 25% enter other graduate study.

FRESHMAN ADMISSIONS. Selection criteria: Academic recommendations. 2.5 GPA recommended. School and community activities and test scores considered. **High school preparation:** 17 units recommended. Recommended units include biological science 2, English 4, foreign language 2, mathematics 3, social science 3 and science 3. **Test requirements:** SAT or ACT; score report by September 1.

1992 FRESHMAN CLASS PROFILE. 277 men applied, 220 accepted, 120 enrolled; 384 women applied, 305 accepted, 163 enrolled. 47% had high school GPA of 3.0 or higher, 45% between 2.0 and 2.99. 17% were in top tenth and 38% were in top quarter of graduating class. **Academic background:** Mid 50% of enrolled freshmen had SAT-V between 390-520, SAT-M between 420-570; ACT composite between 20-25. 57% submitted SAT scores, 43% submitted ACT scores. **Characteristics:** 70% from in state, 84% live in college housing, 9% have minority backgrounds, 5% are foreign students. Average age is 18.

FALL-TERM APPLICATIONS. $25 fee, may be waived for applicants with need. No closing date; applicants notified on a rolling basis. Audition required for music, theater applicants. Interview recommended for academically weak applicants. Essay recommended. CRDA. Deferred and early admission available.

STUDENT LIFE. Housing: Dormitories (men, women); apartment housing available. All students under 20 not living with parents required to live on campus. **Activities:** Student government, student newspaper, yearbook, choral groups, concert band, drama, jazz band, music ensembles, musical theater, symphony orchestra, campus ministries organization. **Additional information:** Students required to donate 200 hours of community service over 4 years. Chapel attendance required of all students.

ATHLETICS. NAIA. **Intercollegiate:** Baseball M, basketball M, golf, soccer M, tennis, volleyball W. **Intramural:** Basketball, bowling, golf, racquetball, softball, swimming, tennis, volleyball.

STUDENT SERVICES. Aptitude testing, career counseling, employment service for undergraduates, freshman orientation, health services, personal counseling, veterans counselor.

ANNUAL EXPENSES. Tuition and fees (projected): $7,200. **Room and board:** $3,000. **Books and supplies:** $500.

FINANCIAL AID. 90% of freshmen receive some form of aid. 35% of grants, 83% of loans, all jobs based on need. Academic, music/drama, athletic, state/district residency, leadership, religious affiliation scholarships available. **Aid applications:** No closing date; priority given to applications received by May 1; applicants notified on a rolling basis.

ADDRESS/TELEPHONE. Rich Grimm, Director of Admissions, Palm Beach Atlantic College, PO Box 24708, 901 S. Flagler Drive, West Palm Beach, FL 33416-4708. (407) 835-4309. (800) 238-3998. Fax: (407) 835-4342.

Palm Beach Community College
Lake Worth, Florida — CB code: 5531

2-year public community college, coed. Founded in 1933. **Accreditation:** Regional. **Undergraduate enrollment:** 2,474 men, 2,806 women full time; 4,225 men, 7,038 women part time. **Faculty:** 723 total (202 full time), 34 with doctorates or other terminal degrees. **Location:** Suburban campus in large town; 60 miles from Miami, 30 miles from Fort Lauderdale. **Calendar:** Two 16-week terms and third term consisting of two 6-week sessions. Saturday and extensive evening/early morning classes. **Microcomputers:** Located in libraries, classrooms, computer centers. **Special facilities:** Watson B. Duncan Performing Arts Center. **Additional facts:** Multilocation institution.

DEGREES OFFERED. AA, AS. 1,624 associate degrees awarded in 1992. 15% in business and management, 17% allied health, 45% multi/interdisciplinary studies, 9% social sciences.

UNDERGRADUATE MAJORS. Accounting, airline piloting and navigation, anthropology, architecture, automotive mechanics, automotive technology, biology, business administration and management, business and management, business and office, business computer/console/peripheral equipment operation, business data processing and related programs, business data programming, business education, business systems analysis, chemistry, child development/care/guidance, communications, computer and information sciences, computer programming, construction, criminal justice studies, dance, data processing, dental hygiene, dietetic aide/assistant, drafting, drafting and design technology, dramatic arts, early childhood education, education, electrical/electronics/communications engineering, electronic technology, elementary education, emergency medical technologies, engineering, fashion design, finance, fine arts, fire control and safety technology, food management, food production/management/services, food science and nutrition, geography, graphic and printing production, graphic arts technology, graphic design, health education, history, home economics, hotel/motel and restaurant management, industrial technology, information sciences and systems, interior design, international relations, journalism, legal assistant/paralegal, liberal/general studies, management information systems, marketing and distribution, marketing management, mathematics, medical laboratory technologies, mental health/human services, music, music education, music performance, nursing, occupational therapy assistant, ornamental horticulture, photographic technology, photography, physical sciences, physical therapy assistant, physics, plant protection, political science and government, psychology, radiograph medical technology, recreation and community services technologies, respiratory therapy technology, retailing, robotics, science education, secretarial and related programs, social science education, social sciences, sociology, survey and mapping technology, systems analysis, ultrasound technology, water and wastewater technology, zoology.

ACADEMIC PROGRAMS. 2-year transfer program, accelerated program, cooperative education, dual enrollment of high school students, honors program, internships, study abroad, weekend college. **Remedial services:** Learning center, preadmission summer program, reduced course load, remedial instruction, tutoring. **Placement/credit:** AP, CLEP General and Subject, institutional tests; 45 credit hours maximum for associate degree.

ACADEMIC REQUIREMENTS. Freshmen must earn minimum GPA of 1.8 to continue in good standing. 62% of freshmen return for sophomore year. Students must declare major by end of first year. **Graduation requirements:** 62 hours for associate (28 in major). Most students required to take courses in English, foreign languages, humanities, mathematics, biological/physical sciences, social sciences.

FRESHMAN ADMISSIONS. Selection criteria: Open admissions. Selective admissions to dental and nursing programs based on test scores and high school GPA. Special requirements for health program applicants. **Test requirements:** SAT or ACT (ACT preferred) for placement and counseling only; score report by July 28. SAT/ACT required for admissions for nursing and dental programs applicants; score report by March 6.

1992 FRESHMAN CLASS PROFILE. 1,181 men, 1,553 women enrolled. **Characteristics:** 80% from in state, 100% commute, 24% have minority backgrounds, 2% are foreign students. Average age is 22.

FALL-TERM APPLICATIONS. $15 fee. No closing date; priority given to applications received by July 27; applicants notified on a rolling basis beginning on or about March 1. Audition required for music applicants. Interview recommended for nursing, dental applicants. Early admission available.

STUDENT LIFE. Activities: Student government, student newspaper, choral groups, concert band, dance, drama, jazz band, music ensembles, Black Student Union, Circle-K, Students for International Understanding.

ATHLETICS. NJCAA. **Intercollegiate:** Baseball M, basketball, golf, softball W, tennis. **Intramural:** Baseball M, basketball, volleyball.

STUDENT SERVICES. Aptitude testing, career counseling, employment service for undergraduates, freshman orientation, health services, on-campus day care, personal counseling, placement service for graduates, veterans counselor, counselor for handicapped students, services/facilities for handicapped.

ANNUAL EXPENSES. Tuition and fees (projected): $939, $2,355 additional for out-of-state students. **Books and supplies:** $600. **Other expenses:** $800.

FINANCIAL AID. 78% of grants, 73% of loans, 68% of jobs based on need. Academic, music/drama, athletic scholarships available. **Aid applications:** No closing date; applicants notified on a rolling basis; must reply within 2 weeks.

ADDRESS/TELEPHONE. Don Lore, Director of Counseling Services, Palm Beach Community College, 4200 Congress Avenue, Lake Worth, FL 33461. (407) 439-8102. Fax: (407) 439-8255.

Pasco-Hernando Community College
Dade City, Florida — CB code: 5562

2-year public community college, coed. Founded in 1972. **Accreditation:** Regional. **Undergraduate enrollment:** 708 men, 1,265 women full time; 1,352 men, 2,559 women part time. **Faculty:** 232 total (76 full time), 21 with doctorates or other terminal degrees. **Location:** Rural campus in large town; 35 miles from Tampa. **Calendar:** Semester, limited summer session. Saturday and extensive evening/early morning classes. **Microcomputers:** 264 located in libraries, classrooms, computer centers.

DEGREES OFFERED. AA, AS. 498 associate degrees awarded in 1992. 7% in business and management, 21% allied health, 68% multi/interdisciplinary studies.

UNDERGRADUATE MAJORS. Business administration and management, business data programming, construction, dental hygiene, emergency medical technologies, fire control and safety technology, food production/management/services, law enforcement and corrections technologies, liberal/general studies, marketing management, mental health/human services, nursing, secretarial and related programs.

ACADEMIC PROGRAMS. 2-year transfer program, accelerated program, dual enrollment of high school students, honors program, independent study, internships, study abroad, telecourses. **Remedial services:** Learning center, reduced course load, remedial instruction, special counselor, tutoring. **ROTC:** Army. **Placement/credit:** AP, CLEP General and Subject, IB, institutional tests; 45 credit hours maximum for associate degree.

ACADEMIC REQUIREMENTS. Freshmen must earn minimum GPA of 1.5 to continue in good standing. 60% of freshmen return for sophomore year. Students must declare major on enrollment. **Graduation requirements:** 62 hours for associate. Most students required to take courses in English, history, humanities, mathematics, biological/physical sciences, social sciences.

FRESHMAN ADMISSIONS. Selection criteria: Open admissions. Special criteria for allied health program. 4 English units, 3 mathematics units, 3 social science units, and 3 science units required for candidates for associate degree. **Test requirements:** Florida MAPS required of all applicants.

1992 FRESHMAN CLASS PROFILE. 387 men, 737 women enrolled. **Characteristics:** 100% commute, 8% have minority backgrounds.

FALL-TERM APPLICATIONS. $15 fee. No closing date; applicants notified on a rolling basis. Deferred and early admission available.

STUDENT LIFE. Activities: Student government, magazine, student newspaper, drama, music ensembles, Uhuru, human services club, drama club, student nursing club, writing club, Spanish club, Phi Beta Lambda (business), student dental organization, horticulture club.

ATHLETICS. NJCAA. **Intercollegiate:** Baseball M, basketball M, softball W, volleyball W.

STUDENT SERVICES. Aptitude testing, career counseling, freshman orientation, personal counseling, veterans counselor, Special adviser for minority students, services/facilities for handicapped.

ANNUAL EXPENSES. Tuition and fees (1992-93): $1,044, $2,838 additional for out-of-state students. **Books and supplies:** $600. **Other expenses:** $1,480.

FINANCIAL AID. 43% of freshmen, 43% of continuing students receive some form of aid. 88% of grants, 60% of loans, 84% of jobs based on need. Academic, athletic, leadership, minority scholarships available. **Aid applications:** No closing date; priority given to applications received by June 1; applicants notified on a rolling basis beginning on or about July 1; must reply within 3 weeks.

ADDRESS/TELEPHONE. Michael Malizia, Director of Admissions and Student Records, Pasco-Hernando Community College, 3401 County Road 41 North, Dade City, FL 34654-5199. (813) 847-2727 ext. 3217. Fax: (813) 847-2727 ext. 3300.

Pensacola Junior College
Pensacola, Florida — CB code: 5535

2-year public community college, coed. Founded in 1948. **Accreditation:** Regional. **Undergraduate enrollment:** 17,397 men and women. **Faculty:** 1,111 total (231 full time), 53 with doctorates or other terminal degrees. **Location:** Urban campus in small city; 60 miles from Mobile, Alabama. **Calendar:** Semester, extensive summer session. **Microcomputers:** Located in libraries, computer centers. **Special facilities:** Planetarium, art gallery.

DEGREES OFFERED. AA, AS. 1,298 associate degrees awarded in 1992.

UNDERGRADUATE MAJORS. Accounting, agribusiness, agricultural education, agricultural sciences, apparel and accessories marketing, art education, art history, astronomy, automotive mechanics, biological and physical sciences, biology, biomedical equipment technology, botany, building design and construction, business administration and management, business and management, business and office, business data entry equipment operation, business data processing and related programs, business education, ceramics, chemistry, child development/care/guidance, civil engineering, civil technology, computer and information sciences, computer servicing technology, construction, contract management and procurement/purchasing, court reporting, criminal justice technology, dance, dental assistant, dental hygiene, dental laboratory technology, drafting, drafting and design technology, dramatic arts, drawing, early childhood education, earth sciences, education, electrical and electronics equipment repair, electronic music production, electronic technology, elementary education, emergency medical technologies, engineering, engineering and other disciplines, English, English education, environmental sampling and analysis, environmental science, fashion design, fashion merchandising, fine arts, fire control and safety technology, food production/management/services, foreign languages education, forest products processing technology, forestry and related sciences, French, geology, German, graphic and printing production, graphic design, hazardous material management, health care administration, health education, history, home economics, home economics education, horticultural science, horticulture, hotel/motel and restaurant management, humanities and social sciences, illustration design, industrial arts education, instrumentation technology, junior high education, Latin, law enforcement and corrections technologies, legal assistant/paralegal, legal secretary, liberal/general studies, management information systems, management science, marine biology, marketing and distributive education, marketing management, mathematics, mathematics education, medical records technology, medical secretary, metal/jewelry, music, music education, music history and appreciation, music performance, music theory and composition, nursing, oceanography, office supervision and management, ornamental horticulture, painting, philosophy, physical education, physical sciences, physical therapy assistant, physics, predentistry, prelaw, premedicine, prepharmacy, preveterinary, printmaking, psychology, radiograph medical technology, reading education, religion, respiratory therapy, respiratory therapy technology, robotics, science education, sculpture, secondary education, secretarial and related programs, small business management and ownership, social science education, social sciences, social studies education, special education, speech/communication/theater education, studio art, technical education, trade and industrial education, trade and industrial supervision and management, visual and performing arts, water and wastewater technology, word processing, zoology.

ACADEMIC PROGRAMS. 2-year transfer program, accelerated program, cooperative education, dual enrollment of high school students, external degree, honors program, independent study, internships, study abroad, telecourses, cross-registration. **Remedial services:** Learning center, remedial instruction, special counselor, tutoring. **ROTC:** Army. **Placement/credit:** AP, CLEP General and Subject, institutional tests; 45 credit hours maximum for associate degree.

ACADEMIC REQUIREMENTS. Freshmen must earn minimum GPA of 2.0 to continue in good standing. Freshmen must pass 50% of courses each term. Students must declare major on application. **Graduation requirements:** 60 hours for associate. Most students required to take courses in arts/fine arts, English, foreign languages, history, humanities, mathematics, biological/physical sciences, social sciences.

FRESHMAN ADMISSIONS. Selection criteria: Open admissions. Academic record and test scores required for nursing, dental hygiene, physical therapy assistant, respiratory therapy, and radiography technology programs. College preparatory program required for associate of arts program: 13 academic units including 4 English, 3 science, 3 mathematics, and 3 social science. **Additional information:** All students must submit SAT, ACT, Florida MAPS, or ASSET test results.

1992 FRESHMAN CLASS PROFILE. 1,926 men and women enrolled. **Characteristics:** 95% from in state, 100% commute, 18% have minority backgrounds. Average age is 20.

FALL-TERM APPLICATIONS. $20 fee. No closing date; applicants notified on a rolling basis. Audition required for music applicants. Portfolio required. Early admission available.

STUDENT LIFE. Activities: Student government, student newspaper, television, choral groups, concert band, dance, drama, jazz band, music ensembles, opera, symphony orchestra, fraternities, sororities, Baptist campus ministry, Florida African-American Student Association.

ATHLETICS. NJCAA. **Intercollegiate:** Baseball M, basketball, golf M, softball W. **Intramural:** Archery, badminton, basketball, bowling, golf, racquetball, sailing, soccer, table tennis, tennis, track and field, volleyball, water polo, wrestling.

STUDENT SERVICES. Career counseling, employment service for undergraduates, freshman orientation, health services, on-campus day care, personal counseling, placement service for graduates, veterans counselor, services/facilities for handicapped.

ANNUAL EXPENSES. Tuition and fees (1992-93): $1,035, $2,838 additional for out-of-state students. **Books and supplies:** $500. **Other expenses:** $1,100.

FINANCIAL AID. 30% of freshmen, 30% of continuing students receive some form of aid. 93% of grants, 78% of loans, 40% of jobs based on need. Academic, music/drama, art, athletic, minority scholarships available. **Aid applications:** No closing date; priority given to applications received by April 1; applicants notified on a rolling basis beginning on or about June 1.

ADDRESS/TELEPHONE. Dr. James B. Callaway, Director of Admissions/Registrar, Pensacola Junior College, 1000 College Boulevard, Pensacola, FL 32504. (904) 484-1600. Fax: (904) 484-1826.

Phillips Junior College: Melbourne
Melbourne, Florida — CB code: 0287

2-year proprietary junior college, coed. Founded in 1970. **Undergraduate enrollment:** 843 men and women. **Faculty:** 55 total (32 full time), 5 with doctorates or other terminal degrees. **Location:** Suburban campus in small city; 2 miles from downtown. **Calendar:** Quarter, extensive summer session. **Microcomputers:** 1 located in libraries, computer centers. **Special facilities:** Video editing suite.

DEGREES OFFERED. AS. 200 associate degrees awarded in 1992. 52% in business and management, 11% business/office and marketing/distribution, 16% computer sciences, 21% allied health.

UNDERGRADUATE MAJORS. Accounting, business administration and management, business and management, criminal justice technology, hotel/motel and restaurant management, information sciences and systems, legal secretary, medical assistant, motion picture technology, office supervision and management, secretarial and related programs, tourism, video.

ACADEMIC PROGRAMS. 2-year transfer program, double major, internships. **Remedial services:** Reduced course load, remedial instruction, tutoring. **Placement/credit:** CLEP General and Subject, institutional tests.

ACADEMIC REQUIREMENTS. Freshmen must earn minimum GPA of 2.0 to continue in good standing. 60% of freshmen return for sophomore year. Students must declare major on enrollment. **Graduation requirements:** 36 hours for associate (12 in major). Most students required to take courses in English.

FRESHMAN ADMISSIONS. Selection criteria: Open admissions. Selective admissions to film and video production and medical programs. **Test requirements:** CPAT required for those without SAT or ACT. **Additional information:** Completion of CPAT enrollment examination with score of 115 for 1-year program and 120 for 2-year program required.

1992 FRESHMAN CLASS PROFILE. 210 men and women enrolled.

Characteristics: 98% from in state, 100% commute, 16% have minority backgrounds, 3% are foreign students. Average age is 23.

FALL-TERM APPLICATIONS. $25 fee, may be waived for applicants with need. No closing date; priority given to applications received by August 1; applicants notified on a rolling basis. Interview required. Deferred and early admission available.

STUDENT LIFE. Activities: Student newspaper, fraternities.

STUDENT SERVICES. Aptitude testing, career counseling, employment service for undergraduates, freshman orientation, personal counseling, placement service for graduates, veterans counselor, services/facilities for handicapped.

ANNUAL EXPENSES. Tuition and fees (projected): $4,995. Books included in tuition and fees.

FINANCIAL AID. 52% of freshmen, 44% of continuing students receive some form of aid. 98% of grants, all loans, all jobs based on need. **Aid applications:** No closing date; applicants notified on a rolling basis; must reply within 2 weeks.

ADDRESS/TELEPHONE. Tony Wallace, Director of Admissions, Phillips Junior College: Melbourne, 2401 North Harbor City Blvd, Melbourne, FL 32935. (407) 254-6459 ext. 11. Fax: (407) 255-2017.

Polk Community College
Winter Haven, Florida — CB code: 5548

2-year public community college, coed. Founded in 1963. **Accreditation:** Regional. **Undergraduate enrollment:** 6,200 men and women. **Faculty:** 119 total, 26 with doctorates or other terminal degrees. **Location:** Suburban campus in large town; 4 miles from Cypress Gardens. **Calendar:** Trimester. **Microcomputers:** Located in computer centers.

DEGREES OFFERED. AA, AS. 540 associate degrees awarded in 1992.

UNDERGRADUATE MAJORS. Accounting, agribusiness, agricultural sciences, architecture, biology, botany, business and management, business and office, business data processing and related programs, chemistry, communications, computer and information sciences, drafting, dramatic arts, education, electrical and electronics equipment repair, elementary education, engineering, engineering and engineering-related technologies, English, finance, graphic arts technology, health sciences, home economics, instrumentation technology, journalism, law enforcement and corrections technologies, liberal/general studies, marketing and distribution, mathematics, music, nursing, physical sciences, psychology, radiograph medical technology, recreation and community services technologies, secondary education, secretarial and related programs, social sciences, visual and performing arts, zoology.

ACADEMIC PROGRAMS. 2-year transfer program, dual enrollment of high school students, independent study, internships, cross-registration. **Remedial services:** Learning center, remedial instruction, special counselor, tutoring. **ROTC:** Army. **Placement/credit:** AP, CLEP Subject, institutional tests; 45 credit hours maximum for associate degree.

ACADEMIC REQUIREMENTS. Freshmen must earn minimum GPA of 2.0 to continue in good standing. 60% of freshmen return for sophomore year. Students must declare major on enrollment. **Graduation requirements:** 60 hours for associate. Most students required to take courses in English, history, humanities, mathematics, biological/physical sciences, social sciences.

FRESHMAN ADMISSIONS. Selection criteria: Open admissions. Limited access to nursing and radiographer programs. Recommended units include English 4, foreign language 2, mathematics 4 and social science 3. College-preparatory track recommended for applicants planning to pursue baccalaureate degree. **Test requirements:** CPT, MAPS, or ASSET may be submitted in place of SAT or ACT. MAPS preferred.

1992 FRESHMAN CLASS PROFILE. 3,200 men and women enrolled. **Characteristics:** 97% from in state, 100% commute, 16% have minority backgrounds, 1% are foreign students. Average age is 22.

FALL-TERM APPLICATIONS. $15 fee. No closing date; applicants notified on a rolling basis. Audition recommended for theater, music applicants. Portfolio recommended for graphic arts applicants. Deferred and early admission available.

STUDENT LIFE. Activities: Student government, magazine, student newspaper, choral groups, concert band, dance, drama, jazz band, music ensembles, symphony orchestra, Baptist Student Union.

ATHLETICS. NJCAA. **Intercollegiate:** Baseball M, basketball, volleyball W. **Intramural:** Basketball, bowling, skin diving, softball, tennis, volleyball.

STUDENT SERVICES. Career counseling, employment service for undergraduates, personal counseling, placement service for graduates, veterans counselor, services/facilities for handicapped.

ANNUAL EXPENSES. Tuition and fees (projected): $1,045, $2,869 additional for out-of-state students. **Books and supplies:** $350. **Other expenses:** $500.

FINANCIAL AID. 45% of freshmen, 45% of continuing students receive some form of aid. 91% of grants, 39% of loans, 26% of jobs based on need. 650 enrolled freshmen were judged to have need, all were offered aid. Academic, music/drama, art, athletic, leadership scholarships available. **Aid applications:** Closing date May 15; applicants notified on or about July 1; must reply by July 15. **Additional information:** Short-term loans available if application made prior to registration.

ADDRESS/TELEPHONE. Michelle T. Wampler, Director of Admissions and Records, Polk Community College, 999 Avenue H Northeast, Winter Haven, FL 33881-4299. (813) 297-1001.

Ringling School of Art and Design
Sarasota, Florida — CB code: 5573

4-year private art college, coed. Founded in 1931. **Accreditation:** Regional. **Undergraduate enrollment:** 362 men, 340 women full time; 1 man, 3 women part time. **Faculty:** 81 total (73 full time), 76 with doctorates or other terminal degrees. **Location:** Suburban campus in small city; 50 miles from Tampa. **Calendar:** Semester. **Microcomputers:** 154 located in classrooms, computer centers. **Special facilities:** Art gallery.

DEGREES OFFERED. BFA. 64 bachelor's degrees awarded in 1992. 100% in visual and performing arts.

UNDERGRADUATE MAJORS. Computer graphics, fine arts, graphic design, illustration design, interior design.

ACADEMIC PROGRAMS. Dual enrollment of high school students, internships, study abroad, visiting/exchange student program. **Placement/credit:** AP, IB; 6 credit hours maximum for bachelor's degree.

ACADEMIC REQUIREMENTS. Freshmen must earn minimum GPA of 2.0 to continue in good standing. 80% of freshmen return for sophomore year. Students must declare major by end of first year. **Graduation requirements:** 123 hours for bachelor's (90 in major). Most students required to take courses in arts/fine arts, English, history, humanities, mathematics, biological/physical sciences, social sciences. **Additional information:** Professional art school granting 3-year certificate and bachelor of fine arts degree.

FRESHMAN ADMISSIONS. Selection criteria: Portfolio, school achievement record, statement of purpose.

1992 FRESHMAN CLASS PROFILE. 240 men and women enrolled. **Characteristics:** 50% from in state, 50% commute, 7% have minority backgrounds, 1% are foreign students. Average age is 21.

FALL-TERM APPLICATIONS. $30 fee, may be waived for applicants with need. No closing date; priority given to applications received by March 15; applicants notified on a rolling basis beginning on or about January 1. Portfolio required. Essay required. Interview recommended. CRDA. Deferred admission available. SAT/ACT recommended.

STUDENT LIFE. Housing: Dormitories (men, women). **Activities:** Student government, magazine, student newspaper, variety/talent show, sidewalk art sale, fraternities.

ATHLETICS. Intramural: Basketball, softball, table tennis, volleyball.

STUDENT SERVICES. Aptitude testing, career counseling, employment service for undergraduates, freshman orientation, personal counseling, placement service for graduates, services/facilities for handicapped.

ANNUAL EXPENSES. Tuition and fees (1992-93): $9,665. **Room and board:** $5,100. **Books and supplies:** $1,500. **Other expenses:** $500.

FINANCIAL AID. 70% of freshmen, 72% of continuing students receive some form of aid. Grants, loans, jobs available. Art scholarships available. **Aid applications:** No closing date; priority given to applications received by March 15; applicants notified on a rolling basis beginning on or about May 1; must reply within 2 weeks.

ADDRESS/TELEPHONE. James H. Dean, Dean of Admissions, Ringling School of Art and Design, 2700 North Tamiami Trail, Sarasota, FL 34234. (813) 359-7523. (800) 255-7695. Fax: (813) 359-7517.

Rollins College
Winter Park, Florida — CB code: 5572

Admissions: 72% of applicants accepted
Based on: ••• Essay, school record
•• Activities, interview, recommendations, special talents, test scores
Completion: 93% of freshmen end year in good standing
75% graduate, 25% of these enter graduate study

4-year private liberal arts college, coed. Founded in 1885. **Accreditation:** Regional. **Undergraduate enrollment:** 662 men, 783 women full time. **Graduate enrollment:** 128 men, 106 women full time; 157 men, 257 women part time. **Faculty:** 298 total (177 full time), 222 with doctorates or other terminal degrees. **Location:** Suburban campus in large town; 5 miles from Orlando. **Calendar:** 4-1-4. **Microcomputers:** 100 located in dormitories, libraries, classrooms, computer centers. **Special facilities:** Art museum, Annie Russell Theater, Fred Stone Theater, child development center, Johnson Center For Psychology.

DEGREES OFFERED. BA, MA, MBA, MEd. 352 bachelor's degrees awarded in 1992. 7% in area and ethnic studies, 6% education, 11% letters/literature, 10% psychology, 42% social sciences, 12% visual and performing arts. Graduate degrees offered in 5 major fields of study.

UNDERGRADUATE MAJORS. Anthropology, art history, biology,

Caribbean studies, chemistry, classics, computer and information sciences, dramatic arts, economics, education, elementary education, English, environmental studies, expressive arts, foreign languages (multiple emphasis), French, German, history, international relations, international studies, Latin American studies, mathematics, music, philosophy, physics, political science and government, predentistry, preengineering, prelaw, premedicine, prepharmacy, preveterinary, psychology, religion, Russian and Slavic studies, sociology, Spanish, studio art.

ACADEMIC PROGRAMS. Accelerated program, double major, dual enrollment of high school students, honors program, independent study, internships, student-designed major, study abroad, teacher preparation, visiting/exchange student program, Washington semester; liberal arts/career combination in engineering, forestry, health sciences; combined bachelor's/graduate program in business administration. **Remedial services:** Learning center, reduced course load, special counselor, tutoring. **Placement/credit:** AP, CLEP General, IB, institutional tests.

ACADEMIC REQUIREMENTS. Freshmen must earn minimum GPA of 2.0 to continue in good standing. 88% of freshmen return for sophomore year. Students must declare major by end of second year. **Graduation requirements:** 120 hours for bachelor's (40 in major). Most students required to take courses in arts/fine arts, English, foreign languages, humanities, mathematics, philosophy/religion, biological/physical sciences, social sciences. **Postgraduate studies:** 6% enter law school, 3% enter medical school, 4% enter MBA programs, 12% enter other graduate study.

FRESHMAN ADMISSIONS. Selection criteria: School achievement record most important, followed by test scores, recommendations, and interview. **High school preparation:** 14 units required. Required and recommended units include biological science 1, English 4, mathematics 3, physical science 1 and social science 3. Foreign language 2 recommended. Student must complete algebra 1, geometry, and algebra 2 sequence as part of mathematics requirement. **Test requirements:** SAT or ACT; score report by February 15.

1992 FRESHMAN CLASS PROFILE. 797 men applied, 570 accepted, 182 enrolled; 986 women applied, 718 accepted, 218 enrolled. 45% had high school GPA of 3.0 or higher, 55% between 2.0 and 2.99. 27% were in top tenth and 43% were in top quarter of graduating class. **Academic background:** Mid 50% of enrolled freshmen had SAT-V between 500-550, SAT-M between 500-610; ACT composite between 23-27. 96% submitted SAT scores, 32% submitted ACT scores. **Characteristics:** 38% from in state, 90% live in college housing, 13% have minority backgrounds, 5% are foreign students, 35% join fraternities/sororities. Average age is 18.

FALL-TERM APPLICATIONS. $35 fee, may be waived for applicants with need. Closing date February 15; applicants notified on or about April 1; must reply by May 1. Essay required. Interview recommended. Audition recommended for music, theatre arts applicants. Portfolio recommended for art applicants. CRDA. Deferred and early admission available. EDP-F. 3 ACH tests recommended.

STUDENT LIFE. Housing: Dormitories (coed); fraternity, sorority housing available. Special interest group housing available. **Activities:** Student government, magazine, radio, student newspaper, television, yearbook, choral groups, dance, drama, music ensembles, musical theater, Rollins Players, fraternities, sororities, campus ministry, Black Student Union, Jewish Student League, Newman Club, international club, outdoor club, Latin American Society, Women at Rollins, Greenhouse, World Hunger Committee.

ATHLETICS. NCAA. **Intercollegiate:** Baseball M, basketball, cross-country, golf, rowing (crew), sailing, skiing, soccer, softball W, swimming, tennis, volleyball W. **Intramural:** Badminton, baseball M, basketball, bowling, diving, sailing, soccer, softball, swimming, table tennis, tennis, volleyball.

STUDENT SERVICES. Aptitude testing, career counseling, employment service for undergraduates, freshman orientation, health services, personal counseling, placement service for graduates, veterans counselor, services/facilities for handicapped.

ANNUAL EXPENSES. Tuition and fees (1992-93): $14,974. **Room and board:** $4,626. **Books and supplies:** $400. **Other expenses:** $550.

FINANCIAL AID. 61% of freshmen, 57% of continuing students receive some form of aid. 55% of grants, 78% of loans based on need. 128 enrolled freshmen were judged to have need, 123 were offered aid. Academic, music/drama, art, athletic, state/district residency, leadership, alumni affiliation, minority scholarships available. **Aid applications:** No closing date; priority given to applications received by March 1; applicants notified on a rolling basis beginning on or about April 15. **Additional information:** Audition required for theater arts and music scholarship applicants. Portfolio required for art scholarships.

ADDRESS/TELEPHONE. David G. Erdmann, Dean of Admissions/Student Financial Planning, Rollins College, 1000 Holt Avenue, Campus Box 2720, Winter Park, FL 32789-4499. (407) 646-2161. Fax: (407) 646-1502.

St. John Vianney College Seminary
Miami, Florida — CB code: 5650

Admissions: 92% of applicants accepted
Based on:
- ••• Interview, recommendations, religious affiliation/commitment
- •• School record
- • Activities, test scores

Completion: 90% of freshmen end year in good standing
80% graduate, 90% of these enter graduate study

4-year private seminary college, men only, affiliated with Roman Catholic Church. Founded in 1959. **Accreditation:** Regional. **Undergraduate enrollment:** 45 men full time; 4 men, 1 woman part time. **Faculty:** 21 total (12 full time), 9 with doctorates or other terminal degrees. **Location:** Suburban campus in large city; 12 miles from downtown. **Calendar:** Semester. **Microcomputers:** 6 located in computer centers. **Additional facts:** College concentrates on preparing students for priesthood. Provides Anglo-Hispanic bicultural setting with many courses taught in Spanish as well as English. Women students admitted on part-time basis.

DEGREES OFFERED. BA. 9 bachelor's degrees awarded in 1992. 100% in philosophy, religion, theology.

UNDERGRADUATE MAJORS. Philosophy.

ACADEMIC PROGRAMS. Independent study. **Remedial services:** Reduced course load, remedial instruction. **Placement/credit:** AP, CLEP General and Subject, institutional tests.

ACADEMIC REQUIREMENTS. Freshmen must earn minimum GPA of 2.0 to continue in good standing. 90% of freshmen return for sophomore year. Students must declare major on application. **Graduation requirements:** 128 hours for bachelor's (35 in major). Most students required to take courses in English, foreign languages, history, humanities, mathematics, philosophy/religion, biological/physical sciences, social sciences. **Additional information:** College is bilingual (Spanish and English). Fluency in both languages must be achieved. Students required to take at least 1 course in the alternate language each semester.

FRESHMAN ADMISSIONS. Selection criteria: Interview, academic record, evidence of vocation for priesthood, psychological evaluation, recommendations. **Test requirements:** SAT or ACT (SAT preferred); score report by August 1. **Additional information:** Applicants referred by home (church) Diocesan Office of Vocations.

1992 FRESHMAN CLASS PROFILE. 12 men applied, 11 accepted, 11 enrolled. 34% had high school GPA of 3.0 or higher, 64% between 2.0 and 2.99. **Characteristics:** 100% from in state, 100% live in college housing, 45% have minority backgrounds, 20% are foreign students. Average age is 22.

FALL-TERM APPLICATIONS. No fee. Closing date July 15; priority given to applications received by June 30; applicants notified on a rolling basis. Interview required. Deferred admission available.

STUDENT LIFE. Housing: Dormitories (men). **Activities:** Student government, yearbook, choral groups, drama, music ensembles, liturgical music, apostolic works program. **Additional information:** All sophomores and upperclassmen assigned weekly apostolic work at various locations. Religious observance required.

ATHLETICS. Intramural: Baseball, basketball, handball, racquetball, soccer, softball, swimming, table tennis, tennis, volleyball.

STUDENT SERVICES. Career counseling, health services, personal counseling, special adviser for adult students, spiritual program, services/facilities for handicapped.

ANNUAL EXPENSES. Tuition and fees: $6,500. **Room and board:** $3,500. **Books and supplies:** $550. **Other expenses:** $990.

FINANCIAL AID. 50% of freshmen, 39% of continuing students receive some form of aid. All grants, all loans based on need. 4 enrolled freshmen were judged to have need, all were offered aid. **Aid applications:** No closing date; applicants notified on a rolling basis beginning on or about February 15.

ADDRESS/TELEPHONE. Office of the President, St. John Vianney College Seminary, 2900 Southwest 87 Avenue, Miami, FL 33165. (305) 223-4561. Fax: (305) 223-0650.

St. Johns River Community College
Palatka, Florida — CB code: 5641

2-year public community college, coed. Founded in 1957. **Accreditation:** Regional. **Undergraduate enrollment:** 3,391 men and women. **Faculty:** 185 total (85 full time), 6 with doctorates or other terminal degrees. **Location:** Rural campus in large town; 55 miles from Jacksonville and Daytona Beach. **Calendar:** Trimester, limited summer session. **Microcomputers:** Located in classrooms.

DEGREES OFFERED. AA, AS. 275 associate degrees awarded in 1992.

UNDERGRADUATE MAJORS. Business administration and management, computer programming, criminal justice technology, electronic technology, emergency medical technologies, fire control and safety technology, instrumentation technology, liberal/general studies, marketing and distribution, secretarial and related programs, visual and performing arts, word processing.

ACADEMIC PROGRAMS. 2-year transfer program, dual enrollment of high school students. **Remedial services:** Remedial instruction, tutoring. **Placement/credit:** AP, CLEP General and Subject; 45 credit hours maximum for associate degree.

ACADEMIC REQUIREMENTS. Graduated GPA based on semester hours attempted. 45% of freshmen return for sophomore year. Students must declare major on application. **Graduation requirements:** 64 hours for associate. Most students required to take courses in English, mathematics. **Additional information:** High school courses available to students in Florida School of Arts program.

FRESHMAN ADMISSIONS. Selection criteria: Open admissions. Selective admission to Florida School of Arts program. **High school preparation:** 24 units recommended. Recommended units include English 4, mathematics 3, social science 3 and science 3. **Test requirements:** SAT or ACT (ACT preferred) for placement and counseling only; score report by August 30.

1992 FRESHMAN CLASS PROFILE. 443 men, 584 women enrolled. **Characteristics:** 92% from in state, 100% commute, 10% have minority backgrounds. Average age is 21.

FALL-TERM APPLICATIONS. $15 fee. No closing date; applicants notified on a rolling basis. Interview, audition, and portfolio required of applicants to Florida School of Arts program. Early admission available.

STUDENT LIFE. Activities: Student government, student newspaper, Black Student Union, Circle-K, Compass Club, Future Educators, cheerleaders, golf club, Phi Beta Lamba, Mathematical Association of America.

ATHLETICS. NJCAA. **Intercollegiate:** Baseball M, basketball M, softball W. **Intramural:** Table tennis.

STUDENT SERVICES. Aptitude testing, career counseling, freshman orientation, personal counseling, placement service for graduates, veterans counselor, services/facilities for handicapped.

ANNUAL EXPENSES. Tuition and fees (projected): $900, $2,700 additional for out-of-state students. **Books and supplies:** $550. **Other expenses:** $781.

FINANCIAL AID. 27% of continuing students receive some form of aid. 92% of grants, 80% of loans, 22% of jobs based on need. Academic, music/drama, art, athletic, leadership, minority scholarships available. **Aid applications:** No closing date; priority given to applications received by May 15; applicants notified on a rolling basis beginning on or about June 15.

ADDRESS/TELEPHONE. O'Neal Williams, Dean of Student Services, St. Johns River Community College, 5001 St. Johns Avenue, Palatka, FL 32177-3897. (904) 328-1571 ext. 134. Fax: (904) 325-6627.

St. Leo College
St. Leo, Florida — CB code: 5638

Admissions: 70% of applicants accepted
Based on:
- ••• Essay, school record, test scores
- •• Activities, recommendations
- • Interview, special talents

Completion: 80% of freshmen end year in good standing
40% graduate, 7% of these enter graduate study

4-year private liberal arts college, coed, affiliated with Roman Catholic Church. Founded in 1889. **Accreditation:** Regional. **Undergraduate enrollment:** 437 men, 390 women full time; 39 men, 78 women part time. **Faculty:** 71 total (53 full time), 30 with doctorates or other terminal degrees. **Location:** Rural campus in rural community; 25 miles from Tampa. **Calendar:** Semester, limited summer session. **Microcomputers:** 40 located in libraries.

DEGREES OFFERED. AA, BA, BS. 47 associate degrees awarded in 1992. 100% in multi/interdisciplinary studies. 176 bachelor's degrees awarded. 39% in business and management, 13% education, 11% teacher education, 6% letters/literature, 11% parks/recreation, protective services, public affairs, 6% psychology, 7% visual and performing arts.

UNDERGRADUATE MAJORS. Associate: Liberal/general studies. **Bachelor's:** Art education, biology, business and management, clinical laboratory science, criminology, dance, dramatic arts, elementary education, English, fine arts, health care administration, history, history education, human resources development, human services, international relations, international studies, mathematics education, music, music education, physical education, political science and government, political science education, prelaw, psychology, public administration, religion, social work, sociology, specific learning disabilities.

ACADEMIC PROGRAMS. Accelerated program, double major, dual enrollment of high school students, honors program, independent study, internships, teacher preparation, weekend college. **Remedial services:** Reduced course load, remedial instruction, special counselor, tutoring, writing center, writing laboratory, mathematics laboratory. **ROTC:** Air Force, Army. **Placement/credit:** AP, CLEP General and Subject, IB, institutional tests; 32 credit hours maximum for associate degree; 40 credit hours maximum for bachelor's degree.

ACADEMIC REQUIREMENTS. Freshmen must earn minimum GPA of 2.0 to continue in good standing. 62% of freshmen return for sophomore year. Students must declare major by end of second year. **Graduation requirements:** 60 hours for associate, 120 hours for bachelor's. Most students required to take courses in arts/fine arts, English, history, humanities, mathematics, philosophy/religion, biological/physical sciences, social sciences. **Postgraduate studies:** 1% enter law school, 1% enter medical school, 3% enter MBA programs, 2% enter other graduate study.

FRESHMAN ADMISSIONS. Selection criteria: SAT or ACT scores, GPA, guidance counselor's recommendation, high school curriculum. **High school preparation:** 16 units recommended. Recommended units include English 4, mathematics 3, social science 3 and science 2. No more than 4 nonacademic units. **Test requirements:** SAT or ACT; score report by August 1.

1992 FRESHMAN CLASS PROFILE. 611 men applied, 428 accepted, 111 enrolled; 499 women applied, 349 accepted, 89 enrolled. 10% had high school GPA of 3.0 or higher, 80% between 2.0 and 2.99. **Academic background:** Mid 50% of enrolled freshmen had SAT-V between 370-450, SAT-M between 400-500. 63% submitted SAT scores. **Characteristics:** 90% live in college housing, 13% have minority backgrounds, 1% are foreign students. Average age is 18.

FALL-TERM APPLICATIONS. $30 fee, may be waived for applicants with need. Closing date August 1; applicants notified on a rolling basis; must reply by May 1 or within 2 weeks if notified thereafter. Audition required for performing arts applicants. Essay required. Interview recommended. Portfolio recommended for art applicants. Deferred and early admission available.

STUDENT LIFE. Housing: Dormitories (men, women, coed). **Activities:** Student government, magazine, student newspaper, television, yearbook, choral groups, concert band, dance, drama, music ensembles, fraternities, sororities, Circle-K, campus ministry, student leadership coalition.

ATHLETICS. NCAA. **Intercollegiate:** Baseball M, basketball, cross-country, soccer M, softball W, tennis, volleyball W. **Intramural:** Archery, basketball, golf, racquetball, soccer, softball, swimming, tennis, volleyball.

STUDENT SERVICES. Aptitude testing, career counseling, employment service for undergraduates, freshman orientation, health services, personal counseling, placement service for graduates, special adviser for adult students, veterans counselor, services/facilities for handicapped.

ANNUAL EXPENSES. Tuition and fees: $9,370. **Room and board:** $4,200. **Books and supplies:** $500. **Other expenses:** $640.

FINANCIAL AID. 75% of freshmen, 75% of continuing students receive some form of aid. 47% of grants, 82% of loans, 17% of jobs based on need. Academic, music/drama, art, athletic scholarships available. **Aid applications:** No closing date; priority given to applications received by March 1; applicants notified on a rolling basis beginning on or about May 1; must reply within 2 weeks.

ADDRESS/TELEPHONE. Bonnie L. Black, Director of Admissions, St. Leo College, PO Box 2008, St. Leo, FL 33574-2008. (904) 588-8283. (800) 247-6559. Fax: (904) 588-8350.

St. Petersburg Junior College
St. Petersburg, Florida — CB code: 5606

2-year public community college, coed. Founded in 1927. **Accreditation:** Regional. **Undergraduate enrollment:** 2,834 men, 3,460 women full time; 6,286 men, 10,908 women part time. **Faculty:** 1,007 total (307 full time), 69 with doctorates or other terminal degrees. **Location:** Suburban campus in small city; 20 miles from Tampa. **Calendar:** Semester, extensive summer session. **Microcomputers:** 950 located in libraries, classrooms, computer centers, campus-wide network. **Special facilities:** Observatory, planetarium, art galleries, DiMaggio Baseball Complex in Clearwater, firing range. **Additional facts:** Campuses in Clearwater, St. Petersburg, and Tarpon Springs; health education center in Pinellas Park; criminal justice/computer complex at Allstate Center in St. Petersburg; Corporate Training Center at Carillon.

DEGREES OFFERED. AA, AS. 2,500 associate degrees awarded in 1992. 7% in business and management, 5% business/office and marketing/distribution, 18% health sciences, 40% allied health.

UNDERGRADUATE MAJORS. Accounting, airline piloting and navigation, architectural technologies, architecture, aviation management, business administration and management, business and office, business data programming, computer programming, construction, criminal justice technology, dental hygiene, early childhood education, electronic technology, emergency medical technologies, fashion merchandising, finance, fire control and safety technology, funeral services/mortuary science, graphic design, health care administration, interior design, legal assistant/paralegal, legal secretary, manufacturing technology, marketing management, medical laboratory technologies, medical records technology, mental health/human services, nursing, office supervision and management, ophthalmic services, physical therapy assistant, radiograph medical technology, respiratory therapy, respiratory therapy technology, systems analysis, veterinarian's assistant, water and wastewater technology.

ACADEMIC PROGRAMS. 2-year transfer program, accelerated program, dual enrollment of high school students, honors program, independent study, internships, telecourses, visiting/exchange student program, weekend college, cross-registration, 3-year program in business and computer science for deaf students, BS program in electrical engrineering with University of South Florida. **Remedial services:** Learning center, reduced course load, remedial instruction, special counselor, tutoring. **ROTC:** Air Force, Army. **Placement/credit:** AP, CLEP General and Subject, institutional tests; 45 credit hours maximum for associate degree.

ACADEMIC REQUIREMENTS. Freshmen must earn minimum GPA of 2.0 to continue in good standing. 55% of freshmen return for sophomore year. Students must declare major on enrollment. **Graduation requirements:** 64 hours for associate. Most students required to take courses in computer science, English, humanities, mathematics, biological/physical sciences, social sciences.

FRESHMAN ADMISSIONS. Selection criteria: Open admissions. Selective admissions to 9 limited enrollment health-related programs. **Test requirements:** Florida MAPS required of all applicants.

1992 FRESHMAN CLASS PROFILE. 1,406 men, 2,034 women enrolled. **Characteristics:** 99% from in state, 100% commute, 12% have minority backgrounds, 1% are foreign students. Average age is 19.

FALL-TERM APPLICATIONS. $20 fee, may be waived for applicants with need. Closing date August 22; applicants notified on a rolling basis. Interview recommended for allied health applicants. Early admission available.

STUDENT LIFE. Activities: Student government, magazine, student newspaper, television, choral groups, concert band, dance, drama, jazz band, music ensembles, symphony orchestra, Circle-K, Phi Theta Kappa.

ATHLETICS. NJCAA. **Intercollegiate:** Baseball M, basketball, golf, softball W, swimming, volleyball W. **Intramural:** Badminton, basketball, bowling, golf, racquetball, skin diving, soccer, softball, swimming, table tennis, tennis, track and field, volleyball, water polo M.

STUDENT SERVICES. Aptitude testing, career counseling, employment service for undergraduates, freshman orientation, health services, personal counseling, placement service for graduates, veterans counselor, services/facilities for handicapped.

ANNUAL EXPENSES. Tuition and fees (1992-93): $1,001, $2,677 additional for out-of-state students. **Books and supplies:** $500. **Other expenses:** $915.

FINANCIAL AID. 60% of freshmen, 60% of continuing students receive some form of aid. 91% of grants, 67% of loans, 61% of jobs based on need. Academic, music/drama, art, athletic, minority scholarships available. **Aid applications:** No closing date; priority given to applications received by April 15; applicants notified on a rolling basis; must reply within 2 weeks.

ADDRESS/TELEPHONE. Dr. Naomi B. Williams, Director of Admissions/Registrar, St. Petersburg Junior College, PO Box 13489, St. Petersburg, FL 33733. (813) 341-3600.

St. Thomas University
Miami, Florida — CB code: 5076

4-year private university, coed, affiliated with Roman Catholic Church. Founded in 1962. **Accreditation:** Regional. **Undergraduate enrollment:** 525 men, 648 women full time; 166 men, 313 women part time. **Graduate enrollment:** 541 men, 479 women full time. **Faculty:** 166 total (101 full time), 78 with doctorates or other terminal degrees. **Location:** Suburban campus in large city; 10 miles from downtown. **Calendar:** Semester, limited summer session. **Microcomputers:** 25 located in computer centers. **Additional facts:** Multilocation institution. Affiliated with archdiocese of Miami.

DEGREES OFFERED. BA, MA, MS, MBA, JD. 288 bachelor's degrees awarded in 1992. 43% in business and management, 11% communications, 13% teacher education, 8% parks/recreation, protective services, public affairs, 8% psychology. Graduate degrees offered in 10 major fields of study.

UNDERGRADUATE MAJORS. Accounting, biology, business administration and management, business and management, chemistry, communications, computer and information sciences, criminal justice studies, elementary education, English, English education, finance, history, hotel/motel and restaurant management, human resources development, information sciences and systems, international business management, international relations, liberal/general studies, marketing management, mathematics, political science and government, psychology, public administration, religion, secondary education, social studies education, sociology, Spanish, sports management, tourism.

ACADEMIC PROGRAMS. Double major, dual enrollment of high school students, education specialist degree, honors program, independent study, internships, study abroad, teacher preparation. **Remedial services:** Learning center, preadmission summer program, reduced course load, remedial instruction, special counselor, tutoring. **ROTC:** Air Force. **Placement/credit:** AP, CLEP General and Subject, IB, institutional tests; 45 credit hours maximum for bachelor's degree.

ACADEMIC REQUIREMENTS. Freshmen must earn minimum GPA of 2.0 to continue in good standing. 70% of freshmen return for sophomore year. Students must declare major by end of second year. **Graduation requirements:** 120 hours for bachelor's. Most students required to take courses in English, history, humanities, mathematics, philosophy/religion, biological/physical sciences, social sciences.

FRESHMAN ADMISSIONS. Selection criteria: High school grades and class rank primary factors. Test scores, interview, school and community activities, and recommendations also considered. **High school preparation:** 16 units required. Required units include biological science 1, English 4, mathematics 3, physical science 1 and social science 2. **Test requirements:** SAT or ACT; score report by August 15.

1992 FRESHMAN CLASS PROFILE. 167 men, 223 women enrolled. 25% had high school GPA of 3.0 or higher, 70% between 2.0 and 2.99. **Characteristics:** 63% from in state, 52% commute, 65% have minority backgrounds, 1% are foreign students, 1% join fraternities/sororities. Average age is 19.

FALL-TERM APPLICATIONS. $30 fee, may be waived for applicants with need. No closing date; priority given to applications received by May 1; applicants notified on a rolling basis; must reply within 4 weeks. Interview recommended. Essay recommended. CRDA. Deferred and early admission available. EDP-F. Applicants needing on-campus housing are strongly encouraged to apply before May 15.

STUDENT LIFE. Housing: Dormitories (men, women, coed). **Activities:** Student government, magazine, student newspaper, television, yearbook, choral groups, liturgical music group, fraternities, sororities, Respect Life, international student organization, political action club, Students for Global Preservation, Circle-K, science fiction club, Best Buddies, prelaw society, premedicine club.

ATHLETICS. NAIA. **Intercollegiate:** Baseball M, basketball M, golf M, lacrosse M, soccer, softball W, tennis W. **Intramural:** Basketball, football M, golf, lacrosse M, racquetball, softball, table tennis, tennis, volleyball.

STUDENT SERVICES. Aptitude testing, career counseling, employment service for undergraduates, freshman orientation, health services, personal counseling, placement service for graduates, special adviser for adult students, services/facilities for handicapped.

ANNUAL EXPENSES. Tuition and fees (1992-93): $8,900. **Room and board:** $4,300. **Books and supplies:** $550. **Other expenses:** $2,000.

FINANCIAL AID. 81% of freshmen, 73% of continuing students receive some form of aid. Grants, loans, jobs available. **Aid applications:** No closing date; priority given to applications received by May 1; applicants notified on a rolling basis beginning on or about April 15; must reply by May 1 or within 3 weeks if notified thereafter. **Additional information:** Deadline for financial aid applications for state residents April 15.

ADDRESS/TELEPHONE. John M. Letvinchuk, Director of Admissions, St. Thomas University, 16400 Northwest 32nd Avenue, Miami, FL 33054. (305) 628-6546. (800) 367-9010. Fax: (305) 628-6510.

Santa Fe Community College
Gainesville, Florida — CB code: 5653

2-year public community college, coed. Founded in 1965. **Accreditation:** Regional. **Undergraduate enrollment:** 2,941 men, 3,038 women full time; 2,667 men, 3,584 women part time. **Faculty:** 587 total (306 full time), 40 with doctorates or other terminal degrees. **Location:** Suburban campus in small city; 80 miles from Jacksonville. **Calendar:** Semester, extensive summer session. Saturday classes. **Microcomputers:** Located in libraries, computer centers. **Special facilities:** Teaching zoo, art gallery. **Additional facts:** Branch campuses located downtown, at airport, and in Starke.

DEGREES OFFERED. AA, AS. 1,400 associate degrees awarded in 1992.

UNDERGRADUATE MAJORS. Accounting, air pollution control technology, automotive technology, business administration and management, business and management, business and office, business data processing and related programs, child development/care/guidance, clothing and textiles management/production/services, computer programming, construction, criminal justjce technology, data processing, dental hygiene, drafting, drafting and design technology, early childhood education, electrodiagnostic technologies, electronic technology, emergency medical technologies, English, environmental science technology, fashion design, fashion merchandising, finance, fire control and safety technology, graphic design, legal assistant/paralegal, legal secretary, liberal/general studies, marketing and distribution, marketing management, medical radiation dosimetry, medical secretary, nuclear medical technology, nursing, ornamental horticulture, parks and recreation management, predentistry, premedicine, prepharmacy, radiograph medical technology, respiratory therapy technology, secretarial and related programs.

ACADEMIC PROGRAMS. 2-year transfer program, computer delivered (on-line) credit-bearing course offerings, cooperative education, dual enrollment of high school students, honors program, independent study, telecourses, cross-registration. **Remedial services:** Learning center, remedial instruction, tutoring. **ROTC:** Air Force, Army, Naval. **Placement/credit:** AP, CLEP General and Subject, institutional tests; 48 credit hours maximum for associate degree.

ACADEMIC REQUIREMENTS. Freshmen must earn minimum GPA

of 2.0 to continue in good standing. 69% of freshmen return for sophomore year. Students must declare major on application. **Graduation requirements:** 64 hours for associate. Most students required to take courses in English, history, humanities, mathematics, biological/physical sciences, social sciences.

FRESHMAN ADMISSIONS. Selection criteria: Open admissions. Nursing program requires five prerequisite courses; radiologic technology and dental hygiene applicants selected by admissions committee; radiation therapy students must have xray or nuclear medicine license and experience. High school diploma not required of applicants to vocational programs. **Test requirements:** SAT or ACT (ACT preferred) for placement and counseling only; score report by August 27. ASSETS, Florida MAPS, or CPT may be submitted in place of SAT or ACT.

1992 FRESHMAN CLASS PROFILE. 800 men, 909 women enrolled. **Characteristics:** 94% from in state, 100% commute, 22% have minority backgrounds, 4% are foreign students. Average age is 19.

FALL-TERM APPLICATIONS. $20 fee. Closing date August 25; priority given to applications received by July 1; applicants notified on a rolling basis. Early admission available.

STUDENT LIFE. Activities: Student government, radio, student newspaper, television, choral groups, dance, drama, music ensembles, musical theater, Black Student Union, Phi Theta Kappa.

ATHLETICS. NJCAA. **Intercollegiate:** Baseball M, basketball, softball W. **Intramural:** Bowling, racquetball.

STUDENT SERVICES. Aptitude testing, career counseling, employment service for undergraduates, freshman orientation, health services, on-campus day care, personal counseling, placement service for graduates, veterans counselor, services/facilities for handicapped.

ANNUAL EXPENSES. Tuition and fees (projected): $990, $2,835 additional for out-of-state students. **Books and supplies:** $690. **Other expenses:** $800.

FINANCIAL AID. 55% of freshmen, 60% of continuing students receive some form of aid. 94% of grants, 80% of loans, 37% of jobs based on need. Academic, music/drama, art, athletic, minority scholarships available. **Aid applications:** Closing date April 1; priority given to applications received by March 1; applicants notified on a rolling basis beginning on or about April 15; must reply within 2 weeks.

ADDRESS/TELEPHONE. Office of Admissions, Santa Fe Community College, PO Box 1530, 3000 NW 83rd Street, Gainesville, FL 32602. (904) 395-5443. Fax: (904) 395-5581.

Schiller International University
Dunedin, Florida

CB code: 0601

4-year proprietary university, coed. Founded in 1964. **Undergraduate enrollment:** 714 men, 476 women full time; 54 men, 36 women part time. **Graduate enrollment:** 176 men, 117 women full time; 13 men, 9 women part time. **Faculty:** 286 total (76 full time), 69 with doctorates or other terminal degrees. **Calendar:** Semester, extensive summer session. **Microcomputers:** Located in computer centers. **Additional facts:** Students from more than 100 nations enrolled on 10 campuses in 6 countries can transfer without loss of credit.

DEGREES OFFERED. AA, AS, AAS, BA, BS, MA, MBA. 120 associate degrees awarded in 1992. 82% in business and management, 15% social sciences. 300 bachelor's degrees awarded. 85% in business and management, 12% social sciences. Graduate degrees offered in 2 major fields of study.

UNDERGRADUATE MAJORS. Associate: Business administration and management, business and management, commercial art, finance, hotel/motel and restaurant management, international business management, legal assistant/paralegal, liberal/general studies, preengineering, premedicine, preveterinary, tourism. **Bachelor's:** Business administration and management, business and management, computer and information sciences, engineering management, European studies, finance, French, geography, German, hotel/motel and restaurant management, humanities and social sciences, international business management, international hotel and tourism management, international relations, international studies, international tourism management, legal assistant/paralegal, liberal/general studies, marketing and distribution, psychology, public administration, tourism.

ACADEMIC PROGRAMS. 2-year transfer program, double major, independent study, internships, study abroad, visiting/exchange student program. **Placement/credit:** AP, CLEP Subject, institutional tests; 16 credit hours maximum for associate degree; 16 credit hours maximum for bachelor's degree.

ACADEMIC REQUIREMENTS. Freshmen must earn minimum GPA of 2.0 to continue in good standing. Students who do not complete 60% of their courses are placed on probation. Students must declare major by end of second year. **Graduation requirements:** 62 hours for associate (15 in major), 124 hours for bachelor's (45 in major). Most students required to take courses in English, foreign languages, history, mathematics, biological/physical sciences, social sciences. **Additional information:** Completion of the intermediate level of at least one foreign language is required in most undergraduate degree programs.

FRESHMAN ADMISSIONS. Selection criteria: Open admissions.

1992 FRESHMAN CLASS PROFILE. 408 men and women enrolled. **Characteristics:** 80% are foreign students. Average age is 18.

FALL-TERM APPLICATIONS. $30 fee. No closing date; applicants notified on a rolling basis; must reply by registration. Deferred admission available.

STUDENT LIFE. Housing: Dormitories (men, women); apartment housing available. **Activities:** Student government, student newspaper, yearbook.

ATHLETICS. Intramural: Tennis.

STUDENT SERVICES. Career counseling, freshman orientation, personal counseling.

ANNUAL EXPENSES. Tuition and fees: $10,740. **Room and board:** $2,800. **Books and supplies:** $350. **Other expenses:** $2,527.

FINANCIAL AID. 35% of freshmen receive some form of aid. 54% of grants, 68% of loans, all jobs based on need. Academic scholarships available. **Aid applications:** No closing date; priority given to applications received by March 30; applicants notified on a rolling basis beginning on or about May 1; must reply within 3 weeks. **Additional information:** Special Scholarship program for U.S. College students studying abroad at European campuses.

ADDRESS/TELEPHONE. Christoper Leibrecht, Director of Admissions, Schiller International University, 453 Edgewater Drive, Dunedin, FL 34698-4964. (813) 736-5082. (800) 336-4133. Fax: (813) 736-6263.

Seminole Community College
Sanford, Florida

CB code: 5662

2-year public community college, coed. Founded in 1965. **Accreditation:** Regional. **Undergraduate enrollment:** 1,539 men, 1,501 women full time; 2,110 men, 3,252 women part time. **Faculty:** 547 total (144 full time), 73 with doctorates or other terminal degrees. **Location:** Suburban campus in large town; 21 miles from Orlando. **Calendar:** Semester, limited summer session. **Microcomputers:** Located in computer centers.

DEGREES OFFERED. AA, AS. 823 associate degrees awarded in 1992.

UNDERGRADUATE MAJORS. Architectural technologies, automotive mechanics, automotive technology, business data processing and related programs, child development/care/guidance, computer programming, computer technology, construction, criminal justice technology, drafting and design technology, education, electronic technology, emergency medical technologies, finance, fire control and safety technology, home furnishings and equipment management/production/services, information sciences and systems, legal assistant/paralegal, liberal/general studies, manufacturing technology, marketing management, microcomputer software, nursing, physical therapy assistant, respiratory therapy technology, word processing.

ACADEMIC PROGRAMS. 2-year transfer program, accelerated program, cooperative education, dual enrollment of high school students, honors program, independent study, study abroad, telecourses, cross-registration. **Remedial services:** Learning center, reduced course load, remedial instruction, special counselor, tutoring. **ROTC:** Army. **Placement/credit:** AP, CLEP General and Subject, institutional tests; 45 credit hours maximum for associate degree.

ACADEMIC REQUIREMENTS. Freshmen must earn minimum GPA of 2.0 to continue in good standing. 60% of freshmen return for sophomore year. Students must declare major on enrollment. **Graduation requirements:** 64 hours for associate. Most students required to take courses in English, humanities, mathematics, social sciences.

FRESHMAN ADMISSIONS. Selection criteria: Open admissions. **High school preparation:** 13 units required. Required and recommended units include English 4, mathematics 3, social science 3 and science 3. Foreign language 2 recommended. **Test requirements:** SAT or ACT (ACT preferred) for placement; score report by August 15. TSWE required if SAT scores submitted.

1992 FRESHMAN CLASS PROFILE. 2,269 men, 2,723 women enrolled. **Characteristics:** 95% from in state, 100% commute, 15% have minority backgrounds, 1% are foreign students. Average age is 19.

FALL-TERM APPLICATIONS. $25 fee, may be waived for applicants with need. No closing date; priority given to applications received by August 1; applicants notified on a rolling basis beginning on or about February 1. Interview recommended for RT program, RN program, international, PT program applicants. Deferred and early admission available.

STUDENT LIFE. Activities: Student government, magazine, choral groups, concert band, drama, jazz band, music ensembles, musical theater, symphony orchestra.

ATHLETICS. NJCAA. **Intercollegiate:** Baseball M, basketball, softball W. **Intramural:** Basketball M, softball, tennis, volleyball.

STUDENT SERVICES. Aptitude testing, career counseling, employment service for undergraduates, freshman orientation, personal counseling, placement service for graduates, veterans counselor, services/facilities for handicapped.

ANNUAL EXPENSES. Tuition and fees (1992-93): $996, $2,580 additional for out-of-state students. **Books and supplies:** $500. **Other expenses:** $918.

FINANCIAL AID. 51% of grants, 64% of loans, 39% of jobs based on need. Academic, music/drama, art, athletic, minority scholarships available. **Aid applications:** No closing date; priority given to applications received by May 1; applicants notified on a rolling basis beginning on or about July 1; must reply within 2 weeks.

ADDRESS/TELEPHONE. Joseph A. Roof, Dean of Admissions and Records Systems, Seminole Community College, 100 Weldon Boulevard, Sanford, FL 32773-6199. (407) 323-1450. Fax: (407) 644-7822.

South College: Palm Beach Campus
West Palm Beach, Florida CB code: 5321

Admissions: 79% of applicants accepted
Based on: ••• Test scores
•• Interview, school record
• Essay
Completion: 98% of freshmen end year in good standing
75% go on to graduate

2-year proprietary junior college, coed. **Undergraduate enrollment:** 350 men and women. **Faculty:** 26 total (6 full time), 20 with doctorates or other terminal degrees. **Location:** Urban campus in small city; 3 miles from downtown. **Calendar:** Quarter, extensive summer session. **Microcomputers:** 12 located in classrooms.

DEGREES OFFERED. AS. 74 associate degrees awarded in 1992. 45% in business and management, 45% computer sciences, 10% allied health.

UNDERGRADUATE MAJORS. Accounting, business administration and management, computer and information sciences, legal assistant/paralegal, medical assistant, office supervision and management.

ACADEMIC PROGRAMS. Double major, dual enrollment of high school students, internships. **Remedial services:** Remedial instruction, tutoring, peer tutoring. **Placement/credit:** Institutional tests.

ACADEMIC REQUIREMENTS. Freshmen must earn minimum GPA of 2.0 to continue in good standing. 75% of freshmen return for sophomore year. Students must declare major on enrollment. **Graduation requirements:** 100 hours for associate (45 in major). Most students required to take courses in computer science, English, mathematics, social sciences.

FRESHMAN ADMISSIONS. Selection criteria: Applicants must achieve satisfactory score on college-administered entrance examination or submit combined score of 550 on SAT or 9 on ACT. Paralegal program requires a higher score on entrance examination and combined score of 750 on SAT or 19 on ACT.

1992 FRESHMAN CLASS PROFILE. 140 men and women applied, 110 accepted; 102 enrolled. **Characteristics:** 100% commute. Average age is 27.

FALL-TERM APPLICATIONS. $25 fee. No closing date; priority given to applications received by October 3; applicants notified on a rolling basis. Interview required.

STUDENT LIFE. Activities: Student government, student newspaper.

STUDENT SERVICES. Employment service for undergraduates, freshman orientation, personal counseling, placement service for graduates, special adviser for adult students, services/facilities for handicapped.

ANNUAL EXPENSES. Tuition and fees (1992-93): $4,525. **Books and supplies:** $650.

FINANCIAL AID. 97% of freshmen, 97% of continuing students receive some form of aid. 99% of grants, 89% of loans, all jobs based on need. **Aid applications:** No closing date.

ADDRESS/TELEPHONE. Dean of Academic Affairs, South College: Palm Beach Campus, 1760 North Congress Avenue, West Palm Beach, FL 33409. (407) 697-9200.

South Florida Community College
Avon Park, Florida CB code: 5666

2-year public community, junior, technical college, coed. Founded in 1965. **Accreditation:** Regional. **Undergraduate enrollment:** 472 men, 474 women full time; 629 men, 1,032 women part time. **Faculty:** 237 total (46 full time), 19 with doctorates or other terminal degrees. **Location:** Rural campus in small town; 90 miles from Orlando. **Calendar:** Semester, limited summer session. Extensive evening/early morning classes. **Microcomputers:** 178 located in libraries, classrooms, computer centers. **Special facilities:** Fully operational hotel and restaurant/conference center used as laboratory for hospitality and culinary programs.

DEGREES OFFERED. AA, AS. 169 associate degrees awarded in 1992. 8% in business/office and marketing/distribution, 39% health sciences, 12% home economics, 24% parks/recreation, protective services, public affairs, 7% trade and industry.

UNDERGRADUATE MAJORS. Accounting, agricultural sciences, biology, business administration and management, business and management, business and office, construction, criminal justice technology, data processing, drafting, drafting and design technology, electronic technology, finance, food management, historic preservation, hotel/motel and restaurant management, legal assistant/paralegal, legal secretary, marketing management, nursing, office supervision and management, physical sciences, psychology, secretarial and related programs, social sciences, teacher aide, trade and industrial supervision and management.

ACADEMIC PROGRAMS. 2-year transfer program, accelerated program, cooperative education, dual enrollment of high school students, independent study, internships, telecourses. **Remedial services:** Learning center, remedial instruction, special counselor, tutoring. **Placement/credit:** AP, CLEP General and Subject, IB, institutional tests; 45 credit hours maximum for associate degree.

ACADEMIC REQUIREMENTS. Freshmen must earn minimum GPA of 2.0 to continue in good standing. Students must declare major on application. **Graduation requirements:** 64 hours for associate. Most students required to take courses in English, foreign languages, history, humanities, mathematics, biological/physical sciences, social sciences.

FRESHMAN ADMISSIONS. Selection criteria: Open admissions. **High school preparation:** 13 units required. Required units include English 4, mathematics 3, social science 3 and science 3. **Test requirements:** SAT or ACT for placement and counseling only; score report by September 1.

1992 FRESHMAN CLASS PROFILE. 151 men, 230 women enrolled. **Characteristics:** 95% from in state, 94% commute, 21% have minority backgrounds. Average age is 22.

FALL-TERM APPLICATIONS. No fee. No closing date; applicants notified on a rolling basis. Interview recommended. Early admission available.

STUDENT LIFE. Housing: Dormitories (coed). **Activities:** Student government, student newspaper, choral groups, drama, jazz band, music ensembles, musical theater.

ATHLETICS. NJCAA. **Intercollegiate:** Basketball M, volleyball W.

STUDENT SERVICES. Aptitude testing, career counseling, employment service for undergraduates, freshman orientation, personal counseling, placement service for graduates, veterans counselor, services/facilities for handicapped.

ANNUAL EXPENSES. Tuition and fees (projected): $1,035, $2,700 additional for out-of-state students. **Room and board:** $1,978. **Books and supplies:** $700. **Other expenses:** $1,000.

FINANCIAL AID. 30% of freshmen, 20% of continuing students receive some form of aid. 73% of grants, all loans, all jobs based on need. Academic, music/drama, athletic, state/district residency, minority scholarships available. **Aid applications:** No closing date; priority given to applications received by April 1; applicants notified on a rolling basis beginning on or about July 15; must reply within 2 weeks.

ADDRESS/TELEPHONE. William L. Rudy, Dean of Student Services, South Florida Community College, 600 West College Drive, Avon Park, FL 33825. (813) 453-6661 ext. 131. Fax: (813) 452-6042.

Southeastern College of the Assemblies of God
Lakeland, Florida CB code: 5621

4-year private Bible, teachers college, coed, affiliated with Assemblies of God. Founded in 1935. **Accreditation:** Regional. **Undergraduate enrollment:** 564 men, 545 women full time; 50 men, 50 women part time. **Faculty:** 80 total (51 full time), 31 with doctorates or other terminal degrees. **Location:** Suburban campus in small city; 30 miles from Tampa, 45 miles from Orlando. **Calendar:** Semester, limited summer session. Extensive evening/early morning classes. **Microcomputers:** 24 located in computer centers. **Special facilities:** Audio and video communications studio.

DEGREES OFFERED. BA. 172 bachelor's degrees awarded in 1992. 40% in teacher education, 50% philosophy, religion, theology, 10% psychology.

UNDERGRADUATE MAJORS. Bible studies, communications, early childhood education, elementary education, English education, mathematics education, missionary studies, music education, psychology, religious education, religious music, science education, secondary education, social science education, social studies education, theological studies.

ACADEMIC PROGRAMS. Double major, dual enrollment of high school students, external degree, independent study. **Remedial services:** Remedial instruction, special counselor, tutoring, writing center. **ROTC:** Army. **Placement/credit:** AP, CLEP General and Subject; 30 credit hours maximum for bachelor's degree.

ACADEMIC REQUIREMENTS. Freshmen must earn minimum GPA of 2.0 to continue in good standing. 65% of freshmen return for sophomore year. Students must declare major on enrollment. **Graduation requirements:** 130 hours for bachelor's. Most students required to take courses in arts/fine arts, English, humanities, mathematics, philosophy/religion, biological/physical sciences, social sciences.

FRESHMAN ADMISSIONS. Selection criteria: Christian character important. **Test requirements:** SAT or ACT; score report by September 1.

1992 FRESHMAN CLASS PROFILE. 280 men and women enrolled. **Characteristics:** 95% live in college housing. Average age is 18.

FALL-TERM APPLICATIONS. $35 fee. No closing date; applicants notified on a rolling basis. Interview required for academically weak applicants. Essay required. Deferred and early admission available.

STUDENT LIFE. Housing: Dormitories (men, women); apartment housing available. **Activities:** Student government, student newspaper, yearbook, weekly news release, choral groups, concert band, drama, music ensembles. **Additional information:** Religious observance required.

ATHLETICS. Intercollegiate: Basketball, soccer M, volleyball W. **Intramural:** Baseball M, basketball, volleyball.

STUDENT SERVICES. Freshman orientation, personal counseling, placement service for graduates, services/facilities for handicapped.

ANNUAL EXPENSES. Tuition and fees (1992-93): $3,600. **Room and board:** $2,860. **Books and supplies:** $600.

FINANCIAL AID. 76% of continuing students receive some form of aid. 89% of grants, 82% of loans, 51% of jobs based on need. 162 enrolled freshmen were judged to have need, all were offered aid. Academic, music/drama, state/district residency, leadership, religious affiliation, minority scholarships available. **Aid applications:** No closing date; priority given to applications received by April 1; applicants notified on a rolling basis beginning on or about May 1; must reply within 3 weeks.

ADDRESS/TELEPHONE. Rev. Royce M. Shelton, Director of Admissions and Records, Southeastern College of the Assemblies of God, 1000 Longfellow Boulevard, Lakeland, FL 33801. (813) 665-4404 ext. 210. Fax: (813) 666-8103.

Southern College
Orlando, Florida — CB code: 5323

2-year proprietary junior college, coed. Founded in 1968. **Undergraduate enrollment:** 124 men, 402 women full time; 64 men, 194 women part time. **Faculty:** 57 total (13 full time), 13 with doctorates or other terminal degrees. **Location:** Urban campus in very large city; 5 miles from center of city. **Calendar:** Quarter, extensive summer session. Saturday and extensive evening/early morning classes. **Microcomputers:** 45 located in libraries, computer centers.

DEGREES OFFERED. AS. 160 associate degrees awarded in 1992. 12% in architecture and environmental design, 13% business and management, 13% business/office and marketing/distribution, 13% computer sciences, 12% engineering technologies, 12% health sciences, 13% allied health, 12% law.

UNDERGRADUATE MAJORS. Business and management, computer programming, dental laboratory technology, dental specialties, electronic technology, interior design, legal assistant/paralegal, microcomputer software, secretarial and related programs.

ACADEMIC PROGRAMS. Independent study, internships. **Remedial services:** Remedial instruction, tutoring. **Placement/credit:** CLEP General and Subject, institutional tests; 50 credit hours maximum for associate degree.

ACADEMIC REQUIREMENTS. Freshmen must earn minimum GPA of 2.0 to continue in good standing. Students must declare major on application. **Graduation requirements:** 101 hours for associate (50 in major). Most students required to take courses in computer science, English, humanities, mathematics, social sciences.

FRESHMAN ADMISSIONS. Selection criteria: Open admissions. **Test requirements:** SAT or ACT for placement; score report by January 5. **Additional information:** If no SAT or ACT scores, students may take TABE exam on campus.

1992 FRESHMAN CLASS PROFILE. 70 men, 210 women enrolled. **Characteristics:** 100% commute, 23% have minority backgrounds. Average age is 33.

FALL-TERM APPLICATIONS. $30 fee. Closing date October 1; priority given to applications received by August 1; applicants notified on a rolling basis. Interview required.

STUDENT LIFE. Activities: Student government, student newspaper.

ATHLETICS. Intramural: Softball.

STUDENT SERVICES. Aptitude testing, career counseling, employment service for undergraduates, freshman orientation, on-campus day care, personal counseling, placement service for graduates, veterans counselor, services/facilities for handicapped.

ANNUAL EXPENSES. Tuition and fees: $4,722. **Books and supplies:** $565. **Other expenses:** $210.

FINANCIAL AID. 87% of freshmen, 89% of continuing students receive some form of aid. All grants, 74% of loans, all jobs based on need. 282 enrolled freshmen were judged to have need, all were offered aid. **Aid applications:** No closing date; applicants notified on a rolling basis.

ADDRESS/TELEPHONE. Stephanie Rizzo, Director of Admissions, Southern College, 5600 Lake Underhill Road, Orlando, FL 32807. (407) 273-1000.

Stetson University
DeLand, Florida — CB code: 5630

Admissions: 82% of applicants accepted
Based on:
- ••• School record
- •• Activities, essay, recommendations, special talents, test scores
- • Interview, religious affiliation/commitment

Completion: 77% of freshmen end year in good standing
60% graduate, 31% of these enter graduate study

4-year private university, coed, affiliated with Baptist Church. Founded in 1883. **Accreditation:** Regional. **Undergraduate enrollment:** 888 men, 1,142 women full time; 33 men, 41 women part time. **Graduate enrollment:** 367 men, 371 women full time; 74 men, 153 women part time. **Faculty:** 276 total (181 full time), 162 with doctorates or other terminal degrees. **Location:** Suburban campus in large town; 20 miles from Daytona Beach, 35 miles from Orlando. **Calendar:** 4-1-4, limited summer session. **Microcomputers:** 175 located in libraries, classrooms, computer centers. **Special facilities:** Geological museum, art gallery, greenhouse with growth chambers. **Additional facts:** Law school located in St. Petersburg.

DEGREES OFFERED. BA, BS, MA, MS, MBA, MEd, JD. 430 bachelor's degrees awarded in 1992. 42% in business and management, 9% education, 7% letters/literature, 8% psychology, 14% social sciences, 7% visual and performing arts. Graduate degrees offered in 17 major fields of study.

UNDERGRADUATE MAJORS. Accounting, American studies, art education, art history, biological and physical sciences, biology, business administration and management, business and management, chemistry, clinical laboratory science, communications, computer and information sciences, dramatic arts, economics, education, elementary education, English, English education, finance, fine arts, foreign languages (multiple emphasis), foreign languages education, forestry and related sciences, French, geography, German, history, humanities, junior high education, management science, marketing management, mathematics, mathematics education, music, music education, music history and appreciation, music performance, music theory and composition, musical theater, philosophy, physical education, physics, political science and government, predentistry, prelaw, premedicine, prepharmacy, preveterinary, psychology, religion, religious music, Russian and Slavic studies, science education, secondary education, social science education, social sciences, sociology, Spanish, speech, speech/communication/theater education, urban studies.

ACADEMIC PROGRAMS. Accelerated program, double major, dual enrollment of high school students, education specialist degree, honors program, independent study, internships, student-designed major, study abroad, teacher preparation, visiting/exchange student program, New York semester, United Nations semester, Washington semester; liberal arts/career combination in engineering, forestry, health sciences. **Remedial services:** Learning center, preadmission summer program, tutoring. **ROTC:** Army. **Placement/credit:** AP, CLEP General and Subject, institutional tests; 64 credit hours maximum for bachelor's degree.

ACADEMIC REQUIREMENTS. Freshmen must earn minimum GPA of 2.0 to continue in good standing. 81% of freshmen return for sophomore year. Students must declare major by end of second year. **Graduation requirements:** 126 hours for bachelor's (30 in major). Most students required to take courses in computer science, English, foreign languages, humanities, mathematics, philosophy/religion, biological/physical sciences, social sciences. **Postgraduate studies:** 7% enter law school, 3% enter medical school, 9% enter MBA programs, 12% enter other graduate study.

FRESHMAN ADMISSIONS. Selection criteria: High school record most important, followed by class rank, standardized test scores, and secondary school's recommendation. Extracurricular activities and particular talents or abilities also important. **High school preparation:** 16 units required. Required units include English 4, foreign language 2, mathematics 3, social science 2 and science 2. **Test requirements:** SAT or ACT (SAT preferred); score report by March 1.

1992 FRESHMAN CLASS PROFILE. 1,630 men and women applied, 1,341 accepted; 221 men enrolled, 282 women enrolled. 74% had high school GPA of 3.0 or higher, 26% between 2.0 and 2.99. 35% were in top tenth and 65% were in top quarter of graduating class. **Academic background:** Mid 50% of enrolled freshmen had SAT-V between 420-540, SAT-M between 470-610; ACT composite between 21-27. 95% submitted SAT scores, 44% submitted ACT scores. **Characteristics:** 77% from in state, 92% live in college housing, 12% have minority backgrounds, 3% are foreign students, 33% join fraternities/sororities. Average age is 18.

FALL-TERM APPLICATIONS. $25 fee, may be waived for applicants with need. Closing date March 1; applicants notified on or about March 15; must reply by May 1. Audition required for music applicants. Essay required. Interview recommended. Portfolio recommended for art applicants. CRDA. Deferred and early admission available. EDP-F.

STUDENT LIFE. Housing: Dormitories (men, women, coed); fraternity, sorority housing available. **Activities:** Student government, magazine, radio, student newspaper, yearbook, choral groups, concert band, dance, drama, jazz band, music ensembles, musical theater, opera, pep band, symphony orchestra, fraternities, sororities, Catholic Campus Ministry, Baptist

Campus Ministry, Canterbury House, Wesley Foundation, Westminister Fellowship, Hillel, Young Democrats, Young Republicans, Amnesty International, NOW, Habitat for Humanity.

ATHLETICS. NCAA. **Intercollegiate:** Baseball M, basketball, cross-country, golf, soccer, softball W, tennis, volleyball W. **Intramural:** Badminton, basketball, racquetball, rowing (crew), soccer, softball, swimming, table tennis, tennis, volleyball.

STUDENT SERVICES. Aptitude testing, career counseling, employment service for undergraduates, freshman orientation, health services, on-campus day care, personal counseling, placement service for graduates, services/facilities for handicapped.

ANNUAL EXPENSES. Tuition and fees: $11,995. **Room and board:** $4,440. **Books and supplies:** $600. **Other expenses:** $825.

FINANCIAL AID. 80% of freshmen, 80% of continuing students receive some form of aid. 38% of grants, 91% of loans, 68% of jobs based on need. 276 enrolled freshmen were judged to have need, 274 were offered aid. Academic, music/drama, athletic, state/district residency, leadership, religious affiliation, minority scholarships available. **Aid applications:** No closing date; priority given to applications received by March 15; applicants notified on a rolling basis beginning on or about April 15; must reply by May 1 or within 15 days if notified thereafter.

ADDRESS/TELEPHONE. Linda Glover, Dean of Admissions, Stetson University, Campus Box 8378, DeLand, FL 32720. (904) 822-7100. (800) 688-0101. Fax: (904) 822-8832.

Tallahassee Community College
Tallahassee, Florida CB code: 5794

2-year public community college, coed. Founded in 1965. **Accreditation:** Regional. **Undergraduate enrollment:** 2,221 men, 2,175 women full time; 2,214 men, 3,097 women part time. **Faculty:** 381 total (141 full time), 42 with doctorates or other terminal degrees. **Location:** Suburban campus in small city; 230 miles from Tampa, 200 miles from Pensacola. **Calendar:** Semester, extensive summer session. Saturday and extensive evening/early morning classes. **Microcomputers:** Located in libraries, classrooms.

DEGREES OFFERED. AA, AS. 1,523 associate degrees awarded in 1992. 94% in multi/interdisciplinary studies.

UNDERGRADUATE MAJORS. Business and management, business and office, business data programming, civil technology, criminal justice studies, data processing, dental hygiene, emergency medical technologies, film arts, fire control and safety technology, landscape architecture, legal assistant/paralegal, liberal/general studies, nursing, ornamental horticulture, radiograph medical technology, respiratory therapy technology, secretarial and related programs, trade and industrial supervision and management.

ACADEMIC PROGRAMS. 2-year transfer program, dual enrollment of high school students, honors program, independent study, study abroad, telecourses, cross-registration. **Remedial services:** Learning center, remedial instruction, special counselor, tutoring. **ROTC:** Air Force, Army, Naval. **Placement/credit:** AP, CLEP General and Subject, IB, institutional tests; 45 credit hours maximum for associate degree.

ACADEMIC REQUIREMENTS. Freshmen must earn minimum GPA of 2.0 to continue in good standing. Students must declare major on application. **Graduation requirements:** 62 hours for associate (23 in major). Most students required to take courses in English, history, humanities, mathematics, biological/physical sciences, social sciences.

FRESHMAN ADMISSIONS. Selection criteria: Open admissions. Selective admissions to nursing, dental hygiene, emergency medical technology, and respiratory therapy programs. **High school preparation:** 13 units required. Required and recommended units include English 4, mathematics 3, social science 3 and science 3. Foreign language 2 recommended. **Test requirements:** National League for Nursing Pre-Nursing and Guidance Examination required of nursing applicants. Entrance examination for schools with health related technologies required of respiratory therapy applicants.

1992 FRESHMAN CLASS PROFILE. 2,686 men, 3,135 women enrolled. **Characteristics:** 95% from in state, 100% commute, 24% have minority backgrounds, 1% are foreign students.

FALL-TERM APPLICATIONS. $15 fee. Closing date July 19; applicants notified on a rolling basis. Early admission available. Separate application procedure for health programs.

STUDENT LIFE. Activities: Student government, magazine, student newspaper, choral groups, concert band, dance, drama, jazz band, marching band, music ensembles, Phi Theta Kappa, Black Student Union, Returning Adults Valuing Education, International Students Club, College Republicans, Baptist Campus Ministries, Alpha Phi Omega, Future Educators of America. Students Interested in Legal Careers, College Democrats.

ATHLETICS. NJCAA. **Intercollegiate:** Baseball M, basketball M, softball W. **Intramural:** Badminton, basketball, bowling, cross-country, diving, golf, racquetball, softball, swimming, table tennis, tennis, volleyball, water polo M.

STUDENT SERVICES. Aptitude testing, career counseling, freshman orientation, personal counseling, special adviser for adult students, veterans counselor, health services offered through Florida State University, services/facilities for handicapped.

ANNUAL EXPENSES. Tuition and fees (1992-93): $900, $2,475 additional for out-of-state students. **Books and supplies:** $500. **Other expenses:** $1,000.

FINANCIAL AID. 18% of freshmen, 17% of continuing students receive some form of aid. 96% of grants, 49% of loans, all jobs based on need. Academic, music/drama, state/district residency, leadership scholarships available. **Aid applications:** No closing date; priority given to applications received by June 1; applicants notified on a rolling basis beginning on or about May 15; must reply within 15 days.

ADDRESS/TELEPHONE. Mike Bussell, Registrar, Tallahassee Community College, 444 Appleyard Drive, Tallahassee, FL 32304-2895. (904) 922-8126. Fax: (904) 488-2203.

Talmudic College of Florida
Miami Beach, Florida CB code: 0514

5-year private rabbinical college, men only, affiliated with Jewish faith. Founded in 1974. **Undergraduate enrollment:** 70 men full time; 40 men part time. **Graduate enrollment:** 10 men full time. **Location:** Urban campus in small city. **Calendar:** Semester.

FRESHMAN ADMISSIONS. Selection criteria: Recommendations and personal interview most important.

ADDRESS/TELEPHONE. Office of Admissions, Talmudic College of Florida, 4014 Chase Avenue, Suite 217, Miami Beach, FL 33140. (305) 534-8444.

Tampa College
Tampa, Florida CB code: 0428

4-year proprietary business college, coed. Founded in 1890. **Undergraduate enrollment:** 1,269 men and women. **Faculty:** 50 total (8 full time). **Location:** Urban campus in large city. **Calendar:** Quarter, extensive summer session. **Microcomputers:** Located in computer centers.

DEGREES OFFERED. AS, BS, MBA. 170 associate degrees awarded in 1992. 150 bachelor's degrees awarded. Graduate degrees offered in 1 major field of study.

UNDERGRADUATE MAJORS. Associate: Accounting, business administration and management, business and management, computer and information sciences, computer programming, criminal justice studies, graphic design, information sciences and systems, legal assistant/paralegal, marketing management, medical assistant. **Bachelor's:** Accounting, business administration and management, business and management, computer and information sciences, computer programming, criminal justice studies, information sciences and systems, marketing management.

ACADEMIC PROGRAMS. Accelerated program, double major, independent study, internships. **Remedial services:** Tutoring. **Placement/credit:** AP, CLEP General and Subject, institutional tests.

ACADEMIC REQUIREMENTS. Freshmen must earn minimum GPA of 2.0 to continue in good standing. Students must declare major on application. **Graduation requirements:** 96 hours for associate, 192 hours for bachelor's. Most students required to take courses in computer science, English, mathematics, social sciences.

FRESHMAN ADMISSIONS. Selection criteria: CPAT, ACT, and SAT scores considered.

1992 FRESHMAN CLASS PROFILE. 485 men and women enrolled. **Characteristics:** 80% from in state, 100% commute, 17% have minority backgrounds, 10% are foreign students. Average age is 24.

FALL-TERM APPLICATIONS. $25 fee. No closing date; applicants notified on a rolling basis; must reply as soon as possible. Deferred and early admission available.

STUDENT LIFE. Activities: Student newspaper.

STUDENT SERVICES. Career counseling, employment service for undergraduates, freshman orientation, placement service for graduates, veterans counselor, services/facilities for handicapped.

ANNUAL EXPENSES. Tuition and fees: $5,225. Tuition includes book loans and laboratory fees (except for graduate students). **Other expenses:** $700.

FINANCIAL AID. 75% of freshmen, 80% of continuing students receive some form of aid. Grants, loans, jobs available. **Aid applications:** No closing date; applicants notified on a rolling basis.

ADDRESS/TELEPHONE. Cyndy Agle, Admissions Coordinator, Tampa College, 3319 West Hillsborough Avenue, Tampa, FL 33614. (813) 879-6000.

Trinity College at Miami
Miami, Florida CB code: 4598

4-year private liberal arts college, coed, affiliated with Evangelical Free Church of America. Founded in 1949. **Accreditation:** Regional. **Under-**

graduate enrollment: 121 men, 82 women full time; 32 men, 27 women part time. **Faculty:** 21 total (7 full time), 5 with doctorates or other terminal degrees. **Location:** Urban campus in very large city. **Calendar:** 4-4-1, limited summer session. **Microcomputers:** 10 located in libraries, computer centers. **Additional facts:** Branch school of Trinity College, Deerfield, Illinois.

DEGREES OFFERED. BA. 54 bachelor's degrees awarded in 1992.

UNDERGRADUATE MAJORS. Bible studies, business and management, communications, counseling psychology, elementary education, missionary studies, psychology, radio/television broadcasting, religious education, religious music, theological studies.

ACADEMIC PROGRAMS. 2-year transfer program, accelerated program, internships, study abroad, teacher preparation. **Remedial services:** Preadmission summer program, reduced course load, remedial instruction. **Placement/credit:** AP, CLEP General and Subject, institutional tests.

ACADEMIC REQUIREMENTS. Freshmen must earn minimum GPA of 1.5 to continue in good standing. 50% of freshmen return for sophomore year. Students must declare major by end of second year. **Graduation requirements:** 126 hours for bachelor's (39 in major). Most students required to take courses in arts/fine arts, English, history, humanities, mathematics, philosophy/religion, biological/physical sciences, social sciences. **Postgraduate studies:** 75% from 2-year programs enter 4-year programs. 1% enter law school, 1% enter MBA programs, 27% enter other graduate study.

FRESHMAN ADMISSIONS. Selection criteria: Applicants should be in top half of class. Personal references and statement of personal Christian faith important. Test scores also considered. **High school preparation:** 16 units required. Required units include biological science 1, English 4, mathematics 2, physical science 1 and social science 3. **Test requirements:** SAT or ACT (ACT preferred); score report by August 25.

1992 FRESHMAN CLASS PROFILE. 38 men and women enrolled. **Characteristics:** 90% from in state. Average age is 21.

FALL-TERM APPLICATIONS. $15 fee. No closing date; priority given to applications received by April 1; applicants notified on a rolling basis; must reply within 4 weeks. Essay required. Interview recommended. Deferred and early admission available.

STUDENT LIFE. Housing: Apartment housing available. **Activities:** Student government, radio, student newspaper, television, yearbook, choral groups, music ensembles, puppet team. **Additional information:** Religious observance required.

ATHLETICS. Intercollegiate: Baseball M, basketball, soccer M, volleyball W.

STUDENT SERVICES. Career counseling, employment service for undergraduates, freshman orientation, health services, personal counseling, placement service for graduates.

ANNUAL EXPENSES. Tuition and fees (1992-93): $6,170. **Room and board:** $3,080. **Books and supplies:** $700. **Other expenses:** $800.

FINANCIAL AID. 80% of freshmen, 78% of continuing students receive some form of aid. Grants, loans, jobs available. Academic, leadership, religious affiliation scholarships available. **Aid applications:** No closing date; priority given to applications received by April 1; applicants notified on a rolling basis beginning on or about July 1; must reply within 2 weeks.

ADDRESS/TELEPHONE. Liam Gillen, Associate Director Admission, Trinity College at Miami, PO Box 019674, 500 NE First Avenue, Miami, FL 33101-9674. (305) 577-4600 ext. 135. (800) 966-2024. Fax: (305) 577-4612.

University of Central Florida
Orlando, Florida — CB code: 5233

Admissions: 29% of applicants accepted
Based on: ••• School record, test scores
• Activities, essay, interview, recommendations, special talents
Completion: 85% of freshmen end year in good standing
39% graduate, 9% of these enter graduate study

4-year public university, coed. Founded in 1963. **Accreditation:** Regional. **Undergraduate enrollment:** 5,212 men, 5,744 women full time; 3,291 men, 3,437 women part time. **Graduate enrollment:** 327 men, 393 women full time; 1,561 men, 1,625 women part time. **Faculty:** 943 total (598 full time), 726 with doctorates or other terminal degrees. **Location:** Suburban campus in large city; 13 miles from downtown. **Calendar:** Semester, extensive summer session. Saturday classes. **Microcomputers:** 295 located in computer centers. **Special facilities:** Central Florida Research Park, Florida Solar Energy Center, Institute for Simulation and Training.

DEGREES OFFERED. AA, BA, BS, BFA, MA, MS, MBA, MEd, MSW, PhD, EdD. 217 associate degrees awarded in 1992. 3,783 bachelor's degrees awarded. 26% in business and management, 8% communications, 19% education, 8% engineering, 8% multi/interdisciplinary studies, 6% psychology. Graduate degrees offered in 48 major fields of study.

UNDERGRADUATE MAJORS. Associate: Liberal/general studies. **Bachelor's:** Accounting, aerospace/aeronautical/astronautical engineering, anthropology, art education, biology, botany, business and management, business economics, business education, chemistry, civil engineering, clinical laboratory science, communications, computer and information sciences, computer engineering, computer technology, criminal justice studies, drafting and design technology, dramatic arts, economics, electrical/electronics/communications engineering, electronic technology, elementary education, English, English education, environmental health engineering, finance, fine arts, foreign languages (multiple emphasis), foreign languages education, forensic studies, French, health care administration, history, hotel/motel and restaurant management, humanities, industrial engineering, information sciences and systems, journalism, legal assistant/paralegal, liberal/general studies, limnology, management science, marketing management, mathematics, mathematics education, mechanical engineering, medical records administration, microbiology, motion picture technology, music education, music performance, nursing, operations technology, philosophy, physical education, physical therapy, physics, political science and government, psychology, public administration, radio/television technology, radiograph medical technology, respiratory therapy, science education, social science education, social work, sociology, Spanish, special education, speech, speech pathology/audiology, statistics, trade and industrial education, visual and performing arts, zoology.

ACADEMIC PROGRAMS. Cooperative education, double major, dual enrollment of high school students, education specialist degree, honors program, independent study, internships, student-designed major, study abroad, teacher preparation, telecourses. **Remedial services:** Learning center, preadmission summer program, reduced course load, tutoring. **ROTC:** Air Force, Army. **Placement/credit:** AP, CLEP General and Subject, institutional tests; 45 credit hours maximum for bachelor's degree.

ACADEMIC REQUIREMENTS. Freshmen must earn minimum GPA of 2.0 to continue in good standing. 74% of freshmen return for sophomore year. Students must declare major on application. **Graduation requirements:** 60 hours for associate, 120 hours for bachelor's (48 in major). Most students required to take courses in English, foreign languages, history, humanities, mathematics, philosophy/religion, biological/physical sciences, social sciences.

FRESHMAN ADMISSIONS. Selection criteria: Priority given to students with minimum academic 3.0 GPA, ACT composite score of 22 or above or SAT combined score of 1000 or above. **High school preparation:** 19 units required. Required units include English 4, foreign language 2, mathematics 3, social science 3 and science 3. **Test requirements:** SAT or ACT; score report by May 15.

1992 FRESHMAN CLASS PROFILE. 6,755 men and women applied, 1,941 accepted; 675 men enrolled, 749 women enrolled. 73% had high school GPA of 3.0 or higher, 27% between 2.0 and 2.99. **Academic background:** Mid 50% of enrolled freshmen had SAT-V between 410-520, SAT-M between 480-600; ACT composite between 21-25. 71% submitted SAT scores, 29% submitted ACT scores. **Characteristics:** 90% from in state, 85% commute, 27% have minority backgrounds. Average age is 18.

FALL-TERM APPLICATIONS. $20 fee. Closing date March 15; applicants notified on a rolling basis. Deferred and early admission available. Institutional early decision plan.

STUDENT LIFE. Housing: Dormitories (men, women, coed); fraternity, sorority housing available. **Activities:** Student government, film, magazine, radio, student newspaper, television, yearbook, choral groups, concert band, dance, drama, jazz band, marching band, music ensembles, musical theater, pep band, symphony orchestra, fraternities, sororities, Campus Activities Board, African-American Student Union, International Student Association, Student Government Association, Orientation Team, Hispanic-American Student Association, Korean Student Association, Indian Student Association.

ATHLETICS. NCAA. **Intercollegiate:** Baseball M, basketball, cross-country, football M, golf, soccer, tennis, track and field, volleyball W. **Intramural:** Basketball, fencing, field hockey, golf, racquetball, rowing (crew), sailing, skiing, soccer, softball, volleyball.

STUDENT SERVICES. Aptitude testing, career counseling, employment service for undergraduates, freshman orientation, health services, on-campus day care, personal counseling, placement service for graduates, veterans counselor, services/facilities for handicapped.

ANNUAL EXPENSES. Tuition and fees (projected): $1,820, $5,000 additional for out-of-state students. **Room and board:** $4,990. **Books and supplies:** $660. **Other expenses:** $1,630.

FINANCIAL AID. 56% of grants, 94% of loans, 71% of jobs based on need. Academic, music/drama, art, athletic, state/district residency, leadership, alumni affiliation, religious affiliation, minority scholarships available. **Aid applications:** No closing date; priority given to applications received by March 15; applicants notified on a rolling basis beginning on or about May 1; must reply within 2 weeks.

ADDRESS/TELEPHONE. Jeanne Rutenkroger, Director of Admissions, University of Central Florida, PO Box 25000, 4000 Central Florida Boulevard, Orlando, FL 32816. (407) 823-3000.

University of Florida
Gainesville, Florida CB code: 5812

Admissions: 66% of applicants accepted
Based on: ••• School record, test scores
•• Special talents
• Activities, essay, interview, recommendations
Completion: 94% of freshmen end year in good standing
51% graduate

4-year public university, coed. Founded in 1853. **Accreditation:** Regional. **Undergraduate enrollment:** 12,535 men, 10,737 women full time; 1,893 men, 1,621 women part time. **Graduate enrollment:** 3,732 men, 2,693 women full time; 1,102 men, 795 women part time. **Faculty:** 3,865 total (3,630 full time), 3,648 with doctorates or other terminal degrees. **Location:** Suburban campus in small city; 75 miles from Jacksonville. **Calendar:** Semester, limited summer session. **Microcomputers:** 947 located in dormitories, libraries, classrooms, computer centers, campus-wide network. **Special facilities:** Natural history museum, astronomical research facility, marine laboratory, art gallery.

DEGREES OFFERED. AA, BA, BS, BFA, BArch, MA, MS, MBA, MFA, MEd, PhD, EdD, DMD, MD, B. Pharm, DVM, JD. 1,411 associate degrees awarded in 1992. 5,459 bachelor's degrees awarded. 20% in business and management, 12% communications, 5% education, 14% engineering, 6% health sciences, 5% letters/literature, 5% psychology, 12% social sciences. Graduate degrees offered in 120 major fields of study.

UNDERGRADUATE MAJORS. Associate: Liberal/general studies. **Bachelor's:** Accounting, advertising, aerospace/aeronautical/astronautical engineering, agricultural economics, agricultural education, agricultural engineering, agronomy, American studies, animal sciences, anthropology, architecture, art education, art history, Asian studies, astronomy, botany, business administration and management, chemical engineering, chemistry, civil engineering, computer and information sciences, construction, criminal justice studies, dairy, dramatic arts, East Asian studies, economics, electrical/electronics/communications engineering, elementary education, engineering, English, entomology, environmental health engineering, finance, food sciences, forestry and related sciences, French, geography, geology, German, graphic design, Greek (classical), health education, history, horticultural science, independent/interdisciplinary studies, industrial engineering, insurance and risk management, interior design, Jewish studies, journalism, landscape architecture, linguistics, marketing management, materials engineering, mathematics, mechanical engineering, microbiology, music, music education, music history and appreciation, nuclear engineering, nursing, occupational therapy, parks and recreation management, pharmacy, philosophy, physical education, physical therapy, physician's assistant, physics, plant pathology, plant sciences, political science and government, Portuguese, poultry, psychology, public relations, radio/television broadcasting, real estate, recreation and community services technologies, recreation therapy, rehabilitation counseling/services, religion, Russian, sociology, soil sciences, Spanish, special education, speech, speech correction, statistics, studio art, surveying and mapping sciences, tourism, zoology.

ACADEMIC PROGRAMS. Cooperative education, dual enrollment of high school students, education specialist degree, honors program, independent study, internships, student-designed major, study abroad, teacher preparation, telecourses; liberal arts/career combination in engineering, business; combined bachelor's/graduate program in law. **Remedial services:** Learning center, reduced course load, special counselor, tutoring. **ROTC:** Air Force, Army, Naval. **Placement/credit:** AP, CLEP General and Subject, IB, institutional tests; 30 credit hours maximum for bachelor's degree.

ACADEMIC REQUIREMENTS. Freshmen must earn minimum GPA of 2.0 to continue in good standing. 88% of freshmen return for sophomore year. Students must declare major by end of second year. **Graduation requirements:** 124 hours for bachelor's. Most students required to take courses in English, humanities, mathematics, biological/physical sciences, social sciences. **Additional information:** Interdisciplinary degrees include joint master's program with new college of environmental sciences and ecology.

FRESHMAN ADMISSIONS. Selection criteria: High school GPA in academic subjects, test scores, and senior year curriculum of primary importance. Class rank, recommendations, and personal record also considered. **High school preparation:** 19 units required. Required units include English 4, foreign language 2, mathematics 3, social science 3 and science 3. Mathematics must include algebra I and II, and geometry. Foreign language must be 2 units of same language. **Test requirements:** SAT or ACT (SAT preferred); score report by January 29.

1992 FRESHMAN CLASS PROFILE. 6,607 men applied, 4,326 accepted, 1,731 enrolled; 5,767 women applied, 3,836 accepted, 1,456 enrolled. 75% had high school GPA of 3.0 or higher, 25% between 2.0 and 2.99. **Academic background:** Mid 50% of enrolled freshmen had SAT-V between 480-580, SAT-M between 560-670; ACT composite between 25-29. 77% submitted SAT scores, 23% submitted ACT scores. **Characteristics:** 91% from in state, 85% live in college housing, 20% have minority backgrounds, 1% are foreign students, 21% join fraternities/sororities. Average age is 18.

FALL-TERM APPLICATIONS. $20 fee. Closing date January 29; applicants notified on or about March 26; must reply within 3 weeks. Early admission available. EDP-S.

STUDENT LIFE. Housing: Dormitories (men, women, coed); apartment, fraternity, sorority, cooperative housing available. **Activities:** Student government, radio, student newspaper, television, yearbook, choral groups, concert band, dance, drama, jazz band, marching band, music ensembles, musical theater, pep band, symphony orchestra, fraternities, sororities, Young Life, Newman Club, Fellowship of Christian Athletes, Hillel, American Civil Liberties Union, National Organization of Women, Baptist Student Union, Black Student Union, Young Americans for Freedom, Hispanic Student Union.

ATHLETICS. NCAA. **Intercollegiate:** Baseball M, basketball, cross-country, diving, football M, golf, gymnastics W, swimming, tennis, track and field, volleyball W. **Intramural:** Archery, basketball, bowling, fencing, golf, handball, lacrosse M, racquetball, rugby M, sailing, soccer M, softball, squash, table tennis, tennis, volleyball.

STUDENT SERVICES. Aptitude testing, career counseling, employment service for undergraduates, freshman orientation, health services, on-campus day care, personal counseling, placement service for graduates, special adviser for adult students, veterans counselor, services/facilities for handicapped.

ANNUAL EXPENSES. Tuition and fees (projected): $1,770, $5,120 additional for out-of-state students. **Room and board:** $4,080. **Books and supplies:** $600. **Other expenses:** $1,130.

FINANCIAL AID. 30% of freshmen, 46% of continuing students receive some form of aid. Grants, loans, jobs available. 899 enrolled freshmen were judged to have need, 893 were offered aid. Academic, music/drama, athletic, minority scholarships available. **Aid applications:** Closing date April 15; priority given to applications received by April 1; applicants notified on a rolling basis beginning on or about April 15; must reply within 2 weeks.

ADDRESS/TELEPHONE. S. William Kolb, Director of Admissions, University of Florida, Gainesville, FL 32611. (904) 392-1365.

University of Miami
Coral Gables, Florida CB code: 5815

4-year private university, coed. Founded in 1925. **Accreditation:** Regional. **Undergraduate enrollment:** 4,276 men, 3,751 women full time; 349 men, 506 women part time. **Graduate enrollment:** 2,384 men, 1,768 women full time; 490 men, 631 women part time. **Faculty:** 2,502 total (1,984 full time), 1,873 with doctorates or other terminal degrees. **Location:** Suburban campus in small city; 7 miles from downtown Miami. **Microcomputers:** 1,000 located in dormitories, libraries, classrooms, computer centers. **Special facilities:** Art museum, cinema, observatory, theater, concert hall, cable television station.

DEGREES OFFERED. BA, BS, BFA, BArch, MA, MS, MBA, MFA, MEd, PhD, EdD, MD, JD. 1,824 bachelor's degrees awarded in 1992. 19% in business and management, 5% business/office and marketing/distribution, 8% communications, 9% engineering, 5% letters/literature, 7% life sciences, 7% psychology, 8% social sciences, 12% visual and performing arts. Graduate degrees offered in 109 major fields of study.

UNDERGRADUATE MAJORS. Accounting, advertising, aerospace/aeronautical/astronautical engineering, anthropology, architectural engineering, architecture, art history, atmospheric sciences and meteorology, biochemistry, biology, business administration and management, business and management, business economics, chemistry, cinematography/film, civil engineering, communications, computer and information sciences, computer engineering, criminology, cytotechnology, developmental psychology, dramatic arts, economics, electrical/electronics/communications engineering, elementary education, engineering science, English, environmental health engineering, environmental science, finance, fine arts, French, geography, geology, German, health sciences, history, human resources development, industrial engineering, information sciences and systems, international business management, international studies, jazz, Jewish studies, journalism, Latin American studies, liberal/general studies, management information systems, marine biology, marketing management, mathematics, mechanical engineering, medical laboratory technologies, microbiology, motion picture technology, music, music business management, music education, music engineering technology, music history and appreciation, music literature, music performance, music theory and composition, music therapy, musical theater, nuclear medical technology, nursing, organization communication, philosophy, photography, physics, political science and government, predentistry, prelaw, premedicine, psychobiology, psychology, public relations, radio/television broadcasting, real estate, religion, secondary education, small business management and ownership, sociology, Spanish, special education, speech, speech communication, studio music, systems analysis, telecommunications, ultrasound technology, video.

ACADEMIC PROGRAMS. Accelerated program, double major, education specialist degree, honors program, independent study, internships, student-designed major, study abroad, teacher preparation, visiting/exchange student program; combined bachelor's/graduate program in business administration, medicine, law. **Remedial services:** Learning center, preadmission summer program, special counselor, tutoring. **ROTC:** Air Force, Army.

Placement/credit: AP, CLEP General and Subject, IB, institutional tests; 60 credit hours maximum for bachelor's degree.

ACADEMIC REQUIREMENTS. Freshmen must earn minimum GPA of 2.0 to continue in good standing. Students must declare major by end of second year. **Graduation requirements:** 120 hours for bachelor's (32 in major). Most students required to take courses in arts/fine arts, English, foreign languages, history, humanities, mathematics, philosophy/religion, biological/physical sciences, social sciences.

FRESHMAN ADMISSIONS. Selection criteria: School achievement record, SAT or ACT scores, recommendations and extracurricular activities considered. **High school preparation:** 16 units required. Required units include English 4, foreign language 2, mathematics 4, social science 3 and science 3. **Test requirements:** SAT or ACT; score report by March 1. 3 ACH required of applicants to honors programs in medical education, engineering, and medicine. Score report by January 15 Prueba de Aptitud Academica for Spanish speaking applicants. SAT required of all students in American schools abroad.

1992 FRESHMAN CLASS PROFILE. 4,244 men applied, 3,342 accepted, 937 enrolled; 3,527 women applied, 2,882 accepted, 853 enrolled. **Academic background:** Mid 50% of enrolled freshmen had ACT composite between 21-28. 30% submitted ACT scores. **Characteristics:** 46% from in state, 75% live in college housing, 39% have minority backgrounds, 9% are foreign students. Average age is 18.

FALL-TERM APPLICATIONS. $35 fee, may be waived for applicants with need. Closing date March 1; applicants notified on a rolling basis beginning on or about March 1; must reply by May 1. Audition required for music, drama applicants. Essay required. Interview required for applicants to honors programs in medical education, law, marine science, international studies, business, engineering and medicine; recommended for all others. CRDA. Deferred and early admission available. EDP-F.

STUDENT LIFE. Housing: Apartment, fraternity housing available. Residential college system available to all undergraduates. Students live with faculty members and their families in five residential colleges. **Activities:** Student government, film, radio, student newspaper, television, yearbook, choral groups, concert band, dance, drama, jazz band, marching band, music ensembles, musical theater, opera, pep band, symphony orchestra, fraternities, sororities, 150 clubs and organizations including peer counseling organization, international student associations, religious organizations.

ATHLETICS. NCAA. **Intercollegiate:** Baseball M, basketball, cross-country, diving, football M, golf W, rowing (crew), swimming, tennis, track and field. **Intramural:** Badminton, baseball M, basketball, bowling, boxing M, diving, fencing, golf, handball, lacrosse, racquetball, rugby, sailing, skin diving, soccer, softball, swimming, tennis, track and field, volleyball, water polo, wrestling M.

STUDENT SERVICES. Aptitude testing, career counseling, employment service for undergraduates, freshman orientation, health services, personal counseling, placement service for graduates, veterans counselor, services/facilities for handicapped.

ANNUAL EXPENSES. Tuition and fees: $15,700. **Room and board:** $6,227. **Books and supplies:** $600. **Other expenses:** $924.

FINANCIAL AID. 83% of freshmen, 75% of continuing students receive some form of aid. 66% of grants, 90% of loans, all jobs based on need. 1,483 enrolled freshmen were judged to have need, all were offered aid. Academic, music/drama, athletic, state/district residency, minority scholarships available. **Aid applications:** No closing date; priority given to applications received by March 1; applicants notified on a rolling basis beginning on or about April 15. **Additional information:** Loans to parents available.

ADDRESS/TELEPHONE. Edward M. Gillis, Director of Admissions, University of Miami, PO Box 248025, Coral Gables, FL 33124. (305) 284-4323. Fax: (305) 284-2507.

University of North Florida
Jacksonville, Florida — CB code: 5490

Admissions: 69% of applicants accepted
Based on:
••• School record, test scores
•• Activities, recommendations
• Essay, interview, special talents
Completion: 90% of freshmen end year in good standing
19% enter graduate study

4-year public university, coed. Founded in 1965. **Accreditation:** Regional. **Undergraduate enrollment:** 6,392 men and women. **Graduate enrollment:** 1,383 men and women. **Faculty:** 214 total, 184 with doctorates or other terminal degrees. **Location:** Urban campus in very large city; 12 miles from downtown. **Calendar:** Semester, extensive summer session. **Microcomputers:** 89 located in computer centers. **Special facilities:** 12 miles of nature trails, designated wildlife preserve and bird sanctuary.

DEGREES OFFERED. AA, BA, BS, BFA, MA, MS, MBA, MEd, EdD. 100% in multi/interdisciplinary studies. 1,331 bachelor's degrees awarded. 36% in business and management, 5% communications, 6% computer sciences, 20% education, 6% engineering technologies, 9% health sciences, 5% psychology, 5% social sciences. Graduate degrees offered in 26 major fields of study.

UNDERGRADUATE MAJORS. Associate: Liberal/general studies. **Bachelor's:** Accounting, allied health, art education, art history, biological and physical sciences, biology, business administration and management, business and management, business economics, chemistry, communications, computer and information sciences, construction, criminal justice studies, criminology, economics, education of the deaf and hearing impaired, electrical technology, electrical/electronics/communications engineering, elementary education, English, English literature, finance, fine arts, health sciences, history, industrial technology, information sciences and systems, insurance and risk management, jazz, liberal/general studies, manufacturing technology, marketing and distributive education, marketing management, mathematics, mathematics education, music education, music history and appreciation, nursing, physical education, physical sciences, physical therapy, political science and government, psychology, science education, secondary education, social science education, sociology, Spanish, special education, speech correction, statistics, technical education, transportation management.

ACADEMIC PROGRAMS. Cooperative education, double major, dual enrollment of high school students, honors program, independent study, internships, teacher preparation, cross-registration. **Remedial services:** Learning center, special counselor, tutoring. **ROTC:** Army. **Placement/credit:** AP, CLEP General and Subject; 45 credit hours maximum for bachelor's degree.

ACADEMIC REQUIREMENTS. Freshmen must earn minimum GPA of 2.0 to continue in good standing. 85% of freshmen return for sophomore year. Students must declare major by end of second year. **Graduation requirements:** 60 hours for associate, 120 hours for bachelor's. Most students required to take courses in English, foreign languages, history, humanities, mathematics, biological/physical sciences, social sciences. **Postgraduate studies:** 3% enter law school, 3% enter medical school, 10% enter MBA programs, 3% enter other graduate study.

FRESHMAN ADMISSIONS. Selection criteria: SAT or ACT score and high school GPA very important. **High school preparation:** 19 units required. Required units include English 4, foreign language 2, mathematics 3, social science 3 and science 3. **Test requirements:** SAT or ACT; score report by March 1.

1992 FRESHMAN CLASS PROFILE. 1,799 men and women applied, 1,247 accepted; 493 enrolled. 65% had high school GPA of 3.0 or higher, 35% between 2.0 and 2.99. **Characteristics:** 96% from in state, 70% commute, 12% have minority backgrounds. Average age is 18.

FALL-TERM APPLICATIONS. $20 fee, may be waived for applicants with need. Closing date July 1; priority given to applications received by March 1; applicants notified on a rolling basis. Audition required for music applicants. Essay recommended. CRDA. Deferred and early admission available.

STUDENT LIFE. Housing: Dormitories (coed); apartment housing available. **Activities:** Student government, student newspaper, yearbook, choral groups, concert band, drama, jazz band, music ensembles, symphony orchestra, fraternities, sororities.

ATHLETICS. Intercollegiate: Baseball M, basketball, cross-country, golf M, softball W, tennis, volleyball W. **Intramural:** Badminton, basketball, bowling, racquetball, sailing, soccer M, softball, swimming, track and field, volleyball.

STUDENT SERVICES. Aptitude testing, career counseling, employment service for undergraduates, freshman orientation, health services, on-campus day care, personal counseling, placement service for graduates, veterans counselor, women's center, services/facilities for handicapped.

ANNUAL EXPENSES. Tuition and fees (1992-93): $1,650, $4,760 additional for out-of-state students. **Room and board:** $1,450 room only. **Books and supplies:** $450. **Other expenses:** $540.

FINANCIAL AID. 30% of freshmen, 21% of continuing students receive some form of aid. 87% of grants, 93% of loans, 73% of jobs based on need. Academic, music/drama, athletic, leadership scholarships available. **Aid applications:** No closing date; priority given to applications received by April 1; applicants notified on a rolling basis.

ADDRESS/TELEPHONE. Mary S. Bolla, Director of Admissions, University of North Florida, 4567 St. Johns Bluff Road, South, Jacksonville, FL 32224-2645. (904) 646-2624.

University of South Florida
Tampa, Florida — CB code: 5828

Admissions: 77% of applicants accepted
Based on:
••• School record, test scores
• Activities, essay, recommendations, special talents
Completion: 88% of freshmen end year in good standing

4-year public university, coed. Founded in 1956. **Accreditation:** Regional. **Undergraduate enrollment:** 6,421 men, 8,160 women full time; 3,795 men, 4,657 women part time. **Graduate enrollment:** 1,059 men, 1,115 women full time; 1,346 men, 2,270 women part time. **Faculty:** 1,870 total (1,654 full time), 1,280 with doctorates or other terminal degrees. **Location:** Suburban campus in large city; 10 miles from downtown. **Calendar:** Semester, extensive summer session. Extensive evening/early morning classes. **Microcomputers:** 250 located in computer centers. **Special facilities:** Planetarium, fine arts rehearsal hall, weather station, botanical garden, 4 art galleries. **Additional facts:** Upper-division campuses located in Fort Myers, St. Petersburg, Sarasota, and Lakeland.

DEGREES OFFERED. BA, BS, BFA, MA, MS, MBA, MFA, MEd, MSW, PhD, EdD, MD. 4,800 bachelor's degrees awarded in 1992. 25% in business and management, 20% education, 8% engineering, 7% letters/literature, 5% psychology, 16% social sciences. Graduate degrees offered in 91 major fields of study.

UNDERGRADUATE MAJORS. Liberal/general studies. accounting, African studies, Afro-American (black) studies, American studies, analytical chemistry, anthropology, art education, art history, biological and physical sciences, biology, biotechnology, botany, business administration and management, business and management, business economics, business education, chemical engineering, chemistry, cinematography/film, civil engineering, classics, clinical laboratory science, communications, computer and information sciences, computer engineering, criminology, dance, dramatic arts, early childhood education, economics, education of exceptional children, education of the emotionally handicapped, education of the mentally handicapped, electrical/electronics/communications engineering, elementary education, engineering, engineering mechanics, engineering science, English education, finance, foreign languages (multiple emphasis), foreign languages education, French, geography, geology, German, gerontology, history, humanities and social sciences, industrial arts education, industrial engineering, information sciences and systems, international studies, Italian, Latin, liberal/general studies, management information systems, marketing and distribution, marketing and distributive education, materials engineering, mathematics, mathematics education, mechanical engineering, medical laboratory technologies, microbiology, music education, music performance, music theory and composition, nursing, philosophy, photography, physical education, physics, political science and government, psychology, religion, Russian, science education, social science education, social sciences, social work, sociology, Spanish, specific learning disabilities, speech, studio art, theater design, women's studies, zoology.

ACADEMIC PROGRAMS. Accelerated program, cooperative education, double major, dual enrollment of high school students, education specialist degree, external degree, honors program, independent study, internships, student-designed major, study abroad, teacher preparation, telecourses, visiting/exchange student program, weekend college, cross-registration. **Remedial services:** Preadmission summer program, special counselor, tutoring. **ROTC:** Air Force, Army. **Placement/credit:** AP, CLEP General and Subject, IB, institutional tests; 45 credit hours maximum for bachelor's degree.

ACADEMIC REQUIREMENTS. Freshmen must earn minimum GPA of 2.0 to continue in good standing. 70% of freshmen return for sophomore year. Students must declare major by end of second year. **Graduation requirements:** 120 hours for bachelor's (30 in major). Most students required to take courses in arts/fine arts, English, foreign languages, humanities, mathematics, biological/physical sciences, social sciences.

FRESHMAN ADMISSIONS. Selection criteria: Combination of high school GPA and SAT or ACT score. A sliding scale with higher grades compensates for lower test scores. **High school preparation:** 19 units required. Required units include English 4, foreign language 2, mathematics 3, social science 3 and science 3. Foreign language units must be in 1 language. **Test requirements:** SAT or ACT; score report by July 1. **Additional information:** Requirements higher for several degree programs.

1992 FRESHMAN CLASS PROFILE. 7,558 men and women applied, 5,836 accepted; 897 men enrolled, 1,133 women enrolled. 55% had high school GPA of 3.0 or higher, 45% between 2.0 and 2.99. 26% were in top tenth and 62% were in top quarter of graduating class. **Academic background:** Mid 50% of enrolled freshmen had SAT-V between 430-540, SAT-M between 490-610; ACT composite between 20-25. 65% submitted SAT scores, 52% submitted ACT scores. **Characteristics:** 85% from in state, 70% live in college housing, 21% have minority backgrounds, 2% are foreign students, 3% join fraternities/sororities. Average age is 19.

FALL-TERM APPLICATIONS. $20 fee, may be waived for applicants with need. Closing date June 1; applicants notified on a rolling basis. Audition required for music applicants. Portfolio required for art applicants. Early admission available.

STUDENT LIFE. Housing: Dormitories (men, women, coed); apartment housing available. Accessible on-campus housing for handicapped students. **Activities:** Student government, film, magazine, radio, student newspaper, television, yearbook, choral groups, concert band, dance, drama, jazz band, music ensembles, musical theater, opera, pep band, symphony orchestra, fraternities, sororities, Black Student Union, Jewish Student Union, over 250 active student organizations.

ATHLETICS. NCAA. **Intercollegiate:** Baseball M, basketball, cross-country, golf, soccer M, softball W, tennis, track and field, volleyball W. **Intramural:** Archery, badminton, baseball M, basketball, bowling, fencing, golf, handball, racquetball, rugby M, sailing, soccer, softball, swimming, table tennis, tennis, track and field, volleyball, wrestling M.

STUDENT SERVICES. Aptitude testing, career counseling, employment service for undergraduates, freshman orientation, health services, on-campus day care, personal counseling, placement service for graduates, special adviser for adult students, veterans counselor, services/facilities for handicapped.

ANNUAL EXPENSES. Tuition and fees (projected): $1,820, $4,759 additional for out-of-state students. **Room and board:** $3,626. **Books and supplies:** $500. **Other expenses:** $2,180.

FINANCIAL AID. 49% of grants, 93% of loans, 8% of jobs based on need. 776 enrolled freshmen were judged to have need, 730 were offered aid. Academic, music/drama, art, athletic, state/district residency, minority scholarships available. **Aid applications:** No closing date; priority given to applications received by April 9; applicants notified on a rolling basis beginning on or about May 1; must reply within 2 weeks. **Additional information:** Deferred tuition payment plan available for late financial aid recipients.

ADDRESS/TELEPHONE. Vicki W. Ahrens, Director of Admissions, University of South Florida, 4202 Fowler Avenue, Tampa, FL 33620-6900. (813) 974-3350. Fax: (813) 974-5271.

University of Tampa
Tampa, Florida — CB code: 5819

Admissions: 84% of applicants accepted
Based on: ••• School record, test scores
•• Activities, essay, special talents
• Interview, recommendations
Completion: 69% of freshmen end year in good standing

4-year private university and liberal arts college, coed. Founded in 1931. **Accreditation:** Regional. **Undergraduate enrollment:** 1,605 men and women full time; 220 men and women part time. **Graduate enrollment:** 360 men and women part time. **Faculty:** 182 total (120 full time), 117 with doctorates or other terminal degrees. **Location:** Urban campus in large city; in center of city. **Calendar:** Semester, limited summer session. **Microcomputers:** 97 located in libraries, computer centers. **Special facilities:** Museum of Victorian art and furniture, art gallery, concert hall, 2 theaters, television studio, dance studio, marine science research vessel.

DEGREES OFFERED. AA, BA, BS, BFA, MBA. 10 associate degrees awarded in 1992. 420 bachelor's degrees awarded. Graduate degrees offered in 3 major fields of study.

UNDERGRADUATE MAJORS. Associate: Biology, chemistry, computer and information sciences, creative writing, English, French, geography, history, mathematics, music, philosophy, political science and government, psychology, sociology, Spanish. **Bachelor's:** Accounting, applied mathematics, art education, arts management, biochemistry, biology, business administration and management, business and management, business economics, chemistry, communications, computer and information sciences, computer programming, creative writing, criminology, education, elementary education, English, English education, finance, fine arts, French, history, international business management, marine biology, marketing management, mathematics, mathematics education, medical laboratory technologies, music, music education, music performance, music theory and composition, nursing, operations research, philosophy, physical education, political science and government, practical nursing, predentistry, preengineering, prelaw, premedicine, preveterinary, psychology, science education, social science education, social sciences, social work, sociology, Spanish, urban studies.

ACADEMIC PROGRAMS. Computer delivered (on-line) credit-bearing course offerings, double major, dual enrollment of high school students, honors program, independent study, internships, study abroad, teacher preparation, Washington semester. **Remedial services:** Learning center, reduced course load, special counselor, tutoring. **ROTC:** Air Force, Army. **Placement/credit:** AP, CLEP General and Subject, institutional tests; 60 credit hours maximum for bachelor's degree.

ACADEMIC REQUIREMENTS. Freshmen must earn minimum GPA of 2.2 to continue in good standing. 67% of freshmen return for sophomore year. Students must declare major by end of second year. **Graduation requirements:** 64 hours for associate (16 in major), 124 hours for bachelor's. Most students required to take courses in arts/fine arts, computer science, English, history, humanities, mathematics, biological/physical sciences, social sciences.

FRESHMAN ADMISSIONS. Selection criteria: Combination of GPA and combined SAT score most important. Recommendations, activities and talents, and essay also considered. **High school preparation:** 15 units required. Required and recommended units include biological science 2, English 4, mathematics 2 and social science 2. Foreign language 2 recommended. **Test requirements:** SAT or ACT.

1992 FRESHMAN CLASS PROFILE. 1,700 men and women applied, 1,430 accepted; 305 enrolled. 50% had high school GPA of 3.0 or higher, 45% between 2.0 and 2.99. **Academic background:** Mid 50% of enrolled freshmen had SAT-V between 400-450, SAT-M between 400-450; ACT composite between 21-24. 80% submitted SAT scores, 20% submitted ACT scores. **Characteristics:** 45% from in state, 70% live in college housing, 16% have minority backgrounds, 6% are foreign students, 12% join fraternities/sororities. Average age is 18.

FALL-TERM APPLICATIONS. $25 fee, may be waived for applicants with need. No closing date; priority given to applications received by May 1; applicants notified on a rolling basis. Audition required for music applicants. Essay required. Interview recommended. Portfolio recommended for art applicants. CRDA. Deferred and early admission available.

STUDENT LIFE. Housing: Dormitories (women, coed); apartment housing available. **Activities:** Student government, magazine, radio, student newspaper, television, yearbook, poetry review, choral groups, concert band, dance, drama, jazz band, music ensembles, musical theater, symphony orchestra, fraternities, sororities, Campus Christian Fellowship, Hillel, International Students, Newman Club, Volunteer Action Center, honor societies and interest groups, diplomat student hosts, Association for Minority Collegiates, Student Political Organization.

ATHLETICS. NCAA. **Intercollegiate:** Baseball M, basketball, cross-country, diving, golf M, rowing (crew), soccer M, softball W, swimming, tennis, volleyball W. **Intramural:** Badminton, baseball M, basketball, bowling, cross-country, diving, golf, gymnastics, soccer, softball, swimming, table tennis, tennis, volleyball.

STUDENT SERVICES. Aptitude testing, career counseling, employment service for undergraduates, freshman orientation, health services, personal counseling, placement service for graduates, special adviser for adult students, services/facilities for handicapped.

ANNUAL EXPENSES. Tuition and fees: $12,280. **Room and board:** $4,450. **Books and supplies:** $775. **Other expenses:** $1,100.

FINANCIAL AID. 70% of freshmen, 75% of continuing students receive some form of aid. 12% of grants, 93% of loans, 47% of jobs based on need. 225 enrolled freshmen were judged to have need, all were offered aid. Academic, music/drama, art, athletic, state/district residency, leadership scholarships available. **Aid applications:** No closing date; priority given to applications received by March 15; applicants notified on a rolling basis beginning on or about March 15; must reply within 30 days.

ADDRESS/TELEPHONE. John F. Dolan, Vice President Admissions/Financial Aid, University of Tampa, 401 West Kennedy Boulevard, Tampa, FL 33606. (813) 253-6228. (800) 733-4773. Fax: (813) 251-0016.

University of West Florida
Pensacola, Florida — CB code: 5833

4-year public university, coed. Founded in 1963. **Accreditation:** Regional. **Undergraduate enrollment:** 6,759 men and women. **Graduate enrollment:** 1,159 men and women. **Faculty:** 383 total (270 full time), 281 with doctorates or other terminal degrees. **Location:** Suburban campus in small city; 10 miles from downtown. **Calendar:** Semester, extensive summer session. **Microcomputers:** 75 located in classrooms, computer centers. **Special facilities:** Art gallery, library special collections focusing on West Florida history. **Additional facts:** Campus located on 1,000-acre nature preserve. School owns 152 acres of undeveloped beaches, used by students for recreation and research.

DEGREES OFFERED. AA, BA, BS, BFA, MA, MS, MBA, MEd. 45 associate degrees awarded in 1992. 1,125 bachelor's degrees awarded. Graduate degrees offered in 25 major fields of study.

UNDERGRADUATE MAJORS. Associate: Liberal/general studies. **Bachelor's:** Accounting, anthropology, applied mathematics, art education, art history, biological and physical sciences, biology, business administration and management, business and management, business economics, chemistry, clinical laboratory science, communications, computer and information sciences, criminal justice studies, dramatic arts, earth sciences, economics, education, education of the emotionally handicapped, education of the gifted and talented, education of the mentally handicapped, electrical technology, elementary education, English, English education, finance, fine arts, foreign languages education, French, history, humanities and social sciences, industrial arts education, industrial technology, information sciences and systems, international relations, international studies, junior high education, legal assistant/paralegal, management information systems, marine biology, marketing and distribution, mathematics, mathematics education, music, music education, nursing, philosophy, physical education, physics, political science and government, prelaw, psychology, public administration, religion, renewable natural resources, science education, secondary education, social science education, social sciences, social work, sociology, Spanish, special education, specific learning disabilities, speech, statistics, studio art, technical education, visual and performing arts.

ACADEMIC PROGRAMS. 2-year transfer program, accelerated program, cooperative education, double major, dual enrollment of high school students, honors program, internships, study abroad, teacher preparation, engineering program with Florida State and Florida Agricultural and Mechanical Universities. **Remedial services:** Learning center, remedial instruction, tutoring. **ROTC:** Army. **Placement/credit:** AP, CLEP General and Subject, institutional tests; 30 credit hours maximum for bachelor's degree.

ACADEMIC REQUIREMENTS. Freshmen must earn minimum GPA of 2.0 to continue in good standing. 85% of freshmen return for sophomore year. Students must declare major by end of second year. **Graduation requirements:** 60 hours for associate (45 in major), 120 hours for bachelor's (33 in major). Most students required to take courses in English, foreign languages, history, humanities, mathematics, philosophy/religion, biological/physical sciences, social sciences.

FRESHMAN ADMISSIONS. Selection criteria: School achievement record, test scores, recommendations. **High school preparation:** 19 units required. Required units include English 4, foreign language 2, mathematics 3, social science 3 and science 3. **Test requirements:** SAT or ACT; score report by June 30.

1992 FRESHMAN CLASS PROFILE. 462 men and women enrolled. **Characteristics:** 77% from in state, 86% commute, 8% have minority backgrounds, 2% are foreign students, 2% join fraternities/sororities. Average age is 18.

FALL-TERM APPLICATIONS. $20 fee. Closing date June 1; applicants notified on a rolling basis. Audition required for music applicants. Portfolio required for fine arts applicants. Early admission available.

STUDENT LIFE. Housing: Dormitories (men, women, coed); apartment, fraternity, sorority housing available. **Activities:** Student government, radio, student newspaper, television, choral groups, drama, jazz band, music ensembles, musical theater, symphony orchestra, fraternities, sororities, 5 registered honor societies, 28 special interest organizations, 4 religious organizations, 1 international professional fraternity, and 6 professional organizations.

ATHLETICS. NAIA. **Intercollegiate:** Baseball M, basketball W, cross-country, golf M, soccer M, softball W, tennis. **Intramural:** Badminton, diving M, handball, sailing, soccer, swimming, volleyball, water polo.

STUDENT SERVICES. Aptitude testing, career counseling, employment service for undergraduates, freshman orientation, health services, on-campus day care, personal counseling, placement service for graduates, veterans counselor, services/facilities for handicapped.

ANNUAL EXPENSES. Tuition and fees (projected): $1,667, $4,760 additional for out-of-state students. **Room and board:** $3,859. **Books and supplies:** $523. **Other expenses:** $1,352.

FINANCIAL AID. 44% of freshmen, 40% of continuing students receive some form of aid. 88% of grants, 95% of loans, 11% of jobs based on need. Academic, music/drama, athletic, minority scholarships available. **Aid applications:** No closing date; priority given to applications received by April 1; applicants notified on a rolling basis beginning on or about March 1; must reply within 2 weeks.

ADDRESS/TELEPHONE. Dr. Linda J. Cox, Director of Admissions, University of West Florida, 11000 University Parkway, Pensacola, FL 32514-5750. (904) 474-2230.

Valencia Community College
Orlando, Florida — CB code: 5869

2-year public community college, coed. Founded in 1967. **Accreditation:** Regional. **Undergraduate enrollment:** 3,293 men, 3,849 women full time; 6,143 men, 8,809 women part time. **Faculty:** 923 total (265 full time), 98 with doctorates or other terminal degrees. **Location:** Suburban campus in large city; 235 miles from Miami, 145 miles from Jacksonville, 90 miles from Tampa. **Calendar:** Semester, extensive summer session. Saturday and extensive evening/early morning classes. **Microcomputers:** 600 located in libraries, classrooms, computer centers. **Additional facts:** Multilocation institution.

DEGREES OFFERED. AA, AS. 1,904 associate degrees awarded in 1992.

UNDERGRADUATE MAJORS. Accounting, architectural technologies, business administration and management, business and office, cardiovascular technology, civil technology, computer programming, criminal justice technology, dental hygiene, drafting and design technology, electronic technology, emergency medical technologies, engineering and engineering-related technologies, film arts, finance, fire control and safety technology, graphic arts technology, graphic design, health care administration, horticulture, hospitality and recreation marketing, laser electro-optic technology, legal assistant/paralegal, legal secretary, liberal/general studies, medical laboratory technologies, medical radiation dosimetry, medical secretary, motion picture technology, nuclear medical technology, nursing, pest control technology, radiograph medical technology, real estate, respiratory therapy technology, robotics, secretarial and related programs, survey and mapping technology, theater entertainment, ultrasound technology, visual and performing arts, water and wastewater technology, word processing.

ACADEMIC PROGRAMS. 2-year transfer program, cooperative education, dual enrollment of high school students, honors program, independent study, internships, study abroad, telecourses, weekend college. **Remedial services:** Learning center, remedial instruction, tutoring. **ROTC:** Army. **Placement/credit:** CLEP General and Subject, IB, institutional tests; 45 credit hours maximum for associate degree.

ACADEMIC REQUIREMENTS. Freshmen must earn minimum GPA of 2.0 to continue in good standing. 45% of freshmen return for sophomore year. Students must declare major on enrollment. **Graduation requirements:** 60 hours for associate (40 in major). Most students required to take courses in English, foreign languages, humanities, mathematics, biological/physical sciences, social sciences.

FRESHMAN ADMISSIONS. Selection criteria: Open admissions.

Test requirements: SAT or ACT for placement. Florida MAPS or ASSET (ASSET preferred) may be submitted in place of SAT or ACT.

1992 FRESHMAN CLASS PROFILE. 1,398 men, 1,732 women enrolled. **Characteristics:** 99% from in state, 100% commute, 34% have minority backgrounds, 2% are foreign students. Average age is 22.

FALL-TERM APPLICATIONS. $20 fee. Closing date August 29; priority given to applications received by August 14; applicants notified on a rolling basis beginning on or about February 15. Deferred and early admission available.

STUDENT LIFE. Activities: Student government, magazine, student newspaper, choral groups, concert band, dance, drama, jazz band, music ensembles, musical theater, opera, symphony orchestra, foreign students club (VISA).

ATHLETICS. NJCAA. **Intercollegiate:** Baseball M, basketball, softball W. **Intramural:** Basketball, football, soccer, tennis, track and field, water polo.

STUDENT SERVICES. Aptitude testing, career counseling, employment service for undergraduates, freshman orientation, health services, personal counseling, placement service for graduates, special adviser for adult students, veterans counselor, services/facilities for handicapped.

ANNUAL EXPENSES. Tuition and fees (projected): $1,043, $2,706 additional for out-of-state students. **Books and supplies:** $500. **Other expenses:** $700.

FINANCIAL AID. 37% of freshmen, 33% of continuing students receive some form of aid. 93% of grants, 74% of loans, 88% of jobs based on need. Academic, music/drama, art, athletic, state/district residency scholarships available. **Aid applications:** No closing date; priority given to applications received by April 1; applicants notified on a rolling basis beginning on or about August 1; must reply within 2 weeks.

ADDRESS/TELEPHONE. Charles H. Drosin, Director of Admissions, Valencia Community College, PO Box 3028, Orlando, FL 32802-3028. (407) 299-1506 ext. 1506.

Warner Southern College
Lake Wales, Florida — CB code: 5883

4-year private liberal arts college, coed, affiliated with Church of God (Anderson, Indiana). Founded in 1968. **Accreditation:** Regional. **Undergraduate enrollment:** 180 men, 217 women full time; 12 men, 32 women part time. **Faculty:** 51 total (22 full time), 13 with doctorates or other terminal degrees. **Location:** Rural campus in large town; 60 miles from Tampa, 55 miles from Orlando. **Calendar:** 2 terms of 16 weeks each followed by 2 sessions of 6 weeks each. **Microcomputers:** 40 located in libraries, computer centers. **Additional facts:** Evening courses offered at branch campuses in Daytona, Orlando, and Lake Wales for bachelor's in organizational management.

DEGREES OFFERED. AA, BA. 7 associate degrees awarded in 1992. 14% in business and management, 57% multi/interdisciplinary studies, 14% philosophy, religion, theology, 14% visual and performing arts. 171 bachelor's degrees awarded. 64% in business and management, 27% teacher education.

UNDERGRADUATE MAJORS. Associate: Bible studies, business administration and management, liberal/general studies, music. **Bachelor's:** Biology, business administration and management, communications, elementary education, English, English education, music education, physical education, psychology, religion, religious music, science education, secondary education, social work, theological studies.

ACADEMIC PROGRAMS. 2-year transfer program, dual enrollment of high school students, internships, student-designed major, teacher preparation, simulated Third World setting for missionary training. **Remedial services:** Remedial instruction, tutoring. **Placement/credit:** AP, CLEP General and Subject.

ACADEMIC REQUIREMENTS. Freshmen must earn minimum GPA of 2.0 to continue in good standing. 49% of freshmen return for sophomore year. Students must declare major by end of second year. **Graduation requirements:** 64 hours for associate (20 in major), 128 hours for bachelor's (30 in major). Most students required to take courses in arts/fine arts, English, foreign languages, history, humanities, mathematics, philosophy/religion, biological/physical sciences, social sciences.

FRESHMAN ADMISSIONS. Selection criteria: Applicants must meet 2 of 3 admission criteria: 2.0 GPA, top half of high school class, or minimum test scores of 18 ACT or 700/SAT. **High school preparation:** 15 units recommended. Recommended units include biological science 2, English 4, foreign language 2, mathematics 2, social science 3 and science 2. **Test requirements:** SAT or ACT (ACT preferred); score report by September 1.

1992 FRESHMAN CLASS PROFILE. 48 men, 48 women enrolled. 24% had high school GPA of 3.0 or higher, 72% between 2.0 and 2.99. **Characteristics:** 65% from in state, 60% live in college housing, 19% have minority backgrounds, 6% are foreign students. Average age is 19.

FALL-TERM APPLICATIONS. $20 fee, may be waived for applicants with need. Closing date August 15; applicants notified on a rolling basis; must reply within 4 weeks. Audition required. Interview recommended. Deferred and early admission available.

STUDENT LIFE. Housing: Dormitories (men, women). **Activities:** Student government, radio, student newspaper, yearbook, choral groups, drama, music ensembles, campus crusade, missions, outreach ministries, Koinonia Agathon (for wives of pastoral ministry students). **Additional information:** Religious observance required.

ATHLETICS. NAIA. **Intercollegiate:** Baseball M, basketball, cross-country, soccer M, volleyball W. **Intramural:** Basketball M, golf, racquetball, table tennis, tennis, volleyball.

STUDENT SERVICES. Career counseling, employment service for undergraduates, freshman orientation, health services, personal counseling, placement service for graduates.

ANNUAL EXPENSES. Tuition and fees (1992-93): $6,200. **Room and board:** $2,920. **Books and supplies:** $600. **Other expenses:** $1,200.

FINANCIAL AID. 83% of freshmen, 89% of continuing students receive some form of aid. 60% of grants, 85% of loans, 67% of jobs based on need. 56 enrolled freshmen were judged to have need, all were offered aid. Academic, athletic, leadership, alumni affiliation, religious affiliation scholarships available. **Aid applications:** No closing date; priority given to applications received by April 1; applicants notified on a rolling basis beginning on or about February 15.

ADDRESS/TELEPHONE. Valerie S. Rutland, Director of Enrollment Management, Warner Southern College, 5301 Highway 27 South, Lake Wales, FL 33853-8725. (813) 638-2109. (800) 949-7248. Fax: (813) 638-1472.

Webber College
Babson Park, Florida — CB code: 5893

Admissions: 63% of applicants accepted
Based on:
- ••• Essay, recommendations, school record, test scores
- •• Interview
- • Activities, special talents

Completion: 82% of freshmen end year in good standing
72% graduate, 15% of these enter graduate study

4-year private business college, coed. Founded in 1927. **Accreditation:** Regional. **Undergraduate enrollment:** 149 men, 172 women full time; 20 men, 29 women part time. **Faculty:** 33 total (22 full time), 15 with doctorates or other terminal degrees. **Location:** Rural campus in rural community; 50 miles from Orlando, 14 miles from Winter Haven. **Calendar:** Semester, limited summer session. Saturday classes. **Microcomputers:** 33 located in libraries, computer centers. **Special facilities:** Audobon Society Nature Preserve.

DEGREES OFFERED. AS, BS. 11 associate degrees awarded in 1992. 96% in business and management. 25 bachelor's degrees awarded. 100% in business and management.

UNDERGRADUATE MAJORS. Associate: Accounting, business administration and management, business and management, finance, hospitality and recreation marketing, hotel/motel and restaurant management, marketing and distribution, marketing management, retailing, tourism, transportation and travel marketing. **Bachelor's:** Accounting, business administration and management, business and management, club management, finance, hospitality and recreation marketing, hotel/motel and restaurant management, marketing and distribution, marketing management, retailing, tourism, transportation and travel marketing.

ACADEMIC PROGRAMS. Double major, dual enrollment of high school students, internships, study abroad, visiting/exchange student program, weekend college, cross-registration. **Remedial services:** Reduced course load, remedial instruction, tutoring. **Placement/credit:** AP, CLEP General and Subject, institutional tests; 15 credit hours maximum for associate degree; 30 credit hours maximum for bachelor's degree.

ACADEMIC REQUIREMENTS. Freshmen must earn minimum GPA of 1.85 to continue in good standing. 77% of freshmen return for sophomore year. Students must declare major on application. **Graduation requirements:** 61 hours for associate (21 in major), 122 hours for bachelor's (36 in major). Most students required to take courses in computer science, English, history, humanities, mathematics, biological/physical sciences, social sciences. **Postgraduate studies:** 83% from 2-year programs enter 4-year programs. 3% enter law school, 12% enter MBA programs.

FRESHMAN ADMISSIONS. Selection criteria: High school record, courses, activities, SAT or ACT scores, essay, and recommendations important. Recommended units include English 4, foreign language 1, mathematics 3, social science 2 and science 2. **Test requirements:** SAT or ACT (SAT preferred); score report by August 15.

1992 FRESHMAN CLASS PROFILE. 133 men applied, 84 accepted, 42 enrolled; 145 women applied, 92 accepted, 40 enrolled. 5% were in top tenth and 22% were in top quarter of graduating class. **Academic background:** Mid 50% of enrolled freshmen had SAT-V between 360-480, SAT-M between 400-520; ACT composite between 11-21. 66% submitted SAT scores, 34% submitted ACT scores. **Characteristics:** 73% from in state, 84% live in college housing, 25% have minority backgrounds, 9% are foreign students, 2% join fraternities/sororities. Average age is 20.

FALL-TERM APPLICATIONS. $25 fee, may be waived for applicants

with need. Closing date August 1; priority given to applications received by June 15; applicants notified on a rolling basis; must reply by August 1. Essay required. Interview recommended. CRDA. Deferred and early admission available.

STUDENT LIFE. Housing: Dormitories (men, women). **Activities:** Student government, student newspaper, yearbook, fraternities, service clubs, professional development organizations.

ATHLETICS. NAIA. **Intercollegiate:** Basketball, cross-country, golf M, soccer M, softball W, tennis, volleyball. **Intramural:** Basketball, bowling, softball, swimming, table tennis, tennis, volleyball.

STUDENT SERVICES. Career counseling, employment service for undergraduates, freshman orientation, health services, personal counseling, placement service for graduates, special adviser for adult students, veterans counselor, services/facilities for handicapped.

ANNUAL EXPENSES. Tuition and fees: $5,950. **Room and board:** $2,900. **Books and supplies:** $500. **Other expenses:** $100.

FINANCIAL AID. 73% of freshmen, 82% of continuing students receive some form of aid. 42% of grants, 93% of loans, 68% of jobs based on need. 55 enrolled freshmen were judged to have need, all were offered aid. Academic, athletic, state/district residency scholarships available. **Aid applications:** Closing date July 15; priority given to applications received by March 31; applicants notified on or about May 15; must reply by August 1.

ADDRESS/TELEPHONE. Dr. Deborah Milliken, Dean of Student Development, Webber College, PO Box 96, 1201 Alt. 27 South, Babson Park, FL 33827-0096. (813) 638-1431. (800) 741-1844. Fax: (813) 638-2823.

Georgia

Abraham Baldwin Agricultural College

Tifton, Georgia CB code: 5001

2-year public agricultural and technical, community college, coed. Founded in 1924. **Accreditation:** Regional. **Undergraduate enrollment:** 1,320 men, 1,531 women full time. **Faculty:** 135 total (113 full time), 30 with doctorates or other terminal degrees. **Location:** Rural campus in large town; 100 miles from Macon, 50 miles from Albany and Valdosta. Saturday and extensive evening/early morning classes. **Microcomputers:** 120 located in libraries, classrooms. **Special facilities:** 200-acre farm. **Additional facts:** Students may pursue programs of study at 3 off-campus sites: Valdosta State College (associate in nursing),Ben-Hill Irwin Technical Institute (associate in applied science), and Moultrie Area Technical Institute.

DEGREES OFFERED. AA, AS, AAS. 352 associate degrees awarded in 1992.

UNDERGRADUATE MAJORS. Accounting, agribusiness, agricultural business and management, agricultural engineering, agricultural sciences, animal sciences, biology, business and management, business and office, business data entry equipment operation, business data processing and related programs, business data programming, chemistry, child development/care/guidance, communications, computer and information sciences, data processing, dental hygiene, education, English, fashion merchandising, fine arts, food production/management/services, forestry and related sciences, history, home economics, home furnishings and equipment management/production/services, journalism, law enforcement and corrections technologies, liberal/general studies, marketing and distribution, mathematics, mechanical design technology, medical records technology, music, nursing, ornamental horticulture, physical sciences, physics, plant sciences, predentistry, prelaw, premedicine, prepharmacy, psychology, recreation and community services technologies, science technologies, social sciences, sociology, sports medicine, visual and performing arts, wildlife management, word processing.

ACADEMIC PROGRAMS. 2-year transfer program, dual enrollment of high school students, external degree, independent study, internships, study abroad. **Remedial services:** Learning center, remedial instruction, special counselor, tutoring. **Placement/credit:** AP, CLEP General and Subject, institutional tests; 45 credit hours maximum for associate degree.

ACADEMIC REQUIREMENTS. Freshmen must earn minimum GPA of 1.5 to continue in good standing. 50% of freshmen return for sophomore year. Students must declare major by end of first year. **Graduation requirements:** 90 hours for associate (45 in major). Most students required to take courses in English, foreign languages, history, mathematics, biological/physical sciences, social sciences.

FRESHMAN ADMISSIONS. Selection criteria: Minimum SAT-verbal score of 250 or ACT English of 15, or SAT-mathematical score of 280 or ACT mathematical of 18, or 1.8 GPA required. **High school preparation:** 16 units required. Required units include English 4, foreign language 2, mathematics 3, social science 3 and science 3. College preparatory program not required for students pursuing AAS degree. **Test requirements:** SAT or ACT; score report by September 1. **Additional information:** Students who score below 350 on SAT-verbal (ACT English 18) or 430 on SAT-mathematical (ACT mathematical 20) required to take collegiate placement examination in English, reading and/or mathematics.

1992 FRESHMAN CLASS PROFILE. 932 men and women enrolled. 34% had high school GPA of 3.0 or higher, 57% between 2.0 and 2.99. **Academic background:** Mid 50% of enrolled freshmen had SAT-V between 320-440, SAT-M between 340-480. 95% submitted SAT scores. **Characteristics:** 90% from in state, 60% live in college housing, 11% have minority backgrounds, 3% are foreign students. Average age is 19.

FALL-TERM APPLICATIONS. $5 fee. Closing date September 1; applicants notified on a rolling basis beginning on or about March 15. Interview recommended for nursing applicants. Deferred and early admission available.

STUDENT LIFE. Housing: Dormitories (men, women, coed). **Activities:** Student government, magazine, radio, student newspaper, choral groups, concert band, drama, jazz band.

ATHLETICS. NJCAA. **Intercollegiate:** Baseball M, basketball M, golf M, softball W, tennis M. **Intramural:** Softball, volleyball.

STUDENT SERVICES. Aptitude testing, career counseling, employment service for undergraduates, freshman orientation, health services, personal counseling, placement service for graduates, veterans counselor, services/facilities for handicapped.

ANNUAL EXPENSES. Tuition and fees (projected): $1,311, $939 additional for out-of-state students. **Room and board:** $2,820. **Books and supplies:** $675. **Other expenses:** $1,146.

FINANCIAL AID. 76% of freshmen, 65% of continuing students receive some form of aid. 83% of grants, 82% of loans, 66% of jobs based on need. 600 enrolled freshmen were judged to have need, all were offered aid. Academic, music/drama, art, athletic, leadership scholarships available. **Aid applications:** No closing date; priority given to applications received by May 1; applicants notified on a rolling basis beginning on or about June 1; must reply within 2 weeks.

ADDRESS/TELEPHONE. Garth L. Webb, Jr, Director of Admissions, Abraham Baldwin Agricultural College, ABAC Station, Box 4, Tifton, GA 31794-2693. (912) 386-3230. (800) 733-3653. Fax: (912) 386-7006.

Agnes Scott College

Decatur, Georgia CB code: 5002

Admissions: 77% of applicants accepted
Based on: ••• School record, test scores
•• Recommendations
• Activities, essay, interview, special talents
Completion: 85% of freshmen end year in good standing
60% graduate, 30% of these enter graduate study

4-year private liberal arts college, women only, affiliated with Presbyterian Church (USA). Founded in 1889. **Accreditation:** Regional. **Undergraduate enrollment:** 538 women full time; 3 men, 64 women part time. **Graduate enrollment:** 12 women full time; 2 women part time. **Faculty:** 93 total (78 full time), 68 with doctorates or other terminal degrees. **Location:** Urban campus in very large city; 6 miles from Atlanta. **Calendar:** Semester. **Microcomputers:** 61 located in dormitories, libraries, classrooms, computer centers. **Special facilities:** Observatory, Robert Frost Collection in library, art collection, electron microscope, 30-inch Beck telescope.

DEGREES OFFERED. BA, M. 123 bachelor's degrees awarded in 1992. 6% in languages, 12% letters/literature, 5% life sciences, 5% multi/interdisciplinary studies, 6% philosophy, religion, theology, 18% psychology, 34% social sciences, 8% visual and performing arts. Graduate degrees offered in 1 major field of study.

UNDERGRADUATE MAJORS. Art history/English, astrophysics, biology, biology/psychology, chemistry, classics, creative writing, dramatic arts, economics, English, English literature, English literature/creative writing, fine arts, French, German, Greek (classical), history, history/English literature, international relations, Latin, Latin American studies, mathematics, mathematics/economics, mathematics/physics, music, philosophy, physics, political science and government, psychology, religion, sociology, sociology/anthropology, Spanish.

ACADEMIC PROGRAMS. Accelerated program, double major, dual enrollment of high school students, independent study, internships, student-designed major, study abroad, teacher preparation, visiting/exchange student program, United Nations semester, Washington semester, cross-registration, Return to College program for women beyond traditional college age; exchange program with Mills College; 3-2 liberal arts and career combination in information and computer science, industrial management, and management science with Georgia Institute of Technology; 3-4 liberal arts and architecture program with Washington University, Missouri; PLEN Public Policy Semester; exchange programs with institutions in France, Germany and Japan; liberal arts/career combination in engineering. **Remedial services:** Learning center, tutoring. **ROTC:** Air Force, Naval. **Placement/credit:** AP, IB, institutional tests.

ACADEMIC REQUIREMENTS. To continue in good academic standing, freshmen must earn a 1.5 GPA, and pass at least 9 credit hours per semester with no more than 1 grade below 1.0 in academic courses. 80% of freshmen return for sophomore year. Students must declare major by end of second year. **Graduation requirements:** 124 hours for bachelor's (30 in major). Most students required to take courses in arts/fine arts, English, foreign languages, history, mathematics, philosophy/religion, biological/physical sciences, social sciences. **Additional information:** Global Awareness Program offers opportunities to visit all regions of the world. Over 300 internships and externships available in Atlanta and other cities. Year 5 program allows graduates to return next year on tuition-free basis.

FRESHMAN ADMISSIONS. Selection criteria: High school record, class rank, test scores, counselor recommendation, personal qualities, and extracurricular activities considered. **High school preparation:** 16 units recommended. Recommended units include English 4, foreign language 2, mathematics 3, social science 1 and science 1. **Test requirements:** SAT or ACT (SAT preferred); score report by April 1.

1992 FRESHMAN CLASS PROFILE. 579 women applied, 445 accepted, 133 enrolled. 84% had high school GPA of 3.0 or higher, 16% between 2.0 and 2.99. 53% were in top tenth and 87% were in top quarter of graduating class. **Academic background:** Mid 50% of enrolled freshmen had SAT-V between 450-580, SAT-M between 500-580. 89% submitted SAT scores. **Characteristics:** 41% from in state, 95% live in college housing, 17% have minority backgrounds, 3% are foreign students. Average age is 18.

FALL-TERM APPLICATIONS. $35 fee. No closing date; priority given to applications received by February 1; applicants notified on a rolling basis beginning on or about February 1. Audition required for music scholarship applicants. Essay required. Interview recommended. Portfolio recommended for art applicants. CRDA. Deferred and early admission available. EDP-S.

STUDENT LIFE. Housing: Dormitories (women). Limited number of college-owned houses available to nontraditional students. **Activities:** Student government, magazine, student newspaper, yearbook, student handbook, choral groups, dance, drama, music ensembles, symphony orchestra, literary festival, Religious Life Council, College Republicans, Young Democrats, Chimo (foreign student group), honor societies, environmental group, Circle-K, Witkaze (African-American student group), Students for a Feminist Awareness, Volunteer Community Service Program.

ATHLETICS. NCAA. **Intercollegiate:** Cross-country, soccer, tennis. **Intramural:** Badminton, basketball, racquetball, softball, swimming, track and field, volleyball.

STUDENT SERVICES. Career counseling, employment service for undergraduates, freshman orientation, health services, personal counseling, placement service for graduates, special adviser for adult students, services/facilities for handicapped.

ANNUAL EXPENSES. Tuition and fees: $12,135. **Room and board:** $5,000. **Books and supplies:** $450. **Other expenses:** $500.

FINANCIAL AID. 94% of freshmen, 92% of continuing students receive some form of aid. 71% of grants, 85% of loans, 85% of jobs based on need. 92 enrolled freshmen were judged to have need, all were offered aid. Academic, music/drama, state/district residency, leadership scholarships available. **Aid applications:** No closing date; priority given to applications received by March 15; applicants notified on a rolling basis beginning on or about March 1; must reply by May 1 or within 2 weeks if notified thereafter. **Additional information:** College-sponsored parent loan program available. Middle Income Assistance Grants available. Auditions recommended for music scholarship applicants.

ADDRESS/TELEPHONE. Office of Admission, Agnes Scott College, 141 East College Avenue, Decatur, GA 30030. (404) 371-6285. (800) 863-8602. Fax: (404) 371-6177.

Albany State College

Albany, Georgia CB code: 5004

4-year public liberal arts college, coed. Founded in 1903. **Accreditation:** Regional. **Undergraduate enrollment:** 881 men, 1,362 women full time; 154 men, 385 women part time. **Graduate enrollment:** 4 men, 5 women full time; 86 men, 229 women part time. **Faculty:** 148 total (135 full time), 73 with doctorates or other terminal degrees. **Location:** Urban campus in small city; 176 miles from Atlanta. **Calendar:** Quarter, limited summer session. **Microcomputers:** Located in libraries, classrooms, computer centers. **Special facilities:** Outdoor classroom and nature trails on Flint River.

DEGREES OFFERED. AA, BA, BS, MS, MBA. 247 bachelor's degrees awarded. 24% in business and management, 10% teacher education, 12% health sciences, 9% allied health, 5% life sciences, 14% parks/recreation, protective services, public affairs, 8% psychology. Graduate degrees offered in 13 major fields of study.

UNDERGRADUATE MAJORS. Associate: Forensic studies, protective services. **Bachelor's:** Accounting, allied health, biology, business administration and management, chemistry, computer and information sciences, criminal justice studies, early childhood education, French, health education, history, junior high education, mathematics, mathematics education, music, music education, nursing, physical education, political science and government, psychology, science education, secondary education, secretarial and related programs, social science education, social work, sociology, Spanish, special education, speech/communication/theater education.

ACADEMIC PROGRAMS. Cooperative education, double major, dual enrollment of high school students, education specialist degree, honors program, internships, teacher preparation, weekend college, cross-registration, engineering program with Georgia Institute of Technology; liberal arts/career combination in engineering, health sciences. **Remedial services:** Learning center, remedial instruction, special counselor, tutoring. **ROTC:** Army. **Placement/credit:** AP, institutional tests; 45 credit hours maximum for bachelor's degree.

ACADEMIC REQUIREMENTS. Freshmen must earn minimum GPA of 2.0 to continue in good standing. 67% of freshmen return for sophomore year. Students must declare major by end of second year. **Graduation requirements:** 95 hours for associate, 186 hours for bachelor's. Most students required to take courses in arts/fine arts, English, history, mathematics, biological/physical sciences, social sciences. **Postgraduate studies:** 3% enter law school, 3% enter medical school, 2% enter MBA programs, 2% enter other graduate study.

FRESHMAN ADMISSIONS. Selection criteria: Minimum SAT-verbal score of 250 or ACT English of 10, or SAT-mathematical score of 280 or ACT mathematical of 5, or 1.8 high school GPA. **High school preparation:** 16 units required. Required units include English 4, foreign language 2, mathematics 3, social science 3 and science 3. Foreign language must have 2 units in same language. **Test requirements:** SAT or ACT; score report by September 1.

1992 FRESHMAN CLASS PROFILE. 529 men, 720 women enrolled. **Academic background:** Mid 50% of enrolled freshmen had SAT-V between 300-400, SAT-M between 350-400. 80% submitted SAT scores. **Characteristics:** 90% from in state, 60% live in college housing, 98% have minority backgrounds. Average age is 18.

FALL-TERM APPLICATIONS. No fee. Closing date September 1; applicants notified on a rolling basis; must reply within 1 week. Interview required for academically weak applicants. Deferred and early admission available.

STUDENT LIFE. Housing: Dormitories (men, women). **Activities:** Student government, film, student newspaper, yearbook, choral groups, concert band, dance, drama, jazz band, marching band, music ensembles, pep band, gospel choir, fraternities, sororities, religious life organization, Black Men in Unity, Black Women in Unity.

ATHLETICS. NCAA. **Intercollegiate:** Baseball M, basketball, cross-country, football M, tennis, track and field. **Intramural:** Basketball, swimming M, volleyball.

STUDENT SERVICES. Aptitude testing, career counseling, freshman orientation, health services, personal counseling, placement service for graduates, veterans counselor, minority student adviser, services/facilities for handicapped.

ANNUAL EXPENSES. Tuition and fees: $1,773, $1,380 additional for out-of-state students. **Room and board:** $2,475. **Books and supplies:** $675. **Other expenses:** $726.

FINANCIAL AID. 88% of freshmen, 88% of continuing students receive some form of aid. Academic, state/district residency, leadership scholarships available. **Aid applications:** No closing date; priority given to applications received by June 1; applicants notified on a rolling basis beginning on or about July 1; must reply within 2 weeks.

ADDRESS/TELEPHONE. Patricia Price, Assistant Director of Admissions, Albany State College, 504 College Drive, Albany, GA 31705-2796. (912) 430-4650 ext. 4650.

American College for the Applied Arts

Atlanta, Georgia CB code: 2486

4-year proprietary art, business college, coed. Founded in 1977. **Accreditation:** Regional. **Undergraduate enrollment:** 96 men, 356 women full time; 17 men, 125 women part time. **Faculty:** 63 total (7 full time), 5 with doctorates or other terminal degrees. **Location:** Urban campus in very large city. **Calendar:** Quarter, extensive summer session. **Microcomputers:** 55 located in libraries, classrooms, computer centers. **Special facilities:** Sewing and darkroom laboratories, interior design library.

DEGREES OFFERED. BA. 40 associate degrees awarded in 1992. 140 bachelor's degrees awarded.

UNDERGRADUATE MAJORS. Associate: Business and management, fashion design, fashion merchandising, graphic design, illustration design, interior design. **Bachelor's:** Business and management, fashion design, fashion merchandising, graphic design, illustration design, interior design.

ACADEMIC PROGRAMS. Double major, internships, study abroad. **Remedial services:** Remedial instruction, tutoring. **Placement/credit:** Institutional tests.

ACADEMIC REQUIREMENTS. Freshmen must earn minimum GPA of 2.0 to continue in good standing. 78% of freshmen return for sophomore year. Students must declare major on enrollment. **Graduation requirements:** 120 hours for associate (90 in major), 190 hours for bachelor's (140 in major). Most students required to take courses in arts/fine arts, computer science, English, history, humanities, mathematics, social sciences. **Postgraduate studies:** 15% from 2-year programs enter 4-year programs.

FRESHMAN ADMISSIONS. Selection criteria: Open admissions. 2 letters of recommendation required. **Test requirements:** Institutional placement tests in English and mathematics required.

1992 FRESHMAN CLASS PROFILE. 28 men, 257 women enrolled. **Characteristics:** 70% commute, 10% are foreign students. Average age is 19.

FALL-TERM APPLICATIONS. $35 fee. No closing date; applicants notified on a rolling basis; must reply within 30 days. Interview recommended. Portfolio recommended.

STUDENT LIFE. Housing: Apartment housing available. **Activities:** Student government, American Society of Interior Designers, Fashion Association, American Marketing Association, Graphic Arts Association.

STUDENT SERVICES. Career counseling, employment service for undergraduates, freshman orientation, personal counseling, placement service for graduates, services/facilities for handicapped.

ANNUAL EXPENSES. Tuition and fees (1992-93): $7,440. Tuition and fees includes use of text books. **Room and board:** $3,375 room only. **Other expenses:** $960.

FINANCIAL AID. 70% of freshmen, 45% of continuing students receive some form of aid. 98% of grants, 44% of loans, all jobs based on need. Academic scholarships available. **Aid applications:** No closing date; priority given to applications received by June 1; applicants notified on a rolling basis; must reply within 30 days.

ADDRESS/TELEPHONE. Suzanne McBride, Director of Admissions, American College for the Applied Arts, 3330 Peachtree Road Northeast, Atlanta, GA 30326. (404) 231-9000. (800) 255-6839. Fax: (404) 231-1062.

Andrew College
Cuthbert, Georgia CB code: 5009

2-year private junior college, coed, affiliated with United Methodist Church. Founded in 1854. **Accreditation:** Regional. **Undergraduate enrollment:** 144 men, 147 women full time; 6 men, 9 women part time. **Faculty:** 24 total (15 full time). **Location:** Rural campus in small town; 60 miles from Columbus, 40 miles from Albany. **Calendar:** Quarter, limited summer session. **Microcomputers:** Located in computer centers.

DEGREES OFFERED. AA, AS. 72 associate degrees awarded in 1992.

UNDERGRADUATE MAJORS. Agricultural sciences, biology, business and management, business and office, business data entry equipment operation, business data processing and related programs, business education, chemistry, education, elementary education, engineering, English, English literature, French, health sciences, humanities, information sciences and systems, junior high education, liberal/general studies, music, pharmacy, physical sciences, physics, predental hygiene, predentistry, preforestry, premedical technology, premedicine, prenursing, prepharmacy, preveterinary, psychology, religion, religious education, secondary education, social sciences, sociology, Spanish, special education, speech.

ACADEMIC PROGRAMS. 2-year transfer program, dual enrollment of high school students, honors program. **Remedial services:** Preadmission summer program, remedial instruction, tutoring. **Placement/credit:** AP, CLEP General, institutional tests; 40 credit hours maximum for associate degree.

ACADEMIC REQUIREMENTS. Freshmen must earn minimum GPA of 2.0 to continue in good standing. Students must declare major by end of first year. **Graduation requirements:** 98 hours for associate (30 in major). Most students required to take courses in English, history, humanities, mathematics, philosophy/religion, biological/physical sciences, social sciences.

FRESHMAN ADMISSIONS. Selection criteria: High school academic record, test scores, and school and community activities important. **High school preparation:** 18 units recommended. **Test requirements:** SAT or ACT; score report by September 1.

1992 FRESHMAN CLASS PROFILE. 105 men, 98 women enrolled. **Characteristics:** 60% from in state, 74% live in college housing, 20% have minority backgrounds, 10% are foreign students, 22% join fraternities/sororities. Average age is 18.

FALL-TERM APPLICATIONS. $15 fee. No closing date; priority given to applications received by June 1; applicants notified on a rolling basis; must reply by July 1 or immediately if notified thereafter. Interview required for academically weak applicants. Audition required for music applicants. Portfolio recommended for art applicants. Essay recommended. CRDA. Deferred and early admission available. EDP-F.

STUDENT LIFE. Housing: Dormitories (men, women, coed). **Activities:** Student government, magazine, yearbook, choral groups, musical theater, fraternities, sororities, Baptist Student Union, Wesley Fellowship, Alpha Omega.

ATHLETICS. NJCAA. **Intercollegiate:** Baseball M, soccer, tennis. **Intramural:** Badminton, basketball, bowling, golf, racquetball, soccer, softball, table tennis, tennis, volleyball.

STUDENT SERVICES. Aptitude testing, career counseling, freshman orientation, health services, personal counseling.

ANNUAL EXPENSES. Tuition and fees: $4,590. **Room and board:** $3,780. **Books and supplies:** $600. **Other expenses:** $1,200.

FINANCIAL AID. 90% of freshmen, 90% of continuing students receive some form of aid. 65% of grants, 94% of loans based on need. Academic, music/drama, art, athletic, state/district residency, leadership, religious affiliation scholarships available. **Aid applications:** No closing date; priority given to applications received by June 1; applicants notified on a rolling basis beginning on or about July 15.

ADDRESS/TELEPHONE. Director of Admissions, Office of Admissions, Andrew College, College Street, Cuthbert, GA 31740-1395. (912) 732-2171 ext. 135.

Armstrong State College
Savannah, Georgia CB code: 5012

4-year public liberal arts college, coed. Founded in 1935. **Accreditation:** Regional. **Undergraduate enrollment:** 840 men, 1,780 women full time; 710 men, 1,510 women part time. **Graduate enrollment:** 327 men and women. **Faculty:** 310 total (210 full time), 97 with doctorates or other terminal degrees. **Location:** Suburban campus in small city; Located in Savannah, 250 miles from Atlanta. **Calendar:** Quarter, extensive summer session. Saturday and extensive evening/early morning classes. **Microcomputers:** 60 located in computer centers.

DEGREES OFFERED. AA, AS, AAS, BA, BS. 163 associate degrees awarded in 1992. 256 bachelor's degrees awarded. Graduate degrees offered in 1 major field of study.

UNDERGRADUATE MAJORS. Associate: Dental hygiene, liberal/general studies, nursing, radiograph medical technology, respiratory therapy technology. **Bachelor's:** Applied mathematics, art education, biology, business education, chemistry, computer and information sciences, criminal justice studies, dental hygiene, dramatic arts, elementary education, English, English education, fine arts, health sciences, history, junior high education, liberal/general studies, mathematics education, medical laboratory technologies, music, music education, nursing, physical education, physical sciences, political science and government, psychology, science education, social science education, special education, specific learning disabilities, speech correction.

ACADEMIC PROGRAMS. 2-year transfer program, accelerated program, cooperative education, double major, dual enrollment of high school students, honors program, independent study, internships, study abroad, teacher preparation, cross-registration, graduate degrees offered in affiliation with Georgia Southern University; liberal arts/career combination in engineering. **Remedial services:** Learning center, remedial instruction, special counselor, tutoring, writing center, math tutorial center, reading center. **ROTC:** Army, Naval. **Placement/credit:** AP, CLEP General and Subject, institutional tests; 45 credit hours maximum for bachelor's degree.

ACADEMIC REQUIREMENTS. 50% of freshmen return for sophomore year. Students must declare major by end of second year. **Graduation requirements:** 93 hours for associate (55 in major), 191 hours for bachelor's (40 in major). Most students required to take courses in arts/fine arts, computer science, English, history, humanities, mathematics, biological/physical sciences, social sciences.

FRESHMAN ADMISSIONS. Selection criteria: Minimum SAT combined score of 760 with minimum SAT-mathematical and verbal scores of 380 each and 2.0 GPA required for regular admissions. 1.8 high school GPA for conditional admissions with lower test scores. **High school preparation:** 18 units required. Required units include biological science 1, English 4, foreign language 2, mathematics 3, physical science 1, social science 3 and science 2. **Test requirements:** SAT or ACT; score report by September 1.

1992 FRESHMAN CLASS PROFILE. Characteristics: 88% from in state, 96% commute, 23% have minority backgrounds, 4% are foreign students, 1% join fraternities/sororities. Average age is 18.

FALL-TERM APPLICATIONS. $10 fee. No closing date; priority given to applications received by September 1; applicants notified on a rolling basis beginning on or about June 15. Deferred and early admission available. EDP-S.

STUDENT LIFE. Housing: Dormitories (coed). **Activities:** Student government, magazine, student newspaper, yearbook, choral groups, concert band, drama, jazz band, music ensembles, pep band, fraternities, sororities, Women of Worth, Ebony Coalition, Baptist Student Union, Hispanic Society.

ATHLETICS. NCAA. **Intercollegiate:** Baseball M, basketball, cross-country, tennis, volleyball W. **Intramural:** Badminton, basketball, bowling, golf, racquetball, soccer M, softball, table tennis, tennis, track and field, volleyball, water polo.

STUDENT SERVICES. Career counseling, employment service for undergraduates, freshman orientation, health services, personal counseling, placement service for graduates, special adviser for adult students, veterans counselor, services/facilities for handicapped.

ANNUAL EXPENSES. Tuition and fees (projected): $1,569, $1,380 additional for out-of-state students. **Room and board:** $3,306. **Books and supplies:** $450. **Other expenses:** $750.

FINANCIAL AID. 25% of freshmen, 25% of continuing students receive some form of aid. 68% of grants, 81% of loans, 29% of jobs based on need. Academic, music/drama, art, athletic, state/district residency, leadership, alumni affiliation, minority scholarships available. **Aid applications:** No closing date; priority given to applications received by May 31; applicants notified on a rolling basis; must reply within 3 weeks.

ADDRESS/TELEPHONE. Kim West, Registrar/Director of Admissions, Armstrong State College, 11935 Abercorn Street, Savannah, GA 31419-1997. (912) 927-5275. (800) 633-2349. Fax: (912) 921-5462.

Art Institute of Atlanta
Atlanta, Georgia CB code: 5429

2-year proprietary technical college, coed. Founded in 1949. **Accreditation:** Regional. **Undergraduate enrollment:** 139 men, 435 women full time; 43 men, 69 women part time. **Faculty:** 44 total (28 full time). **Location:** Suburban campus in very large city; 8 miles from city center. **Calendar:** Quarter, extensive summer session. **Additional facts:** Music Business Institute offers associate degree programs in music and entertainment management.

DEGREES OFFERED. AA. 336 associate degrees awarded in 1992.

UNDERGRADUATE MAJORS. Fashion merchandising, graphic arts technology, photographic technology.

ACADEMIC REQUIREMENTS. Freshmen must earn minimum GPA of 2.0 to continue in good standing. **Additional information:** Career-oriented programs with limited academic offerings.

FRESHMAN ADMISSIONS. Selection criteria: School record, interview very important; portfolio considered if available.

1992 FRESHMAN CLASS PROFILE. 271 men, 122 women enrolled.

Characteristics: 50% from in state, 60% commute, 20% have minority backgrounds, 2% are foreign students.

FALL-TERM APPLICATIONS. $50 fee. No closing date; applicants notified on a rolling basis. Interview recommended. Portfolio recommended.

STUDENT LIFE. Housing: Cooperative housing available. **Activities:** Student government.

STUDENT SERVICES. Placement service for graduates.

ANNUAL EXPENSES. Tuition and fees (1992-93): $7,900. Tuition for photography program is $7,665, music program is $7,825. **Room and board:** $3,000 room only. **Books and supplies:** $1,500. **Other expenses:** $500.

FINANCIAL AID. Grants, loans, jobs available. **Aid applications:** No closing date; applicants notified on a rolling basis beginning on or about March 1; must reply within 3 weeks.

ADDRESS/TELEPHONE. Bob Bouchard, Director of Admissions, Art Institute of Atlanta, 3376 Peachtree Road Northeast, Atlanta, GA 30326. (404) 266-2662. (800) 554-3346. Fax: (404) 266-2662.

Athens Area Technical Institute

Athens, Georgia — CB code: 0462

2-year public technical college, coed. Founded in 1959. **Accreditation:** Regional. **Undergraduate enrollment:** 308 men, 519 women full time; 234 men, 377 women part time. **Faculty:** 77 total, 21 with doctorates or other terminal degrees. **Location:** Suburban campus in small city; 65 miles from Atlanta. **Calendar:** Quarter, extensive summer session. **Microcomputers:** 100 located in classrooms, computer centers.

DEGREES OFFERED. AAS. 47 associate degrees awarded in 1992.

UNDERGRADUATE MAJORS. Accounting, biological laboratory technology, computer programming, electromechanical technology, electronic technology, legal assistant/paralegal, nursing, radiograph medical technology, respiratory therapy technology, retailing, secretarial and related programs.

ACADEMIC PROGRAMS. Internships. **Remedial services:** Learning center, reduced course load, remedial instruction.

ACADEMIC REQUIREMENTS. Freshmen must earn minimum GPA of 2.0 to continue in good standing. Students must declare major on enrollment. **Graduation requirements:** 112 hours for associate (74 in major). Most students required to take courses in English, humanities, mathematics.

FRESHMAN ADMISSIONS. Selection criteria: Open admissions. Selective admissions to radiology, respiratory therapy, and nursing. **Test requirements:** SAT or ACT; score report by August 31. Applicants to nursing program must submit SAT or ACT scores by April 1, radiation technology and respiratory therapy applicants by April 30.

1992 FRESHMAN CLASS PROFILE. 90 men, 230 women enrolled. **Characteristics:** 100% commute.

FALL-TERM APPLICATIONS. $15 fee. No closing date; applicants notified on a rolling basis. Interview required. March 1 deadline for applicants to nursing program, April 1 deadline for radiation technology and respiratory therapy.

STUDENT LIFE. Activities: Student government.

STUDENT SERVICES. Aptitude testing, career counseling, employment service for undergraduates, freshman orientation, on-campus day care, personal counseling, placement service for graduates, special adviser for adult students, veterans counselor, services/facilities for handicapped.

ANNUAL EXPENSES. Tuition and fees (1992-93): $740, $740 additional for out-of-state students.

FINANCIAL AID. 25% of freshmen, 25% of continuing students receive some form of aid. All grants, 47% of jobs based on need.

ADDRESS/TELEPHONE. Carroll D. Humphries, Vice President for Student Services, Athens Area Technical Institute, U.S. Highway 29 North, Athens, GA 30610-0399. (706) 542-8050 ext. 201.

Atlanta Christian College

East Point, Georgia — CB code: 5029

4-year private Bible college, coed, nondenominational. Founded in 1937. **Accreditation:** Regional. **Undergraduate enrollment:** 113 men, 104 women full time; 16 men, 21 women part time. **Faculty:** 26 total (15 full time), 5 with doctorates or other terminal degrees. **Location:** Suburban campus in large town; 10 miles from Atlanta. **Calendar:** Semester, limited summer session. **Microcomputers:** Located in classrooms.

DEGREES OFFERED. AA, BA, BS. 5 associate degrees awarded in 1992. 14 bachelor's degrees awarded.

UNDERGRADUATE MAJORS. Associate: Nursing, secretarial and related programs. **Bachelor's:** Elementary education, human relations, religion, religious education, religious music, secretarial and related programs, theological studies.

ACADEMIC PROGRAMS. Double major, independent study, internships, study abroad, weekend college, cooperative program with Clayton State College in nursing. **Remedial services:** Reduced course load, remedial instruction, special counselor, tutoring. **Placement/credit:** AP, institutional tests; 32 credit hours maximum for associate degree; 32 credit hours maximum for bachelor's degree.

ACADEMIC REQUIREMENTS. Freshmen must earn minimum GPA of 1.5 to continue in good standing. 75% of freshmen return for sophomore year. Students must declare major by end of second year. **Graduation requirements:** 65 hours for associate, 128 hours for bachelor's. Most students required to take courses in English, history, philosophy/religion, biological/physical sciences, social sciences. **Postgraduate studies:** 1% from 2-year programs enter 4-year programs.

FRESHMAN ADMISSIONS. Selection criteria: Recommendations, scholastic ability, and test scores considered. **Test requirements:** SAT or ACT (SAT preferred); score report by June 1.

1992 FRESHMAN CLASS PROFILE. Academic background: Mid 50% of enrolled freshmen had SAT-V between 340-480, SAT-M between 360-540. 95% submitted SAT scores. **Characteristics:** 80% from in state, 65% live in college housing, 25% have minority backgrounds, 7% are foreign students. Average age is 22.

FALL-TERM APPLICATIONS. No fee. Closing date August 1; applicants notified on a rolling basis. Essay required. Deferred and early admission available.

STUDENT LIFE. Housing: Dormitories (men, women); apartment housing available. **Activities:** Student government, yearbook, choral groups, drama, music ensembles, pep band, religious organizations, Christian service clubs, service-oriented fraternities and sororities. **Additional information:** Religious observance required.

ATHLETICS. Intercollegiate: Basketball, soccer, tennis, volleyball W. **Intramural:** Soccer, softball, volleyball.

STUDENT SERVICES. Career counseling, freshman orientation, health services, personal counseling, placement service for graduates, services/facilities for handicapped.

ANNUAL EXPENSES. Tuition and fees: $4,000. **Room and board:** $2,900. **Books and supplies:** $400. **Other expenses:** $500.

FINANCIAL AID. 65% of freshmen, 70% of continuing students receive some form of aid. 50% of grants, 65% of loans, all jobs based on need. Academic, music/drama, leadership, religious affiliation scholarships available. **Aid applications:** Closing date August 1; priority given to applications received by June 1; applicants notified on a rolling basis beginning on or about June 1; must reply within 2 weeks.

ADDRESS/TELEPHONE. Denise Kaiser, Director of Admissions, Atlanta Christian College, 2605 Ben Hill Road, East Point, GA 30344. (404) 761-8861. (800) 886-IACC.

Atlanta College of Art

Atlanta, Georgia — CB code: 5014

4-year private art college, coed. Founded in 1928. **Accreditation:** Regional. **Undergraduate enrollment:** 421 men and women. **Location:** Urban campus in very large city. **Calendar:** Semester. **Additional facts:** Founding member of The Woodruff Arts Center, including the High Museum of Art, Atlanta Symphony Orchestra, and Alliance Theater Company.

FRESHMAN ADMISSIONS. Selection criteria: Transcript, essay portfolio including at least 12-15 samples of work, and SAT or ACT scores all important.

ANNUAL EXPENSES. Tuition and fees: $9,495. **Room and board:** $3,000 room only. **Books and supplies:** $850. **Other expenses:** $1,245.

ADDRESS/TELEPHONE. John Anthony Farkas, Director of Enrollment Management, Atlanta College of Art, 1280 Peachtree Street NE, Atlanta, GA 30309. (404) 898-1163. (800) 832-2104. Fax: (404) 898-9577.

Atlanta Metropolitan College

Atlanta, Georgia — CB code: 5725

Admissions:	60% of applicants accepted
Based on:	••• School record, test scores
Completion:	90% of freshmen end year in good standing 85% enter 4-year programs

2-year public junior college, coed. Founded in 1974. **Accreditation:** Regional. **Undergraduate enrollment:** 358 men, 483 women full time; 358 men, 501 women part time. **Faculty:** 78 total (50 full time). **Location:** Urban campus in very large city; 2 miles from downtown. **Calendar:** Quarter, extensive summer session. **Microcomputers:** Located in libraries.

DEGREES OFFERED. AA, AS, AAS. 185 associate degrees awarded in 1992.

UNDERGRADUATE MAJORS. Accounting, agricultural engineering, agricultural sciences, air conditioning/heating/refrigeration mechanics, aircraft mechanics, anthropology, automotive mechanics, automotive technology, biological and physical sciences, business administration and management, business and office, business data processing and related programs, business data programming, business education, carpentry, chemistry, computer and information sciences, construction, criminology, dental laboratory technology, diesel engine mechanics, drafting, early childhood education, economics, education, electrical and electronics equipment repair, electrical installation, elementary education, engineering and engineering-related technologies, English, fine arts, foreign languages (multiple emphasis), forestry and related sciences, geography, geology, graphic and printing production, history, home economics, humanities, information sciences and systems, journalism, law enforcement and corrections technologies, liberal/general studies, marketing and distribution, masonry/tile setting, mathematics, medical illustrating, medical laboratory technologies, medical records administration, medical records technology, mental health/human services, music, nursing, occupational therapy, office supervision and management, physical therapy, political science and government, protective services, psychology, public affairs, radiograph medical technology, recreation and community services technologies, science technologies, secretarial and related programs, social work, sociology, speech, teacher aide, urban studies.

ACADEMIC PROGRAMS. 2-year transfer program, cooperative education, dual enrollment of high school students, internships, weekend college, cross-registration. **Remedial services:** Learning center, remedial instruction, special counselor, tutoring. **Placement/credit:** Institutional tests.

ACADEMIC REQUIREMENTS. Freshmen must earn minimum GPA of 1.8 to continue in good standing. 80% of freshmen return for sophomore year. Students must declare major on application. **Graduation requirements:** 97 hours for associate (30 in major). Most students required to take courses in English, foreign languages, history, mathematics, biological/physical sciences, social sciences.

FRESHMAN ADMISSIONS. Selection criteria: Test scores and high school GPA. **High school preparation:** 16 units required. Required units include English 4, foreign language 2, mathematics 3, social science 3 and science 3. **Test requirements:** SAT or ACT; score report by May 1.

1992 FRESHMAN CLASS PROFILE. 485 men applied, 325 accepted, 311 enrolled; 741 women applied, 415 accepted, 415 enrolled. **Characteristics:** 85% from in state, 100% commute, 95% have minority backgrounds. Average age is 19.

FALL-TERM APPLICATIONS. $10 fee. Closing date September 8; applicants notified on a rolling basis beginning on or about March 1. Deferred and early admission available.

STUDENT LIFE. Activities: Student government, magazine, student newspaper, yearbook, choral groups, dance, drama, music ensembles, gospel chorus, black and third world cultural club, international students organization, veterans club, social services club.

ATHLETICS. NJCAA. **Intramural:** Basketball M, softball, tennis, track and field.

STUDENT SERVICES. Aptitude testing, career counseling, employment service for undergraduates, health services, personal counseling, placement service for graduates, veterans counselor, services/facilities for handicapped.

ANNUAL EXPENSES. Tuition and fees: $1,164, $939 additional for out-of-state students. **Books and supplies:** $500.

FINANCIAL AID. 25% of freshmen, 35% of continuing students receive some form of aid. All aid based on need. **Aid applications:** No closing date; priority given to applications received by August 20; applicants notified on a rolling basis beginning on or about July 1; must reply within 2 weeks.

ADDRESS/TELEPHONE. Verel V. Wilson, Director of Admissions, Atlanta Metropolitan College, 1630 Stewart Avenue, Southwest, Atlanta, GA 30310. (404) 756-4000. Fax: (404) 756-4460.

Augusta College

Augusta, Georgia — CB code: 5336

Admissions: 79% of applicants accepted
Based on: ••• School record
•• Test scores
Completion: 75% of freshmen end year in good standing

4-year public liberal arts college, coed. Founded in 1925. **Accreditation:** Regional. **Undergraduate enrollment:** 1,186 men, 1,735 women full time; 621 men, 1,203 women part time. **Graduate enrollment:** 84 men, 141 women full time; 205 men, 404 women part time. **Faculty:** 241 total (173 full time), 143 with doctorates or other terminal degrees. **Location:** Urban campus in large town; 145 miles from Atlanta. **Calendar:** Quarter, extensive summer session. **Microcomputers:** 142 located in libraries, classrooms.

DEGREES OFFERED. AA, AS, AAS, BA, BS, BFA, MS, MBA, MEd. 62 associate degrees awarded in 1992. 76% in health sciences, 15% multi/interdisciplinary studies, 5% social sciences. 384 bachelor's degrees awarded. 20% in business and management, 10% business/office and marketing/distribution, 5% communications, 7% computer sciences, 13% teacher education, 5% life sciences, 9% psychology, 16% social sciences. Graduate degrees offered in 12 major fields of study.

UNDERGRADUATE MAJORS. Associate: Criminal justice studies, liberal/general studies, nursing. **Bachelor's:** Accounting, art education, biology, business administration and management, business and management, business economics, business education, chemistry, communications, computer and information sciences, education of the mentally handicapped, elementary education, English, French, history, junior high education, marketing and distribution, mathematics, music, music education, music performance, office supervision and management, physical education, physical sciences, physics, political science and government, psychology, sociology, Spanish, special education, studio art.

ACADEMIC PROGRAMS. Accelerated program, cooperative education, double major, dual enrollment of high school students, education specialist degree, honors program, independent study, internships, study abroad, teacher preparation, cross-registration, pre-engineering and pre-allied health sequences. **Remedial services:** Learning center, remedial instruction, special counselor, tutoring. **ROTC:** Army. **Placement/credit:** AP, CLEP General and Subject, institutional tests; 45 credit hours maximum for bachelor's degree.

ACADEMIC REQUIREMENTS. Freshmen must earn minimum GPA of 2.0 to continue in good standing. 77% of freshmen return for sophomore year. Students must declare major by end of second year. **Graduation requirements:** 90 hours for associate (30 in major), 180 hours for bachelor's (75 in major). Most students required to take courses in English, history, humanities, mathematics, biological/physical sciences, social sciences.

FRESHMAN ADMISSIONS. Selection criteria: Minimum SAT-verbal score of 350 or ACT English of 18, or SAT-mathematical score of 350 or ACT mathematical of 16, and 2.0 high school GPA. **High school preparation:** 16 units required. Required units include English 4, foreign language 2, mathematics 3, social science 3 and science 3. **Test requirements:** SAT or ACT (SAT preferred); score report by August 15. Students with minimum SAT-verbal score of 500 or ACT English score of 27 or minimum SAT-mathematical score of 600 or ACT mathematical score of 29 are invited to take ACH for possible advanced placement or credit. Score report by August 15.

1992 FRESHMAN CLASS PROFILE. 523 men applied, 430 accepted, 328 enrolled; 900 women applied, 699 accepted, 509 enrolled. 25% had high school GPA of 3.0 or higher, 50% between 2.0 and 2.99. **Academic background:** Mid 50% of enrolled freshmen had SAT-V between 320-490, SAT-M between 350-530. 95% submitted SAT scores. **Characteristics:** 86% from in state, 100% commute, 25% have minority backgrounds. Average age is 19.

FALL-TERM APPLICATIONS. $10 fee, may be waived for applicants with need. Closing date August 15; priority given to applications received by May 1; applicants notified on a rolling basis. CRDA. Deferred and early admission available.

STUDENT LIFE. Housing: Private off campus housing reserved for students. **Activities:** Student government, film, magazine, student newspaper, yearbook, choral groups, concert band, dance, drama, jazz band, music ensembles, opera, pep band, fraternities, sororities, Black Student Union, Office to Promote the Independence of Disabled Students, Baptist Student Union.

ATHLETICS. NAIA, NCAA. **Intercollegiate:** Baseball M, basketball, cross-country, diving, golf M, soccer M, softball W, tennis, volleyball W. **Intramural:** Basketball M, softball, table tennis, tennis, volleyball W.

STUDENT SERVICES. Aptitude testing, career counseling, employment service for undergraduates, freshman orientation, on-campus day care, personal counseling, placement service for graduates, special adviser for adult students, veterans counselor, services/facilities for handicapped.

ANNUAL EXPENSES. Tuition and fees (projected): $1,593, $1,380 additional for out-of-state students. **Books and supplies:** $480. **Other expenses:** $4,206.

FINANCIAL AID. 40% of continuing students receive some form of aid. 83% of grants, 75% of loans, 38% of jobs based on need. 607 enrolled freshmen were judged to have need, all were offered aid. Academic, music/drama, art, athletic, leadership, religious affiliation scholarships available. **Aid applications:** No closing date; priority given to applications received by May 1; applicants notified on a rolling basis beginning on or about May 15; must reply within 2 weeks.

ADDRESS/TELEPHONE. Luanne Baroni, Director of Admissions/Assistant Dean for Enrollment Services, Augusta College, 2500 Walton Way, Augusta, GA 30904-2200. (706) 737-1405.

Augusta Technical Institute

Augusta, Georgia — CB code: 2620

2-year public technical college, coed. **Accreditation:** Regional. **Undergraduate enrollment:** 2,629 men and women. **Location:** Suburban campus in large town. **Calendar:** Quarter.

FRESHMAN ADMISSIONS. Selection criteria: Test scores most important. High school diploma or GED required for all medical and associate degree programs.

ANNUAL EXPENSES. Tuition and fees (1992-93): $575, $360 additional for out-of-state students. **Books and supplies:** $450.

ADDRESS/TELEPHONE. Terry Elam, Director of Admissions, Augusta Technical Institute, 3116 Deans Bridge Road, Augusta, GA 30906. (706) 771-4000.

Bainbridge College
Bainbridge, Georgia CB code: 5062

2-year public community college, coed. Founded in 1973. **Accreditation:** Regional. **Undergraduate enrollment:** 192 men, 329 women full time; 199 men, 303 women part time. **Faculty:** 58 total (45 full time), 24 with doctorates or other terminal degrees. **Location:** Rural campus in large town; 43 miles from Tallahassee, Florida. **Calendar:** Quarter, extensive summer session. **Microcomputers:** 35 located in libraries, classrooms, computer centers. **Special facilities:** Nature trail.

DEGREES OFFERED. AA, AAS. 83 associate degrees awarded in 1992.

UNDERGRADUATE MAJORS. Accounting, agricultural sciences, automotive mechanics, biology, business administration and management, business and management, business and office, business data programming, business education, chemistry, drafting, early childhood education, economics, electronic technology, elementary education, English, foreign languages (multiple emphasis), forestry and related sciences, history, home economics, journalism, junior high education, law enforcement and corrections technologies, liberal/general studies, marketing and distribution, mathematics, pharmacy, physics, political science and government, precision metal work, psychology, secondary education, sociology, Spanish, speech.

ACADEMIC PROGRAMS. 2-year transfer program, dual enrollment of high school students, 2-year registered nursing program with Darton College. **Remedial services:** Learning center, reduced course load, remedial instruction, special counselor, tutoring. **Placement/credit:** AP, CLEP General and Subject, institutional tests; 25 credit hours maximum for associate degree.

ACADEMIC REQUIREMENTS. Freshmen must earn minimum GPA of 1.8 to continue in good standing. 50% of freshmen return for sophomore year. Students must declare major by end of first year. **Graduation requirements:** 96 hours for associate (30 in major). Most students required to take courses in arts/fine arts, English, history, humanities, mathematics, biological/physical sciences, social sciences.

FRESHMAN ADMISSIONS. Selection criteria: Minimum SAT-verbal score of 250 or ACT English of 13, or SAT-mathematical score of 280 or ACT mathematical of 14, or 1.8 high school GPA. **High school preparation:** 16 units required. Required units include English 4, foreign language 2, mathematics 3, social science 3 and science 3. **Test requirements:** SAT or ACT; score report by September 15.

1992 FRESHMAN CLASS PROFILE. 49 men, 65 women enrolled. **Academic background:** Mid 50% of enrolled freshmen had SAT-V between 310-460, SAT-M between 330-470. 90% submitted SAT scores. **Characteristics:** 99% from in state, 100% commute. Average age is 25.

FALL-TERM APPLICATIONS. No fee. Closing date September 13; applicants notified on a rolling basis. Interview required for licensed practical nurse applicants. Deferred admission available.

STUDENT LIFE. Activities: Student government.

ATHLETICS. Intramural: Bowling, softball, table tennis, tennis, volleyball.

STUDENT SERVICES. Aptitude testing, career counseling, employment service for undergraduates, freshman orientation, personal counseling, placement service for graduates, special adviser for adult students, veterans counselor, services/facilities for handicapped.

ANNUAL EXPENSES. Tuition and fees: $1,089, $939 additional for out-of-state students. **Books and supplies:** $600. **Other expenses:** $450.

FINANCIAL AID. 39% of freshmen, 35% of continuing students receive some form of aid. All grants, 84% of loans, 41% of jobs based on need. **Aid applications:** No closing date; priority given to applications received by July 1; applicants notified on a rolling basis beginning on or about June 1; must reply within 2 weeks. **Additional information:** 30-day loans available for tuition and fees.

ADDRESS/TELEPHONE. Karen Hill, Director of Admissions and Records, Bainbridge College, Highway 84E, Bainbridge, GA 31717-0953. (912) 248-2500.

Bauder College
Atlanta, Georgia CB code: 5070

2-year proprietary fashion and design college, coed. Founded in 1964. **Accreditation:** Regional. **Undergraduate enrollment:** 12 men, 485 women full time. **Faculty:** 27 total (21 full time), 1 with doctorate or other terminal degree. **Location:** Suburban campus in very large city; about 5 miles from downtown. **Calendar:** Quarter, limited summer session. **Microcomputers:** 35 located in libraries, computer centers.

DEGREES OFFERED. AA. 220 associate degrees awarded in 1992.

UNDERGRADUATE MAJORS. Fashion design, fashion merchandising, interior design.

ACADEMIC PROGRAMS. Double major, internships, study abroad, New York semester. **Remedial services:** Remedial instruction, tutoring.

ACADEMIC REQUIREMENTS. Freshmen must earn minimum GPA of 2.0 to continue in good standing. 70% of freshmen return for sophomore year. **Graduation requirements:** 90 hours for associate (68 in major). Most students required to take courses in arts/fine arts, computer science, English, mathematics, social sciences. **Additional information:** Modeling program available. Students must declare major by end of first quarter.

FRESHMAN ADMISSIONS. Selection criteria: Motivation, 2.0 high school GPA, 2 character reference letters, and written essay very important. **Test requirements:** SAT or ACT not required but highly recommended.

1992 FRESHMAN CLASS PROFILE. 9 men, 301 women enrolled. **Characteristics:** 14% from in state, 89% live in college housing, 40% have minority backgrounds. Average age is 18.

FALL-TERM APPLICATIONS. $35 fee. No closing date; applicants notified on a rolling basis; must reply within 2 weeks. Essay required. Interview recommended. Portfolio recommended for interior and fashion design applicants. Deferred admission available.

STUDENT LIFE. Housing: Dormitories (women). **Activities:** Student government, student newspaper, yearbook, sororities.

STUDENT SERVICES. Career counseling, employment service for undergraduates, freshman orientation, personal counseling, placement service for graduates.

ANNUAL EXPENSES. Tuition and fees (1992-93): $6,120. $496 additional text and supply fee required for all students. **Room and board:** $2,250 room only. **Books and supplies:** $650. **Other expenses:** $1,100.

FINANCIAL AID. 55% of freshmen, 55% of continuing students receive some form of aid. All grants based on need. **Aid applications:** No closing date; applicants notified on a rolling basis beginning on or about July 15; must reply within 10 days.

ADDRESS/TELEPHONE. Lillie Lanier, Director of Admissions, Bauder College, Phipps Plaza, 3500 Peachtree Road NE, Atlanta, GA 30326-9975. (404) 237-7573. (800) 241-3797. Fax: (404) 237-1642.

Berry College
Rome, Georgia CB code: 5059

4-year private liberal arts college, coed. Founded in 1902. **Accreditation:** Regional. **Undergraduate enrollment:** 1,628 men and women. **Graduate enrollment:** 117 men and women. **Location:** Suburban campus in large town; 65 miles from Atlanta, adjacent to Rome. **Calendar:** Semester.

FRESHMAN ADMISSIONS. Selection criteria: School achievement record and test scores most important. Recommendations also considered.

ANNUAL EXPENSES. Tuition and fees: $8,050. **Room and board:** $4,590. **Books and supplies:** $450. **Other expenses:** $1,910.

ADDRESS/TELEPHONE. George Gaddie, Dean of Admissions, Berry College, PO Box 159 Mount Berry Station, Rome, GA 30149. (706) 236-2215. (800) MT-BERRY. Fax: (706) 236-2248.

Brenau University
Gainesville, Georgia CB code: 5066

Admissions:	73% of applicants accepted
Based on:	••• School record
	•• Interview, recommendations, test scores
	• Activities, essay, special talents
Completion:	85% of freshmen end year in good standing
	50% graduate, 19% of these enter graduate study

4-year private university, women only. Founded in 1878. **Accreditation:** Regional. **Undergraduate enrollment:** 125 men, 720 women full time; 183 men, 286 women part time. **Graduate enrollment:** 118 men, 207 women full time; 120 men, 228 women part time. **Faculty:** 159 total (87 full time), 57 with doctorates or other terminal degrees. **Location:** Suburban campus in small city; 52 miles from Atlanta. **Calendar:** Quarter, limited summer session. Saturday classes. **Microcomputers:** 55 located in dormitories, libraries. **Special facilities:** 2 art gallerys. **Additional facts:** Composed of 4 educational units: The Women's College (main campus), The Academy (women's secondary school), Nursing School (coeducational), and The University (coeducational evening and weekend programs). Undergraduate and graduate programs offered in education, business administration, and public administration, both on campus and at off-campus locations. Fine arts daytime program is coeducational.

DEGREES OFFERED. BA, BS, BFA, MS, MBA, MEd. 375 bachelor's degrees awarded in 1992. 30% in business and management, 5% communications, 22% teacher education, 18% health sciences, 7% psychology, 5% social sciences, 9% visual and performing arts. Graduate degrees offered in 7 major fields of study.

UNDERGRADUATE MAJORS. Accounting, applied mathematics, arts management, biology, business administration and management, commercial art, communications, criminal justice studies, dance, dance/theater, dramatic arts, early childhood education, education, education of the mentally handicapped, elementary education, English, English education, equestrian science, graphic design, history, human resources development, interior design, journalism, liberal/general studies, music education, music performance, nursing, personnel management, political science and government, psychology, public administration, public relations, radio/television broadcasting, secondary education, social science education, special education, studio art.

ACADEMIC PROGRAMS. Accelerated program, double major, education specialist degree, honors program, independent study, internships, student-designed major, study abroad, teacher preparation, weekend college, cross-registration. **Remedial services:** Learning center, preadmission summer program, reduced course load, remedial instruction, special counselor, tutoring, learning disability program. **ROTC:** Army. **Placement/credit:** AP, CLEP General and Subject, institutional tests; 80 credit hours maximum for bachelor's degree.

ACADEMIC REQUIREMENTS. Freshmen must earn minimum GPA of 2.0 to continue in good standing. 60% of freshmen return for sophomore year. Students must declare major by end of first year. **Graduation requirements:** 200 hours for bachelor's (85 in major). Most students required to take courses in arts/fine arts, computer science, English, foreign languages, history, humanities, mathematics, philosophy/religion, biological/physical sciences, social sciences. **Postgraduate studies:** 3% enter law school, 2% enter medical school, 7% enter MBA programs, 7% enter other graduate study. **Additional information:** Leadership curriculum available.

FRESHMAN ADMISSIONS. Selection criteria: School achievement record most important, followed by test scores and recommendations. **High school preparation:** 16 units required. Required and recommended units include English 4, mathematics 2-3, social science 3 and science 2-3. **Test requirements:** SAT or ACT; score report by September 1.

1992 FRESHMAN CLASS PROFILE. 3 men applied, 1 accepted, 1 enrolled; 349 women applied, 255 accepted, 132 enrolled. **Characteristics:** 79% from in state, 81% live in college housing, 11% have minority backgrounds, 1% are foreign students, 65% join fraternities/sororities. Average age is 20.

FALL-TERM APPLICATIONS. $30 fee, may be waived for applicants with need. No closing date; applicants notified on a rolling basis. Interview required for academically marginal applicants. Audition required for ballet, theater, music applicants. Portfolio required for commercial, studio art, interior design applicants. CRDA. Deferred and early admission available. Institutional early decision plan. Submit test scores of 1000 or better during junior year with self-reported minimum 3.0 GPA for acceptance under early decision.

STUDENT LIFE. Housing: Dormitories (women); apartment, sorority housing available. No housing for men available. Students under 22 years of age required to live in college housing unless living with family. **Activities:** Student government, magazine, radio, student newspaper, yearbook, choral groups, dance, drama, music ensembles, musical theater, opera, symphony orchestra, sororities, Brenau Fellowship Association, Young Republicians, Rotoract.

ATHLETICS. NAIA. **Intercollegiate:** Tennis. **Intramural:** Basketball, horseback riding, soccer, softball, swimming, tennis, volleyball.

STUDENT SERVICES. Aptitude testing, career counseling, employment service for undergraduates, freshman orientation, health services, on-campus day care, personal counseling, placement service for graduates, special adviser for adult students, veterans counselor, services/facilities for handicapped.

ANNUAL EXPENSES. Tuition and fees: $8,823. **Room and board:** $5,911. **Books and supplies:** $600. **Other expenses:** $800.

FINANCIAL AID. 55% of freshmen, 61% of continuing students receive some form of aid. 51% of grants, 81% of loans, 91% of jobs based on need. 71 enrolled freshmen were judged to have need, all were offered aid. Academic, music/drama, art, athletic, state/district residency, leadership, minority scholarships available. **Aid applications:** No closing date; priority given to applications received by May 15; applicants notified on a rolling basis beginning on or about April 1; must reply within 2 weeks.

ADDRESS/TELEPHONE. Dr. John Upchurch, Dean of Admissions, Brenau University, One Centennial Circle, Gainesville, GA 30501-3697. (706) 534-6100. (800) 252-5119. Fax: (706) 534-6168.

Brewton-Parker College
Mount Vernon, Georgia — CB code: 5068

4-year private liberal arts college, coed, affiliated with Southern Baptist Convention. Founded in 1904. **Accreditation:** Regional. **Undergraduate enrollment:** 1,974 men and women. **Faculty:** 125 total (40 full time), 21 with doctorates or other terminal degrees. **Location:** Rural campus in rural community; 90 miles from Macon or Savannah. **Calendar:** Quarter, limited summer session. **Microcomputers:** Located in libraries, classrooms.

DEGREES OFFERED. AA, BA, BS. 140 associate degrees awarded in 1992. 100% in multi/interdisciplinary studies. 100 bachelor's degrees awarded. 16% in business and management, 53% teacher education, 13% life sciences, 17% multi/interdisciplinary studies.

UNDERGRADUATE MAJORS. Associate: Biology, business administration and management, business education, chemistry, Christianity, criminal justice studies, data processing, dental hygiene, economics, education, elementary education, fine arts, health education, health sciences, history, home economics, legal secretary, liberal/general studies, mathematics, medical assistant, medical records administration, medical records technology, medical secretary, music, nursing, occupational therapy assistant, pharmacy, physical education, physical therapy, physics, political science and government, predentistry, prelaw, premedicine, prepharmacy, preveterinary, psychology, recreation and community services technologies, religious education, religious music, respiratory therapy, respiratory therapy technology, science technologies, secretarial and related programs, social sciences, sociology, statistics, word processing. **Bachelor's:** Accounting, biology, biology education, business administration and management, business and management, business education, Christianity, early childhood education, elementary education, English education, health education, history, history education, information sciences and systems, liberal/general studies, management information systems, marketing management, music, music education, office supervision and management, physical education, psychology, religion, secondary education, sociology.

ACADEMIC PROGRAMS. Dual enrollment of high school students, honors program, independent study, internships, teacher preparation. **Remedial services:** Learning center, reduced course load, remedial instruction, special counselor, tutoring.

ACADEMIC REQUIREMENTS. Freshmen must earn minimum GPA of 1.7 to continue in good standing. 60% of freshmen return for sophomore year. Students must declare major by end of first year. **Graduation requirements:** 95 hours for associate (25 in major), 187 hours for bachelor's (50 in major). Most students required to take courses in English, history, mathematics, philosophy/religion, biological/physical sciences, social sciences. **Postgraduate studies:** 85% from 2-year programs enter 4-year programs.

FRESHMAN ADMISSIONS. Selection criteria: Open admissions. **Test requirements:** SAT or ACT for placement and counseling only; score report by September 1.

1992 FRESHMAN CLASS PROFILE. 710 men and women enrolled. 70% had high school GPA of 3.0 or higher, 20% between 2.0 and 2.99. **Academic background:** Mid 50% of enrolled freshmen had SAT-V between 280-430, SAT-M between 280-460. 98% submitted SAT scores. **Characteristics:** 90% from in state, 60% live in college housing, 19% have minority backgrounds, 1% are foreign students. Average age is 19.

FALL-TERM APPLICATIONS. $15 fee, may be waived for applicants with need. No closing date; priority given to applications received by September 1; applicants notified on a rolling basis. Interview required for music, drama applicants. Audition required for music, drama applicants. CRDA.

STUDENT LIFE. Housing: Dormitories (men, women). **Activities:** Student government, radio, student newspaper, yearbook, choral groups, concert band, drama, jazz band, musical theater, pep band, handbell choir, fraternities, sororities, Baptist Student Union, ministerial association, Fellowship of Christian Athletes, Christian fraternities and sororities. **Additional information:** Religious observance required.

ATHLETICS. NAIA. **Intercollegiate:** Baseball M, basketball, golf M, soccer M, tennis. **Intramural:** Basketball, football M, softball, table tennis, tennis, volleyball.

STUDENT SERVICES. Aptitude testing, career counseling, employment service for undergraduates, freshman orientation, health services, personal counseling, placement service for graduates, veterans counselor.

ANNUAL EXPENSES. Tuition and fees (1992-93): $3,885. **Room and board:** $2,295. **Books and supplies:** $575. **Other expenses:** $1,000.

FINANCIAL AID. 96% of freshmen, 96% of continuing students receive some form of aid. Academic, music/drama, art, athletic, state/district residency, religious affiliation scholarships available. **Aid applications:** No closing date; priority given to applications received by April 1; applicants notified on a rolling basis beginning on or about June 1; must reply by date indicated on award letter.

ADDRESS/TELEPHONE. Jill O'Neal, Director of Admissions, Brewton-Parker College, Highway 280, Mount Vernon, GA 30445. (912) 583-2241. Fax: (912) 583-4498.

Brunswick College
Brunswick, Georgia — CB code: 5078

2-year public community college, coed. Founded in 1961. **Accreditation:** Regional. **Undergraduate enrollment:** 278 men, 583 women full time; 318 men, 656 women part time. **Faculty:** 81 total (67 full time), 18 with doctorates or other terminal degrees. **Location:** Suburban campus in large town; 70 miles from Savannah, 60 miles from Jacksonville, Florida. **Calendar:** Quarter, limited summer session. Saturday and extensive evening/early morning classes. **Microcomputers:** 120 located in libraries, classrooms, computer centers. **Additional facts:** Students may take courses at Camden Center in Kingsland

DEGREES OFFERED. AA, AS, AAS. 187 associate degrees awarded in 1992.

UNDERGRADUATE MAJORS. Accounting, biology, business administration and management, business data processing and related programs, chemistry, criminal justice studies, data processing, drafting and design technology, education, electronic technology, engineering and engineering-related technologies, forestry and related sciences, liberal/general studies, management information systems, manufacturing technology, marketing and distribution, mathematics, mechanical design technology, medical laboratory technologies, nursing, precision metal work, radiograph medical technology, recreation and community services technologies, secretarial and related programs.

ACADEMIC PROGRAMS. 2-year transfer program, double major, dual enrollment of high school students, independent study, teacher preparation. **Remedial services:** Learning center, reduced course load, remedial instruction, special counselor, tutoring. **Placement/credit:** AP, CLEP General and Subject, institutional tests; 30 credit hours maximum for associate degree.

ACADEMIC REQUIREMENTS. Freshmen must earn minimum GPA of 1.5 to continue in good standing. 59% of freshmen return for sophomore year. **Graduation requirements:** 96 hours for associate. Most students required to take courses in arts/fine arts, English, humanities, mathematics, biological/physical sciences, social sciences.

FRESHMAN ADMISSIONS. Selection criteria: Minimum SAT-verbal score of 250 or ACT English of 13, or SAT-mathematical score of 280 or ACT mathematical score of 14, or 1.8 high school GPA. **High school preparation:** 15 units required. Required units include biological science 1, English 4, foreign language 2, mathematics 3, physical science 2 and social science 3. College preparatory program required only of prebaccalaureate transfer program applicants. **Test requirements:** SAT or ACT; score report by August 15. **Additional information:** Students scoring below 350 SAT-verbal or 350 SAT-mathematical or equivalent on enhanced ACT must take Collegiate Placement Examination.

1992 FRESHMAN CLASS PROFILE. 111 men and women enrolled. **Characteristics:** 90% from in state, 100% commute, 19% have minority backgrounds. Average age is 26.

FALL-TERM APPLICATIONS. $5 fee. Closing date September 1; applicants notified on a rolling basis beginning on or about February 15. Interview required for registered nursing, allied health programs applicants. Deferred and early admission available.

STUDENT LIFE. Activities: Student government, magazine, student newspaper, minority club, Baptist student union.

ATHLETICS. NJCAA. **Intercollegiate:** Basketball M, softball W, tennis M. **Intramural:** Archery, badminton, basketball, bowling, cross-country, golf, handball, racquetball, sailing, softball, swimming, table tennis, tennis, volleyball.

STUDENT SERVICES. Aptitude testing, career counseling, employment service for undergraduates, freshman orientation, personal counseling, placement service for graduates, special adviser for adult students, veterans counselor, services/facilities for handicapped.

ANNUAL EXPENSES. Tuition and fees: $1,179, $939 additional for out-of-state students. **Books and supplies:** $600. **Other expenses:** $500.

FINANCIAL AID. 50% of freshmen, 50% of continuing students receive some form of aid. 76% of grants, 86% of loans, 58% of jobs based on need. Academic, athletic, state/district residency, leadership, minority scholarships available. **Aid applications:** No closing date; priority given to applications received by May 1; applicants notified on a rolling basis beginning on or about July 1; must reply within 3 weeks.

ADDRESS/TELEPHONE. Harrison R. Fields, Registrar/Director of Admissions, Brunswick College, Altama Avenue at Fourth Street, Brunswick, GA 31523. (912) 264-7253. Fax: (912) 262-3072.

Chattahoochee Technical Institute

Marietta, Georgia — CB code: 5441

2-year public technical college, coed. **Accreditation:** Regional. **Undergraduate enrollment:** 364 men, 337 women full time; 499 men, 568 women part time. **Faculty:** 83 total (40 full time), 9 with doctorates or other terminal degrees. **Location:** Suburban campus in large town; 20 miles from Atlanta, 2 miles from Marietta. Extensive evening/early morning classes. **Microcomputers:** 178 located in classrooms, computer centers.

DEGREES OFFERED. 33 associate degrees awarded in 1992. 22% in business and management, 25% computer sciences, 43% engineering technologies, 9% parks/recreation, protective services, public affairs.

UNDERGRADUATE MAJORS. Accounting, computer programming, electrical technology, electromechanical engineering technology, law enforcement and corrections, management science, marketing management, secretarial and related programs.

ACADEMIC PROGRAMS. Dual enrollment of high school students, internships. **Remedial services:** Learning center, reduced course load, remedial instruction, special counselor, tutoring. **Placement/credit:** Institutional tests; 15 credit hours maximum for associate degree.

ACADEMIC REQUIREMENTS. Freshmen must earn minimum GPA of 2.0 to continue in good standing. **Graduation requirements:** 105 hours for associate (65 in major). Most students required to take courses in English, mathematics, social sciences.

FRESHMAN ADMISSIONS. Selection criteria: Diploma programs: satisfactory scores on Technical Assessment and Placement Program (TAPP). Associate of Applied Technology (AAT): SAT scores of 400 mathematics, 380 verbal. **Test requirements:** SAT or ACT (SAT preferred); score report by September 25.

1992 FRESHMAN CLASS PROFILE. 499 men, 580 women enrolled. **Characteristics:** 100% from in state, 100% commute. Average age is 20.

FALL-TERM APPLICATIONS. $15 fee. Closing date September 10; priority given to applications received by September 1; applicants notified on a rolling basis beginning on or about September 15. Interview recommended. Deferred and early admission available.

STUDENT LIFE. Activities: Student government, television.

STUDENT SERVICES. Aptitude testing, career counseling, employment service for undergraduates, personal counseling, placement service for graduates, veterans counselor, services/facilities for handicapped.

ANNUAL EXPENSES. Tuition and fees (1992-93): $654, $360 additional for out-of-state students. **Books and supplies:** $850.

FINANCIAL AID. 15% of freshmen, 22% of continuing students receive some form of aid. 97% of grants based on need. 296 enrolled freshmen were judged to have need, all were offered aid. Academic scholarships available. **Aid applications:** No closing date. **Additional information:** We attempt to work out individual situations with students when fees present a hardship.

ADDRESS/TELEPHONE. Boyd Saunders, Director of Admissions, Chattahoochee Technical Institute, 980 South Cobb Drive, Marietta, GA 30060. (706) 528-4545. Fax: (706) 528-4580.

Clark Atlanta University

Atlanta, Georgia — CB code: 5110

Admissions:	49% of applicants accepted
Based on:	••• School record
	•• Test scores
	• Activities, essay, interview, recommendations, special talents
Completion:	85% of freshmen end year in good standing

4-year private university, coed, affiliated with United Methodist Church. Founded in 1869. **Accreditation:** Regional. **Undergraduate enrollment:** 3,251 men and women full time; 113 men and women part time. **Graduate enrollment:** 1,229 men and women full time; 501 men and women part time. **Faculty:** 321 total (251 full time), 199 with doctorates or other terminal degrees. **Location:** Urban campus in very large city; 2 miles from downtown. **Calendar:** Semester. **Microcomputers:** Located in libraries, computer centers, campus-wide network.

DEGREES OFFERED. BA, BS, MA, MS, MBA, PhD, EdD. 360 bachelor's degrees awarded in 1992. 36% in business and management, 18% communications, 9% education, 6% life sciences, 6% psychology, 8% social sciences. Graduate degrees offered in 27 major fields of study.

UNDERGRADUATE MAJORS. Accounting, advertising, allied health, biology, business administration and management, business economics, business education, chemistry, communications, computer and information sciences, criminology, dramatic arts, economics, education, elementary education, engineering and other disciplines, English, English education, fashion merchandising, finance, fine arts, foreign languages (multiple emphasis), French, German, health education, history, journalism, junior high education, marketing management, mass media arts, mathematical and computer sciences, mathematics, mathematics education, medical illustrating, medical laboratory technologies, medical records technology, music, nutritional sciences, philosophy, physical education, physical therapy, physics, political science and government, psychology, public relations, radio/television broadcasting, radio/television technology, religion, secondary education, social science education, social sciences, social work, sociology, Spanish, speech.

ACADEMIC PROGRAMS. Accelerated program, cooperative education, double major, dual enrollment of high school students, education specialist degree, honors program, independent study, internships, study abroad, teacher preparation, visiting/exchange student program, cross-registration; liberal arts/career combination in engineering; combined bachelor's/graduate program in business administration. **Remedial services:** Learning center, reduced course load, remedial instruction, special counselor, tutoring. **ROTC:** Air Force, Army, Naval. **Placement/credit:** Institutional tests.

ACADEMIC REQUIREMENTS. Freshmen must earn minimum GPA of 1.76 to continue in good standing. 80% of freshmen return for sophomore year. Students must declare major by end of second year. **Graduation requirements:** 122 hours for bachelor's (36 in major). Most students required to take courses in computer science, English, foreign languages, history, humanities, mathematics, philosophy/religion, biological/physical sciences, social sciences.

FRESHMAN ADMISSIONS. High school preparation: 16 units required. Required units include biological science 1, English 4, foreign language 1, mathematics 2, physical science 1, social science 2 and science 2. **Test requirements:** SAT or ACT (SAT preferred); score report by August 1. **Additional information:** High school transcripts, 2 recommendations required.

1992 FRESHMAN CLASS PROFILE. 5,749 men and women applied, 2,840 accepted; 797 enrolled. **Characteristics:** 57% from in state, 60% commute, 98% have minority backgrounds, 2% are foreign students. Average age is 18.

FALL-TERM APPLICATIONS. $20 fee, may be waived for applicants with need. Closing date March 1; applicants notified on a rolling basis beginning on or about January 1; must reply within 30 days of notification of acceptance. Interview recommended. Audition recommended for music, drama applicants. Essay recommended. Early admission available.

STUDENT LIFE. Housing: Dormitories (men, women, coed). **Activities:** Student government, film, radio, student newspaper, television, yearbook, choral groups, concert band, dance, drama, jazz band, marching band, musical theater, pep band, symphony orchestra, fraternities, sororities, NAACP, women's resource center, Caribbean-oriented student organization.

ATHLETICS. NCAA. **Intercollegiate:** Basketball, football M, tennis, track and field. **Intramural:** Basketball, track and field.

STUDENT SERVICES. Aptitude testing, career counseling, employment service for undergraduates, freshman orientation, health services, personal counseling, placement service for graduates, veterans counselor, services/facilities for handicapped.

ANNUAL EXPENSES. Tuition and fees (projected): $7,460. **Room and board:** $3,940. **Books and supplies:** $630. **Other expenses:** $945.

FINANCIAL AID. 78% of freshmen, 76% of continuing students receive some form of aid. 82% of grants, 82% of loans, all jobs based on need. 561 enrolled freshmen were judged to have need, all were offered aid. Academic, music/drama, athletic, alumni affiliation scholarships available. **Aid applications:** Closing date April 15; priority given to applications received by April 1; applicants notified on a rolling basis beginning on or about June 30; must reply within 30 days.

ADDRESS/TELEPHONE. Clifton Rawles, Director of Admissions, Clark Atlanta University, James P. Brawley Drive at Fair Street, S.W, Atlanta, GA 30314. (404) 880-8000. Fax: (404) 880-8222.

Clayton State College
Morrow, Georgia CB code: 5145

4-year public college of arts and sciences and business college, coed. Founded in 1969. **Accreditation:** Regional. **Undergraduate enrollment:** 777 men, 996 women full time; 1,110 men, 1,974 women part time. **Faculty:** 208 total (109 full time), 54 with doctorates or other terminal degrees. **Location:** Suburban campus in small city; 12 miles from Atlanta. **Calendar:** Quarter, extensive summer session. Extensive evening/early morning classes. **Microcomputers:** Located in libraries, classrooms, computer centers. **Special facilities:** Spivey Concert Hall. **Additional facts:** Extensive continuing education program available. Various schools include college of nursing, college of health science, and technical college.

DEGREES OFFERED. AA, AS, AAS, BA, BS. 364 associate degrees awarded in 1992. 7% in business and management, 22% engineering technologies, 29% health sciences, 42% social sciences. 110 bachelor's degrees awarded. 74% in business and management, 25% health sciences.

UNDERGRADUATE MAJORS. Associate: Accounting, aeronautical technology, agricultural engineering, agricultural sciences, aircraft mechanics, art education, biology, business administration and management, business and office, business data processing and related programs, chemistry, clinical laboratory science, computer and information sciences, computer servicing technology, criminal justice studies, data processing, dental hygiene, drafting, drafting and design technology, dramatic arts, education, electrical and electronics equipment repair, electromechanical technology, electronic technology, elementary education, engineering, engineering and engineering-related technologies, English, finance, forestry and related sciences, French, history, home economics, journalism, legal secretary, liberal/general studies, marketing and distribution, marketing management, mathematics, mechanical design technology, medical laboratory technologies, medical records administration, music, music performance, music theory and composition, nursing, occupational therapy, philosophy, physical education, physical therapy, physics, political science and government, predentistry, prelaw, premedicine, prepharmacy, preveterinary, psychology, secondary education, secretarial and related programs, sociology, Spanish, studio art, telecommunications, trade and industrial supervision and management, urban studies. **Bachelor's:** Accounting, business administration and management, business and management, management information systems, music performance, music theory and composition, nursing.

ACADEMIC PROGRAMS. 2-year transfer program, cooperative education, dual enrollment of high school students, honors program, internships, study abroad, cross-registration. **Remedial services:** Learning center, remedial instruction, special counselor, tutoring. **Placement/credit:** AP, CLEP General and Subject, institutional tests; 60 credit hours maximum for associate degree; 135 credit hours maximum for bachelor's degree.

ACADEMIC REQUIREMENTS. Freshmen must earn minimum GPA of 2.0 to continue in good standing. 48% of freshmen return for sophomore year. Students must declare major on enrollment. **Graduation requirements:** 90 hours for associate (30 in major), 180 hours for bachelor's (45 in major). Most students required to take courses in English, history, humanities, mathematics, philosophy/religion, biological/physical sciences, social sciences. **Postgraduate studies:** 62% from 2-year programs enter 4-year programs.

FRESHMAN ADMISSIONS. Selection criteria: Open admissions. Selective admissions to health sciences, music, and business programs. **High school preparation:** 15 units required. Required units include English 4, foreign language 2, mathematics 3, physical science 1, social science 3 and science 2. Students not meeting college preparatory requirements must take remedial classes before entering any program. **Test requirements:** SAT or ACT; score report by September 1.

1992 FRESHMAN CLASS PROFILE. 2,710 men and women enrolled. **Academic background:** Mid 50% of enrolled freshmen had SAT-V between 390-490, SAT-M between 400-500. 95% submitted SAT scores. **Characteristics:** 99% from in state, 100% commute, 9% have minority backgrounds, 1% are foreign students. Average age is 20.

FALL-TERM APPLICATIONS. No fee. Closing date September 1; applicants notified on a rolling basis. Audition recommended for music applicants. Deferred and early admission available.

STUDENT LIFE. Activities: Student government, student newspaper, choral groups, concert band, dance, drama, jazz band, music ensembles, musical theater, opera, Black Cultural Awareness Association, Student Political Union, College Republicans, Students Supporting other Students, International Awarness Club, Baptist Student Union, United Methodist Fellowship, Rotoract.

ATHLETICS. NAIA. **Intercollegiate:** Basketball, golf, soccer M. **Intramural:** Badminton, baseball, basketball, cross-country, golf, soccer M, softball, tennis, volleyball.

STUDENT SERVICES. Aptitude testing, career counseling, employment service for undergraduates, freshman orientation, personal counseling, placement service for graduates, veterans counselor, handicapped/special needs student counseling, services/facilities for handicapped.

ANNUAL EXPENSES. Tuition and fees (projected): $1,440, $1,341 additional for out-of-state students. **Books and supplies:** $555. **Other expenses:** $1,080.

FINANCIAL AID. 25% of freshmen, 25% of continuing students receive some form of aid. 98% of grants, 84% of loans, all jobs based on need. 179 enrolled freshmen were judged to have need, all were offered aid. Academic, music/drama, art, athletic scholarships available. **Aid applications:** No closing date; priority given to applications received by April 1; applicants notified on a rolling basis beginning on or about July 1; must reply within 2 weeks. **Additional information:** 30-day emergency loans available for tuition, books.

ADDRESS/TELEPHONE. Tonya R. Hobson, Director of Admissions/Registrar, Clayton State College, PO Box 285, 5900 Lee Street, Morrow, GA 30260-1221. (404) 961-3500. Fax: (404) 961-3700.

Columbus College
Columbus, Georgia CB code: 5123

Admissions: 77% of applicants accepted
Based on: ••• School record, test scores
• Interview, recommendations
Completion: 85% of freshmen end year in good standing
26% graduate, 10% of these enter graduate study

4-year public liberal arts college, coed. Founded in 1958. **Accreditation:** Regional. **Undergraduate enrollment:** 1,051 men, 1,749 women full time; 627 men, 1,027 women part time. **Graduate enrollment:** 99 men, 162 women full time; 103 men, 191 women part time. **Faculty:** 241 total (193 full time), 137 with doctorates or other terminal degrees. **Location:** Suburban campus in small city; 100 miles from Atlanta. **Calendar:** Quarter, extensive summer session. **Microcomputers:** 265 located in libraries, computer centers.

DEGREES OFFERED. AA, AS, AAS, BA, BS, MS, MBA, MEd. 131 associate degrees awarded in 1992. 26% in health sciences, 20% allied health, 12% multi/interdisciplinary studies, 40% parks/recreation, protective services, public affairs. 454 bachelor's degrees awarded. 24% in business and management, 21% teacher education, 13% health sciences, 16% letters/literature, 9% parks/recreation, protective services, public affairs, 5% social sciences. Graduate degrees offered in 16 major fields of study.

UNDERGRADUATE MAJORS. Associate: Criminal justice studies, data processing, dental hygiene, electronic technology, health sciences, liberal/general studies, medical laboratory technologies, medical records technology, nursing, occupational therapy, occupational therapy assistant, physical therapy, recreation and community services technologies, respiratory therapy technology. **Bachelor's:** Accounting, art education, biology, business administration and management, business and management, business economics, chemistry, clinical laboratory science, computer and information sciences, criminal justice studies, dramatic arts, early childhood education, education of the mentally handicapped, elementary education, English, English education, finance, fine arts, geology, health education, health sciences, history, junior high education, liberal/general studies, management information systems, marketing management, mathematics, mathematics education, music, music education, nursing, parks and recreation management, physical education, physician's assistant, political science and government, predentistry, prelaw, premedicine, prepharmacy, preveterinary, psychology, public administration, public health laboratory science, science education, secondary education, social science education, sociology, special education, speech, speech pathology/audiology, speech/communication/theater education.

ACADEMIC PROGRAMS. 2-year transfer program, accelerated program, cooperative education, double major, dual enrollment of high school students, education specialist degree, independent study, internships, study abroad, teacher preparation; liberal arts/career combination in engineering, forestry. **Remedial services:** Learning center, remedial instruction, special counselor, tutoring, summer enrichment program. **ROTC:** Army. **Placement/credit:** AP, CLEP General and Subject, institutional tests; 45 credit hours maximum for associate degree; 90 credit hours maximum for bachelor's degree.

ACADEMIC REQUIREMENTS. Freshmen must earn minimum GPA of 1.45 to continue in good standing. 70% of freshmen return for sophomore year. Students must declare major by end of second year. **Graduation requirements:** 90 hours for associate, 192 hours for bachelor's (30 in major). Most students required to take courses in arts/fine arts, English, history, humanities, mathematics, biological/physical sciences, social sciences.

FRESHMAN ADMISSIONS. Selection criteria: Minimum SAT-mathematical score of 350 or ACT mathematical of 16, or SAT-verbal score of 350 or ACT English of 18 required. Minimum SAT-verbal score of 280 or ACT English of 13, or SAT-mathematical of 250 or ACT mathematical of 14, or high school GPA of 1.8 considered for developmental studies program. **High school preparation:** 16 units required. Required units include English 4, foreign language 2, mathematics 3, physical science 1, social science 3 and science 3. In addition to a physical science, students are required to complete two units of laboratory sciences. **Test requirements:** SAT or ACT (SAT preferred); score report by September 1.

1992 FRESHMAN CLASS PROFILE. 1,297 men and women applied, 996 accepted; 358 enrolled. 35% had high school GPA of 3.0 or higher, 63% between 2.0 and 2.99. **Academic background:** Mid 50% of enrolled freshmen had SAT-V between 350-470, SAT-M between 400-510; ACT composite between 18-23. 87% submitted SAT scores, 16% submitted ACT scores. **Characteristics:** 87% from in state, 97% commute, 42% have minority backgrounds, 2% are foreign students, 2% join fraternities/sororities. Average age is 19.

FALL-TERM APPLICATIONS. $10 fee, may be waived for applicants with need. Closing date September 1; priority given to applications received by July 1; applicants notified on a rolling basis. Interview required for health sciences, nursing, education applicants. Audition required for music applicants. Portfolio recommended for art applicants. Deferred and early admission available. Early admission applicants must have a combined SAT score of 1,000 and a minimum cummulative high school GPA of 3.0 in academic subjects.

STUDENT LIFE. Housing: Apartment, fraternity, sorority, handicapped housing available. **Activities:** Student government, magazine, radio, student newspaper, yearbook, choral groups, concert band, drama, jazz band, music ensembles, musical theater, pep band, symphony orchestra, choral readers, fraternities, sororities, Baptist Student Union, service organizations, African American Student Union.

ATHLETICS. NCAA. **Intercollegiate:** Baseball M, basketball, cross-country, golf M, soccer M, softball W, tennis, volleyball W. **Intramural:** Basketball M, bowling, golf, racquetball, soccer M, softball, table tennis, tennis, volleyball.

STUDENT SERVICES. Aptitude testing, career counseling, employment service for undergraduates, freshman orientation, health services, personal counseling, placement service for graduates, special adviser for adult students, veterans counselor, services/facilities for handicapped.

ANNUAL EXPENSES. Tuition and fees: $1,602, $1,380 additional for out-of-state students. **Books and supplies:** $650. **Other expenses:** $600.

FINANCIAL AID. 37% of freshmen, 33% of continuing students receive some form of aid. 65% of grants, 73% of loans, 41% of jobs based on need. 161 enrolled freshmen were judged to have need, all were offered aid. Academic, music/drama, art, athletic scholarships available. **Aid applications:** No closing date; priority given to applications received by June 1; applicants notified on a rolling basis beginning on or about June 15; must reply within 4 weeks.

ADDRESS/TELEPHONE. Carl Wallman, Director of Admissions and Registrar, Columbus College, 3600 Algonquin Drive, Columbus, GA 31907-2079. (706) 568-2035. Fax: (706) 568-2462.

Columbus Technical Institute
Columbus, Georgia — CB code: 7005

2-year public technical college. **Accreditation:** Regional. **Undergraduate enrollment:** 1,238 men and women. **Location:** Suburban campus in small city. **Calendar:** Quarter.

FRESHMAN ADMISSIONS. Selection criteria: Open admissions.

ANNUAL EXPENSES. Tuition and fees (1992-93): $540.

ADDRESS/TELEPHONE. Columbus Technical Institute, 928 45th Street, Columbus, GA 31995. (706) 649-1800. Fax: (404) 649-1885.

Covenant College
Lookout Mountain, Georgia — CB code: 6124

Admissions:	80% of applicants accepted
Based on:	••• Religious affiliation/commitment, school record, test scores
	•• Essay, interview, recommendations
	• Activities
Completion:	92% of freshmen end year in good standing
	48% graduate

4-year private liberal arts college, coed, affiliated with Presbyterian Church in America. Founded in 1955. **Accreditation:** Regional. **Undergraduate enrollment:** 247 men, 314 women full time; 17 men, 22 women part time. **Graduate enrollment:** 15 men, 10 women full time. **Faculty:** 49 total (48 full time), 26 with doctorates or other terminal degrees. **Location:** Suburban campus in rural community; 5 miles from Chattanooga, Tennessee. **Calendar:** Semester, limited summer session. Extensive evening/early morning classes. **Microcomputers:** 56 located in libraries, computer centers.

DEGREES OFFERED. AA, BA, BS, MEd. 1 associate degree awarded in 1992. 100% in health sciences. 99 bachelor's degrees awarded. 11% in business and management, 15% teacher education, 15% letters/literature, 5% life sciences, 23% multi/interdisciplinary studies, 18% social sciences. Graduate degrees offered in 3 major fields of study.

UNDERGRADUATE MAJORS. Associate: Bible studies, business and management, health sciences. **Bachelor's:** Bible studies, biology, business administration and management, business and management, chemistry, computer and information sciences, elementary education, engineering, English, history, history education, humanities, humanities and social sciences, junior high education, liberal/general studies, music, music education, music performance, physical sciences, psychology, secondary education, sociology.

ACADEMIC PROGRAMS. 2-year transfer program, double major, external degree, honors program, independent study, internships, study abroad, teacher preparation, Washington semester, dual engineering degree with Georgia Institute of Technology; liberal arts/career combination in engineering. **Remedial services:** Reduced course load, remedial instruction, special counselor, tutoring. **ROTC:** Army. **Placement/credit:** AP, CLEP General and Subject, institutional tests; 30 credit hours maximum for bachelor's degree.

ACADEMIC REQUIREMENTS. Freshmen must earn minimum GPA of 1.8 to continue in good standing. 71% of freshmen return for sophomore year. Students must declare major by end of second year. **Graduation requirements:** 62 hours for associate (26 in major), 126 hours for bachelor's (49 in major). Most students required to take courses in arts/fine arts, computer science, English, foreign languages, history, humanities, mathematics, philosophy/religion, biological/physical sciences, social sciences. **Additional information:** Organizational Management Program designed for adult students with minimum of 5 years of work experience who have completed at least 2 years of college. Maximum of 32 credit hours given for assessment of life experience learning. All classes held in evenings, with degree completion taking a little over 1 year.

FRESHMAN ADMISSIONS. Selection criteria: School achievement record, test scores, recommendation, autobiography, personal interview very important. **High school preparation:** 16 units recommended. Recommended units include English 4, foreign language 2, mathematics 3, social science 2 and science 2. 3 electives recommended. **Test requirements:** SAT or ACT (SAT preferred); score report by June 1.

1992 FRESHMAN CLASS PROFILE. 168 men applied, 108 accepted, 65 enrolled; 232 women applied, 210 accepted, 114 enrolled. 79% had high school GPA of 3.0 or higher, 20% between 2.0 and 2.99. 26% were in top tenth and 62% were in top quarter of graduating class. **Academic background:** Mid 50% of enrolled freshmen had SAT-V between 450-560, SAT-M between 480-580; ACT composite between 21-28. 58% submitted SAT scores, 44% submitted ACT scores. **Characteristics:** 15% from in state, 99% live in college housing, 6% have minority backgrounds, 2% are foreign students. Average age is 19.

FALL-TERM APPLICATIONS. $20 fee. No closing date; priority given to applications received by March 31; applicants notified on a rolling basis; must reply by May 1 or within 3 weeks if notified thereafter. Interview required. Audition required for music, voice applicants. Essay required. CRDA. Deferred and early admission available.

STUDENT LIFE. Housing: Dormitories (men, women); apartment housing available. **Activities:** Student government, magazine, student newspaper, yearbook, choral groups, concert band, dance, drama, music ensembles, symphony orchestra, Christian Service Council, Student Missions Fellowship, Rotoract, Young Republicans, Prison Ministries, On and Off Campus Ministries, Inner City Ministries, Pro Life, World Christian Fellowship, Young Life. **Additional information:** Smoking, alcoholic beverages, and drugs prohibited. Approved forms of dance allowed.

ATHLETICS. NAIA. **Intercollegiate:** Basketball, cross-country, soccer M, volleyball W. **Intramural:** Basketball, soccer, softball, tennis, volleyball.

STUDENT SERVICES. Aptitude testing, career counseling, employment service for undergraduates, freshman orientation, health services,

personal counseling, placement service for graduates, special adviser for adult students, services/facilities for handicapped.

ANNUAL EXPENSES. Tuition and fees (1992-93): $8,640. **Room and board:** $3,654. **Books and supplies:** $470. **Other expenses:** $560.

FINANCIAL AID. 86% of freshmen, 85% of continuing students receive some form of aid. 62% of grants, 95% of loans, 90% of jobs based on need. 139 enrolled freshmen were judged to have need, all were offered aid. Academic, music/drama, athletic, state/district residency, leadership, religious affiliation scholarships available. **Aid applications:** No closing date; priority given to applications received by March 31; applicants notified on a rolling basis beginning on or about February 1; must reply within 3 weeks.

ADDRESS/TELEPHONE. Richard Allen, Director of Admissions Counseling, Covenant College, Scenic Highway, Lookout Mountain, GA 30750. (706) 820-1560 ext. 1148. (800) 926-8362. Fax: (706) 820-0672.

Dalton College
Dalton, Georgia — CB code: 5167

2-year public junior college, coed. Founded in 1963. **Accreditation:** Regional. **Undergraduate enrollment:** 590 men, 744 women full time; 608 men, 942 women part time. **Faculty:** 104 total (80 full time), 40 with doctorates or other terminal degrees. **Location:** Suburban campus in large town; 25 miles from Chattanooga, Tennessee, 90 miles from Atlanta. **Calendar:** Quarter, limited summer session. **Microcomputers:** Located in libraries, computer centers.

DEGREES OFFERED. 311 associate degrees awarded in 1992.

UNDERGRADUATE MAJORS. Accounting, allied health, business and office, business computer/console/peripheral equipment operation, business data processing and related programs, business data programming, drafting, electrical and electronics equipment repair, engineering and engineering-related technologies, finance, law enforcement and corrections technologies, liberal/general studies, marketing and distribution, medical laboratory technologies, nursing, science technologies, secretarial and related programs.

ACADEMIC PROGRAMS. 2-year transfer program, independent study, internships. **Remedial services:** Remedial instruction. **Placement/credit:** AP, CLEP General and Subject, institutional tests.

ACADEMIC REQUIREMENTS. Freshmen must earn minimum GPA of 1.8 to continue in good standing. 60% of freshmen return for sophomore year. Students must declare major on application. **Graduation requirements:** 96 hours for associate. Most students required to take courses in English, history, mathematics, biological/physical sciences.

FRESHMAN ADMISSIONS. Selection criteria: Minimum SAT-verbal score of 250 or ACT English of 10, or SAT-mathematical score of 280 or ACT mathematical of 5, or 1.8 high school GPA. **High school preparation:** 16 units required. Required units include English 4, foreign language 2, mathematics 3, social science 3 and science 3. **Test requirements:** SAT or ACT; score report by September 19.

1992 FRESHMAN CLASS PROFILE. 1,465 men and women enrolled. **Characteristics:** 99% from in state, 100% commute, 3% have minority backgrounds, 1% are foreign students.

FALL-TERM APPLICATIONS. No fee. Closing date September 1; applicants notified on a rolling basis. Deferred admission available.

STUDENT LIFE. Activities: Student government, film, magazine, television, Circle-K, Baptist Student Union, service and honor societies.

ATHLETICS. NJCAA. **Intramural:** Badminton, basketball, softball.

STUDENT SERVICES. Aptitude testing, career counseling, employment service for undergraduates, personal counseling, placement service for graduates, services/facilities for handicapped.

ANNUAL EXPENSES. Tuition and fees: $1,074, $939 additional for out-of-state students. **Books and supplies:** $600. **Other expenses:** $200.

FINANCIAL AID. Grants, loans, jobs available. Academic, leadership scholarships available. **Aid applications:** No closing date; priority given to applications received by August 1; applicants notified on a rolling basis beginning on or about July 1.

ADDRESS/TELEPHONE. Dr. David F. Hay, Registrar/Director of Admissions, Dalton College, 213 North College Drive, Dalton, GA 30720. (800) 829-4436. (800) 829-4436. Fax: (706) 272-4588.

Darton College
Albany, Georgia — CB code: 5026

2-year public community college, coed. Founded in 1963. **Accreditation:** Regional. **Undergraduate enrollment:** 2,633 men and women. **Faculty:** 150 total (80 full time), 26 with doctorates or other terminal degrees. **Location:** Urban campus in small city; 175 miles south of Atlanta. **Calendar:** Quarter, limited summer session. Extensive evening/early morning classes. **Microcomputers:** 120 located in libraries, classrooms, computer centers.

DEGREES OFFERED. AA, AS, AAS. 321 associate degrees awarded in 1992. 28% in business and management, 9% teacher education, 30% health sciences, 17% multi/interdisciplinary studies. 15% in psychology.

UNDERGRADUATE MAJORS. Accounting, agricultural sciences, air conditioning/heating/refrigeration mechanics, automotive mechanics, biology, business administration and management, business and management, business and office, business computer/console/peripheral equipment operation, business data processing and related programs, business data programming, carpentry, chemistry, computer and information sciences, computer programming, construction, criminal justice studies, criminology, data processing, dental hygiene, diesel engine mechanics, dramatic arts, education, electrical and electronics equipment repair, elementary education, engineering, engineering and engineering-related technologies, English, English literature, food production/management/services, forestry and related sciences, French, geology, graphic arts technology, history, home economics, information sciences and systems, journalism, law enforcement and corrections technologies, liberal/general studies, marketing and distribution, mathematics, medical assistant, medical laboratory technologies, medical records administration, medical records technology, music, nursing, office supervision and management, physical sciences, physics, political science and government, predentistry, premedicine, prepharmacy, psychology, public administration, public affairs, respiratory therapy, secondary education, secretarial and related programs, small business management and ownership, social sciences, social work, sociology, Spanish, speech, statistics, visual and performing arts.

ACADEMIC PROGRAMS. 2-year transfer program, cooperative education, dual enrollment of high school students, honors program, independent study, student-designed major, study abroad, cross-registration. **Remedial services:** Learning center, preadmission summer program, remedial instruction, special counselor, tutoring. **Placement/credit:** AP, CLEP General and Subject, institutional tests.

ACADEMIC REQUIREMENTS. Freshmen must earn minimum GPA of 1.8 to continue in good standing. Students must declare major by end of first year. **Graduation requirements:** 90 hours for associate (30 in major). Most students required to take courses in English, history, mathematics, biological/physical sciences, social sciences.

FRESHMAN ADMISSIONS. Selection criteria: High school GPA and test scores are most important. **High school preparation:** 16 units required. Required units include English 4, foreign language 2, mathematics 3, social science 3 and science 3. **Test requirements:** SAT or ACT (SAT preferred); score report by August 18.

1992 FRESHMAN CLASS PROFILE. 916 men and women enrolled. 12% had high school GPA of 3.0 or higher, 50% between 2.0 and 2.99. **Characteristics:** 98% from in state. Average age is 25.

FALL-TERM APPLICATIONS. $5 fee. No closing date; priority given to applications received by September 1; applicants notified on a rolling basis; must reply by registration. Deferred and early admission available.

STUDENT LIFE. Activities: Student government, magazine, choral groups, concert band, drama, jazz band, music ensembles, symphony orchestra.

ATHLETICS. NJCAA. **Intercollegiate:** Golf, swimming, table tennis, tennis. **Intramural:** Basketball, bowling, golf, softball, table tennis, tennis, volleyball.

STUDENT SERVICES. Employment service for undergraduates, personal counseling, placement service for graduates.

ANNUAL EXPENSES. Tuition and fees: $1,119, $939 additional for out-of-state students. **Books and supplies:** $300. **Other expenses:** $600.

FINANCIAL AID. 65% of continuing students receive some form of aid. 60% of jobs based on need. Academic, music/drama, art scholarships available. **Aid applications:** No closing date; priority given to applications received by September 1; applicants notified on a rolling basis beginning on or about July 15; must reply within 3 weeks.

ADDRESS/TELEPHONE. Charles T. Edwards, Registrar/Director of Admissions, Darton College, 2400 Gillionville Road, Albany, GA 31707-3098. (912) 888-8740.

DeKalb College
Decatur, Georgia — CB code: 5711

2-year public junior college, coed. Founded in 1964. **Accreditation:** Regional. **Undergraduate enrollment:** 15,976 men and women. **Faculty:** 1,010 total (320 full time), 175 with doctorates or other terminal degrees. **Location:** Urban campus in large town; in Atlanta metropolitan area. **Calendar:** Quarter, extensive summer session. Saturday classes. **Microcomputers:** 150 located in classrooms, computer centers. **Additional facts:** 4 campuses in metropolitan area at Clarkston, Dunwoody, and Decatur, Gwinnett.

DEGREES OFFERED. AA, AS, AAS. 777 associate degrees awarded in 1992. 36% in business and management, 9% teacher education, 25% health sciences, 5% multi/interdisciplinary studies, 11% social sciences.

UNDERGRADUATE MAJORS. Accounting, agricultural engineering, agricultural sciences, anthropology, automotive technology, biological and physical sciences, biology, business administration and management, business and management, business computer/console/peripheral equipment operation, business data processing and related programs, business data programming, chemistry, construction, data processing, dental hygiene, drafting, education, emergency medical technologies, engineering, engineering and engineering-related technologies, engineering and other disciplines, fine arts, fire control and safety technology, foreign languages (multiple emphasis), geology, history, home economics, hotel/motel and restaurant management, humanities and social sciences, industrial technology, information sciences and systems, interpreter for the deaf, journalism, liberal/general studies, management information systems, marketing and distribution, marketing management, mathematics, medical assistant, medical laboratory technologies, medical records technology, medical secretary, music, nursing, office supervision and management, ophthalmic services, philosophy, physics, political science and government, predentistry, premedicine, prepharmacy, psychology, public relations, respiratory therapy technology, science technologies, secretarial and related programs, sociology, surgical technology, trade and industrial supervision and management, urban studies.

ACADEMIC PROGRAMS. 2-year transfer program, accelerated program, double major, dual enrollment of high school students, honors program, telecourses, weekend college. **Remedial services:** Learning center, reduced course load, remedial instruction, special counselor, tutoring. **Placement/credit:** AP, CLEP General and Subject, institutional tests; 35 credit hours maximum for associate degree.

ACADEMIC REQUIREMENTS. Freshmen must earn minimum GPA of 1.75 to continue in good standing. Students must declare major on application. **Graduation requirements:** 100 hours for associate. Most students required to take courses in English, foreign languages, history, humanities, mathematics, biological/physical sciences, social sciences. **Additional information:** Continuing/adult education program.

FRESHMAN ADMISSIONS. Selection criteria: Test scores and high school GPA important. **High school preparation:** 16 units required. Required units include English 4, foreign language 2, mathematics 3, social science 3 and science 3. **Test requirements:** SAT or ACT; score report by August 27.

1992 FRESHMAN CLASS PROFILE. 5,292 men and women enrolled. **Characteristics:** 95% from in state, 100% commute, 19% have minority backgrounds, 5% are foreign students. Average age is 25.

FALL-TERM APPLICATIONS. $15 fee. Closing date August 13; applicants notified on a rolling basis. Interview required for nursing, dental hygiene applicants. Early admission available.

STUDENT LIFE. Activities: Student government, magazine, radio, student newspaper, choral groups, concert band, drama, jazz band, music ensembles, musical theater, symphony orchestra.

ATHLETICS. NJCAA. **Intercollegiate:** Baseball M, basketball M, soccer M, softball W, tennis. **Intramural:** Soccer M, softball, volleyball.

STUDENT SERVICES. Aptitude testing, career counseling, employment service for undergraduates, freshman orientation, personal counseling, placement service for graduates, veterans counselor, services/facilities for handicapped.

ANNUAL EXPENSES. Tuition and fees: $1,160, $630 additional for out-of-state students. **Books and supplies:** $400.

FINANCIAL AID. All grants, 91% of loans, 52% of jobs based on need. **Aid applications:** Closing date July 1; applicants notified on a rolling basis; must reply within 15 days.

ADDRESS/TELEPHONE. William C. Crews, Director of Enrollment Management, DeKalb College, 555 North Indian Creek Drive, Clarkson, GA 30021-2396. (404) 299-4564.

DeKalb Technical Institute

Clarkston, Georgia — CB code: 3226

2-year public technical college, coed. Founded in 1963. **Accreditation:** Regional. **Undergraduate enrollment:** 494 men, 484 women full time; 699 men, 731 women part time. **Faculty:** 418 total (118 full time), 19 with doctorates or other terminal degrees. **Location:** Suburban campus in small town; 8 miles from Atlanta. **Calendar:** Quarter, extensive summer session. **Microcomputers:** 244 located in classrooms, computer centers.

DEGREES OFFERED. AAS. 70 associate degrees awarded in 1992.

UNDERGRADUATE MAJORS. Accounting, automotive mechanics, biomedical equipment technology, business data programming, computer and information sciences, data processing, electromechanical technology, electronic technology, fashion merchandising, marketing and distribution, mechanical engineering, ophthalmic services, practical nursing.

ACADEMIC PROGRAMS. Independent study, internships. **Remedial services:** Learning center, remedial instruction, special counselor. **Placement/credit:** AP, CLEP General and Subject, institutional tests.

ACADEMIC REQUIREMENTS. No policy requiring minimum GPA; records of students having academic difficulty are reviewed individually. Students must declare major on enrollment. **Graduation requirements:** 70 hours for associate (30 in major). Most students required to take courses in English, mathematics.

FRESHMAN ADMISSIONS. Selection criteria: Test scores most important for admission into specific programs. Open admissions for Developmental Studies program (non-credit). Students not passing admissions exams must successfully complete Developmental Studies before entering individual programs. **Test requirements:** SAT or ACT for placement and counseling only; score report by September 18.

1992 FRESHMAN CLASS PROFILE. 608 men, 697 women enrolled. **Characteristics:** 100% commute. Average age is 27.

FALL-TERM APPLICATIONS. $10 fee, may be waived for applicants with need. Closing date September 1; priority given to applications received by May 15; applicants notified on a rolling basis. Interview recommended. Early admission available. Individual programs require admissions test.

STUDENT SERVICES. Aptitude testing, career counseling, employment service for undergraduates, freshman orientation, personal counseling, placement service for graduates, veterans counselor, services/facilities for handicapped.

ANNUAL EXPENSES. Tuition and fees: $840, $180 additional for out-of-state students. **Books and supplies:** $400. **Other expenses:** $600.

FINANCIAL AID. 10% of continuing students receive some form of aid. All grants, 43% of jobs based on need. 400 enrolled freshmen were judged to have need, all were offered aid. Academic, state/district residency scholarships available. **Aid applications:** No closing date; priority given to applications received by April 15; applicants notified on a rolling basis beginning on or about April 30; must reply within 15 days.

ADDRESS/TELEPHONE. Dr. Wilfred Martinez, Recruiter/Admissions Specialist, DeKalb Technical Institute, 495 North Indian Creek Drive, Clarkston, GA 30021. (706) 297-9522. Fax: (706) 294-4234.

DeVry Institute of Technology: Atlanta

Decatur, Georgia — CB code: 5715

Admissions:	90% of applicants accepted
Based on:	••• Test scores
	• Interview
Completion:	26% graduate

4-year proprietary business, technical college, coed. Founded in 1969. **Accreditation:** Regional. **Undergraduate enrollment:** 1,711 men, 594 women full time; 310 men, 186 women part time. **Faculty:** 81 total (63 full time), 2 with doctorates or other terminal degrees. **Location:** Suburban campus in large town; 15 miles from Atlanta. **Calendar:** Three continous calendar terms. Extensive evening/early morning classes. **Microcomputers:** 275 located in computer centers.

DEGREES OFFERED. AAS, BS. 192 associate degrees awarded in 1992. 100% in engineering technologies. 358 bachelor's degrees awarded. 39% in business and management, 35% computer sciences, 26% engineering technologies.

UNDERGRADUATE MAJORS. Associate: Electronic technology. **Bachelor's:** Accounting, business administration and management, electronic technology, information sciences and systems.

ACADEMIC PROGRAMS. Accelerated program. **Remedial services:** Learning center, reduced course load, special counselor, tutoring, developmental coursework. **Placement/credit:** Institutional tests; 30 credit hours maximum for associate degree; 55 credit hours maximum for bachelor's degree.

ACADEMIC REQUIREMENTS. Freshmen must earn minimum GPA of 2.0 to continue in good standing. 33% of freshmen return for sophomore year. Students must declare major on enrollment. **Graduation requirements:** 87 hours for associate, 135 hours for bachelor's. Most students required to take courses in computer science, English, history, humanities, mathematics, social sciences.

FRESHMAN ADMISSIONS. Selection criteria: Applicants must have high school diploma or equivalent, pass institutional entrance examination or submit acceptable ACT/SAT/WPCT scores, and be 17 years of age. **Test requirements:** SAT or ACT. **Additional information:** New students may enter at beginning of any semester.

1992 FRESHMAN CLASS PROFILE. 1,929 men and women applied, 1,739 accepted; 635 men enrolled, 223 women enrolled. **Characteristics:** 57% from in state, 100% commute, 71% have minority backgrounds.

FALL-TERM APPLICATIONS. $25 fee. Closing date November 4; applicants notified on a rolling basis; must reply within 4 weeks. Interview required. Deferred admission available.

STUDENT LIFE. Housing: School-contracted furnished apartments available for single students. **Activities:** Student government, student newspaper, Data Processing Management Association (DPMA), American Production and Inventory Control Society (APICS).

ATHLETICS. NAIA. **Intercollegiate:** Basketball M.

STUDENT SERVICES. Career counseling, employment service for undergraduates, freshman orientation, placement service for graduates, veterans counselor, services/facilities for handicapped.

ANNUAL EXPENSES. Tuition and fees (1992-93): $5,249. **Books and supplies:** $500. **Other expenses:** $1,911.

FINANCIAL AID. 86% of freshmen, 83% of continuing students receive some form of aid. All grants, 73% of loans, all jobs based on need. Academic scholarships available. **Aid applications:** No closing date; applicants notified on a rolling basis; must reply immediately. **Additional information:** Approximately 80% of students work part-time at jobs found through Institute.

ADDRESS/TELEPHONE. Susann Anderson-Hirst, Director of Admissions, DeVry Institute of Technology: Atlanta, 250 North Arcadia Avenue, Decatur, GA 30030-2198. (404) 292-7900. (800) 221-4771. Fax: (706) 292-2321.

East Georgia College
Swainsboro, Georgia CB code: 5200

Admissions: 82% of applicants accepted
Based on: ••• School record, test scores
Completion: 80% of freshmen end year in good standing
88% enter 4-year programs

2-year public community, junior college, coed. Founded in 1973. **Accreditation:** Regional. **Undergraduate enrollment:** 139 men, 226 women full time; 185 men, 342 women part time. **Faculty:** 26 total (19 full time), 11 with doctorates or other terminal degrees. **Location:** Rural campus in small town; 80 miles from Savannah, Augusta, and Macon. **Calendar:** Quarter, limited summer session. Extensive evening/early morning classes. **Microcomputers:** 26 located in libraries, computer centers.

DEGREES OFFERED. AA, AAS. 60 associate degrees awarded in 1992. 38% in business and management, 30% education, 32% multi/interdisciplinary studies.

UNDERGRADUATE MAJORS. Accounting, agricultural sciences, allied health, biology, business and management, chemistry, computer and information sciences, early childhood education, education, elementary education, English, geology, health sciences, junior high education, law enforcement and corrections, liberal/general studies, mathematics, prelaw, psychology, secondary education, secretarial and related programs, social sciences.

ACADEMIC PROGRAMS. 2-year transfer program, dual enrollment of high school students, independent study, study abroad, cross-registration. **Remedial services:** Reduced course load, remedial instruction, tutoring. **Placement/credit:** AP, CLEP Subject, institutional tests; 30 credit hours maximum for associate degree.

ACADEMIC REQUIREMENTS. Freshmen must earn minimum GPA of 1.8 to continue in good standing. 50% of freshmen return for sophomore year. Students must declare major by end of first year. **Graduation requirements:** 90 hours for associate (30 in major). Most students required to take courses in English, history, humanities, mathematics, biological/physical sciences, social sciences.

FRESHMAN ADMISSIONS. Selection criteria: Minimum SAT verbal score of 250/mathemathical score of 280 or ACT English of 10/mathematical of 5 or 1.8 high school GPA. **High school preparation:** 16 units recommended. Recommended units include biological science 1, English 4, foreign language 2, mathematics 3, physical science 2 and social science 3. **Test requirements:** SAT or ACT (SAT preferred); score report by September 20. **Additional information:** Incoming freshmen must take Collegiate Placement Examination.

1992 FRESHMAN CLASS PROFILE. 162 men applied, 130 accepted, 61 enrolled; 266 women applied, 223 accepted, 103 enrolled. **Academic background:** Mid 50% of enrolled freshmen had SAT-V between 350-550, SAT-M between 350-450. 95% submitted SAT scores. **Characteristics:** 98% from in state, 100% commute, 14% have minority backgrounds. Average age is 19.

FALL-TERM APPLICATIONS. No fee. Closing date September 20; applicants notified on a rolling basis. CRDA. Deferred and early admission available.

STUDENT LIFE. Activities: Student government, magazine, radio, student newspaper, yearbook, choral groups, drama, Baptist Student Union, Afro-American Club, Gamma Beta Phi.

STUDENT SERVICES. Aptitude testing, career counseling, freshman orientation, personal counseling, veterans counselor, services/facilities for handicapped.

ANNUAL EXPENSES. Tuition and fees: $1,089, $939 additional for out-of-state students. **Books and supplies:** $400. **Other expenses:** $350.

FINANCIAL AID. 18% of freshmen, 18% of continuing students receive some form of aid. 89% of grants, 77% of loans, 35% of jobs based on need. Academic, leadership scholarships available. **Aid applications:** No closing date; applicants notified on a rolling basis beginning on or about June 15; must reply within 2 weeks.

ADDRESS/TELEPHONE. Wayne E. Smith, Director of Admissions, East Georgia College, 237 Thigpen Drive, Swainsboro, GA 30401-2699. (912) 237-7831. Fax: (912) 237-5161.

Emmanuel College
Franklin Springs, Georgia CB code: 5184

Admissions: 75% of applicants accepted
Based on: ••• School record, test scores
• Special talents
Completion: 75% of freshmen end year in good standing

4-year private liberal arts college, coed, affiliated with Pentecostal Holiness Church. Founded in 1919. **Accreditation:** Regional. **Undergraduate enrollment:** 232 men, 251 women full time; 22 men, 21 women part time. **Faculty:** 36 total (32 full time), 14 with doctorates or other terminal degrees. **Location:** Rural campus in rural community; 30 miles from Athens, 90 miles from Atlanta. **Calendar:** Semester, limited summer session. Saturday and extensive evening/early morning classes. **Microcomputers:** 15 located in classrooms. **Additional facts:** Emphasis on Christian lifestyle.

DEGREES OFFERED. AA, BA, BS. 80 associate degrees awarded in 1992. 16% in business and management, 6% health sciences, 68% multi/interdisciplinary studies, 8% philosophy, religion, theology. 15 bachelor's degrees awarded. 100% in philosophy, religion, theology.

UNDERGRADUATE MAJORS. Associate: Business and office, liberal/general studies, music, prepharmacy, secretarial and related programs. **Bachelor's:** Business administration and management, elementary education, English, history, junior high education, liberal/general studies, religion.

ACADEMIC PROGRAMS. 2-year transfer program, dual enrollment of high school students, independent study, internships. **Remedial services:** Preadmission summer program, remedial instruction, special counselor, tutoring. **Placement/credit:** AP, CLEP General, institutional tests.

ACADEMIC REQUIREMENTS. Freshmen must earn minimum GPA of 1.5 to continue in good standing. 70% of freshmen return for sophomore year. Students must declare major on enrollment. **Graduation requirements:** 64 hours for associate, 127 hours for bachelor's. Most students required to take courses in English, foreign languages, history, humanities, mathematics, philosophy/religion, biological/physical sciences, social sciences. **Postgraduate studies:** 60% from 2-year programs enter 4-year programs.

FRESHMAN ADMISSIONS. Test requirements: SAT or ACT for placement and counseling only; score report by August 1.

1992 FRESHMAN CLASS PROFILE. 250 men applied, 181 accepted, 141 enrolled; 256 women applied, 199 accepted, 153 enrolled. **Characteristics:** 65% from in state, 52% live in college housing, 15% have minority backgrounds. Average age is 19.

FALL-TERM APPLICATIONS. $25 fee, may be waived for applicants with need. No closing date; applicants notified on a rolling basis beginning on or about January 1. Audition required for music applicants. Interview recommended for music applicants. Deferred and early admission available.

STUDENT LIFE. Housing: Dormitories (men, women); apartment housing available. All students not commuting from home must reside in college housing. **Activities:** Student government, student newspaper, yearbook, choral groups, concert band, drama, music ensembles, pep band, ministerial fellowship, missions fellowship, Rotaract. **Additional information:** Religious observance required.

ATHLETICS. NJCAA. **Intercollegiate:** Baseball M, basketball, tennis. **Intramural:** Basketball, soccer, softball, table tennis, tennis, track and field, volleyball.

STUDENT SERVICES. Career counseling, freshman orientation, health services, personal counseling, veterans counselor, services/facilities for handicapped.

ANNUAL EXPENSES. Tuition and fees: $4,360. **Room and board:** $2,990. **Books and supplies:** $550. **Other expenses:** $800.

FINANCIAL AID. 95% of freshmen, 97% of continuing students receive some form of aid. 74% of grants, 94% of loans, 95% of jobs based on need. Academic, music/drama, athletic, state/district residency, leadership, religious affiliation scholarships available. **Aid applications:** No closing date; priority given to applications received by March 15; applicants notified on a rolling basis beginning on or about March 15; must reply within 2 weeks.

ADDRESS/TELEPHONE. Ronald G. White, Director of Admissions, Emmanuel College, PO Box 129, 212 Spring Street, Franklin Springs, GA 30639-0129. (706) 245-7226. (800) 860-8800. Fax: (706) 245-4424.

Emory University
Atlanta, Georgia CB code: 5187

Admissions: 58% of applicants accepted
Based on: ••• Activities, school record, special talents
•• Essay, recommendations, test scores
Completion: 99% of freshmen end year in good standing
80% graduate, 66% of these enter graduate study

4-year private university, coed, affiliated with United Methodist Church. Founded in 1836. **Accreditation:** Regional. **Undergraduate enrollment:** 2,161 men, 2,618 women full time; 13 men, 30 women part time. **Graduate enrollment:** 1,695 men, 1,522 women full time; 373 men, 508 women part time. **Faculty:** 1,647 total (1,537 full time), 1,559 with doctorates or other terminal degrees. **Location:** Suburban campus in very large city; 5 miles from central downtown area. **Calendar:** Semester, limited summer session. **Microcomputers:** 400 located in dormitories, libraries, classrooms, computer centers. **Special facilities:** Michael C. Carlos Museum of Art and Archeology, biological field station, Yerkes primate center, 185-acre park, Carter Presidential Center, satellite dish for Russian television, Rollins Research Center, US Centers for Disease Control. **Additional facts:** Campus life distinguished by high degree of commitment to moral and ethical discourse about issues of academic and student life. Students volunteer for a wide variety of service on campus and in metropolitan area.

DEGREES OFFERED. AS, BA, BS, MA, MS, MBA, MEd, PhD, MD, JD, M.Div. 179 associate degrees awarded in 1992. 96% in multi/interdisciplinary studies. 1,486 bachelor's degrees awarded. 9% in business and management, 5% health sciences, 8% letters/literature, 11% life sciences, 6% philosophy, religion, theology, 14% psychology, 29% social sciences. Graduate degrees offered in 77 major fields of study.

UNDERGRADUATE MAJORS. Associate: Nuclear medical technology. **Bachelor's:** Accounting, African studies, Afro-American (black) studies, American literature, anthropology, art history, biological and physical sciences, biology, business administration and management, business and management, business economics, Caribbean studies, chemistry, classics, comparative literature, computer and information sciences, computer mathematics, creative writing, dramatic arts, Eastern European studies, economics, education, elementary education, English, English literature, film arts, finance, foreign languages (multiple emphasis), French, Greek (classical), history, humanities and social sciences, international relations, international studies, Jewish studies, Latin, Latin American studies, liberal/general studies, marketing management, mathematics, medical radiation dosimetry, medical records administration, medieval studies, music, music history and appreciation, nursing, philosophy, physics, political science and government, psychology, religion, Russian, Russian and Slavic studies, secondary education, sociology, Spanish, women's studies.

ACADEMIC PROGRAMS. 2-year transfer program, accelerated program, double major, dual enrollment of high school students, honors program, independent study, internships, semester at sea, study abroad, teacher preparation, visiting/exchange student program, Washington semester, cross-registration, 3-2 program in engineering with Georgia Institute of Technology; liberal arts/career combination in engineering. **Remedial services:** Learning center, preadmission summer program, tutoring. **Placement/credit:** AP, IB, institutional tests; 32 credit hours maximum for bachelor's degree.

ACADEMIC REQUIREMENTS. Freshmen must pass minimum of 26 semester hours to continue in good academic standing and must have a 1.5 GPA. 90% of freshmen return for sophomore year. Students must declare major by end of second year. **Graduation requirements:** 132 hours for bachelor's (32 in major). Most students required to take courses in arts/fine arts, English, foreign languages, history, humanities, mathematics, philosophy/religion, biological/physical sciences, social sciences. **Postgraduate studies:** 85% from 2-year programs enter 4-year programs. 22% enter law school, 18% enter medical school, 2% enter MBA programs, 24% enter other graduate study.

FRESHMAN ADMISSIONS. Selection criteria: Primarily school achievement record, with careful examination of program content. Standardized test scores (SAT or ACT). Prior academic success, character and maturity important. Diversity of interests, background, and special talents sought. **High school preparation:** 16 units required. Required units include biological science 1, English 4, foreign language 2, mathematics 3, physical science 1 and social science 2. One each additional units in mathematics and science recommended for students intending to concentrate in science or mathematics. At least 3 units laboratory science. **Test requirements:** SAT or ACT; score report by March 1. **Additional information:** Campus visit recommended and noted as indication of interest. Personal interviews not offered. Small group information sessions conducted by members of admission committee. Tours of campus also available.

1992 FRESHMAN CLASS PROFILE. 3,373 men applied, 2,036 accepted, 523 enrolled; 4,327 women applied, 2,394 accepted, 677 enrolled. 93% had high school GPA of 3.0 or higher, 7% between 2.0 and 2.99. **Academic background:** Mid 50% of enrolled freshmen had SAT-V between 520-620, SAT-M between 590-680; ACT composite between 25-29. 82% submitted SAT scores, 21% submitted ACT scores. **Characteristics:** 20% from in state, 99% live in college housing, 24% have minority backgrounds, 3% are foreign students, 45% join fraternities/sororities. Average age is 18.

FALL-TERM APPLICATIONS. $35 fee, may be waived for applicants with need. Closing date February 1; applicants notified on or about April 1; must reply by May 1. Essay required. CRDA. Deferred and early admission available. EDP-F.

STUDENT LIFE. Housing: Dormitories (women, coed); apartment, fraternity, sorority housing available. Theme dormitories available. **Activities:** Student government, magazine, radio, student newspaper, yearbook, choral groups, concert band, dance, drama, jazz band, music ensembles, musical theater, symphony orchestra, fraternities, sororities, over 200 student organizations including Protestant, Catholic, Jewish, and Moslem student organizations, Black Student Alliance, interest clubs, many social service organizations, 27 honorary societies.

ATHLETICS. NCAA. **Intercollegiate:** Baseball M, basketball, cross-country, diving, golf M, soccer, swimming, tennis, track and field, volleyball W. **Intramural:** Badminton, basketball, bowling, cross-country, diving, fencing, field hockey M, golf, handball M, racquetball, rowing (crew) M, soccer, softball, swimming, table tennis, tennis, track and field, volleyball, water polo, wrestling M.

STUDENT SERVICES. Aptitude testing, career counseling, employment service for undergraduates, freshman orientation, health services, personal counseling, placement service for graduates, services/facilities for handicapped.

ANNUAL EXPENSES. Tuition and fees: $16,820. **Room and board:** $5,110. **Books and supplies:** $570. **Other expenses:** $1,100.

FINANCIAL AID. 61% of freshmen, 58% of continuing students receive some form of aid. 69% of grants, 96% of loans, all jobs based on need. 571 enrolled freshmen were judged to have need, all were offered aid. Academic, music/drama, state/district residency, leadership, alumni affiliation, religious affiliation scholarships available. **Aid applications:** Closing date April 1; priority given to applications received by February 15; applicants notified on or about April 15; must reply by May 1. **Additional information:** Emory Parent and Student Loan Programs assist families in financing tuition. A fixed tuition program is also available. Foreign medical school applicants required to submit CSS Foreign Student Financial Aid Application.

ADDRESS/TELEPHONE. Daniel C. Walls, Dean of Admission, Emory University, Boisfeuillet Jones Center, Atlanta, GA 30322. (404) 727-6036. (800) 727-6036.

Floyd College
Rome, Georgia CB code: 5237

2-year public junior college, coed. Founded in 1968. **Accreditation:** Regional. **Undergraduate enrollment:** 1,554 men and women full time; 1,271 men and women part time. **Faculty:** 87 total (52 full time), 15 with doctorates or other terminal degrees. **Location:** Rural campus in large town; 66 miles from Atlanta. **Calendar:** Quarter, limited summer session. Extensive evening/early morning classes. **Microcomputers:** 75 located in libraries, computer centers. **Special facilities:** Art gallery in library, observatory. **Additional facts:** Classes offered at Cartersville and North Metro Technical Institute

DEGREES OFFERED. AA, AS, AAS. 200 associate degrees awarded in 1992.

UNDERGRADUATE MAJORS. Accounting, agricultural sciences, air conditioning/heating/refrigeration mechanics, air conditioning/heating/refrigeration technology, automotive mechanics, automotive technology, biology, business administration and management, business and management, business and office, business economics, carpentry, chemistry, computer and information sciences, computer programming, data processing, dental hygiene, drafting, education, education of the deaf and hearing impaired, electronic technology, elementary education, emergency medical technologies, engineering, engineering and engineering-related technologies, history, horticulture, hotel/motel and restaurant management, information sciences and systems, international studies, interpreter for the deaf, journalism, junior high education, law enforcement and corrections technologies, legal assistant/paralegal, liberal/general studies, machine tool operation/machine shop, marketing and distribution, marketing management, mathematics, medical records administration, mental health/human services, microcomputer software, military science (Army), nursing, ornamental horticulture, philosophy, physics, political science and government, predentistry, premedicine, prepharmacy, preveterinary, psychology, respiratory therapy, science technologies, secondary education, secretarial and related programs, sociology, teacher aide, telecommunications, welding technology.

ACADEMIC PROGRAMS. 2-year transfer program, cooperative education, double major, dual enrollment of high school students, honors program, independent study, study abroad. **Remedial services:** Remedial instruction, tutoring. **Placement/credit:** AP, CLEP General, institutional tests; 15 credit hours maximum for associate degree.

ACADEMIC REQUIREMENTS. Freshmen must earn minimum GPA of 2.0 to continue in good standing. 60% of freshmen return for sophomore year. Students must declare major by end of first year. **Graduation requirements:** 90 hours for associate (60 in major). Most students required to take courses in English, history, humanities, mathematics, biological/physical sciences, social sciences.

FRESHMAN ADMISSIONS. Selection criteria: Open admissions for associate of applied science. For other program, minimum SAT-verbal score of 250 or ACT English of 10, or SAT-mathematical score of 280 or ACT mathematical of 5, or 1.8 high school GPA. **High school preparation:** 16 units required. Required units include English 4, foreign language 2, mathematics 3, social science 3 and science 3. **Test requirements:** SAT or ACT; score report by September 17.

1992 FRESHMAN CLASS PROFILE. 289 men and women enrolled. **Characteristics:** 99% from in state, 100% commute, 10% have minority backgrounds.

FALL-TERM APPLICATIONS. No fee. No closing date; applicants notified on a rolling basis. Early admission available.

STUDENT LIFE. Activities: Student government, magazine, student newspaper, Baptist Student Union, College Bowl Team, Volunteer Opportunity Center.

ATHLETICS. Intramural: Archery, badminton, basketball, bowling, field hockey, golf, sailing, skiing, soccer, softball, table tennis, tennis, volleyball, wrestling M.

STUDENT SERVICES. Aptitude testing, career counseling, employment service for undergraduates, freshman orientation, personal counseling, placement service for graduates, veterans counselor, services/facilities for handicapped.

ANNUAL EXPENSES. Tuition and fees (projected): $1,089, $939 additional for out-of-state students. **Books and supplies:** $495. **Other expenses:** $450.

FINANCIAL AID. 45% of freshmen, 45% of continuing students receive some form of aid. 96% of grants, 91% of loans, 87% of jobs based on need. Academic, music/drama, art, state/district residency, leadership, minority scholarships available. **Aid applications:** Closing date June 30; priority given to applications received by April 30; applicants notified on a rolling basis beginning on or about July 15; must reply within 2 weeks.

ADDRESS/TELEPHONE. William P. Kerr, Director of Admissions and Records, Floyd College, PO Box 1864, 3175 Cedartown Hwy, Rome, GA 30162-1864. (706) 295-6339. Fax: (706) 295-6610.

Fort Valley State College
Fort Valley, Georgia — CB code: 5220

4-year public college of arts and sciences, coed. Founded in 1895. **Accreditation:** Regional. **Undergraduate enrollment:** 858 men, 1,159 women full time; 84 men, 116 women part time. **Graduate enrollment:** 25 men, 102 women full time; 44 men, 149 women part time. **Faculty:** 147 total, 82 with doctorates or other terminal degrees. **Location:** Rural campus in small town; 30 miles from Macon. **Calendar:** Quarter, limited summer session. **Microcomputers:** Located in libraries, classrooms, computer centers.

DEGREES OFFERED. AA, AS, BA, BS, MS. 1 associate degree awarded in 1992. 100% in engineering. 231 bachelor's degrees awarded. 5% in agriculture, 24% business and management, 24% business/office and marketing/distribution, 5% computer sciences, 22% education, 6% languages. Graduate degrees offered in 2 major fields of study.

UNDERGRADUATE MAJORS. Associate: Agricultural engineering, engineering and engineering-related technologies, secretarial and related programs. **Bachelor's:** Accounting, agricultural business and management, agricultural economics, agricultural engineering, agricultural sciences, agronomy, animal sciences, biology, botany, business administration and management, business and management, business economics, chemistry, commercial design, computer and information sciences, criminal justice studies, criminology, early childhood education, economics, education, electronic technology, elementary education, English, food science and nutrition, French, history, home economics, horticultural science, individual and family development, journalism, junior high education, mathematics, nutritional sciences, physical education, physics, political science and government, psychology, school psychology, secondary education, secretarial and related programs, social work, sociology, textiles and clothing, zoology.

ACADEMIC PROGRAMS. Cooperative education, dual enrollment of high school students, external degree, honors program, internships, student-designed major, study abroad, teacher preparation. **Remedial services:** Learning center, reduced course load, remedial instruction, special counselor, tutoring. **ROTC:** Army. **Placement/credit:** Institutional tests; 20 credit hours maximum for associate degree; 45 credit hours maximum for bachelor's degree.

ACADEMIC REQUIREMENTS. Freshmen must earn minimum GPA of 2.0 to continue in good standing. 88% of freshmen return for sophomore year. Students must declare major by end of second year. **Graduation requirements:** 90 hours for associate (20 in major), 180 hours for bachelor's (30 in major). Most students required to take courses in arts/fine arts, computer science, English, foreign languages, history, mathematics, philosophy/religion, biological/physical sciences, social sciences. **Postgraduate studies:** 90% from 2-year programs enter 4-year programs. 3% enter medical school, 7% enter MBA programs, 15% enter other graduate study.

FRESHMAN ADMISSIONS. Selection criteria: High school transcript, SAT scores, physical examination important. **High school preparation:** 18 units required. Required units include English 4, mathematics 2, social science 3 and science 1. **Test requirements:** SAT or ACT; score report by September 5.

1992 FRESHMAN CLASS PROFILE. 322 men, 393 women enrolled. **Characteristics:** 93% from in state, 69% live in college housing, 93% have minority backgrounds, 1% are foreign students, 1% join fraternities/sororities. Average age is 18.

FALL-TERM APPLICATIONS. No fee. Closing date August 25; applicants notified on a rolling basis beginning on or about February 1; must reply within 4 weeks. Audition recommended for music education applicants. Early admission available.

STUDENT LIFE. Housing: Dormitories (men, women); cooperative housing available. **Activities:** Student government, student newspaper, yearbook, choral groups, concert band, dance, drama, jazz band, marching band, music ensembles, musical theater, pep band, fraternities, sororities.

ATHLETICS. NCAA. **Intercollegiate:** Basketball, football M, tennis, track and field, volleyball W. **Intramural:** Basketball, softball, swimming, tennis, track and field, volleyball.

STUDENT SERVICES. Career counseling, health services, personal counseling, placement service for graduates, special adviser for adult students, veterans counselor, services/facilities for handicapped.

ANNUAL EXPENSES. Tuition and fees (projected): $1,779, $1,380 additional for out-of-state students. **Room and board:** $2,460. **Books and supplies:** $630. **Other expenses:** $1,386.

FINANCIAL AID. 96% of freshmen, 96% of continuing students receive some form of aid. Grants, loans, jobs available. 412 enrolled freshmen were judged to have need, 397 were offered aid. Academic, music/drama, athletic, alumni affiliation, religious affiliation, minority scholarships available. **Aid applications:** Closing date May 1; priority given to applications received by April 15; applicants notified on a rolling basis beginning on or about June 1; must reply within 10 days.

ADDRESS/TELEPHONE. Delia W. Taylor, Director of Admissions and Recruitment, Fort Valley State College, 1005 State College Drive, Fort Valley, GA 31030. (912) 825-6307. Fax: (912) 825-6394.

Gainesville College
Gainesville, Georgia — CB code: 5273

2-year public junior college, coed. Founded in 1964. **Accreditation:** Regional. **Undergraduate enrollment:** 1,737 men and women full time; 1,203 men and women part time. **Faculty:** 127 total (99 full time), 31 with doctorates or other terminal degrees. **Location:** Suburban campus in large town; 45 miles from Atlanta. **Calendar:** Quarter, extensive summer session. Extensive evening/early morning classes. **Microcomputers:** 100 located in libraries, classrooms. **Special facilities:** Art gallery.

DEGREES OFFERED. AA, AS, AAS. 330 associate degrees awarded in 1992.

UNDERGRADUATE MAJORS. Accounting, agricultural sciences, allied health, anthropology, art education, biology, business administration and management, business and management, business and office, business economics, business education, chemistry, child development/care/guidance, chiropractic, computer and information sciences, criminal justice studies, dental assistant, dental hygiene, dramatic arts, early childhood education, education, elementary education, emergency medical technologies, engineering, engineering and engineering-related technologies, English, English education, finance, forestry and related sciences, geology, health education, history, hotel/motel and restaurant management, international business management, journalism, legal assistant/paralegal, legal secretary, liberal/general studies, marketing management, mathematics, mathematics education, medical assistant, medical laboratory technologies, medical records administration, medical records technology, music education, music performance, occupational therapy, occupational therapy assistant, optometry, pharmacy, physical education, physical therapy, physical therapy assistant, physics, political science and government, predentistry, premedicine, prepharmacy, preveterinary, psychology, radiograph medical technology, science education, secondary education, secretarial and related programs, social science education, social work, sociology, studio art.

ACADEMIC PROGRAMS. 2-year transfer program, dual enrollment of high school students, honors program, study abroad. **Remedial services:** Learning center, remedial instruction, tutoring. **Placement/credit:** AP, CLEP General and Subject, institutional tests.

ACADEMIC REQUIREMENTS. Freshmen must earn minimum GPA of 2.0 to continue in good standing. 65% of freshmen return for sophomore year. Students must declare major on application. **Graduation requirements:** 90 hours for associate (30 in major). Most students required to take courses in English, history, humanities, mathematics, biological/physical sciences, social sciences.

FRESHMAN ADMISSIONS. Selection criteria: SAT minimum of 250 verbal or 280 math or 1.8 academic GPA required, college preparatory curriculum required. **High school preparation:** 16 units required. Required units include English 4, foreign language 2, mathematics 3, social science 3 and science 3. 2 sciences must be laboratory sciences. **Test requirements:** SAT or ACT; score report by August 16.

1992 FRESHMAN CLASS PROFILE. 1,981 men and women enrolled. **Characteristics:** 98% from in state, 7% have minority backgrounds, 1% are foreign students. Average age is 19.

FALL-TERM APPLICATIONS. $15 fee, may be waived for applicants with need. Closing date August 16. Audition required for music performance applicants. Portfolio required for applied art, art education applicants. Deferred and early admission available.

STUDENT LIFE. Activities: Student government, magazine, student newspaper, choral groups, concert band, drama, jazz band, music ensembles, musical theater, Baptist Student Union, Rotaract, Black Student Association, International Club, Students for Environmental Awareness.

ATHLETICS. Intramural: Badminton, baseball M, basketball, bowling, softball, tennis, volleyball.

STUDENT SERVICES. Aptitude testing, career counseling, employment service for undergraduates, freshman orientation, personal counseling, special adviser for adult students, veterans counselor, services/facilities for handicapped.

ANNUAL EXPENSES. Tuition and fees: $1,104, $939 additional for out-of-state students. **Books and supplies:** $500. **Other expenses:** $1,000.

FINANCIAL AID. 17% of freshmen, 17% of continuing students receive some form of aid. 91% of grants, 75% of loans, 34% of jobs based on need. Academic, music/drama, art, state/district residency, leadership, alumni affiliation, minority scholarships available. **Aid applications:** No closing date; priority given to applications received by April 15; applicants notified on a rolling basis; must reply within 3 weeks.

ADDRESS/TELEPHONE. Carol Nobles, Director of Admissions, Gainesville College, PO Box 1358, Gainesville, GA 30503. (706) 535-6239. (800) 745-5922. Fax: (404) 535-6359.

Georgia College
Milledgeville, Georgia

CB code: 5252

Admissions:	87% of applicants accepted
Based on:	••• School record, test scores
	• Interview
Completion:	80% of freshmen end year in good standing
	37% graduate

4-year public senior college, coed. Founded in 1889. **Accreditation:** Regional. **Undergraduate enrollment:** 1,314 men, 2,107 women full time; 458 men, 623 women part time. **Graduate enrollment:** 150 men, 194 women full time; 239 men, 416 women part time. **Faculty:** 265 total (187 full time). **Location:** Suburban campus in large town; 95 miles from Atlanta, 30 miles from Macon. **Calendar:** Quarter, limited summer session. **Microcomputers:** 120 located in libraries, computer centers. **Special facilities:** Archives, museum, art galleries, greenhouse, challenge/ropes course. **Additional facts:** Centers in Macon, Dublin and Warner Robins.

DEGREES OFFERED. BA, BS, MA, MS, MBA, MEd. 724 bachelor's degrees awarded in 1992. 41% in business and management, 6% computer sciences, 24% education, 8% psychology. Graduate degrees offered in 31 major fields of study.

UNDERGRADUATE MAJORS. Accounting, art education, arts management, biology, business administration and management, business and management, business and office, business computer/console/peripheral equipment operation, business data entry equipment operation, business data processing and related programs, business data programming, business economics, chemistry, commercial art, computer and information sciences, computer mathematics, criminal justice studies, curriculum and instruction, early childhood education, economics, education, education of the mentally handicapped, education of the physically handicapped, elementary education, English, English education, forestry and related sciences, French, health education, history, information sciences and systems, journalism, junior high education, legal assistant/paralegal, liberal/general studies, management information systems, marketing and distribution, marketing management, mathematics, mathematics education, military science (Army), music, music education, music performance, music theory and composition, nursing, office supervision and management, physical education, political science and government, predentistry, preengineering, prelaw, premedicine, prepharmacy, preveterinary, psychology, public administration, remedial education, science education, secondary education, social science education, social sciences, social studies education, sociology, Spanish, special education.

ACADEMIC PROGRAMS. Accelerated program, cooperative education, double major, dual enrollment of high school students, education specialist degree, external degree, honors program, independent study, internships, student-designed major, study abroad, teacher preparation, visiting/exchange student program; liberal arts/career combination in engineering; combined bachelor's/graduate program in business administration. **Remedial services:** Preadmission summer program, remedial instruction, special counselor, tutoring. **ROTC:** Army. **Placement/credit:** AP, CLEP General and Subject, institutional tests; 45 credit hours maximum for bachelor's degree.

ACADEMIC REQUIREMENTS. Freshmen must earn minimum GPA of 1.6 to continue in good standing. 85% of freshmen return for sophomore year. Students must declare major by end of second year. **Graduation requirements:** 186 hours for bachelor's (90 in major). Most students required to take courses in English, history, humanities, mathematics, biological/physical sciences, social sciences. **Additional information:** Preprofessional program offered in 18 areas.

FRESHMAN ADMISSIONS. Selection criteria: Minimum SAT-verbal score of 250 or ACT English of 13, or SAT-mathematical score of 280 or ACT mathematical of 14, 1.8 high school GPA, and completion of at least 4 areas of the Georgia College Preparatory Curriculum. **High school preparation:** 16 units required. Required units include English 4, foreign language 2, mathematics 3, social science 3 and science 3. **Test requirements:** SAT or ACT; score report by August 31. **Additional information:** Remedial, noncredit course work required of applicants with College Placement Exam mathematical score below 80 and/or SAT verbal score below 360.

1992 FRESHMAN CLASS PROFILE. 841 men applied, 714 accepted, 322 enrolled; 1,155 women applied, 1,018 accepted, 476 enrolled. 32% had high school GPA of 3.0 or higher, 57% between 2.0 and 2.99. **Academic background:** Mid 50% of enrolled freshmen had SAT-V between 360-460, SAT-M between 380-500. 98% submitted SAT scores. **Characteristics:** 94% from in state, 55% commute, 18% have minority backgrounds, 1% are foreign students, 15% join fraternities/sororities. Average age is 19.

FALL-TERM APPLICATIONS. $10 fee, may be waived for applicants with need. Closing date August 31; applicants notified on a rolling basis. Audition required for music, drama applicants. Portfolio required for art education, art applicants. Interview recommended. CRDA. Deferred and early admission available. Education, business and nursing programs require special application procedures.

STUDENT LIFE. Housing: Dormitories (men, women); fraternity, sorority, handicapped housing available. Students who choose student housing must remain in dormitories for full academic year. **Activities:** Student government, magazine, radio, student newspaper, television, yearbook, choral groups, concert band, dance, drama, jazz band, music ensembles, musical theater, pep band, fraternities, sororities, Baptist Student Union, Wesley Foundation, Black Student Alliance, and International Student Orgranization.

ATHLETICS. NCAA. **Intercollegiate:** Baseball M, basketball, cross-country, golf M, softball W, tennis. **Intramural:** Badminton, basketball, cross-country, fencing, golf M, racquetball, rugby, skiing, soccer, softball, table tennis, tennis, volleyball.

STUDENT SERVICES. Aptitude testing, career counseling, employment service for undergraduates, freshman orientation, health services, on-campus day care, personal counseling, placement service for graduates, special adviser for adult students, veterans counselor, student support services for physically disabled, services/facilities for handicapped.

ANNUAL EXPENSES. Tuition and fees (projected): $1,695, $1,380 additional for out-of-state students. **Room and board:** $2,829. **Books and supplies:** $400. **Other expenses:** $1,352.

FINANCIAL AID. 62% of freshmen, 56% of continuing students receive some form of aid. 73% of grants, 92% of loans, 46% of jobs based on need. 527 enrolled freshmen were judged to have need, 474 were offered aid. Academic, music/drama, athletic, leadership, minority scholarships available. **Aid applications:** No closing date; priority given to applications received by April 15; applicants notified on a rolling basis beginning on or about May 1; must reply within 2 weeks.

ADDRESS/TELEPHONE. Larry A. Peevy, Associate Vice President for Admissions and Records, Georgia College, Campus PO Box 023, Milledgeville, GA 31061. (912) 453-5004. Fax: (912) 453-1914.

Georgia Institute of Technology
Atlanta, Georgia

CB code: 5248

Admissions:	51% of applicants accepted
Based on:	••• School record, test scores
	• Activities, interview, recommendations, special talents
Completion:	85% of freshmen end year in good standing
	57% graduate, 20% of these enter graduate study

4-year public university and technical college, coed. Founded in 1885. **Accreditation:** Regional. **Undergraduate enrollment:** 6,449 men, 2,220 women full time; 495 men, 155 women part time. **Graduate enrollment:** 2,151 men, 577 women full time; 672 men, 172 women part time. **Faculty:** 712 total (705 full time), 546 with doctorates or other terminal degrees. **Location:** Urban campus in very large city; near downtown area. **Calendar:** Quarter, extensive summer session. **Microcomputers:** 750 located in libraries, computer centers. **Special facilities:** Official depository of the U.S. Government Printing Office and the U.S. Patent and Trademark Office, nuclear reactor, electron microscope.

DEGREES OFFERED. BS, BArch, MS, PhD. 1,829 bachelor's degrees awarded in 1992. 20% in business and management, 6% computer sciences, 64% engineering. Graduate degrees offered in 42 major fields of study.

UNDERGRADUATE MAJORS. Aerospace/aeronautical/astronautical engineering, applied biology, applied mathematics, applied psychology, architecture, biological and physical sciences, biology, business administration and management, business and management, business economics, ceramic engineering, chemical engineering, chemistry, cinematography/film, civil engineering, computer and information sciences, computer engineering, construction, discrete mathematics, economics, electrical/electronics/communications engineering, engineering and other disciplines, engineering mechanics, engineering science, health systems, history, technology and society, industrial and organizational psychology, industrial engineering, international relations, management science, materials engineering, mathematics, mechanical engineering, nuclear engineering, physics, psychology, science technologies, science, technology and culture, systems engineering, textile engineering, textile technology, textiles, textiles and clothing.

ACADEMIC PROGRAMS. Accelerated program, cooperative education, double major, dual enrollment of high school students, honors program, independent study, student-designed major, study abroad, cross-registration, dual degree program (3-2) with approximately 90 liberal arts colleges and universities, Regents Engineering Transfer Program with 9 Georgia colleges. **Remedial services:** Learning center, reduced course load, special counselor, tutoring. **ROTC:** Air Force, Army, Naval. **Placement/credit:** AP, institutional tests; 183 credit hours maximum for bachelor's degree.

ACADEMIC REQUIREMENTS. Freshmen must earn minimum GPA of 1.7 to continue in good standing. 84% of freshmen return for sophomore year. Students must declare major by end of second year. **Graduation requirements:** 200 hours for bachelor's (75 in major). Most students required to take courses in computer science, English, history, humanities, mathematics, biological/physical sciences, social sciences.

FRESHMAN ADMISSIONS. Selection criteria: School achievement record and SAT-mathematical score most important, followed by SAT-verbal score. Activities, leadership, recommendations considered. **High school preparation:** 16 units required. Required units include English 4, foreign language 2, mathematics 4, physical science 3 and social science 3. Physical sciences must include 2 laboratory science, 1 chemistry. Mathematics must include 2 algebra, 1 geometry, 1 precalculus including trigonometry. Foreign language units must be in 1 language. **Test requirements:** SAT or ACT (SAT preferred); score report by February 1.

1992 FRESHMAN CLASS PROFILE. 5,965 men applied, 2,975 accepted, 1,751 enrolled; 2,150 women applied, 1,177 accepted, 640 enrolled. 33% had high school GPA of 3.0 or higher, 55% between 2.0 and 2.99. 70% were in top tenth of graduating class. **Academic background:** Mid 50% of enrolled freshmen had SAT-V between 520-610, SAT-M between 630-720. 99% submitted SAT scores. **Characteristics:** 60% from in state, 80% live in college housing, 17% have minority backgrounds, 1% are foreign students, 24% join fraternities/sororities. Average age is 20.

FALL-TERM APPLICATIONS. $25 fee, may be waived for applicants with need. Closing date February 1; applicants notified on a rolling basis; must reply by May 1. Interview recommended for marginal applicants. CRDA. Deferred and early admission available. Nonresident applicants advised to apply early.

STUDENT LIFE. Housing: Dormitories (men, women); apartment, fraternity, sorority, handicapped housing available. **Activities:** Student government, magazine, radio, student newspaper, yearbook, choral groups, concert band, drama, jazz band, marching band, music ensembles, pep band, symphony orchestra, fraternities, sororities, wide variety of religious and special interest organizations, Afro-American Association.

ATHLETICS. NCAA. **Intercollegiate:** Baseball M, basketball, cross-country, football M, golf M, softball W, swimming, tennis M, track and field, volleyball W, wrestling M. **Intramural:** Archery, basketball, bowling, fencing, field hockey, gymnastics, handball, ice hockey, lacrosse M, racquetball, rifle, rugby, soccer, softball, swimming, tennis, track and field M, volleyball, wrestling M.

STUDENT SERVICES. Aptitude testing, career counseling, employment service for undergraduates, freshman orientation, health services, personal counseling, placement service for graduates, veterans counselor, services/facilities for handicapped.

ANNUAL EXPENSES. Tuition and fees (1992-93): $2,277, $2,610 additional for out-of-state students. **Room and board:** $4,308. **Books and supplies:** $795. **Other expenses:** $1,164.

FINANCIAL AID. 39% of freshmen, 32% of continuing students receive some form of aid. 85% of grants, 86% of loans, all jobs based on need. Academic, state/district residency, leadership, alumni affiliation, minority scholarships available. **Aid applications:** Closing date March 1; applicants notified on or about April 1; must reply by May 1.

ADDRESS/TELEPHONE. Deborah Smith, Director of Admissions, Georgia Institute of Technology, 225 North Avenue, N.W, Atlanta, GA 30332-0320. (404) 894-2000.

Georgia Military College
Milledgeville, Georgia CB code: 5249

2-year public junior, military college, coed. Founded in 1879. **Accreditation:** Regional. **Undergraduate enrollment:** 472 men, 444 women full time; 865 men, 735 women part time. **Faculty:** 107 total (16 full time), 47 with doctorates or other terminal degrees. **Location:** Suburban campus in large town; 90 miles from Atlanta, 30 miles from Macon. **Calendar:** Quarter, limited summer session. Saturday classes. **Microcomputers:** Located in libraries, computer centers. **Additional facts:** Multilocation institution. 2-year ROTC commissioning program on main campus. Military base programs and degree programs for civilians offered.

DEGREES OFFERED. AA, AS. 636 associate degrees awarded in 1992. 19% in business and management, 64% multi/interdisciplinary studies, 6% social sciences.

UNDERGRADUATE MAJORS. Business administration and management, business and office, criminal justice studies, education, engineering, fire control and safety technology, food production/management/services, hospitality and recreation marketing, law enforcement and corrections technologies, liberal/general studies, military science (Army), nursing, preengineering, social sciences.

ACADEMIC PROGRAMS. 2-year transfer program, double major, external degree, cross-registration. **Remedial services:** Learning center, remedial instruction, tutoring. **ROTC:** Army. **Placement/credit:** CLEP General and Subject, institutional tests.

ACADEMIC REQUIREMENTS. Freshmen must earn minimum GPA of 1.9 to continue in good standing. 75% of freshmen return for sophomore year. Students must declare major by end of first year. **Graduation requirements:** 90 hours for associate (30 in major). Most students required to take courses in English, history, mathematics, biological/physical sciences, social sciences.

FRESHMAN ADMISSIONS. Selection criteria: Open admissions. Advanced ROTC applicants must have SAT combined score of 850 or ACT composite score of 19 and minimum 2.0 high school GPA. Selection criteria applies to scholarship candidates only. **Test requirements:** SAT or ACT; score report by September 1.

1992 FRESHMAN CLASS PROFILE. 461 men, 342 women enrolled. **Characteristics:** 71% from in state, 84% commute, 44% have minority backgrounds, 3% are foreign students. Average age is 20.

FALL-TERM APPLICATIONS. $25 fee, may be waived for applicants with need. Closing date August 15; applicants notified on a rolling basis. Interview recommended. Deferred and early admission available. Students interested in attending ROTC Basic Camp must apply by May 1.

STUDENT LIFE. Housing: Dormitories (coed). **Activities:** Student government, student newspaper, yearbook, choral groups, marching band, pep band, drill team, rifle team, Circle-K.

ATHLETICS. NJCAA. **Intercollegiate:** Football M, golf, rifle, tennis. **Intramural:** Baseball, basketball, soccer, softball, swimming, tennis, volleyball.

STUDENT SERVICES. Aptitude testing, freshman orientation, health services, personal counseling, veterans counselor.

ANNUAL EXPENSES. Tuition and fees (1992-93): $3,270. Additional cost of $900 for uniforms for cadets may be applicable. **Room and board:** $3,654. **Books and supplies:** $475. **Other expenses:** $1,025.

FINANCIAL AID. 50% of freshmen, 50% of continuing students receive some form of aid. Grants, loans, jobs available. **Aid applications:** No closing date; priority given to applications received by April 1; applicants notified on a rolling basis beginning on or about August 15. **Additional information:** Institutional aid offered to those enrolled in Cadet Corps who reside in on-campus housing.

ADDRESS/TELEPHONE. CPT David S. Bill, Director of Admissions and Enrollments, Georgia Military College, 201 East Greene Street, Milledgeville, GA 31061. (912) 454-2700. (800) 342-0413. Fax: (912)454-2688.

Georgia Southern University
Statesboro, Georgia CB code: 5253

Admissions: 71% of applicants accepted
Based on: ••• School record, test scores
• Interview, recommendations, special talents
Completion: 54% of freshmen end year in good standing
31% graduate

4-year public university and liberal arts college, coed. Founded in 1906. **Accreditation:** Regional. **Undergraduate enrollment:** 5,335 men, 5,806 women full time; 498 men, 581 women part time. **Graduate enrollment:** 236 men, 443 women full time; 314 men, 817 women part time. **Faculty:** 683 total (604 full time), 385 with doctorates or other terminal degrees. **Location:** Suburban campus in large town; 50 miles from Savannah. **Calendar:** Quarter, extensive summer session. **Microcomputers:** 225 located in dormitories, libraries, classrooms, computer centers. **Special facilities:** Art gallery, science complex including planetarium and electron microscope, Herty Woodland Nature Preserve, elementary laboratory school, museum, Center for Rural Health and Research, eagle sanctuary.

DEGREES OFFERED. AAS, BA, BS, BFA, MA, MS, MBA, MEd, EdD. 1,689 bachelor's degrees awarded. 34% in business and management, 5% communications, 26% education, 11% engineering technologies, 5% social sciences. Graduate degrees offered in 51 major fields of study.

UNDERGRADUATE MAJORS. Associate: Education, teacher aide. **Bachelor's:** Accounting, administration of special education, advertising, anthropology, art education, biology, business administration and management, business and management, business economics, business education, business home economics, chemistry, child development/care/guidance, civil technology, clinical laboratory science, clothing and textiles management/production/services, communications, computer and information sciences, construction, criminal justice studies, criminology, early childhood education, economics, education, education of exceptional children, education of the emotionally handicapped, education of the gifted and talented, education of the mentally handicapped, electrical technology, elementary education, engineering and engineering-related technologies, English, English education, family and community services, family/consumer resource management, fashion design, fashion merchandising, finance, fine arts, food management, food production/management/services, food science and nutrition, foreign languages education, French, geology, German, health education, history, home economics, home economics education, home furnishings and equipment management/production/services, hotel/motel and restaurant management, human environment and housing, human resources development, individual and family development, industrial arts education, industrial technology, information sciences and systems, institutional management, institutional/home management/supporting programs, insurance and risk management, interior design, journalism, junior high education, liberal/general studies, management information systems, managerial accounting, manufacturing technology, marketing and distribution, mathematics, mathematics education, mechanical design technology, medical laboratory technologies, music, music education, music performance, music theory and composition, nursing, parks and recreation management, physical education, physics, political science and government, practical nursing, predentistry, prelaw, premedicine, prepharmacy, preveterinary, psychology, public relations, radio/television broadcasting, radio/television technology, real estate, recreation and community services technologies, retailing, science education, secondary education, secretarial and related programs, social science education, social sciences, sociology, Spanish, special education, specific learning disabilities, speech, speech/communication/theater education, textiles and clothing, trade and industrial education, trade and industrial supervision and management, transportation and travel marketing, transportation management.

ACADEMIC PROGRAMS. 2-year transfer program, cooperative education, double major, dual enrollment of high school students, education specialist degree, honors program, independent study, internships, study abroad, teacher preparation. **Remedial services:** Learning center, reduced course load, remedial instruction, special counselor, tutoring. **ROTC:** Army. **Placement/credit:** AP, CLEP General and Subject, institutional tests; 45 credit hours maximum for bachelor's degree.

ACADEMIC REQUIREMENTS. Freshmen must earn minimum GPA of 2.0 to continue in good standing. 70% of freshmen return for sophomore year. Students must declare major by end of second year. **Graduation requirements:** 190 hours for bachelor's (30 in major). Most students required to take courses in arts/fine arts, English, history, humanities, mathematics, biological/physical sciences, social sciences. **Additional information:** 24-hour library computer lab.

FRESHMAN ADMISSIONS. Selection criteria: Test scores, high school GPA considered. **High school preparation:** 15 units required. Required units include English 4, foreign language 2, mathematics 3, social science 3 and science 3. **Test requirements:** SAT or ACT; score report by September 1.

1992 FRESHMAN CLASS PROFILE. 3,746 men applied, 2,618 accepted, 1,316 enrolled; 4,258 women applied, 3,071 accepted, 1,542 enrolled. 30% had high school GPA of 3.0 or higher, 65% between 2.0 and 2.99. **Academic background:** Mid 50% of enrolled freshmen had SAT-V between 370-450, SAT-M between 400-500. 90% submitted SAT scores. **Characteristics:** 75% from in state, 75% live in college housing, 27% have minority backgrounds, 1% are foreign students. Average age is 19.

FALL-TERM APPLICATIONS. $10 fee, may be waived for applicants with need. Closing date August 1; applicants notified on a rolling basis. Deferred and early admission available.

STUDENT LIFE. Housing: Dormitories (men, women, coed); apartment, fraternity, sorority housing available. **Activities:** Student government, film, magazine, radio, student newspaper, television, yearbook, choral groups, concert band, dance, drama, jazz band, marching band, music ensembles, musical theater, opera, pep band, symphony orchestra, fraternities, sororities, religious organizations, political/civil rights organizations.

ATHLETICS. NCAA. **Intercollegiate:** Baseball M, basketball, cross-country, diving, football M, golf M, soccer M, softball W, swimming, tennis, volleyball W. **Intramural:** Badminton, basketball, bowling, fencing, golf, racquetball, rugby M, soccer, softball, tennis, volleyball.

STUDENT SERVICES. Aptitude testing, career counseling, employment service for undergraduates, freshman orientation, health services, personal counseling, placement service for graduates, veterans counselor, services/facilities for handicapped.

ANNUAL EXPENSES. Tuition and fees: $1,827, $1,380 additional for out-of-state students. **Room and board:** $2,700. **Books and supplies:** $552. **Other expenses:** $735.

FINANCIAL AID. 22% of freshmen, 30% of continuing students receive some form of aid. 67% of grants, 64% of loans, 46% of jobs based on need. Academic, music/drama, athletic, leadership scholarships available. **Aid applications:** Closing date April 15; priority given to applications received by March 1; applicants notified on or about June 15; must reply within 4 weeks.

ADDRESS/TELEPHONE. W. Dale Wasson, Director of Admissions, Georgia Southern University, Landrum Box 8024, Statesboro, GA 30460-8024. (912) 681-5531. Fax: (912) 681-0081.

Georgia Southwestern College
Americus, Georgia CB code: 5250

Admissions: 54% of applicants accepted
Based on: ••• School record, test scores
Completion: 55% of freshmen end year in good standing
25% enter graduate study

4-year public liberal arts college, coed. Founded in 1906. **Accreditation:** Regional. **Undergraduate enrollment:** 2,153 men and women. **Graduate enrollment:** 380 men and women. **Faculty:** 148 total (127 full time), 75 with doctorates or other terminal degrees. **Location:** Suburban campus in large town; 135 miles from Atlanta. **Calendar:** Quarter, limited summer session. **Microcomputers:** 150 located in libraries, classrooms, computer centers. **Special facilities:** Rosalyn Carter Institute of Human Development, Asian Studies Constoritum of State University System, observatory.

DEGREES OFFERED. AA, AAS, BA, BS, BFA, MS, MEd. 33 associate degrees awarded in 1992. 20% in business/office and marketing/distribution, 6% computer sciences, 71% health sciences. 310 bachelor's degrees awarded. 18% in business and management, 7% business/office and marketing/distribution, 6% computer sciences, 43% teacher education, 5% health sciences, 6% psychology, 7% social sciences. Graduate degrees offered in 12 major fields of study.

UNDERGRADUATE MAJORS. Associate: Accounting, aeronautical technology, air conditioning/heating/refrigeration technology, automation manufacturing technology, computer programming, drafting, electronic technology, nursing, office automation. **Bachelor's:** Accounting, agribusiness, art education, behavioral sciences, biology, business administration and management, business and management, business and office, business education, chemistry, computer and information sciences, computer programming, dramatic arts, early childhood education, earth sciences, education, elementary education, English, English education, finance, fine arts, foreign languages education, geology, history, junior high education, management science, marketing management, mathematics, mathematics education, music education, nursing, physical education, physics, political science and government, psychology, public administration, science education, social science education, social sciences, sociology, special education, speech, systems analysis, visual and performing arts.

ACADEMIC PROGRAMS. 2-year transfer program, accelerated program, cooperative education, dual enrollment of high school students, education specialist degree, honors program, internships, study abroad, teacher preparation, cross-registration, associate degree program in trade and industry with South Georgia Technical Institute. **Remedial services:** Learning center, reduced course load, remedial instruction, special counselor, tutoring. **ROTC:** Army. **Placement/credit:** AP, CLEP General and Subject, institutional tests; 45 credit hours maximum for bachelor's degree.

ACADEMIC REQUIREMENTS. Freshmen must earn minimum GPA of 2.0 to continue in good standing. 65% of freshmen return for sophomore year. Students must declare major by end of first year. **Graduation requirements:** 90 hours for associate, 180 hours for bachelor's. Most students required to take courses in English, history, humanities, mathematics, biological/physical sciences, social sciences. **Postgraduate studies:** 20% from 2-year programs enter 4-year programs.

FRESHMAN ADMISSIONS. Selection criteria: School achievement record, test scores. **High school preparation:** 20 units required. Required units include English 4, foreign language 2, mathematics 3, social science 3 and science 3. **Test requirements:** SAT or ACT; score report by September 1.

1992 FRESHMAN CLASS PROFILE. 991 men and women applied, 538 accepted; 485 enrolled. 37% had high school GPA of 3.0 or higher, 48% between 2.0 and 2.99. **Academic background:** Mid 50% of enrolled freshmen had SAT-V between 350-460, SAT-M between 370-500. 96% submitted SAT scores. **Characteristics:** 98% from in state, 55% commute, 17% have minority backgrounds, 1% are foreign students. Average age is 19.

FALL-TERM APPLICATIONS. $10 fee. Closing date September 1; applicants notified on a rolling basis. Early admission available.

STUDENT LIFE. Housing: Dormitories (men, women); fraternity housing available. **Activities:** Student government, magazine, student newspaper, choral groups, concert band, drama, jazz band, marching band, musical theater, fraternities, sororities, Baptist Student Union, Wesley Foundation, Circle K. Blue Key, Young Republicans, Young Democrats, Gamma Beta Phi.

ATHLETICS. NAIA. **Intercollegiate:** Baseball M, basketball, golf M. **Intramural:** Basketball, softball, tennis, volleyball.

STUDENT SERVICES. Career counseling, employment service for undergraduates, freshman orientation, health services, personal counseling, placement service for graduates, special adviser for adult students, veterans counselor, services/facilities for handicapped.

ANNUAL EXPENSES. Tuition and fees (projected): $1,704, $1,380 additional for out-of-state students. **Room and board:** $2,570. **Books and supplies:** $600. **Other expenses:** $750.

FINANCIAL AID. 98% of freshmen, 50% of continuing students receive some form of aid. 77% of grants, 85% of loans, 46% of jobs based on need. 182 enrolled freshmen were judged to have need, 179 were offered aid. Academic, music/drama, art, athletic scholarships available. **Aid appli-**

cations: No closing date; priority given to applications received by April 1; applicants notified on a rolling basis beginning on or about May 1; must reply within 10 days.

ADDRESS/TELEPHONE. Diane Burns, Director of Admissions, Georgia Southwestern College, 800 Wheatly Street, Americus, GA 31709-4693. (912) 928-1273. (800) 338-0082. Fax: (912) 928-1630.

Georgia State University
Atlanta, Georgia — CB code: 5251

Admissions: 73% of applicants accepted
Based on: ••• School record, test scores
• Activities, essay, interview, recommendations, special talents
Completion: 66% of freshmen end year in good standing

4-year public university, coed. Founded in 1913. **Accreditation:** Regional. **Undergraduate enrollment:** 3,225 men, 4,508 women full time; 3,899 men, 5,529 women part time. **Graduate enrollment:** 1,651 men, 1,773 women full time; 1,368 men, 2,148 women part time. **Faculty:** 918 total (865 full time), 772 with doctorates or other terminal degrees. **Location:** Urban campus in very large city; in downtown area. **Calendar:** Quarter, extensive summer session. Saturday and extensive evening/early morning classes. **Microcomputers:** 200 located in libraries, computer centers. **Additional facts:** Courses are offered at North Metro Center and Gwinnett Center.

DEGREES OFFERED. AA, AS, AAS, BA, BS, BFA, MA, MS, MBA, MFA, MEd, PhD. 8 associate degrees awarded in 1992. 25% in business and management, 75% multi/interdisciplinary studies. 2,375 bachelor's degrees awarded. 39% in business and management, 5% computer sciences, 9% education, 6% health sciences, 6% psychology, 12% social sciences, 5% visual and performing arts. Graduate degrees offered in 96 major fields of study.

UNDERGRADUATE MAJORS. Associate: Liberal/general studies. **Bachelor's:** Accounting, actuarial sciences, adult and continuing teacher education, anthropology, art education, biology, business administration and management, business economics, business education, business statistics, chemistry, classics, computer and information sciences, criminal justice studies, dance, dramatic arts, drawing, early childhood education, economics, education of the mentally handicapped, English, film arts, finance, fine arts, food science and nutrition, French, geography, geology, German, health education, history, hotel/motel and restaurant management, information sciences and systems, insurance and risk management, interdisciplinary studies, journalism, junior high education, law enforcement and corrections, marketing and distribution, marketing and distributive education, marketing management, mathematics, medical laboratory technologies, medical records administration, mental health/human services, music, music business management, nursing, office supervision and management, operations research, parks and recreation management, philosophy, physical education, physical therapy, physics, political science and government, psychology, real estate, religion, respiratory therapy, respiratory therapy technology, secondary education, social work, sociology, Spanish, speech, studio art, trade and industrial education, urban studies, video.

ACADEMIC PROGRAMS. 2-year transfer program, accelerated program, cooperative education, double major, dual enrollment of high school students, education specialist degree, honors program, independent study, internships, student-designed major, study abroad, cross-registration. **Remedial services:** Learning center, reduced course load, remedial instruction, special counselor, tutoring. **ROTC:** Army. **Placement/credit:** AP, CLEP Subject, institutional tests; 30 credit hours maximum for associate degree; 45 credit hours maximum for bachelor's degree.

ACADEMIC REQUIREMENTS. Freshmen must earn minimum GPA of 2.0 to continue in good standing. 69% of freshmen return for sophomore year. Students must declare major by end of second year. **Graduation requirements:** 95 hours for associate (35 in major), 185 hours for bachelor's (95 in major). Most students required to take courses in English, foreign languages, history, humanities, mathematics, biological/physical sciences, social sciences.

FRESHMAN ADMISSIONS. Selection criteria: Scholastic record, test scores, personal readiness for college. 2.0 high school GPA, specified college preparatory courses. **High school preparation:** 15 units required. Required units include English 4, foreign language 2, mathematics 3, social science 3 and science 3. **Test requirements:** SAT or ACT; score report by July 15. Combined 600 SAT for developmental studies students, 800 for all others.

1992 FRESHMAN CLASS PROFILE. 1,022 men applied, 735 accepted, 632 enrolled; 1,447 women applied, 1,071 accepted, 921 enrolled. 28% had high school GPA of 3.0 or higher, 71% between 2.0 and 2.99. **Academic background:** Mid 50% of enrolled freshmen had SAT-V between 370-480, SAT-M between 410-490; ACT composite between 19-22. 98% submitted SAT scores, 7% submitted ACT scores. **Characteristics:** 91% from in state, 100% commute, 39% have minority backgrounds, 3% are foreign students, 10% join fraternities/sororities. Average age is 19.

FALL-TERM APPLICATIONS. $10 fee, may be waived for applicants with need. Closing date July 15; applicants notified on a rolling basis; must reply by registration. Audition required for music applicants. Interview recommended for marginal applicants. Portfolio recommended for art applicants. Essay recommended. Deferred and early admission available.

STUDENT LIFE. Activities: Student government, film, magazine, radio, student newspaper, television, yearbook, choral groups, concert band, dance, drama, jazz band, music ensembles, musical theater, pep band, symphony orchestra, fraternities, sororities, World Affairs Council, Black Student Alliance, International Student Association, Ecumenical Council.

ATHLETICS. NCAA. **Intercollegiate:** Baseball M, basketball, cross-country, golf, soccer M, softball W, swimming, tennis, volleyball W, wrestling M. **Intramural:** Badminton, basketball, bowling, cross-country, diving, golf, racquetball, soccer, softball, swimming, tennis, volleyball, wrestling M.

STUDENT SERVICES. Aptitude testing, career counseling, employment service for undergraduates, freshman orientation, health services, on-campus day care, personal counseling, placement service for graduates, veterans counselor, Career Development Center, available to the community, services/facilities for handicapped.

ANNUAL EXPENSES. Tuition and fees: $2,019, $4,433 additional for out-of-state students. **Books and supplies:** $980. **Other expenses:** $800.

FINANCIAL AID. 25% of freshmen, 30% of continuing students receive some form of aid. 88% of grants, 83% of loans, 17% of jobs based on need. Academic, music/drama, art, athletic, state/district residency, minority scholarships available. **Aid applications:** No closing date; priority given to applications received by May 1; applicants notified on a rolling basis beginning on or about July 1; must reply within 2 weeks.

ADDRESS/TELEPHONE. Darryl Johnson, Dean of Admissions, Georgia State University, University Plaza, Atlanta, GA 30303-3083. (404) 651-2365.

Gordon College
Barnesville, Georgia — CB code: 5256

Admissions: 98% of applicants accepted
Based on: ••• School record, test scores
•• Special talents
• Activities, recommendations
Completion: 75% of freshmen end year in good standing
30% graduate, 50% of these enter 4-year programs

2-year public junior college, coed. Founded in 1852. **Accreditation:** Regional. **Undergraduate enrollment:** 505 men, 737 women full time; 183 men, 488 women part time. **Faculty:** 108 total (66 full time), 24 with doctorates or other terminal degrees. **Location:** Rural campus in small town; 57 miles from Atlanta. **Calendar:** Quarter, limited summer session. Extensive evening/early morning classes. **Microcomputers:** 75 located in libraries, classrooms, computer centers. **Special facilities:** Hightower Library Alumni Room housing Gordon memorabilia dating from 1852 and Georgia Collection, books by Georgia authors or about Georgia.

DEGREES OFFERED. AA, AS, AAS. 258 associate degrees awarded in 1992. 39% in business and management, 11% education, 20% health sciences, 5% social sciences.

UNDERGRADUATE MAJORS. Accounting, agricultural engineering, agricultural sciences, anthropology, biology, business administration and management, business and management, business data processing and related programs, business data programming, business economics, chemistry, computer and information sciences, criminal justice studies, dental hygiene, dramatic arts, economics, education, English, fine arts, foreign languages (multiple emphasis), forestry and related sciences, history, home economics, journalism, liberal/general studies, mathematics, medical laboratory technologies, music, nursing, office supervision and management, physics, political science and government, predentistry, preengineering, prelaw, premedicine, prepharmacy, preveterinary, psychology, radiograph medical technology, science technologies, secretarial and related programs, sociology, textile technology, urban studies.

ACADEMIC PROGRAMS. 2-year transfer program, cooperative education, dual enrollment of high school students, study abroad, cooperative associate degree programs with local vocational-technical schools. **Remedial services:** Learning center, preadmission summer program, remedial instruction, special counselor, tutoring. **Placement/credit:** AP, CLEP General and Subject, institutional tests; 45 credit hours maximum for associate degree.

ACADEMIC REQUIREMENTS. Freshmen must earn minimum GPA of 2.0 to continue in good standing. 60% of freshmen return for sophomore year. Students must declare major by end of first year. **Graduation requirements:** 90 hours for associate (30 in major). Most students required to take courses in arts/fine arts, English, foreign languages, history, humanities, mathematics, biological/physical sciences, social sciences.

FRESHMAN ADMISSIONS. Selection criteria: Test scores and GPA most important. Lower test scores and high school GPA used for admission to Developmental Studies Program. **High school preparation:** 16 units required. Required units include English 4, foreign language 2, mathematics 3, social science 3 and science 3. Foreign language units must be in same language. **Test requirements:** SAT or ACT (SAT preferred); score report by September 6.

1992 FRESHMAN CLASS PROFILE. 300 men applied, 292 accepted, 292 enrolled; 463 women applied, 452 accepted, 353 enrolled. 23% had high school GPA of 3.0 or higher, 50% between 2.0 and 2.99. **Academic background:** Mid 50% of enrolled freshmen had SAT-V between 310-430, SAT-M between 330-470; ACT composite between 16-21. 90% submitted SAT scores, 3% submitted ACT scores. **Characteristics:** 90% from in state, 70% commute, 20% have minority backgrounds. Average age is 23.

FALL-TERM APPLICATIONS. No fee. Closing date September 6; applicants notified on a rolling basis. Interview required for nursing applicants. Early admission available.

STUDENT LIFE. Housing: Dormitories (men, women). **Activities:** Student government, magazine, choral groups, dance, drama, jazz band, music ensembles, musical theater, Baptist Student Union, Future science club, art club, Fellowship of Christian Athletes, Fresh Start, Minority Advising Program, Phi Beta Lamda (business), Explorers Club.

ATHLETICS. NJCAA. **Intercollegiate:** Baseball M, basketball M, softball W, tennis W. **Intramural:** Badminton, basketball, handball, racquetball, soccer, softball, table tennis, tennis, volleyball.

STUDENT SERVICES. Aptitude testing, career counseling, employment service for undergraduates, freshman orientation, personal counseling, placement service for graduates, special adviser for adult students, veterans counselor, services/facilities for handicapped.

ANNUAL EXPENSES. Tuition and fees: $1,164, $939 additional for out-of-state students. **Room and board:** $2,430. **Books and supplies:** $379. **Other expenses:** $700.

FINANCIAL AID. 44% of freshmen, 30% of continuing students receive some form of aid. Grants, loans, jobs available. Academic, music/drama, art, athletic, state/district residency, leadership, alumni affiliation scholarships available. **Aid applications:** No closing date; priority given to applications received by June 22; applicants notified on a rolling basis beginning on or about May 1.

ADDRESS/TELEPHONE. Dr. Mary Jean Simmons, Director of Enrollment Services, Gordon College, 419 College Drive, Barnesville, GA 30204. (404) 358-5000.

Gupton Jones College of Funeral Service
Decatur, Georgia — CB code: 6200

2-year private technical college, coed. Founded in 1920. **Undergraduate enrollment:** 325 men and women. **Faculty:** 8 total, 8 with doctorates or other terminal degrees. **Location:** Suburban campus in large town. **Calendar:** Quarter. **Additional facts:** Accredited by American Board of Funeral Service Education.

DEGREES OFFERED. AS. 45 associate degrees awarded in 1992. 100% in allied health.

UNDERGRADUATE MAJORS. Funeral services/mortuary science.

ACADEMIC PROGRAMS. Placement/credit: Institutional tests.

ACADEMIC REQUIREMENTS. Students must declare major on enrollment. **Graduation requirements:** 80 hours for associate (80 in major).

FRESHMAN ADMISSIONS. Selection criteria: Open admissions.

1992 FRESHMAN CLASS PROFILE. 225 men and women enrolled. **Characteristics:** 100% commute.

FALL-TERM APPLICATIONS. Closing date is 2 weeks after registration.

ANNUAL EXPENSES. Tuition and fees: Tuition for 12-month program is $5,200 including fees and books. Associate degree program is an additional $1,200, plus books.

FINANCIAL AID. Aid applications: No closing date.

ADDRESS/TELEPHONE. Daniel E. Buchanan, President, Gupton Jones College of Funeral Service, 5141 Snapfinger Woods Drive, Decatur, GA 30035. (404) 593-2257. (800) 848-5352. Fax: (404) 593-1891.

Gwinnett Technical Institute
Lawrenceville, Georgia — CB code: 5168

2-year public technical college. **Accreditation:** Regional. **Undergraduate enrollment:** 542 men, 567 women full time; 959 men, 1,019 women part time. **Faculty:** 166 total (84 full time), 11 with doctorates or other terminal degrees. **Location:** Suburban campus in large town; 25 miles from Atlanta, GA. Saturday and extensive evening/early morning classes. **Microcomputers:** Located in libraries, classrooms, computer centers. **Special facilities:** New 18000 foot media center, studio, and seminar room contains microcomputers and multimedia compilers. **Additional facts:** Internships available with several manufacturers and companies, among them American Honda, Toyota Nissan, and Chrysler.

DEGREES OFFERED. AAS.

UNDERGRADUATE MAJORS. Accounting, automotive mechanics, automotive technology, business and management, computer programming, construction, electrical and electronics equipment repair, electronic technology, fashion merchandising, horticulture, hotel/motel and restaurant management, manufacturing technology, marketing and distribution, marketing management, photography, physical therapy assistant, radiograph medical technology, robotics, secretarial and related programs, telecommunications, tourism.

ACADEMIC PROGRAMS. Cooperative education, double major, dual enrollment of high school students, internships, weekend college. **Remedial services:** Remedial instruction.

ACADEMIC REQUIREMENTS. Freshmen must earn minimum GPA of 2.0 to continue in good standing. Students must declare major on application. **Graduation requirements:** Most students required to take courses in English, mathematics.

FRESHMAN ADMISSIONS. Test requirements: SAT or ACT.

1992 FRESHMAN CLASS PROFILE. Characteristics: Average age is 28.

FALL-TERM APPLICATIONS. $15 fee. No closing date. Interview required for health science programs applicants. Application closing dates for health sciences programs. Call for information.

STUDENT LIFE. Activities: Student government, student leadership assembly.

STUDENT SERVICES. Aptitude testing, career counseling, freshman orientation, personal counseling, placement service for graduates, special adviser for adult students, veterans counselor.

ANNUAL EXPENSES. Tuition and fees (1992-93):

ADDRESS/TELEPHONE. Pete Atkinson, Director of Admissions, Gwinnett Technical Institute, 1250 Atkinson Road P.O. Box 1505, Lawrenceville, GA 30246-1505. 962-7580 ext. 116. Fax: 962-7985.

Kennesaw State College
Marietta, Georgia — CB code: 5359

Admissions:	74% of applicants accepted
Based on:	••• School record, test scores
Completion:	70% of freshmen end year in good standing
	20% graduate, 6% of these enter graduate study

4-year public community, liberal arts college, coed. Founded in 1963. **Accreditation:** Regional. **Undergraduate enrollment:** 2,061 men, 2,987 women full time; 1,882 men, 3,532 women part time. **Graduate enrollment:** 180 men, 344 women full time; 248 men, 427 women part time. **Faculty:** 438 total (331 full time), 246 with doctorates or other terminal degrees. **Location:** Suburban campus in large town; 20 miles from Atlanta. **Calendar:** Quarter, extensive summer session. **Microcomputers:** 583 located in classrooms, computer centers. **Special facilities:** Center for Excellence in Teaching and Learning, rare book collection, art gallery, physiology laboratory.

DEGREES OFFERED. AS, BA, BS, MBA, MEd. 130 associate degrees awarded in 1992. 27% in business and management, 71% health sciences. 880 bachelor's degrees awarded. 51% in business and management, 6% communications, 13% education, 7% psychology. Graduate degrees offered in 11 major fields of study.

UNDERGRADUATE MAJORS. Associate: Nursing. **Bachelor's:** Accounting, art education, biology, business administration and management, business and management, business economics, business education, chemistry, communications, computer and information sciences, computer programming, early childhood education, economics, education, elementary education, English, English education, finance, fine arts, foreign languages education, French, French education, health and physical education, health education, history, information sciences and systems, international relations, international studies, journalism, junior high education, marketing and distribution, mathematics, mathematics education, music, music education, music performance, nursing, physical education, political science and government, predentistry, prelaw, premedicine, prepharmacy, preveterinary, psychology, public affairs, science education, secondary education, social studies education, Spanish, Spanish education.

ACADEMIC PROGRAMS. Cooperative education, dual enrollment of high school students, honors program, internships, study abroad, teacher preparation, weekend college, cross-registration. **Remedial services:** Learning center, reduced course load, remedial instruction, tutoring. **ROTC:** Army. **Placement/credit:** AP, CLEP Subject, institutional tests; 45 credit hours maximum for associate degree; 45 credit hours maximum for bachelor's degree.

ACADEMIC REQUIREMENTS. Freshmen must earn minimum GPA of 2.0 to continue in good standing. 70% of freshmen return for sophomore year. Students must declare major by end of second year. **Graduation requirements:** 99 hours for associate (45 in major), 186 hours for bachelor's (90 in major). Most students required to take courses in English, foreign languages, history, humanities, mathematics, philosophy/religion, biological/physical sciences, social sciences. **Postgraduate studies:** 1% enter medical school, 3% enter MBA programs, 2% enter other graduate study.

FRESHMAN ADMISSIONS. High school preparation: 21 units required. Required units include biological science 2, English 4, foreign language 2, mathematics 3, physical science 1 and social science 3. Students who have not fulfilled college preparatory requirements must do so in college. **Test requirements:** SAT or ACT; score report by September 3.

1992 FRESHMAN CLASS PROFILE. Characteristics: 97% from in state, 100% commute, 26% have minority backgrounds, 3% are foreign students, 4% join fraternities/sororities. Average age is 20.

FALL-TERM APPLICATIONS. $20 fee. Closing date September 1; priority given to applications received by June 1; applicants notified on a rolling basis. Audition required for music applicants. Portfolio recommended for art applicants. Deferred and early admission available.

STUDENT LIFE. Housing: 2 apartment complexes within walking distance of campus available. **Activities:** Student government, magazine, student newspaper, yearbook, choral groups, concert band, dance, drama, jazz band, music ensembles, musical theater, pep band, symphony orchestra, fraternities, sororities, Baptist Student Union, Black Students Alliance, International Student Association, Student Nurses Association, special interest clubs, College Ambassadors, Fellowship of Christian Athletes, College Chorale, Volunteer Kennesaw State, American Marketing Association.

ATHLETICS. NCAA. **Intercollegiate:** Baseball M, basketball, cross-country, golf M, softball W, tennis W. **Intramural:** Archery, badminton, basketball, bowling, football, golf, handball, racquetball, soccer, softball, swimming, table tennis, tennis, volleyball.

STUDENT SERVICES. Aptitude testing, career counseling, employment service for undergraduates, freshman orientation, personal counseling, placement service for graduates, veterans counselor, writing laboratory, math laboratory, wellness center, adult learning counseling, services/facilities for handicapped.

ANNUAL EXPENSES. Tuition and fees (projected): $1,560, $1,380 additional for out-of-state students. **Books and supplies:** $600. **Other expenses:** $935.

FINANCIAL AID. 15% of freshmen, 17% of continuing students receive some form of aid. 92% of grants, 80% of loans, 2% of jobs based on need. 213 enrolled freshmen were judged to have need, 212 were offered aid. Academic, music/drama, art, athletic, leadership scholarships available. **Aid applications:** Closing date May 1; priority given to applications received by April 15; applicants notified on a rolling basis beginning on or about June 1; must reply within 2 weeks.

ADDRESS/TELEPHONE. Joe F. Head, Director of Admissions, Kennesaw State College, PO Box 444, Marietta, GA 30061. (404) 423-6300. Fax: (404) 423-6541.

LaGrange College
LaGrange, Georgia

CB code: 5362

4-year private liberal arts college, coed, affiliated with United Methodist Church. Founded in 1831. **Accreditation:** Regional. **Undergraduate enrollment:** 259 men, 349 women full time; 105 men, 197 women part time. **Graduate enrollment:** 7 men, 3 women full time; 14 men, 25 women part time. **Faculty:** 81 total (69 full time), 58 with doctorates or other terminal degrees. **Location:** Suburban campus in large town; 70 miles from Atlanta, 45 miles from Columbus. **Calendar:** Quarter, limited summer session. **Microcomputers:** 48 located in dormitories, libraries, classrooms, computer centers, campus-wide network. **Special facilities:** Art gallery, regional theater.

DEGREES OFFERED. AA, BA, BS, MBA, MEd. 28 associate degrees awarded in 1992. 128 bachelor's degrees awarded. Graduate degrees offered in 3 major fields of study.

UNDERGRADUATE MAJORS. Associate: Business and office, law enforcement and corrections technologies, liberal/general studies, nursing, radiograph medical technology, textile technology. **Bachelor's:** Accounting, biology, business administration and management, business and management, business economics, ceramics, chemistry, computer and information sciences, computer programming, dramatic arts, drawing, early childhood education, economics, elementary education, English, environmental science, history, mathematics, painting, photography, physical sciences, political science and government, predentistry, prelaw, premedicine, prepharmacy, preveterinary, psychology, religion, religious education, sculpture, secondary education, social work, theological studies.

ACADEMIC PROGRAMS. Double major, dual enrollment of high school students, education specialist degree, honors program, independent study, internships, study abroad; liberal arts/career combination in engineering; combined bachelor's/graduate program in business administration. **Remedial services:** Tutoring. **Placement/credit:** AP, CLEP General, institutional tests.

ACADEMIC REQUIREMENTS. Freshmen must earn minimum GPA of 2.0 to continue in good standing. 82% of freshmen return for sophomore year. Students must declare major by end of second year. **Graduation requirements:** 95 hours for associate (45 in major), 205 hours for bachelor's (60 in major). Most students required to take courses in arts/fine arts, computer science, English, history, humanities, mathematics, philosophy/religion, biological/physical sciences, social sciences. **Postgraduate studies:** 52% from 2-year programs enter 4-year programs.

FRESHMAN ADMISSIONS. Selection criteria: School achievement record and test scores most important, interview and recommendations considered. **High school preparation:** 15 units required. Required and recommended units include English 4, mathematics 2-3, social science 3 and science 2-3. Foreign language 2 recommended. **Test requirements:** SAT or ACT (SAT preferred); score report by August 1.

1992 FRESHMAN CLASS PROFILE. 200 men and women enrolled. **Characteristics:** 80% from in state, 75% live in college housing, 7% have minority backgrounds, 6% are foreign students, 30% join fraternities/sororities. Average age is 18.

FALL-TERM APPLICATIONS. $20 fee. Closing date August 1; priority given to applications received by June 1; applicants notified on a rolling basis. Interview required for nursing applicants. Early admission available.

STUDENT LIFE. Housing: Dormitories (men, women, coed); fraternity housing available. **Activities:** Student government, magazine, student newspaper, yearbook, choral groups, dance, drama, jazz band, music ensembles, musical theater, symphony orchestra, fraternities, sororities, Wesley Fellowship, Baptist Student Union, Circle-K, Rotoract, Interfaith Council.

ATHLETICS. NAIA. **Intercollegiate:** Baseball M, basketball M, cross-country M, soccer, softball W, tennis, volleyball W. **Intramural:** Archery, badminton, basketball, football M, golf, softball, tennis, volleyball.

STUDENT SERVICES. Career counseling, freshman orientation, health services, personal counseling, placement service for graduates, special adviser for adult students.

ANNUAL EXPENSES. Tuition and fees: $6,375. **Room and board:** $3,480. **Books and supplies:** $600. **Other expenses:** $900.

FINANCIAL AID. 75% of freshmen, 80% of continuing students receive some form of aid. 47% of grants, 85% of loans, all jobs based on need. 115 enrolled freshmen were judged to have need, all were offered aid. Academic, music/drama, art, state/district residency, leadership, religious affiliation scholarships available. **Aid applications:** No closing date; priority given to applications received by May 1; applicants notified on a rolling basis beginning on or about May 1; must reply within 2 weeks.

ADDRESS/TELEPHONE. Phillip Dodson, Director of Admissions, LaGrange College, 601 Broad Street, LaGrange, GA 30240. (706) 882-2911. (800) 476-4925. Fax: (706) 884-6567.

Macon College
Macon, Georgia

CB code: 5439

2-year public junior college, coed. Founded in 1968. **Accreditation:** Regional. **Undergraduate enrollment:** 616 men, 976 women full time; 1,017 men, 2,479 women part time. **Faculty:** 202 total (150 full time), 71 with doctorates or other terminal degrees. **Location:** Suburban campus in small city; 85 miles from Atlanta. **Calendar:** Quarter, extensive summer session. Extensive evening/early morning classes. **Microcomputers:** Located in libraries, computer centers. **Additional facts:** Jointly operated with Georgia College and Fort Valley State resident center through which employees of Robins Air Force Base may receive degrees.

DEGREES OFFERED. AA, AS, AAS. 468 associate degrees awarded in 1992. 31% in business and management, 8% teacher education, 37% health sciences.

UNDERGRADUATE MAJORS. Accounting, agricultural sciences, biology, business administration and management, business and management, business and office, business data processing and related programs, business data programming, business education, chemistry, computer and information sciences, computer programming, criminal justice studies, dental hygiene, economics, electronic technology, elementary education, engineering, engineering and engineering-related technologies, English, fine arts, fire protection, food sciences, foreign languages (multiple emphasis), health sciences, history, information sciences and systems, journalism, law enforcement and corrections, liberal/general studies, mathematics, medical laboratory technologies, music, nursing, physical education, physical therapy, physics, political science and government, predentistry, prelaw, premedicine, prepharmacy, preveterinary, psychology, public administration, renewable natural resources, retailing, secondary education, secretarial and related programs, social work, sociology, speech.

ACADEMIC PROGRAMS. 2-year transfer program, dual enrollment of high school students, honors program, internships, study abroad, telecourses. **Remedial services:** Preadmission summer program, reduced course load, remedial instruction, special counselor, tutoring. **Placement/credit:** AP, CLEP Subject, institutional tests; 60 credit hours maximum for associate degree.

ACADEMIC REQUIREMENTS. Freshmen must earn minimum GPA of 1.5 to continue in good standing. 62% of freshmen return for sophomore year. Students must declare major by end of first year. **Graduation requirements:** 96 hours for associate (30 in major). Most students required to take courses in English, history, humanities, mathematics, biological/physical sciences, social sciences.

FRESHMAN ADMISSIONS. Selection criteria: Minimum SAT-verbal score of 250 or ACT English of 13, or SAT-mathematical score of 280 or ACT mathematical of 14 or 1.8 high school GPA required. Minimum SAT-verbal score of 450, SAT-mathematical of 550 and 3.0 high school GPA required for Regents Engineering Transfer Program applicants. Minimum SAT composite score of 900, SAT-verbal score of 450 and 3.0 academic high school GPA required for high school joint enrollment or early admission applicants. Required units include English 4, foreign language 2, mathematics 3, physical science 1, social science 3 and science 2. **Test requirements:** SAT or ACT; score report by September 16. **Additional information:**

College preparatory requirements waived for students in career or terminal programs and those graduated from high school prior to May 1988. Applicants to A.A. and A.S. transfer programs who have not satisfied precollege curriculum required to make up deficiencies. SAT/ACT requirement waived for freshman applicants who have been out of high school for five years or more. Placement testing is required for these applicants.

1992 FRESHMAN CLASS PROFILE. 1,116 men and women enrolled. **Characteristics:** 100% commute.

FALL-TERM APPLICATIONS. No fee. No closing date; applicants notified on a rolling basis. Interview required for dental hygiene applicants. Early admission available.

STUDENT LIFE. Activities: Student government, magazine, student newspaper, choral groups, drama, music ensembles, musical theater, pep band, Black Student Union, Georgia Association of Nursing Students, nontraditional support group, Circle-K, art club, Spanish club, Baptist Student Union.

ATHLETICS. NJCAA. **Intercollegiate:** Basketball M, softball W. **Intramural:** Basketball, golf, softball, tennis, volleyball.

STUDENT SERVICES. Aptitude testing, career counseling, employment service for undergraduates, freshman orientation, on-campus day care, personal counseling, veterans counselor, services/facilities for handicapped.

ANNUAL EXPENSES. Tuition and fees: $1,113, $939 additional for out-of-state students. **Books and supplies:** $500. **Other expenses:** $950.

FINANCIAL AID. 25% of freshmen, 25% of continuing students receive some form of aid. Grants, loans, jobs available. Academic, leadership, minority scholarships available. **Aid applications:** No closing date; priority given to applications received by April 1; applicants notified on a rolling basis beginning on or about August 1; must reply within 2 weeks.

ADDRESS/TELEPHONE. Dee B. Minter, Director of Admissions, Macon College, 100 College Station Drive, Macon, GA 31297. (912) 474-2800. Fax: (912) 471-2846.

Meadows College of Business
Columbus, Georgia CB code: 0899

2-year proprietary junior college, coed. Founded in 1971. **Undergraduate enrollment:** 60 men, 261 women full time. **Faculty:** 21 total (18 full time). **Location:** Urban campus in small city; 100 miles from Atlanta. **Calendar:** Quarter. **Microcomputers:** 40 located in classrooms, computer centers.

DEGREES OFFERED. AS. 42 associate degrees awarded in 1992. 45% in business/office and marketing/distribution, 30% computer sciences, 25% allied health.

UNDERGRADUATE MAJORS. Accounting, business data processing and related programs, computer and information sciences, engineering and engineering-related technologies, legal secretary, medical assistant, medical secretary, microcomputer software, secretarial and related programs, word processing.

ACADEMIC PROGRAMS. 2-year transfer program, accelerated program, double major, honors program, independent study, internships. **Remedial services:** Learning center, reduced course load, remedial instruction, tutoring. **Placement/credit:** Institutional tests; 24 credit hours maximum for associate degree.

ACADEMIC REQUIREMENTS. Freshmen must earn minimum GPA of 2.0 to continue in good standing. 64% of freshmen return for sophomore year. Students must declare major on enrollment. **Graduation requirements:** 96 hours for associate (40 in major). Most students required to take courses in computer science, English, history, mathematics, social sciences.

FRESHMAN ADMISSIONS. Selection criteria: Open admissions. Interview and recommendations important, school record, test scores, school and community activities considered. All applicants with high school diplomaor GED accepted. **High school preparation:** 18 units recommended. Recommended units include biological science 2, English 4, mathematics 4, physical science 2, social science 4 and science 2. **Test requirements:** Institutionally administered test required for admission. **Additional information:** Applicants without high school diploma or GED may be accepted with passing grade on ACT CPA test.

1992 FRESHMAN CLASS PROFILE. 19 men, 82 women enrolled. **Characteristics:** 75% from in state, 100% commute, 56% have minority backgrounds. Average age is 25.

FALL-TERM APPLICATIONS. $50 fee. Closing date September 17; applicants notified on or about October 1. Interview required.

STUDENT LIFE. Activities: Student government, student newspaper.

ATHLETICS. Intramural: Basketball, volleyball.

STUDENT SERVICES. Career counseling, employment service for undergraduates, freshman orientation, personal counseling, placement service for graduates, special adviser for adult students, veterans counselor, services/facilities for handicapped.

ANNUAL EXPENSES. Tuition and fees (1992-93): $2,775. Tuition and fees includes cost of books.

FINANCIAL AID. 90% of freshmen, 90% of continuing students receive some form of aid. **Aid applications:** No closing date; applicants notified on a rolling basis.

ADDRESS/TELEPHONE. Shirley Spoonemore, Director of Admissions, Meadows College of Business, 1170 Brown Avenue, Columbus, GA 31906. (706) 327-7668.

Medical College of Georgia
Augusta, Georgia CB code: 5406

2-year upper-division public health sciences professional university, coed. Founded in 1828. **Accreditation:** Regional. **Undergraduate enrollment:** 167 men, 666 women full time; 5 men, 47 women part time. **Graduate enrollment:** 636 men, 362 women full time; 47 men, 128 women part time. **Faculty:** 851 total (733 full time), 693 with doctorates or other terminal degrees. **Location:** Urban campus in large town; 157 miles from Atlanta. **Calendar:** Quarter. **Microcomputers:** Located in libraries, classrooms, computer centers. **Special facilities:** 600-bed teaching hospital, over 80 clinics.

DEGREES OFFERED. AS, BS, MS, PhD, DMD, MD. 306 bachelor's degrees awarded. 50% in health sciences, 50% allied health. Graduate degrees offered in 16 major fields of study.

UNDERGRADUATE MAJORS. Associate: Dental hygiene, dental laboratory technology, medical records technology, neurodiagnostic technology, nuclear medical technology, occupational therapy assistant, physical therapy assistant, radiation therapy, radiograph medical technology, respiratory therapy. **Bachelor's:** Clinical laboratory science, dental hygiene, medical laboratory technologies, medical records administration, nuclear medical technology, nursing, occupational therapy, physical therapy, physician's assistant, radiation therapy, radiograph medical technology, respiratory therapy, ultrasound technology.

ACADEMIC PROGRAMS. Internships, cooperative program with Augusta College. **Remedial services:** Learning center, preadmission summer program, remedial instruction, tutoring. **Placement/credit:** CLEP General and Subject; 45 credit hours maximum for bachelor's degree.

ACADEMIC REQUIREMENTS. Students must declare major on application. **Graduation requirements:** 180 hours for bachelor's (90 in major). Most students required to take courses in English, history, mathematics, biological/physical sciences, social sciences.

STUDENT LIFE. Housing: Dormitories (coed); apartment, handicapped housing available. **Activities:** Student government, student newspaper, yearbook, Christian Medical Society, Black Student Medical Alliance.

ATHLETICS. Intramural: Basketball, rowing (crew), rugby M, soccer M, softball, volleyball.

STUDENT SERVICES. Career counseling, employment service for undergraduates, health services, personal counseling, placement service for graduates, services/facilities for handicapped.

ANNUAL EXPENSES. Tuition and fees: $2,085, $1,845 additional for out-of-state students. **Room and board:** $3,807. **Books and supplies:** $700. **Other expenses:** $1,170.

FINANCIAL AID. 77% of continuing students receive some form of aid. 99% of grants, 96% of loans, 17% of jobs based on need. Academic scholarships available. **Aid applications:** No closing date; priority given to applications received by March 2; applicants notified on a rolling basis beginning on or about April 15; must reply within 30 days.

ADDRESS/TELEPHONE. Elizabeth Griffin, Director of Undergraduate Admissions, Medical College of Georgia, Administration Building, Room 170, Augusta, GA 30912. (706) 721-2725. Fax: (706) 721-3461.

Mercer University
Macon, Georgia CB code: 5409

4-year private university, coed, affiliated with Southern Baptist Convention. Founded in 1833. **Accreditation:** Regional. **Undergraduate enrollment:** 1,338 men, 1,484 women full time; 553 men, 390 women part time. **Graduate enrollment:** 361 men, 277 women full time; 178 men, 156 women part time. **Faculty:** 373 total (273 full time), 223 with doctorates or other terminal degrees. **Location:** Suburban campus in small city; 85 miles from Atlanta. **Calendar:** Quarter, limited summer session. **Microcomputers:** 140 located in libraries, classrooms, computer centers.

DEGREES OFFERED. BA, BS, MS, MBA, MEd, PhD, MD, B. Pharm. 457 bachelor's degrees awarded in 1992. 26% in business and management, 9% communications, 14% teacher education, 6% psychology, 21% social sciences. Graduate degrees offered in 19 major fields of study.

UNDERGRADUATE MAJORS. Accounting, aerospace/aeronautical/astronautical engineering, Afro-American (black) studies, art history, bioengineering and biomedical engineering, biological and physical sciences, biology, business administration and management, business and management, business economics, chemistry, communications, computer and information sciences, computer engineering, dramatic arts, early childhood education, earth sciences, economics, education, education of the mentally handicapped, electrical/electronics/communications engineering, elementary education, engineering, English, finance, forestry and related sciences, French, German, Greek (classical), history, industrial administration, industrial engineering, junior high education, Latin, law , management information systems, marketing management, mathematics, mechanical engineering, mental health/human services, music, music education, music performance, pharmacy, philosophy, physics, political science and government, psychology, religion, secondary education, social sciences, social work, sociology, Spanish, special education, specific learning disabilities, studio art, visual and performing arts.

ACADEMIC PROGRAMS. Accelerated program, cooperative education, double major, education specialist degree, independent study, internships, student-designed major, study abroad, teacher preparation, Great Books Program alternative to standard requirements; liberal arts/career combination in forestry; combined bachelor's/graduate program in law. **Remedial services:** Learning center, preadmission summer program, reduced course load, special counselor, tutoring, special services program for disadvantaged students. **ROTC:** Army. **Placement/credit:** AP, CLEP General and Subject, institutional tests; 45 credit hours maximum for bachelor's degree.

ACADEMIC REQUIREMENTS. Freshmen must earn minimum GPA of 2.0 to continue in good standing. 68% of freshmen return for sophomore year. Students must declare major by end of second year. **Graduation requirements:** 180 hours for bachelor's (40 in major). Most students required to take courses in arts/fine arts, English, foreign languages, history, humanities, mathematics, philosophy/religion, biological/physical sciences. **Additional information:** Freshman seminar program, human services program available.

FRESHMAN ADMISSIONS. Selection criteria: School grades most important, class rank, and test scores considered. Counselor's recommendation and extracurricular activities also considered. **High school preparation:** 16 units required; 16 recommended. Recommended units include biological science 1, English 4, foreign language 2, mathematics 3, physical science 1 and social science 3. **Test requirements:** SAT or ACT (SAT preferred); score report by August 31.

1992 FRESHMAN CLASS PROFILE. 368 men, 299 women enrolled. 69% had high school GPA of 3.0 or higher, 29% between 2.0 and 2.99. **Academic background:** Mid 50% of enrolled freshmen had SAT-V between 460-580, SAT-M between 440-620; ACT composite between 19-26. 94% submitted SAT scores, 25% submitted ACT scores. **Characteristics:** 67% from in state, 88% live in college housing, 14% have minority backgrounds, 1% are foreign students, 29% join fraternities/sororities. Average age is 18.

FALL-TERM APPLICATIONS. $25 fee. No closing date; applicants notified on a rolling basis. Essay required. Interview recommended for marginally qualified applicants. Audition recommended for music applicants. CRDA. Deferred and early admission available.

STUDENT LIFE. Housing: Dormitories (men, women); apartment, sorority, handicapped housing available. Sophomore students must live in dormitories unless granted exemption by housing review board. **Activities:** Student government, magazine, student newspaper, yearbook, choral groups, concert band, dance, drama, jazz band, music ensembles, musical theater, symphony orchestra, performances in sign language, fraternities, sororities, Baptist Student Union, Black Students Organization, Wesley Foundation, Catholic folk mass, Jewish youth organization, Reformed University Fellowship. **Additional information:** Limited, specialized services and facilities available to those with learning disabilities.

ATHLETICS. NCAA. **Intercollegiate:** Baseball M, basketball, cross-country, golf, soccer, softball W, tennis, volleyball W. **Intramural:** Basketball, golf M, racquetball, rugby M, softball, swimming, table tennis, tennis, track and field, volleyball, water polo.

STUDENT SERVICES. Aptitude testing, career counseling, employment service for undergraduates, freshman orientation, health services, personal counseling, placement service for graduates, services/facilities for handicapped.

ANNUAL EXPENSES. Tuition and fees (1992-93): $10,287. **Room and board:** $3,780. **Books and supplies:** $450. **Other expenses:** $600.

FINANCIAL AID. 80% of freshmen, 73% of continuing students receive some form of aid. 45% of grants, 95% of loans, 88% of jobs based on need. 380 enrolled freshmen were judged to have need, all were offered aid. Academic, music/drama, art, athletic, state/district residency, leadership, religious affiliation scholarships available. **Aid applications:** No closing date; priority given to applications received by May 1; applicants notified on a rolling basis beginning on or about February 1; must reply within 2 weeks.

ADDRESS/TELEPHONE. Dr. J. Thompson Biggers, Vice President for Enrollment Management, Mercer University, 1400 Coleman Avenue, Macon, GA 31207-0001. (912) 752-2650. (800) 637-2378.

Mercer University Atlanta
Atlanta, Georgia

2-year upper-division private business college, coed, affiliated with Southern Baptist Convention. Founded in 1964. **Accreditation:** Regional. **Undergraduate enrollment:** 17 men, 23 women full time; 89 men, 65 women part time. **Graduate enrollment:** 339 men, 534 women full time; 236 men, 296 women part time. **Faculty:** 121 total (76 full time), 69 with doctorates or other terminal degrees. **Location:** Suburban campus in very large city; 12 miles from downtown. **Calendar:** Quarter, limited summer session. **Microcomputers:** 52 located in classrooms, computer centers. **Special facilities:** Zimmerman Collection of British literature. **Additional facts:** University includes pharmacy school, senior business school providing only upper-division business study, graduate business, graduate engineering, and college of liberal arts offering graduate education only.

DEGREES OFFERED. BS, MS, MBA, B. Pharm. 152 bachelor's degrees awarded in 1992. Graduate degrees offered in 13 major fields of study.

UNDERGRADUATE MAJORS. Accounting, aviation management, business administration and management, business and management, business economics, computer and information sciences, finance, humanities, marketing and distribution, marketing management.

ACADEMIC PROGRAMS. Accelerated program, cooperative education, double major, education specialist degree, independent study, internships, student-designed major, study abroad, teacher preparation, weekend college, cross-registration. **Remedial services:** Preadmission summer program, reduced course load, special counselor, tutoring, English Language Institute. **Placement/credit:** AP, CLEP General and Subject; 90 credit hours maximum for bachelor's degree.

ACADEMIC REQUIREMENTS. Students must declare major by end of second year. **Graduation requirements:** 180 hours for bachelor's (30 in major). Most students required to take courses in arts/fine arts, computer science, English, history, mathematics, biological/physical sciences, social sciences.

ADMISSIONS. Applications accepted until 2 weeks before start of quarter. Transfers with GPA between 2.3 and 2.0 admitted on probation. High School transcript required for those with less than 20 transfer hours.

FALL-TERM APPLICATIONS. $35 fee. Interview recommended for academically weak applicants. Essay recommended. Deferred and early admission available.

STUDENT LIFE. Activities: Student government, Baptist Student Union, International Students Club, Adult Life Support Organization, Black Student Alliance.

ATHLETICS. Intramural: Golf, soccer, softball, swimming, table tennis, tennis, volleyball.

STUDENT SERVICES. Special adviser for adult students, veterans counselor, orientation program/new students, services/facilities for handicapped.

ANNUAL EXPENSES. Tuition and fees (1992-93): $6,435. **Books and supplies:** $450. **Other expenses:** $800.

FINANCIAL AID. 71% of freshmen, 75% of continuing students receive some form of aid. 77% of grants, 80% of loans, 34% of jobs based on need. Academic, state/district residency, leadership, alumni affiliation, religious affiliation scholarships available. **Aid applications:** No closing date; priority given to applications received by May 1; applicants notified on a rolling basis beginning on or about March 15; must reply within 2 weeks.

ADDRESS/TELEPHONE. Laurie W. Taylor, Director of Admissions, Mercer University Atlanta, 3001 Mercer University Drive, Atlanta, GA 30341-4115. (404) 986-3200.

Middle Georgia College
Cochran, Georgia — CB code: 5411

Admissions: 81% of applicants accepted
Based on: ••• Test scores
•• School record
• Interview, recommendations
Completion: 86% of freshmen end year in good standing
63% enter 4-year programs

2-year public junior college, coed. Founded in 1884. **Accreditation:** Regional. **Undergraduate enrollment:** 504 men, 493 women full time; 239 men, 642 women part time. **Faculty:** 103 total (68 full time), 31 with doctorates or other terminal degrees. **Location:** Rural campus in small town; 39 miles from Macon. **Calendar:** Quarter, limited summer session. **Microcomputers:** 186 located in libraries, classrooms, computer centers. **Additional facts:** Branch campus in Dublin.

DEGREES OFFERED. AA, AS, AAS. 269 associate degrees awarded in 1992. 26% in business and management, 21% education, 7% engineering, 11% health sciences, 20% physical sciences, 7% social sciences.

UNDERGRADUATE MAJORS. Accounting, aerospace/aeronautical/astronautical engineering, agricultural engineering, agricultural sciences, American literature, architecture, art education, biology, british literature, business administration and management, business and office, business computer/console/peripheral equipment operation, business data entry equipment operation, business data processing and related programs, business data programming, ceramic engineering, chemical engineering, chemistry, civil engineering, computer and information sciences, creative writing, criminal justice studies, data processing, dramatic arts, education, electrical/electronics/communications engineering, engineering, engineering and engineering-related technologies, English, fashion merchandising, finance, fine arts, foreign languages (multiple emphasis), forestry and related sciences, geology, history, home economics, industrial engineering, industrial technology, journalism, landscape architecture, law enforcement and corrections technologies, liberal/general studies, library science, mathematics, mechanical engineering, medical records administration, music, nursing, occupational therapy, personnel management, physical therapy, physics, political science and government, predentistry, prelaw, premedicine, prepharmacy, preveterinary, psychology, public administration, religious music, respiratory therapy, secretarial and related programs, social sciences, sociology, speech, technical communications, trade and industrial education, zoology.

ACADEMIC PROGRAMS. 2-year transfer program, cooperative education, double major, dual enrollment of high school students, study abroad. **Remedial services:** Learning center, remedial instruction, tutoring. **Placement/credit:** AP, CLEP General and Subject, institutional tests.

ACADEMIC REQUIREMENTS. Freshmen must earn minimum GPA of 1.7 to continue in good standing. 77% of freshmen return for sophomore year. Students must declare major on application. **Graduation requirements:** 100 hours for associate (30 in major). Most students required to take courses in English, history, mathematics, biological/physical sciences, social sciences.

FRESHMAN ADMISSIONS. Selection criteria: Minimum SAT-verbal score of 250 or ACT English score of 13, or SAT-mathematical score of 280 or ACT mathematical of 14, or 1.8 high school GPA. Open admissions to AAS programs. **High school preparation:** 16 units required. Required units include English 4, foreign language 2, mathematics 3, social science 3 and science 3. **Test requirements:** SAT or ACT; score report by August 15.

1992 FRESHMAN CLASS PROFILE. 536 men applied, 473 accepted, 326 enrolled; 629 women applied, 476 accepted, 372 enrolled. 51% had high school GPA of 3.0 or higher, 44% between 2.0 and 2.99. **Academic background:** Mid 50% of enrolled freshmen had SAT-V between 310-440, SAT-M between 340-510; ACT composite between 16-23. 93% submitted SAT scores, 5% submitted ACT scores. **Characteristics:** 98% from in state, 75% commute, 23% have minority backgrounds, 1% are foreign students. Average age is 19.

FALL-TERM APPLICATIONS. $5 fee. Closing date August 15; applicants notified on a rolling basis. Interview recommended. Early admission available.

STUDENT LIFE. Housing: Dormitories (men, women). Students must live with their immediate families or live in college housing unless permission is given to live off campus. **Activities:** Student government, film, magazine, student newspaper, television, yearbook, choral groups, concert band, drama, music ensembles, Baptist Student Union, Newman Center, Wesley Foundation, Black Students Club, Rotoract, Circle-K, International Relations Club, Young Republicans Young Democrats.

ATHLETICS. NJCAA. **Intercollegiate:** Baseball M, basketball M, softball W. **Intramural:** Basketball, soccer M, softball, tennis, volleyball.

STUDENT SERVICES. Aptitude testing, career counseling, freshman orientation, health services, personal counseling, veterans counselor, minority counseling, services/facilities for handicapped.

ANNUAL EXPENSES. Tuition and fees (projected): $1,284, $939 additional for out-of-state students. **Room and board:** $2,520. **Books and supplies:** $515. **Other expenses:** $515.

FINANCIAL AID. 28% of freshmen, 27% of continuing students receive some form of aid. 96% of grants, 74% of loans, 70% of jobs based on need. Academic, music/drama, athletic scholarships available. **Aid applications:** No closing date; priority given to applications received by July 1; applicants notified on a rolling basis beginning on or about May 1; must reply within 10 days.

ADDRESS/TELEPHONE. George K. Hinton, Director of Admissions and Information Services, Middle Georgia College, 1100 Second Street Southeast, Cochran, GA 31014-1599. (912) 934-3136. Fax: (912) 934-3199.

Morehouse College
Atlanta, Georgia — CB code: 5415

Admissions: 42% of applicants accepted
Based on:
- ••• School record
- •• Activities, essay, interview, recommendations, test scores
- • Special talents

Completion: 80% of freshmen end year in good standing
55% graduate, 39% of these enter graduate study

4-year private liberal arts college, men only. Founded in 1867. **Accreditation:** Regional. **Undergraduate enrollment:** 2,787 men full time; 203 men part time. **Faculty:** 178 total (150 full time), 123 with doctorates or other terminal degrees. **Location:** Urban campus in very large city; 2 miles from downtown. **Calendar:** Semester, limited summer session. **Microcomputers:** 250 located in dormitories, libraries, classrooms, computer centers. **Special facilities:** Martin Luther King, Jr. International Chapel. **Additional facts:** One of 6 members of Atlanta University Center sharing facilities including library.

DEGREES OFFERED. BA, BS. 447 bachelor's degrees awarded in 1992. 18% in business and management, 9% business/office and marketing/distribution, 5% health sciences, 10% law, 7% letters/literature, 9% life sciences, 12% mathematics, 5% physical sciences, 5% psychology, 9% social sciences.

UNDERGRADUATE MAJORS. Accounting, architecture, biology, business administration and management, business economics, chemistry, computer and information sciences, dramatic arts, early childhood education, economics, education, elementary education, engineering, English, finance, fine arts, French, German, history, insurance and risk management, international studies, linguistics, marketing management, mathematics, music, philosophy, physics, political science and government, predentistry, prelaw, premedicine, psychology, real estate, religion, secondary education, sociology, Spanish, urban studies.

ACADEMIC PROGRAMS. Cooperative education, double major, dual enrollment of high school students, honors program, independent study, internships, study abroad, visiting/exchange student program, cross-registration. **Remedial services:** Reduced course load, remedial instruction, tutoring. **ROTC:** Air Force, Army, Naval. **Placement/credit:** AP, CLEP Subject, institutional tests; 30 credit hours maximum for bachelor's degree.

ACADEMIC REQUIREMENTS. Freshmen must earn minimum GPA of 2.0 to continue in good standing. 77% of freshmen return for sophomore year. Students must declare major by end of second year. **Graduation requirements:** 124 hours for bachelor's (60 in major). Most students required to take courses in arts/fine arts, English, foreign languages, history, humanities, mathematics, philosophy/religion, biological/physical sciences, social sciences. **Postgraduate studies:** 7% enter law school, 10% enter medical school, 12% enter MBA programs, 10% enter other graduate study.

FRESHMAN ADMISSIONS. Selection criteria: School academic record most important, followed by test scores, school and community activities. Sons of alumni given special consideration. **High school preparation:** 13 units required; 16 recommended. Required and recommended units include biological science 1, English 4, foreign language 2, mathematics 3, physical science 1-2 and social science 2. 3 additional units may be from any academic discipline. **Test requirements:** SAT or ACT (SAT preferred); score report by February 15.

1992 FRESHMAN CLASS PROFILE. 3,526 men applied, 1,491 accepted, 660 enrolled. 83% had high school GPA of 3.0 or higher, 16% between 2.0 and 2.99. **Academic background:** Mid 50% of enrolled freshmen had SAT-V between 400-530, SAT-M between 450-610; ACT composite between 18-27. 79% submitted SAT scores, 21% submitted ACT scores. **Characteristics:** 20% from in state, 82% live in college housing, 98% have minority backgrounds, 2% are foreign students. Average age is 18.

FALL-TERM APPLICATIONS. $35 fee, may be waived for applicants with need. Closing date February 15; priority given to applications received by January 15; applicants notified on or about April 1; must reply by May 1. Essay required. Interview recommended. Deferred and early admission available. Early action applicants must complete process by October 15.

STUDENT LIFE. Housing: Dormitories (men). **Activities:** Student government, student newspaper, yearbook, forensic team, choral groups, dance, drama, jazz band, marching band, musical theater, fraternities, Martin Luther King International Chapel Assistants, International Student Association, Mentoring Program, Frederick Douglass Tutorial Program, Political Science Club.

ATHLETICS. NCAA. **Intercollegiate:** Basketball, cross-country, football, swimming, tennis, track and field. **Intramural:** Baseball, basketball, bowling, softball, swimming, table tennis, tennis.

STUDENT SERVICES. Career counseling, employment service for undergraduates, freshman orientation, health services, personal counseling, placement service for graduates, veterans counselor, services/facilities for handicapped.

ANNUAL EXPENSES. Tuition and fees (1992-93): $7,430. **Room and board:** $4,980. **Books and supplies:** $500. **Other expenses:** $2,500.

FINANCIAL AID. 70% of freshmen, 68% of continuing students receive some form of aid. All jobs based on need. Academic, music/drama, athletic scholarships available. **Aid applications:** Closing date April 1; applicants notified on or about May 1; must reply by May 1 or within 2 weeks if notified thereafter.

ADDRESS/TELEPHONE. Sterling H. Hudson III, Director of Admissions, Morehouse College, 830 Westview Drive SW, Atlanta, GA 30314. (404) 681-2800. (800) 992-0642. Fax: (404) 659-6536.

Morris Brown College
Atlanta, Georgia — CB code: 5417

4-year private liberal arts college, coed, affiliated with African Methodist Episcopal Church. Founded in 1881. **Accreditation:** Regional. **Undergraduate enrollment:** 798 men, 1,154 women full time; 36 men, 42 women part time. **Faculty:** 145 total (102 full time), 102 with doctorates or other terminal degrees. **Location:** Urban campus in very large city; 2 miles from downtown Atlanta. **Calendar:** Semester. **Microcomputers:** Located in libraries, classrooms, computer centers.

DEGREES OFFERED. BA, BS. 115 bachelor's degrees awarded in 1992. 39% in business and management, 5% communications, 12% computer sciences, 6% teacher education, 14% health sciences, 21% social sciences.

UNDERGRADUATE MAJORS. Accounting, African studies, Afro-American (black) studies, allied health, architecture, biology, business administration and management, business and office, business data processing and related programs, business economics, business education, chemical engineering, chemistry, city/community/regional planning, civil engineering, communications, community health work, computer and information sciences, criminal justice studies, criminology, dramatic arts, early childhood education, economics, education of the emotionally handicapped, education of the mentally handicapped, education of the physically handicapped, electrical/electronics/communications engineering, elementary education, English literature, fashion design, fashion merchandising, fine arts, food science and nutrition, French, geography, health education, history, hotel/motel and restaurant management, industrial design, industrial engineering, journalism, legal assistant/paralegal, marketing management, mathematics, mechanical engineering, medical illustrating, medical records technology, music, music performance, nursing, nursing education, philosophy, physical education, physical therapy, physics, political science and government, psychology, public relations, radio/television broadcasting, recreation therapy, religion, secretarial and related programs, sociology, Spanish, specific learning disabilities, speech, textiles and clothing, urban studies.

ACADEMIC PROGRAMS. Accelerated program, cooperative education, double major, honors program, independent study, internships, study abroad, cross-registration; liberal arts/career combination in engineering. **Remedial services:** Preadmission summer program, reduced course load, remedial instruction, special counselor, tutoring, special services program for socioeconomically deprived students. **ROTC:** Army, Naval. **Placement/credit:** AP, CLEP General and Subject, institutional tests; 30 credit hours maximum for bachelor's degree.

ACADEMIC REQUIREMENTS. Freshmen must earn minimum GPA of 2.0 to continue in good standing. 62% of freshmen return for sophomore year. Students must declare major by end of second year. **Graduation requirements:** 124 hours for bachelor's. Most students required to take courses in arts/fine arts, computer science, English, foreign languages, history, humanities, mathematics, philosophy/religion, biological/physical sciences, social sciences.

FRESHMAN ADMISSIONS. **Selection criteria:** High school average, SAT or ACT scores and counselor recommendation strongly considered. Academically weak applicants receive special review. **High school preparation:** 15 units required. Required units include English 4, foreign language 2, mathematics 3, social science 3 and science 3. **Test requirements:** SAT or ACT (SAT preferred); score report by June 30.

1992 FRESHMAN CLASS PROFILE. 1,849 men and women applied, 1,849 accepted; 628 enrolled. 5% had high school GPA of 3.0 or higher, 90% between 2.0 and 2.99. **Academic background:** Mid 50% of enrolled freshmen had SAT-V between 300-340, SAT-M between 320-380. 100% submitted SAT scores. **Characteristics:** 49% from in state, 55% commute, 98% have minority backgrounds. Average age is 18.

FALL-TERM APPLICATIONS. $20 fee, may be waived for applicants with need. No closing date; priority given to applications received by June 30; applicants notified on a rolling basis beginning on or about February 1; must reply within 4 weeks. Essay recommended. Early admission available.

STUDENT LIFE. **Housing:** Dormitories (men, women). **Activities:** Student government, student newspaper, yearbook, choral groups, concert band, dance, drama, jazz band, marching band, music ensembles, opera, pep band, fraternities, sororities.

ATHLETICS. NCAA. **Intercollegiate:** Basketball, football M, tennis, track and field. **Intramural:** Basketball.

STUDENT SERVICES. Career counseling, employment service for undergraduates, freshman orientation, health services, personal counseling, placement service for graduates, veterans counselor, services/facilities for handicapped.

ANNUAL EXPENSES. **Tuition and fees (1992-93):** $7,032. **Room and board:** $4,150. **Books and supplies:** $600. **Other expenses:** $650.

FINANCIAL AID. 95% of freshmen, 92% of continuing students receive some form of aid. 91% of grants, 91% of loans, all jobs based on need. Academic, music/drama, art, athletic scholarships available. **Aid applications:** Closing date June 15; priority given to applications received by April 15; applicants notified on a rolling basis beginning on or about July 1; must reply within 15 days.

ADDRESS/TELEPHONE. Tyrone Fletcher, Director of Admissions, Morris Brown College, 643 Martin Luther King, Jr. Drive, Northwest, Atlanta, GA 30314. (404) 220-0270.

North Georgia College
Dahlonega, Georgia — CB code: 5497

Admissions: 71% of applicants accepted
Based on: ••• School record, test scores
• Interview, recommendations
Completion: 80% of freshmen end year in good standing
40% graduate, 18% of these enter graduate study

4-year public liberal arts, military college, coed. Founded in 1873. **Accreditation:** Regional. **Undergraduate enrollment:** 848 men, 1,187 women full time; 118 men, 273 women part time. **Graduate enrollment:** 30 men, 285 women full time; 48 men, 205 women part time. **Faculty:** 151 total (140 full time), 74 with doctorates or other terminal degrees. **Location:** Rural campus in small town; 70 miles from Atlanta. **Calendar:** Quarter, extensive summer session. **Microcomputers:** 75 located in computer centers. **Special facilities:** Observatory, rapelling tower, planetarium. **Additional facts:** 4 years Army ROTC required of all resident male students. Open to female students. Military service following graduation is not mandatory.

DEGREES OFFERED. AS, BA, BS, MS, MEd. 53 associate degrees awarded in 1992. 100% in health sciences. 362 bachelor's degrees awarded. 29% in business and management, 8% business/office and marketing/distribution, 29% teacher education, 6% parks/recreation, protective services, public affairs, 7% physical sciences, 5% psychology, 7% social sciences. Graduate degrees offered in 12 major fields of study.

UNDERGRADUATE MAJORS. **Associate:** Nursing, secretarial and related programs. **Bachelor's:** Accounting, art education, biology, business administration and management, business and management, business and office, business economics, chemistry, computer and information sciences, criminal justice studies, early childhood education, economics, elementary education, English, English education, finance, fine arts, foreign languages education, French, history, junior high education, marketing and distribution, mathematics, mathematics education, music, music education, nursing, office supervision and management, physical education, physics, political science and government, psychology, recreation and community services technologies, secretarial and related programs, social science education, social sciences, sociology, Spanish, special education.

ACADEMIC PROGRAMS. Accelerated program, cooperative education, double major, dual enrollment of high school students, internships, teacher preparation, cross-registration, dual degree program in engineering with Georgia Institute of Technology and Clemson University; liberal arts/career combination in engineering. **Remedial services:** Learning center, preadmission summer program, reduced course load, remedial instruction, special counselor. **ROTC:** Army. **Placement/credit:** AP, CLEP Subject, institutional tests; 45 credit hours maximum for associate degree; 45 credit hours maximum for bachelor's degree.

ACADEMIC REQUIREMENTS. Freshmen must earn minimum GPA of 1.5 to continue in good standing. 75% of freshmen return for sophomore year. Students must declare major by end of first year. **Graduation requirements:** 95 hours for associate (45 in major), 185 hours for bachelor's (50 in major). Most students required to take courses in computer science, English, history, humanities, mathematics, biological/physical sciences, social sciences. **Postgraduate studies:** 50% from 2-year programs enter 4-year programs. 3% enter law school, 3% enter medical school, 5% enter MBA programs, 7% enter other graduate study.

FRESHMAN ADMISSIONS. **Selection criteria:** High school academic record, test scores, recommendation, good disciplinary record. **High school preparation:** 16 units required. Required units include English 4, foreign language 2, mathematics 3, social science 3 and science 3. **Test requirements:** SAT or ACT; score report by September 1.

1992 FRESHMAN CLASS PROFILE. 45% had high school GPA of 3.0 or higher, 50% between 2.0 and 2.99. **Characteristics:** 95% from in state, 80% live in college housing, 3% have minority backgrounds, 10% join fraternities/sororities. Average age is 19.

FALL-TERM APPLICATIONS. $10 fee. Closing date September 1; priority given to applications received by July 1; applicants notified on a rolling basis; must reply by May 1 or within 2 weeks if notified thereafter. Audition recommended. Portfolio recommended. Deferred and early admission available.

STUDENT LIFE. **Housing:** Dormitories (men, women). Female dormitory space is usually filled by late February. **Activities:** Student government, student newspaper, yearbook, choral groups, concert band, drama, marching band, pep band, fraternities, sororities, mountaineering, military field activities, sport parachuting.

ATHLETICS. NAIA. **Intercollegiate:** Basketball, rifle, soccer, softball W, tennis, track and field. **Intramural:** Basketball, football M, softball, volleyball.

STUDENT SERVICES. Aptitude testing, career counseling, employment service for undergraduates, freshman orientation, health services, personal counseling, placement service for graduates, veterans counselor, services/facilities for handicapped.

ANNUAL EXPENSES. **Tuition and fees:** $1,662, $1,380 additional for out-of-state students. **Room and board:** $2,445. **Books and supplies:** $525. **Other expenses:** $1,191.

FINANCIAL AID. 70% of freshmen, 75% of continuing students receive some form of aid. 75% of grants, 60% of loans, 35% of jobs based on need. 361 enrolled freshmen were judged to have need, all were offered aid. Academic, music/drama, art, athletic, leadership scholarships available. **Aid applications:** No closing date; priority given to applications received by May 15; applicants notified on a rolling basis beginning on or about June 15; must reply within 2 weeks.

ADDRESS/TELEPHONE. Gary R. Steffey, Director of Admissions/Registrar, North Georgia College, Dahlonega, GA 30597. (706) 864-1800.

Oglethorpe University
Atlanta, Georgia — CB code: 5521

Admissions: 84% of applicants accepted
Based on: ••• Recommendations, school record, test scores
•• Activities
• Interview, special talents
Completion: 95% of freshmen end year in good standing
63% graduate, 27% of these enter graduate study

4-year private university and liberal arts college, coed. Founded in 1835. **Accreditation:** Regional. **Undergraduate enrollment:** 298 men, 430 women full time; 96 men, 288 women part time. **Graduate enrollment:** 11 men, 72 women part time. **Faculty:** 102 total (43 full time), 63 with doctorates or other terminal degrees. **Location:** Suburban campus in very large city; 10 miles from downtown Atlanta. **Calendar:** Semester, limited summer session. **Microcomputers:** 44 located in libraries, classrooms, computer centers. **Special facilities:** Art museum. **Additional facts:** Academic buildings feature English gothic architecture, campus is home to the Georgia Shakespeare Festival.

DEGREES OFFERED. BA, BS, MA. 213 bachelor's degrees awarded in 1992. 35% in business and management, 10% communications, 5% teacher education, 6% health sciences, 13% multi/interdisciplinary studies, 7% psychology, 9% social sciences. Graduate degrees offered in 2 major fields of study.

UNDERGRADUATE MAJORS. Accounting, American studies, biology, business administration and behavioral sciences, business administration and computer science, business administration and computers, business administration and management, business and management, business economics, chemistry, clinical laboratory science, communications, computer and information sciences, economics, elementary education, English, fine arts, history, international relations, international studies, junior high education, liberal/general studies, mathematics, philosophy, physics, political science and government, predentistry, preengineering, prelaw, premedicine, prepharmacy, preveterinary, psychology, secondary education, social work, sociology.

ACADEMIC PROGRAMS. Accelerated program, cooperative education, double major, dual enrollment of high school students, honors program, independent study, internships, student-designed major, study abroad, teacher preparation, visiting/exchange student program, Washington semester, cross-registration, dual engineering degree program with Auburn University, Georgia Institute of Technology, University of Florida, and University of Southern California; dual art degree program with Atlanta College of Art; liberal arts/career combination in engineering, health sciences. **ROTC:** Air Force, Army. **Placement/credit:** AP, CLEP General and Subject, institutional tests; 30 credit hours maximum for bachelor's degree.

ACADEMIC REQUIREMENTS. Freshmen must earn minimum GPA of 1.5 to continue in good standing. 76% of freshmen return for sophomore year. Students must declare major by end of second year. **Graduation requirements:** 120 hours for bachelor's (40 in major). Most students required to take courses in arts/fine arts, English, history, humanities, mathematics, philosophy/religion, biological/physical sciences, social sciences. **Postgraduate studies:** 6% enter law school, 5% enter medical school, 3% enter MBA programs, 13% enter other graduate study.

FRESHMAN ADMISSIONS. Selection criteria: Recommendations requried. High school GPA and general academic record most important, followed by test scores. Activities considered. **High school preparation:** 18 units required. Required and recommended units include biological science 1, English 4, mathematics 3, physical science 1, social science 2 and science 2. Foreign language 2 recommended. **Test requirements:** SAT or ACT; score report by July 1. **Additional information:** Students completing application procedures by January 21 will be notified by February 21.

1992 FRESHMAN CLASS PROFILE. 1,123 men and women applied, 942 accepted; 96 men enrolled, 142 women enrolled. 96% had high school GPA of 3.0 or higher, 4% between 2.0 and 2.99. 61% were in top tenth and 83% were in top quarter of graduating class. **Academic background:** Mid 50% of enrolled freshmen had SAT-V between 470-590, SAT-M between 560-680; ACT composite between 24-29. 61% submitted SAT scores, 39% submitted ACT scores. **Characteristics:** 76% from in state, 91% live in college housing, 13% have minority backgrounds, 4% are foreign students, 35% join fraternities/sororities. Average age is 18.

FALL-TERM APPLICATIONS. $25 fee, may be waived for applicants with need. Closing date August 1; priority given to applications received by March 1; applicants notified on a rolling basis beginning on or about February 1; must reply by May 1 or within 3 weeks if notified thereafter. Interview recommended. CRDA. Deferred and early admission available. EDP-F.

STUDENT LIFE. Housing: Dormitories (men, women, coed); fraternity, sorority housing available. Dorms include local phone service. **Activities:** Student government, magazine, student newspaper, television, yearbook, choral groups, dance, drama, music ensembles, musical theater, pep band, fraternities, sororities, Catholic Student Association, Black Student Caucus, Oglethorpe Christian Fellowship, International Club, Environmentally Concerned Oglethorpe Students, Oglethorpe Academic Team.

ATHLETICS. NCAA. **Intercollegiate:** Baseball M, basketball, cross-country, golf M, gymnastics M, soccer, tennis, track and field, volleyball W. **Intramural:** Badminton, basketball, softball, tennis, volleyball.

STUDENT SERVICES. Aptitude testing, career counseling, employment service for undergraduates, freshman orientation, health services, personal counseling, placement service for graduates, special adviser for adult students, veterans counselor, services/facilities for handicapped.

ANNUAL EXPENSES. Tuition and fees (1992-93): $11,150. **Room and board:** $4,150. **Books and supplies:** $500. **Other expenses:** $2,045.

FINANCIAL AID. 81% of freshmen, 76% of continuing students receive some form of aid. 32% of grants, 88% of loans, 71% of jobs based on need. 144 enrolled freshmen were judged to have need, all were offered aid. Academic, music/drama, state/district residency, leadership, religious affiliation scholarships available. **Aid applications:** Closing date May 1; applicants notified on a rolling basis beginning on or about February 1; must reply within 4 weeks. **Additional information:** Investment equivalent plan, two guaranteed rate plans and family discount plan available.

ADDRESS/TELEPHONE. Dennis T. Matthews, Director of Admissions, Oglethorpe University, 4484 Peachtree Road Northeast, Atlanta, GA 30319-2797. (404) 364-8307. (404) 428-4484. Fax: (404) 364-8500.

Oxford College of Emory University
Oxford, Georgia — CB code: 5186

Admissions: 71% of applicants accepted
Based on: ••• School record
•• Recommendations, test scores
• Activities, essay, interview, special talents
Completion: 90% of freshmen end year in good standing
99% enter 4-year programs

2-year private branch campus, liberal arts college, coed, affiliated with United Methodist Church. Founded in 1836. **Accreditation:** Regional candidate. **Undergraduate enrollment:** 213 men, 347 women full time; 6 men, 3 women part time. **Faculty:** 47 total (41 full time), 39 with doctorates or other terminal degrees. **Location:** Suburban campus in large town; 38 miles from Atlanta. **Calendar:** Semester, limited summer session. **Microcomputers:** 40 located in computer centers. **Special facilities:** Opportunities for undergraduate research at Yerkes Regional Primate Center, Centers for Disease Control, American Cancer Society, Emory University & Grady Hospital, Carter Presidential Center for International Studies. **Additional facts:** Automatic continuation to Emory College with junior status. Selective continuation to Emory School of Business and Emory School of Nursing.

DEGREES OFFERED. AA. 211 associate degrees awarded in 1992.

UNDERGRADUATE MAJORS. Anatomy, anthropology, art history, biochemistry, biology, business and management, chemistry, classics, clinical psychology, counseling psychology, creative writing, economics, English, French, German, Hebrew, inorganic chemistry, mathematics, organic chemistry, philosophy, physical sciences, plant genetics, prelaw, psychology, religion.

ACADEMIC PROGRAMS. 2-year transfer program, double major, dual enrollment of high school students, independent study, study abroad, cross-registration, 3-2 program in engineering with Georgia Institute of Technology. **Remedial services:** Preadmission summer program, reduced course load, special counselor, tutoring. **Placement/credit:** AP, IB, institutional tests; 16 credit hours maximum for associate degree.

ACADEMIC REQUIREMENTS. Freshmen must earn minimum GPA of 2.0 to continue in good standing. 85% of freshmen return for sophomore year. Students must declare major by end of second year. **Graduation requirements:** 68 hours for associate. Most students required to take courses in English, foreign languages, history, humanities, mathematics, biological/physical sciences, social sciences.

FRESHMAN ADMISSIONS. Selection criteria: High school record most important, followed by test scores, and extracurriculars. **High school preparation:** 16 units required. Required and recommended units include English 4, mathematics 3, social science 2 and science 2-3. Foreign language 2 recommended. Mathematics units should include Geometry and study through Algebra II. **Test requirements:** SAT or ACT (SAT preferred); score report by August 15.

1992 FRESHMAN CLASS PROFILE. 262 men applied, 164 accepted, 131 enrolled; 359 women applied, 275 accepted, 204 enrolled. **Characteristics:** 52% from in state, 97% live in college housing, 19% have minority backgrounds, 6% are foreign students. Average age is 18.

FALL-TERM APPLICATIONS. $35 fee, may be waived for applicants with need. No closing date; applicants notified on a rolling basis; must reply by May 1 or within 3 weeks if notified thereafter. Interview recommended. Essay recommended. CRDA. Deferred and early admission available. January 7 deadline for scholars program.

STUDENT LIFE. Housing: Dormitories (men, women, coed). **Activities:** Student government, student newspaper, yearbook, choral groups, dance, drama, musical theater, Circle-K, Rotaract, Oxford Fellowship, Union of Jewish Services, community service organizations.

ATHLETICS. Intramural: Badminton, baseball M, basketball, cross-country, football M, gymnastics, horseback riding, soccer, softball, swimming, table tennis, tennis, volleyball, water polo, wrestling M.

STUDENT SERVICES. Aptitude testing, career counseling, freshman orientation, health services, personal counseling, services/facilities for handicapped.

ANNUAL EXPENSES. Tuition and fees: $12,350. **Room and board:** $4,348. **Books and supplies:** $450. **Other expenses:** $750.

FINANCIAL AID. 78% of freshmen, 65% of continuing students receive some form of aid. 50% of grants, 92% of loans, 73% of jobs based on need. 130 enrolled freshmen were judged to have need, all were offered aid. Academic, state/district residency, leadership, minority scholarships available. **Aid applications:** No closing date; priority given to applications received by April 1; applicants notified on a rolling basis beginning on or about April 15; must reply within 2 weeks.

ADDRESS/TELEPHONE. Jennifer B. Taylor, Director of Admissions and Financial Aid, Oxford College of Emory University, 100 Hamill Street, Oxford, GA 30267-1328. (404) 784-8328. (800) 723-8328. Fax: (404) 784-8443.

Paine College
Augusta, Georgia — CB code: 5530

4-year private liberal arts college, coed, affiliated with Christian Methodist Episcopal Church and United Methodist Church. Founded in 1882. **Accreditation:** Regional. **Undergraduate enrollment:** 188 men, 401 women full time; 33 men, 64 women part time. **Faculty:** 61 total (54 full time), 28 with doctorates or other terminal degrees. **Location:** Urban campus in large town; 74 miles from Columbia, South Carolina, 150 miles from Atlanta. **Calendar:** Semester, extensive summer session. **Microcomputers:** 80 located in classrooms, computer centers.

DEGREES OFFERED. BA, BS. 59 bachelor's degrees awarded in 1992. 32% in business and management, 5% teacher education, 7% letters/literature, 10% mathematics, 7% psychology, 32% social sciences.

UNDERGRADUATE MAJORS. Biology, business and management, chemistry, communications, elementary education, English, history, junior high education, mathematics, music education, philosophy, philosophy/religion, psychology, religion, sociology.

ACADEMIC PROGRAMS. Cooperative education, dual enrollment of high school students, honors program, independent study, internships, study abroad, teacher preparation, cross-registration, dual degree in engineering and mathematics with Florida Agriculture and Mechanical University and Georgia Institute of Technology. **Remedial services:** Learning center, preadmission summer program, reduced course load, remedial instruction, special counselor, tutoring. **ROTC:** Army. **Placement/credit:** AP, institutional tests.

ACADEMIC REQUIREMENTS. Freshmen must earn minimum GPA of 1.7 to continue in good standing. 56% of freshmen return for sophomore year. Students must declare major by end of second year. **Graduation requirements:** 124 hours for bachelor's (48 in major). Most students required to take courses in arts/fine arts, computer science, English, foreign languages, history, mathematics, philosophy/religion, biological/physical sciences, social sciences.

FRESHMAN ADMISSIONS. Selection criteria: School achievement record and test scores considered. Minimum 2.0 high school GPA. College preparatory program preferred. Recommended units include English 4, mathematics 2, social science 2 and science 1. Social science recommendation includes 1 history. 6 electives required. **Test requirements:** SAT or ACT; score report by July 15.

1992 FRESHMAN CLASS PROFILE. 66 men, 159 women enrolled. 38% had high school GPA of 3.0 or higher, 61% between 2.0 and 2.99. **Academic background:** Mid 50% of enrolled freshmen had SAT-V between 260-390, SAT-M between 300-430; ACT composite between 14-18. 72% submitted SAT scores, 20% submitted ACT scores. **Characteristics:** 60% from in state, 81% live in college housing, 100% have minority backgrounds. Average age is 18.

FALL-TERM APPLICATIONS. $10 fee. Closing date August 1; applicants notified on a rolling basis. Audition required for music education applicants. Essay required. Interview recommended. CRDA. Deferred and early admission available. EDP-F.

STUDENT LIFE. Housing: Dormitories (men, women). **Activities:** Student government, film, magazine, student newspaper, television, yearbook, choral groups, dance, drama, jazz band, music ensembles, fraternities, sororities, Afro-American Alliance, Christian Methodist Episcopal Club, the Masons.

ATHLETICS. NCAA. **Intercollegiate:** Baseball M, basketball, cross-country, softball W, track and field, volleyball W. **Intramural:** Badminton, baseball M, basketball, cross-country, softball, table tennis, tennis, track and field, volleyball.

STUDENT SERVICES. Aptitude testing, career counseling, employment service for undergraduates, freshman orientation, health services, personal counseling, placement service for graduates, veterans counselor, services/facilities for handicapped.

ANNUAL EXPENSES. Tuition and fees (1992-93): $5,468. **Room and board:** $2,739. **Books and supplies:** $400. **Other expenses:** $485.

FINANCIAL AID. 90% of freshmen, 79% of continuing students receive some form of aid. 45% of grants, all loans, all jobs based on need. Music/drama scholarships available. **Aid applications:** No closing date; priority given to applications received by May 15; applicants notified on a rolling basis beginning on or about June 1; must reply within 2 weeks.

ADDRESS/TELEPHONE. Director of Enrollment Management, Director of Enrollment Management, Paine College, 1235 15th Street, Augusta, GA 30901-3182. (706) 821-8320. (800) 476-7703. Fax: (706) 821-8293.

Piedmont College
Demorest, Georgia — CB code: 5537

Admissions:	90% of applicants accepted
Based on:	••• School record
	•• Activities, interview, special talents, test scores
	• Recommendations
Completion:	91% of freshmen end year in good standing
	25% graduate

4-year private liberal arts college, coed, affiliated with Congregational Christian Churches of America. Founded in 1897. **Accreditation:** Regional. **Undergraduate enrollment:** 281 men, 300 women full time; 19 men, 39 women part time. **Faculty:** 58 total (45 full time), 34 with doctorates or other terminal degrees. **Location:** Rural campus in rural community; 30 miles from Gainesville, 75 miles from Atlanta. **Calendar:** Semester, extensive summer session. **Microcomputers:** 200 located in libraries, classrooms, computer centers. **Special facilities:** Observatory, golf course, art gallery, early childhood development center.

DEGREES OFFERED. BA, BS. 73 bachelor's degrees awarded in 1992. 31% in business and management, 26% teacher education, 9% psychology, 14% social sciences.

UNDERGRADUATE MAJORS. Accounting, art education, biology, business administration and management, business and management, business economics, chemistry, computer and information sciences, computer mathematics, drawing, economics, elementary education, English, English education, fine arts, foreign languages education, history, junior high education, mathematics, mathematics education, music, music education, music performance, painting, predentistry, premedicine, prepharmacy, preveterinary, psychology, science education, secondary education, social science education, social studies education, sociology, Spanish, special education, studio art.

ACADEMIC PROGRAMS. Double major, dual enrollment of high school students, internships, teacher preparation, 3-2 nursing with Emory University. **Remedial services:** Reduced course load, remedial instruction, special counselor, tutoring. **Placement/credit:** AP, CLEP General and Subject, institutional tests; 30 credit hours maximum for bachelor's degree.

ACADEMIC REQUIREMENTS. Freshmen must earn minimum GPA of 2.0 to continue in good standing. 64% of freshmen return for sophomore year. Students must declare major by end of second year. **Graduation requirements:** 124 hours for bachelor's (27 in major). Most students required to take courses in arts/fine arts, English, foreign languages, history, humanities, mathematics, philosophy/religion, biological/physical sciences, social sciences.

FRESHMAN ADMISSIONS. Selection criteria: SAT scores and GPA. **High school preparation:** 21 units recommended. Recommended units include biological science 2, English 4, foreign language 2, mathematics 4, physical science 1 and social science 4. **Test requirements:** SAT or ACT (SAT preferred); score report by August 15.

1992 FRESHMAN CLASS PROFILE. 196 men applied, 175 accepted, 70 enrolled; 230 women applied, 210 accepted, 91 enrolled. 41% had high school GPA of 3.0 or higher, 51% between 2.0 and 2.99. **Characteristics:** 91% from in state, 55% live in college housing, 13% have minority backgrounds, 7% are foreign students. Average age is 22.

FALL-TERM APPLICATIONS. $20 fee, may be waived for applicants with need. Closing date July 31; applicants notified on a rolling basis. Interview recommended for academically weak applicants. CRDA. Deferred and early admission available.

STUDENT LIFE. Housing: Dormitories (men, women); apartment housing available. Unmarried student must live in dormitories or with blood relative, unless they are 21 years of age. **Activities:** Student government, student newspaper, yearbook, choral groups, concert band, drama, music ensembles, Lyceums, fraternities, sororities, Baptist Student Union, Compass Club.

ATHLETICS. NAIA. **Intercollegiate:** Baseball M, basketball, cross-country, golf, soccer, softball W, tennis. **Intramural:** Baseball M, basketball, cross-country, golf, racquetball, soccer, softball, tennis, volleyball.

STUDENT SERVICES. Aptitude testing, career counseling, employment service for undergraduates, freshman orientation, health services, personal counseling, placement service for graduates, special adviser for adult students, veterans counselor, services/facilities for handicapped.

ANNUAL EXPENSES. Tuition and fees (1992-93): $4,430. **Room and board:** $3,320. **Books and supplies:** $600. **Other expenses:** $900.

FINANCIAL AID. 88% of freshmen, 90% of continuing students receive some form of aid. 61% of grants, 97% of loans, 13% of jobs based on need. 80 enrolled freshmen were judged to have need, all were offered aid. Academic, music/drama, art, athletic, state/district residency, leadership, alumni affiliation, religious affiliation scholarships available. **Aid applications:** Closing date July 1; priority given to applications received by June 1; applicants notified on a rolling basis beginning on or about July 1; must reply within 2 weeks.

ADDRESS/TELEPHONE. Martha Kirkland, Director of Admissions, Piedmont College, PO Box 10, Demorest, GA 30535. (706) 778-3000. (800) 277-7020. Fax: (706) 776-2811.

Reinhardt College
Waleska, Georgia — CB code: 5568

Admissions: 84% of applicants accepted
Based on: ••• School record
•• Special talents, test scores
• Activities, essay, interview, recommendations
Completion: 85% of freshmen end year in good standing
68% enter 4-year programs

2-year private junior, liberal arts college, coed, affiliated with United Methodist Church. Founded in 1883. **Accreditation:** Regional. **Undergraduate enrollment:** 333 men, 386 women full time; 45 men, 100 women part time. **Faculty:** 39 total (31 full time), 10 with doctorates or other terminal degrees. **Location:** Rural campus in rural community; 50 miles north of Atlanta. **Calendar:** Quarter. **Microcomputers:** Located in computer centers. **Special facilities:** Indoor tennis courts and AMF bowling lanes. **Additional facts:** Off campus center in Roswell, and Chatsworth.

DEGREES OFFERED. AA, AS. 119 associate degrees awarded in 1992. 40% in business and management, 15% computer sciences, 10% education, 10% mathematics, 5% philosophy, religion, theology, 10% social sciences, 10% visual and performing arts.

UNDERGRADUATE MAJORS. Accounting, American studies, art history, biology, botany, chemistry, communications, criminal justice studies, education, engineering, English, European studies, finance, fine arts, health sciences, history, liberal/general studies, mathematics, music, music history and appreciation, nursing, physical therapy, predentistry, prelaw, premedicine, prepharmacy, preveterinary, psychology, religion, social sciences, visual and performing arts. business administration and management.

ACADEMIC PROGRAMS. 2-year transfer program, dual enrollment of high school students, independent study, internships, study abroad. **Remedial services:** Learning center, preadmission summer program, reduced course load, remedial instruction, tutoring. **Placement/credit:** AP, CLEP General and Subject; 25 credit hours maximum for associate degree.

ACADEMIC REQUIREMENTS. Freshmen must earn minimum GPA of 2.0 to continue in good standing. 85% of freshmen return for sophomore year. Students must declare major by end of first year. **Graduation requirements:** 97 hours for associate. Most students required to take courses in English, history, mathematics, philosophy/religion, biological/physical sciences, social sciences. **Additional information:** BS in business administration offered as of fall 1992.

FRESHMAN ADMISSIONS. Selection criteria: School achievement record most important, followed by test scores, recommendations. **High school preparation:** 10 units required. Required units include English 4, mathematics 2, social science 2 and science 2. Foreign langauage recommended. **Test requirements:** SAT or ACT (SAT preferred); score report by August 1.

1992 FRESHMAN CLASS PROFILE. 225 men applied, 186 accepted, 126 enrolled; 333 women applied, 284 accepted, 200 enrolled. 38% had high school GPA of 3.0 or higher, 60% between 2.0 and 2.99. **Academic background:** Mid 50% of enrolled freshmen had SAT-V between 390-450, SAT-M between 370-450. 95% submitted SAT scores. **Characteristics:** 96% from in state, 80% live in college housing, 8% have minority backgrounds, 3% are foreign students, 50% join fraternities/sororities. Average age is 18.

FALL-TERM APPLICATIONS. $15 fee, may be waived for applicants with need. Closing date August 1; priority given to applications received by May 1; applicants notified on a rolling basis; must reply within 4 weeks. Audition required for music applicants. Portfolio required for art applicants. Essay required. Interview recommended. CRDA. Deferred and early admission available. EDP-F.

STUDENT LIFE. Housing: Dormitories (men, women, coed). Freshmen and sophomores are required to live on campus. **Activities:** Student government, magazine, student newspaper, yearbook, choral groups, drama, jazz band, music ensembles, symphony orchestra, fraternities, sororities, Methodist and Baptist religious groups, Phi Theta Kappa, honors fraternities.

ATHLETICS. NJCAA. **Intercollegiate:** Basketball, golf M, soccer M, softball W, tennis. **Intramural:** Basketball, bowling, football M, soccer W, softball, tennis, volleyball.

STUDENT SERVICES. Aptitude testing, career counseling, freshman orientation, health services, personal counseling, special adviser for adult students, services/facilities for handicapped.

ANNUAL EXPENSES. Tuition and fees (1992-93): $4,140. $72 per credit hour for over 16 credits. **Room and board:** $3,375. **Books and supplies:** $500. **Other expenses:** $1,000.

FINANCIAL AID. 85% of continuing students receive some form of aid. Grants, loans, jobs available. **Aid applications:** Closing date May 1; applicants notified on a rolling basis; must reply within 2 weeks.

ADDRESS/TELEPHONE. C. Ray Tatum, Director of Admissions, Reinhardt College, 250 Canton Street, Waleska, GA 30183. (404) 479-1454. Fax: (404) 479-9007.

Savannah College of Art and Design
Savannah, Georgia — CB code: 5631

4-year private art college, coed. Founded in 1978. **Accreditation:** Regional. **Undergraduate enrollment:** 2,090 men and women. **Graduate enrollment:** 240 men and women. **Faculty:** 127 total (106 full time), 123 with doctorates or other terminal degrees. **Location:** Urban campus in small city; 150 miles from Jacksonville, Florida, 250 miles from Atlanta. **Calendar:** Quarter, extensive summer session. **Microcomputers:** 140 located in computer centers. **Special facilities:** 8 art galleries.

DEGREES OFFERED. BFA, BArch, MFA. 217 bachelor's degrees awarded in 1992. 97% in visual and performing arts. Graduate degrees offered in 10 major fields of study.

UNDERGRADUATE MAJORS. Architecture, art history, computer art, fashion design, fiber/textiles/weaving, graphic design, historic preservation, illustration design, interior design, painting, photography, video.

ACADEMIC PROGRAMS. Double major, dual enrollment of high school students, independent study, internships, study abroad, New York semester. **Remedial services:** Preadmission summer program, reduced course load, tutoring. **Placement/credit:** 15 credit hours maximum for bachelor's degree.

ACADEMIC REQUIREMENTS. Freshmen must earn minimum GPA of 2.0 to continue in good standing. 65% of freshmen return for sophomore year. Students must declare major by end of second year. **Graduation requirements:** 180 hours for bachelor's (60 in major). Most students required to take courses in arts/fine arts, computer science, English, history, humanities, social sciences. **Postgraduate studies:** 10% enter other graduate study.

FRESHMAN ADMISSIONS. Selection criteria: Test scores, 3 letters of recommendation, and high school transcript required. **Test requirements:** SAT or ACT; score report by September 1.

1992 FRESHMAN CLASS PROFILE. 777 men and women enrolled. 75% had high school GPA of 3.0 or higher, 25% between 2.0 and 2.99. **Academic background:** Mid 50% of enrolled freshmen had SAT-V between 470-550, SAT-M between 490-560; ACT composite between 22-24. 95% submitted SAT scores, 5% submitted ACT scores. **Characteristics:** 17% from in state, 80% live in college housing, 11% have minority backgrounds, 6% are foreign students. Average age is 19.

FALL-TERM APPLICATIONS. $50 fee. No closing date; priority given to applications received by April 15; applicants notified on a rolling basis; must reply within 4 weeks. Interview recommended. Portfolio recommended for all except historic preservation applicants. Deferred and early admission available.

STUDENT LIFE. Housing: Dormitories (men, women, coed); apartment housing available. Some apartment-style dormitories with full kitchen facilities available. **Activities:** Student government, magazine, choral groups, dance, drama, graphic design club, fiber arts club, photography club, painting club, video club, illustration, historic preservation club, student chapter of American Institute of Architects, computer club, student chapter of American Society of Interior Designers.

ATHLETICS. NCAA. **Intercollegiate:** Golf, rowing (crew), soccer, softball W, tennis. **Intramural:** Bowling, football M, rowing (crew), rugby M, softball M, volleyball.

STUDENT SERVICES. Career counseling, employment service for undergraduates, freshman orientation, personal counseling, placement service for graduates.

ANNUAL EXPENSES. Tuition and fees: $9,180. **Room and board:** $5,250. **Books and supplies:** $1,200. **Other expenses:** $6,000.

FINANCIAL AID. 55% of freshmen, 60% of continuing students receive some form of aid. 33% of grants, 96% of loans, 24% of jobs based on need. 315 enrolled freshmen were judged to have need, all were offered aid. Academic, art, state/district residency scholarships available. **Aid applications:** No closing date; priority given to applications received by April 1; applicants notified on a rolling basis beginning on or about July 1.

ADDRESS/TELEPHONE. Cissy Rudder, Dean of Admissions, Savannah College of Art and Design, P.O. Box 3146, Savannah, GA 31402-3146. (912) 238-2483. Fax: (912) 238-2456.

Savannah State College
Savannah, Georgia CB code: 5609

4-year public college of arts and sciences and business college, coed. Founded in 1890. **Accreditation:** Regional. **Undergraduate enrollment:** 1,055 men, 1,373 women full time; 184 men, 260 women part time. **Faculty:** 171 total (141 full time), 80 with doctorates or other terminal degrees. **Location:** Urban campus in small city; 250 miles from Atlanta, GA, 120 miles from Jacksonville, FL. **Calendar:** Quarter, extensive summer session. Extensive evening/early morning classes. **Microcomputers:** 300 located in computer centers. **Special facilities:** Marine biology dock, college archives.

DEGREES OFFERED. AS, BA, BS. 1 associate degree awarded in 1992. 100% in computer sciences. 213 bachelor's degrees awarded. 35% in business and management, 6% business/office and marketing/distribution, 8% communications, 8% computer sciences, 7% engineering technologies, 9% life sciences, 8% parks/recreation, protective services, public affairs, 11% social sciences.

UNDERGRADUATE MAJORS. Associate: Chemical manufacturing technology, computer technology, electronic technology. **Bachelor's:** Accounting, biology, business and management, chemical manufacturing technology, chemistry, civil technology, computer and information sciences, criminal justice studies, electronic technology, English, environmental science, history, information sciences and systems, journalism, management information systems, marine biology, marketing and distribution, mathematics, mechanical design technology, medical laboratory technologies, music, parks and recreation management, political science and government, social work, sociology.

ACADEMIC PROGRAMS. Cooperative education, double major, dual enrollment of high school students, honors program, independent study, internships, visiting/exchange student program, cross-registration; liberal arts/career combination in engineering. **Remedial services:** Learning center, remedial instruction, special counselor, tutoring. **ROTC:** Army, Naval. **Placement/credit:** AP, CLEP General and Subject, institutional tests; 45 credit hours maximum for associate degree; 45 credit hours maximum for bachelor's degree.

ACADEMIC REQUIREMENTS. Freshmen must earn minimum GPA of 2.0 to continue in good standing. 63% of freshmen return for sophomore year. Students must declare major by end of second year. **Graduation requirements:** 110 hours for associate (53 in major), 195 hours for bachelor's (100 in major). Most students required to take courses in English, history, humanities, mathematics, biological/physical sciences, social sciences.

FRESHMAN ADMISSIONS. Selection criteria: Open admissions. Test scores and high school GPA considered. **High school preparation:** 16 units required. Required units include English 4, foreign language 2, mathematics 3, social science 3 and science 3. Students lacking complete college-preparatory requirements admitted on provisional basis. **Test requirements:** SAT or ACT; score report by September 1.

1992 FRESHMAN CLASS PROFILE. 311 men, 375 women enrolled. **Characteristics:** 95% from in state, 50% commute, 96% have minority backgrounds, 3% are foreign students. Average age is 19.

FALL-TERM APPLICATIONS. $10 fee, may be waived for applicants with need. Closing date September 1; applicants notified on a rolling basis beginning on or about March 1. Deferred and early admission available.

STUDENT LIFE. Housing: Dormitories (men, women); apartment housing available. **Activities:** Student government, radio, student newspaper, yearbook, choral groups, concert band, drama, jazz band, marching band, music ensembles, fraternities, sororities.

ATHLETICS. NCAA. **Intercollegiate:** Baseball M, basketball, cross-country W, football M, tennis W, track and field. **Intramural:** Baseball M, bowling, softball W, table tennis.

STUDENT SERVICES. Aptitude testing, career counseling, employment service for undergraduates, health services, personal counseling, placement service for graduates, veterans counselor.

ANNUAL EXPENSES. Tuition and fees (projected): $1,743, $1,380 additional for out-of-state students. **Room and board:** $2,310. **Books and supplies:** $575. **Other expenses:** $650.

FINANCIAL AID. 85% of freshmen, 85% of continuing students receive some form of aid. All aid based on need. Academic, music/drama, athletic scholarships available. **Aid applications:** Closing date August 1; priority given to applications received by May 1; applicants notified on a rolling basis beginning on or about June 15; must reply within 10 days.

ADDRESS/TELEPHONE. Roy A. Jackson, Director of Admissions, Savannah State College, State College Branch, Savannah, GA 31404. (912) 356-2181.

Savannah Technical Institute
Savannah, Georgia CB code: 3741

2-year public technical college, coed. **Accreditation:** Regional. **Undergraduate enrollment:** 565 men, 450 women full time; 559 men, 397 women part time. **Faculty:** 171 total (94 full time), 5 with doctorates or other terminal degrees. **Location:** Urban campus in small city. **Calendar:** Quarter, extensive summer session. **Microcomputers:** Located in libraries, classrooms, computer centers. **Additional facts:** Classes offered at off-campus sites located in Hinesville, Ga.

DEGREES OFFERED. AAS. 8 associate degrees awarded in 1992. 40% in business/office and marketing/distribution, 15% computer sciences, 10% engineering technologies, 15% allied health, 20% trade and industry.

UNDERGRADUATE MAJORS. Accounting, apparel and accessories marketing, automotive mechanics, bioengineering and biomedical engineering, biomedical equipment technology, business data processing and related programs, computer and information sciences, drafting and design technology, electrical/electronics/communications engineering, electromechanical technology, electronic technology, mechanical engineering, secretarial and related programs.

ACADEMIC PROGRAMS. Double major, internships. **Remedial services:** Learning center, remedial instruction, special counselor, tutoring. **Placement/credit:** AP, CLEP General and Subject, institutional tests; 50 credit hours maximum for associate degree.

ACADEMIC REQUIREMENTS. Freshmen must earn minimum GPA of 1.9 to continue in good standing. 95% of freshmen return for sophomore year. Students must declare major on enrollment. **Graduation requirements:** 114 hours for associate (50 in major). Most students required to take courses in English, humanities, mathematics.

FRESHMAN ADMISSIONS. Selection criteria: Open admissions. Acceptance to diploma or degree programs on a first come basis. Recommended units include English 4 and mathematics 3. **Test requirements:** SAT or ACT for placement; score report by September 21.

1992 FRESHMAN CLASS PROFILE. 287 men, 173 women enrolled. **Characteristics:** 98% from in state, 100% commute.

FALL-TERM APPLICATIONS. $15 fee. No closing date; applicants notified on a rolling basis.

STUDENT LIFE. Activities: Student government, student newspaper.

STUDENT SERVICES. Aptitude testing, career counseling, employment service for undergraduates, freshman orientation, on-campus day care, personal counseling, placement service for graduates, Peer tutoring program, services/facilities for handicapped.

ANNUAL EXPENSES. Tuition and fees (1992-93): $744, $756 additional for out-of-state students.

FINANCIAL AID. 36% of freshmen, 44% of continuing students receive some form of aid. All grants, all jobs based on need. 183 enrolled freshmen were judged to have need, all were offered aid. Academic scholarships available. **Aid applications:** No closing date; applicants notified on a rolling basis.

ADDRESS/TELEPHONE. Richard W. Swanson, Director of Admissions, Savannah Technical Institute, 5717 White Bluff Road, Savannah, GA 31499. (912) 351-6362. Fax: (912) 352-4382.

Shorter College
Rome, Georgia CB code: 5616

Admissions:	76% of applicants accepted
Based on:	••• School record
	•• Essay, test scores
	• Activities, interview, recommendations
Completion:	69% of freshmen end year in good standing
	42% graduate, 60% of these enter graduate study

4-year private liberal arts college, coed, affiliated with Southern Baptist Convention. Founded in 1873. **Accreditation:** Regional. **Undergraduate enrollment:** 280 men, 476 women full time; 62 men, 62 women part time. **Graduate enrollment:** 5 men, 14 women part time. **Faculty:** 103 total (63 full time), 41 with doctorates or other terminal degrees. **Location:** Urban campus in large town; 70 miles from Atlanta, 65 miles from Chattanooga, Tennessee. **Calendar:** Semester, limited summer session. Extensive evening/early morning classes. **Microcomputers:** 55 located in libraries, classrooms, computer centers. **Special facilities:** Wild-game collection, extensive pathological collection of human organs, extensive music collection, microfilm archive of local history. **Additional facts:** 2 off-campus sites for credit courses. Evening degree completion programs in Marietta, Georgia.

DEGREES OFFERED. BA, BS, BFA, MEd. 126 bachelor's degrees awarded in 1992. 23% in business and management, 17% teacher education, 8% life sciences, 6% mathematics, 6% multi/interdisciplinary studies, 6% parks/recreation, protective services, public affairs, 7% psychology, 15% visual and performing arts. Graduate degrees offered in 6 major fields of study.

UNDERGRADUATE MAJORS. Accounting, art education, biological and physical sciences, biology, business administration and management, business and management, chemistry, clinical laboratory science, communications, computer and information sciences, dramatic arts, economics, elementary education, English, English education, environmental science, finance, French, history, humanities and social sciences, journalism, junior high education, liberal/general studies, management information systems, marketing management, mathematics, mathematics education, music, music business management, music education, music performance, musical theater, parks and recreation management, philosophy, physical sciences, political science and government, predentistry, prelaw, premedicine, prepharmacy, psychology, public relations, radio/television broadcasting, religion, religious music, science education, secondary education, social science education, social sciences, social studies education, sociology, Spanish, speech, speech/communication/theater education, studio art, visual and performing arts.

ACADEMIC PROGRAMS. Double major, dual enrollment of high school students, honors program, independent study, internships, student-designed major, study abroad, teacher preparation, visiting/exchange student program, annual extended seacoast field trips in natural science, joint degree programs in medical technology with Georgia State University and Duke University; liberal arts/career combination in health sciences. **Remedial services:** Reduced course load, remedial instruction, tutoring. **Placement/credit:** AP, CLEP General and Subject, institutional tests; 30 credit hours maximum for bachelor's degree.

ACADEMIC REQUIREMENTS. Freshmen must earn minimum GPA of 2.0 to continue in good standing. 68% of freshmen return for sophomore year. Students must declare major by end of second year. **Graduation requirements:** 126 hours for bachelor's (45 in major). Most students required to take courses in arts/fine arts, computer science, English, history, mathematics, philosophy/religion, biological/physical sciences, social sciences. **Postgraduate studies:** 2% enter law school, 1% enter medical school, 6% enter MBA programs, 51% enter other graduate study.

FRESHMAN ADMISSIONS. Selection criteria: High school achievement and curriculum most important. Test scores and counselor recommendation also considered. **High school preparation:** 16 units required. Required and recommended units include English 4, mathematics 3, social science 3 and science 3. Foreign language 2 recommended. Science units should include 1 laboratory science. Mathematics units should include 2 algebra and 1 geometry. **Test requirements:** SAT or ACT; score report by August 25.

1992 FRESHMAN CLASS PROFILE. 471 men and women applied, 359 accepted; 88 men enrolled, 136 women enrolled. 57% had high school GPA of 3.0 or higher, 38% between 2.0 and 2.99. 30% were in top tenth and 53% were in top quarter of graduating class. **Academic background:** Mid 50% of enrolled freshmen had SAT-V between 380-490, SAT-M between 420-550; ACT composite between 18-25. 96% submitted SAT scores, 18% submitted ACT scores. **Characteristics:** 93% from in state, 69% live in college housing, 7% have minority backgrounds, 4% are foreign students, 25% join fraternities/sororities. Average age is 20.

FALL-TERM APPLICATIONS. $20 fee, may be waived for applicants with need. No closing date; priority given to applications received by June 1; applicants notified on a rolling basis. Audition required for music, drama applicants. Essay required. Interview recommended for borderline applicants. Early admission available.

STUDENT LIFE. Housing: Dormitories (men, women); apartment housing available. **Activities:** Student government, radio, student newspaper, television, yearbook, choral groups, concert band, dance, drama, music ensembles, musical theater, opera, pep band, fraternities, sororities, Baptist Student Union, Black Awareness Society, Shorter Relations Society, Fellowship of Christian Athletes, International Student Organization. **Additional information:** Fraternities and sororities are local, accept all who complete pledge, and must do service projects. Three attendances at chapel required per term. Religious observance required.

ATHLETICS. NAIA. **Intercollegiate:** Baseball M, basketball, cross-country, golf M, softball W, tennis, track and field M. **Intramural:** Basketball, bowling, golf, soccer, softball, table tennis, tennis, track and field, volleyball.

STUDENT SERVICES. Aptitude testing, career counseling, employment service for undergraduates, freshman orientation, health services, personal counseling, placement service for graduates, services/facilities for handicapped.

ANNUAL EXPENSES. Tuition and fees: $6,670. **Room and board:** $3,600. **Books and supplies:** $500. **Other expenses:** $1,400.

FINANCIAL AID. 100% of freshmen, 100% of continuing students receive some form of aid. 20% of grants, 71% of loans, all jobs based on need. Academic, music/drama, art, athletic, state/district residency, leadership, alumni affiliation, religious affiliation, minority scholarships available. **Aid applications:** No closing date; priority given to applications received by April 1; applicants notified on a rolling basis beginning on or about May 1; must reply within 3 weeks. **Additional information:** Cost is reduced for all in-state students by state tuition equalization granted program. College matches this for out-of-state full-time students.

ADDRESS/TELEPHONE. John P. Mc Elveen, Director of Admissions, Shorter College, 315 Shorter Avenue, Rome, GA 30165-4298. (706) 291-2121. (800) 868-6980. Fax: (706) 236-1515.

South College
Savannah, Georgia

CB code: 5157

Admissions: 93% of applicants accepted
Based on: • Interview, school record, test scores
Completion: 10% enter 4-year programs

2-year proprietary community, junior college, coed. Founded in 1899. **Accreditation:** Regional. **Undergraduate enrollment:** 65 men, 340 women full time; 21 men, 105 women part time. **Faculty:** 52 total (20 full time). **Location:** Suburban campus in small city; 225 miles from Atlanta, 165 miles from Jacksonville, Florida. **Calendar:** Quarter, extensive summer session. **Microcomputers:** Located in libraries, classrooms, computer centers. **Additional facts:** Certificate programs in downtown Savannah. Branch campus in West Palm Beach, Florida.

DEGREES OFFERED. AS. 35 associate degrees awarded in 1992. 78% in business and management, 7% computer sciences, 8% allied health, 7% law.

UNDERGRADUATE MAJORS. Accounting, business and management, computer and information sciences, emergency medical technologies, hotel/motel and restaurant management, legal assistant/paralegal, medical assistant, secretarial and related programs.

ACADEMIC PROGRAMS. Double major, internships, teacher preparation. **Remedial services:** Reduced course load, remedial instruction, tutoring. **Placement/credit:** CLEP General and Subject, institutional tests.

ACADEMIC REQUIREMENTS. Freshmen must earn minimum GPA of 1.8 to continue in good standing. Students must declare major on enrollment. **Graduation requirements:** Most students required to take courses in computer science, English, mathematics, social sciences.

FRESHMAN ADMISSIONS. Selection criteria: Test scores and school achievement record considered. **Test requirements:** SAT or ACT; score report by September 20. CPAT may be submitted in place of SAT for admission.

1992 FRESHMAN CLASS PROFILE. 35 men applied, 30 accepted, 10 enrolled; 176 women applied, 166 accepted, 73 enrolled. **Characteristics:** 98% from in state, 100% commute, 50% have minority backgrounds.

FALL-TERM APPLICATIONS. $25 fee. No closing date; applicants notified on a rolling basis beginning on or about January 1. Interview required. Deferred and early admission available.

STUDENT LIFE. Activities: Student newspaper.

STUDENT SERVICES. Aptitude testing, personal counseling, placement service for graduates, veterans counselor.

ANNUAL EXPENSES. Tuition and fees (projected): $4,525. **Books and supplies:** $450. **Other expenses:** $1,260.

FINANCIAL AID. 85% of freshmen, 85% of continuing students receive some form of aid. 99% of grants, 86% of loans, all jobs based on need. Academic scholarships available. **Aid applications:** No closing date; applicants notified on a rolling basis beginning on or about September 1; must reply by registration.

ADDRESS/TELEPHONE. Scott McVicar, Director of Admissions, South College, 709 Mall Boulevard, Savannah, GA 31406. (912) 651-8100. Fax: (912) 356-1609.

South Georgia College
Douglas, Georgia

CB code: 5619

Admissions: 74% of applicants accepted
Based on: •• School record, test scores
Completion: 70% of freshmen end year in good standing
29% graduate, 75% of these enter 4-year programs

2-year public community college, coed. Founded in 1906. **Accreditation:** Regional. **Undergraduate enrollment:** 334 men, 612 women full time; 178 men, 371 women part time. **Faculty:** 59 total (46 full time), 14 with doctorates or other terminal degrees. **Location:** Rural campus in large town; 200 miles from Atlanta, 120 miles from Jacksonville, FL. **Calendar:** Quarter, limited summer session. **Microcomputers:** 80 located in libraries, classrooms.

DEGREES OFFERED. AA, AS, AAS. 223 associate degrees awarded in 1992. 7% in business and management, 16% education, 52% health sciences, 6% physical sciences.

UNDERGRADUATE MAJORS. Accounting, agribusiness, agricultural business and management, agricultural sciences, allied health, biology, business administration and management, business and management, business and office, business data programming, business education, chemistry, communications, computer and information sciences, computer programming, criminal justice studies, education, English, finance, foreign languages (multiple emphasis), health education, history, journalism, law enforcement and corrections, liberal/general studies, marketing and distribution, mathematics, nursing, parks and recreation management, philosophy, physical sciences, physics, political science and government, prelaw, psychology, recreation and community services technologies, secretarial and related programs, social sciences, sociology, Spanish.

ACADEMIC PROGRAMS. 2-year transfer program, dual enrollment of

high school students, independent study. **Remedial services:** Learning center, reduced course load, remedial instruction, special counselor, tutoring, developmental studies. **Placement/credit:** AP, CLEP General and Subject, institutional tests; 45 credit hours maximum for associate degree.

ACADEMIC REQUIREMENTS. Freshmen must earn minimum GPA of 1.4 to continue in good standing. 73% of freshmen return for sophomore year. Students must declare major by end of first year. **Graduation requirements:** 96 hours for associate (30 in major). Most students required to take courses in English, history, humanities, mathematics, biological/physical sciences, social sciences.

FRESHMAN ADMISSIONS. Selection criteria: Minimum SAT-verbal score of 250 or ACT English of 10, or SAT-mathematical score of 280 or ACT mathematical of 5, or high school GPA of 1.8. **High school preparation:** 16 units required. Required units include English 4, foreign language 2, mathematics 3, social science 3 and science 3. **Test requirements:** SAT or ACT; score report by September 15.

1992 FRESHMAN CLASS PROFILE. 280 men applied, 200 accepted, 160 enrolled; 400 women applied, 300 accepted, 251 enrolled. 34% had high school GPA of 3.0 or higher, 58% between 2.0 and 2.99. **Academic background:** Mid 50% of enrolled freshmen had SAT-V between 290-430, SAT-M between 300-460. 88% submitted SAT scores. **Characteristics:** 97% from in state, 85% commute, 22% have minority backgrounds, 1% are foreign students. Average age is 22.

FALL-TERM APPLICATIONS. $5 fee. No closing date; priority given to applications received by August 29; applicants notified on a rolling basis. Interview required for nursing applicants. CRDA. Deferred and early admission available.

STUDENT LIFE. Housing: Dormitories (men, women). **Activities:** Student government, magazine, student newspaper, yearbook, Baptist Student Union, Students of Black Unity.

ATHLETICS. NJCAA. **Intercollegiate:** Baseball M, basketball M, softball W. **Intramural:** Basketball, softball, table tennis, tennis, volleyball.

STUDENT SERVICES. Aptitude testing, career counseling, employment service for undergraduates, freshman orientation, personal counseling, veterans counselor, services/facilities for handicapped.

ANNUAL EXPENSES. Tuition and fees (projected): $1,152, $939 additional for out-of-state students. **Room and board:** $2,880. **Books and supplies:** $600. **Other expenses:** $750.

FINANCIAL AID. 68% of freshmen, 72% of continuing students receive some form of aid. 91% of grants, 72% of loans, 84% of jobs based on need. Academic, athletic, state/district residency, leadership, minority scholarships available. **Aid applications:** Closing date July 12; priority given to applications received by July 13; applicants notified on a rolling basis beginning on or about June 1; must reply within 2 weeks.

ADDRESS/TELEPHONE. Dr. K. H. Foshee, Director of Admissions, Records, and Research, South Georgia College, 100 West College Park Drive, Douglas, GA 31533-5098. (912) 383-4300. Fax: (912) 383-4322.

Southern College of Technology

Marietta, Georgia — CB code: 5626

Admissions: 66% of applicants accepted
Based on: ••• Test scores
•• School record
Completion: 80% of freshmen end year in good standing
15% graduate, 10% of these enter graduate study

4-year public technical college, coed. Founded in 1948. **Accreditation:** Regional. **Undergraduate enrollment:** 1,911 men, 336 women full time; 1,146 men, 188 women part time. **Graduate enrollment:** 58 men, 41 women full time; 143 men, 77 women part time. **Faculty:** 209 total (149 full time), 73 with doctorates or other terminal degrees. **Location:** Suburban campus in large town; 15 miles from Atlanta. **Calendar:** Quarter, extensive summer session. Extensive evening/early morning classes. **Microcomputers:** 500 located in libraries, classrooms, computer centers, campus-wide network.

DEGREES OFFERED. AS, BS, BArch, MS. 31 associate degrees awarded in 1992. 98% in engineering technologies. 456 bachelor's degrees awarded. 10% in computer sciences, 88% engineering technologies. Graduate degrees offered in 1 major field of study.

UNDERGRADUATE MAJORS. Associate: Liberal/general studies. **Bachelor's:** Apparel engineering technology, architecture, civil technology, computer technology, construction, electrical technology, environmental design, industrial distribution, industrial technology, information sciences and systems, manufacturing technology, mathematics, mechanical design technology, physics, technology management, textile technology.

ACADEMIC PROGRAMS. 2-year transfer program, cooperative education, double major, dual enrollment of high school students, honors program, study abroad, weekend college, cross-registration. **Remedial services:** Learning center, reduced course load, remedial instruction, tutoring. **Placement/credit:** AP, CLEP General and Subject, institutional tests.

ACADEMIC REQUIREMENTS. Freshmen must earn minimum GPA of 1.8 to continue in good standing. 62% of freshmen return for sophomore year. Students must declare major by end of first year. **Graduation requirements:** 105 hours for associate (30 in major), 205 hours for bachelor's (60 in major). Most students required to take courses in arts/fine arts, computer science, English, history, humanities, mathematics, biological/physical sciences, social sciences. **Postgraduate studies:** 95% from 2-year programs enter 4-year programs. 4% enter MBA programs, 6% enter other graduate study.

FRESHMAN ADMISSIONS. Selection criteria: Test scores, high school units, and GPA considered. **High school preparation:** 21 units required. Required and recommended units include English 4, foreign language 2, mathematics 3-4, physical science 1-2, social science 3 and science 2. **Test requirements:** SAT or ACT; score report by September 1.

1992 FRESHMAN CLASS PROFILE. 702 men applied, 488 accepted, 296 enrolled; 153 women applied, 80 accepted, 50 enrolled. 42% had high school GPA of 3.0 or higher, 54% between 2.0 and 2.99. **Academic background:** Mid 50% of enrolled freshmen had SAT-V between 370-460, SAT-M between 430-560; ACT composite between 19-20. 90% submitted SAT scores, 2% submitted ACT scores. **Characteristics:** 96% from in state, 87% commute, 23% have minority backgrounds, 3% are foreign students, 5% join fraternities/sororities. Average age is 19.

FALL-TERM APPLICATIONS. No fee. Closing date September 1; applicants notified on a rolling basis. Deferred and early admission available.

STUDENT LIFE. Housing: Dormitories (men, coed); handicapped housing available. **Activities:** Student government, radio, student newspaper, yearbook, drama, jazz band, fraternities, sororities, service organizations, Black Student Union, Fellowship of Christian Athletes, NAACP, Baptist Student Association.

ATHLETICS. NAIA. **Intercollegiate:** Baseball M, basketball M, tennis M. **Intramural:** Basketball, bowling, golf, softball, table tennis, tennis, volleyball.

STUDENT SERVICES. Aptitude testing, career counseling, employment service for undergraduates, freshman orientation, health services, personal counseling, placement service for graduates, veterans counselor, services/facilities for handicapped.

ANNUAL EXPENSES. Tuition and fees: $1,650, $1,380 additional for out-of-state students. **Room and board:** $2,775. **Books and supplies:** $650. **Other expenses:** $750.

FINANCIAL AID. 38% of freshmen, 32% of continuing students receive some form of aid. 88% of grants, 90% of loans, 19% of jobs based on need. Academic, athletic, state/district residency, leadership, alumni affiliation, religious affiliation, minority scholarships available. **Aid applications:** Closing date May 31; priority given to applications received by March 15; applicants notified on a rolling basis beginning on or about July 1; must reply within 3 weeks.

ADDRESS/TELEPHONE. Virginia Head, Director of Admissions, Southern College of Technology, South Marietta Parkway, Marietta, GA 30060-2896. (706) 528-7281. (800) 635-3204. Fax: (404) 528-7292.

Spelman College

Atlanta, Georgia — CB code: 5628

Admissions: 45% of applicants accepted
Based on: ••• School record, test scores
•• Activities, essay, recommendations
• Interview, special talents
Completion: 89% of freshmen end year in good standing
85% graduate, 42% of these enter graduate study

4-year private liberal arts college, women only. Founded in 1881. **Accreditation:** Regional. **Undergraduate enrollment:** 1,925 women full time; 101 women part time. **Faculty:** 174 total (114 full time), 90 with doctorates or other terminal degrees. **Location:** Urban campus in very large city; 2 miles from downtown. **Calendar:** Semester. Saturday and extensive evening/early morning classes. **Microcomputers:** 102 located in libraries, classrooms, computer centers. **Additional facts:** One of 6 members of Atlanta University Center sharing facilities, resources and activities. Students may take courses at the other undergraduate schools in the Atlanta University Consortium.

DEGREES OFFERED. BA, BS. 357 bachelor's degrees awarded in 1992. 5% in teacher education, 16% letters/literature, 11% life sciences, 8% mathematics, 16% psychology, 37% social sciences.

UNDERGRADUATE MAJORS. Biochemistry, biological and physical sciences, biology, chemistry, child development/care/guidance, computer and information sciences, dramatic arts, economics, engineering, English, fine arts, French, history, mathematics, music, philosophy, physics, political science and government, psychology, religion, sociology, Spanish.

ACADEMIC PROGRAMS. Double major, dual enrollment of high school students, honors program, independent study, internships, student-designed major, study abroad, teacher preparation, visiting/exchange student program, New York semester, Washington semester, cross-registration; liberal arts/career combination in engineering. **Remedial services:** Special counselor, tutoring. **ROTC:** Air Force, Army, Naval. **Placement/credit:** AP, CLEP General and Subject, institutional tests; 60 credit hours maximum for bachelor's degree.

ACADEMIC REQUIREMENTS. Freshmen must earn minimum GPA

of 1.5 to continue in good standing. 88% of freshmen return for sophomore year. Students must declare major by end of first year. **Graduation requirements:** 120 hours for bachelor's. Most students required to take courses in arts/fine arts, computer science, English, foreign languages, history, humanities, mathematics, philosophy/religion, biological/physical sciences, social sciences. **Postgraduate studies:** 22% enter law school, 17% enter medical school, 3% enter MBA programs.

FRESHMAN ADMISSIONS. Selection criteria: School achievement record, letters of recommendation, test scores, leadership, activities, essay all important. **High school preparation:** 15 units required; 16 recommended. Required and recommended units include English 4, mathematics 2-3, social science 2 and science 2. Biological science 1, foreign language 4 and physical science 2 recommended. Each science unit must be a laboratory science. Mathematics units must include algebra and geometry. **Test requirements:** SAT or ACT; score report by February 1.

1992 FRESHMAN CLASS PROFILE. 3,250 women applied, 1,452 accepted, 548 enrolled. 86% had high school GPA of 3.0 or higher, 14% between 2.0 and 2.99. **Academic background:** Mid 50% of enrolled freshmen had SAT-V between 410-510, SAT-M between 440-540; ACT composite between 20-24. 88% submitted SAT scores, 42% submitted ACT scores. **Characteristics:** 16% from in state, 93% live in college housing, 100% have minority backgrounds, 1% are foreign students. Average age is 18.

FALL-TERM APPLICATIONS. $35 fee, may be waived for applicants with need. Closing date February 1; applicants notified on or about March 15; must reply by May 1. Essay required. Audition recommended. Portfolio recommended. CRDA. Early admission available. EDP-F.

STUDENT LIFE. Housing: Dormitories (women). **Activities:** Student government, magazine, student newspaper, yearbook, television and radio with Atlanta University Center, choral groups, dance, drama, jazz band, marching band, music ensembles, musical theater, chamber orchestra, sororities, Bible studies, YWCA, subject-related clubs, debate team, music club, dance club, drama club, Community Service Office, gospel choir.

ATHLETICS. Intercollegiate: Basketball, tennis, track and field, volleyball. **Intramural:** Basketball, bowling, softball, swimming, tennis, track and field, volleyball.

STUDENT SERVICES. Aptitude testing, career counseling, employment service for undergraduates, freshman orientation, health services, on-campus day care, personal counseling, placement service for graduates, special adviser for adult students, services/facilities for handicapped.

ANNUAL EXPENSES. Tuition and fees (1992-93): $7,077. **Room and board:** $5,000. **Books and supplies:** $450. **Other expenses:** $1,150.

FINANCIAL AID. 81% of freshmen, 78% of continuing students receive some form of aid. 53% of grants, all loans, all jobs based on need. Academic, music/drama, state/district residency, leadership, religious affiliation scholarships available. **Aid applications:** Closing date April 1; applicants notified on a rolling basis beginning on or about June 1; must reply within 2 weeks.

ADDRESS/TELEPHONE. Deborah Urquhart, Executive Director of Enrollment Management, Spelman College, 350 Spelman Lane Southwest, Atlanta, GA 30314-4399. (404) 681-3643. (800) 241-3421. Fax: (404) 223-1449.

Thomas College
Thomasville, Georgia — CB code: 5072

4-year private liberal arts college, coed. Founded in 1950. **Accreditation:** Regional. **Undergraduate enrollment:** 63 men, 157 women full time; 42 men, 74 women part time. **Faculty:** 27 total (15 full time), 7 with doctorates or other terminal degrees. **Location:** Rural campus in large town; 35 miles from Tallahassee, Florida, 60 miles from Albany, Georgia. **Calendar:** Quarter, limited summer session. Saturday and extensive evening/early morning classes. **Microcomputers:** 24 located in libraries, computer centers.

DEGREES OFFERED. AA, AS, AAS, BS. 25 associate degrees awarded in 1992. 48% in business and management, 24% teacher education, 16% multi/interdisciplinary studies. 10 bachelor's degrees awarded. 100% in business and management.

UNDERGRADUATE MAJORS. Associate: Biology, business and management, early childhood education, education, elementary education, fine arts, history, junior high education, liberal/general studies, mathematics, music, political science and government, prelaw, psychology, science education, secondary education, sociology, special education. **Bachelor's:** Business administration and management.

ACADEMIC PROGRAMS. 2-year transfer program, accelerated program, double major, dual enrollment of high school students. **Remedial services:** Learning center, reduced course load, remedial instruction, special counselor, tutoring, Student support services program. **Placement/credit:** AP, CLEP General and Subject, institutional tests; 60 credit hours maximum for associate degree.

ACADEMIC REQUIREMENTS. Freshmen must earn minimum GPA of 1.8 to continue in good standing. 37% of freshmen return for sophomore year. Students must declare major by end of second year. **Graduation requirements:** 96 hours for associate (30 in major), 183 hours for bachelor's (80 in major). Most students required to take courses in arts/fine arts, computer science, English, foreign languages, history, humanities, mathematics, biological/physical sciences, social sciences. **Postgraduate studies:** 72% from 2-year programs enter 4-year programs.

FRESHMAN ADMISSIONS. Selection criteria: Open admissions for students scoring 900 or above on SAT or 20 or above on ACT. Students with SAT below 900 or ACT below 20 must take comprehensive guidance placement and successfully complete remedial courses before enrolling in academic courses.

1992 FRESHMAN CLASS PROFILE. 53 men applied, 53 accepted, 22 enrolled; 57 women applied, 57 accepted, 56 enrolled. **Characteristics:** 99% from in state, 100% commute, 32% have minority backgrounds. Average age is 23.

FALL-TERM APPLICATIONS. $25 fee. No closing date; applicants notified on a rolling basis. Essay recommended. CRDA. Deferred and early admission available.

STUDENT LIFE. Activities: Student government, student newspaper, choral groups, jazz band, music ensembles.

STUDENT SERVICES. Aptitude testing, career counseling, employment service for undergraduates, freshman orientation, personal counseling, placement service for graduates, special adviser for adult students, veterans counselor, services/facilities for handicapped.

ANNUAL EXPENSES. Tuition and fees (1992-93): $3,084. **Books and supplies:** $525. **Other expenses:** $651.

FINANCIAL AID. 66% of freshmen, 60% of continuing students receive some form of aid. 77% of grants, all loans, all jobs based on need. Academic scholarships available. **Aid applications:** No closing date; priority given to applications received by September 1; applicants notified on a rolling basis; must reply by July 1 or as soon as possible if notified thereafter.

ADDRESS/TELEPHONE. Robert Bohman, Director Student Services, Thomas College, 1501 Millpond Road, Thomasville, GA 31792-7499. (912) 226-1621.

Toccoa Falls College
Toccoa Falls, Georgia — CB code: 5799

4-year private Bible, music, liberal arts, seminary college, coed, interdenominational. Founded in 1907. **Accreditation:** Regional. **Undergraduate enrollment:** 401 men, 393 women full time; 41 men, 76 women part time. **Faculty:** 59 total (39 full time), 22 with doctorates or other terminal degrees. **Location:** Rural campus in large town; 60 miles from Greenville, South Carolina, 90 miles from Atlanta. **Calendar:** 4-1-4, limited summer session. **Microcomputers:** 25 located in computer centers. **Special facilities:** 186-foot waterfall, power house and electric generator built in 1898. **Additional facts:** College committed to providing foundation for careers in Christian world service. Has strong ties with the Christian and Missionary Alliance.

DEGREES OFFERED. AA, BA, BS. 17 associate degrees awarded in 1992. 144 bachelor's degrees awarded. 14% in area and ethnic studies, 15% communications, 11% education, 15% teacher education, 24% philosophy, religion, theology, 7% psychology.

UNDERGRADUATE MAJORS. Associate: Liberal/general studies. **Bachelor's:** Bible studies, biblical languages, children's/family education, Christian education, clinical psychology, communications, counseling psychology, cross-cultural studies, early childhood education, English, English education, journalism, junior high education, missionary studies, music, music education, music performance, music theory and composition, philosophy, psychology, public relations, radio/television broadcasting, religion, religious education, religious music, secondary education, theological studies, youth ministries.

ACADEMIC PROGRAMS. 2-year transfer program, double major, dual enrollment of high school students, honors program, independent study, internships, study abroad, teacher preparation. **Remedial services:** Learning center, reduced course load, remedial instruction, special counselor, tutoring. **Placement/credit:** AP, CLEP General and Subject, institutional tests; 30 credit hours maximum for bachelor's degree.

ACADEMIC REQUIREMENTS. Freshmen must earn minimum GPA of 2.0 to continue in good standing. 80% of freshmen return for sophomore year. Students must declare major by end of second year. **Graduation requirements:** 66 hours for associate, 130 hours for bachelor's (45 in major). Most students required to take courses in arts/fine arts, computer science, English, foreign languages, history, humanities, mathematics, philosophy/religion, biological/physical sciences, social sciences. **Postgraduate studies:** 40% from 2-year programs enter 4-year programs. **Additional information:** All students required to take 6 credit hours of student ministry and at least 30 credit hours of Bible studies.

FRESHMAN ADMISSIONS. Selection criteria: Test scores, school academic record, 3 references, evidence of Christian character required. College-preparatory program recommended. **Test requirements:** SAT or ACT; score report by August 1.

1992 FRESHMAN CLASS PROFILE. 146 men, 154 women enrolled. **Characteristics:** 75% live in college housing. Average age is 19.

FALL-TERM APPLICATIONS. $20 fee, may be waived for applicants with need. Closing date August 15; applicants notified on a rolling basis; must reply within 60 days of notification. Interview recommended for marginal applicants. Audition recommended for music applicants. Essay recommended. Personal statement of Christian faith required of all applicants. Deferred and early admission available. EDP-F.

STUDENT LIFE. Housing: Dormitories (men, women); apartment housing available. 45 trailers available on campus lots for married students. New townhouses built for single female students. **Activities:** Student government, film, radio, student newspaper, yearbook, choral groups, concert band, drama, music ensembles, pep band, missions team, religious and service organizations, missions felowship, Baptist student union, political action committee, foreign student association. **Additional information:** 50 different ministry opportunities for students. Religious observance required.

ATHLETICS. Intercollegiate: Baseball M, basketball, cross-country, soccer M, volleyball W. **Intramural:** Basketball, football M, golf, racquetball, skiing, soccer, softball, table tennis, tennis, volleyball.

STUDENT SERVICES. Aptitude testing, career counseling, employment service for undergraduates, freshman orientation, health services, personal counseling, placement service for graduates, special adviser for adult students, veterans counselor.

ANNUAL EXPENSES. Tuition and fees (1992-93): $5,436. **Room and board:** $3,264. **Books and supplies:** $500. **Other expenses:** $1,354.

FINANCIAL AID. 75% of freshmen, 75% of continuing students receive some form of aid. 165 enrolled freshmen were judged to have need, all were offered aid. Academic, music/drama scholarships available. **Aid applications:** No closing date; priority given to applications received by April 1; applicants notified on a rolling basis beginning on or about April 1.

ADDRESS/TELEPHONE. Matthew King, Director of Admissions, Toccoa Falls College, Toccoa Falls, GA 30598-0368. (706) 886-6831 ext. 5380. (800) 868-3257. Fax: (706) 886-6412.

Truett-McConnell College
Cleveland, Georgia — CB code: 5798

2-year private college of arts and sciences and liberal arts college, coed, affiliated with Southern Baptist Convention. Founded in 1946. **Accreditation:** Regional. **Undergraduate enrollment:** 1,878 men and women. **Faculty:** 37 total (30 full time), 9 with doctorates or other terminal degrees. **Location:** Rural campus in rural community; 85 miles northeast of Atlanta. **Calendar:** Quarter, extensive summer session. **Microcomputers:** 14 located in computer centers.

DEGREES OFFERED. AA, AAS. 92 associate degrees awarded in 1992. 15% in business and management, 80% multi/interdisciplinary studies, 5% visual and performing arts.

UNDERGRADUATE MAJORS. Accounting, Bible studies, business and management, business and office, data processing, drafting, drafting and design technology, education, electrical and electronics equipment repair, history, liberal/general studies, mechanical design technology, medical laboratory technologies, music, music performance, predentistry, prelaw, premedicine, prepharmacy, preveterinary, psychology, religion, secretarial and related programs, sociology.

ACADEMIC PROGRAMS. 2-year transfer program, dual enrollment of high school students, honors program. **Remedial services:** Learning center, preadmission summer program, remedial instruction, tutoring. **Placement/credit:** AP, CLEP Subject, institutional tests.

ACADEMIC REQUIREMENTS. Freshmen must earn minimum GPA of 1.7 to continue in good standing. 71% of freshmen return for sophomore year. Students must declare major by end of first year. **Graduation requirements:** 96 hours for associate (30 in major). Most students required to take courses in arts/fine arts, English, history, humanities, mathematics, philosophy/religion, biological/physical sciences, social sciences.

FRESHMAN ADMISSIONS. Selection criteria: Selective admissions for music applicants. Require 600 combines SAT score or overall GPA of 2.0. **High school preparation:** 18 units recommended. Recommended units include biological science 3, English 4, foreign language 2, mathematics 4, physical science 1 and social science 4. **Test requirements:** SAT or ACT (SAT preferred) for placement and counseling only; score report by September 1.

1992 FRESHMAN CLASS PROFILE. 732 men and women enrolled. **Academic background:** Mid 50% of enrolled freshmen had SAT-V between 330-430, SAT-M between 340-440; ACT composite between 10-14. 40% submitted SAT scores, 2% submitted ACT scores. **Characteristics:** 97% from in state, 80% live in college housing, 10% have minority backgrounds. Average age is 18.

FALL-TERM APPLICATIONS. $25 fee, may be waived for applicants with need. Closing date August 15; applicants notified on a rolling basis; must reply by May 1 or within 1 week if notified thereafter. Audition required for music applicants. CRDA. Deferred and early admission available.

STUDENT LIFE. Housing: Dormitories (men, women). **Activities:** Student government, yearbook, choral groups, concert band, drama, jazz band, music ensembles, musical theater, Baptist Student Union, Key Club.

ATHLETICS. NJCAA. **Intercollegiate:** Baseball M, basketball, soccer M, softball W, tennis. **Intramural:** Basketball, golf M, softball, tennis, volleyball.

STUDENT SERVICES. Career counseling, freshman orientation, health services, personal counseling, veterans counselor, services/facilities for handicapped.

ANNUAL EXPENSES. Tuition and fees (1992-93): $3,885. **Room and board:** $2,475. **Books and supplies:** $450. **Other expenses:** $600.

FINANCIAL AID. 95% of freshmen, 95% of continuing students receive some form of aid. Grants, loans, jobs available. Academic, music/drama, athletic, state/district residency, religious affiliation scholarships available. **Aid applications:** No closing date; applicants notified on a rolling basis beginning on or about June 1; must reply by May 1 or within 2 weeks if notified thereafter.

ADDRESS/TELEPHONE. Lee Ragsdale, Director of Admissions, Truett-McConnell College, Highway 115 East, Cleveland, GA 30528. (706) 865-2138. Fax: (706) 865-0975.

University of Georgia
Athens, Georgia — CB code: 5813

Admissions:	64% of applicants accepted
Based on:	••• School record, test scores
	• Essay, special talents
Completion:	85% of freshmen end year in good standing
	55% graduate, 33% of these enter graduate study

4-year public university, coed. Founded in 1785. **Accreditation:** Regional. **Undergraduate enrollment:** 9,057 men, 10,414 women full time; 1,455 men, 1,281 women part time. **Graduate enrollment:** 2,350 men, 2,397 women full time; 553 men, 986 women part time. **Faculty:** 2,626 total (2,416 full time), 1,804 with doctorates or other terminal degrees. **Location:** Suburban campus in small city; 70 miles from Atlanta. **Calendar:** Quarter, extensive summer session. Extensive evening/early morning classes. **Microcomputers:** 850 located in dormitories, libraries, classrooms, computer centers. **Special facilities:** Museum of Art, Georgia State Botanical Garden, golf course, Biological Sciences Complex.

DEGREES OFFERED. AAS, BA, BS, BFA, MA, MS, MBA, MFA, MEd, MSW, PhD, EdD, Pharm D, DVM, JD. 4 associate degrees awarded in 1992. 100% in business/office and marketing/distribution. 4,418 bachelor's degrees awarded. 22% in business and management, 9% communications, 13% education, 6% home economics, 9% letters/literature, 5% psychology, 11% social sciences. Graduate degrees offered in 157 major fields of study.

UNDERGRADUATE MAJORS. Associate: Business and office, medieval studies, women's studies. **Bachelor's:** Accounting, advertising, African studies, Afro-American (black) studies, agribusiness, agricultural economics, agricultural education, agricultural engineering, agricultural mechanics, agronomy, animal sciences, anthropology, art education, art history, astronomy, biochemistry, biological and physical sciences, biology, botany, business administration and management, business and management, business economics, business education, Caribbean studies, ceramics, chemistry, child development/care/guidance, classics, clothing and textiles management/production/services, comparative literature, computer and information sciences, criminal justice studies, dairy, dance, dramatic arts, drawing, early childhood education, economics, education of the mentally handicapped, education of the multiple handicapped, educational media technology, elementary education, English, English education, English literature, entomology, environmental design, family/consumer resource management, fashion merchandising, finance, fishing and fisheries, food production/management/services, food science and nutrition, food sciences, foreign languages (multiple emphasis), foreign languages education, forestry and related sciences, French, French studies, genetics, human and animal, geography, geology, German, German studies, graphic design, Greek (classical), health education, historic preservation, history, home economics, home economics education, home furnishings and equipment management/production/services, horticultural science, horticulture, hospitality and recreation marketing, hotel/motel and restaurant management, human environment and housing, humanities and social sciences, individual and family development, industrial arts education, institutional/home management/supporting programs, insurance and risk management, interior design, international business management, international studies, Italian, journalism, junior high education, labor/industrial relations, landscape architecture, Latin, Latin American studies, liberal/general studies, linguistics, management information systems, management science, marketing and distribution, marketing and distributive education, mathematics, mathematics education, medieval studies, metal/jewelry, microbiology, music, music education, music history and appreciation, music performance, music theory and composition, music therapy, nutritional sciences, organizational behavior, ornamental horticulture, painting, parks and recreation management, pharmacy, philosophy, photography, physical education, physics, plant pathology, plant physiology, plant protection, plant sciences, political science and government, poultry, predentistry, preengineering, prelaw, premedicine, preveterinary, printmaking, psychology, public relations, radio/television broadcasting, radio/television technology, reading education, real estate, recreation therapy, religion, religious music, renewable natural resources, science education, sculpture, secondary education, Slavic languages, social science education, social sciences, social work, sociology, soil sciences, Spanish, speech, speech correction, speech pathology/audiology, sports management, statistics, telecommunications, textiles and clothing, trade and industrial education, video, Western European studies, wildlife management, zoology.

ACADEMIC PROGRAMS. Accelerated program, cooperative education, double major, dual enrollment of high school students, education specialist degree, honors program, independent study, internships, student-designed major, study abroad, teacher preparation, visiting/exchange student program, Washington semester; liberal arts/career combination in engineering, health sciences; combined bachelor's/graduate program in business administration. **Remedial services:** Learning center, preadmission summer program, reduced course load, remedial instruction, special counselor, tutoring, developmental studies. **ROTC:** Air Force, Army. **Placement/credit:** AP, CLEP General and Subject, institutional tests. Unlimited number of hours of credit by examination may be counted toward bachelor's degree.

ACADEMIC REQUIREMENTS. Freshmen must earn minimum GPA of 1.7 to continue in good standing. 85% of freshmen return for sophomore year. Students must declare major by end of second year. **Graduation requirements:** 50 hours for associate (45 in major), 195 hours for bachelor's (45 in major). Most students required to take courses in arts/fine arts, English, history, mathematics, biological/physical sciences, social sciences. **Postgraduate studies:** 4% enter law school, 4% enter medical school, 10% enter MBA programs, 15% enter other graduate study.

FRESHMAN ADMISSIONS. Selection criteria: Combination of high school GPA, test scores, and college preparatory curriculum. **High school preparation:** 15 units required; 24 recommended. Required and recommended units include English 4, foreign language 2-4, social science 3-4 and science 3-4. Mathematics 4 recommended. **Test requirements:** SAT or ACT (SAT preferred); score report by March 1.

1992 FRESHMAN CLASS PROFILE. 5,066 men applied, 3,076 accepted, 1,390 enrolled; 6,297 women applied, 4,228 accepted, 1,841 enrolled. 77% had high school GPA of 3.0 or higher, 22% between 2.0 and 2.99. **Academic background:** Mid 50% of enrolled freshmen had SAT-V between 460-560, SAT-M between 520-620. 98% submitted SAT scores. **Characteristics:** 85% from in state, 82% live in college housing, 11% have minority backgrounds, 1% are foreign students, 28% join fraternities/sororities. Average age is 19.

FALL-TERM APPLICATIONS. $25 fee, may be waived for applicants with need. Closing date June 1; priority given to applications received by February 1; applicants notified on a rolling basis beginning on or about March 30. Audition required for music applicants. CRDA. Deferred and early admission available. Institutional early decision plan.

STUDENT LIFE. Housing: Dormitories (men, women, coed); apartment, fraternity, sorority housing available. **Activities:** Student government, film, magazine, radio, student newspaper, television, yearbook, choral groups, concert band, dance, drama, jazz band, marching band, music ensembles, musical theater, opera, pep band, symphony orchestra, fraternities, sororities, over 400 student organizations.

ATHLETICS. NCAA. **Intercollegiate:** Baseball M, basketball, cross-country, diving, football M, golf, gymnastics W, swimming, tennis, track and field, volleyball W. **Intramural:** Baseball M, basketball, bowling, cross-country, diving, football, golf, horseback riding, ice hockey M, lacrosse M, racquetball, rugby M, soccer, softball, swimming, tennis, volleyball.

STUDENT SERVICES. Aptitude testing, career counseling, employment service for undergraduates, freshman orientation, health services, personal counseling, placement service for graduates, special adviser for adult students, veterans counselor, services/facilities for handicapped.

ANNUAL EXPENSES. Tuition and fees: $2,250, $1,845 additional for out-of-state students. **Room and board:** $3,165. **Books and supplies:** $525. **Other expenses:** $1,230.

FINANCIAL AID. 30% of freshmen, 50% of continuing students receive some form of aid. Grants, loans, jobs available. Academic, music/drama, minority scholarships available. **Aid applications:** No closing date; priority given to applications received by March 1; applicants notified on a rolling basis beginning on or about May 1; must reply within 2 weeks.

ADDRESS/TELEPHONE. Dr. Claire Swann, Director of Undergraduate Admissions, University of Georgia, Academic Building, Athens, GA 30602. (706) 542-8776.

Valdosta State College
Valdosta, Georgia — CB code: 5855

Admissions:	70% of applicants accepted
Based on:	••• School record, test scores
Completion:	88% of freshmen end year in good standing
	15% enter graduate study

4-year public college of arts and sciences and art, business, music, nursing, liberal arts, teachers college, coed. Founded in 1906. **Accreditation:** Regional. **Undergraduate enrollment:** 5,448 men and women full time; 1,282 men and women part time. **Graduate enrollment:** 430 men and women full time; 738 men and women part time. **Faculty:** 390 total (315 full time), 247 with doctorates or other terminal degrees. **Location:** Suburban campus in large town; 235 miles from Atlanta. **Calendar:** Quarter, extensive summer session. **Microcomputers:** 35 located in libraries, classrooms, computer centers. **Special facilities:** Planetarium, art gallery.

DEGREES OFFERED. AA, AS, BA, BS, MA, MS, MEd. 28 associate degrees awarded in 1992. 939 bachelor's degrees awarded. Graduate degrees offered in 25 major fields of study.

UNDERGRADUATE MAJORS. Associate: Business data processing and related programs, emergency medical technologies, engineering and engineering-related technologies, liberal/general studies. **Bachelor's:** Accounting, anthropology, applied mathematics, art education, astronomy, biology, business administration and management, business economics, business education, chemistry, communications, computer and information sciences, computer programming, criminology, dramatic arts, early childhood education, educational supervision, elementary education, English, English education, finance, foreign languages education, French, history, junior high education, law enforcement and corrections, liberal/general studies, marketing and distribution, marketing management, mathematics, mathematics education, music, music education, music performance, nursing, philosophy, physical education, physics, political science and government, preengineering, prelaw, psychology, radio/television broadcasting, school psychology, science education, secondary education, secretarial and related programs, social studies education, sociology, Spanish, special education, speech correction, sports medicine, telecommunications.

ACADEMIC PROGRAMS. 2-year transfer program, cooperative education, double major, dual enrollment of high school students, education specialist degree, honors program, independent study, internships, study abroad, teacher preparation; liberal arts/career combination in engineering. **Remedial services:** Learning center, remedial instruction, special counselor, tutoring. **ROTC:** Air Force. **Placement/credit:** AP, CLEP Subject, institutional tests; 45 credit hours maximum for bachelor's degree.

ACADEMIC REQUIREMENTS. Freshmen must earn minimum GPA of 1.6 to continue in good standing. 60% of freshmen return for sophomore year. Students must declare major by end of second year. **Graduation requirements:** 183 hours for bachelor's (93 in major). Most students required to take courses in arts/fine arts, English, history, humanities, mathematics, biological/physical sciences, social sciences.

FRESHMAN ADMISSIONS. Selection criteria: Minimum SAT-verbal score of 400 or ACT English of 21, or SAT-mathematical score of 400 or ACT mathematical of 19, or 2.0 high school GPA. **High school preparation:** 15 units required. Required units include English 4, foreign language 2, mathematics 3, social science 3 and science 3. **Test requirements:** SAT or ACT; score report by September 1.

1992 FRESHMAN CLASS PROFILE. 1,415 men applied, 1,042 accepted, 420 enrolled; 1,859 women applied, 1,260 accepted, 504 enrolled. **Characteristics:** 80% from in state, 65% commute, 15% have minority backgrounds, 15% join fraternities/sororities. Average age is 19.

FALL-TERM APPLICATIONS. $10 fee. Closing date September 1; applicants notified on a rolling basis; must reply by September 1. Deferred and early admission available.

STUDENT LIFE. Housing: Dormitories (men, women, coed); apartment, fraternity, sorority, handicapped housing available. **Activities:** Student government, magazine, radio, student newspaper, television, choral groups, concert band, drama, jazz band, marching band, music ensembles, musical theater, pep band, fraternities, sororities, Black Student League, several religious and social service organizations.

ATHLETICS. NCAA. **Intercollegiate:** Baseball M, basketball, cross-country, football M, golf M, softball W, tennis. **Intramural:** Badminton, basketball, cross-country, soccer, softball, tennis, volleyball.

STUDENT SERVICES. Aptitude testing, career counseling, employment service for undergraduates, freshman orientation, health services, personal counseling, placement service for graduates, special adviser for adult students, veterans counselor, services/facilities for handicapped.

ANNUAL EXPENSES. Tuition and fees (projected): $1,731, $1,380 additional for out-of-state students. **Room and board:** $2,913. **Books and supplies:** $600. **Other expenses:** $636.

FINANCIAL AID. 36% of freshmen, 36% of continuing students receive some form of aid. 82% of grants, 84% of loans, 27% of jobs based on need. 575 enrolled freshmen were judged to have need, all were offered aid. Academic, music/drama, art, athletic, leadership, alumni affiliation scholarships available. **Aid applications:** No closing date; priority given to applications received by May 1; applicants notified on a rolling basis beginning on or about June 1; must reply within 2 weeks.

ADDRESS/TELEPHONE. Walter H. Peacock, Director of Admissions, Valdosta State College, Valdosta, GA 31698. (912) 333-5791. Fax: (912) 333-7408.

Waycross College
Waycross, Georgia — CB code: 5889

2-year public community, junior college, coed. Founded in 1976. **Accreditation:** Regional. **Undergraduate enrollment:** 888 men and women. **Faculty:** 44 total (28 full time), 10 with doctorates or other terminal degrees. **Location:** Rural campus in large town; 70 miles from Jacksonville, Florida. **Cal-**

endar: Quarter, limited summer session. **Microcomputers:** 43 located in computer centers. **Special facilities:** Repository of materials about the Okefenokee Swamp.

DEGREES OFFERED. AA, AS, AAS. 90 associate degrees awarded in 1992. 29% in business and management, 20% education, 6% health sciences, 7% allied health, 7% mathematics, 13% psychology, 6% social sciences.

UNDERGRADUATE MAJORS. Biology, business and management, child development/care/guidance, clinical laboratory science, computer programming, criminology, early childhood education, education, education administration, electronic technology, elementary education, English, forest products processing technology, history, junior high education, liberal/general studies, mathematics, medical laboratory technologies, physical sciences, political science and government, psychology, secondary education, secretarial and related programs, social sciences, sociology, speech.

ACADEMIC PROGRAMS. 2-year transfer program, dual enrollment of high school students, independent study, study abroad, 2-2 program in engineering technologies through Southern Technical Institute, cooperative nursing programs (RN) with South Georgia College and Valdosta State College, 2-2 program in Criminal Justice with Albany State College. **Remedial services:** Learning center, reduced course load, remedial instruction, tutoring. **Placement/credit:** AP, CLEP General and Subject, institutional tests; 25 credit hours maximum for associate degree.

ACADEMIC REQUIREMENTS. Freshmen must earn minimum GPA of 1.7 to continue in good standing. 40% of freshmen return for sophomore year. Students must declare major by end of first year. **Graduation requirements:** 97 hours for associate (30 in major). Most students required to take courses in English, history, mathematics, biological/physical sciences, social sciences.

FRESHMAN ADMISSIONS. Selection criteria: Minimum of 200 SAT verbal and 280 SAT math required. **High school preparation:** 15 units required. Required units include English 4, foreign language 2, mathematics 3, social science 3 and science 3. **Test requirements:** SAT or ACT (SAT preferred); score report by September 21.

1992 FRESHMAN CLASS PROFILE. 317 men and women enrolled. 25% had high school GPA of 3.0 or higher, 70% between 2.0 and 2.99. **Characteristics:** 99% from in state, 100% commute, 11% have minority backgrounds, 1% are foreign students. Average age is 19.

FALL-TERM APPLICATIONS. No fee. Closing date September 21; applicants notified on a rolling basis. Essay required of low-scoring SAT-verbal or ACT English applicants and those who have not completed 4 years high school English. Deferred and early admission available. Students not meeting required college-preparatory units may be provisionally admitted.

STUDENT LIFE. Activities: Student government, student newspaper, choral groups, drama, jazz band, music ensembles, Baptist Student Union, Black Student Alliance.

ATHLETICS. NJCAA. **Intercollegiate:** Golf M, softball W, tennis. **Intramural:** Basketball, bowling, racquetball, softball, table tennis, tennis, volleyball.

STUDENT SERVICES. Aptitude testing, career counseling, freshman orientation, personal counseling, veterans counselor, services/facilities for handicapped.

ANNUAL EXPENSES. Tuition and fees: $1,134, $939 additional for out-of-state students. **Books and supplies:** $500. **Other expenses:** $900.

FINANCIAL AID. 26% of continuing students receive some form of aid. 89% of grants, 86% of loans, 45% of jobs based on need. 148 enrolled freshmen were judged to have need, 140 were offered aid. Academic, music/drama, art, athletic, state/district residency scholarships available. **Aid applications:** Closing date September 19; applicants notified on a rolling basis beginning on or about August 1; must reply within 2 weeks.

ADDRESS/TELEPHONE. George E. Norton, Director of Admissions, Waycross College, 2001 Francis Street, Waycross, GA 31501. (912) 285-6133. Fax: (912) 287-4909.

Wesleyan College

Macon, Georgia — CB code: 5895

Admissions: 93% of applicants accepted
Based on:
- ••• Interview, school record
- •• Activities, recommendations, special talents, test scores
- • Essay

Completion: 88% of freshmen end year in good standing
55% graduate, 36% of these enter graduate study

4-year private liberal arts college, women only, affiliated with United Methodist Church. Founded in 1836. **Accreditation:** Regional. **Undergraduate enrollment:** 418 women full time; 66 women part time. **Faculty:** 72 total (47 full time), 33 with doctorates or other terminal degrees. **Location:** Suburban campus in small city; 90 miles from Atlanta. **Calendar:** Semester. **Microcomputers:** 430 located in dormitories, classrooms, computer centers. Lease or purchase required**Special facilities:** Museum, 2 art galleries, equestrian facilities, fitness center.

DEGREES OFFERED. BA. 100 bachelor's degrees awarded in 1992. 11% in business and management, 14% communications, 10% education, 10% letters/literature, 9% life sciences, 12% psychology, 12% social sciences, 9% visual and performing arts.

UNDERGRADUATE MAJORS. Art history, biology, business administration and management, chemistry, communications, early childhood education, education, elementary education, engineering, English, English education, history, international relations, journalism, liberal/general studies, mathematics, mathematics education, music, philosophy, political science and government, predentistry, prelaw, premedicine, prepharmacy, preveterinary, psychology, public relations, religion, science education, secondary education, social science education, sociology, Spanish, speech, studio art, visual and performing arts.

ACADEMIC PROGRAMS. Double major, dual enrollment of high school students, honors program, independent study, internships, student-designed major, study abroad, teacher preparation, visiting/exchange student program, Washington semester; liberal arts/career combination in engineering. **Remedial services:** Reduced course load, special counselor, tutoring. **Placement/credit:** AP, CLEP General and Subject, IB, institutional tests; 30 credit hours maximum for bachelor's degree.

ACADEMIC REQUIREMENTS. Freshmen must earn minimum GPA of 1.7 to continue in good standing. 75% of freshmen return for sophomore year. Students must declare major by end of second year. **Graduation requirements:** 120 hours for bachelor's (30 in major). Most students required to take courses in arts/fine arts, English, foreign languages, history, humanities, mathematics, biological/physical sciences, social sciences. **Postgraduate studies:** 10% enter law school, 10% enter medical school, 6% enter MBA programs, 10% enter other graduate study. **Additional information:** Self-designed interdisciplinary major, honors program.

FRESHMAN ADMISSIONS. Selection criteria: Academic achievement and interview most important, followed by test scores, and recommendations. Leadership achievement is also considered. **High school preparation:** 16 units required. Required units include English 4, mathematics 3, social science 3 and science 2. **Test requirements:** SAT or ACT; score report by August 15.

1992 FRESHMAN CLASS PROFILE. 341 women applied, 316 accepted, 135 enrolled. 67% had high school GPA of 3.0 or higher, 30% between 2.0 and 2.99. **Academic background:** Mid 50% of enrolled freshmen had SAT-V between 450-600, SAT-M between 450-600. 96% submitted SAT scores. **Characteristics:** 47% from in state, 93% live in college housing, 24% have minority backgrounds, 3% are foreign students. Average age is 18.

FALL-TERM APPLICATIONS. $25 fee, may be waived for applicants with need. Closing date March 1; applicants notified on or about April 1; must reply by May 1 or within 4 weeks if notified thereafter. Audition required for music, theater applicants. Portfolio required for art applicants. Essay required. Interview recommended. CRDA. Deferred and early admission available. EDP-S. Early decision application date November 1—notification by December 1. Regular decision application date March 1—notification by April 1.

STUDENT LIFE. Housing: Dormitories (women). Students required to live on campus unless married or living with family in the local area. **Activities:** Student government, magazine, student newspaper, yearbook, choral groups, drama, music ensembles, musical theater, symphony orchestra, washboard band, Student Honor Council, religious council and groups, Mortar Board, honorary fraternities, Black Student Alliance, International Club. **Additional information:** Entering freshmen receive Macintosh Plus and printer as part of their tuition package.

ATHLETICS. Intercollegiate: Basketball, horseback riding, soccer, tennis, volleyball. **Intramural:** Archery, basketball, horseback riding, soccer, softball, swimming, tennis, volleyball.

STUDENT SERVICES. Aptitude testing, career counseling, employment service for undergraduates, freshman orientation, health services, personal counseling, placement service for graduates, special adviser for adult students.

ANNUAL EXPENSES. Tuition and fees (1992-93): $10,495. **Room and board:** $4,100. **Books and supplies:** $515. **Other expenses:** $957.

FINANCIAL AID. 86% of freshmen, 97% of continuing students receive some form of aid. 93% of grants, 96% of loans, 37% of jobs based on need. 111 enrolled freshmen were judged to have need, 82 were offered aid. Academic, music/drama, art, leadership, alumni affiliation, religious affiliation scholarships available. **Aid applications:** No closing date; priority given to applications received by April 1; applicants notified on a rolling basis beginning on or about February 15; must reply by May 1 or within 4 weeks if notified thereafter.

ADDRESS/TELEPHONE. E. Norman Jones, Dean of Admissions and Financial Planning, Wesleyan College, 4760 Forsyth Road, Macon, GA 31297-4299. (912) 477-1110 ext. 206. (800) 447-6610. Fax: (912) 477-7572.

West Georgia College

Carrollton, Georgia CB code: 5900

Admissions: 89% of applicants accepted
Based on: ••• School record, test scores
Completion: 48% of freshmen end year in good standing
29% graduate

4-year public liberal arts college, coed. Founded in 1933. **Accreditation:** Regional. **Undergraduate enrollment:** 1,902 men, 2,610 women full time; 506 men, 1,031 women part time. **Graduate enrollment:** 45 men, 79 women full time; 319 men, 1,225 women part time. **Faculty:** 355 total (307 full time), 209 with doctorates or other terminal degrees. **Location:** Suburban campus in large town; 50 miles from Atlanta. **Calendar:** Quarter, extensive summer session. Extensive evening/early morning classes. **Microcomputers:** 236 located in libraries, classrooms, computer centers. **Special facilities:** Observatory, performing arts center, Anthonio J. Waring, Jr. archaeological laboratory. **Additional facts:** Off-campus sites in Dalton (graduate) and Newman (undergraduate).

DEGREES OFFERED. AS, AAS, BA, BS, BFA, MA, MS, MBA, MEd. 41 associate degrees awarded in 1992. 94% in health sciences. 849 bachelor's degrees awarded. 19% in business and management, 16% business/office and marketing/distribution, 5% communications, 21% teacher education, 11% psychology, 9% social sciences. Graduate degrees offered in 24 major fields of study.

UNDERGRADUATE MAJORS. Associate: Computer and information sciences, criminal justice studies, nursing, secretarial and related programs. **Bachelor's:** Accounting, anthropology, biology, business administration and management, business economics, business education, chemistry, communications, computer and information sciences, criminal justice studies, dramatic arts, earth sciences, economics, education of exceptional children, education of the mentally handicapped, elementary education, English, finance, fine arts, French, geography, geology, history, junior high education, liberal/general studies, management information systems, marketing and distribution, mathematics, music education, music performance, music theory and composition, nursing, office supervision and management, philosophy, physical education, physics, political science and government, psychology, real estate, recreation and community services technologies, science education, secondary education, social science education, sociology, Spanish, special education, speech.

ACADEMIC PROGRAMS. Accelerated program, cooperative education, double major, dual enrollment of high school students, education specialist degree, external degree, honors program, independent study, internships, study abroad, teacher preparation, Washington semester; liberal arts/career combination in engineering, health sciences, business. **Remedial services:** Learning center, preadmission summer program, reduced course load, remedial instruction, special counselor, tutoring. **ROTC:** Army. **Placement/credit:** AP, CLEP General and Subject, institutional tests; 45 credit hours maximum for associate degree; 45 credit hours maximum for bachelor's degree.

ACADEMIC REQUIREMENTS. Freshmen must earn minimum GPA of 1.6 to continue in good standing. 52% of freshmen return for sophomore year. Students must declare major by end of second year. **Graduation requirements:** 90 hours for associate, 190 hours for bachelor's. Most students required to take courses in English, history, humanities, mathematics, philosophy/religion, biological/physical sciences, social sciences.

FRESHMAN ADMISSIONS. Selection criteria: Minimum high school GPA of 2.5 and test scores. **High school preparation:** 18 units required. Required and recommended units include English 4, foreign language 2-4, mathematics 3-3, physical science 1-1, social science 3-4 and science 2-3. Biological science 4 recommended. Mathematics units should include 2 algebra, 1 geometry. Science units should include 2 laboratory science and 1 physical science. Social science units should include 1 American history, 1 world history, .5 economics, .5 government. Additional courses in trigonometry, lab course in science, foreign language, computers, and typing are recommended. **Test requirements:** SAT or ACT; score report by July 1. ACH required if English or math is an area of deficiency.

1992 FRESHMAN CLASS PROFILE. 1,540 men applied, 1,370 accepted, 551 enrolled; 1,961 women applied, 1,743 accepted, 709 enrolled. 28% had high school GPA of 3.0 or higher, 54% between 2.0 and 2.99. **Academic background:** Mid 50% of enrolled freshmen had SAT-V between 340-440, SAT-M between 370-490; ACT composite between 17-21. 93% submitted SAT scores, 7% submitted ACT scores. **Characteristics:** 96% from in state, 67% live in college housing, 23% have minority backgrounds, 1% are foreign students. Average age is 18.

FALL-TERM APPLICATIONS. $10 fee, may be waived for applicants with need. Closing date September 1; applicants notified on a rolling basis beginning on or about October 1. Early admission available.

STUDENT LIFE. Housing: Dormitories (men, women, coed); sorority housing available. All freshmen required to reside on campus unless married or living with parents, relatives, or legal guardians. **Activities:** Student government, magazine, radio, student newspaper, television, choral groups, concert band, dance, drama, jazz band, marching band, music ensembles, musical theater, opera, fraternities, sororities, Baptist, Episcopal, Methodist, and Presbyterian student organizations, Black Students Alliance, Democratic organization, Republican organization.

ATHLETICS. NCAA. **Intercollegiate:** Baseball M, basketball, cross-country, football M, golf M, softball W, tennis, volleyball W. **Intramural:** Badminton, basketball, bowling, cross-country, golf, soccer, softball, swimming, table tennis, tennis, volleyball, water polo, wrestling M.

STUDENT SERVICES. Aptitude testing, career counseling, employment service for undergraduates, freshman orientation, health services, on-campus day care, personal counseling, placement service for graduates, special adviser for adult students, veterans counselor, services/facilities for handicapped.

ANNUAL EXPENSES. Tuition and fees (projected): $1,497, $1,380 additional for out-of-state students. **Room and board:** $2,436. **Books and supplies:** $450. **Other expenses:** $1,000.

FINANCIAL AID. 45% of freshmen, 45% of continuing students receive some form of aid. 73% of grants, 91% of loans, 22% of jobs based on need. 513 enrolled freshmen were judged to have need, all were offered aid. Academic, music/drama, art, athletic, state/district residency, alumni affiliation, minority scholarships available. **Aid applications:** No closing date; priority given to applications received by March 15; applicants notified on a rolling basis beginning on or about June 1; must reply within 3 weeks.

ADDRESS/TELEPHONE. Jennifer W. Payne, Director of Admissions, West Georgia College, Carrollton, GA 30118-0001. (404) 836-6416. Fax: (404) 836-6720.

Young Harris College

Young Harris, Georgia CB code: 5990

Admissions: 86% of applicants accepted
Based on: ••• School record
•• Test scores
• Activities, essay, interview, recommendations
Completion: 82% of freshmen end year in good standing
93% enter 4-year programs

2-year private junior, liberal arts college, coed, affiliated with United Methodist Church. Founded in 1886. **Accreditation:** Regional. **Undergraduate enrollment:** 261 men, 260 women full time. **Faculty:** 32 total (28 full time). **Location:** Rural campus in rural community; 110 miles from Atlanta. **Calendar:** Quarter, limited summer session. **Microcomputers:** 40 located in classrooms, computer centers. **Special facilities:** Planetarium, art gallery.

DEGREES OFFERED. AA, AS. 115 associate degrees awarded in 1992.

UNDERGRADUATE MAJORS. Agribusiness, agricultural economics, agricultural sciences, art history, biological and physical sciences, biology, business and management, chemistry, communications, dramatic arts, education, English, fine arts, forestry and related sciences, French, history, home economics, journalism, liberal/general studies, mathematics, music, music history and appreciation, parks and recreation management, philosophy, physical sciences, physics, political science and government, prelaw, psychology, religion, social sciences, sociology, Spanish, speech, visual and performing arts.

ACADEMIC PROGRAMS. 2-year transfer program, dual enrollment of high school students, independent study, internships, study abroad. **Remedial services:** Preadmission summer program, reduced course load, remedial instruction, English and mathematics laboratory. **Placement/credit:** AP, CLEP Subject, institutional tests.

ACADEMIC REQUIREMENTS. Freshmen must earn minimum GPA of 1.5 to continue in good standing. 72% of freshmen return for sophomore year. **Graduation requirements:** 93 hours for associate. Most students required to take courses in English, history, mathematics, philosophy/religion, biological/physical sciences, social sciences.

FRESHMAN ADMISSIONS. Selection criteria: High school record, test scores, interview considered. Conditional admission possible. **Test requirements:** SAT or ACT (SAT preferred); score report by May 1.

1992 FRESHMAN CLASS PROFILE. 304 men applied, 248 accepted, 168 enrolled; 331 women applied, 301 accepted, 162 enrolled. **Academic background:** Mid 50% of enrolled freshmen had SAT-V between 460-600, SAT-M between 460-500. 85% submitted SAT scores. **Characteristics:** 93% from in state, 90% live in college housing, 1% have minority backgrounds, 1% are foreign students, 36% join fraternities/sororities. Average age is 18.

FALL-TERM APPLICATIONS. $25 fee. No closing date; applicants notified on a rolling basis; must reply by May 1 or within 3 weeks if notified thereafter. Interview recommended for academically weak applicants. CRDA. Deferred and early admission available.

STUDENT LIFE. Housing: Dormitories (men, women, coed). All single freshmen and sophomores not living with family must reside in college dormitories. **Activities:** Student government, student newspaper, yearbook, literary review, choral groups, dance, drama, music ensembles, musical theater, opera, fraternities, sororities, Ministerial Conference, Methodist Youth Fellowship, Baptist Student Union, Vespers, honorary service organizations.

ATHLETICS. NJCAA. **Intercollegiate:** Baseball M, soccer M, softball W, tennis. **Intramural:** Archery, badminton, basketball, cross-country, golf

M, soccer M, softball, swimming, table tennis, tennis, track and field M, volleyball, water polo M.

STUDENT SERVICES. Career counseling, freshman orientation, health services, personal counseling.

ANNUAL EXPENSES. Tuition and fees (projected): $5,000. **Room and board:** $3,605. **Books and supplies:** $500. **Other expenses:** $900.

FINANCIAL AID. 71% of continuing students receive some form of aid. 46% of grants, 93% of loans, 75% of jobs based on need. Academic, music/drama, art, athletic, state/district residency, leadership scholarships available. **Aid applications:** Closing date July 1; priority given to applications received by May 1; applicants notified on a rolling basis beginning on or about March 1; must reply by May 1 or within 2 weeks if notified thereafter.

ADDRESS/TELEPHONE. George L. Dyer, Director of Admissions, Young Harris College, PO Box 116, Young Harris, GA 30582-0116. (706) 379-3111. (800) 241-3754. Fax: (706) 379-4203.

Hawaii

Brigham Young University-Hawaii
Laie, Hawaii CB code: 4106

Admissions: 51% of applicants accepted
Based on: ••• Interview, recommendations, religious affiliation/commitment, school record, test scores
•• Essay
• Activities, special talents
Completion: 80% of freshmen end year in good standing
30% enter graduate study

4-year private liberal arts college, coed, affiliated with Church of Jesus Christ of Latter-day Saints. Founded in 1955. **Accreditation:** Regional. **Undergraduate enrollment:** 818 men, 1,164 women full time; 40 men, 48 women part time. **Faculty:** 149 total (102 full time), 65 with doctorates or other terminal degrees. **Location:** Rural campus in small town; 35 miles from Honolulu. **Calendar:** 4-4-2. **Microcomputers:** 60 located in dormitories, libraries, classrooms, computer centers, campus-wide network. **Special facilities:** Natural history museum, planetarium. **Additional facts:** International campus with students from more than 50 countries.

DEGREES OFFERED. AA, AS, BA, BS. 50 associate degrees awarded in 1992. 17% in business and management, 22% business/office and marketing/distribution, 17% computer sciences, 6% teacher education, 6% home economics, 14% letters/literature, 5% trade and industry, 13% visual and performing arts. 200 bachelor's degrees awarded. 34% in business and management, 13% business/office and marketing/distribution, 11% computer sciences, 11% education, 9% letters/literature, 12% social sciences.

UNDERGRADUATE MAJORS. Associate: Accounting, business and office, business computer/console/peripheral equipment operation, child development/care/guidance, commercial art, communications, computer and information sciences, dramatic arts, graphic arts technology, music, music performance, secretarial and related programs, speech, transportation and travel marketing. **Bachelor's:** Accounting, art education, art history, biology, business administration and management, business and management, business and office, business computer/console/peripheral equipment operation, business data processing and related programs, business education, chemistry, computer and information sciences, education, elementary education, English, fine arts, history, hotel/motel and restaurant management, human resources development, information sciences and systems, junior high education, mathematics, mathematics education, physical education, physical sciences, political science and government, science education, secondary education, secretarial and related programs, social science education, social work, teaching English as a second language/foreign language, transportation and travel marketing, visual and performing arts.

ACADEMIC PROGRAMS. Cooperative education, dual enrollment of high school students, education specialist degree, honors program, internships, teacher preparation, visiting/exchange student program. **Remedial services:** Learning center, preadmission summer program, reduced course load, remedial instruction, special counselor, tutoring. **Placement/credit:** AP, CLEP General and Subject, institutional tests.

ACADEMIC REQUIREMENTS. Freshmen must earn minimum GPA of 2.0 to continue in good standing. 53% of freshmen return for sophomore year. Students must declare major on enrollment. **Graduation requirements:** 64 hours for associate, 128 hours for bachelor's. Most students required to take courses in arts/fine arts, computer science, English, foreign languages, history, humanities, mathematics, philosophy/religion, biological/physical sciences, social sciences. **Postgraduate studies:** 80% from 2-year programs enter 4-year programs. 1% enter law school, 1% enter medical school, 5% enter MBA programs, 23% enter other graduate study. **Additional information:** University has a special mission to educate students from Asia and the Pacific Islands. Polynesian Cultural Center provides employment and educational opportunities.

FRESHMAN ADMISSIONS. Selection criteria: Interview and recommendations very important. Test scores important. 3.0 GPA required for local students, 3.25 for others. **Test requirements:** ACT; score report by August 15.

1992 FRESHMAN CLASS PROFILE. 531 men applied, 243 accepted, 191 enrolled; 767 women applied, 423 accepted, 359 enrolled. 58% had high school GPA of 3.0 or higher, 41% between 2.0 and 2.99. **Academic background:** Mid 50% of enrolled freshmen had ACT composite between 15-22. 60% submitted ACT scores. **Characteristics:** 30% from in state, 85% live in college housing, 49% have minority backgrounds, 40% are foreign students. Average age is 19.

FALL-TERM APPLICATIONS. $10 fee. Closing date March 31; applicants notified on a rolling basis beginning on or about April 15; must reply by August 30. Interview required. Essay required. Portfolio recommended. Early admission available.

STUDENT LIFE. Housing: Dormitories (men, women); apartment housing available. All first-time, nonlocal freshmen required to live on campus until sophomore standing achieved. **Activities:** Student government, film, student newspaper, television, yearbook, choral groups, concert band, dance, drama, jazz band, music ensembles, musical theater, pep band, 17 ethnic and cultural clubs representing the Pacific Islands and Asian rim, 13 Wards and 2 Stakes (church-related). **Additional information:** Religious observance required.

ATHLETICS. NAIA. **Intercollegiate:** Basketball M, cross-country, rugby M, softball W, tennis, volleyball W. **Intramural:** Badminton, basketball, bowling, racquetball, rugby M, soccer M, softball, swimming, table tennis, tennis, track and field, volleyball.

STUDENT SERVICES. Aptitude testing, career counseling, employment service for undergraduates, freshman orientation, health services, personal counseling, placement service for graduates, veterans counselor, peer counseling, services/facilities for handicapped.

ANNUAL EXPENSES. Tuition and fees (1992-93): $2,125. $1000 additional tuition per year for students who are not members of Church of Jesus Christ of Latter-day Saints. $150 per credit hour for nonmembers. **Room and board:** $3,840. **Books and supplies:** $450. **Other expenses:** $1,000.

FINANCIAL AID. 80% of freshmen, 80% of continuing students receive some form of aid. 71% of grants, all loans based on need. All jobs based on criteria other than need. 400 enrolled freshmen were judged to have need, all were offered aid. Academic, music/drama, art, athletic, leadership, religious affiliation, minority scholarships available. **Aid applications:** Closing date July 31; applicants notified on or about July 31; must reply by August 31. **Additional information:** Closing date for scholarship applications May 1.

ADDRESS/TELEPHONE. David Settle, Asst Dean for Admissions/Records, Brigham Young University-Hawaii, BYU Box 1973, Laie, HI 96762-1294. (808) 293-3738.

Cannon's International Business College of Honolulu
Honolulu, Hawaii CB code: 4324

2-year proprietary junior college, coed. **Undergraduate enrollment:** 71 men, 227 women full time; 31 men, 154 women part time. **Location:** Urban campus in large city. **Calendar:** Quarter.

FRESHMAN ADMISSIONS. Selection criteria: Open admissions. Entrance examination used to determine if applicants are accepted in good standing or on provisional status. Placement tests administered for mathematics, reading, or English to determine if remedial courses will be a condition of enrollment.

ANNUAL EXPENSES. Tuition and fees (1992-93): $6,820. Tuition and fees are for 4 quarters (12 months). **Books and supplies:** $1,000. **Other expenses:** $1,200.

ADDRESS/TELEPHONE. Richard S.K. Young, Director of Admissions, Cannon's International Business College of Honolulu, 1500 Kapiolani Boulevard, Honolulu, HI 96814-3715. (808) 955-1500. Fax: (808)955-6964.

Chaminade University of Honolulu
Honolulu, Hawaii CB code: 4105

4-year private university, coed, affiliated with Roman Catholic Church. Founded in 1955. **Accreditation:** Regional. **Undergraduate enrollment:** 1,920 men and women. **Graduate enrollment:** 350 men and women. **Location:** Suburban campus in large city; 2 miles from Waikiki, 4 miles from downtown. **Calendar:** Semester. **Additional facts:** Campus shared with St. Louis School. 9 off-campus sites on Oahu military bases.

FRESHMAN ADMISSIONS. Selection criteria: School achievement record, test scores, statement of purpose.

ANNUAL EXPENSES. Tuition and fees (1992-93): $8,500. **Room and board:** $4,280. **Books and supplies:** $500. **Other expenses:** $800.

ADDRESS/TELEPHONE. Faye E. Conquest, Director of Admissions, Chaminade University of Honolulu, 3140 Waialae Avenue, Honolulu, HI 96816-1578. (808) 735-4735. (800) 735-3733. Fax: (808) 739-4647.

Hawaii Pacific University
Honolulu, Hawaii CB code: 4352

Admissions: 78% of applicants accepted
Based on: ••• School record
•• Activities, interview, recommendations, test scores
• Special talents
Completion: 80% of freshmen end year in good standing
60% enter graduate study

4-year private business, liberal arts college, coed. Founded in 1965. **Accreditation:** Regional. **Undergraduate enrollment:** 2,319 men, 1,797 women full time; 1,196 men, 828 women part time. **Graduate enrollment:** 195 men, 162 women full time; 302 men, 147 women part time. **Faculty:** 396 total (139 full time), 207 with doctorates or other terminal degrees. **Location:** Urban campus in large city. **Calendar:** 4-1-4, limited summer session. Saturday and extensive evening/early morning classes. **Microcomputers:** 200 located in libraries, classrooms, computer centers. **Special facilities:** Art gallery. **Additional facts:** Programs offered for military personnel and their dependents, and for older students. Satellite campus on 8 military installations on the island of Oahu. Branch campus 8 miles from downtown Honolulu.

DEGREES OFFERED. AS, BA, BS, MA, MS, MBA. 324 associate degrees awarded in 1992. 80% in business and management, 20% computer sciences. 557 bachelor's degrees awarded. 42% in business and management, 8% business/office and marketing/distribution, 26% computer sciences, 5% health sciences, 5% psychology, 5% social sciences. Graduate degrees offered in 12 major fields of study.

UNDERGRADUATE MAJORS. Associate: Accounting, business administration and management, business and management, business and office, business computer/console/peripheral equipment operation, business data processing and related programs, business data programming, business economics, computer programming, computer technology, finance, marketing and distribution, mathematics, systems analysis, trade and industrial supervision and management. **Bachelor's:** Accounting, American literature, American studies, anthropology, Asian studies, business administration and management, business and management, business economics, communications, computer and information sciences, computer programming, computer technology, credit management, criminal justice studies, economics, English, English education, entrepreneurial studies, family and community services, finance, history, hotel/motel and restaurant management, human resources development, humanities, humanities and social sciences, industrial and organizational psychology, international business management, international relations, international studies, labor/industrial relations, liberal/general studies, management information systems, marine biology, marketing and distribution, marketing management, mathematics, nursing, organizational behavior, Pacific area studies, personnel management, political science and government, prelaw, psychology, public administration, public relations, small business management and ownership, social sciences, sociology, systems analysis, teaching English as a second language/foreign language.

ACADEMIC PROGRAMS. Accelerated program, cooperative education, double major, dual enrollment of high school students, honors program, independent study, internships, student-designed major, teacher preparation, weekend college; liberal arts/career combination in business; combined bachelor's/graduate program in business administration. **Remedial services:** Learning center, preadmission summer program, reduced course load, remedial instruction, special counselor, tutoring. **ROTC:** Air Force, Army. **Placement/credit:** AP, CLEP General and Subject, IB, institutional tests; 36 credit hours maximum for associate degree; 36 credit hours maximum for bachelor's degree.

ACADEMIC REQUIREMENTS. Freshmen must earn minimum GPA of 2.0 to continue in good standing. 70% of freshmen return for sophomore year. Students must declare major by end of second year. **Graduation requirements:** 60 hours for associate (15 in major), 124 hours for bachelor's (30 in major). Most students required to take courses in computer science, English, history, humanities, mathematics, philosophy/religion, biological/physical sciences, social sciences. **Postgraduate studies:** 65% from 2-year programs enter 4-year programs. 5% enter law school, 45% enter MBA programs, 10% enter other graduate study.

FRESHMAN ADMISSIONS. Selection criteria: High school academic record, test scores, recommendations, and interview of equal importance. **High school preparation:** 20 units recommended. Recommended units include English 4, foreign language 2, mathematics 3 and science 2. Nursing and marine science majors must have additional high school science and mathematics courses.

1992 FRESHMAN CLASS PROFILE. 2,900 men and women applied, 2,266 accepted; 1,016 men enrolled, 783 women enrolled. 38% had high school GPA of 3.0 or higher, 58% between 2.0 and 2.99. **Academic background:** Mid 50% of enrolled freshmen had SAT-V between 400-510, SAT-M between 410-560; ACT composite between 18-23. 65% submitted SAT scores, 4% submitted ACT scores. **Characteristics:** 40% from in state, 90% commute, 36% have minority backgrounds, 15% are foreign students. Average age is 20.

FALL-TERM APPLICATIONS. $50 fee. No closing date; priority given to applications received by August 15; applicants notified on a rolling basis beginning on or about March 1; must reply by registration. Interview recommended. Deferred and early admission available. SAT or ACT strongly recommended.

STUDENT LIFE. Housing: Dormitories (women, coed); apartment housing available. Homestay program also available. **Activities:** Student government, magazine, student newspaper, choral groups, drama, music ensembles, pep band, Rotaract, President's Hosts, International Student Organization, Christian Fellowship, American Marketing Association, Travel Industry Management Student Organization, honors club, student business organization, ethnic clubs.

ATHLETICS. NAIA. **Intercollegiate:** Baseball M, basketball M, cross-country, soccer M, softball W, tennis, volleyball W. **Intramural:** Soccer M.

STUDENT SERVICES. Aptitude testing, career counseling, employment service for undergraduates, freshman orientation, personal counseling, placement service for graduates, special adviser for adult students, veterans counselor, services/facilities for handicapped.

ANNUAL EXPENSES. Tuition and fees: $5,900. **Room and board:** $5,600. **Books and supplies:** $600. **Other expenses:** $900.

FINANCIAL AID. 25% of freshmen, 16% of continuing students receive some form of aid. 60% of grants, 83% of loans, all jobs based on need. 171 enrolled freshmen were judged to have need, all were offered aid. Academic, music/drama, athletic, religious affiliation scholarships available. **Aid applications:** No closing date; priority given to applications received by March 15; applicants notified on a rolling basis beginning on or about April 15.

ADDRESS/TELEPHONE. Don D. Barlow, Director of Admissions, Hawaii Pacific University, 1164 Bishop Street, Honolulu, HI 96813. (808) 544-0249. (800) 669-4724. Fax: (808) 544-1136.

University of Hawaii: Hawaii Community College
Hilo, Hawaii — CB code: 1801

2-year public community college. **Accreditation:** Regional. **Undergraduate enrollment:** 2,287 men and women. **Faculty:** 100 total. **Location:** Rural campus in large town; 200 miles from Honolulu. **Microcomputers:** Located in libraries, classrooms, computer centers.

DEGREES OFFERED. AA, AS. 230 associate degrees awarded in 1992.

UNDERGRADUATE MAJORS. Accounting, agricultural production, automotive mechanics, business data processing and related programs, carpentry, criminal justice studies, diesel engine mechanics, drafting and design technology, early childhood education, electrical installation, electronic technology, fire control and safety technology, food production/management/services, liberal/general studies, marketing and distribution, nursing, precision metal work, secretarial and related programs, welding technology.

ACADEMIC PROGRAMS. 2-year transfer program, cooperative education, double major, dual enrollment of high school students, independent study, cross-registration. **Remedial services:** Learning center, preadmission summer program, reduced course load, remedial instruction, special counselor, tutoring. **Placement/credit:** 15 credit hours maximum for associate degree.

ACADEMIC REQUIREMENTS. Freshmen must earn minimum GPA of 2.0 to continue in good standing. Students must declare major on enrollment. **Graduation requirements:** 60 hours for associate (40 in major). Most students required to take courses in arts/fine arts, English, history, humanities, mathematics, biological/physical sciences, social sciences.

FRESHMAN ADMISSIONS. Selection criteria: Open admissions. Priority to state residents for programs with quotas. College preparatory program required for applicants in electronics technology and nursing programs.

1992 FRESHMAN CLASS PROFILE. 345 men and women enrolled.

FALL-TERM APPLICATIONS. No closing date; applicants notified on a rolling basis.

STUDENT LIFE. Housing: Dormitories (coed); apartment housing available. **Activities:** Student government, student newspaper, Phi Theta Kappa honors society.

STUDENT SERVICES. Career counseling, employment service for undergraduates, freshman orientation, health services, personal counseling, special adviser for adult students, veterans counselor, services/facilities for handicapped.

ANNUAL EXPENSES. Tuition and fees: $510, $2,290 additional for out-of-state students. **Room and board:** $4,151. **Books and supplies:** $554. **Other expenses:** $914.

FINANCIAL AID. 33% of freshmen, 37% of continuing students receive some form of aid. 99% of grants, 91% of loans, 46% of jobs based on need. 375 enrolled freshmen were judged to have need, all were offered aid. Academic, state/district residency, leadership scholarships available. **Aid applications:** No closing date; priority given to applications received by March 1; applicants notified on a rolling basis beginning on or about May 1; must reply within 2 weeks.

ADDRESS/TELEPHONE. Jim Yoshida, Coordinator Admissions/Records, University of Hawaii: Hawaii Community College, 523 West Lanikavla Street, Hilo, HI 96720-4091. (808) 933-3611. Fax: (808) 933-3692.

University of Hawaii at Hilo

Hilo, Hawaii CB code: 4869

Admissions: 61% of applicants accepted
Based on: ••• School record
•• Test scores
• Activities, recommendations, special talents
Completion: 70% of freshmen end year in good standing
25% graduate

4-year public university, coed. Founded in 1970. **Accreditation:** Regional. **Undergraduate enrollment:** 830 men, 1,245 women full time; 240 men, 360 women part time. **Faculty:** 281 total (206 full time), 195 with doctorates or other terminal degrees. **Location:** Rural campus in large town; 200 miles from Honolulu. **Calendar:** Semester, limited summer session. **Microcomputers:** 108 located in dormitories, libraries, classrooms, computer centers. **Special facilities:** Center for Study of Active Volcano, world-class observatory, small business development center, Kalakaua Marine Education Center, 110-acre farm laboratory.

DEGREES OFFERED. BA, BS. 222 bachelor's degrees awarded in 1992. 6% in agriculture, 22% business and management, 20% letters/literature, 15% physical sciences, 25% social sciences. Graduate degrees offered in 3 major fields of study.

UNDERGRADUATE MAJORS. Agricultural sciences, anthropology, aquaculture, Asian studies, biology, business and management, chemistry, computer and information sciences, economics, English, fine arts, geography, geology, Hawaiian studies, history, Japanese studies, liberal/general studies, linguistics, marine biology, marine science, mathematics, music, natural science, nursing, philosophy, physics, political science and government, predentistry, prelaw, premedicine, preveterinary, psychology, sociology, speech.

ACADEMIC PROGRAMS. Double major, dual enrollment of high school students, honors program, independent study, internships, student-designed major, study abroad, teacher preparation, telecourses, visiting/exchange student program. **Remedial services:** Learning center, preadmission summer program, special counselor, tutoring. **Placement/credit:** AP, CLEP General and Subject, institutional tests; 30 credit hours maximum for bachelor's degree.

ACADEMIC REQUIREMENTS. Freshmen must earn minimum GPA of 2.0 to continue in good standing. 63% of freshmen return for sophomore year. Students must declare major by end of second year. **Graduation requirements:** 120 hours for bachelor's (33 in major). Most students required to take courses in English, humanities, mathematics, biological/physical sciences, social sciences.

FRESHMAN ADMISSIONS. Selection criteria: High school GPA in academic subjects, SAT/ACT test scores, class rank, and school recommendation are factors considered. **High school preparation:** 20 units required. Required and recommended units include English 4, mathematics 2, social science 3 and science 2. Foreign language 2 recommended. 2 mathematics beyond prealgebra, 2 additional academic subjects, 7 electives not including physical education or ROTC. **Test requirements:** SAT or ACT (SAT preferred); score report by June 15.

1992 FRESHMAN CLASS PROFILE. 392 men applied, 239 accepted, 123 enrolled; 588 women applied, 359 accepted, 184 enrolled. 47% had high school GPA of 3.0 or higher, 53% between 2.0 and 2.99. 18% were in top tenth and 26% were in top quarter of graduating class. **Academic background:** Mid 50% of enrolled freshmen had SAT-V between 340-440, SAT-M between 400-520. 73% submitted SAT scores. **Characteristics:** 60% commute, 77% have minority backgrounds, 3% are foreign students. Average age is 23.

FALL-TERM APPLICATIONS. $10 fee. Closing date June 15; priority given to applications received by March 1; applicants notified on a rolling basis beginning on or about March 15; must reply within 2 weeks. Deferred admission available.

STUDENT LIFE. Housing: Dormitories (coed); apartment, handicapped housing available. Student housing units available for mobility-impaired students. **Activities:** Student government, magazine, student newspaper, student activities council, choral groups, concert band, dance, drama, jazz band, music ensembles, musical theater, pep band, Hawaiian Club, International Student Association, Circle K Club.

ATHLETICS. NAIA, NCAA. **Intercollegiate:** Baseball M, basketball M, cross-country, golf M, softball W, tennis, volleyball W. **Intramural:** Archery, badminton, basketball, bowling, cross-country, golf, softball, table tennis, tennis, volleyball.

STUDENT SERVICES. Aptitude testing, career counseling, employment service for undergraduates, freshman orientation, health services, personal counseling, placement service for graduates, services/facilities for handicapped.

ANNUAL EXPENSES. Tuition and fees: $510, $2,340 additional for out-of-state students. For upper division, tuition and fees are $1,320, additional out-of-state tuition is $2,600. **Room and board:** $4,151. **Books and supplies:** $687. **Other expenses:** $1,074.

FINANCIAL AID. 49% of freshmen, 42% of continuing students receive some form of aid. 78% of grants, 95% of loans, 15% of jobs based on need. Academic, music/drama, art, athletic, state/district residency, leadership, minority scholarships available. **Aid applications:** No closing date; priority given to applications received by March 1; applicants notified on a rolling basis beginning on or about April 12; must reply within 20 days.

ADDRESS/TELEPHONE. James B. West, Admissions Specialist, University of Hawaii at Hilo, Hilo, HI 96720-4091. (808) 933-3414. Fax: (808) 993-3691.

University of Hawaii: Honolulu Community College

Honolulu, Hawaii CB code: 4350

2-year public community college, coed. Founded in 1920. **Accreditation:** Regional. **Undergraduate enrollment:** 5,203 men and women. **Faculty:** 238 total (145 full time), 20 with doctorates or other terminal degrees. **Location:** Urban campus in large city. **Calendar:** Semester, limited summer session. Saturday and extensive evening/early morning classes. **Microcomputers:** 175 located in libraries, classrooms, computer centers.

DEGREES OFFERED. AA, AS. 522 associate degrees awarded in 1992.

UNDERGRADUATE MAJORS. Aeronautical technology, air conditioning/heating/refrigeration mechanics, air conditioning/heating/refrigeration technology, aircraft mechanics, automotive mechanics, automotive technology, carpentry, community services, criminal justice studies, diesel engine mechanics, drafting, drafting and design technology, early childhood education, electrical and electronics equipment repair, electrical installation, electrical technology, electronic technology, engineering and engineering-related technologies, fashion design, fashion merchandising, fire control and safety technology, food production/management/services, graphic arts technology, industrial arts education, law enforcement and corrections technologies, liberal/general studies, occupational safety and health technology, plastic technology, plumbing/pipefitting/steamfitting, precision metal work, secretarial and related programs, trade and industrial education, welding technology.

ACADEMIC PROGRAMS. 2-year transfer program, cooperative education, dual enrollment of high school students, independent study, internships, cross-registration. **Remedial services:** Learning center, remedial instruction, special counselor, tutoring. **Placement/credit:** AP, CLEP General and Subject, institutional tests; 30 credit hours maximum for associate degree.

ACADEMIC REQUIREMENTS. Freshmen must earn minimum GPA of 2.0 to continue in good standing. Students must declare major on application. **Graduation requirements:** 60 hours for associate (18 in major). Most students required to take courses in English, mathematics, biological/physical sciences, social sciences.

FRESHMAN ADMISSIONS. Selection criteria: Open admissions. Out-of-state and foreign applicants subject to nonresident quota. Minimum age of 18 years required of all applicants without high school diploma. High school diploma required for cosmetology program.

1992 FRESHMAN CLASS PROFILE. 1,058 men and women enrolled. **Characteristics:** 100% commute.

FALL-TERM APPLICATIONS. No fee. No closing date; priority given to applications received by July 1; applicants notified on a rolling basis beginning on or about March 1. Early admission available.

STUDENT LIFE. Activities: Student government, magazine, student newspaper, variety of student clubs.

STUDENT SERVICES. Aptitude testing, career counseling, employment service for undergraduates, health services, on-campus day care, personal counseling, placement service for graduates, veterans counselor, services/facilities for handicapped.

ANNUAL EXPENSES. Tuition and fees: $470, $2,340 additional for out-of-state students. **Books and supplies:** $554. **Other expenses:** $914.

FINANCIAL AID. 7% of freshmen, 9% of continuing students receive some form of aid. 87% of grants, 99% of loans, 14% of jobs based on need. Academic, leadership, minority scholarships available. **Aid applications:** No closing date; priority given to applications received by May 1; applicants notified on a rolling basis beginning on or about July 1; must reply within 3 weeks.

ADDRESS/TELEPHONE. Jill Merl, Director of Enrollment Services, University of Hawaii: Honolulu Community College, 874 Dillingham Boulevard, Honolulu, HI 96817. (808) 845-9129. Fax: (808) 845-2679.

University of Hawaii: Kapiolani Community College

Honolulu, Hawaii CB code: 4377

2-year public community college, coed. Founded in 1957. **Accreditation:** Regional. **Undergraduate enrollment:** 1,121 men, 1,513 women full time; 1,644 men, 2,838 women part time. **Faculty:** 288 total (162 full time), 33 with doctorates or other terminal degrees. **Location:** Urban campus in large city. **Calendar:** Semester, limited summer session. Saturday and extensive evening/early morning classes. **Microcomputers:** 150 located in classrooms, computer centers.

DEGREES OFFERED. AA, AS. 466 associate degrees awarded in

1992. 10% in business and management, 10% business/office and marketing/distribution, 8% computer sciences, 26% allied health, 17% home economics, 6% law, 23% multi/interdisciplinary studies.

UNDERGRADUATE MAJORS. Accounting, business data processing and related programs, data processing, emergency medical technologies, food production/management/services, hospitality and recreation marketing, hotel/motel and restaurant management, legal assistant/paralegal, legal secretary, liberal/general studies, marketing and distribution, medical assistant, medical laboratory technologies, nursing, occupational therapy assistant, physical therapy assistant, radiograph medical technology, respiratory therapy, retailing, secretarial and related programs.

ACADEMIC PROGRAMS. 2-year transfer program, double major, dual enrollment of high school students, external degree, honors program, independent study, internships, study abroad, teacher preparation, visiting/exchange student program, cross-registration. **Remedial services:** Learning center, remedial instruction, special counselor, tutoring. **Placement/credit:** AP, CLEP General and Subject, institutional tests.

ACADEMIC REQUIREMENTS. Freshmen must earn minimum GPA of 2.0 to continue in good standing. 55% of freshmen return for sophomore year. Students must declare major on application. **Graduation requirements:** 60 hours for associate. Most students required to take courses in English, history, humanities, mathematics, biological/physical sciences, social sciences.

FRESHMAN ADMISSIONS. Selection criteria: Open admissions. Selective admissions to allied health, nursing, and legal assistant programs. **Additional information:** Student must be 18 years of age or have a high school diploma. High school diploma required for allied health and nursing programs.

1992 FRESHMAN CLASS PROFILE. 586 men, 803 women enrolled. **Characteristics:** 98% from in state, 100% commute, 75% have minority backgrounds. Average age is 21.

FALL-TERM APPLICATIONS. No fee. Closing date July 1; applicants notified on a rolling basis; must reply within 2 weeks. Interview required for allied health, legal assistant, nursing applicants. Deadline of April 1 for applications to allied health and legal assistant programs. Registered nursing program deadline February 1.

STUDENT LIFE. Activities: Student government, student newspaper, choral groups.

ATHLETICS. Intramural: Basketball, bowling, golf, softball, volleyball.

STUDENT SERVICES. Career counseling, employment service for undergraduates, freshman orientation, on-campus day care, personal counseling, placement service for graduates, veterans counselor, services/facilities for handicapped.

ANNUAL EXPENSES. Tuition and fees: $475, $2,800 additional for out-of-state students. **Books and supplies:** $554. **Other expenses:** $777.

FINANCIAL AID. 20% of freshmen, 20% of continuing students receive some form of aid. 88% of grants, 94% of loans, 6% of jobs based on need. Academic, state/district residency, leadership, minority scholarships available. **Aid applications:** No closing date; priority given to applications received by May 1; applicants notified on a rolling basis; must reply within 2 weeks.

ADDRESS/TELEPHONE. Cynthia N. Kimura, Coordinator of Enrollment Services, University of Hawaii: Kapiolani Community College, 4303 Diamond Head Road, Honolulu, HI 96816-4421. (808) 734-9559.

University of Hawaii: Kauai Community College
Lihue, Hawaii CB code: 4378

2-year public community college, coed. Founded in 1928. **Accreditation:** Regional. **Undergraduate enrollment:** 214 men, 313 women full time; 431 men, 605 women part time. **Faculty:** 86 total (82 full time), 9 with doctorates or other terminal degrees. **Location:** Rural campus in large town; 100 air miles from Honolulu. **Calendar:** Semester, limited summer session. Extensive evening/early morning classes. **Microcomputers:** 60 located in computer centers.

DEGREES OFFERED. AA, AS. 84 associate degrees awarded in 1992.

UNDERGRADUATE MAJORS. Accounting, automotive mechanics, automotive technology, carpentry, early childhood education, electrical and electronics equipment repair, electrical installation, electrical technology, electronic technology, food production/management/services, liberal/general studies, marketing and distribution, nursing, office supervision and management.

ACADEMIC PROGRAMS. 2-year transfer program, dual enrollment of high school students, internships, telecourses. **Remedial services:** Learning center, remedial instruction, special counselor, tutoring. **Placement/credit:** Institutional tests.

ACADEMIC REQUIREMENTS. Freshmen must earn minimum GPA of 2.0 to continue in good standing. 20% of freshmen return for sophomore year. Students must declare major on application. **Graduation requirements:** 60 hours for associate. Most students required to take courses in English, history, mathematics.

FRESHMAN ADMISSIONS. Selection criteria: Open admissions. Selective admissions for out-of-state residents, nursing, electrical installation and maintenance technology, and electronics technology programs.

1992 FRESHMAN CLASS PROFILE. 392 men, 450 women enrolled. **Characteristics:** 95% from in state, 100% commute, 65% have minority backgrounds, 3% are foreign students. Average age is 23.

FALL-TERM APPLICATIONS. No fee. Closing date August 1; applicants notified on a rolling basis beginning on or about March 1. Early admission available.

STUDENT LIFE. Activities: Student government, student newspaper, choral groups, dance, drama, music ensembles, musical theater, symphony orchestra, international club, Hawaiian club, computer club.

ATHLETICS. Intramural: Basketball, bowling, tennis, volleyball.

STUDENT SERVICES. Aptitude testing, career counseling, employment service for undergraduates, freshman orientation, on-campus day care, personal counseling, placement service for graduates, special adviser for adult students, veterans counselor, services/facilities for handicapped.

ANNUAL EXPENSES. Tuition and fees: $470, $2,340 additional for out-of-state students. **Books and supplies:** $554. **Other expenses:** $914.

FINANCIAL AID. 12% of continuing students receive some form of aid. 79% of grants, 71% of loans, 5% of jobs based on need. Academic, music/drama, state/district residency, leadership, minority scholarships available. **Aid applications:** No closing date; priority given to applications received by May 1; applicants notified on a rolling basis; must reply within 2 weeks.

ADDRESS/TELEPHONE. Thomas Baca, Admissions Officer and Registrar, University of Hawaii: Kauai Community College, 3-1901 Kaumualii Highway, Lihue, HI 96766. (808) 245-8212. Fax: (808) 245-8260.

University of Hawaii: Leeward Community College
Pearl City, Hawaii CB code: 4410

2-year public community college, coed. Founded in 1968. **Accreditation:** Regional. **Undergraduate enrollment:** 6,098 men and women. **Location:** Suburban campus in large town; 10 miles from Honolulu. **Calendar:** Semester.

FRESHMAN ADMISSIONS. Selection criteria: Open admissions.

ANNUAL EXPENSES. Tuition and fees: $475, $2,340 additional for out-of-state students. **Books and supplies:** $427. **Other expenses:** $792.

ADDRESS/TELEPHONE. Warren Mau, Registrar, University of Hawaii: Leeward Community College, 96-045 Ala Ike, Pearl City, HI 96782. (808) 455-0217. Fax: (808) 455-0471.

University of Hawaii at Manoa
Honolulu, Hawaii CB code: 4867

4-year public university, coed. Founded in 1907. **Accreditation:** Regional. **Undergraduate enrollment:** 4,881 men, 5,868 women full time; 1,227 men, 1,269 women part time. **Graduate enrollment:** 1,447 men, 1,613 women full time; 1,509 men, 1,957 women part time. **Faculty:** 2,033 total (1,771 full time). **Location:** Urban campus in very large city; 3 miles from downtown. **Calendar:** Semester, limited summer session. **Microcomputers:** Located in libraries, computer centers.

DEGREES OFFERED. BA, BS, BFA, BArch, MA, MS, MBA, MFA, MEd, MSW, PhD, EdD, MD, JD. 2,362 bachelor's degrees awarded in 1992. Graduate degrees offered in 84 major fields of study.

UNDERGRADUATE MAJORS. Accounting, agricultural economics, agricultural sciences, agronomy, American studies, animal sciences, anthropology, architecture, Asian studies, atmospheric sciences and meteorology, biology, botany, business and management, business economics, chemistry, Chinese, civil engineering, classics, communications, computer and information sciences, dance, dental hygiene, dramatic arts, early childhood education, economics, education, electrical/electronics/communications engineering, elementary education, English, entomology, fashion design, fashion merchandising, finance, fine arts, food science and nutrition, food sciences, French, geography, geology, German, Hawaiian, Hawaiian studies, history, home economics, horticulture, human resources development, individual and family development, international business management, Japanese, journalism, liberal/general studies, management information systems, marketing and distribution, marketing research, mathematics, mechanical engineering, medical laboratory technologies, microbiology, music, nursing, operations research, philosophy, physical education, physics, political science and government, psychology, real estate, religion, Russian, secondary education, social work, sociology, soil sciences, Spanish, speech, speech pathology/audiology, tourism, transportation and travel marketing, women's studies, zoology.

ACADEMIC PROGRAMS. Accelerated program, cooperative education, double major, dual enrollment of high school students, honors program, independent study, internships, student-designed major, study abroad, teacher preparation, telecourses, visiting/exchange student program, cross-registration. **Remedial services:** Learning center, tutoring. **ROTC:** Air Force, Army. **Placement/credit:** AP, CLEP General and Subject, institutional tests.

ACADEMIC REQUIREMENTS. Freshmen must earn minimum GPA of 2.0 to continue in good standing. Students must declare major by end of second year. **Graduation requirements:** 124 hours for bachelor's (30 in major). Most students required to take courses in English, foreign languages, history, humanities, mathematics, philosophy/religion, biological/physical sciences, social sciences.

FRESHMAN ADMISSIONS. Selection criteria: School achievement record, test scores, class rank most important. **High school preparation:** 20 units required. Required and recommended units include English 4, mathematics 2, social science 4 and science 2. Foreign language 2 recommended. **Test requirements:** SAT or ACT (SAT preferred); score report by May 1.

1992 FRESHMAN CLASS PROFILE. Characteristics: Average age is 19.

FALL-TERM APPLICATIONS. $10 fee. Closing date May 1; applicants notified on a rolling basis beginning on or about March 1; must reply within 4 weeks. Early admission available to seniors enrolled in local high schools only.

STUDENT LIFE. Housing: Dormitories (men, women, coed); apartment housing available. **Activities:** Student government, magazine, radio, student newspaper, choral groups, concert band, dance, drama, marching band, musical theater, symphony orchestra, fraternities, sororities, 220 honorary, religious, and cultural organizations.

ATHLETICS. NCAA. **Intercollegiate:** Baseball M, basketball, cross-country W, diving, football M, golf, sailing, softball W, swimming, tennis, track and field W, volleyball. **Intramural:** Badminton, basketball, bowling, golf, gymnastics, soccer, softball, swimming, table tennis, tennis, track and field, volleyball, water polo, wrestling.

STUDENT SERVICES. Aptitude testing, career counseling, employment service for undergraduates, freshman orientation, health services, on-campus day care, personal counseling, placement service for graduates, special adviser for adult students, veterans counselor, services/facilities for handicapped.

ANNUAL EXPENSES. Tuition and fees (1992-93): $1,437, $2,730 additional for out-of-state students. **Room and board:** $3,186. **Books and supplies:** $540. **Other expenses:** $1,342.

FINANCIAL AID. 16% of freshmen, 15% of continuing students receive some form of aid. All grants, 85% of loans, 4% of jobs based on need. Academic, music/drama, athletic, leadership scholarships available. **Aid applications:** No closing date; priority given to applications received by March 1; applicants notified on a rolling basis beginning on or about June 1; must reply within 2 weeks.

ADDRESS/TELEPHONE. David Robb, Director of Admissions and Records, University of Hawaii at Manoa, 2530 Dole Street, Room C-200, Honolulu, HI 96822. (808) 956-8975.

University of Hawaii: Maui Community College
Kahului, Hawaii CB code: 4510

2-year public community college, coed. Founded in 1931. **Accreditation:** Regional. **Undergraduate enrollment:** 2,688 men and women. **Location:** Suburban campus in small city; 150 air miles from Honolulu. **Calendar:** Semester.

FRESHMAN ADMISSIONS. Selection criteria: Open admissions. Selective admissions to nursing program.

ANNUAL EXPENSES. Tuition and fees: $480, $2,340 additional for out-of-state students. **Room and board:** $4,525. **Books and supplies:** $554. **Other expenses:** $1,074.

ADDRESS/TELEPHONE. Stephen Kameda, Admissions Officer/Registrar, University of Hawaii: Maui Community College, 310 Kaahumanu Avenue, Kahului, HI 96732. (808) 244-9181. Fax: (808) 242-9618.

University of Hawaii: West Oahu
Pearl City, Hawaii CB code: 1042

2-year upper-division public liberal arts college, coed. Founded in 1976. **Accreditation:** Regional. **Undergraduate enrollment:** 76 men, 143 women full time; 194 men, 275 women part time. **Faculty:** 39 total (19 full time), 20 with doctorates or other terminal degrees. **Location:** Suburban campus in large town; 10 miles from Honolulu. **Calendar:** Semester, limited summer session. Saturday and extensive evening/early morning classes. **Microcomputers:** 5 located in libraries. **Additional facts:** Campus shared with community college.

DEGREES OFFERED. BA. 135 bachelor's degrees awarded in 1992. 32% in business and management, 12% letters/literature, 21% parks/recreation, protective services, public affairs, 21% psychology, 14% social sciences.

UNDERGRADUATE MAJORS. American studies, anthropology, Asian studies, business administration and management, economics, English, European studies, history, international business management, Pacific area studies, philosophy, political science and government, psychology, public administration, social sciences, sociology.

ACADEMIC PROGRAMS. Accelerated program, double major, independent study, internships, student-designed major, weekend college. **Placement/credit:** CLEP General and Subject, institutional tests; 21 credit hours maximum for bachelor's degree.

ACADEMIC REQUIREMENTS. Students must declare major by end of third year. **Graduation requirements:** 120 hours for bachelor's (21 in major). Most students required to take courses in English, history, humanities, mathematics, biological/physical sciences, social sciences.

STUDENT LIFE. Activities: Student government, magazine, student newspaper.

STUDENT SERVICES. Career counseling, employment service for undergraduates, personal counseling, veterans counselor, services/facilities for handicapped.

ANNUAL EXPENSES. Tuition and fees: $870, $1,940 additional for out-of-state students. Foreign students pay out-of-state tuition rates, except for applicants from countries with reciprocity agreements. **Books and supplies:** $687. **Other expenses:** $1,865.

FINANCIAL AID. 10% of continuing students receive some form of aid. 94% of grants, 94% of loans, 15% of jobs based on need. Academic, music/drama, art, leadership, minority scholarships available. **Aid applications:** No closing date; priority given to applications received by May 1; applicants notified on a rolling basis beginning on or about July 1; must reply within 2 weeks.

ADDRESS/TELEPHONE. Phyllis Tsutsui, Student Services Specialist, University of Hawaii: West Oahu, 96-043 Ala Ike, Pearl City, HI 96782. (808) 455-0800. Fax: (808) 456-5208.

University of Hawaii: Windward Community College
Kaneohe, Hawaii CB code: 4976

2-year public community college, coed. Founded in 1972. **Accreditation:** Regional. **Undergraduate enrollment:** 1,643 men and women. **Faculty:** 83 total (46 full time), 9 with doctorates or other terminal degrees. **Location:** Suburban campus in small city; 10 miles from Honolulu. **Calendar:** Semester, limited summer session. **Microcomputers:** 30 located in computer centers.

DEGREES OFFERED. AA. 110 associate degrees awarded in 1992.

UNDERGRADUATE MAJORS. Accounting, business and office, finance, liberal/general studies, secretarial and related programs.

ACADEMIC PROGRAMS. 2-year transfer program, cooperative education, double major, dual enrollment of high school students, independent study, cross-registration. **Remedial services:** Learning center, reduced course load, remedial instruction, special counselor, tutoring. **ROTC:** Air Force, Army. **Placement/credit:** CLEP General and Subject, institutional tests.

ACADEMIC REQUIREMENTS. Freshmen must earn minimum GPA of 2.0 to continue in good standing. Students must declare major on application. **Graduation requirements:** 60 hours for associate. Most students required to take courses in English, humanities, mathematics, biological/physical sciences, social sciences.

FRESHMAN ADMISSIONS. Selection criteria: Open admissions. Students under 18 without high school diploma not admitted. **Test requirements:** Nelson-Denny Reading Test used for placement.

1992 FRESHMAN CLASS PROFILE. 594 men and women enrolled. **Characteristics:** 93% from in state, 100% commute, 50% have minority backgrounds.

FALL-TERM APPLICATIONS. No fee. Closing date August 1; applicants notified on a rolling basis; must reply by registration. Early admission available.

STUDENT LIFE. Activities: Student government, magazine, student newspaper, choral groups, drama.

STUDENT SERVICES. Aptitude testing, career counseling, employment service for undergraduates, personal counseling, placement service for graduates, veterans counselor, services/facilities for handicapped.

ANNUAL EXPENSES. Tuition and fees: $480, $2,340 additional for out-of-state students. **Books and supplies:** $554. **Other expenses:** $914.

FINANCIAL AID. 10% of freshmen, 10% of continuing students receive some form of aid. All grants, 91% of loans based on need. Academic, leadership scholarships available. **Aid applications:** No closing date; priority given to applications received by April 1; must reply within 2 weeks.

ADDRESS/TELEPHONE. Charles Heaukulani, Registrar, University of Hawaii: Windward Community College, 45-720 Keaahala Road, Kaneohe, HI 96817. (808) 235-7432.

Idaho

Albertson College

Caldwell, Idaho CB code: 4060

Admissions: 83% of applicants accepted
Based on: ••• Activities, test scores
•• Essay, interview, school record
• Recommendations, special talents
Completion: 45% graduate

4-year private liberal arts college, coed. Founded in 1891. **Accreditation:** Regional. **Undergraduate enrollment:** 357 men, 331 women full time; 27 men, 19 women part time. **Graduate enrollment:** 69 men, 259 women part time. **Faculty:** 143 total (80 full time), 44 with doctorates or other terminal degrees. **Location:** Rural campus in large town; 30 miles from Boise, 400 miles from Salt Lake City, Utah. **Calendar:** 13-6-13. **Microcomputers:** 90 located in dormitories, libraries, classrooms, computer centers, campus-wide network. **Special facilities:** Natural history museum, mineral and gem collection, planetarium, observatory, Rosenthal Art Gallery, nuclear magnetic resonance spectrometer, Jewett Auditorium, J.A. Albertson Activities Center, Langroise Performing and Fine Arts Center.

DEGREES OFFERED. BA, BS, MA, MEd. 91 bachelor's degrees awarded in 1992. 24% in business and management, 18% life sciences, 7% psychology, 6% visual and performing arts. Graduate degrees offered in 5 major fields of study.

UNDERGRADUATE MAJORS. Accounting, anthropology, biology, business administration and management, chemistry, computer and information sciences, dramatic arts, economics, elementary education, English, English education, fine arts, French, history, international relations, mathematics, mathematics education, music, philosophy, physical education, physics, political science and government, psychology, religion, science education, social studies education, sociology, Spanish, sports medicine, zoology.

ACADEMIC PROGRAMS. Accelerated program, double major, dual enrollment of high school students, honors program, independent study, internships, student-designed major, study abroad, teacher preparation, visiting/exchange student program, Washington semester, cross-registration; liberal arts/career combination in engineering. **Remedial services:** Reduced course load, special counselor. **Placement/credit:** AP, CLEP General and Subject, IB, institutional tests.

ACADEMIC REQUIREMENTS. Freshmen must earn minimum GPA of 1.65 to continue in good standing. 86% of freshmen return for sophomore year. Students must declare major by end of second year. **Graduation requirements:** 124 hours for bachelor's (32 in major). Most students required to take courses in arts/fine arts, English, history, humanities, mathematics, philosophy/religion, biological/physical sciences, social sciences.

FRESHMAN ADMISSIONS. Selection criteria: Academic record, test scores, extracurricular activities, essay written by the student important. Teacher recommendation considered. Recommended units include English 4, foreign language 2, mathematics 3, social science 3 and science 2. **Test requirements:** SAT or ACT; score report by August 31.

1992 FRESHMAN CLASS PROFILE. 508 men and women applied, 423 accepted; 88 men enrolled, 88 women enrolled. 77% had high school GPA of 3.0 or higher, 20% between 2.0 and 2.99. 25% were in top tenth and 69% were in top quarter of graduating class. **Characteristics:** 78% from in state, 85% live in college housing, 7% have minority backgrounds, 5% are foreign students, 15% join fraternities/sororities. Average age is 18.

FALL-TERM APPLICATIONS. $25 fee, may be waived for applicants with need. No closing date; priority given to applications received by March 1; applicants notified on a rolling basis; must reply by registration. Audition required for music applicants. Portfolio required for art applicants. Essay required. Interview recommended. Deferred admission available.

STUDENT LIFE. Housing: Dormitories (women, coed); fraternity housing available. Honors residence available for students with superior academic records. Freshman under age 21 must live on campus unless living with parents, relatives. **Activities:** Student government, student newspaper, yearbook, choral groups, drama, music ensembles, musical theater, symphony orchestra, fraternities, sororities, Intercollegiate Knights, Amnesty International, Best Buddies, Religion In Life Committee. **Additional information:** Emphasis on outdoor sports such as hiking, backpacking, rock climbing, rafting, skiing.

ATHLETICS. NAIA. **Intercollegiate:** Baseball M, basketball M, skiing, soccer, tennis W, volleyball W. **Intramural:** Basketball, softball, swimming, volleyball.

STUDENT SERVICES. Aptitude testing, career counseling, employment service for undergraduates, freshman orientation, health services, personal counseling, placement service for graduates, special adviser for adult students, services/facilities for handicapped.

ANNUAL EXPENSES. Tuition and fees (1992-93): $10,750. **Room and board:** $2,850. **Books and supplies:** $400. **Other expenses:** $675.

FINANCIAL AID. 80% of freshmen, 84% of continuing students receive some form of aid. 35% of grants, 96% of loans, 63% of jobs based on need. Academic, music/drama, art, athletic, state/district residency, alumni affiliation, religious affiliation scholarships available. **Aid applications:** No closing date; priority given to applications received by March 1; applicants notified on a rolling basis beginning on or about April 15; must reply within 30 days. **Additional information:** 35% of students receive honor student scholarships.

ADDRESS/TELEPHONE. Carol Kriz, Director of Enrollment Services, Albertson College, 2112 Cleveland Boulevard, Caldwell, ID 83605. (208) 459-5209. (800) 635-0434. Fax: (208) 454-2077.

Boise Bible College

Boise, Idaho CB code: 0891

4-year private Bible college, coed, nondenominational. Founded in 1945. **Undergraduate enrollment:** 50 men, 35 women full time; 18 men, 9 women part time. **Faculty:** 26 total (9 full time), 2 with doctorates or other terminal degrees. **Location:** Suburban campus in small city. **Calendar:** Semester. Extensive evening/early morning classes.

DEGREES OFFERED. AS, BA, BS. 4 associate degrees awarded in 1992. 100% in philosophy, religion, theology. 9 bachelor's degrees awarded. 100% in philosophy, religion, theology.

UNDERGRADUATE MAJORS. Associate: Bible studies, religious education, religious music, theological studies. **Bachelor's:** Bible studies, biblical languages, Christian ministries, religious education, religious music, theological studies.

ACADEMIC PROGRAMS. 2-year transfer program, double major, internships. **Remedial services:** Remedial instruction. **Placement/credit:** AP, CLEP General, institutional tests.

ACADEMIC REQUIREMENTS. Freshmen must earn minimum GPA of 1.75 to continue in good standing. 50% of freshmen return for sophomore year. Students must declare major on enrollment. **Graduation requirements:** 64 hours for associate (17 in major), 128 hours for bachelor's (24 in major). Most students required to take courses in arts/fine arts, English, foreign languages, history, humanities, philosophy/religion, biological/physical sciences, social sciences. **Postgraduate studies:** 30% enter other graduate study.

FRESHMAN ADMISSIONS. Selection criteria: Christian conduct or ethical code standards based on signed student statement, recommendation of home church minister, 1 employment reference required. **Test requirements:** AABC Bible Knowledge Test, College English Placement Test required.

1992 FRESHMAN CLASS PROFILE. 37 men applied, 37 accepted, 37 enrolled; 23 women applied, 23 accepted, 12 enrolled. 47% had high school GPA of 3.0 or higher, 35% between 2.0 and 2.99. **Characteristics:** 12% from in state, 88% live in college housing, 4% have minority backgrounds. Average age is 18.

FALL-TERM APPLICATIONS. $25 fee. Closing date September 1; priority given to applications received by August 15; applicants notified on a rolling basis; must reply by registration. Essay required. Interview recommended. Deferred admission available.

STUDENT LIFE. Housing: Dormitories (men, women). **Activities:** Student government, student newspaper, yearbook, choral groups, drama, music ensembles, Christian service missions club. **Additional information:** Student activities include speaking and chapel presiding. Religious observance required.

ATHLETICS. Intramural: Basketball, football M, soccer M, softball, table tennis, volleyball.

STUDENT SERVICES. Career counseling, employment service for undergraduates, freshman orientation, health services, personal counseling, placement service for graduates, veterans counselor.

ANNUAL EXPENSES. Tuition and fees (1992-93): $3,261. **Room and board:** $2,840. **Books and supplies:** $400. **Other expenses:** $895.

FINANCIAL AID. 81% of freshmen, 90% of continuing students receive some form of aid. 72% of grants, all loans, all jobs based on need. Academic, leadership scholarships available. **Aid applications:** No closing date; applicants notified on a rolling basis.

ADDRESS/TELEPHONE. Carl A. Anderson, Academic Dean, Boise Bible College, 8695 Marigold Street, Boise, ID 83714-1220. (208) 376-7731. Fax: (208) 376-7743.

Boise State University

Boise, Idaho CB code: 4018

4-year public university, coed. Founded in 1932. **Accreditation:** Regional. **Undergraduate enrollment:** 4,223 men, 4,591 women full time; 1,459 men, 1,954 women part time. **Graduate enrollment:** 134 men, 190 women full time; 867 men, 2,032 women part time. **Faculty:** 744 total (455 full time). **Location:** Urban campus in small city; in downtown area. **Calendar:** Semester, limited summer session. Saturday and extensive evening/early morning classes. **Microcomputers:** 450 located in dormitories, libraries, computer centers. **Special facilities:** Morrison Center for the Performing Arts, Simplot

Micron Technology Center, World Center for Birds of Prey Research, Snake River Birds of Prey natural area.

DEGREES OFFERED. AA, AS, AAS, BA, BS, BFA, MA, MS, MBA, MFA, MSW. 209 associate degrees awarded in 1992. 15% in business/office and marketing/distribution, 41% health sciences, 41% allied health. 987 bachelor's degrees awarded. 26% in business and management, 6% business/office and marketing/distribution, 6% communications, 17% teacher education, 6% health sciences, 16% social sciences, 6% visual and performing arts. Graduate degrees offered in 24 major fields of study.

UNDERGRADUATE MAJORS. Associate: Business and office, business computer/console/peripheral equipment operation, criminal justice studies, drafting, drafting and design technology, electrical and electronics equipment repair, electronic technology, fire control and safety technology, manufacturing technology, marketing and distribution, medical records administration, medical records technology, nursing, ornamental horticulture, radiograph medical technology, respiratory therapy, respiratory therapy technology, secretarial and related programs, social sciences. **Bachelor's:** Accounting, anthropology, applied science, art education, biology, business administration and management, business and management, business economics, chemistry, communications, computer and information sciences, computer engineering, construction, criminal justice studies, dramatic arts, earth sciences, economics, electrical/electronics/communications engineering, elementary education, elementary education-bilingual/multicultural, English, English education, environmental science, finance, fine arts, French, geology, geophysics and seismology, German, health sciences, history, human resources development, liberal/general studies, management information systems, manufacturing technology, marketing and distribution, marketing management, mathematics, mathematics education, medical laboratory technologies, medical records administration, multiethnic studies, music, music education, music performance, music theory and composition, nursing, philosophy, physical education, physics, political science and government, predentistry, premedicine, preveterinary, psychology, radiograph medical technology, respiratory therapy, respiratory therapy technology, science education, social science education, social sciences, social work, sociology, Spanish, speech/communication/theater education.

ACADEMIC PROGRAMS. Computer delivered (on-line) credit-bearing course offerings, double major, honors program, independent study, internships, student-designed major, study abroad, teacher preparation, visiting/exchange student program, weekend college. **Remedial services:** Learning center, reduced course load, remedial instruction, tutoring. **ROTC:** Army. **Placement/credit:** AP, CLEP General and Subject, institutional tests.

ACADEMIC REQUIREMENTS. Freshmen must earn minimum GPA of 2.0 to continue in good standing. 71% of freshmen return for sophomore year. Students must declare major by end of second year. **Graduation requirements:** 128 hours for bachelor's (45 in major). Most students required to take courses in arts/fine arts, English, humanities, mathematics, biological/physical sciences, social sciences. **Additional information:** Basque studies program abroad.

FRESHMAN ADMISSIONS. Selection criteria: Minimum GPA of 2.0 and high school core curriculum most important. If applicants do not meet core curriculm requirements, SAT/ACT scores important. **High school preparation:** 14 units required. Required and recommended units include English 4, mathematics 3, social science 2.5 and science 3. Foreign language 1 recommended. 1 unit, foreign language, humanities, or fine arts also required. **Test requirements:** SAT or ACT; score report by July 28. **Additional information:** Applicants not meeting core requirements considered for provisional admission. Applicants without high school diploma or GED may petition for admission if situation warrants special consideration.

1992 FRESHMAN CLASS PROFILE. 1,408 men applied, 1,165 accepted, 898 enrolled; 1,652 women applied, 1,368 accepted, 971 enrolled. 47% had high school GPA of 3.0 or higher, 50% between 2.0 and 2.99. **Academic background:** Mid 50% of enrolled freshmen had SAT-V between 360-490, SAT-M between 390-530; ACT composite between 14-22. 20% submitted SAT scores, 65% submitted ACT scores. **Characteristics:** 90% from in state, 81% commute, 9% have minority backgrounds, 3% are foreign students, 1% join fraternities/sororities. Average age is 21.

FALL-TERM APPLICATIONS. $15 fee. Closing date July 28; applicants notified on a rolling basis beginning on or about February 15. Interview required for vocational-technical, registered nursing program applicants. Strongly recommended that students apply January-March.

STUDENT LIFE. Housing: Dormitories (men, women, coed); apartment, fraternity, sorority housing available. **Activities:** Student government, magazine, radio, student newspaper, television, choral groups, concert band, dance, drama, jazz band, marching band, music ensembles, musical theater, pep band, symphony orchestra, fraternities, sororities, Black Student Union, Native American Association, Organization de Estudiantes Latino-Americanos, International Student Association, Latter-day Saints Student Association, Alternative Mobility Adventure Seekers.

ATHLETICS. NCAA. **Intercollegiate:** Basketball, cross-country, football M, golf, gymnastics W, tennis, track and field, volleyball W, wrestling M. **Intramural:** Baseball M, basketball, football M, handball, racquetball, soccer M, softball, tennis, volleyball, water polo M. **Clubs:** Bowling MW.

STUDENT SERVICES. Aptitude testing, career counseling, employment service for undergraduates, freshman orientation, health services, on-campus day care, personal counseling, placement service for graduates, special adviser for adult students, veterans counselor, services/facilities for handicapped.

ANNUAL EXPENSES. Tuition and fees: $1,480, $3,050 additional for out-of-state students. **Room and board:** $3,240. **Books and supplies:** $400. **Other expenses:** $928.

FINANCIAL AID. 60% of freshmen, 50% of continuing students receive some form of aid. 87% of grants, 92% of loans, 26% of jobs based on need. Academic, music/drama, art, athletic, state/district residency, leadership, minority scholarships available. **Aid applications:** No closing date; priority given to applications received by March 31; applicants notified on a rolling basis beginning on or about June 1; must reply within 2 weeks.

ADDRESS/TELEPHONE. Stephen E. Spafford, Dean of Admissions, Boise State University, 1910 University Drive, Boise, ID 83725. (208) 385-1820. (800) 824-7017. Fax: (208) 385-4253.

College of Southern Idaho
Twin Falls, Idaho CB code: 4114

2-year public community college, coed. Founded in 1964. **Accreditation:** Regional. **Undergraduate enrollment:** 741 men, 1,030 women full time; 591 men, 1,442 women part time. **Faculty:** 245 total (115 full time), 12 with doctorates or other terminal degrees. **Location:** Suburban campus in large town; 130 miles from Boise. **Calendar:** Semester, limited summer session. Extensive evening/early morning classes. **Microcomputers:** 250 located in classrooms, computer centers. **Special facilities:** Herrett Museum, including anthropology, archeology, fine arts collections. **Additional facts:** Outreach centers in Burley, Gooding, and Hailey.

DEGREES OFFERED. AA, AS, AAS. 243 associate degrees awarded in 1992.

UNDERGRADUATE MAJORS. Accounting, agribusiness, agricultural engineering, agricultural sciences, air conditioning/heating/refrigeration mechanics, air conditioning/heating/refrigeration technology, anthropology, art education, automotive mechanics, automotive technology, biological and physical sciences, biology, botany, business administration and management, business and office, business education, chemical engineering, chemistry, civil engineering, computer and information sciences, computer engineering, diesel engine mechanics, drafting, drafting and design technology, dramatic arts, education, electrical/electronics/communications engineering, elementary education, engineering, engineering and other disciplines, English, English education, equestrian science, finance, geography, history, home economics, home economics education, hotel/motel and restaurant management, law enforcement and corrections technologies, liberal/general studies, library science, marketing and distribution, marketing management, mathematics, mechanical engineering, medical secretary, music, music education, nursing, photography, physical education, physics, political science and government, predentistry, prelaw, premedicine, prepharmacy, preveterinary, psychology, real estate, secondary education, sociology, welding technology, woodworking.

ACADEMIC PROGRAMS. 2-year transfer program, cooperative education, dual enrollment of high school students, honors program, internships, telecourses. **Remedial services:** Learning center, preadmission summer program, reduced course load, remedial instruction, special counselor, tutoring. **Placement/credit:** AP, CLEP Subject, institutional tests; 32 credit hours maximum for associate degree.

ACADEMIC REQUIREMENTS. Freshmen must earn minimum GPA of 1.5 to continue in good standing. 42% of freshmen return for sophomore year. Students must declare major on application. **Graduation requirements:** 64 hours for associate. Most students required to take courses in arts/fine arts, computer science, English, foreign languages, history, humanities, mathematics, biological/physical sciences, social sciences.

FRESHMAN ADMISSIONS. Selection criteria: Open admissions. ACT recommended, letters of reference, letter of intent, special tests required for registered nursing applicants. **Test requirements:** ACT required for nursing applicants. ASSET required of all for placement and counseling.

1992 FRESHMAN CLASS PROFILE. 455 men, 572 women enrolled. **Characteristics:** 91% from in state, 95% commute, 16% have minority backgrounds, 1% are foreign students.

FALL-TERM APPLICATIONS. No fee. No closing date; applicants notified on a rolling basis. Interview required for registered nursing, trade, industrial applicants. Deferred admission available.

STUDENT LIFE. Housing: Dormitories (coed). **Activities:** Student government, choral groups, concert band, drama, jazz band, music ensembles, pep band, symphony orchestra, Campus Democrats, Christian Fellowship, International Students, Latter Day Saints Student Association, Ambassadors.

ATHLETICS. NJCAA. **Intercollegiate:** Baseball M, basketball, cross-country, track and field, volleyball W. **Intramural:** Basketball, golf, racquetball, softball, volleyball.

STUDENT SERVICES. Aptitude testing, career counseling, employment service for undergraduates, freshman orientation, health services, on-campus day care, personal counseling, placement service for graduates,

special adviser for adult students, veterans counselor, class interpreters for deaf students, services/facilities for handicapped.

ANNUAL EXPENSES. Tuition and fees: $900, $1,200 additional for out-of-state students. $1200/$69 per credit additional tuition for out-of-county students paid for by county of residence. **Room and board:** $2,870. **Books and supplies:** $800. **Other expenses:** $1,530.

FINANCIAL AID. 65% of freshmen, 65% of continuing students receive some form of aid. 89% of grants, 95% of loans, 78% of jobs based on need. Academic, music/drama, art, athletic, state/district residency, leadership, alumni affiliation, minority scholarships available. **Aid applications:** No closing date; priority given to applications received by March 1; applicants notified on a rolling basis beginning on or about April 15; must reply within 3 weeks. **Additional information:** Out-of-state tuition waivers based on GPA and activities.

ADDRESS/TELEPHONE. Dr. John S. Martin, Director of Admissions, College of Southern Idaho, PO Box 1238, Twin Falls, ID 83303-1238. (208) 733-9554. Fax: (208) 736-3014.

Eastern Idaho Technical College
Idaho Falls, Idaho

2-year public technical college, coed. Founded in 1969. **Accreditation:** Regional. **Location:** Suburban campus in large town. **Calendar:** Semester.

FRESHMAN ADMISSIONS. Selection criteria: Open admissions.

ANNUAL EXPENSES. Tuition and fees (1992-93): $890, $1,588 additional for out-of-state students.

ADDRESS/TELEPHONE. Steven Aldiston, Student Services Manager, Eastern Idaho Technical College, 1600 South 2500 East, Idaho Falls, ID 83404. (208) 524-3000. Fax: (208) 524-3007.

Idaho State University
Pocatello, Idaho CB code: 4355

Admissions:	82% of applicants accepted
Based on:	••• School record
	•• Test scores
	• Essay, interview, recommendations, special talents
Completion:	69% of freshmen end year in good standing
	43% graduate

4-year public university, coed. Founded in 1901. **Accreditation:** Regional. **Undergraduate enrollment:** 3,186 men, 3,379 women full time; 1,044 men, 1,411 women part time. **Graduate enrollment:** 265 men, 306 women full time; 457 men, 681 women part time. **Faculty:** 587 total (421 full time), 371 with doctorates or other terminal degrees. **Location:** Urban campus in small city; 150 miles from Salt Lake City, Utah. **Calendar:** Semester, limited summer session. Extensive evening/early morning classes. **Microcomputers:** Located in dormitories, libraries, classrooms, computer centers. **Special facilities:** Idaho Museum of Natural History, Holt Arena. **Additional facts:** Designated by State Board of Education as institution specializing in health-related programs. Only college of pharmacy in Idaho.

DEGREES OFFERED. AA, AS, AAS, BA, BS, BFA, MA, MS, MBA, MFA, MEd, PhD, EdD, B. Pharm. 240 associate degrees awarded in 1992. 7% in business/office and marketing/distribution, 16% computer sciences, 33% engineering technologies, 6% allied health, 38% trade and industry. 730 bachelor's degrees awarded. 19% in business and management, 29% education, 10% health sciences, 5% allied health, 6% life sciences, 5% psychology, 5% social sciences. Graduate degrees offered in 41 major fields of study.

UNDERGRADUATE MAJORS. Associate: Aircraft mechanics, automotive technology, business data processing and related programs, business data programming, business systems analysis, civil technology, criminal justice studies, data processing, diesel engine mechanics, drafting, drafting and design technology, electrical technology, electromechanical technology, electronic technology, food production/management/services, graphic and printing production, instrumentation technology, laser electro-optic technology, machine tool operation/machine shop, marketing and distribution, mechanical design technology, radiograph medical technology. **Bachelor's:** Accounting, American studies, anthropology, biochemistry, biology, biophysics, botany, business administration and management, chemistry, clinical laboratory science, communications, computer and information sciences, computer mathematics, dental hygiene, dramatic arts, early childhood education, ecology, economics, elementary education, engineering, engineering and other disciplines, English, finance, fine arts, food science and nutrition, French, geology, German, health care administration, history, home economics, international relations, international studies, journalism, junior high education, liberal/general studies, marketing and distribution, marketing management, marketing research, mathematics, medical radiation dosimetry, medical records technology, microbiology, music, music education, nursing, philosophy, photographic technology, physical education, physics, plant sciences, political science and government, predentistry, prelaw, premedicine, prepharmacy, preveterinary, psychology, radio/television broadcasting, radio/television technology, radiograph medical technology, renewable natural resources, secondary education, social work, sociology, Spanish, special education, speech, speech correction, speech pathology/audiology, sports medicine, technical education, textiles and clothing, trade and industrial education, University studies, zoology.

ACADEMIC PROGRAMS. Double major, dual enrollment of high school students, education specialist degree, honors program, independent study, internships, student-designed major, teacher preparation; combined bachelor's/graduate program in business administration. **Remedial services:** Learning center, remedial instruction, special counselor, tutoring. **Placement/credit:** AP, CLEP General and Subject, institutional tests; 48 credit hours maximum for bachelor's degree.

ACADEMIC REQUIREMENTS. Freshmen must earn minimum GPA of 2.0 to continue in good standing. Students must declare major by end of second year. **Graduation requirements:** 128 hours for bachelor's (50 in major). Most students required to take courses in arts/fine arts, English, foreign languages, history, humanities, mathematics, philosophy/religion, biological/physical sciences, social sciences.

FRESHMAN ADMISSIONS. Selection criteria: For regular admission, applicants must earn an overall 2.0 GPA in college preparatory courses. Applicants not meeting core subject requirements may be considered for provisional admission if their GPA in core subjects completed and test scores predict a 2.0 GPA at Idaho State. **High school preparation:** 15 units required. Required units include English 4, mathematics 3, social science 2.5 and science 3. Science must include 1 unit of laboratory experience, 2 units of mathematics must be taken in 10th, 11th, or 12th grades, 1 unit humanities/foreign language, 1.5 units other college preparatory courses. **Test requirements:** SAT or ACT; score report by August 15. **Additional information:** GED accepted in place of high school diploma only for provisional admission. Minimum ACT composite score of 14 required of GED students completing test after 1989.

1992 FRESHMAN CLASS PROFILE. 1,989 men and women applied, 1,627 accepted; 1,137 enrolled. 51% had high school GPA of 3.0 or higher, 44% between 2.0 and 2.99. **Academic background:** Mid 50% of enrolled freshmen had ACT composite between 17-23. 68% submitted ACT scores. **Characteristics:** 95% from in state, 80% commute, 9% have minority backgrounds, 2% are foreign students, 1% join fraternities/sororities. Average age is 22.

FALL-TERM APPLICATIONS. $15 fee, may be waived for applicants with need. Closing date August 15; priority given to applications received by August 1; applicants notified on a rolling basis. Interview recommended. Audition recommended for music applicants. Portfolio recommended for those seeking experiential credit applicants. Deferred and early admission available. High school students who graduate early may petition admissions committee to enroll full time.

STUDENT LIFE. Housing: Dormitories (men, women, coed); apartment, fraternity, sorority, handicapped housing available. Housing modified for handicapped available on request, subject to waiting list. Students may request roommates with similar academic majors, religious background, and interests. **Activities:** Student government, student newspaper, television, choral groups, concert band, dance, drama, jazz band, music ensembles, musical theater, opera, pep band, symphony orchestra, fraternities, sororities, campus ministry, Newman Center, Latter-Day Saints Institute, student Ambassadors, Spurs, Young Democrats, Young Republicans, Campus Crusade for Christ, Associated Black Students, Native Americans United, Cooperative Wilderness Handicapped Outdoor Group, Hispanic Awareness Leadership Organization.

ATHLETICS. NCAA. **Intercollegiate:** Basketball, cross-country, football M, tennis, track and field, volleyball W. **Intramural:** Archery, badminton, baseball M, basketball, gymnastics, racquetball, rifle, skiing, soccer, softball, tennis, volleyball, wrestling M. **Clubs:** Bowling M,W.

STUDENT SERVICES. Aptitude testing, career counseling, employment service for undergraduates, freshman orientation, health services, on-campus day care, personal counseling, placement service for graduates, special adviser for adult students, veterans counselor, American Indian students counselor, services/facilities for handicapped.

ANNUAL EXPENSES. Tuition and fees: $1,386, $3,614 additional for out-of-state students. **Room and board:** $2,970. **Books and supplies:** $500. **Other expenses:** $1,575.

FINANCIAL AID. 80% of freshmen, 80% of continuing students receive some form of aid. 85% of grants, 91% of loans, 23% of jobs based on need. Academic, music/drama, art, athletic, state/district residency, leadership, alumni affiliation, minority scholarships available. **Aid applications:** No closing date; priority given to applications received by March 15; applicants notified on a rolling basis beginning on or about June 15; must reply within 4 weeks.

ADDRESS/TELEPHONE. Mike Echanis, Associate Director for Admissions, Idaho State University, PO Box 8054, Pocatello, ID 83209. (208) 236-2123. (800) 888-ISU1.

ITT Technical Institute: Boise

Boise, Idaho CB code: 3596

Admissions: 60% of applicants accepted
Based on: ••• Test scores
• School record
Completion: 72% of freshmen end year in good standing
9% enter 4-year programs

2-year proprietary technical college, coed. Founded in 1906. **Undergraduate enrollment:** 156 men, 155 women full time. **Faculty:** 17 total (16 full time). **Location:** Suburban campus in small city. **Calendar:** Quarter. **Microcomputers:** 90 located in classrooms.

DEGREES OFFERED. AAS. 96 associate degrees awarded in 1992. 45% in computer sciences, 55% engineering technologies.

UNDERGRADUATE MAJORS. Computer-aided drafting technology, electronic technology.

ACADEMIC PROGRAMS. Remedial services: Tutoring.

ACADEMIC REQUIREMENTS. Freshmen must earn minimum GPA of 2.0 to continue in good standing. Students must declare major on application. **Graduation requirements:** 124 hours for associate.

FRESHMAN ADMISSIONS. Selection criteria: Satisfactory scores in English and/or mathematics tests required. **Test requirements:** Institutional test in English and mathematics required for admission.

1992 FRESHMAN CLASS PROFILE. 182 men applied, 109 accepted, 109 enrolled; 211 women applied, 127 accepted, 127 enrolled. **Characteristics:** 92% from in state, 100% commute. Average age is 27.

FALL-TERM APPLICATIONS. $100 fee. Application fee refunded if student not accepted. No closing date; applicants notified on a rolling basis.

STUDENT LIFE. Activities: Student newspaper.

STUDENT SERVICES. Personal counseling, placement service for graduates, services/facilities for handicapped.

ANNUAL EXPENSES. Tuition and fees: Tuition for a 12-month period ranges from $6,125 to $9,020 depending on course of study. Laboratory fees, $75 per quarter. **Books and supplies:** $900. **Other expenses:** $1,206.

FINANCIAL AID. Aid applications: No closing date; applicants notified on a rolling basis.

ADDRESS/TELEPHONE. Jennifer Kandler, Director of Education, ITT Technical Institute: Boise, 950 Lusk Street, Boise, ID 83706. (208) 344-8376. Fax: (208) 345-0056.

Lewis Clark State College

Lewiston, Idaho CB code: 4385

4-year public business, nursing, liberal arts, teachers college, coed. Founded in 1893. **Accreditation:** Regional. **Undergraduate enrollment:** 776 men, 1,090 women full time; 355 men, 808 women part time. **Faculty:** 115 total (105 full time), 70 with doctorates or other terminal degrees. **Location:** Urban campus in large town; 300 miles from Boise, 100 miles from Spokane, Washington. **Calendar:** Semester, limited summer session. Saturday and extensive evening/early morning classes. **Microcomputers:** Located in dormitories, libraries, computer centers. **Special facilities:** State of the art educational technology center.

DEGREES OFFERED. AA, AS, AAS, BA, BS. 142 associate degrees awarded in 1992. 36% in business/office and marketing/distribution, 27% health sciences, 33% trade and industry. 228 bachelor's degrees awarded. 44% in business and management, 14% teacher education, 9% health sciences, 16% multi/interdisciplinary studies, 10% social sciences.

UNDERGRADUATE MAJORS. Associate: Accounting, agricultural mechanics, automotive mechanics, automotive technology, behavioral sciences, business and office, computer servicing technology, computer technology, diesel engine mechanics, drafting, drafting and design technology, electrical and electronics equipment repair, electronic technology, English, graphic and printing production, graphic arts technology, hospitality and recreation marketing, industrial equipment maintenance and repair, law enforcement and corrections technologies, legal assistant/paralegal, legal secretary, liberal/general studies, manufacturing technology, marketing and distribution, medical laboratory technologies, medical records technology, medical secretary, nursing, practical nursing, precision metal work, science technologies, secretarial and related programs, welding technology, word processing. **Bachelor's:** Biological and physical sciences, biology, business administration and management, business and management, chemistry, communications, criminal justice studies, earth sciences, education, elementary education, English, English/business, fine arts, geology, history, history/political science, humanities and social sciences, international studies, junior high education, law enforcement and corrections, liberal/general studies, management science, mathematics, nursing, physical education, physical sciences, secondary education, social sciences, social work, special education.

ACADEMIC PROGRAMS. Accelerated program, cooperative education, double major, dual enrollment of high school students, honors program, independent study, internships, student-designed major, study abroad, teacher preparation, telecourses, weekend college, cross-registration. **Remedial services:** Learning center, reduced course load, remedial instruction, special counselor, tutoring. **ROTC:** Army. **Placement/credit:** AP, CLEP General and Subject, institutional tests; 32 credit hours maximum for bachelor's degree.

ACADEMIC REQUIREMENTS. Freshmen must earn minimum GPA of 2.0 to continue in good standing. Students must declare major on enrollment. **Graduation requirements:** 68 hours for associate, 128 hours for bachelor's. Most students required to take courses in arts/fine arts, English, mathematics, biological/physical sciences, social sciences. **Postgraduate studies:** 4% from 2-year programs enter 4-year programs.

FRESHMAN ADMISSIONS. Selection criteria: Specific academic units and test scores important. **High school preparation:** 20 units required. Required units include English 8, mathematics 2, social science 3 and science 2. 4 units from humanities/languages/fine arts and 1 unit of speech also required. **Test requirements:** SAT or ACT (ACT preferred); score report by August 31. Washington Pre-College Test may be used in place of SAT or ACT.

1992 FRESHMAN CLASS PROFILE. 241 men, 288 women enrolled. **Characteristics:** 85% from in state, 80% commute, 5% have minority backgrounds, 3% are foreign students. Average age is 24.

FALL-TERM APPLICATIONS. $10 fee. No closing date; applicants notified on a rolling basis beginning on or about April 1. CRDA. Early admission available. First Monday in March is the deadline for nursing applications.

STUDENT LIFE. Housing: Dormitories (men, women, coed); apartment housing available. Coed dormitories are for honor students only. **Activities:** Student government, student newspaper, choral groups, concert band, dance, drama, jazz band, music ensembles, musical theater, pep band, Native American Indian Student Organization, International Student Club, Ambassadors Club, Criminal Justice Society, Idaho Student Lobby.

ATHLETICS. NAIA. **Intercollegiate:** Baseball M, basketball, tennis, volleyball W. **Intramural:** Badminton, baseball, basketball, golf, skiing, soccer, softball, table tennis, tennis, volleyball.

STUDENT SERVICES. Career counseling, employment service for undergraduates, freshman orientation, health services, on-campus day care, personal counseling, placement service for graduates, special adviser for adult students, veterans counselor, services/facilities for handicapped.

ANNUAL EXPENSES. Tuition and fees: $1,320, $2,920 additional for out-of-state students. **Room and board:** $3,026. **Books and supplies:** $560. **Other expenses:** $1,116.

FINANCIAL AID. 64% of freshmen, 52% of continuing students receive some form of aid. 65% of grants, 95% of loans, 75% of jobs based on need. 256 enrolled freshmen were judged to have need, 232 were offered aid. Academic, music/drama, athletic, state/district residency, leadership, minority scholarships available. **Aid applications:** No closing date; priority given to applications received by March 1; applicants notified on a rolling basis beginning on or about June 1; must reply within 2 weeks.

ADDRESS/TELEPHONE. Steven J. Bussolini, Director of Enrollment Management, Lewis Clark State College, Eighth Avenue and Sixth Street, Lewiston, ID 83501-2698. (208) 799-LCSC. (800) 933-LCSC. Fax: (208) 799-2831.

North Idaho College

Coeur d'Alene, Idaho CB code: 4539

2-year public community college, coed. Founded in 1933. **Accreditation:** Regional. **Undergraduate enrollment:** 853 men, 877 women full time; 361 men, 977 women part time. **Faculty:** 168 total (74 full time), 5 with doctorates or other terminal degrees. **Location:** Urban campus in large town; 30 miles from Spokane, Washington. **Calendar:** Semester, limited summer session. Extensive evening/early morning classes. **Microcomputers:** 120 located in classrooms, computer centers. **Special facilities:** Art gallery, Fort Sherman museum, 3300 feet of beachfront property on shores of Lake Coeur d'Alene and Spokane River.

DEGREES OFFERED. AA, AS, AAS. 239 associate degrees awarded in 1992. 20% in business and management, 71% teacher education, 27% health sciences, 12% allied health, 16% multi/interdisciplinary studies.

UNDERGRADUATE MAJORS. Agricultural engineering, air conditioning/heating/refrigeration mechanics, anthropology, astronomy, automotive mechanics, bacteriology, biology, botany, business administration and management, business and management, business and office, business data processing and related programs, business data programming, business education, business systems analysis, carpentry, chemical engineering, chemistry, child development/care/guidance, civil engineering, clinical laboratory science, commercial art, communications, computer and information sciences, computer programming, computer technology, criminal justice studies, data processing, diesel engine mechanics, drafting, drafting and design technology, early childhood education, education, electrical technology, electrical/electronics/communications engineering, elementary education, engineering, engineering and engineering-related technologies, English, fine arts, fishing and fisheries, foreign languages (multiple emphasis), forestry and related sciences, geological engineering, geology, health sciences, history, industrial equipment maintenance and repair, journalism, junior high education, law enforcement and corrections technologies, legal secretary, liberal/

general studies, machine tool operation/machine shop, mathematics, medical laboratory technologies, medical secretary, mining and mineral engineering, music, music education, music performance, music theory and composition, nursing, physical sciences, physics, political science and government, practical nursing, precision metal work, predentistry, prelaw, premedicine, prepharmacy, preveterinary, psychology, radiograph medical technology, renewable natural resources, respiratory therapy technology, secondary education, secretarial and related programs, small business management and ownership, social sciences, sociology, speech pathology/audiology, welding technology, wildlife management, zoology.

ACADEMIC PROGRAMS. 2-year transfer program, dual enrollment of high school students, independent study, internships, Lewis Clark State College and University of Idaho upper division and graduate classes on campus. **Remedial services:** Learning center, reduced course load, remedial instruction, special counselor, tutoring, counselor for learning disabled. **Placement/credit:** AP, CLEP General and Subject, institutional tests; 24 credit hours maximum for associate degree.

ACADEMIC REQUIREMENTS. Freshmen must earn minimum GPA of 1.75 to continue in good standing. 50% of freshmen return for sophomore year. Students must declare major by end of first year. **Graduation requirements:** 64 hours for associate (17 in major). Most students required to take courses in arts/fine arts, computer science, English, foreign languages, history, humanities, mathematics, philosophy/religion, biological/physical sciences, social sciences. **Additional information:** Guaranteed transfer of credits with junior standing to all Idaho 4-year institutions if student receives Associate of Arts or Associate of Science degree. This agreement also available at Eastern Washington University for students receiving Associate of Arts.

FRESHMAN ADMISSIONS. Selection criteria: Open admissions. RN and LPN nursing program applicants must submit 3 references and supplemental statement. Vocational school applicants must take ASSET test and be interviewed by vocational counselor. Recommended units include English 4, foreign language 2, mathematics 3, social science 2 and science 3. Algebra, biology, 2 years chemistry with laboratory, English, social science with cummulative GPA 2.50 required for registered nursing applicants. Physics, advanced algebra also recommended for nursing applicants.

1992 FRESHMAN CLASS PROFILE. 1,146 men and women enrolled. 33% had high school GPA of 3.0 or higher, 57% between 2.0 and 2.99. 9% were in top tenth and 23% were in top quarter of graduating class. **Characteristics:** 88% from in state, 97% commute, 4% have minority backgrounds, 1% are foreign students. Average age is 22.

FALL-TERM APPLICATIONS. $10 fee, may be waived for applicants with need. No closing date; priority given to applications received by August 1; applicants notified on a rolling basis beginning on or about February 1. Interview required for vocational applicants. Deferred and early admission available. Skills assessment test required in writing, reading, and mathematics for placement and counseling.

STUDENT LIFE. Housing: Dormitories (coed). Apartment complex adjacent to campus. **Activities:** Student government, magazine, student newspaper, television, choral groups, concert band, dance, drama, jazz band, music ensembles, musical theater, pep band, symphony orchestra, Students for Human Equality, Creative Writers Club, Nursing Student Association, Veterans Club, International Student Relations.

ATHLETICS. NJCAA. **Intercollegiate:** Baseball M, basketball, cross-country, track and field, volleyball W, wrestling M. **Intramural:** Badminton, basketball, bowling, golf, racquetball, rowing (crew), sailing, skiing, soccer, softball, tennis, volleyball. **Clubs:** Rowing, skiing.

STUDENT SERVICES. Aptitude testing, career counseling, employment service for undergraduates, freshman orientation, health services, on-campus day care, personal counseling, placement service for graduates, special adviser for adult students, veterans counselor, services/facilities for handicapped.

ANNUAL EXPENSES. Tuition and fees: $942, $1,000 additional for out-of-district students, $1,602 additional for out-of-state students. **Room and board:** $3,064. **Books and supplies:** $500. **Other expenses:** $830.

FINANCIAL AID. 43% of freshmen, 40% of continuing students receive some form of aid. 86% of grants, 94% of loans, all jobs based on need. Academic, music/drama, art, athletic, state/district residency, leadership scholarships available. **Aid applications:** No closing date; priority given to applications received by April 15; applicants notified on a rolling basis beginning on or about May 15; must reply within 2 weeks.

ADDRESS/TELEPHONE. M. Kirk Koenig, Director of Admissions, North Idaho College, 1000 West Garden Avenue, Coeur d'Alene, ID 83814. (208) 769-3311.

Northwest Nazarene College
Nampa, Idaho

CB code: 4544

4-year private liberal arts college, coed, affiliated with Church of the Nazarene. Founded in 1913. **Accreditation:** Regional. **Undergraduate enrollment:** 1,058 men and women full time; 88 men and women part time. **Graduate enrollment:** 92 men and women. **Faculty:** 91 total (87 full time), 44 with doctorates or other terminal degrees. **Location:** Suburban campus in large town; 18 miles from Boise. **Calendar:** Quarter, extensive summer session. **Microcomputers:** Located in computer centers. **Special facilities:** Selective depository for federal government publications.

DEGREES OFFERED. AA, AS, BA, BS, MEd. 5 associate degrees awarded in 1992. 210 bachelor's degrees awarded. Graduate degrees offered in 4 major fields of study.

UNDERGRADUATE MAJORS. Associate: Allied health, Bible studies, business and management, chemical manufacturing technology, computer programming, engineering and engineering-related technologies, fine arts, human resources development, psychology, recreation and community services technologies, religion, religious education, social sciences, social work. **Bachelor's:** Accounting, apparel and accessories marketing, art education, Bible studies, biological and physical sciences, biology, business administration and management, business home economics, chemistry, chemistry education, child development/care/guidance, communications, compassionate ministries, computer and information sciences, elementary education, engineering and other disciplines, engineering physics, English, English education, entrepreneurship, finance, fine arts, foreign languages (multiple emphasis), health education, history, home economics education, humanities, humanities and social sciences, information sciences and systems, international relations, international studies, liberal/general studies, management information systems, managerial accounting, mathematics, mathematics education, music, music education, pastoral ministries, philosophy, physical education, physics, political science and government, predentistry, predietetics, prelaw, premedicine, prepharmacy, preveterinary, psychology, recreation and community services technologies, religion, religious education, religious music, science education, secondary education, social science education, social sciences, social work, sociology, special education, specific learning disabilities, speech, speech correction, speech pathology/audiology, speech/communication/theater education, sports medicine, theological studies.

ACADEMIC PROGRAMS. Accelerated program, double major, dual enrollment of high school students, education specialist degree, independent study, internships, student-designed major, teacher preparation, Washington semester, cross-registration; liberal arts/career combination in engineering. **Remedial services:** Learning center, reduced course load, remedial instruction, special counselor, tutoring. **ROTC:** Army. **Placement/credit:** AP, CLEP General and Subject, institutional tests; 23 credit hours maximum for associate degree; 47 credit hours maximum for bachelor's degree.

ACADEMIC REQUIREMENTS. Freshmen must earn minimum GPA of 1.75 to continue in good standing. 61% of freshmen return for sophomore year. Students must declare major by end of second year. **Graduation requirements:** 92 hours for associate (32 in major), 188 hours for bachelor's (64 in major). Most students required to take courses in arts/fine arts, English, history, humanities, philosophy/religion, biological/physical sciences, social sciences. **Postgraduate studies:** 40% from 2-year programs enter 4-year programs.

FRESHMAN ADMISSIONS. Selection criteria: Character recommendation from pastor or teacher required. **High school preparation:** 16 units recommended. Recommended units include English 4, foreign language 2, mathematics 3, social science 3 and science 4. **Test requirements:** ACT for placement and counseling only; score report by September 15. SAT or ACT scores used for admissions purposes for marginal applicants only.

1992 FRESHMAN CLASS PROFILE. 290 men and women enrolled. **Academic background:** Mid 50% of enrolled freshmen had ACT composite between 16-26. 85% submitted ACT scores. **Characteristics:** 39% from in state, 85% live in college housing, 5% have minority backgrounds. Average age is 18.

FALL-TERM APPLICATIONS. $10 fee, may be waived for applicants with need. No closing date; applicants notified on a rolling basis. Interview recommended for academically weak applicants. Deferred and early admission available.

STUDENT LIFE. Housing: Dormitories (men, women); apartment housing available. All students required to live on campus until senior year, or age 22, unless living with parent(s) or guardian. **Activities:** Student government, film, magazine, student newspaper, yearbook, choral groups, concert band, drama, jazz band, music ensembles, pep band, General Missionary Society, summer ministries, Circle-K, Crusaders in Mission, Athletes in Ministry, Action Against Hunger, urban ministries club, social work clubs.

ATHLETICS. NAIA. **Intercollegiate:** Baseball M, basketball, soccer M, tennis W, track and field, volleyball W. **Intramural:** Archery, badminton, basketball, bowling, cross-country, gymnastics, handball, racquetball, skiing, softball, swimming, table tennis, tennis, track and field, volleyball.

STUDENT SERVICES. Aptitude testing, career counseling, employment service for undergraduates, freshman orientation, health services, personal counseling, placement service for graduates, veterans counselor, vocational rehabilitation, services/facilities for handicapped.

ANNUAL EXPENSES. Tuition and fees (1992-93): $8,160. **Room and board:** $2,590. **Books and supplies:** $675. **Other expenses:** $788.

FINANCIAL AID. 85% of freshmen, 92% of continuing students receive some form of aid. Grants, loans, jobs available. Academic, music/drama, art, athletic, state/district residency, leadership, alumni affiliation, religious affiliation, minority scholarships available. **Aid applications:** No closing date; priority given to applications received by March 1; applicants notified on a rolling basis beginning on or about April 1; must reply within 2 weeks.

ADDRESS/TELEPHONE. Terry Blom, Director of Enrollment Management, Northwest Nazarene College, Dewey at Holly Street, Nampa, ID 83686. (208) 467-8496. (800) NNC-4YOU.

Ricks College
Rexburg, Idaho CB code: 4657

Admissions: 94% of applicants accepted
Based on: ••• Recommendations, religious affiliation/commitment
•• Essay, school record, test scores
• Special talents
Completion: 90% of freshmen end year in good standing
40% graduate, 60% of these enter 4-year programs

2-year private junior college, coed, affiliated with Church of Jesus Christ of Latter-day Saints. Founded in 1888. **Accreditation:** Regional. **Undergraduate enrollment:** 3,115 men, 4,499 women full time; 164 men, 165 women part time. **Faculty:** 414 total (326 full time), 90 with doctorates or other terminal degrees. **Location:** Rural campus in large town; 30 miles from Idaho Falls. **Calendar:** Semester, extensive summer session. Extensive evening/early morning classes. **Microcomputers:** Located in libraries, classrooms, computer centers. **Special facilities:** Observatory, planetarium, livestock center, off-campus outdoor educational facility.

DEGREES OFFERED. AA, AS. 2,041 associate degrees awarded in 1992. 6% in business/office and marketing/distribution, 6% teacher education, 6% home economics, 43% multi/interdisciplinary studies, 6% social sciences.

UNDERGRADUATE MAJORS. Accounting, agricultural business and management, agricultural mechanics, agricultural sciences, agronomy, animal sciences, architectural technologies, automotive mechanics, automotive technology, biology, botany, business administration and management, business and management, business and office, business computer/console/peripheral equipment operation, business data processing and related programs, business data programming, business education, carpentry, chemical engineering, chemistry, child development/care/guidance, civil engineering, clothing and textiles management/production/services, communications, computer and information sciences, computer programming, computer servicing technology, computer technology, construction, criminal justice studies, dairy, dance, data processing, dental hygiene, drafting, drafting and design technology, dramatic arts, early childhood education, ecology, economics, education, electrical and electronics equipment repair, electrical/electronics/communications engineering, electronic technology, elementary education, emergency medical technologies, engineering, engineering and engineering-related technologies, English, fashion design, fashion merchandising, finance, fine arts, food science and nutrition, forestry and related sciences, French, geography, geology, German, health sciences, history, home economics, home economics education, horticultural science, horticulture, humanities, individual and family development, interior design, international business management, journalism, law enforcement and corrections technologies, liberal/general studies, management information systems, manufacturing technology, marine biology, marketing and distribution, marketing management, mathematics, mechanical engineering, medical laboratory technologies, microbiology, music, music education, nursing, ornamental horticulture, photography, physical education, physical sciences, physics, plant sciences, political science and government, predentistry, prelaw, premedicine, prepharmacy, preveterinary, psychology, radio/television broadcasting, recreation and community services technologies, Russian, secretarial and related programs, social work, sociology, soil sciences, Spanish, special education, speech, speech pathology/audiology, sports medicine, technical education, welding technology, wildlife management, woodworking, word processing, zoology.

ACADEMIC PROGRAMS. 2-year transfer program, honors program, internships. **Remedial services:** Learning center, preadmission summer program, reduced course load, remedial instruction, special counselor, tutoring. **ROTC:** Army. **Placement/credit:** AP, CLEP General and Subject, institutional tests.

ACADEMIC REQUIREMENTS. Freshmen must earn minimum GPA of 2.0 to continue in good standing. 60% of freshmen return for sophomore year. Students must declare major on application. **Graduation requirements:** 64 hours for associate. Most students required to take courses in arts/fine arts, English, humanities, philosophy/religion, biological/physical sciences, social sciences.

FRESHMAN ADMISSIONS. Selection criteria: Religious affiliation, recommendations most important. High school record, test scores, and personal essay also important. **Test requirements:** SAT or ACT (ACT preferred); score report by March 1.

1992 FRESHMAN CLASS PROFILE. 60% had high school GPA of 3.0 or higher, 38% between 2.0 and 2.99. **Academic background:** Mid 50% of enrolled freshmen had ACT composite between 17-24. 95% submitted ACT scores. **Characteristics:** 38% from in state, 80% commute, 2% have minority backgrounds, 4% are foreign students. Average age is 18.

FALL-TERM APPLICATIONS. $15 fee. Closing date March 1; applicants notified on or about April 1. Audition required for music, dance applicants. Essay required. Interview with student's church leader required. Early admission available.

STUDENT LIFE. Housing: Dormitories (men, women); apartment, cooperative housing available. **Activities:** Student government, radio, student newspaper, yearbook, choral groups, concert band, dance, drama, jazz band, music ensembles, musical theater, opera, pep band, symphony orchestra, International Student Club, Order of Ammon (Native American Club), Young Republicans, Young Democrats. **Additional information:** Students encouraged to attend weekly devotional at which noted church leaders speak.

ATHLETICS. NAIA, NJCAA. **Intercollegiate:** Baseball M, basketball, cross-country, football M, track and field, volleyball W, wrestling M. **Intramural:** Archery, badminton, basketball, bowling, diving, golf, racquetball, skiing, soccer, softball, swimming, table tennis, tennis, track and field, volleyball, wrestling M.

STUDENT SERVICES. Aptitude testing, career counseling, employment service for undergraduates, freshman orientation, health services, personal counseling, placement service for graduates, veterans counselor, services/facilities for handicapped.

ANNUAL EXPENSES. Tuition and fees (1992-93): $1,550. $770 additional for students not members of Church of Jesus Christ of Latter-day Saints. **Room and board:** $2,760. **Books and supplies:** $550. **Other expenses:** $1,000.

FINANCIAL AID. 78% of freshmen, 70% of continuing students receive some form of aid. All grants, 97% of loans based on need. All jobs based on criteria other than need. Academic, music/drama, art, athletic, leadership scholarships available. **Aid applications:** No closing date; applicants notified on a rolling basis beginning on or about February 1. **Additional information:** Application deadline for merit scholarships March 1.

ADDRESS/TELEPHONE. Gordon Westenskow, Director of Admissions, Ricks College, Rexburg, ID 83460-4104. (208) 356-1020. Fax: (208) 356-1185.

University of Idaho
Moscow, Idaho CB code: 4843

Admissions: 92% of applicants accepted
Based on: ••• School record
•• Test scores
Completion: 92% of freshmen end year in good standing
33% graduate, 33% of these enter graduate study

4-year public university, coed. Founded in 1889. **Accreditation:** Regional. **Undergraduate enrollment:** 4,186 men, 2,828 women full time; 457 men, 331 women part time. **Graduate enrollment:** 746 men, 380 women full time; 805 men, 526 women part time. **Faculty:** 916 total (830 full time), 632 with doctorates or other terminal degrees. **Location:** Rural campus in large town; 85 miles from Spokane, Washington. **Calendar:** Semester, extensive summer session. **Microcomputers:** 225 located in dormitories, libraries, classrooms, computer centers. **Special facilities:** Art gallery, observatory, arboretum, 18-hole golf course. **Additional facts:** Residential land grant university.

DEGREES OFFERED. BA, BS, BFA, BArch, MA, MS, MFA, MEd, PhD, EdD. 1,040 bachelor's degrees awarded in 1992. 5% in architecture and environmental design, 11% business and management, 9% communications, 14% teacher education, 14% engineering, 6% parks/recreation, protective services, public affairs, 7% social sciences. Graduate degrees offered in 71 major fields of study.

UNDERGRADUATE MAJORS. Accounting, actuarial sciences, advertising, agribusiness, agricultural business and management, agricultural economics, agricultural engineering, agricultural mechanics, agricultural sciences, American studies, animal sciences, anthropology, applied mathematics, architecture, bacteriology, biology, botany, business economics, cartography, ceramics, chemical engineering, chemistry, civil engineering, classics, communications, computer and information sciences, computer engineering, criminal justice studies, dance, dramatic arts, drawing, economics, electrical/electronics/communications engineering, elementary education, English, entomology, finance, fine arts, fishing and fisheries, food science and nutrition, forest products processing technology, forestry and related sciences, French, geography, geological engineering, geology, German, graphic design, history, home economics, horticultural science, human resources development, individual and family development, industrial technology, interior design, international studies, journalism, landscape architecture, Latin, Latin American studies, liberal/general studies, management information systems, manufacturing engineering, marketing and distribution, marketing management, mathematics, mechanical engineering, medical laboratory technologies, metal/jewelry, metallurgical engineering, mining and mineral engineering, music, music history and appreciation, music performance, music theory and composition, naval science (Navy, Marines), office supervision and management, operations research, ornamental horticulture, painting, parks and recreation management, philosophy, physical sciences, physics, plant protection, political science and government, poultry, preveterinary, printmaking, psychology, public relations, range management, renewable natural resources, sculpture, secondary education, secretarial and related programs, sociology, soil sciences, Spanish, special education, speech, telecommunications, textiles and clothing, wildlife management, zoology.

ACADEMIC PROGRAMS. Accelerated program, cooperative education, double major, dual enrollment of high school students, education specialist degree, honors program, independent study, internships, student-designed major, study abroad, teacher preparation, telecourses, visiting/exchange student program, cross-registration. **Remedial services:** Learning center, preadmission summer program, reduced course load, remedial instruction, special counselor, tutoring. **ROTC:** Air Force, Army, Naval. **Placement/credit:** AP, CLEP General and Subject, institutional tests; 48 credit hours maximum for bachelor's degree.

ACADEMIC REQUIREMENTS. Freshmen must earn minimum GPA of 1.6 to continue in good standing. 73% of freshmen return for sophomore year. Students must declare major by end of second year. **Graduation requirements:** 128 hours for bachelor's (40 in major). Most students required to take courses in arts/fine arts, computer science, English, history, humanities, mathematics, biological/physical sciences, social sciences. **Postgraduate studies:** 4% enter law school, 2% enter medical school, 2% enter MBA programs, 25% enter other graduate study.

FRESHMAN ADMISSIONS. Selection criteria: Applicants must rank in top three quarters of class. 2.0 GPA in college preparatory courses required. **High school preparation:** 15 units required. Required and recommended units include English 4, mathematics 3, social science 3 and science 3. Foreign language 2 recommended. 1 unit from humanities, arts, foreign language, 1.5 units other college prep. **Test requirements:** SAT or ACT; score report by August 1.

1992 FRESHMAN CLASS PROFILE. 1,638 men applied, 1,508 accepted, 766 enrolled; 1,191 women applied, 1,092 accepted, 587 enrolled. 69% had high school GPA of 3.0 or higher, 31% between 2.0 and 2.99. 23% were in top tenth and 49% were in top quarter of graduating class. **Academic background:** Mid 50% of enrolled freshmen had SAT-V between 390-520, SAT-M between 440-590; ACT composite between 20-25. 57% submitted SAT scores, 69% submitted ACT scores. **Characteristics:** 64% from in state, 98% live in college housing, 6% have minority backgrounds, 1% are foreign students, 40% join fraternities/sororities. Average age is 19.

FALL-TERM APPLICATIONS. $20 fee. Closing date August 1; applicants notified on a rolling basis beginning on or about November 1. CRDA. Deferred admission available. Institutional early decision plan. Admission decision and student notification upon receipt of application, transcripts, and results of ACT or SAT. Student not required to confirm enrollment prior to registation.

STUDENT LIFE. Housing: Dormitories (men, women, coed); apartment, fraternity, sorority, cooperative housing available. **Activities:** Student government, radio, student newspaper, television, yearbook, choral groups, concert band, dance, drama, jazz band, marching band, music ensembles, musical theater, opera, pep band, symphony orchestra, fraternities, sororities, Campus Christian Center, Campus Crusade for Christ, St. Augustine's Catholic Center, Latter-Day Saint Institute, MECHA (Hispanic students), Blue Key Service Honorary, Intercollegiate Knights Services Honorary, Young Republicans, Valkeries Service Organization.

ATHLETICS. NCAA. **Intercollegiate:** Basketball, cross-country, football M, golf M, tennis, track and field, volleyball W. **Intramural:** Badminton, basketball, bowling, golf, racquetball, rifle, skiing, soccer, softball, table tennis, tennis, wrestling M.

STUDENT SERVICES. Aptitude testing, career counseling, employment service for undergraduates, freshman orientation, health services, on-campus day care, personal counseling, placement service for graduates, special adviser for adult students, veterans counselor, services/facilities for handicapped.

ANNUAL EXPENSES. Tuition and fees: $1,426, $3,900 additional for out-of-state students. **Room and board:** $3,400. **Books and supplies:** $770. **Other expenses:** $1,650.

FINANCIAL AID. 65% of freshmen, 60% of continuing students receive some form of aid. 77% of grants, 88% of loans, 31% of jobs based on need. Academic, music/drama, art, athletic, state/district residency, leadership, alumni affiliation, minority scholarships available. **Aid applications:** No closing date; priority given to applications received by February 15; applicants notified on a rolling basis beginning on or about May 1; must reply within 3 weeks.

ADDRESS/TELEPHONE. Peter T. Brown, Director of Admissions, University of Idaho, Moscow, ID 83844-3133. (208) 885-6326. Fax: (208) 885-5752.

Illinois

American Academy of Art
Chicago, Illinois CB code: 1013

2-year proprietary art college, coed. Founded in 1923. **Undergraduate enrollment:** 370 men and women full time; 250 men and women part time. **Faculty:** 46 total (11 full time), 9 with doctorates or other terminal degrees. **Location:** Urban campus in very large city; in downtown Loop area. **Calendar:** Semester, extensive summer session. **Special facilities:** Art gallery.

DEGREES OFFERED. AAS. 106 associate degrees awarded in 1992. 100% in visual and performing arts.

UNDERGRADUATE MAJORS. Advertising design, drawing, electronic design, graphic design, illustration design, painting.

ACADEMIC PROGRAMS. Double major. **Remedial services:** Preadmission summer program.

ACADEMIC REQUIREMENTS. Freshmen must earn minimum GPA of 2.0 to continue in good standing. 85% of freshmen return for sophomore year. Students must declare major by end of first year. **Graduation requirements:** 64 hours for associate (48 in major). Most students required to take courses in arts/fine arts, English, humanities, mathematics, biological/physical sciences.

FRESHMAN ADMISSIONS. Selection criteria: Portfolio and interview important. Prospective students must have strong artistic skills.

1992 FRESHMAN CLASS PROFILE. 185 men and women enrolled. **Characteristics:** 84% from in state, 100% commute, 20% have minority backgrounds. Average age is 18.

FALL-TERM APPLICATIONS. $25 fee. Closing date September 4; priority given to applications received by July 1; applicants notified on a rolling basis. Interview recommended. Essay recommended. Portfolio required of all full-time applicants and of part-time applicants who want to take advanced courses. Deferred admission available.

STUDENT LIFE. Activities: Yearbook, student art shows.

STUDENT SERVICES. Career counseling, employment service for undergraduates, freshman orientation, personal counseling, placement service for graduates, veterans counselor, services/facilities for handicapped.

ANNUAL EXPENSES. Tuition and fees (1992-93): $8,380. **Books and supplies:** $800.

FINANCIAL AID. 45% of freshmen, 43% of continuing students receive some form of aid. 94% of grants, 74% of loans based on need. Art scholarships available. **Aid applications:** No closing date; applicants notified on a rolling basis beginning on or about July 1; must reply by August 15 or by start of classes if notified thereafter.

ADDRESS/TELEPHONE. Mary Ellen Taylor, Chief Admissions Officer, American Academy of Art, 122 South Michigan Avenue, Chicago, IL 60603-6191. (312) 939-3883. Fax: (312) 939-5429.

American Conservatory of Music
Chicago, Illinois CB code: 1014

4-year private music college, coed. Founded in 1886. **Undergraduate enrollment:** 14 men, 13 women full time; 5 men, 3 women part time. **Graduate enrollment:** 4 men, 6 women full time; 2 men, 4 women part time. **Faculty:** 37 total. **Location:** Urban campus in very large city; in geographic center of Chicago. **Calendar:** Semester, extensive summer session. **Microcomputers:** 3 located in libraries. **Special facilities:** Extensive recordings and video holdings. **Additional facts:** Undergraduates may choose between degree programs in jazz or classical studies. Accredited by National Association of Schools of Music.

DEGREES OFFERED. B, M, D. 1 associate degree awarded in 1992. 100% in visual and performing arts. 10 bachelor's degrees awarded. 100% in visual and performing arts. Graduate degrees offered in 2 major fields of study.

UNDERGRADUATE MAJORS. Jazz. jazz, music performance, music theory and composition.

ACADEMIC PROGRAMS. Accelerated program, double major. **Remedial services:** Reduced course load, remedial instruction. **Placement/credit:** Institutional tests; 12 credit hours maximum for associate degree; 12 credit hours maximum for bachelor's degree.

ACADEMIC REQUIREMENTS. Freshmen must earn minimum GPA of 2.0 to continue in good standing. 65% of freshmen return for sophomore year. Students must declare major on enrollment. **Graduation requirements:** 64 hours for associate (16 in major), 134 hours for bachelor's (32 in major). Most students required to take courses in arts/fine arts, English, foreign languages, history, humanities, social sciences. **Postgraduate studies:** 100% from 2-year programs enter 4-year programs.

FRESHMAN ADMISSIONS. Recommended units include English 3, foreign language 2, mathematics 2, social science 2 and science 2. Adequate background in fundamentals of music. Participation in school music program recommended. **Test requirements:** SAT or ACT; score report by June 1. Institutional entrance examinations in music history and music theory.

1992 FRESHMAN CLASS PROFILE. 7 men enrolled. 23% had high school GPA of 3.0 or higher, 77% between 2.0 and 2.99. **Characteristics:** 90% from in state, 100% commute, 22% have minority backgrounds, 19% are foreign students. Average age is 20.

FALL-TERM APPLICATIONS. $25 fee. No closing date; priority given to applications received by April 1; applicants notified on a rolling basis beginning on or about April 1; must reply within 30 days of notification. Interview required. Audition required. Essay required. Deferred and early admission available.

STUDENT LIFE. Activities: Student government, choral groups, concert band, jazz band, music ensembles, opera, symphony orchestra.

STUDENT SERVICES. Employment service for undergraduates, freshman orientation, services/facilities for handicapped.

ANNUAL EXPENSES. Tuition and fees (1992-93): $7,000. **Books and supplies:** $500. **Other expenses:** $1,200.

FINANCIAL AID. 69% of freshmen, 61% of continuing students receive some form of aid. 56% of grants, 97% of loans, all jobs based on need. Music/drama scholarships available. **Aid applications:** No closing date; priority given to applications received by June 1; applicants notified on a rolling basis beginning on or about April 1; must reply within 2 weeks.

ADDRESS/TELEPHONE. Joseph Miller, Director of Admissions, American Conservatory of Music, 16 North Wabash Avenue, suite 1850, Chicago, IL 60602-4792. (312) 263-4161. Fax: (312) 263-8419.

Augustana College
Rock Island, Illinois CB code: 1025

Admissions: 88% of applicants accepted
Based on: ••• School record, test scores
•• Essay, interview
• Activities, recommendations, special talents
Completion: 96% of freshmen end year in good standing
72% graduate, 31% of these enter graduate study

4-year private liberal arts college, coed, affiliated with Evangelical Lutheran Church in America. Founded in 1860. **Accreditation:** Regional. **Undergraduate enrollment:** 911 men, 1,135 women full time; 17 men, 17 women part time. **Faculty:** 173 total (143 full time), 117 with doctorates or other terminal degrees. **Location:** Urban campus in small city; 165 miles from Chicago. **Calendar:** Quarter, limited summer session. **Microcomputers:** 150 located in dormitories, libraries, classrooms, computer centers, campus-wide network. **Special facilities:** Art gallery, planetarium, observatory, map library, geology museum, Swenson Swedish Immigration Research Center, national public radio station, research foundation, language laboratory, link with National Center for Super-Computing Applications at University of Illinois, 400-acre environmental laboratory. **Additional facts:** Ecumenical in nature, founded by Swedish Lutheran immigrants.

DEGREES OFFERED. BA. 582 bachelor's degrees awarded in 1992. 26% in business and management, 6% teacher education, 8% health sciences, 5% languages, 8% letters/literature, 11% life sciences, 5% physical sciences, 6% psychology, 9% social sciences.

UNDERGRADUATE MAJORS. Accounting, art education, art history, Asian studies, biology, business administration and management, business and management, business economics, chemistry, classics, clinical laboratory science, communications, comparative literature, computer and information sciences, computer mathematics, creative writing, cytotechnology, dramatic arts, early childhood education, earth science teaching, earth sciences, economics, education, elementary education, engineering and other disciplines, English, English education, English literature, environmental design, environmental science, finance, fine arts, foreign languages education, forestry and related sciences, French, geography, geology, German, Greek (classical), health sciences, history, international business management, international relations, jazz, junior high education, landscape architecture, Latin, marketing management, mathematics, mathematics education, music, music education, music history and appreciation, music performance, philosophy, physical education, physical sciences, physics, political science and government, predentistry, preengineering, prelaw, premedicine, prepharmacy, preveterinary, psychology, public administration, religion, religious music, Scandinavian languages, Scandinavian studies, secondary education, sociology, Spanish, speech, speech correction, speech pathology/audiology, speech/communication/theater education.

ACADEMIC PROGRAMS. Accelerated program, cooperative education, double major, honors program, independent study, internships, student-designed major, study abroad, teacher preparation, visiting/exchange student program, coordinated degree programs in engineering with University of Illinois at Urbana-Champaign, Washington University; Iowa State University; forestry and environmental management with Duke University; landscape architecture with University of Illinois at Urbana-Champaign; occupational therapy with Washington University; early selection programs in dentistry under Northwestern and University of Iowa; liberal arts/career combination in engineering, health sciences. **Remedial services:** Learning center, reduced course load, special counselor, tutoring. **Placement/credit:** AP, IB, institutional tests; 24 credit hours maximum for bachelor's degree.

ACADEMIC REQUIREMENTS. Freshmen must earn minimum GPA of 2.0 to continue in good standing. 87% of freshmen return for sophomore year. Students must declare major by end of second year. **Graduation requirements:** 123 hours for bachelor's (24 in major). Most students required to take courses in arts/fine arts, English, foreign languages, history, humanities, philosophy/religion, biological/physical sciences, social sciences. **Postgraduate studies:** 4% enter law school, 6% enter medical school, 4% enter MBA programs, 17% enter other graduate study. **Additional information:** Internship programs in cities throughout United States and in South America, Europe, Asia, Africa, and Australia. Exchange programs with universities in People's Republic of China, Germany, Peru, and Sweden. Summer language study programs in Sweden, Germany, France, Ecquador and The Mediterranean.

FRESHMAN ADMISSIONS. Selection criteria: GPA, class rank, test scores, high school curriculum are most important. Academic honors, special qualifications, extracurricular activities, interviews, essays also considered. **High school preparation:** 12 units recommended. Recommended units include English 4, foreign language 1, mathematics 3, social science 2 and science 2. Engineering, science, and mathematics majors should have 3 units mathematics: 1.5 algebra, 1 plane geometry, .5 trigonometry. **Test requirements:** SAT or ACT; score report by June 1.

1992 FRESHMAN CLASS PROFILE. 752 men applied, 645 accepted, 229 enrolled; 1,038 women applied, 938 accepted, 309 enrolled. 78% had high school GPA of 3.0 or higher, 22% between 2.0 and 2.99. 33% were in top tenth and 66% were in top quarter of graduating class. **Academic background:** Mid 50% of enrolled freshmen had SAT-V between 440-560, SAT-M between 480-630; ACT composite between 22-28. 25% submitted SAT scores, 95% submitted ACT scores. **Characteristics:** 80% from in state, 93% live in college housing, 6% have minority backgrounds, 2% are foreign students, 15% join fraternities/sororities. Average age is 18.

FALL-TERM APPLICATIONS. $20 fee, may be waived for applicants with need. No closing date; priority given to applications received by April 1; applicants notified on a rolling basis; must reply by registration. Audition recommended for music, theater applicants. Interview and essay required of freshman honors program applicants, recommended for all applicants. Essay also required of academically marginal applicants and for certain departmental programs. Portfolio required of applicants to certain art programs. CRDA. Deferred admission available.

STUDENT LIFE. Housing: Dormitories (men, women, coed); apartment housing available. Lower-division students not living with parents required to live on campus unless released to live off-campus by student services office. **Activities:** Student government, magazine, radio, student newspaper, yearbook, choral groups, concert band, dance, drama, jazz band, music ensembles, musical theater, opera, pep band, symphony orchestra, Japanese koto ensemble, fraternities, sororities, Black Student Union, Black Culture House, International Club, Global Affect, campus ministry, Intervarsity Christian Fellowship, Promoting Alcohol Responsibility Thru You (PARTY), Amnesty International, College Democrats, College Republicans, Student Volunteer Bureau. **Additional information:** Students represented on all major faculty/administrative committees and act as observers at Board of Trustee meetings. Student life governed by bill of student rigts and code of social conduct. Campus judiciary process includes student participation.

ATHLETICS. NCAA. **Intercollegiate:** Baseball M, basketball, cross-country, diving, football M, golf M, soccer, softball W, swimming, tennis, track and field, volleyball W, wrestling M. **Intramural:** Badminton, basketball, cross-country, racquetball, softball, swimming, table tennis, tennis, track and field, volleyball. **Clubs:** Flag football, water basketball for men and women.

STUDENT SERVICES. Aptitude testing, career counseling, employment service for undergraduates, freshman orientation, health services, personal counseling, placement service for graduates, women's center, services/facilities for handicapped.

ANNUAL EXPENSES. Tuition and fees (1992-93): $12,009. **Room and board:** $3,849. **Books and supplies:** $480. **Other expenses:** $250.

FINANCIAL AID. 88% of freshmen, 83% of continuing students receive some form of aid. 63% of grants, 94% of loans, 45% of jobs based on need. 404 enrolled freshmen were judged to have need, all were offered aid. Academic, music/drama, art, alumni affiliation, religious affiliation scholarships available. **Aid applications:** No closing date; priority given to applications received by April 1; applicants notified on a rolling basis beginning on or about February 15; must reply within 2 weeks.

ADDRESS/TELEPHONE. Harold Velline, Director of Admissions, Augustana College, 639 38th Street, Rock Island, IL 61201-2296. (309) 794-7341. (800) 798-8100. Fax: (309) 794-7422.

Aurora University
Aurora, Illinois — CB code: 1027

4-year private university, coed. Founded in 1893. **Accreditation:** Regional. **Undergraduate enrollment:** 350 men, 470 women full time; 350 men, 450 women part time. **Graduate enrollment:** 495 men and women. **Faculty:** 155 total (95 full time), 53 with doctorates or other terminal degrees. **Location:** Suburban campus in small city; 40 miles from Chicago. **Calendar:** Trimester, limited summer session. **Microcomputers:** Located in libraries, classrooms, computer centers. **Special facilities:** Singoethe Museum of Native American History.

DEGREES OFFERED. BA, BS, MA, MS, MBA, MSW. 320 bachelor's degrees awarded in 1992. 22% in business and management, 17% computer sciences, 9% teacher education, 7% health sciences, 17% multi/interdisciplinary studies, 10% parks/recreation, protective services, public affairs, 6% psychology, 5% social sciences. Graduate degrees offered in 12 major fields of study.

UNDERGRADUATE MAJORS. Accounting, biological and physical sciences, biology, business administration and management, business and management, business economics, chemistry, communications, computer and information sciences, computer mathematics, computer programming, economics, elementary education, engineering and other disciplines, engineering science, English, English education, English literature, environmental science, finance, health sciences, history, humanities, information sciences and systems, junior high education, management science, marketing management, mathematics, mathematics education, medical laboratory technologies, nursing, parks and recreation management, philosophy, physical education, physics, political science and government, predentistry, preengineering, prelaw, premedicine, prepharmacy, preveterinary, psychology, recreation therapy, religion, science education, secondary education, social sciences, social studies education, social work, sociology.

ACADEMIC PROGRAMS. Double major, honors program, independent study, internships, student-designed major, study abroad, teacher preparation, visiting/exchange student program, weekend college, cross-registration. **Remedial services:** Learning center, remedial instruction, special counselor, tutoring. **Placement/credit:** AP, CLEP General and Subject, institutional tests; 30 credit hours maximum for bachelor's degree.

ACADEMIC REQUIREMENTS. Freshmen must earn minimum GPA of 2.0 to continue in good standing. Students must declare major by end of second year. **Graduation requirements:** 120 hours for bachelor's (30 in major). Most students required to take courses in English, humanities, mathematics, biological/physical sciences, social sciences.

FRESHMAN ADMISSIONS. Selection criteria: School achievement record most important, followed by test scores. Interview and recommendation also considered. Recommended units include biological science 1, English 4, foreign language 2, mathematics 2, physical science 1 and social science 2. **Test requirements:** SAT or ACT (ACT preferred); score report by September 1.

1992 FRESHMAN CLASS PROFILE. 458 men and women applied, 379 accepted; 126 enrolled. **Academic background:** Mid 50% of enrolled freshmen had ACT composite between 18-23. 89% submitted ACT scores. **Characteristics:** 91% from in state, 80% live in college housing, 31% have minority backgrounds, 15% join fraternities/sororities. Average age is 18.

FALL-TERM APPLICATIONS. No fee. No closing date; applicants notified on a rolling basis; must reply by May 1 or within 4 weeks if notified thereafter. Interview recommended. Essay recommended. CRDA. Deferred admission available.

STUDENT LIFE. Housing: Dormitories (men, women). **Activities:** Student government, magazine, student newspaper, television, yearbook, choral groups, drama, musical theater, fraternities, sororities, Black Student Association, campus ministries, Latin American Student Organization, International Club, Bahai Club, Student Association.

ATHLETICS. NCAA. **Intercollegiate:** Baseball M, basketball, cross-country, football M, golf M, soccer M, softball W, tennis, volleyball W. **Intramural:** Basketball, football M, racquetball, soccer, softball, tennis, volleyball.

STUDENT SERVICES. Aptitude testing, career counseling, employment service for undergraduates, freshman orientation, health services, personal counseling, placement service for graduates, special adviser for adult students, veterans counselor, services/facilities for handicapped.

ANNUAL EXPENSES. Tuition and fees (1992-93): $9,255. **Room and board:** $3,405. **Books and supplies:** $600. **Other expenses:** $1,415.

FINANCIAL AID. 78% of continuing students receive some form of aid. 72% of grants based on need. Academic, leadership, minority scholarships available. **Aid applications:** No closing date; priority given to applications received by May 1; applicants notified on a rolling basis beginning on or about March 1; must reply by May 1 or within 4 weeks if notified thereafter.

ADDRESS/TELEPHONE. Frank Johnson, Director of Admissions, Aurora University, 347 South Gladstone, Aurora, IL 60506-4892. (708) 896-1975.

Barat College

Lake Forest, Illinois

CB code: 1052

Admissions: 53% of applicants accepted
Based on: ••• Essay, school record, test scores
•• Interview, recommendations, special talents
• Activities
Completion: 85% of freshmen end year in good standing
70% graduate, 38% of these enter graduate study

4-year private liberal arts college, coed, affiliated with Roman Catholic Church. Founded in 1858. **Accreditation:** Regional. **Undergraduate enrollment:** 142 men, 311 women full time; 64 men, 202 women part time. **Faculty:** 95 total (40 full time), 78 with doctorates or other terminal degrees. **Location:** Suburban campus in large town; 29 miles from Chicago, 100 miles from Milwaukee. **Calendar:** Semester, limited summer session. Extensive evening/early morning classes. **Microcomputers:** 20 located in libraries, classrooms, computer centers. **Special facilities:** Art gallery, theater, interfaith chapel.

DEGREES OFFERED. BA, BS, BFA. 104 bachelor's degrees awarded in 1992. 34% in business and management, 7% communications, 13% education, 6% letters/literature, 18% psychology, 8% social sciences, 8% visual and performing arts.

UNDERGRADUATE MAJORS. Accounting, art therapy, behavioral sciences, biology, business administration and management, business and management, business economics, ceramics, chemistry, communications, computer and information sciences, computer mathematics, computer programming, dance, dance education, dramatic arts, economics, education, education of the emotionally handicapped, education of the social/emotional handicapped, elementary education, English, English education, fiber/textiles/weaving, finance, fine arts, health sciences, human resources development, humanities, humanities and social sciences, junior high education, liberal/general studies, marketing management, mathematics, mathematics education, medical laboratory technologies, nursing, personnel management, photography, political science and government, prelaw, premedicine, psychology, secondary education, social science education, social sciences, sociology, special education, specific learning disabilities, speech/communication/theater education, studio art, visual and performing arts.

ACADEMIC PROGRAMS. Double major, dual enrollment of high school students, education specialist degree, independent study, internships, student-designed major, study abroad, teacher preparation, cross-registration, cooperative medical technology program and bachelor of science in nursing completion program with University of Health Sciences, Chicago Medical School. **Remedial services:** Learning center, preadmission summer program, reduced course load, remedial instruction, special counselor, tutoring. **Placement/credit:** AP, CLEP General and Subject, institutional tests; 18 credit hours maximum for bachelor's degree.

ACADEMIC REQUIREMENTS. Freshmen must earn minimum GPA of 2.0 to continue in good standing. 78% of freshmen return for sophomore year. Students must declare major by end of second year. **Graduation requirements:** 120 hours for bachelor's (50 in major). Most students required to take courses in arts/fine arts, computer science, English, foreign languages, history, humanities, mathematics, philosophy/religion, biological/physical sciences, social sciences. **Postgraduate studies:** 6% enter law school, 2% enter medical school, 12% enter MBA programs, 18% enter other graduate study. **Additional information:** Learning Opportunities Program designed to meet needs of college-able men and women with specific learning disabilities.

FRESHMAN ADMISSIONS. Selection criteria: Admission based on candidate's total history presented in application material. School achievement record and test scores most important, followed by faculty recommendations and personal interview. Nursing program is BSN completion only. Applicant must be registered nurse. **High school preparation:** 16 units recommended. Recommended units include English 4, foreign language 2, mathematics 2, social science 3 and science 2. **Test requirements:** SAT or ACT; score report by August 15.

1992 FRESHMAN CLASS PROFILE. 81 men applied, 57 accepted, 40 enrolled; 280 women applied, 135 accepted, 71 enrolled. 60% had high school GPA of 3.0 or higher, 40% between 2.0 and 2.99. 15% were in top tenth and 36% were in top quarter of graduating class. **Academic background:** Mid 50% of enrolled freshmen had SAT-V between 450-550, SAT-M between 420-520; ACT composite between 19-24. 25% submitted SAT scores, 76% submitted ACT scores. **Characteristics:** 76% from in state, 71% live in college housing, 23% have minority backgrounds, 09% are foreign students. Average age is 18.

FALL-TERM APPLICATIONS. $20 fee, may be waived for applicants with need. No closing date; priority given to applications received by April 15; applicants notified on a rolling basis; must reply by May 1 or as soon as possible if notified thereafter. Audition required for dance applicants. Essay required. Interview recommended. Portfolio recommended for art applicants. Interview required of learning disabled applicants. CRDA. Deferred admission available.

STUDENT LIFE. Housing: Dormitories (men, women, coed). **Activities:** Student government, magazine, radio, student newspaper, yearbook, choral groups, dance, drama, musical theater, International Club, religious organizations, volunteer political and social service groups. **Additional information:** College affirms freedom of thought and expression and respect for sacredness of personal and religious belief.

ATHLETICS. NAIA. **Intercollegiate:** Basketball M, volleyball W. **Intramural:** Basketball, table tennis, volleyball.

STUDENT SERVICES. Aptitude testing, career counseling, employment service for undergraduates, freshman orientation, health services, on-campus day care, personal counseling, placement service for graduates, adult reentry admissions counselor, services/facilities for handicapped.

ANNUAL EXPENSES. Tuition and fees: $9,830. **Room and board:** $4,300. **Books and supplies:** $700. **Other expenses:** $1,500.

FINANCIAL AID. 70% of freshmen, 70% of continuing students receive some form of aid. 88% of grants, 88% of loans, all jobs based on need. 95 enrolled freshmen were judged to have need, all were offered aid. Academic, music/drama, art, leadership, alumni affiliation scholarships available. **Aid applications:** No closing date; priority given to applications received by March 15; applicants notified on a rolling basis beginning on or about April 15; must reply within 2 weeks.

ADDRESS/TELEPHONE. Loretta Brickman, Director of Admissions, Barat College, 700 East Westleigh Road, Lake Forest, IL 60045. (708) 234-3000. Fax: (708) 615-5000.

Belleville Area College

Belleville, Illinois

CB code: 1057

2-year public community college, coed. Founded in 1946. **Accreditation:** Regional. **Undergraduate enrollment:** 1,913 men, 2,183 women full time; 4,713 men, 6,824 women part time. **Faculty:** 588 total (113 full time), 52 with doctorates or other terminal degrees. **Location:** Suburban campus in large town; 12 miles from St. Louis, Missouri. **Calendar:** Semester, limited summer session. Saturday and extensive evening/early morning classes. **Microcomputers:** 250 located in libraries, classrooms, computer centers. **Special facilities:** Largest solar collector for a greenhouse in North America; native tree arboretum. **Additional facts:** Campuses at Belleville, Granite City, and Red Bud and extension centers in 22 locations throughout the district.

DEGREES OFFERED. AA, AS, AAS. 1,089 associate degrees awarded in 1992.

UNDERGRADUATE MAJORS. Agricultural business and management, air conditioning/heating/refrigeration mechanics, air conditioning/heating/refrigeration technology, aircraft mechanics, airline piloting and navigation, biology, business administration and management, business and management, business data processing and related programs, business data programming, carpentry, chemistry, child development/care/guidance, computer technology, construction, data processing, drafting, drafting and design technology, electrical installation, electrical/electronics/communications engineering, electronic technology, elementary education, emergency medical technologies, engineering and engineering-related technologies, finance, fire control and safety technology, horticultural science, horticulture, industrial equipment maintenance and repair, industrial technology, information sciences and systems, law enforcement and corrections technologies, legal secretary, liberal/general studies, marketing management, masonry/tile setting, mathematics, medical assistant, medical laboratory technologies, medical records technology, medical secretary, microcomputer software, mining and petroleum technologies, nursing, physical sciences, physical therapy assistant, physics, plumbing/pipefitting/steamfitting, preengineering, psychology, radiograph medical technology, real estate, secondary education, secretarial and related programs, small business management and ownership, welding technology, word processing.

ACADEMIC PROGRAMS. 2-year transfer program, accelerated program, computer delivered (on-line) credit-bearing course offerings, double major, dual enrollment of high school students, independent study, internships, study abroad, telecourses, weekend college. **Remedial services:** Reduced course load, remedial instruction, special counselor, tutoring. **ROTC:** Air Force. **Placement/credit:** AP, CLEP General and Subject, institutional tests; 30 credit hours maximum for associate degree.

ACADEMIC REQUIREMENTS. Freshmen must earn minimum GPA of 2.0 to continue in good standing. Students must declare major on application. **Graduation requirements:** 64 hours for associate. Most students required to take courses in English, humanities, mathematics, biological/physical sciences, social sciences.

FRESHMAN ADMISSIONS. Selection criteria: Test scores required for nursing, allied health, and aviation maintenance programs. Admission requirements for Associate of Arts and Science degree programs, open admissions for certificate and associate of applied science. **High school preparation:** 15 units required. Required units include English 4, mathematics 2, social science 3 and science 3. High school course requirements, including 1 unit of foreign language, music, art, or vocational education, only for associate of arts and science degree programs. **Test requirements:** ACT required for admission to all allied health programs except medical assistant, scores by January 31. National League for Nursing Test required for nursing applicants. ASSET test required for most students.

1992 FRESHMAN CLASS PROFILE. 4,122 men, 5,864 women enrolled. **Characteristics:** 99% from in state, 100% commute, 12% have minority backgrounds. Average age is 29.

FALL-TERM APPLICATIONS. $10 fee. No closing date; applicants notified on a rolling basis beginning on or about April 16. Early admission available.

STUDENT LIFE. Activities: Student government, student newspaper, choral groups, concert band, drama, jazz band.

ATHLETICS. NJCAA. **Intercollegiate:** Baseball M, basketball, soccer M, softball W, tennis, volleyball W, wrestling M. **Intramural:** Badminton, basketball M, bowling, softball, table tennis, volleyball.

STUDENT SERVICES. Aptitude testing, career counseling, employment service for undergraduates, freshman orientation, on-campus day care, personal counseling, placement service for graduates, special adviser for adult students, veterans counselor, services/facilities for handicapped.

ANNUAL EXPENSES. Tuition and fees: $1,060, $2,130 additional for out-of-district students, $3,030 additional for out-of-state students. **Books and supplies:** $500. **Other expenses:** $1,320.

FINANCIAL AID. 50% of freshmen, 50% of continuing students receive some form of aid. 68% of grants, 98% of loans, 27% of jobs based on need. Academic, music/drama, art, athletic, state/district residency scholarships available. **Aid applications:** No closing date; priority given to applications received by May 31; applicants notified on a rolling basis beginning on or about July 1; must reply within 2 weeks.

ADDRESS/TELEPHONE. Jann Haskins Florek, Director of Admissions, Belleville Area College, 2500 Carlyle Road, Belleville, IL 62221-9989. (618) 235-2700 ext. 400. (800) BAC-5131. Fax: (618) 235-1578.

Black Hawk College
Moline, Illinois — CB code: 1483

2-year public community college, coed. Founded in 1946. **Accreditation:** Regional. **Undergraduate enrollment:** 929 men, 1,090 women full time; 1,337 men, 2,426 women part time. **Faculty:** 311 total (136 full time). **Location:** Urban campus in large town; 160 miles from Chicago. **Calendar:** Semester, limited summer session. **Microcomputers:** Located in computer centers.

DEGREES OFFERED. AA, AS, AAS. 638 associate degrees awarded in 1992. 9% in business and management, 8% business/office and marketing/distribution, 14% allied health, 41% multi/interdisciplinary studies, 8% parks/recreation, protective services, public affairs, 15% trade and industry.

UNDERGRADUATE MAJORS. Accounting, air conditioning/heating/refrigeration technology, anthropology, archeology, automotive mechanics, automotive technology, biology, business and management, business and office, business computer/console/peripheral equipment operation, business data entry equipment operation, business data processing and related programs, business data programming, chemistry, child development/care/guidance, civil technology, commercial art, comparative literature, computer and information sciences, computer programming, computer servicing technology, computer technology, data processing, diesel engine mechanics, drafting, drafting and design technology, earth sciences, economics, electronic technology, elementary education, engineering, engineering and engineering-related technologies, English, fashion merchandising, finance, fine arts, French, German, history, hotel/motel and restaurant management, industrial technology, instrumentation technology, interior design, Japanese, journalism, labor/industrial relations, law enforcement and corrections, law enforcement and corrections technologies, legal assistant/paralegal, legal secretary, liberal/general studies, library assistant, manufacturing technology, marketing and distribution, marketing management, mathematics, mechanical design technology, medical assistant, medical secretary, music, nursing, philosophy, physical therapy assistant, political science and government, precision metal work, predentistry, prelaw, premedicine, prepharmacy, protective services, psychology, public affairs, public relations, radio/television broadcasting, radiograph medical technology, real estate, respiratory therapy, respiratory therapy technology, Russian, science technologies, secondary education, secretarial and related programs, sociology, Spanish, technical and business writing, visual and performing arts, word processing.

ACADEMIC PROGRAMS. 2-year transfer program, independent study, internships, study abroad. **Remedial services:** Learning center, reduced course load, remedial instruction, special counselor, tutoring. **Placement/credit:** AP, CLEP General and Subject, institutional tests; 30 credit hours maximum for associate degree.

ACADEMIC REQUIREMENTS. Freshmen must earn minimum GPA of 2.0 to continue in good standing. **Graduation requirements:** 64 hours for associate. Most students required to take courses in English, humanities, mathematics, biological/physical sciences, social sciences.

FRESHMAN ADMISSIONS. Selection criteria: Open admissions.

1992 FRESHMAN CLASS PROFILE. 719 men, 1,059 women enrolled. **Characteristics:** 100% commute, 12% have minority backgrounds. Average age is 28.

FALL-TERM APPLICATIONS. No fee. No closing date; applicants notified on a rolling basis beginning on or about March 1; must reply by registration. Deferred and early admission available.

STUDENT LIFE. Activities: Student government, film, magazine, radio, student newspaper, television, choral groups, drama, jazz band, music ensembles, pep band.

ATHLETICS. NJCAA. **Intercollegiate:** Baseball M, basketball, golf M, softball W, volleyball W. **Intramural:** Basketball M, golf, skiing, soccer M, swimming, tennis, track and field, volleyball, wrestling M.

STUDENT SERVICES. Aptitude testing, career counseling, employment service for undergraduates, health services, personal counseling, placement service for graduates, veterans counselor, services/facilities for handicapped.

ANNUAL EXPENSES. Tuition and fees (1992-93): $1,470, $1,740 additional for out-of-district students, $3,990 additional for out-of-state students. **Books and supplies:** $500. **Other expenses:** $1,418.

FINANCIAL AID. 62% of freshmen, 82% of continuing students receive some form of aid. 90% of grants, all loans, all jobs based on need. Academic, music/drama, art, athletic scholarships available. **Aid applications:** No closing date; priority given to applications received by May 15; applicants notified on a rolling basis beginning on or about June 15; must reply within 10 days.

ADDRESS/TELEPHONE. Barton Schiermeyer, Director of Admissions and Records, Black Hawk College, 6600 34th Avenue, Moline, IL 61265. (309) 796-1311. (800) 798-1311. Fax: (309) 792-5976.

Black Hawk College: East Campus
Kewanee, Illinois — CB code: 0690

2-year public community college, coed. Founded in 1967. **Accreditation:** Regional. **Undergraduate enrollment:** 210 men, 297 women full time; 99 men, 224 women part time. **Faculty:** 48 total (23 full time). **Location:** Rural campus in large town; 40 miles from Peoria. **Calendar:** Semester, extensive summer session. **Microcomputers:** 44 located in classrooms, computer centers.

DEGREES OFFERED. AA, AS, AAS. 100 associate degrees awarded in 1992. 33% in agriculture, 7% business/office and marketing/distribution, 47% multi/interdisciplinary studies, 9% trade and industry.

UNDERGRADUATE MAJORS. Agribusiness, agricultural production, agricultural sciences, automotive mechanics, automotive technology, biological and physical sciences, business and management, business and office, equestrian science, humanities and social sciences, industrial technology, information sciences and systems, legal secretary, liberal/general studies, nursing, science technologies, secretarial and related programs, visual and performing arts, welding technology.

ACADEMIC PROGRAMS. 2-year transfer program, cooperative education, double major, dual enrollment of high school students, independent study, internships, study abroad, cross-registration. **Remedial services:** Learning center, preadmission summer program, reduced course load, remedial instruction. **Placement/credit:** CLEP General and Subject, institutional tests; 30 credit hours maximum for associate degree.

ACADEMIC REQUIREMENTS. Freshmen must earn minimum GPA of 2.0 to continue in good standing. 70% of freshmen return for sophomore year. **Graduation requirements:** 62 hours for associate. Most students required to take courses in English, mathematics, biological/physical sciences, social sciences.

FRESHMAN ADMISSIONS. Selection criteria: Open admissions. Selective admissions to some programs.

1992 FRESHMAN CLASS PROFILE. 164 men, 127 women enrolled. **Characteristics:** 100% from in state, 100% commute, 1% have minority backgrounds. Average age is 28.

FALL-TERM APPLICATIONS. No fee. No closing date; applicants notified on a rolling basis; must reply by registration. Interview required for nursing applicants. Deferred admission available.

STUDENT LIFE. Activities: Student government, drama, musical theater.

ATHLETICS. NJCAA. **Intercollegiate:** Basketball, track and field. **Intramural:** Basketball, volleyball.

STUDENT SERVICES. Aptitude testing, career counseling, employment service for undergraduates, personal counseling, placement service for graduates, veterans counselor, services/facilities for handicapped.

ANNUAL EXPENSES. Tuition and fees: $1,500, $1,740 additional for out-of-district students, $4,110 additional for out-of-state students. **Books and supplies:** $500. **Other expenses:** $1,418.

FINANCIAL AID. 60% of freshmen, 65% of continuing students receive some form of aid. 95% of grants, 92% of loans, all jobs based on need. Academic, athletic, state/district residency, leadership scholarships available. **Aid applications:** No closing date; priority given to applications received by June 1; applicants notified on a rolling basis beginning on or about June 15; must reply within 2 weeks.

ADDRESS/TELEPHONE. Admissions Office, Black Hawk College: East Campus, PO Box 489, Kewanee, IL 61443-0489. (309) 852-5671 ext. 220. Fax: (309) 856-6005.

Blackburn College
Carlinville, Illinois CB code: 1065

Admissions: 65% of applicants accepted
Based on: ••• School record, test scores
•• Activities, essay
• Interview, recommendations, special talents
Completion: 84% of freshmen end year in good standing
35% graduate, 15% of these enter graduate study

4-year private liberal arts college, coed, affiliated with Presbyterian Church (USA). Founded in 1837. **Accreditation:** Regional. **Undergraduate enrollment:** 211 men, 237 women full time; 25 men, 22 women part time. **Faculty:** 50 total (35 full time), 26 with doctorates or other terminal degrees. **Location:** Rural campus in small town; 40 miles from Springfield, 60 miles from St. Louis, Missouri. **Calendar:** Semester. **Microcomputers:** 12 located in libraries, computer centers.

DEGREES OFFERED. BA. 87 bachelor's degrees awarded in 1992. 27% in business and management, 5% computer sciences, 17% teacher education, 13% life sciences, 14% psychology, 9% social sciences.

UNDERGRADUATE MAJORS. Accounting, art education, biological and physical sciences, biology, business administration and management, chemistry, computer and information sciences, elementary education, English, English education, foreign languages education, history, humanities and social sciences, liberal/general studies, mathematics, mathematics education, medical laboratory technologies, music, music education, physical education, political science and government, predentistry, prelaw, premedicine, preveterinary, psychology, public administration, science education, social science education, social studies education, Spanish, speech, studio art.

ACADEMIC PROGRAMS. Accelerated program, cooperative education, double major, dual enrollment of high school students, honors program, independent study, internships, student-designed major, study abroad, teacher preparation, Washington semester. **Remedial services:** Learning center, reduced course load, remedial instruction, special counselor, tutoring. **Placement/credit:** AP, CLEP General and Subject, institutional tests; 30 credit hours maximum for bachelor's degree.

ACADEMIC REQUIREMENTS. Freshmen must earn minimum GPA of 1.8 to continue in good standing. 55% of freshmen return for sophomore year. Students must declare major by end of first year. **Graduation requirements:** 122 hours for bachelor's (32 in major). Most students required to take courses in arts/fine arts, English, foreign languages, humanities, mathematics, philosophy/religion, biological/physical sciences, social sciences. **Postgraduate studies:** 1% enter law school, 1% enter medical school, 1% enter MBA programs, 12% enter other graduate study.

FRESHMAN ADMISSIONS. Selection criteria: School achievement record, substantiated by test scores, most important. **High school preparation:** 16 units recommended. Recommended units include biological science 2, English 4, foreign language 2, mathematics 2, physical science 2 and social science 2. **Test requirements:** SAT or ACT; score report by July 30.

1992 FRESHMAN CLASS PROFILE. 340 men applied, 215 accepted, 99 enrolled; 271 women applied, 182 accepted, 104 enrolled. 35% had high school GPA of 3.0 or higher, 62% between 2.0 and 2.99. **Academic background:** Mid 50% of enrolled freshmen had ACT composite between 18-23. 89% submitted ACT scores. **Characteristics:** 75% from in state, 80% live in college housing, 16% have minority backgrounds, 2% are foreign students. Average age is 18.

FALL-TERM APPLICATIONS. No fee. Closing date July 30; applicants notified on a rolling basis; must reply within 2 weeks. Essay required. Interview recommended. Audition recommended for music applicants. Portfolio recommended for art applicants. Deferred and early admission available.

STUDENT LIFE. Housing: Dormitories (men, women, coed). **Activities:** Student government, student newspaper, yearbook, literary magazine, choral groups, concert band, drama, jazz band, music ensembles. **Additional information:** Small size of college combined with work program encourages extremely close-knit community.

ATHLETICS. NCAA. **Intercollegiate:** Baseball M, basketball, cross-country, football M, golf, soccer M, softball W, tennis, track and field W, volleyball W. **Intramural:** Badminton, basketball, bowling, racquetball, softball, tennis, volleyball, water polo.

STUDENT SERVICES. Aptitude testing, career counseling, employment service for undergraduates, freshman orientation, personal counseling, placement service for graduates, services/facilities for handicapped.

ANNUAL EXPENSES. Tuition and fees: $8,120. **Room and board:** $1,000. **Books and supplies:** $500. **Other expenses:** $800.

FINANCIAL AID. 89% of freshmen, 90% of continuing students receive some form of aid. 99% of grants, 85% of loans, 38% of jobs based on need. Academic, leadership scholarships available. **Aid applications:** No closing date; priority given to applications received by April 1; applicants notified on a rolling basis beginning on or about March 1; must reply within 4 weeks. **Additional information:** Each resident student works 15 hours weekly on campus.

ADDRESS/TELEPHONE. John Malin, Director of Admissions, Blackburn College, 700 College Avenue, Carlinville, IL 62626. (217) 854-3231 ext. 215. Fax: (217) 854-8564. (800)233-3550 (Illinois only).

Blessing-Reiman College of Nursing
Quincy, Illinois CB code: 0139

4-year private nursing college, coed. **Accreditation:** Regional. **Undergraduate enrollment:** 8 men, 131 women full time; 3 men, 44 women part time. **Faculty:** 11 total (8 full time). **Location:** Urban campus in large town; 120 miles from St. Louis, Missouri. **Calendar:** Semester, limited summer session. **Microcomputers:** 10 located in libraries. **Additional facts:** Joint degree program with Culver-Stockton College (MO). Student activities, sports, sororities/fraternities, offered at Culver-Stockton.

DEGREES OFFERED. BS. 21 bachelor's degrees awarded in 1992. 100% in health sciences.

UNDERGRADUATE MAJORS. Nursing.

ACADEMIC REQUIREMENTS. Freshmen must earn minimum GPA of 2.0 to continue in good standing. 86% of freshmen return for sophomore year. Students must declare major on application. **Graduation requirements:** 124 hours for bachelor's (64 in major). Most students required to take courses in arts/fine arts, computer science, English, humanities, mathematics, philosophy/religion, biological/physical sciences, social sciences. **Additional information:** Cross-registration with Culver-Stockton College (MO).

FRESHMAN ADMISSIONS. Selection criteria: Students should rank in upper half of class, have high school GPA of 3.0, and ACT of 20. Required units include biological science 1, English 2, mathematics 1, physical science 1 and social science 1. Biology required, chemistry recommended. **Test requirements:** SAT or ACT (ACT preferred); score report by August 10.

1992 FRESHMAN CLASS PROFILE. 3 men, 52 women enrolled. 100% had high school GPA of 3.0 or higher. **Characteristics:** 85% live in college housing. Average age is 20.

FALL-TERM APPLICATIONS. No fee. No closing date; priority given to applications received by June 15; applicants notified on a rolling basis. Interview required. Essay required.

STUDENT LIFE. Housing: Apartment housing available. Freshman/sophomore housing available at Culver-Stockton College. **Activities:** Student government, Student Nurses Organization (SNO).

STUDENT SERVICES. Career counseling, freshman orientation, health services, on-campus day care, placement service for graduates, services/facilities for handicapped.

ANNUAL EXPENSES. Tuition and fees: $7,850. **Room and board:** $3,075. **Books and supplies:** $400. **Other expenses:** $500.

FINANCIAL AID. 100% of continuing students receive some form of aid. 95% of grants, 39% of loans based on need. Academic, state/district residency, leadership, alumni affiliation scholarships available.

ADDRESS/TELEPHONE. Sharon Wharton, Admissions Coordinator, Blessing-Reiman College of Nursing, Broadway at 11th Street, Quincy, IL 62301. (217) 223-5811 ext. 1382. (800) 877-9140. Fax: (217) 223-6400.

Bradley University
Peoria, Illinois CB code: 1070

Admissions: 94% of applicants accepted
Based on: ••• School record
•• Recommendations, test scores
• Activities, essay, interview, special talents
Completion: 95% of freshmen end year in good standing
61% graduate, 70% of these enter graduate study

4-year private university, coed. Founded in 1897. **Accreditation:** Regional. **Undergraduate enrollment:** 2,412 men, 2,217 women full time; 304 men, 325 women part time. **Graduate enrollment:** 82 men, 64 women full time; 439 men, 348 women part time. **Faculty:** 428 total (298 full time). **Location:** Urban campus in small city; 150 miles from Chicago, 165 miles from St. Louis, Missouri. **Calendar:** Semester, extensive summer session. **Microcomputers:** 1,300 located in dormitories, libraries, classrooms, computer centers. **Special facilities:** 2 art galleries.

DEGREES OFFERED. BA, BS, BFA, MA, MS, MBA, MFA. 1,122 bachelor's degrees awarded in 1992. 26% in business and management, 12% communications, 8% teacher education, 22% engineering, 6% psychology, 8% social sciences. Graduate degrees offered in 32 major fields of study.

UNDERGRADUATE MAJORS. Accounting, actuarial sciences, advertising, art history, biological and physical sciences, biology, business administration and management, business and management, business economics, business systems analysis, ceramics, chemistry, civil engineering, clinical laboratory science, communications, computer and information sciences, computer engineering, construction, criminal justice studies, dramatic arts, early childhood education, earth sciences, economics, education, education of the emotionally handicapped, education of the mentally handicapped, electrical/electronics/communications engineering, elementary education, engineering, engineering and other disciplines, engineering physics, engineering science, English, English literature, environmental science, fashion merchandising, finance, food management, French, geography, geological engineering, geology, German, graphic design, history, home economics, home economics education, humanities, humanities and social sciences, industrial engineering, information sciences and systems, interior design, international business management, international relations, international studies, journalism, junior high education, management information systems, manufacturing technology, marketing management, marketing research, materials engineering, mathematics, mechanical design technology, mechanical engineering, medical laboratory technologies, music, music education, nursing, nursing education, operations research, painting, philosophy, photographic technology, photography, physical sciences, physical therapy, physics, political science and government, printmaking, psychology, public relations, radio/television broadcasting, radio/television technology, religion, sculpture, secondary education, social sciences, social work, sociology, Spanish, special education, specific learning disabilities, speech, speech correction, systems analysis, textiles and clothing, visual and performing arts.

ACADEMIC PROGRAMS. Accelerated program, cooperative education, double major, education specialist degree, honors program, independent study, internships, student-designed major, study abroad, teacher preparation; combined bachelor's/graduate program in business administration. **Remedial services:** Learning center, tutoring. **Placement/credit:** AP, CLEP General and Subject, institutional tests; 60 credit hours maximum for bachelor's degree.

ACADEMIC REQUIREMENTS. Freshmen must earn minimum GPA of 2.0 to continue in good standing. 87% of freshmen return for sophomore year. Students must declare major by end of second year. **Graduation requirements:** 124 hours for bachelor's (26 in major). Most students required to take courses in arts/fine arts, computer science, English, history, humanities, mathematics, philosophy/religion, biological/physical sciences, social sciences. **Postgraduate studies:** 30% enter law school, 10% enter medical school, 30% enter MBA programs. **Additional information:** Academic Exploration Program available to assist undergraduates in choosing major.

FRESHMAN ADMISSIONS. Selection criteria: School achievement record most important, then test scores, class rank, interview, recommendations. **High school preparation:** 16 units required. Required and recommended units include English 3-4, mathematics 2-3, social science 2 and science 1-2. Foreign language 2 recommended. Additional requirements for business, science, engineering, liberal arts, music, nursing and physical therapy majors. **Test requirements:** SAT or ACT; score report by July 1.

1992 FRESHMAN CLASS PROFILE. 1,717 men applied, 1,627 accepted, 632 enrolled; 1,744 women applied, 1,640 accepted, 561 enrolled. 89% had high school GPA of 3.0 or higher, 11% between 2.0 and 2.99. 31% were in top tenth and 59% were in top quarter of graduating class. **Academic background:** Mid 50% of enrolled freshmen had SAT-V between 430-570, SAT-M between 530-650; ACT composite between 21-28. 38% submitted SAT scores, 85% submitted ACT scores. **Characteristics:** 64% from in state, 100% live in college housing, 13% have minority backgrounds, 2% are foreign students, 38% join fraternities/sororities. Average age is 18.

FALL-TERM APPLICATIONS. $35 fee. Closing date August 1; priority given to applications received by March 1; applicants notified on a rolling basis; must reply by May 1 or within 2 weeks if notified thereafter. Audition required for music applicants. Interview recommended. Portfolio recommended for art applicants. CRDA. Deferred and early admission available.

STUDENT LIFE. Housing: Dormitories (men, women, coed); apartment, fraternity, sorority housing available. Dormitories with single occupancy rooms and dormitory with microcomputers linked to university computers available. **Activities:** Student government, magazine, radio, student newspaper, television, yearbook, choral groups, concert band, dance, drama, jazz band, music ensembles, musical theater, opera, pep band, symphony orchestra, fraternities, sororities, Chi Rho House (Protestant), Newman Club, Hillel, Young Republicans, Young Democrats, International Students Organization, Black Student Alliance, Hospitality Corps, Circle-K.

ATHLETICS. NCAA. **Intercollegiate:** Baseball M, basketball, cross-country, diving M, golf, ice hockey M, soccer M, softball W, swimming, tennis, volleyball W. **Intramural:** Badminton, basketball, bowling, diving, football M, golf, racquetball, soccer, softball, swimming, table tennis, tennis, volleyball, water polo, wrestling M.

STUDENT SERVICES. Aptitude testing, career counseling, employment service for undergraduates, freshman orientation, health services, on-campus day care, personal counseling, placement service for graduates, veterans counselor, services/facilities for handicapped.

ANNUAL EXPENSES. Tuition and fees: $10,408. **Room and board:** $4,310. **Books and supplies:** $480. **Other expenses:** $1,322.

FINANCIAL AID. 82% of freshmen, 80% of continuing students receive some form of aid. 68% of grants, 98% of loans, 33% of jobs based on need. 595 enrolled freshmen were judged to have need, all were offered aid. Academic, music/drama, art, athletic, alumni affiliation, minority scholarships available. **Aid applications:** No closing date; priority given to applications received by March 1; applicants notified on a rolling basis beginning on or about February 15; must reply by May 1 or within 2 weeks if notified thereafter.

ADDRESS/TELEPHONE. Gary Bergman, Executive Director of Enrollment Management, Bradley University, 1501 West Bradley Avenue, Peoria, IL 61625. (309) 677-1000. (800) 447-6460. Fax: (309) 677-2797.

Carl Sandburg College
Galesburg, Illinois — CB code: 1982

2-year public community college, coed. Founded in 1966. **Accreditation:** Regional. **Undergraduate enrollment:** 480 men, 621 women full time; 927 men, 1,369 women part time. **Faculty:** 201 total (58 full time), 5 with doctorates or other terminal degrees. **Location:** Rural campus in large town; 200 miles from Chicago, 40 miles from Peoria. **Calendar:** Semester, limited summer session. **Microcomputers:** 105 located in libraries, computer centers. **Special facilities:** Greenhouse for biology and agricultural programs, 22-acre agriculture experience plot. **Additional facts:** Extension campus in Carthage.

DEGREES OFFERED. AA, AS, AAS. 210 associate degrees awarded in 1992.

UNDERGRADUATE MAJORS. Accounting, agribusiness, agricultural business and management, agricultural mechanics, agricultural production, automotive mechanics, automotive technology, business and office, business data entry equipment operation, business data processing and related programs, business data programming, child development/care/guidance, criminal justice studies, data processing, diesel engine mechanics, drafting, electrical and electronics equipment repair, fashion merchandising, finance, fire control and safety technology, law enforcement and corrections technologies, liberal/general studies, machine tool operation/machine shop, marketing and distribution, marketing management, nursing, personal services, practical nursing, precision metal work, protective services, radiograph medical technology, real estate, science technologies, secretarial and related programs, solar heating and cooling technology, trade and industrial supervision and management, transportation management.

ACADEMIC PROGRAMS. 2-year transfer program, honors program, independent study, internships, student-designed major, study abroad, cross-registration. **Remedial services:** Learning center, remedial instruction, tutoring. **ROTC:** Army. **Placement/credit:** CLEP General and Subject, institutional tests; 20 credit hours maximum for associate degree.

ACADEMIC REQUIREMENTS. Freshmen must earn minimum GPA of 2.0 to continue in good standing. **Graduation requirements:** 62 hours for associate. Most students required to take courses in arts/fine arts, English, mathematics, biological/physical sciences, social sciences. **Additional information:** Cross-registration with Southeastern Community College (IA).

FRESHMAN ADMISSIONS. Selection criteria: Open admissions. Selective admissions for allied health program based on test scores. **Test requirements:** ACT required of allied health program applicants; score report by February 1.

1992 FRESHMAN CLASS PROFILE. 2,000 men and women enrolled. **Characteristics:** 99% from in state, 100% commute, 7% have minority backgrounds. Average age is 29.

FALL-TERM APPLICATIONS. No fee. No closing date; applicants notified on a rolling basis; must reply by registration. Interview recommended for allied health applicants.

STUDENT LIFE. Activities: Student government, magazine, student newspaper, literary magazine, choral groups, drama, jazz band, music ensembles.

ATHLETICS. NJCAA. **Intercollegiate:** Baseball M, basketball, softball W, volleyball W. **Intramural:** Basketball M.

STUDENT SERVICES. Aptitude testing, career counseling, employment service for undergraduates, freshman orientation, on-campus day care, personal counseling, placement service for graduates, veterans counselor, services/facilities for handicapped.

ANNUAL EXPENSES. Tuition and fees (1992-93): $1,350, $1,678 additional for out-of-district students, $4,310 additional for out-of-state students. **Books and supplies:** $450. **Other expenses:** $500.

FINANCIAL AID. 60% of freshmen, 65% of continuing students receive some form of aid. 87% of grants, all loans, 67% of jobs based on need. Academic, music/drama, art, athletic, state/district residency scholarships available. **Aid applications:** No closing date; priority given to applications received by May 1; applicants notified on a rolling basis beginning on or about May 1; must reply within 2 weeks.

ADDRESS/TELEPHONE. Carol Kreider, Director of Admissions and Records, Carl Sandburg College, 2232 South Lake Storey Road, Galesburg, IL 61401. (309) 344-2518. Fax: (309) 344-3526.

Chicago State University

Chicago, Illinois CB code: 1118

Admissions: 44% of applicants accepted
Based on: ••• School record, test scores
Completion: 80% of freshmen end year in good standing
9% graduate

4-year public university, coed. Founded in 1867. **Accreditation:** Regional. **Undergraduate enrollment:** 1,295 men, 2,841 women full time; 734 men, 1,672 women part time. **Graduate enrollment:** 41 men, 27 women full time; 675 men, 1,390 women part time. **Faculty:** 431 total (322 full time), 167 with doctorates or other terminal degrees. **Location:** Urban campus in very large city; 12 miles from downtown Chicago. **Calendar:** Semester, limited summer session. Saturday and extensive evening/early morning classes. **Microcomputers:** 40 located in computer centers. **Special facilities:** Electron microscopy laboratory, art gallery.

DEGREES OFFERED. BA, BS, MA, MS, MEd. 571 bachelor's degrees awarded in 1992. 19% in business and management, 10% teacher education, 6% health sciences, 24% multi/interdisciplinary studies, 8% parks/recreation, protective services, public affairs, 9% social sciences. Graduate degrees offered in 21 major fields of study.

UNDERGRADUATE MAJORS. Accounting, anthropology, art history, bilingual/bicultural education, biological and physical sciences, biology, business administration and management, chemistry, computer and information sciences, criminal justice studies, data processing, early childhood education, economics, education of the mentally handicapped, elementary education, English, English literature, fashion design, fashion merchandising, finance, geography, graphic design, history, hotel/motel and restaurant management, humanities and social sciences, information sciences and systems, law enforcement and corrections, library science, linguistics, management information systems, marketing and distribution, mathematics, medical records administration, music, nursing, occupational therapy, physics, political science and government, premedicine, psychology, radio/television broadcasting, secondary education, sociology, Spanish, special education, technical and business writing.

ACADEMIC PROGRAMS. Accelerated program, cooperative education, double major, dual enrollment of high school students, honors program, independent study, internships, student-designed major, study abroad, teacher preparation, visiting/exchange student program, programs for mature adults (University Without Walls, individualized curriculum, Board of Governors degree program). **Remedial services:** Learning center, remedial instruction, special counselor, tutoring. **ROTC:** Air Force, Army. **Placement/credit:** AP, CLEP General and Subject, institutional tests; 60 credit hours maximum for bachelor's degree.

ACADEMIC REQUIREMENTS. Freshmen must earn minimum GPA of 2.0 to continue in good standing. 50% of freshmen return for sophomore year. Students must declare major on application. **Graduation requirements:** 120 hours for bachelor's (42 in major). Most students required to take courses in English, humanities, mathematics, biological/physical sciences, social sciences.

FRESHMAN ADMISSIONS. Selection criteria: High school GPA, class rank, test scores, and subject/units completed important. **High school preparation:** 10 units required. Required units include English 4, mathematics 2, social science 2 and science 2. **Test requirements:** SAT or ACT (ACT preferred); score report by August 1.

1992 FRESHMAN CLASS PROFILE. 3,050 men and women applied, 1,341 accepted; 268 men enrolled, 430 women enrolled. 10% had high school GPA of 3.0 or higher, 41% between 2.0 and 2.99. 12% were in top tenth and 36% were in top quarter of graduating class. **Academic background:** Mid 50% of enrolled freshmen had ACT composite between 15-18. 78% submitted ACT scores. **Characteristics:** 98% from in state, 100% commute, 99% have minority backgrounds, 1% are foreign students. Average age is 21.

FALL-TERM APPLICATIONS. No fee. No closing date; priority given to applications received by August 1; applicants notified on a rolling basis; must reply by registration. Deferred admission available.

STUDENT LIFE. Activities: Student government, magazine, radio, student newspaper, television, yearbook, choral groups, concert band, dance, drama, jazz band, music ensembles, musical theater, pep band, symphony orchestra, fraternities, sororities, Over 65 student clubs and organizations including Campus Ministry, Hispanic Organization, Black Student Psychological Association, honor societies.

ATHLETICS. NAIA, NCAA. **Intercollegiate:** Baseball M, basketball, cross-country, tennis, track and field, volleyball W, wrestling M. **Intramural:** Badminton, basketball, diving, football M, gymnastics, softball, swimming, table tennis, tennis, track and field, volleyball, wrestling M.

STUDENT SERVICES. Aptitude testing, career counseling, employment service for undergraduates, freshman orientation, health services, on-campus day care, personal counseling, placement service for graduates, special adviser for adult students, veterans counselor, counselors for handicapped assigned as needed, services/facilities for handicapped.

ANNUAL EXPENSES. Tuition and fees (1992-93): $2,198, $3,696 additional for out-of-state students. **Books and supplies:** $650. **Other expenses:** $1,700.

FINANCIAL AID. 75% of freshmen, 85% of continuing students receive some form of aid. 88% of grants, 94% of loans, 88% of jobs based on need. 532 enrolled freshmen were judged to have need, all were offered aid. Academic, music/drama, art, athletic, leadership scholarships available. **Aid applications:** No closing date; priority given to applications received by April 15; applicants notified on a rolling basis beginning on or about June 1; must reply within 2 weeks. **Additional information:** Freshmen of outstanding academic ability and talent eligible for Scholars Program full-tuition scholarship.

ADDRESS/TELEPHONE. Romi Lowe, Director of Admissions, Chicago State University, 9501 South King Drive, Chicago, IL 60628. (312) 995-2513. Fax: (312) 995-3820.

City Colleges of Chicago: Harold Washington College

Chicago, Illinois CB code: 1089

2-year public community college, coed. Founded in 1962. **Accreditation:** Regional. **Undergraduate enrollment:** 8,689 men and women. **Faculty:** 182 total (157 full time), 37 with doctorates or other terminal degrees. **Location:** Urban campus in very large city. **Calendar:** Semester, limited summer session. **Microcomputers:** 100 located in classrooms, computer centers. **Additional facts:** Merged with Chicago City-Wide College in 1992.

DEGREES OFFERED. AA, AS, AAS. 288 associate degrees awarded in 1992.

UNDERGRADUATE MAJORS. Accounting, architectural technologies, architecture, automotive mechanics, automotive technology, biology, business administration and management, business and management, business and office, business data processing and related programs, chemical manufacturing technology, chemistry, city/community/regional planning, civil technology, computer and information sciences, computer programming, construction, criminal justice studies, data processing, drafting, drafting and design technology, early childhood education, education, elementary education, emergency medical technologies, engineering, engineering and engineering-related technologies, engineering management, English, finance, fine arts, fire control and safety technology, food management, foreign languages (multiple emphasis), foreign languages education, French, funeral services/mortuary science, German, hotel/motel and restaurant management, international business management, Italian, Japanese, journalism, junior high education, labor/industrial relations, law enforcement and corrections, law enforcement and corrections technologies, legal secretary, liberal/general studies, marketing and distribution, mathematics, medical secretary, music, occupational therapy assistant, philosophy, physical sciences, physician's assistant, physics, predentistry, prelaw, premedicine, prepharmacy, protective services, recreation and community services technologies, retailing, Russian, secondary education, secretarial and related programs, social sciences, Spanish, special education, speech, teacher aide, tourism, transportation and travel marketing, transportation management, water and wastewater technology.

ACADEMIC PROGRAMS. 2-year transfer program, cooperative education, dual enrollment of high school students, independent study, internships, telecourses, cross-registration, courses by videocassette at Chicago public libraries. **Remedial services:** Learning center, reduced course load, remedial instruction, special counselor, tutoring. **ROTC:** Air Force. **Placement/credit:** AP, CLEP General, institutional tests; 30 credit hours maximum for associate degree.

ACADEMIC REQUIREMENTS. Freshmen must earn minimum GPA of 1.5 to continue in good standing. 60% of freshmen return for sophomore year. Students must declare major on enrollment. **Graduation requirements:** 60 hours for associate (18 in major). Most students required to take courses in English, humanities, mathematics, biological/physical sciences, social sciences.

FRESHMAN ADMISSIONS. Selection criteria: Open admissions. Specific admissions criteria for physicians asistant and police progams. **High school preparation:** 15 units required. Required units include English 4, mathematics 3, social science 3 and science 3. 2 additional units in foreign language, art, music, computer science, or other electives required.

1992 FRESHMAN CLASS PROFILE. 2,515 men and women enrolled. 10% had high school GPA of 3.0 or higher, 85% between 2.0 and 2.99. 5% were in top tenth and 40% were in top quarter of graduating class. **Academic background:** Mid 50% of enrolled freshmen had ACT composite between 12-17. 32% submitted ACT scores. **Characteristics:** 91% from in state, 100% commute, 81% have minority backgrounds, 9% are foreign students. Average age is 22.

FALL-TERM APPLICATIONS. No fee. No closing date; applicants notified on a rolling basis. Deferred admission available. ACT recommended for placement and counseling. Score report by August 15.

STUDENT LIFE. Activities: Student government, magazine, student newspaper, choral groups, drama, jazz band, music ensembles, Afro-American Student Association, organization of Latin American students.

ATHLETICS. NJCAA. **Intercollegiate:** Soccer M.

STUDENT SERVICES. Aptitude testing, career counseling, em-

ployment service for undergraduates, freshman orientation, health services, personal counseling, placement service for graduates, special adviser for adult students, veterans counselor, senior citizens adviser, services/facilities for handicapped.

ANNUAL EXPENSES. Tuition and fees (1992-93): $985, $1,895 additional for out-of-district students, $2,940 additional for out-of-state students. **Books and supplies:** $600. **Other expenses:** $1,761.

FINANCIAL AID. 42% of freshmen, 35% of continuing students receive some form of aid. 96% of grants, 96% of loans, 93% of jobs based on need. State/district residency scholarships available. **Aid applications:** No closing date; priority given to applications received by May 1; applicants notified on a rolling basis beginning on or about July 1; must reply within 2 weeks.

ADDRESS/TELEPHONE. Doranne G. Polcrack, Director of Admissions and Outreach, City Colleges of Chicago: Harold Washington College, 30 East Lake Street, Chicago, IL 60601. (312) 984-2800. Fax: (312) 781-9481.

City Colleges of Chicago: Harry S. Truman College
Chicago, Illinois CB code: 1111

2-year public community college, coed. Founded in 1956. **Accreditation:** Regional. **Undergraduate enrollment:** 5,078 men and women. **Location:** Urban campus in very large city; in northeast section of Chicago. **Calendar:** Semester.

FRESHMAN ADMISSIONS. Selection criteria: Open admissions. Selective admissions to nursing and certain allied health programs.

ANNUAL EXPENSES. Tuition and fees (projected): $985, $1,882 additional for out-of-district students, $2,923 additional for out-of-state students. **Books and supplies:** $600. **Other expenses:** $1,761.

ADDRESS/TELEPHONE. Cathryn Battle, Admissions, City Colleges of Chicago: Harry S. Truman College, 1145 West Wilson Street, Chicago, IL 60640. (312) 878-1700. Fax: (312) 980-6135.

City Colleges of Chicago: Kennedy-King College
Chicago, Illinois CB code: 1910

2-year public community college, coed. Founded in 1935. **Accreditation:** Regional. **Undergraduate enrollment:** 285 men, 751 women full time; 484 men, 1,160 women part time. **Faculty:** 389 total (230 full time), 34 with doctorates or other terminal degrees. **Location:** Urban campus in very large city. **Calendar:** Semester, limited summer session. Saturday classes. **Microcomputers:** Located in classrooms, computer centers. **Special facilities:** Theater.

DEGREES OFFERED. AA, AS, AAS. 100 associate degrees awarded in 1992. 5% in business and management, 15% computer sciences, 5% health sciences, 60% parks/recreation, protective services, public affairs, 10% trade and industry, 5% visual and performing arts.

UNDERGRADUATE MAJORS. Accounting, air conditioning/heating/refrigeration mechanics, automotive mechanics, business data processing and related programs, data processing, drafting, dramatic arts, engineering, food production/management/services, graphic and printing production, graphic arts technology, home economics, law enforcement and corrections technologies, liberal/general studies, marketing and distribution, music, practical nursing, prelaw, premedicine, prepharmacy, radio/television broadcasting, real estate, secretarial and related programs, social work.

ACADEMIC PROGRAMS. Cooperative education, dual enrollment of high school students, honors program, independent study, internships, telecourses, weekend college, cross-registration. **Remedial services:** Learning center, preadmission summer program, reduced course load, remedial instruction, special counselor, tutoring. **Placement/credit:** CLEP General, institutional tests; 30 credit hours maximum for associate degree.

ACADEMIC REQUIREMENTS. Freshmen must earn minimum GPA of 1.5 to continue in good standing. 45% of freshmen return for sophomore year. Students must declare major on application. **Graduation requirements:** 60 hours for associate. Most students required to take courses in English, humanities, biological/physical sciences, social sciences.

FRESHMAN ADMISSIONS. Selection criteria: Open admissions. **Additional information:** Applicants admitted without high school diploma must pass GED by end of first school year.

1992 FRESHMAN CLASS PROFILE. 447 men, 1,088 women enrolled. **Characteristics:** 99% from in state, 100% commute, 100% have minority backgrounds. Average age is 29.

FALL-TERM APPLICATIONS. No fee. Closing date August 19; priority given to applications received by June 13; applicants notified on a rolling basis beginning on or about May 1. Deferred admission available.

STUDENT LIFE. Activities: Student government, radio, student newspaper, television, choral groups, musical theater, fraternities.

ATHLETICS. NJCAA. **Intercollegiate:** Basketball, track and field M. **Intramural:** Basketball M, volleyball.

STUDENT SERVICES. Aptitude testing, career counseling, employment service for undergraduates, freshman orientation, on-campus day care, personal counseling, placement service for graduates, special adviser for adult students, veterans counselor, services/facilities for handicapped.

ANNUAL EXPENSES. Tuition and fees (1992-93): $985, $1,895 additional for out-of-district students, $2,940 additional for out-of-state students. **Books and supplies:** $600. **Other expenses:** $1,761.

FINANCIAL AID. Grants, loans, jobs available. **Aid applications:** No closing date; applicants notified on a rolling basis beginning on or about August 15; must reply within 3 weeks.

ADDRESS/TELEPHONE. Welton T. Murphy, Director of Recruitment and Admissions, City Colleges of Chicago: Kennedy-King College, 6800 South Wentworth Avenue, Chicago, IL 60621. (312) 962-3200.

City Colleges of Chicago: Malcolm X College
Chicago, Illinois CB code: 1144

2-year public community college, coed. Founded in 1911. **Accreditation:** Regional. **Undergraduate enrollment:** 2,670 men and women. **Faculty:** 280 total (140 full time), 37 with doctorates or other terminal degrees. **Location:** Urban campus in very large city; 3 miles from downtown Chicago. **Calendar:** Semester, limited summer session. Saturday and extensive evening/early morning classes. **Microcomputers:** Located in libraries, classrooms, computer centers.

DEGREES OFFERED. AA, AS, AAS. 200 associate degrees awarded in 1992.

UNDERGRADUATE MAJORS. Accounting, biology, business administration and management, business and management, business and office, business data entry equipment operation, business data processing and related programs, child development/care/guidance, clinical laboratory science, data processing, early childhood education, food management, food production/management/services, food sciences, funeral services/mortuary science, health sciences, liberal/general studies, marketing and distribution, medical laboratory technologies, medical records technology, nursing, physician's assistant, radiograph medical technology, real estate, renal dialysis technician, respiratory therapy technology, secretarial and related programs, teacher aide, word processing.

ACADEMIC PROGRAMS. 2-year transfer program, accelerated program, cooperative education, double major, dual enrollment of high school students, honors program, independent study, internships, telecourses, weekend college, cross-registration. **Remedial services:** Learning center, preadmission summer program, reduced course load, remedial instruction, special counselor, tutoring, skills training. **Placement/credit:** AP, CLEP General and Subject, IB, institutional tests; 30 credit hours maximum for associate degree.

ACADEMIC REQUIREMENTS. Freshmen must earn minimum GPA of 2.0 to continue in good standing. 55% of freshmen return for sophomore year. Students must declare major on enrollment. **Graduation requirements:** 64 hours for associate (30 in major). Most students required to take courses in English, foreign languages, humanities, mathematics, biological/physical sciences, social sciences.

FRESHMAN ADMISSIONS. Selection criteria: Open admissions. Selective admissions for nursing and allied health applicants. **Additional information:** Adults out of high school 5 years or more may be concurrently registered while obtaining GED.

1992 FRESHMAN CLASS PROFILE. 1,390 men and women enrolled. **Characteristics:** 98% from in state, 100% commute. Average age is 23.

FALL-TERM APPLICATIONS. No fee. No closing date; applicants notified on a rolling basis; must reply by registration. Interview recommended for nursing, allied health applicants. Deferred and early admission available.

STUDENT LIFE. Activities: Student government, radio, student newspaper, television, choral groups, concert band, dance, jazz band, music ensembles, musical theater, fraternities.

ATHLETICS. NJCAA. **Intercollegiate:** Baseball M, basketball M. **Intramural:** Basketball, softball, volleyball.

STUDENT SERVICES. Aptitude testing, career counseling, employment service for undergraduates, freshman orientation, health services, on-campus day care, personal counseling, placement service for graduates, special adviser for adult students, veterans counselor, services/facilities for handicapped.

ANNUAL EXPENSES. Tuition and fees (1992-93): $985, $1,895 additional for out-of-district students, $2,940 additional for out-of-state students. **Books and supplies:** $600. **Other expenses:** $1,761.

FINANCIAL AID. Aid applications: No closing date; priority given to applications received by May 1; applicants notified on a rolling basis; must reply within 3 weeks.

ADDRESS/TELEPHONE. Ivan R. Lane, Registrar, City Colleges of Chicago: Malcolm X College, 1900 West Van Buren Street, Chicago, IL 60612. (312) 850-7055. Fax: (312) 850-7092.

City Colleges of Chicago: Olive-Harvey College
Chicago, Illinois CB code: 1584

2-year public community college, coed. Founded in 1970. **Accreditation:** Regional. **Undergraduate enrollment:** 462 men, 1,156 women full time; 605 men, 1,475 women part time. **Faculty:** 123 total, 16 with doctorates or other terminal degrees. **Location:** Urban campus in very large city; 16 miles from downtown. **Calendar:** Semester, limited summer session. **Microcomputers:** Located in libraries, classrooms, computer centers. **Special facilities:** Child development and high technology centers.

DEGREES OFFERED. AA, AS, AAS. 285 associate degrees awarded in 1992. 15% in business and management, 7% health sciences, 73% multi/interdisciplinary studies.

UNDERGRADUATE MAJORS. Accounting, Afro-American (black) studies, architectural technologies, architecture, biology, business administration and management, business and office, business data processing and related programs, chemistry, child development/care/guidance, computer and information sciences, computer programming, data processing, drawing, earth sciences, electrical/electronics/communications engineering, fine arts, liberal/general studies, mathematics, music, nursing, painting, philosophy, photography, physics, secretarial and related programs, social sciences.

ACADEMIC PROGRAMS. 2-year transfer program, cooperative education, dual enrollment of high school students, honors program, independent study, internships, student-designed major, study abroad, telecourses, cross-registration. **Remedial services:** Learning center, reduced course load, remedial instruction, special counselor, tutoring. **ROTC:** Air Force. **Placement/credit:** AP, CLEP General and Subject, institutional tests; 30 credit hours maximum for associate degree.

ACADEMIC REQUIREMENTS. Freshmen must earn minimum GPA of 1.0 to continue in good standing. 65% of freshmen return for sophomore year. Students must declare major by end of first year. **Graduation requirements:** 60 hours for associate (30 in major). Most students required to take courses in English, history, humanities, philosophy/religion, biological/physical sciences, social sciences.

FRESHMAN ADMISSIONS. Selection criteria: Open admissions. Selective admissions to some programs, including nursing and electronics. **High school preparation:** 15 units required. Required and recommended units include English 4, mathematics 3, social science 3 and science 3. Foreign language 2 recommended.

1992 FRESHMAN CLASS PROFILE. 560 men, 1,386 women enrolled. **Characteristics:** 99% from in state, 100% commute, 97% have minority backgrounds. Average age is 19.

FALL-TERM APPLICATIONS. No fee. No closing date; applicants notified on a rolling basis. Deferred and early admission available. ACT recommended for placement and counseling. Scores must be submitted by August 15.

STUDENT LIFE. Activities: Student government, student newspaper, choral groups, concert band, drama, African-American and Latino student groups.

ATHLETICS. Intercollegiate: Basketball M, softball W, volleyball W. **Intramural:** Basketball, swimming, volleyball.

STUDENT SERVICES. Aptitude testing, career counseling, employment service for undergraduates, freshman orientation, health services, on-campus day care, personal counseling, placement service for graduates, special adviser for adult students, veterans counselor, services/facilities for handicapped.

ANNUAL EXPENSES. Tuition and fees (1992-93): $985, $1,895 additional for out-of-district students, $2,940 additional for out-of-state students. **Books and supplies:** $600. **Other expenses:** $1,761.

FINANCIAL AID. 72% of freshmen, 72% of continuing students receive some form of aid. 98% of grants, all loans, all jobs based on need. Academic, athletic scholarships available. **Aid applications:** No closing date; priority given to applications received by August 10; applicants notified on a rolling basis; must reply within 3 weeks.

ADDRESS/TELEPHONE. Ruby M. Howard, Registrar and Director of Admissions, City Colleges of Chicago: Olive-Harvey College, 10001 South Woodlawn Avenue, Chicago, IL 60628. (312) 291-6349. Fax: (312) 291-6403.

City Colleges of Chicago: Richard J. Daley College
Chicago, Illinois CB code: 1093

2-year public community college, coed. Founded in 1960. **Accreditation:** Regional. **Undergraduate enrollment:** 5,557 men and women. **Location:** Urban campus in very large city. **Calendar:** Semester.

FRESHMAN ADMISSIONS. Selection criteria: Open admissions.

ANNUAL EXPENSES. Tuition and fees: $985, $1,895 additional for out-of-district students, $2,940 additional for out-of-state students. **Books and supplies:** $600. **Other expenses:** $1,761.

ADDRESS/TELEPHONE. Walter A. Calgaro, Registrar, City Colleges of Chicago: Richard J. Daley College, 7500 South Pulaski Road, Chicago, IL 60652. (312) 735-3000.

City Colleges of Chicago: Wright College
Chicago, Illinois CB code: 1925

2-year public community college, coed. Founded in 1934. **Accreditation:** Regional. **Undergraduate enrollment:** 5,602 men and women. **Location:** Urban campus in very large city. **Calendar:** Semester.

FRESHMAN ADMISSIONS. Selection criteria: Open admissions.

ANNUAL EXPENSES. Tuition and fees (projected): $985, $1,882 additional for out-of-district students, $2,923 additional for out-of-state students. **Books and supplies:** $600. **Other expenses:** $1,754.

ADDRESS/TELEPHONE. Michael P. Langley, Dean of Student Services/Registrar, City Colleges of Chicago: Wright College, 3400 North Austin Avenue, Chicago, IL 60634-4276. (312) 794-3100. Fax: (312) 481-8185.

College of DuPage
Glen Ellyn, Illinois CB code: 1083

2-year public community college, coed. Founded in 1966. **Accreditation:** Regional. **Undergraduate enrollment:** 4,380 men, 4,180 women full time; 9,144 men, 13,921 women part time. **Faculty:** 1,877 total (368 full time), 67 with doctorates or other terminal degrees. **Location:** Suburban campus in large town; 25 miles from Chicago. **Calendar:** Quarter, extensive summer session. **Microcomputers:** 930 located in libraries, computer centers. **Special facilities:** Performing and fine arts center, physical education and recreation center, multi-university center, older adult institute. **Additional facts:** Extension division offers courses at more than 80 off-campus locations.

DEGREES OFFERED. AA, AS, AAS. 1,878 associate degrees awarded in 1992. 6% in business and management, 68% multi/interdisciplinary studies.

UNDERGRADUATE MAJORS. Accounting, air conditioning/heating/refrigeration mechanics, air conditioning/heating/refrigeration technology, allied health, automotive mechanics, automotive technology, business and management, business and office, business data processing and related programs, business data programming, business information specialist, child development/care/guidance, commercial art, communications, computer and information sciences, criminal justice technology, data processing, digital microprocessor technology, drafting, drafting and design technology, electromechanical technology, electronic technology, environmental health, environmental science, facilities management, fashion design, fashion merchandising, fire control and safety technology, food management, food production/management/services, graphic and printing production, graphic arts technology, hotel/motel and restaurant management, human services/developmental disabilities, illustration design, information sciences and systems, interior design, law enforcement and corrections, liberal/general studies, library assistant, management science, manufacturing technology, marketing and distribution, marketing management, marriage and family counseling, medical records technology, mental health/human services, nursing, occupational therapy assistant, office supervision and management, ornamental horticulture, photographic technology, photography, plastic technology, radiograph medical technology, real estate, respiratory therapy, respiratory therapy technology, retailing, secretarial and related programs, tourism, transportation and travel marketing, transportation management.

ACADEMIC PROGRAMS. 2-year transfer program, accelerated program, cooperative education, double major, dual enrollment of high school students, honors program, independent study, internships, student-designed major, study abroad, telecourses, weekend college, cross-registration. **Remedial services:** Learning center, preadmission summer program, reduced course load, remedial instruction, special counselor, tutoring. **Placement/credit:** AP, CLEP General and Subject, institutional tests; 65 credit hours maximum for associate degree.

ACADEMIC REQUIREMENTS. Freshmen must earn minimum GPA of 1.75 to continue in good standing. 60% of freshmen return for sophomore year. Students must declare major on application. **Graduation requirements:** 96 hours for associate (30 in major). Most students required to take courses in English, humanities, mathematics, biological/physical sciences, social sciences. **Additional information:** Cross-registration with William Rainey Harper College, Joliet Junior College, Waubonsee Community College, Moraine Valley Community College, Morton College, Elgin Community College, Kishwaukee College, Triton College, Rock Valley College, Prairie State College, and Chicago City Colleges.

FRESHMAN ADMISSIONS. Selection criteria: Open admissions. Selective admissions to allied health programs. **High school preparation:** 15 units recommended. Recommended units include English 4, foreign language 2, mathematics 3, social science 3 and science 3. **Test requirements:** Placement tests required of applicants in certain programs such as nursing.

1992 FRESHMAN CLASS PROFILE. 2,675 men, 3,448 women enrolled. **Characteristics:** 90% from in state, 100% commute, 14% have minority backgrounds. Average age is 32.

FALL-TERM APPLICATIONS. $10 fee. No closing date; applicants notified on a rolling basis; must reply by registration. Deferred and early admission available.

STUDENT LIFE. Activities: Student government, film, magazine, radio, student newspaper, television, forensics, choral groups, concert band, dance, drama, jazz band, marching band, music ensembles, musical theater, opera, pep band, symphony orchestra, Campus Christian Fellowship, International Students Organization, Circolo Culturale Italiano, BASIC (Brothers and Sisters in Christ), Black Awareness Student Association, Cricket club.

ATHLETICS. NJCAA. **Intercollegiate:** Baseball M, basketball, cross-country, diving, football M, golf M, ice hockey M, soccer M, softball W, swimming, tennis, track and field, volleyball W, wrestling M. **Intramural:** Baseball M, basketball, bowling, golf, ice hockey M, racquetball, skiing, soccer, softball, swimming, tennis, track and field, volleyball, wrestling M.

STUDENT SERVICES. Aptitude testing, career counseling, employment service for undergraduates, freshman orientation, health services, on-campus day care, personal counseling, placement service for graduates, services/facilities for handicapped.

ANNUAL EXPENSES. Tuition and fees (1992-93): $990, $2,070 additional for out-of-district students, $3,285 additional for out-of-state students. **Books and supplies:** $860. **Other expenses:** $1,065.

FINANCIAL AID. 10% of freshmen, 19% of continuing students receive some form of aid. 79% of grants, 96% of loans, 1% of jobs based on need. Academic, music/drama, art, state/district residency, leadership, alumni affiliation scholarships available. **Aid applications:** No closing date; priority given to applications received by June 15; applicants notified on a rolling basis beginning on or about July 1; must reply within 2 weeks.

ADDRESS/TELEPHONE. Charles D. Erickson, Director of Admissions, Registration and Records, College of DuPage, 22nd Street and Lambert Road, Glen Ellyn, IL 60137-6599. (708) 858-2800 ext. 2441.

College of Lake County
Grayslake, Illinois — CB code: 1983

2-year public community college, coed. Founded in 1967. **Accreditation:** Regional. **Undergraduate enrollment:** 1,347 men, 1,405 women full time; 5,298 men, 7,594 women part time. **Faculty:** 677 total (187 full time), 26 with doctorates or other terminal degrees. **Location:** Suburban campus in small town; 10 miles from Waukegan. **Calendar:** Semester, extensive summer session. Saturday and extensive evening/early morning classes. **Microcomputers:** 520 located in libraries, classrooms, computer centers, campus-wide network. **Special facilities:** Art gallery, CAD/CAM center, automated industrial center.

DEGREES OFFERED. AA, AS, AAS. 815 associate degrees awarded in 1992.

UNDERGRADUATE MAJORS. Accounting, air conditioning/heating/refrigeration mechanics, air conditioning/heating/refrigeration technology, alcohol/substance abuse/addictive disorders, architectural technologies, architecture, automotive technology, biological and physical sciences, business data processing and related programs, chemical manufacturing technology, child development/care/guidance, civil technology, computer engineering, construction, criminal justice technology, data processing, drafting and design technology, education of exceptional children, electrical and electronics equipment repair, electrical installation, electrical/electronics/communications engineering, electromechanical technology, electronic technology, fire control and safety technology, food management, food production/management/services, geriatric services, horticulture, industrial equipment maintenance and repair, liberal/general studies, library science, machine tool operation/machine shop, marketing and distribution, marketing management, mechanical design technology, medical laboratory technologies, medical records technology, microcomputer software, nursing, ornamental horticulture, production management technology, radiograph medical technology, retailing, secretarial and related programs, technical and business writing, word processing.

ACADEMIC PROGRAMS. 2-year transfer program, accelerated program, cooperative education, dual enrollment of high school students, honors program, independent study, internships, student-designed major, study abroad, cross-registration. **Remedial services:** Learning center, reduced course load, remedial instruction, special counselor, tutoring. **Placement/credit:** AP, CLEP General and Subject, institutional tests; 30 credit hours maximum for associate degree.

ACADEMIC REQUIREMENTS. Freshmen must earn minimum GPA of 1.5 to continue in good standing. Students must declare major on application. **Graduation requirements:** 60 hours for associate. Most students required to take courses in arts/fine arts, English, humanities, mathematics, biological/physical sciences, social sciences. **Additional information:** Cross-registration with McHenry County College, Gateway Technical College (WI), William Rainey Harper College, and Oakton Community College.

FRESHMAN ADMISSIONS. Selection criteria: Open admissions for certificate and associate of applied science degree, college-preparatory high school program required for associate of arts and science degrees. Selective admissions for health career programs. **High school preparation:** 15 units required. Required units include English 4, foreign language 2, mathematics 3, social science 3 and science 3. 2 biology and 1 chemistry required for nursing program; mathematics for medical laboratory technician program; and chemistry for radiology program. **Test requirements:** SAT or ACT required of health career program applicants, recommended for all others for placement. Scores must be received by August 28.

1992 FRESHMAN CLASS PROFILE. 1,321 men, 1,432 women enrolled. **Characteristics:** 100% commute, 28% have minority backgrounds, 4% are foreign students.

FALL-TERM APPLICATIONS. No fee. No closing date; applicants notified on a rolling basis; must reply by registration. Deferred and early admission available. Application deadlines vary for health career programs.

STUDENT LIFE. Activities: Student government, magazine, radio, student newspaper, choral groups, concert band, drama, jazz band.

ATHLETICS. NJCAA. **Intercollegiate:** Baseball M, basketball, cross-country, golf M, soccer M, softball W, tennis, volleyball W, wrestling M. **Intramural:** Basketball, diving, fencing, skiing, swimming, volleyball.

STUDENT SERVICES. Aptitude testing, career counseling, employment service for undergraduates, freshman orientation, health services, on-campus day care, personal counseling, placement service for graduates, veterans counselor, services/facilities for handicapped.

ANNUAL EXPENSES. Tuition and fees: $1,181, $3,931 additional for out-of-district students, $5,206 additional for out-of-state students. **Books and supplies:** $400.

FINANCIAL AID. 77% of grants, 88% of loans, 24% of jobs based on need. Academic, music/drama, art, athletic, state/district residency, leadership scholarships available. **Aid applications:** No closing date; applicants notified on a rolling basis.

ADDRESS/TELEPHONE. Curtis Denny, Director of Admission and Records, College of Lake County, 19351 West Washington Street, Grayslake, IL 60030-1198. (708) 223-6601 ext. 2573. Fax: (708) 223-1017.

College of St. Francis
Joliet, Illinois — CB code: 1130

Admissions:	69% of applicants accepted
Based on:	••• School record
	•• Essay, recommendations, test scores
	• Activities, interview
Completion:	86% of freshmen end year in good standing
	62% graduate, 16% of these enter graduate study

4-year private college of arts and sciences, coed, affiliated with Roman Catholic Church. Founded in 1920. **Accreditation:** Regional. **Undergraduate enrollment:** 370 men, 440 women full time; 140 men, 133 women part time. **Graduate enrollment:** 396 men, 491 women part time. **Faculty:** 97 total (51 full time), 37 with doctorates or other terminal degrees. **Location:** Suburban campus in small city; 45 miles from Chicago. **Calendar:** Semester, limited summer session. Saturday classes. **Microcomputers:** 70 located in dormitories, libraries, classrooms, computer centers. **Additional facts:** Affiliated with Argonne National Laboratories, Morton Arboretum, and Will County Forest Preserve.

DEGREES OFFERED. BA, BS, MS. 234 bachelor's degrees awarded in 1992. 15% in business and management, 10% business/office and marketing/distribution, 10% communications, 10% computer sciences, 13% teacher education, 25% health sciences, 5% allied health, 5% parks/recreation, protective services, public affairs. Graduate degrees offered in 1 major field of study.

UNDERGRADUATE MAJORS. Accounting, actuarial sciences, advertising, biology, business administration and management, business and management, clinical laboratory science, communications, computer and information sciences, computer programming, criminal justice studies, elementary education, English, environmental science, finance, fine arts, health sciences, history, hospitality and recreation marketing, industrial and organizational psychology, information sciences and systems, international relations, journalism, management information systems, marketing and distribution, mathematics, medical laboratory technologies, nuclear medical technology, parks and recreation management, political science and government, psychology, public policy studies, public relations, radio/television broadcasting, recreation and community services technologies, recreation therapy, secondary education, social work, theological studies.

ACADEMIC PROGRAMS. Accelerated program, double major, independent study, internships, student-designed major, study abroad, teacher preparation, weekend college, Washington semester. **Placement/credit:** AP, CLEP General and Subject; 30 credit hours maximum for bachelor's degree.

ACADEMIC REQUIREMENTS. Freshmen must earn minimum GPA of 2.0 to continue in good standing. 83% of freshmen return for sophomore year. Students must declare major by end of first year. **Graduation requirements:** 128 hours for bachelor's (48 in major). Most students required to take courses in arts/fine arts, English, foreign languages, history, mathematics, philosophy/religion, biological/physical sciences, social sciences. **Postgraduate studies:** 2% enter law school, 1% enter medical school, 9% enter MBA programs, 4% enter other graduate study.

FRESHMAN ADMISSIONS. Selection criteria: High school record, rank in top half of class, and test scores important. **High school preparation:** 16 units required. Required units include biological science 1, English 4, mathematics 3, social science 2 and science 1. One unit each in 2 of the following required: foreign language, fine arts, or computer science. **Test requirements:** SAT or ACT (ACT preferred); score report by June 1.

1992 FRESHMAN CLASS PROFILE. 262 men applied, 171 accepted, 86 enrolled; 204 women applied, 149 accepted, 74 enrolled. 66% had high school GPA of 3.0 or higher, 32% between 2.0 and 2.99. 20% were in top tenth and 46% were in top quarter of graduating class. **Academic background:** Mid 50% of enrolled freshmen had ACT composite between 20-25. 95% submitted ACT scores. **Characteristics:** 85% from in state, 65% live in college housing, 11% have minority backgrounds. Average age is 18.

FALL-TERM APPLICATIONS. $15 fee, may be waived for applicants with need. Closing date July 1; priority given to applications received by March 1; applicants notified on a rolling basis; must reply by May 1 or within 4 weeks if notified thereafter. Essay required for academically weak applicants. Interview recommended for academically weak applicants. CRDA. Deferred admission available.

STUDENT LIFE. Housing: Dormitories (coed). **Activities:** Student government, film, magazine, radio, student newspaper, television, yearbook, choral groups, drama, musical theater, pep band, campus ministry, social work club, Circle-K, Minority Student Association.

ATHLETICS. NAIA, NCAA. **Intercollegiate:** Baseball M, basketball, cross-country W, football M, golf M, soccer M, softball W, tennis, volleyball W. **Intramural:** Badminton, baseball M, basketball, bowling, handball M, racquetball, softball, table tennis, volleyball.

STUDENT SERVICES. Aptitude testing, career counseling, employment service for undergraduates, health services, personal counseling, placement service for graduates, special adviser for adult students, services/facilities for handicapped.

ANNUAL EXPENSES. Tuition and fees: $9,100. **Room and board:** $3,970. **Books and supplies:** $400. **Other expenses:** $900.

FINANCIAL AID. 95% of freshmen, 93% of continuing students receive some form of aid. 50% of grants, 87% of loans, all jobs based on need. 117 enrolled freshmen were judged to have need, all were offered aid. Academic, athletic, leadership, minority scholarships available. **Aid applications:** No closing date; priority given to applications received by May 1; applicants notified on a rolling basis beginning on or about February 1; must reply within 2 weeks.

ADDRESS/TELEPHONE. Charles M. Beutel, Director of Admissions, College of St. Francis, 500 Wilcox Street, Joliet, IL 60435-6188. (815) 740-3400. (800) 735-7500. Fax: (815) 740-4285.

Columbia College
Chicago, Illinois — CB code: 1135

4-year private college of arts and sciences, coed. Founded in 1890. **Accreditation:** Regional. **Undergraduate enrollment:** 2,411 men, 2,298 women full time; 988 men, 1,032 women part time. **Graduate enrollment:** 74 men, 99 women full time; 96 men, 135 women part time. **Faculty:** 791 total (163 full time), 70 with doctorates or other terminal degrees. **Location:** Urban campus in very large city; in downtown area. **Calendar:** Semester, limited summer session. **Microcomputers:** 190 located in libraries, classrooms, computer centers. **Special facilities:** Museum of contemporary photography, art gallery, photography studios, film/video sound stage, dance performance space, 11th Street Theater.

DEGREES OFFERED. BA, MA, MFA. 838 bachelor's degrees awarded in 1992. 9% in business and management, 31% business/office and marketing/distribution, 33% communications, 24% visual and performing arts. Graduate degrees offered in 13 major fields of study.

UNDERGRADUATE MAJORS. Advertising, advertising art, art history, arts management, business and management, cinematography/film, commercial art, communications, creative writing, dance, dramatic arts, fashion design, fashion merchandising, film animation, film arts, fine arts, graphic design, illustration design, interior design, journalism, liberal/general studies, marketing and distribution, media management, motion picture technology, music, music business management, music performance, music theory and composition, musical theater, photographic technology, photography, public relations, radio/television broadcasting, radio/television technology, video, visual and performing arts.

ACADEMIC PROGRAMS. Double major, dual enrollment of high school students, independent study, internships, student-designed major. **Remedial services:** Learning center, preadmission summer program, reduced course load, special counselor, tutoring. **Placement/credit:** AP, CLEP General and Subject; 62 credit hours maximum for bachelor's degree.

ACADEMIC REQUIREMENTS. Freshmen must earn minimum GPA of 2.0 to continue in good standing. 50% of freshmen return for sophomore year. **Graduation requirements:** 124 hours for bachelor's (48 in major). Most students required to take courses in computer science, English, history, humanities, mathematics, biological/physical sciences, social sciences. **Postgraduate studies:** 1% enter law school, 1% enter medical school, 9% enter other graduate study. **Additional information:** Students need not declare a major.

FRESHMAN ADMISSIONS. Selection criteria: Open admissions.

1992 FRESHMAN CLASS PROFILE. 556 men, 506 women enrolled. **Characteristics:** 90% from in state, 100% commute, 48% have minority backgrounds, 1% are foreign students. Average age is 19.

FALL-TERM APPLICATIONS. No fee. No closing date; applicants notified on a rolling basis; must reply by registration. Interview recommended. Deferred admission available. ACT or SAT recommended.

STUDENT LIFE. Housing: Student housing available at nearby colleges and universities. **Activities:** Magazine, radio, student newspaper, television, creative writing annual volume, choral groups, dance, drama, jazz band, music ensembles, musical theater, black theater workshop, gospel singers, fraternities, sororities, African-American Alliance, Latino Alliance, Columbia Women's Coalition, League of Black Women, Gay and Lesbian Alliance, bible study group, Students for a Better World.

STUDENT SERVICES. Career counseling, employment service for undergraduates, freshman orientation, personal counseling, placement service for graduates, special adviser for adult students, veterans counselor, services/facilities for handicapped.

ANNUAL EXPENSES. Tuition and fees (1992-93): $6,654. **Books and supplies:** $500. **Other expenses:** $1,612.

FINANCIAL AID. 92% of loans, 23% of jobs based on need. Academic, state/district residency scholarships available. **Aid applications:** No closing date; priority given to applications received by May 1; applicants notified on a rolling basis beginning on or about May 15.

ADDRESS/TELEPHONE. Debra McGrath, Director of Admissions, Columbia College, 600 South Michigan Avenue, Chicago, IL 60605-1996. (312) 663-1600 ext. 129.

Concordia University ⇎
River Forest, Illinois — CB code: 1140

Admissions:	93% of applicants accepted
Based on:	••• Recommendations, school record, test scores
	• Activities, interview, religious affiliation/commitment, special talents
Completion:	92% of freshmen end year in good standing
	60% graduate, 12% of these enter graduate study

4-year private university and college of arts and sciences and nursing, teachers college, coed, affiliated with Lutheran Church—Missouri Synod. Founded in 1864. **Accreditation:** Regional. **Undergraduate enrollment:** 387 men, 732 women full time; 35 men, 126 women part time. **Graduate enrollment:** 11 men, 57 women full time; 86 men, 292 women part time. **Faculty:** 155 total (91 full time), 67 with doctorates or other terminal degrees. **Location:** Suburban campus in large town; 9 miles from Chicago. **Calendar:** Quarter, extensive summer session. **Microcomputers:** 60 located in libraries, computer centers. **Special facilities:** Early childhood education laboratory school, curriculum center (teacher's resource), Elizabeth Fergusen Art Gallery, human performance laboratory.

DEGREES OFFERED. BA, BS, MA, MEd. 220 bachelor's degrees awarded in 1992. 8% in business and management, 59% teacher education, 10% health sciences, 7% social sciences. Graduate degrees offered in 18 major fields of study.

UNDERGRADUATE MAJORS. Accounting, American literature, art education, biblical languages, biological and physical sciences, biology, business administration and management, business and management, chemistry, communications, computer and information sciences, computer mathematics, computer programming, dramatic arts, early childhood education, earth sciences, education, elementary education, English, English education, English literature, environmental science, exercise science and fitness management, fine arts, foreign languages (multiple emphasis), foreign languages education, geography, German, history, information sciences and systems, junior high education, mathematics, mathematics education, music, music education, music history and appreciation, music performance, music theory and composition, nursing, philosophy, physical education, physical sciences, physics, political science and government, predentistry, prelaw, premedicine, prepharmacy, psychology, pure mathematics, religion, religious education, religious music, science education, secondary education, social science education, social work, sociology, speech/communication/theater education, sports management, systems analysis, theological studies.

ACADEMIC PROGRAMS. Double major, education specialist degree, independent study, internships, teacher preparation, weekend college, cross-registration, Adult degree completion program in organizational management. **Remedial services:** Learning center, reduced course load, special counselor, tutoring. **Placement/credit:** AP, CLEP General and Subject, institutional tests; 16 credit hours maximum for bachelor's degree.

ACADEMIC REQUIREMENTS. Freshmen must earn minimum GPA of 2.0 to continue in good standing. 80% of freshmen return for sophomore year. Students must declare major by end of second year. **Graduation requirements:** 188 hours for bachelor's (48 in major). Most students required to take courses in English, history, humanities, mathematics, philosophy/religion, biological/physical sciences, social sciences. **Postgraduate studies:** 1% enter law school, 1% enter medical school, 10% enter other graduate study.

FRESHMAN ADMISSIONS. Selection criteria: School achievement record and character reference most important. 2.0 GPA, rank in top half of class, or minimum ACT composite score of 18 required. **High school preparation:** 15 units required. Required and recommended units include English 3-4, mathematics 1-2, social science 1-2 and science 1-2. Foreign language 2 recommended. One laboratory science required. **Test requirements:** ACT; score report by September 1.

1992 FRESHMAN CLASS PROFILE. 243 men applied, 210 accepted, 88 enrolled; 364 women applied, 353 accepted, 164 enrolled. 61% had high school GPA of 3.0 or higher, 37% between 2.0 and 2.99. **Academic background:** Mid 50% of enrolled freshmen had ACT composite between 18-25. 94% submitted ACT scores. **Characteristics:** 58% from in state, 75% live in college housing, 16% have minority backgrounds, 1% are foreign students. Average age is 18.

FALL-TERM APPLICATIONS. $25 fee. No closing date; applicants notified on a rolling basis; must reply by May 1 or within 60 days if notified thereafter. Interview recommended for nursing applicants. CRDA. Deferred admission available.

STUDENT LIFE. Housing: Dormitories (men, women, coed). **Activities:** Student government, film, radio, student newspaper, yearbook, choral groups, concert band, drama, jazz band, music ensembles, musical theater, pep band, wind symphony, minority students organization, Concordia Youth Ministry, Ambassadors for Christ.

ATHLETICS. NCAA. **Intercollegiate:** Baseball M, basketball, cross-country, football M, softball W, tennis, track and field, volleyball W, wrestling M. **Intramural:** Badminton, basketball, bowling, cross-country, softball, swimming, table tennis, volleyball.

STUDENT SERVICES. Aptitude testing, career counseling, employment service for undergraduates, freshman orientation, health services, on-campus day care, personal counseling, placement service for graduates, services/facilities for handicapped.

ANNUAL EXPENSES. Tuition and fees (1992-93): $8,000. **Room and board:** $3,807. **Books and supplies:** $400. **Other expenses:** $600.

FINANCIAL AID. 81% of freshmen, 83% of continuing students receive some form of aid. Grants, loans, jobs available. 161 enrolled freshmen were judged to have need, all were offered aid. Academic, music/drama, state/district residency, leadership, alumni affiliation, religious affiliation scholarships available. **Aid applications:** No closing date; priority given to applications received by June 1; applicants notified on a rolling basis beginning on or about February 1; must reply within 30 days.

ADDRESS/TELEPHONE. Sara Dahms, Admissions Office, Concordia University, 7400 Augusta Street, River Forest, IL 60305-1499. (708) 209-3100. (800) 735-2668. Fax: (708) 209-3176.

Danville Area Community College
Danville, Illinois — CB code: 1160

2-year public community college, coed. Founded in 1946. **Accreditation:** Regional. **Undergraduate enrollment:** 1,567 men and women full time; 1,862 men and women part time. **Faculty:** 124 total (59 full time), 3 with doctorates or other terminal degrees. **Location:** Urban campus in large town; 150 miles from Chicago. **Calendar:** Semester, limited summer session.

DEGREES OFFERED. AA, AS, AAS. 350 associate degrees awarded in 1992.

UNDERGRADUATE MAJORS. Accounting, agribusiness, agricultural production, agricultural products and processing, agricultural sciences, automotive mechanics, automotive technology, biology, botany, business administration and management, business and management, business and office, business computer/console/peripheral equipment operation, business data entry equipment operation, business data processing and related programs, business data programming, chemistry, communications, computer and information sciences, computer programming, criminal justice studies, data processing, education, electronic technology, engineering, engineering and engineering-related technologies, fine arts, horticulture, industrial technology, law enforcement and corrections technologies, liberal/general studies, marketing and distribution, mathematics, mechanical design technology, medical secretary, microbiology, philosophy, physical sciences, physics, practical nursing, psychology, secretarial and related programs, social sciences, teacher aide, zoology.

ACADEMIC PROGRAMS. 2-year transfer program, dual enrollment of high school students, independent study, internships. **Remedial services:** Learning center, remedial instruction, special counselor, tutoring. **Placement/credit:** AP, CLEP General and Subject, institutional tests; 30 credit hours maximum for associate degree.

ACADEMIC REQUIREMENTS. Freshmen must earn minimum GPA of 2.6 to continue in good standing. 35% of freshmen return for sophomore year. **Graduation requirements:** 62 hours for associate. Most students required to take courses in English, humanities, mathematics, biological/physical sciences, social sciences.

FRESHMAN ADMISSIONS. Selection criteria: Open admissions. Selective admissions to some programs. **High school preparation:** 15 units required. Required units include English 4, mathematics 3, social science 2 and science 2. 2 additional academic units and 2 electives required.

1992 FRESHMAN CLASS PROFILE. 950 men and women enrolled. **Characteristics:** 93% from in state, 100% commute, 16% have minority backgrounds, 1% are foreign students. Average age is 21.

FALL-TERM APPLICATIONS. No fee. No closing date; applicants notified on a rolling basis.

STUDENT LIFE. Activities: Student government, student newspaper, symphony orchestra.

ATHLETICS. NJCAA. **Intercollegiate:** Basketball, cross-country, golf.

STUDENT SERVICES. Aptitude testing, career counseling, employment service for undergraduates, health services, on-campus day care, personal counseling, placement service for graduates, special adviser for adult students, veterans counselor, services/facilities for handicapped.

ANNUAL EXPENSES. Tuition and fees (projected): $1,150, $1,830 additional for out-of-district students, $3,107 additional for out-of-state students. **Books and supplies:** $800. **Other expenses:** $1,400.

FINANCIAL AID. 80% of freshmen, 70% of continuing students receive some form of aid. All grants, 98% of loans, 78% of jobs based on need. 900 enrolled freshmen were judged to have need, all were offered aid. Academic, athletic, minority scholarships available. **Aid applications:** No closing date; priority given to applications received by June 1; applicants notified on a rolling basis beginning on or about July 1; must reply by registration.

ADDRESS/TELEPHONE. Kym Ammons-Scott, Director of Admissions and Records, Danville Area Community College, 2000 East Main Street, Martin Luther King Memorial Way, Danville, IL 61832. (217) 443-8800.

De Paul University
Chicago, Illinois — CB code: 1165

4-year private university, coed, affiliated with Roman Catholic Church. Founded in 1898. **Accreditation:** Regional. **Undergraduate enrollment:** 2,637 men, 3,339 women full time; 1,478 men, 2,329 women part time. **Graduate enrollment:** 1,582 men, 1,440 women full time; 2,037 men, 1,657 women part time. **Faculty:** 1,170 total (494 full time), 435 with doctorates or other terminal degrees. **Location:** Urban campus in very large city; in central city. **Calendar:** Quarter, extensive summer session. Saturday and extensive evening/early morning classes. **Microcomputers:** 750 located in dormitories, libraries, classrooms, computer centers. **Special facilities:** Blackstone theatre in downtown Chicago.

DEGREES OFFERED. BA, BS, BFA, MA, MS, MBA, MFA, MEd, PhD, JD. 1,671 bachelor's degrees awarded in 1992. 37% in business and management, 10% business/office and marketing/distribution, 8% communications, 5% psychology, 8% social sciences, 7% visual and performing arts. Graduate degrees offered in 54 major fields of study.

UNDERGRADUATE MAJORS. Accounting, actuarial sciences, American studies, anthropology, applied mathematics, art history, biology, business administration and management, business and management, business economics, chemistry, clinical laboratory science, communications, comparative literature, computer and information sciences, computer programming, computer science education, dramatic arts, early childhood education, economics, education, elementary education, English, English education, environmental science, finance, foreign languages education, French, geography, German, history, humanities and social sciences, industrial and organizational psychology, information sciences and systems, international relations, international studies, Italian, jazz, Jewish studies, Latin American studies, liberal/general studies, marketing and distribution, marketing management, mathematics, mathematics education, medical laboratory technologies, music, music business management, music education, music performance, music theory and composition, nursing, philosophy, physical education, physics, political science and government, predentistry, prelaw, premedicine, prepharmacy, preveterinary, psychology, pure mathematics, recording and sound technology, religion, science education, secondary education, social science education, social sciences, sociology, Spanish, statistics, studio art, telecommunications, theater design, transportation and travel marketing, urban studies, women's studies.

ACADEMIC PROGRAMS. Accelerated program, double major, dual enrollment of high school students, honors program, independent study, internships, student-designed major, study abroad, teacher preparation, weekend college, nontraditional bachelor's and master's degree programs for adults; liberal arts/career combination in engineering; combined bachelor's/graduate program in business administration. **Remedial services:** Learning center, preadmission summer program, reduced course load, remedial instruction, special counselor, tutoring. **ROTC:** Army. **Placement/credit:** AP, CLEP General and Subject, IB, institutional tests; 90 credit hours maximum for bachelor's degree.

ACADEMIC REQUIREMENTS. Freshmen must earn minimum GPA of 2.0 to continue in good standing. 82% of freshmen return for sophomore year. Students must declare major by end of second year. **Graduation requirements:** 188 hours for bachelor's (48 in major). Most students required to take courses in arts/fine arts, computer science, English, foreign languages, history, humanities, mathematics, philosophy/religion, biological/physical sciences, social sciences. **Additional information:** Honors programs offered in arts and sciences, business. Conservatory program in theater and music provides professional training.

FRESHMAN ADMISSIONS. Selection criteria: High school course selection and recommendations are important. Test scores required. School and community activities encouraged and personal interview with campus visit recommended. **High school preparation:** 16 units required; 16 recommended. Required and recommended units include English 4, foreign language 2, mathematics 2-3, social science 2 and science 2-3. **Test requirements:** SAT or ACT; score report by August 1.

1992 FRESHMAN CLASS PROFILE. 421 men, 540 women enrolled. 32% were in top tenth and 60% were in top quarter of graduating class. **Academic background:** Mid 50% of enrolled freshmen had SAT-V between 440-560, SAT-M between 480-610; ACT composite between 22-27. 37% submitted SAT scores, 85% submitted ACT scores. **Characteristics:** 73% from in state, 50% commute, 29% have minority backgrounds, 1% are foreign students, 3% join fraternities/sororities. Average age is 18.

FALL-TERM APPLICATIONS. $20 fee, may be waived for applicants with need. Closing date August 1; priority given to applications received by November 15; applicants notified on a rolling basis; must reply by May 1 or within 2 weeks if notified thereafter. Interview required for acting, theater technologies, recording sound technology applicants. Audition required for music, acting applicants. Portfolio required for theater technology and design applicants. CRDA. Deferred and early admission available. Institutional early decision plan. Early action program applicants (apply by November 15) receive early financial aid estimates, priority registration and priority housing.

STUDENT LIFE. Housing: Dormitories (coed); apartment, handicapped housing available. Students are encouraged to apply for housing early as space is limited. **Activities:** Student government, magazine, radio, student newspaper, yearbook, choral groups, concert band, drama, jazz band, music ensembles, pep band, symphony orchestra, fraternities, sororities, 18 academic organizations, 10 ethnic clubs, 10 honorary academic groups, 20 special interest clubs, debate team. 15 community service organizations.

ATHLETICS. NCAA. **Intercollegiate:** Basketball, cross-country, golf M, rifle, soccer M, softball W, tennis, track and field, volleyball W. **Intramural:** Badminton, baseball M, basketball, handball, racquetball, skiing, soccer W, softball, swimming, table tennis, tennis, volleyball.

STUDENT SERVICES. Aptitude testing, career counseling, employment service for undergraduates, freshman orientation, health services, personal counseling, placement service for graduates, special adviser for adult students, veterans counselor, services/facilities for handicapped.

ANNUAL EXPENSES. Tuition and fees (1992-93): $10,014. **Room and board:** $4,750. **Books and supplies:** $480. **Other expenses:** $1,300.

FINANCIAL AID. 69% of freshmen, 65% of continuing students receive some form of aid. Grants, loans, jobs available. Academic, music/drama, art, athletic, leadership scholarships available. **Aid applications:** Closing date May 1; applicants notified on a rolling basis beginning on or about February 15; Must reply by May 1 or within 2 weeks if notified after April 15. **Additional information:** Students in top 10%of class, with SAT scores of at least 1100 or ACT of 26, and active in student/community organizations should inquire about scholarships.

ADDRESS/TELEPHONE. Anne M. Kennedy, Vice President for Enrollment Management, De Paul University, 25 East Jackson Boulevard, Chicago, IL 60604. (312) 362-8300. (800) 433-7285. Fax: (312) 362-5749.

DeVry Institute of Technology: Addison

Addison, Illinois — CB code: 3204

Admissions: 92% of applicants accepted
Based on: ••• Test scores
• Interview
Completion: 39% graduate

4-year proprietary business, technical college, coed. Founded in 1982. **Accreditation:** Regional. **Undergraduate enrollment:** 1,537 men, 327 women full time; 636 men, 187 women part time. **Faculty:** 107 total (53 full time). **Location:** Suburban campus in large town; 20 miles from Chicago. **Calendar:** Three continuous calendar terms. Extensive evening/early morning classes. **Microcomputers:** 100 located in computer centers.

DEGREES OFFERED. AAS, BS. 195 associate degrees awarded in 1992. 100% in engineering technologies. 360 bachelor's degrees awarded. 17% in business and management, 23% communications, 30% computer sciences, 30% engineering technologies.

UNDERGRADUATE MAJORS. Associate: Electronic technology. **Bachelor's:** Accounting, business administration and management, electronic technology, information sciences and systems, telecommunications.

ACADEMIC PROGRAMS. Accelerated program. **Remedial services:** Learning center, reduced course load, special counselor, tutoring, developmental coursework. **ROTC:** Army. **Placement/credit:** Institutional tests; 30 credit hours maximum for associate degree. 47 to 55 hours of credit by examination may be counted towards bachelor's degree.

ACADEMIC REQUIREMENTS. Freshmen must earn minimum GPA of 2.0 to continue in good standing. 47% of freshmen return for sophomore year. Students must declare major on enrollment. **Graduation requirements:** 87 hours for associate, 134 hours for bachelor's. Most students required to take courses in computer science, English, history, humanities, mathematics, social sciences.

FRESHMAN ADMISSIONS. Selection criteria: Applicants must have high school diploma or equivalent, pass institutional entrance examination or submit acceptable SAT, ACH, or WPCT scores, and be 17 years of age. **Test requirements:** SAT or ACT; score report by October 25. **Additional information:** New students may enter at the beginning of any semester.

1992 FRESHMAN CLASS PROFILE. 1,392 men and women applied, 1,274 accepted; 647 men enrolled, 118 women enrolled. **Characteristics:** 80% from in state, 100% commute, 23% have minority backgrounds.

FALL-TERM APPLICATIONS. $25 fee. Closing date November 4; applicants notified on a rolling basis; must reply within 4 weeks. Interview required. Deferred admission available.

STUDENT LIFE. Housing: School contracted furnished apartments available for single students. **Activities:** Student government, student newspaper, Institute of Electrical and Electronic Engineers (IEEE), Data Processing Management Association (DPMA).

ATHLETICS. Intramural: Baseball, basketball, golf, volleyball.

STUDENT SERVICES. Career counseling, employment service for undergraduates, freshman orientation, placement service for graduates, veterans counselor, services/facilities for handicapped.

ANNUAL EXPENSES. Tuition and fees: $5,580. **Books and supplies:** $525. **Other expenses:** $1,928.

FINANCIAL AID. 71% of freshmen, 68% of continuing students receive some form of aid. All grants, 77% of loans, all jobs based on need. Academic scholarships available. **Aid applications:** No closing date; applicants notified on a rolling basis; must reply immediately. **Additional information:** Approximately 80% of students work part-time at jobs found through Institute.

ADDRESS/TELEPHONE. Virginia Mechnig, Director of Admissions, DeVry Institute of Technology: Addison, 1221 North Swift Road, Addison, IL 60101-6106. (708) 953-2000. (800) 346-5420. Fax: (708) 953-1236.

DeVry Institute of Technology: Chicago

Chicago, Illinois — CB code: 1171

Admissions: 88% of applicants accepted
Based on: ••• Test scores
• Interview
Completion: 38% graduate

4-year proprietary business, technical college, coed. Founded in 1931. **Accreditation:** Regional. **Undergraduate enrollment:** 1,641 men, 550 women full time; 692 men, 309 women part time. **Faculty:** 114 total (50 full time). **Location:** Urban campus in very large city; 6 miles from downtown Chicago. **Calendar:** Three continuous calendar terms. Extensive evening/early morning classes. **Microcomputers:** 230 located in computer centers.

DEGREES OFFERED. AAS, BS. 259 associate degrees awarded in 1992. 100% in engineering technologies. 323 bachelor's degrees awarded. 17% in business and management, 35% computer sciences, 48% engineering technologies.

UNDERGRADUATE MAJORS. Associate: Electronic technology. **Bachelor's:** Accounting, business administration and management, electronic technology, information sciences and systems.

ACADEMIC PROGRAMS. Accelerated program. **Remedial services:** Learning center, reduced course load, special counselor, tutoring, developmental coursework. **Placement/credit:** Institutional tests; 30 credit hours maximum for associate degree. 47 to 55 hours of credit by examination may be counted toward bachelor's degree.

ACADEMIC REQUIREMENTS. Freshmen must earn minimum GPA of 2.0 to continue in good standing. 45% of freshmen return for sophomore year. Students must declare major on enrollment. **Graduation requirements:** 87 hours for associate, 134 hours for bachelor's. Most students required to take courses in computer science, English, history, humanities, mathematics, social sciences.

FRESHMAN ADMISSIONS. Selection criteria: Applicants must have high school diploma or equivalant, pass institutional entrance examination or submit acceptable SAT, ACT, or WPCT scores, and be 17 years of age. **Test requirements:** SAT or ACT. **Additional information:** New students may enter at beginning of any semester.

1992 FRESHMAN CLASS PROFILE. 1,295 men and women applied, 1,141 accepted; 763 men enrolled, 251 women enrolled. **Characteristics:** 97% from in state, 100% commute, 68% have minority backgrounds, 3% are foreign students.

FALL-TERM APPLICATIONS. $25 fee. Closing date November 4; applicants notified on a rolling basis; must reply within 4 weeks. Interview required. Deferred admission available.

STUDENT LIFE. Activities: Student government, student newspaper, drama, Institute of Electrical and Electronic Engineers (IEEE), Data Processing Management Association (DPMA).

ATHLETICS. Intramural: Basketball, bowling, soccer, softball, table tennis, volleyball.

STUDENT SERVICES. Career counseling, employment service for undergraduates, freshman orientation, placement service for graduates, veterans counselor, services/facilities for handicapped.

ANNUAL EXPENSES. Tuition and fees: $5,580. **Books and supplies:** $525. **Other expenses:** $1,928.

FINANCIAL AID. 77% of freshmen, 82% of continuing students receive some form of aid. All grants, 85% of loans, all jobs based on need. Academic scholarships available. **Aid applications:** No closing date; applicants notified on a rolling basis; must reply immediately. **Additional information:** Approximately 80% of students work part-time at jobs found through Institute.

ADDRESS/TELEPHONE. Rick Yaconis, Director of Admissions, DeVry Institute of Technology: Chicago, 3300 North Campbell Avenue, Chicago, IL 60618-5994. (312) 929-6550. (800) 383-3879. Fax: (312) 348-1780.

Eastern Illinois University
Charleston, Illinois CB code: 1199

Admissions: 75% of applicants accepted
Based on: ••• School record, test scores
Completion: 92% of freshmen end year in good standing
50% graduate

4-year public university and teachers college, coed. Founded in 1895. **Accreditation:** Regional. **Undergraduate enrollment:** 4,085 men, 4,903 women full time; 326 men, 512 women part time. **Graduate enrollment:** 188 men, 226 women full time; 368 men, 803 women part time. **Faculty:** 676 total (628 full time), 483 with doctorates or other terminal degrees. **Location:** Rural campus in large town; 180 miles from Chicago. **Calendar:** Semester, limited summer session. **Microcomputers:** 776 located in dormitories, libraries, classrooms, computer centers. **Special facilities:** Tarble Arts Center, zoology vivarium. **Additional facts:** Off-campus sites in Champaign, Danville, Decatur, Olney, Rantoul.

DEGREES OFFERED. BA, BS, MA, MS, MBA, MEd. 2,466 bachelor's degrees awarded in 1992. 11% in business and management, 5% business/office and marketing/distribution, 19% teacher education, 9% home economics, 11% letters/literature, 6% multi/interdisciplinary studies, 6% psychology, 12% social sciences. Graduate degrees offered in 26 major fields of study.

UNDERGRADUATE MAJORS. Accounting, Afro-American (black) studies, art education, art history, arts management, botany, business administration and management, business education, business home economics, chemistry, clinical laboratory science, computer mathematics, dramatic arts, economics, elementary education, engineering, English, English education, environmental science, family and community services, finance, food science and nutrition, French, geology, German, health education, history, home economics education, industrial arts education, industrial technology, information sciences and systems, journalism, junior high education, liberal/general studies, marketing management, mathematics, mathematics education, music education, music performance, office supervision and management, parks and recreation management, philosophy, physical education, physics, political science and government, psychology, social science education, sociology, Spanish, special education, speech, speech pathology/audiology, speech/communication/theater education, studio art, technical education, zoology.

ACADEMIC PROGRAMS. Double major, dual enrollment of high school students, education specialist degree, honors program, independent study, internships, study abroad, teacher preparation; liberal arts/career combination in engineering; combined bachelor's/graduate program in business administration. **Remedial services:** Learning center, reduced course load, special counselor, tutoring. **ROTC:** Army. **Placement/credit:** AP, CLEP General and Subject.

ACADEMIC REQUIREMENTS. Freshmen must earn minimum GPA of 2.0 to continue in good standing. 81% of freshmen return for sophomore year. Students must declare major by end of second year. **Graduation requirements:** 120 hours for bachelor's (45 in major). Most students required to take courses in arts/fine arts, English, foreign languages, humanities, mathematics, biological/physical sciences, social sciences.

FRESHMAN ADMISSIONS. Selection criteria: Applicants must be in top half of high school class and have ACT score of at least 18 or be in upper three-quarters of high school class and have ACT score of at least 22. **High school preparation:** 13 units required; 15 recommended. Required and recommended units include English 4, mathematics 3, social science 3 and science 3. Foreign language 2 recommended. **Test requirements:** SAT or ACT (ACT preferred); score report by August 15. **Additional information:** Minority admissions program for students with ACT composite score of 14 or above and GPA of 2.0 or above.

1992 FRESHMAN CLASS PROFILE. 2,157 men applied, 1,556 accepted, 605 enrolled; 2,845 women applied, 2,194 accepted, 843 enrolled. 10% were in top tenth and 40% were in top quarter of graduating class. **Characteristics:** 98% from in state, 80% live in college housing, 10% have minority backgrounds. Average age is 19.

FALL-TERM APPLICATIONS. $25 fee. No closing date; applicants notified on a rolling basis; must reply by registration. Audition required for music applicants. Early admission available. Consult university for possible early cut-off date.

STUDENT LIFE. Housing: Dormitories (men, women, coed); apartment, fraternity, sorority housing available. Greek court complex for 12 fraternities/sororities on campus. **Activities:** Student government, magazine, radio, student newspaper, television, yearbook, choral groups, concert band, dance, drama, jazz band, marching band, music ensembles, musical theater, pep band, symphony orchestra, The Collegians swing choir, fraternities, sororities, United Campus Ministry, Newman Community, College Democrats, Veterans Association, Young Republicans, Black Student Union, Hispanic Student Union, Association of International Students.

ATHLETICS. NCAA. **Intercollegiate:** Baseball M, basketball, cross-country, football M, golf M, soccer M, softball W, swimming, tennis, track and field, volleyball W, wrestling M. **Intramural:** Archery, badminton, basketball, bowling, cross-country, racquetball, rifle, soccer, softball, swimming, table tennis, tennis, track and field, volleyball, wrestling M.

STUDENT SERVICES. Aptitude testing, career counseling, employment service for undergraduates, freshman orientation, health services, personal counseling, placement service for graduates, special adviser for adult students, veterans counselor, services/facilities for handicapped.

ANNUAL EXPENSES. Tuition and fees (1992-93): $2,533, $3,696 additional for out-of-state students. **Room and board:** $2,856. **Books and supplies:** $120. **Other expenses:** $1,280.

FINANCIAL AID. 64% of continuing students receive some form of aid. 76% of grants, 98% of loans, 13% of jobs based on need. Academic, music/drama, art, athletic, leadership scholarships available. **Aid applications:** No closing date; priority given to applications received by April 15; applicants notified on a rolling basis beginning on or about July 1; must reply within 2 weeks.

ADDRESS/TELEPHONE. Dale Wolf, Director of Admissions, Eastern Illinois University, 600 Lincoln - Old Main 117, Charleston, IL 61920-3099. (217) 581-2223. (800) 252-5711.

East-West University
Chicago, Illinois CB code: 0798

4-year private university, coed. Founded in 1978. **Accreditation:** Regional. **Undergraduate enrollment:** 129 men, 131 women full time; 5 men, 3 women part time. **Faculty:** 25 total (9 full time), 5 with doctorates or other terminal degrees. **Location:** Urban campus in very large city. **Calendar:** Quarter. **Microcomputers:** Located in computer centers.

DEGREES OFFERED. AA, AS, BA, BS. 6 associate degrees awarded in 1992. 18 bachelor's degrees awarded. 29% in business and management, 40% computer sciences, 30% engineering technologies.

UNDERGRADUATE MAJORS. Associate: Computer and information sciences, electronic technology. **Bachelor's:** Behavioral sciences, business and management, computer and information sciences, electronic technology, liberal/general studies, mathematics.

ACADEMIC PROGRAMS. 2-year transfer program, independent study. **Remedial services:** Tutoring. **Placement/credit:** AP, CLEP Subject, IB, institutional tests.

ACADEMIC REQUIREMENTS. Students must declare major by end of second year. **Graduation requirements:** 90 hours for associate (30 in major), 180 hours for bachelor's (60 in major). Most students required to take courses in English, mathematics, biological/physical sciences, social sciences.

FRESHMAN ADMISSIONS. Selection criteria: Open admissions.

1992 FRESHMAN CLASS PROFILE. 36 men, 40 women enrolled. **Characteristics:** 90% from in state, 100% commute, 82% have minority backgrounds, 17% are foreign students. Average age is 18.

FALL-TERM APPLICATIONS. $25 fee, may be waived for applicants with need. No closing date; applicants notified on a rolling basis. Interview recommended. Deferred admission available. SAT/ACT recommended for placement.

STUDENT LIFE. Activities: Student government, drama.

ATHLETICS. Intramural: Basketball M.

STUDENT SERVICES. Freshman orientation, services/facilities for handicapped.

ANNUAL EXPENSES. Tuition and fees (1992-93): $5,910. **Books and supplies:** $600. **Other expenses:** $1,800.

FINANCIAL AID. Grants, loans, jobs available. Academic scholarships available. **Aid applications:** No closing date; applicants notified on a rolling basis. **Additional information:** Foreign students eligible to apply for Islamic Studies scholarship.

ADDRESS/TELEPHONE. Mettha M. Green, Director of Admissions, East-West University, 816 South Michigan Avenue, Chicago, IL 60605. (312) 939-0111. Fax: (312) 939-0083.

Elgin Community College
Elgin, Illinois CB code: 1203

2-year public community college, coed. Founded in 1949. **Accreditation:** Regional. **Undergraduate enrollment:** 2,077 men and women full time; 6,937 men and women part time. **Faculty:** 410 total (110 full time), 20 with doctorates or other terminal degrees. **Location:** Suburban campus in small city; 40 miles from Chicago. **Calendar:** Semester, extensive summer session.

Microcomputers: 360 located in libraries, classrooms, computer centers. **Special facilities:** Photographic art gallery, E. Von Isser art gallery, greenhouse.

DEGREES OFFERED. AA, AS, AAS. 592 associate degrees awarded in 1992.

UNDERGRADUATE MAJORS. Accounting, air conditioning/heating/refrigeration mechanics, air conditioning/heating/refrigeration technology, airline piloting and navigation, automotive mechanics, automotive technology, aviation management, business administration and management, business and management, business and office, business computer/console/peripheral equipment operation, business data processing and related programs, business data programming, business systems analysis, child development/care/guidance, computer aided machining, computer and information sciences, computer graphics, computer-aided design and drafting, court reporting, criminal justice studies, data processing, drafting, drafting and design technology, electrical/electronics/communications engineering, electronic technology, engineering and engineering-related technologies, finance, fire control and safety technology, food management, food production/management/services, geriatric services, gerontology, graphic arts technology, graphic design, hospitality and recreation marketing, hotel/motel and restaurant management, legal assistant/paralegal, legal secretary, liberal/general studies, management science, manufacturing technology, marketing and distribution, marketing management, mechanical design technology, medical secretary, mental health/human services, nursing, office supervision and management, precision metal work, real estate, retailing, secretarial and related programs, welding technology, word processing.

ACADEMIC PROGRAMS. 2-year transfer program, cooperative education, dual enrollment of high school students, honors program, independent study, internships, study abroad, telecourses, weekend college. **Remedial services:** Learning center, reduced course load, remedial instruction, tutoring. **Placement/credit:** AP, CLEP General and Subject; 30 credit hours maximum for associate degree.

ACADEMIC REQUIREMENTS. Freshmen must earn minimum GPA of 1.6 to continue in good standing. **Graduation requirements:** 60 hours for associate. Most students required to take courses in English, humanities, mathematics, biological/physical sciences, social sciences.

FRESHMAN ADMISSIONS. Selection criteria: Open admissions.

1992 FRESHMAN CLASS PROFILE. 2,497 men and women enrolled. 31% were in top quarter of graduating class. **Characteristics:** 99% from in state, 100% commute. Average age is 19.

FALL-TERM APPLICATIONS. $15 fee, may be waived for applicants with need. No closing date; applicants notified on a rolling basis; must reply by registration.

STUDENT LIFE. Activities: Student government, student newspaper, literary magazine, choral groups, concert band, dance, drama, jazz band, musical theater, symphony orchestra.

ATHLETICS. NJCAA. **Intercollegiate:** Baseball M, basketball, golf M, soccer M, softball W, tennis, volleyball W.

STUDENT SERVICES. Career counseling, employment service for undergraduates, freshman orientation, on-campus day care, personal counseling, placement service for graduates, special adviser for adult students, veterans counselor, minority counselor, bilingual staff, services/facilities for handicapped.

ANNUAL EXPENSES. Tuition and fees (1992-93): $1,110, $2,220 additional for out-of-district students, $3,210 additional for out-of-state students. **Books and supplies:** $550. **Other expenses:** $700.

FINANCIAL AID. 28% of freshmen, 28% of continuing students receive some form of aid. 58% of grants, 94% of loans, 41% of jobs based on need. 378 enrolled freshmen were judged to have need, 245 were offered aid. Academic, music/drama, art, athletic, leadership scholarships available. **Aid applications:** No closing date; priority given to applications received by July 1; applicants notified on a rolling basis beginning on or about April 1; must reply within 2 weeks.

ADDRESS/TELEPHONE. Russ Fahrner, Admissions Advisor, Elgin Community College, 1700 Spartan Drive, Elgin, IL 60123. (708) 888-7385.

Elmhurst College
Elmhurst, Illinois — CB code: 1204

Admissions: 69% of applicants accepted
Based on:
- ••• School record
- •• Test scores
- • Activities, essay, interview, recommendations, special talents

Completion: 82% of freshmen end year in good standing
54% graduate, 13% of these enter graduate study

4-year private liberal arts college, coed, affiliated with United Church of Christ. Founded in 1871. **Accreditation:** Regional. **Undergraduate enrollment:** 659 men, 945 women full time; 476 men, 645 women part time. **Faculty:** 138 total (99 full time), 100 with doctorates or other terminal degrees. **Location:** Suburban campus in large town; 15 miles from downtown Chicago. **Calendar:** 4-1-4, extensive summer session. Saturday and extensive evening/early morning classes. **Microcomputers:** 140 located in libraries, classrooms, computer centers. **Special facilities:** 2 nuclear accelerators, 4 electron microscopes, collection of Impressionist art, computer science and technology center, media center, sound studio, greenhouse. **Additional facts:** Campus designated as national arboretum.

DEGREES OFFERED. BA, BS. 765 bachelor's degrees awarded in 1992. 47% in business and management, 6% communications, 14% education, 9% health sciences, 5% psychology, 6% social sciences.

UNDERGRADUATE MAJORS. Accounting, American studies, art education, arts management, biochemistry, biology, business administration and management, business economics, chemistry, chemistry business management, chemistry education, communications, computer and information sciences, computer graphics, dramatic arts, early childhood education, economics, education, education of the emotionally handicapped, elementary education, English, English education, environmental management, finance, fine arts, foreign languages education, French, geography, German, health care administration, history, interdisciplinary communications, international business management, management information systems, management science, marketing management, mathematics, mathematics education, music, music business management, music education, nursing, organizational behavior, personnel management, philosophy, physical education, physics, piano pedagogy, political science and government, polymer coatings, predentistry, prelaw, premedicine, prepharmacy, preveterinary, psychology, recreation/business management, religion, religious music, science education, social science education, sociology, Spanish, specific learning disabilities, speech, speech pathology/audiology, speech/communication/theater education, sports medicine, theological studies, transportation management, urban studies.

ACADEMIC PROGRAMS. Double major, dual enrollment of high school students, honors program, independent study, internships, study abroad, teacher preparation, weekend college, Washington semester, 3+2 engineering with Illinois Institute of Technology, University of Illinois at Urbana-Champaign, and Washington University (MO). **Remedial services:** Learning center, preadmission summer program, reduced course load, special counselor, tutoring. **ROTC:** Air Force, Army. **Placement/credit:** AP, CLEP General and Subject, IB, institutional tests; 48 credit hours maximum for bachelor's degree.

ACADEMIC REQUIREMENTS. Freshmen must earn minimum GPA of 2.0 to continue in good standing. 72% of freshmen return for sophomore year. Students must declare major by end of second year. **Graduation requirements:** 132 hours for bachelor's (32 in major). Most students required to take courses in arts/fine arts, computer science, English, humanities, mathematics, philosophy/religion, biological/physical sciences, social sciences. **Postgraduate studies:** 2% enter law school, 1% enter medical school, 8% enter MBA programs, 2% enter other graduate study.

FRESHMAN ADMISSIONS. Selection criteria: School achievement record, including grades and course levels, most important followed by test scores. Applicants should rank in top half of class and have 2.0 high school GPA. Activities and counselor recommendations also considered. **High school preparation:** 12 units required; 16 recommended. Required and recommended units include English 4, mathematics 2-3, social science 2-3 and science 2-3. Foreign language 2 recommended. Chemistry required for nursing applicants. 3 mathematics required for most business administration majors and for computer-related specialties applicants. **Test requirements:** SAT or ACT; score report by August 15.

1992 FRESHMAN CLASS PROFILE. 553 men applied, 327 accepted, 101 enrolled; 445 women applied, 363 accepted, 134 enrolled. 38% had high school GPA of 3.0 or higher, 59% between 2.0 and 2.99. 13% were in top tenth and 38% were in top quarter of graduating class. **Academic background:** Mid 50% of enrolled freshmen had SAT-V between 330-420, SAT-M between 350-470; ACT composite between 18-23. 5% submitted SAT scores, 93% submitted ACT scores. **Characteristics:** 92% from in state, 57% live in college housing, 19% have minority backgrounds, 2% are foreign students, 13% join fraternities/sororities. Average age is 18.

FALL-TERM APPLICATIONS. $15 fee, may be waived for applicants with need. Closing date August 1; applicants notified on a rolling basis; must reply by June 1 or within 4 weeks if notified thereafter. Audition required for music applicants. Interview recommended for academically marginal applicants. Portfolio recommended for art applicants. Essay recommended. CRDA. Deferred and early admission available.

STUDENT LIFE. Housing: Dormitories (men, women, coed). Each residence hall is self-governing. **Activities:** Student government, magazine, radio, student newspaper, yearbook, choral groups, concert band, dance, drama, jazz band, music ensembles, musical theater, pep band, symphony orchestra, fraternities, sororities, religious life committee, Young Republicans, Young Democrats, coed service fraternity, Black Student Union, campus ministry, Students for South Africa.

ATHLETICS. NCAA. **Intercollegiate:** Baseball M, basketball, cross-country, football M, golf M, softball W, tennis, track and field, volleyball W, wrestling M. **Intramural:** Basketball, softball, volleyball.

STUDENT SERVICES. Aptitude testing, career counseling, employment service for undergraduates, freshman orientation, health services, on-campus day care, personal counseling, placement service for graduates,

special adviser for adult students, veterans counselor, services/facilities for handicapped.

ANNUAL EXPENSES. Tuition and fees: $9,676. **Room and board:** $3,964. **Books and supplies:** $550. **Other expenses:** $2,000.

FINANCIAL AID. 59% of freshmen, 55% of continuing students receive some form of aid. 97% of grants, 82% of loans, 61% of jobs based on need. 144 enrolled freshmen were judged to have need, all were offered aid. Academic, music/drama, leadership, religious affiliation scholarships available. **Aid applications:** No closing date; priority given to applications received by April 15; applicants notified on a rolling basis beginning on or about March 1; must reply by May 1 or within 2 weeks if notified thereafter. **Additional information:** For needy students, proportion of gift assistance in aid package increases as academic credentials get better.

ADDRESS/TELEPHONE. Michael E. Dessimoz, Director of Enrollment Development, Elmhurst College, 190 Prospect, Elmhurst, IL 60126-3296. (708) 617-3400. (800) 697-1871. Fax: (708) 617-3245.

Eureka College
Eureka, Illinois — CB code: 1206

Admissions: 81% of applicants accepted
Based on: ••• Interview, school record, test scores
•• Recommendations
• Activities
Completion: 80% of freshmen end year in good standing
60% graduate, 36% of these enter graduate study

4-year private college of arts and sciences, coed, affiliated with Christian Church (Disciples of Christ). Founded in 1855. **Accreditation:** Regional. **Undergraduate enrollment:** 237 men, 277 women full time. **Faculty:** 61 total (43 full time), 39 with doctorates or other terminal degrees. **Location:** Rural campus in small town; 140 miles from Chicago, 20 miles from Peoria. **Calendar:** Four 8-week terms. **Microcomputers:** Located in libraries, classrooms, computer centers. **Additional facts:** Classes meet every day, students take 2 or 3 classes in each of four 8-week terms.

DEGREES OFFERED. BA, BS. 108 bachelor's degrees awarded in 1992. 20% in business and management, 5% computer sciences, 30% teacher education, 7% letters/literature, 5% philosophy, religion, theology, 10% physical sciences, 9% psychology, 6% social sciences.

UNDERGRADUATE MAJORS. Accounting, biology, business administration and management, business and management, chemistry, clinical laboratory science, communications, computer and information sciences, dramatic arts, economics, education, elementary education, English, fine arts, history, junior high education, marketing and distribution, mathematics, mathematics education, music, music education, music performance, nursing, philosophy, physical education, physical sciences, political science and government, predentistry, preengineering, prelaw, premedicine, prepharmacy, preveterinary, psychology, religion, science education, secondary education, social sciences, social work, sociology, Spanish, speech, visual and performing arts.

ACADEMIC PROGRAMS. Double major, dual enrollment of high school students, honors program, independent study, internships, student-designed major, study abroad, teacher preparation; liberal arts/career combination in engineering. **Remedial services:** Learning center, reduced course load, tutoring. **Placement/credit:** AP, CLEP General and Subject, institutional tests.

ACADEMIC REQUIREMENTS. Freshmen must earn minimum GPA of 1.7 to continue in good standing. 70% of freshmen return for sophomore year. Students must declare major by end of second year. **Graduation requirements:** 124 hours for bachelor's (32 in major). Most students required to take courses in arts/fine arts, English, history, mathematics, philosophy/religion, biological/physical sciences, social sciences. **Postgraduate studies:** 3% enter law school, 3% enter medical school, 10% enter MBA programs, 20% enter other graduate study.

FRESHMAN ADMISSIONS. Selection criteria: Class rank, high school GPA, ACT scores, and high school subjects studied most important. Recommendations and interviews also important. **High school preparation:** 16 units recommended. Recommended units include biological science 1, English 4, foreign language 2, mathematics 3, physical science 1 and social science 3. **Test requirements:** SAT or ACT (ACT preferred); score report by May 15.

1992 FRESHMAN CLASS PROFILE. 263 men applied, 217 accepted, 59 enrolled; 257 women applied, 204 accepted, 59 enrolled. 32% had high school GPA of 3.0 or higher, 67% between 2.0 and 2.99. 12% were in top tenth and 37% were in top quarter of graduating class. **Academic background:** Mid 50% of enrolled freshmen had ACT composite between 18-24. 98% submitted ACT scores. **Characteristics:** 90% from in state, 92% live in college housing, 7% have minority backgrounds, 2% are foreign students, 30% join fraternities/sororities. Average age is 18.

FALL-TERM APPLICATIONS. No fee. No closing date; priority given to applications received by May 15; applicants notified on a rolling basis; must reply within 4 weeks. Interview required. Audition required for music and drama applicants. Portfolio required for art scholarship applicants. Deferred admission available.

STUDENT LIFE. Housing: Dormitories (men, women, coed); fraternity, sorority housing available. All single students under 24 not living with parents required to live on campus. **Activities:** Student government, magazine, student newspaper, yearbook, choral groups, drama, fraternities, sororities, campus religious organization.

ATHLETICS. NAIA, NCAA. **Intercollegiate:** Baseball M, basketball, diving, football M, golf, softball W, swimming, tennis, track and field, volleyball W. **Intramural:** Badminton, basketball, bowling, golf, softball, swimming, tennis, volleyball.

STUDENT SERVICES. Aptitude testing, career counseling, employment service for undergraduates, freshman orientation, health services, personal counseling.

ANNUAL EXPENSES. Tuition and fees (1992-93): $10,325. **Room and board:** $3,330. **Books and supplies:** $330. **Other expenses:** $510.

FINANCIAL AID. 90% of freshmen, 87% of continuing students receive some form of aid. 96% of grants, 90% of loans, 56% of jobs based on need. Academic, music/drama, art, leadership, religious affiliation scholarships available. **Aid applications:** No closing date; priority given to applications received by May 1; applicants notified on a rolling basis; must reply within 4 weeks.

ADDRESS/TELEPHONE. Susan R. Jordan, Dean of Admissionsand Financial Aid, Eureka College, 300 College Avenue, Eureka, IL 61530. (800) 322-3756. (800) 322-3756. Fax: (309) 467-6386.

Gem City College
Quincy, Illinois — CB code: 0808

2-year proprietary business, technical college, coed. Founded in 1870. **Undergraduate enrollment:** 250 men and women. **Faculty:** 16 total (14 full time). **Location:** Rural campus in large town; 250 miles from Chicago, 120 miles from St. Louis. **Calendar:** Quarter. **Microcomputers:** Located in computer centers.

DEGREES OFFERED. AAS. 10 associate degrees awarded in 1992. 75% in business and management, 25% trade and industry.

UNDERGRADUATE MAJORS. Accounting, business administration and management, jewelry store management.

ACADEMIC REQUIREMENTS. Students must declare major on application. **Graduation requirements:** 94 hours for associate.

FRESHMAN ADMISSIONS. Selection criteria: Open admissions.

1992 FRESHMAN CLASS PROFILE. 25 men, 75 women enrolled. **Characteristics:** 100% commute. Average age is 27.

FALL-TERM APPLICATIONS. $25 fee. No closing date; applicants notified on a rolling basis; must reply by registration. Interview recommended. Deferred admission available. Registration fee of $25 due at time of application.

STUDENT SERVICES. Freshman orientation, personal counseling, placement service for graduates, special adviser for adult students, veterans counselor, services/facilities for handicapped.

ANNUAL EXPENSES. Tuition and fees: $3,150. **Books and supplies:** $400. **Other expenses:** $1,800.

FINANCIAL AID. 65% of continuing students receive some form of aid. All grants based on need. **Aid applications:** No closing date; applicants notified on a rolling basis.

ADDRESS/TELEPHONE. Barbara Goings, Director of Admissions, Gem City College, PO Box 179, Quincy, IL 62306. (217) 222-0391.

Governors State University
University Park, Illinois — CB code: 0807

2-year upper-division public university, coed. Founded in 1969. **Accreditation:** Regional. **Undergraduate enrollment:** 302 men, 544 women full time; 740 men, 1,185 women part time. **Graduate enrollment:** 40 men, 92 women full time; 776 men, 1,815 women part time. **Faculty:** 314 total (160 full time), 180 with doctorates or other terminal degrees. **Location:** Suburban campus in large town; 30 miles from Chicago. **Calendar:** Trimester, extensive summer session. Saturday and extensive evening/early morning classes. **Microcomputers:** 125 located in libraries, computer centers. **Special facilities:** 750-acre campus, nature trails, 6 lakes, sculpture park, art and photo galleries.

DEGREES OFFERED. BA, BS, MA, MS, MBA. 670 bachelor's degrees awarded in 1992. 20% in business and management, 5% communications, 5% computer sciences, 17% teacher education, 15% health sciences, 23% multi/interdisciplinary studies. Graduate degrees offered in 20 major fields of study.

UNDERGRADUATE MAJORS. Biology, business administration and management, business and technology, chemistry, communications, computer and information sciences, criminal justice studies, early childhood education, elementary education, English, English education, fine arts, health care administration, journalism, liberal/general studies, media communications, mental health/human services, music, music education, nursing, predentistry, prelaw, premedicine, preveterinary, psychology, public administration, radio/television broadcasting, science education, social sciences, social work, speech, speech pathology/audiology.

ACADEMIC PROGRAMS. External degree, honors program, independent study, internships, student-designed major, teacher preparation, telecourses, weekend college, cross-registration, Board of Governors degree program, dual enrollment with several community colleges. **Remedial services:** Learning center, reduced course load, remedial instruction, special counselor, tutoring, developmental reading. **ROTC:** Air Force, Army. **Placement/credit:** CLEP General and Subject, institutional tests.

ACADEMIC REQUIREMENTS. Students must declare major on application. **Graduation requirements:** 120 hours for bachelor's (30 in major). Most students required to take courses in computer science, English, humanities, mathematics, biological/physical sciences, social sciences. **Additional information:** Cross-registration with other institutions in Illinois Board of Governors and Educational Administration programs.

STUDENT LIFE. Activities: Student government, film, magazine, student newspaper, television, choral groups, concert band, jazz band, music ensembles, string quartet, veterans organization, several international student organizations, Union of African Peoples, naturalist club, 30-plus co-curricular professional service organizations.

ATHLETICS. Intramural: Badminton, basketball, handball, racquetball, skiing, softball, table tennis, volleyball.

STUDENT SERVICES. Aptitude testing, career counseling, employment service for undergraduates, on-campus day care, personal counseling, placement service for graduates, veterans counselor, campus ministry, services/facilities for handicapped.

ANNUAL EXPENSES. Tuition and fees (1992-93): $1,978, $3,696 additional for out-of-state students. **Books and supplies:** $450. **Other expenses:** $800.

FINANCIAL AID. 40% of freshmen, 60% of continuing students receive some form of aid. 89% of grants, 84% of loans, 26% of jobs based on need. Academic, music/drama, art, state/district residency, leadership, minority scholarships available. **Aid applications:** Closing date October 1; priority given to applications received by May 1; applicants notified on a rolling basis beginning on or about June 15; must reply within 2 weeks.

ADDRESS/TELEPHONE. William Craig, Director of Admissions, Governors State University, University Parkway, University Park, IL 60466. (708) 534-5000 ext. 4490. Fax: (708) 534-8951.

Greenville College
Greenville, Illinois — CB code: 1256

Admissions:	72% of applicants accepted
Based on:	••• Recommendations, school record
	•• Test scores
	• Activities, essay, interview, religious affiliation/commitment, special talents
Completion:	82% of freshmen end year in good standing
	45% graduate, 15% of these enter graduate study

4-year private liberal arts college, coed, affiliated with Free Methodist Church of North America. Founded in 1892. **Accreditation:** Regional. **Undergraduate enrollment:** 422 men, 358 women full time; 40 men, 37 women part time. **Faculty:** 61 total (55 full time), 26 with doctorates or other terminal degrees. **Location:** Rural campus in small town; 50 miles from St. Louis, Missouri. **Calendar:** 4-1-4, limited summer session. **Microcomputers:** 75 located in libraries, classrooms, computer centers. **Special facilities:** Bock Art Museum, Ayers Center in Colorado. **Additional facts:** Academic and Christian values emphasized.

DEGREES OFFERED. BA, BS. 158 bachelor's degrees awarded in 1992. 19% in business and management, 5% communications, 21% teacher education, 11% life sciences, 6% philosophy, religion, theology, 7% psychology, 6% social sciences, 11% visual and performing arts.

UNDERGRADUATE MAJORS. Accounting, art education, biology, business administration and management, business and management, chemistry, communications, computer and information sciences, computer programming, dramatic arts, education, education of the emotionally handicapped, education of the mentally handicapped, elementary education, English, English education, fine arts, foreign languages education, French, gerontology, history, junior high education, liberal/general studies, management information systems, marketing management, mathematics, mathematics education, music, music education, philosophy, physical education, physics, political science and government, psychology, recreation and community services technologies, religion, science education, secondary education, social science education, social studies education, social work, sociology, Spanish, special education, specific learning disabilities, speech/communication/theater education.

ACADEMIC PROGRAMS. Accelerated program, cooperative education, double major, honors program, independent study, internships, student-designed major, study abroad, Washington semester, cross-registration; liberal arts/career combination in engineering, health sciences. **Remedial services:** Learning center, reduced course load, remedial instruction, special counselor, tutoring. **Placement/credit:** AP, CLEP General and Subject, institutional tests; 32 credit hours maximum for bachelor's degree.

ACADEMIC REQUIREMENTS. Freshmen must earn minimum GPA of 1.5 to continue in good standing. 70% of freshmen return for sophomore year. Students must declare major by end of second year. **Graduation requirements:** 132 hours for bachelor's (40 in major). Most students required to take courses in arts/fine arts, English, history, humanities, mathematics, philosophy/religion, biological/physical sciences, social sciences. **Postgraduate studies:** 1% enter law school, 2% enter medical school, 2% enter MBA programs, 10% enter other graduate study.

FRESHMAN ADMISSIONS. Selection criteria: School achievement record, recommendations, test scores very important. Compatibility with college's philosophy of education considered. **High school preparation:** 16 units recommended. Recommended units include English 4, foreign language 2, mathematics 2 and science 1. Mathematics recommendation includes algebra and geometry. One American history also recommended. **Test requirements:** SAT or ACT (ACT preferred); score report by September 1.

1992 FRESHMAN CLASS PROFILE. 289 men applied, 205 accepted, 130 enrolled; 240 women applied, 178 accepted, 98 enrolled. 12% were in top tenth and 25% were in top quarter of graduating class. **Academic background:** Mid 50% of enrolled freshmen had ACT composite between 18-25. 73% submitted ACT scores. **Characteristics:** 40% from in state, 84% live in college housing, 20% have minority backgrounds, 7% are foreign students. Average age is 18.

FALL-TERM APPLICATIONS. $10 fee, may be waived for applicants with need. Closing date August 15; applicants notified on a rolling basis; must reply by July 1 or within 2 weeks if notified thereafter. Interview required for academically weak applicants. Audition recommended for music applicants. CRDA. Deferred and early admission available.

STUDENT LIFE. Housing: Dormitories (men, women). All single students not living at home must live in college housing. **Activities:** Student government, radio, student newspaper, yearbook, choral groups, concert band, drama, jazz band, music ensembles, musical theater, pep band, Missions Fellowship, Rapports, College Republicans, Fellowship of Christian Athletes, student ministry teams, Club GC, Ladies of Elpinice, Agora. **Additional information:** Religious observance required.

ATHLETICS. NAIA. **Intercollegiate:** Baseball M, basketball, cross-country M, golf M, soccer M, softball W, tennis, track and field, volleyball W. **Intramural:** Badminton, basketball, bowling, golf, soccer M, softball, table tennis, tennis, volleyball.

STUDENT SERVICES. Aptitude testing, career counseling, employment service for undergraduates, freshman orientation, health services, personal counseling, placement service for graduates.

ANNUAL EXPENSES. Tuition and fees (1992-93): $9,300. **Room and board:** $3,910. **Books and supplies:** $400. **Other expenses:** $500.

FINANCIAL AID. 94% of freshmen, 87% of continuing students receive some form of aid. 95% of grants, 95% of loans, 43% of jobs based on need. 170 enrolled freshmen were judged to have need, all were offered aid. Academic, leadership, religious affiliation scholarships available. **Aid applications:** No closing date; priority given to applications received by June 1; applicants notified on a rolling basis beginning on or about March 1; must reply within 2 weeks. **Additional information:** Low-interest loans funded by college.

ADDRESS/TELEPHONE. H. Kent Krober, Director of Admissons, Greenville College, 315 East College Avenue, Greenville, IL 62246. (618) 664-1840. (800) 345-4440. Fax: (618) 664-1748.

Harrington Institute of Interior Design
Chicago, Illinois — CB code: 0940

4-year proprietary professional college of interior design, coed. Founded in 1931. **Undergraduate enrollment:** 293 men and women. **Faculty:** 38 total (12 full time), 1 with doctorate or other terminal degree. **Location:** Urban campus in very large city; in downtown Chicago. **Calendar:** Semester. **Special facilities:** Access to Chicago Merchandise Mart wholesale showroom. **Additional facts:** Accredited by Foundation for Interior Design Education Research.

DEGREES OFFERED. AAS, BA. 67 associate degrees awarded in 1992. 100% in architecture and environmental design. 21 bachelor's degrees awarded. 100% in architecture and environmental design.

UNDERGRADUATE MAJORS. Associate: Interior design. **Bachelor's:** Interior design.

ACADEMIC PROGRAMS. Study abroad, visiting/exchange student program. **Placement/credit:** CLEP General.

ACADEMIC REQUIREMENTS. Freshmen must earn minimum GPA of 2.0 to continue in good standing. 83% of freshmen return for sophomore year. Students must declare major on application. **Graduation requirements:** 93 hours for associate (93 in major), 123 hours for bachelor's (93 in major). Most students required to take courses in arts/fine arts, computer science, history, humanities, social sciences. **Additional information:** Student exchange program with Interior Architecture Department, Rotterdam College of Art and Design, The Netherlands.

FRESHMAN ADMISSIONS. Selection criteria: Personal interview, commitment to career, 2.0 GPA most important.

1992 FRESHMAN CLASS PROFILE. 89 men and women enrolled. **Characteristics:** 83% from in state, 97% commute, 12% have minority backgrounds, 2% are foreign students. Average age is 20.

FALL-TERM APPLICATIONS. $50 fee. No closing date; priority given to applications received by June 1; applicants notified on a rolling basis; must reply by registration. Interview required. Essay required. Deferred admission available.

STUDENT LIFE. Housing: Students may reside at Crown Center Residence at nearby Roosevelt University. **Activities:** Student government, student chapter American Society of Interior Design.

STUDENT SERVICES. Career counseling, personal counseling, placement service for graduates, veterans counselor.

ANNUAL EXPENSES. Tuition and fees (1992-93): $8,025. **Books and supplies:** $925. **Other expenses:** $2,000.

FINANCIAL AID. 39% of freshmen, 50% of continuing students receive some form of aid. All grants, 61% of loans based on need. **Aid applications:** No closing date; priority given to applications received by June 1; applicants notified on a rolling basis.

ADDRESS/TELEPHONE. Mary J. Grether, Director of Admissions, Harrington Institute of Interior Design, 410 South Michigan Avenue, Chicago, IL 60605. (312) 939-4975. Fax: (312) 939-8005.

Highland Community College
Freeport, Illinois — CB code: 1233

2-year public community college, coed. Founded in 1961. **Accreditation:** Regional. **Undergraduate enrollment:** 426 men, 600 women full time; 678 men, 1,476 women part time. **Faculty:** 159 total (46 full time), 2 with doctorates or other terminal degrees. **Location:** Rural campus in large town; 100 miles from Chicago, 38 miles from Rockford. **Calendar:** Semester, limited summer session. Extensive evening/early morning classes. **Microcomputers:** Located in libraries, computer centers. **Special facilities:** YMCA with sports complex, regional arboretum.

DEGREES OFFERED. AA, AS, AAS. 271 associate degrees awarded in 1992.

UNDERGRADUATE MAJORS. Accounting, agribusiness, agricultural production, agricultural sciences, automotive mechanics, biology, business administration and management, business data processing and related programs, chemistry, child development/care/guidance, computer and information sciences, education, electronic technology, engineering, engineering and engineering-related technologies, fine arts, geology, history, liberal/general studies, management science, marketing management, mathematics, music, nursing, physics, political science and government, predentistry, premedicine, prepharmacy, preveterinary, psychology, secretarial and related programs, sociology, visual and performing arts, welding technology, word processing.

ACADEMIC PROGRAMS. 2-year transfer program, dual enrollment of high school students, independent study, student-designed major, study abroad, telecourses. **Remedial services:** Learning center, remedial instruction, tutoring. **Placement/credit:** CLEP Subject, institutional tests; 32 credit hours maximum for associate degree.

ACADEMIC REQUIREMENTS. Freshmen must earn minimum GPA of 1.5 to continue in good standing. 68% of freshmen return for sophomore year. Students must declare major by end of first year. **Graduation requirements:** 62 hours for associate (23 in major). Most students required to take courses in English, history, humanities, mathematics, biological/physical sciences, social sciences.

FRESHMAN ADMISSIONS. Selection criteria: Open admissions. **High school preparation:** 15 units recommended. Recommended units include English 4, foreign language 2, mathematics 3, social science 3 and science 3.

1992 FRESHMAN CLASS PROFILE. 1,108 men and women enrolled. **Characteristics:** 100% from in state, 100% commute, 2% have minority backgrounds. Average age is 24.

FALL-TERM APPLICATIONS. No fee. No closing date; applicants notified on a rolling basis; must reply by registration. Interview required for nursing applicants. Deferred and early admission available.

STUDENT LIFE. Housing: Privately owned apartments on edge of campus available. **Activities:** Student government, student newspaper, television, choral groups, concert band, drama, jazz band, music ensembles, musical theater, pep band.

ATHLETICS. NJCAA. **Intercollegiate:** Basketball, golf, volleyball W. **Intramural:** Basketball M, football, racquetball, skiing, soccer M, softball, table tennis, tennis, volleyball.

STUDENT SERVICES. Aptitude testing, career counseling, employment service for undergraduates, freshman orientation, on-campus day care, personal counseling, placement service for graduates, special adviser for adult students, veterans counselor, services/facilities for handicapped.

ANNUAL EXPENSES. Tuition and fees: $1,050, $2,012 additional for out-of-district students, $2,997 additional for out-of-state students. **Books and supplies:** $550. **Other expenses:** $1,045.

FINANCIAL AID. 40% of freshmen, 30% of continuing students receive some form of aid. 90% of grants, all loans, all jobs based on need. Academic, music/drama, art, athletic, state/district residency, leadership scholarships available. **Aid applications:** No closing date; priority given to applications received by June 1; applicants notified on a rolling basis beginning on or about August 1; must reply within 2 weeks.

ADDRESS/TELEPHONE. Karl Richards, Director of Admissions and Records, Highland Community College, Pearl City Road, Freeport, IL 61032-9341. (815) 235-6121 ext 285. Fax: (815) 235-6130.

Illinois Benedictine College
Lisle, Illinois — CB code: 1707

Admissions: 89% of applicants accepted
Based on:
- ••• School record
- •• Test scores
- • Activities, essay, interview, recommendations, special talents

Completion: 92% of freshmen end year in good standing
55% graduate, 35% of these enter graduate study

4-year private liberal arts college, coed, affiliated with Roman Catholic Church. Founded in 1887. **Accreditation:** Regional. **Undergraduate enrollment:** 561 men, 606 women full time; 345 men, 503 women part time. **Graduate enrollment:** 85 men, 102 women full time; 365 men, 415 women part time. **Faculty:** 245 total (88 full time), 87 with doctorates or other terminal degrees. **Location:** Suburban campus in large town; 25 miles from downtown Chicago. **Calendar:** Semester, extensive summer session. **Microcomputers:** 79 located in libraries, classrooms, computer centers, campus-wide network. **Special facilities:** Natural history museum, art gallery, observatory, pond, architectural award winning abbey, Lincoln Collection. **Additional facts:** Affiliated with Morton Arboretum, Fermi Nuclear Accelerator Laboratories, Argonne National Laboratories, Rush University, Illinois Institute of Technology.

DEGREES OFFERED. BA, BS, MS, MBA. 353 bachelor's degrees awarded in 1992. 35% in business and management, 9% education, 10% health sciences, 15% life sciences, 7% psychology, 7% social sciences. Graduate degrees offered in 6 major fields of study.

UNDERGRADUATE MAJORS. Accounting, aerospace/aeronautical/astronautical engineering, basic clinical health sciences, biochemistry, biology, business and management, business economics, chemistry, clinical laboratory science, communications, computer and information sciences, computer engineering, early childhood education, economics, education of the emotionally handicapped, electrical/electronics/communications engineering, elementary education, engineering science, English, finance, health care administration, health sciences, history, international business management, jazz, management science, marketing and distribution, marketing management, mathematics, mechanical engineering, music, music education, nuclear medical technology, nursing, nutritional sciences, philosophy, physical education, physics, political science and government, psychology, religion, religious music, social sciences, sociology, Spanish, special education, specific learning disabilities.

ACADEMIC PROGRAMS. Double major, dual enrollment of high school students, honors program, independent study, internships, study abroad, teacher preparation, telecourses, visiting/exchange student program, cross-registration, engineering degree program with Illinois Institute of Technology; liberal arts/career combination in engineering; combined bachelor's/graduate program in business administration. **Remedial services:** Learning center, preadmission summer program, reduced course load, remedial instruction, special counselor, tutoring. **Placement/credit:** AP, CLEP General and Subject, institutional tests; 30 credit hours maximum for bachelor's degree.

ACADEMIC REQUIREMENTS. Freshmen must earn minimum GPA of 2.0 to continue in good standing. 81% of freshmen return for sophomore year. Students must declare major by end of second year. **Graduation requirements:** 120 hours for bachelor's (36 in major). Most students required to take courses in English, humanities, mathematics, philosophy/religion, biological/physical sciences, social sciences. **Postgraduate studies:** 1% enter law school, 12% enter medical school, 2% enter MBA programs, 20% enter other graduate study.

FRESHMAN ADMISSIONS. Selection criteria: Require rank in top half of class and above average test scores. Candidates falling below these criteria reviewed by faculty admissions committee. **High school preparation:** 16 units required. Required and recommended units include English 4, foreign language 2, mathematics 2-4 and social science 1. One history, 2 science, one of which must be laboratory science, required of both science and business applicants. **Test requirements:** SAT or ACT (ACT preferred).

1992 FRESHMAN CLASS PROFILE. 307 men applied, 273 accepted, 120 enrolled; 251 women applied, 224 accepted, 111 enrolled. 22% were in top tenth and 47% were in top quarter of graduating class. **Academic background:** Mid 50% of enrolled freshmen had ACT composite between 19-25. 98% submitted ACT scores. **Characteristics:** 97% from in state, 68% live in college housing, 21% have minority backgrounds, 1% are foreign students. Average age is 18.

FALL-TERM APPLICATIONS. $25 fee, may be waived for applicants with need. No closing date; applicants notified on a rolling basis. Audition required for musical instruments and voice applicants. Essay required. Interview recommended. CRDA. Deferred and early admission available. Scholars program offers early decision plan.

STUDENT LIFE. Housing: Dormitories (men, women, coed). **Activities:** Student government, film, magazine, student newspaper, television, yearbook, video production, choral groups, concert band, drama, jazz band, music ensembles, Union of Minority Students, Spanish Club, Business Club, Campus MinistryCenter.

ATHLETICS. NCAA. **Intercollegiate:** Baseball M, basketball, cross-country, diving, football M, golf, soccer M, softball W, swimming, tennis, track and field, volleyball W. **Intramural:** Baseball M, basketball, bowling, handball, ice hockey M, racquetball, soccer, softball, table tennis, tennis, volleyball, water polo. **Clubs:** Floor hockey.

STUDENT SERVICES. Aptitude testing, career counseling, employment service for undergraduates, freshman orientation, health services, on-campus day care, personal counseling, placement service for graduates, special adviser for adult students, services/facilities for handicapped.

ANNUAL EXPENSES. Tuition and fees: $10,080. **Room and board:** $4,067. **Books and supplies:** $650. **Other expenses:** $1,500.

FINANCIAL AID. 94% of freshmen, 97% of continuing students receive some form of aid. 58% of grants, 98% of loans, 20% of jobs based on need. Academic, music/drama, art, leadership, alumni affiliation, minority scholarships available. **Aid applications:** No closing date; priority given to applications received by April 15; applicants notified on a rolling basis beginning on or about March 1; must reply within 2 weeks.

ADDRESS/TELEPHONE. Barbara A. Bernhard, VP Enrollment Mgmt/Human Res, Illinois Benedictine College, 5700 College Road, Lisle, IL 60532-0900. (708) 960-1500 ext. 4000. Fax: (708) 960-1126.

Illinois Central College
East Peoria, Illinois — CB code: 1312

2-year public community college, coed. Founded in 1966. **Accreditation:** Regional. **Undergraduate enrollment:** 2,009 men, 2,188 women full time; 3,478 men, 5,381 women part time. **Faculty:** 626 total (176 full time), 25 with doctorates or other terminal degrees. **Location:** Suburban campus in small city; 150 miles from Chicago, 5 miles from Peoria. **Calendar:** Semester, extensive summer session. Saturday and extensive evening/early morning classes. **Microcomputers:** 200 located in computer centers.

DEGREES OFFERED. AA, AS, AAS. 1,202 associate degrees awarded in 1992. 20% in business and management, 6% business/office and marketing/distribution, 7% teacher education, 7% health sciences, 7% allied health, 17% multi/interdisciplinary studies, 5% parks/recreation, protective services, public affairs, 6% trade and industry.

UNDERGRADUATE MAJORS. Accounting, actuarial sciences, agribusiness, agricultural business and management, agricultural mechanics, architectural technologies, architecture, automotive technology, behavioral sciences, biology, business and management, business data programming, chemistry, child development/care/guidance, commercial art, computer and information sciences, court reporting, criminal justice studies, dance, dental hygiene, diesel engine mechanics, dramatic arts, earth sciences, economics, electromechanical technology, electronic technology, elementary education, engineering, English, environmental science, finance, fine arts, fire control and safety technology, food science and nutrition, foreign languages (multiple emphasis), geography, geology, graphic and printing production, health care administration, history, home economics, horticulture, industrial equipment maintenance and repair, industrial technology, institutional management, interior design, international business management, journalism, law enforcement and corrections, legal assistant/paralegal, liberal/general studies, library assistant, manufacturing technology, marketing and distribution, mathematics, mechanical design technology, medical laboratory technologies, medical records administration, medical records technology, music, nursing, occupational therapy, occupational therapy assistant, physical education, physical therapy, physical therapy assistant, physics, political science and government, predentistry, prelaw, premedicine, prepharmacy, preveterinary, protective services, psychology, radio/television broadcasting, radiograph medical technology, real estate, respiratory therapy technology, robotics, secondary education, secretarial and related programs, sociology, special education, speech, welding technology.

ACADEMIC PROGRAMS. 2-year transfer program, honors program, internships, weekend college. **Remedial services:** Learning center, remedial instruction, tutoring. **Placement/credit:** AP, CLEP General and Subject, institutional tests; 30 credit hours maximum for associate degree.

ACADEMIC REQUIREMENTS. Freshmen must earn minimum GPA of 1.7 to continue in good standing. 90% of freshmen return for sophomore year. Students must declare major on application. **Graduation requirements:** 64 hours for associate. Most students required to take courses in English, humanities, mathematics, biological/physical sciences, social sciences. **Additional information:** QUEST (Quality Undergraduate Education for Transfer Students) provides team-taught, multidisciplinary program for transfer students.

FRESHMAN ADMISSIONS. Selection criteria: Open admissions. Selective admissions for arts, science, and some applied science programs. **High school preparation:** 15 units recommended. Recommended units include English 4, mathematics 3, social science 2 and science 2. 2 units of foreign language, fine arts, or vocational education required for admission to transfer program. **Test requirements:** ACT required for admissions and placement in certain programs. Scores must be received by August 9. Basic skills test required of full-time students if ACT not submitted.

1992 FRESHMAN CLASS PROFILE. 1,231 men, 1,315 women enrolled. 12% had high school GPA of 3.0 or higher, 50% between 2.0 and 2.99. 1% were in top tenth and 28% were in top quarter of graduating class. **Academic background:** Mid 50% of enrolled freshmen had ACT composite between 15-21. 42% submitted ACT scores. **Characteristics:** 99% from in state, 100% commute, 7% have minority backgrounds. Average age is 20.

FALL-TERM APPLICATIONS. No fee. No closing date; applicants notified on a rolling basis; must reply by registration. Audition required for music applicants. Essay required.

STUDENT LIFE. Activities: Student government, student newspaper, choral groups, concert band, dance, drama, jazz band, Tomorrow's Black Leaders, College Republicans, College Democrats, Inter-varsity Christian Fellowship.

ATHLETICS. NJCAA. **Intercollegiate:** Baseball M, basketball, golf M, softball W, volleyball W. **Intramural:** Badminton, basketball, golf, table tennis, tennis, volleyball.

STUDENT SERVICES. Aptitude testing, career counseling, employment service for undergraduates, freshman orientation, health services, on-campus day care, personal counseling, placement service for graduates, special adviser for adult students, veterans counselor, services/facilities for handicapped.

ANNUAL EXPENSES. Tuition and fees: $1,350, $2,170 additional for out-of-district students, $3,330 additional for out-of-state students. Fees vary by program. **Room and board:** $3,225. **Books and supplies:** $500. **Other expenses:** $2,335.

FINANCIAL AID. 18% of freshmen, 18% of continuing students receive some form of aid. 62% of grants, 92% of loans, 21% of jobs based on need. 1,000 enrolled freshmen were judged to have need, 950 were offered aid. Academic, athletic, minority scholarships available. **Aid applications:** No closing date; priority given to applications received by April 15; applicants notified on a rolling basis beginning on or about June 1; must reply within 2 weeks.

ADDRESS/TELEPHONE. Joanne Bannon-Gray, Director of Enrollment Management, Illinois Central College, One College Drive, East Peoria, IL 61635. (309) 694-5235. (800) 422-2293 ext. 235. Fax: (309) 694-5450.

Illinois College
Jacksonville, Illinois — CB code: 1315

Admissions:	90% of applicants accepted
Based on:	••• Recommendations, school record, test scores
	•• Activities, interview
	• Essay, special talents
Completion:	92% of freshmen end year in good standing
	65% graduate, 18% of these enter graduate study

4-year private liberal arts college, coed, Affiliated with United Church of Christ and Presbyterian Church (USA). Founded in 1829. **Accreditation:** Regional. **Undergraduate enrollment:** 450 men, 435 women full time; 23 men, 18 women part time. **Faculty:** 85 total (60 full time), 53 with doctorates or other terminal degrees. **Location:** Rural campus in large town; 35 miles from Springfield, 100 miles from St. Louis. **Calendar:** Semester, limited summer session. **Microcomputers:** 80 located in classrooms, computer centers. **Special facilities:** Engelbach Biology Station, Walter A. Balche Observatory.

DEGREES OFFERED. BA, BS. 150 bachelor's degrees awarded in 1992. 33% in business and management, 5% communications, 9% computer sciences, 11% teacher education, 6% engineering, 5% letters/literature, 5% life sciences, 5% physical sciences, 15% social sciences.

UNDERGRADUATE MAJORS. Accounting, art history, Asian studies, biology, business administration and management, business and management, business economics, chemistry, communications, computer and information sciences, cytotechnology, dramatic arts, economics, education, elementary education, engineering, English, English education, English literature, fine arts, foreign languages education, French, German, history, information sciences and systems, international relations, liberal/general studies, mathematics, mathematics education, medical laboratory technologies, music, music history and appreciation, occupational therapy, philosophy, physical education, physics, political science and government, psychology, radio/television broadcasting, radio/television technology, religion, science education, secondary education, social studies education, social work, sociology, Spanish, speech, speech/communication/theater education, visual and performing arts.

ACADEMIC PROGRAMS. Double major, independent study, internships, study abroad, teacher preparation, intercultural exchange program with Ritsumeikan University, Japan; liberal arts/career combination in engineering, health sciences. **Remedial services:** Reduced course load, tutoring. **Placement/credit:** AP, CLEP General and Subject; 60 credit hours maximum for bachelor's degree.

ACADEMIC REQUIREMENTS. Freshmen must earn minimum GPA of 1.7 after completion of 27 credit hours to continue in good academic standing. 85% of freshmen return for sophomore year. Students must declare major by end of second year. **Graduation requirements:** 120 hours for bachelor's (35 in major). Most students required to take courses in arts/fine arts, English, history, mathematics, philosophy/religion, biological/physical sciences, social sciences. **Postgraduate studies:** 5% enter law school, 3% enter medical school, 3% enter MBA programs, 7% enter other graduate study.

FRESHMAN ADMISSIONS. Selection criteria: Test scores, rank in top half of class, and 2 teachers' recommendations most important. **High school preparation:** 15 units required. Required and recommended units include English 3-4. Biological science 1, mathematics 3, physical science 1 and social science 1 recommended. 7 additional units in foreign language, history, laboratory science, mathematics, and social science recommended. **Test requirements:** SAT or ACT; score report by August 1.

1992 FRESHMAN CLASS PROFILE. 348 men applied, 302 accepted, 125 enrolled; 375 women applied, 346 accepted, 136 enrolled. 75% had high school GPA of 3.0 or higher, 23% between 2.0 and 2.99. 32% were in top tenth and 65% were in top quarter of graduating class. **Academic background:** Mid 50% of enrolled freshmen had SAT-V between 480-580, SAT-M between 530-680; ACT composite between 21-26. 10% submitted SAT scores, 90% submitted ACT scores. **Characteristics:** 91% from in state, 79% live in college housing, 3% have minority backgrounds, 1% are foreign students, 35% join fraternities/sororities. Average age is 18.

FALL-TERM APPLICATIONS. $10 fee, may be waived for applicants with need. Closing date August 15; priority given to applications received by May 1; applicants notified on a rolling basis; must reply within 60 days of notification. Interview recommended. Early admission available. Accepted applicants who reply by July 1 will receive preferential treatment.

STUDENT LIFE. Housing: Dormitories (men, women, coed). Apartment suites on campus for juniors and seniors. **Activities:** Student government, magazine, student newspaper, television, yearbook, choral groups, concert band, drama, music ensembles, pep band, symphony orchestra, fraternities, sororities, Young Republicans, Young Democrats, Alpha Phi Omega, Alpha Kappa Phi.

ATHLETICS. NCAA. **Intercollegiate:** Baseball M, basketball, cross-country, football M, golf M, soccer, softball W, tennis, track and field, volleyball W, wrestling M. **Intramural:** Basketball, handball, racquetball, softball, volleyball.

STUDENT SERVICES. Aptitude testing, career counseling, employment service for undergraduates, freshman orientation, health services, personal counseling, placement service for graduates.

ANNUAL EXPENSES. Tuition and fees (1992-93): $7,050. **Room and board:** $3,450. **Books and supplies:** $600. **Other expenses:** $700.

FINANCIAL AID. 85% of freshmen, 89% of continuing students receive some form of aid. 81% of grants, 87% of loans, 37% of jobs based on need. 184 enrolled freshmen were judged to have need, all were offered aid. Academic, music/drama, leadership scholarships available. **Aid applications:** No closing date; priority given to applications received by May 1; applicants notified on a rolling basis beginning on or about April 1; must reply within 8 weeks.

ADDRESS/TELEPHONE. Gale F. Vaughn, Director of Enrollment, Illinois College, 1101 West College Avenue, Jacksonville, IL 62650-9990. (217) 245-3030. Fax: (217) 245-3034.

Illinois Eastern Community Colleges: Frontier Community College

Fairfield, Illinois — CB code: 1894

2-year public community college, coed. Founded in 1976. **Accreditation:** Regional. **Undergraduate enrollment:** 56 men, 189 women full time; 436 men, 1,226 women part time. **Faculty:** 148 total (3 full time). **Location:** Rural campus in small town; 110 miles from St. Louis, Missouri. **Calendar:** Semester, extensive summer session. Saturday classes. **Microcomputers:** Located in classrooms, computer centers.

DEGREES OFFERED. AA, AS, AAS. 76 associate degrees awarded in 1992. 6% in business/office and marketing/distribution, 20% computer sciences, 73% multi/interdisciplinary studies.

UNDERGRADUATE MAJORS. Emergency medical technologies, fine arts, information sciences and systems, liberal/general studies, office supervision and management, physical sciences, secretarial and related programs.

ACADEMIC PROGRAMS. 2-year transfer program, double major, dual enrollment of high school students, honors program, independent study, student-designed major, study abroad. **Remedial services:** Learning center, remedial instruction, tutoring. **Placement/credit:** CLEP Subject, institutional tests; 32 credit hours maximum for associate degree.

ACADEMIC REQUIREMENTS. Freshmen must earn minimum GPA of 1.7 to continue in good standing. 34% of freshmen return for sophomore year. Students must declare major on enrollment. **Graduation requirements:** 64 hours for associate (48 in major). Most students required to take courses in English, humanities, mathematics, biological/physical sciences, social sciences. **Additional information:** Students, with counselor's aid, design own academic programs through nontraditional alternatives to classroom study.

FRESHMAN ADMISSIONS. Selection criteria: Open admissions. Recommended units include English 3, mathematics 2, social science 2 and science 1. **Test requirements:** SAT or ACT (ACT preferred) for placement and counseling only; score report by August 20. ACT Career Planning Program used for placement.

1992 FRESHMAN CLASS PROFILE. 1,255 men and women enrolled. **Characteristics:** 95% commute. Average age is 44.

FALL-TERM APPLICATIONS. $10 fee. No closing date; applicants notified on a rolling basis beginning on or about August 1; must reply by registration. Deferred admission available.

STUDENT SERVICES. Aptitude testing, career counseling, freshman orientation, personal counseling, placement service for graduates, veterans counselor, services/facilities for handicapped.

ANNUAL EXPENSES. Tuition and fees (projected): $820, $2,224 additional for out-of-district students, $3,234 additional for out-of-state students. **Books and supplies:** $600. **Other expenses:** $800.

FINANCIAL AID. 20% of continuing students receive some form of aid. Grants, loans, jobs available. Academic scholarships available. **Aid applications:** No closing date; applicants notified on a rolling basis beginning on or about August 1.

ADDRESS/TELEPHONE. Suzanne Brooks, Coordinator of Admission and Records, Illinois Eastern Community Colleges: Frontier Community College, Lot 2 Frontier Drive, Fairfield, IL 62837-9801. (618) 842-3711. Fax: (618) 842-6340.

Illinois Eastern Community Colleges: Lincoln Trail College

Robinson, Illinois — CB code: 0758

2-year public community college, coed. Founded in 1969. **Accreditation:** Regional. **Undergraduate enrollment:** 288 men, 286 women full time; 223 men, 288 women part time. **Faculty:** 67 total (23 full time). **Location:** Rural campus in small town; 200 miles from Indianapolis, 110 miles from St. Louis, Missouri. **Calendar:** Semester, extensive summer session. Saturday classes. **Microcomputers:** Located in classrooms.

DEGREES OFFERED. AA, AS, AAS. 112 associate degrees awarded in 1992. 6% in computer sciences, 62% multi/interdisciplinary studies, 21% trade and industry.

UNDERGRADUATE MAJORS. Air conditioning/heating/refrigeration mechanics, air conditioning/heating/refrigeration technology, architectural drafting, business and office, business data entry equipment operation, business data processing and related programs, business data programming, construction, drafting, drafting and design technology, finance, fine arts, food production/management/services, hotel/motel and restaurant management, information sciences and systems, liberal/general studies, machine tool operation/machine shop, mining and petroleum technologies, office supervision and management, physical sciences, secretarial and related programs, special education, teacher aide.

ACADEMIC PROGRAMS. 2-year transfer program, double major, dual enrollment of high school students, honors program, independent study, internships, student-designed major, study abroad. **Remedial services:** Learning center, remedial instruction, tutoring. **Placement/credit:** CLEP Subject, institutional tests; 32 credit hours maximum for associate degree.

ACADEMIC REQUIREMENTS. Freshmen must earn minimum GPA of 1.7 to continue in good standing. 31% of freshmen return for sophomore year. Students must declare major on enrollment. **Graduation requirements:** 64 hours for associate (48 in major). Most students required to take courses in English, humanities, mathematics, biological/physical sciences, social sciences.

FRESHMAN ADMISSIONS. Selection criteria: Open admissions. Recommended units include English 3, mathematics 2, social science 2 and science 1. **Test requirements:** SAT or ACT (ACT preferred) for placement and counseling only; score report by August 20. ACT career planning program required for placement and counseling.

1992 FRESHMAN CLASS PROFILE. 749 men and women enrolled. **Characteristics:** Average age is 29.

FALL-TERM APPLICATIONS. $10 fee. No closing date; applicants notified on a rolling basis beginning on or about August 1; must reply by registration. Deferred admission available.

STUDENT LIFE. Activities: Student government, student newspaper, yearbook, choral groups, concert band, drama, jazz band, music ensembles, musical theater, pep band.

ATHLETICS. NJCAA. **Intercollegiate:** Baseball M, basketball, golf M, softball W, volleyball W.

STUDENT SERVICES. Aptitude testing, career counseling, employment service for undergraduates, freshman orientation, personal counsel-

ing, placement service for graduates, veterans counselor, services/facilities for handicapped.

ANNUAL EXPENSES. Tuition and fees (projected): $820, $2,224 additional for out-of-district students, $3,234 additional for out-of-state students. **Books and supplies:** $600. **Other expenses:** $800.

FINANCIAL AID. 44% of continuing students receive some form of aid. Grants, loans, jobs available. Academic scholarships available. **Aid applications:** No closing date; applicants notified on a rolling basis beginning on or about August 1.

ADDRESS/TELEPHONE. Becky Mikeworth, Director of Admissions, Illinois Eastern Community Colleges: Lincoln Trail College, Rural Route 3 Box 82A, Robinson, IL 62454-9803. (618) 544-8657. Fax: (618) 544-7423.

Illinois Eastern Community Colleges: Olney Central College

Olney, Illinois CB code: 0827

2-year public community college, coed. Founded in 1962. **Accreditation:** Regional. **Undergraduate enrollment:** 342 men, 521 women full time; 194 men, 493 women part time. **Faculty:** 92 total (43 full time). **Location:** Rural campus in small town; 200 miles from St. Louis, Missouri. **Calendar:** Semester, extensive summer session. Saturday classes. **Microcomputers:** Located in libraries, classrooms.

DEGREES OFFERED. AA, AS, AAS. 321 associate degrees awarded in 1992. 7% in business/office and marketing/distribution, 29% allied health, 55% multi/interdisciplinary studies, 5% trade and industry.

UNDERGRADUATE MAJORS. Accounting, automotive mechanics, automotive technology, business and office, construction, fine arts, industrial equipment maintenance and repair, information sciences and systems, law enforcement and corrections technologies, liberal/general studies, marketing and distribution, medical secretary, nursing, office supervision and management, prelaw, radiograph medical technology, secretarial and related programs, welding technology, woodworking.

ACADEMIC PROGRAMS. 2-year transfer program, double major, dual enrollment of high school students, honors program, independent study, internships, student-designed major, study abroad. **Remedial services:** Learning center, remedial instruction, tutoring. **Placement/credit:** CLEP Subject, institutional tests; 32 credit hours maximum for associate degree.

ACADEMIC REQUIREMENTS. Freshmen must earn minimum GPA of 1.7 to continue in good standing. 48% of freshmen return for sophomore year. Students must declare major on enrollment. **Graduation requirements:** 64 hours for associate (48 in major). Most students required to take courses in English, humanities, mathematics, biological/physical sciences, social sciences.

FRESHMAN ADMISSIONS. Selection criteria: Open admissions. Selective admissions to nursing program. Recommended units include English 3, mathematics 2, social science 2 and science 1. **Test requirements:** SAT or ACT (ACT preferred) for placement and counseling only; score report by August 20. ACT Career Planning Program used for placement and counseling.

1992 FRESHMAN CLASS PROFILE. 802 men and women enrolled. **Characteristics:** Average age is 28.

FALL-TERM APPLICATIONS. $10 fee. No closing date; applicants notified on a rolling basis beginning on or about August 1; must reply by registration. Interview required for nursing, radiology technology applicants. Deferred admission available.

STUDENT LIFE. Activities: Student government, student newspaper, yearbook, choral groups, concert band, drama, jazz band, music ensembles, musical theater.

ATHLETICS. NJCAA. **Intercollegiate:** Baseball M, basketball, softball W, tennis, volleyball W.

STUDENT SERVICES. Aptitude testing, career counseling, employment service for undergraduates, freshman orientation, on-campus day care, personal counseling, placement service for graduates, veterans counselor, services/facilities for handicapped.

ANNUAL EXPENSES. Tuition and fees (projected): $820, $2,224 additional for out-of-district students, $3,234 additional for out-of-state students. **Books and supplies:** $600. **Other expenses:** $800.

FINANCIAL AID. 30% of continuing students receive some form of aid. Grants, loans, jobs available. Academic scholarships available. **Aid applications:** No closing date; applicants notified on a rolling basis beginning on or about August 1.

ADDRESS/TELEPHONE. Chris Webber, Asst Dean Student Services, Illinois Eastern Community Colleges: Olney Central College, 305 North West Street, Olney, IL 62450. (618) 395-4351. Fax: (618) 392-5212.

Illinois Eastern Community Colleges: Wabash Valley College

Mount Carmel, Illinois CB code: 1936

2-year public community college, coed. Founded in 1960. **Accreditation:** Regional. **Undergraduate enrollment:** 376 men, 340 women full time; 1,324 men, 522 women part time. **Faculty:** 94 total (43 full time). **Location:** Rural campus in small town; 40 miles from Evansville, Indiana. **Calendar:** Semester, extensive summer session. Saturday classes. **Microcomputers:** Located in libraries, classrooms.

DEGREES OFFERED. AA, AS, AAS. 231 associate degrees awarded in 1992. 9% in agriculture, 7% business/office and marketing/distribution, 5% computer sciences, 5% home economics, 40% multi/interdisciplinary studies, 27% trade and industry.

UNDERGRADUATE MAJORS. Agribusiness, agricultural business and management, business and office, child development/care/guidance, court reporting, diesel engine mechanics, electrical/electronics/communications engineering, electronic technology, engineering and engineering-related technologies, fine arts, information sciences and systems, liberal/general studies, library assistant, library science, marketing and distribution, marketing management, mental health/human services, mining and petroleum technologies, office supervision and management, parks and recreation management, physical sciences, radio/television broadcasting, secretarial and related programs, telecommunications.

ACADEMIC PROGRAMS. 2-year transfer program, double major, dual enrollment of high school students, honors program, independent study, internships, student-designed major, study abroad. **Remedial services:** Learning center, remedial instruction, tutoring, peer counselors. **Placement/credit:** CLEP Subject, institutional tests; 32 credit hours maximum for associate degree.

ACADEMIC REQUIREMENTS. Freshmen must earn minimum GPA of 1.7 to continue in good standing. 28% of freshmen return for sophomore year. Students must declare major on enrollment. **Graduation requirements:** 64 hours for associate (48 in major). Most students required to take courses in English, humanities, mathematics, biological/physical sciences, social sciences. **Additional information:** Students design their own academic programs through nontraditional alternatives to classroom study.

FRESHMAN ADMISSIONS. Selection criteria: Open admissions. Recommended units include English 3, mathematics 2, social science 2 and science 1. **Test requirements:** SAT or ACT (ACT preferred) for placement and counseling only; score report by August 20. ACT Career Planning Program required for placement and counseling.

1992 FRESHMAN CLASS PROFILE. 1,834 men and women enrolled. **Characteristics:** Average age is 37.

FALL-TERM APPLICATIONS. $10 fee. No closing date; applicants notified on a rolling basis beginning on or about August 1; must reply by registration. Deferred admission available.

STUDENT LIFE. Activities: Student government, radio, student newspaper, yearbook, choral groups, concert band, drama, jazz band, music ensembles, musical theater.

ATHLETICS. NJCAA. **Intercollegiate:** Baseball M, basketball, softball W, volleyball W.

STUDENT SERVICES. Aptitude testing, career counseling, employment service for undergraduates, freshman orientation, on-campus day care, personal counseling, placement service for graduates, veterans counselor, services/facilities for handicapped.

ANNUAL EXPENSES. Tuition and fees (projected): $820, $2,224 additional for out-of-district students, $3,234 additional for out-of-state students. **Books and supplies:** $600. **Other expenses:** $800.

FINANCIAL AID. 22% of continuing students receive some form of aid. Grants, loans, jobs available. Academic scholarships available. **Aid applications:** No closing date; applicants notified on a rolling basis beginning on or about August 1.

ADDRESS/TELEPHONE. Diana Spear, Assist Dean for Student Services, Illinois Eastern Community Colleges: Wabash Valley College, 2200 College Drive, Mount Carmel, IL 62863-2657. (618) 262-8641. Fax: (618) 262-5347.

Illinois Institute of Technology

Chicago, Illinois CB code: 1318

Admissions: 84% of applicants accepted
Based on: ••• Essay, school record, test scores
•• Recommendations
• Activities, interview, special talents
Completion: 85% of freshmen end year in good standing
53% graduate

4-year private university and engineering college, coed. Founded in 1890. **Accreditation:** Regional. **Undergraduate enrollment:** 1,384 men, 432 women full time. **Graduate enrollment:** 4,187 men and women. **Faculty:** 514 total (288 full time), 189 with doctorates or other terminal degrees. **Location:** Urban campus in very large city; 3 miles from downtown Chicago. **Calendar:** Semester, extensive summer session. Extensive evening/early morning classes. **Microcomputers:** 200 located in dormitories, libraries, computer centers. **Special facilities:** Railroad assimilator, windtunnel, Center on Excellence in Polymers, Center for Study of Ethics in the Professions.

DEGREES OFFERED. BA, BS, BArch, MS, MBA, PhD. 383 bachelor's degrees awarded in 1992. 14% in architecture and environmental design, 12% business and management, 6% computer sciences, 60% engineering. Graduate degrees offered in 31 major fields of study.

UNDERGRADUATE MAJORS. Accounting, aerospace/aeronautical/astronautical engineering, architecture, biochemistry, bioengineering and biomedical engineering, biology, biotechnology, business administration and management, chemical engineering, chemistry, civil engineering, computer and information sciences, electrical/electronics/communications engineering, English, environmental health engineering, graphic design, history, industrial design, mathematics, mechanical engineering, metallurgical engineering, philosophy, physics, political science and government, premedicine, psychology, rehabilitation counseling/services, sociology, sociology and psychology.

ACADEMIC PROGRAMS. Accelerated program, cooperative education, double major, honors program, independent study, internships, student-designed major, study abroad, telecourses, visiting/exchange student program, weekend college; combined bachelor's/graduate program in business administration, medicine, law. **Remedial services:** Learning center, preadmission summer program, reduced course load, special counselor, tutoring. **ROTC:** Air Force, Army, Naval. **Placement/credit:** AP; 18 credit hours maximum for bachelor's degree.

ACADEMIC REQUIREMENTS. Freshmen must earn minimum GPA of 1.85 to continue in good standing. 85% of freshmen return for sophomore year. Students must declare major by end of first year. **Graduation requirements:** 120 hours for bachelor's. Most students required to take courses in computer science, English, humanities, mathematics, biological/physical sciences, social sciences.

FRESHMAN ADMISSIONS. Selection criteria: Academic performance, class rank, test scores, and essay most important. Counselor recommendations and alumni relationship also considered. **High school preparation:** 16 units required. Required units include English 4, mathematics 4 and social science 1. 2 laboratory science courses required, 1 physics and 1 chemistry recommended. **Test requirements:** SAT or ACT; score report by August 1. ACH required of applicants to 7-year honors programs in engineering and medicine. Score report by January 1.

1992 FRESHMAN CLASS PROFILE. 1,092 men applied, 915 accepted, 313 enrolled; 281 women applied, 243 accepted, 96 enrolled. 85% had high school GPA of 3.0 or higher, 15% between 2.0 and 2.99. 40% were in top tenth and 80% were in top quarter of graduating class. **Academic background:** Mid 50% of enrolled freshmen had SAT-V between 450-570, SAT-M between 560-680; ACT composite between 22-27. 28% submitted SAT scores, 75% submitted ACT scores. **Characteristics:** 53% from in state, 75% live in college housing, 19% have minority backgrounds, 7% are foreign students, 25% join fraternities/sororities. Average age is 18.

FALL-TERM APPLICATIONS. $30 fee, may be waived for applicants with need. Applicants notified on a rolling basis beginning on or about January 15. Essay required. Interview recommended. CRDA. Deferred admission available. Institutional early decision plan. Students applying by December 1 are notified January 15 and must reply by May 1. Those applying by March 15 are notified April 1 and must reply by May 1. Those applying by May 15 are notified July 1 and must reply within 2 weeks.

STUDENT LIFE. Housing: Dormitories (men, women, coed); apartment, fraternity, sorority housing available. **Activities:** Student government, radio, student newspaper, television, yearbook, choral groups, drama, jazz band, musical theater, pep band, fraternities, sororities, many cultural, ethnic, and religious organizations.

ATHLETICS. NAIA. **Intercollegiate:** Baseball M, basketball, bowling, cross-country, diving, golf, soccer M, softball W, swimming, tennis, volleyball. **Intramural:** Basketball M, bowling M, diving, handball M, ice hockey M, racquetball, sailing M, soccer M, softball, swimming, table tennis, tennis, volleyball.

STUDENT SERVICES. Aptitude testing, career counseling, employment service for undergraduates, freshman orientation, health services, personal counseling, placement service for graduates, study skills counseling, services/facilities for handicapped.

ANNUAL EXPENSES. Tuition and fees (1992-93): $13,070. Tuition and fees figure allows students unlimited number of courses during academic year and includes summer school, library and computer usage fees. **Room and board:** $4,480. **Books and supplies:** $800. **Other expenses:** $800.

FINANCIAL AID. 96% of freshmen, 85% of continuing students receive some form of aid. All aid based on need. Alumni affiliation scholarships available. **Aid applications:** No closing date; priority given to applications received by May 1; applicants notified on a rolling basis beginning on or about March 1; must reply by registration.

ADDRESS/TELEPHONE. Office of Undergraduate Admissions, Illinois Institute of Technology, 10 West 33rd Street, Chicago, IL 60616. (312) 567-3025. (800) 448-2329. Fax: (312) 567-3304.

Illinois State University
Normal, Illinois — CB code: 1319

Admissions: 79% of applicants accepted
Based on: ••• School record, test scores
• Interview, recommendations, special talents
Completion: 50% graduate

4-year public university, coed. Founded in 1857. **Accreditation:** Regional. **Undergraduate enrollment:** 7,399 men, 9,090 women full time; 958 men, 1,171 women part time. **Graduate enrollment:** 118 men, 174 women full time; 982 men, 1,872 women part time. **Faculty:** 947 total (802 full time), 745 with doctorates or other terminal degrees. **Location:** Suburban campus in small city; 150 miles from Chicago. **Calendar:** Semester, limited summer session. Saturday classes. **Microcomputers:** 1,039 located in dormitories, libraries, classrooms, computer centers. **Special facilities:** 310-acre farm, Eyestone School Museum, planetarium, 2 art galleries, Ewing Museum of Nations, Stevenson Memorial Room, laboratory school.

DEGREES OFFERED. BA, BS, BFA, MA, MS, MBA, MFA, PhD, EdD. 4,171 bachelor's degrees awarded in 1992. 22% in business and management, 9% communications, 12% teacher education, 19% social sciences, 5% visual and performing arts. Graduate degrees offered in 41 major fields of study.

UNDERGRADUATE MAJORS. Accounting, agribusiness, agricultural sciences, anthropology, biology, business administration and management, business and office, business education, chemistry, computer and information sciences, criminal justice studies, dance, dramatic arts, early childhood education, economics, elementary education, English, environmental science, finance, fine arts, French, geography, geology, German, health education, history, home economics, industrial technology, international business management, journalism, junior high education, liberal/general studies, management science, marketing management, mathematics, medical laboratory technologies, medical records administration, music, music education, music performance, occupational safety and health technology, parks and recreation management, philosophy, physical education, physics, political science and government, psychology, public relations, Russian and Slavic studies, social sciences, social work, sociology, Spanish, special education, speech, speech pathology/audiology.

ACADEMIC PROGRAMS. Cooperative education, double major, dual enrollment of high school students, education specialist degree, honors program, independent study, internships, student-designed major, study abroad, teacher preparation, visiting/exchange student program, Washington semester, cross-registration; combined bachelor's/graduate program in business administration. **Remedial services:** Learning center, preadmission summer program, special counselor, tutoring. **ROTC:** Army. **Placement/credit:** AP, CLEP General and Subject, institutional tests; 18 credit hours maximum for bachelor's degree.

ACADEMIC REQUIREMENTS. Freshmen must earn minimum GPA of 1.8 to continue in good standing. 74% of freshmen return for sophomore year. Students must declare major on application. **Graduation requirements:** 120 hours for bachelor's (42 in major). Most students required to take courses in English.

FRESHMAN ADMISSIONS. High school preparation: 15 units required. Required and recommended units include English 4, mathematics 3-3, social science 2-2 and science 2-2. 2 units required in foreign language and/or fine arts, two units of electives. **Test requirements:** SAT or ACT (ACT preferred); score report by August 20.

1992 FRESHMAN CLASS PROFILE. 9,623 men and women applied, 7,642 accepted; 2,900 enrolled. 9% were in top tenth and 33% were in top quarter of graduating class. **Academic background:** Mid 50% of enrolled freshmen had ACT composite between 19-23. 97% submitted ACT scores. **Characteristics:** 98% from in state, 84% live in college housing, 17% have minority backgrounds. Average age is 19.

FALL-TERM APPLICATIONS. No fee. No closing date; applicants notified on a rolling basis; must reply by registration. Interview required for special admission applicants. Audition recommended for music applicants. Portfolio recommended for art applicants. Early admission available.

STUDENT LIFE. Housing: Dormitories (men, women, coed); apartment, fraternity, sorority housing available. **Activities:** Student government, radio, student newspaper, television, yearbook, choral groups, concert band, dance, drama, jazz band, marching band, music ensembles, musical theater, pep band, symphony orchestra, fraternities, sororities.

ATHLETICS. NCAA. **Intercollegiate:** Baseball M, basketball, cross-country, diving W, football M, golf, gymnastics W, soccer M, softball W, swimming W, tennis, track and field, volleyball W, wrestling M. **Intramural:** Badminton, basketball, diving, field hockey, golf, horseback riding, ice hockey, lacrosse, racquetball, rifle, rugby, skin diving, soccer, softball, swimming, tennis, track and field, volleyball, water polo, wrestling.

STUDENT SERVICES. Aptitude testing, career counseling, employment service for undergraduates, freshman orientation, health services, on-campus day care, personal counseling, placement service for graduates, special adviser for adult students, veterans counselor, University Center for Learning Assistance, minority student services, Office of Disability Concerns, services/facilities for handicapped.

ANNUAL EXPENSES. Tuition and fees (1992-93): $2,791, $4,322 additional for out-of-state students. **Room and board:** $2,910. **Books and supplies:** $500. **Other expenses:** $1,867.

FINANCIAL AID. 15% of jobs based on need. Academic, music/drama, art, athletic, leadership, alumni affiliation, minority scholarships available. **Aid applications:** No closing date; priority given to applications received by March 1; applicants notified on a rolling basis beginning on or about May 1; must reply within 2 weeks.

ADDRESS/TELEPHONE. Dave Snyder, Director of Enrollment Management, Illinois State University, North and School Streets, Normal, IL 61761-6901. (309) 438-2181. (800) 366-2478. Fax: (309) 438-2768.

Illinois Valley Community College
Oglesby, Illinois CB code: 1397

2-year public community college, coed. Founded in 1966. **Accreditation:** Regional. **Undergraduate enrollment:** 4,244 men and women. **Faculty:** 161 total (87 full time), 8 with doctorates or other terminal degrees. **Location:** Rural campus in small town; 60 miles from Peoria, 95 miles from Chicago. **Calendar:** Semester, extensive summer session. **Microcomputers:** Located in libraries, classrooms, computer centers. **Special facilities:** Federal, state, and nuclear regulatory commission document depositories.

DEGREES OFFERED. AA, AS, AAS. 240 associate degrees awarded in 1992.

UNDERGRADUATE MAJORS. Accounting, agribusiness, agricultural business and management, agricultural mechanics, agricultural products and processing, agricultural sciences, automotive mechanics, automotive technology, biology, business and management, business and office, business data processing and related programs, business data programming, communications, computer technology, drafting, drafting and design technology, early childhood education, education, electronic technology, elementary education, engineering, engineering and engineering-related technologies, English, fire control and safety technology, home economics, industrial technology, journalism, junior high education, law enforcement and corrections technologies, liberal/general studies, marketing and distribution, marketing management, mathematics, mechanical design technology, medical laboratory technologies, music, nursing, physical sciences, prelaw, psychology, quality control technology, radiograph medical technology, secondary education, secretarial and related programs, social sciences, teacher aide, visual and performing arts.

ACADEMIC PROGRAMS. 2-year transfer program, dual enrollment of high school students, internships, study abroad, cross-registration. **Remedial services:** Learning center, preadmission summer program, reduced course load, remedial instruction, tutoring. **Placement/credit:** CLEP General and Subject, institutional tests; 16 credit hours maximum for associate degree.

ACADEMIC REQUIREMENTS. Freshmen must earn minimum GPA of 1.5 to continue in good standing. Nursing students must earn minimum GPA of 2.0. 60% of freshmen return for sophomore year. Students must declare major on enrollment. **Graduation requirements:** 64 hours for associate (32 in major). Most students required to take courses in English, mathematics.

FRESHMAN ADMISSIONS. Selection criteria: Open admissions. Applicants to nursing programs must have 2.5 GPA and background in laboratory science.

1992 FRESHMAN CLASS PROFILE. 1,084 men and women enrolled. **Characteristics:** 100% from in state, 100% commute, 3% have minority backgrounds. Average age is 19.

FALL-TERM APPLICATIONS. No fee. No closing date; applicants notified on a rolling basis. Deferred and early admission available.

STUDENT LIFE. Activities: Student government, student newspaper, choral groups, concert band, drama, jazz band, musical theater.

ATHLETICS. NJCAA. **Intercollegiate:** Baseball M, basketball, football M, softball W, tennis, volleyball W. **Intramural:** Basketball, softball, volleyball.

STUDENT SERVICES. Aptitude testing, career counseling, employment service for undergraduates, freshman orientation, on-campus day care, personal counseling, placement service for graduates, veterans counselor, services/facilities for handicapped.

ANNUAL EXPENSES. Tuition and fees: $1,004, $1,800 additional for out-of-district students, $2,760 additional for out-of-state students. **Books and supplies:** $450. **Other expenses:** $1,044.

FINANCIAL AID. 88% of grants, 95% of loans, 42% of jobs based on need. Academic, music/drama, art, state/district residency scholarships available. **Aid applications:** No closing date; priority given to applications received by May 1; applicants notified on a rolling basis beginning on or about May 1; must reply within 10 days.

ADDRESS/TELEPHONE. Robert P. Marshall EdD, Director of Admissions and Records, Illinois Valley Community College, 2578 East 350th Road, Oglesby, IL 61348-1099. (815) 224-2720. Fax: (815) 224-3033.

Illinois Wesleyan University
Bloomington, Illinois CB code: 1320

Admissions: 45% of applicants accepted
Based on:
••• Essay, school record, test scores
•• Activities, interview, recommendations
• Special talents
Completion: 98% of freshmen end year in good standing
87% graduate, 33% of these enter graduate study

4-year private university, coed, affiliated with United Methodist Church. Founded in 1850. **Accreditation:** Regional. **Undergraduate enrollment:** 838 men, 971 women full time; 6 men, 7 women part time. **Faculty:** 178 total (143 full time), 136 with doctorates or other terminal degrees. **Location:** Urban campus in small city; 125 miles from Chicago. **Calendar:** 4-1-4, limited summer session. **Microcomputers:** 294 located in dormitories, libraries, classrooms, computer centers, campus-wide network. **Special facilities:** Evans Observatory, Wakely Art Gallery, Merwin Art Gallery, Fort Natatorium. **Additional facts:** Students have access to Illinois State University library, facilities, and activities.

DEGREES OFFERED. BA, BS, BFA. 383 bachelor's degrees awarded in 1992. 26% in business and management, 6% teacher education, 8% health sciences, 10% life sciences, 6% physical sciences, 6% psychology, 12% social sciences, 13% visual and performing arts.

UNDERGRADUATE MAJORS. Accounting, art history, arts management, biological and physical sciences, biology, business administration and management, business and management, business economics, ceramics, chemistry, clinical laboratory science, computer and information sciences, dramatic arts, drawing, economics, elementary education, English, English education, foreign languages education, French, German, graphic design, history, humanities and social sciences, insurance and risk management, international studies, junior high education, mathematics, mathematics and computer science, mathematics education, medical laboratory technologies, music, music business management, music education, music history and appreciation, music performance, music theory and composition, musical theater, nursing, painting, philosophy, physics, political science and government, predentistry, preengineering, premedicine, prepharmacy, preveterinary, printmaking, psychology, religion, religious music, science education, sculpture, secondary education, social science education, social work, sociology, Spanish, studio art, theater design.

ACADEMIC PROGRAMS. Accelerated program, double major, honors program, independent study, internships, student-designed major, study abroad, visiting/exchange student program, New York semester, United Nations semester, Washington semester, cross-registration; liberal arts/career combination in engineering, forestry, health sciences. **Remedial services:** Tutoring. **ROTC:** Army. **Placement/credit:** AP, CLEP General and Subject, institutional tests.

ACADEMIC REQUIREMENTS. Freshmen must earn minimum GPA of 2.0 to continue in good standing. 95% of freshmen return for sophomore year. Students must declare major by end of second year. **Graduation requirements:** 120 hours for bachelor's (35 in major). Most students required to take courses in arts/fine arts, English, foreign languages, history, humanities, mathematics, philosophy/religion, biological/physical sciences, social sciences. **Postgraduate studies:** 4% enter law school, 5% enter medical school, 6% enter MBA programs, 18% enter other graduate study. **Additional information:** Cross-registration with Illinois State University.

FRESHMAN ADMISSIONS. Selection criteria: Test scores, class rank, 3.0 GPA, school achievement record, and essay or personal statement most important. **High school preparation:** 15 units required. Required units include English 4, foreign language 2, mathematics 2, social science 1 and science 2. Biology and chemistry required for admission to nursing and biology. **Test requirements:** SAT or ACT; score report by March 1.

1992 FRESHMAN CLASS PROFILE. 3,344 men and women applied, 1,519 accepted; 270 men enrolled, 283 women enrolled. 90% had high school GPA of 3.0 or higher, 10% between 2.0 and 2.99. 75% were in top tenth and 95% were in top quarter of graduating class. **Academic background:** Mid 50% of enrolled freshmen had SAT-V between 530-630, SAT-M between 590-680; ACT composite between 24-30. 42% submitted SAT scores, 89% submitted ACT scores. **Characteristics:** 83% from in state, 95% live in college housing, 9% have minority backgrounds, 4% are foreign students, 25% join fraternities/sororities. Average age is 18.

FALL-TERM APPLICATIONS. No fee. No closing date; priority given to applications received by March 1; applicants notified on a rolling basis; must reply by May 1 or within 3 weeks if notified thereafter. Audition required for music, music theater, drama performance applicants. Portfolio required for art applicants. Essay required. Interview recommended. Interview recommended for all applicants, required for drama (nonperformance) applicants. CRDA. Deferred and early admission available.

STUDENT LIFE. Housing: Dormitories (men, women, coed); fraternity, sorority housing available. International house available. **Activities:** Student government, magazine, radio, student newspaper, yearbook, choral groups, concert band, dance, drama, jazz band, music ensembles, musical theater, opera, pep band, symphony orchestra, fraternities, sororities, Black Student Union, Inter-Varsity Christian Fellowship, Brothers and Sisters in

Christ, Fellowship of Christian Athletes, other religious organizations, Bread for the World, Amnesty International, Hillel Club, Model United Nations, Circle-K.

ATHLETICS. NCAA. **Intercollegiate:** Baseball M, basketball, cross-country, diving, football M, golf M, soccer M, softball W, swimming, tennis, track and field, volleyball W. **Intramural:** Badminton, basketball, bowling M, golf M, sailing, softball, swimming M, table tennis M, tennis, volleyball.

STUDENT SERVICES. Career counseling, employment service for undergraduates, freshman orientation, health services, personal counseling, placement service for graduates, study skills, writing skills, and time management seminars, services/facilities for handicapped.

ANNUAL EXPENSES. Tuition and fees: $13,295. Per course unit charge is $1343 during year, $761 during summer session. **Room and board:** $3,985. **Books and supplies:** $400. **Other expenses:** $550.

FINANCIAL AID. 85% of freshmen, 85% of continuing students receive some form of aid. 88% of grants, 92% of loans, 86% of jobs based on need. 358 enrolled freshmen were judged to have need, all were offered aid. Academic, music/drama, art, minority scholarships available. **Aid applications:** No closing date; priority given to applications received by March 1; applicants notified on a rolling basis beginning on or about July 1; must reply within 4 to 6 weeks or by September 1.

ADDRESS/TELEPHONE. James Ruoti, Dean of Admissions, Illinois Wesleyan University, 1312 North Park, Bloomington, IL 61702-9965. (309) 556-3031. (800) 332-2498. Fax: (309) 556-3411.

International Academy of Merchandising and Design
Chicago, Illinois CB code: 3363

4-year proprietary Fashion design, merchandizing management, interior design, and advertising design, coed. Founded in 1977. **Undergraduate enrollment:** 37 men, 264 women full time; 40 men, 247 women part time. **Faculty:** 68 total (3 full time), 8 with doctorates or other terminal degrees. **Location:** Urban campus in very large city; in north loop area of Chicago. **Calendar:** Quarter, limited summer session. **Microcomputers:** 11 located in classrooms. **Additional facts:** Located in Chicago's Mart Center (Apparel Center and Merchandise Mart with over 8,000 showrooms). Access to Art Institute of Chicago libraries.

DEGREES OFFERED. AAS, BA, BFA. 18 associate degrees awarded in 1992. 20% in architecture and environmental design, 60% business/office and marketing/distribution, 20% home economics. 34 bachelor's degrees awarded. 20% in architecture and environmental design, 50% business/office and marketing/distribution, 30% home economics.

UNDERGRADUATE MAJORS. Associate: Advertising, fashion design, fashion merchandising, interior design. **Bachelor's:** Advertising, fashion design, fashion merchandising, interior design.

ACADEMIC PROGRAMS. Dual enrollment of high school students, internships, study abroad, weekend college. **Remedial services:** Reduced course load, remedial instruction. **Placement/credit:** CLEP Subject; 24 credit hours maximum for associate degree; 45 credit hours maximum for bachelor's degree.

ACADEMIC REQUIREMENTS. Freshmen must earn minimum GPA of 1.5 to continue in good standing. 65% of freshmen return for sophomore year. Students must declare major on application. **Graduation requirements:** 90 hours for associate, 180 hours for bachelor's. Most students required to take courses in arts/fine arts, computer science, English, history, humanities, mathematics, philosophy/religion, biological/physical sciences, social sciences. **Postgraduate studies:** 10% from 2-year programs enter 4-year programs.

FRESHMAN ADMISSIONS. Selection criteria: School achievement record most important. **Additional information:** Conditional acceptance for applicants with grade-point average less than 2.5. Must earn minimum 2.0 in first term to continue.

1992 FRESHMAN CLASS PROFILE. 32 men, 138 women enrolled. 53% had high school GPA of 3.0 or higher, 30% between 2.0 and 2.99. **Characteristics:** 90% from in state, 100% commute, 51% have minority backgrounds, 1% are foreign students. Average age is 25.

FALL-TERM APPLICATIONS. $50 fee, may be waived for applicants with need. No closing date; applicants notified on a rolling basis; must reply within 10 days. Interview required for local applicants. Deferred and early admission available.

STUDENT LIFE. Housing: Dormitory housing available at nearby Mundelein College and Roosevelt University. **Activities:** Student government, student newspaper, Interior Design Club, Fashion Club, student chapter of American Society of Interior Designers.

STUDENT SERVICES. Career counseling, employment service for undergraduates, freshman orientation, personal counseling, placement service for graduates, veterans counselor, services/facilities for handicapped.

ANNUAL EXPENSES. Tuition and fees (1992-93): $7,040. Tuition higher for certain programs. **Books and supplies:** $500. **Other expenses:** $1,500.

FINANCIAL AID. 35% of freshmen, 20% of continuing students receive some form of aid. All grants, 75% of loans based on need. All jobs based on criteria other than need. 91 enrolled freshmen were judged to have need, all were offered aid. Academic scholarships available. **Aid applications:** No closing date; applicants notified on a rolling basis; must reply no later than 8 weeks before beginning of quarter.

ADDRESS/TELEPHONE. Suzanne Karsten, Director of Admissions, International Academy of Merchandising and Design, 350 North Orleans, Chicago, IL 60654-1596. (312) 828-0202. (800) ACADEMY. Fax: (312) 828-9405.

ITT Technical Institute: Hoffman Estates
Hoffman Estates, Illinois CB code: 4271

Admissions:	50% of applicants accepted
Based on:	••• Interview
	•• School record, test scores
	• Activities, essay, recommendations
Completion:	85% of freshmen end year in good standing
	60% graduate, 15% of these enter 4-year programs

2-year proprietary technical college, coed. Founded in 1986. **Undergraduate enrollment:** 381 men, 20 women full time. **Faculty:** 17 total. **Location:** Suburban campus in small city; 20 miles from Chicago. **Calendar:** Quarter. **Microcomputers:** 20 located in classrooms, computer centers.

DEGREES OFFERED. AAS. 160 associate degrees awarded in 1992. 100% in engineering technologies.

UNDERGRADUATE MAJORS. Computer servicing technology, electronic technology.

ACADEMIC PROGRAMS. Cooperative education. **Remedial services:** Learning center, remedial instruction, tutoring. **Placement/credit:** Institutional tests; 40 credit hours maximum for associate degree.

ACADEMIC REQUIREMENTS. Freshmen must earn minimum GPA of 2.0 to continue in good standing. 70% of freshmen return for sophomore year. Students must declare major on application. **Graduation requirements:** 118 hours for associate. Most students required to take courses in computer science, English, mathematics, social sciences. **Additional information:** Continuous academic counseling available to students experiencing difficulties.

FRESHMAN ADMISSIONS. High school preparation: 16 units recommended. Recommended units include English 4, mathematics 2 and physical science 1. Technical courses recommended: electronics, electricity, computer science, circuits design or analysis, robotics. Algebra recommended for computer-aided drafting. **Test requirements:** Career Performance Assessment Tests (reading and mathematics) required for admission.

1992 FRESHMAN CLASS PROFILE. 286 men applied, 143 accepted, 129 enrolled; 28 women applied, 14 accepted, 2 enrolled. 10% had high school GPA of 3.0 or higher, 20% between 2.0 and 2.99. **Characteristics:** 99% from in state, 100% commute, 34% have minority backgrounds. Average age is 19.

FALL-TERM APPLICATIONS. $100 fee. Application fee refunded if student not accepted. No closing date; priority given to applications received by August 1; applicants notified on a rolling basis. Interview required. Essay recommended.

STUDENT LIFE. Activities: Student government, electronics club, computer club.

STUDENT SERVICES. Career counseling, employment service for undergraduates, freshman orientation, personal counseling, placement service for graduates, services/facilities for handicapped.

ANNUAL EXPENSES. Tuition and fees (1992-93): $7,402. Tuition and fees for 12-month period. Computer-aided drafting program $8544for 12 months. Laboratory fees, $50 per quarter. **Books and supplies:** $1,100.

FINANCIAL AID. 95% of freshmen, 95% of continuing students receive some form of aid. Grants, loans available. **Aid applications:** No closing date; applicants notified on a rolling basis; must reply immediately.

ADDRESS/TELEPHONE. Gregory L. Murakami, Director of Education, ITT Technical Institute: Hoffman Estates, 375 West Higgins Road, Hoffman Estates, IL 60195. (708) 519-9300 ext. 26. Fax: (708) 519-0153.

John A. Logan College
Carterville, Illinois CB code: 1357

2-year public community college, coed. Founded in 1967. **Accreditation:** Regional. **Undergraduate enrollment:** 2,858 men and women full time; 3,675 men and women part time. **Faculty:** 213 total (83 full time), 11 with doctorates or other terminal degrees. **Location:** Rural campus in small town; 10 miles from Carbondale. **Calendar:** Semester, limited summer session. Saturday classes. **Microcomputers:** 160 located in libraries, classrooms, computer centers. **Special facilities:** Museum/art gallery.

DEGREES OFFERED. AA, AS, AAS. 550 associate degrees awarded in 1992. 17% in business and management, 5% business/office and marketing/distribution, 11% education, 7% engineering technologies, 5% allied health, 38% multi/interdisciplinary studies, 9% social sciences, 5% trade and industry.

UNDERGRADUATE MAJORS. Accounting, automotive technology, biology, business and management, business and office, business data processing and related programs, chemistry, computer and information sciences, dental assistant, dental hygiene, dental laboratory technology, drafting, dramatic arts, drawing, electrical/electronics/communications engineering, electronic technology, elementary education, engineering, engineering and engineering-related technologies, fashion merchandising, finance, graphic arts technology, history, industrial technology, journalism, law enforcement and corrections technologies, liberal/general studies, marketing and distribution, mathematics, nursing, painting, philosophy, physical sciences, physics, political science and government, practical nursing, precision metal work, psychology, sculpture, secretarial and related programs, sociology, special education, studio art, teacher aide, tourism.

ACADEMIC PROGRAMS. 2-year transfer program, cooperative education, dual enrollment of high school students, independent study, internships, study abroad, telecourses, weekend college. **Remedial services:** Learning center, remedial instruction, special counselor, tutoring. **ROTC:** Air Force, Army. **Placement/credit:** AP, CLEP General and Subject, institutional tests; 30 credit hours maximum for associate degree.

ACADEMIC REQUIREMENTS. Freshmen must earn minimum GPA of 2.0 to continue in good standing. 64% of freshmen return for sophomore year. Students must declare major on enrollment. **Graduation requirements:** 62 hours for associate. Most students required to take courses in English, mathematics, biological/physical sciences, social sciences.

FRESHMAN ADMISSIONS. Selection criteria: Open admissions. Students entering transfer programs must have 15 high school course units: 4 english, 3 math, 3 laboratory science, 3 social science, 2 electives. **Test requirements:** ACT required of transfer program applicants only. Score report must be received by August 20. Asset.

1992 FRESHMAN CLASS PROFILE. 1,430 men and women enrolled. **Characteristics:** 99% from in state, 100% commute, 7% have minority backgrounds. Average age is 24.

FALL-TERM APPLICATIONS. No fee. No closing date; applicants notified on a rolling basis; must reply by registration. Deferred admission available.

STUDENT LIFE. Activities: Student government, student newspaper, choral groups, drama, music ensembles, musical theater.

ATHLETICS. NJCAA. **Intercollegiate:** Baseball M, basketball, golf M, softball W, tennis, volleyball W.

STUDENT SERVICES. Aptitude testing, career counseling, employment service for undergraduates, on-campus day care, personal counseling, placement service for graduates, special adviser for adult students, veterans counselor, services/facilities for handicapped.

ANNUAL EXPENSES. Tuition and fees (1992-93): $748, $2,192 additional for out-of-district students, $4,896 additional for out-of-state students. **Books and supplies:** $450. **Other expenses:** $550.

FINANCIAL AID. 65% of freshmen, 60% of continuing students receive some form of aid. 89% of grants, 92% of loans, 27% of jobs based on need. Academic, music/drama, art, athletic, minority scholarships available. **Aid applications:** No closing date; priority given to applications received by May 1; applicants notified on a rolling basis beginning on or about August 1.

ADDRESS/TELEPHONE. Dr. Larry A. Chapman, Dean of Student Services, John A. Logan College, Carterville, IL 62918. (618) 985-3741.

John Wood Community College
Quincy, Illinois CB code: 1374

2-year public community college, coed. Founded in 1974. **Accreditation:** Regional. **Undergraduate enrollment:** 3,545 men and women. **Location:** Suburban campus in large town; 140 miles north of St. Louis, Missouri. **Calendar:** Semester. **Additional facts:** College contracts with 2 vocational schools.

FRESHMAN ADMISSIONS. Selection criteria: Open admissions.

ANNUAL EXPENSES. Tuition and fees (projected): $1,380, $1,635 additional for out-of-district students, $3,692 additional for out-of-state students. **Books and supplies:** $450. **Other expenses:** $600.

ADDRESS/TELEPHONE. Mark McNett, Admissions Counselor, John Wood Community College, 150 South 48th Street, Quincy, IL 62301. (217) 224-6500. Fax: (217) 224-4208.

Joliet Junior College
Joliet, Illinois CB code: 1346

2-year public community college, coed. Founded in 1901. **Accreditation:** Regional. **Undergraduate enrollment:** 1,600 men, 1,519 women full time; 2,748 men, 4,560 women part time. **Faculty:** 585 total (155 full time), 38 with doctorates or other terminal degrees. **Location:** Suburban campus in small city; 35 miles from Chicago. **Calendar:** Semester, limited summer session. **Microcomputers:** 120 located on campus. **Special facilities:** Art gallery, planetarium, nature trail, arboretum, working farm, fitness center.

DEGREES OFFERED. AA, AS, AAS. 783 associate degrees awarded in 1992. 5% in agriculture, 12% business and management, 12% health sciences, 52% multi/interdisciplinary studies, 13% trade and industry.

UNDERGRADUATE MAJORS. Accounting, agribusiness, agricultural business and management, agricultural production, agricultural sciences, American literature, automotive mechanics, automotive technology, biological and physical sciences, biology, botany, business administration and management, business and management, business and office, business data processing and related programs, business data programming, business education, chemistry, computer and information sciences, computer programming, construction, criminal justice studies, drafting and design technology, dramatic arts, economics, education, electromechanical technology, electronic technology, elementary education, engineering, engineering and engineering-related technologies, engineering and other disciplines, English, fashion merchandising, finance, fine arts, fire control and safety technology, food production/management/services, food science and nutrition, forestry and related sciences, French, geography, geology, German, history, horticultural science, horticulture, hotel/motel and restaurant management, humanities and social sciences, industrial technology, institutional/home management/supporting programs, interior design, journalism, law enforcement and corrections technologies, liberal/general studies, library assistant, marketing and distribution, mathematics, mechanical design technology, microbiology, microcomputer software, music, nuclear technologies, nursing, ornamental horticulture, physics, political science and government, precision metal work, predentistry, prelaw, premedicine, prepharmacy, preveterinary, protective services, psychology, real estate, science technologies, secondary education, secretarial and related programs, sociology, Spanish, special education, teacher aide, visual and performing arts, water and wastewater technology, word processing, zoology.

ACADEMIC PROGRAMS. 2-year transfer program, cooperative education, honors program, independent study, internships, study abroad. **Remedial services:** Learning center, preadmission summer program, reduced course load, remedial instruction, special counselor, tutoring. **Placement/credit:** AP, CLEP General; 45 credit hours maximum for associate degree.

ACADEMIC REQUIREMENTS. Freshmen must earn minimum GPA of 1.75 to continue in good standing. 67% of freshmen return for sophomore year. **Graduation requirements:** 64 hours for associate (24 in major). Most students required to take courses in English, humanities, mathematics, biological/physical sciences, social sciences.

FRESHMAN ADMISSIONS. Selection criteria: Open admissions. Preference given to cooperative programs and in-district applicants. Selective admissions to some programs: nursing requires ACT score of 20 if in top third of high school class, 21 if in top half. **Test requirements:** ACT required for nursing applicants.

1992 FRESHMAN CLASS PROFILE. 1,259 men, 1,340 women enrolled. **Academic background:** Mid 50% of enrolled freshmen had ACT composite between 13-20. 27% submitted ACT scores. **Characteristics:** 99% from in state, 100% commute, 16% have minority backgrounds. Average age is 25.

FALL-TERM APPLICATIONS. No fee. No closing date; applicants notified on a rolling basis beginning on or about January 1; must reply by registration. Interview recommended. Deferred and early admission available.

STUDENT LIFE. Activities: Student government, student newspaper, television, choral groups, concert band, drama, jazz band, musical theater, skiing clubs.

ATHLETICS. NJCAA. **Intercollegiate:** Baseball M, basketball, football M, softball W, tennis, volleyball W.

STUDENT SERVICES. Aptitude testing, career counseling, employment service for undergraduates, freshman orientation, health services, on-campus day care, personal counseling, placement service for graduates, tutoring and counseling for special-need students, services/facilities for handicapped.

ANNUAL EXPENSES. Tuition and fees: $1,080, $2,780 additional for out-of-district students, $3,400 additional for out-of-state students. **Books and supplies:** $400. **Other expenses:** $1,274.

FINANCIAL AID. 25% of freshmen, 25% of continuing students receive some form of aid. 81% of grants, 47% of loans, 10% of jobs based on need. 1,200 enrolled freshmen were judged to have need, 1,000 were offered aid. Academic, music/drama, art, state/district residency, leadership, alumni affiliation, minority scholarships available. **Aid applications:** No closing date; priority given to applications received by July 1; applicants notified on a rolling basis beginning on or about May 1.

ADDRESS/TELEPHONE. Russell Corey, Director of Enrollment Management, Joliet Junior College, 1216 Houbolt Avenue, Joliet, IL 60436-9985. (815) 729-9020 ext. 2311. Fax: (815) 744-5507.

Judson College
Elgin, Illinois CB code: 1351

Admissions: 67% of applicants accepted
Based on: •• Essay, interview, school record, test scores
• Activities, recommendations, religious affiliation/commitment, special talents
Completion: 85% of freshmen end year in good standing
42% graduate, 32% of these enter graduate study

4-year private liberal arts college, coed, affiliated with American Baptist Churches in the USA. Founded in 1963. **Accreditation:** Regional. **Undergraduate enrollment:** 273 men, 332 women full time. **Faculty:** 105 total (29 full time), 15 with doctorates or other terminal degrees. **Location:** Suburban campus in small city; 40 miles from Chicago. **Calendar:** 4-1-4-1. Extensive evening/early morning classes. **Microcomputers:** 50 located in libraries, computer centers. **Special facilities:** Computer-aided graphics lab, cadaver room, gene splicing lab.

DEGREES OFFERED. BA. 132 bachelor's degrees awarded in 1992. 16% in business and management, 5% communications, 5% computer sciences, 29% teacher education, 11% philosophy, religion, theology, 14% psychology, 9% visual and performing arts.

UNDERGRADUATE MAJORS. Prenursing. accounting, anthropology, Bible studies, biological and physical sciences, biology, business administration and management, chemistry, communications, computer and information sciences, computer programming, dramatic arts, education, elementary education, English, English education, English literature, fine arts, graphic arts technology, history, humanities and social sciences, information sciences and systems, journalism, mathematics, mathematics education, music performance, music theory and composition, parks and recreation management, philosophy, physical education, physical sciences, predentistry, preengineering, prelaw, premedicine, psychology, religion, religious music, science education, secondary education, social sciences, sociology, visual and performing arts.

ACADEMIC PROGRAMS. Accelerated program, cooperative education, double major, honors program, independent study, internships, study abroad, visiting/exchange student program, Washington semester, cooperative program in radio and television with Elgin Community College; liberal arts/career combination in health sciences. **Remedial services:** Reduced course load, remedial instruction, special counselor, tutoring. **Placement/credit:** AP, CLEP General and Subject, institutional tests; 30 credit hours maximum for bachelor's degree.

ACADEMIC REQUIREMENTS. Freshmen must earn minimum GPA of 2.0 to continue in good standing. 67% of freshmen return for sophomore year. Students must declare major by end of second year. **Graduation requirements:** 122 hours for bachelor's (55 in major). Most students required to take courses in arts/fine arts, English, history, humanities, mathematics, philosophy/religion, biological/physical sciences, social sciences.

FRESHMAN ADMISSIONS. Selection criteria: School achievement record, test scores, and essay important. Counselor's reference also considered. **High school preparation:** 8 units required; 15 recommended. Required units include English 4, mathematics 2, physical science 1 and social science 1. **Test requirements:** SAT or ACT; score report by August 15.

1992 FRESHMAN CLASS PROFILE. 156 men applied, 110 accepted, 62 enrolled; 200 women applied, 127 accepted, 71 enrolled. 49% had high school GPA of 3.0 or higher, 49% between 2.0 and 2.99. 10% were in top tenth and 38% were in top quarter of graduating class. **Academic background:** Mid 50% of enrolled freshmen had ACT composite between 18-24. 88% submitted ACT scores. **Characteristics:** 56% from in state, 88% live in college housing, 2% are foreign students. Average age is 18.

FALL-TERM APPLICATIONS. $30 fee, may be waived for applicants with need. Closing date August 15; applicants notified on a rolling basis; must reply by September 1. Essay required. Interview recommended. Audition recommended for performing arts applicants. Portfolio recommended for art applicants. Deferred and early admission available.

STUDENT LIFE. Housing: Dormitories (men, women); apartment housing available. **Activities:** Student government, magazine, radio, yearbook, choral groups, concert band, drama, music ensembles, musical theater, opera, pep band. **Additional information:** Chapel services held three mornings a week.

ATHLETICS. NAIA. **Intercollegiate:** Baseball M, basketball, cross-country, soccer, softball W, tennis, volleyball W. **Intramural:** Badminton, basketball, football M, racquetball, soccer, softball, table tennis M, tennis, volleyball.

STUDENT SERVICES. Aptitude testing, career counseling, employment service for undergraduates, freshman orientation, health services, personal counseling, placement service for graduates, special adviser for adult students, services/facilities for handicapped.

ANNUAL EXPENSES. Tuition and fees: $9,284. **Room and board:** $4,422. **Books and supplies:** $450. **Other expenses:** $1,000.

FINANCIAL AID. 94% of freshmen, 94% of continuing students receive some form of aid. 72% of grants, 83% of loans, 60% of jobs based on need. 102 enrolled freshmen were judged to have need, all were offered aid. Academic, music/drama, art, athletic, state/district residency scholarships available. **Aid applications:** No closing date; priority given to applications received by May 1; applicants notified on a rolling basis beginning on or about March 1; must reply within 2 weeks.

ADDRESS/TELEPHONE. Matthew S. Osborne, Director of Admissions, Judson College, 1151 North State Street, Elgin, IL 60123. (708) 695-2500 ext. 2310. (800) 879-5376. Fax: (708) 695-0216.

Kankakee Community College
Kankakee, Illinois CB code: 1380

2-year public community college, coed. Founded in 1966. **Accreditation:** Regional. **Undergraduate enrollment:** 464 men, 633 women full time; 1,054 men, 1,731 women part time. **Faculty:** 158 total (56 full time), 3 with doctorates or other terminal degrees. **Location:** Rural campus in large town; 60 miles from Chicago. **Calendar:** Semester, extensive summer session. **Microcomputers:** Located in libraries, classrooms, computer centers.

DEGREES OFFERED. AA, AS, AAS. 306 associate degrees awarded in 1992.

UNDERGRADUATE MAJORS. Accounting, agribusiness, agricultural mechanics, agricultural production, agricultural sciences, air conditioning/heating/refrigeration mechanics, air conditioning/heating/refrigeration technology, automotive mechanics, automotive technology, business and management, business and office, child development/care/guidance, computer programming, computer-aided drafting, diesel engine mechanics, electrical technology, electronic technology, emergency medical technologies, engineering, humanities and social sciences, industrial equipment maintenance and repair, industrial technology, information sciences and systems, law enforcement and corrections technologies, legal secretary, liberal/general studies, machine tool operation/machine shop, management science, marketing and distribution, marketing management, mathematics and science, medical laboratory technologies, medical secretary, nursing, predentistry, premedicine, prepharmacy, preveterinary, radiograph medical technology, real estate, secretarial and related programs, visual and performing arts, welding technology.

ACADEMIC PROGRAMS. 2-year transfer program, dual enrollment of high school students, internships, study abroad, cross-registration. **Remedial services:** Learning center, preadmission summer program, reduced course load, remedial instruction, special counselor, tutoring. **Placement/credit:** AP, CLEP General and Subject, institutional tests; 16 credit hours maximum for associate degree.

ACADEMIC REQUIREMENTS. Freshmen must earn minimum GPA of 2.0 to continue in good standing. Students must declare major on application. **Graduation requirements:** 64 hours for associate. Most students required to take courses in English, history, humanities, mathematics, biological/physical sciences, social sciences.

FRESHMAN ADMISSIONS. Selection criteria: Open admissions. Selective admissions to allied health programs and transfer programs to 4-year institutions. ASSET assessment testing required of all students.

1992 FRESHMAN CLASS PROFILE. 1,300 men and women enrolled. **Characteristics:** 99% from in state, 100% commute, 10% have minority backgrounds. Average age is 29.

FALL-TERM APPLICATIONS. No fee. No closing date; applicants notified on a rolling basis. Deferred and early admission available.

STUDENT LIFE. Activities: Student government.

ATHLETICS. NJCAA. **Intercollegiate:** Baseball M, basketball, softball W, volleyball W. **Intramural:** Basketball, golf, tennis.

STUDENT SERVICES. Aptitude testing, career counseling, employment service for undergraduates, freshman orientation, on-campus day care, placement service for graduates, special adviser for adult students, services/facilities for handicapped.

ANNUAL EXPENSES. Tuition and fees: $1,216, $720 additional for out-of-district students, $4,320 additional for out-of-state students. **Books and supplies:** $480. **Other expenses:** $855.

FINANCIAL AID. 55% of freshmen, 55% of continuing students receive some form of aid. 80% of grants, 77% of loans, 24% of jobs based on need. Academic, music/drama, art, athletic, state/district residency, alumni affiliation, minority scholarships available. **Aid applications:** No closing date; priority given to applications received by June 1; applicants notified on a rolling basis; must reply within 1 week.

ADDRESS/TELEPHONE. Thomas D. Dolliger, Assistant Dean of Student Services, Kankakee Community College, PO Box 888, River Road, Kankakee, IL 60901. (815) 933-0200. Fax: (815) 933-0217.

Kaskaskia College
Centralia, Illinois CB code: 1108

2-year public community college, coed. Founded in 1940. **Accreditation:** Regional. **Undergraduate enrollment:** 1,299 men, 2,199 women full time; 361 men, 790 women part time. **Faculty:** 228 total (64 full time), 15 with doctorates or other terminal degrees. **Location:** Rural campus in large town; 60 miles from St. Louis, Missouri. **Calendar:** Semester, extensive summer session. Saturday and extensive evening/early morning classes. **Microcomputers:** 45 located in libraries, computer centers.

DEGREES OFFERED. AA, AS, AAS. 463 associate degrees awarded in 1992.

UNDERGRADUATE MAJORS. Accounting, agribusiness, automotive technology, business and management, business and office, business data entry equipment operation, business data processing and related programs, business data programming, child development/care/guidance, computer programming, drafting, education, electronic technology, engineering, finance, industrial technology, law enforcement and corrections technologies, liberal/general studies, marketing and distribution, marketing management, nursing, personal services, radiograph medical technology, secretarial and related programs, social sciences, teacher aide, trade and industrial supervision and management, visual and performing arts, word processing.

ACADEMIC PROGRAMS. 2-year transfer program, cooperative education, double major, dual enrollment of high school students, independent study, internships, student-designed major, study abroad, cross-registration, cooperative agreements with Rend Lake College, Belleville Area College, Illinois Eastern Community College. **Remedial services:** Learning center, preadmission summer program, remedial instruction, special counselor, tutoring. **Placement/credit:** AP, CLEP General and Subject, institutional tests; 30 credit hours maximum for associate degree.

ACADEMIC REQUIREMENTS. Freshmen must earn minimum GPA of 1.76 to continue in good standing. 80% of freshmen return for sophomore year. Students must declare major on application. **Graduation requirements:** 64 hours for associate. Most students required to take courses in English, history, humanities, mathematics, biological/physical sciences, social sciences.

FRESHMAN ADMISSIONS. Selection criteria: Open admissions. Selective admissions to associate of arts and associate of science degree programs. 4 units English, 2 foreign language, 3 mathematics, 3 social sciences, 3 laboratory sciences required for students pursuing associate degrees in arts or sciences. **Test requirements:** SAT or ACT recommended for all students, required for admission to associate of arts or science degree programs. Nelson-Denny Reading Test required for practical nursing.

1992 FRESHMAN CLASS PROFILE. 1,898 men and women enrolled. **Characteristics:** 100% commute. Average age is 18.

FALL-TERM APPLICATIONS. No fee. No closing date; applicants notified on a rolling basis. Interview recommended for allied health applicants. Early admission available.

STUDENT LIFE. Activities: Student government, student newspaper, choral groups, concert band, jazz band, music ensembles, symphony orchestra.

ATHLETICS. NJCAA. **Intercollegiate:** Baseball M, basketball, soccer W, softball W, volleyball W. **Intramural:** Basketball.

STUDENT SERVICES. Aptitude testing, career counseling, employment service for undergraduates, freshman orientation, on-campus day care, personal counseling, placement service for graduates, veterans counselor, services/facilities for handicapped.

ANNUAL EXPENSES. Tuition and fees (1992-93): $1,013, $1,050 additional for out-of-district students, $3,270 additional for out-of-state students. **Books and supplies:** $500. **Other expenses:** $648.

FINANCIAL AID. 19% of freshmen, 27% of continuing students receive some form of aid. 88% of grants, 97% of loans, 24% of jobs based on need. 313 enrolled freshmen were judged to have need, 299 were offered aid. Academic, music/drama, athletic scholarships available. **Aid applications:** No closing date; priority given to applications received by July 1; applicants notified on a rolling basis beginning on or about July 1; must reply within 2 weeks.

ADDRESS/TELEPHONE. Constance J. Stoneman, Director of Admissions and Public Relations, Kaskaskia College, 27210 College Road, Centralia, IL 62801. (618) 532-1981. Fax: (618) 532-1981 ext. 263. (800) 642-0859 (Illinois only).

Kendall College
Evanston, Illinois — CB code: 1366

4-year private liberal arts college, coed, affiliated with United Methodist Church. Founded in 1934. **Accreditation:** Regional. **Undergraduate enrollment:** 403 men and women. **Faculty:** 29 total (20 full time), 15 with doctorates or other terminal degrees. **Location:** Suburban campus in small city; 15 miles from downtown Chicago. **Calendar:** Quarter, limited summer session. **Microcomputers:** Located in computer centers. **Special facilities:** Mitchell Indian Museum, public dining room operated by students in culinary arts program. **Additional facts:** Associate degree program in culinary arts offered.

DEGREES OFFERED. AA, AAS, BA. 180 associate degrees awarded in 1992. 35% in business and management, 5% teacher education, 35% home economics, 25% multi/interdisciplinary studies. 55 bachelor's degrees awarded. 70% in business and management, 20% teacher education, 10% social sciences.

UNDERGRADUATE MAJORS. Associate: Allied health, business administration and management, business and office, early childhood education, fine arts, food production/management/services, hotel/motel and restaurant management, liberal/general studies, social work. **Bachelor's:** American studies, business administration and management, early childhood education, food management, hotel/motel and restaurant management, human services, liberal/general studies, social sciences, social work.

ACADEMIC PROGRAMS. Independent study, internships, cross-registration, cooperative programs with Evanston Art Center and National-Louis University. **Remedial services:** Learning center, reduced course load, remedial instruction, special counselor, tutoring, Freshman Year Program. **Placement/credit:** AP, institutional tests.

ACADEMIC REQUIREMENTS. Freshmen must earn minimum GPA of 2.0 to continue in good standing. 63% of freshmen return for sophomore year. Students must declare major by end of second year. **Graduation requirements:** 96 hours for associate, 192 hours for bachelor's. Most students required to take courses in English, history, humanities, mathematics, biological/physical sciences, social sciences. **Postgraduate studies:** 80% from 2-year programs enter 4-year programs. **Additional information:** Cooperative programs with Evanston Art Center and National-Louis University.

FRESHMAN ADMISSIONS. Selection criteria: High school record most important, followed by test scores, class rank, recommendations, and interview. Placement test may be required. Recommended units include English 4, mathematics 2, social science 2 and science 2. College-preparatory program recommended. Specific academic units required for certain majors. **Test requirements:** SAT or ACT (ACT preferred); score report by October 1.

1992 FRESHMAN CLASS PROFILE. 158 men and women enrolled. 12% had high school GPA of 3.0 or higher, 69% between 2.0 and 2.99. **Academic background:** Mid 50% of enrolled freshmen had ACT composite between 15-19. 95% submitted ACT scores. **Characteristics:** 70% from in state, 65% commute, 23% have minority backgrounds, 1% are foreign students. Average age is 19.

FALL-TERM APPLICATIONS. $25 fee, may be waived for applicants with need. No closing date; applicants notified on a rolling basis; must reply within 30 days. Essay required. Interview recommended. Deferred admission available.

STUDENT LIFE. Housing: Dormitories (men, women). **Activities:** Student government, student newspaper, yearbook, International Club, NAACP, Helping Professions Club.

ATHLETICS. Intramural: Basketball M, bowling, softball, tennis M, volleyball.

STUDENT SERVICES. Employment service for undergraduates, freshman orientation, personal counseling, placement service for graduates, veterans counselor.

ANNUAL EXPENSES. Tuition and fees (1992-93): $7,500. **Room and board:** $4,600. **Books and supplies:** $400. **Other expenses:** $900.

FINANCIAL AID. 62% of freshmen, 65% of continuing students receive some form of aid. Grants, loans, jobs available. Academic, alumni affiliation scholarships available. **Aid applications:** No closing date; priority given to applications received by June 1; applicants notified on a rolling basis beginning on or about April 1; must reply within 2 weeks. **Additional information:** Tuition guaranteed for culinary arts majors. 10 percent discount applied if tuition for entire program paid in advance.

ADDRESS/TELEPHONE. Ralph Starenko, Director of Enrollment Management, Kendall College, 2408 Orrington Avenue, Evanston, IL 60201. (708) 866-1304. Fax: (708) 866-1320.

Kishwaukee College
Malta, Illinois — CB code: 0599

2-year public community college, coed. Founded in 1967. **Accreditation:** Regional. **Undergraduate enrollment:** 613 men, 665 women full time; 857 men, 1,135 women part time. **Faculty:** 233 total (70 full time), 9 with doctorates or other terminal degrees. **Location:** Rural campus in rural community; 7 miles from De Kalb. **Calendar:** Semester, limited summer session. Saturday and extensive evening/early morning classes. **Microcomputers:** Located in libraries, classrooms, computer centers. **Special facilities:** All-American trial seed garden.

DEGREES OFFERED. AA, AS, AAS. 455 associate degrees awarded in 1992. 7% in agriculture, 21% business and management, 5% business/office and marketing/distribution, 9% teacher education, 10% health sciences, 5% allied health, 10% multi/interdisciplinary studies.

UNDERGRADUATE MAJORS. Accounting, agribusiness, agricultural mechanics, agricultural sciences, architecture, automotive mechanics, automotive technology, biology, business and management, business and office, business data processing and related programs, chemistry, child development/care/guidance, communications, computer and information sciences, crafts, data processing, diesel engine mechanics, drafting, early childhood education, education, electronic technology, elementary education, engineering, engineering and engineering-related technologies, English, fine arts, fire control and safety technology, home economics, horticulture, industrial technology, junior high education, law enforcement and corrections technologies, liberal/general studies, manufacturing technology, marketing and distribution, mathematics, mechanical design technology, music, nursing, ornamental horticulture, philosophy, physical sciences, physics, predentistry, prelaw, premedicine, prepharmacy, preveterinary, psychology, radiograph medical technology, secondary education, secretarial and related programs, social sciences, special education, water and wastewater technology.

ACADEMIC PROGRAMS. 2-year transfer program, accelerated program, double major, dual enrollment of high school students, independent study, internships, study abroad, teacher preparation, telecourses, cross-registration. **Remedial services:** Learning center, preadmission summer program, reduced course load, remedial instruction, special counselor, tutoring. **ROTC:** Army. **Placement/credit:** AP, CLEP General and Subject, institutional tests; 48 credit hours maximum for associate degree.

ACADEMIC REQUIREMENTS. Freshmen must earn minimum GPA of 2.0 to continue in good standing. 60% of freshmen return for sophomore year. **Graduation requirements:** 64 hours for associate. Most students required to take courses in English, humanities, mathematics, biological/physical sciences, social sciences. **Additional information:** Cross-registration with Northern Illinois University and nearby community colleges.

FRESHMAN ADMISSIONS. Selection criteria: Open admissions. Selective admission to nursing and radiologic technology programs. **High school preparation:** 15 units recommended. Recommended units include English 4, foreign language 2, mathematics 3, social science 3 and science 3. High school diploma or equivalency required for nursing and radiologic technology applicants. College-preparatory program strongly recommended for students intending to transfer to 4-year institution.

1992 FRESHMAN CLASS PROFILE. 323 men, 294 women enrolled. **Academic background:** Mid 50% of enrolled freshmen had ACT composite between 15-22. 20% submitted ACT scores. **Characteristics:** 98% from in state, 100% commute, 3% have minority backgrounds, 1% are foreign students. Average age is 24.

FALL-TERM APPLICATIONS. No fee. No closing date; applicants notified on a rolling basis; must reply by registration. Interview required for nursing, radiologic technology applicants. Audition required for music applicants. Portfolio recommended for art applicants. Deferred and early admission available.

STUDENT LIFE. Activities: Student government, magazine, student newspaper, television, forensics, choral groups, drama, music ensembles, musical theater, international student club, Nurses Christian Fellowship, Phi Theta Kappa, African-American self-awareness organization.

ATHLETICS. NJCAA. **Intercollegiate:** Baseball M, basketball, golf, soccer M, softball W, volleyball W. **Intramural:** Badminton, basketball, softball, volleyball.

STUDENT SERVICES. Aptitude testing, career counseling, employment service for undergraduates, freshman orientation, on-campus day care, personal counseling, placement service for graduates, special adviser for adult students, veterans counselor, personal development workshops, services/facilities for handicapped.

ANNUAL EXPENSES. Tuition and fees (1992-93): $1,040, $1,936 additional for out-of-district students, $2,857 additional for out-of-state students. **Books and supplies:** $400. **Other expenses:** $943.

FINANCIAL AID. 40% of continuing students receive some form of aid. 91% of grants, 92% of loans, 62% of jobs based on need. Academic, athletic, leadership scholarships available. **Aid applications:** No closing date; priority given to applications received by June 1; applicants notified on a rolling basis beginning on or about June 15; must reply within 2 weeks.

ADDRESS/TELEPHONE. Jon C. Markin, Director of Admissions, Registration and Records, Kishwaukee College, 21193 Malta Road, Malta, IL 60150-9699. (815) 825-2086 ext. 218. Fax: (815) 825-2072.

Knox College
Galesburg, Illinois — CB code: 1372

Admissions: 84% of applicants accepted
Based on:
- ••• School record
- •• Essay, recommendations
- • Activities, interview, special talents, test scores

Completion: 95% of freshmen end year in good standing
75% graduate, 37% of these enter graduate study

4-year private liberal arts college, coed. Founded in 1837. **Accreditation:** Regional. **Undergraduate enrollment:** 455 men, 475 women full time; 10 men, 14 women part time. **Faculty:** 87 total (84 full time), 75 with doctorates or other terminal degrees. **Location:** Rural campus in large town; 180 miles from Chicago, 200 miles from St.Louis, Missouri. **Calendar:** 3 10-week terms and 1 optional miniterm. **Microcomputers:** 100 located in libraries, classrooms, computer centers. **Special facilities:** Electron microscope, greenhouse, studio and large-scale production theaters, 760-acre biological field station, anthropology, art, and field museums, ceramics, sculpture, painting, and printmaking studios. **Additional facts:** Extensive overseas study centers and more than 30 International and domestic cooperative programs. Repertory theater term, independent research opportunities, and academic honor system.

DEGREES OFFERED. BA. 233 bachelor's degrees awarded in 1992. 6% in languages, 11% letters/literature, 9% life sciences, 8% physical sciences, 7% psychology, 40% social sciences.

UNDERGRADUATE MAJORS. Afro-American (black) studies, American studies, anthropology, art history, biochemistry, biology, chemistry, classics, computer and information sciences, creative writing, dramatic arts, economics, education, elementary education, English, foreign languages (multiple emphasis), French, German, German area studies, history, international relations, junior high education, mathematics, modern languages and classics, music, philosophy, physics, political science and government, psychology, religion, Russian, Russian and Slavic studies, secondary education, sociology, Spanish, studio art, women's studies.

ACADEMIC PROGRAMS. Accelerated program, double major, dual enrollment of high school students, honors program, independent study, internships, student-designed major, study abroad, teacher preparation, visiting/exchange student program, Washington semester; liberal arts/career combination in engineering, forestry, health sciences; combined bachelor's/graduate program in business administration, medicine, law. **Remedial services:** Learning center, reduced course load, remedial instruction, special counselor, tutoring. **Placement/credit:** AP, CLEP Subject, IB, institutional tests. 25% of required credits may be obtained through examination.

ACADEMIC REQUIREMENTS. Freshmen must earn minimum GPA of 2.0 to continue in good standing. 85% of freshmen return for sophomore year. Students must declare major by end of second year. **Graduation requirements:** 120 hours for bachelor's (30 in major). Most students required to take courses in arts/fine arts, English, foreign languages, history, humanities, mathematics, biological/physical sciences, social sciences. **Postgraduate studies:** 5% enter law school, 3% enter medical school, 5% enter MBA programs, 24% enter other graduate study.

FRESHMAN ADMISSIONS. Selection criteria: Course of study, grades, class rank, and recommendations most important. Extracurricular activities, personal statement, special skills, talents and personal qualities, test scores and interview also considered. **High school preparation:** 15 units required; 17 recommended. Required and recommended units include English 4, foreign language 2-3, mathematics 3-4, social science 3 and science 3. Biological science 1 and physical science 2 recommended. Students should have taken honors-level courses if available in their high schools. GED tests may be accepted in place of high school diploma for nontraditional students. **Test requirements:** SAT or ACT; score report by February 15.

1992 FRESHMAN CLASS PROFILE. 492 men applied, 413 accepted, 147 enrolled; 490 women applied, 410 accepted, 145 enrolled. 40% were in top tenth and 70% were in top quarter of graduating class. **Academic background:** Mid 50% of enrolled freshmen had SAT-V between 460-570, SAT-M between 490-630; ACT composite between 22-27. 44% submitted SAT scores, 92% submitted ACT scores. **Characteristics:** 57% from in state, 95% live in college housing, 17% have minority backgrounds, 9% are foreign students, 30% join fraternities/sororities. Average age is 18.

FALL-TERM APPLICATIONS. $20 fee, may be waived for applicants with need. No closing date; priority given to applications received by February 15; applicants notified on or about March 31; must reply by May 1 or within 2 weeks if notified thereafter. Essay required. Interview recommended. CRDA. Deferred and early admission available. Institutional early decision plan. Early action application deadline is December 1 with notification by December 31.

STUDENT LIFE. Housing: Dormitories (men, women, coed); apartment, fraternity, cooperative housing available. International house, black students house available. **Activities:** Student government, magazine, radio, student newspaper, yearbook, choral groups, concert band, dance, drama, jazz band, music ensembles, musical theater, symphony orchestra, fraternities, sororities, Several religious and ethnic organizations, Sexual Equality Awareness Coalition, Political Awareness Coalition, International Club, Amnesty International, Latin American Concerns, United Way on Campus, Allied Blacks for Liberty and Equality, Lo Nuestro (Hispanic student group).

ATHLETICS. NCAA. **Intercollegiate:** Baseball M, basketball, cross-country, diving, football M, golf, soccer, softball W, swimming, tennis, track and field, volleyball W, wrestling M. **Intramural:** Badminton, baseball M, basketball, cross-country, fencing, ice hockey M, lacrosse M, softball, swimming, tennis, track and field, volleyball, water polo.

STUDENT SERVICES. Aptitude testing, career counseling, employment service for undergraduates, freshman orientation, health services, personal counseling, placement service for graduates, services/facilities for handicapped.

ANNUAL EXPENSES. Tuition and fees: $15,132. **Room and board:** $3,858. **Books and supplies:** $350. **Other expenses:** $600.

FINANCIAL AID. 89% of freshmen, 83% of continuing students receive some form of aid. 95% of grants, 95% of loans, all jobs based on need. 212 enrolled freshmen were judged to have need, all were offered aid. Academic, music/drama, art scholarships available. **Aid applications:** No closing date; priority given to applications received by March 1; applicants notified on a rolling basis beginning on or about April 15; must reply by May 1 or within 15 days if notified thereafter. **Additional information:** College offers long-term, low-interest, variable-rate loan program to parents of students.

ADDRESS/TELEPHONE. Paul Steenis, Director of Admissions, Knox College, Box 148, Galesburg, IL 61401-4999. (309) 343-0112 ext. 123. (800) 678-5669. Fax: (309) 343-8921.

Lake Forest College

Lake Forest, Illinois — CB code: 1392

Admissions: 72% of applicants accepted
Based on:
••• Activities, essay, school record
•• Interview, recommendations, special talents
• Test scores
Completion: 95% of freshmen end year in good standing
73% graduate, 39% of these enter graduate study

4-year private liberal arts college, coed, affiliated with Presbyterian Church (USA). Founded in 1857. **Accreditation:** Regional. **Undergraduate enrollment:** 453 men, 482 women full time; 8 men, 16 women part time. **Graduate enrollment:** 17 men and women. **Faculty:** 116 total (92 full time), 83 with doctorates or other terminal degrees. **Location:** Suburban campus in large town; 30 miles from Chicago. **Calendar:** Semester, limited summer session. **Microcomputers:** 246 located in dormitories, libraries, classrooms, computer centers, campus-wide network. **Special facilities:** Art gallery, electron microscope, NMR spectrometer, neutron howitzer, multimedia language laboratory, electronic music studio.

DEGREES OFFERED. BA, M. 262 bachelor's degrees awarded in 1992. 24% in business and management, 6% languages, 11% letters/literature, 7% life sciences, 5% multi/interdisciplinary studies, 5% physical sciences, 10% psychology, 14% social sciences, 8% visual and performing arts. Graduate degrees offered in 1 major field of study.

UNDERGRADUATE MAJORS. African studies, American studies, anthropology, art history, Asian studies, biological and physical sciences, biology, business and management, chemistry, city/community/regional planning, clinical laboratory science, comparative literature, computer and information sciences, creative writing, Eastern European studies, economics, education, elementary education, English, environmental science, European studies, French, German, history, humanities and social sciences, international relations, junior high education, Latin American studies, liberal/general studies, mathematics, Middle Eastern studies, music history and appreciation, music performance, music theory and composition, nursing, philosophy, physics, political science and government, psychology, public policy studies, secondary education, social sciences, sociology, Spanish, studio art.

ACADEMIC PROGRAMS. Double major, honors program, independent study, internships, student-designed major, study abroad, teacher preparation, visiting/exchange student program, Washington semester, cross-registration, international internship program in Paris and Madrid, 3-2 engineering program with Washington University (St. Louis, Missouri); liberal arts/career combination in engineering, forestry. **Remedial services:** Tutoring, writing center. **Placement/credit:** AP, institutional tests.

ACADEMIC REQUIREMENTS. Freshmen must earn minimum GPA of 1.5 to continue in good standing. 88% of freshmen return for sophomore year. Students must declare major by end of second year. **Graduation requirements:** 128 hours for bachelor's. Most students required to take courses in humanities, mathematics, biological/physical sciences, social sciences. **Postgraduate studies:** 8% enter law school, 6% enter medical school, 10% enter MBA programs, 15% enter other graduate study. **Additional information:** Freshman Studies Program: each freshman selects 1 of 4 fall semester courses from designated set, usually 25 to 30, with class size limit of 15 students. Faculty member teaching course serves as student's academic adviser.

FRESHMAN ADMISSIONS. Selection criteria: Secondary school curriculum and record most important, followed by school and community activities and essay. Recommendations considered carefully. **High school preparation:** 16 units required; 20 recommended. Recommended units include English 4, foreign language 3, mathematics 3, social science 2 and science 1. **Test requirements:** SAT or ACT; score report by March 1. **Additional information:** Copy of graded paper required.

1992 FRESHMAN CLASS PROFILE. 408 men applied, 301 accepted, 112 enrolled; 439 women applied, 306 accepted, 123 enrolled. 22% were in top tenth and 61% were in top quarter of graduating class. **Academic background:** Mid 50% of enrolled freshmen had SAT-V between 430-550, SAT-M between 480-580; ACT composite between 22-27. 72% submitted SAT scores, 65% submitted ACT scores. **Characteristics:** 22% from in state, 94% live in college housing, 16% have minority backgrounds, 2% are foreign students, 21% join fraternities/sororities. Average age is 18.

FALL-TERM APPLICATIONS. $20 fee, may be waived for applicants with need. No closing date; priority given to applications received by March 1; applicants notified on a rolling basis; must reply by May 1 or within 3 weeks if notified thereafter. Essay required. Interview recommended. Portfolio recommended for studio art applicants. CRDA. Deferred and early admission available. EDP-F. Early decision deadline February 1.

STUDENT LIFE. Housing: Dormitories (men, women, coed). **Activities:** Student government, film, radio, student newspaper, yearbook, Tusitala (literary magazine), Collages (foreign language, literary magazine), choral groups, drama, jazz band, music ensembles, musical theater, fraternities, sororities, Community Services Program, Christian fellowship group, Interfaith Council, Jewish and international student organizations, film club, Amnesty International, political organizations, League for Environmental Awareness and Protection, African Americans and Others Committed to an Open Community for Equality, Cultural Sensitivity and Service.

ATHLETICS. NCAA. **Intercollegiate:** Basketball, diving, football M, handball, ice hockey M, lacrosse M, sailing, soccer, softball W, swimming, tennis, volleyball W. **Intramural:** Basketball, football M, ice hockey, racquetball, sailing, soccer, softball, squash, tennis, volleyball, water polo M.

STUDENT SERVICES. Career counseling, employment service for undergraduates, freshman orientation, health services, personal counseling, placement service for graduates, special adviser for adult students, services/facilities for handicapped.

ANNUAL EXPENSES. Tuition and fees (1992-93): $15,085. **Room and board:** $3,535. **Books and supplies:** $475. **Other expenses:** $455.

FINANCIAL AID. 58% of freshmen, 57% of continuing students receive some form of aid. Grants, loans, jobs available. 154 enrolled freshmen were judged to have need, all were offered aid. **Aid applications:** No closing date; priority given to applications received by February 15; applicants notified on a rolling basis beginning on or about March 20; must reply by May 1 or within 3 weeks if notified thereafter. **Additional information:** Early Need Analysis provided to students who file the Lake Forest Application for Financial Aid prior to February 1 and notification given within two weeks of its receipt.

ADDRESS/TELEPHONE. Francis B. Gummere Jr, VP for Enrollment Planning, Lake Forest College, 555 North Sheridan Road, Lake Forest, IL 60045-2399. (708) 234-3100. Fax: (708) 735-6291.

Lake Land College

Mattoon, Illinois — CB code: 1424

2-year public community college, coed. Founded in 1966. **Accreditation:** Regional. **Undergraduate enrollment:** 1,043 men, 1,136 women full time; 882 men, 1,482 women part time. **Faculty:** 284 total (106 full time), 11 with doctorates or other terminal degrees. **Location:** Rural campus in large town; 45 miles from Decatur, 45 miles from Champaign. **Calendar:** Semester, extensive summer session. **Microcomputers:** 125 located in libraries, classrooms, computer centers.

DEGREES OFFERED. AA, AS, AAS. 531 associate degrees awarded in 1992.

UNDERGRADUATE MAJORS. Accounting, agribusiness, agricultural business and management, agricultural mechanics, agricultural production, agricultural sciences, architectural technologies, architecture, automotive mechanics, automotive technology, biology, business administration and management, business and management, business and office, business computer/console/peripheral equipment operation, business data processing and related programs, business data programming, civil engineering, civil technology, data processing, dental hygiene, diesel engine mechanics, drafting, drafting and design technology, electrical and electronics equipment repair, electronic technology, engineering, engineering and engineering-related technologies, English, finance, fire control and safety technology, health sciences, industrial equipment maintenance and repair, insurance marketing, law enforcement and corrections, law enforcement and corrections technologies, legal secretary, liberal/general studies, marketing and distribution, mathematics, mechanical design technology, medical secretary, nursing, personal services, practical nursing, psychology, radio/television broadcasting, real estate, secretarial and related programs, special education, sports medicine, teacher aide.

ACADEMIC PROGRAMS. 2-year transfer program, cooperative education, dual enrollment of high school students, honors program, independent study, internships. **Remedial services:** Learning center, reduced course load, remedial instruction, special counselor, tutoring. **Placement/credit:** CLEP General, institutional tests; 30 credit hours maximum for associate degree.

ACADEMIC REQUIREMENTS. Freshmen must earn minimum GPA of 1.7 to continue in good standing. Students must declare major on application. **Graduation requirements:** 64 hours for associate (24 in major). Most students required to take courses in English, humanities, mathematics, biological/physical sciences, social sciences.

FRESHMAN ADMISSIONS. Selection criteria: Open admissions. Special requirements for dental hygiene, dental assistant, practical nursing programs and civil engineering. Mathematics and biology required for dental hygiene, dental assistant, and nursing applicants. **Test requirements:** ACT required of dental hygiene and dental assistant applicants; score report by September 1.

1992 FRESHMAN CLASS PROFILE. 683 men, 755 women enrolled. **Characteristics:** 100% commute, 6% have minority backgrounds.

FALL-TERM APPLICATIONS. $10 fee. No closing date; applicants notified on a rolling basis. Interview required for dental, nursing applicants. Early admission available.

STUDENT LIFE. Activities: Student government, radio, student newspaper, yearbook, Young Democrats, Young Republicans.

ATHLETICS. NJCAA. **Intercollegiate:** Baseball M, basketball, cross-country, softball W, tennis, volleyball W. **Intramural:** Archery, basketball, bowling, golf, tennis, volleyball.

STUDENT SERVICES. Aptitude testing, career counseling, employment service for undergraduates, freshman orientation, health services, on-campus day care, personal counseling, placement service for graduates, services/facilities for handicapped.

ANNUAL EXPENSES. Tuition and fees (projected): $1,209, $990 additional for out-of-district students, $2,850 additional for out-of-state students. **Books and supplies:** $205. **Other expenses:** $830.

FINANCIAL AID. 46% of freshmen, 46% of continuing students receive some form of aid. 85% of grants, 91% of loans, 75% of jobs based on need. Academic, music/drama, art, athletic, leadership scholarships available. **Aid applications:** No closing date; priority given to applications received by May 1; applicants notified on a rolling basis beginning on or about May 15; must reply within 2 weeks. **Additional information:** Estimated costs for commuter student not living at home is $6,870.

ADDRESS/TELEPHONE. Linda Von Behren, Director of Admission Services, Lake Land College, 5001 Lake Land Boulevard, Mattoon, IL 61938. (217) 235-3131 ext. 254. Fax: (217) 258-6459.

Lakeview College of Nursing

Danville, Illinois — CB code: 0149

Admissions: 98% of applicants accepted
Based on: •• Essay, recommendations, school record, test scores
• Activities, interview, special talents
Completion: 98% of freshmen end year in good standing
95% graduate

4-year private nursing college, coed. Founded in 1894. **Accreditation:** Regional candidate. **Undergraduate enrollment:** 3 men, 74 women full time; 33 men, 2 women part time. **Faculty:** 18 total (12 full time). **Location:** Urban campus in large town; 25 miles from Urbana/Champaign, 85 miles from Chicago. **Calendar:** Semester, limited summer session. **Microcomputers:** 7 located in libraries, classrooms, computer centers.

DEGREES OFFERED. BS. 5 bachelor's degrees awarded in 1992. 100% in health sciences.

UNDERGRADUATE MAJORS. Nursing.

ACADEMIC PROGRAMS. Independent study.

ACADEMIC REQUIREMENTS. Freshmen must earn minimum GPA of 2.0 to continue in good standing. 98% of freshmen return for sophomore year. **Graduation requirements:** 124 hours for bachelor's (60 in major). Most students required to take courses in computer science, English, humanities, philosophy/religion, biological/physical sciences, social sciences.

FRESHMAN ADMISSIONS. Selection criteria: Applicants to nursing program must be approved by admission committee. **Test requirements:** ACT recommended for counseling.

1992 FRESHMAN CLASS PROFILE. 10 men applied, 10 accepted, 4 enrolled; 107 women applied, 105 accepted, 30 enrolled. **Characteristics:** 100% commute. Average age is 26.

FALL-TERM APPLICATIONS. $35 fee. Closing date August 31; priority given to applications received by August 1; applicants notified on a rolling basis; must reply by registration. Interview required. Essay required. Deferred and early admission available. Proficiency test, NLN Test required.

STUDENT LIFE. Activities: Student government.

STUDENT SERVICES. Freshman orientation, personal counseling, special adviser for adult students, services/facilities for handicapped.

ANNUAL EXPENSES. Tuition and fees (1992-93): $4,575. **Books and supplies:** $400.

FINANCIAL AID. 100% of continuing students receive some form of aid. All grants, all loans based on need.

ADDRESS/TELEPHONE. Beverly Shelton, Coordinator of Admissions, Lakeview College of Nursing, 812 North Logan Avenue, Danville, IL 61832. (217) 443-5238. Fax: (217) 443-5238.

Lewis and Clark Community College

Godfrey, Illinois — CB code: 0623

2-year public community college, coed. Founded in 1970. **Accreditation:** Regional. **Undergraduate enrollment:** 820 men, 1,046 women full time; 1,369 men, 2,618 women part time. **Faculty:** 307 total (80 full time), 9 with doctorates or other terminal degrees. **Location:** Suburban campus in large town; 30 miles from St. Louis, Missouri. **Calendar:** Semester, limited summer session. **Microcomputers:** Located in computer centers. **Additional facts:** 3 off-campus admissions and registration sites.

DEGREES OFFERED. AA, AS, AAS. 450 associate degrees awarded in 1992. 8% in business and management, 7% business/office and marketing/distribution, 8% computer sciences, 11% engineering technologies, 45% allied health, 7% multi/interdisciplinary studies, 7% parks/recreation, protective services, public affairs.

UNDERGRADUATE MAJORS. Accounting, agribusiness, automotive mechanics, automotive technology, business and management, business and office, business data processing and related programs, business data programming, communications, computer servicing technology, construction, court reporting, criminal justice studies, data processing, desktop media, drafting, drafting and design technology, electromechanical technology, engineering and engineering-related technologies, finance, fire control and safety technology, food management, hotel/motel and restaurant management, interpreter for the deaf, labor/industrial relations, law enforcement and corrections technologies, legal secretary, liberal/general studies, library assistant, machine tool operation/machine shop, marketing and distribution, medical laboratory technologies, nursing, personal services, radio/television broadcasting, real estate, secretarial and related programs.

ACADEMIC PROGRAMS. 2-year transfer program, double major, dual enrollment of high school students, honors program, internships, student-designed major, study abroad, telecourses, weekend college, cross-registration. **Remedial services:** Learning center, remedial instruction, special counselor, tutoring. **ROTC:** Air Force. **Placement/credit:** CLEP General and Subject, institutional tests; 32 credit hours maximum for associate degree.

ACADEMIC REQUIREMENTS. Freshmen must earn minimum GPA of 1.75 to continue in good standing. 60% of freshmen return for sophomore year. Students must declare major on enrollment. **Graduation requirements:** 64 hours for associate. Most students required to take courses in English, mathematics, biological/physical sciences, social sciences. **Additional information:** Cross-registration with Blackburn College, Belleville Area College, Illinois Eastern Community Colleges.

FRESHMAN ADMISSIONS. Selection criteria: Open admissions. Selective admissions to nursing and allied health programs. **High school preparation:** 15 units recommended. Recommended units include English 4, foreign language 2, mathematics 3, social science 3 and science 3. 15 units mandated by Illinois Board of Higher Education for students who plan to transfer.

1992 FRESHMAN CLASS PROFILE. 812 men, 1,191 women enrolled. **Characteristics:** 99% from in state, 100% commute, 14% have minority backgrounds. Average age is 28.

FALL-TERM APPLICATIONS. No fee. No closing date; applicants notified on a rolling basis; must reply by registration. Interview required for medical laboratory technology, radio broadcasting applicants. Audition required. Deferred admission available.

STUDENT LIFE. Activities: Student government, radio, student newspaper, choral groups, concert band, dance, drama, jazz band, music ensembles, veterans organization, Christian Campus Fellowship, Disabled Students Organization, Black Students Association, Political Action Club.

ATHLETICS. NJCAA. **Intercollegiate:** Baseball M, basketball W, soccer M, softball W, tennis, volleyball W. **Intramural:** Basketball, bowling, softball, tennis, volleyball.

STUDENT SERVICES. Aptitude testing, career counseling, employment service for undergraduates, freshman orientation, health services, on-campus day care, personal counseling, placement service for graduates, special adviser for adult students, veterans counselor, student support services, services/facilities for handicapped.

ANNUAL EXPENSES. Tuition and fees: $1,035, $1,875 additional for out-of-district students, $4,011 additional for out-of-state students. **Books and supplies:** $600. **Other expenses:** $1,000.

FINANCIAL AID. 52% of freshmen, 67% of continuing students receive some form of aid. 84% of grants, 99% of loans, 70% of jobs based on need. Academic, music/drama, athletic, state/district residency, leadership, alumni affiliation, minority scholarships available. **Aid applications:** No closing date; priority given to applications received by June 1; applicants notified on a rolling basis beginning on or about August 1; must reply within 3 weeks.

ADDRESS/TELEPHONE. Carla Totten, Director of Admissions, Lewis and Clark Community College, 5800 Godfrey Road, Godfrey, IL 62035-2466. (618) 466-3411. (800) 642-1794 ext. 4202. Fax: (618) 466-2798.

Lewis University

Romeoville, Illinois — CB code: 1404

Admissions: 92% of applicants accepted
Based on: ••• School record
•• Test scores
• Essay, interview, special talents
Completion: 87% of freshmen end year in good standing
12% enter graduate study

4-year private university, coed, affiliated with Roman Catholic Church. Founded in 1932. **Accreditation:** Regional. **Undergraduate enrollment:** 1,071 men, 928 women full time; 849 men, 530 women part time. **Graduate enrollment:** 6 men, 7 women full time; 372 men, 339 women part time. **Faculty:** 108 total, 65 with doctorates or other terminal degrees. **Location:** Rural campus in large town; 30 miles from Chicago. **Calendar:** Semester, limited summer session. **Microcomputers:** 70 located in computer centers. **Spe-**

cial facilities: Campus airport, aeronautical training center. **Additional facts:** Institution conducted by the Brothers of the Christian Schools.

DEGREES OFFERED. AA, AS, BA, BS, MA, MS, MBA. 48 associate degrees awarded in 1992. 100% in trade and industry. 557 bachelor's degrees awarded. 15% in business and management, 17% business/office and marketing/distribution, 15% health sciences, 5% multi/interdisciplinary studies, 17% social sciences, 8% trade and industry, 6% visual and performing arts. Graduate degrees offered in 5 major fields of study.

UNDERGRADUATE MAJORS. Associate: Aeronautical technology, aircraft mechanics. **Bachelor's:** Accounting, aeronautical technology, aircraft mechanics, airline piloting and navigation, art history, aviation equipment nondestructive testing, biology, business administration and management, business and office, business economics, chemistry, clinical laboratory science, communications, computer and information sciences, criminal justice studies, dramatic arts, elementary education, English, finance, history, industrial and organizational psychology, information sciences and systems, journalism, liberal/general studies, management information systems, marketing management, mathematics, music, nursing, operations research, philosophy, physical education, physics, political science and government, psychology, public administration, religion, secondary education, social work, sociology, speech.

ACADEMIC PROGRAMS. Double major, dual enrollment of high school students, honors program, independent study, internships, student-designed major, teacher preparation; combined bachelor's/graduate program in business administration. **Remedial services:** Learning center, reduced course load, remedial instruction, special counselor, tutoring. **ROTC:** Air Force, Army, Naval. **Placement/credit:** AP, CLEP General and Subject, institutional tests.

ACADEMIC REQUIREMENTS. Freshmen must earn minimum GPA of 1.75 to continue in good standing. 76% of freshmen return for sophomore year. Students must declare major by end of second year. **Graduation requirements:** 77 hours for associate (65 in major), 128 hours for bachelor's (63 in major). Most students required to take courses in arts/fine arts, English, history, humanities, mathematics, philosophy/religion, biological/physical sciences, social sciences.

FRESHMAN ADMISSIONS. Selection criteria: Applicants should be in upper 40% of class with 2.0 high school GPA. A composite ACT score of 20 or above preferred although not used as a sole criterion. **High school preparation:** 15 units required. Required units include English 3. **Test requirements:** SAT or ACT (ACT preferred); score report by September 1.

1992 FRESHMAN CLASS PROFILE. 610 men applied, 568 accepted, 403 enrolled; 455 women applied, 412 accepted, 248 enrolled. 45% had high school GPA of 3.0 or higher, 53% between 2.0 and 2.99. **Academic background:** Mid 50% of enrolled freshmen had ACT composite between 18-24. 99% submitted ACT scores. **Characteristics:** 68% commute, 16% have minority backgrounds. Average age is 18.

FALL-TERM APPLICATIONS. $20 fee, may be waived for applicants with need. No closing date; applicants notified on a rolling basis; August 15. Interview recommended. Deferred and early admission available.

STUDENT LIFE. Housing: Dormitories (men, women, coed). Handicapped accessibility in several residence halls. **Activities:** Student government, magazine, radio, student newspaper, television, choral groups, dance, drama, jazz band, music ensembles, musical theater, pep band, symphony orchestra, fraternities, sororities, university ministry, Black Student Union, International Student Association, Pan Hellenic Council, Model UN, Peace Education Committee, Latin American Student Organization, Amnesty International, Cultural Awareness Council, LaSallian Collegiate Group.

ATHLETICS. NCAA. **Intercollegiate:** Baseball M, basketball, cross-country, golf, soccer, softball W, tennis, track and field, volleyball W. **Intramural:** Baseball M, basketball, bowling, handball, softball W, table tennis, volleyball.

STUDENT SERVICES. Aptitude testing, career counseling, employment service for undergraduates, freshman orientation, health services, personal counseling, placement service for graduates, special adviser for adult students, veterans counselor, services/facilities for handicapped.

ANNUAL EXPENSES. Tuition and fees (1992-93): $9,206. **Room and board:** $4,270. **Books and supplies:** $400. **Other expenses:** $1,200.

FINANCIAL AID. 80% of freshmen, 65% of continuing students receive some form of aid. 66% of grants, 81% of loans, 42% of jobs based on need. 290 enrolled freshmen were judged to have need, all were offered aid. Academic, music/drama, art, athletic, religious affiliation scholarships available. **Aid applications:** No closing date; priority given to applications received by April 1; applicants notified on a rolling basis.

ADDRESS/TELEPHONE. Frank Palmasani, Director of Admissions, Lewis University, Route 53, Romeoville, IL 60441-2298. (815) 838-0500 ext. 470. Fax: (815) 838-9456.

Lexington Institute of Hospitality Careers

Chicago, Illinois — CB code: 3843

Admissions:	90% of applicants accepted
Based on:	••• School record
	•• Activities, interview
	• Recommendations, test scores
Completion:	90% of freshmen end year in good standing
	93% graduate, 9% of these enter 4-year programs

2-year private junior college, women only. **Accreditation:** Regional candidate. **Undergraduate enrollment:** 35 women full time; 6 women part time. **Faculty:** 17 total, 4 with doctorates or other terminal degrees. **Location:** Urban campus in very large city; 20 miles from downtown Chicago. **Calendar:** Semester. **Microcomputers:** 5 located in computer centers. **Special facilities:** Computer laboratory, culinary demonstration laboratory. **Additional facts:** Off-campus site at Valparaiso, Indiana.

DEGREES OFFERED. AAS. 16 associate degrees awarded in 1992. 100% in business and management.

UNDERGRADUATE MAJORS. Dietetic aide/assistant, food management, food production/management/services, hotel/motel and restaurant management.

ACADEMIC PROGRAMS. 2-year transfer program, cooperative education, internships. **Remedial services:** Reduced course load, remedial instruction, tutoring.

ACADEMIC REQUIREMENTS. Freshmen must earn minimum GPA of 2.0 to continue in good standing. 85% of freshmen return for sophomore year. Students must declare major by end of first year. **Graduation requirements:** 64 hours for associate (18 in major). Most students required to take courses in computer science, English, history, humanities, mathematics, philosophy/religion.

FRESHMAN ADMISSIONS. Selection criteria: Interviews and high school record important. Test scores, if submitted, also considered. **Test requirements:** SAT or ACT; score report by September 4.

1992 FRESHMAN CLASS PROFILE. 29 women applied, 26 accepted, 26 enrolled. 23% had high school GPA of 3.0 or higher, 64% between 2.0 and 2.99. **Characteristics:** 59% from in state, 78% commute, 35% have minority backgrounds, 27% are foreign students. Average age is 18.

FALL-TERM APPLICATIONS. $25 fee, may be waived for applicants with need. Closing date October 1; applicants notified on a rolling basis; must reply by registration. Interview recommended. Deferred and early admission available. ACT/SAT recommended.

STUDENT LIFE. Housing: Dormitories (women). Student residence located near campus. **Activities:** Student government, student newspaper, campus ministry.

STUDENT SERVICES. Aptitude testing, career counseling, employment service for undergraduates, freshman orientation, health services, personal counseling, placement service for graduates, services/facilities for handicapped.

ANNUAL EXPENSES. Tuition and fees (projected): $4,800. **Room and board:** $3,000. **Books and supplies:** $600. **Other expenses:** $360.

FINANCIAL AID. 76% of freshmen, 83% of continuing students receive some form of aid. 58% of grants, all loans based on need. 14 enrolled freshmen were judged to have need, all were offered aid. Academic scholarships available. **Aid applications:** No closing date; priority given to applications received by June 1; applicants notified on a rolling basis beginning on or about August 1; must reply by registration.

ADDRESS/TELEPHONE. Mary Jane Markel, Admissions Officer, Lexington Institute of Hospitality Careers, 10840 South Western Avenue, Chicago, IL 60643-3294. (312) 779-3800 ext. 11.

Lincoln Christian College and Seminary

Lincoln, Illinois — CB code: 1405

Admissions:	90% of applicants accepted
Based on:	••• Recommendations, religious affiliation/commitment
	•• School record, test scores
	• Essay, interview
Completion:	80% of freshmen end year in good standing
	35% graduate, 50% of these enter graduate study

4-year private Bible, seminary college, coed, affiliated with Church of Christ. Founded in 1944. **Accreditation:** Regional. **Undergraduate enrollment:** 214 men, 187 women full time; 24 men, 36 women part time. **Graduate enrollment:** 59 men, 22 women full time; 108 men, 24 women part time. **Faculty:** 63 total (34 full time), 15 with doctorates or other terminal degrees. **Location:** Suburban campus in large town; 30 miles from Springfield. **Calendar:** Semester, limited summer session. **Microcomputers:** 10 located in libraries.

DEGREES OFFERED. AA, BA, BS, MA, M.Div. 5 associate degrees awarded in 1992. 100% in philosophy, religion, theology. 40 bachelor's degrees awarded. 14% in business and management, 10% teacher education,

76% philosophy, religion, theology. Graduate degrees offered in 7 major fields of study.

UNDERGRADUATE MAJORS. Associate: Bible studies, secretarial and related programs. **Bachelor's:** Bible studies, business administration and management, early childhood education, elementary education, junior high education, linguistics, missionary studies, religious education, religious music, secondary education, secretarial and related programs, theological studies.

ACADEMIC PROGRAMS. 2-year transfer program, double major, independent study, internships, teacher preparation, teacher preparatory program through Sangamon State University, Illinois State University, and Greenville College. **Remedial services:** Learning center, reduced course load, remedial instruction, special counselor, tutoring.

ACADEMIC REQUIREMENTS. Freshmen must earn minimum GPA of 1.7 to continue in good standing. 75% of freshmen return for sophomore year. Students must declare major by end of second year. **Graduation requirements:** 66 hours for associate, 130 hours for bachelor's (44 in major). Most students required to take courses in English, foreign languages, history, humanities, philosophy/religion, biological/physical sciences, social sciences.

FRESHMAN ADMISSIONS. Selection criteria: Recommendation of applicant's church leaders as to suitability for church-related vocations most important. High school record and ACT test scores considered. **Test requirements:** ACT; score report by August 10.

1992 FRESHMAN CLASS PROFILE. 78 men applied, 70 accepted, 57 enrolled; 105 women applied, 95 accepted, 72 enrolled. 13% were in top tenth and 28% were in top quarter of graduating class. **Academic background:** Mid 50% of enrolled freshmen had ACT composite between 13-24. 97% submitted ACT scores. **Characteristics:** 60% from in state, 88% live in college housing, 2% have minority backgrounds, 4% are foreign students. Average age is 19.

FALL-TERM APPLICATIONS. $20 fee. No closing date; applicants notified on a rolling basis; must reply by registration. Audition required for music applicants. Interview recommended. Deferred admission available.

STUDENT LIFE. Housing: Dormitories (men, women); apartment housing available. **Activities:** Student government, yearbook, choral groups, drama, music ensembles, musical theater, pep band, volunteer groups in local health care institutions, missions interest groups, Christian service and outreach groups. **Additional information:** Religious observance required.

ATHLETICS. Intercollegiate: Baseball M, basketball, soccer M, tennis M, volleyball W. **Intramural:** Basketball M, tennis, volleyball.

STUDENT SERVICES. Aptitude testing, career counseling, employment service for undergraduates, freshman orientation, health services, personal counseling, placement service for graduates, services/facilities for handicapped.

ANNUAL EXPENSES. Tuition and fees (1992-93): $3,830. **Room and board:** $2,610. **Books and supplies:** $400. **Other expenses:** $1,600.

FINANCIAL AID. 95% of freshmen, 95% of continuing students receive some form of aid. All aid based on need. Academic, religious affiliation scholarships available. **Aid applications:** No closing date; priority given to applications received by August 10; applicants notified on a rolling basis beginning on or about July 15; must reply within 10 days.

ADDRESS/TELEPHONE. Lynn Laughlin, Director of Admissions, Lincoln Christian College and Seminary, 100 Campus View Drive, Lincoln, IL 62656-2111. (217) 732-3168 ext. 2219. Fax: (217) 732-5914.

Lincoln College
Lincoln, Illinois — CB code: 1406

2-year private junior college, coed. Founded in 1865. **Accreditation:** Regional. **Undergraduate enrollment:** 666 men, 692 women full time. **Faculty:** 46 total (35 full time), 8 with doctorates or other terminal degrees. **Location:** Rural campus in large town; 185 miles from Chicago, 125 miles from St. Louis. **Calendar:** Semester, limited summer session. **Microcomputers:** 45 located in libraries, classrooms, computer centers. **Special facilities:** Museum of the Presidents, art gallery. **Additional facts:** Liberal arts degree program offered only at main campus. Degree and vocational programs available at extension campus in Bloomington.

DEGREES OFFERED. AA, AS, AAS. 500 associate degrees awarded in 1992.

UNDERGRADUATE MAJORS. English literature.

ACADEMIC PROGRAMS. 2-year transfer program, dual enrollment of high school students, honors program, independent study, study abroad. **Remedial services:** Learning center, preadmission summer program, reduced course load, tutoring. **Placement/credit:** CLEP General and Subject, institutional tests; 15 credit hours maximum for associate degree.

ACADEMIC REQUIREMENTS. Freshmen must earn minimum GPA of 2.0 to continue in good standing. Students with 17 or more credit hours must maintain a 2.0 GPA to remain in good academic standing. 70% of freshmen return for sophomore year. **Graduation requirements:** 61 hours for associate. Most students required to take courses in English, humanities, mathematics, biological/physical sciences, social sciences.

FRESHMAN ADMISSIONS. Selection criteria: Test scores and high school transcript most important. Interview considered. **Test requirements:** SAT or ACT (ACT preferred); score report by August 15.

1992 FRESHMAN CLASS PROFILE. 595 men, 545 women enrolled. **Academic background:** Mid 50% of enrolled freshmen had ACT composite between 18-24. 91% submitted ACT scores. **Characteristics:** 98% from in state, 79% live in college housing, 13% have minority backgrounds. Average age is 18.

FALL-TERM APPLICATIONS. $25 fee. Closing date August 18; applicants notified on a rolling basis; must reply within 2 weeks. Interview recommended for academically weak applicants. Deferred and early admission available.

STUDENT LIFE. Housing: Dormitories (men, women). **Activities:** Student government, magazine, radio, student newspaper, yearbook, choral groups, dance, drama, jazz band, music ensembles, musical theater, pep band, symphony orchestra, speech team, readers' theater, children's theater company, Interfaith Committee, Fellowship of Christian Athletes.

ATHLETICS. NJCAA. **Intercollegiate:** Baseball M, basketball, diving, golf, soccer, softball W, swimming, volleyball W, wrestling M. **Intramural:** Badminton, baseball M, basketball, soccer, softball, table tennis, tennis, volleyball.

STUDENT SERVICES. Aptitude testing, career counseling, employment service for undergraduates, freshman orientation, health services, placement service for graduates, special adviser for adult students.

ANNUAL EXPENSES. Tuition and fees: $8,205. **Room and board:** $3,650. **Books and supplies:** $450. **Other expenses:** $1,000.

FINANCIAL AID. 84% of freshmen, 82% of continuing students receive some form of aid. 94% of grants, 92% of loans, 85% of jobs based on need. Academic, music/drama, art, athletic, state/district residency, leadership, alumni affiliation scholarships available. **Aid applications:** No closing date; applicants notified on a rolling basis beginning on or about March 1; must reply within 3 weeks. **Additional information:** Auditions recommended for music, speech, theater, broadcasting, and dance scholarship candidates, portfolios recommended for art and technical theater scholarship candidates.

ADDRESS/TELEPHONE. Michael W. Riley, Director of Admissions, Lincoln College, 300 Keokuk, Lincoln, IL 62656. (217) 732-3155 ext. 250. Fax: (217) 732-8859.

Lincoln Land Community College
Springfield, Illinois — CB code: 1428

2-year public community college, coed. Founded in 1967. **Accreditation:** Regional. **Undergraduate enrollment:** 1,305 men, 1,115 women full time; 3,001 men, 4,197 women part time. **Faculty:** 375 total (125 full time), 23 with doctorates or other terminal degrees. **Location:** Suburban campus in small city; 180 miles from Chicago. **Calendar:** Semester, extensive summer session. Saturday classes. **Microcomputers:** 80 located in libraries, classrooms, computer centers. **Additional facts:** Lincoln Land Community College service centers located at Hillsboro, Litchfield, Taylorville, Jacksonville.

DEGREES OFFERED. AA, AS, AAS. 724 associate degrees awarded in 1992. 18% in business and management, 5% education, 14% allied health, 25% multi/interdisciplinary studies, 6% parks/recreation, protective services, public affairs, 5% trade and industry.

UNDERGRADUATE MAJORS. Accounting, agricultural business and management, agricultural sciences, air traffic control, American literature, anthropology, architectural technologies, architecture, automotive mechanics, automotive technology, aviation management, biological and physical sciences, biology, business administration and management, business and management, business and office, business data processing and related programs, business data programming, chemical engineering, chemistry, child development/care/guidance, communications, data processing, dramatic arts, economics, education, electrical and electronics equipment repair, electronic technology, elementary education, engineering, engineering and engineering-related technologies, engineering and other disciplines, English, fine arts, fire control and safety technology, foreign languages (multiple emphasis), geography, history, humanities and social sciences, journalism, law enforcement and corrections technologies, liberal/general studies, marketing and distribution, marketing management, mathematics, mining and petroleum technologies, music, nursing, office supervision and management, ornamental horticulture, philosophy, physical sciences, physics, political science and government, predentistry, preengineering, prelaw, premedicine, prepharmacy, preveterinary, psychology, public affairs, radiograph medical technology, real estate, respiratory therapy technology, retailing, science technologies, secretarial and related programs, social work, sociology, trade and industrial supervision and management, word processing.

ACADEMIC PROGRAMS. 2-year transfer program, cooperative education, dual enrollment of high school students, honors program, independent study, internships, telecourses, United Nations semester, cross-registration. **Remedial services:** Learning center, remedial instruction, special counselor, tutoring. **Placement/credit:** AP, CLEP General and Subject, institutional tests.

ACADEMIC REQUIREMENTS. Freshmen must earn minimum GPA of 1.75 to continue in good standing. **Graduation requirements:** 60 hours for associate. Most students required to take courses in English, mathematics, biological/physical sciences, social sciences.

FRESHMAN ADMISSIONS. Selection criteria: Open admissions. Applicants to nursing and allied health programs must rank in top half of high school graduating class. **Test requirements:** ACT required for nursing, respiratory therapy, and radiologic technology applicants. Admissions assessment not required for students with ACT composite score of 22 or above.

1992 FRESHMAN CLASS PROFILE. 6,963 men and women enrolled. **Characteristics:** 99% from in state, 100% commute, 7% have minority backgrounds. Average age is 20.

FALL-TERM APPLICATIONS. No fee. No closing date; applicants notified on a rolling basis. Deferred and early admission available.

STUDENT LIFE. Activities: Student government, student newspaper, choral groups, concert band, drama, jazz band, musical theater, pep band, symphony orchestra.

ATHLETICS. NJCAA. **Intercollegiate:** Basketball, soccer M, softball W, volleyball W. **Intramural:** Basketball, bowling, softball, table tennis, tennis, track and field, volleyball.

STUDENT SERVICES. Aptitude testing, career counseling, employment service for undergraduates, freshman orientation, health services, on-campus day care, personal counseling, placement service for graduates, veterans counselor, services/facilities for handicapped.

ANNUAL EXPENSES. Tuition and fees: $1,033, $1,380 additional for out-of-district students, $2,910 additional for out-of-state students. **Books and supplies:** $450. **Other expenses:** $500.

FINANCIAL AID. 92% of grants, 97% of loans, 20% of jobs based on need. Academic, music/drama, art, athletic, state/district residency, leadership, alumni affiliation, minority scholarships available. **Aid applications:** No closing date; priority given to applications received by May 1; applicants notified on a rolling basis beginning on or about June 1; must reply within 2 weeks.

ADDRESS/TELEPHONE. Kim Kirschman, Dean of Enrollment Services, Lincoln Land Community College, Shepherd Road, Springfield, IL 62794-9256. (217) 786-2290.

Loyola University of Chicago
Chicago, Illinois — CB code: 1412

Admissions:	81% of applicants accepted
Based on:	••• School record, test scores
	• Activities, essay, interview, recommendations, special talents
Completion:	94% of freshmen end year in good standing
	66% graduate

4-year private university, coed, affiliated with Roman Catholic Church. Founded in 1870. **Accreditation:** Regional. **Undergraduate enrollment:** 2,299 men, 3,458 women full time; 1,406 men, 2,394 women part time. **Graduate enrollment:** 1,001 men, 1,277 women full time; 1,334 men, 2,129 women part time. **Location:** Urban campus in very large city; Lake Shore and Water Tower campuses are in Chicago, Mallinckrodt campus is in suburb. **Calendar:** Semester, extensive summer session. **Microcomputers:** 207 located in libraries, classrooms, computer centers. **Special facilities:** Martin D'Arcy Gallery of Medieval and Renaissance Art, nursing resource center, seismograph station, theater, electron micropscope. **Additional facts:** Extensive degree program for returning adults.

DEGREES OFFERED. BA, BS, MA, MS, MBA, MEd, MSW, PhD, EdD, DMD, MD, JD, M.Div. 1,588 bachelor's degrees awarded in 1992. 15% in business and management, 8% business/office and marketing/distribution, 11% communications, 6% education, 5% health sciences, 6% letters/literature, 8% life sciences, 5% parks/recreation, protective services, public affairs, 11% psychology, 14% social sciences. Graduate degrees offered in 57 major fields of study.

UNDERGRADUATE MAJORS. Accounting, anthropology, applied psychology, biology, business administration and management, business and management, business economics, chemistry, classics, communications, computer and information sciences, computer mathematics, criminal justice studies, dramatic arts, economics, education, elementary education, English, finance, fine arts, French, German, Greek (classical), history, information sciences and systems, Italian, Latin, linguistics, management information systems, marketing and distribution, marketing management, mathematics, music, nursing, personnel management, philosophy, physics, political science and government, production and operations management, psychology, secondary education, social work, sociology, Spanish, special education, theological studies.

ACADEMIC PROGRAMS. Accelerated program, double major, honors program, independent study, internships, study abroad, teacher preparation, weekend college, Washington semester, cross-registration, cooperative programs with Erikson Institute for Early Education and Niles College (theological seminary); liberal arts/career combination in engineering. **Remedial services:** Learning center, reduced course load, special counselor, tutoring, learning enrichment program. **Placement/credit:** AP, CLEP General and Subject; 15 credit hours maximum for bachelor's degree.

ACADEMIC REQUIREMENTS. Freshmen must earn minimum GPA of 2.0 to continue in good standing. 86% of freshmen return for sophomore year. Students must declare major by end of second year. **Graduation requirements:** 128 hours for bachelor's (36 in major). Most students required to take courses in arts/fine arts, English, foreign languages, history, mathematics, philosophy/religion, biological/physical sciences, social sciences. **Additional information:** Foreign language required if 2 years of same language not taken in high school. ROTC offered through neighboring institutions.

FRESHMAN ADMISSIONS. Selection criteria: Class rank and SAT or ACT scores most important, followed by rigor of high school curriculum, for admission to full-time undergraduate programs. Initial conditional open admission to part-time returning adult programs. **High school preparation:** 15 units required. Required and recommended units include English 4, mathematics 2-4, social science 1-3 and science 1-2. Foreign language 4 recommended. Additional requirements for certain majors. **Test requirements:** SAT or ACT; score report by July 24.

1992 FRESHMAN CLASS PROFILE. 1,407 men applied, 1,143 accepted, 449 enrolled; 2,509 women applied, 2,022 accepted, 631 enrolled. 25% were in top tenth and 57% were in top quarter of graduating class. **Academic background:** Mid 50% of enrolled freshmen had SAT-V between 430-540, SAT-M between 460-590; ACT composite between 21-26. 54% submitted SAT scores, 89% submitted ACT scores. **Characteristics:** 79% from in state, 51% live in college housing, 27% have minority backgrounds. Average age is 18.

FALL-TERM APPLICATIONS. $25 fee, may be waived for applicants with need. Closing date July 10; applicants notified on a rolling basis; must reply by May 1 or by specified date if notified thereafter. Interview recommended. Essay recommended for honor program applicants. CRDA. Honors program applicants must apply by March 1.

STUDENT LIFE. Housing: Dormitories (women, coed); apartment, fraternity housing available. 24-hour quiet facility. **Activities:** Student government, magazine, radio, student newspaper, choral groups, concert band, drama, jazz band, musical theater, fraternities, sororities, over 100 clubs and organizations.

ATHLETICS. NCAA. **Intercollegiate:** Basketball, cross-country, golf M, soccer, softball W, swimming M, track and field, volleyball W. **Intramural:** Badminton, baseball M, basketball, cross-country, golf, racquetball, skiing, soccer, softball, swimming, table tennis, tennis, volleyball.

STUDENT SERVICES. Aptitude testing, career counseling, employment service for undergraduates, freshman orientation, health services, personal counseling, placement service for graduates, special adviser for adult students, veterans counselor, services/facilities for handicapped.

ANNUAL EXPENSES. Tuition and fees (1992-93): $9,930. **Room and board:** $5,154. **Books and supplies:** $700. **Other expenses:** $1,400.

FINANCIAL AID. 75% of freshmen, 85% of continuing students receive some form of aid. Grants, loans, jobs available. Academic, music/drama, art, athletic, leadership scholarships available. **Aid applications:** No closing date; priority given to applications received by April 1; applicants notified on a rolling basis beginning on or about February 1; must reply within 2 weeks.

ADDRESS/TELEPHONE. Allen V. Lentino, Director of Admissions Counseling, Loyola University of Chicago, 820 North Michigan Avenue, Chicago, IL 60611. (312) 915-6500. (800) 262-2373. Fax: (312) 915-6449.

MacCormac Junior College
Chicago, Illinois — CB code: 1520

2-year private junior college, coed. Founded in 1904. **Accreditation:** Regional. **Undergraduate enrollment:** 75 men, 300 women full time; 20 men, 95 women part time. **Faculty:** 46 total (35 full time), 9 with doctorates or other terminal degrees. **Location:** Suburban campus in very large city. **Calendar:** Quarter, limited summer session. **Microcomputers:** 70 located in computer centers. **Additional facts:** Branch campus in suburban Elmhurst.

DEGREES OFFERED. AA, AAS. 115 associate degrees awarded in 1992. 50% in business and management, 20% business/office and marketing/distribution, 10% computer sciences, 20% law.

UNDERGRADUATE MAJORS. Accounting, business administration and management, business and management, business and office, court reporting, fashion merchandising, hospitality and recreation marketing, information sciences and systems, international business management, legal assistant/paralegal, legal secretary, marketing and distribution, prelaw, retailing, secretarial and related programs, tourism, transportation and travel marketing, word processing.

ACADEMIC PROGRAMS. Internships. **Remedial services:** Preadmission summer program. **Placement/credit:** AP, CLEP Subject.

ACADEMIC REQUIREMENTS. Freshmen must earn minimum GPA of 2.0 to continue in good standing. 70% of freshmen return for sophomore year. Students must declare major by end of first year. **Graduation requirements:** 96 hours for associate. Most students required to take courses in computer science, English, social sciences.

FRESHMAN ADMISSIONS. Selection criteria: Test scores and class rank most important. **Test requirements:** SAT or ACT (ACT preferred); score report by May 31.

1992 FRESHMAN CLASS PROFILE. 75 men, 275 women enrolled. **Academic background:** Mid 50% of enrolled freshmen had ACT composite between 19-23. 95% submitted ACT scores. **Characteristics:** 90% from in state, 100% commute, 48% have minority backgrounds, 3% are foreign students. Average age is 19.

FALL-TERM APPLICATIONS. $15 fee, may be waived for applicants with need. No closing date; priority given to applications received by May 31; applicants notified on a rolling basis; must reply within 4 weeks. Interview required. Deferred admission available.

STUDENT LIFE. Activities: Student government, fraternities, sororities.

ATHLETICS. Intramural: Softball, table tennis, volleyball.

STUDENT SERVICES. Aptitude testing, career counseling, employment service for undergraduates, freshman orientation, personal counseling, placement service for graduates, veterans counselor, services/facilities for handicapped.

ANNUAL EXPENSES. Tuition and fees (1992-93): $6,300. **Books and supplies:** $600. **Other expenses:** $1,200.

FINANCIAL AID. 80% of freshmen, 80% of continuing students receive some form of aid. Grants, loans, jobs available. **Aid applications:** No closing date; applicants notified on a rolling basis; must reply within 2 weeks.

ADDRESS/TELEPHONE. Alan B. Solid, Director of Admissions, MacCormac Junior College, 506 South Wabash, Chicago, IL 60605. (312) 922-1884. Fax: (708) 941-0937.

MacMurray College
Jacksonville, Illinois CB code: 1435

Admissions: 74% of applicants accepted
Based on: ••• School record
•• Activities, recommendations
• Essay, interview, test scores
Completion: 91% of freshmen end year in good standing
45% graduate, 15% of these enter graduate study

4-year private liberal arts college, coed, affiliated with United Methodist Church. Founded in 1846. **Accreditation:** Regional. **Undergraduate enrollment:** 274 men, 357 women full time; 25 men, 36 women part time. **Faculty:** 70 total (53 full time), 24 with doctorates or other terminal degrees. **Location:** Rural campus in large town; 235 miles from Chicago, 30 miles from Springfield. **Calendar:** 4-1-4, limited summer session. **Microcomputers:** 30 located in libraries, computer centers. **Special facilities:** Mobil art gallery.

DEGREES OFFERED. AA, AS, BA, BS. 1 associate degree awarded in 1992. 100% in business and management. 122 bachelor's degrees awarded. 24% in business and management, 40% teacher education, 6% health sciences, 10% parks/recreation, protective services, public affairs, 9% social sciences.

UNDERGRADUATE MAJORS. Associate: Business administration and management, law enforcement and corrections. **Bachelor's:** Accounting, art education, art history, biology, business administration and management, chemistry, computer and information sciences, education of the deaf and hearing impaired, education of the emotionally handicapped, elementary education, English, English education, foreign languages education, French, history, journalism, law enforcement and corrections, management information systems, marketing management, mathematics, mathematics education, music, music education, nursing, philosophy, physical education, physics, political science and government, predentistry, preengineering, prelaw, premedicine, preoccupational therapy, preveterinary, psychology, religion, science education, secondary education, social studies education, social work, sociology, Spanish, specific learning disabilities, sports management.

ACADEMIC PROGRAMS. Double major, dual enrollment of high school students, honors program, independent study, internships, student-designed major, study abroad, teacher preparation, Washington semester, cross-registration, 3-2 programs in engineering with Washington University (Missouri) and Columbia University (New York), in occupational therapy with Washington University. **Remedial services:** Reduced course load, special counselor, tutoring, writing center. **Placement/credit:** AP, CLEP Subject, institutional tests; 32 credit hours maximum for bachelor's degree.

ACADEMIC REQUIREMENTS. Freshmen must earn minimum GPA of 2.0 to continue in good standing. 77% of freshmen return for sophomore year. Students must declare major by end of second year. **Graduation requirements:** 60 hours for associate (18 in major), 120 hours for bachelor's (30 in major). Most students required to take courses in arts/fine arts, English, foreign languages, history, humanities, mathematics, philosophy/religion, biological/physical sciences, social sciences. **Postgraduate studies:** 2% enter law school, 3% enter medical school, 1% enter MBA programs, 9% enter other graduate study.

FRESHMAN ADMISSIONS. Selection criteria: 2.5 high school GPA and rank in top half of high school graduating class. Participation in school, community, and church activities, and recommendations are considered. Recommended units include English 4, mathematics 4, social science 2 and science 3. **Test requirements:** SAT or ACT (ACT preferred); score report by August 1. Minimum ACT score of 20 required for nursing applicants.

1992 FRESHMAN CLASS PROFILE. 362 men applied, 250 accepted, 98 enrolled; 280 women applied, 223 accepted, 106 enrolled. 47% had high school GPA of 3.0 or higher, 50% between 2.0 and 2.99. **Academic background:** Mid 50% of enrolled freshmen had ACT composite between 18-23. 97% submitted ACT scores. **Characteristics:** 80% from in state, 90% live in college housing, 9% have minority backgrounds, 1% are foreign students, 4% join fraternities/sororities. Average age is 18.

FALL-TERM APPLICATIONS. $10 fee, may be waived for applicants with need. Closing date August 1; priority given to applications received by January 1; applicants notified on a rolling basis; must reply by May 1 or within 2 weeks of financial aid notification. Essay required. Interview recommended for academically deficient applicants. Audition recommended for music scholarships applicants. Portfolio recommended for art scholarship applicants. CRDA. Deferred and early admission available.

STUDENT LIFE. Housing: Dormitories (men, women, coed). **Activities:** Student government, student newspaper, yearbook, choral groups, concert band, music ensembles, musical theater, pep band, symphony orchestra, fraternities, sororities, NAACP, APO, Circle-K, Newman club, Basic, Holy Fools, religious life committee.

ATHLETICS. NCAA. **Intercollegiate:** Baseball M, basketball, football M, golf, soccer, softball W, tennis, volleyball W, wrestling M. **Intramural:** Basketball, cross-country, softball, swimming, table tennis, volleyball.

STUDENT SERVICES. Aptitude testing, career counseling, employment service for undergraduates, freshman orientation, health services, personal counseling, placement service for graduates, services/facilities for handicapped.

ANNUAL EXPENSES. Tuition and fees: $9,120. **Room and board:** $3,680. **Books and supplies:** $625. **Other expenses:** $500.

FINANCIAL AID. 92% of freshmen, 92% of continuing students receive some form of aid. 70% of grants, 88% of loans, all jobs based on need. Academic, music/drama, art, alumni affiliation, religious affiliation scholarships available. **Aid applications:** Closing date August 1; priority given to applications received by January 1; applicants notified on a rolling basis beginning on or about March 1; must reply within 4 weeks. **Additional information:** Merit scholarships for accepted, enrolled freshman available through academic scholarship competition. Decisions are based on interviews, essays, and other information.

ADDRESS/TELEPHONE. Dr. Ed Hockett, Dean of Admissions, MacMurray College, 447 East College Avenue, Jacksonville, IL 62650-2590. (217) 479-7056. Fax: (217) 245-5214.

McHenry County College
Crystal Lake, Illinois CB code: 1525

2-year public community college, coed. Founded in 1967. **Accreditation:** Regional. **Undergraduate enrollment:** 510 men, 575 women full time; 1,397 men, 2,258 women part time. **Faculty:** 183 total (63 full time), 5 with doctorates or other terminal degrees. **Location:** Rural campus in large town; 40 miles from Chicago. **Calendar:** Semester, limited summer session. Saturday and extensive evening/early morning classes. **Microcomputers:** Located in classrooms, computer centers.

DEGREES OFFERED. AA, AS, AAS. 230 associate degrees awarded in 1992. 6% in business/office and marketing/distribution, 85% multi/interdisciplinary studies.

UNDERGRADUATE MAJORS. Accounting, agricultural business and management, automotive mechanics, business and management, business data programming, drafting, electronic technology, emergency medical technologies, horticulture, industrial technology, law enforcement and corrections technologies, liberal/general studies, marketing and distribution, mechanical design technology, retailing, secretarial and related programs, word processing.

ACADEMIC PROGRAMS. 2-year transfer program, dual enrollment of high school students, honors program, independent study, internships, study abroad, cooperative programs in various technologies with neighboring community colleges. **Remedial services:** Remedial instruction. **Placement/credit:** AP, CLEP General and Subject, institutional tests; 30 credit hours maximum for associate degree.

ACADEMIC REQUIREMENTS. Freshmen must earn minimum GPA of 2.0 to continue in good standing. Students must declare major on enrollment. **Graduation requirements:** 60 hours for associate (15 in major). Most students required to take courses in computer science, English, humanities, mathematics, biological/physical sciences, social sciences.

FRESHMAN ADMISSIONS. Selection criteria: Open admissions.

1992 FRESHMAN CLASS PROFILE. 2,000 men and women enrolled. **Characteristics:** 99% from in state, 2% have minority backgrounds. Average age is 20.

FALL-TERM APPLICATIONS. No fee. No closing date; applicants notified on a rolling basis. Early admission available.

STUDENT LIFE. Activities: Student government, magazine, student newspaper, choral groups, drama.

ATHLETICS. NJCAA. **Intercollegiate:** Baseball M, basketball, soccer M, softball W, tennis, volleyball W.

STUDENT SERVICES. Aptitude testing, career counseling, employment service for undergraduates, freshman orientation, health services, on-campus day care, personal counseling, placement service for graduates, special adviser for adult students, veterans counselor, services/facilities for handicapped.

ANNUAL EXPENSES. Tuition and fees (1992-93): $1,156, $3,810 additional for out-of-district students, $4,740 additional for out-of-state students. **Books and supplies:** $440. **Other expenses:** $1,400.

FINANCIAL AID. 20% of freshmen, 20% of continuing students receive some form of aid. 96% of grants, all loans, all jobs based on need. 300 enrolled freshmen were judged to have need, 250 were offered aid. Academic, art, athletic, leadership scholarships available. **Aid applications:** No closing date; priority given to applications received by July 1; applicants notified on a rolling basis.

ADDRESS/TELEPHONE. Alan Hardersen, Registrar, McHenry County College, Route 14 at Lucas Road, Crystal Lake, IL 60012. (815) 455-3700 ext. #245. Fax: (815) 455-3999.

McKendree College
Lebanon, Illinois — CB code: 1456

Admissions: 66% of applicants accepted
Based on:
- ••• School record, test scores
- •• Interview, recommendations
- • Activities, essay, religious affiliation/commitment, special talents

Completion: 85% of freshmen end year in good standing
50% graduate, 15% of these enter graduate study

4-year private liberal arts college, coed, affiliated with United Methodist Church. Founded in 1828. **Accreditation:** Regional. **Undergraduate enrollment:** 360 men, 466 women full time; 234 men, 390 women part time. **Faculty:** 80 total (45 full time), 45 with doctorates or other terminal degrees. **Location:** Rural campus in small town; 10 miles from Fairview Heights, 23 miles from St. Louis, Missouri. **Calendar:** Semester, limited summer session. **Microcomputers:** 120 located in dormitories, libraries, computer centers, campus-wide network. **Special facilities:** McKendree Archives, greenhouse. **Additional facts:** Charter member of Servicemen's Opportunity Colleges. Participant in Federal Aviation Administration College Opportunity Program.

DEGREES OFFERED. BA, BS, BFA. 336 bachelor's degrees awarded in 1992. 58% in business and management, 10% computer sciences, 7% teacher education, 5% health sciences.

UNDERGRADUATE MAJORS. Accounting, art education, biology, business administration and management, business and management, business education, chemistry, clinical laboratory science, communications, computer and information sciences, criminal justice studies, elementary education, English, fine arts, history, information sciences and systems, international relations, journalism, marketing and distribution, marketing management, mathematics, medical laboratory technologies, nursing, occupational therapy, organization communication, philosophy, physical education, political science and government, prelaw, psychology, religion, religious education, secondary education, social sciences, sociology, speech.

ACADEMIC PROGRAMS. Accelerated program, double major, honors program, independent study, internships, student-designed major, study abroad, teacher preparation, evening programs in accounting, business administration, organizational communication. **Remedial services:** Learning center, reduced course load, special counselor, tutoring. **ROTC:** Air Force. **Placement/credit:** AP, CLEP General and Subject, institutional tests; 70 credit hours maximum for bachelor's degree.

ACADEMIC REQUIREMENTS. Freshmen must earn minimum GPA of 1.75 to continue in good standing. 75% of freshmen return for sophomore year. Students must declare major by end of second year. **Graduation requirements:** 128 hours for bachelor's (32 in major). Most students required to take courses in arts/fine arts, computer science, English, history, humanities, mathematics, philosophy/religion, biological/physical sciences, social sciences. **Postgraduate studies:** 2% enter law school, 1% enter medical school, 2% enter MBA programs, 10% enter other graduate study.

FRESHMAN ADMISSIONS. Selection criteria: High school record, class rank, test scores, and counselor's recommendation most important. **High school preparation:** 12 units recommended. Recommended units include English 4, mathematics 3, social science 2 and science 3. Placement tests given for students entering without college preparatory English or math. **Test requirements:** SAT or ACT (ACT preferred); score report by August 1.

1992 FRESHMAN CLASS PROFILE. 271 men applied, 176 accepted, 56 enrolled; 455 women applied, 303 accepted, 87 enrolled. 54% had high school GPA of 3.0 or higher, 41% between 2.0 and 2.99. 21% were in top tenth and 52% were in top quarter of graduating class. **Academic background:** Mid 50% of enrolled freshmen had ACT composite between 18-23. 97% submitted ACT scores. **Characteristics:** 98% from in state, 63% live in college housing, 11% have minority backgrounds, 25% join fraternities/sororities. Average age is 18.

FALL-TERM APPLICATIONS. No fee. No closing date; priority given to applications received by August 1; applicants notified on a rolling basis; must reply by registration. Interview recommended. Deferred admission available.

STUDENT LIFE. Housing: Dormitories (men, women, coed); apartment housing available. Apartment suites, 6 students per unit, available. **Activities:** Student government, student newspaper, yearbook, choral groups, drama, pep band, fraternities, sororities, Model United Nations, Campus Christian Fellowship, Alpha (minority social organization), Alpha Phi Omega, Students Against Social Injustice, Brothers and Sisters in Christ. **Additional information:** Students encouraged to participate in college activities to gain leadership qualities.

ATHLETICS. NAIA. **Intercollegiate:** Baseball M, basketball, cross-country, golf, soccer, softball W, volleyball W. **Intramural:** Badminton, basketball, bowling, cross-country, softball, table tennis, tennis, volleyball.

STUDENT SERVICES. Aptitude testing, career counseling, employment service for undergraduates, freshman orientation, health services, personal counseling, placement service for graduates, veterans counselor, services/facilities for handicapped.

ANNUAL EXPENSES. Tuition and fees: $7,010. **Room and board:** $3,600. **Books and supplies:** $500. **Other expenses:** $800.

FINANCIAL AID. 85% of freshmen, 80% of continuing students receive some form of aid. 96% of grants, 80% of loans, 78% of jobs based on need. Academic, music/drama, athletic, minority scholarships available. **Aid applications:** No closing date; priority given to applications received by June 1; applicants notified on a rolling basis beginning on or about March 1; must reply by May 1 or within 2 weeks if notified thereafter.

ADDRESS/TELEPHONE. Sue Cordon, Director of Admissions, McKendree College, 701 College Road, Lebanon, IL 62254. (618) 537-4481. Fax: (618) 537-6259. (800) 232-7228 (Illinois and adjoining states).

Mennonite College of Nursing
Bloomington, Illinois — CB code: 0530

2-year upper-division private nursing college, coed. Founded in 1983. **Accreditation:** Regional. **Undergraduate enrollment:** 150 men and women. **Faculty:** 23 total (11 full time), 3 with doctorates or other terminal degrees. **Location:** Urban campus in small city; 150 miles from Chicago. **Calendar:** Semester, extensive summer session. **Microcomputers:** 15 located in computer centers. **Special facilities:** State-of-the-art nursing laboratory, broad clinical agency network.

DEGREES OFFERED. BS. 70 bachelor's degrees awarded in 1992. 100% in health sciences.

UNDERGRADUATE MAJORS. Nursing.

ACADEMIC PROGRAMS. Independent study, study abroad, international nursing experience exchange program. **Placement/credit:** Applicants who have graduated from associate degree or diploma nursing program may receive 33 semester hours of credit based on National League for Nursing Examinations and ACT-PEP examinations.

ACADEMIC REQUIREMENTS. Students must declare major on application. **Graduation requirements:** 122 hours for bachelor's (62 in major). Most students required to take courses in English, humanities, philosophy/religion, biological/physical sciences, social sciences.

STUDENT LIFE. Housing: Dormitories (women). **Activities:** Student government, student newspaper, yearbook, choral groups, Faith and Life Club, Community Service Club, Transcultural Nursing Club, Fitness Club.

STUDENT SERVICES. Career counseling, health services, personal counseling, placement service for graduates.

ANNUAL EXPENSES. Tuition and fees: $7,560. **Room and board:** $2,240. **Books and supplies:** $450. **Other expenses:** $600.

FINANCIAL AID. 79% of continuing students receive some form of aid. 45% of grants, 89% of loans, all jobs based on need. Academic scholarships available. **Aid applications:** No closing date; priority given to applications received by April 1; applicants notified on a rolling basis; must reply within 2 weeks. **Additional information:** Many health care agencies provide up to full tuition to nursing students for a commitment to work for agency following graduation.

ADDRESS/TELEPHONE. Mary Ann Watkins, Director of Admissions and Financial Aid, Mennonite College of Nursing, 804 North East Street, Bloomington, IL 61701. (309) 829-0765. Fax: (309) 829-0707.

Midstate College
Peoria, Illinois — CB code: 3329

2-year proprietary junior college, coed. Founded in 1888. **Accreditation:** Regional. **Undergraduate enrollment:** 38 men, 317 women full time; 16 men, 141 women part time. **Location:** Urban campus in small city; 165 miles southwest of Chicago. **Calendar:** Quarter.

FRESHMAN ADMISSIONS. Selection criteria: Scores on Wonderlic Scholastic level and Iowa Tests of Educational Development in mathematics, English, and vocabulary are most important. School achievement record, interview, and essay also considered.

ANNUAL EXPENSES. Tuition and fees: $4,995. **Room and board:** $1,575 room only. **Books and supplies:** $850. **Other expenses:** $1,430.

ADDRESS/TELEPHONE. Steve Sergeant, Director of Admissions, Midstate College, 244 Southwest Jefferson Street, Peoria, IL 61602-9990. (309) 673-6365. Fax: (309) 673-5814.

Millikin University

Decatur, Illinois CB code: 1470

Admissions: 90% of applicants accepted
Based on: ••• School record, test scores
•• Activities, interview, recommendations, special talents
Completion: 92% of freshmen end year in good standing
63% graduate, 14% of these enter graduate study

4-year private university, coed, affiliated with Presbyterian Church (USA). Founded in 1901. **Accreditation:** Regional. **Undergraduate enrollment:** 762 men, 1,041 women full time; 29 men, 60 women part time. **Faculty:** 198 total (120 full time), 138 with doctorates or other terminal degrees. **Location:** Suburban campus in small city; 180 miles from Chicago, 125 miles from St. Louis, Missouri. **Calendar:** Semester, limited summer session. **Microcomputers:** 110 located in computer centers. **Special facilities:** Museum of porcelain, glass, art, and jewelry and Kirkland Art Gallery.

DEGREES OFFERED. BA, BS, BFA. 416 bachelor's degrees awarded in 1992. 28% in business and management, 6% communications, 8% education, 9% health sciences, 8% life sciences, 5% psychology, 7% social sciences, 20% visual and performing arts.

UNDERGRADUATE MAJORS. Accounting, American studies, art education, art therapy, arts management, biological and physical sciences, biology, business administration and management, business and management, business economics, chemistry, communications, computer and information sciences, computer graphics, creative writing, dramatic arts, driver and safety education, economics, education, elementary education, English, English education, experimental psychology, finance, fine arts, foreign languages (multiple emphasis), foreign languages education, French, German, health sciences, history, humanities and social sciences, information sciences and systems, international business management, international relations, international studies, junior high education, liberal/general studies, management information systems, marketing management, mathematics, mathematics education, mental health/human services, music, music business management, music education, music performance, musical theater, nursing, occupational therapy, personnel management, philosophy, physical education, physics, political science and government, predentistry, preengineering, prelaw, premedicine, preveterinary, production/operations management, psychology, religion, religious music, science education, secondary education, social science education, sociology, Spanish, speech/communication/theater education, trade and industrial supervision and management, visual and performing arts.

ACADEMIC PROGRAMS. Double major, honors program, independent study, internships, student-designed major, study abroad, teacher preparation, United Nations semester, Washington semester. **Remedial services:** Tutoring, writing center. **Placement/credit:** AP, CLEP General, IB, institutional tests; 24 credit hours maximum for bachelor's degree.

ACADEMIC REQUIREMENTS. Freshmen must earn minimum GPA of 2.0 to continue in good standing. 88% of freshmen return for sophomore year. Students must declare major by end of second year. **Graduation requirements:** 124 hours for bachelor's (36 in major). Most students required to take courses in arts/fine arts, English, history, humanities, mathematics, philosophy/religion, biological/physical sciences, social sciences. **Postgraduate studies:** 1% enter law school, 1% enter medical school, 1% enter MBA programs, 11% enter other graduate study.

FRESHMAN ADMISSIONS. Selection criteria: School achievement record and test scores most important. Rank should be in top half of class. School recommendation and character references considered. **High school preparation:** 15 units recommended. Recommended units include English 4, foreign language 2, mathematics 3, physical science 1, social science 2 and science 2. **Test requirements:** SAT or ACT; score report by July 1.

1992 FRESHMAN CLASS PROFILE. 554 men applied, 473 accepted, 217 enrolled; 749 women applied, 699 accepted, 304 enrolled. 57% had high school GPA of 3.0 or higher, 28% between 2.0 and 2.99. 27% were in top tenth and 57% were in top quarter of graduating class. **Academic background:** Mid 50% of enrolled freshmen had SAT-V between 400-540, SAT-M between 450-610; ACT composite between 21-27. 16% submitted SAT scores, 93% submitted ACT scores. **Characteristics:** 87% from in state, 96% live in college housing, 5% have minority backgrounds, 22% join fraternities/sororities. Average age is 18.

FALL-TERM APPLICATIONS. $25 fee, may be waived for applicants with need. No closing date; applicants notified on a rolling basis. Audition required for music, music/theater applicants. Interview recommended. Portfolio recommended for art applicants. Deferred admission available.

STUDENT LIFE. Housing: Dormitories (men, women, coed); apartment, fraternity, sorority housing available. **Activities:** Student government, magazine, radio, student newspaper, yearbook, literary magazine, choral groups, concert band, dance, drama, jazz band, marching band, music ensembles, musical theater, opera, pep band, symphony orchestra, speech and forensics, fraternities, sororities, several denominational, political, and ethnic groups.

ATHLETICS. NCAA. **Intercollegiate:** Baseball M, basketball, cross-country, diving, football M, golf M, soccer M, softball W, swimming, tennis, track and field, volleyball W, wrestling M. **Intramural:** Basketball, bowling, football M, softball, table tennis, tennis, volleyball.

STUDENT SERVICES. Career counseling, employment service for undergraduates, freshman orientation, health services, personal counseling, placement service for graduates, services/facilities for handicapped.

ANNUAL EXPENSES. Tuition and fees: $11,331. **Room and board:** $4,168. **Books and supplies:** $450. **Other expenses:** $765.

FINANCIAL AID. 91% of freshmen, 88% of continuing students receive some form of aid. 89% of grants, 94% of loans, 27% of jobs based on need. 459 enrolled freshmen were judged to have need, all were offered aid. Academic, music/drama, art, religious affiliation scholarships available. **Aid applications:** No closing date; priority given to applications received by June 1; applicants notified on a rolling basis beginning on or about January 1; must reply within 2 weeks. **Additional information:** TERI supplemental loan program (private loan based on credit worthiness) available.

ADDRESS/TELEPHONE. James F. Kettelkamp, Dean of Admissions, Millikin University, 1184 West Main, Decatur, IL 62522-9982. (217) 424-6210. (800) 373-7733. Fax: (217) 424-3993.

Monmouth College

Monmouth, Illinois CB code: 1484

Admissions: 85% of applicants accepted
Based on: ••• Recommendations, school record, test scores
•• Activities, essay, interview, special talents
Completion: 95% of freshmen end year in good standing
73% graduate, 22% of these enter graduate study

4-year private liberal arts college, coed, affiliated with Presbyterian Church (USA). Founded in 1853. **Accreditation:** Regional. **Undergraduate enrollment:** 274 men, 302 women full time; 3 men, 6 women part time. **Faculty:** 71 total (56 full time), 51 with doctorates or other terminal degrees. **Location:** Rural campus in large town; 180 miles from Chicago, 70 miles from Peoria. **Calendar:** Semester, limited summer session. **Microcomputers:** Located in libraries, computer centers. **Special facilities:** Ecological field station on the Mississippi River, Len G. Everett art gallery, Monmouthiana Exhibit.

DEGREES OFFERED. BA. 154 bachelor's degrees awarded in 1992. 24% in business and management, 8% communications, 10% education, 5% teacher education, 6% letters/literature, 15% physical sciences, 8% social sciences, 5% visual and performing arts.

UNDERGRADUATE MAJORS. Accounting, art education, biological and physical sciences, biology, business administration and management, business and management, business economics, chemistry, classics, clinical laboratory science, communications, computer and information sciences, dramatic arts, economics, education, elementary education, English, environmental studies, Greek (classical), history, humanities and social sciences, Latin, liberal/general studies, mathematics, music, music education, nursing, physical education, physical sciences, physics, political science and government, psychology, religion, secondary education, social sciences, sociology, Spanish, specific learning disabilities, visual and performing arts.

ACADEMIC PROGRAMS. Accelerated program, double major, honors program, independent study, internships, student-designed major, study abroad, Washington semester, cross-registration, off-campus programs in cooperation with Associated Colleges of the Midwest; liberal arts/career combination in engineering, health sciences. **Remedial services:** Learning center, special counselor, tutoring. **ROTC:** Army. **Placement/credit:** AP, institutional tests; 30 credit hours maximum for bachelor's degree.

ACADEMIC REQUIREMENTS. Freshmen must earn minimum GPA of 1.8 to continue in good standing. 89% of freshmen return for sophomore year. Students must declare major by end of second year. **Graduation requirements:** 124 hours for bachelor's (24 in major). Most students required to take courses in arts/fine arts, computer science, English, foreign languages, history, humanities, mathematics, philosophy/religion, biological/physical sciences, social sciences. **Postgraduate studies:** 4% enter law school, 5% enter medical school, 6% enter MBA programs, 7% enter other graduate study. **Additional information:** General education courses intertwined throughout 4 years of study, complementing and paralleling major program.

FRESHMAN ADMISSIONS. Selection criteria: School achievement record most important, followed by recommendations of counselor and teacher, test scores, and interview. **High school preparation:** 15 units required. Required and recommended units include English 4, foreign language 2-3, mathematics 3, social science 3 and science 2-3. **Test requirements:** SAT or ACT (ACT preferred); score report by May 1.

1992 FRESHMAN CLASS PROFILE. 247 men applied, 194 accepted,

58 enrolled; 272 women applied, 245 accepted, 66 enrolled. 78% had high school GPA of 3.0 or higher, 22% between 2.0 and 2.99. 26% were in top tenth and 56% were in top quarter of graduating class. **Academic background:** Mid 50% of enrolled freshmen had ACT composite between 23-27. 90% submitted ACT scores. **Characteristics:** 75% from in state, 97% live in college housing, 14% have minority backgrounds, 3% are foreign students, 40% join fraternities/sororities. Average age is 18.

FALL-TERM APPLICATIONS. $25 fee, may be waived for applicants with need. Closing date April 1; priority given to applications received by December 1; applicants notified on or about April 15; must reply by May 1. Audition required for music, drama applicants. Portfolio required for art, creative writing applicants. Essay required. Interview recommended. CRDA. Deferred and early admission available. EDP-F.

STUDENT LIFE. Housing: Dormitories (men, women, coed); fraternity housing available. Single room option available to all students. **Activities:** Student government, film, magazine, radio, student newspaper, yearbook, choral groups, concert band, drama, jazz band, music ensembles, musical theater, pep band, bagpipe band, fraternities, sororities, Black Action and Affairs Council, Christian fellowship groups, interdenominational religious group.

ATHLETICS. NCAA. **Intercollegiate:** Baseball M, basketball, cross-country, football M, soccer, softball W, track and field, volleyball W, wrestling M. **Intramural:** Archery, badminton, basketball, cross-country, golf, racquetball, soccer, softball, swimming, table tennis, tennis, track and field, volleyball, wrestling M.

STUDENT SERVICES. Aptitude testing, career counseling, employment service for undergraduates, freshman orientation, health services, personal counseling, placement service for graduates.

ANNUAL EXPENSES. Tuition and fees: $13,000. **Room and board:** $3,800. **Books and supplies:** $400. **Other expenses:** $150.

FINANCIAL AID. 86% of freshmen, 88% of continuing students receive some form of aid. 73% of grants, 99% of loans, 67% of jobs based on need. 93 enrolled freshmen were judged to have need, all were offered aid. Academic, music/drama, art, religious affiliation, minority scholarships available. **Aid applications:** Closing date March 1; applicants notified on or about April 1; must reply within 4 weeks.

ADDRESS/TELEPHONE. Dr. David Long, Dean of Admission, Monmouth College, Monmouth College, Monmouth, IL 61462-9989. (309) 457-2131. (800) 747-2687. Fax: (309) 457-2141.

Montay College
Chicago, Illinois CB code: 1220

2-year private junior, liberal arts college, coed, affiliated with Roman Catholic Church. Founded in 1926. **Accreditation:** Regional. **Undergraduate enrollment:** 26 men, 41 women full time; 35 men, 133 women part time. **Faculty:** 56 total (5 full time), 3 with doctorates or other terminal degrees. **Location:** Urban campus in very large city; 12 miles from downtown. **Calendar:** Semester, limited summer session. Extensive evening/early morning classes. **Microcomputers:** 12 located in computer centers. **Additional facts:** 3 off-campus sites.

DEGREES OFFERED. AA, AAS. 19 associate degrees awarded in 1992. 21% in business and management, 26% teacher education, 10% health sciences.

UNDERGRADUATE MAJORS. Business and management, computer and information sciences, early childhood education, education, fine arts, gerontology, health sciences, liberal/general studies, music, prelaw, social sciences.

ACADEMIC PROGRAMS. 2-year transfer program, independent study, internships. **Remedial services:** Learning center, preadmission summer program, reduced course load, remedial instruction, special counselor, tutoring. **Placement/credit:** AP, CLEP General and Subject, institutional tests; 15 credit hours maximum for associate degree.

ACADEMIC REQUIREMENTS. Freshmen must earn minimum GPA of 2.0 to continue in good standing. 75% of freshmen return for sophomore year. Students must declare major on application. **Graduation requirements:** 60 hours for associate. Most students required to take courses in arts/fine arts, English, history, humanities, mathematics, philosophy/religion, biological/physical sciences, social sciences.

FRESHMAN ADMISSIONS. Selection criteria: High school GPA most important. **High school preparation:** 16 units required. Required units include English 4, mathematics 3, social science 3 and science 3.

1992 FRESHMAN CLASS PROFILE. 50 men applied, 45 accepted, 30 enrolled; 70 women applied, 88 accepted, 88 enrolled. 1% had high school GPA of 3.0 or higher, 96% between 2.0 and 2.99. **Academic background:** Mid 50% of enrolled freshmen had ACT composite between 8-15. 76% submitted ACT scores. **Characteristics:** 96% from in state, 100% commute, 59% have minority backgrounds, 4% are foreign students. Average age is 19.

FALL-TERM APPLICATIONS. $20 fee, may be waived for applicants with need. Closing date August 31; priority given to applications received by August 1; applicants notified on a rolling basis; must reply by registration. Interview required. Deferred admission available.

STUDENT LIFE. Activities: Student government, choral groups, symphony orchestra, campus ministry.

STUDENT SERVICES. Career counseling, freshman orientation, health services, personal counseling, special adviser for adult students.

ANNUAL EXPENSES. Tuition and fees: $5,630. **Books and supplies:** $500. **Other expenses:** $990.

FINANCIAL AID. 56% of freshmen, 56% of continuing students receive some form of aid. All grants, 75% of loans based on need. 26 enrolled freshmen were judged to have need, all were offered aid. Academic, music/drama, art, minority scholarships available. **Aid applications:** No closing date; priority given to applications received by June 1; applicants notified on a rolling basis; must reply within 2 weeks.

ADDRESS/TELEPHONE. Scott Dalhouse, Director of Admissions and Records, Montay College, 3750 West Peterson Avenue, Chicago, IL 60659-3115. (312) 539-1919. Fax: (312) 539-1913.

Moody Bible Institute
Chicago, Illinois CB code: 1486

4-year private Bible college, coed, interdenominational/evangelical. Founded in 1886. **Accreditation:** Regional. **Undergraduate enrollment:** 834 men, 532 women full time; 34 men, 22 women part time. **Graduate enrollment:** 32 men, 26 women full time; 6 men, 9 women part time. **Faculty:** 96 total (84 full time), 40 with doctorates or other terminal degrees. **Location:** Urban campus in very large city; 1 mile from the Loop. **Calendar:** Semester, limited summer session. **Microcomputers:** 12 located in computer centers.

DEGREES OFFERED. BA, BS, MA. 280 bachelor's degrees awarded in 1992. 12% in communications, 6% engineering technologies, 82% philosophy, religion, theology. Graduate degrees offered in 1 major field of study.

UNDERGRADUATE MAJORS. Aeronautical technology, Bible studies, communications, missionary studies, religious education, religious music, theological studies.

ACADEMIC PROGRAMS. Double major, independent study, internships, study abroad. **Remedial services:** Learning center, reduced course load, remedial instruction, special counselor, tutoring. **Placement/credit:** AP, CLEP General and Subject, institutional tests; 12 credit hours maximum for bachelor's degree.

ACADEMIC REQUIREMENTS. Freshmen must earn minimum GPA of 1.75 to continue in good standing. 73% of freshmen return for sophomore year. Students must declare major by end of first year. **Graduation requirements:** 130 hours for bachelor's (24 in major). Most students required to take courses in arts/fine arts, English, foreign languages, history, mathematics, philosophy/religion, biological/physical sciences, social sciences. **Postgraduate studies:** 10% enter other graduate study.

FRESHMAN ADMISSIONS. Selection criteria: Rank in top half of graduating class and/or high school GPA above 2.3. Applicants must have been Christians for at least 1 year. Membership in Evangelical church required. College-preparatory program recommended. **Test requirements:** ACT; score report by May 15. Numerical Ability Test and Test of Mechanical Comprehension required for missionary aviation applicants.

1992 FRESHMAN CLASS PROFILE. 229 men, 159 women enrolled. **Academic background:** Mid 50% of enrolled freshmen had ACT composite between 19-25. 100% submitted ACT scores. **Characteristics:** 22% from in state, 89% live in college housing, 5% have minority backgrounds, 7% are foreign students. Average age is 18.

FALL-TERM APPLICATIONS. $35 fee. Closing date May 1; applicants notified on a rolling basis; must reply by March 1 if notified before February, by May 1 if notified in February or March, by July 1 if notified in April or May, or as soon as possibleif notified thereafter. Audition required for music applicants. Deferred admission available.

STUDENT LIFE. Housing: Dormitories (men, women); apartment housing available. **Activities:** Student government, radio, student newspaper, yearbook, choral groups, concert band, music ensembles, Student Missionary Fellowship, Gospel teams, Afro Awareness Fellowship, International Student Fellowship, Big Brother/Big Sister Program, pre-aviation club, student wives fellowship, married students fellowship, residence activities coucil.

ATHLETICS. Intercollegiate: Basketball, soccer M, volleyball W. **Intramural:** Badminton, basketball, cross-country, football M, racquetball, soccer, swimming, table tennis, volleyball, water polo, wrestling M. **Clubs:** Volleyball.

STUDENT SERVICES. Aptitude testing, career counseling, employment service for undergraduates, freshman orientation, health services, personal counseling, placement service for graduates, veterans counselor, services/facilities for handicapped.

ANNUAL EXPENSES. Tuition and fees: $754. **Room and board:** $3,750. **Books and supplies:** $400. **Other expenses:** $500.

FINANCIAL AID. 2% of freshmen, 4% of continuing students receive some form of aid. 83% of grants based on need. Leadership scholarships available. **Aid applications:** No closing date; applicants notified on a rolling basis. **Additional information:** No financial aid for freshmen. Some aid available to upperclassmen based on need or merit.

ADDRESS/TELEPHONE. Philip Van Wynen, Dean of Enrollment Management/Registrar, Moody Bible Institute, 820 North La Salle Boulevard, Chicago, IL 60610-3284. (312) 329-4266.

Moraine Valley Community College
Palos Hills, Illinois CB code: 1524

2-year public community college, coed. Founded in 1968. **Accreditation:** Regional. **Undergraduate enrollment:** 2,412 men, 2,364 women full time; 3,688 men, 5,610 women part time. **Faculty:** 636 total (183 full time), 37 with doctorates or other terminal degrees. **Location:** Suburban campus in large town; 7 miles from Chicago. **Calendar:** Semester, limited summer session. Saturday and extensive evening/early morning classes. **Microcomputers:** 419 located in libraries, classrooms, computer centers. **Special facilities:** Nature study area, Center for Contemporary Technology, Fine and Performing Arts Center.

DEGREES OFFERED. AA, AS, AAS. 1,113 associate degrees awarded in 1992. 8% in health sciences, 7% allied health, 70% multi/interdisciplinary studies.

UNDERGRADUATE MAJORS. Automotive mechanics, automotive technology, biological and physical sciences, business administration and management, business and management, business and office, business computer/console/peripheral equipment operation, child development/care/guidance, computer and information sciences, criminal justice studies, drafting and design technology, electrical and electronics equipment repair, electrical installation, electrical technology, electronic technology, energy conservation and use technology, engineering and engineering-related technologies, finance, fire control and safety technology, food management, hotel/motel and restaurant management, industrial equipment maintenance and repair, industrial technology, information sciences and systems, liberal/general studies, management information systems, marketing and distribution, mechanical design technology, medical laboratory technologies, medical records technology, nursing, occupational safety and health technology, parks and recreation management, quality control technology, radiograph medical technology, real estate, recreation therapy, respiratory therapy, respiratory therapy technology, secretarial and related programs, tourism, trade and industrial supervision and management, transportation and travel marketing, transportation management.

ACADEMIC PROGRAMS. 2-year transfer program, dual enrollment of high school students, honors program, independent study, internships, study abroad, weekend college. **Remedial services:** Learning center, reduced course load, remedial instruction, special counselor, tutoring. **Placement/credit:** AP, CLEP General and Subject, institutional tests; 47 credit hours maximum for associate degree.

ACADEMIC REQUIREMENTS. No policy requiring minimum GPA; records of students having academic difficulty are reviewed individually. Health science students must maintain 2.0 GPA in major. **Graduation requirements:** 62 hours for associate. Most students required to take courses in English, humanities, mathematics, biological/physical sciences, social sciences.

FRESHMAN ADMISSIONS. Selection criteria: Open admissions. Selective admissions to allied health and nursing programs. **Test requirements:** ACT required for selected health science programs. **Additional information:** Mathematics and communications assessment required following admission.

1992 FRESHMAN CLASS PROFILE. 1,889 men, 2,030 women enrolled. **Characteristics:** 99% from in state, 100% commute, 15% have minority backgrounds, 1% are foreign students.

FALL-TERM APPLICATIONS. No fee. No closing date; applicants notified on a rolling basis; must reply by registration. Health science applicants must reply within 2 weeks.

STUDENT LIFE. Activities: Student government, magazine, student newspaper, choral groups, concert band, dance, drama, jazz band, BACCHUS (Boost Alcohol Consciousness Concerning the Health of University Students), Alliance of Latin American Students, Black Student Union, Arab Student Union, Young Republicans, Total Access for Students and Community.

ATHLETICS. NJCAA. **Intercollegiate:** Baseball M, basketball, football M, golf M, softball W, volleyball W. **Intramural:** Badminton, basketball, softball, tennis, volleyball.

STUDENT SERVICES. Aptitude testing, career counseling, employment service for undergraduates, freshman orientation, on-campus day care, personal counseling, placement service for graduates, special adviser for adult students, services/facilities for handicapped.

ANNUAL EXPENSES. Tuition and fees (1992-93): $1,172, $2,520 additional for out-of-district students, $3,180 additional for out-of-state students. **Books and supplies:** $405. **Other expenses:** $1,256.

FINANCIAL AID. 25% of continuing students receive some form of aid. 61% of grants, 82% of loans, 7% of jobs based on need. Academic, state/district residency scholarships available. **Aid applications:** No closing date; priority given to applications received by June 1; applicants notified on a rolling basis beginning on or about August 15; must reply within 4 weeks.

ADDRESS/TELEPHONE. Eric Gunnink, Dean of Enrollment Services, Moraine Valley Community College, 10900 South 88th Avenue, Palos Hills, IL 60465-0937. (708) 974-2110.

Morrison Institute of Technology
Morrison, Illinois CB code: 1269

2-year private technical college, coed. Founded in 1973. **Undergraduate enrollment:** 155 men, 17 women full time. **Faculty:** 14 total (10 full time), 5 with doctorates or other terminal degrees. **Location:** Rural campus in small town; 100 miles from Chicago, 50 miles from Quad Cities (Davenport, Moline, East Moline, Bettendorf). **Calendar:** Semester, extensive summer session. **Microcomputers:** Located in classrooms, computer centers. **Special facilities:** 3 computer-aided design (CAD) laboratories. **Additional facts:** Accredited by Accreditation Board of Engineering and Technology.

DEGREES OFFERED. AAS. 86 associate degrees awarded in 1992. 100% in engineering technologies.

UNDERGRADUATE MAJORS. Architectural technologies, civil technology, computer technology, drafting and design technology, electromechanical technology, engineering and engineering-related technologies, industrial technology, instrumentation technology, manufacturing technology, mechanical design technology, survey and mapping technology.

ACADEMIC PROGRAMS. 2-year transfer program, double major, dual enrollment of high school students, student-designed major, cross-registration. **Remedial services:** Reduced course load, tutoring. **Placement/credit:** Institutional tests; 30 credit hours maximum for associate degree.

ACADEMIC REQUIREMENTS. Freshmen must earn minimum GPA of 2.0 to continue in good standing. 70% of freshmen return for sophomore year. Students must declare major on enrollment. **Graduation requirements:** 64 hours for associate (40 in major). Most students required to take courses in computer science, English, mathematics, biological/physical sciences. **Additional information:** 4 semesters of computer-aided design required for all majors.

FRESHMAN ADMISSIONS. Selection criteria: Open admissions. Recommended units include mathematics 2 and physical science 1. College-preparatory program recommended, including mathematics (algebra and geometry) and drafting.

1992 FRESHMAN CLASS PROFILE. 81 men, 10 women enrolled. **Characteristics:** 70% from in state, 60% commute, 17% have minority backgrounds. Average age is 20.

FALL-TERM APPLICATIONS. May be waived for applicants with need. $50 fee applied to first semester tuition. $25 refundable if not accepted or enrolled. Closing date October 15; applicants notified on a rolling basis. Interview recommended. Deferred and early admission available.

STUDENT LIFE. Housing: Apartment, cooperative housing available. **Activities:** Student government, drama, musical theater.

ATHLETICS. Intramural: Baseball M, basketball M, bowling, golf, softball, swimming, table tennis, tennis, track and field, volleyball.

STUDENT SERVICES. Career counseling, employment service for undergraduates, freshman orientation, personal counseling, placement service for graduates.

ANNUAL EXPENSES. Tuition and fees (projected): $6,500. **Room and board:** $2,000. **Books and supplies:** $800. **Other expenses:** $1,200.

FINANCIAL AID. 60% of freshmen, 40% of continuing students receive some form of aid. 99% of grants, 91% of loans, all jobs based on need. Academic scholarships available. **Aid applications:** No closing date; applicants notified on a rolling basis; must reply within 2 weeks.

ADDRESS/TELEPHONE. Dr. Dale W. Trimpe, Director of Admissions, Morrison Institute of Technology, 701 Portland Avenue, Morrison, IL 61270-0410. (815) 772-7218 ext. 15. Fax: (815) 772-7548.

Morton College
Cicero, Illinois CB code: 1489

2-year public community college, coed. Founded in 1924. **Accreditation:** Regional. **Undergraduate enrollment:** 338 men, 506 women full time; 1,542 men, 2,312 women part time. **Faculty:** 275 total (57 full time), 4 with doctorates or other terminal degrees. **Location:** Suburban campus in small city; 9 miles from downtown Chicago. **Calendar:** Semester, limited summer session. Saturday and extensive evening/early morning classes. **Microcomputers:** 106 located in libraries, classrooms, computer centers. **Special facilities:** Planetarium.

DEGREES OFFERED. AA, AS, AAS. 300 associate degrees awarded in 1992.

UNDERGRADUATE MAJORS. Accounting, actuarial sciences, air conditioning/heating/refrigeration mechanics, air conditioning/heating/refrigeration technology, architecture, astronomy, automotive mechanics, automotive technology, biochemistry, biology, business administration and management, business and management, business data processing and related programs, chemistry, data processing, drafting, drafting and design technology, earth sciences, education, electronic technology, engineering, finance, fine arts, geography, health sciences, history, industrial technology, law enforcement and corrections technologies, legal secretary, liberal/general studies, marketing and distribution, marketing management, mathematics, medical secretary, music, nursing, philosophy, physical sciences, physical therapy assistant, physics, political science and government, practical nursing, prelaw, premedicine, prepharmacy, preveterinary, psychology, public administration, real estate, secretarial and related programs, social sciences, social work, sociology, visual and performing arts.

ACADEMIC PROGRAMS. 2-year transfer program, double major, dual enrollment of high school students, honors program, internships, student-designed major. **Remedial services:** Learning center, remedial instruction, tutoring. **Placement/credit:** AP, CLEP General, institutional tests; 30 credit hours maximum for associate degree.

ACADEMIC REQUIREMENTS. Freshmen must earn minimum GPA of 1.5 to continue in good standing. **Graduation requirements:** 62 hours for associate. Most students required to take courses in English, humanities, mathematics, biological/physical sciences, social sciences.

FRESHMAN ADMISSIONS. Selection criteria: Open admissions. Dental assisting, nursing,and physical therapist assisting programs have limited number of spaces. Applicants should file before March 1. Preference given to in-district applicants using class rank, math and science course prerequisites, and placement tests as guides. Recommended units include English 4, foreign language 2, mathematics 3, social science 3 and science 3.

1992 FRESHMAN CLASS PROFILE. 1,385 men and women enrolled. **Characteristics:** 100% from in state, 100% commute.

FALL-TERM APPLICATIONS. $10 fee. No closing date; applicants notified on a rolling basis; must reply by registration. Interview required for dental assistant, nursing, physical therapy assistant applicants.

STUDENT LIFE. Activities: Student government, magazine, student newspaper, choral groups, drama, jazz band, music ensembles, musical theater, Alpha and Omega, Nursing Students Association, Phi Theta Kappa, ecology club, Returning Adult Students Club, College Ambassadors, Hispanic Heritage Club.

ATHLETICS. NJCAA. **Intercollegiate:** Baseball M, basketball, cross-country, golf, softball W, tennis, volleyball W. **Intramural:** Basketball, bowling, cross-country, golf, racquetball, skiing, softball M, table tennis, volleyball. **Clubs:** Volleyball, skiing.

STUDENT SERVICES. Aptitude testing, career counseling, employment service for undergraduates, freshman orientation, personal counseling, placement service for graduates, special adviser for adult students, on-campus child learning center, services/facilities for handicapped.

ANNUAL EXPENSES. Tuition and fees: $1,320, $2,200 additional for out-of-district students, $3,115 additional for out-of-state students. **Books and supplies:** $400. **Other expenses:** $900.

FINANCIAL AID. 20% of continuing students receive some form of aid. 79% of grants, 89% of loans, 8% of jobs based on need. Academic, music/drama, art, athletic, state/district residency, leadership, minority scholarships available. **Aid applications:** No closing date; priority given to applications received by June 1; applicants notified on a rolling basis beginning on or about August 1.

ADDRESS/TELEPHONE. Patricia A. Matijevic, Director of Admissions and Records, Morton College, 3801 South Central Avenue, Cicero, IL 60650. (708) 656-8000 ext.342. Fax: (708) 656-9592.

NAES College
Chicago, Illinois — CB code: 1533

4-year private liberal arts college, coed. Founded in 1974. **Accreditation:** Regional. **Undergraduate enrollment:** 20 men, 38 women full time; 2 men, 14 women part time. **Location:** Urban campus in very large city. **Calendar:** Semester. **Additional facts:** An American Indian community-based liberal arts college. Other campus sites at Fort Peck reservation in Montana and Menominee Reservation in Wisconsin. Two urban campuses (Chicago, Illinois and Minneapolis-St. Paul, Minnesota).

FRESHMAN ADMISSIONS. Selection criteria: Student must be 24 years or older or have 60 hours of transfer credit and be board member, staff member, or volunteer in Indian organization or organization that serves Indian community. Special admissions for some other students.

ANNUAL EXPENSES. Tuition and fees: $4,220. **Books and supplies:** $250.

ADDRESS/TELEPHONE. Registrar, NAES College, 2838 West Peterson Avenue, Chicago, IL 60659. (312) 761-5000. Fax: (312) 761-3808.

National College of Chiropractic
Lombard, Illinois — CB code: 1567

2-year upper-division private health science college, coed. Founded in 1906. **Accreditation:** Regional. **Undergraduate enrollment:** 273 men and women. **Graduate enrollment:** 449 men and women. **Faculty:** 92 total (70 full time), 72 with doctorates or other terminal degrees. **Location:** Suburban campus in large town; 22 miles from Chicago. **Calendar:** Trimester, extensive summer session. **Microcomputers:** Located in libraries.

DEGREES OFFERED. BS, DC. 200 bachelor's degrees awarded in 1992. 100% in health sciences. Graduate degrees offered in 1 major field of study.

UNDERGRADUATE MAJORS. Biology, chiropractic.

ACADEMIC PROGRAMS. Accelerated program. **Remedial services:** Learning center, reduced course load, tutoring. **Placement/credit:** Maximum of 20 semester hours of credit by examination may be counted toward degree in courses other than natural biological and physical sciences.

ACADEMIC REQUIREMENTS. Students must declare major on application. **Graduation requirements:** 202 hours for bachelor's (202 in major). Most students required to take courses in English, humanities, biological/physical sciences, social sciences. **Additional information:** Curriculum primarily 5-year program leading to Doctor of Chiropractic degree.

STUDENT LIFE. Housing: Dormitories (men, women); apartment housing available. **Activities:** Student government, student newspaper, yearbook, fraternities, sororities, 24 student organizations providing a broad spectrum of religious, political, professional, organizational, and social activities.

ATHLETICS. Intercollegiate: Rugby M. **Intramural:** Basketball, bowling, soccer M, softball, volleyball.

STUDENT SERVICES. Employment service for undergraduates, health services, personal counseling, placement service for graduates.

ANNUAL EXPENSES. Tuition and fees (1992-93): $8,000. **Room and board:** $1,800 room only. **Books and supplies:** $800. **Other expenses:** $1,915.

FINANCIAL AID. 85% of continuing students receive some form of aid. Grants, loans, jobs available. Academic, minority scholarships available. **Aid applications:** No closing date; priority given to applications received by August 1; applicants notified on a rolling basis; must reply within 2 weeks.

ADDRESS/TELEPHONE. Jo Beth Castleberry, Director of Admissions, National College of Chiropractic, 200 East Roosevelt Road, Lombard, IL 60148. (708) 629-2000. (800) 826-NATL. Fax: (708) 629-0282.

National-Louis University
Evanston, Illinois — CB code: 1551

Admissions: 75% of applicants accepted
Based on: ••• Interview, school record
•• Activities, recommendations, test scores
• Essay
Completion: 89% of freshmen end year in good standing
45% graduate; 30% of these enter graduate study

4-year private university and teachers college, coed. Founded in 1886. **Accreditation:** Regional. **Undergraduate enrollment:** 938 men, 1,812 women full time; 98 men, 383 women part time. **Graduate enrollment:** 135 men, 626 women full time; 477 men, 3,049 women part time. **Faculty:** 243 total (231 full time), 150 with doctorates or other terminal degrees. **Location:** Suburban campus in small city; 10 miles from Chicago. **Calendar:** Quarter, limited summer session. **Microcomputers:** 300 located in computer centers. **Special facilities:** Elementary demonstration school for practice teaching and observation. **Additional facts:** Branch campuses in downtown Chicago and west suburban Wheaton. Chicago Loop campus houses College of Management and Business. Wheaton campus has upper-division undergraduate and graduate programs only. Programs for employed adults available both on and off campus. Out-of-state academic centers offering selected undergraduate and graduate programs to employed adults are located in Atlanta.

DEGREES OFFERED. BA, BS, MA, MS, MEd, EdD. 957 bachelor's degrees awarded in 1992. 51% in business and management, 27% teacher education, 10% parks/recreation, protective services, public affairs. Graduate degrees offered in 28 major fields of study.

UNDERGRADUATE MAJORS. Accounting, allied health, anthropology, applied mathematics, Asian/bilingual multicultural studies, behavioral sciences, biological and physical sciences, business administration and management, clinical laboratory science, community health work, community services, computer and information sciences, dramatic arts, early childhood education, education, elementary education, English, family and community services, fine arts, gerontology, health care administration, human development, management information systems, mathematics, medical laboratory technologies, mental health/human services, multicultural studies, psychology, radiograph medical technology, rehabilitation counseling/services, respiratory therapy, respiratory therapy technology, social sciences, sports management, visual and performing arts.

ACADEMIC PROGRAMS. Accelerated program, double major, education specialist degree, honors program, independent study, internships, study abroad, teacher preparation; liberal arts/career combination in health sciences. **Remedial services:** Learning center, preadmission summer program, reduced course load, remedial instruction, special counselor, tutoring. **Placement/credit:** AP, CLEP General and Subject, institutional tests; 135 credit hours maximum for bachelor's degree.

ACADEMIC REQUIREMENTS. No policy requiring minimum GPA; records of students having academic difficulty are reviewed individually. 90% of freshmen return for sophomore year. Students must declare major on enrollment. **Graduation requirements:** 180 hours for bachelor's (45 in major). Most students required to take courses in English, history, humanities, mathematics, biological/physical sciences. **Additional information:** Degree-completion programs for certified and/or licensed professionals available in allied health leadership, in management, and in applied behavioral science.

FRESHMAN ADMISSIONS. Selection criteria: Rank in top half of class and interview most important. Test scores, recommendations, and adult student's professional experience also considered. **High school preparation:** 15 units required. Required units include biological science 1, English 4, mathematics 2, physical science 1 and social science 3. One unit U.S. government or U.S. history recommended. **Test requirements:** SAT or ACT; score report by September 1. SAT/ACT not required of adult students. **Additional information:** Entering students whose native language is not English assessed by Language Institute counselors. Such testing may be used in place of TOEFL for nonresident international students.

1992 FRESHMAN CLASS PROFILE. 131 men applied, 95 accepted, 76 enrolled; 339 women applied, 258 accepted, 197 enrolled. **Academic background:** Mid 50% of enrolled freshmen had ACT composite between 12-17. 27% submitted ACT scores. **Characteristics:** 99% from in state, 60% commute, 32% have minority backgrounds. Average age is 24.

FALL-TERM APPLICATIONS. $25 fee, may be waived for applicants with need. No closing date; applicants notified on a rolling basis; must reply by May 1 or within 4 weeks if notified thereafter. Interview required for honors, provisional applicants. Essay required for honors applicants. CRDA. Deferred and early admission available.

STUDENT LIFE. Housing: Dormitories (coed). **Activities:** Student government, student newspaper, yearbook, poetry magazine, choral groups, drama, music ensembles, musical theater, sororities, Council for Exceptional Children, Fellowship of Christian Athletes, international students association, human services forum, early childhood club, Circle-K International.

ATHLETICS. NAIA. **Intercollegiate:** Basketball W, soccer M, softball W, volleyball W. **Intramural:** Swimming, table tennis, tennis, volleyball.

STUDENT SERVICES. Aptitude testing, career counseling, employment service for undergraduates, freshman orientation, health services, personal counseling, placement service for graduates, special adviser for adult students, services/facilities for handicapped.

ANNUAL EXPENSES. Tuition and fees (1992-93): $8,550. **Room and board:** $4,489. **Books and supplies:** $500. **Other expenses:** $1,000.

FINANCIAL AID. 85% of freshmen, 85% of continuing students receive some form of aid. 96% of grants, 72% of loans, 78% of jobs based on need. Academic, athletic scholarships available. **Aid applications:** No closing date; priority given to applications received by June 15; applicants notified on a rolling basis beginning on or about April 1; must reply by May 1 or within 2 weeks if notified thereafter.

ADDRESS/TELEPHONE. Randall Berd, Director Student Enrollment, National-Louis University, 2840 Sheridan Road, Evanston, IL 60201-1796. (708) 256-6771. (800) 443-5522. Fax: (708) 256-1057.

North Central College

Naperville, Illinois — CB code: 1555

Admissions: 78% of applicants accepted
Based on:
- ••• School record, test scores
- •• Interview
- • Activities, essay, recommendations, special talents

Completion: 92% of freshmen end year in good standing
60% graduate, 16% of these enter graduate study

4-year private liberal arts college, coed, affiliated with United Methodist Church. Founded in 1861. **Accreditation:** Regional. **Undergraduate enrollment:** 701 men, 598 women full time; 441 men, 382 women part time. **Graduate enrollment:** 413 men and women. **Faculty:** 178 total (97 full time), 97 with doctorates or other terminal degrees. **Location:** Suburban campus in small city; 29 miles from Chicago. **Calendar:** Trimester, limited summer session. Saturday and extensive evening/early morning classes. **Microcomputers:** 110 located in dormitories, libraries, computer centers. **Additional facts:** Member of the council of West Suburban Colleges, which includes Wheaton College and Illinois Benedictine College. Degree candidates may enroll for courses in other schools without additional tuition.

DEGREES OFFERED. BA, BS, MA, MS, MBA. 480 bachelor's degrees awarded in 1992. 37% in business and management, 9% communications, 15% computer sciences, 6% psychology, 6% social sciences. Graduate degrees offered in 4 major fields of study.

UNDERGRADUATE MAJORS. Accounting, anthropology, art education, biochemistry, biological and physical sciences, biology, business administration and management, business and management, business economics, chemistry, classics, communications, community psychology, computer and information sciences, counseling psychology, creative writing, dramatic arts, earth sciences, economics, education, elementary education, English, English education, English literature, finance, fine arts, foreign languages (multiple emphasis), foreign languages education, French, German, Greek (classical), health education, health sciences, history, humanities and social sciences, industrial and organizational psychology, information sciences and systems, international business management, international relations, international studies, Japanese, journalism, Latin, liberal/general studies, management information systems, marketing and distribution, marketing management, mathematics, mathematics education, medical laboratory technologies, music, organizational communication, philosophy, physical education, physical sciences, physics, political science and government, predentistry, preengineering, prelaw, premedicine, preveterinary, psychology, public relations, radio/television broadcasting, reading education, religion, science education, secondary education, social science education, social studies education, sociology, Spanish, speech, speech/communication/theater education, sports medicine, studio art.

ACADEMIC PROGRAMS. Accelerated program, cooperative education, double major, honors program, independent study, internships, student-designed major, study abroad, teacher preparation, visiting/exchange student program, weekend college, New York semester, United Nations semester, Washington semester, 3+2 programs in nursing and medical technology with Rush University; liberal arts/career combination in engineering, health sciences; combined bachelor's/graduate program in business administration. **Remedial services:** Preadmission summer program, remedial instruction, tutoring. **ROTC:** Air Force, Army, Naval. **Placement/credit:** AP, CLEP General and Subject, institutional tests; 36 credit hours maximum for bachelor's degree.

ACADEMIC REQUIREMENTS. Freshmen must earn minimum GPA of 1.6 to continue in good standing. 76% of freshmen return for sophomore year. Students must declare major by end of second year. **Graduation requirements:** 120 hours for bachelor's (40 in major). Most students required to take courses in arts/fine arts, English, history, humanities, mathematics, philosophy/religion, biological/physical sciences, social sciences. **Additional information:** Students may take botany courses for credit at Morton Arboretum in nearby Lisle.

FRESHMAN ADMISSIONS. Selection criteria: Academic record, rank in top half of class, SAT or ACT scores, personal character all considered. **High school preparation:** 12 units required. Required and recommended units include English 3-4, mathematics 2-3 and science 3-3. Foreign language 2, physical science 2 and social science 2 recommended. **Test requirements:** SAT or ACT; score report by September 1. **Additional information:** Transfer academic scholarship available with 3.3 GPA and 1 year transferrable credit.

1992 FRESHMAN CLASS PROFILE. 522 men applied, 389 accepted, 138 enrolled; 524 women applied, 430 accepted, 157 enrolled. 73% had high school GPA of 3.0 or higher, 22% between 2.0 and 2.99. 30% were in top tenth and 61% were in top quarter of graduating class. **Academic background:** Mid 50% of enrolled freshmen had SAT-V between 430-550, SAT-M between 480-620; ACT composite between 22-27. 32% submitted SAT scores, 87% submitted ACT scores. **Characteristics:** 73% from in state, 84% live in college housing, 12% have minority backgrounds, 1% are foreign students. Average age is 18.

FALL-TERM APPLICATIONS. $20 fee, may be waived for applicants with need. No closing date; priority given to applications received by June 1; applicants notified on a rolling basis; must reply within 4 weeks. Interview recommended for marginal applicants. Essay recommended for marginal applicants. CRDA. Deferred admission available.

STUDENT LIFE. Housing: Dormitories (men, women, coed). Houses available on campus that can be rented to juniors and seniors. **Activities:** Student government, radio, student newspaper, yearbook, literary magazine, choral groups, concert band, drama, jazz band, music ensembles, musical theater, pep band, United Methodist Student Organization, multi-cultural student organization, Fellowship of Christian Athletes, non-traditional student organization, Leadership, Ethics, and Values Program, POLIS, Amnesty International.

ATHLETICS. NCAA. **Intercollegiate:** Baseball M, basketball, cross-country, football M, golf M, soccer, softball W, swimming, tennis, track and field, volleyball W, wrestling M. **Intramural:** Badminton, basketball, bowling, golf, skiing, softball, volleyball.

STUDENT SERVICES. Aptitude testing, career counseling, employment service for undergraduates, freshman orientation, health services, personal counseling, placement service for graduates, special adviser for adult students, campus ministry.

ANNUAL EXPENSES. Tuition and fees: $11,286. Graduate students charged $1150 per course credit. **Room and board:** $4,212. **Books and supplies:** $450. **Other expenses:** $1,180.

FINANCIAL AID. 85% of freshmen, 82% of continuing students receive some form of aid. 62% of grants, 83% of loans, 24% of jobs based on need. Academic, music/drama, art, religious affiliation, minority scholarships available. **Aid applications:** No closing date; priority given to applications received by April 1; applicants notified on a rolling basis beginning on or about April 1; must reply within 4 weeks. **Additional information:** Muhlenberg Tuition Exchange Program and Council of Independent Colleges Tuition Exchange Program available.

ADDRESS/TELEPHONE. Marguerite Waters, Director of Admission, North Central College, 30 North Brainard Street, P.O. Box 3065, Naperville, IL 60566-7065. (708) 420-3414. Fax: (708) 420-4234.

North Park College
Chicago, Illinois CB code: 1556

Admissions: 76% of applicants accepted
Based on: ••• School record, test scores
•• Essay, recommendations
• Activities, interview, special talents
Completion: 90% of freshmen end year in good standing
60% graduate, 25% of these enter graduate study

4-year private liberal arts college, coed, affiliated with Evangelical Covenant Church of America. Founded in 1891. **Accreditation:** Regional. **Undergraduate enrollment:** 398 men, 475 women full time; 42 men, 62 women part time. **Graduate enrollment:** 54 men, 36 women full time; 25 men, 21 women part time. **Faculty:** 89 total (77 full time), 48 with doctorates or other terminal degrees. **Location:** Urban campus in very large city; 6 miles from downtown. **Calendar:** Quarter, limited summer session. Extensive evening/early morning classes. **Microcomputers:** 60 located in libraries, classrooms, computer centers. **Special facilities:** Scandinavian collection, Center for Scandavian Studies, Center for Korean Studies.

DEGREES OFFERED. BA, BS, MA, MS, MBA, M.Div. 170 bachelor's degrees awarded in 1992. 24% in business and management, 11% teacher education, 19% health sciences, 10% letters/literature, 12% psychology, 5% visual and performing arts. Graduate degrees offered in 2 major fields of study.

UNDERGRADUATE MAJORS. Accounting, anthropology, art education, Bible studies, biological and physical sciences, biology, business administration and management, business and management, business economics, chemistry, communications, early childhood education, economics, elementary education, English, fine arts, German, history, international business management, international relations, international studies, marketing management, mathematics, medical laboratory technologies, music, music performance, nursing, philosophy, physical education, physics, political science and government, predentistry, prelaw, premedicine, preveterinary, psychology, religion, Scandinavian languages, science education, secondary education, social science education, social sciences, sociology, Spanish, speech, theological studies, urban studies.

ACADEMIC PROGRAMS. Accelerated program, double major, honors program, independent study, internships, student-designed major, study abroad, teacher preparation, visiting/exchange student program, Washington semester, film studies program in Hollywood, California; liberal arts/career combination in engineering, health sciences; combined bachelor's/graduate program in business administration. **Remedial services:** Learning center, reduced course load, remedial instruction, special counselor, tutoring. **Placement/credit:** AP, CLEP General and Subject, IB, institutional tests; 90 credit hours maximum for bachelor's degree.

ACADEMIC REQUIREMENTS. Freshmen must earn minimum GPA of 1.6 to continue in good standing. 84% of freshmen return for sophomore year. Students must declare major by end of second year. **Graduation requirements:** 180 hours for bachelor's (50 in major). Most students required to take courses in arts/fine arts, English, foreign languages, history, mathematics, philosophy/religion, biological/physical sciences, social sciences.

FRESHMAN ADMISSIONS. Selection criteria: Admission based on achievement record, class rank, test scores, school and community involvement. No statement of faith or religious belief required. Recommended units include English 4, foreign language 2, mathematics 3, social science 3 and science 3. College-preparatory program and work in computer science recommended. **Test requirements:** SAT or ACT; score report by August 1.

1992 FRESHMAN CLASS PROFILE. 292 men applied, 200 accepted, 112 enrolled; 255 women applied, 217 accepted, 99 enrolled. **Academic background:** Mid 50% of enrolled freshmen had SAT-V between 410-560, SAT-M between 460-620; ACT composite between 19-25. 20% submitted SAT scores, 79% submitted ACT scores. **Characteristics:** 48% from in state, 87% live in college housing, 16% have minority backgrounds, 3% are foreign students. Average age is 18.

FALL-TERM APPLICATIONS. $20 fee, may be waived for applicants with need. Closing date August 15; applicants notified on a rolling basis; must reply within 3 weeks. Audition required for music applicants. Essay required. Interview recommended for marginal applicants. Portfolio recommended for art applicants. Deferred and early admission available.

STUDENT LIFE. Housing: Dormitories (men, women); apartment housing available. **Activities:** Student government, magazine, student newspaper, yearbook, choral groups, drama, jazz band, music ensembles, musical theater, opera, pep band, symphony orchestra, chamber orchestra, Gospel teams, Black Student Association, Habitat for Humanity, urban outreach.

ATHLETICS. NCAA. **Intercollegiate:** Baseball M, basketball, cross-country, football M, soccer M, softball W, tennis, track and field, volleyball W. **Intramural:** Basketball, ice hockey M, softball, track and field, volleyball.

STUDENT SERVICES. Aptitude testing, career counseling, employment service for undergraduates, freshman orientation, health services, personal counseling, placement service for graduates, special adviser for adult students, services/facilities for handicapped.

ANNUAL EXPENSES. Tuition and fees (1992-93): $11,295. **Room and board:** $4,140. **Books and supplies:** $475. **Other expenses:** $515.

FINANCIAL AID. 85% of freshmen, 79% of continuing students receive some form of aid. 94% of grants, 86% of loans, 43% of jobs based on need. 160 enrolled freshmen were judged to have need, all were offered aid. Academic, music/drama, art, state/district residency scholarships available. **Aid applications:** Closing date July 1; priority given to applications received by April 1; applicants notified on a rolling basis; must reply within 20 days.

ADDRESS/TELEPHONE. Melissa Morriss-Olson, VP Enrollment Mgmt Planning, North Park College, 3225 West Foster Avenue, Chicago, IL 60625-4987. (312) 583-2700. (800) 888-6728.

Northeastern Illinois University
Chicago, Illinois CB code: 1090

Admissions: 68% of applicants accepted
Based on: ••• School record
•• Test scores
• Recommendations
Completion: 69% of freshmen end year in good standing

4-year public university, coed. Founded in 1961. **Accreditation:** Regional. **Undergraduate enrollment:** 1,662 men, 2,485 women full time; 1,572 men, 2,147 women part time. **Graduate enrollment:** 73 men, 78 women full time; 923 men, 1,880 women part time. **Faculty:** 509 total (359 full time), 275 with doctorates or other terminal degrees. **Location:** Urban campus in very large city. **Calendar:** Semester, limited summer session. **Microcomputers:** 105 located in libraries, computer centers.

DEGREES OFFERED. BA, BS, MA, MS, MBA, MEd. 1,103 bachelor's degrees awarded in 1992. 21% in business and management, 8% computer sciences, 15% teacher education, 19% multi/interdisciplinary studies, 5% psychology, 17% social sciences. Graduate degrees offered in 27 major fields of study.

UNDERGRADUATE MAJORS. Accounting, anthropology, bilingual/bicultural education, biology, business administration and management, chemistry, computer and information sciences, criminal justice studies, dramatic arts, early childhood education, earth sciences, economics, education, education of the emotionally handicapped, education of the mentally handicapped, elementary education, English, environmental science, environmental studies, finance, French, geography, history, human resources development, Jewish studies, leisure studies, linguistics, marketing and distribution, marketing management, mathematics, music, parks and recreation management, philosophy, physical education, physics, political science and government, psychology, secondary education, social sciences, social work, sociology, Spanish, special education, specific learning disabilities, speech, studio art, urban studies.

ACADEMIC PROGRAMS. Accelerated program, double major, honors program, independent study, internships, student-designed major, study abroad, teacher preparation, visiting/exchange student program, cross-registration, Board of Governors degree program, University Without Walls, cooperative program in Judaic studies with Spertus College of Judaica; liberal arts/career combination in health sciences; combined bachelor's/graduate program in business administration. **Remedial services:** Learning center, special counselor, tutoring. **ROTC:** Air Force, Army. **Placement/credit:** AP, CLEP General, institutional tests; 30 credit hours maximum for bachelor's degree.

ACADEMIC REQUIREMENTS. Freshmen must earn minimum GPA of 2.0 to continue in good standing. 64% of freshmen return for sophomore year. Students must declare major by end of second year. **Graduation requirements:** 120 hours for bachelor's (40 in major). Most students required to take courses in arts/fine arts, computer science, English, history, humanities, mathematics, biological/physical sciences, social sciences.

FRESHMAN ADMISSIONS. Selection criteria: Rank in top half of graduating class or minimum enhanced ACT composite of 19 or SAT combined score of 750 required. **High school preparation:** 15 units required. Required and recommended units include English 4-4, mathematics 3-3, social science 3-3 and science 3-3. Biological science 1 and foreign language 2 recommended. 2-additional units in fine arts, foreign languages, or vocational education. **Test requirements:** SAT or ACT (ACT preferred); score report by July 1.

1992 FRESHMAN CLASS PROFILE. 860 men applied, 576 accepted, 329 enrolled; 1,343 women applied, 928 accepted, 462 enrolled. 7% were in top tenth and 23% were in top quarter of graduating class. **Academic background:** Mid 50% of enrolled freshmen had ACT composite between 14-19. 84% submitted ACT scores. **Characteristics:** 99% from in state, 100% commute, 56% have minority backgrounds. Average age is 23.

FALL-TERM APPLICATIONS. No fee. Closing date July 1; applicants notified on a rolling basis. Audition recommended for dance, music applicants. Portfolio recommended for art applicants.

STUDENT LIFE. Activities: Student government, magazine, radio, student newspaper, yearbook, choral groups, concert band, dance, drama, jazz band, music ensembles, musical theater, opera, pep band, symphony orchestra, gospel choir, fraternities, sororities, Aspira; Black Caucus; Black Heritage; Chimexla; Gay, Lesbian and Bisexual Alliance; Hillel; Student

Enviromental Action Coalition; Union for Puerto Rican Students United; Alliance of Student Social Workers.

ATHLETICS. NCAA. **Intercollegiate:** Baseball M, basketball, cross-country, golf M, softball W, swimming, tennis, volleyball W. **Intramural:** Badminton, basketball, racquetball, soccer, softball, swimming, table tennis, tennis, volleyball.

STUDENT SERVICES. Career counseling, employment service for undergraduates, freshman orientation, health services, personal counseling, placement service for graduates, special adviser for adult students, veterans counselor, services/facilities for handicapped.

ANNUAL EXPENSES. Tuition and fees (1992-93): $2,277, $3,696 additional for out-of-state students. **Books and supplies:** $515. **Other expenses:** $2,150.

FINANCIAL AID. 22% of freshmen, 35% of continuing students receive some form of aid. 87% of grants, 92% of loans, 44% of jobs based on need. 433 enrolled freshmen were judged to have need, all were offered aid. Academic, music/drama, art, athletic, state/district residency, leadership, minority scholarships available. **Aid applications:** No closing date; priority given to applications received by April 1; applicants notified on a rolling basis; must reply within 2 weeks. **Additional information:** May 1 application closing date for Pell Grants.

ADDRESS/TELEPHONE. Miriam Rivera, Director of Admissions and Records, Northeastern Illinois University, 5500 North St. Louis Avenue, Chicago, IL 60625. (312) 583-4050. Fax: (312) 794-6246.

Northern Illinois University

DeKalb, Illinois — CB code: 1559

Admissions: 67% of applicants accepted
Based on: ••• School record, test scores
• Special talents
Completion: 71% of freshmen end year in good standing
9% enter graduate study

4-year public university, coed. Founded in 1895. **Accreditation:** Regional. **Undergraduate enrollment:** 7,260 men, 8,345 women full time; 802 men, 1,030 women part time. **Graduate enrollment:** 1,098 men, 1,109 women full time; 1,756 men, 2,652 women part time. **Faculty:** 1,677 total (1,476 full time), 828 with doctorates or other terminal degrees. **Location:** Urban campus in large town; 65 miles from Chicago. **Calendar:** Semester, extensive summer session. **Microcomputers:** 550 located in computer centers. **Special facilities:** Earl W. Hayter Regional History Center, Swen Parsen Art Gallery. **Additional facts:** Classes also held at Loredo Taft Field campus in Oregon.

DEGREES OFFERED. BA, BS, BFA, MA, MS, MBA, MFA, MEd, PhD, EdD, JD. 3,750 bachelor's degrees awarded in 1992. 15% in business and management, 8% business/office and marketing/distribution, 9% communications, 9% teacher education, 5% health sciences, 15% social sciences, 7% visual and performing arts. Graduate degrees offered in 87 major fields of study.

UNDERGRADUATE MAJORS. Accounting, allied health, anthropology, art education, art history, atmospheric sciences and meteorology, biology, business administration and management, business education, business systems analysis, chemistry, clinical laboratory science, computer and information sciences, dramatic arts, early childhood education, economics, education of the deaf and hearing impaired, education of the mentally handicapped, education of the physically handicapped, education of the visually handicapped, electrical/electronics/communications engineering, elementary education, engineering and engineering-related technologies, English, family and community services, fashion merchandising, finance, food science and nutrition, French, geography, geology, German, history, home economics education, individual and family development, industrial arts education, industrial engineering, journalism, liberal/general studies, marketing management, mathematics, mechanical engineering, medical laboratory technologies, music, music education, nursing, office supervision and management, philosophy, physical education, physical therapy, physics, political science and government, psychology, Russian, social science education, social sciences, sociology, Spanish, special education, speech, speech pathology/audiology, studio art, textiles and clothing, visual and performing arts.

ACADEMIC PROGRAMS. Accelerated program, cooperative education, double major, education specialist degree, external degree, honors program, independent study, internships, student-designed major, study abroad, teacher preparation; liberal arts/career combination in engineering; combined bachelor's/graduate program in business administration, law. **Remedial services:** Tutoring, CHANCE (admissions, counseling, tutoring program) for educationally, culturally, socially disadvantaged students. **ROTC:** Army. **Placement/credit:** AP, CLEP General, institutional tests.

ACADEMIC REQUIREMENTS. Freshmen must earn minimum GPA of 2.0 to continue in good standing. 80% of freshmen return for sophomore year. Students must declare major by end of second year. **Graduation requirements:** 124 hours for bachelor's (45 in major). Most students required to take courses in English, humanities, mathematics, biological/physical sciences, social sciences.

FRESHMAN ADMISSIONS. Selection criteria: Minimum ACT composite score of 19 required of applicants who rank in top half of class, 23 of required applicants in top two-thirds of class or with high school equivalency certificate. **High school preparation:** 15 units required. Required and recommended units include English 4-4, mathematics 2-3, social science 2-3 and science 2-3. At least one unit of art, film, music, theater, or foreign language required. Mathematics must include algebra and/or geometry. Social sciences must include U.S. history or a combination of U.S. history and government. **Test requirements:** SAT or ACT (ACT preferred); score report by August 1.

1992 FRESHMAN CLASS PROFILE. 5,084 men applied, 3,324 accepted, 1,220 enrolled; 6,777 women applied, 4,615 accepted, 1,539 enrolled. **Academic background:** Mid 50% of enrolled freshmen had ACT composite between 20-25. 99% submitted ACT scores. **Characteristics:** 97% from in state, 95% live in college housing, 27% have minority backgrounds, 1% are foreign students. Average age is 18.

FALL-TERM APPLICATIONS. No fee. Closing date August 1; priority given to applications received by February 15; applicants notified on a rolling basis; must reply by registration. Interview required for CHANCE program applicants. Audition required for music applicants. Portfolio recommended for art applicants. Early admission available. Institutional early decision plan.

STUDENT LIFE. Housing: Dormitories (coed); apartment, fraternity, sorority, cooperative housing available. **Activities:** Student government, magazine, radio, student newspaper, television, yearbook, choral groups, concert band, dance, drama, jazz band, marching band, music ensembles, musical theater, opera, pep band, symphony orchestra, fraternities, sororities, numerous religious, political, ethnic, and social service organizations.

ATHLETICS. NCAA. **Intercollegiate:** Baseball, basketball, field hockey W, football M, golf, gymnastics W, soccer M, softball W, swimming, tennis, volleyball W, wrestling M. **Intramural:** Badminton, baseball, basketball, football, golf, ice hockey M, racquetball, sailing, soccer, softball, table tennis, tennis, volleyball, wrestling.

STUDENT SERVICES. Career counseling, employment service for undergraduates, health services, on-campus day care, personal counseling, placement service for graduates, veterans counselor, services/facilities for handicapped.

ANNUAL EXPENSES. Tuition and fees (1992-93): $3,041, $4,322 additional for out-of-state students. **Room and board:** $2,841. **Books and supplies:** $450. **Other expenses:** $1,340.

FINANCIAL AID. 67% of freshmen, 67% of continuing students receive some form of aid. Grants, loans, jobs available. Music/drama, art, athletic scholarships available. **Aid applications:** Closing date May 1; priority given to applications received by March 1; applicants notified on a rolling basis beginning on or about June 1; must reply within 2 weeks.

ADDRESS/TELEPHONE. Daniel S. Oborn, Director of Admissions, Northern Illinois University, DeKalb, IL 60115-2854. (815) 753-0446.

Northwestern University

Evanston, Illinois — CB code: 1565

Admissions: 42% of applicants accepted
Based on: ••• Essay, school record
•• Recommendations, test scores
• Activities, interview, special talents
Completion: 97% of freshmen end year in good standing
88% graduate, 45% of these enter graduate study

4-year private university, coed. Founded in 1851. **Accreditation:** Regional. **Undergraduate enrollment:** 3,699 men, 3,725 women full time; 28 men, 20 women part time. **Graduate enrollment:** 3,611 men, 2,583 women full time; 1,004 men, 602 women part time. **Faculty:** 2,124 total (1,739 full time), 2,124 with doctorates or other terminal degrees. **Location:** Suburban campus in small city; 12 miles from the center of Chicago. **Calendar:** Quarter, limited summer session. **Microcomputers:** 250 located in dormitories, libraries, classrooms, computer centers. **Special facilities:** Fine-arts complex, art gallery, dance center, sports and aquatic center, media center, jogging and bicycling paths.

DEGREES OFFERED. BA, BS, MA, MS, MBA, MFA, PhD, DDS, MD. 2,068 bachelor's degrees awarded in 1992. 15% in communications, 14% engineering, 8% letters/literature, 34% social sciences. Graduate degrees offered in 111 major fields of study.

UNDERGRADUATE MAJORS. Afro-American (black) studies, American literature, American studies, analytical chemistry, anthropology, applied mathematics, art education, art history, Asian studies, astronomy, astrophysics, biochemistry, bioengineering and biomedical engineering, biological and physical sciences, biology, cell biology, chemical engineering, chemistry, cinematography/film, civil engineering, classics, communications, comparative literature, computer and information sciences, computer engineering, creative writing, dramatic arts, earth sciences, East Asian studies, economics, education, education of the deaf and hearing impaired, electrical/electronics/communications engineering, engineering physics, engineering science, English, English education, English literature, environmental health engineering, environmental science, film arts, foreign languages education, French, geology, German, Greek (modern), histology, history, industrial engineering, inorganic chemistry, international relations, international studies, Italian, journalism, Latin, Latin American studies, liberal/general studies, linguistics, materials engineering, mathematics, mathematics education, mechanical engineering, metallurgical engineering, microbiology, molecular biology, music, music education, music history and appreciation, music performance, music theory and composition, musical theater, neurosciences, operations research, organizational behavior, painting, philosophy, physical chemistry, physics, political science and government, psychology, public policy studies, radio/television broadcasting, religion, Russian, Russian and Slavic studies, science education, secondary education, social science education, social studies education, sociology, Spanish, specific learning disabilities, speech, speech correction, speech pathology/audiology, speech/communication/theater education, statistics, studio art, urban studies, visual and performing arts.

ACADEMIC PROGRAMS. Accelerated program, cooperative education, double major, dual enrollment of high school students, honors program, independent study, internships, student-designed major, study abroad, teacher preparation, visiting/exchange student program, Washington semester, 7-year program in biomedical engineering leading to bachelor's and dental (DDS) degrees, 3-year integrated science program, 4-year mathematical methods in social sciences bachelor's program, honors program in undergraduate research engineering, engineering and management; combined bachelor's/graduate program in business administration, medicine. **ROTC:** Air Force, Army, Naval. **Placement/credit:** AP, IB, institutional tests.

ACADEMIC REQUIREMENTS. No policy requiring minimum GPA; records of students having academic difficulty are reviewed individually. 95% of freshmen return for sophomore year. Students must declare major by end of second year. **Graduation requirements:** Most students required to take courses in English, foreign languages, humanities, mathematics, biological/physical sciences, social sciences.

FRESHMAN ADMISSIONS. Selection criteria: Academic record, essay, test scores, activity record, and school recommendations important. **High school preparation:** 16 units recommended. Recommended units include English 4, foreign language 2, mathematics 3, social science 4 and science 3. 3.5 units of mathematics recommended for engineering applicants. **Test requirements:** SAT or ACT; score report by February 1. ACH required of applicants in specified honors programs. Score report by January 15.

1992 FRESHMAN CLASS PROFILE. 6,459 men applied, 2,641 accepted, 940 enrolled; 6,172 women applied, 2,616 accepted, 948 enrolled. 82% were in top tenth and 98% were in top quarter of graduating class. **Academic background:** Mid 50% of enrolled freshmen had SAT-V between 540-640, SAT-M between 610-710; ACT composite between 27-31. 92% submitted SAT scores, 46% submitted ACT scores. **Characteristics:** 26% from in state, 96% live in college housing, 25% have minority backgrounds, 3% are foreign students, 40% join fraternities/sororities. Average age is 18.

FALL-TERM APPLICATIONS. $45 fee, may be waived for applicants with need. Closing date January 1; applicants notified on or about April 15; must reply by May 1. Audition required for music applicants. Essay required. Interview recommended. CRDA. Deferred and early admission available. EDP-F. November 1 application deadline for December 15 notification for early decision plan. Accepted applicants must reply by March 1. ACH recommended for all applicants.

STUDENT LIFE. Housing: Dormitories (men, women, coed); fraternity, sorority housing available. Housing options include 9 residential colleges devoted to particular themes (arts, international studies, etc.), 2 nonthematic residential colleges, and wellness dormitory. **Activities:** Student government, film, magazine, radio, student newspaper, television, yearbook, choral groups, concert band, dance, drama, jazz band, marching band, music ensembles, musical theater, opera, pep band, symphony orchestra, fraternities, sororities, more than 100 student organizations.

ATHLETICS. NCAA. **Intercollegiate:** Baseball M, basketball, diving, fencing, field hockey W, football M, golf, soccer M, softball W, swimming, tennis, volleyball W, wrestling M. **Intramural:** Badminton, basketball, bowling, football M, golf, handball, horseback riding, ice hockey M, lacrosse, racquetball, rowing (crew), rugby M, sailing, skiing, soccer, softball, squash, tennis, volleyball, water polo M.

STUDENT SERVICES. Aptitude testing, career counseling, employment service for undergraduates, freshman orientation, health services, personal counseling, placement service for graduates, special adviser for adult students, veterans counselor, services/facilities for handicapped.

ANNUAL EXPENSES. Tuition and fees: $15,804. **Room and board:** $5,289. **Books and supplies:** $723. **Other expenses:** $1,059.

FINANCIAL AID. 60% of freshmen, 60% of continuing students receive some form of aid. All grants, 99% of loans, all jobs based on need. 953 enrolled freshmen were judged to have need, all were offered aid. Music/drama, athletic scholarships available. **Aid applications:** Closing date February 15; applicants notified on or about April 15; must reply by May 1.

ADDRESS/TELEPHONE. Carol Lunkenheimer, Director of Undergraduate Admissions, Northwestern University, 1801 Hinman Avenue, Evanston, IL 60204-3060. (708) 491-7271.

Oakton Community College
Des Plaines, Illinois CB code: 1573

2-year public community college, coed. Founded in 1969. **Accreditation:** Regional. **Undergraduate enrollment:** 1,321 men, 1,316 women full time; 3,478 men, 5,138 women part time. **Faculty:** 519 total (144 full time), 32 with doctorates or other terminal degrees. **Location:** Suburban campus in small city; 15 miles from Chicago. **Calendar:** Semester, limited summer session. **Microcomputers:** Located in computer centers. **Additional facts:** Branch campus in Skokie

DEGREES OFFERED. AA, AS, AAS. 520 associate degrees awarded in 1992.

UNDERGRADUATE MAJORS. Accounting, air conditioning/heating/refrigeration mechanics, air conditioning/heating/refrigeration technology, architectural technologies, architecture, automotive technology, biological and physical sciences, biomedical equipment technology, business administration and management, business and management, business and office, business data processing and related programs, business data programming, child development/care/guidance, computer programming, data processing, electronic technology, engineering, finance, fire control and safety technology, hotel/motel and restaurant management, industrial equipment maintenance and repair, international business management, investments and securities, law enforcement and corrections technologies, liberal/general studies, machine tool operation/machine shop, marketing and distribution, marketing management, mechanical design technology, medical laboratory technologies, medical records technology, nursing, office supervision and management, physical therapy assistant, power plant operation and maintenance, real estate, retailing, secretarial and related programs, trade and industrial supervision and management, word processing.

ACADEMIC PROGRAMS. 2-year transfer program, dual enrollment of high school students, honors program, independent study, internships, study abroad, telecourses, visiting/exchange student program, weekend college. **Remedial services:** Learning center, remedial instruction, special counselor, tutoring, assistance for disabled students. **Placement/credit:** AP, CLEP General and Subject, institutional tests; 45 credit hours maximum for associate degree.

ACADEMIC REQUIREMENTS. Minimum 2.0 GPA required each semester. Students are required to complete more than 50% of their courses successfully. 60% of freshmen return for sophomore year. **Graduation requirements:** 60 hours for associate. Most students required to take courses in English, humanities, mathematics, biological/physical sciences, social sciences.

FRESHMAN ADMISSIONS. Selection criteria: Open admissions. Selective admission to health career programs. **High school preparation:** 15 units recommended. Recommended units include English 4, mathematics 3, social science 3 and science 3. Specific requirements for applicants in health fields. Recommended high school units, including 2 units in foreign language, music, art, or vocational education are required for all students pursuing bachelor's degree. Students not entering with required units must take courses to make up deficiencies.

1992 FRESHMAN CLASS PROFILE. Characteristics: 99% from in state, 100% commute, 16% have minority backgrounds.

FALL-TERM APPLICATIONS. $15 fee. Fee waived for residents over 60. No closing date; applicants notified on a rolling basis; must reply by registration. Interview required for health career applicants. Early admission available. ACT recommended for placement and counseling. SAT accepted.

STUDENT LIFE. Activities: Student government, student newspaper, choral groups, drama, jazz band, music ensembles, Christian Student Association, Indian Student Association, Political Science Forum, wellness committee, fencing club, nursing club, accounting club, photography club.

ATHLETICS. NJCAA. **Intercollegiate:** Baseball M, basketball, cross-country, golf, softball W, tennis, track and field, volleyball W, wrestling M. **Intramural:** Badminton, bowling, ice hockey M, soccer.

STUDENT SERVICES. Career counseling, employment service for undergraduates, health services, personal counseling, placement service for graduates, special adviser for adult students, veterans counselor, services/facilities for handicapped.

ANNUAL EXPENSES. Tuition and fees: $948, $3,750 additional for out-of-district students, $3,798 additional for out-of-state students. **Books and supplies:** $400. **Other expenses:** $1,000.

FINANCIAL AID. 12% of freshmen, 12% of continuing students receive some form of aid. 77% of grants, 83% of loans, 2% of jobs based on need. Academic, music/drama, art, athletic, leadership, alumni affiliation, minority scholarships available. **Aid applications:** No closing date; priority given to applications received by June 1; applicants notified on a rolling basis beginning on or about June 1; must reply within 2 weeks.

ADDRESS/TELEPHONE. Evelyn Burdick, Director of Enrollment Management, Oakton Community College, 1600 East Golf Road, Des Plaines, IL 60016. (708) 635-1700. Fax: (708) 635-1706.

Olivet Nazarene University

Kankakee, Illinois CB code: 1596

Admissions: 95% of applicants accepted
Based on: ••• Recommendations, school record
•• Test scores
• Activities, essay, interview, religious affiliation/commitment
Completion: 80% of freshmen end year in good standing
40% graduate, 10% of these enter graduate study

4-year private university and liberal arts college, coed, affiliated with Church of the Nazarene. Founded in 1907. **Accreditation:** Regional. **Undergraduate enrollment:** 716 men, 805 women full time; 106 men, 202 women part time. **Graduate enrollment:** 17 men, 13 women full time; 64 men, 50 women part time. **Faculty:** 120 total (93 full time), 45 with doctorates or other terminal degrees. **Location:** Suburban campus in small city; 60 miles from Chicago. **Calendar:** Semester, extensive summer session. **Microcomputers:** 80 located in libraries, classrooms, computer centers. **Special facilities:** Planetarium, observatory, art gallery, science museum. **Additional facts:** Evangelical liberal arts institution where Christian values are emphasized.

DEGREES OFFERED. AA, BA, BS, MA, MBA, MEd. 1 associate degree awarded in 1992. 293 bachelor's degrees awarded. 20% in business and management, 24% teacher education, 7% health sciences, 7% philosophy, religion, theology, 9% psychology, 11% social sciences. Graduate degrees offered in 9 major fields of study.

UNDERGRADUATE MAJORS. Associate: Computer and information sciences, dietetic aide/assistant, engineering and engineering-related technologies, science technologies, teacher aide. **Bachelor's:** Accounting, anthropology, art education, Bible studies, biological and physical sciences, biology, business administration and management, business and management, business economics, chemistry, clothing and textiles management/production/services, communications, computer and information sciences, counseling psychology, criminal justice studies, dietetic aide/assistant, early childhood education, economics, education, elementary education, engineering, engineering and other disciplines, English, English education, English literature, environmental science, family and community services, family/consumer resource management, fashion design, fashion merchandising, film arts, finance, fine arts, food science and nutrition, foreign languages (multiple emphasis), foreign languages education, geology, history, home economics, home economics education, humanities, humanities and social sciences, information sciences and systems, interior design, journalism, junior high education, liberal/general studies, marketing management, mathematics, mathematics education, medical laboratory technologies, music, music education, music performance, nursing, philosophy, physical education, physical sciences, political science and government, predentistry, prelaw, premedicine, prepharmacy, preveterinary, psychology, radio/television broadcasting, religion, religious education, religious music, science education, secondary education, social science education, social sciences, social studies education, social work, sociology, speech, studio art, theological studies.

ACADEMIC PROGRAMS. Accelerated program, double major, honors program, independent study, internships, student-designed major, teacher preparation, Washington semester; liberal arts/career combination in health sciences. **Remedial services:** Learning center, preadmission summer program, reduced course load, remedial instruction, special counselor, tutoring. **ROTC:** Army. **Placement/credit:** AP, CLEP General and Subject, institutional tests; 24 credit hours maximum for bachelor's degree.

ACADEMIC REQUIREMENTS. Freshmen must earn minimum GPA of 1.7 to continue in good standing. 70% of freshmen return for sophomore year. Students must declare major by end of second year. **Graduation requirements:** 64 hours for associate (24 in major), 128 hours for bachelor's (32 in major). Most students required to take courses in arts/fine arts, computer science, English, foreign languages, history, humanities, mathematics, philosophy/religion, biological/physical sciences, social sciences. **Postgraduate studies:** 10% from 2-year programs enter 4-year programs. 1% enter law school, 1% enter medical school, 1% enter MBA programs, 7% enter other graduate study.

FRESHMAN ADMISSIONS. Selection criteria: Minimum 2.0 GPA in college-preparatory subjects and ranking in top three-quarters of class required. **High school preparation:** 15 units required. Required units include English 3. Additional units among language, mathematics, natural sciences, and social sciences required. **Test requirements:** ACT for placement and counseling only; score report by August 1.

1992 FRESHMAN CLASS PROFILE. 660 men and women applied, 630 accepted; 186 men enrolled, 202 women enrolled. **Academic background:** Mid 50% of enrolled freshmen had ACT composite between 16-23. 99% submitted ACT scores. **Characteristics:** 35% from in state, 80% live in college housing, 5% have minority backgrounds, 1% are foreign students. Average age is 18.

FALL-TERM APPLICATIONS. No fee. Closing date August 1; applicants notified on a rolling basis. Audition required for music applicants. Interview recommended. Deferred admission available.

STUDENT LIFE. Housing: Dormitories (men, women). **Activities:** Student government, radio, student newspaper, yearbook, choral groups, concert band, drama, jazz band, music ensembles, pep band, symphony orchestra, social service clubs, spiritual life groups. **Additional information:** Chapel convocations held twice weekly. Religious observance required.

ATHLETICS. NAIA. **Intercollegiate:** Baseball M, basketball, cross-country, football M, golf M, soccer M, softball W, tennis, track and field, volleyball W, wrestling M. **Intramural:** Baseball M, basketball, cross-country, football M, golf M, soccer M, softball M, tennis, volleyball.

STUDENT SERVICES. Aptitude testing, career counseling, employment service for undergraduates, freshman orientation, health services, personal counseling, placement service for graduates, special adviser for adult students, veterans counselor, services/facilities for handicapped.

ANNUAL EXPENSES. Tuition and fees: $7,836. **Room and board:** $4,140. **Books and supplies:** $500. **Other expenses:** $900.

FINANCIAL AID. 86% of freshmen, 84% of continuing students receive some form of aid. 48% of grants, 85% of loans, 17% of jobs based on need. 317 enrolled freshmen were judged to have need, all were offered aid. Academic, music/drama, art, athletic, leadership, religious affiliation scholarships available. **Aid applications:** Closing date August 1; priority given to applications received by April 1; applicants notified on a rolling basis beginning on or about May 1; must reply within 2 weeks.

ADDRESS/TELEPHONE. John Mongerson, Director of Admissions, Olivet Nazarene University, PO Box 592, Kankakee, IL 60901-0592. (815) 939-5203. Fax: (815) 939-0416.

Parkland College

Champaign, Illinois CB code: 1619

2-year public community college, coed. Founded in 1966. **Accreditation:** Regional. **Undergraduate enrollment:** 9,343 men and women. **Location:** Suburban campus in small city; 150 miles south of Chicago. **Calendar:** Semester. **Additional facts:** Students have access to resources at University of Illinois and within certain guidelines may enroll in University of Illinois classes.

FRESHMAN ADMISSIONS. Selection criteria: Open admissions. Selective admissions for health programs.

ANNUAL EXPENSES. Tuition and fees: $1,248, $3,072 additional for out-of-district students, $4,640 additional for out-of-state students. **Books and supplies:** $500. **Other expenses:** $860.

ADDRESS/TELEPHONE. Joan Williams, Director of Admissions and Records, Parkland College, 2400 West Bradley, Champaign, IL 61821-1899. (217) 351-2208. (800) 346-8089. Fax: (217) 351-2592.

Parks College of St. Louis University

Cahokia, Illinois CB code: 1621

Admissions: 79% of applicants accepted
Based on: ••• School record
•• Test scores
• Activities, essay, interview, recommendations, special talents
Completion: 75% of freshmen end year in good standing
70% graduate

4-year private engineering, technical college, coed, affiliated with Roman Catholic Church. Founded in 1927. **Accreditation:** Regional. **Undergraduate enrollment:** 857 men, 107 women full time; 94 men, 12 women part time. **Graduate enrollment:** 10 men, 1 woman full time; 9 men, 1 woman part time. **Faculty:** 109 total (59 full time), 25 with doctorates or other terminal degrees. **Location:** Suburban campus in large town; 3 miles from St. Louis, Missouri. **Calendar:** Semester, extensive summer session. **Microcomputers:** 68 located in libraries, classrooms, computer centers. **Special facilities:** Controlled airport for flight instruction, sub- and supersonic wind tunnel laboratory, avionics laboratory. **Additional facts:** Only aviation-aerospace college in Illinois and 1 of 3 in nation.

DEGREES OFFERED. AS, BS, MS. 100 associate degrees awarded in 1992. 250 bachelor's degrees awarded. Graduate degrees offered in 1 major field of study.

UNDERGRADUATE MAJORS. Associate: Aeronautical technology, air traffic control, aircraft mechanics, airline piloting and navigation, aviation management, avionics, electrical technology, electronic technology. **Bachelor's:** Aeronautical technology, aerospace/aeronautical/astronautical engineering, air traffic control, aircraft mechanics, airline piloting and navigation, atmospheric sciences and meteorology, aviation management, avionics, computer and information sciences, electrical/electronics/communications engineering, electronic technology, tourism, transportation and travel marketing.

ACADEMIC PROGRAMS. Accelerated program, double major, dual enrollment of high school students, independent study, internships, study abroad, cross-registration, 3-2 with St. Louis University. **Remedial services:** Learning center, preadmission summer program, reduced course load, remedial instruction, special counselor, tutoring. **ROTC:** Air Force, Army. **Placement/credit:** AP, CLEP General and Subject, institutional tests; 30 credit hours maximum for bachelor's degree.

ACADEMIC REQUIREMENTS. Freshmen must earn minimum GPA of 2.0 to continue in good standing. 85% of freshmen return for sophomore year. Students must declare major on application. **Graduation requirements:** 64 hours for associate, 121 hours for bachelor's. Most students required to take courses in arts/fine arts, English, history, humanities, mathematics, philosophy/religion, biological/physical sciences, social sciences. **Postgraduate studies:** 70% from 2-year programs enter 4-year programs.

FRESHMAN ADMISSIONS. Selection criteria: School achievement record, particularly in mathematics and science, most important. High school GPA, school attended, class rank, and intended college major (for traditional students) are also considered. Nontraditional student requirements differ. **High school preparation:** 16 units recommended. Required and recommended units include mathematics 2-4 and physical science 2-4. English 3 and social science 2 recommended. One chemistry and one physics required for engineering majors. Recommended courses vary for each specific major. **Test requirements:** SAT or ACT; score report by September 1.

1992 FRESHMAN CLASS PROFILE. 518 men applied, 405 accepted, 116 enrolled; 93 women applied, 79 accepted, 22 enrolled. 62% had high school GPA of 3.0 or higher, 36% between 2.0 and 2.99. 18% were in top tenth and 47% were in top quarter of graduating class. **Academic background:** Mid 50% of enrolled freshmen had ACT composite between 21-26. 63% submitted ACT scores. **Characteristics:** 39% from in state, 50% commute, 22% have minority backgrounds, 9% are foreign students, 10% join fraternities/sororities. Average age is 20.

FALL-TERM APPLICATIONS. $25 fee. Closing date September 1; priority given to applications received by May 1; applicants notified on a rolling basis beginning on or about November 1. Interview recommended. Deferred and early admission available. EDP-S.

STUDENT LIFE. Housing: Dormitories (men, women, coed). All single, full-time students under age 20 required to live on campus unless they have completed 4 semesters with at least 2.0 GPA. **Activities:** Student government, radio, student newspaper, yearbook, choral groups, concert band, drama, jazz band, music ensembles, fraternities, sororities, flying team. **Additional information:** Students have access to performing arts activities at main campus of St. Louis University (MO).

ATHLETICS. NCAA. **Intercollegiate:** Baseball M, basketball M, soccer M, tennis M. **Intramural:** Baseball, basketball, handball, ice hockey, racquetball, soccer, softball, tennis, volleyball.

STUDENT SERVICES. Aptitude testing, career counseling, employment service for undergraduates, freshman orientation, health services, personal counseling, placement service for graduates, services/facilities for handicapped.

ANNUAL EXPENSES. Tuition and fees (1992-93): $7,770. **Room and board:** $3,870. **Books and supplies:** $450. **Other expenses:** $800.

FINANCIAL AID. 80% of freshmen, 85% of continuing students receive some form of aid. 93% of grants, 66% of loans, 20% of jobs based on need. Academic, state/district residency, leadership, alumni affiliation scholarships available. **Aid applications:** No closing date; priority given to applications received by January 1; applicants notified on a rolling basis beginning on or about February 17; must reply within 2 weeks.

ADDRESS/TELEPHONE. Kent Hopkins, Director Undergraduate Admissions, Parks College of St. Louis University, Cahokia, IL 62206. (800) 851-7878 ext. 233. (800) 851-3048 ext. 233.

Prairie State College
Chicago Heights, Illinois — CB code: 1077

2-year public community college, coed. Founded in 1957. **Accreditation:** Regional. **Undergraduate enrollment:** 5,785 men and women. **Location:** Suburban campus in large town; 30 miles south of Chicago. **Calendar:** Semester.

FRESHMAN ADMISSIONS. Selection criteria: Open admissions. Selective admissions for nursing and dental hygiene programs based on GPA in required courses and test scores.

ANNUAL EXPENSES. Tuition and fees: $1,500, $1,830 additional for out-of-district students, $2,910 additional for out-of-state students. **Books and supplies:** $700. **Other expenses:** $1,500.

ADDRESS/TELEPHONE. Carol Cleator, Coordinator of Admissions and Records, Prairie State College, 202 South Halsted Street, Chicago Heights, IL 60411. (708) 709-3516.

Principia College
Elsah, Illinois — CB code: 1630

Admissions: 85% of applicants accepted
Based on:
••• Essay, religious affiliation/commitment, school record
•• Interview, recommendations, test scores
• Activities, special talents
Completion: 72% graduate

4-year private college of arts and sciences, coed. Founded in 1910. **Accreditation:** Regional. **Undergraduate enrollment:** 240 men, 330 women full time; 9 men, 10 women part time. **Faculty:** 88 total (59 full time), 43 with doctorates or other terminal degrees. **Location:** Rural campus in rural community; 35 miles from St. Louis, Missouri. **Calendar:** 3 10-week terms. **Microcomputers:** 85 located in libraries, classrooms, computer centers. **Special facilities:** School of Nations Museum, observatory. **Additional facts:** College for Christian Scientists.

DEGREES OFFERED. BA, BS. 140 bachelor's degrees awarded in 1992. 12% in business and management, 6% communications, 5% computer sciences, 5% teacher education, 7% languages, 16% letters/literature, 6% life sciences, 18% social sciences, 18% visual and performing arts.

UNDERGRADUATE MAJORS. Art history, Asian studies, biology, business and management, business economics, chemistry, communications, computer and information sciences, dramatic arts, elementary education, engineering, English, fine arts, foreign languages (multiple emphasis), French, German, history, mathematics, music, philosophy, physics, political science and government, religion, Russian, Russian and Slavic studies, secondary education, sociology, Spanish, sports management, studio art.

ACADEMIC PROGRAMS. Accelerated program, double major, honors program, independent study, internships, student-designed major, study abroad, Washington semester; liberal arts/career combination in engineering. **Remedial services:** Learning center, tutoring, reading workshop. **Placement/credit:** AP, CLEP General and Subject, institutional tests; 45 credit hours maximum for bachelor's degree.

ACADEMIC REQUIREMENTS. Freshmen must earn minimum GPA of 2.0 to continue in good standing. 90% of freshmen return for sophomore year. Students must declare major by end of second year. **Graduation requirements:** 180 hours for bachelor's (60 in major). Most students required to take courses in arts/fine arts, English, foreign languages, history, philosophy/religion, biological/physical sciences, social sciences.

FRESHMAN ADMISSIONS. Selection criteria: School achievement record and essay or personal statement most important. Applicant must be practicing Christian Scientist. **High school preparation:** 16 units required. Required and recommended units include biological science 1, English 4, foreign language 2-3, mathematics 3, physical science 2 and social science 3-4. **Test requirements:** SAT or ACT (SAT preferred); score report by August 1.

1992 FRESHMAN CLASS PROFILE. 92 men applied, 76 accepted, 52 enrolled; 115 women applied, 100 accepted, 69 enrolled. 52% had high school GPA of 3.0 or higher, 45% between 2.0 and 2.99. 11% were in top tenth and 31% were in top quarter of graduating class. **Academic background:** Mid 50% of enrolled freshmen had SAT-V between 430-550, SAT-M between 460-600. 95% submitted SAT scores. **Characteristics:** 10% from in state, 99% live in college housing, 1% have minority backgrounds, 4% are foreign students. Average age is 18.

FALL-TERM APPLICATIONS. $25 fee, may be waived for applicants with need. Closing date August 1; priority given to applications received by December 1; applicants notified on a rolling basis beginning on or about October 1; must reply within 4 weeks. Essay required. Interview recommended. Portfolio recommended for art applicants. Deferred admission available.

STUDENT LIFE. Housing: Dormitories (men, women); apartment housing available. **Activities:** Student government, radio, student newspaper, television, yearbook, choral groups, concert band, dance, drama, jazz band, music ensembles, musical theater, Christian Science Organization. **Additional information:** Students required to comply with standards of Christian Science. No drinking of alcoholic beverages, no smoking, no drugs permitted. High moral standards and behavior expected. Religious observance recommended.

ATHLETICS. NAIA, NCAA. **Intercollegiate:** Baseball M, basketball, cross-country, diving, football M, golf, soccer, softball W, swimming, tennis, track and field, volleyball W. **Intramural:** Basketball, soccer, softball, volleyball.

STUDENT SERVICES. Career counseling, employment service for undergraduates, freshman orientation, on-campus day care, personal counseling, special adviser for adult students.

ANNUAL EXPENSES. Tuition and fees: $12,567. **Room and board:** $5,232. **Books and supplies:** $375. **Other expenses:** $750.

FINANCIAL AID. 82% of freshmen, 70% of continuing students receive some form of aid. 95% of grants, 99% of loans, 43% of jobs based on need. 104 enrolled freshmen were judged to have need, all were offered aid. Academic, leadership, alumni affiliation scholarships available. **Aid applications:** No closing date; priority given to applications received by March 1;

applicants notified on a rolling basis beginning on or about March 15. **Additional information:** Tuition Reduction Work Plan offered combining job and grant.

ADDRESS/TELEPHONE. Martha Green Quirk, Dir Admissions and Enrollment, Principia College, Elsah, IL 62028-9799. (618) 374-5176. (800) 851-1084. Fax: (618) 374-4000.

Quincy University
Quincy, Illinois CB code: 1645

Admissions: 69% of applicants accepted
Based on:
- ••• School record, test scores
- •• Activities, recommendations
- • Essay, interview, special talents

Completion: 90% of freshmen end year in good standing
64% graduate, 22% of these enter graduate study

4-year private university, coed, affiliated with Roman Catholic Church. Founded in 1860. **Accreditation:** Regional. **Undergraduate enrollment:** 538 men, 546 women full time; 41 men, 52 women part time. **Graduate enrollment:** 26 men, 20 women part time. **Faculty:** 103 total (71 full time), 61 with doctorates or other terminal degrees. **Location:** Suburban campus in large town; 280 miles from Chicago, 120 miles from St. Louis, Missouri. **Calendar:** Semester, limited summer session. Extensive evening/early morning classes. **Microcomputers:** 132 located in dormitories, libraries, classrooms, computer centers. **Special facilities:** 80-acre biological field station for environmental studies, art gallery.

DEGREES OFFERED. AA, AS, BA, BS, MS, MBA. 226 bachelor's degrees awarded. 27% in business and management, 6% communications, 17% teacher education, 7% life sciences, 19% social sciences. Graduate degrees offered in 2 major fields of study.

UNDERGRADUATE MAJORS. Associate: Computer programming. **Bachelor's:** Accounting, art education, art history, biology, business administration and management, chemistry, clinical laboratory science, communications, computer and information sciences, elementary education, English, English education, finance, history, humanities, information sciences and systems, international studies, management information systems, marketing management, mathematics, mathematics education, music business management, music education, music performance, personnel management, philosophy, physical education, political science and government, predentistry, prelaw, premedicine, preveterinary, psychology, religious education, science education, social studies education, social work, sociology, specific learning disabilities, studio art, theological studies.

ACADEMIC PROGRAMS. Double major, dual enrollment of high school students, honors program, independent study, internships, student-designed major, study abroad, teacher preparation; liberal arts/career combination in engineering; combined bachelor's/graduate program in business administration. **Remedial services:** Learning center, reduced course load, special counselor, tutoring. **Placement/credit:** AP, CLEP General and Subject, institutional tests; 30 credit hours maximum for bachelor's degree.

ACADEMIC REQUIREMENTS. Freshmen must earn minimum GPA of 2.0 to continue in good standing. 88% of freshmen return for sophomore year. Students must declare major by end of second year. **Graduation requirements:** 64 hours for associate (15 in major), 124 hours for bachelor's (27 in major). Most students required to take courses in arts/fine arts, English, history, humanities, mathematics, philosophy/religion, biological/physical sciences, social sciences. **Postgraduate studies:** 3% enter law school, 3% enter medical school, 3% enter MBA programs, 13% enter other graduate study. **Additional information:** 2 programs, the Mentor Program and the Freshman Year Experience, designed specifically for freshmen to ensure successful transition to university life, are offered.

FRESHMAN ADMISSIONS. Selection criteria: School achievement record and test scores most important. Consideration also given to recommendations, motivation, involvement in nonacademic areas, and seriousness of educational purpose. **High school preparation:** 16 units recommended. Recommended units include biological science 1, English 4, foreign language 2, mathematics 3, physical science 2 and social science 4. **Test requirements:** SAT or ACT; score report by August 1.

1992 FRESHMAN CLASS PROFILE. 1,100 men and women applied, 755 accepted; 167 men enrolled, 150 women enrolled. 66% had high school GPA of 3.0 or higher, 32% between 2.0 and 2.99. 23% were in top tenth and 66% were in top quarter of graduating class. **Academic background:** Mid 50% of enrolled freshmen had ACT composite between 22-28. 95% submitted ACT scores. **Characteristics:** 68% from in state, 86% live in college housing, 8% have minority backgrounds, 1% are foreign students. Average age is 18.

FALL-TERM APPLICATIONS. No fee. No closing date; applicants notified on a rolling basis; must reply within 4 weeks. Audition required for music applicants. Interview recommended. Portfolio recommended for art applicants. Tapes may be accepted in place of live audition. Deferred and early admission available.

STUDENT LIFE. Housing: Dormitories (men, women); apartment housing available. **Activities:** Student government, magazine, radio, student newspaper, television, yearbook, choral groups, concert band, drama, jazz band, music ensembles, pep band, symphony orchestra, campus ministry, Circle-K, Black Student Organization, service clubs, entrepreneur club.

ATHLETICS. NCAA. **Intercollegiate:** Baseball M, basketball, football M, soccer, softball W, tennis, volleyball. **Intramural:** Badminton, baseball M, basketball, bowling, soccer, softball, tennis, volleyball.

STUDENT SERVICES. Career counseling, employment service for undergraduates, freshman orientation, personal counseling, placement service for graduates, services/facilities for handicapped.

ANNUAL EXPENSES. Tuition and fees (1992-93): $9,160. **Room and board:** $3,666. **Books and supplies:** $400. **Other expenses:** $620.

FINANCIAL AID. 98% of freshmen, 93% of continuing students receive some form of aid. 59% of grants, 85% of loans, 65% of jobs based on need. Academic, music/drama, art, athletic, state/district residency, leadership, religious affiliation scholarships available. **Aid applications:** No closing date; applicants notified on a rolling basis beginning on or about March 1; must reply within 3 weeks.

ADDRESS/TELEPHONE. Patrick Olwig, Director of Admissions, Quincy University, 1800 College Avenue, Quincy, IL 62301-2699. (217) 222-8020 ext. 210. (800) 688-4295. Fax: (217) 228-5376.

Ray College of Design
Chicago, Illinois CB code: 2908

Admissions: 91% of applicants accepted
Based on:
- ••• Special talents
- •• Interview
- • Activities, essay, recommendations, school record, test scores

Completion: 92% of freshmen end year in good standing
92% graduate

4-year proprietary art college, coed. Founded in 1916. **Undergraduate enrollment:** 130 men, 350 women full time; 130 men, 240 women part time. **Faculty:** 93 total (14 full time), 5 with doctorates or other terminal degrees. **Location:** Urban campus in very large city; downtown Chicago. **Calendar:** Semester. Saturday and extensive evening/early morning classes. **Microcomputers:** 25 located in classrooms, computer centers. **Special facilities:** Computer graphics laboratories, exhibit galleries, incentive studio. **Additional facts:** Branch campus at Woodfield in Schaumburg.

DEGREES OFFERED. AAS, BA, BFA. 50 associate degrees awarded in 1992. 70 bachelor's degrees awarded.

UNDERGRADUATE MAJORS. Associate: Advertising, apparel and accessories marketing, clothing and textiles management/production/services, fashion design, fashion illustration, fashion merchandising, graphic design, illustration design, interior design, marketing management, photography, public relations, retailing. **Bachelor's:** Advertising, apparel and accessories marketing, clothing and textiles management/production/services, fashion design, fashion merchandising, graphic design, illustration design, interior design, marketing management, public relations, retailing.

ACADEMIC PROGRAMS. Accelerated program, cooperative education, internships. **Remedial services:** Reduced course load.

ACADEMIC REQUIREMENTS. Freshmen must earn minimum GPA of 2.0 to continue in good standing. 92% of freshmen return for sophomore year. Students must declare major by end of first year. **Graduation requirements:** 60 hours for associate (48 in major), 120 hours for bachelor's (90 in major). Most students required to take courses in arts/fine arts, English, history, humanities, mathematics, social sciences. **Postgraduate studies:** 80% from 2-year programs enter 4-year programs.

FRESHMAN ADMISSIONS. Selection criteria: Samples of work required for advertising, design illustration, photography, fashion illustration, and fashion design applicants. Recommended units include biological science 1, English 4, foreign language 1, mathematics 3, physical science 1, social science 2 and science 1. art, interior design, drafting, fashion. **Test requirements:** Institutional examination required for fashion design applicants for admission.

1992 FRESHMAN CLASS PROFILE. 140 men applied, 130 accepted, 80 enrolled; 400 women applied, 360 accepted, 280 enrolled. 30% had high school GPA of 3.0 or higher, 60% between 2.0 and 2.99. 10% were in top quarter of graduating class. **Characteristics:** 80% from in state, 100% commute, 60% have minority backgrounds, 6% are foreign students. Average age is 19.

FALL-TERM APPLICATIONS. $50 fee. No closing date; applicants notified on a rolling basis. Portfolio required for advertising design, illustration, photography, fashion design, fashion illustration applicants. Essay required. Interview recommended. Deferred admission available. SAT or ACT scores recommended for placement and evaluation.

STUDENT LIFE. Activities: Student newspaper, student fashion competitions, art competitions, interior design competitions, Student Positive Action Committee.

STUDENT SERVICES. Employment service for undergraduates, freshman orientation, placement service for graduates, veterans counselor, services/facilities for handicapped.

ANNUAL EXPENSES. Tuition and fees: $8,330. **Books and supplies:** $1,000. **Other expenses:** $1,260.

FINANCIAL AID. 86% of freshmen, 75% of continuing students receive some form of aid. All grants, 94% of loans, all jobs based on need. 66 enrolled freshmen were judged to have need, all were offered aid. Academic, art scholarships available. **Aid applications:** No closing date; priority given to applications received by January 1; applicants notified on a rolling basis; must reply immediately.

ADDRESS/TELEPHONE. Julie Spencer, Director of Admissions, Ray College of Design, 401 North Wabash Avenue, Chicago, IL 60611. (312) 280-3500. Fax: (312) 280-3528.

Rend Lake College
Ina, Illinois CB code: 1673

2-year public community college, coed. Founded in 1955. **Accreditation:** Regional. **Undergraduate enrollment:** 2,966 men and women. **Location:** Rural campus in rural community; 45 miles from Carbondale, 85 miles from St. Louis, Missouri. **Calendar:** Semester.

FRESHMAN ADMISSIONS. Selection criteria: Open admissions.

ANNUAL EXPENSES. Tuition and fees (1992-93): $896, $1,412 additional for out-of-district students, $4,605 additional for out-of-state students. **Books and supplies:** $375. **Other expenses:** $1,031.

ADDRESS/TELEPHONE. Sue Wells, Director of Admissions and Records, Rend Lake College, Route 1, Ina, IL 62846. (618) 437-5321 ext. 230. Fax: (618) 437-5677.

Richland Community College
Decatur, Illinois CB code: 0738

2-year public community college, coed. Founded in 1971. **Accreditation:** Regional. **Undergraduate enrollment:** 563 men, 628 women full time; 1,156 men, 1,763 women part time. **Faculty:** 224 total (49 full time), 11 with doctorates or other terminal degrees. **Location:** Urban campus in small city; 180 miles from Chicago, 120 miles from St. Louis, Missouri. **Calendar:** Semester. Saturday and extensive evening/early morning classes. **Microcomputers:** 130 located in libraries, classrooms, computer centers.

DEGREES OFFERED. AA, AS, AAS. 392 associate degrees awarded in 1992. 25% in business and management, 15% business/office and marketing/distribution, 7% teacher education, 25% social sciences, 22% trade and industry.

UNDERGRADUATE MAJORS. Accounting, aerospace/aeronautical/astronautical engineering, Afro-American (black) studies, agribusiness, agricultural production, American literature, American studies, art history, biological and physical sciences, biology, business and management, business and office, business computer/console/peripheral equipment operation, business data entry equipment operation, business data processing and related programs, business data programming, ceramic engineering, ceramics, chemical engineering, chemistry, civil engineering, communications, comparative literature, computer and information sciences, computer engineering, computer graphics, computer programming, computer technology, creative writing, data processing, drafting and design technology, drawing, East Asian studies, Eastern European studies, education, electrical and electronics equipment repair, electrical/electronics/communications engineering, electronic technology, engineering, engineering and other disciplines, engineering mechanics, engineering physics, English, English literature, European studies, finance, fine arts, French, German, history, humanities, industrial engineering, industrial equipment maintenance and repair, industrial technology, journalism, legal secretary, liberal/general studies, marketing management, mathematics, mechanical engineering, medical secretary, music, nursing, office supervision and management, painting, philosophy, physical sciences, physics, power plant operation and maintenance, preengineering, prelaw, printmaking, psychology, real estate, retailing, secretarial and related programs, social foundations, social sciences, social work, Spanish, speech, teacher aide, transportation management, visual and performing arts, word processing.

ACADEMIC PROGRAMS. 2-year transfer program, dual enrollment of high school students, honors program, independent study. **Remedial services:** Learning center, reduced course load, remedial instruction, special counselor, tutoring. **Placement/credit:** AP, CLEP General and Subject, institutional tests; 30 credit hours maximum for associate degree.

ACADEMIC REQUIREMENTS. Freshmen must earn minimum GPA of 1.8 to continue in good standing. Students must declare major on enrollment. **Graduation requirements:** 60 hours for associate (16 in major). Most students required to take courses in arts/fine arts, English, humanities, mathematics, biological/physical sciences, social sciences.

FRESHMAN ADMISSIONS. Selection criteria: Open admissions.

1992 FRESHMAN CLASS PROFILE. 671 men, 808 women enrolled. **Characteristics:** 100% from in state, 100% commute. Average age is 25.

FALL-TERM APPLICATIONS. No fee. No closing date; applicants notified on a rolling basis; must reply by registration. Early admission available. SAT/ACT recommended for placement.

STUDENT LIFE. Activities: Student government, student newspaper, drama.

ATHLETICS. NJCAA. **Intercollegiate:** Basketball M, volleyball W. **Intramural:** Basketball M, volleyball W.

STUDENT SERVICES. Aptitude testing, career counseling, employment service for undergraduates, freshman orientation, on-campus day care, personal counseling, placement service for graduates, special adviser for adult students, veterans counselor, services/facilities for handicapped.

ANNUAL EXPENSES. Tuition and fees: $1,035, $2,083 additional for out-of-district students, $3,041 additional for out-of-state students. **Books and supplies:** $400.

FINANCIAL AID. 28% of freshmen, 34% of continuing students receive some form of aid. 93% of grants, 96% of loans, 49% of jobs based on need. Academic, athletic scholarships available. **Aid applications:** No closing date; applicants notified on a rolling basis beginning on or about June 1.

ADDRESS/TELEPHONE. D. Michael Beube, Director of Admissions, Richland Community College, One College Park, Decatur, IL 62521. (217) 875-7200 ext. 267. Fax: (217) 875-6965.

Robert Morris College: Chicago
Chicago, Illinois CB code: 1670

2-year private business, junior college, coed. Founded in 1965. **Accreditation:** Regional. **Undergraduate enrollment:** 3,122 men and women. **Faculty:** 105 total (55 full time). **Location:** Urban campus in very large city; In downtown Loop area. **Calendar:** Quarter, extensive summer session. **Microcomputers:** 250 located in libraries, classrooms. **Additional facts:** Additional commuter campuses in Springfield and Orland Park.

DEGREES OFFERED. AS, AAS. 546 associate degrees awarded in 1992. 30% in business and management, 68% business/office and marketing/distribution.

UNDERGRADUATE MAJORS. Accounting, allied health, business administration and management, business data processing and related programs, business data programming, computer graphics, drafting, drafting and design technology, legal assistant/paralegal, legal secretary, medical assistant, medical records technology, microcomputer software, retailing, secretarial and related programs, tourism.

ACADEMIC PROGRAMS. Accelerated program, cooperative education, honors program, internships. **Remedial services:** Learning center, preadmission summer program, reduced course load, tutoring, preadmission program available every quarter. **Placement/credit:** Institutional tests.

ACADEMIC REQUIREMENTS. Freshmen must earn minimum GPA of 2.0 to continue in good standing. Students must declare major on application. **Graduation requirements:** 100 hours for associate (64 in major). Most students required to take courses in English, mathematics. **Additional information:** All students required to comply with college dress and attendance policies.

FRESHMAN ADMISSIONS. Selection criteria: Applicants must interview with counselor and submit high school transcript. Applicants whose academic records are not satisfactory offered tuition-free college-bound program. Upon successful completion, students admitted to career major.

1992 FRESHMAN CLASS PROFILE. 2,343 men and women enrolled. **Characteristics:** 95% from in state, 100% commute, 74% have minority backgrounds. Average age is 20.

FALL-TERM APPLICATIONS. $25 fee. No closing date; applicants notified on a rolling basis; must reply by registration. Interview required.

ATHLETICS. Intramural: Basketball, soccer, softball, volleyball.

STUDENT SERVICES. Career counseling, personal counseling, placement service for graduates, services/facilities for handicapped.

ANNUAL EXPENSES. Tuition and fees: $8,100. **Books and supplies:** $525. **Other expenses:** $1,020.

FINANCIAL AID. 82% of freshmen, 82% of continuing students receive some form of aid. 92% of grants, 81% of loans, all jobs based on need. Academic, leadership scholarships available. **Aid applications:** No closing date; priority given to applications received by June 1; applicants notified on a rolling basis.

ADDRESS/TELEPHONE. Janet S. Day, Senior Vice President for Admissions, Robert Morris College: Chicago, 180 North LaSalle Street, Chicago, IL 60601. (312) 836-4608.

Rock Valley College
Rockford, Illinois CB code: 1674

2-year public community college, coed. Founded in 1964. **Accreditation:** Regional. **Undergraduate enrollment:** 1,131 men, 1,165 women full time; 2,861 men, 4,057 women part time. **Faculty:** 520 total (140 full time), 39 with doctorates or other terminal degrees. **Location:** Suburban campus in small city; 85 miles northwest of Chicago. **Calendar:** Semester, limited summer session. Saturday and extensive evening/early morning classes. **Microcomputers:** 66 located in classrooms, computer centers.

DEGREES OFFERED. AA, AS, AAS. 672 associate degrees awarded in 1992.

UNDERGRADUATE MAJORS. Accounting, aeronautical technology, aircraft mechanics, automotive mechanics, automotive technology, business administration and management, business and office, business data processing and related programs, business data programming, computer and information sciences, construction, electrical installation, electrical/electronics/communications engineering, electronic technology, elementary education, engineering, engineering and engineering-related technologies, finance, fire control and safety technology, hotel/motel and restaurant management, industrial technology, international business management, law enforcement and corrections technologies, legal secretary, liberal/general studies, library assistant, manufacturing technology, marketing and distribution, marketing management, masonry/tile setting, mechanical design technology, medical secretary, nursing, quality control technology, respiratory therapy technology, retailing, secondary education, secretarial and related programs, small business management and ownership, social work, word processing.

ACADEMIC PROGRAMS. 2-year transfer program, cooperative education, dual enrollment of high school students, independent study, internships, student-designed major, study abroad. **Remedial services:** Learning center, reduced course load, remedial instruction, tutoring. **Placement/credit:** AP, CLEP General and Subject, institutional tests; 39 credit hours maximum for associate degree.

ACADEMIC REQUIREMENTS. Freshmen must earn minimum GPA of 1.5 to continue in good standing. 41% of freshmen return for sophomore year. Students must declare major on enrollment. **Graduation requirements:** 64 hours for associate. Most students required to take courses in English, mathematics, biological/physical sciences, social sciences.

FRESHMAN ADMISSIONS. Selection criteria: Open admissions. Selective admissions to nursing and respiratory therapy programs based on test scores. One chemistry required for nursing applicants, 1 chemistry and 1 algebra for respiratory therapy applicants.

1992 FRESHMAN CLASS PROFILE. 1,145 men, 1,391 women enrolled. **Characteristics:** 100% from in state, 100% commute, 11% have minority backgrounds. Average age is 20.

FALL-TERM APPLICATIONS. No fee. No closing date; applicants notified on a rolling basis; must reply by registration. Interview required for respiratory therapy, nursing, aviation maintenance applicants. Audition required for music applicants. Deferred and early admission available.

STUDENT LIFE. Activities: Student government, student newspaper, choral groups, concert band, drama, jazz band, music ensembles, musical theater, 24 student interest groups.

ATHLETICS. NJCAA. **Intercollegiate:** Baseball M, basketball, football M, golf M, softball W, tennis, volleyball W. **Intramural:** Basketball M, bowling, cross-country, racquetball, skiing, table tennis.

STUDENT SERVICES. Aptitude testing, career counseling, employment service for undergraduates, freshman orientation, personal counseling, placement service for graduates, special adviser for adult students, veterans counselor, services/facilities for handicapped.

ANNUAL EXPENSES. Tuition and fees: $1,204, $2,673 additional for out-of-district students, $4,785 additional for out-of-state students. **Books and supplies:** $600. **Other expenses:** $2,400.

FINANCIAL AID. 48% of freshmen, 52% of continuing students receive some form of aid. Grants, loans, jobs available. Academic, music/drama, leadership, alumni affiliation, minority scholarships available. **Aid applications:** No closing date; priority given to applications received by June 1; applicants notified on a rolling basis beginning on or about June 1; must reply within 2 weeks.

ADDRESS/TELEPHONE. Peter Lonsway, Director of Admissions and Records, Rock Valley College, 3301 North Mulford Road, Rockford, IL 61114. (815) 654-4285. Fax: (815) 654-4459.

Rockford College

Rockford, Illinois — CB code: 1665

Admissions: 84% of applicants accepted
Based on:
••• School record, test scores
•• Activities, interview, recommendations
• Essay, special talents
Completion: 85% of freshmen end year in good standing
25% enter graduate study

4-year private liberal arts college, coed. Founded in 1847. **Accreditation:** Regional. **Undergraduate enrollment:** 301 men, 451 women full time; 150 men, 225 women part time. **Graduate enrollment:** 9 men, 13 women full time; 137 men, 205 women part time. **Faculty:** 147 total (72 full time), 45 with doctorates or other terminal degrees. **Location:** Suburban campus in small city; 75 miles from Chicago. **Calendar:** Semester, extensive summer session. Extensive evening/early morning classes. **Microcomputers:** 60 located in libraries, classrooms, computer centers. **Special facilities:** Art gallery, performing arts, theater.

DEGREES OFFERED. BA, BS, BFA, MBA. 258 bachelor's degrees awarded in 1992. 32% in business and management, 5% computer sciences, 16% teacher education, 8% health sciences, 7% psychology, 9% social sciences, 6% visual and performing arts. Graduate degrees offered in 5 major fields of study.

UNDERGRADUATE MAJORS. Accounting, anthropology, art history, biological and physical sciences, biology, business administration and management, business and management, business economics, chemistry, classics, clinical laboratory science, computer and information sciences, creative writing, criminal justice studies, dramatic arts, early childhood education, economics, education, elementary education, English, English literature, finance, fine arts, French, German, history, humanities and social sciences, information sciences and systems, international studies, junior high education, Latin, liberal/general studies, management information systems, marketing management, mathematics, music, musical theater, nursing, philosophy, physical sciences, political science and government, predentistry, preengineering, prelaw, premedicine, prepharmacy, preveterinary, psychology, public administration, religion, secondary education, social sciences, social work, sociology, Spanish, urban studies, visual and performing arts.

ACADEMIC PROGRAMS. Accelerated program, double major, dual enrollment of high school students, honors program, independent study, internships, student-designed major, study abroad, teacher preparation, United Nations semester, Washington semester; liberal arts/career combination in engineering; combined bachelor's/graduate program in business administration. **Remedial services:** Learning center, preadmission summer program, reduced course load, remedial instruction, special counselor, tutoring. **ROTC:** Army. **Placement/credit:** AP, CLEP General and Subject, institutional tests; 64 credit hours maximum for bachelor's degree.

ACADEMIC REQUIREMENTS. Freshmen must earn minimum GPA of 2.0 to continue in good standing. 80% of freshmen return for sophomore year. Students must declare major by end of second year. **Graduation requirements:** 124 hours for bachelor's (44 in major). Most students required to take courses in arts/fine arts, computer science, English, foreign languages, history, humanities, mathematics, philosophy/religion, biological/physical sciences, social sciences.

FRESHMAN ADMISSIONS. Selection criteria: School achievement record, test scores most important. Recommendations, activities, and interview also considered. **High school preparation:** 14 units required. Required and recommended units include biological science 2, English 4, foreign language 1-2, mathematics 2-3, physical science 1-2 and social science 3-4. **Test requirements:** SAT or ACT; score report by September 1.

1992 FRESHMAN CLASS PROFILE. 688 men and women applied, 580 accepted; 143 enrolled. 50% had high school GPA of 3.0 or higher, 50% between 2.0 and 2.99. 24% were in top tenth and 39% were in top quarter of graduating class. **Academic background:** Mid 50% of enrolled freshmen had SAT-V between 450-550, SAT-M between 450-560; ACT composite between 21-26. 2% submitted SAT scores, 98% submitted ACT scores. **Characteristics:** 79% from in state, 60% commute, 13% have minority backgrounds, 4% are foreign students. Average age is 18.

FALL-TERM APPLICATIONS. $35 fee, may be waived for applicants with need. No closing date; applicants notified on a rolling basis; must reply within 3 weeks. Interview recommended. Essay recommended. Deferred and early admission available.

STUDENT LIFE. Housing: Dormitories (men, women, coed). Students not living with family must live on campus. **Activities:** Student government, magazine, radio, student newspaper, yearbook, choral groups, dance, drama, music ensembles, musical theater, pep band, several religious, ethnic, and social service organizations, Phi Beta Kappa.

ATHLETICS. NCAA. **Intercollegiate:** Baseball M, basketball, diving, golf M, soccer, softball W, swimming, tennis, volleyball W. **Intramural:** Archery, badminton, basketball, bowling, diving, golf M, soccer, softball, swimming, table tennis, tennis, track and field, volleyball.

STUDENT SERVICES. Aptitude testing, career counseling, employment service for undergraduates, freshman orientation, health services, personal counseling, placement service for graduates, substance abuse counselor, services/facilities for handicapped.

ANNUAL EXPENSES. Tuition and fees (1992-93): $10,025. **Room and board:** $3,575. **Books and supplies:** $600. **Other expenses:** $1,080.

FINANCIAL AID. 80% of freshmen, 85% of continuing students receive some form of aid. 90% of grants, 95% of loans, all jobs based on need. Academic, music/drama, art, leadership, alumni affiliation scholarships available. **Aid applications:** No closing date; priority given to applications received by April 15; applicants notified on a rolling basis; must reply by date indicated on award notification. **Additional information:** Will meet 100% of student's demonstrated financial need.

ADDRESS/TELEPHONE. Miriam King, VP for Enrollment Management, Rockford College, 5050 East State Street, Rockford, IL 61108-2393. (815) 226-4050. (800) 892-2984. Fax: (815) 226-4119.

Roosevelt University

Chicago, Illinois — CB code: 1666

4-year private university, coed. Founded in 1945. **Accreditation:** Regional. **Undergraduate enrollment:** 716 men, 873 women full time; 1,171 men, 1,759 women part time. **Graduate enrollment:** 141 men, 173 women full time; 629 men, 982 women part time. **Faculty:** 508 total (151 full time), 285 with doctorates or other terminal degrees. **Location:** Urban campus in very large city. **Calendar:** Semester, extensive summer session. **Microcomputers:** 94 located in libraries, classrooms, computer centers. **Special facilities:** Electron microscope. **Additional facts:** Branch campus in Arlington Heights and extension site in Little Village.

DEGREES OFFERED. BA, BS, MA, MS, MBA, MEd, EdD. 825 bachelor's degrees awarded in 1992. 35% in business and management, 18% computer sciences, 13% multi/interdisciplinary studies, 6% psychology, 7% social sciences. Graduate degrees offered in 43 major fields of study.

UNDERGRADUATE MAJORS. Accounting, actuarial sciences, advertising, Afro-American (black) studies, American studies, art history, biology, business administration and management, business economics, business education, chemistry, city/community/regional planning, comparative literature, computer and information sciences, cytotechnology, data processing, dramatic arts, early childhood education, economics, electronic technology, elementary education, English, English education, finance, foreign languages education, French, health care administration, history, histotechnology, hotel/motel and restaurant management, humanities and social sciences, industrial engineering, information sciences and systems, interior design, international relations, international studies, jazz, journalism, liberal/general studies, management science, marketing management, mathematics, mathematics education, medical laboratory technologies, mining and petroleum technologies, music, music business management, music education, music history and appreciation, music performance, music theory and composition, musical theater, nuclear medical technology, operations research, personnel management, philosophy, physics, political science and government, predentistry, prelaw, premedicine, prepharmacy, preveterinary, psychology, public administration, public relations, radiation therapy technology, radio/television broadcasting, secondary education, social sciences, sociology, Spanish, speech, telecommunications, urban studies, visual and performing arts, women's studies.

ACADEMIC PROGRAMS. Accelerated program, double major, dual enrollment of high school students, external degree, honors program, independent study, internships, student-designed major, study abroad, teacher preparation, weekend college, cross-registration; liberal arts/career combination in engineering, health sciences. **Remedial services:** Learning center, preadmission summer program, reduced course load, remedial instruction, special counselor, tutoring, learning support services program for students with learning disabilities. **Placement/credit:** AP, CLEP General and Subject, institutional tests.

ACADEMIC REQUIREMENTS. Freshmen must earn minimum GPA of 2.0 to continue in good standing. 75% of freshmen return for sophomore year. Students must declare major by end of second year. **Graduation requirements:** 120 hours for bachelor's (30 in major). Most students required to take courses in English, humanities, mathematics, biological/physical sciences, social sciences. **Additional information:** Cross-registration with School of Art Institute of Chicago and Spertus College of Judaica.

FRESHMAN ADMISSIONS. Selection criteria: Grades, class rank, and test scores most important. **High school preparation:** 15 units recommended. Extensive work in English, history, mathematics, foreign language, and science recommended. **Test requirements:** SAT or ACT; score report by August 15. Institutional examination accepted in lieu of SAT or ACT. **Additional information:** Placement evaluation required for all admitted, degree-seeking undergraduate students.

1992 FRESHMAN CLASS PROFILE. 90 men, 166 women enrolled. 48% had high school GPA of 3.0 or higher, 25% between 2.0 and 2.99. **Characteristics:** 88% from in state, 94% commute. Average age is 20.

FALL-TERM APPLICATIONS. $20 fee, may be waived for applicants with need. No closing date; priority given to applications received by August 15; applicants notified on a rolling basis; must reply by registration. Interview required for early admission, borderline applicants. Audition required for music, theatre applicants. Portfolio recommended for art, theatre applicants. CRDA. Deferred and early admission available. Institutional early decision plan.

STUDENT LIFE. Housing: Dormitories (coed). Dormitories connected to main building for easy access to classrooms. **Activities:** Student government, magazine, radio, student newspaper, yearbook, choral groups, concert band, drama, jazz band, music ensembles, musical theater, opera, symphony orchestra, fraternities, sororities, Christian Bible Groups, theater club, Black Student Union, Hispanic Organization.

ATHLETICS. Intramural: Archery, badminton, basketball, soccer M, softball, table tennis, tennis M, volleyball.

STUDENT SERVICES. Aptitude testing, career counseling, employment service for undergraduates, freshman orientation, personal counseling, placement service for graduates, special adviser for adult students, veterans counselor, services/facilities for handicapped.

ANNUAL EXPENSES. Tuition and fees (1992-93): $8,280. **Room and board:** $4,800. **Books and supplies:** $528. **Other expenses:** $1,456.

FINANCIAL AID. 60% of freshmen, 65% of continuing students receive some form of aid. 73% of grants, 78% of loans, 12% of jobs based on need. Academic, music/drama, art, leadership scholarships available. **Aid applications:** No closing date; priority given to applications received by May 1; applicants notified on a rolling basis; must reply within 1 week.

ADDRESS/TELEPHONE. Barbara H. Gianneschi, Dean of Enrollment Management, Roosevelt University, 430 South Michigan Avenue, Chicago, IL 60605-1394. (312) 341-3515. Fax: (312) 341-3523.

Rosary College

River Forest, Illinois — CB code: 1667

Admissions:		70% of applicants accepted
Based on:	•••	School record
	••	Essay, interview, recommendations, test scores
	•	Activities, special talents
Completion:		92% of freshmen end year in good standing
		62% graduate

4-year private liberal arts college, coed, affiliated with Roman Catholic Church. Founded in 1901. **Accreditation:** Regional. **Undergraduate enrollment:** 130 men, 462 women full time; 64 men, 199 women part time. **Graduate enrollment:** 67 men, 117 women full time; 227 men, 500 women part time. **Faculty:** 123 total (79 full time), 62 with doctorates or other terminal degrees. **Location:** Suburban campus in large town; 10 miles from downtown Chicago. **Calendar:** Semester, extensive summer session. **Microcomputers:** 60 located in libraries, classrooms, computer centers. **Special facilities:** Art gallery, language laboratory, athletic facilities, new computer classroom.

DEGREES OFFERED. BA, MBA, MEd. 230 bachelor's degrees awarded in 1992. 40% in business and management, 10% communications, 6% home economics, 9% letters/literature, 5% life sciences, 7% psychology, 12% social sciences. Graduate degrees offered in 6 major fields of study.

UNDERGRADUATE MAJORS. Accounting, American studies, biochemistry, biology, British studies, business and management, chemistry, communications, computer and information sciences, computer mathematics, corporate communications, economics, English, environmental science, European studies, fashion design, fashion merchandising, fine arts, food management, food science and nutrition, foreign languages (multiple emphasis), French, German, history, home economics, humanities and social sciences, information sciences and systems, international business management, Italian, Latin American studies, management information systems, mathematics, music, philosophy, political science and government, predentistry, prelaw, premedicine, prepharmacy, psychology, religion, social sciences, sociology, Spanish, technical and business writing, visual and performing arts.

ACADEMIC PROGRAMS. Accelerated program, double major, dual enrollment of high school students, honors program, independent study, internships, student-designed major, study abroad, teacher preparation, Washington semester, cross-registration, 2+2 nursing, medical technology programs with Rush University; combined bachelor's/graduate program in business administration. **Remedial services:** Reduced course load, remedial instruction, special counselor, tutoring. **Placement/credit:** AP, CLEP General and Subject, institutional tests; 28 credit hours maximum for bachelor's degree.

ACADEMIC REQUIREMENTS. Freshmen must earn minimum GPA of 2.0 to continue in good standing. 75% of freshmen return for sophomore year. Students must declare major by end of second year. **Graduation requirements:** 124 hours for bachelor's (50 in major). Most students required to take courses in arts/fine arts, English, foreign languages, history, humanities, mathematics, philosophy/religion, biological/physical sciences, social sciences.

FRESHMAN ADMISSIONS. Selection criteria: Academic record and class rank most important. Test scores, recommendations considered. **High school preparation:** 16 units required. 14 units must be distributed among English, mathematics, laboratory science, social science, and foreign language. **Test requirements:** SAT or ACT; score report by August 15.

1992 FRESHMAN CLASS PROFILE. 81 men applied, 48 accepted, 25 enrolled; 326 women applied, 236 accepted, 120 enrolled. 75% had high school GPA of 3.0 or higher, 25% between 2.0 and 2.99. 28% were in top tenth and 50% were in top quarter of graduating class. **Academic background:** Mid 50% of enrolled freshmen had ACT composite between 18-23. 93% submitted ACT scores. **Characteristics:** 90% from in state, 60% live in college housing, 25% have minority backgrounds, 1% are foreign students. Average age is 18.

FALL-TERM APPLICATIONS. $20 fee, may be waived for applicants with need. No closing date; priority given to applications received by June 15; applicants notified on a rolling basis; must reply by May 1 or within 3 weeks if notified thereafter. Interview recommended. Audition recommended for music applicants. Portfolio recommended for art applicants. Essay recommended. CRDA. Deferred and early admission available.

STUDENT LIFE. Housing: Dormitories (coed). International wing available for international students. **Activities:** Student government, magazine, radio, student newspaper, choral groups, drama, pep band, campus ministry, African-American Association, Organization of Latin Americans.

ATHLETICS. NAIA. **Intercollegiate:** Baseball M, basketball, soccer M, tennis, volleyball W. **Intramural:** Badminton, basketball, bowling, cross-country, field hockey, racquetball, softball, swimming, table tennis, volleyball.

STUDENT SERVICES. Aptitude testing, career counseling, employment service for undergraduates, freshman orientation, health services, on-campus day care, personal counseling, placement service for graduates, special adviser for adult students, veterans counselor, minority student services director, services/facilities for handicapped.

ANNUAL EXPENSES. Tuition and fees: $10,550. **Room and board:** $4,490. **Books and supplies:** $500. **Other expenses:** $900.

FINANCIAL AID. 75% of freshmen, 70% of continuing students receive some form of aid. 83% of grants, all loans, 49% of jobs based on need. 107 enrolled freshmen were judged to have need, all were offered aid. Academic, athletic, leadership, religious affiliation scholarships available. **Aid applications:** No closing date; priority given to applications received by May 1; applicants notified on a rolling basis beginning on or about April 1; must reply within 2 weeks.

ADDRESS/TELEPHONE. Hildegarde Schmidt, Dean of Admissions and Financial Aid, Rosary College, 7900 West Division, River Forest, IL 60305-1099. (708) 524-6800. (800) 828-8475. Fax: (708) 366-5360.

Rush University
Chicago, Illinois — CB code: 3262

2-year upper-division private health professions university, coed. Founded in 1971. **Accreditation:** Regional. **Undergraduate enrollment:** 33 men, 188 women full time; 2 men, 36 women part time. **Graduate enrollment:** 291 men, 430 women full time; 39 men, 278 women part time. **Faculty:** 853 total (828 full time), 479 with doctorates or other terminal degrees. **Location:** Urban campus in very large city; 2 miles from downtown. **Calendar:** Quarter, limited summer session. **Microcomputers:** 85 located in classrooms, computer centers. **Additional facts:** Educational component of Rush Presbyterian-St. Luke's Medical Center. Students use clinical and laboratory facilities of the Medical Center, its affiliated hospitals, and a community health center.

DEGREES OFFERED. BS, MS, D, MD. 91 bachelor's degrees awarded in 1992. 100% in health sciences. Graduate degrees offered in 11 major fields of study.

UNDERGRADUATE MAJORS. Clinical laboratory science, nursing.

ACADEMIC PROGRAMS. Registered nurse completion program; combined bachelor's/graduate program in medicine. **Remedial services:** Learning center. **Placement/credit:** CLEP Subject, institutional tests; 45 credit hours maximum for bachelor's degree.

ACADEMIC REQUIREMENTS. Students must declare major on application. **Graduation requirements:** 180 hours for bachelor's (82 in major).

ADMISSIONS. Admission decisions based on GPA and letters of recommendation.

FALL-TERM APPLICATIONS. $25 fee.

STUDENT LIFE. Housing: Dormitories (coed); apartment housing available. **Activities:** Student government, student newspaper, Christian Fellowship, Rape Victim Advocate Program, med technicians club.

STUDENT SERVICES. Career counseling, employment service for undergraduates, health services, on-campus day care, personal counseling, placement service for graduates, veterans counselor, services/facilities for handicapped.

ANNUAL EXPENSES. Tuition and fees (projected): $9,434. **Room and board:** $2,100 room only. **Books and supplies:** $325. **Other expenses:** $1,100.

FINANCIAL AID. 65% of continuing students receive some form of aid. 87% of grants, 95% of loans, all jobs based on need. Minority scholarships available. **Aid applications:** No closing date; priority given to applications received by April 15; applicants notified on a rolling basis beginning on or about June 1.

ADDRESS/TELEPHONE. Phyllis Peterson, Director of College Admission Services, Rush University, 1743 West Harrison Street #119, Chicago, IL 60612. (312) 942-7100. Fax: (312) 942-2219.

St. Augustine College
Chicago, Illinois — CB code: 0697

2-year private junior college, coed, affiliated with Episcopal Church. Founded in 1980. **Accreditation:** Regional. **Undergraduate enrollment:** 412 men, 881 women full time; 9 men, 39 women part time. **Faculty:** 129 total (11 full time), 9 with doctorates or other terminal degrees. **Location:** Urban campus in very large city. **Calendar:** Semester, limited summer session. **Microcomputers:** 80 located in libraries, computer centers. **Additional facts:** Programs geared to suit a primarily adult Hispanic student population.

DEGREES OFFERED. AA, AAS. 125 associate degrees awarded in 1992. 30% in business and management, 15% business/office and marketing/distribution, 10% computer sciences, 45% social sciences.

UNDERGRADUATE MAJORS. Accounting, business administration and management, business and management, computer and information sciences, liberal/general studies, management information systems, psychology, secretarial and related programs, social sciences.

ACADEMIC PROGRAMS. 2-year transfer program, double major, independent study, internships. **Remedial services:** Learning center, preadmission summer program, remedial instruction, special counselor, tutoring, laboratory for students with low English proficiency. **Placement/credit:** CLEP General and Subject, institutional tests.

ACADEMIC REQUIREMENTS. Minimum grade-point average requirement varies with number of credit hours attempted. 40% of freshmen return for sophomore year. Students must declare major on enrollment. **Graduation requirements:** 60 hours for associate. Most students required to take courses in English, history, humanities, mathematics. **Additional information:** Curriculum offers several elective courses in English language to address the needs of 99% Hispanic student population.

FRESHMAN ADMISSIONS. Selection criteria: Open admissions. Ability to benefit test scores considered for students over 17 years old who have not completed high school. **Test requirements:** Ability to benefit test required for students who have not completed high school or equivalent. **Additional information:** Applicants without high school diploma or GED at time of enrollment must earn GED before completion of degree program.

1992 FRESHMAN CLASS PROFILE. 174 men, 335 women enrolled. **Characteristics:** 99% from in state, 100% commute, 100% have minority backgrounds, 1% are foreign students. Average age is 29.

FALL-TERM APPLICATIONS. No fee. No closing date; applicants notified on a rolling basis; must reply by registration. Deferred admission available.

STUDENT LIFE. Activities: Student government, student newspaper, choral groups.

ATHLETICS. Intercollegiate: Soccer M.

STUDENT SERVICES. Freshman orientation, on-campus day care, personal counseling, placement service for graduates, special adviser for adult students.

ANNUAL EXPENSES. Tuition and fees (1992-93): $4,960. **Books and supplies:** $800. **Other expenses:** $700.

FINANCIAL AID. 97% of freshmen, 97% of continuing students receive some form of aid. 98% of grants, all loans, all jobs based on need. Academic scholarships available. **Aid applications:** No closing date; applicants notified on a rolling basis.

ADDRESS/TELEPHONE. Guadalupe Moreno, Admissions and Records Officer, St. Augustine College, 1333 West Argyle, Chicago, IL 60640-3501. (312) 878-8756. Fax: (312) 878-8756 ext. 181.

St. Francis Medical Center College of Nursing
Peoria, Illinois — CB code: 1756

2-year upper-division private nursing college, coed, affiliated with Roman Catholic Church. Founded in 1905. **Accreditation:** Regional. **Undergraduate enrollment:** 16 men, 101 women full time; 1 man, 35 women part time. **Faculty:** 19 total, 5 with doctorates or other terminal degrees. **Location:** Urban campus in small city. **Calendar:** Semester, limited summer session. **Microcomputers:** 4 located on campus. **Additional facts:** Located at large medical center.

DEGREES OFFERED. BS. 40 bachelor's degrees awarded in 1992. 100% in health sciences.

UNDERGRADUATE MAJORS. Nursing.

ACADEMIC REQUIREMENTS. Students must declare major on application. **Graduation requirements:** 124 hours for bachelor's (62 in major). Most students required to take courses in computer science, English, humanities, mathematics, philosophy/religion, biological/physical sciences, social sciences.

STUDENT LIFE. Housing: Dormitories (coed). **Activities:** Student government, yearbook, choral groups, Christian Fellowship, Student Nurse Association of Illinois.

STUDENT SERVICES. Health services, personal counseling, special adviser for adult students, services/facilities for handicapped.

ANNUAL EXPENSES. Tuition and fees: $6,343. **Room and board:** $3,750. **Books and supplies:** $600. **Other expenses:** $1,257.

FINANCIAL AID. 88% of continuing students receive some form of aid. 75% of grants, 92% of loans based on need. All jobs based on criteria other than need. Academic, state/district residency, leadership, alumni affiliation, religious affiliation, minority scholarships available. **Aid applications:** No closing date; applicants notified on a rolling basis beginning on or about June 1; must reply within 10 days. **Additional information:** Modified Education Employment Program available to full-time students. Tuition waiver program for hospital employees available.

ADDRESS/TELEPHONE. Jan Farquharson, Director of Admissions/Recruitment, St. Francis Medical Center College of Nursing, 511 Greenleaf Street, Peoria, IL 61603. (309) 655-2596.

St. Joseph College of Nursing
Joliet, Illinois — CB code: 0155

2-year upper-division private nursing college, coed, affiliated with Roman Catholic Church. Founded in 1987. **Accreditation:** Regional. **Undergraduate enrollment:** 4 men, 100 women full time; 2 men, 42 women part time. **Fac-**

ulty: 20 total (16 full time), 3 with doctorates or other terminal degrees. **Location:** Suburban campus in small city; 40 miles from Chicago. **Calendar:** Semester, limited summer session. **Microcomputers:** 6 located in libraries. **Additional facts:** Affiliated with Franciscan Sisters of the Sacred Heart.

DEGREES OFFERED. BS. 41 bachelor's degrees awarded in 1992. 100% in health sciences.

UNDERGRADUATE MAJORS. Nursing.

ACADEMIC PROGRAMS. Placement/credit: Institutional tests.

ACADEMIC REQUIREMENTS. Students must declare major on application. **Graduation requirements:** 128 hours for bachelor's (57 in major). Most students required to take courses in English, humanities, mathematics, philosophy/religion, biological/physical sciences, social sciences.

STUDENT LIFE. 1992 freshman class profile: 100% commute. **Activities:** Student government, student newspaper, student volunteer service organization, Christian nurses association, student nurses association, liturgy committee. **Additional information:** Food service lockers and lounges available to accommodate commuter students.

STUDENT SERVICES. Career counseling, health services, personal counseling, services/facilities for handicapped.

ANNUAL EXPENSES. Tuition and fees: $7,460. **Books and supplies:** $750. **Other expenses:** $1,350.

FINANCIAL AID. 67% of continuing students receive some form of aid. 97% of grants, all loans based on need. scholarships available. **Aid applications:** Closing date June 1; applicants notified on or about June 15; must reply within 2 weeks.

ADDRESS/TELEPHONE. Alan Christensen, Director of Admissions, St. Joseph College of Nursing, 290 North Springfield Avenue, Joliet, IL 60435. (815) 741-7382. Fax: (815) 741-7131.

St. Xavier University

Chicago, Illinois CB code: 1708

4-year private university, coed, affiliated with Roman Catholic Church. Founded in 1847. **Accreditation:** Regional. **Undergraduate enrollment:** 332 men, 877 women full time; 242 men, 777 women part time. **Graduate enrollment:** 20 men, 31 women full time; 321 men, 1,250 women part time. **Faculty:** 285 total (165 full time). **Location:** Urban campus in very large city; 20 miles from downtown. **Calendar:** 4-1-4, limited summer session. Saturday classes. **Microcomputers:** Located in dormitories, libraries, classrooms, computer centers. **Special facilities:** Art gallery, music performance studio, theater, reading clinic, speech clinic, learning disabilities clinic, wellness center, learning assistance center, writing center, mathematics laboratory.

DEGREES OFFERED. BA, BS, MA, MS, MBA. 456 bachelor's degrees awarded in 1992. 35% in business and management, 12% teacher education, 20% health sciences, 15% social sciences. Graduate degrees offered in 17 major fields of study.

UNDERGRADUATE MAJORS. Accounting, art history, biological and physical sciences, biology, botany, business administration and management, chemistry, communications, computer and information sciences, criminal justice studies, early childhood education, education, elementary education, English, French, graphic design, history, humanities and social sciences, industrial and organizational psychology, international business management, international relations, international studies, junior high education, liberal/general studies, mathematics, music, music performance, nursing, philosophy, political science and government, predentistry, prelaw, premedicine, prepharmacy, preveterinary, psychology, radio/television technology, religion, religious education, religious music, secondary education, social sciences, sociology, Spanish, speech correction, speech pathology/audiology.

ACADEMIC PROGRAMS. Accelerated program, double major, independent study, internships, student-designed major, study abroad, teacher preparation, visiting/exchange student program, weekend college. **Remedial services:** Learning center, reduced course load, remedial instruction, special counselor, tutoring. **ROTC:** Air Force. **Placement/credit:** AP, CLEP General and Subject, institutional tests.

ACADEMIC REQUIREMENTS. Freshmen must earn minimum GPA of 2.0 to continue in good standing. 74% of freshmen return for sophomore year. Students must declare major by end of second year. **Graduation requirements:** 120 hours for bachelor's (50 in major). Most students required to take courses in arts/fine arts, English, foreign languages, history, humanities, mathematics, philosophy/religion, biological/physical sciences, social sciences.

FRESHMAN ADMISSIONS. Selection criteria: Class rank, GPA, and test scores most important. Counselor recommendation considered. **High school preparation:** 16 units recommended. Recommended units include English 4, foreign language 2, mathematics 3 and social science 4. Chemistry required of nursing applicants. **Test requirements:** SAT or ACT (ACT preferred); score report by August 1.

1992 FRESHMAN CLASS PROFILE. 63 men, 158 women enrolled. **Academic background:** Mid 50% of enrolled freshmen had ACT composite between 17-24. 90% submitted ACT scores. **Characteristics:** 95% from in state, 07% live in college housing, 27% have minority backgrounds, 1% are foreign students. Average age is 20.

FALL-TERM APPLICATIONS. $25 fee, may be waived for applicants with need. Closing date August 15; priority given to applications received by May 1; applicants notified on a rolling basis. Interview recommended for borderline applicants. Early admission available. EDP-S.

STUDENT LIFE. Housing: Dormitories (coed). **Activities:** Student government, film, magazine, radio, student newspaper, television, yearbook, choral groups, concert band, drama, jazz band, marching band, music ensembles, musical theater, opera, pep band, symphony orchestra, Black Student Organization, Lithuanian Club, Hispanic Student Organization.

ATHLETICS. NAIA. **Intercollegiate:** Baseball M, basketball M, football M, soccer M, softball W, volleyball W. **Intramural:** Baseball, basketball, cross-country, football M, softball, volleyball.

STUDENT SERVICES. Aptitude testing, career counseling, employment service for undergraduates, freshman orientation, health services, on-campus day care, personal counseling, placement service for graduates, special adviser for adult students, services/facilities for handicapped.

ANNUAL EXPENSES. Tuition and fees (projected): $10,340. **Room and board:** $4,410. **Books and supplies:** $450. **Other expenses:** $779.

FINANCIAL AID. 34% of freshmen, 75% of continuing students receive some form of aid. 82% of grants, 84% of loans, 41% of jobs based on need. 142 enrolled freshmen were judged to have need, all were offered aid. Academic, music/drama, athletic, leadership scholarships available. **Aid applications:** No closing date; priority given to applications received by March 1; applicants notified on a rolling basis beginning on or about March 15; must reply within 2 weeks.

ADDRESS/TELEPHONE. Mary E. Hendry, Vice President Enrollment Management, St. Xavier University, 3700 West 103rd Street, Chicago, IL 60655. (312) 779-3300. Fax: (312) 779-9061.

Sangamon State University

Springfield, Illinois CB code: 0834

2-year upper-division public university, coed. Founded in 1969. **Accreditation:** Regional. **Undergraduate enrollment:** 548 men, 670 women full time; 571 men, 951 women part time. **Graduate enrollment:** 143 men, 148 women full time; 630 men, 875 women part time. **Faculty:** 233 total (161 full time), 120 with doctorates or other terminal degrees. **Location:** Suburban campus in small city; 95 miles from St. Louis, Missouri. **Calendar:** Semester, extensive summer session. Saturday and extensive evening/early morning classes. **Microcomputers:** 75 located in computer centers. **Special facilities:** Observatory, PLATO laboratory. **Additional facts:** Public affairs university with 4 public affairs centers.

DEGREES OFFERED. BA, BS, MA, MBA. 646 bachelor's degrees awarded in 1992. 41% in business and management, 7% communications, 7% health sciences, 8% home economics, 6% parks/recreation, protective services, public affairs, 12% psychology, 7% social sciences. Graduate degrees offered in 23 major fields of study.

UNDERGRADUATE MAJORS. Accounting, anthropology, biology, business administration and management, business and management, chemistry, clinical laboratory science, communications, computer and information sciences, criminal justice studies, economics, English, environmental studies, family and community services, health care administration, history, labor/industrial relations, liberal/general studies, mathematics, nursing, political science and government, prelaw, psychology, sociology, sociology/anthropology, visual and performing arts.

ACADEMIC PROGRAMS. Double major, independent study, internships, student-designed major, teacher preparation, telecourses, weekend college, cross-registration. **Remedial services:** Learning center, reduced course load, tutoring. **Placement/credit:** CLEP General and Subject, institutional tests; 25 credit hours maximum for bachelor's degree.

ACADEMIC REQUIREMENTS. Graduation requirements: 120 hours for bachelor's. Most students required to take courses in English, humanities, mathematics, biological/physical sciences, social sciences.

STUDENT LIFE. Housing: Apartment housing available. **Activities:** Student government, radio, student newspaper, television, drama, jazz band, music ensembles, Circle-K, Model Illinois Government, 20 other clubs.

ATHLETICS. NAIA. **Intercollegiate:** Sailing, soccer M, tennis, volleyball W. **Intramural:** Baseball, basketball, table tennis, tennis.

STUDENT SERVICES. Aptitude testing, career counseling, employment service for undergraduates, health services, on-campus day care, personal counseling, placement service for graduates, services/facilities for handicapped.

ANNUAL EXPENSES. Tuition and fees (1992-93): $2,284, $4,013 additional for out-of-state students. **Room and board:** $2,664 room only. **Books and supplies:** $500. **Other expenses:** $1,454.

FINANCIAL AID. 36% of continuing students receive some form of aid. 77% of grants, 96% of loans, 12% of jobs based on need. Academic, athletic, state/district residency, leadership, minority scholarships available. **Aid applications:** No closing date; priority given to applications received by April 1; applicants notified on a rolling basis beginning on or about July 1; must reply within 30 days. **Additional information:** Extensive on-campus employment opportunities.

ADDRESS/TELEPHONE. Dr. Jerry Curl, Director of Admissions and Records, Sangamon State University, Shepherd Road, Springfield, IL 62794-9243. (217) 786-6626. Fax: (217) 786-6511.

Sauk Valley Community College
Dixon, Illinois CB code: 1780

2-year public community college, coed. Founded in 1965. **Accreditation:** Regional. **Undergraduate enrollment:** 2,870 men and women. **Faculty:** 256 total (67 full time), 23 with doctorates or other terminal degrees. **Location:** Rural campus in large town; 110 miles from Chicago. **Calendar:** Semester, limited summer session. **Microcomputers:** 40 located on campus. **Special facilities:** Art gallery.

DEGREES OFFERED. AA, AS, AAS. 546 associate degrees awarded in 1992. 20% in business and management, 5% business/office and marketing/distribution, 6% education, 10% teacher education, 15% allied health, 16% multi/interdisciplinary studies, 7% trade and industry.

UNDERGRADUATE MAJORS. Accounting, air conditioning/heating/refrigeration mechanics, air conditioning/heating/refrigeration technology, anthropology, architecture, automotive mechanics, biology, business administration and management, business and management, business data processing and related programs, business data programming, chemistry, communications, criminal justice studies, data processing, diesel engine mechanics, economics, education, electronic technology, elementary education, engineering, English, fine arts, foreign languages (multiple emphasis), history, law enforcement and corrections, law enforcement and corrections technologies, legal secretary, liberal/general studies, marketing and distribution, marketing management, mathematics, mechanical design technology, medical laboratory technologies, medical secretary, mental health/human services, music, nursing, office supervision and management, philosophy, physics, political science and government, predentistry, prelaw, premedicine, prepharmacy, preveterinary, psychology, radiograph medical technology, secondary education, secretarial and related programs, social sciences, sociology, solar heating and cooling technology, special education.

ACADEMIC PROGRAMS. 2-year transfer program, double major, dual enrollment of high school students, honors program, independent study, internships, study abroad. **Remedial services:** Learning center, remedial instruction, special counselor, tutoring. **Placement/credit:** AP, CLEP General and Subject, institutional tests; 30 credit hours maximum for associate degree.

ACADEMIC REQUIREMENTS. Freshmen must earn minimum GPA of 2.0 to continue in good standing. 60% of freshmen return for sophomore year. Students must declare major on enrollment. **Graduation requirements:** 64 hours for associate. Most students required to take courses in English, humanities, mathematics, biological/physical sciences, social sciences.

FRESHMAN ADMISSIONS. Selection criteria: Open admissions. Selective admissions to allied health programs. Special course requirements for allied health programs. **Test requirements:** ACT required for allied health programs.

1992 FRESHMAN CLASS PROFILE. 1,585 men and women enrolled. 5% were in top tenth and 21% were in top quarter of graduating class. **Characteristics:** 99% from in state, 100% commute, 7% have minority backgrounds. Average age is 19.

FALL-TERM APPLICATIONS. No fee. No closing date; applicants notified on a rolling basis. Interview required for allied health applicants. Early admission available.

STUDENT LIFE. Activities: Student government, student newspaper, choral groups, concert band, drama, music ensembles, musical theater, pep band, symphony orchestra.

ATHLETICS. NJCAA. **Intercollegiate:** Baseball M, basketball, golf M, tennis, volleyball W. **Intramural:** Basketball, softball.

STUDENT SERVICES. Aptitude testing, career counseling, employment service for undergraduates, freshman orientation, on-campus day care, personal counseling, placement service for graduates, special adviser for adult students, veterans counselor, services/facilities for handicapped.

ANNUAL EXPENSES. Tuition and fees (projected): $1,110, $1,301 additional for out-of-district students, $2,375 additional for out-of-state students. **Books and supplies:** $500. **Other expenses:** $900.

FINANCIAL AID. 35% of freshmen, 65% of continuing students receive some form of aid. 97% of grants, 95% of loans, all jobs based on need. Academic, music/drama, athletic, state/district residency, leadership, minority scholarships available. **Aid applications:** No closing date; priority given to applications received by May 1; applicants notified on a rolling basis beginning on or about May 15.

ADDRESS/TELEPHONE. Steve Ullrick, Director of Admissions, Records, and Placement, Sauk Valley Community College, 173 Illinois Route 2, Dixon, IL 61021-9110. (815) 288-5511 ext. 297.

School of the Art Institute of Chicago
Chicago, Illinois CB code: 1713

4-year private art college, coed. Founded in 1866. **Accreditation:** Regional. **Undergraduate enrollment:** 558 men, 641 women full time; 58 men, 119 women part time. **Graduate enrollment:** 109 men, 168 women full time; 20 men, 55 women part time. **Faculty:** 304 total (93 full time), 81 with doctorates or other terminal degrees. **Location:** Urban campus in very large city; in downtown area. **Calendar:** Semester, extensive summer session. **Microcomputers:** 40 located in libraries, computer centers. **Special facilities:** Video data bank, Art Institute of Chicago collection, 2 art galleries, slide library, film center. **Additional facts:** Credit/no credit system. Students define their own concentrations of study.

DEGREES OFFERED. BFA, MA, MFA. 288 bachelor's degrees awarded in 1992. 100% in visual and performing arts. Graduate degrees offered in 19 major fields of study.

UNDERGRADUATE MAJORS. Art education, ceramics, cinematography/film, drawing, fashion design, fiber/textiles/weaving, fine arts, graphic design, interior design, painting, photography, printmaking, sculpture, studio art, video, visual and performing arts.

ACADEMIC PROGRAMS. Cooperative education, independent study, internships, student-designed major, study abroad, teacher preparation, visiting/exchange student program, cross-registration. **Remedial services:** Learning center, preadmission summer program, remedial instruction, special counselor, tutoring. **Placement/credit:** AP, CLEP General and Subject; 30 credit hours maximum for bachelor's degree.

ACADEMIC REQUIREMENTS. No policy requiring minimum GPA; records of students having academic difficulty are reviewed individually. 80% of freshmen return for sophomore year. **Graduation requirements:** 132 hours for bachelor's (90 in major). Most students required to take courses in arts/fine arts, English, history, humanities, biological/physical sciences, social sciences. **Additional information:** Bachelor's candidates must take 72 credit hours in studio art and 18 hours in art history.

FRESHMAN ADMISSIONS. Selection criteria: Portfolio most important, then interview. Statement of purpose, test scores, academic credentials, and recommendations also considered. **Test requirements:** SAT or ACT; score report by August 15.

1992 FRESHMAN CLASS PROFILE. 288 men applied, 108 accepted, 102 enrolled; 306 women applied, 110 accepted, 101 enrolled. **Characteristics:** 30% from in state, 100% commute, 23% have minority backgrounds, 1% are foreign students.

FALL-TERM APPLICATIONS. $35 fee, may be waived for applicants with need. No closing date; priority given to applications received by March 15; applicants notified on a rolling basis beginning on or about February 1; must reply by May 1 or within 3 weeks if notified thereafter. Portfolio required. Essay required. Interview recommended. CRDA. Deferred admission available.

STUDENT LIFE. Housing: Dormitories (coed). Housing available nearby at Roosevelt University and Mundelein College. **Activities:** Student government, magazine, student newspaper, film center, school gallery, dance, music ensembles, multicultural organization; artists of color united; lesbian, gay, bisexual union.

STUDENT SERVICES. Career counseling, employment service for undergraduates, freshman orientation, health services, personal counseling, placement service for graduates, veterans counselor, services/facilities for handicapped.

ANNUAL EXPENSES. Tuition and fees (1992-93): $12,450. **Books and supplies:** $1,750. **Other expenses:** $1,080.

FINANCIAL AID. 67% of freshmen, 74% of continuing students receive some form of aid. 89% of grants, 91% of loans, 90% of jobs based on need. Art, minority scholarships available. **Aid applications:** No closing date; priority given to applications received by April 1; applicants notified on a rolling basis; must reply by May 1 or within 3 weeks if notified thereafter.

ADDRESS/TELEPHONE. Ellen Cohen, Director of Admissions, School of the Art Institute of Chicago, 37 South Wabash Avenue, Chicago, IL 60603. (312) 899-5219.

Shawnee Community College
Ullin, Illinois CB code: 0882

2-year public community college, coed. Founded in 1967. **Accreditation:** Regional. **Undergraduate enrollment:** 320 men, 649 women full time; 321 men, 652 women part time. **Faculty:** 182 total (32 full time), 7 with doctorates or other terminal degrees. **Location:** Rural campus in rural community; 40 miles from Paducah, Kentucky. **Calendar:** Semester, extensive summer session. Saturday and extensive evening/early morning classes. **Microcomputers:** 40 located in classrooms. **Additional facts:** Extension centers in Anna, Cairo, Metropolis, and Johnson County.

DEGREES OFFERED. AA, AS, AAS. 223 associate degrees awarded in 1992.

UNDERGRADUATE MAJORS. Accounting, agricultural business and management, agricultural sciences, automotive mechanics, automotive technology, biological and physical sciences, business and management, business computer/console/peripheral equipment operation, dental assistant, drafting, drafting and design technology, electronic technology, family and community services, food science and nutrition, forestry and related sciences, horticulture, law enforcement and corrections, legal secretary, liberal/general studies, management science, medical records administration, medical secretary, nursing, practical nursing, respiratory therapy technology, secretarial and related programs, social work, wildlife management.

ACADEMIC PROGRAMS. 2-year transfer program, dual enrollment of high school students, honors program, independent study, internships, telecourses. **Remedial services:** Learning center, remedial instruction, special counselor, tutoring. **Placement/credit:** AP, CLEP General, institutional tests.

ACADEMIC REQUIREMENTS. Freshmen must earn minimum GPA of 2.0 to continue in good standing. Students must declare major on enrollment. **Graduation requirements:** 64 hours for associate. Most students required to take courses in English, humanities, mathematics, biological/physical sciences, social sciences.

FRESHMAN ADMISSIONS. Selection criteria: Open admissions. Applicants for nursing program selected on basis of entrance examination score. **High school preparation:** 15 units recommended. Recommended units include English 4, foreign language 2, mathematics 3, social science 3 and science 3. 2 units recommended in foreign language, music, or art. Transfer program applicants must have state mandated high school course requirements or demonstrate proficiency through placement tests. **Test requirements:** SAT/ACT recommended for placement and counseling.

1992 FRESHMAN CLASS PROFILE. 228 men, 441 women enrolled. **Characteristics:** 100% from in state, 100% commute, 17% have minority backgrounds. Average age is 23.

FALL-TERM APPLICATIONS. No fee. No closing date; applicants notified on a rolling basis beginning on or about January 15; must reply by registration. Interview recommended for art, music, speech applicants. Audition recommended for speech, music applicants. Portfolio recommended for art applicants.

STUDENT LIFE. Activities: Student government, student newspaper, choral groups, drama, musical theater, Baptist Student Union.

ATHLETICS. NJCAA. **Intercollegiate:** Baseball M, basketball M, golf M, softball W, tennis M, volleyball W. **Intramural:** Baseball, basketball, softball, table tennis, volleyball.

STUDENT SERVICES. Aptitude testing, career counseling, employment service for undergraduates, freshman orientation, on-campus day care, personal counseling, placement service for graduates, veterans counselor, services/facilities for handicapped.

ANNUAL EXPENSES. Tuition and fees: $694, $1,453 additional for out-of-district students, $4,296 additional for out-of-state students. **Books and supplies:** $300. **Other expenses:** $540.

FINANCIAL AID. 72% of freshmen, 60% of continuing students receive some form of aid. 94% of grants, 96% of loans, all jobs based on need. Academic, music/drama, art, athletic, state/district residency scholarships available. **Aid applications:** No closing date; priority given to applications received by September 1; applicants notified on a rolling basis; must reply within 2 weeks.

ADDRESS/TELEPHONE. Dee Blakely, Director of Admissions and Counseling, Shawnee Community College, Route 1 Box 53, Ullin, IL 62992. (618) 634-2242. Fax: (618) 634-9028.

Shimer College
Waukegan, Illinois — CB code: 1717

Admissions:	96% of applicants accepted
Based on:	••• Essay, interview
	•• Activities, recommendations, school record, special talents
	• Test scores
Completion:	80% of freshmen end year in good standing
	40% graduate, 60% of these enter graduate study

4-year private liberal arts college, coed. Founded in 1853. **Accreditation:** Regional. **Undergraduate enrollment:** 41 men, 48 women full time; 7 men, 10 women part time. **Faculty:** 15 total (13 full time), 9 with doctorates or other terminal degrees. **Location:** Suburban campus in small city; 40 miles from Chicago. **Calendar:** Semester, limited summer session. **Microcomputers:** 6 located in computer centers. **Special facilities:** Nature preserves along Lake Michigan.

DEGREES OFFERED. BA, BS. 6 bachelor's degrees awarded in 1992.

UNDERGRADUATE MAJORS. American literature, biological and physical sciences, comparative literature, English literature, humanities, humanities and social sciences, liberal/general studies, physical sciences, prelaw, social sciences.

ACADEMIC PROGRAMS. Accelerated program, double major, dual enrollment of high school students, independent study, internships, study abroad, weekend college, cross-registration, Shimer-in-Oxford Program. **Remedial services:** Reduced course load, special counselor, tutoring. **Placement/credit:** Institutional tests; 35 credit hours maximum for bachelor's degree.

ACADEMIC REQUIREMENTS. Freshmen must earn minimum GPA of 2.2 to continue in good standing. 60% of freshmen return for sophomore year. Students must declare major by end of second year. **Graduation requirements:** 125 hours for bachelor's (40 in major). Most students required to take courses in humanities, mathematics, philosophy/religion, biological/physical sciences, social sciences.

FRESHMAN ADMISSIONS. Selection criteria: Essays and interviews most important. Test scores, GPA, student's interests, motivation, and maturity also considered. **Additional information:** All applicants considered. Those with nontraditional backgrounds should provide materials to demonstrate potential.

1992 FRESHMAN CLASS PROFILE. 20 men applied, 18 accepted, 18 enrolled; 25 women applied, 25 accepted, 24 enrolled. **Characteristics:** 75% from in state, 70% live in college housing, 26% have minority backgrounds, 5% are foreign students. Average age is 21.

FALL-TERM APPLICATIONS. $10 fee, may be waived for applicants with need. Closing date July 1; applicants notified on a rolling basis; must reply by August 1. Interview required. Essay required. Writing portfolio may be required of some applicants. CRDA. Deferred and early admission available. SAT or ACT recommended for financial aid applicants.

STUDENT LIFE. Housing: Dormitories (coed). **Activities:** Student government, student newspaper, creative writing publication, drama.

ATHLETICS. Intramural: Basketball, softball, swimming, table tennis, tennis, volleyball.

STUDENT SERVICES. Career counseling, freshman orientation, on-campus day care, personal counseling, placement service for graduates, special adviser for adult students.

ANNUAL EXPENSES. Tuition and fees: $11,200. **Room and board:** $1,650 room only. **Books and supplies:** $650. **Other expenses:** $1,300.

FINANCIAL AID. 80% of freshmen, 80% of continuing students receive some form of aid. 98% of grants, 97% of loans, all jobs based on need. 10 enrolled freshmen were judged to have need, all were offered aid. Academic, music/drama, art, leadership, alumni affiliation scholarships available. **Aid applications:** Closing date July 31; priority given to applications received by June 1; applicants notified on or about July 31; must reply by September 1.

ADDRESS/TELEPHONE. David Buchanan, Director of Admissions, Shimer College, PO Box A500, 438 North Sheridan Road, Waukegan, IL 60079-0500. (708) 623-8400. Fax: (708) 249-7171.

South Suburban College of Cook County
South Holland, Illinois — CB code: 1806

2-year public community college, coed. Founded in 1927. **Accreditation:** Regional. **Undergraduate enrollment:** 852 men, 1,301 women full time; 1,771 men, 3,728 women part time. **Location:** Suburban campus in large town; 20 miles south of Chicago Loop. **Calendar:** Semester.

FRESHMAN ADMISSIONS. Selection criteria: Open admissions. Selective admission to health career programs.

ANNUAL EXPENSES. Tuition and fees (1992-93): $1,320, $2,820 additional for out-of-district students, $4,560 additional for out-of-state students. **Books and supplies:** $500. **Other expenses:** $1,000.

ADDRESS/TELEPHONE. Ellis G. Falk, Dean of Admissions and Records, South Suburban College of Cook County, 15800 South State Street, South Holland, IL 60473. (708) 596-2000 ext. 417. (800) 248-4SSC. Fax: (708) 596-9957.

Southeastern Illinois College
Harrisburg, Illinois — CB code: 1777

2-year public community college, coed. Founded in 1960. **Accreditation:** Regional. **Undergraduate enrollment:** 3,700 men and women. **Faculty:** 91 total (38 full time), 5 with doctorates or other terminal degrees. **Location:** Rural campus in large town; 45 miles from Carbondale, 65 miles from Evansville, Indiana. **Calendar:** Semester, extensive summer session. Saturday and extensive evening/early morning classes. **Microcomputers:** 35 located in libraries, classrooms. **Special facilities:** Shawnee National forest and Glenn 'O' Jones Lake used as outdoor laboratories for forestry technology program.

DEGREES OFFERED. AA, AS, AAS. 300 associate degrees awarded in 1992.

UNDERGRADUATE MAJORS. Agricultural mechanics, automotive technology, biological and physical sciences, biology, business and management, business and office, business data processing and related programs, business data programming, child development/care/guidance, communications, data processing, diesel engine mechanics, early childhood education, electronic technology, engineering, engineering and other disciplines, English, forest products processing technology, home economics, humanities and social sciences, law enforcement and corrections technologies, liberal/general studies, mathematics, nursing, ornamental horticulture, physical sciences, predentistry, prelaw, premedicine, prepharmacy, preveterinary, psychology, secretarial and related programs, social sciences, visual and performing arts, welding technology.

ACADEMIC PROGRAMS. 2-year transfer program, double major, dual enrollment of high school students, independent study, internships, student-designed major, telecourses, weekend college, cross-registration. **Remedial**

services: Learning center, preadmission summer program, reduced course load, remedial instruction, special counselor, tutoring, disadvantaged student program. **Placement/credit:** AP, CLEP General and Subject, institutional tests; 29 credit hours maximum for associate degree.

ACADEMIC REQUIREMENTS. Freshmen must earn minimum GPA of 2.0 to continue in good standing. Students must declare major on enrollment. **Graduation requirements:** 62 hours for associate. Most students required to take courses in arts/fine arts, English, humanities, mathematics, biological/physical sciences, social sciences.

FRESHMAN ADMISSIONS. Selection criteria: Open admissions. Selective admission to nursing and medical records programs. **Test requirements:** Psychological Corporation Pre-Nursing Examination or Comparative Guidance and Placement Program required of nursing applicants.

1992 FRESHMAN CLASS PROFILE. 2,200 men and women enrolled. **Academic background:** Mid 50% of enrolled freshmen had ACT composite between 14-20. 55% submitted ACT scores. **Characteristics:** 99% from in state, 100% commute, 23% have minority backgrounds. Average age is 23.

FALL-TERM APPLICATIONS. No fee. Closing date August 25; applicants notified on a rolling basis beginning on or about May 1. Interview recommended. Deferred and early admission available. ACT test recommended for all students for placement and counseling.

STUDENT LIFE. Activities: Student government, magazine, student newspaper, choral groups, concert band, jazz band, music ensembles, pep band, Young Republicans, Circle-K, student religious organization.

ATHLETICS. NJCAA. **Intercollegiate:** Baseball M, basketball, softball W. **Intramural:** Basketball.

STUDENT SERVICES. Aptitude testing, career counseling, employment service for undergraduates, on-campus day care, personal counseling, placement service for graduates, veterans counselor, counselor for disadvantaged students, services/facilities for handicapped.

ANNUAL EXPENSES. Tuition and fees: $750, $3,150 additional for out-of-district students, $3,570 additional for out-of-state students. **Books and supplies:** $500. **Other expenses:** $855.

FINANCIAL AID. 68% of freshmen receive some form of aid. 89% of grants, 97% of loans, all jobs based on need. Academic, music/drama, art, athletic, state/district residency, leadership scholarships available. **Aid applications:** No closing date; priority given to applications received by August 19; applicants notified on a rolling basis beginning on or about May 1; must reply within 30 days.

ADDRESS/TELEPHONE. Dr. David Nudo, Director of Counseling, Southeastern Illinois College, 3575 College Road, Harrisburg, IL 62946. (618) 252-6376. Fax: (618) 252-2713.

Southern Illinois University at Carbondale

Carbondale, Illinois CB code: 1726

Admissions: 63% of applicants accepted
Based on: ••• School record, test scores
• Recommendations
Completion: 72% of freshmen end year in good standing
38% graduate

4-year public university, coed. Founded in 1869. **Accreditation:** Regional. **Undergraduate enrollment:** 10,828 men, 7,074 women full time; 1,462 men, 975 women part time. **Graduate enrollment:** 682 men, 652 women full time; 1,560 men, 1,533 women part time. **Faculty:** 1,332 total (1,222 full time), 849 with doctorates or other terminal degrees. **Location:** Rural campus in large town; 100 miles from St. Louis. **Calendar:** Semester, extensive summer session. **Microcomputers:** 3,000 located in dormitories, libraries, classrooms, computer centers, campus-wide network. **Special facilities:** Museum, university press, coal research center, materials technology center, outdoor education laboratory, university farms, center for study of crime, center for electron microscopy, cooperative wildlife research laboratory, cooperative fisheries research laboratory, vivarium, airport training facility, McLeod Theatre and Laboratory Theatre, child development laboratory, center for archaeological investigations, small business incubator.

DEGREES OFFERED. AAS, BA, BS, BFA, MA, MS, MBA, MFA, MSW, PhD, MD, JD. 520 associate degrees awarded in 1992. 8% in architecture and environmental design, 8% business/office and marketing/distribution, 7% engineering technologies, 22% allied health, 52% trade and industry. 4,760 bachelor's degrees awarded. 10% in business and management, 19% teacher education, 11% engineering technologies, 6% parks/recreation, protective services, public affairs, 9% trade and industry. Graduate degrees offered in 85 major fields of study.

UNDERGRADUATE MAJORS. Associate: Aircraft mechanics, airline piloting and navigation, allied health, architectural technologies, automotive technology, avionics, business computer/console/peripheral equipment operation, business data entry equipment operation, business data processing and related programs, business data programming, commercial art, construction, court reporting, criminal justice studies, criminal justice technology, dental hygiene, dental laboratory technology, electronic technology, funeral services/mortuary science, graphic arts technology, graphic design, law enforcement and corrections, law enforcement and corrections technologies, legal secretary, machine tool operation/machine shop, medical secretary, office supervision and management, photographic technology, physical therapy assistant, precision metal work, radiograph medical technology, respiratory therapy, respiratory therapy technology, secretarial and related programs, tool and manufacturing technology. **Bachelor's:** Accounting, advertising, agribusiness, agricultural economics, agricultural education, agricultural mechanics, agricultural production, agricultural sciences, agronomy, analytical chemistry, animal sciences, anthropology, art education, art history, automotive technology, aviation management, biochemistry, biological and physical sciences, biology, botany, business administration and management, business and management, business economics, business education, ceramics, chemistry, cinematography/film, civil engineering, classics, clothing and textiles management/production/services, computer and information sciences, conservation and regulation, creative writing, criminal justice studies, criminal justice technology, criminology, design (interdisciplinary), dramatic arts, drawing, early childhood education, economics, education of the mentally handicapped, education of the physically handicapped, electrical/electronics/communications engineering, electronic technology, elementary education, engineering and engineering-related technologies, English, English education, English literature, environmental science, equestrian science, family/consumer resource management, fashion design, fiber/textiles/weaving, film arts, finance, fine arts, fire protection, fishing and fisheries, food production/management/services, food science and nutrition, foreign language and international trade, foreign languages (multiple emphasis), foreign languages education, forestry and related sciences, forestry production and processing, French, geography, geology, German, glass, graphic design, health care administration, health education, history, home economics education, horticultural science, hotel/motel and restaurant management, industrial arts education, industrial design, industrial technology, interior design, international business management, international studies, jazz, journalism, language arts, law enforcement and corrections, law enforcement and corrections technologies, legal assistant/paralegal, liberal/general studies, linguistics, manufacturing technology, marketing management, mathematics, mathematics education, mechanical engineering, metal/jewelry, microbiology, mining and mineral engineering, motion picture technology, music, music business management, music education, music history and appreciation, music performance, music theory and composition, ornamental horticulture, painting, parks and recreation management, philosophy, photography, physical education, physics, physiology, human and animal, piano pedagogy, plant sciences, political science and government, predentistry, prelaw, premedicine, prepharmacy, preveterinary, printmaking, psychology, public relations, radio/television broadcasting, radio/television technology, reading education, recreation therapy, Russian, science education, sculpture, secondary education, small business management and ownership, social science education, social sciences, social studies education, social work, sociology, soil sciences, Spanish, special education, specific learning disabilities, speech, speech correction, speech pathology/audiology, speech/communication/theater education, statistics, studio art, teaching English as a second language/foreign language, textiles and clothing, theater design, trade and industrial education, visual and performing arts, zoology.

ACADEMIC PROGRAMS. Accelerated program, cooperative education, double major, dual enrollment of high school students, education specialist degree, honors program, independent study, internships, student-designed major, study abroad, teacher preparation, telecourses, weekend college, Washington semester, combined graduate degrees; prenursing, preosteopathy, prephysical therapy, and prepodiatry programs. **Remedial services:** Learning center, special counselor, tutoring. **ROTC:** Air Force, Army. **Placement/credit:** AP, CLEP General and Subject, institutional tests; 15 credit hours maximum for associate degree; 30 credit hours maximum for bachelor's degree.

ACADEMIC REQUIREMENTS. Freshmen must earn minimum GPA of 2.0 to continue in good standing. 72% of freshmen return for sophomore year. Students must declare major by end of second year. **Graduation requirements:** 60 hours for associate (15 in major), 120 hours for bachelor's (30 in major). Most students required to take courses in English, humanities, mathematics, biological/physical sciences, social sciences.

FRESHMAN ADMISSIONS. Selection criteria: High School class rank and ACT scores most important. **High school preparation:** 15 units required; 16 recommended. Required and recommended units include English 4, mathematics 3, social science 3 and science 3-3. Foreign language 2 recommended. Engineering applicants must have 2 algebra, 1 geometry, and 0.5 trigonometry. 2 units of art, music, language, and/or vocational education required for all applicants. **Test requirements:** ACT; score report by August 1.

1992 FRESHMAN CLASS PROFILE. 5,759 men applied, 3,759 accepted, 1,507 enrolled; 5,405 women applied, 3,306 accepted, 1,182 enrolled. 13% were in top tenth and 36% were in top quarter of graduating class. **Academic background:** Mid 50% of enrolled freshmen had ACT composite between 18-23. 88% submitted ACT scores. **Characteristics:** 90% from in state, 55% live in college housing, 21% have minority backgrounds, 3% are foreign students, 6% join fraternities/sororities. Average age is 18.

FALL-TERM APPLICATIONS. No fee. No closing date; applicants notified on a rolling basis; must reply 1 month before classes start. Audition recommended for music/theater applicants.

STUDENT LIFE. Housing: Dormitories (men, women, coed); apartment, fraternity, sorority, handicapped housing available. Freshmen and sophomores under age 21 required to live in approved housing. **Activities:** Student government, film, radio, student newspaper, television, yearbook, advertising agency, public relations agency, choral groups, concert band, dance, drama, jazz band, marching band, music ensembles, musical theater, opera, pep band, symphony orchestra, 400 student organizations, fraternities, sororities, More than 400 student and professional organizations, including several religious groups, Black Affairs Council, Mobilization of Volunteer Effort, Returned Peace Corp Volunteers. **Additional information:** Full-time dietitian available for students with special dietary needs.

ATHLETICS. NCAA. **Intercollegiate:** Baseball M, basketball, cross-country, diving, football M, golf, softball W, swimming, tennis, track and field, volleyball W. **Intramural:** Badminton, basketball, bowling, boxing M, cross-country, fencing, field hockey, golf, handball, horseback riding, racquetball, rugby, sailing, skiing, skin diving, soccer, softball, squash, swimming, table tennis, tennis, track and field, volleyball, water polo, wrestling.

STUDENT SERVICES. Aptitude testing, career counseling, employment service for undergraduates, freshman orientation, health services, on-campus day care, personal counseling, placement service for graduates, special adviser for adult students, veterans counselor, women's services, services/facilities for handicapped.

ANNUAL EXPENSES. Tuition and fees: $3,052, $4,500 additional for out-of-state students. **Room and board:** $3,182. **Books and supplies:** $575. **Other expenses:** $1,900.

FINANCIAL AID. 90% of freshmen, 85% of continuing students receive some form of aid. Grants, loans, jobs available. Academic, music/drama, art, athletic, alumni affiliation, minority scholarships available. **Aid applications:** No closing date; priority given to applications received by April 1; applicants notified on a rolling basis beginning on or about May 1; must reply within 3 weeks.

ADDRESS/TELEPHONE. Roland Keim, Director of Admissions and Records, Southern Illinois University at Carbondale, Woody Hall, Carbondale, IL 62901-4710. (618) 536-4405. Fax: (618) 453-3250.

Southern Illinois University at Edwardsville

Edwardsville, Illinois CB code: 1759

Admissions: 78% of applicants accepted
Based on: ••• School record, test scores
Completion: 65% of freshmen end year in good standing

4-year public university, coed. Founded in 1957. **Accreditation:** Regional. **Undergraduate enrollment:** 2,957 men, 3,825 women full time; 940 men, 1,188 women part time. **Graduate enrollment:** 297 men, 218 women full time; 933 men, 1,312 women part time. **Faculty:** 724 total (519 full time). **Location:** Suburban campus in large town; 18 miles from downtown St. Louis, Missouri. **Calendar:** Semester, extensive summer session. Saturday and extensive evening/early morning classes. **Microcomputers:** Located in libraries, classrooms, computer centers. **Special facilities:** Museum collections, art gallery.

DEGREES OFFERED. BA, BS, BFA, MA, MS, MBA, MFA, MEd, EdD, DDS. 1,566 bachelor's degrees awarded in 1992. 24% in business and management, 6% communications, 20% education, 7% engineering, 9% health sciences, 5% letters/literature, 5% psychology, 10% social sciences. Graduate degrees offered in 51 major fields of study.

UNDERGRADUATE MAJORS. Accounting, American literature, anthropology, art history, biology, business administration and management, business economics, business education, chemistry, civil engineering, clinical laboratory science, communications, computer and information sciences, construction, dance, dramatic arts, early childhood education, earth sciences, ecology, economics, education of the emotionally handicapped, education of the gifted and talented, education of the mentally handicapped, electrical/electronics/communications engineering, elementary education, English, English education, English literature, finance, foreign languages (multiple emphasis), French, genetics, human and animal, geography, German, health education, history, industrial engineering, jazz, journalism, labor/industrial relations, liberal/general studies, management information systems, management science, marketing and distribution, mathematics, mathematics education, mechanical engineering, music, music education, music history and appreciation, music performance, music theory and composition, musical theater, nursing, organizational behavior, personnel management, philosophy, physical sciences, physics, political science and government, psychology, radio/television broadcasting, radio/television technology, recreation and community services technologies, science education, science technologies, secondary education, social work, sociology, Spanish, special education, specific learning disabilities, speech, speech pathology/audiology, statistics, studio art.

ACADEMIC PROGRAMS. Cooperative education, double major, dual enrollment of high school students, education specialist degree, honors program, independent study, internships, student-designed major, study abroad, teacher preparation, weekend college, elementary and secondary teacher certification programs in art, business education, music, social studies, English, and physical education; combined bachelor's/graduate program in business administration. **Remedial services:** Learning center, reduced course load, remedial instruction, special counselor, tutoring. **ROTC:** Air Force, Army. **Placement/credit:** AP, CLEP General and Subject, institutional tests; 32 credit hours maximum for bachelor's degree.

ACADEMIC REQUIREMENTS. Freshmen must earn minimum GPA of 2.0 to continue in good standing. 71% of freshmen return for sophomore year. Students must declare major by end of second year. **Graduation requirements:** 124 hours for bachelor's (32 in major). Most students required to take courses in arts/fine arts, English, history, humanities, mathematics, philosophy/religion, biological/physical sciences, social sciences.

FRESHMAN ADMISSIONS. Selection criteria: Recent high school graduates admitted unconditionally if percentile ranking on college entrance examination plus high school percentile rank equals 100 or greater. Applicants who do not meet this requirement may be considered for admission through the Special Admissions Program. **High school preparation:** 15 units required. Required and recommended units include biological science 1, English 4, mathematics 3, physical science 2 and social science 3. Foreign language 2 recommended. 2 years of foreign language, music, dance, theater, art, or vocational education (1 year maximum) electives required. 2 years of 1 foreign language and 1 year of music and/or art recommended. One year of chemistry should be included in physcial science requirement. Biology and physical science courses should include laboratory. **Test requirements:** SAT or ACT (ACT preferred); score report by August 2.

1992 FRESHMAN CLASS PROFILE. 1,146 men applied, 864 accepted, 426 enrolled; 1,765 women applied, 1,398 accepted, 601 enrolled. 11% were in top tenth and 41% were in top quarter of graduating class. **Academic background:** Mid 50% of enrolled freshmen had ACT composite between 18-23. 92% submitted ACT scores. **Characteristics:** 86% from in state, 75% commute, 24% have minority backgrounds, 1% are foreign students. Average age is 21.

FALL-TERM APPLICATIONS. No fee. Closing date August 2; priority given to applications received by June 30; applicants notified on a rolling basis; must reply by registration. Audition recommended for music applicants. Portfolio recommended for art applicants. Early admission available. Application and all official required documents must be on file 3 weeks prior to beginning of term.

STUDENT LIFE. Housing: Apartment, fraternity, handicapped housing available. Apartments for single students available. **Activities:** Student government, film, magazine, radio, student newspaper, choral groups, concert band, dance, drama, jazz band, music ensembles, musical theater, pep band, symphony orchestra, fraternities, sororities, over 100 departmental, professional, religious, political, ethnic, and social organizations and honor societies. **Additional information:** Leadership Development Program helps students develop leadership skills, citizenship responsibilities, and service commitments.

ATHLETICS. NCAA. **Intercollegiate:** Baseball M, basketball, cross-country, golf M, soccer, softball W, tennis, track and field, wrestling M. **Intramural:** Badminton, basketball, bowling, golf, racquetball, soccer, softball, swimming, table tennis, tennis, volleyball.

STUDENT SERVICES. Aptitude testing, career counseling, employment service for undergraduates, freshman orientation, health services, on-campus day care, personal counseling, placement service for graduates, veterans counselor, services/facilities for handicapped.

ANNUAL EXPENSES. Tuition and fees: $2,199, $3,454 additional for out-of-state students. Required fees for undergraduates include book rental. **Room and board:** $3,300. **Books and supplies:** $215. **Other expenses:** $1,146.

FINANCIAL AID. 70% of freshmen, 60% of continuing students receive some form of aid. 69% of grants, 91% of loans, 11% of jobs based on need. Academic, music/drama, art, athletic scholarships available. **Aid applications:** No closing date; priority given to applications received by April 1; applicants notified on a rolling basis beginning on or about May 15; must reply within 2 weeks.

ADDRESS/TELEPHONE. Christa Oxford, Director Admissions/Registrar, Southern Illinois University at Edwardsville, Box 1600, Edwardsville, IL 62026-1600. (618) 692-3705.

Spoon River College

Canton, Illinois CB code: 1154

2-year public community college, coed. Founded in 1959. **Accreditation:** Regional. **Undergraduate enrollment:** 2,300 men and women. **Faculty:** 174 total (41 full time), 2 with doctorates or other terminal degrees. **Location:** Rural campus in large town; 35 miles from Peoria. **Calendar:** Semester, limited summer session. **Microcomputers:** Located in computer centers.

DEGREES OFFERED. AA, AS, AAS. 200 associate degrees awarded in 1992.

UNDERGRADUATE MAJORS. Accounting, agricultural business and management, automotive mechanics, automotive technology, business and office, business data processing and related programs, data processing, finance, law enforcement and corrections technologies, liberal/general studies, secretarial and related programs, teacher aide.

ACADEMIC PROGRAMS. 2-year transfer program, dual enrollment of high school students, honors program, internships. **Remedial services:** Learning center, reduced course load, remedial instruction, special counselor, tutoring. **Placement/credit:** CLEP General and Subject, institutional tests; 32 credit hours maximum for associate degree.

ACADEMIC REQUIREMENTS. No policy requiring minimum GPA; records of students having academic difficulty are reviewed individually. 75% of freshmen return for sophomore year. **Graduation requirements:** 64 hours for associate. Most students required to take courses in English, mathematics.

FRESHMAN ADMISSIONS. Selection criteria: Open admissions. **High school preparation:** 15 units recommended. Recommended units include English 4, mathematics 3, social science 3 and science 3. **Test requirements:** SAT/ACT scores recommended for counseling. **Additional information:** College-preparatory program required for transfer degree programs. Vocational students not required to have specific high school courses.

1992 FRESHMAN CLASS PROFILE. 1,600 men and women enrolled. **Characteristics:** 99% from in state, 100% commute, 1% have minority backgrounds, 1% are foreign students.

FALL-TERM APPLICATIONS. No fee. No closing date; applicants notified on a rolling basis.

STUDENT LIFE. Activities: Student government, magazine, choral groups, drama, pep band.

ATHLETICS. Intercollegiate: Baseball M, basketball, cross-country, golf M, softball W, track and field.

STUDENT SERVICES. Aptitude testing, career counseling, freshman orientation, on-campus day care, personal counseling, placement service for graduates, special adviser for adult students, services/facilities for handicapped.

ANNUAL EXPENSES. Tuition and fees: $1,170, $300 additional for out-of-district students, $4,170 additional for out-of-state students. **Books and supplies:** $500.

FINANCIAL AID. 80% of freshmen, 85% of continuing students receive some form of aid. Grants, loans, jobs available. Academic, music/drama, art scholarships available. **Aid applications:** No closing date; applicants notified on a rolling basis.

ADDRESS/TELEPHONE. Sharon Wrenn, Associate Dean of Student Development, Spoon River College, Route 1, Canton, IL 61520. (309) 647-4645. (800) 334-7337.

Springfield College in Illinois

Springfield, Illinois CB code: 1734

2-year private junior, liberal arts college, coed, affiliated with Roman Catholic Church. Founded in 1929. **Accreditation:** Regional. **Undergraduate enrollment:** 114 men, 152 women full time; 36 men, 103 women part time. **Faculty:** 45 total (13 full time), 1 with doctorate or other terminal degree. **Location:** Urban campus in small city; 200 miles from Chicago, 100 miles from St. Louis, Missouri. **Calendar:** 4-1-4, limited summer session. Saturday classes. **Microcomputers:** 21 located in libraries, computer centers.

DEGREES OFFERED. AA. 99 associate degrees awarded in 1992.

UNDERGRADUATE MAJORS. Liberal/general studies.

ACADEMIC PROGRAMS. 2-year transfer program, double major, dual enrollment of high school students, independent study, student-designed major, study abroad, teacher preparation, cross-registration, adult program, coordinated programs with St. John's Hospital Schools of Nursing, Respiratory Therapy, EEG Technology, and Histologic Technique. **Remedial services:** Reduced course load, remedial instruction, tutoring, reading techniques and study skills center. **Placement/credit:** AP, CLEP Subject, institutional tests; 15 credit hours maximum for associate degree.

ACADEMIC REQUIREMENTS. Freshmen must earn minimum GPA of 2.0 to continue in good standing. 85% of freshmen return for sophomore year. Students must declare major on enrollment. **Graduation requirements:** 60 hours for associate. Most students required to take courses in English, mathematics, philosophy/religion, biological/physical sciences, social sciences. **Additional information:** For adult program, maximum of 15 credit hours for prior learning counted toward degree, with maximum of 40 credit hours by examination and prior learning combined.

FRESHMAN ADMISSIONS. Selection criteria: High school GPA, test scores, and class rank important. **High school preparation:** 16 units required. Required units include English 3. Mathematics and physical science recommended for all applicants, foreign language for some. **Test requirements:** SAT or ACT (ACT preferred); score report by August 15. Institutional reading and English tests required for applicants with ACT or SAT scores or high school records below those generally required. Mathematics Placement Test required for all students.

1992 FRESHMAN CLASS PROFILE. 40 men, 90 women enrolled. **Academic background:** Mid 50% of enrolled freshmen had ACT composite between 11-28. 78% submitted ACT scores. **Characteristics:** 100% from in state, 91% commute, 14% have minority backgrounds. Average age is 20.

FALL-TERM APPLICATIONS. $15 fee, may be waived for applicants with need. No closing date; applicants notified on a rolling basis; must reply by registration. Audition required for music applicants. Interview recommended for academically weak applicants. Portfolio recommended for art applicants. Deferred and early admission available.

STUDENT LIFE. Housing: Student housing available through St. John's School of Nursing. **Activities:** Student newspaper, choral groups, drama, jazz band, Circle-K, campus ministry, Student Ambassadors, Alpha Phi Omega, Phi Theta Kappa.

ATHLETICS. NJCAA. **Intercollegiate:** Basketball M, soccer M, tennis W. **Intramural:** Basketball, volleyball.

STUDENT SERVICES. Aptitude testing, employment service for undergraduates, freshman orientation, personal counseling, special adviser for adult students, veterans counselor.

ANNUAL EXPENSES. Tuition and fees: $5,540. **Books and supplies:** $400. **Other expenses:** $3,225.

FINANCIAL AID. 89% of freshmen, 86% of continuing students receive some form of aid. 92% of grants, all loans based on need. Academic, music/drama, art, religious affiliation, minority scholarships available. **Aid applications:** No closing date; priority given to applications received by May 1; applicants notified on a rolling basis beginning on or about April 1; must reply within 3 weeks.

ADDRESS/TELEPHONE. Janelle Rinke, Director, Springfield College in Illinois, 1500 North Fifth Street, Springfield, IL 62702-2694. (217) 525-1420 ext. 10. Fax: (217) 789-1698. (800) 635-5555 (instate only).

State Community College

East St. Louis, Illinois CB code: 1749

2-year public community college, coed. Founded in 1969. **Accreditation:** Regional. **Undergraduate enrollment:** 1,268 men and women. **Location:** Urban campus in small city; 1 mile from downtown St.Louis (MO). **Calendar:** Semester. **Microcomputers:** 10 located in classrooms, computer centers.

DEGREES OFFERED. AA, AS, AAS. 85 associate degrees awarded in 1992.

UNDERGRADUATE MAJORS. Accounting, biology, business administration and management, business data processing and related programs, business systems analysis, chemistry, child development/care/guidance, data processing, ecology, engineering, family and community services, history, law enforcement and corrections, mathematics, nursing, physics, political science and government, psychology, religion, secretarial and related programs, sociology, word processing.

ACADEMIC PROGRAMS. Dual enrollment of high school students, internships, teacher preparation, telecourses. **Remedial services:** Learning center, remedial instruction, special counselor, tutoring. **Placement/credit:** CLEP General and Subject, institutional tests; 9 credit hours maximum for associate degree.

ACADEMIC REQUIREMENTS. Freshmen must earn minimum GPA of 2.0 to continue in good standing. 70% of freshmen return for sophomore year. Students must declare major on enrollment. **Graduation requirements:** 63 hours for associate. Most students required to take courses in arts/fine arts, computer science, English, history, humanities, mathematics, philosophy/religion, biological/physical sciences, social sciences.

FRESHMAN ADMISSIONS. Selection criteria: Open admissions. Selective admissions for nursing program.

1992 FRESHMAN CLASS PROFILE. 400 men and women enrolled. **Characteristics:** 100% commute.

FALL-TERM APPLICATIONS. No fee. No closing date; applicants notified on a rolling basis; must reply by registration.

STUDENT LIFE. Activities: Student government, sororities, Black Student Association.

ATHLETICS. NJCAA. **Intercollegiate:** Baseball M, basketball M, track and field M.

STUDENT SERVICES. Aptitude testing, career counseling, employment service for undergraduates, freshman orientation, personal counseling, placement service for graduates, services/facilities for handicapped.

ANNUAL EXPENSES. Tuition and fees (1992-93): $918, $4,620 additional for out-of-state students. **Books and supplies:** $200. **Other expenses:** $1,300.

FINANCIAL AID. 85% of freshmen, 85% of continuing students receive some form of aid. 79% of grants, all loans, all jobs based on need. Minority scholarships available. **Aid applications:** No closing date; priority given to applications received by July 1; applicants notified on a rolling basis.

ADDRESS/TELEPHONE. Lois C. Shelby, Registrar, State Community College, 601 James R. Thompson Boulevard, East St. Louis, IL 62201. (618) 583-2500. Fax: (618) 583-2660.

Telshe Yeshiva-Chicago

Chicago, Illinois CB code: 7009

4-year private institution. **Undergraduate enrollment:** 80 men full time.

ADDRESS/TELEPHONE. Financial Aid Office, Telshe Yeshiva-Chicago, 3535 West Foster Avenue, Chicago, IL 60625. (312) 463-7738.

Trinity Christian College
Palos Heights, Illinois CB code: 1820

Admissions: 75% of applicants accepted
Based on: ••• School record, test scores
•• Interview
• Activities, essay, recommendations, religious affiliation/commitment, special talents
Completion: 93% of freshmen end year in good standing
44% graduate, 20% of these enter graduate study

4-year private nursing, liberal arts, teachers college, coed, affiliated with Christian Reformed Church, Orthodox Presbyterian Church, Reformed Church in America, Presbyterian Church in America, Protestant Reformed Church. Founded in 1959. **Accreditation:** Regional. **Undergraduate enrollment:** 208 men, 318 women full time; 18 men, 27 women part time. **Faculty:** 67 total (40 full time), 23 with doctorates or other terminal degrees. **Location:** Suburban campus in large town; 20 miles from Chicago. **Calendar:** Semester. **Microcomputers:** 50 located in computer centers. **Special facilities:** Art gallery, Dutch Heritage Center. **Additional facts:** Offers personalized Christian education.

DEGREES OFFERED. BA, BS. 105 bachelor's degrees awarded in 1992. 28% in business and management, 16% teacher education, 17% health sciences, 6% physical sciences, 10% psychology, 7% social sciences, 8% visual and performing arts.

UNDERGRADUATE MAJORS. Accounting, allied health, biology, business administration and management, business and management, business education, chemistry, clinical laboratory science, communications, computer and information sciences, counseling psychology, developmental psychology, education, elementary education, English, English education, finance, fine arts, foreign languages education, history, home economics education, industrial arts education, junior high education, marketing and distribution, mathematics, mathematics education, music, music education, music performance, nursing, philosophy, physical education, prelaw, psychology, religion, religious education, science education, secondary education, social science education, social studies education, sociology, Spanish, special education, speech/communication/theater education, studio art, theological studies.

ACADEMIC PROGRAMS. Accelerated program, double major, dual enrollment of high school students, external degree, independent study, internships, study abroad, teacher preparation, Washington semester, cross-registration; liberal arts/career combination in health sciences. **Remedial services:** Learning center, preadmission summer program, reduced course load, remedial instruction, special counselor, tutoring. **Placement/credit:** AP, CLEP General and Subject, institutional tests; 30 credit hours maximum for bachelor's degree.

ACADEMIC REQUIREMENTS. Freshmen must earn minimum GPA of 1.7 to continue in good standing. 68% of freshmen return for sophomore year. Students must declare major by end of second year. **Graduation requirements:** 125 hours for bachelor's (32 in major). Most students required to take courses in arts/fine arts, computer science, English, history, humanities, mathematics, philosophy/religion, biological/physical sciences, social sciences.

FRESHMAN ADMISSIONS. Selection criteria: Minimum 2.1 overall high school GPA, 2.0 in English and mathematics, and ACT composite score of 18 or SAT combined score of 750 required. **High school preparation:** 14 units recommended. Recommended units include biological science 1, English 4, foreign language 2, mathematics 3, physical science 1 and social science 3. One three-year major in mathematics, science, or social studies, and 2 two-year minors in mathematics, science, social studies, or foreign language recommended. **Test requirements:** SAT or ACT (ACT preferred); score report by August 15.

1992 FRESHMAN CLASS PROFILE. 168 men applied, 126 accepted, 59 enrolled; 250 women applied, 189 accepted, 89 enrolled. 44% had high school GPA of 3.0 or higher, 49% between 2.0 and 2.99. **Academic background:** Mid 50% of enrolled freshmen had ACT composite between 18-24. 94% submitted ACT scores. **Characteristics:** 54% from in state, 70% live in college housing, 9% have minority backgrounds. Average age is 18.

FALL-TERM APPLICATIONS. $20 fee, may be waived for applicants with need. Closing date August 15; priority given to applications received by February 15; applicants notified on a rolling basis; must reply by May 1 or within 2 weeks if notified thereafter. Interview required for academically weak applicants. Statement of religious faith recommended. CRDA.

STUDENT LIFE. Housing: Dormitories (men, women); apartment housing available. **Activities:** Student government, student newspaper, yearbook, choral groups, music ensembles, pep band, literary anthology, Christian ministry club, religious drama club, theology club, pro-life, Bread for the World, Inter Varsity Fellowship, Big Brother Big Sister, Adopt a Grandparent, Association for Public Justice.

ATHLETICS. NAIA. **Intercollegiate:** Baseball M, basketball, golf, soccer M, softball W, track and field, volleyball. **Intramural:** Basketball, racquetball, soccer, softball, table tennis, tennis, volleyball.

STUDENT SERVICES. Aptitude testing, career counseling, employment service for undergraduates, freshman orientation, personal counseling, placement service for graduates, services/facilities for handicapped.

ANNUAL EXPENSES. Tuition and fees (1992-93): $8,910. **Room and board:** $3,470. **Books and supplies:** $600. **Other expenses:** $1,050.

FINANCIAL AID. 87% of freshmen, 87% of continuing students receive some form of aid. 61% of grants, 92% of loans, 58% of jobs based on need. Academic, music/drama, art, athletic, state/district residency, leadership, alumni affiliation, religious affiliation, minority scholarships available. **Aid applications:** Closing date August 15; priority given to applications received by February 15; applicants notified on or about April 15; must reply by May 1 or within 2 weeks if notified thereafter.

ADDRESS/TELEPHONE. Jon F. Bontekoe, Director of Admissions and Financial Aid, Trinity Christian College, 6601 West College Drive, Palos Heights, IL 60463. (708) 597-3000 ext. 303. (800) 748-0085. Fax: (708) 385-5665.

Trinity College
Deerfield, Illinois CB code: 1810

Admissions: 74% of applicants accepted
Based on: ••• Essay, recommendations, religious affiliation/commitment, school record, test scores
• Activities, interview
Completion: 87% of freshmen end year in good standing
56% graduate, 12% of these enter graduate study

4-year private liberal arts college, coed, affiliated with Evangelical Free Church of America. Founded in 1897. **Accreditation:** Regional. **Undergraduate enrollment:** 300 men, 316 women full time; 25 men, 32 women part time. **Faculty:** 60 total (40 full time), 22 with doctorates or other terminal degrees. **Location:** Suburban campus in large town; 25 miles from Chicago. **Calendar:** Semester, limited summer session. **Microcomputers:** 23 located in libraries, computer centers. **Additional facts:** Seminary facilities (library and faculty) available to undergraduates.

DEGREES OFFERED. BA. 156 bachelor's degrees awarded in 1992. 9% in business and management, 21% teacher education, 10% parks/recreation, protective services, public affairs, 10% philosophy, religion, theology, 49% psychology.

UNDERGRADUATE MAJORS. Accounting, Bible studies, biology, business administration and management, business economics, chemistry, communications, computer and information sciences, elementary education, English, English education, history, human resources development, humanities, humanities and social sciences, junior high education, liberal/general studies, marketing and distribution, mathematics, mathematics education, music, music education, philosophy, physical education, predentistry, prelaw, premedicine, preveterinary, psychology, pure mathematics, religious education, science education, secondary education, social sciences, sociology, youth ministry.

ACADEMIC PROGRAMS. Double major, honors program, independent study, internships, study abroad, visiting/exchange student program, Washington semester, cross-registration, TIPS (Training Institute for Pastoral Study) and REACH (for nontraditional students with previous college credit). **Remedial services:** Learning center, reduced course load, special counselor, tutoring, GAP Program (credit-bearing remedial work). **Placement/credit:** AP, CLEP Subject, institutional tests; 60 credit hours maximum for bachelor's degree.

ACADEMIC REQUIREMENTS. Freshmen must earn minimum GPA of 2.0 to continue in good standing. 74% of freshmen return for sophomore year. Students must declare major by end of second year. **Graduation requirements:** 126 hours for bachelor's (55 in major). Most students required to take courses in English, history, humanities, philosophy/religion, biological/physical sciences, social sciences. **Postgraduate studies:** 2% enter MBA programs, 10% enter other graduate study. **Additional information:** Cross-registration with other institutions in Christian College Consortium. TIPS (Training for Pastoral Study) and REACH (for nontraditional students with previous college credit) are offered.

FRESHMAN ADMISSIONS. Selection criteria: School achievement record, rank in top half of class, test scores, recommendations, evidence of Christian commitment, and essays are most important. **High school preparation:** 12 units required. **Test requirements:** SAT or ACT (ACT preferred); score report by July 1.

1992 FRESHMAN CLASS PROFILE. 266 men applied, 167 accepted, 92 enrolled; 208 women applied, 183 accepted, 111 enrolled. 48% had high school GPA of 3.0 or higher, 50% between 2.0 and 2.99. **Academic background:** Mid 50% of enrolled freshmen had ACT composite between 17-25. 80% submitted ACT scores. **Characteristics:** 50% from in state, 80% live in college housing, 23% have minority backgrounds, 2% are foreign students. Average age is 18.

FALL-TERM APPLICATIONS. $15 fee, may be waived for applicants with need. No closing date; priority given to applications received by May 1; applicants notified on a rolling basis; must reply by May 1 or within 4 weeks if notified thereafter. Essay required. Interview recommended for borderline applicants. CRDA. Deferred admission available.

STUDENT LIFE. Housing: Dormitories (men, women); apartment housing available. **Activities:** Student government, student newspaper, yearbook, choral groups, concert band, drama, music ensembles, pep band, Christian Life Team, Student Missions Fellowship.

ATHLETICS. NAIA, NSCAA. **Intercollegiate:** Baseball M, basketball, cross-country, football M, golf M, soccer, softball W, tennis, volleyball, wrestling M. **Intramural:** Baseball M, basketball, racquetball, soccer M, softball, table tennis, tennis, track and field, volleyball.

STUDENT SERVICES. Aptitude testing, career counseling, employment service for undergraduates, freshman orientation, health services, on-campus day care, personal counseling, placement service for graduates, services/facilities for handicapped.

ANNUAL EXPENSES. Tuition and fees (1992-93): $9,200. **Room and board:** $4,030. **Books and supplies:** $600. **Other expenses:** $900.

FINANCIAL AID. 87% of freshmen, 87% of continuing students receive some form of aid. Grants, loans, jobs available. Academic, music/drama, athletic, leadership, alumni affiliation, religious affiliation scholarships available. **Aid applications:** Closing date August 1; priority given to applications received by April 1; applicants notified on a rolling basis beginning on or about March 1; must reply by May 1 or within 2 weeks if notified thereafter. **Additional information:** Monthly payment plan to spread cost of the semester evenly over 4 months.

ADDRESS/TELEPHONE. Gary Larson, Director of Admissions, Trinity College, 2077 Half Day Road, Deerfield, IL 60015. (708) 317-7000. (800) 822-3225. Fax: (708) 317-7081.

Triton College

River Grove, Illinois — CB code: 1821

2-year public community college, coed. Founded in 1964. **Accreditation:** Regional. **Undergraduate enrollment:** 2,253 men, 2,093 women full time; 4,086 men, 5,224 women part time. **Faculty:** 835 total (195 full time), 107 with doctorates or other terminal degrees. **Location:** Suburban campus in large town; 3 miles from Chicago. **Calendar:** Semester, extensive summer session. Saturday and extensive evening/early morning classes. **Microcomputers:** 100 located in classrooms, computer centers. **Special facilities:** Cernan Earth and Space Center with planetarium and theater, Richard Burton Performing Arts Center, botanical gardens, art gallery.

DEGREES OFFERED. AA, AS, AAS. 844 associate degrees awarded in 1992.

UNDERGRADUATE MAJORS. Accounting, air conditioning/heating/refrigeration mechanics, air conditioning/heating/refrigeration technology, anthropology, architectural technologies, architecture, astronomy, automotive mechanics, automotive technology, biological and physical sciences, biology, business administration and management, business and management, business and office, business data processing and related programs, business data programming, carpentry, child development/care/guidance, clinical laboratory science, computer and information sciences, computer technology, construction, court reporting, criminal justice studies, criminal justice technology, data processing, dental laboratory technology, diesel engine mechanics, drafting, drafting and design technology, economics, education, electrical and electronics equipment repair, electronic technology, engineering, engineering and engineering-related technologies, English, fashion merchandising, finance, fine arts, fire control and safety technology, geography, geology, graphic and printing production, graphic arts technology, history, hotel/motel and restaurant management, industrial equipment maintenance and repair, intercultural studies, interior design, international business management, journalism, law enforcement and corrections technologies, legal secretary, liberal/general studies, machine tool operation/machine shop, management information systems, manufacturing technology, marketing and distribution, marketing management, mathematics, medical laboratory technologies, music, nuclear medical technology, nursing, ophthalmic services, ornamental horticulture, personnel management, philosophy, physical sciences, physics, plumbing/pipefitting/steamfitting, political science and government, precision metal work, psychology, radiograph medical technology, real estate, respiratory therapy, respiratory therapy technology, retailing, robotics, secretarial and related programs, social sciences, trade and industrial supervision and management, transportation management, ultrasound technology, welding technology, word processing.

ACADEMIC PROGRAMS. 2-year transfer program, cooperative education, dual enrollment of high school students, honors program, independent study, internships, student-designed major, study abroad, telecourses, weekend college. **Remedial services:** Learning center, reduced course load, remedial instruction, special counselor, tutoring. **Placement/credit:** AP, CLEP General and Subject, institutional tests; 49 credit hours maximum for associate degree.

ACADEMIC REQUIREMENTS. Freshmen must earn minimum GPA of 2.0 to continue in good standing. Students must declare major by end of first year. **Graduation requirements:** 64 hours for associate. Most students required to take courses in computer science, English, humanities, mathematics, biological/physical sciences, social sciences.

FRESHMAN ADMISSIONS. Selection criteria: Open admissions. Applicants to allied health program must attend information session. Biology, chemistry, or algebra required for most allied health programs. 15 specified units of high school coursework required for university transfer programs.

1992 FRESHMAN CLASS PROFILE. 6,785 men and women enrolled. **Characteristics:** 99% from in state, 100% commute, 34% have minority backgrounds. Average age is 26.

FALL-TERM APPLICATIONS. No fee. No closing date; applicants notified on a rolling basis beginning on or about January 30; must reply by registration. Deferred and early admission available.

STUDENT LIFE. Activities: Student government, radio, student newspaper, television, choral groups, concert band, dance, drama, jazz band, 50 clubs and organizations.

ATHLETICS. NJCAA. **Intercollegiate:** Baseball M, basketball, cross-country, diving, football M, soccer M, softball W, swimming, tennis, track and field, volleyball W, wrestling M. **Intramural:** Basketball, swimming, volleyball.

STUDENT SERVICES. Aptitude testing, career counseling, employment service for undergraduates, freshman orientation, health services, on-campus day care, personal counseling, placement service for graduates, veterans counselor, developmental education and disabled students adviser, services/facilities for handicapped.

ANNUAL EXPENSES. Tuition and fees (projected): $1,146, $2,550 additional for out-of-district students, $4,470 additional for out-of-state students. **Books and supplies:** $450.

FINANCIAL AID. 44% of freshmen, 40% of continuing students receive some form of aid. 87% of grants, 98% of loans, 59% of jobs based on need. Academic, state/district residency, leadership scholarships available. **Aid applications:** No closing date; priority given to applications received by April 15; applicants notified on a rolling basis beginning on or about May 15; must reply within 15 days. **Additional information:** In-district high school students in top 10% of graduating class eligible for renewable Board of Trustees Honor Scholarship, covering tuition and fees.

ADDRESS/TELEPHONE. Gwen E. Kanelos, Associate Dean of Student Services, Triton College, 2000 Fifth Avenue, River Grove, IL 60171. (708) 456-0300 ext. 253. Fax: (708) 456-0049.

University of Chicago

Chicago, Illinois — CB code: 1832

Admissions: 44% of applicants accepted
Based on:
••• Essay, school record
•• Activities, recommendations, test scores
• Interview, special talents
Completion: 95% of freshmen end year in good standing
85% graduate, 41% of these enter graduate study

4-year private university and liberal arts college, coed. Founded in 1891. **Accreditation:** Regional. **Undergraduate enrollment:** 1,902 men, 1,453 women full time; 36 men, 7 women part time. **Graduate enrollment:** 3,733 men, 2,274 women full time; 543 men, 283 women part time. **Faculty:** 1,843 total, 1,840 with doctorates or other terminal degrees. **Location:** Urban campus in very large city; 7 miles from Chicago's Loop. **Calendar:** Quarter, extensive summer session. **Microcomputers:** 600 located in dormitories, libraries, classrooms, computer centers. **Special facilities:** Oriental Institute, Argonne National Laboratory, Yerkes Observatory, Smart Museum of Art, John Crerar Library of Sciences, Fermi National Accelerator Laboratory, Bergman Gallery, Court Theater, Gerald Mast Center for Film Studies.

DEGREES OFFERED. BA, BS, MA, MS, MBA, MFA, MSW, PhD, MD, JD, M.Div. 882 bachelor's degrees awarded in 1992. 6% in languages, 12% letters/literature, 11% life sciences, 5% mathematics, 6% physical sciences, 9% psychology, 39% social sciences. Graduate degrees offered in 144 major fields of study.

UNDERGRADUATE MAJORS. African studies, Afro-American (black) studies, analytical chemistry, anthropology, applied mathematics, Arabic, art history, Asian studies, atmospheric sciences and meteorology, atomic/molecular physics, bacteriology, behavioral sciences, biochemistry, biological and physical sciences, biology, botany, cell biology, chemistry, Chinese, classics, cognitive psychology, comparative literature, creative writing, developmental psychology, earth sciences, East Asian studies, Eastern European studies, ecology, economics, elementary particle physics, English, English literature, environmental science, experimental psychology; fine arts, foreign languages (multiple emphasis), French, genetics, human and animal, geochemistry, geography, geology, geophysics and seismology, German, Greek (classical), Hebrew, history, humanities, humanities and social sciences, Indic languages, inorganic chemistry, Iranian languages, Italian, Japanese, Jewish studies, Korean, Latin, Latin American studies, liberal/general studies, linguistics, mathematics, medieval studies, metallurgy, microbiology, Middle Eastern studies, molecular biology, music, music history and appreciation, music theory and composition, oceanography, organic chemistry, paleontology, philosophy, physical chemistry, physical sciences, physics, physiology, human and animal, plant genetics, plant physiology, political science and government, Portuguese, psychobiology, psycholinguistics, psychology, public policy studies, pure mathematics, religion, Russian, Russian and Slavic studies, Scandinavian languages, Slavic languages, social sciences, social work, sociology, South Asian studies, Spanish, statistics, urban studies, visual and performing arts, zoology.

ACADEMIC PROGRAMS. Accelerated program, double major, honors program, independent study, internships, student-designed major, study abroad, cross-registration; combined bachelor's/graduate program in business administration, law. **Remedial services:** Reduced course load, special counselor, tutoring. **Placement/credit:** AP, IB, institutional tests.

ACADEMIC REQUIREMENTS. Freshmen must earn minimum GPA of 1.75 to continue in good standing. Students must pass 75% of courses in which they enroll. 93% of freshmen return for sophomore year. Students must declare major by end of second year. **Graduation requirements:** 140 hours for bachelor's (36 in major). Most students required to take courses in arts/fine arts, foreign languages, history, humanities, mathematics, biological/physical sciences, social sciences. **Postgraduate studies:** 7% enter law school, 7% enter medical school, 27% enter other graduate study. **Additional information:** Army and Air Force ROTC offered through agreement with 2 other Chicago area schools.

FRESHMAN ADMISSIONS. Selection criteria: Academic record, essay, test scores, recommendations, extracurricular activities, interview all considered. Admissions decisions made on individual basis. **High school preparation:** 16 units required. Required units include biological science 1, English 4, foreign language 3, mathematics 4, physical science 2 and social science 2. Honors and/or advanced courses considered with greater weight. **Test requirements:** SAT or ACT; score report by February 15.

1992 FRESHMAN CLASS PROFILE. 3,758 men applied, 1,618 accepted, 513 enrolled; 2,915 women applied, 1,330 accepted, 397 enrolled. 71% were in top tenth and 89% were in top quarter of graduating class. **Academic background:** Mid 50% of enrolled freshmen had SAT-V between 570-680, SAT-M between 620-730; ACT composite between 26-31. 80% submitted SAT scores, 50% submitted ACT scores. **Characteristics:** 26% from in state, 98% live in college housing, 34% have minority backgrounds, 3% are foreign students. Average age is 18.

FALL-TERM APPLICATIONS. $55 fee, may be waived for applicants with need. Closing date January 15; applicants notified on or about April 1; must reply by May 1. Essay required. Interview recommended. CRDA. Deferred and early admission available. Institutional early decision plan. Early notification plan application deadline November 15. Applicants notified of admissions decision on or about December 15; must reply by January 15.

STUDENT LIFE. Housing: Dormitories (coed); apartment, fraternity housing available. Housing guaranteed for undergraduates for all 4 years. **Activities:** Student government, film, magazine, radio, student newspaper, yearbook, literary magazine, choral groups, concert band, dance, drama, jazz band, music ensembles, musical theater, pep band, symphony orchestra, fraternities, sororities, over 100 organizations, including Organization of Black Students, Hispanic Cultural Society, debate society, volunteer service organizations.

ATHLETICS. NCAA. **Intercollegiate:** Baseball M, basketball, cross-country, fencing M, football M, lacrosse M, soccer, softball W, swimming, tennis, track and field, wrestling M. **Intramural:** Archery, badminton, basketball, cross-country, handball, racquetball, swimming, table tennis, tennis, track and field, volleyball. **Clubs:** Many club sports available.

STUDENT SERVICES. Aptitude testing, career counseling, employment service for undergraduates, freshman orientation, health services, personal counseling, placement service for graduates, special adviser for adult students, veterans counselor, services/facilities for handicapped.

ANNUAL EXPENSES. Tuition and fees: $18,207. Freshmen pay orientation fee of $180. **Room and board:** $6,130. **Books and supplies:** $652. **Other expenses:** $556.

FINANCIAL AID. 67% of freshmen, 63% of continuing students receive some form of aid. 94% of grants, 81% of loans, all jobs based on need. Academic, music/drama, art, athletic, leadership scholarships available. **Aid applications:** Closing date February 1; applicants notified on or about April 1; must reply by May 1. **Additional information:** SHARE Loan Program available.

ADDRESS/TELEPHONE. Theodore A. O'Neill, Dean of Admissions, University of Chicago, 1116 East 59th Street, Chicago, IL 60637. (312) 702-8650. Fax: (312) 702-5846.

University of Health Sciences: The Chicago Medical School

North Chicago, Illinois CB code: 0768

2-year upper-division private health science college, coed. Founded in 1912. **Accreditation:** Regional. **Undergraduate enrollment:** 27 men, 56 women full time; 1 man, 13 women part time. **Graduate enrollment:** 552 men, 359 women full time; 20 men, 42 women part time. **Location:** Suburban campus in large town; 40 miles north of Chicago. **Calendar:** Quarter.

ADMISSIONS. Minimum 90 quarter hours required for admission. Strong science course background recommended. Interview required.

ANNUAL EXPENSES. Tuition and fees (1992-93): $12,550. **Books and supplies:** $966. **Other expenses:** $2,666.

ADDRESS/TELEPHONE. LaDonna E. Norstrom, Director of Admissions and Records, University of Health Sciences: The Chicago Medical School, 3333 Green Bay Road, North Chicago, IL 60064. (708) 578-3209.

University of Illinois at Chicago

Chicago, Illinois CB code: 1851

Admissions:	69% of applicants accepted
Based on:	••• School record, test scores
	• Essay, special talents
Completion:	51% of freshmen end year in good standing
	28% graduate, 28% of these enter graduate study

4-year public university, coed. Founded in 1965. **Accreditation:** Regional. **Undergraduate enrollment:** 6,546 men, 6,657 women full time; 1,613 men, 1,447 women part time. **Graduate enrollment:** 2,750 men, 2,297 women full time; 1,466 men, 2,209 women part time. **Faculty:** 2,529 total (1,760 full time), 2,063 with doctorates or other terminal degrees. **Location:** Urban campus in very large city; 1 mile from downtown Chicago. **Calendar:** Semester, limited summer session. **Microcomputers:** 885 located in dormitories, libraries, classrooms, computer centers, campus-wide network. **Special facilities:** Jane Addams' Hull House, James Woodworth Prairie Preserve. **Additional facts:** Medical, dental, nursing and pharmacy colleges, and medical center within university complex.

DEGREES OFFERED. BA, BS, BFA, MA, MS, MBA, MFA, MEd, MSW, PhD, DDS, MD, Pharm D. 2,651 bachelor's degrees awarded in 1992. 22% in business and management, 5% communications, 5% education, 12% engineering, 11% health sciences, 5% life sciences, 5% parks/recreation, protective services, public affairs, 7% psychology, 11% social sciences, 5% visual and performing arts. Graduate degrees offered in 73 major fields of study.

UNDERGRADUATE MAJORS. Accounting, Afro-American (black) studies, American literature, anthropology, architecture, art education, art history, biochemistry, biocommunication arts, bioengineering and biomedical engineering, biology, business administration and management, business and management, business statistics, chemical engineering, chemistry, civil engineering, classics, clinical laboratory science, communications, computer engineering, criminal justice studies, criminology, dentistry, design, economics, education, electrical/electronics/communications engineering, elementary education, energy conservation and use technology, engineering, engineering management, engineering mechanics, engineering physics, English education, English literature, finance, fluids engineering, foreign languages education, French, French business studies, geography, geology, German, history, humanities and social sciences, industrial engineering, Italian, Jewish studies, Latin American studies, management science, marketing management, mathematics, mathematics and computer sciences, mathematics education, mechanical engineering, medical records administration, metallurgical engineering, music, nursing, nutrition and medical dietetics, occupational therapy, pharmacy, philosophy, physical education, physical therapy, physics, political science and government, psychology, Russian, science education, secondary education, Slavic languages, social science education, social work, sociology, Spanish, speech/communication/theater education, statistics, studio art, thermo-mechanical engineering.

ACADEMIC PROGRAMS. Accelerated program, cooperative education, double major, dual enrollment of high school students, honors program, independent study, internships, student-designed major, study abroad, teacher preparation, concurrent registration at another campus of University of Illinois, City Colleges of Chicago, and American Conservatory of Music. **Remedial services:** Learning center, preadmission summer program, remedial instruction, special counselor, tutoring, writing center. **ROTC:** Air Force, Army, Naval. **Placement/credit:** AP, CLEP General and Subject, IB, institutional tests; 30 credit hours maximum for bachelor's degree.

ACADEMIC REQUIREMENTS. Individual colleges set minimum grade-point average required of freshmen to continue in good academic standing. 71% of freshmen return for sophomore year. Students must declare major on application. **Graduation requirements:** 120 hours for bachelor's (30 in major). Most students required to take courses in English, humanities, biological/physical sciences, social sciences. **Postgraduate studies:** 1% enter law school, 7% enter medical school, 20% enter other graduate study.

FRESHMAN ADMISSIONS. Selection criteria: Satisfactory combination of class rank and test scores. **High school preparation:** 16 units required. Required and recommended units include English 4, mathematics 3-3.5, social science 3 and science 3. Foreign language 2 recommended. Additional course requirements vary with college and program. **Test requirements:** SAT or ACT (ACT preferred); score report by June 17.

1992 FRESHMAN CLASS PROFILE. 3,816 men applied, 2,596 accepted, 1,300 enrolled; 4,196 women applied, 2,926 accepted, 1,367 enrolled. 51% had high school GPA of 3.0 or higher, 46% between 2.0 and 2.99. 21% were in top tenth and 51% were in top quarter of graduating class. **Academic background:** Mid 50% of enrolled freshmen had SAT-V between 380-490, SAT-M between 430-580; ACT composite between 18-24. 22% submitted SAT scores, 96% submitted ACT scores. **Characteristics:**

97% from in state, 85% commute, 55% have minority backgrounds, 1% are foreign students. Average age is 19.

FALL-TERM APPLICATIONS. $30 fee, may be waived for applicants with need. Closing date June 17; priority given to applications received by February 28; applicants notified on a rolling basis. Interview required for some health and sciences applicants. Portfolio required for architecture applicants. Essay required for some upper division applicants. Deferred and early admission available.

STUDENT LIFE. Housing: Dormitories (coed); apartment, fraternity, sorority housing available. **Activities:** Student government, student newspaper, choral groups, concert band, dance, drama, jazz band, music ensembles, musical theater, fraternities, sororities, 151 student groups including academic, governing, ethnic, religious, literary, political, service, special interest organizations.

ATHLETICS. NCAA. **Intercollegiate:** Baseball M, basketball, cross-country, diving, gymnastics, ice hockey M, soccer M, softball W, swimming, tennis, volleyball W. **Intramural:** Badminton, basketball, cross-country, racquetball, soccer, softball, squash, table tennis, tennis, volleyball, water polo, wrestling M. **Clubs:** Fencing, rugby.

STUDENT SERVICES. Aptitude testing, career counseling, employment service for undergraduates, freshman orientation, health services, on-campus day care, personal counseling, placement service for graduates, veterans counselor, council for women's services, services/facilities for handicapped.

ANNUAL EXPENSES. Tuition and fees: $3,317, $4,194 additional for out-of-state students. $200 tuition surcharge required of engineering students. **Room and board:** $4,988. **Books and supplies:** $630. **Other expenses:** $3,100.

FINANCIAL AID. 86% of freshmen, 64% of continuing students receive some form of aid. Grants, loans, jobs available. Academic, music/drama, athletic, state/district residency, minority scholarships available. **Aid applications:** No closing date; priority given to applications received by March 1; applicants notified on a rolling basis; must reply within 3 weeks.

ADDRESS/TELEPHONE. Marilyn Fiduccia, Executive Director of the Office of Admissions, University of Illinois at Chicago, PO Box 5220, Chicago, IL 60680. (312) 996-4350.

University of Illinois at Urbana-Champaign

Urbana, Illinois — CB code: 1836

Admissions:	72% of applicants accepted
Based on:	••• School record, test scores
	• Essay, recommendations, special talents
Completion:	82% of freshmen end year in good standing
	75% graduate, 38% of these enter graduate study

4-year public university, coed. Founded in 1867. **Accreditation:** Regional. **Undergraduate enrollment:** 13,927 men, 11,020 women full time; 500 men, 399 women part time. **Graduate enrollment:** 4,718 men, 2,857 women full time; 1,264 men, 1,130 women part time. **Faculty:** 2,222 total (2,156 full time), 2,004 with doctorates or other terminal degrees. **Location:** Urban campus in small city; 130 miles from Chicago. **Calendar:** Semester, extensive summer session. **Microcomputers:** 8,000 located in dormitories, libraries, classrooms, computer centers, campus-wide network. **Special facilities:** Krannert Art Museum, Natural History Museum, World Heritage Museum, Krannert Center for the Performing Arts, Robert Allerton Park.

DEGREES OFFERED. BA, BS, BFA, MA, MS, MBA, MFA, MEd, MSW, PhD, EdD, DVM, JD. 6,175 bachelor's degrees awarded in 1992. 16% in business and management, 17% engineering, 8% letters/literature, 8% life sciences, 7% psychology, 13% social sciences. Graduate degrees offered in 147 major fields of study.

UNDERGRADUATE MAJORS. Accounting, actuarial sciences, advertising, aerospace/aeronautical/astronautical engineering, agribusiness, agricultural economics, agricultural education, agricultural engineering, agricultural mechanics, agricultural sciences, agronomy, anatomy, animal sciences, anthropology, architecture, art education, art history, Asian studies, astronomy, biochemistry, bioengineering and biomedical engineering, biology, biophysics, business administration and management, business economics, business education, cell biology, ceramic engineering, chemical engineering, chemistry, city/community/regional planning, civil engineering, classics, clinical psychology, clothing and textiles management/production/services, cognitive psychology, communications, community psychology, comparative literature, comparative psychology, computer and information sciences, computer engineering, computer science education, counseling psychology, crafts, dairy, dance, developmental psychology, dietetic aide/assistant, dramatic arts, early childhood education, ecology, economics, education of the mentally handicapped, electrical/electronics/communications engineering, elementary education, engineering, engineering mechanics, engineering physics, English, English education, entomology, experimental psychology, family/consumer resource management, fashion design, finance, food production/management/services, food science and nutrition, food sciences, foreign languages education, forestry and related sciences, French, genetics, human and animal, geography, geology, German, graphic design, health education, history, home economics, home economics education, horticultural science, hotel/motel and restaurant management, humanities, individual and family development, industrial and organizational psychology, industrial design, industrial engineering, institutional management, institutional/home management/supporting programs, interior design, Italian, journalism, landscape architecture, Latin American studies, leisure studies, linguistics, marketing management, mathematics, mathematics and computer science, mathematics education, mechanical engineering, metallurgical engineering, microbiology, music, music education, music history and appreciation, music performance, music theory and composition, nuclear engineering, ornamental horticulture, painting, philosophy, photography, physical education, physics, physiological psychology, physiology, human and animal, plant biology, political science and government, Portuguese, psychology, quantitative psychology, radio/television broadcasting, religion, rhetoric, Russian, Russian and Slavic studies, science education, sculpture, secondary education, social psychology, social studies education, social work, sociology, soil sciences, Spanish, speech, speech pathology/audiology, speech/communication/theater education, statistics, statistics and computer science, technical education, textiles and clothing, veterinary medicine.

ACADEMIC PROGRAMS. Accelerated program, cooperative education, double major, dual enrollment of high school students, honors program, independent study, internships, student-designed major, study abroad, teacher preparation, visiting/exchange student program, cross-registration; liberal arts/career combination in engineering; combined bachelor's/graduate program in business administration. **Remedial services:** Preadmission summer program, reduced course load, special counselor, tutoring. **ROTC:** Air Force, Army, Naval. **Placement/credit:** AP, CLEP General, IB, institutional tests.

ACADEMIC REQUIREMENTS. Students must maintain 2.0 GPA to remain in good standing. 91% of freshmen return for sophomore year. **Graduation requirements:** 120 hours for bachelor's (30 in major). Most students required to take courses in English, humanities, biological/physical sciences, social sciences. **Postgraduate studies:** 6% enter law school, 4% enter medical school, 28% enter other graduate study. **Additional information:** Students generally declare major upon enrollment. Students without declared major may apply for General Curriculum option in College of Liberal Arts and Science.

FRESHMAN ADMISSIONS. Selection criteria: High school course work, class rank, test scores, and optional essay considered. **High school preparation:** 15 units required; 15 recommended. Required and recommended units include English 4, foreign language 2, mathematics 3-3, social science 2 and science 2-2. Specific subject requirements vary with college and program. **Test requirements:** SAT or ACT; score report by January 1.

1992 FRESHMAN CLASS PROFILE. 8,193 men applied, 5,735 accepted, 2,931 enrolled; 7,076 women applied, 5,188 accepted, 2,573 enrolled. 89% had high school GPA of 3.0 or higher, 11% between 2.0 and 2.99. 55% were in top tenth and 87% were in top quarter of graduating class. **Academic background:** Mid 50% of enrolled freshmen had SAT-V between 470-590, SAT-M between 550-690; ACT composite between 25-29. 49% submitted SAT scores, 94% submitted ACT scores. **Characteristics:** 92% from in state, 72% live in college housing, 27% have minority backgrounds, 20% join fraternities/sororities. Average age is 18.

FALL-TERM APPLICATIONS. $30 fee, may be waived for applicants with need. Closing date January 1; priority given to applications received by November 15; applicants notified on or about March 1; must reply by May 1. Interview required for aviation applicants. Audition required for dance, music, theater (performance) applicants. Professional Interest Statement required of majority of applicants to College of Agriculture. Deferred and early admission available. The applications filing period is October 1 to January 1. Applicants encouraged to have complete application on file by November 15.

STUDENT LIFE. Housing: Dormitories (men, women, coed); apartment, fraternity, sorority, cooperative housing available. Beckwith Center for severely physically disabled individuals unable to live independently in conventional residence halls or other off-campus housing. **Activities:** Student government, magazine, radio, student newspaper, television, yearbook, choral groups, concert band, dance, drama, jazz band, marching band, music ensembles, musical theater, opera, pep band, symphony orchestra, experimental and Kabuki theater, fraternities, sororities, 700 registered student organizations including: Young Democrats, Young Republicans, Latin Cultural House, Afro-American Cultural Program, all major religious student organizations, social service fraternities.

ATHLETICS. NCAA. **Intercollegiate:** Baseball M, basketball, cross-country, diving, fencing M, football M, golf, gymnastics, swimming, tennis, track and field, volleyball W, wrestling M. **Intramural:** Archery, badminton, baseball M, basketball, bowling, cross-country, fencing M, field hockey W, golf, gymnastics, handball M, horseback riding, ice hockey, lacrosse, racquetball, rifle, rugby, sailing, skiing, soccer, softball, squash, swimming, table tennis, tennis, track and field, volleyball, water polo, wrestling M.

STUDENT SERVICES. Aptitude testing, career counseling, employment service for undergraduates, freshman orientation, health services, personal counseling, placement service for graduates, veterans counselor, services/facilities for handicapped.

ANNUAL EXPENSES. Tuition and fees: $3,388, $4,252 additional for

out-of-state students. Upper division tuition is $2746. Tuition surcharges for certain programs: engineering $500, chemical life science $250, lower division fine/applied arts $100, upper division fine/applied arts $200. **Room and board:** $4,358. **Books and supplies:** $500. **Other expenses:** $1,600.

FINANCIAL AID. 78% of freshmen, 84% of continuing students receive some form of aid. 7% of jobs based on need. 2,411 enrolled freshmen were judged to have need, 2,347 were offered aid. Academic, music/drama, art, athletic, state/district residency, leadership, minority scholarships available. **Aid applications:** No closing date; priority given to applications received by March 15; applicants notified on a rolling basis beginning on or about May 15; must reply within 2 weeks.

ADDRESS/TELEPHONE. Patricia E. Askew, Director of Admissions and Records, University of Illinois at Urbana-Champaign, 10 Administration Building, Urbana, IL 61801. (217) 333-0302.

VanderCook College of Music
Chicago, Illinois — CB code: 1872

Admissions: 52% of applicants accepted
Based on:
••• Interview, special talents
•• Activities, essay, school record
• Recommendations, test scores
Completion: 85% of freshmen end year in good standing
70% graduate, 19% of these enter graduate study

4-year private music college, coed. Founded in 1909. **Accreditation:** Regional. **Undergraduate enrollment:** 26 men, 23 women full time; 1 man part time. **Faculty:** 33 total (6 full time), 6 with doctorates or other terminal degrees. **Location:** Urban campus in very large city; in downtown area. **Calendar:** Semester, limited summer session. **Microcomputers:** 9 located in dormitories, libraries, computer centers. **Special facilities:** Listening booths equipped with cassette, compact disc, and LP formats; MIDI/Electronic Music Laboratory. **Additional facts:** Institution devoted solely to preparation of music educators.

DEGREES OFFERED. B, M. 19 bachelor's degrees awarded in 1992. 100% in teacher education. Graduate degrees offered in 2 major fields of study.

UNDERGRADUATE MAJORS. Music, music education.

ACADEMIC PROGRAMS. Independent study, internships, teacher preparation. **Remedial services:** Reduced course load, remedial instruction, tutoring. **Placement/credit:** AP, institutional tests.

ACADEMIC REQUIREMENTS. Freshmen must earn minimum GPA of 2.0 to continue in good standing. 80% of freshmen return for sophomore year. Students must declare major on application. **Graduation requirements:** 134 hours for bachelor's (80 in major). Most students required to take courses in arts/fine arts, computer science, English, history, humanities, mathematics, biological/physical sciences, social sciences. **Postgraduate studies:** 19% enter other graduate study.

FRESHMAN ADMISSIONS. Selection criteria: Primary consideration given to musical ability and background, as demonstrated in the audition and music theory test. 2.0 high school GPA required. **High school preparation:** 13 units required. Required units include English 4, foreign language 2, mathematics 2, physical science 2, social science 2 and science 1. Vocal or instrumental music background and knowledge of music theory also required. **Test requirements:** SAT or ACT; score report by July 1. Institutional test required for admissions.

1992 FRESHMAN CLASS PROFILE. 14 men applied, 7 accepted, 6 enrolled; 11 women applied, 6 accepted, 6 enrolled. 40% had high school GPA of 3.0 or higher, 60% between 2.0 and 2.99. **Characteristics:** 55% from in state, 50% commute, 25% have minority backgrounds, 40% join fraternities/sororities. Average age is 18.

FALL-TERM APPLICATIONS. $25 fee, may be waived for applicants with need. Closing date July 1; priority given to applications received by March 1; applicants notified on a rolling basis; must reply by May 1 or within 3 weeks if notified thereafter. Interview required. Audition required. Essay required. Deferred admission available.

STUDENT LIFE. Housing: Dormitories (men, women, coed); apartment, fraternity, sorority housing available. **Activities:** Student government, student newspaper, choral groups, concert band, jazz band, music ensembles, fraternities, sororities.

STUDENT SERVICES. Employment service for undergraduates, freshman orientation, health services, personal counseling, placement service for graduates.

ANNUAL EXPENSES. Tuition and fees (1992-93): $8,400. **Room and board:** $4,410. **Books and supplies:** $450. **Other expenses:** $250.

FINANCIAL AID. 81% of freshmen, 70% of continuing students receive some form of aid. Grants, loans, jobs available. Music/drama scholarships available. **Aid applications:** Closing date June 1; priority given to applications received by March 1; applicants notified on or about June 15; must reply within 4 weeks. **Additional information:** Musical talent considered for partial tuition waiver.

ADDRESS/TELEPHONE. Admissions Office, VanderCook College of Music, 3209 South Michigan Avenue, Chicago, IL 60616-3886. (312) 225-6288. (800) 448-2655. Fax: (312) 225-5211.

Waubonsee Community College
Sugar Grove, Illinois — CB code: 1938

2-year public community college, coed. Founded in 1966. **Accreditation:** Regional. **Undergraduate enrollment:** 7,550 men and women. **Location:** Suburban campus in rural community; 9 miles from Aurora. **Calendar:** 4-4-1.

FRESHMAN ADMISSIONS. Selection criteria: Open admissions. Selective admissions for nursing program and respiratory therapy.

ANNUAL EXPENSES. Tuition and fees (1992-93): $1,138, $2,880 additional for out-of-district students, $3,819 additional for out-of-state students. **Books and supplies:** $400. **Other expenses:** $900.

ADDRESS/TELEPHONE. Robert Baker, Dean of Student Development, Waubonsee Community College, Route 47 at Harter Road, Sugar Grove, IL 60554. (708) 466-4811. Fax: (708) 466-4964.

West Suburban College of Nursing
Oak Park, Illinois — CB code: 1927

Admissions: 73% of applicants accepted
Based on:
••• Essay, recommendations, school record, test scores
• Activities
Completion: 75% of freshmen end year in good standing
65% graduate

4-year private nursing college, coed. Founded in 1982. **Accreditation:** Regional. **Undergraduate enrollment:** 12 men, 210 women full time. **Faculty:** 17 total, 3 with doctorates or other terminal degrees. **Location:** Suburban campus in small city; 10 miles from Chicago Loop. **Calendar:** Quarter. **Microcomputers:** Located in libraries, computer centers. **Special facilities:** Health sciences library, nursing clinical skills laboratory. **Additional facts:** Facilities located in West Suburban Hospital Medical Center. General education and support courses taken at nearby Concordia University.

DEGREES OFFERED. BS. 18 bachelor's degrees awarded in 1992. 100% in health sciences.

UNDERGRADUATE MAJORS. Nursing.

ACADEMIC PROGRAMS. Independent study, cross-registration, BS completion program for registered nurses. **Remedial services:** Learning center, reduced course load, remedial instruction, special counselor, tutoring. **Placement/credit:** AP, CLEP General; 16 credit hours maximum for bachelor's degree.

ACADEMIC REQUIREMENTS. Freshmen must earn minimum GPA of 2.0 to continue in good standing. 75% of freshmen return for sophomore year. Students must declare major on application. **Graduation requirements:** 192 hours for bachelor's (72 in major). Most students required to take courses in arts/fine arts, English, history, humanities, mathematics, philosophy/religion, biological/physical sciences, social sciences.

FRESHMAN ADMISSIONS. Selection criteria: Rank in top third of class, minimum high school GPA of 2.33, ACT composite score of 20 or higher, essay, and personal recommendation most important. **High school preparation:** 11 units required; 16 recommended. Required and recommended units include biological science 1, English 4-4, mathematics 2-4, physical science 1-3 and social science 3-3. Foreign language 2 recommended. Required science units must include 1 biology and 1 chemistry. **Test requirements:** ACT; score report by August 31.

1992 FRESHMAN CLASS PROFILE. 30% had high school GPA of 3.0 or higher, 70% between 2.0 and 2.99. **Academic background:** Mid 50% of enrolled freshmen had ACT composite between 18-22. 100% submitted ACT scores. **Characteristics:** 60% from in state, 55% commute, 21% have minority backgrounds. Average age is 18.

FALL-TERM APPLICATIONS. $25 fee. Closing date August 31; applicants notified on a rolling basis; must reply within 4 weeks. Essay required. Interview recommended. Deferred admission available.

STUDENT LIFE. Housing: Dormitories (men, women). Students requesting on campus housing must reside on Concordia University campus. **Activities:** Student government, film, radio, student newspaper, television, yearbook, choral groups, drama, marching band, music ensembles, musical theater, symphony orchestra, nursing student organization. **Additional information:** Athletic programs and student activities offered through Concordia University.

ATHLETICS. NCAA. **Intercollegiate:** Baseball M, basketball, cross-country M, field hockey W, football M, tennis, track and field, volleyball W, wrestling M. **Intramural:** Basketball M, field hockey W, soccer, softball, swimming, tennis, volleyball.

STUDENT SERVICES. Aptitude testing, career counseling, employment service for undergraduates, freshman orientation, health services, on-campus day care, personal counseling, placement service for graduates, veterans counselor.

ANNUAL EXPENSES. Tuition and fees: $8,576. **Room and board:** $4,035. **Books and supplies:** $350. **Other expenses:** $525.

FINANCIAL AID. Aid applications: Closing date April 1; applicants notified on a rolling basis beginning on or about June 1; must reply immediately. **Additional information:** Financial aid administered through Concordia University.

ADDRESS/TELEPHONE. Stephen R. Clark, Director of Admissions, West Suburban College of Nursing, Erie at Austin, Oak Park, IL 60302. (708) 383-6200 ext. 6530. (800) 285-2668. Fax: (708) 383-8783.

Western Illinois University
Macomb, Illinois CB code: 1900

Admissions: 75% of applicants accepted
Based on: ••• School record, test scores
Completion: 84% of freshmen end year in good standing
39% graduate, 25% of these enter graduate study

4-year public university, coed. Founded in 1899. **Accreditation:** Regional. **Undergraduate enrollment:** 4,954 men, 4,340 women full time; 774 men, 734 women part time. **Graduate enrollment:** 224 men, 193 women full time; 756 men, 1,402 women part time. **Faculty:** 677 total (642 full time), 422 with doctorates or other terminal degrees. **Location:** Rural campus in large town; 75 miles from Rock Island, and 80 miles from Peoria. **Calendar:** Semester, limited summer session. **Microcomputers:** Located in dormitories, libraries, classrooms, computer centers. **Special facilities:** Geology museum, art gallery.

DEGREES OFFERED. BA, BS, BFA, MA, MS, MBA, MFA. 2,401 bachelor's degrees awarded in 1992. 12% in business and management, 10% communications, 10% education, 6% teacher education, 5% health sciences, 11% multi/interdisciplinary studies, 15% parks/recreation, protective services, public affairs, 5% social sciences. Graduate degrees offered in 29 major fields of study.

UNDERGRADUATE MAJORS. Accounting, agricultural education, agricultural sciences, art education, bilingual/bicultural education, biology, business administration and management, business economics, business education, chemistry, communications, computer and information sciences, corrections education, dramatic arts, economics, education of the emotionally handicapped, education of the mentally handicapped, educational media technology, elementary education, English, English education, finance, fine arts, foreign languages education, French, geography, geology, German, health education, health sciences, history, home economics, home economics education, industrial arts education, industrial technology, journalism, law enforcement and corrections, liberal/general studies, manufacturing technology, marketing and distribution, mathematics, mathematics education, music, music education, office supervision and management, operations management, parks and recreation management, personnel management, philosophy, physical education, physics, political science and government, protective services, psychology, secretarial and related programs, sociology, Spanish, speech pathology/audiology, transportation management.

ACADEMIC PROGRAMS. Cooperative education, double major, dual enrollment of high school students, education specialist degree, external degree, honors program, independent study, internships, student-designed major, study abroad, teacher preparation, telecourses, visiting/exchange student program; combined bachelor's/graduate program in business administration. **Remedial services:** Learning center, special counselor, tutoring. **ROTC:** Army. **Placement/credit:** AP, CLEP General and Subject, institutional tests; 30 credit hours maximum for bachelor's degree.

ACADEMIC REQUIREMENTS. Freshmen must earn minimum GPA of 1.75 to continue in good standing. 69% of freshmen return for sophomore year. Students must declare major by end of first year. **Graduation requirements:** 120 hours for bachelor's (32 in major). Most students required to take courses in English, humanities, biological/physical sciences, social sciences.

FRESHMAN ADMISSIONS. Selection criteria: ACT composite score of 22, or rank in top half of class and ACT composite score of 18 required. **High school preparation:** 13 units required. Required units include English 4, mathematics 3, social science 3 and science 3. 2 units of film, art, theater, or foreign language also required. **Test requirements:** SAT or ACT (ACT preferred); score report by August 1.

1992 FRESHMAN CLASS PROFILE. 3,351 men applied, 2,438 accepted, 842 enrolled; 3,933 women applied, 3,039 accepted, 792 enrolled. 7% were in top tenth and 22% were in top quarter of graduating class. **Academic background:** Mid 50% of enrolled freshmen had ACT composite between 20-24. 91% submitted ACT scores. **Characteristics:** 90% from in state, 88% live in college housing, 16% have minority backgrounds, 3% are foreign students, 10% join fraternities/sororities. Average age is 18.

FALL-TERM APPLICATIONS. No fee. Closing date August 1; applicants notified on a rolling basis; must reply by registration. Audition required for music applicants. Deferred admission available. EDP-S.

STUDENT LIFE. Housing: Dormitories (men, women, coed); apartment, fraternity, sorority housing available. **Activities:** Student government, film, radio, student newspaper, television, yearbook, choral groups, concert band, dance, drama, jazz band, marching band, music ensembles, musical theater, pep band, symphony orchestra, fraternities, sororities, 83 special-interest organizations, 8 service organizations, 25 religious organizations, 34 national honorary and professional fraternities.

ATHLETICS. NCAA. **Intercollegiate:** Baseball M, basketball, cross-country, diving, football M, golf M, soccer M, softball W, swimming, tennis, track and field, volleyball W. **Intramural:** Archery, badminton, baseball M, basketball, bowling, cross-country M, diving, fencing, field hockey W, golf, handball, ice hockey, lacrosse W, racquetball, rifle, rugby M, soccer M, softball, swimming, table tennis, tennis, track and field, volleyball, water polo, wrestling M.

STUDENT SERVICES. Aptitude testing, career counseling, employment service for undergraduates, freshman orientation, health services, on-campus day care, personal counseling, placement service for graduates, veterans counselor, services/facilities for handicapped.

ANNUAL EXPENSES. Tuition and fees (1992-93): $2,454, $3,696 additional for out-of-state students. Residents of nearby counties in Iowa and Missouri pay in-state tuition during first year. **Room and board:** $2,993. **Books and supplies:** $550. **Other expenses:** $1,210.

FINANCIAL AID. 85% of freshmen, 85% of continuing students receive some form of aid. 60% of grants, 99% of loans, 15% of jobs based on need. Academic, music/drama, art, athletic, leadership scholarships available. **Aid applications:** No closing date; priority given to applications received by March 31; applicants notified on a rolling basis beginning on or about April 15; must reply within 2 weeks.

ADDRESS/TELEPHONE. Thomas Streveler, Director of Admissions-Outreach, Western Illinois University, 900 West Adams, Sherman Hall, Room 109, Macomb, IL 61455. (309) 298-1891.

Wheaton College
Wheaton, Illinois CB code: 1905

Admissions: 68% of applicants accepted
Based on: ••• Religious affiliation/commitment, school record
•• Essay, interview, recommendations, special talents, test scores
• Activities
Completion: 98% of freshmen end year in good standing
78% graduate, 25% of these enter graduate study

4-year private liberal arts college, coed, affiliated with nondenominational Christian churches. Founded in 1860. **Accreditation:** Regional. **Undergraduate enrollment:** 1,052 men, 1,185 women full time; 35 men, 32 women part time. **Graduate enrollment:** 107 men, 70 women full time; 56 men, 69 women part time. **Faculty:** 259 total (151 full time), 123 with doctorates or other terminal degrees. **Location:** Suburban campus in small city; 25 miles from Chicago. **Calendar:** Semester, limited summer session. **Microcomputers:** 50 located in libraries, computer centers. **Special facilities:** Billy Graham Museum, science station, Honey Rock Camp.

DEGREES OFFERED. BA, BS, MA, D. 497 bachelor's degrees awarded in 1992. 10% in business and management, 11% communications, 6% teacher education, 5% languages, 7% letters/literature, 16% philosophy, religion, theology, 6% physical sciences, 9% psychology, 16% social sciences. Graduate degrees offered in 7 major fields of study.

UNDERGRADUATE MAJORS. Ancient languages, archeology, art education, art history, Bible studies, biblical languages, biology, business economics, chemistry, communications, computer mathematics, economics, elementary education, English education, English literature, foreign languages (multiple emphasis), foreign languages education, French, geology, German, history, liberal/general studies, mathematics, mathematics education, music, music education, music history and appreciation, music performance, music theory and composition, philosophy, physical education, physics, political science and government, psychology, religion, religious education, science education, secondary education, social science education, social sciences, sociology, Spanish, speech, speech/communication/theater education, studio art.

ACADEMIC PROGRAMS. Accelerated program, double major, independent study, internships, student-designed major, study abroad, teacher preparation, visiting/exchange student program, Washington semester, cross-registration; liberal arts/career combination in engineering, health sciences. **ROTC:** Army. **Placement/credit:** AP, CLEP Subject, institutional tests; 36 credit hours maximum for bachelor's degree.

ACADEMIC REQUIREMENTS. Freshmen must earn minimum GPA of 1.8 to continue in good standing. 93% of freshmen return for sophomore year. Students must declare major by end of first year. **Graduation requirements:** 124 hours for bachelor's (36 in major). Most students required to take courses in arts/fine arts, English, foreign languages, history, humanities, mathematics, philosophy/religion, biological/physical sciences, social sciences. **Postgraduate studies:** 2% enter law school, 4% enter medical school, 1% enter MBA programs, 18% enter other graduate study.

FRESHMAN ADMISSIONS. Selection criteria: Evidence of a vital Christian experience, moral character, personal integrity, social concern, academic ability, and desire for a liberal arts education as defined by the college most important. **High school preparation:** 13 units recommended. Recommended units include English 4, foreign language 2, mathematics 2, social science 2 and science 2. **Test requirements:** SAT or ACT; score report by March 1.

1992 FRESHMAN CLASS PROFILE. 546 men applied, 443 accepted, 254 enrolled; 841 women applied, 502 accepted, 295 enrolled. 93% had high school GPA of 3.0 or higher, 7% between 2.0 and 2.99. 52% were in top tenth and 83% were in top quarter of graduating class. **Academic background:** Mid 50% of enrolled freshmen had SAT-V between 500-610, SAT-M between 550-660; ACT composite between 25-29. 78% submitted SAT scores, 64% submitted ACT scores. **Characteristics:** 21% from in state, 99% live in college housing, 9% have minority backgrounds, 1% are foreign students. Average age is 18.

FALL-TERM APPLICATIONS. $30 fee, may be waived for applicants with need. Closing date February 15; applicants notified on or about April 1; must reply by May 1. Interview required. Audition required for music applicants. Essay required. Portfolio recommended for art applicants. CRDA. Deferred admission available. Institutional early decision plan. ACH recommended for placement purposes; score report by July 1.

STUDENT LIFE. Housing: Dormitories (men, women); apartment, cooperative housing available. **Activities:** Student government, magazine, radio, student newspaper, yearbook, choral groups, concert band, dance, drama, jazz band, music ensembles, opera, pep band, symphony orchestra, Christian Service Council, Student Missionary Project, Youth Hostel Ministries, World Christian Fellowship. **Additional information:** Religious observance required.

ATHLETICS. NCAA. **Intercollegiate:** Baseball M, basketball, cross-country, football M, golf M, soccer, softball W, swimming, tennis, track and field, volleyball W, wrestling M. **Intramural:** Badminton, basketball, football M, ice hockey M, lacrosse M, skiing, soccer, softball, tennis, volleyball, water polo.

STUDENT SERVICES. Aptitude testing, career counseling, employment service for undergraduates, freshman orientation, health services, personal counseling, placement service for graduates, services/facilities for handicapped.

ANNUAL EXPENSES. Tuition and fees: $10,640. **Room and board:** $4,070. **Books and supplies:** $500. **Other expenses:** $1,300.

FINANCIAL AID. 69% of freshmen, 59% of continuing students receive some form of aid. 95% of grants, 99% of loans, 31% of jobs based on need. 302 enrolled freshmen were judged to have need, all were offered aid. Academic, music/drama scholarships available. **Aid applications:** No closing date; priority given to applications received by March 15; applicants notified on a rolling basis beginning on or about March 1.

ADDRESS/TELEPHONE. Dan Crabtree, Director of Admissions, Wheaton College, 501 East College, Wheaton, IL 60187-5593. (708) 752-5005. (800) 222-2419. Fax: (708) 752-5245.

William Rainey Harper College

Palatine, Illinois CB code: 1932

2-year public community college, coed. Founded in 1965. **Accreditation:** Regional. **Undergraduate enrollment:** 2,404 men, 2,367 women full time; 4,103 men, 6,947 women part time. **Faculty:** 1,004 total (204 full time), 40 with doctorates or other terminal degrees. **Location:** Suburban campus in large town; 25 miles from Chicago. **Calendar:** Semester, limited summer session. Saturday and extensive evening/early morning classes. **Microcomputers:** 600 located in libraries, computer centers. **Special facilities:** Observatory. **Additional facts:** Program for hearing-impaired offered.

DEGREES OFFERED. AA, AS, AAS. 1,224 associate degrees awarded in 1992. 19% in business and management, 5% business/office and marketing/distribution, 7% education, 12% allied health, 5% home economics, 23% letters/literature, 8% physical sciences.

UNDERGRADUATE MAJORS. Accounting, air conditioning/heating/refrigeration mechanics, air conditioning/heating/refrigeration technology, architectural technologies, biological and physical sciences, biology, business administration and management, business and management, business and office, business computer/console/peripheral equipment operation, business data processing and related programs, business systems analysis, cardiac exercise technology, chemistry, child development/care/guidance, communications, computer and information sciences, criminal justice technology, dance, data processing, dental hygiene, dietetic aide/assistant, early childhood education, education, electronic technology, engineering and engineering-related technologies, English, fashion design, fashion merchandising, finance, fine arts, fire control and safety technology, food management, food production/management/services, horticulture, hotel/motel and restaurant management, humanities, information sciences and systems, insurance and risk management, interior design, international business management, journalism, law enforcement and corrections technologies, legal assistant/paralegal, legal secretary, liberal/general studies, management information systems, manufacturing technology, marketing and distribution, marketing management, mathematics, mechanical design technology, medical secretary, music, nursing, office supervision and management, parks and recreation management, pharmacy technician, physical sciences, physics, practical nursing, predentistry, preengineering, prelaw, premedicine, prepharmacy, preveterinary, psychology, real estate, secretarial and related programs, small business management and ownership, social sciences, trade and industrial supervision and management, visual and performing arts.

ACADEMIC PROGRAMS. 2-year transfer program, dual enrollment of high school students, honors program, independent study, internships, study abroad, telecourses, weekend college. **Remedial services:** Learning center, reduced course load, remedial instruction, special counselor, tutoring, study skills courses. **Placement/credit:** AP, CLEP General and Subject, institutional tests. Maximum of 50% total hours in any degree program may be earned through credit by examination.

ACADEMIC REQUIREMENTS. Students must maintain a GPA which varies depending on number of credit hours earned. 67% of freshmen return for sophomore year. **Graduation requirements:** 60 hours for associate. Most students required to take courses in English, humanities, mathematics, biological/physical sciences, social sciences. **Additional information:** Cooperative career program with in-district high schools. Students begin specialized training in high school and continue in colleges.

FRESHMAN ADMISSIONS. Selection criteria: Open admissions. Selective admission to some programs. 15 high school units required for transfer program applicants: minimum of 4 English, 1 foreign language, music, or art, 2 mathematics, 2 social studies, and 2 science. **Test requirements:** SAT or ACT (ACT preferred) for counseling. Psychological Corporation Pre-Nursing Examinations for nursing applicants. Watson-Glaser Critical Thinking Test for legal technology applicants. Harper Assessment Test Battery for full-time students and for placement in English and mathematics for part-time students.

1992 FRESHMAN CLASS PROFILE. 1,738 men, 2,076 women enrolled. **Characteristics:** 99% from in state, 100% commute, 17% have minority backgrounds. Average age is 24.

FALL-TERM APPLICATIONS. $15 fee. No closing date; applicants notified on a rolling basis; must reply by registration. Deferred and early admission available. Priority given to applications to nursing program received by December 1. Priority given to applications received by February 1 for all other limited-enrollment programs.

STUDENT LIFE. Activities: Student government, film, magazine, radio, student newspaper, television, choral groups, concert band, dance, drama, jazz band, music ensembles, musical theater, International Student Club, religious organizations, service organizations, professional organizations, Student Ambassadors.

ATHLETICS. NJCAA. **Intercollegiate:** Baseball, basketball, cross-country, diving, football M, golf M, softball W, swimming, tennis, track and field, volleyball W, wrestling M. **Intramural:** Badminton, baseball M, basketball, bowling M, diving, handball, racquetball, skiing, softball, swimming, table tennis, tennis, volleyball W.

STUDENT SERVICES. Aptitude testing, career counseling, employment service for undergraduates, freshman orientation, health services, on-campus day care, personal counseling, placement service for graduates, special adviser for adult students, veterans counselor, services/facilities for handicapped.

ANNUAL EXPENSES. Tuition and fees (1992-93): $1,030, $2,670 additional for out-of-district students, $3,630 additional for out-of-state students. In-district tuition rates available to employees of in-district companies who reside outside college district. **Books and supplies:** $450. **Other expenses:** $1,325.

FINANCIAL AID. 12% of freshmen, 21% of continuing students receive some form of aid. 36% of grants, 88% of loans, 2% of jobs based on need. Academic, music/drama, art, leadership scholarships available. **Aid applications:** No closing date; priority given to applications received by May 1; applicants notified on a rolling basis; must reply within 2 weeks.

ADDRESS/TELEPHONE. Bruce Bohrer, Director of Adimissions, William Rainey Harper College, 1200 West Algonquin Road, Palatine, IL 60067-7398. (708) 397-3000 ext. 2506.

Indiana

Ancilla College
Donaldson, Indiana CB code: 1015

Admissions: 99% of applicants accepted
Based on: ••• School record, test scores
•• Interview
• Activities, recommendations
Completion: 90% of freshmen end year in good standing
50% graduate, 70% of these enter 4-year programs

2-year private junior college, coed, affiliated with Roman Catholic Church. Founded in 1937. **Accreditation:** Regional. **Undergraduate enrollment:** 61 men, 188 women full time; 120 men, 309 women part time. **Faculty:** 46 total (22 full time), 3 with doctorates or other terminal degrees. **Location:** Rural campus in rural community; 30 miles from South Bend. **Calendar:** 4-4-1, limited summer session. Saturday classes. **Microcomputers:** 35 located in computer centers. **Special facilities:** Academic skills center, museum, greenhouse.

DEGREES OFFERED. AA, AS. 56 associate degrees awarded in 1992. 58% in business and management, 6% computer sciences, 32% multi/interdisciplinary studies.

UNDERGRADUATE MAJORS. Accounting, biology, business administration and management, business and management, business and office, business data processing and related programs, business data programming, computer and information sciences, criminology, English, information sciences and systems, liberal/general studies, optometry, secretarial and related programs, sociology, special education.

ACADEMIC PROGRAMS. 2-year transfer program, dual enrollment of high school students, independent study, internships, teacher preparation. **Remedial services:** Learning center, reduced course load, remedial instruction, tutoring. **Placement/credit:** CLEP General and Subject, institutional tests.

ACADEMIC REQUIREMENTS. Freshmen must earn minimum GPA of 2.0 to continue in good standing. 80% of freshmen return for sophomore year. Students must declare major by end of first year. **Graduation requirements:** 60 hours for associate (31 in major). Most students required to take courses in English, history, mathematics, philosophy/religion, biological/physical sciences, social sciences.

FRESHMAN ADMISSIONS. Selection criteria: Class rank, test scores, interview considered. Recommended units include biological science 3, English 4, foreign language 2, mathematics 4 and social science 2. College-preparatory program recommended. **Test requirements:** SAT or ACT (SAT preferred); score report by August 30.

1992 FRESHMAN CLASS PROFILE. 160 men applied, 159 accepted, 142 enrolled; 400 women applied, 395 accepted, 355 enrolled. 20% had high school GPA of 3.0 or higher, 78% between 2.0 and 2.99. **Academic background:** Mid 50% of enrolled freshmen had SAT-V between 360-480, SAT-M between 390-490. 30% submitted SAT scores. **Characteristics:** 99% from in state, 100% commute, 2% have minority backgrounds, 1% are foreign students. Average age is 27.

FALL-TERM APPLICATIONS. $20 fee, may be waived for applicants with need. No closing date; priority given to applications received by May 30; applicants notified on a rolling basis. Interview recommended. CRDA. Deferred and early admission available.

STUDENT LIFE. Activities: Student government, student newspaper, choral groups, drama, Single Parents, Seeking Employment Laying Foundation (SELF) support group.

ATHLETICS. Intercollegiate: Basketball M, volleyball W. **Intramural:** Swimming, table tennis, tennis, volleyball.

STUDENT SERVICES. Aptitude testing, career counseling, employment service for undergraduates, personal counseling, placement service for graduates, special adviser for adult students, services/facilities for handicapped.

ANNUAL EXPENSES. Tuition and fees: $2,460. **Books and supplies:** $400. **Other expenses:** $700.

FINANCIAL AID. 60% of freshmen, 60% of continuing students receive some form of aid. 99% of grants, 72% of loans, all jobs based on need. 145 enrolled freshmen were judged to have need, all were offered aid. Academic, athletic, alumni affiliation scholarships available. **Aid applications:** No closing date; priority given to applications received by May 1; applicants notified on a rolling basis beginning on or about May 15; must reply within 4 weeks.

ADDRESS/TELEPHONE. Kathryn Castle, Director of Admissions and Financial Aid, Ancilla College, Union Road, Donaldson, IN 46513. (219) 936-8898 ext. 350. Fax: (219) 935-1773.

Anderson University
Anderson, Indiana CB code: 1016

Admissions: 83% of applicants accepted
Based on: ••• Religious affiliation/commitment, school record
•• Activities, recommendations, test scores
• Essay, special talents
Completion: 84% of freshmen end year in good standing
45% graduate, 15% of these enter graduate study

4-year private liberal arts college, coed, affiliated with Church of God. Founded in 1917. **Accreditation:** Regional. **Undergraduate enrollment:** 786 men, 1,032 women full time; 90 men, 205 women part time. **Graduate enrollment:** 35 men, 10 women full time; 70 men, 22 women part time. **Faculty:** 191 total (124 full time), 84 with doctorates or other terminal degrees. **Location:** Urban campus in small city; 45 miles from of Indianapolis. **Calendar:** Semester, limited summer session. Saturday and extensive evening/early morning classes. **Microcomputers:** 125 located in libraries, classrooms, computer centers. **Special facilities:** Bible museum, 2 art galleries, observatory.

DEGREES OFFERED. AA, BA, BS, MA, MBA, M.Div. 21 associate degrees awarded in 1992. 34% in business/office and marketing/distribution, 62% teacher education. 326 bachelor's degrees awarded. 18% in business and management, 7% business/office and marketing/distribution, 21% teacher education, 8% health sciences, 5% philosophy, religion, theology, 7% psychology, 12% social sciences, 7% visual and performing arts. Graduate degrees offered in 4 major fields of study.

UNDERGRADUATE MAJORS. Associate: Business and management, business and office, criminal justice studies, early childhood education, secretarial and related programs. **Bachelor's:** Accounting, American studies, art education, Bible studies, biology, business administration and management, chemistry, communications, computer and information sciences, computer mathematics, criminal justice studies, dramatic arts, education, elementary education, English, English education, finance, foreign languages education, French, German, graphic design, history, junior high education, marketing and distribution, marriage and family counseling, mathematics, mathematics education, medical laboratory technologies, music business management, music education, music performance, nursing, philosophy, physical education, physics, political science and government, predentistry, prelaw, premedicine, prepharmacy, preveterinary, psychology, religion, religious education, religious music, science education, secondary education, social studies education, social work, sociology, Spanish, speech, speech/communication/theater education, sports medicine, studio art.

ACADEMIC PROGRAMS. Accelerated program, cooperative education, double major, honors program, independent study, internships, student-designed major, study abroad, cross-registration, summer overseas service program. **Remedial services:** Learning center, preadmission summer program, reduced course load, remedial instruction, special counselor, tutoring. **Placement/credit:** AP, CLEP General and Subject, institutional tests; 30 credit hours maximum for bachelor's degree.

ACADEMIC REQUIREMENTS. Freshmen must earn minimum GPA of 2.0 to continue in good standing. 78% of freshmen return for sophomore year. Students must declare major by end of second year. **Graduation requirements:** 64 hours for associate (32 in major), 124 hours for bachelor's (36 in major). Most students required to take courses in arts/fine arts, English, foreign languages, history, mathematics, philosophy/religion, biological/physical sciences, social sciences.

FRESHMAN ADMISSIONS. Selection criteria: Rank in top half of class, test scores, reference important. School, church, and community activities also considered. **High school preparation:** 4 units required; 11 recommended. Required and recommended units include English 2-4 and mathematics 2-3. Foreign language 2 and science 2 recommended. **Test requirements:** SAT or ACT; score report by September 1.

1992 FRESHMAN CLASS PROFILE. 363 men applied, 283 accepted, 230 enrolled; 485 women applied, 418 accepted, 347 enrolled. 49% had high school GPA of 3.0 or higher, 49% between 2.0 and 2.99. 32% were in top tenth and 51% were in top quarter of graduating class. **Academic background:** Mid 50% of enrolled freshmen had SAT-V between 360-490, SAT-M between 380-540. 55% submitted SAT scores. **Characteristics:** 59% from in state, 90% live in college housing, 7% have minority backgrounds, 4% are foreign students. Average age is 23.

FALL-TERM APPLICATIONS. $20 fee, may be waived for applicants with need. Closing date September 1; priority given to applications received by March 1; applicants notified on a rolling basis; must reply by May 1 or within 3 weeks if notified thereafter. Audition required for music applicants. CRDA. Deferred and early admission available. EDP-F.

STUDENT LIFE. Housing: Dormitories (men, women); apartment, cooperative housing available. All single undergraduate students (except seniors) under 22 years of age and not living with parents required to live on campus. **Activities:** Student government, film, radio, student newspaper, television, yearbook, choral groups, concert band, drama, jazz band, music ensembles, musical theater, pep band, symphony orchestra, Multicultural Student Union, Religious Life Council, business club, women's clubs, men's clubs, international student association.

ATHLETICS. NCAA. **Intercollegiate:** Baseball M, basketball, cross-country, football M, golf M, soccer, softball W, tennis, track and field, volleyball W. **Intramural:** Basketball, softball, table tennis, tennis, track and field, volleyball.

STUDENT SERVICES. Aptitude testing, career counseling, employment service for undergraduates, freshman orientation, health services, personal counseling, placement service for graduates, special adviser for adult students, veterans counselor, services/facilities for handicapped.

ANNUAL EXPENSES. Tuition and fees (1992-93): $8,780. **Room and board:** $3,120. **Books and supplies:** $500. **Other expenses:** $700.

FINANCIAL AID. 87% of freshmen, 87% of continuing students receive some form of aid. 85% of grants, 99% of loans, 68% of jobs based on need. Academic, music/drama, art, leadership, religious affiliation, minority scholarships available. **Aid applications:** No closing date; priority given to applications received by March 1; applicants notified on a rolling basis beginning on or about April 1; must reply by May 1 or within 3 weeks if notified thereafter.

ADDRESS/TELEPHONE. Ann E. Brandon, Director of Admissions, Anderson University, 1100 East Fifth, Anderson, IN 46012-3462. (317) 641-3043. (800) 428-6414. Fax: (317) 641-3851.

Ball State University

Muncie, Indiana CB code: 1051

Admissions: 79% of applicants accepted
Based on:
••• School record, test scores
•• Special talents
• Activities, essay, interview, recommendations
Completion: 77% of freshmen end year in good standing
62% graduate, 20% of these enter graduate study

4-year public university, coed. Founded in 1918. **Accreditation:** Regional. **Undergraduate enrollment:** 7,205 men, 8,806 women full time; 940 men, 1,148 women part time. **Graduate enrollment:** 464 men, 522 women full time; 516 men, 685 women part time. **Faculty:** 1,123 total (943 full time), 592 with doctorates or other terminal degrees. **Location:** Suburban campus in small city; 56 miles from Indianapolis. **Calendar:** Semester, extensive summer session. Saturday and extensive evening/early morning classes. **Microcomputers:** 2,300 located in dormitories, libraries, classrooms, computer centers. **Special facilities:** Art gallery, planetarium, nature preserves, community-university auditoriums for cultural events, wellness institute.

DEGREES OFFERED. AA, AS, BA, BS, BFA, BArch, MA, MS, MBA, PhD, EdD. 215 associate degrees awarded in 1992. 3,175 bachelor's degrees awarded. Graduate degrees offered in 66 major fields of study.

UNDERGRADUATE MAJORS. Associate: Business administration and management, business and office, chemical manufacturing technology, criminal justice studies, food science and nutrition, graphic and printing production, industrial technology, legal assistant/paralegal, liberal/general studies, manufacturing technology, mechanical design technology, nuclear medical technology, nurse anesthetist, nursing, public administration, radiograph medical technology, respiratory therapy technology, secretarial and related programs, teacher aide, word processing. **Bachelor's:** Accounting, actuarial sciences, advertising, allied health, anthropology, architecture, art education, art history, athletic training, biology, botany, business administration and management, business and management, business economics, business education, business statistics, cell biology, ceramics, chemistry, city/community/regional planning, clinical laboratory science, community health work, computer and information sciences, conservation and regulation, consumer home economics, criminal justice studies, dance, dramatic arts, drawing, early childhood education, economics, education of the deaf and hearing impaired, education of the mentally handicapped, education of the multiple handicapped, education of the physically handicapped, elementary education, English, English education, environmental design, environmental science, exercise science and fitness specialist, family/consumer resource management, fashion design, fashion merchandising, fiber/textiles/weaving, finance, finance and management, fishing and fisheries, food management, food production/management/services, food science and nutrition, foreign languages education, forestry and related sciences, French, genetics, human and animal, geography, geology, German, graphic arts technology, graphic design, health education, health sciences, health services supervision, history, home economics, home economics education, home furnishings and equipment management/production/services, human environment and housing, industrial arts education, insurance and risk management, insurance marketing, interior design, international business management, interpretation and public information, journalism, junior high education, landscape architecture, Latin, Latin American studies, legal administration, library science, management information systems, management science, marketing and distribution, marketing management, mathematical economics, mathematics, mathematics education, metal/jewelry, microbiology, molecular biology, music, music education, music engineering technology, music performance, music theory and composition, nursing, occupational home economics, operations research, painting, personnel management, philosophy, photography, photojournalism, physical education, physical sciences, physics, plant genetics, political science and government, predentistry, preengineering, premedicine, prepharmacy, printmaking, production, psychology, public health laboratory science, public relations, radio/television broadcasting, radio/television technology, real estate, religion, renewable natural resources, retailing, sales and advertising, sales and management, sales and promotion, science education, sculpture, secondary education, secretarial and related programs, small business management and ownership, social science education, social sciences, social studies education, social work, sociology, Spanish, special education, speech, speech correction, speech pathology/audiology, speech/communication/theater education, teaching economics, telecommunications, textiles and clothing, theater design, tourism, trade and industrial education, urban design, visual and performing arts, zoology.

ACADEMIC PROGRAMS. 2-year transfer program, accelerated program, cooperative education, double major, dual enrollment of high school students, education specialist degree, honors program, independent study, internships, student-designed major, study abroad, teacher preparation, visiting/exchange student program, Washington semester, cross-registration; liberal arts/career combination in health sciences; combined bachelor's/graduate program in business administration. **Remedial services:** Learning center, preadmission summer program, reduced course load, special counselor, tutoring, writing center; athletic and Greek study tables. **ROTC:** Army. **Placement/credit:** AP, CLEP General and Subject, institutional tests; 15 credit hours maximum for associate degree; 63 credit hours maximum for bachelor's degree.

ACADEMIC REQUIREMENTS. Freshmen must earn minimum GPA of 2.0 to continue in good standing. 82% of freshmen return for sophomore year. Students must declare major by end of second year. **Graduation requirements:** 63 hours for associate, 126 hours for bachelor's. Most students required to take courses in arts/fine arts, English, history, humanities, mathematics, biological/physical sciences, social sciences. **Postgraduate studies:** 32% from 2-year programs enter 4-year programs. 5% enter law school, 4% enter medical school, 4% enter MBA programs, 7% enter other graduate study. **Additional information:** Minimum credit hours in major for associate degree range from 30 to 45; for bachelor's, 45 to 65. All undergraduates must pass writing competency test.

FRESHMAN ADMISSIONS. Selection criteria: School achievement record, test scores, class rank. **High school preparation:** 19 units recommended. Recommended units include English 4, foreign language 2, mathematics 3, social science 3 and science 2. **Test requirements:** SAT or ACT; score report by March 1. **Additional information:** Older adult's credentials evaluated for admission on individual basis.

1992 FRESHMAN CLASS PROFILE. 3,940 men applied, 2,995 accepted, 1,416 enrolled; 4,976 women applied, 4,048 accepted, 1,846 enrolled. 39% were in top quarter of graduating class. **Academic background:** Mid 50% of enrolled freshmen had SAT-V between 370-480, SAT-M between 410-540; ACT composite between 12-25. 87% submitted SAT scores, 9% submitted ACT scores. **Characteristics:** 90% from in state, 87% live in college housing, 7% have minority backgrounds, 1% are foreign students, 15% join fraternities/sororities. Average age is 19.

FALL-TERM APPLICATIONS. $15 fee, may be waived for applicants with need. No closing date; priority given to applications received by March 1; applicants notified on a rolling basis; Students meeting priority deadline must reply by May 1. Essay required. Interview recommended. Audition recommended for music, theater applicants. Portfolio recommended for art, architecture applicants. CRDA. Deferred admission available.

STUDENT LIFE. Housing: Dormitories (men, women, coed); apartment, fraternity, handicapped housing available. Freshmen and new freshman and sophomore transfer students required to live on campus unless living with parents or guardian, or 21 years of age or older. **Activities:** Student government, film, magazine, radio, student newspaper, television, yearbook, choral groups, concert band, dance, drama, jazz band, marching band, music ensembles, musical theater, opera, pep band, symphony orchestra, folk dance group, fraternities, sororities, over 300 student organizations, religious council, student association (political), minority round table, North American Hispanic Association, student voluntary services, nontraditional student association, African Students Association, Young Socialists Alliance.

ATHLETICS. NCAA. **Intercollegiate:** Baseball M, basketball, cross-country, diving, field hockey W, football M, golf M, gymnastics W, horseback riding, softball W, swimming, tennis, track and field, volleyball. **Intramural:** Archery, badminton, baseball M, basketball, bowling, cross-country, diving, fencing, football M, golf M, gymnastics W, handball, lacrosse, racquetball, rowing (crew), rugby, sailing, skiing, soccer, softball, swimming, table tennis, tennis, track and field, volleyball, wrestling M.

STUDENT SERVICES. Aptitude testing, career counseling, employment service for undergraduates, freshman orientation, health services, on-campus day care, personal counseling, placement service for graduates, veterans counselor, peer tutoring, services/facilities for handicapped.

ANNUAL EXPENSES. Tuition and fees (1992-93): $2,464, $3,408 additional for out-of-state students. **Room and board:** $3,376. **Books and supplies:** $500. **Other expenses:** $1,100.

FINANCIAL AID. 60% of freshmen, 70% of continuing students receive some form of aid. 54% of grants, 81% of loans, 7% of jobs based on need. 1,729 enrolled freshmen were judged to have need, 1,674 were offered aid. Academic, music/drama, athletic, leadership, minority scholarships available. **Aid applications:** No closing date; priority given to applications received by March 1; applicants notified on a rolling basis beginning on or about May 1; must reply within 3 weeks.

ADDRESS/TELEPHONE. Ruth A. Vedvik, Director of Admissions, Ball State University, 2000 University Avenue, Muncie, IN 47306-0855. (317) 285-8300. (800) 482-4278.

Bethel College
Mishawaka, Indiana CB code: 1079

4-year private college of arts and sciences and liberal arts college, coed, affiliated with Missionary Church. Founded in 1947. **Accreditation:** Regional. **Undergraduate enrollment:** 268 men, 351 women full time; 96 men, 244 women part time. **Graduate enrollment:** 20 men, 5 women part time. **Faculty:** 89 total (54 full time), 29 with doctorates or other terminal degrees. **Location:** Suburban campus in large town; 90 miles from Chicago, 140 miles from Indianapolis. **Calendar:** Semester, limited summer session. Saturday and extensive evening/early morning classes. **Microcomputers:** 25 located in dormitories, classrooms, computer centers. **Special facilities:** Otis and Elizabeth Bowen Library.

DEGREES OFFERED. AA, AS, BA, BS, M. 32 associate degrees awarded in 1992. 91% in health sciences. 113 bachelor's degrees awarded. 43% in business and management, 19% teacher education, 6% multi/interdisciplinary studies, 6% parks/recreation, protective services, public affairs. Graduate degrees offered in 1 major field of study.

UNDERGRADUATE MAJORS. Associate: Bible studies, biology, business administration and management, chemistry, computer and information sciences, early childhood education, graphic arts technology, journalism, nursing, religious music, secretarial and related programs, social sciences. **Bachelor's:** Accounting, aerospace/aeronautical/astronautical engineering, Bible studies, biology, business administration and management, business education, chemical engineering, chemistry, civil engineering, communications, driver and safety education, electrical/electronics/communications engineering, elementary education, engineering science, English, English education, fine arts, graphic arts technology, human resources development, junior high education, liberal/general studies, mathematics, mathematics education, mechanical engineering, mechanical/industrial engineering, mechanical/nuclear engineering, metallurgical engineering, music, music education, music performance, nursing, parks and recreation management, physical education, predentistry, premedicine, psychology, religious music, science education, secondary education, social sciences, social studies education, sociology.

ACADEMIC PROGRAMS. 2-year transfer program, accelerated program, independent study, internships, study abroad, teacher preparation, weekend college, cross-registration; liberal arts/career combination in engineering. **Remedial services:** Learning center, reduced course load, remedial instruction, special counselor, tutoring. **ROTC:** Naval. **Placement/credit:** AP, CLEP General and Subject, institutional tests; 20 credit hours maximum for bachelor's degree.

ACADEMIC REQUIREMENTS. Freshmen must earn minimum GPA of 2.0 to continue in good standing. 60% of freshmen return for sophomore year. **Graduation requirements:** 62 hours for associate, 124 hours for bachelor's. Most students required to take courses in arts/fine arts, English, foreign languages, history, mathematics, philosophy/religion, biological/physical sciences, social sciences. **Postgraduate studies:** 10% from 2-year programs enter 4-year programs.

FRESHMAN ADMISSIONS. Selection criteria: School achievement record, character recommendations. **High school preparation:** 14 units recommended. Recommended units include biological science 2, English 4, foreign language 2, mathematics 2, physical science 2 and social science 2. **Test requirements:** SAT or ACT; score report by September 1.

1992 FRESHMAN CLASS PROFILE. 131 men, 201 women enrolled. 42% had high school GPA of 3.0 or higher, 49% between 2.0 and 2.99. 13% were in top tenth and 30% were in top quarter of graduating class. **Academic background:** Mid 50% of enrolled freshmen had SAT-V between 350-490, SAT-M between 390-540; ACT composite between 17-23. 68% submitted SAT scores, 32% submitted ACT scores. **Characteristics:** 80% from in state, 52% commute, 22% have minority backgrounds, 1% are foreign students. Average age is 19.

FALL-TERM APPLICATIONS. $25 fee, may be waived for applicants with need. Closing date August 1; priority given to applications received by July 1; applicants notified on a rolling basis; must reply within 4 weeks. Interview recommended. Audition recommended for music students applicants. Portfolio recommended for fine arts students, returning adults who wish to receive life experience credits applicants. Deferred admission available.

STUDENT LIFE. Housing: Dormitories (men, women); apartment housing available. **Activities:** Student government, radio, student newspaper, yearbook, choral groups, drama, music ensembles, pep band, symphony orchestra, Fellowship of Christian Athletes, ministerial association, interest clubs. **Additional information:** Religious observance required.

ATHLETICS. NAIA. **Intercollegiate:** Baseball M, basketball, cross-country, golf M, soccer M, softball W, tennis, track and field, volleyball W. **Intramural:** Basketball M, football M, soccer, table tennis, volleyball.

STUDENT SERVICES. Aptitude testing, career counseling, employment service for undergraduates, freshman orientation, health services, personal counseling, placement service for graduates, special adviser for adult students, services/facilities for handicapped.

ANNUAL EXPENSES. Tuition and fees: $8,500. **Room and board:** $2,900. **Books and supplies:** $600. **Other expenses:** $700.

FINANCIAL AID. 85% of continuing students receive some form of aid. 60% of grants, 79% of loans, 55% of jobs based on need. Academic, music/drama, athletic, leadership, religious affiliation scholarships available. **Aid applications:** No closing date; priority given to applications received by March 1; applicants notified on a rolling basis beginning on or about April 15; must reply within 2 weeks.

ADDRESS/TELEPHONE. Steve Matteson, Director of Admissions, Bethel College, 1001 West McKinley, Mishawaka, IN 46545. (219) 259-8511 ext. 339. (800) 422-4101. Fax: (219) 257-3326.

Butler University
Indianapolis, Indiana CB code: 1073

Admissions:	86% of applicants accepted
Based on:	••• School record, test scores
	•• Recommendations, special talents
	• Activities, essay, interview
Completion:	85% of freshmen end year in good standing
	63% graduate, 10% of these enter graduate study

4-year private university, coed. Founded in 1855. **Accreditation:** Regional. **Undergraduate enrollment:** 1,060 men, 1,520 women full time; 43 men, 122 women part time. **Graduate enrollment:** 58 men, 61 women full time; 440 men, 521 women part time. **Faculty:** 368 total (214 full time), 195 with doctorates or other terminal degrees. **Location:** Suburban campus in very large city. **Calendar:** Semester, limited summer session. **Microcomputers:** 200 located in dormitories, classrooms, computer centers. **Special facilities:** Observatory, planetarium, Holcomb Research Institute (international center for environmental science), Eiteljorg Gallery (African, Oceanic, and American art), Clowes Memorial Hall for the Performing Arts, Institute for Study Abroad in Great Britain and Australia.

DEGREES OFFERED. BA, BS, MA, MS, MBA, B. Pharm. 533 bachelor's degrees awarded in 1992. 21% in business and management, 17% communications, 12% teacher education, 15% allied health, 5% letters/literature, 5% social sciences, 7% visual and performing arts. Graduate degrees offered in 31 major fields of study.

UNDERGRADUATE MAJORS. Accounting, actuarial sciences, American studies, arts management, biological and physical sciences, biology, business administration and management, business economics, chemistry, communications, computer and information sciences, computer programming, dance, dramatic arts, early childhood education, education of exceptional children, education of the emotionally handicapped, education of the gifted and talented, education of the mentally handicapped, elementary education, English, English education, environmental science, foreign languages education, French, German, Greek (classical), health education, history, international relations, international studies, journalism, junior high education, Latin, marketing management, mathematics, mathematics education, medical laboratory technologies, music business management, music education, music history and appreciation, music performance, music theory and composition, pharmacy, philosophy, physical education, physics, political science and government, predentistry, prelaw, premedicine, psychology, public relations, radio/television broadcasting, reading education, religion, science education, secondary education, social science education, social studies education, sociology, Spanish, specific learning disabilities, speech, speech pathology/audiology.

ACADEMIC PROGRAMS. Accelerated program, double major, dual enrollment of high school students, education specialist degree, honors program, independent study, internships, study abroad, teacher preparation, cross-registration; liberal arts/career combination in engineering, forestry. **Remedial services:** Reduced course load, tutoring. **ROTC:** Air Force, Army. **Placement/credit:** AP, CLEP General and Subject, institutional tests.

ACADEMIC REQUIREMENTS. Freshmen must earn minimum GPA of 2.0 to continue in good standing. 82% of freshmen return for sophomore year. Students must declare major by end of second year. **Graduation requirements:** 126 hours for bachelor's (30 in major). Most students required to take courses in arts/fine arts, computer science, English, history, humanities, mathematics, biological/physical sciences, social sciences. **Postgraduate studies:** 2% enter law school, 2% enter medical school, 2% enter MBA programs, 4% enter other graduate study.

FRESHMAN ADMISSIONS. Selection criteria: Test scores, high school record most important. Interview, recommendations, activities considered. **High school preparation:** 13 units required. Required units include biological science 1, English 4, foreign language 2, mathematics 3, physical science 1 and social science 2. 3 science units required for science majors; 4

mathematics units for business administration majors. **Test requirements:** SAT or ACT (SAT preferred); score report by August 15.

1992 FRESHMAN CLASS PROFILE. 978 men applied, 841 accepted, 318 enrolled; 1,400 women applied, 1,204 accepted, 440 enrolled. 65% had high school GPA of 3.0 or higher, 35% between 2.0 and 2.99. **Academic background:** Mid 50% of enrolled freshmen had SAT-V between 420-550, SAT-M between 460-600. 83% submitted SAT scores. **Characteristics:** 63% from in state, 93% live in college housing, 8% have minority backgrounds, 1% are foreign students, 41% join fraternities/sororities. Average age is 18.

FALL-TERM APPLICATIONS. $20 fee, may be waived for applicants with need. Closing date August 1; priority given to applications received by March 1; applicants notified on a rolling basis; must reply by May 1 or within 4 weeks if notified thereafter. Audition required for dance, drama, music, radio/television applicants. Essay required. Interview recommended. CRDA. Deferred and early admission available.

STUDENT LIFE. Housing: Dormitories (men, women, coed); fraternity, sorority housing available. **Activities:** Student government, magazine, radio, student newspaper, television, yearbook, choral groups, concert band, dance, drama, jazz band, marching band, music ensembles, musical theater, opera, pep band, symphony orchestra, stage band, fraternities, sororities, campus ministry, Campus Crusade for Christ, Circle-K, Mortar Board, service organizations, black student union, international students club.

ATHLETICS. NCAA. **Intercollegiate:** Baseball M, basketball, cross-country, diving, football M, golf M, lacrosse M, rowing (crew), soccer M, softball W, swimming, tennis, track and field M, volleyball W. **Intramural:** Badminton, baseball M, basketball, bowling, cross-country, diving, golf M, racquetball, soccer M, softball W, swimming, table tennis, tennis, track and field, volleyball.

STUDENT SERVICES. Aptitude testing, career counseling, employment service for undergraduates, freshman orientation, health services, personal counseling, placement service for graduates, services/facilities for handicapped.

ANNUAL EXPENSES. Tuition and fees: $12,280. **Room and board:** $4,245. **Books and supplies:** $500. **Other expenses:** $1,260.

FINANCIAL AID. 80% of freshmen, 80% of continuing students receive some form of aid. 54% of grants, 86% of loans, 4% of jobs based on need. 520 enrolled freshmen were judged to have need, all were offered aid. Academic, music/drama, athletic, minority scholarships available. **Aid applications:** No closing date; priority given to applications received by March 1; applicants notified on a rolling basis beginning on or about March 1; must reply by May 1 or within 3 weeks if notified thereafter.

ADDRESS/TELEPHONE. Thomas Snider, Vice President Enrollment Management, Butler University, 4600 Sunset Avenue, Indianapolis, IN 46208. (317) 283-9255. (800) 368-6852. Fax: (317) 283-9519.

Calumet College of St. Joseph
Hammond, Indiana — CB code: 1776

4-year private liberal arts college, coed, affiliated with Roman Catholic Church. Founded in 1951. **Accreditation:** Regional. **Undergraduate enrollment:** 147 men, 297 women full time; 212 men, 430 women part time. **Faculty:** 111 total (35 full time), 56 with doctorates or other terminal degrees. **Location:** Suburban campus in small city; 20 miles from downtown Chicago. **Calendar:** Semester, limited summer session. Saturday classes. **Microcomputers:** 72 located in computer centers. **Special facilities:** Art gallery, environmental wetlands study area, teleconference center. **Additional facts:** Satellite campus in Merrillville.

DEGREES OFFERED. AA, AS, BA, BS, BFA. 29 associate degrees awarded in 1992. 30% in business and management, 5% business/office and marketing/distribution, 6% communications, 10% computer sciences, 9% multi/interdisciplinary studies, 26% parks/recreation, protective services, public affairs, 10% philosophy, religion, theology, 10% physical sciences. 175 bachelor's degrees awarded. 72% in business and management, 10% teacher education.

UNDERGRADUATE MAJORS. Associate: Accounting, business administration and management, chemistry, communications, computer and information sciences, criminal justice studies, English, journalism, liberal/general studies, photographic technology, religion, secretarial and related programs, social work. **Bachelor's:** Accounting, art education, biological and physical sciences, biology, business administration and management, business economics, business education, communications, computer and information sciences, criminal justice studies, elementary education, English, English education, fine arts, history, humanities and social sciences, journalism, labor/industrial relations, liberal/general studies, organization management, philosophy, political science and government, psychology, science education, secondary education, social science education, social sciences, social work, sociology, theological studies.

ACADEMIC PROGRAMS. 2-year transfer program, accelerated program, cooperative education, double major, dual enrollment of high school students, honors program, independent study, internships, student-designed major, study abroad, telecourses, weekend college. **Remedial services:** Learning center, reduced course load, remedial instruction, special counselor, tutoring. **Placement/credit:** CLEP General, institutional tests; 30 credit hours maximum for associate degree; 60 credit hours maximum for bachelor's degree.

ACADEMIC REQUIREMENTS. Freshmen must earn minimum GPA of 2.0 to continue in good standing. 63% of freshmen return for sophomore year. Students must declare major by end of second year. **Graduation requirements:** 60 hours for associate (30 in major), 124 hours for bachelor's (36 in major). Most students required to take courses in arts/fine arts, English, history, humanities, mathematics, philosophy/religion, biological/physical sciences, social sciences. **Postgraduate studies:** 70% from 2-year programs enter 4-year programs.

FRESHMAN ADMISSIONS. Selection criteria: High school record most important. Bachelor's degree requirements include rank in top half of class, with minimum 2.0 GPA; for associate degree must rank in top three-quarters of class with 2.0 GPA. **High school preparation:** 15 units recommended. Recommended units include English 4, foreign language 1, mathematics 3, social science 3 and science 2. **Test requirements:** SAT or ACT; score report by September 1.

1992 FRESHMAN CLASS PROFILE. 115 men, 215 women enrolled. 17% had high school GPA of 3.0 or higher, 64% between 2.0 and 2.99. **Academic background:** Mid 50% of enrolled freshmen had SAT-V between 290-410, SAT-M between 300-450. 22% submitted SAT scores. **Characteristics:** 80% from in state, 100% commute, 49% have minority backgrounds. Average age is 23.

FALL-TERM APPLICATIONS. $25 fee, may be waived for applicants with need. No closing date; applicants notified on a rolling basis. Essay required for borderline applicants. Interview recommended. Deferred and early admission available.

STUDENT LIFE. Activities: Student government, student newspaper, drama, Amigos, science clubs, service organization, black student organization, criminal justice club, Students in Free Enterprise, photography club.

ATHLETICS. Intramural: Basketball M, bowling, football M, softball, volleyball.

STUDENT SERVICES. Aptitude testing, career counseling, freshman orientation, personal counseling, placement service for graduates, veterans counselor, services/facilities for handicapped.

ANNUAL EXPENSES. Tuition and fees (projected): $4,250. **Books and supplies:** $400. **Other expenses:** $1,130.

FINANCIAL AID. 62% of freshmen, 72% of continuing students receive some form of aid. 93% of grants, 93% of loans, all jobs based on need. 99 enrolled freshmen were judged to have need, all were offered aid. Academic, religious affiliation, minority scholarships available. **Aid applications:** Closing date October 5; applicants notified on a rolling basis beginning on or about July 1; must reply within 2 weeks. **Additional information:** Immediate computerized estimate of financial aid eligibility available to students applying in person.

ADDRESS/TELEPHONE. Leonor Venegas, Recruitment Counselor, Calumet College of St. Joseph, 2400 New York Avenue, Whiting, IN 46394-2195. (219) 473-4215. Fax: (219) 473-4259.

DePauw University
Greencastle, Indiana — CB code: 1166

Admissions: 85% of applicants accepted
Based on: ••• School record
•• Activities, essay, recommendations, test scores
• Interview, special talents
Completion: 95% of freshmen end year in good standing
78% graduate, 26% of these enter graduate study

4-year private university, coed, affiliated with United Methodist Church. Founded in 1837. **Accreditation:** Regional. **Undergraduate enrollment:** 909 men, 1,120 women full time; 11 men, 18 women part time. **Faculty:** 217 total (159 full time), 165 with doctorates or other terminal degrees. **Location:** Rural campus in small town; 45 miles from Indianapolis. **Calendar:** 4-1-4. **Microcomputers:** 126 located in dormitories, libraries, computer centers. **Special facilities:** Observatory, anthropology museum, art museum, nature preserve.

DEGREES OFFERED. BA. 585 bachelor's degrees awarded in 1992. 12% in communications, 6% teacher education, 13% letters/literature, 7% life sciences, 7% psychology, 32% social sciences, 5% visual and performing arts.

UNDERGRADUATE MAJORS. Anthropology, art history, biological and physical sciences, biology, chemistry, communications, composition, computer and information sciences, earth sciences, East Asian studies, economics, elementary education, English literature, foreign languages (multiple emphasis), French, geography, geology, German, Greek (classical), history, humanities and social sciences, international studies, Latin, mathematics, medical laboratory technologies, music, music education, music performance, music theory and composition, nursing, philosophy, physical education, physics, political science and government, preengineering, psychology, religion, Russian and Slavic studies, sociology, Spanish, studio art, women's studies.

ACADEMIC PROGRAMS. Double major, honors program, independent study, internships, semester at sea, student-designed major, study abroad, teacher preparation, visiting/exchange student program, New York semester, United Nations semester, Washington semester; liberal arts/career combination in engineering, health sciences. **ROTC:** Air Force, Army. **Placement/credit:** AP, CLEP Subject, IB, institutional tests; 32 credit hours maximum for bachelor's degree.

ACADEMIC REQUIREMENTS. Freshmen must earn minimum GPA of 2.0 to continue in good standing. 90% of freshmen return for sophomore year. Students must declare major by end of second year. **Graduation requirements:** 124 hours for bachelor's. Most students required to take courses in arts/fine arts, English, foreign languages, history, humanities, mathematics, philosophy/religion, biological/physical sciences, social sciences. **Postgraduate studies:** 6% enter law school, 4% enter medical school, 3% enter MBA programs, 13% enter other graduate study. **Additional information:** More than 700 students participate each January in off-campus internships. Demonstrated competence in writing, quantitative reasoning, and oral communication required in addition to seminar, thesis, project or comprehensive examination in major.

FRESHMAN ADMISSIONS. Selection criteria: Academic achievement, verbal and quantitative skills, and evidence of commitment to learning important. **High school preparation:** 15 units recommended. Recommended units include English 4, foreign language 2, mathematics 3, social science 3 and science 3. **Test requirements:** SAT or ACT; score report by February 15.

1992 FRESHMAN CLASS PROFILE. 857 men applied, 714 accepted, 240 enrolled; 1,029 women applied, 883 accepted, 326 enrolled. 46% were in top tenth and 71% were in top quarter of graduating class. **Academic background:** Mid 50% of enrolled freshmen had SAT-V between 490-600, SAT-M between 550-670; ACT composite between 23-28. 89% submitted SAT scores, 59% submitted ACT scores. **Characteristics:** 37% from in state, 99% live in college housing, 17% have minority backgrounds, 2% are foreign students, 80% join fraternities/sororities. Average age is 18.

FALL-TERM APPLICATIONS. $25 fee, may be waived for applicants with need. Closing date February 15; priority given to applications received by December 1; applicants notified on or about April 1; must reply by May 1. Audition required for music applicants. Essay required. Interview recommended. Portfolio recommended for art applicants. CRDA. Deferred and early admission available. Institutional early decision plan. Early action notification is second week of January for those who apply by December 1; candidates reply date is May 1.

STUDENT LIFE. Housing: Dormitories (coed); fraternity, sorority housing available. Housing available for special living/learning groups. **Activities:** Student government, film, magazine, radio, student newspaper, television, yearbook, choral groups, concert band, dance, drama, jazz band, music ensembles, musical theater, opera, pep band, symphony orchestra, fraternities, sororities, Young Democrats, Young Republicans, Association of African-American Students, International Students Association, Union Board, Intervarsity Christian Fellowship, Gospel Choir, Coalition for Women's Concerns, Habitat for Humanity, Hispanic Club.

ATHLETICS. NCAA. **Intercollegiate:** Baseball M, basketball, cross-country, diving, fencing, field hockey W, football M, golf, lacrosse M, soccer, swimming, tennis, track and field, volleyball W. **Intramural:** Badminton, basketball, diving, golf, racquetball, soccer, softball W, swimming, table tennis, tennis, track and field, volleyball, wrestling M.

STUDENT SERVICES. Aptitude testing, career counseling, employment service for undergraduates, freshman orientation, health services, personal counseling, placement service for graduates.

ANNUAL EXPENSES. Tuition and fees (projected): $13,700. **Room and board:** $4,830. **Books and supplies:** $550. **Other expenses:** $700.

FINANCIAL AID. 59% of freshmen, 53% of continuing students receive some form of aid. 73% of grants, all loans, 60% of jobs based on need. 243 enrolled freshmen were judged to have need, all were offered aid. Academic, music/drama, art, state/district residency, leadership, alumni affiliation, religious affiliation, minority scholarships available. **Aid applications:** Closing date February 15; applicants notified on or about April 1; must reply by May 1 or within 3 weeks if notified thereafter.

ADDRESS/TELEPHONE. David C. Murray, Dean of Admissions and Associate Provost, DePauw University, 313 South Locust Street, Greencastle, IN 46135-0037. (317) 658-4006. (800) 447-2495. Fax: (317) 658-4177.

Earlham College
Richmond, Indiana

CB code: 1195

Admissions:	68% of applicants accepted
Based on:	••• Essay, recommendations, school record
	•• Activities, interview, test scores
	• Religious affiliation/commitment, special talents
Completion:	90% of freshmen end year in good standing
	67% graduate, 63% of these enter graduate study

4-year private liberal arts college, coed, affiliated with Society of Friends. Founded in 1847. **Accreditation:** Regional. **Undergraduate enrollment:** 445 men, 590 women full time; 10 men, 8 women part time. **Faculty:** 212 total (134 full time), 113 with doctorates or other terminal degrees. **Location:** Suburban campus in large town; 70 miles from Indianapolis, 40 miles from Dayton, Ohio, 60 miles from Cincinnati, Ohio. **Calendar:** Trimester. **Microcomputers:** 100 located in libraries, classrooms, computer centers. **Special facilities:** Natural history museum, observatory, planetarium, conservatory, herbarium, working farm, Conner Prairie Living History Museum, biological field stations, Leeds Art Gallery.

DEGREES OFFERED. BA. 305 bachelor's degrees awarded in 1992. 10% in area and ethnic studies, 8% languages, 8% letters/literature, 12% life sciences, 14% multi/interdisciplinary studies, 5% philosophy, religion, theology, 5% physical sciences, 6% psychology, 22% social sciences, 5% visual and performing arts.

UNDERGRADUATE MAJORS. African studies, Afro-American (black) studies, anthropology, art history, astronomy, biological and physical sciences, biology, business and management, chemistry, classics, computer and information sciences, dance, East Asian studies, economics, education, English, fine arts, foreign languages (multiple emphasis), French, geology, German, history, human development and social relations, international relations, international studies, Japanese studies, mathematics, museum studies, music, peace studies, philosophy, physics, political science and government, psychology, religion, secondary education, sociology, Spanish, visual and performing arts, women's studies.

ACADEMIC PROGRAMS. Accelerated program, double major, dual enrollment of high school students, independent study, internships, student-designed major, study abroad, New York semester, Washington semester; liberal arts/career combination in engineering, forestry, health sciences. **Remedial services:** Learning center, preadmission summer program, reduced course load, special counselor, tutoring. **Placement/credit:** AP, CLEP Subject, institutional tests.

ACADEMIC REQUIREMENTS. Freshmen must earn minimum GPA of 2.0 to continue in good standing. 85% of freshmen return for sophomore year. Students must declare major by end of second year. **Graduation requirements:** 120 hours for bachelor's (40 in major). Most students required to take courses in arts/fine arts, English, foreign languages, history, humanities, mathematics, philosophy/religion, biological/physical sciences, social sciences. **Postgraduate studies:** 4% enter law school, 8% enter medical school, 8% enter MBA programs, 43% enter other graduate study.

FRESHMAN ADMISSIONS. Selection criteria: School achievement record most important, followed by recommendations and test scores. Special consideration to Quakers, minorities, children of state residents. **High school preparation:** 15 units required. Required units include English 4, foreign language 2, mathematics 3, social science 2 and science 2. 3 years of natural science which includes 2 years of lab science, 3 years of mathematics which should include a second year of algebra, 3-4 years of foreign language study and courses in studio or the performing arts recommended. **Test requirements:** SAT or ACT (SAT preferred); score report by February 15.

1992 FRESHMAN CLASS PROFILE. 693 men applied, 379 accepted, 121 enrolled; 720 women applied, 586 accepted, 165 enrolled. 34% were in top tenth and 60% were in top quarter of graduating class. **Academic background:** Mid 50% of enrolled freshmen had SAT-V between 480-600, SAT-M between 490-630; ACT composite between 22-29. 84% submitted SAT scores, 31% submitted ACT scores. **Characteristics:** 22% from in state, 98% live in college housing, 16% have minority backgrounds, 5% are foreign students. Average age is 18.

FALL-TERM APPLICATIONS. $25 fee, may be waived for applicants with need. Closing date February 15; applicants notified on or about April 2; must reply by May 1. Essay required. Interview recommended. CRDA. Deferred and early admission available. EDP-F. Early decision plan applicants must reply by January 15.

STUDENT LIFE. Housing: Dormitories (coed); apartment, cooperative housing available. 27 college-owned off-campus language and special interest houses (Japan House, German House, Peace House) available to upperclass students. Also Living/Learning halls in some residence halls. **Activities:** Student government, film, magazine, radio, student newspaper, yearbook, women's programs newspaper, literary magazine, choral groups, concert band, dance, drama, jazz band, music ensembles, musical theater, opera, symphony orchestra, Earlham Christian Fellowship, Jewish Students' Union, Council on Religion at Earlham, Amnesty International, Apartheid Action Coalition, Black Leadership Action Coalition, Committee in Solidarity with Latin America, Habitat for Humanity, the Earlham Volunteer Exchange,

Service Learning Center. **Additional information:** Community and academic honor codes exist based on such values as peace & social justice, respect for the individual, simplicity and cooperative learning.

ATHLETICS. NAIA, NCAA. **Intercollegiate:** Baseball M, basketball, cross-country, field hockey W, football M, golf M, lacrosse W, soccer, softball W, tennis, track and field, volleyball W. **Intramural:** Basketball, horseback riding, lacrosse M, racquetball, sailing, softball, swimming, volleyball.

STUDENT SERVICES. Aptitude testing, career counseling, employment service for undergraduates, freshman orientation, health services, on-campus day care, personal counseling, placement service for graduates, individualized programs/services, services/facilities for handicapped.

ANNUAL EXPENSES. Tuition and fees: $15,326. **Room and board:** $4,056. **Books and supplies:** $550. **Other expenses:** $600.

FINANCIAL AID. 72% of freshmen, 72% of continuing students receive some form of aid. 95% of grants, 85% of loans, 98% of jobs based on need. 209 enrolled freshmen were judged to have need, all were offered aid. Academic, state/district residency, leadership, religious affiliation, minority scholarships available. **Aid applications:** Closing date April 1; priority given to applications received by March 1; applicants notified on a rolling basis beginning on or about March 2; must reply by May 1 or within 2 weeks if notified thereafter.

ADDRESS/TELEPHONE. Robert L. de Veer, Dean of Admissions, Earlham College, National Road West, Richmond, IN 47374. (317) 983-1600. (800) EARLHAM. Fax: (317) 983-1560.

Franklin College
Franklin, Indiana CB code: 1228

Admissions: 78% of applicants accepted
Based on: ••• Essay, school record
•• Interview, recommendations, test scores
• Activities, special talents
Completion: 95% of freshmen end year in good standing
20% enter graduate study

4-year private liberal arts college, coed, affiliated with American Baptist Churches in the USA. Founded in 1834. **Accreditation:** Regional. **Undergraduate enrollment:** 375 men, 461 women full time; 24 men, 39 women part time. **Faculty:** 98 total (64 full time), 49 with doctorates or other terminal degrees. **Location:** Rural campus in large town; 20 miles from Indianapolis. **Calendar:** 4-1-4, limited summer session. **Microcomputers:** 60 located in dormitories, libraries, classrooms, computer centers.

DEGREES OFFERED. AA, BA, BS. 115 bachelor's degrees awarded.

UNDERGRADUATE MAJORS. Associate: Studio art. **Bachelor's:** Accounting, advertising, allied health, American studies, applied mathematics, art education, biology, business administration and management, business and management, business education, chemistry, clinical laboratory science, computer and information sciences, dramatic arts, economics, elementary education, English, English education, finance, foreign languages education, French, health education, history, information sciences and systems, international business management, journalism, junior high education, labor/industrial relations, marketing management, mathematics, mathematics education, nursing, philosophy, physical education, physics, political science and government, predentistry, prelaw, premedicine, prepharmacy, preveterinary, psychology, public relations, pure mathematics, radio/television broadcasting, religion, science education, secondary education, social studies education, sociology, Spanish, studio art.

ACADEMIC PROGRAMS. Accelerated program, double major, honors program, independent study, internships, study abroad, teacher preparation, visiting/exchange student program, United Nations semester, Washington semester, cross-registration; liberal arts/career combination in engineering, forestry, health sciences. **Remedial services:** Special counselor, tutoring, writing workshop. **ROTC:** Army. **Placement/credit:** AP, CLEP Subject, institutional tests; 30 credit hours maximum for bachelor's degree.

ACADEMIC REQUIREMENTS. Freshmen must earn minimum GPA of 1.5 to continue in good standing. 82% of freshmen return for sophomore year. Students must declare major by end of second year. **Graduation requirements:** 136 hours for bachelor's (24 in major). Most students required to take courses in English, history, humanities, mathematics, philosophy/religion, biological/physical sciences, social sciences. **Postgraduate studies:** 5% enter law school, 5% enter medical school, 10% enter other graduate study.

FRESHMAN ADMISSIONS. Selection criteria: Class rank, test scores, and counselor recommendations required, and extracurricular activities considered. Recommended units include English 4, foreign language 2, mathematics 4, social science 2 and science 2. **Test requirements:** SAT or ACT; score report by July 15.

1992 FRESHMAN CLASS PROFILE. 723 men and women applied, 567 accepted; 147 men enrolled, 162 women enrolled. 27% were in top tenth and 62% were in top quarter of graduating class. **Academic background:** Mid 50% of enrolled freshmen had SAT-V between 450-550, SAT-M between 550-650; ACT composite between 23-25. 75% submitted SAT scores, 25% submitted ACT scores. **Characteristics:** 92% from in state, 95% live in college housing, 2% have minority backgrounds, 2% are foreign students, 40% join fraternities/sororities. Average age is 18.

FALL-TERM APPLICATIONS. $15 fee, may be waived for applicants with need. Closing date August 15; applicants notified on a rolling basis; must reply by May 1 or within 2 weeks if notified thereafter. Essay required. Interview recommended. Interview required of borderline applicants. CRDA. EDP-F.

STUDENT LIFE. Housing: Dormitories (men, women, coed); apartment, fraternity housing available. Residence facility housing 4 men or women in suite of living room, 2 bedrooms, private bath available. All students under 21 must live on campus unless living with family. **Activities:** Student government, magazine, radio, student newspaper, television, yearbook, choral groups, dance, drama, music ensembles, musical theater, pep band, fraternities, sororities, Campus Christian Fellowship, Young Democrats, International Club, Fellowship of Christian Athletes, Young Republicans, Religious Life Committee.

ATHLETICS. NCAA. **Intercollegiate:** Baseball M, basketball, cross-country, field hockey W, football M, golf, soccer M, softball W, tennis, track and field, volleyball W. **Intramural:** Badminton, basketball, bowling, softball, tennis, volleyball.

STUDENT SERVICES. Aptitude testing, career counseling, employment service for undergraduates, freshman orientation, health services, personal counseling, placement service for graduates, special adviser for adult students, veterans counselor, services/facilities for handicapped.

ANNUAL EXPENSES. Tuition and fees: $10,090. **Room and board:** $3,870. **Books and supplies:** $525. **Other expenses:** $895.

FINANCIAL AID. 95% of freshmen, 90% of continuing students receive some form of aid. 47% of grants, 95% of loans, all jobs based on need. 223 enrolled freshmen were judged to have need, all were offered aid. Academic, music/drama, art, state/district residency, leadership, alumni affiliation, religious affiliation, minority scholarships available. **Aid applications:** No closing date; priority given to applications received by March 1; applicants notified on a rolling basis beginning on or about April 1; must reply by May 1 or within 2 weeks if notified thereafter.

ADDRESS/TELEPHONE. B. Stephen Richards, Vice President for Enrollment Management, Franklin College, 501 East Monroe Street, Franklin, IN 46131-2598. (317) 738-8062. (800) 852-0232. Fax: (317) 736-6030.

Goshen College
Goshen, Indiana CB code: 1251

Admissions: 82% of applicants accepted
Based on: ••• Recommendations, school record, test scores
•• Activities
• Interview, religious affiliation/commitment, special talents
Completion: 93% of freshmen end year in good standing
60% graduate, 18% of these enter graduate study

4-year private liberal arts college, coed, affiliated with Mennonite Church. Founded in 1894. **Accreditation:** Regional. **Undergraduate enrollment:** 416 men, 495 women full time; 47 men, 99 women part time. **Faculty:** 168 total (132 full time), 60 with doctorates or other terminal degrees. **Location:** Rural campus in large town; 25 miles from South Bend, 150 miles from Chicago. **Calendar:** Trimester, limited summer session. **Microcomputers:** 80 located in dormitories, computer centers. **Special facilities:** Turner X-ray Precision Laboratory, art gallery, nature preserve, marine biology laboratory in Florida Keys.

DEGREES OFFERED. BA, BS. 226 bachelor's degrees awarded in 1992. 16% in business and management, 15% teacher education, 9% health sciences, 6% letters/literature, 9% life sciences, 9% psychology, 13% social sciences, 5% visual and performing arts.

UNDERGRADUATE MAJORS. Accounting, art education, biological and physical sciences, biology, business administration and management, business and management, business education, chemistry, clinical laboratory science, communications, computer and information sciences, dramatic arts, early childhood education, economics, education, elementary education, English, English education, fine arts, food science and nutrition, foreign languages education, German, history, humanities, humanities and social sciences, individual and family development, junior high education, liberal/general studies, mathematics, mathematics education, music, music education, nursing, physical education, physical sciences, physics, political science and government, predentistry, prelaw, premedicine, prepharmacy, preveterinary, psychology, religion, science education, secondary education, social sciences, social studies education, social work, sociology, Spanish, speech/communication/theater education, teaching English as a second language/foreign language, theological studies.

ACADEMIC PROGRAMS. Accelerated program, double major, dual enrollment of high school students, independent study, internships, student-designed major, study abroad, teacher preparation; liberal arts/career combination in engineering, health sciences. **Remedial services:** Learning center, reduced course load, remedial instruction, special counselor, tutoring. **Place-**

ment/credit: AP, CLEP General and Subject, IB, institutional tests; 12 credit hours maximum for bachelor's degree.

ACADEMIC REQUIREMENTS. Freshmen must earn minimum GPA of 2.0 to continue in good standing. Freshmen must successfully complete 20 semester hours during first year. 78% of freshmen return for sophomore year. Students must declare major by end of second year. **Graduation requirements:** 120 hours for bachelor's (40 in major). Most students required to take courses in arts/fine arts, English, foreign languages, history, humanities, philosophy/religion, biological/physical sciences, social sciences. **Postgraduate studies:** 2% enter law school, 4% enter medical school, 2% enter MBA programs, 10% enter other graduate study. **Additional information:** General education practicum and ethics course required in major.

FRESHMAN ADMISSIONS. Selection criteria: School achievement record most important. Applicants should rank in top half of class and have minimum GPA of 2.0. Must have SAT of 800 or ACT or 21. Personal references important. Recommended units include English 4, foreign language 2, mathematics 2, social science 2 and science 2. **Test requirements:** SAT or ACT (SAT preferred); score report by September 10.

1992 FRESHMAN CLASS PROFILE. 536 men and women applied, 439 accepted; 108 men enrolled, 118 women enrolled. 64% had high school GPA of 3.0 or higher, 35% between 2.0 and 2.99. 27% were in top tenth and 28% were in top quarter of graduating class. **Academic background:** Mid 50% of enrolled freshmen had SAT-V between 420-570, SAT-M between 450-590. 54% submitted SAT scores. **Characteristics:** 37% from in state, 88% live in college housing, 12% have minority backgrounds, 7% are foreign students. Average age is 19.

FALL-TERM APPLICATIONS. $15 fee, may be waived for applicants with need. No closing date; priority given to applications received by May 1; applicants notified on a rolling basis. Interview recommended. CRDA. Deferred and early admission available.

STUDENT LIFE. Housing: Dormitories (men, women, coed); apartment, cooperative housing available. **Activities:** Student government, radio, student newspaper, television, yearbook, choral groups, concert band, drama, jazz band, music ensembles, musical theater, opera, symphony orchestra, Peace Society, black student union, Latin student union, student senate, international student club, Goshen Student Women's Association.

ATHLETICS. NAIA. **Intercollegiate:** Baseball M, basketball, cross-country, golf M, soccer, softball W, tennis, track and field, volleyball W. **Intramural:** Badminton, basketball, cross-country, ice hockey M, skiing, soccer, softball, table tennis, tennis, volleyball.

STUDENT SERVICES. Aptitude testing, career counseling, employment service for undergraduates, freshman orientation, health services, personal counseling, placement service for graduates, services/facilities for handicapped.

ANNUAL EXPENSES. Tuition and fees: $8,770. **Room and board:** $3,590. **Books and supplies:** $560. **Other expenses:** $960.

FINANCIAL AID. 97% of freshmen, 92% of continuing students receive some form of aid. 46% of grants, 76% of loans, all jobs based on need. 130 enrolled freshmen were judged to have need, all were offered aid. Academic, music/drama, athletic scholarships available. **Aid applications:** No closing date; priority given to applications received by March 1; applicants notified on a rolling basis beginning on or about February 15; must reply within 3 weeks.

ADDRESS/TELEPHONE. Martha Lehman, Director of Admissions, Goshen College, 1700 South Main Street, Goshen, IN 46526-9988. (219) 535-7535. (800) 348-7422. Fax: (212) 535-7660.

Grace College
Winona Lake, Indiana

CB code: 1252

Admissions: 77% of applicants accepted
Based on:
- ••• Recommendations, religious affiliation/commitment
- •• School record, test scores
- • Activities, interview, special talents

Completion: 90% of freshmen end year in good standing
41% graduate, 36% of these enter graduate study

4-year private liberal arts college, coed, affiliated with Brethren Church. Founded in 1948. **Accreditation:** Regional. **Undergraduate enrollment:** 255 men, 326 women full time; 40 men, 52 women part time. **Faculty:** 67 total (34 full time), 18 with doctorates or other terminal degrees. **Location:** Rural campus in small town; 40 miles from Fort Wayne. **Calendar:** Semester, limited summer session. **Microcomputers:** 55 located in libraries, computer centers. **Special facilities:** Billy Sunday's home.

DEGREES OFFERED. AS, BA, BS. 140 bachelor's degrees awarded. 19% in business and management, 25% teacher education, 7% life sciences, 25% psychology, 6% social sciences.

UNDERGRADUATE MAJORS. Associate: Fine arts. **Bachelor's:** Accounting, Bible studies, biblical languages, biology, business and management, communications, counseling psychology, criminology, elementary education, English, French, German, graphic design, mathematics, music, physical education, prelaw, psychology, religious music, Russian, secondary education, sociology, Spanish, speech.

ACADEMIC PROGRAMS. Double major, dual enrollment of high school students, internships, study abroad, teacher preparation; liberal arts/career combination in engineering. **Remedial services:** Reduced course load, remedial instruction, special counselor, tutoring. **Placement/credit:** AP, CLEP Subject, institutional tests; 10 credit hours maximum for associate degree; 30 credit hours maximum for bachelor's degree.

ACADEMIC REQUIREMENTS. Freshmen must earn minimum GPA of 1.6 to continue in good standing. 72% of freshmen return for sophomore year. Students must declare major by end of first year. **Graduation requirements:** 62 hours for associate (20 in major), 124 hours for bachelor's (40 in major). Most students required to take courses in arts/fine arts, English, history, mathematics, philosophy/religion, biological/physical sciences, social sciences. **Postgraduate studies:** 4% from 2-year programs enter 4-year programs. 2% enter law school, 1% enter medical school, 3% enter MBA programs, 30% enter other graduate study.

FRESHMAN ADMISSIONS. Selection criteria: High school class rank in top half, ACT scores in top 75%, references most important. **High school preparation:** 17 units recommended. Recommended units include biological science 2, English 4, foreign language 2, mathematics 3, physical science 3 and social science 3. **Test requirements:** SAT or ACT (ACT preferred); score report by September 1.

1992 FRESHMAN CLASS PROFILE. 190 men applied, 142 accepted, 73 enrolled; 228 women applied, 179 accepted, 94 enrolled. 66% had high school GPA of 3.0 or higher, 31% between 2.0 and 2.99. 16% were in top tenth and 41% were in top quarter of graduating class. **Characteristics:** 31% from in state, 94% live in college housing, 1% have minority backgrounds, 1% are foreign students. Average age is 18.

FALL-TERM APPLICATIONS. $20 fee, may be waived for applicants with need. Closing date August 1; priority given to applications received by April 1; applicants notified on a rolling basis; must reply by June 1 or within 2 weeks if notified thereafter. Interview recommended for music, art applicants. Audition recommended for music applicants. Portfolio recommended for art applicants. CRDA. Deferred and early admission available. EDP-F.

STUDENT LIFE. Housing: Dormitories (men, women); apartment housing available. **Activities:** Student government, student newspaper, choral groups, concert band, drama, music ensembles, pep band, symphony orchestra, brass choir, hand bell choir, Christian outreach groups. **Additional information:** Religious observance required.

ATHLETICS. NAIA. **Intercollegiate:** Baseball M, basketball, golf M, soccer M, softball W, tennis M, track and field, volleyball W. **Intramural:** Basketball, softball, volleyball.

STUDENT SERVICES. Aptitude testing, career counseling, employment service for undergraduates, freshman orientation, health services, personal counseling, placement service for graduates, veterans counselor, services/facilities for handicapped.

ANNUAL EXPENSES. Tuition and fees: $8,450. **Room and board:** $3,670. **Books and supplies:** $400. **Other expenses:** $800.

FINANCIAL AID. 85% of freshmen, 85% of continuing students receive some form of aid. 56% of grants, 96% of loans, 59% of jobs based on need. 144 enrolled freshmen were judged to have need, all were offered aid. Academic, music/drama, art, athletic, leadership, religious affiliation, minority scholarships available. **Aid applications:** No closing date; priority given to applications received by April 1; applicants notified on a rolling basis beginning on or about March 15; must reply by May 1 or within 3 weeks if notified thereafter.

ADDRESS/TELEPHONE. Ron Henry, Director of Admissions, Grace College, Omega Center 200 Seminary Drive, Winona Lake, IN 46590. (219) 372-5131. (800) 544-7223. Fax: (219) 372-5265.

Hanover College ⇎
Hanover, Indiana

CB code: 1290

Admissions: 72% of applicants accepted
Based on:
- ••• School record
- •• Activities, essay, interview, test scores
- • Recommendations, special talents

Completion: 95% of freshmen end year in good standing
60% graduate, 40% of these enter graduate study

4-year private liberal arts college, coed, affiliated with Presbyterian Church (USA). Founded in 1827. **Accreditation:** Regional. **Undergraduate enrollment:** 495 men, 570 women full time; 3 men, 3 women part time. **Faculty:** 103 total (92 full time), 76 with doctorates or other terminal degrees. **Location:** Rural campus in small town; 85 miles from Indianapolis, 40 miles from Louisville, Kentucky, 65 miles from Cincinnati, Ohio. **Calendar:** 4-4-1. **Microcomputers:** 22 located in libraries, classrooms, computer centers. **Special facilities:** Geology museum, observatory.

DEGREES OFFERED. BA. 258 bachelor's degrees awarded in 1992. 30% in business and management, 12% communications, 8% teacher education, 6% languages, 12% life sciences, 7% psychology, 14% social sciences.

UNDERGRADUATE MAJORS. Anthropology, biology, business administration and management, chemistry, communications, dramatic arts, East Asian studies, economics, elementary education, engineering, English, fine arts, French, geology, German, history, international studies, mathematics, music, philosophy, physics, political science and government, prelaw, psychology, secondary education, sociology, Spanish, theological studies.

ACADEMIC PROGRAMS. Double major, honors program, independent study, internships, student-designed major, study abroad, teacher preparation, visiting/exchange student program, United Nations semester, Washington semester; liberal arts/career combination in engineering. **Remedial services:** Reduced course load, tutoring, writing center. **Placement/credit:** AP, institutional tests.

ACADEMIC REQUIREMENTS. Freshmen must earn minimum GPA of 2.0 to continue in good standing. 85% of freshmen return for sophomore year. Students must declare major by end of second year. **Graduation requirements:** 136 hours for bachelor's (38 in major). Most students required to take courses in arts/fine arts, English, foreign languages, history, humanities, mathematics, philosophy/religion, biological/physical sciences, social sciences. **Postgraduate studies:** 4% enter law school, 5% enter medical school, 5% enter MBA programs, 26% enter other graduate study. **Additional information:** Students take only 1 course in spring term, permitting variety of study methods and field trips on or off campus.

FRESHMAN ADMISSIONS. Selection criteria: Selection of and performance in academic courses most important. **High school preparation:** 16 units required. Required and recommended units include biological science 2, English 4, foreign language 2, mathematics 2-3, physical science 1-2, social science 2-3 and science 2. Science requirements must include 2 laboratory sciences. **Test requirements:** SAT or ACT (SAT preferred); score report by March 15.

1992 FRESHMAN CLASS PROFILE. 595 men applied, 411 accepted, 141 enrolled; 564 women applied, 424 accepted, 193 enrolled. 75% had high school GPA of 3.0 or higher, 25% between 2.0 and 2.99. 52% were in top tenth and 76% were in top quarter of graduating class. **Academic background:** Mid 50% of enrolled freshmen had SAT-V between 500-550, SAT-M between 490-600; ACT composite between 20-28. 94% submitted SAT scores, 5% submitted ACT scores. **Characteristics:** 60% from in state, 95% live in college housing, 2% have minority backgrounds, 3% are foreign students, 62% join fraternities/sororities. Average age is 18.

FALL-TERM APPLICATIONS. $20 fee, may be waived for applicants with need. Closing date March 15; priority given to applications received by February 15; applicants notified on a rolling basis; must reply within 4 weeks. Essay required. Interview recommended. CRDA. Deferred and early admission available.

STUDENT LIFE. Housing: Dormitories (men, women); fraternity, sorority housing available. **Activities:** Student government, film, magazine, radio, student newspaper, television, yearbook, choral groups, concert band, dance, drama, jazz band, music ensembles, musical theater, pep band, chamber orchestra, fraternities, sororities, Campus Fellowship, political and social service organizations, international club.

ATHLETICS. NCAA. **Intercollegiate:** Baseball M, basketball, cross-country, field hockey W, football M, golf, soccer M, softball W, tennis, track and field M, volleyball W. **Intramural:** Badminton, basketball, bowling, cross-country W, field hockey W, football M, golf, racquetball M, soccer M, softball, swimming, table tennis, tennis, track and field, volleyball.

STUDENT SERVICES. Aptitude testing, career counseling, employment service for undergraduates, freshman orientation, health services, on-campus day care, personal counseling, placement service for graduates, services/facilities for handicapped.

ANNUAL EXPENSES. Tuition and fees: $7,750. **Room and board:** $3,200. **Books and supplies:** $500. **Other expenses:** $800.

FINANCIAL AID. 70% of freshmen, 70% of continuing students receive some form of aid. 82% of grants, 62% of loans, all jobs based on need. Academic, leadership scholarships available. **Aid applications:** No closing date; priority given to applications received by April 15; applicants notified on a rolling basis beginning on or about February 15; must reply within 2 weeks.

ADDRESS/TELEPHONE. C. Eugene McLemore, Director of Admissions, Hanover College, Hanover, IN 47243-0108. (812) 866-7021. Fax: (812) 866-2164.

Holy Cross College
Notre Dame, Indiana — CB code: 1309

Admissions: 96% of applicants accepted
Based on:
- ••• School record
- •• Interview, recommendations
- • Activities, essay, special talents, test scores

Completion: 85% of freshmen end year in good standing
25% graduate, 90% of these enter 4-year programs

2-year private junior college, coed, affiliated with Roman Catholic Church. Founded in 1966. **Accreditation:** Regional. **Undergraduate enrollment:** 205 men, 159 women full time; 44 men, 22 women part time. **Faculty:** 32 total (17 full time), 5 with doctorates or other terminal degrees. **Location:** Suburban campus in small city; one mile from South Bend, 80 miles from Chicago, 120 miles from Indianapolis. **Calendar:** Semester. **Microcomputers:** 8 located in computer centers.

DEGREES OFFERED. AA. 47 associate degrees awarded in 1992. 100% in multi/interdisciplinary studies.

UNDERGRADUATE MAJORS. Liberal/general studies.

ACADEMIC PROGRAMS. 2-year transfer program, cross-registration. **Remedial services:** Reduced course load, remedial instruction, special counselor. **ROTC:** Air Force, Army. **Placement/credit:** AP, CLEP Subject; 30 credit hours maximum for associate degree.

ACADEMIC REQUIREMENTS. Freshmen must earn minimum GPA of 2.0 to continue in good standing. 55% of freshmen return for sophomore year. **Graduation requirements:** 61 hours for associate. Most students required to take courses in English, humanities, mathematics, philosophy/religion, biological/physical sciences, social sciences.

FRESHMAN ADMISSIONS. Selection criteria: School achievement and student's perception of value of program for future plans most important. Required and recommended units include English 4, mathematics 2-4, social science 2-4 and science 2-4. Foreign language 2 recommended. **Test requirements:** SAT or ACT (SAT preferred) for counseling; score report by August 1. ACH required.

1992 FRESHMAN CLASS PROFILE. 154 men applied, 146 accepted, 108 enrolled; 108 women applied, 105 accepted, 92 enrolled. **Characteristics:** 70% from in state, 100% commute, 8% have minority backgrounds, 3% are foreign students. Average age is 18.

FALL-TERM APPLICATIONS. $25 fee. Closing date July 1; priority given to applications received by March 1; applicants notified on a rolling basis. Interview required for local applicants. Deferred admission available.

STUDENT LIFE. Activities: Student government, student newspaper. **Additional information:** Students participate in nonathletic activities at University of Notre Dame.

ATHLETICS. Intramural: Bowling, volleyball.

STUDENT SERVICES. Aptitude testing, career counseling, freshman orientation, personal counseling, services/facilities for handicapped.

ANNUAL EXPENSES. Tuition and fees (1992-93): $4,550. **Books and supplies:** $500. **Other expenses:** $1,441.

FINANCIAL AID. 47% of freshmen, 40% of continuing students receive some form of aid. All grants, all jobs based on need. **Aid applications:** No closing date; priority given to applications received by March 1; applicants notified on a rolling basis beginning on or about June 1; must reply within 2 weeks.

ADDRESS/TELEPHONE. Vincent M. Duke, Director of Admissions, Holy Cross College, PO Box 308, Notre Dame, IN 46556-0308. (219) 233-6813. Fax: (219) 233-7427.

Huntington College
Huntington, Indiana — CB code: 1304

Admissions: 90% of applicants accepted
Based on:
- ••• School record
- •• Test scores
- • Activities, essay, recommendations, religious affiliation/commitment, special talents

Completion: 80% of freshmen end year in good standing
50% graduate, 14% of these enter graduate study

4-year private liberal arts college, coed, affiliated with United Brethren in Christ. Founded in 1897. **Accreditation:** Regional. **Undergraduate enrollment:** 242 men, 273 women full time; 24 men, 38 women part time. **Graduate enrollment:** 14 men, 1 woman full time; 21 men, 1 woman part time. **Faculty:** 80 total (50 full time), 2 with doctorates or other terminal degrees. **Location:** Rural campus in large town; 25 miles from Fort Wayne. **Calendar:** 4-1-4, limited summer session. **Microcomputers:** 80 located in dormitories, libraries, classrooms, computer centers. **Special facilities:** Thornhill Nature Preserve, Pinkerton Resource Area, Upper Wabash Basin Regional Resource Center, Robert E. Wilson Art Gallery.

DEGREES OFFERED. AA, BA, BS, M. 3 associate degrees awarded in 1992. 33% in business and management, 67% business/office and marketing/distribution. 91 bachelor's degrees awarded. 27% in business and management, 36% teacher education, 8% philosophy, religion, theology, 13% psychology, 8% social sciences. Graduate degrees offered in 2 major fields of study.

UNDERGRADUATE MAJORS. Associate: Accounting, office supervision and management. **Bachelor's:** Accounting, art education, biology, business administration and management, business economics, business education, chemistry, clinical laboratory science, computer and information sciences, elementary education, English, English education, graphic design, history, journalism, junior high education, mathematics, mathematics education, music education, music performance, parks and recreation management, philosophy, physical education, predentistry, prelaw, premedicine, psychology, radio/television broadcasting, religious education, science education, secondary education, social studies education, sociology, studio art, theological studies.

ACADEMIC PROGRAMS. Double major, dual enrollment of high school students, independent study, internships, study abroad, teacher preparation, Washington semester, cross-registration. **Remedial services:** Learning center, preadmission summer program, reduced course load, remedial instruction, special counselor, tutoring, writing center. **Placement/credit:** AP, CLEP Subject; 38 credit hours maximum for bachelor's degree.

ACADEMIC REQUIREMENTS. Freshmen must earn minimum GPA of 1.8 to continue in good standing. 75% of freshmen return for sophomore year. Students must declare major by end of second year. **Graduation requirements:** 64 hours for associate (36 in major), 128 hours for bachelor's (36 in major). Most students required to take courses in arts/fine arts, computer science, English, history, humanities, mathematics, philosophy/religion, biological/physical sciences, social sciences. **Postgraduate studies:** 80% from 2-year programs enter 4-year programs. 1% enter law school, 1% enter medical school, 2% enter MBA programs, 10% enter other graduate study.

FRESHMAN ADMISSIONS. **Selection criteria:** Class rank in top half, satisfactory SAT or ACT scores, and GPA of 2.3 most important. **High school preparation:** 16 units recommended. Recommended units include biological science 1, foreign language 4, mathematics 3, physical science 2 and social science 2. **Test requirements:** SAT or ACT for placement; score report by August 15. **Additional information:** Selected students with combined SAT score of 750 or more, GPA of 2.0, or rank in top 50% of class may be admitted on minimum load.

1992 FRESHMAN CLASS PROFILE. 255 men applied, 219 accepted, 60 enrolled; 271 women applied, 252 accepted, 95 enrolled. 56% had high school GPA of 3.0 or higher, 44% between 2.0 and 2.99. 22% were in top tenth and 50% were in top quarter of graduating class. **Academic background:** Mid 50% of enrolled freshmen had SAT-V between 370-490, SAT-M between 400-550; ACT composite between 19-25. 95% submitted SAT scores, 63% submitted ACT scores. **Characteristics:** 65% from in state, 94% live in college housing, 3% have minority backgrounds, 6% are foreign students, 5% join fraternities/sororities. Average age is 18.

FALL-TERM APPLICATIONS. $15 fee. Closing date August 15; priority given to applications received by April 1; applicants notified on a rolling basis; must reply by May 1 or within 4 weeks if notified thereafter. Audition required for music applicants. Essay required. Interview required of applicants potentially unsuited to Christian (nondenominational) atmosphere. CRDA. Deferred and early admission available.

STUDENT LIFE. **Housing:** Dormitories (men, women); apartment housing available. Single undergraduates must live in resident halls or with parents. **Activities:** Student government, radio, student newspaper, yearbook, choral groups, concert band, drama, jazz band, music ensembles, musical theater, symphony orchestra, fraternities, sororities, college outreach, Minority Student Fellowship, Collegians for Life, Christian service organization, international club. **Additional information:** Chapel/convocation attendance required at 2 out of 3 weekly programs. Use of alcohol prohibited.

ATHLETICS. NAIA. **Intercollegiate:** Baseball M, basketball, cross-country, golf, soccer M, softball W, tennis, track and field, volleyball W. **Intramural:** Badminton, basketball M, bowling, football M, racquetball, softball, swimming, table tennis, tennis, volleyball.

STUDENT SERVICES. Aptitude testing, career counseling, employment service for undergraduates, freshman orientation, health services, on-campus day care, personal counseling, placement service for graduates, veterans counselor, services/facilities for handicapped.

ANNUAL EXPENSES. **Tuition and fees:** $9,490. **Room and board:** $3,730. **Books and supplies:** $500. **Other expenses:** $800.

FINANCIAL AID. 89% of freshmen, 91% of continuing students receive some form of aid. 64% of grants, 96% of loans, 63% of jobs based on need. 119 enrolled freshmen were judged to have need, all were offered aid. Academic, music/drama, art, athletic, state/district residency, leadership, alumni affiliation, religious affiliation, minority scholarships available. **Aid applications:** Closing date September 1; priority given to applications received by March 1; applicants notified on or about September 1; must reply within 3 weeks.

ADDRESS/TELEPHONE. Chantler Thompson, Dean of Admissions and Financial Aid, Huntington College, 2303 College Avenue, Huntington, IN 46750. (219) 356-6000 ext. 1076. (800) 642-6493. Fax: (219) 356-9448.

Indiana Institute of Technology

Fort Wayne, Indiana — CB code: 1323

4-year private business, engineering college, coed. Founded in 1930. **Accreditation:** Regional. **Undergraduate enrollment:** 1,054 men and women. **Location:** Urban campus in small city; 180 miles east of Chicago. **Calendar:** Semester.

FRESHMAN ADMISSIONS. **Selection criteria:** GPA and test scores required.

ANNUAL EXPENSES. **Tuition and fees:** $8,204. **Room and board:** $3,540. **Books and supplies:** $600. **Other expenses:** $600.

ADDRESS/TELEPHONE. Don St. Clair, Vice President of Marketing, Indiana Institute of Technology, 1600 East Washington Boulevard, Fort Wayne, IN 46803. (219) 422-5561. Fax: (219) 422-7696.

Indiana State University

Terre Haute, Indiana — CB code: 1322

Admissions: 84% of applicants accepted
Based on:
••• School record
•• Test scores
• Essay, interview, recommendations, special talents
Completion: 75% of freshmen end year in good standing
35% graduate, 11% of these enter graduate study

4-year public university, coed. Founded in 1865. **Accreditation:** Regional. **Undergraduate enrollment:** 4,438 men, 4,233 women full time; 828 men, 1,151 women part time. **Graduate enrollment:** 1,621 men and women full time. **Faculty:** 718 total (591 full time), 445 with doctorates or other terminal degrees. **Location:** Urban campus in small city; 70 miles from Indianapolis. **Calendar:** Semester, extensive summer session. **Microcomputers:** 514 located in dormitories, libraries, classrooms, computer centers. **Special facilities:** Observatory, nature preserves, Turman Art Gallery.

DEGREES OFFERED. AA, AS, AAS, BA, BS, BFA, MA, MS, MBA, MFA, MEd, PhD, EdD. 160 associate degrees awarded in 1992. 10% in business/office and marketing/distribution, 6% engineering technologies, 65% health sciences, 9% parks/recreation, protective services, public affairs. 1,320 bachelor's degrees awarded. 24% in business and management, 19% education, 15% engineering technologies, 6% health sciences, 12% social sciences. Graduate degrees offered in 109 major fields of study.

UNDERGRADUATE MAJORS. **Associate:** Airline piloting and navigation, architectural technologies, architecture, criminology, drafting, drafting and design technology, instrumentation technology, liberal/general studies, manufacturing technology, medical laboratory technologies, nursing, secretarial and related programs, teacher aide, trade and industrial supervision and management. **Bachelor's:** Accounting, Afro-American (black) studies, airline piloting and navigation, anthropology, art education, art history, automotive technology, aviation management, biological and physical sciences, biology, business administration and management, business education, chemistry, child development/care/guidance, city/community/regional planning, clinical laboratory science, clinical psychology, clothing and textiles management/production/services, communications, computer and information sciences, computer graphics, computer programming, computer servicing technology, computer technology, construction, creative writing, criminology, dental assistant, dramatic arts, early childhood education, earth sciences, economics, education of the deaf and hearing impaired, educational media technology, electromechanical technology, electronic technology, elementary education, English, English education, English literature, family/consumer resource management, finance, fine arts, food production/management/services, food science and nutrition, foreign languages (multiple emphasis), foreign languages education, French, geography, geology, German, graphic and printing production, graphic design, health education, health sciences, history, home economics, home economics education, home furnishings and equipment management/production/services, hotel/motel and restaurant management, human environment and housing, humanities, humanities and social sciences, individual and family development, industrial arts education, industrial technology, information sciences and systems, insurance and risk management, interior design, international studies, journalism, junior high education, Latin, Latin American studies, library science, management information systems, management science, manufacturing technology, marketing and distributive education, marketing management, mathematics, mathematics education, mechanical design technology, medical laboratory technologies, music, music business management, music education, music performance, music theory and composition, nursing, occupational safety and health technology, office supervision and management, parks and recreation management, philosophy, physical education, physical sciences, physics, political science and government, predentistry, prelaw, premedicine, prepharmacy, preveterinary, psychology, public health laboratory science, public relations, radio/television broadcasting, radio/television technology, recreation therapy, religion, Russian, science education, secondary education, social science education, social sciences, social studies education, social work, sociology, Spanish, special education, speech, speech correction, speech pathology/audiology, speech/communication/theater education, sports management, sports medicine, systems analysis, taxation, technical education, textiles and clothing, trade and industrial education, trade and industrial supervision and management, urban studies, visual and performing arts.

ACADEMIC PROGRAMS. 2-year transfer program, accelerated program, cooperative education, double major, dual enrollment of high school students, education specialist degree, honors program, independent study, internships, study abroad, teacher preparation, telecourses, cross-registration; liberal arts/career combination in health sciences; combined bachelor's/graduate program in business administration. **Remedial services:** Learning center, tutoring. **ROTC:** Air Force, Army. **Placement/credit:** AP, CLEP General and Subject, institutional tests; 31 credit hours maximum for bachelor's degree.

ACADEMIC REQUIREMENTS. Freshmen must earn minimum GPA of 2.0 to continue in good standing. 68% of freshmen return for sophomore year. Students must declare major on application. **Graduation requirements:** 62 hours for associate, 124 hours for bachelor's. Most students required to take courses in arts/fine arts, English, history, mathematics, philosophy/religion, biological/physical sciences, social sciences. **Postgraduate studies:** 60% from 2-year programs enter 4-year programs.

FRESHMAN ADMISSIONS. Selection criteria: Students who rank in top 50% of high school class granted admission, others reviewed on individual basis. High school curriculum, GPA, test scores, class rank, type of high school, and interview all considered when students rank in lower 50% of high school class. **High school preparation:** 20 units recommended. Recommended units include English 4, foreign language 4, mathematics 4, social science 4 and science 4. One speech and one typing or word processing recommended. **Test requirements:** SAT or ACT; score report by August 31.

1992 FRESHMAN CLASS PROFILE. 5,718 men and women applied, 4,802 accepted; 1,151 men enrolled, 1,198 women enrolled. 27% had high school GPA of 3.0 or higher, 66% between 2.0 and 2.99. **Academic background:** Mid 50% of enrolled freshmen had SAT-V between 330-440, SAT-M between 350-500; ACT composite between 16-22. 81% submitted SAT scores, 15% submitted ACT scores. **Characteristics:** 88% from in state, 75% live in college housing, 8% have minority backgrounds, 3% are foreign students, 11% join fraternities/sororities. Average age is 19.

FALL-TERM APPLICATIONS. $20 fee, may be waived for applicants with need. Closing date August 15; priority given to applications received by May 1; applicants notified on a rolling basis. Audition required for music applicants. Interview recommended. Portfolio recommended for art applicants. Essay recommended. Interviews recommended for applicants below 50th percentile of high school graduating class. Required for certain scholarship applicants. Deferred admission available.

STUDENT LIFE. Housing: Dormitories (men, women, coed); apartment, fraternity, sorority housing available. Honors floors, quiet floors, age 21-and-over floors. **Activities:** Student government, film, radio, student newspaper, television, yearbook, choral groups, concert band, dance, drama, jazz band, marching band, music ensembles, musical theater, opera, pep band, symphony orchestra, fraternities, sororities, over 150 student organizations.

ATHLETICS. NCAA. **Intercollegiate:** Baseball M, basketball, cross-country, football M, softball W, tennis, track and field, volleyball W. **Intramural:** Archery, badminton, basketball, bowling, golf, racquetball, soccer, softball, swimming, table tennis, tennis, track and field, volleyball, water polo, wrestling M.

STUDENT SERVICES. Aptitude testing, career counseling, employment service for undergraduates, freshman orientation, health services, on-campus day care, personal counseling, placement service for graduates, special adviser for adult students, veterans counselor, services/facilities for handicapped.

ANNUAL EXPENSES. Tuition and fees (1992-93): $2,452, $3,508 additional for out-of-state students. **Room and board:** $3,468. **Books and supplies:** $530. **Other expenses:** $1,100.

FINANCIAL AID. 76% of freshmen, 49% of continuing students receive some form of aid. 70% of grants, 95% of loans, 20% of jobs based on need. Academic, music/drama, art, athletic, state/district residency, leadership, alumni affiliation scholarships available. **Aid applications:** Closing date March 1; applicants notified on or about June 1; must reply by June 15.

ADDRESS/TELEPHONE. Richard Riehl, Director of Admissions, Indiana State University, 217 North Sixth Street, Terre Haute, IN 47809. (812) 237-2121. Fax: (812) 237-4292.

Indiana University Bloomington
Bloomington, Indiana CB code: 1324

Admissions: 84% of applicants accepted
Based on: ••• School record
• Activities, essay, recommendations, special talents, test scores
Completion: 96% of freshmen end year in good standing
65% graduate

4-year public university, coed. Founded in 1820. **Accreditation:** Regional. **Undergraduate enrollment:** 11,423 men, 13,619 women full time; 873 men, 1,040 women part time. **Graduate enrollment:** 1,993 men, 1,946 women full time; 1,062 men, 941 women part time. **Faculty:** 1,575 total (1,405 full time), 2,395 with doctorates or other terminal degrees. **Location:** Urban campus in small city; 50 miles from Indianapolis. **Calendar:** Semester, extensive summer session. Extensive evening/early morning classes. **Microcomputers:** 900 located in dormitories, libraries, classrooms, computer centers. **Special facilities:** Art museum, cyclotron, 2 observatories, museum of anthropology, history, and folklore, rare book library, outdoor educational center, musical arts center, center for excellence in education.

DEGREES OFFERED. AS, BA, BS, BFA, MA, MS, MBA, MFA, MEd, PhD, EdD, OD. 74 associate degrees awarded in 1992. 5,421 bachelor's degrees awarded. Graduate degrees offered in 175 major fields of study.

UNDERGRADUATE MAJORS. Associate: Dental hygiene, hazard control, labor/industrial relations, liberal/general studies, ophthalmic services, optical technology, public affairs, textiles and clothing, theater design, women's studies. **Bachelor's:** Accounting, actuarial sciences, Afro-American (black) studies, American literature, anthropology, applied mathematics, Arabic, art history, Asian studies, astronomy, bilingual/bicultural education, biochemistry, biology, botany, business administration and management, business analysis, business economics, business education, ceramics, chemistry, Chinese, city/community/regional planning, classics, cognitive psychology, cognitive science, communications, comparative literature, computer and information sciences, creative writing, criminal justice studies, criminology, curriculum and instruction, dance, dramatic arts, drawing, driver and safety education, early childhood education, East Asian studies, economics, education, education of the deaf and hearing impaired, education of the emotionally handicapped, education of the mentally handicapped, educational psychology, elementary education, English, English education, English literature, environmental affairs, environmental design, environmental science, family/consumer resource management, fashion design, fashion merchandising, fiber/textiles/weaving, finance, fine arts, folklore and mythology, food science and nutrition, foreign languages (multiple emphasis), foreign languages education, forensic studies, French, geography, geology, German, graphic design, Greek (classical), health education, health sciences, Hebrew, history, human environment and housing, individual and family development, insurance and risk management, interior design, Italian, Japanese, jazz, journalism, journalism education, junior high education, labor/industrial relations, Latin, liberal/general studies, linguistics, management information systems, management science, marketing and distributive education, marketing management, marketing/advertising, mathematics, mathematics education, media services, medical records technology, metal/jewelry, microbiology, Middle Eastern studies, music, music education, music history and appreciation, music performance, music theory and composition, nursing, nutritional education, nutritional sciences, operations research, optometry, painting, parks and recreation management, personnel management, philosophy, photography, physical education, physics, political science and government, Portuguese, predentistry, prelaw, premedicine, prepharmacy, preveterinary, printmaking, psychology, public administration, public affairs, public health laboratory science, public policy studies, public utilities, radio/television broadcasting, radio/television technology, real estate, religion, Russian, Russian and Slavic studies, school library/audio visual services, science education, sculpture, secondary education, Slavic languages, small business management and ownership, social science education, social studies education, social work, sociology, Spanish, special education, speech, speech and hearing sciences, speech pathology/audiology, sports management, sports medicine, sports science, telecommunications, textiles and clothing, transportation management, urban studies, visual and performing arts.

ACADEMIC PROGRAMS. 2-year transfer program, accelerated program, cooperative education, double major, dual enrollment of high school students, education specialist degree, external degree, honors program, independent study, internships, semester at sea, student-designed major, study abroad, teacher preparation, United Nations semester, Washington semester; liberal arts/career combination in health sciences. **Remedial services:** Learning center, preadmission summer program, reduced course load, remedial instruction, special counselor, tutoring. **ROTC:** Air Force, Army. **Placement/credit:** AP, CLEP General and Subject, institutional tests.

ACADEMIC REQUIREMENTS. Freshmen must earn minimum GPA of 2.0 to continue in good standing. 82% of freshmen return for sophomore year. Students must declare major by end of second year. **Graduation requirements:** 62 hours for associate (31 in major), 122 hours for bachelor's (38 in major). Most students required to take courses in arts/fine arts, English, humanities, mathematics, biological/physical sciences, social sciences.

FRESHMAN ADMISSIONS. Selection criteria: Strength of college-preparatory program, including senior year; grade trends in college-preparatory subjects, student's rank in class most important. In-state students must be in top half of class, out-of-state students in top third. Additional factors include recommendations of high school counselors and teachers and extracurricular activities. **High school preparation:** 16 units required; 17 recommended. Required and recommended units include English 4-4, mathematics 3-4, social science 2-3 and science 1-3. Foreign language 2 recommended. Residents must have at least 3 year-long academic courses in different subject areas in senior year. Nonresidents must schedule 4. **Test requirements:** SAT or ACT; score report by February 15.

1992 FRESHMAN CLASS PROFILE. 6,864 men applied, 5,563 accepted, 2,508 enrolled; 9,012 women applied, 7,770 accepted, 3,578 enrolled. 24% were in top tenth and 62% were in top quarter of graduating class. **Characteristics:** 67% from in state, 87% live in college housing, 10% have minority backgrounds, 1% are foreign students. Average age is 19.

FALL-TERM APPLICATIONS. $30 fee, may be waived for applicants with need. Closing date February 15; applicants notified on a rolling basis; must reply by May 1. Audition required for music applicants. CRDA. Deferred admission available. Foreign language ACH recommended for those who intend to major in a language.

STUDENT LIFE. Housing: Dormitories (men, women, coed); apartment, fraternity, sorority, cooperative housing available. Residential language houses and living/learning centers available, wellness center. **Activities:** Student government, film, magazine, radio, student newspaper, television, yearbook, choral groups, concert band, dance, drama, jazz band, marching band, music ensembles, musical theater, opera, pep band, symphony orchestra, fraternities, sororities, over 200 political, religious, and ethnic organizations.

ATHLETICS. NCAA. **Intercollegiate:** Baseball M, basketball, cross-country, diving, football M, golf, soccer M, softball W, swimming, tennis, track and field, volleyball W, wrestling M. **Intramural:** Badminton, basketball, bowling, cross-country, fencing, field hockey W, gymnastics, handball, horseback riding, ice hockey M, lacrosse, racquetball, rifle, rowing (crew), rugby, sailing, skiing, skin diving, soccer, softball, squash, swimming, table tennis, tennis, volleyball, water polo, wrestling M.

STUDENT SERVICES. Aptitude testing, career counseling, employment service for undergraduates, freshman orientation, health services, on-campus day care, personal counseling, placement service for graduates, special adviser for adult students, veterans counselor, vocational rehabilitation for veterans, services/facilities for handicapped.

ANNUAL EXPENSES. Tuition and fees (projected): $2,828, $5,712 additional for out-of-state students. **Room and board:** $3,630. **Books and supplies:** $584. **Other expenses:** $1,486.

FINANCIAL AID. 70% of freshmen, 69% of continuing students receive some form of aid. 74% of grants, 88% of loans, 46% of jobs based on need. 1,914 enrolled freshmen were judged to have need, 1,757 were offered aid. Academic, music/drama, art, athletic, state/district residency, leadership, alumni affiliation, minority scholarships available. **Aid applications:** No closing date; priority given to applications received by March 1; applicants notified on a rolling basis beginning on or about March 1; must reply by May 1 or within 3 weeks if notified thereafter.

ADDRESS/TELEPHONE. Robert S. Magee, Director of Admissions, Indiana University Bloomington, 300 North Jordan Avenue, Bloomington, IN 47405-7700. (812) 855-0661.

Indiana University East
Richmond, Indiana — CB code: 1194

4-year public university and college of arts and sciences and branch campus college, coed. Founded in 1971. **Accreditation:** Regional. **Undergraduate enrollment:** 292 men, 714 women full time; 391 men, 992 women part time. **Graduate enrollment:** 9 men, 13 women full time. **Faculty:** 179 total (64 full time), 51 with doctorates or other terminal degrees. **Location:** Rural campus in large town; 70 miles from Indianapolis, 40 miles from Dayton, Ohio, 60 miles from Cincinnati, Ohio. **Calendar:** Semester, limited summer session. Saturday and extensive evening/early morning classes. **Microcomputers:** 60 located in libraries, classrooms, computer centers.

DEGREES OFFERED. AA, AS, AAS, BA, BS. 87 associate degrees awarded in 1992. 22% in business and management, 36% health sciences, 36% multi/interdisciplinary studies, 5% parks/recreation, protective services, public affairs. 80 bachelor's degrees awarded. 28% in business and management, 21% teacher education, 26% health sciences, 24% multi/interdisciplinary studies.

UNDERGRADUATE MAJORS. Associate: Accounting, biological and physical sciences, biology, business administration and management, chemistry, computer and information sciences, criminal justice studies, earth sciences, liberal/general studies, mathematics, nursing, social work. **Bachelor's:** Accounting, business administration and management, elementary education, English, junior high education, liberal/general studies, nursing, psychology, secondary education, social work, sociology.

ACADEMIC PROGRAMS. 2-year transfer program, double major, dual enrollment of high school students, external degree, independent study, internships, teacher preparation, weekend college, state-wide technology program with Purdue University. **Remedial services:** Remedial instruction, special counselor, tutoring. **Placement/credit:** AP, CLEP General and Subject, institutional tests.

ACADEMIC REQUIREMENTS. Freshmen must earn minimum GPA of 2.0 to continue in good standing. 54% of freshmen return for sophomore year. Students must declare major by end of second year. **Graduation requirements:** 68 hours for associate (15 in major), 122 hours for bachelor's (32 in major). Most students required to take courses in computer science, English, humanities, biological/physical sciences, social sciences.

FRESHMAN ADMISSIONS. Selection criteria: Open admissions. **High school preparation:** 14 units required. Required units include English 4, mathematics 3, social science 2 and science 1. 4 units in some combination of foreign language, additional mathematics, laboratory science, social science, and/or computer science. Foreign language strongly recommended. **Test requirements:** SAT or ACT; score report by August 15. **Additional information:** College preparatory program recommended.

1992 FRESHMAN CLASS PROFILE. 238 men applied, 238 accepted, 238 enrolled; 547 women applied, 547 accepted, 547 enrolled. 6% were in top tenth and 24% were in top quarter of graduating class. **Academic background:** Mid 50% of enrolled freshmen had SAT-V between 350-470, SAT-M between 350-520. 56% submitted SAT scores. **Characteristics:** 97% from in state, 100% commute, 3% have minority backgrounds.

FALL-TERM APPLICATIONS. $25 fee. Closing date August 1; applicants notified on a rolling basis. Interview recommended. Deferred admission available.

STUDENT LIFE. Activities: Student government, student newspaper, drama.

ATHLETICS. Intramural: Basketball M, soccer, softball, volleyball.

STUDENT SERVICES. Career counseling, freshman orientation, personal counseling, placement service for graduates, services/facilities for handicapped.

ANNUAL EXPENSES. Tuition and fees (projected): $2,354, $3,450 additional for out-of-state students. **Books and supplies:** $587. **Other expenses:** $1,052.

FINANCIAL AID. 55% of freshmen, 70% of continuing students receive some form of aid. 96% of grants, 93% of loans, 66% of jobs based on need. 307 enrolled freshmen were judged to have need, 294 were offered aid. Academic, state/district residency, alumni affiliation, minority scholarships available. **Aid applications:** No closing date; priority given to applications received by March 1; applicants notified on a rolling basis beginning on or about July 15; must reply within 2 weeks.

ADDRESS/TELEPHONE. Patricia E. Lemmons, Director of Admissions and Financial Aid, Indiana University East, 2325 Chester Boulevard, Richmond, IN 47374-1289. (317) 973-8208. (800) 959-3278. Fax: (317) 973-8388.

Indiana University at Kokomo
Kokomo, Indiana — CB code: 1337

4-year public university, coed. Founded in 1945. **Accreditation:** Regional. **Undergraduate enrollment:** 3,356 men and women. **Graduate enrollment:** 166 men and women. **Location:** Urban campus in small city; 50 miles from Indianapolis. **Calendar:** Semester.

FRESHMAN ADMISSIONS. Selection criteria: Test scores, class rank, course work. 2 out of 3 criteria should be met for admission. In-state applicants should be in top half of graduating class (top third for out-of-state applicants).

ANNUAL EXPENSES. Tuition and fees (1992-93): $2,189, $3,195 additional for out-of-state students. **Books and supplies:** $658. **Other expenses:** $1,108.

ADDRESS/TELEPHONE. Director of Admissions, Office of Admissions, Indiana University at Kokomo, PO Box 9003, Kokomo, IN 46904-9003. (317) 453-2000.

Indiana University Northwest
Gary, Indiana — CB code: 1338

Admissions:	78% of applicants accepted
Based on:	••• School record
	•• Test scores
	• Recommendations
Completion:	75% of freshmen end year in good standing
	30% enter graduate study

4-year public university, coed. Founded in 1922. **Accreditation:** Regional. **Undergraduate enrollment:** 854 men, 1,618 women full time; 1,082 men, 2,050 women part time. **Graduate enrollment:** 703 men and women. **Faculty:** 372 total (184 full time), 136 with doctorates or other terminal degrees. **Location:** Urban campus in small city; 35 miles from Chicago. **Calendar:** Semester, limited summer session. **Microcomputers:** Located in classrooms, computer centers. **Special facilities:** Art gallery.

DEGREES OFFERED. AA, AS, BA, BS, MS, MBA. 172 associate degrees awarded in 1992. 333 bachelor's degrees awarded. Graduate degrees offered in 7 major fields of study.

UNDERGRADUATE MAJORS. Associate: Clinical laboratory science, criminal justice studies, dental hygiene, labor/industrial relations, liberal/general studies, medical laboratory technologies, medical records technology, nursing, public affairs, radiograph medical technology, respiratory therapy technology. **Bachelor's:** Accounting, actuarial sciences, Afro-American (black) studies, biology, business administration and management, business and management, business economics, chemistry, clinical laboratory science, communications, criminal justice studies, data processing, dramatic arts, economics, education, elementary education, English, fine arts, French, geology, history, information sciences and systems, junior high education, labor/industrial relations, law enforcement and corrections, liberal/general studies, mathematics, minority studies, nursing, philosophy, political science and government, psychology, public administration, public affairs, public policy studies, secondary education, sociology, Spanish, visual and performing arts.

ACADEMIC PROGRAMS. 2-year transfer program, accelerated program, cooperative education, double major, dual enrollment of high school students, external degree, honors program, independent study, internships, student-designed major, study abroad, teacher preparation, weekend college. **Remedial services:** Learning center, preadmission summer program, reduced course load, remedial instruction, special counselor, tutoring, counselor for handicapped students. **ROTC:** Army. **Placement/credit:** AP, CLEP General and Subject, institutional tests.

ACADEMIC REQUIREMENTS. Freshmen must earn minimum GPA of 2.0 to continue in good standing. 50% of freshmen return for sophomore year. Students must declare major by end of second year. **Graduation requirements:** 60 hours for associate (15 in major), 120 hours for bachelor's (30 in major). Most students required to take courses in English, foreign languages, humanities, mathematics, biological/physical sciences, social sciences.

FRESHMAN ADMISSIONS. Selection criteria: School achievement record and test scores most important. Applicants should be in top half of class and have 2.0 high school GPA or better. **High school preparation:** 13 units required. Required units include English 4, mathematics 3 and science 1. **Test requirements:** SAT or ACT; score report by July 15.

1992 FRESHMAN CLASS PROFILE. 809 men applied, 617 accepted, 457 enrolled; 1,532 women applied, 1,203 accepted, 793 enrolled. **Characteristics:** 99% from in state, 100% commute, 30% have minority backgrounds. Average age is 23.

FALL-TERM APPLICATIONS. $25 fee. No closing date; applicants notified on a rolling basis. Deferred admission available.

STUDENT LIFE. Activities: Student government, magazine, student newspaper, choral groups, dance, drama, fraternities, sororities, Christian Student Fellowship, Young Republicans, Young Democrats, Women With a Challenge, Student Guide Services, Black Student Union.

ATHLETICS. Intramural: Baseball M, basketball M, softball, table tennis, volleyball.

STUDENT SERVICES. Career counseling, employment service for undergraduates, on-campus day care, personal counseling, placement service for graduates, special adviser for adult students, veterans counselor, services/facilities for handicapped.

ANNUAL EXPENSES. Tuition and fees (1992-93): $2,156, $3,195 additional for out-of-state students. **Books and supplies:** $500. **Other expenses:** $1,436.

FINANCIAL AID. 40% of freshmen, 45% of continuing students receive some form of aid. 97% of grants, all loans, 42% of jobs based on need. Academic scholarships available. **Aid applications:** No closing date; priority given to applications received by March 1; applicants notified on a rolling basis beginning on or about May 1; must reply within 2 weeks.

ADDRESS/TELEPHONE. William D. Lee, Director of Admissions, Indiana University Northwest, 3400 Broadway, Gary, IN 46408. (219) 980-6991. (800) 437-5409. Fax: (219) 980-6624.

Indiana University South Bend

South Bend, Indiana — CB code: 1339

Admissions: 76% of applicants accepted
Based on: ••• School record
• Activities, interview, recommendations, test scores
Completion: 65% of freshmen end year in good standing

4-year public university, coed. Founded in 1940. **Accreditation:** Regional. **Undergraduate enrollment:** 1,127 men, 1,692 women full time; 1,378 men, 2,069 women part time. **Graduate enrollment:** 77 men, 107 women full time; 537 men, 814 women part time. **Faculty:** 557 total (219 full time), 162 with doctorates or other terminal degrees. **Location:** Urban campus in small city; 90 miles from Chicago, 120 miles from Indianapolis. **Calendar:** Semester, limited summer session. **Microcomputers:** 300 located in libraries, classrooms, computer centers.

DEGREES OFFERED. BA, BS, BFA, MA, MS, MBA. 90 associate degrees awarded in 1992. 370 bachelor's degrees awarded. Graduate degrees offered in 11 major fields of study.

UNDERGRADUATE MAJORS. Associate: Computer and information sciences, criminal justice studies, dental hygiene, early childhood education, finance, jazz, labor/industrial relations, law enforcement and corrections technologies, legal assistant/paralegal, liberal/general studies, marketing and distribution, nursing, public affairs, radiograph medical technology. **Bachelor's:** Accounting, advertising, American literature, applied mathematics, art history, biology, business administration and management, business economics, chemistry, comparative literature, computer and information sciences, criminal justice studies, dental hygiene, dramatic arts, economics, education of the multiple handicapped, elementary education, English, English education, fine arts, French, German, history, junior high education, labor/industrial relations, law enforcement and corrections, liberal/general studies, mathematics, music, music education, music performance, music theory and composition, nursing, personnel management, philosophy, physics, political science and government, psychology, public administration, public affairs, science education, secondary education, social studies education, sociology, Spanish, special education, speech, visual and performing arts.

ACADEMIC PROGRAMS. 2-year transfer program, double major, dual enrollment of high school students, external degree, honors program, independent study, internships, student-designed major, study abroad, visiting/exchange student program, weekend college, cross-registration, electrical, mechanical engineering, and computer technology with Purdue University on Indiana University campus; liberal arts/career combination in health sciences. **Remedial services:** Learning center, preadmission summer program, reduced course load, remedial instruction, tutoring, special services for handicapped and for older students returning to school after a long absence. **ROTC:** Air Force, Army. **Placement/credit:** CLEP Subject, institutional tests; 90 credit hours maximum for bachelor's degree.

ACADEMIC REQUIREMENTS. Freshmen must earn minimum GPA of 2.0 to continue in good standing. 70% of freshmen return for sophomore year. Students must declare major by end of second year. **Graduation requirements:** 60 hours for associate (18 in major), 124 hours for bachelor's (30 in major). Most students required to take courses in arts/fine arts, English, humanities, mathematics, biological/physical sciences, social sciences. **Additional information:** Most allied health programs must be completed at Indianapolis campus.

FRESHMAN ADMISSIONS. Selection criteria: Applicants should rank in top half of class. **High school preparation:** 13 units required. Required units include English 4 and mathematics 2. Strong preparation in mathematics and sciences recommended. **Test requirements:** SAT or ACT; score report by August 1.

1992 FRESHMAN CLASS PROFILE. 554 men applied, 419 accepted, 199 enrolled; 831 women applied, 629 accepted, 324 enrolled. 30% had high school GPA of 3.0 or higher, 69% between 2.0 and 2.99. **Characteristics:** 97% from in state, 100% commute, 7% have minority backgrounds. Average age is 23.

FALL-TERM APPLICATIONS. $25 fee. Closing date August 1; priority given to applications received by June 1; applicants notified on a rolling basis. Audition required for music applicants. Interview recommended for academically weak applicants. Deferred and early admission available.

STUDENT LIFE. Housing: Special housing for international students. **Activities:** Student government, film, magazine, student newspaper, choral groups, drama, jazz band, music ensembles, musical theater, opera, pep band, symphony orchestra, fraternities, Student Educational Association, Black Student Union, Student Council for Exceptional Children, campus ministry.

ATHLETICS. NAIA. **Intercollegiate:** Basketball M, soccer W. **Intramural:** Baseball M, basketball, golf, table tennis, volleyball.

STUDENT SERVICES. Aptitude testing, career counseling, employment service for undergraduates, freshman orientation, on-campus day care, personal counseling, placement service for graduates, special adviser for adult students, veterans counselor, professional practice program, career testing and evaluation services, services/facilities for handicapped.

ANNUAL EXPENSES. Tuition and fees (1992-93): $2,255, $3,195 additional for out-of-state students. **Books and supplies:** $574. **Other expenses:** $1,356.

FINANCIAL AID. 40% of freshmen, 35% of continuing students receive some form of aid. Grants, loans, jobs available. Academic, music/drama, art, leadership scholarships available. **Aid applications:** No closing date; priority given to applications received by March 1; applicants notified on a rolling basis beginning on or about April 15; must reply within 2 weeks.

ADDRESS/TELEPHONE. Esker E. Ligon, Director of Admissions, Indiana University South Bend, PO Box 7111, 1700 Mishawaka Avenue, South Bend, IN 46634-7111. (219) 237-4839. Fax: (219) 237-4599.

Indiana University Southeast ⇎

New Albany, Indiana — CB code: 1314

4-year public university, coed. Founded in 1941. **Accreditation:** Regional. **Undergraduate enrollment:** 5,611 men and women. **Graduate enrollment:** 331 men and women. **Location:** Suburban campus in large town; 10 miles from Louisville, Kentucky. **Calendar:** Semester.

FRESHMAN ADMISSIONS. Selection criteria: School achievement record, test scores. Rank in top half of class for in-state applicants, top third for out-of-state applicants.

ANNUAL EXPENSES. Tuition and fees (projected): $2,115, $3,195 additional for out-of-state students. **Books and supplies:** $470. **Other expenses:** $1,166.

ADDRESS/TELEPHONE. David Campbell, Director of Admissions, Indiana University Southeast, 4201 Grant Line Road, New Albany, IN 47150. (812) 941-2212. Fax: (812) 941-2493.

Indiana University—Purdue University at Fort Wayne ⇎

Fort Wayne, Indiana — CB code: 1336

Admissions: 74% of applicants accepted
Based on: •• School record, test scores
Completion: 90% of freshmen end year in good standing
15% enter graduate study

4-year public university, coed. Founded in 1964. **Accreditation:** Regional. **Undergraduate enrollment:** 2,312 men, 2,754 women full time; 2,921 men, 4,103 women part time. **Graduate enrollment:** 678 men and women. **Faculty:** 662 total (345 full time), 292 with doctorates or other terminal degrees. **Location:** Suburban campus in small city; 110 miles from Indianapolis. **Calendar:** Semester, limited summer session. **Microcomputers:** Located in libraries, classrooms, computer centers. Lease or purchase required**Additional facts:** Degree awarded through Indiana University or Purdue University, depending on course of study.

DEGREES OFFERED. AA, AS, AAS, BA, BS, BFA, MA, MS, MBA, MEd. 574 associate degrees awarded in 1992. 679 bachelor's degrees awarded. Graduate degrees offered in 13 major fields of study.

UNDERGRADUATE MAJORS. Associate: Accounting, architectural technologies, business and office, business data programming, civil technology, computer and information sciences, criminal justice studies, dental assistant, dental hygiene, dental laboratory technology, drafting, drafting and design technology, electrical technology, engineering and engineering-related technologies, graphic arts technology, hotel/motel and restaurant management, industrial technology, interior design, liberal/general studies, marketing and distribution, mechanical design technology, medical records technology, mental health/human services, nursing, office supervision and management, public affairs, radiograph medical technology, teacher aide. **Bachelor's:** Accounting, anthropology, biology, business administration and management, business and management, business economics, chemistry, clinical laboratory science, communications, computer and information sciences, criminal justice studies, dental hygiene, dramatic arts, earth sciences, economics, electrical technology, elementary education, engineering, engineering and engineering-related technologies, English, English education, English literature, finance, fine arts, foreign languages education, French, geology, German, history, industrial technology, junior high education, labor/industrial relations, liberal/general studies, marketing management, mathematics, mathematics education, medical laboratory technologies, music, music education, nursing, personnel management, philosophy, physical sciences, physics, political science and government, psychology, public affairs, radio/television broadcasting, science education, secondary education, social studies education, sociology, Spanish, visual and performing arts.

ACADEMIC PROGRAMS. 2-year transfer program, accelerated program, cooperative education, double major, dual enrollment of high school students, external degree, honors program, independent study, internships, student-designed major, study abroad, teacher preparation, visiting/exchange student program, weekend college; combined bachelor's/graduate program in business administration. **Remedial services:** Learning center, remedial instruction, special counselor, tutoring. **Placement/credit:** AP, institutional tests.

ACADEMIC REQUIREMENTS. Freshmen must earn minimum GPA of 2.0 to continue in good standing. 50% of freshmen return for sophomore year. **Graduation requirements:** 63 hours for associate, 123 hours for bachelor's. Most students required to take courses in English, mathematics. **Postgraduate studies:** 20% from 2-year programs enter 4-year programs.

FRESHMAN ADMISSIONS. Selection criteria: In-state applicants should rank in top half of high school class, out-of-state in top third. **High school preparation:** 13 units required. Required units include English 4, mathematics 3, social science 2 and science 2. One chemistry, 4 mathematics (including trigonometry) required for engineering applicants. **Test requirements:** SAT or ACT; score report by July 1.

1992 FRESHMAN CLASS PROFILE. 2,306 men and women applied, 1,714 accepted; 1,714 enrolled. **Academic background:** Mid 50% of enrolled freshmen had SAT-V between 350-500, SAT-M between 400-550; ACT composite between 16-20. 80% submitted SAT scores, 20% submitted ACT scores. **Characteristics:** 95% from in state, 100% commute, 5% have minority backgrounds, 1% are foreign students, 2% join fraternities/sororities.

FALL-TERM APPLICATIONS. $20 fee for Indiana University applicants only. Closing date August 1; applicants notified on a rolling basis. Audition required for music applicants. Portfolio required for fine arts applicants. Deferred admission available.

STUDENT LIFE. Activities: Student government, student newspaper, television, choral groups, concert band, drama, jazz band, music ensembles, pep band, symphony orchestra, fraternities, sororities.

ATHLETICS. NCAA. **Intercollegiate:** Baseball M, basketball, cross-country, golf, soccer M, softball W, tennis, volleyball. **Intramural:** Basketball, football M, handball, racquetball, softball, table tennis, track and field M, volleyball.

STUDENT SERVICES. Aptitude testing, career counseling, employment service for undergraduates, freshman orientation, health services, on-campus day care, personal counseling, placement service for graduates, veterans counselor, services/facilities for handicapped.

ANNUAL EXPENSES. Tuition and fees (projected): $2,330, $3,324 additional for out-of-state students. **Books and supplies:** $500. **Other expenses:** $900.

FINANCIAL AID. 65% of continuing students receive some form of aid. Grants, loans, jobs available. Academic, music/drama, art, athletic, state/district residency, leadership, alumni affiliation scholarships available. **Aid applications:** No closing date; priority given to applications received by March 1; applicants notified on a rolling basis beginning on or about May 1; must reply within 4 weeks.

ADDRESS/TELEPHONE. Karl F. Zimmerman, Director of Admissions, Indiana University—Purdue University at Fort Wayne, 2101 Coliseum Boulevard East, Fort Wayne, IN 46805. (219) 481-6812.

Indiana University—Purdue University at Indianapolis

Indianapolis, Indiana — CB code: 1325

Admissions: 89% of applicants accepted
Based on: ••• School record
• Essay, interview, recommendations, special talents, test scores
Completion: 60% of freshmen end year in good standing
12% graduate

4-year public university, coed. Founded in 1969. **Accreditation:** Regional. **Undergraduate enrollment:** 4,074 men, 5,751 women full time; 4,475 men, 7,146 women part time. **Graduate enrollment:** 1,518 men, 1,317 women full time; 1,728 men, 2,336 women part time. **Faculty:** 2,066 total (1,273 full time), 1,399 with doctorates or other terminal degrees. **Location:** Urban campus in very large city. **Calendar:** Semester, extensive summer session. Saturday and extensive evening/early morning classes. **Microcomputers:** 400 located in libraries, classrooms, computer centers.

DEGREES OFFERED. AA, AS, AAS, BA, BS, BFA, MA, MS, MBA, MEd, MSW, PhD, EdD, DDS, MD, JD. 673 associate degrees awarded in 1992. 30% in engineering technologies, 25% health sciences, 11% allied health, 28% multi/interdisciplinary studies. 1,919 bachelor's degrees awarded. 18% in business and management, 10% teacher education, 6% engineering technologies, 15% health sciences, 6% allied health, 5% letters/literature, 7% multi/interdisciplinary studies, 7% parks/recreation, protective services, public affairs, 5% psychology, 5% social sciences. Graduate degrees offered in 46 major fields of study.

UNDERGRADUATE MAJORS. Associate: Architectural technologies, biomedical equipment technology, civil technology, computer technology, criminal justice studies, dental hygiene, drafting and design technology, early childhood education, electrical technology, emergency medical technologies, environmental science, food production/management/services, humanities, labor/industrial relations, liberal/general studies, manufacturing technology, mechanical design technology, nursing, occupational therapy assistant, public administration, public affairs, radiograph medical technology, respiratory therapy, social sciences, trade and industrial supervision and management. **Bachelor's:** Accounting, anthropology, art education, art history, biology, business administration and management, business and management, business economics, ceramics, chemistry, computer and information sciences, computer technology, construction, criminal justice studies, cytotechnology, dental hygiene, economics, electrical technology, electrical/electronics/communications engineering, elementary education, engineering and other disciplines, English, English education, environmental science, finance, fine arts, foreign languages education, French, geography, geology, German, graphic design, health care administration, health education, history, insurance and risk management, journalism, labor/industrial relations, liberal/general studies, manufacturing technology, marketing management, mathematics, mechanical design technology, mechanical engineering, medical laboratory technologies, medical radiation dosimetry, medical records administration, nuclear medical technology, nursing, occupational therapy, painting, personnel management, philosophy, photography, physical education, physical therapy, physics, political science and government, printmaking, psychology, public administration, public affairs, real estate, religion, respiratory therapy, sculpture, secondary education, social studies education, social work, sociology, Spanish, speech, speech/communication/theater education, trade and industrial supervision and management, woodworking.

ACADEMIC PROGRAMS. 2-year transfer program, cooperative education, double major, education specialist degree, external degree, honors program, independent study, internships, study abroad, teacher preparation, weekend college, cross-registration. **Remedial services:** Learning center, reduced course load, remedial instruction, special counselor, tutoring. **ROTC:** Army. **Placement/credit:** AP, CLEP General and Subject, institutional tests.

ACADEMIC REQUIREMENTS. No policy requiring minimum GPA; records of students having academic difficulty are reviewed individually. 56% of freshmen return for sophomore year. **Graduation requirements:** 60 hours for associate, 120 hours for bachelor's. Most students required to take courses in English, mathematics.

FRESHMAN ADMISSIONS. Selection criteria: Rank in top half of class, completion of required academic units, SAT or ACT scores, school record. Interview and recommendations considered for academically weak students. **High school preparation:** 14 units required. Required and recommended units include English 4, mathematics 3, social science 2 and science 1. Foreign language 2 recommended. Additional mathematics and science units required for science, engineering, and nursing programs. 4 additional units required in some combination of foreign language, laboratory science, mathematics, social science; or computer science. Courses that develop writing composition skills strongly recommended. **Test requirements:** SAT or ACT; score report by June 15. **Additional information:** Test scores waived for adults 21 or older and applicants out of high school 2 years.

1992 FRESHMAN CLASS PROFILE. 2,483 men applied, 2,238 accepted, 1,280 enrolled; 3,492 women applied, 3,077 accepted, 1,684 enrolled. 5% were in top tenth and 20% were in top quarter of graduating class. **Academic background:** Mid 50% of enrolled freshmen had SAT-V between 320-440, SAT-M between 350-480; ACT composite between 16-21. 68% submitted SAT scores, 14% submitted ACT scores. **Characteristics:** 97% from in state, 99% commute, 13% have minority backgrounds, 1% are foreign students, 1% join fraternities/sororities. Average age is 22.

FALL-TERM APPLICATIONS. $25 fee, may be waived for applicants with need. Closing date June 15; applicants notified on a rolling basis. Interview required for allied health science applicants. Portfolio required for art applicants. Deferred admission available. Application deadlines for nursing and allied health programs range from October 15 to February 1.

STUDENT LIFE. Housing: Dormitories (coed); apartment, cooperative housing available. **Activities:** Student government, student newspaper, yearbook, literary magazine, choral groups, dance, drama, musical theater, pep band, fraternities, sororities.

ATHLETICS. NAIA. **Intercollegiate:** Baseball M, basketball, softball W, tennis M, volleyball W. **Intramural:** Badminton, baseball M, basketball, cross-country, diving, football M, golf, racquetball, soccer, softball, swimming, table tennis, tennis, track and field, volleyball, water polo.

STUDENT SERVICES. Aptitude testing, career counseling, employment service for undergraduates, freshman orientation, health services, on-campus day care, personal counseling, placement service for graduates, special adviser for adult students, veterans counselor, services/facilities for handicapped.

ANNUAL EXPENSES. Tuition and fees (1992-93): $2,611, $4,863 additional for out-of-state students. **Room and board:** $2,925. **Books and supplies:** $528. **Other expenses:** $1,359.

FINANCIAL AID. 65% of freshmen, 60% of continuing students receive some form of aid. 98% of grants, 86% of loans, all jobs based on need. Academic, art, athletic scholarships available. **Aid applications:** Closing date March 1; applicants notified on or about May 1; must reply within 2 weeks.

ADDRESS/TELEPHONE. Dr. Alan N. Crist, Director of Admissions, Indiana University—Purdue University at Indianapolis, Cavanaugh Hall, Room 129, 425 University Boulevard, Indianapolis, IN 46202-5143. (317) 274-4591.

Indiana Vocational Technical College: Central Indiana

Indianapolis, Indiana CB code: 1311

2-year public technical college, coed. Founded in 1966. **Accreditation:** Regional. **Undergraduate enrollment:** 569 men, 1,049 women full time; 1,882 men, 2,280 women part time. **Faculty:** 363 total (115 full time), 11 with doctorates or other terminal degrees. **Location:** Urban campus in very large city; in downtown area. **Calendar:** Semester. **Microcomputers:** 120 located in computer centers.

DEGREES OFFERED. AAS. 274 associate degrees awarded in 1992. 12% in business and management, 8% business/office and marketing/distribution, 12% computer sciences, 12% engineering technologies, 24% allied health, 7% law, 23% trade and industry.

UNDERGRADUATE MAJORS. Accounting, air conditioning/heating/refrigeration mechanics, automotive mechanics, computer programming, drafting, drafting and design technology, electronic technology, fire control and safety technology, food production/management/services, health care administration, hotel/motel and restaurant management, industrial equipment maintenance and repair, industrial laboratory technology, information sciences and systems, legal assistant/paralegal, marketing and distribution, medical assistant, mental health/human services, nursing, radiograph medical technology, respiratory therapy technology, robotics, secretarial and related programs, small business management and ownership, trade and industrial supervision and management.

ACADEMIC PROGRAMS. 2-year transfer program, cooperative education, internships, weekend college. **Remedial services:** Reduced course load, special counselor, tutoring, developmental classes. **Placement/credit:** Institutional tests.

ACADEMIC REQUIREMENTS. Freshmen must earn minimum GPA of 2.0 to continue in good standing. 70% of freshmen return for sophomore year. **Graduation requirements:** 65 hours for associate. Most students required to take courses in English, mathematics, social sciences.

FRESHMAN ADMISSIONS. Selection criteria: Open admissions. Selective admissions to health programs.

1992 FRESHMAN CLASS PROFILE. 390 men, 535 women enrolled. **Characteristics:** 100% commute, 30% have minority backgrounds. Average age is 29.

FALL-TERM APPLICATIONS. No fee. No closing date; applicants notified on a rolling basis. Deferred admission available.

STUDENT LIFE. Activities: Student government, radio, Phi Theta Kappa, human services club, National Issues Forum, paralegal club, radio club, secretarial club.

STUDENT SERVICES. Aptitude testing, career counseling, employment service for undergraduates, freshman orientation, on-campus day care, personal counseling, placement service for graduates, veterans counselor, services/facilities for handicapped.

ANNUAL EXPENSES. Tuition and fees (1992-93): $1,509, $1,236 additional for out-of-state students. **Books and supplies:** $484. **Other expenses:** $1,340.

FINANCIAL AID. 25% of freshmen, 54% of continuing students receive some form of aid. All grants, 68% of loans, all jobs based on need. Academic scholarships available. **Aid applications:** No closing date; priority given to applications received by March 1; applicants notified on a rolling basis.

ADDRESS/TELEPHONE. Sonia Dickerson, Enrollment Manager, Indiana Vocational Technical College: Central Indiana, PO Box 1763, One West 26th Street, Indianapolis, IN 46206-1763. (317) 921-4800.

Indiana Vocational Technical College: Columbus

Columbus, Indiana CB code: 1286

2-year public technical college, coed. Founded in 1963. **Accreditation:** Regional. **Undergraduate enrollment:** 290 men, 608 women full time; 779 men, 939 women part time. **Faculty:** 198 total (51 full time). **Location:** Urban campus in large town; 40 miles from Indianapolis. **Calendar:** Semester, extensive summer session. **Microcomputers:** Located in libraries, classrooms, computer centers. **Special facilities:** Graphic design and commercial photography gallery.

DEGREES OFFERED. AAS. 155 associate degrees awarded in 1992. 23% in business and management, 12% business/office and marketing/distribution, 5% communications, 22% computer sciences, 25% engineering technologies, 10% visual and performing arts.

UNDERGRADUATE MAJORS. Accounting, air conditioning/heating/refrigeration mechanics, automotive mechanics, computer programming, drafting, drafting and design technology, electronic technology, graphic design, information sciences and systems, nursing, photographic technology, quality control technology, robotics, secretarial and related programs, small business management and ownership.

ACADEMIC PROGRAMS. 2-year transfer program, internships. **Remedial services:** Learning center, reduced course load, remedial instruction, special counselor, tutoring. **Placement/credit:** Institutional tests.

ACADEMIC REQUIREMENTS. Freshmen must earn minimum GPA of 2.0 to continue in good standing. 74% of freshmen return for sophomore year. Students must declare major on enrollment. **Graduation requirements:** 60 hours for associate. Most students required to take courses in English, mathematics.

FRESHMAN ADMISSIONS. Selection criteria: Open admissions. Selective admissions to health programs.

1992 FRESHMAN CLASS PROFILE. 220 men, 374 women enrolled. **Characteristics:** 1% from in state, 100% commute, 3% have minority backgrounds. Average age is 26.

FALL-TERM APPLICATIONS. No fee. No closing date; applicants notified on a rolling basis. Interview recommended for health occupations applicants. Portfolio recommended for graphic design applicants.

STUDENT LIFE. Activities: Student government, Phi Theta Kappa.

ATHLETICS. Intramural: Softball, volleyball.

STUDENT SERVICES. Aptitude testing, career counseling, employment service for undergraduates, freshman orientation, on-campus day care, personal counseling, placement service for graduates, special adviser for adult students, veterans counselor, services/facilities for handicapped.

ANNUAL EXPENSES. Tuition and fees (1992-93): $1,509, $1,236 additional for out-of-state students. **Books and supplies:** $484. **Other expenses:** $1,340.

FINANCIAL AID. 60% of freshmen, 60% of continuing students receive some form of aid. All grants, 84% of loans, all jobs based on need. Academic scholarships available. **Aid applications:** No closing date; priority given to applications received by March 1; applicants notified on a rolling basis beginning on or about July 1; must reply within 3 weeks.

ADDRESS/TELEPHONE. Lucinda J. Casey, Director of Student Services, Indiana Vocational Technical College: Columbus, 4475 Central Avenue, Columbus, IN 47203. (812) 372-9925.

Indiana Vocational Technical College: Eastcentral

Muncie, Indiana CB code: 1279

2-year public technical college, coed. Founded in 1968. **Accreditation:** Regional. **Undergraduate enrollment:** 378 men, 698 women full time; 550 men, 689 women part time. **Faculty:** 169 total (46 full time), 1 with doctorate or other terminal degree. **Location:** Suburban campus in small city; 50 miles from Indianapolis. **Calendar:** Semester, extensive summer session. **Microcomputers:** Located in computer centers.

DEGREES OFFERED. AAS. 139 associate degrees awarded in 1992. 7% in business and management, 9% business/office and marketing/distribution, 25% computer sciences, 11% engineering technologies, 24% allied health, 24% trade and industry.

UNDERGRADUATE MAJORS. Accounting, air conditioning/heating/refrigeration mechanics, automotive mechanics, child development/care/guidance, computer programming, construction, drafting, electronic technology, industrial equipment maintenance and repair, information sciences and systems, machine tool operation/machine shop, marketing and distribution, medical assistant, mental health/human services, robotics, secretarial and related programs, small business management and ownership, trade and industrial supervision and management.

ACADEMIC PROGRAMS. Dual enrollment of high school students, internships. **Remedial services:** Learning center, remedial instruction, special counselor, tutoring. **Placement/credit:** Institutional tests.

ACADEMIC REQUIREMENTS. No policy requiring minimum GPA; records of students having academic difficulty are reviewed individually. 70% of freshmen return for sophomore year. Students must declare major on application. **Graduation requirements:** 65 hours for associate. Most students required to take courses in English, humanities, mathematics.

FRESHMAN ADMISSIONS. Selection criteria: Open admissions.

1992 FRESHMAN CLASS PROFILE. 268 men, 459 women enrolled. **Characteristics:** 100% from in state, 100% commute, 9% have minority backgrounds. Average age is 28.

FALL-TERM APPLICATIONS. No fee. No closing date; applicants notified on a rolling basis. Deferred and early admission available.

STUDENT LIFE. Activities: Student government, Phi Theta Kappa.

STUDENT SERVICES. Aptitude testing, career counseling, employment service for undergraduates, freshman orientation, personal counseling, placement service for graduates, veterans counselor, services/facilities for handicapped.

ANNUAL EXPENSES. Tuition and fees (projected): $1,509, $1,236 additional for out-of-state students. **Books and supplies:** $515. **Other expenses:** $1,236.

FINANCIAL AID. 35% of freshmen, 68% of continuing students receive some form of aid. All aid based on need. **Aid applications:** No closing date; priority given to applications received by March 1; applicants notified on a rolling basis beginning on or about August 22. **Additional information:** HEA, CDV, IVTC scholarships and grants, vocational rehabilitation and veteran's assistance are available. None require repayment.

ADDRESS/TELEPHONE. Student Services, Indiana Vocational Technical College: Eastcentral, PO Box 3100, 4301 Cowan Road, Muncie, IN 47307. (317) 289-2291. Fax: (317) 289-2291 ext. 502.

Indiana Vocational Technical College: Kokomo

Kokomo, Indiana — CB code: 1329

2-year public technical college, coed. Founded in 1968. **Accreditation:** Regional. **Undergraduate enrollment:** 187 men, 335 women full time; 563 men, 655 women part time. **Faculty:** 125 total (30 full time). **Location:** Suburban campus in small city; 50 miles from Indianapolis. **Calendar:** Semester, extensive summer session. **Microcomputers:** 350 located in libraries, classrooms, computer centers. **Additional facts:** Branch location at Logansport.

DEGREES OFFERED. AAS. 106 associate degrees awarded in 1992. 19% in business and management, 8% business/office and marketing/distribution, 29% computer sciences, 11% engineering technologies, 8% allied health, 21% trade and industry.

UNDERGRADUATE MAJORS. Accounting, air conditioning/heating/refrigeration mechanics, automotive mechanics, computer programming, construction, drafting, drafting and design technology, electronic technology, industrial equipment maintenance and repair, information sciences and systems, interior design, machine tool operation/machine shop, marketing and distribution, medical assistant, quality control technology, robotics, secretarial and related programs.

ACADEMIC PROGRAMS. Dual enrollment of high school students, independent study, internships, weekend college. **Remedial services:** Learning center, reduced course load, remedial instruction, special counselor, tutoring. **Placement/credit:** Institutional tests.

ACADEMIC REQUIREMENTS. Freshmen must earn minimum GPA of 2.0 to continue in good standing. 50% of freshmen return for sophomore year. Students must declare major on application. **Graduation requirements:** 65 hours for associate. Most students required to take courses in English, mathematics, biological/physical sciences.

FRESHMAN ADMISSIONS. Selection criteria: Open admissions. Selective admissions to medical assistant program.

1992 FRESHMAN CLASS PROFILE. 183 men, 334 women enrolled. **Characteristics:** 100% from in state, 100% commute, 8% have minority backgrounds. Average age is 25.

FALL-TERM APPLICATIONS. No fee. No closing date; priority given to applications received by August 1; applicants notified on a rolling basis. Deferred admission available.

STUDENT LIFE. Activities: Student government, Phi Theta Kappa.

STUDENT SERVICES. Aptitude testing, career counseling, employment service for undergraduates, freshman orientation, personal counseling, placement service for graduates, veterans counselor, services/facilities for handicapped.

ANNUAL EXPENSES. Tuition and fees (1992-93): $1,509, $1,236 additional for out-of-state students. **Books and supplies:** $484. **Other expenses:** $1,340.

FINANCIAL AID. 45% of freshmen, 81% of continuing students receive some form of aid. All grants, 94% of loans, all jobs based on need. Academic, state/district residency, leadership, minority scholarships available. **Aid applications:** No closing date; priority given to applications received by March 1; applicants notified on a rolling basis beginning on or about February 1; must reply within 4 weeks.

ADDRESS/TELEPHONE. Jane Wilson, Enrollment Manager, Indiana Vocational Technical College: Kokomo, 1815 East Morgan Street, P.O. Box 1373, Kokomo, IN 46903-1373. (317) 459-0561. Fax: (317) 454-5111.

Indiana Vocational Technical College: Lafayette

Lafayette, Indiana — CB code: 1282

2-year public technical college, coed. Founded in 1968. **Accreditation:** Regional. **Undergraduate enrollment:** 190 men, 381 women full time; 526 men, 736 women part time. **Faculty:** 128 total (40 full time), 2 with doctorates or other terminal degrees. **Location:** Suburban campus in small city; 60 miles from Indianapolis. **Calendar:** Semester, extensive summer session. **Microcomputers:** Located in classrooms, computer centers. **Special facilities:** Multimedia laboratory.

DEGREES OFFERED. AS, AAS. 110 associate degrees awarded in 1992. 20% in business and management, 15% business/office and marketing/distribution, 13% computer sciences, 24% engineering technologies, 18% health sciences, 10% trade and industry.

UNDERGRADUATE MAJORS. Accounting, air conditioning/heating/refrigeration mechanics, automotive mechanics, computer programming, drafting, drafting and design technology, electrical and electronics equipment repair, electronic technology, industrial equipment maintenance and repair, machine tool operation/machine shop, marketing and distribution, nursing, robotics, secretarial and related programs, small business management and ownership, trade and industrial supervision and management.

ACADEMIC PROGRAMS. 2-year transfer program, double major, dual enrollment of high school students, internships, cross-registration. **Remedial services:** Learning center, reduced course load, remedial instruction, special counselor, tutoring. **Placement/credit:** Institutional tests.

ACADEMIC REQUIREMENTS. Freshmen must earn minimum GPA of 2.0 to continue in good standing. 45% of freshmen return for sophomore year. Students must declare major on application. **Graduation requirements:** 70 hours for associate. Most students required to take courses in English, mathematics.

FRESHMAN ADMISSIONS. Selection criteria: Open admissions. Limited enrollment to health programs.

1992 FRESHMAN CLASS PROFILE. 143 men, 239 women enrolled. 35% had high school GPA of 3.0 or higher, 50% between 2.0 and 2.99. **Characteristics:** 100% from in state, 100% commute, 3% have minority backgrounds. Average age is 25.

FALL-TERM APPLICATIONS. No fee. No closing date; applicants notified on a rolling basis. Interview required for allied health applicants.

STUDENT LIFE. Activities: Student government, student newspaper, Phi Theta Kappa.

STUDENT SERVICES. Aptitude testing, career counseling, employment service for undergraduates, freshman orientation, personal counseling, placement service for graduates, special adviser for adult students, veterans counselor, adult re-entry outreach coordinator, services/facilities for handicapped.

ANNUAL EXPENSES. Tuition and fees (1992-93): $1,509, $1,236 additional for out-of-state students. **Books and supplies:** $484. **Other expenses:** $1,340.

FINANCIAL AID. 64% of freshmen, 51% of continuing students receive some form of aid. All grants, 80% of loans, all jobs based on need. Academic scholarships available. **Aid applications:** No closing date; priority given to applications received by March 1; applicants notified on a rolling basis beginning on or about July 1.

ADDRESS/TELEPHONE. James S. Jovanovic, Admissions Manger, Indiana Vocational Technical College: Lafayette, PO Box 6299, Lafayette, IN 47903. (317) 477-9100. Fax: (317) 477-9214.

Indiana Vocational Technical College: Northcentral

South Bend, Indiana — CB code: 1280

2-year public technical college, coed. Founded in 1967. **Accreditation:** Regional. **Undergraduate enrollment:** 254 men, 445 women full time; 920 men, 1,070 women part time. **Faculty:** 219 total (57 full time), 1 with doctorate or other terminal degree. **Location:** Urban campus in small city; 100 miles from Chicago. **Calendar:** Semester, extensive summer session. **Microcomputers:** 70 located in classrooms, computer centers. **Additional facts:** Off-campus sites at Warsaw and Elkhart. Distance learning through computer.

DEGREES OFFERED. AS, AAS. 142 associate degrees awarded in 1992. 5% in architecture and environmental design, 15% business and management, 6% business/office and marketing/distribution, 22% computer sciences, 14% engineering technologies, 13% health sciences, 17% trade and industry, 10% visual and performing arts.

UNDERGRADUATE MAJORS. Accounting, air conditioning/heating/refrigeration mechanics, automotive mechanics, communications, computer programming, drafting, drafting and design technology, electronic technology, graphic arts technology, graphic design, industrial equipment maintenance and repair, information sciences and systems, interior design, machine tool operation/machine shop, marketing and distribution, medical assistant, medical laboratory technologies, nursing, photographic technology, photography, plastic technology, radio/television technology, robotics, secretarial and related programs, small business management and ownership, trade and industrial supervision and management, video.

ACADEMIC PROGRAMS. 2-year transfer program, computer delivered (on-line) credit-bearing course offerings, dual enrollment of high school students, internships, telecourses, cross-registration. **Remedial services:** Learning center, reduced course load, remedial instruction, special counselor, tutoring. **Placement/credit:** Institutional tests.

ACADEMIC REQUIREMENTS. Freshmen must earn minimum GPA of 2.0 to continue in good standing. 50% of freshmen return for sophomore year. Students must declare major on enrollment. **Graduation requirements:** 65 hours for associate (51 in major). Most students required to take courses in English, social sciences. **Additional information:** Our industrial training division offers customized courses and seminars to companies and corporations in the surrounding community.

FRESHMAN ADMISSIONS. Selection criteria: Open admissions. Selective admission to allied health programs. Medical laboratory assistant program requires 1 chemistry and 1 algebra. **Test requirements:** Comparative Guidance and Placement Program required for admission of allied health applicants. MAPS test administered to all degree seeking students.

1992 FRESHMAN CLASS PROFILE. 211 men, 326 women enrolled. **Characteristics:** 99% from in state, 100% commute, 11% have minority backgrounds.

FALL-TERM APPLICATIONS. No fee. No closing date; applicants notified on a rolling basis beginning on or about April 1. Interview required for allied health applicants. Portfolio recommended for photographic technology, graphic arts technology applicants. Early admission available. Health occupations applicants should complete application requirements 3 months prior to enrollment date.

STUDENT LIFE. Activities: Student government, Phi Theta Kappa.

STUDENT SERVICES. Aptitude testing, career counseling, employment service for undergraduates, freshman orientation, personal counseling, placement service for graduates, veterans counselor, counselor for disabled students, services/facilities for handicapped.

ANNUAL EXPENSES. Tuition and fees (1992-93): $1,509, $1,236 additional for out-of-state students. **Books and supplies:** $484. **Other expenses:** $1,340.

FINANCIAL AID. 45% of continuing students receive some form of aid. All grants, 79% of loans, all jobs based on need. Academic, state/district residency scholarships available. **Aid applications:** No closing date; priority given to applications received by March 1; applicants notified on a rolling basis; must reply immediately.

ADDRESS/TELEPHONE. Larry C. Bartek, Director of Student Services, Indiana Vocational Technical College: Northcentral, 1534 West Sample Street, South Bend, IN 46619. (219) 289-7001.

Indiana Vocational Technical College: Northeast
Fort Wayne, Indiana CB code: 1278

2-year public technical college, coed. Founded in 1963. **Accreditation:** Regional. **Undergraduate enrollment:** 337 men, 1,433 women full time; 683 men, 1,749 women part time. **Faculty:** 290 total (58 full time), 2 with doctorates or other terminal degrees. **Location:** Urban campus in small city; 120 miles from Indianapolis. **Calendar:** Semester, extensive summer session. **Microcomputers:** Located in computer centers.

DEGREES OFFERED. AAS. 196 associate degrees awarded in 1992. 9% in business and management, 11% business/office and marketing/distribution, 13% computer sciences, 33% engineering technologies, 14% allied health, 17% trade and industry.

UNDERGRADUATE MAJORS. Accounting, air conditioning/heating/refrigeration mechanics, automotive mechanics, child development/care/guidance, computer programming, construction, drafting, drafting and design technology, electronic technology, fire control and safety technology, food production/management/services, industrial equipment maintenance and repair, information sciences and systems, machine tool operation/machine shop, marketing and distribution, medical assistant, quality control technology, respiratory therapy technology, robotics, secretarial and related programs, small business management and ownership, trade and industrial supervision and management.

ACADEMIC PROGRAMS. Dual enrollment of high school students, internships, student-designed major, telecourses. **Remedial services:** Learning center, reduced course load, remedial instruction, special counselor. **Placement/credit:** Institutional tests.

ACADEMIC REQUIREMENTS. Freshmen must earn minimum GPA of 2.0 to continue in good standing. 30% of freshmen return for sophomore year. Students must declare major on application. **Graduation requirements:** 65 hours for associate. Most students required to take courses in English, mathematics, social sciences.

FRESHMAN ADMISSIONS. Selection criteria: Open admissions.

1992 FRESHMAN CLASS PROFILE. 261 men, 507 women enrolled. **Characteristics:** 100% commute, 14% have minority backgrounds.

FALL-TERM APPLICATIONS. No fee. No closing date; applicants notified on a rolling basis. Deferred admission available.

STUDENT LIFE. Activities: Student government, accounting club, Phi Theta Kappa.

STUDENT SERVICES. Aptitude testing, career counseling, employment service for undergraduates, freshman orientation, on-campus day care, personal counseling, placement service for graduates, veterans counselor.

ANNUAL EXPENSES. Tuition and fees (projected): $1,610, $1,380 additional for out-of-state students. **Books and supplies:** $515. **Other expenses:** $2,800.

FINANCIAL AID. 56% of freshmen, 62% of continuing students receive some form of aid. All grants, 96% of loans, all jobs based on need. Academic, leadership, minority scholarships available. **Aid applications:** No closing date; priority given to applications received by March 1; applicants notified on a rolling basis beginning on or about June 1.

ADDRESS/TELEPHONE. Jim Aschliman, Admissions Coordinator, Indiana Vocational Technical College: Northeast, 3800 North Anthony Boulevard, Fort Wayne, IN 46805. (219) 482-9171.

Indiana Vocational Technical College: Northwest
Gary, Indiana CB code: 1281

2-year public technical college, coed. Founded in 1968. **Accreditation:** Regional. **Undergraduate enrollment:** 410 men, 635 women full time; 802 men, 657 women part time. **Faculty:** 213 total (76 full time), 3 with doctorates or other terminal degrees. **Location:** Urban campus in small city; 30 miles from Chicago. **Calendar:** Semester. **Microcomputers:** 150 located in libraries, classrooms, computer centers. **Additional facts:** Campuses also at Hammond and Valparaiso

DEGREES OFFERED. AS, AAS. 160 associate degrees awarded in 1992. 16% in business and management, 24% business/office and marketing/distribution, 13% computer sciences, 14% engineering technologies, 31% trade and industry.

UNDERGRADUATE MAJORS. Accounting, air conditioning/heating/refrigeration mechanics, automotive mechanics, computer programming, drafting, drafting and design technology, electronic technology, fire control and safety technology, food production/management/services, industrial equipment maintenance and repair, information sciences and systems, machine tool operation/machine shop, manufacturing technology, marketing and distribution, medical assistant, respiratory therapy technology, robotics, secretarial and related programs, small business management and ownership, trade and industrial supervision and management, water and wastewater technology.

ACADEMIC PROGRAMS. 2-year transfer program, double major, dual enrollment of high school students, internships, weekend college. **Remedial services:** Learning center, reduced course load, remedial instruction, special counselor, tutoring. **Placement/credit:** Institutional tests; 75 credit hours maximum for associate degree.

ACADEMIC REQUIREMENTS. Freshmen must earn minimum GPA of 2.0 to continue in good standing. 40% of freshmen return for sophomore year. Students must declare major on enrollment. **Graduation requirements:** 64 hours for associate. Most students required to take courses in English, mathematics.

FRESHMAN ADMISSIONS. Selection criteria: Open admissions. Selective admissions for human services and health technology programs based on test scores, interview, recommendations, and essay.

1992 FRESHMAN CLASS PROFILE. 349 men, 425 women enrolled. **Characteristics:** 100% commute, 45% have minority backgrounds.

FALL-TERM APPLICATIONS. No fee. No closing date; applicants notified on a rolling basis.

STUDENT LIFE. Activities: Student government, Phi Theta Kappa.

ATHLETICS. Intramural: Basketball M, bowling, softball M.

STUDENT SERVICES. Career counseling, employment service for undergraduates, freshman orientation, personal counseling, placement service for graduates, veterans counselor, services/facilities for handicapped.

ANNUAL EXPENSES. Tuition and fees (1992-93): $1,509, $1,236 additional for out-of-state students. **Books and supplies:** $484. **Other expenses:** $1,340.

FINANCIAL AID. 89% of continuing students receive some form of aid. All grants, 93% of loans, all jobs based on need. **Aid applications:** No closing date; applicants notified on a rolling basis.

ADDRESS/TELEPHONE. Ramona Calhoun, Manager of Student Services/Financial Aid, Indiana Vocational Technical College: Northwest, 1440 East 35th Avenue, Gary, IN 46409-1499. (219) 981-1111.

Indiana Vocational Technical College: Southcentral
Sellersburg, Indiana CB code: 1273

2-year public technical college, coed. Founded in 1968. **Accreditation:** Regional. **Undergraduate enrollment:** 241 men, 526 women full time; 623 men, 704 women part time. **Faculty:** 124 total (36 full time). **Location:** Suburban campus in small town; 10 miles from Louisville, Kentucky. **Calendar:** Semester, extensive summer session. **Microcomputers:** 73 located in classrooms, computer centers.

DEGREES OFFERED. AAS. 81 associate degrees awarded in 1992. 26% in business and management, 9% business/office and marketing/distribution, 11% computer sciences, 15% engineering technologies, 34% trade and industry.

UNDERGRADUATE MAJORS. Accounting, air conditioning/heating/refrigeration mechanics, automotive mechanics, computer and information sciences, computer programming, construction, electronic technology, graphic arts technology, industrial equipment maintenance and repair, information sciences and systems, medical assistant, nursing, robotics, secretarial and related programs, small business management and ownership, welding technology.

ACADEMIC PROGRAMS. 2-year transfer program, accelerated program, cooperative education, double major, internships. **Remedial services:** Learning center, preadmission summer program, reduced course load, remedial instruction, special counselor, tutoring. **Placement/credit:** Institutional tests; 45 credit hours maximum for associate degree.

ACADEMIC REQUIREMENTS. Freshmen must earn minimum GPA of 2.0 to continue in good standing. 75% of freshmen return for sophomore year. Students must declare major on enrollment. **Graduation requirements:** 64 hours for associate. Most students required to take courses in computer science, English, mathematics, biological/physical sciences.

FRESHMAN ADMISSIONS. Selection criteria: Open admissions. Selective admissions to licensed practical nursing program.

1992 FRESHMAN CLASS PROFILE. 212 men, 427 women enrolled. **Characteristics:** 100% commute, 5% have minority backgrounds. Average age is 27.

FALL-TERM APPLICATIONS. No fee. No closing date; applicants notified on a rolling basis. Deferred and early admission available. MAPS test recommended for all programs.

STUDENT LIFE. Activities: Student government, Phi Theta Kappa.

STUDENT SERVICES. Aptitude testing, career counseling, employment service for undergraduates, freshman orientation, personal counseling, placement service for graduates, veterans counselor, services/facilities for handicapped.

ANNUAL EXPENSES. Tuition and fees (projected): $1,674, $1,371 additional for out-of-state students. **Books and supplies:** $515. **Other expenses:** $1,975.

FINANCIAL AID. 70% of freshmen, 68% of continuing students receive some form of aid. 96% of grants, 88% of loans, all jobs based on need. **Aid applications:** No closing date; priority given to applications received by March 1; applicants notified on a rolling basis beginning on or about August 1.

ADDRESS/TELEPHONE. Randy Emily, Admissions Coordinator, Indiana Vocational Technical College: Southcentral, 8204 Highway 31 West, Sellersburg, IN 47172. (812) 246-3301.

Indiana Vocational Technical College: Southeast

Madison, Indiana CB code: 1334

2-year public technical college, coed. Founded in 1968. **Accreditation:** Regional. **Undergraduate enrollment:** 78 men, 266 women full time; 179 men, 431 women part time. **Faculty:** 91 total (35 full time), 1 with doctorate or other terminal degree. **Location:** Suburban campus in large town; 46 miles from Columbus, Indiana, 88 miles from Indianapolis. **Calendar:** Semester, extensive summer session. **Microcomputers:** Located in computer centers.

DEGREES OFFERED. AS, AAS. 66 associate degrees awarded in 1992. 15% in business and management, 8% business/office and marketing/distribution, 29% computer sciences, 15% engineering technologies, 32% health sciences.

UNDERGRADUATE MAJORS. Accounting, automotive mechanics, business administration and management, computer programming, electronic technology, information sciences and systems, nursing, robotics, secretarial and related programs, small business management and ownership.

ACADEMIC PROGRAMS. 2-year transfer program, dual enrollment of high school students, internships, weekend college. **Remedial services:** Learning center, remedial instruction. **Placement/credit:** Institutional tests.

ACADEMIC REQUIREMENTS. Freshmen must earn minimum GPA of 2.0 to continue in good standing. 74% of freshmen return for sophomore year. Students must declare major on enrollment. **Graduation requirements:** 64 hours for associate. Most students required to take courses in English, mathematics, social sciences.

FRESHMAN ADMISSIONS. Selection criteria: Open admissions. Selective admission to nursing program.

1992 FRESHMAN CLASS PROFILE. 64 men, 143 women enrolled. **Characteristics:** 100% commute, 1% have minority backgrounds. Average age is 25.

FALL-TERM APPLICATIONS. No fee. No closing date; applicants notified on a rolling basis beginning on or about July 1; must reply within 4 weeks.

STUDENT LIFE. Activities: Student government, Phi Theta Kappa.

ATHLETICS. Intramural: Basketball M, bowling, softball, table tennis, volleyball.

STUDENT SERVICES. Aptitude testing, career counseling, personal counseling, placement service for graduates, veterans counselor, services/facilities for handicapped.

ANNUAL EXPENSES. Tuition and fees (1992-93): $1,509, $1,236 additional for out-of-state students. **Books and supplies:** $484. **Other expenses:** $1,340.

FINANCIAL AID. 66% of freshmen, 75% of continuing students receive some form of aid. All grants, 96% of loans, all jobs based on need. **Aid applications:** No closing date; priority given to applications received by March 1; applicants notified on a rolling basis beginning on or about July 1; must reply within 4 weeks.

ADDRESS/TELEPHONE. Donald L. Heiderman, Director of Student Services, Indiana Vocational Technical College: Southeast, 590 Ivy Tech Drive, Madison, IN 47250. (812) 265-2580.

Indiana Vocational Technical College: Southwest

Evansville, Indiana CB code: 1277

2-year public technical college, coed. Founded in 1968. **Accreditation:** Regional. **Undergraduate enrollment:** 388 men, 528 women full time; 830 men, 1,015 women part time. **Faculty:** 185 total (50 full time). **Location:** Urban campus in small city; 100 miles from Terre Haute. **Calendar:** Semester, extensive summer session. **Microcomputers:** Located in libraries, classrooms, computer centers.

DEGREES OFFERED. AS, AAS. 170 associate degrees awarded in 1992. 12% in business and management, 12% business/office and marketing/distribution, 5% communications, 10% engineering technologies, 23% health sciences, 5% allied health, 24% trade and industry, 5% visual and performing arts.

UNDERGRADUATE MAJORS. Accounting, air conditioning/heating/refrigeration mechanics, automotive mechanics, computer programming, drafting, drafting and design technology, electronic technology, graphic arts technology, industrial equipment maintenance and repair, information sciences and systems, interior design, marketing and distribution, medical assistant, nursing, photographic technology, plastic technology, robotics, secretarial and related programs, small business management and ownership, trade and industrial supervision and management.

ACADEMIC PROGRAMS. 2-year transfer program, cooperative education, double major, independent study, internships, cross-registration. **Remedial services:** Learning center, preadmission summer program, reduced course load, remedial instruction, special counselor, tutoring. **Placement/credit:** Institutional tests; 15 credit hours maximum for associate degree.

ACADEMIC REQUIREMENTS. Freshmen must earn minimum GPA of 2.0 to continue in good standing. 72% of freshmen return for sophomore year. Students must declare major on enrollment. **Graduation requirements:** 65 hours for associate. Most students required to take courses in English, mathematics.

FRESHMAN ADMISSIONS. Selection criteria: Open admissions. Selective admissions to certain programs. Degree-seeking students strongly directed to take MAPS.

1992 FRESHMAN CLASS PROFILE. 336 men, 468 women enrolled. **Characteristics:** 100% commute, 8% have minority backgrounds.

FALL-TERM APPLICATIONS. No fee. No closing date; priority given to applications received by June 1; applicants notified on a rolling basis beginning on or about August 20. Interview required for medical assistant, practical nursing, surgical technician, nursing applicants. CRDA. Deferred and early admission available.

STUDENT LIFE. Housing: Housing available at University of Southern Indiana. **Activities:** Student government, Phi Theta Kappa.

ATHLETICS. Intramural: Softball.

STUDENT SERVICES. Career counseling, employment service for undergraduates, freshman orientation, on-campus day care, personal counseling, placement service for graduates, veterans counselor, services/facilities for handicapped.

ANNUAL EXPENSES. Tuition and fees (projected): $1,674, $1,371 additional for out-of-state students. **Books and supplies:** $515. **Other expenses:** $1,109.

FINANCIAL AID. 65% of freshmen, 65% of continuing students receive some form of aid. 95% of grants, 78% of loans, all jobs based on need. 1,470 enrolled freshmen were judged to have need, 1,400 were offered aid. Academic, state/district residency, leadership, minority scholarships available. **Aid applications:** No closing date; priority given to applications received by August 31; applicants notified on a rolling basis beginning on or about June 1; must reply by registration.

ADDRESS/TELEPHONE. Philip A. Hesson, Enrollment Services Manager, Indiana Vocational Technical College: Southwest, 3501 First Avenue, Evansville, IN 47710. (812) 426-2865.

Indiana Vocational Technical College: Wabash Valley
Terre Haute, Indiana CB code: 1284

2-year public technical college, coed. Founded in 1966. **Accreditation:** Regional. **Undergraduate enrollment:** 456 men, 652 women full time; 511 men, 691 women part time. **Faculty:** 181 total (59 full time). **Location:** Urban campus in small city; 80 miles from Indianapolis. **Calendar:** Semester, extensive summer session. **Microcomputers:** Located in libraries, classrooms, computer centers. **Special facilities:** Plastics productivity center, advanced technology center. **Additional facts:** Extension centers at Bloomfield, Greencastle, Hyte Community Center, North Central High School, Rockville, South Vermillion, and Sullivan.

DEGREES OFFERED. AS, AAS. 179 associate degrees awarded in 1992. 16% in business and management, 7% business/office and marketing/distribution, 12% computer sciences, 13% engineering technologies, 17% allied health, 32% trade and industry.

UNDERGRADUATE MAJORS. Accounting, automotive mechanics, computer programming, drafting, drafting and design technology, electronic technology, graphic and printing production, industrial equipment maintenance and repair, industrial laboratory technology, information sciences and systems, marketing and distribution, medical assistant, medical laboratory technologies, mining and petroleum technologies, plastic technology, quality control technology, radiograph medical technology, robotics, secretarial and related programs, small business management and ownership.

ACADEMIC PROGRAMS. 2-year transfer program, double major, dual enrollment of high school students, internships. **Remedial services:** Learning center, preadmission summer program, reduced course load, remedial instruction, special counselor, tutoring. **Placement/credit:** Institutional tests.

ACADEMIC REQUIREMENTS. Freshmen must earn minimum GPA of 2.0 to continue in good standing. 66% of freshmen return for sophomore year. Students must declare major on enrollment. **Graduation requirements:** 62 hours for associate. Most students required to take courses in computer science, English, mathematics.

FRESHMAN ADMISSIONS. Selection criteria: Open admissions. Selective admissions to allied health programs.

1992 FRESHMAN CLASS PROFILE. 325 men, 410 women enrolled. **Characteristics:** 100% commute, 12% have minority backgrounds. Average age is 24.

FALL-TERM APPLICATIONS. No fee. No closing date; applicants notified on a rolling basis. Interview required for health occupations applicants. Deferred and early admission available.

STUDENT LIFE. Activities: Student government, Phi Theta Kappa.

ATHLETICS. Intramural: Badminton, basketball, bowling, softball.

STUDENT SERVICES. Career counseling, employment service for undergraduates, freshman orientation, personal counseling, placement service for graduates, veterans counselor, minority outreach specialist, single parents/displaced homemaker project, services/facilities for handicapped.

ANNUAL EXPENSES. Tuition and fees (projected): $1,509, $1,236 additional for out-of-state students. **Books and supplies:** $515. **Other expenses:** $1,109.

FINANCIAL AID. 80% of freshmen, 56% of continuing students receive some form of aid. All grants, 99% of loans, all jobs based on need. **Aid applications:** No closing date; priority given to applications received by March 1; applicants notified on a rolling basis beginning on or about June 18; must reply immediately.

ADDRESS/TELEPHONE. Ron Maxwell, Director of Student Services, Indiana Vocational Technical College: Wabash Valley, 7999 US Highway 41 South, Terre Haute, IN 47802. (812) 299-1121 ext. 207. Fax: (812) 299-1121 ext. 325.

Indiana Vocational Technical College: Whitewater
Richmond, Indiana CB code: 1283

2-year public technical college, coed. Founded in 1968. **Accreditation:** Regional. **Undergraduate enrollment:** 112 men, 327 women full time; 321 men, 429 women part time. **Faculty:** 108 total (31 full time), 1 with doctorate or other terminal degree. **Location:** Suburban campus in large town; 70 miles from Indianapolis, 45 miles from Dayton, Ohio. **Calendar:** Semester, extensive summer session. **Microcomputers:** 80 located in classrooms, computer centers. **Special facilities:** Student operated restaurant. **Additional facts:** Library shared with Indiana University East.

DEGREES OFFERED. AS, AAS. 42 associate degrees awarded in 1992. 31% in business and management, 14% business/office and marketing/distribution, 26% computer sciences, 9% engineering technologies, 9% health sciences, 11% trade and industry.

UNDERGRADUATE MAJORS. Accounting, automotive mechanics, child development/care/guidance, computer programming, construction, electronic technology, industrial equipment maintenance and repair, information sciences and systems, machine tool operation/machine shop, medical assistant, nursing, robotics, secretarial and related programs, small business management and ownership.

ACADEMIC PROGRAMS. 2-year transfer program, dual enrollment of high school students, independent study, internships, weekend college. **Remedial services:** Learning center, preadmission summer program, reduced course load, remedial instruction, special counselor, tutoring, computer assisted instruction facility for remediation/PC work. **Placement/credit:** Institutional tests.

ACADEMIC REQUIREMENTS. Freshmen must earn minimum GPA of 2.0 to continue in good standing. 66% of freshmen return for sophomore year. Students must declare major on enrollment. **Graduation requirements:** 60 hours for associate. Most students required to take courses in English, mathematics, social sciences.

FRESHMAN ADMISSIONS. Selection criteria: Open admissions. Selective admissions for registered nursing and practical nursing. **Test requirements:** MAPS test required of applicants without high school diploma or GED.

1992 FRESHMAN CLASS PROFILE. 135 men, 256 women enrolled. **Characteristics:** 100% commute, 18% have minority backgrounds.

FALL-TERM APPLICATIONS. No fee. No closing date; applicants notified on a rolling basis. Deferred admission available.

STUDENT LIFE. Activities: Student government, student newspaper, business/computer club, accounting club, automotive service club, Phi Theta Kappa.

ATHLETICS. Intramural: Softball.

STUDENT SERVICES. Aptitude testing, career counseling, employment service for undergraduates, freshman orientation, personal counseling, placement service for graduates, veterans counselor, financial aid counseling, services/facilities for handicapped.

ANNUAL EXPENSES. Tuition and fees (projected): $1,675, $1,384 additional for out-of-state students. **Books and supplies:** $515.

FINANCIAL AID. 80% of freshmen, 81% of continuing students receive some form of aid. All aid based on need. **Aid applications:** No closing date; priority given to applications received by March 1; applicants notified on a rolling basis beginning on or about June 30; must reply within 3 weeks.

ADDRESS/TELEPHONE. Charles Tillman, Manager of Admissions and Placement, Indiana Vocational Technical College: Whitewater, PO Box 1145, 2325 Chester Boulevard, Richmond, IN 47374. (317) 966-2656. Fax: (317) 966-2656.

Indiana Wesleyan University
Marion, Indiana CB code: 1446

4-year private liberal arts college, coed, affiliated with Wesleyan Church. Founded in 1920. **Accreditation:** Regional. **Undergraduate enrollment:** 990 men, 1,144 women full time; 154 men, 294 women part time. **Graduate enrollment:** 527 men, 228 women full time; 30 men, 18 women part time. **Faculty:** 128 total (92 full time), 55 with doctorates or other terminal degrees. **Location:** Suburban campus in large town; 65 miles from Indianapolis. **Calendar:** 4-1-4, limited summer session. **Microcomputers:** Located in dormitories, classrooms, computer centers. **Special facilities:** History museum and nature preserve. **Additional facts:** Adult and professional studies division offers undergraduate business, nursing, and addictions counseling courses, as well as graduate education and business courses at Indianapolis, Fort Wayne, and other cities in central Indiana.

DEGREES OFFERED. AA, AS, BA, BS, MA, MS, MBA. 21 associate degrees awarded in 1992. 61% in business and management, 14% health sciences, 20% allied health, 5% multi/interdisciplinary studies. 570 bachelor's degrees awarded. 72% in business and management, 7% teacher education, 7% health sciences. Graduate degrees offered in 7 major fields of study.

UNDERGRADUATE MAJORS. Associate: Accounting, addictions counseling, Bible studies, business and management, business and office, business data processing and related programs, business data programming, law enforcement and corrections technologies, medical laboratory technologies, philosophy, religion, religious education. **Bachelor's:** Accounting, addictions counseling, art education, art history, Bible studies, biology, business administration and management, business and management, business economics, business education, chemistry, clinical laboratory science, communications, computer and information sciences, creative writing, criminal justice studies, criminology, economics, elementary education, English, English education, finance, history, junior high education, marketing management, mathematics, mathematics education, music, music education, music performance, nursing, parks and recreation management, philosophy, physical education, political science and government, predentistry, prelaw, premedicine, prepharmacy, preveterinary, psychology, religion, religious education, religious music, science education, secondary education, social sciences, social studies education, social work, sociology, Spanish, studio art, theological studies, writing.

ACADEMIC PROGRAMS. 2-year transfer program, double major, dual enrollment of high school students, honors program, independent study, internships, student-designed major, study abroad, teacher preparation, cross-registration; combined bachelor's/graduate program in business administration. **Remedial services:** Learning center, reduced course load, special counselor, tutoring. **Placement/credit:** AP, CLEP General and Subject, institutional tests.

ACADEMIC REQUIREMENTS. Freshmen must earn minimum GPA of 1.8 to continue in good standing. 70% of freshmen return for sophomore

year. Students must declare major by end of second year. **Graduation requirements:** 62 hours for associate (24 in major), 124 hours for bachelor's (40 in major). Most students required to take courses in arts/fine arts, English, foreign languages, history, humanities, mathematics, philosophy/religion, biological/physical sciences, social sciences.

FRESHMAN ADMISSIONS. Selection criteria: High school record, class rank and test scores. Recommendations required. **High school preparation:** 10 units recommended. Recommended college-preparatory subjects include English, science, social science, mathematics, and foreign language. **Test requirements:** SAT or ACT (SAT preferred); score report by September 1.

1992 FRESHMAN CLASS PROFILE. 180 men, 235 women enrolled. **Academic background:** Mid 50% of enrolled freshmen had SAT-V between 310-440, SAT-M between 330-510; ACT composite between 17-23. 56% submitted SAT scores, 37% submitted ACT scores. **Characteristics:** 60% from in state, 70% live in college housing, 10% have minority backgrounds. Average age is 20.

FALL-TERM APPLICATIONS. $15 fee, may be waived for applicants with need. Closing date September 1; applicants notified on a rolling basis. Interview recommended. Audition recommended for music applicants. Portfolio recommended for art applicants. Essay recommended for writing applicants. CRDA. Deferred and early admission available.

STUDENT LIFE. Housing: Dormitories (men, women); apartment, handicapped housing available. **Activities:** Student government, radio, student newspaper, television, yearbook, choral groups, concert band, drama, jazz band, music ensembles, pep band, Christian service teams, Student Missions Outreach, community outreach, international student organization, collegions for life, ministry director program. **Additional information:** Significant emphasis on leadership development and Christian service.

ATHLETICS. NAIA. **Intercollegiate:** Baseball M, basketball, cross-country, golf M, soccer, softball W, tennis, track and field, volleyball W. **Intramural:** Badminton, basketball, bowling, golf, racquetball, softball, table tennis, tennis, volleyball.

STUDENT SERVICES. Aptitude testing, career counseling, employment service for undergraduates, freshman orientation, health services, personal counseling, placement service for graduates, services/facilities for handicapped.

ANNUAL EXPENSES. Tuition and fees: $8,660. **Room and board:** $3,672. **Books and supplies:** $640. **Other expenses:** $528.

FINANCIAL AID. 82% of freshmen, 85% of continuing students receive some form of aid. 62% of grants, 85% of loans, 54% of jobs based on need. 286 enrolled freshmen were judged to have need, all were offered aid. Academic, music/drama, art, athletic, state/district residency, leadership, alumni affiliation, religious affiliation, minority scholarships available. **Aid applications:** No closing date; priority given to applications received by April 1; applicants notified on a rolling basis beginning on or about March 1; must reply within 3 weeks.

ADDRESS/TELEPHONE. J. Charles Mealy, Director of Admissions, Indiana Wesleyan University, 4201 South Washington Street, Marion, IN 46953-9980. (317) 677-2138. (800) 332-6901. Fax: (317) 677-2499.

International Business College
Fort Wayne, Indiana — CB code: 1330

2-year proprietary business, junior college, coed. Founded in 1889. **Undergraduate enrollment:** 40 men, 341 women full time; 30 men, 101 women part time. **Location:** Suburban campus in small city; 4 miles from downtown. **Calendar:** Trimester.

FRESHMAN ADMISSIONS. Selection criteria: School achievement record and personal interview most important. Recommendations important.

ANNUAL EXPENSES. Tuition and fees: $8,490. Tuition and fees for legal secretary $9,590, medical assisting $8,790. **Room and board:** $3,500 room only. **Books and supplies:** $725.

ADDRESS/TELEPHONE. Marianne Likens, Director of Admissions, International Business College, 3811 Illinois Road, Fort Wayne, IN 46804. (219) 432-8702. (800) 589-6363.

ITT Technical Institute: Evansville
Evansville, Indiana — CB code: 7311

2-year proprietary technical college, coed. Founded in 1966. **Undergraduate enrollment:** 413 men and women. **Faculty:** 15 total. **Location:** Suburban campus in small city; 170 miles from Indianapolis, 120 miles from Louisville, Kentucky. **Calendar:** Quarter. Extensive evening/early morning classes. **Microcomputers:** Located in classrooms.

DEGREES OFFERED. AAS. 195 associate degrees awarded in 1992.

UNDERGRADUATE MAJORS. Electronic technology, tool engineering technology.

ACADEMIC PROGRAMS. Accelerated program, cross-registration. **Remedial services:** Learning center, remedial instruction, tutoring.

ACADEMIC REQUIREMENTS. Freshmen must earn minimum GPA of 2.0 to continue in good standing. Students must declare major on enrollment. **Graduation requirements:** 124 hours for associate (124 in major). Most students required to take courses in biological/physical sciences.

FRESHMAN ADMISSIONS. Selection criteria: Specialized on-site test results considered for certain programs. Recommended units include mathematics 2.

1992 FRESHMAN CLASS PROFILE. 240 men and women enrolled. **Characteristics:** 100% commute.

FALL-TERM APPLICATIONS. $100 fee. Application fee refunded if student not accepted. No closing date; applicants notified on a rolling basis. Interview required.

ATHLETICS. Intramural: Basketball M.

STUDENT SERVICES. Aptitude testing, career counseling, employment service for undergraduates, freshman orientation, personal counseling, placement service for graduates, services/facilities for handicapped.

ANNUAL EXPENSES. Tuition and fees (1992-93): Tuition for 2-year electronics program $14,405, books and supplies, $1,100. Laboratory fees, $50 per quarter. **Books and supplies:** $1,500.

FINANCIAL AID. Aid applications: No closing date; applicants notified on a rolling basis.

ADDRESS/TELEPHONE. Joseph J. Sweeney, Director of Education, ITT Technical Institute: Evansville, 5115 Oak Grove Road, Evansville, IN 47715-2340. (812) 479-1441. Fax: (812) 479-1446.

ITT Technical Institute: Fort Wayne
Fort Wayne, Indiana — CB code: 0650

3-year proprietary technical college, coed. Founded in 1967. **Undergraduate enrollment:** 1,212 men, 125 women full time. **Faculty:** 39 total (36 full time), 1 with doctorate or other terminal degree. **Location:** Urban campus in large city; 122 miles from Indianapolis. **Calendar:** Quarter (4 terms of 12 weeks each; students attend 4 quarters per year to complete one full academic year.).

DEGREES OFFERED. AAS, B. 305 associate degrees awarded in 1992. 100% in engineering technologies. 162 bachelor's degrees awarded. 100% in engineering technologies.

UNDERGRADUATE MAJORS. Architectural technologies, architecture, automotive technology, electronic technology, tool engineering technology. automated manufacturing technology.

ACADEMIC REQUIREMENTS. Freshmen must earn minimum GPA of 1.5 to continue in good standing. Students must declare major on enrollment. **Graduation requirements:** 120 hours for associate, 180 hours for bachelor's.

FRESHMAN ADMISSIONS. Selection criteria: Specialized on-site test results considered for all programs.

1992 FRESHMAN CLASS PROFILE. 768 men and women enrolled. **Characteristics:** 60% from in state, 100% commute, 10% have minority backgrounds. Average age is 19.

FALL-TERM APPLICATIONS. $100 fee. Application fee refunded if student not accepted. No closing date; applicants notified on a rolling basis.

STUDENT LIFE. Activities: Student government.

ATHLETICS. Intramural: Basketball M, bowling M.

STUDENT SERVICES. Freshman orientation, placement service for graduates, services/facilities for handicapped.

ANNUAL EXPENSES. Tuition and fees (1992-93): Tuition for 12-month period ranges from $6,877 to $7,202 depending on course of study. Lab

FINANCIAL AID. Aid applications: No closing date; applicants notified on a rolling basis.

ADDRESS/TELEPHONE. Admissions Office, ITT Technical Institute: Fort Wayne, 4919 Coldwater Road, Fort Wayne, IN 46825-5532. (219) 484-4107.

ITT Technical Institute: Indianapolis
Indianapolis, Indiana — CB code: 0640

3-year proprietary technical college, coed. Founded in 1956. **Undergraduate enrollment:** 1,287 men, 158 women full time. **Faculty:** 41 total (37 full time), 1 with doctorate or other terminal degree. **Location:** Suburban campus in very large city; 10 miles from center of city. **Calendar:** Quarter (4 terms of 12 weeks each; students attend 4 quarters per year to complete one full year). Extensive evening/early morning classes. **Microcomputers:** 100 located in libraries, classrooms. **Additional facts:** Extensions in Austin, Houston, Milwaukee, and Chicago.

DEGREES OFFERED. AAS, B. 203 associate degrees awarded in 1992. 30% in architecture and environmental design, 10% business and management, 60% engineering technologies. 160 bachelor's degrees awarded. 100% in engineering technologies.

UNDERGRADUATE MAJORS. Accounting, architectural technologies, business and management, business data programming, drafting, electronic technology. electronic technology, manufacturing technology.

ACADEMIC PROGRAMS. Remedial services: Tutoring. **Placement/credit:** Institutional tests; 30 credit hours maximum for associate degree.

ACADEMIC REQUIREMENTS. Freshmen must earn minimum GPA of 1.5 to continue in good standing. 70% of freshmen return for sophomore year. Students must declare major on application. **Graduation requirements:** 126 hours for associate (120 in major), 72 hours for bachelor's (60 in major). Most students required to take courses in mathematics. **Postgraduate studies:** 1% from 2-year programs enter 4-year programs.

FRESHMAN ADMISSIONS. Selection criteria: Specialized on-site admissions test results, high school diploma or GED required.

1992 FRESHMAN CLASS PROFILE. 420 men and women enrolled. 20% had high school GPA of 3.0 or higher, 40% between 2.0 and 2.99. 1% were in top tenth and 10% were in top quarter of graduating class. **Characteristics:** 75% from in state, 100% commute, 9% have minority backgrounds. Average age is 23.

FALL-TERM APPLICATIONS. $100 fee. Fee refunded if student not accepted. No closing date; applicants notified on a rolling basis. Interview recommended for academically weak applicants.

STUDENT LIFE. Activities: Student government, student newspaper.

ATHLETICS. Intramural: Basketball M, bowling.

STUDENT SERVICES. Career counseling, employment service for undergraduates, personal counseling, placement service for graduates, services/facilities for handicapped.

ANNUAL EXPENSES. Tuition and fees (1992-93): Tuition for 12-month period ranges from $5,398 to $7,202, depending on course of study. Laboratory fees, $50 per quarter. **Books and supplies:** $750.

FINANCIAL AID. 85% of freshmen, 85% of continuing students receive some form of aid. Grants, loans, jobs available. **Aid applications:** No closing date; priority given to applications received by July 22; applicants notified on a rolling basis.

ADDRESS/TELEPHONE. Director of Education, ITT Technical Institute: Indianapolis, 9511 Angola Court, Indianapolis, IN 46268. (317) 875-8640. (800) 937-4488 ext. 249. Fax: (317) 875-8641.

Lutheran College of Health Professions
Fort Wayne, Indiana — CB code: 1416

Admissions: 56% of applicants accepted
Based on:
••• School record, test scores
•• Essay, interview, recommendations
• Activities
Completion: 85% of freshmen end year in good standing
15% enter graduate study

4-year private health science college, coed, affiliated with Lutheran Church—Missouri Synod. Founded in 1987. **Accreditation:** Regional candidate. **Undergraduate enrollment:** 14 men, 188 women full time; 26 men, 351 women part time. **Faculty:** 56 total (40 full time), 6 with doctorates or other terminal degrees. **Location:** Urban campus in small city. **Calendar:** Semester, extensive summer session. **Microcomputers:** 14 located in computer centers. **Additional facts:** Only hospital-based college in Indiana.

DEGREES OFFERED. AS, BS. 104 associate degrees awarded in 1992. 100% in health sciences. 8 bachelor's degrees awarded.

UNDERGRADUATE MAJORS. Associate: Nursing, radiograph medical technology. **Bachelor's:** Nursing.

ACADEMIC PROGRAMS. Placement/credit: AP, CLEP General and Subject; 9 credit hours maximum for associate degree; 19 credit hours maximum for bachelor's degree.

ACADEMIC REQUIREMENTS. Freshmen must earn minimum GPA of 2.0 to continue in good standing. 82% of freshmen return for sophomore year. Students must declare major on application. **Graduation requirements:** 73 hours for associate (46 in major), 123 hours for bachelor's (70 in major). Most students required to take courses in English, philosophy/religion, biological/physical sciences, social sciences. **Postgraduate studies:** 20% from 2-year programs enter 4-year programs. 15% enter other graduate study.

FRESHMAN ADMISSIONS. Selection criteria: Rank in upper half of high school class, test scores, academic courses most important. **High school preparation:** 8 units required; 12 recommended. Required and recommended units include biological science 1-2, English 4, mathematics 2-3 and physical science 1-2. Foreign language 1 recommended. One year of algebra and chemistry required for nursing. 2 years mathematics required for radiologic technology. College preparatory program should be followed for all programs. Students who have taken GED in place of high school graduation must have minimum score of 50. **Test requirements:** SAT or ACT; score report by June 1.

1992 FRESHMAN CLASS PROFILE. 9 men applied, 5 accepted, 5 enrolled; 117 women applied, 65 accepted, 51 enrolled. 12% were in top tenth and 23% were in top quarter of graduating class. **Academic background:** Mid 50% of enrolled freshmen had SAT-V between 430-490, SAT-M between 440-490; ACT composite between 20-22. 57% submitted SAT scores, 20% submitted ACT scores. **Characteristics:** 86% from in state, 95% commute, 2% have minority backgrounds. Average age is 20.

FALL-TERM APPLICATIONS. $30 fee. Closing date May 1; priority given to applications received by March 1; applicants notified on a rolling basis; must reply within 2 weeks. Essay required. Interview recommended. Deferred admission available.

STUDENT LIFE. Housing: Dormitories (men, women). **Activities:** Student government.

STUDENT SERVICES. Career counseling, freshman orientation, health services, on-campus day care.

ANNUAL EXPENSES. Tuition and fees: $4,914. **Room and board:** $1,728 room only. **Books and supplies:** $486. **Other expenses:** $1,800.

FINANCIAL AID. 51% of freshmen, 56% of continuing students receive some form of aid. All grants, 96% of loans based on need. Academic scholarships available. **Aid applications:** No closing date; priority given to applications received by April 15; applicants notified on a rolling basis; must reply within 1 week.

ADDRESS/TELEPHONE. Frank C. Guzik, Director of Admissions, Lutheran College of Health Professions, 535 Home Avenue, Fort Wayne, IN 46807. (219) 458-2447. Fax: (219) 458-3077.

Manchester College
North Manchester, Indiana — CB code: 1440

Admissions: 75% of applicants accepted
Based on:
••• Recommendations, school record, test scores
•• Interview, special talents
• Activities, essay, religious affiliation/commitment
Completion: 85% of freshmen end year in good standing
58% graduate, 20% of these enter graduate study

4-year private liberal arts college, coed, affiliated with Church of the Brethren. Founded in 1889. **Accreditation:** Regional. **Undergraduate enrollment:** 503 men, 530 women full time; 18 men, 31 women part time. **Graduate enrollment:** 11 men, 4 women full time; 4 women part time. **Faculty:** 110 total (92 full time), 50 with doctorates or other terminal degrees. **Location:** Rural campus in small town; 35 miles from Fort Wayne. **Calendar:** 4-1-4, limited summer session. **Microcomputers:** 70 located in classrooms, computer centers, campus-wide network. **Special facilities:** Observatory, environmental studies and retreat center.

DEGREES OFFERED. AA, BA, BS, MA. 11 associate degrees awarded in 1992. 18% in business/office and marketing/distribution, 18% communications, 28% education, 18% allied health, 18% social sciences. 217 bachelor's degrees awarded. 39% in business and management, 9% teacher education, 8% health sciences, 8% multi/interdisciplinary studies, 9% psychology, 12% social sciences. Graduate degrees offered in 1 major field of study.

UNDERGRADUATE MAJORS. Associate: Accounting, business administration and management, business and management, computer and information sciences, criminal justice studies, criminology, early childhood education, English literature, fine arts, gerontology, journalism, radio/television broadcasting, sports medicine, technical and business writing. **Bachelor's:** Accounting, allied health, anthropology, art education, biology, business administration and management, business and management, chemistry, clinical laboratory science, communications, computer and information sciences, dramatic arts, economics, education, elementary education, engineering science, English, English education, environmental science, finance, fine arts, foreign languages education, French, German, health education, health sciences, history, international business management, junior high education, marketing management, mathematics, mathematics education, medical laboratory technologies, music, music education, peace studies, philosophy, physical education, physics, political science and government, predentistry, prelaw, premedicine, preveterinary, psychology, radio/television broadcasting, religion, science education, secondary education, social science education, social studies education, social work, sociology, Spanish, speech, speech/communication/theater education, sports medicine.

ACADEMIC PROGRAMS. Double major, dual enrollment of high school students, honors program, independent study, internships, student-designed major, study abroad, teacher preparation, medical technology programs with area hospitals; liberal arts/career combination in engineering, health sciences. **Remedial services:** Learning center, reduced course load, remedial instruction, special counselor, tutoring. **Placement/credit:** AP, CLEP Subject, IB, institutional tests.

ACADEMIC REQUIREMENTS. Freshmen must earn minimum GPA of 1.75 to continue in good standing. 80% of freshmen return for sophomore year. Students must declare major by end of second year. **Graduation requirements:** 64 hours for associate (27 in major), 128 hours for bachelor's (40 in major). Most students required to take courses in arts/fine arts, computer science, English, history, humanities, mathematics, philosophy/religion, biological/physical sciences, social sciences. **Postgraduate studies:** 50% from 2-year programs enter 4-year programs. 1% enter law school, 3% enter medical school, 2% enter MBA programs, 14% enter other graduate study.

FRESHMAN ADMISSIONS. Selection criteria: School achievement record most important, with emphasis on college preparatory courses, followed by SAT or ACT scores and recommendations. Musical, artistic and other special talents and abilities considered. **High school preparation:** 19

units recommended. Recommended units include English 4, foreign language 2, mathematics 3, social science 2 and science 3. **Test requirements:** SAT or ACT (SAT preferred); score report by August 1.

1992 FRESHMAN CLASS PROFILE. 454 men applied, 330 accepted, 126 enrolled; 434 women applied, 338 accepted, 121 enrolled. 57% had high school GPA of 3.0 or higher, 43% between 2.0 and 2.99. 20% were in top tenth and 52% were in top quarter of graduating class. **Academic background:** Mid 50% of enrolled freshmen had SAT-V between 380-500, SAT-M between 440-580; ACT composite between 19-28. 83% submitted SAT scores, 26% submitted ACT scores. **Characteristics:** 82% from in state, 93% live in college housing, 9% have minority backgrounds, 2% are foreign students. Average age is 19.

FALL-TERM APPLICATIONS. $20 fee, may be waived for applicants with need. No closing date; priority given to applications received by August 1; applicants notified on a rolling basis. Interview recommended for all applicants. Audition recommended for music applicants. Essay recommended for borderline applicants. Deferred admission available.

STUDENT LIFE. Housing: Dormitories (men, women, coed); apartment, handicapped housing available. All students over 21 may live off-campus. Other students required to live on campus unless living with family. **Activities:** Student government, film, magazine, radio, student newspaper, yearbook, literary magazine, choral groups, concert band, drama, jazz band, music ensembles, musical theater, symphony orchestra, Campus Ministry Board, political clubs, Black Student Union, Hispanos Unidos, Manchester College International Association, Habitat for Humanity, volunteer corps. **Additional information:** Significant student involvement in governance, programming, activities, and administrative services such as security, health, and residence hall management.

ATHLETICS. NCAA. **Intercollegiate:** Baseball M, basketball, cross-country, football M, golf M, soccer M, softball W, tennis, track and field, volleyball W, wrestling M. **Intramural:** Badminton, basketball, bowling, racquetball, soccer, softball, swimming, table tennis, tennis, volleyball, wrestling.

STUDENT SERVICES. Aptitude testing, career counseling, employment service for undergraduates, freshman orientation, health services, personal counseling, placement service for graduates, special adviser for adult students, veterans counselor, services/facilities for handicapped.

ANNUAL EXPENSES. Tuition and fees: $9,600. **Room and board:** $3,640. **Books and supplies:** $425. **Other expenses:** $900.

FINANCIAL AID. 82% of freshmen, 85% of continuing students receive some form of aid. 83% of grants, all loans, all jobs based on need. Academic, state/district residency, alumni affiliation, religious affiliation, minority scholarships available. **Aid applications:** No closing date; priority given to applications received by May 1; applicants notified on a rolling basis beginning on or about May 1; must reply within 4 weeks.

ADDRESS/TELEPHONE. Greg Miller, Dean of Admissions and Financial Aid, Manchester College, 604 College Avenue, North Manchester, IN 46962-0365. (219) 982-5055. Fax: (219) 982-6868.

Marian College
Indianapolis, Indiana

CB code: 1442

4-year private liberal arts college, coed, affiliated with Roman Catholic Church. Founded in 1851. **Accreditation:** Regional. **Undergraduate enrollment:** 314 men, 588 women full time; 62 men, 324 women part time. **Faculty:** 140 total (77 full time), 37 with doctorates or other terminal degrees. **Location:** Urban campus in very large city. **Calendar:** Semester, limited summer session. **Microcomputers:** 55 located in libraries, computer centers. **Special facilities:** Rare stamp collection, archives (materials on development of education in the Archdiocese).

DEGREES OFFERED. AA, AS, BA, BS. 110 associate degrees awarded in 1992. 5% in business and management, 6% teacher education, 80% health sciences, 8% allied health. 120 bachelor's degrees awarded. 28% in business and management, 20% teacher education, 6% health sciences, 9% letters/literature, 7% psychology, 11% visual and performing arts.

UNDERGRADUATE MAJORS. Associate: Accounting, business administration and management, early childhood education, fashion merchandising, finance, nursing. **Bachelor's:** Accounting, allied health, art education, art history, art therapy, biology, business administration and management, chemistry, clinical laboratory science, communications, dramatic arts, early childhood education, elementary education, English, English education, fashion merchandising, finance, food science and nutrition, foreign languages education, French, German, history, interior design, mathematics, mathematics education, medical laboratory technologies, music, music education, nursing, philosophy, physical education, predentistry, prelaw, premedicine, preveterinary, psychology, religious education, science education, secondary education, social studies education, sociology, Spanish, speech, studio art, theological studies, visual and performing arts.

ACADEMIC PROGRAMS. Double major, dual enrollment of high school students, honors program, independent study, internships, study abroad, teacher preparation, cross-registration. **Remedial services:** Learning center, reduced course load, remedial instruction, special counselor, tutoring. **ROTC:** Army. **Placement/credit:** AP, CLEP General and Subject, institutional tests; 30 credit hours maximum for associate degree; 62 credit hours maximum for bachelor's degree.

ACADEMIC REQUIREMENTS. Freshmen must earn minimum GPA of 1.75 to continue in good standing. 76% of freshmen return for sophomore year. Students must declare major by end of second year. **Graduation requirements:** 64 hours for associate, 128 hours for bachelor's. Most students required to take courses in arts/fine arts, computer science, English, foreign languages, history, humanities, mathematics, philosophy/religion, biological/physical sciences, social sciences.

FRESHMAN ADMISSIONS. Selection criteria: School achievement record, test scores, recommendations important. Recommended units include English 3, foreign language 2, mathematics 2, social science 1 and science 1. **Test requirements:** SAT or ACT; score report by August 15.

1992 FRESHMAN CLASS PROFILE. 103 men, 175 women enrolled. 42% had high school GPA of 3.0 or higher, 53% between 2.0 and 2.99. 15% were in top tenth and 35% were in top quarter of graduating class. **Academic background:** Mid 50% of enrolled freshmen had SAT-V between 360-470, SAT-M between 380-530. 72% submitted SAT scores. **Characteristics:** 90% from in state, 75% live in college housing, 12% have minority backgrounds, 2% are foreign students. Average age is 19.

FALL-TERM APPLICATIONS. $20 fee, may be waived for applicants with need. No closing date; applicants notified on a rolling basis. Interview recommended. Essay recommended for academically weak applicants. CRDA.

STUDENT LIFE. Housing: Dormitories (men, women); apartment housing available. **Activities:** Student government, magazine, student newspaper, yearbook, choral groups, drama, jazz band, music ensembles, musical theater, pep band, campus ministry, service organization.

ATHLETICS. NAIA. **Intercollegiate:** Baseball M, basketball, cross-country, golf, softball W, tennis, track and field, volleyball W. **Intramural:** Basketball M, racquetball, softball, swimming, volleyball.

STUDENT SERVICES. Aptitude testing, career counseling, employment service for undergraduates, freshman orientation, health services, personal counseling, placement service for graduates, services/facilities for handicapped.

ANNUAL EXPENSES. Tuition and fees (1992-93): $8,628. **Room and board:** $3,412. **Books and supplies:** $450. **Other expenses:** $900.

FINANCIAL AID. 89% of freshmen, 72% of continuing students receive some form of aid. 73% of grants, 93% of loans, all jobs based on need. 165 enrolled freshmen were judged to have need, all were offered aid. Academic, music/drama, art, athletic, leadership, alumni affiliation, religious affiliation scholarships available. **Aid applications:** No closing date; priority given to applications received by August 15; applicants notified on a rolling basis beginning on or about April 1.

ADDRESS/TELEPHONE. Dr. Brent E. Smith, Dean for Enrollment Management, Marian College, 3200 Cold Spring Road, Indianapolis, IN 46222. (317) 929-0321. (800) 772-7264.

Martin University
Indianapolis, Indiana

CB code: 1379

4-year private university, coed. Founded in 1977. **Accreditation:** Regional. **Undergraduate enrollment:** 79 men, 200 women full time; 64 men, 130 women part time. **Graduate enrollment:** 5 men, 7 women full time; 7 men, 1 woman part time. **Faculty:** 56 total (24 full time), 27 with doctorates or other terminal degrees. **Location:** Urban campus in very large city; in downtown area. **Calendar:** Semester, extensive summer session. Saturday classes. **Microcomputers:** 14 located in computer centers. **Special facilities:** Specialized hematology laboratory (sickle cell anemia research). **Additional facts:** Campus in Indiana Women's Prison.

DEGREES OFFERED. BA, BS, MA, MS. 72 bachelor's degrees awarded in 1992. 39% in business and management, 7% letters/literature, 9% philosophy, religion, theology, 36% psychology.

UNDERGRADUATE MAJORS. Accounting, Afro-American (black) studies, art education, biology, business administration and management, business education, chemistry, communications, community psychology, computer and information sciences, computer programming, counseling psychology, creative writing, education, elementary education, English, English education, history, humanities, humanities and social sciences, information sciences and systems, insurance and risk management, journalism, junior high education, marketing and distribution, mathematics, mathematics education, medieval studies, music, music education, physics, political science and government, psychology, religion, renewable natural resources, science education, secondary education, social science education, social studies education, sociology, speech/communication/theater education, theological studies, urban religious study.

ACADEMIC PROGRAMS. Accelerated program, double major, internships, student-designed major, cross-registration, program with University of Indianapolis in teacher education and nursing. **Remedial services:** Learning center, remedial instruction, special counselor, tutoring, summer mathematics workshops. **Placement/credit:** CLEP General and Subject.

ACADEMIC REQUIREMENTS. Freshmen must earn minimum GPA of 2.0 to continue in good standing. 90% of freshmen return for sophomore

year. Students must declare major by end of first year. **Graduation requirements:** 134 hours for bachelor's (38 in major). Most students required to take courses in arts/fine arts, computer science, English, history, humanities, mathematics, philosophy/religion, biological/physical sciences, social sciences. **Additional information:** Assessment of prior learning for college credit.

FRESHMAN ADMISSIONS. Selection criteria: Open admissions.

1992 FRESHMAN CLASS PROFILE. 70 men applied, 70 accepted, 70 enrolled; 181 women applied, 181 accepted, 181 enrolled. **Characteristics:** 100% from in state, 100% commute, 90% have minority backgrounds. Average age is 36.

FALL-TERM APPLICATIONS. $10 fee, may be waived for applicants with need. Closing date September 12; applicants notified on a rolling basis. Interview required. Applicants tested with WRAT and Wonderlic.

STUDENT LIFE. Activities: Student government, student newspaper, choral groups, dance, opera, GIFT of Brightwood (neighborhood youth services), Healthy Babies (pre and post-natal education).

STUDENT SERVICES. Aptitude testing, career counseling, employment service for undergraduates, freshman orientation, health services, personal counseling, placement service for graduates, special adviser for adult students, veterans counselor, services/facilities for handicapped.

ANNUAL EXPENSES. Tuition and fees: $6,060. **Books and supplies:** $400. **Other expenses:** $2,400.

FINANCIAL AID. 80% of freshmen, 65% of continuing students receive some form of aid. 6% of loans, all jobs based on need. 60 enrolled freshmen were judged to have need, all were offered aid. Academic, leadership, minority scholarships available. **Aid applications:** No closing date; priority given to applications received by March 1; applicants notified on a rolling basis beginning on or about August 1; must reply within 2 weeks.

ADDRESS/TELEPHONE. Bobbye Jean Craig, Director of Admissions, Martin University, PO Box 18567, 2171 Avondale, Indianapolis, IN 46218. (317) 543-3238. Fax: (317) 543-3257.

Mid-America College of Funeral Service
Jeffersonville, Indiana CB code: 0644

2-year proprietary college of mortuary science, coed. Founded in 1905. **Undergraduate enrollment:** 69 men, 17 women full time. **Faculty:** 5 total (4 full time). **Location:** Suburban campus in large town; 5 miles from Louisville, Kentucky. **Calendar:** Quarter.

DEGREES OFFERED. AAS. 28 associate degrees awarded in 1992. 100% in parks/recreation, protective services, public affairs.

UNDERGRADUATE MAJORS. Funeral services/mortuary science.

ACADEMIC REQUIREMENTS. Freshmen must earn minimum GPA of 2.0 to continue in good standing. 86% of freshmen return for sophomore year. Students must declare major on application. **Graduation requirements:** 125 hours for associate.

FRESHMAN ADMISSIONS. Selection criteria: Open admissions.

1992 FRESHMAN CLASS PROFILE. 69 men, 17 women enrolled. **Characteristics:** 100% commute, 55% join fraternities/sororities. Average age is 23.

FALL-TERM APPLICATIONS. $25 fee. No closing date; applicants notified on a rolling basis.

STUDENT LIFE. Activities: Student government, fraternities.

STUDENT SERVICES. Employment service for undergraduates, personal counseling, placement service for graduates, services/facilities for handicapped.

ANNUAL EXPENSES. Tuition and fees (projected): Tuition for 12-month certificate program is $5,200 including fees and books. Associate degree program is an additional $3,950.

FINANCIAL AID. 70% of freshmen receive some form of aid. All grants, 65% of loans based on need. **Aid applications:** No closing date; applicants notified on a rolling basis.

ADDRESS/TELEPHONE. Renee M. Fischer, Director of Admissions, Mid-America College of Funeral Service, 3111 Hamburg Pike, Jeffersonville, IN 47130. (812) 288-8878. (800) 221-6158. Fax: (812) 288-5942.

Oakland City College
Oakland City, Indiana CB code: 1585

Admissions: 96% of applicants accepted
Based on: ••• School record, test scores
•• Interview
• Recommendations, special talents
Completion: 86% of freshmen end year in good standing
65% graduate, 36% of these enter graduate study

4-year private liberal arts college, coed, affiliated with General Association of General Baptists. Founded in 1885. **Accreditation:** Regional. **Undergraduate enrollment:** 263 men, 319 women full time; 73 men, 130 women part time. **Graduate enrollment:** 6 men full time; 10 men, 2 women part time. **Faculty:** 41 total (25 full time), 19 with doctorates or other terminal degrees. **Location:** Rural campus in small town; 30 miles from Evansville. **Calendar:** Semester, limited summer session. **Microcomputers:** Located in libraries, classrooms, computer centers. **Additional facts:** Nontraditional adult bachelor's degree completion program designed for adults with 64 or more prior semester hours. Associate degree in business administration offered in accelerated format.

DEGREES OFFERED. AA, AS, AAS, BA, BS, M, M.Div. 14 associate degrees awarded in 1992. 50% in business and management, 25% multi/interdisciplinary studies, 25% trade and industry. 98 bachelor's degrees awarded. 38% in business and management, 23% teacher education, 35% multi/interdisciplinary studies. Graduate degrees offered in 2 major fields of study.

UNDERGRADUATE MAJORS. Associate: Accounting, air conditioning/heating/refrigeration mechanics, air conditioning/heating/refrigeration technology, automotive mechanics, automotive technology, business administration and management, business and management, business and office, business data programming, computer programming, liberal/general studies, prelaw, secretarial and related programs, welding technology. **Bachelor's:** Accounting, applied mathematics, art education, biological and physical sciences, biology, business administration and management, business and management, business and office, business education, chemistry, elementary education, English, English education, fine arts, human resources development, humanities, humanities and social sciences, junior high education, mathematics education, music, music education, physical education, pure mathematics, religion, science education, secondary education, social studies education, visual and performing arts.

ACADEMIC PROGRAMS. 2-year transfer program, accelerated program, cooperative education, double major, dual enrollment of high school students, external degree, independent study, teacher preparation, telecourses. **Remedial services:** Learning center, reduced course load, remedial instruction, special counselor, tutoring, GED preparation classes, Project Opportunity developmental program, Upward Bound, student support services. **Placement/credit:** AP, CLEP General and Subject, institutional tests; 3 credit hours maximum for associate degree; 9 credit hours maximum for bachelor's degree.

ACADEMIC REQUIREMENTS. Freshmen must earn minimum GPA of 1.75 to continue in good standing. 70% of freshmen return for sophomore year. Students must declare major on enrollment. **Graduation requirements:** 64 hours for associate (24 in major), 128 hours for bachelor's (36 in major). Most students required to take courses in arts/fine arts, computer science, English, history, humanities, mathematics, philosophy/religion, biological/physical sciences, social sciences. **Postgraduate studies:** 35% from 2-year programs enter 4-year programs. 1% enter MBA programs, 35% enter other graduate study.

FRESHMAN ADMISSIONS. Selection criteria: High School GPA and test scores most important. Interviews and recommendations also considered. Recommended units include biological science 2, English 4, mathematics 3, physical science 1 and social science 2. **Test requirements:** SAT or ACT; score report by August 1.

1992 FRESHMAN CLASS PROFILE. 125 men applied, 120 accepted, 101 enrolled; 110 women applied, 105 accepted, 105 enrolled. 40% had high school GPA of 3.0 or higher, 50% between 2.0 and 2.99. **Characteristics:** 70% from in state, 70% commute, 3% have minority backgrounds. Average age is 20.

FALL-TERM APPLICATIONS. $15 fee, may be waived for applicants with need. Closing date September 1; priority given to applications received by April 1; applicants notified on a rolling basis; must reply by May 1 or within 4 weeks if notified thereafter. Interview recommended. CRDA. Deferred and early admission available. EDP-F.

STUDENT LIFE. Housing: Dormitories (men, women); apartment housing available. **Activities:** Student government, student newspaper, yearbook, choral groups, drama, music ensembles, pep band, mental health assistance group, ministerial students group, Circle-K, Young Republicans, Young Democrats.

ATHLETICS. NCAA. **Intercollegiate:** Baseball M, basketball, cross-country, golf, softball W, tennis, volleyball W. **Intramural:** Archery, badminton, basketball, bowling, cross-country, golf, softball, table tennis, tennis, volleyball, wrestling M.

STUDENT SERVICES. Aptitude testing, career counseling, employment service for undergraduates, freshman orientation, health services, personal counseling, placement service for graduates, veterans counselor, services/facilities for handicapped.

ANNUAL EXPENSES. Tuition and fees (1992-93): $6,726. **Room and board:** $2,720. **Books and supplies:** $650. **Other expenses:** $1,800.

FINANCIAL AID. 97% of freshmen, 80% of continuing students receive some form of aid. 98% of grants, all loans, all jobs based on need. 140 enrolled freshmen were judged to have need, all were offered aid. Academic, music/drama, art, athletic, religious affiliation scholarships available. **Aid applications:** No closing date; priority given to applications received by March 1; applicants notified on a rolling basis beginning on or about March 15; must reply within 2 weeks.

ADDRESS/TELEPHONE. Tracy Siekman, Director of Admissions, Oakland City College, Lucretia Street, Oakland City, IN 47660. (812) 749-4781.

Purdue University

West Lafayette, Indiana CB code: 1631

Admissions: 83% of applicants accepted
Based on: ••• School record, test scores
• Interview, recommendations
Completion: 95% of freshmen end year in good standing
60% graduate, 20% of these enter graduate study

4-year public university, coed. Founded in 1869. **Accreditation:** Regional. **Undergraduate enrollment:** 15,116 men, 11,409 women full time; 1,378 men, 1,408 women part time. **Graduate enrollment:** 3,005 men, 1,558 women full time; 1,165 men, 794 women part time. **Faculty:** 2,171 total (2,081 full time), 99 with doctorates or other terminal degrees. **Location:** Suburban campus in small city; 65 miles from Indianapolis. **Calendar:** Semester, extensive summer session. **Microcomputers:** 750 located in dormitories, libraries, computer centers. **Special facilities:** Art galleries, linear accelerator, horticultural park, concert hall, 3 theaters, outdoor concert facility.

DEGREES OFFERED. AS, AAS, BA, BS, MA, MS, MEd, PhD, B. Pharm, Pharm D, DVM. 492 associate degrees awarded in 1992. 5% in business/office and marketing/distribution, 18% computer sciences, 69% engineering technologies. 5,706 bachelor's degrees awarded. 6% in agriculture, 12% business and management, 6% business/office and marketing/distribution, 6% communications, 8% teacher education, 22% engineering, 9% engineering technologies, 5% health sciences, 7% social sciences. Graduate degrees offered in 194 major fields of study.

UNDERGRADUATE MAJORS. Associate: Aeronautical technology, agricultural economics, agricultural mechanics, agricultural sciences, agronomy, air traffic control, aircraft mechanics, airline piloting and navigation, animal sciences, aviation management, business data processing and related programs, business data programming, civil technology, computer graphics, computer technology, drafting, drafting and design technology, electrical technology, electromechanical technology, food management, food production/management/services, horticulture, hotel/motel and restaurant management, industrial technology, mechanical design technology, office supervision and management, physics, renewable natural resources, trade and industrial education, trade and industrial supervision and management, veterinarian's assistant. **Bachelor's:** Accounting, actuarial sciences, advertising, aeronautical technology, aerospace/aeronautical/astronautical engineering, Afro-American (black) studies, agribusiness, agricultural business and management, agricultural economics, agricultural education, agricultural engineering, agricultural mechanics, agricultural sciences, agronomy, air traffic control, aircraft mechanics, airline piloting and navigation, American literature, American studies, animal sciences, anthropology, apparel and accessories marketing, applied mathematics, art education, art history, atmospheric sciences and meteorology, aviation management, biochemistry, bioengineering and biomedical engineering, biological and physical sciences, biology, biophysics, botany, business administration and management, business data processing and related programs, business data programming, business economics, cell biology, ceramics, chemical engineering, chemistry, child development/care/guidance, city/community/regional planning, civil engineering, civil technology, clinical laboratory science, clinical psychology, clothing and textiles management/production/services, cognitive psychology, communications, communications research, community health work, community psychology, comparative literature, computer and information sciences, computer engineering, computer graphics, computer programming, computer technology, crafts, creative writing, criminal justice studies, criminology, data processing, developmental psychology, drafting, drafting and design technology, dramatic arts, drawing, driver and safety education, early childhood education, earth sciences, ecology, economics, education of the emotionally handicapped, education of the gifted and talented, education of the mentally handicapped, education of the physically handicapped, educational media technology, educational psychology, electrical technology, electrical/electronics/communications engineering, electromechanical technology, elementary education, engineering, engineering and other disciplines, engineering management, engineering science, English, English education, entomology, environmental design, environmental health engineering, environmental science, family and community services, family/consumer resource management, fashion design, fashion merchandising, fiber/textiles/weaving, fine arts, fishing and fisheries, food management, food production/management/services, food science and nutrition, food sciences, foreign languages education, forest products processing technology, forestry and related sciences, forestry production and processing, French, genetics, human and animal, geochemistry, geological engineering, geology, geophysics and seismology, German, health education, health physics, health sciences, history, home economics, home economics education, home furnishings and equipment management/production/services, horticultural science, horticulture, hotel/motel and restaurant management, human environment and housing, humanities and social sciences, individual and family development, industrial and organizational psychology, industrial arts education, industrial design, industrial engineering, industrial technology, information sciences and systems, institutional management, institutional/home management/supporting programs, interior design, international agriculture, international studies, journalism, junior high education, labor/industrial relations, landscape architecture, linguistics, materials engineering, mathematics, mathematics education, mechanical design technology, mechanical engineering, medical laboratory technologies, medieval studies, metal/jewelry, metallurgical engineering, microbiology, molecular biology, nuclear engineering, nuclear medical technology, nursing, occupational safety and health technology, office supervision and management, ornamental horticulture, painting, paleontology, parks and recreation management, personality psychology, personnel management, pharmacy, philosophy, photographic technology, photography, physical education, physics, physiology, human and animal, plant genetics, plant pathology, plant protection, plant sciences, political science and government, predentistry, prelaw, premedicine, printmaking, psychobiology, psychology, public relations, quantitative psychology, radio/television broadcasting, range management, reading education, religion, renewable natural resources, retailing, robotics, Russian, science education, sculpture, secondary education, social psychology, social studies education, sociology, soil sciences, Spanish, special education, speech correction, speech pathology/audiology, speech/communication/theater education, sports medicine, statistics, surveying and mapping sciences, systems analysis, telecommunications, textiles and clothing, theater design, tourism, trade and industrial education, trade and industrial supervision and management, urban design, visual and performing arts, wildlife management.

ACADEMIC PROGRAMS. Accelerated program, cooperative education, double major, dual enrollment of high school students, education specialist degree, honors program, independent study, internships, student-designed major, study abroad, teacher preparation, telecourses, cross-registration; liberal arts/career combination in engineering; combined bachelor's/graduate program in business administration. **Remedial services:** Learning center, preadmission summer program, reduced course load, remedial instruction, special counselor, tutoring. **ROTC:** Air Force, Army, Naval. **Placement/credit:** AP, CLEP General and Subject, institutional tests.

ACADEMIC REQUIREMENTS. Freshmen must earn minimum GPA of 1.5 to continue in good standing. 84% of freshmen return for sophomore year. Students must declare major on application. **Graduation requirements:** 65 hours for associate, 130 hours for bachelor's. Most students required to take courses in English, mathematics, biological/physical sciences, social sciences. **Postgraduate studies:** 95% from 2-year programs enter 4-year programs. **Additional information:** Minimal amount of course work outside student's major can be taken on pass-fail basis, not to exceed 20% of total credit hours required.

FRESHMAN ADMISSIONS. Selection criteria: Class rank, curriculum, high school GPA, test scores, recommendation are most important. In-state applicants generally must be in top half of senior class, out-of-state applicants must rank in top third, engineering applicants in top 15%. Out-of-state students with alumni affiliation reviewed on in-state basis. **High school preparation:** 15 units required. Required and recommended units include English 4, mathematics 2-4 and science 1-3. Foreign language 2 and social science 1 recommended. Additional requirements include 2-3 laboratory science, 2 additional units of mathematics required for some programs. **Test requirements:** SAT or ACT; score report by December 15. English, mathematics, science ACH required of students schooled at home or graduating from unaccredited high schools. **Additional information:** Admissions competitive, especially for out-of-state applicants. Some programs close without notice. Early application recommended.

1992 FRESHMAN CLASS PROFILE. 34% were in top tenth and 57% were in top quarter of graduating class. **Academic background:** Mid 50% of enrolled freshmen had SAT-V between 400-520, SAT-M between 480-630; ACT composite between 22-27. 84% submitted SAT scores, 16% submitted ACT scores. **Characteristics:** 69% from in state, 90% live in college housing, 13% have minority backgrounds, 1% are foreign students. Average age is 18.

FALL-TERM APPLICATIONS. No fee. No closing date; applicants notified on a rolling basis; must reply by May 1 if notified by then, if notified after must reply within 21 days. Interview required of veterinary medicine, veterinary technology and pharmacy applicants; recommended for flight technology and nursing applicants. CRDA. Early admission available. Engineering, nursing, flight technology, programs have November 15 deadline. Veterinary technology deadline is December 15.

STUDENT LIFE. Housing: Dormitories (men, women, coed); apartment, fraternity, sorority, cooperative housing available. **Activities:** Student government, magazine, radio, student newspaper, television, yearbook, choral groups, concert band, dance, drama, jazz band, marching band, music ensembles, pep band, symphony orchestra, fraternities, sororities, over 500 religious, political, ethnic, and social service organizations.

ATHLETICS. NCAA. **Intercollegiate:** Baseball M, basketball, cross-country, diving, football M, golf, swimming, tennis, track and field, volleyball W, wrestling M. **Intramural:** Archery, badminton, basketball, bowling, cross-country, diving, golf, handball, ice hockey M, racquetball, rifle, soccer W, softball, squash M, swimming, table tennis, tennis, track and field, volleyball, water polo.

STUDENT SERVICES. Aptitude testing, career counseling, employment service for undergraduates, freshman orientation, health services, on-campus day care, personal counseling, placement service for graduates, special adviser for adult students, veterans counselor, services/facilities for handicapped.

ANNUAL EXPENSES. Tuition and fees (projected): $2,720, $6,130 additional for out-of-state students. **Room and board:** $4,450. **Books and supplies:** $570. **Other expenses:** $1,060.

FINANCIAL AID. 60% of freshmen, 50% of continuing students receive some form of aid. 69% of grants, 91% of loans, all jobs based on need. 3,400 enrolled freshmen were judged to have need, 2,900 were offered aid. Academic, athletic, state/district residency, leadership, minority scholarships available. **Aid applications:** No closing date; priority given to applications received by March 1; applicants notified on a rolling basis beginning on or about March 20; must reply within 3 weeks. **Additional information:** Student cooperative housing available to reduce housing costs. Room and board installment payment plan available. Co-operative work for credit is available in many programs.

ADDRESS/TELEPHONE. William J. Murray, Director of Admissions, Purdue University, Schleman Hall, West Lafayette, IN 47907-1080. (317) 494-1776. Fax: (317) 494-0544.

Purdue University: Calumet
Hammond, Indiana CB code: 1638

4-year public university, coed. Founded in 1943. **Accreditation:** Regional. **Undergraduate enrollment:** 1,810 men, 1,906 women full time; 2,154 men, 2,763 women part time. **Graduate enrollment:** 24 men, 69 women full time; 285 men, 485 women part time. **Faculty:** 457 total (250 full time), 181 with doctorates or other terminal degrees. **Location:** Urban campus in small city; 20 miles from Chicago. **Calendar:** Semester, extensive summer session. **Microcomputers:** 453 located in computer centers.

DEGREES OFFERED. AA, AS, AAS, BA, BS, MA, MS. 300 associate degrees awarded in 1992. 550 bachelor's degrees awarded. Graduate degrees offered in 13 major fields of study.

UNDERGRADUATE MAJORS. Associate: Business and management, business data programming, chemical manufacturing technology, civil technology, computer and information sciences, computer technology, electrical technology, engineering and engineering-related technologies, food production/management/services, food science and nutrition, hospitality and recreation marketing, humanities and social sciences, industrial technology, liberal/general studies, manufacturing technology, mechanical technology, nursing, supervision, women's studies. **Bachelor's:** Accounting, applied mathematics, biology, biotechnology, botany, business administration and management, business and management, chemistry, civil technology, clinical laboratory science, clinical psychology, communications, computer and information sciences, computer engineering, computer programming, computer technology, developmental psychology, education, electrical technology, electrical/electronics/communications engineering, elementary education, engineering, engineering and engineering-related technologies, engineering and other disciplines, English, English literature, French, German, gerontology, history, hotel/motel and restaurant management, industrial and organizational psychology, industrial technology, manufacturing technology, mathematics, mechanical engineering, mechanical technology, microbiology, nursing, philosophy, physics, political science and government, predentistry, premedicine, prepharmacy, preveterinary, psychology, radio/television broadcasting, school media services, secondary education, sociology, Spanish, special education, speech, statistics, supervision, zoology.

ACADEMIC PROGRAMS. 2-year transfer program, cooperative education, dual enrollment of high school students, honors program, internships, teacher preparation, weekend college. **Remedial services:** Learning center, reduced course load, remedial instruction, special counselor, tutoring. **Placement/credit:** AP, CLEP General and Subject, institutional tests.

ACADEMIC REQUIREMENTS. Freshmen must earn minimum GPA of 2.0 to continue in good standing. 65% of freshmen return for sophomore year. Students must declare major by end of second year. **Graduation requirements:** 66 hours for associate, 126 hours for bachelor's. Most students required to take courses in English, mathematics, biological/physical sciences, social sciences. **Postgraduate studies:** 90% from 2-year programs enter 4-year programs.

FRESHMAN ADMISSIONS. Selection criteria: Students must submit SAT or ACT scores and high school transcript. Students who do not meet admission requirements may possibly be admitted through the developmental program of the University Division. **High school preparation:** 16 units required. Course requirements vary according to program. **Test requirements:** SAT or ACT; score report by August 21.

1992 FRESHMAN CLASS PROFILE. 2,942 men and women enrolled. **Academic background:** Mid 50% of enrolled freshmen had SAT-V between 390-470, SAT-M between 440-520. 93% submitted SAT scores. **Characteristics:** 91% from in state, 100% commute, 15% have minority backgrounds. Average age is 19.

FALL-TERM APPLICATIONS. No fee. No closing date; priority given to applications received by August 1; applicants notified on a rolling basis.

STUDENT LIFE. Activities: Student government, magazine, student newspaper, choral groups, drama, musical theater, pep band, fraternities, sororities, Black Student Union, Los Latinos, Minority Assistance Club.

ATHLETICS. NAIA. **Intercollegiate:** Basketball, golf M, soccer M, volleyball W. **Intramural:** Badminton, basketball, racquetball, softball, tennis, volleyball.

STUDENT SERVICES. Aptitude testing, career counseling, employment service for undergraduates, freshman orientation, health services, on-campus day care, personal counseling, placement service for graduates, veterans counselor, services/facilities for handicapped.

ANNUAL EXPENSES. Tuition and fees (projected): $2,269, $3,339 additional for out-of-state students. **Books and supplies:** $490. **Other expenses:** $1,169.

FINANCIAL AID. 41% of freshmen, 39% of continuing students receive some form of aid. 98% of grants, 95% of loans, 28% of jobs based on need. Academic, athletic, minority scholarships available. **Aid applications:** No closing date; priority given to applications received by March 1; applicants notified on a rolling basis beginning on or about June 1; must reply within 3 weeks.

ADDRESS/TELEPHONE. John P. Fruth, Director of Admissions, Purdue University: Calumet, 171 Street and Woodmar Avenue, Hammond, IN 46323-2094. (219) 989-2213. Fax: (219) 989-2775.

Purdue University: North Central Campus
Westville, Indiana CB code: 1640

4-year public branch campus, community college, coed. Founded in 1943. **Accreditation:** Regional. **Undergraduate enrollment:** 509 men, 682 women full time; 890 men, 1,396 women part time. **Graduate enrollment:** 7 men, 56 women part time. **Faculty:** 218 total (88 full time), 56 with doctorates or other terminal degrees. **Location:** Rural campus in rural community; 10 miles From Michigan City, 13 miles from Laporte. **Calendar:** Semester, limited summer session. **Microcomputers:** 135 located in classrooms, computer centers.

DEGREES OFFERED. AS, AAS, BA, BS, MS. 272 associate degrees awarded in 1992. 50% in business and management, 12% engineering technologies, 35% health sciences. 96 bachelor's degrees awarded. 19% in business and management, 27% teacher education, 7% engineering technologies, 46% multi/interdisciplinary studies. Graduate degrees offered in 1 major field of study.

UNDERGRADUATE MAJORS. Associate: Accounting, architectural technologies, business and management, business and office, business data programming, civil technology, computer and information sciences, computer technology, construction, electrical technology, health care administration, hotel/motel and restaurant management, industrial technology, labor/industrial relations, marketing and distribution, marketing management, mechanical design technology, nursing, personnel management, robotics, trade and industrial supervision and management. **Bachelor's:** Accounting, business and management, elementary education, English, labor/industrial relations, liberal/general studies, mechanical design technology, personnel management, trade and industrial supervision and management.

ACADEMIC PROGRAMS. 2-year transfer program, dual enrollment of high school students, teacher preparation, weekend college. **Remedial services:** Learning center, reduced course load, remedial instruction, special counselor, tutoring. **Placement/credit:** AP, CLEP General and Subject, institutional tests.

ACADEMIC REQUIREMENTS. Freshmen must earn minimum GPA of 1.5 to continue in good standing. 53% of freshmen return for sophomore year. Students must declare major by end of first year. **Graduation requirements:** 60 hours for associate, 123 hours for bachelor's. Most students required to take courses in computer science, English, humanities, mathematics, biological/physical sciences, social sciences. **Postgraduate studies:** 3% from 2-year programs enter 4-year programs.

FRESHMAN ADMISSIONS. Selection criteria: High school record and class rank. Open admissions for community college division. **High school preparation:** 10 units required. Required and recommended units include biological science 1-2, English 4, mathematics 2-4, physical science 1-4 and social science 2-4. Foreign language 4 recommended. **Test requirements:** SAT or ACT; score report by August 1.

1992 FRESHMAN CLASS PROFILE. 980 men and women enrolled. **Academic background:** Mid 50% of enrolled freshmen had SAT-V between 380-490, SAT-M between 410-560. 75% submitted SAT scores. **Characteristics:** 99% from in state, 100% commute, 7% have minority backgrounds, 1% are foreign students.

FALL-TERM APPLICATIONS. No fee. No closing date; applicants notified on a rolling basis. Interview recommended for academically weak applicants. Deferred admission available.

STUDENT LIFE. Activities: Student government, student newspaper, Campus Crusade for Christ, computer club, photography club, accounting club, Student Cultural Society, Students in Fall Enterprise.

ATHLETICS. Intramural: Basketball, bowling, cross-country, football M, golf, skiing, softball, table tennis, tennis, volleyball.

STUDENT SERVICES. Aptitude testing, career counseling, employment service for undergraduates, freshman orientation, on-campus day care, personal counseling, placement service for graduates, services/facilities for handicapped.

ANNUAL EXPENSES. Tuition and fees (projected): $2,200, $3,200

additional for out-of-state students. **Books and supplies:** $485. **Other expenses:** $1,200.

FINANCIAL AID. 25% of freshmen, 22% of continuing students receive some form of aid. 96% of grants, 98% of loans, 62% of jobs based on need. 675 enrolled freshmen were judged to have need, all were offered aid. Academic scholarships available. **Aid applications:** No closing date; priority given to applications received by March 1; applicants notified on a rolling basis.

ADDRESS/TELEPHONE. Bill Barnett, Director of Admissions and Placement, Purdue University: North Central Campus, 1401 South U.S. 421, Westville, IN 46391-9528. (219) 785-5458. (800) 533-1112. Fax: (219) 785-5355.

Rose-Hulman Institute of Technology

Terre Haute, Indiana — CB code: 1668

Admissions: 64% of applicants accepted
Based on: ••• School record, test scores
•• Recommendations
• Activities, interview
Completion: 90% of freshmen end year in good standing
75% graduate, 21% of these enter graduate study

4-year private engineering college, men only. Founded in 1874. **Accreditation:** Regional. **Undergraduate enrollment:** 1,360 men full time. **Graduate enrollment:** 51 men, 2 women full time; 40 men part time. **Faculty:** 100 total (95 full time), 87 with doctorates or other terminal degrees. **Location:** Rural campus in small city. **Calendar:** Quarter, limited summer session. **Microcomputers:** Located in libraries, computer centers. **Special facilities:** Art collection.

DEGREES OFFERED. BS, MS. 275 bachelor's degrees awarded in 1992. 80% in engineering, 5% mathematics, 15% physical sciences. Graduate degrees offered in 6 major fields of study.

UNDERGRADUATE MAJORS. Applied mathematics, chemical engineering, chemistry, civil engineering, computer and information sciences, computer engineering, economics, electrical/electronics/communications engineering, mechanical engineering, optics, physics.

ACADEMIC PROGRAMS. Accelerated program, double major, independent study, study abroad, cross-registration. **Remedial services:** Preadmission summer program, reduced course load, tutoring. **ROTC:** Air Force, Army. **Placement/credit:** AP, institutional tests.

ACADEMIC REQUIREMENTS. Freshmen must earn minimum GPA of 1.75 to continue in good standing. 82% of freshmen return for sophomore year. Students must declare major by end of first year. **Graduation requirements:** 195 hours for bachelor's. Most students required to take courses in English, mathematics, biological/physical sciences, social sciences. **Postgraduate studies:** 2% enter law school, 2% enter medical school, 5% enter MBA programs, 12% enter other graduate study. **Additional information:** Area minor programs in humanities and social sciences.

FRESHMAN ADMISSIONS. Selection criteria: Primary consideration given to school achievement record and subjects taken. Test scores also considered. Applicants must rank in top quarter of graduating class. Extracurricular and leadership activities, alumni ties considered. Interviews, although not required, can be determining factor. Some preference given to in-state applicants; out-of-state applications more competitive. **High school preparation:** 18 units required. Required units include English 4, mathematics 4, physical science 2 and social science 2. **Test requirements:** SAT or ACT; score report by March 1.

1992 FRESHMAN CLASS PROFILE. 3,190 men applied, 2,050 accepted, 364 enrolled. 100% had high school GPA of 3.0 or higher. 70% were in top tenth and 100% were in top quarter of graduating class. **Academic background:** Mid 50% of enrolled freshmen had SAT-V between 500-600, SAT-M between 620-730; ACT composite between 27-30. 75% submitted SAT scores, 25% submitted ACT scores. **Characteristics:** 58% from in state, 90% live in college housing, 4% have minority backgrounds, 2% are foreign students. Average age is 18.

FALL-TERM APPLICATIONS. $20 fee, may be waived for applicants with need. Closing date March 1; priority given to applications received by December 1; applicants notified on a rolling basis; must reply by May 1. Interview recommended. Deferred admission available.

STUDENT LIFE. Housing: Dormitories (men); fraternity housing available. **Activities:** Student government, magazine, radio, student newspaper, yearbook, choral groups, concert band, drama, jazz band, music ensembles, pep band, fraternities, astronomy society, debate, mathematics, and computer teams, service organization.

ATHLETICS. NCAA. **Intercollegiate:** Baseball, basketball, cross-country, football, golf, rifle, soccer, tennis, track and field, wrestling. **Intramural:** Badminton, basketball, bowling, cross-country, football, handball, racquetball, rifle, soccer, softball, table tennis, tennis, track and field, volleyball.

STUDENT SERVICES. Career counseling, employment service for undergraduates, freshman orientation, health services, personal counseling, placement service for graduates, services/facilities for handicapped.

ANNUAL EXPENSES. Tuition and fees: $12,495. **Room and board:** $3,984. **Books and supplies:** $500. **Other expenses:** $600.

FINANCIAL AID. 90% of freshmen, 90% of continuing students receive some form of aid. 77% of grants, 94% of loans, 77% of jobs based on need. 285 enrolled freshmen were judged to have need, all were offered aid. Academic, minority scholarships available. **Aid applications:** Closing date March 1; priority given to applications received by December 1; applicants notified on a rolling basis; must reply by May 1 or within 2 weeks if notified thereafter.

ADDRESS/TELEPHONE. Charles Howard, Dean of Admissions, Rose-Hulman Institute of Technology, 5500 Wabash Avenue, Terre Haute, IN 47803-9989. (812) 877-1511 ext. 213. (800) 248-7448. Fax: (812) 877-3198.

St. Francis College

Fort Wayne, Indiana — CB code: 1693

4-year private liberal arts college, coed, affiliated with Roman Catholic Church. Founded in 1890. **Accreditation:** Regional. **Undergraduate enrollment:** 144 men, 331 women full time; 69 men, 165 women part time. **Graduate enrollment:** 10 men, 24 women full time; 66 men, 141 women part time. **Faculty:** 79 total (39 full time), 42 with doctorates or other terminal degrees. **Location:** Suburban campus in small city; 125 miles from Indianapolis, 150 miles from Chicago. **Calendar:** Semester, limited summer session. **Microcomputers:** 15 located in computer centers. **Special facilities:** Art gallery, planetarium, nature preserve.

DEGREES OFFERED. AA, AS, BA, BS, MS, MBA. 21 associate degrees awarded in 1992. 10% in business and management, 57% health sciences, 33% visual and performing arts. 75 bachelor's degrees awarded. 29% in business and management, 23% education, 10% health sciences, 5% letters/literature, 9% parks/recreation, protective services, public affairs, 6% social sciences, 6% visual and performing arts. Graduate degrees offered in 15 major fields of study.

UNDERGRADUATE MAJORS. Associate: Accounting, business and management, commercial art, environmental science, graphic arts technology, graphic design, radiograph medical technology. **Bachelor's:** Accounting, allied health, American studies, art education, biology, business administration and management, business and management, business education, chemistry, clinical laboratory science, commercial art, communications, education, education of the emotionally handicapped, education of the mentally handicapped, elementary education, English, English education, environmental science, fine arts, health education, liberal/general studies, nursing, physical sciences, predentistry, prelaw, premedicine, preveterinary, psychology, religion, science education, secondary education, social sciences, social studies education, social work, special education, specific learning disabilities.

ACADEMIC PROGRAMS. Double major, dual enrollment of high school students, honors program, independent study, internships, study abroad, teacher preparation. **Remedial services:** Learning center, reduced course load, remedial instruction, special counselor, tutoring. **Placement/credit:** AP, CLEP General and Subject, institutional tests; 16 credit hours maximum for associate degree; 32 credit hours maximum for bachelor's degree.

ACADEMIC REQUIREMENTS. Freshmen must earn minimum GPA of 2.0 to continue in good standing. 68% of freshmen return for sophomore year. Students must declare major by end of first year. **Graduation requirements:** 64 hours for associate (30 in major), 128 hours for bachelor's (45 in major). Most students required to take courses in arts/fine arts, computer science, English, history, humanities, mathematics, philosophy/religion, biological/physical sciences, social sciences. **Postgraduate studies:** 75% from 2-year programs enter 4-year programs.

FRESHMAN ADMISSIONS. Selection criteria: School achievement record, rank in top half of class, and test scores most important. Recommended units include foreign language 2, mathematics 3 and social science 2. For nursing program, minimum of 1 year high school algebra, biology, chemistry required. **Test requirements:** SAT or ACT; score report by July 1.

1992 FRESHMAN CLASS PROFILE. 38% had high school GPA of 3.0 or higher, 53% between 2.0 and 2.99. 16% were in top tenth and 43% were in top quarter of graduating class. **Academic background:** Mid 50% of enrolled freshmen had SAT-V between 370-470, SAT-M between 400-540; ACT composite between 17-23. 72% submitted SAT scores, 33% submitted ACT scores. **Characteristics:** 33% live in college housing. Average age is 22.

FALL-TERM APPLICATIONS. No fee. Closing date August 10; priority given to applications received by March 1; applicants notified on a rolling basis. Essay required. Interview recommended for underprepared applicants. Portfolio recommended. CRDA. Deferred admission available.

STUDENT LIFE. Housing: Dormitories (men, women). Full-time students under 21 not living at home or with adult relatives must live in residence halls. **Activities:** Student government, literary publication, drama, pep band, sororities, campus ministry, Council for Exceptional Children, social work organization, Circle-K, Mission Club, New Horizons.

ATHLETICS. NAIA. **Intercollegiate:** Baseball M, basketball, golf M, soccer M, softball W, tennis, volleyball W. **Intramural:** Basketball, bowling, fencing, swimming, volleyball.

STUDENT SERVICES. Career counseling, freshman orientation, health services, personal counseling, placement service for graduates, academic counseling, special services program for variety of age groups, women's support group, services/facilities for handicapped.

ANNUAL EXPENSES. Tuition and fees: $8,300. **Room and board:** $3,630. **Books and supplies:** $450. **Other expenses:** $1,000.

FINANCIAL AID. 80% of freshmen, 88% of continuing students receive some form of aid. 77% of grants, 92% of loans, 48% of jobs based on need. 92 enrolled freshmen were judged to have need, all were offered aid. Academic, art, athletic scholarships available. **Aid applications:** No closing date; priority given to applications received by March 1; applicants notified on a rolling basis beginning on or about March 1; must reply by May 1 or within 2 weeks if notified thereafter.

ADDRESS/TELEPHONE. Debra A. Dotterer, Dean of Admissions, St. Francis College, 2701 Spring Street, Fort Wayne, IN 46808. (219) 434-3279. (800) 729-4732. Fax: (219) 434-3194.

St. Joseph's College

Rensselaer, Indiana — CB code: 1697

Admissions: 82% of applicants accepted
Based on:
- ••• School record
- •• Test scores
- • Activities, essay, interview, recommendations, special talents

Completion: 85% of freshmen end year in good standing
59% graduate

4-year private liberal arts college, coed, affiliated with Roman Catholic Church. Founded in 1889. **Accreditation:** Regional. **Undergraduate enrollment:** 403 men, 399 women full time; 25 men, 173 women part time. **Graduate enrollment:** 2 men, 23 women full time; 1 man, 3 women part time. **Faculty:** 83 total (59 full time), 27 with doctorates or other terminal degrees. **Location:** Rural campus in small town; 80 miles from Chicago, 90 miles from Indianapolis. **Calendar:** Semester, limited summer session. **Microcomputers:** 20 located in dormitories, libraries, classrooms, computer centers, campus-wide network.

DEGREES OFFERED. AA, AS, BA, BS, MA. 1 associate degree awarded in 1992. 100% in business and management. 190 bachelor's degrees awarded. 35% in business and management, 11% communications, 6% education, 6% teacher education, 6% mathematics, 7% psychology, 11% social sciences. Graduate degrees offered in 1 major field of study.

UNDERGRADUATE MAJORS. Associate: Biochemistry, business computer/console/peripheral equipment operation, business data processing and related programs, business/computer science, computer and information sciences, humanities, management/marketing/information systems, music theory and composition. **Bachelor's:** Accounting, accounting/finance, accounting/information systems, biochemistry, biology, business administration and management, business and management, business computer/console/peripheral equipment operation, business data processing and related programs, business economics, business education, chemistry, communications, communications/theater arts, computer and information sciences, computer mathematics, computer programming, creative writing, economics, education, elementary education, English, English education, finance, finance/accounting, finance/information systems, geobiology, geochemistry, geophysics and seismology, history, humanities and social sciences, information sciences and systems, international business management, international relations, international studies, junior high education, management information systems, management/marketing/information systems, marketing and distribution, marketing management, math/computer science, math/physics, mathematics, mathematics education, medical laboratory technologies, music, music business management, music education, nursing, nursing education, philosophy, philosophy/religious studies, physical education, political science and government, practical nursing, predentistry, prelaw, premedicine, preoccupational therapy, preveterinary, psychology, radio/television broadcasting, science education, secondary education, social science education, social studies education, sociology, speech, speech/communication/theater education.

ACADEMIC PROGRAMS. 2-year transfer program, accelerated program, double major, dual enrollment of high school students, honors program, independent study, internships, student-designed major, study abroad, teacher preparation, Washington semester; liberal arts/career combination in engineering, health sciences. **Remedial services:** Reduced course load, special counselor, tutoring, writing clinic, freshman academic support program. **Placement/credit:** AP, CLEP General and Subject; 15 credit hours maximum for associate degree; 30 credit hours maximum for bachelor's degree.

ACADEMIC REQUIREMENTS. Freshmen must earn minimum GPA of 1.8 to continue in good standing. 76% of freshmen return for sophomore year. Students must declare major by end of second year. **Graduation requirements:** 60 hours for associate, 120 hours for bachelor's (36 in major). Most students required to take courses in arts/fine arts, English, history, humanities, philosophy/religion, biological/physical sciences, social sciences. **Additional information:** Core program of progressive liberal arts curriculum integrates history, art, music, literature, social science, political science, and communication skills into sequence of 10 interdisciplinary courses and seeks to examine mankind in civilization and the human condition.

FRESHMAN ADMISSIONS. Selection criteria: High school GPA in academic subjects most important factor. Class rank and SAT or ACT scores should support grade average. **High school preparation:** 15 units required. At least 10 units must be from English, foreign language, social studies, mathematics and natural science. Not all fields need to be represented. **Test requirements:** SAT or ACT; score report by August 1. Prueba de Aptitud Academica for Spanish speaking applicants.

1992 FRESHMAN CLASS PROFILE. 517 men applied, 411 accepted, 115 enrolled; 267 women applied, 231 accepted, 85 enrolled. 32% had high school GPA of 3.0 or higher, 59% between 2.0 and 2.99. **Academic background:** Mid 50% of enrolled freshmen had SAT-V between 370-480, SAT-M between 400-550; ACT composite between 18-24. 64% submitted SAT scores, 36% submitted ACT scores. **Characteristics:** 67% from in state, 89% live in college housing, 6% have minority backgrounds. Average age is 18.

FALL-TERM APPLICATIONS. $15 fee, may be waived for applicants with need. No closing date; priority given to applications received by June 1; applicants notified on a rolling basis; must reply by May 1 or within 4 weeks if notified thereafter. Interview recommended. CRDA. Deferred and early admission available. Essays required for Presidential scholarships.

STUDENT LIFE. Housing: Dormitories (men, women). **Activities:** Student government, film, magazine, radio, student newspaper, television, yearbook, choral groups, concert band, drama, jazz band, marching band, musical theater, pep band, black student union, Gallagher Charitable Society, campus ministry, Blue Key, Alpha Phi Omega.

ATHLETICS. NCAA. **Intercollegiate:** Baseball M, basketball, cross-country, football M, golf, soccer, softball W, tennis, track and field, volleyball W. **Intramural:** Basketball, bowling, cross-country, racquetball, soccer, softball, swimming, tennis, volleyball, water polo.

STUDENT SERVICES. Career counseling, employment service for undergraduates, freshman orientation, health services, personal counseling, placement service for graduates, special adviser for adult students, services/facilities for handicapped.

ANNUAL EXPENSES. Tuition and fees: $10,830. **Room and board:** $3,900. **Books and supplies:** $500. **Other expenses:** $500.

FINANCIAL AID. 93% of freshmen, 70% of continuing students receive some form of aid. 61% of grants, 90% of loans, 55% of jobs based on need. 148 enrolled freshmen were judged to have need, all were offered aid. Academic, music/drama, athletic, leadership scholarships available. **Aid applications:** Closing date August 1; priority given to applications received by May 1; applicants notified on a rolling basis beginning on or about April 1; must reply by May 1 or within 2 weeks if notified thereafter.

ADDRESS/TELEPHONE. Brian Kesse, Director of Admissions, St. Joseph's College, PO Box 890, Rensselaer, IN 47978. (800) 447-8781. (800) 447-8781. Fax: (219) 866-4497.

St. Mary-of-the-Woods College

St. Mary-of-the-Woods, Indiana — CB code: 1704

Admissions: 98% of applicants accepted
Based on:
- ••• School record
- •• Test scores
- • Activities, essay, interview, recommendations, special talents

Completion: 90% of freshmen end year in good standing
65% graduate, 13% of these enter graduate study

4-year private liberal arts college, women only, affiliated with Roman Catholic Church. Founded in 1840. **Accreditation:** Regional. **Undergraduate enrollment:** 389 women full time; 836 women part time. **Graduate enrollment:** 77 women. **Faculty:** 78 total (56 full time), 30 with doctorates or other terminal degrees. **Location:** Suburban campus in rural community; 4 miles from Terre Haute, 70 miles from Indianapolis. **Calendar:** Semester. Saturday classes. **Microcomputers:** Located in dormitories, libraries, computer centers. **Special facilities:** Law library, collection of rare books and art objects, learning resource center, equine indoor and outdoor arena, fitness trail, art gallery. **Additional facts:** Special program for single mothers to live on campus with their children.

DEGREES OFFERED. AA, AS, BA, BS, MA. 1 associate degree awarded in 1992. 94 bachelor's degrees awarded. 24% in business and management, 13% communications, 14% education, 7% parks/recreation, protective services, public affairs, 9% philosophy, religion, theology, 9% psychology, 5% social sciences. Graduate degrees offered in 1 major field of study.

UNDERGRADUATE MAJORS. Associate: Business administration and management, business and management, early childhood education, equestrian science, gerontology, legal assistant/paralegal, liberal/general studies, speech, theological studies. **Bachelor's:** Accounting, advertising, art education, biology, business administration and management, business and management, Chinese, computer and information sciences, dramatic arts, early childhood education, elementary education, English, English education, equestrian science, fine arts, foreign languages education, French, history, humanities, intercultural communications, journalism, legal assistant/paralegal, liberal/general studies, marketing and distribution, marketing management, mathematics, mathematics education, medical laboratory technologies, music, music education, music performance, music therapy, musical theater, political science and government, predentistry, prelaw, premedicine, preveterinary, psychology, public relations, religion, religious education, religious music, science education, secondary education, social studies education, social work, Spanish, special education, speech, speech/communication/theater education, studio art, theological studies, visual and performing arts.

ACADEMIC PROGRAMS. 2-year transfer program, accelerated program, double major, external degree, honors program, independent study, internships, student-designed major, study abroad, teacher preparation, visiting/exchange student program, weekend college, cross-registration, Women's External Degree Program. **Remedial services:** Learning center, reduced course load, special counselor, tutoring, restricted status-student is required to carry 12 credits and participate in placement testing and tutoring. **ROTC:** Army. **Placement/credit:** AP, CLEP General and Subject, institutional tests; 30 credit hours maximum for bachelor's degree.

ACADEMIC REQUIREMENTS. Freshmen must earn minimum GPA of 1.7 to continue in good standing. 90% of freshmen return for sophomore year. Students must declare major by end of second year. **Graduation requirements:** 61 hours for associate (36 in major), 122 hours for bachelor's (36 in major). Most students required to take courses in arts/fine arts, computer science, English, foreign languages, history, humanities, mathematics, philosophy/religion, biological/physical sciences, social sciences. **Postgraduate studies:** 10% from 2-year programs enter 4-year programs. 3% enter law school, 3% enter medical school, 7% enter other graduate study. **Additional information:** Women's External Degree Program, for nontraditional women; 850 students throughout country visit campus 1 or 2 days twice a year and do course work at home. Exchange program with Providence University in Taiwan. Other study abroad opportunities.

FRESHMAN ADMISSIONS. Selection criteria: School achievement record, test scores, extracurricular activities, work experience, recommendations, individual review and evaluation of potential for college success considered. **High school preparation:** 16 units recommended. Recommended units include English 4, foreign language 2, mathematics 3, social science 2 and science 3. 2 units of academic electives recommended. **Test requirements:** SAT or ACT; score report by August 15.

1992 FRESHMAN CLASS PROFILE. 508 women applied, 496 accepted, 341 enrolled. 48% had high school GPA of 3.0 or higher, 51% between 2.0 and 2.99. **Academic background:** Mid 50% of enrolled freshmen had SAT-V between 410-520, SAT-M between 390-520; ACT composite between 16-21. 73% submitted SAT scores, 20% submitted ACT scores. **Characteristics:** 59% from in state, 50% commute, 7% have minority backgrounds, 7% are foreign students. Average age is 26.

FALL-TERM APPLICATIONS. $30 fee. No closing date; applicants notified on a rolling basis. Audition required for theater, music applicants. Portfolio required for art, journalism applicants. Interview recommended. Essay recommended. CRDA. Deferred and early admission available.

STUDENT LIFE. Housing: Dormitories (women). Single parents with children 3-10 may live in college housing. **Activities:** Student government, magazine, student newspaper, yearbook, choral groups, drama, music ensembles, musical theater, symphony orchestra, campus ministry, Circle-K, Bacchus, Amnesty International, Habitat for Humanity, literacy volunteers, environmentalist activities.

ATHLETICS. NAIA. **Intercollegiate:** Basketball, cross-country, horseback riding, softball, swimming, tennis, volleyball.

STUDENT SERVICES. Career counseling, employment service for undergraduates, freshman orientation, health services, on-campus day care, personal counseling, special adviser for adult students, services/facilities for handicapped.

ANNUAL EXPENSES. Tuition and fees (1992-93): $9,920. External degree program has different tuition structure, $195 per credit hour **Room and board:** $3,970. **Books and supplies:** $775. **Other expenses:** $900.

FINANCIAL AID. 82% of freshmen, 87% of continuing students receive some form of aid. 29% of jobs based on need. 64 enrolled freshmen were judged to have need, all were offered aid. Academic, music/drama, art, state/district residency, leadership, alumni affiliation, religious affiliation scholarships available. **Aid applications:** No closing date; priority given to applications received by March 1; applicants notified on a rolling basis beginning on or about April 1. **Additional information:** Portfolio or audition required of applicants who wish to be considered for Creative Arts Scholarship.

ADDRESS/TELEPHONE. Katherine K. Satchwill, Vice President for External Affairs, St. Mary-of-the-Woods College, Office of Admissions, St. Mary-of-the-Woods, IN 47876-0068. (812) 535-5106. (800) 926-SMWC. Fax: (812) 535-4613.

St. Mary's College
Notre Dame, Indiana

CB code: 1702

Admissions: 84% of applicants accepted
Based on: ••• Essay, school record, test scores
•• Activities, recommendations, special talents
• Interview
Completion: 98% of freshmen end year in good standing
77% graduate, 20% of these enter graduate study

4-year private liberal arts college, women only, affiliated with Roman Catholic Church. Founded in 1844. **Accreditation:** Regional. **Undergraduate enrollment:** 1,510 women full time; 2 men, 6 women part time. **Faculty:** 196 total (116 full time), 109 with doctorates or other terminal degrees. **Location:** Suburban campus in small city; 1 mile from South Bend. **Calendar:** Semester. **Microcomputers:** 180 located in dormitories, libraries, classrooms, computer centers. **Special facilities:** Art gallery, nature trail. **Additional facts:** College has campus in Rome, Italy, and sponsors programs in Ireland and India. Enrolls a few part-time male students on campus and a few full-time in programs abroad.

DEGREES OFFERED. BA, BS, BFA. 425 bachelor's degrees awarded in 1992. 21% in business and management, 10% communications, 6% teacher education, 10% letters/literature, 5% life sciences, 9% parks/recreation, protective services, public affairs, 6% psychology, 12% social sciences, 5% visual and performing arts.

UNDERGRADUATE MAJORS. Biology, business administration and management, chemistry, communications, creative writing, cytotechnology, dramatic arts, economics, elementary education, English literature, fine arts, French, history, humanities, mathematics, medical laboratory technologies, music, music education, music performance, music theory and composition, nursing, philosophy, political science and government, psychology, religion, social work, sociology, Spanish, studio art.

ACADEMIC PROGRAMS. Accelerated program, double major, independent study, internships, study abroad, teacher preparation, Washington semester, cross-registration; liberal arts/career combination in engineering. **Remedial services:** Reduced course load, tutoring. **ROTC:** Air Force, Army, Naval. **Placement/credit:** AP, CLEP Subject, IB, institutional tests; 30 credit hours maximum for bachelor's degree.

ACADEMIC REQUIREMENTS. Grade-point average of 1.8 end of first semester, 1.9 end of second semester required. 90% of freshmen return for sophomore year. Students must declare major by end of second year. **Graduation requirements:** 128 hours for bachelor's (24 in major). Most students required to take courses in arts/fine arts, English, foreign languages, history, mathematics, philosophy/religion, biological/physical sciences, social sciences. **Postgraduate studies:** 5% enter law school, 2% enter medical school, 3% enter MBA programs, 10% enter other graduate study. **Additional information:** Religious studies and theater departments operate in conjunction with University of Notre Dame.

FRESHMAN ADMISSIONS. Selection criteria: School achievement record, including high school transcript listing GPA, class rank, test scores and activities most important; school recommendations considered. **High school preparation:** 16 units required. Required units include English 4, foreign language 2, mathematics 3, social science 2 and science 1. Science and nursing programs require more science and mathematics. **Test requirements:** SAT or ACT; score report by March 1. 3 ACH required including English Composition, Mathematics Level I or II, and foreign language. Score report by June 15 Prueba de Aptitud Academica for Spanish speaking applicants.

1992 FRESHMAN CLASS PROFILE. 889 women applied, 750 accepted, 393 enrolled. 71% had high school GPA of 3.0 or higher, 29% between 2.0 and 2.99. 26% were in top tenth and 60% were in top quarter of graduating class. **Academic background:** Mid 50% of enrolled freshmen had SAT-V between 430-530, SAT-M between 460-570; ACT composite between 22-27. 62% submitted SAT scores, 38% submitted ACT scores. **Characteristics:** 15% from in state, 99% live in college housing, 7% have minority backgrounds, 1% are foreign students. Average age is 18.

FALL-TERM APPLICATIONS. $30 fee, may be waived for applicants with need. No closing date; priority given to applications received by March 1; applicants notified on a rolling basis beginning on or about January 15; must reply within 2 weeks. Essay required. Interview recommended. Audition recommended for music applicants. Portfolio recommended for art applicants. CRDA. Deferred and early admission available. EDP-F. Early decision applications deadline November 15. Notification December 15.

STUDENT LIFE. Housing: Dormitories (women). One small dormitory available to juniors and seniors only. **Activities:** Student government, magazine, yearbook, student newspaper, and radio and television in conjunction with University of Notre Dame, choral groups, dance, drama, music ensembles, musical theater, opera, band activities with University of Notre Dame, Neighborhood Study Help Program, Community of International Lay Apostolate, Urban Plunge, Circle K, World Hunger Coalition, Student Alliance for Women's Colleges, Right to Life, Women for the Environment, Best Buddies.

ATHLETICS. NCAA. **Intercollegiate:** Basketball, diving, soccer, softball, swimming, tennis, track and field, volleyball. **Intramural:** Basketball, cross-country, golf, gymnastics, horseback riding, racquetball, rowing (crew), sailing, skiing, soccer, softball, swimming, tennis, volleyball.

STUDENT SERVICES. Career counseling, employment service for undergraduates, freshman orientation, health services, on-campus day care, personal counseling, placement service for graduates, special adviser for adult students, services/facilities for handicapped.

ANNUAL EXPENSES. Tuition and fees (projected): $12,885. **Room and board:** $4,244. **Books and supplies:** $500. **Other expenses:** $1,250.

FINANCIAL AID. 52% of freshmen, 41% of continuing students receive some form of aid. All grants, 76% of loans, all jobs based on need. 200 enrolled freshmen were judged to have need, all were offered aid. **Aid applications:** No closing date; priority given to applications received by March 1; applicants notified on a rolling basis beginning on or about February 1; must reply within 2 weeks.

ADDRESS/TELEPHONE. Mary Ann Rowan, Director of Admissions, St. Mary's College, Notre Dame, IN 46556. (219) 284-4587.

St. Meinrad College

St. Meinrad, Indiana CB code: 1705

Admissions:	74% of applicants accepted
Based on:	••• Essay, recommendations, religious affiliation/commitment, school record, test scores
	•• Activities, interview
	• Special talents
Completion:	90% of freshmen end year in good standing
	43% graduate, 70% of these enter graduate study

4-year private liberal arts, seminary college, men only, affiliated with Roman Catholic Church. Founded in 1857. **Accreditation:** Regional. **Undergraduate enrollment:** 112 men full time; 41 men part time. **Faculty:** 39 total (16 full time), 20 with doctorates or other terminal degrees. **Location:** Rural campus in rural community; 50 miles from Evansville, 60 miles from Louisville, Kentucky. **Calendar:** Semester. **Microcomputers:** Located in computer centers. **Special facilities:** Abbey Press, Benedictine monastic community.

DEGREES OFFERED. BA, BS. 26 bachelor's degrees awarded in 1992. 11% in languages, 23% letters/literature, 23% philosophy, religion, theology, 35% psychology.

UNDERGRADUATE MAJORS. Biological and physical sciences, classics, English, history, philosophy, psychology, Spanish.

ACADEMIC PROGRAMS. Honors program, independent study. **Remedial services:** Learning center, reduced course load, remedial instruction, special counselor, tutoring. **Placement/credit:** AP, CLEP General and Subject; 24 credit hours maximum for bachelor's degree.

ACADEMIC REQUIREMENTS. Freshmen must earn minimum GPA of 1.75 to continue in good standing. 60% of freshmen return for sophomore year. Students must declare major by end of second year. **Graduation requirements:** 128 hours for bachelor's (28 in major). Most students required to take courses in arts/fine arts, English, foreign languages, history, mathematics, philosophy/religion, biological/physical sciences, social sciences.

FRESHMAN ADMISSIONS. Selection criteria: Academic performance, 2.0 high school GPA, recommendations most important, followed by test scores. **High school preparation:** 12 units recommended. Recommended units include English 4, foreign language 2, mathematics 2, social science 2 and science 2. **Test requirements:** SAT or ACT (ACT preferred); score report by August 15.

1992 FRESHMAN CLASS PROFILE. 57 men applied, 42 accepted, 29 enrolled. 31% had high school GPA of 3.0 or higher, 59% between 2.0 and 2.99. 7% were in top tenth and 26% were in top quarter of graduating class. **Academic background:** Mid 50% of enrolled freshmen had ACT composite between 18-24. 100% submitted ACT scores. **Characteristics:** 24% from in state, 100% live in college housing, 10% have minority backgrounds. Average age is 18.

FALL-TERM APPLICATIONS. $10 fee. No closing date; priority given to applications received by April 1; applicants notified on a rolling basis. Interview recommended. Essay recommended.

STUDENT LIFE. Housing: Dormitories (men). **Activities:** Student government, film, magazine, radio, student newspaper, television, choral groups, concert band, drama, music ensembles, pep band, community social service projects. **Additional information:** Religious observance required.

ATHLETICS. NSCAA. **Intercollegiate:** Basketball, cross-country, tennis. **Intramural:** Basketball, bowling, cross-country, field hockey, golf, handball, racquetball, soccer, softball, swimming, table tennis, tennis, volleyball.

STUDENT SERVICES. Aptitude testing, career counseling, health services, personal counseling, special adviser for adult students, veterans counselor.

ANNUAL EXPENSES. Tuition and fees: $6,003. **Room and board:** $4,227. **Books and supplies:** $500. **Other expenses:** $900.

FINANCIAL AID. 100% of freshmen, 100% of continuing students receive some form of aid. 87% of grants, all loans, all jobs based on need. Academic scholarships available. **Aid applications:** No closing date; priority given to applications received by March 1; applicants notified on a rolling basis beginning on or about June 1; must reply within 3 weeks.

ADDRESS/TELEPHONE. Rev. Kieran Kleczewski, OSB, Director of Enrollment Office, St. Meinrad College, St. Meinrad, IN 47577-1030. (812) 357-6575. (800) 752-9384. Fax: (812) 357-6964.

Taylor University

Upland, Indiana CB code: 1802

Admissions:	58% of applicants accepted
Based on:	••• Essay, recommendations, religious affiliation/commitment, school record, test scores
	•• Activities, interview, special talents
Completion:	97% of freshmen end year in good standing
	12% enter graduate study

4-year private liberal arts college, coed, interdenominational. Founded in 1846. **Accreditation:** Regional. **Undergraduate enrollment:** 827 men, 916 women full time; 33 men, 41 women part time. **Faculty:** 144 total (112 full time), 71 with doctorates or other terminal degrees. **Location:** Rural campus in small town; 20 miles from Muncie, 50 miles from Fort Wayne, 65 miles from Indianapolis. **Calendar:** 4-1-4, limited summer session. **Microcomputers:** 171 located in dormitories, libraries, computer centers, campus-wide network. **Special facilities:** 65-acre arboretum, 19,000 square-foot environmental studies laboratory. **Additional facts:** Evangelical Christian education. Branch campuses in Singapore and Fort Wayne, Indiana.

DEGREES OFFERED. AA, BA, BS, BFA. 6 associate degrees awarded in 1992. 50% in business and management, 17% computer sciences, 33% teacher education. 407 bachelor's degrees awarded. 20% in business and management, 6% communications, 29% teacher education, 7% philosophy, religion, theology, 10% psychology, 9% social sciences.

UNDERGRADUATE MAJORS. Associate: Business administration and management, liberal/general studies, management information systems. **Bachelor's:** Accounting, art education, artificial intelligence, Bible studies, biology, biology/environmental science, business administration and management, business economics, chemistry, chemistry/environmental science, communications, computer and information sciences, computer programming, creative writing, criminal justice studies, dramatic arts, early childhood education, economics, elementary education, English, English education, English literature, environmental economics, environmental management, environmental science, fine arts, foreign languages education, French, health education, history, information sciences and systems, international studies, journalism, junior high education, mathematics, mathematics education, mathematics/computer science, mathematics/environmental science, medical laboratory technologies, missionary studies, music, music education, music performance, music theory and composition, philosophy, physical education, physics, physics/environmental science, political science and government, predentistry, preengineering, prelaw, premedicine, prepharmacy, preveterinary, psychology, public relations, radio/television broadcasting, recreation and community services technologies, religion, religious education, religious music, science education, secondary education, social science education, social studies education, social work, sociology, Spanish, special education, speech/communication/theater education, urban ministry, visual and performing arts.

ACADEMIC PROGRAMS. 2-year transfer program, accelerated program, cooperative education, double major, dual enrollment of high school students, honors program, independent study, internships, student-designed major, study abroad, teacher preparation, telecourses, visiting/exchange student program, Washington semester, cross-registration; liberal arts/career combination in engineering. **Remedial services:** Learning center, preadmission summer program, reduced course load, remedial instruction, special counselor, tutoring. **Placement/credit:** AP, CLEP Subject, institutional tests. Unlimited number of hours of credit by examination may be counted toward degree.

ACADEMIC REQUIREMENTS. Freshmen must earn minimum GPA of 1.7 to continue in good standing. 95% of freshmen return for sophomore year. Students must declare major by end of second year. **Graduation requirements:** 64 hours for associate (42 in major), 128 hours for bachelor's (42 in major). Most students required to take courses in arts/fine arts, computer science, English, foreign languages, history, humanities, mathematics, philosophy/religion, biological/physical sciences, social sciences. **Postgraduate studies:** 3% enter medical school, 1% enter MBA programs, 8% enter other graduate study.

FRESHMAN ADMISSIONS. Selection criteria: High school transcript, test scores important. Recommend rank in top 25% of graduating class with GPA of 3.3 and SAT combined score of 1000. Recommendations from applicant's pastor and counselor required. Co-curricular activities considered. Interview may be required. **High school preparation:** 10 units required. Required and recommended units include English 4, mathematics 3-4, social science 2 and science 3-4. Foreign language 2 recommended. Required units include laboratory science, algebra, and geometry. **Test requirements:** SAT or ACT; score report by May 1.

1992 FRESHMAN CLASS PROFILE. 711 men applied, 480 accepted, 235 enrolled; 1,075 women applied, 552 accepted, 258 enrolled. 85% had high school GPA of 3.0 or higher, 15% between 2.0 and 2.99. 57% were in top tenth and 81% were in top quarter of graduating class. **Characteristics:** 33% from in state, 100% live in college housing, 5% have minority backgrounds, 2% are foreign students. Average age is 18.

FALL-TERM APPLICATIONS. $20 fee, may be waived for applicants with need. No fee if applying before December 15. No closing date; priority given to applications received by February 15; applicants notified on a rolling basis; must reply by May 1 or within 2 weeks if notified thereafter. Audition required for music applicants. Essay required. Interview recommended. Portfolio recommended for art applicants. CRDA. Deferred admission available. Early admission criteria include 3.3 GPA, SAT combined score of 1000 or ACT composite of 24, and rank in top quarter of class.

STUDENT LIFE. Housing: Dormitories (men, women); apartment housing available. 7 residence halls available. Some off-campus apartments available for upperclassmen with special permission. **Activities:** Student government, film, magazine, radio, student newspaper, television, yearbook, choral groups, concert band, drama, jazz band, music ensembles, musical theater, opera, pep band, symphony orchestra, summer missions service program, Multi-Cultural Society, Missionary Kids Organizations, Big Brother-Big Sister, community outreach, Campus Life Young Life, Youth for Christ, gospel choir, International Student Society, Young Republicans. **Additional information:** Students and faculty sign Life Together Covenant explaining expectations, responsibilities of living in Christian community where faith is integrated with academic progress.

ATHLETICS. NAIA. **Intercollegiate:** Baseball M, basketball, cross-country, football M, golf M, soccer M, softball W, tennis, track and field, volleyball W. **Intramural:** Archery, badminton, basketball M, bowling, football, golf M, handball, horseback riding, racquetball, soccer, softball, table tennis M, tennis, volleyball.

STUDENT SERVICES. Aptitude testing, career counseling, employment service for undergraduates, freshman orientation, health services, personal counseling, placement service for graduates, learning skills center, services/facilities for handicapped.

ANNUAL EXPENSES. Tuition and fees: $10,650. **Room and board:** $3,800. **Books and supplies:** $400. **Other expenses:** $1,100.

FINANCIAL AID. 75% of freshmen, 75% of continuing students receive some form of aid. Grants, loans, jobs available. 284 enrolled freshmen were judged to have need, all were offered aid. Academic, music/drama, athletic, leadership, religious affiliation, minority scholarships available. **Aid applications:** Closing date March 1; applicants notified on a rolling basis beginning on or about March 1; must reply by registration. **Additional information:** Reduced rates for high school students during academic year. Tuition waivers for children of alumni during summer session.

ADDRESS/TELEPHONE. Herb Frye, Dean of Enrollment Management, Taylor University, 500 West Reade Avenue, Upland, IN 46989-1001. (317) 998-2751. (800) 882-3456. Fax: (317) 998-4925.

Tri-State University
Angola, Indiana — CB code: 1811

Admissions: 91% of applicants accepted
Based on:
- ••• School record
- •• Test scores
- • Activities, interview, recommendations, special talents

Completion: 94% of freshmen end year in good standing
52% graduate

4-year private university, coed. Founded in 1884. **Accreditation:** Regional. **Undergraduate enrollment:** 653 men, 280 women full time; 83 men, 35 women part time. **Faculty:** 92 total (80 full time), 39 with doctorates or other terminal degrees. **Location:** Rural campus in small town; 40 miles from Fort Wayne. **Calendar:** Quarter, extensive summer session. **Microcomputers:** 280 located in libraries, computer centers. **Special facilities:** Golf course, General Lewis B. Hershey Museum.

DEGREES OFFERED. AA, AS, BA, BS. 15 associate degrees awarded in 1992. 20% in business and management, 67% engineering technologies, 8% life sciences. 175 bachelor's degrees awarded. 17% in business/office and marketing/distribution, 5% computer sciences, 13% teacher education, 56% engineering.

UNDERGRADUATE MAJORS. Associate: Accounting, biological and physical sciences, business administration and management, computer programming, computer technology, criminal justice studies, drafting, drafting and design technology, manufacturing technology, secretarial and related programs. **Bachelor's:** Accounting, aerospace/aeronautical/astronautical engineering, biology, business administration and management, business and humanities, business and management, business education, chemical engineering, chemistry, civil engineering, communications, computer and information sciences, computer programming, corporate English, criminal justice studies, drafting and design technology, economics, electrical/electronics/communications engineering, elementary education, engineering administration, engineering management, English, English education, environmental science, history, information sciences and systems, junior high education, liberal/general studies, management information systems, marketing and distribution, marketing management, mathematics, mathematics education, mechanical engineering, office supervision and management, physical education, physical sciences, premedicine, psychology, science education, secondary education, social science education, social sciences, social studies education.

ACADEMIC PROGRAMS. 2-year transfer program, cooperative education, double major, dual enrollment of high school students, internships, teacher preparation. **Remedial services:** Learning center, reduced course load, remedial instruction, tutoring. **Placement/credit:** AP, CLEP Subject, institutional tests.

ACADEMIC REQUIREMENTS. Freshmen must earn minimum GPA of 2.0 to continue in good standing. 64% of freshmen return for sophomore year. Students must declare major by end of first year. **Graduation requirements:** 102 hours for associate, 206 hours for bachelor's. Most students required to take courses in computer science, English, history, humanities, mathematics, biological/physical sciences, social sciences.

FRESHMAN ADMISSIONS. Selection criteria: School achievement, class rank, test scores, school and community activities, and recommendations important. Required units include English 4, mathematics 2, social science 3 and science 2. Engineering and computer science majors require 3 1/2 years of Mathematics, physics, and chemistry. **Test requirements:** SAT or ACT (SAT preferred); score report by August 1.

1992 FRESHMAN CLASS PROFILE. 830 men applied, 750 accepted, 157 enrolled; 323 women applied, 301 accepted, 68 enrolled. **Characteristics:** 52% from in state, 90% live in college housing, 6% have minority backgrounds, 11% are foreign students, 10% join fraternities/sororities. Average age is 21.

FALL-TERM APPLICATIONS. $20 fee, may be waived for applicants with need. No closing date; priority given to applications received by June 1; applicants notified on a rolling basis. Interview recommended. CRDA. Deferred and early admission available.

STUDENT LIFE. Housing: Dormitories (men, women, coed); apartment, fraternity, sorority housing available. Single-room residence housing available for upper-division students. **Activities:** Student government, film, radio, student newspaper, yearbook, drama, musical theater, pep band, fraternities, sororities, Circle-K, Newman Fellowship, Inter-Varsity Christian Fellowship, International Association, Society for Black Engineers, Muslim Student Association.

ATHLETICS. NAIA. **Intercollegiate:** Baseball M, basketball, cross-country, fencing, golf M, soccer, softball W, tennis, track and field, volleyball. **Intramural:** Basketball, bowling, golf, handball, racquetball, skiing, soccer, softball, swimming, table tennis, tennis, volleyball, water polo M.

STUDENT SERVICES. Aptitude testing, career counseling, employment service for undergraduates, freshman orientation, health services, personal counseling, placement service for graduates, special adviser for adult students, veterans counselor.

ANNUAL EXPENSES. Tuition and fees: $9,642. $230 per credit hour for engineering; $197 for others. **Room and board:** $4,200. **Books and supplies:** $469. **Other expenses:** $850.

FINANCIAL AID. 90% of freshmen, 79% of continuing students receive some form of aid. 60% of grants, 95% of loans, all jobs based on need. 164 enrolled freshmen were judged to have need, all were offered aid. Academic, athletic scholarships available. **Aid applications:** No closing date; priority given to applications received by March 1; applicants notified on a rolling basis beginning on or about April 1; must reply by May 1 or within 3 weeks if notified thereafter.

ADDRESS/TELEPHONE. Walter Lilley, Director or Admission, Tri-State University, 320 South Darling, Angola, IN 46703-0307. (219) 665-4133. (800) 347-4878. Fax: (219) 665-4292.

University of Evansville
Evansville, Indiana — CB code: 1208

Admissions: 96% of applicants accepted
Based on:
- ••• School record
- •• Essay, recommendations, special talents, test scores
- • Activities, interview

Completion: 96% of freshmen end year in good standing
60% graduate, 40% of these enter graduate study

4-year private university, coed, affiliated with United Methodist Church. Founded in 1854. **Accreditation:** Regional. **Undergraduate enrollment:** 1,055 men, 1,396 women full time; 160 men, 192 women part time. **Graduate enrollment:** 1 man, 8 women full time; 23 men, 93 women part time. **Faculty:** 165 total, 132 with doctorates or other terminal degrees. **Location:** Suburban campus in small city; 150 miles from Indianapolis and St. Louis, Missouri; 100 miles from Louisville, Kentucky. **Calendar:** Semester, extensive summer session. **Microcomputers:** 100 located in dormitories, libraries, classrooms, computer centers. **Special facilities:** Ceramic studio, art gallery, gerontology center, simulated hospital laboratory, Shanklin Theatre.

DEGREES OFFERED. BA, BS, BFA, MA, MS. 503 bachelor's degrees awarded. 15% in business and management, 6% communications, 7% education, 17% engineering, 13% health sciences, 6% life sciences, 11% multi/interdisciplinary studies, 5% social sciences, 9% visual and performing arts. Graduate degrees offered in 5 major fields of study.

UNDERGRADUATE MAJORS. Associate: Finance, physical therapy assistant. **Bachelor's:** Accounting, applied mathematics, archeology, art education, art history, biology, business economics, business education, chemistry, civil engineering, commercial art, communications, computer engineering, computer programming, creative writing, dramatic arts, economics, education, education of the emotionally handicapped, education of the mentally handicapped, education of the multiple handicapped, electrical/electronics/communications engineering, elementary education, engineering management, English, English education, English literature, environmental administration, environmental science, exercise science, finance, French, German, history, international business management, international studies, journalism, junior high education, legal administration, legal assistant/paralegal, liberal/general studies, management science, marketing and distribution, mathematics, mathematics education, mechanical engineering, medical laboratory technologies, music, music business management, music education, music performance, music therapy, nursing, philosophy, physical education, physics, political science and government, predentistry, prelaw, premedicine, prepharmacy, preveterinary, psychobiology, psychology, public relations, religion, science education, secondary education, social studies education, sociology, Spanish, special education, speech/communication/theater education, studio art, theater business management, theater design, theological studies.

ACADEMIC PROGRAMS. Cooperative education, double major, dual enrollment of high school students, honors program, independent study, internships, study abroad, teacher preparation, visiting/exchange student program, Italian archeological excavation program; liberal arts/career combination in engineering. **Remedial services:** Reduced course load, tutoring. **Placement/credit:** AP, CLEP General and Subject, institutional tests; 6 credit hours maximum for associate degree; 6 credit hours maximum for bachelor's degree. Credits granted for all AP exams with score of 4 or better. Maximum of 6 credits allowed for CLEP exams.

ACADEMIC REQUIREMENTS. Freshmen must earn minimum GPA of 1.6 to continue in good standing. Student must complete minimum of 24 semester hours during academic year for full-time status. 81% of freshmen return for sophomore year. Students must declare major by end of second year. **Graduation requirements:** 124 hours for bachelor's (40 in major). Most students required to take courses in arts/fine arts, English, foreign languages, history, humanities, mathematics, philosophy/religion, biological/physical sciences, social sciences.

FRESHMAN ADMISSIONS. Selection criteria: High school rank in top half of class, college preparatory curriculum. Special talents, recommendations, essay important. **High school preparation:** 14 units required; 17 recommended. Required and recommended units include English 4, mathematics 3-4, social science 2-3 and science 2-3. Biological science 1 and foreign language 2 recommended. Chemistry required for health programs. Chemistry, physics, and 4 units mathematics required for engineering programs. **Test requirements:** SAT or ACT; score report by August 25. **Additional information:** Students seeking admission under early notification calender will get priority consideration for housing, scholarship, advising.

1992 FRESHMAN CLASS PROFILE. 934 men applied, 876 accepted, 299 enrolled; 1,183 women applied, 1,147 accepted, 404 enrolled. 34% were in top tenth and 70% were in top quarter of graduating class. **Academic background:** Mid 50% of enrolled freshmen had SAT-V between 430-530, SAT-M between 480-630; ACT composite between 21-27. 72% submitted SAT scores, 59% submitted ACT scores. **Characteristics:** 53% from in state, 90% live in college housing, 6% have minority backgrounds, 2% are foreign students, 35% join fraternities/sororities. Average age is 18.

FALL-TERM APPLICATIONS. $30 fee, may be waived for applicants with need. Closing date February 15; priority given to applications received by December 1; applicants notified on a rolling basis beginning on or about December 15; must reply by May 1. Audition required for music, theater applicants. Portfolio required for art applicants. Essay required. Interview recommended. Interviews required for academically weak applicants, recommended for all others. Deferred and early admission available. Early closing date required for some programs having limited enrollment. December 15 notification for December 1 applicants. Rolling notification begins February 15 for others.

STUDENT LIFE. Housing: Dormitories (men, women, coed); fraternity, cooperative housing available. **Activities:** Student government, film, magazine, radio, student newspaper, television, yearbook, literary magazine, choral groups, concert band, dance, drama, jazz band, marching band, music ensembles, musical theater, pep band, symphony orchestra, fraternities, sororities, Baptist Student Union, Minority Student Association, Inter-Varsity Christian Fellowship, Hillel, Newman Foundation, Outward Bound International Students Club, Kappa Chi (Service), Amnesty International, Habitat for Humanity.

ATHLETICS. NCAA. **Intercollegiate:** Baseball M, basketball, cross-country, diving, football M, golf M, soccer, softball W, swimming, tennis, volleyball W. **Intramural:** Badminton W, basketball, bowling, cross-country, football M, golf, racquetball, soccer, softball, swimming, table tennis, tennis, track and field, volleyball, wrestling M.

STUDENT SERVICES. Aptitude testing, career counseling, employment service for undergraduates, freshman orientation, health services, personal counseling, placement service for graduates, special adviser for adult students, veterans counselor, international student services, services/facilities for handicapped.

ANNUAL EXPENSES. Tuition and fees: $11,330. **Room and board:** $4,170. **Books and supplies:** $600. **Other expenses:** $450.

FINANCIAL AID. 95% of freshmen, 72% of continuing students receive some form of aid. 47% of grants, 95% of loans, all jobs based on need. 529 enrolled freshmen were judged to have need, all were offered aid. Academic, music/drama, art, athletic, religious affiliation, minority scholarships available. **Aid applications:** No closing date; priority given to applications received by March 1; applicants notified on a rolling basis beginning on or about March 1; must reply by May 1 or within 3 weeks if notified thereafter. **Additional information:** Early financial planning service allows prospective students to get free estimate of aid available to them.

ADDRESS/TELEPHONE. Dr. John Burd, Vice President of Academic Services, University of Evansville, 1800 Lincoln Avenue, Evansville, IN 47722. (812) 479-2468. (800) 423-8633. Fax: (812) 479-2320.

University of Indianapolis
Indianapolis, Indiana — CB code: 1321

Admissions:	84% of applicants accepted
Based on:	••• School record
	•• Test scores
	• Activities, interview, recommendations, special talents
Completion:	90% of freshmen end year in good standing
	13% enter graduate study

4-year private university, coed, affiliated with United Methodist Church. Founded in 1902. **Accreditation:** Regional. **Undergraduate enrollment:** 590 men, 812 women full time; 339 men, 1,129 women part time. **Graduate enrollment:** 100 men, 147 women full time; 181 men, 280 women part time. **Faculty:** 276 total (121 full time), 56 with doctorates or other terminal degrees. **Location:** Suburban campus in very large city; 5 miles from downtown. **Calendar:** 2 terms of 15 weeks followed by spring term of 3 weeks. Saturday and extensive evening/early morning classes. **Microcomputers:** 200 located in libraries, classrooms, computer centers. **Special facilities:** Observatory, art gallery.

DEGREES OFFERED. AA, AS, BA, BS, MA, MS, MBA. 90 associate degrees awarded in 1992. 37% in business and management, 35% health sciences, 20% law, 5% social sciences. 258 bachelor's degrees awarded. 32% in business and management, 7% communications, 15% teacher education, 17% health sciences, 19% social sciences. Graduate degrees offered in 9 major fields of study.

UNDERGRADUATE MAJORS. Associate: Business and management, business and office, business data processing and related programs, chemistry, contract management and procurement/purchasing, credit management, criminal justice studies, data processing, finance, hotel/motel and restaurant management, law enforcement and corrections, legal assistant/paralegal, liberal/general studies, nursing, tourism, transportation and travel marketing. **Bachelor's:** Accounting, art education, art history, art therapy, biology, business administration and management, business and management, business economics, business education, chemistry, communications, communications in business, computer and information sciences, criminal justice studies, data processing, dramatic arts, early childhood education, earth sciences, economics, electrical/electronics/communications engineering, elementary education, English, English education, finance, foreign languages education, French, German, graphic design, history, human biology, information sciences and systems, international business management, journalism, junior high education, law enforcement and corrections, management information systems, marketing management, mathematics, mathematics education, mechanical engineering, medical laboratory technologies, music, music education, music performance, nursing, philosophy, physical education, physical sciences, physics, political science and government, predentistry, preforestry, prelaw, premedicine, preveterinary, psychology, radio/television broadcasting, religion, science education, secondary education, social studies education, social work, sociology, Spanish, specific learning disabilities, speech/communication/theater education, sports information, studio art.

ACADEMIC PROGRAMS. Accelerated program, cooperative education, double major, dual enrollment of high school students, honors program, independent study, internships, study abroad, teacher preparation, visiting/exchange student program, weekend college, cross-registration, third-year medical technology program at Methodist Hospital, Baccalaureate for University of Indianapolis for Learning Disabled (BUILD); liberal arts/career combination in engineering. **Remedial services:** Learning center, reduced course load, remedial instruction, special counselor, tutoring, limited college preparation workshop. **ROTC:** Army. **Placement/credit:** AP, CLEP General and Subject, institutional tests.

ACADEMIC REQUIREMENTS. Freshmen must earn minimum GPA of 1.8 to continue in good standing. 75% of freshmen return for sophomore year. Students must declare major by end of first year. **Graduation require-**

ments: 62 hours for associate (20 in major), 124 hours for bachelor's (24 in major). Most students required to take courses in arts/fine arts, computer science, English, history, humanities, mathematics, philosophy/religion, biological/physical sciences, social sciences. **Postgraduate studies:** 50% from 2-year programs enter 4-year programs.

FRESHMAN ADMISSIONS. Selection criteria: High school class rank and academic record considered, test scores required. **High school preparation:** 12 units required. Required and recommended units include biological science 1, English 4, foreign language 2-2, mathematics 2-3, social science 2 and science 1-2. **Test requirements:** SAT or ACT; score report by August 15.

1992 FRESHMAN CLASS PROFILE. 569 men applied, 464 accepted, 163 enrolled; 723 women applied, 626 accepted, 202 enrolled. 39% had high school GPA of 3.0 or higher, 52% between 2.0 and 2.99. 26% were in top tenth and 45% were in top quarter of graduating class. **Academic background:** Mid 50% of enrolled freshmen had SAT-V between 360-490, SAT-M between 410-560; ACT composite between 18-25. 93% submitted SAT scores, 29% submitted ACT scores. **Characteristics:** 90% from in state, 87% live in college housing, 10% have minority backgrounds, 1% are foreign students. Average age is 18.

FALL-TERM APPLICATIONS. $20 fee, may be waived for applicants with need. Closing date August 15; priority given to applications received by March 1; applicants notified on a rolling basis; must reply by May 1 or within 2 weeks if notified thereafter. Audition required for music applicants. Interview recommended for borderline applicants. Portfolio recommended for art applicants. CRDA. Deferred and early admission available.

STUDENT LIFE. Housing: Dormitories (women, coed); apartment housing available. **Activities:** Student government, magazine, radio, student newspaper, television, yearbook, choral groups, concert band, dance, drama, jazz band, music ensembles, musical theater, opera, pep band, symphony orchestra, Young Democrats, Young Republicans, Fellowship of Christian Athletes, Circle-K, social service and honorary societies.

ATHLETICS. NCAA. **Intercollegiate:** Baseball M, basketball, cross-country, diving, football M, golf, soccer M, softball W, swimming, tennis, track and field, volleyball W, wrestling M. **Intramural:** Badminton, basketball, racquetball, softball, table tennis, tennis, volleyball.

STUDENT SERVICES. Aptitude testing, career counseling, employment service for undergraduates, freshman orientation, health services, personal counseling, placement service for graduates, services/facilities for handicapped.

ANNUAL EXPENSES. Tuition and fees: $10,590. **Room and board:** $3,920. **Books and supplies:** $515. **Other expenses:** $975.

FINANCIAL AID. 76% of freshmen, 85% of continuing students receive some form of aid. 53% of grants, 85% of loans, 20% of jobs based on need. 252 enrolled freshmen were judged to have need, all were offered aid. Academic, music/drama, art, athletic, state/district residency, leadership, alumni affiliation, religious affiliation scholarships available. **Aid applications:** No closing date; priority given to applications received by March 1; applicants notified on a rolling basis beginning on or about March 1; must reply by May 1 or within 2 weeks if notified thereafter. **Additional information:** Participant in Council of Independent Colleges Tuition Exchange and National Tuition Exchange.

ADDRESS/TELEPHONE. Mark Weigand, Director of Admissions, University of Indianapolis, 1400 East Hanna Avenue, Indianapolis, IN 46227-3697. (317) 788-3216. (800) 232-8634. Fax: (317) 788-3300.

University of Notre Dame
Notre Dame, Indiana — CB code: 1841

Admissions: 49% of applicants accepted
Based on: ••• School record
•• Activities, essay, recommendations, special talents, test scores
Completion: 99% of freshmen end year in good standing
93% graduate, 42% of these enter graduate study

4-year private university, coed; affiliated with Roman Catholic Church. Founded in 1842. **Accreditation:** Regional. **Undergraduate enrollment:** 4,700 men, 2,900 women full time. **Graduate enrollment:** 1,480 men, 820 women full time; 100 men, 100 women part time. **Faculty:** 960 total (700 full time), 850 with doctorates or other terminal degrees. **Location:** Suburban campus in small city; 90 miles from Chicago. **Calendar:** Semester, extensive summer session. **Microcomputers:** 1,000 located in dormitories, classrooms, computer centers, campus-wide network. **Special facilities:** Art museum, theater, germ-free research facility, radiation laboratory, preserve for biological research in Land O' Lakes, Wisconsin, international studies center.

DEGREES OFFERED. BA, BS, BFA, BArch, MA, MS, MBA, MFA, PhD, JD, M.Div. 1,910 bachelor's degrees awarded in 1992. 26% in business and management, 17% engineering, 8% letters/literature, 10% life sciences, 5% multi/interdisciplinary studies, 17% social sciences. Graduate degrees offered in 74 major fields of study.

UNDERGRADUATE MAJORS. Accounting, aerospace/aeronautical/astronautical engineering, African studies, Afro-American (black) studies, American literature, American studies, anthropology, applied mathematics, architecture, art history, Asian studies, biochemistry, biology, biophysics, business administration and management, business economics, cell biology, ceramics, chemical engineering, chemistry, cinematography/film, civil engineering, classics, communications, comparative literature, computer and information sciences, computer engineering, computer mathematics, dramatic arts, drawing, earth sciences, Eastern European studies, economics, electrical/electronics/communications engineering, engineering, engineering and other disciplines, English, English literature, European studies, film arts, finance, foreign languages (multiple emphasis), French, geological engineering, geology, German, graphic design, Greek (classical), history, international business management, international relations, international studies, Italian, Japanese, Latin, Latin American studies, liberal/general studies, management information systems, management science, marketing management, marketing research, mathematics, mechanical engineering, medieval studies, microbiology, molecular biology, music, music performance, music theory and composition, painting, philosophy, photography, physical sciences, physics, political science and government, predentistry, premedicine, prepharmacy, preveterinary, psychology, pure mathematics, religion, Russian, sculpture, secondary education, sociology, Spanish, studio art, theological studies, video, visual and performing arts, Western European studies.

ACADEMIC PROGRAMS. Accelerated program, double major, honors program, independent study, internships, student-designed major, study abroad, teacher preparation, visiting/exchange student program, Washington semester, cross-registration; liberal arts/career combination in engineering, business; combined bachelor's/graduate program in business administration. **Remedial services:** Learning center, reduced course load, special counselor, tutoring. **ROTC:** Air Force, Army, Naval. **Placement/credit:** AP, IB, institutional tests.

ACADEMIC REQUIREMENTS. Freshmen must earn minimum GPA of 1.85 to continue in good standing. 97% of freshmen return for sophomore year. Students must declare major by end of second year. **Graduation requirements:** 120 hours for bachelor's (30 in major). Most students required to take courses in English, history, humanities, mathematics, philosophy/religion, biological/physical sciences, social sciences. **Postgraduate studies:** 9% enter law school, 10% enter medical school, 3% enter MBA programs, 20% enter other graduate study. **Additional information:** Research opportunities for undergraduates majoring in science.

FRESHMAN ADMISSIONS. Selection criteria: Demonstrated academic achievement and test scores most important. Essay, teacher recommendations, extracurricular activities, and personal statement also considered. Alumni children receive some additional consideration. **High school preparation:** 16 units required; 20 recommended. Required and recommended units include biological science 1-2, English 4, foreign language 2-4, mathematics 3-4, physical science 1-2 and social science 2-4. 1 history required. Mathematics units must include 1 algebra, 1 geometry, 1 advanced algebra with trigenometry. Additional units required of engineering and science majors: 1 advanced mathematics, 1 chemistry, 1 physics. **Test requirements:** SAT or ACT (SAT preferred); score report by February 28. ACH required for high school foreign language for continuation of study. Score report by February 28. **Additional information:** Freshman admission extremely competitive.

1992 FRESHMAN CLASS PROFILE. 4,400 men applied, 2,100 accepted, 1,058 enrolled; 3,300 women applied, 1,700 accepted, 824 enrolled. 98% had high school GPA of 3.0 or higher, 2% between 2.0 and 2.99. 78% were in top tenth and 96% were in top quarter of graduating class. **Academic background:** Mid 50% of enrolled freshmen had SAT-V between 540-650, SAT-M between 620-720. 97% submitted SAT scores. **Characteristics:** 9% from in state, 99% live in college housing, 14% have minority backgrounds, 3% are foreign students. Average age is 18.

FALL-TERM APPLICATIONS. $35 fee, may be waived for applicants with need. Closing date January 4; priority given to applications received by December 1; applicants notified on or about April 5; must reply by May 1. Essay required. Audition recommended for music applicants. Portfolio recommended for art applicants. CRDA. Deferred admission available. Institutional early decision plan. Nonbinding Early Action plan: apply by November 1, notification before December 20. Accepted applicants must reply by May 1.

STUDENT LIFE. Housing: Dormitories (men, women); apartment, handicapped housing available. Most students live in same residence hall for duration of stay on campus. **Activities:** Student government, film, magazine, radio, student newspaper, television, yearbook, student weekly magazine, choral groups, concert band, dance, drama, jazz band, marching band, music ensembles, musical theater, pep band, symphony orchestra, over 20 community social service programs, Hispanic and black organizations.

ATHLETICS. NCAA. **Intercollegiate:** Baseball M, basketball, cross-country, diving, fencing, football M, golf, gymnastics, ice hockey M, lacrosse M, rowing (crew), sailing, soccer, softball W, swimming, tennis, track and field, volleyball. **Intramural:** Badminton, baseball M, basketball, bowling, boxing M, cross-country, football M, golf, handball, ice hockey M, lacrosse M, racquetball, skiing, soccer, softball, squash, swimming, table tennis, tennis, track and field, volleyball, water polo. **Clubs:** Rugby, sailing, skiing, water polo, horseback riding.

STUDENT SERVICES. Aptitude testing, career counseling, em-

ployment service for undergraduates, freshman orientation, health services, personal counseling, placement service for graduates, academic counseling required for all freshmen, services/facilities for handicapped.

ANNUAL EXPENSES. Tuition and fees (projected): $16,010. **Room and board:** $4,150. **Books and supplies:** $550. **Other expenses:** $1,165.

FINANCIAL AID. 67% of freshmen, 71% of continuing students receive some form of aid. 37% of grants, 99% of loans, 47% of jobs based on need. 813 enrolled freshmen were judged to have need, all were offered aid. Athletic scholarships available. **Aid applications:** Closing date February 28; applicants notified on or about April 15; must reply by May 1.

ADDRESS/TELEPHONE. Kevin M. Rooney, Director of Admissions, University of Notre Dame, Office of Admissions, Notre Dame, IN 46556-5602. (219) 631-7505.

University of Southern Indiana
Evansville, Indiana — CB code: 1335

4-year public university and college of arts and sciences, coed. Founded in 1965. **Accreditation:** Regional. **Undergraduate enrollment:** 7,430 men and women. **Graduate enrollment:** 98 men and women. **Faculty:** 319 total (164 full time), 92 with doctorates or other terminal degrees. **Location:** Suburban campus in small city; 175 miles from Indianapolis, 150 miles from Louisville, Kentucky. **Calendar:** Semester, limited summer session. Extensive evening/early morning classes. **Microcomputers:** Located in dormitories, libraries, classrooms, computer centers. **Special facilities:** New Harmony, a restored historic town managed by the university. **Additional facts:** Credit courses offered at various off-campus sites in Evansville and surrounding areas.

DEGREES OFFERED. AA, AS, BA, BS, MA, MS, MBA. 133 associate degrees awarded in 1992. 25% in business and management, 69% allied health. 625 bachelor's degrees awarded. 31% in business and management, 7% communications, 22% teacher education, 14% social sciences. Graduate degrees offered in 5 major fields of study.

UNDERGRADUATE MAJORS. Associate: Business and management, business and office, business computer/console/peripheral equipment operation, business data programming, civil technology, communications, dental assistant, dental hygiene, early childhood education, electrical technology, engineering and engineering-related technologies, forestry and related sciences, information sciences and systems, mechanical engineering technology, nursing, preforestry, preosteopathy, prepodiatry, pretheology, radiograph medical technology, respiratory therapy technology, secretarial and related programs, social sciences. **Bachelor's:** Accounting, art education, biology, biophysics, business administration and management, business and management, business economics, business education, chemistry, civil technology, communications, dental hygiene education, education, electrical technology, elementary education, English, English education, finance, foreign languages education, French, geology, German, health sciences, history, industrial supervision, information sciences and systems, junior high education, marketing management, mathematics, mathematics education, mechanical engineering technology, medical laboratory technologies, nursing, occupational therapy, office supervision and management, philosophy, physical education, political science and government, predentistry, preengineering, prelaw, premedicine, preosteopathy, prepharmacy, preveterinary, psychology, science education, secondary education, social science education, social sciences, social studies education, social work, sociology, Spanish, speech/communication/theater education, visual and performing arts.

ACADEMIC PROGRAMS. 2-year transfer program, cooperative education, double major, dual enrollment of high school students, independent study, internships, student-designed major, teacher preparation; combined bachelor's/graduate program in business administration. **Remedial services:** Learning center, reduced course load, remedial instruction, special counselor, tutoring. **Placement/credit:** AP, CLEP General and Subject, institutional tests; 46 credit hours maximum for associate degree; 94 credit hours maximum for bachelor's degree.

ACADEMIC REQUIREMENTS. Freshmen must earn minimum GPA of 2.0 to continue in good standing. Students must declare major by end of second year. **Graduation requirements:** 64 hours for associate (38 in major), 124 hours for bachelor's (78 in major). Most students required to take courses in English, humanities, mathematics, biological/physical sciences, social sciences. **Postgraduate studies:** 30% from 2-year programs enter 4-year programs. 1% enter law school, 2% enter medical school, 4% enter MBA programs, 12% enter other graduate study.

FRESHMAN ADMISSIONS. Selection criteria: Open admissions. 2.0 GPA for out-of-state applicants. Recommended units include English 4, foreign language 2, mathematics 2, social science 2 and science 2. **Test requirements:** SAT or ACT for placement and counseling only; score report by August 15.

1992 FRESHMAN CLASS PROFILE. 2,412 men and women applied, 2,317 accepted; 1,399 enrolled. 24% had high school GPA of 3.0 or higher, 49% between 2.0 and 2.99. 13% were in top tenth and 37% were in top quarter of graduating class. **Characteristics:** 95% from in state, 78% commute, 5% have minority backgrounds, 1% are foreign students, 20% join fraternities/sororities. Average age is 19.

FALL-TERM APPLICATIONS. No fee. No closing date; priority given to applications received by August 15; applicants notified on a rolling basis. Interview recommended. Early admission available. Applicants accepted through first week of classes, but encouraged to apply by August 15 for fall and January 1 for spring.

STUDENT LIFE. Housing: Apartment, fraternity housing available. Apartments located on campus. **Activities:** Student government, film, magazine, radio, student newspaper, television, yearbook, choral groups, drama, music ensembles, musical theater, pep band, fraternities, sororities, Black Student Union, campus ministry, over 70 other clubs and organizations.

ATHLETICS. NCAA. **Intercollegiate:** Baseball M, basketball, cross-country, golf M, soccer M, softball W, tennis, volleyball W. **Intramural:** Basketball, bowling, golf, softball, tennis, volleyball, water polo.

STUDENT SERVICES. Aptitude testing, employment service for undergraduates, counselor for handicapped students, services/facilities for handicapped.

ANNUAL EXPENSES. Tuition and fees (projected): $2,118, $3,062 additional for out-of-state students. **Room and board:** $1,660 room only. **Books and supplies:** $500. **Other expenses:** $925.

FINANCIAL AID. 53% of freshmen, 45% of continuing students receive some form of aid. 70% of grants, 78% of loans, 12% of jobs based on need. 807 enrolled freshmen were judged to have need, 690 were offered aid. Academic, music/drama, art, athletic, state/district residency, leadership, minority scholarships available. **Aid applications:** No closing date; priority given to applications received by March 1; applicants notified on a rolling basis; must reply within 2 weeks.

ADDRESS/TELEPHONE. Timothy K. Buecher, Director of Admissions, University of Southern Indiana, 8600 University Boulevard, Evansville, IN 47712. (812) 464-1765. (800) 467-1965. Fax: A.

Valparaiso University
Valparaiso, Indiana — CB code: 1874

4-year private university, coed, affiliated with Lutheran Church—Missouri Synod. Founded in 1859. **Accreditation:** Regional. **Undergraduate enrollment:** 1,232 men, 1,533 women full time; 54 men, 174 women part time. **Graduate enrollment:** 313 men, 219 women full time; 66 men, 166 women part time. **Faculty:** 310 total (230 full time), 180 with doctorates or other terminal degrees. **Location:** Suburban campus in large town; 45 miles from Chicago. **Microcomputers:** 225 located in dormitories, libraries, classrooms, computer centers. **Special facilities:** Nuclear reactor, planetarium, observatory, speech and hearing clinic.

DEGREES OFFERED. AS, BA, BS, MA, MS, MEd, JD. 100% in multi/interdisciplinary studies. 763 bachelor's degrees awarded. 17% in business and management, 8% communications, 6% education, 11% engineering, 11% health sciences, 5% letters/literature, 5% multi/interdisciplinary studies, 6% psychology, 9% social sciences. Graduate degrees offered in 13 major fields of study.

UNDERGRADUATE MAJORS. Associate: Allied health, biological and physical sciences. **Bachelor's:** Accounting, American studies, astronomy, biological and physical sciences, biology, business administration and management, chemistry, civil engineering, classics, communications, computer and information sciences, computer engineering, criminal justice studies, East Asian studies, economics, education, electrical/electronics/communications engineering, elementary education, English, fine arts, food science and nutrition, French, geography, geology, German, Greek (classical), history, home economics, home furnishings and equipment management/production/services, humanities and social sciences, international studies, journalism, Latin, liberal/general studies, mathematics, mechanical engineering, music, music education, music history and appreciation, music theory and composition, nursing, philosophy, physical education, physics, political science and government, psychology, public relations, religion, social work, sociology, Spanish, speech pathology/audiology, theological studies, visual and performing arts.

ACADEMIC PROGRAMS. 2-year transfer program, accelerated program, cooperative education, double major, dual enrollment of high school students, honors program, independent study, internships, student-designed major, study abroad, teacher preparation, visiting/exchange student program, United Nations semester, Washington semester, cross-registration; liberal arts/career combination in engineering, health sciences. **Remedial services:** Learning center, reduced course load, special counselor, tutoring, writing center. **Placement/credit:** AP, CLEP General and Subject, IB, institutional tests.

ACADEMIC REQUIREMENTS. Freshmen must earn minimum GPA of 2.0 to continue in good standing. 93% of freshmen return for sophomore year. Students must declare major by end of second year. **Graduation requirements:** 60 hours for associate (30 in major), 124 hours for bachelor's (30 in major). Most students required to take courses in English, foreign languages, history, mathematics, philosophy/religion, biological/physical sciences, social sciences.

FRESHMAN ADMISSIONS. Selection criteria: High school record most important. Test scores next in importance, followed by recommendations and activities. Nature of high school program considered. **High school**

preparation: 14 units recommended. Recommended units include biological science 1, English 4, foreign language 2, mathematics 3, physical science 2 and social science 2. **Test requirements:** SAT or ACT; score report by August 15.

1992 FRESHMAN CLASS PROFILE. 273 men, 357 women enrolled. 38% were in top tenth and 69% were in top quarter of graduating class. **Academic background:** Mid 50% of enrolled freshmen had SAT-V between 440-560, SAT-M between 510-650; ACT composite between 23-29. 49% submitted SAT scores, 51% submitted ACT scores. **Characteristics:** 29% from in state, 92% live in college housing, 4% have minority backgrounds, 1% are foreign students, 34% join fraternities/sororities. Average age is 18.

FALL-TERM APPLICATIONS. $30 fee, may be waived for applicants with need. No closing date; priority given to applications received by April 1; applicants notified on a rolling basis; must reply by May 1 or within 4 weeks if notified thereafter. Audition required for music applicants. Interview recommended. Portfolio recommended for art applicants. Essay recommended. CRDA. Deferred and early admission available. EDP-F.

STUDENT LIFE. Housing: Dormitories (men, women, coed); fraternity, sorority housing available. **Activities:** Student government, magazine, radio, student newspaper, television, yearbook, choral groups, concert band, dance, drama, jazz band, music ensembles, musical theater, pep band, symphony orchestra, fraternities, sororities, Lutheran Campus Ministry, Fellowship of Christian Athletes, Alpha Phi Omega, Conservative Voice, St. Teresa of Avila, Black Student Organization, International Student Association, One in the Spirit, Circle-K.

ATHLETICS. NCAA. **Intercollegiate:** Baseball M, basketball, cross-country, diving, football M, soccer, softball W, swimming, tennis, volleyball W, wrestling M. **Intramural:** Badminton, basketball, bowling, cross-country, diving, golf, handball, racquetball, rugby M, soccer, softball, swimming, table tennis, tennis, track and field, volleyball, water polo M, wrestling M.

STUDENT SERVICES. Aptitude testing, career counseling, employment service for undergraduates, freshman orientation, health services, personal counseling, placement service for graduates, wellness program, services/facilities for handicapped.

ANNUAL EXPENSES. Tuition and fees: $11,720. **Room and board:** $3,090. **Books and supplies:** $500. **Other expenses:** $600.

FINANCIAL AID. 80% of freshmen, 75% of continuing students receive some form of aid. 48% of grants, 89% of loans, 27% of jobs based on need. Academic, music/drama, athletic, leadership, alumni affiliation, religious affiliation, minority scholarships available. **Aid applications:** No closing date; priority given to applications received by March 1; applicants notified on a rolling basis; must reply by May 1 or within 4 weeks if notified thereafter.

ADDRESS/TELEPHONE. Katharine Wehling, Vice President for Admissions/Student Financial Planning, Valparaiso University, Office of Admissions, Valparaiso, IN 46383-6493. (219) 464-5011. (800) 348-2611. Fax: (219) 464-5381.

Vincennes University
Vincennes, Indiana

CB code: 1877

2-year public junior college, coed. Founded in 1801. **Accreditation:** Regional. **Undergraduate enrollment:** 4,329 men, 2,692 women full time; 375 men, 625 women part time. **Faculty:** 408 total (402 full time), 45 with doctorates or other terminal degrees. **Location:** Suburban campus in large town; 120 miles from Indianapolis, 55 miles from Evansville, IN. **Calendar:** Semester, extensive summer session. Extensive evening/early morning classes. **Microcomputers:** 200 located in dormitories, libraries, classrooms, computer centers, campus-wide network. **Special facilities:** Planetarium, nature trails, 2 college-owned airports, television station.

DEGREES OFFERED. AA, AS, AAS. 1,495 associate degrees awarded in 1992. 5% in agriculture, 20% business and management, 10% health sciences, 5% law, 5% life sciences, 5% mathematics, 5% social sciences, 25% trade and industry, 5% visual and performing arts.

UNDERGRADUATE MAJORS. Accounting, aeronautical technology, agribusiness, agricultural economics, agricultural education, agricultural engineering, agricultural mechanics, agricultural products and processing, agricultural sciences, agronomy, aircraft mechanics, airline piloting and navigation, American sign language, animal sciences, anthropology, archeology, architectural technologies, art education, autobody repair, automotive mechanics, automotive technology, behavioral sciences, biological and physical sciences, biology, biomedical equipment technology, botany, bowling lane mechanics, business administration and management, business and management, business and office, business computer/console/peripheral equipment operation, business data entry equipment operation, business data processing and related programs, business data programming, business education, carpentry, ceramics, chemical engineering, chemistry, child development/care/guidance, civil engineering, civil technology, clinical laboratory science, clothing and textiles management/production/services, commercial art, computer and information sciences, computer graphics, computer programming, computer servicing technology, computer technology, construction, criminal justice studies, data processing, dental hygiene, diesel engine mechanics, drafting, drafting and design technology, dramatic arts, drawing, driver and safety education, early childhood education, earth sciences, economics, education, education of the deaf and hearing impaired, education of the emotionally handicapped, electrical and electronics equipment repair, electrical technology, electrical/electronics/communications engineering, electronic technology, elementary education, engineering, engineering and other disciplines, English, English education, fashion design, fashion merchandising, finance, fine arts, fishing and fisheries, food management, food production/management/services, food science and nutrition, food sciences, foreign languages education, forestry and related sciences, forestry production and processing, French, funeral services/mortuary science, geography, geology, German, gerontology, graphic and printing production, graphic arts technology, graphic design, health education, history, home economics, home economics education, horticultural science, horticulture, hospitality and recreation marketing, hotel/motel and restaurant management, human resources development, humanities, humanities and social sciences, illustration design, industrial arts education, industrial equipment maintenance and repair, information sciences and systems, injection tool mold, instrumentation technology, insurance and risk management, insurance marketing, interior design, international business management, interpreter for the deaf, journalism, junior high education, laser electro-optic technology, law enforcement and corrections, law enforcement and corrections technologies, legal assistant/paralegal, legal secretary, liberal/general studies, library science, machine tool operation/machine shop, management information systems, marketing and distribution, marketing and distributive education, marketing management, mathematics, mathematics education, mechanical design technology, mechanical engineering, medical assistant, medical laboratory technologies, medical records administration, medical records technology, medical secretary, music, music education, music theory and composition, musical theater, nuclear medical technology, nursing, nursing education, nutritional education, occupational therapy, office supervision and management, optometry, ornamental horticulture, painting, personal services, pharmaceutical chemistry, pharmacy, philosophy, physical education, physical sciences, physical therapy assistant, physics, plant pharmacology, plastic technology, political science and government, precision metal work, predentistry, prelaw, premedicine, prepharmacy, preveterinary, printmaking, psychology, public affairs, public relations, radio/television broadcasting, radio/television technology, reading education, recreation and community services technologies, recreation therapy, remedial education, renewable natural resources, respiratory therapy, respiratory therapy technology, retailing, robotics, science education, science technologies, sculpture, secondary education, secretarial and related programs, small business management and ownership, social science education, social sciences, social studies education, social work, sociology, soil sciences, solar heating and cooling technology, Spanish, special education, specific learning disabilities, speech, speech correction, speech/communication/theater education, sports management, sports medicine, studio art, survey and mapping technology, surveying and mapping sciences, teacher aide, teaching English as a second language/foreign language, technical education, textiles and clothing, tool and die, trade and industrial education, visual and performing arts, welding technology, wildlife management, word processing, zoology.

ACADEMIC PROGRAMS. 2-year transfer program, double major, dual enrollment of high school students, external degree, honors program, independent study, internships, student-designed major, telecourses. **Remedial services:** Learning center, preadmission summer program, reduced course load, remedial instruction, special counselor, tutoring. **Placement/credit:** AP, CLEP General and Subject, institutional tests; 18 credit hours maximum for associate degree.

ACADEMIC REQUIREMENTS. Freshmen must earn minimum GPA of 2.0 to continue in good standing. 72% of freshmen return for sophomore year. Students must declare major on enrollment. **Graduation requirements:** 64 hours for associate (40 in major). Most students required to take courses in English, humanities, mathematics, biological/physical sciences, social sciences.

FRESHMAN ADMISSIONS. Selection criteria: Open admissions. Selective admissions to health occupation programs. **Test requirements:** SAT or ACT (SAT preferred) required for health occupation programs.

1992 FRESHMAN CLASS PROFILE. 2,145 men, 1,384 women enrolled. 15% had high school GPA of 3.0 or higher, 55% between 2.0 and 2.99. **Academic background:** Mid 50% of enrolled freshmen had SAT-V between 290-420, SAT-M between 310-450; ACT composite between 15-29. 60% submitted SAT scores, 5% submitted ACT scores. **Characteristics:** 90% from in state, 55% commute, 5% have minority backgrounds, 3% are foreign students, 5% join fraternities/sororities. Average age is 18.

FALL-TERM APPLICATIONS. $20 fee. Closing date August 28; priority given to applications received by July 14; applicants notified on a rolling basis; must reply within 4 weeks. Audition required for music applicants. Portfolio recommended for fine arts, commercial art, design applicants. Deferred and early admission available.

STUDENT LIFE. Housing: Dormitories (men, women, coed); fraternity housing available. **Activities:** Student government, film, magazine, radio, student newspaper, television, yearbook, choral groups, concert band, dance, drama, jazz band, music ensembles, musical theater, pep band, fraternities, sororities.

ATHLETICS. NJCAA. **Intercollegiate:** Baseball M, basketball, bowling, cross-country, diving, golf, soccer M, swimming, tennis M, track and field, volleyball W. **Intramural:** Archery, badminton, baseball, basketball, bowling, cross-country, golf, gymnastics, handball, racquetball, skiing, soccer, softball, swimming, table tennis, tennis, track and field, volleyball, wrestling.

STUDENT SERVICES. Aptitude testing, career counseling, employment service for undergraduates, health services, on-campus day care, personal counseling, placement service for graduates, special adviser for adult students, veterans counselor, services/facilities for handicapped.

ANNUAL EXPENSES. Tuition and fees (projected): $2,220, $1,110 additional for out-of-district students, $3,270 additional for out-of-state students. **Room and board:** $3,480. **Books and supplies:** $500. **Other expenses:** $550.

FINANCIAL AID. 60% of freshmen, 55% of continuing students receive some form of aid. 99% of grants, 90% of loans, all jobs based on need. Academic, music/drama, art, athletic, leadership, alumni affiliation scholarships available. **Aid applications:** No closing date; priority given to applications received by March 1; applicants notified on a rolling basis beginning on or about June 1; must reply by May 1 or within 2 weeks if notified thereafter.

ADDRESS/TELEPHONE. Stephen M. Simonds, Director of Admissions, Vincennes University, 1002 First Street, Vincennes, IN 47591. (812) 885-4313. (800) 742-9198. Fax: (812) 885-5868.

Wabash College

Crawfordsville, Indiana — CB code: 1895

Admissions: 77% of applicants accepted
Based on:
- ••• School record
- •• Recommendations, test scores
- • Activities, essay, interview, special talents

Completion: 90% of freshmen end year in good standing
75% graduate, 46% of these enter graduate study

4-year private liberal arts college, men only. Founded in 1832. **Accreditation:** Regional. **Undergraduate enrollment:** 768 men full time; 4 men part time. **Faculty:** 80 total (74 full time), 71 with doctorates or other terminal degrees. **Location:** Rural campus in large town; 45 miles from Indianapolis. **Calendar:** Semester. **Microcomputers:** 103 located in libraries, classrooms, computer centers. **Special facilities:** 2 art galleries, 180-acre biology field station.

DEGREES OFFERED. BA. 195 bachelor's degrees awarded in 1992. 13% in letters/literature, 7% life sciences, 7% mathematics, 9% philosophy, religion, theology, 10% physical sciences, 13% psychology, 33% social sciences.

UNDERGRADUATE MAJORS. Biology, chemistry, classics, dramatic arts, economics, English, fine arts, French, German, Greek (classical), history, Latin, mathematics, music, philosophy, physics, political science and government, psychology, religion, Spanish, speech.

ACADEMIC PROGRAMS. Double major, independent study, internships, semester at sea, study abroad, teacher preparation, visiting/exchange student program, New York semester, Washington semester, cooperative law program with Columbia University (NY), International and Domestic Study Program of Great Lakes Colleges Association; liberal arts/career combination in engineering; combined bachelor's/graduate program in law. **Remedial services:** Special counselor, tutoring, writing center, quantitative skills center. **Placement/credit:** AP, CLEP General and Subject, IB, institutional tests.

ACADEMIC REQUIREMENTS. Freshmen must earn minimum GPA of 1.1 to continue in good standing. 90% of freshmen return for sophomore year. Students must declare major by end of second year. **Graduation requirements:** 136 hours for bachelor's (28 in major). Most students required to take courses in arts/fine arts, English, foreign languages, history, humanities, mathematics, philosophy/religion, biological/physical sciences, social sciences. **Postgraduate studies:** 13% enter law school, 6% enter medical school, 1% enter MBA programs, 26% enter other graduate study.

FRESHMAN ADMISSIONS. Selection criteria: In order of importance: school achievement record, test scores, essay, and school's recommendation required. Alumni relation and extracurricular activities also considered. **High school preparation:** 13 units recommended. Recommended units include English 4, foreign language 2, mathematics 3, social science 2 and science 2. Typing and computer literacy strongly recommended. **Test requirements:** SAT or ACT; score report by May 1.

1992 FRESHMAN CLASS PROFILE. 694 men applied, 533 accepted, 219 enrolled. 78% had high school GPA of 3.0 or higher, 22% between 2.0 and 2.99. 47% were in top tenth and 70% were in top quarter of graduating class. **Academic background:** Mid 50% of enrolled freshmen had SAT-V between 460-580, SAT-M between 540-650. 98% submitted SAT scores. **Characteristics:** 75% from in state, 100% live in college housing, 15% have minority backgrounds, 4% are foreign students, 68% join fraternities/sororities. Average age is 18.

FALL-TERM APPLICATIONS. $15 fee, may be waived for applicants with need. Closing date July 15; priority given to applications received by February 1; applicants notified on a rolling basis; must reply by May 1 or within 3 weeks if notified thereafter. Essay required. Interview recommended. CRDA. Deferred and early admission available.

STUDENT LIFE. Housing: Dormitories (men); fraternity, cooperative housing available. International House and limited wheelchair accessibility available. **Activities:** Student government, magazine, radio, student newspaper, yearbook, literary review, satire magazine, choral groups, concert band, drama, jazz band, music ensembles, musical theater, pep band, fraternities, Malcolm X Institute for Black Studies, political groups, Newman Center, Alpha Phi Omega, Fellowship of Christian Athletes, International Club, Mortar Board, Moslem Student Association, Wabash Christian Fellowship.

ATHLETICS. NCAA. **Intercollegiate:** Baseball, basketball, cross-country, diving, football, golf, sailing, soccer, swimming, tennis, track and field, wrestling. **Intramural:** Badminton, basketball, bowling, boxing, cross-country, diving, golf, handball, ice hockey, racquetball, skiing, soccer, softball, swimming, table tennis, tennis, track and field, volleyball, water polo, wrestling.

STUDENT SERVICES. Career counseling, employment service for undergraduates, freshman orientation, health services, personal counseling, placement service for graduates, minority counseling, services/facilities for handicapped.

ANNUAL EXPENSES. Tuition and fees: $12,450. **Room and board:** $4,000. **Books and supplies:** $500. **Other expenses:** $635.

FINANCIAL AID. 90% of freshmen, 87% of continuing students receive some form of aid. 63% of grants, 98% of loans, all jobs based on need. 180 enrolled freshmen were judged to have need, all were offered aid. Academic, music/drama, art, state/district residency, leadership scholarships available. **Aid applications:** No closing date; priority given to applications received by March 15; applicants notified on a rolling basis beginning on or about January 1; must reply by May 1 or within 3 weeks if notified thereafter. **Additional information:** Unlimited President's Scholarships based on class rank, SAT scores. Extensive merit awards.

ADDRESS/TELEPHONE. Greg Birk, Director of Admissions, Wabash College, PO Box 352, Crawfordsville, IN 47933-0352. (317) 364-4225. (800) 345-5385. Fax: (317) 364-4295.

Iowa

American Institute of Business

Des Moines, Iowa CB code: 7302

2-year private junior, technical college, coed. Founded in 1921. **Accreditation:** Regional. **Undergraduate enrollment:** 144 men, 521 women full time; 67 men, 224 women part time. **Faculty:** 44 total (28 full time), 1 with doctorate or other terminal degree. **Location:** Urban campus in large city. **Calendar:** Quarter, extensive summer session. **Microcomputers:** 101 located in libraries, classrooms. **Special facilities:** Dictation tape library for court reporting speed development, video collection. **Additional facts:** Court-reporting program approved by National Court Reporters Association.

DEGREES OFFERED. 261 associate degrees awarded in 1992. 57% in business and management, 25% business/office and marketing/distribution, 14% law.

UNDERGRADUATE MAJORS. Accounting, business administration and management, business and management, business and office, business computer/console/peripheral equipment operation, business data processing and related programs, court reporting, data processing, finance, hospitality and recreation marketing, hotel/motel and restaurant management, information sciences and systems, legal secretary, marketing and distribution, marketing management, medical secretary, office supervision and management, secretarial and related programs, transportation and travel marketing, word processing.

ACADEMIC PROGRAMS. Double major, dual enrollment of high school students, internships. **Remedial services:** Reduced course load, remedial instruction, special counselor, tutoring. **Placement/credit:** Institutional tests.

ACADEMIC REQUIREMENTS. Freshmen must earn minimum GPA of 2.0 to continue in good standing. 67% of freshmen return for sophomore year. Students must declare major on application. **Graduation requirements:** 120 hours for associate. Most students required to take courses in computer science, English, mathematics, social sciences.

FRESHMAN ADMISSIONS. Selection criteria: High school record, interview, and test scores important. **Test requirements:** Wonderlic Scholastic Inventory, Nelson-Denny Reading Test, College Math Inventory, Career Interest Inventory required for placement. **Additional information:** 18 composite ACT score or higher used in place of college entrance tests.

1992 FRESHMAN CLASS PROFILE. 54 men, 223 women enrolled. 17% were in top quarter of graduating class. **Academic background:** Mid 50% of enrolled freshmen had ACT composite between 18-21. 66% submitted ACT scores. **Characteristics:** 94% from in state, 83% live in college housing, 4% have minority backgrounds, 1% join fraternities/sororities. Average age is 19.

FALL-TERM APPLICATIONS. $25 fee. No closing date; applicants notified on a rolling basis; must reply by registration. Interview required. ACT recommended.

STUDENT LIFE. Housing: Dormitories (coed); apartment, fraternity, sorority, handicapped housing available. Housing available for single-parent, married students, families. **Activities:** Student government, yearbook, fraternities, sororities. **Additional information:** Campus setting conducive to close interaction between students and staff.

ATHLETICS. Intramural: Basketball, bowling, golf, softball, tennis, volleyball.

STUDENT SERVICES. Aptitude testing, career counseling, employment service for undergraduates, freshman orientation, on-campus day care, personal counseling, placement service for graduates, special adviser for adult students, services/facilities for handicapped.

ANNUAL EXPENSES. Tuition and fees: $5,000. **Room and board:** $2,760. **Books and supplies:** $720. **Other expenses:** $990.

FINANCIAL AID. 77% of freshmen, 77% of continuing students receive some form of aid. 94% of grants, 89% of loans, 57% of jobs based on need. 200 enrolled freshmen were judged to have need, all were offered aid. Academic, minority scholarships available. **Aid applications:** No closing date; priority given to applications received by April 1; applicants notified on a rolling basis beginning on or about March 15; must reply within 3 weeks.

ADDRESS/TELEPHONE. Tom Shively, Director of Admissions, American Institute of Business, 2500 Fleur Drive, Des Moines, IA 50321. (515) 244-4221. (800) 444-1921. Fax: (515) 244-6773.

American Institute of Commerce

Davenport, Iowa CB code: 5848

2-year proprietary business, junior college, coed. Founded in 1937. **Accreditation:** Regional candidate. **Undergraduate enrollment:** 40 men, 146 women full time; 34 men, 127 women part time. **Faculty:** 43 total (16 full time). **Location:** Suburban campus in small city. **Calendar:** Quarter, extensive summer session. Extensive evening/early morning classes. **Microcomputers:** Located in classrooms, campus-wide network.

DEGREES OFFERED. 72 associate degrees awarded in 1992.

UNDERGRADUATE MAJORS. Accounting, business administration and management, court reporting, hotel/motel and restaurant management, office supervision and management, systems analysis.

ACADEMIC PROGRAMS. Double major, internships. **Remedial services:** Learning center, remedial instruction, tutoring.

ACADEMIC REQUIREMENTS. Freshmen must earn minimum GPA of 1.7 to continue in good standing. Students must declare major on application. **Graduation requirements:** 90 hours for associate (66 in major). Most students required to take courses in computer science, English, humanities, mathematics, social sciences.

FRESHMAN ADMISSIONS. Selection criteria: Open admissions. **Test requirements:** Career program assessment test required.

1992 FRESHMAN CLASS PROFILE. 39 men, 101 women enrolled. **Characteristics:** 100% commute.

FALL-TERM APPLICATIONS. $25 fee. No closing date; applicants notified on a rolling basis. Interview recommended.

STUDENT LIFE. Activities: Student government, student newspaper.

STUDENT SERVICES. Career counseling, employment service for undergraduates, freshman orientation, personal counseling, placement service for graduates, services/facilities for handicapped.

ANNUAL EXPENSES. Tuition and fees (1992-93): $5,095. **Books and supplies:** $850. **Other expenses:** $1,206.

FINANCIAL AID. 80% of freshmen, 80% of continuing students receive some form of aid. All aid based on need. **Aid applications:** No closing date.

ADDRESS/TELEPHONE. Carol Mannon, Admissions Coordinator, American Institute of Commerce, 1801 East Kimberly Road, Davenport, IA 52807-2095. (319) 355-3500. (800) 747-1035. Fax: (319) 355-1320.

Briar Cliff College

Sioux City, Iowa CB code: 6046

Admissions:	84% of applicants accepted
Based on:	••• School record, test scores
	•• Activities
	• Essay, interview, recommendations
Completion:	88% of freshmen end year in good standing
	47% graduate, 13% of these enter graduate study

4-year private liberal arts college, coed, affiliated with Roman Catholic Church. Founded in 1930. **Accreditation:** Regional. **Undergraduate enrollment:** 272 men, 425 women full time; 71 men, 170 women part time. **Faculty:** 72 total (65 full time), 52 with doctorates or other terminal degrees. **Location:** Suburban campus in small city; 90 miles from Omaha, Nebraska. **Calendar:** 3-term system plus 2 summer sessions. Saturday and extensive evening/early morning classes. **Microcomputers:** 50 located in dormitories, libraries, classrooms, computer centers, campus-wide network. **Special facilities:** Art gallery, natural prairie nature preserve, cadaver laboratory. **Additional facts:** Academic calendar consists of three 10-week terms (Sept-May) with two five-week summer sessions also available.

DEGREES OFFERED. AA, AS, BA, BS. 1 associate degree awarded in 1992. 100% in multi/interdisciplinary studies. 198 bachelor's degrees awarded. 35% in business and management, 9% communications, 8% health sciences, 12% parks/recreation, protective services, public affairs, 13% psychology, 5% social sciences, 5% visual and performing arts.

UNDERGRADUATE MAJORS. Associate: Liberal/general studies, pastoral ministry, theological studies. **Bachelor's:** Accounting, art education, biological and physical sciences, biology, business and management, chemistry, communications, computer and information sciences, elementary education, English, English education, fine arts, health education, history, human resources development, junior high education, mathematics, mathematics education, medical laboratory technologies, medical radiation dosimetry, music, music education, nursing, parks and recreation management, pastoral ministry, physical education, predentistry, prelaw, premedicine, prepharmacy, preveterinary, psychology, reading education, science education, secondary education, social science education, social work, sociology, Spanish, theological studies, visual and performing arts.

ACADEMIC PROGRAMS. 2-year transfer program, double major, dual enrollment of high school students, independent study, internships, student-designed major, study abroad, teacher preparation, weekend college, Washington semester, cross-registration, radiologic technology 1-2-1 program, medical technology 3-1 program; liberal arts/career combination in engineering, health sciences. **Remedial services:** Learning center, preadmission summer program, reduced course load, remedial instruction, special counselor, tutoring, English as a second language. **Placement/credit:** AP, CLEP General and Subject, institutional tests; 30 credit hours maximum for associate degree; 30 credit hours maximum for bachelor's degree.

ACADEMIC REQUIREMENTS. Freshmen must earn minimum GPA of 2.0 to continue in good standing. 69% of freshmen return for sophomore year. Students must declare major by end of second year. **Graduation re-**

quirements: 60 hours for associate, 120 hours for bachelor's (30 in major). Most students required to take courses in arts/fine arts, English, history, humanities, mathematics, philosophy/religion, biological/physical sciences, social sciences. **Postgraduate studies:** 1% enter law school, 5% enter medical school, 2% enter MBA programs, 5% enter other graduate study.

FRESHMAN ADMISSIONS. Selection criteria: GPA of 2.25, top half of class, ACT score of 19 recommended. For full acceptance students must meet 2 of the 3 criteria. Students not meeting requirement may be accepted conditionally or may not be accepted with right to appeal. **High school preparation:** 16 units recommended. Recommended units include English 4, foreign language 2, mathematics 2, social science 3 and science 2. **Test requirements:** SAT or ACT (ACT preferred); score report by September 1. Prueba de Aptitud Academica for Spanish speaking applicants.

1992 FRESHMAN CLASS PROFILE. 422 men and women applied, 353 accepted; 65 men enrolled, 94 women enrolled. 60% had high school GPA of 3.0 or higher, 38% between 2.0 and 2.99. 15% were in top tenth and 36% were in top quarter of graduating class. **Academic background:** Mid 50% of enrolled freshmen had SAT-V between 340-430, SAT-M between 360-510; ACT composite between 20-23. 6% submitted SAT scores, 91% submitted ACT scores. **Characteristics:** 55% from in state, 87% live in college housing, 9% have minority backgrounds, 3% are foreign students. Average age is 19.

FALL-TERM APPLICATIONS. $20 fee, may be waived for applicants with need. No closing date; priority given to applications received by April 1; applicants notified on a rolling basis; must reply by April 15 or within 2 weeks if notified thereafter. Interview recommended. Essay recommended. CRDA. Deferred and early admission available.

STUDENT LIFE. Housing: Dormitories (men, women, coed); handicapped housing available. **Activities:** Student government, film, magazine, radio, student newspaper, television, choral groups, drama, jazz band, music ensembles, musical theater, pep band, Young Republicans, Antioch (religious), Protestant Union, volunteer bureau, ethnic relations, wellness program, Knights of Columbus, BACCHUS, BCCares.

ATHLETICS. NAIA. **Intercollegiate:** Baseball M, basketball, golf, soccer M, softball W, volleyball W. **Intramural:** Badminton, basketball, bowling, cross-country, golf, gymnastics, handball, racquetball, soccer, softball, table tennis, tennis, volleyball, wrestling M.

STUDENT SERVICES. Aptitude testing, career counseling, employment service for undergraduates, freshman orientation, health services, personal counseling, placement service for graduates, special adviser for adult students, spiritual counseling, services/facilities for handicapped.

ANNUAL EXPENSES. Tuition and fees: $9,930. **Room and board:** $3,445. **Books and supplies:** $600. **Other expenses:** $1,000.

FINANCIAL AID. 94% of freshmen, 94% of continuing students receive some form of aid. 74% of grants, 86% of loans, 71% of jobs based on need. Academic, music/drama, art, athletic, state/district residency, leadership, religious affiliation, minority scholarships available. **Aid applications:** No closing date; priority given to applications received by March 1; applicants notified on a rolling basis beginning on or about March 15; must reply within 2 weeks. **Additional information:** Auditions/interviews required for art, theater, and music scholarships. Slides of work required for art scholarships. Interviews required for departmental scholarships.

ADDRESS/TELEPHONE. Sharisue Wilcoxon, Exec Dir Admissions/Marketing, Briar Cliff College, 3303 Rebecca Street, Sioux City, IA 51104-2100. (712) 279-5200. (800) 662-3303. Fax: (712) 279-5410.

Buena Vista College

Storm Lake, Iowa — CB code: 6047

Admissions: 92% of applicants accepted
Based on: ••• School record
•• Activities, essay, interview, test scores
• Recommendations, special talents
Completion: 96% of freshmen end year in good standing
62% graduate, 15% of these enter graduate study

4-year private liberal arts college, coed, affiliated with Presbyterian Church (USA). Founded in 1891. **Accreditation:** Regional. **Undergraduate enrollment:** 476 men, 460 women full time; 10 men, 25 women part time. **Faculty:** 78 total (67 full time), 43 with doctorates or other terminal degrees. **Location:** Rural campus in large town; 150 miles from Des Moines, 70 miles from Sioux City. **Calendar:** 4-1-4, limited summer session. **Microcomputers:** 100 located in dormitories, libraries, classrooms, computer centers. **Special facilities:** Broadband telecommunications system, electron microscope, one of world's largest butterfly collections, business/forum/computer center. **Additional facts:** 9 branch campuses throughout Iowa provide educational opportunities for nontraditional students.

DEGREES OFFERED. BA, BS. 218 bachelor's degrees awarded in 1992. 38% in business and management, 12% communications, 21% teacher education, 10% social sciences.

UNDERGRADUATE MAJORS. Accounting, allied health, art education, biology, business administration and management, business and management, business economics, business education, chemistry, communications, computer and information sciences, corporate communications, criminal justice studies, dramatic arts, economics, education, education of the emotionally handicapped, education of the mentally handicapped, elementary education, English, English education, finance, fine arts, foreign languages (multiple emphasis), foreign languages education, history, information sciences and systems, international business management, journalism, junior high education, liberal/general studies, management information systems, management science, marketing management, mathematics, mathematics education, medical laboratory technologies, music, music education, philosophy, physical education, physical sciences, physics, political science and government, predentistry, prelaw, premedicine, prepharmacy, preveterinary, psychology, public relations, radio/television broadcasting, reading education, religion, science education, secondary education, small business management and ownership, social science education, social sciences, social studies education, social work, sociology, Spanish, special education, speech.

ACADEMIC PROGRAMS. Accelerated program, double major, dual enrollment of high school students, honors program, independent study, internships, semester at sea, student-designed major, study abroad, visiting/exchange student program, cross-registration; liberal arts/career combination in engineering. **Remedial services:** Learning center, reduced course load, special counselor, tutoring. **Placement/credit:** AP, CLEP General and Subject, institutional tests; 20 credit hours maximum for bachelor's degree.

ACADEMIC REQUIREMENTS. Freshmen must earn minimum GPA of 2.0 to continue in good standing. 75% of freshmen return for sophomore year. Students must declare major by end of second year. **Graduation requirements:** 128 hours for bachelor's (40 in major). Most students required to take courses in arts/fine arts, English, history, humanities, mathematics, philosophy/religion, biological/physical sciences, social sciences. **Postgraduate studies:** 3% enter law school, 4% enter medical school, 1% enter MBA programs, 7% enter other graduate study. **Additional information:** Students must earn credit (3 hours) toward graduation by attending the Academic and Cultural Events Series.

FRESHMAN ADMISSIONS. Selection criteria: High school GPA, rank in class, test scores, interview, school and community activities, high school curriculum important. **High school preparation:** 15 units required. Required and recommended units include biological science 1, English 4, mathematics 3, physical science 1 and social science 2. Foreign language 1 recommended. One unit computer science also recommended. **Test requirements:** SAT or ACT; score report by April 1.

1992 FRESHMAN CLASS PROFILE. 464 men applied, 414 accepted, 158 enrolled; 404 women applied, 381 accepted, 139 enrolled. 83% had high school GPA of 3.0 or higher, 17% between 2.0 and 2.99. 29% were in top tenth and 60% were in top quarter of graduating class. **Academic background:** Mid 50% of enrolled freshmen had ACT composite between 22-26. 96% submitted ACT scores. **Characteristics:** 76% from in state, 93% live in college housing, 2% have minority backgrounds, 5% are foreign students. Average age is 18.

FALL-TERM APPLICATIONS. $25 fee. Closing date May 31; priority given to applications received by February 1; applicants notified on a rolling basis beginning on or about November 1; must reply by May 1 or as soon as possible if notified thereafter. Interview recommended. Essay recommended. CRDA. Deferred and early admission available.

STUDENT LIFE. Housing: Dormitories (men, women, coed); handicapped housing available. **Activities:** Student government, magazine, radio, student newspaper, television, yearbook, choral groups, concert band, drama, jazz band, marching band, music ensembles, musical theater, pep band, Academic Cultural Events Series, Over 50 organizations including Circle-K, People for People, political society during election year.

ATHLETICS. NCAA. **Intercollegiate:** Baseball M, basketball, cross-country, diving, football M, golf, softball W, swimming, tennis, track and field, volleyball W, wrestling M. **Intramural:** Basketball, football M, handball, racquetball, softball, table tennis, volleyball.

STUDENT SERVICES. Aptitude testing, career counseling, employment service for undergraduates, freshman orientation, health services, personal counseling, placement service for graduates, veterans counselor, services/facilities for handicapped.

ANNUAL EXPENSES. Tuition and fees: $12,565. **Room and board:** $3,585. **Books and supplies:** $450. **Other expenses:** $950.

FINANCIAL AID. 95% of freshmen, 94% of continuing students receive some form of aid. 23% of grants, 96% of loans, 84% of jobs based on need. Academic, music/drama, art, state/district residency, leadership, religious affiliation scholarships available. **Aid applications:** No closing date; priority given to applications received by April 20; applicants notified on a rolling basis beginning on or about January 20; must reply by May 1 or as soon as possible if notified thereafter. **Additional information:** Portfolio required of art scholarship applicants, audition required of music and drama scholarship applicants.

ADDRESS/TELEPHONE. Joanne Loonan, Director of Admissions, Buena Vista College, 610 West Fourth Street, Storm Lake, IA 50588-1798. (712) 749-2235. (800) 383-9600. Fax: (712) 749-2037.

Central College

Pella, Iowa CB code: 6087

4-year private liberal arts college, coed, affiliated with Reformed Church in America. Founded in 1853. **Accreditation:** Regional. **Undergraduate enrollment:** 618 men, 815 women full time; 17 men, 23 women part time. **Faculty:** 135 total (81 full time), 87 with doctorates or other terminal degrees. **Location:** Rural campus in small town; 45 miles from Des Moines. **Calendar:** Quarter, limited summer session. **Microcomputers:** 227 located in libraries, classrooms, computer centers. **Special facilities:** Mills art gallery, glass blowing studio, cross-cultural study center, Kruidenier Center for Communication and Theater, nature conservancy. **Additional facts:** Study centers in France, Austria, Spain, England, Wales, Mexico, China and the Netherlands. More than 40 percent of students spend a semester or year outside the United States.

DEGREES OFFERED. BA. 338 bachelor's degrees awarded in 1992. 20% in business and management, 8% communications, 14% teacher education, 7% languages, 6% letters/literature, 5% life sciences, 10% multi/interdisciplinary studies, 7% psychology, 6% social sciences.

UNDERGRADUATE MAJORS. Accounting, anthropology, art history, biology, business and management, business economics, chemistry, communications, computer and information sciences, dramatic arts, economics, elementary education, English, environmental science, environmental studies/global public policy, French, German, history, information sciences and systems, international business management, international relations, international studies, Latin American studies, liberal/general studies, linguistics, mathematics, music, music education, occupational therapy, philosophy, physics, political science and government, pre-architecture, predentistry, preengineering, prelaw, premedicine, prepharmacy, preveterinary, psychology, recreation and community services technologies, religion, sociology, Spanish, systems analysis, urban studies, Western European studies.

ACADEMIC PROGRAMS. Double major, dual enrollment of high school students, honors program, independent study, internships, student-designed major, study abroad, teacher preparation, Washington semester, Chicago semester; liberal arts/career combination in engineering, health sciences. **Remedial services:** Learning center, reduced course load, special counselor, tutoring. **Placement/credit:** AP, CLEP Subject, institutional tests; 66 credit hours maximum for bachelor's degree.

ACADEMIC REQUIREMENTS. Freshmen must earn minimum GPA of 1.65 to continue in good standing. 76% of freshmen return for sophomore year. Students must declare major by end of second year. **Graduation requirements:** 180 hours for bachelor's (45 in major). Most students required to take courses in arts/fine arts, computer science, English, foreign languages, history, humanities, mathematics, philosophy/religion, biological/physical sciences, social sciences. **Postgraduate studies:** 3% enter law school, 2% enter medical school, 2% enter MBA programs, 14% enter other graduate study. **Additional information:** All students must satisfy a departmental communication skills requirement.

FRESHMAN ADMISSIONS. Selection criteria: High school curriculum, GPA, class rank, test scores, and interview most important. Recommendations, school and community activities and alumni affiliation also considered. Recommended units include English 4, foreign language 2, mathematics 3, social science 3 and science 3. **Test requirements:** SAT or ACT (ACT preferred); score report by August 15.

1992 FRESHMAN CLASS PROFILE. 195 men, 236 women enrolled. 82% had high school GPA of 3.0 or higher, 18% between 2.0 and 2.99. 30% were in top tenth and 62% were in top quarter of graduating class. **Academic background:** Mid 50% of enrolled freshmen had ACT composite between 20-27. 96% submitted ACT scores. **Characteristics:** 78% from in state, 99% live in college housing, 6% have minority backgrounds, 1% are foreign students. Average age is 18.

FALL-TERM APPLICATIONS. $20 fee, may be waived for applicants with need. No closing date; priority given to applications received by January 1; applicants notified on a rolling basis; must reply within 1 month. Interview recommended. Audition recommended for music applicants. Portfolio recommended for art applicants. Essay recommended. CRDA. Deferred admission available.

STUDENT LIFE. Housing: Dormitories (men, women, coed); apartment, fraternity, sorority housing available. 22 town houses, each housing 16 to 32 students, available to juniors and seniors. French, German, and Spanish houses available to language majors. **Activities:** Student government, magazine, radio, student newspaper, yearbook, writing anthology, choral groups, concert band, dance, drama, jazz band, marching band, music ensembles, musical theater, opera, pep band, symphony orchestra, fraternities, sororities, Young Democrats, Young Republicans, Fellowship of Christian Athletes, Inter-Varsity Christian Fellowship, Alcohol Awareness Committee, Coalition for a Multicultural Campus, Circle-K, Amnesty International, Students Against Apartheid, Students Concerned About the Environment.

ATHLETICS. NCAA. **Intercollegiate:** Baseball M, basketball, cross-country, football M, golf, softball W, tennis, track and field, volleyball W, wrestling M. **Intramural:** Archery, baseball M, basketball, bowling, gymnastics, handball, racquetball, rugby M, soccer, softball, swimming, tennis, volleyball.

STUDENT SERVICES. Aptitude testing, career counseling, employment service for undergraduates, freshman orientation, health services, personal counseling, placement service for graduates, services/facilities for handicapped.

ANNUAL EXPENSES. Tuition and fees (projected): $10,363. **Room and board:** $3,660. **Books and supplies:** $650. **Other expenses:** $52.

FINANCIAL AID. 98% of freshmen, 98% of continuing students receive some form of aid. 94% of grants, all loans, 61% of jobs based on need. 363 enrolled freshmen were judged to have need, all were offered aid. Academic, music/drama, art, state/district residency, leadership, alumni affiliation, religious affiliation, minority scholarships available. **Aid applications:** No closing date; priority given to applications received by March 1; applicants notified on a rolling basis beginning on or about March 15; must reply within 2 weeks. **Additional information:** Institutional parent loan program and interest-earning, tuition prepayment savings account available. Auditions required for music and theater scholarships, portfolios required for art scholarships.

ADDRESS/TELEPHONE. Eric Sickler, Director of Admission, Central College, 812 University Avenue, Pella, IA 50219-9989. (800) 458-5503. (800) 458-5503. Fax: (515) 628-5316.

Clarke College

Dubuque, Iowa CB code: 6099

Admissions:	73% of applicants accepted
Based on:	••• Essay, recommendations, school record, test scores
	•• Interview
	• Activities, special talents
Completion:	96% of freshmen end year in good standing
	64% graduate, 15% of these enter graduate study

4-year private liberal arts college, coed, affiliated with Roman Catholic Church. Founded in 1843. **Accreditation:** Regional. **Undergraduate enrollment:** 186 men, 380 women full time; 111 men, 226 women part time. **Graduate enrollment:** 1 man, 23 women part time. **Faculty:** 84 total (54 full time), 56 with doctorates or other terminal degrees. **Location:** Urban campus in small city; 180 miles west of Chicago. **Calendar:** Semester, extensive summer session. Saturday and extensive evening/early morning classes. **Microcomputers:** 121 located in dormitories, libraries, classrooms, computer centers. **Special facilities:** Art gallery, planetarium, electron microscope, online library catalog available from any terminal on campus, communications laboratory, writing center, academic support center, art slide library, mathematics laboratory, nursing laboratory, multimedia classroom.

DEGREES OFFERED. AA, BA, BS, BFA, MEd. 1 associate degree awarded in 1992. 129 bachelor's degrees awarded. 17% in business and management, 7% communications, 15% computer sciences, 18% teacher education, 5% physical sciences, 11% social sciences, 13% visual and performing arts. Graduate degrees offered in 7 major fields of study.

UNDERGRADUATE MAJORS. Associate: Communications, liberal/general studies, studio art. **Bachelor's:** Accounting, advertising, art education, art history, biochemistry, biology, business administration and management, chemistry, communications, computer and information sciences, computer programming, dramatic arts, early childhood education, elementary education, English, English education, fine arts, foreign languages education, French, German, history, information sciences and systems, international business management, journalism, management information systems, marketing management, mathematics, mathematics education, medical laboratory technologies, molecular biology, music, music education, musical theater, nursing, peace studies, philosophy, physical education, physical therapy, political science and government, prechiropractic, predentistry, preengineering, prelaw, premedicine, prepharmacy, preveterinary, print media, psychology, public relations, religion, science education, secondary education, social science education, social studies education, social work, sociology, Spanish, special education, speech/communication/theater education, studio art, theological studies.

ACADEMIC PROGRAMS. Accelerated program, cooperative education, double major, dual enrollment of high school students, honors program, independent study, internships, student-designed major, study abroad, teacher preparation, cross-registration, 3-2 engineering program with Washington University and University of Southern California; liberal arts/career combination in engineering. **Remedial services:** Learning center, reduced course load, remedial instruction, tutoring, mentor system. **Placement/credit:** AP, CLEP General and Subject; 15 credit hours maximum for associate degree; 30 credit hours maximum for bachelor's degree.

ACADEMIC REQUIREMENTS. Freshmen must earn minimum GPA of 1.8 to continue in good standing. 89% of freshmen return for sophomore year. Students must declare major by end of second year. **Graduation requirements:** 62 hours for associate (20 in major), 124 hours for bachelor's (35 in major). Most students required to take courses in arts/fine arts, computer science, English, foreign languages, history, humanities, mathematics, philosophy/religion, biological/physical sciences, social sciences. **Postgraduate studies:** 1% enter law school, 1% enter medical school, 13% enter other graduate study. **Additional information:** A limited number of students who do not meet admissions requirements are granted a probationary admission and participate in mentor program.

FRESHMAN ADMISSIONS. Selection criteria: High school record of primary importance. Particular attention paid to cumulative high school rank (top half of class) in relation to overall type of academic program pursued. Test scores also considered. Required essay and recommendations reviewed carefully. **High school preparation:** 19 units required. Required units include English 4, foreign language 2, mathematics 3, social science 2 and science 3. Mathematics requirement includes 2 units algebra and 1 unit geometry. Science requirement must include 2 laboratory sciences. **Test requirements:** SAT or ACT (ACT preferred); score report by August 15. **Additional information:** Personal interview can be very important in admissions decisions. Applicants considered on individual basis.

1992 FRESHMAN CLASS PROFILE. 117 men applied, 86 accepted, 65 enrolled; 225 women applied, 164 accepted, 133 enrolled. 54% had high school GPA of 3.0 or higher, 45% between 2.0 and 2.99. 20% were in top tenth and 44% were in top quarter of graduating class. **Academic background:** Mid 50% of enrolled freshmen had ACT composite between 22-25. 98% submitted ACT scores. **Characteristics:** 51% from in state, 65% live in college housing, 13% have minority backgrounds, 4% are foreign students. Average age is 18.

FALL-TERM APPLICATIONS. $20 fee, may be waived for applicants with need. No closing date; applicants notified on a rolling basis; must reply by May 1 or within 3 weeks if notified thereafter. Interview required for academically weak applicants. Essay required. CRDA. Deferred and early admission available.

STUDENT LIFE. Housing: Dormitories (women, coed). All students under age 23 must live on campus unless residing with parents or relatives. **Activities:** Student government, magazine, student newspaper, choral groups, dance, drama, jazz band, music ensembles, musical theater, pep band, symphony orchestra, campus ministry, Amnesty International, Peace and Justice, Phoenix, Peer Ministry Program, Union Board, Minority Student Organization, Walden Society (political discussion group). **Additional information:** Opportunities for community service for students. Volunteer service is a component of freshman seminar.

ATHLETICS. NAIA. **Intercollegiate:** Baseball M, basketball, cross-country, golf, skiing, soccer M, softball W, tennis, volleyball. **Intramural:** Badminton, basketball, bowling, golf, skiing, soccer, softball, swimming, tennis, volleyball.

STUDENT SERVICES. Aptitude testing, career counseling, employment service for undergraduates, freshman orientation, health services, personal counseling, placement service for graduates, special adviser for adult students, mentors for "at risk" students, services/facilities for handicapped.

ANNUAL EXPENSES. Tuition and fees: $10,455. **Room and board:** $3,500. **Books and supplies:** $400. **Other expenses:** $600.

FINANCIAL AID. 89% of freshmen, 75% of continuing students receive some form of aid. Grants, loans, jobs available. Academic, music/drama, art, state/district residency, leadership, alumni affiliation scholarships available. **Aid applications:** No closing date; priority given to applications received by March 1; applicants notified on a rolling basis beginning on or about March 1; must reply by May 1 or within 3 weeks if notified thereafter. **Additional information:** Financial aid program meets 100% of student needs as determined by the processing center for those who file applications by March 1.

ADDRESS/TELEPHONE. Bobbe Ames, Vice President of Institutional Marketing and Recruitment, Clarke College, 1550 Clarke Drive, Dubuque, IA 52001-3198. (319) 588-6316. (800) 383-2345. Fax: (319) 588-6789.

Clinton Community College
Clinton, Iowa — CB code: 6100

2-year public community college, coed. Founded in 1946. **Accreditation:** Regional. **Undergraduate enrollment:** 252 men, 380 women full time; 158 men, 484 women part time. **Faculty:** 75 total (33 full time), 6 with doctorates or other terminal degrees. **Location:** Suburban campus in large town; 40 miles from Davenport. **Calendar:** Semester, limited summer session. **Microcomputers:** 70 located in libraries, classrooms, computer centers. **Additional facts:** Part of Eastern Iowa Community College distict, which also includes Muscatine and Scott Community Colleges.

DEGREES OFFERED. AA, AS, AAS. 216 associate degrees awarded in 1992. 8% in engineering technologies, 20% health sciences, 57% multi/interdisciplinary studies, 12% trade and industry.

UNDERGRADUATE MAJORS. Accounting, biology, business administration and management, business and management, business and office, chemistry, computer and information sciences, computer programming, criminal justice technology, drafting, drafting and design technology, education, electronic technology, English, finance, fine arts, history, humanities and social sciences, journalism, liberal/general studies, marketing and distribution, mathematics, medical laboratory technologies, nursing, physics, predentistry, preengineering, prelaw, premedicine, prepharmacy, preveterinary, psychology, retailing, secretarial and related programs, social sciences, social work, sociology.

ACADEMIC PROGRAMS. 2-year transfer program, accelerated program, double major, dual enrollment of high school students, honors program, independent study, internships, telecourses. **Remedial services:** Learning center, preadmission summer program, reduced course load, remedial instruction, special counselor, tutoring. **Placement/credit:** AP, CLEP General and Subject; 30 credit hours maximum for associate degree.

ACADEMIC REQUIREMENTS. Freshmen must earn minimum GPA of 1.75 to continue in good standing. 40% of freshmen return for sophomore year. Students must declare major on application. **Graduation requirements:** 64 hours for associate (21 in major). Most students required to take courses in English, humanities, mathematics, biological/physical sciences, social sciences.

FRESHMAN ADMISSIONS. Selection criteria: Open admissions. Selective admissions to nursing program.

1992 FRESHMAN CLASS PROFILE. 160 men, 320 women enrolled. **Characteristics:** 90% from in state, 100% commute, 2% have minority backgrounds. Average age is 24.

FALL-TERM APPLICATIONS. $20 fee. No closing date; applicants notified on a rolling basis beginning on or about September 1. Interview recommended. Early admission available.

STUDENT LIFE. Activities: Student government, student newspaper, literary magazine, drama, Circle-K, Phi Beta Lambda, skiing club, drafting club, art club.

ATHLETICS. NJCAA. **Intercollegiate:** Basketball M, volleyball W. **Intramural:** Basketball, bowling, softball, table tennis, tennis, volleyball.

STUDENT SERVICES. Aptitude testing, career counseling, employment service for undergraduates, freshman orientation, personal counseling, placement service for graduates, veterans counselor, vocational rehabilitation counselor, services/facilities for handicapped.

ANNUAL EXPENSES. Tuition and fees (1992-93): $1,455, $645 additional for out-of-state students. **Books and supplies:** $900. **Other expenses:** $900.

FINANCIAL AID. 50% of freshmen, 50% of continuing students receive some form of aid. 96% of grants, 91% of loans, all jobs based on need. Academic, art, athletic, state/district residency, leadership, alumni affiliation scholarships available. **Aid applications:** No closing date; priority given to applications received by April 20; applicants notified on a rolling basis beginning on or about May 15; must reply within 2 weeks.

ADDRESS/TELEPHONE. Susan Carmody, Assistant Dean for Enrollment Services, Clinton Community College, 1000 Lincoln Boulevard, Clinton, IA 52732-6299. (319) 242-6841 ext. 348. Fax: (319) 242-7868.

Coe College
Cedar Rapids, Iowa — CB code: 6101

Admissions: 82% of applicants accepted
Based on:
••• Recommendations, school record
•• Essay, test scores
• Activities, interview, special talents
Completion: 90% of freshmen end year in good standing
65% graduate, 25% of these enter graduate study

4-year private liberal arts college, coed, affiliated with Presbyterian Church (USA). Founded in 1851. **Accreditation:** Regional. **Undergraduate enrollment:** 501 men, 567 women full time; 88 men, 129 women part time. **Faculty:** 109 total (83 full time), 61 with doctorates or other terminal degrees. **Location:** Urban campus in small city; 230 miles from Chicago. **Calendar:** 4-1-4, limited summer session. Extensive evening/early morning classes. **Microcomputers:** 207 located in libraries, classrooms, computer centers. **Special facilities:** Bird museum, art gallery, fine arts studio, American art collection, electron microscopes, IBM 6152 academic computing system, racquet center, infrared spectrometer, foreign language computer laboratory, Thornton Analytical Physiology Units.

DEGREES OFFERED. BA, M. 248 bachelor's degrees awarded in 1992. 35% in business and management, 7% teacher education, 8% health sciences, 8% life sciences, 14% psychology, 8% visual and performing arts.

UNDERGRADUATE MAJORS. Accounting, Afro-American (black) studies, American studies, architecture, art education, Asian studies, biological and physical sciences, biology, business administration and management, business and management, business economics, chemistry, computer and information sciences, dramatic arts, economics, elementary education, engineering and other disciplines, English, English literature, fine arts, French, German, history, humanities and social sciences, international studies, liberal/general studies, mathematics, music, music education, nursing, philosophy, physical education, physics, political science and government, predentistry, preengineering, prelaw, premedicine, psychology, religion, secondary education, sociology, Spanish.

ACADEMIC PROGRAMS. Accelerated program, double major, dual enrollment of high school students, honors program, independent study, internships, student-designed major, study abroad, teacher preparation, New York semester, Washington semester, cross-registration, Oak Ridge science semester, research program in wilderness field stations in Costa Rica, Canadian boundary waters, England, Hong Kong, India, Italy, Japan, Russia,

Zimbabwe, Latin America, and Chicago; liberal arts/career combination in engineering, health sciences. **Remedial services:** Preadmission summer program, reduced course load, special counselor, tutoring. **ROTC:** Army. **Placement/credit:** AP, CLEP Subject, IB, institutional tests; 30 credit hours maximum for bachelor's degree.

ACADEMIC REQUIREMENTS. Freshmen must earn minimum GPA of 2.0 to continue in good standing. 83% of freshmen return for sophomore year. Students must declare major by end of second year. **Graduation requirements:** 120 hours for bachelor's (33 in major). Most students required to take courses in arts/fine arts, English, foreign languages, history, humanities, biological/physical sciences, social sciences. **Postgraduate studies:** 5% enter law school, 3% enter medical school, 5% enter MBA programs, 12% enter other graduate study. **Additional information:** Writing emphasis courses required, writing center, foreign language computer laboratory available.

FRESHMAN ADMISSIONS. Selection criteria: School achievement record most important. Test scores, recommendations, interview, school and community activities also considered. **High school preparation:** 13 units recommended. Recommended units include English 4, foreign language 2, mathematics 3, social science 2 and science 2. **Test requirements:** SAT or ACT; score report by April 1.

1992 FRESHMAN CLASS PROFILE. 458 men applied, 331 accepted, 135 enrolled; 459 women applied, 418 accepted, 168 enrolled. 85% had high school GPA of 3.0 or higher, 15% between 2.0 and 2.99. 27% were in top tenth and 62% were in top quarter of graduating class. **Academic background:** Mid 50% of enrolled freshmen had SAT-V between 430-550, SAT-M between 490-580; ACT composite between 22-26. 31% submitted SAT scores, 92% submitted ACT scores. **Characteristics:** 51% from in state, 98% live in college housing, 8% have minority backgrounds, 6% are foreign students, 25% join fraternities/sororities. Average age is 18.

FALL-TERM APPLICATIONS. $25 fee, may be waived for applicants with need. No closing date; priority given to applications received by December 1; applicants notified on a rolling basis; must reply by May 1 or within 2 weeks if notified thereafter. Audition required for music, theater, fine arts applicants. Portfolio required for art, writing applicants. Essay required. Interview recommended. CRDA. Deferred and early admission available. EDP-S.

STUDENT LIFE. Housing: Dormitories (men, women, coed); apartment housing available. All students must live on campus unless residing with relatives or granted off-campus permission by Department of Residential Life. **Activities:** Student government, magazine, student newspaper, yearbook, choral groups, concert band, dance, drama, jazz band, music ensembles, musical theater, pep band, symphony orchestra, fraternities, sororities, Black Self-Education Organization, Volunteer Bureau, International Club, Shalom, Young Democrats, Young Republicans, Coe Action for Peace. **Additional information:** Students drawn from 41 states.

ATHLETICS. NCAA. **Intercollegiate:** Baseball M, basketball, cross-country, diving, football M, golf M, soccer, softball W, swimming, tennis, track and field, volleyball W, wrestling M. **Intramural:** Basketball, football, handball, racquetball, soccer, softball, squash, swimming, table tennis, tennis, track and field, volleyball, water polo, wrestling M.

STUDENT SERVICES. Aptitude testing, career counseling, employment service for undergraduates, freshman orientation, health services, personal counseling, placement service for graduates, special adviser for adult students, veterans counselor.

ANNUAL EXPENSES. Tuition and fees: $12,805. **Room and board:** $4,280. **Books and supplies:** $500. **Other expenses:** $1,200.

FINANCIAL AID. 85% of freshmen, 88% of continuing students receive some form of aid. 87% of grants, 96% of loans, 70% of jobs based on need. 287 enrolled freshmen were judged to have need, all were offered aid. Academic, music/drama, art, leadership, alumni affiliation, religious affiliation scholarships available. **Aid applications:** No closing date; priority given to applications received by March 1; applicants notified on a rolling basis beginning on or about March 1; must reply by May 1 or within 2 weeks if notified thereafter.

ADDRESS/TELEPHONE. Michael White, Vice President for Admissions, Coe College, 1220 First Avenue Northeast, Cedar Rapids, IA 52402-9983. (319) 399-8500. (800) 332-8404. Fax: (319) 399-8816.

Cornell College
Mount Vernon, Iowa — CB code: 6119

Admissions:	87% of applicants accepted
Based on:	••• Activities, essay, interview, recommendations, school record
	•• Special talents, test scores
Completion:	100% of freshmen end year in good standing
	100% graduate, 32% of these enter graduate study

4-year private liberal arts college, coed, affiliated with United Methodist Church. Founded in 1853. **Accreditation:** Regional. **Undergraduate enrollment:** 516 men, 636 women full time; 4 men, 6 women part time. **Faculty:** 139 total (89 full time), 74 with doctorates or other terminal degrees. **Location:** Rural campus in small town; 15 miles from Cedar Rapids, 20 miles from Iowa City. **Calendar:** Nine terms of 3.5 weeks, one course per term. **Microcomputers:** 125 located in dormitories, libraries, classrooms, computer centers. **Special facilities:** Geology museum, nearby state park for biology and environmental science research.

DEGREES OFFERED. BA. 270 bachelor's degrees awarded in 1992. 5% in area and ethnic studies, 15% business and management, 9% teacher education, 12% letters/literature, 9% life sciences, 5% philosophy, religion, theology, 9% psychology, 15% social sciences, 7% visual and performing arts.

UNDERGRADUATE MAJORS. Allied health, anthropology, art education, art history, behavioral sciences, biochemistry, biological and physical sciences, biology, business economics, business education, chemistry, classics, communications, computer and information sciences, dramatic arts, earth sciences, economics, elementary education, engineering, engineering and other disciplines, English, English education, environmental science, fine arts, foreign languages (multiple emphasis), foreign languages education, French, geology, German, health education, history, humanities, humanities and social sciences, international business management, international relations, Latin, Latin American studies, liberal/general studies, mathematics, mathematics education, medical laboratory technologies, molecular biology, music, music education, music performance, musical theater, occupational therapy, philosophy, physical education, physics, political science and government, predentistry, preengineering, prelaw, premedicine, prepharmacy, preveterinary, psychology, religion, Russian, Russian and Slavic studies, science education, secondary education, social science education, social studies education, sociology, Spanish, speech, speech/communication/theater education, women's studies.

ACADEMIC PROGRAMS. Accelerated program, double major, independent study, internships, student-designed major, study abroad, teacher preparation, Washington semester; liberal arts/career combination in engineering, forestry, health sciences; combined bachelor's/graduate program in business administration. **Remedial services:** Learning center, special counselor, tutoring. **Placement/credit:** AP, CLEP Subject, institutional tests; 28 credit hours maximum for bachelor's degree.

ACADEMIC REQUIREMENTS. Freshmen must earn minimum GPA of 2.0 to continue in good standing. 80% of freshmen return for sophomore year. Students must declare major by end of second year. **Graduation requirements:** 128 hours for bachelor's (36 in major). Most students required to take courses in arts/fine arts, English, foreign languages, humanities, mathematics, biological/physical sciences, social sciences. **Postgraduate studies:** 5% enter law school, 4% enter medical school, 3% enter MBA programs, 20% enter other graduate study.

FRESHMAN ADMISSIONS. Selection criteria: Academic record, statement of purpose, and interview weighed on individual basis. Test scores often secondary. **High school preparation:** 15 units required. Required units include English 4, foreign language 2, mathematics 3, social science 4 and science 2. **Test requirements:** SAT or ACT; score report by March 15.

1992 FRESHMAN CLASS PROFILE. 665 men applied, 554 accepted, 175 enrolled; 817 women applied, 739 accepted, 208 enrolled. 76% had high school GPA of 3.0 or higher, 24% between 2.0 and 2.99. 31% were in top tenth and 69% were in top quarter of graduating class. **Academic background:** Mid 50% of enrolled freshmen had SAT-V between 450-580, SAT-M between 490-630; ACT composite between 23-28. 45% submitted SAT scores, 97% submitted ACT scores. **Characteristics:** 24% from in state, 98% live in college housing, 9% have minority backgrounds, 5% are foreign students. Average age is 18.

FALL-TERM APPLICATIONS. $25 fee, may be waived for applicants with need. No closing date; priority given to applications received by March 1; applicants notified on a rolling basis beginning on or about April 1; must reply by May 1 or within 2 weeks if notified thereafter. Essay required. Interview recommended. CRDA. Deferred and early admission available. EDP-F.

STUDENT LIFE. Housing: Dormitories (men, women, coed). **Activities:** Student government, magazine, radio, student newspaper, yearbook, choral groups, concert band, dance, drama, jazz band, music ensembles, musical theater, pep band, symphony orchestra, koto ensemble, chamber ensembles, fraternities, sororities, Alpha Phi Omega.

ATHLETICS. NCAA. **Intercollegiate:** Baseball M, basketball, cross-country, diving, football M, golf, ice hockey M, soccer, softball W, swimming, tennis, track and field, volleyball W, wrestling M. **Intramural:** Badminton, basketball, bowling, golf, ice hockey, racquetball, softball, swimming, table tennis, tennis, track and field, volleyball, water polo, wrestling M.

STUDENT SERVICES. Aptitude testing, career counseling, employment service for undergraduates, freshman orientation, health services, personal counseling, placement service for graduates, special adviser for adult students, services/facilities for handicapped.

ANNUAL EXPENSES. Tuition and fees: $14,228. **Room and board:** $4,197. **Books and supplies:** $550. **Other expenses:** $1,000.

FINANCIAL AID. 80% of freshmen, 75% of continuing students receive some form of aid. 93% of grants, 97% of loans, 91% of jobs based on need. 352 enrolled freshmen were judged to have need, all were offered aid. Academic, music/drama, art, leadership, religious affiliation scholarships available. **Aid applications:** Closing date March 1; applicants notified on or about April 1; must reply by May 1 or within 2 weeks if notified thereafter. **Additional information:** Portfolio recommended for art scholarship applicants.

ADDRESS/TELEPHONE. Kevin Crockett, Dean of Admissions and Enrollment Services, Cornell College, 600 First Street West, Mount Vernon, IA 52314-1098. (319) 895-4477. (800) 747-1112. Fax: (319) 895-4451.

Des Moines Area Community College
Ankeny, Iowa — CB code: 6177

2-year public community college, coed. Founded in 1966. **Accreditation:** Regional. **Undergraduate enrollment:** 2,224 men, 2,594 women full time; 2,165 men, 4,231 women part time. **Faculty:** 257 total (245 full time), 20 with doctorates or other terminal degrees. **Location:** Suburban campus in large town; 15 miles from downtown. **Calendar:** Semester, extensive summer session. Saturday and extensive evening/early morning classes. **Microcomputers:** 200 located in libraries, classrooms, computer centers. **Additional facts:** Multilocation institution with campuses at Boone, Des Moines, and Carroll. Ankeny campus is primary location and administrative center.

DEGREES OFFERED. AA, AS, AAS. 1,092 associate degrees awarded in 1992. 10% in business and management, 15% business/office and marketing/distribution, 5% computer sciences, 18% health sciences, 25% multi/interdisciplinary studies, 17% trade and industry.

UNDERGRADUATE MAJORS. Accounting, agribusiness, apparel and accessories marketing, automotive mechanics, automotive technology, biomedical equipment technology, business administration and management, business and management, business and office, business data processing and related programs, business data programming, child development/care/guidance, clinical laboratory science, commercial art, community services, computer programming, computer servicing technology, computer technology, criminal justice studies, dental hygiene, diesel engine mechanics, electrical and electronics equipment repair, electrical/electronics/communications engineering, electromechanical technology, electronic technology, fashion merchandising, finance, fire control and safety technology, food production/management/services, health care administration, horticulture, hotel/motel and restaurant management, insurance and risk management, law enforcement and corrections technologies, legal assistant/paralegal, legal secretary, liberal/general studies, marketing and distribution, marketing management, medical assistant, medical laboratory technologies, medical secretary, nursing, office supervision and management, ornamental horticulture, precision metal work, recreation and community services technologies, respiratory therapy, respiratory therapy technology, retailing, robotics, secretarial and related programs, social work, teacher aide, telecommunications.

ACADEMIC PROGRAMS. 2-year transfer program, cooperative education, dual enrollment of high school students, honors program, independent study, internships, telecourses, weekend college, cross-registration. **Remedial services:** Learning center, preadmission summer program, reduced course load, remedial instruction, special counselor, tutoring. **Placement/credit:** CLEP General and Subject, institutional tests; 28 credit hours maximum for associate degree.

ACADEMIC REQUIREMENTS. Freshmen must earn minimum GPA of 2.0 to continue in good standing. 66% of freshmen return for sophomore year. Students must declare major on application. **Graduation requirements:** 64 hours for associate. Most students required to take courses in English, mathematics.

FRESHMAN ADMISSIONS. Selection criteria: Open admissions. Recommended units include biological science 1, English 3, mathematics 3 and social science 1. Specific course requirements for some programs. **Test requirements:** Dental Hygiene Aptitude Test required for dental hygiene applicants. Assest test for nursing.

1992 FRESHMAN CLASS PROFILE. 3,008 men and women enrolled. **Characteristics:** 98% from in state, 100% commute, 6% have minority backgrounds, 2% are foreign students. Average age is 27.

FALL-TERM APPLICATIONS. $10 fee. No closing date; applicants notified on a rolling basis; must reply within 4 weeks. Interview required for dental hygiene, commercial art applicants. Portfolio required for commercial art applicants. Deferred admission available.

STUDENT LIFE. Activities: Student government, student newspaper, choral groups, drama.

ATHLETICS. NJCAA. **Intercollegiate:** Baseball M, basketball, golf M, softball W. **Intramural:** Basketball M, soccer M, softball, table tennis, tennis, volleyball.

STUDENT SERVICES. Aptitude testing, career counseling, employment service for undergraduates, freshman orientation, health services, on-campus day care, personal counseling, placement service for graduates, special adviser for adult students, veterans counselor, services/facilities for handicapped.

ANNUAL EXPENSES. Tuition and fees (projected): $1,377, $1,230 additional for out-of-state students. **Books and supplies:** $500. **Other expenses:** $640.

FINANCIAL AID. 60% of freshmen, 73% of continuing students receive some form of aid. 99% of grants, 89% of loans, 63% of jobs based on need. Academic, athletic scholarships available. **Aid applications:** No closing date; priority given to applications received by March 1; applicants notified on a rolling basis beginning on or about March 1; must reply within 2 weeks.

ADDRESS/TELEPHONE. Lynn Albrecht, Dean, Student Records and Services, Des Moines Area Community College, 2006 South Ankeny Boulevard, Ankeny, IA 50021. (515) 964-6241.

Divine Word College
Epworth, Iowa — CB code: 6174

Admissions:	37% of applicants accepted
Based on:	••• Interview, religious affiliation/commitment
	•• Essay, recommendations, school record, test scores
	• Activities
Completion:	95% of freshmen end year in good standing
	33% graduate, 60% of these enter graduate study

4-year private liberal arts, seminary college, men only, affiliated with Roman Catholic Church. Founded in 1912. **Accreditation:** Regional. **Undergraduate enrollment:** 54 men full time; 3 men, 6 women part time. **Faculty:** 45 total (40 full time), 7 with doctorates or other terminal degrees. **Location:** Rural campus in rural community; 15 miles from Dubuque. **Calendar:** Semester. **Microcomputers:** 26 located in computer centers. **Special facilities:** Fr. Weyland Art Gallery.

DEGREES OFFERED. AA, BA, BS. 3 associate degrees awarded in 1992. 100% in multi/interdisciplinary studies. 14 bachelor's degrees awarded. 50% in philosophy, religion, theology, 50% social sciences.

UNDERGRADUATE MAJORS. Associate: Liberal/general studies. **Bachelor's:** Biological and physical sciences, computer and information sciences, English, mathematics, philosophy, sociology, theological studies.

ACADEMIC PROGRAMS. Double major, dual enrollment of high school students, independent study, student-designed major, study abroad. **Remedial services:** Reduced course load, remedial instruction, special counselor, tutoring. **Placement/credit:** AP, CLEP Subject, institutional tests.

ACADEMIC REQUIREMENTS. Freshmen must earn minimum GPA of 1.9 to continue in good standing. 73% of freshmen return for sophomore year. Students must declare major by end of second year. **Graduation requirements:** 60 hours for associate, 128 hours for bachelor's (36 in major). Most students required to take courses in arts/fine arts, English, foreign languages, history, humanities, mathematics, philosophy/religion, biological/physical sciences, social sciences. **Postgraduate studies:** 60% enter other graduate study.

FRESHMAN ADMISSIONS. Selection criteria: Interview and religious commitment most important. School achievement record, test scores, recommendations, and school and community activities also considered. **High school preparation:** 16 units required. Required units include English 4, mathematics 2, social science 1 and science 1. **Test requirements:** SAT or ACT; score report by July 15. Minnesota Multiphasic Personality Inventory (MMPI) for admission and counseling.

1992 FRESHMAN CLASS PROFILE. 30 men applied, 11 accepted, 9 enrolled. 86% had high school GPA of 3.0 or higher, 14% between 2.0 and 2.99. 66% were in top tenth and 66% were in top quarter of graduating class. **Academic background:** Mid 50% of enrolled freshmen had SAT-V between 360-430, SAT-M between 550-570. 38% submitted SAT scores. **Characteristics:** 1% from in state, 100% live in college housing, 78% have minority backgrounds, 2% are foreign students. Average age is 19.

FALL-TERM APPLICATIONS. $25 fee, may be waived for applicants with need. Closing date August 1; priority given to applications received by July 1; applicants notified on a rolling basis beginning on or about January 1; must reply by August 1. Interview required. Essay required.

STUDENT LIFE. Housing: Dormitories (men). All students live in dormitories on campus. **Activities:** Student government, choral groups, drama, Social Justice Committee. **Additional information:** Religious observance required.

ATHLETICS. Intramural: Baseball, basketball, handball, ice hockey, soccer, softball, swimming, table tennis, tennis, volleyball.

STUDENT SERVICES. Aptitude testing, career counseling, freshman orientation, health services, personal counseling, services/facilities for handicapped.

ANNUAL EXPENSES. Tuition and fees (1992-93): $5,535. **Room and board:** $1,200. **Books and supplies:** $400. **Other expenses:** $800.

FINANCIAL AID. 100% of freshmen, 100% of continuing students receive some form of aid. All grants, 96% of loans, 96% of jobs based on need. 9 enrolled freshmen were judged to have need, all were offered aid. **Aid applications:** No closing date; priority given to applications received by August 31; applicants notified on a rolling basis beginning on or about August 1.

ADDRESS/TELEPHONE. Rev. Robert Kelly, SVD, Director of Admissions, Divine Word College, South Center Avenue, Epworth, IA 52045. (319) 876-3332. (800) 553-3321.

Dordt College
Sioux Center, Iowa CB code: 6171

Admissions: 95% of applicants accepted
Based on: ••• School record, test scores
•• Religious affiliation/commitment
• Special talents
Completion: 88% of freshmen end year in good standing
52% graduate, 16% of these enter graduate study

4-year private liberal arts college, coed, affiliated with Christian Reformed Church. Founded in 1955. **Accreditation:** Regional. **Undergraduate enrollment:** 506 men, 524 women full time; 16 men, 31 women part time. **Faculty:** 105 total (86 full time), 47 with doctorates or other terminal degrees. **Location:** Rural campus in small town; 45 miles from Sioux City. **Calendar:** Semester. **Microcomputers:** 100 located in dormitories, libraries, classrooms, computer centers. **Special facilities:** 2 farms for training, experimentation, and research.

DEGREES OFFERED. AA, BA, BS. 32 associate degrees awarded in 1992. 15% in agriculture, 30% business/office and marketing/distribution, 50% multi/interdisciplinary studies. 203 bachelor's degrees awarded. 6% in agriculture, 18% business and management, 35% teacher education, 8% engineering, 8% multi/interdisciplinary studies, 5% psychology, 7% social sciences.

UNDERGRADUATE MAJORS. Associate: Agricultural sciences, business data processing and related programs, data processing, liberal/general studies, secretarial and related programs, teacher aide. **Bachelor's:** Accounting, agribusiness, agricultural sciences, animal sciences, biology, business administration and management, business and management, business education, chemistry, clinical laboratory science, communications, computer and information sciences, dramatic arts, Dutch, electrical/electronics/communications engineering, elementary education, engineering, engineering science, English, environmental science, fine arts, foreign languages education, German, history, information sciences and systems, journalism, liberal/general studies, management information systems, mathematics, medical laboratory technologies, music, philosophy, physical education, physical sciences, physics, plant sciences, political science and government, predentistry, prelaw, premedicine, prepharmacy, preveterinary, psychology, radio/television broadcasting, secondary education, social sciences, social work, sociology, Spanish, speech, theological studies.

ACADEMIC PROGRAMS. Double major, independent study, internships, study abroad, teacher preparation, Washington semester, Chicago semester, Iowa Legislative Intern program. **Remedial services:** Learning center, tutoring. **Placement/credit:** AP, CLEP General and Subject, institutional tests.

ACADEMIC REQUIREMENTS. Freshmen must earn minimum GPA of 2.0 to continue in good standing. 82% of freshmen return for sophomore year. Students must declare major by end of first year. **Graduation requirements:** 60 hours for associate (27 in major), 120 hours for bachelor's (42 in major). Most students required to take courses in arts/fine arts, computer science, English, foreign languages, history, humanities, mathematics, philosophy/religion, biological/physical sciences, social sciences. **Postgraduate studies:** 35% from 2-year programs enter 4-year programs. 2% enter law school, 1% enter medical school, 1% enter MBA programs, 12% enter other graduate study.

FRESHMAN ADMISSIONS. Selection criteria: School achievement record, high school GPA, test scores, religious affiliation or commitment. **High school preparation:** 17 units required. Required and recommended units include English 3-4 and mathematics 2. Biological science 2, foreign language 2, physical science 2 and social science 2 recommended. 17 units required. 10 units must be in social science, English, foreign language, natural science, or mathematics; 3 units English and 2 units algebra/geometry required. One half typing/word processing recommended. **Test requirements:** ACT; score report by September 5.

1992 FRESHMAN CLASS PROFILE. 257 men applied, 245 accepted, 159 enrolled; 267 women applied, 255 accepted, 168 enrolled. 66% had high school GPA of 3.0 or higher, 33% between 2.0 and 2.99. 25% were in top tenth and 49% were in top quarter of graduating class. **Characteristics:** 39% from in state, 98% live in college housing, 2% have minority backgrounds, 15% are foreign students. Average age is 18.

FALL-TERM APPLICATIONS. $10 fee. Closing date August 31; applicants notified on a rolling basis beginning on or about October 1; must reply by May 1 or within 3 weeks if notified thereafter. Interview recommended for academically borderline applicants. Deferred admission available. Applicants with high school GPA under 2.0 considered on individual basis, may be admitted on probation.

STUDENT LIFE. Housing: Dormitories (men, women, coed); apartment, cooperative housing available. **Activities:** Student government, magazine, radio, student newspaper, yearbook, choral groups, concert band, drama, music ensembles, musical theater, opera, pep band, symphony orchestra. **Additional information:** Religious observance required.

ATHLETICS. NAIA. **Intercollegiate:** Baseball M, basketball, cross-country, golf, ice hockey M, soccer M, softball W, swimming, tennis, track and field, volleyball W. **Intramural:** Badminton, basketball, bowling, cross-country, field hockey, golf, racquetball, soccer, softball, swimming, tennis, volleyball.

STUDENT SERVICES. Employment service for undergraduates, freshman orientation, personal counseling, placement service for graduates, veterans counselor, services/facilities for handicapped.

ANNUAL EXPENSES. Tuition and fees: $9,200. **Room and board:** $2,490. **Books and supplies:** $610. **Other expenses:** $1,700.

FINANCIAL AID. 98% of freshmen, 98% of continuing students receive some form of aid. 54% of grants, 96% of loans, 97% of jobs based on need. 280 enrolled freshmen were judged to have need, all were offered aid. Academic, music/drama, art, athletic, state/district residency, leadership, alumni affiliation, religious affiliation, minority scholarships available. **Aid applications:** No closing date; priority given to applications received by April 1; applicants notified on a rolling basis beginning on or about March 15; must reply within 2 weeks.

ADDRESS/TELEPHONE. Quentin Van Essen, Director of Admissions, Dordt College, 498 Fourth Avenue, Northeast, Sioux Center, IA 51250. (712) 722-6080. (800) 34DORDT. Fax: (712) 722-1967.

Drake University
Des Moines, Iowa CB code: 6168

Admissions: 90% of applicants accepted
Based on: ••• School record
•• Essay, interview, recommendations, test scores
• Activities, special talents
Completion: 88% of freshmen end year in good standing
76% graduate, 19% of these enter graduate study

4-year private university, coed. Founded in 1881. **Accreditation:** Regional. **Undergraduate enrollment:** 1,498 men, 1,971 women full time; 260 men, 531 women part time. **Graduate enrollment:** 333 men, 252 women full time; 723 men, 765 women part time. **Faculty:** 278 total, 259 with doctorates or other terminal degrees. **Location:** Urban campus in large city. **Calendar:** Semester, extensive summer session. Extensive evening/early morning classes. **Microcomputers:** 1,000 located in dormitories, libraries, classrooms, computer centers. **Special facilities:** Observatory, Weeks Art Gallery.

DEGREES OFFERED. BA, BS, BFA, MA, MS, MBA, MFA, MEd, EdD, B. Pharm, Pharm D, JD. 866 bachelor's degrees awarded in 1992. 27% in business and management, 17% communications, 12% education, 11% health sciences, 6% life sciences, 5% psychology, 9% social sciences. Graduate degrees offered in 46 major fields of study.

UNDERGRADUATE MAJORS. Accounting, actuarial sciences, advertising, American literature, art education, art history, astronomy, biology, broadcast sales and management, business administration and management, business and management, business education, chemistry, clinical laboratory science, communications, comparative literature, computer and information sciences, creative writing, dramatic arts, drawing, early childhood education, earth sciences, economics, education, elementary education, English, English education, English literature, environmental science, finance, foreign languages education, French, geography, German, graphic design, history, history education, information sciences and systems, insurance and risk management, interior design, international business management, international relations, investments and securities, journalism, journalism education, journalism teaching, Latin American studies, liberal/general studies, management information systems, management science, marine biology, marketing management, mathematics, mathematics education, music, music business management, music education, music history and appreciation, music performance, music theory and composition, musical theater, nursing, painting, pharmacy, philosophy, physics, physics education, political science and government, predentistry, prelaw, premedicine, preveterinary, printmaking, psychology, public administration, public relations, radio/television broadcasting, reading education, religion, religious music, science education, sculpture, secondary education, social science education, social sciences, social studies education, sociology, Spanish, speech/communication/theater education, studio art, theater design.

ACADEMIC PROGRAMS. Accelerated program, double major, dual enrollment of high school students, education specialist degree, honors program, independent study, internships, semester at sea, student-designed major, study abroad, teacher preparation, visiting/exchange student program, weekend college, United Nations semester, Washington semester, cross-registration; liberal arts/career combination in engineering; combined bachelor's/graduate program in business administration, law. **Remedial services:** Learning center, reduced course load, special counselor, tutoring. **ROTC:** Air Force, Army. **Placement/credit:** AP, CLEP General and Subject, IB, institutional tests.

ACADEMIC REQUIREMENTS. Freshmen must earn minimum GPA of 2.0 to continue in good standing. 84% of freshmen return for sophomore year. Students must declare major by end of second year. **Graduation requirements:** 124 hours for bachelor's (32 in major). Most students required to take courses in computer science, English, history, humanities, mathematics, biological/physical sciences, social sciences. **Postgraduate studies:** 4%

enter law school, 3% enter medical school, 4% enter MBA programs, 8% enter other graduate study.

FRESHMAN ADMISSIONS. Selection criteria: Consideration given to school academic record, test scores, interview, extracurricular activities, counselor recommendation, optional essay, other special factors. Admission committee reviews full record of each candidate and makes decision based upon qualifications of each individual. **High school preparation:** 16 units recommended. Recommended units include English 4, foreign language 2, mathematics 3, social science 4 and science 2. College of Business and Public Administration and College of Pharmacy and Health Sciences recommend 2 algebra, 1 geometry. College of Pharmacy and Health Sciences recommends 1 biology, 1 chemistry. **Test requirements:** SAT or ACT; score report by August 1.

1992 FRESHMAN CLASS PROFILE. 1,131 men applied, 1,005 accepted, 367 enrolled; 1,525 women applied, 1,397 accepted, 474 enrolled. 75% had high school GPA of 3.0 or higher, 25% between 2.0 and 2.99. 34% were in top tenth and 65% were in top quarter of graduating class. **Academic background:** Mid 50% of enrolled freshmen had SAT-V between 410-540, SAT-M between 480-620; ACT composite between 22-28. 9% submitted SAT scores, 91% submitted ACT scores. **Characteristics:** 25% from in state, 90% live in college housing, 10% have minority backgrounds, 3% are foreign students, 29% join fraternities/sororities. Average age is 18.

FALL-TERM APPLICATIONS. $25 fee, may be waived for applicants with need. No closing date; priority given to applications received by March 1; applicants notified on a rolling basis beginning on or about November 1; must reply by May 1 or within 2 weeks if notified thereafter. Audition required for music applicants. Interview recommended. Portfolio recommended for art applicants. Essay recommended. Deferred and early admission available.

STUDENT LIFE. Housing: Dormitories (coed); apartment, fraternity, sorority housing available. Freshmen residence hall rooms equipped with computers, printers, and word processing and spreadsheet software. **Activities:** Student government, magazine, radio, student newspaper, television, yearbook, choral groups, concert band, dance, drama, jazz band, marching band, music ensembles, musical theater, opera, pep band, symphony orchestra, fraternities, sororities, Newman Community, United Ministries in Higher Education, Inter-Varsity Fellowship, Hillel, volunteer programs, Landlord-Tenant Association, Black Student Organization, Black American Law Students Association, International Students Association, Amnesty International. **Additional information:** Students communiate with faculty, business and government through computer voice network, electronic mail, and file transfer services.

ATHLETICS. NCAA. **Intercollegiate:** Basketball, cross-country, football M, golf M, rowing (crew), soccer M, softball W, tennis, track and field, volleyball W, wrestling M. **Intramural:** Badminton, baseball M, basketball, bowling, golf, lacrosse M, racquetball, rugby M, soccer, softball, swimming, table tennis, tennis, track and field, volleyball, water polo.

STUDENT SERVICES. Aptitude testing, career counseling, employment service for undergraduates, freshman orientation, health services, personal counseling, placement service for graduates, special adviser for adult students, veterans counselor, wellness program, lifetime sports instruction, services/facilities for handicapped.

ANNUAL EXPENSES. Tuition and fees: $12,780. Room rates reduced by $290 per year for students bringing their own Apple Macintosh, IBM or IBM compatible computer. **Room and board:** $4,520. **Books and supplies:** $550. **Other expenses:** $1,500.

FINANCIAL AID. 75% of freshmen, 75% of continuing students receive some form of aid. 64% of grants, 72% of loans, 63% of jobs based on need. 405 enrolled freshmen were judged to have need, all were offered aid. Academic, music/drama, art, athletic, state/district residency, religious affiliation, minority scholarships available. **Aid applications:** No closing date; priority given to applications received by March 1; applicants notified on a rolling basis beginning on or about March 1; must reply within 3 weeks.

ADDRESS/TELEPHONE. Thomas F. Willoughby, Director of Admission, Drake University, 2507 University Avenue, Des Moines, IA 50311-4505. (515) 271-3181. (800) 44-DRAKE. Fax: (515) 271-2831.

Ellsworth Community College
Iowa Falls, Iowa — CB code: 5528

2-year public community college, coed. Founded in 1890. **Accreditation:** Regional. **Undergraduate enrollment:** 340 men, 310 women full time; 70 men, 100 women part time. **Faculty:** 65 total (59 full time), 3 with doctorates or other terminal degrees. **Location:** Rural campus in small town; 70 miles from Des Moines. **Calendar:** Semester, limited summer session. Extensive evening/early morning classes. **Microcomputers:** 30 located in libraries, classrooms, computer centers. **Special facilities:** 80-acre wildlife area. **Additional facts:** Founded in 1890 as independent private four-year preparatory academy and college. Became public junior college in 1930. Now part of Iowa Valley Community College District.

DEGREES OFFERED. AA, AS, AAS. 245 associate degrees awarded in 1992.

UNDERGRADUATE MAJORS. Accounting, agribusiness, agricultural production, agricultural sciences, air pollution control technology, allied health, behavioral sciences, bioengineering and biomedical engineering, biological laboratory technology, biology, biotechnology, business administration and management, business and management, business and office, business computer/console/peripheral equipment operation, business data processing and related programs, business data programming, carpentry, chemistry, clothing and textiles management/production/services, commercial art, conservation and regulation, construction, criminal justice studies, data processing, education, education of the emotionally handicapped, education of the mentally handicapped, education of the physically handicapped, elementary education, engineering, engineering and engineering-related technologies, equestrian science, fashion merchandising, fine arts, home economics, humanities and social sciences, law enforcement and corrections, law enforcement and corrections technologies, legal secretary, liberal/general studies, marketing and distribution, marketing management, mathematics, medical secretary, mental health/human services, nursing, physical sciences, prelaw, premedicine, prepharmacy, preveterinary, psychology, recreation and community services technologies, retailing, science technologies, secondary education, secretarial and related programs, social sciences, teacher aide, veterinarian's assistant, wildlife management.

ACADEMIC PROGRAMS. 2-year transfer program, cooperative education, dual enrollment of high school students, internships. **Remedial services:** Learning center, remedial instruction, special counselor, tutoring. **Placement/credit:** CLEP General, institutional tests; 24 credit hours maximum for associate degree.

ACADEMIC REQUIREMENTS. Freshmen must earn minimum GPA of 1.5 to continue in good standing. 55% of freshmen return for sophomore year. Students must declare major on application. **Graduation requirements:** 64 hours for associate (20 in major). Most students required to take courses in English, history, humanities, mathematics, biological/physical sciences, social sciences.

FRESHMAN ADMISSIONS. Selection criteria: Open admissions. School achievement record considered for out-of-state applicants. Selective admission to some programs. Recommended units include biological science 1, English 3, mathematics 2 and social science 2. Typing also recommended. **Test requirements:** SAT or ACT (ACT preferred) for placement and counseling only; score report by August 15.

1992 FRESHMAN CLASS PROFILE. 303 men, 292 women enrolled. **Academic background:** Mid 50% of enrolled freshmen had ACT composite between 17-22. 60% submitted ACT scores. **Characteristics:** 90% from in state, 50% commute, 9% have minority backgrounds. Average age is 22.

FALL-TERM APPLICATIONS. $25 fee, may be waived for applicants with need. Closing date August 1; priority given to applications received by May 1; applicants notified on a rolling basis; must reply by registration. Interview required for human services applicants. Deferred admission available. Applicants without ACT test must take ASSET test.

STUDENT LIFE. Housing: Dormitories (men, women). **Activities:** Student government, student newspaper, choral groups, drama, jazz band, music ensembles, musical theater, pep band, Bible study group, Young Democrats, Young Republicans.

ATHLETICS. NJCAA. **Intercollegiate:** Baseball M, basketball, football M, softball W, volleyball W, wrestling M. **Intramural:** Badminton, basketball, bowling, handball, racquetball, swimming, tennis, volleyball.

STUDENT SERVICES. Aptitude testing, career counseling, employment service for undergraduates, freshman orientation, health services, personal counseling, placement service for graduates, special adviser for adult students, veterans counselor, services/facilities for handicapped.

ANNUAL EXPENSES. Tuition and fees (1992-93): $1,865, $1,750 additional for out-of-state students. **Room and board:** $2,700. **Books and supplies:** $400. **Other expenses:** $1,800.

FINANCIAL AID. 70% of freshmen, 70% of continuing students receive some form of aid. 93% of grants, 99% of loans, 78% of jobs based on need. Academic, music/drama, athletic, leadership scholarships available. **Aid applications:** No closing date; priority given to applications received by April 1; applicants notified on a rolling basis beginning on or about February 15; must reply within 3 weeks.

ADDRESS/TELEPHONE. Philip Rusley, Director of Admissions and Registrar, Ellsworth Community College, 1100 College, Iowa Falls, IA 50126. (515) 648-4611. (800) 322-9235. Fax: (515) 648-3128.

Emmaus Bible College
Dubuque, Iowa — CB code: 1215

4-year private Bible college, coed, nondenominational. Founded in 1942. **Undergraduate enrollment:** 97 men, 77 women full time; 9 men, 6 women part time. **Faculty:** 14 total, 13 with doctorates or other terminal degrees. **Location:** Urban campus in small city; 90 miles from Waterloo, 150 miles from Chicago Illinois. **Calendar:** Semester. **Microcomputers:** 4 located in libraries.

DEGREES OFFERED. AA, AS, BS. 15 associate degrees awarded in 1992. 100% in philosophy, religion, theology. 10 bachelor's degrees awarded. 100% in philosophy, religion, theology.

UNDERGRADUATE MAJORS. Associate: Bible studies. **Bachelor's:** Bible studies.

ACADEMIC PROGRAMS. Cross-registration.

ACADEMIC REQUIREMENTS. Freshmen must earn minimum GPA of 2.0 to continue in good standing. 50% of freshmen return for sophomore year. Students must declare major by end of second year. **Graduation requirements:** 100 hours for associate (74 in major), 130 hours for bachelor's (94 in major). Most students required to take courses in philosophy/religion.

FRESHMAN ADMISSIONS. Selection criteria: Recommendations and essay most important. Test scores and GPA also important. **Test requirements:** SAT or ACT for placement; score report by August 1.

1992 FRESHMAN CLASS PROFILE. 47 men, 42 women enrolled. **Academic background:** Mid 50% of enrolled freshmen had SAT-V between 380-480, SAT-M between 340-540; ACT composite between 13-25. 28% submitted SAT scores, 25% submitted ACT scores. **Characteristics:** 98% live in college housing, 3% have minority backgrounds, 10% are foreign students. Average age is 19.

FALL-TERM APPLICATIONS. $10 fee. No closing date; priority given to applications received by August 1; applicants notified on a rolling basis; must reply within 2 weeks. Interview recommended. Deferred admission available.

STUDENT LIFE. Housing: Dormitories (men, women). **Activities:** Radio, yearbook, choral groups, drama.

ATHLETICS. Intercollegiate: Basketball M. **Intramural:** Basketball W, field hockey M, handball, racquetball, soccer M, softball, table tennis, tennis, volleyball.

STUDENT SERVICES. Aptitude testing, career counseling, employment service for undergraduates, freshman orientation, health services, personal counseling, veterans counselor.

ANNUAL EXPENSES. Tuition and fees: $1,820. **Room and board:** $3,900. **Books and supplies:** $400. **Other expenses:** $1,770.

FINANCIAL AID. 65% of freshmen, 67% of continuing students receive some form of aid. All grants, all loans, 5% of jobs based on need. 30 enrolled freshmen were judged to have need, 27 were offered aid. Academic, leadership scholarships available. **Aid applications:** Closing date August 1; priority given to applications received by May 15; applicants notified on a rolling basis; must reply within 2 weeks.

ADDRESS/TELEPHONE. Philip K. Leverentz, Director of Admissions, Emmaus Bible College, 2570 Asbury Road, Dubuque, IA 52001. (319) 588-8000. Fax: (319) 588-1216.

Faith Baptist Bible College and Theological Seminary
Ankeny, Iowa CB code: 6214

Admissions: 62% of applicants accepted
Based on:
••• Recommendations, religious affiliation/commitment
•• Essay, school record, test scores
• Activities, interview
Completion: 85% of freshmen end year in good standing
38% graduate, 25% of these enter graduate study

4-year private Bible, seminary college, coed, affiliated with General Association of Regular Baptist Churches. Founded in 1921. **Accreditation:** Regional candidate. **Undergraduate enrollment:** 95 men, 100 women full time; 7 men, 22 women part time. **Graduate enrollment:** 9 men, 1 woman full time; 14 men, 2 women part time. **Faculty:** 30 total (23 full time), 12 with doctorates or other terminal degrees. **Location:** Suburban campus in large town; 6 miles from Des Moines. **Calendar:** Semester, limited summer session. **Microcomputers:** 4 located in libraries.

DEGREES OFFERED. AA, BA, BS, MA, M.Div. 9 associate degrees awarded in 1992. 35 bachelor's degrees awarded. Graduate degrees offered in 4 major fields of study.

UNDERGRADUATE MAJORS. Associate: Bible studies, missionary studies, secretarial and related programs. **Bachelor's:** Bible studies, elementary education, missionary studies, religious education, religious music, theological studies.

ACADEMIC PROGRAMS. Double major, internships. **Remedial services:** Reduced course load. **Placement/credit:** AP, CLEP General and Subject, institutional tests.

ACADEMIC REQUIREMENTS. Freshmen must earn minimum GPA of 2.0 to continue in good standing. 61% of freshmen return for sophomore year. Students must declare major by end of second year. **Graduation requirements:** 64 hours for associate (64 in major), 130 hours for bachelor's (50 in major). Most students required to take courses in arts/fine arts, English, history, philosophy/religion, biological/physical sciences.

FRESHMAN ADMISSIONS. Selection criteria: Recommendations, church affiliation, high school record, test scores important. **Test requirements:** SAT or ACT (ACT preferred); score report by August 15.

1992 FRESHMAN CLASS PROFILE. 62 men applied, 43 accepted, 24 enrolled; 90 women applied, 51 accepted, 34 enrolled. 52% had high school GPA of 3.0 or higher, 44% between 2.0 and 2.99. 38% were in top quarter of graduating class. **Characteristics:** 55% from in state, 93% live in college housing, 1% have minority backgrounds. Average age is 18.

FALL-TERM APPLICATIONS. $20 fee. Closing date August 1; applicants notified on a rolling basis; must reply by August 15. Essay required. Interview recommended for borderline applicants. Deferred admission available.

STUDENT LIFE. Housing: Dormitories (men, women); apartment housing available. **Activities:** Student government, yearbook, choral groups, concert band, drama, music ensembles, pep band, Sign Co. Fellowship, FATJ Ministries Fellowship, Men in Ministry, Families of Faith, Student Missionary Fellowship, Missionary Kids Fellowship, Missions Ambassadors, Student Association, Future Christian Teachers Association. **Additional information:** Religious observance required.

ATHLETICS. Intercollegiate: Basketball, cross-country M, soccer M, tennis M, volleyball W. **Intramural:** Basketball, soccer M, softball M, table tennis, volleyball.

STUDENT SERVICES. Career counseling, freshman orientation, health services, personal counseling, placement service for graduates, veterans counselor, services/facilities for handicapped.

ANNUAL EXPENSES. Tuition and fees (1992-93): $4,436. **Room and board:** $2,964. **Books and supplies:** $345. **Other expenses:** $1,000.

FINANCIAL AID. 87% of freshmen, 85% of continuing students receive some form of aid. 85% of grants, all loans based on need. All jobs based on criteria other than need. Academic, leadership scholarships available. **Aid applications:** No closing date; priority given to applications received by February 15; applicants notified on a rolling basis beginning on or about May 15; must reply within 30 days.

ADDRESS/TELEPHONE. Jeffery Newman, Admissions Coordinator, Faith Baptist Bible College and Theological Seminary, 1900 Northwest Fourth Street, Ankeny, IA 50021. (515) 964-0601 ext. 216. (800) 352-0147. Fax: (515) 964-1638.

Graceland College
Lamoni, Iowa CB code: 6249

Admissions: 78% of applicants accepted
Based on:
••• School record, test scores
•• Special talents
• Activities, interview, recommendations
Completion: 90% of freshmen end year in good standing
14% enter graduate study

4-year private liberal arts college, coed, affiliated with Reorganized Church of Jesus Christ of Latter-day Saints. Founded in 1895. **Accreditation:** Regional. **Undergraduate enrollment:** 450 men, 483 women full time; 31 men, 94 women part time. **Faculty:** 97 total (83 full time), 40 with doctorates or other terminal degrees. **Location:** Rural campus in small town; 110 miles from Kansas City, Missouri, 75 miles from Des Moines. **Calendar:** 4-1-4, limited summer session. **Microcomputers:** 62 located in computer centers.

DEGREES OFFERED. BA, BS. 225 bachelor's degrees awarded in 1992. 20% in business and management, 16% teacher education, 26% health sciences, 9% multi/interdisciplinary studies, 9% social sciences, 5% visual and performing arts.

UNDERGRADUATE MAJORS. Accounting, art history, biology, business administration and management, business economics, chemistry, communications, computer and information sciences, computer engineering, dramatic arts, economics, education, elementary education, English, English literature, French, German, graphic design, health sciences, history, information sciences and systems, international studies, liberal/general studies, mathematics, medical laboratory technologies, music, music education, nursing, parks and recreation management, physical sciences, predentistry, prelaw, premedicine, psychology, religion, secondary education, social sciences, sociology, Spanish, speech, studio art.

ACADEMIC PROGRAMS. Double major, external degree, honors program, independent study, internships, student-designed major, study abroad, teacher preparation, visiting/exchange student program, cross-registration. **Remedial services:** Learning center, reduced course load, remedial instruction, special counselor, tutoring, Chance Program for students with learning dysfunctions. **Placement/credit:** AP, CLEP General and Subject, institutional tests.

ACADEMIC REQUIREMENTS. Freshmen must earn minimum GPA of 1.7 to continue in good standing. 69% of freshmen return for sophomore year. Students must declare major by end of second year. **Graduation requirements:** 128 hours for bachelor's (36 in major). Most students required to take courses in arts/fine arts, computer science, English, history, humanities, mathematics, philosophy/religion, biological/physical sciences, social sciences. **Postgraduate studies:** 2% enter law school, 3% enter medical school, 3% enter MBA programs, 6% enter other graduate study. **Additional information:** Outreach program available for registered nurses seeking Bachelor of Science in nursing or Bachelor of Arts to complete program through home study and 2-week residencies.

FRESHMAN ADMISSIONS. Selection criteria: GPA and curriculum most important, followed by test scores. Applicants should have 2 of following: 2.0 GPA, SAT combined score of 840 or ACT composite score of 21, rank in top half of class. Recommendations and extracurricular activities considered. Exceptions are international students, Chance candidates, and students out of high school 1 year or more. **Test requirements:** SAT or ACT; score report by August 15.

1992 FRESHMAN CLASS PROFILE. 235 men applied, 183 accepted, 108 enrolled; 255 women applied, 198 accepted, 122 enrolled. 60% had high school GPA of 3.0 or higher, 38% between 2.0 and 2.99. 18% were in top tenth and 43% were in top quarter of graduating class. **Academic background:** Mid 50% of enrolled freshmen had SAT-V between 420-560, SAT-M between 450-620; ACT composite between 19-25. 24% submitted SAT scores, 77% submitted ACT scores. **Characteristics:** 32% from in state, 96% live in college housing, 8% have minority backgrounds, 7% are foreign students. Average age is 18.

FALL-TERM APPLICATIONS. $20 fee. No closing date; priority given to applications received by June 1; applicants notified on a rolling basis; must reply by registration. Audition required. Portfolio required for art applicants. Interview recommended. Interview required of applicants who do not meet admissions requirements, recommended for others. Deferred and early admission available.

STUDENT LIFE. Housing: Dormitories (men, women); apartment housing available. Students required to live on campus through sophomore year unless married or living with relatives. **Activities:** Student government, student newspaper, yearbook, choral groups, concert band, drama, jazz band, marching band, music ensembles, musical theater, pep band, symphony orchestra, stage band, Religious Life Program (social service projects), peace organization, Amnesty International. **Additional information:** Non-alcoholic night spot available.

ATHLETICS. NAIA. **Intercollegiate:** Baseball M, basketball, cross-country, football M, soccer, softball W, tennis, track and field, volleyball. **Intramural:** Badminton, baseball, basketball, bowling, cross-country, football, golf, handball, racquetball, soccer, softball, swimming, table tennis, tennis, track and field, volleyball.

STUDENT SERVICES. Aptitude testing, career counseling, employment service for undergraduates, freshman orientation, health services, personal counseling, placement service for graduates, special adviser for adult students, veterans counselor, services/facilities for handicapped.

ANNUAL EXPENSES. Tuition and fees: $8,680. **Room and board:** $2,920. **Books and supplies:** $550. **Other expenses:** $880.

FINANCIAL AID. 85% of freshmen, 87% of continuing students receive some form of aid. 26% of grants, 91% of loans, 42% of jobs based on need. 166 enrolled freshmen were judged to have need, 165 were offered aid. Academic, music/drama, art, athletic, leadership scholarships available. **Aid applications:** No closing date; priority given to applications received by March 1; applicants notified on a rolling basis beginning on or about March 20; must reply within 3 weeks.

ADDRESS/TELEPHONE. Bonita A. Booth, Dean of Admissions, Graceland College, 700 College Avenue, Lamoni, IA 50140. (800) 638-0053. (800) 346-9208. Fax: (515) 784-5480.

Grand View College
Des Moines, Iowa CB code: 6251

4-year private liberal arts college, coed, affiliated with Evangelical Lutheran Church in America. Founded in 1896. **Accreditation:** Regional. **Undergraduate enrollment:** 1,477 men and women. **Faculty:** 131 total (75 full time), 21 with doctorates or other terminal degrees. **Location:** Urban campus in large city; 200 miles from Kansas City, Missouri. **Calendar:** 4-4-1, limited summer session. **Microcomputers:** Located in dormitories, libraries, computer centers.

DEGREES OFFERED. AA, BA, BS. 200 bachelor's degrees awarded.

UNDERGRADUATE MAJORS. Associate: Criminal justice studies, engineering, liberal/general studies. **Bachelor's:** Accounting, applied mathematics, behavioral sciences, biology, business administration and management, business and management, business education, communications, computer and information sciences, computer programming, dramatic arts, education, elementary education, English, English education, fine arts, graphic design, health sciences, humanities, humanities and social sciences, journalism, liberal/general studies, mathematics education, nursing, nursing education, prelaw, radio/television broadcasting, religion, science education, secondary education, social science education, social sciences, social studies education, social work.

ACADEMIC PROGRAMS. 2-year transfer program, double major, dual enrollment of high school students, honors program, independent study, internships, student-designed major, study abroad, teacher preparation, Washington semester, cross-registration; liberal arts/career combination in health sciences. **Remedial services:** Learning center, preadmission summer program, reduced course load, remedial instruction, special counselor, tutoring. **ROTC:** Army. **Placement/credit:** AP, CLEP Subject, institutional tests; 32 credit hours maximum for bachelor's degree.

ACADEMIC REQUIREMENTS. Freshmen must earn minimum GPA of 1.5 to continue in good standing. 82% of freshmen return for sophomore year. Students must declare major on application. **Graduation requirements:** 62 hours for associate, 124 hours for bachelor's (52 in major). Most students required to take courses in English, history, humanities, mathematics, philosophy/religion, biological/physical sciences, social sciences. **Postgraduate studies:** 96% from 2-year programs enter 4-year programs. 1% enter law school, 1% enter medical school, 2% enter MBA programs, 8% enter other graduate study.

FRESHMAN ADMISSIONS. Selection criteria: Applicant should show evidence of ability to do satisfactory college work. **High school preparation:** 16 units recommended. Recommended units include biological science 1, English 2, foreign language 1, mathematics 1 and social science 2. **Test requirements:** SAT or ACT; score report by August 15.

1992 FRESHMAN CLASS PROFILE. 244 men and women enrolled. **Characteristics:** 93% from in state, 83% commute, 14% have minority backgrounds, 1% are foreign students. Average age is 18.

FALL-TERM APPLICATIONS. $20 fee, may be waived for applicants with need. Closing date August 1; applicants notified on a rolling basis; must reply within 8 weeks. Interview recommended for nursing, education, human services applicants. Portfolio recommended for commercial and fine arts applicants. Early admission available.

STUDENT LIFE. Housing: Dormitories (men, women). **Activities:** Student government, film, radio, student newspaper, television, choral groups, dance, drama, musical theater, Concerned Black Students, international students club, Student Political Awareness Alliance, campus Bible fellowship, art club, literary club.

ATHLETICS. NAIA. **Intercollegiate:** Baseball M, basketball, cross-country, golf, soccer M, softball W, tennis, track and field, volleyball W. **Intramural:** Badminton, basketball, bowling, softball, table tennis, tennis, volleyball.

STUDENT SERVICES. Aptitude testing, career counseling, employment service for undergraduates, freshman orientation, personal counseling, placement service for graduates, special adviser for adult students, veterans counselor, services/facilities for handicapped.

ANNUAL EXPENSES. Tuition and fees: $9,870. **Room and board:** $3,360. **Books and supplies:** $450. **Other expenses:** $625.

FINANCIAL AID. 98% of freshmen, 72% of continuing students receive some form of aid. Grants, loans, jobs available. Academic, music/drama, art, athletic, alumni affiliation, religious affiliation, minority scholarships available. **Aid applications:** No closing date; priority given to applications received by April 20; applicants notified on a rolling basis beginning on or about February 15; must reply within 10 days.

ADDRESS/TELEPHONE. Lori Hanson, Director of Admissiions and Financial Aid, Grand View College, 1200 Grandview Avenue, Des Moines, IA 50316. (515) 263-2800.

Grinnell College
Grinnell, Iowa CB code: 6252

Admissions: 62% of applicants accepted
Based on:
- ••• School record
- •• Activities, essay, recommendations, special talents, test scores
- • Interview

Completion: 92% of freshmen end year in good standing
82% graduate, 30% of these enter graduate study

4-year private liberal arts college, coed. Founded in 1846. **Accreditation:** Regional. **Undergraduate enrollment:** 583 men, 650 women full time; 7 men, 24 women part time. **Faculty:** 183 total (157 full time), 124 with doctorates or other terminal degrees. **Location:** Rural campus in small town; 55 miles from Des Moines. **Calendar:** Semester. **Microcomputers:** 224 located in dormitories, libraries, classrooms, computer centers. **Special facilities:** 365-acre environmental research area, 24-inch research telescope, 2 theaters.

DEGREES OFFERED. BA. 226 bachelor's degrees awarded in 1992. 11% in languages, 9% letters/literature, 11% life sciences, 6% mathematics, 9% physical sciences, 6% psychology, 33% social sciences.

UNDERGRADUATE MAJORS. American literature, American studies, anthropology, art history, biological and physical sciences, biology, chemistry, Chinese, classics, computer and information sciences, dramatic arts, economics, English, English literature, French, German, Greek (classical), history, international studies, Latin, mathematics, music, philosophy, physics, political science and government, predentistry, premedicine, prepharmacy, preveterinary, psychology, religion, Russian, sociology, Spanish, studio art.

ACADEMIC PROGRAMS. Double major, independent study, internships, student-designed major, study abroad, teacher preparation, Washington semester; liberal arts/career combination in engineering; combined bachelor's/graduate program in business administration, law. **Remedial services:** Tutoring, reading, writing, mathematics laboratories. **Placement/credit:** AP, IB, institutional tests.

ACADEMIC REQUIREMENTS. Freshmen must earn minimum GPA of 1.8 to continue in good standing. 93% of freshmen return for sophomore year. Students must declare major by end of second year. **Graduation requirements:** 124 hours for bachelor's (32 in major). **Postgraduate studies:**

4% enter law school, 3% enter medical school, 23% enter other graduate study. **Additional information:** Internships available in public agencies, private organizations, and corporations. Students may have no more than 48 credits in 1 department and 92 credits in 1 division.

FRESHMAN ADMISSIONS. Selection criteria: Scholastic ability, personal pursuits and accomplishments, interest in educational experience. Curiosity, motivation, and persistence stressed. Applicants should rank in top 20% of class. **High school preparation:** 16 units required. Required and recommended units include English 4, foreign language 2-3, mathematics 3, social science 3 and science 3. **Test requirements:** SAT or ACT; score report by February 1.

1992 FRESHMAN CLASS PROFILE. 849 men applied, 505 accepted, 127 enrolled; 993 women applied, 635 accepted, 170 enrolled. **Academic background:** Mid 50% of enrolled freshmen had SAT-V between 530-660, SAT-M between 580-700; ACT composite between 26-31. 82% submitted SAT scores, 59% submitted ACT scores. **Characteristics:** 16% from in state, 100% live in college housing, 10% have minority backgrounds, 11% are foreign students. Average age is 18.

FALL-TERM APPLICATIONS. $25 fee, may be waived for applicants with need. Closing date February 1; applicants notified on or about March 15; must reply by May 1. Essay required. Interview recommended. CRDA. Deferred and early admission available. EDP-F. Closing date for early decision applications December 1, notification January 15.

STUDENT LIFE. Housing: Dormitories (coed); cooperative housing available. Students required to live in college housing 2 years. Limited number upperclass students may reside off campus. **Activities:** Student government, film, magazine, radio, student newspaper, yearbook, video studio, choral groups, dance, drama, jazz band, music ensembles, musical theater, opera, symphony orchestra, gospel choir, 66 ethnic, political, religious, women's, and social service organizations.

ATHLETICS. NCAA. **Intercollegiate:** Baseball M, basketball, cross-country, diving, football M, golf M, soccer, softball W, swimming, tennis, track and field, volleyball W. **Intramural:** Basketball, soccer, softball, volleyball.

STUDENT SERVICES. Aptitude testing, career counseling, employment service for undergraduates, freshman orientation, health services, personal counseling, placement service for graduates, services/facilities for handicapped.

ANNUAL EXPENSES. Tuition and fees: $15,404. **Room and board:** $4,386. **Books and supplies:** $400. **Other expenses:** $400.

FINANCIAL AID. 79% of freshmen, 69% of continuing students receive some form of aid. Grants, loans, jobs available. Academic scholarships available. **Aid applications:** Closing date February 1; applicants notified on or about March 15; must reply by May 1. **Additional information:** Students may apply financial aid to off-campus study programs.

ADDRESS/TELEPHONE. Vincent Cuser, Director of Admission, Grinnell College, PO Box 805, Grinnell, IA 50112-0807. (515) 269-3600. Fax: (515) 269-4800.

Hamilton Technical College
Davenport, Iowa — CB code: 1588

3-year proprietary technical college, coed. Founded in 1969. **Undergraduate enrollment:** 309 men, 89 women full time. **Faculty:** 15 total (12 full time). **Location:** Suburban campus in small city; 175 miles from Chicago, 190 miles from Des Moines. **Calendar:** Semester.

DEGREES OFFERED. AS, AAS, BS. 172 associate degrees awarded in 1992. 32 bachelor's degrees awarded.

UNDERGRADUATE MAJORS. Associate: Aviation computer technology, electrical and electronics equipment repair, electronic technology. **Bachelor's:** Electronic technology.

ACADEMIC PROGRAMS. 2-year transfer program. **Remedial services:** Tutoring. **Placement/credit:** Institutional tests; 60 credit hours maximum for associate degree; 120 credit hours maximum for bachelor's degree.

ACADEMIC REQUIREMENTS. Freshmen must earn minimum GPA of 2.0 to continue in good standing. 99% of freshmen return for sophomore year. Students must declare major on enrollment. **Graduation requirements:** 60 hours for associate, 120 hours for bachelor's. Most students required to take courses in computer science, English, humanities, mathematics. **Postgraduate studies:** 10% from 2-year programs enter 4-year programs.

FRESHMAN ADMISSIONS. Selection criteria: Admission tests and interview required. **Test requirements:** Pseudoisochromatic Color Plates and Wonderlic required.

1992 FRESHMAN CLASS PROFILE. 314 men, 42 women enrolled. **Characteristics:** 60% from in state, 100% commute, 12% have minority backgrounds. Average age is 22.

FALL-TERM APPLICATIONS. $25 fee. No closing date; applicants notified on a rolling basis. Interview required. Deferred and early admission available.

STUDENT LIFE. Activities: Student government.

ATHLETICS. Intramural: Softball M.

STUDENT SERVICES. Aptitude testing, career counseling, employment service for undergraduates, personal counseling, placement service for graduates, services/facilities for handicapped.

ANNUAL EXPENSES. Tuition and fees (1992-93): $5,010. **Other expenses:** $750.

FINANCIAL AID. 90% of freshmen, 90% of continuing students receive some form of aid. Grants, loans available. **Aid applications:** No closing date; applicants notified on a rolling basis; must reply immediately.

ADDRESS/TELEPHONE. Maryanne Hamilton, Vice President, Hamilton Technical College, 1011 East 53rd Street, Davenport, IA 52807. (319) 386-3570. Fax: (319) 386-6756.

Hawkeye Community College
Waterloo, Iowa — CB code: 6288

2-year public community college, coed. Founded in 1966. **Accreditation:** Regional. **Undergraduate enrollment:** 1,030 men, 880 women full time; 190 men, 370 women part time. **Faculty:** 165 total (109 full time), 5 with doctorates or other terminal degrees. **Location:** Rural campus in small city; 120 miles from Des Moines, 90 miles from Cedar Rapids. **Calendar:** Semester, limited summer session. Saturday and extensive evening/early morning classes. **Microcomputers:** 160 located in libraries, classrooms.

DEGREES OFFERED. AA, AAS. 414 associate degrees awarded in 1992. 10% in agriculture, 16% business/office and marketing/distribution, 11% engineering technologies, 10% allied health, 5% home economics, 13% parks/recreation, protective services, public affairs, 20% trade and industry.

UNDERGRADUATE MAJORS. Accounting, agricultural business and management, agricultural production, aircraft mechanics, animal sciences, automotive mechanics, automotive technology, business administration and management, child development/care/guidance, civil technology, clothing and textiles management/production/services, commercial art, computer servicing technology, dental hygiene, diesel engine mechanics, drafting and design technology, electronic technology, farm equipment mechanics, fashion merchandising, graphic arts technology, home furnishings and equipment management/production/services, horticultural science, horticulture, industrial technology, interior design, law enforcement and corrections technologies, liberal/general studies, machine tool operation/machine shop, manufacturing technology, marketing and distribution, marketing management, mechanical design technology, medical laboratory technologies, nursing, office supervision and management, photographic technology, photography, precision metal work, protective services, robotics, secretarial and related programs, survey and mapping technology, tool and die making, tool and die/moldmaking.

ACADEMIC PROGRAMS. 2-year transfer program, external degree, internships, dental hygiene, nursing, and laboratory technology with University of Northern Iowa. **Remedial services:** Learning center, reduced course load, remedial instruction, special counselor, tutoring. **Placement/credit:** CLEP General and Subject, institutional tests; 30 credit hours maximum for associate degree.

ACADEMIC REQUIREMENTS. Freshmen must earn minimum GPA of 2.0 to continue in good standing. 60% of freshmen return for sophomore year. Students must declare major on application. **Graduation requirements:** 60 hours for associate. Most students required to take courses in computer science, English, mathematics.

FRESHMAN ADMISSIONS. Selection criteria: Open admissions. One biology required for nursing. One algebra required for electronics engineering technology, architectural and construction drafting, mechanical drafting, civil engineering technology and mechanical engineering technology. **Test requirements:** ACT required for admission to medical laboratory technician and dental hygiene programs only. SAT or ACT suggested for other applicants.

1992 FRESHMAN CLASS PROFILE. 444 men, 426 women enrolled. 18% were in top quarter of graduating class. **Academic background:** Mid 50% of enrolled freshmen had ACT composite between 16-21. 12% submitted ACT scores. **Characteristics:** 99% from in state, 100% commute, 8% have minority backgrounds, 1% are foreign students. Average age is 21.

FALL-TERM APPLICATIONS. No fee. No closing date; applicants notified on a rolling basis. Portfolio required for commercial art applicants. Deferred and early admission available. Accepted students asked to pay first-semester tuition in August to confirm fall enrollment.

STUDENT LIFE. Housing: Students in coordinate programs with University of Northern Iowa (nursing, medical lab technology, dental hygiene) may live in University of Northern Iowa housing. **Activities:** Student government.

ATHLETICS. Intramural: Basketball, bowling, cross-country, diving, golf, skiing, softball, swimming, volleyball, wrestling.

STUDENT SERVICES. Aptitude testing, career counseling, employment service for undergraduates, freshman orientation, personal counseling, placement service for graduates, services/facilities for handicapped.

ANNUAL EXPENSES. Tuition and fees (1992-93): $1,643, $1,575 additional for out-of-state students. **Books and supplies:** $700. **Other expenses:** $2,182.

FINANCIAL AID. 75% of freshmen, 80% of continuing students receive some form of aid. 93% of grants, 87% of loans, 96% of jobs based on

need. Academic, state/district residency, minority scholarships available. **Aid applications:** Closing date June 30; priority given to applications received by April 20; applicants notified on a rolling basis beginning on or about June 1; must reply within 2 weeks.

ADDRESS/TELEPHONE. David Fish, Director, Enrollment Services, Hawkeye Community College, PO Box 8015, Waterloo, IA 50704. (319) 296-2320 ext. 4000. Fax: (319) 296-2874.

Indian Hills Community College
Ottumwa, Iowa CB code: 6312

2-year public community college, coed. Founded in 1966. **Accreditation:** Regional. **Undergraduate enrollment:** 1,216 men, 1,318 women full time; 224 men, 578 women part time. **Faculty:** 134 total (125 full time), 7 with doctorates or other terminal degrees. **Location:** Rural campus in large town; 90 miles from of Des Moines. **Calendar:** 4 terms of about 12 weeks each; semester credits issued. **Microcomputers:** 112 located in libraries, classrooms, computer centers. **Special facilities:** Art gallery, nature preserve, outdoor amphitheater. **Additional facts:** Multilocation institution. Classes also available at Centerville. No Friday classes.

DEGREES OFFERED. AA, AS, AAS. 784 associate degrees awarded in 1992. 6% in computer sciences, 20% engineering technologies, 10% health sciences, 5% allied health, 42% multi/interdisciplinary studies, 13% trade and industry.

UNDERGRADUATE MAJORS. Aircraft mechanics, airline piloting and navigation, automotive technology, business systems analysis, child development/care/guidance, computer servicing technology, computer technology, criminal justice technology, diesel engine mechanics, drafting and design technology, electronic technology, food production/management/services, health care administration, laser electro-optic technology, liberal/general studies, machine tool operation/machine shop, medical records technology, nursing, physical therapy assistant, radiograph medical technology, robotics.

ACADEMIC PROGRAMS. 2-year transfer program, cooperative education, dual enrollment of high school students, honors program, independent study, internships. **Remedial services:** Learning center, reduced course load, remedial instruction, tutoring. **Placement/credit:** AP, CLEP General and Subject; 30 credit hours maximum for associate degree.

ACADEMIC REQUIREMENTS. Freshmen must earn minimum GPA of 2.0 to continue in good standing. 68% of freshmen return for sophomore year. Students must declare major on enrollment. **Graduation requirements:** 60 hours for associate. Most students required to take courses in English, history, humanities, mathematics, biological/physical sciences, social sciences.

FRESHMAN ADMISSIONS. Selection criteria: Open admissions. High school GPA and test scores considered for limited enrollment programs. Recommended units include English 2 and mathematics 2. Mathematics background required for some technology programs; recommended for arts and sciences majors. **Test requirements:** ACT required for technology programs. College Qualification Test required for nursing program applicants.

1992 FRESHMAN CLASS PROFILE. 576 men, 587 women enrolled. **Characteristics:** 93% from in state, 83% commute, 2% have minority backgrounds. Average age is 23.

FALL-TERM APPLICATIONS. No fee. No closing date; applicants notified on a rolling basis. Deferred and early admission available.

STUDENT LIFE. Housing: Dormitories (men, women, coed). **Activities:** Student government, choral groups, dance, drama, jazz band, music ensembles, musical theater, pep band, symphony orchestra.

ATHLETICS. NJCAA. **Intercollegiate:** Baseball M, basketball M, golf M, softball W, volleyball W. **Intramural:** Basketball, bowling, fencing, football M, racquetball, softball, tennis, volleyball.

STUDENT SERVICES. Aptitude testing, career counseling, employment service for undergraduates, freshman orientation, on-campus day care, personal counseling, placement service for graduates, special adviser for adult students, veterans counselor, services/facilities for handicapped.

ANNUAL EXPENSES. Tuition and fees (1992-93): $1,330, $600 additional for out-of-state students. **Room and board:** $2,115. **Books and supplies:** $675. **Other expenses:** $750.

FINANCIAL AID. 80% of freshmen, 80% of continuing students receive some form of aid. 71% of grants, 76% of loans, 31% of jobs based on need. Academic, music/drama, art, athletic, state/district residency, leadership, minority scholarships available. **Aid applications:** No closing date; priority given to applications received by April 1; applicants notified on a rolling basis beginning on or about June 1; must reply within 2 weeks.

ADDRESS/TELEPHONE. Jane Sapp, Admissions Officer, Indian Hills Community College, 525 Grandview, Ottumwa, IA 52501. (515) 683-5153. (800) 726-2585 ext.153. Fax: (516) 683-5184.

Iowa Central Community College
Fort Dodge, Iowa CB code: 6217

2-year public community college, coed. Founded in 1966. **Accreditation:** Regional. **Undergraduate enrollment:** 2,738 men and women. **Faculty:** 175 total (166 full time). **Location:** Rural campus in large town; 90 miles from Des Moines. **Calendar:** Semester, limited summer session. **Microcomputers:** Located in libraries, classrooms.

DEGREES OFFERED. AA, AS, AAS. 423 associate degrees awarded in 1992.

UNDERGRADUATE MAJORS. Accounting, agribusiness, airline piloting and navigation, automotive mechanics, automotive technology, aviation management, business data entry equipment operation, business data processing and related programs, business data programming, child development/care/guidance, communications, data processing, dental assistant, diesel engine mechanics, electronic technology, fashion merchandising, horticultural science, industrial technology, law enforcement and corrections technologies, liberal/general studies, management information systems, marketing and distribution, medical laboratory technologies, nursing, protective services, public affairs, radio/television broadcasting, retailing, secretarial and related programs, teacher aide, telecommunications.

ACADEMIC PROGRAMS. 2-year transfer program, accelerated program, cooperative education, dual enrollment of high school students, honors program, independent study, internships, telecourses. **Remedial services:** Learning center, preadmission summer program, reduced course load, remedial instruction, special counselor, tutoring. **Placement/credit:** AP, CLEP General and Subject.

ACADEMIC REQUIREMENTS. No policy requiring minimum GPA; records of students having academic difficulty are reviewed individually. 40% of freshmen return for sophomore year. **Graduation requirements:** 60 hours for associate. Most students required to take courses in arts/fine arts, English, history, humanities, mathematics, biological/physical sciences, social sciences.

FRESHMAN ADMISSIONS. Selection criteria: Open admissions. **Test requirements:** ACT for placement. ASSET may be submitted in place of ACT.

1992 FRESHMAN CLASS PROFILE. 1,834 men and women enrolled. **Academic background:** Mid 50% of enrolled freshmen had ACT composite between 17-22. 30% submitted ACT scores. **Characteristics:** 95% from in state, 85% commute, 5% have minority backgrounds, 1% are foreign students. Average age is 23.

FALL-TERM APPLICATIONS. No fee. No closing date; applicants notified on a rolling basis. Early admission available.

STUDENT LIFE. Housing: Dormitories (men, women). **Activities:** Student government, film, radio, student newspaper, yearbook, choral groups, concert band, drama, jazz band, music ensembles, pep band.

ATHLETICS. NJCAA. **Intercollegiate:** Baseball M, basketball, football M, golf, softball W, volleyball W, wrestling M. **Intramural:** Archery, badminton, bowling, softball, swimming, table tennis, tennis.

STUDENT SERVICES. Aptitude testing, career counseling, employment service for undergraduates, freshman orientation, health services, on-campus day care, personal counseling, placement service for graduates, special adviser for adult students, veterans counselor, services/facilities for handicapped.

ANNUAL EXPENSES. Tuition and fees (projected): $2,040, $910 additional for out-of-state students. **Room and board:** $2,860. **Books and supplies:** $500. **Other expenses:** $1,240.

FINANCIAL AID. 75% of freshmen, 75% of continuing students receive some form of aid. Grants, loans, jobs available. Academic, music/drama, athletic scholarships available. **Aid applications:** No closing date; applicants notified on a rolling basis beginning on or about May 15; must reply within 2 weeks.

ADDRESS/TELEPHONE. Dale Daggy, Director of Admissions, Iowa Central Community College, 330 Avenue M, Fort Dodge, IA 50501. (515) 576-7201 ext. 2400. (800) 362-2793 ext. 2400.

Iowa Lakes Community College
Estherville, Iowa CB code: 6196

2-year public college of arts and sciences and agricultural and technical, nursing, community, junior, technical college, coed. Founded in 1967. **Accreditation:** Regional. **Undergraduate enrollment:** 1,798 men and women. **Faculty:** 76 total (68 full time), 12 with doctorates or other terminal degrees. **Location:** Urban campus in small town; 100 miles from Sioux Falls, South Dakota. **Calendar:** Semester, limited summer session. **Microcomputers:** Located in classrooms, computer centers. **Special facilities:** Lakeside laboratory, 360-acre farm, print collection. **Additional facts:** Classes also held at Emmetsburg, Spencer, Algona, and Spirit Lake.

DEGREES OFFERED. AA, AS, AAS. 550 associate degrees awarded in 1992. 7% in agriculture, 5% education, 10% teacher education, 5% engineering technologies, 10% health sciences, 6% allied health, 10% life sciences, 6% parks/recreation, protective services, public affairs, 10% physical sciences, 5% psychology, 10% social sciences.

UNDERGRADUATE MAJORS. Accounting, agribusiness, agricultural business and management, agricultural education, agricultural production, air pollution control technology, airline piloting and navigation, apparel and accessories marketing, art education, automotive mechanics, aviation management, biology, botany, business administration and management, business and management, business and office, business computer/console/peripheral equipment operation, business data processing and related programs, business data programming, business education, chemistry, child development/care/guidance, commercial art, communications, computer and information sciences, computer programming, computer-aided drafting and design, conservation and regulation, criminal justice studies, data processing, drafting, drafting and design technology, early childhood education, ecology, education, elementary education, English, English education, environmental science, fashion merchandising, fine arts, fishing and fisheries, forestry and related sciences, health care administration, health education, horticulture, hospitality and recreation marketing, hotel/motel and restaurant management, industrial arts education, jazz, journalism, junior high education, law enforcement and corrections, legal assistant/paralegal, liberal/general studies, marketing and distribution, marketing and distributive education, mathematics, mathematics education, mental health/human services, music, music education, music performance, nursing, office supervision and management, parks and recreation management, personal services, physical education, physical sciences, physics, predentistry, prelaw, premedicine, prepharmacy, preveterinary, psychology, radio/television broadcasting, recreation and community services technologies, science education, science technologies, secondary education, small business management and ownership, social science education, social sciences, social studies education, speech, studio art, tourism, trade and industrial education, transportation and travel marketing, water and wastewater technology, wildlife management, zoology.

ACADEMIC PROGRAMS. 2-year transfer program, cooperative education, dual enrollment of high school students, honors program, internships, telecourses, weekend college, evening college. **Remedial services:** Learning center, preadmission summer program, reduced course load, remedial instruction, special counselor, tutoring, developmental studies and special help for those with learning disabilities. **Placement/credit:** CLEP General and Subject, institutional tests.

ACADEMIC REQUIREMENTS. Freshmen must earn minimum GPA of 2.0 to continue in good standing. 62% of freshmen return for sophomore year. Students must declare major on enrollment. **Graduation requirements:** 64 hours for associate (38 in major). Most students required to take courses in computer science, English, humanities, mathematics, biological/physical sciences, social sciences.

FRESHMAN ADMISSIONS. Selection criteria: Open admissions. Selective admissions to nursing, aviation/airport management, and computer-aided drafting and design programs.

1992 FRESHMAN CLASS PROFILE. 594 men and women enrolled. **Characteristics:** 95% from in state, 85% commute, 5% have minority backgrounds, 1% are foreign students. Average age is 20.

FALL-TERM APPLICATIONS. No fee. No closing date; applicants notified on a rolling basis. Interview required for career programs applicants. Audition recommended for music applicants. Portfolio recommended for commercial art applicants. Deferred and early admission available.

STUDENT LIFE. Housing: Dormitories (coed); apartment, cooperative housing available. **Activities:** Student government, radio, student newspaper, television, choral groups, concert band, jazz band, marching band, music ensembles, pep band, swing choir.

ATHLETICS. NJCAA. **Intercollegiate:** Baseball M, basketball M, football M, golf, softball W, volleyball W. **Intramural:** Basketball, bowling, golf, racquetball, skiing, softball, table tennis, volleyball.

STUDENT SERVICES. Aptitude testing, career counseling, freshman orientation, personal counseling, placement service for graduates, special adviser for adult students, veterans counselor, services/facilities for handicapped.

ANNUAL EXPENSES. Tuition and fees (1992-93): $1,557, $605 additional for out-of-state students. **Room and board:** $2,205. **Books and supplies:** $405. **Other expenses:** $455.

FINANCIAL AID. 80% of freshmen, 80% of continuing students receive some form of aid. All grants, 98% of loans, all jobs based on need. Academic, music/drama, art, athletic scholarships available. **Aid applications:** No closing date; applicants notified on a rolling basis beginning on or about April 15; must reply within 10 days.

ADDRESS/TELEPHONE. John G. Nelson, Director of Admissions and Marketing, Iowa Lakes Community College, 300 South 18th Street, Estherville, IA 51334. (712) 362-2604. Fax: (712) 362-2260.

Iowa State University

Ames, Iowa — CB code: 6306

Admissions: 88% of applicants accepted
Based on:
- ••• School record
- •• Test scores
- • Essay, interview, recommendations, special talents

Completion: 91% of freshmen end year in good standing
54% graduate, 16% of these enter graduate study

4-year public university, coed. Founded in 1858. **Accreditation:** Regional. **Undergraduate enrollment:** 11,057 men, 7,746 women full time; 849 men, 767 women part time. **Graduate enrollment:** 1,861 men, 969 women full time; 1,059 men, 955 women part time. **Faculty:** 1,759 total (1,590 full time), 1,465 with doctorates or other terminal degrees. **Location:** Suburban campus in small city; 30 miles north of Des Moines. **Calendar:** Semester, extensive summer session. **Microcomputers:** 1,000 located in dormitories, libraries, classrooms, computer centers, campus-wide network. **Special facilities:** Brunier Gallery, Iowa State Center, Erwin W. Fick observatory, Pammel Woods nature preserve, research park, molecular biology building, Durham Computation Center, center for designing foods. **Additional facts:** Classes also offered at numerous off-campus sites, including Des Moines.

DEGREES OFFERED. BA, BS, BFA, BArch, MA, MS, MBA, MFA, MEd, PhD, DVM. 3,837 bachelor's degrees awarded in 1992. 9% in agriculture, 20% business and management, 12% teacher education, 17% engineering, 5% letters/literature, 6% social sciences. Graduate degrees offered in 106 major fields of study.

UNDERGRADUATE MAJORS. Accounting, advertising, aerospace/aeronautical/astronautical engineering, agribusiness, agricultural biochemistry, agricultural business and management, agricultural education, agricultural engineering, agricultural mechanics, agricultural microbiology, agronomy, animal sciences, anthropology, architecture, atmospheric sciences and meteorology, biochemistry, biology, biophysics, botany, ceramic engineering, chemical engineering, chemistry, child development/care/guidance, city/community/regional planning, civil engineering, computer and information sciences, computer engineering, construction engineering, crafts, dairy, design, distributed studies, early childhood education, earth sciences, ecology, economics, electrical/electronics/communications engineering, elementary education, engineering operations, engineering science, English, entomology, family and community services, family/consumer resource management, fashion design, fashion merchandising, finance, fine arts, fishing and fisheries, food production/management/services, food science and nutrition, food sciences, food technology, forestry and related sciences, forestry production and processing, French, genetics, human and animal, geology, German, graphic design, health education, history, home economics, home economics education, horticultural science, horticulture, hotel/motel and restaurant management, human environment and housing, individual and family development, industrial engineering, institutional/home management/supporting programs, interior design, international/comparative home economics, journalism, landscape architecture, liberal/general studies, linguistics, management information systems, management science, marketing management, mathematics, mechanical engineering, medical illustrating, metallurgy, microbiology, music, music education, naval science (Navy, Marines), ornamental horticulture, parks and recreation management, philosophy, physical education, physics, plant sciences, political science and government, predentistry, prelaw, premedicine, prepharmacy, preveterinary, psychology, public administration, range management, religion, Russian, social work, sociology, Spanish, speech, statistics, textiles and clothing, transportation management, wildlife management, zoology.

ACADEMIC PROGRAMS. Accelerated program, computer delivered (on-line) credit-bearing course offerings, cooperative education, double major, dual enrollment of high school students, external degree, honors program, independent study, internships, student-designed major, study abroad, teacher preparation, telecourses, Washington semester, cross-registration. **Remedial services:** Reduced course load, tutoring, academic support services. **ROTC:** Air Force, Army, Naval. **Placement/credit:** AP, CLEP General and Subject, IB, institutional tests. No limit on number of hours of credit by examination that may be counted toward degree.

ACADEMIC REQUIREMENTS. Freshmen must earn minimum GPA of 1.67 to continue in good standing. 82% of freshmen return for sophomore year. Students must declare major by end of first year. **Graduation requirements:** 125 hours for bachelor's. Most students required to take courses in English, humanities, mathematics, biological/physical sciences, social sciences. **Postgraduate studies:** 1% enter law school, 1% enter medical school, 2% enter MBA programs, 12% enter other graduate study.

FRESHMAN ADMISSIONS. Selection criteria: Rank in top half of graduating class and completion of a prescribed set of college-preparatory high school courses.Test scores considered as alternative criterion to class rank in some instances. **High school preparation:** 12 units required. Required units include English 4, mathematics 3, social science 2 and science 3. College of Liberal Arts and Sciences requires 1 additional social sciences unit and 2 units of a single foreign language for total of 15 units. **Test re-**

quirements: SAT or ACT (ACT preferred); score report by August 23. Test results used for admission in some instances.

1992 FRESHMAN CLASS PROFILE. 4,454 men applied, 3,884 accepted, 1,931 enrolled; 3,345 women applied, 3,003 accepted, 1,453 enrolled. 76% had high school GPA of 3.0 or higher, 24% between 2.0 and 2.99. 27% were in top tenth and 57% were in top quarter of graduating class. **Academic background:** Mid 50% of enrolled freshmen had SAT-V between 370-530, SAT-M between 460-630; ACT composite between 22-27. 9% submitted SAT scores, 91% submitted ACT scores. **Characteristics:** 70% from in state, 76% live in college housing, 9% have minority backgrounds, 3% are foreign students, 9% join fraternities/sororities. Average age is 18.

FALL-TERM APPLICATIONS. $20 fee. Fee may be deferred for some educationally disadvantaged applicants. No closing date; applicants notified on a rolling basis. Deferred admission available.

STUDENT LIFE. Housing: Dormitories (men, women, coed); apartment, fraternity, sorority, handicapped housing available. Special academic, cross-cultural, and no-alcohol housing available. **Activities:** Student government, film, magazine, radio, student newspaper, television, yearbook, choral groups, concert band, dance, drama, jazz band, marching band, music ensembles, musical theater, pep band, symphony orchestra, fraternities, sororities, more than 500 clubs and organizations including Black Student Organization, United Native American Student Association, Hispanic American Student Union, Young Democrats, Young Republicans. **Additional information:** Quality of student life rated very high in Eli Lilly Foundation study.

ATHLETICS. NCAA. **Intercollegiate:** Baseball M, basketball, cross-country, diving, football M, golf, gymnastics, softball W, swimming, tennis, track and field, volleyball W, wrestling M. **Intramural:** Archery, badminton, baseball, basketball, bowling, diving, fencing, golf, horseback riding, ice hockey, lacrosse M, racquetball, rifle, rugby M, sailing, skiing, soccer, softball, squash, swimming, table tennis, tennis, track and field, volleyball, water polo, wrestling.

STUDENT SERVICES. Aptitude testing, career counseling, employment service for undergraduates, freshman orientation, health services, personal counseling, placement service for graduates, special adviser for adult students, veterans counselor, services/facilities for handicapped.

ANNUAL EXPENSES. Tuition and fees (1992-93): $2,228, $4,768 additional for out-of-state students. **Room and board:** $3,044. **Books and supplies:** $520. **Other expenses:** $1,690.

FINANCIAL AID. 75% of freshmen, 71% of continuing students receive some form of aid. 69% of grants, 23% of jobs based on need. Academic, music/drama, art, athletic, state/district residency, leadership, alumni affiliation, minority scholarships available. **Aid applications:** No closing date; priority given to applications received by March 1; applicants notified on a rolling basis beginning on or about March 1; must reply by May 1 or within 2 weeks if notified thereafter. **Additional information:** Short-term loan program available to meet unplanned needs. Financial counseling clinic available to discuss budget preparation and money concerns.

ADDRESS/TELEPHONE. Karsten Smedal, Director of Admissions, Iowa State University, Alumni Hall, Ames, IA 50011-2010. (515) 294-5836. (800) 262-3810. Fax: (515) 294-1088.

Iowa Wesleyan College
Mount Pleasant, Iowa — CB code: 6308

Admissions:	66% of applicants accepted
Based on:	••• School record
	•• Recommendations, test scores
	• Activities, essay, interview, special talents
Completion:	75% of freshmen end year in good standing
	14% enter graduate study

4-year private liberal arts college, coed, affiliated with United Methodist Church. Founded in 1842. **Accreditation:** Regional. **Undergraduate enrollment:** 278 men, 306 women full time; 412 men and women part time. **Faculty:** 60 total (43 full time). **Location:** Rural campus in small town; 47 miles from Iowa City, 25 miles from Burlington. **Calendar:** 4-1-4, limited summer session. Extensive evening/early morning classes. **Microcomputers:** Located in libraries, classrooms, computer centers. **Special facilities:** Radio station, media center, art gallery.

DEGREES OFFERED. BA, BS. 173 bachelor's degrees awarded in 1992. 33% in business and management, 17% teacher education, 19% health sciences, 6% visual and performing arts.

UNDERGRADUATE MAJORS. Accounting, art education, behavioral sciences, biology, business administration and management, business and management, business economics, chemistry, clinical laboratory science, communications, computer and information sciences, criminal justice studies, early childhood education, elementary education, English, English education, junior high education, liberal/general studies, mathematics, mathematics education, music, music education, nursing, physical education, physical therapy, predentistry, prelaw, premedicine, prepharmacy, preveterinary, psychology, science education, secondary education, sociology.

ACADEMIC PROGRAMS. Double major, dual enrollment of high school students, independent study, internships, student-designed major, study abroad, teacher preparation, telecourses, visiting/exchange student program, cross-registration; liberal arts/career combination in engineering, forestry, health sciences. **Remedial services:** Learning center, reduced course load, special counselor, tutoring. **Placement/credit:** AP, CLEP Subject, institutional tests; 30 credit hours maximum for bachelor's degree.

ACADEMIC REQUIREMENTS. Freshmen must earn minimum GPA of 2.0 to continue in good standing. 68% of freshmen return for sophomore year. Students must declare major by end of second year. **Graduation requirements:** 124 hours for bachelor's (36 in major). Most students required to take courses in arts/fine arts, computer science, English, history, humanities, mathematics, philosophy/religion, biological/physical sciences, social sciences. **Postgraduate studies:** 1% enter law school, 1% enter medical school, 4% enter MBA programs, 8% enter other graduate study.

FRESHMAN ADMISSIONS. Selection criteria: Rank in top half of class preferred. Test scores and recommendations considered. **High school preparation:** 16 units recommended. Recommended units include biological science 2, English 4, foreign language 1, mathematics 2, physical science 2 and social science 2. **Test requirements:** SAT or ACT; score report by August 20.

1992 FRESHMAN CLASS PROFILE. 298 men applied, 171 accepted, 88 enrolled; 145 women applied, 120 accepted, 63 enrolled. 7% were in top tenth and 29% were in top quarter of graduating class. **Academic background:** Mid 50% of enrolled freshmen had ACT composite between 17-23. 90% submitted ACT scores. **Characteristics:** 61% from in state, 85% live in college housing, 23% have minority backgrounds, 1% are foreign students, 25% join fraternities/sororities. Average age is 18.

FALL-TERM APPLICATIONS. $15 fee, may be waived for applicants with need. Closing date August 15; applicants notified on a rolling basis; must reply within 4 weeks. Audition required for music applicants. Essay required. Interview recommended. Portfolio recommended for art, creative programs applicants. Deferred and early admission available. Institutional early decision plan.

STUDENT LIFE. Housing: Dormitories (men, women). **Activities:** Student government, radio, student newspaper, television, yearbook, literary magazine, choral groups, concert band, drama, jazz band, music ensembles, musical theater, pep band, symphony orchestra, fraternities, sororities, Campus Crusade for Christ, black awareness board, international club.

ATHLETICS. NAIA. **Intercollegiate:** Baseball M, basketball, cross-country, football M, golf, softball W, track and field, volleyball W. **Intramural:** Basketball, bowling, softball, table tennis, volleyball.

STUDENT SERVICES. Career counseling, employment service for undergraduates, freshman orientation, health services, personal counseling, placement service for graduates, special adviser for adult students.

ANNUAL EXPENSES. Tuition and fees: $9,850. **Room and board:** $3,400. **Books and supplies:** $500. **Other expenses:** $1,448.

FINANCIAL AID. 85% of freshmen, 85% of continuing students receive some form of aid. Grants, loans, jobs available. Academic, music/drama, art, athletic, state/district residency, religious affiliation scholarships available. **Aid applications:** No closing date; priority given to applications received by July 1; applicants notified on a rolling basis beginning on or about January 25; must reply within 20 days.

ADDRESS/TELEPHONE. Karen Conrad, Director of Admissions, Iowa Wesleyan College, 601 North Main Street, Mount Pleasant, IA 52641. (319) 385-8021. (800) 582-2383. Fax: (319) 385-6296.

Iowa Western Community College
Council Bluffs, Iowa — CB code: 6302

2-year public community college, coed. Founded in 1966. **Accreditation:** Regional. **Undergraduate enrollment:** 881 men, 963 women full time; 645 men, 1,134 women part time. **Faculty:** 186 total (171 full time), 10 with doctorates or other terminal degrees. **Location:** Suburban campus in small city; 10 miles from Omaha, Nebraska. **Calendar:** Semester, extensive summer session. Saturday and extensive evening/early morning classes. **Microcomputers:** 75 located in libraries, classrooms, computer centers. **Additional facts:** Branch campus at Clarinda offers liberal arts and vocational programs in practical nursing, secretarial, mechanical technology, and electromechanical technology. Attendance centers in Harlan and Atlantic offer evening programs in liberal arts and business administration. Practical nursing offered at Harlan attendance center.

DEGREES OFFERED. AA, AS, AAS. 492 associate degrees awarded in 1992. 18% in business and management, 8% computer sciences, 12% education, 16% health sciences, 5% parks/recreation, protective services, public affairs, 8% social sciences, 13% trade and industry.

UNDERGRADUATE MAJORS. Accounting, agricultural business and management, aircraft mechanics, architectural technologies, automotive mechanics, automotive technology, business and management, civil technology, computer and information sciences, computer programming, criminal justice studies, criminology, diesel engine mechanics, education, electronic technology, fashion merchandising, fire control and safety technology, food management, food production/management/services, interpreter for the deaf, journalism, law enforcement and corrections technologies, legal assistant/paralegal, legal secretary, liberal/general studies, machine tool operation/machine shop, mathematics, mechanical design technology, medical secretary, nursing, physical sciences, psychology, retailing, secretarial and related programs, social sciences, social work, substance abuse counseling.

ACADEMIC PROGRAMS. 2-year transfer program, cooperative education, dual enrollment of high school students, independent study, internships, telecourses, weekend college. **Remedial services:** Learning center, reduced course load, remedial instruction, special counselor, tutoring, interpreter services for deaf students. **ROTC:** Air Force, Army. **Placement/credit:** CLEP General and Subject, institutional tests.

ACADEMIC REQUIREMENTS. Freshmen must earn minimum GPA of 1.75 to continue in good standing. Minimum GPA of 2.0 required in nursing programs. 62% of freshmen return for sophomore year. Students must declare major by end of first year. **Graduation requirements:** 60 hours for associate. Most students required to take courses in English, humanities, mathematics, biological/physical sciences, social sciences.

FRESHMAN ADMISSIONS. Selection criteria: Open admissions. Selective criteria for career programs, with test scores most important. School achievement record considered. Specific subject requirements for some career programs. **Test requirements:** Career Planning Program test required for placement of all full-time freshmen and for admission to limited enrollment career programs. **Additional information:** Developmental courses available to assist applicants gain proficiency needed for admission to specific programs.

1992 FRESHMAN CLASS PROFILE. 646 men, 768 women enrolled. **Characteristics:** 85% commute. Average age is 24.

FALL-TERM APPLICATIONS. $15 fee. No closing date; priority given to applications received by July 1; applicants notified on a rolling basis; must reply within 4 weeks. Interview required of vocational-technical applicants, recommended for all. Early admission available. Applicants for limited-enrollment programs considered on first applied, first accepted basis.

STUDENT LIFE. Housing: Dormitories (coed); apartment housing available. **Activities:** Student government, magazine, radio, student newspaper, choral groups, concert band, drama, christian fellowships, special interest clubs.

ATHLETICS. NJCAA. **Intercollegiate:** Baseball M, basketball M, softball W, volleyball W. **Intramural:** Basketball, softball, tennis, volleyball.

STUDENT SERVICES. Aptitude testing, career counseling, employment service for undergraduates, freshman orientation, on-campus day care, personal counseling, placement service for graduates, veterans counselor, services/facilities for handicapped.

ANNUAL EXPENSES. Tuition and fees (projected): $1,800, $810 additional for out-of-state students. **Room and board:** $3,000. **Books and supplies:** $325. **Other expenses:** $900.

FINANCIAL AID. 76% of freshmen, 66% of continuing students receive some form of aid. 93% of grants, 93% of loans, 60% of jobs based on need. 647 enrolled freshmen were judged to have need, 595 were offered aid. Academic, athletic, state/district residency scholarships available. **Aid applications:** No closing date; priority given to applications received by May 1; applicants notified on a rolling basis beginning on or about June 1; must reply within 2 weeks.

ADDRESS/TELEPHONE. Thomas O. Dutch, Director of Admissions, Iowa Western Community College, 2700 College Road, Box 4C, Council Bluffs, IA 51502. (712) 325-3200 ext. 277. Fax: (712) 325-3424. For admissions to branch campus: Director of Admissions, Iowa Western Community College: Clarinda, 923 East Washington, Clarinda, IA 51632. Telephone: (712) 542-5117.

Kirkwood Community College
Cedar Rapids, Iowa — CB code: 6027

2-year public community college, coed. Founded in 1966. **Accreditation:** Regional. **Undergraduate enrollment:** 2,407 men, 2,631 women full time; 1,649 men, 2,925 women part time. **Faculty:** 542 total (203 full time), 25 with doctorates or other terminal degrees. **Location:** Suburban campus in small city; 280 miles from Chicago, 285 miles from Minneapolis-St. Paul. **Calendar:** Semester, extensive summer session. Saturday and extensive evening/early morning classes. **Microcomputers:** 450 located in classrooms, computer centers. **Special facilities:** Telecommunications center, computer center, student development center, raptor center.

DEGREES OFFERED. AA, AS, AAS. 1,031 associate degrees awarded in 1992. 7% in agriculture, 7% business and management, 5% engineering technologies, 19% health sciences, 39% multi/interdisciplinary studies, 7% parks/recreation, protective services, public affairs.

UNDERGRADUATE MAJORS. Accounting, agribusiness, agricultural business and management, agricultural economics, agricultural education, agricultural mechanics, agricultural production, agricultural sciences, agronomy, air conditioning/heating/refrigeration mechanics, air conditioning/heating/refrigeration technology, anatomy, animal sciences, automated manufacturing technology, automotive mechanics, automotive technology, biology, botany, business administration and management, business and management, business and office, business computer/console/peripheral equipment operation, business data processing and related programs, business data programming, business education, chemistry, computer and information sciences, computer programming, computerized numerical control technology, construction, dairy, dental assistant, dental laboratory technology, diesel engine mechanics, early childhood education, education, electrical and electronics equipment repair, electrical/electronics/communications engineering, electrodiagnostic technologies, electromechanical technology, electronic technology, elementary education, engineering, engineering and engineering-related technologies, English, equestrian science, fashion merchandising, finance, fine arts, fire control and safety technology, food management, food production/management/services, French, graphic and printing production, graphic arts technology, horticultural science, horticulture, humanities, industrial equipment maintenance and repair, institutional/home management/supporting programs, integrated career studies, interior design, international business management, journalism, junior high education, landscape architecture, law enforcement and corrections technologies, legal assistant/paralegal, liberal/general studies, machine tool operation/machine shop, marine maintenance, marketing and distribution, marketing and distributive education, marketing management, mathematics, mathematics education, mechanical design technology, mechanical engineering, medical assistant, medical records technology, music, music education, nursing, nursing education, occupational therapy assistant, ornamental horticulture, parks and recreation management, photographic technology, physical education, physical sciences, physics, practical nursing, predentistry, preengineering, prelaw, premedicine, prepharmacy, preveterinary, protective services, psychology, public affairs, public relations, radio/television broadcasting, radio/television technology, recreation and community services technologies, renewable natural resources, respiratory therapy, respiratory therapy technology, retailing, science technologies, secondary education, secretarial and related programs, small business management and ownership, social sciences, social work, soil sciences, Spanish, teacher aide, telecommunications, veterinarian's assistant, visual and performing arts, water and wastewater technology, zoology.

ACADEMIC PROGRAMS. 2-year transfer program, accelerated program, cooperative education, dual enrollment of high school students, honors program, independent study, internships, student-designed major, telecourses, visiting/exchange student program, weekend college, cross-registration. **Remedial services:** Learning center, preadmission summer program, reduced course load, remedial instruction, special counselor, tutoring. **Placement/credit:** AP, CLEP General and Subject, institutional tests; 66 credit hours maximum for associate degree.

ACADEMIC REQUIREMENTS. Freshmen must earn minimum GPA of 2.0 to continue in good standing. Students must declare major on application. **Graduation requirements:** 62 hours for associate (21 in major). Most students required to take courses in English, history, humanities, mathematics, biological/physical sciences, social sciences.

FRESHMAN ADMISSIONS. Selection criteria: Open admissions. Selective admissions to some programs. **Test requirements:** SAT or ACT (ACT preferred) for placement; score report by August 27. ASSET required for vocational-technical program counseling. Either SAT or ACT required for placement for Arts and Sciences division applicants.

1992 FRESHMAN CLASS PROFILE. 1,595 men, 1,759 women enrolled. **Characteristics:** 95% from in state, 100% commute, 5% have minority backgrounds, 3% are foreign students. Average age is 24.

FALL-TERM APPLICATIONS. No fee. No closing date; applicants notified on a rolling basis. Interview required for vocational-technical, career option applicants.

STUDENT LIFE. Activities: Student government, film, magazine, radio, student newspaper, television, videotape, choral groups, concert band, dance, drama, jazz band, music ensembles, musical theater, pep band, symphony orchestra, Circle-K, Newman Club, 39 other organizations.

ATHLETICS. NJCAA. **Intercollegiate:** Baseball M, basketball, golf M, soccer M, softball W. **Intramural:** Basketball, golf, handball, racquetball, soccer, softball, table tennis, tennis, volleyball.

STUDENT SERVICES. Aptitude testing, career counseling, employment service for undergraduates, freshman orientation, health services, on-campus day care, personal counseling, placement service for graduates, special adviser for adult students, veterans counselor, tutoring program, services/facilities for handicapped.

ANNUAL EXPENSES. Tuition and fees (1992-93): $1,410, $1,230 additional for out-of-state students. **Books and supplies:** $400. **Other expenses:** $850.

FINANCIAL AID. 65% of freshmen, 75% of continuing students receive some form of aid. All aid based on need. **Aid applications:** No closing date; priority given to applications received by March 15; applicants notified on a rolling basis beginning on or about June 1; must reply within 10 days.

ADDRESS/TELEPHONE. Jim Miller, Director of Admissions, Kirkwood Community College, 6301 Kirkwood Boulevard, Southwest, Cedar Rapids, IA 52406. (319) 398-5517. Fax: (319) 398-1244 ext.5517.

Loras College
Dubuque, Iowa CB code: 6370

Admissions: 75% of applicants accepted
Based on: ••• School record, test scores
•• Essay, recommendations
• Activities, interview, religious affiliation/commitment, special talents
Completion: 85% of freshmen end year in good standing
60% graduate, 15% of these enter graduate study

4-year private liberal arts college, coed, affiliated with Roman Catholic Church. Founded in 1839. **Accreditation:** Regional. **Undergraduate enrollment:** 793 men, 743 women full time; 102 men, 138 women part time. **Graduate enrollment:** 81 men and women. **Faculty:** 133 total (115 full time), 90 with doctorates or other terminal degrees. **Location:** Urban campus in small city; 180 miles from Chicago. **Calendar:** Semester, extensive summer session. Extensive evening/early morning classes. **Microcomputers:** 95 located in dormitories, classrooms, computer centers. **Special facilities:** Planetarium.

DEGREES OFFERED. AA, AS, BA, BS, MA. 311 bachelor's degrees awarded. Graduate degrees offered in 10 major fields of study.

UNDERGRADUATE MAJORS. **Associate:** Liberal/general studies. **Bachelor's:** Accounting, art education, art history, biological and physical sciences, biology, business administration and management, business and management, business economics, chemistry, classics, clinical psychology, communications, computer and information sciences, computer programming, creative writing, economics, education, education of the mentally handicapped, elementary education, engineering physics, English, English education, finance, foreign languages education, French, German, health sciences, history, human resources development, international business management, international studies, journalism, Latin, liberal/general studies, management information systems, marketing management, mathematics, mathematics education, music, music education, music theory and composition, nuclear medical technology, philosophy, physical education, physical sciences, physics, political science and government, predentistry, premedicine, prepharmacy, preveterinary, psychology, public relations, radio/television broadcasting, religion, religious education, science education, secondary education, social sciences, social work, sociology, Spanish, special education, speech, speech/communication/theater education, sports management, sports medicine, studio art.

ACADEMIC PROGRAMS. Accelerated program, double major, dual enrollment of high school students, honors program, independent study, internships, student-designed major, study abroad, teacher preparation, cross-registration. **Remedial services:** Learning center, reduced course load, remedial instruction, special counselor, tutoring. **Placement/credit:** AP, CLEP General and Subject; 30 credit hours maximum for bachelor's degree.

ACADEMIC REQUIREMENTS. Freshmen must earn minimum GPA of 2.0 to continue in good standing. 90% of freshmen return for sophomore year. Students must declare major by end of second year. **Graduation requirements:** 60 hours for associate (20 in major), 120 hours for bachelor's (40 in major). Most students required to take courses in arts/fine arts, computer science, English, foreign languages, history, humanities, mathematics, philosophy/religion, biological/physical sciences, social sciences. **Postgraduate studies:** 80% from 2-year programs enter 4-year programs. 5% enter law school, 5% enter medical school, 5% enter MBA programs.

FRESHMAN ADMISSIONS. Selection criteria: High school academic record and test scores most important. **High school preparation:** 10 units recommended. Recommended units include English 4, mathematics 2, social science 2 and science 2. **Test requirements:** SAT or ACT (ACT preferred); score report by August 15. ACH required of some applicants.

1992 FRESHMAN CLASS PROFILE. 672 men applied, 484 accepted, 234 enrolled; 600 women applied, 470 accepted, 206 enrolled. 10% were in top tenth and 23% were in top quarter of graduating class. **Academic background:** Mid 50% of enrolled freshmen had ACT composite between 17-24. 90% submitted ACT scores. **Characteristics:** 60% from in state, 80% live in college housing, 3% have minority backgrounds, 5% are foreign students. Average age is 18.

FALL-TERM APPLICATIONS. $25 fee, may be waived for applicants with need. Closing date August 15; applicants notified on a rolling basis; must reply within 2 weeks. Interview recommended. Essay recommended. CRDA. Deferred admission available.

STUDENT LIFE. Housing: Dormitories (men, women, coed); apartment, handicapped housing available. **Activities:** Student government, magazine, radio, student newspaper, television, yearbook, choral groups, concert band, drama, jazz band, music ensembles, musical theater, pep band, fraternities, sororities.

ATHLETICS. NCAA. **Intercollegiate:** Baseball M, basketball, cross-country, diving, football M, golf, ice hockey M, soccer M, softball W, swimming, tennis, track and field, volleyball W, wrestling M. **Intramural:** Badminton, baseball M, basketball, cross-country, diving, golf, handball, racquetball, softball, swimming, tennis, track and field, volleyball. **Clubs:** Skiing, rugby.

STUDENT SERVICES. Aptitude testing, career counseling, employment service for undergraduates, freshman orientation, health services, personal counseling, placement service for graduates, special adviser for adult students, veterans counselor, services/facilities for handicapped.

ANNUAL EXPENSES. Tuition and fees: $10,580. **Room and board:** $3,660. **Books and supplies:** $600. **Other expenses:** $450.

FINANCIAL AID. 80% of freshmen, 80% of continuing students receive some form of aid. Grants, loans, jobs available. Academic, music/drama, art, athletic, leadership, religious affiliation, minority scholarships available. **Aid applications:** Closing date April 15; applicants notified on a rolling basis beginning on or about February 1; must reply within 3 weeks. **Additional information:** Audition or portfolio recommended for music and art financial aid applicants.

ADDRESS/TELEPHONE. Kelly Myers, Director of Admissions, Loras College, 1450 Alta Vista, Dubuque, IA 52001. (319) 588-7236. (800) 245-6727. Fax: (319) 588-7964.

Luther College
Decorah, Iowa CB code: 6375

Admissions: 88% of applicants accepted
Based on: ••• School record, test scores
•• Essay
• Activities, interview, recommendations, special talents
Completion: 96% of freshmen end year in good standing
76% graduate, 26% of these enter graduate study

4-year private liberal arts college, coed, affiliated with Evangelical Lutheran Church in America. Founded in 1861. **Accreditation:** Regional. **Undergraduate enrollment:** 924 men, 1,329 women full time; 29 men, 45 women part time. **Faculty:** 193 total (155 full time), 138 with doctorates or other terminal degrees. **Location:** Rural campus in small town; 70 miles from Rochester, Minnesota, 50 miles from LaCrosse, Wisconsin. **Calendar:** 4-1-4, limited summer session. **Microcomputers:** 274 located in dormitories, libraries, classrooms, computer centers. **Special facilities:** Live animal center, planetarium, art galleries, Norwegian-American museum, 5 downhill ski runs, extensive biology field study areas.

DEGREES OFFERED. BA. 521 bachelor's degrees awarded in 1992. 19% in business and management, 5% communications, 7% teacher education, 7% health sciences, 6% letters/literature, 11% life sciences, 7% psychology, 18% social sciences, 6% visual and performing arts.

UNDERGRADUATE MAJORS. Accounting, African studies, Afro-American (black) studies, anthropology, art education, arts management, biological and physical sciences, biology, business administration and management, business and management, business economics, chemistry, classics, clinical laboratory science, communications, computer and information sciences, cytotechnology, economics, education, education of the mentally handicapped, elementary education, engineering, English, English education, English literature, environmental science, fine arts, foreign languages education, French, German, Greek (classical), health education, Hebrew, Hispanic American studies, history, humanities and social sciences, international business management, international studies, Latin, Latin American studies, liberal/general studies, management information systems, marine biology, mathematics, mathematics education, medical laboratory technologies, music, music business management, music education, norwegian, nursing, nursing/physical therapy, occupational therapy, philosophy, physical education, physical sciences, physics, political science and government, predentistry, prelaw, premedicine, prepharmacy, preveterinary, psychobiology, psychology, reading education, religion, Russian and Slavic studies, Scandinavian languages, Scandinavian studies, secondary education, social sciences, social studies education, social work, sociology, sociology/political science, Spanish, special education, speech, sports management, theater/dance, theological studies.

ACADEMIC PROGRAMS. Accelerated program, double major, honors program, independent study, internships, student-designed major, study abroad, teacher preparation, visiting/exchange student program, Washington semester; liberal arts/career combination in engineering, forestry, health sciences. **Remedial services:** Learning center, reduced course load, remedial instruction, special counselor, tutoring. **Placement/credit:** AP, CLEP Subject, IB, institutional tests; 64 credit hours maximum for bachelor's degree.

ACADEMIC REQUIREMENTS. Freshmen must earn minimum GPA of 2.0 to continue in good standing. 89% of freshmen return for sophomore year. Students must declare major by end of second year. **Graduation requirements:** 128 hours for bachelor's. Most students required to take courses in arts/fine arts, English, foreign languages, history, humanities, mathematics, philosophy/religion, biological/physical sciences, social sciences. **Postgraduate studies:** 2% enter law school, 7% enter medical school, 2% enter MBA programs, 15% enter other graduate study.

FRESHMAN ADMISSIONS. Selection criteria: Rigor of high school curriculum most important, followed by SAT or ACT scores and interview. Applicants should rank in top half of high school class. Recommendations and extracurricular activities considered. Required and recommended units include English 4, mathematics 3, social science 3 and science 2. Foreign language 2 recommended. **Test requirements:** SAT or ACT (ACT preferred); score report by March 1.

1992 FRESHMAN CLASS PROFILE. 592 men applied, 499 accepted, 239 enrolled; 908 women applied, 827 accepted, 365 enrolled. 37% were in top tenth and 67% were in top quarter of graduating class. **Academic background:** Mid 50% of enrolled freshmen had SAT-V between 460-560, SAT-M between 520-650; ACT composite between 22-28. 21% submitted SAT scores, 98% submitted ACT scores. **Characteristics:** 35% from in state, 99% live in college housing, 3% have minority backgrounds, 3% are foreign students. Average age is 18.

FALL-TERM APPLICATIONS. $20 fee, may be waived for applicants with need. No closing date; priority given to applications received by March 1; applicants notified on a rolling basis beginning on or about December 15; applicants select reply date from several possibilities. Essay required. Interview recommended. Audition recommended for music applicants. Portfolio recommended for art applicants. CRDA. Deferred and early admission available.

STUDENT LIFE. Housing: Dormitories (coed); apartment, handicapped housing available. International language houses available. **Activities:** Student government, film, magazine, radio, student newspaper, yearbook, choral groups, concert band, dance, drama, jazz band, music ensembles, musical theater, opera, pep band, symphony orchestra, fraternities, sororities, major religious denominations and political parties represented, Black Student Union, Asian Student Association, International Student Association.

ATHLETICS. NCAA. **Intercollegiate:** Baseball M, basketball, cross-country, football M, golf, soccer, softball W, swimming, tennis, track and field, volleyball W, wrestling M. **Intramural:** Archery, badminton, basketball, bowling, cross-country, fencing, field hockey W, football M, golf, racquetball, rugby, skiing, soccer, softball, table tennis, tennis, track and field, volleyball, water polo.

STUDENT SERVICES. Aptitude testing, career counseling, employment service for undergraduates, freshman orientation, health services, personal counseling, placement service for graduates, services/facilities for handicapped.

ANNUAL EXPENSES. Tuition and fees (projected): $12,375. **Room and board:** $3,525. **Books and supplies:** $600. **Other expenses:** $400.

FINANCIAL AID. 83% of freshmen, 87% of continuing students receive some form of aid. 93% of grants, 93% of loans, 36% of jobs based on need. 424 enrolled freshmen were judged to have need, all were offered aid. Academic, music/drama, art, minority scholarships available. **Aid applications:** Closing date June 1; priority given to applications received by March 1; applicants notified on a rolling basis beginning on or about March 15; must reply within 4 weeks.

ADDRESS/TELEPHONE. Dennis R. Johnson, Dean for Enrollment, Luther College, 700 College Drive, Decorah, IA 52101-1042. (319) 387-1287. (800) 458-8437. Fax: (319) 387-2159.

Maharishi International University
Fairfield, Iowa CB code: 4497

Admissions: 51% of applicants accepted
Based on: ••• Recommendations
•• Essay, interview, school record
• Activities, special talents
Completion: 87% of freshmen end year in good standing
48% graduate, 40% of these enter graduate study

4-year private university, coed. Founded in 1971. **Accreditation:** Regional. **Undergraduate enrollment:** 224 men, 190 women full time; 22 men, 23 women part time. **Graduate enrollment:** 126 men, 108 women full time; 44 men, 59 women part time. **Faculty:** 170 total (150 full time), 103 with doctorates or other terminal degrees. **Location:** Rural campus in large town; 60 miles south of Iowa City, 110 miles southeast of Des Moines. **Calendar:** 10 terms of 4 weeks each plus two 2-week blocks. **Microcomputers:** 55 located in libraries, computer centers. **Special facilities:** Scanning electron microscope, real time cell imaging system, DNA synthesizer, two large domes for meditation, art gallery. **Additional facts:** Students, faculty, and staff practice Transcendental Meditation (TM) and TM-Sidhi daily.

DEGREES OFFERED. AA, BA, BS, BFA, MA, MS, MBA, MFA, PhD. 5 associate degrees awarded in 1992. 100% in multi/interdisciplinary studies. 54 bachelor's degrees awarded. 30% in business and management, 7% computer sciences, 9% engineering, 9% letters/literature, 17% multi/interdisciplinary studies, 24% visual and performing arts. Graduate degrees offered in 14 major fields of study.

UNDERGRADUATE MAJORS. Associate: Ayur-ved (holistic preventive medicine), biology, business administration and management, chemistry, computer and information sciences, education, English literature, fine arts, French, Indic languages, liberal/general studies, mathematics, music, physics, political science and government, science of creative intelligence, Spanish, visual and performing arts. **Bachelor's:** Ayur-ved (holistic preventive medicine), biochemistry, biology, business administration and management, chemistry, computer and information sciences, electrical/electronics/communications engineering, English literature, fine arts, mathematics, physics, political science and government, psychology, science of creative intelligence.

ACADEMIC PROGRAMS. 2-year transfer program, double major, honors program, independent study, internships, study abroad, teacher preparation, visiting/exchange student program; combined bachelor's/graduate program in business administration. **Remedial services:** Learning center, remedial instruction, special counselor, tutoring. **Placement/credit:** AP, CLEP General and Subject, institutional tests; 12 credit hours maximum for associate degree; 12 credit hours maximum for bachelor's degree.

ACADEMIC REQUIREMENTS. Freshmen must earn minimum GPA of 2.0 to continue in good standing. 61% of freshmen return for sophomore year. Students must declare major by end of first year. **Graduation requirements:** 80 hours for associate (28 in major), 160 hours for bachelor's (60 in major). Most students required to take courses in arts/fine arts, computer science, English, humanities, mathematics, philosophy/religion, biological/physical sciences, social sciences. **Additional information:** Innovative modular block system in which students study one subject at a time.

FRESHMAN ADMISSIONS. Selection criteria: Academics, grades, recommendations, personal and academic performance and promise. Recommended units include English 4, foreign language 2, mathematics 2 and science 2.

1992 FRESHMAN CLASS PROFILE. 190 men and women applied, 97 accepted; 35 men enrolled, 38 women enrolled. 52% had high school GPA of 3.0 or higher, 35% between 2.0 and 2.99. 13% were in top tenth and 19% were in top quarter of graduating class. **Characteristics:** 21% from in state, 98% live in college housing, 5% have minority backgrounds, 44% are foreign students. Average age is 26.

FALL-TERM APPLICATIONS. $25 fee, may be waived for applicants with need. No closing date; applicants notified on a rolling basis. Essay required. Interview recommended. Deferred admission available.

STUDENT LIFE. Housing: Dormitories (men, women); apartment housing available. **Activities:** Student government, film, magazine, student newspaper, television, yearbook, choral groups, dance, drama, music ensembles, musical theater, improvisation group, World Congress, Association des Quepeccois de MIU, African Students Association, Club UNO, Association of Students for Invincibility of Asia, Organization for a New Earth (ONE), International Cultural Exchange Club, International Student Organization. **Additional information:** Daily practice of transcendental meditation by all students, faculty and staff fosters a fulfilling and harmonious campus life.

ATHLETICS. Intercollegiate: Soccer M, volleyball. **Intramural:** Archery, badminton, basketball M, diving, golf, gymnastics, ice hockey M, racquetball, sailing, skiing, soccer M, softball, swimming, table tennis, tennis, track and field.

STUDENT SERVICES. Aptitude testing, career counseling, freshman orientation, personal counseling, veterans counselor, preschool, services/facilities for handicapped.

ANNUAL EXPENSES. Tuition and fees (1992-93): $7,890. **Room and board:** $2,760. **Books and supplies:** $400. **Other expenses:** $660.

FINANCIAL AID. 79% of freshmen, 82% of continuing students receive some form of aid. All grants, 82% of loans, all jobs based on need. 63 enrolled freshmen were judged to have need, all were offered aid. **Aid applications:** No closing date; priority given to applications received by February 28; applicants notified on a rolling basis beginning on or about May 1; must reply within 6 weeks or by fall registration, whichever is earlier. **Additional information:** Students may earn scholarships through volunteer staff program. International students must agree to return to native country in order to be eligible for scholarship.

ADDRESS/TELEPHONE. Harry Bright, Director of Admissions, Maharishi International University, 1000 North Fourth Street DB1155, Fairfield, IA 52557-1155. (515) 472-1166. Fax: (515) 472-1189.

Marshalltown Community College
Marshalltown, Iowa CB code: 6394

2-year public community college, coed. Founded in 1927. **Accreditation:** Regional. **Undergraduate enrollment:** 1,227 men and women. **Faculty:** 116 total (47 full time), 4 with doctorates or other terminal degrees. **Location:** Suburban campus in large town; 50 miles from of Des Moines. **Calendar:** Semester, limited summer session. **Microcomputers:** Located in computer centers.

DEGREES OFFERED. AA, AS, AAS. 199 associate degrees awarded in 1992.

UNDERGRADUATE MAJORS. Accounting, agribusiness, agricultural sciences, architecture, biology, botany, business and management, business and office, child development/care/guidance, community services, computer and information sciences, dental assistant, drafting, drafting and design technology, education, elementary education, engineering, English, English literature, fine arts, forestry and related sciences, home economics, liberal/general studies, marketing and distribution, mathematics, medical assistant, nursing, physical sciences, practical nursing, psychology, secondary education, secretarial and related programs, social sciences, Spanish, surgical technology, visual and performing arts, zoology.

ACADEMIC PROGRAMS. 2-year transfer program, cooperative educa-

tion, independent study, internships. **Remedial services:** Learning center, reduced course load, remedial instruction, special counselor, tutoring. **Placement/credit:** CLEP General and Subject, institutional tests; 30 credit hours maximum for associate degree.

ACADEMIC REQUIREMENTS. No policy requiring minimum GPA; records of students having academic difficulty are reviewed individually. 70% of freshmen return for sophomore year. **Graduation requirements:** 62 hours for associate. Most students required to take courses in English, humanities, mathematics, biological/physical sciences, social sciences.

FRESHMAN ADMISSIONS. Selection criteria: Open admissions. Selective admissions to health career programs. **Test requirements:** SAT or ACT (ACT preferred) for placement and counseling only; score report by August 20.

1992 FRESHMAN CLASS PROFILE. 739 men and women enrolled. **Characteristics:** 98% from in state, 100% commute, 3% have minority backgrounds.

FALL-TERM APPLICATIONS. $25 fee. No closing date; applicants notified on a rolling basis. Interview recommended for health careers, child care applicants. Deferred admission available.

STUDENT LIFE. Activities: Student government, student newspaper, choral groups, concert band, drama, jazz band, music ensembles, musical theater, Circle-K, international student organization.

ATHLETICS. NJCAA. **Intercollegiate:** Baseball M, basketball, golf, racquetball M, softball W, tennis. **Intramural:** Basketball, bowling, cross-country, golf, racquetball, soccer M, swimming, table tennis, tennis, volleyball.

STUDENT SERVICES. Aptitude testing, career counseling, employment service for undergraduates, health services, on-campus day care, personal counseling, placement service for graduates, special adviser for adult students, veterans counselor, services/facilities for handicapped.

ANNUAL EXPENSES. Tuition and fees (1992-93): $1,865, $1,760 additional for out-of-state students. **Books and supplies:** $425. **Other expenses:** $690.

FINANCIAL AID. 50% of freshmen, 45% of continuing students receive some form of aid. 93% of grants, 81% of loans, 94% of jobs based on need. 480 enrolled freshmen were judged to have need, 410 were offered aid. Academic, leadership scholarships available. **Aid applications:** No closing date; priority given to applications received by March 15; applicants notified on a rolling basis beginning on or about April 30; must reply within 2 weeks.

ADDRESS/TELEPHONE. Sylvia Grandgeorge, Director of Admissions and Registrar, Marshalltown Community College, 3700 South Center Street, Marshalltown, IA 50158. (515) 752-7106. (800) 456-3633. Fax: (515) 752-8194.

Morningside College
Sioux City, Iowa

CB code: 6415

Admissions:	88% of applicants accepted
Based on:	••• School record, test scores
	•• Activities, interview, recommendations
	• Essay, special talents
Completion:	85% of freshmen end year in good standing
	55% graduate, 12% of these enter graduate study

4-year private liberal arts college, coed, affiliated with United Methodist Church. Founded in 1894. **Accreditation:** Regional. **Undergraduate enrollment:** 419 men, 545 women full time; 52 men, 153 women part time. **Graduate enrollment:** 2 men, 3 women full time; 20 men, 94 women part time. **Faculty:** 106 total (70 full time), 52 with doctorates or other terminal degrees. **Location:** Suburban campus in small city; 90 miles from Omaha, Nebraska. **Calendar:** Semester, limited summer session. **Microcomputers:** 150 located in dormitories, libraries, classrooms, computer centers. **Special facilities:** Observatory, biology research station sponsored by Midwest Energy, HPER facility, art gallery, wild flower and prairie gra.

DEGREES OFFERED. AA, BA, BS, M. 219 bachelor's degrees awarded. 34% in business and management, 6% communications, 21% teacher education, 11% health sciences, 7% life sciences, 6% parks/recreation, protective services, public affairs. Graduate degrees offered in 9 major fields of study.

UNDERGRADUATE MAJORS. Associate: Criminal justice studies. **Bachelor's:** Accounting, agribusiness, American Indian studies, art education, biological and physical sciences, biology, business administration and management, business and management, business education, chemistry, communications, comparative literature, computer and information sciences, computer programming, creative writing, criminal justice studies, dramatic arts, early childhood education, economics, education of the emotionally handicapped, education of the mentally handicapped, education of the multiple handicapped, elementary education, English education, English literature, finance, foreign languages (multiple emphasis), foreign languages education, French, graphic design, history, humanities and social sciences, industrial and organizational psychology, international business management, journalism, junior high education, liberal/general studies, marketing management, mathematics, mathematics education, medical laboratory technologies, music, music education, music performance, nursing, office supervision and management, parks and recreation management, personnel management, philosophy, photography, physical education, physics, political science and government, preengineering, prelaw, premedicine, psychology, radio/television broadcasting, reading education, religion, science education, secondary education, secretarial and related programs, social science education, social studies education, sociology, Spanish, specific learning disabilities, speech/communication/theater education, studio art, teaching English as a second language/foreign language.

ACADEMIC PROGRAMS. 2-year transfer program, accelerated program, double major, honors program, independent study, internships, student-designed major, study abroad, teacher preparation, visiting/exchange student program, United Nations semester, Washington semester; liberal arts/career combination in engineering, health sciences. **Remedial services:** Learning center, reduced course load, remedial instruction, special counselor, tutoring. **Placement/credit:** AP, CLEP General and Subject, institutional tests; 30 credit hours maximum for associate degree; 30 credit hours maximum for bachelor's degree.

ACADEMIC REQUIREMENTS. Freshmen must earn minimum GPA of 2.0 to continue in good standing. 74% of freshmen return for sophomore year. Students must declare major by end of second year. **Graduation requirements:** 62 hours for associate, 124 hours for bachelor's (36 in major). Most students required to take courses in arts/fine arts, computer science, English, foreign languages, history, humanities, mathematics, philosophy/religion, biological/physical sciences, social sciences. **Postgraduate studies:** 1% enter law school, 5% enter medical school, 1% enter MBA programs, 5% enter other graduate study.

FRESHMAN ADMISSIONS. Selection criteria: High school academic record most important; test data supplemental. High school recommendation also considered. **High school preparation:** 20 units recommended. Recommended units include biological science 1, English 3, foreign language 2, mathematics 2, physical science 2 and social science 2. **Test requirements:** SAT or ACT (ACT preferred); score report by August 15.

1992 FRESHMAN CLASS PROFILE. 282 men applied, 246 accepted, 95 enrolled; 383 women applied, 340 accepted, 102 enrolled. 51% had high school GPA of 3.0 or higher, 49% between 2.0 and 2.99. 16% were in top tenth and 37% were in top quarter of graduating class. **Academic background:** Mid 50% of enrolled freshmen had ACT composite between 19-25. 89% submitted ACT scores. **Characteristics:** 76% from in state, 77% live in college housing, 5% have minority backgrounds, 4% are foreign students, 4% join fraternities/sororities. Average age is 18.

FALL-TERM APPLICATIONS. $15 fee, may be waived for applicants with need. No closing date; applicants notified on a rolling basis; must reply within 2 weeks of notification or 2 weeks after receiving a financial aid award, if appropriate. Audition required for music applicants. Interview recommended. Portfolio recommended for art applicants. Audition or audition tape recommended for theater applicants. Early admission available. EDP-S.

STUDENT LIFE. Housing: Dormitories (men, women, coed); apartment, sorority housing available. **Activities:** Student government, magazine, radio, student newspaper, television, yearbook, choral groups, concert band, drama, jazz band, marching band, music ensembles, musical theater, pep band, symphony orchestra, fraternities, sororities, Fellowship of Christian Athletes, Newman Club, Young Democrats, Young Republicans, Morningside Christian Fellowship, All-Campus Worship, Fellowship of women in Ministry, International Association.

ATHLETICS. NCAA. **Intercollegiate:** Baseball M, basketball, cross-country M, football M, softball W, track and field, volleyball W. **Intramural:** Basketball, cross-country, racquetball, soccer M, swimming, table tennis, tennis, volleyball, water polo.

STUDENT SERVICES. Aptitude testing, career counseling, employment service for undergraduates, freshman orientation, health services, on-campus day care, personal counseling, placement service for graduates, special adviser for adult students, services/facilities for handicapped.

ANNUAL EXPENSES. Tuition and fees: $10,376. **Room and board:** $3,520. **Books and supplies:** $500. **Other expenses:** $1,000.

FINANCIAL AID. 88% of freshmen, 97% of continuing students receive some form of aid. 45% of grants, 87% of loans, 77% of jobs based on need. 157 enrolled freshmen were judged to have need, all were offered aid. Academic, music/drama, art, athletic, state/district residency, religious affiliation scholarships available. **Aid applications:** No closing date; priority given to applications received by March 1; applicants notified on a rolling basis beginning on or about March 15; must reply within 2 weeks.

ADDRESS/TELEPHONE. Lora Vander Zwaag, Director of Admissions, Morningside College, 1501 Morningside Avenue, Sioux City, IA 51106-1751. (712) 274-5111. (800) 831-0806. Fax: (712) 274-5101.

Mount Mercy College
Cedar Rapids, Iowa CB code: 6417

Admissions: 64% of applicants accepted
Based on: ••• School record
•• Test scores
• Interview, recommendations
Completion: 90% of freshmen end year in good standing
56% graduate, 8% of these enter graduate study

4-year private liberal arts college, coed, affiliated with Roman Catholic Church. Founded in 1928. **Accreditation:** Regional. **Undergraduate enrollment:** 236 men, 690 women full time; 207 men, 259 women part time. **Faculty:** 110 total (63 full time), 65 with doctorates or other terminal degrees. **Location:** Urban campus in small city; 230 miles from Chicago. **Calendar:** 4-1-4, limited summer session. Saturday and extensive evening/early morning classes. **Microcomputers:** 48 located in dormitories, libraries, computer centers.

DEGREES OFFERED. BA, BS. 334 bachelor's degrees awarded in 1992. 42% in business and management, 7% computer sciences, 10% teacher education, 9% health sciences, 5% psychology, 11% social sciences.

UNDERGRADUATE MAJORS. Accounting, art education, biology, business administration and management, business and management, business education, computer and information sciences, criminal justice studies, dramatic arts, education, elementary education, English, English education, fine arts, history, liberal/general studies, marketing and distribution, marketing management, mathematics, mathematics education, medical laboratory technologies, music, music education, nursing, political science and government, prelaw, psychology, public relations, religion, science education, secondary education, social science education, social work, sociology, speech, speech/communication/theater education.

ACADEMIC PROGRAMS. Accelerated program, double major, dual enrollment of high school students, honors program, independent study, internships, student-designed major, study abroad, teacher preparation, visiting/exchange student program, weekend college, cross-registration. **Remedial services:** Learning center, reduced course load, remedial instruction, tutoring. **Placement/credit:** AP, CLEP General and Subject, institutional tests; 30 credit hours maximum for bachelor's degree.

ACADEMIC REQUIREMENTS. Freshmen must earn minimum GPA of 2.0 to continue in good standing. 78% of freshmen return for sophomore year. Students must declare major by end of second year. **Graduation requirements:** 123 hours for bachelor's (30 in major). Most students required to take courses in arts/fine arts, English, history, mathematics, philosophy/religion, biological/physical sciences, social sciences. **Postgraduate studies:** 3% enter law school, 1% enter medical school, 2% enter MBA programs, 2% enter other graduate study.

FRESHMAN ADMISSIONS. Selection criteria: Class rank in top 50%, 2.0 high school GPA, test scores most important. **High school preparation:** 16 units required. Required units include English 4, mathematics 2 and social science 2. One laboratory science also required. **Test requirements:** SAT or ACT; score report by August 15.

1992 FRESHMAN CLASS PROFILE. 141 men applied, 93 accepted, 74 enrolled; 421 women applied, 269 accepted, 205 enrolled. 65% had high school GPA of 3.0 or higher, 35% between 2.0 and 2.99. 35% were in top tenth and 60% were in top quarter of graduating class. **Academic background:** Mid 50% of enrolled freshmen had ACT composite between 20-26. 98% submitted ACT scores. **Characteristics:** 85% from in state, 80% live in college housing, 1% have minority backgrounds, 1% are foreign students. Average age is 18.

FALL-TERM APPLICATIONS. $20 fee, may be waived for applicants with need. Closing date August 15; priority given to applications received by April 1; applicants notified on a rolling basis; must reply by May 1 or within 1 week if notified thereafter. Audition required for music applicants. Portfolio required for art applicants. Interview recommended. CRDA. Deferred and early admission available.

STUDENT LIFE. Housing: Dormitories (coed); apartment housing available. **Activities:** Student government, student newspaper, choral groups, drama, pep band, volunteer association, campus ministry, Amnesty International, social work organization.

ATHLETICS. NAIA. **Intercollegiate:** Baseball M, basketball, cross-country, golf, soccer M, softball W, track and field, volleyball W. **Intramural:** Basketball, football, racquetball, soccer, softball, table tennis, tennis, volleyball.

STUDENT SERVICES. Career counseling, employment service for undergraduates, freshman orientation, health services, personal counseling, placement service for graduates, veterans counselor, services/facilities for handicapped.

ANNUAL EXPENSES. Tuition and fees: $9,900. **Room and board:** $3,330. **Books and supplies:** $500.

FINANCIAL AID. 85% of freshmen, 90% of continuing students receive some form of aid. Grants, loans, jobs available. Academic, music/drama, art, alumni affiliation, minority scholarships available. **Aid applications:** No closing date; priority given to applications received by March 1; applicants notified on a rolling basis beginning on or about February 15; must reply by May 1 or within 2 weeks if notified thereafter.

ADDRESS/TELEPHONE. Rebecca Thomas, Director of Admissions, Mount Mercy College, 1330 Elmhurst Drive Northeast, Cedar Rapids, IA 52402. (319) 363-8213. (800) 248-4504. Fax: (319) 363-5270 ext. 221.

Mount St. Clare College
Clinton, Iowa CB code: 6418

Admissions: 71% of applicants accepted
Based on: ••• School record, test scores
•• Recommendations
• Activities, essay, interview, special talents
Completion: 79% of freshmen end year in good standing
26% graduate, 12% of these enter graduate study

4-year private liberal arts college, coed, affiliated with Roman Catholic Church. Founded in 1895. **Accreditation:** Regional. **Undergraduate enrollment:** 411 men and women. **Faculty:** 37 total (18 full time), 7 with doctorates or other terminal degrees. **Location:** Urban campus in large town; 35 miles from Davenport, 138 miles from Chicago. **Calendar:** Semester, extensive summer session. **Microcomputers:** 19 located in libraries, computer centers.

DEGREES OFFERED. AA, AAS, BA. 40 associate degrees awarded in 1992. 17% in business/office and marketing/distribution, 10% teacher education, 86% multi/interdisciplinary studies. 50 bachelor's degrees awarded. 64% in business and management, 10% computer sciences, 26% multi/interdisciplinary studies.

UNDERGRADUATE MAJORS. Associate: Child development/care/guidance, early childhood education, liberal/general studies, prelaw. **Bachelor's:** Accounting, business administration and management, computer and information sciences, cytotechnology, elementary education, liberal/general studies, office supervision and management, social sciences.

ACADEMIC PROGRAMS. 2-year transfer program, double major, dual enrollment of high school students, honors program, independent study, internships, student-designed major, teacher preparation, cross-registration. **Remedial services:** Learning center, reduced course load, remedial instruction, special counselor, tutoring, developmental reading and mathematics. **Placement/credit:** AP, CLEP General and Subject, institutional tests; 32 credit hours maximum for associate degree; 32 credit hours maximum for bachelor's degree.

ACADEMIC REQUIREMENTS. Freshmen must earn minimum GPA of 1.65 to continue in good standing. 54% of freshmen return for sophomore year. Students must declare major by end of second year. **Graduation requirements:** 62 hours for associate, 122 hours for bachelor's (30 in major). Most students required to take courses in arts/fine arts, English, history, mathematics, philosophy/religion, biological/physical sciences, social sciences. **Postgraduate studies:** 64% from 2-year programs enter 4-year programs.

FRESHMAN ADMISSIONS. Selection criteria: High school record, GPA, class rank, test scores all considered. Rank in top three-fourths of class required. Applicants not meeting selection criteria may be admitted based on committee's evaluation, high school record, evidence of potential. Must provide recommendation. Science students should complete 1 unit each of chemistry and biology, plus minimum 3 of mathematics. **Test requirements:** SAT or ACT (ACT preferred); score report by August 15.

1992 FRESHMAN CLASS PROFILE. 465 men and women applied, 330 accepted; 270 enrolled. 24% had high school GPA of 3.0 or higher, 61% between 2.0 and 2.99. **Characteristics:** 66% from in state, 51% live in college housing, 12% have minority backgrounds, 2% are foreign students. Average age is 18.

FALL-TERM APPLICATIONS. $20 fee, may be waived for applicants with need. Closing date August 15; applicants notified on a rolling basis beginning on or about October 1; must reply within 4 weeks. Interview recommended for music applicants. Essay recommended for academically weak applicants. Deferred and early admission available.

STUDENT LIFE. Housing: Dormitories (men, women). **Activities:** Student government, student newspaper, yearbook, choral groups, musical theater, campus ministry, Student Iowa State Education Association, business organization, language clubs, Circle-K, Student Ambassadors, international club.

ATHLETICS. NAIA. **Intercollegiate:** Baseball M, basketball, cross-country, golf, soccer M, softball W, tennis, volleyball W. **Intramural:** Basketball, golf, tennis, track and field, volleyball.

STUDENT SERVICES. Aptitude testing, career counseling, employment service for undergraduates, freshman orientation, on-campus day care, personal counseling, placement service for graduates, special adviser for adult students, on-campus pre-school, speech and hearing clinic, services/facilities for handicapped.

ANNUAL EXPENSES. Tuition and fees: $9,280. **Room and board:** $3,600. **Books and supplies:** $600. **Other expenses:** $700.

FINANCIAL AID. 90% of freshmen, 95% of continuing students re-

ceive some form of aid. Grants, loans, jobs available. Academic, music/drama, art, athletic, leadership, alumni affiliation scholarships available. **Aid applications:** Closing date August 1; priority given to applications received by April 1; applicants notified on a rolling basis beginning on or about February 15; must reply within 4 weeks. **Additional information:** Commitment to meet 100% of student need. Scholarships and grants also available for students without financial need.

ADDRESS/TELEPHONE. Arthur Belair, Director of Enrollment, Mount St. Clare College, 400 North Bluff Boulevard, Clinton, IA 52732. (319) 242-4153. Fax: (319) 242-2003.

Muscatine Community College

Muscatine, Iowa CB code: 6422

2-year public community college, coed. Founded in 1929. **Accreditation:** Regional. **Undergraduate enrollment:** 257 men, 325 women full time; 215 men, 458 women part time. **Faculty:** 71 total (31 full time), 4 with doctorates or other terminal degrees. **Location:** Rural campus in large town; 30 miles from Quad Cities (Moline, Davenport, Rock Island, Bettendorf). **Calendar:** Semester, limited summer session. **Microcomputers:** Located in libraries, classrooms, computer centers. **Additional facts:** Part of Eastern Iowa Community College District, which also includes Clinton and Scott Community Colleges.

DEGREES OFFERED. AA, AS, AAS. 186 associate degrees awarded in 1992. 5% in agriculture, 5% business/office and marketing/distribution, 5% engineering technologies, 80% multi/interdisciplinary studies, 5% trade and industry.

UNDERGRADUATE MAJORS. Accounting, agribusiness, agricultural business and management, agricultural production, biology, business administration and management, business and management, business and office, chemistry, child development/care/guidance, dramatic arts, education, English, finance, fine arts, history, home economics, humanities and social sciences, industrial technology, journalism, liberal/general studies, manufacturing technology, mathematics, music, predentistry, preengineering, premedicine, prepharmacy, preveterinary, psychology, renewable natural resources, secretarial and related programs, social sciences, sociology, visual and performing arts.

ACADEMIC PROGRAMS. 2-year transfer program, cooperative education, dual enrollment of high school students, honors program, independent study, internships, telecourses, cross-registration. **Remedial services:** Learning center, remedial instruction, special counselor, tutoring. **Placement/credit:** AP, CLEP General and Subject, institutional tests; 30 credit hours maximum for associate degree.

ACADEMIC REQUIREMENTS. Freshmen must earn minimum GPA of 1.75 to continue in good standing. 40% of freshmen return for sophomore year. Students must declare major on application. **Graduation requirements:** 64 hours for associate. Most students required to take courses in English, humanities, mathematics, biological/physical sciences, social sciences.

FRESHMAN ADMISSIONS. Selection criteria: Open admissions. Selective admissions to nursing program.

1992 FRESHMAN CLASS PROFILE. 168 men, 239 women enrolled. **Characteristics:** 92% from in state, 100% commute, 10% have minority backgrounds, 1% are foreign students. Average age is 26.

FALL-TERM APPLICATIONS. $20 fee. No closing date; applicants notified on a rolling basis. Early admission available.

STUDENT LIFE. Activities: Student government, student newspaper, television, choral groups, drama, music ensembles.

ATHLETICS. NJCAA. **Intercollegiate:** Baseball M, softball W. **Intramural:** Basketball, bowling, softball, table tennis, volleyball.

STUDENT SERVICES. Aptitude testing, career counseling, employment service for undergraduates, freshman orientation, on-campus day care, personal counseling, placement service for graduates, veterans counselor, vocational rehabilitation counselor, services/facilities for handicapped.

ANNUAL EXPENSES. Tuition and fees (1992-93): $1,455, $645 additional for out-of-state students. **Books and supplies:** $900. **Other expenses:** $900.

FINANCIAL AID. 40% of freshmen, 60% of continuing students receive some form of aid. 91% of grants, 86% of loans, all jobs based on need. Academic, music/drama, athletic, state/district residency, leadership scholarships available. **Aid applications:** No closing date; priority given to applications received by April 20; applicants notified on a rolling basis beginning on or about May 15; must reply within 2 weeks.

ADDRESS/TELEPHONE. Beverly Knoernschild, Coordinator of Admissions, Muscatine Community College, 152 Colorado Street, Muscatine, IA 52761-5396. (319) 263-8250 ext. 122. Fax: (319) 264-8341.

National Education Center: National Institute of Technology Campus

West Des Moines, Iowa CB code: 0400

2-year proprietary technical college, coed. Founded in 1964. **Undergraduate enrollment:** 300 men and women. **Location:** Suburban campus in large town; 5 miles from downtown Des Moines. **Calendar:** 8-week terms.

FRESHMAN ADMISSIONS. Selection criteria: Admission is predicated upon the ACT/CPAT scores and high school record.

ANNUAL EXPENSES. Tuition and fees (1992-93): $5,725. Tuition and required fees include books and some supplies. $9060 tuition for 12-month medical program.

ADDRESS/TELEPHONE. Jeff Marcus, Admissions Director, National Education Center: National Institute of Technology Campus, 1119 Fifth Street, West Des Moines, IA 50265. (515) 223-1486. (800) 445-4279.

North Iowa Area Community College

Mason City, Iowa CB code: 6400

2-year public community college, coed. **Accreditation:** Regional. **Undergraduate enrollment:** 986 men, 1,112 women full time; 296 men, 680 women part time. **Faculty:** 100 total (86 full time), 8 with doctorates or other terminal degrees. **Location:** Suburban campus in large town; 120 miles from Des Moines, 140 miles from Minneapolis-St. Paul. **Calendar:** Semester, limited summer session. **Microcomputers:** 200 located in dormitories, libraries, classrooms, computer centers. **Special facilities:** Art gallery. **Additional facts:** 4 branch campuses at Charles City, Lake Mills, Hampton, and Garner

DEGREES OFFERED. AA, AS, AAS. 641 associate degrees awarded in 1992. 9% in business and management, 8% education, 10% health sciences, 49% multi/interdisciplinary studies, 5% trade and industry.

UNDERGRADUATE MAJORS. Accounting, agribusiness, agricultural business and management, agricultural economics, agricultural sciences, air conditioning/heating/refrigeration mechanics, air conditioning/heating/refrigeration technology, apparel and accessories marketing, automated systems technology, automotive mechanics, automotive technology, biology, botany, business and management, business and office, business data processing and related programs, business data programming, chemistry, clinical laboratory science, communications, computer and information sciences, computer programming, criminal justice studies, drafting, drafting and design technology, early childhood education, education, electromechanical technology, electronic technology, elementary education, engineering, engineering and engineering-related technologies, English, fashion merchandising, finance, fine arts, German, health sciences, home economics, industrial equipment maintenance and repair, insurance and risk management, journalism, law enforcement and corrections technologies, legal secretary, liberal/general studies, manufacturing technology, marketing and distribution, marketing management, mathematics, mechanical design technology, medical assistant, medical secretary, music, nursing, office supervision and management, ophthalmic services, physical sciences, physics, practical nursing, predentistry, prelaw, premedicine, prepharmacy, preveterinary, psychology, retailing, robotics, secondary education, secretarial and related programs, social sciences, Spanish, teacher aide, visual and performing arts, word processing, zoology.

ACADEMIC PROGRAMS. 2-year transfer program, dual enrollment of high school students, honors program, independent study, student-designed major, telecourses. **Remedial services:** Learning center, preadmission summer program, reduced course load, remedial instruction, special counselor, tutoring. **Placement/credit:** AP, CLEP General and Subject; 30 credit hours maximum for associate degree.

ACADEMIC REQUIREMENTS. Freshmen must earn minimum GPA of 1.5 to continue in good standing. 45% of freshmen return for sophomore year. Students must declare major on application. **Graduation requirements:** 60 hours for associate (40 in major). Most students required to take courses in arts/fine arts, English, humanities, mathematics, biological/physical sciences, social sciences.

FRESHMAN ADMISSIONS. Selection criteria: Open admissions. Selective admissions to nursing program. **Test requirements:** ACT required of nursing applicants for placement and counseling, recommended for others.

1992 FRESHMAN CLASS PROFILE. 869 men, 1,217 women enrolled. 14% were in top tenth and 29% were in top quarter of graduating class. **Characteristics:** 97% from in state, 89% commute, 2% have minority backgrounds. Average age is 20.

FALL-TERM APPLICATIONS. No fee. Closing date September 3; applicants notified on a rolling basis. Deferred admission available. Nelson-Denny, Myers Briggs Trait Inventory, Asset mathematics required.

STUDENT LIFE. Housing: Dormitories (men, women, coed); apartment housing available. **Activities:** Student government, student newspaper, choral groups, concert band, drama, jazz band, music ensembles, pep band, symphony orchestra, OK House (ecumenical religious organization).

ATHLETICS. NJCAA. **Intercollegiate:** Baseball M, basketball, football M, golf, softball W, volleyball W. **Intramural:** Basketball, bowling, cross-country, golf, skiing, skin diving, softball, tennis, volleyball.

STUDENT SERVICES. Aptitude testing, career counseling, employment service for undergraduates, freshman orientation, on-campus day care, personal counseling, placement service for graduates, veterans counselor, personality inventory, services/facilities for handicapped.

ANNUAL EXPENSES. Tuition and fees: $1,620, $735 additional for

out-of-state students. **Room and board:** $2,570. **Books and supplies:** $600. **Other expenses:** $1,125.

FINANCIAL AID. 60% of freshmen, 65% of continuing students receive some form of aid. 94% of grants, 78% of loans, 63% of jobs based on need. 960 enrolled freshmen were judged to have need, 910 were offered aid. Academic, music/drama, art, athletic, state/district residency, leadership, minority scholarships available. **Aid applications:** No closing date; priority given to applications received by March 1; applicants notified on a rolling basis beginning on or about April 10; must reply within 2 weeks.

ADDRESS/TELEPHONE. Tom Dunn, Enrollment Specialist, North Iowa Area Community College, 500 College Drive, Mason City, IA 50401. (515) 421-4253. Fax: (515) 423-1711.

Northeast Iowa Community College
Calmar, Iowa CB code: 6751

2-year public community college, coed. Founded in 1966. **Accreditation:** Regional. **Undergraduate enrollment:** 573 men, 818 women full time; 251 men, 641 women part time. **Faculty:** 148 total (120 full time), 1 with doctorate or other terminal degree. **Location:** Rural campus in rural community; 60 miles from Waterloo. **Calendar:** Semester, limited summer session. **Microcomputers:** Located in classrooms, computer centers. **Special facilities:** State-of-the-art computer laboratories. **Additional facts:** Second location at Peosta, 10 miles from Dubuque.

DEGREES OFFERED. AA, AS, AAS. 249 associate degrees awarded in 1992.

UNDERGRADUATE MAJORS. Accounting, agribusiness, allied health, automotive technology, business and office, business data processing and related programs, clinical laboratory science, computer technology, electrical installation, electrical technology, electrical/electronics/communications engineering, electronic technology, industrial technology, marketing and distribution, marketing management, mechanical design technology, medical records administration, medical records technology, nursing, office supervision and management, personal services, practical nursing, precision metal work, radiograph medical technology.

ACADEMIC PROGRAMS. 2-year transfer program, dual enrollment of high school students, independent study, internships. **Remedial services:** Learning center, remedial instruction, tutoring.

ACADEMIC REQUIREMENTS. Freshmen must earn minimum GPA of 2.0 to continue in good standing. Students must declare major on application. **Graduation requirements:** 65 hours for associate. Most students required to take courses in English, mathematics, biological/physical sciences, social sciences.

FRESHMAN ADMISSIONS. Selection criteria: Open admissions.

1992 FRESHMAN CLASS PROFILE. 824 men, 1,459 women enrolled. **Characteristics:** 96% from in state, 100% commute. Average age is 26.

FALL-TERM APPLICATIONS. No fee. No closing date; applicants notified on a rolling basis. Early admission available. No applications accepted before October 1 of year before entrance.

STUDENT LIFE. Activities: Student government, student newspaper, yearbook.

ATHLETICS. Intramural: Basketball, bowling, cross-country, golf, skiing, softball, swimming, table tennis, tennis, volleyball.

STUDENT SERVICES. Aptitude testing, career counseling, on-campus day care, personal counseling, placement service for graduates, services/facilities for handicapped.

ANNUAL EXPENSES. Tuition and fees: $1,943, $1,695 additional for out-of-state students. **Books and supplies:** $1,000. **Other expenses:** $945.

FINANCIAL AID. 76% of freshmen, 79% of continuing students receive some form of aid. 97% of grants, 86% of loans, 88% of jobs based on need. Academic, leadership scholarships available. **Aid applications:** No closing date; priority given to applications received by April 1; applicants notified on a rolling basis beginning on or about June 1; must reply within 2 weeks.

ADDRESS/TELEPHONE. Martha Keune, Coordinator of Admissions, Northeast Iowa Community College, PO Box 400, Calmar, IA 52132. (319) 562-3263. (800) 728-2256 ext. 307.

Northwest Iowa Community College
Sheldon, Iowa CB code: 1359

2-year public community college, coed. Founded in 1966. **Accreditation:** Regional. **Undergraduate enrollment:** 352 men, 154 women full time; 28 men, 69 women part time. **Faculty:** 44 total (36 full time), 2 with doctorates or other terminal degrees. **Location:** Rural campus in small town; 60 miles from Sioux City, 65 miles from Sioux Falls. **Calendar:** 010. Extensive evening/early morning classes. **Microcomputers:** 50 located in libraries, classrooms, computer centers.

DEGREES OFFERED. AA, AS, AAS. 57 associate degrees awarded in 1992. 28% in business and management, 14% business/office and marketing/distribution, 7% computer sciences, 37% engineering technologies, 14% trade and industry.

UNDERGRADUATE MAJORS. Accounting, agribusiness, agricultural business and management, air conditioning/heating/refrigeration mechanics, automotive mechanics, automotive technology, building automation systems, business and management, computer programming, drafting and design technology, electrical and electronics equipment repair, electrical installation, electrical technology, electromechanical technology, electronic technology, finance, instrumentation technology, insurance and risk management, manufacturing technology, marketing and distribution, marketing management, mechanical design technology, nursing.

ACADEMIC PROGRAMS. 2-year transfer program, cooperative education, dual enrollment of high school students, independent study, telecourses, nursing program in conjunction with Western Iowa Tech Community College. **Remedial services:** Learning center, preadmission summer program, reduced course load, remedial instruction, special counselor, tutoring. **Placement/credit:** Institutional tests; 30 credit hours maximum for associate degree.

ACADEMIC REQUIREMENTS. Freshmen must earn minimum GPA of 2.0 to continue in good standing. 91% of freshmen return for sophomore year. Students must declare major on application. **Graduation requirements:** 90 hours for associate (45 in major). Most students required to take courses in English, humanities, mathematics.

FRESHMAN ADMISSIONS. Selection criteria: Open admissions. GPA of 2.0 and 2 units science required for LPN program. **Test requirements:** ASSET required for placement.

1992 FRESHMAN CLASS PROFILE. 191 men, 89 women enrolled. 10% had high school GPA of 3.0 or higher, 75% between 2.0 and 2.99. 6% were in top tenth and 15% were in top quarter of graduating class. **Characteristics:** 90% from in state, 95% commute, 3% have minority backgrounds. Average age is 19.

FALL-TERM APPLICATIONS. $10 fee. No closing date; applicants notified on a rolling basis; must reply within 4 weeks. Interview required. Early admission available.

STUDENT LIFE. Housing: Apartment housing available. **Activities:** Student government, student newspaper, choral groups.

ATHLETICS. Intramural: Basketball, bowling, racquetball, softball, swimming, tennis, volleyball.

STUDENT SERVICES. Aptitude testing, career counseling, employment service for undergraduates, freshman orientation, personal counseling, placement service for graduates, veterans counselor, services/facilities for handicapped.

ANNUAL EXPENSES. Tuition and fees (1992-93): $1,575, $675 additional for out-of-state students. **Books and supplies:** $525. **Other expenses:** $675.

FINANCIAL AID. 78% of freshmen, 80% of continuing students receive some form of aid. 99% of grants, 93% of loans, all jobs based on need. Academic, state/district residency, leadership scholarships available. **Aid applications:** No closing date; priority given to applications received by April 20; applicants notified on a rolling basis beginning on or about April 1; must reply within 2 weeks.

ADDRESS/TELEPHONE. Bonnie Brands, Director of Admissions, Northwest Iowa Community College, 603 W Park Street, Sheldon, IA 51201. (712) 324-5061. (800) 352-4907. Fax: (712) 324-4136.

Northwestern College
Orange City, Iowa CB code: 6490

Admissions: 97% of applicants accepted
Based on: ••• School record, test scores
•• Recommendations
• Activities, essay, interview, religious affiliation/commitment
Completion: 90% of freshmen end year in good standing
56% graduate, 15% of these enter graduate study

4-year private liberal arts college, coed, affiliated with Reformed Church in America. Founded in 1882. **Accreditation:** Regional. **Undergraduate enrollment:** 432 men, 559 women full time; 21 men, 26 women part time. **Graduate enrollment:** 5 men, 16 women part time. **Faculty:** 84 total (57 full time), 37 with doctorates or other terminal degrees. **Location:** Rural campus in small town; 40 miles from Sioux City, 140 miles from Omaha, Nebraska. **Calendar:** Semester, limited summer session. **Microcomputers:** 220 located in dormitories, libraries, classrooms, computer centers. **Additional facts:** Christian liberal arts college striving to integrate Christian faith with living and learning.

DEGREES OFFERED. AA, BA, MA. 11 associate degrees awarded in 1992. 100% in business/office and marketing/distribution. 193 bachelor's degrees awarded. 25% in business and management, 20% teacher education, 10% health sciences, 6% life sciences, 5% parks/recreation, protective services, public affairs, 5% philosophy, religion, theology, 10% psychology, 10% social sciences, 6% visual and performing arts. Graduate degrees offered in 1 major field of study.

UNDERGRADUATE MAJORS. Associate: Office supervision and management, secretarial and related programs. **Bachelor's:** Accounting, biological and physical sciences, biology, business administration and management, business and management, chemistry, clinical laboratory science, communications, computer and information sciences, dramatic arts, education of the mentally handicapped, elementary education, English, French, history, humanities and social sciences, junior high education, library science, mathematics, music, philosophy, physics, political science and government, psychology, recreation and community services technologies, religion, secondary education, social sciences, social work, sociology, Spanish, speech, theological studies.

ACADEMIC PROGRAMS. Accelerated program, double major, honors program, independent study, internships, student-designed major, study abroad, teacher preparation, Washington semester. **Remedial services:** Learning center, reduced course load, tutoring. **Placement/credit:** AP, CLEP Subject; 24 credit hours maximum for bachelor's degree.

ACADEMIC REQUIREMENTS. Freshmen must earn minimum GPA of 1.5 to continue in good standing. 75% of freshmen return for sophomore year. Students must declare major by end of second year. **Graduation requirements:** 62 hours for associate (26 in major), 124 hours for bachelor's (30 in major). Most students required to take courses in arts/fine arts, English, foreign languages, history, humanities, mathematics, philosophy/religion, biological/physical sciences, social sciences. **Postgraduate studies:** 50% from 2-year programs enter 4-year programs. 2% enter law school, 5% enter medical school, 1% enter MBA programs, 7% enter other graduate study. **Additional information:** Internship possibilites available through Chicago and Washington, DC, study programs.

FRESHMAN ADMISSIONS. Selection criteria: Top half of class and test scores above 50th percentile. Recommendations also important. **High school preparation:** 16 units recommended. Recommended units include English 4, mathematics 3, social science 3 and science 2. **Test requirements:** SAT or ACT (ACT preferred); score report by August 15.

1992 FRESHMAN CLASS PROFILE. 297 men applied, 284 accepted, 153 enrolled; 443 women applied, 433 accepted, 181 enrolled. 65% had high school GPA of 3.0 or higher, 34% between 2.0 and 2.99. 24% were in top tenth and 41% were in top quarter of graduating class. **Academic background:** Mid 50% of enrolled freshmen had ACT composite between 20-27. 98% submitted ACT scores. **Characteristics:** 64% from in state, 92% live in college housing, 1% have minority backgrounds, 4% are foreign students. Average age is 18.

FALL-TERM APPLICATIONS. $20 fee, may be waived for applicants with need. Closing date June 1; applicants notified on a rolling basis beginning on or about November 1; must reply within 2 weeks. Audition required for theater, music applicants. Portfolio required for art applicants. Interview recommended. Essay recommended. Deferred admission available.

STUDENT LIFE. Housing: Dormitories (men, women); apartment housing available. **Activities:** Student government, radio, student newspaper, television, yearbook, choral groups, concert band, drama, jazz band, music ensembles, pep band, symphony orchestra, many religious clubs and organizations. **Additional information:** Religious observance required.

ATHLETICS. NAIA. **Intercollegiate:** Baseball M, basketball, cross-country, football M, golf, soccer, softball W, tennis, track and field, volleyball W, wrestling M. **Intramural:** Badminton, basketball, bowling, golf, racquetball, soccer, softball, table tennis, tennis, volleyball.

STUDENT SERVICES. Aptitude testing, career counseling, employment service for undergraduates, freshman orientation, health services, personal counseling, placement service for graduates, services/facilities for handicapped.

ANNUAL EXPENSES. Tuition and fees: $9,300. **Room and board:** $2,950. **Books and supplies:** $450. **Other expenses:** $950.

FINANCIAL AID. 95% of freshmen, 95% of continuing students receive some form of aid. 96% of grants, 95% of loans, 57% of jobs based on need. 260 enrolled freshmen were judged to have need, all were offered aid. Academic, music/drama, art, athletic, leadership, alumni affiliation, religious affiliation scholarships available. **Aid applications:** No closing date; priority given to applications received by April 1; applicants notified on a rolling basis beginning on or about February 1; must reply within 2 weeks.

ADDRESS/TELEPHONE. Ron De Jong, Director of Admissions, Northwestern College, 101 College Lane, Orange City, IA 51041. (712) 737-4821. (800) 747-4757. Fax: (712) 737-8847.

St. Ambrose University
Davenport, Iowa

CB code: 6617

4-year private liberal arts college, coed, affiliated with Roman Catholic Church. Founded in 1882. **Accreditation:** Regional. **Undergraduate enrollment:** 573 men, 696 women full time; 195 men, 252 women part time. **Graduate enrollment:** 41 men, 24 women full time; 385 men, 251 women part time. **Faculty:** 197 total (92 full time), 59 with doctorates or other terminal degrees. **Location:** Urban campus in small city; in metropolitan Quad Cities area. **Calendar:** Semester, extensive summer session. **Microcomputers:** 62 located in libraries, classrooms, computer centers. **Special facilities:** Art gallery, transmission electron microscope, FM radio station, cable television channel, observatory.

DEGREES OFFERED. BA, BS, MBA, MEd. 357 bachelor's degrees awarded in 1992. 51% in business and management, 8% communications, 5% teacher education, 5% parks/recreation, protective services, public affairs, 5% psychology, 8% social sciences. Graduate degrees offered in 4 major fields of study.

UNDERGRADUATE MAJORS. Accounting, advertising, agricultural business and management, art education, art/multimedia, biology, business administration and management, business and management, chemistry, communications, computer and information sciences, contract management and procurement/purchasing, criminal justice studies, dramatic arts, economics, education, elementary education, engineering physics, English, finance, French, German, graphic design, history, industrial engineering, information sciences and systems, journalism, law enforcement and corrections, liberal/general studies, marketing management, mathematics, mathematics education, music, music education, occupational therapy, peace studies, philosophy, physical education, physics, political science and government, psychology, public administration, public relations, radio/television broadcasting, recreation therapy, Russian, secondary education, sociology, Spanish, speech, studio art, theological studies.

ACADEMIC PROGRAMS. Cooperative education, double major, dual enrollment of high school students, honors program, independent study, internships, student-designed major, study abroad, teacher preparation, weekend college, course-a-month program in which students complete course through intensive weekend classes; liberal arts/career combination in engineering, health sciences. **Remedial services:** Learning center, preadmission summer program, reduced course load, remedial instruction, special counselor, tutoring. **Placement/credit:** AP, CLEP General and Subject, institutional tests; 60 credit hours maximum for bachelor's degree.

ACADEMIC REQUIREMENTS. Freshmen must earn minimum GPA of 2.0 to continue in good standing. 88% of freshmen return for sophomore year. Students must declare major by end of second year. **Graduation requirements:** 120 hours for bachelor's (30 in major). Most students required to take courses in arts/fine arts, English, foreign languages, history, humanities, mathematics, philosophy/religion, biological/physical sciences, social sciences. **Postgraduate studies:** 2% enter MBA programs, 6% enter other graduate study.

FRESHMAN ADMISSIONS. Selection criteria: Minimum high school GPA 2.5; SAT combined score 780 or ACT 20 required. **High school preparation:** 15 units recommended. Recommended units include biological science 1, English 4, foreign language 2, mathematics 3, physical science 2 and social science 3. **Test requirements:** SAT or ACT (ACT preferred); score report by August 1. **Additional information:** Admission requirements designed to select individuals capable of graduation.

1992 FRESHMAN CLASS PROFILE. 140 men, 118 women enrolled. 43% had high school GPA of 3.0 or higher, 57% between 2.0 and 2.99. **Characteristics:** 70% from in state, 56% live in college housing, 17% have minority backgrounds, 1% are foreign students. Average age is 19.

FALL-TERM APPLICATIONS. $15 fee, may be waived for applicants with need. No closing date; priority given to applications received by August 1; applicants notified on a rolling basis; must reply within 2 weeks. Audition required for music, drama applicants. Portfolio required for art applicants. Interview recommended. Deferred admission available.

STUDENT LIFE. Housing: Dormitories (men, women, coed). Townhouses for seniors. **Activities:** Student government, magazine, radio, student newspaper, television, choral groups, concert band, dance, drama, jazz band, music ensembles, musical theater, pep band, music ministry, Fellowship of Christian Athletes, Black Student Union, philosophy club, Young Republicans, Young Democrats, veterans club, art club, music club, psychology club.

ATHLETICS. NAIA. **Intercollegiate:** Baseball M, basketball, cross-country, football M, golf, soccer M, softball W, tennis, track and field, volleyball W. **Intramural:** Basketball, handball, racquetball, softball, volleyball.

STUDENT SERVICES. Aptitude testing, career counseling, employment service for undergraduates, freshman orientation, health services, on-campus day care, personal counseling, placement service for graduates, special adviser for adult students, veterans counselor, Freshman mentor program, services/facilities for handicapped.

ANNUAL EXPENSES. Tuition and fees: $9,850. **Room and board:** $3,830. **Books and supplies:** $500. **Other expenses:** $940.

FINANCIAL AID. 92% of freshmen, 90% of continuing students receive some form of aid. 72% of grants, 84% of loans, 81% of jobs based on need. 175 enrolled freshmen were judged to have need, all were offered aid. Academic, music/drama, art, athletic, alumni affiliation, religious affiliation scholarships available. **Aid applications:** No closing date; priority given to applications received by March 15; applicants notified on a rolling basis beginning on or about April 1; must reply by May 1 or within 2 weeks if notified thereafter. **Additional information:** Iowa applicants must apply for financial aid by April 1. University has policy of meeting established need and minimizing future indebtedness.

ADDRESS/TELEPHONE. Patrick O'Connor, Dean of Admissions, St. Ambrose University, 518 West Locust Street, Davenport, IA 52803. (319) 383-8888. (800) 383-2627.

Scott Community College
Bettendorf, Iowa CB code: 0282

2-year public community college, coed. Founded in 1966. **Accreditation:** Regional. **Undergraduate enrollment:** 912 men, 1,151 women full time; 631 men, 1,161 women part time. **Faculty:** 232 total (78 full time), 17 with doctorates or other terminal degrees. **Location:** Suburban campus in small city; 3 miles from Davenport, part of Iowa-Illinois Quad Cities region. **Calendar:** Semester, extensive summer session. **Microcomputers:** Located in computer centers. **Additional facts:** Part of Eastern Iowa Community College District, which also includes Muscatine and Clinton Community Colleges.

DEGREES OFFERED. AA, AS, AAS. 327 associate degrees awarded in 1992. 6% in business and management, 6% business/office and marketing/distribution, 19% health sciences, 5% allied health, 44% multi/interdisciplinary studies, 8% trade and industry.

UNDERGRADUATE MAJORS. Accounting, automotive mechanics, automotive technology, biology, business administration and management, business and management, business and office, business data programming, chemical laboratory techinican, chemistry, communications, computer and information sciences, computer programming, criminal justice studies, diesel engine mechanics, education, electrodiagnostic technologies, electronic technology, English, fashion merchandising, finance, fine arts, food production/management/services, home furnishings and equipment management/production/services, humanities and social sciences, interior design, law enforcement and corrections technologies, liberal/general studies, mathematics, medical laboratory technologies, nursing, physical therapy, physics, prechiropractic, preengineering, premedicine, prepharmacy, preveterinary, psychology, radio/television broadcasting, radiograph medical technology, respiratory therapy, respiratory therapy technology, science technologies, secretarial and related programs, social sciences, social work, sociology.

ACADEMIC PROGRAMS. 2-year transfer program, accelerated program, double major, dual enrollment of high school students, internships, telecourses, cross-registration. **Remedial services:** Learning center, reduced course load, remedial instruction, special counselor, tutoring. **Placement/credit:** CLEP General and Subject; 30 credit hours maximum for associate degree.

ACADEMIC REQUIREMENTS. Freshmen must earn minimum GPA of 1.75 to continue in good standing. 40% of freshmen return for sophomore year. Students must declare major on application. **Graduation requirements:** 64 hours for associate. Most students required to take courses in English, humanities, mathematics, biological/physical sciences, social sciences.

FRESHMAN ADMISSIONS. Selection criteria: Open admissions. Selective admissions, based on academic achievement and previous courses, to some programs, particularly health occupations.

1992 FRESHMAN CLASS PROFILE. 647 men, 735 women enrolled. **Characteristics:** 90% from in state, 100% commute, 9% have minority backgrounds, 1% are foreign students. Average age is 26.

FALL-TERM APPLICATIONS. $20 fee. No closing date; applicants notified on a rolling basis; must reply within 2 weeks. Interview required for radiologic technology and medical laboratory technician; recommended for nursing, electroneuro diagnostic technology and pharmacy technician. Early admission available.

STUDENT LIFE. Activities: Student government.

ATHLETICS. Intramural: Basketball, bowling, golf, racquetball, skiing, softball, table tennis, tennis, volleyball, wrestling.

STUDENT SERVICES. Aptitude testing, career counseling, employment service for undergraduates, freshman orientation, personal counseling, placement service for graduates, veterans counselor, special support services for disadvantaged students, services/facilities for handicapped.

ANNUAL EXPENSES. Tuition and fees (1992-93): $1,455, $645 additional for out-of-state students. **Books and supplies:** $900. **Other expenses:** $900.

FINANCIAL AID. 49% of freshmen, 52% of continuing students receive some form of aid. 98% of grants, 73% of loans, all jobs based on need. Academic, state/district residency, leadership scholarships available. **Aid applications:** No closing date; priority given to applications received by April 20; applicants notified on a rolling basis beginning on or about May 15; must reply within 2 weeks.

ADDRESS/TELEPHONE. Steve Norton, Dean of Student Development, Scott Community College, 500 Belmont Road, Bettendorf, IA 52722-6804. (319) 359-7531 ext. 202. Fax: (319) 359-8139.

Simpson College
Indianola, Iowa CB code: 6650

Admissions: 81% of applicants accepted
Based on: ••• School record, test scores
•• Activities, recommendations
• Interview
Completion: 96% of freshmen end year in good standing
60% graduate, 15% of these enter graduate study

4-year private liberal arts college, coed, affiliated with United Methodist Church. Founded in 1860. **Accreditation:** Regional. **Undergraduate enrollment:** 519 men, 575 women full time; 202 men, 394 women part time. **Faculty:** 154 total (77 full time), 54 with doctorates or other terminal degrees. **Location:** Suburban campus in large town; 12 miles from Des Moines. **Calendar:** 4-4-1, limited summer session. **Microcomputers:** 180 located in libraries, classrooms, computer centers. **Special facilities:** Barborka Gallery, Lekberg Recital Hall, Farnham Art Gallery, Pote Theater, Craven Room (specialized book collections).

DEGREES OFFERED. BA. 317 bachelor's degrees awarded in 1992. 40% in business and management, 19% education, 5% mathematics, 5% psychology, 8% social sciences.

UNDERGRADUATE MAJORS. Accounting, art education, biology, business administration and management, business and management, business economics, business education, chemistry, commercial art, communications, computer and information sciences, criminal justice studies, dramatic arts, economics, education, elementary education, English, English education, environmental science, fine arts, foreign languages education, French, German, history, international business management, international relations, junior high education, mathematics, mathematics education, medical laboratory technologies, music, music education, music performance, philosophy, physical education, political science and government, predentistry, preengineering, prelaw, premedicine, prepharmacy, preveterinary, psychology, religion, science education, secondary education, social science education, social studies education, sociology, Spanish, speech/communication/theater education, theological studies.

ACADEMIC PROGRAMS. Accelerated program, double major, honors program, independent study, internships, student-designed major, study abroad, teacher preparation, weekend college, United Nations semester, Washington semester; liberal arts/career combination in engineering. **Remedial services:** Learning center, tutoring. **Placement/credit:** AP, CLEP General and Subject, institutional tests; 24 credit hours maximum for bachelor's degree.

ACADEMIC REQUIREMENTS. Freshmen must earn minimum GPA of 1.8 to continue in good standing. 78% of freshmen return for sophomore year. Students must declare major by end of second year. **Graduation requirements:** 128 hours for bachelor's (30 in major). Most students required to take courses in arts/fine arts, computer science, English, foreign languages, history, humanities, mathematics, philosophy/religion, biological/physical sciences, social sciences. **Postgraduate studies:** 2% enter law school, 2% enter medical school, 3% enter MBA programs, 8% enter other graduate study.

FRESHMAN ADMISSIONS. Selection criteria: High school record most important, followed by test scores, recommendations, interview. **High school preparation:** 18 units recommended. Recommended units include English 4, foreign language 2, mathematics 3, social science 2 and science 2. 3 units laboratory science and 3 units electives also recommended. **Test requirements:** SAT or ACT; score report by August 15.

1992 FRESHMAN CLASS PROFILE. 519 men applied, 410 accepted, 135 enrolled; 450 women applied, 377 accepted, 149 enrolled. 28% were in top tenth and 60% were in top quarter of graduating class. **Academic background:** Mid 50% of enrolled freshmen had ACT composite between 22-27. 98% submitted ACT scores. **Characteristics:** 95% from in state, 98% live in college housing, 1% have minority backgrounds, 1% are foreign students, 35% join fraternities/sororities. Average age is 18.

FALL-TERM APPLICATIONS. No fee. No closing date; priority given to applications received by April 15; applicants notified on a rolling basis. Interview recommended. Audition recommended for music, drama applicants. Deferred and early admission available.

STUDENT LIFE. Housing: Dormitories (men, women, coed); apartment, fraternity, sorority housing available. Theme houses available. **Activities:** Student government, student newspaper, yearbook, student literary publication, choral groups, concert band, drama, jazz band, music ensembles, musical theater, opera, pep band, fraternities, sororities, Religious Life Council, Concerned Multicultural Students, Alpha Phi Omega, Young Democrats, Young Republicans, Fellowship of Christian Athletes, SCAF(Student-Counselor-Adviser-Friend). Students Embracing Responsible Volunteer Experiences. Habitat for Humanity, Amnesty International. **Additional information:** Campus Activities Board responsible for planning and implementing social activities.

ATHLETICS. NCAA. **Intercollegiate:** Baseball M, basketball, cross-country, football M, golf, softball W, tennis, track and field, volleyball W, wrestling M. **Intramural:** Basketball, bowling, football M, soccer, softball, swimming, volleyball, water polo.

STUDENT SERVICES. Career counseling, employment service for undergraduates, freshman orientation, health services, personal counseling, placement service for graduates, special adviser for adult students, services/facilities for handicapped.

ANNUAL EXPENSES. Tuition and fees: $10,825. **Room and board:** $3,810. **Books and supplies:** $550. **Other expenses:** $1,100.

FINANCIAL AID. 90% of freshmen, 90% of continuing students receive some form of aid. 83% of grants, 83% of loans, 60% of jobs based on need. 236 enrolled freshmen were judged to have need, all were offered aid. Academic, music/drama, art, alumni affiliation, minority scholarships available. **Aid applications:** No closing date; priority given to applications received by April 20; applicants notified on a rolling basis beginning on or about March 1; must reply within 30 days up to May 1 and within 2 weeks if notified thereafter. **Additional information:** Music and theater scholarships based on audition.Art scholarships based on portfolio.

ADDRESS/TELEPHONE. John A. Kellogg, Vice President for Enrollment and Planning, Simpson College, 701 North C Street, Indianola, IA 50125-1299. (515) 961-1624. (800) 362-2454. Fax: (515) 961-1498.

Southeastern Community College: North Campus
West Burlington, Iowa CB code: 6048

2-year public community college, coed. Founded in 1966. **Accreditation:** Regional. **Undergraduate enrollment:** 608 men, 786 women full time; 255 men, 514 women part time. **Faculty:** 94 total (82 full time), 6 with doctorates or other terminal degrees. **Location:** Suburban campus in large town; 200 miles from Des Moines, 200 miles from Chicago. **Calendar:** Semester, limited summer session. **Microcomputers:** 40 located in libraries, computer centers.

DEGREES OFFERED. AA, AS, AAS. 360 associate degrees awarded in 1992.

UNDERGRADUATE MAJORS. Accounting, agribusiness, agricultural production, automotive mechanics, automotive technology, business and management, business data entry equipment operation, business data processing and related programs, clinical laboratory science, computer programming, construction, criminal justice studies, drafting and design technology, electronic technology, emergency medical technologies, engineering and engineering-related technologies, gunsmithing, industrial technology, law enforcement and corrections, liberal/general studies, machine tool operation/machine shop, manufacturing technology, mechanical design technology, microcomputer software, nursing, robotics.

ACADEMIC PROGRAMS. 2-year transfer program, dual enrollment of high school students, independent study, internships, telecourses, cross-registration, BA in conjunction with Western Illinois Univerity, MBA with St. Ambrose College. **Remedial services:** Learning center, preadmission summer program, reduced course load, remedial instruction, special counselor, tutoring. **Placement/credit:** CLEP General and Subject; 30 credit hours maximum for associate degree.

ACADEMIC REQUIREMENTS. Freshmen must earn minimum GPA of 1.8 to continue in good standing. 48% of freshmen return for sophomore year. Students must declare major by end of first year. **Graduation requirements:** 62 hours for associate. Most students required to take courses in English, humanities, mathematics, biological/physical sciences, social sciences.

FRESHMAN ADMISSIONS. Selection criteria: Open admissions. Selective admissions to nursing, computer programming, electronic technology, automated manufacturing, medical assistant, and design engineering technology programs. Recommended units include English 3, mathematics 3, social science 3 and science 3.

1992 FRESHMAN CLASS PROFILE. 1,610 men and women enrolled. 22% had high school GPA of 3.0 or higher, 66% between 2.0 and 2.99. **Characteristics:** 95% from in state, 5% have minority backgrounds. Average age is 21.

FALL-TERM APPLICATIONS. No fee. No closing date; applicants notified on a rolling basis beginning on or about January 1; must reply by registration. Interview required for nursing, medical assistant applicants. Deferred and early admission available.

STUDENT LIFE. Housing: Dormitories (men, women). **Activities:** Student government, choral groups, minority organization.

ATHLETICS. NJCAA. **Intercollegiate:** Baseball M, basketball M, golf M, softball W, volleyball W. **Intramural:** Basketball, bowling, softball, volleyball.

STUDENT SERVICES. Aptitude testing, career counseling, employment service for undergraduates, freshman orientation, on-campus day care, personal counseling, placement service for graduates, veterans counselor, services/facilities for handicapped.

ANNUAL EXPENSES. Tuition and fees (1992-93): $1,302, $600 additional for out-of-state students. **Room and board:** $2,392. **Books and supplies:** $300.

FINANCIAL AID. 76% of freshmen, 72% of continuing students receive some form of aid. Grants, loans, jobs available. 469 enrolled freshmen were judged to have need, all were offered aid. Academic scholarships available. **Aid applications:** No closing date; applicants notified on a rolling basis beginning on or about June 1; must reply within 4 weeks.

ADDRESS/TELEPHONE. Dana Feinberg, Admissions Coordinator, Southeastern Community College: North Campus, Drawer F, West Burlington, IA 52655-0605. (319) 752-2731 ext. 163. Fax: (319) 752-4957.

Southeastern Community College: South Campus
Keokuk, Iowa CB code: 6340

2-year public community college, coed. Founded in 1966. **Accreditation:** Regional. **Undergraduate enrollment:** 116 men, 308 women full time; 84 men, 189 women part time. **Faculty:** 26 total (19 full time), 2 with doctorates or other terminal degrees. **Location:** Rural campus in large town; 45 miles from Burlington, 45 miles from Quincy, Illinois. **Calendar:** Semester, limited summer session. **Microcomputers:** 40 located in computer centers.

DEGREES OFFERED. AA, AS, AAS. 80 associate degrees awarded in 1992.

UNDERGRADUATE MAJORS. Business and management, liberal/general studies, nursing.

ACADEMIC PROGRAMS. 2-year transfer program, dual enrollment of high school students, independent study, cross-registration, cooperative degree programs with Western Illinois University. **Remedial services:** Learning center, reduced course load, remedial instruction, special counselor, tutoring. **Placement/credit:** CLEP General and Subject; 30 credit hours maximum for associate degree.

ACADEMIC REQUIREMENTS. Freshmen must earn minimum GPA of 1.8 to continue in good standing. 50% of freshmen return for sophomore year. **Graduation requirements:** 62 hours for associate. Most students required to take courses in English, humanities, mathematics, biological/physical sciences, social sciences.

FRESHMAN ADMISSIONS. Selection criteria: Open admissions. Selective admissions to nursing program. Applicants must meet specific scores on reading and numerical skills parts of ASSET test. **Test requirements:** ASSET required for placement.

1992 FRESHMAN CLASS PROFILE. 152 men, 405 women enrolled. **Characteristics:** 100% commute.

FALL-TERM APPLICATIONS. No fee. No closing date; applicants notified on a rolling basis; must reply by registration. Interview required for nursing applicants. Deferred and early admission available. Nursing program begins in June. Students should apply for nursing program at least 1 year in advance.

STUDENT LIFE. Activities: Student government, student newspaper, student nurses association, drama club, computer club.

ATHLETICS. Intramural: Basketball M, soccer M, volleyball. **Clubs:** Pool.

STUDENT SERVICES. Aptitude testing, career counseling, freshman orientation, on-campus day care, personal counseling, veterans counselor, services/facilities for handicapped.

ANNUAL EXPENSES. Tuition and fees (1992-93): $1,302, $600 additional for out-of-state students. **Books and supplies:** $500.

FINANCIAL AID. 63% of freshmen, 63% of continuing students receive some form of aid. All aid based on need. Academic scholarships available. **Aid applications:** No closing date; applicants notified on a rolling basis beginning on or about June 1; must reply within 2 weeks.

ADDRESS/TELEPHONE. Kristin Mische, Admissions Coordinator, Southeastern Community College: South Campus, 335 Messenger Road, Keokuk, IA 52632-1088. (319) 524-3221 ext. 18. Fax: (319) 524-3221.

Southwestern Community College
Creston, Iowa CB code: 6122

2-year public community college, coed. Founded in 1966. **Accreditation:** Regional. **Undergraduate enrollment:** 385 men, 518 women full time; 167 men, 302 women part time. **Faculty:** 54 total (44 full time), 1 with doctorate or other terminal degree. **Location:** Rural campus in small town; 75 miles from Des Moines. **Calendar:** Semester, limited summer session. **Microcomputers:** 80 located in libraries, computer centers.

DEGREES OFFERED. AA, AS, AAS. 170 associate degrees awarded in 1992. 45% in business and management, 8% computer sciences, 20% education, 15% health sciences, 8% multi/interdisciplinary studies.

UNDERGRADUATE MAJORS. Accounting, automotive mechanics, automotive technology, business administration and management, business and management, business and office, business computer/console/peripheral equipment operation, clinical laboratory science, computer programming, drafting and design technology, education, electronic technology, liberal/general studies, marketing management, medical laboratory technologies, music, music performance, music theory and composition, nursing, secretarial and related programs.

ACADEMIC PROGRAMS. 2-year transfer program, cooperative education, dual enrollment of high school students, internships, telecourses. **Remedial services:** Learning center, reduced course load, remedial instruction, special counselor, tutoring. **Placement/credit:** CLEP General; 30 credit hours maximum for associate degree.

ACADEMIC REQUIREMENTS. Freshmen must earn minimum GPA of 1.75 to continue in good standing. 60% of freshmen return for sophomore year. **Graduation requirements:** 60 hours for associate. Most students required to take courses in English, humanities, mathematics, biological/physical sciences, social sciences.

FRESHMAN ADMISSIONS. Selection criteria: Open admissions. Selective admissions to nursing program. One unit chemistry required for all health programs, 1 unit algebra for medical laboratory technology. **Test requirements:** ASSET required for placement.

1992 FRESHMAN CLASS PROFILE. 300 men, 334 women enrolled. **Characteristics:** 94% from in state, 93% commute, 1% have minority backgrounds. Average age is 19.

FALL-TERM APPLICATIONS. No fee. No closing date; applicants notified on a rolling basis.

STUDENT LIFE. Housing: Dormitories (men, women). **Activities:** Student government, student newspaper, choral groups, concert band, jazz band, music ensembles, pep band.

ATHLETICS. NJCAA. **Intercollegiate:** Baseball M, basketball, softball W, volleyball W. **Intramural:** Basketball, table tennis, tennis, volleyball.

STUDENT SERVICES. Aptitude testing, career counseling, employment service for undergraduates, freshman orientation, health services, personal counseling, placement service for graduates, special adviser for adult students, veterans counselor, services/facilities for handicapped.

ANNUAL EXPENSES. Tuition and fees (1992-93): $1,590, $690 additional for out-of-state students. **Room and board:** $2,400. **Books and supplies:** $500. **Other expenses:** $968.

FINANCIAL AID. 75% of freshmen, 75% of continuing students receive some form of aid. 94% of grants, 65% of loans, 73% of jobs based on need. Academic, music/drama, athletic, leadership scholarships available. **Aid applications:** No closing date; priority given to applications received by April 15; applicants notified on a rolling basis.

ADDRESS/TELEPHONE. Bill Hitesman, Admissions Coordinator, Southwestern Community College, 1501 West Townline, Creston, IA 50801. (515) 782-7081. Fax: (515) 782-4164.

Teikyo Marycrest University
Davenport, Iowa CB code: 6397

Admissions:	73% of applicants accepted
Based on:	••• School record, test scores
	•• Interview, recommendations, special talents
	• Activities, essay
Completion:	81% of freshmen end year in good standing
	48% graduate, 11% of these enter graduate study

4-year private university, coed, Christian heritage. Founded in 1939. **Accreditation:** Regional. **Undergraduate enrollment:** 215 men, 446 women full time; 146 men, 456 women part time. **Graduate enrollment:** 8 men, 3 women full time; 15 men, 194 women part time. **Faculty:** 101 total (54 full time), 39 with doctorates or other terminal degrees. **Location:** Suburban campus in small city; part of Iowa-Illinois Quad-Cities region. **Calendar:** Semester, limited summer session. Saturday classes. **Microcomputers:** 35 located in libraries, computer centers. **Special facilities:** Computer graphics laboratory. **Additional facts:** Courses offered in Cedar Rapids, Clinton, and Ottumwa.

DEGREES OFFERED. AA, AS, BA, BS, MA, MS. 14 associate degrees awarded in 1992. 214 bachelor's degrees awarded. 26% in business and management, 12% communications, 11% computer sciences, 9% education, 19% health sciences, 11% parks/recreation, protective services, public affairs, 9% social sciences. Graduate degrees offered in 4 major fields of study.

UNDERGRADUATE MAJORS. Associate: American studies, English, environmental management, liberal/general studies, philosophy, religion, social work. **Bachelor's:** Accounting, advertising, American studies, art education, art history, biological and physical sciences, biology, business administration and management, business and management, business education, chemistry, communications, computer and information sciences, computer graphics, computer programming, dramatic arts, early childhood education, education, elementary education, English, English education, environmental management, fine arts, food science and nutrition, foreign languages education, global studies, graphic design, history, humanities and social sciences, information sciences and systems, international business management, journalism, junior high education, liberal/general studies, marketing and distribution, mathematics, mathematics education, nursing, painting, predentistry, prelaw, premedicine, preveterinary, psychology, public relations, radio/television broadcasting, radio/television technology, reading education, science education, sculpture, secondary education, social studies education, social work, speech/communication/theater education, systems analysis, technical and business writing, telecommunications, visual and performing arts.

ACADEMIC PROGRAMS. Accelerated program, cooperative education, double major, dual enrollment of high school students, external degree, independent study, internships, student-designed major, study abroad, teacher preparation, telecourses, weekend college. **Remedial services:** Learning center, preadmission summer program, reduced course load, special counselor, tutoring. **Placement/credit:** AP, CLEP General and Subject, institutional tests; 30 credit hours maximum for bachelor's degree.

ACADEMIC REQUIREMENTS. Freshmen must earn minimum GPA of 2.0 to continue in good standing. 77% of freshmen return for sophomore year. Students must declare major by end of second year. **Graduation requirements:** 60 hours for associate, 120 hours for bachelor's. Most students required to take courses in arts/fine arts, computer science, English, foreign languages, history, humanities, mathematics, philosophy/religion, biological/physical sciences, social sciences. **Postgraduate studies:** 5% enter law school, 6% enter MBA programs.

FRESHMAN ADMISSIONS. Selection criteria: Test scores, high school GPA, academic record most important. 2 letters of recommendation also considered. **High school preparation:** 16 units recommended. Recommended units include biological science 1, English 4, foreign language 3, mathematics 3, physical science 1 and social science 2. **Test requirements:** SAT or ACT (ACT preferred); score report by August 25.

1992 FRESHMAN CLASS PROFILE. 320 men and women applied, 232 accepted; 87 men enrolled, 181 women enrolled. **Characteristics:** 65% from in state. Average age is 18.

FALL-TERM APPLICATIONS. $25 fee. No closing date; priority given to applications received by April 1; applicants notified on a rolling basis; must reply by May 1 or within 4 weeks if notified thereafter. Interview recommended for all applicants applicants. Audition recommended for dramatic arts applicants. Portfolio recommended for art students applicants. Essay recommended for academically weak or scholarship students applicants. CRDA. Deferred and early admission available.

STUDENT LIFE. Housing: Dormitories (men, women, coed). Limited number of apartments available for single parents and children. **Activities:** Student government, magazine, radio, student newspaper, television, choral groups, dance, drama, jazz band, musical theater, campus ministry, voluntary action center, international student organization, minority student union, Marycrest International Culture Association.

ATHLETICS. NAIA. **Intercollegiate:** Baseball M, basketball, cross-country, soccer, softball W, volleyball W. **Intramural:** Basketball, bowling, golf, soccer, softball, tennis, volleyball.

STUDENT SERVICES. Aptitude testing, career counseling, employment service for undergraduates, freshman orientation, health services, on-campus day care, personal counseling, placement service for graduates, special adviser for adult students, services/facilities for handicapped.

ANNUAL EXPENSES. Tuition and fees: $9,800. **Room and board:** $3,400. **Books and supplies:** $525. **Other expenses:** $700.

FINANCIAL AID. 90% of freshmen, 90% of continuing students receive some form of aid. 57% of grants, 87% of loans, all jobs based on need. Academic, music/drama, art, athletic, leadership, alumni affiliation scholarships available. **Aid applications:** No closing date; priority given to applications received by March 1; applicants notified on a rolling basis beginning on or about April 1; must reply within 2 weeks.

ADDRESS/TELEPHONE. Suellen Ofe, Executive Director of Admissions and Financial Aid, Teikyo Marycrest University, 1607 West Twelfth Street, Davenport, IA 52804-4096. (319) 326-9512. (800) 728-9705. Fax: (319) 326-9250.

Teikyo Westmar University
Le Mars, Iowa CB code: 6936

Admissions:	64% of applicants accepted
Based on:	••• School record, test scores
	• Activities, essay, interview, recommendations, special talents
Completion:	87% of freshmen end year in good standing
	6% enter graduate study

4-year private liberal arts college, coed. Founded in 1890. **Accreditation:** Regional. **Undergraduate enrollment:** 514 men, 247 women full time. **Faculty:** 70 total (60 full time), 29 with doctorates or other terminal degrees. **Location:** Rural campus in small town; 20 miles from Sioux City, 90 miles from Omaha, Nebraska. **Calendar:** 4-1-4, limited summer session. **Microcomputers:** Located in dormitories, libraries, classrooms, computer centers. **Special facilities:** Danner Arboretum, lifesports center. **Additional facts:** Global Plus Program offers students opportunity to gain leadership and community service experience and to travel abroad.

DEGREES OFFERED. BA, BFA. 84 bachelor's degrees awarded in 1992. 40% in business and management, 23% education, 7% physical sciences, 24% social sciences.

UNDERGRADUATE MAJORS. Accounting, art education, biology, business administration and management, business and management, business economics, business education, chemistry, Christian education, communications, computer and information sciences, computer programming, court reporting, cultural sciences, dance, dramatic arts, economics, education, elementary education, English, English education, fine arts, foreign languages education, German, health education, history, international business management, Japanese, journalism, junior high education, liberal/general studies, marketing and distribution, marketing management, mathematics, mathematics education, music, music education, philosophy, physical education, physics, precytotechnology, predentistry, prelaw, premedicine, preveterinary, psychology, radio/television broadcasting, recreation and community services technologies, religion, science education, secondary education, social science education, social sciences, sociology, speech, telecommunications, theater design.

ACADEMIC PROGRAMS. Accelerated program, cooperative education, double major, dual enrollment of high school students, honors program, independent study, internships, student-designed major, study abroad, teacher preparation, visiting/exchange student program, cross-registration, international internships; liberal arts/career combination in engineering, health sciences. **Remedial services:** Learning center, reduced course load, remedial instruction, special counselor, tutoring. **Placement/credit:** AP, CLEP General and Subject, institutional tests; 43 credit hours maximum for bachelor's degree.

ACADEMIC REQUIREMENTS. Freshmen must earn minimum GPA of 2.0 to continue in good standing. 78% of freshmen return for sophomore year. Students must declare major by end of second year. **Graduation requirements:** 128 hours for bachelor's. Most students required to take courses in computer science, English, history, humanities, mathematics, biological/physical sciences, social sciences. **Postgraduate studies:** 2% enter MBA programs, 4% enter other graduate study.

FRESHMAN ADMISSIONS. Selection criteria: School achievement record, rank in top half of class, test scores. **High school preparation:** 16 units recommended. Recommended units include biological science 2, English 4, foreign language 2, mathematics 4, physical science 2 and social science 2. Foreign language strongly recommended for intercultural communication and international business majors. **Test requirements:** SAT or ACT (ACT preferred); score report by August 15.

1992 FRESHMAN CLASS PROFILE. 345 men applied, 217 accepted, 62 enrolled; 126 women applied, 86 accepted, 23 enrolled. 37% had high school GPA of 3.0 or higher, 58% between 2.0 and 2.99. 4% were in top tenth and 25% were in top quarter of graduating class. **Characteristics:** 53% from in state, 91% live in college housing. Average age is 18.

FALL-TERM APPLICATIONS. No fee. No closing date; applicants notified on a rolling basis; must reply within 2 weeks. Audition required for voice, instrumental music, theater, dance applicants. Interview recommended for marginal applicants. Deferred and early admission available.

STUDENT LIFE. Housing: Dormitories (men, women, coed); apartment housing available. Students under 21 need housing director approval to live-off campus. **Activities:** Student government, student newspaper, yearbook, choral groups, concert band, dance, drama, jazz band, music ensembles, musical theater, pep band, Fellowship of Christian Athletes, Black Student Association, Christian Outreach, Biosphere Club, Phi Kappa Delta, Peer Assistance Leaders, Student Ambassadors.

ATHLETICS. NAIA. **Intercollegiate:** Baseball M, basketball, football M, golf, soccer, softball W, tennis, track and field, volleyball W, wrestling M. **Intramural:** Baseball, basketball, bowling, racquetball, soccer, softball, tennis, track and field, volleyball.

STUDENT SERVICES. Aptitude testing, career counseling, employment service for undergraduates, freshman orientation, health services, personal counseling, placement service for graduates, special adviser for adult students, veterans counselor.

ANNUAL EXPENSES. Tuition and fees: $9,780. **Room and board:** $3,350. **Books and supplies:** $560. **Other expenses:** $880.

FINANCIAL AID. 99% of freshmen, 98% of continuing students receive some form of aid. 83% of grants, 93% of loans, 60% of jobs based on need. 77 enrolled freshmen were judged to have need, all were offered aid. Academic, music/drama, athletic, religious affiliation scholarships available. **Aid applications:** No closing date; priority given to applications received by April 1; applicants notified on a rolling basis beginning on or about March 1; must reply within 2 weeks. **Additional information:** Scholarships available for cheerleading and danceline for men and women.

ADDRESS/TELEPHONE. Richard Phillips, Vice President of Enrollment Management, Teikyo Westmar University, 1002 Third Avenue SE, Le Mars, IA 51031. (712) 546-2070. (800) 352-4634. Fax: (712) 546-2080.

University of Dubuque

Dubuque, Iowa — CB code: 6869

Admissions:	73% of applicants accepted
Based on:	••• School record, test scores
	•• Interview
	• Activities, essay, recommendations
Completion:	75% of freshmen end year in good standing
	78% graduate

4-year private university and liberal arts, seminary college, coed, affiliated with Presbyterian Church (USA). Founded in 1852. **Accreditation:** Regional. **Undergraduate enrollment:** 359 men, 332 women full time; 63 men, 126 women part time. **Graduate enrollment:** 148 men, 61 women full time; 104 men, 71 women part time. **Faculty:** 82 total (58 full time), 53 with doctorates or other terminal degrees. **Location:** Suburban campus in small city; 180 miles from Chicago. **Calendar:** Semester, extensive summer session. Saturday and extensive evening/early morning classes. **Microcomputers:** 45 located in libraries, classrooms, computer centers. **Special facilities:** Floating laboratory on Mississippi River, alumni art gallery, curriculum laboratory for teachers, aviation operation.

DEGREES OFFERED. AA, AS, BA, BS, MBA, MEd, M.Div. 4 associate degrees awarded in 1992. 50% in business and management, 25% computer sciences, 25% social sciences. 174 bachelor's degrees awarded. 35% in business and management, 13% teacher education, 15% health sciences, 6% life sciences, 11% social sciences. Graduate degrees offered in 17 major fields of study.

UNDERGRADUATE MAJORS. Associate: Accounting, business administration and management, liberal/general studies. **Bachelor's:** Accounting, aviation management, biology, business administration and management, business and management, business economics, chemistry, computer and information sciences, computer programming, early childhood education, earth sciences, economics, education, education of the mentally handicapped, education of the multiple handicapped, elementary education, English, English education, environmental science, foreign languages education, French, German, history, junior high education, marketing management, marketing research, mathematics, mathematics education, music, nursing, philosophy, physical education, physics, political science and government, prelaw, premedicine, psychology, religion, science education, secondary education, social work, sociology, Spanish, special education, speech, theological studies.

ACADEMIC PROGRAMS. 2-year transfer program, accelerated program, cooperative education, double major, dual enrollment of high school students, honors program, independent study, internships, student-designed major, study abroad, teacher preparation, weekend college, cross-registration. **Remedial services:** Learning center, preadmission summer program, reduced course load, remedial instruction, special counselor, tutoring. **Placement/credit:** AP, CLEP Subject, institutional tests; 24 credit hours maximum for bachelor's degree.

ACADEMIC REQUIREMENTS. Freshmen must earn minimum GPA of 2.0 to continue in good standing. 65% of freshmen return for sophomore year. Students must declare major by end of second year. **Graduation requirements:** 64 hours for associate, 124 hours for bachelor's. Most students required to take courses in computer science, English, history, humanities, mathematics, biological/physical sciences, social sciences.

FRESHMAN ADMISSIONS. Selection criteria: Minimum ACT score 18, SAT 740 for admission. GPA in college preparatory classes also considered. **High school preparation:** 15 units required. Required and recommended units include English 4, mathematics 3, social science 3 and science 3. Foreign language 2 recommended. **Test requirements:** SAT or ACT (ACT preferred); score report by August 15.

1992 FRESHMAN CLASS PROFILE. 389 men applied, 270 accepted, 96 enrolled; 330 women applied, 254 accepted, 81 enrolled. 9% were in top tenth and 43% were in top quarter of graduating class. **Academic background:** Mid 50% of enrolled freshmen had ACT composite between 18-24. 89% submitted ACT scores. **Characteristics:** 49% from in state, 75% live in college housing, 8% have minority backgrounds, 8% are foreign students, 13% join fraternities/sororities. Average age is 20.

FALL-TERM APPLICATIONS. $15 fee, may be waived for applicants with need. Closing date March 1; applicants notified on a rolling basis; must reply by May 1 or within 4 weeks if notified thereafter. Interview recommended for all applicants applicants. Essay recommended. CRDA. Deferred and early admission available.

STUDENT LIFE. Housing: Dormitories (men, women, coed); apartment housing available. **Activities:** Student government, student newspaper, yearbook, choral groups, concert band, dance, drama, jazz band, music ensembles, musical theater, pep band, fraternities, sororities, religious, social service and international organizations, national service fraternity.

ATHLETICS. NCAA. **Intercollegiate:** Baseball M, basketball, cross-country, football M, golf, softball W, tennis, track and field, volleyball W, wrestling M. **Intramural:** Archery, badminton, basketball, bowling, golf, racquetball, skiing, soccer M, softball, swimming, table tennis, tennis, volleyball.

STUDENT SERVICES. Aptitude testing, career counseling, employment service for undergraduates, freshman orientation, health services, personal counseling, placement service for graduates, special adviser for adult students, services/facilities for handicapped.

ANNUAL EXPENSES. Tuition and fees: $10,530. **Room and board:** $3,620. **Books and supplies:** $500. **Other expenses:** $600.

FINANCIAL AID. 85% of freshmen, 80% of continuing students receive some form of aid. 79% of grants, 88% of loans, 82% of jobs based on need. 136 enrolled freshmen were judged to have need, all were offered aid. Academic, music/drama, state/district residency, leadership, religious affiliation scholarships available. **Aid applications:** No closing date; priority given to applications received by April 1; applicants notified on a rolling basis beginning on or about March 15; must reply within 3 weeks.

ADDRESS/TELEPHONE. Christine Chapin Tilton, Di of Undergraduate Admission, University of Dubuque, 2000 University Avenue, Dubuque, IA 52001. (319) 589-3200. (800) 7-CALLUD. Fax: (319) 556-8633.

University of Iowa

Iowa City, Iowa CB code: 6681

Admissions:	87% of applicants accepted
Based on:	••• School record, test scores
	• Essay, interview, recommendations, special talents
Completion:	56% graduate

4-year public university, coed. Founded in 1847. **Accreditation:** Regional. **Undergraduate enrollment:** 7,652 men, 8,120 women full time; 1,374 men, 1,527 women part time. **Graduate enrollment:** 3,219 men, 2,313 women full time; 1,477 men, 1,781 women part time. **Faculty:** 1,729 total (1,674 full time), 1,640 with doctorates or other terminal degrees. **Location:** Urban campus in small city; 20 miles from Cedar Rapids, 100 miles from Des Moines. **Calendar:** Semester, extensive summer session. Saturday and extensive evening/early morning classes. **Microcomputers:** 930 located in dormitories, libraries, classrooms, computer centers. **Special facilities:** Art museum, field campus, accelerator, observatory, natural history museum.

DEGREES OFFERED. BA, BS, BFA, MA, MS, MBA, MFA, MSW, PhD, DDS, MD, Pharm D, JD. 3,649 bachelor's degrees awarded in 1992. 16% in business and management, 11% communications, 7% teacher education, 6% engineering, 9% health sciences, 7% letters/literature, 5% psychology, 15% social sciences. Graduate degrees offered in 149 major fields of study.

UNDERGRADUATE MAJORS. Accounting, actuarial sciences, Afro-American (black) studies, American studies, anthropology, applied mathematics, art education, art history, Asian languages, Asian literature, Asian studies, astronomy, biochemistry, bioengineering and biomedical engineering, biology, botany, business administration and management, business and management, business economics, ceramics, chemical engineering, chemistry, cinematography/film, civil engineering, classics, communications, comparative literature, computer and information sciences, computer engineering, dance, dental hygiene, dramatic arts, drawing, Eastern European studies, economics, education of the mentally handicapped, education of the physically handicapped, electrical/electronics/communications engineering, elementary education, engineering, English, English education, fiber/textiles/weaving, finance, fine arts, foreign languages education, French, geography, geology, German, Greek (classical), health occupations education, history, human resources development, humanities, industrial engineering, Italian, jazz, journalism, labor/industrial relations, Latin, liberal/general studies, linguistics, management science, marketing and distribution, mathematics, mathematics education, mechanical engineering, medical laboratory technologies, metal/jewelry, microbiology, music, music education, music history and appreciation, music performance, music theory and composition, music therapy, nuclear medical technology, nursing, painting, parks and recreation management, pharmacy, philosophy, physical education, physics, political science and government, Portuguese, printmaking, psychology, pure mathematics, radio/television broadcasting, recreation therapy, religion, Russian, science education, sculpture, secondary education, social science education, social sciences, social studies education, social work, sociology, Spanish, speech pathology/audiology, speech/communication/theater education, statistics, studio art.

ACADEMIC PROGRAMS. Accelerated program, cooperative education, double major, dual enrollment of high school students, education specialist degree, external degree, honors program, independent study, internships, student-designed major, study abroad, teacher preparation, telecourses, visiting/exchange student program, Washington semester, cross-registration; liberal arts/career combination in engineering, health sciences; combined bachelor's/graduate program in business administration, medicine. **Remedial services:** Learning center, preadmission summer program, reduced course load, remedial instruction, special counselor, tutoring. **ROTC:** Air Force, Army. **Placement/credit:** AP, CLEP General and Subject, IB, institutional tests; 32 credit hours maximum for bachelor's degree.

ACADEMIC REQUIREMENTS. Freshmen must earn minimum GPA of 1.7 to continue in good standing. 89% of freshmen return for sophomore year. **Graduation requirements:** 124 hours for bachelor's. Most students required to take courses in English, foreign languages, history, humanities, mathematics, biological/physical sciences, social sciences.

FRESHMAN ADMISSIONS. Selection criteria: For in-state applicants, rank in top half of class or an acceptable admission index score (a combination of class rank and ACT or SAT). For nonresidents, rank in top 30% or acceptable admission index score. Students must have completed specific high school course units. **High school preparation:** 15 units required. Required and recommended units include English 4, foreign language 2-4, mathematics 3, social science 3 and science 3. Mathematics units must include 2 algebra, 1 geometry; engineering majors require fourth unit of higher mathematics. Science units must include 1 from any 2 of the following: biology, chemistry, and physics; engineering requires 1 unit chemistry and 1 unit physics. Engineering majors require only 2 units social studies. **Test requirements:** SAT or ACT; score report by May 15.

1992 FRESHMAN CLASS PROFILE. 4,283 men applied, 3,600 accepted, 1,485 enrolled; 4,587 women applied, 4,112 accepted, 1,768 enrolled. 79% had high school GPA of 3.0 or higher, 21% between 2.0 and 2.99. 23% were in top tenth of graduating class. **Academic background:** Mid 50% of enrolled freshmen had ACT composite between 22-27. 92% submitted ACT scores. **Characteristics:** 62% from in state, 89% live in college housing, 16% have minority backgrounds, 1% are foreign students, 18% join fraternities/sororities. Average age is 18.

FALL-TERM APPLICATIONS. $20 fee, may be waived for applicants with need. Closing date May 15; applicants notified on a rolling basis. Interview required for physical therapy, physician's assistant, dentistry applicants. Audition required for music applicants. Deferred and early admission available. Early application for engineering students strongly recommended.

STUDENT LIFE. Housing: Dormitories (coed); apartment, fraternity, sorority, cooperative housing available. Foreign language, honors, and quiet houses available. Housing reserved for juniors, seniors, and graduate students. **Activities:** Student government, film, magazine, radio, student newspaper, television, yearbook, choral groups, concert band, dance, drama, jazz band, marching band, music ensembles, musical theater, opera, pep band, symphony orchestra, fraternities, sororities, College Republicans, University Democrats, Afro-American Cultural Center, Chicano/Indian American Cultural Center.

ATHLETICS. NCAA. **Intercollegiate:** Baseball M, basketball, cross-country, diving, field hockey W, football M, golf, gymnastics, softball W, swimming, tennis, track and field, volleyball W, wrestling M. **Intramural:** Badminton, basketball, bowling, diving, fencing, golf, ice hockey, lacrosse, racquetball, rifle, rowing (crew), rugby, sailing, skiing, soccer, softball, squash, swimming, table tennis, tennis, track and field, volleyball, water polo, wrestling M.

STUDENT SERVICES. Aptitude testing, career counseling, employment service for undergraduates, freshman orientation, health services, personal counseling, placement service for graduates, special adviser for adult students, veterans counselor, special services for minority students, services/facilities for handicapped.

ANNUAL EXPENSES. Tuition and fees (projected): $2,352, $5,388 additional for out-of-state students. **Room and board:** $3,306. **Books and supplies:** $610. **Other expenses:** $1,854.

FINANCIAL AID. 75% of freshmen, 75% of continuing students receive some form of aid. 88% of grants, 89% of loans, 10% of jobs based on need. Academic, music/drama, art, athletic, minority scholarships available. **Aid applications:** No closing date; applicants notified on a rolling basis beginning on or about April 1; must reply within 2 weeks.

ADDRESS/TELEPHONE. Michael Barron, Director of Admissions, University of Iowa, 107 Calvin Hall, Iowa City, IA 52242-1396. (319) 335-3847. (800) 553-IOWA.

University of Northern Iowa

Cedar Falls, Iowa CB code: 6307

Admissions:	88% of applicants accepted
Based on:	••• School record, test scores
	• Interview, recommendations, special talents
Completion:	85% of freshmen end year in good standing
	48% graduate, 6% of these enter graduate study

4-year public university, coed. Founded in 1876. **Accreditation:** Regional. **Undergraduate enrollment:** 4,507 men, 5,726 women full time; 613 men, 979 women part time. **Graduate enrollment:** 187 men, 266 women full time; 287 men, 480 women part time. **Faculty:** 808 total (661 full time). **Location:** Suburban campus in large town; 110 miles from Des Moines. **Calendar:** Semester, extensive summer session. **Microcomputers:** 421 located in dormitories, libraries, classrooms, computer centers. **Special facilities:** Museum, art gallery, observatory, nature preserves, domed stadium, NASA teacher resource center.

DEGREES OFFERED. BA, BS, BFA, MA, MS, MBA, MFA, MEd, EdD. 2,244 bachelor's degrees awarded in 1992. 23% in business and management, 6% communications, 28% education, 6% letters/literature, 6% social sciences. Graduate degrees offered in 53 major fields of study.

UNDERGRADUATE MAJORS. Accounting, American studies, anthropology, applied physics, architectural design and construction technology, Asian studies, biological and physical sciences, biology, biotechnology, business administration and management, business and management, business education, chemistry, chemistry marketing, communications, community health work, computer and information sciences, criminology, drafting and design technology, dramatic arts, driver and safety education, early childhood, early childhood education, earth sciences, economics, education of the emotionally handicapped, education of the mentally handicapped, elementary education, energy conservation and use technology, engineering and engineering-related technologies, English, European studies, family and community services, finance, fine arts, food production/management/services, food science and nutrition, French, geography, geology, German, graphic design, health education, history, home economics, home economics education, human environment and housing, humanities, industrial arts education, industrial technology, information sciences and systems, journalism, junior high education, Latin American studies, leisure services: youth agency administration, liberal/general studies, life sciences, manufacturing technology, marketing management, mathematics, mechanical design technology, music, music education, music performance, musical theater, office information systems, parks and recreation management, philosophy, philosophy and religion, physical education, physics, political science and government, psychology, public administration, public relations, radio/television broadcasting, reading education, real estate, recreation therapy, religion, Russian and Slavic studies, science education, social science education, social sciences, social work, sociology, Spanish, special education, speech, speech pathology/audiology, teaching English as a second language/foreign language, textiles and clothing, theater design, trade and industrial education.

ACADEMIC PROGRAMS. Cooperative education, double major, dual enrollment of high school students, education specialist degree, external degree, honors program, independent study, internships, student-designed major, study abroad, teacher preparation, visiting/exchange student program, Washington semester, cross-registration; combined bachelor's/graduate program in business administration. **Remedial services:** Learning center, reduced course load, remedial instruction, special counselor, tutoring, Educational Opportunity Program. **ROTC:** Army. **Placement/credit:** AP, CLEP General and Subject, IB, institutional tests; 32 credit hours maximum for bachelor's degree.

ACADEMIC REQUIREMENTS. Freshmen must earn minimum GPA of 2.0 to continue in good standing. Freshmen must maintain GPA not more than 13 grade points below 2.0 according to special university scale. 82% of freshmen return for sophomore year. Students must declare major by end of first year. **Graduation requirements:** 124 hours for bachelor's (40 in major). Most students required to take courses in arts/fine arts, English, foreign languages, history, humanities, mathematics, philosophy/religion, biological/physical sciences, social sciences.

FRESHMAN ADMISSIONS. Selection criteria: Rank in top half of class, test scores. **High school preparation:** 15 units required. Required units include English 4, mathematics 3, social science 3 and science 3. English units must include 1 compostion. Mathematics units must include 1 algebra. One unit foreign language credit awarded for 2.0 GPA in 2 high school language units. **Test requirements:** SAT or ACT (ACT preferred); score report by August 15.

1992 FRESHMAN CLASS PROFILE. 3,640 men and women applied, 3,211 accepted; 1,076 men enrolled, 1,531 women enrolled. 17% were in top tenth and 49% were in top quarter of graduating class. **Academic background:** Mid 50% of enrolled freshmen had ACT composite between 21-26. 97% submitted ACT scores. **Characteristics:** 96% from in state, 73% live in college housing, 4% have minority backgrounds, 2% join fraternities/sororities. Average age is 18.

FALL-TERM APPLICATIONS. $20 fee. Closing date August 15; applicants notified on a rolling basis. Audition required for music applicants. Interview recommended for academically weak applicants. Deferred admission available.

STUDENT LIFE. Housing: Dormitories (men, women, coed); apartment, fraternity, sorority housing available. **Activities:** Student government, magazine, radio, student newspaper, yearbook, choral groups, concert band, dance, drama, jazz band, marching band, music ensembles, musical theater, opera, pep band, symphony orchestra, drill team, fraternities, sororities, Young Democrats, Young Republicans, religious organizations.

ATHLETICS. NCAA. **Intercollegiate:** Baseball M, basketball, cross-country, diving, football M, golf, softball W, swimming, tennis, track and field, volleyball W, wrestling M. **Intramural:** Badminton, basketball, bowling, cross-country, golf, racquetball, softball, swimming, table tennis, tennis, track and field, volleyball, wrestling M.

STUDENT SERVICES. Aptitude testing, career counseling, employment service for undergraduates, freshman orientation, health services, on-campus day care, personal counseling, placement service for graduates, special adviser for adult students, veterans counselor, services/facilities for handicapped.

ANNUAL EXPENSES. Tuition and fees (1992-93): $2,228, $3,342 additional for out-of-state students. **Room and board:** $2,620. **Books and supplies:** $565. **Other expenses:** $1,735.

FINANCIAL AID. 65% of freshmen, 61% of continuing students receive some form of aid. 73% of grants, 95% of loans, 96% of jobs based on need. 899 enrolled freshmen were judged to have need, 807 were offered aid. Academic, music/drama, art, athletic, state/district residency, leadership scholarships available. **Aid applications:** No closing date; priority given to applications received by February 15; applicants notified on a rolling basis beginning on or about April 1; must reply within 2 weeks.

ADDRESS/TELEPHONE. Clark K. Elmer, Director of Admissions, University of Northern Iowa, 120 Gilchrist Hall, Cedar Falls, IA 50614-0018. (319) 273-2281. (800) 772-2037. Fax: (319) 273-6792.

University of Osteopathic Medicine and Health Sciences
Des Moines, Iowa — CB code: 1767

2-year upper-division private health science university, coed. Founded in 1898. **Accreditation:** Regional. **Undergraduate enrollment:** 21 men, 24 women full time; 2 men, 26 women part time. **Graduate enrollment:** 751 men, 347 women full time; 33 men, 107 women part time. **Faculty:** 75 total (65 full time), 61 with doctorates or other terminal degrees. **Location:** Urban campus in small city; 220 miles from Chicago. **Calendar:** Trimester. **Microcomputers:** 6 located in libraries. **Special facilities:** Museum.

DEGREES OFFERED. BS, MS, DO. 32 bachelor's degrees awarded in 1992. 100% in health sciences. Graduate degrees offered in 4 major fields of study.

UNDERGRADUATE MAJORS. Health care administration, physician's assistant.

ACADEMIC PROGRAMS. Accelerated program. **Remedial services:** Special counselor. **Placement/credit:** 6 credit hours maximum for bachelor's degree.

ACADEMIC REQUIREMENTS. Students must declare major on application. **Graduation requirements:** 120 hours for bachelor's (30 in major). Most students required to take courses in English, history, philosophy/religion, biological/physical sciences, social sciences.

STUDENT LIFE. Activities: Student government, yearbook.

STUDENT SERVICES. Health services, personal counseling.

ANNUAL EXPENSES. Tuition and fees: $7,870. **Books and supplies:** $1,100.

FINANCIAL AID. 90% of continuing students receive some form of aid. All grants, 75% of loans, all jobs based on need. **Aid applications:** No closing date; applicants notified on a rolling basis.

ADDRESS/TELEPHONE. Dennis L. Bates, PhD, Director, University of Osteopathic Medicine and Health Sciences, 3200 Grand Avenue, Des Moines, IA 50312. (515) 271-1450. Fax: (515) 271-1532.

Upper Iowa University
Fayette, Iowa — CB code: 6885

Admissions: 75% of applicants accepted
Based on: ••• Activities, school record
•• Interview, test scores
• Essay, recommendations, special talents
Completion: 85% of freshmen end year in good standing
13% enter graduate study

4-year private liberal arts college, coed. Founded in 1857. **Accreditation:** Regional. **Undergraduate enrollment:** 2,641 men and women. **Faculty:** 214 total (34 full time), 10 with doctorates or other terminal degrees. **Location:** Rural campus in rural community; 150 miles from Des Moines, 50 miles from Waterloo. **Calendar:** Quarter, limited summer session. **Microcomputers:** Located in computer centers. **Special facilities:** Electron microscopy laboratory, Volga Lake Project. **Additional facts:** Alternatives to traditional classroom method of earning a baccalaureate degree offered through external degree program and through various off-campus centers: in Des Moines, Waterloo and Newton, Iowa, and in Madison and Prairie du Chien, Wisconsin.

DEGREES OFFERED. AA, AS, BA, BS. 5 associate degrees awarded in 1992. 533 bachelor's degrees awarded.

UNDERGRADUATE MAJORS. Associate: Business and management, computer and information sciences, liberal/general studies. **Bachelor's:** Accounting, art education, biology, business administration and management, business and management, business education, commercial art, communications, computer and information sciences, earth sciences, education, elementary education, English, English education, fine arts, foreign languages education, health education, junior high education, marketing and distribution, marketing and distributive education, marketing management, mathematics, mathematics education, music, music education, parks and recreation management, physical education, predentistry, prelaw, premedicine, prepharmacy, preveterinary, psychology, reading education, science education, secondary education, social science education, social sciences, social studies education, sociology, speech/communication/theater education, sports medicine.

ACADEMIC PROGRAMS. Accelerated program, double major, dual enrollment of high school students, external degree, independent study, internships, teacher preparation. **Remedial services:** Learning center, remedial instruction, special counselor, tutoring. **Placement/credit:** AP, CLEP Subject, institutional tests; 30 credit hours maximum for bachelor's degree.

ACADEMIC REQUIREMENTS. Freshmen must earn minimum GPA of 2.0 to continue in good standing. 87% of freshmen return for sophomore year. Students must declare major by end of second year. **Graduation requirements:** 60 hours for associate (18 in major), 120 hours for bachelor's. Most students required to take courses in computer science, English, history, humanities, mathematics, biological/physical sciences, social sciences.

FRESHMAN ADMISSIONS. Selection criteria: Minimum 2.0 high school GPA, ACT composite score of 16, SAT composite test score of 630 important. **High school preparation:** 16 units required. Required units include biological science 1, English 4, foreign language 1, mathematics 2, physical science 1 and social science 3. **Test requirements:** SAT or ACT; score report by May 30. **Additional information:** Early application is recommended because of a limited enrollment policy.

1992 FRESHMAN CLASS PROFILE. 666 men and women applied, 502 accepted; 226 enrolled. **Academic background:** Mid 50% of enrolled freshmen had SAT-V between 400-450, SAT-M between 450-500; ACT composite between 21-24. 6% submitted SAT scores, 94% submitted ACT scores. **Characteristics:** 65% from in state, 100% live in college housing, 12% have minority backgrounds, 2% are foreign students. Average age is 19.

FALL-TERM APPLICATIONS. $15 fee, may be waived for applicants with need. Closing date August 1; priority given to applications received by June 30; applicants notified on a rolling basis; must reply within 3 weeks. Interview recommended for academically weak applicants. Audition recommended for music applicants. Portfolio recommended for art applicants. Deferred and early admission available.

STUDENT LIFE. Housing: Dormitories (men, women). **Activities:** Student government, student newspaper, yearbook, choral groups, concert band, drama, jazz band, music ensembles, pep band, sororities, various political, academic, religious, and ethnic organizations.

ATHLETICS. NCAA. **Intercollegiate:** Baseball M, basketball, cross-country, football M, golf, rugby M, softball W, tennis, track and field, volleyball W, wrestling M. **Intramural:** Badminton, basketball, bowling, softball, table tennis, volleyball.

STUDENT SERVICES. Aptitude testing, career counseling, employment service for undergraduates, freshman orientation, health services, personal counseling, placement service for graduates, services/facilities for handicapped.

ANNUAL EXPENSES. Tuition and fees: $8,840. **Room and board:** $3,060. **Books and supplies:** $500. **Other expenses:** $600.

FINANCIAL AID. 99% of freshmen, 97% of continuing students receive some form of aid. 92% of grants, 98% of loans, all jobs based on need. 156 enrolled freshmen were judged to have need, all were offered aid. Academic, alumni affiliation, religious affiliation scholarships available. **Aid applications:** No closing date; priority given to applications received by April 20; applicants notified on a rolling basis; must reply within 3 weeks.

ADDRESS/TELEPHONE. Debra Sanborn, Director of Admission, Upper Iowa University, Carter Hall, Box 1859, Fayette, IA 52142-1859. (319) 425-5281. (800) 553-4150. Fax: (319) 425-5271.

Vennard College
University Park, Iowa
CB code: 6094

4-year private Bible college, coed, interdenominational. Founded in 1910. **Undergraduate enrollment:** 70 men, 62 women full time; 8 men, 10 women part time. **Faculty:** 14 total (10 full time), 3 with doctorates or other terminal degrees. **Location:** Rural campus in large town; 65 miles from Des Moines. **Calendar:** Semester, limited summer session. **Microcomputers:** 11 located in computer centers. **Additional facts:** Dedicated to education in basic Christian doctrine and to preparing students for service in church-related ministries, or as lay persons in a Christian context.

DEGREES OFFERED. BA, MA. 1 associate degree awarded in 1992. 22 bachelor's degrees awarded.

UNDERGRADUATE MAJORS. Associate: Bible studies, liberal/general studies, sacred music, teacher aide. **Bachelor's:** Bible studies, biblical languages, business and management, early childhood education, education, elementary education, humanities and social sciences, missionary studies, music, music performance, music theory and composition, nursing, philosophy, presecondary education, psychology, religious education, religious music, sacred music, social sciences, theological studies.

ACADEMIC PROGRAMS. 2-year transfer program, double major, honors program, independent study, internships, teacher preparation, Salvation Army 2-2 cooperative program, Association of Christian Schools, international 5-year teacher certification program, 5-year Pastoral Theology program, 5-year nursing program. **Remedial services:** Learning center, preadmission summer program, reduced course load, remedial instruction, special counselor, tutoring. **Placement/credit:** Institutional tests.

ACADEMIC REQUIREMENTS. Freshmen must earn minimum GPA of 1.6 to continue in good standing. 85% of freshmen return for sophomore year. Students must declare major by end of first year. **Graduation requirements:** 64 hours for associate (18 in major), 128 hours for bachelor's (34 in major). Most students required to take courses in arts/fine arts, English, foreign languages, history, humanities, mathematics, philosophy/religion, biological/physical sciences, social sciences. **Postgraduate studies:** 17% from 2-year programs enter 4-year programs. **Additional information:** All students choose double major: Bible and 1 of 20 other majors.

FRESHMAN ADMISSIONS. Selection criteria: Applicant's statement of Christian experience and recommendation of pastor major factors. **Test requirements:** SAT or ACT (ACT preferred); score report by August 20. **Additional information:** Minimum required ACT score and GPA are flexible, depending on other factors as considered by admissions office and academic departments.

1992 FRESHMAN CLASS PROFILE. 17 men, 24 women enrolled. 23% had high school GPA of 3.0 or higher, 62% between 2.0 and 2.99. **Academic background:** Mid 50% of enrolled freshmen had ACT composite between 16-22. 87% submitted ACT scores. **Characteristics:** 30% from in state, 85% live in college housing. Average age is 19.

FALL-TERM APPLICATIONS. $10 fee, may be waived for applicants with need. Closing date August 20; priority given to applications received by July 12; applicants notified on a rolling basis. Essay recommended. Deferred admission available.

STUDENT LIFE. Housing: Dormitories (men, women); apartment housing available. Single students 28 years of age or older may petition for permission to live off campus. **Activities:** Student government, student newspaper, yearbook, choral groups, concert band, music ensembles, pep band, World Christian Fellowship, Ministerial Association. **Additional information:** College emphasizes social life disciplines as they relate to Christian life. Religious observance required.

ATHLETICS. Intercollegiate: Basketball, soccer M, tennis M, volleyball W. **Intramural:** Basketball, bowling, golf, soccer M, softball, table tennis, tennis, volleyball.

STUDENT SERVICES. Career counseling, employment service for undergraduates, freshman orientation, health services, on-campus day care, personal counseling, placement service for graduates, special adviser for adult students.

ANNUAL EXPENSES. Tuition and fees: $5,590. **Room and board:** $2,680. **Books and supplies:** $448. **Other expenses:** $1,280.

FINANCIAL AID. 85% of freshmen, 90% of continuing students receive some form of aid. Grants, loans, jobs available. Academic, music/drama, state/district residency, alumni affiliation, religious affiliation scholarships available. **Aid applications:** Closing date August 1; priority given to applications received by May 1; applicants notified on a rolling basis; must reply within 10 days.

ADDRESS/TELEPHONE. Mark Becker, Director of Admissions, Vennard College, Box 29, University Park, IA 52595. (515) 673-8391. (800) 338-2407.

Waldorf College
Forest City, Iowa
CB code: 6925

Admissions:	85% of applicants accepted
Based on:	••• School record
	•• Interview
	• Recommendations, test scores
Completion:	80% of freshmen end year in good standing
	90% enter 4-year programs

2-year private junior, liberal arts college, coed, affiliated with Evangelical Lutheran Church in America. Founded in 1903. **Accreditation:** Regional. **Undergraduate enrollment:** 234 men, 213 women full time; 25 men, 27 women part time. **Faculty:** 46 total (35 full time), 6 with doctorates or other terminal degrees. **Location:** Rural campus in small town; 125 miles from Des Moines and Minneapolis-St. Paul. **Calendar:** Semester. **Microcomputers:** 85 located in libraries, computer centers. **Special facilities:** Art gallery.

DEGREES OFFERED. AA. 189 associate degrees awarded in 1992.

UNDERGRADUATE MAJORS. Accounting, agribusiness, Bible studies, biology, business and management, business and office, business data programming, child development/care/guidance, communications, computer and information sciences, data processing, drafting, early childhood education, education, journalism, law enforcement and corrections technologies, legal secretary, liberal/general studies, marketing and distribution, mathematics, medical records technology, medical secretary, music, precision metal work, radio/television broadcasting, recreation and community services technologies, secretarial and related programs, social sciences, special education, telecommunications, visual and performing arts, word processing.

ACADEMIC PROGRAMS. 2-year transfer program, cooperative education, dual enrollment of high school students, honors program, independent study, internships. **Remedial services:** Learning center, preadmission summer program, reduced course load, remedial instruction, special counselor, tutoring. **Placement/credit:** AP, CLEP General and Subject; 8 credit hours maximum for associate degree.

ACADEMIC REQUIREMENTS. Freshmen must earn minimum GPA of 1.5 to continue in good standing. 58% of freshmen return for sophomore year. Students must declare major by end of first year. **Graduation requirements:** 64 hours for associate (12 in major). Most students required to take courses in English, history, humanities, mathematics, philosophy/religion, biological/physical sciences, social sciences.

FRESHMAN ADMISSIONS. Selection criteria: School achievement record and school recommendation. 2.0 high school GPA suggested. Test scores considered. **Test requirements:** SAT or ACT; score report by August 15.

1992 FRESHMAN CLASS PROFILE. 399 men applied, 328 accepted, 171 enrolled; 313 women applied, 278 accepted, 153 enrolled. 26% had high school GPA of 3.0 or higher, 60% between 2.0 and 2.99. **Academic background:** Mid 50% of enrolled freshmen had ACT composite between 19-25. 90% submitted ACT scores. **Characteristics:** 65% from in state, 95% live in college housing, 4% have minority backgrounds, 8% are foreign students. Average age is 18.

FALL-TERM APPLICATIONS. $15 fee. No application fee prior to January 1. No closing date; applicants notified on a rolling basis beginning on or about October 1; must reply within 4 weeks. Interview recommended. Audition recommended for music applicants. Early admission available.

STUDENT LIFE. Housing: Dormitories (men, women, coed). **Activities:** Student government, radio, student newspaper, yearbook, choral groups, concert band, drama, jazz band, music ensembles, musical theater, pep band, Lutheran Youth Encounter, Fellowship of Christian Athletes.

ATHLETICS. NJCAA. **Intercollegiate:** Baseball M, basketball, football M, golf M, softball W, volleyball W, wrestling M. **Intramural:** Badminton, basketball, racquetball, soccer, table tennis, volleyball.

STUDENT SERVICES. Aptitude testing, career counseling, employment service for undergraduates, freshman orientation, health services, personal counseling, placement service for graduates, veterans counselor.

ANNUAL EXPENSES. Tuition and fees: $9,620. **Room and board:** $3,250. **Books and supplies:** $495. **Other expenses:** $940.

FINANCIAL AID. 95% of freshmen, 95% of continuing students receive some form of aid. 82% of grants, all loans, all jobs based on need. 209 enrolled freshmen were judged to have need, all were offered aid. Academic, music/drama, art, athletic, leadership, religious affiliation scholarships available. **Aid applications:** Closing date August 1; priority given to applications received by April 20; applicants notified on a rolling basis beginning on or about March 1; must reply within 2 weeks.

ADDRESS/TELEPHONE. Steve Lovik, Director of Admission, Waldorf College, 106 South Sixth Street, Forest City, IA 50436. (515) 582-8112. Fax: (515) 582-8111.

Wartburg College
Waverly, Iowa — CB code: 6926

Admissions:	87% of applicants accepted
Based on:	••• School record
	•• Interview, recommendations, test scores
	• Activities, essay, special talents
Completion:	95% of freshmen end year in good standing
	66% graduate, 18% of these enter graduate study

4-year private liberal arts college, coed, affiliated with Evangelical Lutheran Church in America. Founded in 1852. **Accreditation:** Regional. **Undergraduate enrollment:** 604 men, 748 women full time; 39 men, 54 women part time. **Faculty:** 149 total (98 full time), 72 with doctorates or other terminal degrees. **Location:** Rural campus in small town; 15 miles from Waterloo-Cedar Falls. **Calendar:** 4-4-1, limited summer session. **Microcomputers:** 200 located in dormitories, libraries, classrooms, computer centers. **Special facilities:** Planetarium, Prairie Preserve, Schield Museum, Institute for Leadership Education. **Additional facts:** Students govern themselves through student senate, residence hall councils, and Student Judicial Board. Off-campus academic internship program for all majors in Denver, CO, and Washington, DC. Intercultural certification program encourages students to study all over the world.

DEGREES OFFERED. BA. 263 bachelor's degrees awarded in 1992. 27% in business and management, 19% teacher education, 7% letters/literature, 8% life sciences, 5% mathematics, 7% parks/recreation, protective services, public affairs, 5% social sciences.

UNDERGRADUATE MAJORS. Accounting, art education, arts management, biology, business administration and management, business and management, business economics, chemistry, chiropractic, clinical laboratory science, communications, computer and information sciences, computer programming, drawing, early childhood education, economics, education, elementary education, English, English education, English literature, finance, foreign languages education, French, German, Greek (classical), history, information sciences and systems, international business management, journalism, junior high education, law enforcement and corrections, leisure services, liberal/general studies, marketing management, marketing research, mathematics, mathematics education, music, music education, music performance, music theory and composition, music therapy, occupational therapy, optometry, pharmacy, philosophy, physical education, physical therapy, physics, political science and government, predentistry, preengineering, premedicine, prepharmacy, preveterinary, psychology, public relations, radio/television broadcasting, reading education, religion, religious education, science education, secondary education, social science education, social sciences, social studies education, social work, sociology, Spanish, speech/communication/theater education, theological studies.

ACADEMIC PROGRAMS. Double major, dual enrollment of high school students, independent study, internships, student-designed major, study abroad, teacher preparation, visiting/exchange student program, New York semester, Washington semester, Spring term consortium (students may enroll at any of 11 member colleges for spring term), Wartburg West urban academic internship experience in Denver, CO. **Remedial services:** Learning center, reduced course load, remedial instruction, special counselor, tutoring, reading and study skills consultant. **Placement/credit:** AP, CLEP Subject, institutional tests; 43 credit hours maximum for bachelor's degree.

ACADEMIC REQUIREMENTS. Freshmen must earn minimum GPA of 1.6 to continue in good standing. 78% of freshmen return for sophomore year. Students must declare major by end of second year. **Graduation requirements:** 128 hours for bachelor's (28 in major). Most students required to take courses in arts/fine arts, English, humanities, mathematics, philosophy/religion, biological/physical sciences, social sciences.

FRESHMAN ADMISSIONS. Selection criteria: Class rank, GPA, courses taken, test scores, recommendations are important. **High school preparation:** 14 units recommended. Recommended units include biological science 3, English 4, foreign language 2, mathematics 3 and social science 2. One unit computer science also recommended. **Test requirements:** SAT or ACT (ACT preferred); score report by August 1. **Additional information:** Students with 18 ACT composite and below or who rank in the lower half of their high school class are reviewed by the admission and scholarship committee for a final decision.

1992 FRESHMAN CLASS PROFILE. 589 men applied, 495 accepted, 223 enrolled; 653 women applied, 580 accepted, 269 enrolled. 81% had high school GPA of 3.0 or higher, 19% between 2.0 and 2.99. 33% were in top tenth and 68% were in top quarter of graduating class. **Academic background:** Mid 50% of enrolled freshmen had SAT-V between 400-540, SAT-M between 490-650; ACT composite between 22-29. 12% submitted SAT scores, 88% submitted ACT scores. **Characteristics:** 74% from in state, 95% live in college housing, 2% have minority backgrounds, 3% are foreign students. Average age is 18.

FALL-TERM APPLICATIONS. $20 fee, may be waived for applicants with need. No closing date; priority given to applications received by March 1; applicants notified on a rolling basis; must reply by May 1 or within 2 weeks if notified thereafter. Interview recommended. Audition recommended for music applicants. Portfolio recommended for art applicants. Essay recommended. Deferred admission available.

STUDENT LIFE. Housing: Dormitories (men, women, coed). **Activities:** Student government, magazine, radio, student newspaper, yearbook, choral groups, concert band, drama, jazz band, music ensembles, musical theater, opera, pep band, symphony orchestra, Castle Singers, touring theater, chamber orchestra, drum corp, religious organizations, Young Democrats, Young Republicans, Black Culture House, Afro-American Society, social service environmental, and leadership organizations. **Additional information:** Students actively assist in residential-life design and food-service planning.

ATHLETICS. NCAA. **Intercollegiate:** Baseball M, basketball, cross-country, football M, golf, soccer, softball W, tennis, track and field, volleyball W, wrestling M. **Intramural:** Badminton, basketball, bowling, golf, racquetball, soccer, softball W, tennis, volleyball, wrestling M.

STUDENT SERVICES. Aptitude testing, career counseling, employment service for undergraduates, freshman orientation, health services, personal counseling, placement service for graduates, special adviser for adult students, veterans counselor, services/facilities for handicapped.

ANNUAL EXPENSES. Tuition and fees: $11,080. **Room and board:** $3,450. **Books and supplies:** $300. **Other expenses:** $520.

FINANCIAL AID. 89% of freshmen, 89% of continuing students receive some form of aid. 55% of grants, 91% of loans, 71% of jobs based on need. 266 enrolled freshmen were judged to have need, all were offered aid. Academic, music/drama, art, state/district residency, leadership, alumni affiliation, religious affiliation, minority scholarships available. **Aid applications:** No closing date; priority given to applications received by March 1; applicants notified on a rolling basis beginning on or about March 1; must reply within 2 weeks.

ADDRESS/TELEPHONE. Dee Katko-Roquet, Director of Admissions, Wartburg College, 222 Ninth Street Northwest, Waverly, IA 50677. (319) 352-8200. (800) 772-2085. Fax: (319) 352-8514.

Western Iowa Tech Community College
Sioux City, Iowa — CB code: 6950

2-year public community college, coed. Founded in 1966. **Accreditation:** Regional. **Undergraduate enrollment:** 2,575 men and women. **Faculty:** 99 total (84 full time), 1 with doctorate or other terminal degree. **Location:** Suburban campus in small city. **Calendar:** 4 12-week semester-term sessions. **Microcomputers:** Located in libraries. **Additional facts:** Most programs require attendance for at least 4 semester terms.

DEGREES OFFERED. AA, AS, AAS. 275 associate degrees awarded in 1992.

UNDERGRADUATE MAJORS. Accounting, automotive technology, business and office, business data processing and related programs, business data programming, diesel engine mechanics, drafting, engineering and engineering-related technologies, graphic arts technology, law enforcement and corrections technologies, liberal/general studies, marketing and distribution, mechanical design technology, nursing, precision metal work, secretarial and related programs.

ACADEMIC PROGRAMS. Independent study, internships. **Remedial services:** Learning center, preadmission summer program, reduced course load, remedial instruction, special counselor, tutoring. **Placement/credit:** CLEP General and Subject, institutional tests.

ACADEMIC REQUIREMENTS. Freshmen must earn minimum GPA of 1.8 to continue in good standing.

FRESHMAN ADMISSIONS. Selection criteria: Open admissions. Selective admissions to nursing, surgical technician, and dental assistant programs. **Test requirements:** ACT required for health services applicants; GATB for dental assistant applicants. Computer Programmer Aptitude Battery for data processing applicants.

1992 FRESHMAN CLASS PROFILE. 1,000 men and women enrolled. **Characteristics:** 90% from in state, 85% commute, 5% have minority backgrounds, 1% are foreign students. Average age is 24.

FALL-TERM APPLICATIONS. No fee. No closing date; applicants notified on a rolling basis. Deferred and early admission available.

STUDENT LIFE. Housing: Apartment housing available. **Activities:** Student government.

ATHLETICS. Intramural: Basketball, bowling, softball, table tennis, volleyball.

STUDENT SERVICES. Aptitude testing, career counseling, employment service for undergraduates, health services, on-campus day care, personal counseling, placement service for graduates, services/facilities for handicapped.

ANNUAL EXPENSES. Tuition and fees (1992-93): $1,365, $1,290 additional for out-of-state students. **Room and board:** $1,275 room only. **Books and supplies:** $425. **Other expenses:** $800.

FINANCIAL AID. 75% of freshmen, 75% of continuing students receive some form of aid. Grants, loans, jobs available. **Aid applications:** No closing date; applicants notified on a rolling basis; must reply within 4 weeks.

ADDRESS/TELEPHONE. Walt J. Brockamp, Admissions Coordinator, Western Iowa Tech Community College, PO Box 265, Sioux City, IA 51102. (712) 274-6400. (800) 352-4649. Fax: (712) 274-6238.

William Penn College

Oskaloosa, Iowa CB code: 6943

Admissions: 86% of applicants accepted
Based on: ••• Test scores
•• Recommendations, school record
• Activities, essay, interview
Completion: 92% of freshmen end year in good standing
45% graduate, 9% of these enter graduate study

4-year private liberal arts college, coed, affiliated with Friends United Meeting. Founded in 1873. **Accreditation:** Regional. **Undergraduate enrollment:** 317 men, 316 women full time; 23 men, 33 women part time. **Faculty:** 65 total (40 full time), 14 with doctorates or other terminal degrees. **Location:** Rural campus in large town; 60 miles from Des Moines, 300 miles from Chicago. **Calendar:** Semester, extensive summer session. **Microcomputers:** Located in libraries, computer centers. **Special facilities:** Mideast art collection. **Additional facts:** Founded by members of Society of Friends (Quakers) committed to quest for spiritual and intellectual growth and maturity.

DEGREES OFFERED. BA. 140 bachelor's degrees awarded in 1992.

UNDERGRADUATE MAJORS. Accounting, agricultural mechanics, art education, biological and physical sciences, biology, business administration and management, business and management, business education, chemistry, communications, computer and information sciences, drafting and design technology, driver and safety education, early childhood education, earth sciences, economics, education, elementary education, engineering and engineering-related technologies, English, English education, environmental science, fine arts, foreign languages education, health education, history, human resources development, humanities and social sciences, industrial arts education, industrial technology, junior high education, law enforcement and corrections, liberal/general studies, management information systems, manufacturing technology, marketing and distributive education, marketing management, mathematics, mathematics education, music, music education, philosophy, physical education, physical sciences, political science and government, predentistry, prelaw, premedicine, prepharmacy, preveterinary, psychology, religion, science education, secondary education, social science education, social sciences, social studies education, sociology, special education, special education for elementary education, speech/communication/theater education, sports management, trade and industrial education, visual and performing arts.

ACADEMIC PROGRAMS. Accelerated program, double major, dual enrollment of high school students, independent study, internships, student-designed major, study abroad, teacher preparation, Washington semester; liberal arts/career combination in health sciences. **Remedial services:** Preadmission summer program, reduced course load, special counselor, tutoring. **Placement/credit:** AP, CLEP General and Subject; 28 credit hours maximum for bachelor's degree.

ACADEMIC REQUIREMENTS. Freshmen must earn minimum GPA of 1.6 to continue in good standing. 65% of freshmen return for sophomore year. Students must declare major by end of second year. **Graduation requirements:** 124 hours for bachelor's (56 in major). Most students required to take courses in arts/fine arts, English, foreign languages, history, humanities, mathematics, philosophy/religion, biological/physical sciences, social sciences.

FRESHMAN ADMISSIONS. Selection criteria: Class rank, test scores, high school recommendation important. Extracurricular activities, alumni relationship, geographical distribution considered. **High school preparation:** 15 units required. Required units include English 4, foreign language 2, mathematics 2, social science 2 and science 2. **Test requirements:** SAT or ACT; score report by August 15.

1992 FRESHMAN CLASS PROFILE. 202 men applied, 168 accepted, 113 enrolled; 150 women applied, 133 accepted, 84 enrolled. **Characteristics:** 77% from in state, 75% live in college housing, 8% have minority backgrounds, 2% are foreign students, 30% join fraternities/sororities. Average age is 19.

FALL-TERM APPLICATIONS. $15 fee. No closing date; applicants notified on a rolling basis; must reply within 3 weeks. Interview recommended for academically marginal applicants. Audition recommended for music applicants. Essay recommended. Deferred and early admission available. EDP-F.

STUDENT LIFE. Housing: Dormitories (men, women, coed). **Activities:** Student government, magazine, radio, student newspaper, yearbook, choral groups, concert band, drama, jazz band, music ensembles, musical theater, pep band, symphony orchestra, fraternities, sororities, Fellowship of Christian Athletes.

ATHLETICS. NCAA. **Intercollegiate:** Baseball M, basketball, cross-country, football M, golf, softball W, tennis, track and field, volleyball W, wrestling M. **Intramural:** Badminton, basketball, bowling, softball, swimming, table tennis, tennis, volleyball, wrestling M.

STUDENT SERVICES. Aptitude testing, career counseling, employment service for undergraduates, freshman orientation, health services, on-campus day care, personal counseling, placement service for graduates, veterans counselor, services/facilities for handicapped.

ANNUAL EXPENSES. Tuition and fees: $10,290. **Room and board:** $3,100. **Books and supplies:** $500. **Other expenses:** $750.

FINANCIAL AID. 98% of freshmen, 98% of continuing students receive some form of aid. 84% of grants, all loans based on need. Academic, music/drama, art, leadership, religious affiliation scholarships available. **Aid applications:** Closing date August 15; priority given to applications received by August 1; applicants notified on or about April 1; must reply within 2 weeks. **Additional information:** Academic scholarships up to $8,000 per year for students who were in top half of graduating class, above 19 on ACT. Auditions required for music scholarships; portfolios recommended for art scholarships.

ADDRESS/TELEPHONE. Eric Otto, Director of Admissions, William Penn College, 201 Trueblood Avenue, Oskaloosa, IA 52577. (515) 673-1012. (800) 779-7366. Fax: (515) 673-1396.

Kansas

Allen County Community College
Iola, Kansas CB code: 6305

2-year public community college, coed. Founded in 1923. **Accreditation:** Regional. **Undergraduate enrollment:** 282 men, 295 women full time; 303 men, 837 women part time. **Faculty:** 190 total (35 full time), 2 with doctorates or other terminal degrees. **Location:** Rural campus in small town; 100 miles from Wichita and Kansas City, Missouri. **Calendar:** Semester. **Microcomputers:** 25 located in computer centers. **Special facilities:** College-operated farm.

DEGREES OFFERED. AA, AS, AAS. 135 associate degrees awarded in 1992. 7% in agriculture, 15% business and management, 5% business/office and marketing/distribution, 12% education, 5% engineering technologies, 6% health sciences, 7% letters/literature, 30% multi/interdisciplinary studies.

UNDERGRADUATE MAJORS. Agribusiness, agricultural business and management, allied health, biology, business administration and management, business and management, business and office, chemistry, child development/care/guidance, computer and information sciences, construction, early childhood education, education, education of the deaf and hearing impaired, electrical and electronics equipment repair, electrical/electronics/communications engineering, electronic technology, elementary education, engineering, English, equestrian science, farm and ranch management/production, finance, fine arts, geriatric aide, health care administration, history, home economics, industrial technology, journalism, law enforcement and corrections, liberal/general studies, library science, manufacturing technology, marketing and distribution, mathematics, mechanical design technology, music, physical sciences, physics, predentistry, preengineering, prelaw, premedicine, prepharmacy, preveterinary, psychology, secondary education, secretarial and related programs, social sciences, sociology, trade and industrial supervision and management.

ACADEMIC PROGRAMS. 2-year transfer program, dual enrollment of high school students, external degree, honors program, independent study, internships, student-designed major. **Remedial services:** Learning center, reduced course load, remedial instruction, special counselor, tutoring, developmental courses in English, mathematics, and reading. **Placement/credit:** AP, CLEP General and Subject, institutional tests; 48 credit hours maximum for associate degree.

ACADEMIC REQUIREMENTS. Freshmen must earn minimum GPA of 1.6 to continue in good standing. 65% of freshmen return for sophomore year. Students must declare major by end of first year. **Graduation requirements:** 64 hours for associate. Most students required to take courses in arts/fine arts, English, history, humanities, mathematics, biological/physical sciences, social sciences.

FRESHMAN ADMISSIONS. Selection criteria: Open admissions. **Test requirements:** SAT or ACT (ACT preferred) for placement and counseling only; score report by August 21.

1992 FRESHMAN CLASS PROFILE. 232 men, 441 women enrolled. 42% had high school GPA of 3.0 or higher, 53% between 2.0 and 2.99. **Characteristics:** 85% from in state, 70% commute, 7% have minority backgrounds. Average age is 23.

FALL-TERM APPLICATIONS. No fee. Closing date September 6; applicants notified on a rolling basis; must reply by registration. Early admission available. ASSET test used for placement in English and mathematics.

STUDENT LIFE. Housing: Dormitories (coed). **Activities:** Student government, student newspaper, yearbook, choral groups, drama, jazz band, music ensembles, musical theater, pep band, Republican club, Democratic club.

ATHLETICS. NJCAA. **Intercollegiate:** Baseball M, basketball, cross-country, golf M, soccer M, softball W, track and field, volleyball W. **Intramural:** Basketball, softball, table tennis, tennis, volleyball.

STUDENT SERVICES. Aptitude testing, career counseling, employment service for undergraduates, freshman orientation, on-campus day care, personal counseling, placement service for graduates, special adviser for adult students, veterans counselor, services/facilities for handicapped.

ANNUAL EXPENSES. Tuition and fees (projected): $1,088, $1,429 additional for out-of-state students. **Room and board:** $2,600. **Books and supplies:** $200. **Other expenses:** $1,620.

FINANCIAL AID. 48% of freshmen, 40% of continuing students receive some form of aid. 74% of grants, 89% of loans, 27% of jobs based on need. Academic, music/drama, athletic scholarships available. **Aid applications:** No closing date; applicants notified on a rolling basis beginning on or about June 1; must reply within 2 weeks. **Additional information:** Scholarships for horse judging, livestock judging, cheerleading/pom-pom, choir, drama, and journalism.

ADDRESS/TELEPHONE. Mike Schlies, Dean of Student Services, Allen County Community College, 1801 North Cottonwood, Iola, KS 66749. (316) 365-5116. Fax: (316) 365-3284.

Baker University
Baldwin City, Kansas CB code: 6031

4-year private liberal arts college, coed, affiliated with United Methodist Church. Founded in 1858. **Accreditation:** Regional. **Undergraduate enrollment:** 725 men, 700 women full time; 3 men, 7 women part time. **Graduate enrollment:** 219 men, 196 women full time. **Faculty:** 134 total (64 full time). **Location:** Rural campus in small town; 14 miles from Lawrence, 45 miles from Kansas City, MO. **Calendar:** 4-1-4, limited summer session. **Microcomputers:** 79 located in dormitories, libraries, classrooms, computer centers, campus-wide network. **Special facilities:** Quayle Rare Bible Collection.

DEGREES OFFERED. BA, BS, MS, MBA. 152 bachelor's degrees awarded in 1992. 41% in business and management, 9% communications, 9% teacher education, 5% languages, 9% life sciences, 6% psychology. Graduate degrees offered in 2 major fields of study.

UNDERGRADUATE MAJORS. Accounting, art education, biology, business and management, business economics, chemistry, communications, computer and information sciences, dramatic arts, economics, education, elementary education, English, English education, English literature, environmental science, fashion merchandising, fine arts, foreign languages education, forestry and related sciences, French, German, history, international business management, journalism, mathematics, mathematics education, music, music education, music performance, music therapy, nursing, philosophy, physical education, physics, political science and government, practical nursing, predentistry, preengineering, prelaw, premedicine, prepharmacy, preveterinary, psychology, religion, science education, secondary education, social sciences, social studies education, sociology, Spanish, speech, speech/communication/theater education.

ACADEMIC PROGRAMS. Accelerated program, double major, dual enrollment of high school students, honors program, independent study, internships, study abroad, teacher preparation, cross-registration; liberal arts/career combination in engineering, forestry. **Remedial services:** Learning center, reduced course load, tutoring. **ROTC:** Air Force, Army. **Placement/credit:** AP, CLEP General; 15 credit hours maximum for bachelor's degree.

ACADEMIC REQUIREMENTS. Freshmen must earn minimum GPA of 2.0 to continue in good standing. 84% of freshmen return for sophomore year. Students must declare major by end of second year. **Graduation requirements:** 132 hours for bachelor's (29 in major). Most students required to take courses in arts/fine arts, computer science, English, history, mathematics, philosophy/religion, biological/physical sciences, social sciences. **Postgraduate studies:** 2% enter law school, 3% enter medical school, 9% enter MBA programs, 21% enter other graduate study.

FRESHMAN ADMISSIONS. Selection criteria: Minimum 2.5 GPA, 19 ACT composite, counselor recommendation, class rank in top half. Recommended units include English 4, foreign language 2, mathematics 2, social science 2 and science 2. **Test requirements:** SAT or ACT; score report by August 15.

1992 FRESHMAN CLASS PROFILE. 121 men, 124 women enrolled. 77% had high school GPA of 3.0 or higher, 23% between 2.0 and 2.99. 20% were in top tenth and 49% were in top quarter of graduating class. **Academic background:** Mid 50% of enrolled freshmen had ACT composite between 20-27. 96% submitted ACT scores. **Characteristics:** 65% from in state, 97% live in college housing, 18% have minority backgrounds, 3% are foreign students, 69% join fraternities/sororities. Average age is 18.

FALL-TERM APPLICATIONS. $20 fee, may be waived for applicants with need. No closing date; applicants notified on a rolling basis. Interview recommended. Audition recommended for music, theater applicants. Portfolio recommended for art applicants. Essay recommended. Deferred and early admission available.

STUDENT LIFE. Housing: Dormitories (men, women, coed); fraternity, sorority housing available. **Activities:** Student government, magazine, radio, student newspaper, television, yearbook, choral groups, concert band, drama, jazz band, marching band, music ensembles, musical theater, pep band, fraternities, sororities, religious life council.

ATHLETICS. NAIA. **Intercollegiate:** Baseball M, basketball, cross-country, football M, golf M, soccer, softball W, tennis, track and field, volleyball W. **Intramural:** Archery, badminton, basketball, golf, racquetball, soccer, softball, swimming, table tennis, tennis, volleyball.

STUDENT SERVICES. Career counseling, employment service for undergraduates, freshman orientation, health services, personal counseling, placement service for graduates, special adviser for adult students, services/facilities for handicapped.

ANNUAL EXPENSES. Tuition and fees: $8,234. **Room and board:** $4,050. **Books and supplies:** $586. **Other expenses:** $1,350.

FINANCIAL AID. 92% of freshmen, 92% of continuing students receive some form of aid. 55% of grants, 79% of loans, 68% of jobs based on need. 149 enrolled freshmen were judged to have need, all were offered aid. Academic, music/drama, art, athletic, leadership, religious affiliation, minority scholarships available. **Aid applications:** No closing date; priority given to applications received by March 1; applicants notified on a rolling basis beginning on or about March 15; must reply within 3 weeks. **Additional information:** Special loan program available to returning students filing family financial statements and meeting grade criteria. Loans advanced annually become grants upon graduation and do not have to be repaid.

ADDRESS/TELEPHONE. John D. Haynes, Director of Admissions, Baker University, PO P.O. Box 65, Baldwin City, KS 66006. (913) 594-6451. (800) 873-4282. Fax: (913) 594-6721.

Barclay College
Haviland, Kansas CB code: 6228

Admissions: 75% of applicants accepted
Based on: ••• Recommendations
•• Religious affiliation/commitment
• Interview, school record
Completion: 95% of freshmen end year in good standing
40% graduate, 3% of these enter graduate study

4-year private Bible college, coed, affiliated with Evangelical Friends Alliance and Friends United Meeting. Founded in 1917. **Undergraduate enrollment:** 35 men, 43 women full time; 5 men, 15 women part time. **Faculty:** 19 total (9 full time), 1 with doctorate or other terminal degree. **Location:** Rural campus in rural community; 100 miles from Wichita, 55 miles from Dodge City. **Calendar:** Semester, limited summer session. **Microcomputers:** 6 located in libraries.

DEGREES OFFERED. BA, BS. 10 bachelor's degrees awarded in 1992. 20% in business and management, 20% teacher education, 60% philosophy, religion, theology.

UNDERGRADUATE MAJORS. Bible studies, business administration and management, Christian ministry, elementary education, missionary studies, music, pastoral ministry, religious education, religious music, theological studies.

ACADEMIC PROGRAMS. Double major, independent study, internships, study abroad, teacher preparation, cross-registration, cooperative classes with Pratt Community College. **Remedial services:** Remedial instruction, tutoring. **Placement/credit:** CLEP General and Subject, institutional tests; 30 credit hours maximum for bachelor's degree.

ACADEMIC REQUIREMENTS. Freshmen must earn minimum GPA of 1.75 to continue in good standing. 80% of freshmen return for sophomore year. Students must declare major by end of second year. **Graduation requirements:** 128 hours for bachelor's (34 in major). Most students required to take courses in English, history, humanities, mathematics, philosophy/religion, biological/physical sciences, social sciences. **Additional information:** Each student has Bible major in addition to individually chosen major. Teaching certification available through cross-registration.

FRESHMAN ADMISSIONS. Selection criteria: Personal references and commitment to Christian vocation important. Interview and previous academic record also considered. **Test requirements:** SAT or ACT (ACT preferred) for placement and counseling only; score report by July 30.

1992 FRESHMAN CLASS PROFILE. 78% had high school GPA of 3.0 or higher, 22% between 2.0 and 2.99. **Academic background:** Mid 50% of enrolled freshmen had ACT composite between 10-13. 67% submitted ACT scores. **Characteristics:** 55% from in state, 100% live in college housing. Average age is 18.

FALL-TERM APPLICATIONS. $10 fee. No closing date; applicants notified on a rolling basis. Interview recommended. Audition recommended for music applicants. Early admission available.

STUDENT LIFE. Housing: Dormitories (men, women). **Activities:** Student government, student newspaper, yearbook, choral groups, drama, music ensembles, Christian and social work in prisons and in state institutions for mentally disturbed. **Additional information:** Religious observance required.

ATHLETICS. Intercollegiate: Basketball, golf M, soccer M, tennis M, volleyball W. **Intramural:** Softball, volleyball.

STUDENT SERVICES. Aptitude testing, employment service for undergraduates, health services, personal counseling, placement service for graduates.

ANNUAL EXPENSES. Tuition and fees (1992-93): $6,225. **Room and board:** $2,650. **Books and supplies:** $300. **Other expenses:** $600.

FINANCIAL AID. 99% of freshmen, 100% of continuing students receive some form of aid. 26% of grants, 74% of loans, 14% of jobs based on need. 10 enrolled freshmen were judged to have need, all were offered aid. Academic, music/drama, state/district residency, leadership, alumni affiliation scholarships available. **Aid applications:** No closing date; priority given to applications received by May 15; applicants notified on a rolling basis beginning on or about July 15.

ADDRESS/TELEPHONE. Lonny Choate, Director of Admissions, Barclay College, PO Box 288, Haviland, KS 67059. (316) 862-5252. Fax: (316) 862-5403.

Barton County Community College
Great Bend, Kansas CB code: 0784

2-year public community college, coed. Founded in 1965. **Accreditation:** Regional. **Undergraduate enrollment:** 479 men, 766 women full time; 2,307 men, 2,965 women part time. **Faculty:** 287 total (66 full time), 14 with doctorates or other terminal degrees. **Location:** Rural campus in large town; 125 miles from Wichita. **Calendar:** Semester, limited summer session. **Microcomputers:** 70 located in libraries, classrooms, computer centers. **Special facilities:** Art gallery, planetarium.

DEGREES OFFERED. AA, AS, AAS. 395 associate degrees awarded in 1992. 11% in business and management, 9% education, 20% health sciences, 28% multi/interdisciplinary studies, 5% parks/recreation, protective services, public affairs.

UNDERGRADUATE MAJORS. Accounting, agricultural production, agricultural sciences, aircraft mechanics, animal sciences, automotive technology, biology, business and management, business data processing and related programs, child development/care/guidance, communications, computer technology, diesel engine mechanics, dietetic aide/assistant, drafting, education, emergency medical technologies, engineering, finance, fire control and safety technology, foreign languages (multiple emphasis), geriatric aide, home economics, institutional/home management/supporting programs, law enforcement and corrections technologies, legal secretary, liberal/general studies, library science, machine tool operation/machine shop, mathematics, medical assistant, medical laboratory technologies, mining and petroleum technologies, music, nursing, personal services, philosophy, physical sciences, practical nursing, predentistry, prelaw, premedicine, prepharmacy, preveterinary, psychology, religion, retailing, secretarial and related programs, social sciences, speech, trade and industrial supervision and management, visual and performing arts, word processing.

ACADEMIC PROGRAMS. 2-year transfer program, cooperative education, independent study, internships, telecourses. **Remedial services:** Learning center, remedial instruction, tutoring. **Placement/credit:** AP, CLEP General and Subject, institutional tests.

ACADEMIC REQUIREMENTS. Freshmen must earn minimum GPA of 1.5 to continue in good standing. 67% of freshmen return for sophomore year. Students must declare major by end of first year. **Graduation requirements:** 64 hours for associate (33 in major). Most students required to take courses in English, humanities, mathematics, biological/physical sciences, social sciences.

FRESHMAN ADMISSIONS. Selection criteria: Open admissions.

1992 FRESHMAN CLASS PROFILE. 861 men, 1,033 women enrolled. 32% had high school GPA of 3.0 or higher, 52% between 2.0 and 2.99. **Characteristics:** 99% from in state, 85% commute, 16% have minority backgrounds. Average age is 32.

FALL-TERM APPLICATIONS. No fee. No closing date; applicants notified on a rolling basis; must reply by registration. Interview required for nursing applicants. Early admission available.

STUDENT LIFE. Housing: Dormitories (men, women, coed). **Activities:** Student government, magazine, radio, student newspaper, television, yearbook, choral groups, concert band, drama, jazz band, music ensembles, musical theater, pep band, Newman Club, Fellowship of Christian Athletes.

ATHLETICS. NJCAA. **Intercollegiate:** Baseball M, basketball, cross-country, golf M, softball W, tennis W, track and field, volleyball W. **Intramural:** Basketball, bowling, golf, horseback riding, skin diving, softball, swimming, table tennis, tennis, track and field, volleyball.

STUDENT SERVICES. Aptitude testing, career counseling, employment service for undergraduates, freshman orientation, health services, on-campus day care, personal counseling, placement service for graduates, veterans counselor, services/facilities for handicapped.

ANNUAL EXPENSES. Tuition and fees (projected): $896, $1,456 additional for out-of-state students. **Room and board:** $2,000. **Books and supplies:** $500. **Other expenses:** $1,000.

FINANCIAL AID. 40% of freshmen, 28% of continuing students receive some form of aid. 82% of grants, 84% of loans, 20% of jobs based on need. Academic, music/drama, art, athletic, state/district residency, leadership, alumni affiliation, religious affiliation, minority scholarships available. **Aid applications:** No closing date; priority given to applications received by March 1; applicants notified on a rolling basis beginning on or about April 1.

ADDRESS/TELEPHONE. Lori Crowther, Coordinator of Admissions, Barton County Community College, Route 3, Great Bend, KS 67530-9283. (316) 792-2701. Fax: (316) 792-3238.

Benedictine College
Atchison, Kansas CB code: 6056

Admissions: 78% of applicants accepted
Based on: ••• School record, test scores
• Activities, essay, interview, recommendations, special talents
Completion: 93% of freshmen end year in good standing
44% graduate, 20% of these enter graduate study

4-year private liberal arts college, coed, affiliated with Roman Catholic Church. Founded in 1858. **Accreditation:** Regional. **Undergraduate enrollment:** 388 men, 314 women full time; 93 men, 408 women part time. **Graduate enrollment:** 9 men, 13 women part time. **Faculty:** 68 total (45 full time), 36 with doctorates or other terminal degrees. **Location:** Rural campus in large town; 45 miles from Kansas City. **Calendar:** Semester, limited summer session. **Microcomputers:** 60 located in dormitories, libraries, classrooms, computer centers. **Additional facts:** Evening degree program offered in Salina, Kansas.

DEGREES OFFERED. AA, BA, MA. 1 associate degree awarded in 1992. 100% in computer sciences. 144 bachelor's degrees awarded. 28% in business and management, 5% communications, 19% teacher education, 10% letters/literature, 6% life sciences, 5% physical sciences, 18% social sciences. Graduate degrees offered in 1 major field of study.

UNDERGRADUATE MAJORS. Associate: Accounting, business administration and management, health care administration, information sciences and systems. **Bachelor's:** Accounting, astronomy, biological and physical sciences, biology, business administration and management, chemistry, classics, clinical pastoral care, computer and information sciences, dramatic arts, economics, elementary education, English, English education, foreign languages (multiple emphasis), foreign languages education, French, health care administration, health education, history, humanities, humanities and social sciences, information sciences and systems, journalism, junior high education, Latin, liberal/general studies, marketing and distribution, mathematics, mathematics education, music, music education, philosophy, physical education, physics, political science and government, prelaw, psychology, religion, science education, social science education, social sciences, social work, sociology, Spanish, special education, speech/communication/theater education, youth ministry.

ACADEMIC PROGRAMS. Accelerated program, double major, dual enrollment of high school students, honors program, independent study, internships, student-designed major, study abroad, teacher preparation, visiting/exchange student program, cross-registration; liberal arts/career combination in engineering, health sciences. **Remedial services:** Reduced course load, remedial instruction, special counselor, tutoring. **ROTC:** Army. **Placement/credit:** AP, CLEP General and Subject, institutional tests; 30 credit hours maximum for bachelor's degree.

ACADEMIC REQUIREMENTS. Freshmen must earn minimum GPA of 1.8 to continue in good standing. Students must complete 24 credit hours per year to maintain satisfactory academic progress. 69% of freshmen return for sophomore year. Students must declare major by end of second year. **Graduation requirements:** 65 hours for associate, 124 hours for bachelor's (30 in major). Most students required to take courses in arts/fine arts, English, foreign languages, history, humanities, mathematics, philosophy/religion, biological/physical sciences, social sciences. **Postgraduate studies:** 2% enter law school, 3% enter medical school, 1% enter MBA programs, 14% enter other graduate study.

FRESHMAN ADMISSIONS. Selection criteria: GPA, test scores, class rank, counselor recommendation considered. **High school preparation:** 16 units required. Required and recommended units include English 4, foreign language 2-4, mathematics 3-4, social science 2 and science 2-4. 1 unit of history. **Test requirements:** SAT or ACT (ACT preferred); score report by August 15. Prueba de Aptitud Academica for Spanish speaking applicants.

1992 FRESHMAN CLASS PROFILE. 424 men applied, 325 accepted, 146 enrolled; 222 women applied, 180 accepted, 87 enrolled. 60% had high school GPA of 3.0 or higher, 38% between 2.0 and 2.99. 15% were in top tenth and 39% were in top quarter of graduating class. **Academic background:** Mid 50% of enrolled freshmen had SAT-V between 430-540, SAT-M between 400-470; ACT composite between 19-27. 34% submitted SAT scores, 83% submitted ACT scores. **Characteristics:** 30% from in state, 96% live in college housing, 11% have minority backgrounds, 1% are foreign students. Average age is 18.

FALL-TERM APPLICATIONS. $25 fee, may be waived for applicants with need. Closing date August 1; priority given to applications received by May 1; applicants notified on a rolling basis; must reply by May 1 or within 4 weeks if notified thereafter. Audition required for music applicants. Interview recommended for academically weak applicants. CRDA. Deferred and early admission available.

STUDENT LIFE. Housing: Dormitories (men, women). **Activities:** Student government, magazine, student newspaper, yearbook, choral groups, concert band, dance, drama, jazz band, music ensembles, musical theater, opera, pep band, symphony orchestra, Ravens Respect Life, Young Democrats, Young Republicans, Knights of Columbus, Hunger Coalition, AASU, Greenwich Club, Environmental Club.

ATHLETICS. NAIA. **Intercollegiate:** Baseball M, basketball, football M, golf M, soccer, softball W, track and field, volleyball W. **Intramural:** Baseball M, basketball, field hockey W, handball, racquetball, soccer, softball, table tennis, tennis, volleyball.

STUDENT SERVICES. Aptitude testing, career counseling, employment service for undergraduates, freshman orientation, health services, personal counseling, placement service for graduates, veterans counselor, services/facilities for handicapped.

ANNUAL EXPENSES. Tuition and fees (1992-93): $8,480. **Room and board:** $3,810. **Books and supplies:** $500. **Other expenses:** $1,200.

FINANCIAL AID. 90% of freshmen, 92% of continuing students receive some form of aid. 41% of grants, 87% of loans, 67% of jobs based on need. Academic, music/drama, athletic, leadership scholarships available. **Aid applications:** No closing date; priority given to applications received by April 15; applicants notified on a rolling basis beginning on or about February 1; must reply by May 1 or within 2 weeks if notified thereafter.

ADDRESS/TELEPHONE. James Hoffman, Dean of Enrollment Management, Benedictine College, 1020 North Second Street, Atchison, KS 66002-1499. (913) 367-5340 ext. 2475. Fax: (913) 367-6102.

Bethany College
Lindsborg, Kansas

CB code: 6034

Admissions: 72% of applicants accepted
Based on:
••• School record, test scores
•• Interview
• Activities, essay, recommendations
Completion: 85% of freshmen end year in good standing
42% graduate, 21% of these enter graduate study

4-year private liberal arts college, coed, affiliated with Evangelical Lutheran Church in America. Founded in 1881. **Accreditation:** Regional. **Undergraduate enrollment:** 365 men, 280 women full time; 14 men, 35 women part time. **Faculty:** 71 total (54 full time), 33 with doctorates or other terminal degrees. **Location:** Rural campus in small town; 20 miles from Salina, 70 miles from Wichita. **Calendar:** 4-1-4, limited summer session. **Microcomputers:** 58 located in libraries, classrooms, computer centers. **Special facilities:** Art gallery.

DEGREES OFFERED. BA. 108 bachelor's degrees awarded in 1992. 18% in business and management, 5% computer sciences, 25% teacher education, 5% life sciences, 11% mathematics, 7% psychology, 16% social sciences, 6% visual and performing arts.

UNDERGRADUATE MAJORS. Accounting, art education, biology, business administration and management, business economics, business education, chemistry, computer and information sciences, criminal justice studies, education of the emotionally handicapped, education of the mentally handicapped, elementary education, English, English education, fine arts, health education, history, information sciences and systems, junior high education, mathematics, mathematics education, medical laboratory technologies, music, music education, philosophy, physical education, political science and government, predentistry, prelaw, premedicine, prepharmacy, preveterinary, psychology, recreation and community services technologies, religion, science education, secondary education, social science education, social studies education, social work, sociology, special education, specific learning disabilities, sports medicine.

ACADEMIC PROGRAMS. Double major, dual enrollment of high school students, independent study, internships, student-designed major, study abroad, teacher preparation, Washington semester, cross-registration, special education program with Associated Colleges of Central Kansas, various engineering programs with Witchita State University; liberal arts/career combination in engineering. **Remedial services:** Learning center, reduced course load, special counselor, tutoring. **Placement/credit:** AP, CLEP General and Subject, IB, institutional tests; 32 credit hours maximum for bachelor's degree.

ACADEMIC REQUIREMENTS. Freshmen must earn minimum GPA of 1.7 to continue in good standing. 62% of freshmen return for sophomore year. Students must declare major by end of second year. **Graduation requirements:** 128 hours for bachelor's (55 in major). Most students required to take courses in arts/fine arts, English, history, humanities, mathematics, philosophy/religion, biological/physical sciences, social sciences. **Postgraduate studies:** 2% enter law school, 3% enter medical school, 3% enter MBA programs, 13% enter other graduate study.

FRESHMAN ADMISSIONS. Selection criteria: Courses taken, high school GPA, class rank, test scores, references, interviews considered. Recommended units include biological science 2, English 4, foreign language 2, mathematics 3, physical science 1 and social science 3. **Test requirements:** SAT or ACT (ACT preferred); score report by July 1.

1992 FRESHMAN CLASS PROFILE. 584 men applied, 394 accepted, 124 enrolled; 270 women applied, 217 accepted, 74 enrolled. 64% had high school GPA of 3.0 or higher, 35% between 2.0 and 2.99. 12% were in top tenth and 31% were in top quarter of graduating class. **Academic background:** Mid 50% of enrolled freshmen had ACT composite between 19-25. 95% submitted ACT scores. **Characteristics:** 51% from in state, 90% live in college housing, 14% have minority backgrounds, 2% are foreign students, 10% join fraternities/sororities. Average age is 18.

FALL-TERM APPLICATIONS. $10 fee. No closing date; applicants notified on a rolling basis. Audition required for music, theater applicants. Portfolio required for art applicants. Interview recommended for borderline applicants. Essay recommended. Deferred admission available.

STUDENT LIFE. Housing: Dormitories (men, women, coed); apartment housing available. **Activities:** Student government, student newspaper, yearbook, choral groups, concert band, drama, jazz band, music ensembles, musical theater, pep band, symphony orchestra, fraternities, sororities, SOAR (Students Organized For Active Response).

ATHLETICS. NAIA. **Intercollegiate:** Baseball M, basketball, cross-country, football M, golf, soccer M, softball W, tennis, track and field, volleyball W. **Intramural:** Archery, badminton, basketball, bowling, cross-country, football M, golf, handball, racquetball, soccer, softball, swimming, table tennis, tennis, track and field, volleyball.

STUDENT SERVICES. Career counseling, employment service for undergraduates, freshman orientation, health services, personal counseling, placement service for graduates, multicultural student adviser, services/facilities for handicapped.

ANNUAL EXPENSES. Tuition and fees: $8,105. **Room and board:** $3,225. **Books and supplies:** $550. **Other expenses:** $1,092.

FINANCIAL AID. 97% of freshmen, 96% of continuing students receive some form of aid. 52% of grants, 94% of loans, 40% of jobs based on need. 162 enrolled freshmen were judged to have need, all were offered aid. Academic, music/drama, art, athletic, leadership scholarships available. **Aid applications:** No closing date; priority given to applications received by March 15; applicants notified on a rolling basis beginning on or about March 15; must reply within 2 weeks.

ADDRESS/TELEPHONE. Louise Cummings Simmons, Dean of Admissions and Financial Aid, Bethany College, 421 North First Street, Lindsborg, KS 67456-1897. (913) 227-3311. (800) 826-2281. Fax: (913) 227-2860.

Bethel College
North Newton, Kansas CB code: 6037

Admissions:	96% of applicants accepted
Based on:	••• School record, test scores
	•• Interview, recommendations
	• Activities, essay, religious affiliation/commitment, special talents
Completion:	90% of freshmen end year in good standing
	15% enter graduate study

4-year private liberal arts college, coed, affiliated with General Conference, Mennonite Church. Founded in 1887. **Accreditation:** Regional. **Undergraduate enrollment:** 239 men, 282 women full time; 28 men, 76 women part time. **Faculty:** 61 total (43 full time), 33 with doctorates or other terminal degrees. **Location:** Suburban campus in large town; 25 miles from Wichita. **Calendar:** 4-1-4, limited summer session. **Microcomputers:** 25 located in dormitories, classrooms, computer centers. **Special facilities:** Natural history museum, 80-acre natural history field laboratory, Kansas Institute for Peace and Conflict Resolution. **Additional facts:** Anabaptist-Mennonite tradition provides base for strong interest in peace and social concerns.

DEGREES OFFERED. BA, BS. 65 bachelor's degrees awarded in 1992. 5% in area and ethnic studies, 11% business and management, 20% education, 11% health sciences, 7% languages, 6% mathematics, 6% physical sciences, 5% psychology, 14% social sciences, 6% visual and performing arts.

UNDERGRADUATE MAJORS. Accounting, biological and physical sciences, biology, business administration and management, chemistry, communications, dramatic arts, economics, elementary education, English, environmental science, fine arts, German, history, home economics, humanities and social sciences, international development, international studies, liberal/general studies, mathematics, music, nursing, peace studies, philosophy, physics, predentistry, prelaw, premedicine, preveterinary, psychology, recreation and community services technologies, religion, social sciences, social work, speech, theological studies, visual and performing arts.

ACADEMIC PROGRAMS. Double major, dual enrollment of high school students, external degree, honors program, independent study, internships, student-designed major, study abroad, teacher preparation, visiting/exchange student program, cross-registration; liberal arts/career combination in engineering. **Remedial services:** Learning center, preadmission summer program, remedial instruction, special counselor, tutoring. **Placement/credit:** AP, CLEP General and Subject, institutional tests; 15 credit hours maximum for bachelor's degree.

ACADEMIC REQUIREMENTS. Freshmen must earn minimum GPA of 2.0 to continue in good standing. 67% of freshmen return for sophomore year. Students must declare major by end of second year. **Graduation requirements:** 62 hours for associate (30 in major), 124 hours for bachelor's (40 in major). Most students required to take courses in arts/fine arts, computer science, English, history, humanities, mathematics, philosophy/religion, biological/physical sciences, social sciences. **Postgraduate studies:** 1% enter law school, 3% enter medical school, 1% enter MBA programs, 10% enter other graduate study.

FRESHMAN ADMISSIONS. Selection criteria: Rank in top third of class, SAT combined score of 770 or ACT composite score of 19 important. Letters of recommendation also considered. **High school preparation:** 15 units recommended. Recommended units include biological science 1, English 4, foreign language 2, mathematics 3, physical science 2 and social science 2. **Test requirements:** SAT or ACT; score report by August 15.

1992 FRESHMAN CLASS PROFILE. 222 men applied, 215 accepted, 50 enrolled; 162 women applied, 152 accepted, 56 enrolled. 74% had high school GPA of 3.0 or higher, 25% between 2.0 and 2.99. 23% were in top tenth and 46% were in top quarter of graduating class. **Academic background:** Mid 50% of enrolled freshmen had ACT composite between 19-26. 100% submitted ACT scores. **Characteristics:** 64% from in state, 90% live in college housing, 6% have minority backgrounds, 3% are foreign students. Average age is 19.

FALL-TERM APPLICATIONS. No fee. Closing date August 15; applicants notified on a rolling basis. Essay required for academically weak applicants. Interview recommended for those applying for scholarships applicants. Audition recommended for fine arts, forensics, drama, music, athletics applicants. Deferred and early admission available.

STUDENT LIFE. Housing: Dormitories (men, women, coed); apartment housing available. Limited on-campus housing in addition to 3 dormitories available. **Activities:** Student government, film, radio, student newspaper, yearbook, forensics, choral groups, concert band, dance, drama, jazz band, music ensembles, musical theater, opera, pep band, symphony orchestra, Student Community Action Network for voluntary services, Peace Club, Bethel Christian Fellowship, Circle-K, Service Corps-Disaster Response, Fellowship of Christian Athletes. **Additional information:** Chapel services voluntary. 2 weekly convocations required and credited as part of general education.

ATHLETICS. NAIA. **Intercollegiate:** Basketball, football M, soccer M, tennis, track and field, volleyball W. **Intramural:** Badminton, basketball, racquetball, softball, table tennis, tennis, volleyball.

STUDENT SERVICES. Career counseling, employment service for undergraduates, freshman orientation, health services, personal counseling, services/facilities for handicapped.

ANNUAL EXPENSES. Tuition and fees (1992-93): $7,980. **Room and board:** $3,000. **Books and supplies:** $450. **Other expenses:** $900.

FINANCIAL AID. 57% of freshmen, 97% of continuing students receive some form of aid. 53% of grants, 98% of loans, 46% of jobs based on need. 60 enrolled freshmen were judged to have need, all were offered aid. Academic, music/drama, art, athletic, leadership, religious affiliation scholarships available. **Aid applications:** No closing date; priority given to applications received by January 1; applicants notified on a rolling basis beginning on or about April 1; must reply within 2 weeks. **Additional information:** Aid to farmers who have been foreclosed available.

ADDRESS/TELEPHONE. J. Michael Lamb, Director of Admissions, Bethel College, 300 East 27th Street, North Newton, KS 67117-9899. (316) 283-2500 ext. 230. (800) 522-1887. Fax: (316) 283-5284.

Brown Mackie College
Salina, Kansas CB code: 3366

2-year proprietary business, junior college, coed. **Accreditation:** Regional. **Undergraduate enrollment:** 79 men, 188 women full time. **Faculty:** 26 total (12 full time), 4 with doctorates or other terminal degrees. **Location:** Urban campus in large town; 90 miles from Wichita, 108 miles from Topeka. **Calendar:** 6 and 12 wee modules, using quarter credit hours. **Microcomputers:** 38 located in computer centers. **Additional facts:** Branch campus in Kansas City.

DEGREES OFFERED. AAS. 47 associate degrees awarded in 1992. 70% in business and management, 19% business/office and marketing/distribution, 11% law.

UNDERGRADUATE MAJORS. Accounting, administrative assistant, business administration and management, court reporting, legal assistant/paralegal, marketing and distribution, marketing management.

ACADEMIC PROGRAMS. Double major, internships. **Remedial services:** Learning center, remedial instruction, tutoring. **Placement/credit:** Institutional tests.

ACADEMIC REQUIREMENTS. Freshmen must earn minimum GPA of 1.0 for 4 to 12 attempted credit hours, 1.2 for 13 to 22 attempted credit hours. Students must declare major on application. **Graduation requirements:** 96 hours for associate (96 in major). Most students required to take courses in English, history, mathematics, social sciences.

FRESHMAN ADMISSIONS. Selection criteria: Open admissions.

1992 FRESHMAN CLASS PROFILE. Characteristics: 100% commute.

FALL-TERM APPLICATIONS. No fee. No closing date; applicants notified on a rolling basis; must reply by registration. Interview required.

STUDENT LIFE. Activities: Student government, student newspaper.

ATHLETICS. NJCAA. **Intercollegiate:** Baseball M, basketball, softball W, volleyball W. **Intramural:** Softball, volleyball.

STUDENT SERVICES. Career counseling, employment service for undergraduates, freshman orientation, placement service for graduates, services/facilities for handicapped.

ANNUAL EXPENSES. Tuition and fees: $6,870. **Books and supplies:** $700. **Other expenses:** $1,008.

FINANCIAL AID. 98% of freshmen, 98% of continuing students receive some form of aid. 99% of grants, 60% of loans, all jobs based on need. 530 enrolled freshmen were judged to have need, all were offered aid. Academic, athletic scholarships available. **Aid applications:** No closing date; applicants notified on a rolling basis.

ADDRESS/TELEPHONE. Larry D. Schafer, Director of Admissions, Brown Mackie College, 126 South Santa Fe, Salina, KS 67402-1787. (913) 825-5422. (800) 365-0433.

Butler County Community College
Eldorado, Kansas CB code: 6191

2-year public community college, coed. Founded in 1927. **Accreditation:** Regional. **Undergraduate enrollment:** 947 men, 1,000 women full time; 1,737 men, 2,943 women part time. **Faculty:** 548 total (98 full time), 8 with doctorates or other terminal degrees. **Location:** Rural campus in large town; 25 miles from Wichita. **Calendar:** Semester, extensive summer session. Saturday and extensive evening/early morning classes. **Microcomputers:** 65 located in libraries, classrooms, computer centers. **Additional facts:** Off-campus sites at Andover, McConnell, Sedgwick, and Augusta.

DEGREES OFFERED. AA, AS, AAS. 425 associate degrees awarded in 1992. 20% in business and management, 22% health sciences, 28% multi/interdisciplinary studies, 6% trade and industry.

UNDERGRADUATE MAJORS. Agribusiness, agricultural business and management, agricultural production, agricultural sciences, automotive mechanics, automotive technology, behavioral sciences, biology, business administration and management, business and management, business and office, business computer/console/peripheral equipment operation, business data entry equipment operation, business data processing and related programs, business data programming, business education, ceramics, chemistry, child development/care/guidance, data processing, drafting, drafting and design technology, dramatic arts, drawing, early childhood education, education, electrical and electronics equipment repair, electrical technology, electronic technology, engineering, engineering and engineering-related technologies, English, fire control and safety technology, graphic arts technology, history, hotel/motel and restaurant management, humanities and social sciences, industrial technology, journalism, law enforcement and corrections technologies, legal secretary, liberal/general studies, marketing and distribution, marketing management, mathematics, mechanical design technology, medical secretary, music, nursing, nursing education, painting, photographic technology, physical sciences, physics, political science and government, practical nursing, predentistry, prelaw, premedicine, prepharmacy, preveterinary, psychology, public affairs, real estate, recreation and community services technologies, science technologies, secretarial and related programs, small business management and ownership, social sciences, sociology, trade and industrial education, welding technology, zoology.

ACADEMIC PROGRAMS. 2-year transfer program, cooperative education, dual enrollment of high school students, honors program, independent study, telecourses. **Remedial services:** Learning center, reduced course load, remedial instruction, special counselor, tutoring. **Placement/credit:** CLEP General and Subject, institutional tests; 30 credit hours maximum for associate degree.

ACADEMIC REQUIREMENTS. Freshmen must earn minimum GPA of 1.5 to continue in good standing. 60% of freshmen return for sophomore year. Students must declare major on application. **Graduation requirements:** 62 hours for associate (24 in major). Most students required to take courses in arts/fine arts, English, humanities, mathematics, biological/physical sciences, social sciences.

FRESHMAN ADMISSIONS. Selection criteria: Open admissions. GPA and test scores considered for out-of-state applicants. **Test requirements:** SAT or ACT (ACT preferred) for counseling; score report by August 20. ASSET required for placement.

1992 FRESHMAN CLASS PROFILE. 699 men, 858 women enrolled. **Characteristics:** 92% from in state, 82% commute, 14% have minority backgrounds, 2% are foreign students. Average age is 20.

FALL-TERM APPLICATIONS. No fee. No closing date; applicants notified on a rolling basis; must reply by registration.

STUDENT LIFE. Housing: Dormitories (men, women, coed). **Activities:** Student government, student newspaper, yearbook, choral groups, concert band, drama, jazz band, music ensembles, musical theater, pep band, fraternities, sororities.

ATHLETICS. NJCAA. **Intercollegiate:** Basketball, cross-country, football M, golf M, softball W, tennis, track and field, volleyball W. **Intramural:** Badminton, basketball, bowling, golf M, soccer M, softball, table tennis, tennis, volleyball.

STUDENT SERVICES. Aptitude testing, career counseling, employment service for undergraduates, personal counseling, placement service for graduates, services/facilities for handicapped.

ANNUAL EXPENSES. Tuition and fees (1992-93): $878, $1,470 additional for out-of-state students. **Room and board:** $2,748. **Books and supplies:** $500. **Other expenses:** $1,200.

FINANCIAL AID. 80% of grants, 78% of loans, 71% of jobs based on need. Academic, music/drama, art, athletic, leadership scholarships available. **Aid applications:** No closing date; priority given to applications received by May 1; applicants notified on a rolling basis beginning on or about May 30; must reply within 2 weeks.

ADDRESS/TELEPHONE. Neal Holting, Director, Admissions, Butler County Community College, Towanda Avenue and Haverhill Road, Eldorado, KS 67042-3280. (316) 321-5083. Fax: (316) 321-5122.

Central College
McPherson, Kansas CB code: 6088

2-year private junior college, coed, affiliated with Free Methodist Church of North America. Founded in 1884. **Accreditation:** Regional. **Undergraduate enrollment:** 191 men, 136 women full time; 4 men, 4 women part time. **Faculty:** 31 total (20 full time), 5 with doctorates or other terminal degrees. **Location:** Suburban campus in large town; 55 miles from Wichita. **Calendar:** 4-1-4. **Microcomputers:** Located in libraries, classrooms, computer centers, campus-wide network. **Additional facts:** 4-year bachelor's degree in religious studies also available.

DEGREES OFFERED. AA, BS. 90 associate degrees awarded in 1992. 7 bachelor's degrees awarded.

UNDERGRADUATE MAJORS. Associate: Accounting, aeronautical technology, agribusiness, airline piloting and navigation, allied health, architecture, automotive mechanics, automotive technology, behavioral sciences, Bible studies, biological and physical sciences, biology, botany, business administration and management, business and management, business and office, business computer/console/peripheral equipment operation, business data entry equipment operation, business data processing and related programs, business data programming, business economics, carpentry, chemistry, child development/care/guidance, communications, computer and information sciences, construction, creative writing, criminal justice studies, data processing, dietetic aide/assistant, drafting and design technology, economics, education, elementary education, engineering, engineering and engineering-related technologies, English, fashion design, fashion merchandising, finance, fine arts, food production/management/services, food science and nutrition, health sciences, history, home economics, hotel/motel and restaurant management, journalism, law , legal secretary, liberal/general studies, library assistant, library science, marketing and distribution, marketing management, mathematics, medical secretary, missionary studies, music, parks and recreation management, philosophy, preengineering, prelaw, psychology, recreation and community services technologies, religion, religious music, science technologies, secondary education, secretarial and related programs, small business management and ownership, social sciences, sociology, solid state physics, special education, studio art, theological studies, welding technology, zoology. **Bachelor's:** Missionary studies, pastoral studies, religion, religious music, theological studies.

ACADEMIC PROGRAMS. 2-year transfer program, cooperative education, double major, independent study, student-designed major, cross-registration. **Remedial services:** Learning center, reduced course load, remedial instruction, special counselor, tutoring. **Placement/credit:** AP, CLEP General and Subject; 30 credit hours maximum for associate degree.

ACADEMIC REQUIREMENTS. Freshmen must earn minimum GPA of 1.75 to continue in good standing. 70% of freshmen return for sophomore year. Students must declare major by end of first year. **Graduation requirements:** 64 hours for associate (27 in major). Most students required to take courses in English, humanities, philosophy/religion, biological/physical sciences, social sciences.

FRESHMAN ADMISSIONS. Selection criteria: Christian lifestyle important; student achievement record considered. **High school preparation:** 16 units recommended. Recommended units include English 4, mathematics 1 and science 1. One American history unit also recommended. **Test requirements:** SAT or ACT (ACT preferred) for placement and counseling only; score report by September 1.

1992 FRESHMAN CLASS PROFILE. 106 men, 71 women enrolled. 25% had high school GPA of 3.0 or higher, 70% between 2.0 and 2.99. **Academic background:** Mid 50% of enrolled freshmen had ACT composite between 14-22. 100% submitted ACT scores. **Characteristics:** 22% from in state, 95% live in college housing, 21% have minority backgrounds. Average age is 18.

FALL-TERM APPLICATIONS. $5 fee, may be waived for applicants with need. No closing date; applicants notified on a rolling basis. Interview recommended. Essay recommended. Deferred and early admission available.

STUDENT LIFE. Housing: Dormitories (men, women); apartment housing available. **Activities:** Student government, student newspaper, yearbook, choral groups, concert band, drama, jazz band, music ensembles, pep band, symphony orchestra, Christian service organization.

ATHLETICS. NJCAA, NSCAA. **Intercollegiate:** Baseball M, basketball, cross-country, soccer, softball W, tennis, volleyball W. **Intramural:** Badminton, basketball, bowling, golf, soccer, softball, swimming, table tennis, tennis, volleyball.

STUDENT SERVICES. Aptitude testing, career counseling, employment service for undergraduates, freshman orientation, health services, personal counseling, placement service for graduates.

ANNUAL EXPENSES. Tuition and fees: $7,250. **Room and board:** $3,050. **Books and supplies:** $400. **Other expenses:** $500.

FINANCIAL AID. 90% of freshmen, 90% of continuing students receive some form of aid. 46% of grants, 98% of loans, 41% of jobs based on need. 128 enrolled freshmen were judged to have need, all were offered aid. Academic, music/drama, athletic scholarships available. **Aid applications:** No closing date; priority given to applications received by June 1; applicants notified on a rolling basis beginning on or about March 1.

ADDRESS/TELEPHONE. Greg Gossell, Director of Admissions and Financial Aid, Central College, 1200 South Main, McPherson, KS 67460-5740. (316) 241-0723. (800) 835-0078. Fax: (316) 241-6032.

Cloud County Community College
Concordia, Kansas CB code: 6137

2-year public community college, coed. Founded in 1965. **Accreditation:** Regional. **Undergraduate enrollment:** 2,939 men and women. **Location:** Rural campus in small town; 200 miles from Kansas City, 140 miles from Topeka. **Calendar:** Semester.

FRESHMAN ADMISSIONS. Selection criteria: Open admissions. School record, test scores, and recommendations considered for out-of-state applicants.

ANNUAL EXPENSES. Tuition and fees (1992-93): $900, $1,425 additional for out-of-state students. **Room and board:** $2,650. **Books and supplies:** $350. **Other expenses:** $900.

ADDRESS/TELEPHONE. John W. Carlson, Dean of Admissions, Cloud County Community College, 2221 Campus Drive, PO Box 1002, Concordia, KS 66901-1002. (913) 243-1435. (800) 729-5101. Fax: (913) 243-1459.

Coffeyville Community College
Coffeyville, Kansas CB code: 6102

2-year public community college, coed. Founded in 1923. **Accreditation:** Regional. **Faculty:** 75 total (50 full time), 1 with doctorate or other terminal degree. **Location:** Urban campus in large town; 75 miles from Tulsa, Oklahoma. **Calendar:** Semester, limited summer session. **Microcomputers:** 75 located in classrooms, computer centers. **Special facilities:** Greenhouse commerical television station.

DEGREES OFFERED. AA, AS, AAS. 235 associate degrees awarded in 1992.

UNDERGRADUATE MAJORS. Accounting, advertising, agribusiness, agricultural business and management, agricultural economics, agricultural production, agricultural products and processing, agricultural sciences, air conditioning/heating/refrigeration mechanics, anatomy, animal sciences, architecture, art history, automotive mechanics, automotive technology, biological and physical sciences, biology, botany, business administration and management, business and management, business and office, business data entry equipment operation, business data processing and related programs, business economics, carpentry, chemistry, computer and information sciences, computer programming, diesel engine mechanics, drafting, dramatic arts, drawing, economics, education, electrical installation, elementary education, emergency medical technologies, engineering, engineering and engineering-related technologies, engineering and other disciplines, English, fashion design, fashion merchandising, fine arts, health sciences, history, home economics, horticultural science, horticulture, humanities and social sciences, information sciences and systems, interior design, journalism, legal secretary, liberal/general studies, management information systems, masonry/tile setting, mathematics, medical secretary, microbiology, microcomputer software, music, music history and appreciation, music performance, music theory and composition, nursing, painting, physical sciences, physics, plant sciences, political science and government, practical nursing, precision metal work, predentistry, prelaw, premedicine, prepharmacy, preveterinary, psychology, radio/television broadcasting, radio/television technology, retailing, sculpture, secondary education, secretarial and related programs, small business management and ownership, social sciences, social work, sociology, speech, sports medicine, textiles and clothing, word processing, zoology.

ACADEMIC PROGRAMS. 2-year transfer program, dual enrollment of high school students, independent study, internships. **Remedial services:** Learning center, remedial instruction, special counselor, tutoring. **Placement/credit:** CLEP General, institutional tests.

ACADEMIC REQUIREMENTS. Freshmen must earn minimum GPA of 2.0 to continue in good standing. Students must declare major by end of first year. **Graduation requirements:** 64 hours for associate. Most students required to take courses in computer science, English, humanities, mathematics, biological/physical sciences, social sciences.

FRESHMAN ADMISSIONS. Selection criteria: Open admissions.

1992 FRESHMAN CLASS PROFILE. 349 men, 403 women enrolled. **Characteristics:** 80% from in state, 70% commute, 15% have minority backgrounds, 3% are foreign students. Average age is 26.

FALL-TERM APPLICATIONS. No fee. No closing date; applicants notified on a rolling basis.

STUDENT LIFE. Housing: Dormitories (men, women). **Activities:** Student government, magazine, student newspaper, television, choral groups, concert band, drama, jazz band, marching band, music ensembles, musical theater, pep band, symphony orchestra, bible study group.

ATHLETICS. NJCAA. **Intercollegiate:** Baseball M, basketball, cross-country, football M, golf M, soccer M, softball W, track and field, volleyball W. **Intramural:** Basketball, bowling, racquetball, table tennis.

STUDENT SERVICES. Aptitude testing, career counseling, freshman orientation, health services, on-campus day care, personal counseling, special adviser for adult students, veterans counselor, services/facilities for handicapped.

ANNUAL EXPENSES. Tuition and fees (projected): $960, $1,536 additional for out-of-state students. **Room and board:** $2,400. **Books and supplies:** $350. **Other expenses:** $1,200.

FINANCIAL AID. 66% of freshmen, 66% of continuing students receive some form of aid. 78% of grants, all loans, 80% of jobs based on need. Academic, music/drama, art, athletic, leadership scholarships available. **Aid applications:** No closing date; applicants notified on a rolling basis; must reply within 30 days. **Additional information:** Serves as conduit for Central American Scholarship Program. Provides aid to under- and unemployed women.

ADDRESS/TELEPHONE. Helen Ellerman, Director of Admissions and Financial Aid, Coffeyville Community College, 11th and Willow, Coffeyville, KS 67337. (316) 251-7700 ext. 2057. (800) 782-4732. Fax: (316) 251-7798.

Colby Community College
Colby, Kansas CB code: 6129

2-year public community college, coed. Founded in 1964. **Accreditation:** Regional. **Undergraduate enrollment:** 331 men, 404 women full time; 139 men, 169 women part time. **Faculty:** 74 total (52 full time), 12 with doctorates or other terminal degrees. **Location:** Rural campus in small town; 100 miles from Hays, 200 miles from Denver, Colorado. **Calendar:** Semester, limited summer session. Extensive evening/early morning classes. **Microcomputers:** 20 located in dormitories, libraries, computer centers. **Special facilities:** 64-acre farm, Cultural Arts Center.

DEGREES OFFERED. AA, AS, AAS. 250 associate degrees awarded in 1992. 8% in agriculture, 15% business and management, 10% communications, 8% education, 5% engineering, 15% allied health.

UNDERGRADUATE MAJORS. Accounting, advertising, agribusiness, agricultural business and management, agricultural economics, agricultural education, agricultural products and processing, agricultural sciences, allied health, anatomy, animal sciences, art education, biology, botany, business administration and management, business and management, business and office, business computer/console/peripheral equipment operation, business data entry equipment operation, business data processing and related programs, business data programming, business economics, chemistry, child development/care/guidance, communications, computer and information sciences, computer programming, criminal justice studies, criminology, drawing, education, elementary education, engineering, engineering and engineering-related technologies, English, English education, equestrian science, fashion design, finance, fine arts, food production/management/services, forestry and related sciences, graphic and printing production, graphic arts technology, graphic design, health sciences, home economics, home economics education, information sciences and systems, journalism, law enforcement and corrections, legal secretary, liberal/general studies, library assistant, library science, management science, marketing and distribution, mathematics, mathematics education, medical secretary, mental health/human services, motion picture technology, music, nursing, painting, photographic technology, physical education, physical sciences, physical therapy assistant, physics, practical nursing, predentistry, prelaw, premedicine, prepharmacy, preveterinary, psychology, public administration, public relations, radio/television broadcasting, radio/television technology, range management, recreation and community services technologies, respiratory therapy technology, science education, science technologies, secondary education, secretarial and related programs, social science education, social sciences, social studies education, social work, soil sciences, speech/communication/theater education, teacher aide, telecommunications, veterinarian's assistant, visual and performing arts, word processing.

ACADEMIC PROGRAMS. 2-year transfer program, dual enrollment of high school students, independent study, internships, telecourses. **Remedial services:** Learning center, preadmission summer program, reduced course load, remedial instruction, special counselor, tutoring. **Placement/credit:** CLEP General and Subject, institutional tests; 30 credit hours maximum for associate degree.

ACADEMIC REQUIREMENTS. Freshmen must earn minimum GPA of 2.0 to continue in good standing. 82% of freshmen return for sophomore year. Students must declare major by end of first year. **Graduation requirements:** 62 hours for associate (28 in major). Most students required to take courses in English, history, humanities, mathematics, biological/physical sciences, social sciences.

FRESHMAN ADMISSIONS. Selection criteria: Open admissions. Selective admissions to physical therapy assistant, veterinary technology, horse and sheep production, and nursing programs.

1992 FRESHMAN CLASS PROFILE. 248 men, 304 women enrolled. 40% had high school GPA of 3.0 or higher, 49% between 2.0 and 2.99. 10% were in top tenth and 28% were in top quarter of graduating class. **Academic background:** Mid 50% of enrolled freshmen had ACT composite between 17-23. 50% submitted ACT scores. **Characteristics:** 70% from in state, 70%

commute, 16% have minority backgrounds, 2% are foreign students. Average age is 19.

FALL-TERM APPLICATIONS. $10 fee. No closing date; applicants notified on a rolling basis; must reply by registration. Interview required for most health, nursing, agricultural applicants. Audition recommended for music applicants. Portfolio recommended for art applicants. Deferred and early admission available.

STUDENT LIFE. Housing: Dormitories (men, women, coed); handicapped housing available. **Activities:** Student government, film, magazine, radio, student newspaper, television, yearbook, choral groups, concert band, drama, jazz band, music ensembles, musical theater, pep band, characters club, Cowboys for Christ, Gold Key.

ATHLETICS. NJCAA. **Intercollegiate:** Baseball M, basketball, cross-country, softball W, track and field, volleyball W, wrestling M. **Intramural:** Baseball M, basketball, bowling, golf, handball, racquetball, skiing, softball, swimming, table tennis, tennis, volleyball, water polo.

STUDENT SERVICES. Aptitude testing, career counseling, employment service for undergraduates, freshman orientation, health services, personal counseling, placement service for graduates, special adviser for adult students, veterans counselor, services/facilities for handicapped.

ANNUAL EXPENSES. Tuition and fees (1992-93): $870, $1,395 additional for out-of-state students. **Room and board:** $2,500. **Books and supplies:** $400. **Other expenses:** $500.

FINANCIAL AID. 88% of continuing students receive some form of aid. 77% of loans, all jobs based on need. Academic, music/drama, art, athletic, state/district residency, leadership scholarships available. **Aid applications:** No closing date; priority given to applications received by June 1; applicants notified on a rolling basis beginning on or about May 1.

ADDRESS/TELEPHONE. Theron Johnson, Director of Admissions, Colby Community College, 1255 South Range, Colby, KS 67701. (913) 462-3984 ext. 285.

Cowley County Community College
Arkansas City, Kansas CB code: 6008

2-year public community, technical college, coed. Founded in 1922. **Accreditation:** Regional. **Undergraduate enrollment:** 489 men, 531 women full time; 476 men, 1,293 women part time. **Location:** Rural campus in large town; 50 miles from Wichita. **Calendar:** Semester. **Additional facts:** Area Vocational-Technical School programs available.

FRESHMAN ADMISSIONS. Selection criteria: Open admissions.

ANNUAL EXPENSES. Tuition and fees (projected): $900, $1,455 additional for out-of-state students. **Room and board:** $2,390. **Books and supplies:** $500. **Other expenses:** $1,000.

ADDRESS/TELEPHONE. Margaret Picking, Dean of Students, Cowley County Community College, 125 South Second, Arkansas City, KS 67005. (316) 442-0430. (800) 593-2220. Fax: (316) 442-0713.

Dodge City Community College
Dodge City, Kansas CB code: 6166

2-year public community, technical college, coed. Founded in 1935. **Accreditation:** Regional. **Undergraduate enrollment:** 1,825 men and women. **Faculty:** 162 total (54 full time), 2 with doctorates or other terminal degrees. **Location:** Rural campus in large town; 150 miles from Wichita. **Calendar:** Semester, limited summer session. Saturday and extensive evening/early morning classes. **Microcomputers:** 125 located in libraries, classrooms, computer centers. **Special facilities:** Federal depository of books and documents, horse barn, rodeo practice arena. **Additional facts:** Outreach programs in: Ness City, Ashland, Kinsley, Jetmore, Fowler, Coldwater, Protection, Spearville, Ford, Lewis, Mullinville, Bazine, Bucklin, Cimmaron, Minneola.

DEGREES OFFERED. AA, AS, AAS. 393 associate degrees awarded in 1992. 5% in agriculture, 20% business/office and marketing/distribution, 15% health sciences, 5% life sciences, 7% mathematics, 20% multi/interdisciplinary studies, 5% social sciences, 5% trade and industry.

UNDERGRADUATE MAJORS. Accounting, agribusiness, agricultural mechanics, agricultural sciences, animal sciences, art history, automotive mechanics, automotive technology, biology, business administration and management, business and management, business and office, business data entry equipment operation, business data processing and related programs, business systems analysis, chemistry, child development/care/guidance, data processing, diesel engine mechanics, drafting, dramatic arts, education, electrical and electronics equipment repair, electronic technology, English, equestrian science, fashion merchandising, finance, fire control and safety technology, food production/management/services, food science and nutrition, funeral services/mortuary science, graphic arts technology, individual and family development, insurance and risk management, insurance marketing, investments and securities, journalism, legal secretary, liberal/general studies, library science, marketing and distribution, marketing research, mathematics, mechanical design technology, medical records technology, medical secretary, music, music history and appreciation, nursing, parks and recreation management, personal services, physical sciences, physical therapy assistant, physics, practical nursing, precision metal work, predentistry, prelaw, premedicine, prepharmacy, preveterinary, psychology, radio/television broadcasting, radio/television technology, real estate, recreation and community services technologies, rehabilitation counseling/services, science technologies, secretarial and related programs, small business management and ownership, social sciences, social work, sports medicine, teacher aide, visual and performing arts, water and wastewater technology.

ACADEMIC PROGRAMS. 2-year transfer program, cooperative education, double major, dual enrollment of high school students, honors program, independent study, internships, cross-registration. **Remedial services:** Learning center, remedial instruction, tutoring. **Placement/credit:** CLEP General and Subject; 30 credit hours maximum for associate degree.

ACADEMIC REQUIREMENTS. Freshmen must earn minimum GPA of 1.6 to continue in good standing. 65% of freshmen return for sophomore year. Students must declare major by end of first year. **Graduation requirements:** 62 hours for associate. Most students required to take courses in computer science, English, humanities, mathematics, biological/physical sciences, social sciences.

FRESHMAN ADMISSIONS. Selection criteria: Open admissions. Students without GED or high school diploma must take a test to demonstrate ability. **Test requirements:** SAT or ACT (ACT preferred) for placement and counseling only; score report by September 1. ASSET test required for placement.

1992 FRESHMAN CLASS PROFILE. 504 men, 702 women enrolled. **Characteristics:** 95% from in state, 67% commute, 15% have minority backgrounds, 1% are foreign students. Average age is 22.

FALL-TERM APPLICATIONS. No fee. No closing date; applicants notified on a rolling basis. Interview recommended for nursing applicants. Audition recommended for music applicants. Portfolio recommended for art applicants. Deferred and early admission available.

STUDENT LIFE. Housing: Dormitories (men, women, coed). **Activities:** Student government, radio, student newspaper, television, yearbook, choral groups, concert band, drama, jazz band, music ensembles, pep band, fraternities, sororities, Black Student Union, Fellowship of Christian Athletes, Hispanic American Leadership Organization, Newman Club.

ATHLETICS. NJCAA. **Intercollegiate:** Baseball M, basketball, cross-country, football M, golf, softball W, track and field, volleyball W. **Intramural:** Basketball, handball, racquetball, soccer, softball, table tennis.

STUDENT SERVICES. Aptitude testing, career counseling, employment service for undergraduates, freshman orientation, health services, on-campus day care, personal counseling, placement service for graduates, special adviser for adult students, services/facilities for handicapped.

ANNUAL EXPENSES. Tuition and fees (1992-93): $975, $1,275 additional for out-of-state students. **Room and board:** $2,600. **Books and supplies:** $400. **Other expenses:** $900.

FINANCIAL AID. 69% of grants, 89% of loans, 41% of jobs based on need. Academic, music/drama, athletic, leadership, alumni affiliation, minority scholarships available. **Aid applications:** No closing date; applicants notified on a rolling basis beginning on or about May 1; must reply within 3 weeks.

ADDRESS/TELEPHONE. Deborah Lloyd, Director of Admissions, Dodge City Community College, 2501 North 14th, Dodge City, KS 67801-2399. (316) 225-1321. (800) 262-4565. Fax: (316) 225-0918.

Donnelly College
Kansas City, Kansas CB code: 6167

2-year private community, liberal arts college, coed, affiliated with Roman Catholic Church. Founded in 1949. **Accreditation:** Regional. **Undergraduate enrollment:** 136 men, 208 women full time; 66 men, 101 women part time. **Faculty:** 67 total (33 full time), 2 with doctorates or other terminal degrees. **Location:** Urban campus in small city; 5 miles from downtown. **Calendar:** Semester, limited summer session. Saturday classes. **Microcomputers:** 62 located in libraries, classrooms, computer centers.

DEGREES OFFERED. AA, AS, AAS. 45 associate degrees awarded in 1992.

UNDERGRADUATE MAJORS. Business and management, data processing, early childhood education, health sciences, liberal/general studies, nursing.

ACADEMIC PROGRAMS. 2-year transfer program, dual enrollment of high school students, external degree, honors program, independent study. **Remedial services:** Learning center, reduced course load, remedial instruction, special counselor, tutoring. **Placement/credit:** Institutional tests; 20 credit hours maximum for associate degree.

ACADEMIC REQUIREMENTS. Freshmen must earn minimum GPA of 2.0 to continue in good standing. 54% of freshmen return for sophomore year. **Graduation requirements:** 64 hours for associate (15 in major). Most students required to take courses in computer science, English, humanities, mathematics, philosophy/religion, biological/physical sciences, social sciences.

FRESHMAN ADMISSIONS. Selection criteria: Open admissions.

1992 FRESHMAN CLASS PROFILE. 27 men, 70 women enrolled.

Characteristics: 90% from in state, 100% commute, 77% have minority backgrounds, 5% are foreign students. Average age is 26.

FALL-TERM APPLICATIONS. No fee. No closing date; applicants notified on a rolling basis. Deferred and early admission available. Michigan Proficiency Test required of foreign applicants.

STUDENT SERVICES. Aptitude testing, career counseling, employment service for undergraduates, freshman orientation, personal counseling, placement service for graduates, veterans counselor, services/facilities for handicapped.

ANNUAL EXPENSES. Tuition and fees: $2,600. **Books and supplies:** $500.

FINANCIAL AID. 85% of freshmen, 75% of continuing students receive some form of aid. 99% of grants, 99% of loans, all jobs based on need. Academic, religious affiliation scholarships available. **Aid applications:** Closing date August 1; priority given to applications received by June 1; applicants notified on a rolling basis beginning on or about July 1.

ADDRESS/TELEPHONE. Delia Hernandez, Coordinator of College Relations, Donnelly College, 608 North 18th Street, Kansas City, KS 66102. (913) 621-6070 ext. 74.

Emporia State University
Emporia, Kansas — CB code: 6335

4-year public university, coed. Founded in 1863. **Accreditation:** Regional. **Undergraduate enrollment:** 1,720 men, 2,178 women full time; 260 men, 318 women part time. **Graduate enrollment:** 170 men, 237 women full time; 292 men, 831 women part time. **Faculty:** 405 total (346 full time), 211 with doctorates or other terminal degrees. **Location:** Rural campus in large town; 100 miles from Kansas City, Missouri, 85 miles from Wichita. **Calendar:** Semester, extensive summer session. **Microcomputers:** 696 located in dormitories, classrooms, computer centers. **Special facilities:** Planetarium, natural history reservation, natural history museum, art gallery, Jones Institute for Educational Excellence, National Teachers Hall of Fame.

DEGREES OFFERED. AS, BA, BS, BFA, MA, MS, MBA. 10 associate degrees awarded in 1992. 16% in business and management, 83% business/office and marketing/distribution. 659 bachelor's degrees awarded. 26% in business and management, 7% business/office and marketing/distribution, 23% teacher education, 5% life sciences, 7% psychology, 9% social sciences. Graduate degrees offered in 24 major fields of study.

UNDERGRADUATE MAJORS. Associate: Business and management, secretarial and related programs. **Bachelor's:** Accounting, art education, biology, business administration and management, business and management, business data processing and related programs, business education, chemistry, clinical laboratory science, communications, computer and information sciences, dramatic arts, earth sciences, economics, elementary education, English, English education, finance, fine arts, foreign languages (multiple emphasis), foreign languages education, geography, health education, history, information sciences and systems, liberal/general studies, marketing and distribution, marketing management, mathematics, mathematics education, medical laboratory technologies, music, music education, nursing, office supervision and management, physical education, physical sciences, physics, political science and government, psychology, recreation and community services technologies, rehabilitation counseling/services, science education, secondary education, social science education, social sciences, sociology, speech/communication/theater education.

ACADEMIC PROGRAMS. Accelerated program, cooperative education, double major, dual enrollment of high school students, education specialist degree, honors program, independent study, internships, student-designed major, study abroad, teacher preparation, telecourses, visiting/exchange student program; liberal arts/career combination in health sciences. **Remedial services:** Learning center, reduced course load, remedial instruction, special counselor, tutoring. **ROTC:** Army. **Placement/credit:** AP, CLEP General and Subject, institutional tests; 30 credit hours maximum for bachelor's degree.

ACADEMIC REQUIREMENTS. Freshmen must earn minimum GPA of 1.7 to continue in good standing. 65% of freshmen return for sophomore year. Students must declare major by end of second year. **Graduation requirements:** 62 hours for associate (35 in major), 124 hours for bachelor's (50 in major). Most students required to take courses in arts/fine arts, computer science, English, foreign languages, history, humanities, mathematics, biological/physical sciences, social sciences. **Postgraduate studies:** 1% enter law school, 1% enter medical school, 3% enter MBA programs, 11% enter other graduate study.

FRESHMAN ADMISSIONS. Selection criteria: Open admissions. Test scores and interviews considered for out-of-state applicants. Recommended units include English 4, mathematics 3, social science 3 and science 3. **Test requirements:** ACT for placement and counseling only; score report by August 1. **Additional information:** Open Admissions for in-State residents. Out of state applicants have a minimum GPA requirement.

1992 FRESHMAN CLASS PROFILE. 253 men, 415 women enrolled. 52% had high school GPA of 3.0 or higher, 45% between 2.0 and 2.99. **Characteristics:** 95% from in state, 70% live in college housing, 5% have minority backgrounds, 4% are foreign students, 19% join fraternities/sororities. Average age is 20.

FALL-TERM APPLICATIONS. $15 fee. No closing date; applicants notified on a rolling basis. Deferred and early admission available. High School GPA and ACT results considered for early admissions.

STUDENT LIFE. Housing: Dormitories (men, women, coed); apartment, fraternity, sorority, handicapped housing available. **Activities:** Magazine, student newspaper, yearbook, choral groups, concert band, dance, drama, jazz band, marching band, music ensembles, musical theater, opera, pep band, symphony orchestra, fraternities, sororities, Black Student Union, international student organization, Spurs, Hispanic American Leadership Organization, Cardinal Key, Native American Student Association.

ATHLETICS. NCAA. **Intercollegiate:** Baseball M, basketball, cross-country, football M, golf M, softball W, tennis, track and field, volleyball W. **Intramural:** Archery, badminton, basketball, bowling, cross-country, golf, handball, racquetball, soccer, softball, swimming, table tennis, tennis, track and field, volleyball, water polo, wrestling M.

STUDENT SERVICES. Aptitude testing, career counseling, employment service for undergraduates, freshman orientation, health services, on-campus day care, personal counseling, placement service for graduates, special adviser for adult students, veterans counselor, services/facilities for handicapped.

ANNUAL EXPENSES. Tuition and fees (1992-93): $1,584, $2,880 additional for out-of-state students. **Room and board:** $2,790. **Books and supplies:** $450. **Other expenses:** $1,018.

FINANCIAL AID. 85% of freshmen, 70% of continuing students receive some form of aid. 73% of grants, 95% of loans, 39% of jobs based on need. Academic, music/drama, art, athletic, state/district residency, leadership, alumni affiliation, religious affiliation, minority scholarships available. **Aid applications:** No closing date; priority given to applications received by March 15; applicants notified on a rolling basis beginning on or about March 15; must reply within 3 weeks.

ADDRESS/TELEPHONE. Barbara Tarter, Director of Admissions, Emporia State University, 1200 Commercial, Emporia, KS 66801-5087. (316) 341-5465, Fax: (316) 341-5073.

Fort Hays State University
Hays, Kansas — CB code: 6218

4-year public university, coed. Founded in 1902. **Accreditation:** Regional. **Undergraduate enrollment:** 1,759 men, 1,881 women full time; 222 men, 484 women part time. **Graduate enrollment:** 132 men, 194 women full time; 262 men, 669 women part time. **Faculty:** 388 total (311 full time), 127 with doctorates or other terminal degrees. **Location:** Rural campus in large town; 170 miles from Wichita, 270 miles from Kansas City. **Calendar:** Semester, extensive summer session. Saturday and extensive evening/early morning classes. **Microcomputers:** 490 located in dormitories, libraries, classrooms, computer centers. **Special facilities:** Art gallery, observatory, paleontology, natural history, archeology, history, geology, botanical-zoological museums.

DEGREES OFFERED. AS, BA, BS, BFA, MA, MS, MBA, MFA. 44 associate degrees awarded in 1992. 64% in business/office and marketing/distribution, 36% allied health. 642 bachelor's degrees awarded. 17% in business and management, 7% communications, 27% teacher education, 9% health sciences, 6% psychology, 9% social sciences, 6% visual and performing arts. Graduate degrees offered in 22 major fields of study.

UNDERGRADUATE MAJORS. Associate: Radiograph medical technology, secretarial and related programs. **Bachelor's:** Accounting, agricultural business and management, agricultural sciences, biological and physical sciences, biology, business administration and management, business and management, business education, chemistry, communications, computer and information sciences, economics, elementary education, English, finance, fine arts, foreign languages (multiple emphasis), geology, history, home economics, industrial arts education, marketing management, marketing research, mathematics, music, nursing, office supervision and management, philosophy, physical education, physical sciences, physics, political science and government, psychology, sociology.

ACADEMIC PROGRAMS. 2-year transfer program, accelerated program, double major, dual enrollment of high school students, education specialist degree, independent study, internships, teacher preparation, visiting/exchange student program, United Nations semester, cross-registration; liberal arts/career combination in engineering; combined bachelor's/graduate program in business administration. **Remedial services:** Learning center, preadmission summer program, reduced course load, remedial instruction, special counselor, tutoring, reading improvement courses. **Placement/credit:** AP, CLEP General and Subject, institutional tests.

ACADEMIC REQUIREMENTS. Freshmen must earn minimum GPA of 2.0 to continue in good standing. 60% of freshmen return for sophomore year. Students must declare major by end of second year. **Graduation requirements:** 62 hours for associate (44 in major), 124 hours for bachelor's (33 in major). Most students required to take courses in computer science, English, foreign languages, mathematics, biological/physical sciences, social sciences. **Postgraduate studies:** 40% from 2-year programs enter 4-year programs.

FRESHMAN ADMISSIONS. Selection criteria: Open admissions. High school GPA and test scores considered for out-of-state applicants. Recommended units include English 4, foreign language 2, mathematics 3, social science 3 and science 3. **Test requirements:** SAT or ACT (ACT preferred) for placement and counseling only; score report by August 25.

1992 FRESHMAN CLASS PROFILE. 371 men, 435 women enrolled. 87% had high school GPA of 3.0 or higher, 13% between 2.0 and 2.99. **Academic background:** Mid 50% of enrolled freshmen had ACT composite between 14-22. 74% submitted ACT scores. **Characteristics:** 91% from in state, 63% live in college housing, 2% have minority backgrounds, 4% are foreign students, 1% join fraternities/sororities. Average age is 19.

FALL-TERM APPLICATIONS. $15 fee. No closing date; applicants notified on a rolling basis. Audition recommended for music applicants. Deferred admission available.

STUDENT LIFE. Housing: Dormitories (men, women, coed); apartment, fraternity, sorority, cooperative housing available. **Activities:** Student government, film, radio, student newspaper, television, yearbook, research publications (The Fort Hays Studies), choral groups, concert band, dance, drama, jazz band, marching band, music ensembles, musical theater, opera, pep band, symphony orchestra, fraternities, sororities, many ethnic, religious, and political organizations.

ATHLETICS. NCAA. **Intercollegiate:** Baseball M, basketball, bowling, cross-country, football M, gymnastics W, softball W, tennis, track and field, volleyball W, wrestling M. **Intramural:** Archery, badminton, baseball, basketball, bowling, cross-country, diving, fencing, field hockey, football M, golf M, gymnastics W, handball, racquetball, soccer, softball, swimming, table tennis, tennis, track and field, volleyball, water polo, wrestling M.

STUDENT SERVICES. Aptitude testing, career counseling, employment service for undergraduates, freshman orientation, health services, on-campus day care, personal counseling, placement service for graduates, special adviser for adult students, veterans counselor, services/facilities for handicapped.

ANNUAL EXPENSES. Tuition and fees (projected): $1,711, $3,052 additional for out-of-state students. **Room and board:** $2,941. **Books and supplies:** $500. **Other expenses:** $1,250.

FINANCIAL AID. 70% of freshmen, 65% of continuing students receive some form of aid. 88% of grants, 94% of loans, 36% of jobs based on need. Academic, music/drama, art, athletic scholarships available. **Aid applications:** No closing date; priority given to applications received by March 15; applicants notified on a rolling basis beginning on or about March 15; must reply within 2 weeks.

ADDRESS/TELEPHONE. Pat Mahon, Director of Admissions Counseling, Fort Hays State University, 600 Park Street, Hays, KS 67601-4099. (913) 628-4222. Fax: (913) 628-4046.

Fort Scott Community College
Fort Scott, Kansas — CB code: 6219

2-year public community college, coed. Founded in 1919. **Accreditation:** Regional. **Undergraduate enrollment:** 441 men, 497 women full time; 413 men, 464 women part time. **Faculty:** 163 total (67 full time), 4 with doctorates or other terminal degrees. **Location:** Rural campus in small town; 25 miles north of Pittsburg. **Calendar:** Semester, limited summer session. **Microcomputers:** 60 located in computer centers.

DEGREES OFFERED. AA, AS, AAS. 221 associate degrees awarded in 1992.

UNDERGRADUATE MAJORS. Accounting, agribusiness, agricultural business and management, agricultural economics, agricultural education, agricultural sciences, airline piloting and navigation, allied health, animal sciences, architectural technologies, architecture, art education, aviation management, Bible studies, business administration and management, business and management, business and office, business computer/console/peripheral equipment operation, business data entry equipment operation, business data processing and related programs, business data programming, business economics, business statistics, chemistry, city/community/regional planning, civil engineering, communications, computer and information sciences, computer graphics, computer programming, criminal justice studies, criminology, data processing, drafting, drafting and design technology, early childhood education, economics, education, elementary education, engineering, engineering and engineering-related technologies, engineering management, English education, environmental health engineering, finance, graphic and printing production, graphic arts technology, history, industrial arts education, junior high education, law enforcement and corrections, law enforcement and corrections technologies, legal secretary, liberal/general studies, marketing and distribution, mathematics education, medical assistant, music education, nursing, nursing education, photographic technology, physical education, physical sciences, physics, political science and government, practical nursing, precision metal work, psychology, public administration, public relations, reading education, recreation and community services technologies, renewable natural resources, science education, science technologies, secondary education, secretarial and related programs, small business management and ownership, social science education, social sciences, social studies education, sociology, special education, speech/communication/theater education, water and wastewater technology, water resources, woodworking.

ACADEMIC PROGRAMS. 2-year transfer program, dual enrollment of high school students, independent study, internships, teacher preparation, telecourses. **Remedial services:** Learning center, preadmission summer program, remedial instruction, special counselor, tutoring. **Placement/credit:** CLEP General and Subject; 18 credit hours maximum for associate degree.

ACADEMIC REQUIREMENTS. Freshmen must earn minimum GPA of 2.0 to continue in good standing. 70% of freshmen return for sophomore year. Students must declare major by end of first year. **Graduation requirements:** 60 hours for associate. Most students required to take courses in English, humanities, mathematics, biological/physical sciences.

FRESHMAN ADMISSIONS. Selection criteria: Open admissions.

1992 FRESHMAN CLASS PROFILE. 519 men, 724 women enrolled. **Characteristics:** 60% from in state, 90% commute, 4% have minority backgrounds, 2% are foreign students. Average age is 19.

FALL-TERM APPLICATIONS. No fee. No closing date; applicants notified on a rolling basis. Interview recommended. CRDA. Deferred and early admission available. EDP-F.

STUDENT LIFE. Housing: Dormitories (coed). **Activities:** Student government, student newspaper, yearbook, choral groups, concert band, dance, drama, jazz band, marching band, music ensembles, musical theater, pep band, symphony orchestra, Fellowship of Christian Athletes.

ATHLETICS. NJCAA. **Intercollegiate:** Baseball M, basketball, cross-country, football M, softball W, track and field, volleyball W. **Intramural:** Basketball, bowling, racquetball, softball, table tennis, tennis, track and field, volleyball.

STUDENT SERVICES. Aptitude testing, career counseling, employment service for undergraduates, freshman orientation, veterans counselor, services/facilities for handicapped.

ANNUAL EXPENSES. Tuition and fees (projected): $750, $2,430 additional for out-of-state students. **Room and board:** $2,480. **Books and supplies:** $500. **Other expenses:** $2,100.

FINANCIAL AID. 40% of freshmen, 80% of continuing students receive some form of aid. All grants, 96% of loans, all jobs based on need. 500 enrolled freshmen were judged to have need, all were offered aid. **Aid applications:** No closing date; priority given to applications received by May 1; applicants notified on a rolling basis beginning on or about October 1.

ADDRESS/TELEPHONE. Pat Flynn, Director of Admissions, Fort Scott Community College, 2108 South Horton, Fort Scott, KS 66701. (316) 223-2700 ext. 77. (800) 774-3722. Fax: (316) 223-6530.

Friends University
Wichita, Kansas — CB code: 6224

4-year private college of arts and sciences and business college, coed, affiliated with Religious Society of Friends. Founded in 1898. **Accreditation:** Regional. **Undergraduate enrollment:** 443 men, 579 women full time; 56 men, 61 women part time. **Graduate enrollment:** 194 men, 200 women full time. **Faculty:** 65 total (50 full time), 27 with doctorates or other terminal degrees. **Location:** Urban campus in large city; 1 mile from downtown. **Calendar:** Semester, limited summer session. **Microcomputers:** 125 located in libraries, classrooms, computer centers. **Special facilities:** Fellow-Reeve Museum, Quaker Collection, Whittier Art Gallery, Garvey Art Center, laboratory school for teacher education, observatory.

DEGREES OFFERED. AA, AS, BA, BS, BFA, MA, MS, MBA. 4 associate degrees awarded in 1992. 322 bachelor's degrees awarded. 62% in business and management, 14% teacher education, 6% psychology. Graduate degrees offered in 3 major fields of study.

UNDERGRADUATE MAJORS. Associate: Accounting, Bible studies, business and office, business data processing and related programs, fashion merchandising, recreation and community services technologies, science technologies, secretarial and related programs, teacher aide. **Bachelor's:** Accounting, art education, biological and physical sciences, biology, business administration and management, business and management, business education, chemistry, communications, computer and information sciences, dance, dramatic arts, education, elementary education, English education, environmental science, fine arts, foreign languages (multiple emphasis), foreign languages education, history, human resources development, humanities and social sciences, individual and family development, international business management, junior high education, liberal/general studies, management information systems, mathematics, mathematics education, music, music education, music performance, physical education, political science and government, predentistry, prelaw, premedicine, preveterinary, psychology, religion, religious music, science education, secondary education, secretarial and related programs, social science education, social sciences, social studies education, social work, sociology, Spanish, sports communications, theological studies.

ACADEMIC PROGRAMS. Double major, dual enrollment of high school students, external degree, honors program, independent study, internships, student-designed major, teacher preparation, cross-registration, degree completion program for working adults; liberal arts/career combination in business. **Remedial services:** Reduced course load, special counselor, tutoring. **Placement/credit:** AP, CLEP General; 60 credit hours maximum for bachelor's degree.

ACADEMIC REQUIREMENTS. Freshmen must earn minimum GPA of 2.0 to continue in good standing. 65% of freshmen return for sophomore year. Students must declare major by end of second year. **Graduation requirements:** 62 hours for associate, 124 hours for bachelor's. Most students required to take courses in arts/fine arts, computer science, English, history, humanities, mathematics, philosophy/religion, biological/physical sciences, social sciences. **Additional information:** Friends English Language school offered.

FRESHMAN ADMISSIONS. Selection criteria: ACT score multiplied by GPA must equal 45 or above for admission. Those with score between 20 and 29 admitted provisionally. **High school preparation:** 11 units required. Required units include biological science 1, English 4, mathematics 2, physical science 1 and social science 2. **Test requirements:** SAT or ACT (ACT preferred); score report by August 20.

1992 FRESHMAN CLASS PROFILE. 82 men, 112 women enrolled. **Characteristics:** 80% from in state, 76% commute, 8% have minority backgrounds, 6% are foreign students. Average age is 18.

FALL-TERM APPLICATIONS. $10 fee. No closing date; applicants notified on a rolling basis beginning on or about January 1. Audition required for music applicants. Interview recommended. Portfolio recommended for art applicants.

STUDENT LIFE. Housing: Dormitories (men, women); apartment housing available. **Activities:** Student government, radio, student newspaper, yearbook, choral groups, concert band, dance, drama, jazz band, marching band, music ensembles, musical theater, opera, pep band, symphony orchestra, fraternities, sororities, International Relations Club.

ATHLETICS. NAIA. **Intercollegiate:** Baseball M, basketball, cross-country, football M, soccer M, softball W, tennis, volleyball W. **Intramural:** Basketball M, racquetball, soccer M, table tennis, volleyball.

STUDENT SERVICES. Aptitude testing, career counseling, employment service for undergraduates, freshman orientation, health services, personal counseling, placement service for graduates, special adviser for adult students, veterans counselor, services/facilities for handicapped.

ANNUAL EXPENSES. Tuition and fees: $8,230. **Room and board:** $2,890. **Books and supplies:** $575. **Other expenses:** $2,300.

FINANCIAL AID. 87% of freshmen, 83% of continuing students receive some form of aid. 25% of grants, 92% of loans, 45% of jobs based on need. Academic, music/drama, art, athletic, leadership, alumni affiliation, religious affiliation scholarships available. **Aid applications:** No closing date; priority given to applications received by April 15; applicants notified on a rolling basis beginning on or about April 30; must reply within 3 weeks.

ADDRESS/TELEPHONE. Cheryl Wilson, Enrollment Management, Friends University, 2100 University Avenue, Wichita, KS 67213. (316) 261-5842.

Garden City Community College
Garden City, Kansas — CB code: 6246

2-year public community, liberal arts college, coed. Founded in 1919. **Accreditation:** Regional. **Undergraduate enrollment:** 550 men, 549 women full time; 439 men, 678 women part time. **Faculty:** 138 total (68 full time), 6 with doctorates or other terminal degrees. **Location:** Rural campus in large town; 200 miles from Wichita. **Calendar:** Semester, limited summer session. Extensive evening/early morning classes. **Microcomputers:** 50 located in dormitories, libraries, classrooms, computer centers. **Special facilities:** Art galleries, learning center, wellness center.

DEGREES OFFERED. AA, AS, AAS. 224 associate degrees awarded in 1992. 16% in business and management, 16% education, 20% health sciences, 11% letters/literature, 12% trade and industry, 5% visual and performing arts.

UNDERGRADUATE MAJORS. Accounting, advertising, agribusiness, agricultural business and management, agricultural mechanics, agricultural production, agricultural products and processing, agricultural sciences, animal sciences, apparel and accessories marketing, architectural technologies, automotive mechanics, automotive technology, aviation management, biological and physical sciences, biology, business administration and management, business and management, business and office, business computer/console/peripheral equipment operation, business data entry equipment operation, business data processing and related programs, business data programming, carpentry, chemistry, child development/care/guidance, clothing and textiles management/production/services, communications, computer and information sciences, computer programming, computer technology, construction, crafts, criminal justice studies, criminal justice technology, dance, data processing, drafting, drafting and design technology, dramatic arts, drawing, early childhood education, education, electrical installation, elementary education, emergency medical technologies, emergency/disaster science, engineering, engineering and engineering-related technologies, engineering and other disciplines, English, fashion design, fashion merchandising, fine arts, food management, food science and nutrition, food sciences, geriatric aide, graphic and printing production, graphic arts technology, graphic design, health sciences, history, home economics, humanities and social sciences, industrial technology, interior design, junior high education, law enforcement and corrections, law enforcement and corrections technologies, liberal/general studies, marketing and distribution, masonry/tile setting, mathematics, mechanical design technology, medical assistant, medical secretary, microcomputer software, music, music performance, music theory and composition, nursing, painting, personal services, photographic technology, photography, physical sciences, physics, predentistry, prelaw, premedicine, prepharmacy, preveterinary, psychology, public administration, public relations, retailing, robotics, science technologies, sculpture, secondary education, secretarial and related programs, small business management and ownership, social sciences, social work, special education, speech, sports medicine, studio art, teacher aide, theater design, visual and performing arts, woodworking, word processing.

ACADEMIC PROGRAMS. 2-year transfer program, cooperative education, dual enrollment of high school students, internships, student-designed major, cross-registration. **Remedial services:** Learning center, reduced course load, remedial instruction, special counselor, tutoring. **Placement/credit:** AP, CLEP General and Subject, institutional tests; 30 credit hours maximum for associate degree.

ACADEMIC REQUIREMENTS. Freshmen must earn minimum GPA of 1.5 to continue in good standing. 71% of freshmen return for sophomore year. Students must declare major by end of first year. **Graduation requirements:** 64 hours for associate (32 in major). Most students required to take courses in English, history, humanities, mathematics, biological/physical sciences, social sciences.

FRESHMAN ADMISSIONS. Selection criteria: Open admissions. **Test requirements:** SAT or ACT for placement and counseling only; score report by August 15.

1992 FRESHMAN CLASS PROFILE. 277 men, 229 women enrolled. 18% had high school GPA of 3.0 or higher, 44% between 2.0 and 2.99. **Academic background:** Mid 50% of enrolled freshmen had ACT composite between 9-18. 80% submitted ACT scores. **Characteristics:** 41% from in state, 85% commute, 22% have minority backgrounds, 2% are foreign students. Average age is 19.

FALL-TERM APPLICATIONS. No fee. No closing date; applicants notified on a rolling basis beginning on or about January 5. Audition recommended for music applicants. Portfolio recommended for art, photography applicants. Early admission available.

STUDENT LIFE. Housing: Dormitories (coed). **Activities:** Student government, magazine, choral groups, concert band, dance, drama, jazz band, music ensembles, musical theater, pep band, Mecha, Baptist Student Union, Christian Fellowship Organization, Newman Club.

ATHLETICS. NJCAA. **Intercollegiate:** Baseball M, basketball, cross-country, football M, golf M, soccer M, volleyball W, wrestling M. **Intramural:** Archery, basketball, bowling, racquetball, rifle, softball, swimming, table tennis, tennis, track and field, volleyball.

STUDENT SERVICES. Career counseling, employment service for undergraduates, freshman orientation, health services, on-campus day care, personal counseling, placement service for graduates, veterans counselor, services/facilities for handicapped.

ANNUAL EXPENSES. Tuition and fees (1992-93): $894, $1,305 additional for out-of-state students. **Room and board:** $2,500. **Books and supplies:** $420. **Other expenses:** $500.

FINANCIAL AID. 75% of freshmen, 50% of continuing students receive some form of aid. Grants, loans, jobs available. Academic, music/drama, art, athletic, state/district residency, leadership scholarships available. **Aid applications:** No closing date; priority given to applications received by July 15; applicants notified on a rolling basis beginning on or about July 15.

ADDRESS/TELEPHONE. Larry Fowler, Director of Admissions, Garden City Community College, 801 Campus Drive, Garden City, KS 67846. (316) 276-7611. (800) 658-1696. Fax: (316) 276-9630.

Haskell Indian Junior College
Lawrence, Kansas — CB code: 0919

2-year public junior college, coed. Founded in 1884. **Accreditation:** Regional. **Undergraduate enrollment:** 476 men, 334 women full time; 31 men, 39 women part time. **Faculty:** 60 total (54 full time), 5 with doctorates or other terminal degrees. **Location:** Suburban campus in small city; 38 miles from Kansas City, Missouri. **Calendar:** Semester. **Microcomputers:** 45 located in libraries, classrooms, computer centers. **Additional facts:** Federally owned and operated college provides educational benefits to North American Indians who are under jurisdiction of Bureau of Indian Affairs. Students receive tuition, books, and some college housing.

DEGREES OFFERED. AA, AS, AAS. 78 associate degrees awarded in 1992.

UNDERGRADUATE MAJORS. Accounting, American Indian studies, business administration and management, business and management, business and office, business computer/console/peripheral equipment operation, business data processing and related programs, communications, data processing, English, industrial equipment maintenance and repair, industrial technology, journalism, liberal/general studies, office supervision and management, power plant operation and maintenance, renewable natural resources, secretarial and related programs, social work.

ACADEMIC PROGRAMS. 2-year transfer program, cooperative education, independent study, internships. **Remedial services:** Learning center, reduced course load, remedial instruction, special counselor, tutoring. **Placement/credit:** 8 credit hours maximum for associate degree.

ACADEMIC REQUIREMENTS. Freshmen must earn minimum GPA of 1.75 to continue in good standing. 50% of freshmen return for sophomore year. Students must declare major on application. **Graduation requirements:** 62 hours for associate. Most students required to take courses in English, history, humanities, mathematics, biological/physical sciences, social sciences.

FRESHMAN ADMISSIONS. Selection criteria: Open admissions. Students must be certified by Bureau of Indian Affairs as member of federally recognized tribe, or quarter degree descendant of tribal member. **Test requirements:** ACT; score report by August 20.

1992 FRESHMAN CLASS PROFILE. 284 men, 225 women enrolled. 8% had high school GPA of 3.0 or higher, 66% between 2.0 and 2.99. **Characteristics:** 10% from in state, 90% live in college housing, 100% have minority backgrounds. Average age is 20.

FALL-TERM APPLICATIONS. No fee. Closing date July 31; priority given to applications received by July 15; applicants notified on a rolling basis beginning on or about March 15.

STUDENT LIFE. Housing: Dormitories (men, women, coed). Haskell graduates who attend Kansas University may work as residential assistants for room and board at Haskell. **Activities:** Student government, student newspaper, yearbook, choral groups, dance, drama, Native American dancing, Native American clubs, rodeo club, Phi Beta Lambda (service organization), Baptist Student Union, Thunderbird Theatre, LIGHT House (Lutheran organization), Catholic Center.

ATHLETICS. NJCAA. **Intercollegiate:** Basketball, cross-country, football M, track and field, volleyball. **Intramural:** Basketball, bowling, racquetball, softball, volleyball, wrestling M.

STUDENT SERVICES. Aptitude testing, career counseling, employment service for undergraduates, freshman orientation, health services, personal counseling, placement service for graduates, special adviser for adult students, veterans counselor, services/facilities for handicapped.

ANNUAL EXPENSES. Tuition and fees (1992-93): $70. **Books and supplies:** $70. **Other expenses:** $989.

FINANCIAL AID. 65% of freshmen, 65% of continuing students receive some form of aid. All grants, all jobs based on need. **Aid applications:** No closing date; priority given to applications received by May 15; applicants notified on a rolling basis beginning on or about March 15; must reply within 9 weeks. **Additional information:** Some personal expenses may be offset by Bureau of Indian Affairs grants. Most students qualify for only the minimum Pell grant.

ADDRESS/TELEPHONE. Esther J. Geary, Director of Admissions and Records, Haskell Indian Junior College, PO Box 1282, 155 Indian Ave, Lawrence, KS 66046-4800. (913) 749-8454. Fax: (913) 749-8429.

Hesston College
Hesston, Kansas CB code: 6274

2-year private junior college, coed, affiliated with Mennonite Church. Founded in 1909. **Accreditation:** Regional. **Undergraduate enrollment:** 229 men, 209 women full time; 23 men, 47 women part time. **Faculty:** 62 total (45 full time), 6 with doctorates or other terminal degrees. **Location:** Rural campus in small town; 30 miles from Wichita. **Calendar:** 4-1-4, limited summer session. **Microcomputers:** 34 located in classrooms, computer centers.

DEGREES OFFERED. AA. 192 associate degrees awarded in 1992. 20% in engineering technologies, 17% health sciences, 46% multi/interdisciplinary studies, 7% philosophy, religion, theology.

UNDERGRADUATE MAJORS. Aeronautical technology, automotive technology, Bible studies, business and office, business data processing and related programs, business data programming, early childhood education, electronic technology, hotel/motel and restaurant management, liberal/general studies, medical secretary, nursing, secretarial and related programs.

ACADEMIC PROGRAMS. Cooperative education, independent study, cross-registration. **Remedial services:** Learning center, preadmission summer program, reduced course load, remedial instruction, special counselor, tutoring. **Placement/credit:** 10 credit hours maximum for associate degree.

ACADEMIC REQUIREMENTS. No policy requiring minimum GPA; records of students having academic difficulty are reviewed individually. 70% of freshmen return for sophomore year. Students must declare major by end of first year. **Graduation requirements:** 64 hours for associate. Most students required to take courses in arts/fine arts, English, history, humanities, philosophy/religion, biological/physical sciences.

FRESHMAN ADMISSIONS. Selection criteria: Applicant carefully screened to determine lifestyle. **Test requirements:** SAT or ACT for placement and counseling only; score report by September 1.

1992 FRESHMAN CLASS PROFILE. 108 men, 80 women enrolled. 48% had high school GPA of 3.0 or higher, 42% between 2.0 and 2.99. 15% were in top tenth and 28% were in top quarter of graduating class. **Academic background:** Mid 50% of enrolled freshmen had ACT composite between 18-25. 46% submitted ACT scores. **Characteristics:** 16% from in state, 90% live in college housing, 7% have minority backgrounds, 20% are foreign students. Average age is 21.

FALL-TERM APPLICATIONS. $10 fee. No closing date; applicants notified on a rolling basis. Deferred admission available.

STUDENT LIFE. Housing: Dormitories (men, women). **Activities:** Student government, yearbook, choral groups, drama, music ensembles, social service organizations.

ATHLETICS. NJCAA, NSCAA. **Intercollegiate:** Baseball M, basketball, soccer M, tennis, volleyball W. **Intramural:** Basketball, racquetball, soccer, softball, table tennis, tennis, volleyball.

STUDENT SERVICES. Career counseling, employment service for undergraduates, personal counseling, services/facilities for handicapped.

ANNUAL EXPENSES. Tuition and fees: $7,500. **Room and board:** $3,450. **Books and supplies:** $600. **Other expenses:** $1,000.

FINANCIAL AID. 92% of freshmen, 92% of continuing students receive some form of aid. 73% of grants, 78% of loans, 46% of jobs based on need. 153 enrolled freshmen were judged to have need, all were offered aid. Academic, music/drama, art, athletic scholarships available. **Aid applications:** No closing date; priority given to applications received by May 1; applicants notified on a rolling basis beginning on or about March 15; must reply within 4 weeks.

ADDRESS/TELEPHONE. Diane Yoder, Director of Admissions, Hesston College, PO Box 3000, Hesston, KS 67062-2093. (316) 327-4221. Fax: (316) 327-8300.

Highland Community College
Highland, Kansas CB code: 6276

2-year public community college, coed. Founded in 1857. **Accreditation:** Regional. **Undergraduate enrollment:** 335 men, 263 women full time; 468 men, 1,094 women part time. **Faculty:** 128 total (32 full time), 11 with doctorates or other terminal degrees. **Location:** Rural campus in rural community; 26 miles from St. Joseph, Missouri. **Calendar:** Semester, limited summer session. Extensive evening/early morning classes. **Microcomputers:** 71 located in libraries, classrooms, computer centers. **Special facilities:** Art gallery, photography studio, sports medicine/athletic trainer facilities, learning skills center, communication technology complex.

DEGREES OFFERED. AA, AAS. 100 associate degrees awarded in 1992.

UNDERGRADUATE MAJORS. Accounting, advertising, agribusiness, agricultural sciences, allied health, American studies, biological and physical sciences, biology, business administration and management, business and management, business and office, business data processing and related programs, chiropractic, commercial art, communications, community services, computer and information sciences, early childhood education, education, engineering, English, fashion merchandising, fine arts, graphic arts technology, health sciences, home economics, journalism, law enforcement and corrections technologies, legal secretary, liberal/general studies, mathematics, medical secretary, music, nursing, physical sciences, practical nursing, prelaw, psychology, public relations, recreation and community services technologies, science technologies, secretarial and related programs, social sciences, speech, sports medicine, visual and performing arts.

ACADEMIC PROGRAMS. 2-year transfer program, cooperative education, dual enrollment of high school students, independent study, student-designed major. **Remedial services:** Learning center, preadmission summer program, reduced course load, remedial instruction, special counselor, tutoring. **Placement/credit:** AP, CLEP General and Subject, institutional tests; 15 credit hours maximum for associate degree.

ACADEMIC REQUIREMENTS. Freshmen must earn minimum GPA of 1.8 to continue in good standing. 71% of freshmen return for sophomore year. Students must declare major on enrollment. **Graduation requirements:** 62 hours for associate (20 in major). Most students required to take courses in arts/fine arts, English, humanities, mathematics, biological/physical sciences, social sciences.

FRESHMAN ADMISSIONS. Selection criteria: Open admissions. Out-of-state applicants must be in top two-thirds of graduating class or have ACT composite score of 14 or SAT combined score of 660. Placement tests determine program eligibility. **High school preparation:** 11 units recommended. Recommended units include biological science 1, English 3, mathematics 2, physical science 1, social science 2 and science 2.

1992 FRESHMAN CLASS PROFILE. 411 men, 462 women enrolled. 39% had high school GPA of 3.0 or higher, 50% between 2.0 and 2.99. 3% were in top tenth and 10% were in top quarter of graduating class. **Academic background:** Mid 50% of enrolled freshmen had ACT composite between 15-20. 69% submitted ACT scores. **Characteristics:** 92% from in state, 82% commute, 8% have minority backgrounds. Average age is 22.

FALL-TERM APPLICATIONS. No fee. No closing date; priority given to applications received by July 1; applicants notified on a rolling basis beginning on or about April 1; must reply by registration. Interview recommended. Deferred and early admission available. Application deadline for out-of-state applicants August 1, must reply within 2 weeks. SAT or ACT recommended, ACT preferred. Score report by August 1.

STUDENT LIFE. Housing: Dormitories (men, women, coed); apartment housing available. **Activities:** Student government, student newspaper, yearbook, choral groups, concert band, drama, jazz band, music ensembles, musical theater, pep band, forensics, Campus Christian Fellowship, Christian Athletes Association.

ATHLETICS. NJCAA. **Intercollegiate:** Baseball M, basketball, cross-country, football M, softball W, track and field, volleyball W. **Intramural:** Badminton, basketball, softball, table tennis, tennis, volleyball.

STUDENT SERVICES. Aptitude testing, career counseling, employment service for undergraduates, freshman orientation, placement service for graduates, special adviser for adult students, veterans counselor.

ANNUAL EXPENSES. Tuition and fees (1992-93): $930, $1,410 additional for out-of-state students. **Room and board:** $2,600. **Books and supplies:** $350. **Other expenses:** $400.

FINANCIAL AID. 39% of freshmen, 35% of continuing students receive some form of aid. 71% of grants, 71% of loans, 80% of jobs based on need. Academic, music/drama, art, athletic, leadership scholarships available. **Aid applications:** No closing date; priority given to applications received by April 1; applicants notified on a rolling basis beginning on or about April 15. **Additional information:** Auditions and portfolios important for certain scholarship candidates.

ADDRESS/TELEPHONE. David E. Reist, Dean of Student Services, Highland Community College, Main at Elmira, Highland, KS 66035-0068. (913) 442-3236. Fax: (913) 442-3599.

Hutchinson Community College
Hutchinson, Kansas — CB code: 6281

2-year public community college, coed. Founded in 1928. **Accreditation:** Regional. **Undergraduate enrollment:** 893 men, 844 women full time; 736 men, 1,365 women part time. **Faculty:** 267 total (95 full time), 23 with doctorates or other terminal degrees. **Location:** Urban campus in large town; 45 miles from Wichita. **Calendar:** Semester, limited summer session. Saturday and extensive evening/early morning classes. **Microcomputers:** 175 located in libraries, classrooms, computer centers, campus-wide network. **Special facilities:** Kansas Cosmosphere and Space Discovery Center. **Additional facts:** 2 campuses.

DEGREES OFFERED. AA, AAS. 350 associate degrees awarded in 1992. 6% in agriculture, 20% business and management, 7% business/office and marketing/distribution, 7% education, 6% engineering technologies, 11% allied health, 16% multi/interdisciplinary studies.

UNDERGRADUATE MAJORS. Accounting, agricultural business and management, agricultural mechanics, agricultural sciences, architecture, automotive mechanics, automotive technology, biological and physical sciences, biology, business administration and management, business and management, business and office, business data processing and related programs, business data programming, chemistry, child development/care/guidance, chiropractic, clinical laboratory science, commercial art, computer and information sciences, computer servicing technology, computer technology, construction, cytotechnology, data processing, dental assistant, dental hygiene, diesel engine mechanics, drafting, drafting and design technology, dramatic arts, education, electrical technology, electronic technology, elementary education, emergency medical technologies, emergency/disaster science, engineering, engineering and engineering-related technologies, English, fashion merchandising, finance, fine arts, fire control and safety technology, foreign languages (multiple emphasis), forestry and related sciences, funeral services/mortuary science, geology, graphic design, history, home economics, hotel/motel and restaurant management, industrial arts education, industrial technology, insurance and risk management, journalism, law enforcement and corrections, legal assistant/paralegal, legal secretary, liberal/general studies, library science, manufacturing technology, marketing and distribution, mathematics, mechanical design technology, medical laboratory technologies, medical records administration, medical records technology, medical secretary, mining and petroleum technologies, music, music education, nursing, occupational therapy, office supervision and management, optometry, parks and recreation management, pharmacy, physical education, physical sciences, physical therapy, physics, political science and government, predentistry, prelaw, premedicine, prepharmacy, preveterinary, psychology, public administration, public affairs, radio/television broadcasting, radiograph medical technology, recreation and community services technologies, retailing, science technologies, secondary education, secretarial and related programs, small business management and ownership, social sciences, sociology, speech, sports medicine, tourism, transportation and travel marketing, word processing.

ACADEMIC PROGRAMS. 2-year transfer program, dual enrollment of high school students, internships, telecourses. **Remedial services:** Learning center, remedial instruction, special counselor, tutoring. **Placement/credit:** AP, CLEP General and Subject, institutional tests; 16 credit hours maximum for associate degree.

ACADEMIC REQUIREMENTS. Freshmen must earn minimum GPA of 1.69 to continue in good standing. **Graduation requirements:** 64 hours for associate. Most students required to take courses in English, humanities, mathematics, philosophy/religion, biological/physical sciences, social sciences.

FRESHMAN ADMISSIONS. Selection criteria: Open admissions. Selective admissions to associate degree programs in nursing and radiology. **Test requirements:** ACT required for nursing program applicants; score report by March 1.

1992 FRESHMAN CLASS PROFILE. 1,224 men, 1,515 women enrolled. **Characteristics:** 93% from in state, 84% commute, 8% have minority backgrounds. Average age is 20.

FALL-TERM APPLICATIONS. No fee. No closing date; applicants notified on a rolling basis. Interview required for allied health applicants. Audition recommended. March 1 priority date for nursing applicants.

STUDENT LIFE. Housing: Dormitories (men, women). **Activities:** Student government, magazine, student newspaper, yearbook, choral groups, concert band, drama, jazz band, music ensembles, pep band, symphony orchestra.

ATHLETICS. NJCAA. **Intercollegiate:** Baseball M, basketball, cross-country, football M, golf M, softball W, tennis, track and field, volleyball W. **Intramural:** Badminton, basketball, bowling, racquetball, soccer, softball, table tennis, tennis, track and field, volleyball.

STUDENT SERVICES. Aptitude testing, career counseling, employment service for undergraduates, freshman orientation, health services, on-campus day care, personal counseling, placement service for graduates, special adviser for adult students, veterans counselor, services/facilities for handicapped.

ANNUAL EXPENSES. Tuition and fees (1992-93): $840, $1,335 additional for out-of-state students. **Room and board:** $2,200. **Books and supplies:** $500. **Other expenses:** $900.

FINANCIAL AID. 28% of freshmen, 21% of continuing students receive some form of aid. Grants, loans, jobs available. 919 enrolled freshmen were judged to have need, 585 were offered aid. Academic, music/drama, art, athletic, state/district residency, leadership, alumni affiliation, minority scholarships available. **Aid applications:** No closing date; priority given to applications received by March 1; applicants notified on a rolling basis beginning on or about April 1; must reply within 2 weeks.

ADDRESS/TELEPHONE. C. Duane Halpain, Director of Admissions and Records, Hutchinson Community College, 1300 North Plum, Hutchinson, KS 67501. (316) 665-3535. (800) 289-3501. Fax: (316) 655-3310.

Independence Community College
Independence, Kansas — CB code: 6304

2-year public community college, coed. Founded in 1925. **Accreditation:** Regional. **Undergraduate enrollment:** 337 men, 317 women full time; 532 men, 1,065 women part time. **Faculty:** 160 total (30 full time), 11 with doctorates or other terminal degrees. **Location:** Urban campus in large town; 90 miles from Tulsa, Oklahoma. **Calendar:** Semester, limited summer session. **Microcomputers:** 52 located in libraries, classrooms, computer centers. **Special facilities:** William Inge collection including manuscripts and memorabilia.

DEGREES OFFERED. AA, AS, AAS. 97 associate degrees awarded in 1992.

UNDERGRADUATE MAJORS. Accounting, automotive mechanics, automotive technology, biology, business and management, business and office, business computer/console/peripheral equipment operation, business data entry equipment operation, business data processing and related programs, business data programming, chemistry, child development/care/guidance, civil technology, computer and information sciences, drafting, drafting and design technology, engineering, engineering and engineering-related technologies, finance, fine arts, foreign languages (multiple emphasis), French, journalism, liberal/general studies, management science, marketing and distribution, mathematics, music, nursing, office supervision and management, practical nursing, secretarial and related programs, small business management and ownership, social sciences, Spanish, word processing.

ACADEMIC PROGRAMS. 2-year transfer program, double major, dual enrollment of high school students, independent study, internships, telecourses. **Remedial services:** Learning center, reduced course load, remedial instruction, special counselor, tutoring. **Placement/credit:** Institutional tests.

ACADEMIC REQUIREMENTS. Freshmen must earn minimum GPA of 1.5 to continue in good standing. 30% of freshmen return for sophomore year. Students must declare major by end of first year. **Graduation requirements:** 64 hours for associate. Most students required to take courses in arts/fine arts, computer science, English, history, humanities, mathematics, biological/physical sciences, social sciences.

FRESHMAN ADMISSIONS. Selection criteria: Open admissions.

1992 FRESHMAN CLASS PROFILE. 87 men and women enrolled. **Characteristics:** 91% from in state, 88% commute, 9% have minority backgrounds. Average age is 21.

FALL-TERM APPLICATIONS. No fee. No closing date; applicants

notified on a rolling basis. Interview recommended for music applicants. Audition recommended for music applicants.

STUDENT LIFE. Housing: Dormitories (coed). **Activities:** Student government, radio, student newspaper, yearbook, choral groups, concert band, drama, jazz band, music ensembles, musical theater, pep band.

ATHLETICS. NJCAA. **Intercollegiate:** Baseball M, basketball, football M, golf, tennis, track and field, volleyball W. **Intramural:** Archery, badminton, basketball, bowling, softball, table tennis, tennis, volleyball.

STUDENT SERVICES. Aptitude testing, career counseling, employment service for undergraduates, freshman orientation, on-campus day care, personal counseling, placement service for graduates, special adviser for adult students, veterans counselor, services/facilities for handicapped.

ANNUAL EXPENSES. Tuition and fees (1992-93): $780, $1,455 additional for out-of-state students. **Room and board:** $2,500. **Books and supplies:** $400. **Other expenses:** $700.

FINANCIAL AID. 40% of continuing students receive some form of aid. 94% of grants, all loans, 77% of jobs based on need. Academic, music/drama, art, athletic, state/district residency, leadership, alumni affiliation, minority scholarships available. **Aid applications:** No closing date; applicants notified on a rolling basis.

ADDRESS/TELEPHONE. Paula Hastings, Director of Admissions, Independence Community College, Brookside Drive and College Avenue, Independence, KS 67301. (316) 331-4100 ext. 295. Fax: (316) 331-5344.

Johnson County Community College
Overland Park, Kansas — CB code: 6325

2-year public community college, coed. Founded in 1967. **Accreditation:** Regional. **Undergraduate enrollment:** 2,339 men, 2,536 women full time; 4,342 men, 6,275 women part time. **Faculty:** 715 total (279 full time), 33 with doctorates or other terminal degrees. **Location:** Suburban campus in small city; 20 miles from Kansas City, Missouri. **Calendar:** Semester, extensive summer session. Saturday and extensive evening/early morning classes. **Microcomputers:** 160 located in classrooms, computer centers.

DEGREES OFFERED. AA, AS, AAS. 700 associate degrees awarded in 1992. 10% in business and management, 8% health sciences, 5% law, 52% multi/interdisciplinary studies, 5% trade and industry.

UNDERGRADUATE MAJORS. Accounting, aeronautical technology, air conditioning/heating/refrigeration technology, automotive technology, biomedical equipment technology, business administration and management, business data processing and related programs, civil technology, commercial art, computer and information sciences, computer programming, computer technology, data processing, dental hygiene, drafting, drafting and design technology, electronic technology, emergency medical technologies, energy conservation and use technology, fashion merchandising, fire control and safety technology, fire protection, food production/management/services, home furnishings and equipment management/production/services, hotel/motel and restaurant management, interpreter for the deaf, law enforcement and corrections technologies, legal assistant/paralegal, legal secretary, liberal/general studies, manufacturing technology, marketing management, medical records technology, medical secretary, nursing, occupational therapy assistant, office supervision and management, physical therapy assistant, radiograph medical technology, respiratory therapy, respiratory therapy technology, science technologies, secretarial and related programs, veterinarian's assistant, word processing.

ACADEMIC PROGRAMS. 2-year transfer program, cooperative education, double major, dual enrollment of high school students, honors program, independent study, internships, study abroad, telecourses, visiting/exchange student program, weekend college, cross-registration. **Remedial services:** Learning center, reduced course load, remedial instruction, special counselor, tutoring, mathematics resource center, writing center, learning strategies program, new student assessment. **Placement/credit:** AP, CLEP Subject, institutional tests; 30 credit hours maximum for associate degree.

ACADEMIC REQUIREMENTS. No policy requiring minimum GPA; records of students having academic difficulty are reviewed individually. **Graduation requirements:** 64 hours for associate. Most students required to take courses in arts/fine arts, English, humanities, mathematics, biological/physical sciences, social sciences. **Additional information:** Wide variety of telecourses and courses offered by special arrangement.

FRESHMAN ADMISSIONS. Selection criteria: Open admissions. Selective admissions to some allied health programs. **Test requirements:** ACT recommended for all applicants, required for nursing and dental hygiene applicants (score report by February 1).

1992 FRESHMAN CLASS PROFILE. 959 men, 1,051 women enrolled. 32% had high school GPA of 3.0 or higher, 56% between 2.0 and 2.99. **Characteristics:** 93% from in state, 100% commute, 9% have minority backgrounds. Average age is 24.

FALL-TERM APPLICATIONS. $10 fee. No closing date; applicants notified on a rolling basis; must reply by registration. Interview required for nursing, dental hygiene, emergency medical intensive care technician, respiratory therapy, paralegal applicants. Portfolio required for art applicants.

STUDENT LIFE. Activities: Student newspaper, choral groups, concert band, drama, jazz band.

ATHLETICS. NJCAA. **Intercollegiate:** Baseball M, basketball, cross-country, golf M, soccer M, softball W, tennis, track and field, volleyball W. **Intramural:** Basketball M, bowling, handball, racquetball, softball M, table tennis M, tennis M, volleyball M.

STUDENT SERVICES. Aptitude testing, career counseling, employment service for undergraduates, freshman orientation, on-campus day care, personal counseling, placement service for graduates, special adviser for adult students, veterans counselor, services/facilities for handicapped.

ANNUAL EXPENSES. Tuition and fees (1992-93): $990, $1,980 additional for out-of-state students. **Books and supplies:** $400. **Other expenses:** $1,620.

FINANCIAL AID. 25% of freshmen, 25% of continuing students receive some form of aid. 75% of grants, 86% of loans, 34% of jobs based on need. Academic, music/drama, art, athletic, leadership scholarships available. **Aid applications:** No closing date; priority given to applications received by April 15; applicants notified on a rolling basis beginning on or about May 1; must reply within 2 weeks.

ADDRESS/TELEPHONE. Patricia N. Long, Director of Admissions and Records, Johnson County Community College, 12345 College Boulevard, Overland Park, KS 66210-1299. (913) 469-8500. Fax: (913) 469-4409.

Kansas City Kansas Community College
Kansas City, Kansas — CB code: 6333

2-year public community college, coed. Founded in 1923. **Accreditation:** Regional. **Undergraduate enrollment:** 5,876 men and women. **Faculty:** 395 total (122 full time), 38 with doctorates or other terminal degrees. **Location:** Suburban campus in small city; 10 miles from Kansas City, Missouri. **Calendar:** 4-4-1, limited summer session. **Microcomputers:** 75 located in computer centers.

DEGREES OFFERED. AA, AS, AAS. 595 associate degrees awarded in 1992.

UNDERGRADUATE MAJORS. Accounting, agricultural sciences, air conditioning/heating/refrigeration mechanics, air conditioning/heating/refrigeration technology, allied health, automotive mechanics, automotive technology, biology, business and management, business and office, business computer/console/peripheral equipment operation, business data entry equipment operation, business data processing and related programs, business data programming, carpentry, chemistry, computer and information sciences, computer technology, creative writing, data processing, drafting, electrical and electronics equipment repair, electronic technology, elementary education, engineering, finance, fine arts, fire control and safety technology, French, funeral services/mortuary science, German, graphic arts technology, history, home economics, industrial equipment maintenance and repair, jazz, journalism, law enforcement and corrections technologies, marketing and distribution, mathematics, medical assistant, music, nursing, physical sciences, physical therapy assistant, predentistry, prelaw, premedicine, prepharmacy, printmaking, psychology, recreation and community services technologies, recreation therapy, respiratory therapy, respiratory therapy technology, robotics, science technologies, secondary education, secretarial and related programs, social sciences, social work, sociology, Spanish, word processing.

ACADEMIC PROGRAMS. 2-year transfer program, double major, dual enrollment of high school students, external degree, honors program, independent study, internships, telecourses, weekend college, PACE (program for adult college education). **Remedial services:** Learning center, remedial instruction, tutoring. **Placement/credit:** AP, CLEP General, institutional tests; 15 credit hours maximum for associate degree.

ACADEMIC REQUIREMENTS. Freshmen must earn minimum GPA of 1.5 to continue in good standing. 38% of freshmen return for sophomore year. Students must declare major on enrollment. **Graduation requirements:** 60 hours for associate (30 in major). Most students required to take courses in arts/fine arts, computer science, English, history, humanities, mathematics, philosophy/religion, biological/physical sciences, social sciences.

FRESHMAN ADMISSIONS. Selection criteria: Open admissions.

1992 FRESHMAN CLASS PROFILE. 1,144 men and women enrolled. **Characteristics:** 98% from in state, 100% commute, 3% have minority backgrounds. Average age is 24.

FALL-TERM APPLICATIONS. No closing date; applicants notified on a rolling basis; must reply by registration.

STUDENT LIFE. Activities: Student government, student newspaper, choral groups, concert band, drama, jazz band, music ensembles, pep band, symphony orchestra.

ATHLETICS. NJCAA. **Intercollegiate:** Baseball M, basketball, cross-country, golf, softball W, tennis, track and field, volleyball W. **Intramural:** Baseball, basketball, bowling, soccer.

STUDENT SERVICES. Aptitude testing, career counseling, employment service for undergraduates, health services, on-campus day care, personal counseling, placement service for graduates, special adviser for adult students, veterans counselor, services/facilities for handicapped.

ANNUAL EXPENSES. Tuition and fees (projected): $672, $1,080 additional for out-of-state students. **Books and supplies:** $750.

FINANCIAL AID. 17% of freshmen, 66% of continuing students re-

ceive some form of aid. 96% of grants, 77% of loans, 71% of jobs based on need. 841 enrolled freshmen were judged to have need, 593 were offered aid. Academic, music/drama, athletic, state/district residency, leadership, alumni affiliation, minority scholarships available. **Aid applications:** No closing date; priority given to applications received by April 15; applicants notified on a rolling basis beginning on or about April 15; must reply within 4 weeks.

ADDRESS/TELEPHONE. B. Buaurer, Director of Admissions/Registrar, Kansas City Kansas Community College, 7250 State Avenue, Kansas City, KS 66112. (913) 596-9600.

Kansas Newman College
Wichita, Kansas — CB code: 6615

Admissions: 80% of applicants accepted
Based on:
••• School record
•• Activities, interview, test scores
• Essay, recommendations, special talents

Completion: 90% of freshmen end year in good standing
29% graduate, 19% of these enter graduate study

4-year private liberal arts college, coed, affiliated with Roman Catholic Church. Founded in 1933. **Accreditation:** Regional. **Undergraduate enrollment:** 215 men, 593 women full time; 333 men, 477 women part time. **Faculty:** 71 total (68 full time), 18 with doctorates or other terminal degrees. **Location:** Urban campus in large city; 160 miles from Oklahoma City, Oklahoma, 180 miles from Kansas City. **Calendar:** Semester, limited summer session. Saturday and extensive evening/early morning classes. **Microcomputers:** 30 located in libraries, classrooms, computer centers. **Special facilities:** Planetarium, photography laboratory.

DEGREES OFFERED. AS, BA, BS, MEd. 75 associate degrees awarded in 1992. 78% in health sciences, 20% life sciences. 346 bachelor's degrees awarded. 56% in business and management, 19% teacher education, 6% health sciences.

UNDERGRADUATE MAJORS. Associate: Addictions counseling, computer and information sciences, health sciences, information sciences and systems, liberal/general studies, medical laboratory technologies, nursing, radiograph medical technology, ultrasound technology. **Bachelor's:** Accounting, addictions counseling, biology, business administration and management, business and management, chemistry, clinical laboratory science, communications, cytotechnology, education, elementary education, English, fine arts, fitness management, graphic design, health care administration, health sciences, history, information sciences and systems, marketing and distribution, marketing management, mathematics, medical radiation dosimetry, nuclear medical technology, nursing, occupational therapy, pastoral ministry, predentistry, prelaw, premedicine, prepharmacy, preveterinary, psychology, secondary education, sociology, statistics, theological studies.

ACADEMIC PROGRAMS. 2-year transfer program, accelerated program, cooperative education, double major, dual enrollment of high school students, honors program, independent study, internships, study abroad, weekend college, cross-registration; liberal arts/career combination in engineering, health sciences. **Remedial services:** Learning center, reduced course load, remedial instruction, special counselor, tutoring. **Placement/credit:** AP, CLEP General and Subject, institutional tests; 30 credit hours maximum for bachelor's degree.

ACADEMIC REQUIREMENTS. Freshmen must earn minimum GPA of 1.6 to continue in good standing. 60% of freshmen return for sophomore year. Students must declare major by end of second year. **Graduation requirements:** 62 hours for associate (18 in major), 124 hours for bachelor's (30 in major). Most students required to take courses in arts/fine arts, English, history, humanities, mathematics, philosophy/religion, biological/physical sciences, social sciences. **Postgraduate studies:** 2% enter law school, 3% enter medical school, 4% enter MBA programs, 10% enter other graduate study.

FRESHMAN ADMISSIONS. Selection criteria: Caliber of high school curriculum, GPA, class rank, interview important. Special consideration given to veterans and to applicants involved in school and community activities. **High school preparation:** 23 units recommended. Recommended units include biological science 1, English 4, foreign language 2, mathematics 3, physical science 1 and social science 2. **Test requirements:** SAT or ACT (ACT preferred); score report by August 15.

1992 FRESHMAN CLASS PROFILE. 107 men applied, 85 accepted, 28 enrolled; 160 women applied, 129 accepted, 72 enrolled. 53% had high school GPA of 3.0 or higher, 43% between 2.0 and 2.99. **Academic background:** Mid 50% of enrolled freshmen had ACT composite between 18-24. 59% submitted ACT scores. **Characteristics:** 87% from in state, 75% commute, 6% have minority backgrounds. Average age is 18.

FALL-TERM APPLICATIONS. $15 fee, may be waived for applicants with need. No closing date; priority given to applications received by May 1; applicants notified on a rolling basis. Portfolio recommended for art applicants. Interview recommended for all applicants, required for applicants with grade-point average below 2.0. CRDA. Deferred and early admission available. EDP-F.

STUDENT LIFE. Housing: Dormitories (coed). Freshmen required to live in college housing first 2 years if not living with parents. **Activities:** Student government, magazine, student newspaper, television, choral groups, music ensembles, musical theater, campus ministries.

ATHLETICS. NAIA. **Intercollegiate:** Baseball M, basketball W, golf M, soccer, softball W, volleyball W. **Intramural:** Basketball, bowling, racquetball, soccer, softball, table tennis, volleyball.

STUDENT SERVICES. Aptitude testing, career counseling, employment service for undergraduates, freshman orientation, personal counseling, placement service for graduates, special adviser for adult students.

ANNUAL EXPENSES. Tuition and fees (projected): $7,380. **Room and board:** $3,486. **Books and supplies:** $586. **Other expenses:** $1,458.

FINANCIAL AID. 88% of freshmen, 70% of continuing students receive some form of aid. 65% of grants, 70% of loans based on need. 55 enrolled freshmen were judged to have need, all were offered aid. **Aid applications:** No closing date; priority given to applications received by March 15; applicants notified on a rolling basis beginning on or about March 1; must reply within 2 weeks.

ADDRESS/TELEPHONE. Ken R. Rasp, Dean of Admissions, Kansas Newman College, 3100 McCormick Avenue, Wichita, KS 67213-2097. (316) 942-4291 ext. 144. (800) 736-7585 ext. 144. Fax: (316) 942-4483.

Kansas State University
Manhattan, Kansas — CB code: 6334

4-year public university and technical college, coed. Founded in 1863. **Accreditation:** Regional. **Undergraduate enrollment:** 8,234 men, 6,913 women full time; 1,296 men, 1,144 women part time. **Graduate enrollment:** 1,072 men, 724 women full time; 791 men, 1,050 women part time. **Faculty:** 1,843 total (1,430 full time), 840 with doctorates or other terminal degrees. **Location:** Suburban campus in large town; 120 miles from Kansas City. **Calendar:** Semester, extensive summer session. Saturday and extensive evening/early morning classes. **Microcomputers:** 350 located in dormitories, classrooms, computer centers. **Special facilities:** Trigma Mark II nuclear reactor, Konza Prairie for biological research, laser laboratory, Center for Basic Cancer Research. **Additional facts:** Associate/bachelor's degrees available at Kansas State University at Salina.

DEGREES OFFERED. AA, AS, BA, BS, MA, MS, MBA, MFA, MEd, PhD, EdD, DVM. 87 associate degrees awarded in 1992. 5% in agriculture, 71% engineering technologies, 22% multi/interdisciplinary studies. 3,013 bachelor's degrees awarded. 11% in agriculture, 18% business and management, 6% communications, 14% education, 12% engineering, 8% home economics, 5% life sciences, 11% social sciences. Graduate degrees offered in 120 major fields of study.

UNDERGRADUATE MAJORS. Associate: Aeronautical technology, air traffic control, aircraft mechanics, Airframe and power plant, airline piloting and navigation, chemical manufacturing technology, civil technology, computer technology, electronic technology, industrial technology, information sciences and systems, manufacturing technology, mechanical design technology, prenursing, preoccupational therapy, prerespiratory therapy, retail floriculture, survey and mapping technology. **Bachelor's:** Accounting, advertising, agribusiness, agricultural business and management, agricultural economics, agricultural education, agricultural engineering, agricultural mechanics, agricultural sciences, agronomy, animal sciences, anthropology, apparel and accessories marketing, architectural engineering, architecture, art education, bakery science, biochemistry, biological and physical sciences, biology, business administration and management, business and management, business economics, business education, chemical engineering, chemistry, civil engineering, commercial art, community health work, computer and information sciences, computer engineering, conservation and regulation, creative writing, criminal justice studies, dairy, dance, dramatic arts, economics, electrical/electronics/communications engineering, elementary education, engineering and engineering-related technologies, English, English education, English literature, equestrian science, family and community services, fashion design, fashion merchandising, feed science and management, finance, fine arts, fishing and fisheries, food production/management/services, food science and nutrition, food sciences, foreign languages education, forestry and related sciences, French, genetics, human and animal, geography, geology, geophysics and seismology, German, graphic and printing production, history, home economics, home economics education, horticultural science, horticulture, hotel/motel and restaurant management, human environment and housing, human resources development, humanities, humanities and social sciences, individual and family development, industrial engineering, information sciences and systems, interior design, journalism, landscape architecture, leisure and recreational studies, management information systems, marketing management, mathematics, mathematics education, mechanical engineering, medical laboratory technologies, microbiology, milling science and management, music, music education, nuclear engineering, nuclear technologies, nutrition and exercise science, nutritional sciences, ornamental horticulture, parks and recreation management, pathology, human and animal, philosophy, physical education, physical sciences, physics, physiology, human and animal, plant protection, plant sciences, political science and government, poultry, predentistry, prelaw, premedicine, prepharmacy, preveterinary, psychology, public relations, radio/television broadcasting, radio/television technology, range management, renewable natural resources, Russian, science education, secondary education, social sciences, social studies education, social work, sociology, soil sciences, Spanish, speech, speech pathology/audiology, speech/communication/theater education, statistics, textiles and clothing, water and wastewater technology, word processing.

ACADEMIC PROGRAMS. 2-year transfer program, accelerated program, cooperative education, double major, dual enrollment of high school students, external degree, honors program, independent study, internships, study abroad, teacher preparation, visiting/exchange student program, weekend college; liberal arts/career combination in forestry, health sciences, business; combined bachelor's/graduate program in business administration. **Remedial services:** Learning center, preadmission summer program, reduced course load, remedial instruction, special counselor, tutoring, academic assistance center. **ROTC:** Air Force, Army. **Placement/credit:** AP, CLEP General and Subject, IB, institutional tests.

ACADEMIC REQUIREMENTS. Freshmen must earn minimum GPA of 2.0 to continue in good standing. 76% of freshmen return for sophomore year. Students must declare major by end of second year. **Graduation requirements:** 60 hours for associate, 120 hours for bachelor's. Most students required to take courses in English, humanities, mathematics, biological/physical sciences, social sciences. **Postgraduate studies:** 5% enter law school, 2% enter medical school, 1% enter MBA programs, 24% enter other graduate study.

FRESHMAN ADMISSIONS. Selection criteria: Open admissions. Out-of-state applicants must be in top half of class and show academic promise on basis of ACT scores. Architecture students must meet additional selective criteria. **High school preparation:** 15 units recommended. Recommended units include English 4, foreign language 2, mathematics 3, social science 3 and science 3. **Test requirements:** SAT or ACT (ACT preferred); score report by August 1. SAT or ACT used for admissions for out-of-state applicants only.

1992 FRESHMAN CLASS PROFILE. 5,679 men and women applied, 3,931 accepted; 1,594 men enrolled, 1,506 women enrolled. 69% had high school GPA of 3.0 or higher, 28% between 2.0 and 2.99. **Academic background:** Mid 50% of enrolled freshmen had ACT composite between 19-25. 90% submitted ACT scores. **Characteristics:** 88% from in state, 55% live in college housing, 12% have minority backgrounds, 1% are foreign students, 18% join fraternities/sororities. Average age is 19.

FALL-TERM APPLICATIONS. $15 fee. No closing date; priority given to applications received by August 1; applicants notified on a rolling basis. Interview recommended for academically weak applicants. Audition recommended for music, theater applicants. Portfolio recommended for art, architecture applicants.

STUDENT LIFE. Housing: Dormitories (men, women, coed); apartment, fraternity, sorority, cooperative housing available. **Activities:** Student government, film, magazine, radio, student newspaper, television, yearbook, choral groups, concert band, dance, drama, jazz band, marching band, music ensembles, musical theater, opera, pep band, symphony orchestra, fraternities, sororities, 340 religious, political, ethnic, and social service clubs and organizations.

ATHLETICS. NCAA. **Intercollegiate:** Baseball M, basketball, cross-country, football M, golf, tennis W, track and field, volleyball W. **Intramural:** Archery M, badminton, basketball, bowling, cross-country, golf, handball, racquetball, rifle, rowing (crew), rugby, soccer, softball, swimming, table tennis, tennis, track and field, volleyball, water polo, wrestling.

STUDENT SERVICES. Aptitude testing, career counseling, employment service for undergraduates, freshman orientation, health services, on-campus day care, personal counseling, placement service for graduates, special adviser for adult students, veterans counselor, services/facilities for handicapped.

ANNUAL EXPENSES. Tuition and fees (1992-93): $1,841, $4,172 additional for out-of-state students. **Room and board:** $2,840. **Books and supplies:** $572. **Other expenses:** $1,710.

FINANCIAL AID. 38% of freshmen, 63% of continuing students receive some form of aid. All grants, 92% of loans, all jobs based on need. 1,450 enrolled freshmen were judged to have need, all were offered aid. Academic, music/drama, art, athletic, state/district residency, leadership, alumni affiliation, minority scholarships available. **Aid applications:** No closing date; priority given to applications received by March 15; applicants notified on a rolling basis beginning on or about April 15; must reply within 10 days.

ADDRESS/TELEPHONE. Richard Elkins, Director of Admissions, Kansas State University, Anderson Hall, Room 119, Manhattan, KS 66506. (913) 532-6250. Fax: (913) 532-6393.

Kansas State University-Salina
Salina, Kansas — CB code: 1172

2-year public engineering college. **Accreditation:** Regional. **Undergraduate enrollment:** 850 men and women. **Location:** Large town.

FRESHMAN ADMISSIONS. Selection criteria: Open admissions.

ADDRESS/TELEPHONE. Bonnie Scranton, Director of College Advancement, Kansas State University-Salina, 2409 Scanlon Avenue, Salina, KS 67401-8196. (913) 825-0575. Fax: (913) 825-8475.

Kansas Wesleyan University
Salina, Kansas — CB code: 6337

4-year private liberal arts college, coed, affiliated with United Methodist Church. Founded in 1886. **Accreditation:** Regional. **Undergraduate enrollment:** 753 men and women. **Faculty:** 56 total (38 full time), 23 with doctorates or other terminal degrees. **Location:** Suburban campus in large town; 90 miles from Wichita, 180 miles from Kansas City. **Calendar:** Semester, limited summer session. Extensive evening/early morning classes. **Microcomputers:** 50 located in libraries, classrooms, computer centers. **Special facilities:** Observatory with a "16" Cassegrain telescope.

DEGREES OFFERED. AA, AAS, BA, BS. 51 associate degrees awarded in 1992. 7% in business and management, 90% health sciences. 73 bachelor's degrees awarded. 20% in business and management, 31% education, 5% mathematics, 8% parks/recreation, protective services, public affairs, 8% psychology, 5% social sciences, 5% visual and performing arts.

UNDERGRADUATE MAJORS. Associate: Business and management, computer and information sciences, criminal justice studies, early childhood education, nursing, practical nursing. **Bachelor's:** Accounting, advertising art, art education, arts management, biology, business administration and management, business and management, chemistry, clinical laboratory science, commercial art, communications, computer and information sciences, counseling psychology, criminal justice studies, cytotechnology, dramatic arts, elementary education, English, history, mathematics, medical laboratory technologies, music, music education, nursing, physics, practical nursing, prelaw, psychology, religion, religious education, sociology, Spanish, speech, studio art.

ACADEMIC PROGRAMS. Double major, dual enrollment of high school students, independent study, internships, student-designed major, teacher preparation, cross-registration, bachelor of applied science in business offered in association with Brown Mackie College; liberal arts/career combination in engineering, health sciences. **Remedial services:** Learning center, reduced course load, remedial instruction, special counselor, tutoring, one-to-one study skills instruction. **Placement/credit:** AP, CLEP General and Subject, institutional tests; 30 credit hours maximum for bachelor's degree.

ACADEMIC REQUIREMENTS. Freshmen must earn minimum GPA of 1.7 to continue in good standing. Students must declare major by end of second year. **Graduation requirements:** 65 hours for associate (20 in major), 126 hours for bachelor's (36 in major). Most students required to take courses in arts/fine arts, computer science, English, foreign languages, history, humanities, mathematics, philosophy/religion, biological/physical sciences, social sciences.

FRESHMAN ADMISSIONS. Selection criteria: Test scores and rank in class most important, followed by GPA, reference letter, interview. Applicant must have ACT composite score of 18 or SAT combined score of 700 and high school GPA of 2.5 or rank in top half of class. **Test requirements:** SAT or ACT (ACT preferred); score report by August 28.

1992 FRESHMAN CLASS PROFILE. 141 men and women enrolled. 45% had high school GPA of 3.0 or higher, 55% between 2.0 and 2.99. 10% were in top tenth and 15% were in top quarter of graduating class. **Characteristics:** 54% from in state, 57% live in college housing, 26% have minority backgrounds, 1% are foreign students. Average age is 18.

FALL-TERM APPLICATIONS. $15 fee. No closing date; applicants notified on a rolling basis. Interview recommended for academically weak applicants. Audition recommended for music applicants. Portfolio recommended for art applicants. Deferred and early admission available.

STUDENT LIFE. Housing: Dormitories (men, women); apartment housing available. **Activities:** Student government, magazine, radio, student newspaper, yearbook, choral groups, drama, jazz band, music ensembles, musical theater, pep band, stage band, brass choir, sororities, Campus Council on Ministry, Fellowship of Christian Athletes, Theophiles multicultural organization.

ATHLETICS. NAIA. **Intercollegiate:** Baseball M, basketball, cross-country, football M, golf M, softball W, track and field, volleyball W. **Intramural:** Basketball, softball, tennis, volleyball.

STUDENT SERVICES. Aptitude testing, career counseling, employment service for undergraduates, freshman orientation, health services, personal counseling, placement service for graduates, special adviser for adult students, veterans counselor, services/facilities for handicapped.

ANNUAL EXPENSES. Tuition and fees: $8,020. **Room and board:** $3,200. **Books and supplies:** $500. **Other expenses:** $500.

FINANCIAL AID. 97% of freshmen, 97% of continuing students receive some form of aid. 75% of grants, 86% of loans, 50% of jobs based on need. Academic, music/drama, art, athletic, leadership, alumni affiliation, religious affiliation scholarships available. **Aid applications:** No closing date; priority given to applications received by March 1; applicants notified on a rolling basis beginning on or about April 1; must reply by May 1 or within 2 weeks if notified thereafter.

ADDRESS/TELEPHONE. Valerie Robinson, Director of Admissions, Kansas Wesleyan University, 100 East Claflin, Salina, KS 67401-6196. (913) 827-5541 ext. 307. (800) 874-1154.

Labette Community College

Parsons, Kansas CB code: 6576

2-year public community college, coed. Founded in 1923. **Accreditation:** Regional. **Undergraduate enrollment:** 315 men, 406 women full time; 411 men, 1,111 women part time. **Faculty:** 139 total (33 full time), 9 with doctorates or other terminal degrees. **Location:** Rural campus in large town; 130 miles from Kansas City. **Calendar:** Semester, extensive summer session. **Microcomputers:** 110 located in libraries, computer centers.

DEGREES OFFERED. AA, AS. 224 associate degrees awarded in 1992. 27% in health sciences, 39% multi/interdisciplinary studies, 34% visual and performing arts.

UNDERGRADUATE MAJORS. Accounting, air conditioning/heating/refrigeration mechanics, biology, business administration and management, business and management, chemistry, commercial art, communications, computer and information sciences, criminal justice studies, data processing, elementary education, engineering, fire control and safety technology, journalism, law enforcement and corrections technologies, legal secretary, liberal/general studies, mathematics, medical secretary, music, nursing, psychology, radiograph medical technology, respiratory therapy, secondary education, secretarial and related programs, social sciences.

ACADEMIC PROGRAMS. 2-year transfer program, dual enrollment of high school students, telecourses. **Remedial services:** Learning center, reduced course load, remedial instruction, tutoring. **Placement/credit:** AP, CLEP General and Subject, institutional tests; 30 credit hours maximum for associate degree.

ACADEMIC REQUIREMENTS. Freshmen must earn minimum GPA of 1.6 to continue in good standing. 75% of freshmen return for sophomore year. Students must declare major on enrollment. **Graduation requirements:** 60 hours for associate (15 in major). Most students required to take courses in English, history, humanities, mathematics, biological/physical sciences, social sciences.

FRESHMAN ADMISSIONS. Selection criteria: Open admissions. **Test requirements:** ACT for placement; score report by August 1. ACT and School and College Ability Tests required of nursing applicants.

1992 FRESHMAN CLASS PROFILE. 175 men, 347 women enrolled. 40% had high school GPA of 3.0 or higher, 40% between 2.0 and 2.99. **Characteristics:** 95% from in state, 99% commute, 10% have minority backgrounds, 1% are foreign students.

FALL-TERM APPLICATIONS. No fee. No closing date; applicants notified on a rolling basis; must reply by registration. Interview required for nursing, radiology, respiratory therapy applicants. Deferred and early admission available.

STUDENT LIFE. Housing: Dormitories (men, women). **Activities:** Student government, student newspaper, student directory, choral groups, concert band, drama, jazz band, Young Democrats, Young Republicans, Circle-K.

ATHLETICS. NJCAA. **Intercollegiate:** Baseball M, basketball, tennis W, volleyball W, wrestling M. **Intramural:** Basketball, bowling, boxing, tennis, volleyball.

STUDENT SERVICES. Career counseling, employment service for undergraduates, personal counseling, placement service for graduates, veterans counselor, services/facilities for handicapped.

ANNUAL EXPENSES. Tuition and fees (1992-93): $690, $1,800 additional for out-of-state students. **Room and board:** $2,160. **Books and supplies:** $320. **Other expenses:** $425.

FINANCIAL AID. 44% of freshmen, 45% of continuing students receive some form of aid. 90% of loans, 51% of jobs based on need. **Aid applications:** No closing date; applicants notified on a rolling basis; must reply by registration.

ADDRESS/TELEPHONE. Janet Eads, Associate Dean of Student Services, Labette Community College, 200 South 14th Street, Parsons, KS 67357. (316) 421-6700. Fax: (316) 421-0180.

Manhattan Christian College

Manhattan, Kansas CB code: 6392

4-year private Bible college, coed, affiliated with Christian Church. Founded in 1927. **Undergraduate enrollment:** 96 men, 77 women full time; 44 men, 41 women part time. **Faculty:** 21 total (11 full time), 4 with doctorates or other terminal degrees. **Location:** Suburban campus in large town; 130 miles from Kansas City. **Calendar:** Semester, limited summer session. **Additional facts:** Students have access to Kansas State University library.

DEGREES OFFERED. AA, BA, BS. 5 associate degrees awarded in 1992. 100% in philosophy, religion, theology. 15 bachelor's degrees awarded. 100% in philosophy, religion, theology.

UNDERGRADUATE MAJORS. Associate: Bible studies, missionary studies, religious education. **Bachelor's:** Bible studies, missionary studies, religion, religious education, religious music, theological studies.

ACADEMIC PROGRAMS. Double major, internships, dual degree program with Kansas State University. **Remedial services:** Reduced course load, special counselor, tutoring. **Placement/credit:** AP, CLEP Subject, institutional tests; 18 credit hours maximum for bachelor's degree.

ACADEMIC REQUIREMENTS. Freshmen must earn minimum GPA of 1.75 to continue in good standing. 74% of freshmen return for sophomore year. Students must declare major by end of first year. **Graduation requirements:** 65 hours for associate (37 in major), 179 hours for bachelor's (36 in major). Most students required to take courses in English, history, humanities, philosophy/religion, biological/physical sciences, social sciences. **Postgraduate studies:** 26% from 2-year programs enter 4-year programs. **Additional information:** Joint programs with Kansas State University available.

FRESHMAN ADMISSIONS. Selection criteria: High school record, SAT/ACT scores, recommendations. **Test requirements:** SAT or ACT; score report by May 15.

1992 FRESHMAN CLASS PROFILE. 37 men, 24 women enrolled. 15% had high school GPA of 3.0 or higher, 53% between 2.0 and 2.99. **Characteristics:** 63% from in state, 98% live in college housing, 4% have minority backgrounds, 3% are foreign students. Average age is 18.

FALL-TERM APPLICATIONS. $20 fee. No closing date; priority given to applications received by March 15; applicants notified on a rolling basis. Interview recommended. Audition recommended for music applicants. Essay recommended. Character recommendations required. Deferred admission available.

STUDENT LIFE. Housing: Dormitories (men, women); apartment housing available. **Activities:** Student government, student newspaper, yearbook, missions group, choral groups, concert band, drama, music ensembles, pep band.

ATHLETICS. Intercollegiate: Basketball, golf, soccer M, volleyball W. **Intramural:** Baseball, basketball, racquetball, softball, table tennis, tennis, volleyball.

STUDENT SERVICES. Career counseling, employment service for undergraduates, freshman orientation, health services, personal counseling, services/facilities for handicapped.

ANNUAL EXPENSES. Tuition and fees: $4,140. **Room and board:** $2,670. **Books and supplies:** $600. **Other expenses:** $800.

FINANCIAL AID. 70% of freshmen, 78% of continuing students receive some form of aid. 83% of grants, 87% of loans, all jobs based on need. Academic scholarships available. **Aid applications:** No closing date; priority given to applications received by April 1; applicants notified on a rolling basis beginning on or about June 15; must reply within 2 weeks.

ADDRESS/TELEPHONE. John Poulson, Vice President of Admissions, Manhattan Christian College, 1415 Anderson Avenue, Manhattan, KS 66502. (913) 539-3571. Fax: (913) 539-3571.

McPherson College

McPherson, Kansas CB code: 6404

4-year private liberal arts college, coed, affiliated with Church of the Brethren. Founded in 1887. **Accreditation:** Regional. **Undergraduate enrollment:** 199 men, 165 women full time; 30 men, 85 women part time. **Faculty:** 51 total (38 full time), 27 with doctorates or other terminal degrees. **Location:** Suburban campus in large town; 60 miles from Wichita. **Calendar:** 4-1-4, limited summer session. **Microcomputers:** 25 located in dormitories, classrooms, computer centers. **Special facilities:** College and community-operated museum. **Additional facts:** Only degree program in antique auto restoration in United States.

DEGREES OFFERED. AA, BA, BS. 5 associate degrees awarded in 1992. 100% in trade and industry. 80 bachelor's degrees awarded. 32% in business and management, 15% teacher education, 5% life sciences, 8% philosophy, religion, theology, 12% trade and industry.

UNDERGRADUATE MAJORS. Associate: Antique automobile restoration, automotive technology. **Bachelor's:** Accounting, agribusiness, agricultural economics, agricultural sciences, art education, biology, business administration and management, business education, chemistry, computer and information sciences, dramatic arts, early childhood education, education of the mentally handicapped, education of the physically handicapped, elementary education, English, English education, environmental science, fine arts, foreign languages (multiple emphasis), foreign languages education, German, health sciences, history, industrial arts education, industrial technology, interior design, junior high education, mathematics, mathematics education, music, music education, music performance, philosophy, physical education, physical sciences, physics, prelaw, psychology, religion, science education, secondary education, social science education, social sciences, social studies education, sociology, Spanish, special education, specific learning disabilities, speech, speech/communication/theater education.

ACADEMIC PROGRAMS. Cooperative education, double major, dual enrollment of high school students, independent study, internships, student-designed major, study abroad, teacher preparation, visiting/exchange student program, cross-registration, cooperative degree program with Kansas State University in agriculture. **Remedial services:** Learning center, reduced course load, remedial instruction, tutoring. **Placement/credit:** AP, CLEP General and Subject, institutional tests.

ACADEMIC REQUIREMENTS. Freshmen must earn minimum GPA of 2.0 to continue in good standing. 71% of freshmen return for sophomore year. Students must declare major by end of second year. **Graduation requirements:** 65 hours for associate (56 in major), 124 hours for bachelor's (32 in major). Most students required to take courses in arts/fine arts, computer science, English, history, humanities, mathematics, philosophy/religion, biological/physical sciences, social sciences. **Postgraduate studies:** 10% from 2-year programs enter 4-year programs.

FRESHMAN ADMISSIONS. Selection criteria: Applicants must meet 2 of the following 3 criteria: rank in top third of high school class, 2.25 high school GPA, or ACT composite score of 19. **Test requirements:** SAT or ACT (ACT preferred); score report by September 1.

1992 FRESHMAN CLASS PROFILE. 92 men, 39 women enrolled. 68% had high school GPA of 3.0 or higher, 29% between 2.0 and 2.99. **Academic background:** Mid 50% of enrolled freshmen had ACT composite between 15-30. 70% submitted ACT scores. **Characteristics:** 45% from in state, 92% live in college housing, 5% have minority backgrounds, 5% are foreign students. Average age is 18.

FALL-TERM APPLICATIONS. $15 fee, may be waived for applicants with need. No closing date; applicants notified on a rolling basis; must reply within 4 weeks. Interview recommended. Deferred and early admission available.

STUDENT LIFE. Housing: Dormitories (men, women, coed); apartment housing available. Unmarried students under 23 years old not living with parents required to live in residence halls. **Activities:** Student government, student newspaper, yearbook, choral groups, concert band, dance, drama, jazz band, music ensembles, musical theater, 44 clubs and organizations including Minority Student Union, Brethren Identity Group, Peace Awareness Group, Circle-K, Fellowship of Christian Athletes.

ATHLETICS. NAIA. **Intercollegiate:** Basketball, cross-country, football M, golf, soccer, tennis, track and field, volleyball W. **Intramural:** Badminton, handball, racquetball, table tennis, tennis, volleyball.

STUDENT SERVICES. Career counseling, employment service for undergraduates, freshman orientation, health services, personal counseling, placement service for graduates.

ANNUAL EXPENSES. Tuition and fees (1992-93): $7,500. **Room and board:** $3,420. **Books and supplies:** $530. **Other expenses:** $1,536.

FINANCIAL AID. 91% of freshmen, 83% of continuing students receive some form of aid. 42% of grants, 95% of loans based on need. 58 enrolled freshmen were judged to have need, all were offered aid. Academic, music/drama, athletic, leadership, alumni affiliation, religious affiliation, minority scholarships available. **Aid applications:** No closing date; priority given to applications received by April 15; applicants notified on a rolling basis beginning on or about January 15; must reply within 2 weeks. **Additional information:** Early estimate of financial aid called Priority Award upon receipt of financial aid estimator form.

ADDRESS/TELEPHONE. Frederick Schmidt, Director of Admissions, McPherson College, 1600 East Euclid Street, McPherson, KS 67460. (316) 241-0731 ext. 255. Fax: (316) 241-0731 ext. 1664.

MidAmerica Nazarene College
Olathe, Kansas — CB code: 6437

4-year private liberal arts college, coed, affiliated with Church of the Nazarene. Founded in 1966. **Accreditation:** Regional. **Undergraduate enrollment:** 424 men, 523 women full time. **Faculty:** 120 total (83 full time), 40 with doctorates or other terminal degrees. **Location:** Suburban campus in small city; 19 miles from Kansas City, Missouri. **Calendar:** Semester, limited summer session. **Microcomputers:** Located in libraries, classrooms, computer centers.

DEGREES OFFERED. AA, BA, MBA, MEd. 6 associate degrees awarded in 1992. 60% in business/office and marketing/distribution, 40% philosophy, religion, theology. 257 bachelor's degrees awarded. 39% in business and management, 14% teacher education, 5% health sciences, 18% philosophy, religion, theology, 6% psychology. Graduate degrees offered in 2 major fields of study.

UNDERGRADUATE MAJORS. Associate: Agribusiness, agricultural sciences, Bible studies, business and management, early childhood education, humanities and social sciences, religious education, religious music. **Bachelor's:** Accounting, agribusiness, agricultural sciences, biology, business administration and management, business and management, business education, chemistry, communications, computer and information sciences, education, elementary education, English, English education, English literature, foreign languages (multiple emphasis), foreign languages education, history, human resources development, humanities and social sciences, international agriculture, mathematics, mathematics education, music, music education, nursing, physical education, physics, psychology, public relations, religion, religious education, religious music, science education, social science education, social studies education, Spanish, speech/communication/theater education.

ACADEMIC PROGRAMS. Accelerated program, double major, independent study, internships, study abroad, Washington semester, cross-registration, dual degree program with Kansas State University. **Remedial services:** Learning center, reduced course load, remedial instruction, tutoring. **ROTC:** Air Force, Army, Naval. **Placement/credit:** AP, CLEP General and Subject, institutional tests; 25 credit hours maximum for bachelor's degree.

ACADEMIC REQUIREMENTS. Freshmen must earn minimum GPA of 1.6 to continue in good standing. 66% of freshmen return for sophomore year. Students must declare major by end of second year. **Graduation requirements:** 60 hours for associate (30 in major), 126 hours for bachelor's (30 in major). Most students required to take courses in English, humanities, mathematics, philosophy/religion, biological/physical sciences, social sciences. **Postgraduate studies:** 1% enter law school, 2% enter medical school, 5% enter MBA programs, 15% enter other graduate study. **Additional information:** Adults, 25 and older, may earn bachelor's degree through evening division.

FRESHMAN ADMISSIONS. Selection criteria: Open admissions. Selective admissions to nursing, elementary education, and secondary education programs. Recommended units include English 4, mathematics 3, social science 3 and science 3. **Test requirements:** SAT or ACT (ACT preferred) for placement and counseling only; score report by August 1.

1992 FRESHMAN CLASS PROFILE. 225 men and women enrolled. 50% had high school GPA of 3.0 or higher, 36% between 2.0 and 2.99. 17% were in top tenth and 41% were in top quarter of graduating class. **Characteristics:** 51% from in state, 63% live in college housing, 4% have minority backgrounds, 3% are foreign students. Average age is 21.

FALL-TERM APPLICATIONS. $15 fee. No closing date; priority given to applications received by March 1; applicants notified on a rolling basis; must reply within 30 days. Interview recommended for music, nursing, elementary and secondary education applicants. Audition recommended for music applicants. Deferred and early admission available.

STUDENT LIFE. Housing: Dormitories (men, women); apartment housing available. **Activities:** Student government, student newspaper, yearbook, choral groups, concert band, drama, music ensembles, pep band, symphony orchestra.

ATHLETICS. NAIA. **Intercollegiate:** Baseball M, basketball, cross-country, football M, track and field, volleyball W. **Intramural:** Basketball, bowling, softball, volleyball.

STUDENT SERVICES. Career counseling, employment service for undergraduates, freshman orientation, health services, personal counseling, placement service for graduates, placement for education majors, services/facilities for handicapped.

ANNUAL EXPENSES. Tuition and fees (1992-93): $5,838. **Room and board:** $3,390. **Books and supplies:** $600. **Other expenses:** $1,000.

FINANCIAL AID. 87% of freshmen, 81% of continuing students receive some form of aid. Grants, loans, jobs available. Academic, music/drama, athletic, state/district residency scholarships available. **Aid applications:** No closing date; priority given to applications received by March 1; applicants notified on a rolling basis beginning on or about March 30; must reply within 2 weeks.

ADDRESS/TELEPHONE. Dennis Troyer, Director of Admissions, MidAmerica Nazarene College, PO Box 1776, 2030 East College Way, Olathe, KS 66062-1899. (913) 782-3750 ext. 481. (800) 800-8887.

Neosho County Community College
Chanute, Kansas — CB code: 6093

2-year public community college, coed. Founded in 1936. **Accreditation:** Regional. **Undergraduate enrollment:** 236 men, 196 women full time; 290 men, 590 women part time. **Faculty:** 100 total (40 full time), 5 with doctorates or other terminal degrees. **Location:** Rural campus in large town; 110 miles from Kansas City, 100 miles from Wichita. **Calendar:** Semester, limited summer session. **Microcomputers:** 120 located in dormitories, libraries, classrooms, computer centers.

DEGREES OFFERED. AA, AS, AAS. 140 associate degrees awarded in 1992. 30% in business/office and marketing/distribution, 40% education, 20% health sciences, 10% allied health.

UNDERGRADUATE MAJORS. Accounting, air conditioning/heating/refrigeration mechanics, air conditioning/heating/refrigeration technology, automotive mechanics, automotive technology, biological and physical sciences, biology, business and management, business and office, business computer/console/peripheral equipment operation, business data entry equipment operation, business data processing and related programs, business data programming, carpentry, chemistry, communications, computer and information sciences, computer servicing technology, construction, criminal justice studies, diesel engine mechanics, drafting, education, electrical and electronics equipment repair, electronic technology, elementary education, engineering, engineering and engineering-related technologies, English, finance, fine arts, foreign languages (multiple emphasis), home economics, humanities and social sciences, junior high education, law enforcement and corrections, liberal/general studies, marketing and distribution, marketing management, mathematics, music, nursing, office supervision and management, physical sciences, physics, plumbing/pipefitting/steamfitting, predentistry, preengineering, prelaw, premedicine, prepharmacy, preveterinary, psychology, science technologies, secondary education, secretarial and related programs, social sciences, social work, speech, sports medicine, teacher aide, visual and performing arts, woodworking, word processing.

ACADEMIC PROGRAMS. 2-year transfer program, dual enrollment of high school students. **Remedial services:** Learning center, reduced course load, remedial instruction, tutoring. **Placement/credit:** CLEP General, institutional tests; 15 credit hours maximum for associate degree.

ACADEMIC REQUIREMENTS. Freshmen must earn minimum GPA of 1.5 to continue in good standing. 60% of freshmen return for sophomore year. Students must declare major by end of first year. **Graduation requirements:** 61 hours for associate. Most students required to take courses in arts/fine arts, English, history, humanities, mathematics, biological/physical sciences, social sciences.

FRESHMAN ADMISSIONS. Selection criteria: Open admissions. Selective admissions to nursing program.

1992 FRESHMAN CLASS PROFILE. 290 men, 404 women enrolled. 30% had high school GPA of 3.0 or higher, 60% between 2.0 and 2.99. **Academic background:** Mid 50% of enrolled freshmen had ACT composite between 15-20. 40% submitted ACT scores. **Characteristics:** 98% from in state, 90% commute, 9% have minority backgrounds. Average age is 21.

FALL-TERM APPLICATIONS. No fee. No closing date; priority given to applications received by August 15; applicants notified on a rolling basis; must reply by registration. Early admission available. Either SAT or ACT recommended, ACT preferred. Score report by June 1.

STUDENT LIFE. Housing: Dormitories (coed). **Activities:** Student government, choral groups, drama, jazz band, music ensembles, pep band.

ATHLETICS. NJCAA. **Intercollegiate:** Baseball M, basketball, cross-country, softball W, track and field, volleyball W. **Intramural:** Basketball, softball, table tennis, volleyball.

STUDENT SERVICES. Aptitude testing, career counseling, freshman orientation, personal counseling, veterans counselor, services/facilities for handicapped.

ANNUAL EXPENSES. Tuition and fees (projected): $705, $1,440 additional for out-of-state students. **Room and board:** $2,400. **Books and supplies:** $300. **Other expenses:** $350.

FINANCIAL AID. 65% of freshmen, 70% of continuing students receive some form of aid. 84% of grants, 85% of loans, 50% of jobs based on need. Academic, music/drama, art, athletic, state/district residency scholarships available. **Aid applications:** No closing date; applicants notified on a rolling basis; must reply within 4 weeks.

ADDRESS/TELEPHONE. Gary D. Royse, Director of Admissions and Counseling, Neosho County Community College, 1000 South Allen, Chanute, KS 66720. (316) 431-6222. Fax: (316) 431-0082.

Ottawa University
Ottawa, Kansas — CB code: 6547

4-year private liberal arts college, coed, affiliated with American Baptist Churches in the USA. Founded in 1865. **Accreditation:** Regional. **Undergraduate enrollment:** 274 men, 228 women full time; 27 men, 16 women part time. **Faculty:** 45 total (35 full time), 26 with doctorates or other terminal degrees. **Location:** Urban campus in large town; 50 miles from Kansas City. **Calendar:** Semester, limited summer session. **Microcomputers:** Located in classrooms, computer centers. **Special facilities:** Asian art collection. **Additional facts:** Branch campuses in Phoenix, Arizona, and Kansas City.

DEGREES OFFERED. BA. 96 bachelor's degrees awarded in 1992. 28% in business and management, 5% computer sciences, 23% teacher education, 5% letters/literature, 8% life sciences, 6% psychology, 15% social sciences.

UNDERGRADUATE MAJORS. Accounting, American studies, behavioral sciences, biological and physical sciences, biology, business administration and management, business and management, chemistry, communications, computer and information sciences, dramatic arts, economics, education, elementary education, English, fine arts, health care administration, history, humanities, humanities and social sciences, junior high education, mathematics, music, music performance, philosophy, political science and government, prelaw, psychology, religion, religious music, secondary education, social sciences, social work, visual and performing arts.

ACADEMIC PROGRAMS. Accelerated program, double major, independent study, internships, student-designed major, teacher preparation; liberal arts/career combination in engineering, forestry, health sciences. **Remedial services:** Learning center, reduced course load, remedial instruction, tutoring. **Placement/credit:** AP, CLEP General and Subject, institutional tests.

ACADEMIC REQUIREMENTS. Freshmen must earn minimum GPA of 1.6 to continue in good standing. 60% of freshmen return for sophomore year. Students must declare major by end of second year. **Graduation requirements:** 124 hours for bachelor's (24 in major). Most students required to take courses in arts/fine arts, computer science, English, history, humanities, mathematics, philosophy/religion, biological/physical sciences, social sciences.

FRESHMAN ADMISSIONS. Selection criteria: Rank in top half of class, 2.0 high school GPA and ACT composite score of 17 or above required. Personal recommendation and school and community achievements also considered. **Test requirements:** SAT or ACT; score report by August 15.

1992 FRESHMAN CLASS PROFILE. 91 men, 45 women enrolled. 28% had high school GPA of 3.0 or higher, 69% between 2.0 and 2.99. **Academic background:** Mid 50% of enrolled freshmen had ACT composite between 17-23. 80% submitted ACT scores. **Characteristics:** 53% from in state, 95% live in college housing. Average age is 19.

FALL-TERM APPLICATIONS. $15 fee, may be waived for applicants with need. Deposit fee of $100, $50 toward tuition and $50 against potential property damages, refunded. No closing date; priority given to applications received by May 1; applicants notified on a rolling basis; must reply within 4 weeks. Interview required. Audition recommended for music, drama applicants. Portfolio recommended for art applicants. Deferred and early admission available.

STUDENT LIFE. Housing: Dormitories (men, women); apartment housing available. **Activities:** Student government, radio, student newspaper, yearbook, choral groups, concert band, drama, jazz band, music ensembles, musical theater, pep band, Christian Faith in Action, Voluntary Service Organization, Whole Earth Club, Black Student Union, Circle-K.

ATHLETICS. NAIA. **Intercollegiate:** Baseball M, basketball, cross-country, football M, golf M, soccer M, tennis, track and field, volleyball W. **Intramural:** Basketball, soccer, softball, volleyball.

STUDENT SERVICES. Aptitude testing, career counseling, employment service for undergraduates, freshman orientation, health services, personal counseling, placement service for graduates.

ANNUAL EXPENSES. Tuition and fees: $7,290. **Room and board:** $1,620. **Books and supplies:** $600. **Other expenses:** $1,780.

FINANCIAL AID. 92% of freshmen, 95% of continuing students receive some form of aid. All grants, 97% of loans, 49% of jobs based on need. 109 enrolled freshmen were judged to have need, all were offered aid. **Aid applications:** No closing date; priority given to applications received by April 1; applicants notified on a rolling basis beginning on or about February 1; must reply within 8 weeks or within 2 weeks if notified after July 1.

ADDRESS/TELEPHONE. Tim Adams, Director of Admissions, Ottawa University, 1001 South Cedar Street, Ottawa, KS 66067-3399. (913) 242-5200 ext. 5557. (800) 447-4797. Fax: (913) 242-7429.

Pittsburg State University
Pittsburg, Kansas — CB code: 6336

4-year public university, coed. Founded in 1903. **Accreditation:** Regional. **Undergraduate enrollment:** 2,256 men, 2,053 women full time; 255 men, 261 women part time. **Graduate enrollment:** 202 men, 209 women full time; 340 men, 665 women part time. **Faculty:** 305 total (250 full time), 144 with doctorates or other terminal degrees. **Location:** Rural campus in large town; 100 miles from Kansas City. **Calendar:** Semester with 8-week summer session. Extensive evening/early morning classes. **Microcomputers:** 256 located in dormitories, libraries, classrooms, computer centers, campus-wide network. **Special facilities:** Planetarium, observatory, field biology reserve, art gallery, physical education and recreation building. **Additional facts:** Academic service centers in Iola, Coffeyville, Chanute, Parsons, Ft. Scott, and Independence offer courses and some complete degree programs.

DEGREES OFFERED. AAS, BA, BS, MA, MS, MBA, MEd. 851 bachelor's degrees awarded. 16% in business and management, 5% communications, 9% education, 18% teacher education, 12% engineering technologies, 15% psychology, 7% social sciences. Graduate degrees offered in 34 major fields of study.

UNDERGRADUATE MAJORS. Associate: Engineering and engineering-related technologies. **Bachelor's:** Accounting, advertising, art education, art therapy, automotive technology, biological and physical sciences, biology, business administration and management, business and management, business economics, chemistry, child development/care/guidance, clinical laboratory science, communications, computer and information sciences, computer programming, construction, curriculum and instruction, economics, education, electronic technology, elementary education, engineering and engineering-related technologies, English, English education, environmental science, family and community services, fashion design, fashion merchandising, finance, fine arts, food production/management/services, food science and nutrition, French, geography, graphic and printing production, graphic arts technology, health education, history, home economics, industrial arts education, industrial technology, information sciences and systems, interior design, liberal/general studies, manufacturing technology, marketing management, mathematics, mathematics education, mechanical design technology, medical laboratory technologies, music, music performance, nursing, parks and recreation management, physical education, physical sciences, physics, plastic technology, political science and government, predentistry, preengineering, prelaw, premedicine, prepharmacy, preveterinary, psychology, public relations, radio/television broadcasting, recreation therapy, retailing, school psychology, science education, secondary education, social science education, social sciences, social work, sociology, Spanish, speech, textiles and clothing, trade and industrial education, woodworking.

ACADEMIC PROGRAMS. 2-year transfer program, cooperative education, double major, dual enrollment of high school students, education specialist degree, external degree, honors program, independent study, internships, student-designed major, study abroad, telecourses, visiting/exchange student program; liberal arts/career combination in engineering; combined bachelor's/graduate program in business administration. **Remedial services:** Preadmission summer program, reduced course load, remedial instruction, special counselor, tutoring, writing laboratory, intensive English program for international students. **ROTC:** Army. **Placement/credit:** AP, CLEP General and Subject, IB, institutional tests; 24 credit hours maximum for bachelor's degree.

ACADEMIC REQUIREMENTS. Freshmen must earn minimum GPA of 2.0 to continue in good standing. 69% of freshmen return for sophomore year. Students must declare major by end of second year. **Graduation requirements:** 60 hours for associate, 124 hours for bachelor's (30 in major). Most students required to take courses in computer science, English, history, humanities, mathematics, biological/physical sciences, social sciences. **Postgraduate studies:** 50% from 2-year programs enter 4-year programs. 1% enter law school, 2% enter medical school, 5% enter MBA programs, 14% enter other graduate study.

FRESHMAN ADMISSIONS. Selection criteria: Open admissions. Out-of-state students must rank in top half of class or have a 2.0 school GPA. International students must have 520 TOEFL or go to intensive English only. Recommended units include English 4, foreign language 2, mathematics 3 and science 3. **Test requirements:** ACT for counseling; score report by August 16.

1992 FRESHMAN CLASS PROFILE. 490 men, 455 women enrolled. 39% had high school GPA of 3.0 or higher, 31% between 2.0 and 2.99. **Characteristics:** 85% from in state, 59% commute. Average age is 19.

FALL-TERM APPLICATIONS. $15 fee. $55 fee for foreign applicants. No closing date; applicants notified on a rolling basis. Interview recommended. Deferred and early admission available.

STUDENT LIFE. Housing: Dormitories (men, women, coed); apartment, fraternity, sorority housing available. **Activities:** Student government, film, magazine, radio, student newspaper, television, yearbook, choral groups, concert band, dance, drama, jazz band, marching band, music ensembles, musical theater, opera, pep band, symphony orchestra, summer stock theater, fraternities, sororities, 100 organizations: 9 religious organizations, 2 political groups, 36 departmental organizations and professional societies, several ethnic groups. **Additional information:** CARES (campus advisement registration and enrollment sessions) assists new students and parents to adjust to new environment. PINNACLE for adult older student.

ATHLETICS. NCAA. **Intercollegiate:** Baseball M, basketball, cross-country, football M, golf M, softball W, track and field, volleyball W. **Intramural:** Archery M, badminton, basketball, bowling, cross-country, diving, racquetball, rugby, soccer, softball, swimming M, table tennis, tennis, track and field, volleyball, water polo, wrestling M.

STUDENT SERVICES. Aptitude testing, career counseling, employment service for undergraduates, freshman orientation, health services, personal counseling, placement service for graduates, special adviser for adult students, veterans counselor, services/facilities for handicapped.

ANNUAL EXPENSES. Tuition and fees (1992-93): $1,564, $2,880 additional for out-of-state students. **Room and board:** $2,704. **Books and supplies:** $450. **Other expenses:** $1,000.

FINANCIAL AID. 71% of freshmen, 52% of continuing students receive some form of aid. 80% of grants, 89% of loans, 46% of jobs based on need. 329 enrolled freshmen were judged to have need, all were offered aid. Academic, music/drama, art, athletic, state/district residency, leadership, minority scholarships available. **Aid applications:** No closing date; priority given to applications received by March 15; applicants notified on a rolling basis beginning on or about May 15; must reply within 2 weeks.

ADDRESS/TELEPHONE. Ange Peterson, Assistant Director of Enrollment Services, Pittsburg State University, 1701 South Broadway, Pittsburg, KS 66762. (316) 235-4251. (800) 854-PITT. Fax: (316) 232-7515.

Pratt Community College
Pratt, Kansas CB code: 6581

2-year public community college, coed. Founded in 1938. **Accreditation:** Regional. **Undergraduate enrollment:** 1,672 men and women. **Faculty:** 80 total (30 full time), 3 with doctorates or other terminal degrees. **Location:** Rural campus in small town; 70 miles from Wichita. **Calendar:** Semester, limited summer session. **Microcomputers:** 125 located in libraries, classrooms, computer centers. **Special facilities:** Art gallery, indoor and outdoor rodeo facilities.

DEGREES OFFERED. AA, AS, AAS. 135 associate degrees awarded in 1992.

UNDERGRADUATE MAJORS. Accounting, agribusiness, agricultural business and management, agricultural mechanics, agricultural production, agricultural sciences, aircraft mechanics, architectural engineering, automotive mechanics, automotive technology, biological and physical sciences, biology, botany, business administration and management, business and management, business and office, business data processing and related programs, ceramics, chemistry, chiropractic, communications, diesel engine mechanics, dramatic arts, drawing, early childhood education, education, elementary education, engineering, English, fine arts, French, graphic design, health sciences, history, home economics, humanities, humanities and social sciences, inorganic chemistry, journalism, legal secretary, liberal/general studies, marketing and distribution, marketing management, mathematics, medical secretary, music, nursing, office supervision and management, painting, physical therapy, physics, political science and government, practical nursing, precision metal work, predentistry, prelaw, premedicine, prepharmacy, preveterinary, psychology, range management, secondary education, secretarial and related programs, small business management and ownership, social sciences, sociology, Spanish, speech, sports medicine, trade and industrial supervision and management, visual and performing arts, wildlife management, word processing, zoology.

ACADEMIC PROGRAMS. 2-year transfer program, dual enrollment of high school students, independent study, internships, telecourses. **Remedial services:** Learning center, remedial instruction, tutoring. **Placement/credit:** CLEP Subject; 15 credit hours maximum for associate degree.

ACADEMIC REQUIREMENTS. No policy requiring minimum GPA; records of students having academic difficulty are reviewed individually. 65% of freshmen return for sophomore year. Students must declare major on enrollment. **Graduation requirements:** 64 hours for associate. Most students required to take courses in English, foreign languages, history, humanities, mathematics, biological/physical sciences, social sciences.

FRESHMAN ADMISSIONS. Selection criteria: Open admissions. Selective admissions to health occupation programs. **Test requirements:** SAT or ACT (ACT preferred) for placement and counseling only; score report by September 1.

1992 FRESHMAN CLASS PROFILE. 480 men and women enrolled. **Characteristics:** 89% from in state, 60% commute, 7% have minority backgrounds, 1% are foreign students.

FALL-TERM APPLICATIONS. No fee. No closing date; applicants notified on a rolling basis beginning on or about January 1. Interview required. Audition required for music, drama applicants. Deferred and early admission available.

STUDENT LIFE. Housing: Dormitories (men, women, coed). **Activities:** Student government, magazine, student newspaper, choral groups, concert band, drama, jazz band, music ensembles, musical theater, pep band, show choir, sororities, Newman Club, Black Student Union.

ATHLETICS. NJCAA. **Intercollegiate:** Baseball M, basketball, cross-country, tennis, track and field, volleyball W. **Intramural:** Basketball, softball, table tennis, volleyball.

STUDENT SERVICES. Aptitude testing, career counseling, employment service for undergraduates, freshman orientation, health services, on-campus day care, personal counseling, placement service for graduates, special adviser for adult students, veterans counselor, services/facilities for handicapped.

ANNUAL EXPENSES. Tuition and fees (projected): $900, $1,560 additional for out-of-state students. **Room and board:** $2,500. **Books and supplies:** $400. **Other expenses:** $1,125.

FINANCIAL AID. 65% of freshmen, 65% of continuing students receive some form of aid. All grants, 95% of loans, all jobs based on need. Academic, music/drama, art, athletic, alumni affiliation, minority scholarships available. **Aid applications:** No closing date; priority given to applications received by May 1; applicants notified on a rolling basis beginning on or about May 1.

ADDRESS/TELEPHONE. Lisa Miller, Director of Admissions, Pratt Community College, Highway 61, Pratt, KS 67124. (316) 672-5641. Fax: (316) 672-5288 ext. 222.

St. Mary College
Leavenworth, Kansas CB code: 6630

Admissions: 85% of applicants accepted
Based on: ••• School record
•• Activities, recommendations, test scores
• Interview, special talents
Completion: 90% of freshmen end year in good standing
40% graduate, 8% of these enter graduate study

4-year private liberal arts college, coed, affiliated with Roman Catholic Church. Founded in 1923. **Accreditation:** Regional. **Undergraduate enrollment:** 146 men, 276 women full time; 265 men, 336 women part time. **Faculty:** 102 total (41 full time), 35 with doctorates or other terminal degrees. **Location:** Suburban campus in large town; 26 miles from Kansas City. **Calendar:** Semester, extensive summer session. **Microcomputers:** 45 located in libraries, classrooms, computer centers.

DEGREES OFFERED. AA, BA, BS. 29 associate degrees awarded in 1992. 104 bachelor's degrees awarded. 25% in business and management, 10% teacher education, 5% health sciences, 6% letters/literature, 6% psychology, 32% social sciences, 6% visual and performing arts.

UNDERGRADUATE MAJORS. Associate: Liberal/general studies. **Bachelor's:** Accounting, biology, business administration and management, chemistry, clinical laboratory science, computer and information sciences, dramatic arts, elementary education, English, English education, foreign languages education, history, mathematics, mathematics education, music, music performance, political science and government, premedicine, prepharmacy, preveterinary, psychology, public affairs, religion, science education, social science education, sociology, Spanish, speech/communication/theater education, studio art, theological studies.

ACADEMIC PROGRAMS. 2-year transfer program, double major, dual enrollment of high school students, honors program, independent study, internships, student-designed major, study abroad, teacher preparation, visiting/exchange student program, weekend college, cross-registration, 2+2 programs with Donnelly College in human services, business administration, accounting, public affairs, and computer science, bachelor's degree program in nursing for registered nurses, 2+2 program with Kansas City Kansas Community College in elementary education and with Johnson County Community College in public affairs and human services. **Remedial services:** Learning center, remedial instruction, tutoring. **Placement/credit:** AP, CLEP General and Subject, institutional tests; 32 credit hours maximum for bachelor's degree.

ACADEMIC REQUIREMENTS. Freshmen must earn minimum GPA of 2.0 to continue in good standing. 87% of freshmen return for sophomore year. Students must declare major by end of second year. **Graduation requirements:** 64 hours for associate (12 in major), 128 hours for bachelor's (30 in major). Most students required to take courses in arts/fine arts, English, foreign languages, history, mathematics, philosophy/religion, biological/physical sciences, social sciences.

FRESHMAN ADMISSIONS. Selection criteria: Minimum 2.5 high school GPA, test scores, recommendations. **High school preparation:** 16 units recommended. Recommended units include English 4, foreign language 2, mathematics 2, social science 2 and science 1. College-preparatory program recommended. **Test requirements:** SAT or ACT (ACT preferred); score report by September 1.

1992 FRESHMAN CLASS PROFILE. 129 men applied, 104 accepted, 141 enrolled; 216 women applied, 190 accepted, 109 enrolled. 74% had high school GPA of 3.0 or higher, 26% between 2.0 and 2.99. **Academic background:** Mid 50% of enrolled freshmen had ACT composite between 17-25. 85% submitted ACT scores. **Characteristics:** 65% from in state, 65% live in college housing, 17% have minority backgrounds, 6% are foreign students. Average age is 19.

FALL-TERM APPLICATIONS. $20 fee, may be waived for applicants with need. No closing date; applicants notified on a rolling basis. Interview recommended. Portfolio recommended for fine arts, applied arts applicants. Deferred and early admission available.

STUDENT LIFE. Housing: Dormitories (coed). **Activities:** Student government, student newspaper, yearbook, choral groups, dance, drama, music ensembles, musical theater, opera, music club, campus ministry, International Club, political clubs.

ATHLETICS. NAIA. **Intercollegiate:** Soccer M, volleyball W. **Intramural:** Basketball, softball, tennis, volleyball W.

STUDENT SERVICES. Aptitude testing, career counseling, employment service for undergraduates, freshman orientation, health services, on-campus day care, personal counseling, placement service for graduates, special adviser for adult students, services/facilities for handicapped.

ANNUAL EXPENSES. Tuition and fees: $7,550. **Room and board:** $3,700. **Books and supplies:** $500. **Other expenses:** $910.

FINANCIAL AID. 80% of freshmen, 80% of continuing students receive some form of aid. 89% of grants, 92% of loans, all jobs based on need. 48 enrolled freshmen were judged to have need, all were offered aid. Academic, music/drama, art, athletic, leadership, alumni affiliation, minority scholarships available. **Aid applications:** No closing date; priority given to applications received by March 16; applicants notified on a rolling basis beginning on or about March 16; must reply within 2 weeks. **Additional information:** Essays recommended for scholarship applicants. Auditions recommended for music and drama scholarship applicants.

ADDRESS/TELEPHONE. Domenic Teti, Director of Admissions, St. Mary College, 4100 South Fourth Street Trafficway, Leavenworth, KS 66048-5082. (913) 682-5151. (800) 752-7043. Fax: (913) 682-2406.

Seward County Community College
Liberal, Kansas — CB code: 0286

2-year public community college, coed. Founded in 1967. **Accreditation:** Regional. **Undergraduate enrollment:** 232 men, 314 women full time; 321 men, 632 women part time. **Faculty:** 166 total (68 full time), 2 with doctorates or other terminal degrees. **Location:** Rural campus in large town; 210 miles from Wichita, 150 miles from Amarillo, Texas. **Calendar:** Semester, limited summer session. Saturday and extensive evening/early morning classes. **Microcomputers:** 65 located in libraries, classrooms, computer centers. **Special facilities:** Swine management laboratory, wellness center. **Additional facts:** Off-campus classes offered in 7 locations, adult learning center with ESL classes.

DEGREES OFFERED. AA, AS, AAS. 107 associate degrees awarded in 1992. 20% in business and management, 5% business/office and marketing/distribution, 5% education, 18% teacher education, 35% allied health.

UNDERGRADUATE MAJORS. Accounting, agribusiness, agricultural sciences, biology, business administration and management, business and management, business and office, business computer/console/peripheral equipment operation, business data entry equipment operation, business data processing and related programs, business data programming, computer and information sciences, computer programming, data processing, education, elementary education, engineering, English, finance, fine arts, fishing and fisheries, journalism, law enforcement and corrections technologies, liberal/general studies, machine tool operation/machine shop, marketing and distribution, mathematics, medical laboratory technologies, music, nursing, physical sciences, practical nursing, psychology, respiratory therapy technology, science technologies, secondary education, secretarial and related programs, social sciences, visual and performing arts, wildlife management.

ACADEMIC PROGRAMS. 2-year transfer program, double major, dual enrollment of high school students, external degree, internships, cross-registration. **Remedial services:** Learning center, remedial instruction, special counselor, tutoring. **Placement/credit:** CLEP Subject; 24 credit hours maximum for associate degree.

ACADEMIC REQUIREMENTS. Freshmen must earn minimum GPA of 1.75 to continue in good standing. 64% of freshmen return for sophomore year. Students must declare major by end of first year. **Graduation requirements:** 64 hours for associate (12 in major). Most students required to take courses in arts/fine arts, English, history, humanities, mathematics, biological/physical sciences, social sciences.

FRESHMAN ADMISSIONS. Selection criteria: Open admissions. Selective admissions to health occupation programs.

1992 FRESHMAN CLASS PROFILE. 591 men applied, 501 accepted, 274 enrolled; 824 women applied, 792 accepted, 570 enrolled. 20% had high school GPA of 3.0 or higher, 80% between 2.0 and 2.99. **Characteristics:** 85% from in state, 60% commute, 8% have minority backgrounds. Average age is 18.

FALL-TERM APPLICATIONS. No fee. Closing date August 20; applicants notified on a rolling basis. CRDA. Deferred and early admission available.

STUDENT LIFE. Housing: Dormitories (coed). **Activities:** Student government, film, magazine, student newspaper, television, choral groups, concert band, drama, jazz band, music ensembles, musical theater, pep band, symphony orchestra, 2 religious groups.

ATHLETICS. NJCAA. **Intercollegiate:** Baseball M, basketball, tennis, volleyball W. **Intramural:** Basketball, volleyball.

STUDENT SERVICES. Aptitude testing, career counseling, employment service for undergraduates, freshman orientation, personal counseling, special adviser for adult students, veterans counselor, services/facilities for handicapped.

ANNUAL EXPENSES. Tuition and fees (projected): $960, $1,440 additional for out-of-state students. **Room and board:** $2,700. **Books and supplies:** $600. **Other expenses:** $700.

FINANCIAL AID. 91% of freshmen, 91% of continuing students receive some form of aid. 88% of grants, 91% of loans, 18% of jobs based on need. 301 enrolled freshmen were judged to have need, all were offered aid. **Aid applications:** No closing date; priority given to applications received by May 1; applicants notified on a rolling basis beginning on or about June 15; must reply within 2 weeks.

ADDRESS/TELEPHONE. Jerry Headrick, Director of Guidance Services, Seward County Community College, PO Box 1137, 1801 North Kansas Avenue, Liberal, KS 67905-1137. (316) 624-1951. (800) 373-9951. Fax: (316) 624-0637.

Southwestern College
Winfield, Kansas — CB code: 6670

Admissions:	61% of applicants accepted
Based on:	••• School record, test scores
	• Activities, essay, interview, recommendations, special talents
Completion:	90% of freshmen end year in good standing
	30% enter graduate study

4-year private liberal arts college, coed, affiliated with United Methodist Church. Founded in 1885. **Accreditation:** Regional. **Undergraduate enrollment:** 275 men, 302 women full time; 40 men, 59 women part time. **Graduate enrollment:** 6 men, 20 women part time. **Faculty:** 59 total (43 full time), 27 with doctorates or other terminal degrees. **Location:** Suburban campus in large town; 40 miles from Wichita. **Calendar:** 4-1-4, limited summer session. **Microcomputers:** 35 located in dormitories, libraries, computer centers. **Special facilities:** Science hall with 8,000-specimen bird skin research collection.

DEGREES OFFERED. BA, BS, MEd. 144 bachelor's degrees awarded in 1992. 17% in business and management, 21% teacher education, 19%

health sciences, 7% letters/literature, 9% life sciences, 11% social sciences. Graduate degrees offered in 2 major fields of study.

UNDERGRADUATE MAJORS. Art education, biological and physical sciences, biology, business administration and management, business economics, business education, chemistry, clinical laboratory science, communications, computer and information sciences, criminal justice studies, criminology, cytotechnology, dramatic arts, economics, elementary education, engineering and engineering-related technologies, English, English education, film arts, foreign languages (multiple emphasis), foreign languages education, French, health education, history, humanities, humanities and social sciences, international business management, liberal/general studies, manufacturing technology, marine biology, mathematics, mathematics education, medical laboratory technologies, music, music education, music performance, music theory and composition, nuclear medical technology, nursing, philosophy, physical education, physical sciences, physics, political science and government, psychology, radiograph medical technology, religion, respiratory therapy technology, secretarial and related programs, social sciences, social work, Spanish, speech, speech/communication/theater education, visual and performing arts.

ACADEMIC PROGRAMS. Accelerated program, double major, dual enrollment of high school students, honors program, independent study, internships, student-designed major, study abroad, teacher preparation, visiting/exchange student program; liberal arts/career combination in health sciences. **Remedial services:** Learning center, reduced course load, remedial instruction, special counselor, tutoring. **Placement/credit:** AP, CLEP General and Subject, institutional tests; 30 credit hours maximum for bachelor's degree.

ACADEMIC REQUIREMENTS. Freshmen must earn minimum GPA of 2.0 to continue in good standing. 65% of freshmen return for sophomore year. Students must declare major by end of second year. **Graduation requirements:** 124 hours for bachelor's (30 in major). Most students required to take courses in arts/fine arts, computer science, English, foreign languages, history, humanities, mathematics, philosophy/religion, biological/physical sciences. **Postgraduate studies:** 5% enter law school, 8% enter medical school, 7% enter MBA programs, 10% enter other graduate study.

FRESHMAN ADMISSIONS. Selection criteria: Minimum 2.0 high school GPA required. Test scores considered. Admission calculated on selection index with weighted average for test scores and GPA, high school curriculum. **High school preparation:** 9 units recommended. Recommended units include biological science 1, English 4, foreign language 1, mathematics 2 and social science 2. **Test requirements:** SAT or ACT (ACT preferred); score report by August 1.

1992 FRESHMAN CLASS PROFILE. 188 men and women applied, 115 accepted; 106 enrolled. 65% had high school GPA of 3.0 or higher, 35% between 2.0 and 2.99. **Academic background:** Mid 50% of enrolled freshmen had ACT composite between 18-26. 82% submitted ACT scores. **Characteristics:** 74% from in state, 90% live in college housing, 23% have minority backgrounds, 1% are foreign students. Average age is 18.

FALL-TERM APPLICATIONS. $15 fee, may be waived for applicants with need. Closing date August 1; priority given to applications received by July 15; applicants notified on a rolling basis; Students should reply as soon as possible after notification. Interview recommended for emergency medical intensive care training, nursing applicants. Audition recommended for music, debate, drama applicants. Essay recommended. CRDA. Deferred and early admission available.

STUDENT LIFE. Housing: Dormitories (men, women, coed); apartment, handicapped housing available. Freshmen and sophomores under 20 years old, not veteran or living with parent or guardian, must live on campus. **Activities:** Student government, film, radio, student newspaper, television, yearbook, choral groups, concert band, drama, jazz band, music ensembles, musical theater, pep band, symphony orchestra, fraternities, sororities, Student Christian Association, Black Student Union, Campus Council on Ministries, Sharp Ambassadors.

ATHLETICS. NAIA. **Intercollegiate:** Basketball, cross-country, football M, golf M, tennis, track and field, volleyball W. **Intramural:** Basketball, bowling, softball, swimming, tennis, volleyball.

STUDENT SERVICES. Aptitude testing, career counseling, employment service for undergraduates, freshman orientation, health services, personal counseling, placement service for graduates, services/facilities for handicapped.

ANNUAL EXPENSES. Tuition and fees: $6,500. **Room and board:** $3,532. **Books and supplies:** $550. **Other expenses:** $900.

FINANCIAL AID. 83% of freshmen, 87% of continuing students receive some form of aid. 55% of grants, 91% of loans, 58% of jobs based on need. Academic, music/drama, art, athletic, leadership, religious affiliation scholarships available. **Aid applications:** No closing date; priority given to applications received by April 1; applicants notified on a rolling basis beginning on or about May 15; must reply within 2 weeks.

ADDRESS/TELEPHONE. Douglas M. Mason, Director of Admissions, Southwestern College, 100 College Street, Winfield, KS 67156-9988. (316) 221-4150 ext. 236. Fax: (316) 221-3725.

Sterling College
Sterling, Kansas

CB code: 6684

Admissions:	78% of applicants accepted
Based on:	••• School record, test scores
	•• Recommendations
	• Activities, interview, religious affiliation/commitment
Completion:	82% of freshmen end year in good standing
	35% graduate, 6% of these enter graduate study

4-year private liberal arts college, coed, affiliated with Presbyterian Church (USA). Founded in 1887. **Accreditation:** Regional. **Undergraduate enrollment:** 481 men and women. **Faculty:** 48 total (31 full time), 17 with doctorates or other terminal degrees. **Location:** Rural campus in rural community; 80 miles from Wichita. **Calendar:** 4-1-4. **Microcomputers:** Located in computer centers. **Additional facts:** Christian values of faith and service stressed.

DEGREES OFFERED. AA, BA, BS. 95 bachelor's degrees awarded.

UNDERGRADUATE MAJORS. Associate: Music. **Bachelor's:** Accounting, agronomy, behavioral sciences, biological and physical sciences, biology, business administration and management, chemistry, computer and information sciences, dramatic arts, education, elementary education, English, fine arts, food science and nutrition, history, home economics, individual and family development, junior high education, liberal/general studies, mathematics, music, philosophy, political science and government, prelaw, psychology, religion, religious education, secondary education, special education, speech, theological studies.

ACADEMIC PROGRAMS. Accelerated program, double major, dual enrollment of high school students, honors program, independent study, student-designed major, study abroad, cross-registration. **Remedial services:** Learning center, reduced course load, remedial instruction, tutoring. **Placement/credit:** AP, CLEP General and Subject; 30 credit hours maximum for bachelor's degree.

ACADEMIC REQUIREMENTS. Freshmen must earn minimum GPA of 1.7 to continue in good standing. 51% of freshmen return for sophomore year. **Graduation requirements:** 124 hours for bachelor's. Most students required to take courses in arts/fine arts, English, history, humanities, philosophy/religion, biological/physical sciences. **Postgraduate studies:** 1% enter law school, 1% enter MBA programs, 4% enter other graduate study. **Additional information:** Curriculum composed of academic and applied courses.

FRESHMAN ADMISSIONS. Selection criteria: High school record, test scores, recommendations from school counselor and pastor. Commitment to Christian values and service important. **Test requirements:** SAT or ACT; score report by August 31.

1992 FRESHMAN CLASS PROFILE. 271 men applied, 199 accepted, 66 enrolled; 208 women applied, 174 accepted, 61 enrolled. 62% had high school GPA of 3.0 or higher, 38% between 2.0 and 2.99. 17% were in top tenth and 36% were in top quarter of graduating class. **Academic background:** Mid 50% of enrolled freshmen had ACT composite between 17-22. 85% submitted ACT scores. **Characteristics:** 58% from in state, 80% live in college housing, 14% have minority backgrounds. Average age is 18.

FALL-TERM APPLICATIONS. $10 fee. No closing date; priority given to applications received by May 15; applicants notified on a rolling basis. Audition required for music, theater applicants. Interview recommended. Portfolio recommended for art applicants. Deferred and early admission available.

STUDENT LIFE. Housing: Dormitories (men, women). All students required to live in campus dormitories unless married or living at home with parents. **Activities:** Student government, student newspaper, yearbook, choral groups, concert band, dance, drama, music ensembles, musical theater, pep band, stage band, science club, Minority Cultural Organization, Political Science Union, Alpha Phi Omega, Fellowship of Christian Athletes, psychology club.

ATHLETICS. NAIA. **Intercollegiate:** Baseball M, basketball, cross-country, football M, soccer, softball W, tennis, track and field, volleyball W. **Intramural:** Golf, racquetball, soccer, softball, tennis, volleyball.

STUDENT SERVICES. Career counseling, employment service for undergraduates, health services, personal counseling, placement service for graduates, services/facilities for handicapped.

ANNUAL EXPENSES. Tuition and fees (1992-93): $7,230. **Room and board:** $3,100. **Books and supplies:** $450. **Other expenses:** $600.

FINANCIAL AID. 90% of freshmen, 90% of continuing students receive some form of aid. 91% of grants, 95% of loans, 78% of jobs based on need. 98 enrolled freshmen were judged to have need, all were offered aid. Academic, music/drama, art, athletic, leadership, alumni affiliation, religious affiliation scholarships available. **Aid applications:** No closing date; priority given to applications received by May 1; applicants notified on a rolling basis beginning on or about June 1; must reply within 2 weeks.

ADDRESS/TELEPHONE. Dennis Dutton, Admissions Director, Sterling College, Box 98, Sterling, KS 67579-9989. (316) 278-2173. (800) 346-1017. Fax: (316) 278-3188.

Tabor College
Hillsboro, Kansas CB code: 6815

4-year private liberal arts college, coed, affiliated with Mennonite Brethren Church. Founded in 1908. **Accreditation:** Regional. **Undergraduate enrollment:** 235 men, 179 women full time; 13 men, 21 women part time. **Faculty:** 85 total (51 full time), 19 with doctorates or other terminal degrees. **Location:** Rural campus in small town; 50 miles from Wichita. **Calendar:** 4-1-4. **Microcomputers:** Located in libraries, classrooms.

DEGREES OFFERED. AA, BA. 1 associate degree awarded in 1992. 100% in multi/interdisciplinary studies. 67 bachelor's degrees awarded. 22% in business and management, 28% teacher education, 8% letters/literature, 8% life sciences, 5% philosophy, religion, theology, 7% physical sciences, 16% social sciences.

UNDERGRADUATE MAJORS. Associate: Bible studies, liberal/general studies, secretarial and related programs. **Bachelor's:** Accounting, actuarial sciences, applied mathematics, biology, business and management, business economics, business education, chemistry, computer and information sciences, computer programming, education, education of the emotionally handicapped, education of the mentally handicapped, elementary education, English, English education, humanities, international relations, international studies, junior high education, legal secretary, liberal/general studies, mathematics, mathematics education, medical laboratory technologies, medical secretary, music, music education, office supervision and management, physical education, predentistry, premedicine, preveterinary, recreation and community services technologies, religion, science education, secondary education, secretarial and related programs, social science education, social sciences, special education, specific learning disabilities.

ACADEMIC PROGRAMS. Double major, independent study, internships, student-designed major, study abroad, Washington semester, cross-registration. **Remedial services:** Reduced course load, special counselor. **Placement/credit:** AP, CLEP General and Subject, institutional tests; 30 credit hours maximum for bachelor's degree.

ACADEMIC REQUIREMENTS. Freshmen must earn minimum GPA of 1.7 to continue in good standing. 57% of freshmen return for sophomore year. Students must declare major by end of second year. **Graduation requirements:** 64 hours for associate, 124 hours for bachelor's (40 in major). Most students required to take courses in arts/fine arts, computer science, English, history, humanities, mathematics, philosophy/religion, biological/physical sciences, social sciences.

FRESHMAN ADMISSIONS. Selection criteria: Life values and objectives, desire for Christian growth, interview, references, and formula that combines GPA and ACT composite score to yield admissions standing. **Test requirements:** SAT or ACT (ACT preferred); score report by July 15.

1992 FRESHMAN CLASS PROFILE. 64 men, 66 women enrolled. 75% had high school GPA of 3.0 or higher, 23% between 2.0 and 2.99. 19% were in top tenth and 54% were in top quarter of graduating class. **Academic background:** Mid 50% of enrolled freshmen had ACT composite between 18-26. 97% submitted ACT scores. **Characteristics:** 45% from in state, 99% live in college housing, 5% have minority backgrounds. Average age is 18.

FALL-TERM APPLICATIONS. $10 fee. No closing date; priority given to applications received by April 1; applicants notified on a rolling basis. Essay required. Interview recommended. Audition recommended for music applicants. Deferred admission available.

STUDENT LIFE. Housing: Dormitories (men, women). **Activities:** Student government, student newspaper, yearbook, choral groups, concert band, drama, jazz band, music ensembles, pep band, social work club, science club, student music association, Christian student organizations, minority student union, international student club.

ATHLETICS. NAIA. **Intercollegiate:** Baseball M, basketball, cross-country, football M, soccer M, softball W, tennis, track and field, volleyball W. **Intramural:** Badminton, basketball, bowling, football M, golf, handball, racquetball, soccer, softball, table tennis, tennis, track and field, volleyball.

STUDENT SERVICES. Aptitude testing, career counseling, employment service for undergraduates, freshman orientation, personal counseling, placement service for graduates.

ANNUAL EXPENSES. Tuition and fees (1992-93): $7,520. **Room and board:** $3,290. **Books and supplies:** $550. **Other expenses:** $2,500.

FINANCIAL AID. 100% of freshmen, 100% of continuing students receive some form of aid. 46% of grants, 98% of loans, 75% of jobs based on need. Academic, music/drama, athletic, leadership scholarships available. **Aid applications:** No closing date; priority given to applications received by April 15; applicants notified on a rolling basis beginning on or about March 1.

ADDRESS/TELEPHONE. Glenn Lygrisse, VP Enrollment Management, Tabor College, 400 South Jefferson, Hillsboro, KS 67063. (316) 947-3121. Fax: (316) 947-2607.

University of Kansas
Lawrence, Kansas CB code: 6871

Admissions: 70% of applicants accepted
Based on:
••• School record
•• Test scores
• Recommendations, special talents
Completion: 49% graduate

4-year public university, coed. Founded in 1866. **Accreditation:** Regional. **Undergraduate enrollment:** 8,993 men, 8,556 women full time; 888 men, 850 women part time. **Graduate enrollment:** 1,488 men, 1,654 women full time; 1,821 men, 2,215 women part time. **Faculty:** 1,223 total (1,028 full time). **Location:** Suburban campus in small city; 40 miles from Kansas City, Missouri. **Calendar:** Semester, extensive summer session. **Microcomputers:** 500 located in dormitories, classrooms, computer centers. **Special facilities:** Natural history, art, anthropology, entomological and invertebrate paleontology museums, space technology center, Kansas Geological Survey, observatory, herbarium, music library, Bureau of Child Research, Crafton-Preyer Theater, Institute for Life Span Studies, Ernest F. Lied Center for the Performing Arts.

DEGREES OFFERED. BA, BS, BFA, BArch, MA, MS, MBA, MFA, MEd, MSW, PhD, EdD, MD, B. Pharm, Pharm D, JD. 3,340 bachelor's degrees awarded in 1992. 12% in business and management, 13% communications, 9% teacher education, 7% engineering, 7% letters/literature, 6% life sciences, 10% psychology, 11% social sciences, 7% visual and performing arts. Graduate degrees offered in 104 major fields of study.

UNDERGRADUATE MAJORS. Accounting, advertising, aerospace/aeronautical/astronautical engineering, African studies, Afro-American (black) studies, American studies, anthropology, archeology, architectural engineering, architectural studies, architecture, art education, art history, astronomy, atmospheric sciences and meteorology, biochemistry, biological and physical sciences, biology, business and management, cell biology, ceramics, chemical engineering, chemistry, Chinese, civil engineering, classics, cognitive psychology, communication disorders, comparative literature, computer and information sciences, computer engineering, cytotechnology, dance, design, design theory, developmental psychology, dramatic arts, East Asian studies, ecology, economics, electrical/electronics/communications engineering, elementary education, engineering physics, English, English education, environmental studies, fiber/textiles/weaving, film arts, foreign languages education, French, geography, geology, geophysics and seismology, German, Greek (classical), health education, history, history and philosophy of science, humanities and social sciences, industrial design, interior design, Italian, Japanese, journalism, junior high education, Latin, Latin American studies, leisure and recreational studies, liberal/general studies, linguistics, mathematics, mathematics education, mechanical engineering, medical laboratory technologies, medical records administration, metal/jewelry, microbiology, music, music education, music history and appreciation, music performance, music theory and composition, music therapy, nursing, occupational therapy, painting, petroleum engineering, pharmacy, philosophy, physical education, physics, political science and government, predentistry, premedicine, printmaking, psychology, radio/television broadcasting, radiograph medical technology, religion, respiratory therapy, Russian, Russian and Slavic studies, science education, sculpture, secondary education, Slavic languages, social studies education, social work, sociology, Spanish, speech, speech pathology/audiology, theater design, toxicology, visual and performing arts, visual communication, voice, women's studies.

ACADEMIC PROGRAMS. Cooperative education, double major, dual enrollment of high school students, education specialist degree, honors program, independent study, internships, student-designed major, study abroad, teacher preparation, visiting/exchange student program, Washington semester, dual enrollment with University of Kansas College of Health Science; Regents Center offers KU courses in Kansas City area; liberal arts/career combination in engineering, business. **Remedial services:** Learning center, remedial instruction, tutoring, study skills workshops. **ROTC:** Air Force, Army, Naval. **Placement/credit:** AP, CLEP General and Subject, institutional tests.

ACADEMIC REQUIREMENTS. Freshmen must earn minimum GPA of 1.0 to continue in good standing. 80% of freshmen return for sophomore year. Students must declare major by end of second year. **Graduation requirements:** 124 hours for bachelor's (20 in major). Most students required to take courses in English, humanities, mathematics, biological/physical sciences, social sciences.

FRESHMAN ADMISSIONS. Selection criteria: Open admission for graduates of accredited Kansas high schools who have not previously attended college. Selective admissions for architecture and all engineering programs. Selective out-of-state admissions for fine arts, and health, physical education, recreation department of School of Education. Out-of-state applicants must have minimum 2.0 high school GPA, ACT scores of 24, or SAT score of at least 990, or 2.0 GPA and 4 units English, 3 units mathematics, 3 units science, 3 units social science, and 2 units foreign language, or GPA of 3.0 for admission to liberal arts and sciences. **High school preparation:** 15 units recommended. Recommended units include English 4, foreign language 2, mathematics 3, social science 3 and science 3. 4 units mathematics recommended for mathematics, engineering and architecture majors. **Test requirements:** SAT or ACT; score report by August 20.

1992 FRESHMAN CLASS PROFILE. 8,103 men and women applied, 5,662 accepted; 1,746 men enrolled, 1,807 women enrolled. 25% were in top tenth and 50% were in top quarter of graduating class. **Academic background:** Mid 50% of enrolled freshmen had ACT composite between 20-26. 92% submitted ACT scores. **Characteristics:** 61% from in state, 53% commute, 10% have minority backgrounds, 6% are foreign students. Average age is 19.

FALL-TERM APPLICATIONS. $15 fee. Closing date February 1; applicants notified on a rolling basis. Audition required for piano, voice applicants. Early admission available. Out-of-state applicants must apply by February 1.

STUDENT LIFE. Housing: Dormitories (men, women, coed); apartment, fraternity, sorority, cooperative housing available. Scholarship halls (5 male, 4 female) available to students with high ACT scores and good high school or college grades. **Activities:** Student government, film, magazine, radio, student newspaper, television, yearbook, choral groups, concert band, dance, drama, jazz band, marching band, music ensembles, musical theater, opera, pep band, symphony orchestra, fraternities, sororities, over 300 student organizations and activities.

ATHLETICS. NCAA. **Intercollegiate:** Baseball M, basketball, cross-country, diving, football M, golf, softball W, swimming, tennis, track and field, volleyball W. **Intramural:** Badminton, basketball, bowling, golf, racquetball, soccer, softball, table tennis, tennis, volleyball, wrestling M. **Clubs:** 34 club sports available.

STUDENT SERVICES. Aptitude testing, career counseling, employment service for undergraduates, freshman orientation, health services, on-campus day care, personal counseling, placement service for graduates, special adviser for adult students, veterans counselor, women's and minority resource centers, services/facilities for handicapped.

ANNUAL EXPENSES. Tuition and fees (projected): $1,914, $4,506 additional for out-of-state students. **Room and board:** $3,376. **Books and supplies:** $700. **Other expenses:** $1,600.

FINANCIAL AID. 43% of freshmen, 34% of continuing students receive some form of aid. 93% of grants, 78% of loans, 12% of jobs based on need. 1,876 enrolled freshmen were judged to have need, all were offered aid. Academic, music/drama, art, athletic, state/district residency, leadership, minority scholarships available. **Aid applications:** No closing date; priority given to applications received by March 1; applicants notified on a rolling basis beginning on or about April 25; must reply within 2 weeks.

ADDRESS/TELEPHONE. Deborah Castrop, Director of Admissions, University of Kansas, 222 Strong Hall, Lawrence, KS 66045. (913) 864-3301.

University of Kansas Medical Center
Kansas City, Kansas — CB code: 0414

2-year upper-division public university and nursing college, coed. Founded in 1905. **Accreditation:** Regional. **Undergraduate enrollment:** 80 men, 461 women full time; 4 men, 41 women part time. **Graduate enrollment:** 1,027 men, 626 women full time; 75 men, 382 women part time. **Faculty:** 779 total (614 full time), 653 with doctorates or other terminal degrees. **Location:** Urban campus in very large city; On state line of Kansas City, Missouri. **Calendar:** Semester, limited summer session. **Microcomputers:** 44 located in libraries, computer centers. **Additional facts:** Provides health professional education and training programs for University of Kansas at Lawrence, 40 miles from Medical Center.

DEGREES OFFERED. BS, MA, MS, PhD, EdD, MD. 218 bachelor's degrees awarded in 1992. 57% in health sciences, 43% allied health. Graduate degrees offered in 18 major fields of study.

UNDERGRADUATE MAJORS. Cytotechnology, medical laboratory technologies, medical records administration, nursing, occupational therapy, radiograph medical technology, respiratory therapy.

ACADEMIC PROGRAMS. Double major, honors program, internships, visiting/exchange student program; liberal arts/career combination in health sciences; combined bachelor's/graduate program in medicine. **Remedial services:** Learning center, remedial instruction, special counselor.

ACADEMIC REQUIREMENTS. Students must declare major on application. **Graduation requirements:** 124 hours for bachelor's. Most students required to take courses in English, humanities, mathematics, biological/physical sciences, social sciences.

STUDENT LIFE. 1992 freshman class profile: 100% commute. **Activities:** Student government, student newspaper, yearbook, choral groups, music ensembles, symphony orchestra, art show, Christian Medical Society. **Additional information:** 4 clusters of satellite personal computer stations with link to mainframe available to students; 2 clusters on 24-hour basis.

ATHLETICS. Intramural: Basketball, golf, softball, swimming, table tennis, volleyball.

STUDENT SERVICES. Career counseling, health services, personal counseling, services/facilities for handicapped.

ANNUAL EXPENSES. Tuition and fees (projected): $1,696, $4,506 additional for out-of-state students. **Books and supplies:** $500. **Other expenses:** $2,025.

FINANCIAL AID. 49% of continuing students receive some form of aid. 74% of grants, 81% of loans, all jobs based on need. 281 enrolled freshmen were judged to have need, all were offered aid. Academic, state/district residency, minority scholarships available. **Aid applications:** No closing date; priority given to applications received by April 15; applicants notified on a rolling basis beginning on or about July 1; must reply within 2 weeks.

ADDRESS/TELEPHONE. Donna Kempin, Director of Student Records and Registration, University of Kansas Medical Center, 3901 Rainbow Boulevard, Kansas City, KS 66160. (913) 588-7055.

Washburn University of Topeka
Topeka, Kansas — CB code: 6928

4-year public university, coed. Founded in 1865. **Accreditation:** Regional. **Undergraduate enrollment:** 1,321 men, 1,867 women full time; 982 men, 1,743 women part time. **Graduate enrollment:** 271 men, 190 women full time; 105 men, 151 women part time. **Faculty:** 443 total (255 full time), 169 with doctorates or other terminal degrees. **Location:** Urban campus in small city; 60 miles from Kansas City. **Calendar:** Semester, extensive summer session. **Microcomputers:** 150 located in libraries, classrooms. **Special facilities:** 2 art galleries, observatory, nature preserve and laboratory.

DEGREES OFFERED. AA, AS, AAS, BA, BS, BFA, MA, MBA. 166 associate degrees awarded in 1992. 29% in business and management, 7% computer sciences, 35% allied health, 15% law. 669 bachelor's degrees awarded. 23% in business and management, 10% communications, 5% computer sciences, 11% education, 7% allied health, 9% parks/recreation, protective services, public affairs, 5% psychology, 16% social sciences, 5% visual and performing arts. Graduate degrees offered in 8 major fields of study.

UNDERGRADUATE MAJORS. Associate: Business and office, business data processing and related programs, computer and information sciences, court reporting, electronic technology, gerontology, hospitality and recreation marketing, hotel/motel and restaurant management, law enforcement and corrections technologies, legal assistant/paralegal, legal secretary, liberal/general studies, medical records administration, medical records technology, medical secretary, mental health/human services, office supervision and management, physical sciences, physical therapy assistant, radiograph medical technology, respiratory therapy technology, secretarial and related programs. **Bachelor's:** Accounting, anthropology, biology, business administration and management, business and management, business economics, business education, chemistry, communications, computer and information sciences, criminal justice studies, dramatic arts, economics, education, elementary education, English, English education, finance, fine arts, foreign languages education, French, German, health education, history, journalism, law enforcement and corrections, liberal/general studies, marketing management, mathematics, mathematics education, medical laboratory technologies, military science (Army), music education, nursing, philosophy, physical education, physics, political science and government, predentistry, prelaw, premedicine, prepharmacy, preveterinary, psychology, public administration, public relations, radio/television broadcasting, religion, science education, secondary education, social science education, social studies education, social work, sociology, Spanish, speech, speech/communication/theater education, theological studies, visual and performing arts.

ACADEMIC PROGRAMS. 2-year transfer program, double major, dual enrollment of high school students, honors program, independent study, internships, student-designed major, study abroad, teacher preparation; liberal arts/career combination in engineering. **Remedial services:** Remedial instruction, tutoring. **ROTC:** Air Force, Army. **Placement/credit:** AP, CLEP General, institutional tests; 40 credit hours maximum for bachelor's degree.

ACADEMIC REQUIREMENTS. Freshmen must earn minimum GPA of 2.0 to continue in good standing. 50% of freshmen return for sophomore year. Students must declare major by end of second year. **Graduation requirements:** 62 hours for associate (15 in major), 124 hours for bachelor's (30 in major). Most students required to take courses in English, humanities, mathematics, biological/physical sciences, social sciences. **Postgraduate studies:** 35% from 2-year programs enter 4-year programs.

FRESHMAN ADMISSIONS. Selection criteria: Open admissions. Out-of-state applicants need 2.0 high school GPA. Selective admissions to health science programs. Recommended units include biological science 2, English 4, mathematics 2, physical science 1 and social science 2.

1992 FRESHMAN CLASS PROFILE. 381 men, 525 women enrolled. **Academic background:** Mid 50% of enrolled freshmen had ACT composite between 15-23. 70% submitted ACT scores. **Characteristics:** 95% from in state, 94% commute, 21% have minority backgrounds, 1% are foreign students, 15% join fraternities/sororities. Average age is 21.

FALL-TERM APPLICATIONS. No fee. Closing date August 8; priority given to applications received by July 1; applicants notified on a rolling basis. Deferred admission available.

STUDENT LIFE. Housing: Dormitories (men, women, coed); apartment, fraternity, sorority housing available. **Activities:** Student government, radio, student newspaper, television, yearbook, choral groups, concert band, dance, drama, jazz band, marching band, music ensembles, musical theater, opera, pep band, fraternities, sororities.

ATHLETICS. NAIA, NCAA. **Intercollegiate:** Baseball M, basketball, football M, golf M, softball W, tennis, volleyball W. **Intramural:** Basketball, bowling, softball, swimming, table tennis, tennis.

STUDENT SERVICES. Aptitude testing, career counseling, employment service for undergraduates, freshman orientation, health services, personal counseling, placement service for graduates, veterans counselor, athletic adviser, services/facilities for handicapped.

ANNUAL EXPENSES. Tuition and fees (1992-93): $2,762, $1,380 additional for out-of-state students. **Room and board:** $2,995. **Books and supplies:** $450. **Other expenses:** $755.

FINANCIAL AID. 80% of freshmen, 78% of continuing students receive some form of aid. 71% of grants, 77% of loans, 47% of jobs based on need. Academic, music/drama, art, athletic, leadership, alumni affiliation scholarships available. **Aid applications:** No closing date; priority given to applications received by March 15; applicants notified on a rolling basis beginning on or about April 15; must reply within 2 weeks.

ADDRESS/TELEPHONE. Greg Greider, Director of Admissions, Washburn University of Topeka, 1700 College, Topeka, KS 66621. (913) 231-1010 ext. 1625. (800) 332-0291.

Wichita State University
Wichita, Kansas — CB code: 6884

4-year public university and college of arts and sciences and art, business, engineering, health science, music, nursing, liberal arts, teachers college, coed. Founded in 1895. **Accreditation:** Regional. **Undergraduate enrollment:** 3,334 men, 3,389 women full time; 2,477 men, 2,768 women part time. **Graduate enrollment:** 397 men, 308 women full time; 813 men, 1,209 women part time. **Faculty:** 488 total (467 full time), 403 with doctorates or other terminal degrees. **Location:** Urban campus in large city. **Calendar:** Semester, extensive summer session. Saturday and extensive evening/early morning classes. **Microcomputers:** 1,500 located in dormitories, libraries, classrooms, computer centers. **Special facilities:** Art museum, sculpture garden, wind tunnels, observatory, first Marcusson pipe organ in the western hemisphere, flow-visualization water tunnel, National Institute for Aviation Research, Ablah Library.

DEGREES OFFERED. AS, BA, BS, BFA, MA, MS, MBA, MFA, MEd, PhD, EdD. 86 associate degrees awarded in 1992. 53% in health sciences, 35% law, 12% multi/interdisciplinary studies. 1,598 bachelor's degrees awarded. 25% in business and management, 11% education, 10% engineering, 13% health sciences, 11% life sciences, 10% social sciences. Graduate degrees offered in 47 major fields of study.

UNDERGRADUATE MAJORS. Associate: Dental hygiene, legal assistant/paralegal, respiratory therapy technology. **Bachelor's:** Accounting, aerospace/aeronautical/astronautical engineering, Afro-American (black) studies, American Indian studies, American studies, anthropology, art education, art history, aviation management, biology, business administration and management, business and management, business economics, chemistry, communications, computer and information sciences, criminal justice studies, economics, electrical/electronics/communications engineering, elementary education, English, entrepreneurship, finance, fine arts, French, geology, German, gerontology, graphic design, health care administration, health sciences, Hispanic American studies, history, industrial engineering, industrial technology, international business management, Latin, liberal/general studies, marketing management, mathematics, mechanical engineering, medical laboratory technologies, medical records administration, Mexican American studies, music, music education, nursing, painting, personnel management, philosophy, physical education, physician's assistant, physics, political science and government, psychology, real estate, secondary education, social work, sociology, Spanish, speech pathology/audiology, studio art, visual and performing arts, women's studies.

ACADEMIC PROGRAMS. Cooperative education, double major, dual enrollment of high school students, education specialist degree, honors program, independent study, internships, student-designed major, study abroad, teacher preparation, telecourses, Washington semester; combined bachelor's/graduate program in business administration. **Remedial services:** Learning center, preadmission summer program, reduced course load, remedial instruction, special counselor, tutoring. **Placement/credit:** AP, CLEP General and Subject, IB, institutional tests.

ACADEMIC REQUIREMENTS. Freshmen must earn minimum GPA of 2.0 to continue in good standing. 41% of freshmen return for sophomore year. Students must declare major by end of second year. **Graduation requirements:** 64 hours for associate, 124 hours for bachelor's (30 in major). Most students required to take courses in English, humanities, mathematics, biological/physical sciences, social sciences.

FRESHMAN ADMISSIONS. Selection criteria: Open admissions. Selective admissions for out-of-state applicants and foreign students. **High school preparation:** 12 units recommended. Recommended units include English 4, foreign language 2, mathematics 2, social science 2 and science 2. College-preparatory program recommended. **Test requirements:** SAT or ACT (ACT preferred) for placement; score report by December 15.

1992 FRESHMAN CLASS PROFILE. 1,211 men and women enrolled. 47% had high school GPA of 3.0 or higher, 44% between 2.0 and 2.99. **Characteristics:** 86% from in state, 22% commute, 22% have minority backgrounds, 2% are foreign students. Average age is 20.

FALL-TERM APPLICATIONS. $15 fee. No closing date; applicants notified on a rolling basis. Deferred and early admission available.

STUDENT LIFE. Housing: Dormitories (coed); fraternity, sorority housing available. Student housing accessible to handicapped persons. **Activities:** Student government, magazine, radio, student newspaper, television, choral groups, concert band, dance, drama, jazz band, music ensembles, musical theater, opera, pep band, symphony orchestra, fraternities, sororities, many religious and social service organizations. **Additional information:** Traditional and nontraditional students; more than one third married, and more than 84% work full or part time.

ATHLETICS. NCAA. **Intercollegiate:** Baseball M, basketball, bowling, cross-country, golf, softball W, tennis, track and field, volleyball W. **Intramural:** Badminton, basketball, fencing, golf, lacrosse, racquetball, rowing (crew), soccer, softball, swimming, tennis, volleyball.

STUDENT SERVICES. Aptitude testing, career counseling, employment service for undergraduates, freshman orientation, health services, on-campus day care, personal counseling, placement service for graduates, special adviser for adult students, veterans counselor, services/facilities for handicapped.

ANNUAL EXPENSES. Tuition and fees (projected): $2,018, $4,506 additional for out-of-state students. **Room and board:** $3,005. **Books and supplies:** $600. **Other expenses:** $900.

FINANCIAL AID. 27% of freshmen, 40% of continuing students receive some form of aid. 76% of grants, all loans, all jobs based on need. 580 enrolled freshmen were judged to have need, all were offered aid. Academic, music/drama, art, athletic, state/district residency, leadership scholarships available. **Aid applications:** No closing date; priority given to applications received by March 15; applicants notified on a rolling basis beginning on or about March 15; must reply by May 1 or within 4 weeks if notified thereafter. **Additional information:** Top 200 freshman applicants admitted by February 1 invited to university scholarship competition.

ADDRESS/TELEPHONE. Glenn Lygrisse, Director of Admissions, Wichita State University, 111 Jardine Hall, Wichita, KS 67208-1595. (316) 689-3085. (800) 362-2594. Fax: (316) 689-3770.

Kentucky

Alice Lloyd College
Pippa Passes, Kentucky CB code: 1098

4-year private liberal arts college, coed. Founded in 1923. **Accreditation:** Regional. **Undergraduate enrollment:** 579 men and women. **Faculty:** 46 total (45 full time), 30 with doctorates or other terminal degrees. **Location:** Rural campus in rural community; 35 miles from Hazard, 150 miles from Lexington. **Calendar:** Semester. **Microcomputers:** 25 located in libraries, classrooms, computer centers. **Special facilities:** Appalachian history collection, photographic archives. **Additional facts:** Required work/study program.

DEGREES OFFERED. BA, BS. 60 bachelor's degrees awarded in 1992. 18% in business and management, 68% teacher education, 10% social sciences.

UNDERGRADUATE MAJORS. Accounting, biology, business administration and management, elementary education, history, mathematics education, physical education, science education, secondary education, social studies education.

ACADEMIC PROGRAMS. Independent study, teacher preparation, required work-study program. **Remedial services:** Learning center, reduced course load, remedial instruction, special counselor, tutoring. **Placement/credit:** AP, CLEP General and Subject, institutional tests. Limited number of hours of credit by examination may be counted toward degree, decided on individual basis.

ACADEMIC REQUIREMENTS. Freshmen must earn minimum GPA of 2.0 to continue in good standing. 58% of freshmen return for sophomore year. Students must declare major by end of second year. **Graduation requirements:** 128 hours for bachelor's (36 in major). Most students required to take courses in arts/fine arts, English, history, humanities, mathematics, philosophy/religion, biological/physical sciences, social sciences. **Postgraduate studies:** 3% enter law school, 2% enter medical school, 2% enter MBA programs, 33% enter other graduate study.

FRESHMAN ADMISSIONS. Selection criteria: 2.25 GPA. ACT scores considered. **High school preparation:** 12 units required. Required units include biological science 2, English 4, mathematics 2, physical science 2 and social science 2. **Test requirements:** SAT or ACT (ACT preferred); score report by August 1.

1992 FRESHMAN CLASS PROFILE. 60% had high school GPA of 3.0 or higher, 40% between 2.0 and 2.99. **Academic background:** Mid 50% of enrolled freshmen had ACT composite between 18-22. 98% submitted ACT scores. **Characteristics:** 85% from in state, 75% live in college housing. Average age is 20.

FALL-TERM APPLICATIONS. No fee. No closing date; priority given to applications received by August 1; applicants notified on a rolling basis; must reply by registration. Interview recommended for academically marginal applicants. CRDA. Deferred admission available.

STUDENT LIFE. Housing: Dormitories (men, women). **Activities:** Student government, radio, student newspaper, yearbook, choral groups, drama, pep band, Students for Christ.

ATHLETICS. NAIA. **Intercollegiate:** Baseball M, basketball, cross-country, softball W, tennis. **Intramural:** Basketball, softball, swimming, table tennis, tennis, volleyball.

STUDENT SERVICES. Aptitude testing, career counseling, employment service for undergraduates, freshman orientation, health services, on-campus day care, personal counseling, placement service for graduates, veterans counselor.

ANNUAL EXPENSES. Tuition and fees (1992-93): $270, $3,960 additional for out-of-district students, $3,360 additional for out-of-state students. Free tuition for students from the Appalachian areas in Kentucky, West Virginia, Virginia, Tennessee, and Ohio **Room and board:** $2,480. **Books and supplies:** $450. **Other expenses:** $500.

FINANCIAL AID. 100% of freshmen, 100% of continuing students receive some form of aid. 65% of grants, all loans, 59% of jobs based on need. Academic, athletic, state/district residency, leadership scholarships available. **Aid applications:** Closing date August 31; priority given to applications received by February 15; applicants notified on a rolling basis beginning on or about May 1; must reply as soon as possible. **Additional information:** For students residing in specific geographic region, all costs met from financial resources other than students'. For students outside region, 25% payment at registration, balance in monthly payments first three months of school. All students receive financial aid through work study program. No student denied admission because of inability to pay.

ADDRESS/TELEPHONE. Bill Melton, Director of Admissions, Alice Lloyd College, Purpose Road, Pippa Passes, KY 41844. (606) 368-2101 ext. 246. Fax: (606) 368-2125.

Asbury College
Wilmore, Kentucky CB code: 1019

Admissions: 76% of applicants accepted
Based on:
••• Recommendations, school record
•• Activities, religious affiliation/commitment, test scores
• Essay, interview
Completion: 82% of freshmen end year in good standing
45% enter graduate study

4-year private liberal arts college, coed, interdenominational. Founded in 1890. **Accreditation:** Regional. **Undergraduate enrollment:** 484 men, 589 women full time; 27 men, 29 women part time. **Faculty:** 125 total (85 full time), 68 with doctorates or other terminal degrees. **Location:** Rural campus in small town; 14 miles from Lexington. **Calendar:** Semester, limited summer session. **Microcomputers:** 40 located in classrooms, computer centers. **Additional facts:** Evangelical Christian institution with a Wesleyan emphasis.

DEGREES OFFERED. BA, BS. 195 bachelor's degrees awarded in 1992. 15% in business and management, 8% communications, 24% teacher education, 5% languages, 8% life sciences, 15% philosophy, religion, theology, 7% psychology, 8% social sciences.

UNDERGRADUATE MAJORS. Applied mathematics, art education, Bible studies, biochemistry, biology, business and management, chemistry, classics, computer graphics, computer programming, elementary education, English, English education, foreign languages (multiple emphasis), foreign languages education, French, health sciences, history, human services, journalism, junior high education, mathematics, mathematics education, medical laboratory technologies, missionary studies, music, music education, parks and recreation management, philosophy, physical education, physical sciences, psychology, radio/television broadcasting, religious education, science education, secondary education, social studies education, social work, sociology, Spanish, speech, studio art.

ACADEMIC PROGRAMS. Double major, dual enrollment of high school students, independent study, internships, study abroad, teacher preparation, visiting/exchange student program, Washington semester, cross-registration, exchange program with colleges in Christian College Consortium; liberal arts/career combination in engineering, health sciences. **Remedial services:** Learning center, preadmission summer program, reduced course load, remedial instruction, special counselor, tutoring. **Placement/credit:** AP, institutional tests.

ACADEMIC REQUIREMENTS. Freshmen must earn minimum GPA of 2.0 to continue in good standing. 2.5 GPA required for education majors. 74% of freshmen return for sophomore year. Students must declare major by end of second year. **Graduation requirements:** 124 hours for bachelor's (36 in major). Most students required to take courses in arts/fine arts, computer science, English, foreign languages, history, humanities, mathematics, philosophy/religion, biological/physical sciences, social sciences.

FRESHMAN ADMISSIONS. Selection criteria: School achievement record most important, followed by recommendations from minister, an adult, and high school along with average or above-average test scores. Recommended units include English 4, foreign language 2, mathematics 3, social science 3 and science 2. **Test requirements:** SAT or ACT; score report by August 15. **Additional information:** Students must agree to abide by campus social and religious policies.

1992 FRESHMAN CLASS PROFILE. 254 men applied, 180 accepted, 103 enrolled; 384 women applied, 305 accepted, 165 enrolled. 21% were in top tenth and 57% were in top quarter of graduating class. **Academic background:** Mid 50% of enrolled freshmen had SAT-V between 410-520, SAT-M between 420-560; ACT composite between 20-25. 56% submitted SAT scores, 60% submitted ACT scores. **Characteristics:** 15% from in state, 94% live in college housing, 1% have minority backgrounds, 2% are foreign students. Average age is 18.

FALL-TERM APPLICATIONS. $25 fee. Closing date August 1; applicants notified on a rolling basis beginning on or about October 1; must reply by May 1. Audition required for music applicants. Interview recommended for music, academically weak, scholarships applicants. Portfolio recommended for art applicants. Essay recommended. CRDA. Deferred admission available. EDP-S. Probationary acceptance possible if GPA is below 2.0 or test results fall below minimum.

STUDENT LIFE. Housing: Dormitories (men, women); apartment housing available. Apartments for single parents available. **Activities:** Student government, film, magazine, radio, student newspaper, television, yearbook, choral groups, concert band, drama, jazz band, music ensembles, chamber orchestra, Christian Service Association, Community Involvement, Foreign Missions Council, Fellowship of Christian Athletes, College Republicans, Young Democrats; Salvation Army Student Fellowship, Oriental Missionary Society Student Fellowship, World Gospel Mission Student Fellowship, Christian Missionary Alliance Student Fellowship, Brothers and Sisters In Christ. **Additional information:** Christian values stressed. Religious observance required.

ATHLETICS. NAIA, NCAA. **Intercollegiate:** Baseball M, basketball, cross-country, soccer M, softball W, swimming, tennis, volleyball W. **Intra-**

mural: Basketball, gymnastics, soccer, softball, swimming, table tennis, tennis, volleyball.

STUDENT SERVICES. Aptitude testing, career counseling, employment service for undergraduates, freshman orientation, health services, personal counseling, placement service for graduates, veterans counselor, special adviser for minority and missionary students, services/facilities for handicapped.

ANNUAL EXPENSES. Tuition and fees: $8,445. **Room and board:** $2,660. **Books and supplies:** $500. **Other expenses:** $750.

FINANCIAL AID. 92% of freshmen, 89% of continuing students receive some form of aid. 85% of grants, 91% of loans, all jobs based on need. 202 enrolled freshmen were judged to have need, all were offered aid. Academic, music/drama, art, state/district residency, leadership, alumni affiliation, religious affiliation, minority scholarships available. **Aid applications:** No closing date; priority given to applications received by March 15; applicants notified on a rolling basis beginning on or about April 1; must reply by May 1 or within 4 weeks if notified thereafter.

ADDRESS/TELEPHONE. Stan F. Wiggam, Dean of Admissions, Asbury College, 1 Macklem Drive, Wilmore, KY 40390-1198. (606) 858-3511. Fax: (606) 858-3921.

Ashland Community College
Ashland, Kentucky CB code: 0703

2-year public community college, coed. Founded in 1957. **Accreditation:** Regional. **Undergraduate enrollment:** 1,854 men and women full time; 1,413 men and women part time. **Faculty:** 142 total (90 full time), 15 with doctorates or other terminal degrees. **Location:** Suburban campus in large town; 15 miles from Huntington, West Virginia, 120 miles from Lexington. **Calendar:** Semester, limited summer session. Saturday and extensive evening/early morning classes. **Microcomputers:** 120 located in libraries, classrooms, computer centers. **Additional facts:** Comprehensive course offerings in evening program. Off-campus classes in surrounding counties.

DEGREES OFFERED. AA, AS, AAS. 216 associate degrees awarded in 1992.

UNDERGRADUATE MAJORS. Accounting, business and management, business and office, computer and information sciences, engineering and engineering-related technologies, finance, legal secretary, liberal/general studies, management information systems, medical secretary, nursing, real estate, secretarial and related programs.

ACADEMIC PROGRAMS. 2-year transfer program, cooperative education, dual enrollment of high school students, honors program, internships, telecourses, cross-registration. **Remedial services:** Learning center, preadmission summer program, reduced course load, remedial instruction, special counselor, tutoring, academic success program. **Placement/credit:** AP, CLEP General and Subject, institutional tests; 40 credit hours maximum for associate degree.

ACADEMIC REQUIREMENTS. Freshmen must earn minimum GPA of 2.0 to continue in good standing. 60% of freshmen return for sophomore year. Students must declare major on enrollment. **Graduation requirements:** 64 hours for associate. Most students required to take courses in English, history, humanities, mathematics, biological/physical sciences, social sciences.

FRESHMAN ADMISSIONS. Selection criteria: Open admissions. Selective admissions to nursing program based on test scores and academic record. **High school preparation:** 11 units recommended. Recommended units include English 4, mathematics 3, social science 2 and science 2. **Test requirements:** ACT for placement and counseling only; score report by August 20.

1992 FRESHMAN CLASS PROFILE. 243 men, 446 women enrolled. 6% were in top tenth and 22% were in top quarter of graduating class. **Academic background:** Mid 50% of enrolled freshmen had ACT composite between 34-21. 53% submitted ACT scores. **Characteristics:** 89% from in state, 100% commute, 1% have minority backgrounds. Average age is 24.

FALL-TERM APPLICATIONS. No fee. Closing date August 20; applicants notified on a rolling basis. Interview recommended. Deferred and early admission available. Nursing applications due by March 1.

STUDENT LIFE. Activities: Student government, student newspaper, choral groups, drama, Baptist Student Union/Students for Christ.

ATHLETICS. Intramural: Basketball, bowling, fencing, softball, table tennis, tennis, volleyball.

STUDENT SERVICES. Aptitude testing, career counseling, employment service for undergraduates, freshman orientation, personal counseling, placement service for graduates, veterans counselor, special services for veterans, services/facilities for handicapped.

ANNUAL EXPENSES. Tuition and fees (projected): $840, $1,680 additional for out-of-state students. **Books and supplies:** $450. **Other expenses:** $848.

FINANCIAL AID. 40% of freshmen, 40% of continuing students receive some form of aid. 93% of grants, all loans, 60% of jobs based on need. 376 enrolled freshmen were judged to have need, all were offered aid. Academic, state/district residency, minority scholarships available. **Aid applications:** No closing date; priority given to applications received by April 1; applicants notified on a rolling basis beginning on or about June 15; must reply within 3 weeks. **Additional information:** In-state 100% disabled or deceased veterans' children receive tuition waiver from state.

ADDRESS/TELEPHONE. Willie G. McCullough, Dean for Student Affairs, Ashland Community College, 1400 College Drive, Ashland, KY 41101-3683. (606) 329-2999. Fax: (606) 325-8124.

Bellarmine College
Louisville, Kentucky CB code: 1056

Admissions: 91% of applicants accepted
Based on:
- ••• Essay, recommendations, school record, test scores
- •• Activities
- • Interview, special talents

Completion: 85% of freshmen end year in good standing
78% graduate, 37% of these enter graduate study

4-year private liberal arts college, coed, affiliated with Roman Catholic Church. Founded in 1950. **Accreditation:** Regional. **Undergraduate enrollment:** 468 men, 635 women full time; 167 men, 456 women part time. **Graduate enrollment:** 9 men, 6 women full time; 213 men, 369 women part time. **Faculty:** 175 total (88 full time), 131 with doctorates or other terminal degrees. **Location:** Suburban campus in large city; Seven miles from downtown Louisville. **Calendar:** Semester, extensive summer session. Saturday and extensive evening/early morning classes. **Microcomputers:** 200 located in dormitories, libraries, classrooms, computer centers. **Special facilities:** Thomas Merton Collection, Data Courier (world's largest on-line business periodical service), 9-hole golf course, on-campus tennis center.

DEGREES OFFERED. BA, BS, MA, MS, MBA, MEd. 9 associate degrees awarded in 1992. 80% in business and management, 20% computer sciences. 303 bachelor's degrees awarded in 1992. 37% in business and management, 6% communications, 7% education, 14% health sciences, 5% letters/literature, 5% life sciences, 9% psychology, 6% social sciences. Graduate degrees offered in 5 major fields of study.

UNDERGRADUATE MAJORS. Accounting, actuarial sciences, art education, biology, business administration and management, chemistry, communications, computer and information sciences, computer engineering, computer mathematics, early childhood education, economics, elementary education, English, English education, history, junior high education, liberal/general studies, mathematics, mathematics education, music, music education, music performance, nursing, philosophy, political science and government, predentistry, prelaw, premedicine, prepharmacy, preveterinary, psychology, secondary education, social studies education, sociology, special education, specific learning disabilities, studio art, theological studies.

ACADEMIC PROGRAMS. 2-year transfer program, accelerated program, cooperative education, double major, dual enrollment of high school students, honors program, independent study, internships, study abroad, teacher preparation, cross-registration; combined bachelor's/graduate program in business administration. **Remedial services:** Reduced course load, tutoring. **ROTC:** Air Force, Army. **Placement/credit:** AP, CLEP General and Subject, institutional tests; 30 credit hours maximum for bachelor's degree.

ACADEMIC REQUIREMENTS. Freshmen must earn minimum GPA of 2.0 to continue in good standing. 89% of freshmen return for sophomore year. Students must declare major by end of second year. **Graduation requirements:** 126 hours for bachelor's (36 in major). Most students required to take courses in arts/fine arts, English, history, humanities, mathematics, philosophy/religion, biological/physical sciences, social sciences. **Postgraduate studies:** 7% enter law school, 10% enter medical school, 6% enter MBA programs, 14% enter other graduate study.

FRESHMAN ADMISSIONS. Selection criteria: Admission standards: minimum GPA 2.5, rank in top half of class, college preparatory curriculum, 21 ACT, or 900 SAT, strong high school recommendation, submission of acceptable essay. Applicants not meeting requirements may be admitted on strength of each criterion. School activities also considered. **High school preparation:** 16 units required; 18 recommended. Required and recommended units include English 4, mathematics 3, social science 2-3 and science 2. Biological science 1 and foreign language 2 recommended. One unit computer science recommended. **Test requirements:** SAT or ACT; score report by August 15.

1992 FRESHMAN CLASS PROFILE. 309 men applied, 276 accepted, 155 enrolled; 394 women applied, 365 accepted, 236 enrolled. 63% had high school GPA of 3.0 or higher, 35% between 2.0 and 2.99. 35% were in top tenth and 59% were in top quarter of graduating class. **Academic background:** Mid 50% of enrolled freshmen had SAT-V between 440-510, SAT-M between 490-540; ACT composite between 20-25. 42% submitted SAT scores, 86% submitted ACT scores. **Characteristics:** 74% from in state, 60% live in college housing, 5% have minority backgrounds, 1% are foreign students. Average age is 19.

FALL-TERM APPLICATIONS. $20 fee, may be waived for applicants with need. No closing date; priority given to applications received by May 1; applicants notified on a rolling basis; must reply by orientation. Essay required. Interview recommended. Audition recommended for music applicants. Portfolio recommended for art applicants. CRDA. Deferred and early admission available. Institutional early decision plan.

STUDENT LIFE. Housing: Dormitories (men, women, coed). Juniors and seniors live in dormitory suites of three rooms each. **Activities:** Student government, magazine, student newspaper, yearbook, choral groups, concert band, dance, drama, jazz band, music ensembles, musical theater, pep band, fraternities, sororities, Campus Ministry Council, Amnesty International, Bellarmine Scholars, Student Ambassadors, Student Ass'n for Equality. **Additional information:** 40 clubs and organizations available. Mock-trial team nationally ranked.

ATHLETICS. NCAA. **Intercollegiate:** Baseball M, basketball, cross-country, field hockey W, golf M, soccer, softball W, tennis, track and field, volleyball W. **Intramural:** Badminton, basketball, bowling, golf, soccer, softball, table tennis, tennis, volleyball.

STUDENT SERVICES. Aptitude testing, career counseling, employment service for undergraduates, freshman orientation, health services, personal counseling, placement service for graduates, special adviser for adult students, veterans counselor, services/facilities for handicapped.

ANNUAL EXPENSES. Tuition and fees: $8,172. **Room and board:** $4,505. **Books and supplies:** $750. **Other expenses:** $750.

FINANCIAL AID. 90% of freshmen, 76% of continuing students receive some form of aid. 38% of grants, 90% of loans, 95% of jobs based on need. 181 enrolled freshmen were judged to have need, all were offered aid. Academic, music/drama, art, athletic, leadership, alumni affiliation, minority scholarships available. **Aid applications:** No closing date; priority given to applications received by April 1; applicants notified on a rolling basis beginning on or about March 15; must reply by May 1 or within 2 weeks if notified thereafter.

ADDRESS/TELEPHONE. Dr. Leonard Moisan, Vice President for Institutional Advancement, Bellarmine College, 2001 Newburg Road, Louisville, KY 40205-0671. (502) 452-8131. (800) 274-4723. Fax: (502) 456-1844.

Berea College

Berea, Kentucky — CB code: 1060

Admissions: 32% of applicants accepted
Based on: ••• Essay, school record
•• Activities, interview, recommendations, special talents, test scores
Completion: 88% of freshmen end year in good standing
50% graduate

4-year private liberal arts college, coed, nondenominational. Founded in 1855. **Accreditation:** Regional. **Undergraduate enrollment:** 664 men, 850 women full time; 17 men, 32 women part time. **Faculty:** 148 total (133 full time), 92 with doctorates or other terminal degrees. **Location:** Rural campus in small town; 40 miles from Lexington. **Calendar:** 4-1-4, limited summer session. **Microcomputers:** 165 located in dormitories, libraries, classrooms, computer centers, campus-wide network. **Special facilities:** Special Appalachian library collection, Appalachian museum, geology museum, planetarium with observatory. **Additional facts:** 80% of students come from southern Appalachia and Kentucky. All students participate in work program.

DEGREES OFFERED. BA, BS. 274 bachelor's degrees awarded in 1992. 5% in agriculture, 10% business and management, 12% teacher education, 9% home economics, 9% letters/literature, 7% life sciences, 6% mathematics, 12% social sciences, 5% trade and industry, 7% visual and performing arts.

UNDERGRADUATE MAJORS. Agribusiness, agricultural sciences, art education, art history, biology, business administration and management, chemistry, early childhood education, economics, elementary education, English, English education, fine arts, food science and nutrition, foreign languages education, French, German, history, home economics, home economics education, hotel/motel and restaurant management, individual and family development, industrial arts education, junior high education, Latin, mathematics, mathematics education, music, music education, music performance, nursing, philosophy, physical education, physics, political science and government, psychology, religion, science education, secondary education, social science education, sociology, Spanish, studio art, technology and industrial arts, visual and performing arts.

ACADEMIC PROGRAMS. Double major, dual enrollment of high school students, independent study, internships, student-designed major, study abroad, teacher preparation, visiting/exchange student program, 3-2 engineering program with Washington University (MO); liberal arts/career combination in engineering. **Remedial services:** Learning center, remedial instruction, tutoring. **Placement/credit:** AP, CLEP General and Subject, institutional tests. Unlimited number of credit hours may be counted toward degree.

ACADEMIC REQUIREMENTS. Passing grade in 7 courses (28 semester hours) required to remain in good standing. If on academic probation, must earn grades of "C" or better in 3 full credit courses and a minimum term GPA of 1.67. 70% of freshmen return for sophomore year. Students must declare major by end of second year. **Graduation requirements:** 132 hours for bachelor's (48 in major). Most students required to take courses in arts/fine arts, computer science, English, history, humanities, mathematics, philosophy/religion, biological/physical sciences, social sciences.

FRESHMAN ADMISSIONS. Selection criteria: Rank in top half of class with good recommendations, involvement in community and school activities important. Financial need absolute prerequisite for admission. Recommended units include English 4, foreign language 2, mathematics 3, social science 2 and science 2. **Test requirements:** SAT or ACT; score report by April 15.

1992 FRESHMAN CLASS PROFILE. 802 men applied, 258 accepted, 191 enrolled; 893 women applied, 291 accepted, 206 enrolled. **Characteristics:** 47% from in state, 94% live in college housing, 12% have minority backgrounds, 6% are foreign students. Average age is 18.

FALL-TERM APPLICATIONS. $5 fee. No closing date; priority given to applications received by February 28; August 15. Essay required. Interview recommended for academically borderline applicants. Portfolio recommended for art applicants. CRDA. Early admission available. April 15 latest acceptance date for SAT/ACT scores. Applicants advised to submit scores earlier since openings filled quickly.

STUDENT LIFE. Housing: Dormitories (men, women); apartment, cooperative housing available. Unmarried students under 25 (except for local students) required to live in college housing. Limited housing available for single parents and their children and for married students. **Activities:** Student government, student newspaper, yearbook, magazine (Twenty Writers Club), choral groups, concert band, drama, jazz band, music ensembles, pep band, symphony orchestra, religious organizations, People Who Care, Students for Appalachia, Country Dancers, Habitat for Humanity.

ATHLETICS. NAIA, NCAA. **Intercollegiate:** Baseball M, basketball, cross-country, field hockey W, golf M, soccer M, softball W, swimming, tennis, track and field, volleyball W. **Intramural:** Basketball, racquetball, soccer M, softball M, volleyball W.

STUDENT SERVICES. Aptitude testing, career counseling, employment service for undergraduates, freshman orientation, health services, on-campus day care, personal counseling, placement service for graduates, veterans counselor, services/facilities for handicapped.

ANNUAL EXPENSES. Tuition and fees: $183. **Room and board:** $2,700. **Books and supplies:** $400. **Other expenses:** $788.

FINANCIAL AID. 100% of freshmen, 100% of continuing students receive some form of aid. All aid based on need. **Aid applications:** No closing date; priority given to applications received by February 28; applicants notified on a rolling basis.

ADDRESS/TELEPHONE. John S. Cook, Director of Admissions, Berea College, CPO 2344, Berea, KY 40404. (606) 986-9341 ext. 5083. Fax: (606) 986-4506.

Brescia College

Owensboro, Kentucky — CB code: 1071

4-year private liberal arts college, coed, affiliated with Roman Catholic Church. Founded in 1950. **Accreditation:** Regional. **Undergraduate enrollment:** 168 men, 335 women full time; 103 men, 194 women part time. **Faculty:** 68 total (41 full time), 22 with doctorates or other terminal degrees. **Location:** Urban campus in small city; 45 miles from Evansville, Indiana, 120 miles from Nashville, Tennessee. **Calendar:** Semester, extensive summer session. Saturday classes. **Microcomputers:** 99 located in libraries, computer centers. **Special facilities:** Speech and hearing clinic.

DEGREES OFFERED. AA, AS, BA, BS. 14 associate degrees awarded in 1992. 64% in business and management, 7% philosophy, religion, theology, 29% social sciences. 125 bachelor's degrees awarded. 33% in business and management, 15% teacher education, 6% health sciences, 5% life sciences, 8% mathematics, 6% psychology, 9% social sciences, 6% visual and performing arts.

UNDERGRADUATE MAJORS. Associate: Business and management, chemical manufacturing technology, engineering, engineering and engineering-related technologies, human relations, ministry formation, photographic technology, photography, religious education. **Bachelor's:** Accounting, applied mathematics, art education, biological and physical sciences, biology, business and management, chemistry, computer and information sciences, elementary education, English, graphic design, history, junior high education, liberal/general studies, medical laboratory technologies, ministry formation, pre-art therapy, prelaw, psychology, religion, secondary education, social sciences, social studies education, sociology, special education, speech correction, studio art, theological studies.

ACADEMIC PROGRAMS. Cooperative education, double major, honors program, independent study, internships, student-designed major, teacher preparation, weekend college, cross-registration. **Remedial services:** Learning center, reduced course load, remedial instruction, special counselor, tutoring. **Placement/credit:** AP, CLEP General and Subject, institutional tests; 18 credit hours maximum for associate degree; 36 credit hours maximum for bachelor's degree.

ACADEMIC REQUIREMENTS. Freshmen must earn minimum GPA of 1.75 to continue in good standing. 70% of freshmen return for sophomore

year. Students must declare major by end of second year. **Graduation requirements:** 63 hours for associate (30 in major), 128 hours for bachelor's (42 in major). Most students required to take courses in arts/fine arts, computer science, English, history, humanities, mathematics, philosophy/religion, biological/physical sciences, social sciences.

FRESHMAN ADMISSIONS. Selection criteria: GPA, class rank, test scores, and intended major considered. Recommended units include English 4, mathematics 3 and social science 2. **Test requirements:** SAT or ACT (ACT preferred); score report by August 15.

1992 FRESHMAN CLASS PROFILE. 30 men, 63 women enrolled. 54% had high school GPA of 3.0 or higher, 44% between 2.0 and 2.99. 28% were in top tenth and 54% were in top quarter of graduating class. **Academic background:** Mid 50% of enrolled freshmen had ACT composite between 18-24. 93% submitted ACT scores. **Characteristics:** Average age is 19.

FALL-TERM APPLICATIONS. $15 fee, may be waived for applicants with need. No closing date; applicants notified on a rolling basis beginning on or about January 15. Audition required for music applicants. Portfolio required for art, photography applicants. Interview recommended. Essay recommended. Deferred and early admission available.

STUDENT LIFE. Housing: Dormitories (women); apartment housing available. Students live in small groups in family-style houses around perimeter of campus. **Activities:** Student government, magazine, yearbook, choral groups, drama, Council for Exceptional Children, Circle-K, campus ministry, Christian Student Union, International Student Organization.

ATHLETICS. NAIA. **Intercollegiate:** Basketball, golf M, soccer M, softball W, tennis M, volleyball W. **Intramural:** Badminton, basketball, bowling, soccer, softball, table tennis, tennis, volleyball.

STUDENT SERVICES. Aptitude testing, career counseling, employment service for undergraduates, freshman orientation, personal counseling, placement service for graduates, special adviser for adult students, veterans counselor, services/facilities for handicapped.

ANNUAL EXPENSES. Tuition and fees: $6,760. **Room and board:** $3,100. **Books and supplies:** $650. **Other expenses:** $650.

FINANCIAL AID. 39% of freshmen, 59% of continuing students receive some form of aid. 90% of grants, 87% of loans, 73% of jobs based on need. Academic, music/drama, art, athletic, state/district residency, leadership, alumni affiliation, religious affiliation scholarships available. **Aid applications:** No closing date; priority given to applications received by April 1; applicants notified on a rolling basis beginning on or about May 1; must reply within 4 weeks.

ADDRESS/TELEPHONE. Dennis Vessels, Director of Admissions, Brescia College, 717 Frederica Street, Owensboro, KY 42301-3023. (502) 685-3131. (800) 284-1962. Fax: (502) 686-4213.

Campbellsville College
Campbellsville, Kentucky — CB code: 1097

4-year private college of arts and sciences and business, liberal arts, teachers college, coed, affiliated with Kentucky Southern Baptist Convention. Founded in 1906. **Accreditation:** Regional. **Undergraduate enrollment:** 413 men, 397 women full time; 93 men, 104 women part time. **Graduate enrollment:** 2 men, 29 women full time. **Faculty:** 70 total (50 full time), 25 with doctorates or other terminal degrees. **Location:** Rural campus in large town; 80 miles from Louisville, Lexington, and Bowling Green; 140 miles from Nashville, TN. **Calendar:** Semester, extensive summer session. **Microcomputers:** 30 located in libraries, classrooms, computer centers. **Special facilities:** Gosser Fine Arts Center and art gallery, Kentuckiana Room and Collection.

DEGREES OFFERED. AA, AS, BA, BS, MA. 3 associate degrees awarded in 1992. 100% in business and management. 112 bachelor's degrees awarded. 29% in business and management, 40% teacher education, 5% philosophy, religion, theology, 7% psychology. Graduate degrees offered in 1 major field of study.

UNDERGRADUATE MAJORS. Associate: Business administration and management, business and office, business data processing and related programs, criminal justice studies, data processing, law enforcement and corrections technologies, office supervision and management, professional assistant, social sciences. **Bachelor's:** Accounting, art education, art history, biological and physical sciences, biology, business administration and management, business and management, business economics, business education, chemistry, christian studies, church recreation, communications, computer and information sciences, economics, elementary education, English, English education, health education, history, institutional management, journalism, junior high education, mathematics, mathematics education, medical laboratory technologies, music, music education, music performance, office supervision and management, organizational administration, physical education, political science and government, predentistry, preengineering, prelaw, premedicine, prepharmacy, preveterinary, psychology, radio/television broadcasting, religion, religious education, religious music, science education, secondary education, social sciences, social studies education, sociology, theological studies.

ACADEMIC PROGRAMS. Accelerated program, double major, dual enrollment of high school students, independent study, internships, study abroad, teacher preparation, visiting/exchange student program, Washington semester, 3-2 program with the University of Kentucky for engineering; liberal arts/career combination in engineering, health sciences, business. **Remedial services:** Learning center, preadmission summer program, reduced course load, remedial instruction, tutoring, teacher learning resource room. **Placement/credit:** AP, CLEP General and Subject, institutional tests; 36 credit hours maximum for bachelor's degree.

ACADEMIC REQUIREMENTS. Freshmen must earn minimum GPA of 1.8 to continue in good standing. 2.0 GPA at end of third semester. 60% of freshmen return for sophomore year. Students must declare major by end of second year. **Graduation requirements:** 64 hours for associate (20 in major), 128 hours for bachelor's (30 in major). Most students required to take courses in arts/fine arts, computer science, English, history, humanities, mathematics, philosophy/religion, biological/physical sciences, social sciences. **Postgraduate studies:** 2% enter law school, 1% enter medical school, 5% enter MBA programs, 30% enter other graduate study.

FRESHMAN ADMISSIONS. Selection criteria: Achievement in strong high school program and satisfactory ACT or SAT scores most important. Special consideration for entry to basic skills program may be given by Admissions Committee to other highly motivated and potentially successful applicants. **Test requirements:** SAT or ACT; score report by August 20.

1992 FRESHMAN CLASS PROFILE. 270 men and women enrolled. 50% had high school GPA of 3.0 or higher, 49% between 2.0 and 2.99. **Academic background:** Mid 50% of enrolled freshmen had SAT-V between 300-600, SAT-M between 300-580; ACT composite between 19-25. 5% submitted SAT scores, 95% submitted ACT scores. **Characteristics:** 80% from in state, 70% live in college housing, 11% have minority backgrounds. Average age is 18.

FALL-TERM APPLICATIONS. $10 fee, may be waived for applicants with need. No closing date; applicants notified on a rolling basis. Interview recommended. Portfolio recommended. Essay recommended. CRDA. Deferred admission available.

STUDENT LIFE. Housing: Dormitories (men, women); apartment housing available. Campus houses available for single parents and married couples. **Activities:** Student government, magazine, student newspaper, television, yearbook, literary publications, choral groups, concert band, drama, jazz band, marching band, music ensembles, musical theater, pep band, contemporary Christian vocal ensembles, handbell choir, collegiate chorale, Baptist Student Union, Young Republicans, Young Democrats, Student Government Association, Student Foundation, Fellowship of Christian Athletes.

ATHLETICS. NAIA. **Intercollegiate:** Baseball M, basketball, cross-country, diving, football M, golf M, soccer M, softball W, swimming, tennis, volleyball W. **Intramural:** Basketball, soccer, softball, table tennis, tennis, volleyball.

STUDENT SERVICES. Career counseling, employment service for undergraduates, freshman orientation, health services, personal counseling, placement service for graduates, veterans counselor, services/facilities for handicapped.

ANNUAL EXPENSES. Tuition and fees: $5,720. **Room and board:** $3,000. **Books and supplies:** $600. **Other expenses:** $1,000.

FINANCIAL AID. 88% of freshmen, 88% of continuing students receive some form of aid. 69% of grants, 91% of loans, 93% of jobs based on need. Academic, music/drama, art, athletic, leadership, religious affiliation scholarships available. **Aid applications:** No closing date; priority given to applications received by April 1; applicants notified on a rolling basis beginning on or about May 15; must reply within 10 days. **Additional information:** Matching scholarships available for students whose church contributes $200 annually.

ADDRESS/TELEPHONE. Trent Argo, Director of Admissions, Campbellsville College, 200 West College Street, Campbellsville, KY 42718-2799. (502) 789-5220. (800) 264-6014. Fax: (502) 789-5020.

CareerCom Junior College of Business
Hopkinsville, Kentucky — CB code: 5375

2-year proprietary business, junior college, coed. **Undergraduate enrollment:** 195 men and women. **Location:** Suburban campus in large town. **Calendar:** Quarter.

FRESHMAN ADMISSIONS. Selection criteria: All applicants must pass interest evaluation test. Test scores and interview also important.

ANNUAL EXPENSES. Tuition and fees (1992-93): $7,805.

ADDRESS/TELEPHONE. Diane Suver, Director of Admissions, CareerCom Junior College of Business, 1102 South Virginia Street, Hopkinsville, KY 42240. (502) 886-1302.

Centre College

Danville, Kentucky — CB code: 1109

Admissions: 90% of applicants accepted
Based on:
- ••• Recommendations, school record
- •• Activities, essay, interview, special talents, test scores

Completion: 95% of freshmen end year in good standing
72% graduate, 39% of these enter graduate study

4-year private college of arts and sciences, coed, affiliated with Presbyterian Church (USA). Founded in 1819. **Accreditation:** Regional. **Undergraduate enrollment:** 465 men, 439 women full time. **Faculty:** 94 total (87 full time), 82 with doctorates or other terminal degrees. **Location:** Rural campus in large town; 35 miles from Lexington. **Calendar:** 4-2-4. **Microcomputers:** 80 located in dormitories, libraries, classrooms, computer centers, campus-wide network. **Special facilities:** Norton Center for the Arts, Olin Physical Science Center. **Additional facts:** Affiliate of Regents College in London.

DEGREES OFFERED. BA, BS. 198 bachelor's degrees awarded in 1992. 5% in languages, 13% letters/literature, 16% life sciences, 5% mathematics, 5% physical sciences, 6% psychology, 39% social sciences, 6% visual and performing arts.

UNDERGRADUATE MAJORS. Anthropology, biochemistry, biology, chemical physics, chemistry, computer and information sciences, dramatic arts, economics, elementary education, English, fine arts, French, German, history, mathematics, molecular biology, music, philosophy, physics, political science and government, predentistry, prelaw, premedicine, preveterinary, psychobiology, psychology, religion, sociology, Spanish.

ACADEMIC PROGRAMS. Double major, independent study, internships, student-designed major, study abroad, teacher preparation, science semester at Oak Ridge National Laboratories, Tennessee, and five other national science laboratories, 3-2 engineering program with Columbia University, New York, Washington University, Missouri, Vanderbilt University, Tennessee, Georgia Tech, and University of Kentucky; liberal arts/career combination in engineering. **Remedial services:** Preadmission summer program, reduced course load, tutoring. **ROTC:** Air Force, Army. **Placement/credit:** AP, CLEP General, IB, institutional tests.

ACADEMIC REQUIREMENTS. Freshmen must earn minimum GPA of 1.5 to continue in good standing. 87% of freshmen return for sophomore year. Students must declare major by end of second year. **Graduation requirements:** 115 hours for bachelor's (30 in major). Most students required to take courses in arts/fine arts, English, foreign languages, history, humanities, mathematics, philosophy/religion, biological/physical sciences, social sciences. **Postgraduate studies:** 8% enter law school, 7% enter medical school, 2% enter MBA programs, 22% enter other graduate study. **Additional information:** Experimental courses and off-campus study options offered during 6-week winter term.

FRESHMAN ADMISSIONS. Selection criteria: Achievement and quality of high school program most important. Recommendations, test scores, academic and nonacademic interests, experiences, and interview also considered. **High school preparation:** 14 units required; 16 recommended. Required and recommended units include English 4, foreign language 2, mathematics 4, social science 2-3 and science 2-3. Fine art courses recommended. **Test requirements:** SAT or ACT; score report by March 1.

1992 FRESHMAN CLASS PROFILE. 428 men applied, 392 accepted, 165 enrolled; 544 women applied, 479 accepted, 123 enrolled. 65% were in top tenth and 88% were in top quarter of graduating class. **Academic background:** Mid 50% of enrolled freshmen had SAT-V between 480-600, SAT-M between 530-650; ACT composite between 25-29. 63% submitted SAT scores, 88% submitted ACT scores. **Characteristics:** 63% from in state, 99% live in college housing, 6% have minority backgrounds, 1% are foreign students, 65% join fraternities/sororities. Average age is 18.

FALL-TERM APPLICATIONS. $25 fee, may be waived for applicants with need. Closing date March 1; applicants notified on or about March 15; must reply by May 1. Essay required. Interview recommended. CRDA. Deferred and early admission available. EDP-F. Early Action Plan available. November 15 application deadline; December15 notification; May 1 response. Early decision plan available. November 15 application deadline; December 15 notification; January 15 response.

STUDENT LIFE. Housing: Dormitories (men, women, coed); fraternity housing available. **Activities:** Student government, magazine, radio, student newspaper, yearbook, literary publications, choral groups, drama, jazz band, music ensembles, musical theater, pep band, symphony orchestra, fraternities, sororities, CARE (Volunteer Services), Black Student Union, Fellowship of Christian Athletes, Circle-K, Catholic Campus Ministry, Baptist Campus Ministry, College Life, Centrecycle (environmental), LIFT (tutoring and mentoring for at-risk elementary students).

ATHLETICS. NCAA. **Intercollegiate:** Baseball M, basketball, cross-country, diving, field hockey W, football M, golf M, soccer, swimming, tennis, track and field, volleyball W. **Intramural:** Archery, badminton, basketball, bowling, cross-country, fencing, field hockey W, golf, racquetball, rugby M, soccer, softball, swimming, table tennis, tennis, track and field, volleyball, wrestling M.

STUDENT SERVICES. Aptitude testing, career counseling, employment service for undergraduates, freshman orientation, health services, personal counseling, placement service for graduates, services/facilities for handicapped.

ANNUAL EXPENSES. Tuition and fees: $11,600. **Room and board:** $4,200. **Books and supplies:** $600. **Other expenses:** $600.

FINANCIAL AID. 79% of freshmen, 67% of continuing students receive some form of aid. 70% of grants, 99% of loans, all jobs based on need. 169 enrolled freshmen were judged to have need, all were offered aid. Academic, state/district residency, leadership, minority scholarships available. **Aid applications:** Closing date March 15; applicants notified on or about April 1; must reply by May 1 or within 2 weeks if notified thereafter.

ADDRESS/TELEPHONE. John W. Rogers, Director of Admission, Centre College, 600 West Walnut Street, Danville, KY 40422. (606) 238-5350. (800) 423-6236. Fax: (606) 238-5507.

Clear Creek Baptist Bible College

Pineville, Kentucky — CB code: 5975

4-year private Bible, seminary college, coed, affiliated with Southern Baptist Convention. Founded in 1926. **Undergraduate enrollment:** 111 men, 15 women full time; 11 men, 15 women part time. **Location:** Rural campus in small town; 76 miles north of Knoxville. **Calendar:** Semester. **Additional facts:** An adult family Bible college that trains individuals for ministry in the local church. Students required to be at least 21 years of age.

FRESHMAN ADMISSIONS. Selection criteria: Open admissions. Demonstrated clear call to Christian ministry necessary.

ANNUAL EXPENSES. Tuition and fees (projected): $2,110. Health/hospital insurance required. Students who are not Southern Baptists pay additional tuition of $220/semester or $23 per credit hour. **Room and board:** $2,100. **Books and supplies:** $200.

ADDRESS/TELEPHONE. Jayson P. Barnett, Director of Admissions, Clear Creek Baptist Bible College, 300 Clear Creek Road, Pineville, KY 40977. (606) 337-3196 ext. 108. Fax: (606) 337-2372.

Cumberland College

Williamsburg, Kentucky — CB code: 1145

4-year private liberal arts college, coed, affiliated with Southern Baptist Convention. Founded in 1889. **Accreditation:** Regional. **Undergraduate enrollment:** 589 men, 728 women full time; 44 men, 40 women part time. **Graduate enrollment:** 2 men, 2 women full time; 22 men, 71 women part time. **Faculty:** 100 total (94 full time), 47 with doctorates or other terminal degrees. **Location:** Rural campus in small town; 100 miles from Lexington, 65 miles from Knoxville, Tennessee. **Calendar:** Semester, extensive summer session. Extensive evening/early morning classes. **Microcomputers:** 150 located in dormitories, libraries, classrooms, computer centers. **Special facilities:** Natural history museum, greenhouse, art gallery.

DEGREES OFFERED. BA, BS, MEd. 237 bachelor's degrees awarded in 1992. 13% in business and management, 19% teacher education, 8% health sciences, 5% letters/literature, 6% life sciences, 6% mathematics, 9% physical sciences, 10% psychology, 10% social sciences. Graduate degrees offered in 4 major fields of study.

UNDERGRADUATE MAJORS. Accounting, allied health, art education, biology, business administration and management, business education, chemistry, clinical laboratory science, communications, computer and information sciences, dramatic arts, early childhood education, education, elementary education, English, English education, fine arts, health education, history, junior high education, mathematics, mathematics education, medical laboratory technologies, military science (Army), movement and leisure studies, movement and leisure studies/health, music, music education, music performance, physics, political science and government, predentistry, prelaw, premedicine, prepharmacy, preveterinary, psychology, religion, religious education, religious music, secondary education, secretarial and related programs, sociology, special education.

ACADEMIC PROGRAMS. Accelerated program, double major, dual enrollment of high school students, education specialist degree, honors program, independent study, internships, study abroad, teacher preparation; liberal arts/career combination in engineering. **Remedial services:** Learning center, preadmission summer program, reduced course load, remedial instruction, special counselor, tutoring, writing laboratory. **ROTC:** Army. **Placement/credit:** AP, CLEP General and Subject, institutional tests; 50 credit hours maximum for bachelor's degree.

ACADEMIC REQUIREMENTS. Freshmen must earn minimum GPA of 2.0 to continue in good standing. 70% of freshmen return for sophomore year. Students must declare major by end of second year. **Graduation requirements:** 128 hours for bachelor's (36 in major). Most students required to take courses in arts/fine arts, computer science, English, history, humanities, mathematics, philosophy/religion, biological/physical sciences, social sciences. **Postgraduate studies:** 2% enter law school, 5% enter medical school, 6% enter MBA programs, 40% enter other graduate study.

FRESHMAN ADMISSIONS. Selection criteria: Evaluation of Counselor recommendation and other recommendations only after admissions requirements for ACT/SAT and GPA have been met. Recommended units include English 4, mathematics 3, physical science 1, social science 1 and science 2. **Test requirements:** SAT or ACT; score report by August 26.

1992 FRESHMAN CLASS PROFILE. 152 men, 188 women enrolled. 63% had high school GPA of 3.0 or higher, 25% between 2.0 and 2.99. 39% were in top tenth and 49% were in top quarter of graduating class. **Academic background:** Mid 50% of enrolled freshmen had ACT composite between 19-27. 70% submitted ACT scores. **Characteristics:** 45% from in state, 80% live in college housing, 8% have minority backgrounds, 5% are foreign students. Average age is 19.

FALL-TERM APPLICATIONS. $25 fee, may be waived for applicants with need. No closing date; priority given to applications received by July 1; applicants notified on a rolling basis; must reply by May 1 or within 2 weeks if notified thereafter. Audition required for music applicants. Interview recommended. Portfolio recommended for art applicants. CRDA. Deferred and early admission available.

STUDENT LIFE. Housing: Dormitories (men, women). Freshmen must live on campus. **Activities:** Student government, radio, student newspaper, television, yearbook, choral groups, concert band, dance, drama, jazz band, marching band, music ensembles, musical theater, opera, pep band, handbell choir, chamber orchestra, show choir, Baptist Student Union, Fellowship of Christian Athletes, International Students Club, Young Democrats, Appalachian Ministries. **Additional information:** Religious observance required.

ATHLETICS. NAIA. **Intercollegiate:** Baseball M, basketball, cross-country, football M, golf, skin diving, soccer, softball W, tennis, track and field W, volleyball W. **Intramural:** Archery, badminton, basketball, bowling, golf, racquetball, soccer, softball, squash, table tennis, tennis, track and field, volleyball, wrestling M.

STUDENT SERVICES. Aptitude testing, career counseling, employment service for undergraduates, freshman orientation, health services, personal counseling, placement service for graduates, services/facilities for handicapped.

ANNUAL EXPENSES. Tuition and fees: $6,230. **Room and board:** $3,526. **Books and supplies:** $400. **Other expenses:** $500.

FINANCIAL AID. 85% of freshmen, 85% of continuing students receive some form of aid. 46% of grants, 92% of loans, all jobs based on need. 298 enrolled freshmen were judged to have need, all were offered aid. Academic, music/drama, art, athletic scholarships available. **Aid applications:** No closing date; priority given to applications received by March 15; applicants notified on a rolling basis beginning on or about May 1; must reply within 2 weeks.

ADDRESS/TELEPHONE. Danny E. Hall, Dean of Admissions, Cumberland College, 6178 College Station Drive, Williamsburg, KY 40769-6178. (606) 549-2200 ext. 4241. (800) 343-1609. Fax: (606) 549-2200 ext. 4250.

Eastern Kentucky University
Richmond, Kentucky CB code: 1200

4-year public university, coed. Founded in 1906. **Accreditation:** Regional. **Undergraduate enrollment:** 5,022 men, 6,612 women full time; 1,185 men, 2,103 women part time. **Graduate enrollment:** 199 men, 287 women full time; 403 men, 1,055 women part time. **Faculty:** 829 total (610 full time), 397 with doctorates or other terminal degrees. **Location:** Rural campus in large town; 28 miles from Lexington, 110 miles from Louisville and Cincinnati, Ohio. **Calendar:** Semester, extensive summer session. **Microcomputers:** 150 located in dormitories, libraries, computer centers. **Special facilities:** Planetarium, nature preserves, law enforcement facilities, art gallery, music library. **Additional facts:** Courses offered at additional sites in Corbin, Manchester, London, Somerset and Barbourville.

DEGREES OFFERED. AA, BA, BS, BFA, MA, MS, MBA, MEd. 240 associate degrees awarded in 1992. 1,583 bachelor's degrees awarded. Graduate degrees offered in 54 major fields of study.

UNDERGRADUATE MAJORS. Associate: Agricultural mechanics, agricultural sciences, air conditioning/heating/refrigeration technology, clinical laboratory science, commercial art, computer servicing technology, computer technology, drafting, drafting and design technology, education of the deaf and hearing impaired, electrical and electronics equipment repair, emergency medical technologies, fire control and safety technology, graphic and printing production, graphic arts technology, horticulture, interior design, interpreter for the deaf, landscape architecture, legal assistant/paralegal, machine tool operation/machine shop, mechanical design technology, medical assistant, medical laboratory technologies, medical records administration, medical records technology, nursing, ornamental horticulture, parks and recreation management, physician's assistant, practical nursing, quality control technology, radio/television technology, robotics, secretarial and related programs, sports management. **Bachelor's:** Accounting, administrative communication services, advertising, agribusiness, agricultural business and management, agricultural education, agricultural mechanics, agricultural sciences, air conditioning/heating/refrigeration mechanics, aircraft mechanics, animal sciences, anthropology, art education, automotive mechanics, aviation administration, biology, business administration and management, business and management, business and office, business computer/console/peripheral equipment operation, business economics, business education, carpentry, ceramics, chemistry, city/community/regional planning, clinical laboratory science, commercial art, community health work, computer and information sciences, computer graphics, computer programming, computer technology, conservation and regulation, construction, cytotechnology, dairy, diesel engine mechanics, drafting, drafting and design technology, dramatic arts, drawing, early childhood education, earth sciences, economics, education, education of the deaf and hearing impaired, education of the emotionally handicapped, education of the mentally handicapped, education of the physically handicapped, electrical and electronics equipment repair, elementary education, English, English education, environmental science, fashion merchandising, finance, fine arts, fire control and safety technology, fishing and fisheries, food management, food science and nutrition, foreign languages education, forensic studies, French, geography, geography education, geology, German, graphic and printing production, graphic design, health care administration, health education, history, home economics, home economics education, horticultural science, horticulture, industrial arts education, industrial design, information sciences and systems, insurance and risk management, interior design, interpreter for the deaf, investments and securities, journalism, junior high education, landscape architecture, law enforcement and corrections, legal assistant/paralegal, machine tool operation/machine shop, marketing management, masonry/tile setting, mathematics, mathematics education, medical laboratory technologies, medical records administration, medical records technology, metal/jewelry, microbiology, music, music business management, music education, music performance, music theory and composition, musical theater, nursing, occupational therapy, ornamental horticulture, painting, parks and recreation management, personnel management, philosophy, physical education, physics, plumbing/pipefitting/steamfitting, political science and government, practical nursing, prelaw, printmaking, psychology, public health laboratory science, public relations, quality control technology, radio/television broadcasting, radio/television technology, real estate, religion, renewable natural resources, robotics, science education, sculpture, secondary education, secretarial and related programs, social science education, social studies education, social work, sociology, soil sciences, Spanish, special education, specific learning disabilities, speech, speech correction, speech/communication/theater education, sports management, sports medicine, statistics, textiles and clothing, trade and industrial education, transportation and travel marketing, transportation management, wildlife management, woodworking.

ACADEMIC PROGRAMS. 2-year transfer program, cooperative education, double major, dual enrollment of high school students, education specialist degree, honors program, independent study, internships, student-designed major, study abroad, teacher preparation; liberal arts/career combination in engineering. **Remedial services:** Learning center, preadmission summer program, remedial instruction, tutoring. **ROTC:** Air Force, Army. **Placement/credit:** AP, CLEP General and Subject, institutional tests; 30 credit hours maximum for associate degree; 65 credit hours maximum for bachelor's degree.

ACADEMIC REQUIREMENTS. Freshmen must earn minimum GPA of 1.4 to continue in good standing. 63% of freshmen return for sophomore year. Students must declare major by end of second year. **Graduation requirements:** 64 hours for associate (18 in major), 128 hours for bachelor's (30 in major). Most students required to take courses in arts/fine arts, English, history, humanities, biological/physical sciences, social sciences. **Postgraduate studies:** 10% from 2-year programs enter 4-year programs.

FRESHMAN ADMISSIONS. Selection criteria: Open admissions. Out-of-state applicants must rank in top half of graduating class or have ACT composite score of 21 or SAT combined score of 890. Interview also considered. Resident applicants must have completed specified high school curriculum. **High school preparation:** 20 units recommended. Recommended units include English 4, foreign language 2, mathematics 4, social science 2 and science 3. Art, drama, music and computer science also recommended. **Test requirements:** ACT; score report by August 15. ACT scores used for placement and counseling of state residents and for admission of out-of-state applicants. **Additional information:** Applicants without college preparatory courses subject to remediation.

1992 FRESHMAN CLASS PROFILE. 1,095 men, 1,404 women enrolled. 25% had high school GPA of 3.0 or higher, 65% between 2.0 and 2.99. **Academic background:** Mid 50% of enrolled freshmen had ACT composite between 13-20. 95% submitted ACT scores. **Characteristics:** 88% from in state, 63% live in college housing, 5% have minority backgrounds, 1% are foreign students, 11% join fraternities/sororities. Average age is 19.

FALL-TERM APPLICATIONS. No fee. No closing date; applicants notified on a rolling basis. Interview recommended. Audition recommended for music applicants. Portfolio recommended for graphic art, art applicants.

STUDENT LIFE. Housing: Dormitories (men, women, coed); apartment, handicapped housing available. Students required to live on campus until age 21 unless living with parent or guardian. **Activities:** Student government, film, magazine, radio, student newspaper, television, yearbook, choral groups, concert band, dance, drama, jazz band, marching band, music ensembles, musical theater, pep band, symphony orchestra, fraternities, sororities, 160 religious, political, ethnic, social service, and special interest organizations, Black Student Union.

ATHLETICS. NCAA. **Intercollegiate:** Baseball M, basketball, cross-country, football M, golf M, tennis, track and field, volleyball W. **Intramu-**

ral: Basketball, bowling, football M, golf, horseback riding, racquetball, rugby M, soccer, softball, tennis, volleyball.

STUDENT SERVICES. Aptitude testing, career counseling, employment service for undergraduates, freshman orientation, health services, personal counseling, placement service for graduates, veterans counselor, services/facilities for handicapped.

ANNUAL EXPENSES. Tuition and fees (1992-93): $1,460, $2,680 additional for out-of-state students. **Room and board:** $3,046. **Books and supplies:** $250. **Other expenses:** $600.

FINANCIAL AID. 71% of freshmen, 65% of continuing students receive some form of aid. 77% of grants, 90% of loans, 48% of jobs based on need. Academic, music/drama, art, athletic, alumni affiliation, minority scholarships available. **Aid applications:** No closing date; priority given to applications received by April 15; applicants notified on a rolling basis; must reply within 2 weeks.

ADDRESS/TELEPHONE. James L. Grigsby, Director of Admissions, Eastern Kentucky University, Coates Box 2A, 203 Jones Building, Richmond, KY 40475-3101. (606) 622-2106.

Elizabethtown Community College
Elizabethtown, Kentucky CB code: 1211

2-year public community college, coed. Founded in 1964. **Accreditation:** Regional. **Undergraduate enrollment:** 1,718 men and women full time; 2,579 men and women part time. **Faculty:** 146 total (81 full time), 10 with doctorates or other terminal degrees. **Location:** Suburban campus in large town; 40 miles from Louisville. **Calendar:** Semester, limited summer session. Saturday and extensive evening/early morning classes. **Microcomputers:** 50 located in computer centers. **Special facilities:** Regional Home for the Arts center. **Additional facts:** Off-campus locations at Fort Knox, Bardstown, Leitchfield, and Hardinsburg.

DEGREES OFFERED. AA, AS, AAS. 261 associate degrees awarded in 1992.

UNDERGRADUATE MAJORS. Business and management, business and office, finance, information sciences and systems, liberal/general studies, nursing, real estate, secretarial and related programs.

ACADEMIC PROGRAMS. 2-year transfer program, honors program, internships, weekend college. **Remedial services:** Learning center, remedial instruction, special counselor, tutoring. **Placement/credit:** AP, CLEP General and Subject, institutional tests.

ACADEMIC REQUIREMENTS. Freshmen must earn minimum GPA of 2.0 to continue in good standing. **Graduation requirements:** 60 hours for associate. Most students required to take courses in English, history, humanities, mathematics, biological/physical sciences, social sciences.

FRESHMAN ADMISSIONS. Selection criteria: Open admissions. **Test requirements:** ACT for placement and counseling only. Enrolled freshmen must take ACT or ACT/Career Planning Profile by start of second semester.

1992 FRESHMAN CLASS PROFILE. 337 men, 614 women enrolled. **Characteristics:** 99% from in state, 100% commute. Average age is 24.

FALL-TERM APPLICATIONS. No fee. No closing date; priority given to applications received by August 1; applicants notified on a rolling basis beginning on or about April 1. Early admission available for specially qualified high school students on part-time basis.

STUDENT LIFE. Activities: Student government, student newspaper, choral groups, drama, Fellowship of Christian Athletes, Baptist Student Union, foreign language club, Newman Club, Black Student Interest Group.

ATHLETICS. Intramural: Basketball, soccer M, softball W, table tennis, tennis W, volleyball.

STUDENT SERVICES. Career counseling, employment service for undergraduates, freshman orientation, health services, personal counseling, placement service for graduates, veterans counselor, services/facilities for handicapped.

ANNUAL EXPENSES. Tuition and fees: $840, $1,680 additional for out-of-state students. **Books and supplies:** $450.

FINANCIAL AID. 60% of freshmen, 74% of continuing students receive some form of aid. 84% of grants, all loans, 70% of jobs based on need. Academic, minority scholarships available. **Aid applications:** No closing date; priority given to applications received by April 1; applicants notified on a rolling basis beginning on or about June 1; must reply within 2 weeks.

ADDRESS/TELEPHONE. Ronald B. Thomas, Dean of Student Affairs, Elizabethtown Community College, 600 College Street Road, Elizabethtown, KY 42701. (502) 769-1632. Fax: (502) 769-1618.

Franklin College
Paducah, Kentucky CB code: 2161

2-year proprietary business, junior college, coed. Founded in 1895. **Undergraduate enrollment:** 170 men and women. **Location:** Urban campus in large town; 145 miles northwest of Nashville, Tennessee, 160 miles southeast of St. Louis, Missouri. **Calendar:** Quarter.

FRESHMAN ADMISSIONS. Selection criteria: Interview required. Certain programs require score of 11 or better on entrance examination.

ANNUAL EXPENSES. Tuition and fees (1992-93): $4,200. **Books and supplies:** $400. **Other expenses:** $900.

ADDRESS/TELEPHONE. Carolyn West, Director of Education, Franklin College, 218 North Fifth Street, Paducah, KY 42001. (502) 443-8478. Fax: (502) 442-5329.

Georgetown College
Georgetown, Kentucky CB code: 1249

Admissions: 83% of applicants accepted
Based on:
- ••• School record
- •• Test scores
- • Activities, essay, interview, recommendations, special talents

Completion: 82% of freshmen end year in good standing
42% graduate, 44% of these enter graduate study

4-year private liberal arts college, coed, affiliated with Southern Baptist Convention. Founded in 1829. **Accreditation:** Regional. **Undergraduate enrollment:** 536 men, 620 women full time; 17 men, 39 women part time. **Graduate enrollment:** 1 woman full time; 39 men, 228 women part time. **Faculty:** 94 total (68 full time), 56 with doctorates or other terminal degrees. **Location:** Suburban campus in large town; 12 miles from Lexington, 70 miles from Cincinnati, Ohio. **Calendar:** Semester, limited summer session. **Microcomputers:** 46 located in libraries, classrooms, computer centers. **Special facilities:** Planetarium, art gallery, full Nautilus center, Foucault pendulum.

DEGREES OFFERED. BA, BS, MA. 189 bachelor's degrees awarded in 1992. 17% in business and management, 13% business/office and marketing/distribution, 6% communications, 7% computer sciences, 12% teacher education, 11% life sciences, 5% psychology, 11% social sciences. Graduate degrees offered in 2 major fields of study.

UNDERGRADUATE MAJORS. Accounting, American studies, art education, biology, business administration and management, business and management, business education, business systems analysis, chemistry, clinical laboratory science, clinical psychology, communications, computer and information sciences, computer programming, dramatic arts, early childhood education, elementary education, engineering, engineering science, English, English education, environmental science, European studies, finance, fine arts, foreign languages (multiple emphasis), foreign languages education, French, German, health, physical education and recreation, history, home economics, information sciences and systems, international business management, international studies, marketing and distribution, marketing management, mathematics, mathematics education, music, music education, nursing, philosophy, physical education, physics, political science and government, predentistry, preengineering, prelaw, premedicine, prepharmacy, preveterinary, psychology, religion, science education, secondary education, social science education, sociology, Spanish, speech, speech/communication/theater education.

ACADEMIC PROGRAMS. Accelerated program, double major, honors program, independent study, internships, student-designed major, study abroad, teacher preparation, visiting/exchange student program, cross-registration, 3-2 nursing program with University of Kentucky; liberal arts/career combination in engineering. **Remedial services:** Learning center, reduced course load, special counselor, tutoring. **ROTC:** Air Force, Army. **Placement/credit:** AP, CLEP Subject, institutional tests.

ACADEMIC REQUIREMENTS. Freshmen must earn minimum GPA of 1.7 to continue in good standing. 70% of freshmen return for sophomore year. Students must declare major by end of second year. **Graduation requirements:** 128 hours for bachelor's (33 in major). Most students required to take courses in arts/fine arts, English, foreign languages, history, humanities, mathematics, philosophy/religion, biological/physical sciences, social sciences. **Postgraduate studies:** 4% enter law school, 3% enter medical school, 7% enter MBA programs, 30% enter other graduate study.

FRESHMAN ADMISSIONS. Selection criteria: School achievement record, test scores, rank in top half of class considered. **High school preparation:** 20 units required. Required and recommended units include English 4, mathematics 2, social science 2 and science 2. Foreign language 2 recommended. **Test requirements:** SAT or ACT (ACT preferred); score report by July 31.

1992 FRESHMAN CLASS PROFILE. 382 men applied, 299 accepted, 153 enrolled; 438 women applied, 379 accepted, 173 enrolled. 58% had high school GPA of 3.0 or higher, 42% between 2.0 and 2.99. **Academic background:** Mid 50% of enrolled freshmen had ACT composite between 19-25. 99% submitted ACT scores. **Characteristics:** 73% from in state, 93% live in college housing, 3% have minority backgrounds, 1% are foreign students. Average age is 18.

FALL-TERM APPLICATIONS. $20 fee, may be waived for applicants with need. Closing date July 1; priority given to applications received by April 1; applicants notified on a rolling basis; must reply by May 1 or within 4 weeks if notified thereafter. Essay required. Interview recommended for academically weak, specially needy applicants. Audition recommended for music, communication arts applicants. Portfolio recommended for art applicants. CRDA. Early admission available.

STUDENT LIFE. Housing: Dormitories (men, women); apartment, fraternity, sorority housing available. Most students housed in minidorms of fewer than 80 students each. **Activities:** Student government, radio, student newspaper, yearbook, choral groups, concert band, drama, jazz band, music ensembles, musical theater, pep band, fraternities, sororities, Baptist Student Union, Fellowship of Christian Athletes.

ATHLETICS. NAIA. **Intercollegiate:** Baseball M, basketball, cross-country, football M, golf M, soccer M, softball W, tennis, volleyball W. **Intramural:** Basketball, bowling, racquetball, softball, table tennis, volleyball.

STUDENT SERVICES. Aptitude testing, career counseling, employment service for undergraduates, health services, personal counseling, placement service for graduates, services/facilities for handicapped.

ANNUAL EXPENSES. Tuition and fees: $7,390, $100 additional for out-of-state students. **Room and board:** $3,600. **Books and supplies:** $550. **Other expenses:** $550.

FINANCIAL AID. 85% of freshmen, 90% of continuing students receive some form of aid. 47% of grants, 95% of loans, 46% of jobs based on need. 227 enrolled freshmen were judged to have need, all were offered aid. Academic, music/drama, art, athletic, leadership, religious affiliation scholarships available. **Aid applications:** No closing date; priority given to applications received by April 1; applicants notified on a rolling basis beginning on or about April 1; must reply by May 1 or within 4 weeks if notified thereafter.

ADDRESS/TELEPHONE. Garvel R. Kindrick, Director of Admissions, Georgetown College, 400 East Avenue of Champions, Georgetown, KY 40324-1696. (502) 863-8009. (800) 788-9985.

Hazard Community College
Hazard, Kentucky — CB code: 0815

2-year public community college, coed. Founded in 1968. **Accreditation:** Regional. **Undergraduate enrollment:** 1,803 men and women. **Location:** Rural campus in small town; 100 miles from Lexington. **Calendar:** Semester.

FRESHMAN ADMISSIONS. Selection criteria: Open admissions. Selective admissions to nursing, radiology, and medical laboratory technology. Out-of-state applicants must rank in top half of high school class or have 3.0 GPA.

ANNUAL EXPENSES. Tuition and fees (projected): $840, $1,680 additional for out-of-state students. **Books and supplies:** $450. **Other expenses:** $848.

ADDRESS/TELEPHONE. Virgil Lykins, Admissions Counselor, Hazard Community College, One Community College Drive, Hazard, KY 41701. (606) 436-5721.

Henderson Community College
Henderson, Kentucky — CB code: 1307

2-year public community college, coed. Founded in 1960. **Accreditation:** Regional. **Undergraduate enrollment:** 1,500 men and women. **Faculty:** 83 total (42 full time), 7 with doctorates or other terminal degrees. **Location:** Rural campus in large town; 10 miles from Evansville, Indiana. **Calendar:** Semester, limited summer session. Extensive evening/early morning classes. **Microcomputers:** Located in computer centers. **Special facilities:** New 1,000-seat auditorium.

DEGREES OFFERED. AA, AS, AAS. 132 associate degrees awarded in 1992.

UNDERGRADUATE MAJORS. Business and management, business and office, business data processing and related programs, communications, data processing, electrical technology, liberal/general studies, medical laboratory technologies, nursing, recreation and community services technologies, secretarial and related programs, social work.

ACADEMIC PROGRAMS. 2-year transfer program, cooperative education, dual enrollment of high school students. **Remedial services:** Learning center, remedial instruction, special counselor, tutoring. **Placement/credit:** AP, CLEP Subject, institutional tests.

ACADEMIC REQUIREMENTS. To continue in good academic standing freshmen must earn grade-point average within 5 quality points of 2.0. Students must declare major on application. **Graduation requirements:** 60 hours for associate (32 in major). Most students required to take courses in computer science, English, biological/physical sciences, social sciences.

FRESHMAN ADMISSIONS. Selection criteria: Open admissions. Required units include physical science 1. **Test requirements:** ACT for placement and counseling only; score report by September 1.

1992 FRESHMAN CLASS PROFILE. 187 men, 439 women enrolled. **Characteristics:** 99% from in state, 100% commute, 5% have minority backgrounds, 1% are foreign students. Average age is 23.

FALL-TERM APPLICATIONS. No fee. No closing date; applicants notified on a rolling basis beginning on or about March 1. Interview required for nursing applicants.

STUDENT LIFE. Activities: Student government, magazine, student newspaper, Baptist Student Union.

ATHLETICS. Intercollegiate: Golf M. **Intramural:** Basketball, bowling, football M, golf, softball.

STUDENT SERVICES. Career counseling, freshman orientation, personal counseling, placement service for graduates, veterans counselor, services/facilities for handicapped.

ANNUAL EXPENSES. Tuition and fees (1992-93): $840, $1,680 additional for out-of-state students. **Books and supplies:** $475.

FINANCIAL AID. 55% of freshmen, 42% of continuing students receive some form of aid. 76% of grants, 89% of loans, all jobs based on need. Academic, athletic, state/district residency, minority scholarships available. **Aid applications:** No closing date; applicants notified on a rolling basis beginning on or about May 1; must reply immediately.

ADDRESS/TELEPHONE. Bob Park, Dean for Student Affairs, Henderson Community College, 2660 South Green Street, Henderson, KY 42420. (502) 827-1867.

Hopkinsville Community College
Hopkinsville, Kentucky — CB code: 1274

2-year public community college, coed. Founded in 1965. **Accreditation:** Regional. **Undergraduate enrollment:** 3,020 men and women. **Faculty:** 145 total (45 full time), 8 with doctorates or other terminal degrees. **Location:** Suburban campus in large town; 70 miles from Nashville, Tennessee. **Calendar:** Semester, limited summer session. **Microcomputers:** 82 located in libraries, classrooms, computer centers.

DEGREES OFFERED. AA, AS, AAS. 228 associate degrees awarded in 1992.

UNDERGRADUATE MAJORS. Business and management, business and office, finance, law enforcement and corrections technologies, liberal/general studies, management information systems, mental health/human services, nursing, secretarial and related programs.

ACADEMIC PROGRAMS. 2-year transfer program, dual enrollment of high school students, honors program. **Remedial services:** Learning center, remedial instruction, special counselor, tutoring. **Placement/credit:** AP, CLEP General and Subject, institutional tests.

ACADEMIC REQUIREMENTS. Freshmen must earn minimum GPA of 2.0 to continue in good standing. Students must declare major on application. **Graduation requirements:** 60 hours for associate. Most students required to take courses in English, history, humanities, mathematics, biological/physical sciences, social sciences.

FRESHMAN ADMISSIONS. Selection criteria: Open admissions. **Test requirements:** ACT for placement and counseling only; score report by August 1.

1992 FRESHMAN CLASS PROFILE. 683 men and women enrolled. **Characteristics:** 99% from in state, 100% commute, 5% have minority backgrounds, 5% join fraternities/sororities.

FALL-TERM APPLICATIONS. No fee. No closing date; applicants notified on a rolling basis. Early admission available.

STUDENT LIFE. Activities: Student government, fraternities, sororities.

ATHLETICS. Intramural: Basketball, table tennis, volleyball.

STUDENT SERVICES. Aptitude testing, career counseling, employment service for undergraduates, freshman orientation, personal counseling, placement service for graduates, veterans counselor, services/facilities for handicapped.

ANNUAL EXPENSES. Tuition and fees (projected): $840, $1,680 additional for out-of-state students. **Books and supplies:** $450. **Other expenses:** $2,808.

FINANCIAL AID. 97% of grants, 94% of loans, all jobs based on need. Academic, state/district residency, leadership, minority scholarships available. **Aid applications:** No closing date; priority given to applications received by April 1; applicants notified on a rolling basis beginning on or about July 1; must reply within 3 weeks.

ADDRESS/TELEPHONE. Ruth Ann Rettie, Registrar, Hopkinsville Community College, PO Box 2100, North Drive, Hopkinsville, KY 42241-2100. (502) 886-3921. Fax: (502) 886-0239.

Institute of Electronic Technology
Paducah, Kentucky — CB code: 0669

2-year proprietary technical college, coed. Founded in 1964. **Undergraduate enrollment:** 170 men, 5 women full time. **Faculty:** 6 total. **Location:** Suburban campus in large town; 150 miles from Nashville, Tennessee and St. Louis, Missouri. **Calendar:** Trimester. **Microcomputers:** 18 located in computer centers.

DEGREES OFFERED. AAS. 45 associate degrees awarded in 1992. 100% in engineering technologies.

UNDERGRADUATE MAJORS. Electrical and electronics equipment repair, electronic technology, engineering and engineering-related technologies.

ACADEMIC PROGRAMS. Remedial services: Special counselor, tutoring.

ACADEMIC REQUIREMENTS. Freshmen must earn minimum GPA of 2.0 to continue in good standing. 92% of freshmen return for sophomore year. Students must declare major on application. **Graduation requirements:** 72 hours for associate (72 in major). Most students required to take courses in mathematics.

FRESHMAN ADMISSIONS. Selection criteria: School achievement record very important. Interview, special talents important.

1992 FRESHMAN CLASS PROFILE. 89 men applied, 89 accepted, 84 enrolled; 9 women applied, 9 accepted, 5 enrolled. **Characteristics:** 70% from in state, 100% commute, 3% have minority backgrounds. Average age is 19.

FALL-TERM APPLICATIONS. $50 fee, may be waived for applicants with need. No closing date; applicants notified on a rolling basis beginning on or about January 1. Interview required. Deferred admission available.

STUDENT LIFE. Activities: Film.

STUDENT SERVICES. Career counseling, employment service for undergraduates, personal counseling, placement service for graduates, services/facilities for handicapped.

ANNUAL EXPENSES. Tuition and fees: $4,975. **Books and supplies:** $100. **Other expenses:** $1,000.

FINANCIAL AID. 80% of freshmen, 85% of continuing students receive some form of aid. All grants, 76% of loans based on need. **Aid applications:** No closing date; applicants notified on a rolling basis beginning on or about June 15; must reply within 3 weeks.

ADDRESS/TELEPHONE. Arnold Harris, Director of Admission, Institute of Electronic Technology, 509 South 30th Street, Paducah, KY 42001. (502) 444-9676. (800) 995-4438. Fax: (502) 441-7201.

Jefferson Community College
Louisville, Kentucky — CB code: 1328

2-year public community college, coed. Founded in 1968. **Accreditation:** Regional. **Undergraduate enrollment:** 1,502 men, 2,058 women full time; 2,808 men, 5,493 women part time. **Faculty:** 410 total (243 full time), 44 with doctorates or other terminal degrees. **Location:** Urban campus in large city. **Calendar:** Semester, extensive summer session. Saturday and extensive evening/early morning classes. **Microcomputers:** 100 located in libraries, classrooms, computer centers. **Additional facts:** 2 campuses: downtown Louisville and southwestern Jefferson County. Courses offered off-campus and in Carrolton, Kentucky.

DEGREES OFFERED. AA, AS, AAS. 519 associate degrees awarded in 1992. 20% in business and management, 20% business/office and marketing/distribution, 13% computer sciences, 9% teacher education, 10% health sciences, 17% allied health, 5% multi/interdisciplinary studies.

UNDERGRADUATE MAJORS. Accounting, advertising, automotive technology, business and management, business data processing and related programs, business data programming, chemical manufacturing technology, commercial art, data processing, early childhood education, electronic technology, engineering and engineering-related technologies, finance, fire control and safety technology, food management, food production/management/services, graphic arts technology, industrial equipment maintenance and repair, industrial technology, law enforcement and corrections technologies, liberal/general studies, mental health/human services, nursing, office supervision and management, photographic technology, physical therapy assistant, real estate, respiratory therapy, respiratory therapy technology, secretarial and related programs.

ACADEMIC PROGRAMS. 2-year transfer program, cooperative education, dual enrollment of high school students, education specialist degree, independent study, internships, weekend college, cross-registration, interdisciplinary studies curriculum. **Remedial services:** Learning center, reduced course load, remedial instruction, special counselor, tutoring. **Placement/credit:** CLEP General and Subject, institutional tests.

ACADEMIC REQUIREMENTS. Freshmen must earn minimum GPA of 2.0 to continue in good standing. Students must declare major on enrollment. **Graduation requirements:** 60 hours for associate. Most students required to take courses in English, history, humanities, mathematics, biological/physical sciences, social sciences.

FRESHMAN ADMISSIONS. Selection criteria: Open admissions. Selective admission to allied health programs. **Test requirements:** ACT for counseling. Entering freshmen required to take ACT before start of second semester.

1992 FRESHMAN CLASS PROFILE. 852 men, 1,236 women enrolled. **Academic background:** Mid 50% of enrolled freshmen had ACT composite between 15-19. 35% submitted ACT scores. **Characteristics:** 97% from in state, 100% commute, 15% have minority backgrounds, 1% are foreign students.

FALL-TERM APPLICATIONS. No fee. No closing date; applicants notified on a rolling basis. Interview required for nursing, physical therapy, respiratory therapy applicants. Early admission available.

STUDENT LIFE. Activities: Student government, student newspaper, choral groups, drama, music ensembles, Black Student Union, Baptist Student Union, Student Senate, Earth-Ecology Club.

STUDENT SERVICES. Aptitude testing, career counseling, employment service for undergraduates, freshman orientation, health services, personal counseling, placement service for graduates, special adviser for adult students, veterans counselor, services/facilities for handicapped.

ANNUAL EXPENSES. Tuition and fees (projected): $840, $1,680 additional for out-of-state students. **Books and supplies:** $450. **Other expenses:** $848.

FINANCIAL AID. 35% of freshmen, 35% of continuing students receive some form of aid. 97% of grants, 92% of loans, 20% of jobs based on need. Academic, minority scholarships available. **Aid applications:** No closing date; priority given to applications received by April 1; applicants notified on a rolling basis beginning on or about June 15; must reply within 3 weeks.

ADDRESS/TELEPHONE. Ron Walford, Admissions Officer/Registrar, Jefferson Community College, 109 East Broadway, Louisville, KY 40202. (502) 584-0181.

Kentucky Christian College
Grayson, Kentucky — CB code: 1377

4-year private Bible college, coed, affiliated with Christian Church. Founded in 1919. **Accreditation:** Regional. **Undergraduate enrollment:** 234 men, 231 women full time; 8 men, 10 women part time. **Location:** Rural campus in small town; 25 miles from Ashland, 100 miles east of Lexington. **Calendar:** Semester.

FRESHMAN ADMISSIONS. Selection criteria: High school grades, rank, ACT or SAT, and personal references given equal weight.

ANNUAL EXPENSES. Tuition and fees: $4,288. **Room and board:** $3,420. **Books and supplies:** $600. **Other expenses:** $1,413.

ADDRESS/TELEPHONE. Sandra Deakins, Director of Admissions, Kentucky Christian College, 617 North Carol Malone Boulevard, Grayson, KY 41143-1199. (606) 474-3266. (800) 522-3181. Fax: (606) 474-3155.

Kentucky College of Business
Lexington, Kentucky — CB code: 0987

2-year proprietary business, junior college, coed. Founded in 1941. **Undergraduate enrollment:** 771 men and women. **Location:** Urban campus in small city. **Calendar:** Quarter.

FRESHMAN ADMISSIONS. Selection criteria: Interview, school achievement record important. Test scores, recommendations considered.

ANNUAL EXPENSES. Tuition and fees (1992-93): $4,748. **Books and supplies:** $475.

ADDRESS/TELEPHONE. Larry Steele, Vice President of Admissions, Kentucky College of Business, 628 East Main Street, Lexington, KY 40508. (606) 253-0621. Fax: (606) 233-3054.

Kentucky State University
Frankfort, Kentucky — CB code: 1368

4-year public university, coed. Founded in 1886. **Accreditation:** Regional. **Undergraduate enrollment:** 1,630 men and women full time; 835 men and women part time. **Graduate enrollment:** 22 men and women full time; 58 men and women part time. **Faculty:** 130 total (124 full time), 77 with doctorates or other terminal degrees. **Location:** Urban campus in large town; 50 miles from Louisville, 25 miles west of Lexington. **Calendar:** Semester, limited summer session. **Microcomputers:** Located in libraries, classrooms, computer centers. **Special facilities:** Art gallery.

DEGREES OFFERED. AA, AS, BA, BS, M. 72 associate degrees awarded in 1992. 65% in health sciences, 21% multi/interdisciplinary studies, 5% parks/recreation, protective services, public affairs. 146 bachelor's degrees awarded. 20% in business and management, 10% computer sciences, 10% teacher education, 7% home economics, 5% letters/literature, 7% life sciences, 7% mathematics, 10% parks/recreation, protective services, public affairs, 5% psychology, 6% social sciences. Graduate degrees offered in 1 major field of study.

UNDERGRADUATE MAJORS. Associate: Child development/care/guidance, computer and information sciences, criminal justice studies, drafting, drafting and design technology, electronic technology, food management, liberal/general studies, manufacturing technology, nursing, office supervision and management. **Bachelor's:** Accounting, applied mathematics, art education, biology, business administration and management, business economics, business education, chemistry, child development/care/guidance, clothing and textiles management/production/services, computer and information sciences, criminal justice studies, early childhood education, elementary education, English, history, liberal/general studies, mathematics, medical laboratory technologies, music education, music performance, physical education, political science and government, psychology, public administration, social studies education, social work, sociology, studio art, textiles and clothing.

ACADEMIC PROGRAMS. 2-year transfer program, cooperative education, double major, dual enrollment of high school students, internships, student-designed major, study abroad, teacher preparation, visiting/exchange student program, weekend college, Whitney M. Young, Jr. College of Leadership Studies, Liberal Studies Great Books Program; liberal arts/career combination in engineering, health sciences. **Remedial services:** Learning center, preadmission summer program, reduced course load, remedial instruction, special counselor, tutoring. **ROTC:** Air Force, Army. **Placement/credit:** AP, CLEP Subject, institutional tests; 16 credit hours maximum for associate degree; 32 credit hours maximum for bachelor's degree.

ACADEMIC REQUIREMENTS. Freshmen must earn minimum GPA of 1.6 by end of first semester, 1.8 by end of second semester, and 2.0 thereafter. 56% of freshmen return for sophomore year. Students must declare major by end of second year. **Graduation requirements:** 64 hours for associate, 128 hours for bachelor's (30 in major). Most students required to take courses in arts/fine arts, English, foreign languages, history, humanities, mathematics, philosophy/religion, biological/physical sciences, social sciences. **Postgraduate studies:** 1% enter law school, 1% enter medical school, 8% enter other graduate study.

FRESHMAN ADMISSIONS. Selection criteria: Unconditional admission for graduates of accredited high schools meeting Pre-College Curriculum (PCC) requirements established by Kentucky Council on Higher Education and having admission index of 430. Nontraditional applicants (25 or older) may substitute results of Career Planning and Placement test (CPP-II) for ACT or SAT results if pursuing associate degree. **High school preparation:** 21 units required. Required and recommended units include English 4, mathematics 3, social science 2 and science 2. Foreign language 2 recommended. **Test requirements:** ACT; score report by July 15.

1992 FRESHMAN CLASS PROFILE. 421 men and women enrolled. **Academic background:** Mid 50% of enrolled freshmen had SAT-V between 290-420, SAT-M between 350-480; ACT composite between 12-20. 93% submitted SAT scores. **Characteristics:** 69% from in state, 70% live in college housing, 51% have minority backgrounds. Average age is 20.

FALL-TERM APPLICATIONS. $5 fee. No closing date; applicants notified on a rolling basis. Essay required for Whitney M. Young, Jr. College of Leadership Studies applicants. Interview recommended for nursing, Whitney M. Young, Jr. College of Leadership Studies applicants. Audition recommended for music applicants. Portfolio recommended for art applicants. Early admission available.

STUDENT LIFE. Housing: Dormitories (men, women). **Activities:** Student government, student newspaper, yearbook, literary journal, choral groups, concert band, dance, drama, jazz band, marching band, music ensembles, musical theater, opera, pep band, fraternities, sororities, Alpha Phi Omega, Gamma Sigma Sigma, Wesley Club, Baptist Student Union, Circle-K, International Student Association, Baha'i Club, NAACP.

ATHLETICS. NCAA. **Intercollegiate:** Baseball M, basketball, cross-country, football M, golf M, softball W, tennis, track and field, volleyball W. **Intramural:** Archery, badminton, basketball, bowling, football M, soccer, softball W, swimming, table tennis, tennis, track and field, volleyball.

STUDENT SERVICES. Aptitude testing, career counseling, employment service for undergraduates, freshman orientation, health services, on-campus day care, personal counseling, placement service for graduates, special adviser for adult students, veterans counselor, marriage and family counseling, services/facilities for handicapped.

ANNUAL EXPENSES. Tuition and fees (projected): $1,600, $3,000 additional for out-of-state students. **Room and board:** $2,682. **Books and supplies:** $510. **Other expenses:** $800.

FINANCIAL AID. 82% of freshmen, 80% of continuing students receive some form of aid. 65% of grants, 75% of loans, 73% of jobs based on need. Academic, music/drama, athletic, leadership scholarships available. **Aid applications:** Closing date April 15; priority given to applications received by March 15; applicants notified on a rolling basis beginning on or about March 1; must reply within 2 weeks.

ADDRESS/TELEPHONE. Myra Jackson, Associate Director of Admissions, Kentucky State University, East Main Street, Frankfort, KY 40601. (502) 227-6813. (800) 325-1716. Fax: (502) 227-6412.

Kentucky Wesleyan College

Owensboro, Kentucky — CB code: 1369

Admissions:	73% of applicants accepted
Based on:	••• Essay, school record, test scores
	• Activities, interview, recommendations, special talents
Completion:	83% of freshmen end year in good standing
	52% graduate, 27% of these enter graduate study

4-year private liberal arts college, coed, affiliated with United Methodist Church. Founded in 1858. **Accreditation:** Regional. **Undergraduate enrollment:** 316 men, 333 women full time; 29 men, 89 women part time. **Faculty:** 77 total (52 full time), 35 with doctorates or other terminal degrees. **Location:** Suburban campus in small city; 115 miles from Louisville, and 125 miles from Nashville, Tennessee. **Calendar:** Semester, limited summer session. Extensive evening/early morning classes. **Microcomputers:** 80 located in dormitories, libraries, classrooms, computer centers, campus-wide network.

DEGREES OFFERED. AA, AS, AAS, BA, BS. 42 associate degrees awarded in 1992. 97% in health sciences. 116 bachelor's degrees awarded. 21% in business and management, 10% communications, 12% teacher education, 5% letters/literature, 12% life sciences, 6% mathematics, 6% psychology, 19% social sciences.

UNDERGRADUATE MAJORS. Associate: Business administration and management, law enforcement and corrections technologies, nursing. **Bachelor's:** Accounting, advertising, art education, biology, business administration and management, business and management, chemistry, communications, computer and information sciences, creative writing, criminal justice studies, criminology, dramatic arts, early childhood education, education, elementary education, English, English literature, fine arts, foreign languages (multiple emphasis), history, human resources development, journalism, junior high education, mathematics, medical laboratory technologies, music, music education, nursing, philosophy, physical education, physics, political science and government, predentistry, prelaw, premedicine, prepharmacy, preveterinary, psychology, public relations, radio/television broadcasting, religion, religious music, secondary education, sociology, special education, telecommunications, theological studies.

ACADEMIC PROGRAMS. Double major, dual enrollment of high school students, independent study, internships, study abroad, teacher preparation, cross-registration; liberal arts/career combination in engineering. **Remedial services:** Learning center, reduced course load, special counselor, tutoring. **Placement/credit:** AP, CLEP General and Subject, IB, institutional tests; 42 credit hours maximum for bachelor's degree.

ACADEMIC REQUIREMENTS. Freshmen must earn minimum GPA of 1.5 to continue in good standing. 60% of freshmen return for sophomore year. Students must declare major by end of second year. **Graduation requirements:** 64 hours for associate (28 in major), 128 hours for bachelor's (40 in major). Most students required to take courses in arts/fine arts, computer science, English, foreign languages, history, humanities, mathematics, philosophy/religion, biological/physical sciences, social sciences. **Postgraduate studies:** 50% from 2-year programs enter 4-year programs. 4% enter law school, 8% enter medical school, 6% enter MBA programs, 9% enter other graduate study.

FRESHMAN ADMISSIONS. Selection criteria: Test scores, GPA, class rank, and school activities considered. **High school preparation:** 12 units required; 14 recommended. Required and recommended units include English 4, mathematics 3-3, social science 2-3 and science 3. Biological science 1 and physical science 2 recommended. **Test requirements:** SAT or ACT; score report by August 25.

1992 FRESHMAN CLASS PROFILE. 511 men applied, 342 accepted, 78 enrolled; 193 women applied, 169 accepted, 74 enrolled. 69% had high school GPA of 3.0 or higher, 27% between 2.0 and 2.99. 35% were in top tenth and 62% were in top quarter of graduating class. **Academic background:** Mid 50% of enrolled freshmen had ACT composite between 19-26. 97% submitted ACT scores. **Characteristics:** 65% from in state, 78% live in college housing, 6% have minority backgrounds, 1% are foreign students, 30% join fraternities/sororities. Average age is 18.

FALL-TERM APPLICATIONS. $15 fee, may be waived for applicants with need. Closing date August 20; applicants notified on a rolling basis; must reply by May 1 or within 3 weeks if notified thereafter. Portfolio required for art applicants. Interview recommended. Audition recommended for music applicants. Essay recommended. CRDA. Deferred admission available.

STUDENT LIFE. Housing: Dormitories (men, women, coed); apartment housing available. **Activities:** Student government, film, magazine, radio, student newspaper, yearbook, choral groups, drama, jazz band, music ensembles, musical theater, opera, pep band, fraternities, sororities, Baptist Student Union, United Methodist Student Fellowship, Fellowship of Christian Athletes, Newman Club, Black Student Union.

ATHLETICS. NCAA. **Intercollegiate:** Baseball M, basketball, cross-country M, football M, golf, soccer M, softball W, tennis, volleyball W. **Intramural:** Badminton, basketball, cross-country, golf, handball, racquetball, soccer, softball, swimming, table tennis, tennis, volleyball.

STUDENT SERVICES. Aptitude testing, employment service for undergraduates, health services, services/facilities for handicapped.

ANNUAL EXPENSES. Tuition and fees (1992-93): $7,170. **Books and supplies:** $400. **Other expenses:** $700.

FINANCIAL AID. 85% of freshmen, 84% of continuing students receive some form of aid. 44% of grants, 99% of loans, 68% of jobs based on need. 180 enrolled freshmen were judged to have need, all were offered aid. Academic, music/drama, art, athletic, leadership, minority scholarships available. **Aid applications:** Closing date April 1; applicants notified on or about April 15; must reply within 3 weeks. **Additional information:** On-campus scholarship competitions (held in fall and spring) allow students to compete for scholarships that range from $1000 to the full cost of tuition.

ADDRESS/TELEPHONE. Richard G. Ernst, Director of Enrollment Services, Kentucky Wesleyan College, 3000 Frederica Street, Owensboro, KY 42302-1039. (502) 926-3111. (800) 999-0592. Fax: (502) 926-3196.

Lees College
Jackson, Kentucky CB code: 1402

Admissions: 75% of applicants accepted
Based on: ••• School record, test scores
•• Interview
• Recommendations
Completion: 80% of freshmen end year in good standing
80% enter 4-year programs

2-year private nursing, liberal arts college, coed, affiliated with Presbyterian Church (USA). Founded in 1883. **Accreditation:** Regional. **Undergraduate enrollment:** 130 men, 291 women full time. **Faculty:** 25 total (18 full time), 4 with doctorates or other terminal degrees. **Location:** Rural campus in small town; 80 miles from Lexington. **Calendar:** Semester, extensive summer session. **Microcomputers:** Located in libraries, computer centers. **Additional facts:** Strong tradition of service to Appalachian section of Kentucky.

DEGREES OFFERED. AA, AS. 4 associate degrees awarded in 1992.

UNDERGRADUATE MAJORS. Allied health, business administration and management, business and office, business data processing and related programs, computer and information sciences, education, history, legal secretary, liberal/general studies, medical secretary, nursing, philosophy, practical nursing, predentistry, prelaw, premedicine, prepharmacy, preveterinary, psychology, religion, secretarial and related programs, sociology.

ACADEMIC PROGRAMS. 2-year transfer program, cooperative education, dual enrollment of high school students, honors program, independent study, teacher preparation, telecourses, Washington semester. **Remedial services:** Learning center, reduced course load, remedial instruction, special counselor, tutoring. **ROTC:** Army. **Placement/credit:** AP, institutional tests; 12 credit hours maximum for associate degree.

ACADEMIC REQUIREMENTS. Freshmen must earn minimum GPA of 2.0 to continue in good standing. 50% of freshmen return for sophomore year. Students must declare major by end of first year. **Graduation requirements:** 66 hours for associate (18 in major). Most students required to take courses in arts/fine arts, English, history, humanities, mathematics, philosophy/religion, biological/physical sciences, social sciences.

FRESHMAN ADMISSIONS. Selection criteria: ACT and high school GPA of 2.0 required. Interview required for those with high school GPA below 2.0 or ACT scores below 14. Those with GPA below 2.0 also need ACT score of 14. **Test requirements:** ACT; score report by August 21.

1992 FRESHMAN CLASS PROFILE. Characteristics: 85% from in state, 50% commute, 5% have minority backgrounds. Average age is 19.

FALL-TERM APPLICATIONS. No fee. No closing date; applicants notified on a rolling basis. Interview required for academically weak applicants. Deferred admission available.

STUDENT LIFE. Housing: Dormitories (men, women). **Activities:** Student government, radio, student newspaper, television, yearbook, choral groups, drama, music ensembles, Appalachian Leadership in Community Outreach (social service in remote Appalachian communities). **Additional information:** Religious observance required.

ATHLETICS. NJCAA, NSCAA. **Intercollegiate:** Baseball M, basketball, cross-country M, softball W, tennis M, volleyball W. **Intramural:** Basketball, handball, softball, table tennis, tennis, volleyball.

STUDENT SERVICES. Career counseling, freshman orientation, personal counseling.

ANNUAL EXPENSES. Tuition and fees: $3,900. **Room and board:** $2,700. **Books and supplies:** $400. **Other expenses:** $650.

FINANCIAL AID. 90% of freshmen, 90% of continuing students receive some form of aid. 88% of grants, all loans, 92% of jobs based on need. 290 enrolled freshmen were judged to have need, all were offered aid. Academic, athletic, leadership scholarships available. **Aid applications:** No closing date; priority given to applications received by April 1; applicants notified on a rolling basis beginning on or about April 1; must reply immediately.

ADDRESS/TELEPHONE. Jerry McIntosh, Director of Admissions, Lees College, 601 Jefferson Avenue, Jackson, KY 41339. (606) 666-7521 ext. 30. Fax: (606) 666-8910.

Lexington Community College
Lexington, Kentucky CB code: 0645

2-year public community, technical college, coed. Founded in 1965. **Accreditation:** Regional. **Undergraduate enrollment:** 1,169 men, 1,389 women full time; 783 men, 1,522 women part time. **Faculty:** 302 total (132 full time), 14 with doctorates or other terminal degrees. **Location:** Suburban campus in small city; 75 miles from Cincinnati, Ohio. **Calendar:** Semester, limited summer session. **Microcomputers:** Located in libraries, computer centers. **Additional facts:** Located on University of Kentucky's main campus with social and cultural activity privileges.

DEGREES OFFERED. AA, AS, AAS. 377 associate degrees awarded in 1992. 7% in architecture and environmental design, 13% business and management, 6% computer sciences, 6% engineering technologies, 42% allied health, 22% multi/interdisciplinary studies.

UNDERGRADUATE MAJORS. Accounting, architectural technologies, architecture, business and management, data processing, dental hygiene, dental laboratory technology, electrical technology, electronic technology, engineering and engineering-related technologies, liberal/general studies, mechanical engineering technology, nuclear medical technology, nursing, radiograph medical technology, real estate, respiratory therapy technology, secretarial and related programs.

ACADEMIC PROGRAMS. 2-year transfer program, cooperative education, independent study, internships, telecourses, cross-registration. **Remedial services:** Remedial instruction, special counselor, tutoring. **ROTC:** Air Force, Army. **Placement/credit:** AP, CLEP General and Subject, institutional tests.

ACADEMIC REQUIREMENTS. Freshmen must earn minimum GPA of 2.0 to continue in good standing. 43% of freshmen return for sophomore year. Students must declare major on application. **Graduation requirements:** 66 hours for associate (21 in major). Most students required to take courses in English, history, humanities, philosophy/religion, biological/physical sciences, social sciences.

FRESHMAN ADMISSIONS. Selection criteria: Open admissions. Selective admissions to associate health technology programs. Recommended units include biological science 2, English 4, mathematics 3, social science 2 and science 2. Students are strongly encouraged to follow Kentucky's pre-college curriculum. **Test requirements:** ACT for placement and counseling only; score report by August 27. ACT required for admission to some health programs. Dental Laboratory Aptitude Test required for dental laboratory technology applicants for admission.

1992 FRESHMAN CLASS PROFILE. 405 men, 537 women enrolled. **Academic background:** Mid 50% of enrolled freshmen had ACT composite between 16-20. 90% submitted ACT scores. **Characteristics:** 97% from in state, 85% commute, 6% have minority backgrounds. Average age is 22.

FALL-TERM APPLICATIONS. No fee. Closing date August 12; applicants notified on a rolling basis.

STUDENT LIFE. Housing: Dormitories (men, women, coed); apartment housing available. Students apply for and are assigned housing at University of Kentucky. Applications submitted to Office of Student Housing, University of Kentucky. **Activities:** Student government, radio, student newspaper, yearbook, choral groups, concert band, dance, drama, marching band, music ensembles, pep band, fraternities, Handicapped Student Organization.

ATHLETICS. Intramural: Badminton, basketball, fencing, field hockey, golf, lacrosse, racquetball, rugby, skiing, soccer, softball, swimming, table tennis, tennis, track and field, volleyball, wrestling.

STUDENT SERVICES. Aptitude testing, career counseling, employment service for undergraduates, freshman orientation, health services, personal counseling, placement service for graduates, veterans counselor, services for those with emotional disabilities, services/facilities for handicapped.

ANNUAL EXPENSES. Tuition and fees (projected): $1,938, $3,240 additional for out-of-state students. **Room and board:** $3,534. **Books and supplies:** $450.

FINANCIAL AID. 5% of freshmen, 15% of continuing students receive some form of aid. 94% of grants, 91% of loans, all jobs based on need. Academic, state/district residency, minority scholarships available. **Aid applications:** No closing date; priority given to applications received by April 1; applicants notified on a rolling basis beginning on or about June 1; must reply within 3 weeks.

ADDRESS/TELEPHONE. Toni Bishop, Admissions Officer, Lexington Community College, 206 Oswald Building, Cooper Drive, Lexington, KY 40506-0235. (606) 257-4872.

Lindsey Wilson College
Columbia, Kentucky CB code: 1409

4-year private liberal arts college, coed, affiliated with United Methodist Church. Founded in 1903. **Accreditation:** Regional. **Undergraduate enrollment:** 455 men, 462 women full time; 58 men, 116 women part time. **Faculty:** 47 total, 18 with doctorates or other terminal degrees. **Location:** Rural campus in small town; 100 miles from Louisville. **Calendar:** Semester, extensive summer session. **Microcomputers:** 65 located in libraries, classrooms, computer centers. **Special facilities:** Art gallery.

DEGREES OFFERED. AA, BA. 87 associate degrees awarded in 1992. 102 bachelor's degrees awarded. 26% in business and management, 45% teacher education, 29% multi/interdisciplinary studies.

UNDERGRADUATE MAJORS. Associate: Agribusiness, biology, business administration and management, business and management, business and office, chemistry, computer and information sciences, English, liberal/general studies, mathematics, prelaw, premedicine, secretarial and related programs, social sciences, studio art. **Bachelor's:** Accounting, biology, business administration and management, elementary education, English, history, humanities and social sciences, junior high education, liberal/general studies, social sciences.

ACADEMIC PROGRAMS. 2-year transfer program, dual enrollment of high school students, independent study, internships, teacher preparation, on-campus and extension evening program for associate degree in business management and computer science. **Remedial services:** Learning center, reduced course load, remedial instruction, special counselor, tutoring. **Placement/credit:** AP, CLEP General and Subject; 16 credit hours maximum for associate degree; 32 credit hours maximum for bachelor's degree.

ACADEMIC REQUIREMENTS. Freshmen must earn minimum GPA of 1.7 to continue in good standing. 60% of freshmen return for sophomore year. Students must declare major by end of first year. **Graduation requirements:** 64 hours for associate (15 in major), 128 hours for bachelor's (60 in major). Most students required to take courses in arts/fine arts, English, history, humanities, mathematics, philosophy/religion, biological/physical sciences, social sciences. **Postgraduate studies:** 75% from 2-year programs enter 4-year programs.

FRESHMAN ADMISSIONS. Selection criteria: Open admissions. School achievement record and test scores considered for placement. ASSET test used for placement for those with low SAT/ACT scores. **Test requirements:** SAT or ACT (ACT preferred) for placement and counseling only; score report by August 15.

1992 FRESHMAN CLASS PROFILE. 306 men and women enrolled. 30% had high school GPA of 3.0 or higher, 40% between 2.0 and 2.99. **Academic background:** Mid 50% of enrolled freshmen had ACT composite between 10-28. 100% submitted ACT scores. **Characteristics:** 90% from in state, 55% live in college housing, 6% have minority backgrounds, 1% are foreign students. Average age is 18.

FALL-TERM APPLICATIONS. No fee. No closing date; priority given to applications received by June 1; applicants notified on a rolling basis beginning on or about January 1; must reply by registration. Interview recommended. Early admission available.

STUDENT LIFE. Housing: Dormitories (men, women); apartment housing available. All students not living with family must live in campus housing. **Activities:** Student government, yearbook, choral groups, drama, music ensembles, musical theater, Christian students organizations, Young Republicans, Young Democrats, Student Ambassadors.

ATHLETICS. NAIA. **Intercollegiate:** Baseball M, basketball, cross-country M, golf M, soccer, softball W. **Intramural:** Basketball, softball, table tennis, tennis, volleyball.

STUDENT SERVICES. Aptitude testing, career counseling, employment service for undergraduates, freshman orientation, health services, personal counseling, placement service for graduates, services/facilities for handicapped.

ANNUAL EXPENSES. Tuition and fees (1992-93): $5,552. **Room and board:** $3,250. **Books and supplies:** $450. **Other expenses:** $960.

FINANCIAL AID. 96% of freshmen, 96% of continuing students receive some form of aid. All grants, 96% of loans, 86% of jobs based on need. Academic, music/drama, art, athletic, leadership, religious affiliation scholarships available. **Aid applications:** No closing date; priority given to applications received by April 15; applicants notified on a rolling basis beginning on or about May 1; must reply within 2 weeks.

ADDRESS/TELEPHONE. Kevin Thompson, Director of Admissions, Lindsey Wilson College, 210 Lindsey Wilson Street, Columbia, KY 42728. (502) 384-2126 ext. 8100. (800) 264-0138. Fax: (502) 384-8200.

Louisville Technical Institute
Louisville, Kentucky CB code: 1501

2-year proprietary technical college, coed. Founded in 1961. **Undergraduate enrollment:** 467 men and women. **Faculty:** 48 total (12 full time), 2 with doctorates or other terminal degrees. **Location:** Suburban campus in large city; 7 miles from downtown. **Calendar:** Quarter. Extensive evening/early morning classes.

DEGREES OFFERED. AAS. 200 associate degrees awarded in 1992. 5% in architecture and environmental design, 20% engineering technologies, 75% trade and industry.

UNDERGRADUATE MAJORS. Architectural technologies, computer engineering, computer servicing technology, drafting, drafting and design technology, electrical and electronics equipment repair, electrical/electronics/communications engineering, electronic technology, engineering and engineering-related technologies, industrial equipment maintenance and repair, interior design, mechanical design technology, robotics.

ACADEMIC PROGRAMS. Accelerated program, cooperative education, internships. **Remedial services:** Learning center, tutoring. **Placement/credit:** Institutional tests; 16 credit hours maximum for associate degree.

ACADEMIC REQUIREMENTS. Freshmen must earn minimum GPA of 1.8 to continue in good standing. 75% of freshmen return for sophomore year. Students must declare major on application. **Graduation requirements:** 103 hours for associate (103 in major). Most students required to take courses in computer science, English, mathematics.

FRESHMAN ADMISSIONS. Selection criteria: Test scores most important. School achievement record also important. **Test requirements:** Comparative Guidance and Placement Program required. Scores on Differential Aptitude Tests (numerical and verbal) and Wonderlic required for admissions.

1992 FRESHMAN CLASS PROFILE. 244 men and women enrolled. 28% had high school GPA of 3.0 or higher, 36% between 2.0 and 2.99. **Characteristics:** 90% from in state, 95% commute. Average age is 20.

FALL-TERM APPLICATIONS. $100 fee. Closing date October 1; priority given to applications received by August 1; applicants notified on a rolling basis; must reply by registration. Interview required.

STUDENT LIFE. Housing: Apartment housing available. **Activities:** Student government, student newspaper.

ATHLETICS. Intramural: Basketball M, bowling, softball M.

STUDENT SERVICES. Placement service for graduates, services/facilities for handicapped.

ANNUAL EXPENSES. Tuition and fees (1992-93): $6,360. **Room and board:** $2,520 room only. **Books and supplies:** $500. **Other expenses:** $1,830.

FINANCIAL AID. 82% of freshmen, 83% of continuing students receive some form of aid. 98% of grants, 64% of loans, all jobs based on need. Academic scholarships available. **Aid applications:** No closing date; applicants notified on a rolling basis; must reply within 2 weeks.

ADDRESS/TELEPHONE. G. Sam Nunley, Director of Admissions, Louisville Technical Institute, 3901 Atkinson Drive, Louisville, KY 40218-4524. (502) 456-6509. (800) 844-6528. Fax: (502) 456-2341.

Madisonville Community College
Madisonville, Kentucky CB code: 1606

2-year public community college, coed. Founded in 1968. **Accreditation:** Regional. **Undergraduate enrollment:** 2,403 men and women. **Faculty:** 155 total (63 full time), 8 with doctorates or other terminal degrees. **Location:** Rural campus in large town; 50 miles from Evansville, Indiana. **Calendar:** Semester, limited summer session. Saturday and extensive evening/early morning classes. **Microcomputers:** 35 located in classrooms. **Special facilities:** Fine arts center.

DEGREES OFFERED. AA, AS, AAS. 179 associate degrees awarded in 1992. 14% in business and management, 6% business/office and marketing/distribution, 44% health sciences, 6% allied health, 28% multi/interdisciplinary studies.

UNDERGRADUATE MAJORS. Accounting, biomedical equipment technology, business and management, business and office, business data processing and related programs, clinical laboratory science, education, electrical technology, finance, information sciences and systems, laser electro-optic technology, liberal/general studies, mechanical design technology, nursing, radiograph medical technology, real estate, respiratory therapy technology, retailing, secretarial and related programs.

ACADEMIC PROGRAMS. 2-year transfer program, cooperative education, honors program, independent study, internships, weekend college. **Remedial services:** Learning center, remedial instruction, special counselor, tutoring. **Placement/credit:** AP, CLEP General and Subject.

ACADEMIC REQUIREMENTS. Freshmen must earn minimum GPA of 2.0 to continue in good standing. **Graduation requirements:** 60 hours for associate. Most students required to take courses in English, history, humanities, mathematics, biological/physical sciences, social sciences. **Additional information:** Students must declare major upon enrollment or by end of first semester. Adult and continuing education programs available.

FRESHMAN ADMISSIONS. Selection criteria: Open admissions. **Test requirements:** ACT for placement and counseling only; score report by August 26.

1992 FRESHMAN CLASS PROFILE. 1,656 men and women enrolled. **Characteristics:** 98% from in state, 100% commute, 4% have minority backgrounds. Average age is 26.

FALL-TERM APPLICATIONS. No fee. No closing date; applicants notified on a rolling basis. Interview recommended for nursing applicants.

STUDENT LIFE. Activities: Student government, student newspaper, choral groups, drama, social service club, Fellowship of Christian Students, Circle-K.

ATHLETICS. Intramural: Badminton, basketball M, bowling, football M, golf, racquetball, softball, table tennis, tennis, volleyball.

STUDENT SERVICES. Career counseling, employment service for undergraduates, freshman orientation, health services, personal counseling, placement service for graduates, veterans counselor, services/facilities for handicapped.

ANNUAL EXPENSES. Tuition and fees (1992-93): $840, $1,680 additional for out-of-state students. **Books and supplies:** $450. **Other expenses:** $250.

FINANCIAL AID. 54% of freshmen, 63% of continuing students receive some form of aid. Grants, loans, jobs available. Academic scholarships available. **Aid applications:** No closing date; priority given to applications received by April 1; applicants notified on a rolling basis beginning on or about June 15; must reply within 3 weeks.

ADDRESS/TELEPHONE. Robert Renn, Admissions Officer, Madisonville Community College, College Drive, Madisonville, KY 42431. (502) 821-2250. Fax: (502) 825-8553.

Maysville Community College
Maysville, Kentucky CB code: 0693

2-year public community college, coed. Founded in 1968. **Accreditation:** Regional. **Undergraduate enrollment:** 146 men, 400 women full time; 187 men, 590 women part time. **Faculty:** 112 total (44 full time), 22 with doctorates or other terminal degrees. **Location:** Rural campus in small town; 60 miles from Cincinnati, Ohio, 60 miles from Lexington, Kentucky. **Calendar:** Semester, limited summer session. **Microcomputers:** 40 located in libraries, computer centers. **Special facilities:** Access to University of Kentucky library through automated system.

DEGREES OFFERED. AA, AS, AAS. 123 associate degrees awarded in 1992. 25% in business and management, 13% business/office and marketing/distribution, 7% engineering technologies, 32% health sciences, 22% multi/interdisciplinary studies.

UNDERGRADUATE MAJORS. Business administration and management, business data processing and related programs, data processing, dental hygiene, electronic technology, liberal/general studies, management information systems, management science, marketing and distribution, marketing management, nursing, secretarial and related programs.

ACADEMIC PROGRAMS. 2-year transfer program, cooperative education, dual enrollment of high school students, independent study, internships, telecourses. **Remedial services:** Learning center, reduced course load, remedial instruction, special counselor, tutoring. **Placement/credit:** AP, CLEP General and Subject, institutional tests.

ACADEMIC REQUIREMENTS. No policy requiring minimum GPA; records of students having academic difficulty are reviewed individually. 58% of freshmen return for sophomore year. **Graduation requirements:** 60 hours for associate. Most students required to take courses in English, history, humanities, mathematics, biological/physical sciences, social sciences. **Additional information:** Can qraduate without specific major.

FRESHMAN ADMISSIONS. Selection criteria: Open admissions. High school diploma required and ACT scores considered for nursing and dental hygiene programs. Out-of-state applicants must rank in top half of class and have ACT scores in 50th percentile. **Test requirements:** ACT for placement and counseling only; score report by August 20. ACT required for admission to nursing and dental hygiene programs. ASSET required for all new freshmen.

1992 FRESHMAN CLASS PROFILE. 62 men, 184 women enrolled. **Academic background:** Mid 50% of enrolled freshmen had ACT composite between 13-18. 50% submitted ACT scores. **Characteristics:** 90% from in state, 100% commute, 1% have minority backgrounds. Average age is 23.

FALL-TERM APPLICATIONS. No fee. No closing date; applicants notified on a rolling basis. Interview required for nursing, dental hygiene applicants. Early admission available. March 1st priority date for nursing applicants.

STUDENT LIFE. Activities: Student government, television, choral groups, drama, Association of Nontraditional Students.

STUDENT SERVICES. Aptitude testing, career counseling, employment service for undergraduates, freshman orientation, health services, personal counseling, placement service for graduates, special adviser for adult students, veterans counselor, services/facilities for handicapped.

ANNUAL EXPENSES. Tuition and fees (projected): $840, $1,680 additional for out-of-state students. **Books and supplies:** $450. **Other expenses:** $848.

FINANCIAL AID. 51% of freshmen, 56% of continuing students receive some form of aid. 99% of grants, 95% of loans, 91% of jobs based on need. Academic, state/district residency, minority scholarships available. **Aid applications:** No closing date; priority given to applications received by April 1; applicants notified on a rolling basis beginning on or about July 1; must reply within 3 weeks.

ADDRESS/TELEPHONE. John F. Meyers, Registrar/Admissions Officer, Maysville Community College, 1755 US 68, Maysville, KY 41056. (606) 759-7141 ext. 117. Fax: (606) 759-7176.

Mid-Continent Baptist Bible College
Mayfield, Kentucky CB code: 0254

4-year private Bible college, coed, affiliated with Southern Baptist Convention. Founded in 1949. **Accreditation:** Regional. **Undergraduate enrollment:** 48 men, 12 women full time; 38 men, 15 women part time. **Faculty:** 16 total (3 full time), 4 with doctorates or other terminal degrees. **Location:** Rural campus in large town; 20 miles from Paducah, 125 from Nashville, Tennessee. **Calendar:** Semester, limited summer session. **Microcomputers:** 10 located in libraries, classrooms.

DEGREES OFFERED. BA. 17 bachelor's degrees awarded in 1992. 100% in philosophy, religion, theology.

UNDERGRADUATE MAJORS. Bible studies, christian education, religion.

ACADEMIC PROGRAMS. Placement/credit: AP.

ACADEMIC REQUIREMENTS. Freshmen must earn minimum GPA of 1.8 to continue in good standing. 84% of freshmen return for sophomore year. Students must declare major on enrollment. **Graduation requirements:** 128 hours for bachelor's (33 in major). Most students required to take courses in arts/fine arts, computer science, English, foreign languages, history, humanities, mathematics, philosophy/religion, biological/physical sciences, social sciences. **Postgraduate studies:** 29% enter other graduate study.

FRESHMAN ADMISSIONS. Selection criteria: Open admissions. **High school preparation:** 16 units recommended. Recommended units include English 4, mathematics 2, social science 2 and science 2. **Test requirements:** SAT or ACT (ACT preferred) for placement and counseling only; score report by August 6.

1992 FRESHMAN CLASS PROFILE. 11 men, 6 women enrolled. **Academic background:** Mid 50% of enrolled freshmen had ACT composite between 16-20. 100% submitted ACT scores. **Characteristics:** 62% from in state, 60% live in college housing, 1% have minority backgrounds, 1% are foreign students. Average age is 28.

FALL-TERM APPLICATIONS. $10 fee. No closing date; priority given to applications received by August 1; applicants notified on a rolling basis; must reply by registration. Interview required.

STUDENT LIFE. Housing: Dormitories (men, women). **Activities:** Student government, student newspaper, yearbook, Baptist Student Union. **Additional information:** Religious observance required.

STUDENT SERVICES. Personal counseling, veterans counselor, services/facilities for handicapped.

ANNUAL EXPENSES. Tuition and fees: $1,740. **Room and board:** $3,382. **Books and supplies:** $250. **Other expenses:** $600.

FINANCIAL AID. 65% of freshmen, 50% of continuing students receive some form of aid. All grants, all loans based on need. All jobs based on criteria other than need. 9 enrolled freshmen were judged to have need, all were offered aid. Leadership scholarships available. **Aid applications:** No closing date; priority given to applications received by May 1; applicants notified on a rolling basis beginning on or about June 29; must reply within 4 weeks.

ADDRESS/TELEPHONE. Yvonne Yates, Director of Admissions/Registrar, Mid-Continent Baptist Bible College, PO Box 7010, Route 2 Highway 45 North, Mayfield, KY 42066-0357. (502) 247-8521.

Midway College
Midway, Kentucky CB code: 1467

4-year private liberal arts college, women only, affiliated with Christian Church (Disciples of Christ). Founded in 1847. **Accreditation:** Regional. **Undergraduate enrollment:** 798 women. **Faculty:** 48 total (26 full time), 14 with doctorates or other terminal degrees. **Location:** Rural campus in rural community; 12 miles from Lexington, 60 miles from Louisville. **Calendar:** Semester, limited summer session. Saturday and extensive evening/early morning classes. **Microcomputers:** 18 located in libraries, classrooms, computer centers. **Special facilities:** Law library, equine science center, riding arena, campus farm. **Additional facts:** Men admitted to extension program in nursing located at Ephrim McDowell Regional Medical Center, Danville, and to extension program in business (evening only, on-campus).

DEGREES OFFERED. AA, BA. 122 associate degrees awarded in 1992. 24% in business and management, 8% teacher education, 48% health sciences, 10% law, 8% multi/interdisciplinary studies. 23 bachelor's degrees awarded. 50% in business and management, 50% health sciences.

UNDERGRADUATE MAJORS. Associate: Child development/care/guidance, computer and information sciences, early childhood, early childhood education, elementary education, equestrian science, equine science, general science studies, humanities, legal assistant/paralegal, liberal/general studies, nursing, secondary education. **Bachelor's:** Accounting, agricultural business and management, behavioral sciences, business administration and management, business and management, business economics, communications, early childhood, early childhood education, equestrian science, finance, legal assistant/paralegal, marketing management, nursing, religion.

ACADEMIC PROGRAMS. 2-year transfer program, independent study, internships, student-designed major, evening business program. **Remedial services:** Learning center, preadmission summer program, reduced course load, remedial instruction, special counselor, tutoring. **Placement/credit:** AP, CLEP General and Subject, institutional tests; 12 credit hours maximum for associate degree.

ACADEMIC REQUIREMENTS. Freshmen must earn minimum GPA of 1.85 to continue in good standing. 70% of freshmen return for sophomore year. Students must declare major by end of first year. **Graduation requirements:** 69 hours for associate (36 in major). Most students required to take courses in computer science, English, humanities, mathematics, philosophy/religion, biological/physical sciences, social sciences. **Postgraduate studies:** 40% from 2-year programs enter 4-year programs.

FRESHMAN ADMISSIONS. Selection criteria: Test scores, GPA important. **High school preparation:** 11 units required. Required units include English 4, mathematics 2, social science 3 and science 2. Specific college-preparatory program required for some majors. **Test requirements:** SAT or ACT; score report by August 15.

1992 FRESHMAN CLASS PROFILE. 235 men and women enrolled. 43% had high school GPA of 3.0 or higher, 51% between 2.0 and 2.99. **Academic background:** Mid 50% of enrolled freshmen had ACT composite between 17-23. 62% submitted ACT scores. **Characteristics:** 86% from in state, 55% commute, 9% have minority backgrounds, 1% are foreign students. Average age is 23.

FALL-TERM APPLICATIONS. $15 fee, may be waived for applicants with need. No closing date; applicants notified on a rolling basis. Interview required for in-home child care specialist, nursing, early childhood education, paralegal, academically weak applicants. CRDA. Deferred and early admission available.

STUDENT LIFE. Housing: Dormitories (women). All students under 21, unmarried, and not living at home required to live in campus housing. **Activities:** Student government, student newspaper, yearbook, choral groups, drama, vespers committee, international student organization.

ATHLETICS. NAIA. **Intercollegiate:** Basketball, horseback riding, softball, volleyball. **Intramural:** Badminton, racquetball, softball, tennis, volleyball.

STUDENT SERVICES. Aptitude testing, career counseling, employment service for undergraduates, freshman orientation, health services, on-campus day care, personal counseling, special adviser for adult students.

ANNUAL EXPENSES. Tuition and fees (1992-93): $6,200. **Room and board:** $3,700. **Books and supplies:** $600. **Other expenses:** $500.

FINANCIAL AID. 80% of freshmen, 76% of continuing students receive some form of aid. 88% of grants, 80% of loans, all jobs based on need. Academic, music/drama, art, athletic, leadership, religious affiliation, minority scholarships available. **Aid applications:** Closing date August 1; applicants notified on a rolling basis; must reply by May 1 or within 2 weeks if notified thereafter.

ADDRESS/TELEPHONE. Carl P. Rollins II, Director of Admissions, Midway College, 512 East Stephen Street, Midway, KY 40347-1120. (606) 846-4221. (800) 755-0031. Fax: (606) 846-5349.

Morehead State University
Morehead, Kentucky CB code: 1487

Admissions: 91% of applicants accepted
Based on: ••• School record, test scores
• Interview, special talents
Completion: 70% of freshmen end year in good standing
35% graduate

4-year public university, coed. Founded in 1922. **Accreditation:** Regional. **Undergraduate enrollment:** 2,833 men, 3,678 women full time; 260 men, 761 women part time. **Graduate enrollment:** 136 men, 143 women full time; 353 men, 1,005 women part time. **Faculty:** 392 total (329 full time). **Location:** Rural campus in small town; 65 miles from Lexington, 70 miles from Huntington, West Virginia. **Calendar:** Semester, extensive summer session. **Microcomputers:** 1,118 located in dormitories, libraries, classrooms, computer centers. **Special facilities:** Art gallery, planetarium, 320-acre agriculture complex, 50-acre outdoor learning center at Cave Run, Eagle Lake recreation area.

DEGREES OFFERED. AA, AS, AAS, BA, BS, MA, MS, MBA, MEd. 167 associate degrees awarded in 1992. 16% in agriculture, 18% business/office and marketing/distribution, 7% engineering technologies, 20% allied health, 16% multi/interdisciplinary studies, 15% trade and industry. 955 bachelor's degrees awarded. 11% in business and management, 6% business/office and marketing/distribution, 8% communications, 6% education, 16% teacher education, 10% social sciences, 12% trade and industry. Graduate degrees offered in 19 major fields of study.

UNDERGRADUATE MAJORS. Associate: Agribusiness, agricultural production, architectural technologies, business and office, business data processing and related programs, child development/care/guidance, drafting, electromechanical technology, electronic technology, fashion merchandising, food management, food production/management/services, graphic and printing production, home furnishings and equipment management/production/services, industrial technology, journalism, law enforcement and corrections, liberal/general studies, manufacturing technology, nursery operation and management, office supervision and management, power technology, practical nursing, radio/television broadcasting, radio/television technology, radiograph medical technology, real estate, reclamation technology, respiratory therapy, respiratory therapy technology, secretarial and related programs, small business management and ownership, social work, technical education, trade and industrial supervision and management, veterinarian's assistant, welding technology. **Bachelor's:** Accounting, advertising, agricultural education, agricultural sciences, biology, business administration and management, business and management, business data processing and related programs, business economics, business education, chemistry, commercial art, communications, computer and information sciences, dramatic arts, earth sciences, ecology, elementary education, English, finance, food production/management/services, food science and nutrition, French, geography, geology, health education, history, home economics, home economics education, hotel/motel and restaurant management, human environment and housing, industrial arts education, industrial technology, journalism, junior high education, legal assistant/paralegal, liberal/general studies, management science, marketing and distribution, marketing management, math and physical sciences education, mathematics, mathematics and computer programming, medical laboratory technologies, music, music education, nursing, parks and recreation management, philosophy, photography, physical education, physics, political science and government, product management, psychology, radio/television broadcasting, real estate, science education, social sciences, social work, sociology, Spanish, special education, speech, speech and theater, studio art, textiles and clothing, trade and industrial education, veterinarian's assistant.

ACADEMIC PROGRAMS. Accelerated program, computer delivered (on-line) credit-bearing course offerings, cooperative education, double major, dual enrollment of high school students, education specialist degree, honors program, independent study, internships, student-designed major, study abroad, teacher preparation, telecourses, visiting/exchange student program, weekend college, Washington semester; liberal arts/career combination in engineering. **Remedial services:** Learning center, preadmission summer program, remedial instruction, special counselor, tutoring, Developmental Studies Program. **ROTC:** Army. **Placement/credit:** AP, CLEP General and Subject, institutional tests; 16 credit hours maximum for associate degree; 32 credit hours maximum for bachelor's degree.

ACADEMIC REQUIREMENTS. Freshmen must earn minimum GPA of 1.65 to continue in good standing. 63% of freshmen return for sophomore year. Students must declare major by end of second year. **Graduation requirements:** 64 hours for associate (15 in major), 128 hours for bachelor's (30 in major). Most students required to take courses in English, history, humanities, mathematics, biological/physical sciences, social sciences. **Additional information:** 2-year transfer programs in prechiropractic, predentistry, preengineering, preforestry, prelaw, premedicine, preoptometry, prepharmacy, prephysical therapy, preveterinary medicine offered.

FRESHMAN ADMISSIONS. Selection criteria: ACT/SAT scores and GPA used to calculate index to determine admission. Status and review of precollege curriculum important. **High school preparation:** 20 units required. Required and recommended units include English 4, mathematics 3, social science 2 and science 2. Foreign language 2 recommended. **Test requirements:** SAT or ACT (ACT preferred); score report by August 15.

1992 FRESHMAN CLASS PROFILE. 2,965 men and women applied, 2,706 accepted; 593 men enrolled, 800 women enrolled. **Academic background:** Mid 50% of enrolled freshmen had ACT composite between 16-22. 94% submitted ACT scores. **Characteristics:** 82% from in state, 78% live in college housing, 6% have minority backgrounds, 1% are foreign students, 12% join fraternities/sororities. Average age is 19.

FALL-TERM APPLICATIONS. No fee. No closing date; applicants notified on a rolling basis beginning on or about September 1. Interview recommended for specialized allied health programs applicants. Audition recommended for music applicants.

STUDENT LIFE. Housing: Dormitories (men, women, coed); apartment housing available. Limited housing available at agriculture complex for agriculture science students. Housing for handicapped students and private rooms available. **Activities:** Student government, film, magazine, radio, student newspaper, television, yearbook, choral groups, concert band, dance, drama, jazz band, marching band, music ensembles, musical theater, pep band, symphony orchestra, fraternities, sororities, seven religious organizations, Young Democrats, Young Republicans, several service organizations.

ATHLETICS. NCAA. **Intercollegiate:** Baseball M, basketball, cross-country, diving, football M, golf M, soccer M, softball W, swimming, tennis, track and field, volleyball W. **Intramural:** Archery, badminton, basketball, bowling, golf, handball, racquetball, softball, swimming, table tennis, tennis, volleyball.

STUDENT SERVICES. Aptitude testing, career counseling, employment service for undergraduates, freshman orientation, health services, personal counseling, placement service for graduates, special adviser for adult students, veterans counselor, services/facilities for handicapped.

ANNUAL EXPENSES. Tuition and fees (projected): $1,790, $3,000 additional for out-of-state students. **Room and board:** $2,800. **Books and supplies:** $500. **Other expenses:** $800.

FINANCIAL AID. 68% of freshmen, 70% of continuing students receive some form of aid. 71% of grants, 80% of loans, 64% of jobs based on need. Academic, music/drama, art, athletic, state/district residency, leadership, alumni affiliation, minority scholarships available. **Aid applications:** No closing date; priority given to applications received by April 1; applicants notified on a rolling basis beginning on or about May 15; must reply within 2 to 4 weeks, as specified.

ADDRESS/TELEPHONE. Charles Myers, Director of Admissions, Morehead State University, University Boulevard, Morehead, KY 40351. (606) 783-2000. (800) 354-2090. Fax: (606) 783-2678.

Murray State University

Murray, Kentucky CB code: 1494

Admissions:	82% of applicants accepted
Based on:	••• School record, test scores
	•• Activities, special talents
	• Essay, interview, recommendations
Completion:	75% of freshmen end year in good standing
	42% graduate, 25% of these enter graduate study

4-year public university, coed. Founded in 1922. **Accreditation:** Regional. **Undergraduate enrollment:** 2,811 men, 3,194 women full time; 376 men, 591 women part time. **Graduate enrollment:** 189 men, 170 women full time; 284 men, 575 women part time. **Faculty:** 371 total (368 full time), 226 with doctorates or other terminal degrees. **Location:** Rural campus in large town; 115 miles from Nashville, Tennessee. **Calendar:** Semester, limited summer session. Extensive evening/early morning classes. **Microcomputers:** Located in dormitories, libraries, classrooms, computer centers. **Special facilities:** Biological research station, aquatic wildlife area, veterinary diagnostic research center, Center of Excellence for Reservoir Research, NASA-related technology-transfer station, 2 farms, National Museum of Boy Scouts of America, archaeological research and excavation site, regional museum. **Additional facts:** Composed of 6 academic colleges offering 136 programs of study.

DEGREES OFFERED. AA, AS, BA, BS, BFA, MA, MS, MBA, MEd. 26 associate degrees awarded in 1992. 5% in agriculture, 17% business and management, 21% business/office and marketing/distribution, 24% engineering technologies, 7% health sciences, 5% letters/literature, 14% trade and industry. 1,043 bachelor's degrees awarded. 5% in agriculture, 15% business and management, 6% business/office and marketing/distribution, 7% communications, 15% teacher education, 9% engineering technologies, 6% health sciences, 5% parks/recreation, protective services, public affairs, 5% social sciences. Graduate degrees offered in 33 major fields of study.

UNDERGRADUATE MAJORS. Associate: Business and office, business data processing and related programs, business data programming, child development/care/guidance, civil technology, drafting, drafting and design technology, electrical and electronics equipment repair, electrical technology, engineering and engineering-related technologies, equestrian science, fashion merchandising, food production/management/services, graphic and printing production, graphic arts technology, horticultural science, industrial technology, law enforcement and corrections technologies, marketing and distribution, mechanical design technology, medical laboratory technologies, occupational safety and health technology, secretarial and related programs, trade and industrial education. **Bachelor's:** Accounting, agribusiness, agricultural economics, agricultural education, agricultural mechanics, agricultural sciences, agronomy, animal sciences, applied mathematics, art education, biochemistry, biology, business administration and management, business and management, business and office, business economics, business education, chemistry, civil technology, clinical laboratory science, computer and information sciences, computer programming, computer technology, creative writing, criminal justice studies, criminology, dramatic arts, earth sciences, economics, education of the emotionally handicapped, education of the mentally handicapped, electrical technology, elementary education, engineering and engineering-related technologies, engineering physics, English, English education, family/consumer resource management, finance, food science and nutrition, foreign languages education, French, geography, geology, German, graphic arts technology, health education, history, home economics, home economics education, horticultural science, human environment and housing, individual and family development, industrial arts education, industrial technology, information sciences and systems, interior design, journalism, junior high education, law enforcement and corrections, library science, manufacturing technology, marketing and distribution, marketing and distributive education, mathematics, mathematics education, mechanical design technology, mining and petroleum technologies, music, music education, music performance, nursing, occupational safety and health technology, ornamental horticulture, parks and recreation management, philosophy, physical education, physics, political science and government, psychology, radio/television broadcasting, rehabilitation counseling/services, science education, secretarial and related programs, social science education, social work, sociology, soil sciences, Spanish, special education, specific learning disabilities, speech, speech correction, speech pathology/audiology, speech/communication/theater education, studio art, textiles and clothing, trade and industrial education, urban studies.

ACADEMIC PROGRAMS. 2-year transfer program, cooperative education, double major, dual enrollment of high school students, education specialist degree, external degree, honors program, independent study, internships, semester at sea, study abroad, teacher preparation, telecourses, visiting/exchange student program, Cooperative Center for Study in Britain, Kentucky Institute for European Studies. **Remedial services:** Learning center, preadmission summer program, reduced course load, remedial instruction, special counselor, tutoring. **ROTC:** Army. **Placement/credit:** AP, CLEP General and Subject, institutional tests; 30 credit hours maximum for bachelor's degree.

ACADEMIC REQUIREMENTS. Freshmen must earn minimum GPA of 2.0 to continue in good standing. 68% of freshmen return for sophomore year. Students must declare major by end of second year. **Graduation requirements:** 64 hours for associate (18 in major), 128 hours for bachelor's (30 in major). Most students required to take courses in arts/fine arts, English, history, humanities, mathematics, biological/physical sciences, social sciences.

FRESHMAN ADMISSIONS. Selection criteria: Out-of-state applicants must have completed precollege curriculum and be in top third of high school class with minimum ACT composite of 18, or have ACT composite score of 21. In-state applicants must have completed precollege curriculum and be in top half of class with ACT composite of 18, or have ACT composite score of 20. Selective admissions to nursing program. **High school preparation:** 20 units required. Required and recommended units include English 4, mathematics 3-4, social science 2 and science 3. Foreign language 2 recommended. Social sciences must include US history and world civilization. One arts and 1 computer science recommended. Mathematics must include 3 units algebra I and above. **Test requirements:** ACT; score report by July 1.

1992 FRESHMAN CLASS PROFILE. 2,125 men and women applied, 1,750 accepted; 547 men enrolled, 598 women enrolled. 66% had high school GPA of 3.0 or higher, 32% between 2.0 and 2.99. 30% were in top tenth and 77% were in top quarter of graduating class. **Academic background:** Mid 50% of enrolled freshmen had ACT composite between 19-25. 100% submitted ACT scores. **Characteristics:** 75% from in state, 50% commute, 7% have minority backgrounds, 1% are foreign students, 25% join fraternities/sororities. Average age is 18.

FALL-TERM APPLICATIONS. $10 fee. Closing date August 15; applicants notified on a rolling basis; must reply by July 1 or within 2 weeks if notified thereafter. Interview recommended for art, music, nursing applicants. Audition recommended for music applicants. Portfolio recommended for art applicants. Deferred and early admission available.

STUDENT LIFE. Housing: Dormitories (men, women, coed); apartment, fraternity, sorority, handicapped housing available. **Activities:** Student government, radio, student newspaper, television, yearbook, choral groups, concert band, dance, drama, jazz band, marching band, music ensembles, musical theater, opera, pep band, symphony orchestra, fraternities, sororities, intercollegiate rodeo, equestrian team.

ATHLETICS. NCAA. **Intercollegiate:** Baseball M, basketball, bowling M, cross-country, football M, golf M, horseback riding, rifle, softball W, tennis, track and field, volleyball W. **Intramural:** Archery, badminton, basketball, bowling, cross-country, fencing, golf, gymnastics, handball, horseback riding, racquetball, sailing, skin diving, soccer, softball, swimming, table tennis, tennis, volleyball.

STUDENT SERVICES. Aptitude testing, career counseling, employment service for undergraduates, freshman orientation, health services, personal counseling, placement service for graduates, special adviser for adult students, veterans counselor, services/facilities for handicapped.

ANNUAL EXPENSES. Tuition and fees (projected): $1,780, $3,000 additional for out-of-state students. Reciprocity with certain Tennessee counties. **Room and board:** $3,022. **Books and supplies:** $500. **Other expenses:** $600.

FINANCIAL AID. 60% of freshmen, 60% of continuing students receive some form of aid. 50% of grants, 88% of loans, 19% of jobs based on need. 535 enrolled freshmen were judged to have need, 475 were offered aid. Academic, music/drama, art, athletic, state/district residency, leadership, alumni affiliation, minority scholarships available. **Aid applications:** No closing date; priority given to applications received by April 1; applicants notified on a rolling basis beginning on or about May 1; must reply within 2 weeks.

ADDRESS/TELEPHONE. Phil Bryan, Dean of Admissions/Registrar, Murray State University, One Murray Street, Murray, KY 42071. (502) 762-3741. (800) 272-4678. Fax: (502) 762-3050.

National Education Center: Kentucky College of Technology Campus

Louisville, Kentucky CB code: 3951

2-year proprietary technical college, coed. Founded in 1946. **Undergraduate enrollment:** 380 men and women. **Location:** Suburban campus in large city; 10 miles from downtown. **Calendar:** Quarter.

FRESHMAN ADMISSIONS. Selection criteria: Interview to determine interest in the field and motivation to complete curriculum.

ANNUAL EXPENSES. Tuition and fees (1992-93): For 21-month associate program in electronics, total cost of $13,285 includes books, supplies, and tuition (roughly $100 per credit hour). For 18-month associate program in business technology, total cost is $11,175 (roughly $103 per credit hour).

ADDRESS/TELEPHONE. Greg Gawthon, Director of Admissions, National Education Center: Kentucky Coll of Technology, 300 High Rise Drive, Louisville, KY 40213. (502) 966-5555. (800) 666-2500. Fax: (502) 964-0967.

Northern Kentucky University
Highland Heights, Kentucky CB code: 1574

4-year public university, coed. Founded in 1968. **Accreditation:** Regional. **Undergraduate enrollment:** 3,168 men, 3,617 women full time; 1,446 men, 1,926 women part time. **Graduate enrollment:** 135 men, 147 women full time; 264 men, 515 women part time. **Faculty:** 661 total (363 full time), 241 with doctorates or other terminal degrees. **Location:** Suburban campus in small town; 8 miles from Cincinnati, Ohio. **Calendar:** Semester, extensive summer session. **Microcomputers:** 144 located in dormitories, classrooms, computer centers. **Special facilities:** Anthropology museum, biology museum, geology exhibit, art gallery. **Additional facts:** Introductory-level courses and some graduate-level courses and business seminars available at University College Campus in Covington.

DEGREES OFFERED. AAS, BA, BS, BFA, MA, MBA, JD. 257 associate degrees awarded in 1992. 17% in business and management, 5% business/office and marketing/distribution, 35% health sciences, 21% allied health, 15% trade and industry. 799 bachelor's degrees awarded. 24% in business and management, 9% communications, 7% computer sciences, 13% education, 5% letters/literature, 6% psychology, 14% social sciences, 8% visual and performing arts. Graduate degrees offered in 9 major fields of study.

UNDERGRADUATE MAJORS. Associate: Aviation management, business administration and management, chemical manufacturing technology, construction, dental hygiene, electronic technology, fire control and safety technology, labor/industrial relations, law enforcement and corrections technologies, manufacturing technology, mental health/human services, nursing, office supervision and management, radiograph medical technology, real estate, respiratory therapy. **Bachelor's:** Accounting, anthropology, applied sociology/anthropology, art education, biology, business administration and management, business and management, business education, chemistry, dramatic arts, economics, electronic technology, elementary education, English, finance, fine arts, French, geography, geology, graphic design, history, industrial arts education, industrial technology, information sciences and systems, international studies, journalism, labor/industrial relations, manufacturing technology, marketing management, mathematics, medical laboratory technologies, mental health/human services, music, music education, nursing, office supervision and management, philosophy, physical education, physics, political science and government, psychology, public administration, radio/television broadcasting, radiograph medical technology, secondary education, social work, sociology, Spanish, special education, speech, speech/theater arts, studio art.

ACADEMIC PROGRAMS. Cooperative education, double major, dual enrollment of high school students, honors program, independent study, internships, student-designed major, study abroad, teacher preparation, telecourses, visiting/exchange student program, weekend college, United Nations semester, cross-registration. **Remedial services:** Learning center, preadmission summer program, reduced course load, remedial instruction, special counselor, tutoring. **ROTC:** Army. **Placement/credit:** AP, CLEP General and Subject, IB, institutional tests.

ACADEMIC REQUIREMENTS. Freshmen must earn minimum GPA of 2.0 to continue in good standing. 56% of freshmen return for sophomore year. Students must declare major by end of second year. **Graduation requirements:** 64 hours for associate, 128 hours for bachelor's. Most students required to take courses in arts/fine arts, English, foreign languages, history, mathematics, biological/physical sciences, social sciences. **Postgraduate studies:** 2% enter law school, 1% enter medical school, 4% enter MBA programs, 10% enter other graduate study. **Additional information:** For bachelor's degree 6 semester hours must by taken from 2 of the following groups: arts; foreign language; religion/philosophy; social science. Must take oral communication or demonstrate speech competency. Also must take 3 hours in nonwestern subject area.

FRESHMAN ADMISSIONS. Selection criteria: Open admissions. Required and recommended units include social science 2-2. Biological science 1, English 4, foreign language 2, mathematics 4 and science 4 recommended. Chemistry and biology required for nursing program. Computer science recommended for all. **Test requirements:** ACT for placement and counseling only; score report by August 20.

1992 FRESHMAN CLASS PROFILE. 1,636 men and women enrolled. **Characteristics:** 74% from in state, 5% have minority backgrounds. Average age is 19.

FALL-TERM APPLICATIONS. $25 fee, may be waived for applicants with need. Closing date August 30; priority given to applications received by May 1; applicants notified on a rolling basis; must reply by August 30. Interview recommended. Early admission available. January 31 application closing date for nursing program. March 31 closing date for radiologic technology program.

STUDENT LIFE. Housing: Dormitories (men, women, coed); apartment, handicapped housing available. One-third of all college housing accessible to handicapped. **Activities:** Student government, magazine, radio, student newspaper, television, Literature Collage Collection Book, choral groups, concert band, dance, drama, jazz band, music ensembles, musical theater, opera, fraternities, sororities, Young Democrats, Young Republicans, religious fellowship organizations, minority organizations.

ATHLETICS. NCAA. **Intercollegiate:** Baseball M, basketball, cross-country, golf M, soccer M, softball W, tennis, volleyball W. **Intramural:** Archery, badminton, baseball, basketball, racquetball, skiing, soccer, softball, swimming, table tennis, tennis, volleyball, water polo.

STUDENT SERVICES. Aptitude testing, career counseling, employment service for undergraduates, freshman orientation, health services, on-campus day care, personal counseling, placement service for graduates, special adviser for adult students, veterans counselor, women's center, services/facilities for handicapped.

ANNUAL EXPENSES. Tuition and fees (projected): $1,720, $3,000 additional for out-of-state students. **Room and board:** $3,240. **Books and supplies:** $500. **Other expenses:** $800.

FINANCIAL AID. 21% of freshmen, 79% of continuing students receive some form of aid. 79% of grants, 87% of loans, 25% of jobs based on need. 568 enrolled freshmen were judged to have need, all were offered aid. Academic, music/drama, art, athletic, state/district residency, minority scholarships available. **Aid applications:** No closing date; priority given to applications received by April 1; applicants notified on a rolling basis beginning on or about May 15; must reply within 2 weeks.

ADDRESS/TELEPHONE. Gregory Stewart, Director of Admissions, Northern Kentucky University, Highland Heights, KY 41099-7010. (606) 572-5220. (800) 637-9948. Fax: (606) 572-5566 ext. 5220.

Owensboro Community College
Owensboro, Kentucky CB code: 0613

2-year public institution. **Accreditation:** Regional. **Undergraduate enrollment:** 3,000 men and women.

FRESHMAN ADMISSIONS. Selection criteria: Open admissions.

ADDRESS/TELEPHONE. Gretta McDonough, Admissions Officer, Owensboro Community College, 4800 New Hartford Road, Owensboro, KY 42303. (502) 686-4400. Fax: (502) 686-4496.

Owensboro Junior College of Business
Owensboro, Kentucky CB code: 0772

2-year proprietary business, junior college, coed. Founded in 1963. **Undergraduate enrollment:** 29 men, 246 women full time; 2 men, 7 women part time. **Faculty:** 13 total (10 full time). **Location:** Urban campus in small city; 120 miles from Louisville, 35 miles from Evansville, Indiana. **Calendar:** Quarter. Extensive evening/early morning classes. **Microcomputers:** 65 located in classrooms, computer centers.

DEGREES OFFERED. AS. 80 associate degrees awarded in 1992. 30% in business and management, 15% business/office and marketing/distribution, 45% computer sciences, 10% allied health.

UNDERGRADUATE MAJORS. Business and office, business data entry equipment operation, business data processing and related programs, computer and information sciences, data processing, fashion merchandising, legal assistant/paralegal, legal secretary, management information systems, marketing and distribution, medical assistant, medical secretary, microcomputer software, secretarial and related programs, word processing.

ACADEMIC PROGRAMS. 2-year transfer program, accelerated program, double major, dual enrollment of high school students, honors program, independent study. **Remedial services:** Remedial instruction, special counselor, tutoring. **Placement/credit:** AP, institutional tests; 12 credit hours maximum for associate degree.

ACADEMIC REQUIREMENTS. Freshmen must earn minimum GPA of 2.0 to continue in good standing. 79% of freshmen return for sophomore year. Students must declare major on application. **Graduation requirements:** 96 hours for associate (72 in major). Most students required to take courses in English, humanities, mathematics, social sciences.

FRESHMAN ADMISSIONS. Selection criteria: School achievement record most important; test scores and interview important. **High school preparation:** 6 units recommended. Recommended units include English 3, mathematics 1, physical science 1 and social science 1. One human relations also recommended. **Test requirements:** SAT or ACT; score report by October 1. Institutional tests required for placement. Skadron test required for admission.

1992 FRESHMAN CLASS PROFILE. 175 men and women enrolled. **Characteristics:** 85% from in state, 100% commute, 15% have minority backgrounds. Average age is 21.

FALL-TERM APPLICATIONS. $10 fee, may be waived for applicants with need. Closing date October 1; applicants notified on or about September 1. Interview required.

STUDENT LIFE. Activities: Student government, student newspaper.

ATHLETICS. Intercollegiate: Bowling, softball.

STUDENT SERVICES. Aptitude testing, career counseling, employment service for undergraduates, freshman orientation, on-campus day care, personal counseling, placement service for graduates, veterans counselor, services/facilities for handicapped.

ANNUAL EXPENSES. Tuition and fees: $3,668. **Books and supplies:** $600.

FINANCIAL AID. 96% of freshmen, 96% of continuing students receive some form of aid. All grants, 97% of loans, all jobs based on need. Academic, state/district residency, leadership scholarships available. **Aid applications:** No closing date; applicants notified on a rolling basis; must reply by registration.

ADDRESS/TELEPHONE. W. Shane Wilson, President, Owensboro Junior College of Business, 1515 East 18th Street, Owensboro, KY 42303. (502) 926-4040. Fax: (502) 685-4090.

Paducah Community College
Paducah, Kentucky CB code: 1620

2-year public community college, coed. Founded in 1932. **Accreditation:** Regional. **Undergraduate enrollment:** 3,133 men and women. **Faculty:** 107 total (55 full time), 7 with doctorates or other terminal degrees. **Location:** Suburban campus in large town; 140 miles from Nashville, Tennessee. **Calendar:** Semester, limited summer session. Saturday classes. **Microcomputers:** 70 located in libraries, classrooms, computer centers.

DEGREES OFFERED. AA, AS, AAS. 223 associate degrees awarded in 1992. 6% in business and management, 7% business/office and marketing/distribution, 31% health sciences, 49% multi/interdisciplinary studies.

UNDERGRADUATE MAJORS. Accounting, business and management, business and office, business computer/console/peripheral equipment operation, business data entry equipment operation, business data processing and related programs, business data programming, communications, computer and information sciences, finance, food management, liberal/general studies, nursing, physical therapy assistant, real estate, secretarial and related programs.

ACADEMIC PROGRAMS. 2-year transfer program, computer delivered (on-line) credit-bearing course offerings, dual enrollment of high school students, honors program, telecourses, weekend college. **Remedial services:** Learning center, reduced course load, remedial instruction, special counselor, tutoring. **Placement/credit:** AP, CLEP General and Subject.

ACADEMIC REQUIREMENTS. Freshmen must earn minimum GPA of 2.0 to continue in good standing. 40% of freshmen return for sophomore year. Students must declare major by end of first year. **Graduation requirements:** 60 hours for associate (24 in major). Most students required to take courses in arts/fine arts, computer science, English, history, humanities, mathematics, biological/physical sciences, social sciences.

FRESHMAN ADMISSIONS. Selection criteria: Open admissions. ACT score of 19 required for nursing and physical therapist assistant applicants. Interview required of nursing applicants. **High school preparation:** 20 units required. Required units include English 4, mathematics 3, social science 2 and science 2. **Test requirements:** ACT for placement and counseling only; score report by August 25.

1992 FRESHMAN CLASS PROFILE. 2,167 men and women enrolled. **Characteristics:** 96% from in state, 100% commute, 6% have minority backgrounds. Average age is 20.

FALL-TERM APPLICATIONS. No fee. No closing date; priority given to applications received by August 15; applicants notified on a rolling basis beginning on or about April 1. Interview required for nursing applicants. Early admission available.

STUDENT LIFE. Activities: Student government, radio, student newspaper, television, choral groups, drama, musical theater, fraternities, sororities.

ATHLETICS. NJCAA. **Intercollegiate:** Baseball M, softball W. **Intramural:** Golf, volleyball.

STUDENT SERVICES. Aptitude testing, career counseling, employment service for undergraduates, freshman orientation, personal counseling, placement service for graduates, veterans counselor, services/facilities for handicapped.

ANNUAL EXPENSES. Tuition and fees (1992-93): $840, $1,680 additional for out-of-state students. **Books and supplies:** $375. **Other expenses:** $400.

FINANCIAL AID. 49% of continuing students receive some form of aid. Grants, loans, jobs available. 493 enrolled freshmen were judged to have need, all were offered aid. Academic, athletic, leadership, minority scholarships available. **Aid applications:** No closing date; priority given to applications received by April 1; applicants notified on a rolling basis beginning on or about July 15; must reply within 4 weeks.

ADDRESS/TELEPHONE. Jerry Anderson, Career Counselor and Student Service Officer, Paducah Community College, PO Box 7380, Paducah, KY 42002-7380. (502) 554-9200. Fax: (502) 554-6218.

Pikeville College
Pikeville, Kentucky CB code: 1625

4-year private liberal arts college, coed, affiliated with Presbyterian Church (USA). Founded in 1889. **Accreditation:** Regional. **Undergraduate enrollment:** 254 men, 598 women full time; 32 men, 107 women part time. **Faculty:** 68 total (56 full time), 27 with doctorates or other terminal degrees. **Location:** Rural campus in small town; 140 miles from Lexington. **Calendar:** Semester, limited summer session. **Microcomputers:** 50 located in classrooms, computer centers. **Special facilities:** Weber Art Gallery.

DEGREES OFFERED. AS, BA, BS. 17 associate degrees awarded in 1992. 100% in health sciences. 132 bachelor's degrees awarded. 22% in business and management, 48% teacher education, 7% psychology, 17% social sciences.

UNDERGRADUATE MAJORS. Associate: Business administration and management, nursing. **Bachelor's:** Art education, biology, business administration and management, business education, chemistry, computer and information sciences, early childhood education, education, elementary education, English, English education, fine arts, history, junior high education, mathematics, mathematics education, medical laboratory technologies, political science and government, psychology, religion, science education, secondary education, social science education, social sciences, social studies education, special education.

ACADEMIC PROGRAMS. Double major, dual enrollment of high school students, internships, teacher preparation. **Remedial services:** Learning center, preadmission summer program, reduced course load, remedial instruction, special counselor, tutoring. **Placement/credit:** AP, CLEP General and Subject, institutional tests; 15 credit hours maximum for bachelor's degree.

ACADEMIC REQUIREMENTS. Freshmen must earn minimum GPA of 2.0 to continue in good standing. 65% of freshmen return for sophomore year. Students must declare major by end of second year. **Graduation requirements:** 64 hours for associate (36 in major), 128 hours for bachelor's (30 in major). Most students required to take courses in arts/fine arts, computer science, English, foreign languages, history, humanities, mathematics, philosophy/religion, biological/physical sciences, social sciences. **Postgraduate studies:** 1% from 2-year programs enter 4-year programs.

FRESHMAN ADMISSIONS. Selection criteria: Open admissions. Composite ACT score of 19 required of nursing applicants. **High school preparation:** 20 units recommended. Recommended units include biological science 3, English 4, foreign language 1, mathematics 3, physical science 2 and social science 3. **Test requirements:** ACT for placement and counseling only; score report by November 1.

1992 FRESHMAN CLASS PROFILE. 69 men, 131 women enrolled. 45% had high school GPA of 3.0 or higher, 50% between 2.0 and 2.99. **Academic background:** Mid 50% of enrolled freshmen had ACT composite between 15-18. 100% submitted ACT scores. **Characteristics:** 92% from in state, 80% commute, 2% have minority backgrounds. Average age is 20.

FALL-TERM APPLICATIONS. $10 fee, may be waived for applicants with need. Closing date September 1; applicants notified on a rolling basis; must reply by registration. Interview recommended for academically weak applicants. CRDA. Deferred and early admission available. EDP-F. ACT score reports for fall freshman applicants must be received by registration.

STUDENT LIFE. Housing: Dormitories (men, women); apartment housing available. **Activities:** Student government, magazine, student newspaper, yearbook, dance, drama, Social Science Club, Fellowship of Christian Athletes. **Additional information:** Weekly chapel service available.

ATHLETICS. NAIA. **Intercollegiate:** Baseball M, basketball, softball W, tennis. **Intramural:** Baseball M, basketball, bowling, football M, golf, softball, table tennis, tennis, volleyball.

STUDENT SERVICES. Aptitude testing, career counseling, freshman orientation, health services, personal counseling, placement service for graduates, veterans counselor, off-campus daycare, services/facilities for handicapped.

ANNUAL EXPENSES. Tuition and fees: $5,500. **Room and board:** $3,000. **Books and supplies:** $600. **Other expenses:** $800.

FINANCIAL AID. 80% of freshmen, 78% of continuing students receive some form of aid. Grants, loans, jobs available. Academic, athletic scholarships available. **Aid applications:** No closing date; priority given to applications received by March 15; applicants notified on a rolling basis beginning on or about May 1; must reply within 2 weeks.

ADDRESS/TELEPHONE. Dr. John Sanders, Director of Admissions and Financial Aid, Pikeville College, Box 187, Pikeville, KY 41501-1194. (606) 432-9322. Fax: (606) 432-9328.

Prestonburg Community College
Prestonburg, Kentucky CB code: 0869

2-year public community college, coed. Founded in 1964. **Accreditation:** Regional. **Undergraduate enrollment:** 659 men, 1,130 women full time; 268 men, 830 women part time. **Faculty:** 124 total (83 full time), 26 with doctorates or other terminal degrees. **Location:** Rural campus in small town; 120 miles from Lexington. **Calendar:** Semester, limited summer session. Saturday and extensive evening/early morning classes. **Microcomputers:** 40 located in computer centers. **Special facilities:** Art gallery. **Additional facts:** Off-campus site in Pikeville, Kentucky.

DEGREES OFFERED. AA, AS, AAS. 203 associate degrees awarded in 1992.

UNDERGRADUATE MAJORS. Accounting, accounting technology, business administration and management, liberal/general studies, management information systems, nursing, real estate.

ACADEMIC PROGRAMS. 2-year transfer program, cooperative education, independent study, telecourses. **Remedial services:** Learning center, remedial instruction, tutoring. **Placement/credit:** AP, CLEP General and Subject, institutional tests; 36 credit hours maximum for associate degree.

ACADEMIC REQUIREMENTS. Freshmen must earn minimum GPA of 2.0 to continue in good standing. 55% of freshmen return for sophomore year. Students must declare major on application. **Graduation requirements:** 60 hours for associate. Most students required to take courses in English, history, humanities, mathematics, biological/physical sciences, social sciences.

FRESHMAN ADMISSIONS. Selection criteria: Open admissions. Restricted admission to nursing program. **High school preparation:** 20 units recommended. Recommended units include English 4, mathematics 3, social science 2 and science 2. **Test requirements:** ACT for placement and counseling only; score report by August 15.

1992 FRESHMAN CLASS PROFILE. 261 men, 396 women enrolled. **Characteristics:** 99% from in state, 100% commute, 1% have minority backgrounds. Average age is 22.

FALL-TERM APPLICATIONS. No fee. No closing date; applicants notified on a rolling basis. Early admission available. Must have completed junior year of high school prior to enrolling full-time; may audit courses if junior or sophomore, except English 101/102.

STUDENT LIFE. Activities: Student government, student newspaper, choral groups, concert band, dance, drama, Baptist Student Union, Caucus Club, Phi Theta Kappa.

ATHLETICS. Intramural: Archery, badminton, basketball, bowling, football, softball, table tennis, tennis, volleyball.

STUDENT SERVICES. Career counseling, freshman orientation, personal counseling, placement service for graduates, veterans counselor, services/facilities for handicapped.

ANNUAL EXPENSES. Tuition and fees (projected): $840, $1,680 additional for out-of-state students. **Books and supplies:** $450. **Other expenses:** $2,808.

FINANCIAL AID. 60% of freshmen, 70% of continuing students receive some form of aid. All aid based on need. Academic scholarships available. **Aid applications:** No closing date; priority given to applications received by April 1; applicants notified on a rolling basis beginning on or about July 15; must reply within 10 days.

ADDRESS/TELEPHONE. Gia Rae Hall, Admissions Officer/Registrar, Prestonburg Community College, 1 Bert T. Combs Drive, Prestonburg, KY 41653. (606) 886-3863. Fax: (606) 886-2677.

RETS Electronic Institute
Louisville, Kentucky — CB code: 0305

2-year proprietary technical college, coed. Founded in 1974. **Undergraduate enrollment:** 495 men, 48 women full time. **Faculty:** 22 total (21 full time). **Location:** Suburban campus in large city. **Calendar:** Trimester.

DEGREES OFFERED. AS. 200 associate degrees awarded in 1992. 100% in engineering technologies.

UNDERGRADUATE MAJORS. Electronic technology.

ACADEMIC PROGRAMS. Remedial services: Tutoring. **Placement/credit:** 16 hours of credit by Engineering Technologies CLEP examination may be counted toward associate degree.

ACADEMIC REQUIREMENTS. Freshmen must earn minimum GPA of 2.0 to continue in good standing. 85% of freshmen return for sophomore year. Students must declare major on application. **Graduation requirements:** 90 hours for associate (90 in major).

FRESHMAN ADMISSIONS. Selection criteria: Open admissions.

1992 FRESHMAN CLASS PROFILE. 128 men, 10 women enrolled. **Characteristics:** 99% from in state, 100% commute, 7% have minority backgrounds. Average age is 22.

FALL-TERM APPLICATIONS. $165 fee. No closing date; applicants notified on a rolling basis. Interview required.

STUDENT LIFE. Housing: Apartment housing available. **Activities:** Fraternities.

ATHLETICS. Intercollegiate: Basketball M, softball M.

STUDENT SERVICES. Career counseling, personal counseling, placement service for graduates, services/facilities for handicapped.

ANNUAL EXPENSES. Tuition and fees (1992-93): $6,065. **Other expenses:** $896.

FINANCIAL AID. 85% of freshmen, 80% of continuing students receive some form of aid. All grants, 99% of loans, all jobs based on need. **Aid applications:** No closing date; applicants notified on a rolling basis; must reply by registration.

ADDRESS/TELEPHONE. Dwealt H. Martin, Director of Admissions, RETS Electronic Institute, 4146 Outer Loop, Louisville, KY 40219. (502) 968-7191. Fax: (502) 968-1727.

St. Catharine College
St. Catharine, Kentucky — CB code: 1690

2-year private junior, liberal arts college, coed, affiliated with Roman Catholic Church. Founded in 1931. **Accreditation:** Regional. **Undergraduate enrollment:** 83 men, 139 women full time; 37 men, 94 women part time. **Location:** Rural campus in small town; 60 miles from Louisville and Lexington. **Calendar:** Semester.

FRESHMAN ADMISSIONS. Selection criteria: Open admissions.

ANNUAL EXPENSES. Tuition and fees: $4,350. **Room and board:** $2,720. **Books and supplies:** $400. **Other expenses:** $900.

ADDRESS/TELEPHONE. Frank Sallee, Director of Admissions, St. Catharine College, Highway 150, St. Catharine, KY 40061. (606) 336-5082 ext. 223. Fax: (606) 336-5031.

Somerset Community College
Somerset, Kentucky — CB code: 1779

2-year public community college, coed. Founded in 1965. **Accreditation:** Regional. **Undergraduate enrollment:** 2,528 men and women. **Location:** Rural campus in large town; 80 miles south of Lexington. **Calendar:** Semester. **Additional facts:** One of 14 community colleges affiliated with University of Kentucky.

FRESHMAN ADMISSIONS. Selection criteria: Open admissions. Test scores and interview considered for limited enrollment programs. Selective admissions for out-of-state students.

ANNUAL EXPENSES. Tuition and fees (projected): $840, $1,680 additional for out-of-state students. **Books and supplies:** $450.

ADDRESS/TELEPHONE. Charles Hansel, Dean of Student Affairs, Somerset Community College, 808 Monticello Road, Somerset, KY 42501. (606) 679-8501 ext. 3209. Fax: (606) 679-5139.

Southeast Community College
Cumberland, Kentucky — CB code: 1770

2-year public community college, coed. Founded in 1960. **Accreditation:** Regional. **Undergraduate enrollment:** 495 men, 1,097 women full time; 270 men, 591 women part time. **Faculty:** 140 total (52 full time), 6 with doctorates or other terminal degrees. **Location:** Rural campus in small town; 150 miles from Lexington. **Calendar:** Semester, limited summer session. **Microcomputers:** Located in classrooms, computer centers. **Additional facts:** Branch campuses at Middlesboro and Whitesburg.

DEGREES OFFERED. AA, AS, AAS. 179 associate degrees awarded in 1992. 19% in business/office and marketing/distribution, 20% health sciences, 57% multi/interdisciplinary studies.

UNDERGRADUATE MAJORS. Business and management, business and office, business systems analysis, computer servicing technology, electrical/electronics/communications engineering, elementary education, finance, liberal/general studies, mining and petroleum technologies, nursing, secretarial and related programs.

ACADEMIC PROGRAMS. 2-year transfer program, cooperative education, dual enrollment of high school students, internships, telecourses. **Remedial services:** Learning center, preadmission summer program, reduced course load, remedial instruction, special counselor, tutoring. **Placement/credit:** AP, CLEP Subject, institutional tests.

ACADEMIC REQUIREMENTS. No policy requiring minimum GPA; records of students having academic difficulty are reviewed individually. 82% of freshmen return for sophomore year. Students must declare major by end of first year. **Graduation requirements:** 60 hours for associate (32 in major). Most students required to take courses in English, history, humanities, mathematics, biological/physical sciences, social sciences.

FRESHMAN ADMISSIONS. Selection criteria: Open admissions. Selective admissions to nursing program. **High school preparation:** 22 units recommended. Recommended units include biological science 1, English 4, mathematics 3, physical science 1 and social science 2. **Test requirements:** ACT for placement and counseling only; score report by August 15.

1992 FRESHMAN CLASS PROFILE. 174 men, 435 women enrolled. **Academic background:** Mid 50% of enrolled freshmen had ACT composite between 16-20. 75% submitted ACT scores. **Characteristics:** 96% from in state, 100% commute, 8% have minority backgrounds. Average age is 21.

FALL-TERM APPLICATIONS. No fee. No closing date; applicants notified on a rolling basis beginning on or about February 1. Interview required for nursing applicants. Early admission available.

STUDENT LIFE. Activities: Student government, student newspaper, choral groups, dance, drama, Christian Student Union, Black Student Union.

ATHLETICS. Intramural: Basketball, volleyball.

STUDENT SERVICES. Aptitude testing, career counseling, freshman orientation, personal counseling, placement service for graduates, veterans counselor, services/facilities for handicapped.

ANNUAL EXPENSES. Tuition and fees (1992-93): $840, $1,680 additional for out-of-state students. **Books and supplies:** $450. **Other expenses:** $425.

FINANCIAL AID. 70% of freshmen, 68% of continuing students receive some form of aid. 99% of grants, all loans, 81% of jobs based on need. Academic scholarships available. **Aid applications:** No closing date; priority given to applications received by April 15; applicants notified on a rolling basis beginning on or about May 1; must reply within 3 weeks.

ADDRESS/TELEPHONE. James Blair, Director of Admissions, Southeast Community College, 300 College Road, Cumberland, KY 40823. (606) 589-2145 ext. 40. Fax: (606) 589-2149.

Spalding University
Louisville, Kentucky CB code: 1552

4-year private university, coed, affiliated with Roman Catholic Church. Founded in 1814. **Accreditation:** Regional. **Undergraduate enrollment:** 58 men, 511 women full time; 51 men, 215 women part time. **Graduate enrollment:** 19 men, 34 women full time; 64 men, 189 women part time. **Faculty:** 107 total (72 full time), 58 with doctorates or other terminal degrees. **Location:** Urban campus in large city; in downtown area. **Calendar:** Semester, extensive summer session. **Microcomputers:** 50 located in dormitories, libraries, computer centers. **Special facilities:** Art gallery, historic Victorian mansion.

DEGREES OFFERED. AA, BA, BS, MA, MS, EdD. 3 associate degrees awarded in 1992. 100% in business and management. 127 bachelor's degrees awarded. 18% in business and management, 8% communications, 20% education, 34% health sciences, 7% social sciences. Graduate degrees offered in 10 major fields of study.

UNDERGRADUATE MAJORS. Associate: Business and management. **Bachelor's:** Biology, business and management, chemistry, communications, computer and information sciences, early childhood education, elementary education, English, history, liberal/general studies, library science, mathematics, nursing, philosophy, predentistry, prelaw, premedicine, prepharmacy, preveterinary, psychology, religion, secondary education, social work, sociology, studio art.

ACADEMIC PROGRAMS. Double major, dual enrollment of high school students, education specialist degree, independent study, internships, study abroad, teacher preparation, weekend college, cross-registration; liberal arts/career combination in health sciences. **Remedial services:** Learning center, reduced course load, remedial instruction, special counselor, tutoring. **ROTC:** Army. **Placement/credit:** AP, CLEP General and Subject, institutional tests; 16 credit hours maximum for associate degree; 32 credit hours maximum for bachelor's degree.

ACADEMIC REQUIREMENTS. Freshmen must earn minimum GPA of 2.0 to continue in good standing. 75% of freshmen return for sophomore year. Students must declare major by end of second year. **Graduation requirements:** 64 hours for associate (24 in major), 128 hours for bachelor's (38 in major). Most students required to take courses in arts/fine arts, computer science, English, history, mathematics, philosophy/religion, biological/physical sciences, social sciences.

FRESHMAN ADMISSIONS. Selection criteria: Class rank (top half), academic preparation, and SAT or ACT test scores. **High school preparation:** 16 units recommended. Recommended units include biological science 1, English 4, foreign language 2, mathematics 2, physical science 1 and social science 2. **Test requirements:** SAT or ACT; score report by August 15. Comprehensive Test of Basic Skills (CTBS).

1992 FRESHMAN CLASS PROFILE. 20 men, 90 women enrolled. 50% had high school GPA of 3.0 or higher, 45% between 2.0 and 2.99. 12% were in top tenth and 41% were in top quarter of graduating class. **Characteristics:** 91% from in state, 90% commute, 3% have minority backgrounds. Average age is 26.

FALL-TERM APPLICATIONS. $20 fee, may be waived for applicants with need. Closing date August 15; applicants notified on a rolling basis; must reply by June 1. Interview recommended. CRDA. Deferred and early admission available.

STUDENT LIFE. Housing: Dormitories (coed). **Activities:** Student government, magazine, student newspaper, choral groups, drama.

ATHLETICS. NAIA. **Intercollegiate:** Basketball. **Intramural:** Table tennis, volleyball.

STUDENT SERVICES. Career counseling, employment service for undergraduates, freshman orientation, health services, on-campus day care, personal counseling, placement service for graduates, special adviser for adult students, services/facilities for handicapped.

ANNUAL EXPENSES. Tuition and fees (1992-93): $7,295. **Room and board:** $2,400. **Books and supplies:** $265. **Other expenses:** $1,000.

FINANCIAL AID. 95% of freshmen, 93% of continuing students receive some form of aid. 92% of grants, 92% of loans, 98% of jobs based on need. Academic, music/drama, art, leadership, minority scholarships available. **Aid applications:** No closing date; priority given to applications received by March 15; applicants notified on a rolling basis beginning on or about March 31; must reply by May 1 or within 3 weeks if notified thereafter.

ADDRESS/TELEPHONE. Dorothy Allen, Director of Admissions, Spalding University, 851 South Fourth Street, Louisville, KY 40203. (502) 585-9911. Fax: (502) 585-0108.

Sue Bennett College
London, Kentucky CB code: 1741

4-year private junior college, coed, affiliated with United Methodist Church. Founded in 1897. **Accreditation:** Regional. **Undergraduate enrollment:** 131 men, 226 women full time; 23 men, 75 women part time. **Faculty:** 40 total (24 full time), 4 with doctorates or other terminal degrees. **Location:** Rural campus in large town; 70 miles from Lexington. **Calendar:** Semester, limited summer session. **Microcomputers:** 25 located in computer centers.

DEGREES OFFERED. AA, BA. 58 associate degrees awarded in 1992.

UNDERGRADUATE MAJORS. Associate: Accounting, allied health, American studies, biology, business administration and management, business and management, business and office, business education, chemistry, communications, communications research, community health work, computer and information sciences, elementary education, engineering, engineering and engineering-related technologies, English, English education, English literature, fine arts, foreign languages education, history, humanities and social sciences, information sciences and systems, legal assistant/paralegal, liberal/general studies, marriage and family counseling, mathematics, mathematics education, nursing, physical sciences, predentistry, prelaw, premedicine, prepharmacy, preveterinary, psychology, science education, secondary education, social science education, social sciences, social work, speech/communication/theater education. **Bachelor's:** Accounting, business administration and management, business and management, gerontology.

ACADEMIC PROGRAMS. 2-year transfer program, cooperative education, honors program, independent study, internships, teacher preparation, cross-registration. **Remedial services:** Learning center, reduced course load, remedial instruction, special counselor, tutoring. **Placement/credit:** CLEP General, institutional tests; 16 credit hours maximum for associate degree.

ACADEMIC REQUIREMENTS. Freshmen must earn minimum GPA of 2.0 to continue in good standing. 40% of freshmen return for sophomore year. **Graduation requirements:** 64 hours for associate, 128 hours for bachelor's. Most students required to take courses in arts/fine arts, English, history, humanities, mathematics, philosophy/religion, biological/physical sciences, social sciences. **Postgraduate studies:** 75% from 2-year programs enter 4-year programs.

FRESHMAN ADMISSIONS. Selection criteria: Open admissions. **Test requirements:** SAT or ACT (ACT preferred) for placement and counseling only; score report by August 1. Nelson-Denny Reading Test for placement.

1992 FRESHMAN CLASS PROFILE. 67 men, 106 women enrolled. **Characteristics:** 99% from in state, 12% live in college housing, 10% have minority backgrounds. Average age is 20.

FALL-TERM APPLICATIONS. $15 fee, may be waived for applicants with need. No closing date; applicants notified on a rolling basis. Interview recommended. Audition recommended for music applicants. Essay recommended for academic scholarship applicants applicants. Deferred and early admission available.

STUDENT LIFE. Housing: Dormitories (men, women). **Activities:** Student government, student newspaper, yearbook, news and yearbook photography staff, choral groups, dance, drama, music ensembles, Young Adults for Christ, Circle-K.

ATHLETICS. NAIA. **Intercollegiate:** Baseball M, basketball, cross-country, football M, golf, soccer, softball W, tennis, volleyball W. **Intramural:** Basketball, football M, softball, table tennis, tennis, volleyball.

STUDENT SERVICES. Aptitude testing, career counseling, freshman orientation, personal counseling, veterans counselor, services/facilities for handicapped.

ANNUAL EXPENSES. Tuition and fees: $4,800. **Room and board:** $3,580. **Books and supplies:** $500. **Other expenses:** $700.

FINANCIAL AID. 93% of freshmen, 85% of continuing students receive some form of aid. All aid based on need. **Aid applications:** No closing date; applicants notified on a rolling basis beginning on or about June 1; must reply by registration.

ADDRESS/TELEPHONE. Pamela Jarrett, Director of Admissions, Sue Bennett College, 151 College Street, London, KY 40741. (606) 864-2238 ext. 1113. Fax: (606) 864-2238 ext. 1198.

Sullivan College
Louisville, Kentucky CB code: 0811

4-year proprietary business, technical college, coed. Founded in 1962. **Accreditation:** Regional. **Undergraduate enrollment:** 384 men, 874 women full time; 188 men, 468 women part time. **Faculty:** 70 total (37 full time), 8 with doctorates or other terminal degrees. **Location:** Suburban campus in large city; 6 miles from downtown. **Calendar:** Quarter, extensive summer session. Saturday and extensive evening/early morning classes. **Microcomputers:** 75 located in libraries, classrooms. **Special facilities:** All students may use Lexis/Nexis on-line database for class assignments. **Additional facts:** Classes meet Monday to Thursday only; special program on Friday for additional help.

DEGREES OFFERED. AS, BS. 216 associate degrees awarded in 1992. 70% in business and management, 21% business/office and marketing/distribution, 9% computer sciences. 4 bachelor's degrees awarded. 100% in business and management.

UNDERGRADUATE MAJORS. Associate: Accounting, business and management, business and office, business data processing and related programs, business data programming, computer programming, food management, food production/management/services, hospitality management, hotel/motel and restaurant management, legal assistant/paralegal, legal secretary, marketing and distribution, office supervision and management, secretarial and related programs, tourism. **Bachelor's:** Accounting, business and management, computer and information sciences, marketing and distribution.

ACADEMIC PROGRAMS. 2-year transfer program, accelerated program, double major, independent study, internships. **Remedial services:** Reduced course load, remedial instruction, tutoring. **Placement/credit:** Institutional tests.

ACADEMIC REQUIREMENTS. Freshmen must earn minimum GPA of 1.8 to continue in good standing. 60% of freshmen return for sophomore year. Students must declare major on application. **Graduation requirements:** 95 hours for associate, 181 hours for bachelor's. Most students required to take courses in arts/fine arts, computer science, English, history, humanities, mathematics, philosophy/religion, biological/physical sciences, social sciences. **Postgraduate studies:** 10% from 2-year programs enter 4-year programs.

FRESHMAN ADMISSIONS. Selection criteria: Test scores, interview, high school record considered. **Test requirements:** SAT or ACT. ACT Career Programs Assessment test required for placement. Reading and English comprehension tests required of paralegal applicants.

1992 FRESHMAN CLASS PROFILE. 437 men and women enrolled. **Characteristics:** 89% from in state, 90% commute, 26% have minority backgrounds.

FALL-TERM APPLICATIONS. $100 fee. Closing date October 1; applicants notified on a rolling basis. Interview required. Deferred admission available.

STUDENT LIFE. Housing: Apartment housing available. **Activities:** Student government, student newspaper, choral groups, pep band, sororities, Baptist Student Union, national student business organization, women's service organization, minority student affairs organization.

ATHLETICS. NJCAA, NSCAA. **Intercollegiate:** Basketball, bowling, golf. **Intramural:** Basketball, bowling, golf, softball, tennis, volleyball.

STUDENT SERVICES. Aptitude testing, career counseling, employment service for undergraduates, freshman orientation, personal counseling, placement service for graduates, special adviser for adult students, veterans counselor, services/facilities for handicapped.

ANNUAL EXPENSES. Tuition and fees (1992-93): Tuition, fees and per-credit-hour charges vary by program. $8,640 tuition for 12-month business programs; $6,480 tuition for 9-month business programs. Somewhat higher for hospitality-related programs. **Room and board:** $2,610 room only. **Books and supplies:** $600. **Other expenses:** $1,143.

FINANCIAL AID. 87% of freshmen, 87% of continuing students receive some form of aid. 99% of grants, 71% of loans, all jobs based on need. 250 enrolled freshmen were judged to have need, 235 were offered aid. Academic, athletic scholarships available. **Aid applications:** No closing date; priority given to applications received by September 24; applicants notified on a rolling basis.

ADDRESS/TELEPHONE. James P. Crick, Director of Admissions, Sullivan College, PO Box 33308, 3101 Bardstown Road, Louisville, KY 40232. (502) 456-6504. (800) 844-1354. Fax: (502) 454-4880.

Thomas More College
Crestview Hills, Kentucky — CB code: 1876

4-year private liberal arts college, coed, affiliated with Roman Catholic Church. Founded in 1921. **Accreditation:** Regional. **Undergraduate enrollment:** 1,300 men and women. **Faculty:** 110 total (60 full time), 33 with doctorates or other terminal degrees. **Location:** Suburban campus in small town; 8 miles from Cincinnati, Ohio. **Calendar:** Semester, extensive summer session. Saturday and extensive evening/early morning classes. **Microcomputers:** Located in computer centers. **Special facilities:** Art gallery, sports country club.

DEGREES OFFERED. AA, BA, BS. 88 associate degrees awarded in 1992. 55% in business and management, 5% computer sciences, 8% law, 10% mathematics, 10% physical sciences, 6% psychology. 139 bachelor's degrees awarded. 40% in business and management, 6% computer sciences, 6% teacher education, 5% allied health, 12% physical sciences, 9% psychology, 12% social sciences.

UNDERGRADUATE MAJORS. Associate: Accounting, business administration and management, business and management, business economics, chemistry, communications, computer and information sciences, criminal justice studies, data processing, dramatic arts, economics, English, exercise science, gerontology, history, humanities and social sciences, international studies, law enforcement and corrections, mathematics, philosophy, physics, political science and government, prelaw, psychology, religion, sociology, studio art, theological studies. **Bachelor's:** Accounting, American studies, art education, biology, business administration and management, business and management, business economics, business education, chemistry, clinical laboratory science, communications, computer and information sciences, criminal justice studies, data processing, dramatic arts, economics, education, elementary education, English, English education, history, humanities and social sciences, insurance and risk management, international studies, junior high education, law enforcement and corrections, liberal/general studies, mathematics, mathematics education, medical laboratory technologies, nursing, philosophy, physics, predentistry, preengineering, prelaw, premedicine, prepharmacy, preveterinary, psychology, religion, science education, secondary education, social science education, sociology, studio art, theological studies.

ACADEMIC PROGRAMS. Accelerated program, cooperative education, double major, dual enrollment of high school students, honors program, internships, teacher preparation, weekend college, cross-registration; liberal arts/career combination in engineering, health sciences. **Remedial services:** Learning center, preadmission summer program, reduced course load, remedial instruction, special counselor, tutoring. **ROTC:** Air Force, Army. **Placement/credit:** AP, CLEP General and Subject, institutional tests; 30 credit hours maximum for bachelor's degree.

ACADEMIC REQUIREMENTS. Freshmen must earn minimum GPA of 1.75 to continue in good standing. 75% of freshmen return for sophomore year. Students must declare major by end of second year. **Graduation requirements:** 64 hours for associate, 128 hours for bachelor's. Most students required to take courses in arts/fine arts, English, foreign languages, history, philosophy/religion, biological/physical sciences, social sciences. **Postgraduate studies:** 95% from 2-year programs enter 4-year programs.

FRESHMAN ADMISSIONS. Selection criteria: Rank in top half of graduating class, 2.0 GPA (admissions based on college-preparatory curriculum), and ACT composite score of 20 with at least 20 English score, or SAT combined score of 900 with at least 450 verbal score important. **High school preparation:** 16 units recommended. Recommended units include English 4, foreign language 2, mathematics 2, social science 2 and science 2. **Test requirements:** SAT or ACT; score report by August 15. **Additional information:** Test scores required prior to registration.

1992 FRESHMAN CLASS PROFILE. 265 men and women enrolled. 78% had high school GPA of 3.0 or higher, 22% between 2.0 and 2.99. **Academic background:** Mid 50% of enrolled freshmen had ACT composite between 18-24. 90% submitted ACT scores. **Characteristics:** 67% from in state, 75% commute. Average age is 18.

FALL-TERM APPLICATIONS. $15 fee, may be waived for applicants with need. Closing date September 1; priority given to applications received by August 15; applicants notified on a rolling basis. Essay recommended for special admissions applicants. CRDA. Deferred and early admission available.

STUDENT LIFE. Housing: Dormitories (men, women, coed). **Activities:** Student government, student newspaper, yearbook, student literary magazine, drama, fraternities, sororities, Youth for Life, campus ministry.

ATHLETICS. NCAA. **Intercollegiate:** Baseball M, basketball, football M, soccer, softball W, tennis, volleyball W. **Intramural:** Baseball M, basketball M, bowling, cross-country M, racquetball, soccer, softball, table tennis, tennis M, track and field, volleyball.

STUDENT SERVICES. Aptitude testing, career counseling, employment service for undergraduates, freshman orientation, health services, personal counseling, placement service for graduates, special adviser for adult students, services/facilities for handicapped.

ANNUAL EXPENSES. Tuition and fees (1992-93): $8,455. **Room and board:** $3,600. **Books and supplies:** $400. **Other expenses:** $500.

FINANCIAL AID. 70% of freshmen, 65% of continuing students receive some form of aid. 43% of grants, 96% of loans, all jobs based on need. Academic, music/drama, art, leadership scholarships available. **Aid applications:** No closing date; priority given to applications received by March 1; applicants notified on a rolling basis beginning on or about April 15; must reply within 2 weeks.

ADDRESS/TELEPHONE. Victoria Thompson-Campbell, Director of Admissions, Thomas More College, Thomas More Parkway, Crestview Hills, KY 41017. (606) 344-3332 ext. 3327. (800) 825-4557.

Transylvania University
Lexington, Kentucky — CB code: 1808

Admissions: 95% of applicants accepted
Based on:
- ••• Essay, interview, school record, test scores
- •• Activities, recommendations
- • Religious affiliation/commitment, special talents

Completion: 80% of freshmen end year in good standing
70% graduate, 45% of these enter graduate study

4-year private liberal arts college, coed, affiliated with Christian Church (Disciples of Christ). Founded in 1780. **Accreditation:** Regional. **Undergraduate enrollment:** 399 men, 500 women full time; 34 men, 41 women part time. **Faculty:** 98 total (63 full time), 63 with doctorates or other terminal degrees. **Location:** Urban campus in small city; 80 miles from Louisville, 80 miles from Cincinnati, Ohio. **Calendar:** 4-4-1, limited summer session. **Microcomputers:** 180 located in dormitories, libraries, classrooms. **Special facilities:** Museum of early scientific apparatus, special library collections of early medical and scientific works, and Kentucky books, Morlan Art Gallery.

DEGREES OFFERED. BA. 208 bachelor's degrees awarded in 1992. 24% in business and management, 5% computer sciences, 8% teacher education, 18% life sciences, 12% psychology, 14% social sciences.

UNDERGRADUATE MAJORS. Anthropology, art education, biology, business and management, chemistry, computer and information sciences, dramatic arts, early childhood education, economics, elementary education, English, English education, foreign languages education, French, history, junior high education, mathematics, mathematics education, music education, music performance, philosophy, physical education, physics, political science and government, preengineering, psychology, religion, science education, secondary education, social science education, sociology, sociology/anthropology, Spanish, studio art.

ACADEMIC PROGRAMS. Double major, independent study, internships, student-designed major, study abroad, teacher preparation, visiting/exchange student program, Washington semester; liberal arts/career combination in engineering. **Remedial services:** Writing laboratory. **ROTC:** Air Force, Army. **Placement/credit:** AP, CLEP Subject.

ACADEMIC REQUIREMENTS. Freshmen must earn minimum GPA of 1.75 to continue in good standing. 78% of freshmen return for sophomore year. Students must declare major by end of second year. **Graduation requirements:** 144 hours for bachelor's (48 in major). Most students required to take courses in arts/fine arts, English, foreign languages, history, humanities, mathematics, biological/physical sciences, social sciences. **Postgraduate studies:** 9% enter law school, 8% enter medical school, 8% enter MBA programs, 20% enter other graduate study.

FRESHMAN ADMISSIONS. Selection criteria: Rigor of high school curriculum most important. Minimum 2.25 GPA, 840 SAT, 21 ACT. Academic recommendations required and extracurricular activities considered. Interview recommended for marginal students. **High school preparation:** 12 units required. Required and recommended units include English 4, mathematics 3, social science 2 and science 2. Foreign language 2 recommended. Broad high school curriculum important to allow full participation in required liberal arts course work. Solid background in English highly recommended. **Test requirements:** SAT or ACT; score report by June 1. **Additional information:** Early Decision application deadline for first-choice decision is November 1; notification by December 1.

1992 FRESHMAN CLASS PROFILE. 326 men applied, 302 accepted, 106 enrolled; 450 women applied, 436 accepted, 149 enrolled. 76% had high school GPA of 3.0 or higher, 23% between 2.0 and 2.99. 61% were in top tenth and 78% were in top quarter of graduating class. **Academic background:** Mid 50% of enrolled freshmen had SAT-V between 490-620, SAT-M between 530-650; ACT composite between 23-30. 65% submitted SAT scores, 93% submitted ACT scores. **Characteristics:** 75% from in state, 87% live in college housing, 6% have minority backgrounds, 1% are foreign students, 68% join fraternities/sororities. Average age is 18.

FALL-TERM APPLICATIONS. $20 fee, may be waived for applicants with need. Closing date June 1; priority given to applications received by March 15; applicants notified on or about April 15; must reply by May 1. Audition required for music and drama scholarships applicants. Portfolio required for art scholarships applicants. Essay required. Interview recommended. CRDA. Deferred and early admission available. EDP-F. Applications received after March 15 considered on an individual basis.

STUDENT LIFE. Housing: Dormitories (men, women, coed); apartment housing available. Rosenthal Complex (with handicapped facilities in two apartments) and honors houses provide efficiency apartment option for upperclassmen. 24 suites (2 rooms with common bath) available. **Activities:** Student government, magazine, radio, student newspaper, yearbook, choral groups, concert band, drama, jazz band, music ensembles, pep band, fraternities, sororities, Intercultural Awareness Group, Amnesty International, Environmental Awareness Group, Democrats on Campus, Transylvania College Republicans, Transy Line of Care (TLC), Fellowship of Christian Athletes, Bacchus, Taylortown Tutors, Transylvania University Community Action Network. **Additional information:** All students allowed registered automobiles on campus. Greek members all live in residence halls and have their chapter rooms there.

ATHLETICS. NAIA. **Intercollegiate:** Basketball, diving, field hockey W, golf M, soccer M, softball W, swimming, tennis. **Intramural:** Archery, badminton, basketball, bowling, cross-country M, golf M, racquetball, softball, swimming, table tennis, tennis, track and field, volleyball.

STUDENT SERVICES. Aptitude testing, career counseling, employment service for undergraduates, freshman orientation, health services, personal counseling, veterans counselor, services/facilities for handicapped.

ANNUAL EXPENSES. Tuition and fees: $10,670. **Room and board:** $4,300. **Books and supplies:** $500. **Other expenses:** $800.

FINANCIAL AID. 94% of freshmen, 82% of continuing students receive some form of aid. 14% of grants, 97% of loans, 72% of jobs based on need. 220 enrolled freshmen were judged to have need, all were offered aid. Academic, music/drama, art, athletic, leadership, religious affiliation, minority scholarships available. **Aid applications:** Closing date August 1; priority given to applications received by March 15; applicants notified on a rolling basis beginning on or about March 1; must reply by May 1. **Additional information:** Auditions and portfolios required for music and art scholarships respectively. Essays required for other scholarship programs.

ADDRESS/TELEPHONE. Thomas Nowack, Director of Enrollment Mgmnt, Transylvania University, 300 North Broadway, Lexington, KY 40508-1797. (606) 233-8242. (800) 872-6798. Fax: (606) 233-8797.

Union College
Barbourville, Kentucky — CB code: 1825

Admissions: 76% of applicants accepted
Based on:
- ••• School record
- •• Activities, test scores
- • Essay, interview, recommendations, religious affiliation/commitment, special talents

Completion: 83% of freshmen end year in good standing
53% graduate, 30% of these enter graduate study

4-year private liberal arts college, coed, affiliated with United Methodist Church. Founded in 1879. **Accreditation:** Regional. **Undergraduate enrollment:** 337 men, 301 women full time; 36 men, 65 women part time. **Graduate enrollment:** 3 men, 7 women full time; 73 men, 177 women part time. **Faculty:** 66 total (54 full time), 31 with doctorates or other terminal degrees. **Location:** Rural campus in small town; 95 miles from Lexington and from Knoxville, Tennessee. **Calendar:** Semester, extensive summer session. Extensive evening/early morning classes. **Microcomputers:** 55 located in libraries, classrooms, computer centers. **Special facilities:** Conway Boatman Chapel, greenhouse, Abraham Lincoln library collection, US government depository.

DEGREES OFFERED. AA, BA, BS, MEd. 3 associate degrees awarded in 1992. 67% in business and management, 33% computer sciences. 124 bachelor's degrees awarded. 30% in business and management, 33% teacher education, 5% letters/literature, 10% psychology, 11% social sciences. Graduate degrees offered in 6 major fields of study.

UNDERGRADUATE MAJORS. Associate: Accounting, business administration and management, computer and information sciences, information sciences and systems, law enforcement and corrections, office supervision and management, teacher aide. **Bachelor's:** Accounting, biology, business administration and management, business education, chemistry, computer and information sciences, criminology, dramatic arts, elementary education, English, English education, history, journalism, junior high education, law enforcement and corrections, mathematics, mathematics education, music, music business management, music education, music performance, office supervision and management, physical education, physics, political science and government, predentistry, preengineering, prelaw, premedicine, prepharmacy, preveterinary, psychology, religion, religious education, religious music, science education, secondary education, social studies education, sociology.

ACADEMIC PROGRAMS. 2-year transfer program, double major, dual enrollment of high school students, independent study, internships, student-designed major, study abroad, teacher preparation; liberal arts/career combination in engineering, health sciences. **Remedial services:** Learning center, reduced course load, remedial instruction, special counselor, tutoring. **ROTC:** Army. **Placement/credit:** AP, CLEP General and Subject, institutional tests; 30 credit hours maximum for bachelor's degree.

ACADEMIC REQUIREMENTS. Freshmen must earn minimum GPA of 1.8 to continue in good standing. 68% of freshmen return for sophomore year. Students must declare major by end of second year. **Graduation requirements:** 64 hours for associate (30 in major), 128 hours for bachelor's (30 in major). Most students required to take courses in arts/fine arts, computer science, English, history, humanities, mathematics, philosophy/religion, biological/physical sciences, social sciences. **Postgraduate studies:** 66% from 2-year programs enter 4-year programs. 3% enter law school, 3% enter medical school, 6% enter MBA programs, 18% enter other graduate study. **Additional information:** Appalachian Studies Program, including Appalachian Semester and Environmental Studies of the Region.

FRESHMAN ADMISSIONS. Selection criteria: School achievement record, caliber of course work, class rank, SAT or ACT scores, and interview should confirm potential for academic achievement and for positive contribution to college community; special consideration given to out-of-state applicants. **High school preparation:** 20 units recommended. Required and recommended units include biological science 1, English 4, mathematics 3, physical science 1 and social science 3. Foreign language 1 recommended. ACT test must be taken for the education program. **Test requirements:** SAT or ACT (ACT preferred); score report by August 25.

1992 FRESHMAN CLASS PROFILE. 442 men applied, 314 accepted, 108 enrolled; 248 women applied, 212 accepted, 93 enrolled. 35% had high school GPA of 3.0 or higher, 62% between 2.0 and 2.99. **Characteristics:** 69% from in state, 69% live in college housing, 14% have minority backgrounds, 1% are foreign students. Average age is 19.

FALL-TERM APPLICATIONS. $20 fee, may be waived for applicants

with need. Closing date August 20; priority given to applications received by July 1; applicants notified on a rolling basis; must reply by June 1. Audition required for music applicants. Portfolio required. Interview recommended. CRDA. Deferred and early admission available. Permission of secondary school principal required.

STUDENT LIFE. Housing: Dormitories (men, women); apartment housing available. **Activities:** Student government, student newspaper, yearbook, choral groups, dance, drama, jazz band, music ensembles, pep band, 21 student groups, including Fellowship of Christian Athletes, Appalachian Wilderness Club, drama, science, philosophy societies, several service organizations, Baptist Student Union, Methodist Student Organizations, Newman Club, Student Ambassadors, Academic Team. **Additional information:** Religious counseling/advising available.

ATHLETICS. NAIA. **Intercollegiate:** Baseball M, basketball, cross-country, diving, football M, golf M, soccer, softball W, swimming, tennis, track and field, volleyball W. **Intramural:** Basketball, softball, swimming, table tennis, tennis, track and field, volleyball.

STUDENT SERVICES. Aptitude testing, career counseling, employment service for undergraduates, freshman orientation, personal counseling, placement service for graduates, special adviser for adult students, veterans counselor, services/facilities for handicapped.

ANNUAL EXPENSES. Tuition and fees: $7,000. **Room and board:** $2,790. **Books and supplies:** $500. **Other expenses:** $600.

FINANCIAL AID. 85% of freshmen, 89% of continuing students receive some form of aid. 84% of grants, 98% of loans, 95% of jobs based on need. 152 enrolled freshmen were judged to have need, all were offered aid. Academic, music/drama, athletic, leadership, alumni affiliation, religious affiliation scholarships available. **Aid applications:** No closing date; priority given to applications received by April 1; applicants notified on a rolling basis beginning on or about May 1; must reply within 2 weeks.

ADDRESS/TELEPHONE. Donald Hapward, Dean of Admissions, Union College, 310 College Street, Barbourville, KY 40906. (606) 546-4223. (800) 489-8646. Fax: (606) 546-2215.

University of Kentucky
Lexington, Kentucky CB code: 1837

Admissions: 76% of applicants accepted
Based on:
••• School record, test scores
•• Activities
• Essay, special talents
Completion: 75% of freshmen end year in good standing
42% graduate

4-year public university, coed. Founded in 1865. **Accreditation:** Regional. **Undergraduate enrollment:** 7,421 men, 7,324 women full time; 1,124 men, 1,598 women part time. **Graduate enrollment:** 2,325 men, 1,678 women full time; 1,128 men, 1,576 women part time. **Faculty:** 2,081 total (1,658 full time), 1,600 with doctorates or other terminal degrees. **Location:** Urban campus in small city; 80 miles from Louisville; 70 miles from Cincinnati, Ohio. **Calendar:** Semester, limited summer session. **Microcomputers:** 250 located in dormitories, libraries, classrooms, computer centers. **Special facilities:** Center for the arts, Van de Graaff accelerator, equine research center, center for the humanities.

DEGREES OFFERED. BA, BS, BFA, BArch, MA, MS, MBA, MFA, MEd, MSW, PhD, EdD, DMD, MD, B. Pharm, Pharm D, JD. 2,859 bachelor's degrees awarded in 1992. 16% in business and management, 6% business/office and marketing/distribution, 9% communications, 7% education, 8% engineering, 7% health sciences, 5% allied health, 5% home economics, 5% psychology, 8% social sciences. Graduate degrees offered in 105 major fields of study.

UNDERGRADUATE MAJORS. Accounting, advertising, agricultural economics, agricultural education, agricultural engineering, agricultural production, agronomy, animal sciences, anthropology, architecture, art education, art history, arts management, biology, botany, business administration and management, business economics, business education, chemical engineering, chemistry, civil engineering, classics, clinical laboratory science, communications, community health work, computer and information sciences, dramatic arts, economics, education of the emotionally handicapped, education of the mentally handicapped, electrical/electronics/communications engineering, elementary education, English, English education, entomology, family/consumer resource management, finance, food management, food science and nutrition, food sciences, foreign languages education, forestry and related sciences, French, geography, geology, German, health care administration, health education, history, home economics education, horticultural science, horticulture, hotel/motel and restaurant management, human environment and housing, individual and family development, industrial arts education, information sciences and systems, interior design, Italian, journalism, junior high education, labor/industrial relations, landscape architecture, Latin American studies, liberal/general studies, library science, linguistics, management science, marketing and distribution, marketing and distributive education, marketing management, materials engineering, mathematics, mathematics education, mechanical engineering, medical laboratory technologies, microbiology, mining and mineral engineering, music, music education, music performance, nursing, personnel management, pharmacy, philosophy, physical education, physical therapy, physician's assistant, physics, political science and government, poultry, psychology, radiograph medical technology, recreation and community services technologies, Russian, Russian and Slavic studies, science education, social studies education, social work, sociology, Spanish, specific learning disabilities, speech, speech correction, speech pathology/audiology, speech/communication/theater education, studio art, telecommunications, textiles and clothing, topical major, visual and performing arts, zoology.

ACADEMIC PROGRAMS. Accelerated program, cooperative education, double major, dual enrollment of high school students, education specialist degree, honors program, independent study, internships, student-designed major, study abroad, teacher preparation, telecourses, visiting/exchange student program, weekend college; combined bachelor's/graduate program in business administration. **Remedial services:** Learning center, reduced course load, special counselor, tutoring, writing center. **ROTC:** Air Force, Army. **Placement/credit:** AP, CLEP General and Subject, IB, institutional tests.

ACADEMIC REQUIREMENTS. Freshmen must earn minimum GPA of 2.0 to continue in good standing. 76% of freshmen return for sophomore year. Students must declare major by end of second year. **Graduation requirements:** 120 hours for bachelor's. Most students required to take courses in English, foreign languages, history, humanities, mathematics, biological/physical sciences, social sciences.

FRESHMAN ADMISSIONS. Selection criteria: Test scores and GPA should indicate potential for academic success. Required course work and extracurricular activities also considered. **High school preparation:** 11 units required. Required and recommended units include biological science 1, English 4, mathematics 3-4, physical science 1 and social science 2. Foreign language 2 recommended. Social science units should include US history and world civilization. One fine arts also recommended. 2 sciences must be chosen from biology, chemistry, and physics. **Test requirements:** SAT or ACT; score report by June 1. Architectural School Aptitude Test required for architecture applicants for admission. **Additional information:** Students out of high school 2 years or more with no college credit admitted on probationary basis.

1992 FRESHMAN CLASS PROFILE. 3,270 men applied, 2,498 accepted, 1,188 enrolled; 3,690 women applied, 2,767 accepted, 1,379 enrolled. 74% had high school GPA of 3.0 or higher, 26% between 2.0 and 2.99. **Academic background:** Mid 50% of enrolled freshmen had ACT composite between 22-27. 87% submitted ACT scores. **Characteristics:** 84% from in state, 90% live in college housing, 11% have minority backgrounds, 1% are foreign students, 17% join fraternities/sororities. Average age is 18.

FALL-TERM APPLICATIONS. $15 fee, may be waived for applicants with need. Closing date June 1; priority given to applications received by February 15; applicants notified on a rolling basis beginning on or about November 1; must reply by May 1 or within 2 weeks if notified thereafter. Audition required for music applicants. CRDA. Early admission available.

STUDENT LIFE. Housing: Dormitories (men, women, coed); apartment, fraternity, sorority, handicapped housing available. Students not required to live on campus. On-campus apartments available. **Activities:** Student government, magazine, radio, student newspaper, television, yearbook, choral groups, concert band, dance, drama, jazz band, marching band, music ensembles, musical theater, opera, pep band, symphony orchestra, fraternities, sororities, Baha'i, Baptist Student Union, Canterbury Fellowship, Hillel Foundation, Newman Center, Wesley Foundation, student government association, more than 250 organized student clubs.

ATHLETICS. NCAA. **Intercollegiate:** Baseball M, basketball, cross-country, diving, football M, golf, gymnastics W, rifle, soccer, swimming, tennis, track and field, volleyball W. **Intramural:** Archery, badminton, basketball, bowling, cross-country, fencing, field hockey W, golf, handball, ice hockey M, lacrosse, racquetball, rugby M, skiing, soccer, softball, squash, swimming, table tennis, tennis, track and field, volleyball, wrestling M.

STUDENT SERVICES. Aptitude testing, career counseling, employment service for undergraduates, freshman orientation, health services, personal counseling, placement service for graduates, special adviser for adult students, veterans counselor, services/facilities for handicapped.

ANNUAL EXPENSES. Tuition and fees (projected): $2,290, $3,920 additional for out-of-state students. **Room and board:** $4,190. **Books and supplies:** $450. **Other expenses:** $850.

FINANCIAL AID. 48% of freshmen, 52% of continuing students receive some form of aid. 39% of grants, 90% of loans, all jobs based on need. Academic, music/drama, art, athletic, alumni affiliation, minority scholarships available. **Aid applications:** No closing date; priority given to applications received by April 1; applicants notified on a rolling basis beginning on or about June 1; must reply within 3 weeks.

ADDRESS/TELEPHONE. Dr. Joseph L. Fink, III, Associate Vice Chancellor of Administration, University of Kentucky, 100 Funkhouser Building, Lexington, KY 40506-0054. (606) 257-2000. Fax: (606) 257-3823.

University of Louisville

Louisville, Kentucky CB code: 1838

Admissions: 71% of applicants accepted
Based on: ••• School record, test scores
• Activities, essay, recommendations, special talents
Completion: 24% graduate, 49% of these enter graduate study

4-year public university, coed. Founded in 1798. **Accreditation:** Regional. **Undergraduate enrollment:** 5,052 men, 5,300 women full time; 3,008 men, 3,621 women part time. **Graduate enrollment:** 688 men, 731 women full time; 943 men, 1,446 women part time. **Faculty:** 1,710 total (1,184 full time). **Location:** Urban campus in large city; 92 miles from Cincinnati, Ohio, 110 miles from Indianapolis, Indiana. **Calendar:** Semester, extensive summer session. Saturday and extensive evening/early morning classes. **Microcomputers:** Located in classrooms, computer centers. **Special facilities:** J. B. Speed Art Museum, Rauch Memorial Planetarium, computer-aided engineering building with robotics laboratory.

DEGREES OFFERED. AA, AAS, BA, BS, BFA, MA, MS, MBA, MFA, MEd, MSW, PhD, EdD, DDS, MD. 153 associate degrees awarded in 1992. 9% in computer sciences, 21% engineering technologies, 8% health sciences, 23% allied health, 23% law, 9% multi/interdisciplinary studies. 1,951 bachelor's degrees awarded. 26% in business and management, 6% communications, 15% education, 9% engineering, 6% health sciences, 5% life sciences, 5% psychology, 8% social sciences. Graduate degrees offered in 66 major fields of study.

UNDERGRADUATE MAJORS. Associate: Clinical laboratory science, data processing, dental hygiene, electrical technology, health sciences, labor/industrial relations, law enforcement and corrections technologies, legal assistant/paralegal, liberal/general studies, mechanical design technology, office supervision and management, radiograph medical technology, respiratory therapy technology, trade and industrial supervision and management. **Bachelor's:** Accounting, Afro-American (black) studies, American studies, anthropology, art history, biology, botany, business administration and management, business economics, chemical engineering, chemistry, civil engineering, clinical laboratory science, communications, computer engineering, cytotechnology, dental hygiene, dramatic arts, economics, electrical/electronics/communications engineering, elementary education, English, finance, food science and nutrition, French, geography, geology, German, health education, health sciences, history, humanities and social sciences, industrial engineering, information sciences and systems, interior design, junior high education, law enforcement and corrections, liberal/general studies, linguistics, marketing management, mathematics, mechanical engineering, medical laboratory technologies, music education, music history and appreciation, music performance, music theory and composition, nuclear medical technology, nursing, parks and recreation management, philosophy, physical education, physical therapy, physics, political science and government, psychology, respiratory therapy technology, Russian, Russian and Slavic studies, secretarial and related programs, sociology, Spanish, speech, student counseling and personnel services, studio art, systems analysis, trade and industrial education, urban studies, zoology.

ACADEMIC PROGRAMS. Accelerated program, cooperative education, double major, dual enrollment of high school students, education specialist degree, honors program, independent study, internships, student-designed major, study abroad, teacher preparation, visiting/exchange student program, weekend college, cross-registration; liberal arts/career combination in health sciences. **Remedial services:** Learning center, preadmission summer program, reduced course load, remedial instruction, special counselor, tutoring. **ROTC:** Air Force, Army. **Placement/credit:** AP, CLEP Subject, institutional tests; 24 credit hours maximum for bachelor's degree.

ACADEMIC REQUIREMENTS. Freshmen must earn minimum GPA of 2.0 to continue in good standing. 68% of freshmen return for sophomore year. Students must declare major by end of second year. **Graduation requirements:** 64 hours for associate (14 in major), 128 hours for bachelor's (29 in major). Most students required to take courses in English, history, mathematics, biological/physical sciences, social sciences.

FRESHMAN ADMISSIONS. Selection criteria: High school grades, curriculum, class rank, and test scores. Rank in top half of graduating class. Minimum admissions to preparatory (remedial) program for those not meeting degree unit admissions requirements. Diagnostic testing/interview option for those failing to meet minimum. 95% of freshmen must have completed state's precollege curriculum. **High school preparation:** 20 units required. Required and recommended units include English 4, mathematics 3, social science 2 and science 2. Biological science 1 and foreign language 2 recommended. Special mathematics and science requirements for engineering applicants. Social science limited to United States history and world civilization. One laboratory science required. **Test requirements:** SAT or ACT (ACT preferred); score report by August 10. SAT/ACT score reports must be received by registration.

1992 FRESHMAN CLASS PROFILE. 2,274 men applied, 1,646 accepted, 934 enrolled; 2,294 women applied, 1,617 accepted, 881 enrolled. 50% had high school GPA of 3.0 or higher, 43% between 2.0 and 2.99. 19% were in top tenth and 53% were in top quarter of graduating class. **Academic background:** Mid 50% of enrolled freshmen had ACT composite between 19-26. 68% submitted ACT scores. **Characteristics:** 93% from in state, 90% commute, 20% have minority backgrounds, 1% are foreign students. Average age is 20.

FALL-TERM APPLICATIONS. $25 fee, may be waived for applicants with need. No closing date; priority given to applications received by May 1; applicants notified on a rolling basis. Interview required for minimum admission applicants applicants. Audition required for music applicants. Early admission available.

STUDENT LIFE. Housing: Dormitories (men, women, coed); apartment, fraternity, sorority housing available. Special dormitory with in-house computer facilities available for honors students. **Activities:** Student government, magazine, radio, student newspaper, yearbook, debate program, choral groups, concert band, dance, drama, jazz band, marching band, music ensembles, pep band, symphony orchestra, fraternities, sororities, 114 clubs and organizations.

ATHLETICS. NCAA. **Intercollegiate:** Baseball M, basketball, cross-country, diving, field hockey W, football M, golf M, soccer, swimming, tennis, track and field, volleyball W. **Intramural:** Badminton, basketball, bowling, cross-country, diving, fencing, golf, racquetball, rowing (crew), rugby M, skiing, soccer, softball, swimming, table tennis, tennis, track and field, volleyball, water polo.

STUDENT SERVICES. Career counseling, employment service for undergraduates, freshman orientation, health services, on-campus day care, personal counseling, placement service for graduates, special adviser for adult students, veterans counselor, life planning center, special services for adult students, services/facilities for handicapped.

ANNUAL EXPENSES. Tuition and fees (projected): $2,080, $3,920 additional for out-of-state students. **Room and board:** $3,426. **Books and supplies:** $510. **Other expenses:** $1,680.

FINANCIAL AID. 49% of freshmen, 46% of continuing students receive some form of aid. 61% of grants, 50% of loans, all jobs based on need. 1,228 enrolled freshmen were judged to have need, 1,162 were offered aid. Academic, music/drama, art, athletic, state/district residency, alumni affiliation, minority scholarships available. **Aid applications:** No closing date; priority given to applications received by April 15; applicants notified on a rolling basis beginning on or about June 1; must reply within 3 weeks.

ADDRESS/TELEPHONE. Robert W. Parrent, Director of Admissions, University of Louisville, 2211 South Brook Street, Louisville, KY 40292. (502) 588-6525.

Western Kentucky University

Bowling Green, Kentucky CB code: 1901

4-year public university, coed. Founded in 1906. **Accreditation:** Regional. **Undergraduate enrollment:** 4,746 men, 5,939 women full time; 933 men, 1,096 women part time. **Graduate enrollment:** 175 men, 244 women full time; 384 men, 1,236 women part time. **Faculty:** 805 total (594 full time), 427 with doctorates or other terminal degrees. **Location:** Suburban campus in small city; 110 miles from Louisville, 65 miles from Nashville, Tennessee. **Calendar:** Semester, limited summer session. Extensive evening/early morning classes. **Microcomputers:** 487 located in dormitories, libraries, computer centers, campus-wide network. **Special facilities:** Kentucky Museum and Library, Hardin Planetarium. **Additional facts:** Branch campus located in Glasgow, Kentucky offering general education, nursing, and elementary education programs.

DEGREES OFFERED. AAS, BA, BS, BFA, MA, MS. 278 associate degrees awarded in 1992. 12% in business and management, 6% business/office and marketing/distribution, 5% engineering technologies, 40% health sciences, 26% multi/interdisciplinary studies. 1,724 bachelor's degrees awarded. 14% in business and management, 12% communications, 22% teacher education, 5% health sciences, 5% multi/interdisciplinary studies, 5% psychology, 8% social sciences. Graduate degrees offered in 48 major fields of study.

UNDERGRADUATE MAJORS. Associate: Agricultural mechanics, agricultural production, atmospheric sciences and meteorology, computer and information sciences, dental hygiene, drafting, electrical technology, finance, graphic and printing production, industrial technology, liberal/general studies, manufacturing technology, medical records technology, nursing, occupational safety and health technology, real estate, retailing, secretarial and related programs, small business management and ownership, survey and mapping technology, technical education. **Bachelor's:** Accounting, advertising, agricultural sciences, anthropology, art education, biochemistry, biology, biotechnology, business administration and management, business and management, business economics, business education, chemistry, civil technology, commercial art, communications, community health work, computer and information sciences, dental hygiene, dramatic arts, earth sciences, economics, education of the emotionally handicapped, education of the mentally handicapped, electrical technology, elementary education, English, environmental science, finance, food science and nutrition, French, geography, geology, German, health care administration, health education, history, home economics education, human environment and housing, industrial arts education, industrial technology, institutional management, journalism, junior high education, liberal/general studies, library science, management information systems, marketing management, mathematics, mechanical design technology, medical laboratory technologies, music, music education, music performance, nursing, parks and recreation management, philosophy, photojournalism, physical education, physical sciences, physics, political science and government, predentistry, prelaw, premedicine, prepharmacy, preveterinary, psychology, public relations, radio/television broadcasting, religion, science education, social sciences, social work, sociology, Spanish, special education, specific learning disabilities, speech, speech correction, speech pathology/audiology, speech/communication/theater education, studio art, technical education, textiles and clothing, trade and industrial education, visual and performing arts.

ACADEMIC PROGRAMS. 2-year transfer program, cooperative education, double major, dual enrollment of high school students, education specialist degree, honors program, independent study, internships, student-designed major, study abroad, teacher preparation, telecourses, New York semester. **Remedial services:** Learning center, reduced course load, remedial instruction, tutoring. **ROTC:** Air Force, Army. **Placement/credit:** AP, CLEP General and Subject, institutional tests. Unlimited number of hours of credit by examination may be counted toward a degree. Student must complete residency requirement.

ACADEMIC REQUIREMENTS. Freshmen must earn minimum GPA of 1.8 to continue in good standing. 65% of freshmen return for sophomore year. Students must declare major by end of second year. **Graduation requirements:** 64 hours for associate, 128 hours for bachelor's (30 in major). Most students required to take courses in English, history, mathematics, biological/physical sciences, social sciences.

FRESHMAN ADMISSIONS. Selection criteria: Class rank, GPA, ACT test scores, and completion of pre-college curriculum recommended. **High school preparation:** 20 units required. Required units include English 4, mathematics 3, social science 2 and science 2. **Test requirements:** ACT; score report by August 1. **Additional information:** Part-time students not required to provide ACT scores. Course requirements differ for nursing, medical records technology, dental hygiene and electro-mechanical engineering technology applicants.

1992 FRESHMAN CLASS PROFILE. 4,960 men and women applied, 3,896 accepted; 1,016 men enrolled, 1,401 women enrolled. 46% had high school GPA of 3.0 or higher, 50% between 2.0 and 2.99. **Academic background:** Mid 50% of enrolled freshmen had ACT composite between 18-23. 100% submitted ACT scores. **Characteristics:** 79% from in state, 96% live in college housing, 8% have minority backgrounds, 1% are foreign students. Average age is 19.

FALL-TERM APPLICATIONS. No fee. Closing date August 1; applicants notified on a rolling basis. Interview recommended. Deferred admission available. Closing date for fall-term applications is June 1 for out-of-state applicants.

STUDENT LIFE. Housing: Dormitories (men, women, coed); fraternity, sorority, handicapped housing available. Freshmen required to live on campus. Local students may receive exemption. **Activities:** Student government, magazine, radio, student newspaper, television, yearbook, choral groups, concert band, dance, drama, jazz band, marching band, music ensembles, musical theater, opera, pep band, symphony orchestra, fraternities, sororities, Black Student Alliance, Fellowship of Christian Athletes, United Campuses to Prevent Nuclear War, College Republicans, Young Democrats, Campus Crusade, Alpha Phi Omega, Gamma Sigma Sigma, Women in Transition, International Student Committee.

ATHLETICS. NCAA. **Intercollegiate:** Baseball M, basketball, cross-country, diving M, football M, golf, horseback riding, rugby M, soccer M, swimming M, tennis, track and field, volleyball W. **Intramural:** Archery, badminton, basketball, bowling, fencing, golf, handball, racquetball, softball, swimming, table tennis, tennis, track and field, volleyball, water polo, wrestling M.

STUDENT SERVICES. Aptitude testing, career counseling, freshman orientation, health services, on-campus day care, personal counseling, placement service for graduates, special adviser for adult students, veterans counselor, services/facilities for handicapped.

ANNUAL EXPENSES. Tuition and fees (projected): $1,704, $3,000 additional for out-of-state students. **Room and board:** $3,096. **Books and supplies:** $500. **Other expenses:** $1,100.

FINANCIAL AID. 41% of freshmen, 73% of continuing students receive some form of aid. 50% of grants, 91% of loans, 43% of jobs based on need. 1,076 enrolled freshmen were judged to have need, 1,008 were offered aid. Academic, music/drama, art, athletic, state/district residency, leadership, alumni affiliation scholarships available. **Aid applications:** No closing date; priority given to applications received by April 1; applicants notified on a rolling basis beginning on or about May 1; must reply within 2 weeks. **Additional information:** Freshman priority financial aid applicants notified on or about June 1.

ADDRESS/TELEPHONE. Cheryl Chambless, Director of Admissions, Western Kentucky University, 101 Cravens Building, Bowling Green, KY 42101. (502) 745-2551.

Louisiana

Bossier Parish Community College
Bossier City, Louisiana CB code: 0787

2-year public community college, coed. Founded in 1966. **Accreditation:** Regional. **Undergraduate enrollment:** 605 men, 792 women full time; 928 men, 1,851 women part time. **Faculty:** 133 total (78 full time), 5 with doctorates or other terminal degrees. **Location:** Suburban campus in small city; 3 miles from Shreveport. **Calendar:** Semester, limited summer session. **Microcomputers:** 54 located in classrooms.

DEGREES OFFERED. AS. 105 associate degrees awarded in 1992. 39% in business and management, 20% business/office and marketing/distribution, 5% allied health, 24% multi/interdisciplinary studies, 10% parks/recreation, protective services, public affairs.

UNDERGRADUATE MAJORS. Business administration and management, business and management, business and office, business data processing and related programs, criminal justice studies, data processing, industrial control systems, law enforcement and corrections technologies, liberal/general studies, medical assistant, respiratory therapy, secretarial and related programs.

ACADEMIC PROGRAMS. Dual enrollment of high school students, internships. **Remedial services:** Learning center, remedial instruction. **Placement/credit:** CLEP General and Subject.

ACADEMIC REQUIREMENTS. Freshmen must earn minimum GPA of 2.0 to continue in good standing. Students must declare major on application. **Graduation requirements:** 66 hours for associate (36 in major). Most students required to take courses in English, history, mathematics, biological/physical sciences, social sciences.

FRESHMAN ADMISSIONS. Selection criteria: Open admissions. **Test requirements:** ACT for placement and counseling only; score report by September 1.

1992 FRESHMAN CLASS PROFILE. 502 men, 764 women enrolled. **Characteristics:** 98% from in state, 100% commute, 15% have minority backgrounds.

FALL-TERM APPLICATIONS. $5 fee. No closing date; priority given to applications received by August 15; applicants notified on a rolling basis.

STUDENT LIFE. Activities: Student government, magazine, student newspaper, choral groups, dance, drama, jazz band, Baptist Union.

ATHLETICS. NJCAA. **Intercollegiate:** Baseball M, basketball M, golf M, tennis. **Intramural:** Badminton, basketball, bowling, table tennis, tennis, volleyball.

STUDENT SERVICES. Career counseling, employment service for undergraduates, freshman orientation, personal counseling, placement service for graduates, veterans counselor, services/facilities for handicapped.

ANNUAL EXPENSES. Tuition and fees (1992-93): $605, $90 additional for out-of-district students, $600 additional for out-of-state students. **Books and supplies:** $575. **Other expenses:** $1,000.

FINANCIAL AID. 10% of freshmen, 25% of continuing students receive some form of aid. 98% of grants, 74% of loans, all jobs based on need. 150 enrolled freshmen were judged to have need, all were offered aid. Academic, athletic, state/district residency, minority scholarships available. **Aid applications:** No closing date; priority given to applications received by June 1; applicants notified on a rolling basis beginning on or about August 1.

ADDRESS/TELEPHONE. Ann Jampole, Admissions Officer, Bossier Parish Community College, 2719 Airline Drive North, Bossier City, LA 71111. (318) 746-9851. Fax: (318) 742-8664.

Centenary College of Louisiana
Shreveport, Louisiana CB code: 6082

Admissions:	89% of applicants accepted
Based on:	••• Interview, school record, test scores
	•• Activities, essay, recommendations, special talents
	• Religious affiliation/commitment
Completion:	90% of freshmen end year in good standing
	60% graduate, 57% of these enter graduate study

4-year private liberal arts college, coed, affiliated with United Methodist Church. Founded in 1825. **Accreditation:** Regional. **Undergraduate enrollment:** 338 men, 421 women full time; 18 men, 40 women part time. **Graduate enrollment:** 5 women full time; 74 men, 146 women part time. **Faculty:** 92 total (72 full time), 58 with doctorates or other terminal degrees. **Location:** Suburban campus in small city; 325 miles from New Orleans, 189 miles from Dallas. **Calendar:** 4-1-4, limited summer session. **Microcomputers:** Located in libraries, classrooms, computer centers. **Special facilities:** Art museum, amphitheater, playhouse, music library.

DEGREES OFFERED. B, MA, MS, MBA. 166 bachelor's degrees awarded in 1992. 21% in area and ethnic studies, 21% business and management, 10% teacher education, 8% life sciences, 8% multi/interdisciplinary studies, 5% philosophy, religion, theology, 7% physical sciences, 8% psychology, 16% social sciences, 8% visual and performing arts. Graduate degrees offered in 4 major fields of study.

UNDERGRADUATE MAJORS. Accounting, allied health, biology, business and management, chemistry, computer and information sciences, dramatic arts, economics, elementary education, engineering, English, fine arts, foreign languages (multiple emphasis), forestry and related sciences, French, geology, history, humanities and social sciences, journalism, liberal/general studies, mathematics, military science (Army), music, music education, music performance, musical theater, philosophy, physical education, physics, political science and government, psychology, religion, religious education, religious music, science education, secondary education, social studies education, sociology, Spanish, speech, theological studies.

ACADEMIC PROGRAMS. Accelerated program, double major, dual enrollment of high school students, honors program, independent study, internships, student-designed major, study abroad, teacher preparation, visiting/exchange student program, Washington semester, Oak Ridge National Laboratory semester; liberal arts/career combination in engineering, forestry, health sciences. **Remedial services:** Reduced course load, tutoring. **ROTC:** Army. **Placement/credit:** AP, CLEP General and Subject, institutional tests; 24 credit hours maximum for bachelor's degree.

ACADEMIC REQUIREMENTS. Freshmen must earn minimum GPA of 1.5 to continue in good standing. 79% of freshmen return for sophomore year. Students must declare major by end of second year. **Graduation requirements:** 124 hours for bachelor's (30 in major). Most students required to take courses in arts/fine arts, English, foreign languages, history, humanities, mathematics, philosophy/religion, biological/physical sciences, social sciences. **Postgraduate studies:** 6% enter law school, 6% enter medical school, 15% enter MBA programs, 30% enter other graduate study. **Additional information:** Writing and speaking skills enhanced in designated courses with individualized criticism by faculty.

FRESHMAN ADMISSIONS. Selection criteria: Academic achievement record, test scores, and interview required. Must be in top half of class. Extracurricular activities and leadership ability considered. Special consideration given to minority applicants and children of alumni. **High school preparation:** 13 units required. Required and recommended units include English 4, mathematics 3, physical science 2, social science 2 and science 2. Foreign language 2 recommended. **Test requirements:** SAT or ACT; score report by August 1. **Additional information:** Applications evaluated on individual basis.

1992 FRESHMAN CLASS PROFILE. 203 men applied, 185 accepted, 104 enrolled; 257 women applied, 224 accepted, 132 enrolled. 71% had high school GPA of 3.0 or higher, 28% between 2.0 and 2.99. **Academic background:** Mid 50% of enrolled freshmen had SAT-V between 410-540, SAT-M between 480-610; ACT composite between 21-28. 56% submitted SAT scores, 88% submitted ACT scores. **Characteristics:** 60% from in state, 66% live in college housing, 15% have minority backgrounds, 2% are foreign students, 32% join fraternities/sororities. Average age is 18.

FALL-TERM APPLICATIONS. $30 fee. Closing date August 15; priority given to applications received by February 15; applicants notified on a rolling basis; must reply by May 1 or within 4 weeks if notified thereafter. Interview required. Audition required for music, theater applicants. Essay required. Portfolio recommended for art applicants. CRDA. Deferred and early admission available.

STUDENT LIFE. Housing: Dormitories (men, women); fraternity housing available. **Activities:** Student government, film, magazine, radio, student newspaper, television, yearbook, choral groups, concert band, dance, drama, jazz band, music ensembles, musical theater, opera, pep band, symphony orchestra, chamber singers, fraternities, sororities, Baptist Student Union, Methodist Student Movement, Canterbury Club, Newman Club, Open Ear crisis telephone service, Circle-K, and service organizations. **Additional information:** Students participate on enrollment management task force and educational policy committee. Honor code monitored by students.

ATHLETICS. NAIA, NCAA. **Intercollegiate:** Baseball M, basketball M, cross-country, golf, gymnastics W, rifle, soccer M, tennis, volleyball. **Intramural:** Archery, badminton, basketball, bowling, football M, golf M, racquetball, softball, table tennis, tennis, volleyball.

STUDENT SERVICES. Aptitude testing, career counseling, employment service for undergraduates, freshman orientation, health services, personal counseling, placement service for graduates, veterans counselor, services/facilities for handicapped.

ANNUAL EXPENSES. Tuition and fees: $8,400. **Room and board:** $3,420. **Books and supplies:** $600. **Other expenses:** $1,200.

FINANCIAL AID. 86% of freshmen, 75% of continuing students receive some form of aid. 18% of grants, 83% of loans, 79% of jobs based on need. 134 enrolled freshmen were judged to have need, all were offered aid. Academic, music/drama, art, athletic, state/district residency, religious affiliation, minority scholarships available. **Aid applications:** No closing date; priority given to applications received by March 15; applicants notified on a rolling basis beginning on or about April 15; must reply by May 1 or within 2 weeks if notified thereafter. **Additional information:** Merit scholarships offered on Scholarship Day by invitation only.

ADDRESS/TELEPHONE. Caroline S. Kelsey, Director of Admissions, Centenary College of Louisiana, PO Box 41188, Shreveport, LA 71134-1188. (318) 869-5131. (800) 234-4448. Fax: (318) 869-5026.

Delgado Community College
New Orleans, Louisiana CB code: 6176

2-year public community college, coed. Founded in 1921. **Accreditation:** Regional. **Undergraduate enrollment:** 14,781 men and women. **Location:** Urban campus in very large city. **Calendar:** Semester. Saturday classes.

FRESHMAN ADMISSIONS. Selection criteria: Open admissions.

ANNUAL EXPENSES. Tuition and fees (1992-93): $1,021, $1,200 additional for out-of-state students. **Room and board:** $800 room only. **Books and supplies:** $500. **Other expenses:** $930.

ADDRESS/TELEPHONE. Marena L. Leinhard, Admissions Director, Delgado Community College, 615 City Park Avenue, New Orleans, LA 70119-4399. (504) 483-4114.

Dillard University
New Orleans, Louisiana CB code: 6164

4-year private liberal arts college, coed, affiliated with United Church of Christ and United Methodist Church. Founded in 1869. **Accreditation:** Regional. **Undergraduate enrollment:** 1,522 men and women. **Faculty:** 120 total (104 full time), 48 with doctorates or other terminal degrees. **Location:** Urban campus in very large city. **Calendar:** Semester, limited summer session. **Microcomputers:** 212 located in libraries, classrooms, computer centers. **Special facilities:** Video encyclopedia of 20th century.

DEGREES OFFERED. BA, BS. 200 bachelor's degrees awarded in 1992.

UNDERGRADUATE MAJORS. Accounting, allied health, art education, biology, business administration and management, business and management, business economics, chemistry, communications, computer and information sciences, criminology, dramatic arts, early childhood education, economics, education, education of the deaf and hearing impaired, education of the emotionally handicapped, education of the gifted and talented, education of the mentally handicapped, elementary education, engineering, English, English education, fine arts, foreign languages education, French, German, health education, history, Japanese, junior high education, mathematics, mathematics education, music, music education, nursing, philosophy, physical education, physics, political science and government, predentistry, prelaw, premedicine, prepharmacy, preveterinary, psychology, reading education, science education, secondary education, social science education, social studies education, social work, sociology, Spanish, special education, specific learning disabilities, urban studies.

ACADEMIC PROGRAMS. Double major, dual enrollment of high school students, honors program, independent study, internships, study abroad, teacher preparation; liberal arts/career combination in engineering. **Remedial services:** Learning center, preadmission summer program, reduced course load, remedial instruction, special counselor, tutoring. **ROTC:** Air Force, Army, Naval. **Placement/credit:** AP, CLEP Subject, institutional tests; 20 credit hours maximum for bachelor's degree.

ACADEMIC REQUIREMENTS. Freshmen must earn minimum GPA of 2.0 to continue in good standing. 67% of freshmen return for sophomore year. Students must declare major by end of first year. **Graduation requirements:** 130 hours for bachelor's (36 in major). Most students required to take courses in arts/fine arts, computer science, English, foreign languages, history, humanities, mathematics, biological/physical sciences, social sciences. **Postgraduate studies:** 12% enter law school, 11% enter medical school, 6% enter MBA programs, 10% enter other graduate study. **Additional information:** Must acquire computer literacy through use of computers as research tool in courses.

FRESHMAN ADMISSIONS. Selection criteria: Preference to applicants in top 25% of class, 2.0 minimum GPA. Test scores, class rank, and participation in extracurricular activities and community projects considered. **High school preparation:** 18 units required. Required units include English 4, mathematics 4, social science 2 and science 4. **Test requirements:** SAT or ACT; score report by June 15.

1992 FRESHMAN CLASS PROFILE. 133 men and women enrolled. 54% had high school GPA of 3.0 or higher, 39% between 2.0 and 2.99. **Academic background:** Mid 50% of enrolled freshmen had SAT-V between 330-500, SAT-M between 370-460; ACT composite between 10-20. 9% submitted SAT scores, 84% submitted ACT scores. **Characteristics:** 66% from in state, 54% live in college housing, 99% have minority backgrounds, 1% are foreign students. Average age is 18.

FALL-TERM APPLICATIONS. $10 fee, may be waived for applicants with need. Closing date May 15; priority given to applications received by April 15; applicants notified on a rolling basis; must reply within 2 weeks. Essay required. Interview recommended. Audition recommended. Deferred and early admission available.

STUDENT LIFE. Housing: Dormitories (men, women). **Activities:** Student government, radio, student newspaper, television, yearbook, choral groups, concert band, dance, drama, jazz band, music ensembles, fraternities, sororities, service sororities and fraternities, honor societies, religious groups, NAACP.

ATHLETICS. NAIA. **Intercollegiate:** Basketball. **Intramural:** Basketball, bowling, football, golf, gymnastics, softball, swimming, table tennis, tennis, track and field, volleyball.

STUDENT SERVICES. Aptitude testing, career counseling, employment service for undergraduates, freshman orientation, health services, personal counseling, placement service for graduates.

ANNUAL EXPENSES. Tuition and fees: $6,400. $400 additional tuition for nursing students. **Room and board:** $3,750. **Books and supplies:** $600. **Other expenses:** $1,166.

FINANCIAL AID. 85% of freshmen, 90% of continuing students receive some form of aid. 63% of grants, 98% of loans, all jobs based on need. Academic, athletic, religious affiliation scholarships available. **Aid applications:** Closing date June 1; priority given to applications received by April 15; applicants notified on a rolling basis beginning on or about June 1; must reply within 2 weeks.

ADDRESS/TELEPHONE. Vernese B. O'Neal, Director of Admissions, Dillard University, 2601 Gentilly Boulevard, New Orleans, LA 70122-3097. (504) 283-8822.

Grambling State University
Grambling, Louisiana CB code: 6250

4-year public university, coed. Founded in 1901. **Accreditation:** Regional. **Undergraduate enrollment:** 2,790 men and women full time; 4,007 men and women part time. **Graduate enrollment:** 208 men and women full time; 497 men and women part time. **Faculty:** 289 total. **Location:** Rural campus in small town; 35 miles from Monroe, 70 miles from Shreveport. **Calendar:** Semester, limited summer session. Saturday and extensive evening/early morning classes. **Microcomputers:** 175 located in classrooms.

DEGREES OFFERED. AA, AS, BA, BS, MA, MS, MBA, MEd, MSW, EdD. 40 associate degrees awarded in 1992. 7% in business/office and marketing/distribution, 7% computer sciences, 22% home economics, 61% parks/recreation, protective services, public affairs. 591 bachelor's degrees awarded. 22% in business and management, 7% communications, 13% computer sciences, 7% education, 5% engineering technologies, 9% health sciences, 18% parks/recreation, protective services, public affairs. Graduate degrees offered in 14 major fields of study.

UNDERGRADUATE MAJORS. Associate: Accounting, automotive mechanics, automotive technology, business and office, business data processing and related programs, child development/care/guidance, computer and information sciences, construction, criminal justice studies, drafting, electrical technology, secretarial and related programs, word processing. **Bachelor's:** Accounting, anthropology, applied mathematics, art education, art history, automotive mechanics, automotive technology, biology, business administration and management, business and management, business economics, business education, chemistry, computer and information sciences, computer programming, construction, criminal justice studies, drafting, drafting and design technology, dramatic arts, early childhood education, electrical technology, electronic technology, elementary education, English, English education, fine arts, foreign languages education, French, geography, health education, history, home economics, home economics education, hotel/motel and restaurant management, industrial arts education, industrial technology, information sciences and systems, institutional/home management/supporting programs, journalism, marketing and distribution, marketing and distributive education, mathematics, mathematics education, music, music education, music theory and composition, nursing, parks and recreation management, philosophy, physical education, physics, political science and government, prelaw, psychology, public administration, science education, secretarial and related programs, social science education, social sciences, social studies education, social work, sociology, Spanish, special education, speech correction, speech pathology/audiology, speech/communication/theater education, statistics, trade and industrial education.

ACADEMIC PROGRAMS. Cooperative education, double major, education specialist degree, honors program, independent study, internships, study abroad, teacher preparation, visiting/exchange student program, weekend college, cross-registration. **Remedial services:** Learning center, reduced course load, remedial instruction, special counselor, tutoring. **ROTC:** Air Force, Army. **Placement/credit:** CLEP General and Subject.

ACADEMIC REQUIREMENTS. Freshmen must earn minimum GPA of 2.0 to continue in good standing. 73% of freshmen return for sophomore year. Students must declare major by end of second year. **Graduation requirements:** 70 hours for associate, 131 hours for bachelor's. Most students required to take courses in arts/fine arts, computer science, English, foreign languages, history, humanities, mathematics, biological/physical sciences, social sciences. **Postgraduate studies:** 80% from 2-year programs enter 4-year programs. **Additional information:** Advanced specialist degree in developmental education available.

FRESHMAN ADMISSIONS. Selection criteria: Open admissions. Out-of-state students must have 2.0 high school GPA. **Test requirements:**

SAT or ACT (ACT preferred) for placement and counseling only; score report by July 15.

1992 FRESHMAN CLASS PROFILE. 618 men, 786 women enrolled. 17% had high school GPA of 3.0 or higher, 68% between 2.0 and 2.99. **Characteristics:** 65% from in state, 70% live in college housing, 98% have minority backgrounds, 1% are foreign students, 4% join fraternities/sororities. Average age is 18.

FALL-TERM APPLICATIONS. $5 fee. Closing date July 15; applicants notified on a rolling basis. Audition recommended for music applicants. Deferred and early admission available.

STUDENT LIFE. Housing: Dormitories (men, women). **Activities:** Student government, film, radio, student newspaper, television, yearbook, choral groups, concert band, dance, drama, jazz band, marching band, music ensembles, opera, pep band, symphony orchestra, fraternities, sororities.

ATHLETICS. NCAA. **Intercollegiate:** Baseball M, basketball, cross-country, football M, golf M, tennis, track and field. **Intramural:** Badminton, baseball M, basketball, bowling, cross-country, golf, gymnastics M, softball W, swimming, tennis, track and field, volleyball.

STUDENT SERVICES. Career counseling, employment service for undergraduates, freshman orientation, health services, personal counseling, placement service for graduates, veterans counselor, services/facilities for handicapped.

ANNUAL EXPENSES. Tuition and fees (1992-93): $2,088, $1,650 additional for out-of-state students. **Room and board:** $2,612. **Books and supplies:** $576. **Other expenses:** $1,259.

FINANCIAL AID. 95% of freshmen, 98% of continuing students receive some form of aid. 91% of grants, 80% of loans, 58% of jobs based on need. Academic, music/drama, athletic scholarships available. **Aid applications:** No closing date; priority given to applications received by April 15; applicants notified on a rolling basis beginning on or about May 1; must reply within 10 days.

ADDRESS/TELEPHONE. Karen Lewis, Director of Admission, Grambling State University, P.O. Box 864, Grambling, LA 71245. (318) 274-2435.

Grantham College of Engineering
Slidell, Louisiana — CB code: 2244

4-year proprietary engineering college, coed. Founded in 1951. **Undergraduate enrollment:** 1,000 men and women. **Faculty:** 5 total (4 full time), 1 with doctorate or other terminal degree. **Location:** Suburban campus in small city. **Calendar:** Year round. **Additional facts:** Offers home study only.

DEGREES OFFERED. AS, BS. 15 associate degrees awarded in 1992. 100% in engineering technologies. 9 bachelor's degrees awarded. 100% in engineering technologies.

UNDERGRADUATE MAJORS. Associate: Computer engineering, computer technology, electrical/electronics/communications engineering, electronic technology. **Bachelor's:** Computer engineering, computer technology, electrical/electronics/communications engineering, electronic technology.

ACADEMIC PROGRAMS. Independent study; liberal arts/career combination in engineering.

ACADEMIC REQUIREMENTS. Students must declare major on enrollment. **Graduation requirements:** 67 hours for associate (61 in major), 122 hours for bachelor's (83 in major). Most students required to take courses in computer science, English, history, mathematics, biological/physical sciences, social sciences.

FRESHMAN ADMISSIONS. Selection criteria: Open admissions.

FALL-TERM APPLICATIONS. No fee. No closing date; applicants notified on a rolling basis. All students admitted on trial basis for first 16 lessons.

STUDENT LIFE. Activities: Quarterly newsletter.

ANNUAL EXPENSES. Tuition and fees: $2,050. Tuition and fees includes books and supplies for all students.

FINANCIAL AID. Additional information: Defense Activity for Non Traditional Education Support (DANTES) and some employer reimbursement programs available.

ADDRESS/TELEPHONE. Mark P. Dean, Dir of Student Services, Grantham College of Engineering, 34641 Grautham College Road, P.O. Box 5700, Slidell, LA 70469-5700. (504) 649-4191. Fax: (504) 649-4183.

Louisiana College
Pineville, Louisiana — CB code: 6371

Admissions: 41% of applicants accepted
Based on:
- ••• School record, test scores
- •• Recommendations
- • Activities, interview

Completion: 80% of freshmen end year in good standing
38% graduate, 50% of these enter graduate study

4-year private liberal arts college, coed, affiliated with Southern Baptist Convention. Founded in 1906. **Accreditation:** Regional. **Undergraduate enrollment:** 367 men, 646 women full time; 49 men, 123 women part time. **Faculty:** 81 total (61 full time), 57 with doctorates or other terminal degrees. **Location:** Suburban campus in large town; less than 1 mile from Alexandria. **Calendar:** Semester, extensive summer session. **Microcomputers:** 60 located in libraries, classrooms, computer centers. **Special facilities:** Museum, art gallery.

DEGREES OFFERED. AS, BA, BS. 1 associate degree awarded in 1992. 188 bachelor's degrees awarded.

UNDERGRADUATE MAJORS. Associate: Business and office, early childhood education, law enforcement and corrections technologies, secretarial and related programs, teacher aide. **Bachelor's:** Accounting, advertising, applied mathematics, art education, biological and physical sciences, biology, business administration and management, business and management, business education, chemistry, classics, clinical laboratory science, communications, computer and information sciences, computer programming, criminology, dramatic arts, economics, education, education of the physically handicapped, elementary education, English, English education, finance, fine arts, foreign languages (multiple emphasis), foreign languages education, French, graphic design, health education, health sciences, history, humanities and social sciences, information sciences and systems, journalism, junior high education, liberal/general studies, management information systems, marketing and distribution, marketing management, mathematics, mathematics education, music, music education, music performance, music theory and composition, nursing, office supervision and management, philosophy, physical education, political science and government, predentistry, prelaw, premedicine, prepharmacy, preveterinary, psychology, public administration, radio/television broadcasting, religion, religious education, religious music, science education, secondary education, secretarial and related programs, social sciences, social studies education, social work, sociology, special education.

ACADEMIC PROGRAMS. Accelerated program, double major, dual enrollment of high school students, honors program, independent study, internships, student-designed major, study abroad, teacher preparation. **Remedial services:** Preadmission summer program, reduced course load, remedial instruction, special counselor, tutoring. **Placement/credit:** AP, institutional tests; 30 credit hours maximum for bachelor's degree.

ACADEMIC REQUIREMENTS. Freshmen must earn minimum GPA of 2.0 to continue in good standing. 68% of freshmen return for sophomore year. Students must declare major by end of second year. **Graduation requirements:** 65 hours for associate (27 in major), 127 hours for bachelor's (45 in major). Most students required to take courses in English, foreign languages, history, humanities, mathematics, philosophy/religion, biological/physical sciences, social sciences.

FRESHMAN ADMISSIONS. Selection criteria: SAT combined score of 800 or ACT composite score of 20. Those not meeting these criteria must have 2.0 GPA, rank in top half of graduating class, and ACT composite score of 14 or better. **High school preparation:** 17 units required. Required and recommended units include English 4, mathematics 3, social science 3 and science 3. Foreign language 1 recommended. **Test requirements:** SAT or ACT (ACT preferred); score report by July 31.

1992 FRESHMAN CLASS PROFILE. 719 men applied, 245 accepted, 116 enrolled; 1,213 women applied, 547 accepted, 192 enrolled. 41% had high school GPA of 3.0 or higher, 59% between 2.0 and 2.99. **Academic background:** Mid 50% of enrolled freshmen had ACT composite between 19-29. 100% submitted ACT scores. **Characteristics:** 90% from in state, 50% commute, 9% have minority backgrounds, 15% join fraternities/sororities. Average age is 19.

FALL-TERM APPLICATIONS. No fee. No closing date; priority given to applications received by July 31; applicants notified on a rolling basis; must reply by August 1 or within 10 days if notified thereafter. Audition required for music applicants. Interview recommended. Portfolio recommended for art applicants. Deferred and early admission available.

STUDENT LIFE. Housing: Dormitories (men, women); apartment housing available. **Activities:** Student government, student newspaper, yearbook, choral groups, concert band, drama, jazz band, music ensembles, musical theater, opera, pep band, fraternities, sororities, Baptist Student Union, Circle-K.

ATHLETICS. NAIA. **Intercollegiate:** Baseball M, basketball, cross-country, tennis W. **Intramural:** Badminton, basketball, bowling, golf, softball, swimming, table tennis, tennis, volleyball.

STUDENT SERVICES. Aptitude testing, career counseling, employment service for undergraduates, freshman orientation, health services,

personal counseling, placement service for graduates, services/facilities for handicapped.

ANNUAL EXPENSES. Tuition and fees (1992-93): $4,870. **Room and board:** $2,944. **Books and supplies:** $520. **Other expenses:** $1,011.

FINANCIAL AID. 75% of freshmen, 65% of continuing students receive some form of aid. Grants, loans, jobs available. Academic, athletic, leadership scholarships available. **Aid applications:** Closing date May 15; applicants notified on a rolling basis beginning on or about June 1; must reply within 4 weeks.

ADDRESS/TELEPHONE. Byron McGee, Director of Admissions, Louisiana College, PO Box 560, 1140 College Drive, Pineville, LA 71359-0560. (318) 487-7386. Fax: (318) 487-7191.

Louisiana State University and Agricultural and Mechanical College

Baton Rouge, Louisiana — CB code: 6373

Admissions: 79% of applicants accepted
Based on: ••• School record, test scores
• Activities, essay, interview, recommendations, special talents
Completion: 89% of freshmen end year in good standing
31% graduate

4-year public university and agricultural and technical college, coed. Founded in 1860. **Accreditation:** Regional. **Undergraduate enrollment:** 8,694 men, 8,621 women full time; 1,569 men, 2,302 women part time. **Graduate enrollment:** 2,072 men, 1,381 women full time; 882 men, 1,071 women part time. **Faculty:** 1,512 total (1,383 full time), 1,270 with doctorates or other terminal degrees. **Location:** Urban campus in small city; 80 miles from New Orleans. **Calendar:** Semester, extensive summer session. Saturday and extensive evening/early morning classes. **Microcomputers:** 1,725 located in dormitories, libraries, classrooms, computer centers, campus-wide network. **Special facilities:** Mycological herbarium, lichenological herbarium, natural science museum, geoscience museum, rural life museum, Anglo-American Art Museum.

DEGREES OFFERED. BA, BS, BFA, BArch, MA, MS, MBA, MFA, MEd, MSW, PhD, EdD, DVM, JD. 3,189 bachelor's degrees awarded in 1992. 18% in business and management, 5% communications, 10% education, 9% engineering, 6% letters/literature, 11% multi/interdisciplinary studies, 7% psychology, 10% social sciences. Graduate degrees offered in 95 major fields of study.

UNDERGRADUATE MAJORS. Accounting, advertising, agribusiness, agricultural economics, agricultural education, agricultural engineering, agronomy, animal sciences, anthropology, architectural technologies, architecture, biochemistry, botany, business administration and management, business and management, business economics, business education, ceramics, chemical engineering, chemistry, civil engineering, computer and information sciences, computer engineering, construction, dramatic arts, drawing, economics, electrical/electronics/communications engineering, elementary education, English, fashion merchandising, finance, food science and nutrition, food sciences, forestry and related sciences, French, geography, geology, German, graphic design, history, home economics education, horticultural science, horticulture, individual and family development, industrial arts education, industrial engineering, industrial technology, insurance and risk management, interior design, international business management, journalism, landscape architecture, Latin, liberal/general studies, marketing management, mathematics, mechanical engineering, microbiology, music education, music performance, music theory and composition, operations research, painting, petroleum engineering, petroleum land management, philosophy, physical education, physics, plant physiology, political science and government, predentistry, prelaw, premedicine, printmaking, psychology, public administration, radio/television broadcasting, real estate, religion, rural sociology, Russian and Slavic studies, sculpture, sociology, Spanish, speech, speech pathology/audiology, speech/communication/theater education, textiles and clothing, wildlife management, zoology.

ACADEMIC PROGRAMS. Accelerated program, cooperative education, double major, dual enrollment of high school students, education specialist degree, honors program, independent study, internships, study abroad, teacher preparation, cross-registration; combined bachelor's/graduate program in medicine. **Remedial services:** Learning center, remedial instruction, special counselor, tutoring. **ROTC:** Air Force, Army, Naval. **Placement/credit:** AP, CLEP Subject, institutional tests; 30 credit hours maximum for bachelor's degree.

ACADEMIC REQUIREMENTS. Freshmen must earn minimum GPA of 2.0 to continue in good standing. 76% of freshmen return for sophomore year. Students must declare major by end of first year. **Graduation requirements:** 128 hours for bachelor's (30 in major). Most students required to take courses in arts/fine arts, English, humanities, mathematics, biological/physical sciences, social sciences.

FRESHMAN ADMISSIONS. Selection criteria: Specific course units, school achievement record, class rank, and SAT or ACT scores considered. **High school preparation:** 17.5 units required. Required units include English 4, foreign language 2, mathematics 3, social science 3 and science 3. .5 computer studies also required. Specific courses required in some subject areas. 2 additional units from any of the required categories and/or advanced course work in the visual and performing arts. **Test requirements:** SAT or ACT; score report by April 30. **Additional information:** Applicants not meeting course units and/or grades or test score minimum may be considered by Admissions Committee.

1992 FRESHMAN CLASS PROFILE. 3,204 men applied, 2,437 accepted, 1,648 enrolled; 3,503 women applied, 2,829 accepted, 1,916 enrolled. 47% had high school GPA of 3.0 or higher, 52% between 2.0 and 2.99. 26% were in top tenth and 54% were in top quarter of graduating class. **Academic background:** Mid 50% of enrolled freshmen had ACT composite between 20-26. 93% submitted ACT scores. **Characteristics:** 84% from in state, 15% have minority backgrounds, 2% are foreign students. Average age is 19.

FALL-TERM APPLICATIONS. $25 fee, may be waived for applicants with need. Closing date June 1; applicants notified on a rolling basis. Audition required for music applicants. Portfolio required for fine arts, interior design, architecture applicants. Interview recommended. Early admission available. Concurrent enrollment program available for high school students with above average record and test scores.

STUDENT LIFE. Housing: Dormitories (men, women); apartment, fraternity, sorority housing available. **Activities:** Student government, film, magazine, radio, student newspaper, yearbook, choral groups, concert band, dance, drama, jazz band, marching band, music ensembles, musical theater, opera, pep band, symphony orchestra, fraternities, sororities, religious organizations and centers, professional honorary organizations, intrafraternity council, Panhellenic council.

ATHLETICS. NCAA. **Intercollegiate:** Baseball M, basketball, cross-country, football M, golf, gymnastics W, swimming, tennis, track and field, volleyball W. **Intramural:** Badminton, basketball, bowling, golf W, racquetball, soccer, softball, swimming, table tennis, tennis, track and field, volleyball, wrestling M.

STUDENT SERVICES. Aptitude testing, career counseling, employment service for undergraduates, freshman orientation, health services, personal counseling, placement service for graduates, special adviser for adult students, veterans counselor, services/facilities for handicapped.

ANNUAL EXPENSES. Tuition and fees (1992-93): $2,170. **Room and board:** $2,900. **Books and supplies:** $576. **Other expenses:** $1,544.

FINANCIAL AID. 50% of freshmen, 53% of continuing students receive some form of aid. 40% of grants, 63% of loans, 7% of jobs based on need. 1,911 enrolled freshmen were judged to have need, 1,706 were offered aid. Academic, music/drama, athletic scholarships available. **Aid applications:** No closing date; priority given to applications received by April 1; applicants notified on a rolling basis beginning on or about March 1; must reply within 10 days.

ADDRESS/TELEPHONE. Lisa Harris, Director of Undergraduate Admissions, Louisiana State University and Agricultural and Mechanical College, 110 T. Boyd Hall, Baton Rouge, LA 70803-2750. (504) 388-1175.

Louisiana State University at Alexandria

Alexandria, Louisiana — CB code: 1632

2-year public branch campus college, coed. Founded in 1959. **Accreditation:** Regional. **Undergraduate enrollment:** 2,771 men and women. **Faculty:** 91 total (72 full time), 57 with doctorates or other terminal degrees. **Location:** Rural campus in small city; 10 miles from downtown. **Calendar:** Semester, extensive summer session. **Microcomputers:** Located in libraries, computer centers, campus-wide network.

DEGREES OFFERED. AS. 178 associate degrees awarded in 1992. 15% in business and management, 15% computer sciences, 70% health sciences.

UNDERGRADUATE MAJORS. Business administration and management, business data programming, computer and information sciences, liberal/general studies, nursing, science technologies, secretarial and related programs, teacher aide.

ACADEMIC PROGRAMS. 2-year transfer program, dual enrollment of high school students. **Remedial services:** Learning center, remedial instruction, tutoring. **Placement/credit:** AP, CLEP Subject, institutional tests; 15 credit hours maximum for associate degree. Maximum of 25% of total credits required for degree may be earned through examination.

ACADEMIC REQUIREMENTS. Freshmen must earn minimum GPA of 2.0 to continue in good standing. Students must declare major by end of first year. **Graduation requirements:** 60 hours for associate. Most students required to take courses in English, mathematics. **Additional information:** Students may major in any 4-year degree program offered at main campus of Louisiana State University at Baton Rouge.

FRESHMAN ADMISSIONS. Selection criteria: Open admissions. Selective admissions for out-of-state applicants. **Test requirements:** ACT for placement; score report by July 15.

1992 FRESHMAN CLASS PROFILE. 175 men, 291 women enrolled. **Academic background:** Mid 50% of enrolled freshmen had ACT composite between 12-19. 99% submitted ACT scores. **Characteristics:** 99% from in state, 100% commute.

FALL-TERM APPLICATIONS. $20 fee. No closing date; priority given to applications received by July 15; applicants notified on a rolling basis. Early admission available.

STUDENT LIFE. Activities: Student government, student newspaper, television, yearbook, choral groups, drama, musical theater.

ATHLETICS. Intramural: Badminton, basketball, golf, soccer, softball, swimming, table tennis, tennis, volleyball.

STUDENT SERVICES. Aptitude testing, career counseling, employment service for undergraduates, freshman orientation, personal counseling, placement service for graduates, special adviser for adult students, veterans counselor, services/facilities for handicapped.

ANNUAL EXPENSES. Tuition and fees: $924, $1,472 additional for out-of-state students. **Books and supplies:** $520. **Other expenses:** $1,011.

FINANCIAL AID. 43% of freshmen, 56% of continuing students receive some form of aid. 86% of grants, 90% of loans, 47% of jobs based on need. Academic, music/drama, art, state/district residency, leadership, alumni affiliation, minority scholarships available. **Aid applications:** No closing date; priority given to applications received by June 15; applicants notified on a rolling basis beginning on or about July 1; must reply within 4 weeks.

ADDRESS/TELEPHONE. Richard W. Averitt, Registrar, Louisiana State University at Alexandria, 8100 Highway 71 South, Alexandria, LA 71302-9633. (318) 473-6413. Fax: (318) 473-6418.

Louisiana State University at Eunice
Eunice, Louisiana CB code: 6386

2-year public community college, coed. Founded in 1964. **Accreditation:** Regional. **Undergraduate enrollment:** 469 men, 840 women full time; 477 men, 1,075 women part time. **Faculty:** 120 total (73 full time), 36 with doctorates or other terminal degrees. **Location:** Rural campus in large town; 40 miles from Lafayette, 90 miles from Baton Rouge. **Calendar:** Semester, limited summer session. **Microcomputers:** 92 located in classrooms, computer centers.

DEGREES OFFERED. 170 associate degrees awarded in 1992. 6% in business and management, 51% allied health, 21% multi/interdisciplinary studies, 15% parks/recreation, protective services, public affairs.

UNDERGRADUATE MAJORS. Business and management, computer and information sciences, criminal justice studies, fire control and safety technology, liberal/general studies, practical nursing, protective services, radiograph medical technology, respiratory therapy technology, secretarial and related programs.

ACADEMIC PROGRAMS. 2-year transfer program, dual enrollment of high school students, honors program, independent study. **Remedial services:** Learning center, remedial instruction, special counselor, tutoring. **Placement/credit:** AP, CLEP Subject, institutional tests; 30 credit hours maximum for associate degree.

ACADEMIC REQUIREMENTS. Freshmen must earn minimum GPA of 2.0 to continue in good standing. Students must declare major on application. **Graduation requirements:** 66 hours for associate. Most students required to take courses in arts/fine arts, computer science, English, history, humanities, mathematics, biological/physical sciences, social sciences.

FRESHMAN ADMISSIONS. Selection criteria: Open admissions. Test scores, school achievement record, interview considered for admission to nursing and respiratory care programs. **Test requirements:** ACT for placement and counseling only; score report by August 20.

1992 FRESHMAN CLASS PROFILE. 271 men, 473 women enrolled. **Characteristics:** 99% from in state, 100% commute, 13% have minority backgrounds, 20% join fraternities/sororities.

FALL-TERM APPLICATIONS. No fee. No closing date; applicants notified on a rolling basis. Interview required for nursing, respiratory care applicants. Early admission available.

STUDENT LIFE. Activities: Student government, student newspaper, yearbook, drama, fraternities, sororities, Circle-K, Baptist Student Union, Newman Club, Wesley Foundation.

ATHLETICS. Intramural: Archery, basketball, golf, softball, table tennis, tennis, volleyball.

STUDENT SERVICES. Career counseling, health services, personal counseling, placement service for graduates, special adviser for adult students, veterans counselor, services/facilities for handicapped.

ANNUAL EXPENSES. Tuition and fees (1992-93): $960, $1,200 additional for out-of-state students. **Books and supplies:** $650.

FINANCIAL AID. 60% of freshmen, 48% of continuing students receive some form of aid. 92% of grants, 87% of loans, 35% of jobs based on need. Academic scholarships available. **Aid applications:** No closing date; priority given to applications received by July 1; applicants notified on a rolling basis; must reply within 2 weeks.

ADDRESS/TELEPHONE. Arlene C. Tucker, Director of Admissions/Registrar, Louisiana State University at Eunice, PO Box 1129, Eunice, LA 70535. (318) 457-7311.

Louisiana State University Medical Center
New Orleans, Louisiana CB code: 1192

2-year upper-division public medical education campus of university system, coed. Founded in 1931. **Accreditation:** Regional. **Undergraduate enrollment:** 176 men, 741 women full time; 14 men, 92 women part time. **Graduate enrollment:** 999 men, 632 women full time; 60 men, 194 women part time. **Faculty:** 1,047 total (720 full time). **Location:** Urban campus in very large city. **Calendar:** Semester, limited summer session. **Microcomputers:** Located in libraries, classrooms, computer centers. **Additional facts:** Louisiana State University Medical Center has teaching, research and health-care functions statewide, through its 6 professional schools, as well as the more than 100 hospitals and other health-science related institutions worldwide with which they maintain affiliations, providing health care for approximately 75 percent of Louisiana's indigent population. Component professional schools, include: School of Medicine in New Orleans; School of Graduate Studies of the Medical Center; School of Denstistry; School of Medicine in Shreveport; School of Nursing; School of Allied Health Professions.

DEGREES OFFERED. BS, MS, PhD, DMD, MD. 282 bachelor's degrees awarded. Graduate degrees offered in 20 major fields of study.

UNDERGRADUATE MAJORS. Bachelor's: Clinical laboratory science, dental hygiene, dental laboratory technology, medical laboratory technologies, nursing, occupational therapy, ophthalmic services, physical therapy, rehabilitation counseling/services, respiratory therapy technology.

ACADEMIC PROGRAMS. Honors program, independent study, internships, cross-registration. **Remedial services:** Reduced course load, special counselor, tutoring. **Placement/credit:** Institutional tests. Maximum of 60 semester hours of credit by examination may be counted toward degree in the school of nursing only.

ACADEMIC REQUIREMENTS. Students must declare major on application. **Graduation requirements:** 135 hours for bachelor's (65 in major). Most students required to take courses in English, foreign languages, history, humanities, mathematics, philosophy/religion, biological/physical sciences, social sciences.

STUDENT LIFE. Housing: Dormitories (men, women, coed); apartment housing available. **Activities:** Student government, student newspaper, yearbook, choral groups, concert band, jazz band.

ATHLETICS. Intramural: Baseball M, basketball M, golf M, softball M, volleyball.

STUDENT SERVICES. Aptitude testing, health services, personal counseling, services/facilities for handicapped.

ANNUAL EXPENSES. Tuition and fees (1992-93): $1,802, $2,400 additional for out-of-state students. Tuition and fees for nursing program $1,629 ($2,000 additional for out-of-state students), for dental auxiliary program, $1,200 in-state ($1,300 additional for out-of-state students). Allied Health programs: $2,209.00 in-state students an additional $3,000 for out-of-state **Room and board:** $1,500 room only. **Books and supplies:** $1,658. **Other expenses:** $2,492.

FINANCIAL AID. 85% of continuing students receive some form of aid. 88% of grants, 81% of loans, all jobs based on need. Academic scholarships available. **Aid applications:** No closing date; priority given to applications received by May 1; applicants notified on a rolling basis; must reply within 10 days.

ADDRESS/TELEPHONE. Office of the Registrar, Louisiana State University Medical Center, 433 Bolivar Street, New Orleans, LA 70112-2223. (504) 568-4829. Fax: (504) 568-7399 ext. 4829.

Louisiana State University in Shreveport
Shreveport, Louisiana CB code: 6355

4-year public university, coed. Founded in 1965. **Accreditation:** Regional. **Undergraduate enrollment:** 1,155 men, 1,437 women full time; 576 men, 849 women part time. **Graduate enrollment:** 20 men, 25 women full time; 221 men, 382 women part time. **Faculty:** 234 total (167 full time), 140 with doctorates or other terminal degrees. **Location:** Urban campus in small city; 180 miles from Dallas, Texas. **Calendar:** Semester, extensive summer session. **Microcomputers:** 130 located in classrooms, computer centers. **Special facilities:** Life science museum.

DEGREES OFFERED. BA, BS, MA, MS, MBA, MEd. 400 bachelor's degrees awarded in 1992. Graduate degrees offered in 7 major fields of study.

UNDERGRADUATE MAJORS. Accounting, art education, biochemistry, biology, business administration and management, business and management, business economics, business education, chemistry, clinical laboratory science, communications, computer and information sciences, economics, education, education of the deaf and hearing impaired, education of the emotionally handicapped, education of the physically handicapped, elementary education, English, English education, finance, fine arts, foreign languages education, French, geography, health education, history, journalism, law enforcement and corrections, liberal/general studies, marketing management, mathematics, mathematics education, philosophy, physics, political science and government, psychology, public administration, public relations, school psychology, science and medicine, science education, secondary education, social studies education, sociology, Spanish, special education, speech, speech correction, speech pathology/audiology.

ACADEMIC PROGRAMS. Accelerated program, cooperative education, double major, dual enrollment of high school students, education specialist degree, honors program, independent study, internships, study abroad, teacher preparation, Washington semester, cooperative education program with Southern University at Shreveport; combined bachelor's/graduate program in medicine. **Remedial services:** Learning center, remedial instruction, tutoring. **ROTC:** Army. **Placement/credit:** AP, CLEP General and Subject, institutional tests; 62 credit hours maximum for bachelor's degree.

ACADEMIC REQUIREMENTS. Freshmen must earn minimum GPA of 2.0 to continue in good standing. 60% of freshmen return for sophomore year. Students must declare major on enrollment. **Graduation requirements:** 128 hours for bachelor's. Most students required to take courses in arts/fine arts, computer science, English, history, humanities, mathematics, biological/physical sciences, social sciences.

FRESHMAN ADMISSIONS. Selection criteria: Open admissions. **High school preparation:** 18 units recommended. Recommended units include biological science 1, English 4, foreign language 2, mathematics 3, social science 3 and science 2. arts and humanities 1 unit, computer science 1 unit, speech 1 unit. **Test requirements:** ACT for placement; score report by August 15.

1992 FRESHMAN CLASS PROFILE. 587 men, 664 women enrolled. **Academic background:** Mid 50% of enrolled freshmen had ACT composite between 17-22. 95% submitted ACT scores. **Characteristics:** 98% from in state, 100% commute, 14% have minority backgrounds, 10% join fraternities/sororities. Average age is 20.

FALL-TERM APPLICATIONS. $10 fee. Closing date August 10; applicants notified on a rolling basis. Deferred admission available.

STUDENT LIFE. Activities: Student government, radio, student newspaper, music ensembles, fraternities, sororities, Baptist Student Union, Republican Club, Democratic Club, Government and Law Society, Drama Club, Wesley Foundation.

ATHLETICS. NAIA. **Intercollegiate:** Baseball M, basketball, cross-country W, golf, soccer M, tennis, volleyball W. **Intramural:** Badminton, basketball, bowling, golf, racquetball, softball, swimming, table tennis, tennis, track and field, volleyball.

STUDENT SERVICES. Aptitude testing, career counseling, employment service for undergraduates, freshman orientation, personal counseling, placement service for graduates, veterans counselor, services/facilities for handicapped.

ANNUAL EXPENSES. Tuition and fees (1992-93): $1,480, $2,190 additional for out-of-state students. **Books and supplies:** $575. **Other expenses:** $1,025.

FINANCIAL AID. 15% of continuing students receive some form of aid. Grants, loans, jobs available. Academic, state/district residency, leadership, alumni affiliation, minority scholarships available. **Aid applications:** No closing date; applicants notified on a rolling basis; must reply within 2 weeks.

ADDRESS/TELEPHONE. Kathleen G. Plante, Registrar and Director of Admissions, Louisiana State University in Shreveport, One University Place, Shreveport, LA 71115. (318) 797-5207.

Louisiana Tech University
Ruston, Louisiana — CB code: 6372

Admissions:	89% of applicants accepted
Based on:	••• School record, test scores
	•• Special talents
	• Activities, recommendations
Completion:	35% graduate, 36% of these enter graduate study

4-year public university, coed. Founded in 1894. **Accreditation:** Regional. **Undergraduate enrollment:** 4,075 men, 3,114 women full time; 859 men, 910 women part time. **Graduate enrollment:** 480 men, 299 women full time; 167 men, 293 women part time. **Faculty:** 513 total (438 full time), 319 with doctorates or other terminal degrees. **Location:** Rural campus in large town; 70 miles from Shreveport, 30 miles from Monroe. **Calendar:** Quarter, extensive summer session. Extensive evening/early morning classes. **Microcomputers:** 1,000 located in dormitories, libraries, classrooms, computer centers. **Special facilities:** La Tech Museum, School of Art and Architecture Gallery, Center for Rehabilitation Science and Biomedical Engineering, Lomax Arboretum, planetarium.

DEGREES OFFERED. AS, BA, BS, BFA, BArch, MA, MS, MBA, MFA, MEd, PhD. 158 associate degrees awarded in 1992. 19% in business and management, 48% allied health, 31% multi/interdisciplinary studies. 1,265 bachelor's degrees awarded. 5% in agriculture, 27% business and management, 12% education, 15% engineering, 18% multi/interdisciplinary studies. Graduate degrees offered in 46 major fields of study.

UNDERGRADUATE MAJORS. Associate: Business and office, food production/management/services, liberal/general studies, medical records technology, nursing, secretarial and related programs. **Bachelor's:** Accounting, agribusiness, agricultural education, agronomy, airline piloting and navigation, animal sciences, architecture, art education, bioengineering and biomedical engineering, biology, botany, business administration and management, business economics, business education, chemical engineering, chemistry, civil engineering, civil technology, clinical laboratory science, computer and information sciences, computer engineering, early childhood education, education of the emotionally handicapped, education of the mentally handicapped, education of the physically handicapped, electrical/electronics/communications engineering, electronic technology, elementary education, English, English education, family/consumer resource management, finance, food science and nutrition, foreign languages education, forestry and related sciences, forestry production and processing, French, geography, geology, graphic design, history, home economics education, human resources development, individual and family development, industrial engineering, interior design, journalism, liberal/general studies, management information systems, management science, marketing management, mathematics, mathematics education, mechanical engineering, medical records administration, microbiology, music, music education, music performance, operations research, ornamental horticulture, parks and recreation management, personnel management, petroleum engineering, photography, physical education, physics, plant sciences, political science and government, prelaw, psychology, science education, social studies education, social work, sociology, Spanish, specific learning disabilities, speech, speech correction, speech pathology/audiology, speech/communication/theater education, studio art, technical and business writing, textiles and clothing, trade and industrial supervision and management, wildlife management, zoology.

ACADEMIC PROGRAMS. Cooperative education, double major, dual enrollment of high school students, education specialist degree, honors program, independent study, internships, study abroad, teacher preparation, telecourses, cross-registration, cooperative programs with Grambling State University. **Remedial services:** Remedial instruction, tutoring. **ROTC:** Air Force. **Placement/credit:** AP, CLEP Subject, institutional tests; 60 credit hours maximum for bachelor's degree.

ACADEMIC REQUIREMENTS. Freshmen must earn minimum GPA of 2.0 to continue in good standing. 65% of freshmen return for sophomore year. Students must declare major by end of first year. **Graduation requirements:** 62 hours for associate, 130 hours for bachelor's. Most students required to take courses in arts/fine arts, computer science, English, history, humanities, mathematics, biological/physical sciences, social sciences.

FRESHMAN ADMISSIONS. Selection criteria: High school record, test scores most important. Special talents, school and community activities, and recommendations also considered. **High school preparation:** 17 units required. Required and recommended units include English 4, mathematics 3, social science 3 and science 3. Foreign language 2 recommended. Mathematics includeds 2 units Algebra Social Studies includes 1 unit American History, 4.5 units of Electives from: foreign language social Studies, sciences mathematics, speech advanced fine arts, computer literacy. **Test requirements:** SAT or ACT (ACT preferred); score report by August 15. **Additional information:** Provisional admission available.

1992 FRESHMAN CLASS PROFILE. 2,821 men and women applied, 2,501 accepted; 853 men enrolled, 743 women enrolled. 21% were in top tenth and 44% were in top quarter of graduating class. **Academic background:** Mid 50% of enrolled freshmen had ACT composite between 18-24. 90% submitted ACT scores. **Characteristics:** 85% from in state, 80% live in college housing, 20% have minority backgrounds, 20% join fraternities/sororities. Average age is 18.

FALL-TERM APPLICATIONS. $15 fee. Closing date August 15; applicants notified on a rolling basis beginning on or about June 1. Early admission available.

STUDENT LIFE. Housing: Dormitories (men, women); apartment, fraternity, handicapped housing available. **Activities:** Student government, radio, student newspaper, yearbook, choral groups, concert band, dance, drama, jazz band, marching band, music ensembles, musical theater, opera, pep band, symphony orchestra, fraternities, sororities, various religious organizations.

ATHLETICS. NCAA. **Intercollegiate:** Baseball M, basketball, cross-country, football M, golf M, softball W, tennis W, track and field, volleyball W. **Intramural:** Badminton, basketball, bowling, golf M, handball, racquetball, soccer, softball, tennis, volleyball.

STUDENT SERVICES. Aptitude testing, career counseling, employment service for undergraduates, freshman orientation, health services, personal counseling, placement service for graduates, veterans counselor, services/facilities for handicapped.

ANNUAL EXPENSES. Tuition and fees (projected): $2,256, $1,455 additional for out-of-state students. **Room and board:** $3,654. **Books and supplies:** $600. **Other expenses:** $1,166.

FINANCIAL AID. 77% of freshmen, 77% of continuing students receive some form of aid. 50% of grants, 88% of loans, 22% of jobs based on need. 635 enrolled freshmen were judged to have need, all were offered aid. Academic, music/drama, art, athletic, state/district residency, leadership, minority scholarships available. **Aid applications:** No closing date; priority given to applications received by April 1; applicants notified on a rolling basis beginning on or about June 1; must reply within 2 weeks.

ADDRESS/TELEPHONE. Karen Akin, Director of Admissions, Louisiana Tech University, PO Box 3178, Tech Station, Ruston, LA 71272. (318) 257-3036. Fax: (318) 257-4041.

Loyola University
New Orleans, Louisiana CB code: 6374

Admissions: 84% of applicants accepted
Based on: ••• Essay, recommendations, school record
•• Special talents, test scores
• Activities, interview
Completion: 84% of freshmen end year in good standing
56% graduate

4-year private university and college of arts and sciences and business, music, liberal arts college, coed, affiliated with Roman Catholic Church. Founded in 1912. **Accreditation:** Regional. **Undergraduate enrollment:** 1,141 men, 1,506 women full time; 244 men, 623 women part time. **Graduate enrollment:** 439 men, 368 women full time; 264 men, 326 women part time. **Faculty:** 391 total (240 full time), 228 with doctorates or other terminal degrees. **Location:** Urban campus in very large city. **Calendar:** Semester, limited summer session. Saturday and extensive evening/early morning classes. **Microcomputers:** 260 located in dormitories, libraries, classrooms, computer centers. **Special facilities:** Concert hall, small business development center, experimental theater, psychology research laboratories, media center, institute of politics art gallery. **Additional facts:** Largest Catholic university in southern United States. Dedicated to Jesuit academic tradition of liberal education.

DEGREES OFFERED. BA, BS, MA, MS, MBA, MEd, JD. 552 bachelor's degrees awarded in 1992. 24% in business and management, 24% communications, 5% education, 8% psychology, 16% social sciences, 5% visual and performing arts. Graduate degrees offered in 13 major fields of study.

UNDERGRADUATE MAJORS. Accounting, advertising, biology, business administration and management, business and management, business economics, chemistry, communications, computer and information sciences, criminal justice studies, dramatic arts, economics, education, elementary education, English, finance, French, German, history, humanities, humanities and social sciences, information sciences and systems, international business management, jazz, journalism, liberal/general studies, management science, marketing management, mathematics, music, music performance, music theory and composition, music therapy, nursing, philosophy, physics, political science and government, predentistry, prelaw, premedicine, prepharmacy, preveterinary, psychology, public relations, radio/television broadcasting, religion, Russian, social sciences, sociology, Spanish, speech, visual and performing arts.

ACADEMIC PROGRAMS. Accelerated program, double major, honors program, independent study, internships, student-designed major, study abroad, teacher preparation, telecourses, weekend college, cross-registration; liberal arts/career combination in business; combined bachelor's/graduate program in business administration, law. **Remedial services:** Learning center, preadmission summer program, reduced course load, remedial instruction, special counselor, tutoring. **ROTC:** Army. **Placement/credit:** AP, CLEP General and Subject, institutional tests; 30 credit hours maximum for bachelor's degree.

ACADEMIC REQUIREMENTS. Freshmen must earn minimum GPA of 2.0 to continue in good standing. 79% of freshmen return for sophomore year. Students must declare major by end of second year. **Graduation requirements:** 128 hours for bachelor's (30 in major). Most students required to take courses in English, foreign languages, history, humanities, mathematics, philosophy/religion, biological/physical sciences, social sciences.

FRESHMAN ADMISSIONS. Selection criteria: High school performance, test scores, extracurricular activity, community involvement, and work experience. **High school preparation:** 10 units required; 17 recommended. Required and recommended units include English 4, mathematics 2-3, social science 2-3 and science 2-3. Foreign language 2 recommended. **Test requirements:** SAT or ACT; score report by August 15. Prueba de Aptitud Academica for Spanish speaking applicants. Highest ACT scores for single test date used when subscores are considered; Highest SAT individual scores used when subscores are considered. **Additional information:** Adults 22 and over must have minimum high school GPA of 2.0 or a GED score of 50.

1992 FRESHMAN CLASS PROFILE. 1,696 men and women applied, 1,424 accepted; 661 enrolled. 55% had high school GPA of 3.0 or higher, 41% between 2.0 and 2.99. 23% were in top tenth and 50% were in top quarter of graduating class. **Academic background:** Mid 50% of enrolled freshmen had SAT-V between 450-560, SAT-M between 470-570; ACT composite between 23-27. 40% submitted SAT scores, 50% submitted ACT scores. **Characteristics:** 48% from in state, 65% live in college housing, 31% have minority backgrounds, 3% are foreign students, 6% join fraternities/sororities. Average age is 18.

FALL-TERM APPLICATIONS. $20 fee, may be waived for applicants with need. Closing date August 1; priority given to applications received by May 1; applicants notified on a rolling basis; must reply by August 1. Audition required for music applicants. Portfolio required for visual arts, graphic arts applicants. Essay required. Interview recommended for borderline, scholarship applicants. CRDA. Deferred and early admission available.

STUDENT LIFE. Housing: Dormitories (men, women, coed). Conselors live in each hall to provide spiritual/counseling assistance. **Activities:** Student government, film, magazine, radio, student newspaper, television, yearbook, choral groups, concert band, dance, drama, jazz band, music ensembles, musical theater, opera, symphony orchestra, fraternities, sororities, Black Student Union, community action program, law clinic.

ATHLETICS. NAIA. **Intercollegiate:** Baseball M, basketball M. **Intramural:** Badminton, baseball, basketball, bowling, handball, racquetball, sailing, soccer, softball, swimming, table tennis, tennis, volleyball, water polo.

STUDENT SERVICES. Aptitude testing, career counseling, employment service for undergraduates, freshman orientation, health services, on-campus day care, personal counseling, placement service for graduates, special adviser for adult students, commuter services center, services/facilities for handicapped.

ANNUAL EXPENSES. Tuition and fees: $10,625. **Room and board:** $5,190. **Books and supplies:** $600. **Other expenses:** $750.

FINANCIAL AID. 50% of freshmen, 52% of continuing students receive some form of aid. 63% of grants, 85% of loans, all jobs based on need. 372 enrolled freshmen were judged to have need, 365 were offered aid. Academic, music/drama, art scholarships available. **Aid applications:** Closing date August 1; priority given to applications received by May 1; applicants notified on a rolling basis beginning on or about March 5; must reply by May 1 or within 4 weeks if notified thereafter. **Additional information:** Interview recommended for scholarship applicants.

ADDRESS/TELEPHONE. Nan Massingill, Director Admissions, Loyola University, 7214 St. Charles Avenue, New Orleans, LA 70118-6143. (504) 861-5888. (800)4-LOYOLA. Fax: (504) 861-5990.

McNeese State University
Lake Charles, Louisiana CB code: 6403

4-year public university, coed. Founded in 1939. **Accreditation:** Regional. **Undergraduate enrollment:** 7,316 men and women. **Graduate enrollment:** 1,158 men and women. **Faculty:** 397 total (335 full time), 174 with doctorates or other terminal degrees. **Location:** Suburban campus in small city; 150 miles from Houston. **Calendar:** Semester, extensive summer session. **Microcomputers:** Located in dormitories, libraries, classrooms, computer centers. **Special facilities:** Planetarium, vertebrate museum, art gallery.

DEGREES OFFERED. AA, AS, BA, BS, MA, MS, MBA, MFA, MEd. 140 associate degrees awarded in 1992. 700 bachelor's degrees awarded. Graduate degrees offered in 27 major fields of study.

UNDERGRADUATE MAJORS. Associate: Computer and information sciences, criminal justice studies, drafting and design technology, electrical technology, electronic technology, funeral services/mortuary science, instrumentation technology, legal assistant/paralegal, liberal/general studies, secretarial and related programs, word processing. **Bachelor's:** Accounting, agribusiness, agricultural sciences, agronomy, animal sciences, art education, botany, business administration and management, business and management, business economics, business education, business home economics, chemical engineering, chemistry, civil engineering, computer and information sciences, criminal justice studies, dramatic arts, drawing, early childhood education, economics, electrical technology, electrical/electronics/communications engineering, electronic technology, elementary education, English, English education, environmental science, finance, foreign languages education, French, geology, history, home economics education, horticultural science, liberal/general studies, marketing management, mathematics, mathematics education, mechanical engineering, medical laboratory technologies, medical radiation dosimetry, microbiology, music, music education, music performance, music theory and composition, nursing, painting, physical education, physics, political science and government, predentistry, premedicine, psychology, radio/television broadcasting, school psychology, science education, sculpture, secondary education, secretarial and related programs, social studies education, sociology, Spanish, special education, speech, speech/communication/theater education, statistics, wildlife management, zoology.

ACADEMIC PROGRAMS. 2-year transfer program, accelerated program, cooperative education, double major, dual enrollment of high school students, education specialist degree, honors program, internships, teacher preparation, telecourses; liberal arts/career combination in engineering, health sciences. **Remedial services:** Remedial instruction, tutoring. **ROTC:** Army. **Placement/credit:** AP, CLEP General and Subject, institutional tests; 24 credit hours maximum for associate degree; 45 credit hours maximum for bachelor's degree.

ACADEMIC REQUIREMENTS. Freshmen must earn minimum GPA of 1.5 to continue in good standing. 66% of freshmen return for sophomore year. Students must declare major by end of second year. **Graduation requirements:** 60 hours for associate (30 in major), 130 hours for bachelor's (35 in major). Most students required to take courses in arts/fine arts, computer science, English, history, mathematics, biological/physical sciences, social sciences.

FRESHMAN ADMISSIONS. Selection criteria: Open admissions.

Selective admissions for out-of-state applicants based on high school GPA, ACT or SAT scores, class rank, and extracurricular activities. **High school preparation:** 24 units recommended. Recommended units include English 4, foreign language 3, mathematics 3, social science 3 and science 3. **Test requirements:** ACT for placement and counseling only; score report by July 31.

1992 FRESHMAN CLASS PROFILE. 684 men, 838 women enrolled. **Academic background:** Mid 50% of enrolled freshmen had ACT composite between 16-21. 100% submitted ACT scores. **Characteristics:** 95% from in state, 72% commute, 14% have minority backgrounds, 18% join fraternities/sororities. Average age is 18.

FALL-TERM APPLICATIONS. $10 fee. No closing date; priority given to applications received by July 24; applicants notified on a rolling basis beginning on or about March 15. Audition required for music applicants. Early admission available.

STUDENT LIFE. Housing: Dormitories (men, women, coed); apartment, fraternity, sorority housing available. **Activities:** Student government, magazine, student newspaper, television, yearbook, choral groups, concert band, dance, drama, jazz band, marching band, music ensembles, musical theater, opera, pep band, symphony orchestra, fraternities, sororities.

ATHLETICS. NCAA. **Intercollegiate:** Baseball M, basketball, cross-country, football M, golf M, rifle M, softball W, track and field M, volleyball W. **Intramural:** Archery, badminton, basketball, bowling, boxing, cross-country, golf, handball, racquetball, rifle, rowing (crew), soccer, softball, swimming, table tennis, tennis, track and field, volleyball, water polo.

STUDENT SERVICES. Aptitude testing, career counseling, employment service for undergraduates, freshman orientation, health services, personal counseling, placement service for graduates, special adviser for adult students, veterans counselor, services/facilities for handicapped.

ANNUAL EXPENSES. Tuition and fees (projected): $1,864, $1,550 additional for out-of-state students. **Room and board:** $2,412. **Books and supplies:** $600. **Other expenses:** $1,166.

FINANCIAL AID. 60% of freshmen, 52% of continuing students receive some form of aid. 77% of grants, 91% of loans, 45% of jobs based on need. 791 enrolled freshmen were judged to have need, all were offered aid. Academic, music/drama, art, athletic, state/district residency, leadership, alumni affiliation scholarships available. **Aid applications:** No closing date; priority given to applications received by May 1; applicants notified on a rolling basis beginning on or about April 15; must reply within 2 weeks. **Additional information:** Books may be charged and paid in 3 installments during semester.

ADDRESS/TELEPHONE. Kathy Bond, Admissions Counselor, McNeese State University, PO Box 92495, Lake Charles, LA 70609-2495. (318) 475-5000.

New Orleans Baptist Theological Seminary: School of Christian Education

New Orleans, Louisiana CB code: 5034

2-year private Bible college, coed, affiliated with Southern Baptist Convention. **Accreditation:** Regional. **Undergraduate enrollment:** 481 men and women. **Location:** Suburban campus in very large city. **Calendar:** Semester.

FRESHMAN ADMISSIONS. Selection criteria: Must be 25 years old or over and a Christian for at least one year.

ANNUAL EXPENSES. Tuition and fees (1992-93): $1,050. Students not associated with Baptist Convention pay an additional $1000 per academic year.

ADDRESS/TELEPHONE. New Orleans Baptist Theological Seminary: School of Christian Education, 3939 Gentilly Boulevard, New Orleans, LA 70126-4858. (504) 282-4455. (800) 662-8701.

Nicholls State University

Thibodaux, Louisiana CB code: 6221

4-year public university, coed. Founded in 1948. **Accreditation:** Regional. **Undergraduate enrollment:** 2,164 men, 3,058 women full time; 484 men, 1,069 women part time. **Graduate enrollment:** 46 men, 67 women full time; 175 men, 542 women part time. **Faculty:** 297 total, 160 with doctorates or other terminal degrees. **Location:** Suburban campus in large town; 60 miles from New Orleans. **Calendar:** Semester, limited summer session. **Microcomputers:** 180 located in dormitories, classrooms, computer centers. **Special facilities:** Louisiana University Consortium Research Facility in Cocodrie.

DEGREES OFFERED. AS, BA, BS, MA, MS, MBA, MEd. 242 associate degrees awarded in 1992. 8% in business and management, 6% business/office and marketing/distribution, 21% engineering technologies, 38% allied health, 11% home economics, 14% law. 663 bachelor's degrees awarded. 18% in business and management, 20% teacher education, 5% engineering technologies, 22% health sciences, 5% home economics, 5% life sciences, 10% multi/interdisciplinary studies. Graduate degrees offered in 11 major fields of study.

UNDERGRADUATE MAJORS. Associate: Airline piloting and navigation, business and management, business and office, clothing and textiles management/production/services, criminal justice technology, engineering and engineering-related technologies, food production/management/services, legal assistant/paralegal, nursing, ornamental horticulture, petroleum safety technology, petroleum service technology, respiratory therapy, respiratory therapy technology, secretarial and related programs. **Bachelor's:** Accounting, agribusiness, allied health, art education, biology, business administration and management, business and management, business and office, business economics, business education, business home economics, chemistry, civil technology, communications, computer and information sciences, early childhood education, economics, education of the mentally handicapped, electrical technology, elementary education, English, English education, finance, fine arts, food science and nutrition, foreign languages education, French, geology, health education, history, home economics, home economics education, liberal/general studies, marketing and distribution, marketing management, mathematics, mathematics education, mechanical design technology, mining and petroleum technologies, music education, music performance, nursing, operations research, personnel management, petroleum engineering technology, petroleum service technology, physical education, political science and government, predentistry, preengineering, premedicine, production management, psychology, science education, secondary education, secretarial and related programs, social studies education, sociology, speech pathology/audiology, speech, language and hearing.

ACADEMIC PROGRAMS. Internships, study abroad, teacher preparation, visiting/exchange student program. **Remedial services:** Learning center, reduced course load, remedial instruction, special counselor, tutoring. **Placement/credit:** AP, CLEP Subject, institutional tests; 30 credit hours maximum for bachelor's degree.

ACADEMIC REQUIREMENTS. Freshmen must earn minimum GPA of 1.5 to continue in good standing. 60% of freshmen return for sophomore year. Students must declare major on application. **Graduation requirements:** 60 hours for associate (24 in major), 130 hours for bachelor's (24 in major). Most students required to take courses in arts/fine arts, computer science, English, history, humanities, mathematics, biological/physical sciences, social sciences. **Postgraduate studies:** 25% from 2-year programs enter 4-year programs.

FRESHMAN ADMISSIONS. Selection criteria: Open admissions. ACT composite score of 20 required of nursing program applicants. **High school preparation:** 23 units recommended. Recommended units include English 4, mathematics 3, social science 3 and science 3. 10 electives including 2 physical education and .5 computer literacy. **Test requirements:** ACT for placement; score report by August 20.

1992 FRESHMAN CLASS PROFILE. 2,046 men and women applied, 1,944 accepted; 543 men enrolled, 760 women enrolled. **Academic background:** Mid 50% of enrolled freshmen had ACT composite between 16-21. 100% submitted ACT scores. **Characteristics:** 97% from in state, 80% commute, 18% have minority backgrounds, 1% are foreign students, 10% join fraternities/sororities. Average age is 21.

FALL-TERM APPLICATIONS. $10 fee. No closing date; priority given to applications received by August 15; applicants notified on a rolling basis beginning on or about June 1. Interview required for art, music applicants. Audition required for music applicants. Portfolio recommended for art applicants. Early admission available.

STUDENT LIFE. Housing: Dormitories (men, women, coed); apartment housing available. **Activities:** Student government, film, magazine, radio, student newspaper, television, yearbook, choral groups, concert band, dance, drama, jazz band, marching band, music ensembles, musical theater, pep band, Artists and Lecturers Series, fraternities, sororities, Baptist Student Union, St. Thomas Aquinas Catholic Community, Rotaract, Circle K, Young Democrats, Support for Older Students, African American Males, African American Voices, Chi Alpha, Order of Athena.

ATHLETICS. NCAA. **Intercollegiate:** Baseball M, basketball, cross-country, football M, golf M, softball W, tennis W, track and field, volleyball W. **Intramural:** Badminton, baseball M, basketball, bowling, boxing M, cross-country, football M, golf, racquetball, soccer, softball W, swimming, table tennis, tennis, track and field, volleyball.

STUDENT SERVICES. Aptitude testing, career counseling, employment service for undergraduates, freshman orientation, health services, on-campus day care, personal counseling, placement service for graduates, special adviser for adult students, veterans counselor, minority student services, student assistance programs, services/facilities for handicapped.

ANNUAL EXPENSES. Tuition and fees (projected): $1,862, $1,800 additional for out-of-state students. **Room and board:** $2,650. **Books and supplies:** $520. **Other expenses:** $1,000.

FINANCIAL AID. 59% of freshmen, 51% of continuing students receive some form of aid. 72% of grants, 97% of loans, 27% of jobs based on need. Academic, music/drama, athletic, state/district residency scholarships available. **Aid applications:** Closing date May 29; priority given to applications received by February 14; applicants notified on or about July 15; must reply by July 30.

ADDRESS/TELEPHONE. Dr. Walker Allen, Executive Director of Enrollment Services, Nicholls State University, PO Box 2004, College Station, Thibodaux, LA 70310. (504) 448-4139. Fax: (504) 448-4139.

Northeast Louisiana University
Monroe, Louisiana CB code: 6482

4-year public university, coed. Founded in 1931. **Accreditation:** Regional. **Undergraduate enrollment:** 3,699 men, 5,013 women full time; 679 men, 1,226 women part time. **Graduate enrollment:** 258 men, 304 women full time; 115 men, 438 women part time. **Faculty:** 562 total (496 full time), 287 with doctorates or other terminal degrees. **Location:** Urban campus in small city; 250 miles from New Orleans. **Calendar:** Semester, extensive summer session. **Microcomputers:** Located in libraries, classrooms.

DEGREES OFFERED. AA, AS, BA, BS, BFA, MA, MS, MBA, MEd, PhD. 48 associate degrees awarded in 1992. 6% in business/office and marketing/distribution, 60% allied health, 15% multi/interdisciplinary studies, 13% parks/recreation, protective services, public affairs. 1,241 bachelor's degrees awarded. 16% in business and management, 15% teacher education, 22% health sciences, 8% allied health, 9% multi/interdisciplinary studies, 6% parks/recreation, protective services, public affairs. Graduate degrees offered in 27 major fields of study.

UNDERGRADUATE MAJORS. Associate: Building inspection technology, child development/care/guidance, criminal justice technology, education of the multiple handicapped, flight attendants, forest products processing technology, liberal/general studies, occupational therapy assistant, radio/television technology, secretarial and related programs. **Bachelor's:** Accounting, agribusiness, agricultural aviation, air traffic control, airline piloting and navigation, architectural technologies, art education, atmospheric sciences and meteorology, biology, botany, business administration and management, business and management, business economics, business education, business systems analysis, chemistry, computer and information sciences, criminal justice studies, dental hygiene, early childhood education, elementary education, English, English education, finance, fine arts, food science and nutrition, foreign languages education, French, geography, geology, geophysics and seismology, history, home economics education, human environment and housing, individual and family development, insurance and risk management, journalism, liberal/general studies, marketing management, mathematics, mathematics education, medical laboratory technologies, microbiology, music, music education, music performance, nursing, occupational therapy, office supervision and management, pharmacy, physical education, physics, physiology, human and animal, political science and government, predentistry, prelaw, premedicine, psychology, public relations, radio/television broadcasting, radiograph medical technology, real estate, science education, social studies education, social work, sociology, Spanish, speech, speech pathology/audiology, speech/communication/theater education, textiles and clothing, toxicology, zoology.

ACADEMIC PROGRAMS. Accelerated program, double major, education specialist degree, honors program, internships, study abroad, teacher preparation, telecourses. **Remedial services:** Reduced course load, remedial instruction, special counselor, tutoring. **ROTC:** Army. **Placement/credit:** AP, CLEP Subject, institutional tests. Maximum of one-third of credits required for degree may be earned through examination, military experience, and correspondence courses.

ACADEMIC REQUIREMENTS. Freshmen must earn minimum GPA of 1.5 to continue in good standing. 66% of freshmen return for sophomore year. Students must declare major on application. **Graduation requirements:** 60 hours for associate, 128 hours for bachelor's. Most students required to take courses in arts/fine arts, computer science, English, humanities, mathematics, biological/physical sciences, social sciences.

FRESHMAN ADMISSIONS. Selection criteria: Open admissions. Selective admissions for international students. Recommended units include English 4, foreign language 2, mathematics 3, social science 3 and science 3. .5 unit computer science and 1 unit in arts recommended. **Test requirements:** ACT for placement and counseling only; score report by August 15.

1992 FRESHMAN CLASS PROFILE. 753 men, 1,132 women enrolled. **Characteristics:** 92% from in state, 53% commute, 27% have minority backgrounds, 1% are foreign students. Average age is 20.

FALL-TERM APPLICATIONS. $5 fee. No closing date; priority given to applications received by August 15; applicants notified on a rolling basis. Early admission available.

STUDENT LIFE. Housing: Dormitories (men, women); sorority housing available. **Activities:** Student government, magazine, radio, student newspaper, yearbook, choral groups, concert band, dance, drama, jazz band, marching band, music ensembles, musical theater, opera, pep band, symphony orchestra, fraternities, sororities, United Campus Ministries, Black Caucus Association.

ATHLETICS. NCAA. **Intercollegiate:** Baseball M, basketball, cross-country, football M, golf M, softball W, swimming, tennis, track and field, volleyball W. **Intramural:** Archery, badminton, basketball, bowling, diving, golf, softball, swimming, table tennis, tennis, track and field, volleyball.

STUDENT SERVICES. Aptitude testing, career counseling, employment service for undergraduates, freshman orientation, health services, on-campus day care, personal counseling, placement service for graduates, veterans counselor, services/facilities for handicapped.

ANNUAL EXPENSES. Tuition and fees (1992-93): $1,626, $1,584 additional for out-of-state students. **Room and board:** $1,980. **Books and supplies:** $520. **Other expenses:** $1,011.

FINANCIAL AID. 65% of freshmen, 50% of continuing students receive some form of aid. 59% of grants, all loans, 55% of jobs based on need. 1,000 enrolled freshmen were judged to have need, all were offered aid. Academic, music/drama, art, athletic, state/district residency, leadership, alumni affiliation scholarships available. **Aid applications:** No closing date; priority given to applications received by April 1; applicants notified on a rolling basis beginning on or about June 1; must reply within 2 weeks.

ADDRESS/TELEPHONE. James Robertson, Director of Admissions, Northeast Louisiana University, 700 University Avenue, Monroe, LA 71209-0730. (318) 342-5252. Fax: (318) 342-5161.

Northwestern State University
Natchitoches, Louisiana CB code: 6492

4-year public university, coed. Founded in 1884. **Accreditation:** Regional. **Undergraduate enrollment:** 2,153 men, 3,370 women full time; 773 men, 1,368 women part time. **Graduate enrollment:** 23 men, 36 women full time; 145 men, 580 women part time. **Faculty:** 286 total (225 full time), 123 with doctorates or other terminal degrees. **Location:** Suburban campus in large town; 75 miles from Shreveport, 57 miles from Alexandria. **Calendar:** Semester, extensive summer session. Extensive evening/early morning classes. **Microcomputers:** 312 located in dormitories, libraries, classrooms, computer centers. **Special facilities:** Center for History of Education in Louisiana, Louisiana Archives, Williamson Museum, Orvel Hanchey Art Gallery, Louisiana Honors College.

DEGREES OFFERED. AA, AS, BA, BS, MA, MS, MBA, MFA, MEd. 171 associate degrees awarded in 1992. 10% in business/office and marketing/distribution, 63% health sciences, 17% multi/interdisciplinary studies. 629 bachelor's degrees awarded. 24% in business and management, 15% teacher education, 19% health sciences, 7% letters/literature, 9% social sciences. Graduate degrees offered in 22 major fields of study.

UNDERGRADUATE MAJORS. Associate: Accounting, business administration and management, business and management, business data processing and related programs, computer servicing technology, computer technology, data processing, drafting and design technology, electronic technology, liberal/general studies, marketing and distribution, nursing, secretarial and related programs, veterinarian's assistant. **Bachelor's:** Accounting, advertising, anthropology, art education, biology, business administration and management, business and management, business and office, business data processing and related programs, business education, chemistry, child development/care/guidance, computer and information sciences, data processing, dramatic arts, early childhood education, economics, electronic technology, elementary education, engineering and engineering-related technologies, English, English education, fine arts, geology, history, home economics, home economics education, industrial arts education, industrial technology, information sciences and systems, journalism, liberal/general studies, marketing and distributive education, mathematics, mathematics education, medical laboratory technologies, medical radiation dosimetry, music, music education, music performance, music theory and composition, nursing, physical education, physical sciences, physics, political science and government, prelaw, psychology, public relations, radio/television broadcasting, science education, secretarial and related programs, social science education, social sciences, social work, sociology, special education, speech.

ACADEMIC PROGRAMS. 2-year transfer program, accelerated program, double major, dual enrollment of high school students, education specialist degree, honors program, internships, student-designed major, study abroad, teacher preparation, visiting/exchange student program. **Remedial services:** Learning center, remedial instruction, special counselor, tutoring. **ROTC:** Army. **Placement/credit:** AP, CLEP General and Subject, institutional tests. Maximum semester hours of credit by examination may not exceed half the number of credits required for degree.

ACADEMIC REQUIREMENTS. Freshmen must earn minimum GPA of 1.5 to continue in good standing. 51% of freshmen return for sophomore year. Students must declare major by end of second year. **Graduation requirements:** 63 hours for associate (25 in major), 124 hours for bachelor's (30 in major). Most students required to take courses in arts/fine arts, English, foreign languages, history, mathematics, biological/physical sciences, social sciences. **Postgraduate studies:** 24% from 2-year programs enter 4-year programs. 5% enter law school, 3% enter medical school, 7% enter MBA programs, 13% enter other graduate study.

FRESHMAN ADMISSIONS. Selection criteria: Open admissions. **High school preparation:** 17 units recommended. Recommended units include English 4, foreign language 3, mathematics 3, social science 4 and science 3. **Test requirements:** ACT for placement and counseling only; score report by August 1.

1992 FRESHMAN CLASS PROFILE. 618 men, 910 women enrolled. **Characteristics:** 96% from in state, 100% commute, 27% have minority backgrounds, 1% are foreign students, 19% join fraternities/sororities. Average age is 18.

FALL-TERM APPLICATIONS. $5 fee. $15 fee for foreign applicants. No closing date; priority given to applications received by August 1; applicants notified on a rolling basis. Interview recommended. Early admission available.

STUDENT LIFE. Housing: Dormitories (men, women); apartment, fraternity housing available. **Activities:** Student government, film, magazine, radio, student newspaper, television, yearbook, choral groups, concert band, dance, drama, marching band, music ensembles, musical theater, opera, pep band, symphony orchestra, fraternities, sororities, Wesley Foundation, Baptist Student Union.

ATHLETICS. NCAA. **Intercollegiate:** Baseball M, basketball, cross-country, football M, golf M, rifle M, softball W, tennis W, track and field, volleyball W. **Intramural:** Archery, badminton, basketball, bowling, golf, horseback riding, racquetball, soccer, softball, swimming, tennis, track and field, volleyball.

STUDENT SERVICES. Aptitude testing, career counseling, employment service for undergraduates, freshman orientation, health services, on-campus day care, personal counseling, placement service for graduates, veterans counselor, services/facilities for handicapped.

ANNUAL EXPENSES. Tuition and fees (1992-93): $1,772, $1,800 additional for out-of-state students. **Room and board:** $2,093. **Books and supplies:** $550. **Other expenses:** $1,051.

FINANCIAL AID. 70% of freshmen, 77% of continuing students receive some form of aid. Grants, loans, jobs available. 1,030 enrolled freshmen were judged to have need, 1,020 were offered aid. Academic, music/drama, art, athletic, state/district residency, leadership, alumni affiliation, minority scholarships available. **Aid applications:** No closing date; priority given to applications received by April 1; applicants notified on a rolling basis beginning on or about June 1; must reply within 2 weeks.

ADDRESS/TELEPHONE. Marsha Zulick, Director of Admissions and Recruiting, Northwestern State University, Natchitoches, LA 71497. (318) 357-4503. (800) 327 1903. Fax: (318) 357-4257.

Nunez Community College
Chalmette, Louisiana — CB code: 0295

2-year public community college, coed. Founded in 1967. **Accreditation:** Regional. **Undergraduate enrollment:** 1,887 men and women. **Faculty:** 62 total (40 full time), 3 with doctorates or other terminal degrees. **Location:** Suburban campus in small city; 11 miles from New Orleans. **Calendar:** Semester. Extensive evening/early morning classes. **Microcomputers:** Located in libraries, classrooms, computer centers. **Additional facts:** Formed through 1992 merger of St. Bernard Community College and Elaine P. Nunez Technical Institute.

DEGREES OFFERED. AA, AS, AAS. 13 associate degrees awarded in 1992. 54% in business and management, 46% business/office and marketing/distribution.

UNDERGRADUATE MAJORS. Accounting, air conditioning/heating/refrigeration mechanics, business administration and management, business and office, computer and information sciences, drafting and design technology, early childhood education, electronic technology, food production/management/services, general science, health sciences, information sciences and systems, liberal/general studies, office supervision and management.

ACADEMIC PROGRAMS. 2-year transfer program, double major, dual enrollment of high school students, honors program, student-designed major, high school cooperative, senior citizens courses. **Remedial services:** Learning center, remedial instruction. **Placement/credit:** Institutional tests; 17 credit hours maximum for associate degree.

ACADEMIC REQUIREMENTS. Freshmen must earn minimum GPA of 2.0 to continue in good standing. 80% of freshmen return for sophomore year. Students must declare major by end of first year. **Graduation requirements:** 63 hours for associate (18 in major). Most students required to take courses in arts/fine arts, English, humanities, mathematics, biological/physical sciences.

FRESHMAN ADMISSIONS. Selection criteria: Open admissions. Special admissions requirements for nursing and emergency medical techologies programs. **Test requirements:** ACT for placement; score report by August 1.

1992 FRESHMAN CLASS PROFILE. 122 men and women enrolled. **Characteristics:** 99% from in state, 100% commute.

FALL-TERM APPLICATIONS. $10 fee. Closing date August 1; applicants notified on a rolling basis. Early admission available.

STUDENT LIFE. Activities: Student government, magazine, student newspaper, drama, service organizations.

ATHLETICS. Intramural: Basketball M, volleyball.

STUDENT SERVICES. Aptitude testing, career counseling, freshman orientation, personal counseling, veterans counselor, services/facilities for handicapped.

ANNUAL EXPENSES. Tuition and fees (1992-93): $520. **Books and supplies:** $300. **Other expenses:** $300.

FINANCIAL AID. 5% of freshmen receive some form of aid. All grants based on need. **Aid applications:** Closing date June 30; applicants notified on a rolling basis; must reply within 3 weeks.

ADDRESS/TELEPHONE. Donna Clark, Director of Admissions, Nunez Community College, 3700 La Fontaine Street, Chalmette, LA 70043. (504) 278-7440.

Our Lady of Holy Cross College
New Orleans, Louisiana — CB code: 6002

4-year private liberal arts college, coed, affiliated with Roman Catholic Church. Founded in 1916. **Accreditation:** Regional. **Undergraduate enrollment:** 139 men, 476 women full time; 96 men, 305 women part time. **Graduate enrollment:** 5 men, 23 women full time; 30 men, 68 women part time. **Faculty:** 91 total (33 full time), 51 with doctorates or other terminal degrees. **Location:** Suburban campus in very large city; 3 miles from downtown. **Calendar:** Semester, limited summer session. **Microcomputers:** 20 located in computer centers. **Special facilities:** Curriculum library, children and young adult collection, Louisiana collection, government document collection, genealogy collection.

DEGREES OFFERED. AS, BA, BS, MA, MEd. 7 associate degrees awarded in 1992. 100% in social sciences. 101 bachelor's degrees awarded. 7% in business and management, 32% teacher education, 27% health sciences, 15% allied health, 15% social sciences. Graduate degrees offered in 4 major fields of study.

UNDERGRADUATE MAJORS. Associate: Law enforcement and corrections technologies. **Bachelor's:** Allied health, behavioral sciences, biology, business administration and management, business education, elementary education, English, English education, health sciences, history, mathematics education, nursing, reading education, respiratory therapy technology, science education, secondary education, social science education, social sciences, social work.

ACADEMIC PROGRAMS. Double major, dual enrollment of high school students, education specialist degree, independent study, internships, study abroad, teacher preparation, visiting/exchange student program, cross-registration; liberal arts/career combination in health sciences. **Remedial services:** Learning center, preadmission summer program, reduced course load, remedial instruction, special counselor, tutoring. **ROTC:** Air Force, Army. **Placement/credit:** CLEP General and Subject, institutional tests; 60 credit hours maximum for bachelor's degree.

ACADEMIC REQUIREMENTS. Freshmen must earn minimum GPA of 2.0 to continue in good standing. Students must declare major by end of first year. **Graduation requirements:** 68 hours for associate (30 in major), 128 hours for bachelor's (33 in major). Most students required to take courses in arts/fine arts, computer science, English, history, humanities, mathematics, philosophy/religion, biological/physical sciences, social sciences.

FRESHMAN ADMISSIONS. Selection criteria: Those with 2.0 GPA and 20 ACT composite unconditionally accepted. Students with less than 2.0 and 16-19 ACT must take learning contract or institutionally-designed schedule. **High school preparation:** 17.5 units recommended. Recommended units include biological science 2, English 4, foreign language 2, mathematics 2, physical science 2 and social science 3. .5 unit of computer literacy recommended. **Test requirements:** SAT or ACT (ACT preferred) for placement and counseling only. ACH required of applicants with no test scores.

1992 FRESHMAN CLASS PROFILE. 28 men, 110 women enrolled. **Characteristics:** 99% from in state, 100% commute, 32% have minority backgrounds. Average age is 26.

FALL-TERM APPLICATIONS. $15 fee. Closing date July 20; applicants notified on a rolling basis beginning on or about February 1. Deferred and early admission available.

STUDENT LIFE. Activities: Student government, student newspaper, choral groups, drama, fraternities, sororities, Blue Key, chess club, social counseling club, drama club, Circle-K.

ATHLETICS. Intramural: Softball, volleyball.

STUDENT SERVICES. Career counseling, employment service for undergraduates, freshman orientation, health services, personal counseling, placement service for graduates, special adviser for adult students, veterans counselor, student support services, services/facilities for handicapped.

ANNUAL EXPENSES. Tuition and fees: $4,694. **Books and supplies:** $600. **Other expenses:** $1,166.

FINANCIAL AID. 65% of freshmen, 59% of continuing students receive some form of aid. 88% of grants, 77% of loans, all jobs based on need. Academic, leadership, religious affiliation scholarships available. **Aid applications:** No closing date; priority given to applications received by April 15; applicants notified on a rolling basis beginning on or about July 31. **Additional information:** 30% discount to in-service teachers.

ADDRESS/TELEPHONE. Steven Bays, Director of Student Affairs, Our Lady of Holy Cross College, 4123 Woodland Drive, New Orleans, LA 70131-7399. (504) 394-7744. Fax: (504) 391-2421.

Phillips Junior College: New Orleans
New Orleans, Louisiana — CB code: 0357

2-year proprietary junior college, coed. Founded in 1970. **Undergraduate enrollment:** 600 men and women. **Location:** Urban campus in very large city. **Calendar:** Quarter. Extensive evening/early morning classes. **Microcomputers:** 40 located in computer centers.

DEGREES OFFERED. AAS. 240 associate degrees awarded in 1992.

UNDERGRADUATE MAJORS. Apparel and accessories marketing, business administration and management, business and management, business computer/console/peripheral equipment operation, electronic technology, fashion merchandising, hotel/motel and restaurant management, information sciences and systems, legal assistant/paralegal, marketing management, medical assistant, secretarial and related programs, word processing.

ACADEMIC REQUIREMENTS. Freshmen must earn minimum GPA of 2.0 to continue in good standing. Students must declare major on enrollment. **Graduation requirements:** 96 hours for associate. Most students required to take courses in computer science, English.

FRESHMAN ADMISSIONS. Selection criteria: Entrance test required. High school diploma or GED required for federal funding.

1992 FRESHMAN CLASS PROFILE. 300 men and women enrolled. **Characteristics:** 100% commute.

FALL-TERM APPLICATIONS. No fee. No closing date; applicants notified on a rolling basis. Interview required.

STUDENT LIFE. Activities: Student government, student newspaper.

STUDENT SERVICES. Services/facilities for handicapped.

ANNUAL EXPENSES. Tuition and fees (1992-93): $4,665.

FINANCIAL AID. Aid applications: No closing date; applicants notified on a rolling basis.

ADDRESS/TELEPHONE. Lorraine McIntire, Director of Admissions, Phillips Junior College: New Orleans, 822 South Clearview Parkway, New Orleans, LA 70121. (504) 734-0123.

St. Joseph Seminary College

St. Benedict, Louisiana — CB code: 6689

Admissions:	88% of applicants accepted
Based on:	••• Recommendations, religious affiliation/commitment
	•• Interview, school record
	• Essay, test scores
Completion:	92% of freshmen end year in good standing
	62% graduate, 63% of these enter graduate study

4-year private liberal arts, seminary college, men only, affiliated with Roman Catholic Church. Founded in 1891. **Accreditation:** Regional. **Undergraduate enrollment:** 50 men full time; 22 men, 37 women part time. **Faculty:** 36 total, 13 with doctorates or other terminal degrees. **Location:** Rural campus in rural community; 3 miles from Covington, 40 miles from New Orleans. **Calendar:** Semester. **Additional facts:** Non-seminarian, non-degree-seeking women and men may attend part-time.

DEGREES OFFERED. BA. 14 bachelor's degrees awarded in 1992. 100% in multi/interdisciplinary studies.

UNDERGRADUATE MAJORS. Liberal/general studies.

ACADEMIC PROGRAMS. Dual enrollment of high school students. **Remedial services:** Reduced course load, remedial instruction, tutoring. **Placement/credit:** AP, CLEP General and Subject; 24 credit hours maximum for bachelor's degree.

ACADEMIC REQUIREMENTS. Freshmen must earn minimum GPA of 2.0 to continue in good standing. 87% of freshmen return for sophomore year. **Graduation requirements:** 130 hours for bachelor's. Most students required to take courses in arts/fine arts, English, foreign languages, history, humanities, mathematics, philosophy/religion, biological/physical sciences, social sciences. **Additional information:** Non-resident, nondegree students may take courses at seminary.

FRESHMAN ADMISSIONS. Selection criteria: Recommendation by diocesan bishop, academic standing, and test scores required. **High school preparation:** 10 units required. Required and recommended units include biological science 1, English 3-4, foreign language 2, mathematics 2-3, physical science 1 and social science 1-2. Second foreign language recommended. **Test requirements:** ACT; score report by August 26.

1992 FRESHMAN CLASS PROFILE. 16 men applied, 14 accepted, 12 enrolled. 50% had high school GPA of 3.0 or higher, 50% between 2.0 and 2.99. 43% were in top tenth and 57% were in top quarter of graduating class. **Academic background:** Mid 50% of enrolled freshmen had ACT composite between 18-36. 100% submitted ACT scores. **Characteristics:** 75% from in state, 100% live in college housing, 17% have minority backgrounds. Average age is 22.

FALL-TERM APPLICATIONS. $10 fee. No closing date; applicants notified on a rolling basis beginning on or about May 1; August 24. Essay required. Interview recommended for academically weak applicants. Deferred and early admission available.

STUDENT LIFE. Housing: Dormitories (men). All students live on campus. **Activities:** Student government, choral groups, drama, music ensembles, musical theater, community, religious, and social service activities.

ATHLETICS. Intramural: Baseball, basketball, handball, racquetball, soccer, softball, squash, swimming, table tennis, tennis, volleyball, water polo.

STUDENT SERVICES. Career counseling, freshman orientation, health services, personal counseling, veterans counselor, religious counseling.

ANNUAL EXPENSES. Tuition and fees (1992-93): $5,530. **Room and board:** $4,200. **Books and supplies:** $780.

FINANCIAL AID. 72% of freshmen, 63% of continuing students receive some form of aid. All aid based on need. 6 enrolled freshmen were judged to have need, all were offered aid. **Aid applications:** No closing date; applicants notified on a rolling basis; must reply by May 1 or within 2 weeks if notified thereafter.

ADDRESS/TELEPHONE. Thomas A. Siegrist, Director of Admissions/Registrar, St. Joseph Seminary College, St. Benedict, LA 70457-9990. (504) 892-1800. Fax: (504) 892-3723.

Southeastern Louisiana University

Hammond, Louisiana — CB code: 6656

4-year public university, coed. Founded in 1925. **Accreditation:** Regional. **Undergraduate enrollment:** 10,999 men and women. **Graduate enrollment:** 1,282 men and women. **Faculty:** 425 total (319 full time), 197 with doctorates or other terminal degrees. **Location:** Suburban campus in large town; 50 miles from New Orleans. **Calendar:** Semester, extensive summer session. Extensive evening/early morning classes. **Microcomputers:** Located in classrooms, computer centers.

DEGREES OFFERED. AA, AS, AAS, BA, BS, MA, MS, MBA, MEd. 36 associate degrees awarded in 1992. 33% in business/office and marketing/distribution, 17% engineering technologies, 22% health sciences, 25% social sciences. 785 bachelor's degrees awarded. 32% in business and management, 21% education, 14% health sciences, 8% social sciences. Graduate degrees offered in 13 major fields of study.

UNDERGRADUATE MAJORS. Associate: Business data programming, criminal justice studies, drafting, drafting and design technology, industrial technology, law enforcement and corrections technologies, respiratory therapy, respiratory therapy technology, secretarial and related programs. **Bachelor's:** Accounting, art education, biology, business and management, business economics, business education, chemistry, communications, computer and information sciences, criminal justice studies, dance, dramatic arts, early childhood education, education of the deaf and hearing impaired, education of the emotionally handicapped, education of the mentally handicapped, education of the multiple handicapped, education of the physically handicapped, elementary education, English, English education, family/consumer resource management, fashion design, fashion merchandising, fine arts, foreign languages education, French, health education, history, home economics, home economics education, industrial arts education, industrial technology, law enforcement and corrections, liberal/general studies, marketing and distribution, mathematics, mathematics education, music, music education, nursing, nutritional education, physical education, physics, plant sciences, political science and government, predentistry, prelaw, premedicine, prepharmacy, psychology, science education, secondary education, secretarial and related programs, social studies education, social work, sociology, Spanish, speech, speech correction, speech/communication/theater education, trade and industrial education.

ACADEMIC PROGRAMS. 2-year transfer program, cooperative education, double major, dual enrollment of high school students, education specialist degree, honors program, internships, student-designed major, study abroad, teacher preparation, telecourses. **Remedial services:** Learning center, remedial instruction, special counselor, tutoring. **ROTC:** Army. **Placement/credit:** AP, CLEP General and Subject, institutional tests; 60 credit hours maximum for bachelor's degree.

ACADEMIC REQUIREMENTS. Freshmen must earn a cumulative average fewer than 10 quality points below 2.0 average. 50% of freshmen return for sophomore year. Students must declare major by end of first year. **Graduation requirements:** 66 hours for associate (18 in major), 130 hours for bachelor's (36 in major). Most students required to take courses in arts/fine arts, computer science, English, foreign languages, history, humanities, mathematics, philosophy/religion, biological/physical sciences, social sciences.

FRESHMAN ADMISSIONS. Selection criteria: Open admissions. **High school preparation:** 24 units recommended. Recommended units include English 4, foreign language 3, mathematics 3, social science 3 and science 3. **Test requirements:** ACT for placement and counseling only; score report by August 1.

1992 FRESHMAN CLASS PROFILE. 2,551 men and women enrolled. **Characteristics:** 95% from in state, 65% live in college housing, 13% have minority backgrounds, 1% are foreign students, 2% join fraternities/sororities.

FALL-TERM APPLICATIONS. $10 fee. Closing date July 15; applicants notified on a rolling basis. Audition recommended for music applicants. Early admission available.

STUDENT LIFE. Housing: Dormitories (men, women, coed); apartment, fraternity housing available. **Activities:** Student government, radio, student newspaper, yearbook, choral groups, concert band, dance, drama, jazz band, music ensembles, musical theater, opera, pep band, symphony orchestra, fraternities, sororities.

ATHLETICS. NCAA. **Intercollegiate:** Baseball M, basketball, cross-country M, golf M, tennis, track and field, volleyball W. **Intramural:** Badminton, baseball, basketball, racquetball, softball, tennis, volleyball.

STUDENT SERVICES. Aptitude testing, career counseling, em-

ployment service for undergraduates, freshman orientation, health services, personal counseling, placement service for graduates, special adviser for adult students, veterans counselor, services/facilities for handicapped.

ANNUAL EXPENSES. Tuition and fees (1992-93): $1,615, $1,800 additional for out-of-state students. **Room and board:** $2,200. **Books and supplies:** $520. **Other expenses:** $972.

FINANCIAL AID. 55% of freshmen, 55% of continuing students receive some form of aid. 50% of grants, 87% of loans, all jobs based on need. Academic, music/drama, athletic, state/district residency, leadership scholarships available. **Aid applications:** No closing date; priority given to applications received by May 1; applicants notified on a rolling basis beginning on or about June 1; must reply within 2 weeks.

ADDRESS/TELEPHONE. Iris S. Wiggins, Director of Admissions, Southeastern Louisiana University, PO SLU Box 703, Hammond, LA 70402-0752. (504) 549-2123. Fax: (504) 549-5095.

Southern University and Agricultural and Mechanical College

Baton Rouge, Louisiana CB code: 6663

4-year public university, coed. Founded in 1880. **Accreditation:** Regional. **Undergraduate enrollment:** 3,694 men, 4,681 women full time; 303 men, 514 women part time. **Graduate enrollment:** 296 men, 273 women full time; 153 men, 489 women part time. **Faculty:** 639 total (534 full time), 305 with doctorates or other terminal degrees. **Location:** Suburban campus in small city; 85-90 miles from New Orleans. **Calendar:** Semester, extensive summer session. **Microcomputers:** 400 located in libraries, computer centers. **Special facilities:** Experimental (laboratory) farm, outdoor learning resource center (nature trail), meat processing plant.

DEGREES OFFERED. AA, AS, AAS, BA, BS, BArch, MA, MS, MEd, PhD, EdD. 28 associate degrees awarded in 1992. 100% in parks/recreation, protective services, public affairs. 844 bachelor's degrees awarded. 22% in business and management, 10% communications, 6% computer sciences, 10% teacher education, 8% engineering, 14% social sciences. Graduate degrees offered in 21 major fields of study.

UNDERGRADUATE MAJORS. Associate: Electronic technology, law enforcement and corrections, mechanical engineering technology. **Bachelor's:** Accounting, agribusiness, agricultural economics, agricultural education, animal sciences, architecture, art education, biochemistry, biology, botany, business and management, business economics, business education, cardiopulmonary therapy, chemistry, civil engineering, computer and information sciences, counseling psychology, cytotechnology, dramatic arts, education of the deaf and hearing impaired, education of the mentally handicapped, electrical/electronics/communications engineering, electronic technology, elementary education, English, English education, fine arts, food science and nutrition, foreign languages education, forestry and related sciences, French, health education, history, home economics education, individual and family development, industrial arts education, journalism, junior high education, library science, marketing management, mathematics, mathematics education, mechanical engineering, mechanical engineering technology, medical laboratory technologies, microbiology, music, music education, nursing, occupational therapy, parks and recreation management, physical education, physical sciences, physical therapy, physics, plant sciences, political science and government, premedicine, psychology, radio/television broadcasting, rehabilitation counseling/services, science education, secondary education, social studies education, social work, sociology, soil sciences, Spanish, special education, speech, speech correction, speech pathology/audiology, speech/communication/theater education, textiles and clothing, visual and performing arts, zoology.

ACADEMIC PROGRAMS. Cooperative education, double major, dual enrollment of high school students, education specialist degree, honors program, independent study, internships, teacher preparation, cross-registration; liberal arts/career combination in engineering. **Remedial services:** Learning center, preadmission summer program, reduced course load, remedial instruction, special counselor, tutoring. **ROTC:** Army, Naval. **Placement/credit:** AP, CLEP General and Subject, institutional tests; 30 credit hours maximum for bachelor's degree.

ACADEMIC REQUIREMENTS. Freshmen must earn minimum GPA of 1.51 to continue in good standing. 56% of freshmen return for sophomore year. Students must declare major by end of first year. **Graduation requirements:** 66 hours for associate (28 in major), 124 hours for bachelor's (40 in major). Most students required to take courses in arts/fine arts, computer science, English, foreign languages, history, humanities, mathematics, philosophy/religion, biological/physical sciences, social sciences. **Postgraduate studies:** 85% from 2-year programs enter 4-year programs.

FRESHMAN ADMISSIONS. Selection criteria: Open admissions. .5 computer literacy and fine arts recommended. **Test requirements:** SAT or ACT (ACT preferred) for placement and counseling only; score report by August 1.

1992 FRESHMAN CLASS PROFILE. 1,134 men applied, 1,134 accepted, 993 enrolled; 1,178 women applied, 1,178 accepted, 1,102 enrolled. 42% had high school GPA of 3.0 or higher, 57% between 2.0 and 2.99. 37% were in top tenth of graduating class. **Academic background:** Mid 50% of enrolled freshmen had ACT composite between 12-18. 93% submitted ACT scores. **Characteristics:** 74% from in state, 51% live in college housing, 98% have minority backgrounds, 1% are foreign students. Average age is 18.

FALL-TERM APPLICATIONS. $5 fee. Closing date July 2; priority given to applications received by June 30; applicants notified on a rolling basis. Early admission available.

STUDENT LIFE. Housing: Dormitories (men, women); apartment housing available. **Activities:** Student government, film, magazine, radio, student newspaper, television, yearbook, choral groups, concert band, dance, drama, jazz band, marching band, music ensembles, musical theater, pep band, fraternities, sororities, Baptist Student Center, Catholic Student Center, Methodist Student Center.

ATHLETICS. NCAA. **Intercollegiate:** Baseball M, basketball, football M, golf M, tennis M, track and field, volleyball W. **Intramural:** Badminton, basketball M, softball M, table tennis, tennis M, volleyball.

STUDENT SERVICES. Aptitude testing, career counseling, employment service for undergraduates, freshman orientation, health services, on-campus day care, personal counseling, placement service for graduates, veterans counselor, services/facilities for handicapped.

ANNUAL EXPENSES. Tuition and fees (1992-93): $1,588, $1,522 additional for out-of-state students. **Room and board:** $2,865. **Books and supplies:** $500. **Other expenses:** $500.

FINANCIAL AID. 90% of freshmen, 82% of continuing students receive some form of aid. 91% of grants, all loans, all jobs based on need. Academic, athletic scholarships available. **Aid applications:** No closing date; priority given to applications received by April 15; applicants notified on a rolling basis; must reply within 10 days.

ADDRESS/TELEPHONE. Henry J. Bellaire, Director of Admissions and Recruitment, Southern University and Agricultural and Mechanical College, Southern Branch Post Office, Baton Rouge, LA 70813. (504) 771-2430. Fax: (504) 771-2495.

Southern University at New Orleans

New Orleans, Louisiana CB code: 1647

4-year public university, coed. Founded in 1959. **Accreditation:** Regional. **Undergraduate enrollment:** 4,500 men and women. **Graduate enrollment:** 500 men and women. **Faculty:** 250 total (200 full time). **Location:** Urban campus in very large city. **Calendar:** Semester, limited summer session. Saturday and extensive evening/early morning classes.

DEGREES OFFERED. AA, AS, BA, BS, M. 30 associate degrees awarded in 1992. 300 bachelor's degrees awarded. Graduate degrees offered in 1 major field of study.

UNDERGRADUATE MAJORS. Associate: Business data programming, real estate, secretarial and related programs. **Bachelor's:** Accounting, biology, business administration and management, business and management, business economics, chemistry, clinical laboratory science, economics, elementary education, English, French, history, mathematics, physics, political science and government, psychology, secondary education, secretarial and related programs, social sciences, social work, sociology, Spanish, visual and performing arts.

ACADEMIC PROGRAMS. Cooperative education, internships, cross-registration. **Remedial services:** Remedial instruction, special counselor, tutoring. **ROTC:** Air Force, Army. **Placement/credit:** 30 credit hours maximum for bachelor's degree.

ACADEMIC REQUIREMENTS. No policy requiring minimum GPA; records of students having academic difficulty are reviewed individually. **Graduation requirements:** 62 hours for associate, 124 hours for bachelor's. **Postgraduate studies:** 15% from 2-year programs enter 4-year programs.

FRESHMAN ADMISSIONS. Selection criteria: Open admissions. Selective admissions to allied health and various technical programs. 2.5 high school GPA recommended. **Test requirements:** ACT for placement and counseling only; score report by August 10.

1992 FRESHMAN CLASS PROFILE. 550 men and women enrolled. **Characteristics:** 99% from in state, 100% commute, 99% have minority backgrounds, 1% are foreign students.

FALL-TERM APPLICATIONS. $5 fee. Closing date July 1; applicants notified on a rolling basis. Deferred and early admission available.

STUDENT LIFE. Activities: Student government, student newspaper, yearbook, choral groups, drama, jazz band, musical theater, symphony orchestra, fraternities, sororities.

STUDENT SERVICES. Health services, personal counseling, placement service for graduates.

ANNUAL EXPENSES. Tuition and fees (1992-93): $1,456, $1,558 additional for out-of-state students. **Books and supplies:** $400.

FINANCIAL AID. 80% of freshmen, 80% of continuing students receive some form of aid. Grants, loans, jobs available. **Aid applications:** Closing date May 1; applicants notified on or about May 15; must reply within 1 week.

ADDRESS/TELEPHONE. Melvin Hodges, Registrar/Director of Admissions, Southern University at New Orleans, 6400 Press Drive, New Orleans, LA 70126. (504) 286-5000.

Southern University in Shreveport
Shreveport, Louisiana CB code: 0322

2-year public community college, coed. Founded in 1964. **Accreditation:** Regional. **Undergraduate enrollment:** 229 men, 483 women full time; 73 men, 269 women part time. **Faculty:** 73 total (63 full time), 6 with doctorates or other terminal degrees. **Location:** Suburban campus in small city. **Calendar:** Semester, limited summer session.

DEGREES OFFERED. AA, AS, AAS. 65 associate degrees awarded in 1992. 9% in business and management, 7% computer sciences, 20% teacher education, 34% allied health, 8% life sciences, 15% social sciences.

UNDERGRADUATE MAJORS. Accounting, aviation management, biology, business administration and management, chemistry, computer and information sciences, early childhood education, electronic technology, finance, hotel/motel and restaurant management, legal assistant/paralegal, marketing and distribution, mathematics, medical assistant, medical laboratory technologies, medical records technology, mental health/human services, radiograph medical technology, respiratory therapy technology, science technologies, secretarial and related programs, small business management and ownership, social sciences, surgical technology, teacher aide, word processing.

ACADEMIC PROGRAMS. 2-year transfer program, internships, cross-registration. **Remedial services:** Remedial instruction, special counselor, tutoring. **Placement/credit:** Institutional tests.

ACADEMIC REQUIREMENTS. Freshmen must earn minimum GPA of 1.5 to continue in good standing. 50% of freshmen return for sophomore year. Students must declare major by end of first year. **Graduation requirements:** 62 hours for associate. Most students required to take courses in English, mathematics, social sciences.

FRESHMAN ADMISSIONS. Selection criteria: Open admissions. **High school preparation:** 15 units recommended. Recommended units include biological science 2, English 3, mathematics 2, physical science 1, social science 2 and science 2. **Test requirements:** ACT for placement and counseling only; score report by August 3.

1992 FRESHMAN CLASS PROFILE. 231 men and women enrolled. **Characteristics:** 98% from in state, 100% commute, 97% have minority backgrounds. Average age is 19.

FALL-TERM APPLICATIONS. No fee. No closing date; applicants notified on a rolling basis. Early admission available.

STUDENT LIFE. Activities: Student government, student newspaper, yearbook, choral groups, dance, Baptist Student Union and Afro-American Society.

ATHLETICS. NJCAA. **Intercollegiate:** Basketball M.

STUDENT SERVICES. Health services, personal counseling, placement service for graduates, veterans counselor.

ANNUAL EXPENSES. Tuition and fees (1992-93): $910, $1,130 additional for out-of-state students. **Books and supplies:** $500. **Other expenses:** $1,420.

FINANCIAL AID. 90% of freshmen, 90% of continuing students receive some form of aid. All aid based on need. 136 enrolled freshmen were judged to have need, all were offered aid. Academic, leadership, alumni affiliation, minority scholarships available. **Aid applications:** No closing date; applicants notified on a rolling basis beginning on or about July 15; must reply within 2 weeks.

ADDRESS/TELEPHONE. Clifton Jones, Registrar, Southern University in Shreveport, 3050 Martin L. King, Jr. Drive, Shreveport, LA 71107. (318) 674-3342. Fax: (318) 674-3489.

Tulane University
New Orleans, Louisiana CB code: 6832

Admissions:	73% of applicants accepted
Based on:	••• Recommendations, school record, test scores
	•• Activities, essay
	• Special talents
Completion:	85% of freshmen end year in good standing
	75% graduate, 57% of these enter graduate study

4-year private university, coed. Founded in 1834. **Accreditation:** Regional. **Undergraduate enrollment:** 2,668 men, 2,485 women full time; 698 men, 911 women part time. **Graduate enrollment:** 2,027 men, 1,636 women full time; 227 men, 231 women part time. **Faculty:** 1,260 total (934 full time), 915 with doctorates or other terminal degrees. **Location:** Urban campus in very large city; 5 miles from downtown. **Calendar:** Semester, limited summer session. **Microcomputers:** 350 located in dormitories, libraries, classrooms, computer centers. **Special facilities:** William Ransom Hogan Jazz Archive, Louisiana Collection of historical materials, Latin American Library, Southeastern Architecture Archive, Newcomb College Center for Research on Women, Amistad Research Center on ethnic minorities, Murphy Institute of Political Economy, Roger Thayer Stone Center for Latin American Studies, Newcomb Art Gallery, Middle American Research Institute.

DEGREES OFFERED. BA, BS, BFA, BArch, MA, MS, MBA, MFA, MEd, MSW, PhD, MD. 36 associate degrees awarded in 1992. 31% in computer sciences, 69% law. 1,423 bachelor's degrees awarded in 1992. 12% in business and management, 10% engineering, 7% letters/literature, 8% life sciences, 8% psychology, 31% social sciences. Graduate degrees offered in 71 major fields of study.

UNDERGRADUATE MAJORS. Accounting, American studies, anthropology, architecture, art history, Asian studies, biochemistry, bioengineering and biomedical engineering, biological and physical sciences, biological chemistry, biology, business and management, chemical engineering, chemistry, civil engineering, classics, cognitive studies, communications, computer and information sciences, computer engineering, dramatic arts, earth sciences, economics, electrical/electronics/communications engineering, engineering, English, environmental studies, foreign languages (multiple emphasis), French, geology, German, Greek (classical), history, humanities and social sciences, Italian, Jewish studies, Latin, Latin American studies, legal assistant/paralegal, linguistics, marketing management, mathematical economics, mathematics, mathematics/computer science, mechanical engineering, medieval studies, music, philosophy, physics, political economy, political science and government, Portuguese, psychology, religion, Russian, Russian and Slavic studies, sociology, Spanish, special education, studio art, women's studies.

ACADEMIC PROGRAMS. Accelerated program, double major, dual enrollment of high school students, honors program, independent study, internships, student-designed major, study abroad, teacher preparation, visiting/exchange student program, Washington semester, cross-registration; liberal arts/career combination in engineering; combined bachelor's/graduate program in business administration, medicine, law. **Remedial services:** Education resource center. **ROTC:** Air Force, Army, Naval. **Placement/credit:** AP, institutional tests.

ACADEMIC REQUIREMENTS. Freshmen must earn minimum GPA of 2.0 to continue in good standing. 90% of freshmen return for sophomore year. Students must declare major by end of second year. **Graduation requirements:** 128 hours for bachelor's (32 in major). Most students required to take courses in arts/fine arts, English, foreign languages, humanities, mathematics, biological/physical sciences, social sciences. **Postgraduate studies:** 16% enter law school, 9% enter medical school, 7% enter MBA programs, 25% enter other graduate study. **Additional information:** Liberal arts majors must satisfy distribution requirements in humanities and fine arts, social sciences, and sciences/mathematics. Among distribution requirements, 1 course must be selected from a list of courses in Foundations of Western Civilization and one from a list in Non-Western and Latin American Cultures.

FRESHMAN ADMISSIONS. Selection criteria: High school achievement record most important, followed by test scores, recommendation, personal qualities; special consideration for children of alumni and minority applicants. Candidates should be in top third of graduating class with at least B+ average. **High school preparation:** 18 units recommended. Recommended units include English 4, foreign language 4, mathematics 4, social science 2 and science 4. 2 laboratory science also recommended. **Test requirements:** SAT or ACT; score report by January 15. Prueba de Aptitud Academica for Spanish speaking applicants. Puerto Rico students must submit PAA. **Additional information:** Offer early notification option: apply November 1, notified December 15, commit May 1.

1992 FRESHMAN CLASS PROFILE. 6,643 men and women applied, 4,864 accepted; 1,213 enrolled. 72% had high school GPA of 3.0 or higher, 28% between 2.0 and 2.99. 47% were in top tenth and 75% were in top quarter of graduating class. **Academic background:** Mid 50% of enrolled freshmen had SAT-V between 490-620, SAT-M between 540-660. 80% submitted SAT scores. **Characteristics:** 20% from in state, 98% live in college housing, 19% have minority backgrounds, 4% are foreign students. Average age is 18.

FALL-TERM APPLICATIONS. $35 fee, may be waived for applicants with need. Closing date January 15; applicants notified on or about April 15; must reply by May 1. Essay required. Audition recommended for music applicants. Portfolio recommended for architecture, art applicants. CRDA. Deferred and early admission available. Institutional early decision plan.

STUDENT LIFE. Housing: Dormitories (women, coed); apartment, fraternity housing available. Honors program residence hall, language floors, special interest floors, quiet-study floors, and international living floors. **Activities:** Student government, film, magazine, radio, student newspaper, television, yearbook, videotape-video center and literary magazine, choral groups, concert band, dance, drama, jazz band, marching band, music ensembles, musical theater, opera, pep band, chamber orchestra and summer lyric theater, fraternities, sororities, Hillel, Episcopal Center, Inter-Varsity Christian Fellowship, Catholic Center, Baptist Student Union, African-American Congress, Latin American Students Association, International Students Organization, Community Action Council, sports clubs. **Additional information:** Numerous cocurricular, social, recreational, organizational activities, opportunities, and programs that enhance the academic and intellectual environment.

ATHLETICS. NCAA. **Intercollegiate:** Baseball M, basketball, cross-country, football M, golf, tennis, track and field, volleyball W. **Intramural:** Badminton M, basketball, cross-country M, football M, golf M, handball M, racquetball M, soccer, softball, swimming M, table tennis M, tennis, track and field M, volleyball, wrestling M.

STUDENT SERVICES. Aptitude testing, career counseling, employment service for undergraduates, freshman orientation, health services, on-campus day care, personal counseling, placement service for graduates, special adviser for adult students, veterans counselor, international student adviser, services/facilities for handicapped.

ANNUAL EXPENSES. Tuition and fees (projected): $18,735. **Room and board:** $5,780. **Books and supplies:** $350. **Other expenses:** $800.

FINANCIAL AID. 56% of freshmen, 55% of continuing students receive some form of aid. 65% of grants, 90% of loans, 86% of jobs based on need. 594 enrolled freshmen were judged to have need, 592 were offered aid. Academic, athletic scholarships available. **Aid applications:** No closing date; priority given to applications received by March 1; applicants notified on a rolling basis beginning on or about February 1; must reply by May 1 or within 2 weeks if notified thereafter. **Additional information:** Application deadline for merit scholarships December 15.

ADDRESS/TELEPHONE. Nancy G. McDuff, Dean of Admission, Tulane University, 210 Gibson Hall, New Orleans, LA 70118-5680. (504) 865-5731.

University of New Orleans
New Orleans, Louisiana CB code: 6379

4-year public university, coed. Founded in 1956. **Accreditation:** Regional. **Undergraduate enrollment:** 4,011 men, 4,528 women full time; 1,548 men, 2,228 women part time. **Graduate enrollment:** 535 men, 487 women full time; 1,772 men, 2,221 women part time. **Faculty:** 819 total (557 full time). **Location:** Urban campus in very large city. **Calendar:** Semester, extensive summer session. Saturday and extensive evening/early morning classes. **Microcomputers:** 1,020 located in libraries, classrooms, computer centers.

DEGREES OFFERED. BA, BS, MA, MS, MBA, MFA, MEd, PhD, EdD. 1 associate degree awarded in 1992. 100% in business/office and marketing/distribution. 1,324 bachelor's degrees awarded in 1992. 32% in business and management, 7% communications, 13% teacher education, 8% engineering, 6% multi/interdisciplinary studies, 14% social sciences. Graduate degrees offered in 41 major fields of study.

UNDERGRADUATE MAJORS. Accounting, anthropology, art history, biology, business administration and management, business and management, business economics, chemistry, civil engineering, communications, computer and information sciences, dramatic arts, economics, electrical/electronics/communications engineering, elementary education, English, English education, finance, fine arts, foreign languages education, French, geography, geology, geophysics and seismology, history, hotel/motel and restaurant management, liberal/general studies, marketing and distribution, mathematics, mathematics education, mechanical engineering, medical laboratory technologies, music, music education, music theory and composition, naval architecture and marine engineering, philosophy, physical education, physics, political science and government, psychology, real estate, science education, secondary education, social studies education, sociology, Spanish, speech/communication/theater education, studio art.

ACADEMIC PROGRAMS. Cooperative education, double major, dual enrollment of high school students, honors program, independent study, internships, student-designed major, study abroad, teacher preparation, telecourses, weekend college, Washington semester, cross-registration; liberal arts/career combination in engineering. **Remedial services:** Learning center, remedial instruction, tutoring, developmental studies. **ROTC:** Air Force, Army. **Placement/credit:** AP, CLEP Subject, IB, institutional tests; 30 credit hours maximum for bachelor's degree.

ACADEMIC REQUIREMENTS. Freshmen must earn minimum GPA of 2.0 to continue in good standing. Students must declare major on enrollment. **Graduation requirements:** 68 hours for associate (30 in major), 128 hours for bachelor's (45 in major). Most students required to take courses in English, humanities, mathematics, biological/physical sciences, social sciences.

FRESHMAN ADMISSIONS. Selection criteria: Admission based on minimum ACT score of 20 or combined SAT score of 810, graduation from high school. If test score below the minimum, admission is based on 2.0 GPA in 17.5 units of high school core coursework. Applicants with ACT of 15 or SAT of 630 may be considered for developmental College Life program. **High school preparation:** 15 units required. Required units include biological science 1, English 4, foreign language 2, mathematics 3, physical science 2 and social science 3. 2 academic electives, .5 computer literacy or computer science. **Test requirements:** SAT or ACT (ACT preferred); score report by August 15.

1992 FRESHMAN CLASS PROFILE. 2,613 men and women applied, 2,263 accepted; 742 men enrolled, 933 women enrolled. **Academic background:** Mid 50% of enrolled freshmen had ACT composite between 18-23. 76% submitted ACT scores. **Characteristics:** 93% from in state, 32% have minority backgrounds, 2% are foreign students. Average age is 20.

FALL-TERM APPLICATIONS. $20 fee. $20 fee before July 1; $50 thereafter. Closing date August 15; priority given to applications received by July 1; applicants notified on a rolling basis; no reply necessary. Audition required for music students applicants. Portfolio required for fine arts/studio applicants. Interview recommended. Essay recommended. Deferred and early admission available.

STUDENT LIFE. Housing: Dormitories (coed); apartment, fraternity, handicapped housing available. Apartment referral and roommate locator services available. **Activities:** Student government, film, magazine, radio, student newspaper, yearbook, choral groups, concert band, dance, drama, jazz band, marching band, music ensembles, musical theater, opera, pep band, wind ensemble, fraternities, sororities, NAACP, African American Student Union, Circle K, Amnesty International, College Republicans, Young Democrats, International Student Organization, Latin American Student Association, Muslim Student Association, religious council.

ATHLETICS. NCAA. **Intercollegiate:** Baseball M, basketball, cross-country, golf M, swimming, tennis W, track and field, volleyball W. **Intramural:** Badminton, basketball, golf, racquetball, soccer M, softball, swimming, table tennis, tennis, track and field, volleyball.

STUDENT SERVICES. Aptitude testing, career counseling, employment service for undergraduates, freshman orientation, health services, on-campus day care, personal counseling, placement service for graduates, special adviser for adult students, veterans counselor, services/facilities for handicapped.

ANNUAL EXPENSES. Tuition and fees (1992-93): $2,024, $2,792 additional for out-of-state students. **Room and board:** $2,972. **Books and supplies:** $600. **Other expenses:** $1,055.

FINANCIAL AID. 49% of freshmen, 51% of continuing students receive some form of aid. 89% of grants, 88% of loans, all jobs based on need. 596 enrolled freshmen were judged to have need, 511 were offered aid. Academic, music/drama, athletic, state/district residency, leadership, alumni affiliation, religious affiliation, minority scholarships available. **Aid applications:** No closing date; priority given to applications received by May 1; applicants notified on a rolling basis; must reply within 4 weeks. **Additional information:** Lousiana Opportunity Loan available for middle-income families.

ADDRESS/TELEPHONE. Roslyn Sheley, Assoc. Director of Admissions, University of New Orleans, Lakefront, New Orleans, LA 70148. (504) 286-6595.

University of Southwestern Louisiana
Lafayette, Louisiana CB code: 6672

4-year public university, coed. Founded in 1898. **Accreditation:** Regional. **Undergraduate enrollment:** 14,782 men and women. **Graduate enrollment:** 1,562 men and women. **Faculty:** 635 total (585 full time), 387 with doctorates or other terminal degrees. **Location:** Urban campus in small city; 130 miles from New Orleans, 200 miles from Houston. **Calendar:** Semester, extensive summer session. Extensive evening/early morning classes. **Microcomputers:** 500 located in dormitories, computer centers. **Special facilities:** 2 nuclear accelerators, 2 electron microscopes, CAD/CAM laboratory, art museum, Acadiana Folklore Archives.

DEGREES OFFERED. AS, BA, BS, BFA, BArch, MA, MS, MBA, MEd, PhD. 70 associate degrees awarded in 1992. 8% in business/office and marketing/distribution, 10% engineering technologies, 21% health sciences, 51% multi/interdisciplinary studies, 10% social sciences. 1,500 bachelor's degrees awarded. 20% in business and management, 14% teacher education, 6% engineering, 7% health sciences, 21% multi/interdisciplinary studies. Graduate degrees offered in 37 major fields of study.

UNDERGRADUATE MAJORS. Associate: Criminal justice technology, emergency/disaster science, engineering and engineering-related technologies, liberal/general studies, precision metal work, recreation and community services technologies, secretarial and related programs. **Bachelor's:** Accounting, agribusiness, agricultural business and management, agricultural education, agricultural engineering, agricultural sciences, anthropology, architecture, art education, biological and physical sciences, biology, business administration and management, business and management, business economics, business education, chemical engineering, chemistry, city/community/regional planning, civil engineering, clinical laboratory science, communications, computer and information sciences, criminal justice studies, dance, dramatic arts, Eastern European studies, economics, electrical/electronics/communications engineering, elementary education, English, English education, family/consumer resource management, fashion design, fashion merchandising, finance, fine arts, food science and nutrition, foreign languages (multiple emphasis), foreign languages education, French area studies, geography, geology, history, home economics, home economics education, horticultural science, hotel/motel and restaurant management, industrial arts education, institutional/home management/supporting programs, interior design, journalism, liberal/general studies, marketing and distribution, marketing and distributive education, mathematics, mathematics education, mechanical engineering, medical records administration, music education, music history and appreciation, music theory and composition, nursing, optometry, ornamental horticulture, personnel management, petroleum engineering, petroleum land management, philosophy, physical education, physics, piano pedagogy, political science and government, predentistry, prelaw, premedicine, preveterinary, psychology, public relations, radio/television broadcasting, science education, secretarial and related programs, social studies education, sociology, speech, speech correction, speech pathology/audiology, statistics, trade and industrial education, wildlife management.

ACADEMIC PROGRAMS. Accelerated program, double major, dual enrollment of high school students, education specialist degree, honors program, independent study, internships, student-designed major, study abroad, teacher preparation, visiting/exchange student program, Washington semester. **Remedial services:** Learning center, reduced course load, remedial instruction, special counselor, tutoring. **ROTC:** Army. **Placement/credit:** AP, CLEP General and Subject, institutional tests; 15 credit hours maximum for associate degree; 30 credit hours maximum for bachelor's degree.

ACADEMIC REQUIREMENTS. Freshmen must earn minimum GPA of 2.0 to continue in good standing. 60% of freshmen return for sophomore year. Students must declare major by end of first year. **Graduation requirements:** 65 hours for associate, 132 hours for bachelor's (33 in major). Most students required to take courses in arts/fine arts, computer science, English, history, humanities, mathematics, biological/physical sciences, social sciences. **Postgraduate studies:** 5% enter law school, 2% enter medical school, 5% enter MBA programs, 10% enter other graduate study.

FRESHMAN ADMISSIONS. Selection criteria: Open admissions. Selective admissions to most programs after first year. **Test requirements:** SAT or ACT (ACT preferred) for placement and counseling only; score report by August 20. **Additional information:** Those without diploma from accredited high school or equivalency certificate must have ACT composite score of 17 and be at least 19 years of age.

1992 FRESHMAN CLASS PROFILE. 2,513 men and women enrolled. **Characteristics:** 95% from in state, 60% commute, 23% have minority backgrounds, 3% are foreign students, 9% join fraternities/sororities. Average age is 19.

FALL-TERM APPLICATIONS. $5 fee. No closing date; priority given to applications received by July 18; applicants notified on a rolling basis. Audition required for music applicants. Portfolio required for art, architecture applicants. Deferred and early admission available.

STUDENT LIFE. Housing: Dormitories (men, women); apartment, fraternity, sorority housing available. **Activities:** Student government, film, radio, student newspaper, yearbook, choral groups, concert band, dance, drama, marching band, musical theater, opera, fraternities, sororities, Wesley Foundation, Catholic Student Center, Baptist Student Union, Young Republicans, Young Democrats, International Student Organization, Circle-K, Afro-American student groups.

ATHLETICS. NCAA. **Intercollegiate:** Baseball M, basketball, cross-country, football M, golf M, softball W, tennis, track and field, volleyball W. **Intramural:** Badminton, basketball, bowling, golf, horseback riding, racquetball, rugby M, sailing, skin diving, soccer, softball, swimming, table tennis, tennis, volleyball.

STUDENT SERVICES. Aptitude testing, career counseling, employment service for undergraduates, health services, on-campus day care, personal counseling, placement service for graduates, special adviser for adult students, veterans counselor, services/facilities for handicapped.

ANNUAL EXPENSES. Tuition and fees (1992-93): $1,598, $1,800 additional for out-of-state students. **Room and board:** $2,136. **Books and supplies:** $500. **Other expenses:** $930.

FINANCIAL AID. 75% of freshmen, 44% of continuing students receive some form of aid. 97% of grants, 96% of loans, 57% of jobs based on need. 1,260 enrolled freshmen were judged to have need, 1,046 were offered aid. Academic, music/drama, art, athletic, state/district residency, leadership, alumni affiliation, religious affiliation, minority scholarships available. **Aid applications:** No closing date; priority given to applications received by March 1; applicants notified on a rolling basis beginning on or about April 1; must reply within 2 weeks.

ADDRESS/TELEPHONE. Leroy Broussard, Director of Admissions, University of Southwestern Louisiana, East University Avenue, Lafayette, LA 70504. (318) 231-6457. Fax: (318) 231-6195.

Xavier University of Louisiana
New Orleans, Louisiana — CB code: 6975

Admissions:	77% of applicants accepted
Based on:	••• School record, test scores
	•• Recommendations
	• Interview, special talents
Completion:	65% of freshmen end year in good standing
	36% graduate, 40% of these enter graduate study

4-year private university, coed, affiliated with Roman Catholic Church. Founded in 1915. **Accreditation:** Regional. **Undergraduate enrollment:** 882 men, 1,938 women full time; 93 men, 165 women part time. **Graduate enrollment:** 46 men, 118 women full time; 49 men, 113 women part time. **Faculty:** 253 total (209 full time), 166 with doctorates or other terminal degrees. **Location:** Urban campus in very large city; 1 mile from downtown. **Calendar:** Semester, limited summer session. Saturday classes. **Microcomputers:** 136 located in libraries, classrooms, computer centers.

DEGREES OFFERED. BA, BS, MA, MS, Pharm D. 353 bachelor's degrees awarded in 1992. 14% in business and management, 7% communications, 25% health sciences, 16% life sciences, 10% physical sciences, 7% psychology, 11% social sciences. Graduate degrees offered in 7 major fields of study.

UNDERGRADUATE MAJORS. Accounting, art education, biochemistry, biology, business administration and management, business economics, chemistry, computer and information sciences, early childhood education, elementary education, English, English education, fine arts, French, history, information sciences and systems, journalism, mathematics, mathematics education, microbiology, music, music education, music performance, pharmacy, philosophy, physical education, physics, political science and government, predentistry, preengineering, prelaw, premedicine, psychology, radio/television broadcasting, science education, social science education, sociology, Spanish, special education, speech correction, speech pathology/audiology, statistics, theological studies.

ACADEMIC PROGRAMS. Cooperative education, double major, dual enrollment of high school students, honors program, independent study, internships, teacher preparation, telecourses, visiting/exchange student program, cross-registration; liberal arts/career combination in engineering; combined bachelor's/graduate program in business administration. **Remedial services:** Learning center, preadmission summer program, reduced course load, remedial instruction, special counselor, tutoring. **ROTC:** Air Force, Army, Naval. **Placement/credit:** AP, CLEP Subject, institutional tests; 30 credit hours maximum for bachelor's degree.

ACADEMIC REQUIREMENTS. Freshmen must earn minimum GPA of 2.0 to continue in good standing. 79% of freshmen return for sophomore year. Students must declare major by end of second year. **Graduation requirements:** 128 hours for bachelor's (24 in major). Most students required to take courses in arts/fine arts, English, foreign languages, history, mathematics, philosophy/religion, biological/physical sciences, social sciences. **Postgraduate studies:** 3% enter law school, 17% enter medical school, 2% enter MBA programs, 18% enter other graduate study.

FRESHMAN ADMISSIONS. Selection criteria: High school record or GED test scores, standardized test results, and recommendation from counselor. **High school preparation:** 18 units required. Required and recommended units include English 4, mathematics 2-4, social science 1-2 and science 1-2. Foreign language 2 recommended. One history also recommended. 8 academic electives required. **Test requirements:** SAT or ACT; score report by July 15.

1992 FRESHMAN CLASS PROFILE. 839 men applied, 613 accepted, 215 enrolled; 1,848 women applied, 1,461 accepted, 529 enrolled. 38% had high school GPA of 3.0 or higher, 54% between 2.0 and 2.99. 25% were in top tenth and 56% were in top quarter of graduating class. **Academic background:** Mid 50% of enrolled freshmen had SAT-V between 370-490, SAT-M between 390-520; ACT composite between 18-23. 44% submitted SAT scores, 84% submitted ACT scores. **Characteristics:** 65% from in state, 70% commute, 99% have minority backgrounds, 1% are foreign students. Average age is 18.

FALL-TERM APPLICATIONS. $25 fee, may be waived for applicants with need. Closing date March 1; applicants notified on or about April 1; must reply by May 1. Interview recommended for academically weak applicants. Audition recommended for music applicants. Portfolio recommended for art applicants. CRDA. Deferred admission available.

STUDENT LIFE. Housing: Dormitories (men, women). **Activities:** Student government, student newspaper, television, yearbook, choral groups, concert band, jazz band, music ensembles, pep band, gospel choir, fraternities, sororities, service organizations, National Organization of Black College and University Students, Christian Life Community, NAACP.

ATHLETICS. NAIA. **Intercollegiate:** Basketball. **Intramural:** Badminton, basketball, softball, swimming, table tennis, tennis, track and field, volleyball.

STUDENT SERVICES. Aptitude testing, career counseling, employment service for undergraduates, freshman orientation, health services, personal counseling, placement service for graduates, special adviser for adult students, veterans counselor, services/facilities for handicapped.

ANNUAL EXPENSES. Tuition and fees (1992-93): $6,300. **Room and board:** $3,400. **Books and supplies:** $576. **Other expenses:** $1,119.

FINANCIAL AID. 90% of freshmen, 85% of continuing students receive some form of aid. 75% of grants, 79% of loans, all jobs based on need. Academic, music/drama, art, athletic, religious affiliation scholarships available. **Aid applications:** No closing date; priority given to applications received by May 1; applicants notified on a rolling basis beginning on or about June 1; must reply within 2 weeks.

ADDRESS/TELEPHONE. Winston B. Brown, Dean of Admissions and Financial Aid, Xavier University of Louisiana, 7325 Palmetto Street, New Orleans, LA 70125-1098. (504) 486-7411. Fax: (504) 486-4577.

Maine

Andover College
Portland, Maine CB code: 0688

2-year proprietary business, junior college, coed. Founded in 1966. **Undergraduate enrollment:** 83 men, 406 women full time; 6 men, 26 women part time. **Faculty:** 22 total (9 full time), 4 with doctorates or other terminal degrees. **Location:** Urban campus in small city; 115 miles from Boston. **Calendar:** Six 8-week terms. **Microcomputers:** 42 located in libraries, computer centers.

DEGREES OFFERED. AAS. 182 associate degrees awarded in 1992. 46% in business and management, 21% business/office and marketing/distribution, 15% computer sciences, 18% allied health.

UNDERGRADUATE MAJORS. Accounting, business administration and management, business and management, business and office, business data processing and related programs, business data programming, computer and information sciences, computer programming, legal assistant/paralegal, legal secretary, medical assistant, office supervision and management, real estate, secretarial and related programs.

ACADEMIC PROGRAMS. Accelerated program, double major, dual enrollment of high school students, independent study, internships. **Remedial services:** Learning center, reduced course load, remedial instruction, special counselor, tutoring. **Placement/credit:** AP, CLEP General and Subject, institutional tests; 12 credit hours maximum for associate degree.

ACADEMIC REQUIREMENTS. Freshmen must earn minimum GPA of 2.0 to continue in good standing. 70% of freshmen return for sophomore year. Students must declare major on application. **Graduation requirements:** 60 hours for associate (30 in major). Most students required to take courses in computer science, English.

FRESHMAN ADMISSIONS. Selection criteria: Open admissions.

1992 FRESHMAN CLASS PROFILE. 39 men, 193 women enrolled. **Characteristics:** 99% from in state, 100% commute, 1% have minority backgrounds, 1% are foreign students. Average age is 25.

FALL-TERM APPLICATIONS. $25 fee. No closing date; applicants notified on a rolling basis; must reply within 4 weeks. Interview recommended. Deferred and early admission available.

STUDENT LIFE. Activities: Student government, student newspaper, drama.

STUDENT SERVICES. Career counseling, employment service for undergraduates, freshman orientation, personal counseling, placement service for graduates, special adviser for adult students, services/facilities for handicapped.

ANNUAL EXPENSES. Tuition and fees: $4,700. **Books and supplies:** $700. **Other expenses:** $1,000.

FINANCIAL AID. 70% of freshmen, 60% of continuing students receive some form of aid. 91% of grants, 92% of loans, all jobs based on need. Academic scholarships available. **Aid applications:** No closing date; applicants notified on a rolling basis; must reply within 10 days.

ADDRESS/TELEPHONE. Sheri Harrison Leavitt, Director of Admissions, Andover College, 901 Washington Avenue, Portland, ME 04103. (207) 774-6126. (800) 639-3110. Fax: (207) 774-1715.

Bates College
Lewiston, Maine CB code: 3076

Admissions:	36% of applicants accepted
Based on:	••• Essay, interview, recommendations, school record
	•• Activities, special talents
	• Test scores
Completion:	95% of freshmen end year in good standing
	89% graduate

4-year private liberal arts college, coed. Founded in 1855. **Accreditation:** Regional. **Undergraduate enrollment:** 757 men, 758 women full time. **Faculty:** 176 total (148 full time), 154 with doctorates or other terminal degrees. **Location:** Suburban campus in large town; 135 miles from Boston. **Calendar:** 4-4-1. **Microcomputers:** 250 located in libraries, classrooms, computer centers, campus-wide network. **Special facilities:** Bates-Morse Mountain Seacoast Conservation Area, Edmund S. Muskie Archives.

DEGREES OFFERED. BA, BS. 402 bachelor's degrees awarded in 1992. 7% in languages, 13% letters/literature, 8% life sciences, 11% multi/interdisciplinary studies, 6% philosophy, religion, theology, 8% psychology, 36% social sciences, 6% visual and performing arts.

UNDERGRADUATE MAJORS. Afro-American (black) studies, American studies, anthropology, art history, biology, chemistry, classics, dramatic arts, East Asian studies, economics, English, French, geology, German, history, mathematics, medieval studies, music, philosophy, physics, political science and government, psychology, religion, rhetoric, Russian, sociology, Spanish, studio art, women's studies.

ACADEMIC PROGRAMS. Accelerated program, double major, dual enrollment of high school students, honors program, independent study, internships, semester at sea, student-designed major, study abroad, teacher preparation, visiting/exchange student program, Washington semester, marine biology program at Mystic Seaport; liberal arts/career combination in engineering. **Remedial services:** Tutoring. **Placement/credit:** AP, institutional tests.

ACADEMIC REQUIREMENTS. Freshmen must earn minimum GPA of 1.5 to continue in good standing. 97% of freshmen return for sophomore year. Students must declare major by end of second year. **Graduation requirements:** Most students required to take courses in humanities, biological/physical sciences, social sciences.

FRESHMAN ADMISSIONS. Selection criteria: School achievement record, recommendations, special talents, leadership, essay, interview all important. Recommended units include biological science 1, English 4, foreign language 2, mathematics 3, physical science 1 and social science 3. **Test requirements:** Test of Standard Written English required of those who submit SAT.

1992 FRESHMAN CLASS PROFILE. 1,654 men applied, 581 accepted, 189 enrolled; 1,874 women applied, 705 accepted, 215 enrolled. 55% were in top tenth and 90% were in top quarter of graduating class. **Academic background:** Mid 50% of enrolled freshmen had SAT-V between 560-630, SAT-M between 590-670. 70% submitted SAT scores. **Characteristics:** 13% from in state, 100% live in college housing, 13% have minority backgrounds, 3% are foreign students. Average age is 18.

FALL-TERM APPLICATIONS. $40 fee, may be waived for applicants with need. Closing date February 1; applicants notified on or about April 7; must reply by May 1. Essay required. Interview recommended. CRDA. Deferred and early admission available. EDP-F.

STUDENT LIFE. Housing: Dormitories (men, women, coed). On-campus housing guaranteed for four years. **Activities:** Student government, magazine, radio, student newspaper, television, yearbook, choral groups, concert band, dance, drama, jazz band, music ensembles, symphony orchestra, volunteer organizations, political organizations, religious organizations, Afro/American/Hispanic/International Asian groups.

ATHLETICS. NCAA. **Intercollegiate:** Baseball M, basketball, cross-country, diving, field hockey W, football M, golf, ice hockey, lacrosse, rowing (crew), rugby, sailing, skiing, soccer, softball W, squash, swimming, tennis, track and field, volleyball, water polo. **Intramural:** Badminton, basketball, fencing, golf, handball, horseback riding, racquetball, soccer, softball, squash, table tennis, tennis, volleyball, water polo. **Clubs:** Outing clubs.

STUDENT SERVICES. Aptitude testing, career counseling, employment service for undergraduates, freshman orientation, health services, personal counseling, placement service for graduates, services/facilities for handicapped.

ANNUAL EXPENSES. Tuition and fees: Comprehensive fee: $23,990. **Books and supplies:** $610. **Other expenses:** $900.

FINANCIAL AID. 50% of freshmen, 51% of continuing students receive some form of aid. All grants, 99% of loans, 62% of jobs based on need. 178 enrolled freshmen were judged to have need, all were offered aid. **Aid applications:** Closing date February 12; applicants notified on or about April 15; must reply by May 1.

ADDRESS/TELEPHONE. William C. Hiss, Vice President for Administrative Services and Dean of Admissions, Bates College, Lindholm House, 23 Campus Avenue, Lewiston, ME 04240-9917. (207) 786-6000. Fax: (207) 786-6025.

Beal College
Bangor, Maine CB code: 3114

2-year proprietary business, junior college, coed. Founded in 1891. **Undergraduate enrollment:** 32 men, 316 women full time; 17 men, 114 women part time. **Faculty:** 27 total (9 full time), 8 with doctorates or other terminal degrees. **Location:** Urban campus in large town; 250 miles from Boston. **Calendar:** Six 8-week modules per year. Extensive evening/early morning classes. **Microcomputers:** 45 located in libraries, computer centers. **Special facilities:** Law library. **Additional facts:** Extensive business-oriented continuing education evening program.

DEGREES OFFERED. AS. 130 associate degrees awarded in 1992.

UNDERGRADUATE MAJORS. Accounting, business administration and management, business and office, data processing, hotel/motel and restaurant management, legal assistant/paralegal, legal secretary, medical assistant, medical secretary, office supervision and management, radio/television broadcasting, secretarial and related programs, tourism, transportation and travel marketing.

ACADEMIC PROGRAMS. Accelerated program, double major, independent study, internships. **Remedial services:** Reduced course load, remedial instruction, tutoring. **Placement/credit:** Institutional tests; 30 credit hours maximum for associate degree.

ACADEMIC REQUIREMENTS. Freshmen must earn minimum GPA of 2.0 to continue in good standing. Freshmen must earn minimum grade-point average of 1.75 in first semester, 2.0 in second semester to continue in good academic standing. 82% of freshmen return for sophomore year. **Graduation requirements:** 72 hours for associate (48 in major). Most students required to take courses in computer science, English, mathematics, social sciences. **Additional information:** Students in travel and tourism and hotel/motel management programs required to complete travel requirements and 150-hour externship; students in medical administrative assisting program must complete 150-hour practicum.

FRESHMAN ADMISSIONS. Selection criteria: Open admissions. Recommended units include biological science 1, English 4 and mathematics 4. **Additional information:** All students born after January 1, 1957 required to submit proof of immunizations according to state standards.

1992 FRESHMAN CLASS PROFILE. 165 men and women enrolled. **Characteristics:** Average age is 25.

FALL-TERM APPLICATIONS. $25 fee. No closing date; applicants notified on a rolling basis; must reply within 5 weeks. Interview recommended. Deferred admission available. Mathematics and English pre-admission tests required.

STUDENT LIFE. Housing: Dormitories (coed). **Activities:** Student government, student newspaper.

ATHLETICS. Intramural: Volleyball.

STUDENT SERVICES. Career counseling, employment service for undergraduates, freshman orientation, placement service for graduates, special adviser for adult students, veterans counselor, services/facilities for handicapped.

ANNUAL EXPENSES. Tuition and fees (1992-93): $3,610. **Room and board:** $1,600 room only. **Books and supplies:** $750. **Other expenses:** $1,400.

FINANCIAL AID. 70% of freshmen, 83% of continuing students receive some form of aid. 97% of grants, 95% of loans based on need. 85 enrolled freshmen were judged to have need, all were offered aid. Academic scholarships available. **Aid applications:** No closing date; priority given to applications received by May 1; applicants notified on a rolling basis beginning on or about June 15; must reply within 2 weeks.

ADDRESS/TELEPHONE. Louise G. Grant, Admissions Administrator, Beal College, 629 Main Street, Bangor, ME 04401. (207) 947-4591. (800) 432-7351. Fax: (207) 947-0208.

Bowdoin College
Brunswick, Maine

CB code: 3089

Admissions:	34% of applicants accepted
Based on:	••• Essay, recommendations, school record
	•• Activities, special talents
	• Interview, test scores
Completion:	99% of freshmen end year in good standing
	90% graduate, 18% of these enter graduate study

4-year private liberal arts college, coed. Founded in 1794. **Accreditation:** Regional. **Undergraduate enrollment:** 754 men, 671 women full time; 6 men, 14 women part time. **Faculty:** 161 total (148 full time), 123 with doctorates or other terminal degrees. **Location:** Suburban campus in large town; 120 miles from Boston, 26 miles from Portland. **Calendar:** Semester. **Microcomputers:** 90 located in classrooms, computer centers, campus-wide network. **Special facilities:** Art museum, Peary-MacMillan Artic Museum, Bethel Point Marine Research Station, Hawthorne-Longfellow Library, Hatch Science Library, Bowdoin Scientific Station on Kent Island, Breckinridge Public Affairs Center, Coleman Farm Banding Station.

DEGREES OFFERED. BA. 360 bachelor's degrees awarded in 1992. 8% in languages, 9% letters/literature, 14% life sciences, 5% physical sciences, 43% social sciences, 6% visual and performing arts.

UNDERGRADUATE MAJORS. Afro-American (black) studies, anthropology, archeology, art history, art history and archeology, art history and religion, Asian studies, biochemistry, biology, chemistry, classics, classics and archeology, computer and information sciences, computer science and mathematics, economics, English, environmental science, French, geology, geology and chemistry, geology and physics, German, history, mathematics, mathematics and economics, music, neurosciences, philosophy, physics, political science and government, psychology, religion, Romance Languages, Russian, self designed; chemical physics, sociology, Spanish, studio art.

ACADEMIC PROGRAMS. Accelerated program, double major, independent study, semester at sea, student-designed major, study abroad, teacher preparation, visiting/exchange student program, Washington semester; liberal arts/career combination in engineering; combined bachelor's/graduate program in law. **Remedial services:** Reduced course load, special counselor, tutoring. **Placement/credit:** AP, IB, institutional tests; 8 credit hours maximum for bachelor's degree.

ACADEMIC REQUIREMENTS. Freshmen who have failed 4 or more courses by end of first semester or 2 at end of second semester are suspended for 2 semesters. 93% of freshmen return for sophomore year. Students must declare major by end of second year. **Graduation requirements:** Most students required to take courses in arts/fine arts, humanities, mathematics, biological/physical sciences, social sciences. **Postgraduate studies:** 3% enter law school, 3% enter medical school, 1% enter MBA programs, 11% enter other graduate study. **Additional information:** Students must satisfactorily complete 32 courses to graduate, 8 to 10 courses major. Some course work in non-Eurocentric studies required.

FRESHMAN ADMISSIONS. Selection criteria: School achievement record, rigor of course program, quality of application and essay, extracurricular activities, recommendations and interview are most important. Test scores considered at student's request but not required. Motivation of applicants and academic potential also considered. **High school preparation:** 18 units recommended. Recommended units include English 4, foreign language 3, mathematics 4, social science 3 and science 4.

1992 FRESHMAN CLASS PROFILE. 1,598 men applied, 472 accepted, 185 enrolled; 1,483 women applied, 586 accepted, 225 enrolled. 77% were in top tenth of graduating class. **Academic background:** Mid 50% of enrolled freshmen had SAT-V between 540-640, SAT-M between 590-690. 77% submitted SAT scores. **Characteristics:** 13% from in state, 100% live in college housing, 14% have minority backgrounds, 3% are foreign students, 31% join fraternities/sororities. Average age is 18.

FALL-TERM APPLICATIONS. $45 fee, may be waived for applicants with need. Closing date January 15; applicants notified on or about April 15; must reply by May 1. Essay required. Interview recommended. Audition recommended for music applicants. Portfolio recommended for art applicants. CRDA. Deferred admission available. EDP-F. Early decision plan application priority date November 15.

STUDENT LIFE. Housing: Dormitories (coed); apartment housing available. 4 years of housing guaranteed for all students. Wellness House available to those interested in pursuing healthy lifestyle. **Activities:** Student government, film, magazine, radio, student newspaper, yearbook, literary magazines, choral groups, dance, drama, jazz band, marching band, music ensembles, musical theater, pep band, community orchestra, wind ensemble, chamber choir, other vocal ensembles, brass quintet, improvisational comedy, volunteer services, women's association, Afro-American society, foreign student and foreign language associations, religious organizations, coeducational fraternities, peer support. **Additional information:** Students may join recognized coeducational fraternities and live in coeducational fraternity housing.

ATHLETICS. NCAA. **Intercollegiate:** Baseball M, basketball, cross-country, diving, field hockey W, football M, golf, ice hockey, lacrosse, sailing, skiing, soccer, softball W, squash, swimming, tennis, track and field, volleyball W. **Intramural:** Baseball M, basketball M, cross-country, football M, ice hockey, soccer, softball, tennis, volleyball. **Clubs:** Crew, rugby.

STUDENT SERVICES. Career counseling, employment service for undergraduates, freshman orientation, health services, on-campus day care, personal counseling, placement service for graduates, services/facilities for handicapped.

ANNUAL EXPENSES. Tuition and fees: $18,300. **Room and board:** $5,855. **Books and supplies:** $620. **Other expenses:** $875.

FINANCIAL AID. 55% of freshmen, 60% of continuing students receive some form of aid. All grants, 93% of loans, 64% of jobs based on need. 175 enrolled freshmen were judged to have need, all were offered aid. **Aid applications:** Closing date March 1; applicants notified on or about April 5; must reply by May 1.

ADDRESS/TELEPHONE. Richard E. Steele, Dean of Admissions, Bowdoin College, Brunswick, ME 04011-2595. (207) 725-3100. Fax: (207) 725-3123.

Casco Bay College
Portland, Maine

CB code: 3700

2-year proprietary business, junior college, coed. Founded in 1863. **Undergraduate enrollment:** 45 men, 305 women full time; 40 men, 100 women part time. **Faculty:** 22 total (11 full time), 13 with doctorates or other terminal degrees. **Location:** Urban campus in small city; 115 miles from Boston. **Calendar:** Semester, extensive summer session. Extensive evening/early morning classes. **Microcomputers:** 40 located in libraries, classrooms, computer centers. **Special facilities:** College-run travel agency.

DEGREES OFFERED. AS. 95 associate degrees awarded in 1992. 10% in business and management, 85% business/office and marketing/distribution, 5% computer sciences.

UNDERGRADUATE MAJORS. Accounting, business administration and management, business and management, business and office, business computer/console/peripheral equipment operation, business data entry equipment operation, business data processing and related programs, business data programming, business education, computer and information sciences, data processing, legal secretary, medical secretary, secretarial and related programs.

ACADEMIC PROGRAMS. Double major, dual enrollment of high school students, internships, study abroad, teacher preparation. **Remedial services:** Learning center, reduced course load, remedial instruction, special counselor, tutoring. **Placement/credit:** CLEP Subject, institutional tests; 27 credit hours maximum for associate degree.

ACADEMIC REQUIREMENTS. Freshmen must earn minimum GPA

of 1.75 to continue in good standing. 85% of freshmen return for sophomore year. Students must declare major on enrollment. **Graduation requirements:** 60 hours for associate (21 in major). Most students required to take courses in computer science, English, mathematics, biological/physical sciences, social sciences.

FRESHMAN ADMISSIONS. Selection criteria: Open admissions.

1992 FRESHMAN CLASS PROFILE. 50 men, 290 women enrolled. **Characteristics:** 85% from in state, 70% commute. Average age is 20.

FALL-TERM APPLICATIONS. $25 fee, may be waived for applicants with need. No closing date; applicants notified on a rolling basis; must reply within 2 weeks. Interview recommended. Deferred and early admission available.

STUDENT LIFE. Housing: Apartment housing available. **Activities:** Student government, magazine, student newspaper, television, yearbook.

ATHLETICS. Intramural: Basketball, racquetball, skiing, softball, swimming, table tennis, volleyball.

STUDENT SERVICES. Aptitude testing, career counseling, employment service for undergraduates, freshman orientation, personal counseling, placement service for graduates, services/facilities for handicapped.

ANNUAL EXPENSES. Tuition and fees (projected): $5,370. **Room and board:** $3,200. **Books and supplies:** $650. **Other expenses:** $800.

FINANCIAL AID. 80% of freshmen, 75% of continuing students receive some form of aid. All grants, 71% of loans, all jobs based on need. 142 enrolled freshmen were judged to have need, all were offered aid. Leadership scholarships available. **Aid applications:** No closing date; applicants notified on a rolling basis beginning on or about June 1.

ADDRESS/TELEPHONE. Norman E. Gordon, Director of Admissions, Casco Bay College, 477 Congress Street, Portland, ME 04101-3483. (207) 772-0196.

Central Maine Medical Center School of Nursing
Lewiston, Maine CB code: 3302

Admissions: 17% of applicants accepted
Based on: ••• Essay, recommendations, school record, test scores
• Activities
Completion: 90% of freshmen end year in good standing
75% go on to graduate

2-year private nursing college, coed. Founded in 1891. **Accreditation:** Regional. **Undergraduate enrollment:** 7 men, 72 women full time; 7 women part time. **Faculty:** 11 total (8 full time). **Location:** Urban campus in large town; 35 miles from Portland. **Calendar:** Semester. **Microcomputers:** 3 located on campus.

DEGREES OFFERED. AAS. 37 associate degrees awarded in 1992. 100% in health sciences.

UNDERGRADUATE MAJORS. Nursing.

ACADEMIC PROGRAMS. Remedial services: Learning center, remedial instruction. **Placement/credit:** CLEP General and Subject; 27 credit hours maximum for associate degree.

ACADEMIC REQUIREMENTS. Freshmen must earn minimum GPA of 2.0 to continue in good standing. 90% of freshmen return for sophomore year. Students must declare major on application. **Graduation requirements:** 67 hours for associate (40 in major). Most students required to take courses in English, humanities, biological/physical sciences, social sciences.

FRESHMAN ADMISSIONS. Selection criteria: High school GPA of 2.0 and test scores required. Recommendations, essay very important. Recommended units include biological science 1 and physical science 1. Chemistry course required. **Test requirements:** SAT; score report by January 1.

1992 FRESHMAN CLASS PROFILE. 25 men applied, 5 accepted, 5 enrolled; 217 women applied, 37 accepted, 35 enrolled. 67% had high school GPA of 3.0 or higher, 33% between 2.0 and 2.99. 14% were in top tenth and 57% were in top quarter of graduating class. **Academic background:** Mid 50% of enrolled freshmen had SAT-V between 470-550, SAT-M between 420-530. 50% submitted SAT scores. **Characteristics:** 100% from in state, 92% commute, 5% have minority backgrounds. Average age is 29.

FALL-TERM APPLICATIONS. $20 fee. Closing date June 1; priority given to applications received by January 1; applicants notified on or about March 15; must reply by May 1 or within 2 weeks if notified thereafter. Essay required. Deferred admission available. Institutional early decision plan.

STUDENT LIFE. Housing: Dormitories (coed). Single rooms available at extra cost.

STUDENT SERVICES. Freshman orientation, health services, personal counseling, Academic adviser for each student.

ANNUAL EXPENSES. Tuition and fees: $5,066. **Room and board:** $1,220 room only. **Books and supplies:** $879. **Other expenses:** $700.

FINANCIAL AID. 68% of freshmen, 71% of continuing students receive some form of aid. All grants, 85% of loans based on need. 31 enrolled freshmen were judged to have need, all were offered aid. **Aid applications:** Closing date July 1; priority given to applications received by March 15; applicants notified on a rolling basis beginning on or about April 1; must reply within 2 weeks.

ADDRESS/TELEPHONE. Marilyn Brackett, Admissions Committee Chairperson, Central Maine Medical Center School of Nursing, 300 Main Street, Lewiston, ME 04240-9986. (207) 795-2843. Fax: (207) 795-2303.

Central Maine Technical College
Auburn, Maine CB code: 3309

2-year public technical college, coed. Founded in 1964. **Accreditation:** Regional. **Undergraduate enrollment:** 410 men, 186 women full time; 671 men, 205 women part time. **Faculty:** 52 total (49 full time). **Location:** Suburban campus in small city; one mile from downtown. **Calendar:** Semester. **Microcomputers:** 50 located in libraries, computer centers.

DEGREES OFFERED. AAS. 88 associate degrees awarded in 1992. 25% in engineering technologies, 25% health sciences, 50% trade and industry.

UNDERGRADUATE MAJORS. Architectural technologies, automotive mechanics, automotive technology, civil technology, construction, diesel engine mechanics, electromechanical technology, electronic technology, general educational technology, graphic and printing production, graphic arts technology, instrumentation technology, machine tool operation/machine shop, mechanical design technology, nursing, occupational safety and health technology, office supervision and management, precision metal work, trade and technical occupations.

ACADEMIC PROGRAMS. Independent study, internships. **Remedial services:** Learning center, reduced course load, remedial instruction, tutoring. **Placement/credit:** CLEP General and Subject, institutional tests; 9 credit hours maximum for associate degree.

ACADEMIC REQUIREMENTS. Freshmen must earn minimum GPA of 2.0 to continue in good standing. 80% of freshmen return for sophomore year. Students must declare major on application. **Graduation requirements:** 60 hours for associate (39 in major). Most students required to take courses in English, humanities, mathematics, social sciences.

FRESHMAN ADMISSIONS. Selection criteria: Admissions decisions made by program chairpersons on basis of prerequisite qualifications, recommendations, and applicant goals. One physical science, 2 mathematics required for some programs.

1992 FRESHMAN CLASS PROFILE. 347 men, 260 women enrolled. 20% had high school GPA of 3.0 or higher, 31% between 2.0 and 2.99. **Characteristics:** 96% from in state, 75% commute. Average age is 20.

FALL-TERM APPLICATIONS. $15 fee, may be waived for applicants with need. No closing date; applicants notified on a rolling basis; must reply within 30 days. Interview recommended. Deferred admission available.

STUDENT LIFE. Housing: Dormitories (men, women). **Activities:** Student government, yearbook.

ATHLETICS. Intercollegiate: Basketball, golf, soccer. **Intramural:** Baseball M, basketball, bowling, golf, ice hockey M, racquetball, skiing, soccer, softball, swimming, tennis.

STUDENT SERVICES. Aptitude testing, career counseling, employment service for undergraduates, freshman orientation, health services, personal counseling, placement service for graduates, special adviser for adult students, veterans counselor, services/facilities for handicapped.

ANNUAL EXPENSES. Tuition and fees: $1,950, $1,980 additional for out-of-state students. **Room and board:** $3,200. **Books and supplies:** $500. **Other expenses:** $1,000.

FINANCIAL AID. All grants, 95% of loans, 32% of jobs based on need. **Aid applications:** No closing date; priority given to applications received by May 1; applicants notified on a rolling basis beginning on or about August 1; must reply within 2 weeks.

ADDRESS/TELEPHONE. Darcy Stevens, Associate Director of Admissions, Central Maine Technical College, 1250 Turner Street, Auburn, ME 04210-6498. (207) 784-2385. Fax: (207) 777-7353.

Colby College
Waterville, Maine CB code: 3280

Admissions: 47% of applicants accepted
Based on: ••• Essay, school record
•• Activities, recommendations, special talents
• Interview, test scores
Completion: 98% of freshmen end year in good standing
87% graduate, 20% of these enter graduate study

4-year private liberal arts college, coed. Founded in 1813. **Accreditation:** Regional. **Undergraduate enrollment:** 833 men, 914 women full time; 2 women part time. **Faculty:** 227 total (195 full time), 151 with doctorates or other terminal degrees. **Location:** Rural campus in large town; 180 miles from Boston, 75 miles from Portland. **Calendar:** 4-1-4. **Microcomputers:** 130 located in libraries, classrooms, computer centers. **Special facilities:** Art museum, observatory, satellite dish (for foreign TV/radio), art/music library.

Additional facts: 714-acre campus, state wildlife management area including arboretum and bird sanctuary.

DEGREES OFFERED. BA. 456 bachelor's degrees awarded in 1992. 11% in area and ethnic studies, 6% languages, 12% letters/literature, 10% life sciences, 8% psychology, 35% social sciences, 7% visual and performing arts.

UNDERGRADUATE MAJORS. Afro-American (black) studies, American studies, anthropology, art history, biochemistry, biology, biology/environmental science, business and management, chemistry, Chemistry-Environmental Science, classics, East Asian studies, economics, English, environmental science, fine arts, French, geology, Geology-Environmental Science, German, history, international studies, mathematics, mathematics/computer science, music, philosophy, physics, political science and government, psychology, religion, Russian and Slavic studies, sociology, Spanish, studio art, visual and performing arts.

ACADEMIC PROGRAMS. Accelerated program, double major, honors program, independent study, internships, semester at sea, student-designed major, study abroad, teacher preparation, visiting/exchange student program, Washington semester, cross-registration, summer research assistantships, exchange programs with Pomona College (CA), Pitzer College, Howard University (DC), Claremont McKenna College (CA), and Scripps College (CA), Williams-Mystic Seaport, 3-2 programs with Dartmouth College, University of Rochester (NY), Case Western Reserve University (OH); liberal arts/career combination in engineering. **Remedial services:** Reading improvement program, writing center. **ROTC:** Army. **Placement/credit:** AP, IB, institutional tests; 12 credit hours maximum for bachelor's degree.

ACADEMIC REQUIREMENTS. Freshmen must earn minimum GPA of 2.0 to continue in good standing. 94% of freshmen return for sophomore year. Students must declare major by end of second year. **Graduation requirements:** 120 hours for bachelor's. Most students required to take courses in arts/fine arts, English, foreign languages, history, mathematics, biological/physical sciences, social sciences. **Postgraduate studies:** 2% enter law school, 2% enter medical school, 1% enter MBA programs, 15% enter other graduate study.

FRESHMAN ADMISSIONS. Selection criteria: School record, recommendations, potential contribution to college life, and personal qualities, including school or community involvement, important. Test scores considered. Social, economic, racial, geographic diversity considered. **High school preparation:** 16 units recommended. Recommended units include English 4, foreign language 3, mathematics 3, social science 2 and science 2. 2 additional units of college preparatory work recommended. **Test requirements:** SAT or ACT; score report by March 1. 3 ACH (including English Composition, with or without essay) required of applicants who did not take ACT. Score report by March 1.

1992 FRESHMAN CLASS PROFILE. 1,480 men applied, 607 accepted, 195 enrolled; 1,481 women applied, 785 accepted, 260 enrolled. 46% were in top tenth and 78% were in top quarter of graduating class. **Characteristics:** 13% from in state, 99% live in college housing, 6% have minority backgrounds, 6% are foreign students. Average age is 18.

FALL-TERM APPLICATIONS. $40 fee, may be waived for applicants with need. Closing date January 15; applicants notified on or about April 1; must reply by May 1. Essay required. Interview recommended. CRDA. Deferred and early admission available. EDP-F. 2 early admission options available, applications by November 15 and January 1. Notification by December 15 and February 1.

STUDENT LIFE. Housing: Dormitories (coed). Residence halls divided into 4 commons, each with its own dining hall, student government, and faculty associates. Several quiet floors. Chemical free hall. **Activities:** Student government, film, magazine, radio, student newspaper, yearbook, journal of political opinion, literary magazine, choral groups, concert band, dance, drama, jazz band, music ensembles, musical theater, pep band, symphony orchestra, Black and Hispanic student groups, Environmental Council, public interest research group, religious, social service, and political organizations, volunteer center, international student group.

ATHLETICS. NCAA. **Intercollegiate:** Baseball M, basketball, cross-country, diving, field hockey W, football M, golf, ice hockey, lacrosse, rowing (crew), rugby, sailing, skiing, soccer, softball W, squash, swimming, tennis, track and field, volleyball M, water polo. **Intramural:** Archery, badminton, basketball, fencing, field hockey W, golf, horseback riding, ice hockey, lacrosse, racquetball, sailing, skiing, skin diving, soccer, softball, squash, swimming, table tennis, tennis, volleyball, water polo.

STUDENT SERVICES. Career counseling, employment service for undergraduates, freshman orientation, health services, personal counseling, placement service for graduates, veterans counselor, minority student adviser, international student adviser, services/facilities for handicapped.

ANNUAL EXPENSES. Tuition and fees: $18,690. **Room and board:** $5,540. **Books and supplies:** $500. **Other expenses:** $800.

FINANCIAL AID. 75% of freshmen, 70% of continuing students receive some form of aid. All grants, 99% of loans, 52% of jobs based on need. 179 enrolled freshmen were judged to have need, all were offered aid. **Aid applications:** Closing date February 1; priority given to applications received by January 15; applicants notified on or about April 1; must reply by May 1.

ADDRESS/TELEPHONE. Parker J. Beverage, Dean of Admissions and Financial Aid, Colby College, 150 Mayflower Hill Drive, Waterville, ME 04901-4799. (207) 872-3168. (800) 723-3032. Fax: (207) 872-3555.

College of the Atlantic
Bar Harbor, Maine — CB code: 3305

Admissions: 72% of applicants accepted
Based on:
- ••• Activities, essay, interview, recommendations, school record
- •• Special talents
- • Test scores

Completion: 90% of freshmen end year in good standing
23% graduate

4-year private college of human ecology, coed. Founded in 1969. **Accreditation:** Regional. **Undergraduate enrollment:** 88 men, 119 women full time; 7 men, 18 women part time. **Graduate enrollment:** 3 men, 3 women full time. **Faculty:** 38 total (16 full time), 20 with doctorates or other terminal degrees. **Location:** Rural campus in small town; 300 miles from Boston, 150 miles from Portland. **Calendar:** Trimester, limited summer session. **Microcomputers:** 18 located in libraries, classrooms, computer centers. **Special facilities:** Natural history museum, herbarium, greenhouse, pier. **Additional facts:** 24-acre ocean-front campus on Mount Desert Island adjacent to Acadia National Park, facilitating environmental and human ecological studies.

DEGREES OFFERED. BA, MA. 61 bachelor's degrees awarded in 1992. 10% in education, 90% multi/interdisciplinary studies. Graduate degrees offered in 1 major field of study.

UNDERGRADUATE MAJORS. Biological and physical sciences, elementary education, home economics, human ecology, humanities and social sciences, liberal/general studies, science education, social studies education.

ACADEMIC PROGRAMS. Independent study, internships, student-designed major, study abroad, teacher preparation, visiting/exchange student program, cross-registration. **Remedial services:** Special counselor, tutoring, writing clinic. **Placement/credit:** AP, CLEP General and Subject, institutional tests; 30 credit hours maximum for bachelor's degree.

ACADEMIC REQUIREMENTS. No policy requiring minimum GPA; records of students having academic difficulty are reviewed individually. 69% of freshmen return for sophomore year. **Graduation requirements:** 120 hours for bachelor's. Most students required to take courses in English, history, humanities, mathematics, biological/physical sciences, social sciences. **Additional information:** Curriculum is interdisciplinary and consists of problem-solving course work, seminars, independent study, tutorials, specialized skill courses, and supervised internships away from college.

FRESHMAN ADMISSIONS. Selection criteria: Academic ability, motivation, intellectual enthusiasm, independence, creativity, and commitment to ecological concerns and to goals and philosophies of the college as demonstrated by high school record, recommendations, interview. **High school preparation:** 15 units required; 16 recommended. Required and recommended units include English 4, mathematics 3-4, social science 3 and science 3-4. Foreign language 2 recommended. **Additional information:** Applications reviewed by committee of students, staff, and faculty.

1992 FRESHMAN CLASS PROFILE. 63 men applied, 43 accepted, 16 enrolled; 85 women applied, 64 accepted, 17 enrolled. 56% had high school GPA of 3.0 or higher, 44% between 2.0 and 2.99. 24% were in top tenth and 41% were in top quarter of graduating class. **Academic background:** Mid 50% of enrolled freshmen had SAT-V between 460-580, SAT-M between 490-590. 67% submitted SAT scores. **Characteristics:** 12% from in state, 97% live in college housing, 1% have minority backgrounds. Average age is 19.

FALL-TERM APPLICATIONS. $35 fee, may be waived for applicants with need. No closing date; priority given to applications received by March 1; applicants notified on a rolling basis; must reply by May 1 or within 2 weeks if notified thereafter. Essay required. Interview recommended. Portfolio recommended. CRDA. Deferred and early admission available.

STUDENT LIFE. Housing: Dormitories (coed); cooperative housing available. **Activities:** Student government, film, magazine, student newspaper, publication of student research, choral groups, dance, drama, jazz band, music ensembles, Environmental Awareness Resource Network (EARN). **Additional information:** Students participate in developing college policy through committees and all-college meetings.

ATHLETICS. Intramural: Basketball, sailing, skiing, skin diving, softball, swimming, volleyball.

STUDENT SERVICES. Career counseling, employment service for undergraduates, freshman orientation, health services, personal counseling, placement service for graduates, veterans counselor.

ANNUAL EXPENSES. Tuition and fees: $13,287. **Room and board:** $3,860. **Books and supplies:** $420. **Other expenses:** $430.

FINANCIAL AID. 66% of freshmen, 47% of continuing students receive some form of aid. All aid based on need. **Aid applications:** Closing date May 1; priority given to applications received by February 15; applicants notified on a rolling basis beginning on or about April 15; must reply by May 1 or within 2 weeks if notified thereafter.

ADDRESS/TELEPHONE. Thomas S. Thomas, Director of Admissions and Financial Aid, College of the Atlantic, 105 Eden Street, Bar Harbor, ME 04609. (207) 288-5015 ext. 230. (800) 528-0025. Fax: (207) 288-2328.

Eastern Maine Technical College
Bangor, Maine CB code: 3372

2-year public technical college, coed. Founded in 1966. **Accreditation:** Regional. **Undergraduate enrollment:** 507 men and women full time; 771 men and women part time. **Faculty:** 134 total (54 full time), 4 with doctorates or other terminal degrees. **Location:** Urban campus in small city; 250 miles from Boston, 100 miles from Portland. **Calendar:** Semester, limited summer session. **Microcomputers:** Located in dormitories, libraries, classrooms, computer centers.

DEGREES OFFERED. AAS. 155 associate degrees awarded in 1992. 21% in business and management, 10% engineering technologies, 25% allied health, 44% trade and industry.

UNDERGRADUATE MAJORS. Air conditioning/heating/refrigeration mechanics, air conditioning/heating/refrigeration technology, automotive mechanics, automotive technology, business administration and management, business and management, carpentry, clinical laboratory science, construction, diesel engine mechanics, electrical and electronics equipment repair, electrical technology, electronic technology, industrial equipment maintenance and repair, machine tool operation/machine shop, medical laboratory technologies, nursing, practical nursing, precision metal work, radiograph medical technology, welding technology.

ACADEMIC PROGRAMS. 2-year transfer program, internships. **Remedial services:** Learning center, reduced course load, remedial instruction, special counselor, tutoring, Technical studies; one year developmental program. **Placement/credit:** AP, CLEP Subject, institutional tests; 24 credit hours maximum for associate degree.

ACADEMIC REQUIREMENTS. Freshmen must earn minimum GPA of 1.75 to continue in good standing. 70% of freshmen return for sophomore year. Students must declare major on application. **Graduation requirements:** 68 hours for associate. Most students required to take courses in computer science, English, humanities, mathematics, biological/physical sciences, social sciences.

FRESHMAN ADMISSIONS. Selection criteria: School record, recommendations, and test scores considered. Interviews may be required. Entrance requirements vary by program. Recommended units include biological science 1, English 4, mathematics 3 and physical science 1. Academic requirements vary by program. **Test requirements:** SAT; score report by August 1. SAT required for engineering technologies, medical laboratory, and medical radiography applicants; score report preferred by April 30.

1992 FRESHMAN CLASS PROFILE. 287 men, 141 women enrolled. **Characteristics:** 99% from in state, 67% commute, 3% have minority backgrounds.

FALL-TERM APPLICATIONS. $15 fee, may be waived for applicants with need. Closing date August 15; priority given to applications received by February 1; applicants notified on a rolling basis; must reply by May 1 or within 4 weeks if notified thereafter. Essay required. Interview recommended for allied health applicants. CRDA. Deposit refundable up to 60 days before program begins.

STUDENT LIFE. Housing: Dormitories (coed). **Activities:** Student government, student newspaper, yearbook, Inter-Varsity Christian Fellowship.

ATHLETICS. Intercollegiate: Basketball M, golf M, soccer M. **Intramural:** Badminton, basketball, bowling, handball, ice hockey M, racquetball, skiing, soccer, softball, swimming, table tennis, volleyball.

STUDENT SERVICES. Aptitude testing, career counseling, employment service for undergraduates, freshman orientation, health services, personal counseling, placement service for graduates, special adviser for adult students, veterans counselor, services/facilities for handicapped.

ANNUAL EXPENSES. Tuition and fees: $1,880, $1,980 additional for out-of-state students. **Room and board:** $3,200. **Books and supplies:** $600. **Other expenses:** $1,200.

FINANCIAL AID. 76% of freshmen, 66% of continuing students receive some form of aid. 94% of grants, 92% of loans, 51% of jobs based on need. **Aid applications:** No closing date; priority given to applications received by April 1; applicants notified on a rolling basis beginning on or about May 1; must reply within 2 weeks.

ADDRESS/TELEPHONE. Terri Krass, Director of Admissions, Eastern Maine Technical College, 354 Hogan Road, Bangor, ME 04401. (207) 941-4600. Fax: (207) 941-4608.

Husson College
Bangor, Maine CB code: 3440

Admissions: 96% of applicants accepted
Based on:
- ••• School record
- •• Activities, interview, recommendations, special talents
- • Test scores

Completion: 85% of freshmen end year in good standing
2% enter graduate study

4-year private business, nursing college, coed. Founded in 1898. **Accreditation:** Regional. **Undergraduate enrollment:** 261 men, 382 women full time; 342 men, 883 women part time. **Graduate enrollment:** 35 men, 39 women full time; 74 men, 64 women part time. **Faculty:** 67 total (44 full time), 21 with doctorates or other terminal degrees. **Location:** Suburban campus in large town; 140 miles from Portland. **Calendar:** Semester, extensive summer session. Saturday and extensive evening/early morning classes. **Microcomputers:** 76 located in classrooms, computer centers.

DEGREES OFFERED. AS, BS, MS. 92 associate degrees awarded in 1992. 70% in business and management, 15% business/office and marketing/distribution, 5% allied health, 8% law. 235 bachelor's degrees awarded. 75% in business and management, 6% teacher education, 15% health sciences. Graduate degrees offered in 1 major field of study.

UNDERGRADUATE MAJORS. Associate: Accounting, business and management, business and office, business data processing and related programs, court reporting, data processing, information sciences and systems, legal assistant/paralegal, legal secretary, management information systems, medical assistant, medical secretary, radio/television broadcasting, secretarial and related programs, word processing. **Bachelor's:** Accounting, business administration and management, business and management, business education, court reporting, data processing, finance, information sciences and systems, management information systems, nursing, secretarial and related programs, sports management.

ACADEMIC PROGRAMS. Cooperative education, double major, independent study, internships, teacher preparation, weekend college. **Remedial services:** Learning center, preadmission summer program, reduced course load, remedial instruction, special counselor, tutoring. **ROTC:** Air Force, Army, Naval. **Placement/credit:** AP, CLEP General and Subject, institutional tests; 30 credit hours maximum for bachelor's degree.

ACADEMIC REQUIREMENTS. Freshmen must earn minimum GPA of 2.0 to continue in good standing. 77% of freshmen return for sophomore year. Students must declare major on application. **Graduation requirements:** 60 hours for associate (33 in major), 120 hours for bachelor's (69 in major). Most students required to take courses in English, mathematics. **Postgraduate studies:** 40% from 2-year programs enter 4-year programs. 2% enter MBA programs. **Additional information:** Strong liberal arts core within business programs.

FRESHMAN ADMISSIONS. Selection criteria: Class rank and school achievement record most important. Counselor recommendation considered. Test scores considered for nursing applicants only. 4 English, 2 mathematics, 2 science (including chemistry), 1 social science required of nursing applicants. **Test requirements:** SAT or ACT for placement; score report by September 7. SAT or ACT (SAT preferred) required for nursing applicants for admission.

1992 FRESHMAN CLASS PROFILE. 289 men applied, 278 accepted, 119 enrolled; 432 women applied, 417 accepted, 241 enrolled. **Academic background:** Mid 50% of enrolled freshmen had SAT-V between 330-400, SAT-M between 350-500. 62% submitted SAT scores. **Characteristics:** 88% from in state, 50% commute, 4% have minority backgrounds, 3% are foreign students, 13% join fraternities/sororities. Average age is 20.

FALL-TERM APPLICATIONS. $25 fee, may be waived for applicants with need. Closing date September 1; priority given to applications received by March 1; applicants notified on a rolling basis; must reply within 4 weeks. Interview recommended. CRDA. Deferred and early admission available. EDP-F.

STUDENT LIFE. Housing: Dormitories (coed); fraternity, sorority housing available. **Activities:** Student government, radio, student newspaper, yearbook, drama, music ensembles, fraternities, sororities, Young Republicans, Young Democrats.

ATHLETICS. NAIA. **Intercollegiate:** Baseball M, basketball, golf, soccer, softball W, volleyball W. **Intramural:** Archery, basketball, bowling, football M, handball, racquetball, soccer, softball, swimming, volleyball.

STUDENT SERVICES. Aptitude testing, career counseling, employment service for undergraduates, freshman orientation, health services, personal counseling, placement service for graduates, services/facilities for handicapped.

ANNUAL EXPENSES. Tuition and fees (1992-93): $7,630. **Room and board:** $3,880. **Books and supplies:** $375. **Other expenses:** $1,100.

FINANCIAL AID. 88% of freshmen, 85% of continuing students receive some form of aid. 95% of grants, 82% of loans, all jobs based on need. Academic scholarships available. **Aid applications:** No closing date; priority given to applications received by March 15; applicants notified on a rolling basis beginning on or about February 15; must reply within 4 weeks.

ADDRESS/TELEPHONE. Jane Goodwin, Director of Admissions, Husson College, One College Circle, Bangor, ME 04401. (207) 947-1121 ext. 218. (800) 448-7766. Fax: (207) 947-6024.

Kennebec Valley Technical College
Fairfield, Maine CB code: 3475

2-year public technical college, coed. Founded in 1969. **Accreditation:** Regional. **Undergraduate enrollment:** 600 men and women. **Location:** Suburban campus in small town. **Calendar:** Semester.

FRESHMAN ADMISSIONS. Selection criteria: Open admissions. Selective admissions for certain programs.

ANNUAL EXPENSES. Tuition and fees (1992-93): $1,560, $1,860 additional for out-of-state students. **Books and supplies:** $400.

ADDRESS/TELEPHONE. Eric Hasenfus, Dean of Students, Kennebec Valley Technical College, 92 Western Avenue, Fairfield, ME 04937. (207) 453-9762.

Maine College of Art
Portland, Maine CB code: 3701

Admissions: 93% of applicants accepted
Based on: ••• Essay, interview, school record, special talents
•• Recommendations
• Activities, test scores
Completion: 95% of freshmen end year in good standing
15% enter graduate study

4-year private art college, coed. Founded in 1882. **Accreditation:** Regional. **Undergraduate enrollment:** 99 men, 153 women full time; 13 men, 30 women part time. **Faculty:** 42 total (19 full time), 24 with doctorates or other terminal degrees. **Location:** Urban campus in small city; 100 miles from Boston. **Calendar:** 4-1-4. **Microcomputers:** 5 located in libraries, classrooms. **Special facilities:** Photography gallery, general gallery, student gallery. **Additional facts:** Structured 2-year foundation program in drawing, color, and 2-and 3-dimensional design, followed by 2 years in major. Personal studio space with 24-hour access for all juniors and seniors.

DEGREES OFFERED. BFA. 55 bachelor's degrees awarded in 1992. 100% in visual and performing arts.

UNDERGRADUATE MAJORS. Ceramics, graphic design, metal/jewelry, painting, photography, printmaking, sculpture.

ACADEMIC PROGRAMS. Independent study, internships, study abroad, visiting/exchange student program, New York semester, cross-registration, Mobility Program with 28 art colleges across the country. **Remedial services:** Preadmission summer program, tutoring. **Placement/credit:** AP, CLEP General and Subject, institutional tests.

ACADEMIC REQUIREMENTS. Freshmen must earn minimum GPA of 2.0 to continue in good standing. 70% of freshmen return for sophomore year. Students must declare major by end of second year. **Graduation requirements:** 134 hours for bachelor's (36 in major). Most students required to take courses in arts/fine arts, English, humanities, biological/physical sciences, social sciences.

FRESHMAN ADMISSIONS. Selection criteria: Interview and portfolio in conjunction with high school achievement record and essay basis for decision. Recommendations and test scores considered. Recommended units include English 4, foreign language 2, mathematics 2, social science 2 and science 2. 3 units of art also strongly encouraged. **Test requirements:** SAT or ACT (SAT preferred); score report by August 1.

1992 FRESHMAN CLASS PROFILE. 69 men applied, 62 accepted, 33 enrolled; 90 women applied, 86 accepted, 54 enrolled. 3% had high school GPA of 3.0 or higher, 63% between 2.0 and 2.99. **Academic background:** Mid 50% of enrolled freshmen had SAT-V between 450-510, SAT-M between 440-500. 75% submitted SAT scores. **Characteristics:** 43% from in state, 51% commute, 1% have minority backgrounds, 1% are foreign students. Average age is 23.

FALL-TERM APPLICATIONS. $30 fee, may be waived for applicants with need. Closing date August 1; priority given to applications received by March 1; applicants notified on a rolling basis; must reply by May 1 or within 2 weeks if accepted after April 16. Portfolio required. Essay required. Interview recommended. CRDA. Deferred and early admission available.

STUDENT LIFE. Housing: Dormitories (coed); apartment housing available. **Activities:** Student government, film, student newspaper, visiting artists series, PSA film society (weekly movies), outing club.

ATHLETICS. Intramural: Volleyball.

STUDENT SERVICES. Career counseling, employment service for undergraduates, freshman orientation, personal counseling, placement service for graduates, special adviser for adult students.

ANNUAL EXPENSES. Tuition and fees: $10,645. **Room and board:** $5,020. **Books and supplies:** $1,490.

FINANCIAL AID. 75% of freshmen, 73% of continuing students receive some form of aid. 93% of grants, 83% of loans, 84% of jobs based on need. 38 enrolled freshmen were judged to have need, all were offered aid. Academic, art scholarships available. **Aid applications:** No closing date; priority given to applications received by March 1; applicants notified on a rolling basis beginning on or about March 15; must reply by May 1 or within 2 weeks if notified thereafter.

ADDRESS/TELEPHONE. Elizabeth Shea, Director of Admissions, Maine College of Art, 97 Spring Street, Portland, ME 04101-3987. (207) 775-3052. (800) 639-4808. Fax: (207) 772-5069.

Maine Maritime Academy
Castine, Maine CB code: 3505

Admissions: 74% of applicants accepted
Based on: ••• School record, test scores
•• Activities, interview, recommendations
• Essay, special talents
Completion: 85% of freshmen end year in good standing
75% graduate, 2% of these enter graduate study

4-year public engineering, technical college, coed. Founded in 1941. **Accreditation:** Regional. **Undergraduate enrollment:** 627 men, 36 women full time. **Graduate enrollment:** 20 men, 2 women full time; 27 men, 1 woman part time. **Faculty:** 68 total (60 full time), 21 with doctorates or other terminal degrees. **Location:** Rural campus in rural community; 38 miles from Bangor. **Calendar:** 2 semesters and 1 summer term involving 2-month sea training cruise or internship. **Microcomputers:** 15 located in dormitories, libraries, computer centers. **Special facilities:** 530-foot training ship, 100 sailing craft of various sizes, oceanic research vessel, tug, Schooner Bowdoin. **Additional facts:** Graduation can lead to Coast Guard license as third mate or third assistant engineer and/or to a Maine third class stationary power plant license.

DEGREES OFFERED. AS, BS, MS. 10 associate degrees awarded in 1992. 90 bachelor's degrees awarded. Graduate degrees offered in 3 major fields of study.

UNDERGRADUATE MAJORS. Yacht operations and boatyard management. **Bachelor's:** Engineering and engineering-related technologies, environmental science, marine engineering technology, maritime transportation and management, Merchant Marine, nautical science, naval architecture and marine engineering, naval science (Navy, Marines), oceanographic technologies, oceanography, power engineering technology, power plant operation and maintenance, transportation management.

ACADEMIC PROGRAMS. Cooperative education, internships, semester at sea, study abroad. **Remedial services:** Special counselor, tutoring. **ROTC:** Naval. **Placement/credit:** AP, CLEP Subject, institutional tests.

ACADEMIC REQUIREMENTS. Freshmen must earn minimum GPA of 1.8 to continue in good standing. 75% of freshmen return for sophomore year. Students must declare major on enrollment. **Graduation requirements:** 78 hours for associate, 145 hours for bachelor's. Most students required to take courses in computer science, English, history, humanities, mathematics, biological/physical sciences, social sciences.

FRESHMAN ADMISSIONS. Selection criteria: Academic record, test scores most important. Interview, school and community activities, and recommendations also considered. **High school preparation:** 8 units required. Required units include English 4, mathematics 3 and physical science 1. **Test requirements:** SAT or ACT (SAT preferred); score report by May 15.

1992 FRESHMAN CLASS PROFILE. 552 men applied, 406 accepted, 235 enrolled; 47 women applied, 40 accepted, 15 enrolled. **Characteristics:** 65% from in state, 95% live in college housing, 2% have minority backgrounds, 3% are foreign students, 10% join fraternities/sororities. Average age is 19.

FALL-TERM APPLICATIONS. $15 fee, may be waived for applicants with need. Closing date July 1; applicants notified on a rolling basis beginning on or about January 1; must reply by May 1 or within 2 weeks if notified thereafter. Interview recommended. Essay recommended. CRDA. Deferred admission available.

STUDENT LIFE. Housing: Dormitories (coed). Students required to live on campus unless married or over age 24 or have completed 2 or more years of active military service. **Activities:** Student government, student newspaper, yearbook, drama, marching band, musical theater, pep band, Alpha Phi Omega, other service organizations. **Additional information:** Regimental lifestyle optional for all 2-year programs and those majoring in power engineering and ocean studies (mandatory for United States Coast Guard license programs).

ATHLETICS. NCAA. **Intercollegiate:** Basketball M, cross-country, football M, lacrosse M, sailing, soccer. **Intramural:** Basketball, bowling, field hockey, golf, handball, ice hockey M, lacrosse M, racquetball, rifle, rugby, sailing, skiing, skin diving, soccer, softball, squash, swimming, tennis, volleyball, water polo.

STUDENT SERVICES. Aptitude testing, career counseling, employment service for undergraduates, freshman orientation, health services, personal counseling, placement service for graduates, veterans counselor.

ANNUAL EXPENSES. Tuition and fees (1992-93): $4,210, $905 additional for out-of-district students, $2,720 additional for out-of-state students.

Room and board: $4,245. **Books and supplies:** $400. **Other expenses:** $1,000.

FINANCIAL AID. 82% of freshmen, 91% of continuing students receive some form of aid. 82% of grants, all loans, 67% of jobs based on need. 154 enrolled freshmen were judged to have need, 149 were offered aid. Academic, state/district residency, leadership scholarships available. **Aid applications:** No closing date; priority given to applications received by April 15; applicants notified on a rolling basis beginning on or about March 1; must reply by May 1 or within 2 weeks if notified thereafter.

ADDRESS/TELEPHONE. Daniel J. Jones, Director of Admissions, Maine Maritime Academy, Castine, ME 04420-5000. (207) 326-4311. (800) 227-8465. Fax: (207) 326-9703.

Northern Maine Technical College
Presque Isle, Maine — CB code: 3631

2-year public technical college, coed. Founded in 1961. **Accreditation:** Regional. **Undergraduate enrollment:** 378 men, 266 women full time; 56 men, 141 women part time. **Faculty:** 100 total (50 full time). **Location:** Urban campus in large town; 165 miles from Bangor. **Calendar:** Semester, limited summer session. **Microcomputers:** Located in dormitories, libraries, computer centers.

DEGREES OFFERED. AAS. 137 associate degrees awarded in 1992. 37% in business and management, 8% computer sciences, 19% allied health, 36% trade and industry.

UNDERGRADUATE MAJORS. Accounting, agribusiness, air conditioning/heating/refrigeration mechanics, air conditioning/heating/refrigeration technology, automotive mechanics, automotive technology, business administration and management, business and office, business computer/console/peripheral equipment operation, business data entry equipment operation, carpentry, computer electronics, computer programming, computer servicing technology, computer technology, diesel engine mechanics, drafting, drafting and design technology, electrical and electronics equipment repair, electrical installation, electrical technology, electronic technology, industrial equipment maintenance and repair, legal secretary, masonry/tile setting, medical secretary, nursing, plumbing/pipefitting/steamfitting, practical nursing, precision metal work, secretarial and related programs, woodworking.

ACADEMIC PROGRAMS. Double major, internships, cross-registration. **Remedial services:** Learning center, preadmission summer program, reduced course load, remedial instruction, tutoring. **Placement/credit:** CLEP General and Subject; 15 credit hours maximum for associate degree.

ACADEMIC REQUIREMENTS. Freshmen must earn minimum GPA of 1.91 to continue in good standing. 75% of freshmen return for sophomore year. Students must declare major on application. **Graduation requirements:** 64 hours for associate (32 in major). Most students required to take courses in arts/fine arts, English, mathematics.

FRESHMAN ADMISSIONS. Selection criteria: School achievement record important. Recommended units include mathematics 2.

1992 FRESHMAN CLASS PROFILE. 251 men, 287 women enrolled. **Characteristics:** 96% from in state, 70% commute, 5% have minority backgrounds, 3% are foreign students. Average age is 19.

FALL-TERM APPLICATIONS. $15 fee. No closing date; applicants notified on a rolling basis; must reply within 4 weeks. Interview required. Essay required.

STUDENT LIFE. Housing: Dormitories (coed); apartment housing available. **Activities:** Student government, student newspaper, yearbook.

ATHLETICS. Intercollegiate: Basketball M, ice hockey M, soccer M. **Intramural:** Archery, badminton, baseball, field hockey, racquetball, softball, table tennis, tennis, volleyball.

STUDENT SERVICES. Health services, personal counseling, placement service for graduates, special adviser for adult students, services/facilities for handicapped.

ANNUAL EXPENSES. Tuition and fees: $1,950, $1,980 additional for out-of-state students. **Room and board:** $3,200. **Books and supplies:** $750. **Other expenses:** $3,285.

FINANCIAL AID. 83% of freshmen, 75% of continuing students receive some form of aid. All grants, all jobs based on need. Academic scholarships available. **Aid applications:** No closing date; priority given to applications received by April 1; applicants notified on a rolling basis beginning on or about June 1; must reply within 2 weeks.

ADDRESS/TELEPHONE. John G. Krass, Director of Admissions, Northern Maine Technical College, 33 Edgemont Drive, Presque Isle, ME 04769. (207) 769-2461 ext. 237. Fax: (207) 764-8465.

St. Joseph's College
Windham, Maine — CB code: 3755

Admissions: 77% of applicants accepted
Based on:
••• School record, special talents, test scores
•• Activities, recommendations
• Essay, interview
Completion: 89% of freshmen end year in good standing
77% graduate, 34% of these enter graduate study

4-year private liberal arts college, coed, affiliated with Roman Catholic Church. Founded in 1912. **Accreditation:** Regional. **Undergraduate enrollment:** 256 men, 436 women full time; 48 men, 79 women part time. **Graduate enrollment:** 1,475 men and women part time. **Faculty:** 88 total (42 full time), 62 with doctorates or other terminal degrees. **Location:** Rural campus in large town; 16 miles from Portland, 120 miles from Boston. **Calendar:** Semester, limited summer session. **Microcomputers:** 35 located in libraries, computer centers, campus-wide network. **Special facilities:** Private beach on Sebago Lake, lighted baseball, softball and intramural athletic complex. **Additional facts:** One of the largest external degree programs in country with over 5,000 students enrolled in undergraduate programs and over 1,000 enrolled in master's program.

DEGREES OFFERED. AA, AS, BA, BS, MS. 8 associate degrees awarded in 1992. 100% in allied health. 120 bachelor's degrees awarded. 17% in business and management, 13% communications, 19% teacher education, 21% health sciences, 11% life sciences, 15% social sciences. Graduate degrees offered in 1 major field of study.

UNDERGRADUATE MAJORS. Associate: Radiograph medical technology. **Bachelor's:** Accounting, biology, business administration and management, business and management, communications, elementary education, English, English education, environmental science, history, international business management, junior high education, marketing management, mathematics, mathematics education, nursing, philosophy, physical education, physical sciences, predentistry, prelaw, premedicine, prepharmacy, preveterinary, psychology, radio/television broadcasting, radiograph medical technology, religion, science education, secondary education, social studies education, sociology.

ACADEMIC PROGRAMS. Double major, external degree, honors program, independent study, internships, study abroad, teacher preparation, Washington semester, 2-3 pre-pharmacy program with Massachusetts College of Pharmacy. **Remedial services:** Special counselor, tutoring, freshman writer's workshop. **ROTC:** Army. **Placement/credit:** AP, CLEP General and Subject, institutional tests; 15 credit hours maximum for associate degree; 30 credit hours maximum for bachelor's degree.

ACADEMIC REQUIREMENTS. Freshmen must earn minimum GPA of 1.75 to continue in good standing. 89% of freshmen return for sophomore year. Students must declare major by end of first year. **Graduation requirements:** 66 hours for associate (66 in major), 128 hours for bachelor's (36 in major). Most students required to take courses in arts/fine arts, computer science, English, foreign languages, history, humanities, mathematics, philosophy/religion, biological/physical sciences, social sciences. **Postgraduate studies:** 10% from 2-year programs enter 4-year programs. 5% enter law school, 5% enter medical school, 8% enter MBA programs, 16% enter other graduate study.

FRESHMAN ADMISSIONS. Selection criteria: School record, class rank, test scores, recommendations, interview, essays, extracurricular activities considered. **High school preparation:** 18 units required. Required and recommended units include biological science 1, English 4, mathematics 3, physical science 1, social science 2 and science 2. Foreign language 2 recommended. Biology, chemistry, and 3-4 units of mathematics required of nursing and science applicants. **Test requirements:** SAT or ACT (SAT preferred).

1992 FRESHMAN CLASS PROFILE. 354 men applied, 261 accepted, 80 enrolled; 577 women applied, 456 accepted, 153 enrolled. 58% had high school GPA of 3.0 or higher, 40% between 2.0 and 2.99. 10% were in top tenth and 43% were in top quarter of graduating class. **Academic background:** Mid 50% of enrolled freshmen had SAT-V between 410-460, SAT-M between 440-510. 99% submitted SAT scores. **Characteristics:** 53% from in state, 90% live in college housing, 9% have minority backgrounds, 1% are foreign students. Average age is 18.

FALL-TERM APPLICATIONS. $25 fee, may be waived for applicants with need. No closing date; priority given to applications received by April 1; applicants notified on a rolling basis; must reply by May 1 or within 3 weeks if notified thereafter. Essay required. Interview recommended. CRDA. Deferred and early admission available.

STUDENT LIFE. Housing: Dormitories (men, women). **Activities:** Student government, magazine, radio, student newspaper, yearbook, choral groups, drama, musical theater, Campus Ministry Committee, Political Action Club, Wellness Committee, Social Concerns, Super Kids.

ATHLETICS. NAIA, NCAA. **Intercollegiate:** Baseball M, basketball, cross-country, golf M, soccer, softball W, volleyball W. **Intramural:** Basketball, bowling, cross-country, handball, racquetball, skiing, soccer, softball, swimming, table tennis, tennis, volleyball.

STUDENT SERVICES. Career counseling, employment service for

undergraduates, freshman orientation, health services, personal counseling, placement service for graduates, special adviser for adult students, veterans counselor, Myers - Briggs Testing.

ANNUAL EXPENSES. Tuition and fees: $9,670. **Room and board:** $4,850. **Books and supplies:** $550. **Other expenses:** $1,200.

FINANCIAL AID. 88% of freshmen, 73% of continuing students receive some form of aid. 85% of grants, 96% of loans, 87% of jobs based on need. 177 enrolled freshmen were judged to have need, all were offered aid. Academic, leadership scholarships available. **Aid applications:** No closing date; priority given to applications received by March 15; applicants notified on a rolling basis beginning on or about April 1; must reply within 2 weeks.

ADDRESS/TELEPHONE. Fredric V. Stone, Director of Admissions, St Joseph's College, Windham, ME 04062-1198. (207) 892-6766 ext. 1741. (800) 338-7057. Fax: (207) 892-7746.

Southern Maine Technical College
South Portland, Maine — CB code: 3535

Admissions: 56% of applicants accepted
Based on: ••• School record
•• Essay, test scores
• Activities, interview, recommendations
Completion: 75% of freshmen end year in good standing
90% graduate, 5% of these enter 4-year programs

2-year public technical college, coed. Founded in 1946. **Accreditation:** Regional. **Undergraduate enrollment:** 729 men, 328 women full time; 721 men, 610 women part time. **Faculty:** 148 total (98 full time), 7 with doctorates or other terminal degrees. **Location:** Suburban campus in large town; 3 miles from Portland. **Calendar:** Semester, limited summer session. **Microcomputers:** Located in computer centers. **Additional facts:** Located on grounds of Fort Preble, a historic landmark. Oceanside campus.

DEGREES OFFERED. AAS. 291 associate degrees awarded in 1992.

UNDERGRADUATE MAJORS. Air conditioning/heating/refrigeration mechanics, air conditioning/heating/refrigeration technology, automotive mechanics, automotive technology, business data processing and related programs, carpentry, computer and information sciences, computer servicing technology, computer technology, construction, criminal justice studies, criminal justice technology, dietetic aide/assistant, drafting, electrical and electronics equipment repair, electrical installation, electrical technology, electronic technology, environmental science, fire control and safety technology, food production/management/services, food science and nutrition, hospitality and recreation marketing, hotel/motel and restaurant management, information sciences and systems, landscape architecture, law enforcement and corrections technologies, machine tool operation/machine shop, marine biology, marine maintenance, mechanical design technology, medical radiation dosimetry, nursing, oceanography, office supervision and management, plant sciences, practical nursing, radiograph medical technology, respiratory therapy, respiratory therapy technology, secretarial and related programs, soil sciences, surgical technology.

ACADEMIC PROGRAMS. Double major, internships, cross-registration, joint programs leading to associate degree in hotel, motel, and restaurant management and in plant and soil technology with members of the University of Maine system. **Remedial services:** Learning center, reduced course load, remedial instruction, tutoring. **Placement/credit:** CLEP General and Subject, institutional tests.

ACADEMIC REQUIREMENTS. Freshmen must earn minimum GPA of 2.0 to continue in good standing. 80% of freshmen return for sophomore year. Students must declare major on application. **Graduation requirements:** 65 hours for associate (32 in major). Most students required to take courses in English, mathematics, biological/physical sciences, social sciences.

FRESHMAN ADMISSIONS. Selection criteria: High school GPA of primary importance. Test scores and essay considered for admission to degree programs. Priority given to Maine residents. Recommended units include English 4, mathematics 2 and physical science 1. Academic subject requirements vary by program. **Test requirements:** SAT or ACT (SAT preferred); score report by May 1. Psychological Corporation Entrance Examination for Schools of Practical/Vocational Nursing required for admission to all nursing programs. NLN/PN (Proficiency Examination Program) required for admission to upward mobility program (LPN to RN) if from out-of-state practical nursing program. Assessment and Placement Services for Community Colleges test required for placement of all academically weak applicants.

1992 FRESHMAN CLASS PROFILE. 2,218 men and women applied, 1,250 accepted; 570 men enrolled, 245 women enrolled. 20% had high school GPA of 3.0 or higher, 60% between 2.0 and 2.99. 20% were in top tenth and 40% were in top quarter of graduating class. **Characteristics:** 90% from in state, 85% commute, 1% have minority backgrounds. Average age is 24.

FALL-TERM APPLICATIONS. $15 fee, may be waived for applicants with need. Closing date August 15; applicants notified on a rolling basis; must reply within 4 weeks. Interview required for practical nursing, respiratory therapy, radiologic technology, radiation therapy, registered nursing, cardiovascular technology applicants. Essay required.

STUDENT LIFE. Housing: Dormitories (men, coed). **Activities:** Student government, student newspaper, yearbook.

ATHLETICS. Intercollegiate: Baseball M, basketball, cross-country M, soccer M, softball W, volleyball. **Intramural:** Basketball, golf, skiing, skin diving, softball, volleyball.

STUDENT SERVICES. Aptitude testing, career counseling, employment service for undergraduates, freshman orientation, health services, on-campus day care, personal counseling, placement service for graduates, veterans counselor, services/facilities for handicapped.

ANNUAL EXPENSES. Tuition and fees (1992-93): $1,620, $1,860 additional for out-of-state students. **Room and board:** $3,200. **Books and supplies:** $600. **Other expenses:** $832.

FINANCIAL AID. 55% of freshmen, 55% of continuing students receive some form of aid. All grants, 89% of loans, all jobs based on need. 250 enrolled freshmen were judged to have need, all were offered aid. **Aid applications:** Closing date August 15; priority given to applications received by April 15; applicants notified on a rolling basis beginning on or about May 1; must reply within 10 days.

ADDRESS/TELEPHONE. Robert A. Weimont, Director of Admissions, Southern Maine Technical College, Fort Road, South Portland, ME 04106. (207) 767-9500. Fax: (207) 799-8117.

Thomas College
Waterville, Maine — CB code: 3903

4-year private business college, coed. Founded in 1894. **Accreditation:** Regional. **Undergraduate enrollment:** 175 men, 232 women full time; 114 men, 253 women part time. **Graduate enrollment:** 90 men, 56 women part time. **Faculty:** 38 total (27 full time), 8 with doctorates or other terminal degrees. **Location:** Rural campus in large town; 75 miles from Portland. **Calendar:** Semester, limited summer session. **Microcomputers:** 64 located in computer centers. **Additional facts:** Undergraduate courses offered in Portland, Augusta, Rockland, Showhegan, Camden, Pittsfield, and Jay. Graduate courses available in Portland, Augusta, Jay, Rumfield, and Woodland.

DEGREES OFFERED. AS, BS, MBA. 26 associate degrees awarded in 1992. 99% in business and management. 80 bachelor's degrees awarded. 70% in business and management, 16% business/office and marketing/distribution, 14% computer sciences. Graduate degrees offered in 8 major fields of study.

UNDERGRADUATE MAJORS. Associate: Business and office, fashion merchandising, finance, information sciences and systems, legal secretary, liberal/general studies, medical secretary, office supervision and management, retailing, secretarial and related programs. **Bachelor's:** Accounting, business administration and management, business and management, business and office, business economics, business education, economics, fashion merchandising, information sciences and systems, management science, marketing and distribution, marketing management, mathematics education, retailing.

ACADEMIC PROGRAMS. 2-year transfer program, accelerated program, dual enrollment of high school students, education specialist degree, independent study, internships, student-designed major, teacher preparation, visiting/exchange student program, cross-registration; combined bachelor's/graduate program in business administration. **Remedial services:** Reduced course load, tutoring. **ROTC:** Army. **Placement/credit:** AP, CLEP Subject; 9 credit hours maximum for associate degree; 15 credit hours maximum for bachelor's degree.

ACADEMIC REQUIREMENTS. Freshmen must earn minimum GPA of 2.0 to continue in good standing. 85% of freshmen return for sophomore year. Students must declare major on application. **Graduation requirements:** 63 hours for associate (18 in major), 123 hours for bachelor's (24 in major). Most students required to take courses in computer science, English, history, humanities, mathematics, philosophy/religion, biological/physical sciences, social sciences. **Postgraduate studies:** 10% from 2-year programs enter 4-year programs. 10% enter MBA programs.

FRESHMAN ADMISSIONS. Selection criteria: School record, test scores, recommendation, interview considered. Applicants should be in top half of class. **High school preparation:** 18 units recommended. Recommended units include English 4, mathematics 3, social science 2 and science 2. **Test requirements:** SAT or ACT (SAT preferred); score report by August 15.

1992 FRESHMAN CLASS PROFILE. 62 men, 95 women enrolled. 60% had high school GPA of 3.0 or higher, 38% between 2.0 and 2.99. **Academic background:** Mid 50% of enrolled freshmen had SAT-V between 340-460, SAT-M between 350-520. 80% submitted SAT scores. **Characteristics:** 70% from in state, 75% live in college housing, 2% have minority backgrounds, 1% are foreign students, 5% join fraternities/sororities. Average age is 19.

FALL-TERM APPLICATIONS. $15 fee, may be waived for applicants with need. No closing date; priority given to applications received by May 1; applicants notified on a rolling basis; must reply by May 1 or within 4 weeks if notified thereafter. Interview recommended. CRDA. Deferred and early admission available.

STUDENT LIFE. Housing: Dormitories (coed). **Activities:** Student government, student newspaper, yearbook, choral groups, drama, fraternities, sororities, Newman Club, Circle-K, veterans club, marketing group.

ATHLETICS. NAIA. **Intercollegiate:** Basketball, cross-country, golf M, soccer, softball W, tennis M, volleyball W. **Intramural:** Basketball, bowling, ice hockey M, lacrosse M, skiing, soccer, softball, tennis, volleyball. **Clubs:** Skiing, outing.

STUDENT SERVICES. Career counseling, employment service for undergraduates, freshman orientation, health services, personal counseling, placement service for graduates.

ANNUAL EXPENSES. Tuition and fees: $9,050. **Room and board:** $4,450. **Books and supplies:** $600. **Other expenses:** $1,000.

FINANCIAL AID. 92% of freshmen, 90% of continuing students receive some form of aid. 82% of grants, 86% of loans, all jobs based on need. 240 enrolled freshmen were judged to have need, all were offered aid. Academic, leadership scholarships available. **Aid applications:** No closing date; priority given to applications received by February 15; applicants notified on a rolling basis beginning on or about March 15; must reply by May 1 or within 2 weeks if notified thereafter.

ADDRESS/TELEPHONE. Susan Potter, Director of Admissions, Thomas College, 180 West River Road, Waterville, ME 04901-9986. (207) 877-0101. Fax: (207) 873-6120.

Unity College
Unity, Maine CB code: 3925

Admissions: 92% of applicants accepted
Based on: ••• Essay, interview, recommendations, school record
•• Activities, special talents, test scores
Completion: 70% of freshmen end year in good standing
14% enter graduate study

4-year private liberal arts college, coed. Founded in 1965. **Accreditation:** Regional. **Undergraduate enrollment:** 345 men, 115 women full time. **Faculty:** 56 total (29 full time), 17 with doctorates or other terminal degrees. **Location:** Rural campus in rural community; 20 miles from Waterville. **Calendar:** 4-1-4, limited summer session. **Microcomputers:** 4 located in computer centers. **Special facilities:** Indian museum, art gallery, wetlands research area. **Additional facts:** Environmental science and natural resource management offered on 185-acre wooded campus with access to 500-acre woodlot with sawmill and 50 acres of wetland. Research along Lake Winnicook, 1/4 mile from campus.

DEGREES OFFERED. AA, AS, AAS, BA, BS. 31 associate degrees awarded in 1992. 54 bachelor's degrees awarded.

UNDERGRADUATE MAJORS. Associate: Forestry and related sciences, forestry production and processing, liberal/general studies. **Bachelor's:** Biological and physical sciences, city/community/regional planning, conservation and regulation, ecology, environmental science, fishing and fisheries, forestry and related sciences, landscape architecture, law enforcement and corrections, liberal/general studies, marine biology, parks and recreation management, prelaw, range management, renewable natural resources, wildlife management.

ACADEMIC PROGRAMS. 2-year transfer program, accelerated program, cooperative education, double major, dual enrollment of high school students, independent study, internships, student-designed major, Washington semester; liberal arts/career combination in forestry. **Remedial services:** Learning center, preadmission summer program, reduced course load, remedial instruction, special counselor, tutoring, full-time learning disabilities specialist. **ROTC:** Army. **Placement/credit:** AP, CLEP General and Subject, institutional tests; 60 credit hours maximum for bachelor's degree.

ACADEMIC REQUIREMENTS. Freshmen must earn minimum GPA of 1.7 to continue in good standing. 92% of freshmen return for sophomore year. Students must declare major by end of second year. **Graduation requirements:** 60 hours for associate (36 in major), 120 hours for bachelor's (75 in major). Most students required to take courses in arts/fine arts, computer science, English, history, humanities, mathematics, philosophy/religion, biological/physical sciences, social sciences. **Postgraduate studies:** 45% from 2-year programs enter 4-year programs.

FRESHMAN ADMISSIONS. Selection criteria: Academic record, essay, plus motivation and potential to succeed. Letters of recommendation, on-campus interview also considered. SAT scores not required but highly recommended. **High school preparation:** 18 units recommended. Required and recommended units include English 4, mathematics 2-4 and physical science 2. Biological science 2, foreign language 2 and social science 4 recommended.

1992 FRESHMAN CLASS PROFILE. 298 men applied, 268 accepted, 120 enrolled; 97 women applied, 95 accepted, 40 enrolled. **Academic background:** Mid 50% of enrolled freshmen had SAT-V between 400-500, SAT-M between 400-500. 45% submitted SAT scores. **Characteristics:** 90% live in college housing. Average age is 18.

FALL-TERM APPLICATIONS. $25 fee, may be waived for applicants with need. No closing date; priority given to applications received by March 1; applicants notified on a rolling basis. Essay required. Interview recommended. CRDA. Deferred and early admission available. SAT or ACT recommended.

STUDENT LIFE. Housing: Dormitories (men, coed). **Activities:** Student government, radio, student newspaper, yearbook, philosophical and literary journals, drama, fire-fighting crew, photography club, Environmental Awareness, recycling.

ATHLETICS. NAIA. **Intercollegiate:** Basketball M, cross-country, soccer, volleyball W. **Intramural:** Basketball, cross-country, football M, horseback riding, ice hockey, lacrosse M, skiing, soccer, softball, volleyball. **Clubs:** Skiing, woodsman, kayaking.

STUDENT SERVICES. Aptitude testing, career counseling, employment service for undergraduates, freshman orientation, health services, personal counseling, placement service for graduates, veterans counselor, services/facilities for handicapped.

ANNUAL EXPENSES. Tuition and fees: $7,910, $1,100 additional for out-of-state students. **Room and board:** $4,660. **Books and supplies:** $450. **Other expenses:** $600.

FINANCIAL AID. 73% of freshmen, 56% of continuing students receive some form of aid. 85% of grants, 92% of loans, all jobs based on need. 105 enrolled freshmen were judged to have need, all were offered aid. Academic, athletic scholarships available. **Aid applications:** No closing date; priority given to applications received by April 15; applicants notified on a rolling basis beginning on or about April 1; must reply within 4 weeks.

ADDRESS/TELEPHONE. John M.B Craig, Vice President/Dean for Admissions, Unity College, HC 78 Box 1, Unity, ME 04988. (207) 948-3131. Fax: (207) 948-5626.

University of Maine
Orono, Maine CB code: 3916

Admissions: 85% of applicants accepted
Based on: ••• School record
•• Activities, recommendations, test scores
• Essay, interview, special talents
Completion: 49% graduate, 25% of these enter graduate study

4-year public university, coed. Founded in 1865. **Accreditation:** Regional. **Undergraduate enrollment:** 4,224 men, 3,651 women full time; 898 men, 1,433 women part time. **Graduate enrollment:** 573 men, 505 women full time; 360 men, 669 women part time. **Faculty:** 737 total (575 full time). **Location:** Rural campus in small town; 8 miles from Bangor. **Calendar:** Semester, extensive summer session. **Microcomputers:** 500 located in dormitories, libraries, classrooms, computer centers, campus-wide network. **Special facilities:** Planetarium, anthropology museum, woodland preserve, botanical garden, art gallery, Maine Center for the Arts, observatory, Alfond Sports Arena (hockey, basketball).

DEGREES OFFERED. AA, AS, BA, BS, MA, MS, MBA, MEd, MSW, PhD, EdD. 328 associate degrees awarded in 1992. 1,706 bachelor's degrees awarded. Graduate degrees offered in 71 major fields of study.

UNDERGRADUATE MAJORS. Associate: Business and management, business and office, civil technology, dental hygiene, electrical technology, fashion merchandising, forest products processing technology, forestry and related sciences, law enforcement and corrections technologies, liberal/general studies, mechanical design technology, medical records administration, medical records technology, mental health/human services, ornamental horticulture. **Bachelor's:** Accounting, agribusiness, agricultural business and management, agricultural economics, agricultural engineering, agricultural sciences, animal sciences, anthropology, art education, art history, biochemistry, biological and physical sciences, biology, botany, business administration and management, business and management, business economics, cell biology, chemical engineering, chemistry, child development/care/guidance, civil engineering, civil technology, clinical laboratory science, communications, computer and information sciences, computer engineering, dramatic arts, economics, education, electrical technology, electrical/electronics/communications engineering, elementary education, engineering, engineering and other disciplines, engineering physics, English, entomology, finance, fine arts, food science and nutrition, food sciences, foreign languages (multiple emphasis), forest products processing technology, forestry and related sciences, French, geology, German, history, home economics, home economics education, horticulture, humanities and social sciences, international relations, journalism, Latin, liberal/general studies, management information systems, marketing management, mathematics, mechanical design technology, mechanical engineering, microbiology, molecular biology, music, music education, music performance, nursing, ornamental horticulture, paper engineering, parks and recreation management, personnel management, philosophy, physical education, physics, plant pathology, plant sciences, political science and government, psychology, public administration, radio/television broadcasting, renewable natural resources, secondary education, social work, sociology, soil sciences, Spanish, speech, speech pathology/audiology, studio art, surveying and mapping sciences, wildlife management, zoology.

ACADEMIC PROGRAMS. 2-year transfer program, accelerated program, cooperative education, double major, dual enrollment of high school students, education specialist degree, honors program, independent study, internships, student-designed major, study abroad, teacher preparation, telecourses, visiting/exchange student program, cross-registration; liberal arts/career combination in engineering. **Remedial services:** Preadmission summer program, reduced course load, remedial instruction, special counselor, tutoring. **ROTC:** Air Force, Army, Naval. **Placement/credit:** AP, CLEP General and Subject, institutional tests; 60 credit hours maximum for bachelor's degree.

ACADEMIC REQUIREMENTS. Freshmen must earn minimum GPA of 1.7 to continue in good standing. 77% of freshmen return for sophomore year. Students must declare major by end of second year. **Graduation requirements:** 60 hours for associate, 120 hours for bachelor's (60 in major). Most students required to take courses in English, humanities, mathematics, biological/physical sciences, social sciences.

FRESHMAN ADMISSIONS. Selection criteria: School record, test scores, and school recommendations important. **High school preparation:** 16 units required. Required and recommended units include English 4, mathematics 3 and social science 1. Biological science 1, foreign language 2 and physical science 2 recommended. One fine arts and 1 computer science recommended. **Test requirements:** SAT or ACT (SAT preferred); score report by March 15.

1992 FRESHMAN CLASS PROFILE. 2,722 men applied, 2,268 accepted, 817 enrolled; 2,228 women applied, 1,933 accepted, 683 enrolled. 20% were in top tenth and 50% were in top quarter of graduating class. **Academic background:** Mid 50% of enrolled freshmen had SAT-V between 420-520, SAT-M between 470-580. 99% submitted SAT scores. **Characteristics:** 79% from in state, 99% live in college housing, 4% have minority backgrounds, 3% are foreign students, 11% join fraternities/sororities. Average age is 18.

FALL-TERM APPLICATIONS. $20 fee, may be waived for applicants with need. No closing date; priority given to applications received by February 1; applicants notified on a rolling basis beginning on or about February 1; must reply by May 1 or within 2 weeks if notified thereafter. Audition required for music applicants. Interview recommended. Essay recommended. CRDA. Deferred and early admission available.

STUDENT LIFE. Housing: Dormitories (men, women, coed); apartment, fraternity, sorority, cooperative housing available. **Activities:** Student government, radio, student newspaper, television, yearbook, choral groups, concert band, dance, drama, jazz band, marching band, music ensembles, musical theater, opera, pep band, symphony orchestra, fraternities, sororities, wide variety of religious, political, ethnic, and social service organizations.

ATHLETICS. NCAA. **Intercollegiate:** Baseball M, basketball, cross-country, diving, field hockey W, football M, golf M, ice hockey M, soccer, softball W, swimming, tennis, track and field. **Intramural:** Badminton, basketball, bowling, cross-country, fencing, football M, golf, ice hockey W, lacrosse, racquetball, rugby, skiing, soccer, squash, swimming, tennis, track and field, volleyball, water polo, wrestling M.

STUDENT SERVICES. Aptitude testing, career counseling, employment service for undergraduates, freshman orientation, health services, on-campus day care, personal counseling, placement service for graduates, special adviser for adult students, veterans counselor, services/facilities for handicapped.

ANNUAL EXPENSES. Tuition and fees (projected): $3,286, $5,130 additional for out-of-state students. **Room and board:** $4,580. **Books and supplies:** $500. **Other expenses:** $1,150.

FINANCIAL AID. 60% of freshmen, 57% of continuing students receive some form of aid. 89% of grants, 67% of loans, 33% of jobs based on need. Academic, music/drama, art, athletic, state/district residency, leadership, alumni affiliation, minority scholarships available. **Aid applications:** No closing date; priority given to applications received by March 1; applicants notified on a rolling basis beginning on or about April 1; must reply by May 1 or within 2 weeks if notified thereafter.

ADDRESS/TELEPHONE. Joyce Henckler, Assistant VP Enrollment Management, University of Maine, 5713 Chadbourne Hall, Orono, ME 04469-5713. (207) 581-1561. Fax: (207) 581-1556.

University of Maine at Augusta

Augusta, Maine — CB code: 3929

4-year public university and community college, coed. Founded in 1965. **Accreditation:** Regional. **Undergraduate enrollment:** 416 men, 481 women full time; 541 men, 1,460 women part time. **Faculty:** 169 total (64 full time), 24 with doctorates or other terminal degrees. **Location:** Suburban campus in large town; 65 miles from Portland, 75 miles from Bangor. **Calendar:** Semester, extensive summer session. Extensive evening/early morning classes. **Microcomputers:** 89 located in libraries, computer centers, campus-wide network. **Special facilities:** Jewett Hall Art Gallery, outdoor leisure center. **Additional facts:** Additional centers in Lewiston, Thomaston, Brunswick, and Rumford.

DEGREES OFFERED. AA, AS, BA, BS. 212 associate degrees awarded in 1992. 27% in business and management, 23% allied health, 10% multi/interdisciplinary studies, 23% social sciences, 10% visual and performing arts. 87 bachelor's degrees awarded. 94% in business and management, 6% visual and performing arts.

UNDERGRADUATE MAJORS. Associate: Accounting, architecture, business administration and management, computer and information sciences, criminal justice studies, fine arts, graphic arts technology, jazz, liberal/general studies, medical laboratory technologies, nursing, photographic technology, photography, small business management and ownership, social sciences. **Bachelor's:** Accounting, business administration and management, jazz, mathematics, public administration, small business management and ownership.

ACADEMIC PROGRAMS. 2-year transfer program, dual enrollment of high school students, honors program, independent study, internships, telecourses, cross-registration. **Remedial services:** Reduced course load, remedial instruction, special counselor, tutoring, placement testing. **Placement/credit:** CLEP General and Subject, institutional tests; 45 credit hours maximum for associate degree; 45 credit hours maximum for bachelor's degree.

ACADEMIC REQUIREMENTS. Freshmen must earn minimum GPA of 1.8 to continue in good standing. Continuation in good academic standing determined by number of credits attempted and GPA earned. 60% of freshmen return for sophomore year. Students must declare major on enrollment. **Graduation requirements:** 60 hours for associate, 120 hours for bachelor's. Most students required to take courses in English, humanities, mathematics, biological/physical sciences, social sciences. **Postgraduate studies:** 40% from 2-year programs enter 4-year programs.

FRESHMAN ADMISSIONS. Selection criteria: Open admissions. High school achievement record, and test scores, considered for admission to allied health and bachelor's degree programs. **High school preparation:** 16 units recommended. Applicants to health science programs must have biology, chemistry, and algebra II; business administration and public administration applicants must have algebra II and geometry.

1992 FRESHMAN CLASS PROFILE. 97 men, 107 women enrolled. 12% were in top tenth and 37% were in top quarter of graduating class. **Academic background:** Mid 50% of enrolled freshmen had SAT-V between 300-500, SAT-M between 300-500. 70% submitted SAT scores. **Characteristics:** 98% from in state, 100% commute, 1% have minority backgrounds, 1% are foreign students. Average age is 27.

FALL-TERM APPLICATIONS. $20 fee, may be waived for applicants with need. No closing date; applicants notified on a rolling basis; must reply by May 1 or within 2 weeks if notified thereafter. Interview required for medical laboratory technology, architectural studies applicants. Audition required for music applicants. CRDA. Deferred and early admission available. EDP-S. SAT tests requested of medical laboratory technology, nursing, architectural studies, and baccalaureate degree applicants.

STUDENT LIFE. Activities: Student government, jazz band, music ensembles.

ATHLETICS. NAIA. **Intercollegiate:** Basketball W. **Intramural:** Basketball W, bowling, fencing, golf, racquetball, rifle, sailing, skiing, soccer, softball, table tennis, tennis, volleyball.

STUDENT SERVICES. Aptitude testing, career counseling, freshman orientation, on-campus day care, personal counseling, veterans counselor, services/facilities for handicapped.

ANNUAL EXPENSES. Tuition and fees (projected): $2,715, $3,720 additional for out-of-state students. **Books and supplies:** $520. **Other expenses:** $600.

FINANCIAL AID. 50% of freshmen, 45% of continuing students receive some form of aid. All grants, 81% of loans, all jobs based on need. 267 enrolled freshmen were judged to have need, all were offered aid. Academic, music/drama, art, state/district residency scholarships available. **Aid applications:** No closing date; priority given to applications received by April 1; applicants notified on a rolling basis beginning on or about April 1; must reply within 2 weeks.

ADDRESS/TELEPHONE. Clayton Smith, Director of Admissions and Records, University of Maine at Augusta, University Heights, Augusta, ME 04330. (207) 621-3185. Fax: (207) 621-3116.

University of Maine at Farmington

Farmington, Maine — CB code: 3506

Admissions:	70% of applicants accepted
Based on:	••• Recommendations, school record
	•• Activities, essay, interview
	• Special talents, test scores
Completion:	82% of freshmen end year in good standing
	60% graduate, 10% of these enter graduate study

4-year public liberal arts, teachers college, coed. Founded in 1864. **Accreditation:** Regional. **Undergraduate enrollment:** 589 men, 1,287 women full time; 54 men, 223 women part time. **Faculty:** 148 total (114 full time), 87 with doctorates or other terminal degrees. **Location:** Rural campus in small town; 18 miles from Augusta. **Calendar:** Semester, limited summer session. Extensive evening/early morning classes. **Microcomputers:** 120 located in libraries, classrooms, computer centers. **Special facilities:** Art gallery, archaeology research center. **Additional facts:** May term consisting of two 5-week summer terms.

DEGREES OFFERED. BA, BS, BFA. 39 associate degrees awarded in 1992. 15% in business and management, 31% education, 18% home economics, 36% letters/literature. 392 bachelor's degrees awarded in 1992. 5% in education, 48% teacher education, 14% allied health, 15% multi/interdisciplinary studies, 8% psychology.

UNDERGRADUATE MAJORS. Biological and physical sciences, biology, biology education, business economics, community health work, creative writing, dramatic arts, early childhood education, early childhood special education, economics/business, education of the emotionally handicapped, education of the mentally handicapped, elementary education, English, English education, environmental science, geography, geography education, geology/chemistry, geology/geography, health education, history, history education, humanities, international relations, international studies, language arts education, liberal/general studies, mathematics education, mathematics/computer science, mathematics/computer science education, music/arts, physical science education, political science/social science, psychology, pure mathematics, rehabilitation counseling/services, science education, secondary education, social science education, sociology/anthropology, specific learning disabilities, speech correction, speech pathology/audiology, visual and performing arts.

ACADEMIC PROGRAMS. 2-year transfer program, accelerated program, double major, dual enrollment of high school students, honors program, independent study, internships, student-designed major, study abroad, teacher preparation, visiting/exchange student program, cross-registration. **Remedial services:** Learning center, reduced course load, remedial instruction, special counselor, tutoring, program of basic studies. **Placement/credit:** AP, CLEP Subject, IB, institutional tests; 30 credit hours maximum for bachelor's degree.

ACADEMIC REQUIREMENTS. Freshmen must earn minimum GPA of 2.0 to continue in good standing. 82% of freshmen return for sophomore year. Students must declare major by end of second year. **Graduation requirements:** 120 hours for bachelor's (30 in major). Most students required to take courses in arts/fine arts, computer science, English, humanities, mathematics, biological/physical sciences, social sciences. **Postgraduate studies:** 42% from 2-year programs enter 4-year programs. 1% enter MBA programs, 9% enter other graduate study.

FRESHMAN ADMISSIONS. Selection criteria: School achievement record and recommendation most important. School and community activities, interviews, and personal essay considered. Test scores optional. **High school preparation:** 16 units required; 18 recommended. Required and recommended units include biological science 1, English 4, foreign language 2, mathematics 3-4, physical science 1-2 and social science 2. **Test requirements:** Institutional placement tests required of applicants who do not submit SAT scores, those with SAT mathematical scores below 400 or Test of Standard Written English scores below 44, and those who submit SAT for placement purposes.

1992 FRESHMAN CLASS PROFILE. 1,200 men and women applied, 840 accepted; 141 men enrolled, 302 women enrolled. 19% were in top tenth and 43% were in top quarter of graduating class. **Characteristics:** 81% from in state, 85% live in college housing, 2% have minority backgrounds. Average age is 18.

FALL-TERM APPLICATIONS. $20 fee, may be waived for applicants with need. No closing date; priority given to applications received by May 1; applicants notified on a rolling basis; must reply within 3 weeks (fully refundable deposits until May 1). Essay required. Interview recommended for early childhood, elementary education applicants. Deferred and early admission available. Institutional early decision plan. Early Action acceptances issued to applicants in top 15% of high school class who apply by late December.

STUDENT LIFE. Housing: Dormitories (women, coed); apartment housing available. Limited number of apartments available to students maintaining certain GPA. **Activities:** Student government, magazine, radio, student newspaper, yearbook, choral groups, concert band, dance, drama, music ensembles, musical theater, symphony orchestra, Justice Uniting Students Together, Students for Day Care, Young Democrats, Veterans Organization, Student Environmental and Political Awareness Club, Amnesty International, International Club, Inter-Varsity Christian Fellowship, Student Alcohol Educators.

ATHLETICS. NAIA. **Intercollegiate:** Baseball M, basketball, field hockey W, golf, soccer, softball W, volleyball W. **Intramural:** Badminton, basketball, bowling, field hockey, football M, golf, ice hockey, lacrosse, rugby, skiing, soccer, softball, squash, table tennis, tennis, volleyball.

STUDENT SERVICES. Career counseling, employment service for undergraduates, freshman orientation, health services, on-campus day care, personal counseling, placement service for graduates, special adviser for adult students, services/facilities for handicapped.

ANNUAL EXPENSES. Tuition and fees (1992-93): $2,670, $3,540 additional for out-of-state students. New England Regional agreement with 6 states for eligible programs, additional tuition $1148. **Room and board:** $3,566. **Books and supplies:** $450. **Other expenses:** $1,400.

FINANCIAL AID. 65% of freshmen, 65% of continuing students receive some form of aid. Grants, loans, jobs available. Academic, state/district residency, leadership, minority scholarships available. **Aid applications:** No closing date; priority given to applications received by March 15; applicants notified on a rolling basis beginning on or about February 1; must reply within 2 weeks.

ADDRESS/TELEPHONE. J. Anthony McLaughlin, Director of Admissions, University of Maine at Farmington, 102 Main Street, Farmington, ME 04938-1994. (207) 778-7050. Fax: (207) 778-7247.

University of Maine at Fort Kent
Fort Kent, Maine — CB code: 3393

Admissions: 75% of applicants accepted
Based on:
- ••• School record
- •• Test scores
- • Activities, essay, interview, recommendations, special talents

Completion: 98% of freshmen end year in good standing
51% graduate, 5% of these enter graduate study

4-year public university, coed. Founded in 1878. **Accreditation:** Regional. **Undergraduate enrollment:** 641 men and women. **Faculty:** 33 total (32 full time), 20 with doctorates or other terminal degrees. **Location:** Rural campus in small town; 43 miles from Caribou, 21 miles from Edmundston, New Brunswick, Canada. **Calendar:** Semester, limited summer session. **Microcomputers:** 50 located in dormitories, libraries, classrooms, computer centers. **Special facilities:** 16-acre biological park, Acadian Archives, interactive television site. **Additional facts:** Bilingual Franco-American region.

DEGREES OFFERED. AA, BA, BS. 24 associate degrees awarded in 1992. 29% in agriculture, 12% business and management, 17% allied health, 34% parks/recreation, protective services, public affairs. 66 bachelor's degrees awarded. 18% in teacher education, 15% health sciences, 15% letters/literature, 23% life sciences, 23% social sciences.

UNDERGRADUATE MAJORS. Associate: Bicultural studies, business and management, computer and information sciences, criminal justice studies, forestry and related sciences, liberal/general studies, mental health/human services, teacher aide. **Bachelor's:** Agribusiness, behavioral sciences, bilingual/bicultural studies, biology, business and management, computer and information sciences, education, elementary education, English, environmental science, French, history, mathematics/science field, multidisciplinary studies, nursing, social sciences, university studies.

ACADEMIC PROGRAMS. Double major, dual enrollment of high school students, honors program, independent study, internships, student-designed major, study abroad, teacher preparation, telecourses, cross-registration. **Remedial services:** Learning center, preadmission summer program, reduced course load, remedial instruction, special counselor, tutoring. **Placement/credit:** AP, CLEP General and Subject, institutional tests; 57 credit hours maximum for bachelor's degree.

ACADEMIC REQUIREMENTS. Freshmen must earn minimum GPA of 1.75 to continue in good standing. 60% of freshmen return for sophomore year. Students must declare major by end of second year. **Graduation requirements:** 60 hours for associate (15 in major), 120 hours for bachelor's (30 in major). Most students required to take courses in arts/fine arts, computer science, English, foreign languages, history, humanities, mathematics, biological/physical sciences, social sciences. **Additional information:** 4-year Bachelor of University Student Program allows students to develop individualized programs of study.

FRESHMAN ADMISSIONS. Selection criteria: High school courses and achievement record most important. Recommendations considered. SAT scores required for all programs. **High school preparation:** 16 units required. Required and recommended units include biological science 1, English 4, mathematics 2, physical science 1 and social science 2. Foreign language 2 recommended. Biology and chemistry required for nursing and environmental studies. **Test requirements:** SAT or ACT (SAT preferred); score report by August 15. **Additional information:** Each student evaluated individually.

1992 FRESHMAN CLASS PROFILE. 225 men and women applied, 168 accepted; 104 enrolled. 26% had high school GPA of 3.0 or higher, 65% between 2.0 and 2.99. 5% were in top tenth and 28% were in top quarter of graduating class. **Academic background:** Mid 50% of enrolled freshmen had SAT-V between 320-450, SAT-M between 360-480. 64% submitted SAT scores. **Characteristics:** 80% from in state, 64% commute, 1% have minority backgrounds, 6% are foreign students, 5% join fraternities/sororities. Average age is 20.

FALL-TERM APPLICATIONS. $20 fee, may be waived for applicants with need. Closing date August 15; applicants notified on a rolling basis; must reply by May 1 or within 4 weeks if notified thereafter. Interview recommended. Essay recommended. CRDA. Deferred and early admission available. EDP-F.

STUDENT LIFE. Housing: Dormitories (coed). **Activities:** Student government, radio, choral groups, dance, drama, jazz band, music ensembles, musical theater, fraternities, sororities, Christian Fellowship.

ATHLETICS. NAIA. **Intercollegiate:** Basketball, soccer. **Intramural:**

Baseball M, basketball, cross-country, field hockey W, gymnastics W, ice hockey M, racquetball, skiing, soccer, softball, table tennis, tennis, volleyball.

STUDENT SERVICES. Aptitude testing, career counseling, freshman orientation, on-campus day care, personal counseling, placement service for graduates, special adviser for adult students, veterans counselor, services/facilities for handicapped.

ANNUAL EXPENSES. Tuition and fees (projected): $2,650, $3,720 additional for out-of-state students. **Room and board:** $3,600. **Books and supplies:** $500. **Other expenses:** $1,000.

FINANCIAL AID. 75% of freshmen, 75% of continuing students receive some form of aid. All grants, 94% of loans, 78% of jobs based on need. 78 enrolled freshmen were judged to have need, all were offered aid. Academic scholarships available. **Aid applications:** No closing date; priority given to applications received by March 15; applicants notified on a rolling basis beginning on or about April 15; must reply within 2 weeks.

ADDRESS/TELEPHONE. Jerald R. Nadeau, Director of Admissions, University of Maine at Fort Kent, 25 Pleasant Street, Fort Kent, ME 04743-1292. (207) 834-3162 ext. 135. Fax: (207) 834-3144.

University of Maine at Machias
Machias, Maine — CB code: 3956

Admissions: 85% of applicants accepted
Based on:
••• Recommendations, school record
•• Essay, interview, test scores
• Activities, special talents
Completion: 69% of freshmen end year in good standing
40% graduate, 10% of these enter graduate study

4-year public university, coed. Founded in 1909. **Accreditation:** Regional. **Undergraduate enrollment:** 235 men, 405 women full time; 89 men, 229 women part time. **Faculty:** 62 total (43 full time), 14 with doctorates or other terminal degrees. **Location:** Rural campus in small town; 85 miles from Bangor, 65 miles from Bar Harbor. **Calendar:** Semester, limited summer session. **Microcomputers:** 175 located in dormitories, libraries, classrooms, computer centers. **Special facilities:** Greenland Point Center, Outdoor Education Center, lobster and shellfish hatcheries.

DEGREES OFFERED. AA, AS, BA, BS. 30 associate degrees awarded in 1992. 66 bachelor's degrees awarded.

UNDERGRADUATE MAJORS. Associate: Accounting, business and management, business and office, business computer/console/peripheral equipment operation, business data processing and related programs, business data programming, business systems analysis, computer and information sciences, electronic communications and business, information sciences and systems, liberal/general studies, management information systems, marketing management, office supervision and management, parks and recreation management, recreation and community services technologies, secretarial and related programs, small business management and ownership. **Bachelor's:** Accounting, behavioral sciences, biological and physical sciences, biology, business administration and management, business and management, business education, community health work, ecology, education, elementary education, English, environmental science, environmental studies, health education, history, humanities, humanities and social sciences, junior high education, liberal/general studies, marine biology, marketing management, parks and recreation management, recreation and community services technologies, secondary education.

ACADEMIC PROGRAMS. Cooperative education, independent study, internships, student-designed major, teacher preparation, telecourses, cross-registration. **Remedial services:** Learning center, reduced course load, tutoring, learning skills course. **Placement/credit:** AP, CLEP General and Subject, institutional tests.

ACADEMIC REQUIREMENTS. Freshmen must earn minimum GPA of 2.0 to continue in good standing. 68% of freshmen return for sophomore year. Students must declare major on application. **Graduation requirements:** 60 hours for associate (30 in major), 120 hours for bachelor's (45 in major). Most students required to take courses in arts/fine arts, computer science, English, history, humanities, mathematics, biological/physical sciences, social sciences. **Postgraduate studies:** 50% from 2-year programs enter 4-year programs. 2% enter MBA programs, 8% enter other graduate study. **Additional information:** Practicums in elementary education and office management. Internships and/or cooperative program available in business studies, recreation management, biology, and environmental studies.

FRESHMAN ADMISSIONS. Selection criteria: Applicants should rank in top half of class and have overall 3.0 GPA. Recommendations, essay, outstanding nonacademic achievement (extracurricular, community, military, life, or work) also considered. **High school preparation:** 16 units recommended. Recommended units include English 4, mathematics 3, social science 2 and science 2. **Test requirements:** SAT or ACT (SAT preferred); score report by September 5. SAT not required of applicants for associate of science degree.

1992 FRESHMAN CLASS PROFILE. 479 men and women applied, 406 accepted; 186 enrolled. 55% had high school GPA of 3.0 or higher, 45% between 2.0 and 2.99. **Characteristics:** 80% from in state, 58% commute, 5% have minority backgrounds, 1% are foreign students. Average age is 20.

FALL-TERM APPLICATIONS. $20 fee, may be waived for applicants with need. No closing date; priority given to applications received by April 1; applicants notified on a rolling basis; must reply within 2 weeks. Interview recommended. Essay recommended. Deferred and early admission available.

STUDENT LIFE. Housing: Dormitories (women, coed). **Activities:** Student government, student newspaper, yearbook, prose and poetry publication, choral groups, drama, music ensembles, musical theater, pep band, fraternities, sororities, campus ministry.

ATHLETICS. NAIA. **Intercollegiate:** Basketball, soccer M, volleyball W. **Intramural:** Archery, badminton, basketball, cross-country, golf, handball, ice hockey M, racquetball, sailing, soccer W, softball, table tennis M, tennis, volleyball, wrestling M.

STUDENT SERVICES. Career counseling, employment service for undergraduates, health services, personal counseling, placement service for graduates, veterans counselor, services/facilities for handicapped.

ANNUAL EXPENSES. Tuition and fees (1992-93): $2,605, $3,540 additional for out-of-state students. **Room and board:** $3,410. **Books and supplies:** $460. **Other expenses:** $1,100.

FINANCIAL AID. 65% of freshmen, 65% of continuing students receive some form of aid. All grants, 82% of loans, all jobs based on need. **Aid applications:** No closing date; priority given to applications received by May 1; applicants notified on a rolling basis beginning on or about June 15; must reply within 2 weeks.

ADDRESS/TELEPHONE. David Baldwin, Director of Admissions, University of Maine at Machias, 9 O'Brien Avenue, Machias, ME 04654. (207) 255-3313 ext. 318. Fax: (207) 255-4864.

University of Maine at Presque Isle
Presque Isle, Maine — CB code: 3008

Admissions: 77% of applicants accepted
Based on:
••• School record
•• Essay, interview, recommendations, test scores
• Activities, special talents
Completion: 70% of freshmen end year in good standing
18% enter graduate study

4-year public university, coed. Founded in 1903. **Accreditation:** Regional. **Undergraduate enrollment:** 401 men, 492 women full time; 311 men, 373 women part time. **Graduate enrollment:** 3 men, 6 women full time; 8 women part time. **Faculty:** 105 total (66 full time), 42 with doctorates or other terminal degrees. **Location:** Rural campus in large town; 165 miles from Bangor. **Calendar:** Semester, extensive summer session. **Microcomputers:** Located in dormitories, libraries, classrooms, computer centers. **Special facilities:** Art gallery, small business institute, kinesiology laboratory, local history center, human services laboratory.

DEGREES OFFERED. AA, AS, BA, BFA. 23 associate degrees awarded in 1992. 32% in allied health, 23% multi/interdisciplinary studies, 45% parks/recreation, protective services, public affairs. 132 bachelor's degrees awarded. 17% in business and management, 21% teacher education, 7% letters/literature, 30% multi/interdisciplinary studies, 13% social sciences.

UNDERGRADUATE MAJORS. Associate: Communications, creative writing, criminal justice technology, environmental science, graphic arts technology, liberal/general studies, medical laboratory technologies, recreation and community services technologies. **Bachelor's:** Accounting, agricultural sciences, behavioral sciences, biology, business administration and management, communications, criminal justice technology, early childhood education, education, elementary education, English, English education, environmental science, fine arts, food sciences, foreign languages education, forestry and related sciences, French, health education, history, humanities, humanities and social sciences, industrial technology, liberal/general studies, mathematics, mathematics education, physical education, political science and government, psychology, recreation and community services technologies, science education, secondary education, social science education, social sciences, social work, sociology, speech, speech/communication/theater education, wildlife management.

ACADEMIC PROGRAMS. 2-year transfer program, accelerated program, double major, dual enrollment of high school students, honors program, independent study, internships, study abroad, teacher preparation, telecourses, visiting/exchange student program, cross-registration, transfer programs in sciences with University of Maine at Orono and University of Southern Maine, master's programs in education and public administration available on campus through University of Maine at Orono and University of Southern Maine; liberal arts/career combination in engineering, forestry, health sciences. **Remedial services:** Learning center, reduced course load, remedial instruction, special counselor, tutoring, disadvantaged students program. **Placement/credit:** AP, CLEP General and Subject, institutional tests;

30 credit hours maximum for associate degree; 60 credit hours maximum for bachelor's degree.

ACADEMIC REQUIREMENTS. Freshmen must earn minimum GPA of 1.6 to continue in good standing. 54% of freshmen return for sophomore year. Students must declare major by end of second year. **Graduation requirements:** 60 hours for associate (30 in major), 120 hours for bachelor's (45 in major). Most students required to take courses in arts/fine arts, computer science, English, foreign languages, history, humanities, mathematics, biological/physical sciences, social sciences.

FRESHMAN ADMISSIONS. Selection criteria: School achievement record, class rank, test scores, interview counselor's recommendation. Nursing and medical laboratory technician applicants must be in top third of class and have minimum combined SAT score of 800. **High school preparation:** 13 units required; 15 recommended. Required and recommended units include English 4, mathematics 3, social science 3 and science 3. Foreign language 2 recommended. Nursing and medical laboratory technician applicants should have 1 unit each of biology and chemistry, 2 mathematics, and 4 English. **Test requirements:** SAT or ACT (SAT preferred); score report by August 6.

1992 FRESHMAN CLASS PROFILE. 469 men and women applied, 361 accepted; 118 men enrolled, 128 women enrolled. **Academic background:** Mid 50% of enrolled freshmen had SAT-V between 330-460, SAT-M between 330-480. 95% submitted SAT scores. **Characteristics:** 91% from in state, 55% live in college housing, 6% have minority backgrounds, 7% are foreign students. Average age is 21.

FALL-TERM APPLICATIONS. $20 fee, may be waived for applicants with need. Closing date August 6; priority given to applications received by March 1; applicants notified on a rolling basis. Portfolio required for bachelor of fine arts applicants. Interview recommended for academically borderline applicants. Essay recommended. CRDA. Deferred and early admission available. EDP-F.

STUDENT LIFE. Housing: Dormitories (coed); apartment housing available. **Activities:** Student government, magazine, radio, student newspaper, television, yearbook, Northern Lights (experimental journal on creativity), Foxtail (literary magazine) IMAGE (campus newsletter), choral groups, drama, music ensembles, musical theater, fraternities, sororities, various religious organizations, nontraditional student organization.

ATHLETICS. NAIA. **Intercollegiate:** Baseball M, basketball, cross-country, soccer, softball W. **Intramural:** Badminton, baseball M, basketball, bowling, cross-country, field hockey W, golf, handball, ice hockey M, racquetball, skiing, soccer, softball, tennis, volleyball, wrestling M.

STUDENT SERVICES. Aptitude testing, career counseling, employment service for undergraduates, freshman orientation, health services, on-campus day care, personal counseling, placement service for graduates, veterans counselor, adult student learning center, services/facilities for handicapped.

ANNUAL EXPENSES. Tuition and fees (projected): $2,820, $3,720 additional for out-of-state students. **Room and board:** $3,494. **Books and supplies:** $400. **Other expenses:** $975.

FINANCIAL AID. 72% of freshmen, 78% of continuing students receive some form of aid. 93% of grants, 71% of loans, 92% of jobs based on need. 141 enrolled freshmen were judged to have need, 139 were offered aid. Academic, music/drama, art, athletic, minority scholarships available. **Aid applications:** No closing date; priority given to applications received by May 1; applicants notified on a rolling basis beginning on or about March 1; must reply within 2 weeks.

ADDRESS/TELEPHONE. Dr. Gerald Wuori, Director of Admissions, University of Maine at Presque Isle, 181 Main Street, Presque Isle, ME 04769-2888. (207) 764-0311. Fax: (207) 764-0311 ext. 215.

University of New England
Biddeford, Maine

CB code: 3751

4-year private university and college of arts and sciences, coed. Founded in 1939. **Accreditation:** Regional. **Undergraduate enrollment:** 239 men, 512 women full time; 150 men and women part time. **Graduate enrollment:** 421 men and women full time; 111 men and women part time. **Faculty:** 137 total (83 full time). **Location:** Rural campus in large town; 20 miles from Portland, 90 miles from Boston, Massachusetts. **Calendar:** 4-1-4, limited summer session. **Microcomputers:** Located in libraries, computer centers. **Additional facts:** University consists of College of Osteopathic Medicine for physicians and nurse anesthetists and College of Arts and Sciences for undergraduate programs in life and health sciences, human services, management and psychology, and graduate study in social work and psychology, and College of Professional and Continuing Studies.

DEGREES OFFERED. AS, BA, BS, MS, DO. 21 associate degrees awarded in 1992. 100% in health sciences. 135 bachelor's degrees awarded. 7% in business and management, 68% allied health, 8% life sciences, 5% psychology, 7% social sciences. Graduate degrees offered in 4 major fields of study.

UNDERGRADUATE MAJORS. Associate: Nursing. **Bachelor's:** Biological and physical sciences, biology, business administration and management, education, elementary education, environmental science, environmental studies, health care administration, health sciences, human services, humanities, humanities and social sciences, liberal/general studies, marine biology, medical laboratory technologies, mental health/human services, nursing, occupational therapy, parks and recreation management, physical therapy, premedicine, prepharmacy, psychology, science education, social work, special education, sports medicine.

ACADEMIC PROGRAMS. 2-year transfer program, accelerated program, double major, dual enrollment of high school students, independent study, internships, student-designed major, study abroad, teacher preparation, visiting/exchange student program, 2-3 prepharmacy program; liberal arts/career combination in health sciences. **Remedial services:** Learning center, reduced course load, remedial instruction, special counselor, tutoring, program for learning disabled. **Placement/credit:** AP, CLEP Subject, institutional tests; 38 credit hours maximum for bachelor's degree.

ACADEMIC REQUIREMENTS. Freshmen must earn minimum GPA of 1.7 to continue in good standing. 88% of freshmen return for sophomore year. Students must declare major by end of second year. **Graduation requirements:** 70 hours for associate (39 in major), 129 hours for bachelor's (45 in major). Most students required to take courses in computer science, English, history, humanities, mathematics, philosophy/religion, biological/physical sciences, social sciences. **Postgraduate studies:** 65% from 2-year programs enter 4-year programs. 7% enter medical school, 1% enter MBA programs, 12% enter other graduate study.

FRESHMAN ADMISSIONS. Selection criteria: School achievement record, class rank, recommendations, interview, test scores, and school and community activities considered. Must have related work experience to be considered for occupational and physical therapy programs. Can be volunteer service in the field. **High school preparation:** 16 units required; 23 recommended. Required and recommended units include biological science 1-2, English 4, mathematics 3-4, physical science 1-2 and social science 2-4. Foreign language 2 recommended. Life science, health science, and allied health applicants must have 3 units in science including 1 laboratory science, 1 chemistry, 1 algebra. **Test requirements:** SAT or ACT (SAT preferred); score report by September 1. Wechsler Adult Intelligence Scale Revised, Woodcock Johnson or similar type achievement tests required for individual learning program.

1992 FRESHMAN CLASS PROFILE. 249 men and women enrolled. 65% had high school GPA of 3.0 or higher, 31% between 2.0 and 2.99. **Academic background:** Mid 50% of enrolled freshmen had SAT-V between 370-470, SAT-M between 400-520. 90% submitted SAT scores. **Characteristics:** 49% from in state, 84% live in college housing, 1% have minority backgrounds, 2% are foreign students. Average age is 19.

FALL-TERM APPLICATIONS. $30 fee, may be waived for applicants with need. No closing date; priority given to applications received by February 1; applicants notified on a rolling basis beginning on or about November 1; must reply by May 1 or within 4 weeks if notified thereafter. Interview recommended. Essay recommended. Interview required for individual learning program applicants, strongly recommended for academically weak, physical therapy, and occupational therapy applicants, recommended for all others. CRDA. Deferred and early admission available. EDP-F.

STUDENT LIFE. Housing: Dormitories (men, women, coed). Off-campus housing available to qualified students, beach front rentals available. **Activities:** Student government, magazine, student newspaper, yearbook, drama, music ensembles, musical theater, psychology club, alcohol support team.

ATHLETICS. NAIA. **Intercollegiate:** Basketball, lacrosse M, soccer, softball W, volleyball W. **Intramural:** Basketball, bowling, cross-country, golf, ice hockey M, racquetball, sailing, skiing, skin diving M, softball, swimming, table tennis, tennis, volleyball, water polo. **Clubs:** Scuba.

STUDENT SERVICES. Aptitude testing, career counseling, freshman orientation, health services, on-campus day care, personal counseling, placement service for graduates, veterans counselor, services/facilities for handicapped.

ANNUAL EXPENSES. Tuition and fees: $11,200. **Room and board:** $4,870. **Books and supplies:** $850. **Other expenses:** $600.

FINANCIAL AID. 85% of freshmen, 87% of continuing students receive some form of aid. 77% of grants, 79% of loans, all jobs based on need. 193 enrolled freshmen were judged to have need, all were offered aid. Academic, leadership, alumni affiliation scholarships available. **Aid applications:** No closing date; priority given to applications received by March 1; applicants notified on a rolling basis beginning on or about March 1; must reply by May 1 or within 4 weeks if notified thereafter.

ADDRESS/TELEPHONE. Patricia Cribby, Dean of Admissions, University of New England, 11 Hills Beach Road, Biddeford, ME 04005. (207) 283-0171. Fax: (207) 282-6379.

University of Southern Maine
Portland, Maine CB code: 3691

Admissions: 77% of applicants accepted
Based on: ••• School record
•• Essay, recommendations, test scores
• Activities, interview
Completion: 70% of freshmen end year in good standing
52% graduate, 12% of these enter graduate study

4-year public university, coed. Founded in 1878. **Accreditation:** Regional. **Undergraduate enrollment:** 3,855 men and women full time; 4,436 men and women part time. **Graduate enrollment:** 556 men and women full time; 968 men and women part time. **Faculty:** 574 total (329 full time), 223 with doctorates or other terminal degrees. **Location:** Urban campus in small city; 115 miles from Boston. **Calendar:** Semester, limited summer session. Extensive evening/early morning classes. **Microcomputers:** 250 located in dormitories, libraries, classrooms, computer centers, campus-wide network. **Special facilities:** Art gallery, anthropology museum, planetarium, 250-acre farm in Freeport, Smith-Osher cartographic collection. **Additional facts:** Gorham campus located in suburb 10 miles from downtown Portland campus.

DEGREES OFFERED. AA, AS, BA, BS, BFA, MA, MS, MBA, MEd, JD. 85 associate degrees awarded in 1992. 690 bachelor's degrees awarded. Graduate degrees offered in 15 major fields of study.

UNDERGRADUATE MAJORS. Associate: Business administration and management, liberal/general studies, recreation therapy. **Bachelor's:** Accounting, anthropology, biological and physical sciences, biology, business administration and management, chemistry, classics, communications, computer and information sciences, criminology, dramatic arts, economics, electrical/electronics/communications engineering, English, fine arts, French, geography, geology, Hispanic American studies, history, humanities and social sciences, industrial arts education, industrial technology, liberal/general studies, mathematics, music, music education, music performance, nursing, philosophy, physics, political science and government, psychology, recreation therapy, Russian and Slavic studies, social work, sociology, trade and industrial education, women's studies.

ACADEMIC PROGRAMS. Cooperative education, double major, dual enrollment of high school students, honors program, independent study, internships, student-designed major, study abroad, teacher preparation, telecourses, visiting/exchange student program, Washington semester, cross-registration, preengineering program with Orono branch. **Remedial services:** Learning center, reduced course load, remedial instruction, tutoring. **Placement/credit:** AP, CLEP General and Subject, institutional tests.

ACADEMIC REQUIREMENTS. To continue in good academic standing, freshmen must earn the following minimum GPA: 1.8 in 4-year degree programs, 2.0 in 2-year degree programs. 60% of freshmen return for sophomore year. Students must declare major by end of second year. **Graduation requirements:** 60 hours for associate, 120 hours for bachelor's. Most students required to take courses in arts/fine arts, English, history, humanities, mathematics, philosophy/religion, biological/physical sciences, social sciences. **Postgraduate studies:** 1% enter law school, 1% enter medical school, 2% enter MBA programs, 8% enter other graduate study.

FRESHMAN ADMISSIONS. Selection criteria: School achievement record most important, followed by class rank, test scores, and counselor recommendation. Interview considered. **High school preparation:** 16 units required. Required units include English 4, foreign language 2, mathematics 3, social science 2 and science 2. Science units must include 2 laboratory. Languages optional for applied science, business, and nursing applicants. Curriculum requirements more flexible for associate degree programs. **Test requirements:** SAT or ACT (SAT preferred); score report by June 1.

1992 FRESHMAN CLASS PROFILE. 1,087 men applied, 804 accepted, 397 enrolled; 1,271 women applied, 1,010 accepted, 492 enrolled. **Academic background:** Mid 50% of enrolled freshmen had SAT-V between 410-510, SAT-M between 440-550. 91% submitted SAT scores. **Characteristics:** 87% from in state, 54% live in college housing. Average age is 20.

FALL-TERM APPLICATIONS. $20 fee, may be waived for applicants with need. Closing date July 15; priority given to applications received by April 15; applicants notified on a rolling basis; must reply within 2 weeks; deposit refundable until May 1. Audition required for music applicants. Essay required. Interview required for industrial arts and technology applicants, recommended for all others. Deferred and early admission available.

STUDENT LIFE. Housing: Dormitories (coed); apartment, fraternity, handicapped housing available. Housing guaranteed for four years. **Activities:** Student government, magazine, radio, student newspaper, television, literary magazine, choral groups, concert band, dance, drama, jazz band, music ensembles, musical theater, symphony orchestra, fraternities, sororities, Minority Student Organization, Inter-Varsity Christian Fellowship, Public Interest Research Group.

ATHLETICS. NCAA. **Intercollegiate:** Baseball M, basketball, cross-country, field hockey W, golf, ice hockey M, soccer, softball W, tennis. **Intramural:** Basketball, racquetball, soccer, softball, squash, table tennis, tennis, volleyball.

STUDENT SERVICES. Aptitude testing, career counseling, employment service for undergraduates, freshman orientation, health services, on-campus day care, personal counseling, placement service for graduates, special adviser for adult students, veterans counselor, services/facilities for handicapped.

ANNUAL EXPENSES. Tuition and fees (1992-93): $2,814, $4,890 additional for out-of-state students. **Room and board:** $4,038. **Books and supplies:** $500. **Other expenses:** $1,533.

FINANCIAL AID. 40% of freshmen, 44% of continuing students receive some form of aid. 93% of grants, 79% of loans, all jobs based on need. 455 enrolled freshmen were judged to have need, 425 were offered aid. Academic, music/drama, leadership, alumni affiliation, minority scholarships available. **Aid applications:** No closing date; priority given to applications received by March 1; applicants notified on a rolling basis beginning on or about March 15; must reply within 2 weeks.

ADDRESS/TELEPHONE. Dan Palubniak, Director of Admissions, University of Southern Maine, 96 Falmouth Street, Portland, ME 04103. (207) 780-4970. Fax: (207) 780-4933.

Westbrook College
Portland, Maine CB code: 3960

Admissions: 33% of applicants accepted
Based on: ••• School record
•• Activities, essay, interview, recommendations, test scores
• Special talents
Completion: 70% of freshmen end year in good standing
3% enter graduate study

4-year private liberal arts college, coed. Founded in 1831. **Accreditation:** Regional. **Undergraduate enrollment:** 34 men, 215 women full time; 34 men, 104 women part time. **Faculty:** 55 total (34 full time), 17 with doctorates or other terminal degrees. **Location:** Urban campus in small city; 100 miles from Boston. **Calendar:** Semester, limited summer session. **Microcomputers:** 50 located in dormitories, libraries, classrooms, computer centers. **Special facilities:** Westbrook College Children's Center, Maine Women Writer's Collection.

DEGREES OFFERED. BA, BS. 57 associate degrees awarded in 1992. 16% in business and management, 17% business/office and marketing/distribution, 9% computer sciences, 56% allied health. 39 bachelor's degrees awarded in 1992. 28% in business and management, 33% business/office and marketing/distribution, 16% computer sciences, 23% health sciences.

UNDERGRADUATE MAJORS. Dental hygiene. American studies, business administration and management, child development/care/guidance, clinical laboratory science, dental hygiene, early childhood education, English, medical laboratory technologies, nursing, psychology.

ACADEMIC PROGRAMS. Cooperative education, honors program, independent study, internships, student-designed major, teacher preparation; liberal arts/career combination in health sciences, business. **Remedial services:** Learning center, reduced course load, tutoring. **Placement/credit:** AP, CLEP General and Subject, institutional tests; 15 credit hours maximum for associate degree; 15 credit hours maximum for bachelor's degree.

ACADEMIC REQUIREMENTS. Freshmen must earn minimum GPA of 1.9 to continue in good standing. 65% of freshmen return for sophomore year. Students must declare major by end of first year. **Graduation requirements:** 81 hours for associate (41 in major), 120 hours for bachelor's (39 in major). Most students required to take courses in arts/fine arts, computer science, English, history, humanities, mathematics, biological/physical sciences, social sciences. **Postgraduate studies:** 10% from 2-year programs enter 4-year programs. 1% enter law school, 1% enter MBA programs, 1% enter other graduate study. **Additional information:** All career programs include field work, clinical affiliations, or externships during school year.

FRESHMAN ADMISSIONS. Selection criteria: School achievement record, test scores, experience in field of interest, school and community activities, recommendations important. Interview recommended. Recommended units include biological science 1, English 4, mathematics 3, physical science 1 and social science 2. 3 mathematics required for business administration. 3 mathematics, 2 laboratory science (including chemistry) for nursing and dental hygiene. 3 mathematics, 2 laboratory science (including chemistry) for medical technology. Physics highly recommended. **Test requirements:** SAT or ACT (SAT preferred); score report by September 1.

1992 FRESHMAN CLASS PROFILE. 49 men applied, 14 accepted, 7 enrolled; 280 women applied, 93 accepted, 54 enrolled. 24% had high school GPA of 3.0 or higher, 67% between 2.0 and 2.99. 6% were in top tenth and 22% were in top quarter of graduating class. **Characteristics:** 52% live in college housing, 2% have minority backgrounds, 2% are foreign students. Average age is 18.

FALL-TERM APPLICATIONS. $25 fee, may be waived for applicants with need. Closing date August 21; priority given to applications received by March 15; applicants notified on a rolling basis beginning on or about December 1; must reply by May 1 or within 4 weeks if notified thereafter. Essay required. Interview recommended. CRDA. Deferred and early admission available.

STUDENT LIFE. Housing: Dormitories (women, coed). Upperclass dormitory available for junior and seniors. **Activities:** Student government, student newspaper, newsletter, drama.

ATHLETICS. NAIA. **Intercollegiate:** Basketball, cross-country, golf M, soccer, softball W, volleyball W. **Intramural:** Tennis.

STUDENT SERVICES. Aptitude testing, career counseling, employment service for undergraduates, freshman orientation, health services, personal counseling, placement service for graduates, special adviser for adult students.

ANNUAL EXPENSES. Tuition and fees: $11,000. **Room and board:** $4,900. **Books and supplies:** $550. **Other expenses:** $800.

FINANCIAL AID. 86% of freshmen, 86% of continuing students receive some form of aid. All grants, 75% of loans, all jobs based on need. 59 enrolled freshmen were judged to have need, all were offered aid. **Aid applications:** No closing date; priority given to applications received by May 1; applicants notified on a rolling basis beginning on or about March 15; must reply by May 1 or within 2 weeks if notified thereafter.

ADDRESS/TELEPHONE. David D. Anthony, Director of Admissions, Westbrook College, 716 Stevens Avenue, Portland, ME 04103. (207) 797-7261 ext. 225. Fax: (207) 797-7225.

Maryland

Allegany Community College
Cumberland, Maryland CB code: 5028

2-year public community college, coed. Founded in 1961. **Accreditation:** Regional. **Undergraduate enrollment:** 655 men, 1,010 women full time; 341 men, 909 women part time. **Faculty:** 210 total (81 full time), 10 with doctorates or other terminal degrees. **Location:** Suburban campus in large town; 150 miles from Baltimore and Washington, DC, 130 miles from Pittsburgh, Pennsylvania. **Calendar:** Semester, limited summer session. Extensive evening/early morning classes. **Microcomputers:** 200 located in computer centers. **Special facilities:** Art gallery, greenhouse, arboretum, fitness center. **Additional facts:** Two off-campus centers in Somerset and Everett, Pennsylvania, offer credit courses and limited number of associate degree programs.

DEGREES OFFERED. AA. 478 associate degrees awarded in 1992. 9% in business and management, 8% business/office and marketing/distribution, 35% allied health, 31% multi/interdisciplinary studies.

UNDERGRADUATE MAJORS. Automotive technology, biology, business administration and management, business and office, business computer/console/peripheral equipment operation, business data processing and related programs, business data programming, chemistry, computer and information sciences, computer programming, criminal justice technology, data processing, dental hygiene, education, electromechanical technology, engineering, engineering and engineering-related technologies, engineering and other disciplines, finance, food management, food production/management/services, forestry and related sciences, legal secretary, liberal/general studies, medical laboratory technologies, medical secretary, mental health/human services, nursing, psychology, radio/television technology, radiograph medical technology, recreation and community services technologies, respiratory therapy technology, retailing, secretarial and related programs, social work, sociology, teacher aide.

ACADEMIC PROGRAMS. 2-year transfer program, dual enrollment of high school students, honors program, independent study, internships, telecourses, cross-registration. **Remedial services:** Learning center, reduced course load, remedial instruction, tutoring. **ROTC:** Army. **Placement/credit:** CLEP General and Subject, institutional tests; 30 credit hours maximum for associate degree.

ACADEMIC REQUIREMENTS. Freshmen must earn minimum GPA of 2.0 to continue in good standing. 75% of freshmen return for sophomore year. Students must declare major on enrollment. **Graduation requirements:** 65 hours for associate. Most students required to take courses in arts/fine arts, English, humanities, mathematics, biological/physical sciences, social sciences.

FRESHMAN ADMISSIONS. Selection criteria: Open admissions. Admission to allied health programs based on high school records, test scores. **Test requirements:** ACT required of allied health applicants only; score report by March 15.

1992 FRESHMAN CLASS PROFILE. 366 men, 486 women enrolled. **Characteristics:** 70% from in state, 100% commute, 3% have minority backgrounds. Average age is 26.

FALL-TERM APPLICATIONS. No fee. No closing date; applicants notified on a rolling basis. Interview recommended for allied health applicants. Early admission available. High school and/or college transcript and placement tests in English, reading, and mathematics required.

STUDENT LIFE. Activities: Student government, forestry club, electromechanical technology club, older and wiser club, Phi Theta Kappa-Honors Society.

ATHLETICS. NJCAA. **Intercollegiate:** Baseball M, basketball, soccer M, tennis. **Intramural:** Badminton, basketball M, handball, skiing, soccer M, softball W, swimming, tennis, volleyball.

STUDENT SERVICES. Aptitude testing, career counseling, employment service for undergraduates, freshman orientation, on-campus day care, personal counseling, placement service for graduates, veterans counselor, services/facilities for handicapped.

ANNUAL EXPENSES. Tuition and fees (projected): $1,865, $540 additional for out-of-district students, $1,290 additional for out-of-state students. **Books and supplies:** $500. **Other expenses:** $966.

FINANCIAL AID. 54% of freshmen, 60% of continuing students receive some form of aid. All jobs based on need. Academic, state/district residency, leadership scholarships available. **Aid applications:** No closing date; priority given to applications received by March 15; applicants notified on a rolling basis beginning on or about May 15; must reply within 2 weeks.

ADDRESS/TELEPHONE. Gloria Stafford, Director of Admissions and Registration, Allegany Community College, Willow Brook Road, Cumberland, MD 21502. (301) 724-7700 ext. 202. Fax: (301) 724-6892.

Anne Arundel Community College
Arnold, Maryland CB code: 5019

2-year public community college, coed. Founded in 1961. **Accreditation:** Regional. **Undergraduate enrollment:** 1,665 men, 1,734 women full time; 3,163 men, 5,515 women part time. **Faculty:** 522 total (197 full time). **Location:** Suburban campus in large town; 20 miles from Baltimore, 8 miles from Annapolis. **Calendar:** Semester, limited summer session. **Microcomputers:** Located in libraries, computer centers. **Special facilities:** Environmental center, astronomy laboratory, center for performing arts, art gallery.

DEGREES OFFERED. AA. 1,063 associate degrees awarded in 1992.

UNDERGRADUATE MAJORS. Accounting, American studies, architectural technologies, architecture, biological and physical sciences, business administration and management, business and management, business and office, business computer/console/peripheral equipment operation, business data processing and related programs, business data programming, communications, computer and information sciences, data processing, education, electrical technology, elementary education, emergency medical technologies, engineering, engineering and engineering-related technologies, European studies, finance, fine arts, food production/management/services, hotel/motel and restaurant management, information sciences and systems, law enforcement and corrections technologies, legal assistant/paralegal, liberal/general studies, mechanical design technology, medical assistant, nursing, predentistry, premedicine, prepharmacy, preveterinary, radiograph medical technology, recreation and community services technologies, retailing, secondary education.

ACADEMIC PROGRAMS. 2-year transfer program, cooperative education, double major, dual enrollment of high school students, honors program, independent study, internships, student-designed major, telecourses, weekend college. **Remedial services:** Learning center, reduced course load, remedial instruction, special counselor, tutoring. **Placement/credit:** AP, CLEP General and Subject, institutional tests; 30 credit hours maximum for associate degree.

ACADEMIC REQUIREMENTS. Freshmen must earn minimum GPA of 2.0 to continue in good standing. 39% of freshmen return for sophomore year. Students must declare major on application. **Graduation requirements:** 60 hours for associate. Most students required to take courses in English, mathematics, biological/physical sciences.

FRESHMAN ADMISSIONS. Selection criteria: Open admissions. **Test requirements:** SAT or ACT for placement; score report by September 5.

1992 FRESHMAN CLASS PROFILE. 1,260 men, 1,683 women enrolled. **Characteristics:** 99% from in state, 100% commute, 11% have minority backgrounds, 1% are foreign students. Average age is 19.

FALL-TERM APPLICATIONS. No fee. No closing date; applicants notified on a rolling basis. Interview recommended for nursing, human services, radiologic technology applicants. Early admission available.

STUDENT LIFE. Activities: Student government, film, radio, student newspaper, choral groups, concert band, dance, drama, jazz band, music ensembles, musical theater, Black Student Union, International Student Association.

ATHLETICS. NJCAA. **Intercollegiate:** Baseball, basketball, cross-country, field hockey, golf, lacrosse, soccer, softball, swimming, tennis, track and field, volleyball. **Intramural:** Archery, badminton, basketball, fencing, golf, racquetball, softball, table tennis, tennis, volleyball.

STUDENT SERVICES. Career counseling, employment service for undergraduates, freshman orientation, health services, on-campus day care, personal counseling, placement service for graduates, special adviser for adult students, veterans counselor, services/facilities for handicapped.

ANNUAL EXPENSES. Tuition and fees (1992-93): $1,720, $1,320 additional for out-of-district students, $3,960 additional for out-of-state students. **Books and supplies:** $500. **Other expenses:** $1,200.

FINANCIAL AID. All grants, 90% of loans based on need. Academic, athletic, state/district residency scholarships available. **Aid applications:** No closing date; priority given to applications received by April 15; applicants notified on a rolling basis beginning on or about July 1; must reply within 2 weeks.

ADDRESS/TELEPHONE. Herbert Curkin, Director of Admissions, Anne Arundel Community College, 101 College Parkway, Arnold, MD 21012. (301) 647-7100. Fax: (301) 541-2489.

Baltimore City Community College
Baltimore, Maryland CB code: 5051

2-year public community college, coed. Founded in 1947. **Accreditation:** Regional. **Undergraduate enrollment:** 2,437 men and women full time; 4,419 men and women part time. **Faculty:** 393 total (110 full time), 62 with doctorates or other terminal degrees. **Location:** Urban campus in very large city; 50 miles from Washington, D.C., 75 miles from Philadelphia. **Calendar:** Semester, limited summer session. Saturday and extensive evening/early morning classes. **Microcomputers:** 100 located in classrooms. **Special facilities:** Greenhouse, planetarium. **Additional facts:** Second campus in Inner Harbor area.

DEGREES OFFERED. AA. 444 associate degrees awarded in 1992. 12% in business and management, 5% computer sciences, 7% education, 12% health sciences, 23% allied health, 26% multi/interdisciplinary studies.

UNDERGRADUATE MAJORS. Accounting, biotechnology, business administration and management, business and management, business and office, computer and information sciences, dental hygiene, dietetic aide/assistant, drafting, drafting and design technology, early childhood education, electronic technology, emergency medical technologies, engineering, fashion design, fashion merchandising, law enforcement and corrections technologies, legal assistant/paralegal, legal secretary, liberal/general studies, marketing and distribution, medical records technology, medical secretary, nursing, office supervision and management, physical therapy assistant, respiratory therapy, science technologies, secretarial and related programs, word processing.

ACADEMIC PROGRAMS. 2-year transfer program, double major, dual enrollment of high school students, independent study, internships, telecourses. **Remedial services:** Learning center, reduced course load, remedial instruction, tutoring, individual study laboratories. **Placement/credit:** CLEP General and Subject, institutional tests; 15 credit hours maximum for associate degree.

ACADEMIC REQUIREMENTS. Freshmen must earn minimum GPA of 1.5 to continue in good standing. 44% of freshmen return for sophomore year. Students must declare major on enrollment. **Graduation requirements:** 62 hours for associate (38 in major). Most students required to take courses in English, humanities, mathematics, biological/physical sciences, social sciences. **Additional information:** Adults without diploma or GED become eligible for degree programs after successfully completing 15 college-level credits.

FRESHMAN ADMISSIONS. Selection criteria: Open admissions. Selective admission to some programs, particularly in health sciences.

1992 FRESHMAN CLASS PROFILE. 824 men, 1,653 women enrolled. **Characteristics:** 90% from in state, 100% commute, 74% have minority backgrounds, 1% are foreign students. Average age is 24.

FALL-TERM APPLICATIONS. No fee. Closing date August 12; applicants notified on a rolling basis; must reply by registration. Interview recommended for allied health, legal assistant, emergency medical services applicants. Audition recommended for music applicants. Portfolio recommended for art, fashion design applicants. Deferred and early admission available.

STUDENT LIFE. Activities: Student government, radio, student newspaper, television, student handbook, choral groups, Fashion Club, Human Services Club, Media Club, civic organizations.

ATHLETICS. NJCAA. **Intercollegiate:** Baseball M, basketball M, cross-country, track and field. **Intramural:** Basketball M, soccer M, softball M, tennis, volleyball.

STUDENT SERVICES. Career counseling, employment service for undergraduates, freshman orientation, health services, personal counseling, placement service for graduates, veterans counselor, services/facilities for handicapped.

ANNUAL EXPENSES. Tuition and fees: $1,320, $3,210 additional for out-of-state students. **Books and supplies:** $500. **Other expenses:** $2,000.

FINANCIAL AID. 75% of freshmen, 75% of continuing students receive some form of aid. 92% of grants, all loans, all jobs based on need. Academic, athletic, state/district residency scholarships available. **Aid applications:** No closing date; priority given to applications received by June 1; applicants notified on a rolling basis beginning on or about July 1; must reply within 2 weeks.

ADDRESS/TELEPHONE. Marlene Downes, Director of Admissions, Baltimore City Community College, 2901 Liberty Heights Avenue, Baltimore, MD 21215. (410) 333-5393. Fax: (410) 547-1610.

Baltimore Hebrew University
Baltimore, Maryland CB code: 2165

4-year private university specializing in Judaic and Hebraic studies, coed. Founded in 1919. **Accreditation:** Regional. **Undergraduate enrollment:** 4 men, 9 women full time; 66 men, 112 women part time. **Graduate enrollment:** 28 men, 51 women full time. **Faculty:** 30 total (12 full time), 30 with doctorates or other terminal degrees. **Location:** Urban campus in very large city. **Calendar:** Semester, limited summer session.

DEGREES OFFERED. BA, MA, PhD. 5 bachelor's degrees awarded in 1992. 100% in area and ethnic studies. Graduate degrees offered in 6 major fields of study.

UNDERGRADUATE MAJORS. Arabic, Aramaic and other Near Eastern languages, Hebrew, Jewish studies, Middle Eastern studies, social work, Yiddish.

ACADEMIC PROGRAMS. Accelerated program, cooperative education, double major, dual enrollment of high school students, education specialist degree, honors program, independent study, internships, study abroad, teacher preparation, cross-registration. **Remedial services:** Preadmission summer program. **Placement/credit:** CLEP General and Subject, institutional tests; 12 credit hours maximum for bachelor's degree.

ACADEMIC REQUIREMENTS. Freshmen must earn minimum GPA of 2.5 to continue in good standing. Students must declare major on application. **Graduation requirements:** 120 hours for bachelor's (30 in major). Most students required to take courses in English, foreign languages, history, humanities, mathematics, philosophy/religion, biological/physical sciences, social sciences.

FRESHMAN ADMISSIONS. Selection criteria: Academic record and motivation important. **High school preparation:** 18 units required. Required units include biological science 2, English 4, foreign language 3, mathematics 3, physical science 2 and social science 4. **Test requirements:** SAT or ACT (SAT preferred); score report by April 15.

1992 FRESHMAN CLASS PROFILE. 3 men, 9 women enrolled. **Characteristics:** 90% from in state, 100% commute.

FALL-TERM APPLICATIONS. $20 fee. Closing date April 15; applicants notified on or about May 1; must reply by August 15. Interview required. Deferred and early admission available.

STUDENT SERVICES. Career counseling, freshman orientation, on-campus day care, personal counseling, placement service for graduates, special adviser for adult students, services/facilities for handicapped.

ANNUAL EXPENSES. Tuition and fees (1992-93): $3,230. **Books and supplies:** $800. **Other expenses:** $100.

FINANCIAL AID. 33% of continuing students receive some form of aid. All grants, all loans based on need. **Aid applications:** Closing date July 1; applicants notified on or about August 1; must reply by September 1.

ADDRESS/TELEPHONE. Office of the Dean, School of Undergraduate Studies, Baltimore Hebrew University, 5800 Park Heights Avenue, Baltimore, MD 21215-3996. (410) 578-6903. Fax: (410) 578-6940.

Baltimore International Culinary College
Baltimore, Maryland CB code: 5086

Admissions: 95% of applicants accepted
Based on: ••• Interview, school record, test scores
•• Recommendations, special talents
• Activities
Completion: 79% of freshmen end year in good standing

1-year private college of culinary arts, food service management, and innkeeping management, coed. Founded in 1972. **Undergraduate enrollment:** 305 men, 111 women full time; 15 men, 7 women part time. **Faculty:** 32 total (22 full time), 4 with doctorates or other terminal degrees. **Location:** Urban campus in very large city. **Calendar:** Quarter. **Microcomputers:** 20 located in dormitories, libraries, computer centers.

DEGREES OFFERED. AA. 130 associate degrees awarded in 1992. 22% in business and management, 78% home economics.

UNDERGRADUATE MAJORS. Food management, food production/management/services, food science and nutrition, hotel/motel and restaurant management.

ACADEMIC PROGRAMS. Accelerated program, cooperative education, double major, internships, study abroad, study option available at European Educational Center in Ireland. **Remedial services:** Remedial instruction, special counselor, tutoring. **Placement/credit:** CLEP General and Subject, institutional tests.

ACADEMIC REQUIREMENTS. Freshmen must earn minimum GPA of 1.75 to continue in good standing. Students must declare major on enrollment. **Graduation requirements:** 70 hours for associate (34 in major). Most students required to take courses in English, history, humanities, mathematics, biological/physical sciences, social sciences.

FRESHMAN ADMISSIONS. Selection criteria: Institutionally designed placement evaluation most important. School achievement record and interview also important. **High school preparation:** 18 units recommended. Recommended units include English 4, mathematics 2, social science 1 and science 2. **Test requirements:** SAT or ACT. SAT with minimum mathematical score of 350 and minimum verbal score of 350 or ACT with minimum of 15. **Additional information:** Automatic acceptance (placement evaluation waived) for those with postsecondary degree or 16 units of college credit including minimum 2.0 in mathematics and English.

1992 FRESHMAN CLASS PROFILE. 208 men applied, 198 accepted, 99 enrolled; 74 women applied, 70 accepted, 35 enrolled. **Characteristics:** 48% from in state, 41% live in college housing, 30% have minority backgrounds. Average age is 24.

FALL-TERM APPLICATIONS. $25 fee. Closing date September 15; priority given to applications received by May 1; applicants notified on a rolling basis. Interview recommended. Deferred admission available. Applicants accepted for entrance any quarter. Application and payments must be complete 2 weeks prior to start of quarter to avoid late charge.

STUDENT LIFE. Housing: Dormitories (coed); apartment housing available. **Activities:** Student government, yearbook, newsletter. **Additional information:** Freshmen required to live in college housing for first academic year.

STUDENT SERVICES. Career counseling, employment service for undergraduates, health services, personal counseling, placement service for graduates, veterans counselor, services/facilities for handicapped.

ANNUAL EXPENSES. Tuition and fees: $12,255. Fees include use of computer, culinary supplies, upgrading and maintenance of kitchen equipment and facilities. Day students provided one full meal daily. **Room and board:** $3,825 room only. **Books and supplies:** $650. **Other expenses:** $3,627.

FINANCIAL AID. 90% of freshmen, 89% of continuing students receive some form of aid. 84% of grants, 45% of loans, all jobs based on need. 134 enrolled freshmen were judged to have need, all were offered aid. Academic, state/district residency, alumni affiliation scholarships available. **Aid applications:** No closing date; applicants notified on a rolling basis; must reply by registration.

ADDRESS/TELEPHONE. Raymond Joll, Director of Admissions, Baltimore International Culinary College, 25 South Calvert Street, Baltimore, MD 21202-1503. (410) 752-4710 ext. 302. (800) 624-9926 ext. 302. Fax: (410) 752-3730.

Bowie State University
Bowie, Maryland — CB code: 5401

Admissions: 52% of applicants accepted
Based on:
••• School record
•• Recommendations, test scores
• Interview, special talents
Completion: 17% graduate, 15% of these enter graduate study

4-year public university, coed. Founded in 1865. **Accreditation:** Regional. **Undergraduate enrollment:** 894 men, 1,283 women full time; 379 men, 653 women part time. **Graduate enrollment:** 225 men, 196 women full time; 408 men, 771 women part time. **Faculty:** 220 total (126 full time), 71 with doctorates or other terminal degrees. **Location:** Suburban campus in large town; 25 miles from Baltimore, 17 miles from Washington, D.C. **Calendar:** Semester, limited summer session. Saturday and extensive evening/early morning classes. **Microcomputers:** 138 located in computer centers. **Additional facts:** University offers courses at Fort Meade and Andrews military bases.

DEGREES OFFERED. BA, BS, MA, MS, MEd. 307 bachelor's degrees awarded in 1992. 38% in business and management, 10% communications, 6% computer sciences, 11% teacher education, 5% health sciences, 6% psychology, 10% social sciences. Graduate degrees offered in 19 major fields of study.

UNDERGRADUATE MAJORS. Applied mathematics, biology, business administration and management, business and human services, business and management, communications, computer and information sciences, criminal justice studies, dramatic arts, education, English, fine arts, history, international studies, journalism, law enforcement and corrections, linguistics, nursing, office supervision and management, physical education, political science and government, psychology, public administration, pure mathematics, social work, sociology, speech.

ACADEMIC PROGRAMS. Accelerated program, cooperative education, dual enrollment of high school students, honors program, independent study, internships, teacher preparation, telecourses, cross-registration, dual degree programs in engineering and dentistry with cooperating universities. **Remedial services:** Learning center, preadmission summer program, reduced course load, remedial instruction, special counselor, tutoring. **ROTC:** Air Force, Army. **Placement/credit:** AP, CLEP General and Subject, institutional tests; 60 credit hours maximum for bachelor's degree.

ACADEMIC REQUIREMENTS. Freshmen must earn minimum GPA of 2.0 to continue in good standing. 70% of freshmen return for sophomore year. Students must declare major by end of second year. **Graduation requirements:** 120 hours for bachelor's. Most students required to take courses in English, history, humanities, mathematics, biological/physical sciences, social sciences.

FRESHMAN ADMISSIONS. Selection criteria: School achievement record in college preparatory curriculum, test scores, minimum GPA of 2.0, counselor/school recommendation. **High school preparation:** 20 units required. Required units include English 4, foreign language 2, mathematics 3, social science 3 and science 2. **Test requirements:** SAT or ACT (SAT preferred); score report by June 1.

1992 FRESHMAN CLASS PROFILE. 678 men applied, 341 accepted, 185 enrolled; 906 women applied, 480 accepted, 259 enrolled. **Academic background:** Mid 50% of enrolled freshmen had SAT-V between 320-400, SAT-M between 340-430. 92% submitted SAT scores. **Characteristics:** 85% from in state, 61% live in college housing, 94% have minority backgrounds, 2% are foreign students. Average age is 20.

FALL-TERM APPLICATIONS. $10 fee, may be waived for applicants with need. Closing date April 1; priority given to applications received by January 1; applicants notified on a rolling basis; must reply by June 1 or within 7 days if notified thereafter. Interview recommended. Audition recommended for music education applicants. Portfolio recommended for art applicants. Deferred and early admission available. EDP-S.

STUDENT LIFE. Housing: Dormitories (men, women); apartment housing available. Special interest floors/sections available in residence halls. **Activities:** Student government, radio, student newspaper, television, yearbook, choral groups, concert band, dance, drama, jazz band, marching band, music ensembles, musical theater, pep band, fraternities, sororities, International Student Association, Commuter Senate, Bowie Gospel Choir.

ATHLETICS. NCAA. **Intercollegiate:** Baseball M, basketball, cross-country, football M, softball W, track and field, volleyball W. **Intramural:** Basketball, football M, soccer M, softball, volleyball.

STUDENT SERVICES. Career counseling, employment service for undergraduates, freshman orientation, health services, personal counseling, placement service for graduates, special adviser for adult students, veterans counselor, peer counseling for returning adults (women), services/facilities for handicapped.

ANNUAL EXPENSES. Tuition and fees (projected): $2,736, $2,392 additional for out-of-state students. **Room and board:** $3,799. **Books and supplies:** $600. **Other expenses:** $1,300.

FINANCIAL AID. 64% of freshmen, 70% of continuing students receive some form of aid. 91% of grants, 94% of loans, all jobs based on need. Academic, music/drama, athletic, state/district residency, minority scholarships available. **Aid applications:** No closing date; priority given to applications received by June 1; applicants notified on a rolling basis beginning on or about June 1; must reply within 2 weeks.

ADDRESS/TELEPHONE. Lawrence Waters, Director of Admissions, Records, and Registration, Bowie State University, 14000 Jericho Park Road, Bowie, MD 20715. (301) 464-6570. Fax: (301) 464-9350.

Capitol College
Laurel, Maryland — CB code: 5101

Admissions: 90% of applicants accepted
Based on:
••• School record
•• Recommendations
• Activities, essay, interview, test scores
Completion: 70% of freshmen end year in good standing
30% graduate, 21% of these enter graduate study

4-year private engineering, technical college, coed. Founded in 1964. **Accreditation:** Regional. **Undergraduate enrollment:** 233 men, 34 women full time; 307 men, 36 women part time. **Graduate enrollment:** 89 men, 31 women part time. **Faculty:** 74 total (21 full time), 15 with doctorates or other terminal degrees. **Location:** Suburban campus in large town; 19 miles from Washington, D.C., 22 miles from Baltimore. **Calendar:** Semester, extensive summer session. Saturday and extensive evening/early morning classes. **Microcomputers:** 51 located in classrooms, computer centers. **Special facilities:** Telecommunications switching center.

DEGREES OFFERED. AA, BS, MS. 23 associate degrees awarded in 1992. 100% in engineering technologies. 104 bachelor's degrees awarded. 95% in engineering technologies. Graduate degrees offered in 2 major fields of study.

UNDERGRADUATE MAJORS. Associate: Computer programming, computer technology, electrical/electronics/communications engineering, electronic technology, laser electro-optic technology, telecommunications, telecommunications technology. **Bachelor's:** Business administration and management, computer and information sciences, computer programming, computer technology, electrical/electronics/communications engineering, electronic technology, telecommunications, telecommunications technology.

ACADEMIC PROGRAMS. Accelerated program, cooperative education, double major, dual enrollment of high school students, independent study, internships, weekend college. **Remedial services:** Learning center, reduced course load, special counselor, tutoring, developmental mathematics and English program. **Placement/credit:** AP, CLEP General and Subject, institutional tests.

ACADEMIC REQUIREMENTS. Freshmen must earn minimum GPA of 1.75 to continue in good standing. 64% of freshmen return for sophomore year. Students must declare major by end of first year. **Graduation requirements:** 66 hours for associate (30 in major), 133 hours for bachelor's (70 in major). Most students required to take courses in English, history, humanities, mathematics, biological/physical sciences, social sciences. **Postgraduate studies:** 78% from 2-year programs enter 4-year programs.

FRESHMAN ADMISSIONS. Selection criteria: Academic preparation and school record most important. Mathematics foundation necessary for successful completion of programs. Test scores considered. **High school preparation:** 20 units required. Required units include English 4, mathematics 3, physical science 2, social science 2 and science 2. Mathematic units include algebra I, geometry, algebra II/trigonometry. Calculus recommended for advanced standing. **Test requirements:** SAT or ACT (SAT preferred); score report by August 30.

1992 FRESHMAN CLASS PROFILE. 100 men and women applied, 90 accepted; 47 enrolled. 28% had high school GPA of 3.0 or higher, 63% between 2.0 and 2.99. **Characteristics:** 70% from in state, 80% commute, 28% have minority backgrounds, 2% are foreign students. Average age is 19.

FALL-TERM APPLICATIONS. $25 fee, may be waived for applicants with need. No closing date; priority given to applications received by April 1; applicants notified on a rolling basis; must reply by May 1 or within 6 weeks if notified thereafter. Interview recommended. Essay recommended. CRDA. Deferred and early admission available.

STUDENT LIFE. Housing: Apartment housing available. **Activities:** Student government, student newspaper, yearbook, computer club, chess club, robotics club, music club, karate club.

ATHLETICS. NCAA. **Intercollegiate:** Basketball M, soccer M. **Intramural:** Basketball M, bowling M, golf M, softball M, table tennis.

STUDENT SERVICES. Aptitude testing, career counseling, employment service for undergraduates, freshman orientation, personal counseling, placement service for graduates, special adviser for adult students, veterans counselor, services/facilities for handicapped.

ANNUAL EXPENSES. Tuition and fees: $8,013. **Room and board:** $2,730 room only. **Books and supplies:** $600. **Other expenses:** $1,175.

FINANCIAL AID. 39% of freshmen, 36% of continuing students receive some form of aid. 49% of grants, 87% of loans, 55% of jobs based on need. 37 enrolled freshmen were judged to have need, all were offered aid. Academic scholarships available. **Aid applications:** No closing date; priority given to applications received by March 15; applicants notified on a rolling basis beginning on or about May 15; must reply within 2 weeks.

ADDRESS/TELEPHONE. Anthony G. Miller, Coordinator of Admissions, Capitol College, 11301 Springfield Road, Laurel, MD 20708. (301) 953-3200. (800) 950-1992. Fax: (301) 953-3876.

Catonsville Community College
Catonsville, Maryland — CB code: 5137

2-year public community college, coed. Founded in 1956. **Accreditation:** Regional. **Undergraduate enrollment:** 1,384 men, 1,487 women full time; 3,308 men, 4,140 women part time. **Faculty:** 669 total (215 full time), 94 with doctorates or other terminal degrees. **Location:** Suburban campus in small city; 8 miles from Baltimore. **Calendar:** 4-1-4, limited summer session. **Microcomputers:** 200 located in computer centers. **Special facilities:** Planetarium, occupational training center, performing arts theater, computer integrated manufacturing center, art gallery. **Additional facts:** Courses offered at Hunt Valley, Owings Mills, Campfield, Carroll County and other off-campus sites.

DEGREES OFFERED. AA, AS. 936 associate degrees awarded in 1992. 25% in business and management, 13% computer sciences, 8% engineering technologies, 16% allied health, 26% multi/interdisciplinary studies, 7% parks/recreation, protective services, public affairs.

UNDERGRADUATE MAJORS. Accounting, air traffic control, airline piloting and navigation, allied health, automated manufacturing technology, automotive mechanics, automotive technology, aviation management, business administration and management, business and management, business and office, business data programming, chemical manufacturing technology, cinematography/film, civil technology, commercial art, computer and information sciences, computer graphics, computer programming, computer servicing technology, construction, criminal justice studies, data processing, drafting, drafting and design technology, dramatic arts, education, electronic technology, elementary education, engineering, fire protection, flight attendants, funeral services/mortuary science, graphic and printing production, graphic arts technology, industrial technology, information sciences and systems, international studies, law enforcement and corrections, law enforcement and corrections technologies, legal secretary, liberal/general studies, machine tool operation/machine shop, marketing and distribution, marketing management, medical laboratory technologies, medical secretary, mental health/human services, music, nursing, occupational safety and health technology, occupational therapy assistant, office supervision and management, parks and recreation management, photography, prelaw, radio/television technology, real estate, recreation and community services technologies, secondary education, secretarial and related programs, survey and mapping technology, systems analysis.

ACADEMIC PROGRAMS. 2-year transfer program, cooperative education, dual enrollment of high school students, honors program, independent study, study abroad, cross-registration. **Remedial services:** Learning center, reduced course load, remedial instruction, special counselor, tutoring, career development courses, achieving academic success courses. **Placement/credit:** CLEP General and Subject, institutional tests; 30 credit hours maximum for associate degree.

ACADEMIC REQUIREMENTS. Freshmen must earn minimum GPA of 2.0 to continue in good standing. 54% of freshmen return for sophomore year. **Graduation requirements:** 62 hours for associate (24 in major). Most students required to take courses in English, humanities, mathematics, biological/physical sciences, social sciences.

FRESHMAN ADMISSIONS. Selection criteria: Open admissions. Selective admissions to nursing, automotive technology program, and honors program. **High school preparation:** 20 units recommended. Recommended units include English 4, foreign language 2, mathematics 2, social science 4 and science 2. **Additional information:** Early application is encouraged.

1992 FRESHMAN CLASS PROFILE. 1,129 men, 1,240 women enrolled. **Characteristics:** 99% from in state, 100% commute, 37% have minority backgrounds, 1% are foreign students. Average age is 24.

FALL-TERM APPLICATIONS. $10 fee, may be waived for applicants with need. No closing date; applicants notified on a rolling basis beginning on or about March 1. Interview required for early admission, under age 16 applicants. Early admission available. SAT or ACT recommended for placement and counseling. Score report preferred by July 1. Applicants not presenting SAT or ACT score required to take in-house placement tests. 3.0 GPA required for early admission applicants.

STUDENT LIFE. Activities: Student government, magazine, radio, student newspaper, television, yearbook, choral groups, concert band, dance, drama, music ensembles, musical theater, Black Student Union, International Club, Adventure Society, Christian Fellowship. **Additional information:** Special emphasis on leadership within student clubs and organizations.

ATHLETICS. NJCAA. **Intercollegiate:** Baseball M, basketball, bowling, cross-country, diving, lacrosse M, soccer, softball W, swimming, tennis, track and field, volleyball W. **Intramural:** Basketball, cross-country, diving, handball, racquetball, skiing, swimming, table tennis, tennis, track and field, volleyball.

STUDENT SERVICES. Aptitude testing, career counseling, employment service for undergraduates, freshman orientation, health services, on-campus day care, personal counseling, placement service for graduates, veterans counselor, special programs for women and first generation college students, services/facilities for handicapped.

ANNUAL EXPENSES. Tuition and fees (1992-93): $1,510, $1,290 additional for out-of-district students, $3,090 additional for out-of-state students. **Books and supplies:** $500. **Other expenses:** $900.

FINANCIAL AID. 10% of freshmen, 15% of continuing students receive some form of aid. 96% of grants, 87% of loans, 42% of jobs based on need. Academic, athletic, leadership, alumni affiliation scholarships available. **Aid applications:** No closing date; priority given to applications received by March 1; applicants notified on a rolling basis beginning on or about May 1; must reply within 2 weeks. **Additional information:** On-campus employment typically available.

ADDRESS/TELEPHONE. Linda Emmerich, Director of Admissions/Outreach, Catonsville Community College, 800 South Rolling Road, Catonsville, MD 21228. (410) 455-4304. Fax: (410) 455-4411.

Cecil Community College
North East, Maryland — CB code: 5091

2-year public community college, coed. Founded in 1968. **Accreditation:** Regional. **Undergraduate enrollment:** 167 men, 216 women full time; 378 men, 698 women part time. **Faculty:** 123 total (49 full time), 6 with doctorates or other terminal degrees. **Location:** Rural campus in rural community; 50 miles from Baltimore, 50 miles from Philadelphia. **Calendar:** Semester, limited summer session. **Microcomputers:** 50 located in computer centers.

DEGREES OFFERED. AA. 98 associate degrees awarded in 1992. 18% in business and management, 32% health sciences, 21% multi/interdisciplinary studies, 12% visual and performing arts.

UNDERGRADUATE MAJORS. Accounting, air conditioning/heating/refrigeration mechanics, business administration and management, business and management, business and office, business data processing and related programs, carpentry, criminology, data processing, electrical and electronics equipment repair, electrical installation, electromechanical technology, electronic technology, elementary education, finance, law enforcement and corrections technologies, liberal/general studies, marketing and distribution, masonry/tile setting, nursing, photographic technology, plumbing/pipefitting/steamfitting, protective services, science technologies, secondary education, secretarial and related programs, word processing.

ACADEMIC PROGRAMS. 2-year transfer program, dual enrollment of high school students, internships, teacher preparation, telecourses. **Remedial services:** Learning center, reduced course load, remedial instruction, tutoring. **Placement/credit:** CLEP General and Subject, institutional tests; 45 credit hours maximum for associate degree.

ACADEMIC REQUIREMENTS. Freshmen must earn minimum GPA of 2.0 to continue in good standing. 50% of freshmen return for sophomore year. Students must declare major on application. **Graduation requirements:** 62 hours for associate (30 in major). Most students required to take courses in computer science, English, history, humanities, mathematics, biological/physical sciences, social sciences.

FRESHMAN ADMISSIONS. Selection criteria: Open admissions. Selective admission to nursing programs based on high school record, test scores.

1992 FRESHMAN CLASS PROFILE. 202 men, 312 women enrolled. **Characteristics:** 84% from in state, 100% commute, 7% have minority backgrounds, 1% are foreign students. Average age is 26.

FALL-TERM APPLICATIONS. $25 fee. No closing date; applicants notified on a rolling basis. Interview required for nursing applicants. Deferred and early admission available. Institutional early decision plan. Application deadline for nursing program March 1.

STUDENT LIFE. Activities: Student government, student newspaper, drama.

ATHLETICS. NJCAA. **Intercollegiate:** Baseball, basketball, bowling, soccer M, softball W, tennis, volleyball W.

STUDENT SERVICES. Aptitude testing, career counseling, em-

ployment service for undergraduates, personal counseling, placement service for graduates, veterans counselor, services/facilities for handicapped.

ANNUAL EXPENSES. Tuition and fees (projected): $1,674, $1,590 additional for out-of-district students, $2,640 additional for out-of-state students. **Books and supplies:** $660. **Other expenses:** $900.

FINANCIAL AID. 18% of continuing students receive some form of aid. Grants, loans, jobs available. Academic, music/drama, art, athletic, state/district residency, leadership scholarships available. **Aid applications:** No closing date; priority given to applications received by August 1; applicants notified on a rolling basis; must reply within 2 weeks.

ADDRESS/TELEPHONE. Rosemary A. Castelli, Dean of Student Services, Cecil Community College, 1000 North East Road, North East, MD 21901-1999. (410) 287-6060. Fax: (410) 287-1026.

Charles County Community College
La Plata, Maryland — CB code: 5144

2-year public community college, coed. Founded in 1958. **Accreditation:** Regional. **Undergraduate enrollment:** 576 men, 807 women full time; 1,463 men, 2,923 women part time. **Faculty:** 289 total (68 full time), 27 with doctorates or other terminal degrees. **Location:** Rural campus in small town; 30 miles from Washington, D.C. **Calendar:** Semester, limited summer session. Saturday and extensive evening/early morning classes. **Microcomputers:** Located in libraries, classrooms, computer centers. **Additional facts:** Other campuses located at Smallwood Village Center in Charles County and at various locations in Calvert and St. Mary's counties.

DEGREES OFFERED. AA. 362 associate degrees awarded in 1992. 29% in business and management, 13% computer sciences, 13% health sciences, 33% multi/interdisciplinary studies.

UNDERGRADUATE MAJORS. Accounting, biological and physical sciences, business administration and management, business and management, business data processing and related programs, business data programming, care provider, chemistry, child development/care/guidance, computer and information sciences, computer programming, data processing, dental hygiene, drafting, education, electronic technology, elementary education, engineering, engineering and engineering-related technologies, humanities, humanities and social sciences, information sciences and systems, legal assistant/paralegal, liberal/general studies, mathematics, nursing, physical sciences, physics, science technologies, secondary education, social sciences, visual and performing arts.

ACADEMIC PROGRAMS. 2-year transfer program, cooperative education, dual enrollment of high school students, study abroad, teacher preparation, telecourses, weekend college. **Remedial services:** Learning center, reduced course load, remedial instruction, tutoring. **Placement/credit:** AP, CLEP Subject, institutional tests; 30 credit hours maximum for associate degree.

ACADEMIC REQUIREMENTS. Freshmen must earn minimum GPA of 1.5 to continue in good standing. **Graduation requirements:** 60 hours for associate. Most students required to take courses in English, humanities, mathematics, biological/physical sciences, social sciences. **Additional information:** Students must successfully complete any remedial courses required before registering for regular courses.

FRESHMAN ADMISSIONS. Selection criteria: Open admissions. 2.0 GPA and special testing required of nursing applicants. Placement tests required for all full-time students. Applicants to nursing program must have completed biology course with laboratory within 5 years prior to application. **Test requirements:** Nelson-Denny Reading test and institutional tests in mathematics and English used for placement.

1992 FRESHMAN CLASS PROFILE. 726 men, 1,106 women enrolled. **Characteristics:** 99% from in state, 100% commute, 13% have minority backgrounds, 1% are foreign students. Average age is 25.

FALL-TERM APPLICATIONS. $20 fee, may be waived for applicants with need. No closing date; applicants notified on a rolling basis. Interview required for nursing, early admission applicants. Deferred and early admission available. Placement test for full-time students-course specific for part-time students.

STUDENT LIFE. Activities: Student government, student newspaper, choral groups, dance, drama, jazz band, music ensembles, musical theater, pep band, Black Americans for Democracy, Black Student Union, BACCHUS, Christian Student Fellowship, Women's Bible Study.

ATHLETICS. NJCAA. **Intercollegiate:** Baseball M, basketball, golf, soccer M, softball W, tennis, volleyball W.

STUDENT SERVICES. Career counseling, employment service for undergraduates, freshman orientation, health services, personal counseling, placement service for graduates, veterans counselor, services/facilities for handicapped.

ANNUAL EXPENSES. Tuition and fees (projected): $1,580, $1,500 additional for out-of-district students, $3,000 additional for out-of-state students. **Books and supplies:** $650. **Other expenses:** $400.

FINANCIAL AID. 24% of freshmen, 20% of continuing students receive some form of aid. 77% of grants, 81% of loans, 14% of jobs based on need. 325 enrolled freshmen were judged to have need, 300 were offered aid. Academic, music/drama, art, athletic, state/district residency, minority scholarships available. **Aid applications:** No closing date; priority given to applications received by April 1; applicants notified on a rolling basis beginning on or about May 15; must reply within 2 weeks.

ADDRESS/TELEPHONE. Robert R. St. Pierre, Director of Student Development, Charles County Community College, PO Box 910, Mitchell Road, La Plata, MD 20646. (301) 934-2251. Fax: (301) 934-5255.

Chesapeake College
Wye Mills, Maryland — CB code: 5143

2-year public community college, coed. Founded in 1965. **Accreditation:** Regional. **Undergraduate enrollment:** 228 men, 293 women full time; 445 men, 1,165 women part time. **Faculty:** 132 total (42 full time), 17 with doctorates or other terminal degrees. **Location:** Rural campus in rural community; 50 miles from Washington, D.C., and Baltimore. **Calendar:** Semester, limited summer session. Saturday and extensive evening/early morning classes. **Microcomputers:** 37 located in classrooms, computer centers.

DEGREES OFFERED. AA. 121 associate degrees awarded in 1992. 6% in business and management, 8% business/office and marketing/distribution, 8% computer sciences, 14% teacher education, 10% allied health, 40% multi/interdisciplinary studies, 8% social sciences.

UNDERGRADUATE MAJORS. Accounting, aircraft mechanics, business and office, business data programming, child development/care/guidance, computer and information sciences, computer servicing technology, computer technology, data processing, electronic technology, elementary education, fine arts, humanities and social sciences, law , law enforcement and corrections technologies, legal assistant/paralegal, legal secretary, liberal/general studies, mathematics, medical secretary, mental health/human services, physical education, radiograph medical technology, science/mathematics, secondary education, secretarial and related programs, social sciences, teacher aide, word processing.

ACADEMIC PROGRAMS. 2-year transfer program, double major, dual enrollment of high school students, honors program, independent study, internships, student-designed major, teacher preparation, telecourses, cross-registration. **Remedial services:** Learning center, reduced course load, remedial instruction, special counselor, tutoring. **Placement/credit:** CLEP General and Subject, institutional tests; 32 credit hours maximum for associate degree.

ACADEMIC REQUIREMENTS. Freshmen must earn minimum GPA of 1.5 to continue in good standing. 40% of freshmen return for sophomore year. Students must declare major on application. **Graduation requirements:** 64 hours for associate. Most students required to take courses in English, mathematics, biological/physical sciences, social sciences.

FRESHMAN ADMISSIONS. Selection criteria: Open admissions.

1992 FRESHMAN CLASS PROFILE. 235 men, 361 women enrolled. **Characteristics:** 99% from in state, 100% commute, 11% have minority backgrounds. Average age is 27.

FALL-TERM APPLICATIONS. No fee. No closing date; applicants notified on a rolling basis. Deferred and early admission available. Early application advised for radiologic technology program.

STUDENT LIFE. Activities: Student government, choral groups, drama, black student organization.

ATHLETICS. NJCAA. **Intercollegiate:** Baseball M, basketball, soccer M, tennis. **Intramural:** Baseball, basketball, softball, swimming, table tennis, tennis.

STUDENT SERVICES. Career counseling, employment service for undergraduates, freshman orientation, on-campus day care, personal counseling, placement service for graduates, veterans counselor, services/facilities for handicapped.

ANNUAL EXPENSES. Tuition and fees: $1,502, $1,820 additional for out-of-district students, $4,480 additional for out-of-state students. **Books and supplies:** $475. **Other expenses:** $1,720.

FINANCIAL AID. 33% of freshmen, 40% of continuing students receive some form of aid. 81% of grants, all loans, 90% of jobs based on need. Academic, athletic, state/district residency, minority scholarships available. **Aid applications:** No closing date; priority given to applications received by June 1; applicants notified on a rolling basis beginning on or about August 1; must reply within 2 weeks.

ADDRESS/TELEPHONE. Timothy Albert, Director of Admissions, Chesapeake College, PO Box 8, Wye Mills, MD 21679-0008. (410) 827-5400. Fax: (410) 827-9466.

College of Notre Dame of Maryland

Baltimore, Maryland CB code: 5114

Admissions: 78% of applicants accepted
Based on: ••• Essay, interview, recommendations, school record, test scores
•• Activities, special talents
Completion: 94% of freshmen end year in good standing
73% graduate, 21% of these enter graduate study

4-year private liberal arts college, women only, affiliated with Roman Catholic Church. Founded in 1873. **Accreditation:** Regional. **Undergraduate enrollment:** 3 men, 642 women full time; 201 men, 1,692 women part time. **Graduate enrollment:** 4 men, 8 women full time; 55 men, 342 women part time. **Faculty:** 82 total (69 full time), 46 with doctorates or other terminal degrees. **Location:** Suburban campus in very large city; 4 miles from downtown, 37 miles from Washington, D.C. **Calendar:** 4-1-4, limited summer session. Saturday classes. **Microcomputers:** 125 located in libraries, computer centers, campus-wide network. **Special facilities:** Planetarium, art gallery, photography laboratories. **Additional facts:** Men admitted only to undergraduate and graduate weekend college programs.

DEGREES OFFERED. BA, BS, MA. 295 bachelor's degrees awarded in 1992. 29% in business and management, 9% communications, 6% education, 12% health sciences, 9% multi/interdisciplinary studies, 6% psychology, 10% social sciences, 6% visual and performing arts. Graduate degrees offered in 2 major fields of study.

UNDERGRADUATE MAJORS. Aerospace/aeronautical/astronautical engineering, bioengineering and biomedical engineering, biological and physical sciences, biology, business administration and management, business and management, chemical engineering, chemistry, civil engineering, classics, communications, computer and information sciences, computer programming, early childhood education, economics, education, electrical/electronics/communications engineering, elementary education, engineering, English, fine arts, foreign languages (multiple emphasis), French, history, humanities and social sciences, information sciences and systems, international relations, journalism, liberal/general studies, materials engineering, mathematics, mechanical engineering, music, music history and appreciation, music performance, music theory and composition, nuclear engineering, nursing, photography, physical sciences, physics, political science and government, predentistry, prelaw, premedicine, prepharmacy, preveterinary, psychology, radio/television technology, religion, secondary education, social sciences, Spanish.

ACADEMIC PROGRAMS. Accelerated program, double major, dual enrollment of high school students, honors program, independent study, internships, student-designed major, study abroad, teacher preparation, weekend college, cross-registration; liberal arts/career combination in engineering, health sciences. **Remedial services:** Reduced course load, tutoring. **ROTC:** Army. **Placement/credit:** AP, institutional tests; 30 credit hours maximum for bachelor's degree.

ACADEMIC REQUIREMENTS. Freshmen must earn minimum GPA of 2.0 to continue in good standing. 80% of freshmen return for sophomore year. Students must declare major by end of second year. **Graduation requirements:** 128 hours for bachelor's (48 in major). Most students required to take courses in arts/fine arts, computer science, English, foreign languages, history, humanities, mathematics, philosophy/religion, biological/physical sciences, social sciences. **Postgraduate studies:** 4% enter law school, 4% enter medical school, 2% enter MBA programs, 11% enter other graduate study.

FRESHMAN ADMISSIONS. Selection criteria: School achievement record, SAT scores, class rank, letter of recommendation, interview are all very important. **High school preparation:** 18 units required. Required units include biological science 1, English 4, foreign language 3, mathematics 3, physical science 1 and social science 2. **Test requirements:** SAT or ACT (SAT preferred); score report by February 15. Prueba de Aptitud Academica for Spanish speaking applicants.

1992 FRESHMAN CLASS PROFILE. 66% had high school GPA of 3.0 or higher, 34% between 2.0 and 2.99. 27% were in top tenth and 49% were in top quarter of graduating class. **Characteristics:** 70% from in state, 78% live in college housing, 29% have minority backgrounds, 4% are foreign students. Average age is 18.

FALL-TERM APPLICATIONS. $25 fee, may be waived for applicants with need. Closing date February 15; priority given to applications received by November 15; applicants notified on a rolling basis; must reply by May 1. Essay required. Interview recommended. CRDA. Deferred and early admission available.

STUDENT LIFE. Housing: Dormitories (women). **Activities:** Student government, film, magazine, radio, student newspaper, television, yearbook, literary journal, choral groups, dance, drama, music ensembles, musical theater, campus ministries, community service organization, black student organization.

ATHLETICS. NCAA. **Intercollegiate:** Basketball, field hockey, lacrosse, soccer, swimming, tennis, volleyball. **Intramural:** Badminton, basketball, field hockey, lacrosse, racquetball, soccer, softball, tennis, volleyball.

STUDENT SERVICES. Aptitude testing, career counseling, employment service for undergraduates, freshman orientation, health services, on-campus day care, personal counseling, placement service for graduates, special adviser for adult students, services/facilities for handicapped.

ANNUAL EXPENSES. Tuition and fees: $10,650. **Room and board:** $5,400. **Books and supplies:** $450. **Other expenses:** $700.

FINANCIAL AID. 90% of freshmen, 80% of continuing students receive some form of aid. 66% of grants, 92% of loans, 41% of jobs based on need. 128 enrolled freshmen were judged to have need, all were offered aid. Academic, music/drama, art, leadership scholarships available. **Aid applications:** No closing date; priority given to applications received by February 15; applicants notified on a rolling basis beginning on or about April 1; must reply by May 1 or within 2 weeks if notified thereafter.

ADDRESS/TELEPHONE. Sharon Houst, Director of Admissions, College of Notre Dame of Maryland, 4701 North Charles Street, Baltimore, MD 21210-2476. (410) 532-5330. (800) 435-0300. Fax: (410) 435-5937.

Columbia Union College

Takoma Park, Maryland CB code: 5890

Admissions: 65% of applicants accepted
Based on: ••• Recommendations, school record, test scores
•• Essay, interview, special talents
• Activities, religious affiliation/commitment
Completion: 75% of freshmen end year in good standing
21% graduate, 25% of these enter graduate study

4-year private liberal arts college, coed, affiliated with Seventh-day Adventists. Founded in 1904. **Accreditation:** Regional. **Undergraduate enrollment:** 223 men, 317 women full time; 205 men, 376 women part time. **Faculty:** 56 total (50 full time), 31 with doctorates or other terminal degrees. **Location:** Suburban campus in large town; 7 miles from Washington, D.C. **Calendar:** Semester, limited summer session. Extensive evening/early morning classes. **Microcomputers:** 38 located in computer centers.

DEGREES OFFERED. AA, BA, BS. 15 associate degrees awarded in 1992. 7% in business/office and marketing/distribution, 7% computer sciences, 7% education, 64% allied health, 15% multi/interdisciplinary studies. 296 bachelor's degrees awarded. 34% in business and management, 17% health sciences, 19% allied health, 16% psychology.

UNDERGRADUATE MAJORS. Associate: Accounting, computer programming, early childhood education, education, engineering, health sciences, industrial technology, liberal/general studies, medical laboratory technologies, respiratory therapy technology, secretarial and related programs. **Bachelor's:** Accounting, art education, biochemistry, biology, business administration and management, business and management, chemistry, clinical laboratory science, communications, computer and information sciences, counseling psychology, early childhood education, education, elementary education, English, English education, graphic arts technology, health care administration, health sciences, health/fitness management, history, information sciences and systems, journalism, liberal/general studies, mathematics, mathematics education, music, music education, nursing, organizational behavior, physics, predentistry, premedicine, prepharmacy, preveterinary, psychology, radio/television broadcasting, religion, respiratory therapy, science education, secondary education, social work, theological studies.

ACADEMIC PROGRAMS. Cooperative education, double major, dual enrollment of high school students, external degree, independent study, internships, student-designed major, study abroad, teacher preparation, cross-registration. **Remedial services:** Learning center, preadmission summer program, reduced course load, remedial instruction, special counselor. **Placement/credit:** AP, CLEP Subject, institutional tests; 12 credit hours maximum for associate degree; 24 credit hours maximum for bachelor's degree.

ACADEMIC REQUIREMENTS. Freshmen must earn minimum GPA of 2.0 to continue in good standing. 67% of freshmen return for sophomore year. Students must declare major by end of second year. **Graduation requirements:** 64 hours for associate (18 in major), 128 hours for bachelor's (30 in major). Most students required to take courses in English, history, humanities, mathematics, philosophy/religion, biological/physical sciences, social sciences. **Postgraduate studies:** 62% from 2-year programs enter 4-year programs.

FRESHMAN ADMISSIONS. Selection criteria: High school GPA of 2.5, school achievement record, test scores, recommendations, and interviews. **High school preparation:** 14 units required. Required and recommended units include English 4, mathematics 2, social science 2-3 and science 2. Foreign language 2 recommended. Computer science also recommended. **Test requirements:** SAT or ACT (ACT preferred); score report by August 1.

1992 FRESHMAN CLASS PROFILE. 528 men and women applied, 342 accepted; 40 men enrolled, 72 women enrolled. 54% had high school GPA of 3.0 or higher, 41% between 2.0 and 2.99. **Academic background:** Mid 50% of enrolled freshmen had SAT-V between 370-490, SAT-M between 360-590; ACT composite between 17-23. 61% submitted SAT scores, 40% submitted ACT scores. **Characteristics:** 30% from in state, 50% commute, 62% have minority backgrounds, 12% are foreign students. Average age is 20.

FALL-TERM APPLICATIONS. $15 fee, may be waived for applicants with need. Closing date August 15; applicants notified on a rolling basis. Interview required for non-Seventh-day Adventist applicants. Audition required for music applicants. Essay recommended. Deferred and early admission available. Applications accepted until last day of registration, applications should be completed by August 1 to insure processing by registration.

STUDENT LIFE. Housing: Dormitories (men, women). **Activities:** Student government, radio, student newspaper, television, yearbook, choral groups, concert band, drama, music ensembles, Metro Ministries, Humanitas. **Additional information:** Attendance required at weekly chapel service. Dormitories have daily worship. Religious observance required.

ATHLETICS. NAIA. **Intercollegiate:** Basketball, cross-country, gymnastics, soccer M, softball W, tennis, track and field, volleyball W. **Intramural:** Badminton, basketball, racquetball, soccer M, softball, volleyball.

STUDENT SERVICES. Career counseling, employment service for undergraduates, freshman orientation, health services, personal counseling, placement service for graduates, special adviser for adult students, services/facilities for handicapped.

ANNUAL EXPENSES. Tuition and fees: $9,760. **Room and board:** $3,450. **Books and supplies:** $750. **Other expenses:** $1,000.

FINANCIAL AID. 85% of freshmen, 76% of continuing students receive some form of aid. 31% of grants, 74% of loans, 6% of jobs based on need. Academic, music/drama, athletic, leadership scholarships available. **Aid applications:** Closing date May 31; priority given to applications received by March 31; applicants notified on a rolling basis beginning on or about July 1; must reply within 2 weeks.

ADDRESS/TELEPHONE. Sheila Burnette, Director of Admissions, Columbia Union College, 7600 Flower Avenue, Takoma Park, MD 20912. (301) 891-4080. (800) 835-4212. Fax: (301) 270-1618.

Coppin State College
Baltimore, Maryland — CB code: 5122

4-year public nursing, liberal arts, teachers college, coed. Founded in 1900. **Accreditation:** Regional. **Undergraduate enrollment:** 710 men, 1,153 women full time; 212 men, 563 women part time. **Graduate enrollment:** 5 men, 17 women full time; 83 men, 201 women part time. **Faculty:** 105 total. **Location:** Urban campus in very large city; 50 miles from Washington, D.C. **Calendar:** Semester, extensive summer session. **Microcomputers:** 90 located in libraries, classrooms, computer centers. **Special facilities:** Cab Calloway museum.

DEGREES OFFERED. BA, BS, MA, MS. 235 bachelor's degrees awarded in 1992. 18% in business and management, 6% education, 22% health sciences, 10% parks/recreation, protective services, public affairs, 17% psychology, 13% social sciences. Graduate degrees offered in 9 major fields of study.

UNDERGRADUATE MAJORS. African studies, Afro-American (black) studies, biology, business administration and management, chemistry, computer and information sciences, counseling psychology, criminal justice studies, education of the emotionally handicapped, education of the mentally handicapped, education of the multiple handicapped, education of the physically handicapped, elementary education, English, English literature, history, law enforcement and corrections, mathematics, nursing, philosophy, predentistry, premedicine, prepharmacy, psychology, secondary education, social sciences, social work, special education, specific learning disabilities.

ACADEMIC PROGRAMS. Cooperative education, double major, dual enrollment of high school students, honors program, independent study, internships, teacher preparation, weekend college, cross-registration; liberal arts/career combination in engineering. **Remedial services:** Learning center, remedial instruction, tutoring. **ROTC:** Army. **Placement/credit:** AP, CLEP General and Subject, institutional tests; 30 credit hours maximum for bachelor's degree.

ACADEMIC REQUIREMENTS. Freshmen must earn minimum GPA of 2.0 to continue in good standing. 65% of freshmen return for sophomore year. Students must declare major by end of second year. **Graduation requirements:** 120 hours for bachelor's (43 in major). Most students required to take courses in arts/fine arts, English, foreign languages, history, humanities, mathematics, philosophy/religion, biological/physical sciences, social sciences.

FRESHMAN ADMISSIONS. Selection criteria: Minimum GPA of 2.0 and predictive index based on test scores and school achievement record. **High school preparation:** 20 units required. Required units include biological science 1, English 4, mathematics 3, physical science 1, social science 3 and science 1. **Test requirements:** SAT or ACT (SAT preferred); score report by August 1. SAT required of applicants to nursing school.

1992 FRESHMAN CLASS PROFILE. 204 men, 245 women enrolled. **Characteristics:** 96% from in state, 96% have minority backgrounds, 3% are foreign students. Average age is 19.

FALL-TERM APPLICATIONS. $15 fee, may be waived for applicants with need. Closing date July 15; applicants notified on a rolling basis. Interview recommended for nursing applicants. Portfolio recommended for art applicants. Deferred and early admission available.

STUDENT LIFE. Housing: Dormitories (coed). **Activities:** Student government, film, radio, student newspaper, television, yearbook, choral groups, dance, drama, music ensembles, fraternities, sororities, Muslim Student Association, Korean club.

ATHLETICS. NCAA. **Intercollegiate:** Baseball M, basketball, cross-country, tennis, track and field, volleyball W, wrestling M. **Intramural:** Basketball, racquetball, softball, swimming, tennis, volleyball.

STUDENT SERVICES. Aptitude testing, career counseling, health services, personal counseling, placement service for graduates, veterans counselor, services/facilities for handicapped.

ANNUAL EXPENSES. Tuition and fees (1992-93): $2,605, $2,072 additional for out-of-state students. **Books and supplies:** $500. **Other expenses:** $1,031.

FINANCIAL AID. 48% of freshmen, 80% of continuing students receive some form of aid. 86% of grants, all loans, 68% of jobs based on need. 353 enrolled freshmen were judged to have need, all were offered aid. Athletic, state/district residency scholarships available. **Aid applications:** No closing date; priority given to applications received by April 1; applicants notified on a rolling basis beginning on or about June 1; must reply within 2 weeks. **Additional information:** Funds allocated by State of Maryland for minority students enrolled for at least 6 credits who are Maryland residents and U.S. citizens (Other Race Grant).

ADDRESS/TELEPHONE. Allen Mosley, Director of Admissions, Coppin State College, 2500 West North Avenue, Baltimore, MD 21216. (410) 383-5990. Fax: (410) 333-5894.

Dundalk Community College
Baltimore, Maryland — CB code: 5176

2-year public community college, coed. Founded in 1970. **Accreditation:** Regional. **Undergraduate enrollment:** 268 men, 323 women full time; 1,115 men, 1,677 women part time. **Faculty:** 237 total (58 full time), 19 with doctorates or other terminal degrees. **Location:** Urban campus in very large city; 10 miles from downtown. **Calendar:** Semester, extensive summer session. Saturday and extensive evening/early morning classes. **Microcomputers:** 150 located in classrooms, computer centers. **Special facilities:** Art gallery, college/community theater.

DEGREES OFFERED. AA. 230 associate degrees awarded in 1992. 15% in business and management, 10% computer sciences, 8% allied health, 10% law, 27% multi/interdisciplinary studies, 10% trade and industry, 7% visual and performing arts.

UNDERGRADUATE MAJORS. Accounting, air conditioning/heating/refrigeration mechanics, arts and sciences, business administration and management, business and management, child development/care/guidance, computer programming, educational media technology, electrical and electronics equipment repair, elementary education, geriatric services, industrial equipment maintenance and repair, labor/industrial relations, legal assistant/paralegal, liberal/general studies, ornamental horticulture, photographic technology, power plant operation and maintenance, real estate, rehabilitation counseling/services, secondary education, secretarial and related programs, special education.

ACADEMIC PROGRAMS. 2-year transfer program, cooperative education, dual enrollment of high school students, honors program, independent study, internships, teacher preparation, telecourses, weekend college, cross-registration. **Remedial services:** Learning center, reduced course load, remedial instruction, tutoring. **Placement/credit:** AP, CLEP General and Subject, institutional tests; 30 credit hours maximum for associate degree.

ACADEMIC REQUIREMENTS. Freshmen must earn minimum GPA of 2.0 to continue in good standing. 55% of freshmen return for sophomore year. Students must declare major on enrollment. **Graduation requirements:** 60 hours for associate. Most students required to take courses in English, mathematics, biological/physical sciences, social sciences. **Additional information:** Assessment of Prior Learning Program enables students to have prior learning evaluated for college credit (on-the-job experiences, apprenticeship programs, military experience, technical school training, courses required by employer, or high school vocational and academic classes).

FRESHMAN ADMISSIONS. Selection criteria: Open admissions.

1992 FRESHMAN CLASS PROFILE. 331 men, 457 women enrolled. **Characteristics:** 100% commute, 19% have minority backgrounds.

FALL-TERM APPLICATIONS. $10 fee. No closing date; applicants notified on a rolling basis. Early admission available.

STUDENT LIFE. Activities: Student government, student newspaper, television, literary magazine, choral groups, dance, drama, musical theater, Black Student Union, Political Science Club, Service Club, Computer Club, Paralegal Club, International Club, Honors Club, Peer Couseling Club, Programming Board, Students for a Brighter Tomorrow.

ATHLETICS. NJCAA. **Intercollegiate:** Baseball M, basketball, bowling, soccer, softball W, tennis, volleyball W.

STUDENT SERVICES. Aptitude testing, career counseling, on-campus day care, personal counseling, placement service for graduates, veterans counselor, services for disabled peer tutoring, services/facilities for handicapped.

ANNUAL EXPENSES. Tuition and fees (projected): $1,570, $1,290

additional for out-of-district students, $3,090 additional for out-of-state students. **Books and supplies:** $600. **Other expenses:** $1,000.

FINANCIAL AID. 29% of continuing students receive some form of aid. 95% of grants, 67% of jobs based on need. Academic, athletic, state/district residency, leadership scholarships available. **Aid applications:** No closing date; priority given to applications received by April 15; applicants notified on a rolling basis beginning on or about June 1; must reply within 4 weeks.

ADDRESS/TELEPHONE. Karen McKenney, Director of Admissions and Enrollment Development, Dundalk Community College, 7200 Sollers Point Road, Baltimore, MD 21222-4692. (410) 282-6700. Fax: (410) 285-9903.

Essex Community College
Baltimore, Maryland CB code: 5192

2-year public community college, coed. Founded in 1957. **Accreditation:** Regional. **Undergraduate enrollment:** 1,427 men, 1,600 women full time; 2,983 men, 4,752 women part time. **Faculty:** 565 total (185 full time), 93 with doctorates or other terminal degrees. **Location:** Suburban campus in very large city; 8 miles from downtown. **Calendar:** 4-1-4, limited summer session. **Microcomputers:** 100 located in classrooms, computer centers. **Special facilities:** Recital hall.

DEGREES OFFERED. AA. 886 associate degrees awarded in 1992. 17% in business/office and marketing/distribution, 17% health sciences, 54% multi/interdisciplinary studies.

UNDERGRADUATE MAJORS. Accounting, business and management, business and office, computer and information sciences, computer servicing technology, computer technology, criminal justice technology, data processing, drafting and design technology, early childhood education, electrodiagnostic technologies, electronic technology, emergency medical technologies, engineering, histology, hotel/motel and restaurant management, liberal/general studies, marketing management, medical laboratory technologies, medical radiation dosimetry, medical records technology, mental health/human services, nuclear medical technology, nursing, personnel management, physician's assistant, radiograph medical technology, secondary education, secretarial and related programs, ultrasound technology, veterinarian's assistant.

ACADEMIC PROGRAMS. 2-year transfer program, cooperative education, dual enrollment of high school students, honors program, independent study, internships, telecourses. **Remedial services:** Learning center, remedial instruction, special counselor, tutoring, structured reading and writing career for non-English speaking students. **ROTC:** Army. **Placement/credit:** AP, CLEP General and Subject, institutional tests; 45 credit hours maximum for associate degree.

ACADEMIC REQUIREMENTS. Freshmen must earn minimum GPA of 1.6 to continue in good standing. **Graduation requirements:** 60 hours for associate. Most students required to take courses in arts/fine arts, English, mathematics, biological/physical sciences, social sciences.

FRESHMAN ADMISSIONS. Selection criteria: Open admissions. Selective admission to some programs. Biology, chemistry, and algebra required of all allied health applicants.

1992 FRESHMAN CLASS PROFILE. 841 men, 944 women enrolled.

FALL-TERM APPLICATIONS. $10 fee. No closing date; applicants notified on a rolling basis. Interview required for allied health applicants. Audition required for some music applicants. Early admission available.

STUDENT LIFE. Activities: Student government, radio, student newspaper, television, choral groups, concert band, dance, drama, music ensembles, musical theater, symphony orchestra, fraternities.

ATHLETICS. NJCAA. **Intercollegiate:** Basketball, bowling, cross-country, field hockey, golf M, lacrosse, soccer, softball W, track and field, volleyball W.

STUDENT SERVICES. Aptitude testing, career counseling, on-campus day care, personal counseling, placement service for graduates, veterans counselor, services/facilities for handicapped.

ANNUAL EXPENSES. Tuition and fees (1992-93): $1,418, $1,162 additional for out-of-district students, $2,738 additional for out-of-state students. **Books and supplies:** $500.

FINANCIAL AID. 98% of grants, 70% of loans, 74% of jobs based on need. Academic, music/drama, athletic, leadership, minority scholarships available. **Aid applications:** No closing date; priority given to applications received by July 1; applicants notified on a rolling basis beginning on or about April 15; must reply within 2 weeks. **Additional information:** Tuition waiver for handicapped applicants.

ADDRESS/TELEPHONE. Diane C. Lane, Director of Admissions, Essex Community College, 7201 Rossville Boulevard, Baltimore, MD 21237-3899. (410) 780-6840. Fax: (410) 686-9503.

Frederick Community College
Frederick, Maryland CB code: 5230

2-year public community college, coed. Founded in 1957. **Accreditation:** Regional. **Undergraduate enrollment:** 4,336 men and women. **Faculty:** 278 total (78 full time), 13 with doctorates or other terminal degrees. **Location:** Suburban campus in large town; 40 miles from Washington, D.C. and Baltimore. **Calendar:** Semester, limited summer session. **Microcomputers:** Located in computer centers.

DEGREES OFFERED. AA. 389 associate degrees awarded in 1992. 25% in business and management, 5% education, 8% health sciences, 50% multi/interdisciplinary studies.

UNDERGRADUATE MAJORS. Accounting, aeronautical technology, agribusiness, agricultural sciences, aircraft mechanics, biological laboratory technology, biology, business administration and management, business and management, business and office, business computer/console/peripheral equipment operation, business data processing and related programs, communications, computer and information sciences, computer programming, computer technology, construction management, criminal justice studies, data processing, drafting, drafting and design technology, early childhood education, education, electronic technology, elementary education, engineering, English, finance, fine arts, history, information sciences and systems, legal assistant/paralegal, legal secretary, liberal/general studies, management information systems, marketing and distribution, mathematics, mathematics education, medical secretary, mental health/human services, music, music education, nursing, parks and recreation management, philosophy, political science and government, psychology, secretarial and related programs, wildlife management.

ACADEMIC PROGRAMS. 2-year transfer program, cooperative education, honors program, independent study, cross-registration. **Remedial services:** Learning center, reduced course load, remedial instruction, tutoring. **Placement/credit:** AP, CLEP General and Subject; 30 credit hours maximum for associate degree.

ACADEMIC REQUIREMENTS. No policy requiring minimum GPA; records of students having academic difficulty are reviewed individually. **Graduation requirements:** 60 hours for associate. Most students required to take courses in English, humanities, mathematics, biological/physical sciences, social sciences.

FRESHMAN ADMISSIONS. Selection criteria: Open admissions. RN nursing, LPN nursing, respiratory therapy, and aviation maintenance technology have selective admission. Students must show successful completion of appropriate general education requirements.

1992 FRESHMAN CLASS PROFILE. 528 men, 834 women enrolled. **Characteristics:** 99% from in state, 100% commute, 9% have minority backgrounds, 1% are foreign students. Average age is 23.

FALL-TERM APPLICATIONS. $15 fee, may be waived for applicants with need. No closing date; applicants notified on a rolling basis beginning on or about January 1. Interview required of nursing, aviation, respiratory therapy applicants, recommended for all others. Application deadline for nursing applicants December 15, Aviation Applicants March 1.

STUDENT LIFE. Activities: Student government, magazine, student newspaper, choral groups, drama, jazz band, music ensembles, Circle-K, Phi Theta Kappa.

ATHLETICS. NJCAA. **Intercollegiate:** Baseball M, basketball, golf M, soccer M, volleyball W.

STUDENT SERVICES. Aptitude testing, career counseling, employment service for undergraduates, freshman orientation, personal counseling, placement service for graduates, special adviser for adult students, veterans counselor, services/facilities for handicapped.

ANNUAL EXPENSES. Tuition and fees: $2,003, $1,800 additional for out-of-district students, $3,990 additional for out-of-state students. **Books and supplies:** $600. **Other expenses:** $775.

FINANCIAL AID. 15% of freshmen, 22% of continuing students receive some form of aid. 91% of grants, 68% of loans, 47% of jobs based on need. Academic, music/drama, art, athletic, state/district residency, minority scholarships available. **Aid applications:** No closing date; priority given to applications received by June 15; applicants notified on a rolling basis beginning on or about June 1; must reply within 2 weeks.

ADDRESS/TELEPHONE. Dr. James M. Holton, Director of Admissions and Records, Frederick Community College, 7932 Opossumtown Pike, Frederick, MD 21702. (301) 846-2430. Fax: (301) 846-2498.

Frostburg State University
Frostburg, Maryland CB code: 5402

Admissions: 69% of applicants accepted
Based on: ••• School record, test scores
• Activities, interview, recommendations, special talents
Completion: 41% graduate, 24% of these enter graduate study

4-year public university and college of arts and sciences, coed. Founded in 1898. **Accreditation:** Regional. **Undergraduate enrollment:** 2,024 men, 2,015 women full time; 182 men, 270 women part time. **Graduate enrollment:** 79 men, 90 women full time; 290 men, 345 women part time. **Faculty:** 305 total (234 full time), 169 with doctorates or other terminal degrees. **Location:** Rural campus in small town; 10 miles from Cumberland, 150 miles from

Baltimore and Washington, D.C. **Calendar:** Semester, extensive summer session. **Microcomputers:** 165 located in libraries, classrooms, computer centers. **Special facilities:** Art gallery, planetarium, arboretum. **Additional facts:** Center in Hagerstown, MD, offers upper-division undergraduate and graduate courses. MBA courses offered in Frederick, MD.

DEGREES OFFERED. BA, BS, BFA, MA, MS, MBA, MEd. 857 bachelor's degrees awarded in 1992. 30% in business and management, 11% teacher education, 8% multi/interdisciplinary studies, 7% psychology, 17% social sciences. Graduate degrees offered in 16 major fields of study.

UNDERGRADUATE MAJORS. Accounting, actuarial sciences, art education, biology, business and management, business education, chemistry, computer and information sciences, criminal justice studies, early childhood education, earth sciences, economics, elementary education, English, English education, environmental science, fine arts, fishing and fisheries, French, geography, graphic design, history, international studies, journalism, junior high education, mathematics, mathematics education, music, music education, parks and recreation management, philosophy, physical education, physical sciences, physics, political science and government, predentistry, preengineering, prelaw, premedicine, prepharmacy, preveterinary, psychology, secondary education, social science education, social sciences, social work, sociology, Spanish, speech, speech/communication/theater education, visual and performing arts, wildlife management.

ACADEMIC PROGRAMS. Double major, honors program, independent study, internships, study abroad, teacher preparation, telecourses, visiting/exchange student program, cross-registration; liberal arts/career combination in engineering, health sciences; combined bachelor's/graduate program in law. **Remedial services:** Learning center, reduced course load, remedial instruction, special counselor, tutoring. **ROTC:** Army. **Placement/credit:** AP, CLEP General and Subject, institutional tests; 30 credit hours maximum for bachelor's degree.

ACADEMIC REQUIREMENTS. Freshmen must earn minimum GPA of 2.0 to continue in good standing. 78% of freshmen return for sophomore year. Students must declare major by end of second year. **Graduation requirements:** 120 hours for bachelor's (30 in major). Most students required to take courses in arts/fine arts, computer science, English, history, humanities, mathematics, philosophy/religion, biological/physical sciences, social sciences.

FRESHMAN ADMISSIONS. Selection criteria: High school record most important. SAT scores also considered. **High school preparation:** 14 units required. Required units include English 4, foreign language 2, mathematics 3, social science 3 and science 2. **Test requirements:** SAT or ACT (SAT preferred); score report by June 1.

1992 FRESHMAN CLASS PROFILE. 1,646 men applied, 1,058 accepted, 392 enrolled; 1,817 women applied, 1,326 accepted, 469 enrolled. 30% had high school GPA of 3.0 or higher, 66% between 2.0 and 2.99. **Academic background:** Mid 50% of enrolled freshmen had SAT-V between 380-480, SAT-M between 420-530. 99% submitted SAT scores. **Characteristics:** 84% from in state, 81% live in college housing, 14% have minority backgrounds, 1% are foreign students. Average age is 19.

FALL-TERM APPLICATIONS. $30 fee, may be waived for applicants with need. No closing date; priority given to applications received by April 1; applicants notified on a rolling basis beginning on or about December 1; must reply by April 1st or within 4 weeks if notified thereafter. Audition required for music applicants. Portfolio required for art applicants. Interview recommended. Early admission available.

STUDENT LIFE. Housing: Dormitories (men, women, coed). **Activities:** Student government, magazine, radio, student newspaper, yearbook, choral groups, concert band, dance, drama, jazz band, marching band, music ensembles, musical theater, pep band, fraternities, sororities, social, religious, political, and ethnic organizations.

ATHLETICS. NCAA. **Intercollegiate:** Baseball M, basketball, cross-country, diving, field hockey W, football M, lacrosse W, soccer M, swimming, tennis, track and field. **Intramural:** Badminton, basketball, bowling, field hockey W, lacrosse M, racquetball, rugby, skiing, soccer, softball, squash, tennis, volleyball.

STUDENT SERVICES. Aptitude testing, career counseling, employment service for undergraduates, freshman orientation, health services, on-campus day care, personal counseling, placement service for graduates, veterans counselor, services/facilities for handicapped.

ANNUAL EXPENSES. Tuition and fees (projected): $2,666, $2,628 additional for out-of-state students. **Room and board:** $4,198. **Books and supplies:** $550. **Other expenses:** $750.

FINANCIAL AID. 58% of freshmen, 63% of continuing students receive some form of aid. 93% of grants, 94% of loans, 50% of jobs based on need. 400 enrolled freshmen were judged to have need, all were offered aid. Academic, music/drama, art, leadership, alumni affiliation, minority scholarships available. **Aid applications:** No closing date; priority given to applications received by April 1; applicants notified on a rolling basis beginning on or about May 1; must reply within 2 weeks.

ADDRESS/TELEPHONE. David L. Sanford, Dean of Admissions, Frostburg State University, Frostburg, MD 21532-1099. (301) 689-4201. Fax: (301) 689-4737.

Garrett Community College
McHenry, Maryland — CB code: 5279

2-year public community college, coed. Founded in 1971. **Accreditation:** Regional. **Undergraduate enrollment:** 664 men and women. **Location:** Rural campus in rural community; 45 miles from Cumberland, 40 miles from Morgantown, West Virginia. **Calendar:** Semester.

FRESHMAN ADMISSIONS. Selection criteria: Open admissions.

ANNUAL EXPENSES. Tuition and fees (projected): $1,650, $540 additional for out-of-district students, $2,040 additional for out-of-state students. **Books and supplies:** $500. **Other expenses:** $750.

ADDRESS/TELEPHONE. Darlene Tressler, Administrative Assistant, Garrett Community College, Mosser Road, McHenry, MD 21541. (301) 387-6666. Fax: (301) 387-3055.

Goucher College
Baltimore, Maryland — CB code: 5257

Admissions:	71% of applicants accepted
Based on:	••• Essay, interview, school record
	•• Activities, recommendations, test scores
	• Special talents
Completion:	87% of freshmen end year in good standing
	70% graduate, 24% of these enter graduate study

4-year private liberal arts college, coed. Founded in 1885. **Accreditation:** Regional. **Undergraduate enrollment:** 247 men, 539 women full time; 5 men, 62 women part time. **Graduate enrollment:** 15 women full time; 3 men, 58 women part time. **Faculty:** 135 total (80 full time), 95 with doctorates or other terminal degrees. **Location:** Suburban campus in very large city; 8 miles from downtown Baltimore. **Calendar:** Semester. **Microcomputers:** 100 located in dormitories, libraries, classrooms, computer centers. **Special facilities:** Observatory, art gallery, Hughes Field Politics Center, Decker Center for Information Technology, Thormann International Center, Meyerhoff Arts Center, Todd Dance Studio. **Additional facts:** Students must complete one off-campus program such as an internship or study abroad.

DEGREES OFFERED. BA, MEd. 181 bachelor's degrees awarded in 1992. 8% in business and management, 10% communications, 6% education, 5% languages, 16% letters/literature, 6% physical sciences, 13% psychology, 17% social sciences, 10% visual and performing arts. Graduate degrees offered in 4 major fields of study.

UNDERGRADUATE MAJORS. American studies, biocomputing, biology, business administration and management, chemistry, cognitive studies, communications, computer and information sciences, dance, dramatic arts, early childhood education, economics, education, elementary education, English, European studies, fine arts, French, historic preservation, history, international relations, international studies, Latin American studies, mathematics, music, philosophy, political science and government, predentistry, prelaw, premedicine, psychology, religion, Russian, Russian and Slavic studies, sociology, Spanish, special education, women's studies.

ACADEMIC PROGRAMS. Accelerated program, double major, dual enrollment of high school students, honors program, independent study, internships, student-designed major, study abroad, teacher preparation, visiting/exchange student program, cross-registration, Teachers Institute, post-baccalaureate premedical program; liberal arts/career combination in health sciences. **Remedial services:** Learning center, reduced course load, special counselor, tutoring. **ROTC:** Army. **Placement/credit:** AP, CLEP General and Subject, institutional tests; 30 credit hours maximum for bachelor's degree.

ACADEMIC REQUIREMENTS. Freshmen must earn minimum GPA of 1.6 to continue in good standing. 84% of freshmen return for sophomore year, Students must declare major by end of second year. **Graduation requirements:** 120 hours for bachelor's (30 in major). Most students required to take courses in arts/fine arts, computer science, English, foreign languages, history, humanities, mathematics, philosophy/religion, biological/physical sciences, social sciences. **Postgraduate studies:** 4% enter law school, 3% enter medical school, 2% enter MBA programs, 15% enter other graduate study. **Additional information:** Study abroad programs at the University of Exeter in England and the Russian Summer Institute at Odessa State Univesity in the Ukraine.

FRESHMAN ADMISSIONS. Selection criteria: Record in traditional college-preparatory program, interview, and essay most important. **High school preparation:** 13 units required; 16 recommended. Required and recommended units include English 4, foreign language 2-3, mathematics 2-3, social science 3 and science 2-3. **Test requirements:** SAT or ACT; score report by February 1.

1992 FRESHMAN CLASS PROFILE. 272 men applied, 170 accepted, 68 enrolled; 627 women applied, 467 accepted, 155 enrolled. 66% had high school GPA of 3.0 or higher, 34% between 2.0 and 2.99. 51% were in top tenth and 62% were in top quarter of graduating class. **Academic background:** Mid 50% of enrolled freshmen had SAT-V between 470-610, SAT-M between 510-630. 100% submitted SAT scores. **Characteristics:** 37% from in state, 90% live in college housing, 11% have minority backgrounds. Average age is 19.

FALL-TERM APPLICATIONS. $35 fee, may be waived for applicants with need. Closing date February 1; priority given to applications received by December 15; applicants notified on or about April 1; must reply by May 1. Essay required. Interview recommended. CRDA. Deferred and early admission available. EDP-F. Achievement tests are strongly recommended.

STUDENT LIFE. Housing: Dormitories (women, coed). Kosher kitchen, cooperative kitchen available. **Activities:** Student government, magazine, student newspaper, yearbook, choral groups, concert band, dance, drama, music ensembles, musical theater, symphony orchestra, Christian Fellowship, Jewish Students Organization, International Students Organization, RAISE (tutorial project), women's center, Black Student Association, CAUSE (community action program), Environmental Concerns Organization, Amnesty International.

ATHLETICS. NCAA. **Intercollegiate:** Basketball, cross-country, diving, field hockey W, horseback riding, lacrosse W, soccer, swimming, tennis, volleyball W. **Intramural:** Archery, basketball, cross-country, diving, fencing, golf, horseback riding, lacrosse, racquetball, rowing (crew), sailing, skiing, soccer, softball, swimming, tennis, volleyball.

STUDENT SERVICES. Aptitude testing, career counseling, employment service for undergraduates, freshman orientation, health services, on-campus day care, personal counseling, placement service for graduates, special adviser for adult students, services/facilities for handicapped.

ANNUAL EXPENSES. Tuition and fees: $14,525. **Room and board:** $5,995. **Books and supplies:** $500. **Other expenses:** $1,100.

FINANCIAL AID. 53% of freshmen, 70% of continuing students receive some form of aid. 67% of grants, 91% of loans, 68% of jobs based on need. 150 enrolled freshmen were judged to have need, all were offered aid. Academic, music/drama, art, leadership scholarships available. **Aid applications:** No closing date; priority given to applications received by February 15; applicants notified on a rolling basis beginning on or about April 1; must reply by May 1 or within 2 weeks if notified thereafter.

ADDRESS/TELEPHONE. Elise A. Seraydarian, Director of Admissions, Goucher College, Dulaney Valley Road, Baltimore, MD 21204. (410) 337-6100. (800) 638-4278. Fax: (410) 337-6123.

Hagerstown Business College
Hagerstown, Maryland — CB code: 0804

2-year proprietary business, junior college, coed. Founded in 1938. **Undergraduate enrollment:** 18 men, 276 women full time; 12 men, 200 women part time. **Faculty:** 29 total (13 full time). **Location:** Suburban campus in large town; 70 miles from Baltimore and Washington, D.C. **Calendar:** Trimester, limited summer session. **Microcomputers:** 72 located in libraries, classrooms. **Additional facts:** College includes medical, legal, business, and office technologies divisions.

DEGREES OFFERED. AAS. 84 associate degrees awarded in 1992. 23% in business/office and marketing/distribution, 21% computer sciences, 29% allied health, 27% law.

UNDERGRADUATE MAJORS. Accounting, business administration and management, court reporting, legal assistant/paralegal, marketing and distribution, medical assistant, medical receptionist transcriptionist, medical records technology, medical secretary, microcomputer software, secretarial and related programs.

ACADEMIC PROGRAMS. Double major, dual enrollment of high school students, internships. **Remedial services:** Remedial instruction, tutoring. **Placement/credit:** CLEP General and Subject, institutional tests; 40 credit hours maximum for associate degree.

ACADEMIC REQUIREMENTS. Freshmen must earn minimum GPA of 1.0 to continue in good standing. 71% of freshmen return for sophomore year. Students must declare major on application. **Graduation requirements:** 68 hours for associate. Most students required to take courses in English.

FRESHMAN ADMISSIONS. Selection criteria: Open admissions.

1992 FRESHMAN CLASS PROFILE. 23 men, 243 women enrolled. **Characteristics:** 42% from in state, 93% commute, 3% have minority backgrounds. Average age is 20.

FALL-TERM APPLICATIONS. $25 fee. No closing date; applicants notified on a rolling basis; must reply within 25 days. Interview recommended. Deferred admission available.

STUDENT LIFE. Housing: Dormitories (coed). **Activities:** Student government, sororities.

STUDENT SERVICES. Career counseling, freshman orientation, health services, personal counseling, placement service for graduates, services/facilities for handicapped.

ANNUAL EXPENSES. Tuition and fees (1992-93): $3,560. **Room and board:** $1,590 room only. **Books and supplies:** $650. **Other expenses:** $325.

FINANCIAL AID. 92% of freshmen, 90% of continuing students receive some form of aid. 89% of grants, 91% of loans, all jobs based on need. 160 enrolled freshmen were judged to have need, all were offered aid. Academic, state/district residency, leadership scholarships available. **Aid applications:** No closing date; priority given to applications received by October 31; applicants notified on a rolling basis beginning on or about June 1; must reply within 2 weeks.

ADDRESS/TELEPHONE. Teresa Adams, Director of Admissions, Hagerstown Business College, 18618 Crestwood Drive, Hagerstown, MD 21742. (301) 739-2670. (800) 422-2670. Fax: (301) 791-7661.

Hagerstown Junior College
Hagerstown, Maryland — CB code: 5290

2-year public community college, coed. Founded in 1946. **Accreditation:** Regional. **Undergraduate enrollment:** 685 men, 537 women full time; 735 men, 1,232 women part time. **Faculty:** 187 total (57 full time), 26 with doctorates or other terminal degrees. **Location:** Suburban campus in large town; 70 miles from Washington, D.C. and Baltimore. **Calendar:** Semester, extensive summer session. Saturday and extensive evening/early morning classes. **Microcomputers:** 130 located in classrooms, computer centers. **Special facilities:** Advanced technology center.

DEGREES OFFERED. AA. 427 associate degrees awarded in 1992. 28% in business and management, 9% education, 10% allied health, 24% multi/interdisciplinary studies, 10% parks/recreation, protective services, public affairs.

UNDERGRADUATE MAJORS. Accounting, biology, business administration and management, business data processing and related programs, chemistry, computer and information sciences, data processing, education, electronic technology, engineering, engineering and engineering-related technologies, hotel/motel and restaurant management, human services technologies, law enforcement and corrections technologies, liberal/general studies, management science, mathematics, mechanical design technology, mechanical technology with energy option, nursing, physical education, physics, radio/television broadcasting, radiograph medical technology, secretarial and related programs, teacher aide.

ACADEMIC PROGRAMS. 2-year transfer program, accelerated program, cooperative education, dual enrollment of high school students, independent study, internships, telecourses, cross-registration. **Remedial services:** Learning center, preadmission summer program, remedial instruction, tutoring. **Placement/credit:** AP, CLEP General and Subject, institutional tests; 32 credit hours maximum for associate degree.

ACADEMIC REQUIREMENTS. Freshmen must earn minimum GPA of 1.8 to continue in good standing. 70% of freshmen return for sophomore year. Students must declare major on enrollment. **Graduation requirements:** 64 hours for associate. Most students required to take courses in English, humanities, mathematics, social sciences.

FRESHMAN ADMISSIONS. Selection criteria: Open admissions. Selective admissions to nursing and radiologic technologies programs based on 2.0 GPA, ACT composite score of 20, 1 laboratory chemistry and algebra. One chemistry, 1 biology, 2 algebra required of nursing applicants; 1 physics, 1 chemistry, 2 algebra required of radiologic technologies applicants. **Test requirements:** SAT or ACT for placement and counseling only; score report by September 1.

1992 FRESHMAN CLASS PROFILE. 426 men, 418 women enrolled. **Academic background:** Mid 50% of enrolled freshmen had ACT composite between 20-33. 35% submitted ACT scores. **Characteristics:** 80% from in state, 100% commute, 11% have minority backgrounds. Average age is 27.

FALL-TERM APPLICATIONS. $10 fee. Closing date September 1; applicants notified on a rolling basis. Interview required for nursing, radiologic technology applicants. Deferred and early admission available.

STUDENT LIFE. Activities: Student government, student newspaper, choral groups, drama, jazz band.

ATHLETICS. NJCAA. **Intercollegiate:** Baseball M, basketball, cross-country, soccer M, tennis, track and field, volleyball W. **Intramural:** Bowling, racquetball, softball, table tennis.

STUDENT SERVICES. Aptitude testing, career counseling, employment service for undergraduates, freshman orientation, personal counseling, placement service for graduates, veterans counselor, services/facilities for handicapped.

ANNUAL EXPENSES. Tuition and fees: $1,950, $750 additional for out-of-district students, $1,530 additional for out-of-state students. **Books and supplies:** $480. **Other expenses:** $200.

FINANCIAL AID. 50% of freshmen, 42% of continuing students receive some form of aid. 93% of grants, 67% of loans, 58% of jobs based on need. 550 enrolled freshmen were judged to have need, all were offered aid. Academic, athletic scholarships available. **Aid applications:** No closing date; priority given to applications received by June 15; applicants notified on a rolling basis beginning on or about June 15; must reply within 2 weeks.

ADDRESS/TELEPHONE. Dr. Max E. Creager, Director of Admissions/Registrar, Hagerstown Junior College, 11400 Robinwood Drive, Hagerstown, MD 21742-6590. (301) 790-2800. Fax: (301) 733-4229.

Harford Community College
Bel Air, Maryland — CB code: 5303

2-year public community college, coed. Founded in 1957. **Accreditation:**

Regional. **Undergraduate enrollment:** 625 men, 779 women full time; 1,518 men, 2,586 women part time. **Faculty:** 364 total (82 full time), 24 with doctorates or other terminal degrees. **Location:** Suburban campus in small town; 25 miles from Baltimore. **Calendar:** Semester, limited summer session. Saturday and extensive evening/early morning classes. **Microcomputers:** 150 located in libraries, classrooms, computer centers. **Special facilities:** Observatory, art gallery.

DEGREES OFFERED. AA, AS. 374 associate degrees awarded in 1992. 23% in business and management, 8% computer sciences, 5% teacher education, 15% health sciences, 7% allied health, 18% multi/interdisciplinary studies.

UNDERGRADUATE MAJORS. Accounting, automotive technology, behavioral sciences, biology, business administration and management, business and management, business and office, chemistry, commercial art, computer and information sciences, criminal justice technology, early childhood education, electrodiagnostic technologies, electronic technology, elementary education, engineering, English, fine arts, histology, history, hotel/motel and restaurant management, humanities and social sciences, information sciences and systems, interior design, legal assistant/paralegal, liberal/general studies, mathematics, medical laboratory technologies, music, nursing, philosophy, photography, physics, political science and government, psychology, public relations, radio/television broadcasting, retailing, science technologies, secondary education, secretarial and related programs, sociology.

ACADEMIC PROGRAMS. 2-year transfer program, cooperative education, double major, dual enrollment of high school students, independent study, internships, telecourses. **Remedial services:** Learning center, reduced course load, remedial instruction, special counselor, tutoring. **Placement/credit:** AP, CLEP General and Subject, institutional tests; 30 credit hours maximum for associate degree.

ACADEMIC REQUIREMENTS. Freshmen must earn minimum GPA of 2.0 to continue in good standing. Students must declare major on enrollment. **Graduation requirements:** 62 hours for associate. Most students required to take courses in English, history, humanities, mathematics, biological/physical sciences, social sciences.

FRESHMAN ADMISSIONS. Selection criteria: Open admissions. Some restrictions apply for applicants under 16 years old and non-U.S. citizens. Nursing program has specific selection criteria. Recommended units include English 4 and mathematics 2. Several degree programs require additional preparation. Students not meeting basic requirements must complete transitional courses.

1992 FRESHMAN CLASS PROFILE. 510 men, 645 women enrolled. **Characteristics:** 99% from in state, 100% commute, 12% have minority backgrounds.

FALL-TERM APPLICATIONS. No fee. No closing date; applicants notified on a rolling basis beginning on or about February 1. Interview recommended. Early admission available. Application deadline for nursing students August 1, notification August 15, accepted applicants must reply within 2 weeks.

STUDENT LIFE. Activities: Student government, film, magazine, radio, student newspaper, television, student handbook, quarterly calendar, choral groups, concert band, dance, drama, jazz band, music ensembles, musical theater, Campus Christian Life Club, Black Student Union.

ATHLETICS. NJCAA. **Intercollegiate:** Baseball M, basketball, cross-country M, field hockey W, golf, lacrosse, soccer M, softball W, tennis.

STUDENT SERVICES. Aptitude testing, career counseling, employment service for undergraduates, freshman orientation, on-campus day care, personal counseling, placement service for graduates, veterans counselor, services/facilities for handicapped.

ANNUAL EXPENSES. Tuition and fees: $1,814, $1,020 additional for out-of-district students, $2,310 additional for out-of-state students. **Books and supplies:** $600. **Other expenses:** $800.

FINANCIAL AID. 35% of continuing students receive some form of aid. 74% of grants, 51% of loans, all jobs based on need. Academic, music/drama, athletic, state/district residency, leadership scholarships available. **Aid applications:** No closing date; priority given to applications received by May 1; applicants notified on a rolling basis beginning on or about May 15; must reply within 2 weeks. **Additional information:** 2 emergency loan programs offered. Repayment in 2 to 4 installments.

ADDRESS/TELEPHONE. Jackie Strzelczyk, Director of Admissions, Harford Community College, 401 Thomas Run Road, Bel Air, MD 21015. (410) 836-4223. Fax: (410) 836-4197.

Hood College
Frederick, Maryland

CB code: 5296

Admissions: 79% of applicants accepted
Based on:
••• School record, test scores
•• Essay, recommendations
• Activities, interview, special talents
Completion: 95% of freshmen end year in good standing
65% graduate, 30% of these enter graduate study

4-year private liberal arts college, women only, affiliated with United Church of Christ. Founded in 1893. **Accreditation:** Regional. **Undergraduate enrollment:** 42 men, 666 women full time; 110 men, 256 women part time. **Graduate enrollment:** 13 men, 14 women full time; 322 men, 582 women part time. **Faculty:** 87 total (74 full time), 79 with doctorates or other terminal degrees. **Location:** Suburban campus in small city; 45 miles from Washington, D.C., and Baltimore. **Calendar:** Semester, limited summer session. **Microcomputers:** 116 located in dormitories, libraries, classrooms, computer centers, campus-wide network. **Special facilities:** Language, biology, statistics and psychology laboratories, art gallery, aquatic center, solar heated resource management house, observatory. **Additional facts:** Men living in local area may attend as nonresident students.

DEGREES OFFERED. BA, BS, MA, MS, MBA. 298 bachelor's degrees awarded in 1992. 22% in business and management, 7% communications, 8% teacher education, 7% home economics, 8% letters/literature, 7% life sciences, 6% psychology, 20% social sciences. Graduate degrees offered in 5 major fields of study.

UNDERGRADUATE MAJORS. Biochemistry, biology, business and management, chemistry, communications, computer and information sciences, early childhood education, economics, English, environmental science, fine arts, French, German, history, home economics, Latin American studies, law , mathematics, philosophy, political science and government, psychobiology, psychology, religion, religion and philosophy, social work, sociology, Spanish, special education.

ACADEMIC PROGRAMS. Accelerated program, double major, dual enrollment of high school students, honors program, independent study, internships, student-designed major, study abroad, teacher preparation, Washington semester, interdisciplinary Japanese study course at Tohoku Gakuin University, Japan; liberal arts/career combination in engineering. **Remedial services:** Learning center, reduced course load, remedial instruction, special counselor, tutoring. **Placement/credit:** AP, CLEP Subject, IB, institutional tests; 30 credit hours maximum for bachelor's degree.

ACADEMIC REQUIREMENTS. Freshmen must earn minimum GPA of 2.0 to continue in good standing. 85% of freshmen return for sophomore year. Students must declare major by end of second year. **Graduation requirements:** 124 hours for bachelor's (24 in major). Most students required to take courses in arts/fine arts, computer science, English, foreign languages, history, humanities, mathematics, philosophy/religion, biological/physical sciences, social sciences. **Postgraduate studies:** 2% enter law school, 2% enter medical school, 8% enter MBA programs, 18% enter other graduate study. **Additional information:** Academically exceptional students may participate in 4-year honors program with interdisciplinary courses, seminars, and community service projects. Students in all fields may earn academic credits for internships.

FRESHMAN ADMISSIONS. Selection criteria: High school record, class rank, test scores, personal statement, recommendations, interview, and extracurricular activities considered, as well as contributions to school, family, and community. **High school preparation:** 16 units required. **Test requirements:** SAT or ACT (SAT preferred); score report by March 31. **Additional information:** Applicants may participate in a one-day admissions seminar.

1992 FRESHMAN CLASS PROFILE. 570 men and women applied, 450 accepted; 7 men enrolled, 143 women enrolled. 32% were in top tenth and 66% were in top quarter of graduating class. **Academic background:** Mid 50% of enrolled freshmen had SAT-V between 440-560, SAT-M between 470-600. 97% submitted SAT scores. **Characteristics:** 50% from in state, 92% live in college housing, 35% have minority backgrounds, 5% are foreign students. Average age is 18.

FALL-TERM APPLICATIONS. $20 fee, may be waived for applicants with need. Closing date March 31; applicants notified on or about April 15; must reply by May 1. Essay required. Interview recommended. Portfolio recommended for art applicants. CRDA. Deferred and early admission available. Early reply plan: application closing dates November 15 and January 31; notification dates December 15 and February 15.

STUDENT LIFE. Housing: Dormitories (women). French, Spanish, and German language houses available. **Activities:** Student government, magazine, student newspaper, yearbook, radio club, choral groups, dance, drama, music ensembles, Tambo, Amnesty International, Black Student Union, leadership course, various community service projects, Circle-K, environment club, town hall; Catholic campus ministry. **Additional information:** Students responsible for governing themselves through honor code.

ATHLETICS. NCAA. **Intercollegiate:** Field hockey, lacrosse, swimming, tennis, volleyball. **Intramural:** Archery, badminton, basketball, bowling, fencing, field hockey, horseback riding, lacrosse, racquetball, skiing, softball, swimming, tennis, volleyball.

STUDENT SERVICES. Career counseling, freshman orientation, health services, personal counseling, placement service for graduates, special adviser for adult students, Financial aid counselor; library services; transportation services; learning assessment & resource center; workshops; placement testing.

ANNUAL EXPENSES. Tuition and fees: $13,258. **Room and board:** $5,752. **Books and supplies:** $400. **Other expenses:** $700.

FINANCIAL AID. 80% of freshmen, 78% of continuing students receive some form of aid. 72% of grants, 85% of loans, all jobs based on need. 104 enrolled freshmen were judged to have need, all were offered aid. Academic, leadership, minority scholarships available. **Aid applications:** No closing date; priority given to applications received by March 31; applicants notified on a rolling basis beginning on or about March 1; must reply by May 1 or within 2 weeks if notified thereafter. **Additional information:** Loans for students who need additional assistance but are not eligible for federal programs, and institutional scholarships not based on need including scholarships targeted for African-Americans and Hispanics.

ADDRESS/TELEPHONE. Nancy Gillece, Director of Admissions, Hood College, 401 Rosemont Avenue, Frederick, MD 21701-8575. (301) 696-3400. (800) 922-1599. Fax: (301) 694-7653.

Howard Community College
Columbia, Maryland CB code: 5308

2-year public community college, coed. Founded in 1966. **Accreditation:** Regional. **Undergraduate enrollment:** 618 men, 618 women full time; 1,302 men, 2,423 women part time. **Faculty:** 289 total (84 full time), 34 with doctorates or other terminal degrees. **Location:** Suburban campus in small city; 31 miles from Washington, D.C., 18 miles from Baltimore. **Calendar:** Semester, limited summer session. Saturday classes. **Microcomputers:** 250 located in libraries, computer centers. **Special facilities:** Learning resource center, theater.

DEGREES OFFERED. AA. 243 associate degrees awarded in 1992. 26% in business and management, 6% computer sciences, 11% teacher education, 19% health sciences, 32% multi/interdisciplinary studies.

UNDERGRADUATE MAJORS. Accounting, art history, astronomy, atmospheric sciences and meteorology, bacteriology, biological and physical sciences, biology, biomedical equipment technology, botany, business administration and management, business and management, business and office, business computer/console/peripheral equipment operation, business data processing and related programs, business data programming, business education, ceramics, chemical manufacturing technology, chemistry, civil technology, computer and information sciences, computer programming, computer servicing technology, computer technology, crafts, data processing, dramatic arts, drawing, economics, education, electrical technology, electrical/electronics/communications engineering, electronic technology, elementary education, engineering and engineering-related technologies, English, fiber/textiles/weaving, fine arts, health sciences, history, information sciences and systems, international business management, legal secretary, liberal/general studies, marketing and distribution, medical secretary, microbiology, microcomputer software, music, music performance, nursing, office supervision and management, painting, photography, physical sciences, physics, physiology, human and animal, political science and government, predentistry, preengineering, prelaw, premedicine, prepharmacy, preveterinary, psychology, retailing, sculpture, secondary education, secretarial and related programs, social sciences, sociology, studio art, theater design, word processing, zoology.

ACADEMIC PROGRAMS. 2-year transfer program, cooperative education, double major, dual enrollment of high school students, honors program, independent study, internships, teacher preparation, telecourses, weekend college. **Remedial services:** Learning center, reduced course load, remedial instruction, special counselor, tutoring. **Placement/credit:** AP, CLEP General and Subject, institutional tests; 30 credit hours maximum for associate degree.

ACADEMIC REQUIREMENTS. No policy requiring minimum GPA; records of students having academic difficulty are reviewed individually. 47% of freshmen return for sophomore year. Students must declare major by end of first year. **Graduation requirements:** 62 hours for associate (40 in major). Most students required to take courses in arts/fine arts, English, humanities, mathematics, social sciences. **Additional information:** Mandatory Assessment Policy-all students must complete placement testing by the time they have completed 12 credits, or take communications or mathmatics courses.

FRESHMAN ADMISSIONS. Selection criteria: Open admissions. Clinical nursing applicants must complete any college preparatory courses indicated by placement results and our first science course (Integrated Science). High school diploma required for clinical nursing. **Additional information:** Nursing applicants must have high school diploma or equivalency certificate (GED) prior to entry into clinical courses. Howard County residents receive priority consideration.

1992 FRESHMAN CLASS PROFILE. 350 men, 398 women enrolled. **Characteristics:** 100% commute, 28% have minority backgrounds. Average age is 19.

FALL-TERM APPLICATIONS. $10 fee, may be waived for applicants with need. No closing date; applicants notified on a rolling basis. Interview recommended. Deferred and early admission available.

STUDENT LIFE. Activities: Student government, film, student newspaper, television, choral groups, dance, drama, jazz band, music ensembles, musical theater, guitar ensemble, chamber choir, cheerleading group, Christian fellowship club, Black Student Union, Environmental Club, Cultural Club, Jewish Student Union, Nursing Club.

ATHLETICS. NJCAA. **Intercollegiate:** Basketball, cross-country, golf, soccer M, tennis, track and field. **Intramural:** Badminton, basketball, golf, softball, table tennis, tennis, volleyball.

STUDENT SERVICES. Career counseling, employment service for undergraduates, freshman orientation, personal counseling, placement service for graduates, special adviser for adult students, veterans counselor, services/facilities for handicapped.

ANNUAL EXPENSES. Tuition and fees (projected): $1,663, $696 additional for out-of-district students, $1,368 additional for out-of-state students. **Books and supplies:** $450. **Other expenses:** $700.

FINANCIAL AID. 25% of continuing students receive some form of aid. All grants, 65% of loans, 23% of jobs based on need. **Aid applications:** No closing date; priority given to applications received by March 1; applicants notified on a rolling basis beginning on or about July 15; must reply within 2 weeks.

ADDRESS/TELEPHONE. Barbara C. Greenfeld, Director of Admissions, Howard Community College, Little Patuxent Parkway, Columbia, MD 21044. (410) 992-4856. Fax: (410) 992-4803.

Johns Hopkins University
Baltimore, Maryland CB code: 5332

Admissions:	43% of applicants accepted
Based on:	••• School record, test scores
	•• Activities, essay, recommendations
	• Interview, special talents
Completion:	97% of freshmen end year in good standing
	87% graduate, 62% of these enter graduate study

4-year private university, coed. Founded in 1876. **Accreditation:** Regional. **Undergraduate enrollment:** 2,043 men, 1,350 women full time; 47 men, 50 women part time. **Graduate enrollment:** 825 men, 499 women full time; 110 men, 160 women part time. **Faculty:** 480 total (340 full time), 419 with doctorates or other terminal degrees. **Location:** Urban campus in very large city; 4 miles from downtown. **Calendar:** 4-1-4, limited summer session. Extensive evening/early morning classes. **Microcomputers:** 62 located in dormitories, libraries, computer centers. **Special facilities:** Space Telescope Science Institute, center in Bologna, Italy. **Additional facts:** School of Nursing is two-year upper-division institution which also offers graduate degree. Graduate divisions include School of Hygience and Public Health, Medical School, and School of Advanced International Studies in Washington, DC, and Nan'jing Center, China. The School of Continuing Studies offers undergraduate and graduate degree programs in business, education and the liberal arts to adult, part-time, evening students.

DEGREES OFFERED. BA, BS, MA, MS, PhD, MD. 796 bachelor's degrees awarded in 1992. 20% in engineering, 15% letters/literature, 20% life sciences, 5% physical sciences, 29% social sciences. Graduate degrees offered in 57 major fields of study.

UNDERGRADUATE MAJORS. American literature, anthropology, applied mathematics, art history, astronomy, behavioral sciences, biochemistry, bioengineering and biomedical engineering, biological and physical sciences, biology, biomedical science, biophysics, chemical engineering, chemistry, civil engineering, classics, cognitive psychology, comparative literature, computer and information sciences, computer engineering, creative writing, earth sciences, economics, electrical/electronics/communications engineering, engineering, engineering and other disciplines, engineering mechanics, English, English literature, experimental psychology, French, geography, geology, German, Greek (classical), Hispanic American studies, history, humanities, humanities and social sciences, international relations, international studies, Italian, Latin, linguistics, materials engineering, mathematics, mechanical engineering, medieval studies, Middle Eastern studies, music, nuclear physics, nursing, philosophy, physics, planetary science, political science and government, psychology, public health laboratory science, social sciences, sociology, Spanish.

ACADEMIC PROGRAMS. Accelerated program, cooperative education, double major, honors program, independent study, internships, student-designed major, study abroad, teacher preparation, Washington semester, cross-registration; liberal arts/career combination in engineering, health sciences. **Remedial services:** Preadmission summer program, reduced course load, special counselor, tutoring. **ROTC:** Air Force, Army. **Placement/credit:** AP, IB, institutional tests.

ACADEMIC REQUIREMENTS. Freshmen must earn minimum GPA of 2.0 to continue in good standing. 95% of freshmen return for sophomore

year. Students must declare major by end of second year. **Graduation requirements:** 120 hours for bachelor's (85 in major). Most students required to take courses in humanities, mathematics, biological/physical sciences, social sciences. **Postgraduate studies:** 7% enter law school, 26% enter medical school, 8% enter MBA programs, 21% enter other graduate study. **Additional information:** Undergraduate curriculum offers flexibility, research opportunities, and ability to take graduate level courses.

FRESHMAN ADMISSIONS. Selection criteria: School achievement record most important (emphasis on course grades related to applicant's major field of academic interest). Intellectual interests and accomplishments, recommendations, personal character, extracurricular activities also significant. Interview important. SAT and ACH scores very important, but ACT scores also considered. **High school preparation:** 14 units recommended. Recommended units include biological science 1, English 4, foreign language 2, mathematics 4, physical science 1 and social science 2. High level of skill in use of English language, solid foundation in mathematics required. 3 or 4 years of college-preparatory work preferred, with or without high school diploma. **Test requirements:** SAT or ACT (SAT preferred); score report by February 15. 3 ACH required of students not taking ACT. Score report by February 15.

1992 FRESHMAN CLASS PROFILE. 4,638 men applied, 2,050 accepted, 525 enrolled; 3,182 women applied, 1,320 accepted, 331 enrolled. 98% had high school GPA of 3.0 or higher, 2% between 2.0 and 2.99. 78% were in top tenth and 94% were in top quarter of graduating class. **Academic background:** Mid 50% of enrolled freshmen had SAT-V between 570-660, SAT-M between 650-740. 98% submitted SAT scores. **Characteristics:** 15% from in state, 97% live in college housing, 38% have minority backgrounds, 5% are foreign students, 25% join fraternities/sororities. Average age is 18.

FALL-TERM APPLICATIONS. $50 fee, may be waived for applicants with need. Closing date January 1; applicants notified on or about April 2; must reply by May 1. Audition required for dual degree program with Peabody Institute applicants. Essay required. Interview recommended. CRDA. Deferred and early admission available. EDP-F. Freshmen admitted in fall semester only.

STUDENT LIFE. Housing: Dormitories (men, women, coed); apartment, fraternity, handicapped housing available. All freshmen and sophomores are required to live on campus. Two major residence halls recently renovated for undergraduates with state of the art facilities and amenities. **Activities:** Student government, film, magazine, radio, student newspaper, yearbook, student scholarly journals, choral groups, concert band, dance, drama, jazz band, music ensembles, musical theater, opera, pep band, symphony orchestra, fraternities, sororities, Jewish Students Association, Catholic Community, Hopkins Christian Fellowship, Black Student Union, Organizacion Latina Estudiantil, 4 Asian-American student associations, 5 political associations, inner-city tutoring, first-aid squad, peer counseling.

ATHLETICS. NCAA. **Intercollegiate:** Baseball M, basketball, cross-country, diving M, fencing, field hockey W, football M, golf M, lacrosse, rifle, rowing (crew), soccer M, squash W, swimming, tennis, track and field, volleyball W, water polo, wrestling M. **Intramural:** Basketball, cross-country, football, golf, ice hockey M, lacrosse, racquetball, rugby M, sailing, skiing, soccer, softball, squash, swimming, table tennis, tennis, track and field, volleyball, wrestling M.

STUDENT SERVICES. Career counseling, employment service for undergraduates, freshman orientation, health services, personal counseling, placement service for graduates, veterans counselor, chaplain (nondenominational), services/facilities for handicapped.

ANNUAL EXPENSES. Tuition and fees: $17,900. Tuition and fees for School of Nursing $13,440. **Room and board:** $6,460. **Books and supplies:** $450. **Other expenses:** $1,050.

FINANCIAL AID. 50% of freshmen, 50% of continuing students receive some form of aid. 89% of grants, 96% of loans, 48% of jobs based on need. 367 enrolled freshmen were judged to have need, all were offered aid. Academic, music/drama, athletic, leadership scholarships available. **Aid applications:** Closing date February 1; priority given to applications received by January 15; applicants notified on or about April 15; must reply by May 1.

ADDRESS/TELEPHONE. Richard M. Fuller, Director of Admissions, Johns Hopkins University, 3400 North Charles St., 140 Garland Hall, Baltimore, MD 21218. (410) 516-8171. Fax: (410) 516-4495. For Johns Hopkins University: School of Nursing, send correspondence to Office of Admissions, 600 North Wolfe Street, Baltimore, MD 21205 or call (410) 955-7548, Fax (410) 955-7463.

Johns Hopkins University: Peabody Conservatory of Music

Baltimore, Maryland — CB code: 5532

4-year private music college, coed. **Accreditation:** Regional. **Undergraduate enrollment:** 111 men, 136 women full time; 2 women part time. **Graduate enrollment:** 120 men, 146 women full time; 7 men, 7 women part time. **Faculty:** 126 total (71 full time). **Location:** Urban campus in very large city. **Calendar:** Semester. **Microcomputers:** Located in libraries. **Special facilities:** Small gallery, concert halls.

DEGREES OFFERED. B, MA, D. 56 bachelor's degrees awarded in 1992. 100% in visual and performing arts. Graduate degrees offered in 3 major fields of study.

UNDERGRADUATE MAJORS. Music, music performance, music theory and composition, recording arts.

ACADEMIC PROGRAMS. Internships, cross-registration. **Remedial services:** Remedial instruction, special counselor, tutoring. **Placement/credit:** AP, institutional tests.

ACADEMIC REQUIREMENTS. Graduation requirements: 143 hours for bachelor's (108 in major).

FRESHMAN ADMISSIONS. Selection criteria: Performance audition required. Sometimes GPA and test scores also considered. **Test requirements:** SAT or ACT (SAT preferred).

1992 FRESHMAN CLASS PROFILE. 22 men, 25 women enrolled. **Characteristics:** 100% live in college housing.

FALL-TERM APPLICATIONS. $40 fee. Closing date April 1; priority given to applications received by January 1; applicants notified on or about April 1; must reply by May 1. Audition required. Interview recommended. Deferred admission available. Must apply by January 1 for sholarship consideration.

STUDENT LIFE. Housing: Dormitories (men, women, coed). **Activities:** Student government, choral groups, concert band, jazz band, music ensembles, opera, symphony orchestra, fraternities, sororities.

STUDENT SERVICES. Career counseling, employment service for undergraduates, freshman orientation, health services, personal counseling, placement service for graduates, services/facilities for handicapped.

ANNUAL EXPENSES. Tuition and fees (1992-93): $13,000. **Room and board:** $5,450. **Books and supplies:** $450. **Other expenses:** $700.

FINANCIAL AID. 97% of freshmen, 97% of continuing students receive some form of aid. 30% of grants, 80% of loans, 39% of jobs based on need. Music/drama scholarships available. **Aid applications:** No closing date; priority given to applications received by February 17; applicants notified on or about April 7; must reply by May 1.

ADDRESS/TELEPHONE. David Lane, Director of Admissions, Johns Hopkins University: Peabody Conservatory of Music, 1 East Mount Vernon Place, Baltimore, MD 21202. (401) 659-8110. (800) 368-2521.

Loyola College in Maryland

Baltimore, Maryland — CB code: 5370

Admissions:	65% of applicants accepted
Based on:	••• School record, test scores
	•• Essay, recommendations, special talents
	• Activities, interview
Completion:	96% of freshmen end year in good standing
	73% graduate, 33% of these enter graduate study

4-year private university and college of arts and sciences, coed, affiliated with Roman Catholic Church. Founded in 1852. **Accreditation:** Regional. **Undergraduate enrollment:** 1,355 men, 1,680 women full time; 115 men, 97 women part time. **Graduate enrollment:** 263 men, 348 women full time; 1,059 men, 1,304 women part time. **Faculty:** 406 total (220 full time), 193 with doctorates or other terminal degrees. **Location:** Urban campus in very large city. **Calendar:** Semester, extensive summer session. Extensive evening/early morning classes. **Microcomputers:** 195 located in dormitories, libraries, computer centers. **Special facilities:** Art gallery, theater, new mathematics and computing building. **Additional facts:** College in the Jesuit tradition.

DEGREES OFFERED. BA, BS, MA, MS, MBA, MEd, PhD. 831 bachelor's degrees awarded in 1992. 34% in business and management, 8% communications, 5% education, 5% health sciences, 5% letters/literature, 8% psychology, 17% social sciences. Graduate degrees offered in 17 major fields of study.

UNDERGRADUATE MAJORS. Accounting, biology, business administration and management, chemistry, classics, communications, computer and information sciences, creative writing, economics, education, electrical/electronics/communications engineering, elementary education, engineering and other disciplines, engineering science, English, fine arts, French, German, Greek (classical), history, humanities, humanities and social sciences, Latin, mathematics, philosophy, physics, political science and government, psychology, sociology, Spanish, speech pathology/audiology, theological studies.

ACADEMIC PROGRAMS. Accelerated program, double major, honors program, independent study, internships, study abroad, teacher preparation, cross-registration; liberal arts/career combination in engineering; combined bachelor's/graduate program in business administration. **Remedial services:** Reduced course load, special counselor, tutoring. **ROTC:** Army. **Placement/credit:** AP, CLEP Subject, institutional tests; 30 credit hours maximum for bachelor's degree.

ACADEMIC REQUIREMENTS. Freshmen must earn minimum GPA of 1.8 to continue in good standing. 90% of freshmen return for sophomore year. Students must declare major by end of second year. **Graduation requirements:** 120 hours for bachelor's (45 in major). Most students required

to take courses in English, foreign languages, history, humanities, mathematics, philosophy/religion, biological/physical sciences, social sciences. **Postgraduate studies:** 4% enter law school, 2% enter medical school, 4% enter MBA programs, 23% enter other graduate study.

FRESHMAN ADMISSIONS. Selection criteria: Test scores and academic qualifications most important. Extracurricular activities, recommendations, school record, personal background, class rank also considered. **High school preparation:** 16 units required. Required units include biological science 1, English 4, foreign language 2, mathematics 3, physical science 2 and social science 2. **Test requirements:** SAT; score report by August 1. **Additional information:** Midyear senior grades and additional SAT scores may be required for academically borderline applicants.

1992 FRESHMAN CLASS PROFILE. 1,553 men applied, 1,094 accepted, 342 enrolled; 2,499 women applied, 1,553 accepted, 450 enrolled. 75% had high school GPA of 3.0 or higher, 24% between 2.0 and 2.99. 31% were in top tenth and 63% were in top quarter of graduating class. **Academic background:** Mid 50% of enrolled freshmen had SAT-V between 470-580, SAT-M between 520-620. 100% submitted SAT scores. **Characteristics:** 42% from in state, 84% live in college housing, 10% have minority backgrounds, 2% are foreign students. Average age is 18.

FALL-TERM APPLICATIONS. $25 fee, may be waived for applicants with need. Closing date February 1; applicants notified on or about April 15. Essay required. Interview recommended. Deferred and early admission available. Institutional early decision plan. A limited number of outstanding high school students admitted early in their senior year. With an early acceptance there is no obligation to make an immediate decision. Students not selected remain as candidates for admission and are notified of final decision by April 15.

STUDENT LIFE. Housing: Dormitories (men, women, coed); apartment, handicapped housing available. Honors housing available. Most students remain on campus all 4 years. Special interest housing available includes community service, leadership and wellness houses. **Activities:** Student government, film, radio, student newspaper, yearbook, anthology of student papers, choral groups, dance, drama, jazz band, music ensembles, musical theater, pep band, drill team, campus ministries, Black Students' Association, Young Democrats, College Republicans, Korean Students Association, Circle K, Amnesty International, Young Feminist, Jewish Students Association.

ATHLETICS. NCAA. **Intercollegiate:** Basketball, cross-country, diving, golf M, lacrosse, soccer, swimming, tennis, volleyball W. **Intramural:** Badminton, basketball, bowling, cross-country, golf, lacrosse, racquetball, soccer, softball, squash, table tennis, tennis, volleyball, water polo M. **Clubs:** Baseball, rowing (crew), rugby, volleyball, women's soccer, sailing, track, field hockey, martial arts, dance, fencing, outdoor recreation, golf, tennis, racquetball, swimming.

STUDENT SERVICES. Aptitude testing, career counseling, employment service for undergraduates, freshman orientation, health services, personal counseling, placement service for graduates, special adviser for adult students, services/facilities for handicapped.

ANNUAL EXPENSES. Tuition and fees: $12,465. **Room and board:** $6,060. **Books and supplies:** $550. **Other expenses:** $650.

FINANCIAL AID. 62% of freshmen, 58% of continuing students receive some form of aid. 47% of grants, all loans, 57% of jobs based on need. 396 enrolled freshmen were judged to have need, 387 were offered aid. Academic, athletic, minority scholarships available. **Aid applications:** Closing date March 1; priority given to applications received by February 15; applicants notified on or about April 15; must reply by May 1.

ADDRESS/TELEPHONE. William J. Bossemeyer, Director of Admissions, Loyola College in Maryland, 4501 North Charles Street, Baltimore, MD 21210-2699. (410) 617-5012. (800) 221-9107. Fax: (410) 617-2768.

Maryland College of Art and Design
Silver Spring, Maryland — CB code: 5394

2-year private art college, coed. Founded in 1957. **Undergraduate enrollment:** 30 men, 25 women full time; 3 men, 2 women part time. **Location:** Suburban campus in small city; 3 miles from Washington, D.C. **Calendar:** Semester. **Additional facts:** Accredited by NASAD.

FRESHMAN ADMISSIONS. Selection criteria: High school transcript, interview, portfolio presentation of 12-20 works of art, letter of recommendation from art teacher.

ANNUAL EXPENSES. Tuition and fees: $7,930. **Books and supplies:** $1,000. **Other expenses:** $1,200.

ADDRESS/TELEPHONE. Joseph Kabriel, Director of Admissions, Maryland College of Art and Design, 10500 Georgia Avenue, Silver Spring, MD 20902. (301) 649-4454. Fax: (301) 649-2940.

Maryland Institute College of Art
Baltimore, Maryland — CB code: 5399

Admissions: 69% of applicants accepted
Based on:
- ••• Special talents
- •• Essay, interview, school record
- • Activities, recommendations, test scores

Completion: 93% of freshmen end year in good standing
50% graduate, 25% of these enter graduate study

4-year private art college, coed. Founded in 1826. **Accreditation:** Regional. **Undergraduate enrollment:** 360 men, 437 women full time; 21 men, 37 women part time. **Graduate enrollment:** 30 men, 46 women full time; 5 men, 9 women part time. **Faculty:** 136 total (60 full time), 43 with doctorates or other terminal degrees. **Location:** Urban campus in very large city; 180 miles from New York City, 50 miles from Washington, D.C. **Calendar:** Semester, extensive summer session. **Microcomputers:** 31 located in computer centers. **Special facilities:** 6 art galleries, nature library, extensive slide library, graphics laboratory.

DEGREES OFFERED. BFA, MFA. 194 bachelor's degrees awarded in 1992. 98% in visual and performing arts. Graduate degrees offered in 4 major fields of study.

UNDERGRADUATE MAJORS. Art education, ceramics, drawing, fiber/textiles/weaving, fine arts, graphic design, illustration design, interior design, painting, photography, printmaking, sculpture.

ACADEMIC PROGRAMS. Accelerated program, double major, honors program, independent study, internships, student-designed major, study abroad, teacher preparation, visiting/exchange student program, New York semester, cross-registration, cooperative exchange programs with Johns Hopkins University, Goucher College, University of Baltimore, and Loyola College. **Remedial services:** Learning center, preadmission summer program, reduced course load, special counselor, tutoring. **Placement/credit:** AP, institutional tests; 31 credit hours maximum for bachelor's degree.

ACADEMIC REQUIREMENTS. Freshmen must earn minimum GPA of 2.0 to continue in good standing. 76% of freshmen return for sophomore year. Students must declare major by end of first year. **Graduation requirements:** 126 hours for bachelor's (63 in major). Most students required to take courses in arts/fine arts, English, history, humanities, biological/physical sciences, social sciences. **Additional information:** Students fulfill graduation requirement by taking one-third of course work in liberal arts and two-thirds in studio art.

FRESHMAN ADMISSIONS. Selection criteria: Portfolio and school record most important. Essay, recommendations, extracurricular art and community activities, interview, and test scores also considered. Concentration in art, humanities and social sciences courses recommended. **Test requirements:** SAT or ACT; score report by September 2.

1992 FRESHMAN CLASS PROFILE. 291 men applied, 192 accepted, 94 enrolled; 321 women applied, 228 accepted, 107 enrolled. **Characteristics:** 26% from in state, 90% live in college housing, 11% have minority backgrounds, 6% are foreign students. Average age is 18.

FALL-TERM APPLICATIONS. $35 fee, may be waived for applicants with need. Closing date May 15; priority given to applications received by March 1; applicants notified on a rolling basis; must reply by May 1. Portfolio required. Essay required. Interview recommended. CRDA. Deferred and early admission available. EDP-F.

STUDENT LIFE. Housing: Dormitories (coed). Co-ed housing available for 350 students. First year students guaranteed housing. **Activities:** Student government, student newspaper, dance, drama.

STUDENT SERVICES. Career counseling, employment service for undergraduates, freshman orientation, health services, personal counseling, placement service for graduates, services/facilities for handicapped.

ANNUAL EXPENSES. Tuition and fees (1992-93): $12,400. **Room and board:** $4,825. **Books and supplies:** $1,300. **Other expenses:** $600.

FINANCIAL AID. 65% of freshmen, 67% of continuing students receive some form of aid. 85% of grants, 91% of loans, 85% of jobs based on need. 121 enrolled freshmen were judged to have need, all were offered aid. Academic, art scholarships available. **Aid applications:** No closing date; priority given to applications received by March 1; applicants notified on a rolling basis beginning on or about March 31; must reply by May 1 or within 2 weeks if notified thereafter.

ADDRESS/TELEPHONE. Theresa Lynch Bedoya, Vice President Admissions, Maryland Institute College of Art, 1300 Mount Royal Avenue, Baltimore, MD 21217. (410) 225-2222. Fax: (410) 669-9206.

Montgomery College: Germantown Campus
Germantown, Maryland — CB code: 5393

2-year public community college, coed. Founded in 1946. **Accreditation:** Regional. **Undergraduate enrollment:** 395 men, 384 women full time; 1,295 men, 1,856 women part time. **Faculty:** 176 total (54 full time), 31 with doctorates or other terminal degrees. **Location:** Suburban campus in large town; 20 miles from Washington, D.C. **Calendar:** Semester, limited summer session. **Microcomputers:** Located in libraries, classrooms, computer centers. **Special facilities:** Multidisciplinary science laboratory.

DEGREES OFFERED. AA, AAS. 119 associate degrees awarded in 1992. 21% in business and management, 9% business/office and marketing/distribution, 6% computer sciences, 7% teacher education, 7% engineering, 6% engineering technologies, 44% multi/interdisciplinary studies.

UNDERGRADUATE MAJORS. Accounting, art education, biological and physical sciences, business and management, business and office, business data processing and related programs, business data programming, business education, business systems analysis, computer and information sciences, computer programming, data processing, drafting and design technology, early childhood education, education, electromechanical technology, elementary education, engineering, engineering and engineering-related technologies, finance, fine arts, human resources development, humanities, humanities and social sciences, information sciences and systems, liberal/general studies, marketing and distribution, marketing management, mathematics, mathematics education, music education, physical education, physical sciences, predentistry, premedicine, prepharmacy, retailing, science education, secondary education, secretarial and related programs, social science education, social sciences, telecommunications, word processing.

ACADEMIC PROGRAMS. 2-year transfer program, accelerated program, double major, dual enrollment of high school students, honors program, independent study, internships, student-designed major, weekend college. **Remedial services:** Learning center, remedial instruction, special counselor, tutoring, Study Skills Development Course. **Placement/credit:** AP, CLEP General and Subject, institutional tests; 45 credit hours maximum for associate degree.

ACADEMIC REQUIREMENTS. Freshmen must earn minimum GPA of 1.7 to continue in good standing. **Graduation requirements:** 60 hours for associate (32 in major). Most students required to take courses in English, mathematics, biological/physical sciences, social sciences. **Additional information:** Televised courses presented by Maryland Center for Public Broadcasting available for credit to registered students through Takoma Park campus.

FRESHMAN ADMISSIONS. Selection criteria: Open admissions. **Test requirements:** Comprehensive English Language Test (CELT) required for foreign applicants. TOEFL may be substituted with minimum score of 550.

1992 FRESHMAN CLASS PROFILE. 351 men, 481 women enrolled. **Characteristics:** 99% from in state, 100% commute, 24% have minority backgrounds, 2% are foreign students.

FALL-TERM APPLICATIONS. No fee. No closing date; applicants notified on a rolling basis. Early admission available.

STUDENT LIFE. Activities: Student government, magazine, student newspaper, dance, Christian Fellowship.

ATHLETICS. NJCAA. **Intercollegiate:** Baseball M, basketball, tennis, volleyball W. **Intramural:** Badminton, golf, softball, swimming, table tennis, tennis, volleyball.

STUDENT SERVICES. Aptitude testing, career counseling, employment service for undergraduates, on-campus day care, personal counseling, placement service for graduates, veterans counselor, services/facilities for handicapped.

ANNUAL EXPENSES. Tuition and fees: $1,911, $1,560 additional for out-of-district students, $2,880 additional for out-of-state students. **Books and supplies:** $500. **Other expenses:** $1,100.

FINANCIAL AID. Aid applications: No closing date; priority given to applications received by February 15; applicants notified on a rolling basis beginning on or about June 15; must reply within 2 weeks.

ADDRESS/TELEPHONE. Sherman Helberg, Director of Admissions, Registration, and Records, Montgomery College: Germantown Campus, 20200 Observation Drive, Germantown, MD 20876. (301) 353-7818.

Montgomery College: Rockville Campus
Rockville, Maryland CB code: 5440

2-year public community college, coed. Founded in 1946. **Accreditation:** Regional. **Undergraduate enrollment:** 2,496 men, 2,241 women full time; 4,176 men, 5,442 women part time. **Faculty:** 705 total (254 full time), 163 with doctorates or other terminal degrees. **Location:** Suburban campus in small city; 12 miles from Washington, D.C. **Calendar:** Semester, limited summer session. **Microcomputers:** Located in libraries, classrooms, computer centers. **Special facilities:** Performing arts center, child care center.

DEGREES OFFERED. AA, AAS. 474 associate degrees awarded in 1992. 18% in business and management, 13% business/office and marketing/distribution, 6% communications, 5% computer sciences, 7% engineering technologies, 31% multi/interdisciplinary studies, 7% parks/recreation, protective services, public affairs.

UNDERGRADUATE MAJORS. Accounting, advertising, architectural technologies, art education, art history, automotive technology, biological and physical sciences, business administration and management, business and office, business computer/console/peripheral equipment operation, business data processing and related programs, business data programming, business education, child development/care/guidance, city/community/regional planning, civil technology, computer and information sciences, computer programming, computer servicing technology, construction, criminal justice studies, dance, dietetic aide/assistant, drafting, early childhood education, education, electrical and electronics equipment repair, electronic technology, elementary education, engineering, engineering and engineering-related technologies, engineering and other disciplines, fashion merchandising, fire control and safety technology, fire protection, food management, food production/management/services, graphic and printing production, graphic arts technology, hospitality and recreation marketing, hotel/motel and restaurant management, humanities and social sciences, illustration design, information sciences and systems, interior design, international business management, law enforcement and corrections, law enforcement and corrections technologies, legal secretary, liberal/general studies, management science, marketing and distribution, marketing management, mechanical design technology, merchandising, music, music education, photographic technology, photography, physical education, physical sciences, predentistry, premedicine, prepharmacy, protective services, radio/television broadcasting, radio/television technology, rehabilitation counseling/services, science education, secondary education, secretarial and related programs, social sciences, social studies education, studio art, survey and mapping technology, teacher aide, urban planning technology, visual and performing arts.

ACADEMIC PROGRAMS. 2-year transfer program, accelerated program, double major, dual enrollment of high school students, honors program, independent study, internships, student-designed major, study abroad, telecourses, weekend college. **Remedial services:** Learning center, remedial instruction, special counselor, tutoring. **Placement/credit:** AP, CLEP General and Subject, institutional tests; 45 credit hours maximum for associate degree.

ACADEMIC REQUIREMENTS. Freshmen must earn minimum GPA of 1.7 to continue in good standing. 50% of freshmen return for sophomore year. **Graduation requirements:** 60 hours for associate (32 in major). Most students required to take courses in arts/fine arts, computer science, English, history, humanities, mathematics, biological/physical sciences, social sciences.

FRESHMAN ADMISSIONS. Selection criteria: Open admissions. **Test requirements:** Comprehensive English Language Test (CELT) required for foreign applicants. TOEFL may be substituted with minimum score of 550.

1992 FRESHMAN CLASS PROFILE. 1,761 men, 1,780 women enrolled. **Characteristics:** 92% from in state, 100% commute, 43% have minority backgrounds, 12% are foreign students. Average age is 26.

FALL-TERM APPLICATIONS. No fee. No closing date; applicants notified on a rolling basis. Audition required for music applicants. Early admission available.

STUDENT LIFE. Activities: Student government, magazine, radio, student newspaper, television, choral groups, concert band, dance, drama, musical theater, opera, Jewish Student Association, Progressive Student Alliance, Christian Fellowship, International Student Association, Lesbian Student Alliance, Students Against Driving Drunk.

ATHLETICS. NJCAA. **Intercollegiate:** Baseball, basketball, cross-country, field hockey W, football M, golf M, soccer, softball W, swimming, tennis, track and field, volleyball W. **Intramural:** Baseball, basketball, bowling, cross-country, fencing, football M, golf, soccer, softball, swimming, tennis, volleyball, wrestling.

STUDENT SERVICES. Aptitude testing, career counseling, employment service for undergraduates, freshman orientation, on-campus day care, personal counseling, placement service for graduates, special adviser for adult students, veterans counselor, crisis intervention, services/facilities for handicapped.

ANNUAL EXPENSES. Tuition and fees: $1,911, $1,560 additional for out-of-district students, $2,880 additional for out-of-state students. **Books and supplies:** $500. **Other expenses:** $1,100.

FINANCIAL AID. Aid applications: No closing date; priority given to applications received by February 15; applicants notified on a rolling basis beginning on or about June 15; must reply within 2 weeks.

ADDRESS/TELEPHONE. Sherman Helberg, Director of Admissions, Registration, and Records, Montgomery College: Rockville Campus, Mannakee Street, Rockville, MD 20850. (301) 279-5046.

Montgomery College: Takoma Park Campus
Takoma Park, Maryland CB code: 5414

2-year public community college, coed. Founded in 1946. **Accreditation:** Regional. **Undergraduate enrollment:** 449 men, 689 women full time; 1,073 men, 2,619 women part time. **Faculty:** 219 total (80 full time), 44 with doctorates or other terminal degrees. **Location:** Urban campus in large town; adjacent to Washington, D.C. **Calendar:** Semester, limited summer session. **Microcomputers:** Located in libraries, computer centers.

DEGREES OFFERED. AA, AAS. 188 associate degrees awarded in 1992. 12% in business and management, 9% business/office and marketing/distribution, 5% computer sciences, 56% allied health, 16% multi/interdisciplinary studies.

UNDERGRADUATE MAJORS. Accounting, art education, biological and physical sciences, biotechnology, business administration and management, business and office, business data processing and related programs, business data programming, business education, computer and information sciences, dental assistant, early childhood education, education, elementary education, engineering, engineering and engineering-related technologies, engineering and other disciplines, finance, fine arts, humanities, humanities and social sciences, information sciences and systems, international business management, legal assistant/paralegal, liberal/general studies, management science, marketing and distribution, marketing management, medical assistant, medical laboratory technologies, medical records technology, medical secretary, mental health/human services, nursing, physical sciences, predentistry, premedicine, prepharmacy, science education, secondary education, secretarial and related programs, social sciences, social studies education.

ACADEMIC PROGRAMS. 2-year transfer program, accelerated program, double major, dual enrollment of high school students, honors program, independent study, internships, student-designed major, telecourses, weekend college, Washington semester. **Remedial services:** Learning center, remedial instruction, special counselor, tutoring. **Placement/credit:** AP, CLEP General and Subject, institutional tests; 45 credit hours maximum for associate degree.

ACADEMIC REQUIREMENTS. Freshmen must earn minimum GPA of 1.7 to continue in good standing. **Graduation requirements:** 60 hours for associate (32 in major). Most students required to take courses in arts/fine arts, English, humanities, mathematics, biological/physical sciences, social sciences.

FRESHMAN ADMISSIONS. Selection criteria: Open admissions. Selective admission to allied health programs. **Test requirements:** Comprehensive English Language Test (CELT) required for foreign applicants. TOEFL may be substituted with minimum score of 550.

1992 FRESHMAN CLASS PROFILE. 337 men, 609 women enrolled. **Characteristics:** 100% commute, 71% have minority backgrounds, 9% are foreign students.

FALL-TERM APPLICATIONS. No fee. No closing date; applicants notified on a rolling basis. Interview required for mental health associate applicants. Early admission available.

STUDENT LIFE. Activities: Student government, magazine, student newspaper, television, choral groups, concert band, dance, drama, musical theater, religious and political organizations.

ATHLETICS. NJCAA. **Intercollegiate:** Basketball M, soccer M, swimming M, tennis, volleyball W. **Intramural:** Basketball M, racquetball, table tennis, tennis, volleyball.

STUDENT SERVICES. Aptitude testing, career counseling, employment service for undergraduates, on-campus day care, personal counseling, placement service for graduates, veterans counselor, services/facilities for handicapped.

ANNUAL EXPENSES. Tuition and fees: $1,911, $1,560 additional for out-of-district students, $2,880 additional for out-of-state students. **Books and supplies:** $500. **Other expenses:** $1,100.

FINANCIAL AID. Aid applications: No closing date; priority given to applications received by February 15; applicants notified on a rolling basis beginning on or about June 15; must reply within 2 weeks.

ADDRESS/TELEPHONE. Sherman Helberg, Director of Admissions, Registration, and Records, Montgomery College: Takoma Park Campus, Takoma Avenue and Fenton Street, Takoma Park, MD 20912. (301) 650-1300.

Morgan State University
Baltimore, Maryland CB code: 5416

4-year public university and college of arts and sciences and business, engineering, teachers college, coed. Founded in 1867. **Accreditation:** Regional. **Undergraduate enrollment:** 5,219 men and women. **Graduate enrollment:** 482 men and women. **Faculty:** 330 total (200 full time), 138 with doctorates or other terminal degrees. **Location:** Urban campus in very large city; 45 miles from Washington, D.C., 100 miles from Philadelphia. **Calendar:** Semester, limited summer session. Saturday and extensive evening/early morning classes. **Microcomputers:** 65 located in libraries, computer centers. **Special facilities:** 2 art galleries, historical and government documents collections, special collections of African-American History. **Additional facts:** Historically black/multicultural university, attracting students from 32 foreign countries, 32 states, and District of Columbia.

DEGREES OFFERED. BA, BS, MA, MS, MBA, EdD. 515 bachelor's degrees awarded in 1992. Graduate degrees offered in 25 major fields of study.

UNDERGRADUATE MAJORS. Accounting, African studies, Afro-American (black) studies, art education, art history, Asian studies, biology, business administration and management, business and management, business and office, business economics, business education, Caribbean studies, chemistry, civil engineering, clinical laboratory science, communications, computer and information sciences, dietetic aide/assistant, dramatic arts, economics, education, electrical/electronics/communications engineering, elementary education, engineering physics, English, English education, environmental design, European studies, fine arts, food science and nutrition, foreign languages education, French, geography, gerontology, graphic design, health education, history, home economics, industrial engineering, information sciences and systems, international business management, international studies, Latin American studies, management information systems, marketing management, mathematics, mathematics education, Middle Eastern studies, music, music education, music performance, office supervision and management, philosophy, photography, physical education, physics, political science and government, predentistry, prelaw, premedicine, prepharmacy, psychology, radio/television broadcasting, reading education, recreation and community services technologies, religion, remedial education, science education, secondary education, secretarial and related programs, social studies education, social work, sociology, Spanish, special education, speech, telecommunications, urban studies.

ACADEMIC PROGRAMS. Cooperative education, double major, dual enrollment of high school students, honors program, independent study, internships, teacher preparation, weekend college, cross-registration; combined bachelor's/graduate program in business administration. **Remedial services:** Learning center, preadmission summer program, reduced course load, remedial instruction, special counselor, tutoring. **ROTC:** Army. **Placement/credit:** AP, CLEP General and Subject, institutional tests; 45 credit hours maximum for bachelor's degree.

ACADEMIC REQUIREMENTS. Freshmen must earn minimum GPA of 2.0 to continue in good standing. 64% of freshmen return for sophomore year. Students must declare major by end of second year. **Graduation requirements:** 120 hours for bachelor's (54 in major). Most students required to take courses in arts/fine arts, English, history, humanities, mathematics, philosophy/religion, biological/physical sciences, social sciences.

FRESHMAN ADMISSIONS. Selection criteria: School achievement record and test scores most important. **High school preparation:** 13 units recommended. Recommended units include biological science 1, English 4, foreign language 1, mathematics 3, physical science 1 and social science 3. **Test requirements:** SAT or ACT; score report by August 1.

1992 FRESHMAN CLASS PROFILE. 1,242 men and women enrolled. **Characteristics:** Average age is 19.

FALL-TERM APPLICATIONS. $20 fee, may be waived for applicants with need. No closing date; priority given to applications received by April 15; applicants notified on a rolling basis; must reply by May 1 or within 4 weeks if notified thereafter. Interview recommended. Audition recommended for music applicants. CRDA. Deferred and early admission available. 750 SAT or 18 ACT, 85 high school GPA, principal's recommendation, and parents' consent form (for minors) required.

STUDENT LIFE. Housing: Dormitories (men, women, coed). **Activities:** Student government, film, radio, student newspaper, yearbook, choral groups, concert band, dance, drama, jazz band, marching band, music ensembles, pep band, fraternities, sororities, Council on Religious Life.

ATHLETICS. NCAA. **Intercollegiate:** Basketball, cross-country, football M, tennis, track and field, volleyball W, wrestling M. **Intramural:** Basketball, bowling, cross-country, racquetball, rifle, soccer, softball, swimming, table tennis, tennis, track and field, volleyball.

STUDENT SERVICES. Aptitude testing, career counseling, employment service for undergraduates, freshman orientation, health services, on-campus day care, personal counseling, placement service for graduates, veterans counselor, services/facilities for handicapped.

ANNUAL EXPENSES. Tuition and fees: $2,526, $2,536 additional for out-of-state students. **Room and board:** $4,840. **Books and supplies:** $1,000. **Other expenses:** $1,600.

FINANCIAL AID. 79% of freshmen, 76% of continuing students receive some form of aid. 64% of grants, 87% of loans, 74% of jobs based on need. 933 enrolled freshmen were judged to have need, 899 were offered aid. Academic, athletic, state/district residency scholarships available. **Aid applications:** No closing date; priority given to applications received by April 1; applicants notified on a rolling basis beginning on or about June 1; must reply within 2 weeks.

ADDRESS/TELEPHONE. Chelseia Harold-Miller, Director of Admissions and Recruitment, Morgan State University, Cold Spring Lane and Hillen Road, Baltimore, MD 21239. (410) 319-3000. (800) 332-6674. Fax: (410) 319-3698.

Mount St. Mary's College
Emmitsburg, Maryland CB code: 5421

Admissions:	90% of applicants accepted
Based on:	••• Recommendations, school record
	•• Activities, essay, test scores
	• Interview, special talents
Completion:	94% of freshmen end year in good standing
	73% graduate, 30% of these enter graduate study

4-year private liberal arts college, coed, affiliated with Roman Catholic Church. Founded in 1808. **Accreditation:** Regional. **Undergraduate enrollment:** 590 men, 659 women full time; 60 men, 31 women part time. **Graduate enrollment:** 152 men, 11 women full time; 149 men, 91 women part time. **Faculty:** 169 total (102 full time), 89 with doctorates or other terminal degrees. **Location:** Rural campus in rural community; 65 miles from Washington, D.C., 50 miles from Baltimore. **Calendar:** Semester, limited summer session. **Microcomputers:** 100 located in libraries, classrooms, computer centers. **Special facilities:** State-of-the-art athletic facility, 300 acres of mountain forest for hiking and recreation. **Additional facts:** Oldest independent Catholic college in United States.

DEGREES OFFERED. BA, BS, MA, MBA, MEd, M.Div. 321 bachelor's degrees awarded in 1992. 39% in business and management, 7% teacher education, 7% letters/literature, 8% psychology, 24% social sciences. Graduate degrees offered in 4 major fields of study.

UNDERGRADUATE MAJORS. Accounting, American studies, biochemistry, biology, business and finance, chemistry, classics, economics, elementary education, English, English education, fine arts, foreign languages (multiple emphasis), French, German, history, international relations, international studies, liberal/general studies, mathematics, philosophy, political science and government, predentistry, prelaw, premedicine, psychobiology, psychology, rhetoric, rhetoric and writing, secondary education, social studies education, sociology, Spanish, theological studies.

ACADEMIC PROGRAMS. Double major, dual enrollment of high school students, honors program, independent study, internships, student-designed major, study abroad, teacher preparation, Washington semester, cross-registration, 3-2 with Catholic University in computer engineering; 3-2 with John's Hopkins University in nursing; liberal arts/career combination in engineering. **Remedial services:** Learning center, remedial instruction, tutoring. **ROTC:** Army. **Placement/credit:** AP, CLEP General and Subject, institutional tests; 30 credit hours maximum for bachelor's degree.

ACADEMIC REQUIREMENTS. Freshmen must earn minimum GPA of 1.5 to continue in good standing. 84% of freshmen return for sophomore year. Students must declare major by end of second year. **Graduation requirements:** 120 hours for bachelor's (36 in major). Most students required to take courses in arts/fine arts, English, foreign languages, history, humanities, mathematics, philosophy/religion, biological/physical sciences, social sciences. **Postgraduate studies:** 3% enter law school, 3% enter medical school, 4% enter MBA programs, 20% enter other graduate study. **Additional information:** Liberal arts core curriculum integrated over four years includes: western civilization (clustered with literature and art courses) American experience, philosophy, theology, ethics, and non-western cultures.

FRESHMAN ADMISSIONS. Selection criteria: High school record most important (including grades, class rank, and curriculum strength), followed by standardized test scores, recommendations, extracurricular activities and essay. **High school preparation:** 16 units required. Required and recommended units include English 4, foreign language 2, mathematics 3, social science 3 and science 3. Biological science 1 and physical science 1 recommended. **Test requirements:** SAT or ACT (SAT preferred); score report by February 15.

1992 FRESHMAN CLASS PROFILE. 546 men applied, 472 accepted, 158 enrolled; 648 women applied, 597 accepted, 190 enrolled. 56% had high school GPA of 3.0 or higher, 43% between 2.0 and 2.99. 14% were in top tenth and 33% were in top quarter of graduating class. **Academic background:** Mid 50% of enrolled freshmen had SAT-V between 410-520, SAT-M between 440-570. 99% submitted SAT scores. **Characteristics:** 46% from in state, 91% live in college housing, 9% have minority backgrounds, 1% are foreign students. Average age is 18.

FALL-TERM APPLICATIONS. $25 fee, may be waived for applicants with need. Closing date March 1; applicants notified on or about April 1; must reply by May 1. Essay required. Interview recommended. Portfolio recommended. CRDA. Deferred and early admission available. Institutional early decision plan. Early Action program deadline December 1, notification on a rolling basis until December 15.

STUDENT LIFE. Housing: Dormitories (coed); apartment housing available. All students guaranteed housing all 4 years. **Activities:** Student government, magazine, radio, student newspaper, television, yearbook, choral groups, dance, drama, music ensembles, musical theater, pep band, Academic Honor Societies, social service groups, Young Democrats, Young Republicans, Amnesty International, Campus Ministy, Circle K, Organization for Student Cultural Awareness, Commuter Association, admissions student assistants.

ATHLETICS. NCAA. **Intercollegiate:** Baseball M, basketball, cross-country, golf, lacrosse M, soccer, softball W, tennis, track and field. **Intramural:** Basketball, lacrosse W, racquetball, softball, swimming, table tennis, tennis, volleyball.

STUDENT SERVICES. Aptitude testing, career counseling, freshman orientation, health services, personal counseling, placement service for graduates, special advisers for health professions and prelaw students, services/facilities for handicapped.

ANNUAL EXPENSES. Tuition and fees (1992-93): $10,675. **Room and board:** $5,750. **Books and supplies:** $450. **Other expenses:** $525.

FINANCIAL AID. 50% of grants, 62% of loans, 50% of jobs based on need. 161 enrolled freshmen were judged to have need; all were offered aid. Academic, athletic, state/district residency, religious affiliation, minority scholarships available. **Aid applications:** Closing date March 15; applicants notified on or about April 1; must reply by May 1. **Additional information:** College guarantees to meet the full need of any student who scores above 1000 on the SAT and ranks in the top 40% of high school class.

ADDRESS/TELEPHONE. Michael D. Kennedy, Director of Admissions, Mount St. Mary's College, Emmitsburg, MD 21727-7796. (301) 447-5214. (800) 448-4347. Fax: (301) 447-5755.

Ner Israel Rabbinical College
Baltimore, Maryland CB code: 0839

4-year private seminary, teachers college, men only, affiliated with Jewish faith. Founded in 1933. **Undergraduate enrollment:** 185 men full time. **Graduate enrollment:** 119 men full time; 1 man part time. **Faculty:** 39 total, 30 with doctorates or other terminal degrees. **Location:** Urban campus in very large city. **Calendar:** Semester.

DEGREES OFFERED. BA, MA, PhD, B.Div, M.Div. 52 bachelor's degrees awarded in 1992. 100% in philosophy, religion, theology. Graduate degrees offered in 2 major fields of study.

UNDERGRADUATE MAJORS. Talmudic law, theological studies.

ACADEMIC PROGRAMS. Study abroad.

ACADEMIC REQUIREMENTS. 85% of freshmen return for sophomore year. Students must declare major on enrollment. **Graduation requirements:** 120 hours for bachelor's (80 in major). Most students required to take courses in foreign languages, philosophy/religion.

FRESHMAN ADMISSIONS. Selection criteria: Interview most important.

1992 FRESHMAN CLASS PROFILE. 42 men enrolled. **Characteristics:** 95% live in college housing. Average age is 17.

FALL-TERM APPLICATIONS. No fee. No closing date; applicants notified on a rolling basis; must reply within 30 days. Interview required.

STUDENT LIFE. Housing: Dormitories (men). **Additional information:** Religious observance required.

STUDENT SERVICES. Services/facilities for handicapped.

ANNUAL EXPENSES. Tuition and fees: $3,200. **Room and board:** $4,000. **Books and supplies:** $500. **Other expenses:** $1,600.

FINANCIAL AID. 28% of freshmen, 64% of continuing students receive some form of aid. 96% of grants, all loans, all jobs based on need. 17 enrolled freshmen were judged to have need, all were offered aid. Academic, alumni affiliation scholarships available. **Aid applications:** No closing date; priority given to applications received by June 1; applicants notified on a rolling basis; must reply within 30 days.

ADDRESS/TELEPHONE. Beryl Weisgord, Dean of Admissions, Ner Israel Rabbinical College, 400 Mount Wilson Lane, Baltimore, MD 21208-9964. (410) 484-7200. Fax: (410) 484-3060.

Prince George's Community College
Largo, Maryland CB code: 5545

2-year public community college, coed. Founded in 1958. **Accreditation:** Regional. **Undergraduate enrollment:** 1,218 men, 1,986 women full time; 3,844 men, 6,270 women part time. **Faculty:** 612 total (234 full time). **Location:** Suburban campus in large town; 10 miles from Washington, D.C. **Calendar:** Semester, limited summer session. Saturday and extensive evening/early morning classes. **Additional facts:** Extension center at Andrews Air Force Base serves both military and civilian personnel.

DEGREES OFFERED. AA. 798 associate degrees awarded in 1992. 28% in business and management, 10% computer sciences, 7% teacher education, 18% allied health, 21% multi/interdisciplinary studies, 10% parks/recreation, protective services, public affairs.

UNDERGRADUATE MAJORS. Accounting, American studies, business administration and management, business and management, business and office, business data processing and related programs, business education, child development/care/guidance, computer and information sciences, computer programming, computer servicing technology, computer technology, criminal justice technology, drafting, drafting and design technology, electronic technology, elementary education, engineering, engineering and engineering-related technologies, fine arts, food production/management/services, health education, hotel/motel and restaurant management, information sciences and systems, legal assistant/paralegal, legal secretary, liberal/general studies, marketing and distribution, marketing management, medical records technology, medical secretary, microcomputer software, music, nuclear medical technology, nursing, physical education, radiograph medical technology, respiratory therapy technology, secondary education, secretarial and related programs, systems analysis, word processing.

ACADEMIC PROGRAMS. 2-year transfer program, cooperative education, dual enrollment of high school students, honors program, independent study, telecourses, weekend college. **Remedial services:** Learning center, remedial instruction, tutoring, writing center. **Placement/credit:** AP, CLEP General and Subject, institutional tests; 30 credit hours maximum for associate degree.

ACADEMIC REQUIREMENTS. Freshmen must earn minimum GPA of 1.5 to continue in good standing. 50% of freshmen return for sophomore year. Students must declare major on application. **Graduation requirements:**

62 hours for associate. Most students required to take courses in English, history, humanities, mathematics, biological/physical sciences, social sciences.

FRESHMAN ADMISSIONS. Selection criteria: Open admissions. Selective admissions to health technology programs and for international students. High school diploma or GED required for admission to health technology programs. **Test requirements:** Descriptive Tests of Language and Mathematics Skills (DTLS/DTMS) required of all degree-seeking applicants.

1992 FRESHMAN CLASS PROFILE. 2,730 men and women enrolled.

FALL-TERM APPLICATIONS. No fee. No closing date; applicants notified on a rolling basis. Deferred and early admission available.

STUDENT LIFE. Activities: Student government, film, magazine, student newspaper, literary magazine, debate tean, choral groups, concert band, dance, drama, jazz band, musical theater, opera, symphony orchestra, Union of Black Scholars, Active Seniors (for senior citizens), Student Program Board.

ATHLETICS. NJCAA. **Intercollegiate:** Baseball M, basketball, golf M, soccer M, tennis, volleyball W. **Intramural:** Baseball, basketball, bowling, tennis.

STUDENT SERVICES. Aptitude testing, career counseling, employment service for undergraduates, freshman orientation, health services, on-campus day care, personal counseling, placement service for graduates, veterans counselor, special advisors for handicapped students, services/facilities for handicapped.

ANNUAL EXPENSES. Tuition and fees (1992-93): $2,290, $2,040 additional for out-of-district students, $4,490 additional for out-of-state students. **Books and supplies:** $500. **Other expenses:** $800.

FINANCIAL AID. 57% of freshmen, 35% of continuing students receive some form of aid. 95% of grants based on need. 1,200 enrolled freshmen were judged to have need, all were offered aid. Academic, music/drama, athletic scholarships available. **Aid applications:** No closing date; priority given to applications received by June 15; applicants notified on a rolling basis beginning on or about June 1; must reply within 10 days.

ADDRESS/TELEPHONE. Vera Bagley, Director of Admissions and Records, Prince George's Community College, 301 Largo Road, Largo, MD 20772-2199. (301) 322-0801. Fax: (301) 808-0960.

St. John's College

Annapolis, Maryland — CB code: 5598

Admissions:	84% of applicants accepted
Based on:	••• Essay, interview, school record
	•• Recommendations
	• Activities, special talents, test scores
Completion:	90% of freshmen end year in good standing
	60% graduate, 20% of these enter graduate study

4-year private liberal arts college, coed. Founded in 1784. **Accreditation:** Regional. **Undergraduate enrollment:** 236 men, 165 women full time; 2 men, 5 women part time. **Graduate enrollment:** 29 men, 26 women full time; 8 men, 5 women part time. **Faculty:** 69 total (63 full time), 41 with doctorates or other terminal degrees. **Location:** Urban campus in large town; 30 miles from Washington, D.C. and Baltimore. **Calendar:** Semester, limited summer session. **Microcomputers:** 12 located in libraries, computer centers. **Special facilities:** Art gallery, boathouse, planetarium. **Additional facts:** Second campus in Sante Fe, New Mexico. Students can transfer between campuses. Great Books Program: rigorous interdisciplinary program based on reading and discussion of seminal works of Western civilization in fields of philosophy, mathematics, literature, political theory, theology, the sciences, history, language (classical Greek and French), and music. Work progresses through use of original sources, small discussion classes, written essays, oral final examinations, and individual student progress evaluations.

DEGREES OFFERED. BA, MA. 76 bachelor's degrees awarded in 1992. 100% in multi/interdisciplinary studies. Graduate degrees offered in 2 major fields of study.

UNDERGRADUATE MAJORS. European studies, liberal/general studies.

ACADEMIC REQUIREMENTS. No policy requiring minimum GPA; records of students having academic difficulty are reviewed individually. 81% of freshmen return for sophomore year. **Graduation requirements:** 132 hours for bachelor's (132 in major). Most students required to take courses in arts/fine arts, English, foreign languages, history, humanities, mathematics, philosophy/religion, biological/physical sciences, social sciences. **Postgraduate studies:** 5% enter law school, 2% enter medical school, 2% enter MBA programs, 11% enter other graduate study.

FRESHMAN ADMISSIONS. Selection criteria: One optional and 3 required essays most important. School achievement record and teacher recommendations also considered. 2-day campus visit very important. **High school preparation:** 16 units required. Required units include English 4, foreign language 2, mathematics 3 and physical science 2. Additional mathematics, sciences, and foreign language units recommended.

1992 FRESHMAN CLASS PROFILE. 165 men applied, 137 accepted, 63 enrolled; 138 women applied, 117 accepted, 44 enrolled. 29% were in top tenth and 53% were in top quarter of graduating class. **Academic background:** Mid 50% of enrolled freshmen had SAT-V between 540-650, SAT-M between 520-640. 84% submitted SAT scores. **Characteristics:** 19% from in state, 100% live in college housing, 10% have minority backgrounds, 7% are foreign students. Average age is 18.

FALL-TERM APPLICATIONS. No fee. No closing date; priority given to applications received by March 1; applicants notified on a rolling basis. Essay required. Interview recommended. CRDA. Deferred and early admission available. Early application encouraged as class generally fills by first week in May.

STUDENT LIFE. Housing: Dormitories (coed). **Activities:** Student government, magazine, student newspaper, yearbook, choral groups, dance, drama, music ensembles, musical theater, opera, Political Forum, Circle K.

ATHLETICS. Intramural: Badminton, basketball, boxing M, fencing, handball, racquetball, rowing (crew), sailing, soccer, softball, squash, table tennis, tennis, track and field, volleyball.

STUDENT SERVICES. Aptitude testing, career counseling, employment service for undergraduates, freshman orientation, health services, personal counseling, placement service for graduates, veterans counselor, on-campus health care, services/facilities for handicapped.

ANNUAL EXPENSES. Tuition and fees: $16,350. **Room and board:** $5,450. **Books and supplies:** $275. **Other expenses:** $700.

FINANCIAL AID. 48% of freshmen, 50% of continuing students receive some form of aid. All grants, 94% of loans, all jobs based on need. 55 enrolled freshmen were judged to have need, all were offered aid. **Aid applications:** No closing date; priority given to applications received by March 1; applicants notified on a rolling basis beginning on or about January 15; must reply by May 1 or within 3 weeks if notified thereafter.

ADDRESS/TELEPHONE. John Christensen, Director of Admissions, St. John's College, PO Box 2800, Annapolis, MD 21404-2800. (410) 263-2371 ext.222. (800) 727-9238.

St. Mary's College of Maryland

St. Mary's City, Maryland — CB code: 5601

Admissions:	44% of applicants accepted
Based on:	••• School record
	•• Recommendations, test scores
	• Activities, essay, interview, special talents
Completion:	94% of freshmen end year in good standing
	68% graduate, 26% of these enter graduate study

4-year public liberal arts college, coed. Founded in 1840. **Accreditation:** Regional. **Undergraduate enrollment:** 577 men, 695 women full time; 82 men, 156 women part time. **Faculty:** 145 total (94 full time), 111 with doctorates or other terminal degrees. **Location:** Rural campus in rural community; 70 miles from Washington, DC, 100 miles from Baltimore. **Calendar:** Semester, limited summer session. Extensive evening/early morning classes. **Microcomputers:** 70 located in libraries, classrooms, computer centers. **Special facilities:** 40-foot biology research boat, 17th-century archeological site, art gallery, waterfront facilities, aquatic animal research facilities, electron microscopes, tissue culture facilities.

DEGREES OFFERED. BA. 391 bachelor's degrees awarded in 1992. 12% in letters/literature, 11% life sciences, 17% psychology, 47% social sciences, 6% visual and performing arts.

UNDERGRADUATE MAJORS. Anthropology, biological and physical sciences, biology, chemistry, developmental psychology, dramatic arts, economics, English, fine arts, foreign languages (multiple emphasis), history, liberal/general studies, mathematics, music, philosophy, physics, political science and government, psychology, public policy studies, sociology.

ACADEMIC PROGRAMS. Double major, dual enrollment of high school students, honors program, independent study, internships, student-designed major, study abroad, visiting/exchange student program, cross-registration, exchange program with Johns Hopkins University. **Remedial services:** Learning center, reduced course load, remedial instruction, special counselor, tutoring. **Placement/credit:** AP, CLEP General and Subject, IB, institutional tests; 45 credit hours maximum for bachelor's degree.

ACADEMIC REQUIREMENTS. Freshmen must earn minimum GPA of 2.0 to continue in good standing. 90% of freshmen return for sophomore year. Students must declare major by end of second year. **Graduation requirements:** 128 hours for bachelor's (44 in major). Most students required to take courses in arts/fine arts, English, history, humanities, mathematics, philosophy/religion, biological/physical sciences, social sciences. **Postgraduate studies:** 3% enter law school, 2% enter MBA programs, 21% enter other graduate study. **Additional information:** Preprofessional advising available in medicine, dentistry, veterinary medicine, law, and education.

FRESHMAN ADMISSIONS. Selection criteria: High school record of prime importance. SAT scores, recommendations by counselors/teachers, activities and essay carefully considered. Special consideration given to minority, foreign, and out-of-state applicants. **High school preparation:** 13 units required; 20 recommended. Required and recommended units include biological science 1-4, English 4, mathematics 3-4, physical science 2-4 and social science 3-4. Foreign language 4 and science 4 recommended. **Test requirements:** SAT or ACT (SAT preferred); score report by March 15.

1992 FRESHMAN CLASS PROFILE. 503 men applied, 248 accepted, 101 enrolled; 926 women applied, 378 accepted, 134 enrolled. 72% had high school GPA of 3.0 or higher, 28% between 2.0 and 2.99. 39% were in top tenth and 72% were in top quarter of graduating class. **Academic background:** Mid 50% of enrolled freshmen had SAT-V between 520-630, SAT-M between 560-650. 91% submitted SAT scores. **Characteristics:** 84% from in state, 97% live in college housing, 20% have minority backgrounds, 4% are foreign students. Average age is 18.

FALL-TERM APPLICATIONS. $25 fee, may be waived for applicants with need. Closing date March 15; priority given to applications received by January 15; applicants notified on or about April 1; must reply by May 1. Essay required. Interview recommended. Audition recommended for music and dramatic arts applicants. Portfolio recommended for art applicants. CRDA. Early admission available. EDP-F. In order to be considered for housing students should submit application by priority date. Early decision (1) application date is December 1 with notification date January 1. Early decision (2) application date is January 1 with notification February 15.

STUDENT LIFE. Housing: Dormitories (men, women, coed); apartment housing available. Town houses available for single students, 4 students to town house. **Activities:** Student government, magazine, radio, student newspaper, television, yearbook, arts annual, choral groups, concert band, dance, drama, jazz band, music ensembles, musical theater, symphony orchestra, Black Student Union, Christian Fellowship, International Club, Young Democrats, Amnesty International, Coalition for Global Responsibility, For Goodness Sake, BACCHUS, WAGE SADD.

ATHLETICS. NCAA. **Intercollegiate:** Baseball M, basketball, field hockey W, lacrosse, sailing, soccer, swimming, tennis, volleyball W. **Intramural:** Basketball, fencing, lacrosse, rowing (crew), rugby M, sailing, soccer, swimming, tennis, volleyball M. **Clubs:** Touch football.

STUDENT SERVICES. Aptitude testing, career counseling, employment service for undergraduates, freshman orientation, health services, personal counseling, placement service for graduates, special adviser for adult students, veterans counselor, minority affairs counselor, services/facilities for handicapped.

ANNUAL EXPENSES. Tuition and fees: $4,400, $2,300 additional for out-of-state students. **Room and board:** $4,500. **Books and supplies:** $650. **Other expenses:** $1,000.

FINANCIAL AID. 53% of freshmen, 50% of continuing students receive some form of aid. 52% of grants, 82% of loans, 11% of jobs based on need. 61 enrolled freshmen were judged to have need, 56 were offered aid. Academic, music/drama, alumni affiliation, minority scholarships available. **Aid applications:** Closing date March 1; applicants notified on or about April 1; must reply by May 1.

ADDRESS/TELEPHONE. James Antonio, Dean of Admissions, St. Mary's College of Maryland, St. Mary's City, MD 20686-9998. (301) 862-0292. (800) 492-7181. Fax: (301) 862-0906.

Salisbury State University
Salisbury, Maryland

CB code: 5403

Admissions: 54% of applicants accepted
Based on: ••• School record, test scores
• Activities, essay, interview, recommendations, special talents
Completion: 85% of freshmen end year in good standing
52% graduate, 33% of these enter graduate study

4-year public liberal arts college, coed. Founded in 1925. **Accreditation:** Regional. **Undergraduate enrollment:** 1,956 men, 2,389 women full time; 435 men, 617 women part time. **Graduate enrollment:** 41 men, 87 women full time; 123 men, 374 women part time. **Faculty:** 319 total (238 full time), 210 with doctorates or other terminal degrees. **Location:** Suburban campus in small city; 110 miles from Baltimore, and Washington, D.C. **Calendar:** 4-1-4, extensive summer session. **Microcomputers:** 75 located in libraries, classrooms, computer centers. **Special facilities:** Arboretum, research center for Delmarva history and culture, small business development center network.

DEGREES OFFERED. BA, BS, BFA, MA, MS, MBA, MEd. 958 bachelor's degrees awarded in 1992. 23% in business and management, 9% communications, 12% teacher education, 7% health sciences, 5% life sciences, 12% multi/interdisciplinary studies, 5% psychology, 8% social sciences. Graduate degrees offered in 12 major fields of study.

UNDERGRADUATE MAJORS. Accounting, anthropology, applied mathematics, biological and physical sciences, biology, business administration and management, chemistry, clinical laboratory science, communications, dramatic arts, earth sciences, economics, education, English, English education, English literature, Environmental health, environmental science, fine arts, French, geography, history, humanities and social sciences, liberal/general studies, management information systems, mathematics, mathematics education, music, music education, nursing, philosophy, physical education, physical sciences, physics, physics/microelectronics, political science and government, predentistry, prelaw, premedicine, prepharmacy, preveterinary, psychology, radio/television broadcasting, recreation and community services technologies, respiratory therapy, science education, social science education, social sciences, social studies education, social work, sociology, Spanish, speech, speech/communication/theater education, sports medicine.

ACADEMIC PROGRAMS. Accelerated program, cooperative education, double major, dual enrollment of high school students, honors program, independent study, internships, student-designed major, study abroad, teacher preparation, cross-registration; liberal arts/career combination in engineering, health sciences; combined bachelor's/graduate program in law. **Remedial services:** Learning center, remedial instruction, special counselor, tutoring. **ROTC:** Army. **Placement/credit:** AP, CLEP General and Subject, institutional tests; 60 credit hours maximum for bachelor's degree.

ACADEMIC REQUIREMENTS. Freshmen must earn minimum GPA of 2.0 to continue in good standing. 80% of freshmen return for sophomore year. Students must declare major by end of second year. **Graduation requirements:** 120 hours for bachelor's (33 in major). Most students required to take courses in arts/fine arts, English, history, humanities, mathematics, biological/physical sciences, social sciences. **Postgraduate studies:** 2% enter law school, 1% enter medical school, 5% enter MBA programs, 25% enter other graduate study.

FRESHMAN ADMISSIONS. Selection criteria: High school record most important, followed by test scores. **High school preparation:** 14 units required. Required units include English 4, foreign language 2, mathematics 3, social science 3 and science 2. **Test requirements:** SAT or ACT (SAT preferred); score report by March 1.

1992 FRESHMAN CLASS PROFILE. 1,609 men applied, 930 accepted, 263 enrolled; 2,254 women applied, 1,170 accepted, 374 enrolled. 67% had high school GPA of 3.0 or higher, 33% between 2.0 and 2.99. 22% were in top tenth and 62% were in top quarter of graduating class. **Academic background:** Mid 50% of enrolled freshmen had SAT-V between 460-540, SAT-M between 510-600; ACT composite between 21-23. 98% submitted SAT scores, 3% submitted ACT scores. **Characteristics:** 80% from in state, 80% live in college housing, 7% have minority backgrounds, 1% are foreign students, 16% join fraternities/sororities. Average age is 18.

FALL-TERM APPLICATIONS. $25 fee, may be waived for applicants with need. Closing date March 1; priority given to applications received by January 15; applicants notified on or about March 15; must reply by May 1. Audition required for music applicants. Portfolio required for art applicants. Interview recommended. CRDA. Early admission available.

STUDENT LIFE. Housing: Dormitories (men, women, coed). Academic housing, honors groupings available. **Activities:** Student government, film, magazine, radio, student newspaper, television, yearbook, choral groups, concert band, dance, drama, jazz band, music ensembles, musical theater, pep band, symphony orchestra, fraternities, sororities, Afro-American Union.

ATHLETICS. NCAA. **Intercollegiate:** Baseball M, basketball, cross-country, field hockey M, football M, lacrosse, soccer M, softball W, swimming W, tennis, track and field, volleyball W. **Intramural:** Archery, badminton, basketball, bowling, cross-country, golf, gymnastics, handball, ice hockey M, lacrosse, racquetball, rifle, rugby, sailing, skiing, soccer, softball, swimming, table tennis, tennis, volleyball, water polo.

STUDENT SERVICES. Aptitude testing, career counseling, employment service for undergraduates, freshman orientation, health services, personal counseling, placement service for graduates, veterans counselor, services/facilities for handicapped.

ANNUAL EXPENSES. Tuition and fees (projected): $3,026, $2,668 additional for out-of-state students. **Room and board:** $4,490. **Books and supplies:** $550. **Other expenses:** $750.

FINANCIAL AID. 19% of freshmen, 68% of continuing students receive some form of aid. 74% of grants, all loans, 7% of jobs based on need. 310 enrolled freshmen were judged to have need, 275 were offered aid. Academic, state/district residency, minority scholarships available. **Aid applications:** No closing date; priority given to applications received by March 1; applicants notified on a rolling basis beginning on or about April 1; must reply within 2 weeks. **Additional information:** Job opportunities provided for almost 30% of full-time undergraduate students (over 900 jobs). Students can expect to earn between $1,200 and $2,000 per academic year by working 10 to 15 hours per week.

ADDRESS/TELEPHONE. Jane H. Dane', Dean of Admissions, Salisbury State University, Camden and College Avenues, Salisbury, MD 21801-6862. (410) 543-6160. Fax: (410) 543-6068.

Sojourner-Douglass College
Baltimore, Maryland

CB code: 0504

4-year private liberal arts college, coed. Founded in 1980. **Accreditation:** Regional. **Undergraduate enrollment:** 262 men and women. **Faculty:** 67 total (14 full time), 12 with doctorates or other terminal degrees. **Location:** Urban campus in very large city. **Calendar:** Trimester. **Microcomputers:** Located in computer centers.

DEGREES OFFERED. BA. 46 bachelor's degrees awarded in 1992.

54% in business and management, 18% education, 5% health sciences, 11% parks/recreation, protective services, public affairs, 14% psychology.

UNDERGRADUATE MAJORS. Accounting, business administration and management, business economics, counseling psychology, criminal justice studies, early childhood education, elementary education, health care administration, public administration, social work.

ACADEMIC PROGRAMS. Accelerated program, cooperative education, honors program, independent study, internships. **Remedial services:** Learning center, remedial instruction, tutoring.

ACADEMIC REQUIREMENTS. Freshmen must earn minimum GPA of 2.0 to continue in good standing. 48% of freshmen return for sophomore year. **Graduation requirements:** Most students required to take courses in English, history, humanities, social sciences.

FRESHMAN ADMISSIONS. Selection criteria: Evaluation of interview, autobiographical sketch, resume, and institutional test.

1992 FRESHMAN CLASS PROFILE. 72 men and women enrolled. **Characteristics:** 100% from in state, 100% commute, 99% have minority backgrounds, 2% are foreign students. Average age is 32.

FALL-TERM APPLICATIONS. $10 fee, may be waived for applicants with need. No closing date; applicants notified on a rolling basis. Interview required.

STUDENT LIFE. Activities: Student government, student newspaper.

STUDENT SERVICES. Career counseling, on-campus day care, personal counseling.

ANNUAL EXPENSES. Tuition and fees (1992-93): $4,950. **Books and supplies:** $450. **Other expenses:** $1,400.

FINANCIAL AID. 48% of freshmen, 98% of continuing students receive some form of aid. 99% of grants, all loans, all jobs based on need. 33 enrolled freshmen were judged to have need, all were offered aid. Academic, state/district residency scholarships available. **Aid applications:** No closing date; applicants notified on a rolling basis.

ADDRESS/TELEPHONE. Brenda Edmundson, Coordinator of Admissions, Sojourner-Douglass College, 500 North Caroline Street, Baltimore, MD 21205. (410) 276-0306. Fax: (410) 675-1811.

Towson State University

Towson, Maryland CB code: 5404

Admissions:	61% of applicants accepted
Based on:	••• School record, test scores
	• Activities, essay, interview, recommendations, special talents
Completion:	96% of freshmen end year in good standing
	51% graduate, 31% of these enter graduate study

4-year public university, coed. Founded in 1866. **Accreditation:** Regional. **Undergraduate enrollment:** 3,969 men, 5,725 women full time; 1,500 men, 2,210 women part time. **Graduate enrollment:** 96 men, 293 women full time; 324 men, 1,115 women part time. **Faculty:** 903 total (481 full time), 390 with doctorates or other terminal degrees. **Location:** Suburban campus in small city; 1.5 miles from Baltimore. **Calendar:** 4-1-4, extensive summer session. Saturday and extensive evening/early morning classes. **Microcomputers:** 500 located in dormitories, libraries, classrooms, computer centers. **Special facilities:** Watson-King Planetarium, Holtzman Art Gallery, Asian art collection, theaters, concert hall, greenhouse, herbarium, observatory, animal museum, writing laboratory, English language center, athletic center.

DEGREES OFFERED. BA, BS, BFA, MA, MS, MFA, MEd. 2,712 bachelor's degrees awarded in 1992. 28% in business and management, 10% communications, 18% teacher education, 6% health sciences, 6% life sciences, 7% psychology, 8% social sciences, 5% visual and performing arts. Graduate degrees offered in 21 major fields of study.

UNDERGRADUATE MAJORS. Accounting, anthropology, art education, biology, biology education, business administration and management, chemistry, chemistry education, communications, computer and information sciences, dance, dance education, dramatic arts, early childhood education, economics, education, elementary education, English, English education, fine arts, foreign languages education, French, geography, geography education, German, health education, health sciences, history, history education, humanities and social sciences, interdisciplinary studies, international studies, journalism, mathematics, mathematics education, medical laboratory technologies, music, music education, natural science education, nursing, occupational therapy, philosophy, physical education, physics, physics education, political science and government, psychology, secondary education, social sciences, social studies education, sociology, Spanish, speech pathology/audiology, studio art, women's studies.

ACADEMIC PROGRAMS. Accelerated program, cooperative education, double major, dual enrollment of high school students, honors program, independent study, internships, student-designed major, study abroad, teacher preparation, telecourses, visiting/exchange student program, weekend college, cross-registration; liberal arts/career combination in engineering. **Remedial services:** Learning center, remedial instruction, special counselor, tutoring. **ROTC:** Air Force, Army. **Placement/credit:** AP, CLEP General and Subject, institutional tests; 32 credit hours maximum for bachelor's degree.

ACADEMIC REQUIREMENTS. Freshmen must earn minimum GPA of 1.5 to continue in good standing. 81% of freshmen return for sophomore year. **Graduation requirements:** 120 hours for bachelor's (36 in major). Most students required to take courses in arts/fine arts, computer science, English, foreign languages, history, humanities, mathematics, biological/physical sciences, social sciences.

FRESHMAN ADMISSIONS. Selection criteria: Admission assured for freshman applicants with GPA of 3.0 and SAT-verbal and mathematical scores of at least 500 each. Applications of other students are evaluated on probable success grid. Out-of-state and foreign student enrollment limited to 25% of the total undergraduate student body. **High school preparation:** 20 units required. Required units include biological science 1, English 4, foreign language 2, mathematics 3, social science 3 and science 1. **Test requirements:** SAT or ACT (SAT preferred); score report by March 1.

1992 FRESHMAN CLASS PROFILE. 2,607 men applied, 1,522 accepted, 518 enrolled; 4,141 women applied, 2,586 accepted, 830 enrolled. 44% had high school GPA of 3.0 or higher, 55% between 2.0 and 2.99. **Academic background:** Mid 50% of enrolled freshmen had SAT-V between 430-510, SAT-M between 460-560. 99% submitted SAT scores. **Characteristics:** 69% from in state, 56% live in college housing, 15% have minority backgrounds, 1% are foreign students. Average age is 19.

FALL-TERM APPLICATIONS. $25 fee, may be waived for applicants with need. Closing date March 1; applicants notified on a rolling basis; must reply by May 1 or within 4 weeks if notified thereafter. Audition required for music, dance applicants. Portfolio recommended for art applicants. Essay recommended. Interview recommended for early admissions candidates, junior entry. CRDA. Early admission available.

STUDENT LIFE. Housing: Dormitories (women, coed); apartment, handicapped housing available. Although no fraternity or sorority houses on campus, one dormitory caters to such members. **Activities:** Student government, film, magazine, radio, student newspaper, television, yearbook, international relations journal, choral groups, concert band, dance, drama, jazz band, marching band, music ensembles, musical theater, pep band, symphony orchestra, mime, technical/crew, fraternities, sororities, Black Student Union, Jewish Student Union, Circle-K, Student Ambassadors, International Club, Lutheran Student Movement, Newman Club, Korean student organization, Asian Studies Club, Campus Cruscades, Graduate Student Association. **Additional information:** Students play active role in university governance.

ATHLETICS. NCAA. **Intercollegiate:** Baseball M, basketball, cross-country, diving, field hockey W, football M, golf M, gymnastics W, lacrosse, soccer, softball W, swimming, tennis, track and field, volleyball W. **Intramural:** Basketball, lacrosse, racquetball, soccer, softball, table tennis, tennis, volleyball, water polo, wrestling M.

STUDENT SERVICES. Aptitude testing, career counseling, employment service for undergraduates, freshman orientation, health services, on-campus day care, personal counseling, placement service for graduates, special adviser for adult students, veterans counselor, Women's Center, African-American Cultural Center, Minority Affairs, Commuter Affairs, Handicapped Student Services, Tuitorial Services, International Student Center, services/facilities for handicapped.

ANNUAL EXPENSES. Tuition and fees (projected): $3,123, $2,502 additional for out-of-state students. **Room and board:** $4,400. **Books and supplies:** $600. **Other expenses:** $922.

FINANCIAL AID. 22% of freshmen, 36% of continuing students receive some form of aid. 83% of grants, 86% of loans, 11% of jobs based on need. 330 enrolled freshmen were judged to have need, 290 were offered aid. Academic, music/drama, art, athletic, leadership, alumni affiliation, minority scholarships available. **Aid applications:** No closing date; priority given to applications received by March 15; applicants notified on a rolling basis beginning on or about April 1; must reply within 2 weeks. **Additional information:** Special scholarship available for those handicapped individuals who meet certain academic criteria. Resident assistant program for selected students with small salary and 14-meal board provided.

ADDRESS/TELEPHONE. Linda Strating, Director of Undergraduate Admissions, Towson State University, Administration Building, Towson, MD 21204-7097. (410) 830-3333. (800) 225-5878.

United States Naval Academy

Annapolis, Maryland CB code: 5809

Admissions:	13% of applicants accepted
Based on:	••• Activities, essay, interview, recommendations, school record, test scores
	•• Special talents
Completion:	87% of freshmen end year in good standing
	74% graduate, 2% of these enter graduate study

4-year public military college, coed. Founded in 1845. **Accreditation:** Regional. **Undergraduate enrollment:** 3,794 men, 476 women full time. **Faculty:** 600 total, 270 with doctorates or other terminal degrees. **Location:**

Suburban campus in large town; 35 miles from Washington, D.C., 20 miles from Baltimore. **Calendar:** Semester, limited summer session. **Microcomputers:** Located in dormitories, libraries, computer centers. Lease or purchase required**Special facilities:** Observatory, planetarium, satellite dish, oceanographic research vessel, weather station, towing tanks, propulsion laboratory, transonic and hypersonic sound tunnels, sub-critical reactor. **Additional facts:** Military environment and organization under student leadership with officer supervision. Professional training at US bases and with units of fleet during summer months. Graduates receive BS degree, plus a commission as ensign in US Navy or second lieutenant in US Marine Corps.

DEGREES OFFERED. BS. 1,027 bachelor's degrees awarded in 1992. 6% in computer sciences, 37% engineering, 6% letters/literature, 18% physical sciences, 30% social sciences.

UNDERGRADUATE MAJORS. Aerospace/aeronautical/astronautical engineering, chemistry, computer and information sciences, economics, electrical/electronics/communications engineering, engineering, English, history, mathematics, mechanical engineering, naval architecture and marine engineering, ocean engineering, oceanography, physical sciences, physics, political science and government, systems engineering.

ACADEMIC PROGRAMS. Double major, honors program, independent study. **Remedial services:** Learning center, remedial instruction, special counselor, tutoring, writing skills center. **Placement/credit:** AP, institutional tests.

ACADEMIC REQUIREMENTS. Freshmen must earn minimum GPA of 2.0 to continue in good standing. 90% of freshmen return for sophomore year. Students must declare major by end of first year. **Graduation requirements:** 140 hours for bachelor's. Most students required to take courses in English, history, mathematics, biological/physical sciences. **Postgraduate studies:** 1% enter medical school, 1% enter other graduate study.

FRESHMAN ADMISSIONS. Selection criteria: Test scores, school achievement record, recommendations of school officials, participation in sports and school and community activities important. Rank in top 40% of class usually required. Limited number of foreign students accepted. Recommended units include English 4, foreign language 2, mathematics 4 and physical science 2. One chemistry, 1 physics, 1 world or European history, introductory computer and typing courses also recommended. **Test requirements:** SAT or ACT; score report by March 15.

1992 FRESHMAN CLASS PROFILE. 12,268 men and women applied, 1,595 accepted; 1,070 men enrolled, 170 women enrolled. **Characteristics:** 4% from in state, 100% live in college housing, 18% have minority backgrounds. Average age is 18.

FALL-TERM APPLICATIONS. No fee. Closing date March 1; applicants notified on a rolling basis; must reply by May 1. Essay required. Interview recommended. Medical examination, physical aptitude examination required. CRDA. Nomination essential prior to consideration for appointment. Nominating authorities include President, Vice President, Secretary of Navy, members of Congress, delegates to Congress, governors of United States Territories, and resident commissioner of Puerto Rico. Address request directly to official concerned. Applicants for presidential appointments (limited by law to sons and daughters of military personnel, active or retired) contact Director of Candidate Guidance, United States Naval Academy. Applicants encouraged to apply to the Academy and nominating authority by May of junior year. Application deadline for noncongressional nominations, December 1; for congressional nominations, January 31.

STUDENT LIFE. Housing: Dormitories (coed). **Activities:** Student government, film, magazine, radio, television, yearbook, choral groups, concert band, drama, jazz band, marching band, music ensembles, pep band, Fellowship of Christian Athletes, Big Brothers, Naval Academy Christian Association, Newman Club, Big Sisters. **Additional information:** Honor concept conceived and administered by students with decision to separate made by Secretary of the Navy on recommendation of Superintendent of the Academy.

ATHLETICS. NCAA. **Intercollegiate:** Baseball M, basketball, cross-country, diving, fencing, football M, golf M, gymnastics M, lacrosse M, rifle M, rowing (crew), sailing, soccer M, squash M, swimming, tennis M, track and field, volleyball, water polo M, wrestling M. **Intramural:** Basketball, boxing M, cross-country M, fencing W, football M, gymnastics, handball, ice hockey M, lacrosse, racquetball M, rowing (crew), rugby M, sailing, skin diving, soccer, softball, squash M, swimming, tennis, track and field M, volleyball M, water polo M, wrestling M.

STUDENT SERVICES. Career counseling, freshman orientation, health services, personal counseling.

ANNUAL EXPENSES. Tuition and fees (1992-93): $0. First-year students pay deposit of $1,500 for initial outfitting of uniforms and other supplies. Tuition, room and board, and medical and dental care provided by United States government. Each midshipman receives monthly salary of about $560 to cover costs of books, supplies, uniforms, laundry, and equipment, including microcomputer.

ADDRESS/TELEPHONE. Captain John W. Renard, USN (Retired), Dean of Admissions, United States Naval Academy, 117 Decatur Road, Annapolis, MD 21402-5018. (800) 638-9156.

University of Baltimore
Baltimore, Maryland CB code: 5810

2-year upper-division public university, coed. Founded in 1925. **Accreditation:** Regional. **Undergraduate enrollment:** 638 men, 593 women full time; 881 men, 989 women part time. **Graduate enrollment:** 718 men, 617 women full time; 699 men, 655 women part time. **Faculty:** 277 total (171 full time), 205 with doctorates or other terminal degrees. **Location:** Urban campus in very large city; downtown Baltimore. **Calendar:** Semester, extensive summer session. Saturday and extensive evening/early morning classes. **Microcomputers:** 100 located in libraries, computer centers.

DEGREES OFFERED. BA, BS, MA, MS, MBA, JD. 690 bachelor's degrees awarded in 1992. 60% in business and management, 6% communications, 5% law, 5% multi/interdisciplinary studies, 15% social sciences. Graduate degrees offered in 16 major fields of study.

UNDERGRADUATE MAJORS. Accounting, advertising, business administration and management, business and management, business economics, communications, computer and information sciences, computer programming, creative writing, criminal justice studies, criminology, data processing, dramatic arts, economics, English, English literature, finance, history, humanities and social sciences, information sciences and systems, law enforcement and corrections, liberal/general studies, management information systems, marketing management, political science and government, prelaw, psychology, social sciences, sociology.

ACADEMIC PROGRAMS. Accelerated program, cooperative education, double major, honors program, independent study, internships, student-designed major, study abroad, cross-registration; combined bachelor's/graduate program in business administration, law. **Remedial services:** Learning center, preadmission summer program, reduced course load, remedial instruction, special counselor, tutoring. **ROTC:** Army. **Placement/credit:** CLEP General and Subject, institutional tests; 30 credit hours maximum for bachelor's degree.

ACADEMIC REQUIREMENTS. Students must declare major on application. **Graduation requirements:** 120 hours for bachelor's (21 in major). Most students required to take courses in arts/fine arts, computer science, English, humanities, mathematics, biological/physical sciences, social sciences. **Postgraduate studies:** 3% enter law school, 5% enter MBA programs, 5% enter other graduate study. **Additional information:** All undergraduate students take 12 hours in an upper-level core curriculum in a general humanities-based general education.

ADMISSIONS. Admission based on transcript evaluation. Notification on rolling basis. Minimum of 56 transferable credits required. 30-hour residency requirement. Credit will be given for grades of 1.0 for some programs if cumulative GPA is 2.0 or higher.

FALL-TERM APPLICATIONS. $15 fee, may be waived for applicants with need.

STUDENT LIFE. Activities: Student government, magazine, student newspaper, fraternities, Black Student Association, International Student Association, various other organizations.

ATHLETICS. Intramural: Basketball, rowing (crew), volleyball.

STUDENT SERVICES. Aptitude testing, career counseling, employment service for undergraduates, health services, placement service for graduates, veterans counselor, services/facilities for handicapped.

ANNUAL EXPENSES. Tuition and fees (projected): $2,874, $2,240 additional for out-of-state students. **Books and supplies:** $550. **Other expenses:** $1,776.

FINANCIAL AID. 17% of continuing students receive some form of aid. 84% of grants, 80% of loans, all jobs based on need. Academic scholarships available. **Aid applications:** No closing date; priority given to applications received by April 1; applicants notified on a rolling basis beginning on or about June 30; must reply by date noted on acceptance letter. **Additional information:** Full need met for dependent students only.

ADDRESS/TELEPHONE. Dorothy Umans, Director of Admissions, University of Baltimore, 1420 North Charles Street, Baltimore, MD 21201-5779. (410) 625-3350. Fax: (410) 234-3947.

University of Maryland: Baltimore
Baltimore, Maryland CB code: 0527

2-year upper-division public professional schools campus, coed. Founded in 1807. **Accreditation:** Regional. **Undergraduate enrollment:** 153 men, 672 women full time; 19 men, 93 women part time. **Graduate enrollment:** 1,162 men, 1,723 women full time; 299 men, 943 women part time. **Faculty:** 1,453 total (1,138 full time). **Location:** Urban campus in very large city. **Calendar:** 4-1-4. **Microcomputers:** 23 located in libraries, classrooms, computer centers. **Special facilities:** Dental, medical, and pharmacy museums.

DEGREES OFFERED. BS, MS, MSW, PhD, DDS, MD, Pharm D, JD. 363 bachelor's degrees awarded in 1992. 68% in health sciences, 32% allied health. Graduate degrees offered in 24 major fields of study.

UNDERGRADUATE MAJORS. Clinical laboratory science, dental laboratory technology, emergency/disaster science, medical laboratory technologies, nursing.

ACADEMIC PROGRAMS. Combined bachelor's/graduate program in medicine, law. **Remedial services:** Learning center, preadmission summer program, reduced course load, tutoring. **Placement/credit:** CLEP Subject, institutional tests; 30 credit hours maximum for bachelor's degree.

ACADEMIC REQUIREMENTS. Students must declare major on enrollment. **Graduation requirements:** 120 hours for bachelor's (60 in major).

STUDENT LIFE. Housing: Apartment housing available. **Activities:** Student government, student newspaper, campuswide tabloid and magazine (not for students only), Newman Center, International Student Group, African-American student association.

ATHLETICS. Intramural: Basketball, racquetball, squash, volleyball.

STUDENT SERVICES. Employment service for undergraduates, health services, personal counseling, services/facilities for handicapped.

ANNUAL EXPENSES. Tuition and fees (projected): $3,006, $5,390 additional for out-of-state students. Fees vary by program. Nursing tuition and fees $4,030. **Room and board:** $1,780 room only. **Books and supplies:** $1,145. **Other expenses:** $1,200.

FINANCIAL AID. 85% of continuing students receive some form of aid. 99% of grants, 81% of loans, all jobs based on need. **Aid applications:** No closing date; priority given to applications received by March 15; applicants notified on a rolling basis beginning on or about May 1; must reply within 2 weeks.

ADDRESS/TELEPHONE. Wayne A. Smith, Director of Records and Registration, University of Maryland: Baltimore, Baltimore Student Union, 621 West Lombard Street, Baltimore, MD 21201. (410) 706-7480.

University of Maryland: Baltimore County
Baltimore, Maryland CB code: 5835

Admissions: 58% of applicants accepted
Based on: ••• School record, test scores
• Activities, essay, interview, recommendations, special talents
Completion: 89% of freshmen end year in good standing
36% graduate, 32% of these enter graduate study

4-year public university, coed. Founded in 1966. **Accreditation:** Regional. **Undergraduate enrollment:** 3,183 men, 3,201 women full time; 1,203 men, 1,497 women part time. **Graduate enrollment:** 339 men, 350 women full time; 430 men, 451 women part time. **Faculty:** 623 total (384 full time), 410 with doctorates or other terminal degrees. **Location:** Suburban campus in very large city; 5 miles from downtown Baltimore. **Calendar:** 4-1-4, extensive summer session. Saturday and extensive evening/early morning classes. **Microcomputers:** 225 located in dormitories, libraries, classrooms, computer centers. **Special facilities:** Art gallery, greenhouse, research spectrometers, nuclear magnetic resonance machines, electron microscope facility, computer art laboratory, new engineering/computer science building.

DEGREES OFFERED. BA, BS, MA, MS, MFA, PhD. 1,555 bachelor's degrees awarded in 1992. 19% in computer sciences, 13% health sciences, 5% letters/literature, 6% life sciences, 7% parks/recreation, protective services, public affairs, 11% psychology, 20% social sciences, 7% visual and performing arts. Graduate degrees offered in 30 major fields of study.

UNDERGRADUATE MAJORS. Afro-American (black) studies, American studies, ancient studies, biochemical engineering, biochemistry, biology, chemical engineering, chemistry, classics, computer and information sciences, dance, dramatic arts, economics, emergency/disaster science, English, French, geography, German, health care administration, history, information sciences and systems, liberal/general studies, linguistics, mathematics, mechanical engineering, molecular biology, music, nursing, philosophy, physics, political science and government, psychology, Russian, social work, sociology, Spanish, visual and performing arts.

ACADEMIC PROGRAMS. Accelerated program, cooperative education, double major, dual enrollment of high school students, honors program, independent study, internships, student-designed major, study abroad, teacher preparation, telecourses, visiting/exchange student program, cross-registration; combined bachelor's/graduate program in law. **Remedial services:** Learning center, preadmission summer program, special counselor, tutoring. **ROTC:** Air Force, Army. **Placement/credit:** AP, CLEP General and Subject, institutional tests; 60 credit hours maximum for bachelor's degree.

ACADEMIC REQUIREMENTS. Freshmen must earn minimum GPA of 2.0 to continue in good standing. 81% of freshmen return for sophomore year. Students must declare major by end of second year. **Graduation requirements:** 120 hours for bachelor's (36 in major). Most students required to take courses in arts/fine arts, English, foreign languages, humanities, mathematics, biological/physical sciences, social sciences. **Postgraduate studies:** 2% enter law school, 3% enter medical school, 2% enter MBA programs, 25% enter other graduate study. **Additional information:** A limited number of programs have off-campus components that serve Cumberland, Hagerstown, Southern Maryland, Harford County, Montgomery County, and the Eastern Shore.

FRESHMAN ADMISSIONS. High school preparation: 20 units required. Required and recommended units include English 4, foreign language 2, mathematics 3-4, social science 3 and science 2. Algebra I and II, geometry and two years of laboratory-based science required. **Test requirements:** SAT or ACT (SAT preferred); score report by May 1.

1992 FRESHMAN CLASS PROFILE. 1,875 men applied, 1,119 accepted, 467 enrolled; 2,531 women applied, 1,415 accepted, 466 enrolled. 53% had high school GPA of 3.0 or higher, 46% between 2.0 and 2.99. 31% were in top tenth and 60% were in top quarter of graduating class. **Academic background:** Mid 50% of enrolled freshmen had SAT-V between 440-560, SAT-M between 510-620. 97% submitted SAT scores. **Characteristics:** 93% from in state, 51% commute, 30% have minority backgrounds, 2% are foreign students, 15% join fraternities/sororities. Average age is 19.

FALL-TERM APPLICATIONS. $25 fee, may be waived for applicants with need. Closing date May 1; priority given to applications received by December 1; applicants notified on or about December 30; must reply by May 1. Audition recommended for music, dance, theatre applicants. Essay recommended. CRDA. Deferred and early admission available. Notification of decisions after the following review dates: December 1, February 1, April 1 and May 1.

STUDENT LIFE. Housing: Dormitories (men, women, coed); apartment housing available. Residential floors for honors college students. **Activities:** Student government, film, magazine, radio, student newspaper, television, choral groups, concert band, dance, drama, jazz band, music ensembles, musical theater, pep band, symphony orchestra, fraternities, sororities, Black Student Union, Chinese Students Association, Jewish Student Association, Korean Club, International Students Association, Gay and Lesbian Organization, Progressive Action Committee, Christian Fellowship, Women's Union, Amnesty International.

ATHLETICS. NCAA. **Intercollegiate:** Baseball M, basketball, cross-country, diving, golf M, lacrosse, soccer, softball W, swimming, tennis, track and field, volleyball W. **Intramural:** Badminton, basketball, cross-country, soccer, softball, table tennis, tennis, volleyball.

STUDENT SERVICES. Career counseling, employment service for undergraduates, freshman orientation, health services, personal counseling, placement service for graduates, special adviser for adult students, veterans counselor, services/facilities for handicapped.

ANNUAL EXPENSES. Tuition and fees: $3,338, $5,256 additional for out-of-state students. **Room and board:** $4,556. **Books and supplies:** $494. **Other expenses:** $1,085.

FINANCIAL AID. 66% of freshmen, 42% of continuing students receive some form of aid. 59% of grants, 84% of loans, 12% of jobs based on need. 615 enrolled freshmen were judged to have need, 505 were offered aid. Academic, music/drama, art, athletic, minority scholarships available. **Aid applications:** No closing date; priority given to applications received by March 1; applicants notified on a rolling basis beginning on or about April 15; must reply within 2 weeks. **Additional information:** Mayerhoff Scholarship program targets outstanding minority students in science and technology, and provides full scholarships plus computers, stipends, and various academic support services.

ADDRESS/TELEPHONE. Mindy Hand, Director of Admissions, University of Maryland: Baltimore County, 5401 Wilkens Avenue, Baltimore, MD 21228-5398. (410) 455-2291. Fax: (410) 455-1210.

University of Maryland: College Park
College Park, Maryland CB code: 5814

4-year public university, coed. Founded in 1856. **Accreditation:** Regional. **Undergraduate enrollment:** 10,281 men, 9,439 women full time; 2,114 men, 1,796 women part time. **Graduate enrollment:** 2,429 men, 1,890 women full time; 2,378 men, 2,531 women part time. **Faculty:** 2,543 total (1,999 full time), 1,879 with doctorates or other terminal degrees. **Location:** Suburban campus in large town; 30 miles from Baltimore, 9 miles from Washington, D.C. **Calendar:** Semester, extensive summer session. **Microcomputers:** 576 located in dormitories, libraries, classrooms, computer centers. **Special facilities:** Radiation research laboratories, nuclear reactor, engineering-design wind tunnel, super conductivity research center and cartographic laboratory.

DEGREES OFFERED. BA, BS, BArch, MA, MS, MBA, MFA, MEd, PhD, EdD. 5,565 bachelor's degrees awarded in 1992. 15% in business and management, 8% communications, 7% education, 11% engineering, 6% home economics, 7% letters/literature, 5% life sciences, 5% psychology, 20% social sciences. Graduate degrees offered in 93 major fields of study.

UNDERGRADUATE MAJORS. Accounting, advertising, aerospace/aeronautical/astronautical engineering, Afro-American (black) studies, agribusiness, agricultural economics, agricultural engineering, agricultural sciences, agronomy, American studies, animal sciences, anthropology, architecture, art history, astronomy, biochemistry, biology, botany, business administration and management, business and management, business statistics, chemical engineering, chemistry, civil engineering, classics, community services, computer and information sciences, criminal justice studies, criminology, dance, dramatic arts, East Asian studies, economics, education, education of the physically handicapped, electrical/electronics/communications engineering, engineering, English, English literature, entomology, family/consumer resource management, fashion merchandising, finance, fire protection, food science and nutrition, food sciences, French, geography, geology, German, history, home economics education, horticultural science, horticulture, human environment and housing, individual and family development, industrial arts education, information sciences and systems, institutional/home management/supporting programs, interior design, Italian, Japanese, Jewish studies, journalism, labor/industrial relations, liberal/general studies, linguistics, management information systems, marketing and distributive education, marketing management, materials engineering, mathematics, mathematics education, mechanical engineering, microbiology, music, music history and appreciation, music performance, music theory and composition, nuclear engineering, ornamental horticulture, parks and recreation management, personnel management, philosophy, physical sciences, physics, political science and government, Portuguese, poultry, prepharmacy, preveterinary, psychology, public relations, radio/television broadcasting, radio/television technology, renewable natural resources, Russian, Russian and Slavic studies, science education, Slavic languages, social science education, sociology, soil sciences, Spanish, special education, speech, speech correction, speech pathology/audiology, speech/communication/theater education, studio art, textiles and clothing, transportation management, urban design, urban studies, wildlife management, zoology.

ACADEMIC PROGRAMS. Cooperative education, double major, dual enrollment of high school students, honors program, independent study, internships, student-designed major, study abroad, teacher preparation, telecourses, visiting/exchange student program, cross-registration; combined bachelor's/graduate program in business administration. **Remedial services:** Learning center, preadmission summer program, reduced course load, remedial instruction, special counselor, tutoring. **ROTC:** Air Force. **Placement/credit:** AP, CLEP General and Subject, institutional tests; 60 credit hours maximum for bachelor's degree.

ACADEMIC REQUIREMENTS. Freshmen must earn minimum GPA of 2.0 to continue in good standing. 85% of freshmen return for sophomore year. Students must declare major by end of second year. **Graduation requirements:** 120 hours for bachelor's. Most students required to take courses in arts/fine arts, English, history, humanities, mathematics, biological/physical sciences, social sciences. **Postgraduate studies:** 4% enter law school, 2% enter medical school, 3% enter MBA programs, 27% enter other graduate study.

FRESHMAN ADMISSIONS. Selection criteria: High school GPA and SAT scores most important. Standards for out-of-state slightly higher than in-state. Special abilities, school and community activities considered. **High school preparation:** 12 units required. Required units include English 4, foreign language 2, mathematics 3, social science 3 and science 2. Algebra I and II, plane geometry required. **Test requirements:** SAT; score report by April 30.

1992 FRESHMAN CLASS PROFILE. 1,681 men, 1,602 women enrolled. 68% had high school GPA of 3.0 or higher, 32% between 2.0 and 2.99. 24% were in top tenth and 61% were in top quarter of graduating class. **Academic background:** Mid 50% of enrolled freshmen had SAT-V between 450-570, SAT-M between 530-660. 87% submitted SAT scores. **Characteristics:** 68% from in state, 56% commute, 33% have minority backgrounds, 2% are foreign students. Average age is 19.

FALL-TERM APPLICATIONS. $30 fee, may be waived for applicants with need. Closing date April 30; priority given to applications received by December 1; applicants notified on a rolling basis; must reply by May 1. Audition required for music applicants. Essay recommended. CRDA. Early admission available. Institutional early decision plan. Students completing applications by December 1 will be notified no later than January 2.

STUDENT LIFE. Housing: Dormitories (men, women, coed); apartment, fraternity, sorority housing available. Language, honors, and international residence halls available. **Activities:** Student government, film, magazine, radio, student newspaper, television, yearbook, choral groups, concert band, dance, drama, jazz band, marching band, music ensembles, musical theater, opera, pep band, symphony orchestra, fraternities, sororities, more than 275 religious, political, ethnic, and social service organizations.

ATHLETICS. NCAA. **Intercollegiate:** Baseball M, basketball, cross-country, field hockey W, football M, golf M, gymnastics W, lacrosse, soccer, swimming, tennis, track and field, volleyball W, wrestling M. **Intramural:** Badminton, basketball, bowling, racquetball, soccer, softball, table tennis, volleyball.

STUDENT SERVICES. Aptitude testing, career counseling, employment service for undergraduates, freshman orientation, health services, on-campus day care, personal counseling, placement service for graduates, special adviser for adult students, veterans counselor, placement center for alumni, international education services, housing service, crisis center, services/facilities for handicapped.

ANNUAL EXPENSES. Tuition and fees (projected): $3,179, $5,604 additional for out-of-state students. **Room and board:** $5,003. **Books and supplies:** $550. **Other expenses:** $1,550.

FINANCIAL AID. 34% of freshmen, 66% of continuing students receive some form of aid. 58% of grants, 89% of loans, 6% of jobs based on need. 1,176 enrolled freshmen were judged to have need, 1,098 were offered aid. Academic, music/drama, art, athletic, state/district residency, leadership, alumni affiliation, minority scholarships available. **Aid applications:** No closing date; priority given to applications received by February 15; applicants notified on a rolling basis beginning on or about April 15; must reply within 2 weeks.

ADDRESS/TELEPHONE. Dr. Linda M. Clement, Director of Undergraduate Admissions, University of Maryland: College Park, Mitchell Building, College Park, MD 20742-5235. (301) 314-8385. Fax: (301) 314-9693.

University of Maryland: Eastern Shore
Princess Anne, Maryland — CB code: 5400

Admissions: 80% of applicants accepted
Based on: ••• School record, test scores
• Activities, essay, interview, recommendations, special talents
Completion: 75% of freshmen end year in good standing
30% graduate

4-year public university, coed. Founded in 1886. **Accreditation:** Regional. **Undergraduate enrollment:** 1,072 men, 995 women full time; 95 men, 104 women part time. **Graduate enrollment:** 38 men, 17 women full time; 51 men, 58 women part time. **Faculty:** 196 total (125 full time), 91 with doctorates or other terminal degrees. **Location:** Rural campus in rural community; 12 miles from Salisbury. **Calendar:** Semester, limited summer session. Extensive evening/early morning classes. **Microcomputers:** 75 located in libraries, classrooms, computer centers. **Special facilities:** Art gallery, technology center, performing arts center, greenhouse, Richard Henson Education Center.

DEGREES OFFERED. BA, BS, MA, MS, PhD. 217 bachelor's degrees awarded in 1992. 33% in business and management, 7% computer sciences, 14% education, 11% allied health, 5% letters/literature, 10% social sciences. Graduate degrees offered in 7 major fields of study.

UNDERGRADUATE MAJORS. Accounting, aerospace/aeronautical/astronautical engineering, agricultural sciences, biology, business administration and management, business and management, chemistry, clinical laboratory science, communications, computer and information sciences, construction, criminal justice studies, criminology, education, electrical technology, electronic technology, engineering and engineering-related technologies, English, environmental science, fashion design, fashion merchandising, fine arts, food science and nutrition, history, home economics, hotel/motel and restaurant management, interior design, liberal/general studies, marine biology, mathematics, music, physical therapy, poultry, predentistry, prelaw, premedicine, prepharmacy, preveterinary, rehabilitation counseling/services, social sciences, social work, sociology, special education.

ACADEMIC PROGRAMS. Accelerated program, cooperative education, double major, dual enrollment of high school students, honors program, independent study, internships, teacher preparation, visiting/exchange student program, weekend college, cross-registration; liberal arts/career combination in engineering, forestry. **Remedial services:** Learning center, reduced course load, remedial instruction, special counselor, tutoring. **ROTC:** Army. **Placement/credit:** AP, CLEP General and Subject, institutional tests; 60 credit hours maximum for bachelor's degree.

ACADEMIC REQUIREMENTS. Freshmen must earn minimum GPA of 1.65 to continue in good standing. 72% of freshmen return for sophomore year. Students must declare major by end of second year. **Graduation requirements:** 120 hours for bachelor's (60 in major). Most students required to take courses in arts/fine arts, computer science, English, history, humanities, mathematics, biological/physical sciences, social sciences. **Additional information:** General Honors Program and Pre-Professional Honors Program offered in cooperation with University of Maryland at Baltimore. Students who complete all program requirements are admitted to respective professional school without competing with students from regular application pool.

FRESHMAN ADMISSIONS. Selection criteria: Class rank, high school GPA, test scores. **High school preparation:** 20 units required. Required units include biological science 1, English 4, foreign language 2, mathematics 3, physical science 1 and social science 3. **Test requirements:** SAT or ACT (SAT preferred); score report by June 30. ACH required of some applicants. Score report by June 30.

1992 FRESHMAN CLASS PROFILE. 750 men applied, 562 accepted, 257 enrolled; 865 women applied, 735 accepted, 251 enrolled. 18% had high school GPA of 3.0 or higher, 67% between 2.0 and 2.99. **Academic background:** Mid 50% of enrolled freshmen had SAT-V between 350-500, SAT-M between 350-500. 95% submitted SAT scores. **Characteristics:** 72% from in state, 70% live in college housing, 75% have minority backgrounds, 4% are foreign students. Average age is 18.

FALL-TERM APPLICATIONS. $25 fee, may be waived for applicants with need. Closing date July 1; priority given to applications received by May 1; applicants notified on a rolling basis; must reply within 2 weeks. Audition required for music applicants. Interview recommended for honors program, physical therapy applicants. Essay recommended. Deferred and early admission available. ACH recommended for applicants to certain programs, for counseling and placement.

STUDENT LIFE. Housing: Dormitories (men, women, coed); apartment, handicapped housing available. **Activities:** Student government, radio, student newspaper, yearbook, choral groups, concert band, drama, jazz band, music ensembles, pep band, fraternities, sororities, Ecumenical Campus Ministry, NAACP.

ATHLETICS. NCAA. **Intercollegiate:** Baseball M, basketball, cross-country, soccer M, softball W, tennis, track and field, volleyball W. **Intramural:** Basketball, bowling, soccer, softball W, swimming, table tennis, volleyball.

STUDENT SERVICES. Aptitude testing, career counseling, employment service for undergraduates, freshman orientation, health services, personal counseling, placement service for graduates, special adviser for adult students, veterans counselor, services/facilities for handicapped.

ANNUAL EXPENSES. Tuition and fees: $2,674, $4,727 additional for out-of-state students. **Room and board:** $3,580. **Books and supplies:** $500. **Other expenses:** $1,000.

FINANCIAL AID. 80% of freshmen, 86% of continuing students receive some form of aid. 42% of jobs based on need. Academic, music/drama, art, athletic, leadership, alumni affiliation, religious affiliation, minority scholarships available. **Aid applications:** No closing date; priority given to applications received by March 1; applicants notified on a rolling basis beginning on or about April 1; must reply within 2 weeks.

ADDRESS/TELEPHONE. Rochell Peoples, Director of Admissions and Registrations, University of Maryland: Eastern Shore, Princess Anne, MD 21853-1299. (410) 651-2200. (800) 232-8637. Fax: (410) 651-6105.

University of Maryland: University College
College Park, Maryland — CB code: 0551

4-year public university, coed. Founded in 1947. **Accreditation:** Regional. **Undergraduate enrollment:** 447 men, 476 women full time; 4,888 men, 5,455 women part time. **Graduate enrollment:** 72 men, 45 women full time; 1,794 men, 1,541 women part time. **Faculty:** 667 total (18 full time). **Location:** Suburban campus in large town; 9 miles from Washington, D. C. **Calendar:** Semester, extensive summer session. Saturday and extensive evening/early morning classes. **Microcomputers:** 200 located in classrooms, computer centers. **Additional facts:** Courses held at over 30 locations throughout Maryland, Virginia and Washington, D.C. and Germany. Associate degree programs available only to active military personnel. Resources of all state-supported, four-year University of Maryland libraries available.

DEGREES OFFERED. AA, BA, BS, MS. 83 associate degrees awarded in 1992. 100% in multi/interdisciplinary studies. 1,816 bachelor's degrees awarded. 100% in multi/interdisciplinary studies. Graduate degrees offered in 3 major fields of study.

UNDERGRADUATE MAJORS. Associate: Liberal/general studies. **Bachelor's:** Liberal/general studies.

ACADEMIC PROGRAMS. Computer delivered (on-line) credit-bearing course offerings, cooperative education, dual enrollment of high school students, external degree, independent study, telecourses, weekend college. **Remedial services:** Developmental assistance, tutoring on fee basis. **Placement/credit:** AP, CLEP General and Subject, institutional tests; 30 credit hours maximum for associate degree; 60 credit hours maximum for bachelor's degree.

ACADEMIC REQUIREMENTS. Freshmen must earn minimum GPA of 1.65 to continue in good standing. **Graduation requirements:** 60 hours for associate, 120 hours for bachelor's. Most students required to take courses in computer science, English, foreign languages, humanities, mathematics, biological/physical sciences, social sciences. **Additional information:** Degree programs offered primarily for adults attending part-time. No traditional freshman class.

FRESHMAN ADMISSIONS. Selection criteria: Open admissions.

FALL-TERM APPLICATIONS. $25 fee. No closing date; applicants notified on a rolling basis. Deferred admission available.

STUDENT LIFE. Activities: Newsletter.

STUDENT SERVICES. Aptitude testing, career counseling, freshman orientation, personal counseling, special adviser for adult students, veterans counselor, academic support center, on campus interviews with employers, services/facilities for handicapped.

ANNUAL EXPENSES. Tuition and fees: $4,850, $450 additional for out-of-state students. **Books and supplies:** $800. **Other expenses:** $1,159.

FINANCIAL AID. 93% of grants, 83% of loans, 12% of jobs based on need. Academic, state/district residency scholarships available. **Aid applications:** Closing date May 1; applicants notified on or about August 15; must reply within 3 weeks.

ADDRESS/TELEPHONE. Admissions Office, University of Maryland: University College, University Boulevard at Adelphi Road, College Park, MD 20742-1672. (301) 985-7265. (800) 888-UMUC.

Villa Julie College ⇐⇒
Stevenson, Maryland — CB code: 5856

4-year private college of arts and sciences, coed. Founded in 1947. **Accreditation:** Regional. **Undergraduate enrollment:** 197 men, 878 women full time; 100 men, 601 women part time. **Faculty:** 141 total (54 full time), 80 with doctorates or other terminal degrees. **Location:** Suburban campus in very large city; 8 miles from Baltimore. **Calendar:** Semester, limited summer session. Saturday and extensive evening/early morning classes. **Microcomputers:** 140 located in libraries, classrooms, computer centers. **Additional facts:** Nursing program offered in cooperation with Union Memorial Hospital.

DEGREES OFFERED. AA, BS. 148 associate degrees awarded in 1992. 17% in business and management, 7% business/office and marketing/distribution, 5% communications, 11% computer sciences, 11% teacher education, 23% law, 19% multi/interdisciplinary studies. 99 bachelor's degrees awarded. 39% in business and management, 32% computer sciences, 22% law, 7% multi/interdisciplinary studies.

UNDERGRADUATE MAJORS. Associate: Accounting, allied health, biology, biotechnology, business administration and management, business and management, business and office, business communications, business data processing and related programs, chemistry, child development/care/guidance, communications, computer and information sciences, court reporting, dental hygiene, early childhood education, elementary education, fine arts, geriatric aide, geriatric services, graphic design, institutional management, institutional/home management/supporting programs, legal assistant/paralegal, legal secretary, liberal/general studies, medical assistant, medical laboratory technologies, medical secretary, office supervision and management, public affairs, real estate, secretarial and related programs, tourism, transportation and travel marketing, video, visual and performing arts, word processing. **Bachelor's:** Accounting, biological and physical sciences, business administration and management, clinical laboratory science, computer and information sciences, early childhood education, elementary education, humanities, information sciences and systems, legal assistant/paralegal, liberal/general studies, management information systems, nursing, predentistry, prelaw, premedicine, prepharmacy, preveterinary, radio/television technology, science technologies, video.

ACADEMIC PROGRAMS. 2-year transfer program, accelerated program, cooperative education, double major, dual enrollment of high school students, honors program, independent study, internships, student-designed major, study abroad, teacher preparation, weekend college. **Remedial services:** Learning center, preadmission summer program, reduced course load, remedial instruction, special counselor, tutoring, communication skills center. **ROTC:** Army. **Placement/credit:** AP, CLEP General and Subject, institutional tests; 15 credit hours maximum for associate degree; 30 credit hours maximum for bachelor's degree.

ACADEMIC REQUIREMENTS. Freshmen must earn minimum GPA of 1.9 to continue in good standing. Students must declare major by end of first year. **Graduation requirements:** 60 hours for associate (30 in major), 120 hours for bachelor's (60 in major). Most students required to take courses in arts/fine arts, computer science, English, history, humanities, mathematics, philosophy/religion, biological/physical sciences, social sciences. **Postgraduate studies:** 70% from 2-year programs enter 4-year programs. 16% enter law school, 12% enter MBA programs.

FRESHMAN ADMISSIONS. Recommended units include English 4, mathematics 3, social science 3 and science 2. **Test requirements:** SAT or ACT (SAT preferred); score report by May 1. ACH required.

1992 FRESHMAN CLASS PROFILE. 48 men, 194 women enrolled. **Characteristics:** 98% from in state, 15% have minority backgrounds, 12% join fraternities/sororities. Average age is 19.

FALL-TERM APPLICATIONS. $25 fee, may be waived for applicants with need. No closing date; priority given to applications received by February 15; applicants notified on a rolling basis; must reply by May 1 or within 2 weeks if notified thereafter. Interview required. Essay required. CRDA. Deferred and early admission available.

STUDENT LIFE. Housing: Apartment housing available. Listings of room and apartment rentals available to students. Student housing available near campus in apartment complex. **Activities:** Student government, magazine, student newspaper, drama, sororities, Young Republicans, Black Student Union, Phi Sigma Sigma Sorority.

ATHLETICS. Intercollegiate: Cross-country, field hockey W, golf, lacrosse, soccer M, tennis. **Intramural:** Badminton, basketball, bowling, fencing, field hockey W, softball, table tennis, tennis, volleyball.

STUDENT SERVICES. Aptitude testing, career counseling, employment service for undergraduates, freshman orientation, health services, personal counseling, placement service for graduates, special adviser for adult students, veterans counselor, services/facilities for handicapped.

ANNUAL EXPENSES. Tuition and fees (1992-93): $6,320. **Books and supplies:** $500. **Other expenses:** $1,000.

FINANCIAL AID. 82% of freshmen, 74% of continuing students receive some form of aid. 65% of grants, 90% of loans, 73% of jobs based on need. Academic, leadership scholarships available. **Aid applications:** No closing date; priority given to applications received by March 1; applicants notified on a rolling basis beginning on or about May 15; must reply within 2 weeks.

ADDRESS/TELEPHONE. Orsia Young, Director of Admissions, Villa Julie College, Green Spring Valley Road, Stevenson, MD 21153. (410) 486-7001. Fax: (410) 486-1995.

Washington Bible College
Lanham, Maryland — CB code: 5884

4-year private Bible, seminary college, coed, nondenominational. Founded in

1921. **Undergraduate enrollment:** 74 men, 50 women full time; 105 men, 81 women part time. **Graduate enrollment:** 38 men, 4 women full time; 71 men, 19 women part time. **Location:** Suburban campus in large town; 10 miles from Washington, D.C. **Calendar:** Semester. **Additional facts:** Provides Biblical and professional education to equip students for Christian ministry worldwide.

FRESHMAN ADMISSIONS. Selection criteria: Student's spiritual qualifications most important followed by academic achievement.

ADDRESS/TELEPHONE. Stephen A. Salvas, Director of Admissions, Washington Bible College, 6511 Princess Garden Parkway, Lanham, MD 20706. (301) 552-1400 ext. 280. (800) 787-0256.

Washington College
Chestertown, Maryland — CB code: 5888

Admissions: 75% of applicants accepted
Based on: ••• School record
•• Test scores
• Activities, essay, interview, recommendations, special talents
Completion: 95% of freshmen end year in good standing
65% graduate, 30% of these enter graduate study

4-year private liberal arts college, coed. Founded in 1782. **Accreditation:** Regional. **Undergraduate enrollment:** 417 men, 451 women full time; 3 men, 15 women part time. **Graduate enrollment:** 17 men, 34 women part time. **Faculty:** 84 total (64 full time), 57 with doctorates or other terminal degrees. **Location:** Rural campus in small town; 75 miles from Washington, D.C., 70 miles from Baltimore. **Calendar:** Semester. **Microcomputers:** 75 located in dormitories, libraries, computer centers. **Special facilities:** O'Neill Literary House for creative writing program, Larrabee Creative Arts Center, Decker Laboratory Science Center, Casey Academic Center. **Additional facts:** Tenth oldest college in United States.

DEGREES OFFERED. BA, BS, MA. 179 bachelor's degrees awarded in 1992. 13% in business and management, 19% letters/literature, 9% life sciences, 5% multi/interdisciplinary studies, 6% psychology, 34% social sciences, 7% visual and performing arts. Graduate degrees offered in 3 major fields of study.

UNDERGRADUATE MAJORS. American studies, art history, biology, business administration and management, chemistry, computer and information sciences, dramatic arts, economics, English literature, French, German, history, humanities, international relations, international studies, mathematics, music, philosophy, physics, political science and government, psychology, sociology, Spanish.

ACADEMIC PROGRAMS. Double major, dual enrollment of high school students, honors program, independent study, internships, student-designed major, study abroad, teacher preparation, visiting/exchange student program, Washington semester; liberal arts/career combination in engineering, health sciences. **Remedial services:** Learning center, reduced course load, tutoring. **Placement/credit:** AP, CLEP General and Subject, IB; 32 credit hours maximum for bachelor's degree.

ACADEMIC REQUIREMENTS. Freshmen must earn minimum GPA of 2.0 to continue in good standing. 88% of freshmen return for sophomore year. Students must declare major by end of second year. **Graduation requirements:** 128 hours for bachelor's (40 in major). Most students required to take courses in English, humanities, biological/physical sciences, social sciences. **Postgraduate studies:** 5% enter law school, 2% enter medical school, 3% enter MBA programs, 20% enter other graduate study.

FRESHMAN ADMISSIONS. Selection criteria: Primarily grades, high school program, class rank. SAT scores, recommendations, extracurricular activities also considered. **High school preparation:** 15 units required. Required units include English 4, foreign language 2, mathematics 3, social science 3 and science 3. **Test requirements:** SAT or ACT (SAT preferred); score report by March 15.

1992 FRESHMAN CLASS PROFILE. 611 men applied, 421 accepted, 144 enrolled; 525 women applied, 430 accepted, 156 enrolled. 70% had high school GPA of 3.0 or higher, 30% between 2.0 and 2.99. 30% were in top tenth and 64% were in top quarter of graduating class. **Academic background:** Mid 50% of enrolled freshmen had SAT-V between 480-600, SAT-M between 500-620. 99% submitted SAT scores. **Characteristics:** 51% from in state, 96% live in college housing, 13% have minority backgrounds, 2% are foreign students, 20% join fraternities/sororities. Average age is 18.

FALL-TERM APPLICATIONS. $30 fee, may be waived for applicants with need. Closing date June 1; priority given to applications received by March 1; applicants notified on a rolling basis beginning on or about February 1; must reply by May 1. Essay required. Interview recommended. CRDA. Deferred and early admission available. EDP-F. Applicants applying by March 1 notified between February 1 and April 1 must reply by May 1. Applicants applying after March 1 and no later than May 30, wait-listed, notified between May 1 and June 1 must reply within 15 days of notification.

STUDENT LIFE. Housing: Dormitories (men, women, coed); fraternity, sorority housing available. Special interest housing for writers, language majors, international studies majors, and science majors available. **Activities:** Student government, magazine, student newspaper, yearbook, biweekly poetry publications, quarterly prose publications, choral groups, dance, drama, jazz band, music ensembles, Renaissance ensemble, fraternities, sororities, College Republicans, Christian Fellowship, Amnesty International, International Relations Club, Hillel, Hands Out (volunteer group), Dale Adams Society (multi-racial club), environmental club, Newman Club, Big Brothers/Big Sisters.

ATHLETICS. NCAA. **Intercollegiate:** Baseball M, basketball, lacrosse, rowing (crew), soccer M, softball W, swimming, tennis, volleyball W. **Intramural:** Basketball, golf M, racquetball, rugby M, sailing, soccer W, softball M, squash, swimming, tennis, volleyball.

STUDENT SERVICES. Career counseling, employment service for undergraduates, freshman orientation, health services, personal counseling, placement service for graduates, special adviser for adult students, veterans counselor.

ANNUAL EXPENSES. Tuition and fees: $13,952. **Room and board:** $5,318. **Books and supplies:** $500. **Other expenses:** $300.

FINANCIAL AID. 80% of freshmen, 61% of continuing students receive some form of aid. 80% of grants, 95% of loans, 61% of jobs based on need. 189 enrolled freshmen were judged to have need, all were offered aid. Academic, art, state/district residency, minority scholarships available. **Aid applications:** Closing date February 15; applicants notified on or about April 15; must reply by May 1 or within 2 weeks if notified thereafter.

ADDRESS/TELEPHONE. Kevin Coveney, Vice President for Admissions, Washington College, 300 Washington Avenue, Chestertown, MD 21620-1197. (410) 778-7700. (800) 422-1782. Fax: (410) 778-7287.

Western Maryland College
Westminster, Maryland — CB code: 5898

Admissions: 82% of applicants accepted
Based on: ••• Essay, school record
•• Activities, special talents, test scores
• Interview, recommendations
Completion: 73% of freshmen end year in good standing
68% graduate, 35% of these enter graduate study

4-year private liberal arts college, coed. Founded in 1867. **Accreditation:** Regional. **Undergraduate enrollment:** 519 men, 599 women full time; 42 men, 67 women part time. **Graduate enrollment:** 18 men, 60 women full time; 132 men, 706 women part time. **Faculty:** 128 total (83 full time), 74 with doctorates or other terminal degrees. **Location:** Rural campus in large town; 30 miles from Baltimore, 60 miles from Washington, D.C. **Calendar:** 4-1-4, limited summer session. **Microcomputers:** 160 located in libraries, computer centers. **Special facilities:** Art gallery, 9-hole golf course, film/video production laboratory, photography studio, audiology laboratory, human performance laboratory.

DEGREES OFFERED. BA, MS. 272 bachelor's degrees awarded in 1992. 8% in business and management, 13% communications, 9% letters/literature, 11% life sciences, 10% physical sciences, 10% psychology, 26% social sciences, 7% visual and performing arts. Graduate degrees offered in 13 major fields of study.

UNDERGRADUATE MAJORS. American literature, American studies, art education, art history, art therapy, biochemistry, biology, business administration and management, business and management, business economics, chemistry, communications, comparative literature, dramatic arts, economics, English, English education, English literature, fine arts, foreign languages education, French, German, history, mathematics, mathematics and computer science, mathematics education, music, philosophy, physical education, physics, political science and government, predentistry, prelaw, premedicine, preveterinary, psychology, religion, science education, social studies education, social work, sociology, Spanish, sports medicine, studio art, visual and performing arts.

ACADEMIC PROGRAMS. Accelerated program, double major, honors program, independent study, internships, student-designed major, study abroad, teacher preparation, visiting/exchange student program, New York semester, United Nations semester, Washington semester; liberal arts/career combination in engineering, forestry, health sciences. **Remedial services:** Preadmission summer program, reduced course load, special counselor. **ROTC:** Army. **Placement/credit:** AP, CLEP Subject, institutional tests; 30 credit hours maximum for bachelor's degree.

ACADEMIC REQUIREMENTS. Freshmen must earn minimum GPA of 2.0 to continue in good standing. 80% of freshmen return for sophomore year. Students must declare major by end of second year. **Graduation requirements:** 120 hours for bachelor's (36 in major). Most students required to take courses in arts/fine arts, English, foreign languages, history, humanities, mathematics, biological/physical sciences, social sciences. **Postgraduate studies:** 3% enter law school, 3% enter medical school, 5% enter MBA programs, 24% enter other graduate study. **Additional information:** 15% of students have dual majors.

FRESHMAN ADMISSIONS. Selection criteria: Class rank, course work and grades, test results, personal traits, goals, motivation, recommendations by counselors, and participation in nonacademic activities considered. **High school preparation:** 16 units required. Required and recommended units include biological science 2, English 4, foreign language 2-3, mathematics 3, physical science 2 and social science 3. **Test requirements:** SAT or ACT (SAT preferred); score report by March 15. Foreign language ACH required for placement or exemption from 1-year language requirement; score report by August 1.

1992 FRESHMAN CLASS PROFILE. 697 men applied, 536 accepted, 141 enrolled; 592 women applied, 523 accepted, 160 enrolled. 49% had high school GPA of 3.0 or higher, 49% between 2.0 and 2.99. 30% were in top tenth and 50% were in top quarter of graduating class. **Academic background:** Mid 50% of enrolled freshmen had SAT-V between 420-520, SAT-M between 420-570; ACT composite between 19-23. 100% submitted SAT scores. **Characteristics:** 59% from in state, 90% live in college housing, 4% have minority backgrounds, 2% are foreign students, 35% join fraternities/sororities. Average age is 18.

FALL-TERM APPLICATIONS. $30 fee, may be waived for applicants with need. Closing date March 15; applicants notified on or about April 1; must reply by May 1. Essay required. Interview recommended. Portfolio recommended for studio art applicants. CRDA. Deferred and early admission available. EDP-F. Early decision applications due December 1.

STUDENT LIFE. Housing: Dormitories (men, women, coed); apartment, fraternity, sorority housing available. Special housing available for honors students and special interest groups. Freshman residence halls not coeducational. **Activities:** Student government, film, magazine, radio, student newspaper, television, yearbook, choral groups, concert band, drama, jazz band, music ensembles, musical theater, fraternities, sororities, Catholic Ministry, Jewish Student Union, Western Maryland Christian Fellowship, political clubs, Black Student Union, Ukrainian Club, social work club, Coalition for Environmental Concerns, Amnesty International.

ATHLETICS. NCAA. **Intercollegiate:** Baseball M, basketball, cross-country, field hockey W, football M, golf, ice hockey M, lacrosse, soccer, softball W, swimming, tennis, track and field, volleyball W, wrestling M. **Intramural:** Badminton, basketball, football, golf, soccer, softball, table tennis, tennis, volleyball.

STUDENT SERVICES. Aptitude testing, career counseling, employment service for undergraduates, freshman orientation, health services, personal counseling, placement service for graduates, special adviser for adult students, services/facilities for handicapped.

ANNUAL EXPENSES. Tuition and fees: $13,750. **Room and board:** $5,240. **Books and supplies:** $400. **Other expenses:** $500.

FINANCIAL AID. 78% of freshmen, 78% of continuing students receive some form of aid. 51% of grants, 94% of loans, 88% of jobs based on need. 181 enrolled freshmen were judged to have need, all were offered aid. Academic scholarships available. **Aid applications:** No closing date; priority given to applications received by March 1; applicants notified on a rolling basis; must reply by May 1 or within 2 weeks if notified thereafter.

ADDRESS/TELEPHONE. Martha O'Connell, Director of Admissions, Western Maryland College, 2 College Hill, Westminster, MD 21157-4390. (410) 857-2230. (800) 638-5005. Fax: (410) 857-2729.

Wor-Wic Community College
Salisbury, Maryland — CB code: 1613

2-year public community college, coed. Founded in 1975. **Accreditation:** Regional. **Undergraduate enrollment:** 127 men, 195 women full time; 380 men, 1,176 women part time. **Faculty:** 99 total (30 full time), 7 with doctorates or other terminal degrees. **Location:** Suburban campus in large town; 110 miles from Baltimore, 120 miles from Washington, D.C. **Calendar:** Semester, limited summer session. Saturday classes. **Microcomputers:** 67 located in classrooms, computer centers. **Additional facts:** Open-walled college with vocational-technical orientation. Access to library facilities at Salisbury State University and University of Maryland: Eastern Shore.

DEGREES OFFERED. AA. 94 associate degrees awarded in 1992. 18% in business and management, 10% business/office and marketing/distribution, 32% health sciences, 10% allied health, 13% multi/interdisciplinary studies, 5% parks/recreation, protective services, public affairs.

UNDERGRADUATE MAJORS. Accounting, business administration and management, business and office, business computer/console/peripheral equipment operation, chemical dependency counseling, computer programming, criminal justice technology, finance, hotel/motel and restaurant management, law enforcement and corrections technologies, legal secretary, liberal/general studies, medical secretary, nursing, office supervision and management, radiograph medical technology, secretarial and related programs.

ACADEMIC PROGRAMS. 2-year transfer program, double major, internships, telecourses, cross-registration. **Remedial services:** Learning center, reduced course load, remedial instruction, special counselor, tutoring. **Placement/credit:** AP, CLEP General and Subject, institutional tests; 30 credit hours maximum for associate degree.

ACADEMIC REQUIREMENTS. Freshmen must earn minimum GPA of 1.5 to continue in good standing. 60% of freshmen return for sophomore year. Students must declare major by end of first year. **Graduation requirements:** 60 hours for associate (24 in major). Most students required to take courses in English, humanities, mathematics, biological/physical sciences, social sciences.

FRESHMAN ADMISSIONS. Selection criteria: Open admissions. Selective admission to nursing and radiologic technologies programs. Recommended units include English 4 and mathematics 2. High school diploma or equivalent required for nursing and radiologic technology programs. **Test requirements:** ACT required of nursing and radiologic technologies applicants; score report by April 1.

1992 FRESHMAN CLASS PROFILE. 128 men, 312 women enrolled. **Characteristics:** 99% from in state, 100% commute, 23% have minority backgrounds, 1% are foreign students. Average age is 26.

FALL-TERM APPLICATIONS. No fee. No closing date; applicants notified on a rolling basis. Interview required for nursing, radiologic technologies applicants.

STUDENT LIFE. Activities: Student government, film, magazine, student newspaper.

STUDENT SERVICES. Aptitude testing, career counseling, employment service for undergraduates, freshman orientation, personal counseling, placement service for graduates, veterans counselor, services/facilities for handicapped.

ANNUAL EXPENSES. Tuition and fees (projected): $1,615, $2,130 additional for out-of-district students, $2,760 additional for out-of-state students. **Books and supplies:** $450. **Other expenses:** $450.

FINANCIAL AID. 30% of freshmen, 38% of continuing students receive some form of aid. 95% of grants, 90% of loans, all jobs based on need. 140 enrolled freshmen were judged to have need, all were offered aid. Academic, state/district residency, minority scholarships available. **Aid applications:** No closing date; applicants notified on a rolling basis beginning on or about August 1.

ADDRESS/TELEPHONE. Holly E. Smith, Director of Admissions, Wor-Wic Community College, 1409 Wesley Drive, Salisbury, MD 21801-7164. (410) 749-8181 ext. 40. Fax: (410) 543-6569.

Massachusetts

American International College
Springfield, Massachusetts CB code: 3002

Admissions: 76% of applicants accepted
Based on: ••• School record
•• Recommendations, test scores
• Activities, essay, interview, special talents
Completion: 82% of freshmen end year in good standing
59% graduate, 28% of these enter graduate study

4-year private college of arts and sciences and business college, coed. Founded in 1885. **Accreditation:** Regional. **Undergraduate enrollment:** 517 men, 493 women full time; 127 men, 199 women part time. **Graduate enrollment:** 57 men, 86 women full time; 136 men, 200 women part time. **Faculty:** 122 total (74 full time), 52 with doctorates or other terminal degrees. **Location:** Urban campus in small city; 3 miles from downtown. **Calendar:** Semester, extensive summer session. **Microcomputers:** 40 located in libraries, computer centers. **Special facilities:** State-of-the-art Nautilus fitness center, cultural arts center, theater for performing arts.

DEGREES OFFERED. AA, AS, BA, BS, MA, MS, MBA, MEd, EdD. 17 associate degrees awarded in 1992. 292 bachelor's degrees awarded. 42% in business and management, 7% business/office and marketing/distribution, 5% education, 6% health sciences, 13% parks/recreation, protective services, public affairs, 6% psychology, 5% social sciences. Graduate degrees offered in 19 major fields of study.

UNDERGRADUATE MAJORS. Associate: Business administration and management, liberal/general studies. **Bachelor's:** Accounting, administration of special education, biochemistry, biology, business administration and management, business and management, business economics, business education, chemistry, clinical laboratory science, communications, criminal justice studies, criminology, cytotechnology, early childhood education, economics, education of the emotionally handicapped, education of the mentally handicapped, elementary education, English, finance, history, information sciences and systems, international business management, international relations, journalism, junior high education, liberal/general studies, management information systems, marketing and distribution, mathematics, mathematics education, medical laboratory technologies, nursing, personnel management, philosophy, political science and government, predentistry, prelaw, premedicine, preveterinary, psychology, public administration, science education, secondary education, social science education, social studies education, sociology, Spanish, special education.

ACADEMIC PROGRAMS. Accelerated program, double major, dual enrollment of high school students, honors program, independent study, internships, study abroad, teacher preparation, weekend college, Washington semester, cross-registration; combined bachelor's/graduate program in business administration. **Remedial services:** Learning center, reduced course load, special counselor, tutoring, Supportive Learning Services program for learning disabled students. **ROTC:** Air Force, Army. **Placement/credit:** AP, CLEP General and Subject, institutional tests; 30 credit hours maximum for bachelor's degree.

ACADEMIC REQUIREMENTS. Freshmen must earn minimum GPA of 1.68 to continue in good standing. 81% of freshmen return for sophomore year. Students must declare major by end of second year. **Graduation requirements:** 120 hours for bachelor's (30 in major). Most students required to take courses in English, humanities, biological/physical sciences, social sciences. **Postgraduate studies:** 3% enter law school, 4% enter medical school, 10% enter MBA programs, 11% enter other graduate study.

FRESHMAN ADMISSIONS. Selection criteria: School achievement record most important, recommendations and test scores also important. **High school preparation:** 16 units required. Required and recommended units include English 4, mathematics 2, social science 2 and science 2. Foreign language 2 recommended. **Test requirements:** SAT or ACT (SAT preferred); score report by August 15. Wechsler Adult Intelligence Scale revised required for learning disabled applicants.

1992 FRESHMAN CLASS PROFILE. 1,245 men and women applied, 945 accepted; 142 men enrolled, 122 women enrolled. 24% had high school GPA of 3.0 or higher, 61% between 2.0 and 2.99. 6% were in top tenth and 24% were in top quarter of graduating class. **Academic background:** Mid 50% of enrolled freshmen had SAT-V between 350-480, SAT-M between 380-490. 93% submitted SAT scores. **Characteristics:** 57% from in state, 52% live in college housing, 21% have minority backgrounds, 6% are foreign students, 15% join fraternities/sororities. Average age is 19.

FALL-TERM APPLICATIONS. $20 fee, may be waived for applicants with need. No closing date; applicants notified on a rolling basis; must reply by May 1 or within 2 weeks if notified thereafter. Interview recommended. Essay recommended. Interview recommended for all applicants, required for supportive services applicants. CRDA. Deferred and early admission available. EDP-F.

STUDENT LIFE. Housing: Dormitories (men, women, coed). Y. **Activities:** Student government, magazine, radio, student newspaper, yearbook, choral groups, drama, musical theater, pep band, fraternities, sororities, Hillel, United Protestant Fellowship, Newman Club, Persons ready in defense of Ebony (pride a minority student organization).

ATHLETICS. NCAA. **Intercollegiate:** Baseball M, basketball, football M, golf M, ice hockey M, lacrosse M, soccer, softball W, tennis, volleyball W, wrestling M. **Intramural:** Basketball, horseback riding, skiing, soccer, softball, swimming, volleyball.

STUDENT SERVICES. Career counseling, employment service for undergraduates, freshman orientation, health services, personal counseling, placement service for graduates, special adviser for adult students, veterans counselor, writing center, peer tutoring, services/facilities for handicapped.

ANNUAL EXPENSES. Tuition and fees: $9,414. **Room and board:** $4,553. **Books and supplies:** $535. **Other expenses:** $900.

FINANCIAL AID. 70% of freshmen, 77% of continuing students receive some form of aid. 94% of grants, 85% of loans, 53% of jobs based on need. Academic, athletic, leadership scholarships available. **Aid applications:** No closing date; priority given to applications received by April 15; applicants notified on a rolling basis beginning on or about March 20; must reply by May 1 or within 2 weeks if notified thereafter.

ADDRESS/TELEPHONE. Peter J. Miller, Dean of Admissions, American International College, 1000 State Street, Springfield, MA 01109-3184. (413) 747-6201. Fax: (413) 737-2803.

Amherst College
Amherst, Massachusetts CB code: 3003

Admissions: 21% of applicants accepted
Based on: ••• School record
•• Activities, essay, recommendations, test scores
• Interview, special talents
Completion: 99% of freshmen end year in good standing
97% graduate, 30% of these enter graduate study

4-year private liberal arts college, coed. Founded in 1821. **Accreditation:** Regional. **Undergraduate enrollment:** 888 men, 707 women full time; 2 men, 3 women part time. **Faculty:** 167 total (159 full time), 156 with doctorates or other terminal degrees. **Location:** Suburban campus in large town; 90 miles from Boston, 150 miles from New York City. **Calendar:** 2 semesters with 3-week January term, no credit. **Microcomputers:** 61 located in libraries, classrooms, computer centers. **Special facilities:** Art galleries, recital hall, observatory, planetarium, theater, geology museum.

DEGREES OFFERED. BA. 366 bachelor's degrees awarded in 1992. 6% in area and ethnic studies, 8% languages, 20% letters/literature, 7% life sciences, 7% physical sciences, 7% psychology, 30% social sciences, 7% visual and performing arts.

UNDERGRADUATE MAJORS. Afro-American (black) studies, American studies, anthropology, Asian studies, astronomy, biology, chemistry, classics, computer and information sciences, economics, English, European studies, fine arts, foreign languages (multiple emphasis), French, geology, German, Greek (classical), history, Latin, law juris prudence and social thought, mathematics, music, neurosciences, philosophy, physics, political science and government, psychology, religion, Russian, sociology, Spanish, theatre and dance, women's studies.

ACADEMIC PROGRAMS. Double major, honors program, independent study, student-designed major, study abroad, visiting/exchange student program, cross-registration. **Remedial services:** Tutoring, writing counselor. **Placement/credit:** IB, institutional tests.

ACADEMIC REQUIREMENTS. No policy requiring minimum GPA; records of students having academic difficulty are reviewed individually. 97% of freshmen return for sophomore year. Students must declare major by end of second year. **Graduation requirements:** 128 hours for bachelor's (32 in major). **Postgraduate studies:** 7% enter law school, 7% enter medical school, 1% enter MBA programs, 15% enter other graduate study. **Additional information:** 27% of seniors enrolled in interdisciplinary, self-designed, or double majors.

FRESHMAN ADMISSIONS. Selection criteria: Grades, test scores, essays, recommendations, independent work, quality of individual's secondary school program and achievements outside classroom are among factors used to evaluate intellectual promise. Recommended units include English 4, foreign language 3, mathematics 3, social science 1 and science 1. **Test requirements:** SAT or ACT; score report by February 15. 3 ACH required. Score report by February 15.

1992 FRESHMAN CLASS PROFILE. 2,242 men applied, 483 accepted, 218 enrolled; 2,330 women applied, 469 accepted, 176 enrolled. 84% were in top tenth of graduating class. **Characteristics:** 12% from in state, 100% live in college housing, 26% have minority backgrounds, 2% are foreign students. Average age is 18.

FALL-TERM APPLICATIONS. $50 fee, may be waived for applicants with need. Closing date January 1; applicants notified on or about April 15; must reply by May 1. Essay required. CRDA. Deferred and early admission available. EDP-F.

STUDENT LIFE. Housing: Dormitories (coed); cooperative housing available. Language and other theme houses available. **Activities:** Student government, magazine, radio, student newspaper, yearbook, choral groups, dance, drama, jazz band, music ensembles, musical theater, symphony orchestra, chamber orchestras, Hillel, Boltwood House (service), Christian Association, Newman Club, Black Student Union, Association of Asian Students, Cambodian Family Tutoring.

ATHLETICS. NCAA. **Intercollegiate:** Baseball M, basketball, cross-country, field hockey W, football M, golf, ice hockey M, lacrosse, rowing (crew), skiing M, soccer, squash, swimming, tennis, track and field, volleyball W. **Intramural:** Basketball, cross-country, golf, racquetball, skiing, soccer, softball, squash, tennis, volleyball.

STUDENT SERVICES. Career counseling, employment service for undergraduates, freshman orientation, health services, personal counseling, placement service for graduates, special adviser for adult students, services/facilities for handicapped.

ANNUAL EXPENSES. Tuition and fees (1992-93): $18,177. **Room and board:** $4,800. **Books and supplies:** $660. **Other expenses:** $1,285.

FINANCIAL AID. 61% of freshmen, 52% of continuing students receive some form of aid. All grants, all loans, 92% of jobs based on need. 202 enrolled freshmen were judged to have need, all were offered aid. **Aid applications:** Closing date February 1; applicants notified on or about April 15; must reply by May 1.

ADDRESS/TELEPHONE. Jane E. Reynolds, Dean of Admissions, Amherst College, PO Box 2231, Amherst, MA 01002. (413) 542-2328. Fax: (413) 542-2040.

Anna Maria College for Men and Women
Paxton, Massachusetts — CB code: 3005

4-year private liberal arts college, coed, affiliated with Roman Catholic Church. Founded in 1946. **Accreditation:** Regional. **Undergraduate enrollment:** 163 men, 306 women full time; 69 men, 172 women part time. **Graduate enrollment:** 15 men, 34 women full time; 386 men, 335 women part time. **Faculty:** 84 total (39 full time), 20 with doctorates or other terminal degrees. **Location:** Suburban campus in small town; 8 miles from Worcester, 40 miles from Boston. **Calendar:** 4-1-4, limited summer session. **Microcomputers:** Located in classrooms, computer centers. **Special facilities:** Art gallery, multi-media center, recreational facilities. **Additional facts:** Bachelor's degree program for Massachusetts Air and Army National Guard offered at armories/military facilities.

DEGREES OFFERED. AA, AS, BA, BS, BFA, MA, MS, MBA. 4 associate degrees awarded in 1992. 109 bachelor's degrees awarded. Graduate degrees offered in 9 major fields of study.

UNDERGRADUATE MAJORS. Associate: Business administration and management, clinical laboratory science, legal assistant/paralegal, medical laboratory technologies. **Bachelor's:** Accounting, art education, art therapy, arts management, biology, business administration and management, business and management, business and office, clinical laboratory science, criminal justice studies, early childhood education, elementary education, engineering, English, environmental science, finance, fine arts, French, history, humanities and social sciences, legal assistant/paralegal, liberal/general studies, management information systems, marketing and distribution, marketing management, medical laboratory technologies, music, music education, music performance, music therapy, nursing, political science and government, predentistry, prelaw, premedicine, preveterinary, psychology, social work, Spanish, studio art.

ACADEMIC PROGRAMS. Accelerated program, double major, independent study, internships, student-designed major, study abroad, teacher preparation, visiting/exchange student program, weekend college, Washington semester, cross-registration; liberal arts/career combination in engineering. **Remedial services:** Learning center, reduced course load, remedial instruction, special counselor, tutoring. **ROTC:** Air Force, Army, Naval. **Placement/credit:** AP, CLEP General and Subject, institutional tests; 30 credit hours maximum for bachelor's degree.

ACADEMIC REQUIREMENTS. Freshmen must earn minimum GPA of 2.0 to continue in good standing. 88% of freshmen return for sophomore year. Students must declare major by end of second year. **Graduation requirements:** 60 hours for associate (30 in major), 120 hours for bachelor's (60 in major). Most students required to take courses in English, foreign languages, history, mathematics, philosophy/religion, biological/physical sciences, social sciences. **Postgraduate studies:** 90% from 2-year programs enter 4-year programs. 2% enter law school, 1% enter medical school, 4% enter MBA programs, 10% enter other graduate study. **Additional information:** Upper-division transfer program for registered nurses.

FRESHMAN ADMISSIONS. Selection criteria: High school record, rank in top half of class important, test scores, recommendations, interview considered. **High school preparation:** 16 units required. Required units include biological science 1, English 4, foreign language 2, mathematics 2 and physical science 1. One history also required. **Test requirements:** SAT; score report by June 1. Prueba de Aptitud Academica for Spanish speaking applicants.

1992 FRESHMAN CLASS PROFILE. 206 men, 453 women enrolled. **Academic background:** Mid 50% of enrolled freshmen had SAT-V between 410-430, SAT-M between 420-470. 88% submitted SAT scores. **Characteristics:** 75% from in state, 80% live in college housing, 5% have minority backgrounds, 4% are foreign students. Average age is 18.

FALL-TERM APPLICATIONS. $30 fee, may be waived for applicants with need. Closing date June 1; priority given to applications received by May 1; applicants notified on a rolling basis; must reply by August 1. Audition required for music applicants. Portfolio required for art applicants. Essay required. Interview recommended. CRDA. Deferred and early admission available.

STUDENT LIFE. Housing: Dormitories (coed). **Activities:** Student government, student newspaper, yearbook, choral groups, drama, music ensembles, Society for Peace and Justice, campus ministry, Social Action Club.

ATHLETICS. NCAA. **Intercollegiate:** Baseball M, basketball, field hockey W, golf M, soccer, softball W, volleyball W. **Intramural:** Archery, badminton, table tennis, volleyball.

STUDENT SERVICES. Aptitude testing, career counseling, employment service for undergraduates, freshman orientation, health services, personal counseling, placement service for graduates, services/facilities for handicapped.

ANNUAL EXPENSES. Tuition and fees: $10,800. **Room and board:** $4,835. **Books and supplies:** $513. **Other expenses:** $995.

FINANCIAL AID. 78% of freshmen, 73% of continuing students receive some form of aid. 93% of grants, 98% of loans, 98% of jobs based on need. 66 enrolled freshmen were judged to have need, all were offered aid. Academic, music/drama, alumni affiliation scholarships available. **Aid applications:** No closing date; priority given to applications received by March 1; applicants notified on a rolling basis beginning on or about April 1; must reply within 3 weeks.

ADDRESS/TELEPHONE. John Wilbur, Director of Admissions, Anna Maria College for Men and Women, Sunset Lane, Paxton, MA 01612-1198. (508) 849-3362. (800) 344-4586. Fax: (508) 756-2970.

Aquinas College at Milton
Milton, Massachusetts — CB code: 3011

Admissions: 87% of applicants accepted
Based on:
- ••• Interview, school record
- •• Recommendations
- • Activities, essay, test scores

Completion: 90% of freshmen end year in good standing
24% enter 4-year programs

2-year private business, junior college, women only, affiliated with Roman Catholic Church. Founded in 1956. **Accreditation:** Regional. **Undergraduate enrollment:** 204 women full time; 150 women part time. **Faculty:** 21 total (18 full time), 3 with doctorates or other terminal degrees. **Location:** Suburban campus in large town; 10 miles from Boston. **Calendar:** Modular schedule (5 modules of 6 weeks each). **Microcomputers:** 56 located in classrooms.

DEGREES OFFERED. AS. 106 associate degrees awarded in 1992. 32% in business and management, 60% business/office and marketing/distribution, 8% allied health.

UNDERGRADUATE MAJORS. Accounting, business administration and management, business and management, business and office, business computer/console/peripheral equipment operation, business data entry equipment operation, business data processing and related programs, data processing, fashion merchandising, information sciences and systems, legal secretary, liberal/general studies, medical assistant, medical secretary, microcomputer software, office supervision and management, public relations, recreation therapy, retailing, secretarial and related programs, word processing.

ACADEMIC PROGRAMS. 2-year transfer program, internships, visiting/exchange student program. **Remedial services:** Learning center, reduced course load, remedial instruction, tutoring. **Placement/credit:** Institutional tests.

ACADEMIC REQUIREMENTS. Freshmen must earn minimum GPA of 2.0 to continue in good standing. 90% of freshmen return for sophomore year. **Graduation requirements:** 60 hours for associate. Most students required to take courses in computer science, English, humanities, philosophy/religion, social sciences.

FRESHMAN ADMISSIONS. Selection criteria: School achievement record and interview most important. Business courses recommended but not required.

1992 FRESHMAN CLASS PROFILE. 195 women applied, 170 accepted, 103 enrolled. 25% had high school GPA of 3.0 or higher, 75% between 2.0 and 2.99. **Characteristics:** 100% from in state, 100% commute, 25% have minority backgrounds. Average age is 18.

FALL-TERM APPLICATIONS. $25 fee, may be waived for applicants with need. No closing date; applicants notified on a rolling basis beginning on or about December 1; must reply within 3 weeks. Interview recommended. Deferred admission available. SAT or ACT tests are recommended.

STUDENT LIFE. Activities: Student government, yearbook, campus ministry, accounting club.

STUDENT SERVICES. Career counseling, employment service for

undergraduates, freshman orientation, personal counseling, placement service for graduates, special adviser for adult students.

ANNUAL EXPENSES. Tuition and fees (1992-93): $7,400. **Books and supplies:** $400. **Other expenses:** $1,000.

FINANCIAL AID. 73% of freshmen, 72% of continuing students receive some form of aid. 93% of grants, 86% of loans, all jobs based on need. 75 enrolled freshmen were judged to have need, all were offered aid. Academic scholarships available. **Aid applications:** No closing date; priority given to applications received by March 1; applicants notified on a rolling basis beginning on or about April 15; must reply within 2 weeks.

ADDRESS/TELEPHONE. Steven E Kesman, Director of Admissions, Aquinas College at Milton, 303 Adams Street, Milton, MA 02186. (617) 696-3100.

Aquinas College at Newton

Newton, Massachusetts CB code: 3013

Admissions: 96% of applicants accepted
Based on: ••• Interview, recommendations, school record
• Activities, essay, special talents, test scores
Completion: 90% of freshmen end year in good standing
25% enter 4-year programs

2-year private junior college, women only, affiliated with Roman Catholic Church. Founded in 1961. **Accreditation:** Regional. **Undergraduate enrollment:** 1 man, 233 women full time; 3 men, 7 women part time. **Faculty:** 24 total (13 full time), 2 with doctorates or other terminal degrees. **Location:** Suburban campus in small city; 7 miles from Boston. **Calendar:** 4-1-4, limited summer session. Saturday and extensive evening/early morning classes. **Microcomputers:** 54 located in classrooms, computer centers. **Additional facts:** Men admitted to certificate program.

DEGREES OFFERED. AS. 40 associate degrees awarded in 1992. 75% in business and management, 20% teacher education, 5% allied health.

UNDERGRADUATE MAJORS. Accounting, business administration and management, business and management, business and office, early childhood education, human services secretary, legal assistant/paralegal, legal secretary, liberal/general studies, medical assistant, medical secretary, office supervision and management, secretarial and related programs, teacher aide.

ACADEMIC PROGRAMS. 2-year transfer program, double major, independent study, internships, weekend college. **Remedial services:** Learning center, reduced course load, remedial instruction, special counselor, tutoring, evaluation and testing, books on tape. **Placement/credit:** Institutional tests.

ACADEMIC REQUIREMENTS. Freshmen must earn minimum GPA of 1.7 to continue in good standing. 85% of freshmen return for sophomore year. Students must declare major on enrollment. **Graduation requirements:** 60 hours for associate (45 in major). Most students required to take courses in English, philosophy/religion, social sciences. **Additional information:** Focus is on career planning and placement in a comfortable learning environment.

FRESHMAN ADMISSIONS. Selection criteria: Interview and academic performance most important. **High school preparation:** 10 units recommended. Recommended units include biological science 1, English 4, mathematics 2, physical science 1 and social science 2. Business or early childhood courses recommended.

1992 FRESHMAN CLASS PROFILE. 5 men applied, 4 accepted, 4 enrolled; 168 women applied, 162 accepted, 96 enrolled. **Characteristics:** 100% from in state, 100% commute, 10% have minority backgrounds. Average age is 20.

FALL-TERM APPLICATIONS. $15 fee, may be waived for applicants with need. Closing date September 1; applicants notified on a rolling basis; must reply by May 1 or within 2 weeks if notified thereafter. Interview recommended. Essay recommended. CRDA. Deferred and early admission available.

STUDENT LIFE. Activities: Student government, yearbook, quarterly bulletin, campus ministry, Aquinas Student Association, Legal Association, Early Childhood Education Association.

ATHLETICS. Intramural: Softball, volleyball.

STUDENT SERVICES. Aptitude testing, career counseling, employment service for undergraduates, freshman orientation, health services, on-campus day care, personal counseling, placement service for graduates, special adviser for adult students, services/facilities for handicapped.

ANNUAL EXPENSES. Tuition and fees (1992-93): $6,950. **Books and supplies:** $375. **Other expenses:** $1,600.

FINANCIAL AID. 64% of freshmen, 63% of continuing students receive some form of aid. 97% of grants, 72% of loans, all jobs based on need. Academic, state/district residency, leadership, alumni affiliation scholarships available. **Aid applications:** Applicants notified on a rolling basis beginning on or about May 15; must reply within 2 weeks.

ADDRESS/TELEPHONE. Martha Rodweller, Director of Admissions, Aquinas College at Newton, 15 Walnut Park, Newton, MA 02158-9990. (617) 969-4400. Fax: (617) 965-6393.

Assumption College

Worcester, Massachusetts CB code: 3009

Admissions: 79% of applicants accepted
Based on: ••• School record
•• Test scores
• Activities, essay, interview, recommendations, special talents
Completion: 93% of freshmen end year in good standing
80% graduate, 29% of these enter graduate study

4-year private liberal arts college, coed, affiliated with Roman Catholic Church. Founded in 1904. **Accreditation:** Regional. **Undergraduate enrollment:** 680 men, 1,018 women full time; 6 men, 9 women part time. **Graduate enrollment:** 25 men, 44 women full time; 130 men, 216 women part time. **Faculty:** 189 total (115 full time), 102 with doctorates or other terminal degrees. **Location:** Suburban campus in small city; 45 miles from Boston. **Calendar:** Semester, limited summer session. **Microcomputers:** Located in libraries, computer centers.

DEGREES OFFERED. BA, MA, MBA. 406 bachelor's degrees awarded in 1992. 15% in business and management, 5% education, 5% languages, 6% law, 20% letters/literature, 5% mathematics, 5% philosophy, religion, theology, 15% psychology, 15% social sciences, 5% visual and performing arts. Graduate degrees offered in 11 major fields of study.

UNDERGRADUATE MAJORS. Accounting, art/music, biology, business administration and management, business and management, business economics, chemistry, classics, clinical laboratory science, computer and information sciences, economics, education, education of exceptional children, elementary education, English, English literature, foreign languages (multiple emphasis), French, history, information sciences and systems, international business management, international relations, junior high education, liberal/general studies, marketing management, mathematics, philosophy, political science and government, predentistry, prelaw, premedicine, psychology, religion, religious education, secondary education, social and rehabilitation services, social work, sociology, Spanish, theological studies.

ACADEMIC PROGRAMS. Double major, independent study, internships, semester at sea, student-designed major, study abroad, teacher preparation, Washington semester, cross-registration, 3:2 engineering, with Worcester Polytechnic Institute. **Remedial services:** Learning center, reduced course load, remedial instruction, special counselor, tutoring. **ROTC:** Army, Naval. **Placement/credit:** AP, institutional tests; 15 credit hours maximum for bachelor's degree.

ACADEMIC REQUIREMENTS. Freshmen must earn minimum GPA of 2.00 to continue in good standing. 90% of freshmen return for sophomore year. Students must declare major by end of second year. **Graduation requirements:** 120 hours for bachelor's (30 in major). Most students required to take courses in arts/fine arts, English, foreign languages, history, humanities, mathematics, philosophy/religion, biological/physical sciences, social sciences. **Postgraduate studies:** 8% enter law school, 4% enter medical school, 7% enter MBA programs, 10% enter other graduate study.

FRESHMAN ADMISSIONS. Selection criteria: School achievement, class rank in top 40%, test scores, extracurricular activities, and interview considered. **High school preparation:** 15 units required. Required units include English 4, foreign language 2, mathematics 2, social science 1 and science 1. 5 additional academic units from English, foreign language, mathematics, social science, or sciences required. **Test requirements:** SAT or ACT (SAT preferred); score report by March 1.

1992 FRESHMAN CLASS PROFILE. 890 men applied, 700 accepted, 164 enrolled; 1,335 women applied, 1,050 accepted, 290 enrolled. 65% had high school GPA of 3.0 or higher, 35% between 2.0 and 2.99. 15% were in top tenth and 25% were in top quarter of graduating class. **Academic background:** Mid 50% of enrolled freshmen had SAT-V between 400-550, SAT-M between 430-550. 98% submitted SAT scores. **Characteristics:** 60% from in state, 88% live in college housing, 3% have minority backgrounds, 2% are foreign students. Average age is 18.

FALL-TERM APPLICATIONS. $25 fee, may be waived for applicants with need. Closing date March 1; applicants notified on a rolling basis; must reply by May 1. Interview recommended. Essay recommended. CRDA. Deferred and early admission available. EDP-F.

STUDENT LIFE. Housing: Dormitories (men, women, coed); apartment, handicapped housing available. Substance free housing available. Four year housing available. **Activities:** Student government, film, magazine, student newspaper, yearbook, choral groups, drama, jazz band, musical theater, chapel choir, choral scholars, Communitas, peace and justice committee, student volunteer center, International Student Organization, College Democrats, College Republicans, Mexico Mission, politics club, Students for Life, Bible study. **Additional information:** Comprehensive student volunteer program (including 2 week immersion program in Mexico), active student government, new comprehensive recreation facility/complex.

ATHLETICS. NCAA. **Intercollegiate:** Baseball M, basketball, cross-country, field hockey W, football M, golf M, ice hockey M, lacrosse M, rowing (crew), soccer, softball W, tennis, volleyball W. **Intramural:** Basketball, soccer M, softball, volleyball.

STUDENT SERVICES. Career counseling, employment service for

undergraduates, freshman orientation, health services, personal counseling, placement service for graduates, alcohol/substance education adviser for foreign/minority students, services/facilities for handicapped.

ANNUAL EXPENSES. Tuition and fees (1992-93): $10,470. **Room and board:** $5,240. **Books and supplies:** $400. **Other expenses:** $500.

FINANCIAL AID. 60% of freshmen, 60% of continuing students receive some form of aid. All aid based on need. 230 enrolled freshmen were judged to have need, all were offered aid. Athletic scholarships available. **Aid applications:** Closing date February 1; applicants notified on a rolling basis beginning on or about April 5; must reply by May 1.

ADDRESS/TELEPHONE. Thomas E. Dunn, VP Enrollment Management, Assumption College, 500 Salisbury Street, Worcester, MA 01615-0005. (508) 752-5615 ext. 285. Fax: (508) 799-4412.

Atlantic Union College
South Lancaster, Massachusetts CB code: 3010

4-year private liberal arts college, coed, affiliated with Seventh-day Adventists. Founded in 1882. **Accreditation:** Regional. **Undergraduate enrollment:** 303 men, 351 women full time; 528 men, 268 women part time. **Faculty:** 89 total (54 full time), 27 with doctorates or other terminal degrees. **Location:** Rural campus in small town; 45 miles from Boston. **Calendar:** Semester, limited summer session. **Microcomputers:** Located in classrooms, computer centers. **Special facilities:** Art gallery, music conservatory, reading center.

DEGREES OFFERED. AS, BA, BS, MEd. 24 associate degrees awarded in 1992. 130 bachelor's degrees awarded. Graduate degrees offered in 3 major fields of study.

UNDERGRADUATE MAJORS. Associate: Accounting, Bible studies, computer and information sciences, computer programming, legal assistant/paralegal, legal secretary, library assistant, medical secretary, nursing, office supervision and management, secretarial and related programs, teacher aide. **Bachelor's:** Accounting, biology, business administration and management, chemistry, clinical laboratory science, computer and information sciences, elementary education, English, fine arts, food science and nutrition, French, history, home economics, humanities and social sciences, interior design, mathematics, music, nursing, nutritional sciences, office supervision and management, psychology, religion, religious education, secondary education, secretarial and related programs, social work, Spanish, theological studies.

ACADEMIC PROGRAMS. Accelerated program, computer delivered (on-line) credit-bearing course offerings, cooperative education, double major, dual enrollment of high school students, external degree, honors program, independent study, internships, study abroad, teacher preparation; liberal arts/career combination in engineering, health sciences. **Remedial services:** Learning center, reduced course load, remedial instruction, tutoring. **Placement/credit:** AP, CLEP General and Subject, institutional tests; 32 credit hours maximum for bachelor's degree.

ACADEMIC REQUIREMENTS. Freshmen must earn minimum GPA of 2.0 to continue in good standing. Students must declare major by end of second year. **Graduation requirements:** 64 hours for associate, 128 hours for bachelor's (40 in major). Most students required to take courses in arts/fine arts, computer science, English, foreign languages, history, humanities, mathematics, philosophy/religion, biological/physical sciences, social sciences. **Additional information:** External degree program of directed independent study for those 25 and over.Master of education program available summer session only.

FRESHMAN ADMISSIONS. Selection criteria: School achievement record, interview, recommendations, test scores important. **High school preparation:** 14 units required. Required and recommended units include biological science 1, English 4, foreign language 2, mathematics 2-3, physical science 1-2 and social science 2. Science 3 recommended. One science unit must be laboratory science, .5 unit computer science also required. **Test requirements:** SAT or ACT (ACT preferred); score report by August 15.

1992 FRESHMAN CLASS PROFILE. 76 men, 144 women enrolled. **Characteristics:** 27% from in state, 93% live in college housing, 47% have minority backgrounds, 17% are foreign students. Average age is 19.

FALL-TERM APPLICATIONS. $15 fee. No closing date; applicants notified on a rolling basis. Interview required for non-Seventh-day Adventist applicants. Audition recommended for music applicants. Portfolio recommended for art applicants. Deferred and early admission available.

STUDENT LIFE. Housing: Dormitories (men, women); apartment housing available. **Activities:** Student government, student newspaper, yearbook, poetry publication, choral groups, concert band, drama, music ensembles, symphony orchestra, campus community outreach, Big Brother, Adopt-A-Grandparent. **Additional information:** Religious observance required.

ATHLETICS. NAIA. **Intercollegiate:** Basketball M. **Intramural:** Cross-country, golf, gymnastics, racquetball, sailing, skiing, skin diving, softball, swimming, tennis, track and field, volleyball.

STUDENT SERVICES. Aptitude testing, career counseling, employment service for undergraduates, freshman orientation, health services, personal counseling, placement service for graduates, veterans counselor, services/facilities for handicapped.

ANNUAL EXPENSES. Tuition and fees: $10,700. **Room and board:** $3,550. **Books and supplies:** $500. **Other expenses:** $800.

FINANCIAL AID. 95% of freshmen, 95% of continuing students receive some form of aid. 32% of grants, 84% of loans, 17% of jobs based on need. Academic, music/drama, athletic, leadership scholarships available. **Aid applications:** No closing date; priority given to applications received by April 15; applicants notified on a rolling basis beginning on or about May 1; must reply within 10 days.

ADDRESS/TELEPHONE. James Norcliffe, Director of Admissions, Atlantic Union College, Main Street, South Lancaster, MA 01561. (508) 368-2000. (800) AUC-2030. Fax: (508) 368-2015.

Babson College
Babson Park, Massachusetts CB code: 3075

Admissions:	71% of applicants accepted
Based on:	••• School record
	•• Activities, essay, recommendations, special talents, test scores
	• Interview
Completion:	94% of freshmen end year in good standing
	85% graduate, 3% of these enter graduate study

4-year private business college, coed. Founded in 1919. **Accreditation:** Regional. **Undergraduate enrollment:** 1,078 men, 601 women full time. **Graduate enrollment:** 208 men, 111 women full time; 683 men, 476 women part time. **Faculty:** 177 total (126 full time), 127 with doctorates or other terminal degrees. **Location:** Suburban campus in large town; 14 miles from Boston. **Calendar:** Semester, limited summer session. **Microcomputers:** 120 located in dormitories, libraries, computer centers, campus-wide network. **Special facilities:** Sir Isaac Newton Collection, Roger Babson Museum and Archives.

DEGREES OFFERED. BS, MBA. 429 bachelor's degrees awarded in 1992. 100% in business and management. Graduate degrees offered in 14 major fields of study.

UNDERGRADUATE MAJORS. Accounting, American studies, business administration and management, business and management, business economics, communications, economics, entrepreneurial studies, finance, information sciences and systems, international business management, investments and securities, management information systems, marketing management, mathematics, operations research, small business management and ownership.

ACADEMIC PROGRAMS. Accelerated program, double major, honors program, independent study, internships, semester at sea, student-designed major, study abroad, cross-registration. **Remedial services:** Learning center, reduced course load, tutoring, writing center, mathematics resource center. **Placement/credit:** AP, CLEP General and Subject, IB, institutional tests; 64 credit hours maximum for bachelor's degree.

ACADEMIC REQUIREMENTS. Freshmen must earn minimum GPA of 2.0 to continue in good standing. 94% of freshmen return for sophomore year. Students must declare major by end of second year. **Graduation requirements:** 128 hours for bachelor's. Most students required to take courses in computer science, English, history, humanities, mathematics, philosophy/religion, biological/physical sciences, social sciences. **Postgraduate studies:** 1% enter law school, 1% enter MBA programs, 1% enter other graduate study.

FRESHMAN ADMISSIONS. Selection criteria: School performance record, test scores, interview, activities, recommendations, personal statements considered. **High school preparation:** 16 units required. Required and recommended units include English 4, mathematics 3, social science 2 and science 1. Foreign language 2 recommended. Science unit should be laboratory science. Additional units in science recommended. **Test requirements:** SAT or ACT (SAT preferred); score report by February 1. 2 ACH required, including English (with essay preferred) and Mathematics. Score report by June 1.

1992 FRESHMAN CLASS PROFILE. 1,104 men applied, 769 accepted, 292 enrolled; 527 women applied, 386 accepted, 145 enrolled. 22% were in top tenth and 60% were in top quarter of graduating class. **Academic background:** Mid 50% of enrolled freshmen had SAT-V between 440-520, SAT-M between 530-630. 99% submitted SAT scores. **Characteristics:** 41% from in state, 94% live in college housing, 8% have minority backgrounds, 22% are foreign students. Average age is 18.

FALL-TERM APPLICATIONS. $40 fee, may be waived for applicants with need. Closing date February 1; applicants notified on or about April 1; must reply by May 1. Essay required. Interview recommended. CRDA. Deferred admission available. EDP-F; institutional early decision plan. Early action and early decision deadline is December 1; notification by January 1.

STUDENT LIFE. Housing: Dormitories (men, coed); apartment housing available. Freshmen are required to live on campus unless commuting from home. **Activities:** Student government, film, student newspaper, yearbook, dance, drama, jazz band, music ensembles, musical theater, fraternities, sororities, Hillel Babson, International Student Organization, Christian Fellowship, Circle-K, Gay/Lesbian Alliance, Babson Asian Student Association, Black Student Association, get into the volunteer experience (GIVE).

Additional information: More than 50 student-owned and operated businesses on campus, and 51 student-run organizations.

ATHLETICS. NCAA. **Intercollegiate:** Baseball M, basketball, cross-country, diving, field hockey W, golf, ice hockey M, lacrosse, rugby M, sailing, skiing, soccer, softball W, squash, swimming, tennis, volleyball. **Intramural:** Basketball, ice hockey M, racquetball, soccer, softball, squash, tennis, track and field, volleyball, water polo.

STUDENT SERVICES. Career counseling, employment service for undergraduates, freshman orientation, health services, personal counseling, placement service for graduates, veterans counselor, services/facilities for handicapped.

ANNUAL EXPENSES. Tuition and fees: $16,445. **Room and board:** $6,715. **Books and supplies:** $450. **Other expenses:** $1,000.

FINANCIAL AID. 48% of freshmen, 46% of continuing students receive some form of aid. 99% of grants, 93% of loans, 32% of jobs based on need. 194 enrolled freshmen were judged to have need, all were offered aid. Academic scholarships available. **Aid applications:** Closing date February 1; applicants notified on or about April 1; must reply by May 1.

ADDRESS/TELEPHONE. Charles S. Nolan, Dean of Undergraduate Admission, Babson College, Mustard Hall, Babson Park, MA 02157-0310. (617) 239-5522. (800) 488-3696. Fax: (617) 239-4006.

Bay Path College

Longmeadow, Massachusetts — CB code: 3078

Admissions: 80% of applicants accepted
Based on: ••• Interview, school record
•• Recommendations
• Activities, essay, special talents, test scores
Completion: 80% of freshmen end year in good standing

4-year private business, junior college, women only. Founded in 1897. **Accreditation:** Regional. **Undergraduate enrollment:** 534 women full time; 76 women part time. **Faculty:** 54 total (30 full time), 19 with doctorates or other terminal degrees. **Location:** Suburban campus in large town; 3 miles from Springfield, 26 miles from Hartford, Connecticut. **Calendar:** Semester, limited summer session. **Microcomputers:** 65 located in libraries, classrooms, computer centers. **Special facilities:** Art center, academic support center. **Additional facts:** Member of the Cooperating Colleges of Greater Springfield, a consortium of eight colleges.

DEGREES OFFERED. AA, AS, BA, BS. 210 associate degrees awarded in 1992. 6% in business and management, 54% business/office and marketing/distribution, 7% teacher education, 15% law, 14% multi/interdisciplinary studies. 62% in business and management, 19% law, 19% psychology.

UNDERGRADUATE MAJORS. Associate: Accounting, business administration and management, business and office, criminal justice studies, criminology, early childhood education, elementary education, fashion design, fashion merchandising, health care administration, hospitality and recreation marketing, hotel/motel and restaurant management, interior design, legal assistant/paralegal, liberal/general studies, marketing management, mental health/human services, retailing, tourism, transportation and travel marketing. **Bachelor's:** Accounting, business administration and management, criminal justice studies, criminology, elementary education, law psychology.

ACADEMIC PROGRAMS. 2-year transfer program, dual enrollment of high school students, independent study, internships, cross-registration; liberal arts/career combination in business. **Remedial services:** Learning center, reduced course load, remedial instruction, special counselor, tutoring. **ROTC:** Army. **Placement/credit:** AP, CLEP General and Subject, institutional tests; 30 credit hours maximum for associate degree.

ACADEMIC REQUIREMENTS. Freshmen must earn minimum GPA of 1.9 to continue in good standing. 80% of freshmen return for sophomore year. Students must declare major by end of first year. **Graduation requirements:** 60 hours for associate, 120 hours for bachelor's. Most students required to take courses in arts/fine arts, computer science, English, humanities, mathematics, biological/physical sciences, social sciences.

FRESHMAN ADMISSIONS. Selection criteria: Admission based on applicant's ability to succeed. High school transcript, recommendation, and interview required. SAT or ACT scores considered. Recommended units include English 4, mathematics 2, social science 1 and science 1. **Test requirements:** SAT or ACT for placement.

1992 FRESHMAN CLASS PROFILE. 665 women applied, 533 accepted, 278 enrolled. 16% had high school GPA of 3.0 or higher, 74% between 2.0 and 2.99. **Academic background:** Mid 50% of enrolled freshmen had SAT-V between 320-430, SAT-M between 340-440. 67% submitted SAT scores. **Characteristics:** 42% from in state, 71% live in college housing, 12% have minority backgrounds, 7% are foreign students. Average age is 18.

FALL-TERM APPLICATIONS. $25 fee, may be waived for applicants with need. No closing date; applicants notified on a rolling basis. Interview required. CRDA. Deferred and early admission available. EDP-S.

STUDENT LIFE. Housing: Dormitories (women). **Activities:** Student government, yearbook, choral groups, dance, drama, music ensembles, musical theater, Red Cross volunteers, Interfaith Council, Day Student's Club, Golden Zonta, Phi Beta Lambda, Wellness Club, Law Club.

ATHLETICS. Intramural: Bowling, field hockey, horseback riding, skiing, soccer, softball, swimming, table tennis, tennis, volleyball. **Clubs:** Skiing, outing clubs.

STUDENT SERVICES. Aptitude testing, career counseling, employment service for undergraduates, freshman orientation, health services, personal counseling, placement service for graduates, special adviser for adult students, services/facilities for handicapped.

ANNUAL EXPENSES. Tuition and fees: $9,600. **Room and board:** $6,100. **Books and supplies:** $550. **Other expenses:** $900.

FINANCIAL AID. 75% of freshmen, 82% of continuing students receive some form of aid. 80% of grants, 91% of loans, 94% of jobs based on need. 157 enrolled freshmen were judged to have need, all were offered aid. Academic, music/drama, state/district residency, leadership scholarships available. **Aid applications:** No closing date; priority given to applications received by February 28; applicants notified on a rolling basis; must reply within 2 weeks.

ADDRESS/TELEPHONE. Paula A. DesRoberts, Director of Admissions, Bay Path College, 588 Longmeadow Street, Longmeadow, MA 01106. (413) 567-0621. (800) 782-7284. Fax: (413) 567-9324.

Bay State College

Boston, Massachusetts — CB code: 3120

Admissions: 90% of applicants accepted
Based on: ••• Interview
•• Recommendations, school record
• Activities, essay, test scores
Completion: 80% of freshmen end year in good standing
32% enter 4-year programs

2-year private junior college, coed. Founded in 1946. **Accreditation:** Regional. **Undergraduate enrollment:** 148 men, 550 women full time; 6 men, 27 women part time. **Faculty:** 36 total (20 full time), 1 with doctorate or other terminal degree. **Location:** Urban campus in very large city; located in Back Bay section. **Calendar:** Semester, limited summer session. **Microcomputers:** 60 located in computer centers.

DEGREES OFFERED. AAS. 250 associate degrees awarded in 1992. 21% in business and management, 77% business/office and marketing/distribution.

UNDERGRADUATE MAJORS. Accounting, business administration and management, business and office, fashion merchandising, hospitality and recreation marketing, hotel/motel and restaurant management, legal secretary, medical assistant, medical laboratory technologies, medical secretary, occupational therapy assistant, physical therapy assistant, retailing, secretarial and related programs, tourism, transportation and travel marketing.

ACADEMIC PROGRAMS. 2-year transfer program, double major, independent study, internships. **Remedial services:** Learning center, reduced course load, remedial instruction, tutoring. **Placement/credit:** Institutional tests.

ACADEMIC REQUIREMENTS. Freshmen must earn minimum GPA of 1.6 to continue in good standing. 80% of freshmen return for sophomore year. Students must declare major on application. **Graduation requirements:** 60 hours for associate (20 in major). Most students required to take courses in computer science, English, mathematics.

FRESHMAN ADMISSIONS. Selection criteria: Minimum 2.0 GPA. Decision made on individual basis. Interviews and 2 recommendations from guidance counselors may be weighed more heavily for students with lower GPA. Second interviews may be requested.

1992 FRESHMAN CLASS PROFILE. 239 men applied, 215 accepted, 82 enrolled; 954 women applied, 858 accepted, 340 enrolled. **Characteristics:** 75% from in state, 65% commute, 10% have minority backgrounds, 1% are foreign students. Average age is 18.

FALL-TERM APPLICATIONS. $25 fee, may be waived for applicants with need. Closing date August 31; applicants notified on a rolling basis; must reply within 3 weeks. Interview required. Deferred admission available.

STUDENT LIFE. Housing: Dormitories (men, women). **Activities:** Student government, magazine, yearbook, travel club, student activities counsel, Delta Epsilon Chi, student leader organization.

STUDENT SERVICES. Aptitude testing, career counseling, employment service for undergraduates, freshman orientation, health services, personal counseling, placement service for graduates.

ANNUAL EXPENSES. Tuition and fees: $7,825. **Room and board:** $5,900. **Books and supplies:** $500. **Other expenses:** $1,460.

FINANCIAL AID. 75% of freshmen, 75% of continuing students receive some form of aid. 99% of grants, 69% of loans, all jobs based on need. Academic scholarships available. **Aid applications:** No closing date; priority given to applications received by March 1; applicants notified on a rolling basis beginning on or about March 15; must reply within 3 weeks. **Additional information:** Financial planning available to prospective students.

ADDRESS/TELEPHONE. Ruth W. Carrigan, Director of Admissions, Bay State College, 122 Commonwealth Avenue, Boston, MA 02116. (617) 236-8000. Fax: (617) 536-1735.

Becker College: Leicester Campus
Leicester, Massachusetts CB code: 3482

Admissions: 90% of applicants accepted
Based on: ••• Interview, school record
•• Activities
• Essay, recommendations, special talents, test scores
Completion: 75% of freshmen end year in good standing
65% graduate, 60% of these enter 4-year programs

2-year private junior college, coed. Founded in 1784. **Accreditation:** Regional. **Undergraduate enrollment:** 120 men, 282 women full time; 2 men, 11 women part time. **Faculty:** 32 total (21 full time), 1 with doctorate or other terminal degree. **Location:** Suburban campus in small town; 6 miles from Worcester. **Calendar:** Semester, limited summer session. **Microcomputers:** 40 located in classrooms, computer centers, campus-wide network. **Additional facts:** 4-year degree program in business administration, legal studies, and psychology available fall 1993.

DEGREES OFFERED. AS. 147 associate degrees awarded in 1992. 8% in agriculture, 20% business and management, 9% communications, 17% teacher education, 16% allied health, 19% multi/interdisciplinary studies, 11% trade and industry.

UNDERGRADUATE MAJORS. Accounting, animal sciences, business administration and management, communications, early childhood education, hotel/motel and restaurant management, liberal/general studies, marketing and distribution, physical education, sports management, tourism, transportation and travel marketing, veterinarian's assistant.

ACADEMIC PROGRAMS. 2-year transfer program, cooperative education, internships, study abroad, visiting/exchange student program, cross-registration. **Remedial services:** Learning center, reduced course load, remedial instruction, tutoring. **Placement/credit:** AP, CLEP Subject; 30 credit hours maximum for associate degree.

ACADEMIC REQUIREMENTS. Freshmen must earn minimum GPA of 1.3 to continue in good standing. 75% of freshmen return for sophomore year. Students must declare major on enrollment. **Graduation requirements:** 60 hours for associate. Most students required to take courses in arts/fine arts, English, humanities, mathematics.

FRESHMAN ADMISSIONS. Selection criteria: High school record, extracurricular activities, and interview considered. 2 units laboratory science and 2 units of mathematics strongly recommended for veterinary technician programs.

1992 FRESHMAN CLASS PROFILE. 187 men applied, 171 accepted, 76 enrolled; 404 women applied, 359 accepted, 144 enrolled. **Characteristics:** 48% from in state, 75% live in college housing, 16% have minority backgrounds, 8% are foreign students. Average age is 18.

FALL-TERM APPLICATIONS. $25 fee, may be waived for applicants with need. No closing date; priority given to applications received by August 15; applicants notified on a rolling basis; must reply within 30 days, deposit refundable to May 1. Interview recommended. CRDA. Deferred and early admission available.

STUDENT LIFE. Housing: Dormitories (men, women, coed). Substance-free dormitory available. **Activities:** Student government, radio, yearbook, choral groups, drama.

ATHLETICS. NJCAA. **Intercollegiate:** Baseball M, basketball, field hockey W, horseback riding, soccer, softball W, tennis M, volleyball W. **Intramural:** Basketball, horseback riding, skiing, volleyball.

STUDENT SERVICES. Career counseling, employment service for undergraduates, freshman orientation, health services, personal counseling, placement service for graduates, special adviser for adult students, veterans counselor.

ANNUAL EXPENSES. Tuition and fees: $7,935. **Room and board:** $4,210. **Books and supplies:** $500. **Other expenses:** $600.

FINANCIAL AID. 71% of freshmen, 66% of continuing students receive some form of aid. 94% of grants, 89% of loans, all jobs based on need. 145 enrolled freshmen were judged to have need, 140 were offered aid. Athletic scholarships available. **Aid applications:** No closing date; priority given to applications received by February 15; applicants notified on a rolling basis beginning on or about April 1; must reply by May 1 or within 2 weeks if notified thereafter.

ADDRESS/TELEPHONE. Brian P. Davis, Dean of Admissions, Becker College: Leicester Campus, 3 Paxton Street, Leicester, MA 01524. (508) 791-9241. Fax: (508) 892-0330.

Becker College: Worcester Campus
Worcester, Massachusetts CB code: 3079

2-year private junior college, coed. Founded in 1887. **Accreditation:** Regional. **Undergraduate enrollment:** 155 men, 405 women full time; 24 men, 98 women part time. **Faculty:** 53 total (28 full time), 4 with doctorates or other terminal degrees. **Location:** Urban campus in small city; in downtown area. **Calendar:** Semester, limited summer session. Saturday classes. **Microcomputers:** 40 located in computer centers. **Additional facts:** Member of 10 college consortium, member of Worcester Art Museum. 4-year degree programs in business administration and legal studies available in fall 1993.

DEGREES OFFERED. AS. 203 associate degrees awarded in 1992. 40% in business and management, 20% business/office and marketing/distribution, 12% teacher education, 26% health sciences.

UNDERGRADUATE MAJORS. Accounting, business administration and management, business and management, business and office, business computer/console/peripheral equipment operation, business data processing and related programs, business data programming, computer and information sciences, criminal justice studies, criminal justice technology, criminology, early childhood education, fashion merchandising, graphic arts technology, interior design, law enforcement and corrections, law enforcement and corrections technologies, legal assistant/paralegal, legal secretary, liberal/general studies, medical secretary, nursing, occupational therapy assistant, physical therapy assistant, retailing, secretarial and related programs, word processing.

ACADEMIC PROGRAMS. 2-year transfer program, cooperative education, double major, internships, study abroad, visiting/exchange student program, cross-registration, semester internship at Disney World available. **Remedial services:** Learning center, reduced course load, remedial instruction, tutoring. **ROTC:** Air Force, Army, Naval. **Placement/credit:** AP, CLEP General and Subject; 30 credit hours maximum for associate degree.

ACADEMIC REQUIREMENTS. Freshmen must earn minimum GPA of 1.5 to continue in good standing. 70% of freshmen return for sophomore year. Students must declare major on enrollment. **Graduation requirements:** 60 hours for associate. Most students required to take courses in arts/fine arts, English, humanities, mathematics.

FRESHMAN ADMISSIONS. Selection criteria: High school record, extracurricular activities, and interview considered. 2 units science required (including 1 biology) for physical and occupational therapy. Nursing program requires 2 units of science and 2 units algebra.

1992 FRESHMAN CLASS PROFILE. 112 men, 286 women enrolled. **Characteristics:** 60% from in state, 51% live in college housing, 4% have minority backgrounds, 7% are foreign students. Average age is 18.

FALL-TERM APPLICATIONS. $25 fee, may be waived for applicants with need. No closing date; priority given to applications received by August 15; applicants notified on a rolling basis; must reply within 30 days, deposit refundable to May 1. Interview recommended. CRDA. Deferred and early admission available.

STUDENT LIFE. Housing: Dormitories (men, women). Coed dormitory for non-traditional adult students. **Activities:** Student government, radio, yearbook, drama, Student Program for Urban Development.

ATHLETICS. NJCAA. **Intercollegiate:** Basketball, field hockey W, horseback riding, soccer, softball W, tennis, volleyball W. **Intramural:** Basketball, skiing, tennis, volleyball.

STUDENT SERVICES. Career counseling, employment service for undergraduates, freshman orientation, health services, personal counseling, placement service for graduates, special adviser for adult students.

ANNUAL EXPENSES. Tuition and fees: $7,935. **Room and board:** $4,210. **Books and supplies:** $500. **Other expenses:** $600.

FINANCIAL AID. 87% of freshmen, 86% of continuing students receive some form of aid. 90% of grants, 75% of loans, all jobs based on need. 390 enrolled freshmen were judged to have need, 259 were offered aid. Academic, athletic scholarships available. **Aid applications:** No closing date; priority given to applications received by February 15; applicants notified on a rolling basis beginning on or about April 1; must reply within 2 weeks.

ADDRESS/TELEPHONE. Brian P. Davis, Dean of Admissions, Becker College: Worcester Campus, 61 Sever Street, Worcester, MA 01615-0071. (508) 791-9241ext. 245. Fax: (508) 831-7505.

Bentley College
Waltham, Massachusetts CB code: 3096

Admissions: 68% of applicants accepted
Based on: ••• School record
•• Activities, essay, recommendations, test scores
• Interview, special talents
Completion: 95% of freshmen end year in good standing
74% graduate, 4% of these enter graduate study

4-year private business college, coed. Founded in 1917. **Accreditation:** Regional. **Undergraduate enrollment:** 1,861 men, 1,438 women full time; 755 men, 866 women part time. **Graduate enrollment:** 162 men, 116 women full time; 1,079 men, 831 women part time. **Faculty:** 374 total (203 full time), 181 with doctorates or other terminal degrees. **Location:** Suburban campus in small city; 9 miles from Boston. **Calendar:** Semester, extensive summer session. **Microcomputers:** 3,500 located in dormitories, libraries, classrooms, computer centers, campus-wide network. Lease or purchase required**Special facilities:** Art gallery, observatory.

DEGREES OFFERED. BA, BS, MS, MBA. 968 bachelor's degrees awarded in 1992. 90% in business and management, 6% computer sciences. Graduate degrees offered in 6 major fields of study.

UNDERGRADUATE MAJORS. Accounting, applied mathematics, business administration and management, business economics, communications, English, finance, history, information sciences and systems, international studies, liberal/general studies, marketing management, philosophy.

ACADEMIC PROGRAMS. Accelerated program, honors program, independent study, internships, student-designed major, study abroad, cross-registration; combined bachelor's/graduate program in business administration. **Remedial services:** Learning center, remedial instruction, special counselor, tutoring. **ROTC:** Air Force, Army. **Placement/credit:** AP, CLEP General and Subject, institutional tests; 30 credit hours maximum for bachelor's degree.

ACADEMIC REQUIREMENTS. Freshmen must earn minimum GPA of 1.7 to continue in good standing. 87% of freshmen return for sophomore year. Students must declare major by end of second year. **Graduation requirements:** 120 hours for bachelor's (27 in major). Most students required to take courses in computer science, English, history, humanities, mathematics, philosophy/religion, biological/physical sciences, social sciences. **Post-graduate studies:** 1% enter law school, 3% enter MBA programs.

FRESHMAN ADMISSIONS. Selection criteria: Test scores, class rank, GPA, activities, and recommendations all considered. **High school preparation:** 16 units required. Required units include English 4, foreign language 2, mathematics 4, social science 2 and science 1. 3 units in additional English, mathematics, social science, or laboratory science, foreign language, speech, or advanced accounting required. **Test requirements:** SAT or ACT; score report by February 15.

1992 FRESHMAN CLASS PROFILE. 1,761 men applied, 1,181 accepted, 427 enrolled; 1,339 women applied, 928 accepted, 362 enrolled. 20% were in top tenth and 55% were in top quarter of graduating class. **Academic background:** Mid 50% of enrolled freshmen had SAT-V between 410-490, SAT-M between 480-590. 100% submitted SAT scores. **Characteristics:** 56% from in state, 89% live in college housing, 16% have minority backgrounds, 8% are foreign students. Average age is 18.

FALL-TERM APPLICATIONS. $35 fee, may be waived for applicants with need. Closing date February 15; priority given to applications received by December 1; applicants notified on or about April 1; must reply by May 1. Essay required. Interview recommended. CRDA. Deferred and early admission available. EDP-F; institutional early decision plan.

STUDENT LIFE. Housing: Dormitories (coed); apartment, handicapped housing available. **Activities:** Student government, magazine, radio, student newspaper, television, yearbook, choral groups, dance, drama, jazz band, pep band, fraternities, sororities, Hillel, Black United Body, Catholic and Asian-American student groups, Circle-K, International Club, World Affairs Club, Business Ethics Club, Service Learning, Amnesty International, LA Latina Cultura Club.

ATHLETICS. NCAA. **Intercollegiate:** Baseball M, basketball, cross-country, field hockey W, football M, golf M, ice hockey M, lacrosse M, soccer, softball W, tennis, track and field, volleyball W. **Intramural:** Basketball, racquetball, soccer, softball, volleyball. **Clubs:** Swimming.

STUDENT SERVICES. Career counseling, employment service for undergraduates, freshman orientation, health services, personal counseling, placement service for graduates, special adviser for adult students, veterans counselor, services/facilities for handicapped.

ANNUAL EXPENSES. Tuition and fees: $12,880. **Room and board:** $5,200. **Books and supplies:** $400. **Other expenses:** $850.

FINANCIAL AID. 66% of freshmen, 70% of continuing students receive some form of aid. 84% of grants, 91% of loans, 62% of jobs based on need. 450 enrolled freshmen were judged to have need, all were offered aid. Academic, athletic, minority scholarships available. **Aid applications:** Closing date February 1; applicants notified on or about April 1; must reply by May 1 or within 3 weeks if notified thereafter. **Additional information:** 20% discount on tuition and fees for senior citizens.

ADDRESS/TELEPHONE. Office of Undergraduate Admissions, Bentley College, 175 Forest Street, Waltham, MA 02154-4705. (617) 891-2244. (800) 523-2354. Fax: (617) 891-3414.

Berklee College of Music
Boston, Massachusetts — CB code: 3107

Admissions: 70% of applicants accepted
Based on:
- ••• Special talents
- •• Activities, interview, recommendations, school record
- • Essay, test scores

Completion: 85% of freshmen end year in good standing

4-year private music college, coed. Founded in 1945. **Accreditation:** Regional. **Undergraduate enrollment:** 1,884 men, 337 women full time; 341 men, 101 women part time. **Faculty:** 263 total (149 full time). **Location:** Urban campus in very large city; Located in Back Bay area of Boston. **Calendar:** Semester, extensive summer session. **Special facilities:** Concert performance center, synthesizer laboratories, recording studios, film scoring laboratories, library with over 6000 recordings and 14,000 scores, Macintosh-equipped Learning Assistance Laboratory. **Additional facts:** Emphasis on contemporary musical idioms.

DEGREES OFFERED. B. 295 bachelor's degrees awarded in 1992. 5% in teacher education, 95% visual and performing arts.

UNDERGRADUATE MAJORS. Jazz, music business management, music education, music performance, music theory and composition.

ACADEMIC PROGRAMS. Accelerated program, double major, student-designed major, teacher preparation, exchange program with Rotterdan Conservatory in the Netherlands. **Remedial services:** Learning center, preadmission summer program, special counselor, tutoring. **Placement/credit:** AP, CLEP General and Subject, institutional tests; 60 credit hours maximum for bachelor's degree.

ACADEMIC REQUIREMENTS. Freshmen must earn minimum GPA of 2.0 to continue in good standing. 67% of freshmen return for sophomore year. Students must declare major by end of first year. **Graduation requirements:** 120 hours for bachelor's (30 in major). Most students required to take courses in arts/fine arts, English, history, humanities, biological/physical sciences, social sciences. **Additional information:** Degree program includes general education courses.

FRESHMAN ADMISSIONS. Selection criteria: Musical training and experience, recommendations, academic record, test scores, extracurricular music activities, interview important. Cassette tape considered but not required. **High school preparation:** 16 units required. Music training and/or experience required. **Test requirements:** SAT or ACT.

1992 FRESHMAN CLASS PROFILE. Characteristics: 30% from in state, 67% live in college housing, 38% are foreign students.

FALL-TERM APPLICATIONS. $50 fee, may be waived for applicants with need. No closing date; priority given to applications received by March 1; applicants notified on a rolling basis. Interview recommended. Deferred admission available. No specific reply dates but size of freshman class and available housing limited.

STUDENT LIFE. Housing: Dormitories (coed). Residence space limited. Priority given to freshman under 21. Usually filled by June. **Activities:** Student government, choral groups, concert band, drama, jazz band, music ensembles, musical theater, Fine arts programs through Mass College of Art, Emerson College, and The Museum School, Black Student Union, International Club, Environmental Club, Instrumental Clubs, Christian Fellowship, Women's Network, Yoga Society.

ATHLETICS. Intramural: Baseball M, basketball, ice hockey, soccer M, table tennis.

STUDENT SERVICES. Career counseling, employment service for undergraduates, freshman orientation, personal counseling, veterans counselor, placement service for music education graduates.

ANNUAL EXPENSES. Tuition and fees (1992-93): $9,950. **Room and board:** $6,560. **Books and supplies:** $550. **Other expenses:** $800.

FINANCIAL AID. 68% of freshmen, 61% of continuing students receive some form of aid. 43% of grants, 63% of loans, all jobs based on need. 393 enrolled freshmen were judged to have need, 322 were offered aid. Academic, music/drama scholarships available. **Aid applications:** No closing date; priority given to applications received by March 31; applicants notified on a rolling basis beginning on or about April 15; must reply within 2 weeks.

ADDRESS/TELEPHONE. Steven Lipman, Assistant Dean Of Students/Director of Admissions, Berklee College of Music, 1140 Boylston Street, Boston, MA 02215. (617) 266-1400. (800) 421-0084. Fax: (617) 536-2632.

Berkshire Community College
Pittsfield, Massachusetts — CB code: 3102

2-year public community college, coed. Founded in 1960. **Accreditation:** Regional. **Undergraduate enrollment:** 2,580 men and women. **Location:** Suburban campus in small city; 40 miles from Albany, New York. **Calendar:** Semester.

FRESHMAN ADMISSIONS. Selection criteria: Open admissions. Selective admission to nursing and allied health programs.

ANNUAL EXPENSES. Tuition and fees (1992-93): $1,898, $3,882 additional for out-of-state students. **Books and supplies:** $434. **Other expenses:** $900.

ADDRESS/TELEPHONE. Michael Bullock, Director of Admissions, Berkshire Community College, 1350 West Street, Pittsfield, MA 01201-5786. (413) 499-4660 ext. 242. Fax: (413) 448-2700.

Boston Architectural Center
Boston, Massachusetts — CB code: 1168

5-year private professional school of architecture, coed. Founded in 1889. **Accreditation:** Regional. **Undergraduate enrollment:** 422 men, 109 women full time; 53 men, 29 women part time. **Faculty:** 258 total, 190 with doctorates or other terminal degrees. **Location:** Urban campus in very large city; in Back Bay of Boston. **Calendar:** Semester, limited summer session. Extensive evening/early morning classes. **Microcomputers:** Located in classrooms, computer centers. **Special facilities:** On-campus gallery featuring exhibits of architectural interest. **Additional facts:** Bachelor of architecture awarded after 6-year program of concurrent work and academic curriculum. Most new students transfer into the BAC in sophomore or junior years. Approximately 200 new students enter each academic year. Accredited by National Architectural Accrediting Board.

DEGREES OFFERED. BArch. 43 bachelor's degrees awarded in 1992. 100% in architecture and environmental design.

UNDERGRADUATE MAJORS. Architecture.

ACADEMIC PROGRAMS. Independent study, internships, cross-registration, concurrent academic/work curriculum. **Remedial services:** Reduced course load. **Placement/credit:** AP, CLEP Subject, IB, institutional tests; 30 credit hours maximum for bachelor's degree.

ACADEMIC REQUIREMENTS. Freshmen must earn minimum GPA of 2.5 to continue in good standing. 70% of freshmen return for sophomore year. Students must declare major on application. **Graduation requirements:** 123 hours for bachelor's. Most students required to take courses in arts/fine arts, computer science, English, history, humanities, mathematics, biological/physical sciences, social sciences.

FRESHMAN ADMISSIONS. Selection criteria: Open admissions.

1992 FRESHMAN CLASS PROFILE. 91 men, 28 women enrolled. **Characteristics:** 50% from in state, 100% commute. Average age is 24.

FALL-TERM APPLICATIONS. $50 fee. No closing date; applicants notified on a rolling basis. Interview recommended. Portfolio recommended. Deferred admission available.

STUDENT LIFE. Housing: Dormitory space, when available, at Pro Arts Consortium schools. **Activities:** Student government, student newspaper, yearbook, Our House Your House (assistance for homeless), Community Design Studio.

STUDENT SERVICES. Career counseling, employment service for undergraduates, freshman orientation, placement service for graduates, services/facilities for handicapped.

ANNUAL EXPENSES. Tuition and fees (1992-93): $3,084. **Books and supplies:** $1,210. **Other expenses:** $935.

FINANCIAL AID. 47% of freshmen, 37% of continuing students receive some form of aid. 65% of grants, 80% of loans based on need. 55 enrolled freshmen were judged to have need, all were offered aid. Academic, art, leadership scholarships available. **Aid applications:** No closing date; applicants notified on a rolling basis. **Additional information:** Deferred payments available after 1 semester.

ADDRESS/TELEPHONE. Ellen Driscoll, Admissions Coordinator, Boston Architectural Center, 320 Newbury Street, Boston, MA 02115-2795. (617) 536-3170. Fax: (617) 536-5829.

Boston College
Chestnut Hill, Massachusetts — CB code: 3083

Admissions:	46% of applicants accepted
Based on:	••• Essay, school record, test scores
	•• Recommendations, special talents
	• Activities, interview
Completion:	99% of freshmen end year in good standing
	88% graduate, 28% of these enter graduate study

4-year private university, coed, affiliated with Roman Catholic Church. Founded in 1863. **Accreditation:** Regional. **Undergraduate enrollment:** 4,011 men, 4,656 women full time. **Graduate enrollment:** 904 men, 1,186 women full time; 896 men, 1,311 women part time. **Faculty:** 957 total (585 full time), 585 with doctorates or other terminal degrees. **Location:** Suburban campus in small city; 6 miles from downtown Boston. **Calendar:** Semester, extensive summer session. Saturday and extensive evening/early morning classes. **Microcomputers:** 250 located in dormitories, libraries, classrooms, computer centers. **Special facilities:** Art Gallery, Weston Observatory, Robsham Theater Arts Center, Conte Forum (athletic complex). **Additional facts:** Independent institution in Jesuit tradition.

DEGREES OFFERED. BA, BS, MA, MS, MBA, MEd, MSW, PhD, EdD, JD. 2,432 bachelor's degrees awarded in 1992. 25% in business and management, 6% communications, 5% teacher education, 13% letters/literature, 6% psychology, 25% social sciences. Graduate degrees offered in 55 major fields of study.

UNDERGRADUATE MAJORS. Accounting, art history, biochemistry, biology, business administration and management, business and management, business economics, chemistry, classics, communications, computer and information sciences, dramatic arts, early childhood education, economics, education, education of the multiple handicapped, elementary and special needs, elementary education, English, English education, environmental science, finance, foreign languages (multiple emphasis), foreign languages education, French, geology, geophysics and seismology, German, Greek (classical), history, human development, human resources development, information sciences and systems, Italian, Latin, linguistics, marketing management, mathematics, mathematics education, music, nursing, operations research, philosophy, physics, political science and government, psychology, Russian, Russian and Slavic studies, science education, secondary education, Slavic languages, social science education, sociology, Spanish, special education, studio art, theological studies, theology education.

ACADEMIC PROGRAMS. Accelerated program, double major, honors program, independent study, internships, student-designed major, study abroad, teacher preparation, visiting/exchange student program, Washington semester, cross-registration. **Remedial services:** Learning center, preadmission summer program, reduced course load, special counselor, tutoring. **ROTC:** Air Force, Army, Naval. **Placement/credit:** AP; 30 credit hours maximum for bachelor's degree.

ACADEMIC REQUIREMENTS. Freshmen must earn minimum GPA of 1.5 to continue in good standing. 93% of freshmen return for sophomore year. Students must declare major by end of second year. **Graduation requirements:** 114 hours for bachelor's (30 in major). Most students required to take courses in arts/fine arts, English, history, humanities, mathematics, philosophy/religion, biological/physical sciences, social sciences. **Postgraduate studies:** 11% enter law school, 2% enter medical school, 6% enter MBA programs, 9% enter other graduate study.

FRESHMAN ADMISSIONS. Selection criteria: School achievement record, test scores, essays, indications of excellence, recommendations, interview important. Special consideration given to children of alumni. College committed to increasing the number of underrepresented minority group members. **High school preparation:** 18 units recommended. Recommended units include English 4, foreign language 4, mathematics 4, social science 3 and science 3. 4 mathematics strongly recommended for School of Management applicants. 2 laboratory science (including 1 chemistry) required of nursing applicants. **Test requirements:** SAT or ACT; score report by February 1. 3 ACH required (including English Composition and Mathematics Level I or II). Score report by February 1.

1992 FRESHMAN CLASS PROFILE. 5,345 men applied, 2,831 accepted, 1,124 enrolled; 6,938 women applied, 2,760 accepted, 1,091 enrolled. 69% were in top tenth and 96% were in top quarter of graduating class. **Academic background:** Mid 50% of enrolled freshmen had SAT-V between 520-610, SAT-M between 590-680. 93% submitted SAT scores. **Characteristics:** 31% from in state, 94% live in college housing, 21% have minority backgrounds, 3% are foreign students. Average age is 19.

FALL-TERM APPLICATIONS. $45 fee, may be waived for applicants with need. Closing date January 10; applicants notified on or about April 15; must reply by May 1. Essay required. Interview recommended. Portfolio recommended for studio art applicants. CRDA. Deferred and early admission available. Early action plan available. Application closing date November 15; notification date no later than December 15, but commitment not required until May 1.

STUDENT LIFE. Housing: Dormitories (men, women, coed); apartment, handicapped housing available. Undergraduate housing for honors program students and romance language students and 24-hour quiet housing. Special housing available for community living, also intercultural living with international students; substance free floor. **Activities:** Student government, film, magazine, radio, student newspaper, television, yearbook, choral groups, concert band, dance, drama, jazz band, marching band, music ensembles, musical theater, pep band, symphony orchestra, broad range of religious, political, ethnic, and volunteer groups.

ATHLETICS. NCAA. **Intercollegiate:** Baseball M, basketball, cross-country, diving, fencing, field hockey W, football M, golf, ice hockey M, lacrosse, sailing, skiing, soccer, softball W, swimming, tennis, track and field, volleyball W, water polo M, wrestling M. **Intramural:** Basketball, cross-country M, handball M, ice hockey M, racquetball, softball, squash, swimming, table tennis, tennis, track and field, volleyball, water polo M.

STUDENT SERVICES. Career counseling, employment service for undergraduates, freshman orientation, health services, on-campus day care, personal counseling, placement service for graduates, chaplain's office, services/facilities for handicapped.

ANNUAL EXPENSES. Tuition and fees (1992-93): $15,002. **Room and board:** $6,470. **Books and supplies:** $475. **Other expenses:** $800.

FINANCIAL AID. 61% of freshmen, 57% of continuing students receive some form of aid. 73% of grants, 99% of loans, all jobs based on need. 861 enrolled freshmen were judged to have need, all were offered aid. Academic, athletic, leadership scholarships available. **Aid applications:** Closing date February 1; applicants notified on or about April 1; must reply by May 1.

ADDRESS/TELEPHONE. John L. Mahoney, Jr, Director of Undergraduate Admission, Boston College, Lyons Hall 120, Chestnut Hill, MA 02167-3804. (617) 552-3100. Fax: (617) 552-4975.

Boston Conservatory
Boston, Massachusetts — CB code: 3084

4-year private college of music, musical theater, and dance, coed. Founded in 1867. **Accreditation:** Regional. **Undergraduate enrollment:** 80 men, 200 women full time; 5 men, 9 women part time. **Graduate enrollment:** 15 men,

41 women full time; 5 men, 6 women part time. **Faculty:** 92 total (40 full time), 3 with doctorates or other terminal degrees. **Location:** Urban campus in very large city. **Calendar:** Semester, limited summer session. **Microcomputers:** Located in libraries.

DEGREES OFFERED. BFA, MFA. 58 bachelor's degrees awarded in 1992. 100% in visual and performing arts. Graduate degrees offered in 5 major fields of study.

UNDERGRADUATE MAJORS. Dance, music education, music performance, music theory and composition, musical theater.

ACADEMIC PROGRAMS. Double major, independent study, teacher preparation, cross-registration. **Placement/credit:** AP, CLEP General and Subject, institutional tests; 75 credit hours maximum for bachelor's degree.

ACADEMIC REQUIREMENTS. Freshmen must earn minimum GPA of 1.7 to continue in good standing. 82% of freshmen return for sophomore year. Students must declare major on application. **Graduation requirements:** 122 hours for bachelor's (90 in major). Most students required to take courses in English, history.

FRESHMAN ADMISSIONS. Selection criteria: Academic record, artistic background, and audition all considered. Audition carries most weight. **High school preparation:** 16 units recommended. Recommended units include English 4, foreign language 2, mathematics 3, social science 4 and science 3. Participation in school ensembles, productions, and community schools of the arts, private lessons in performance area recommended.

1992 FRESHMAN CLASS PROFILE. 18 men, 66 women enrolled. **Characteristics:** 37% from in state, 67% commute, 7% have minority backgrounds, 8% are foreign students. Average age is 19.

FALL-TERM APPLICATIONS. $40 fee, may be waived for applicants with need. No closing date; priority given to applications received by March 1; applicants notified on a rolling basis; must reply by May 1 or within 30 days if notified thereafter. Audition required. Essay required. Interview recommended for music education, composition applicants. CRDA. Deferred and early admission available. EDP-F.

STUDENT LIFE. Housing: Dormitories (men, women, coed). **Activities:** Student government, student newspaper, yearbook, choral groups, concert band, dance, drama, jazz band, music ensembles, musical theater, opera, symphony orchestra, chamber music, fraternities, African-American Artists' Association, Community Services Association, Christian Fellowship, International Student Organization, Environmental Awareness Group, Commuter Club, Peer Support Aides, Taiwan Chinese Student Association.

ATHLETICS. Intramural: Basketball M.

STUDENT SERVICES. Freshman orientation, health services, personal counseling.

ANNUAL EXPENSES. Tuition and fees: $11,980. **Room and board:** $5,925. **Books and supplies:** $475. **Other expenses:** $1,000.

FINANCIAL AID. 79% of freshmen, 76% of continuing students receive some form of aid. 42% of grants, 87% of loans, 82% of jobs based on need. 62 enrolled freshmen were judged to have need, 56 were offered aid. Music/drama scholarships available. **Aid applications:** Closing date March 1; applicants notified on or about April 1; must reply within 30 days.

ADDRESS/TELEPHONE. Allison Ball, Director of Admissions, Boston Conservatory, 8 The Fenway, Boston, MA 02215. (617) 536-6340. Fax: (617) 536-3176.

Boston University
Boston, Massachusetts CB code: 3087

Admissions: 70% of applicants accepted
Based on:
- ••• School record
- •• Essay, recommendations, special talents, test scores
- • Activities, interview

Completion: 90% of freshmen end year in good standing; 70% graduate

4-year private university, coed. Founded in 1839. **Accreditation:** Regional. **Undergraduate enrollment:** 6,330 men, 7,362 women full time; 341 men, 301 women part time. **Graduate enrollment:** 3,541 men, 3,492 women full time; 1,626 men, 1,775 women part time. **Faculty:** 2,556 total (1,676 full time), 2,071 with doctorates or other terminal degrees. **Location:** Urban campus in very large city; Back Bay area. **Calendar:** Semester, extensive summer session. **Microcomputers:** 400 located in dormitories, libraries, computer centers. **Special facilities:** Science and Engineering center, Proscenium Theater, Coit Observatory, 2 art galleries, Tsai Performance Center, Center for Remote Sensing, Huntington Theatre.

DEGREES OFFERED. AA, AS, BA, BS, BFA, MA, MS, MBA, MFA, MEd, MSW, PhD, EdD, DMD, MD, JD, M.Div. 8 associate degrees awarded in 1992. 63% in business and management, 25% computer sciences, 12% parks/recreation, protective services, public affairs. 3,526 bachelor's degrees awarded. 20% in business and management, 16% communications, 8% engineering, 5% allied health, 6% psychology, 19% social sciences, 5% visual and performing arts. Graduate degrees offered in 125 major fields of study.

UNDERGRADUATE MAJORS. Associate: Accounting, biomedical science, business administration and management, computer and information sciences, criminal justice studies. **Bachelor's:** Accounting, advertising, aerospace/aeronautical/astronautical engineering, African studies, American studies, anthropology, applied mathematics, archeology, art education, art history, astronomy, astrophysics, bilingual/bicultural education, bioengineering and biomedical engineering, biological and physical sciences, biology, business administration and management, business and management, chemistry, classics, communications, computer and information sciences, computer engineering, dental laboratory technology, dramatic arts, early childhood education, East Asian studies, Eastern European studies, economics, education of the deaf and hearing impaired, electrical/electronics/communications engineering, elementary education, engineering, engineering and other disciplines, engineering management, English, English education, environmental science, finance, foreign languages education, French, geography, geology, German, graphic design, Greek (classical), Greek (modern), health education, history, hotel/motel and restaurant management, humanities, humanities and social sciences, international business management, international relations, Italian, journalism, Latin, Latin American studies, legal assistant/paralegal, leisure education studies, liberal/general studies, linguistics, management information systems, manufacturing engineering, marine biology, marketing management, mathematics, mathematics education, mechanical engineering, medical laboratory technologies, music, music education, music history and appreciation, music performance, music theory and composition, occupational therapy, operations research, painting, philosophy, physical education, physical therapy, physics, physiology, human and animal, planetary science, political science and government, predentistry, prelaw, premedicine, professional studies, psychology, public relations, pure mathematics, radio/television broadcasting, recreation therapy, rehabilitation counseling/services, religion, Russian, Russian and Slavic studies, science education, sculpture, social studies education, social work, sociology, Spanish, special education, speech/communication/theater education, sports medicine, statistics, systems engineering, teaching English as a second language/foreign language, urban studies, visual and performing arts.

ACADEMIC PROGRAMS. Accelerated program, cooperative education, double major, honors program, independent study, internships, semester at sea, student-designed major, study abroad, teacher preparation, telecourses, visiting/exchange student program, Washington semester, cross-registration; liberal arts/career combination in engineering, health sciences; combined bachelor's/graduate program in business administration, medicine. **ROTC:** Air Force, Army, Naval. **Placement/credit:** AP, CLEP Subject, IB, institutional tests; 32 credit hours maximum for bachelor's degree.

ACADEMIC REQUIREMENTS. Freshmen must earn minimum GPA of 2.0 to continue in good standing. 84% of freshmen return for sophomore year. Students must declare major by end of second year. **Graduation requirements:** 128 hours for bachelor's. Most students required to take courses in English, foreign languages, humanities, mathematics, biological/physical sciences, social sciences. **Additional information:** University Professors Program offers cross-disciplinary degree to academically gifted students.

FRESHMAN ADMISSIONS. Selection criteria: Overall academic record most important. Attention given to level of courses taken, trends in grades, overall GPA, class rank, and standardized test scores. Essays, teacher/counselor recommendations, extracurricular activities also important. Demonstrated artistic abilities in theater, music and art are very important for admissions to School for the Arts. Interview for accelerated medical and dental programs are by invitation only. Recommended units include biological science 1, English 4, foreign language 3, mathematics 4, physical science 2 and social science 3. **Test requirements:** SAT or ACT; score report by March 15. English, Mathematics, and foreign language ACH required for admission to University Professors Program. Foreign language ACH recommended for liberal arts and communications. English with essay recommended for communications. Chemistry, English with essay, Mathematics recommended for accelerated medical programs, foreign language ACH recommended. Score report by March 15.

1992 FRESHMAN CLASS PROFILE. 8,521 men applied, 5,875 accepted, 1,738 enrolled; 9,628 women applied, 6,811 accepted, 2,050 enrolled. 70% had high school GPA of 3.0 or higher, 30% between 2.0 and 2.99. 32% were in top tenth and 73% were in top quarter of graduating class. **Academic background:** Mid 50% of enrolled freshmen had SAT-V between 500-600, SAT-M between 550-650; ACT composite between 24-29. 98% submitted SAT scores. **Characteristics:** 21% from in state, 93% live in college housing, 27% have minority backgrounds, 10% are foreign students, 4% join fraternities/sororities. Average age is 18.

FALL-TERM APPLICATIONS. $45 fee, may be waived for applicants with need. No closing date; priority given to applications received by January 15; applicants notified on a rolling basis beginning on or about March 15; must reply by May 1 or within 2 weeks if notified thereafter. Interview required for accelarated medical, dental program, University Professors Program, Hahnemann medical program, New Jersey Medical program, all nonperformance theater arts applicants. Audition required for music, theater applicants. Portfolio required for visual arts, theatrical design applicants. Essay required. CRDA. Deferred and early admission available. EDP-F. Early Decision program not applicable for College of Basic Studies, accelerated programs in Dentistry and Medicine, School of Theatre Arts, and the University Professors Program. Applications should be recieved before November 15. Applicants notified between December 15 and December 31. Early decision is considered binding and accepted students should withdraw other applications. Deposits are expected by January 15.

STUDENT LIFE. Housing: Dormitories (women, coed); apartment, cooperative housing available. Undergraduate housing guaranteed for 4 years. More than 100 different residences including small townhouses, high rises, on-campus apartments. Specialty housing residences or floors, for students with common academic, cultural or extra-curricular interests. **Activities:** Student government, film, magazine, radio, student newspaper, television, yearbook, scholarly student journals, choral groups, concert band, dance, drama, jazz band, marching band, music ensembles, musical theater, opera, pep band, symphony orchestra, chamber music groups, early-music performance groups, gospel choir, fraternities, sororities, more than 280 student organizations. **Additional information:** Muir String Quartet, Empire Brass Quintet, Huntington Theatre Company in residence. The Martin Luther King, Jr. Center and Undergraduate Resource Center provide counseling as well as planning and placement services.

ATHLETICS. NCAA. **Intercollegiate:** Baseball M, basketball, cross-country, diving, field hockey W, football M, horseback riding W, ice hockey, rowing (crew), soccer M, softball W, swimming, tennis, track and field, wrestling M. **Intramural:** Basketball, field hockey W, ice hockey, soccer, softball, volleyball, water polo. **Clubs:** Archery, badminton, bowling, fencing, gymnastics, horseback riding, ice hockey W, lacrosse M, rugby M, sailing, skiing, soccer W, volleyball, water polo.

STUDENT SERVICES. Career counseling, employment service for undergraduates, freshman orientation, health services, on-campus day care, personal counseling, placement service for graduates, religious counselor, services/facilities for handicapped.

ANNUAL EXPENSES. Tuition and fees: $17,650. **Room and board:** $6,480. **Books and supplies:** $465. **Other expenses:** $735.

FINANCIAL AID. 75% of freshmen, 66% of continuing students receive some form of aid. 71% of grants, 96% of loans, all jobs based on need. 2,088 enrolled freshmen were judged to have need, 2,066 were offered aid. Academic, music/drama, art, athletic, state/district residency, leadership, religious affiliation, minority scholarships available. **Aid applications:** No closing date; priority given to applications received by March 1; applicants notified on a rolling basis beginning on or about March 15; must reply by May 1 or within 2 weeks if notified thereafter.

ADDRESS/TELEPHONE. Thomas M. Rajala, Director of Admissions, Boston University, 121 Bay State Road, Boston, MA 02215. (617) 353-2300. Fax: (617) 353-9695.

Bradford College

Bradford, Massachusetts — CB code: 3091

Admissions:	78% of applicants accepted
Based on:	••• Essay, recommendations, school record, special talents
	•• Activities, interview
	• Test scores
Completion:	84% of freshmen end year in good standing
	38% graduate, 23% of these enter graduate study

4-year private liberal arts college, coed. Founded in 1803. **Accreditation:** Regional. **Undergraduate enrollment:** 192 men, 302 women full time; 49 men and women part time. **Faculty:** 70 total (34 full time), 40 with doctorates or other terminal degrees. **Location:** Suburban campus in small city; 35 miles from Boston. **Calendar:** Semester. **Microcomputers:** 23 located in dormitories, libraries, computer centers. **Special facilities:** Laura Knott Art Gallery. **Additional facts:** Program for students with learning disabilities. ESL program (full-time residential) available. Students may take classes at Northern Essex Community College.

DEGREES OFFERED. BA. 70 bachelor's degrees awarded in 1992. 23% in business and management, 25% letters/literature, 10% life sciences, 20% social sciences, 22% visual and performing arts.

UNDERGRADUATE MAJORS. American studies, art history, biological and physical sciences, biology, business and management, chemistry, communications, comparative literature, creative writing, dance, dramatic arts, English, English literature, environmental science, European studies, fine arts, French, history, humanities, humanities and social sciences, international relations, international studies, marine biology, marketing management, music, philosophy, political science and government, psychology, social sciences, sociology, Spanish, studio art, visual and performing arts.

ACADEMIC PROGRAMS. Honors program, independent study, internships, semester at sea, student-designed major, study abroad, teacher preparation, Washington semester, cross-registration. **Remedial services:** Learning center, reduced course load, tutoring. **Placement/credit:** AP, CLEP General and Subject, institutional tests.

ACADEMIC REQUIREMENTS. Freshmen must earn minimum GPA of 1.50 to continue in good standing. 68% of freshmen return for sophomore year. Students must declare major by end of second year. **Graduation requirements:** 121 hours for bachelor's (60 in major). Most students required to take courses in arts/fine arts, English, history, humanities, mathematics, biological/physical sciences, social sciences. **Postgraduate studies:** 2% enter law school, 13% enter MBA programs, 8% enter other graduate study.

FRESHMAN ADMISSIONS. Selection criteria: Specific course grades, recommendations, student's personal statement, personal interview considered. Grades and recommendations count most heavily. Recommended units include English 4, foreign language 2, mathematics 3, social science 2 and science 2. **Test requirements:** SAT or ACT (SAT preferred) for counseling.

1992 FRESHMAN CLASS PROFILE. 577 men and women applied, 450 accepted; 150 enrolled. 50% had high school GPA of 3.0 or higher, 50% between 2.0 and 2.99. **Academic background:** Mid 50% of enrolled freshmen had SAT-V between 450-530, SAT-M between 420-500. 90% submitted SAT scores. **Characteristics:** 26% from in state, 80% live in college housing, 4% have minority backgrounds, 7% are foreign students. Average age is 18.

FALL-TERM APPLICATIONS. No fee. No closing date; applicants notified on a rolling basis beginning on or about January 1. Essay required. Interview recommended. Portfolio recommended. CRDA. Deferred admission available. Standardized test scores considered if submitted, score report by March 1. Additional essays, recommendations, or portfolios accepted in place of standardized testing.

STUDENT LIFE. Housing: Dormitories (coed). **Activities:** Student government, film, magazine, radio, student newspaper, television, yearbook, choral groups, dance, drama, music ensembles, musical theater, Nuclear Awareness Group, Foreign Student Association, Young Republicans, Massachusetts Public Interest Research Group, Kane School Volunteers, African-American History Club, International Club, Student Senate Community Committee, Women's Resource Network, Maspirg.

ATHLETICS. Intercollegiate: Basketball M, lacrosse M, soccer, softball W, volleyball W. **Intramural:** Badminton, basketball, soccer, swimming, table tennis, tennis, volleyball, water polo, wrestling M.

STUDENT SERVICES. Career counseling, employment service for undergraduates, freshman orientation, health services, personal counseling, placement service for graduates, services/facilities for handicapped.

ANNUAL EXPENSES. Tuition and fees (1992-93): $12,415. **Room and board:** $5,950. **Books and supplies:** $425. **Other expenses:** $950.

FINANCIAL AID. 71% of freshmen, 67% of continuing students receive some form of aid. 91% of grants, 92% of loans, 82% of jobs based on need. 87 enrolled freshmen were judged to have need, all were offered aid. Academic, leadership scholarships available. **Aid applications:** No closing date; priority given to applications received by March 1; applicants notified on a rolling basis beginning on or about April 1; must reply by May 1 or within 2 weeks if notified thereafter.

ADDRESS/TELEPHONE. William Dunfey, Dean of Admissions, Bradford College, 320 South Main Street, Bradford, MA 01835-7393. (508) 372-7161 ext. 271. (800) 336-6448. Fax: (508) 521-0480.

Brandeis University

Waltham, Massachusetts — CB code: 3092

Admissions:	72% of applicants accepted
Based on:	••• School record
	•• Activities, recommendations, test scores
	• Essay, interview, special talents
Completion:	77% graduate, 40% of these enter graduate study

4-year private university, coed. Founded in 1948. **Accreditation:** Regional. **Undergraduate enrollment:** 1,321 men, 1,520 women full time; 36 men, 38 women part time. **Graduate enrollment:** 416 men, 441 women full time; 20 men, 57 women part time. **Faculty:** 472 total (351 full time), 336 with doctorates or other terminal degrees. **Location:** Suburban campus in small city; 10 miles from Boston and Cambridge. **Calendar:** Semester, limited summer session. **Microcomputers:** 65 located in libraries, classrooms, computer centers, campus-wide network. **Special facilities:** Basic Medical Sciences Research Center, Rose Art Museum, spatial orientation laboratory, Spingold Theater Arts Center, National Center for Complex Systems, Grunebaum Astronomical Observatory.

DEGREES OFFERED. BA, MA, MFA, PhD. 733 bachelor's degrees awarded in 1992. 13% in area and ethnic studies, 15% letters/literature, 9% life sciences, 11% psychology, 39% social sciences, 5% visual and performing arts. Graduate degrees offered in 27 major fields of study.

UNDERGRADUATE MAJORS. African studies, Afro-American (black) studies, American literature, American studies, anthropology, biochemistry, biological and physical sciences, biology, chemistry, classics, comparative literature, computer and information sciences, creative writing, dramatic arts, economics, engineering physics, English, English literature, European studies, fine arts, foreign languages (multiple emphasis), French, German, Greek (classical), history, history of ideas, international economics and finance, Islamic studies, Italian, Jewish studies, Latin, Latin American studies, linguistics, linguistics and cognitive science, mathematics, Middle Eastern studies, music, near Eastern and Judaic studies, neurosciences, philosophy, physics, political science and government, psychology, Russian, Russian and Slavic studies, sociology, Spanish, visual and performing arts.

ACADEMIC PROGRAMS. Double major, honors program, independent study, internships, student-designed major, study abroad, teacher preparation, visiting/exchange student program, cross-registration, seminars at Boston Museum of Fine Arts under auspices of Massachusetts Bay Marine Studies Consortium. **Remedial services:** Reduced course load, tutoring, transitional year program, writing center, student support services. **Placement/credit:** AP, IB, institutional tests.

ACADEMIC REQUIREMENTS. Freshmen must earn minimum GPA of 2.0 to continue in good standing. 90% of freshmen return for sophomore year. Students must declare major by end of second year. **Graduation requirements:** 128 hours for bachelor's. Most students required to take courses in arts/fine arts, English, foreign languages, history, humanities, biological/physical sciences, social sciences. **Postgraduate studies:** 17% enter law school, 9% enter medical school, 3% enter MBA programs, 11% enter other graduate study.

FRESHMAN ADMISSIONS. Selection criteria: Evidence of accomplishment and development most important. School and teacher statements. Relevance of test results, impressions gained through application also considered. **High school preparation:** 12 units required. Required units include English 4, foreign language 3, mathematics 3 and science 1. One history also required. **Test requirements:** SAT or ACT; score report by February 15. 3 ACH required of applicants submitting SAT scores. Score report by February 15.

1992 FRESHMAN CLASS PROFILE. 1,891 men applied, 1,258 accepted, 348 enrolled; 1,936 women applied, 1,494 accepted, 413 enrolled. 36% were in top tenth and 74% were in top quarter of graduating class. **Characteristics:** 27% from in state, 97% live in college housing, 15% have minority backgrounds, 4% are foreign students. Average age is 18.

FALL-TERM APPLICATIONS. $50 fee, may be waived for applicants with need. Applicants notified on or about April 11; must reply by May 1. Essay required. Interview recommended. Portfolio recommended for art applicants. CRDA. Deferred and early admission available. EDP-F.

STUDENT LIFE. Housing: Dormitories (coed); apartment housing available. Housing guaranteed, but not required, for freshman and sophomores. **Activities:** Student government, magazine, radio, student newspaper, television, yearbook, science fiction, literary, feminist, political, and humor journals, choral groups, concert band, dance, drama, jazz band, music ensembles, musical theater, opera, symphony orchestra, student bands, theater companies, Hillel, Student Christian Association, Nosotros (Hispanic student organization), Black Student Organization, Asian American Association, Korean Student Association, Catholic Student Organization, Waltham Group (community service), Brandeis Democrats, College Republicans, Amnesty International.

ATHLETICS. NCAA. **Intercollegiate:** Baseball M, basketball, cross-country, diving, fencing, field hockey W, golf M, ice hockey M, sailing, soccer, softball W, swimming, tennis, track and field, volleyball W, wrestling M. **Intramural:** Basketball, cross-country, golf, lacrosse M, softball, squash, tennis, volleyball, water polo M.

STUDENT SERVICES. Career counseling, freshman orientation, health services, on-campus day care, personal counseling, placement service for graduates, special adviser for adult students, denominational chaplains, residence advisers, services/facilities for handicapped.

ANNUAL EXPENSES. Tuition and fees: $17,726. **Room and board:** $6,505. **Books and supplies:** $410. **Other expenses:** $1,000.

FINANCIAL AID. 49% of freshmen, 44% of continuing students receive some form of aid. 92% of grants, 98% of loans, all jobs based on need. 375 enrolled freshmen were judged to have need, all were offered aid. Academic scholarships available. **Aid applications:** Closing date April 15; priority given to applications received by February 15; applicants notified on a rolling basis beginning on or about April 1; must reply by May 1.

ADDRESS/TELEPHONE. David Gould, Dean of Admissions, Brandeis University, 415 South Street, Waltham, MA 02254-9110. (617) 736-3500. (800) 622-0622. Fax: (617) 736-3485.

Bridgewater State College
Bridgewater, Massachusetts

CB code: 3517

Admissions: 68% of applicants accepted
Based on:
- ••• School record, test scores
- •• Activities, recommendations
- • Essay, interview, special talents

Completion: 85% of freshmen end year in good standing
49% graduate, 8% of these enter graduate study

4-year public liberal arts college, coed. Founded in 1840. **Accreditation:** Regional. **Undergraduate enrollment:** 2,355 men, 3,054 women full time; 217 men, 325 women part time. **Graduate enrollment:** 1,350 men and women. **Faculty:** 336 total (244 full time), 187 with doctorates or other terminal degrees. **Location:** Suburban campus in large town; 30 miles from Boston, 35 miles from Providence, Rhode Island. **Calendar:** Semester, extensive summer session. Extensive evening/early morning classes. **Microcomputers:** 300 located in libraries, classrooms, computer centers, campus-wide network. **Special facilities:** On-campus teacher-training school, electron microscope, observatory, human performance laboratory, flight simulators, speech and hearing clinic, art gallery, outdoor classroom. **Additional facts:** One of the oldest public colleges (153th anniversary) and the second oldest teacher training institution in the country.

DEGREES OFFERED. BA, BS, MA, MS, MEd. 1,191 bachelor's degrees awarded in 1992. 21% in area and ethnic studies, 28% business and management, 8% communications, 27% teacher education, 5% health sciences, 9% psychology, 8% social sciences. Graduate degrees offered in 39 major fields of study.

UNDERGRADUATE MAJORS. Accounting, airline piloting and navigation, anthropology, archeology, aviation management, biology, business administration and management, chemistry, communications, computer and information sciences, crafts, criminology, dramatic arts, early childhood education, earth sciences, economics, elementary education, energy and environmental resource management, English, finance, fine arts, French, geochemistry, geography, geology, graphic design, history, industrial and organizational psychology, international public service, international relations, legal assistant/paralegal, management information systems, management science, marketing management, mathematics, medical psychology, music, oceanography, philosophy, physical education, physics, political science and government, prelaw, psychology, recreation and community services technologies, secondary education, social work, sociology, Spanish, special education, speech, speech correction, speech pathology/audiology, sports medicine, studio art, transportation management.

ACADEMIC PROGRAMS. Double major, dual enrollment of high school students, education specialist degree, honors program, independent study, internships, student-designed major, study abroad, teacher preparation, telecourses, visiting/exchange student program, cross-registration. **Remedial services:** Learning center, reduced course load, remedial instruction, special counselor, tutoring. **ROTC:** Air Force, Army. **Placement/credit:** AP, CLEP General and Subject, IB, institutional tests.

ACADEMIC REQUIREMENTS. Freshmen must earn minimum GPA of 1.5 to continue in good standing. 74% of freshmen return for sophomore year. Students must declare major by end of second year. **Graduation requirements:** 120 hours for bachelor's (30 in major). Most students required to take courses in arts/fine arts, computer science, English, foreign languages, history, humanities, mathematics, philosophy/religion, biological/physical sciences, social sciences. **Postgraduate studies:** 1% enter law school, 1% enter MBA programs, 6% enter other graduate study.

FRESHMAN ADMISSIONS. Selection criteria: High school achievement most important. SAT scores, class rank, extracurricular activities, recommendations also considered. **High school preparation:** 16 units required. Required units include English 4, foreign language 2, mathematics 3, social science 2 and science 2. Sciences should be laboratory sciences. Foreign language units must be from same language. Three units of college preparatory electives. **Test requirements:** SAT; score report by March 1.

1992 FRESHMAN CLASS PROFILE. 2,138 men applied, 1,359 accepted, 398 enrolled; 2,707 women applied, 1,924 accepted, 576 enrolled. **Academic background:** Mid 50% of enrolled freshmen had SAT-V between 410-510, SAT-M between 430-530. 98% submitted SAT scores. **Characteristics:** 94% from in state, 59% live in college housing, 7% have minority backgrounds, 1% are foreign students, 11% join fraternities/sororities. Average age is 18.

FALL-TERM APPLICATIONS. $10 fee, may be waived for applicants with need. $40 fee for out-of-state applicants. Closing date March 1; applicants notified on a rolling basis beginning on or about February 1; must reply by May 1. Essay recommended. CRDA. Deferred and early admission available. Institutional early decision plan. Early action deadline November 15; notified by December 15; must respond by May 1.

STUDENT LIFE. Housing: Dormitories (men, women, coed); apartment housing available. Special rooms available for handicapped students. Quiet floor, nonsmoking floor available in residence hall. Housing application deadline March 1. **Activities:** Student government, magazine, radio, student newspaper, television, yearbook, choral groups, dance, drama, jazz band, music ensembles, musical theater, stage band, fraternities, sororities, 90 clubs and groups, including several religious, ethnic, and nationality groups, disabled students organization.

ATHLETICS. NCAA. **Intercollegiate:** Baseball M, basketball, cross-country, diving, field hockey W, football M, lacrosse W, soccer, softball W, swimming, tennis, track and field, volleyball W, wrestling M. **Intramural:** Badminton, basketball M, football M, lacrosse M, soccer, softball, tennis, volleyball.

STUDENT SERVICES. Aptitude testing, career counseling, employment service for undergraduates, freshman orientation, health services, on-campus day care, personal counseling, placement service for graduates, special adviser for adult students, veterans counselor, counseling for physically challenged, international student advisor, services/facilities for handicapped.

ANNUAL EXPENSES. Tuition and fees (1992-93): $3,000, $3,864 additional for out-of-state students. **Room and board:** $3,590. **Books and supplies:** $500. **Other expenses:** $1,250.

FINANCIAL AID. 52% of freshmen, 54% of continuing students receive some form of aid. 97% of grants, 78% of loans, all jobs based on need. Academic, leadership, minority scholarships available. **Aid applications:** No closing date; priority given to applications received by May 1; applicants notified on a rolling basis; must reply within 4 weeks.

ADDRESS/TELEPHONE. James F. Plotner, Jr, Dean of Admission, Bridgewater State College, Gates House, Bridgewater, MA 02325. (508) 697-1237. Fax: (508) 697-1746.

Bristol Community College
Fall River, Massachusetts CB code: 3110

2-year public community college, coed. Founded in 1965. **Accreditation:** Regional. **Undergraduate enrollment:** 917 men, 1,290 women full time; 1,062 men, 1,952 women part time. **Faculty:** 202 total (88 full time), 24 with doctorates or other terminal degrees. **Location:** Urban campus in small city; 50 miles from Boston, 30 miles from Providence, Rhode Island. **Calendar:** Semester, extensive summer session. **Microcomputers:** 40 located in libraries, computer centers. **Special facilities:** Planetarium, greenhouse, robotics laboratory.

DEGREES OFFERED. AA, AS. 572 associate degrees awarded in 1992.

UNDERGRADUATE MAJORS. Accounting, business administration and management, business and management, child development/care/guidance, civil technology, communications, computer and information sciences, computer programming, criminal justice studies, dental hygiene, electromechanical technology, electronic technology, elementary education, engineering, engineering and engineering-related technologies, fine arts, fire control and safety technology, information sciences and systems, legal secretary, liberal/general studies, library science, marketing and distribution, marketing management, mathematics, mechanical design technology, medical laboratory technologies, medical secretary, microcomputer software, nursing, real estate, retailing, secretarial and related programs, social work, word processing.

ACADEMIC PROGRAMS. 2-year transfer program, cooperative education, independent study, internships, telecourses, cross-registration. **Remedial services:** Learning center, preadmission summer program, reduced course load, remedial instruction, special counselor, tutoring. **Placement/credit:** CLEP Subject, institutional tests; 30 credit hours maximum for associate degree.

ACADEMIC REQUIREMENTS. Freshmen must earn minimum GPA of 2.0 to continue in good standing. **Graduation requirements:** 60 hours for associate. Most students required to take courses in English, history, mathematics, biological/physical sciences, social sciences.

FRESHMAN ADMISSIONS. Selection criteria: Open admissions. SAT required of allied health applicants. Specific programs have varying course requirements.

1992 FRESHMAN CLASS PROFILE. 376 men, 572 women enrolled. **Characteristics:** 91% from in state, 100% commute, 11% have minority backgrounds, 1% are foreign students. Average age is 21.

FALL-TERM APPLICATIONS. $10 fee, may be waived for applicants with need. $35 fee for out-of-state applicants. No closing date; applicants notified on a rolling basis beginning on or about December 1; must reply by May 1 or within 2 weeks if notified thereafter. Interview recommended for health services applicants. Essay recommended for health services applicants. CRDA. Early admission available. Priority given to applications for health services programs received by January 15.

STUDENT LIFE. Activities: Student government, magazine, student newspaper, choral groups, drama, minority student organization.

STUDENT SERVICES. Career counseling, employment service for undergraduates, freshman orientation, health services, on-campus day care, personal counseling, placement service for graduates, veterans counselor, transfer counseling, services/facilities for handicapped.

ANNUAL EXPENSES. Tuition and fees (1992-93): $2,040, $3,822 additional for out-of-state students. **Books and supplies:** $500. **Other expenses:** $1,175.

FINANCIAL AID. 48% of freshmen, 54% of continuing students receive some form of aid. 99% of grants, all loans, all jobs based on need. Academic, art, leadership, minority scholarships available. **Aid applications:** No closing date; priority given to applications received by April 15; applicants notified on a rolling basis beginning on or about May 1; must reply within 2 weeks.

ADDRESS/TELEPHONE. Frank Noble, Director of Admissions, Bristol Community College, 777 Elsbree Street, Fall River, MA 02720. (508) 678-2811 ext. 2179.

Bunker Hill Community College
Boston, Massachusetts CB code: 3123

2-year public community college, coed. Founded in 1973. **Accreditation:** Regional. **Undergraduate enrollment:** 1,109 men, 1,443 women full time; 1,469 men, 2,099 women part time. **Faculty:** 620 total (120 full time), 19 with doctorates or other terminal degrees. **Location:** Urban campus in very large city. **Calendar:** Semester, extensive summer session. Extensive evening/early morning classes. **Microcomputers:** Located in classrooms, computer centers.

DEGREES OFFERED. AA, AS. 449 associate degrees awarded in 1992. 26% in business and management, 6% business/office and marketing/distribution, 7% communications, 8% computer sciences, 6% engineering technologies, 9% allied health, 20% multi/interdisciplinary studies, 18% parks/recreation, protective services, public affairs.

UNDERGRADUATE MAJORS. Accounting, biology, business administration and management, business and management, business and office, business computer/console/peripheral equipment operation, business data processing and related programs, business data programming, commercial art, communications, computer and information sciences, computer programming, criminal justice studies, dental assistant, education, educational media technology, electrical and electronics equipment repair, electronic technology, English, fashion merchandising, fire control and safety technology, food production/management/services, graphic arts technology, hotel/motel and restaurant management, humanities and social sciences, information sciences and systems, international business management, laser electro-optic technology, law enforcement and corrections technologies, legal secretary, liberal/general studies, mathematics, medical secretary, microcomputer software, nuclear medical technology, nursing, office supervision and management, psychology, radiograph medical technology, secretarial and related programs, social work, word processing.

ACADEMIC PROGRAMS. 2-year transfer program, computer delivered (on-line) credit-bearing course offerings, cooperative education, double major, honors program, independent study, internships, study abroad, telecourses, cross-registration. **Remedial services:** Learning center, preadmission summer program, reduced course load, remedial instruction, tutoring. **Placement/credit:** CLEP General and Subject, institutional tests; 45 credit hours maximum for associate degree.

ACADEMIC REQUIREMENTS. Freshmen must earn minimum GPA of 2.0 to continue in good standing. 65% of freshmen return for sophomore year. Students must declare major on application. **Graduation requirements:** 60 hours for associate. Most students required to take courses in English, mathematics. **Additional information:** Some courses taught off-campus in the community.

FRESHMAN ADMISSIONS. Selection criteria: Open admissions. Selective admissions to nursing, medical radiography, and nuclear medical technology programs. **Test requirements:** Entrance Examination for Schools of Nursing for nursing applicants.

1992 FRESHMAN CLASS PROFILE. 1,114 men and women enrolled. **Characteristics:** 94% from in state, 100% commute, 34% have minority backgrounds, 6% are foreign students. Average age is 22.

FALL-TERM APPLICATIONS. $10 fee, may be waived for applicants with need. $35 fee for out-of-state applicants. No closing date; applicants notified on a rolling basis beginning on or about December 15; must reply by May 1 or within 2 weeks if notified thereafter. Interview recommended for allied health applicants. CRDA. Deferred admission available. Limited enrollment in allied health programs.

STUDENT LIFE. Activities: Student government, magazine, radio, student newspaper, choral groups, drama, jazz band.

ATHLETICS. NJCAA. **Intercollegiate:** Baseball M, basketball M, soccer M, softball W. **Intramural:** Tennis.

STUDENT SERVICES. Career counseling, employment service for undergraduates, freshman orientation, health services, personal counseling, placement service for graduates, services/facilities for handicapped.

ANNUAL EXPENSES. Tuition and fees (1992-93): $1,800, $3,822 additional for out-of-state students. **Books and supplies:** $400. **Other expenses:** $1,000.

FINANCIAL AID. 50% of continuing students receive some form of aid. 16% of grants, all loans, all jobs based on need. **Aid applications:** No closing date; priority given to applications received by May 1; applicants notified on a rolling basis beginning on or about June 1; must reply within 2 weeks.

ADDRESS/TELEPHONE. Janice Bonanno, Director of Admissions, Bunker Hill Community College, Rutherford Avenue, Boston, MA 02129. (617) 241-8600.

Cape Cod Community College
West Barnstable, Massachusetts CB code: 3289

2-year public community college, coed. Founded in 1961. **Accreditation:** Regional. **Undergraduate enrollment:** 553 men, 756 women full time; 356 men, 849 women part time. **Faculty:** 307 total (86 full time), 48 with doctorates or other terminal degrees. **Location:** Rural campus in small town; 3 miles from Hyannis. **Calendar:** Semester, limited summer session. **Microcomputers:** 80 located in classrooms, computer centers. **Special facilities:** Source collection for Cape Cod history, marshland nature preserve. **Additional facts:** College situated on 120 acres of pine and oak forest.

DEGREES OFFERED. AA, AS. 422 associate degrees awarded in 1992. 13% in business and management, 6% teacher education, 24% health sciences, 41% multi/interdisciplinary studies, 9% parks/recreation, protective services, public affairs.

UNDERGRADUATE MAJORS. Accounting, business administration and management, business and management, business data processing and related programs, computer and information sciences, construction, criminal justice studies, dental hygiene, early childhood education, engineering, fire control and safety technology, hotel/motel and restaurant management, information sciences and systems, legal secretary, liberal/general studies, management science, medical secretary, nursing, physical therapy assistant, retailing, secretarial and related programs.

ACADEMIC PROGRAMS. 2-year transfer program, cooperative education, dual enrollment of high school students, independent study, internships, study abroad, telecourses, cross-registration. **Remedial services:** Learning center, reduced course load, remedial instruction, special counselor, tutoring. **Placement/credit:** AP, CLEP General and Subject, institutional tests; 30 credit hours maximum for associate degree.

ACADEMIC REQUIREMENTS. Freshmen must earn minimum GPA of 1.75 to continue in good standing. 57% of freshmen return for sophomore year. Students must declare major on application. **Graduation requirements:** 60 hours for associate. Most students required to take courses in arts/fine arts, English, humanities, mathematics, biological/physical sciences, social sciences.

FRESHMAN ADMISSIONS. Selection criteria: Open admissions. Selective admissions to dental hygiene and nursing programs, with priority to Massachusetts residents. Special mathematics and science requirements for dental hygiene, nursing, engineering sciences, and computer science programs. **Additional information:** High school documentation may be waived.

1992 FRESHMAN CLASS PROFILE. 1,109 men and women enrolled. **Characteristics:** 99% from in state, 100% commute, 17% have minority backgrounds. Average age is 23.

FALL-TERM APPLICATIONS. $10 fee, may be waived for applicants with need. $35 fee for out-of-state applicants. Closing date August 10; priority given to applications received by May 1; applicants notified on a rolling basis; must reply by May 1 or within 4 weeks if notified thereafter. Interview recommended for nursing, dental hygiene applicants. CRDA. Deferred admission available. Recommended priority date for applications for dental hygiene February 1. Nursing application must be received by January 5.

STUDENT LIFE. Housing: Housing directory lists apartments, rooms, and houses for rent. **Activities:** Student government, magazine, radio, student newspaper, television, choral groups, dance, drama, Model United Nations, Third World United, Phi Theta Kappa, Earth workers Club, Criminal Justice Club, Cultural Affairs Club.

ATHLETICS. Intramural: Baseball M, basketball, handball, racquetball, rowing (crew), skiing, soccer, softball, tennis, volleyball.

STUDENT SERVICES. Career counseling, employment service for undergraduates, freshman orientation, health services, on-campus day care, personal counseling, placement service for graduates, special adviser for adult students, veterans counselor, services/facilities for handicapped.

ANNUAL EXPENSES. Tuition and fees (1992-93): $1,865, $3,822 additional for out-of-state students. **Books and supplies:** $500. **Other expenses:** $1,000.

FINANCIAL AID. 47% of freshmen, 47% of continuing students receive some form of aid. All grants, 89% of loans, all jobs based on need. **Aid applications:** No closing date; priority given to applications received by April 1; applicants notified on a rolling basis beginning on or about June 15; must reply by registration. **Additional information:** Aid applications may be accepted after May 1, pending availability of funds.

ADDRESS/TELEPHONE. Susan Kline-Symington, Director of Admissions, Cape Cod Community College, Route 132, West Barnstable, MA 02668-1599. (508) 362-2131 ext. 311. Fax: (508) 362-8638.

Clark University
Worcester, Massachusetts — CB code: 3279

Admissions:	67% of applicants accepted
Based on:	••• Recommendations, school record
	•• Activities, essay, test scores
	• Interview, special talents
Completion:	87% of freshmen end year in good standing
	73% graduate, 48% of these enter graduate study

4-year private university, coed. **Accreditation:** Regional. **Undergraduate enrollment:** 877 men, 1,171 women full time; 11 men, 12 women part time. **Graduate enrollment:** 152 men, 139 women full time; 200 men, 195 women part time. **Faculty:** 179 total, 174 with doctorates or other terminal degrees. **Location:** Urban campus in small city; 38 miles from Boston. **Calendar:** Semester, limited summer session. **Microcomputers:** 100 located in libraries, classrooms, computer centers, campus-wide network. **Special facilities:** Cartography laboratory, map library, Robert Goddard exhibition, NMR spectrometer, electron microscope, art gallery, observatory, rare book room, Language Arts Resource Center with satellite dish, state-of-the-art music facility, university arboretum, crafts studio, darkrooms, VAX cluster, 2 theaters. **Additional facts:** Clark European Center in Luxembourg offers intensive May term including classes and field work, Bermuda Biological Station for research site for 2 biology courses, School for Field Studies offers semester programs in Africa, Mexico and Virgin Islands. Other study abroad opportunities is Europe and Asia.

DEGREES OFFERED. BA, BS, MA, MBA, MEd, PhD, EdD. 575 bachelor's degrees awarded in 1992. 8% in business and management, 5% letters/literature, 6% life sciences, 23% psychology, 42% social sciences, 7% visual and performing arts. Graduate degrees offered in 26 major fields of study.

UNDERGRADUATE MAJORS. American literature, ancient civilization, art history, biochemistry, biology, business and management, chemistry, cinematography/film, city/community/regional planning, classics, comparative literature, computer and information sciences, dramatic arts, economics, engineering, English, English literature, environmental science, environmental, technology and society, fine arts, foreign languages (multiple emphasis), French, geography, German, government and international relations, history, international development, international relations, international studies, mathematics, molecular biology, music, music performance, music theory and composition, neurosciences, philosophy, physical sciences, physics, political science and government, predentistry, prelaw, premedicine, preveterinary, psychology, romance languages, screen studies, sociology, Spanish, studio art, video.

ACADEMIC PROGRAMS. Accelerated program, double major, honors program, independent study, internships, student-designed major, study abroad, teacher preparation, visiting/exchange student program, New York semester, Washington semester, cross-registration, 3-2 engineering program with Columbia University (NY), environmental internship in Rehovot, Israel; liberal arts/career combination in engineering; combined bachelor's/graduate program in business administration. **Remedial services:** Learning center, special counselor, tutoring, services for learning disabled students. **ROTC:** Army. **Placement/credit:** AP, institutional tests; 16 credit hours maximum for bachelor's degree.

ACADEMIC REQUIREMENTS. No policy requiring minimum GPA; records of students having academic difficulty are reviewed individually. 5 courses must be satisfactorily completed in first 2 semesters. 87% of freshmen return for sophomore year. Students must declare major by end of second year. **Graduation requirements:** 128 hours for bachelor's. Most students required to take courses in arts/fine arts, English, foreign languages, history, humanities, mathematics, philosophy/religion, biological/physical sciences, social sciences. **Postgraduate studies:** 14% enter law school, 14% enter medical school, 10% enter MBA programs, 10% enter other graduate study. **Additional information:** Program of Liberal Studies encourages critical thinking and broadens perspectives. Interdisciplinary majors and special programs available.

FRESHMAN ADMISSIONS. Selection criteria: School achievement record and courses, recommendations, and test scores most important. Special talents, accomplishments, motivation, and individual circumstances also considered. How applicants have challenged themselves in course selection, outside activities, jobs where they gained responsibilities considered. **High school preparation:** 16 units required. Required units include English 4, foreign language 2, mathematics 3, social science 2 and science 3. **Test requirements:** SAT or ACT (SAT preferred); score report by March 1. English ACH required, 2 others recommended. Score report by March 1.

1992 FRESHMAN CLASS PROFILE. 1,530 men applied, 946 accepted, 213 enrolled; 1,862 women applied, 1,325 accepted, 320 enrolled. 62% had high school GPA of 3.0 or higher, 38% between 2.0 and 2.99. **Academic background:** Mid 50% of enrolled freshmen had SAT-V between 450-570, SAT-M between 510-620. 96% submitted SAT scores. **Characteristics:** 32% from in state, 98% live in college housing, 11% have minority backgrounds, 20% are foreign students. Average age is 18.

FALL-TERM APPLICATIONS. $40 fee, may be waived for applicants with need. Closing date February 15; applicants notified on or about April 1; must reply by May 1. Essay required. Interview recommended. Portfolio recommended for art applicants. CRDA. Deferred and early admission available. EDP-F.

STUDENT LIFE. Housing: Dormitories (women, coed); apartment, handicapped housing available. Some university owned off-campus housing. On-campus housing includes special interest houses, global environmental house, language house. **Activities:** Student government, film, magazine, student newspaper, television, yearbook, videotape, choral groups, concert band, dance, drama, jazz band, music ensembles, musical theater, symphony orchestra, electronic music, experimental theater, recitals, Big Brother/Sister, Clark Outreach Unified Neighborhood Team, Black Student Union, Asian Society, Main South Tutoring Project, International Relations Club, Jewish Student Coalition, campus ministries.

ATHLETICS. NCAA. **Intercollegiate:** Baseball M, basketball, cross-country, diving, field hockey W, golf M, rowing (crew), soccer, softball W, swimming, tennis, track and field, volleyball W. **Intramural:** Badminton, basketball, bowling, football M, handball, racquetball, soccer, softball, squash, table tennis, volleyball, water polo.

STUDENT SERVICES. Aptitude testing, career counseling, employment service for undergraduates, freshman orientation, health services, personal counseling, placement service for graduates, special adviser for adult students, services/facilities for handicapped.

ANNUAL EXPENSES. Tuition and fees (1992-93): $16,200. **Room and board:** $4,500. **Books and supplies:** $500. **Other expenses:** $700.

FINANCIAL AID. 51% of freshmen, 43% of continuing students receive some form of aid. 97% of grants, all loans, 95% of jobs based on need. 233 enrolled freshmen were judged to have need, all were offered aid. Academic, state/district residency, leadership scholarships available. **Aid applications:** Closing date February 1; applicants notified on or about April 1; must reply by May 1. **Additional information:** Application fee waivers available for all low income students who request it.

ADDRESS/TELEPHONE. Richard W. Pierson, Dean of Admissions, Clark University, 950 Main Street, Worcester, MA 01610-1477. (508) 793-7431. Fax: (508) 793-8821.

College of the Holy Cross
Worcester, Massachusetts CB code: 3282

Admissions: 50% of applicants accepted
Based on: ••• Recommendations, school record, test scores
•• Activities, essay, interview
• Special talents
Completion: 99% of freshmen end year in good standing
96% graduate, 28% of these enter graduate study

4-year private liberal arts college, coed, affiliated with Roman Catholic Church. Founded in 1843. **Accreditation:** Regional. **Undergraduate enrollment:** 1,356 men, 1,386 women full time. **Faculty:** 265 total (212 full time), 218 with doctorates or other terminal degrees. **Location:** Suburban campus in small city; 45 miles from Boston. **Calendar:** Semester. **Microcomputers:** 130 located in libraries, computer centers. **Special facilities:** Art gallery, greenhouse, facilities for aquatic research.

DEGREES OFFERED. BA. 650 bachelor's degrees awarded in 1992. 7% in languages, 20% letters/literature, 7% life sciences, 6% mathematics, 5% physical sciences, 13% psychology, 35% social sciences.

UNDERGRADUATE MAJORS. Accounting, art history, biology, chemistry, classics, dramatic arts, economics, English, foreign languages (multiple emphasis), French, German, Greek (classical), history, Latin, mathematics, music, music history and appreciation, philosophy, physics, political science and government, psychology, religion, Russian, sociology, Spanish, studio art, visual and performing arts.

ACADEMIC PROGRAMS. Accelerated program, double major, honors program, independent study, internships, student-designed major, study abroad, visiting/exchange student program, Washington semester, cross-registration; liberal arts/career combination in engineering; combined bachelor's/graduate program in business administration. **ROTC:** Naval. **Placement/credit:** AP; 32 credit hours maximum for bachelor's degree.

ACADEMIC REQUIREMENTS. Freshmen must earn minimum GPA of 2.0 to continue in good standing. 99% of freshmen return for sophomore year. Students must declare major by end of second year. **Graduation requirements:** 128 hours for bachelor's (40 in major). Most students required to take courses in arts/fine arts, English, foreign languages, history, mathematics, philosophy/religion, biological/physical sciences, social sciences. **Postgraduate studies:** 9% enter law school, 8% enter medical school, 1% enter MBA programs, 10% enter other graduate study. **Additional information:** Optional first year program explores variety of disciplines, examines intellectual and ethical questions from common theme. Features include seminar, shared texts, co-curricular events, special housing.

FRESHMAN ADMISSIONS. Selection criteria: Academic record, test scores, recommendations, interview, essay, and extracurricular activities considered. **High school preparation:** 20 units recommended. Recommended units include biological science 1, English 4, foreign language 4, mathematics 4, physical science 3 and social science 4. **Test requirements:** SAT; score report by February 10. 3 ACH (including English Composition) required. Mathematics Level I or II recommended for science, economics, accounting, and biology applicants. Chemistry or physics recommended for science and pre-med applicants. Score report by February 10.

1992 FRESHMAN CLASS PROFILE. 1,896 men applied, 844 accepted, 338 enrolled; 1,750 women applied, 964 accepted, 431 enrolled. 65% were in top tenth and 92% were in top quarter of graduating class. **Characteristics:** 41% from in state, 99% live in college housing, 5% have minority backgrounds. Average age is 18.

FALL-TERM APPLICATIONS. $50 fee, may be waived for applicants with need. Closing date February 1; applicants notified on or about April 10; must reply by May 1. Essay required. Interview recommended. CRDA. Deferred and early admission available. EDP-F. Interview rquired for Early Decision applicants.

STUDENT LIFE. Housing: Dormitories (coed); handicapped housing available. Suites on campus available for juniors and seniors. Fit-for-life program house. First year program house. **Activities:** Student government, magazine, radio, student newspaper, yearbook, choral groups, concert band, dance, drama, jazz band, marching band, music ensembles, musical theater, pep band, Black Student Union, Purple Key Society, Student Program for Urban Development, Committee for Campus Ministry, multi-cultural awareness group, women's forum, Latin American Student Organization, Asian Students for International Awareness.

ATHLETICS. NAIA, NCAA. **Intercollegiate:** Baseball M, basketball, cross-country, diving, field hockey W, football M, golf M, ice hockey, lacrosse, rowing (crew), rugby, sailing, soccer, softball W, swimming, tennis, track and field, volleyball W. **Intramural:** Basketball, field hockey W, ice hockey M, racquetball, skiing, soccer, softball, squash, swimming, volleyball, water polo.

STUDENT SERVICES. Career counseling, employment service for undergraduates, freshman orientation, health services, personal counseling, placement service for graduates, services/facilities for handicapped.

ANNUAL EXPENSES. Tuition and fees: $17,550. **Room and board:** $6,300. **Books and supplies:** $400. **Other expenses:** $960.

FINANCIAL AID. 61% of freshmen, 56% of continuing students receive some form of aid. 98% of grants, all loans, 95% of jobs based on need. 475 enrolled freshmen were judged to have need, all were offered aid. Academic scholarships available. **Aid applications:** No closing date; priority given to applications received by February 1; applicants notified on a rolling basis beginning on or about April 15; must reply by May 1 or within 2 weeks if notified thereafter.

ADDRESS/TELEPHONE. William R. Mason, Director of Admissions, College of the Holy Cross, One College Street, Worcester, MA 01610-2395. (508) 793-2443. Fax: (508) 793-3030.

Curry College
Milton, Massachusetts CB code: 3285

Admissions: 76% of applicants accepted
Based on: ••• School record
•• Activities, essay, recommendations, special talents
• Interview, test scores
Completion: 78% of freshmen end year in good standing
55% graduate

4-year private liberal arts college, coed. Founded in 1879. **Accreditation:** Regional. **Undergraduate enrollment:** 427 men, 401 women full time; 101 men, 175 women part time. **Graduate enrollment:** 6 men, 33 women part time. **Faculty:** 178 total (79 full time), 44 with doctorates or other terminal degrees. **Location:** Suburban campus in large town; 7 miles from downtown Boston. **Calendar:** Semester, limited summer session. **Microcomputers:** 70 located in libraries, computer centers.

DEGREES OFFERED. BA, BS, MEd. 192 bachelor's degrees awarded in 1992. 29% in business and management, 22% communications, 12% teacher education, 13% health sciences, 13% allied health, 7% psychology, 9% social sciences. Graduate degrees offered in 1 major field of study.

UNDERGRADUATE MAJORS. Biology, business and management, chemistry, communications, early childhood education, education, elementary education, English, fine arts, history, humanities and social sciences, nursing, philosophy, physics, political science and government, prelaw, psychology, sociology, visual and performing arts.

ACADEMIC PROGRAMS. Double major, dual enrollment of high school students, education specialist degree, honors program, independent study, internships, student-designed major, study abroad, teacher preparation, Washington semester. **Remedial services:** Learning center, reduced course load, tutoring, program for learning disabled students. **ROTC:** Army. **Placement/credit:** AP, CLEP General and Subject, institutional tests; 60 credit hours maximum for bachelor's degree.

ACADEMIC REQUIREMENTS. Freshmen must earn minimum GPA of 2.0 to continue in good standing. 70% of freshmen return for sophomore year. Students must declare major by end of second year. **Graduation requirements:** 120 hours for bachelor's (30 in major). Most students required to take courses in arts/fine arts, English, history, humanities, philosophy/religion, biological/physical sciences, social sciences.

FRESHMAN ADMISSIONS. Selection criteria: High school record, recommendations, and extracurricular activities most important. Test scores also considered. **High school preparation:** 16 units required. Required units include biological science 1, English 4, foreign language 2, mathematics 3, physical science 1 and social science 2. 3 mathematics through algebra II, 1 chemistry, and 1 biology required for nursing applicants. **Test requirements:** SAT or ACT (SAT preferred); score report by April 1. Wechsler Adult Intelligence Scale required for learning disabled applicants for admission.

1992 FRESHMAN CLASS PROFILE. 570 men applied, 420 accepted, 113 enrolled; 549 women applied, 436 accepted, 101 enrolled. 23% had high school GPA of 3.0 or higher, 65% between 2.0 and 2.99. **Academic background:** Mid 50% of enrolled freshmen had SAT-V between 400-500, SAT-M between 420-500. 95% submitted SAT scores. **Characteristics:** 48% from in state, 82% live in college housing, 5% have minority backgrounds, 3% are foreign students. Average age is 18.

FALL-TERM APPLICATIONS. $25 fee, may be waived for applicants with need. Closing date April 1; applicants notified on a rolling basis beginning on or about January 20; must reply by May 1. Essay required. Interview recommended. CRDA. Deferred and early admission available. EDP-F.

STUDENT LIFE. Housing: Dormitories (men, women, coed). **Activities:** Student government, radio, student newspaper, yearbook, literary journal, choral groups, dance, drama, music ensembles, musical theater, religious clubs, nursing association, international club, student activities board, community service organization.

ATHLETICS. NCAA. **Intercollegiate:** Baseball M, basketball, football M, ice hockey M, lacrosse M, soccer, softball W, tennis. **Intramural:** Basketball, rugby M, softball, tennis, volleyball.

STUDENT SERVICES. Aptitude testing, career counseling, employment service for undergraduates, freshman orientation, health services, on-campus day care, personal counseling, placement service for graduates, special adviser for adult students, veterans counselor, services/facilities for handicapped.

ANNUAL EXPENSES. Tuition and fees (1992-93): $12,945. **Room and board:** $5,900. **Books and supplies:** $600. **Other expenses:** $800.

FINANCIAL AID. 45% of freshmen, 52% of continuing students receive some form of aid. All grants, 98% of loans based on need. **Aid applications:** Closing date April 15; applicants notified on a rolling basis beginning on or about March 10; must reply by May 1.

ADDRESS/TELEPHONE. Janet Cromie Kelly, Dean of Admissions, Curry College, 1071 Blue Hill Avenue, Milton, MA 02186-9984. (617) 333-0500 ext. 2210. (800) 669-0686. Fax: (617) 333-6860.

Dean Junior College
Franklin, Massachusetts — CB code: 3352

Admissions: 96% of applicants accepted
Based on:
••• Recommendations, school record
•• Interview
• Activities, essay, special talents, test scores
Completion: 90% of freshmen end year in good standing
70% enter 4-year programs

2-year private junior college, coed. Founded in 1865. **Accreditation:** Regional. **Undergraduate enrollment:** 568 men, 434 women full time; 484 men, 864 women part time. **Faculty:** 126 total (49 full time), 5 with doctorates or other terminal degrees. **Location:** Suburban campus in large town; 25 miles from Boston. **Calendar:** Semester, limited summer session. Saturday and extensive evening/early morning classes. **Microcomputers:** 170 located in libraries, classrooms, computer centers. **Special facilities:** Writing center, telecommunication center.

DEGREES OFFERED. AA, AS. 496 associate degrees awarded in 1992. 24% in business and management, 8% business/office and marketing/distribution, 9% communications, 8% education, 24% multi/interdisciplinary studies, 10% parks/recreation, protective services, public affairs, 7% visual and performing arts.

UNDERGRADUATE MAJORS. Accounting, biology, business administration and management, business and management, business and office, business data programming, communications, computer and information sciences, criminal justice studies, dance, drafting, dramatic arts, early childhood education, education, elementary education, English, fashion merchandising, fine arts, hotel/motel and restaurant management, humanities, humanities and social sciences, law enforcement and corrections, legal assistant/paralegal, legal secretary, liberal/general studies, marketing and distribution, music, office supervision and management, parks and recreation management, physical education, preengineering, protective services, radio/television broadcasting, radio/television technology, retailing, science technologies, secretarial and related programs, small business management and ownership, social sciences, social work, sports management, teacher aide, tourism, transportation and travel marketing, visual and performing arts, word processing.

ACADEMIC PROGRAMS. 2-year transfer program, honors program, internships, student-designed major, study abroad. **Remedial services:** Learning center, preadmission summer program, reduced course load, remedial instruction, special counselor, tutoring, learning disabilities program. **Placement/credit:** AP, CLEP General and Subject; 30 credit hours maximum for associate degree.

ACADEMIC REQUIREMENTS. Freshmen must earn minimum GPA of 1.5 to continue in good standing. 67% of freshmen return for sophomore year. Students must declare major on application. **Graduation requirements:** 60 hours for associate. Most students required to take courses in arts/fine arts, English, humanities, mathematics, biological/physical sciences, social sciences.

FRESHMAN ADMISSIONS. Selection criteria: School achievement record, test scores if available, recommendations interview considered. **High school preparation:** 16 units required. Required and recommended units include English 4. Mathematics 2, social science 1 and science 1 recommended.

1992 FRESHMAN CLASS PROFILE. 1,066 men applied, 1,002 accepted, 599 enrolled; 888 women applied, 865 accepted, 597 enrolled. 15% had high school GPA of 3.0 or higher, 70% between 2.0 and 2.99. **Academic background:** Mid 50% of enrolled freshmen had SAT-V between 300-400, SAT-M between 300-420. 80% submitted SAT scores. **Characteristics:** 50% from in state, 85% live in college housing, 6% have minority backgrounds, 1% are foreign students. Average age is 18.

FALL-TERM APPLICATIONS. $20 fee, may be waived for applicants with need. No closing date; applicants notified on a rolling basis; must reply by May 1 or within 4 weeks if notified thereafter. Interview recommended. Deferred and early admission available. SAT or ACT recommended for placement. Score report by July 30.

STUDENT LIFE. Housing: Dormitories (men, women, coed). **Activities:** Student government, radio, student newspaper, television, yearbook, choral groups, concert band, dance, drama, jazz band, music ensembles, musical theater, Hillel, Christian Fellowship.

ATHLETICS. NJCAA. **Intercollegiate:** Baseball M, basketball M, field hockey W, football M, lacrosse M, soccer, softball W, tennis M, volleyball W. **Intramural:** Badminton, basketball, golf, ice hockey M, soccer W, softball, swimming, table tennis, tennis, volleyball.

STUDENT SERVICES. Career counseling, employment service for undergraduates, freshman orientation, health services, personal counseling, special adviser for adult students, veterans counselor, services/facilities for handicapped.

ANNUAL EXPENSES. Tuition and fees (1992-93): $9,460. **Room and board:** $5,700. **Books and supplies:** $400. **Other expenses:** $500.

FINANCIAL AID. 48% of freshmen, 48% of continuing students receive some form of aid. 93% of grants, 63% of loans, all jobs based on need. 279 enrolled freshmen were judged to have need, all were offered aid. **Aid applications:** No closing date; priority given to applications received by January 31; applicants notified on a rolling basis beginning on or about February 20; must reply within 2 weeks. **Additional information:** Tuition freeze available for commuting students.

ADDRESS/TELEPHONE. Kathleen Teehan, Dean of Admission/Financial Aid, Dean Junior College, 99 Main Street, Franklin, MA 02038-1994. (508) 528-9100 ext. 300. Fax: (508) 528-7846.

Eastern Nazarene College
Quincy, Massachusetts — CB code: 3365

Admissions: 75% of applicants accepted
Based on:
••• School record
•• Recommendations, test scores
• Activities, essay, interview, religious affiliation/commitment, special talents
Completion: 57% graduate

4-year private liberal arts college, coed, affiliated with Church of the Nazarene. Founded in 1900. **Accreditation:** Regional. **Undergraduate enrollment:** 267 men, 318 women full time; 5 men, 6 women part time. **Graduate enrollment:** 10 men, 16 women full time; 45 men, 80 women part time. **Faculty:** 110 total (82 full time), 34 with doctorates or other terminal degrees. **Location:** Suburban campus in small city; 7 miles from Boston. **Calendar:** 4-1-4, limited summer session. **Microcomputers:** 30 located in libraries, computer centers. **Special facilities:** College-operated preschool. **Additional facts:** Degree-completion program in business offered to professional with equivalent of 2 years college work and professional experience.

DEGREES OFFERED. AA, AS, BA, BS, MA, MEd. 13 associate degrees awarded in 1992. 158 bachelor's degrees awarded. Graduate degrees offered in 14 major fields of study.

UNDERGRADUATE MAJORS. Associate: Bible studies, early childhood education, liberal/general studies, religion. **Bachelor's:** Aerospace/aeronautical/astronautical engineering, bioengineering and biomedical engineering, biological and physical sciences, biology, business administration and management, chemistry, communications, computer and information sciences, computer engineering, early childhood education, education, electrical/electronics/communications engineering, elementary education, engineering physics, English, English education, foreign languages (multiple emphasis), foreign languages education, French, history, information sciences and systems, mathematics, mathematics education, mechanical engineering, music, music education, music performance, physical education, physics, predentistry, prelaw, premedicine, prepharmacy, preveterinary, psychology, religion, religious education, science education, secondary education, social sciences, social studies education, social work, sociology, Spanish, systems engineering, theological studies.

ACADEMIC PROGRAMS. Double major, dual enrollment of high school students, independent study, internships, teacher preparation, Washington semester; liberal arts/career combination in engineering. **Remedial services:** Learning center, reduced course load, remedial instruction, special counselor, tutoring. **Placement/credit:** AP, CLEP General and Subject, institutional tests.

ACADEMIC REQUIREMENTS. Freshmen must earn minimum GPA of 1.7 to continue in good standing. 66% of freshmen return for sophomore year. Students must declare major by end of second year. **Graduation requirements:** 66 hours for associate, 130 hours for bachelor's (32 in major). Most students required to take courses in arts/fine arts, English, foreign languages, history, humanities, mathematics, philosophy/religion, biological/physical sciences, social sciences.

FRESHMAN ADMISSIONS. Selection criteria: School achievement record, test scores, character references, pastor's recommendation important. Recommended units include English 4, foreign language 2, mathematics 2, social science 2 and science 1. 2 algebra for mathematics majors. **Test requirements:** SAT or ACT (SAT preferred); score report by July 15.

1992 FRESHMAN CLASS PROFILE. 289 men applied, 207 accepted, 70 enrolled; 328 women applied, 253 accepted, 98 enrolled. 14% were in top tenth and 30% were in top quarter of graduating class. **Academic background:** Mid 50% of enrolled freshmen had SAT-V between 370-520, SAT-M between 390-550. 87% submitted SAT scores. **Characteristics:** 36% from in state, 86% live in college housing, 11% have minority backgrounds, 4% are foreign students. Average age is 18.

FALL-TERM APPLICATIONS. $20 fee, may be waived for applicants with need. No closing date; priority given to applications received by March 15; applicants notified on a rolling basis; must reply by May 1 or within 4 weeks if notified thereafter. Audition required for music applicants. Interview recommended. Essay recommended. CRDA. Deferred and early admission available.

STUDENT LIFE. Housing: Dormitories (men, women); apartment, handicapped housing available. **Activities:** Student government, radio, student newspaper, yearbook, choral groups, concert band, drama, jazz band, music ensembles, musical theater, opera, pep band, Nursing Home Outreach, church ministry teams, Ministeral Association, Overseas Work and Witness, Boston City Outreach.

ATHLETICS. NCAA. **Intercollegiate:** Baseball M, basketball, cross-country M, soccer M, softball W, tennis, volleyball. **Intramural:** Basketball, soccer M, softball, volleyball.

STUDENT SERVICES. Aptitude testing, career counseling, employment service for undergraduates, freshman orientation, health services, on-campus day care, personal counseling, placement service for graduates, services/facilities for handicapped.

ANNUAL EXPENSES. Tuition and fees: $8,765. **Room and board:** $3,400. **Books and supplies:** $450. **Other expenses:** $700.

FINANCIAL AID. 80% of freshmen, 78% of continuing students receive some form of aid. 87% of loans, all jobs based on need. 118 enrolled freshmen were judged to have need, all were offered aid. Academic, music/drama, leadership, religious affiliation scholarships available. **Aid applications:** No closing date; priority given to applications received by March 1; applicants notified on a rolling basis beginning on or about April 15; must reply within 2 weeks.

ADDRESS/TELEPHONE. William Nichols, Director of Enrollment Management, Eastern Nazarene College, 23 East Elm Avenue, Quincy, MA 02170. (617) 773-2373. (800) 883-6288. Fax: (617) 773-6324.

Elms College
Chicopee, Massachusetts — CB code: 3283

Admissions: 91% of applicants accepted
Based on: ••• School record
•• Activities, essay, interview, recommendations, test scores
• Special talents
Completion: 95% of freshmen end year in good standing
70% graduate, 28% of these enter graduate study

4-year private liberal arts college, women only, affiliated with Roman Catholic Church. Founded in 1928. **Accreditation:** Regional. **Undergraduate enrollment:** 550 women full time; 79 men, 1,027 women part time. **Graduate enrollment:** 27 women full time; 17 men, 108 women part time. **Faculty:** 96 total (47 full time), 31 with doctorates or other terminal degrees. **Location:** Suburban campus in small city; 2 miles from Springfield. **Calendar:** Semester, limited summer session. Saturday and extensive evening/early morning classes. **Microcomputers:** 50 located in dormitories, libraries, computer centers. **Special facilities:** Borgia Art Gallery, rare book gallery, alumnae library (including government documents). **Additional facts:** Only college in Massachusetts with American Bar Association approved paralegal major.

DEGREES OFFERED. AA, BA, M, MSW. 5 associate degrees awarded in 1992. 246 bachelor's degrees awarded. Graduate degrees offered in 4 major fields of study.

UNDERGRADUATE MAJORS. Associate: Legal assistant/paralegal, philosophy. **Bachelor's:** Accounting, American studies, art education, art therapy, biochemistry, biological and physical sciences, biology, business administration and management, business and management, chemistry, early childhood education, education, education of the deaf and hearing impaired, elementary education, English, English education, English literature, foreign languages (multiple emphasis), foreign languages education, French, graphic design, history, humanities, humanities and social sciences, international business management, international relations, international studies, junior high education, legal assistant/paralegal, liberal/general studies, marketing and distribution, marketing management, mathematics, mathematics education, medical laboratory technologies, nursing, predentistry, prelaw, premedicine, preveterinary, psychology, religion, science education, secondary education, social psychology, social science education, social sciences, social studies education, social work, sociology, Spanish, speech correction, speech pathology/audiology, teaching English as a second language/foreign language.

ACADEMIC PROGRAMS. Accelerated program, double major, education specialist degree, honors program, independent study, internships, student-designed major, study abroad, teacher preparation, visiting/exchange student program, weekend college, cross-registration. **Remedial services:** Learning center, preadmission summer program, reduced course load, remedial instruction, special counselor, tutoring. **ROTC:** Air Force, Army. **Placement/credit:** AP, CLEP General and Subject, institutional tests; 30 credit hours maximum for bachelor's degree.

ACADEMIC REQUIREMENTS. Freshmen must earn minimum GPA of 1.9 to continue in good standing. 80% of freshmen return for sophomore year. Students must declare major by end of second year. **Graduation requirements:** 120 hours for bachelor's (40 in major). Most students required to take courses in arts/fine arts, computer science, English, foreign languages, history, humanities, mathematics, philosophy/religion, biological/physical sciences, social sciences. **Postgraduate studies:** 2% enter law school, 1% enter medical school, 5% enter MBA programs, 20% enter other graduate study.

FRESHMAN ADMISSIONS. Selection criteria: Student should rank in the top half of high school class. Interview and alumnae relationship considered. **High school preparation:** 16 units required. Required units include biological science 1, English 4, foreign language 2, mathematics 2, physical science 1 and social science 1. Biology and chemistry required for nursing and medical technology applicants. **Test requirements:** SAT or ACT (SAT preferred); score report by April 15. Prueba de Aptitud Academica for Spanish speaking applicants.

1992 FRESHMAN CLASS PROFILE. 330 women applied, 301 accepted, 112 enrolled. 55% had high school GPA of 3.0 or higher, 42% between 2.0 and 2.99. 12% were in top tenth and 40% were in top quarter of graduating class. **Academic background:** Mid 50% of enrolled freshmen had SAT-V between 450-510, SAT-M between 450-510. 95% submitted SAT scores. **Characteristics:** 50% from in state, 70% live in college housing, 20% have minority backgrounds. Average age is 18.

FALL-TERM APPLICATIONS. $25 fee, may be waived for applicants with need. Closing date May 1; priority given to applications received by April 1; applicants notified on a rolling basis; must reply by May 1 or within 2 weeks if notified thereafter. Essay required. Interview recommended. Portfolio recommended for art applicants. CRDA. Deferred and early admission available.

STUDENT LIFE. Housing: Dormitories (women). On-campus dormitory housing guaranteed for 4 years. **Activities:** Student government, student newspaper, yearbook, choral groups, dance, drama, music ensembles, musical theater, social work club, campus ministry, Big Sister Program with disadvantaged children, foreign language club, speech pathology and audiology club, Student Ambassadors Organization, Organization of Students of Color, Affirmative Action Committee.

ATHLETICS. NCAA. **Intercollegiate:** Basketball, field hockey, horseback riding, lacrosse, soccer, softball. **Intramural:** Basketball, bowling, cross-country, field hockey, golf, horseback riding, lacrosse, racquetball, skiing, soccer, softball, swimming, volleyball, water polo.

STUDENT SERVICES. Career counseling, employment service for undergraduates, freshman orientation, health services, personal counseling, placement service for graduates, special adviser for adult students, services/facilities for handicapped.

ANNUAL EXPENSES. Tuition and fees (1992-93): $10,375. **Room and board:** $4,665. **Books and supplies:** $450. **Other expenses:** $800.

FINANCIAL AID. 80% of freshmen, 80% of continuing students receive some form of aid. 84% of grants, 92% of loans, 56% of jobs based on need. 80 enrolled freshmen were judged to have need, all were offered aid. Academic, state/district residency, religious affiliation scholarships available. **Aid applications:** No closing date; priority given to applications received by February 15; applicants notified on a rolling basis; must reply by May 1 or within 2 weeks if notified thereafter.

ADDRESS/TELEPHONE. Coleen S. Nauman, Director of Admissions, Elms College, 291 Springfield Street, Chicopee, MA 01013-2839. (413) 592-3189. (800) 255-ELMS. Fax: (413) 592-4871.

Emerson College
Boston, Massachusetts — CB code: 3367

Admissions: 72% of applicants accepted
Based on: ••• Essay, recommendations, school record
•• Activities, special talents, test scores
• Interview
Completion: 95% of freshmen end year in good standing
65% graduate

4-year private college of communication, and performing arts, coed. Founded in 1880. **Accreditation:** Regional. **Undergraduate enrollment:** 794 men, 1,130 women full time; 65 men, 98 women part time. **Graduate enrollment:** 160 men, 308 women full time; 57 men, 164 women part time. **Faculty:** 247 total (94 full time), 121 with doctorates or other terminal degrees. **Location:** Urban campus in very large city; in Back Bay section of city. **Calendar:** Semester, limited summer session. Saturday and extensive evening/

early morning classes. **Microcomputers:** 85 located in computer centers. **Special facilities:** Speech and hearing clinic, parent-centered nursery for hearing impaired children, historic proscenium-stage theater, TV studios, film production, 2 radio stations. **Additional facts:** Only four-year, private, residential institution in the United States with curriculum devoted entirely to communication and performing arts. Opportunities to study at 3 off-campus sites: Los Angeles (internships available), Kaasteel Well, The Netherlands, and Maastricht, The Netherlands.

DEGREES OFFERED. BA, BS, BFA, MA, MS, MFA, PhD. 555 bachelor's degrees awarded in 1992. 81% in communications, 8% letters/literature, 11% visual and performing arts. Graduate degrees offered in 16 major fields of study.

UNDERGRADUATE MAJORS. Advertising, business and organizational communications, children's theater, cinematography/film, communication/politics/law, communication, politics and law, communications, creative writing, dance, design/technical theatre, dramatic arts, film arts, journalism, motion picture technology, musical theater, public relations, radio/television broadcasting, radio/television technology, speech, speech correction, speech pathology/audiology, speech/communication/theater education, theater design, theatre production, video, visual and performing arts, writing and publishing.

ACADEMIC PROGRAMS. Accelerated program, double major, dual enrollment of high school students, honors program, independent study, internships, student-designed major, study abroad, teacher preparation, Washington semester, cross-registration, Los Angeles semester, 2 overseas programs in Netherlands. **Remedial services:** Learning center, special counselor, tutoring. **Placement/credit:** AP, CLEP General and Subject, IB, institutional tests; 12 credit hours maximum for bachelor's degree.

ACADEMIC REQUIREMENTS. Freshmen must earn minimum GPA of 1.7 to continue in good standing. 85% of freshmen return for sophomore year. Students must declare major by end of second year. **Graduation requirements:** 128 hours for bachelor's (40 in major). Most students required to take courses in arts/fine arts, English, history, humanities, mathematics, philosophy/religion, biological/physical sciences, social sciences. **Additional information:** Cocurricular involvement in areas of interest highly encouraged.

FRESHMAN ADMISSIONS. Selection criteria: Academic achievement emphasized. Test scores, references, personal essay and extracurricular activities also considered. Interview recommended but not required. Portfolio accepted but not required. Audition required for acting or musical theatre majors. **High school preparation:** 10 units required; 16 recommended. Required and recommended units include English 4, mathematics 2-3, social science 2-4 and science 2-3. Foreign language 2 recommended. Applicants to communication disorders major recommended to take 3 units mathematics and 3 science. **Test requirements:** SAT or ACT.

1992 FRESHMAN CLASS PROFILE. 645 men applied, 440 accepted, 168 enrolled; 1,073 women applied, 802 accepted, 337 enrolled. 50% had high school GPA of 3.0 or higher, 50% between 2.0 and 2.99. 18% were in top tenth and 49% were in top quarter of graduating class. **Academic background:** Mid 50% of enrolled freshmen had SAT-V between 460-570, SAT-M between 450-570. 94% submitted SAT scores. **Characteristics:** 33% from in state, 90% live in college housing, 11% have minority backgrounds, 3% are foreign students, 5% join fraternities/sororities. Average age is 18.

FALL-TERM APPLICATIONS. $45 fee, may be waived for applicants with need. No closing date; priority given to applications received by February 1; applicants notified on a rolling basis. Audition required for acting, musical theatre applicants. Essay required. Interview recommended. Portfolio recommended. CRDA. Deferred and early admission available. Institutional early decision plan. Early action application deadline December 1, decisions sent January 15 (non-binding).

STUDENT LIFE. Housing: Dormitories (coed). **Activities:** Student government, film, magazine, radio, student newspaper, television, yearbook, forensic society, photography, oral interpretation, choral groups, dance, drama, musical theater, opera, comedy, fraternities, sororities, EBONI, religious activities office, international club, Hillel, political awareness organization, Students Offering Service, Catholic organization.

ATHLETICS. NAIA, NCAA. **Intercollegiate:** Baseball M, basketball, golf M, ice hockey M, soccer, softball W, tennis. **Intramural:** Basketball, football M, softball.

STUDENT SERVICES. Aptitude testing, career counseling, employment service for undergraduates, freshman orientation, health services, personal counseling, placement service for graduates, special adviser for adult students, AHANA coordinator, services/facilities for handicapped.

ANNUAL EXPENSES. Tuition and fees (1992-93): $13,894. **Room and board:** $7,285. **Books and supplies:** $500. **Other expenses:** $932.

FINANCIAL AID. 80% of freshmen, 78% of continuing students receive some form of aid. 96% of grants, 97% of loans, 47% of jobs based on need. 261 enrolled freshmen were judged to have need, all were offered aid. Academic, music/drama scholarships available. **Aid applications:** No closing date; priority given to applications received by March 1; applicants notified on a rolling basis beginning on or about April 1; must reply by May 1 or within 3 weeks if notified thereafter. **Additional information:** Massachusetts Family Education Loan Program available for parents of dependent undergraduates.

ADDRESS/TELEPHONE. Jane Bode Brown, Dean of Admission, Emerson College, 100 Beacon Street, Boston, MA 02116-1596. (617) 578-8600. Fax: (617) 578-8609.

Emmanuel College
Boston, Massachusetts — CB code: 3368

Admissions:	78% of applicants accepted
Based on:	••• School record
	•• Activities, essay, interview, recommendations
	• Special talents, test scores
Completion:	87% of freshmen end year in good standing
	68% graduate

4-year private liberal arts college, women only, affiliated with Roman Catholic Church. Founded in 1919. **Accreditation:** Regional. **Undergraduate enrollment:** 43 men, 682 women full time; 74 men, 400 women part time. **Graduate enrollment:** 5 men, 29 women full time; 21 men, 137 women part time. **Faculty:** 92 total (50 full time), 40 with doctorates or other terminal degrees. **Location:** Urban campus in very large city; in downtown area. **Calendar:** Semester, extensive summer session. **Microcomputers:** 43 located in dormitories, libraries, computer centers. **Special facilities:** Academic resource center, science center, art gallery. **Additional facts:** Men may enroll in graduate and adult learner programs. Degree completion opportunites are available at corporate sites.

DEGREES OFFERED. BA, BS, BFA, MA, MS, MEd. 160 bachelor's degrees awarded in 1992. 12% in business and management, 10% communications, 10% teacher education, 6% allied health, 5% life sciences, 31% multi/interdisciplinary studies, 8% psychology, 7% visual and performing arts. Graduate degrees offered in 8 major fields of study.

UNDERGRADUATE MAJORS. Accounting, American literature, art education, art history, art therapy, biochemistry, biology, biotechnology, business administration and management, business economics, chemistry, clinical laboratory science, communications, computer and information sciences, counseling psychology, developmental psychology, economics, elementary education, engineering, engineering and other disciplines, English, English literature, experimental psychology, fine arts, foreign languages (multiple emphasis), gerontology, graphic design, health care administration, history, international relations, international studies, mathematics, nursing, philosophy, physics, political science and government, predentistry, prelaw, premedicine, psychology, rehabilitation counseling/services, religion, secondary education, sociology, Spanish, studio art, theological studies, women's studies.

ACADEMIC PROGRAMS. Accelerated program, double major, independent study, internships, study abroad, teacher preparation, visiting/exchange student program, weekend college, Washington semester, cross-registration, 3-1 program with Cambridge City Hospital in medical technology, 3-2 dual degree program in engineering with Northeastern University; nursing program with New England Baptist School of Nursing; liberal arts/career combination in engineering. **Remedial services:** Reduced course load, remedial instruction, special counselor, tutoring, Academic Resource Center. **ROTC:** Army. **Placement/credit:** AP, CLEP General and Subject, IB, institutional tests; 32 credit hours maximum for bachelor's degree.

ACADEMIC REQUIREMENTS. Freshmen must earn minimum GPA of 2.0 to continue in good standing. 87% of freshmen return for sophomore year. Students must declare major by end of second year. **Graduation requirements:** 128 hours for bachelor's (40 in major). Most students required to take courses in arts/fine arts, English, foreign languages, history, humanities, mathematics, philosophy/religion, biological/physical sciences, social sciences. **Additional information:** Interdepartmental program allows students to concentrate in 2 departments. Internship offerings available in many areas of study, and residence halls are open 12 months of year to accommodate students participating in these programs.

FRESHMAN ADMISSIONS. Selection criteria: High school curriculum and record, recommendations, test results, interview, creativity, initiative considered. **High school preparation:** 16 units required. Required units include English 4, foreign language 3, mathematics 3, social science 2 and science 2. **Test requirements:** SAT or ACT (SAT preferred).

1992 FRESHMAN CLASS PROFILE. 368 women applied, 286 accepted, 165 enrolled. 27% had high school GPA of 3.0 or higher, 59% between 2.0 and 2.99. **Characteristics:** 66% from in state, 75% live in college housing, 24% have minority backgrounds, 1% are foreign students. Average age is 18.

FALL-TERM APPLICATIONS. $30 fee, may be waived for applicants with need. No closing date; applicants notified on a rolling basis; must reply by May 1 or immediately if notified thereafter. Interview required. Essay required. CRDA. Deferred and early admission available. EDP-F.

STUDENT LIFE. Housing: Dormitories (women). Some coeducational dormitory space leased to neighboring colleges. **Activities:** Student government, magazine, student newspaper, yearbook, choral groups, drama, music ensembles, Campus Ministry, Key Club, Peace and Justice, Black Student Organization, International Student Club, Student Ambassadors Club, Environmental Awareness Club.

ATHLETICS. NCAA. **Intercollegiate:** Basketball, softball, tennis, volleyball. **Intramural:** Basketball, soccer, volleyball.

STUDENT SERVICES. Aptitude testing, career counseling, employment service for undergraduates, freshman orientation, health services, personal counseling, placement service for graduates, special adviser for adult students, Peer tutoring, services/facilities for handicapped.

ANNUAL EXPENSES. Tuition and fees: $11,973. **Room and board:** $5,800. **Books and supplies:** $500. **Other expenses:** $900.

FINANCIAL AID. 80% of freshmen, 75% of continuing students receive some form of aid. 98% of grants, all loans, all jobs based on need. Academic scholarships available. **Aid applications:** No closing date; priority given to applications received by March 1; applicants notified on a rolling basis beginning on or about February 15; must reply by May 1 or within 2 weeks if notified thereafter. **Additional information:** 010 020 050.

ADDRESS/TELEPHONE. Margaret Spillane Bonilla, Senior Director of Admissions and Marketing, Emmanuel College, 400 The Fenway, Boston, MA 02115. (617) 735-9715. Fax: (617) 735-9877.

Endicott College

Beverly, Massachusetts CB code: 3369

Admissions:	91% of applicants accepted
Based on:	••• Recommendations, school record
	•• Essay, interview, test scores
	• Activities, special talents
Completion:	84% of freshmen end year in good standing

4-year private junior, liberal arts college, women only. Founded in 1939. **Accreditation:** Regional. **Undergraduate enrollment:** 709 women full time; 46 women part time. **Faculty:** 90 total (45 full time), 18 with doctorates or other terminal degrees. **Location:** Suburban campus in large town; 24 miles from Boston. **Calendar:** 4-1-4. **Microcomputers:** 45 located in libraries, computer centers. **Special facilities:** Art center, children's center, center for creative living. **Additional facts:** In addition to the day women's college also conducts coeducational School of Continuing Education and coeducational International School of Hotel, Restaurant and Travel Administration.

DEGREES OFFERED. AA, AS, BS, BFA. 268 associate degrees awarded in 1992. 22% in architecture and environmental design, 13% business and management, 8% business/office and marketing/distribution, 9% communications, 14% education, 8% health sciences, 7% multi/interdisciplinary studies, 8% psychology. 40 bachelor's degrees awarded. 35% in architecture and environmental design, 30% business and management, 22% business/office and marketing/distribution, 6% teacher education, 5% psychology.

UNDERGRADUATE MAJORS. Associate: Accounting, advertising, allied health, apparel and accessories marketing, arts management, athletic training, biological and physical sciences, business administration and management, business and management, business and office, business computer/console/peripheral equipment operation, child development/care/guidance, clothing and textiles management/production/services, commercial art, communications, computer and information sciences, crafts, criminal justice studies, dental hygiene, early childhood education, education, elementary education, fashion design, fashion merchandising, gerontology, graphic arts technology, graphic design, health sciences, home furnishings and equipment management/production/services, hospitality and recreation marketing, hotel/motel and restaurant management, humanities, humanities and social sciences, interior design, journalism, legal assistant/paralegal, legal secretary, liberal/general studies, marketing management, medical secretary, mental health/human services, nursing, office supervision and management, photographic technology, photography, physical education, physical therapy assistant, pre-occupational therapy, psychology, public relations, radio/television broadcasting, radio/television technology, retailing, secretarial and related programs, small business management and ownership, social sciences, social work, sociology, sports management, teacher aide, textiles and clothing, tourism, transportation and travel marketing. **Bachelor's:** Advertising, early childhood education, elementary education, fashion merchandising, fine arts, graphic arts technology, graphic design, hospitality and recreation marketing, hotel/motel and restaurant management, interior design, nursing, psychology, public relations, retailing, small business management and ownership, tourism, transportation and travel marketing.

ACADEMIC PROGRAMS. 2-year transfer program, double major, dual enrollment of high school students, honors program, internships, student-designed major, study abroad, cross-registration. **Remedial services:** Learning center, preadmission summer program, reduced course load, remedial instruction, special counselor, tutoring, English for foreign students. **Placement/credit:** Institutional tests.

ACADEMIC REQUIREMENTS. Freshmen must earn minimum GPA of 1.6 to continue in good standing. 80% of freshmen return for sophomore year. Students must declare major by end of first year. **Graduation requirements:** 64 hours for associate (30 in major), 128 hours for bachelor's (80 in major). Most students required to take courses in English, mathematics, biological/physical sciences, social sciences. **Postgraduate studies:** 60% from 2-year programs enter 4-year programs.

FRESHMAN ADMISSIONS. Selection criteria: School achievement record, motivation, teacher or counselor recommendation required. SAT scores and interviews strongly recommended, but not required. Recommended units include English 4, mathematics 1, social science 1 and science 1. 1 unit chemistry with laboratory required for nursing program. Hospitality majors encouraged to have background in foreign language. 1 unit chemistry with laboratory required for physical therapy assistant program.

1992 FRESHMAN CLASS PROFILE. 898 women applied, 814 accepted, 307 enrolled. 6% were in top tenth and 20% were in top quarter of graduating class. **Characteristics:** 46% from in state, 75% live in college housing, 17% have minority backgrounds, 8% are foreign students. Average age is 18.

FALL-TERM APPLICATIONS. $25 fee, may be waived for applicants with need. No closing date; applicants notified on a rolling basis; must reply by May 1 or within 2 weeks if notified thereafter. Interview recommended. Portfolio recommended for art, photography and design applicants. Essay recommended. CRDA. Deferred admission available. SAT or ACT recommended.

STUDENT LIFE. Housing: Dormitories (women); apartment housing available. **Activities:** Student government, radio, student newspaper, television, yearbook, choral groups, dance, drama, music ensembles, Student Fellowship, international club. **Additional information:** Development of leadership in all areas of college life stressed.

ATHLETICS. NCAA. **Intercollegiate:** Basketball, cross-country, field hockey, soccer, softball, tennis, volleyball. **Intramural:** Basketball, horseback riding, lacrosse, sailing, skiing, soccer, softball, swimming, tennis, volleyball.

STUDENT SERVICES. Aptitude testing, career counseling, employment service for undergraduates, freshman orientation, health services, on-campus day care, personal counseling, placement service for graduates, transfer counseling, services/facilities for handicapped.

ANNUAL EXPENSES. Tuition and fees: $11,110. **Room and board:** $5,890. **Books and supplies:** $400. **Other expenses:** $1,000.

FINANCIAL AID. 57% of freshmen, 63% of continuing students receive some form of aid. 99% of grants, 85% of loans, 98% of jobs based on need. 283 enrolled freshmen were judged to have need, all were offered aid. **Aid applications:** No closing date; priority given to applications received by March 15; applicants notified on a rolling basis beginning on or about March 1; must reply by May 1 or within 2 weeks if notified thereafter.

ADDRESS/TELEPHONE. Thomas J. Redman, Vice President for Admissions and Financial Aid, Endicott College, 376 Hale Street, Beverly, MA 01915-9985. (508) 921-1000. (800) 325-1114. Fax: (508) 927-0084.

Essex Agricultural and Technical Institute

Hathorne, Massachusetts CB code: 3375

2-year public agricultural and technical college, coed. **Accreditation:** Regional. **Undergraduate enrollment:** 131 men, 224 women full time; 109 men, 86 women part time. **Faculty:** 39 total, 1 with doctorate or other terminal degree. **Location:** Suburban campus in rural community; 18 miles from Boston. **Calendar:** Semester. **Microcomputers:** 30 located in libraries, classrooms, computer centers.

DEGREES OFFERED. AAS. 130 associate degrees awarded in 1992.

UNDERGRADUATE MAJORS. Animal technology, fashion merchandising, food production/management/services, food sciences, forestry and related sciences, horticultural science, horticulture.

ACADEMIC PROGRAMS. Remedial services: Learning center, reduced course load, remedial instruction.

ACADEMIC REQUIREMENTS. Freshmen must earn minimum GPA of 1.7 to continue in good standing. 65% of freshmen return for sophomore year. Students must declare major on application. **Graduation requirements:** 62 hours for associate (35 in major). Most students required to take courses in computer science, English, mathematics, biological/physical sciences, social sciences.

FRESHMAN ADMISSIONS. Selection criteria: Open admissions. Preentrance examination required for LPN and cosmetology programs. Interview is key component of admissions process for other programs. **Additional information:** $30 acceptance fee payable within 15 days of acceptance letter receipt.

1992 FRESHMAN CLASS PROFILE. 151 men, 217 women enrolled. **Characteristics:** 100% from in state, 100% commute, 2% have minority backgrounds, 1% are foreign students. Average age is 25.

FALL-TERM APPLICATIONS. No fee. No closing date; applicants notified on a rolling basis; must reply within 2 weeks. Interview required.

STUDENT LIFE. Activities: Student government, yearbook.

STUDENT SERVICES. Career counseling, freshman orientation, health services, personal counseling, placement service for graduates, veterans counselor, services/facilities for handicapped.

ANNUAL EXPENSES. Tuition and fees: $1,785, $3,700 additional for out-of-district students. **Books and supplies:** $500.

FINANCIAL AID. 25% of freshmen, 15% of continuing students receive some form of aid. All grants, 89% of loans, all jobs based on need. 90 enrolled freshmen were judged to have need, 75 were offered aid. **Aid applications:** No closing date; priority given to applications received by May 1;

applicants notified on a rolling basis beginning on or about June 15; must reply within 15 days.

ADDRESS/TELEPHONE. G. Don Glazier, Jr, Director of Admissions, Essex Agricultural and Technical Institute, 562 Maple Street, Hathorne, MA 01937. (508) 774-0050.

Fisher College
Boston, Massachusetts — CB code: 3391

Admissions: 87% of applicants accepted
Based on:
••• Recommendations
•• Essay, interview, school record, special talents
• Activities, test scores
Completion: 80% of freshmen end year in good standing
50% enter 4-year programs

2-year private junior college, women only. Founded in 1903. **Accreditation:** Regional. **Undergraduate enrollment:** 371 women full time; 3 women part time. **Faculty:** 36 total (14 full time), 3 with doctorates or other terminal degrees. **Location:** Urban campus in very large city; in downtown area. **Calendar:** Semester, limited summer session. **Microcomputers:** 60 located in dormitories, classrooms, computer centers.

DEGREES OFFERED. AA, AS. 109 associate degrees awarded in 1992.

UNDERGRADUATE MAJORS. Accounting, business administration and management, child development/care/guidance, criminology, early childhood education, hotel/motel and restaurant management, information sciences and systems, international business management, journalism, legal assistant/paralegal, legal secretary, liberal/general studies, medical assistant, office supervision and management, secretarial and related programs, tourism, transportation and travel marketing.

ACADEMIC PROGRAMS. 2-year transfer program, internships. **Remedial services:** Learning center, reduced course load, remedial instruction, tutoring. **Placement/credit:** AP, CLEP General and Subject, institutional tests; 30 credit hours maximum for associate degree.

ACADEMIC REQUIREMENTS. Freshmen must earn minimum GPA of 1.7 to continue in good standing. 65% of freshmen return for sophomore year. Students must declare major on enrollment. **Graduation requirements:** 60 hours for associate (36 in major). Most students required to take courses in computer science, English, humanities, mathematics, social sciences. **Additional information:** All associate in science degree programs have computer literacy component. Free lifetime job placement service for graduates.

FRESHMAN ADMISSIONS. Selection criteria: High school GPA and counselor recommendation, interviews considered.

1992 FRESHMAN CLASS PROFILE. 788 women applied, 687 accepted, 249 enrolled. **Characteristics:** 75% from in state, 57% live in college housing, 14% are foreign students. Average age is 18.

FALL-TERM APPLICATIONS. $25 fee, may be waived for applicants with need. No closing date; priority given to applications received by August 1; applicants notified on a rolling basis; must reply within 4 weeks. Interview recommended. Essay recommended. Deferred admission available.

STUDENT LIFE. Housing: Dormitories (women). Single, double, triple, and quadruple dormitory rooms available. **Activities:** Student government, magazine, yearbook, choral groups, dance, drama.

STUDENT SERVICES. Career counseling, employment service for undergraduates, freshman orientation, health services, personal counseling, placement service for graduates, special adviser for adult students.

ANNUAL EXPENSES. Tuition and fees: $10,300. **Room and board:** $6,000. **Books and supplies:** $600. **Other expenses:** $900.

FINANCIAL AID. 76% of freshmen, 70% of continuing students receive some form of aid. 98% of grants, all loans, all jobs based on need. **Aid applications:** No closing date; priority given to applications received by March 1; applicants notified on a rolling basis beginning on or about March 1; must reply within 2 weeks.

ADDRESS/TELEPHONE. Sandra M. Robbins, Director of Admissions, Fisher College, 118 Beacon Street, Boston, MA 02116. (617) 236-8800. (800) 446-1226. Fax: (617) 236-8858.

Fitchburg State College
Fitchburg, Massachusetts — CB code: 3518

Admissions: 66% of applicants accepted
Based on:
••• School record
•• Recommendations, special talents, test scores
• Activities, essay, interview
Completion: 74% of freshmen end year in good standing
49% graduate, 10% of these enter graduate study

4-year public college of arts and sciences, coed. Founded in 1894. **Accreditation:** Regional. **Undergraduate enrollment:** 1,350 men, 1,852 women full time; 588 men, 663 women part time. **Graduate enrollment:** 17 men, 26 women full time; 223 men, 598 women part time. **Faculty:** 389 total (239 full time), 150 with doctorates or other terminal degrees. **Location:** Urban campus in large town; 55 miles from Boston. **Calendar:** Semester, limited summer session. **Microcomputers:** 450 located in dormitories, libraries, computer centers. **Special facilities:** Complete manuscript collection of writer Robert Cormier.

DEGREES OFFERED. BA, BS, MA, MS, MEd. 848 bachelor's degrees awarded in 1992. 20% in business and management, 12% communications, 24% teacher education, 8% engineering technologies, 8% health sciences, 10% social sciences. Graduate degrees offered in 8 major fields of study.

UNDERGRADUATE MAJORS. Accounting, biology, business administration and management, business and management, chemistry, clinical laboratory science, communications, computer and information sciences, construction, early childhood education, economics, educational media technology, electronic technology, elementary education, English education, English literature, environmental science, exercise and sport science, geography, graphic and printing production, graphic arts technology, history, industrial arts education, management information systems, manufacturing technology, marketing management, mathematics, mathematics education, motion picture technology, nursing, photographic technology, psychology, radio/television technology, science education, secondary education, social science education, social work, sociology, special education, technical and business writing, trade and industrial education.

ACADEMIC PROGRAMS. Accelerated program, double major, honors program, independent study, internships, student-designed major, teacher preparation, telecourses. **Remedial services:** Learning center, reduced course load, remedial instruction, tutoring, Access. **ROTC:** Army. **Placement/credit:** AP, CLEP General and Subject, institutional tests; 60 credit hours maximum for bachelor's degree.

ACADEMIC REQUIREMENTS. Freshmen must earn minimum GPA of 1.6 to continue in good standing. 70% of freshmen return for sophomore year. Students must declare major on application. **Graduation requirements:** 120 hours for bachelor's (30 in major). Most students required to take courses in arts/fine arts, computer science, English, history, humanities, mathematics, biological/physical sciences, social sciences. **Postgraduate studies:** 1% enter law school, 1% enter medical school, 1% enter MBA programs, 7% enter other graduate study.

FRESHMAN ADMISSIONS. Selection criteria: School achievement record, SAT scores, proposed major, class rank considered. **High school preparation:** 16 units required. Required units include English 4, foreign language 2, mathematics 3, social science 2 and science 2. Additional units of mathematics, science required for nursing, medical technology, and computer science applicants. **Test requirements:** SAT or ACT (SAT preferred); score report by March 1.

1992 FRESHMAN CLASS PROFILE. 1,383 men applied, 850 accepted, 255 enrolled; 1,897 women applied, 1,325 accepted, 309 enrolled. 18% were in top tenth and 25% were in top quarter of graduating class. **Academic background:** Mid 50% of enrolled freshmen had SAT-V between 370-460, SAT-M between 370-500. 98% submitted SAT scores. **Characteristics:** 97% from in state, 48% live in college housing, 10% have minority backgrounds, 1% are foreign students, 10% join fraternities/sororities. Average age is 19.

FALL-TERM APPLICATIONS. $10 fee, may be waived for applicants with need. $40 fee for out-of-state applicants. Closing date March 1; priority given to applications received by January 15; applicants notified on a rolling basis beginning on or about January 2; must reply by May 1. Interview recommended for nursing, undeclared major, computer science, business administration, communications/media applicants. CRDA. Deferred and early admission available.

STUDENT LIFE. Housing: Dormitories (women, coed); apartment housing available. **Activities:** Student government, film, magazine, radio, student newspaper, yearbook, choral groups, concert band, drama, jazz band, fraternities, sororities, Christian Fellowship, Newman Club, Voluntary Action Center, Amnesty International, Hispanic Student Union, Cultural Society.

ATHLETICS. NCAA. **Intercollegiate:** Baseball M, basketball, cross-country, field hockey W, football M, ice hockey M, soccer M, softball W, track and field, volleyball W. **Intramural:** Badminton, baseball M, basketball, bowling, cross-country, ice hockey M, soccer, softball, table tennis, tennis, track and field, volleyball.

STUDENT SERVICES. Career counseling, employment service for undergraduates, freshman orientation, health services, on-campus day care, personal counseling, placement service for graduates, veterans counselor, services/facilities for handicapped.

ANNUAL EXPENSES. Tuition and fees (1992-93): $3,206, $3,864 additional for out-of-state students. **Room and board:** $3,232. **Books and supplies:** $450. **Other expenses:** $1,538.

FINANCIAL AID. 53% of freshmen, 41% of continuing students receive some form of aid. Grants, loans, jobs available. 139 enrolled freshmen were judged to have need, all were offered aid. Academic, music/drama, art, alumni affiliation scholarships available. **Aid applications:** Closing date July 1; priority given to applications received by March 30; applicants notified on a rolling basis beginning on or about April 15; must reply by May 1 or within 2 weeks if notified thereafter.

ADDRESS/TELEPHONE. Marke M. Vickers, Director of Admissions, Fitchburg State College, 160 Pearl Street, Fitchburg, MA 01420. (508) 345-2151. Fax: (508)343 8603.

Forsyth School for Dental Hygienists
Boston, Massachusetts CB code: 3392

4-year private health science college, coed. Founded in 1916. **Undergraduate enrollment:** 2 men, 104 women full time. **Faculty:** 18 total (8 full time). **Location:** Urban campus in very large city. **Calendar:** Quarter. **Microcomputers:** Located in libraries, computer centers. **Additional facts:** Associate and bachelor's degrees in dental hygiene granted by Northeastern University. Accredited by the American Dental Association: Dental Hygiene, Commission on Dental Education.

DEGREES OFFERED. AS, BS. 44 associate degrees awarded in 1992. 100% in allied health. 2 bachelor's degrees awarded.

UNDERGRADUATE MAJORS. Associate: Dental hygiene. **Bachelor's:** Dental hygiene.

ACADEMIC PROGRAMS. Internships, cross-registration; liberal arts/career combination in health sciences. **Placement/credit:** CLEP General and Subject.

ACADEMIC REQUIREMENTS. 88% of freshmen return for sophomore year. Students must declare major on application. **Graduation requirements:** 100 hours for associate, 180 hours for bachelor's. Most students required to take courses in arts/fine arts, computer science, English, humanities, mathematics, biological/physical sciences, social sciences. **Postgraduate studies:** 18% from 2-year programs enter 4-year programs.

FRESHMAN ADMISSIONS. Selection criteria: School achievement record and test scores most important. **High school preparation:** 10 units required. Required units include biological science 2, English 4, foreign language 2 and mathematics 2. 2 biological sciences must include 1 biology with laboratory and 1 chemistry with laboratory. **Test requirements:** SAT; score report by August 31.

1992 FRESHMAN CLASS PROFILE. 42 women enrolled. **Characteristics:** 85% commute, 1% have minority backgrounds, 4% are foreign students. Average age is 19.

FALL-TERM APPLICATIONS. $35 fee, may be waived for applicants with need. No closing date; applicants notified on a rolling basis; must reply by May 1 or within 3 weeks if notified thereafter. CRDA. Deferred admission available.

STUDENT LIFE. Housing: Dormitories (men, women, coed); apartment housing available. **Activities:** Student government, yearbook.

ANNUAL EXPENSES. Tuition and fees (1992-93): $11,616. **Room and board:** $6,815. **Books and supplies:** $400. **Other expenses:** $450.

FINANCIAL AID. 22% of freshmen, 78% of continuing students receive some form of aid. 94% of grants, 87% of loans based on need. 28 enrolled freshmen were judged to have need, all were offered aid. Academic scholarships available. **Aid applications:** No closing date; priority given to applications received by March 1; applicants notified on a rolling basis beginning on or about May 5; must reply within 15 days.

ADDRESS/TELEPHONE. Judith S. Harvey, Director of Admissions, Forsyth School for Dental Hygienists, 140 The Fenway, Boston, MA 02115. (617) 262-5200 ext. 212. Fax: (617) 262-4021.

Framingham State College
Framingham, Massachusetts CB code: 3519

Admissions:	73% of applicants accepted
Based on:	••• School record
	•• Test scores
	• Activities, essay, recommendations, special talents
Completion:	75% of freshmen end year in good standing
	60% graduate, 20% of these enter graduate study

4-year public liberal arts college, coed. Founded in 1839. **Accreditation:** Regional. **Undergraduate enrollment:** 1,095 men, 2,034 women full time; 693 men, 847 women part time. **Graduate enrollment:** 5 men, 20 women full time; 153 men, 299 women part time. **Faculty:** 219 total (170 full time), 133 with doctorates or other terminal degrees. **Location:** Suburban campus in small city; 20 miles from Boston, 20 miles from Worcester. **Calendar:** Semester, limited summer session. Saturday and extensive evening/early morning classes. **Microcomputers:** 150 located in computer centers. **Special facilities:** Art gallery, media center, planetarium, New England Philharmonic (orchestra in residence), Danforth Art Museum, greenhouse.

DEGREES OFFERED. BA, BS, MA, MS, MEd. 609 bachelor's degrees awarded in 1992. 15% in business and management, 5% communications, 13% teacher education, 12% home economics, 8% letters/literature, 13% psychology, 18% social sciences. Graduate degrees offered in 15 major fields of study.

UNDERGRADUATE MAJORS. Art education, art history, biology, business administration and management, business and management, chemistry, communications, computer and information sciences, early childhood education, earth sciences, economics, elementary education, English, English education, family/consumer resource management, food science and nutrition, food sciences, foreign languages education, French, geography, history, home economics, home economics education, liberal/general studies, mathematics, mathematics education, medical laboratory technologies, nursing, philosophy, political science and government, predentistry, preengineering, prelaw, premedicine, preveterinary, psychology, science education, secondary education, social studies education, sociology, Spanish, studio art, textiles and clothing.

ACADEMIC PROGRAMS. Double major, honors program, independent study, internships, student-designed major, study abroad, teacher preparation, visiting/exchange student program, Washington semester, preengineering in conjunction with: University of Massachusetts at Amherst, University of Massachusetts at Dartmouth, University of Massachusetts at Lowell. **Remedial services:** Learning center, reduced course load, tutoring, disadvantaged student progam. **Placement/credit:** AP, CLEP General and Subject, institutional tests; 64 credit hours maximum for bachelor's degree.

ACADEMIC REQUIREMENTS. Freshmen must earn minimum GPA of 1.8 to continue in good standing. 71% of freshmen return for sophomore year. Students must declare major by end of second year. **Graduation requirements:** 128 hours for bachelor's (48 in major). Most students required to take courses in English, humanities, mathematics, biological/physical sciences, social sciences. **Postgraduate studies:** 1% enter law school, 1% enter MBA programs, 18% enter other graduate study. **Additional information:** Liberal studies degree program for returning adult learners with significant work and career experience offered through Division of Graduate and Continuing Education.

FRESHMAN ADMISSIONS. Selection criteria: Strength of high school curriculum, class rank, and test scores most important. Some attention given to organized and volunteer activities, recommendations, and special talents. **High school preparation:** 16 units required. Required units include English 4, foreign language 2, mathematics 3, social science 2 and science 2. Sciences must include laboratory science. Mathematics must include algebra I and II, and geometry. Additional unit of mathematics strongly recommended for computer science, mathematics, preengineering, science majors. Additional units of biology, chemistry, physics, recommended for science majors. Foreign language must be 2 units of same language. **Test requirements:** SAT; score report by March 15. **Additional information:** Admissions standards policy of Massachusetts Higher Education Coordinating Council requires students to take minimum of 16 college preparatory courses in designated areas and to meet certain minimum standards on admissions eligibility index based on SAT scores and weighted class rank. These are minimum standards and do not guarantee admission.

1992 FRESHMAN CLASS PROFILE. 1,116 men applied, 730 accepted, 195 enrolled; 1,848 women applied, 1,436 accepted, 387 enrolled. 6% were in top tenth and 30% were in top quarter of graduating class. **Academic background:** Mid 50% of enrolled freshmen had SAT-V between 380-480, SAT-M between 380-500. 100% submitted SAT scores. **Characteristics:** 93% from in state, 70% live in college housing, 8% have minority backgrounds, 1% are foreign students. Average age is 18.

FALL-TERM APPLICATIONS. $10 fee, may be waived for applicants with need. $40 fee for out-of-state and foreign applicants. Closing date June 15; priority given to applications received by March 15; applicants notified on a rolling basis beginning on or about February 1; must reply by May 1 or within 2 weeks if notified thereafter. Portfolio required for studio art applicants. CRDA. Deferred and early admission available. Late applications may be considered. Some majors and on-campus housing may be filled by priority filing date of March 15.

STUDENT LIFE. Housing: Dormitories (women, coed); handicapped housing available. **Activities:** Student government, magazine, radio, student newspaper, yearbook, literary magazine, choral groups, drama, music ensembles, Culture in Effect (multicultural student organization), International Students' Club, Christian Fellowship, Hillel.

ATHLETICS. NCAA. **Intercollegiate:** Baseball M, basketball, cross-country, field hockey W, football M, horseback riding, ice hockey M, soccer, softball W, volleyball W. **Intramural:** Basketball, golf, racquetball, softball, volleyball.

STUDENT SERVICES. Aptitude testing, career counseling, employment service for undergraduates, freshman orientation, health services, on-campus day care, personal counseling, placement service for graduates, special adviser for adult students, veterans counselor, services/facilities for handicapped.

ANNUAL EXPENSES. Tuition and fees (1992-93): $3,017, $3,864 additional for out-of-state students. **Room and board:** $3,466. **Books and supplies:** $475. **Other expenses:** $1,200.

FINANCIAL AID. 50% of freshmen, 45% of continuing students receive some form of aid. All grants, 94% of loans, 24% of jobs based on need. 136 enrolled freshmen were judged to have need, all were offered aid. Academic, leadership scholarships available. **Aid applications:** No closing date; priority given to applications received by March 1; applicants notified on a rolling basis beginning on or about April 1; must reply by May 1 or within 3 weeks if notified thereafter.

ADDRESS/TELEPHONE. Dr. Philip M. Dooher, Dean of Admissions Services, Framingham State College, 100 State Street, Framingham, MA 01701. (508) 626-4500. Fax: (508) 626-4592.

Franklin Institute of Boston
Boston, Massachusetts CB code: 3394

2-year private engineering, technical college, coed. Founded in 1908. **Accreditation:** Regional. **Undergraduate enrollment:** 303 men, 14 women full time; 1 woman part time. **Faculty:** 39 total (34 full time). **Location:** Urban campus in very large city. **Calendar:** Semester, limited summer session. **Microcomputers:** 70 located in libraries, classrooms, computer centers. **Additional facts:** Founded under provisions of will of Benjamin Franklin and managed by Franklin Foundation.

DEGREES OFFERED. AS. 97 associate degrees awarded in 1992. 45% in engineering technologies, 55% trade and industry.

UNDERGRADUATE MAJORS. Architectural engineering, architectural technologies, automotive mechanics, automotive technology, biomedical equipment technology, civil engineering, civil technology, computer and information sciences, computer engineering, computer programming, computer servicing technology, computer technology, drafting, drafting and design technology, electrical technology, electrical/electronics/communications engineering, electromechanical technology, electronic technology, engineering and engineering-related technologies, industrial technology, manufacturing technology, mechanical design technology, mechanical engineering, medical electronic engineering.

ACADEMIC PROGRAMS. Remedial services: Preadmission summer program, reduced course load, 5 semester and 6 semester preparatory programs for engineering technology. **Placement/credit:** AP, CLEP Subject.

ACADEMIC REQUIREMENTS. Freshmen must earn minimum GPA of 1.7 to continue in good standing. 75% of freshmen return for sophomore year. Students must declare major on application. **Graduation requirements:** 80 hours for associate. Most students required to take courses in English, mathematics, biological/physical sciences, social sciences.

FRESHMAN ADMISSIONS. Selection criteria: School achievement record, particularly in mathematics and science, considered. **High school preparation:** 16 units required. Required units include English 4, mathematics 2 and physical science 1. Level of mathematics and science required varies by program.

1992 FRESHMAN CLASS PROFILE. 174 men and women enrolled. **Characteristics:** 90% commute, 1% are foreign students. Average age is 19.

FALL-TERM APPLICATIONS. $20 fee, may be waived for applicants with need. No closing date; applicants notified on a rolling basis; must reply by May 1 or within 2 weeks if notified thereafter. Interview required for academically weak applicants. Essay recommended. CRDA. Deferred admission available. SAT recommended for admissions.

STUDENT LIFE. Housing: Dormitories (coed). Student housing at Boston University. **Activities:** Student government, yearbook.

STUDENT SERVICES. Career counseling, employment service for undergraduates, freshman orientation, personal counseling, placement service for graduates, veterans counselor.

ANNUAL EXPENSES. Tuition and fees: $8,231. **Room and board:** $7,300. **Books and supplies:** $600. **Other expenses:** $1,390.

FINANCIAL AID. 90% of freshmen, 85% of continuing students receive some form of aid. 68% of grants, 81% of loans, all jobs based on need. 126 enrolled freshmen were judged to have need, all were offered aid. State/district residency, alumni affiliation scholarships available. **Aid applications:** No closing date; priority given to applications received by April 1; applicants notified on a rolling basis beginning on or about April 19; must reply by May 1 or within 2 weeks if notified thereafter.

ADDRESS/TELEPHONE. Brian Kenny, Director of Admissions, Franklin Institute of Boston, 41 Berkeley Street, Boston, MA 02116. (617) 423-4630.

Gordon College
Wenham, Massachusetts CB code: 3417

Admissions:	88% of applicants accepted
Based on:	••• Activities, essay, interview, recommendations, religious affiliation/commitment, school record
	•• Test scores
	• Special talents
Completion:	60% graduate

4-year private liberal arts college, coed, Interdenominational (Christian). Founded in 1889. **Accreditation:** Regional. **Undergraduate enrollment:** 437 men, 713 women full time; 19 men, 22 women part time. **Faculty:** 97 total (71 full time), 55 with doctorates or other terminal degrees. **Location:** Suburban campus in small town; 20 miles from Boston. **Calendar:** Semester. **Microcomputers:** 95 located in libraries, computer centers. **Special facilities:** Multidisciplinary Jenks Learning Resource Center.

DEGREES OFFERED. BA, BS. 276 bachelor's degrees awarded in 1992.

UNDERGRADUATE MAJORS. Accounting, Bible studies, biology, business administration and management, chemistry, computer and information sciences, early childhood education, economics, education, elementary education, English, foreign languages (multiple emphasis), French, history, international relations, junior high education, leisure recreation, mathematics, movement science, music, music education, music performance, philosophy, physics, political science and government, prelaw, psychology, social work, sociology, Spanish, special education, theological studies.

ACADEMIC PROGRAMS. Accelerated program, cooperative education, double major, honors program, independent study, internships, study abroad, teacher preparation, visiting/exchange student program, Washington semester, cross-registration; liberal arts/career combination in engineering, health sciences. **Remedial services:** Learning center, reduced course load, remedial instruction, tutoring. **ROTC:** Air Force. **Placement/credit:** AP, CLEP General and Subject, institutional tests; 20 credit hours maximum for bachelor's degree.

ACADEMIC REQUIREMENTS. Freshmen must earn minimum GPA of 2.0 to continue in good standing. 90% of freshmen return for sophomore year. Students must declare major by end of first year. **Graduation requirements:** 128 hours for bachelor's (44 in major). Most students required to take courses in arts/fine arts, computer science, English, foreign languages, history, humanities, mathematics, philosophy/religion, biological/physical sciences, social sciences.

FRESHMAN ADMISSIONS. Selection criteria: High school grades, rank in class, essay of Christian commitment, SAT scores, references, interview, school and community activities considered. **High school preparation:** 14 units required. Required units include English 4, foreign language 2, mathematics 2, social science 2 and science 2. **Test requirements:** SAT or ACT (SAT preferred); score report by July 1.

1992 FRESHMAN CLASS PROFILE. 204 men applied, 167 accepted, 100 enrolled; 389 women applied, 352 accepted, 194 enrolled. **Academic background:** Mid 50% of enrolled freshmen had SAT-V between 430-540, SAT-M between 450-580. 85% submitted SAT scores. **Characteristics:** 24% from in state, 97% live in college housing, 17% have minority backgrounds, 6% are foreign students. Average age is 18.

FALL-TERM APPLICATIONS. $40 fee, may be waived for applicants with need. Closing date April 1; priority given to applications received by February 1; applicants notified on a rolling basis; must reply by May 1. Interview required. Audition required for music applicants. Essay required. CRDA. Deferred and early admission available. EDP-F.

STUDENT LIFE. Housing: Dormitories (men, women); apartment housing available. **Activities:** Student government, magazine, student newspaper, yearbook, choral groups, concert band, drama, jazz band, music ensembles, musical theater, pep band, symphony orchestra, Hunger Awareness Committee, student missions, student emergency, religious, political, tutoring organizations, student ministries (15 different groups/activities), Society for a New Politics, Young Republicans. **Additional information:** Religious observance required.

ATHLETICS. NCAA. **Intercollegiate:** Baseball M, basketball, cross-country, field hockey W, soccer, softball W, tennis, volleyball W. **Intramural:** Basketball M, ice hockey M, softball W, volleyball W.

STUDENT SERVICES. Career counseling, employment service for undergraduates, freshman orientation, health services, personal counseling, placement service for graduates, minority students counselor, services/facilities for handicapped.

ANNUAL EXPENSES. Tuition and fees (1992-93): $12,090. **Room and board:** $3,750. **Books and supplies:** $400. **Other expenses:** $400.

FINANCIAL AID. 86% of freshmen, 90% of continuing students receive some form of aid. 74% of grants, 98% of loans, 56% of jobs based on need. Academic, music/drama, leadership scholarships available. **Aid applications:** Closing date June 15; priority given to applications received by March 15; applicants notified on or about April 1; must reply by May 1.

ADDRESS/TELEPHONE. Mark R. Sylvester, Dean of Admissions and Financial Aid, Gordon College, 255 Grapevine Road, Wenham, MA 01984-1899. (508) 927-2300. (800) 343-1379. Fax: (508) 921-1398.

Greenfield Community College
Greenfield, Massachusetts CB code: 3420

2-year public community college, coed. Founded in 1962. **Accreditation:** Regional. **Undergraduate enrollment:** 522 men, 680 women full time; 448 men, 965 women part time. **Faculty:** 207 total (66 full time), 18 with doctorates or other terminal degrees. **Location:** Rural campus in large town; 40 miles from Springfield. **Calendar:** Semester, extensive summer session. **Microcomputers:** 125 located in libraries, classrooms, computer centers. **Special facilities:** Archibald MacLeish Collection, Pioneer Valley Resource Center, Yankee-Rowe Local Public Document Collection. **Additional facts:** Students may enroll in credit courses taught at Smith Vocational High School, Northampton.

DEGREES OFFERED. AA, AS. 327 associate degrees awarded in 1992. 13% in business and management, 18% business/office and marketing/distribution, 5% engineering technologies, 14% health sciences, 28% multi/interdisciplinary studies, 9% parks/recreation, protective services, public affairs, 6% visual and performing arts.

UNDERGRADUATE MAJORS. Accounting, American studies, business administration and management, business and management, communications, computer and information sciences, computer programming, criminal justice studies, early childhood education, education, engineering science, fine arts, fire control and safety technology, food sciences, graphic design, humanities, humanities and social sciences, industrial technology, liberal/general studies, marketing and distribution, mental health/human services, nursing, photography, production management technology, recreation and community services technologies, renewable natural resources, secretarial and related programs, social sciences.

ACADEMIC PROGRAMS. 2-year transfer program, dual enrollment of high school students, honors program, independent study, internships. **Remedial services:** Learning center, reduced course load, remedial instruction, special counselor, tutoring. **Placement/credit:** AP, CLEP General and Subject, institutional tests; 15 credit hours maximum for associate degree.

ACADEMIC REQUIREMENTS. Freshmen must earn minimum GPA of 2.0 to continue in good standing. Students must declare major on application. **Graduation requirements:** 60 hours for associate. Most students required to take courses in English, history, humanities, mathematics, biological/physical sciences, social sciences.

FRESHMAN ADMISSIONS. Selection criteria: Open admissions. Selective admissions to registered nursing program based on class rank in top third. Selective admission to practical nursing program based on examination. College-preparatory chemistry required of registered nursing applicants. High school diploma required for all nursing applicants.

1992 FRESHMAN CLASS PROFILE. 235 men, 297 women enrolled. **Characteristics:** 93% from in state, 100% commute, 7% have minority backgrounds, 1% are foreign students. Average age is 24.

FALL-TERM APPLICATIONS. $10 fee, may be waived for applicants with need. $35 fee for out-of-state applicants. No closing date; applicants notified on a rolling basis. Interview required for nursing applicants. CRDA. Early admission available. Limited space available in nursing, art, and graphic design programs. Application priority date February 1.

STUDENT LIFE. Activities: Student government, choral groups, drama, jazz band, music ensembles, musical theater.

ATHLETICS. NJCAA. **Intercollegiate:** Baseball M, soccer M, softball W, volleyball W.

STUDENT SERVICES. Career counseling, employment service for undergraduates, freshman orientation, health services, on-campus day care, personal counseling, placement service for graduates, veterans counselor, services/facilities for handicapped.

ANNUAL EXPENSES. Tuition and fees (1992-93): $2,006, $3,882 additional for out-of-state students. **Books and supplies:** $550. **Other expenses:** $1,351.

FINANCIAL AID. 76% of freshmen, 60% of continuing students receive some form of aid. All grants, 82% of loans, all jobs based on need. **Aid applications:** No closing date; priority given to applications received by April 15; applicants notified on a rolling basis beginning on or about May 15; must reply within 4 weeks.

ADDRESS/TELEPHONE. Donald W. Brown, Director Admissions/Student Records, Greenfield Community College, One College Drive, Greenfield, MA 01301. (413) 774-3131 ext. 233.

Hampshire College
Amherst, Massachusetts — CB code: 3447

Admissions: 66% of applicants accepted
Based on: ••• School record
•• Activities, essay, interview, recommendations
• Special talents
Completion: 95% of freshmen end year in good standing
60% graduate

4-year private liberal arts college, coed. Founded in 1965. **Accreditation:** Regional. **Undergraduate enrollment:** 486 men, 687 women full time. **Faculty:** 99 total (91 full time), 89 with doctorates or other terminal degrees. **Location:** Rural campus in large town; 90 miles from Boston, 20 miles from Springfield. **Calendar:** 4-1-4. **Microcomputers:** 70 located in libraries, computer centers. **Special facilities:** Bioshelter for hydroponic projects, aquaculture, and solar energy research, 3 art galleries, extensive film, videotape, and photography facilities and equipment, Hampshire College Farm Center.

DEGREES OFFERED. BA. 307 bachelor's degrees awarded in 1992. 14% in letters/literature, 7% life sciences, 13% multi/interdisciplinary studies, 5% philosophy, religion, theology, 8% psychology, 14% social sciences, 24% visual and performing arts.

UNDERGRADUATE MAJORS. African studies, Afro-American (black) studies, agricultural sciences, American Indian studies, American literature, American studies, animal sciences, anthropology, applied mathematics, archeology, architecture, art education, art history, Asian studies, astronomy, behavioral sciences, biochemistry, biological and physical sciences, biology, biomedical science, biophysics, botany, business and society, Caribbean studies, cell biology, chemistry, child development/care/guidance, cinematography/film, cognitive psychology, communications, communications research, comparative literature, computer and information sciences, computer graphics, computer mathematics, computer programming, creative writing, dance, demography, developmental psychology, dramatic arts, drawing, earth sciences, East Asian studies, Eastern European studies, ecology, economics, education, educational statistics and research, elementary education, English, English education, English literature, environmental design, environmental science, European studies, film animation, film arts, fine arts, folklore and mythology, food science and nutrition, genetics, human and animal, geography, geology, gerontology, graphic arts technology, health sciences, higher education research, Hispanic American studies, history, humanities, humanities and social sciences, individual and family development, information sciences and systems, inorganic chemistry, international and comparative education, international development, international relations, international studies, Islamic studies, jazz, Jewish studies, journalism, labor/industrial relations, Latin American studies, liberal/general studies, linguistics, marine biology, mathematics, mathematics education, medieval studies, Mexican American studies, microbiology, Middle Eastern studies, molecular biology, motion picture technology, music, music education, music history and appreciation, music performance, music theory and composition, musical theater, neurosciences, nutritional sciences, oceanography, optics, organic chemistry, Pacific area studies, painting, peace studies, personality psychology, philosophy, photographic technology, photography, physical sciences, physics, physiological psychology, physiology, human and animal, plant genetics, plant physiology, plant sciences, political science and government, population and family planning, predentistry, prelaw, premedicine, preveterinary, psychobiology, psycholinguistics, psychology, public policy studies, pure mathematics, radio/television broadcasting, radio/television technology, reading education, religion, Russian and Slavic studies, Scandinavian studies, science education, science technologies, sculpture, secondary education, social foundations, social psychology, social science education, social sciences, social work, sociology, South Asian studies, Southeast Asian studies, statistics, studio art, systems analysis, theater design, theological studies, urban studies, video, visual and performing arts, Western European studies, women's studies.

ACADEMIC PROGRAMS. Accelerated program, independent study, internships, student-designed major, study abroad, visiting/exchange student program, cross-registration. **Remedial services:** Reading and writing program.

ACADEMIC REQUIREMENTS. No policy requiring minimum GPA; records of students having academic difficulty are reviewed individually. 85% of freshmen return for sophomore year. **Graduation requirements:** Most students required to take courses in humanities, biological/physical sciences, social sciences.

FRESHMAN ADMISSIONS. Selection criteria: Criteria include desire to do rigorous independent work, school record, academic writing samples, recommendations, school and community activities. **High school preparation:** 18 units recommended. Recommended units include English 4, foreign language 2, mathematics 3, social science 4 and science 3.

1992 FRESHMAN CLASS PROFILE. 494 men applied, 306 accepted, 129 enrolled; 831 women applied, 562 accepted, 210 enrolled. 47% had high school GPA of 3.0 or higher, 53% between 2.0 and 2.99. **Characteristics:** 11% from in state, 100% live in college housing, 8% have minority backgrounds, 3% are foreign students. Average age is 18.

FALL-TERM APPLICATIONS. $40 fee, may be waived for applicants with need. Closing date February 1; applicants notified on or about April 1; must reply by May 1. Essay required. Interview recommended. CRDA. Deferred and early admission available. EDP-F.

STUDENT LIFE. Housing: Dormitories (coed); apartment, cooperative housing available. Housing for older students available. **Activities:** Student government, film, magazine, radio, student newspaper, television, academic journals, choral groups, dance, drama, jazz band, music ensembles, musical theater, symphony orchestra, Counselor Advocates Against Sexual Abuse, Asian Pacific Students, Christian Fellowship, Lesbian/Gay/Bisexual Alliance, Source (students of color organization), Responsible Ecology, Umoja (African American student group), United Islam, Students for Progressive Judaism, Raices (Latino Student Group).

ATHLETICS. Intercollegiate: Baseball M, basketball, soccer, volleyball. **Intramural:** Archery, badminton, bowling, fencing, softball, tennis.

STUDENT SERVICES. Career counseling, freshman orientation, health services, on-campus day care, personal counseling, women's center, office of multicultural affairs, services/facilities for handicapped.

ANNUAL EXPENSES. Tuition and fees: $19,490. **Room and board:** $5,160. **Books and supplies:** $375. **Other expenses:** $1,120.

FINANCIAL AID. 52% of freshmen, 51% of continuing students receive some form of aid. Grants, loans, jobs available. Academic, minority scholarships available. **Aid applications:** No closing date; priority given to applications received by February 15; applicants notified on a rolling basis beginning on or about April 2; must reply by May 1 or within 2 weeks if notified thereafter.

ADDRESS/TELEPHONE. Audrey Y. Smith, Director of Admissions, Hampshire College, Amherst, MA 01002. (413) 549-4600 ext. 471.

Harvard and Radcliffe Colleges

Cambridge, Massachusetts CB code: 3434

Admissions: 16% of applicants accepted
Based on: ••• School record
•• Activities, essay, interview, recommendations, special talents, test scores
Completion: 98% of freshmen end year in good standing
97% graduate, 62% of these enter graduate study

4-year private liberal arts college, coed. Founded in 1636. **Accreditation:** Regional. **Undergraduate enrollment:** 4,007 men, 2,792 women full time. **Faculty:** 2,167 total, 2,167 with doctorates or other terminal degrees. **Location:** Urban campus in small city; 3 miles from Boston. **Calendar:** Semester, extensive summer session. **Microcomputers:** 250 located in dormitories, classrooms, computer centers. **Special facilities:** Fogg Museum of Art, Busch-Reisinger Museum of Scandinavian and Germanic Art, Sackler Art Museum, experimental forest in New York State, Center for Study of the Italian Renaissance in Florence, Italy, Center for Byzantine Studies in Washington, DC, Smithsonian Astrophysical Observatory.

DEGREES OFFERED. BA, BS. 1,746 bachelor's degrees awarded in 1992.

UNDERGRADUATE MAJORS. African languages, African studies, Afro-American (black) studies, American literature, American studies, anthropology, applied mathematics, Arabic, archeology, art history, Asian studies, astronomy, astrophysics, biochemistry, bioengineering and biomedical engineering, biological and physical sciences, biology, business economics, chemistry, Chinese, classics, comparative literature, computer and information sciences, computer engineering, creative writing, earth sciences, East Asian studies, Eastern European studies, economics, electrical/electronics/communications engineering, engineering, engineering and other disciplines, engineering physics, engineering science, English, English literature, environmental design, environmental science, European studies, folklore and mythology, foreign languages (multiple emphasis), French, geology, geophysical engineering, geophysics and seismology, German, Greek (classical), Greek (modern), Hebrew, Hispanic American studies, history, humanities and social sciences, Indic languages, Islamic studies, Italian, Japanese, Jewish studies, Korean, Latin, linguistics, materials engineering, mathematics, mechanical engineering, medieval studies, Middle Eastern studies, music, music history and appreciation, philosophy, physical sciences, physics, planetary science, political science and government, Portuguese, psychology, pure mathematics, religion, Russian, Russian and Slavic studies, Scandinavian languages, Scandinavian studies, Slavic languages, social sciences, sociology, South Asian studies, Southeast Asian studies, Spanish, statistics, systems engineering, visual and performing arts, women's studies.

ACADEMIC PROGRAMS. Accelerated program, double major, honors program, independent study, internships, student-designed major, study abroad, teacher preparation, visiting/exchange student program, cross-registration; liberal arts/career combination in engineering. **Remedial services:** Special counselor, tutoring, optional reading course. **ROTC:** Air Force, Army, Naval. **Placement/credit:** AP, IB, institutional tests.

ACADEMIC REQUIREMENTS. No policy requiring minimum GPA; records of students having academic difficulty are reviewed individually. Passing grades in all courses with no more than one 1.0 grade in any term required to remain in good standing. 98% of freshmen return for sophomore year. Students must declare major by end of first year. **Graduation requirements:** Most students required to take courses in English, foreign languages, history, humanities, mathematics, philosophy/religion, biological/physical sciences, social sciences.

FRESHMAN ADMISSIONS. Selection criteria: Character, creative ability in some discipline or activity, leadership, liveliness of mind, demonstrated stamina and ability to carry out a demanding college program, and strong sense of social responsibility. Recommended units include English 4, foreign language 3, mathematics 4, social science 3 and science 3. One fine arts also recommended. Applicants encouraged to take rigorous courses and make the most of any opportunities for enrichment. **Test requirements:** SAT or ACT (SAT preferred); score report by February 15. 3 ACH required. Score report by February 15.

1992 FRESHMAN CLASS PROFILE. 7,322 men applied, 1,196 accepted, 921 enrolled; 5,707 women applied, 939 accepted, 685 enrolled. 100% had high school GPA of 3.0 or higher. **Academic background:** Mid 50% of enrolled freshmen had SAT-V between 620-720, SAT-M between 650-750. 99% submitted SAT scores. **Characteristics:** 16% from in state, 99% live in college housing, 34% have minority backgrounds, 7% are foreign students. Average age is 18.

FALL-TERM APPLICATIONS. $55 fee, may be waived for applicants with need. Closing date January 1; applicants notified on or about April 1; must reply by May 1. Interview required. Essay required. Interview with an alumnus/alumna required of all applicants; documentation of special talents encouraged. CRDA. Deferred admission available. Institutional early decision plan.

STUDENT LIFE. Housing: Dormitories (coed); apartment, cooperative housing available. All freshmen live together. Other students and some faculty members reside in 13 on-campus houses, self-contained communities offering seminars and tutorials. **Activities:** Student government, magazine, radio, student newspaper, yearbook, choral groups, concert band, dance, drama, jazz band, marching band, music ensembles, musical theater, opera, pep band, symphony orchestra, Gilbert and Sullivan Society, 175 official clubs, Phillips Brooks House (largest undergraduate social service organization), political, ethnic, and religious groups.

ATHLETICS. NCAA. **Intercollegiate:** Baseball M, basketball, cross-country, diving, fencing, field hockey W, football M, golf, ice hockey, lacrosse, rowing (crew), sailing, skiing, soccer, softball W, squash, swimming, tennis, track and field, volleyball, water polo, wrestling M. **Intramural:** Badminton, basketball, cross-country, fencing, field hockey W, football M, gymnastics W, ice hockey, rowing (crew), rugby, sailing, skiing, soccer, softball, squash, swimming, table tennis, tennis, track and field, volleyball, wrestling M.

STUDENT SERVICES. Aptitude testing, career counseling, employment service for undergraduates, freshman orientation, health services, on-campus day care, personal counseling, services/facilities for handicapped.

ANNUAL EXPENSES. Tuition and fees: $18,745. **Room and board:** $6,135. **Other expenses:** $1,820.

FINANCIAL AID. 74% of freshmen, 74% of continuing students receive some form of aid. All grants, all loans, 36% of jobs based on need. 797 enrolled freshmen were judged to have need, all were offered aid. **Aid applications:** No closing date; priority given to applications received by February 15; applicants notified on a rolling basis beginning on or about April 10; must reply by May 1 or within 2 weeks if notified thereafter. **Additional information:** Financial aid based solely on need. Admissions process is need blind. Institution meets full need of all admitted students.

ADDRESS/TELEPHONE. William R. Fitzsimmons, Dean of Admissions and Financial Aid, Harvard and Radcliffe Colleges, Byerly Hall, 8 Garden Street, Cambridge, MA 02138. (617) 495-1551. Fax: (617) 495-8821.

Hebrew College

Brookline, Massachusetts CB code: 3435

4-year private liberal arts, teachers college, coed, affiliated with Jewish faith. Founded in 1921. **Accreditation:** Regional. **Undergraduate enrollment:** 2 men, 2 women full time; 7 men, 18 women part time. **Graduate enrollment:** 4 men, 7 women full time; 6 men, 34 women part time. **Faculty:** 22 total (5 full time), 18 with doctorates or other terminal degrees. **Location:** Suburban campus in small city; 2 miles from Boston. **Calendar:** Semester, limited summer session. Extensive evening/early morning classes. **Special facilities:** Museum of Judaic items, periodic art exhibits.

DEGREES OFFERED. BA, MA. 1 bachelor's degrees awarded in 1992. Graduate degrees offered in 3 major fields of study.

UNDERGRADUATE MAJORS. Hebrew, Jewish education, Jewish studies, religious education.

ACADEMIC PROGRAMS. Accelerated program, dual enrollment of high school students, independent study, student-designed major, teacher preparation, cross-registration.

ACADEMIC REQUIREMENTS. Freshmen must earn minimum GPA of 2.0 to continue in good standing. 80% of freshmen return for sophomore year. Students must declare major by end of second year. **Graduation requirements:** 120 hours for bachelor's (18 in major). Most students required to take courses in foreign languages.

FRESHMAN ADMISSIONS. Selection criteria: Open admissions.

1992 FRESHMAN CLASS PROFILE. Characteristics: 85% from in state, 100% commute, 20% are foreign students. Average age is 22.

FALL-TERM APPLICATIONS. No fee. No closing date; priority given to applications received by June 30; applicants notified on a rolling basis beginning on or about May 1; must reply by August 15 or within 4 weeks if notified thereafter. Deferred and early admission available.

STUDENT SERVICES. Career counseling, personal counseling.

ANNUAL EXPENSES. Tuition and fees (1992-93): $150 per credit plus $70 annual in fees. **Books and supplies:** $300.

FINANCIAL AID. 25% of freshmen, 30% of continuing students receive some form of aid. Grants, loans available. **Aid applications:** No closing date; priority given to applications received by June 15; applicants notified on a rolling basis beginning on or about July 1; must reply within 3 weeks.

ADDRESS/TELEPHONE. Norma Frankel, Registrar, Hebrew College, 43 Hawes Street, Brookline, MA 02146. (617) 232-8710. Fax: (617) 734-9769.

Hellenic College

Brookline, Massachusetts CB code: 3449

4-year private liberal arts, seminary college, coed, affiliated with Greek Orthodox Archdiocese of North and South America. Founded in 1937. **Accreditation:** Regional. **Undergraduate enrollment:** 64 men and women. **Graduate enrollment:** 114 men and women. **Faculty:** 17 total (13 full time), 13 with doctorates or other terminal degrees. **Location:** Suburban campus in large town; 4 miles from Boston. **Calendar:** Semester, limited summer session. **Microcomputers:** Located in dormitories, libraries.

DEGREES OFFERED. BA, M, M.Div. 9 bachelor's degrees awarded in 1992. Graduate degrees offered in 2 major fields of study.

UNDERGRADUATE MAJORS. Classics, elementary education, Greek (modern), human resources development, religion, religion and humanities.

ACADEMIC PROGRAMS. Double major, independent study, internships, study abroad, visiting/exchange student program, cross-registration. **Remedial services:** Reduced course load, tutoring. **Placement/credit:** AP, CLEP General and Subject, institutional tests.

ACADEMIC REQUIREMENTS. Freshmen must earn minimum GPA of 2.0 to continue in good standing. 85% of freshmen return for sophomore year. Students must declare major on application. **Graduation requirements:** 128 hours for bachelor's. Most students required to take courses in English, foreign languages, history, philosophy/religion, biological/physical sciences, social sciences. **Postgraduate studies:** 45% enter other graduate study.

FRESHMAN ADMISSIONS. Selection criteria: High school achievement, GPA, test scores, 2 recommendations from instructors, 2 from clergy, school and community activities important. Recommended units include English 4, foreign language 2, mathematics 2, physical science 2 and science 1. 2-3 social studies also recommended. **Test requirements:** SAT or ACT; score report by May 1. California Psychological Inventory for pre-theology applicants.

1992 FRESHMAN CLASS PROFILE. 23 men and women enrolled. **Characteristics:** 98% live in college housing, 29% are foreign students. Average age is 22.

FALL-TERM APPLICATIONS. $35 fee. No closing date; priority given to applications received by May 1; applicants notified on a rolling basis; must reply within 2 weeks. Interview required. Essay required. Deferred and early admission available.

STUDENT LIFE. Housing: Dormitories (men, women). **Activities:** Student government, yearbook, student journal, choral groups, drama, music ensembles, several Orthodox groups, campus ministry, prison ministry, missions group.

ATHLETICS. Intramural: Basketball, bowling, football M, racquetball, skiing, soccer M, softball M, table tennis, tennis, volleyball.

STUDENT SERVICES. Aptitude testing, career counseling, employment service for undergraduates, freshman orientation, health services, personal counseling, placement service for graduates.

ANNUAL EXPENSES. Tuition and fees (1992-93): $6,515. **Room and board:** $4,480. **Books and supplies:** $500. **Other expenses:** $1,300.

FINANCIAL AID. 80% of freshmen, 90% of continuing students receive some form of aid. 32% of grants, 92% of loans, all jobs based on need. 17 enrolled freshmen were judged to have need, all were offered aid. Academic, alumni affiliation, religious affiliation scholarships available. **Aid applications:** Closing date April 1; applicants notified on or about July 15; must reply by August 1.

ADDRESS/TELEPHONE. Rev. Constantine Newman, Director of Admissions and Records, Hellenic College, 50 Goddard Avenue, Brookline, MA 02146. (617) 731-3500 ext. 260. Fax: (617) 738-9169.

Holyoke Community College
Holyoke, Massachusetts — CB code: 3437

2-year public community college, coed. Founded in 1946. **Accreditation:** Regional. **Undergraduate enrollment:** 1,072 men, 1,391 women full time; 946 men, 2,150 women part time. **Faculty:** 158 total (117 full time), 35 with doctorates or other terminal degrees. **Location:** Suburban campus in large town; 8 miles from Springfield. **Calendar:** Semester, extensive summer session. **Microcomputers:** 200 located in libraries, classrooms, computer centers. **Special facilities:** Nature preserves, art gallery.

DEGREES OFFERED. AA, AS. 642 associate degrees awarded in 1992. 27% in business and management, 8% business/office and marketing/distribution, 8% health sciences, 10% home economics, 25% multi/interdisciplinary studies, 7% parks/recreation, protective services, public affairs.

UNDERGRADUATE MAJORS. Accounting, accounting and computing, business administration and management, business data programming, business education, child development/care/guidance, electronic technology, elementary education, engineering, environmental control technologies, environmental science, food production/management/services, hotel/motel and restaurant management, information sciences and systems, institutional management, law enforcement and corrections technologies, legal secretary, liberal/general studies, medical records technology, medical secretary, mental health/human services, music, nursing, radiograph medical technology, retailing, secretarial and related programs, studio art, veterinarian's assistant.

ACADEMIC PROGRAMS. 2-year transfer program, cooperative education, dual enrollment of high school students, honors program, independent study, internships, study abroad, cross-registration. **Remedial services:** Learning center, reduced course load, remedial instruction, special counselor, tutoring. **Placement/credit:** AP, CLEP General and Subject, institutional tests; 30 credit hours maximum for associate degree.

ACADEMIC REQUIREMENTS. Freshmen must earn minimum GPA of 1.25 to continue in good standing. 60% of freshmen return for sophomore year. Students must declare major on application. **Graduation requirements:** 60 hours for associate (20 in major). Most students required to take courses in English, biological/physical sciences, social sciences.

FRESHMAN ADMISSIONS. Selection criteria: Open admissions. Selective admissions to some programs.

1992 FRESHMAN CLASS PROFILE. 729 men, 1,261 women enrolled. **Characteristics:** 99% from in state, 100% commute, 21% have minority backgrounds, 1% are foreign students. Average age is 25.

FALL-TERM APPLICATIONS. $10 fee, may be waived for applicants with need. $35 fee for out-of-state applicants. No closing date; priority given to applications received by March 1; applicants notified on a rolling basis; must reply within 2 weeks. Audition required for music applicants. Portfolio required for fine arts applicants. Deferred and early admission available.

STUDENT LIFE. Activities: Student government, magazine, radio, student newspaper, choral groups, concert band, drama, jazz band, music ensembles, musical theater, symphony orchestra, religious, international student, Afro-American, Hispanic, gay and lesbian clubs, naturalists.

ATHLETICS. NJCAA. **Intercollegiate:** Baseball M, basketball M, golf M, soccer, softball W, tennis. **Clubs:** Skiing, scuba clubs.

STUDENT SERVICES. Aptitude testing, career counseling, employment service for undergraduates, freshman orientation, health services, on-campus day care, personal counseling, placement service for graduates, special adviser for adult students, veterans counselor, ESL Coordinator, Bridge Counselor, Retention Counselor, services/facilities for handicapped.

ANNUAL EXPENSES. Tuition and fees (1992-93): $2,112, $3,822 additional for out-of-state students. **Books and supplies:** $480. **Other expenses:** $1,600.

FINANCIAL AID. 99% of grants, 91% of loans, all jobs based on need. Academic, music/drama, art, athletic, leadership scholarships available. **Aid applications:** No closing date; priority given to applications received by May 15; applicants notified on a rolling basis beginning on or about June 30; must reply within 2 weeks.

ADDRESS/TELEPHONE. Therese Labine, Director of Admissions, Holyoke Community College, 303 Homestead Avenue, Holyoke, MA 01040. (413) 538-7000 ext. 240. Fax: (413) 534-8975.

Katharine Gibbs School
Boston, Massachusetts — CB code: 3473

2-year proprietary business, junior college, coed. Founded in 1911. **Undergraduate enrollment:** 10 men, 420 women full time; 10 men, 110 women part time. **Faculty:** 28 total (18 full time), 2 with doctorates or other terminal degrees. **Location:** Urban campus in very large city; located in Back Bay area of downtown Boston. **Calendar:** Quarter. **Microcomputers:** Located in classrooms. **Additional facts:** Lifetime placement service and refresher courses available.

DEGREES OFFERED. AAS. 102 associate degrees awarded in 1992. 100% in business/office and marketing/distribution.

UNDERGRADUATE MAJORS. Business and management, secretarial and related programs.

ACADEMIC PROGRAMS. Internships. **Remedial services:** Preadmission summer program, tutoring. **Placement/credit:** CLEP General and Subject.

ACADEMIC REQUIREMENTS. Freshmen must earn minimum GPA of 1.7 to continue in good standing. 77% of freshmen return for sophomore year. Students must declare major on enrollment. **Graduation requirements:** 65 hours for associate. Most students required to take courses in English, history, mathematics, social sciences.

FRESHMAN ADMISSIONS. Selection criteria: School achievement record, entrance test, interview, and references are required. **Test requirements:** CPAT required for admission.

1992 FRESHMAN CLASS PROFILE. 393 men and women enrolled. **Characteristics:** Average age is 24.

FALL-TERM APPLICATIONS. $25 fee, may be waived for applicants with need. No closing date; applicants notified on a rolling basis. Interview required. Essay required.

STUDENT LIFE. Housing: Dormitories (coed). **Activities:** Student government, yearbook.

STUDENT SERVICES. Aptitude testing, career counseling, employment service for undergraduates, personal counseling, placement service for graduates.

ANNUAL EXPENSES. Tuition and fees (1992-93): $7,545. **Room and board:** $5,600 room only. **Books and supplies:** $450.

FINANCIAL AID. 58% of freshmen, 50% of continuing students receive some form of aid. Grants, loans, jobs available. 87 enrolled freshmen were judged to have need, all were offered aid. **Aid applications:** No closing date; applicants notified on a rolling basis; must reply within 2 weeks.

ADDRESS/TELEPHONE. Kate Stinelour, Director of Admissions, Katharine Gibbs School, 126 Newbury Street, Boston, MA 02116. (617) 578-7150. (800) 675-4557. Fax: (617) 262-6210.

Laboure College
Boston, Massachusetts CB code: 3287

2-year private junior college of allied health services and nursing, coed, affiliated with Roman Catholic Church. Founded in 1971. **Accreditation:** Regional. **Undergraduate enrollment:** 625 men and women. **Location:** Urban campus in very large city; 5 miles from downtown. **Calendar:** Semester. **Additional facts:** Affiliated with more than 75 health care agencies in the Greater Boston area.

FRESHMAN ADMISSIONS. Selection criteria: School achievement record, recommendations, interview, and work experience important.

ANNUAL EXPENSES. Tuition and fees (1992-93): $7,640. **Room and board:** $2,100 room only. **Books and supplies:** $800. **Other expenses:** $900.

ADDRESS/TELEPHONE. James DuPont, Director of Admissions, Laboure College, 2120 Dorchester Avenue, Boston, MA 02124. (617) 296-8300. Fax: (617) 296-7947.

Lasell College
Newton, Massachusetts CB code: 3481

Admissions: 90% of applicants accepted
Based on: ••• Interview, recommendations, school record
•• Activities
• Essay, special talents, test scores
Completion: 85% of freshmen end year in good standing

4-year private business, liberal arts college, women only. Founded in 1851. **Accreditation:** Regional. **Undergraduate enrollment:** 489 women full time; 50 women part time. **Faculty:** 89 total (32 full time), 17 with doctorates or other terminal degrees. **Location:** Suburban campus in small city; 8 miles from Boston. **Calendar:** Semester. **Microcomputers:** 50 located in libraries, classrooms, computer centers. **Special facilities:** Yamawaki Cultural Center, bed & breakfast facility, retail management center, day care center, simulated travel laboratory, advertising agency and travel agency.

DEGREES OFFERED. AA, AS, AAS, BA, BS. 106 associate degrees awarded in 1992. 42% in business and management, 8% business/office and marketing/distribution, 9% teacher education, 13% allied health, 28% multi/interdisciplinary studies. 41 bachelor's degrees awarded. 46% in business and management, 21% teacher education, 17% allied health, 16% multi/interdisciplinary studies.

UNDERGRADUATE MAJORS. Associate: Accounting, business administration and management, business and management, child development/care/guidance, early childhood education, fashion merchandising, fine arts, hotel/motel and restaurant management, interior design, liberal/general studies, marketing management, mental health/human services, physical therapy assistant, retailing, small business management and ownership, tourism, transportation and travel marketing. **Bachelor's:** Business administration and management, business and management, child development/care/guidance, early childhood education, elementary education, fashion design, fashion merchandising, hotel and travel administration, hotel/motel and restaurant management, liberal/general studies, mental health/human services, retailing, tourism, transportation and travel marketing.

ACADEMIC PROGRAMS. 2-year transfer program, honors program, independent study, internships, student-designed major, study abroad, teacher preparation, visiting/exchange student program. **Remedial services:** Learning center, reduced course load, remedial instruction, tutoring, GATE Program. **Placement/credit:** Institutional tests; 30 credit hours maximum for associate degree; 75 credit hours maximum for bachelor's degree.

ACADEMIC REQUIREMENTS. Freshmen must earn minimum GPA of 2.0 to continue in good standing. 81% of freshmen return for sophomore year. Students must declare major on enrollment. **Graduation requirements:** 63 hours for associate, 125 hours for bachelor's. Most students required to take courses in computer science, English, mathematics, social sciences. **Postgraduate studies:** 72% from 2-year programs enter 4-year programs.

FRESHMAN ADMISSIONS. Selection criteria: GPA, class rank, interview, recommendations important. Recommended units include English 4, mathematics 3, social science 2 and science 2. Chemistry or biology required of physical therapist assistant applicants.

1992 FRESHMAN CLASS PROFILE. 623 women applied, 562 accepted, 263 enrolled. **Characteristics:** 46% from in state, 70% live in college housing, 7% have minority backgrounds, 12% are foreign students. Average age is 18.

FALL-TERM APPLICATIONS. $20 fee, may be waived for applicants with need. No closing date; applicants notified on a rolling basis; must reply within 4 weeks. Interview recommended. Essay recommended. CRDA. Deferred admission available.

STUDENT LIFE. Housing: Dormitories (women). Housing available in Victorian houses or modern brick residences; buildings house from 10 to 128 students; 23% of rooms are singles, 96% are single or double. **Activities:** Student government, student newspaper, yearbook, choral groups, dance, drama, Community Outreach Program, Student Judicial Court, Student Activities Council.

ATHLETICS. Intercollegiate: Basketball, cross-country, rowing (crew), soccer, softball, volleyball.

STUDENT SERVICES. Aptitude testing, career counseling, employment service for undergraduates, freshman orientation, health services, personal counseling, placement service for graduates, special adviser for adult students, services/facilities for handicapped.

ANNUAL EXPENSES. Tuition and fees: $11,675. **Room and board:** $6,000. **Books and supplies:** $600. **Other expenses:** $1,700.

FINANCIAL AID. 76% of freshmen, 62% of continuing students receive some form of aid. 98% of grants, all loans, 81% of jobs based on need. 144 enrolled freshmen were judged to have need, all were offered aid. Academic, leadership scholarships available. **Aid applications:** No closing date; priority given to applications received by May 1; applicants notified on a rolling basis beginning on or about January 1; must reply within 2 weeks.

ADDRESS/TELEPHONE. Adrienne Asiaf, Director of Admissions, Lasell College, 1844 Commonwealth Avenue, Newton, MA 02166. (617) 243-2225. Fax: (617) 243-2389.

Lesley College
Cambridge, Massachusetts CB code: 3483

Admissions: 83% of applicants accepted
Based on: ••• Interview, recommendations, school record
•• Activities, essay, test scores
• Special talents
Completion: 85% of freshmen end year in good standing
60% graduate, 8% of these enter graduate study

4-year private college specializing in human services, management, arts and education, women only. Founded in 1909. **Accreditation:** Regional. **Undergraduate enrollment:** 532 women full time; 22 women part time. **Graduate enrollment:** 185 men, 412 women full time; 587 men, 2,691 women part time. **Faculty:** 648 total (122 full time). **Location:** Urban campus in small city; 4 miles from Boston. **Calendar:** Semester. **Microcomputers:** 75 located in dormitories, libraries, classrooms, computer centers. **Special facilities:** Learning resources center. **Additional facts:** Three schools within college: Undergraduate School (residential college for women that emphasizes education, human services, and management); Graduate School; and School of Programs in Management for Business and Industry. Adult learner programs available. Men admitted to graduate programs and Adult Baccalaureate Programs.

DEGREES OFFERED. BS, MA, MS, MEd, PhD. 2 associate degrees awarded in 1992. 100% in multi/interdisciplinary studies. 515 bachelor's degrees awarded. 43% in business and management, 34% teacher education, 23% allied health. Graduate degrees offered in 29 major fields of study.

UNDERGRADUATE MAJORS. Associate: Liberal/general studies. **Bachelor's:** Adult and continuing education research, American studies, art therapy, behavioral sciences, biological and physical sciences, business administration and management, business and management, clinical pastoral care, counseling psychology, creative writing, developmental psychology, early childhood education, education, education of the emotionally handicapped, education of the mentally handicapped, elementary education, environmental science, health care administration, human resources development, humanities, humanities and social sciences, junior high education, liberal/general studies, management science, mathematics education, mental health/human services, organizational behavior, psychology, science education, social sciences, social work, special education, women's studies.

ACADEMIC PROGRAMS. Accelerated program, double major, education specialist degree, external degree, independent study, internships, student-designed major, study abroad, teacher preparation, visiting/exchange student program, weekend college, Washington semester, cross-registration. **Remedial services:** Learning center, reduced course load, special counselor, tutoring. **Placement/credit:** AP; 16 credit hours maximum for bachelor's degree.

ACADEMIC REQUIREMENTS. Freshmen must earn minimum GPA of 2.0 to continue in good standing. 75% of freshmen return for sophomore year. Students must declare major by end of first year. **Graduation requirements:** 128 hours for bachelor's (30 in major). Most students required to take courses in arts/fine arts, computer science, English, history, humanities, mathematics, philosophy/religion, biological/physical sciences, social sciences. **Postgraduate studies:** 1% enter law school, 7% enter other graduate study. **Additional information:** Field experience in student teaching, human services, or management required of all students beginning freshman year. Accelerated and individualized majors offered through adult bachelor programs.

FRESHMAN ADMISSIONS. Selection criteria: Academic record, interview, recommendations, SAT scores, work with children or community service, character considered. **High school preparation:** 16 units required. Required units include English 4, mathematics 2 and science 1. One American history also required. Science requirement must be laboratory science. **Test requirements:** SAT or ACT; score report by April 1.

1992 FRESHMAN CLASS PROFILE. 299 women applied, 249 accepted, 124 enrolled. 22% had high school GPA of 3.0 or higher, 71% between 2.0 and 2.99. **Academic background:** Mid 50% of enrolled freshmen had SAT-V between 380-480, SAT-M between 370-510. 99% submitted SAT scores. **Characteristics:** 63% from in state, 90% live in college housing, 20% have minority backgrounds, 5% are foreign students. Average age is 18.

FALL-TERM APPLICATIONS. $35 fee, may be waived for applicants with need. No closing date; priority given to applications received by April 1; applicants notified on a rolling basis beginning on or about January 15; must reply by May 1 or immediately if notified thereafter. Essay required. Interview recommended. CRDA. Deferred admission available. EDP-F.

STUDENT LIFE. Housing: Dormitories (women). **Activities:** Student government, magazine, yearbook, choral groups, dance, drama, musical theater, preprofessional and service organizations, Hillel, Catholic Student Organization, Christian Fellowship, AMANA, SOAR.

ATHLETICS. Intramural: Soccer, softball, tennis.

STUDENT SERVICES. Career counseling, employment service for undergraduates, freshman orientation, health services, personal counseling, placement service for graduates, special adviser for adult students, services/facilities for handicapped.

ANNUAL EXPENSES. Tuition and fees: $12,450. **Room and board:** $5,300. **Books and supplies:** $550. **Other expenses:** $850.

FINANCIAL AID. 65% of freshmen, 63% of continuing students receive some form of aid. 95% of grants, 99% of loans, 80% of jobs based on need. 104 enrolled freshmen were judged to have need, all were offered aid. Academic, leadership, minority scholarships available. **Aid applications:** No closing date; priority given to applications received by March 1; applicants notified on a rolling basis beginning on or about March 15; must reply by May 1 or within 3 weeks if notified thereafter.

ADDRESS/TELEPHONE. Carol Streit, Dean Undergraduate School, Lesley College, 29 Everett Street, Cambridge, MA 02138-2790. (617) 349-8800. (800) 999-1959. Fax: (617) 349-8717.

Marian Court Junior College
Swampscott, Massachusetts — CB code: 9100

Admissions:	89% of applicants accepted
Based on:	••• Interview, school record
	•• Activities, recommendations
	• Essay
Completion:	85% of freshmen end year in good standing
	80% graduate, 25% of these enter 4-year programs

2-year private junior college, coed, affiliated with Roman Catholic Church. Founded in 1964. **Accreditation:** Regional. **Undergraduate enrollment:** 172 women full time; 2 men, 20 women part time. **Faculty:** 36 total (8 full time), 3 with doctorates or other terminal degrees. **Location:** Suburban campus in large town; 5 miles from Lynn, 20 miles from Boston. **Calendar:** Semester, limited summer session. **Microcomputers:** 24 located in libraries, computer centers. **Additional facts:** Evening division on quarter system.

DEGREES OFFERED. AS. 67 associate degrees awarded in 1992. 100% in business/office and marketing/distribution.

UNDERGRADUATE MAJORS. Accounting, business and management, human resources development, legal secretary, liberal/general studies, medical secretary, microcomputer software, secretarial and related programs, tourism, word processing.

ACADEMIC PROGRAMS. 2-year transfer program, double major, honors program, independent study, internships, cross-registration. **Remedial services:** Reduced course load, tutoring, academic advising. **Placement/credit:** CLEP General and Subject, institutional tests; 15 credit hours maximum for associate degree.

ACADEMIC REQUIREMENTS. Freshmen must earn minimum GPA of 2.0 to continue in good standing. 85% of freshmen return for sophomore year. Students must declare major by end of first year. **Graduation requirements:** 60 hours for associate. Most students required to take courses in computer science, English, humanities, mathematics, social sciences.

FRESHMAN ADMISSIONS. Selection criteria: Overall high school performance considered.

1992 FRESHMAN CLASS PROFILE. 98 women applied, 87 accepted, 75 enrolled. **Characteristics:** 100% from in state, 100% commute, 5% have minority backgrounds. Average age is 18.

FALL-TERM APPLICATIONS. $25 fee, may be waived for applicants with need. No closing date; priority given to applications received by April 15; applicants notified on a rolling basis; must reply by May 1 or within 2 weeks if notified thereafter. Interview required. CRDA. Deferred admission available.

STUDENT LIFE. Activities: Student government, yearbook, Mercy Outreach, Travel Club, campus ministry.

ATHLETICS. Intramural: Bowling W.

STUDENT SERVICES. Career counseling, employment service for undergraduates, freshman orientation, health services, personal counseling, placement service for graduates, special adviser for adult students, services/facilities for handicapped.

ANNUAL EXPENSES. Tuition and fees: $6,850. Tuition costs lower for evening division degree program. **Books and supplies:** $450. **Other expenses:** $1,393.

FINANCIAL AID. 58% of freshmen, 55% of continuing students receive some form of aid. All grants, 93% of loans, 78% of jobs based on need. **Aid applications:** No closing date; priority given to applications received by April 1; applicants notified on a rolling basis beginning on or about April 15; must reply by May 1 or within 2 weeks if notified thereafter.

ADDRESS/TELEPHONE. Maryelizabeth K. Amico, Director of Admissions, Marian Court Junior College, 35 Little's Point Road, Swampscott, MA 01907-2896. (617) 595-6768. Fax: (617) 595-3560.

Massachusetts Bay Community College
Wellesley Hills, Massachusetts — CB code: 3294

2-year public community college, coed. Founded in 1961. **Accreditation:** Regional. **Undergraduate enrollment:** 1,141 men, 1,406 women full time; 819 men, 1,868 women part time. **Faculty:** 291 total (78 full time), 28 with doctorates or other terminal degrees. **Location:** Suburban campus in large town; 13 miles from Boston. **Calendar:** Semester, extensive summer session. Saturday and extensive evening/early morning classes. **Microcomputers:** 230 located in classrooms, computer centers. **Special facilities:** Art gallery, Center for Innovation (educational services facilty).

DEGREES OFFERED. AA, AS, AAS. 518 associate degrees awarded in 1992. 18% in business and management, 9% business/office and marketing/distribution, 7% engineering technologies, 21% health sciences, 5% allied health, 6% law, 22% multi/interdisciplinary studies, 6% parks/recreation, protective services, public affairs.

UNDERGRADUATE MAJORS. Accounting, automotive technology, biotechnology, business administration and management, business and management, business and office, chemical manufacturing technology, chemical technology, child development/care/guidance, communications, computer and information sciences, computer programming, computer servicing technology, court reporting, criminal justice studies, electronic technology, engineering, engineering and engineering-related technologies, finance, fire protection, information sciences and systems, instrumentation technology, international studies, laser electro-optic technology, legal assistant/paralegal, liberal/general studies, management information systems, marketing management, medical laboratory technologies, medical records technology, nursing, occupational therapy assistant, office supervision and management, pharmacy technology, plastic technology, predentistry, premedicine, prepharmacy, preveterinary, radiograph medical technology, real estate, retailing, secretarial and related programs, social work, speech pathology/audiology, teacher aide, tourism, visual and performing arts.

ACADEMIC PROGRAMS. 2-year transfer program, accelerated program, cooperative education, double major, dual enrollment of high school students, honors program, independent study, internships, study abroad, telecourses. **Remedial services:** Learning center, preadmission summer program, reduced course load, remedial instruction, special counselor, tutoring, developmental program in basic academic skills. **Placement/credit:** CLEP Subject, institutional tests; 30 credit hours maximum for associate degree.

ACADEMIC REQUIREMENTS. Freshmen must earn minimum GPA of 2.0 to continue in good standing. 44% of freshmen return for sophomore year. Students must declare major on application. **Graduation requirements:** 60 hours for associate. Most students required to take courses in computer science, English, humanities, mathematics, social sciences.

FRESHMAN ADMISSIONS. Selection criteria: Open admissions. Some programs require special academic preparation. **Test requirements:** ACT for placement.

1992 FRESHMAN CLASS PROFILE. 715 men, 878 women enrolled. 37% had high school GPA of 3.0 or higher, 61% between 2.0 and 2.99. **Characteristics:** 99% from in state, 100% commute, 18% have minority backgrounds, 3% are foreign students. Average age is 19.

FALL-TERM APPLICATIONS. No fee. $35 fee for out-of-state applicants. No closing date; applicants notified on a rolling basis beginning on or about November 1; must reply within 2 weeks. Deferred and early admission available.

STUDENT LIFE. Activities: Student government, student newspaper, yearbook, student handbook, choral groups, drama, musical theater, Volunteer Service Corps, Christian Fellowship, Hillel.

ATHLETICS. NJCAA. **Intercollegiate:** Baseball M, basketball, soccer M, softball W. **Intramural:** Basketball, field hockey, golf, ice hockey, racquetball, soccer, softball, tennis, track and field.

STUDENT SERVICES. Aptitude testing, career counseling, employment service for undergraduates, freshman orientation, health services, personal counseling, placement service for graduates, special adviser for adult students, veterans counselor, services/facilities for handicapped.

ANNUAL EXPENSES. Tuition and fees (1992-93): $1,980, $3,822 additional for out-of-state students. **Books and supplies:** $400. **Other expenses:** $860.

FINANCIAL AID. 12% of freshmen, 19% of continuing students receive some form of aid. 98% of grants, 59% of loans, all jobs based on need. 567 enrolled freshmen were judged to have need, all were offered aid. Academic, music/drama, art, athletic scholarships available. **Aid applications:**

Closing date May 1; applicants notified on a rolling basis; must reply within 4 weeks.

ADDRESS/TELEPHONE. James R. Regan, Exe Dir Enrollment Svcs, Massachusetts Bay Community College, 50 Oakland Street, Wellesley Hills, MA 02181. (617) 237-0165. Fax: (617) 239-1047.

Massachusetts College of Art

Boston, Massachusetts CB code: 3516

Admissions: 44% of applicants accepted
Based on: ••• Essay, school record, special talents
•• Interview, recommendations, test scores
• Activities
Completion: 91% of freshmen end year in good standing
32% graduate, 10% of these enter graduate study

4-year public art college, coed. Founded in 1873. **Accreditation:** Regional. **Undergraduate enrollment:** 408 men, 585 women full time; 41 men, 89 women part time. **Graduate enrollment:** 27 men, 39 women full time; 7 men, 31 women part time. **Faculty:** 92 total (62 full time), 65 with doctorates or other terminal degrees. **Location:** Urban campus in very large city. **Calendar:** Semester, limited summer session. **Microcomputers:** 60 located in computer centers. **Special facilities:** 7 art galleries, computer arts learning center, foundry, glass furnaces, video and film studios, performance space, Polaroid 20X24 camera, ceramic kiln. **Additional facts:** Individual studio spaces available for students in most major departments.

DEGREES OFFERED. BFA, MFA, MEd. 143 bachelor's degrees awarded in 1992. 7% in teacher education, 90% visual and performing arts. Graduate degrees offered in 15 major fields of study.

UNDERGRADUATE MAJORS. Architecture, art education, art history, ceramics, cinematography/film, crafts, fashion design, fiber/textiles/weaving, fine arts, glass, graphic design, illustration design, industrial design, interrelated media, metal/jewelry, painting, photography, printmaking, sculpture, studio art, video, visual and performing arts.

ACADEMIC PROGRAMS. Double major, independent study, internships, student-designed major, study abroad, teacher preparation, visiting/exchange student program, cross-registration, A.I.C.A.D. and east coast art schools visiting semester programs, foreign exchange programs, foreign summer study abroad. **Remedial services:** Preadmission summer program, reduced course load, remedial instruction, tutoring. **Placement/credit:** AP, CLEP General and Subject, institutional tests.

ACADEMIC REQUIREMENTS. No policy requiring minimum GPA; records of students having academic difficulty are reviewed individually. 84% of freshmen return for sophomore year. Students must declare major by end of first year. **Graduation requirements:** 132 hours for bachelor's (39 in major). Most students required to take courses in arts/fine arts, English, history, humanities, biological/physical sciences, social sciences.

FRESHMAN ADMISSIONS. Selection criteria: Emphasis on portfolio, academic record, essay, SAT scores, and recommendations. **High school preparation:** 16 units required. Required units include English 4, foreign language 2, mathematics 3, social science 2 and science 2. 3 additional units from above or computer science, humanities, or visual and performing arts also required. **Test requirements:** SAT; score report by April 1. **Additional information:** Applicants must meet Massachusetts public college admission standards.

1992 FRESHMAN CLASS PROFILE. 662 men and women applied, 292 accepted; 70 men enrolled, 97 women enrolled. 4% were in top tenth and 32% were in top quarter of graduating class. **Academic background:** Mid 50% of enrolled freshmen had SAT-V between 410-550, SAT-M between 410-560. 100% submitted SAT scores. **Characteristics:** 76% from in state, 70% commute, 13% have minority backgrounds, 6% are foreign students. Average age is 21.

FALL-TERM APPLICATIONS. $10 fee, may be waived for applicants with need. $40 fee for out-of-state applicants. Closing date April 1; applicants notified on a rolling basis beginning on or about February 1; must reply by May 1 or within 4 weeks if notified thereafter. Portfolio required. Essay required. Interview recommended. CRDA. Deferred admission available. EDP-F.

STUDENT LIFE. Housing: Dormitories (coed). **Activities:** Student government, film, student newspaper, yearbook, literary magazine, dance, drama, Spectrum, international students.

ATHLETICS. Intercollegiate: Basketball, field hockey M, golf M, ice hockey M, soccer. **Intramural:** Basketball, table tennis, wrestling M.

STUDENT SERVICES. Career counseling, employment service for undergraduates, freshman orientation, health services, personal counseling, placement service for graduates, veterans counselor, services/facilities for handicapped.

ANNUAL EXPENSES. Tuition and fees (1992-93): $4,318, $4,740 additional for out-of-state students. **Room and board:** $5,827. **Books and supplies:** $1,700. **Other expenses:** $2,200.

FINANCIAL AID. 41% of freshmen, 43% of continuing students receive some form of aid. All grants, 66% of loans, all jobs based on need. 92 enrolled freshmen were judged to have need, all were offered aid. **Aid applications:** No closing date; priority given to applications received by May 1; applicants notified on a rolling basis beginning on or about March 15; must reply by May 1 or within 3 weeks if notified thereafter. **Additional information:** Tuition waiver available to Vietnam veterans, some state employees.

ADDRESS/TELEPHONE. Kay Ransdell, Associate Dean for Admissions and Retention, Massachusetts College of Art, 621 Huntington Avenue, Boston, MA 02115-5882. (617) 232-1555 ext. 235. Fax: (617) 566-4034.

Massachusetts College of Pharmacy and Allied Health Sciences

Boston, Massachusetts CB code: 3512

5-year private health science, pharmacy college, coed. Founded in 1823. **Accreditation:** Regional. **Undergraduate enrollment:** 1,088 men and women. **Graduate enrollment:** 237 men and women. **Faculty:** 122 total (64 full time), 39 with doctorates or other terminal degrees. **Location:** Urban campus in very large city. **Calendar:** Quarter, limited summer session. **Microcomputers:** 14 located in dormitories, libraries, computer centers. **Additional facts:** Access to Harvard Medical School library. Joint pharmacy program offered in conjunction with Western New England College, Springfield

DEGREES OFFERED. AS, BS, MS, PhD, Pharm D. 5 associate degrees awarded in 1992. 249 bachelor's degrees awarded. Graduate degrees offered in 5 major fields of study.

UNDERGRADUATE MAJORS. Associate: Nuclear medical technology, radiograph medical technology. **Bachelor's:** Allied health, chemistry, health sciences, nuclear medical technology, nuclear technologies, nursing, pharmacy, predentistry, premedicine, radiograph medical technology.

ACADEMIC PROGRAMS. Double major, dual enrollment of high school students, independent study, internships, cross-registration; liberal arts/career combination in health sciences. **Remedial services:** Learning center, reduced course load, special counselor, tutoring. **ROTC:** Army. **Placement/credit:** AP, CLEP Subject, institutional tests.

ACADEMIC REQUIREMENTS. Freshmen must earn minimum GPA of 2.0 to continue in good standing. 75% of freshmen return for sophomore year. Students must declare major on enrollment. **Graduation requirements:** 131 hours for associate, 189 hours for bachelor's. Most students required to take courses in English, history, humanities, mathematics, biological/physical sciences, social sciences. **Postgraduate studies:** 20% from 2-year programs enter 4-year programs.

FRESHMAN ADMISSIONS. Selection criteria: School academic record and class rank most important, with emphasis on mathematics and science courses. Counselor's recommendation may be important. Student's interest and aptitude for pharmacy and allied health fields also considered. Interview highly recommended. **High school preparation:** 16 units required. Required and recommended units include biological science 1, English 4, mathematics 3 and social science 1. Physical science 1 recommended. 2 units laboratory science also required. Additional units of mathematics and laboratory science recommended. **Test requirements:** SAT or ACT; score report by June 1.

1992 FRESHMAN CLASS PROFILE. 113 men and women enrolled. 80% had high school GPA of 3.0 or higher, 20% between 2.0 and 2.99. **Characteristics:** 65% from in state, 50% commute, 24% have minority backgrounds, 8% are foreign students, 20% join fraternities/sororities. Average age is 18.

FALL-TERM APPLICATIONS. $25 fee, may be waived for applicants with need. Closing date June 1; priority given to applications received by February 1; applicants notified on a rolling basis beginning on or about January 1; must reply by May 1 or within 2 weeks if notified thereafter. Interview recommended. Essay recommended. CRDA. Deferred and early admission available. EDP-F. Early admission may apply end of junior year. Early decision must apply by December 1.

STUDENT LIFE. Housing: Dormitories (coed). **Activities:** Student government, radio, student newspaper, yearbook, drama, fraternities, sororities, international students association, Black Student Union, Academy of Students of Pharmacy.

ATHLETICS. Intercollegiate: Baseball M, basketball, soccer M. **Intramural:** Field hockey W, skiing, softball, table tennis, volleyball.

STUDENT SERVICES. Aptitude testing, career counseling, employment service for undergraduates, freshman orientation, health services, personal counseling, placement service for graduates, veterans counselor.

ANNUAL EXPENSES. Tuition and fees (1992-93): $10,630. **Room and board:** $6,495. **Books and supplies:** $500. **Other expenses:** $1,600.

FINANCIAL AID. 75% of freshmen, 75% of continuing students receive some form of aid. Grants, loans, jobs available. 92 enrolled freshmen were judged to have need, 89 were offered aid. Academic, leadership scholarships available. **Aid applications:** No closing date; priority given to applications received by April 1; applicants notified on a rolling basis.

ADDRESS/TELEPHONE. Leslie C. Jacobs, Director of Admissions, Massachusetts College of Pharmacy and Allied Health Sciences, 179 Longwood Avenue, Boston, MA 02115. (617) 732-2850. (800) 225-5506. Fax: (617) 732-2801.

Massachusetts Institute of Technology
Cambridge, Massachusetts CB code: 3514

Admissions: 33% of applicants accepted
Based on: ••• Activities, school record, test scores
•• Essay, interview, recommendations
• Special talents
Completion: 97% of freshmen end year in good standing
88% graduate, 55% of these enter graduate study

4-year private university and engineering college, coed. Founded in 1861. **Accreditation:** Regional. **Undergraduate enrollment:** 2,980 men, 1,499 women full time; 34 men, 7 women part time. **Graduate enrollment:** 3,827 men, 1,138 women full time; 235 men, 78 women part time. **Faculty:** 975 total (957 full time), 947 with doctorates or other terminal degrees. **Location:** Urban campus in small city; 1 mile from Boston. **Calendar:** 4-1-4, limited summer session. **Microcomputers:** 1,100 located in dormitories, libraries, classrooms, computer centers, campus-wide network. **Special facilities:** Artificial Intelligence Laboratory, Bates Linear Accelerator, Nuclear Reactor. Woods Hole Oceanographic Institution, Wallace Observatory, Media Laboratory, Plasma Fusion Laboratory, Research Laboratory of Electronics, Dibner Institute for the History of Science/Burndy Library, MIT Museum, List Visual Arts Center. **Additional facts:** Extensive research opportunities for undergraduates.

DEGREES OFFERED. BS, MS, PhD. 1,039 bachelor's degrees awarded in 1992. 5% in business and management, 9% computer sciences, 49% engineering, 8% life sciences, 7% mathematics, 9% physical sciences, 6% social sciences. Graduate degrees offered in 92 major fields of study.

UNDERGRADUATE MAJORS. Aerospace/aeronautical/astronautical engineering, American studies, analytical chemistry, anthropology, applied mathematics, archeology, architecture, art history, astronomy, astrophysics, atomic/molecular physics, bacteriology, biochemistry, bioengineering and biomedical engineering, biological and physical sciences, biology, biophysics, biotechnology, business administration and management, business and management, business economics, cell biology, chemical engineering, chemistry, cinematography/film, city/community/regional planning, civil engineering, cognitive psychology, computer and information sciences, computer mathematics, computer programming, dramatic arts, earth sciences, economics, electrical/electronics/communications engineering, electron physics, elementary particle physics, engineering and other disciplines, environmental design, environmental health engineering, environmental science, fluids and plasmas, French, genetics, human and animal, geochemistry, geology, geophysics and seismology, German, history, humanities, information sciences and systems, inorganic chemistry, international relations, Latin American studies, literature, materials engineering, mathematics, mechanical engineering, metallurgy, microbiology, molecular biology, music, naval architecture and marine engineering, nuclear engineering, nuclear physics, ocean engineering, organic chemistry, pharmaceutical chemistry, philosophy, physical chemistry, physical sciences, physics, planetary science, political science and government, predentistry, prelaw, premedicine, preveterinary, psycholinguistics, psychology, pure mathematics, Russian, Russian and Slavic studies, solid state physics, Spanish, statistics, systems analysis, urban design, urban studies, women's studies, writing.

ACADEMIC PROGRAMS. Accelerated program, cooperative education, double major, independent study, internships, student-designed major, study abroad, cross-registration, Undergraduate Research Opportunities Program, Independent Activities Period, Freshman Year Special Programs: Integrated Studies Program, Concourse Program, Experimental Study Group. **Remedial services:** Learning center, preadmission summer program, tutoring. **ROTC:** Air Force, Army, Naval. **Placement/credit:** AP, IB, institutional tests.

ACADEMIC REQUIREMENTS. No policy requiring minimum GPA; records of students having academic difficulty are reviewed individually. 97% of freshmen return for sophomore year. Students must declare major by end of second year. **Graduation requirements:** Most students required to take courses in English, humanities, mathematics, biological/physical sciences. **Postgraduate studies:** 4% enter law school, 80% enter medical school, 3% enter MBA programs, 40% enter other graduate study. **Additional information:** Freshman non-passing grades not recorded.

FRESHMAN ADMISSIONS. Selection criteria: Intention is to admit candidates whose qualities of intellect, initiative, and energy demonstrate desire for intellectual and personal fulfillment. School achievement record, mathematics and science achievement tests important. Activities, recommendations, and interview also considered. Sensitive evaluation of test scores of minority or educationally disadvantaged applicants. **High school preparation:** 15 units recommended. Recommended units include English 4, foreign language 1, mathematics 4, social science 2 and science 4. Science including chemistry, biology, and physics recommended. **Test requirements:** SAT or ACT (SAT preferred); score report by February 20. 3 ACH required (English with or without composition or American History or European History; Mathematics Level I, II, or IIC; and Chemistry or Physics or Biology). Score report by February 20 Early action candidates must complete all required tests by November test date; other applicants must complete required tests by January test date.

1992 FRESHMAN CLASS PROFILE. 4,919 men applied, 1,414 accepted, 740 enrolled; 1,743 women applied, 806 accepted, 399 enrolled. 95% were in top tenth and 100% were in top quarter of graduating class. **Academic background:** Mid 50% of enrolled freshmen had SAT-V between 580-680, SAT-M between 710-780; ACT composite between 30-33. 99% submitted SAT scores, 21% submitted ACT scores. **Characteristics:** 8% from in state, 99% live in college housing, 36% have minority backgrounds, 7% are foreign students, 45% join fraternities/sororities. Average age is 18.

FALL-TERM APPLICATIONS. $50 fee, may be waived for applicants with need. Closing date January 1; applicants notified on or about April 1; must reply by May 1. Interview required. Essay required. CRDA. Deferred and early admission available. Institutional early decision plan. Early action closing date November 1, notification before Christmas, reconsideration in March.

STUDENT LIFE. Housing: Dormitories (women, coed); apartment, fraternity, sorority, cooperative housing available. **Activities:** Student government, film, magazine, radio, student newspaper, television, yearbook, choral groups, concert band, dance, drama, jazz band, marching band, music ensembles, musical theater, pep band, symphony orchestra, chamber music, early music, brass, gospel, bell ringers, and classical guitar groups, fraternities, sororities, 213 organizations including religious groups, National Society of Black Engineers, Society of Hispanic Professional Engineers, American Indian Science and Engineering Society, Chinese Students Club, African Students Association, Korean Students Association, Association of Women Students, Technology Community Association, Alpha Phi Omega.

ATHLETICS. NAIA, NCAA. **Intercollegiate:** Baseball M, basketball, cross-country, diving, fencing, field hockey W, football M, golf M, gymnastics, ice hockey, lacrosse, rifle, rowing (crew), rugby, sailing, skiing, soccer, softball W, squash M, swimming, tennis, track and field, volleyball, water polo, wrestling M. **Intramural:** Badminton, basketball, cross-country, fencing, ice hockey, rowing (crew), rugby, soccer, softball, squash, table tennis, tennis, volleyball, water polo, wrestling M.

STUDENT SERVICES. Career counseling, employment service for undergraduates, freshman orientation, health services, on-campus day care, personal counseling, placement service for graduates, academic and freshman advisers, services/facilities for handicapped.

ANNUAL EXPENSES. Tuition and fees: $19,000. **Room and board:** $5,800. **Books and supplies:** $700. **Other expenses:** $1,550.

FINANCIAL AID. 62% of freshmen, 55% of continuing students receive some form of aid. All grants, 92% of loans, 66% of jobs based on need. 731 enrolled freshmen were judged to have need, all were offered aid. **Aid applications:** No closing date; priority given to applications received by February 1; applicants notified on a rolling basis beginning on or about April 1; must reply by May 1 or within 2 weeks if notified thereafter.

ADDRESS/TELEPHONE. Michael C. Behnke, Director of Admissions, Massachusetts Institute of Technology, 77 Massachusetts Avenue, Cambridge, MA 02139. (617) 253-4791. Fax: (617) 253-8000.

Massachusetts Maritime Academy
Buzzards Bay, Massachusetts CB code: 3515

Admissions: 40% of applicants accepted
Based on: ••• School record, test scores
•• Activities, essay
• Interview, recommendations, special talents
Completion: 80% of freshmen end year in good standing
78% graduate, 5% of these enter graduate study

4-year public maritime college and college of engineering, coed. Founded in 1891. **Accreditation:** Regional. **Undergraduate enrollment:** 680 men, 44 women full time; 10 men part time. **Faculty:** 49 total (48 full time), 34 with doctorates or other terminal degrees. **Location:** Rural campus in large town; 55 miles from Boston, 50 miles from Providence, Rhode Island. **Calendar:** 2 academic semesters and 2-month sea term. **Microcomputers:** 30 located in dormitories, libraries, classrooms, computer centers. **Special facilities:** Slow-speed diesel simulator, video full-function bridge navigation simulator, modern training ship, commercial fishing simulator, spill management simulator, cargo handling simulator. **Additional facts:** Annual 9-week sea cruise, 12-15 foreign ports of call by graduation. Offer study in business management, commercial fisheries, mechanical engineering and plant/facilities engineering marine safety and enviromental protection.

DEGREES OFFERED. BS. 121 bachelor's degrees awarded in 1992. 70% in engineering, 30% military sciences.

UNDERGRADUATE MAJORS. Industrial technology, marine safety and environmental protection, Merchant Marine, naval architecture and marine engineering, transportation management.

ACADEMIC PROGRAMS. Double major, internships, semester at sea. **Remedial services:** Tutoring. **Placement/credit:** AP, CLEP General and Subject, institutional tests; 6 credit hours maximum for bachelor's degree.

ACADEMIC REQUIREMENTS. Freshmen must earn minimum GPA of 1.5 to continue in good standing. 85% of freshmen return for sophomore year. Students must declare major by end of first year. **Graduation requirements:** 164 hours for bachelor's (64 in major). Most students required to take courses in computer science, English, history, humanities, mathematics, biological/physical sciences. **Additional information:** Technical and practical training for third assistant engineer and third mate licenses. Graduates may apply for commissions in US Navy, Coast Guard, Marine Reserve, Army, or Air Force.

FRESHMAN ADMISSIONS. Selection criteria: School achievement record, test scores, extracurricular accomplishments. Character and personality emphasized, leadership potential desirable. Physical examination required. Campus visit encouraged for in-state students. **High school preparation:** 16 units required. Required and recommended units include biological science 1, English 4, mathematics 3-4 and physical science 1-2. Foreign language 2 recommended. Mathematics units must include 2 algebra, 1 plane geometry. 1 chemistry required. Physics recommended. **Test requirements:** SAT or ACT (SAT preferred); score report by June 1.

1992 FRESHMAN CLASS PROFILE. 611 men applied, 240 accepted, 240 enrolled; 44 women applied, 20 accepted, 20 enrolled. **Academic background:** Mid 50% of enrolled freshmen had SAT-V between 360-480, SAT-M between 400-530. 98% submitted SAT scores. **Characteristics:** 71% from in state, 95% live in college housing, 7% have minority backgrounds, 6% are foreign students. Average age is 19.

FALL-TERM APPLICATIONS. $10 fee, may be waived for applicants with need. $40 fee for out-of-state applicants. No closing date; applicants notified on a rolling basis beginning on or about January 1. Essay required. Interview recommended. CRDA. Deferred admission available. EDP-F.

STUDENT LIFE. Housing: Dormitories (coed). All maritime and environmental protection marine safety majors required to live on campus. Other students may commute. **Activities:** Student government, yearbook, concert band, jazz band, marching band, Newman Club, marine careers group, Association of Industrial Plant Engineers.

ATHLETICS. NCAA. **Intercollegiate:** Baseball M, cross-country, football M, lacrosse M, rifle, rowing (crew), sailing, soccer M, softball W, tennis, volleyball W. **Intramural:** Basketball, boxing M, cross-country, diving, football M, golf, ice hockey M, racquetball, rifle, rugby M, sailing, skin diving, soccer, softball, swimming, table tennis, tennis, volleyball, water polo, wrestling M.

STUDENT SERVICES. Career counseling, employment service for undergraduates, freshman orientation, health services, placement service for graduates, veterans counselor, services/facilities for handicapped.

ANNUAL EXPENSES. Tuition and fees (1992-93): $3,203, $4,740 additional for out-of-state students. **Room and board:** $3,710. **Books and supplies:** $450. **Other expenses:** $1,250.

FINANCIAL AID. 77% of freshmen, 68% of continuing students receive some form of aid. 89% of grants, 51% of loans, all jobs based on need. 58 enrolled freshmen were judged to have need, all were offered aid. Academic, state/district residency scholarships available. **Aid applications:** No closing date; priority given to applications received by May 1; applicants notified on a rolling basis beginning on or about June 1; must reply within 2 weeks.

ADDRESS/TELEPHONE. Cdr. Roy Fulgueras, Director of Admissions, Massachusetts Maritime Academy, Academy Drive, Buzzards Bay, MA 02532-1803. (508) 759-5761 ext. 314. Fax: (508) 759-4117.

Massasoit Community College
Brockton, Massachusetts — CB code: 3549

2-year public community college, coed. Founded in 1966. **Accreditation:** Regional. **Undergraduate enrollment:** 1,552 men, 1,680 women full time; 1,475 men, 2,076 women part time. **Faculty:** 514 total (153 full time), 20 with doctorates or other terminal degrees. **Location:** Urban campus in small city; 25 miles from Boston. **Calendar:** Semester, extensive summer session. Saturday and extensive evening/early morning classes. **Microcomputers:** Located in classrooms, computer centers. **Additional facts:** Second campus located in suburban Canton, 10 miles south of Boston.

DEGREES OFFERED. AA, AS, AAS. 815 associate degrees awarded in 1992. 29% in business and management, 11% engineering technologies, 6% health sciences, 6% allied health, 30% multi/interdisciplinary studies, 11% parks/recreation, protective services, public affairs.

UNDERGRADUATE MAJORS. Accounting, air conditioning/heating/refrigeration technology, architectural technologies, business and management, business and office, business data programming, civil technology, commercial art, communications, computer and information sciences, computer programming, court reporting, criminal justice technology, data processing, diesel engine mechanics, early childhood education, electromechanical technology, electronic technology, engineering and engineering-related technologies, fire control and safety technology, food production/management/services, hotel/motel and restaurant management, law enforcement and corrections technologies, legal secretary, liberal/general studies, marketing and distribution, medical laboratory technologies, medical secretary, mental health/human services, nursing, occupational therapy assistant, radiograph medical technology, respiratory therapy technology, secretarial and related programs, social work, tourism, transportation and travel marketing.

ACADEMIC PROGRAMS. 2-year transfer program, cross-registration. **Remedial services:** Learning center, reduced course load, remedial instruction, special counselor, tutoring, Latch Program for students who have been away from school or college for several years. **Placement/credit:** CLEP General and Subject, institutional tests; 30 credit hours maximum for associate degree.

ACADEMIC REQUIREMENTS. Freshmen must earn minimum GPA of 1.5 to continue in good standing. 50% of freshmen return for sophomore year. Students must declare major on enrollment. **Graduation requirements:** 60 hours for associate. Most students required to take courses in English, humanities, mathematics, biological/physical sciences, social sciences.

FRESHMAN ADMISSIONS. Selection criteria: Open admissions. Selective admissions to allied health programs.

1992 FRESHMAN CLASS PROFILE. 639 men, 556 women enrolled. **Characteristics:** 98% from in state, 100% commute, 12% have minority backgrounds. Average age is 21.

FALL-TERM APPLICATIONS. $10 fee, may be waived for applicants with need. $35 fee for out-of-state applicants. No closing date; applicants notified on a rolling basis beginning on or about February 1; must reply within 4 weeks. Interview recommended for allied health applicants.

STUDENT LIFE. Activities: Student government, magazine, student newspaper, yearbook, drama, jazz band.

ATHLETICS. NJCAA. **Intercollegiate:** Baseball M, basketball, soccer, softball W, volleyball W. **Intramural:** Volleyball.

STUDENT SERVICES. Aptitude testing, career counseling, employment service for undergraduates, freshman orientation, health services, on-campus day care, personal counseling, placement service for graduates, special adviser for adult students, veterans counselor, special adviser for handicapped students, services/facilities for handicapped.

ANNUAL EXPENSES. Tuition and fees (1992-93): $1,804, $3,822 additional for out-of-state students. **Books and supplies:** $400. **Other expenses:** $900.

FINANCIAL AID. 65% of freshmen, 65% of continuing students receive some form of aid. All grants, 70% of loans, all jobs based on need. Academic, athletic scholarships available. **Aid applications:** No closing date; priority given to applications received by April 15; applicants notified on a rolling basis beginning on or about June 1; must reply within 2 weeks.

ADDRESS/TELEPHONE. Roberta Noodell, Director of Admissions, Massasoit Community College, 1 Massasoit Boulevard, Brockton, MA 02402. (617) 588-9100.

Merrimack College
North Andover, Massachusetts — CB code: 3525

Admissions:	90% of applicants accepted	
Based on:	•••	School record
	••	Recommendations, test scores
	•	Activities, essay, interview, special talents
Completion:	90% of freshmen end year in good standing	

4-year private college of arts and sciences, coed, affiliated with Roman Catholic Church. Founded in 1947. **Accreditation:** Regional. **Undergraduate enrollment:** 950 men, 955 women full time; 487 men, 560 women part time. **Faculty:** 169 total (129 full time), 85 with doctorates or other terminal degrees. **Location:** Suburban campus in large town; 25 miles from Boston. **Calendar:** Semester, limited summer session. Extensive evening/early morning classes. **Microcomputers:** 150 located in dormitories, libraries, classrooms, computer centers, campus-wide network. **Special facilities:** Art gallery, observatory, urban institute (for urban social studies). **Additional facts:** Associate degree programs offered through continuing education division only.

DEGREES OFFERED. AA, AS, BA, BS. 29 associate degrees awarded in 1992. 47% in business and management, 33% engineering, 10% letters/literature, 7% philosophy, religion, theology. 586 bachelor's degrees awarded. 52% in business and management, 7% engineering, 6% letters/literature, 5% psychology, 15% social sciences.

UNDERGRADUATE MAJORS. Associate: Accounting, business administration and management, computer and information sciences, engineering science, English. **Bachelor's:** Accounting, allied health, biochemistry, biology, biotechnology, business administration and management, business and management, business economics, chemistry, civil engineering, clinical laboratory science, computer and information sciences, computer engineering, economics, electrical/electronics/communications engineering, elementary education, engineering physics, English, English education, environmental science, finance, health sciences, history, history education, international business management, marketing management, mathematics, mathematics education, medical laboratory technologies, philosophy, physics, political science and government, predentistry, premedicine, psychology, religion, science education, secondary education, social science education, sociology, theological studies.

ACADEMIC PROGRAMS. Cooperative education, double major, dual enrollment of high school students, independent study, internships, student-designed major, study abroad, teacher preparation, Washington semester, cross-registration, 5-year combined BA/BS program. **Placement/credit:** AP, CLEP General and Subject, institutional tests.

ACADEMIC REQUIREMENTS. Freshmen must earn minimum GPA

of 1.5 to continue in good standing. 84% of freshmen return for sophomore year. Students must declare major by end of second year. **Graduation requirements:** 60 hours for associate, 120 hours for bachelor's. Most students required to take courses in computer science, English, humanities, mathematics, philosophy/religion, biological/physical sciences, social sciences. **Additional information:** Freshman seminars, Civilization and inquiry and conversation for all entering students.

FRESHMAN ADMISSIONS. Selection criteria: School achievement record, course selection, class rank, test scores, recommendations, considered. **High school preparation:** 16 units required. Required units include English 4, mathematics 3, social science 2 and science 1. Mathematics units must include algebra I and II and plane geometry. Additional 1 unit mathematics, and 2 science, including physics, required of mathematics, science, engineering, and computer science applicants. **Test requirements:** SAT or ACT (SAT preferred); score report by March 1.

1992 FRESHMAN CLASS PROFILE. 1,021 men applied, 902 accepted, 226 enrolled; 1,082 women applied, 989 accepted, 241 enrolled. **Academic background:** Mid 50% of enrolled freshmen had SAT-V between 450-550, SAT-M between 470-580. 99% submitted SAT scores. **Characteristics:** 77% from in state, 68% live in college housing, 5% have minority backgrounds, 2% are foreign students. Average age is 18.

FALL-TERM APPLICATIONS. $35 fee, may be waived for applicants with need. Closing date March 1; applicants notified on a rolling basis beginning on or about January 15; must reply by May 1. Essay required. Interview recommended. CRDA. Deferred and early admission available. EDP-F.

STUDENT LIFE. Housing: Dormitories (coed); apartment, handicapped housing available. Town houses available for upper class students. **Activities:** Student government, magazine, student newspaper, television, yearbook, choral groups, drama, music ensembles, musical theater, fraternities, sororities, student tutoring group, community service organizations, campus ministry, College Democrats, College Republicans, Society Organized Against Racism (SOAR).

ATHLETICS. NCAA. **Intercollegiate:** Baseball M, basketball, cross-country, field hockey W, golf, ice hockey M, lacrosse M, soccer, softball W, tennis, volleyball W. **Intramural:** Badminton, basketball, ice hockey M, lacrosse W, racquetball, skiing, squash, table tennis, tennis, volleyball.

STUDENT SERVICES. Career counseling, employment service for undergraduates, freshman orientation, health services, personal counseling, placement service for graduates, services/facilities for handicapped.

ANNUAL EXPENSES. Tuition and fees (1992-93): $11,000. **Room and board:** $6,100. **Books and supplies:** $550. **Other expenses:** $450.

FINANCIAL AID. 70% of freshmen, 62% of continuing students receive some form of aid. 69% of grants, 99% of loans, 45% of jobs based on need. 341 enrolled freshmen were judged to have need, all were offered aid. Athletic, religious affiliation, minority scholarships available. **Aid applications:** Closing date March 1; applicants notified on or about April 1; must reply by May 1.

ADDRESS/TELEPHONE. Dennis P. Farrell, Dean of Admissions and Financial Aid, Merrimack College, 315 Turnpike Street, North Andover, MA 01845. (508) 837-5100. Fax: (508) 837-5222.

Middlesex Community College
Bedford, Massachusetts — CB code: 3554

2-year public community college, coed. Founded in 1969. **Accreditation:** Regional. **Undergraduate enrollment:** 1,461 men, 1,875 women full time. **Faculty:** 299 total (122 full time), 25 with doctorates or other terminal degrees. **Location:** Suburban campus in small city; 16 miles from Boston. **Calendar:** Semester, extensive summer session. Saturday and extensive evening/early morning classes. **Microcomputers:** Located in classrooms, computer centers. **Special facilities:** Fitness center, dental clinic. **Additional facts:** Second main campus located in Lowell.

DEGREES OFFERED. AS. 595 associate degrees awarded in 1992.

UNDERGRADUATE MAJORS. Accounting, automotive technology, business administration and management, business and management, business computer/console/peripheral equipment operation, business data entry equipment operation, business data programming, communications, computer and information sciences, computer programming, computer technology, criminal justice studies, dental assistant, dental hygiene, dental laboratory technology, drafting, drafting and design technology, early childhood education, electrodiagnostic technologies, electronic technology, elementary education, emergency medical technologies, engineering science, fashion merchandising, fine arts, fire control and safety technology, hotel/motel and restaurant management, law enforcement and corrections technologies, legal secretary, liberal/general studies, marketing and distribution, medical assistant, medical laboratory technologies, medical secretary, mental health/human services, nursing, radiograph medical technology, retailing, secretarial and related programs, studio art, surgical technology, tourism, ultrasound technology, word processing.

ACADEMIC PROGRAMS. 2-year transfer program, cooperative education, dual enrollment of high school students, independent study, internships, study abroad, visiting/exchange student program, cross-registration. **Remedial services:** Learning center, preadmission summer program, reduced course load, remedial instruction, special counselor, tutoring, Transition Program: a post-secondary program for students with learning disabilities. **ROTC:** Air Force. **Placement/credit:** AP, CLEP General, institutional tests; 45 credit hours maximum for associate degree.

ACADEMIC REQUIREMENTS. Freshmen must earn minimum GPA of 2.0 to continue in good standing. 51% of freshmen return for sophomore year. Students must declare major on application. **Graduation requirements:** 60 hours for associate. Most students required to take courses in English, humanities, mathematics, biological/physical sciences, social sciences. **Additional information:** One of 5 community colleges chosen for a pilot project of dual admissions with University of Massachusetts at Amherst.

FRESHMAN ADMISSIONS. Selection criteria: Open admissions. Selective admissions to health programs based on 3.0 high school GPA and prerequisite courses in mathematics and science. Some health program applicants must submit essays and letters of reference. For health programs, 1 unit each of algebra, biology, chemistry required.

1992 FRESHMAN CLASS PROFILE. 1,176 men, 1,917 women enrolled. **Characteristics:** 99% from in state, 100% commute, 14% have minority backgrounds. Average age is 20.

FALL-TERM APPLICATIONS. No fee. No closing date; applicants notified on a rolling basis beginning on or about March 1; Applicants to health programs must reply within 2 weeks of acceptance. February 1 closing date for dental hygiene, nursing, ultra sound and radiology applications.

STUDENT LIFE. Housing: Housing arrangement available through University of Massachusetts at Lowel. **Activities:** Student government, student newspaper, yearbook, drama. **Additional information:** College sponsors a wellness program.

STUDENT SERVICES. Career counseling, employment service for undergraduates, health services, personal counseling, placement service for graduates, special adviser for adult students, veterans counselor, fitness center, services/facilities for handicapped.

ANNUAL EXPENSES. Tuition and fees (1992-93): $1,924, $3,822 additional for out-of-state students. **Books and supplies:** $405. **Other expenses:** $936.

FINANCIAL AID. 40% of freshmen, 40% of continuing students receive some form of aid. 99% of grants, 77% of loans, all jobs based on need. 249 enrolled freshmen were judged to have need, 207 were offered aid. **Aid applications:** No closing date; priority given to applications received by March 31; applicants notified on a rolling basis beginning on or about May 15; must reply within 2 weeks.

ADDRESS/TELEPHONE. Nina Anton, Asst Dean of Enrollment Services, Middlesex Community College, Springs Road, Bedford, MA 01730. (617) 275-8910 ext. 4501.

Montserrat College of Art
Beverly, Massachusetts — CB code: 9101

Admissions:	87% of applicants accepted
Based on:	••• Interview, school record, special talents
	•• Activities, essay
	• Recommendations, test scores
Completion:	90% of freshmen end year in good standing
	47% graduate, 10% of these enter graduate study

4-year private art college, coed. Founded in 1970. **Accreditation:** Regional. **Undergraduate enrollment:** 126 men, 82 women full time; 12 men, 18 women part time. **Faculty:** 40 total (13 full time), 20 with doctorates or other terminal degrees. **Location:** Suburban campus in large town; 20 miles from Boston. **Calendar:** Semester, limited summer session. **Microcomputers:** 13 located on campus. **Special facilities:** Montserrat Gallery, North Shore Music Theater, Paul Scott Library. **Additional facts:** Summer program in Trieste, Italy. Sister school in Niigata, Japan.

DEGREES OFFERED. BFA. 36 bachelor's degrees awarded in 1992. 100% in visual and performing arts.

UNDERGRADUATE MAJORS. Drawing, film arts, fine arts, graphic design, illustration design, painting, photography, printmaking, sculpture, studio art, video.

ACADEMIC PROGRAMS. Accelerated program, double major, dual enrollment of high school students, independent study, internships, student-designed major, study abroad, visiting/exchange student program, cross-registration. **Remedial services:** Remedial instruction, tutoring. **Placement/credit:** AP.

ACADEMIC REQUIREMENTS. 70% of freshmen return for sophomore year. Students must declare major by end of second year. **Graduation requirements:** 120 hours for bachelor's. Most students required to take courses in arts/fine arts, English, history, humanities, biological/physical sciences, social sciences. **Postgraduate studies:** 10% enter other graduate study. **Additional information:** Senior seminar program offers individual studio spaces, faculty adviser and weekly visiting critics. Student's work reviewed by faculty panel in semester-end evaluations. Courses in continuing education program free for full-time students.

FRESHMAN ADMISSIONS. Selection criteria: Student portfolio most important. High school record, interview (when practical), statement on application also considered. English and communication courses recommended with strong program in drawing, painting, and/or design. **Additional information:** Portfolio may be sent to college if personal visit is impractical.

1992 FRESHMAN CLASS PROFILE. 246 men and women applied, 213 accepted; 77 enrolled. **Characteristics:** 50% commute, 2% have minority backgrounds. Average age is 20.

FALL-TERM APPLICATIONS. $30 fee, may be waived for applicants with need. No closing date; priority given to applications received by May 1; applicants notified on a rolling basis beginning on or about January 1; must reply within 30 days. Portfolio required. Essay required. Interview recommended. Deferred and early admission available. ACT or SAT recommended.

STUDENT LIFE. Housing: Apartment housing available. Student service department helps students relocate to North Shore of Boston. Most first-time students live in nearby apartment complex where four students share two-bedroom apartments. **Activities:** Student government, student newspaper. **Additional information:** College-sponsored weekly lectures by outside artists, film series, and coffee houses.

STUDENT SERVICES. Career counseling, employment service for undergraduates, freshman orientation, personal counseling, special adviser for adult students.

ANNUAL EXPENSES. Tuition and fees: $8,800. **Books and supplies:** $800. **Other expenses:** $600.

FINANCIAL AID. 60% of freshmen, 60% of continuing students receive some form of aid. 99% of grants, 88% of loans, all jobs based on need. 39 enrolled freshmen were judged to have need, all were offered aid. Art scholarships available. **Aid applications:** No closing date; priority given to applications received by April 15; applicants notified on a rolling basis beginning on or about May 1; must reply within 2 weeks. **Additional information:** Limited on-campus employment for students not receiving financial aid.

ADDRESS/TELEPHONE. James Sawyer, Director of Admissions, Montserrat College of Art, PO Box 26, Dunham Road, Beverly, MA 01915. (508) 922-8222. (800) 836-0487. Fax: (508) 921-0793.

Mount Holyoke College
South Hadley, Massachusetts — CB code: 3529

Admissions: 76% of applicants accepted
Based on: ••• Essay, recommendations, school record
•• Activities, interview, special talents
• Test scores
Completion: 99% of freshmen end year in good standing
81% graduate, 20% of these enter graduate study

4-year private liberal arts college, women only. Founded in 1837. **Accreditation:** Regional. **Undergraduate enrollment:** 1,859 women full time; 55 women part time. **Graduate enrollment:** 16 women full time; 2 women part time. **Faculty:** 240 total (198 full time), 179 with doctorates or other terminal degrees. **Location:** Suburban campus in large town; 90 miles from Boston. **Calendar:** 4-1-4. **Microcomputers:** 245 located in dormitories, libraries, classrooms, computer centers. **Special facilities:** Nuclear accelerator, nuclear magnetic resonance equipment, electron microscope, bronze-casting foundry, art museum with permanent collection, solar greenhouse, Japanese meditation garden and tea house, equestrian center, language learning center with satellite communication and interactive video. **Additional facts:** Member of 5-college consortium with Amherst College, Hampshire College, Smith College, and University of massachusetts. Extensive internship programs in US and abroad.

DEGREES OFFERED. BA, M. 526 bachelor's degrees awarded in 1992. 7% in area and ethnic studies, 7% languages, 14% letters/literature, 9% life sciences, 8% psychology, 33% social sciences, 8% visual and performing arts. Graduate degrees offered in 2 major fields of study.

UNDERGRADUATE MAJORS. Afro-American (black) studies, American studies, anthropology, art history, Asian studies, astronomy, biochemistry, biology, biophysics, chemistry, classics, dance, dramatic arts, ecology, economics, English, English literature, European studies, French, geography, geology, German, Greek (classical), history, international relations, Italian, Jewish studies, Latin, Latin American studies, mathematics, medieval studies, music, philosophy, physics, political science and government, psychobiology, psychology, religion, Romance languages and literature, Russian, Russian and Slavic studies, sociology, Spanish, statistics, studio art, women's studies.

ACADEMIC PROGRAMS. Accelerated program, double major, honors program, independent study, internships, student-designed major, study abroad, teacher preparation, visiting/exchange student program, Washington semester, cross-registration, Williams College-Mystic Seaport Program in American maritime studies; liberal arts/career combination in engineering. **Remedial services:** Tutoring. **ROTC:** Air Force, Army. **Placement/credit:** AP, institutional tests; 32 credit hours maximum for bachelor's degree.

ACADEMIC REQUIREMENTS. Freshmen must earn minimum GPA of 2.0 to continue in good standing. 96% of freshmen return for sophomore year. Students must declare major by end of second year. **Graduation requirements:** 128 hours for bachelor's (32 in major). Most students required to take courses in foreign languages, humanities, biological/physical sciences, social sciences. **Additional information:** Honor system and self-scheduled examinations practiced. Third world course and physical education requirements; all students must complete a minor; opportunity for self-designed majors.

FRESHMAN ADMISSIONS. Selection criteria: School record and recommendations most important, then test results, special talents, particular goals, and evidence of determination considered. Students of all races and backgrounds welcomed. Recommended units include English 4, foreign language 4, mathematics 3, social science 3 and science 3. 4 foreign language (or 3 of 1, and 2 of another). **Test requirements:** SAT or ACT; score report by March 1. 3 ACH required (including English Composition). Score report by March 1.

1992 FRESHMAN CLASS PROFILE. 1,782 women applied, 1,351 accepted, 514 enrolled. 44% were in top tenth and 75% were in top quarter of graduating class. **Academic background:** Mid 50% of enrolled freshmen had SAT-V between 470-600, SAT-M between 500-620. 100% submitted SAT scores. **Characteristics:** 21% from in state, 99% live in college housing, 26% have minority backgrounds, 14% are foreign students. Average age is 18.

FALL-TERM APPLICATIONS. $40 fee, may be waived for applicants with need. Closing date February 1; applicants notified on or about April 1; must reply by May 1. Interview required. Essay required. Personal interview on campus required if candidate lives within 200 miles of college or with an alumna admissions representative if applicant resides outside of this area. CRDA. Deferred and early admission available. EDP-F. Two rounds of early decision plans available. Round I-deadline November 15, notification December 15. Round II-deadline January 15, notification February 15.

STUDENT LIFE. Housing: Dormitories (women). Housing guaranteed for all 4 years. Kosher Hallal kitchen available. **Activities:** Student government, magazine, radio, student newspaper, yearbook, choral groups, dance, drama, jazz band, music ensembles, musical theater, symphony orchestra, handbell choir, Association of Pan-African Unity, Asian Student Association, La Unidad, Baha'i Association, Jewish Student Union, Korean Student Association, Newman Club, Islamic Cultural Alliance, International Club, Amnesty International, Cambodian Tutoring Program, Mosaic. **Additional information:** Free bus service connects students with neighboring Amherst College, Hampshire College, Smith College, and University of Massachusetts at Amherst.

ATHLETICS. NCAA. **Intercollegiate:** Basketball, cross-country, diving, field hockey, golf, horseback riding, lacrosse, rowing (crew), soccer, softball, squash, swimming, tennis, track and field, volleyball. **Intramural:** Badminton, basketball, fencing, horseback riding, racquetball, rugby, skiing, soccer, softball, squash, swimming, tennis, volleyball, water polo.

STUDENT SERVICES. Aptitude testing, career counseling, employment service for undergraduates, freshman orientation, health services, personal counseling, placement service for graduates, special adviser for adult students, deans of first year students, international affairs, and third world affairs, Protestant, Catholic, Jewish Chaplains; student advisers, services/facilities for handicapped.

ANNUAL EXPENSES. Tuition and fees: $18,110. **Room and board:** $5,520. **Books and supplies:** $700. **Other expenses:** $700.

FINANCIAL AID. 64% of freshmen, 65% of continuing students receive some form of aid. 95% of grants, all loans, 77% of jobs based on need. 320 enrolled freshmen were judged to have need, all were offered aid. **Aid applications:** Closing date February 1; applicants notified on or about April 1; must reply by May 1. **Additional information:** Parent loan plans available includes SHARE and Massachusetts Family Education loan.

ADDRESS/TELEPHONE. Anita Smith, Director of Admissions, Mount Holyoke College, College Street, South Hadley, MA 01075-1488. (413) 538-2023. Fax: (413) 538-2409.

Mount Ida College
Newton Centre, Massachusetts — CB code: 3530

4-year private college of arts and sciences, coed. Founded in 1899. **Accreditation:** Regional. **Undergraduate enrollment:** 742 men, 907 women full time; 135 men, 165 women part time. **Faculty:** 182 total (66 full time), 40 with doctorates or other terminal degrees. **Location:** Suburban campus in small city; 8 miles from Boston. **Calendar:** Semester, limited summer session. **Microcomputers:** 50 located in classrooms, computer centers. **Special facilities:** Communications laboratory, darkroom, blueprint making facility, veterinary kennel and operating facility, technical electricity laboratory, radio station, TV laboratory. **Additional facts:** Freshmen and sophomores enroll in junior college division. Students may apply to senior college division upon completion of associate degree. Both divisions on same campus.

DEGREES OFFERED. AS, AAS, BA, BS. 425 associate degrees awarded in 1992. 17% in business and management, 21% allied health, 12% life sciences, 17% trade and industry, 21% visual and performing arts. 100 bachelor's degrees awarded. 23% in business and management, 31% allied health, 5% life sciences, 41% visual and performing arts.

UNDERGRADUATE MAJORS. Associate: Accounting, advertising, allied health, animal sciences, apparel and accessories marketing, biological laboratory technology, biology, business administration and management, business and management, business and office, business computer/console/peripheral equipment operation, business data processing and related programs, business data programming, child development/care/guidance, commercial art, communications, computer and information sciences, criminal justice studies, dental assistant, early childhood education, education, electrical and electronics equipment repair, electrical installation, electrical technology, elementary education, equestrian science, fashion design, fashion merchandising, finance, funeral services/mortuary science, graphic arts technology, graphic design, health sciences, hotel/motel and restaurant management, illustration design, information sciences and systems, institutional management, interior design, journalism, legal assistant/paralegal, liberal/general studies, management information systems, marketing and distribution, marketing management, marketing research, medical social work, mental health/human services, occupational therapy assistant, physical education, preengineering, radio/television broadcasting, recreation and community services technologies, retailing, science technologies, social work, teacher aide, textiles and clothing, tourism, transportation and travel marketing, veterinarian's assistant. **Bachelor's:** Animal sciences, business administration and management, business and management, business and office, communications, education, elementary education, fashion design, fashion merchandising, graphic design, hotel/motel and restaurant management, illustration design, institutional management, journalism, legal assistant/paralegal, liberal/general studies, mental health/human services, retailing, veterinarian's assistant.

ACADEMIC PROGRAMS. 2-year transfer program, independent study, internships, student-designed major, study abroad, teacher preparation, affiliation with Tufts Veterinary School and Tufts University School of Dental Medicine. **Remedial services:** Learning center, reduced course load, remedial instruction, special counselor, tutoring, writing skills laboratory, mini courses in study skills. **Placement/credit:** AP, CLEP General and Subject, institutional tests; 12 credit hours maximum for bachelor's degree.

ACADEMIC REQUIREMENTS. No policy requiring minimum GPA; records of students having academic difficulty are reviewed individually. 60% of freshmen return for sophomore year. Students must declare major on application. **Graduation requirements:** 60 hours for associate, 120 hours for bachelor's. Most students required to take courses in English, mathematics, social sciences. **Postgraduate studies:** 50% from 2-year programs enter 4-year programs. **Additional information:** Career focused courses of study offered.

FRESHMAN ADMISSIONS. Selection criteria: Open admissions. Special requirements for science applicants and students interested in the Learning Opportunities Program. Minimum 2.0 GPA required for admission into all bachelor's degree programs, except interior design which requires 2.5 GPA. Veterinary science students must have some science background. Prefer art students to have art background. **High school preparation:** 16 units recommended. Recommended units include English 4, mathematics 4, social science 4 and science 4. 2 units of mathematics and 2 units of physical science recommended for science majors. **Additional information:** Different admissions criteria for different programs.

1992 FRESHMAN CLASS PROFILE. 378 men, 462 women enrolled. 12% had high school GPA of 3.0 or higher, 75% between 2.0 and 2.99. **Characteristics:** 60% from in state, 52% live in college housing, 28% have minority backgrounds. Average age is 19.

FALL-TERM APPLICATIONS. $25 fee, may be waived for applicants with need. No closing date; applicants notified on a rolling basis; must reply within 30 days. Interview recommended. Portfolio recommended for art, interior design, fashion illustration applicants. Essay recommended. Deferred admission available. If submitted, SAT/ACT used for placement and counseling.

STUDENT LIFE. Housing: Dormitories (men, women, coed); cooperative housing available. **Activities:** Student government, radio, student newspaper, yearbook, choral groups, fraternities, sororities, Foreign Students Club, veterinary technology club, multicultural club, judicial board.

ATHLETICS. NJCAA. **Intercollegiate:** Basketball M, horseback riding, lacrosse M, soccer, softball W, volleyball W. **Intramural:** Badminton, basketball, lacrosse M, rugby M, soccer, softball, tennis, volleyball.

STUDENT SERVICES. Aptitude testing, career counseling, employment service for undergraduates, freshman orientation, health services, personal counseling, placement service for graduates, special adviser for adult students, Structured program for learning disabled students, services/facilities for handicapped.

ANNUAL EXPENSES. Tuition and fees: $10,025. **Room and board:** $6,890. **Books and supplies:** $715. **Other expenses:** $525.

FINANCIAL AID. 52% of continuing students receive some form of aid. All grants, 75% of loans, 97% of jobs based on need. **Aid applications:** No closing date; priority given to applications received by May 1; applicants notified on a rolling basis beginning on or about March 1.

ADDRESS/TELEPHONE. Harold Durall, Director of Admission, Mount Ida College, 777 Dedham Street, Newton Centre, MA 02159. (800) 969-7000 ext. 135. (800) 769-7001. Fax: (617) 969-6993.

Mount Wachusett Community College

Gardner, Massachusetts — CB code: 3545

2-year public community college, coed. Founded in 1963. **Accreditation:** Regional. **Undergraduate enrollment:** 2,200 men and women. **Faculty:** 120 total (85 full time), 40 with doctorates or other terminal degrees. **Location:** Rural campus in large town; 50 miles from Boston. **Calendar:** Semester, extensive summer session. **Microcomputers:** 120 located in classrooms, computer centers. **Special facilities:** Modern theater, physical education plant.

DEGREES OFFERED. AA, AS. 535 associate degrees awarded in 1992.

UNDERGRADUATE MAJORS. Accounting, automotive mechanics, automotive technology, business administration and management, business and management, business and office, business data processing and related programs, business data programming, child development/care/guidance, computer programming, electronic technology, fine arts, information sciences and systems, law enforcement and corrections technologies, liberal/general studies, marketing and distribution, marketing management, medical laboratory technologies, nursing, radio/television broadcasting, radio/television technology, science technologies, secretarial and related programs, small business management and ownership, word processing.

ACADEMIC PROGRAMS. 2-year transfer program, cooperative education, dual enrollment of high school students, honors program, internships. **Remedial services:** Learning center, preadmission summer program, remedial instruction, tutoring. **ROTC:** Army. **Placement/credit:** AP, CLEP General and Subject, institutional tests; 24 credit hours maximum for associate degree.

ACADEMIC REQUIREMENTS. Freshmen must earn minimum GPA of 1.7 to continue in good standing. 57% of freshmen return for sophomore year. Students must declare major on enrollment. **Graduation requirements:** 60 hours for associate. Most students required to take courses in English, history, humanities, mathematics, biological/physical sciences, social sciences.

FRESHMAN ADMISSIONS. Selection criteria: Open admissions. Recommendations required for nursing program. Recommended units include biological science 1, English 4 and mathematics 2.

1992 FRESHMAN CLASS PROFILE. 1,200 men and women enrolled. **Characteristics:** 95% from in state, 100% commute, 4% have minority backgrounds, 1% are foreign students. Average age is 23.

FALL-TERM APPLICATIONS. $10 fee, may be waived for applicants with need. $35 fee for out-of-state applicants. Closing date September 5; applicants notified on a rolling basis. Interview recommended. CRDA. Early admission available. Nursing applicants must apply by March 1.

STUDENT LIFE. Activities: Student government, film, radio, student newspaper, television, yearbook, choral groups, drama, musical theater, Newman Club.

ATHLETICS. NJCAA. **Intercollegiate:** Baseball M, basketball, soccer M, softball W, tennis. **Intramural:** Baseball M, basketball, cross-country, golf, racquetball, skiing, soccer, softball, squash, swimming, tennis, volleyball.

STUDENT SERVICES. Career counseling, employment service for undergraduates, freshman orientation, health services, on-campus day care, personal counseling, placement service for graduates, special adviser for adult students, veterans counselor, services/facilities for handicapped.

ANNUAL EXPENSES. Tuition and fees (1992-93): $2,190, $3,822 additional for out-of-state students. **Books and supplies:** $500. **Other expenses:** $1,165.

FINANCIAL AID. 63% of freshmen, 60% of continuing students receive some form of aid. 99% of grants, 85% of loans, 97% of jobs based on need. 850 enrolled freshmen were judged to have need, 750 were offered aid. **Aid applications:** No closing date; applicants notified on a rolling basis beginning on or about July 1; must reply within 4 weeks.

ADDRESS/TELEPHONE. Sidney Goldfader, Director of Admissions, Mount Wachusett Community College, 444 Green Street, Gardner, MA 01440. (508) 632-6600. Fax: (508) 632-1210.

New England Banking Institute

Boston, Massachusetts — CB code: 3376

2-year private business college, coed. Founded in 1909. **Accreditation:** Regional. **Undergraduate enrollment:** 316 men, 847 women part time. **Faculty:** 202 total (2 full time), 17 with doctorates or other terminal degrees. **Location:** Urban campus in very large city; in downtown area. **Calendar:** Semester, limited summer session. Saturday and extensive evening/early morning classes. **Microcomputers:** 24 located in computer centers. **Additional facts:** Access to libraries in major Boston banks and local colleges and universities. 75% of faculty come from banking industry.

DEGREES OFFERED. AS. 23 associate degrees awarded in 1992. 100% in business and management.

UNDERGRADUATE MAJORS. Accounting, business administration and management, computer and information sciences, finance, management information systems, marketing management.

ACADEMIC PROGRAMS. Accelerated program, dual enrollment of high school students. **Remedial services:** Remedial instruction, tutoring. **Placement/credit:** AP, CLEP General and Subject; 9 credit hours maximum for associate degree.

ACADEMIC REQUIREMENTS. Freshmen must earn minimum GPA of 2.0 to continue in good standing. Students must declare major on application. **Graduation requirements:** 63 hours for associate (21 in major). Most students required to take courses in computer science, English, history, humanities, mathematics, biological/physical sciences, social sciences.

FRESHMAN ADMISSIONS. Selection criteria: Academic background, professional recommendation, demonstrated commitment to program and banking, and interview considered.

1992 FRESHMAN CLASS PROFILE. 460 men and women enrolled.

FALL-TERM APPLICATIONS. No fee. No closing date; applicants notified on a rolling basis; must reply within 20 days. Interview required.

STUDENT LIFE. Activities: Film, magazine.

STUDENT SERVICES. Personal counseling, services/facilities for handicapped.

ANNUAL EXPENSES. Tuition and fees (1992-93): $1,782. Per-credit-hour charges: $99/hour member, $145/hour nonmember. **Books and supplies:** $300.

FINANCIAL AID. Additional information: No college-administered financial aid. 90% of students receive tuition reimbursement from employer.

ADDRESS/TELEPHONE. Lynn C. Fitzgerald, Associate Dean of Administration, New England Banking Institute, One Lincoln Plaza, Boston, MA 02111. (617) 951-2350. Fax: (617) 951-2533.

New England Conservatory of Music
Boston, Massachusetts CB code: 3659

4-year private music college, coed. Founded in 1867. **Accreditation:** Regional. **Undergraduate enrollment:** 373 men and women. **Graduate enrollment:** 363 men and women. **Faculty:** 178 total (55 full time), 10 with doctorates or other terminal degrees. **Location:** Urban campus in very large city; 2 miles from downtown. **Calendar:** Semester, limited summer session. **Microcomputers:** Located in libraries. **Special facilities:** Listening library of 18,000 recordings. **Additional facts:** In close proximity to Symphony Hall. Faculty includes members of the Boston Symphony Orchestra.

DEGREES OFFERED. B, M, D. 80 bachelor's degrees awarded in 1992. 100% in visual and performing arts. Graduate degrees offered in 6 major fields of study.

UNDERGRADUATE MAJORS. Jazz, music, music history and appreciation, music performance, music theory and composition.

ACADEMIC PROGRAMS. Double major, honors program, independent study, internships, teacher preparation, cross-registration, artists' diploma (professional degree) offered, 5-year double degree program with Tufts. **Remedial services:** Tutoring, remedial music theory for graduate students. **Placement/credit:** AP, CLEP General and Subject, institutional tests; 12 credit hours maximum for bachelor's degree.

ACADEMIC REQUIREMENTS. Freshmen must earn minimum GPA of 2.0 to continue in good standing. 90% of freshmen return for sophomore year. Students must declare major on application. **Graduation requirements:** 120 hours for bachelor's (32 in major). Most students required to take courses in English, history, humanities.

FRESHMAN ADMISSIONS. Selection criteria: Audition, school record, recommendations, SAT or ACT scores, in that order. **Test requirements:** SAT or ACT; score report by March 1. **Additional information:** Accepted students permitted to postpone admission one-half year.

1992 FRESHMAN CLASS PROFILE. 74 women enrolled. **Characteristics:** 30% from in state, 95% live in college housing, 8% have minority backgrounds, 10% are foreign students. Average age is 18.

FALL-TERM APPLICATIONS. $60 fee, may be waived for applicants with need. Closing date January 15; applicants notified on or about April 1; must reply by May 1 or within 4 weeks if notified thereafter. Audition required. Essay required. CRDA. Deferred admission available.

STUDENT LIFE. Housing: Dormitories (coed). **Activities:** Student government, choral groups, concert band, jazz band, music ensembles, opera, symphony orchestra, chamber music ensembles, fraternities, Christian Fellowship, feminist and minority student organizations. **Additional information:** Students participate in student government and professional fraternities.

STUDENT SERVICES. Career counseling, employment service for undergraduates, freshman orientation, health services, personal counseling, placement service for graduates, services/facilities for handicapped.

ANNUAL EXPENSES. Tuition and fees: $15,290. **Room and board:** $6,990. **Books and supplies:** $400. **Other expenses:** $1,350.

FINANCIAL AID. 70% of freshmen, 70% of continuing students receive some form of aid. All grants, 81% of loans, 70% of jobs based on need. Music/drama scholarships available. **Aid applications:** No closing date; priority given to applications received by January 15; applicants notified on a rolling basis beginning on or about April 1; must reply by May 1 or within 4 weeks if notified thereafter.

ADDRESS/TELEPHONE. Robert L. Annis, Dean of Enrollment Services, New England Conservatory of Music, 290 Huntington Avenue, Boston, MA 02115. (617) 262-1120 ext. 430. Fax: (617) 262-0500.

Newbury College
Brookline, Massachusetts CB code: 3639

2-year private junior college, coed. Founded in 1962. **Accreditation:** Regional. **Undergraduate enrollment:** 476 men, 460 women full time; 966 men, 3,518 women part time. **Faculty:** 369 total (47 full time), 54 with doctorates or other terminal degrees. **Location:** Suburban campus in small city; 4 miles from downtown Boston. **Calendar:** Semester, extensive summer session. Saturday and extensive evening/early morning classes. **Microcomputers:** 40 located in computer centers. **Special facilities:** 7 culinary arts production kitchens, computerized airline reservations system. **Additional facts:** A.A.S. Degree programs offered at 12 off-campus sites throughout eastern Massachusetts, in addition to the main campus.

DEGREES OFFERED. AAS. 767 associate degrees awarded in 1992. 6% in architecture and environmental design, 52% business and management, 15% business/office and marketing/distribution, 8% allied health, 15% home economics.

UNDERGRADUATE MAJORS. Accounting, business administration and management, business and management, computer and information sciences, educational media technology, fashion design, fashion merchandising, finance, food management, food production/management/services, hotel/motel and restaurant management, interior design, legal assistant/paralegal, marketing and distribution, media management, media technology, ophthalmic services, physical therapy assistant, radio/television broadcasting, radio/television technology, respiratory therapy, retailing, tourism.

ACADEMIC PROGRAMS. 2-year transfer program, double major, internships, weekend college. **Remedial services:** Learning center, remedial instruction, special counselor, tutoring. **Placement/credit:** CLEP Subject, institutional tests; 30 credit hours maximum for associate degree.

ACADEMIC REQUIREMENTS. Freshmen must earn minimum GPA of 1.50 to continue in good standing. 70% of freshmen return for sophomore year. Students must declare major on enrollment. **Graduation requirements:** 60 hours for associate (24 in major). Most students required to take courses in computer science, English, humanities, mathematics, social sciences.

FRESHMAN ADMISSIONS. Selection criteria: High school GPA important. Interviews also important. In some cases, recommendations considered.

1992 FRESHMAN CLASS PROFILE. 868 men, 2,303 women enrolled. 23% had high school GPA of 3.0 or higher, 75% between 2.0 and 2.99. **Academic background:** Mid 50% of enrolled freshmen had SAT-V between 380-440, SAT-M between 390-420. 60% submitted SAT scores. **Characteristics:** 80% from in state, 80% commute, 25% have minority backgrounds, 4% are foreign students. Average age is 19.

FALL-TERM APPLICATIONS. $30 fee, may be waived for applicants with need. No closing date; priority given to applications received by May 1; applicants notified on a rolling basis. Interview recommended. Deferred admission available.

STUDENT LIFE. Housing: Dormitories (men, women, coed). **Activities:** Student government, radio, student newspaper, television, yearbook, drama, international student club, culinary club, DECA drama club.

ATHLETICS. NJCAA. **Intercollegiate:** Baseball M, basketball, soccer, softball W. **Intramural:** Badminton W, basketball, ice hockey M, softball, volleyball.

STUDENT SERVICES. Aptitude testing, career counseling, employment service for undergraduates, freshman orientation, personal counseling, placement service for graduates, veterans counselor, services/facilities for handicapped.

ANNUAL EXPENSES. Tuition and fees (1992-93): $9,350. **Room and board:** $5,600. **Books and supplies:** $350. **Other expenses:** $425.

FINANCIAL AID. 60% of freshmen, 53% of continuing students receive some form of aid. 75% of grants, 88% of loans, all jobs based on need. 216 enrolled freshmen were judged to have need, all were offered aid. **Aid applications:** No closing date; priority given to applications received by August 1; applicants notified on a rolling basis beginning on or about March 15; must reply within 2 weeks.

ADDRESS/TELEPHONE. Dr. David Costello, Dean of Enrollment Planning, Newbury College, 129 Fisher Avenue, Brookline, MA 02146. (617) 730-7007. Fax: (617) 731-9618.

Nichols College
Dudley, Massachusetts CB code: 3666

4-year private business, liberal arts college, coed. Founded in 1931. **Accreditation:** Regional. **Undergraduate enrollment:** 462 men, 260 women full time; 266 men, 469 women part time. **Graduate enrollment:** 237 men, 171 women part time. **Faculty:** 50 total (35 full time), 29 with doctorates or other terminal degrees. **Location:** Rural campus in small town; 50 miles from Boston, 20 miles from Worcester. **Calendar:** Semester, limited summer session.

Microcomputers: 850 located in dormitories, libraries, classrooms, computer centers, campus-wide network. Lease or purchase required**Additional facts:** Institute of American Values program of business, economics, and public policy seminars includes experts from private and public sectors.

DEGREES OFFERED. AS, BA, BS, MBA. 13 associate degrees awarded in 1992. 100% in business and management. 204 bachelor's degrees awarded. 70% in business and management, 15% business/office and marketing/distribution, 7% computer sciences, 5% psychology. Graduate degrees offered in 2 major fields of study.

UNDERGRADUATE MAJORS. Associate: Business and management. **Bachelor's:** Accounting, business administration and management, business and management, business economics, economics, finance, history, human resources development, industrial and organizational psychology, information sciences and systems, investments and securities, management information systems, marketing and distribution, marketing management, psychology, public administration, real estate, social work, sociology.

ACADEMIC PROGRAMS. Double major, honors program, independent study, internships, study abroad, Washington semester. **Remedial services:** Reduced course load, tutoring. **ROTC:** Army. **Placement/credit:** AP, CLEP General and Subject; 30 credit hours maximum for bachelor's degree.

ACADEMIC REQUIREMENTS. Freshmen must earn minimum GPA of 1.65 to continue in good standing. Students must declare major by end of second year. **Graduation requirements:** 61 hours for associate (12 in major), 122 hours for bachelor's (21 in major). Most students required to take courses in English, history, mathematics, biological/physical sciences, social sciences.

FRESHMAN ADMISSIONS. Selection criteria: Minimum 2.0 GPA in academic subjects important. SAT or ACT scores required. **High school preparation:** 16 units required. Required units include English 4, mathematics 3, social science 2 and science 2. **Test requirements:** SAT or ACT (SAT preferred); score report by August 15.

1992 FRESHMAN CLASS PROFILE. 497 men applied, 444 accepted, 119 enrolled; 208 women applied, 190 accepted, 68 enrolled. **Characteristics:** 64% from in state, 80% live in college housing, 5% have minority backgrounds, 1% are foreign students. Average age is 18.

FALL-TERM APPLICATIONS. $25 fee, may be waived for applicants with need. No closing date; applicants notified on a rolling basis; must reply by May 1 or within 3 weeks if notified thereafter. Interview recommended. CRDA. Deferred and early admission available. EDP-F.

STUDENT LIFE. Housing: Dormitories (men, women). Substance-free housing available. **Activities:** Student government, radio, student newspaper, yearbook, drama.

ATHLETICS. NCAA. **Intercollegiate:** Baseball M, basketball, field hockey W, football M, golf, ice hockey M, lacrosse M, soccer, softball W, tennis, track and field. **Intramural:** Basketball, football M, horseback riding, rowing (crew) M, rugby M, sailing, skiing, soccer W, softball M, swimming, table tennis, volleyball.

STUDENT SERVICES. Aptitude testing, career counseling, freshman orientation, health services, personal counseling, placement service for graduates, services/facilities for handicapped.

ANNUAL EXPENSES. Tuition and fees: $9,040. **Room and board:** $5,160. **Books and supplies:** $500. **Other expenses:** $650.

FINANCIAL AID. 80% of freshmen, 70% of continuing students receive some form of aid. 91% of grants, 59% of loans, all jobs based on need. Academic, leadership, alumni affiliation scholarships available. **Aid applications:** No closing date; priority given to applications received by April 1; applicants notified on a rolling basis beginning on or about March 1; must reply by May 1 or within 2 weeks if notified thereafter. **Additional information:** Tuition plus 41/2% at time of first enrollment guarantees rate for 4 years.

ADDRESS/TELEPHONE. Charlene Lowell Nemeth, Director of Admissions and Financial Aid, Nichols College, PO Box 5000, Dudley, MA 01570-5000. (617) 943-2055. Fax: (508) 943-1560 ext. 102.

North Adams State College
North Adams, Massachusetts — CB code: 3521

4-year public business, liberal arts college, coed. Founded in 1894. **Accreditation:** Regional. **Undergraduate enrollment:** 756 men, 836 women full time; 49 men, 53 women part time. **Faculty:** 127 total (104 full time), 70 with doctorates or other terminal degrees. **Location:** Rural campus in large town; 50 miles from Albany, New York, 120 miles from Boston. **Calendar:** 4-1-4, limited summer session. **Microcomputers:** 60 located in computer centers.

DEGREES OFFERED. BA, BS, MEd. 400 bachelor's degrees awarded in 1992. Graduate degrees offered in 2 major fields of study.

UNDERGRADUATE MAJORS. Accounting, anthropology, biological and physical sciences, biology, business administration and management, business and management, chemistry, clinical laboratory science, communications, computer and information sciences, computer programming, creative writing, early childhood education, economics, education, elementary education, English, English literature, finance, history, humanities and social sciences, information sciences and systems, journalism, junior high education, liberal/general studies, management science, marketing management, mathematics, medical laboratory technologies, philosophy, physics, political science and government, prelaw, psychology, public relations, radio/television broadcasting, secondary education, sociology, sports medicine.

ACADEMIC PROGRAMS. Accelerated program, double major, independent study, internships, student-designed major, study abroad, teacher preparation, cross-registration. **Remedial services:** Learning center, preadmission summer program, reduced course load, remedial instruction, special counselor, tutoring. **Placement/credit:** AP, CLEP General and Subject, institutional tests.

ACADEMIC REQUIREMENTS. Freshmen must earn minimum GPA of 1.5 to continue in good standing. 70% of freshmen return for sophomore year. Students must declare major by end of second year. **Graduation requirements:** 122 hours for bachelor's. Most students required to take courses in English, history, mathematics, philosophy/religion, biological/physical sciences, social sciences.

FRESHMAN ADMISSIONS. Selection criteria: High school transcript, test scores, recommendations, awards considered. **High school preparation:** 16 units required. Required units include English 4, foreign language 2, mathematics 3, social science 2 and science 2. **Test requirements:** SAT; score report by April 1.

1992 FRESHMAN CLASS PROFILE. 98 men, 106 women enrolled. 32% had high school GPA of 3.0 or higher, 68% between 2.0 and 2.99. 5% were in top tenth and 28% were in top quarter of graduating class. **Academic background:** Mid 50% of enrolled freshmen had SAT-V between 400-500, SAT-M between 400-500. 99% submitted SAT scores. **Characteristics:** 95% from in state, 95% live in college housing, 3% have minority backgrounds, 1% are foreign students. Average age is 18.

FALL-TERM APPLICATIONS. $10 fee, may be waived for applicants with need. Closing date June 1; priority given to applications received by April 1; applicants notified on a rolling basis beginning on or about January 1; must reply by May 1 or within 4 weeks if notified thereafter. CRDA. Deferred admission available.

STUDENT LIFE. Housing: Dormitories (coed); apartment, handicapped housing available. **Activities:** Student government, film, magazine, radio, student newspaper, television, yearbook, choral groups, concert band, dance, drama, jazz band, musical theater, fraternities, sororities, interfaith association, Campus Christian Fellowship, Jewish Student Organization, Newman Club, Gay and Lesbian Allied Student Society, Multicultural Society.

ATHLETICS. NAIA, NCAA. **Intercollegiate:** Baseball M, basketball, cross-country, ice hockey M, lacrosse M, soccer, softball W, tennis, volleyball W. **Intramural:** Badminton, basketball, golf M, ice hockey M, racquetball, rugby M, soccer, softball, squash, swimming, table tennis, tennis, volleyball, water polo.

STUDENT SERVICES. Aptitude testing, career counseling, employment service for undergraduates, freshman orientation, health services, on-campus day care, personal counseling, placement service for graduates, special adviser for adult students, veterans counselor, services/facilities for handicapped.

ANNUAL EXPENSES. Tuition and fees (1992-93): $3,361, $3,279 additional for out-of-state students. **Room and board:** $3,920. **Books and supplies:** $500. **Other expenses:** $1,150.

FINANCIAL AID. 36% of freshmen, 50% of continuing students receive some form of aid. 99% of grants, 62% of loans, 51% of jobs based on need. 230 enrolled freshmen were judged to have need, 218 were offered aid. **Aid applications:** No closing date; priority given to applications received by May 1; applicants notified on a rolling basis beginning on or about May 1; must reply within 2 weeks.

ADDRESS/TELEPHONE. Gerald F. Desmarais, Director of Admissions, North Adams State College, Church Street, North Adams, MA 01247. (413) 664-4511. (800) 292-6632. Fax: (413) 663-3033.

North Shore Community College
Danvers, Massachusetts — CB code: 3651

2-year public community college, coed. Founded in 1965. **Accreditation:** Regional. **Undergraduate enrollment:** 831 men, 1,093 women full time; 1,530 men, 2,853 women part time. **Faculty:** 348 total (122 full time), 20 with doctorates or other terminal degrees. **Location:** Suburban campus in large town; 25 miles from Boston. **Calendar:** Semester, limited summer session. Saturday and extensive evening/early morning classes. **Microcomputers:** 100 located in classrooms, computer centers.

DEGREES OFFERED. AA, AS, AAS. 679 associate degrees awarded in 1992.

UNDERGRADUATE MAJORS. Accounting, air traffic control, airline piloting and navigation, business administration and management, business and office, business data processing and related programs, business data programming, computer and information sciences, computer programming, criminal justice studies, drafting and design technology, early childhood education, electronic technology, engineering, engineering and engineering-related technologies, fire control and safety technology, gerontology, industrial technology, information sciences and systems, legal assistant/paralegal, legal secretary, liberal/general studies, manufacturing technology, marketing and distribution, marketing management, medical secretary, mental health/

human services, microcomputer software, nursing, occupational therapy assistant, office supervision and management, physical therapy assistant, radiograph medical technology, real estate, respiratory therapy, secretarial and related programs, word processing.

ACADEMIC PROGRAMS. 2-year transfer program, accelerated program, dual enrollment of high school students, honors program, independent study, internships, study abroad, telecourses, cross-registration. **Remedial services:** Learning center, remedial instruction, special counselor, tutoring, motivation to Education Program (1-semester core program for handicapped, minority, low-income, or non-English speaking students); ESL Program. **Placement/credit:** CLEP General and Subject, institutional tests; 30 credit hours maximum for associate degree.

ACADEMIC REQUIREMENTS. Freshmen must earn minimum GPA of 2.0 to continue in good standing. 65% of freshmen return for sophomore year. Students must declare major on application. **Graduation requirements:** 60 hours for associate. Most students required to take courses in computer science, English, humanities, mathematics, biological/physical sciences, social sciences. **Additional information:** Massachusetts Transfer Compact facilitates transfer process for graduates who wish to enter 4-year programs at state colleges. Numerous 2+2 agreements with area colleges.

FRESHMAN ADMISSIONS. Selection criteria: Open admissions. School achievement record considered for health, engineering, and computer programs, and some prerequisite course requirements exist. Interviews are required in some health and human service programs. One algebra, 1 biology, and 1 chemistry required for some health programs and for biotechnology. Trigonometry, physics, and chemistry required for engineering. **Test requirements:** Psychological Corporation Pre-Nursing Examination required for nursing applicants.

1992 FRESHMAN CLASS PROFILE. 375 men, 557 women enrolled. **Characteristics:** 99% from in state, 100% commute, 11% have minority backgrounds. Average age is 24.

FALL-TERM APPLICATIONS. No fee. No closing date; applicants notified on a rolling basis beginning on or about February 1. Interview required for health and human service applicants. Early admission available. Applications, with required documents, reviewed on a first-come, first-served basis.

STUDENT LIFE. Activities: Student government, student newspaper, drama, musical theater, Community Service Committee, Haitian Club, African Club.

ATHLETICS. NJCAA. **Intercollegiate:** Baseball M, basketball M, softball W. **Intramural:** Basketball, golf, softball, table tennis, volleyball.

STUDENT SERVICES. Career counseling, employment service for undergraduates, freshman orientation, health services, on-campus day care, personal counseling, placement service for graduates, services/facilities for handicapped.

ANNUAL EXPENSES. Tuition and fees (1992-93): $2,044, $3,822 additional for out-of-state students. **Books and supplies:** $600. **Other expenses:** $1,056.

FINANCIAL AID. 30% of freshmen, 30% of continuing students receive some form of aid. 98% of grants, 90% of loans, all jobs based on need. **Aid applications:** No closing date; priority given to applications received by March 1; applicants notified on a rolling basis beginning on or about July 1; must reply within 2 weeks.

ADDRESS/TELEPHONE. Dr. Cheryl Finkelstein, Assistant Dean of Enrollment Management, North Shore Community College, 1 Ferncroft Road, Danvers, MA 01923. (508) 762-4000 ext. 5484. Fax: (508) 921-4496.

Northeastern University
Boston, Massachusetts — CB code: 3667

Admissions:	74% of applicants accepted
Based on:	••• School record
	•• Recommendations, special talents, test scores
	• Activities, essay, interview
Completion:	80% of freshmen end year in good standing
	46% graduate

5-year private university, coed. Founded in 1898. **Accreditation:** Regional. **Undergraduate enrollment:** 7,029 men, 4,719 women full time; 4,985 men, 5,550 women part time. **Graduate enrollment:** 1,542 men, 1,311 women full time; 1,437 men, 1,046 women part time. **Faculty:** 2,205 total (797 full time), 645 with doctorates or other terminal degrees. **Location:** Urban campus in very large city; in downtown area. **Calendar:** Quarter, extensive summer session. Saturday and extensive evening/early morning classes. **Microcomputers:** 500 located in dormitories, libraries, computer centers. **Special facilities:** Marine Science Center, African American Institute, Barnett Institute of Chemical Analysis and Materials, cardiovascular health and exercise center, Center for Electromagnetic Research, thinking machine in computer science. **Additional facts:** 8 undergraduate colleges, 9 graduate and professional schools, several suburban campuses, and an extensive research division.

DEGREES OFFERED. AS, BA, BS, MA, MS, MBA, MEd, PhD, EdD, B. Pharm, Pharm D, JD. 338 associate degrees awarded in 1992. 63% in business and management, 12% engineering technologies, 21% allied health. 2,979 bachelor's degrees awarded. 32% in business and management, 7% communications, 14% engineering, 5% engineering technologies, 6% health sciences, 6% parks/recreation, protective services, public affairs, 9% social sciences. Graduate degrees offered in 55 major fields of study.

UNDERGRADUATE MAJORS. Associate: Accounting, architectural technologies, biotechnology, business administration and management, clinical laboratory science, computer technology, contract management and procurement/purchasing, criminal justice studies, electrical technology, emergency medical technologies, energy systems program, environmental engineering technology, finance, hotel/motel and restaurant management, human resources development, liberal/general studies, management information systems, marketing management, mechanical design technology, medical laboratory technologies, medical records technology, radiograph medical technology, real estate, recreation therapy, survey and mapping technology, surveying and highway engineering technology, transportation management. **Bachelor's:** Accounting, aerospace/aeronautical/astronautical engineering, Afro-American (black) studies, American sign language-English interpretating, anthropology, athletic training, biochemistry, biology, biotechnology, business administration and management, business and management, chemical engineering, chemistry, civil engineering, clinical exercise physiology, clinical laboratory science, communications, computer and information sciences, computer engineering, computer technology, criminal justice studies, dramatic arts, early childhood education, economics, education, electrical technology, electrical/electronics/communications engineering, elementary education, engineering, English, entrepreneurship and new venture management, finance, fine arts, French, geology, German, health care administration, history, industrial engineering, insurance and risk management, international business management, Italian, journalism, liberal/general studies, linguistics, management information systems, marketing management, mathematics, mechanical design technology, mechanical engineering, medical laboratory technologies, mental health/human services, music, nursing, pharmacy, philosophy, physical therapy, physics, physiology, political science and government, psychology, psychology: applied behavior analysis, Russian, sociology, Spanish, toxicology, transportation management.

ACADEMIC PROGRAMS. 2-year transfer program, accelerated program, cooperative education, double major, dual enrollment of high school students, honors program, independent study, internships, student-designed major, study abroad, teacher preparation, telecourses, visiting/exchange student program, cross-registration, American Sign Language, marine biology program, international cooperative experience; combined bachelor's/graduate program in business administration, law. **Remedial services:** Learning center, preadmission summer program, reduced course load, remedial instruction, special counselor, tutoring, Alternative Freshman Year Program (self-paced program) in basic skills, Project UJIMA (support program to assist minority students). **ROTC:** Air Force, Army, Naval. **Placement/credit:** AP, CLEP General and Subject, IB, institutional tests.

ACADEMIC REQUIREMENTS. Freshmen must earn minimum GPA of 1.4 to continue in good standing. 70% of freshmen return for sophomore year. Students must declare major by end of first year. **Graduation requirements:** 96 hours for associate, 176 hours for bachelor's. Most students required to take courses in English, mathematics, social sciences. **Additional information:** The Cooperative Plan of Education enables students to alternate periods of work and study while offering an opportunity to gain valuable practical experience. The Cooperative Plan also enables students to contribute to the financing of their education.

FRESHMAN ADMISSIONS. Selection criteria: School achievement, recommendations most important. Applicants should rank in top 40% of class in typical comprehensive high school. School and community activities also considered. **High school preparation:** 17 units recommended. Recommended units include biological science 1, English 4, foreign language 2, mathematics 3, physical science 2 and social science 3. Each college of the university and each major have specific requirements that are not standard for all the colleges. **Test requirements:** SAT or ACT (SAT preferred); score report by May 1.

1992 FRESHMAN CLASS PROFILE. 6,191 men applied, 4,691 accepted, 1,547 enrolled; 4,760 women applied, 3,437 accepted, 961 enrolled. 13% were in top tenth and 38% were in top quarter of graduating class. **Academic background:** Mid 50% of enrolled freshmen had SAT-V between 410-510, SAT-M between 460-570; ACT composite between 19-25. 92% submitted SAT scores, 5% submitted ACT scores. **Characteristics:** 54% from in state, 61% live in college housing, 20% have minority backgrounds, 7% are foreign students. Average age is 19.

FALL-TERM APPLICATIONS. $30 fee. No closing date; priority given to applications received by March 1; applicants notified on a rolling basis; must reply by May 1 or within 4 weeks if notified thereafter. Essay required. Interview recommended. CRDA. Deferred and early admission available.

STUDENT LIFE. Housing: Dormitories (men, women, coed); apartment, fraternity housing available. Honors, engineering, computer science housing, international halls, substance free hall, living-learning center, combines residential experience with freshman academic program. **Activities:** Student government, magazine, radio, student newspaper, yearbook, choral groups, concert band, dance, drama, jazz band, marching band, music ensembles, musical theater, pep band, symphony orchestra, fraternities, sororities, numerous educational, political, social action, religious, and ethnic organizations.

ATHLETICS. NCAA. **Intercollegiate:** Baseball M, basketball, cross-country, diving, field hockey W, football M, golf M, gymnastics W, ice hockey, rowing (crew), soccer M, swimming, tennis M, track and field, volleyball W. **Intramural:** Basketball, ice hockey, racquetball, soccer, softball, tennis, volleyball.

STUDENT SERVICES. Aptitude testing, career counseling, employment service for undergraduates, freshman orientation, health services, on-campus day care, personal counseling, placement service for graduates, special adviser for adult students, veterans counselor, International Student Office (advising, workshops, orientation), services/facilities for handicapped.

ANNUAL EXPENSES. Tuition and fees (projected): $12,359. **Room and board:** $7,155. **Books and supplies:** $600. **Other expenses:** $900.

FINANCIAL AID. 76% of freshmen, 64% of continuing students receive some form of aid. 75% of grants, 99% of loans, all jobs based on need. 1,893 enrolled freshmen were judged to have need, all were offered aid. Academic, athletic scholarships available. **Aid applications:** No closing date; priority given to applications received by March 1; applicants notified on a rolling basis beginning on or about March 20; must reply by May 1 or within 4 weeks if notified thereafter.

ADDRESS/TELEPHONE. Kevin Kelly, Dean and Director of Admissions, Northeastern University, 360 Huntington Avenue, Boston, MA 02115-9959. (617) 373-2200. Fax: (617) 373-8780.

Northern Essex Community College

Haverhill, Massachusetts — CB code: 3674

Admissions: 68% of applicants accepted
Based on:
- ••• School record
- •• Recommendations
- • Essay

Completion: 80% of freshmen end year in good standing
65% graduate, 48% of these enter 4-year programs

2-year public community college, coed. Founded in 1960. **Accreditation:** Regional. **Undergraduate enrollment:** 1,082 men, 1,518 women full time; 1,386 men, 2,623 women part time. **Faculty:** 473 total (130 full time). **Location:** Suburban campus in large town; 40 miles from Boston. **Calendar:** Semester, extensive summer session. Saturday and extensive evening/early morning classes. **Microcomputers:** 225 located in classrooms, computer centers. **Special facilities:** Bentley Library Art Gallery, Top Notch Theater, dance studio, fitness center. **Additional facts:** Other campus in Lawrence.

DEGREES OFFERED. AA, AS. 567 associate degrees awarded in 1992. 17% in business and management, 12% business/office and marketing/distribution, 10% engineering technologies, 8% health sciences, 20% allied health, 5% law, 16% multi/interdisciplinary studies, 5% parks/recreation, protective services, public affairs.

UNDERGRADUATE MAJORS. Accounting, biological and physical sciences, biology, business and management, business and office, business computer/console/peripheral equipment operation, business data processing and related programs, business data programming, business education, chemistry, commercial art, computer and information sciences, computer programming, computer servicing technology, computer technology, contract management and procurement/purchasing, criminal justice studies, dance, dramatic arts, early childhood education, earth sciences, education, electronic technology, engineering and engineering-related technologies, finance, graphic and printing production, history, hotel/motel and restaurant management, illustration design, information sciences and systems, international relations, international studies, interpreter for the deaf, journalism, legal assistant/paralegal, legal secretary, liberal/general studies, machine tool operation/machine shop, marketing management, medical records technology, medical secretary, mental health/human services, music, nursing, office supervision and management, philosophy, physics, political science and government, psychology, radiograph medical technology, respiratory therapy technology, retailing, secretarial and related programs, social sciences, visual and performing arts, women's studies, word processing.

ACADEMIC PROGRAMS. 2-year transfer program, accelerated program, computer delivered (on-line) credit-bearing course offerings, cooperative education, double major, dual enrollment of high school students, internships, study abroad, weekend college, cross-registration, 2-2 Capstone Program (graduates granted junior status at Bradford College, University of Massachusetts Lowell). **Remedial services:** Learning center, preadmission summer program, reduced course load, remedial instruction, special counselor, tutoring. **ROTC:** Air Force. **Placement/credit:** AP, CLEP General and Subject, institutional tests; 36 credit hours maximum for associate degree.

ACADEMIC REQUIREMENTS. Freshmen must earn minimum GPA of 1.5 to continue in good standing. 74% of freshmen return for sophomore year. Students must declare major on application. **Graduation requirements:** 60 hours for associate (20 in major). Most students required to take courses in English. **Additional information:** Freshmen undergo regime of testing, evaluation, and planned course placement.

FRESHMAN ADMISSIONS. Selection criteria: Selective admissions for technology studies (engineering, computer, computer maintenance, electronics) and health and human services. Health and technologies have specific mathematics and/or science requirements. **Test requirements:** Entrance Examination for Schools of Practical/Vocational Nursing required for nursing applicants.

1992 FRESHMAN CLASS PROFILE. 2,871 men and women applied, 1,960 accepted; 665 men enrolled, 992 women enrolled. **Characteristics:** 86% from in state, 100% commute, 24% have minority backgrounds, 1% are foreign students. Average age is 24.

FALL-TERM APPLICATIONS. No fee. Closing date September 1; priority given to applications received by February 1; applicants notified on a rolling basis. Interview required for health and human services applicants. CRDA. Deferred and early admission available. EDP-F.

STUDENT LIFE. Activities: Student government, film, magazine, student newspaper, television, choral groups, dance, drama, American Sign Language Club, Hispanic Cultural Club, Womens' Resource Network, Social Club (students with disabilities), Agape Fellowship (Bible Club).

ATHLETICS. NJCAA. **Intercollegiate:** Baseball M, basketball, golf, soccer M, softball W. **Intramural:** Basketball, cross-country, football M, golf, racquetball, skiing, softball, table tennis, volleyball.

STUDENT SERVICES. Aptitude testing, career counseling, employment service for undergraduates, freshman orientation, health services, on-campus day care, personal counseling, placement service for graduates, special adviser for adult students, veterans counselor, services/facilities for handicapped.

ANNUAL EXPENSES. Tuition and fees (1992-93): $1,813, $3,822 additional for out-of-state students. **Books and supplies:** $500. **Other expenses:** $1,400.

FINANCIAL AID. 50% of freshmen, 50% of continuing students receive some form of aid. All grants, 94% of loans, all jobs based on need. **Aid applications:** No closing date; priority given to applications received by April 1; applicants notified on a rolling basis beginning on or about June 15; must reply within 2 weeks.

ADDRESS/TELEPHONE. Elizabeth Huntley Cole, Director of Admissions, Northern Essex Community College, Elliott Way, Haverhill, MA 01830-2399. (508) 374-3900.

Pine Manor College

Chestnut Hill, Massachusetts — CB code: 3689

Admissions: 85% of applicants accepted
Based on:
- ••• School record
- •• Activities, essay, recommendations, special talents, test scores
- • Interview

Completion: 80% of freshmen end year in good standing
55% graduate, 10% of these enter graduate study

4-year private liberal arts college, women only. Founded in 1911. **Accreditation:** Regional. **Undergraduate enrollment:** 425 women full time; 50 women part time. **Faculty:** 61 total (36 full time), 45 with doctorates or other terminal degrees. **Location:** Suburban campus in small city; 5 miles from Boston. **Calendar:** Semester, limited summer session. **Microcomputers:** 70 located in libraries, classrooms, computer centers. **Special facilities:** Hess Art Gallery, Annenberg Library and Communications Center.

DEGREES OFFERED. AA, AS, BA. 38 associate degrees awarded in 1992. 111 bachelor's degrees awarded. 30% in business and management, 20% communications, 10% teacher education, 8% letters/literature, 13% psychology, 10% social sciences, 5% visual and performing arts.

UNDERGRADUATE MAJORS. Associate: Art history, biology, business administration and management, dramatic arts, English, health sciences, history, liberal/general studies, political science and government, psychology, visual and performing arts. **Bachelor's:** Accounting, American studies, art history, biology, business administration and management, communications, developmental psychology, early childhood education, elementary education, English, English education, French, interior design, international business management, marketing management, psychobiology, psychology, sociology, visual and performing arts.

ACADEMIC PROGRAMS. 2-year transfer program, accelerated program, double major, honors program, independent study, internships, semester at sea, student-designed major, study abroad, teacher preparation, visiting/exchange student program, Washington semester, cross-registration, Marine Studies Consortium. **Remedial services:** Learning center, reduced course load, remedial instruction, special counselor, tutoring. **Placement/credit:** AP, CLEP Subject, institutional tests.

ACADEMIC REQUIREMENTS. Freshmen must earn minimum GPA of 1.8 to continue in good standing. 75% of freshmen return for sophomore year. Students must declare major by end of second year. **Graduation requirements:** 64 hours for associate, 128 hours for bachelor's (48 in major). Most students required to take courses in arts/fine arts, English, humanities, mathematics, biological/physical sciences, social sciences. **Postgraduate**

studies: 3% enter law school, 2% enter MBA programs, 5% enter other graduate study.

FRESHMAN ADMISSIONS. Selection criteria: School achievement record, counselor recommendation, test scores, school and community activities important. Special consideration to children of alumnae. **High school preparation:** 16 units required. Required and recommended units include English 4, mathematics 2 and science 2. Biological science 1, foreign language 2 and social science 2 recommended. **Test requirements:** SAT or ACT; score report by September 1.

1992 FRESHMAN CLASS PROFILE. 386 women applied, 328 accepted, 136 enrolled. 6% had high school GPA of 3.0 or higher, 80% between 2.0 and 2.99. **Characteristics:** 20% from in state, 95% live in college housing, 15% have minority backgrounds, 19% are foreign students. Average age is 18.

FALL-TERM APPLICATIONS. $25 fee, may be waived for applicants with need. No closing date; priority given to applications received by April 1; applicants notified on a rolling basis beginning on or about December 15; must reply by May 1 or within 2 weeks if notified thereafter. Essay required. Interview recommended. Portfolio recommended for art applicants. CRDA. Deferred admission available. EDP-F.

STUDENT LIFE. Housing: Dormitories (women). Students live in 1 of 3 villages each composed of 5 houses surrounding central courtyard. French language house, nonsmoking and quiet dormitories available. **Activities:** Student government, film, magazine, radio, student newspaper, television, yearbook, choral groups, dance, drama, musical theater, black student organization, international club, political clubs, service clubs.

ATHLETICS. NCAA. **Intercollegiate:** Basketball, cross-country, field hockey, lacrosse, soccer, softball, swimming, tennis. **Intramural:** Golf, soccer, softball, tennis, volleyball.

STUDENT SERVICES. Aptitude testing, career counseling, employment service for undergraduates, freshman orientation, health services, on-campus day care, personal counseling, placement service for graduates, special adviser for adult students, services/facilities for handicapped.

ANNUAL EXPENSES. Tuition and fees: $15,865. **Room and board:** $6,460. **Books and supplies:** $500. **Other expenses:** $450.

FINANCIAL AID. 41% of freshmen, 39% of continuing students receive some form of aid. All grants, 87% of loans, all jobs based on need. 64 enrolled freshmen were judged to have need, all were offered aid. **Aid applications:** No closing date; priority given to applications received by March 15; applicants notified on a rolling basis beginning on or about March 15; must reply by May 1 or within 2 weeks if notified thereafter.

ADDRESS/TELEPHONE. Laura McPhie, Director of Admissions, Pine Manor College, 400 Heath Street, Chestnut Hill, MA 02167. (617) 731-7104. (800) 762-1357. Fax: (617) 731-7199.

Quincy College
Quincy, Massachusetts — CB code: 3713

2-year public community college, coed. Founded in 1956. **Accreditation:** Regional. **Undergraduate enrollment:** 1,545 men and women full time; 788 men and women part time. **Faculty:** 107 total (47 full time), 4 with doctorates or other terminal degrees. **Location:** Suburban campus in small city; 10 miles from downtown Boston. **Calendar:** Semester, extensive summer session. Saturday and extensive evening/early morning classes. **Microcomputers:** 60 located in classrooms.

DEGREES OFFERED. AA, AS. 360 associate degrees awarded in 1992. 39% in business and management, 5% teacher education, 24% health sciences, 9% law, 5% letters/literature, 6% multi/interdisciplinary studies.

UNDERGRADUATE MAJORS. Accounting, behavioral sciences, biological and physical sciences, business administration and management, business and management, business and office, communications, computer and information sciences, computer programming, criminal justice studies, data processing, early childhood education, English, history, hotel/motel and restaurant management, humanities and social sciences, journalism, law enforcement and corrections technologies, legal assistant/paralegal, legal secretary, liberal/general studies, marketing and distribution, marketing management, mathematics, medical secretary, nursing, office supervision and management, political science and government, psychology, retailing, secretarial and related programs, social sciences, sociology, tourism.

ACADEMIC PROGRAMS. 2-year transfer program, accelerated program, dual enrollment of high school students, independent study, internships. **Remedial services:** Learning center, preadmission summer program, reduced course load, remedial instruction. **Placement/credit:** AP, CLEP Subject, institutional tests; 30 credit hours maximum for associate degree.

ACADEMIC REQUIREMENTS. 71% of freshmen return for sophomore year. Students must declare major by end of first year. **Graduation requirements:** 60 hours for associate. Most students required to take courses in English, history, humanities, mathematics, biological/physical sciences, social sciences.

FRESHMAN ADMISSIONS. Selection criteria: Open admissions. Selective admission to health careers programs based on test scores and high school record. College-preparatory program with biology and chemistry required for registered nursing program.

1992 FRESHMAN CLASS PROFILE. 1,425 men and women enrolled. **Characteristics:** 100% from in state, 100% commute, 8% have minority backgrounds, 5% are foreign students. Average age is 24.

FALL-TERM APPLICATIONS. $15 fee, may be waived for applicants with need. No closing date; priority given to applications received by May 1; applicants notified on a rolling basis beginning on or about April 1. CRDA. Deferred and early admission available.

STUDENT LIFE. Activities: Student government, student newspaper, yearbook.

STUDENT SERVICES. Aptitude testing, career counseling, employment service for undergraduates, freshman orientation, on-campus day care, personal counseling, placement service for graduates, special adviser for adult students, veterans counselor, services/facilities for handicapped.

ANNUAL EXPENSES. Tuition and fees (1992-93): $1,880. Tuition $2,500 for computer science, $3,400 for allied health programs. **Books and supplies:** $400. **Other expenses:** $400.

FINANCIAL AID. 75% of freshmen, 75% of continuing students receive some form of aid. 99% of grants, 84% of loans, all jobs based on need. **Aid applications:** Closing date June 15; priority given to applications received by May 1; applicants notified on a rolling basis beginning on or about May 1; must reply within 2 weeks.

ADDRESS/TELEPHONE. Lori Tomassetti, Director of Admissions, Quincy College, 34 Coddington Street, Quincy, MA 02169. (617) 984-1700. Fax: (617) 984-1789.

Quinsigamond Community College
Worcester, Massachusetts — CB code: 3714

Admissions: 62% of applicants accepted
Based on:
••• School record
•• Interview
• Recommendations
Completion: 75% of freshmen end year in good standing
40% enter 4-year programs

2-year public community college, coed. Founded in 1963. **Accreditation:** Regional. **Undergraduate enrollment:** 763 men, 964 women full time; 1,102 men, 1,950 women part time. **Faculty:** 215 total (93 full time), 23 with doctorates or other terminal degrees. **Location:** Urban campus in small city; 45 miles from Boston. **Calendar:** Semester, extensive summer session. Saturday and extensive evening/early morning classes. **Microcomputers:** 75 located in libraries, computer centers. **Special facilities:** Art gallery, dental hygiene clinic.

DEGREES OFFERED. AA, AS, AAS. 600 associate degrees awarded in 1992. 24% in business and management, 5% business/office and marketing/distribution, 9% engineering technologies, 26% allied health, 17% multi/interdisciplinary studies, 12% parks/recreation, protective services, public affairs.

UNDERGRADUATE MAJORS. Accounting, automotive technology, biomedical equipment technology, business administration and management, business and management, business and office, business data processing and related programs, business data programming, computer and information sciences, computer servicing technology, crafts, data processing, dental hygiene, early childhood education, electrical and electronics equipment repair, electronic technology, engineering, finance, fire control and safety technology, hotel/motel and restaurant management, law enforcement and corrections technologies, legal secretary, liberal/general studies, marketing and distribution, marketing management, medical secretary, nursing, occupational therapy assistant, radiograph medical technology, respiratory therapy technology, retailing, secretarial and related programs, small business management and ownership, tourism, visual and performing arts.

ACADEMIC PROGRAMS. 2-year transfer program, cooperative education, double major, dual enrollment of high school students, independent study, internships, weekend college, cross-registration. **Remedial services:** Learning center, reduced course load, remedial instruction, special counselor, tutoring, preparation for health sciences study. **Placement/credit:** CLEP General and Subject, institutional tests. Unlimited number of hours of credit by examination may be counted toward degree.

ACADEMIC REQUIREMENTS. Freshmen must earn minimum GPA of 1.5 to continue in good standing. 65% of freshmen return for sophomore year. Students must declare major on application. **Graduation requirements:** 63 hours for associate (30 in major). Most students required to take courses in English, humanities, mathematics, biological/physical sciences, social sciences.

FRESHMAN ADMISSIONS. Selection criteria: Selective admissions to most programs. Open admissions to some liberal arts and business technologies programs. English, college mathematics, and laboratory sciences required for health programs. English and mathematics required for business, technology, engineering, and early childhood education.

1992 FRESHMAN CLASS PROFILE. 866 men applied, 591 accepted, 423 enrolled; 1,228 women applied, 713 accepted, 536 enrolled. **Characteristics:** 98% from in state, 100% commute. Average age is 22.

FALL-TERM APPLICATIONS. $10 fee, may be waived for applicants

with need. $35 fee for out-of-state-applicants. No closing date; applicants notified on a rolling basis beginning on or about January 30; must reply by May 1 or within 2 weeks if notified thereafter. Interview required for health sciences and early childhood education applicants. CRDA. Early admission available. January 15 closing date for dental hygiene, nursing, radiologic technology, respiratory therapy, occupational therapy, early childhood education applicants.

STUDENT LIFE. Activities: Student government, film, student newspaper, student handbook, coffeehouse for talent performances, multicultural club, several occupational groups.

ATHLETICS. NJCAA. **Intercollegiate:** Baseball M, basketball, softball W. **Intramural:** Badminton, golf, racquetball, swimming, table tennis, volleyball.

STUDENT SERVICES. Aptitude testing, career counseling, employment service for undergraduates, freshman orientation, health services, on-campus day care, personal counseling, placement service for graduates, veterans counselor, Campus Ministry, services/facilities for handicapped.

ANNUAL EXPENSES. Tuition and fees (1992-93): $2,104, $3,822 additional for out-of-state students. **Books and supplies:** $400. **Other expenses:** $1,448.

FINANCIAL AID. 25% of freshmen, 23% of continuing students receive some form of aid. 98% of grants, 45% of loans, all jobs based on need. Academic, music/drama, art, athletic, leadership scholarships available. **Aid applications:** No closing date; priority given to applications received by May 1; applicants notified on a rolling basis beginning on or about July 1; must reply within 2 weeks.

ADDRESS/TELEPHONE. Ronald Smith, Director of Admissions, Quinsigamond Community College, 670 West Boylston Street, Worcester, MA 01606. (508) 852-6365. Fax: (508) 852-6943.

Regis College
Weston, Massachusetts — CB code: 3723

Admissions: 91% of applicants accepted
Based on: ••• School record
•• Activities, interview, recommendations, special talents, test scores
• Essay
Completion: 90% of freshmen end year in good standing
70% graduate, 11% of these enter graduate study

4-year private liberal arts college, women only, affiliated with Roman Catholic Church. Founded in 1927. **Accreditation:** Regional. **Undergraduate enrollment:** 601 women full time; 495 women part time. **Graduate enrollment:** 25 women part time. **Faculty:** 106 total (53 full time), 60 with doctorates or other terminal degrees. **Location:** Suburban campus in large town; 12 miles from Boston. **Calendar:** Semester, limited summer session. **Microcomputers:** 55 located in computer centers. **Special facilities:** Philatelic museum, Walters Art Gallery.

DEGREES OFFERED. BA, BS, MS. 205 bachelor's degrees awarded in 1992. 22% in business and management, 17% communications, 14% letters/literature, 7% psychology, 23% social sciences, 8% visual and performing arts.

UNDERGRADUATE MAJORS. Biology, business and management, chemistry, classics, communications, economics, English, fine arts, French, German, history, mathematics, political science and government, psychology, social work, sociology, Spanish.

ACADEMIC PROGRAMS. Double major, honors program, independent study, internships, student-designed major, study abroad, teacher preparation, visiting/exchange student program, Washington semester, cross-registration; liberal arts/career combination in engineering. **Remedial services:** Learning center, reduced course load, remedial instruction, tutoring. **Placement/credit:** AP, CLEP Subject, institutional tests.

ACADEMIC REQUIREMENTS. Freshmen must earn minimum GPA of 1.75 to continue in good standing. 80% of freshmen return for sophomore year. Students must declare major by end of first year. **Graduation requirements:** Most students required to take courses in English, foreign languages, humanities, philosophy/religion, biological/physical sciences, social sciences. **Postgraduate studies:** 4% enter law school, 1% enter medical school, 1% enter MBA programs, 5% enter other graduate study. **Additional information:** 38 courses (4 credits each) with 10 courses in major field, required for bachelor's degree.

FRESHMAN ADMISSIONS. Selection criteria: School achievement record most important, then recommendations, interview, test scores, school and community activities. **High school preparation:** 16 units required. Required units include English 4, foreign language 2, mathematics 3, social science 2 and science 2. 2 laboratory sciences required. **Test requirements:** SAT; score report by June 1.

1992 FRESHMAN CLASS PROFILE. 423 women applied, 385 accepted, 138 enrolled. 68% had high school GPA of 3.0 or higher, 32% between 2.0 and 2.99. 11% were in top tenth and 28% were in top quarter of graduating class. **Academic background:** Mid 50% of enrolled freshmen had SAT-V between 380-470, SAT-M between 390-510. 98% submitted SAT scores. **Characteristics:** 76% from in state, 87% live in college housing, 15% have minority backgrounds, 3% are foreign students. Average age is 18.

FALL-TERM APPLICATIONS. $30 fee, may be waived for applicants with need. Closing date June 1; applicants notified on a rolling basis beginning on or about December 1; must reply by May 1 or within 2 weeks if notified thereafter. Interview recommended. Essay recommended. CRDA. Deferred and early admission available.

STUDENT LIFE. Housing: Dormitories (women). **Activities:** Student government, magazine, student newspaper, yearbook, choral groups, drama, music ensembles, cultural, social, political, religious organizations.

ATHLETICS. NCAA. **Intercollegiate:** Basketball, cross-country, diving, field hockey, soccer, softball, swimming, tennis, volleyball. **Intramural:** Tennis, volleyball.

STUDENT SERVICES. Aptitude testing, career counseling, employment service for undergraduates, freshman orientation, health services, personal counseling, placement service for graduates, special adviser for adult students, services/facilities for handicapped.

ANNUAL EXPENSES. Tuition and fees: $11,850. **Room and board:** $5,600. **Books and supplies:** $450. **Other expenses:** $700.

FINANCIAL AID. 70% of freshmen, 64% of continuing students receive some form of aid. 96% of grants, 94% of loans, 98% of jobs based on need. 106 enrolled freshmen were judged to have need, 99 were offered aid. Academic, leadership, alumni affiliation, religious affiliation scholarships available. **Aid applications:** No closing date; priority given to applications received by February 15; applicants notified on a rolling basis beginning on or about March 15; must reply by May 1 or within 2 weeks if notified thereafter.

ADDRESS/TELEPHONE. Mary E. Dunn, Director of Admissions, Regis College, 235 Wellesley Street, Weston, MA 02193. (617) 893-1820.

Roxbury Community College
Boston, Massachusetts — CB code: 3740

2-year public community college, coed. Founded in 1972. **Accreditation:** Regional. **Undergraduate enrollment:** 348 men, 732 women full time; 371 men, 589 women part time. **Faculty:** 147 total (65 full time). **Location:** Urban campus in very large city. **Calendar:** Semester, limited summer session. **Microcomputers:** 52 located in classrooms.

DEGREES OFFERED. AA, AS. 170 associate degrees awarded in 1992.

UNDERGRADUATE MAJORS. Accounting, aeronautical technology, business administration and management, business and office, business computer/console/peripheral equipment operation, business data processing and related programs, business data programming, computer and information sciences, drafting and design technology, engineering and engineering-related technologies, English, English literature, French, humanities and social sciences, legal secretary, liberal/general studies, marketing and distribution, mathematics, mechanical design technology, medical secretary, nursing, secretarial and related programs, word processing.

ACADEMIC PROGRAMS. 2-year transfer program, honors program, independent study, internships, cross-registration. **Remedial services:** Learning center, remedial instruction, special counselor, tutoring. **Placement/credit:** Institutional tests.

ACADEMIC REQUIREMENTS. Freshmen must earn minimum GPA of 1.79 to continue in good standing. Minimum 2.0 average for 44 credits and above. 70% of freshmen return for sophomore year. Students must declare major on enrollment. **Graduation requirements:** 60 hours for associate. Most students required to take courses in arts/fine arts, computer science, English, foreign languages, history, humanities, mathematics, philosophy/religion, biological/physical sciences, social sciences.

FRESHMAN ADMISSIONS. Selection criteria: Open admissions. Recommendations and/or interviews for specialized programs. **Additional information:** Serious, highly motivated applicants may be admitted without high school diploma or GED.

1992 FRESHMAN CLASS PROFILE. 226 men, 440 women enrolled. **Characteristics:** 100% commute.

FALL-TERM APPLICATIONS. $10 fee, may be waived for applicants with need. $35 fee for out-of-state applicants. Closing date September 1; priority given to applications received by June 30; applicants notified on a rolling basis beginning on or about March 15. Interview required of candidates for readmission and nongraduates without GED certificate. Deferred admission available.

STUDENT LIFE. Activities: Student government, student newspaper, yearbook, choral groups, dance, drama, Union Estudiantil Latina, International Students Association, Christian ministry.

ATHLETICS. NJCAA. **Intercollegiate:** Basketball, soccer M.

STUDENT SERVICES. Career counseling, employment service for undergraduates, freshman orientation, health services, on-campus day care, personal counseling, placement service for graduates, services/facilities for handicapped.

ANNUAL EXPENSES. Tuition and fees (1992-93): $1,400, $3,822 additional for out-of-state students. **Books and supplies:** $525. **Other expenses:** $1,470.

FINANCIAL AID. 85% of freshmen, 85% of continuing students receive some form of aid. All grants, all jobs based on need. **Aid applications:** No closing date; priority given to applications received by May 1; applicants notified on a rolling basis beginning on or about July 15; must reply within 2 weeks.

ADDRESS/TELEPHONE. Michael Rice, Director of Admissions, Roxbury Community College, 1234 Columbus Avenue, Roxbury Crossing, MA 02120-3400. (617) 541-5304. Fax: (617) 541-5351.

St. Hyacinth College and Seminary
Granby, Massachusetts CB code: 3772

4-year private liberal arts, seminary college, men only, affiliated with Roman Catholic Church. Founded in 1927. **Accreditation:** Regional. **Undergraduate enrollment:** 26 men full time; 12 men, 12 women part time. **Faculty:** 21 total (9 full time), 9 with doctorates or other terminal degrees. **Location:** Suburban campus in small town; 15 miles from Springfield. **Calendar:** Semester. Extensive evening/early morning classes. **Microcomputers:** Located in computer centers. **Special facilities:** Natural history museum. **Additional facts:** Students preparing for brotherhood or priesthood within Conventual Franciscan Order spend 1 year in spiritual life-training program at Staten Island, New York after second year of academic program in Granby.

DEGREES OFFERED. AA, BA. 2 bachelor's degrees awarded. 100% in philosophy, religion, theology.

UNDERGRADUATE MAJORS. Associate: Philosophy, religion. **Bachelor's:** Philosophy.

ACADEMIC PROGRAMS. Independent study. **Remedial services:** Reduced course load, remedial instruction, special counselor, tutoring. **Placement/credit:** AP, CLEP General and Subject, institutional tests.

ACADEMIC REQUIREMENTS. Freshmen must earn minimum GPA of 2.0 to continue in good standing. 100% of freshmen return for sophomore year. Students must declare major by end of second year. **Graduation requirements:** 60 hours for associate, 120 hours for bachelor's (30 in major). Most students required to take courses in English, foreign languages, history, mathematics, philosophy/religion, biological/physical sciences, social sciences.

FRESHMAN ADMISSIONS. Selection criteria: Interview and recommendations most important. Evidence of academic ability, intellectual curiosity, strength of character, motivation, promise for personal growth and development important. School record and test scores considered. **High school preparation:** 16 units required. Required units include biological science 2, English 4, foreign language 2, mathematics 2 and social science 2. **Test requirements:** SAT or ACT (SAT preferred); score report by June 1.

1992 FRESHMAN CLASS PROFILE. 5 men applied, 5 accepted, 4 enrolled. 25% had high school GPA of 3.0 or higher, 50% between 2.0 and 2.99.

FALL-TERM APPLICATIONS. $25 fee, may be waived for applicants with need. No closing date; applicants notified on a rolling basis. Interview required. Essay required. Deferred admission available. Applications assessed and decisions submitted within one month of application.

STUDENT LIFE. Housing: Dormitories (men). Residency available only for students preparing for priesthood and brotherhood. **Activities:** Student government, magazine, student newspaper, choral groups, drama, music ensembles, various service programs for youth, mentally retarded, aged, and poor.

ATHLETICS. Intramural: Baseball, basketball, golf, soccer, softball, swimming, tennis, volleyball.

STUDENT SERVICES. Aptitude testing, career counseling, freshman orientation, health services, personal counseling, placement service for graduates, services/facilities for handicapped.

ANNUAL EXPENSES. Tuition and fees: $3,795. **Room and board:** $4,500. **Books and supplies:** $425. **Other expenses:** $725.

FINANCIAL AID. 60% of freshmen, 50% of continuing students receive some form of aid. All grants, all loans based on need. Academic, state/district residency scholarships available. **Aid applications:** No closing date; priority given to applications received by June 1; applicants notified on a rolling basis beginning on or about June 15; must reply within 15 days. **Additional information:** All academic expenses beyond aid available paid by the Order of Friars Minor Conventual for students who are members of a Franciscan community. Other students must meet their own expenses or secure outside aid.

ADDRESS/TELEPHONE. Rev. Richard-Jacob Forcier, OFM Conv, Admissions Officer, St. Hyacinth College and Seminary, 66 School Street, Granby, MA 01033-9742. (413) 467-7191. Students interested in seeking affiliation with Franciscan Community should contact Admissions Officer, St. Joseph Cupertino Novitiate, 12290 Folly Quarter Road, Ellicott City, MD 21042; (301) 988-9833.

St. John's Seminary College
Brighton, Massachusetts CB code: 3295

Admissions: 70% of applicants accepted
Based on: ••• Interview, religious affiliation/commitment
•• Essay, recommendations, school record, test scores
• Activities
Completion: 90% of freshmen end year in good standing
75% graduate, 80% of these enter graduate study

4-year private college of arts and sciences and seminary college, men only, affiliated with Roman Catholic Church. Founded in 1883. **Accreditation:** Regional. **Undergraduate enrollment:** 31 men full time; 5 men part time. **Faculty:** 28 total (9 full time), 27 with doctorates or other terminal degrees. **Location:** Urban campus in very large city; 5 miles from center of Boston. **Calendar:** Semester. **Microcomputers:** 2 located in libraries, computer centers. **Special facilities:** Sports complex at Boston College.

DEGREES OFFERED. AA, BA. 100% in philosophy, religion, theology. 8 bachelor's degrees awarded. 100% in philosophy, religion, theology.

UNDERGRADUATE MAJORS. Associate: Philosophy. **Bachelor's:** Biological and physical sciences, humanities and social sciences, liberal/general studies, philosophy.

ACADEMIC PROGRAMS. Double major, independent study, study abroad. **Remedial services:** Reduced course load, special counselor, tutoring. **Placement/credit:** AP, institutional tests.

ACADEMIC REQUIREMENTS. Freshmen must earn minimum GPA of 1.7 to continue in good standing. 85% of freshmen return for sophomore year. Students must declare major by end of first year. **Graduation requirements:** 120 hours for bachelor's (27 in major). Most students required to take courses in arts/fine arts, English, foreign languages, history, philosophy/religion, biological/physical sciences, social sciences.

FRESHMAN ADMISSIONS. Selection criteria: Adequate religious vocational discernment. Interviews most important, followed by school achievement record, test scores, and letters of recommendation. **High school preparation:** 16 units required. Required and recommended units include English 4 and mathematics 3. Foreign language 3 and social science 2 recommended. **Test requirements:** SAT for counseling; score report by June 15. Otis Lennon Mental Ability Test, Iowa Silent Reading Tests required. **Additional information:** Applicants must be sponsored by their local bishops.

1992 FRESHMAN CLASS PROFILE. 10 men applied, 7 accepted, 5 enrolled. 40% had high school GPA of 3.0 or higher, 40% between 2.0 and 2.99. 20% were in top quarter of graduating class. **Academic background:** Mid 50% of enrolled freshmen had SAT-V between 290-410, SAT-M between 300-370. 100% submitted SAT scores. **Characteristics:** 100% from in state, 100% live in college housing. Average age is 22.

FALL-TERM APPLICATIONS. No fee. Closing date July 15; applicants notified on or about May 1; must reply within 5 weeks. Interview required. Essay required. Deferred admission available.

STUDENT LIFE. Housing: Dormitories (men). **Activities:** Student government, choral groups, participation in Harvard's Model UN (representing the Vatican). **Additional information:** Religious observance required.

ATHLETICS. Intramural: Basketball, softball, table tennis, tennis.

STUDENT SERVICES. Career counseling, health services, personal counseling, services/facilities for handicapped.

ANNUAL EXPENSES. Tuition and fees (1992-93): $4,400. **Room and board:** $2,600. **Books and supplies:** $400. **Other expenses:** $600.

FINANCIAL AID. 60% of freshmen, 75% of continuing students receive some form of aid. All grants, all jobs based on need. 4 enrolled freshmen were judged to have need, all were offered aid. **Aid applications:** Closing date July 1; applicants notified on a rolling basis beginning on or about August 15; must reply within 3 weeks.

ADDRESS/TELEPHONE. Rev. William P. Fay, Dean of the College, Dean of Admissions, St. John's Seminary College, 197 Foster Street, Brighton, MA 02135. (617) 254-2610 ext. 273.

Salem State College
Salem, Massachusetts CB code: 3522

Admissions: 78% of applicants accepted
Based on: ••• Recommendations, school record
•• Special talents, test scores
• Activities, interview
Completion: 85% of freshmen end year in good standing
47% graduate, 20% of these enter graduate study

4-year public university, coed. Founded in 1854. **Accreditation:** Regional. **Undergraduate enrollment:** 2,364 men, 3,123 women full time; 1,142 men, 2,237 women part time. **Graduate enrollment:** 46 men, 115 women full time; 350 men, 1,072 women part time. **Faculty:** 422 total (293 full time), 177 with doctorates or other terminal degrees. **Location:** Suburban campus in large town; 20 miles from Boston. **Calendar:** Semester, extensive summer session. Saturday and extensive evening/early morning classes. **Microcom-**

puters: 217 located in dormitories, libraries, classrooms, computer centers. **Special facilities:** Multipurpose library, media facility.

DEGREES OFFERED. BA, BS, BFA, MA, MS, MBA, MEd, MSW. 1,120 bachelor's degrees awarded in 1992. 34% in business and management, 17% teacher education, 6% health sciences, 10% multi/interdisciplinary studies, 5% parks/recreation, protective services, public affairs, 5% psychology, 5% social sciences. Graduate degrees offered in 16 major fields of study.

UNDERGRADUATE MAJORS. Accounting, advertising, applied mathematics, aviation management, biology, business administration and management, business and office, business economics, chemistry, clinical laboratory science, communications, comparative literature, computer and information sciences, computer programming, criminal justice studies, dramatic arts, early childhood education, earth sciences, economics, education, elementary education, English, English literature, finance, fine arts, geography, geology, graphic design, history, liberal/general studies, linguistics, management information systems, marine biology, marketing management, mathematics, music education, nuclear medical technology, nursing, office supervision and management, photography, physical education, political science and government, predentistry, premedicine, preveterinary, professional writing, psychology, public relations, pure mathematics, secretarial and related programs, social work, sociology.

ACADEMIC PROGRAMS. Double major, dual enrollment of high school students, honors program, independent study, internships, student-designed major, study abroad, teacher preparation, visiting/exchange student program, cross-registration; combined bachelor's/graduate program in business administration. **Remedial services:** Learning center, preadmission summer program, reduced course load, remedial instruction, special counselor, tutoring. **Placement/credit:** AP, CLEP General and Subject, institutional tests.

ACADEMIC REQUIREMENTS. Freshmen must earn minimum GPA of 1.5 to continue in good standing. 75% of freshmen return for sophomore year. Students must declare major on application. **Graduation requirements:** 126 hours for bachelor's (36 in major). Most students required to take courses in computer science, English, history, humanities, biological/physical sciences, social sciences.

FRESHMAN ADMISSIONS. Selection criteria: Class rank most important. High school GPA, test scores, counselor's recommendations considered. **High school preparation:** 16 units required. Required units include biological science 1, English 4, foreign language 2, mathematics 3, physical science 1 and social science 2. Additional requirements for some programs, including 1 biology and 1 chemistry for nursing. **Test requirements:** SAT or ACT (SAT preferred); score report by April 1.

1992 FRESHMAN CLASS PROFILE. 1,666 men applied, 1,272 accepted, 428 enrolled; 2,388 women applied, 1,870 accepted, 582 enrolled. 10% had high school GPA of 3.0 or higher, 70% between 2.0 and 2.99. **Academic background:** Mid 50% of enrolled freshmen had SAT-V between 420-460, SAT-M between 430-500. 87% submitted SAT scores. **Characteristics:** 98% from in state, 60% commute, 11% have minority backgrounds, 1% are foreign students. Average age is 18.

FALL-TERM APPLICATIONS. $10 fee, may be waived for applicants with need. $40 fee for out-of-state applicants. Closing date March 1; priority given to applications received by January 15; applicants notified on a rolling basis; must reply within 4 weeks or request May 1 option date. Portfolio required for art applicants. Interview recommended. CRDA. Early admission available.

STUDENT LIFE. Housing: Dormitories (coed); apartment, handicapped housing available. **Activities:** Student government, film, magazine, radio, student newspaper, television, yearbook, choral groups, concert band, dance, drama, jazz band, music ensembles, musical theater, pep band, symphony orchestra, Hillel, women's center, international students association, Political Science Academy, Catholic Student Community, African-American Student Association, Hispanic-American Society, Student Nurses Association, Mass Prig, Criminal Justice Academy. **Additional information:** Student Life Division offers broad range of co-curricular programs which provide learning opportunities.

ATHLETICS. NCAA. **Intercollegiate:** Baseball M, basketball, cross-country, diving, field hockey W, golf M, ice hockey M, sailing, soccer, softball W, swimming, tennis, track and field, volleyball. **Intramural:** Archery, badminton, basketball, fencing, field hockey W, golf, gymnastics, handball, ice hockey, racquetball, sailing, skin diving, soccer, softball, squash, swimming, table tennis, tennis, track and field, volleyball, water polo.

STUDENT SERVICES. Aptitude testing, career counseling, employment service for undergraduates, freshman orientation, health services, on-campus day care, personal counseling, placement service for graduates, special adviser for adult students, veterans counselor, services/facilities for handicapped.

ANNUAL EXPENSES. Tuition and fees (1992-93): $3,073, $3,864 additional for out-of-state students. **Room and board:** $3,514. **Books and supplies:** $450. **Other expenses:** $900.

FINANCIAL AID. 55% of freshmen, 40% of continuing students receive some form of aid. 96% of grants, 78% of loans, 54% of jobs based on need. 618 enrolled freshmen were judged to have need, 460 were offered aid. Academic, music/drama, art, leadership, alumni affiliation scholarships available. **Aid applications:** No closing date; priority given to applications received by April 15; applicants notified on a rolling basis beginning on or about April 15; must reply within 2 weeks. **Additional information:** Tuition waivers for qualified veterans and National Guard members. Grant assistance available for eligible adult students.

ADDRESS/TELEPHONE. Dr. David Sartwell, Director of Admissions, Salem State College, 352 Lafayette Street, Salem, MA 01970. (508) 741-6200. Fax: (508) 741-6126.

School of the Museum of Fine Arts
Boston, Massachusetts CB code: 3794

4-year private art college, coed. Founded in 1876. **Undergraduate enrollment:** 219 men, 306 women full time; 31 men, 72 women part time. **Graduate enrollment:** 57 men and women. **Faculty:** 126 total (56 full time). **Location:** Urban campus in very large city; 1 mile from downtown area. **Calendar:** Semester, limited summer session. Saturday and extensive evening/early morning classes. **Special facilities:** 80,000 slide collection, studio wing adjacent to Museum of Fine Arts. **Additional facts:** Students have access to curatorial departments and other facilities of Boston's Museum of Fine Arts. Degree programs offered in affiliation with Tufts University. Accredited by National Association of Schools of Art and Design.

DEGREES OFFERED. BA, BS, BFA, MFA, MEd. 146 bachelor's degrees awarded in 1992. 100% in visual and performing arts. Graduate degrees offered in 10 major fields of study.

UNDERGRADUATE MAJORS. Art education, art history, ceramics, cinematography/film, drawing, enameling, film animation, film arts, fine arts, glass, graphic design, illustration design, metal/jewelry, painting, photography, printmaking, sculpture, studio art, video, visual and performing arts.

ACADEMIC PROGRAMS. Double major, honors program, independent study, student-designed major, teacher preparation, visiting/exchange student program, cross-registration, 5-year bachelor of fine arts/liberal arts with Tufts University. **Remedial services:** Preadmission summer program.

ACADEMIC REQUIREMENTS. No policy requiring minimum GPA; records of students having academic difficulty are reviewed individually. **Graduation requirements:** 144 hours for bachelor's. Most students required to take courses in arts/fine arts. **Additional information:** Art history only academic subject required of freshmen. Extra credit for exceptional development at end of any semester.

FRESHMAN ADMISSIONS. Selection criteria: Art portfolio and personal motivation most important. Appropriateness of school to applicant's goals considered. **Additional information:** Students admitted first to diploma program and placed at studio art level. Admitted later to degree program with Tufts University.

1992 FRESHMAN CLASS PROFILE. 87 men and women enrolled. **Characteristics:** 37% from in state, 100% commute, 3% have minority backgrounds, 7% are foreign students. Average age is 24.

FALL-TERM APPLICATIONS. $30 fee, may be waived for applicants with need. No closing date; priority given to applications received by March 15; applicants notified on a rolling basis; must reply by May 1 or within 3 weeks if notified thereafter. Portfolio required. Interview recommended. Essay recommended. CRDA. Deferred admission available.

STUDENT SERVICES. Career counseling, employment service for undergraduates, freshman orientation, personal counseling, placement service for graduates, services/facilities for handicapped.

ANNUAL EXPENSES. Tuition and fees: $13,285. **Books and supplies:** $1,000. **Other expenses:** $1,500.

FINANCIAL AID. 60% of freshmen, 63% of continuing students receive some form of aid. 95% of grants, 82% of loans, 53% of jobs based on need. 78 enrolled freshmen were judged to have need, all were offered aid. **Aid applications:** No closing date; priority given to applications received by March 15; applicants notified on a rolling basis beginning on or about April 15; must reply by May 1 or within 2 weeks if notified thereafter.

ADDRESS/TELEPHONE. Alan H. Van Reed, Dean of Admissions, School of the Museum of Fine Arts, 230 The Fenway, Boston, MA 02115. (617) 267-1218. (800) 643-6078. Fax: (617) 424-6271.

Simmons College
Boston, Massachusetts CB code: 3761

Admissions:	78% of applicants accepted
Based on:	••• School record
	•• Recommendations, test scores
	• Activities, essay, interview, special talents
Completion:	97% of freshmen end year in good standing
	75% graduate, 10% of these enter graduate study

4-year private college of arts and sciences, women only. Founded in 1899. **Accreditation:** Regional. **Undergraduate enrollment:** 1,154 women full time; 178 women part time. **Graduate enrollment:** 65 men, 472 women full time; 115 men, 1,095 women part time. **Faculty:** 337 total (168 full time), 257 with doctorates or other terminal degrees. **Location:** Urban campus in very large city; 2 miles from downtown. **Calendar:** Semester, limited summer session. **Microcomputers:** 90 located in dormitories, libraries, computer centers. **Special facilities:** Audiovisual media center, art gallery, sports center.

DEGREES OFFERED. BA, BS, MA, MS, MBA, MSW, PhD. 361 bachelor's degrees awarded in 1992. 20% in business and management, 16% communications, 5% teacher education, 6% allied health, 8% letters/literature, 6% life sciences, 8% psychology, 14% social sciences. Graduate degrees offered in 18 major fields of study.

UNDERGRADUATE MAJORS. Accounting, advertising, Afro-American (black) studies, American literature, art history, arts management, biochemistry, biological and physical sciences, biology, business administration and management, business and management, chemistry, chemistry management, communications, comparative literature, computer and information sciences, economics, education, elementary education, English, English literature, environmental science, finance, French, graphic design, history, humanities and social sciences, international business management, international relations, junior high education, liberal/general studies, management information systems, marketing management, mathematics, mental health/human services, music, music history and appreciation, music performance, music theory and composition, nursing, nutritional sciences, pharmacy, philosophy, physical therapy, political science and government, prelaw, premedicine, psychobiology, psychology, public relations, retailing, secondary education, sociology, Spanish, special education, women's studies.

ACADEMIC PROGRAMS. Accelerated program, double major, dual enrollment of high school students, honors program, independent study, internships, semester at sea, student-designed major, study abroad, teacher preparation, visiting/exchange student program, Washington semester, cross-registration, exchange program with Mills College (CA), Spelman College (GA), Fisk University (TN), American University (DC), New England colleges/Quebec exchange program, joint program with Massachussetts College of Pharmacy. **Remedial services:** Reduced course load, remedial instruction, special counselor, tutoring. **ROTC:** Army. **Placement/credit:** AP, CLEP General and Subject, institutional tests.

ACADEMIC REQUIREMENTS. Freshmen must earn minimum GPA of 1.67 to continue in good standing. 83% of freshmen return for sophomore year. Students must declare major by end of second year. **Graduation requirements:** 128 hours for bachelor's (40 in major). Most students required to take courses in English, foreign languages, humanities, mathematics, biological/physical sciences, social sciences. **Postgraduate studies:** 1% enter law school, 1% enter medical school, 2% enter MBA programs, 6% enter other graduate study.

FRESHMAN ADMISSIONS. Selection criteria: School achievement record most important. Test scores, 2 recommendations, interview (if available), personal qualities, interests, and accomplishments considered. **High school preparation:** 15 units required. Required and recommended units include English 4, foreign language 3, mathematics 3, social science 3 and science 2-3. **Test requirements:** SAT or ACT; score report by February 1.

1992 FRESHMAN CLASS PROFILE. 961 women applied, 745 accepted, 292 enrolled. 20% were in top tenth and 45% were in top quarter of graduating class. **Academic background:** Mid 50% of enrolled freshmen had SAT-V between 410-550, SAT-M between 410-550; ACT composite between 22-26. 95% submitted SAT scores, 5% submitted ACT scores. **Characteristics:** 56% from in state, 83% live in college housing, 20% have minority backgrounds, 4% are foreign students. Average age is 18.

FALL-TERM APPLICATIONS. $35 fee, may be waived for applicants with need. Closing date February 1; applicants notified on or about April 15; must reply by May 1. Essay required. Interview recommended. CRDA. Deferred and early admission available. EDP-F. Two early decision plans available: application closing date November 15, notification by December 15 or application closing date January 1, notification by February 1.

STUDENT LIFE. Housing: Dormitories (women). Housing guaranteed on campus all four years. **Activities:** Student government, film, magazine, student newspaper, yearbook, choral groups, dance, Asian, black, and international students clubs, Catholic women's association, Christian fellowship, Hillel, Amnesty International, Society Organized Against Racism, Feminist Union.

ATHLETICS. NCAA. **Intercollegiate:** Basketball, cross-country, field hockey, rowing (crew), sailing, soccer, swimming, tennis, track and field, volleyball. **Intramural:** Basketball, racquetball, volleyball.

STUDENT SERVICES. Aptitude testing, career counseling, employment service for undergraduates, freshman orientation, health services, personal counseling, placement service for graduates, special adviser for adult students, services/facilities for handicapped.

ANNUAL EXPENSES. Tuition and fees: $15,794. **Room and board:** $6,740. **Books and supplies:** $482. **Other expenses:** $1,124.

FINANCIAL AID. 80% of freshmen, 64% of continuing students receive some form of aid. 90% of grants, 88% of loans, 68% of jobs based on need. 225 enrolled freshmen were judged to have need, all were offered aid. Academic, leadership, minority scholarships available. **Aid applications:** Closing date February 1; applicants notified on or about April 15; must reply by May 1.

ADDRESS/TELEPHONE. Deborah Wright, Dean of Admission, Simmons College, 300 The Fenway, Boston, MA 02115-5898. (617) 738-2107. (800) 345-8468. Fax: (617) 738-2099.

Simon's Rock College of Bard
Great Barrington, Massachusetts — CB code: 3795

Admissions:	63% of applicants accepted
Based on:	••• Essay, interview, recommendations, school record
	•• Test scores
	• Activities, special talents
Completion:	90% of freshmen end year in good standing
	30% graduate

4-year private college of arts and sciences, coed. Founded in 1964. **Accreditation:** Regional. **Undergraduate enrollment:** 162 men, 159 women full time; 3 men, 2 women part time. **Faculty:** 41 total (31 full time), 31 with doctorates or other terminal degrees. **Location:** Rural campus in small town; 140 miles from New York City and Boston. **Calendar:** Semester. **Microcomputers:** 20 located in dormitories, libraries, classrooms, computer centers. **Special facilities:** Arts center. **Additional facts:** Opportunity for highly motivated students who have completed 10th or 11th grade to begin college careers 1 or 2 years ahead of schedule.

DEGREES OFFERED. AA, BA. 70 associate degrees awarded in 1992. 18 bachelor's degrees awarded. 16% in letters/literature, 11% life sciences, 33% social sciences, 38% visual and performing arts.

UNDERGRADUATE MAJORS. Associate: Humanities, liberal/general studies. **Bachelor's:** Arabic, biological and physical sciences, comparative literature, English, English literature, environmental science, fine arts, foreign languages (multiple emphasis), French, German, humanities, humanities and social sciences, liberal/general studies, mathematics, music, predentistry, prelaw, premedicine, prepharmacy, preveterinary, Russian, social sciences, women's studies.

ACADEMIC PROGRAMS. 2-year transfer program, accelerated program, dual enrollment of high school students, independent study, internships, study abroad, visiting/exchange student program, cross-registration; liberal arts/career combination in engineering. **Remedial services:** Reduced course load, tutoring. **Placement/credit:** Institutional tests.

ACADEMIC REQUIREMENTS. Freshmen must earn minimum GPA of 2.0 to continue in good standing. 2.0 GPA required of sophomores, juniors, seniors. 85% of freshmen return for sophomore year. Students must declare major by end of second year. **Graduation requirements:** 60 hours for associate, 120 hours for bachelor's. Most students required to take courses in arts/fine arts, English, foreign languages, humanities, mathematics, biological/physical sciences, social sciences. **Postgraduate studies:** 95% from 2-year programs enter 4-year programs.

FRESHMAN ADMISSIONS. Selection criteria: School achievement record, essays, recommendations (counselor and teacher), test scores, interview considered. Recommended units include biological science 2, English 2, foreign language 2, mathematics 2, physical science 2 and social science 2. Applicants who have completed 10th or 11th grade should have 2 or 3 years college-preparatory curriculum respectively. **Test requirements:** SAT or ACT; score report by June 15. **Additional information:** On-campus interview with parents recommended.

1992 FRESHMAN CLASS PROFILE. 164 men applied, 95 accepted, 74 enrolled; 171 women applied, 116 accepted, 67 enrolled. **Academic background:** Mid 50% of enrolled freshmen had SAT-V between 520-630, SAT-M between 520-650. 44% submitted SAT scores. **Characteristics:** 20% from in state, 98% live in college housing, 19% have minority backgrounds. Average age is 16.

FALL-TERM APPLICATIONS. $25 fee, may be waived for applicants with need. Closing date June 15; applicants notified on a rolling basis beginning on or about January 15; must reply within 2 weeks contingent on financial notification. Interview required. Essay required. Deferred and early admission available.

STUDENT LIFE. Housing: Dormitories (men, women, coed). **Activities:** Student government, magazine, radio, student newspaper, yearbook, choral groups, dance, drama, jazz band, music ensembles, musical theater, community service, religious, social, and cultural organizations.

ATHLETICS. NSCAA. **Intercollegiate:** Basketball, soccer, volleyball. **Intramural:** Badminton, bowling, fencing, skiing, softball, swimming, tennis, volleyball.

STUDENT SERVICES. Career counseling, employment service for undergraduates, freshman orientation, health services, personal counseling, services/facilities for handicapped.

ANNUAL EXPENSES. Tuition and fees (1992-93): $16,590. **Room and board:** $5,620. **Books and supplies:** $400. **Other expenses:** $450.

FINANCIAL AID. 70% of freshmen, 70% of continuing students receive some form of aid. 91% of grants, 96% of loans, all jobs based on need. 89 enrolled freshmen were judged to have need, all were offered aid. **Aid applications:** No closing date; applicants notified on a rolling basis beginning on or about April 1; must reply within 2 weeks.

ADDRESS/TELEPHONE. Brian R. Hopewell, Director of Admissions, Simon's Rock College of Bard, 84 Alford Road, Great Barrington, MA 01230. (413) 528-0771. (800) 235-7186. Fax: (413) 528-4676.

Smith College
Northampton, Massachusetts CB code: 3762

Admissions: 57% of applicants accepted
Based on: ••• Essay, school record
•• Activities, interview, recommendations, test scores
• Special talents
Completion: 97% of freshmen end year in good standing
86% graduate, 20% of these enter graduate study

4-year private liberal arts college, women only. Founded in 1871. **Accreditation:** Regional. **Undergraduate enrollment:** 2,418 women full time; 105 women part time. **Graduate enrollment:** 7 men, 62 women full time; 4 men, 34 women part time. **Faculty:** 276 total (248 full time), 267 with doctorates or other terminal degrees. **Location:** Suburban campus in large town; 90 miles from Boston, 165 miles from New York City. **Calendar:** Semester. **Microcomputers:** 230 located in libraries, classrooms, computer centers. **Special facilities:** Center for performing arts, art museum, plant house, Sophia Smith Collection (women's history archive), electron microscopes, lithographic press, language laboratory.

DEGREES OFFERED. BA, MA, MS, MFA, MEd, MSW, PhD. 767 bachelor's degrees awarded in 1992. 5% in languages, 11% letters/literature, 6% life sciences, 7% multi/interdisciplinary studies, 9% psychology, 35% social sciences, 12% visual and performing arts. Graduate degrees offered in 21 major fields of study.

UNDERGRADUATE MAJORS. Afro-American (black) studies, American studies, anthropology, architecture, art history, astronomy, biochemistry, biology, chemistry, classics, comparative literature, computer and information sciences, dance, dramatic arts, early childhood education, economics, education, elementary education, English, English literature, French, geology, German, Greek (classical), history, Italian, Latin, Latin American studies, mathematics, medieval studies, music, music history and appreciation, philosophy, physics, political science and government, psychology, religion, Russian, secondary education, sociology, Spanish, Spanish and Portuguese, studio art, women's studies.

ACADEMIC PROGRAMS. Accelerated program, double major, honors program, independent study, internships, semester at sea, student-designed major, study abroad, teacher preparation, visiting/exchange student program, Washington semester, cross-registration, Public Policy Program, Smithsonian Internship, Ada Comstock Program for returning students, 12-college exchange program, Pomona College exchange. **Remedial services:** Tutoring, Accommodations made for students with disabilities in their courses. **ROTC:** Air Force, Army. **Placement/credit:** AP, IB, institutional tests; 32 credit hours maximum for bachelor's degree.

ACADEMIC REQUIREMENTS. Freshmen must earn minimum GPA of 2.0 to continue in good standing. 90% of freshmen return for sophomore year. Students must declare major by end of second year. **Graduation requirements:** 128 hours for bachelor's. **Postgraduate studies:** 5% enter law school, 1% enter medical school, 14% enter other graduate study.

FRESHMAN ADMISSIONS. Selection criteria: Review of secondary school record, including rank in class, difficulty of courses, and grade average, accompanied by recommendations and test scores. Interview and essay also important. **High school preparation:** 16 units recommended. Recommended units include English 4, foreign language 3, mathematics 3, social science 2 and science 2. 3 units foreign language or 2 each of 2 languages and 2 history recommended. **Test requirements:** SAT or ACT; score report by February 1. 3 ACH (including English Composition) required of applicants who did not take ACT. Score report by February 1.

1992 FRESHMAN CLASS PROFILE. 2,685 women applied, 1,533 accepted, 641 enrolled. 55% were in top tenth and 88% were in top quarter of graduating class. **Academic background:** Mid 50% of enrolled freshmen had SAT-V between 510-630, SAT-M between 540-650. 98% submitted SAT scores. **Characteristics:** 15% from in state, 100% live in college housing, 24% have minority backgrounds, 9% are foreign students. Average age is 18.

FALL-TERM APPLICATIONS. $40 fee, may be waived for applicants with need. Closing date January 15; applicants notified on or about April 1; must reply by May 1. Essay required. Interview recommended. Interview Strongly recommended, may be conducted off campus by an alumna. CRDA. Deferred and early admission available. EDP-F. Fall early application deadline is November 15; winter early application deadline is January 1.

STUDENT LIFE. Housing: Dormitories (women); apartment, cooperative housing available. Most have individual dining rooms and all have their own policies, governments, and traditions. Housing available for handicapped students. French house available. **Activities:** Student government, magazine, radio, student newspaper, yearbook, Science fiction club, choral groups, dance, drama, music ensembles, musical theater, symphony orchestra, Service Organization of Smith, Women's Resource Center, Black Students Alliance, Asian Students Association, Hillel, Newman Club, Christian Council, International Relations Club, political clubs. **Additional information:** Academic honor code.

ATHLETICS. NCAA. **Intercollegiate:** Basketball, cross-country, diving, field hockey, horseback riding, lacrosse, rowing (crew), skiing, soccer, softball, squash, swimming, tennis, track and field, volleyball. **Intramural:** Badminton, basketball, cross-country, rowing (crew), soccer, softball, squash, tennis, volleyball.

STUDENT SERVICES. Career counseling, employment service for undergraduates, freshman orientation, health services, on-campus day care, personal counseling, placement service for graduates, special adviser for adult students, Special Needs Services Coordinator, services/facilities for handicapped.

ANNUAL EXPENSES. Tuition and fees: $18,136. **Room and board:** $6,100. **Books and supplies:** $400. **Other expenses:** $700.

FINANCIAL AID. 51% of freshmen, 54% of continuing students receive some form of aid. 99% of grants, 97% of loans, 90% of jobs based on need. 317 enrolled freshmen were judged to have need, all were offered aid. State/district residency scholarships available. **Aid applications:** Closing date January 15; applicants notified on or about April 15; must reply by May 1.

ADDRESS/TELEPHONE. B. Ann Wright, Dean of Enrollment, Smith College, Garrison Hall, Northampton, MA 01063. (413) 585-2500. Fax: (413) 585-2527.

Springfield College
Springfield, Massachusetts CB code: 3763

4-year private college of arts and sciences, coed. Founded in 1885. **Accreditation:** Regional. **Undergraduate enrollment:** 2,481 men and women. **Graduate enrollment:** 488 men and women full time; 239 men and women part time. **Faculty:** 184 total (134 full time), 77 with doctorates or other terminal degrees. **Location:** Suburban campus in small city; 90 miles from Boston, 30 miles from Hartford, Connecticut. **Calendar:** Semester, limited summer session. **Microcomputers:** 50 located in computer centers. **Special facilities:** 81-acre nature preserve.

DEGREES OFFERED. BA, BS, MS, MEd, MSW, D. 525 bachelor's degrees awarded in 1992. 15% in business and management, 25% teacher education, 10% health sciences, 40% allied health, 10% social sciences. Graduate degrees offered in 20 major fields of study.

UNDERGRADUATE MAJORS. American studies, athletic training, biological and physical sciences, biology, business administration and management, chemistry, clinical laboratory science, community health work, community services, computer and information sciences, counseling psychology, early childhood education, education of the physically handicapped, elementary education, English, English education, environmental science, gerontology, health care administration, health education, health sciences, history, human resources development, humanities and social sciences, information sciences and systems, liberal/general studies, mathematics, mathematics education, medical illustrating, medical laboratory technologies, mental health/human services, parks and recreation management, physical education, physical therapy, physician's assistant, political science and government, predentistry, prelaw, premedicine, preveterinary, psychology, public health laboratory science, recreation therapy, rehabilitation counseling/services, renewable natural resources, science education, secondary education, social science education, social studies education, sociology, sports management.

ACADEMIC PROGRAMS. Cooperative education, double major, honors program, independent study, internships, study abroad, teacher preparation, cross-registration; liberal arts/career combination in health sciences. **Remedial services:** Learning center, reduced course load, special counselor, tutoring, writing laboratory. **ROTC:** Air Force, Army. **Placement/credit:** AP, CLEP General; 31 credit hours maximum for bachelor's degree.

ACADEMIC REQUIREMENTS. Freshmen must earn minimum GPA of 1.7 to continue in good standing. 89% of freshmen return for sophomore year. Students must declare major by end of first year. **Graduation requirements:** 130 hours for bachelor's. Most students required to take courses in arts/fine arts, English, history, philosophy/religion, biological/physical sciences, social sciences. **Additional information:** Emphasis on practical field-work experiences to supplement classroom learning.

FRESHMAN ADMISSIONS. Selection criteria: School achievement record, interview, extracurricular activities, personal references test scores important. Special consideration given to minorities, children of alumni, handicapped individuals, and international students. **High school preparation:** 16 units required. Required units include biological science 1, English 4, mathematics 2, physical science 1 and social science 2. Emphasis on science for majors in allied health fields. **Test requirements:** SAT or ACT (SAT preferred); score report by April 1.

1992 FRESHMAN CLASS PROFILE. 494 men and women enrolled. **Characteristics:** 35% from in state, 85% live in college housing, 8% have minority backgrounds, 1% are foreign students. Average age is 18.

FALL-TERM APPLICATIONS. $30 fee, may be waived for applicants with need. Closing date April 1; applicants notified on a rolling basis; must reply by May 1. Interview required. Portfolio required for art applicants. Essay required. CRDA. Deferred and early admission available. EDP-F. Application closing date for athletic training, physical therapy majors January 15, for physician assistant majors, February 15; SAT or ACT score reports must be received by February 1.

STUDENT LIFE. Housing: Dormitories (men, women, coed). **Activities:** Student government, magazine, radio, student newspaper, yearbook, campus newsletter, choral groups, dance, drama, music ensembles, musical theater, pep band, stage band, women's group, Afro-American Organization, Hot Line, Foundation for Retarded Individuals, Alpha Phi Omega, service-oriented organizations.

ATHLETICS. NCAA. **Intercollegiate:** Baseball M, basketball, cross-country, diving, field hockey W, football M, golf, gymnastics, lacrosse, soccer, softball W, swimming, tennis, track and field, volleyball, wrestling M. **Intramural:** Basketball, field hockey W, handball, horseback riding, lacrosse, racquetball, rowing (crew), soccer, softball, swimming, tennis, track and field, volleyball, wrestling M.

STUDENT SERVICES. Aptitude testing, career counseling, employment service for undergraduates, health services, personal counseling, placement service for graduates, special adviser for adult students, veterans counselor.

ANNUAL EXPENSES. Tuition and fees (1992-93): $9,870. **Room and board:** $4,300. **Books and supplies:** $400. **Other expenses:** $1,000.

FINANCIAL AID. 70% of freshmen, 75% of continuing students receive some form of aid. All grants, 76% of loans, 30% of jobs based on need. 331 enrolled freshmen were judged to have need, all were offered aid. **Aid applications:** Closing date April 1; applicants notified on or about April 15; must reply by May 1.

ADDRESS/TELEPHONE. Frederick O. Bartlett, Director of Admissions, Springfield College, 263 Alden Street, Springfield, MA 01109. (413) 748-3136.

Springfield Technical Community College

Springfield, Massachusetts CB code: 3791

2-year public community, technical college, coed. Founded in 1967. **Accreditation:** Regional. **Undergraduate enrollment:** 1,216 men, 1,458 women full time; 880 men, 1,139 women part time. **Faculty:** 234 total (177 full time), 31 with doctorates or other terminal degrees. **Location:** Urban campus in small city; 90 miles from Boston, 30 miles from Hartford. **Calendar:** Semester, limited summer session. **Microcomputers:** 305 located in computer centers. **Additional facts:** National Historic Landmark campus.

DEGREES OFFERED. AA, AS. 681 associate degrees awarded in 1992. 16% in business and management, 5% business/office and marketing/distribution, 8% engineering technologies, 26% allied health, 14% multi/interdisciplinary studies, 8% parks/recreation, protective services, public affairs, 6% trade and industry.

UNDERGRADUATE MAJORS. Accounting, air conditioning/heating/refrigeration mechanics, air conditioning/heating/refrigeration technology, allied health, automotive mechanics, automotive technology, bioengineering and biomedical engineering, biomedical equipment technology, business administration and management, business and management, business and office, business data processing and related programs, business data programming, civil engineering, civil technology, computer and information sciences, cosmetology management, court reporting, data processing, dental hygiene, diagnostic medical sonography, drafting, drafting and design technology, early childhood education, electrical and electronics equipment repair, electrical technology, electrical/electronics/communications engineering, electromechanical technology, electronic technology, engineering, engineering and engineering-related technologies, engineering and other disciplines, environmental health engineering, finance, fire control and safety technology, graphic arts technology, horticulture, industrial engineering, industrial technology, landscape architecture, laser electro-optic technology, law enforcement and corrections technologies, legal secretary, liberal/general studies, marketing management, mechanical design technology, mechanical engineering, medical assistant, medical laboratory technologies, medical secretary, mental health/human services, nuclear medical technology, nursing, occupational therapy assistant, physical therapy assistant, plant sciences, predentistry, premedicine, prepharmacy, preveterinary, radiograph medical technology, respiratory therapy, respiratory therapy technology, secretarial and related programs, surgical technology, telecommunications, word processing.

ACADEMIC PROGRAMS. 2-year transfer program, cooperative education, dual enrollment of high school students, honors program, independent study, cross-registration. **Remedial services:** Learning center, reduced course load, remedial instruction, special counselor, tutoring, student development in English and Spanish. **Placement/credit:** CLEP Subject, institutional tests; 30 credit hours maximum for associate degree.

ACADEMIC REQUIREMENTS. Freshmen must earn minimum GPA of 1.7 to continue in good standing. 60% of freshmen return for sophomore year. Students must declare major on application. **Graduation requirements:** 60 hours for associate. Most students required to take courses in English, mathematics, biological/physical sciences, social sciences.

FRESHMAN ADMISSIONS. Selection criteria: Open admissions. Selective admissions to certain health, engineering and science programs. Course prerequisites vary with program. Mathematics, chemistry, biology recommended. 2 units English also recommended. **Test requirements:** SAT/ACT required for some programs.

1992 FRESHMAN CLASS PROFILE. 931 men, 1,182 women enrolled. **Academic background:** Mid 50% of enrolled freshmen had SAT-V between 350-640, SAT-M between 360-650. 10% submitted SAT scores. **Characteristics:** 98% from in state, 100% commute, 25% have minority backgrounds, 1% are foreign students. Average age is 18.

FALL-TERM APPLICATIONS. $10 fee, may be waived for applicants with need. $35 fee for out-of-state applicants. No closing date; priority given to applications received by January 31; applicants notified on a rolling basis beginning on or about December 1; must reply by May 1 or within 2 weeks if notified thereafter. Interview required for for some programs applicants. CRDA. Deferred and early admission available.

STUDENT LIFE. Activities: Student government, radio, student newspaper, yearbook, concert band, drama, Afro-American, American Indian, Spanish, Italian-American ethnic organizations, international student organization.

ATHLETICS. NJCAA. **Intercollegiate:** Baseball M, basketball, soccer, softball M, tennis. **Intramural:** Basketball, bowling, golf, softball, volleyball, wrestling M.

STUDENT SERVICES. Aptitude testing, career counseling, freshman orientation, health services, on-campus day care, personal counseling, placement service for graduates, veterans counselor, bilingual counselor, learning disabilities specialist, services/facilities for handicapped.

ANNUAL EXPENSES. Tuition and fees (1992-93): $1,856, $207 additional for out-of-district students, $3,822 additional for out-of-state students. **Books and supplies:** $400. **Other expenses:** $1,500.

FINANCIAL AID. 45% of continuing students receive some form of aid. All grants, 73% of loans, all jobs based on need. Academic, music/drama, art, athletic, leadership scholarships available. **Aid applications:** No closing date; priority given to applications received by April 1; applicants notified on a rolling basis; must reply by May 1 or within 1 week if notified thereafter.

ADDRESS/TELEPHONE. Patrick Tique, Assistant Dean Enrollment Management, Springfield Technical Community College, 1 Armory Square, Springfield, MA 01105-1296. (413) 781-7822 ext. 3855.

Stonehill College

North Easton, Massachusetts CB code: 3770

Admissions:	61% of applicants accepted
Based on:	••• School record
	•• Test scores
	• Activities, essay, interview, recommendations, special talents
Completion:	93% of freshmen end year in good standing
	80% graduate

4-year private college of arts and sciences, coed, affiliated with Roman Catholic Church. Founded in 1948. **Accreditation:** Regional. **Undergraduate enrollment:** 853 men, 1,083 women full time; 368 men, 735 women part time. **Faculty:** 282 total (112 full time), 182 with doctorates or other terminal degrees. **Location:** Suburban campus in large town; 25 miles from Boston. **Calendar:** Semester, limited summer session. **Microcomputers:** 96 located in classrooms, computer centers. **Special facilities:** Observatory, Joseph W. Martin, Jr. Institute for Law and Society.

DEGREES OFFERED. BA, BS, M. 575 bachelor's degrees awarded in 1992. 28% in business and management, 10% communications, 7% teacher education, 6% health sciences, 7% letters/literature, 6% life sciences, 10% parks/recreation, protective services, public affairs, 9% psychology, 10% social sciences.

UNDERGRADUATE MAJORS. Accounting, American studies, biology, business administration and management, chemistry, clinical laboratory science, college studies, communications, computer and information sciences, criminal justice studies, early childhood education, economics, elementary education, English literature, finance, foreign languages (multiple emphasis), health care administration, history, international studies, managerial economics, marketing management, mathematics, mathematics/computer science, philosophy, political science and government, predentistry, prelaw, premedicine, psychology, public administration, religion, sociology.

ACADEMIC PROGRAMS. Dual enrollment of high school students, honors program, independent study, internships, student-designed major, study abroad, teacher preparation, visiting/exchange student program, Washington semester, cross-registration, international internship sites in London, Madrid, Dublin, Paris, Montreal; semester at University College, Dublin; Stonehill-Quebec exchange program. **Remedial services:** Learning center, reduced course load, special counselor, tutoring, writing center. **ROTC:** Army. **Placement/credit:** AP, CLEP General and Subject, institutional tests; 30 credit hours maximum for bachelor's degree.

ACADEMIC REQUIREMENTS. Freshmen must earn minimum GPA of 2.0 to continue in good standing. 84% of freshmen return for sophomore year. Students must declare major by end of second year. **Graduation requirements:** 120 hours for bachelor's. Most students required to take courses in English, foreign languages, philosophy/religion, social sciences.

FRESHMAN ADMISSIONS. Selection criteria: School achievement record and class rank most important. Test scores considered. Activities, essay, campus visit, and letters of recommendation also considered. **High school preparation:** 16 units required. Required units include English 4, foreign language 2, mathematics 2, social science 1 and science 1. Foreign language units must be in same language. 6 electives with maximum 3 units in business subjects. Mathematics units should consist of algebra and geometry. Additional units in science and mathematics required of science applicants. **Test requirements:** SAT or ACT (SAT preferred); score report by February 15.

1992 FRESHMAN CLASS PROFILE. 1,534 men applied, 919 accepted, 201 enrolled; 2,239 women applied, 1,382 accepted, 313 enrolled. 25% were in top tenth and 66% were in top quarter of graduating class. **Academic background:** Mid 50% of enrolled freshmen had SAT-V between 430-510, SAT-M between 470-570. 99% submitted SAT scores. **Characteristics:** 61% from in state, 88% live in college housing, 4% have minority backgrounds, 1% are foreign students. Average age is 18.

FALL-TERM APPLICATIONS. $40 fee, may be waived for applicants with need. Closing date February 15; applicants notified on or about April 1; must reply by May 1. Essay required. CRDA. Deferred and early admission available.

STUDENT LIFE. Housing: Dormitories (men, women, coed). Coed townhouse residences for upperclass students. **Activities:** Student government, magazine, radio, student newspaper, yearbook, choral groups, drama, Campus Ministry, Alliance for Justice and Peace, Ames Society (service organization), Amnesty International, International Club, College Democrats, College Republicans, alcohol and environmental awareness groups, Into the Streets (volunteer network).

ATHLETICS. NCAA. **Intercollegiate:** Baseball M, basketball, cross-country, football M, horseback riding, ice hockey M, sailing, soccer, softball W, tennis, track and field, volleyball W. **Intramural:** Basketball, golf, racquetball, soccer, softball, volleyball. **Clubs:** Rugby.

STUDENT SERVICES. Career counseling, employment service for undergraduates, freshman orientation, health services, personal counseling, placement service for graduates, services/facilities for handicapped.

ANNUAL EXPENSES. Tuition and fees: $11,440. **Room and board:** $5,996. **Books and supplies:** $480. **Other expenses:** $724.

FINANCIAL AID. 69% of freshmen, 68% of continuing students receive some form of aid. 78% of grants, 91% of loans, 90% of jobs based on need. 310 enrolled freshmen were judged to have need, 306 were offered aid. Academic, music/drama, athletic scholarships available. **Aid applications:** No closing date; priority given to applications received by February 15; applicants notified on a rolling basis beginning on or about April 15; must reply by May 1 or within 2 weeks if notified thereafter.

ADDRESS/TELEPHONE. Brian P. Murphy, Dean of Admissions and Enrollment, Stonehill College, 320 Washington Street, North Easton, MA 02357-5610. (508) 230-1373. Fax: (508) 230-3732.

Suffolk University
Boston, Massachusetts CB code: 3771

Admissions: 80% of applicants accepted
Based on: ••• School record
•• Interview, recommendations, test scores
• Activities, essay, special talents
Completion: 93% of freshmen end year in good standing
60% graduate, 10% of these enter graduate study

4-year private university, coed. Founded in 1906. **Accreditation:** Regional. **Undergraduate enrollment:** 1,010 men, 1,170 women full time; 315 men, 508 women part time. **Graduate enrollment:** 596 men, 606 women full time; 1,008 men, 854 women part time. **Faculty:** 378 total (205 full time), 194 with doctorates or other terminal degrees. **Location:** Urban campus in very large city; Located in the heart of downtown Boston. **Calendar:** Semester, extensive summer session. Extensive evening/early morning classes. **Microcomputers:** 196 located in libraries, classrooms, computer centers, campus-wide network. **Special facilities:** Marine biology station at Cobscook Bay, Maine, C. Walsh Theatre.

DEGREES OFFERED. AA, AS, BA, BS, BFA, MA, MS, MBA, MEd, JD. 543 bachelor's degrees awarded. 45% in business and management, 11% communications, 6% letters/literature, 5% psychology, 22% social sciences. Graduate degrees offered in 23 major fields of study.

UNDERGRADUATE MAJORS. Associate: Legal assistant/paralegal, liberal/general studies. **Bachelor's:** Accounting, biochemistry, biological and physical sciences, biology, biotechnology, business administration and management, business and management, business education, chemistry, clinical psychology, communications, computer and information sciences, computer engineering, criminal justice studies, criminology, cytotechnology, developmental psychology, dramatic arts, economics, electrical/electronics/communications engineering, elementary education, English, finance, fine arts, French, graphic design, history, humanities and social sciences, industrial and organizational psychology, information sciences and systems, international business management, journalism, legal assistant/paralegal, liberal/general studies, management information systems, management science, marine biology, marketing and distribution, marketing management, mathematics, mathematics education, medical laboratory technologies, office supervision and management, personality psychology, philosophy, physics, political science and government, predentistry, premedicine, preveterinary, psychology, public policy studies, public relations, radio/television broadcasting, radio/television technology, science education, secondary education, social psychology, social work, sociology, Spanish, speech.

ACADEMIC PROGRAMS. Cooperative education, double major, dual enrollment of high school students, honors program, independent study, internships, study abroad, teacher preparation, visiting/exchange student program, Washington semester, cross-registration, combined degree (BFA) with New England School of Art and Design, program with Massachusetts General Hospital, international interships and exchanges; liberal arts/career combination in engineering, business; combined bachelor's/graduate program in business administration, law. **Remedial services:** Learning center, reduced course load, remedial instruction, tutoring, mathematics support center, writing center. **Placement/credit:** AP, CLEP General and Subject, IB, institutional tests; 30 credit hours maximum for associate degree; 60 credit hours maximum for bachelor's degree.

ACADEMIC REQUIREMENTS. Freshmen must earn minimum GPA of 2.0 to continue in good standing. 89% of freshmen return for sophomore year. Students must declare major on enrollment. **Graduation requirements:** 62 hours for associate, 122 hours for bachelor's (30 in major). Most students required to take courses in English, history, humanities, mathematics, philosophy/religion, biological/physical sciences, social sciences. **Postgraduate studies:** 5% enter law school, 1% enter medical school, 3% enter MBA programs, 1% enter other graduate study. **Additional information:** Joint engineering program with Boston University and Case Western Reserve University.

FRESHMAN ADMISSIONS. Selection criteria: Consider intended major, class rank, SAT scores, and counselor recommendation. **High school preparation:** 16 units required. Required units include biological science 2, English 4, foreign language 2, mathematics 3, physical science 1 and social science 4. **Test requirements:** SAT; score report by June 1.

1992 FRESHMAN CLASS PROFILE. 549 men applied, 510 accepted, 198 enrolled; 735 women applied, 516 accepted, 195 enrolled. 85% had high school GPA of 3.0 or higher, 15% between 2.0 and 2.99. 10% were in top tenth and 28% were in top quarter of graduating class. **Academic background:** Mid 50% of enrolled freshmen had SAT-V between 390-540, SAT-M between 400-550. 95% submitted SAT scores. **Characteristics:** 94% from in state, 98% commute, 25% have minority backgrounds, 12% are foreign students, 3% join fraternities/sororities. Average age is 19.

FALL-TERM APPLICATIONS. $30 fee, may be waived for applicants with need. Closing date June 1; priority given to applications received by May 1; applicants notified on a rolling basis beginning on or about December 20; must reply by May 1 or within 2 weeks if notified thereafter. Essay required. Interview recommended. CRDA. Deferred and early admission available. 3 ACH recommended.

STUDENT LIFE. Housing: Dormitories (coed). **Activities:** Student government, magazine, radio, student newspaper, television, yearbook, drama, fraternities, sororities, Hillel, Political Science Association, Black Student Union, Hispanic Association, Asian American Association, Alpha Phi Omega, Gamma Sigma Sigma, International Student Association.

ATHLETICS. NCAA. **Intercollegiate:** Baseball M, basketball, cross-country, golf, ice hockey M, soccer, softball W, tennis. **Intramural:** Basketball, softball, volleyball.

STUDENT SERVICES. Aptitude testing, career counseling, employment service for undergraduates, freshman orientation, health services, personal counseling, placement service for graduates, special adviser for adult students, veterans counselor, services/facilities for handicapped.

ANNUAL EXPENSES. Tuition and fees (1992-93): $9,200. **Room and board:** $5,600. **Books and supplies:** $500. **Other expenses:** $2,450.

FINANCIAL AID. 60% of freshmen, 56% of continuing students receive some form of aid. 91% of grants, 94% of loans, 91% of jobs based on need. Academic, leadership scholarships available. **Aid applications:** Closing date March 1; applicants notified on or about April 1; must reply by May 1 or within 2 weeks if notified thereafter.

ADDRESS/TELEPHONE. William F. Coughlin, Director of Admissions, Suffolk University, Beacon Hill, 8 Ashburton Place, Boston, MA 02108-2772. (617) 573-8460. (800) 6-SUFFOLK. Fax: (617) 573-8703.

Tufts University
Medford, Massachusetts

CB code: 3901

Admissions: 45% of applicants accepted
Based on: ••• School record
•• Activities, essay, recommendations, special talents, test scores
• Interview
Completion: 99% of freshmen end year in good standing
90% graduate, 35% of these enter graduate study

4-year private university, coed. Founded in 1852. **Accreditation:** Regional. **Undergraduate enrollment:** 2,126 men, 2,306 women full time. **Graduate enrollment:** 1,321 men, 1,420 women full time; 201 men, 268 women part time. **Faculty:** 572 total (338 full time). **Location:** Suburban campus in small city; 5 miles from Boston. **Calendar:** Semester, limited summer session. **Microcomputers:** 140 located in libraries, computer centers, campus-wide network. **Special facilities:** Computer-aided design laboratory, European center in Talloires, France, center for the arts. **Additional facts:** Schools of medicine, dentistry, veterinary medicine, and Sackler School of Biomedical Sciences in Boston. Graduate School of Nutrition, Graduate School of Arts and Science, and Fletcher School of Law and Diplomacy

DEGREES OFFERED. BA, BS, BFA, MA, MS, MFA, PhD, DMD, MD, DVM. 1,175 bachelor's degrees awarded in 1992. Graduate degrees offered in 100 major fields of study.

UNDERGRADUATE MAJORS. African studies, Afro-American (black) studies, American literature, American studies, anthropology, applied mathematics, archeology, architectural engineering, art education, art history, Asian studies, astronomy, biological and physical sciences, biology, chemical engineering, chemistry, Chinese, civil engineering, classics, clinical psychology, cognitive psychology, comparative literature, computer and information sciences, computer engineering, computer programming, curriculum and instruction, developmental psychology, dramatic arts, East Asian studies, Eastern European studies, ecology, economics, electrical/electronics/communications engineering, elementary education, engineering, engineering and other disciplines, engineering mechanics, engineering physics, engineering science, English, English education, English literature, environmental health engineering, environmental science, European studies, experimental psychology, fine arts, foreign languages (multiple emphasis), French, geology, geophysical engineering, German, Greek (classical), health sciences, history, human factors engineering, humanities and social sciences, information sciences and systems, international relations, Italian, Latin, Latin American studies, liberal/general studies, mathematics, mathematics education, mechanical engineering, Middle Eastern studies, music, music education, music history and appreciation, philosophy, physics, political science and government, psychology, public health laboratory science, reading education, religion, Russian, Russian and Slavic studies, science education, social psychology, social studies education, sociology, Spanish, systems analysis, visual and performing arts, Western European studies.

ACADEMIC PROGRAMS. Accelerated program, double major, honors program, independent study, internships, semester at sea, student-designed major, study abroad, teacher preparation, Washington semester, cross-registration, experimental college, semester exchange with Swarthmore College, 3-2 programs with New England Conservatory of Music (BA/BM) and School of the Museum of Fine Arts (BA/BFA) European Center in Talloires, France; liberal arts/career combination in engineering. **Remedial services:** Learning center, tutoring. **ROTC:** Air Force, Army, Naval. **Placement/credit:** AP, IB, institutional tests.

ACADEMIC REQUIREMENTS. No policy requiring minimum GPA; records of students having academic difficulty are reviewed individually. 99% of freshmen return for sophomore year. Students must declare major by end of second year. **Graduation requirements:** Most students required to take courses in arts/fine arts, English, foreign languages, humanities, mathematics, biological/physical sciences, social sciences. **Additional information:** For bachelor's degree, liberal arts students required to complete minimum 10 courses in major and 34 courses for graduation. Engineering students required minimum 12 courses in major and 38 courses for graduation.

FRESHMAN ADMISSIONS. Selection criteria: School achievement record and test scores most important. Character, personality, extracurricular participation, and special talents also considered. Special attention to geographical distribution, alumni relationship, minority status. Recommended units include English 4 and science 1. 3-4 mathematics, 3-4 foreign language, and 1 history also recommended. 4 mathematics, 2 laboratory science recommended for engineering, mathematics, and science majors. **Test requirements:** SAT or ACT; score report by March 1. For students submitting SAT, 3 ACH (including English Composition) required. Mathematics Level I or II, and Physics or Chemistry required of engineering applicants who submit the SAT. Score report by March 1.

1992 FRESHMAN CLASS PROFILE. 3,786 men applied, 1,680 accepted, 570 enrolled; 4,143 women applied, 1,849 accepted, 625 enrolled. 62% were in top tenth and 89% were in top quarter of graduating class. **Academic background:** Mid 50% of enrolled freshmen had SAT-V between 540-630, SAT-M between 610-700. 85% submitted SAT scores. **Characteristics:** 25% from in state, 98% live in college housing, 19% have minority backgrounds, 7% are foreign students. Average age is 18.

FALL-TERM APPLICATIONS. $50 fee, may be waived for applicants with need. Closing date January 1; applicants notified on or about April 1; must reply by May 1. Essay required. Interview recommended. CRDA. Deferred and early admission available. EDP-F. First round of early decision, apply by November 15, decisions rendered December 15. Second round of early decision, apply by January 1, decisions rendered February 1.

STUDENT LIFE. Housing: Dormitories (women, coed); fraternity, sorority, cooperative housing available. Culture, special interest, and language houses available. **Activities:** Student government, film, magazine, radio, student newspaper, television, yearbook, choral groups, concert band, dance, drama, jazz band, marching band, music ensembles, musical theater, opera, symphony orchestra, fraternities, sororities, 140 student organizations including volunteer community service organizations, religious and cultural organizations, Afro-American Society, International Club, Asian Students Club, Hispanic-American Society, political action and media groups, environmental action groups.

ATHLETICS. NCAA. **Intercollegiate:** Baseball M, basketball, cross-country, diving, field hockey W, football M, golf M, horseback riding, ice hockey M, lacrosse, rowing (crew), rugby, sailing, soccer, softball W, squash, swimming, tennis, track and field, volleyball W. **Intramural:** Badminton, basketball, cross-country, diving, fencing, handball, racquetball, skiing, skin diving, softball, squash, swimming, tennis, track and field, volleyball, wrestling M.

STUDENT SERVICES. Aptitude testing, career counseling, employment service for undergraduates, freshman orientation, health services, on-campus day care, personal counseling, placement service for graduates, special adviser for adult students, services/facilities for handicapped.

ANNUAL EXPENSES. Tuition and fees: $19,269. **Room and board:** $5,693. **Books and supplies:** $600. **Other expenses:** $938.

FINANCIAL AID. 39% of freshmen, 39% of continuing students receive some form of aid. All grants, 98% of loans, all jobs based on need. 416 enrolled freshmen were judged to have need, all were offered aid. Academic scholarships available. **Aid applications:** Closing date February 1; applicants notified on or about April 15; must reply by May 1.

ADDRESS/TELEPHONE. David Cuttino, Dean of Admissions, Tufts University, Medford, MA 02155-5555. (617) 627-3170. Fax: (617) 627-3860.

University of Massachusetts at Amherst
Amherst, Massachusetts

CB code: 3917

Admissions: 88% of applicants accepted
Based on: ••• School record, test scores
•• Essay
• Activities, recommendations, special talents
Completion: 94% of freshmen end year in good standing
60% graduate

4-year public university, coed. Founded in 1863. **Accreditation:** Regional. **Undergraduate enrollment:** 8,496 men, 7,887 women full time; 354 men, 392 women part time. **Graduate enrollment:** 1,021 men, 1,065 women full time; 1,308 men, 1,311 women part time. **Faculty:** 1,254 total (1,154 full time), 1,119 with doctorates or other terminal degrees. **Location:** Rural campus in large town; 90 miles from Boston, 30 miles from Springfield. **Calendar:** Semester, limited summer session. **Microcomputers:** 200 located in dormitories, libraries, classrooms, computer centers. **Special facilities:** Fine Art Center complex with concert hall, gallery, Rand Theater and Benzanson Recital Hall. 6 additional art galleries, Mullins Sports Arena, observatory, botanical gardens, Robsham Vistor's Center. **Additional facts:** Five college interchange program with Amherst, Hampshire, Mount Holyoke and Smith Colleges.

DEGREES OFFERED. AS, BA, BS, BFA, MA, MS, MBA, MFA, MEd. 30 associate degrees awarded in 1992. 100% in agriculture. 4,212 bachelor's degrees awarded. 5% in agriculture, 16% business and management, 7% communications, 7% engineering, 7% letters/literature, 6% psychology, 19% social sciences. Graduate degrees offered in 72 major fields of study.

UNDERGRADUATE MAJORS. Associate: Agricultural production, animal sciences, equestrian science, horticulture, landscape contracting, ornamental horticulture, turf management. **Bachelor's:** Accounting, Afro-American (black) studies, animal sciences, anthropology, apparel and accessories marketing, applied and resource economic, art education, art history, astronomy, biochemistry, biological and physical sciences, biology, building materials technology and management, business administration and management, chemical engineering, chemistry, Chinese, civil engineering, classics, communications, comparative literature, computer and information sciences, computer engineering, dance, dramatic arts, Eastern European studies, economics, education, electrical/electronics/communications engineering, English, entomology, environmental design, environmental science, exercise science, family/consumer resource management, finance, fishing and fisheries, food science and nutrition, food sciences, forestry and related sciences, French, geography, geology, German, history, hotel/motel and restaurant management, humanities, humanities and social sciences, individual and family development, industrial engineering, interior design, international hospitality management, Italian, Japanese, Jewish studies, journalism, landscape architecture, legal studies, liberal/general studies, linguistics, marketing management, mathematics, mechanical engineering, medical laboratory technologies, microbiology, Middle Eastern studies, music, music performance, nursing, parks and recreation management, philosophy, physical education, physics, plant pathology, plant protection, plant sciences, political science and government, Portuguese, predentistry, prelaw, premedicine, preveterinary, psychology, public health laboratory science, renewable natural resources, Russian, sociology, soil sciences, Spanish, speech pathology/audiology, sports management, studio art, women's studies, woodscience technology, woodscience/technology.

ACADEMIC PROGRAMS. Cooperative education, education specialist degree, internships, study abroad, teacher preparation, visiting/exchange student program, Washington semester, cross-registration, bilingual program. **Remedial services:** Learning center, preadmission summer program, remedial instruction, special counselor, tutoring. **ROTC:** Air Force, Army. **Placement/credit:** AP, CLEP General and Subject, institutional tests; 30 credit hours maximum for bachelor's degree.

ACADEMIC REQUIREMENTS. Freshmen must earn minimum GPA of 2.0 to continue in good standing. 77% of freshmen return for sophomore year. Students must declare major by end of second year. **Graduation requirements:** 60 hours for associate (60 in major), 120 hours for bachelor's (30 in major). Most students required to take courses in English, foreign languages, history, humanities, mathematics, biological/physical sciences, social sciences.

FRESHMAN ADMISSIONS. Selection criteria: Primarily high school grades and class rank, followed by test scores, recommendations, essay, activities, quality of school. Special consideration given to minority students. **High school preparation:** 16 units required. Required units include English 4, foreign language 2, mathematics 3, social science 2 and science 2. 4 units mathematics required for business management, engineering, computer science applicants. Strong mathematics and science background recommended for engineering. **Test requirements:** SAT or ACT (SAT preferred); score report by February 15.

1992 FRESHMAN CLASS PROFILE. 6,653 men applied, 5,718 accepted, 1,965 enrolled; 7,221 women applied, 6,425 accepted, 1,929 enrolled. 13% were in top tenth and 40% were in top quarter of graduating class. **Academic background:** Mid 50% of enrolled freshmen had SAT-V between 410-520, SAT-M between 460-580. 99% submitted SAT scores. **Characteristics:** 76% from in state, 98% live in college housing, 15% have minority backgrounds, 2% are foreign students. Average age is 18.

FALL-TERM APPLICATIONS. $20 fee, may be waived for applicants with need. $35 fee for out-of-state applicants. Closing date February 15; applicants notified on a rolling basis beginning on or about January 1; must reply by May 1. Audition required for music, and dance applicants. Portfolio required for art applicants. Essay required. CRDA. Early admission available.

STUDENT LIFE. Housing: Dormitories (men, women, coed); apartment, fraternity, sorority housing available. Freshmen and sophomores living on campus must purchase meal plan. Vegetarian and Kosher plans available. **Activities:** Student government, film, magazine, radio, student newspaper, television, yearbook, choral groups, concert band, dance, drama, jazz band, marching band, music ensembles, musical theater, pep band, symphony orchestra, fraternities, sororities, 189 registered social, religious, political, ethnic, and social service student organizations, and several student-run cooperatives.

ATHLETICS. NCAA. **Intercollegiate:** Baseball M, basketball, cross-country, diving, field hockey W, football M, gymnastics, lacrosse, skiing, soccer, softball W, swimming, tennis W, track and field, volleyball W, water polo M. **Intramural:** Archery, badminton, basketball, cross-country, diving, fencing, football, golf, gymnastics, ice hockey, racquetball, rowing (crew), rugby, soccer, softball, squash, swimming, table tennis, tennis, track and field, volleyball, wrestling M. **Clubs:** Bicycle racing, volleyball, crew, croquet, fencing, golf, rugby, water polo.

STUDENT SERVICES. Aptitude testing, career counseling, employment service for undergraduates, freshman orientation, health services, on-campus day care, personal counseling, placement service for graduates, special adviser for adult students, veterans counselor, counselors for married and handicapped students, handicapped support group, services/facilities for handicapped.

ANNUAL EXPENSES. Tuition and fees (projected): $5,467, $6,346 additional for out-of-state students. New England residents outside of Massachusetts pay reduced tuition plus applicable fees in selected majors. **Room and board:** $3,828. **Books and supplies:** $500. **Other expenses:** $1,000.

FINANCIAL AID. 47% of freshmen, 49% of continuing students receive some form of aid. 87% of grants, 90% of loans, 30% of jobs based on need. Academic, music/drama, art, athletic, state/district residency, leadership, alumni affiliation, minority scholarships available. **Aid applications:** No closing date; priority given to applications received by March 1; applicants notified on a rolling basis beginning on or about April 1; must reply by May 1 or within 2 weeks if notified thereafter.

ADDRESS/TELEPHONE. Timm Rinehart, Director of Undergraduate Admissions, University of Massachusetts at Amherst, University Admissions Center, Amherst, MA 01003. (413) 545-0222. Fax: (413) 545-4312.

University of Massachusetts at Boston

Boston, Massachusetts CB code: 3924

Admissions: 57% of applicants accepted
Based on: ••• School record
•• Essay, recommendations, test scores
• Activities, interview, special talents
Completion: 22% enter graduate study

4-year public university, coed. Founded in 1964. **Accreditation:** Regional. **Undergraduate enrollment:** 2,756 men, 3,061 women full time; 1,241 men, 1,635 women part time. **Graduate enrollment:** 215 men, 366 women full time; 485 men, 831 women part time. **Faculty:** 820 total (457 full time). **Location:** Urban campus in very large city; 3 miles from downtown. **Calendar:** Semester, extensive summer session. Extensive evening/early morning classes. **Microcomputers:** 390 located in libraries. **Special facilities:** Harbor Art Gallery, tropical greenhouse, observatory, adaptive computer laboratory.

DEGREES OFFERED. BA, BS, MA, MS, MBA, MEd, PhD, EdD. 1,636 bachelor's degrees awarded in 1992. 16% in business and management, 8% teacher education, 11% health sciences, 10% letters/literature, 6% parks/recreation, protective services, public affairs, 9% psychology, 24% social sciences. Graduate degrees offered in 24 major fields of study.

UNDERGRADUATE MAJORS. Afro-American (black) studies, anthropology, applied mathematics, biology, business and management, chemistry, classics, community services, computer and information sciences, criminal justice studies, dramatic arts, economics, engineering physics, English, fine arts, foreign languages (multiple emphasis), French, geography, German, gerontology, Greek (classical), history, human services, humanities and social sciences, Italian, labor/industrial relations, Latin, law , medical laboratory technologies, music, nursing, philosophy, physical education, physics, political science and government, psychology, public policy studies, pure mathematics, Russian, sociology, Spanish, women's studies.

ACADEMIC PROGRAMS. Computer delivered (on-line) credit-bearing course offerings, cooperative education, double major, honors program, independent study, internships, student-designed major, study abroad, teacher preparation, visiting/exchange student program, cross-registration, 2-2 programs in engineering with area institutions; combined bachelor's/graduate program in business administration. **Remedial services:** Learning center, preadmission summer program, reduced course load, remedial instruction, special counselor, tutoring, support services for learning and physically disabled students, adaptive computer laboratory. **Placement/credit:** AP, CLEP General and Subject, institutional tests; 90 credit hours maximum for bachelor's degree.

ACADEMIC REQUIREMENTS. Freshmen must earn minimum GPA of 1.65 to continue in good standing. 72% of freshmen return for sophomore year. Students must declare major by end of second year. **Graduation requirements:** 120 hours for bachelor's. Most students required to take courses in arts/fine arts, computer science, English, foreign languages, history, humanities, mathematics, philosophy/religion, biological/physical sciences, social sciences. **Postgraduate studies:** 22% enter other graduate study.

FRESHMAN ADMISSIONS. Selection criteria: School achievement record, sliding scale of test scores and high school rank, extracurricular activities, and recommendations important. **High school preparation:** 16 units required. Required units include English 4, foreign language 2, mathematics 3, social science 2 and science 2. **Test requirements:** SAT or ACT (SAT preferred); score report by June 15.

1992 FRESHMAN CLASS PROFILE. 1,197 men applied, 694 accepted, 386 enrolled; 1,181 women applied, 672 accepted, 348 enrolled. **Academic background:** Mid 50% of enrolled freshmen had SAT-V between 300-460, SAT-M between 360-520. 58% submitted SAT scores. **Characteristics:** 94% from in state, 100% commute, 38% have minority backgrounds, 3% are foreign students. Average age is 23.

FALL-TERM APPLICATIONS. $15 fee, may be waived for applicants with need. $30 fee for out-of-state applicants. Closing date June 15; priority given to applications received by March 15; applicants notified on a rolling basis. Interview recommended for nontraditional applicants. Essay recommended. CRDA. Deferred admission available.

STUDENT LIFE. Activities: Student government, magazine, radio, student newspaper, yearbook, choral groups, dance, drama, jazz band, music ensembles, musical theater, more than 30 religious, political, ethnic, and special-interest organizations.

ATHLETICS. NCAA. **Intercollegiate:** Baseball M, basketball, cross-country, diving, football M, ice hockey M, lacrosse M, soccer M, softball W, swimming, tennis M, volleyball W, wrestling M. **Intramural:** Basketball, ice hockey M, racquetball, sailing, softball, squash, tennis, volleyball.

STUDENT SERVICES. Aptitude testing, career counseling, employment service for undergraduates, freshman orientation, health services, on-campus day care, personal counseling, placement service for graduates,

special adviser for adult students, veterans counselor, birth control counseling, women's center, advising center, services/facilities for handicapped.

ANNUAL EXPENSES. Tuition and fees (1992-93): $4,087, $6,103 additional for out-of-state students. New England residents outside of Massachusetts pay $4,007 tuition plus applicable fees. **Books and supplies:** $540. **Other expenses:** $1,182.

FINANCIAL AID. 64% of freshmen, 42% of continuing students receive some form of aid. 99% of grants, 83% of loans, 37% of jobs based on need. 402 enrolled freshmen were judged to have need, 361 were offered aid. Academic, leadership scholarships available. **Aid applications:** No closing date; priority given to applications received by March 15; applicants notified on a rolling basis beginning on or about April 15; must reply by May 1 or within 3 weeks if notified thereafter. **Additional information:** Some Massachusetts state employees and Massachusetts Vietnam veterans eligible for tuition waiver. Some waivers available based on talent and academic excellence.

ADDRESS/TELEPHONE. David M. Norris, Director of Undergraduate Admissions, University of Massachusetts at Boston, 100 Morrissey Boulevard, Boston, MA 02125-3393. (617) 287-6000. Fax: (617) 287-6242.

University of Massachusetts at Dartmouth
North Dartmouth, Massachusetts — CB code: 3786

Admissions: 67% of applicants accepted
Based on:
- ••• School record
- •• Recommendations, test scores
- • Activities, special talents

Completion: 50% graduate

4-year public university, coed. Founded in 1895. **Accreditation:** Regional. **Undergraduate enrollment:** 2,314 men, 2,264 women full time; 139 men, 167 women part time. **Graduate enrollment:** 79 men, 46 women full time; 115 men, 118 women part time. **Faculty:** 413 total (325 full time), 298 with doctorates or other terminal degrees. **Location:** Suburban campus in large town; 50 miles from Boston, 25 miles from Providence, Rhode Island. **Calendar:** Semester, extensive summer session. **Microcomputers:** 250 located in dormitories, libraries, classrooms, computer centers, campus-wide network. **Special facilities:** Art gallery, observatory, marine research vessel.

DEGREES OFFERED. BA, BS, BFA, MA, MS, MBA, MFA. 1,085 bachelor's degrees awarded in 1992. 30% in business and management, 11% engineering, 5% engineering technologies, 7% health sciences, 6% psychology, 15% social sciences, 11% visual and performing arts. Graduate degrees offered in 19 major fields of study.

UNDERGRADUATE MAJORS. Accounting, art education, art history, biology, business administration and management, business and management, ceramics, chemistry, civil engineering, computer and information sciences, computer engineering, cytotechnology, economics, electrical technology, electrical/electronics/communications engineering, engineering, engineering and engineering-related technologies, English, English literature, fiber/textiles/weaving, finance, French, graphic design, history, humanities and social sciences, illustration design, information sciences and systems, inorganic chemistry, marine biology, marketing and distribution, mathematics, mechanical engineering, medical laboratory technologies, metal/jewelry, motion picture technology, music, nursing, painting, philosophy, photography, physics, political science and government, Portuguese, printmaking, sculpture, sociology, Spanish, technical and business writing, textile chemistry, textile technology.

ACADEMIC PROGRAMS. Accelerated program, double major, dual enrollment of high school students, honors program, independent study, internships, student-designed major, study abroad, teacher preparation, visiting/exchange student program, Washington semester, cross-registration. **Remedial services:** Learning center, reduced course load, remedial instruction, special counselor, tutoring. **Placement/credit:** AP, institutional tests; 30 credit hours maximum for bachelor's degree.

ACADEMIC REQUIREMENTS. Freshmen must earn minimum GPA of 1.5 to continue in good standing. 85% of freshmen return for sophomore year. Students must declare major by end of second year. **Graduation requirements:** 120 hours for bachelor's (30 in major). Most students required to take courses in English, humanities, biological/physical sciences, social sciences. **Additional information:** Alternative admissions program for academically disadvantaged Massachusetts residents. Program offers special freshman curriculum and counseling support. Applicants must be low income; limited English proficiency; or ethnic minority. The S.T.A.R.T. program offers women and minorities interested in scientific or technical majors a freshmen year of special courses. Those who select science or engineering as first choice are automatically considered.

FRESHMAN ADMISSIONS. Selection criteria: Selective admissions based on the university's ability to predict probable academic success. Decision based on school record, test scores, and counselor/teacher recommendation. Minority applicants actively sought. Alternative admissions programs include College Now and S.T.A.R.T. **High school preparation:** 16 units required. Required units include English 4, foreign language 2, mathematics 3, social science 2 and science 2. One unit of American history required. Programs in science, engineering and business require additional mathematics. Science and engineering require physical science. **Test requirements:** SAT. **Additional information:** Freshman applicants advised to apply before end of December and not later than March.

1992 FRESHMAN CLASS PROFILE. 3,590 men and women applied, 2,422 accepted; 418 men enrolled, 451 women enrolled. 10% were in top tenth and 50% were in top quarter of graduating class. **Academic background:** Mid 50% of enrolled freshmen had SAT-V between 380-480, SAT-M between 430-560. 95% submitted SAT scores. **Characteristics:** 96% from in state, 60% live in college housing, 6% have minority backgrounds, 1% are foreign students. Average age is 19.

FALL-TERM APPLICATIONS. $20 fee, may be waived for applicants with need. $40 fee for out-of-state applicants. No closing date; applicants notified on a rolling basis beginning on or about January 15; must reply by May 1 or within 3 weeks if notified thereafter. Audition required for music applicants. Portfolio recommended. CRDA. Deferred and early admission available. EDP-F. Competitive programs may be filled by March 1.

STUDENT LIFE. Housing: Dormitories (coed). Quiet substance free housing available. Apartment style living for upper classmen and graduate students only. **Activities:** Student government, film, magazine, radio, student newspaper, yearbook, literary magazine, women's journal, choral groups, concert band, drama, jazz band, music ensembles, pep band, symphony orchestra, Protestant, Catholic, and Jewish organizations, United Brothers and Sisters Women's center, Public Interest Research Group.

ATHLETICS. NCAA. **Intercollegiate:** Baseball M, basketball, cross-country, diving, field hockey W, football M, golf M, horseback riding W, ice hockey M, lacrosse M, soccer, softball W, swimming, tennis, track and field, volleyball W. **Intramural:** Basketball, cross-country, racquetball, skiing, softball, tennis, volleyball, water polo.

STUDENT SERVICES. Aptitude testing, career counseling, employment service for undergraduates, freshman orientation, health services, on-campus day care, personal counseling, placement service for graduates, special adviser for adult students, veterans counselor, disabled student services, academic assistance center, services/facilities for handicapped.

ANNUAL EXPENSES. Tuition and fees (1992-93): $3,153, $4,886 additional for out-of-state students. New England residents outside of Massachusetts pay $2,649 plus applicable fees. **Room and board:** $4,471. **Books and supplies:** $500. **Other expenses:** $1,000.

FINANCIAL AID. 40% of freshmen, 38% of continuing students receive some form of aid. 82% of grants, 31% of loans, all jobs based on need. Academic, state/district residency, minority scholarships available. **Aid applications:** No closing date; priority given to applications received by May 1; applicants notified on a rolling basis beginning on or about May 1; must reply within 2 weeks. **Additional information:** Tuition payment plan offered by external finance company.

ADDRESS/TELEPHONE. Raymond M. Barrows, Director of Admissions, University of Massachusetts at Dartmouth, Old Westport Road, North Dartmouth, MA 02747-2300. (508) 999-8605. Fax: (508) 999-8901.

University of Massachusetts at Lowell
Lowell, Massachusetts — CB code: 3911

4-year public university, coed. Founded in 1894. **Accreditation:** Regional. **Undergraduate enrollment:** 7,104 men and women. **Graduate enrollment:** 2,269 men and women. **Faculty:** 620 total (508 full time), 413 with doctorates or other terminal degrees. **Location:** Urban campus in small city; 25 miles from Boston. **Calendar:** Semester, extensive summer session. **Microcomputers:** 1,000 located in dormitories, libraries, classrooms, computer centers.

DEGREES OFFERED. AS, BA, BS, BFA, MA, MS, MBA, MEd, PhD, EdD. 60 associate degrees awarded in 1992. 1,644 bachelor's degrees awarded. Graduate degrees offered in 38 major fields of study.

UNDERGRADUATE MAJORS. Associate: Accounting, applied mathematics, business and management, chemistry, civil technology, criminal justice studies, electronic technology, finance, information sciences and systems, mechanical design technology. **Bachelor's:** Accounting, American studies, applied mathematics, atmospheric sciences and meteorology, basic clinical health sciences, biology, biotechnology, business administration and management, chemical engineering, chemistry, civil engineering, civil technology, computer and information sciences, criminal justice studies, earth sciences, economics, electrical/electronics/communications engineering, electronic technology, engineering and other disciplines, English, environmental science, finance, fine arts, foreign languages (multiple emphasis), French, geology, graphic design, health education, history, industrial technology, information sciences and systems, liberal/general studies, management information systems, marketing management, mathematics, mechanical design technology, mechanical engineering, medical laboratory technologies, music, music business management, music education, music history and appreciation, music performance, music theory and composition, nuclear engineering, nursing, philosophy, physics, plastics engineering, political science and government, psychology, sociology, Spanish, statistics, trade and industrial supervision and management.

ACADEMIC PROGRAMS. 2-year transfer program, cooperative educa-

tion, double major, honors program, internships, study abroad, teacher preparation, cross-registration; liberal arts/career combination in engineering. **Remedial services:** Learning center, preadmission summer program, reduced course load, remedial instruction, special counselor, tutoring. **ROTC:** Air Force, Army. **Placement/credit:** AP, CLEP General and Subject, institutional tests; 30 credit hours maximum for bachelor's degree.

ACADEMIC REQUIREMENTS. Freshmen must earn minimum GPA of 1.5 to continue in good standing. 77% of freshmen return for sophomore year. Students must declare major on application. **Graduation requirements:** 60 hours for associate, 120 hours for bachelor's. Most students required to take courses in English, humanities, mathematics, biological/physical sciences, social sciences.

FRESHMAN ADMISSIONS. Selection criteria: School record, test scores, class rank, and recommendations most important. **High school preparation:** 16 units required. Required units include English 4, foreign language 2, mathematics 3, social science 3 and science 2. **Test requirements:** SAT or ACT (SAT preferred).

1992 FRESHMAN CLASS PROFILE. 1,053 men and women enrolled. **Characteristics:** 92% from in state, 75% commute, 19% have minority backgrounds, 3% are foreign students. Average age is 18.

FALL-TERM APPLICATIONS. $10 fee, may be waived for applicants with need. $25 for out-of-state applicants. No closing date; priority given to applications received by April 1; applicants notified on a rolling basis beginning on or about January 15; must reply within 3 weeks. Audition required for music applicants. Interview recommended. Deferred admission available.

STUDENT LIFE. Housing: Dormitories (men, women, coed); apartment housing available. **Activities:** Student government, radio, student newspaper, yearbook, choral groups, concert band, drama, marching band, music ensembles, musical theater, pep band.

ATHLETICS. NCAA. **Intercollegiate:** Baseball M, basketball, bowling, cross-country, field hockey W, football M, golf M, ice hockey M, lacrosse M, rowing (crew), skiing, soccer, softball W, swimming, tennis, track and field, volleyball W, wrestling M. **Intramural:** Badminton, basketball, bowling, diving, horseback riding W, ice hockey, racquetball, rowing (crew), soccer, softball, swimming, table tennis, tennis, volleyball.

STUDENT SERVICES. Career counseling, freshman orientation, health services, personal counseling, placement service for graduates, special adviser for adult students, veterans counselor, services/facilities for handicapped.

ANNUAL EXPENSES. Tuition and fees (1992-93): $4,513, $4,911 additional for out-of-state students. New England residents outside of Massachusetts pay $2,771 tuition plus applicable fees. **Room and board:** $4,223. **Books and supplies:** $400. **Other expenses:** $1,160.

FINANCIAL AID. 40% of freshmen, 40% of continuing students receive some form of aid. **Aid applications:** Closing date May 1; applicants notified on or about May 1; must reply within 2 weeks.

ADDRESS/TELEPHONE. Lawrence R. Martin, Director of Admissions, University of Massachusetts at Lowell, 1 University Avenue, Lowell, MA 01854. (508) 934-3930.

Wellesley College

Wellesley, Massachusetts CB code: 3957

Admissions: 49% of applicants accepted
Based on: ••• School record
•• Activities, essay, recommendations, test scores
• Interview, special talents
Completion: 96% of freshmen end year in good standing
85% graduate, 95% of these enter graduate study

4-year private liberal arts college, women only. Founded in 1870. **Accreditation:** Regional. **Undergraduate enrollment:** 2,123 women full time; 204 women part time. **Faculty:** 314 total (241 full time), 274 with doctorates or other terminal degrees. **Location:** Suburban campus in large town; 12 miles from Boston. **Calendar:** 4-1-4. **Microcomputers:** 150 located in dormitories, libraries, classrooms, computer centers. **Special facilities:** Science center, Center for Research on Women, Child Study Center, art and music center, art museum, observatory, botanic gardens, sports complex.

DEGREES OFFERED. BA. 540 bachelor's degrees awarded in 1992. 7% in area and ethnic studies, 10% languages, 11% letters/literature, 9% life sciences, 8% multi/interdisciplinary studies, 5% physical sciences, 9% psychology, 27% social sciences, 5% visual and performing arts.

UNDERGRADUATE MAJORS. Afro-American (black) studies, American studies, anthropology, archeology, architecture, art history, Asian studies, astronomy, biochemistry, biological and physical sciences, biology, chemistry, Chinese, classical and Near Eastern archeology, classics, cognitive science, computer and information sciences, East Asian studies, economics, engineering, English, European studies, foreign languages (multiple emphasis), French, geology, German, Greek (classical), history, humanities and social sciences, international relations, Italian, Japanese, Jewish studies, language studies, Latin, Latin American studies, mathematics, medieval studies, music, music history and appreciation, peace studies, philosophy, physics, political science and government, prelaw, premedicine, psychobiology, psychology, religion, Russian, Russian and Slavic studies, sociology, Spanish, studio art, technology studies, Western European studies, women's studies.

ACADEMIC PROGRAMS. Accelerated program, double major, honors program, independent study, internships, semester at sea, student-designed major, study abroad, teacher preparation, visiting/exchange student program, Washington semester, cross-registration, dual degree program in engineering with Massachusetts Institute of Technology, Technology Studies Program, exchanges with Mills College and Spelman College. **Remedial services:** Reduced course load, special counselor, tutoring, peer counselors in academic skills. **ROTC:** Air Force, Army. **Placement/credit:** AP, IB, institutional tests; 32 credit hours maximum for bachelor's degree.

ACADEMIC REQUIREMENTS. Freshmen must earn minimum GPA of 2.0 to continue in good standing. 97% of freshmen return for sophomore year. Students must declare major by end of second year. **Graduation requirements:** 128 hours for bachelor's (32 in major). Most students required to take courses in English, foreign languages, humanities, mathematics, biological/physical sciences, social sciences. **Postgraduate studies:** 23% enter law school, 16% enter medical school, 3% enter MBA programs, 53% enter other graduate study.

FRESHMAN ADMISSIONS. Selection criteria: Academic success and potential and school achievement record are most important. Test scores, recommendations, essays, school activities, and interview also reviewed. Students from all geographic areas, all ethnic groups, and all income categories are actively encouraged. **High school preparation:** 17 units recommended. Recommended units include English 4, foreign language 4, mathematics 4, social science 3 and science 3. **Test requirements:** SAT; score report by January 15. 3 ACH required (including English Composition, with or without essay), except for students from mainland China who must take TOEFL. Score report by January 15.

1992 FRESHMAN CLASS PROFILE. 2,509 women applied, 1,230 accepted, 619 enrolled. 74% were in top tenth and 95% were in top quarter of graduating class. **Academic background:** Mid 50% of enrolled freshmen had SAT-V between 540-640, SAT-M between 570-670. 99% submitted SAT scores. **Characteristics:** 16% from in state, 99% live in college housing, 35% have minority backgrounds, 8% are foreign students. Average age is 18.

FALL-TERM APPLICATIONS. $45 fee, may be waived for applicants with need. Closing date January 15; applicants notified on or about April 2; must reply by May 1. Essay required. Interview recommended. CRDA. Deferred and early admission available. EDP-S. Early decision plan deadline November 1. Early evaluation program available for students who requested credentials by January 1. Notifications of admission are sent by end of February with final decision sent in early-April.

STUDENT LIFE. Housing: Dormitories (women); cooperative housing available. French and Spanish houses available. **Activities:** Student government, film, magazine, radio, student newspaper, yearbook, choral groups, dance, drama, jazz band, music ensembles, symphony orchestra, chamber music society, Carilloneers, acappella groups, Ethos (black students), Alianza and Mezcla (Latina students), Newman Catholic Association, Hillel, Christian Fellowship, Slater International Organization, Young Democrats, Young Republicans, Asian Association, Fiske Outreach Program (social service).

ATHLETICS. NCAA. **Intercollegiate:** Basketball, cross-country, diving, fencing, field hockey, lacrosse, rowing (crew), soccer, squash, swimming, tennis, volleyball. **Intramural:** Archery, badminton, basketball, cross-country, golf, racquetball, rowing (crew), rugby, sailing, skiing, soccer, softball, squash, swimming, table tennis, tennis, volleyball, water polo.

STUDENT SERVICES. Aptitude testing, career counseling, employment service for undergraduates, freshman orientation, health services, on-campus day care, personal counseling, placement service for graduates, special adviser for adult students, preventive mental health center, services/facilities for handicapped.

ANNUAL EXPENSES. Tuition and fees: $17,725. **Room and board:** $6,090. **Books and supplies:** $500. **Other expenses:** $700.

FINANCIAL AID. 50% of freshmen, 52% of continuing students receive some form of aid. All grants, 98% of loans, 65% of jobs based on need. 317 enrolled freshmen were judged to have need, all were offered aid. **Aid applications:** Closing date February 1; applicants notified on or about April 5; must reply by May 1. **Additional information:** Various loan programs.

ADDRESS/TELEPHONE. Janet A. Lavin, Director of Admission, Wellesley College, 106 Central Street, Wellesley, MA 02181-8292. (617) 283-2270. Fax: (617) 283-3678.

Wentworth Institute of Technology

Boston, Massachusetts CB code: 3958

Admissions: 86% of applicants accepted
Based on: ••• School record
•• Test scores
• Interview, recommendations, special talents
Completion: 85% of freshmen end year in good standing
45% graduate, 3% of these enter graduate study

4-year private technical college, coed. Founded in 1904. **Accreditation:** Regional. **Undergraduate enrollment:** 2,092 men, 320 women full time; 173 men, 16 women part time. **Faculty:** 231 total (124 full time). **Location:** Urban campus in very large city; 2 miles from downtown. **Calendar:** Semester, limited summer session. Saturday and extensive evening/early morning classes. **Microcomputers:** 186 located in libraries, classrooms, computer centers. **Special facilities:** 141-acre field laboratory for construction and civil engineering technology projects located in Plainville, Massachusetts. **Additional facts:** Member of Fenway Library Consortium (provides access to over 2.5 million volumes and thousands of periodicals at area educational institutions). 5-year bachelor of architecture program accredited by the National Architectural Accrediting Board.

DEGREES OFFERED. AAS, BS, BArch. 544 associate degrees awarded in 1992. 25% in architecture and environmental design, 72% engineering technologies. 601 bachelor's degrees awarded. 16% in architecture and environmental design, 8% business and management, 7% computer sciences, 7% engineering, 62% engineering technologies.

UNDERGRADUATE MAJORS. Associate: Aeronautical technology, aircraft mechanics, architectural technologies, architecture, civil technology, computer and information sciences, computer servicing technology, computer technology, construction, electrical and electronics equipment repair, electrical technology, electromechanical technology, electronic technology, engineering and engineering-related technologies, engineering and other disciplines, environmental health engineering, industrial design, interior design, manufacturing technology, mechanical design technology. **Bachelor's:** Architectural technologies, architecture, civil technology, communications, computer and information sciences, computer servicing technology, computer technology, construction, construction management, electrical/electronics/communications engineering, electronic technology, engineering and engineering-related technologies, engineering and other disciplines, environmental health engineering, facilities management, industrial design, information sciences and systems, interior design, management science, manufacturing technology, mechanical engineering, technical and business writing, technical management.

ACADEMIC PROGRAMS. Cooperative education, double major, dual enrollment of high school students, student-designed major, study abroad, weekend college, cross-registration. **Remedial services:** Learning center, preadmission summer program, reduced course load, tutoring, year-long pretechnology curriculum for under-prepared students. **ROTC:** Air Force, Army. **Placement/credit:** AP, CLEP Subject, IB, institutional tests.

ACADEMIC REQUIREMENTS. Freshmen must earn minimum GPA of 2.0 to continue in good standing. 70% of freshmen return for sophomore year. Students must declare major on application. **Graduation requirements:** 80 hours for associate (50 in major), 144 hours for bachelor's (102 in major). Most students required to take courses in computer science, English, humanities, mathematics, biological/physical sciences, social sciences. **Postgraduate studies:** 70% from 2-year programs enter 4-year programs.

FRESHMAN ADMISSIONS. Selection criteria: Minimum 2.0 GPA in mathematics, science, and English. School achievement record most important, followed by test scores. **High school preparation:** 16 units required. Required units include English 4, mathematics 3 and science 1. Most programs require at least 3 units of college-preparatory mathematics and 1 year of laboratory science. Many programs require 4 units of college-preparatory mathematics and 1 unit of physics; the architecture program requires drafting. **Test requirements:** SAT or ACT (SAT preferred); score report by August 1. SAT scores may be waived for students not applying directly from high school. **Additional information:** Preparatory, certificate and some associate programs are available for students whose backgrounds have not included a college preparatory curriculum.

1992 FRESHMAN CLASS PROFILE. 1,378 men applied, 1,175 accepted, 472 enrolled; 195 women applied, 178 accepted, 64 enrolled. 8% were in top tenth and 26% were in top quarter of graduating class. **Academic background:** Mid 50% of enrolled freshmen had SAT-V between 310-470, SAT-M between 370-520. 81% submitted SAT scores. **Characteristics:** 60% commute. Average age is 18.

FALL-TERM APPLICATIONS. $30 fee, may be waived for applicants with need. Closing date August 1; applicants notified on a rolling basis; must reply by May 1 or within 3 weeks if notified thereafter. Portfolio required for interior design, industrial design, architecture applicants. Interview recommended. CRDA. Deferred admission available. TOEFL required for applicants for whom English is a second language.

STUDENT LIFE. Housing: Dormitories (coed); apartment housing available. Apartments available for upperclassmen. **Activities:** Student government, student newspaper, yearbook, academic honor society, student chapter of American Society of Civil Engineers, Solar Club, student chapter of American Welding Society, Society of Manufacturing Engineers, Associated Builders and Contractors.

ATHLETICS. NCAA. **Intercollegiate:** Baseball M, basketball, ice hockey M, rifle, rugby M, soccer M, softball W, tennis, volleyball, wrestling M. **Intramural:** Badminton, basketball, skiing, softball, tennis, volleyball.

STUDENT SERVICES. Career counseling, employment service for undergraduates, freshman orientation, health services, personal counseling, placement service for graduates, veterans counselor, Special consideration for adult students, services/facilities for handicapped.

ANNUAL EXPENSES. Tuition and fees: $9,250. **Room and board:** $5,950. **Books and supplies:** $800. **Other expenses:** $450.

FINANCIAL AID. 62% of freshmen, 43% of continuing students receive some form of aid. 97% of grants, 85% of loans, all jobs based on need. Academic, leadership scholarships available. **Aid applications:** No closing date; priority given to applications received by March 1; applicants notified on a rolling basis; must reply within 2 weeks.

ADDRESS/TELEPHONE. Thomas McGinn III, Dean of Enrollment Management, Wentworth Institute of Technology, 550 Huntington Avenue, Boston, MA 02115. (617) 442-9010 ext. 220. (800) 556-0610. Fax: (617) 427-2852.

Western New England College

Springfield, Massachusetts CB code: 3962

Admissions: 91% of applicants accepted
Based on: ••• Recommendations, school record, test scores
•• Essay, interview
• Activities, special talents
Completion: 75% of freshmen end year in good standing
52% graduate, 15% of these enter graduate study

4-year private college of arts and sciences and business college, coed. Founded in 1919. **Accreditation:** Regional. **Undergraduate enrollment:** 1,132 men, 768 women full time; 620 men, 473 women part time. **Graduate enrollment:** 263 men, 255 women full time; 792 men, 532 women part time. **Faculty:** 306 total (135 full time), 133 with doctorates or other terminal degrees. **Location:** Suburban campus in small city; 3 miles from downtown, 95 miles from Boston. **Calendar:** Semester, limited summer session. **Microcomputers:** 251 located in libraries, classrooms, computer centers. **Special facilities:** Art gallery, writing center. **Additional facts:** College includes school of law and division of continuing higher education.

DEGREES OFFERED. BA, BS, MS, MBA, JD. 6 associate degrees awarded in 1992. 100% in multi/interdisciplinary studies. 643 bachelor's degrees awarded. 43% in business and management, 12% engineering, 15% parks/recreation, protective services, public affairs, 7% psychology, 10% social sciences. Graduate degrees offered in 11 major fields of study.

UNDERGRADUATE MAJORS. Associate: Liberal/general studies. **Bachelor's:** Accounting, bioengineering and biomedical engineering, biological and physical sciences, biology, business administration and management, business and management, chemistry, computer and information sciences, computer engineering, criminal justice studies, economics, electrical/electronics/communications engineering, engineering, engineering and other disciplines, engineering management, English, finance, history, human resources development, humanities and social sciences, industrial engineering, information sciences and systems, journalism, law enforcement and corrections, liberal/general studies, manufacturing and design, marketing management, mathematics, mechanical engineering, personnel management, pharmacy, political science and government, prelaw, psychology, secondary education, social work, sociology, Technical management.

ACADEMIC PROGRAMS. Accelerated program, double major, dual enrollment of high school students, independent study, internships, student-designed major, study abroad, teacher preparation, Washington semester, cross-registration, 3-2 program in pharmacy with Massachusetts College of Pharmacy and Allied Health Sciences. **Remedial services:** Reduced course load, tutoring. **ROTC:** Air Force, Army. **Placement/credit:** AP, CLEP General and Subject, institutional tests; 60 credit hours maximum for bachelor's degree.

ACADEMIC REQUIREMENTS. Freshmen must earn minimum GPA of 2.0 to continue in good standing. 75% of freshmen return for sophomore year. Students must declare major by end of second year. **Graduation requirements:** 60 hours for associate, 120 hours for bachelor's (54 in major). Most students required to take courses in computer science, English, history, humanities, mathematics, biological/physical sciences, social sciences. **Postgraduate studies:** 2% enter law school, 1% enter medical school, 4% enter MBA programs, 8% enter other graduate study. **Additional information:** Interdisciplinary cultures program offered.

FRESHMAN ADMISSIONS. Selection criteria: School achievement record, class rank, SAT scores, and recommendation most important. Interview, extracurricular activities, and essay also considered. **High school preparation:** 9 units required. Required and recommended units include English 4, mathematics 2-4, physical science 1 and social science 1-2. Biological science 1 and foreign language 2 recommended. One American history and 1 laboratory science required. Additional science and mathematics required for certain programs. **Test requirements:** SAT or ACT.

1992 FRESHMAN CLASS PROFILE. 976 men applied, 869 accepted, 270 enrolled; 644 women applied, 600 accepted, 194 enrolled. 11% had high school GPA of 3.0 or higher, 60% between 2.0 and 2.99. **Academic background:** Mid 50% of enrolled freshmen had SAT-V between 360-450, SAT-M between 400-530. 99% submitted SAT scores. **Characteristics:** 51% from in state, 76% live in college housing, 7% have minority backgrounds, 2% are foreign students. Average age is 18.

FALL-TERM APPLICATIONS. $30 fee, may be waived for applicants with need. No closing date; applicants notified on a rolling basis; must reply by May 1 or within 2 weeks if notified thereafter. Essay required. Interview recommended. CRDA. Deferred and early admission available.

STUDENT LIFE. Housing: Dormitories (men, women, coed); apartment, handicapped housing available. **Activities:** Student government, magazine, radio, student newspaper, yearbook, drama, musical theater, Minority Group Alliance, campus ministry, and international, nontraditional, and continuing education student groups.

ATHLETICS. NCAA. **Intercollegiate:** Baseball M, basketball, bowling, field hockey W, football M, golf M, ice hockey M, lacrosse M, skiing M, soccer, softball W, tennis M, wrestling M. **Intramural:** Basketball, football M, softball, tennis, volleyball.

STUDENT SERVICES. Aptitude testing, career counseling, employment service for undergraduates, freshman orientation, health services, personal counseling, placement service for graduates, special adviser for adult students, veterans counselor, services/facilities for handicapped.

ANNUAL EXPENSES. Tuition and fees: $9,354. **Room and board:** $5,400. **Books and supplies:** $475. **Other expenses:** $800.

FINANCIAL AID. 55% of freshmen, 49% of continuing students receive some form of aid. 71% of grants, 82% of loans, 36% of jobs based on need. 313 enrolled freshmen were judged to have need, 253 were offered aid. **Aid applications:** No closing date; priority given to applications received by April 1; applicants notified on a rolling basis beginning on or about March 1; must reply by May 1 or within 2 weeks if notified thereafter.

ADDRESS/TELEPHONE. Lori-Ann Paterwic, Director of Admissions, Western New England College, 1215 Wilbraham Road, Springfield, MA 01119-2688. (413) 782-3111 ext. 1321. (800) 325-1122. Fax: (413) 782-1746.

Westfield State College
Westfield, Massachusetts — CB code: 3523

Admissions: 67% of applicants accepted
Based on:
••• School record
•• Activities, test scores
• Recommendations, special talents
Completion: 94% of freshmen end year in good standing
60% graduate, 21% of these enter graduate study

4-year public liberal arts college, coed. Founded in 1838. **Accreditation:** Regional. **Undergraduate enrollment:** 1,582 men, 1,689 women full time; 480 men, 528 women part time. **Graduate enrollment:** 38 men, 74 women full time; 187 men, 525 women part time. **Faculty:** 371 total (167 full time), 122 with doctorates or other terminal degrees. **Location:** Suburban campus in large town; 10 miles from Springfield. **Calendar:** Semester, extensive summer session. **Microcomputers:** 175 located in dormitories, libraries, classrooms, computer centers. **Special facilities:** Electron microscope, museum of rocks and minerals, Arno Maris art gallery.

DEGREES OFFERED. BA, BS, MA, MS, MEd. 948 bachelor's degrees awarded in 1992. 23% in business and management, 7% communications, 25% teacher education, 15% parks/recreation, protective services, public affairs, 10% psychology. Graduate degrees offered in 15 major fields of study.

UNDERGRADUATE MAJORS. Applied chemistry, art education, biological and physical sciences, biology, business administration and management, business and management, business economics, business education, chemical manufacturing technology, city/community/regional planning, communications, computer and information sciences, criminal justice studies, early childhood education, economics, education, elementary education, English, English education, fine arts, foreign languages education, French, history, humanities and social sciences, industrial arts education, information sciences and systems, junior high education, law enforcement and corrections, liberal/general studies, mathematics, mathematics education, music, music education, physical education, physical sciences, political science and government, psychology, science education, secondary education, social science education, social sciences, social work, Spanish, special education, speech/communication/theater education, urban studies.

ACADEMIC PROGRAMS. Cooperative education, double major, education specialist degree, independent study, internships, study abroad, teacher preparation, visiting/exchange student program, Washington semester, cross-registration. **Remedial services:** Learning center, preadmission summer program, reduced course load, remedial instruction, special counselor, tutoring. **ROTC:** Army. **Placement/credit:** AP, CLEP General and Subject, institutional tests; 60 credit hours maximum for bachelor's degree.

ACADEMIC REQUIREMENTS. Freshmen must earn minimum GPA of 1.5 to continue in good standing. 80% of freshmen return for sophomore year. Students must declare major by end of second year. **Graduation requirements:** 120 hours for bachelor's (40 in major). Most students required to take courses in arts/fine arts, English, history, humanities, mathematics, biological/physical sciences, social sciences. **Postgraduate studies:** 1% enter law school, 5% enter MBA programs, 15% enter other graduate study.

FRESHMAN ADMISSIONS. Selection criteria: School achievement record most important. SAT scores, school and community activities, recommendations also considered. **High school preparation:** 16 units required. Required units include English 4, foreign language 2, mathematics 3, social science 2 and science 2. One unit United States history required. 4 mathematics required of mathematics and computer science majors. **Test requirements:** SAT; score report by March 1. **Additional information:** SAT scores not required for students with documented learning disability.

1992 FRESHMAN CLASS PROFILE. 3,140 men and women applied, 2,100 accepted; 396 men enrolled, 428 women enrolled. 5% were in top tenth and 29% were in top quarter of graduating class. **Academic background:** Mid 50% of enrolled freshmen had SAT-V between 400-500, SAT-M between 400-500. 99% submitted SAT scores. **Characteristics:** 97% from in state, 89% live in college housing, 6% have minority backgrounds. Average age is 18.

FALL-TERM APPLICATIONS. $10 fee, may be waived for applicants with need. $40 fee for out-of-state applicants. Closing date March 1; applicants notified on a rolling basis beginning on or about January 15; must reply by May 1. Audition required for music applicants. Portfolio required for art applicants. CRDA.

STUDENT LIFE. Housing: Dormitories (men, women, coed); apartment housing available. Specially designed dormitory rooms for handicapped students. **Activities:** Student government, film, magazine, radio, student newspaper, television, yearbook, choral groups, concert band, dance, drama, jazz band, music ensembles, musical theater, symphony orchestra, Third World group, public interest research, Campus Crusade, Circle-K.

ATHLETICS. NCAA. **Intercollegiate:** Baseball M, basketball, cross-country, field hockey W, football M, soccer, softball W, swimming W, track and field. **Intramural:** Badminton, basketball, bowling, diving, gymnastics, racquetball, soccer, softball, swimming, tennis, volleyball, water polo.

STUDENT SERVICES. Aptitude testing, career counseling, employment service for undergraduates, freshman orientation, health services, personal counseling, placement service for graduates, special adviser for adult students, veterans counselor, services/facilities for handicapped.

ANNUAL EXPENSES. Tuition and fees (1992-93): $3,026, $3,864 additional for out-of-state students. **Room and board:** $3,542. **Books and supplies:** $450. **Other expenses:** $1,280.

FINANCIAL AID. 50% of freshmen, 52% of continuing students receive some form of aid. 97% of grants, 64% of loans, 54% of jobs based on need. 311 enrolled freshmen were judged to have need, all were offered aid. Academic, leadership scholarships available. **Aid applications:** No closing date; priority given to applications received by April 1; applicants notified on a rolling basis beginning on or about April 15; must reply within 2 weeks.

ADDRESS/TELEPHONE. John F. Marcus, Director of Admission and Financial Aid, Westfield State College, Western Avenue, Westfield, MA 01086. (413) 568-3311 ext. 218.

Wheaton College
Norton, Massachusetts — CB code: 3963

Admissions: 79% of applicants accepted
Based on:
••• School record
•• Activities, essay, recommendations
• Interview, special talents, test scores
Completion: 93% of freshmen end year in good standing
67% graduate, 20% of these enter graduate study

4-year private liberal arts college, coed. Founded in 1834. **Accreditation:** Regional. **Undergraduate enrollment:** 452 men, 839 women full time; 6 men, 22 women part time. **Faculty:** 110 total (88 full time), 99 with doctorates or other terminal degrees. **Location:** Rural campus in large town; 35 miles from Boston, 15 miles from Providence, Rhode Island. **Calendar:** Semester. **Microcomputers:** 40 located in computer centers. **Special facilities:** Observatory, Watson Art Gallery, Gebbie Archives and Special Collections language laboratory receiving international broadcasts via satellite.

DEGREES OFFERED. BA. 332 bachelor's degrees awarded in 1992. 5% in area and ethnic studies, 15% letters/literature, 8% multi/interdisciplinary studies, 14% psychology, 38% social sciences, 6% visual and performing arts.

UNDERGRADUATE MAJORS. American studies, anthropology, art history, Asian studies, astronomy, biochemistry, biological and physical sciences, biology, chemistry, classics, comparative literature, computer mathematics, economics, English, English literature, fine arts, foreign languages (multiple emphasis), French, German, Greek (classical), history, humanities and social sciences, international relations, Italian, Latin, liberal/general studies, mathematics, music, philosophy, physics, political science and government, prelaw, premedicine, psychology, religion, Russian, Russian and Slavic studies, sociology, Spanish.

ACADEMIC PROGRAMS. Double major, honors program, independent study, internships, student-designed major, study abroad, teacher preparation, Washington semester, cross-registration, dual degree programs with Georgia Institute of Technology in engineering, computer science, and management science; George Washington University in engineering; Emerson College in communications, and New England School of Optometry. Williams College Mystic Seaport semester, semester at National Theater Institute (Waterford), MBA program with Graduate School of Management at University of Rochester; MA program with Andover-Newton Theological School; combined bachelor's/graduate program in business administration. **Remedial services:** Reduced course load, special counselor, tutoring. **Placement/credit:** AP, institutional tests; 32 credit hours maximum for bachelor's degree.

ACADEMIC REQUIREMENTS. Freshmen must earn minimum GPA of 1.67 to continue in good standing. 87% of freshmen return for sophomore year. Students must declare major by end of second year. **Graduation requirements:** 128 hours for bachelor's (40 in major). Most students required to take courses in arts/fine arts, English, foreign languages, history, humanities, mathematics, philosophy/religion, biological/physical sciences, social sciences. **Postgraduate studies:** 8% enter law school, 4% enter medical school, 4% enter MBA programs, 4% enter other graduate study. **Additional information:** Filene Center for Work and Learning offers programs and services designed to help students define educational, career and life goals through internships, mentor program, and alumni network activities.

FRESHMAN ADMISSIONS. Selection criteria: School record, essay/writing sample, personal academic portfolio, extracurricular activities, recommendations. Standardized testing optional. Recommended units include English 4, foreign language 4, mathematics 3, social science 3 and science 3. English with emphasis on composition skills, science must include 2 laboratory science.

1992 FRESHMAN CLASS PROFILE. 571 men applied, 444 accepted, 138 enrolled; 1,126 women applied, 905 accepted, 277 enrolled. 39% had high school GPA of 3.0 or higher, 55% between 2.0 and 2.99. 18% were in top tenth and 50% were in top quarter of graduating class. **Academic background:** Mid 50% of enrolled freshmen had SAT-V between 470-580, SAT-M between 490-600; ACT composite between 22-27. 42% submitted SAT scores, 7% submitted ACT scores. **Characteristics:** 38% from in state, 99% live in college housing, 9% have minority backgrounds, 3% are foreign students. Average age is 18.

FALL-TERM APPLICATIONS. $40 fee, may be waived for applicants with need. Closing date February 1; applicants notified on or about April 1; must reply by May 1. Essay required. Interview recommended. CRDA. Deferred and early admission available. EDP-S; institutional early decision plan. Early action available. SAT/ACT tests optional. Applicants who want tests considered for admissions must submit scores by February 1.

STUDENT LIFE. Housing: Dormitories (women, coed). **Activities:** Student government, film, magazine, radio, student newspaper, yearbook, choral groups, dance, drama, music ensembles, pep band, chamber group, Christian Fellowship, Black Students Association, Amnesty International, Catholic Club, Imani Gospel Choir, International Students Association, Jewish Students Association, Latin American Students Organization, Wheaton Asian Students Association.

ATHLETICS. NCAA. **Intercollegiate:** Basketball, cross-country, diving, field hockey W, lacrosse, soccer, softball W, swimming, tennis, track and field, volleyball W. **Intramural:** Archery, badminton, basketball, cross-country, fencing, field hockey, golf, horseback riding, lacrosse, skiing, soccer, softball, swimming, table tennis, tennis, volleyball, water polo.

STUDENT SERVICES. Career counseling, employment service for undergraduates, freshman orientation, health services, personal counseling, placement service for graduates, special adviser for adult students, graduate adviser, career skills workshop, services/facilities for handicapped.

ANNUAL EXPENSES. Tuition and fees: $17,790. **Room and board:** $6,050. **Books and supplies:** $660. **Other expenses:** $800.

FINANCIAL AID. 59% of freshmen, 60% of continuing students receive some form of aid. All grants, 98% of loans, 68% of jobs based on need. 225 enrolled freshmen were judged to have need, all were offered aid. **Aid applications:** Closing date February 15; applicants notified on or about April 1; must reply by May 1. **Additional information:** Long-term financing plans available. Committed to working with families in planning the financing of education.

ADDRESS/TELEPHONE. Gail Berson, Executive Director of Admission and Student Aid, Wheaton College, Norton, MA 02766. (508) 285-7722 ext. 251. (800) 394-6003. Fax: (508) 285-3479.

Wheelock College

Boston, Massachusetts — CB code: 3964

Admissions: 78% of applicants accepted
Based on:
••• School record
•• Essay, interview, recommendations, test scores
• Activities
Completion: 85% of freshmen end year in good standing
74% graduate, 6% of these enter graduate study

4-year private liberal arts, teachers college, coed. Founded in 1888. **Accreditation:** Regional. **Undergraduate enrollment:** 12 men, 757 women full time; 22 women part time. **Graduate enrollment:** 4 men, 126 women full time; 9 men, 200 women part time. **Faculty:** 203 total (58 full time), 92 with doctorates or other terminal degrees. **Location:** Urban campus in very large city; 2 miles from downtown. **Calendar:** Semester. **Microcomputers:** 56 located in dormitories, libraries, computer centers. **Special facilities:** Fully equipped workshop for development of original curriculum materials.

DEGREES OFFERED. BA, BS, MS. 173 bachelor's degrees awarded in 1992. 74% in teacher education, 26% parks/recreation, protective services, public affairs. Graduate degrees offered in 9 major fields of study.

UNDERGRADUATE MAJORS. Child development/care/guidance, early childhood education, elementary education, social work.

ACADEMIC PROGRAMS. Double major, honors program, independent study, internships, study abroad, teacher preparation, cross-registration. **Remedial services:** Reduced course load, remedial instruction, special counselor, tutoring. **Placement/credit:** AP, CLEP General and Subject, institutional tests; 32 credit hours maximum for bachelor's degree.

ACADEMIC REQUIREMENTS. Freshmen must earn minimum GPA of 1.5 to continue in good standing. 81% of freshmen return for sophomore year. Students must declare major by end of second year. **Graduation requirements:** 136 hours for bachelor's (32 in major). Most students required to take courses in arts/fine arts, computer science, English, history, humanities, mathematics, biological/physical sciences, social sciences. **Postgraduate studies:** 6% enter other graduate study. **Additional information:** Fieldwork, throughout all four years, supplements classwork in day care, infant and toddler behavior, museum teaching, children in health care settings, elementary education, special education, and social work.

FRESHMAN ADMISSIONS. Selection criteria: School achievement record, experience in and motivation for working with children and other people, employer and academic recommendations, SAT or ACT scores, interview, school and community activities. **High school preparation:** 16 units required. Required and recommended units include biological science 1, English 4, mathematics 2-3, physical science 1 and social science 2. Child development course recommended. **Test requirements:** SAT or ACT; score report by February 15.

1992 FRESHMAN CLASS PROFILE. 10 men applied, 5 accepted, 2 enrolled; 450 women applied, 355 accepted, 175 enrolled. 27% had high school GPA of 3.0 or higher, 69% between 2.0 and 2.99. 2% were in top tenth and 24% were in top quarter of graduating class. **Academic background:** Mid 50% of enrolled freshmen had SAT-V between 360-480, SAT-M between 370-500. 98% submitted SAT scores. **Characteristics:** 50% from in state, 90% live in college housing, 16% have minority backgrounds, 1% are foreign students. Average age is 18.

FALL-TERM APPLICATIONS. $30 fee, may be waived for applicants with need. Closing date February 15; applicants notified on a rolling basis beginning on or about January 1; must reply by May 1. Interview required. Essay required. CRDA. Deferred admission available. EDP-F.

STUDENT LIFE. Housing: Dormitories (women, coed); cooperative housing available. **Activities:** Student government, magazine, student newspaper, yearbook, Noon News Bulletin, choral groups, drama, musical theater, Hillel, Social Work Club, Students of Faith, Peace and Social Action Committee, Women's Center, Boston Association for the Education of Young Children, Students Organized Against Racism, Student Child Life Council, Starlight Foundation, Council for Exceptional Children.

ATHLETICS. Intercollegiate: Field hockey W. **Intramural:** Badminton, basketball, cross-country, racquetball, skiing, soccer, softball, squash, tennis, volleyball, water polo.

STUDENT SERVICES. Career counseling, employment service for undergraduates, freshman orientation, health services, personal counseling, placement service for graduates, services/facilities for handicapped.

ANNUAL EXPENSES. Tuition and fees: $12,640. **Room and board:** $5,360. **Books and supplies:** $300. **Other expenses:** $700.

FINANCIAL AID. 78% of freshmen, 65% of continuing students receive some form of aid. 99% of grants, 99% of loans, all jobs based on need. 125 enrolled freshmen were judged to have need, all were offered aid. **Aid applications:** Closing date March 1; applicants notified on a rolling basis; must reply by May 1.

ADDRESS/TELEPHONE. Joan Wexler, Dean of Admissions and Financial Aid, Wheelock College, 200 The Riverway, Boston, MA 02215-4176. (617) 734-5200 ext. 206.

Williams College
Williamstown, Massachusetts CB code: 3965

Admissions: 25% of applicants accepted
Based on: ••• Recommendations, school record, test scores
•• Activities, essay, special talents
Completion: 98% of freshmen end year in good standing
94% graduate, 19% of these enter graduate study

4-year private liberal arts college, coed. Founded in 1793. **Accreditation:** Regional. **Undergraduate enrollment:** 1,034 men, 951 women full time; 13 men, 15 women part time. **Graduate enrollment:** 20 men, 31 women full time. **Faculty:** 262 total (233 full time). **Location:** Rural campus in small town; 150 miles from Boston and New York City. **Calendar:** 4-1-4. **Microcomputers:** 185 located in libraries, computer centers. **Special facilities:** 2,000-acre experimental forest, environmental studies center, art museum, observatory, electron-scanning microscope, 2 transmission microscopes.

DEGREES OFFERED. BA, MA. 520 bachelor's degrees awarded in 1992. 16% in letters/literature, 5% philosophy, religion, theology, 8% physical sciences, 7% psychology, 38% social sciences, 8% visual and performing arts. Graduate degrees offered in 1 major field of study.

UNDERGRADUATE MAJORS. American studies, anthropology, art history, Asian studies, astronomy, astrophysics, biology, chemistry, classics, computer and information sciences, dramatic arts, East Asian studies, economics, engineering and other disciplines, English, French, geology, German, history, mathematics, music, philosophy, physics, political economy, political science and government, psychology, religion, Russian, sociology, Spanish, visual and performing arts.

ACADEMIC PROGRAMS. Accelerated program, double major, honors program, independent study, internships, semester at sea, student-designed major, study abroad, visiting/exchange student program, cross-registration, preadmission summer program for premedical, engineering, and science students; summer science research program; Williams in Oxford; tutorials; liberal arts/career combination in engineering. **Remedial services:** Tutoring. **Placement/credit:** AP, IB, institutional tests.

ACADEMIC REQUIREMENTS. No policy requiring minimum GPA; records of students having academic difficulty are reviewed individually. 96% of freshmen return for sophomore year. Students must declare major by end of second year. **Postgraduate studies:** 4% enter law school, 5% enter medical school, 10% enter other graduate study. **Additional information:** 3 courses required in each of 3 divisions: languages and the arts, social studies, science and mathematics. 9 to 10 courses required in major, 32 courses plus 4 winter study courses required for graduation.

FRESHMAN ADMISSIONS. Selection criteria: School achievement record, applicant's character and personal promise, and essay considered. College seeks diversity of social, economic, and geographic backgrounds. **High school preparation:** 16 units required. Required units include biological science 1, English 4, foreign language 3, mathematics 4, physical science 1 and social science 2. Writing skills stressed. **Test requirements:** SAT or ACT; score report by February 1. 3 ACH required (including English Composition). Score report by February 1.

1992 FRESHMAN CLASS PROFILE. 2,406 men applied, 574 accepted, 260 enrolled; 2,185 women applied, 591 accepted, 259 enrolled. 81% were in top tenth and 96% were in top quarter of graduating class. **Academic background:** Mid 50% of enrolled freshmen had SAT-V between 590-710, SAT-M between 640-730; ACT composite between 27-32. 98% submitted SAT scores, 15% submitted ACT scores. **Characteristics:** 10% from in state, 100% live in college housing, 24% have minority backgrounds, 3% are foreign students. Average age is 18.

FALL-TERM APPLICATIONS. $50 fee, may be waived for applicants with need. Closing date January 1; applicants notified on or about April 7; must reply by May 1. Essay required. CRDA. Deferred and early admission available. EDP-F.

STUDENT LIFE. Housing: Dormitories (coed); cooperative housing available. **Activities:** Student government, magazine, radio, student newspaper, television, yearbook, choral groups, dance, drama, jazz band, marching band, music ensembles, musical theater, pep band, symphony orchestra, early music groups, service and religious organizations, Black Student Union, Purple Key, Asian Link, VISTA (Hispanic students), Koreans of Williams Minority Coalition, Nonviolent Alternatives Committee.

ATHLETICS. NCAA. **Intercollegiate:** Baseball M, basketball, cross-country, diving, field hockey W, football M, golf M, ice hockey, lacrosse, rowing (crew), rugby, skiing, soccer, softball W, squash, swimming, tennis, track and field, volleyball W, water polo, wrestling M. **Intramural:** Badminton, basketball, cross-country, fencing, golf, horseback riding, ice hockey M, racquetball, sailing, soccer, softball, squash, swimming, tennis, track and field, volleyball, water polo.

STUDENT SERVICES. Career counseling, employment service for undergraduates, freshman orientation, health services, on-campus day care, personal counseling, placement service for graduates, special adviser for adult students, services/facilities for handicapped.

ANNUAL EXPENSES. Tuition and fees: $18,795. **Room and board:** $5,795. **Books and supplies:** $500. **Other expenses:** $800.

FINANCIAL AID. 37% of freshmen, 35% of continuing students receive some form of aid. All aid based on need. 191 enrolled freshmen were judged to have need, all were offered aid. **Aid applications:** Closing date February 1; applicants notified on or about April 3; must reply by May 1.

ADDRESS/TELEPHONE. Thomas H. Parker, Director of Admission, Williams College, PO Box 487, Williamstown, MA 01267. (413) 597-2211.

Worcester Polytechnic Institute
Worcester, Massachusetts CB code: 3969

4-year private college of arts and sciences and engineering college, coed. Founded in 1865. **Accreditation:** Regional. **Undergraduate enrollment:** 2,268 men, 518 women full time; 67 men, 15 women part time. **Graduate enrollment:** 299 men, 79 women full time; 537 men, 130 women part time. **Faculty:** 345 total (228 full time), 200 with doctorates or other terminal degrees. **Location:** Suburban campus in small city; 45 miles from Boston. **Calendar:** 4 terms of 7 weeks each. **Microcomputers:** 620 located in dormitories, libraries, classrooms, computer centers, campus-wide network. **Special facilities:** Nuclear reactor, computer-aided design and manufacturing laboratories, robotics laboratory, center for holographic studies and laser technology, hydraulics laboratory, wind tunnel, Very Large Scale Integrated circuit (VLSI) design laboratory, bioprocessing laboratory. **Additional facts:** Off-campus project sites include Digital Equipment Corporation University of Massachusetts Medical Center, Tufts School of Veterinary Medicine. Foreign project centers include universities or research facilities in Puerto Rico, England, Italy, Ecuador, Thailand, Hong Kong.

DEGREES OFFERED. BS, MS, MBA, PhD. 539 bachelor's degrees awarded in 1992. 6% in business and management, 6% computer sciences, 77% engineering, 7% physical sciences. Graduate degrees offered in 25 major fields of study.

UNDERGRADUATE MAJORS. Actuarial sciences, aerospace/aeronautical/astronautical engineering, analytical chemistry, applied mathematics, biochemistry, bioengineering and biomedical engineering, biological and physical sciences, biology, biomedical science, biotechnology, business administration and management, cell biology, chemical engineering, chemistry, city/community/regional planning, civil engineering, computer and information sciences, computer engineering, computer mathematics, ecology, economics, electrical/electronics/communications engineering, engineering, engineering and other disciplines, engineering management, engineering mechanics, engineering physics, environmental health engineering, environmental science, genetics, human and animal, humanities, humanities and social sciences, humanities and technology, industrial engineering, information sciences and systems, inorganic chemistry, manufacturing engineering, materials engineering, mathematics, mechanical engineering, microbiology, molecular biology, nuclear engineering, nuclear physics, ocean engineering, operations research, optics, organic chemistry, pharmaceutical chemistry, physical chemistry, physical sciences, physics, physiology, human and animal, predentistry, prelaw, premedicine, preveterinary, pure mathematics, society and technology, society/technology, solid state physics, statistics, systems analysis, systems engineering, technical and business writing, urban studies.

ACADEMIC PROGRAMS. Accelerated program, cooperative education, double major, dual enrollment of high school students, independent study, internships, student-designed major, study abroad, visiting/exchange student program, Washington semester, cross-registration, International Scholars Program; liberal arts/career combination in engineering; combined bachelor's/graduate program in business administration. **Remedial services:** Reduced course load, tutoring, writing resource center. **ROTC:** Air Force, Army, Naval. **Placement/credit:** AP, IB, institutional tests.

ACADEMIC REQUIREMENTS. No policy requiring minimum GPA; records of students having academic difficulty are reviewed individually. 94% of freshmen return for sophomore year. Students must declare major by end of second year. **Graduation requirements:** 135 hours for bachelor's (54 in major). Most students required to take courses in humanities, mathematics, biological/physical sciences, social sciences. **Postgraduate studies:** 1% enter law school, 1% enter medical school, 3% enter MBA programs, 12% enter other graduate study. **Additional information:** Programs are student-designed and stress projects and individualized study that combine classroom and professional experience.

FRESHMAN ADMISSIONS. Selection criteria: High school record, including evidence of independent study, most important. Test scores, extracurricular activities, recommendations important. No specific rank or grade average required; motivation, creativity, and initiative important. **High school preparation:** 10 units required. Required units include English 4, mathematics 4 and physical science 2. Mathematics requirement should include trigonometry and analytic geometry. Physical science should include physics and chemistry. **Test requirements:** SAT or ACT; score report by March 1. 3 ACH (including English Composition, Mathematics Level I or II, and a science) required of applicants who took SAT. Score report by March 1.

1992 FRESHMAN CLASS PROFILE. 480 men, 130 women enrolled. 58% were in top tenth and 89% were in top quarter of graduating class. **Academic background:** Mid 50% of enrolled freshmen had SAT-V between 490-600, SAT-M between 610-700; ACT composite between 27-31. 95% submitted SAT scores, 11% submitted ACT scores. **Characteristics:** 43%

from in state, 98% live in college housing, 8% have minority backgrounds, 7% are foreign students, 35% join fraternities/sororities. Average age is 18.

FALL-TERM APPLICATIONS. $35 fee, may be waived for applicants with need. Closing date February 15; applicants notified on or about April 1; must reply by May 1. Interview recommended. Essay recommended. CRDA. Deferred and early admission available. EDP-F. Early decision application deadline December 1. Notification within 1 month though usually not prior to December 15.

STUDENT LIFE. Housing: Dormitories (men, coed); apartment, fraternity, sorority housing available. Freshmen guaranteed housing. Quiet floors available upon request. **Activities:** Student government, magazine, student newspaper, yearbook, choral groups, concert band, dance, drama, jazz band, music ensembles, musical theater, pep band, symphony orchestra, fraternities, sororities, African American Cultural Society, volunteer tutoring group, Big Brother/Big Sister, World House, European Students Association, Asian Society, Hispanic student association, women's awareness group, Students for Social Awareness, Amnesty International.

ATHLETICS. NCAA. **Intercollegiate:** Baseball M, basketball, bowling, cross-country, fencing, field hockey W, football M, golf, ice hockey M, lacrosse, rifle, rowing (crew), rugby, sailing, skiing, soccer, softball W, swimming, tennis, track and field, volleyball, water polo M, wrestling M. **Intramural:** Basketball, bowling, cross-country, golf, ice hockey M, skiing, soccer, softball, swimming, table tennis, track and field, volleyball, wrestling M.

STUDENT SERVICES. Aptitude testing, career counseling, employment service for undergraduates, freshman orientation, health services, personal counseling, placement service for graduates, special adviser for adult students, veterans counselor, major selection program, services/facilities for handicapped.

ANNUAL EXPENSES. Tuition and fees: $15,290. **Room and board:** $5,060. **Books and supplies:** $520. **Other expenses:** $905.

FINANCIAL AID. 80% of freshmen, 82% of continuing students receive some form of aid. 99% of grants, 96% of loans, 80% of jobs based on need. **Aid applications:** Closing date March 1; applicants notified on or about April 1; must reply by May 1.

ADDRESS/TELEPHONE. Robert G. Voss, Executive Director for Enrollment Management, Worcester Polytechnic Institute, 100 Institute Road, Worcester, MA 01609-2280. (508) 831-5286. Fax: (508) 831-5753.

Worcester State College
Worcester, Massachusetts — CB code: 3524

Admissions: 66% of applicants accepted
Based on: ••• School record, test scores
•• Interview, recommendations
• Activities, special talents
Completion: 75% of freshmen end year in good standing
22% enter graduate study

4-year public liberal arts college, coed. Founded in 1874. **Accreditation:** Regional. **Undergraduate enrollment:** 1,269 men, 1,757 women full time; 438 men, 790 women part time. **Graduate enrollment:** 8 men, 48 women full time; 40 men, 184 women part time. **Faculty:** 240 total (174 full time), 94 with doctorates or other terminal degrees. **Location:** Urban campus in small city; 40 miles from Boston. **Calendar:** Semester, limited summer session. **Microcomputers:** 160 located in libraries, computer centers.

DEGREES OFFERED. BA, BS, MS, MEd. 701 bachelor's degrees awarded in 1992. 25% in business and management, 7% communications, 12% teacher education, 12% health sciences, 5% allied health, 5% letters/literature, 12% psychology, 12% social sciences. Graduate degrees offered in 3 major fields of study.

UNDERGRADUATE MAJORS. Biological and physical sciences, biology, business and management, chemistry, computer and information sciences, early childhood education, economics, elementary education, English, French, geography, health sciences, history, mathematics, nursing, occupational therapy, physics, psychology, radio/television technology, sociology, Spanish, speech pathology/audiology, urban studies.

ACADEMIC PROGRAMS. Double major, independent study, internships, study abroad, teacher preparation, cross-registration. **Remedial services:** Learning center, preadmission summer program, reduced course load, remedial instruction, special counselor, tutoring. **ROTC:** Air Force, Army, Naval. **Placement/credit:** AP, institutional tests; 30 credit hours maximum for bachelor's degree.

ACADEMIC REQUIREMENTS. Freshmen must earn minimum GPA of 1.5 to continue in good standing. 66% of freshmen return for sophomore year. Students must declare major by end of second year. **Graduation requirements:** 120 hours for bachelor's (33 in major). Most students required to take courses in arts/fine arts, English, history, humanities, mathematics, biological/physical sciences, social sciences. **Postgraduate studies:** 2% enter law school, 1% enter medical school, 2% enter MBA programs, 17% enter other graduate study.

FRESHMAN ADMISSIONS. Selection criteria: High school achievement and test scores important. **High school preparation:** 16 units required. Required units include English 4, foreign language 2, mathematics 3, social science 2 and science 2. One American history recommended. **Test requirements:** SAT; score report by August 10.

1992 FRESHMAN CLASS PROFILE. 2,193 men and women applied, 1,453 accepted; 217 men enrolled, 336 women enrolled. 6% were in top tenth and 24% were in top quarter of graduating class. **Characteristics:** 96% from in state, 50% commute, 12% have minority backgrounds, 1% are foreign students. Average age is 19.

FALL-TERM APPLICATIONS. $10 fee, may be waived for applicants with need. $40 fee for out-of-state applicants. Closing date July 15; priority given to applications received by May 1; applicants notified on a rolling basis beginning on or about December 1; must reply within 30 days or ask for May 1 deferment. Interview recommended for academically weak applicants. CRDA. Deferred admission available.

STUDENT LIFE. Housing: Dormitories (men, women, coed); apartment housing available. **Activities:** Student government, film, magazine, radio, student newspaper, television, yearbook, choral groups, concert band, drama, musical theater, United Campus Ministry, Third World Alliance.

ATHLETICS. NCAA. **Intercollegiate:** Baseball M, basketball, cross-country, field hockey W, football M, golf M, ice hockey M, soccer, softball W, tennis, track and field, volleyball W. **Intramural:** Basketball, football M, horseback riding W, soccer M, softball, tennis, volleyball.

STUDENT SERVICES. Aptitude testing, career counseling, employment service for undergraduates, freshman orientation, health services, personal counseling, placement service for graduates, veterans counselor, services/facilities for handicapped.

ANNUAL EXPENSES. Tuition and fees (1992-93): $2,536, $3,864 additional for out-of-state students. **Room and board:** $3,690. **Books and supplies:** $500. **Other expenses:** $1,150.

FINANCIAL AID. 42% of freshmen, 49% of continuing students receive some form of aid. 97% of grants, 76% of loans, all jobs based on need. 204 enrolled freshmen were judged to have need, 189 were offered aid. Academic, state/district residency, leadership, alumni affiliation, minority scholarships available. **Aid applications:** No closing date; priority given to applications received by April 17; applicants notified on a rolling basis beginning on or about May 1; must reply within 2 weeks. **Additional information:** Tuition waived for in-state National Guard members and eligible veterans.

ADDRESS/TELEPHONE. E. Jay Tierney, Director of Admissions, Worcester State College, 486 Chandler Street, Worcester, MA 01602-2597. (508) 793-8040. Fax: (508) 793-8191.

Michigan

Adrian College

Adrian, Michigan CB code: 1001

Admissions: 78% of applicants accepted
Based on: ••• School record, test scores
• Activities, essay, interview, recommendations
Completion: 80% of freshmen end year in good standing
58% graduate, 17% of these enter graduate study

4-year private liberal arts college, coed, affiliated with United Methodist Church. Founded in 1859. **Accreditation:** Regional. **Undergraduate enrollment:** 501 men, 540 women full time; 36 men, 67 women part time. **Faculty:** 115 total (81 full time), 52 with doctorates or other terminal degrees. **Location:** Suburban campus in large town; 75 miles from Detroit, 35 miles from Ann Arbor. **Calendar:** Semester, limited summer session. **Microcomputers:** 45 located in libraries, computer centers. **Special facilities:** Observatory, planetarium, arboretum, solar greenhouse, education resource center, multicultural resource center, human anatomy laboratory, writing laboratory, acoustics laboratory, animal behavior center, Merillat Sports and Fitness Center. **Additional facts:** International awareness important part of education.

DEGREES OFFERED. AA, BA, BS. 5 associate degrees awarded in 1992. 75% in computer sciences, 25% health sciences. 180 bachelor's degrees awarded. 33% in business and management, 12% teacher education, 11% letters/literature, 8% life sciences, 7% mathematics, 12% social sciences.

UNDERGRADUATE MAJORS. Associate: Accounting, biology, business administration and management, business and management, chemistry, communications, computer programming, creative writing, earth sciences, economics, English, English literature, fine arts, French, German, history, home economics, human services, international business management, international studies, marketing management, mathematics, music, philosophy, physics, political science and government, psychology, radio/television broadcasting, religion, sociology, Spanish, speech, sports medicine. **Bachelor's:** Accounting, art education, arts management, biology, business administration and management, business and management, business education, chemistry, communications, computer programming, creative writing, criminal justice studies, earth sciences, economics, elementary education, English, English education, English literature, environmental science, family and community services, family/consumer resource management, fashion merchandising, fine arts, foreign languages education, French, German, history, home economics, home economics education, human services, individual and family development, interior design, international business management, international studies, marketing management, mathematics, mathematics education, music, music education, philosophy, physical education, physics, political science and government, preseminary studies, psychology, public relations, radio/television broadcasting, religion, science education, social science education, social sciences, social studies education, sociology, Spanish, speech, speech/communication/theater education.

ACADEMIC PROGRAMS. 2-year transfer program, double major, dual enrollment of high school students, honors program, independent study, internships, semester at sea, student-designed major, study abroad, teacher preparation, Washington semester, cross-registration, Appalachian semester; Philadelphia semester; bilingual multicultural program. Study arrangements with Fashion Institute of Technology, New York; Urban Life Center, Chicago; American College, London, England; Washington Center, Washington, D.C; liberal arts/career combination in engineering. **Remedial services:** Learning center, reduced course load, remedial instruction, special counselor, tutoring, learning development program. **ROTC:** Army. **Placement/credit:** AP, CLEP General and Subject, institutional tests; 15 credit hours maximum for associate degree; 30 credit hours maximum for bachelor's degree.

ACADEMIC REQUIREMENTS. Freshmen must earn minimum GPA of 2.0 to continue in good standing. 72% of freshmen return for sophomore year. Students must declare major by end of second year. **Graduation requirements:** 62 hours for associate, 124 hours for bachelor's (30 in major). Most students required to take courses in arts/fine arts, English, history, humanities, mathematics, philosophy/religion, biological/physical sciences, social sciences. **Postgraduate studies:** 2% enter law school, 2% enter medical school, 1% enter MBA programs, 12% enter other graduate study.

FRESHMAN ADMISSIONS. Selection criteria: Academic record in high school most important, followed by SAT or ACT scores. Applicants should rank in top half of high school class. School recommendations and extracurricular activities considered. Each applicant reviewed individually. **High school preparation:** 15 units required; 18 recommended. Required and recommended units include English 4, mathematics 2-3, social science 2-3 and science 2-3. Foreign language 2 recommended. **Test requirements:** SAT or ACT (ACT preferred); score report by August 15.

1992 FRESHMAN CLASS PROFILE. 646 men applied, 450 accepted, 148 enrolled; 683 women applied, 583 accepted, 143 enrolled. 65% had high school GPA of 3.0 or higher, 35% between 2.0 and 2.99. **Academic background:** Mid 50% of enrolled freshmen had ACT composite between 19-23. 95% submitted ACT scores. **Characteristics:** 75% from in state, 90% live in college housing, 10% have minority backgrounds, 3% are foreign students, 15% join fraternities/sororities. Average age is 18.

FALL-TERM APPLICATIONS. $15 fee, may be waived for applicants with need. Closing date August 15; priority given to applications received by June 1; applicants notified on a rolling basis beginning on or about September 1; must reply by May 1 or within 4 weeks if notified thereafter. Audition required for music applicants. Essay required for nontraditional applicants. Interview recommended. Portfolio recommended for art applicants. CRDA. Deferred admission available.

STUDENT LIFE. Housing: Dormitories (men, women, coed); fraternity, sorority housing available. Freshmen and sophomores required to live on campus unless living with family. **Activities:** Student government, magazine, radio, student newspaper, television, yearbook, literary magazine, choral groups, concert band, drama, jazz band, marching band, music ensembles, musical theater, pep band, symphony orchestra, Mime Troupe, fraternities, sororities, Newman Associates, Wesley Fellowship, Inter-Varsity Christian Fellowship, Hispanic Student Organization, International Club, Circle-K, A-Care, Campus Compact, Religious Life Council, A.L.P.H.A.

ATHLETICS. NCAA. **Intercollegiate:** Baseball M, basketball, cross-country, diving, football M, golf, soccer, softball W, swimming, tennis, track and field, volleyball W. **Intramural:** Badminton, basketball, golf M, handball M, ice hockey M, racquetball, soccer M, softball, swimming, tennis, volleyball.

STUDENT SERVICES. Career counseling, employment service for undergraduates, freshman orientation, health services, personal counseling, placement service for graduates, special adviser for adult students, services/facilities for handicapped.

ANNUAL EXPENSES. Tuition and fees: $10,700. **Room and board:** $3,540. **Books and supplies:** $400. **Other expenses:** $694.

FINANCIAL AID. 93% of freshmen, 89% of continuing students receive some form of aid. 94% of grants, 94% of loans, 43% of jobs based on need. 240 enrolled freshmen were judged to have need, 238 were offered aid. Academic, music/drama, art scholarships available. **Aid applications:** No closing date; priority given to applications received by March 15; applicants notified on a rolling basis beginning on or about March 15; must reply by May 1 or within 2 weeks if notified thereafter.

ADDRESS/TELEPHONE. George Wolf, Director of Admissions, Adrian College, 110 South Madison Street, Adrian, MI 49221-2575. (517) 265-5161 ext. 4326. (800) 877-2246. Fax: (517) 264-3331.

Albion College

Albion, Michigan CB code: 1007

Admissions: 89% of applicants accepted
Based on: ••• School record
•• Interview, recommendations, test scores
• Activities
Completion: 85% of freshmen end year in good standing
69% graduate, 47% of these enter graduate study

4-year private liberal arts college, coed, affiliated with United Methodist Church. Founded in 1835. **Accreditation:** Regional. **Undergraduate enrollment:** 847 men, 805 women full time; 11 men, 14 women part time. **Faculty:** 131 total (110 full time), 87 with doctorates or other terminal degrees. **Location:** Rural campus in large town; 90 miles from Detroit. **Calendar:** Semester, limited summer session. **Microcomputers:** 83 located in libraries, classrooms, computer centers. **Special facilities:** 135-acre nature center adjacent to campus.

DEGREES OFFERED. BA, BFA. 346 bachelor's degrees awarded in 1992. 26% in business and management, 5% communications, 5% languages, 16% letters/literature, 8% life sciences, 8% psychology, 17% social sciences, 5% visual and performing arts.

UNDERGRADUATE MAJORS. American studies, anthropology, biology, business administration and management, chemistry, communications, computer mathematics, economics, English, fine arts, French, geology, German, history, humanities and social sciences, mathematics, music, philosophy, physics, political science and government, psychology, religion, sociology, Spanish.

ACADEMIC PROGRAMS. Accelerated program, double major, honors program, independent study, internships, student-designed major, study abroad, teacher preparation, New York semester, Washington semester; liberal arts/career combination in engineering, forestry, health sciences. **Remedial services:** Learning center, tutoring. **Placement/credit:** AP, CLEP Subject, institutional tests; 32 credit hours maximum for bachelor's degree.

ACADEMIC REQUIREMENTS. No policy requiring minimum GPA; records of students having academic difficulty are reviewed individually. 85% of freshmen return for sophomore year. Students must declare major by end of second year. **Graduation requirements:** 124 hours for bachelor's (32 in major). Most students required to take courses in arts/fine arts, humanities, biological/physical sciences, social sciences. **Postgraduate studies:** 7%

enter law school, 5% enter medical school, 2% enter MBA programs, 33% enter other graduate study.

FRESHMAN ADMISSIONS. Selection criteria: Admissions based on school achievement record, test scores, and recommendations from counselor or principal. **Test requirements:** SAT or ACT; score report by August 22.

1992 FRESHMAN CLASS PROFILE. 890 men applied, 765 accepted, 282 enrolled; 1,016 women applied, 938 accepted, 248 enrolled. 36% were in top tenth and 70% were in top quarter of graduating class. **Academic background:** Mid 50% of enrolled freshmen had SAT-V between 560-500, SAT-M between 610-550; ACT composite between 23-27. 24% submitted SAT scores, 89% submitted ACT scores. **Characteristics:** 86% from in state, 99% live in college housing, 7% have minority backgrounds. Average age is 18.

FALL-TERM APPLICATIONS. $20 fee, may be waived for applicants with need. No closing date; applicants notified on a rolling basis; must reply by May 1 or within 3 weeks if notified thereafter. Interview recommended. Audition recommended for music applicants. Deferred and early admission available.

STUDENT LIFE. Housing: Dormitories (men, women, coed); apartment, fraternity, cooperative housing available. **Activities:** Student government, radio, student newspaper, yearbook, choral groups, concert band, dance, drama, jazz band, marching band, music ensembles, musical theater, opera, pep band, symphony orchestra, fraternities, sororities, Student Volunteer Bureau, Black Student Alliance, Appalachian Service Project, Committee on Responsible Drinking, Ecological Awareness Club, Campus Religious Council including: Wesley Fellowship (Methodist), Catholic Campus Ministry, Simcha (Jewish), Fellowship of Christian Athletes.

ATHLETICS. NCAA. **Intercollegiate:** Baseball M, basketball, cross-country, football M, golf, soccer, softball W, swimming, tennis, track and field, volleyball W. **Intramural:** Badminton, basketball, bowling, diving, football M, golf, soccer, softball, swimming, table tennis, tennis, track and field, volleyball, water polo, wrestling M.

STUDENT SERVICES. Career counseling, employment service for undergraduates, freshman orientation, health services, personal counseling, placement service for graduates.

ANNUAL EXPENSES. Tuition and fees (1992-93): $12,294. **Room and board:** $4,316. **Books and supplies:** $500. **Other expenses:** $400.

FINANCIAL AID. 80% of freshmen, 73% of continuing students receive some form of aid. 78% of grants, all loans, 54% of jobs based on need. 300 enrolled freshmen were judged to have need, all were offered aid. Academic, music/drama, art, leadership scholarships available. **Aid applications:** No closing date; priority given to applications received by March 1; applicants notified on a rolling basis beginning on or about March 15; must reply within 2 weeks.

ADDRESS/TELEPHONE. Dr. Frank Bonta, Dean of Admissions, Albion College, Albion, MI 49224. (517) 629-0321. Fax: (517) 629-0509.

Alma College

Alma, Michigan CB code: 1010

Admissions: 85% of applicants accepted
Based on: ••• School record, test scores
• Activities, essay, interview, recommendations
Completion: 95% of freshmen end year in good standing
70% graduate, 28% of these enter graduate study

4-year private liberal arts college, coed, affiliated with Presbyterian Church (USA). Founded in 1886. **Accreditation:** Regional. **Undergraduate enrollment:** 552 men, 713 women full time; 14 men, 16 women part time. **Faculty:** 110 total (77 full time), 62 with doctorates or other terminal degrees. **Location:** Rural campus in large town; 50 miles north of Lansing, 45 miles from Saginaw. **Calendar:** 4-4-1. **Microcomputers:** 113 located in dormitories, libraries, computer centers. **Special facilities:** Eddy Music Center, Clack Art Building, Kapp Science Laboratory Center.

DEGREES OFFERED. BA, BS, BFA. 284 bachelor's degrees awarded in 1992. 20% in business and management, 9% teacher education, 5% health sciences, 7% letters/literature, 12% life sciences, 5% mathematics, 5% physical sciences, 5% psychology, 18% social sciences.

UNDERGRADUATE MAJORS. Applied mathematics, art history, biochemistry, biology, business administration and management, business and management, chemistry, communications, computer and information sciences, computer programming, creative writing, dance, dramatic arts, drawing, economics, education, elementary education, English, English literature, exercise and health science, fine arts, French, German, graphic design, history, international business management, international relations, junior high education, liberal/general studies, management information systems, marketing management, mathematics, medical illustrating, music, occupational therapy, painting, philosophy, physics, political science and government, predentistry, preengineering, prelaw, premedicine, preveterinary, psychology, public administration, public affairs, religion, sculpture, secondary education, sociology, Spanish, speech, sports medicine, systems analysis.

ACADEMIC PROGRAMS. Accelerated program, double major, dual enrollment of high school students, honors program, independent study, internships, student-designed major, study abroad, teacher preparation, visiting/exchange student program, Washington semester, cross-registration; liberal arts/career combination in engineering, forestry, health sciences. **Remedial services:** Reduced course load, special counselor, tutoring, reading program, study skills course. **ROTC:** Army. **Placement/credit:** AP, CLEP General and Subject, institutional tests; 32 credit hours maximum for bachelor's degree.

ACADEMIC REQUIREMENTS. Freshmen must earn minimum GPA of 2.0 to continue in good standing. 85% of freshmen return for sophomore year. Students must declare major by end of second year. **Graduation requirements:** 136 hours for bachelor's (36 in major). Most students required to take courses in arts/fine arts, English, history, humanities, mathematics, philosophy/religion, biological/physical sciences, social sciences. **Postgraduate studies:** 5% enter law school, 4% enter medical school, 4% enter MBA programs, 15% enter other graduate study. **Additional information:** One-month spring term provides special opportunties for study in United States or overseas.

FRESHMAN ADMISSIONS. Selection criteria: Applicant should preferably be in top half of class, have 3.0 high school GPA, or ACT composite score of 22, or combined SAT score of 1000. Cocurricular activities considered. **High school preparation:** 16 units required. Required and recommended units include English 3, mathematics 2, social science 2 and science 2. Foreign language 2 recommended. **Test requirements:** SAT or ACT (ACT preferred); score report by May 1.

1992 FRESHMAN CLASS PROFILE. 547 men applied, 458 accepted, 175 enrolled; 575 women applied, 499 accepted, 238 enrolled. 79% had high school GPA of 3.0 or higher, 21% between 2.0 and 2.99. **Academic background:** Mid 50% of enrolled freshmen had ACT composite between 23-27. 99% submitted ACT scores. **Characteristics:** 93% from in state, 95% live in college housing, 6% have minority backgrounds, 1% are foreign students, 40% join fraternities/sororities. Average age is 18.

FALL-TERM APPLICATIONS. $20 fee, may be waived for applicants with need. Closing date August 30; priority given to applications received by February 1; applicants notified on a rolling basis; must reply by May 1 or within 2 weeks if notified thereafter. Interview recommended. Portfolio recommended for art applicants. Essay recommended. Interview recommended for all applicants, strongly recommended for academically weak applicants and for those whose grades and test scores show discrepancies. Audition, protfolio required of performance scholars. CRDA. Deferred and early admission available. EDP-F. Academically weak applicants may be admitted through special action.

STUDENT LIFE. Housing: Dormitories (men, women, coed); apartment, fraternity, sorority housing available. Small housing units available. Kirk International Center houses students of international experience. Selected students of French or Spanish language and literature reside in the French or Spanish House. **Activities:** Student government, film, magazine, radio, student newspaper, television, yearbook, literary publications, choral groups, concert band, dance, drama, jazz band, marching band, music ensembles, musical theater, pep band, symphony orchestra, bagpipe band and highland dancing, fraternities, sororities, Women's Awareness Organization, Alumni Student Association, Chapel Affairs Committee, Circle-K, Bagpipe Band, Kiltie Dancers, Students for Peace and Nonviolence, Amnesty International, Association for Intercultural Understanding. **Additional information:** Preterm, a special orientation program for freshmen, includes an academic seminar and social activities.

ATHLETICS. NCAA. **Intercollegiate:** Baseball M, basketball, cross-country, diving, football M, golf, soccer, softball W, swimming, tennis, track and field, volleyball W. **Intramural:** Basketball, racquetball, softball, volleyball, water polo.

STUDENT SERVICES. Aptitude testing, career counseling, employment service for undergraduates, freshman orientation, health services, personal counseling, placement service for graduates, services/facilities for handicapped.

ANNUAL EXPENSES. Tuition and fees: $12,046. **Room and board:** $4,334. **Books and supplies:** $700. **Other expenses:** $625.

FINANCIAL AID. 95% of freshmen, 95% of continuing students receive some form of aid. 86% of grants, 98% of loans, 55% of jobs based on need. 321 enrolled freshmen were judged to have need, all were offered aid. Academic, music/drama, art, leadership, religious affiliation scholarships available. **Aid applications:** Closing date May 1; priority given to applications received by February 15; applicants notified on a rolling basis beginning on or about February 15; must reply by May 1. **Additional information:** Auditions required for music, drama, dance scholarship candidates. Portfolios required for art scholarship candidates.

ADDRESS/TELEPHONE. John W. Seveland, Vice President of Enrollment and Student Affairs, Alma College, 614 West Superior Street, Alma, MI 48801-1599. (517) 463-7139. (800) 321-ALMA. Fax: (517) 463-7277.

Alpena Community College
Alpena, Michigan CB code: 1011

2-year public community college, coed. Founded in 1952. **Accreditation:** Regional. **Undergraduate enrollment:** 437 men, 552 women full time; 459 men, 670 women part time. **Faculty:** 117 total (52 full time), 3 with doctorates or other terminal degrees. **Location:** Suburban campus in large town; 240 miles from Detroit. **Calendar:** Semester, limited summer session. **Microcomputers:** 60 located in classrooms, computer centers.

DEGREES OFFERED. AA, AS, AAS. 337 associate degrees awarded in 1992.

UNDERGRADUATE MAJORS. Accounting, business administration and management, business and management, business and office, concrete construction technology, data processing, drafting and design technology, graphic and printing production, graphic arts technology, industrial technology, law enforcement and corrections technologies, liberal/general studies, machine tool operation/machine shop, marketing and distribution, nursing, secretarial and related programs.

ACADEMIC PROGRAMS. 2-year transfer program, double major, dual enrollment of high school students, internships, telecourses. **Remedial services:** Learning center, reduced course load, remedial instruction, special counselor, tutoring. **Placement/credit:** AP, CLEP General and Subject, institutional tests; 30 credit hours maximum for associate degree.

ACADEMIC REQUIREMENTS. Freshmen must earn minimum GPA of 1.7 to continue in good standing. 65% of freshmen return for sophomore year. Students must declare major on application. **Graduation requirements:** 60 hours for associate (30 in major). Most students required to take courses in English, history, humanities, mathematics, biological/physical sciences, social sciences.

FRESHMAN ADMISSIONS. Selection criteria: Open admissions. Selective admissions criteria used in pratical nursing, registered nursing, and utility technician programs. High school diploma or equivalent required for nursing applicants. **Additional information:** Placement testing required of all freshmen.

1992 FRESHMAN CLASS PROFILE. 500 men applied, 500 accepted, 378 enrolled; 650 women applied, 650 accepted, 430 enrolled. **Academic background:** Mid 50% of enrolled freshmen had ACT composite between 14-22. 25% submitted ACT scores. **Characteristics:** 99% from in state, 100% commute, 4% have minority backgrounds. Average age is 29.

FALL-TERM APPLICATIONS. No fee. No closing date; applicants notified on a rolling basis.

STUDENT LIFE. Activities: Student government, student newspaper, drama.

ATHLETICS. NJCAA. **Intercollegiate:** Basketball, cross-country M, golf M, softball W. **Intramural:** Basketball, bowling, field hockey, softball, volleyball.

STUDENT SERVICES. Career counseling, employment service for undergraduates, freshman orientation, personal counseling, placement service for graduates, veterans counselor, services/facilities for handicapped.

ANNUAL EXPENSES. Tuition and fees (projected): $1,460, $630 additional for out-of-district students, $1,260 additional for out-of-state students. **Books and supplies:** $300. **Other expenses:** $600.

FINANCIAL AID. 57% of freshmen, 55% of continuing students receive some form of aid. 99% of grants, 94% of loans, 88% of jobs based on need. 450 enrolled freshmen were judged to have need, all were offered aid. Academic, athletic, leadership scholarships available. **Aid applications:** No closing date; priority given to applications received by May 15; applicants notified on a rolling basis beginning on or about May 15; must reply within 3 weeks.

ADDRESS/TELEPHONE. Max Lindsay, Assistant Dean of Students, Alpena Community College, 666 Johnson Street, Alpena, MI 49707. (517) 356-9021 ext. 200. Fax: (517) 356-0980.

Andrews University
Berrien Springs, Michigan CB code: 1030

4-year private university, coed, affiliated with Seventh-day Adventists. Founded in 1874. **Accreditation:** Regional. **Undergraduate enrollment:** 822 men, 899 women full time; 123 men, 299 women part time. **Graduate enrollment:** 424 men, 174 women full time; 158 men, 135 women part time. **Faculty:** 266 total, 126 with doctorates or other terminal degrees. **Location:** Rural campus in rural community; 10 miles from St. Joseph-Benton Harbor, 25 miles from South Bend, Indiana. **Calendar:** Quarter, limited summer session. **Microcomputers:** Located in dormitories, classrooms, computer centers.

DEGREES OFFERED. AS, BA, BS, BFA, BArch, MA, MS, MBA, PhD, EdD, B.Div, M.Div. 30 associate degrees awarded in 1992. 17% in business and management, 7% home economics, 32% life sciences, 11% multi/interdisciplinary studies, 25% trade and industry. 340 bachelor's degrees awarded. 10% in business and management, 6% teacher education, 20% health sciences, 9% letters/literature, 5% philosophy, religion, theology, 13% social sciences, 5% trade and industry. Graduate degrees offered in 40 major fields of study.

UNDERGRADUATE MAJORS. Associate: Accounting, aeronautical technology, architectural technologies, automotive technology, business and management, drafting, electrical technology, engineering and engineering-related technologies, food production/management/services, graphic and printing production, graphic arts technology, horticultural science, industrial technology, liberal/general studies, mechanical design technology, medical laboratory technologies, radiograph medical technology, secretarial and related programs. **Bachelor's:** Accounting, agricultural sciences, allied health, architecture, automotive technology, behavioral sciences, biochemistry, biology, biophysics, botany, business administration and management, business economics, chemistry, clinical laboratory science, communications, computer and information sciences, educational media technology, elementary education, engineering, engineering and engineering-related technologies, English, family/consumer resource management, fine arts, French, German, graphic and printing production, graphic arts technology, health psychology, health sciences, history, home economics, information sciences and systems, interior design, journalism, marketing and distribution, mathematics, media technology, medical radiation dosimetry, music, nursing, office supervision and management, physical therapy, physics, psychology, radiograph medical technology, religion, religious education, secretarial and related programs, social sciences, social work, sociology, Spanish, speech correction, speech pathology/audiology, teaching English as a second language/foreign language, theological studies, visual and performing arts, zoology.

ACADEMIC PROGRAMS. Accelerated program, cooperative education, double major, dual enrollment of high school students, education specialist degree, honors program, independent study, internships, study abroad, teacher preparation. **Remedial services:** Learning center, reduced course load, remedial instruction, special counselor, tutoring. **Placement/credit:** AP, CLEP General and Subject, institutional tests; 48 credit hours maximum for bachelor's degree.

ACADEMIC REQUIREMENTS. Freshmen must earn minimum GPA of 2.0 to continue in good standing. 64% of freshmen return for sophomore year. Students must declare major by end of first year. **Graduation requirements:** 96 hours for associate (45 in major), 190 hours for bachelor's (60 in major). Most students required to take courses in arts/fine arts, computer science, English, history, humanities, mathematics, philosophy/religion, biological/physical sciences, social sciences.

FRESHMAN ADMISSIONS. Selection criteria: School achievement record, test scores, recommendations considered. **High school preparation:** 13 units required; 13 recommended. 13 academic units generally required, in mathematics, science, English, foreign language, and social sciences. **Test requirements:** ACT; score report by September 26. **Additional information:** Portfolios recommended for credit-seeking continuing education students.

1992 FRESHMAN CLASS PROFILE. 368 men and women enrolled. 55% had high school GPA of 3.0 or higher, 40% between 2.0 and 2.99. **Academic background:** Mid 50% of enrolled freshmen had ACT composite between 14-23. 80% submitted ACT scores. **Characteristics:** 35% from in state, 82% live in college housing, 36% have minority backgrounds, 15% are foreign students. Average age is 18.

FALL-TERM APPLICATIONS. $30 fee, may be waived for applicants with need. No closing date; applicants notified on a rolling basis beginning on or about January 1; must reply by registration. Interview recommended. Audition recommended for music applicants. Portfolio recommended for art applicants. Deferred admission available.

STUDENT LIFE. Housing: Dormitories (men, women); apartment housing available. **Activities:** Student government, radio, student newspaper, yearbook, choral groups, concert band, drama, music ensembles, symphony orchestra, Christian Youth Action.

ATHLETICS. Intramural: Basketball, field hockey M, gymnastics, racquetball, soccer, softball, volleyball.

STUDENT SERVICES. Aptitude testing, career counseling, employment service for undergraduates, freshman orientation, health services, on-campus day care, personal counseling, placement service for graduates, special adviser for adult students, veterans counselor, services/facilities for handicapped.

ANNUAL EXPENSES. Tuition and fees: $11,250. **Room and board:** $3,990. **Books and supplies:** $1,050.

FINANCIAL AID. 90% of freshmen, 90% of continuing students receive some form of aid. Grants, loans, jobs available. Academic, leadership scholarships available. **Aid applications:** Closing date January 31; applicants notified on a rolling basis beginning on or about April 15; must reply within 3 weeks.

ADDRESS/TELEPHONE. John F. Mentges, Executive Director, Andrews University, Berrien Springs, MI 49104. (616) 471-3353 ext. 0740. (800) 253-2874. Fax: (616) 473-9434.

Aquinas College
Grand Rapids, Michigan CB code: 1018

Admissions: 84% of applicants accepted
Based on: ••• School record
•• Special talents, test scores
• Activities, essay, interview, recommendations
Completion: 85% of freshmen end year in good standing
43% graduate, 27% of these enter graduate study

4-year private liberal arts college, coed, affiliated with Roman Catholic Church. Founded in 1922. **Accreditation:** Regional. **Undergraduate enrollment:** 459 men, 830 women full time; 252 men, 545 women part time. **Graduate enrollment:** 1 man, 6 women full time; 232 men, 219 women part time. **Faculty:** 197 total (87 full time), 48 with doctorates or other terminal degrees. **Location:** Suburban campus in small city; 140 miles from Detroit. **Calendar:** Semester, extensive summer session. Saturday and extensive evening/early morning classes. **Microcomputers:** 99 located in dormitories, computer centers. **Special facilities:** Greenhouse, astronomy tower, nature trails.

DEGREES OFFERED. AA, AS, BA, BS, BFA, MBA. 14 associate degrees awarded in 1992. 97% in letters/literature. 389 bachelor's degrees awarded. 42% in business and management, 13% communications, 6% education, 6% letters/literature, 5% psychology, 5% visual and performing arts. Graduate degrees offered in 2 major fields of study.

UNDERGRADUATE MAJORS. Associate: Liberal/general studies, religious music. **Bachelor's:** Accounting, art history, biological and physical sciences, biology, business administration and management, business and management, chemistry, clinical laboratory science, communications, computer and information sciences, earth sciences, economics, education, elementary education, English, environmental design, environmental science, fine arts, French, geography, geology, German, graphic design, history, illustration design, interior design, international business management, international relations, jazz, liberal/general studies, mathematics, music, music education, music performance, philosophy, physical sciences, physics, political science and government, preengineering, premedicine, psychology, reading education, religion, religious music, secondary education, social science education, social sciences, sociology, Spanish, urban studies.

ACADEMIC PROGRAMS. 2-year transfer program, accelerated program, cooperative education, double major, dual enrollment of high school students, honors program, independent study, internships, student-designed major, study abroad, teacher preparation, visiting/exchange student program, cross-registration, applied arts program with Kendall School of Design. **Remedial services:** Tutoring, writing center. **Placement/credit:** AP, CLEP General and Subject, institutional tests; 30 credit hours maximum for bachelor's degree.

ACADEMIC REQUIREMENTS. Freshmen must earn minimum GPA of 2.0 to continue in good standing. Successful completion of 12 credit hours each semester required. 78% of freshmen return for sophomore year. Students must declare major by end of second year. **Graduation requirements:** 64 hours for associate, 124 hours for bachelor's (33 in major). Most students required to take courses in English, humanities, biological/physical sciences.

FRESHMAN ADMISSIONS. Selection criteria: 2.5 high school GPA in academic subjects. Test scores also considered. **High school preparation:** 15 units required. Required units include biological science 1, English 4, mathematics 3, physical science 2 and social science 4. **Test requirements:** SAT or ACT (ACT preferred); score report by August 1.

1992 FRESHMAN CLASS PROFILE. 222 men applied, 174 accepted, 70 enrolled; 437 women applied, 378 accepted, 163 enrolled. 57% had high school GPA of 3.0 or higher, 43% between 2.0 and 2.99. 30% were in top tenth and 70% were in top quarter of graduating class. **Academic background:** Mid 50% of enrolled freshmen had ACT composite between 18-25. 96% submitted ACT scores. **Characteristics:** 91% from in state, 78% live in college housing, 17% have minority backgrounds, 1% are foreign students. Average age is 18.

FALL-TERM APPLICATIONS. $20 fee, may be waived for applicants with need. Closing date August 15; priority given to applications received by February 1; applicants notified on a rolling basis; must reply within 4 weeks. Audition recommended for music applicants. Portfolio recommended for art applicants. Interview required for applicants with above average test scores but less than 2.5 high school GPA in academic subjects; recommended for others. CRDA. Deferred and early admission available.

STUDENT LIFE. Housing: Dormitories (coed). **Activities:** Student government, student newspaper, yearbook, choral groups, concert band, drama, jazz band, music ensembles, musical theater, pep band, community action volunteers, minority and international student unions, campus ministry, social action commission, blood pressure screening group. **Additional information:** Students serve on administrative and faculty committees.

ATHLETICS. NAIA. **Intercollegiate:** Baseball M, basketball, cross-country, golf M, soccer, softball W, tennis, track and field, volleyball W. **Intramural:** Basketball, bowling, fencing M, golf, ice hockey M, skiing, soccer, softball, tennis, volleyball.

STUDENT SERVICES. Aptitude testing, career counseling, employment service for undergraduates, freshman orientation, health services, on-campus day care, personal counseling, placement service for graduates, special adviser for adult students, veterans counselor, special counselor for older women students, services/facilities for handicapped.

ANNUAL EXPENSES. Tuition and fees (1992-93): $9,722. **Room and board:** $4,070. **Books and supplies:** $345. **Other expenses:** $635.

FINANCIAL AID. 91% of freshmen, 87% of continuing students receive some form of aid. 98% of grants, 91% of loans, 18% of jobs based on need. 211 enrolled freshmen were judged to have need, all were offered aid. Academic, music/drama, art, athletic, leadership, alumni affiliation, religious affiliation, minority scholarships available. **Aid applications:** No closing date; priority given to applications received by February 15; applicants notified on a rolling basis beginning on or about April 1; must reply within 4 weeks.

ADDRESS/TELEPHONE. Paula Meehan, Dean of Admissions, Aquinas College, 1607 Robinson Road, Southeast, Grand Rapids, MI 49506-1799. (616) 732-4460. (800) 678-9593.

Baker College of Auburn Hills
Auburn Hills, Michigan CB code: 1457

2-year private business college, coed. Founded in 1888. **Accreditation:** Regional. **Undergraduate enrollment:** 25 men, 159 women full time; 34 men, 78 women part time. **Faculty:** 21 total (3 full time), 4 with doctorates or other terminal degrees. **Location:** Suburban campus in very large city; 30 miles north of Detroit. **Calendar:** Quarter, limited summer session. **Microcomputers:** Located in computer centers.

DEGREES OFFERED. AS, AAS. 140 associate degrees awarded in 1992.

UNDERGRADUATE MAJORS. Accounting, business administration and management, business and management, business and office, business data entry equipment operation, business data processing and related programs, computer and information sciences, data processing, information sciences and systems, management science, marketing and distribution, marketing management, medical assistant, medical records administration, medical secretary, office supervision and management, secretarial and related programs, word processing.

ACADEMIC PROGRAMS. Dual enrollment of high school students, internships. **Remedial services:** Remedial instruction, tutoring, weekly faculty tutor, laboratory days.

ACADEMIC REQUIREMENTS. Freshmen must earn minimum GPA of 2.0 to continue in good standing. 83% of freshmen return for sophomore year. Students must declare major by end of second year. **Graduation requirements:** Most students required to take courses in computer science, English, mathematics.

FRESHMAN ADMISSIONS. Selection criteria: Open admissions.

1992 FRESHMAN CLASS PROFILE. 39 men, 172 women enrolled. 20% had high school GPA of 3.0 or higher, 80% between 2.0 and 2.99. **Characteristics:** 100% from in state, 100% commute, 40% have minority backgrounds. Average age is 24.

FALL-TERM APPLICATIONS. $20 fee, may be waived for applicants with need. No closing date; must reply immediately. Deferred and early admission available.

STUDENT LIFE. Activities: Accounting Club, Management Club, Medical Record Techincal Professionals.

STUDENT SERVICES. Aptitude testing, career counseling, employment service for undergraduates, freshman orientation, personal counseling, special adviser for adult students, services/facilities for handicapped.

ANNUAL EXPENSES. Tuition and fees (1992-93): $4,815. **Books and supplies:** $600.

FINANCIAL AID. 70% of freshmen, 70% of continuing students receive some form of aid. All grants, 91% of loans, all jobs based on need. Academic, leadership scholarships available. **Aid applications:** No closing date; priority given to applications received by February 15; applicants notified on a rolling basis.

ADDRESS/TELEPHONE. Victoria M. Fisher, Director of Admissions, Baker College of Auburn Hills, 1500 University Drive, Auburn Hills, MI 48326. (313) 340-0600. Fax: (313) 340-0608.

Baker College of Cadillac
Cadillac, Michigan CB code: 1381

4-year private business, technical college, coed. Founded in 1888. **Accreditation:** Regional. **Undergraduate enrollment:** 279 men and women full time; 143 men and women part time. **Faculty:** 51 total (1 full time), 2 with doctorates or other terminal degrees. **Location:** Rural campus in large town; 90 miles from Grand Rapids, 45 miles from Traverse City. **Calendar:** Quarter, limited summer session. **Microcomputers:** 48 located in computer centers.

DEGREES OFFERED. AAS, B. 10 associate degrees awarded in 1992. 24% in business and management, 47% business/office and marketing/distribution, 8% computer sciences, 21% allied health. 1 bachelor's degrees awarded. 100% in business and management.

UNDERGRADUATE MAJORS. Accounting, business administration and management, business and management, marketing management, medical assistant, medical secretary, microcomputer software, secretarial and related programs, word processing. business administration and management.

ACADEMIC PROGRAMS. Cooperative education, dual enrollment of high school students, internships. **Remedial services:** Remedial instruction, tutoring.

ACADEMIC REQUIREMENTS. Students must declare major by end of first year. **Graduation requirements:** 99 hours for associate, 195 hours for bachelor's. Most students required to take courses in computer science, English, mathematics.

FRESHMAN ADMISSIONS. **Selection criteria:** Open admissions.

1992 FRESHMAN CLASS PROFILE. 187 men and women applied, 187 accepted; 187 enrolled. **Characteristics:** 100% commute.

FALL-TERM APPLICATIONS. $20 fee. No closing date; applicants notified on a rolling basis; must reply by registration. Interview recommended.

STUDENT SERVICES. Aptitude testing, career counseling, employment service for undergraduates, freshman orientation, placement service for graduates, services/facilities for handicapped.

ANNUAL EXPENSES. **Tuition and fees:** $5,040, $1,575 additional for out-of-state students. **Books and supplies:** $750.

FINANCIAL AID. 88% of freshmen, 86% of continuing students receive some form of aid. All grants, 98% of loans, all jobs based on need. Academic scholarships available. **Aid applications:** No closing date; applicants notified on a rolling basis beginning on or about May 15; must reply by registration.

ADDRESS/TELEPHONE. C. Michael Boedy, VP for Marketing/Admissions, Baker College of Cadillac, 9600 East 13th Street, Cadillac, MI 49601. (616) 775-8458. Fax: (616) 775-8505.

Baker College: Flint
Flint, Michigan CB code: 0806

4-year private business, technical college, coed. Founded in 1911. **Accreditation:** Regional. **Undergraduate enrollment:** 741 men, 2,059 women full time; 407 men, 972 women part time. **Faculty:** 127 total (27 full time), 16 with doctorates or other terminal degrees. **Location:** Urban campus in small city; 60 miles from Detroit. **Calendar:** Quarter, limited summer session. **Microcomputers:** 180 located in libraries, classrooms, computer centers. **Special facilities:** Day care center. **Additional facts:** Corporate services division offers degree-granting programs on campus and/or at work site, coordinated with corporate training and professional development programs.

DEGREES OFFERED. AAS, BA, BS. 349 associate degrees awarded in 1992. 20% in business and management, 40% business/office and marketing/distribution, 20% computer sciences, 20% allied health. 94 bachelor's degrees awarded. 49% in business and management, 30% business/office and marketing/distribution, 21% computer sciences.

UNDERGRADUATE MAJORS. **Associate:** Accounting, airline piloting and navigation, architectural technologies, bioengineering and biomedical engineering, biomedical equipment technology, business administration and management, business and management, business and office, business computer/console/peripheral equipment operation, business data processing and related programs, business data programming, computer graphics, computer programming, computer servicing technology, data processing, drafting, drafting and design technology, electrical and electronics equipment repair, electrical/electronics/communications engineering, electronic technology, fashion merchandising, hotel/motel and restaurant management, interior design, labor/industrial relations, legal secretary, liberal/general studies, marketing management, medical assistant, medical records technology, medical secretary, medical transcription, microcomputer software, physical therapy assistant, secretarial and related programs, SPC/quality improvement, surgical technology, tourism, transportation and travel marketing, word processing. **Bachelor's:** Accounting, airline piloting and navigation, aviation management, business administration and management, business and management, business data programming, computer graphics, computer programming, data processing, drafting and design technology, electronic technology, health information management, industrial technology, information sciences and systems, marketing management, occupational therapy, office supervision and management, SPC/quality improvement, word processing.

ACADEMIC PROGRAMS. 2-year transfer program, accelerated program, cooperative education, double major, dual enrollment of high school students, independent study, internships. **Remedial services:** Learning center, reduced course load, remedial instruction, special counselor, tutoring. **Placement/credit:** Institutional tests; 32 credit hours maximum for associate degree; 32 credit hours maximum for bachelor's degree.

ACADEMIC REQUIREMENTS. Freshmen must earn minimum GPA of 2.0 to continue in good standing. 65% of freshmen return for sophomore year. Students must declare major on application. **Graduation requirements:** 97 hours for associate (24 in major), 189 hours for bachelor's (24 in major). Most students required to take courses in English, mathematics, social sciences. **Postgraduate studies:** 20% from 2-year programs enter 4-year programs.

FRESHMAN ADMISSIONS. **Selection criteria:** Open admissions.

1992 FRESHMAN CLASS PROFILE. 423 men, 950 women enrolled. **Characteristics:** 99% from in state, 95% commute, 18% have minority backgrounds.

FALL-TERM APPLICATIONS. $20 fee. Closing date September 27; applicants notified on a rolling basis. Interview recommended. Deferred and early admission available.

STUDENT LIFE. **Housing:** Dormitories (coed). **Activities:** Choral groups, National Association of Accountants, Data Processing Management Association, American Marketing Association, Interior Design Society, Fashion Association, Travel Club, Environmental Club.

ATHLETICS. **Intramural:** Basketball, volleyball.

STUDENT SERVICES. Aptitude testing, career counseling, employment service for undergraduates, freshman orientation, on-campus day care, personal counseling, placement service for graduates, veterans counselor, services/facilities for handicapped.

ANNUAL EXPENSES. **Tuition and fees:** $5,376. **Room and board:** $1,575 room only. **Books and supplies:** $650. **Other expenses:** $2,500.

FINANCIAL AID. 63% of freshmen, 63% of continuing students receive some form of aid. Grants, loans, jobs available. Academic, leadership scholarships available. **Aid applications:** No closing date; priority given to applications received by February 15; applicants notified on a rolling basis; must reply within 2 weeks.

ADDRESS/TELEPHONE. Mark Heaton, Director of Admissions, Baker College: Flint, 1050 West Bristol Road, Flint, MI 48507-5508. (313) 766-4000. (800) 822-2537. Fax: (313) 766-4049.

Baker College of Mount Clemens
Clinton Township, Michigan CB code: 1386

2-year private business, technical college, coed. Founded in 1990. **Accreditation:** Regional. **Undergraduate enrollment:** 450 men and women. **Faculty:** 40 total (10 full time). **Location:** Large city. **Calendar:** Quarter.

DEGREES OFFERED. 20 associate degrees awarded in 1992.

UNDERGRADUATE MAJORS. Accounting, accounting information systems, business administration and management, business and office, data processing, management science, marketing management, medical assistant, medical records administration, medical records technology, medical secretary, office supervision and management, word processing.

FRESHMAN ADMISSIONS. **Selection criteria:** Open admissions.

1992 FRESHMAN CLASS PROFILE. 250 men and women enrolled. **Characteristics:** 100% commute.

FALL-TERM APPLICATIONS. $20 fee. No closing date; applicants notified on a rolling basis; must reply by registration.

ANNUAL EXPENSES. **Tuition and fees (1992-93):** $5,136.

FINANCIAL AID. **Aid applications:** No closing date.

ADDRESS/TELEPHONE. Heidi Wisby, Director of Admissions, Baker College of Mount Clemens, 34950 Little Mack Avenue, Mount Clemens, MI 48043. Fax: (313) 791-6611.

Baker College of Muskegon
Muskegon, Michigan CB code: 1527

4-year private business college, coed. Founded in 1888. **Accreditation:** Regional. **Undergraduate enrollment:** 2,240 men and women. **Faculty:** 103 total (28 full time). **Location:** Urban campus in large town; 40 miles from Grand Rapids. **Calendar:** Quarter, extensive summer session. **Microcomputers:** 85 located in classrooms, computer centers.

DEGREES OFFERED. AAS, B. 191 associate degrees awarded in 1992. 56% in business and management, 25% business/office and marketing/distribution, 11% engineering technologies, 6% allied health. 34 bachelor's degrees awarded. 98% in business and management.

UNDERGRADUATE MAJORS. Accounting, aeronautical technology, aviation management, business and management, business and office, business computer/console/peripheral equipment operation, business data processing and related programs, business data programming, computer programming, engineering and engineering-related technologies, fashion merchandising, hospitality and recreation marketing, interior design, legal secretary, marketing and distribution, marketing management, medical assistant, medical records technology, medical secretary, secretarial and related programs, surgical technology, tourism, word processing. accounting, aeronautical technology, aviation management, business administration and management, business and management, business data programming, computer programming, data processing, hotel/motel and restaurant management, labor/industrial relations, marketing management, office supervision and management.

ACADEMIC PROGRAMS. 2-year transfer program, cooperative education, double major, internships. **Remedial services:** Learning center, reduced course load, remedial instruction, tutoring. **Placement/credit:** Institutional tests; 43 credit hours maximum for associate degree.

ACADEMIC REQUIREMENTS. Freshmen must earn minimum GPA of 2.0 to continue in good standing. 72% of freshmen return for sophomore year. Students must declare major by end of second year. **Graduation re-**

quirements: 97 hours for associate, 195 hours for bachelor's (52 in major). Most students required to take courses in computer science, English, mathematics. **Postgraduate studies:** 12% from 2-year programs enter 4-year programs.

FRESHMAN ADMISSIONS. Selection criteria: Open admissions.

1992 FRESHMAN CLASS PROFILE. 1,305 men and women enrolled. **Characteristics:** 99% from in state, 89% commute, 12% have minority backgrounds. Average age is 26.

FALL-TERM APPLICATIONS. $20 fee, may be waived for applicants with need. No closing date; applicants notified on a rolling basis. Interview recommended.

STUDENT LIFE. Housing: Dormitories (men, women). **Activities:** Student government, student newspaper.

ATHLETICS. Intramural: Baseball, basketball, bowling, softball, volleyball.

STUDENT SERVICES. Aptitude testing, career counseling, employment service for undergraduates, personal counseling, placement service for graduates, services/facilities for handicapped.

ANNUAL EXPENSES. Tuition and fees: $5,040. **Room and board:** $1,575 room only. **Books and supplies:** $750. **Other expenses:** $2,000.

FINANCIAL AID. 85% of freshmen, 83% of continuing students receive some form of aid. 96% of grants, 88% of loans, all jobs based on need. Academic, state/district residency scholarships available. **Aid applications:** No closing date; priority given to applications received by September 1; applicants notified on a rolling basis beginning on or about June 1; must reply within 2 weeks.

ADDRESS/TELEPHONE. Kathy Jacobson, Vice President of Admissions, Baker College of Muskegon, 141 Hartford, Muskegon, MI 49442. (616) 726-4904. (800) 937-0337.

Baker College of Owosso
Owosso, Michigan CB code: 5270

4-year private business, technical college, coed. **Accreditation:** Regional. **Undergraduate enrollment:** 242 men, 660 women full time; 98 men, 271 women part time. **Faculty:** 68 total (8 full time), 8 with doctorates or other terminal degrees. **Location:** Rural campus in large town; 30 miles from Lansing and Flint. **Calendar:** Quarter. Saturday and extensive evening/early morning classes. **Microcomputers:** 63 located in classrooms.

DEGREES OFFERED. AA, AAS, B. 110 associate degrees awarded in 1992. 19% in business and management, 57% business/office and marketing/distribution, 12% computer sciences, 12% allied health. 15 bachelor's degrees awarded. 85% in business/office and marketing/distribution, 15% computer sciences.

UNDERGRADUATE MAJORS. Accounting, airline piloting and navigation, business administration and management, business data processing and related programs, computer programming, data processing, drafting, drafting and design technology, fashion merchandising, hotel/motel and restaurant management, interior design, labor/industrial relations, legal secretary, medical assistant, medical laboratory technologies, medical records technology, medical secretary, radiograph medical technology, secretarial and related programs, surgical technology, transportation and travel marketing, word processing. accounting, airline piloting and navigation, computer and information sciences, drafting, information sciences and systems, marketing management, office supervision and management.

ACADEMIC PROGRAMS. Accelerated program, cooperative education, dual enrollment of high school students, independent study, internships; liberal arts/career combination in business. **Remedial services:** Learning center, reduced course load, special counselor, tutoring. **Placement/credit:** Institutional tests.

ACADEMIC REQUIREMENTS. Freshmen must earn minimum GPA of 1.65 to continue in good standing. Students must declare major on application. **Graduation requirements:** 96 hours for associate, 192 hours for bachelor's. Most students required to take courses in computer science, English, humanities, mathematics, social sciences.

FRESHMAN ADMISSIONS. Selection criteria: Open admissions.

1992 FRESHMAN CLASS PROFILE. 142 men, 387 women enrolled. 15% had high school GPA of 3.0 or higher, 65% between 2.0 and 2.99. **Characteristics:** 85% commute. Average age is 23.

FALL-TERM APPLICATIONS. $20 fee, may be waived for applicants with need. No closing date; applicants notified on a rolling basis; must reply by registration. Interview recommended for all freshmen applicants. Deferred admission available. Applicants lacking high school diploma or GED may take entrance test for admission.

STUDENT LIFE. Housing: Dormitories (coed). **Activities:** Student newspaper, yearbook.

ATHLETICS. Intramural: Basketball, football M, softball, volleyball.

STUDENT SERVICES. Aptitude testing, career counseling, employment service for undergraduates, freshman orientation, on-campus day care, personal counseling, placement service for graduates, special adviser for adult students, veterans counselor, services/facilities for handicapped.

ANNUAL EXPENSES. Tuition and fees (1992-93): $5,136. **Room and board:** $1,575. **Books and supplies:** $700. **Other expenses:** $400.

FINANCIAL AID. 50% of continuing students receive some form of aid. 99% of grants, 96% of loans, all jobs based on need. Academic scholarships available. **Aid applications:** No closing date; priority given to applications received by May 1; applicants notified on a rolling basis.

ADDRESS/TELEPHONE. Bruce A. Lundeen, Director of Admissions, Baker College of Owosso, 1020 South Washington Street, Owosso, MI 48867. (517) 723-5251. (800) 879-3797. Fax: (517) 723-3355.

Baker College of Port Huron
Port Huron, Michigan CB code: 1413

4-year private business, health science college, coed. Founded in 1888. **Accreditation:** Regional. **Undergraduate enrollment:** 48 men, 307 women full time; 31 men, 115 women part time. **Faculty:** 32 total, 8 with doctorates or other terminal degrees. **Location:** Urban campus in large town; 60 miles from Detroit. **Calendar:** Quarter, limited summer session. Saturday classes. **Microcomputers:** 80 located in libraries, classrooms, computer centers.

DEGREES OFFERED. AAS, B. 12 associate degrees awarded in 1992. 73% in business and management, 27% business/office and marketing/distribution.

UNDERGRADUATE MAJORS. Accounting, business administration and management, business and management, business and office, business computer/console/peripheral equipment operation, business data processing and related programs, computer and information sciences, data processing, marketing management, medical assistant, medical records administration, medical records technology, medical secretary, secretarial and related programs, word processing. business administration and management, business and management.

ACADEMIC PROGRAMS. Accelerated program, cooperative education, double major, dual enrollment of high school students, external degree, independent study, internships, weekend college. **Remedial services:** Reduced course load, special counselor, tutoring. **Placement/credit:** Institutional tests; 49 credit hours maximum for associate degree; 49 credit hours maximum for bachelor's degree.

ACADEMIC REQUIREMENTS. Freshmen must earn minimum GPA of 1.80 to continue in good standing. 72% of freshmen return for sophomore year. Students must declare major on enrollment. **Graduation requirements:** 97 hours for associate (28 in major), 190 hours for bachelor's (52 in major). Most students required to take courses in computer science, English, mathematics. **Postgraduate studies:** 56% from 2-year programs enter 4-year programs.

FRESHMAN ADMISSIONS. Selection criteria: Open admissions. Some allied health programs require a health appraisal form signed by a physician.

1992 FRESHMAN CLASS PROFILE. 41 men, 179 women enrolled. **Characteristics:** 98% from in state, 100% commute, 3% have minority backgrounds. Average age is 21.

FALL-TERM APPLICATIONS. $20 fee. No closing date; applicants notified on a rolling basis beginning on or about September 20; must reply within 10 days. Interview required.

STUDENT SERVICES. Aptitude testing, career counseling, employment service for undergraduates, freshman orientation, personal counseling, placement service for graduates, services/facilities for handicapped.

ANNUAL EXPENSES. Tuition and fees (1992-93): $4,815. **Books and supplies:** $500. **Other expenses:** $2,000.

FINANCIAL AID. 50% of freshmen, 75% of continuing students receive some form of aid. 99% of grants, 98% of loans, all jobs based on need. 98 enrolled freshmen were judged to have need, all were offered aid. Academic, state/district residency scholarships available. **Aid applications:** No closing date; must reply within 10 days.

ADDRESS/TELEPHONE. David Hickman, Associate Director of Admissions, Baker College of Port Huron, 3403 Lapeer Street, Port Huron, MI 48060. (313) 985-7000. Fax: (313) 985-7066.

Bay de Noc Community College
Escanaba, Michigan CB code: 1049

2-year public community college, coed. Founded in 1962. **Accreditation:** Regional. **Faculty:** 116 total (46 full time), 5 with doctorates or other terminal degrees. **Location:** Rural campus in large town; 240 miles from Milwaukee, Wisconsin. **Calendar:** Semester, limited summer session. Saturday and extensive evening/early morning classes. **Microcomputers:** Located in libraries, classrooms, computer centers.

DEGREES OFFERED. AA, AS, AAS. 280 associate degrees awarded in 1992.

UNDERGRADUATE MAJORS. Accounting, American literature, automotive mechanics, biology, business administration and management, business and management, business and office, business computer/console/peripheral equipment operation, business data processing and related programs, business data programming, chemistry, computer and information sciences, computer programming, data processing, diesel engine mechanics, drafting, drafting and design technology, education, electrical and electronics equipment repair, electrical technology, electronic technology, elementary education, engineering, English, English literature, graphic arts technology, history, law enforcement and corrections, liberal/general studies, marketing and distribution, marketing management, mathematics, mental health/human services, physics, political science and government, practical nursing, precision metal work, predentistry, preengineering, prelaw, premedicine, prepharmacy, preveterinary, psychology, secondary education, secretarial and related programs, social sciences, sociology, water and wastewater technology, word processing.

ACADEMIC PROGRAMS. Cooperative education, dual enrollment of high school students, internships. **Remedial services:** Remedial instruction, tutoring. **Placement/credit:** Institutional tests.

ACADEMIC REQUIREMENTS. No policy requiring minimum GPA; records of students having academic difficulty are reviewed individually. 70% of freshmen return for sophomore year. **Graduation requirements:** 62 hours for associate. Most students required to take courses in English, history, humanities, mathematics, biological/physical sciences, social sciences.

FRESHMAN ADMISSIONS. Selection criteria: Open admissions. **Test requirements:** ACT for placement and counseling only.

1992 FRESHMAN CLASS PROFILE. 578 men and women enrolled. **Characteristics:** 99% from in state, 95% commute, 2% have minority backgrounds.

FALL-TERM APPLICATIONS. No fee. No closing date; applicants notified on a rolling basis.

STUDENT LIFE. Housing: Apartment housing available. **Activities:** Student government, magazine, student newspaper.

ATHLETICS. Intramural: Basketball, bowling, golf, skiing, softball, table tennis, tennis, volleyball.

STUDENT SERVICES. Career counseling, employment service for undergraduates, personal counseling, placement service for graduates, veterans counselor.

ANNUAL EXPENSES. Tuition and fees (1992-93): $1,364, $510 additional for out-of-district students, $1,620 additional for out-of-state students. **Room and board:** $1,542 room only. **Books and supplies:** $400. **Other expenses:** $586.

FINANCIAL AID. 75% of freshmen, 75% of continuing students receive some form of aid. 95% of grants, all loans, all jobs based on need. Academic scholarships available. **Aid applications:** No closing date; priority given to applications received by April 15; applicants notified on a rolling basis beginning on or about June 1; must reply within 2 weeks.

ADDRESS/TELEPHONE. David Johnson, Admissions Counselor, Bay de Noc Community College, Escanaba, MI 49829. (906) 786-5802.

Calvin College
Grand Rapids, Michigan — CB code: 1095

Admissions:	95% of applicants accepted
Based on:	••• School record, test scores
	•• Essay, recommendations, religious affiliation/commitment
	• Activities, special talents
Completion:	90% of freshmen end year in good standing
	60% graduate, 22% of these enter graduate study

4-year private liberal arts college, coed, affiliated with Christian Reformed Church. Founded in 1876. **Accreditation:** Regional. **Undergraduate enrollment:** 1,549 men, 1,847 women full time; 58 men, 83 women part time. **Graduate enrollment:** 42 men, 52 women full time; 39 men, 55 women part time. **Faculty:** 303 total (254 full time), 210 with doctorates or other terminal degrees. **Location:** Suburban campus in small city; 150 miles from Detroit. **Calendar:** 4-1-4, extensive summer session. **Microcomputers:** 242 located in dormitories, libraries, classrooms, computer centers. **Special facilities:** Art gallery, nature preserve, Heritage Hall Museum, electron microscope, Broene Center for Counseling and Career Development, Rhetoric Center.

DEGREES OFFERED. BA, BS, BFA, M. 846 bachelor's degrees awarded in 1992. 12% in business and management, 6% communications, 21% teacher education, 7% engineering, 5% health sciences, 6% letters/literature, 6% life sciences, 6% psychology, 18% social sciences. Graduate degrees offered in 10 major fields of study.

UNDERGRADUATE MAJORS. Accounting, American studies, art education, art history, bilingual/bicultural education, biochemistry, biological and physical sciences, biology, business administration and management, business and management, business economics, chemistry, civil engineering, classics, communication disorders, communications, computer and information sciences, criminal justice studies, earth sciences, economics, education, education of the deaf and hearing impaired, education of the emotionally handicapped, education of the mentally handicapped, education of the physically handicapped, electrical/electronics/communications engineering, elementary education, engineering, engineering and other disciplines, engineering science, English, English education, European studies, fine arts, foreign languages education, French, geography, geology, German, Greek (classical), history, humanities and social sciences, junior high education, Latin, liberal/general studies, mathematics, mathematics education, mechanical engineering, medical laboratory technologies, music, music education, music history and appreciation, nursing, occupational therapy, philosophy, physical education, physical sciences, physics, political science and government, predentistry, prelaw, premedicine, prepharmacy, psychology, recreation and community services technologies, religion, religious education, science education, secondary education, social sciences, social studies education, social work, sociology, Spanish, special education, specific learning disabilities, speech, speech pathology/audiology, speech/communication/theater education, telecommunications, theological studies, visual and performing arts.

ACADEMIC PROGRAMS. Double major, dual enrollment of high school students, honors program, independent study, internships, student-designed major, study abroad, teacher preparation, visiting/exchange student program, Washington semester, overseas programs with Central College, January interim and interim exchange with other colleges; liberal arts/career combination in health sciences. **Remedial services:** Learning center, reduced course load, remedial instruction, special counselor, tutoring, student academic services. **Placement/credit:** AP, CLEP Subject, institutional tests.

ACADEMIC REQUIREMENTS. Freshmen must earn minimum GPA of 1.5 to continue in good standing. 81% of freshmen return for sophomore year. Students must declare major by end of second year. **Graduation requirements:** 126 hours for bachelor's (32 in major). Most students required to take courses in arts/fine arts, English, foreign languages, history, mathematics, philosophy/religion, biological/physical sciences, social sciences. **Postgraduate studies:** 3% enter law school, 4% enter medical school, 4% enter MBA programs, 11% enter other graduate study. **Additional information:** Importance of faith perspective in all disciplines and cocurricular activities emphasized.

FRESHMAN ADMISSIONS. Selection criteria: Applicants must have genuine interest in Christian goals of college. 2.5 high school GPA. Special consideration to minority applicants. Enhanced ACT composite score above 20 or SAT-V above 390 and SAT-M score above 420 recommended. **High school preparation:** 15 units recommended. Recommended units include biological science 1, English 4, foreign language 2, mathematics 3, physical science 1, social science 2 and science 2. Mathematics must include algebra and geometry. **Test requirements:** SAT or ACT (ACT preferred); score report by July 1. **Additional information:** GED accepted only for those aged 19 years or more.

1992 FRESHMAN CLASS PROFILE. 584 men applied, 553 accepted, 332 enrolled; 852 women applied, 809 accepted, 476 enrolled. 78% had high school GPA of 3.0 or higher, 22% between 2.0 and 2.99. 30% were in top tenth and 65% were in top quarter of graduating class. **Academic background:** Mid 50% of enrolled freshmen had SAT-V between 460-570, SAT-M between 480-640; ACT composite between 22-28. 31% submitted SAT scores, 100% submitted ACT scores. **Characteristics:** 49% from in state, 90% live in college housing, 5% have minority backgrounds, 7% are foreign students. Average age is 19.

FALL-TERM APPLICATIONS. $25 fee, may be waived for applicants with need. No closing date; priority given to applications received by March 1; applicants notified on a rolling basis; Accepted applicants must reply by May 1 or within 4 weeks if notified thereafter. Essay required. CRDA. Deferred and early admission available.

STUDENT LIFE. Housing: Dormitories (men, women); apartment housing available. 1st and 2nd year students (under 21) not living at home are required to live in residence halls. **Activities:** Student government, magazine, radio, student newspaper, yearbook, choral groups, concert band, drama, music ensembles, musical theater, symphony orchestra, religious and community service organizations, Amnesty International, C.O.L.O.R.S., Progessives, Student Senate, Campus Crusade for Christ, Environmental Stewardship, Republicans Club, InterVarsity, Student Volunteer Services.

ATHLETICS. NCAA. **Intercollegiate:** Baseball M, basketball, cross-country, diving, golf, soccer, softball W, swimming, tennis, track and field, volleyball W. **Intramural:** Badminton, basketball, gymnastics, handball, ice hockey M, racquetball, soccer, softball, tennis, volleyball.

STUDENT SERVICES. Aptitude testing, career counseling, employment service for undergraduates, freshman orientation, health services, personal counseling, placement service for graduates, special adviser for adult students, services/facilities for handicapped.

ANNUAL EXPENSES. Tuition and fees: $9,450. **Room and board:** $3,570. **Books and supplies:** $390. **Other expenses:** $660.

FINANCIAL AID. 88% of freshmen, 88% of continuing students receive some form of aid. 74% of grants, 95% of loans, 66% of jobs based on need. 512 enrolled freshmen were judged to have need, all were offered aid. Academic, music/drama, art, leadership, religious affiliation, minority scholarships available. **Aid applications:** No closing date; priority given to applications received by February 15; applicants notified on a rolling basis beginning on or about March 20; must reply by May 1 or within 3 weeks if notified thereafter.

ADDRESS/TELEPHONE. Thomas E. McWhertor, Director of Admissions, Calvin College, 3201 Burton SE, Grand Rapids, MI 49546. (616) 957-6106. (800) 748-0122. Fax: (616) 957-8551.

Center for Creative Studies: College of Art and Design ⇎
Detroit, Michigan CB code: 1035

Admissions: 69% of applicants accepted
Based on: ••• Interview, school record, special talents, test scores
•• Essay
• Recommendations
Completion: 86% of freshmen end year in good standing
36% graduate, 10% of these enter graduate study

4-year private art college, coed. Founded in 1926. **Accreditation:** Regional. **Undergraduate enrollment:** 371 men, 206 women full time; 171 men, 112 women part time. **Faculty:** 166 total (48 full time), 12 with doctorates or other terminal degrees. **Location:** Urban campus in very large city; 4 miles from downtown. **Calendar:** Semester, limited summer session. Saturday and extensive evening/early morning classes. **Microcomputers:** Located in libraries, classrooms, computer centers. **Special facilities:** Extensive studio space, art gallery for student exhibitions.

DEGREES OFFERED. BFA. 182 bachelor's degrees awarded in 1992. 100% in visual and performing arts.

UNDERGRADUATE MAJORS. Art direction, ceramics, crafts, drawing, environmental design, fiber/textiles/weaving, fine arts, glass, graphic design, illustration design, industrial design, interior design, metal/jewelry, painting, photography, printmaking, sculpture, transportation design.

ACADEMIC PROGRAMS. Double major, independent study, internships, study abroad, visiting/exchange student program, New York semester, cross-registration, advanced students may petition for 1 semester in New York studio space. **Remedial services:** Learning center, reduced course load, special counselor, tutoring. **Placement/credit:** AP, CLEP General and Subject; 6 credit hours maximum for bachelor's degree.

ACADEMIC REQUIREMENTS. Freshmen must earn minimum GPA of 2.0 to continue in good standing. 83% of freshmen return for sophomore year. Students must declare major on application. **Graduation requirements:** 144 hours for bachelor's (63 in major). Most students required to take courses in arts/fine arts, English, history, philosophy/religion, social sciences. **Additional information:** Studio space for advanced students in photography, fine arts, ceramics, and metals and jewelry given to juniors and seniors. Computer studio and advanced computer lab available.

FRESHMAN ADMISSIONS. Selection criteria: Art portfolio, test scores, and high school record important. Minimum 2.5 high school GPA for applicants. ACT or SAT scores required. College-preparatory program recommended. **Test requirements:** SAT or ACT; score report by August 1.

1992 FRESHMAN CLASS PROFILE. 179 men applied, 125 accepted, 58 enrolled; 105 women applied, 70 accepted, 28 enrolled. 46% had high school GPA of 3.0 or higher, 54% between 2.0 and 2.99. **Academic background:** Mid 50% of enrolled freshmen had SAT-V between 400-540, SAT-M between 420-540; ACT composite between 16-23. 80% submitted SAT scores, 62% submitted ACT scores. **Characteristics:** 71% from in state, 68% commute, 17% have minority backgrounds, 3% are foreign students. Average age is 20.

FALL-TERM APPLICATIONS. $35 fee, may be waived for applicants with need. Closing date June 30; priority given to applications received by March 15; applicants notified on a rolling basis beginning on or about September 15; must reply by May 1. Portfolio required. Interview recommended. Essay recommended. Interview required of applicants living within 250 mile radius, recommended for all others. CRDA. Deferred admission available. Classes usually full by June 1.

STUDENT LIFE. Housing: Apartment, cooperative housing available. Furnished, college-owned apartments available. **Activities:** Student government, film, student newspaper, dance, jazz band, music ensembles, Black Students, Women Artists, Industrial Design Students, Alcoholics Anonymous, Children of Alcoholics, Dreammakers.

STUDENT SERVICES. Career counseling, employment service for undergraduates, freshman orientation, personal counseling, placement service for graduates, services/facilities for handicapped.

ANNUAL EXPENSES. Tuition and fees (1992-93): $9,853. **Room and board:** $4,100. **Books and supplies:** $1,926. **Other expenses:** $636.

FINANCIAL AID. 58% of freshmen, 60% of continuing students receive some form of aid. 79% of grants, 93% of loans, 54% of jobs based on need. Art, leadership scholarships available. **Aid applications:** No closing date; priority given to applications received by February 15; applicants notified on a rolling basis; must reply within 2 weeks.

ADDRESS/TELEPHONE. Eddie Kent Tallent, Asst Dean for Enrollment Svcs, Center for Creative Studies: College of Art and Design, 201 East Kirby, Detroit, MI 48202-4034. (313) 872-3118. (800) 952-ARTS. Fax: (313) 872-8377.

Central Michigan University ⇎
Mount Pleasant, Michigan CB code: 1106

Admissions: 86% of applicants accepted
Based on: ••• School record
•• Activities, recommendations, test scores
• Interview, special talents
Completion: 92% of freshmen end year in good standing
31% graduate

4-year public university, coed. Founded in 1892. **Accreditation:** Regional. **Undergraduate enrollment:** 5,866 men, 7,362 women full time; 535 men, 752 women part time. **Graduate enrollment:** 233 men, 279 women full time. **Faculty:** 813 total (608 full time), 588 with doctorates or other terminal degrees. **Location:** Rural campus in large town; 70 miles from Lansing. **Calendar:** Semester, limited summer session. **Microcomputers:** 600 located in dormitories, computer centers. **Special facilities:** Center for Cultural and Natural History, Self-Instructional Systems Center, Brooks Observatory, Creative Arts Gallery, University Art Gallery, Wellness Resource Center, Center for Learning Assesment Services.

DEGREES OFFERED. BA, BS, BFA, MA, MS, MBA, MFA, MEd, PhD. 2,880 bachelor's degrees awarded in 1992. 12% in business and management, 14% business/office and marketing/distribution, 7% communications, 18% education, 7% home economics, 6% letters/literature, 6% psychology, 9% social sciences. Graduate degrees offered in 68 major fields of study.

UNDERGRADUATE MAJORS. Accounting, actuarial sciences, American studies, anthropology, art education, art history, automotive technology, bilingual/bicultural education, biology, business administration and management, business and management, business economics, business education, ceramics, chemistry, child development/care/guidance, cinematography/film, communications, computer and information sciences, computer technology, court reporting, drafting and design technology, dramatic arts, drawing, early childhood education, earth sciences, economics, education, education of the emotionally handicapped, education of the mentally handicapped, electronic technology, elementary education, English, family/consumer resource management, fiber/textiles/weaving, finance, food science and nutrition, French, geography, geology, German, graphic design, health education, history, home economics, home economics education, hotel/motel and restaurant management, individual and family development, industrial arts education, industrial technology, institutional/home management/supporting programs, journalism, legal secretary, liberal/general studies, linguistics, management information systems, management science, manufacturing technology, marketing research, mathematics, mathematics education, mechanical design technology, medical laboratory technologies, medical secretary, metal/jewelry, microbiology, music, music education, music theory and composition, operations research, painting, parks and recreation management, personnel management, philosophy, photography, physical education, physical sciences, physics, political science and government, printmaking, psychology, public administration, radio/television broadcasting, radio/television technology, real estate, religion, science education, sculpture, secondary education, secretarial and related programs, social sciences, sociology, Spanish, special education, speech, speech correction, speech pathology/audiology, sports medicine, statistics, textiles and clothing, visual and performing arts.

ACADEMIC PROGRAMS. Double major, dual enrollment of high school students, education specialist degree, external degree, honors program, independent study, internships, student-designed major, study abroad, teacher preparation, joint engineering programs with Michigan Technological University. **Remedial services:** Learning center, preadmission summer program, remedial instruction, special counselor, tutoring. **ROTC:** Army. **Placement/credit:** AP, CLEP General and Subject, institutional tests.

ACADEMIC REQUIREMENTS. Freshmen must earn minimum GPA of 2.0 to continue in good standing. 73% of freshmen return for sophomore year. **Graduation requirements:** 124 hours for bachelor's (30 in major). Most students required to take courses in English, humanities, mathematics, biological/physical sciences, social sciences.

FRESHMAN ADMISSIONS. Selection criteria: School achievement record, test scores, recommendations. **High school preparation:** 16 units required. Required units include biological science 1, English 4, foreign language 2, mathematics 4, physical science 2 and social science 3. **Test requirements:** ACT; score report by April 1.

1992 FRESHMAN CLASS PROFILE. 7,304 men and women applied, 6,263 accepted; 1,063 men enrolled, 1,476 women enrolled. 61% had high school GPA of 3.0 or higher, 31% between 2.0 and 2.99. **Academic background:** Mid 50% of enrolled freshmen had ACT composite between 19-23. 95% submitted ACT scores. **Characteristics:** 98% from in state, 6% have minority backgrounds, 1% are foreign students. Average age is 18.

FALL-TERM APPLICATIONS. $25 fee, may be waived for applicants with need. No closing date; priority given to applications received by March 1; applicants notified on a rolling basis; must reply within 6 weeks. Audition required for music applicants. Interview recommended. Deferred and early admission available.

STUDENT LIFE. Housing: Dormitories (men, women, coed); apart-

ment, fraternity, sorority housing available. **Activities:** Student government, radio, student newspaper, television, yearbook, choral groups, concert band, dance, drama, jazz band, marching band, music ensembles, pep band, symphony orchestra, fraternities, sororities.

ATHLETICS. NCAA. **Intercollegiate:** Baseball M, basketball, cross-country, field hockey W, football M, gymnastics W, soccer M, softball W, track and field, volleyball W, wrestling M. **Intramural:** Badminton, basketball, bowling, cross-country, fencing M, golf, ice hockey M, racquetball, rugby M, skiing, soccer, softball, swimming, table tennis, tennis, track and field, volleyball, water polo, wrestling.

STUDENT SERVICES. Career counseling, employment service for undergraduates, freshman orientation, health services, personal counseling, placement service for graduates, veterans counselor, services/facilities for handicapped.

ANNUAL EXPENSES. Tuition and fees (1992-93): $2,653, $3,836 additional for out-of-state students. **Room and board:** $3,724. **Books and supplies:** $600. **Other expenses:** $1,000.

FINANCIAL AID. 55% of freshmen, 60% of continuing students receive some form of aid. 73% of grants, 79% of loans, 32% of jobs based on need. 1,250 enrolled freshmen were judged to have need, 1,238 were offered aid. Academic, music/drama, art, athletic, leadership scholarships available. **Aid applications:** No closing date; priority given to applications received by March 1; applicants notified on a rolling basis beginning on or about April 1; must reply within 2 weeks. **Additional information:** Tuition waiver for American Indian students qualifying under state program criteria.

ADDRESS/TELEPHONE. Michael A. Owens, Director of Admissions, Central Michigan University, 105 Warriner Hall, Mount Pleasant, MI 48859. (517) 774-3076.

Charles Stewart Mott Community College
Flint, Michigan CB code: 1225

2-year public community college, coed. Founded in 1923. **Accreditation:** Regional. **Undergraduate enrollment:** 1,351 men, 1,685 women full time; 3,190 men, 4,996 women part time. **Faculty:** 477 total (178 full time), 24 with doctorates or other terminal degrees. **Location:** Urban campus in small city; 65 miles from Detroit. **Calendar:** Semester, extensive summer session. Saturday and extensive evening/early morning classes. **Microcomputers:** Located in libraries, classrooms, computer centers.

DEGREES OFFERED. AA, AS. 996 associate degrees awarded in 1992. 15% in business and management, 7% business/office and marketing/distribution, 9% computer sciences, 12% engineering technologies, 9% health sciences, 6% allied health, 33% multi/interdisciplinary studies.

UNDERGRADUATE MAJORS. Accounting, air conditioning/heating/refrigeration technology, architectural technologies, automotive technology, biological and physical sciences, business and management, business and office, business data processing and related programs, child development/care/guidance, computer programming, computer technology, criminal justice technology, dental assistant, dental hygiene, drafting and design technology, electromechanical technology, electronic technology, engineering and engineering-related technologies, finance, fine arts, fire control and safety technology, food management, food production/management/services, gerontology, histology, humanities and social sciences, industrial technology, interpreter for the deaf, legal assistant/paralegal, legal secretary, liberal/general studies, marketing and distribution, marketing management, mechanical design technology, medical secretary, music, nursing, practical nursing, recreation and community services technologies, respiratory therapy, respiratory therapy technology, robotics, science technologies, secretarial and related programs, social work, trade and industrial supervision and management, word processing.

ACADEMIC PROGRAMS. 2-year transfer program, double major, dual enrollment of high school students, honors program, internships, study abroad, telecourses. **Remedial services:** Learning center, reduced course load, remedial instruction, special counselor, tutoring. **Placement/credit:** Institutional tests.

ACADEMIC REQUIREMENTS. Freshmen must earn minimum GPA of 2.0 to continue in good standing. Students must declare major on application. **Graduation requirements:** 62 hours for associate (30 in major). Most students required to take courses in computer science, English, social sciences.

FRESHMAN ADMISSIONS. Selection criteria: Open admissions. **Test requirements:** ACT.

1992 FRESHMAN CLASS PROFILE. 759 men, 947 women enrolled. **Characteristics:** 99% from in state, 100% commute, 17% have minority backgrounds, 1% are foreign students.

FALL-TERM APPLICATIONS. No fee. Closing date August 27; applicants notified on a rolling basis. Portfolio required for advanced placement art applicants. Audition recommended for music applicants. Deferred and early admission available. If submitted, SAT or ACT scores will be used for placement and couseling.

STUDENT LIFE. Activities: Student government, film, magazine, radio, student newspaper, television, choral groups, drama, jazz band, music ensembles.

ATHLETICS. NJCAA. **Intercollegiate:** Baseball M, basketball, golf M, softball W, volleyball W. **Intramural:** Basketball, golf M, racquetball, softball, swimming, table tennis, tennis, volleyball.

STUDENT SERVICES. Aptitude testing, career counseling, employment service for undergraduates, freshman orientation, health services, on-campus day care, personal counseling, placement service for graduates, services/facilities for handicapped.

ANNUAL EXPENSES. Tuition and fees (1992-93): $1,420, $570 additional for out-of-district students, $1,230 additional for out-of-state students. **Books and supplies:** $550. **Other expenses:** $600.

FINANCIAL AID. 40% of continuing students receive some form of aid. 95% of grants, all loans, 40% of jobs based on need. Academic, music/drama, art, athletic, state/district residency, minority scholarships available. **Aid applications:** Closing date May 31; applicants notified on a rolling basis beginning on or about June 1; must reply by August 15.

ADDRESS/TELEPHONE. Robert Seay, Director of Admissions, Charles Stewart Mott Community College, 1401 East Court Street, Flint, MI 48503. (313) 762-0241. Fax: (313) 762-0257.

Cleary College
Ypsilanti, Michigan CB code: 1123

4-year private business college, coed. Founded in 1883. **Accreditation:** Regional. **Undergraduate enrollment:** 170 men, 268 women full time; 197 men, 305 women part time. **Faculty:** 84 total (17 full time), 3 with doctorates or other terminal degrees. **Location:** Urban campus in large town; 30 miles from Detroit, 7 miles from Ann Arbor. **Calendar:** Quarter, extensive summer session. Saturday and extensive evening/early morning classes. **Microcomputers:** 60 located in libraries, computer centers. **Special facilities:** Knostman Tax Center Research Library. **Additional facts:** Branch campus at Howell. Accelerated degree program offered at various commuity campuses in Michigan.

DEGREES OFFERED. B. 66 associate degrees awarded in 1992. 68% in business and management, 17% business/office and marketing/distribution, 12% computer sciences. 132 bachelor's degrees awarded. 25% in business and management, 6% business/office and marketing/distribution, 9% computer sciences.

UNDERGRADUATE MAJORS. Accounting, business administration and management, business and management, business data processing and related programs, data processing, management information systems, marketing and distribution, marketing management, office supervision and management, secretarial and related programs. accounting, business administration and management, business and management, computer programming, information sciences and systems, management information systems, marketing and distribution, marketing management, secretarial and related programs, total quality management.

ACADEMIC PROGRAMS. Accelerated program, cooperative education, double major, dual enrollment of high school students, independent study, internships, visiting/exchange student program. **Remedial services:** Learning center, reduced course load, remedial instruction, special counselor, tutoring. **Placement/credit:** AP, CLEP General and Subject, institutional tests; 30 credit hours maximum for associate degree; 45 credit hours maximum for bachelor's degree.

ACADEMIC REQUIREMENTS. Freshmen must earn minimum GPA of 2.0 to continue in good standing. 80% of freshmen return for sophomore year. Students must declare major on enrollment. **Graduation requirements:** 90 hours for associate (18 in major), 180 hours for bachelor's (39 in major). Most students required to take courses in computer science, English, history, mathematics, philosophy/religion, social sciences. **Postgraduate studies:** 55% from 2-year programs enter 4-year programs. 10% enter MBA programs.

FRESHMAN ADMISSIONS. Additional information: Regular, special, guest, dual, provisional, transfer, and international admissions available. Applicants with below 2.0 GPA may be accepted if probable success in chosen program indicated.

1992 FRESHMAN CLASS PROFILE. 326 men and women enrolled. **Characteristics:** 98% from in state, 100% commute, 23% have minority backgrounds, 2% are foreign students. Average age is 21.

FALL-TERM APPLICATIONS. $25 fee. No closing date; applicants notified on a rolling basis. Interview recommended. Deferred and early admission available. Applicants accepted for fall term admission up to last day of late registration.

STUDENT LIFE. Housing: Student Services Office can provide list of rental units available in area. **Activities:** Student government, student newspaper.

ATHLETICS. Intramural: Softball, volleyball.

STUDENT SERVICES. Aptitude testing, career counseling, employment service for undergraduates, freshman orientation, on-campus day care, personal counseling, placement service for graduates, special adviser for adult students, services/facilities for handicapped.

ANNUAL EXPENSES. Tuition and fees (1992-93): $5,790. **Books and supplies:** $800. **Other expenses:** $1,000.

FINANCIAL AID. 64% of freshmen, 63% of continuing students re-

ceive some form of aid. 95% of grants, 88% of loans, 67% of jobs based on need. 32 enrolled freshmen were judged to have need, all were offered aid. Academic, leadership, alumni affiliation scholarships available. **Aid applications:** Closing date August 31; priority given to applications received by March 1; applicants notified on a rolling basis beginning on or about May 1; must reply within 2 weeks.

ADDRESS/TELEPHONE. Donna Franklin, Dean of Student Svcs, Cleary College, 2170 Washtenaw Avenue, Ypsilanti, MI 48197. (313) 483-4400 ext. 342. (800) 686-1883. Fax: (313) 483-0090.

Concordia College
Ann Arbor, Michigan — CB code: 1094

Admissions: 84% of applicants accepted
Based on:
- ••• School record
- •• Interview, religious affiliation/commitment, test scores
- • Activities, recommendations, special talents

Completion: 85% of freshmen end year in good standing

4-year private liberal arts college, coed, affiliated with Lutheran Church—Missouri Synod. Founded in 1962. **Accreditation:** Regional. **Undergraduate enrollment:** 222 men, 302 women full time. **Faculty:** 64 total (43 full time), 27 with doctorates or other terminal degrees. **Location:** Suburban campus in small city; 40 miles from Detroit. **Calendar:** Semester, limited summer session. **Microcomputers:** 30 located in libraries, computer centers. **Special facilities:** Fine arts building with studios, gallery, and black box theater. **Additional facts:** Life-Long Learning degree completion program for mature students who have 2 or more years college.

DEGREES OFFERED. AA, BA. 5 associate degrees awarded in 1992. 130 bachelor's degrees awarded. 62% in business and management, 19% teacher education, 6% psychology.

UNDERGRADUATE MAJORS. Associate: Liberal/general studies. **Bachelor's:** Art education, biblical languages, biological and physical sciences, biology, business and management, classics, communications, early childhood education, elementary education, English, English education, fine arts, foreign languages (multiple emphasis), Greek (classical), health care administration, Hebrew, history/political science, human resources development, humanities and social sciences, liberal/general studies, mathematics education, music, music education, physical education, physical sciences, premedicine, psychology, psychology/sociology, science education, secondary education, social science education, social sciences, social studies education, sociology, speech/communication/theater education, sports management, theological studies.

ACADEMIC PROGRAMS. 2-year transfer program, double major, dual enrollment of high school students, independent study, internships, student-designed major, study abroad, teacher preparation, visiting/exchange student program, cross-registration. **Remedial services:** Learning center, reduced course load, special counselor, tutoring. **Placement/credit:** AP, CLEP General and Subject, institutional tests.

ACADEMIC REQUIREMENTS. Freshmen must earn minimum GPA of 2.0 to continue in good standing. 70% of freshmen return for sophomore year. Students must declare major by end of second year. **Graduation requirements:** 60 hours for associate, 128 hours for bachelor's (30 in major). Most students required to take courses in arts/fine arts, English, foreign languages, history, humanities, mathematics, philosophy/religion, biological/physical sciences, social sciences. **Postgraduate studies:** 90% from 2-year programs enter 4-year programs.

FRESHMAN ADMISSIONS. Selection criteria: School achievement record most important. Test scores and rank in top half of class also considered. **High school preparation:** 15 units required. Required and recommended units include English 3-4, mathematics 1-2, social science 1 and science 1-2. Foreign language 2 recommended. 2 or more years piano recommended for teacher education applicants. 11 total units out of required 15 must be presented in English, social studies, mathematics, science, and foreign language. **Test requirements:** SAT or ACT (ACT preferred); score report by September 1.

1992 FRESHMAN CLASS PROFILE. 165 men and women applied, 139 accepted; 121 enrolled. **Characteristics:** 95% live in college housing, 43% have minority backgrounds. Average age is 18.

FALL-TERM APPLICATIONS. $15 fee. Fee may be waived with special request on individual basis. No closing date; applicants notified on a rolling basis; must reply within 4 weeks. Interview recommended. Audition recommended for music applicants. CRDA. Deferred and early admission available.

STUDENT LIFE. Housing: Dormitories (men, women); apartment housing available. **Activities:** Student government, student newspaper, choral groups, drama, jazz band, music ensembles, musical theater, pep band, several religious and service groups.

ATHLETICS. NAIA. **Intercollegiate:** Baseball M, basketball, soccer M, softball W, volleyball W. **Intramural:** Badminton, basketball, cross-country, skiing, softball, tennis, track and field, volleyball.

STUDENT SERVICES. Aptitude testing, career counseling, employment service for undergraduates, freshman orientation, health services, on-campus day care, personal counseling, placement service for graduates, special adviser for adult students, services/facilities for handicapped.

ANNUAL EXPENSES. Tuition and fees (1992-93): $8,680. **Room and board:** $3,750. **Books and supplies:** $500. **Other expenses:** $1,200.

FINANCIAL AID. 85% of freshmen, 87% of continuing students receive some form of aid. 92% of grants, 89% of loans, all jobs based on need. 75 enrolled freshmen were judged to have need, all were offered aid. Academic, music/drama, art, athletic, alumni affiliation scholarships available. **Aid applications:** Closing date May 31; applicants notified on or about July 1; must reply within 3 weeks.

ADDRESS/TELEPHONE. Fred A. Shebor, Director of Admissions, Concordia College, 4090 Geddes Road, Ann Arbor, MI 48105. (313) 995-7322. (800) 253-0680. Fax: (313) 995-4610.

Davenport College of Business
Grand Rapids, Michigan — CB code: 1183

4-year private business college, coed. Founded in 1866. **Accreditation:** Regional. **Undergraduate enrollment:** 551 men, 1,070 women full time; 869 men, 2,034 women part time. **Faculty:** 214 total (41 full time), 22 with doctorates or other terminal degrees. **Location:** Urban campus in small city; 150 miles from Detroit, 175 miles from Chicago. **Calendar:** Quarter, limited summer session. Saturday and extensive evening/early morning classes. **Microcomputers:** 80 located in computer centers. **Additional facts:** Branch campuses at Kalamazoo and Lansing, Detroit College of Business at Warren, Flint, Dearborn. Davenport branches also in Holland, Merriville, South Bend, Indiana.

DEGREES OFFERED. AS, BS. 333 associate degrees awarded in 1992. 68% in business and management, 23% business/office and marketing/distribution, 5% allied health. 235 bachelor's degrees awarded. 86% in business and management, 9% business/office and marketing/distribution, 5% computer sciences.

UNDERGRADUATE MAJORS. Associate: Accounting, business administration and management, business and management, business and office, business data entry equipment operation, business data processing and related programs, business data programming, computer programming, emergency medical technologies, fashion merchandising, legal assistant/paralegal, legal secretary, marketing and distribution, medical assistant, medical records technology, medical secretary, retailing, sales and marketing, secretarial and related programs, word processing. **Bachelor's:** Accounting, business administration and management, business and management, computer programming, hotel/motel and restaurant management, international business management, marketing and distribution, office supervision and management.

ACADEMIC PROGRAMS. Accelerated program, cooperative education, independent study, internships, study abroad, weekend college. **Remedial services:** Learning center, preadmission summer program, tutoring, developmental instruction. **Placement/credit:** AP, CLEP General and Subject, institutional tests; 27 credit hours maximum for associate degree; 27 credit hours maximum for bachelor's degree.

ACADEMIC REQUIREMENTS. Freshmen must earn minimum GPA of 2.0 to continue in good standing. 50% of freshmen return for sophomore year. Students must declare major on application. **Graduation requirements:** 90 hours for associate (45 in major), 185 hours for bachelor's (59 in major). Most students required to take courses in computer science, English, mathematics, social sciences. **Postgraduate studies:** 20% from 2-year programs enter 4-year programs. 10% enter MBA programs.

FRESHMAN ADMISSIONS. Selection criteria: Open admissions.

1992 FRESHMAN CLASS PROFILE. 422 men, 892 women enrolled. **Characteristics:** 98% from in state, 88% commute, 12% have minority backgrounds, 1% are foreign students. Average age is 19.

FALL-TERM APPLICATIONS. $20 fee, may be waived for applicants with need. No closing date; applicants notified on a rolling basis. Interview recommended. Deferred and early admission available.

STUDENT LIFE. Housing: Dormitories (men, women). **Activities:** Student government, student newspaper, sororities, Minority Student Association, hospitality club, organizations for women students and mature women.

ATHLETICS. Intramural: Bowling, racquetball, softball.

STUDENT SERVICES. Aptitude testing, career counseling, employment service for undergraduates, freshman orientation, personal counseling, placement service for graduates, veterans counselor, services/facilities for handicapped.

ANNUAL EXPENSES. Tuition and fees: $6,890. **Room and board:** $3,023. **Books and supplies:** $675. **Other expenses:** $785.

FINANCIAL AID. 75% of freshmen, 75% of continuing students receive some form of aid. 94% of grants, 90% of loans, all jobs based on need. Academic scholarships available. **Aid applications:** No closing date; priority given to applications received by March 15; applicants notified on a rolling basis beginning on or about July 1; must reply within 2 weeks. **Additional information:** Institutional tuition plan available.

ADDRESS/TELEPHONE. Barbara Mieras, PhD, Vice President of Enrollment, Davenport College of Business, 415 East Fulton Street, Grand Rapids, MI 49503. (616) 451-3511. (800) 632-9569. Fax: (616) 732-1144.

Delta College
University Center, Michigan CB code: 1816

2-year public community college, coed. Founded in 1957. **Accreditation:** Regional. **Undergraduate enrollment:** 3,572 men and women full time; 7,656 men and women part time. **Faculty:** 666 total (227 full time). **Location:** Suburban campus in small town; 10 miles from Saginaw, 5 miles from Bay City, and 12 miles from Midland. **Calendar:** Trimester, limited summer session. Saturday and extensive evening/early morning classes. **Microcomputers:** 250 located in classrooms, computer centers. **Special facilities:** Planetarium, natural habitat, television and radio broadcasting studios. **Additional facts:** Classes offered at 35 off-campus sites; 3 majors off-campus facilities in operation.

DEGREES OFFERED. AA, AS, AAS. 1,300 associate degrees awarded in 1992. 25% in business and management, 9% business/office and marketing/distribution, 11% education, 5% engineering technologies, 7% health sciences, 8% allied health, 5% multi/interdisciplinary studies, 5% parks/recreation, protective services, public affairs, 5% social sciences, 5% trade and industry.

UNDERGRADUATE MAJORS. Accounting, agribusiness, agricultural business and management, agriculture enterprise, architectural technologies, automotive mechanics, automotive technology, business and management, business and office, business computer/console/peripheral equipment operation, business data processing and related programs, business data programming, child development/care/guidance, computer programming, construction, criminal justice studies, data processing, dental assistant, dental hygiene, electronic technology, engineering and engineering-related technologies, fashion design, fashion merchandising, finance, fire control and safety technology, industrial technology, information sciences and systems, interior design, law enforcement and corrections, legal assistant/paralegal, legal secretary, liberal/general studies, machine tool operation/machine shop, marketing and distribution, marketing management, mechanical design technology, medical assistant, medical secretary, nursing, office supervision and management, physical therapy assistant, practical nursing, radio/television broadcasting, radiograph medical technology, respiratory therapy, respiratory therapy technology, secretarial and related programs, small business management and ownership, surgical technology, trade and industrial supervision and management, welding technology, word processing.

ACADEMIC PROGRAMS. 2-year transfer program, cooperative education, dual enrollment of high school students, honors program, independent study, internships, telecourses, cross-registration, bachelor's in business with Northwood Institute. **Remedial services:** Learning center, preadmission summer program, reduced course load, remedial instruction, special counselor, tutoring. **Placement/credit:** AP, CLEP General and Subject, institutional tests.

ACADEMIC REQUIREMENTS. Freshmen must earn minimum GPA of 2.0 to continue in good standing. Students must declare major by end of first year. **Graduation requirements:** 62 hours for associate. Most students required to take courses in English, humanities, mathematics, biological/physical sciences, social sciences.

FRESHMAN ADMISSIONS. Selection criteria: Open admissions. Selective admissions for foreign students. **Test requirements:** ACT ASSET required of all students for counseling purposes.

1992 FRESHMAN CLASS PROFILE. 6,697 men and women enrolled. **Characteristics:** 99% from in state, 100% commute, 15% have minority backgrounds. Average age is 24.

FALL-TERM APPLICATIONS. No fee. No closing date; applicants notified on a rolling basis. Deferred and early admission available.

STUDENT LIFE. Activities: Radio, student newspaper, television, yearbook, choral groups, drama, music ensembles.

ATHLETICS. NJCAA. **Intercollegiate:** Basketball, golf, soccer M, softball W, tennis M, volleyball W. **Intramural:** Badminton, basketball, golf, racquetball, softball W, swimming, tennis, volleyball, water polo.

STUDENT SERVICES. Aptitude testing, career counseling, employment service for undergraduates, freshman orientation, health services, on-campus day care, personal counseling, placement service for graduates, veterans counselor, services/facilities for handicapped.

ANNUAL EXPENSES. Tuition and fees (1992-93): $1,440, $570 additional for out-of-district students, $1,470 additional for out-of-state students. **Books and supplies:** $420. **Other expenses:** $600.

FINANCIAL AID. 44% of continuing students receive some form of aid. 97% of grants, 86% of loans, all jobs based on need. Academic scholarships available. **Aid applications:** No closing date; applicants notified on a rolling basis; must reply within 2 weeks.

ADDRESS/TELEPHONE. Margaret Mosequeda, Director of Admissions, Delta College, University Center, MI 48710. (517) 686-9092. Fax: (517) 686-8736.

Detroit College of Business
Dearborn, Michigan CB code: 1181

4-year private business college, coed. Founded in 1962. **Accreditation:** Regional. **Undergraduate enrollment:** 658 men, 2,258 women full time; 499 men, 1,607 women part time. **Faculty:** 316 total (43 full time), 35 with doctorates or other terminal degrees. **Location:** Suburban campus in small city; 10 miles from downtown Detroit. **Calendar:** Quarter, limited summer session. Saturday and extensive evening/early morning classes. **Microcomputers:** 73 located in libraries, classrooms. **Special facilities:** Greenfield Village Museum. **Additional facts:** Campuses in Flint and Warren.

DEGREES OFFERED. B. 341 associate degrees awarded in 1992. 55% in business and management, 34% business/office and marketing/distribution, 11% computer sciences. 291 bachelor's degrees awarded. 67% in business and management, 19% business/office and marketing/distribution, 14% computer sciences.

UNDERGRADUATE MAJORS. Accounting, business and management, business and office, data processing, finance, legal secretary, liberal/general studies, marketing and distribution, medical assistant, medical secretary, secretarial and related programs, tourism, word processing. accounting, business administration and management, business and management, computer programming, health care administration, information sciences and systems, marketing and distribution, microcomputer software, office supervision and management, secretarial and related programs, systems analysis.

ACADEMIC PROGRAMS. Accelerated program, cooperative education, double major, dual enrollment of high school students, independent study, internships, telecourses. **Remedial services:** Learning center, reduced course load, remedial instruction, special counselor, tutoring. **Placement/credit:** CLEP Subject, institutional tests; 16 credit hours maximum for associate degree; 16 credit hours maximum for bachelor's degree.

ACADEMIC REQUIREMENTS. Freshmen must earn minimum GPA of 2.0 to continue in good standing. 70% of freshmen return for sophomore year. Students must declare major on application. **Graduation requirements:** 100 hours for associate (20 in major), 196 hours for bachelor's (60 in major). Most students required to take courses in English, humanities, mathematics, social sciences. **Additional information:** Course work in major begins in first year. Accounting BBA graduates can take CPA examinations immediately.

FRESHMAN ADMISSIONS. Selection criteria: Open admissions. Recommended units include English 3 and mathematics 1.

1992 FRESHMAN CLASS PROFILE. 365 men, 1,220 women enrolled. **Characteristics:** 99% from in state, 100% commute, 49% have minority backgrounds, 2% are foreign students, 1% join fraternities/sororities. Average age is 26.

FALL-TERM APPLICATIONS. $20 fee, may be waived for applicants with need. Closing date September 19; applicants notified on a rolling basis; must reply within 4 weeks. Interview recommended. Deferred and early admission available. Letter required from principal or high school counselor verifying ability to complete classes.

STUDENT LIFE. Activities: Student government, student newspaper, yearbook, fraternities, sororities, Business club, Data Processing Management Association student chapter, Amnesty International.

ATHLETICS. NAIA. **Intercollegiate:** Golf M, soccer M. **Intramural:** Basketball M, bowling, rugby M, softball.

STUDENT SERVICES. Career counseling, employment service for undergraduates, freshman orientation, personal counseling, placement service for graduates, Student Development Center for individualized registration and advisement, friend-peer mentoring program, services/facilities for handicapped.

ANNUAL EXPENSES. Tuition and fees (1992-93): $6,095. **Books and supplies:** $575. **Other expenses:** $825.

FINANCIAL AID. 37% of freshmen, 63% of continuing students receive some form of aid. 86% of grants, 85% of loans, 77% of jobs based on need. Academic, athletic, leadership, alumni affiliation scholarships available. **Aid applications:** No closing date; priority given to applications received by February 15; applicants notified on a rolling basis beginning on or about April 15; must reply before September 1 to assure state aid.

ADDRESS/TELEPHONE. James Farmer, Vice President for Admissions/Placement, Detroit College of Business, 4800 Oakman Boulevard, Dearborn, MI 48126-3799. (313) 581-4400. Fax: (313) 581-1985.

Eastern Michigan University
Ypsilanti, Michigan CB code: 1201

Admissions: 80% of applicants accepted
Based on: ••• School record, test scores
• Activities, essay, interview, recommendations, special talents
Completion: 73% of freshmen end year in good standing

4-year public university, coed. Founded in 1849. **Accreditation:** Regional. **Undergraduate enrollment:** 5,461 men, 7,635 women full time; 2,896 men, 3,723 women part time. **Graduate enrollment:** 314 men, 448 women full time; 1,561 men, 3,096 women part time. **Faculty:** 1,046 total (687 full time), 780 with doctorates or other terminal degrees. **Location:** Suburban campus in large town; 6 miles from Ann Arbor, 30 miles from Detroit, 45 miles from Toledo. **Calendar:** Semester, limited summer session. Saturday and extensive evening/early morning classes. **Microcomputers:** 550 located in dormitories, libraries, classrooms, computer centers. **Special facilities:** Coatings Research Center, corporate education center, golf course.

DEGREES OFFERED. BA, BS, BFA, MA, MS, MBA, MFA, MEd, MSW, EdD. 3,065 bachelor's degrees awarded in 1992. 20% in business and management, 5% business/office and marketing/distribution, 5% communications, 7% education, 9% teacher education, 5% engineering technologies, 5% health sciences, 5% letters/literature, 8% social sciences, 5% visual and performing arts. Graduate degrees offered in 93 major fields of study.

UNDERGRADUATE MAJORS. Accounting, accounting information systems, actuarial sciences, aerospace science (Air Force), African studies, allied health, American literature, analytical chemistry, anthropology, art education, arts management, Asian studies, aviation management, bilingual/bicultural education, biochemistry, biological and physical sciences, biology, business administration and management, business and management, business and office, business computer/console/peripheral equipment operation, business economics, business education, business home economics, ceramics, chemistry, child development/care/guidance, cinematography/film, clinical laboratory science, communications, computer and information sciences, computer technology, computer-aided design, computer-aided design, computer-aided manufacturing, computer-aided manufacturing, construction, construction technology, creative writing, criminal justice studies, criminology, dance, dramatic arts, drawing, early childhood education, earth sciences, East Asian studies, ecology, economics, ecosystem biology (aquatic and terrestrial), education of the deaf and hearing impaired, education of the emotionally handicapped, education of the mentally handicapped, education of the multiple handicapped, education of the physically handicapped, education of the visually handicapped, elementary education, engineering and engineering-related technologies, engineering physics, English, English education, English literature, family/consumer resource management, fashion merchandising, finance, fine arts, food science and nutrition, foreign languages (multiple emphasis), foreign languages education, forestry and related sciences, French, geography, geology, geophysics and seismology, German, graphic and printing production, graphic arts technology, graphic design, health care administration, health education, history, home economics, home economics education, human resources development, humanities, humanities and social sciences, individual and family development, industrial arts education, industrial distribution, industrial technology, information sciences and systems, institutional management, institutional/home management/supporting programs, interdisciplinary technology, interior design, international business management, investments and securities, Japanese, journalism, labor/industrial relations, language and international trade, language and world business, Latin American studies, legal assistant/paralegal, liberal/general studies, linguistics, management information systems, manufacturing technology, marketing and distribution, marketing and distributive education, mathematics, mathematics education, medical laboratory technologies, metal/jewelry, metallurgical chemistry, metallurgy, microbiology, Middle Eastern studies, military science (Army), music, music education, music performance, music therapy, naval science (Navy, Marines), nursing, nutritional sciences, occupational therapy, office supervision and management, operations research, organic chemistry, painting, parks and recreation management, philosophy, physical chemistry, physical education, physical sciences, physics, physiology, human and animal, plastic technology, plastics technology, political science and government, polymers and coatings, pre-architecture, predentistry, preengineering, prelaw, premedicine, prepharmacy, preveterinary, printmaking, psychology, public administration, public relations, radio/television broadcasting, radio/television technology, real estate, recreation therapy, robotics, Russian and Slavic studies, science education, sculpture, secondary education, secretarial and related programs, small business management and ownership, social science education, social sciences, social studies education, social work, sociology, solar heating and cooling technology, Spanish, special education, speech, speech/communication/theater education, sports medicine, statistics, systems analysis, technical and business writing, telecommunications, theater design, tourism, toxicology, trade and industrial education, video, visual and performing arts, word processing.

ACADEMIC PROGRAMS. Accelerated program, cooperative education, double major, dual enrollment of high school students, education specialist degree, honors program, independent study, internships, student-designed major, study abroad, teacher preparation, visiting/exchange student program, weekend college, Washington semester, cross-registration; liberal arts/career combination in forestry. **Remedial services:** Learning center, preadmission summer program, reduced course load, special counselor, tutoring, minority retention program, alternative admissions programs. **ROTC:** Air Force, Army, Naval. **Placement/credit:** AP, CLEP Subject, institutional tests; 30 credit hours maximum for bachelor's degree.

ACADEMIC REQUIREMENTS. Freshmen must earn minimum GPA of 2.0 to continue in good standing. 70% of freshmen return for sophomore year. Students must declare major by end of second year. **Graduation requirements:** 124 hours for bachelor's (30 in major). Most students required to take courses in arts/fine arts, computer science, English, history, humanities, mathematics, philosophy/religion, biological/physical sciences, social sciences. **Additional information:** Full-time students must maintain 12 credit hours.

FRESHMAN ADMISSIONS. Selection criteria: School achievement record and ACT or SAT scores. Grades and test results combined to predict academic success. **High school preparation:** 20 units recommended. Recommended units include biological science 1, English 4, foreign language 3, mathematics 4, physical science 2, social science 3 and science 3. 2 units fine arts and 1 computer literacy also recommended. **Test requirements:** SAT or ACT; score report by July 31.

1992 FRESHMAN CLASS PROFILE. 4,726 men applied, 3,718 accepted, 992 enrolled; 6,226 women applied, 4,991 accepted, 1,255 enrolled. 38% had high school GPA of 3.0 or higher, 60% between 2.0 and 2.99. **Academic background:** Mid 50% of enrolled freshmen had SAT-V between 380-500, SAT-M between 410-540; ACT composite between 17-23. 15% submitted SAT scores, 85% submitted ACT scores. **Characteristics:** 88% from in state, 74% live in college housing, 21% have minority backgrounds, 2% are foreign students. Average age is 18.

FALL-TERM APPLICATIONS. $20 fee, may be waived for applicants with need. Closing date July 31; priority given to applications received by February 1; applicants notified on a rolling basis. Audition required for music applicants. Portfolio required for art applicants. Essay recommended. CRDA. Deferred admission available. EDP-SEDP-F. High school students may enroll, but generally not full-time.

STUDENT LIFE. Housing: Dormitories (men, women, coed); apartment, fraternity, sorority, handicapped housing available. Over 21 floors providing freshman housing, honors halls, in-hall academic services, transfer halls. **Activities:** Student government, film, magazine, radio, student newspaper, television, yearbook, choral groups, concert band, dance, drama, jazz band, marching band, music ensembles, musical theater, opera, pep band, symphony orchestra, symphonic band, Drama for the Young, gospel choir, fraternities, sororities, University Ambassadors Society, Mortar Board. **Additional information:** Office of Student Life and Residence Hall Association provide services to enhance the quality of student life.

ATHLETICS. NCAA. **Intercollegiate:** Baseball M, basketball, bowling, cross-country, diving, football M, golf M, gymnastics W, ice hockey M, rifle, skiing, soccer M, softball W, swimming, tennis, track and field, volleyball W, water polo, wrestling M. **Intramural:** Badminton, basketball, bowling, cross-country, diving, fencing, golf, gymnastics M, handball, ice hockey M, racquetball, sailing, skiing, softball, squash, swimming, table tennis, tennis, track and field, volleyball, water polo, wrestling M.

STUDENT SERVICES. Aptitude testing, career counseling, employment service for undergraduates, freshman orientation, health services, on-campus day care, personal counseling, placement service for graduates, special adviser for adult students, veterans counselor, services/facilities for handicapped.

ANNUAL EXPENSES. Tuition and fees (1992-93): $2,529, $3,585 additional for out-of-state students. **Room and board:** $3,850. **Books and supplies:** $450. **Other expenses:** $1,200.

FINANCIAL AID. 58% of freshmen, 54% of continuing students receive some form of aid. 71% of grants, 84% of loans, 20% of jobs based on need. 1,275 enrolled freshmen were judged to have need, all were offered aid. Academic, music/drama, art, athletic, state/district residency, leadership, alumni affiliation, minority scholarships available. **Aid applications:** No closing date; priority given to applications received by April 1; applicants notified on a rolling basis beginning on or about April 1.

ADDRESS/TELEPHONE. M. Dolan Evanovich, Director of Admissions, Eastern Michigan University, 400 Pierce Hall, Ypsilanti, MI 48197-2260. (313) 487-3060. (800) 468-6368. Fax: (313) 487-1484.

Ferris State University
Big Rapids, Michigan

CB code: 1222

Admissions: 87% of applicants accepted
Based on: ••• School record
• Activities, interview, recommendations, special talents, test scores
Completion: 65% of freshmen end year in good standing
5% enter graduate study

4-year public college of arts and sciences and business, nursing, pharmacy college, coed. Founded in 1884. **Accreditation:** Regional. **Undergraduate enrollment:** 6,097 men, 4,084 women full time; 840 men, 823 women part time. **Graduate enrollment:** 88 men, 56 women full time; 40 men, 43 women part time. **Faculty:** 709 total (495 full time), 200 with doctorates or other terminal degrees. **Location:** Rural campus in large town; 50 miles from Grand Rapids. **Calendar:** Semester, limited summer session. **Microcomputers:** 452 located in libraries, classrooms.

DEGREES OFFERED. AA, AS, AAS, BS, MS, OD, Pharm D. 1,185 associate degrees awarded in 1992. 1,811 bachelor's degrees awarded. Graduate degrees offered in 4 major fields of study.

UNDERGRADUATE MAJORS. Associate: Air conditioning/heating/refrigeration technology, architectural technologies, automotive technology, child development/care/guidance, civil technology, construction, court reporting, dental hygiene, dental laboratory technology, drafting and design technology, early childhood education, engineering and engineering-related technologies, fashion merchandising, food management, food production/management/services, funeral services/mortuary science, graphic and printing production, industrial chemistry technology, industrial equipment maintenance and repair, industrial technology, journalism, legal assistant/paralegal, legal secretary, liberal/general studies, mechanical design technology, medical laboratory technologies, medical records technology, nuclear medical technology, nursing, ophthalmic services, optical technology, optometry, ornamental horticulture, plastic technology, pre-arts, predentistry, prelaw, premedicine, prepharmacy, preveterinary, real estate, respiratory therapy, secondary education, secretarial and related programs, survey and mapping technology, welding technology. **Bachelor's:** Accounting, advertising, allied health education, applied mathematics, automotive and heavy equipment management, biology, biotechnology, business administration and management, business and management, business economics, business education, community services, computer and information sciences, construction management, electrical technology, electronic technology, finance, graphic and printing production, graphic design, health care administration, home economics education, hospitality and recreation marketing, hotel/motel and restaurant management, insurance and risk management, international business management, law enforcement and corrections, manufacturing technology, marketing management, mathematics education, medical records administration, nuclear medical technology, nursing, office supervision and management, operations research, optometry, parks and recreation management, personnel management, pharmacy, plastic technology, production management, professional golf management, professional tennis management, public relations, radio/television technology, real estate, retailing, science education, small business management and ownership, social work, survey and mapping technology, technical communications, technical education, welding technology.

ACADEMIC PROGRAMS. Double major, external degree, internships, teacher preparation; liberal arts/career combination in business. **Remedial services:** Learning center, remedial instruction, special counselor, tutoring. **ROTC:** Army. **Placement/credit:** AP, CLEP General and Subject, institutional tests.

ACADEMIC REQUIREMENTS. Freshmen must earn minimum GPA of 2.0 to continue in good standing. 63% of freshmen return for sophomore year. Students must declare major on application. **Graduation requirements:** 96 hours for associate, 185 hours for bachelor's. Most students required to take courses in English, humanities, mathematics, biological/physical sciences. **Postgraduate studies:** 30% from 2-year programs enter 4-year programs.

FRESHMAN ADMISSIONS. Selection criteria: School achievement record most important. 3.0 GPA in mathematics, biology, and chemistry required of some allied health applicants. **High school preparation:** 19 units recommended. Recommended units include biological science 3, English 4, foreign language 2, mathematics 4 and social science 3. 2 units in fine arts and 1 unit in computer literacy recommended. **Test requirements:** ACT for placement and counseling only; score report by May 1. ACT scores used for admissions purposes for marginal applicants.

1992 FRESHMAN CLASS PROFILE. 3,515 men applied, 3,069 accepted, 1,429 enrolled; 2,814 women applied, 2,464 accepted, 1,057 enrolled. **Academic background:** Mid 50% of enrolled freshmen had ACT composite between 12-20. 97% submitted ACT scores. **Characteristics:** 95% from in state, 97% live in college housing, 15% have minority backgrounds, 1% are foreign students. Average age is 19.

FALL-TERM APPLICATIONS. $20 fee. No closing date; applicants notified on a rolling basis; must reply within 2 weeks. Interview recommended. Portfolio recommended for visual communication applicants. Deferred admission available.

STUDENT LIFE. Housing: Dormitories (men, women, coed); apartment, fraternity housing available. **Activities:** Student government, radio, student newspaper, television, yearbook, choral groups, concert band, drama, jazz band, marching band, music ensembles, musical theater, pep band, symphony orchestra, fraternities, sororities, debate society.

ATHLETICS. NCAA. **Intercollegiate:** Baseball M, basketball, cross-country, football M, golf, ice hockey M, softball W, swimming, tennis, track and field, volleyball W, wrestling M. **Intramural:** Badminton, baseball M, basketball, bowling M, cross-country, football M, golf, ice hockey M, racquetball, softball, swimming, table tennis, tennis, track and field, volleyball, water polo, wrestling M.

STUDENT SERVICES. Aptitude testing, career counseling, employment service for undergraduates, freshman orientation, health services, on-campus day care, personal counseling, placement service for graduates, special adviser for adult students, veterans counselor, services/facilities for handicapped.

ANNUAL EXPENSES. Tuition and fees (1992-93): $3,000, $3,780 additional for out-of-state students. **Room and board:** $3,707. **Books and supplies:** $525. **Other expenses:** $630.

FINANCIAL AID. 65% of freshmen, 60% of continuing students receive some form of aid. All jobs based on need. Academic, music/drama, athletic, leadership, minority scholarships available. **Aid applications:** No closing date; priority given to applications received by April 1; applicants notified on a rolling basis beginning on or about May 1; must reply within 2 weeks.

ADDRESS/TELEPHONE. Dr. Duncan Sargent, Dean of Enrollment Services, Ferris State University, 901 South State Street, Big Rapids, MI 49307-2295. (616) 592-2100. Fax: (616) 592-2990.

Glen Oaks Community College
Centreville, Michigan CB code: 1261

2-year public community college, coed. Founded in 1965. **Accreditation:** Regional. **Undergraduate enrollment:** 1,387 men and women. **Faculty:** 95 total (32 full time), 2 with doctorates or other terminal degrees. **Location:** Rural campus in rural community; 35 miles from Kalamazoo. **Calendar:** Semester, limited summer session. **Microcomputers:** 60 located in classrooms, computer centers.

DEGREES OFFERED. AA, AS, AAS. 149 associate degrees awarded in 1992. 27% in business/office and marketing/distribution, 13% engineering technologies, 13% health sciences, 10% physical sciences, 37% social sciences.

UNDERGRADUATE MAJORS. Automotive technology, business and office, business data processing and related programs, fine arts, liberal/general studies, nursing, practical nursing, social sciences.

ACADEMIC PROGRAMS. 2-year transfer program, accelerated program, honors program, independent study, internships. **Remedial services:** Learning center, remedial instruction, special counselor, tutoring. **Placement/credit:** AP, CLEP General and Subject, institutional tests; 47 credit hours maximum for associate degree.

ACADEMIC REQUIREMENTS. Freshmen must earn minimum GPA of 1.5 to continue in good standing. 47% of freshmen return for sophomore year. **Graduation requirements:** 62 hours for associate (32 in major). Most students required to take courses in English, humanities, mathematics, social sciences.

FRESHMAN ADMISSIONS. Selection criteria: Open admissions. Admission to nursing program based on pre-admissions test, high school grades, and health form.

1992 FRESHMAN CLASS PROFILE. 895 men and women enrolled. **Characteristics:** 90% from in state, 100% commute, 2% have minority backgrounds, 2% are foreign students. Average age is 21.

FALL-TERM APPLICATIONS. No fee. 2. No closing date; applicants notified on a rolling basis. Deferred admission available.

STUDENT LIFE. Activities: Student government, magazine, student newspaper, choral groups, music ensembles, musical theater, academic honorary society, Phi Theta Kappa, student government.

ATHLETICS. NJCAA. **Intercollegiate:** Baseball M, basketball, golf M, volleyball W. **Intramural:** Basketball M, table tennis.

STUDENT SERVICES. Aptitude testing, career counseling, employment service for undergraduates, freshman orientation, personal counseling, placement service for graduates, services/facilities for handicapped.

ANNUAL EXPENSES. Tuition and fees (1992-93): $1,170, $120 additional for out-of-district students, $420 additional for out-of-state students. **Books and supplies:** $460. **Other expenses:** $773.

FINANCIAL AID. 81% of grants, 98% of loans, 76% of jobs based on need. Academic, music/drama, art, athletic, state/district residency, leadership scholarships available. **Aid applications:** No closing date; priority given to applications received by May 15; applicants notified on a rolling basis beginning on or about June 15; must reply within 2 weeks.

ADDRESS/TELEPHONE. Beverly Andrews, Admissions Coordinator/Registrar, Glen Oaks Community College, 62249 Shimmel Road, Centreville, MI 49032. (616) 467-9945. Fax: (616) 467-4114.

GMI Engineering & Management Institute
Flint, Michigan CB code: 1246

Admissions: 74% of applicants accepted
Based on: ••• School record, test scores
•• Activities, essay, interview
• Recommendations, special talents
Completion: 95% of freshmen end year in good standing
74% graduate, 16% of these enter graduate study

5-year private business, engineering college, coed. Founded in 1919. **Accreditation:** Regional. **Undergraduate enrollment:** 1,874 men, 493 women full time. **Graduate enrollment:** 634 men, 140 women part time. **Faculty:** 130 total, 84 with doctorates or other terminal degrees. **Location:** Suburban campus in small city; 70 miles from Detroit. **Calendar:** 2 twelve-week school terms and 2 twelve-week work-experience terms. **Microcomputers:** 250 located in libraries, classrooms, computer centers. **Special facilities:** Alumni collection of industrial history, art gallery.

DEGREES OFFERED. BS, MS. 338 bachelor's degrees awarded in 1992. 11% in business and management, 89% engineering. Graduate degrees offered in 3 major fields of study.

UNDERGRADUATE MAJORS. Accounting, applied mathematics, business administration and management, business and management, computer engineering, electrical/electronics/communications engineering, engineering, engineering management, industrial engineering, information sciences and systems, management information systems, marketing management, mechanical engineering, statistics, systems engineering, trade and industrial supervision and management.

ACADEMIC PROGRAMS. Accelerated program, cooperative education, double major, honors program, independent study; liberal arts/career combination in engineering. **Remedial services:** Special counselor, tutoring. **Placement/credit:** AP, institutional tests; 27 credit hours maximum for bachelor's degree.

ACADEMIC REQUIREMENTS. Freshmen must earn minimum GPA of 2.0 to continue in good standing. 95% of freshmen return for sophomore year. Students must declare major by end of first year. **Graduation requirements:** 180 hours for bachelor's (54 in major). Most students required to take courses in computer science, English, history, humanities, mathematics, biological/physical sciences, social sciences. **Postgraduate studies:** 2% enter law school, 8% enter MBA programs, 6% enter other graduate study. **Additional information:** Extensive cooperative educational opportunities available.

FRESHMAN ADMISSIONS. Selection criteria: Admission based on strength of preparation, performance in school and on standardized tests (ACT or SAT) and non-scholastic activities and achievements. Students accepted are assisted by college staff in obtaining employment as GMI co-op student. Employers are interested in academic ability, leadership, activities and experiences, career objectives, etc. Co-op employers interview students before making a job offer. Students not admitted as freshmen encouraged to re-apply as transfers. **High school preparation:** 16 units required; 20 recommended. Required and recommended units include English 3-4, mathematics 4 and physical science 2-3. Foreign language 2 recommended. At least 1 unit of either chemistry or physics, with laboratory work required of all students. Both chemistry and physics are strongly recommended. Algebra 1 & 2 and geometry or trigonometry required. **Test requirements:** SAT or ACT. Achievement tests, while not required, are welcome and helpful when presented. **Additional information:** Accepted students must choose an enrollment/co-op placement option. Enrollment is confirmed by paying a $200 deposit which is refundable until May 1st or within 30 days after an offer of admission. Many students get jobs before classes start, but the search process continues until each enrolled student secures employment.

1992 FRESHMAN CLASS PROFILE. 1,433 men applied, 1,052 accepted, 403 enrolled; 320 women applied, 247 accepted, 105 enrolled. 90% had high school GPA of 3.0 or higher, 10% between 2.0 and 2.99. **Academic background:** Mid 50% of enrolled freshmen had SAT-V between 450-570, SAT-M between 580-690; ACT composite between 25-29. 50% submitted SAT scores, 70% submitted ACT scores. **Characteristics:** 44% from in state, 100% live in college housing, 15% have minority backgrounds, 8% are foreign students, 40% join fraternities/sororities. Average age is 18.

FALL-TERM APPLICATIONS. $25 fee, may be waived for applicants with need. No closing date; priority given to applications received by February 1; applicants notified on a rolling basis; must reply within 3 weeks. Essay required. Interview recommended. Deferred admission available. Mathematics level II and chemistry or physics ACH tests recommended. Applications considered as long as corporate employment opportunities exist. As new companies join program throughout year, candidates can be considered through early summer.

STUDENT LIFE. Housing: Dormitories (coed); fraternity, sorority housing available. Upperclassmen and women may live in college residence hall if space allows. Freshmen required to live in residence hall. Approximately 50% of upperclass students live in fraternity and sorority housing. **Activities:** Student government, magazine, radio, student newspaper, yearbook, choral groups, drama, jazz band, music ensembles, fraternities, sororities, International Club, Black Unity Congress, Bacchus, Intervarsity Christian Fellowship, Christians in Action, professional and honor societies, special interest clubs. **Additional information:** Approximately 75% of students participate in intramural athletic activities.

ATHLETICS. Intercollegiate: Ice hockey M, soccer M. **Intramural:** Archery, badminton, basketball, bowling, cross-country, golf, racquetball, sailing, skiing, skin diving, soccer, softball, swimming, table tennis, tennis, track and field M, volleyball, wrestling M.

STUDENT SERVICES. Aptitude testing, career counseling, employment service for undergraduates, freshman orientation, health services, personal counseling, placement service for graduates, tutoring services, services/facilities for handicapped.

ANNUAL EXPENSES. Tuition and fees: $11,000. $908 per course tuition for graduate students, $45 per course registration fee. Books and supplies included in per course charge. **Room and board:** $3,166. **Books and supplies:** $575. **Other expenses:** $2,205.

FINANCIAL AID. 66% of freshmen, 54% of continuing students receive some form of aid. 89% of grants, 93% of loans, 70% of jobs based on need. 283 enrolled freshmen were judged to have need, all were offered aid. Academic, state/district residency, leadership, minority scholarships available. **Aid applications:** No closing date; priority given to applications received by March 15; applicants notified on a rolling basis beginning on or about March 15. **Additional information:** All students participate in paid cooperative work experience in 2 12-week segments each year. Average freshman earnings $8,000. Student earnings over 5-year program average $56,000 (range $35,000 to $75,000).

ADDRESS/TELEPHONE. Kevin A. Pollock, Director of Admissions, GMI Engineering & Management Institute, 1700 West Third Avenue, Flint, MI 48504-4898. (313) 762-7865. (800) 955-4464. Fax: (313) 762-9837.

Gogebic Community College
Ironwood, Michigan — CB code: 1250

2-year public community college, coed. Founded in 1932. **Accreditation:** Regional. **Undergraduate enrollment:** 1,200 men and women. **Faculty:** 89 total (32 full time), 3 with doctorates or other terminal degrees. **Location:** Rural campus in small town; 100 miles from Duluth, Minnesota, 100 miles from Marquette. **Calendar:** 4-1-4, limited summer session. **Microcomputers:** 80 located in classrooms, computer centers. **Special facilities:** Arboretum, ski hill.

DEGREES OFFERED. AA, AS, AAS. 155 associate degrees awarded in 1992. 14% in business and management, 24% business/office and marketing/distribution, 13% teacher education, 18% allied health, 16% trade and industry.

UNDERGRADUATE MAJORS. Accounting, automotive mechanics, automotive technology, biology, business administration and management, business and management, business and office, business computer/console/peripheral equipment operation, business data processing and related programs, business data programming, chemistry, child development/care/guidance, commercial art, computer and information sciences, computer graphics, conservation and regulation, construction, court reporting, criminal justice studies, data processing, drafting, drafting and design technology, early childhood education, education, elementary education, engineering, engineering and engineering-related technologies, food production/management/services, graphic and printing production, graphic arts technology, industrial equipment maintenance and repair, industrial technology, legal assistant/paralegal, legal secretary, liberal/general studies, mathematics, medical assistant, medical records technology, medical secretary, nursing, practical nursing, predentistry, prelaw, premedicine, prepharmacy, preveterinary, psychology, secondary education, secretarial and related programs, social sciences, social work, special education, teacher aide, word processing.

ACADEMIC PROGRAMS. 2-year transfer program, computer delivered (on-line) credit-bearing course offerings, cooperative education, double major, dual enrollment of high school students, honors program, independent study, internships, student-designed major, telecourses. **Remedial services:** Learning center, reduced course load, remedial instruction, special counselor, tutoring, study skills course. **Placement/credit:** CLEP General and Subject, institutional tests; 12 credit hours maximum for associate degree.

ACADEMIC REQUIREMENTS. Freshmen must earn minimum GPA of 1.75 to continue in good standing. 82% of freshmen return for sophomore year. **Graduation requirements:** 62 hours for associate (32 in major). Most students required to take courses in English, mathematics, social sciences.

FRESHMAN ADMISSIONS. Selection criteria: Open admissions. Nursing applicants must have background in chemistry, mathematics, and biology.

1992 FRESHMAN CLASS PROFILE. 300 men and women enrolled. **Characteristics:** 80% from in state, 95% commute, 16% have minority backgrounds. Average age is 20.

FALL-TERM APPLICATIONS. $5 fee, may be waived for applicants with need. No closing date; priority given to applications received by August 1; applicants notified on a rolling basis. Deferred admission available.

STUDENT LIFE. Housing: Apartment, cooperative housing available. **Activities:** Student government, student newspaper, choral groups, concert band, drama, Intervarsity Christian Fellowship, Phi Theta Kappa, drama club.

ATHLETICS. NAIA, NJCAA. **Intercollegiate:** Basketball. **Intramural:** Basketball, bowling, golf, skiing, soccer, softball, tennis, volleyball.

STUDENT SERVICES. Aptitude testing, career counseling, employment service for undergraduates, freshman orientation, personal counseling, placement service for graduates, veterans counselor, services/facilities for handicapped.

ANNUAL EXPENSES. Tuition and fees (1992-93): $900, $360 additional for out-of-district students, $360 additional for out-of-state students. **Room and board:** $1,110 room only. **Books and supplies:** $350. **Other expenses:** $750.

FINANCIAL AID. 75% of freshmen, 79% of continuing students receive some form of aid. 96% of grants, 98% of loans, 97% of jobs based on need. Academic, athletic, state/district residency, minority scholarships available. **Aid applications:** No closing date; priority given to applications received by March 15; applicants notified on a rolling basis beginning on or about May 15; must reply within 2 weeks.

ADDRESS/TELEPHONE. Jeffery Daugherty, Director Admissions/Housing, Gogebic Community College, East 4946 Jackson Road, Ironwood, MI 49938. (906) 932-4231. Fax: (906) 932-0868.

Grace Bible College
Grand Rapids, Michigan CB code: 0809

Admissions: 53% of applicants accepted
Based on: ••• School record
•• Religious affiliation/commitment, test scores
• Activities, interview, recommendations, special talents
Completion: 93% of freshmen end year in good standing
20% graduate, 15% of these enter graduate study

4-year private Bible college, coed, affiliated with Grace Gospel Fellowship. Founded in 1945. **Accreditation:** Regional. **Undergraduate enrollment:** 51 men, 33 women full time; 6 men, 10 women part time. **Faculty:** 27 total (9 full time), 7 with doctorates or other terminal degrees. **Location:** Suburban campus in small city; located on the southwest side of Grand Rapids, northwest of 28th street and Clyde Park Avenue. **Calendar:** Semester. **Microcomputers:** 1 located in libraries. **Additional facts:** Goal is to integrate general education and theological studies stressing faith and learning.

DEGREES OFFERED. AA, B. 17 associate degrees awarded in 1992. 6% in business and management, 65% philosophy, religion, theology, 29% social sciences. 7 bachelor's degrees awarded. 14% in business and management, 72% philosophy, religion, theology, 14% social sciences.

UNDERGRADUATE MAJORS. Bible studies, business and management, human services, liberal/general studies, religious education. business and management, human services, missionary studies, music, religious education, religious music, theological studies.

ACADEMIC PROGRAMS. 2-year transfer program, double major, independent study, internships, cross-registration; liberal arts/career combination in business. **Remedial services:** Reduced course load, tutoring. **Placement/credit:** AP, CLEP General and Subject, institutional tests.

ACADEMIC REQUIREMENTS. Freshmen must earn minimum GPA of 1.75 to continue in good standing. 75% of freshmen return for sophomore year. Students must declare major by end of second year. **Graduation requirements:** 64 hours for associate (19 in major), 124 hours for bachelor's (31 in major). Most students required to take courses in English, history, humanities, mathematics, philosophy/religion, biological/physical sciences, social sciences. **Postgraduate studies:** 20% from 2-year programs enter 4-year programs. **Additional information:** All students must major in Bible and theology, with optional additional major.

FRESHMAN ADMISSIONS. Selection criteria: Evidence of personal salvation through Jesus Christ. Rank in top half of class for regular admission. Probationary admission for those in third quarter of class. **High school preparation:** 11 units recommended. **Test requirements:** ACT; score report by August 1.

1992 FRESHMAN CLASS PROFILE. 81 men and women applied, 43 accepted; 13 men enrolled, 17 women enrolled. 41% had high school GPA of 3.0 or higher, 48% between 2.0 and 2.99. 10% were in top tenth and 40% were in top quarter of graduating class. **Characteristics:** 54% from in state, 90% live in college housing, 11% have minority backgrounds, 4% are foreign students. Average age is 18.

FALL-TERM APPLICATIONS. $20 fee for applications submitted after March 1. Additional $20 penalty if submitted after July 15. Closing date July 15; applicants notified on a rolling basis. Interview recommended. Deferred and early admission available.

STUDENT LIFE. Housing: Dormitories (men, women); apartment housing available. **Activities:** Student government, yearbook, literary publication, choral groups, drama, music ensembles, Christian ministry organization, missionary fellowship.

ATHLETICS. Intercollegiate: Basketball, soccer M, volleyball W. **Intramural:** Basketball M, bowling, golf, handball, racquetball, skiing, table tennis, tennis, volleyball.

STUDENT SERVICES. Aptitude testing, career counseling, employment service for undergraduates, freshman orientation, health services, personal counseling, placement service for graduates, services/facilities for handicapped.

ANNUAL EXPENSES. Tuition and fees: $4,850. **Room and board:** $3,100. **Books and supplies:** $300. **Other expenses:** $650.

FINANCIAL AID. 74% of freshmen, 93% of continuing students receive some form of aid. 81% of grants, all loans, 47% of jobs based on need. Academic, music/drama, leadership scholarships available. **Aid applications:** No closing date; priority given to applications received by July 15; applicants notified on a rolling basis beginning on or about July 15.

ADDRESS/TELEPHONE. Linda K. Siler, Admissions Director, Grace Bible College, 1101 Aldon Street, Southwest P.O. box 910, Grand Rapids, MI 49509-0910. (616) 538-2330. Fax: (616) 538-0599.

Grand Rapids Baptist College and Seminary
Grand Rapids, Michigan CB code: 1253

Admissions: 91% of applicants accepted
Based on: ••• Essay, recommendations, religious affiliation/commitment, school record, test scores
•• Interview
• Activities, special talents
Completion: 97% of freshmen end year in good standing
34% graduate

4-year private liberal arts college, coed, affiliated with General Association of Regular Baptist Churches. Founded in 1941. **Accreditation:** Regional. **Undergraduate enrollment:** 311 men, 371 women full time; 49 men, 46 women part time. **Graduate enrollment:** 52 men, 2 women full time; 85 men, 12 women part time. **Faculty:** 64 total (40 full time), 19 with doctorates or other terminal degrees. **Location:** Suburban campus in small city; 4 miles from downtown. **Calendar:** Semester, limited summer session. **Microcomputers:** 34 located in classrooms, computer centers.

DEGREES OFFERED. AAS, BA, M, M.Div. 9 associate degrees awarded in 1992. 75% in business/office and marketing/distribution, 13% communications, 12% philosophy, religion, theology. 125 bachelor's degrees awarded. 16% in business and management, 6% business/office and marketing/distribution, 18% teacher education, 11% letters/literature, 8% life sciences, 17% philosophy, religion, theology, 8% psychology, 6% social sciences, 6% visual and performing arts. Graduate degrees offered in 5 major fields of study.

UNDERGRADUATE MAJORS. Associate: Bible studies, legal secretary, medical secretary, radio/television broadcasting, secretarial and related programs, word processing. **Bachelor's:** Accounting, Bible studies, biblical languages, biology, business and management, business education, English, history, management information systems, management science, marketing management, mathematics, music, music education, music performance, music theory and composition, office supervision and management, physical education, prelaw, psychology, religion, science education, social science education, social work, sociology, speech, speech/communication/theater education.

ACADEMIC PROGRAMS. Double major, dual enrollment of high school students, independent study, internships, study abroad, teacher preparation, Washington semester. **Remedial services:** Learning center, reduced course load, remedial instruction, special counselor, tutoring. **ROTC:** Army. **Placement/credit:** AP, CLEP Subject, institutional tests; 30 credit hours maximum for bachelor's degree.

ACADEMIC REQUIREMENTS. Freshmen must earn minimum GPA of 1.5 to continue in good standing. 67% of freshmen return for sophomore year. Students must declare major by end of second year. **Graduation requirements:** 64 hours for associate (36 in major), 129 hours for bachelor's (30 in major). Most students required to take courses in arts/fine arts, English, history, humanities, mathematics, philosophy/religion, biological/physical sciences, social sciences. **Additional information:** Students must complete internship in major field.

FRESHMAN ADMISSIONS. Selection criteria: Personal Christian commitment, pastoral reference, 2.0 school GPA, and ACT scores. Students with lower scores and GPA may be admitted conditionally. Recommended units include English 4, mathematics 3, social science 2 and science 2. 5 units of academic electives recommended. **Test requirements:** ACT; score report by August 25.

1992 FRESHMAN CLASS PROFILE. 136 men applied, 123 accepted, 83 enrolled; 148 women applied, 136 accepted, 87 enrolled. 59% had high school GPA of 3.0 or higher, 40% between 2.0 and 2.99. 18% were in top tenth and 38% were in top quarter of graduating class. **Academic background:** Mid 50% of enrolled freshmen had ACT composite between 18-25. 96% submitted ACT scores. **Characteristics:** 75% from in state, 100% commute, 1% have minority backgrounds. Average age is 19.

FALL-TERM APPLICATIONS. $25 fee. Closing date August 15; priority given to applications received by May 1; applicants notified on a rolling basis. Audition required for music applicants. Essay required. Interview recommended. Deferred and early admission available.

STUDENT LIFE. Housing: Dormitories (men, women); apartment housing available. Students under 21 must live on campus unless living with immediate family. **Activities:** Student government, radio, student newspaper, yearbook, choral groups, concert band, drama, jazz band, music ensembles, musical theater, pep band, symphony orchestra, student ministries in community and churches. **Additional information:** Religious observance required.

ATHLETICS. NAIA. **Intercollegiate:** Baseball M, basketball, cross-country, golf M, soccer M, softball W, tennis M, track and field, volleyball W. **Intramural:** Basketball, soccer, softball, volleyball.

STUDENT SERVICES. Aptitude testing, career counseling, employment service for undergraduates, freshman orientation, health services, personal counseling, placement service for graduates, veterans counselor, services/facilities for handicapped.

ANNUAL EXPENSES. Tuition and fees (1992-93): $5,920. **Room and board:** $3,738. **Books and supplies:** $500. **Other expenses:** $1,150.

FINANCIAL AID. 73% of freshmen, 79% of continuing students re-

ceive some form of aid. 85% of grants, 96% of loans, 30% of jobs based on need. 147 enrolled freshmen were judged to have need, all were offered aid. Academic, music/drama, athletic, leadership, religious affiliation scholarships available. **Aid applications:** Closing date September 1; priority given to applications received by March 1; applicants notified on a rolling basis beginning on or about March 1; must reply within 2 weeks. **Additional information:** Audition required for music scholarship applicants.

ADDRESS/TELEPHONE. Kay Landrum, Director of Admissions, Grand Rapids Baptist College and Seminary, 1001 East Beltline Northeast, Grand Rapids, MI 49505. (616) 285-9426. (800) 968-4722.

Grand Rapids Community College
Grand Rapids, Michigan — CB code: 1254

2-year public community, junior college, coed. Founded in 1914. **Accreditation:** Regional. **Undergraduate enrollment:** 2,849 men, 2,493 women full time; 4,374 men, 4,578 women part time. **Faculty:** 561 total (241 full time), 49 with doctorates or other terminal degrees. **Location:** Urban campus in small city; 167 miles from Detroit. **Calendar:** Semester, extensive summer session. Saturday and extensive evening/early morning classes. **Microcomputers:** 210 located in libraries, classrooms, computer centers. **Special facilities:** Mezzanine Art Gallery, Lincoln Library Collection, Applied Technology Center. **Additional facts:** Off-campus sites in Rockford and Zeeland, The Netherlands.

DEGREES OFFERED. AA, AS. 1,184 associate degrees awarded in 1992.

UNDERGRADUATE MAJORS. Accounting, air conditioning/heating/refrigeration mechanics, air conditioning/heating/refrigeration technology, architecture, automotive mechanics, automotive technology, business administration and management, business and management, business and office, business computer/console/peripheral equipment operation, business data processing and related programs, business data programming, chemical manufacturing technology, child development/care/guidance, computer programming, computer servicing technology, computer technology, data processing, dental assistant, dental hygiene, drafting, drafting and design technology, electrical and electronics equipment repair, electronic technology, engineering and engineering-related technologies, fashion merchandising, fire control and safety technology, food production/management/services, graphic arts technology, home furnishings and equipment management/production/services, hotel/motel and restaurant management, industrial technology, law enforcement and corrections, legal secretary, liberal/general studies, manufacturing technology, marketing and distribution, marketing management, mechanical design technology, medical secretary, microcomputer software, music, nursing, occupational therapy assistant, plastic technology, precision metal work, quality control technology, radiograph medical technology, secretarial and related programs, water and wastewater technology, welding technology, word processing.

ACADEMIC PROGRAMS. 2-year transfer program, cooperative education, dual enrollment of high school students, independent study, internships, study abroad, telecourses, weekend college. **Remedial services:** Learning center, reduced course load, remedial instruction, special counselor, tutoring, learning laboratories. **Placement/credit:** AP, CLEP Subject, institutional tests; 30 credit hours maximum for associate degree.

ACADEMIC REQUIREMENTS. No policy requiring minimum GPA; records of students having academic difficulty are reviewed individually. 62% of freshmen return for sophomore year. **Graduation requirements:** 62 hours for associate. Most students required to take courses in arts/fine arts, English, humanities, mathematics, biological/physical sciences, social sciences.

FRESHMAN ADMISSIONS. Selection criteria: Open admissions. Selective admissions to occupational health programs. In general, occupational health applicants must be high school graduate or have 2.5 high school GPA and minimum ACT composite score of 16. For specific requirements of each program consult school catalog. Recommended units include biological science 1, English 4, mathematics 3, physical science 1, social science 2 and science 1. **Additional information:** Students strongly encouraged to take ACT for placement and counseling. Those without ACT scores must take ACT ASSET.

1992 FRESHMAN CLASS PROFILE. 5,254 men, 5,008 women enrolled. **Characteristics:** 99% from in state, 100% commute, 13% have minority backgrounds, 1% are foreign students. Average age is 18.

FALL-TERM APPLICATIONS. $20 fee, may be waived for applicants with need. Closing date August 30; applicants notified on a rolling basis. Deferred and early admission available.

STUDENT LIFE. Activities: Student government, film, magazine, student newspaper, television, choral groups, concert band, dance, drama, jazz band, marching band, music ensembles, musical theater, pep band, symphony orchestra, Black, Hispanic, Native American and Vietnamese student organizations, Community College Christian Fellowship, content area student organizations.

ATHLETICS. NJCAA. **Intercollegiate:** Baseball M, basketball, cross-country, diving, football M, golf M, softball W, swimming, tennis, track and field, volleyball W, wrestling M. **Intramural:** Basketball, ice hockey M, racquetball, skiing, soccer M, swimming.

STUDENT SERVICES. Aptitude testing, career counseling, employment service for undergraduates, freshman orientation, on-campus day care, personal counseling, placement service for graduates, special adviser for adult students, single parent services, services/facilities for handicapped.

ANNUAL EXPENSES. Tuition and fees: $1,384, $672 additional for out-of-district students, $1,120 additional for out-of-state students. **Books and supplies:** $420. **Other expenses:** $460.

FINANCIAL AID. 40% of freshmen, 45% of continuing students receive some form of aid. 92% of grants, 88% of loans, 54% of jobs based on need. 1,850 enrolled freshmen were judged to have need, all were offered aid. Academic, music/drama, art, athletic, leadership, alumni affiliation, minority scholarships available. **Aid applications:** Closing date August 1; priority given to applications received by April 1; applicants notified on a rolling basis; must reply within 3 weeks. **Additional information:** Tuition reimbursement and/or child-care services for single parents and homemakers who meet Perkins guidelines.

ADDRESS/TELEPHONE. Diane DeFelice-Patrick, Director of Admissions, Grand Rapids Community College, 143 Bostwick Northeast, Grand Rapids, MI 49503. (616) 771-4101.

Grand Valley State University
Allendale, Michigan — CB code: 1258

Admissions:	73% of applicants accepted
Based on:	••• School record, test scores
	• Activities, essay, interview, recommendations, special talents
Completion:	77% of freshmen end year in good standing
	35% graduate, 35% of these enter graduate study

4-year public university, coed. Founded in 1960. **Accreditation:** Regional. **Undergraduate enrollment:** 3,398 men, 4,680 women full time; 1,004 men, 1,445 women part time. **Graduate enrollment:** 96 men, 190 women full time; 722 men, 1,332 women part time. **Faculty:** 599 total (371 full time), 467 with doctorates or other terminal degrees. **Location:** Suburban campus in small town; 12 miles from Grand Rapids. **Calendar:** Semester, limited summer session. **Microcomputers:** 1,200 located in dormitories, libraries, classrooms, computer centers, campus-wide network. **Special facilities:** Art gallery, cross-country fitness trail, recital hall. **Additional facts:** 4 divisions: Seidman School of Business and Administration, Humanities and Arts Division, Social Science Division, and Division of Mathematics and Science.

DEGREES OFFERED. BA, BS, BFA, MS, MBA, MEd, MSW. 1,332 bachelor's degrees awarded in 1992. 7% in business and management, 15% business/office and marketing/distribution, 7% communications, 16% health sciences, 5% letters/literature, 10% parks/recreation, protective services, public affairs, 10% psychology, 9% social sciences. Graduate degrees offered in 32 major fields of study.

UNDERGRADUATE MAJORS. Accounting, advertising, anthropology, applied mathematics, art education, behavioral sciences, biological and physical sciences, biological laboratory technology, biology, biomedical science, business administration and management, business and management, business economics, ceramics, chemistry, cinematography/film, city/community/regional planning, clinical laboratory science, communications, community services, computer and information sciences, computer programming, creative writing, criminal justice studies, criminology, data processing, dramatic arts, drawing, earth sciences, economics, education, education of the deaf and hearing impaired, education of the emotionally handicapped, education of the mentally handicapped, education of the multiple handicapped, electrical/electronics/communications engineering, elementary education, engineering, English, English education, English literature, environmental design, environmental science, finance, fine arts, foreign languages (multiple emphasis), foreign languages education, French, geochemistry, geology, German, graphic design, health sciences, history, hotel/motel and restaurant management, industrial technology, information sciences and systems, international relations, journalism, junior high education, labor/industrial relations, law enforcement and corrections, liberal/general studies, marketing and distribution, marketing management, mathematics, mathematics education, mechanical engineering, metal/jewelry, music, music education, music performance, nursing, operations research, painting, personnel management, philosophy, photography, physical education, physical sciences, physics, political science and government, predentistry, prelaw, premedicine, printmaking, psychology, public administration, public health laboratory science, public relations, radio/television broadcasting, reading education, recreation therapy, renewable natural resources, Russian and Slavic studies, science education, sculpture, secondary education, social science education, social sciences, social studies education, social work, sociology, soil sciences, Spanish, special education, specific learning disabilities, sports medicine, statistics, urban studies, visual and performing arts.

ACADEMIC PROGRAMS. Cooperative education, double major, dual enrollment of high school students, honors program, independent study, internships, student-designed major, study abroad, teacher preparation, telecourses, visiting/exchange student program, Washington semester, cross-registration. **Remedial services:** Learning center, remedial instruction, special counselor, tutoring. **Placement/credit:** AP, CLEP Subject, institutional tests; 32 credit hours maximum for bachelor's degree.

ACADEMIC REQUIREMENTS. Freshmen must earn minimum GPA of 2.0 to continue in good standing. 77% of freshmen return for sophomore year. Students must declare major by end of second year. **Graduation requirements:** 120 hours for bachelor's (36 in major). Most students required to take courses in arts/fine arts, computer science, English, history, humanities, mathematics, biological/physical sciences, social sciences.

FRESHMAN ADMISSIONS. Selection criteria: Academic performance and test results. Interview and recommendations used for borderline applicants. **High school preparation:** 20 units required. Required units include English 4, mathematics 3 and science 3. Mathematics must include 2 algebra. Science must include 2 laboratory science. English must include 1 composition. Recommend 2 foreign language, 2 fine arts, and computer literacy. **Test requirements:** SAT or ACT (ACT preferred); score report by July 30.

1992 FRESHMAN CLASS PROFILE. 2,110 men applied, 1,533 accepted, 609 enrolled; 3,164 women applied, 2,301 accepted, 1,018 enrolled. 66% had high school GPA of 3.0 or higher, 33% between 2.0 and 2.99. 22% were in top tenth and 52% were in top quarter of graduating class. **Academic background:** Mid 50% of enrolled freshmen had ACT composite between 20-24. 96% submitted ACT scores. **Characteristics:** 98% from in state, 62% live in college housing, 10% have minority backgrounds, 1% are foreign students. Average age is 18.

FALL-TERM APPLICATIONS. $20 fee, may be waived for applicants with need. Closing date July 30; priority given to applications received by February 1; applicants notified on a rolling basis. Audition required for music applicants. Portfolio required for art applicants. CRDA. Deferred and early admission available. Application closing date February 1 for campus housing, scholarships.

STUDENT LIFE. Housing: Dormitories (coed); apartment housing available. Living centers provide 2 bedroom, 4 person suites. **Activities:** Student government, film, radio, student newspaper, television, literary magazine, choral groups, concert band, dance, drama, jazz band, marching band, music ensembles, musical theater, pep band, symphony orchestra, fraternities, sororities, strong Christian Fellowship, Black Student Union, El Renacimiento, Kappa Alpha Psi, Delta Sigma Theta, Alpha Phi Alpha.

ATHLETICS. NCAA. **Intercollegiate:** Baseball M, basketball, cross-country, football M, softball, swimming, tennis, track and field, volleyball W, wrestling M. **Intramural:** Baseball M, basketball, bowling, golf, ice hockey M, racquetball, rowing (crew), soccer, softball, squash, table tennis, tennis, wrestling M.

STUDENT SERVICES. Aptitude testing, career counseling, employment service for undergraduates, freshman orientation, health services, on-campus day care, personal counseling, placement service for graduates, special adviser for adult students, veterans counselor, services/facilities for handicapped.

ANNUAL EXPENSES. Tuition and fees (projected): $2,658, $3,202 additional for out-of-state students. **Room and board:** $3,930. **Books and supplies:** $600. **Other expenses:** $450.

FINANCIAL AID. 66% of freshmen, 66% of continuing students receive some form of aid. 79% of grants, 87% of loans, 43% of jobs based on need. 908 enrolled freshmen were judged to have need, all were offered aid. Academic, music/drama, art, athletic, alumni affiliation, minority scholarships available. **Aid applications:** No closing date; priority given to applications received by February 15; applicants notified on a rolling basis beginning on or about April 1; must reply by May 1 or within 10 days if notified thereafter. **Additional information:** College traditionally funds 100% of each student's demonstrated need.

ADDRESS/TELEPHONE. Jo Ann Foerster, Director of Admissions, Grand Valley State University, 1 Campus Drive, Allendale, MI 49401-9403. (616) 895-6611. (800) 748-0246. Fax: (616) 895-3180.

Great Lakes Christian College
Lansing, Michigan — CB code: 7320

4-year private Bible college, coed, affiliated with Church of Christ (Christian). Founded in 1949. **Undergraduate enrollment:** 207 men and women. **Faculty:** 18 total (10 full time), 3 with doctorates or other terminal degrees. **Location:** Suburban campus in small city; 90 miles from Detroit. **Calendar:** Semester. **Microcomputers:** Located in libraries.

DEGREES OFFERED. AA, B. 5 associate degrees awarded in 1992. 100% in philosophy, religion, theology. 12 bachelor's degrees awarded. 100% in philosophy, religion, theology.

UNDERGRADUATE MAJORS. Bible studies. Bible studies, education, religious education, religious music.

ACADEMIC PROGRAMS. Independent study, internships, 18-month accelerated program in ministries for men over 30, cooperative programs with Michigan State University and other colleges. **Remedial services:** Reduced course load, tutoring.

ACADEMIC REQUIREMENTS. Freshmen must earn minimum GPA of 1.7 to continue in good standing. 65% of freshmen return for sophomore year. Students must declare major by end of second year. **Graduation requirements:** 64 hours for associate, 128 hours for bachelor's (30 in major). Most students required to take courses in English, history, philosophy/religion, biological/physical sciences. **Postgraduate studies:** 15% from 2-year programs enter 4-year programs.

FRESHMAN ADMISSIONS. Selection criteria: Recommendations of character from applicant's church minister and elders required. Students with school GPA below 2.0 admitted on probation. **Test requirements:** ACT; score report by September 1.

1992 FRESHMAN CLASS PROFILE. 80 men and women enrolled. 26% had high school GPA of 3.0 or higher, 63% between 2.0 and 2.99. **Characteristics:** 84% from in state, 95% live in college housing, 2% have minority backgrounds, 1% are foreign students. Average age is 19.

FALL-TERM APPLICATIONS. $30 fee. Closing date July 31; applicants notified on a rolling basis. Interview required for accelerated ministries program applicants. Audition required for music applicants. Essay recommended. Deferred admission available.

STUDENT LIFE. Housing: Dormitories (men, women); apartment housing available. **Activities:** Student government, yearbook, choral groups, drama, music ensembles. **Additional information:** Regular Christian service participation required of all full-time students. Religious observance required.

ATHLETICS. Intercollegiate: Baseball M, basketball, softball W, volleyball W. **Intramural:** Volleyball.

STUDENT SERVICES. Freshman orientation, personal counseling, services/facilities for handicapped.

ANNUAL EXPENSES. Tuition and fees: $4,037. **Room and board:** $3,635. **Books and supplies:** $500. **Other expenses:** $1,500.

FINANCIAL AID. 91% of freshmen, 90% of continuing students receive some form of aid. All aid based on need. 51 enrolled freshmen were judged to have need, all were offered aid. Academic, music/drama, leadership, religious affiliation, minority scholarships available. **Aid applications:** No closing date; priority given to applications received by August 1; applicants notified on a rolling basis beginning on or about August 15; must reply within 2 weeks.

ADDRESS/TELEPHONE. Nancy Hooper, Admissions Director, Great Lakes Christian College, 6211 West Willow Highway, Lansing, MI 48917. (517) 321-0242 ext. 27. Fax: (517) 321-5902.

Great Lakes Junior College of Business
Saginaw, Michigan — CB code: 3378

2-year private business, junior college, coed. Founded in 1907. **Accreditation:** Regional candidate. **Undergraduate enrollment:** 151 men, 870 women full time; 191 men, 885 women part time. **Faculty:** 136 total (48 full time), 6 with doctorates or other terminal degrees. **Location:** Urban campus in small city; 100 miles from Detroit. **Calendar:** Quarter, extensive summer session. **Microcomputers:** 102 located in libraries, classrooms, computer centers. **Additional facts:** Campuses in Saginaw, Midland, Bay City, Caro, and Bad Axe.

DEGREES OFFERED. AAS. 367 associate degrees awarded in 1992. 36% in business and management, 23% business/office and marketing/distribution, 7% computer sciences, 10% allied health, 16% law, 8% trade and industry.

UNDERGRADUATE MAJORS. Accounting, agricultural business and management, allied health, business administration and management, business and management, business and office, business computer/console/peripheral equipment operation, business data processing and related programs, business data programming, computer programming, court reporting, electrical and electronics equipment repair, emergency medical technologies, finance, legal assistant/paralegal, legal secretary, medical assistant, medical secretary, nursing, office supervision and management, secretarial and related programs, word processing.

ACADEMIC PROGRAMS. Accelerated program, double major, dual enrollment of high school students, independent study, internships. **Remedial services:** Reduced course load, remedial instruction, special counselor, tutoring. **Placement/credit:** Institutional tests; 32 credit hours maximum for associate degree.

ACADEMIC REQUIREMENTS. Freshmen must earn minimum GPA of 2.0 to continue in good standing. 60% of freshmen return for sophomore year. Students must declare major on enrollment. **Graduation requirements:** 100 hours for associate (62 in major). Most students required to take courses in computer science, English, mathematics, social sciences.

FRESHMAN ADMISSIONS. Selection criteria: Open admissions.

1992 FRESHMAN CLASS PROFILE. 90 men, 376 women enrolled. **Characteristics:** 100% from in state, 100% commute, 9% have minority backgrounds. Average age is 28.

FALL-TERM APPLICATIONS. $20 fee. No closing date; priority given to applications received by June 15; applicants notified on a rolling basis. Interview recommended. Early admission available. All students must take ASSET for placement purposes.

STUDENT SERVICES. Career counseling, employment service for

undergraduates, freshman orientation, personal counseling, placement service for graduates, veterans counselor, services/facilities for handicapped.

ANNUAL EXPENSES. Tuition and fees (projected): $4,695. **Books and supplies:** $450. **Other expenses:** $490.

FINANCIAL AID. 72% of freshmen, 72% of continuing students receive some form of aid. All grants, 91% of loans, all jobs based on need. Academic scholarships available. **Aid applications:** No closing date; applicants notified on a rolling basis beginning on or about May 15; must reply within 4 weeks.

ADDRESS/TELEPHONE. Office of Admissions, Great Lakes Junior College of Business, 310 South Washington Avenue, Saginaw, MI 48607. (517) 755-3444. Fax: (517) 752-3453.

Henry Ford Community College
Dearborn, Michigan — CB code: 1293

2-year public community college, coed. Founded in 1938. **Accreditation:** Regional. **Undergraduate enrollment:** 14,975 men and women. **Faculty:** 1,005 total (225 full time), 38 with doctorates or other terminal degrees. **Location:** Suburban campus in small city; 8 miles from downtown Detroit. **Calendar:** Semester, limited summer session. Saturday and extensive evening/early morning classes. **Microcomputers:** Located in libraries, classrooms.

DEGREES OFFERED. AA, AS. 1,177 associate degrees awarded in 1992. 21% in business and management, 5% computer sciences, 25% engineering technologies, 17% allied health, 5% law, 17% letters/literature.

UNDERGRADUATE MAJORS. Accounting, air conditioning/heating/refrigeration technology, architectural technologies, architecture-construction, automotive mechanics, automotive technology, business administration and management, business and management, business and office, business data processing and related programs, commercial art, computer and information sciences, computer programming, crafts, drafting, drafting and design technology, dramatic arts, drawing, electrical and electronics equipment repair, electrical technology, electronic technology, emergency medical technologies, energy conservation and use technology, engineering, fire control and safety technology, food management, food production/management/services, graphic arts technology, hotel/motel and restaurant management, industrial technology, institutional management, instrumentation technology, interior design, journalism, law enforcement and corrections, law enforcement and corrections technologies, legal assistant/paralegal, legal secretary, liberal/general studies, management science, manufacturing technology, medical records technology, music, nursing, painting, physical therapy assistant, power plant operation and maintenance, quality control technology, radio/television broadcasting, respiratory therapy, respiratory therapy technology, retailing, robotics, secretarial and related programs, speech, transportation management.

ACADEMIC PROGRAMS. 2-year transfer program, cooperative education, dual enrollment of high school students, honors program, independent study, telecourses. **Remedial services:** Learning center, preadmission summer program, reduced course load, remedial instruction, special counselor, tutoring. **Placement/credit:** AP, institutional tests.

ACADEMIC REQUIREMENTS. Freshmen must earn minimum GPA of 2.0 to continue in good standing. 39% of freshmen return for sophomore year. Students must declare major on application. **Graduation requirements:** 62 hours for associate (20 in major). Most students required to take courses in English, humanities, social sciences.

FRESHMAN ADMISSIONS. Selection criteria: Open admissions. Selective admissions to specific allied health programs. For allied health programs: 1 year high school biology, chemistry, and algebra.

1992 FRESHMAN CLASS PROFILE. 5,000 men and women enrolled. **Characteristics:** 99% from in state, 100% commute, 30% have minority backgrounds, 1% are foreign students.

FALL-TERM APPLICATIONS. $20 fee, may be waived for applicants with need. No closing date; applicants notified on a rolling basis. Deferred admission available.

STUDENT LIFE. Activities: Student government, film, magazine, radio, student newspaper, art exhibits, choral groups, concert band, drama, jazz band, music ensembles, forensics, fraternities, sororities.

ATHLETICS. NJCAA. **Intercollegiate:** Baseball M, basketball, golf M, softball W, tennis, volleyball W. **Intramural:** Basketball, bowling, sailing, table tennis.

STUDENT SERVICES. Aptitude testing, career counseling, employment service for undergraduates, on-campus day care, personal counseling, placement service for graduates, special adviser for adult students, veterans counselor, services/facilities for handicapped.

ANNUAL EXPENSES. Tuition and fees (1992-93): $1,450, $690 additional for out-of-district students, $690 additional for out-of-state students. **Books and supplies:** $500. **Other expenses:** $520.

FINANCIAL AID. 33% of freshmen, 33% of continuing students receive some form of aid. 90% of grants, 89% of loans, 45% of jobs based on need. 2,007 enrolled freshmen were judged to have need, all were offered aid. Academic, music/drama, art, athletic scholarships available. **Aid applications:** No closing date; priority given to applications received by April 1; applicants notified on a rolling basis beginning on or about May 1.

ADDRESS/TELEPHONE. Dorothy Murphy, Coordinator of Admissions, Henry Ford Community College, 5101 Evergreen Road, Dearborn, MI 48128. (313) 845-9766. Fax: (313) 845-9658.

Highland Park Community College
Highland Park, Michigan — CB code: 1294

2-year public community college, coed. Founded in 1918. **Accreditation:** Regional. **Undergraduate enrollment:** 1,918 men and women. **Faculty:** 171 total (40 full time), 31 with doctorates or other terminal degrees. **Location:** Urban campus in large town; in Detroit metropolitan area. **Calendar:** Semester, limited summer session. **Microcomputers:** 30 located in classrooms, computer centers.

DEGREES OFFERED. AA, AS, AAS. 498 associate degrees awarded in 1992.

UNDERGRADUATE MAJORS. Automotive mechanics, automotive technology, business and office, business data processing and related programs, business data programming, computer and information sciences, drafting and design technology, electronic technology, liberal/general studies, medical assistant, medical laboratory technologies, nursing, practical nursing, respiratory therapy technology, secretarial and related programs, surgical technology, word processing.

ACADEMIC PROGRAMS. 2-year transfer program, cooperative education, dual enrollment of high school students, honors program, internships, United Nations semester. **Remedial services:** Learning center, preadmission summer program, remedial instruction, special counselor, tutoring. **Placement/credit:** Institutional tests; 45 credit hours maximum for associate degree.

ACADEMIC REQUIREMENTS. Freshmen must earn minimum GPA of 1.5 to continue in good standing. Students must declare major by end of first year. **Graduation requirements:** 60 hours for associate. Most students required to take courses in English, social sciences.

FRESHMAN ADMISSIONS. Selection criteria: Open admissions. Selective admission to nursing and respiratory therapy programs. **Test requirements:** National League for Nursing Pre-Admissions and Classification Test required of nursing and respiratory therapy applicants.

1992 FRESHMAN CLASS PROFILE. 950 men and women enrolled. **Characteristics:** 98% from in state, 100% commute, 86% have minority backgrounds, 2% are foreign students. Average age is 27.

FALL-TERM APPLICATIONS. $10 fee, may be waived for applicants with need. No closing date; applicants notified on a rolling basis. Interview required for nursing and respiratory therapy applicants. Early admission available.

STUDENT LIFE. Activities: Student government, magazine, student newspaper, television, choral groups, fraternities, sororities.

ATHLETICS. NJCAA. **Intercollegiate:** Baseball M, basketball, cross-country.

STUDENT SERVICES. Aptitude testing, career counseling, employment service for undergraduates, on-campus day care, personal counseling, placement service for graduates, veterans counselor, services/facilities for handicapped.

ANNUAL EXPENSES. Tuition and fees (1992-93): $1,700, $300 additional for out-of-state students. **Books and supplies:** $250. **Other expenses:** $1,300.

FINANCIAL AID. 95% of freshmen, 85% of continuing students receive some form of aid. Grants, loans, jobs available. **Aid applications:** No closing date; applicants notified on a rolling basis.

ADDRESS/TELEPHONE. Ameenah E. P. Omar, Director of Admissions/Registrar, Highland Park Community College, Glendale at Second, Highland Park, MI 48203. (313) 252-0475 ext. 238.

Hillsdale College
Hillsdale, Michigan — CB code: 1295

Admissions: 79% of applicants accepted
Based on:
- ••• School record
- •• Activities, essay, interview, recommendations, test scores
- • Special talents

Completion: 95% of freshmen end year in good standing
75% graduate, 45% of these enter graduate study

4-year private liberal arts college, coed. Founded in 1844. **Accreditation:** Regional. **Undergraduate enrollment:** 480 men, 550 women full time; 10 men, 35 women part time. **Faculty:** 108 total (79 full time), 80 with doctorates or other terminal degrees. **Location:** Suburban campus in small town; 100 miles from Detroit. **Calendar:** Semester, limited summer session. **Microcomputers:** 150 located in libraries, classrooms, computer centers. **Special facilities:** Slayton Arboretum, preschool laboratory, kindergarten through eighth grade academy, Ludwig Von Mises Economic Library. **Additional facts:** Opportunity for highly qualified students to study 1 semester at Oxford University, England.

DEGREES OFFERED. BA, BS. 237 bachelor's degrees awarded in 1992. 35% in business and management, 12% teacher education, 14% letters/literature, 9% life sciences, 5% psychology, 15% social sciences.

UNDERGRADUATE MAJORS. Accounting, American studies, art education, art history, biology, business administration and management, chemistry, Christian studies, Christian studies, classics, comparative literature, dramatic arts, early childhood education, economics, elementary education, English, English education, environmental science, European studies, finance, foreign languages education, French, German, history, international business management, junior high education, marketing management, mathematics, mathematics education, music, music education, philosophy, physical education, physics, political economy, political science and government, psychology, religion, science education, secondary education, social studies education, social work, sociology, Spanish, theological studies, visual and performing arts.

ACADEMIC PROGRAMS. Accelerated program, double major, dual enrollment of high school students, honors program, independent study, internships, study abroad, teacher preparation, visiting/exchange student program, Washington semester. **Remedial services:** Reduced course load, tutoring. **Placement/credit:** AP, CLEP Subject, institutional tests.

ACADEMIC REQUIREMENTS. Freshmen must earn minimum GPA of 1.75 to continue in good standing. 90% of freshmen return for sophomore year. Students must declare major by end of second year. **Graduation requirements:** 124 hours for bachelor's (36 in major). Most students required to take courses in arts/fine arts, English, foreign languages, history, humanities, mathematics, philosophy/religion, biological/physical sciences, social sciences. **Postgraduate studies:** 8% enter law school, 5% enter medical school, 18% enter MBA programs, 14% enter other graduate study.

FRESHMAN ADMISSIONS. Selection criteria: Minimum 3.0 high school GPA, class rank in top third preferred. Test scores, recommendations, interview and personal essay are important. Recommended units include biological science 2, English 4, foreign language 2, mathematics 3, physical science 1 and social science 2. **Test requirements:** SAT or ACT; score report by June 15.

1992 FRESHMAN CLASS PROFILE. 442 men applied, 336 accepted, 135 enrolled; 498 women applied, 403 accepted, 165 enrolled. 73% had high school GPA of 3.0 or higher, 27% between 2.0 and 2.99. 33% were in top tenth and 63% were in top quarter of graduating class. **Academic background:** Mid 50% of enrolled freshmen had SAT-V between 470-580, SAT-M between 490-600; ACT composite between 20-26. 25% submitted SAT scores, 75% submitted ACT scores. **Characteristics:** 55% from in state, 100% live in college housing, 3% have minority backgrounds, 1% are foreign students, 35% join fraternities/sororities. Average age is 18.

FALL-TERM APPLICATIONS. $15 fee. Closing date July 15; priority given to applications received by January 15; applicants notified on a rolling basis. Essay required. Interview recommended. Audition recommended for music applicants. Portfolio recommended. Interview recommended for all applicants, required at discretion of admission committee. CRDA. Deferred admission available. High school students may take limited number of classes before high school graduation.

STUDENT LIFE. Housing: Dormitories (men, women); fraternity, sorority housing available. **Activities:** Student government, film, magazine, radio, student newspaper, yearbook, literary magazine, choral groups, concert band, dance, drama, jazz band, music ensembles, musical theater, pep band, symphony orchestra, fraternities, sororities, Catholic Student Council, H-Club, Acropolis, International Relations Club, Student Activities Board, student federation, Enterprising Leaders.

ATHLETICS. NAIA, NCAA. **Intercollegiate:** Baseball M, basketball, cross-country, diving W, football M, golf M, softball W, swimming W, tennis, track and field, volleyball W. **Intramural:** Basketball, football, golf, handball, ice hockey M, lacrosse M, racquetball, skin diving, soccer, softball, squash, swimming, table tennis, tennis, track and field, volleyball, water polo, wrestling M.

STUDENT SERVICES. Career counseling, employment service for undergraduates, freshman orientation, health services, personal counseling, placement service for graduates.

ANNUAL EXPENSES. Tuition and fees (1992-93): $10,170. **Room and board:** $4,230. **Books and supplies:** $500. **Other expenses:** $800.

FINANCIAL AID. 70% of freshmen, 80% of continuing students receive some form of aid. Grants, loans, jobs available. Academic, music/drama, art, athletic, leadership scholarships available. **Aid applications:** No closing date; priority given to applications received by March 15; applicants notified on a rolling basis beginning on or about March 15; must reply within 4 weeks.

ADDRESS/TELEPHONE. Jeffrey S. Lantis, Director of Admissions, Hillsdale College, 33 East College Street, Hillsdale, MI 49242. (517) 437-7341 ext. 327. Fax: (517) 437-3923.

Hope College
Holland, Michigan

CB code: 1301

Admissions: 88% of applicants accepted
Based on:
- ••• School record, test scores
- •• Activities
- • Essay, interview, recommendations, special talents

Completion: 90% of freshmen end year in good standing
69% graduate, 27% of these enter graduate study

4-year private liberal arts college, coed, affiliated with Reformed Church in America. Founded in 1862. **Accreditation:** Regional. **Undergraduate enrollment:** 1,054 men, 1,412 women full time; 115 men, 174 women part time. **Faculty:** 233 total (173 full time), 154 with doctorates or other terminal degrees. **Location:** Suburban campus in small city; 30 miles from Grand Rapids, 160 miles from Chicago and Detroit. **Calendar:** Semester, limited summer session. **Microcomputers:** 260 located in dormitories, libraries, classrooms, computer centers, campus-wide network. **Special facilities:** Museum, 2.5 million volt accelerator, biological field station, art gallery, electron microscopes, laser research.

DEGREES OFFERED. BA, BS. 587 bachelor's degrees awarded in 1992. 19% in business and management, 5% communications, 13% teacher education, 8% letters/literature, 9% life sciences, 6% physical sciences, 5% psychology, 14% social sciences, 5% visual and performing arts.

UNDERGRADUATE MAJORS. Accounting, art history, athletic training, biochemistry, biological and physical sciences, biology, business administration and management, business and management, business economics, chemistry, classics, clinical laboratory science, communications, computer and information sciences, dance, earth sciences, economics, education, education of the emotionally handicapped, elementary education, engineering and other disciplines, engineering physics, English, fine arts, foreign languages (multiple emphasis), French, geochemistry, geology, geophysics and seismology, German, Greek (classical), history, humanities and social sciences, junior high education, Latin, liberal/general studies, mathematics, music, music history and appreciation, music performance, music theory and composition, nursing, philosophy, physical sciences, physics, political science and government, predentistry, preengineering, prelaw, premedicine, preveterinary, psychology, religion, religious music, secondary education, social sciences, sociology, Spanish, specific learning disabilities, sports medicine.

ACADEMIC PROGRAMS. Accelerated program, double major, dual enrollment of high school students, education specialist degree, independent study, internships, student-designed major, study abroad, teacher preparation, visiting/exchange student program, New York semester, Washington semester; liberal arts/career combination in engineering, health sciences. **Remedial services:** Tutoring. **Placement/credit:** AP, CLEP Subject, institutional tests; 32 credit hours maximum for bachelor's degree.

ACADEMIC REQUIREMENTS. Freshmen must earn minimum GPA of 1.6 to continue in good standing. 87% of freshmen return for sophomore year. Students must declare major by end of second year. **Graduation requirements:** 126 hours for bachelor's (30 in major). Most students required to take courses in arts/fine arts, English, foreign languages, history, humanities, mathematics, philosophy/religion, biological/physical sciences, social sciences. **Postgraduate studies:** 3% enter law school, 4% enter medical school, 2% enter MBA programs, 18% enter other graduate study. **Additional information:** Extensive undergraduate scientific research opportunities available. All fine arts divisions nationally accredited.

FRESHMAN ADMISSIONS. Selection criteria: High school achievement record, recommendations, activities, and test scores considered. Class rank in top half preferred. **High school preparation:** 16 units required. Required and recommended units include biological science 1, English 4, mathematics 2, physical science 1 and social science 2. Foreign language 2 recommended. **Test requirements:** SAT or ACT (ACT preferred).

1992 FRESHMAN CLASS PROFILE. 685 men applied, 581 accepted, 279 enrolled; 917 women applied, 823 accepted, 408 enrolled. 80% had high school GPA of 3.0 or higher, 20% between 2.0 and 2.99. 35% were in top tenth and 63% were in top quarter of graduating class. **Academic background:** Mid 50% of enrolled freshmen had SAT-V between 440-560, SAT-M between 500-640; ACT composite between 21-27. 37% submitted SAT scores, 87% submitted ACT scores. **Characteristics:** 76% from in state, 96% live in college housing, 4% have minority backgrounds, 4% are foreign students, 17% join fraternities/sororities. Average age is 18.

FALL-TERM APPLICATIONS. $25 fee, may be waived for applicants with need. No closing date; priority given to applications received by April 1; applicants notified on a rolling basis; must reply by May 1 or within 2 weeks if notified thereafter. Essay required. Interview recommended. Audition recommended for music, theater, dance applicants. Portfolio recommended for art applicants. CRDA. Deferred and early admission available.

STUDENT LIFE. Housing: Dormitories (men, women, coed); apartment, fraternity, sorority housing available. **Activities:** Student government, magazine, radio, student newspaper, television, yearbook, cable television programs, choral groups, concert band, dance, drama, jazz band, music ensembles, musical theater, pep band, symphony orchestra, fraternities, sororities, Ministry of Christ's People, Fellowship of Christian Athletes, Inter-Varsity Christian Fellowship, Fellowship of Christian Students, College Republicans, International Relations Club, Higher Horizons, academic honorary societies, Black Coalition, Hispanic Students Organization, Union of Catholic Students. **Additional information:** Strong emphasis on residential life. Some faculty and staff live on campus.

ATHLETICS. NCAA. **Intercollegiate:** Baseball M, basketball, cross-country, diving, football M, golf, lacrosse M, sailing, soccer, softball W, swimming, tennis, track and field, volleyball. **Intramural:** Badminton, basketball, fencing, racquetball, skiing, soccer W, softball, table tennis, track and field, volleyball, water polo M.

STUDENT SERVICES. Aptitude testing, career counseling, employment service for undergraduates, freshman orientation, health services, personal counseling, placement service for graduates, special adviser for adult students, services/facilities for handicapped.

ANNUAL EXPENSES. Tuition and fees (1992-93): $10,792. **Room and board:** $3,926. **Books and supplies:** $435. **Other expenses:** $800.

FINANCIAL AID. 73% of freshmen, 73% of continuing students receive some form of aid. Grants, loans, jobs available. 371 enrolled freshmen were judged to have need, all were offered aid. Academic, music/drama, art, leadership, minority scholarships available. **Aid applications:** No closing date; priority given to applications received by February 15; applicants notified on a rolling basis beginning on or about April 1; must reply by May 1 or within 4 weeks if notified thereafter.

ADDRESS/TELEPHONE. Gary Camp, Director of Admissions, Hope College, 69 East Tenth Street, Holland, MI 49423-3698. (616) 394-7850. (800) 968-7850. Fax: (616) 394-7922.

Jackson Community College
Jackson, Michigan CB code: 1340

2-year public community college, coed. Founded in 1928. **Accreditation:** Regional. **Undergraduate enrollment:** 8,000 men, 1,000 women full time; 2,000 men, 3,000 women part time. **Faculty:** 435 total (110 full time), 55 with doctorates or other terminal degrees. **Location:** Suburban campus in large town; 6 miles from downtown. **Calendar:** Semester, limited summer session. Saturday and extensive evening/early morning classes. **Microcomputers:** 140 located in libraries, classrooms, computer centers. **Special facilities:** Michigan Space Center, Dalham Environmental (nature) Center.

DEGREES OFFERED. AA, AS, AAS. 450 associate degrees awarded in 1992.

UNDERGRADUATE MAJORS. Accounting, aeronautical technology, air conditioning/heating/refrigeration mechanics, air conditioning/heating/refrigeration technology, automotive technology, business administration and management, business and management, business and office, business computer/console/peripheral equipment operation, business data entry equipment operation, business data processing and related programs, business data programming, data processing, drafting, drafting and design technology, electronic technology, engineering and engineering-related technologies, finance, fire control and safety technology, hazardous waste material technology, hotel/motel and restaurant management, industrial technology, information sciences and systems, laser electro-optic technology, law enforcement and corrections, law enforcement and corrections technologies, legal secretary, liberal/general studies, machine tool operation/machine shop, marketing and distribution, mechanical design technology, medical assistant, medical secretary, nursing, power plant operation and maintenance, precision metal work, protective services, quality control technology, radiograph medical technology, robotics, secretarial and related programs, solar heating and cooling technology, ultrasound technology, welding technology, word processing.

ACADEMIC PROGRAMS. 2-year transfer program, accelerated program, dual enrollment of high school students, independent study, internships, telecourses, weekend college. **Remedial services:** Learning center, remedial instruction, special counselor, tutoring. **Placement/credit:** AP, institutional tests.

ACADEMIC REQUIREMENTS. No policy requiring minimum GPA; records of students having academic difficulty are reviewed individually. Students must declare major by end of first year. **Graduation requirements:** 63 hours for associate. Most students required to take courses in English, humanities, mathematics, biological/physical sciences, social sciences.

FRESHMAN ADMISSIONS. Selection criteria: Open admissions. Special admissions to all allied health programs.

1992 FRESHMAN CLASS PROFILE. 512 men, 697 women enrolled. **Characteristics:** 99% from in state, 100% commute, 8% have minority backgrounds, 1% are foreign students. Average age is 28.

FALL-TERM APPLICATIONS. No fee. No closing date; applicants notified on a rolling basis. Deferred and early admission available.

STUDENT LIFE. Activities: Student government, magazine, student newspaper, choral groups, concert band, drama, jazz band, music ensembles, musical theater.

ATHLETICS. Intramural: Baseball, basketball, golf, racquetball, soccer, softball, table tennis, tennis, wrestling M.

STUDENT SERVICES. Aptitude testing, career counseling, employment service for undergraduates, freshman orientation, personal counseling, placement service for graduates, veterans counselor, services/facilities for handicapped.

ANNUAL EXPENSES. Tuition and fees (1992-93): $1,371, $346 additional for out-of-district students, $598 additional for out-of-state students. **Books and supplies:** $386. **Other expenses:** $634.

FINANCIAL AID. 92% of grants, 23% of loans, 54% of jobs based on need. Academic, music/drama, state/district residency scholarships available. **Aid applications:** No closing date; priority given to applications received by April 1; applicants notified on a rolling basis beginning on or about May 1; must reply within 2 weeks.

ADDRESS/TELEPHONE. Mark Ulseth, Director of Enrollment Services/Registrar, Jackson Community College, 2111 Emmons Road, Jackson, MI 49201. (517) 787-0800 ext. 131.

Jordan College
Cedar Springs, Michigan CB code: 1952

4-year private community, technical college, coed. Founded in 1967. **Accreditation:** Regional candidate. **Undergraduate enrollment:** 374 men, 997 women full time; 156 men, 591 women part time. **Faculty:** 183 total (51 full time), 26 with doctorates or other terminal degrees. **Location:** Rural campus in small town. **Calendar:** Semester, limited summer session. Saturday and extensive evening/early morning classes. **Microcomputers:** 200 located in libraries, classrooms. **Additional facts:** Multi-location institution with campuses in Benton Harbor, Cass City, Comstock Park, site of the Jordan Energy Institute, Detroit, Flint, Fremont, and Grand Rapids.

DEGREES OFFERED. AA, AAS, BS. 247 associate degrees awarded in 1992. 13% in business and management, 40% business/office and marketing/distribution, 11% computer sciences, 6% home economics, 16% multi/interdisciplinary studies, 11% parks/recreation, protective services, public affairs. 10 bachelor's degrees awarded. 10% in agriculture, 90% engineering technologies.

UNDERGRADUATE MAJORS. Associate: Accounting, allied health, business administration and management, business data processing and related programs, child development/care/guidance, computer programming, electromechanical technology, energy conservation and use technology, legal secretary, liberal/general studies, medical secretary, microcomputer software, recreation and community services technologies, renewable natural resources, secretarial and related programs, social work, solar heating and cooling technology, word processing. **Bachelor's:** Energy conservation and use technology, renewable natural resources.

ACADEMIC PROGRAMS. 2-year transfer program, double major, dual enrollment of high school students, independent study, internships. **Remedial services:** Reduced course load, remedial instruction, special counselor, tutoring. **Placement/credit:** AP, CLEP General and Subject, institutional tests; 15 credit hours maximum for associate degree; 30 credit hours maximum for bachelor's degree.

ACADEMIC REQUIREMENTS. Freshmen must earn minimum GPA of 1.5 to continue in good standing. 37% of freshmen return for sophomore year. Students must declare major on enrollment. **Graduation requirements:** 60 hours for associate (42 in major), 120 hours for bachelor's (85 in major). Most students required to take courses in English, humanities, mathematics, social sciences.

FRESHMAN ADMISSIONS. Selection criteria: Open admissions. **Additional information:** High school and postsecondary performance evaluated to determine student's abilities.

1992 FRESHMAN CLASS PROFILE. 450 men applied, 450 accepted, 215 enrolled; 1,091 women applied, 1,091 accepted, 484 enrolled. **Characteristics:** 99% from in state, 100% commute, 64% have minority backgrounds, 1% are foreign students. Average age is 27.

FALL-TERM APPLICATIONS. No fee. No closing date; applicants notified on a rolling basis; must reply by September 1. Interview recommended. Deferred and early admission available. ACT/ASSET scores used for course placement only.

STUDENT LIFE. Activities: Student government, student newspaper.

ATHLETICS. NSCAA. **Intercollegiate:** Basketball M. **Intramural:** Basketball M.

STUDENT SERVICES. Career counseling, employment service for undergraduates, freshman orientation, on-campus day care, personal counseling, placement service for graduates.

ANNUAL EXPENSES. Tuition and fees: $5,760. **Books and supplies:** $1,050.

FINANCIAL AID. 99% of freshmen, 99% of continuing students receive some form of aid. 70% of grants, all loans, 93% of jobs based on need. Academic, athletic scholarships available. **Aid applications:** No closing date; applicants notified on a rolling basis beginning on or about April 1; must reply within 2 weeks.

ADDRESS/TELEPHONE. Brian Yancey, Vice President of Student Services, Jordan College, 360 West Pine, Cedar Springs, MI 49319. (616) 696-1180. (800) 968-0330. Fax: (616) 696-3790.

Kalamazoo College

Kalamazoo, Michigan CB code: 1365

4-year private liberal arts college, coed, affiliated with American Baptist Churches in the USA. Founded in 1833. **Accreditation:** Regional. **Undergraduate enrollment:** 568 men, 677 women full time. **Faculty:** 110 total (90 full time), 86 with doctorates or other terminal degrees. **Location:** Suburban campus in small city; 130 miles from Detroit and Chicago. **Calendar:** Quarter, extensive summer session. **Microcomputers:** 42 located in classrooms, computer centers. **Special facilities:** 3 theaters, rare book collection, 15 foreign centers for study abroad. **Additional facts:** Foreign study centers located in Kenya, Senegal, Sierra Leone, Ecuador, Spain, France, Germany, Mexico, China, and Swaziland.

DEGREES OFFERED. BA. 250 bachelor's degrees awarded in 1992. 20% in business and management, 6% languages, 7% letters/literature, 9% life sciences, 10% physical sciences, 9% psychology, 18% social sciences, 9% visual and performing arts.

UNDERGRADUATE MAJORS. Anthropology, art history, biology, business economics, chemistry, computer and information sciences, dramatic arts, economics, English, French, German, health sciences, history, human resources development, international relations, international studies, Latin, mathematics, music, philosophy, physics, political science and government, psychology, religion, sociology, Spanish, studio art.

ACADEMIC PROGRAMS. Double major, dual enrollment of high school students, independent study, internships, study abroad, teacher preparation, visiting/exchange student program, New York semester, cross-registration; liberal arts/career combination in engineering. **Remedial services:** Tutoring. **Placement/credit:** AP, IB, institutional tests.

ACADEMIC REQUIREMENTS. Freshmen must earn minimum GPA of 2.0 to continue in good standing. 90% of freshmen return for sophomore year. Students must declare major by end of second year. **Graduation requirements:** Most students required to take courses in arts/fine arts, computer science, English, foreign languages, history, humanities, mathematics, philosophy/religion, biological/physical sciences, social sciences. **Postgraduate studies:** 3% enter law school, 4% enter medical school, 1% enter MBA programs, 9% enter other graduate study. **Additional information:** 90% of students study abroad, 85% participate in career internships at nearly 900 sites. College subsidizes foreign study expenses.

FRESHMAN ADMISSIONS. Selection criteria: Curriculum, grades, essay, recommendations, and special accomplishments influence decision. **High school preparation:** 16 units required. Recommended units include English 4, foreign language 3, mathematics 4, social science 2 and science 3. **Test requirements:** SAT or ACT; score report by April 15. ACH required of graduates of nonaccredited high schools.

1992 FRESHMAN CLASS PROFILE. 91% had high school GPA of 3.0 or higher, 9% between 2.0 and 2.99. 56% were in top tenth and 84% were in top quarter of graduating class. **Academic background:** Mid 50% of enrolled freshmen had SAT-V between 480-610, SAT-M between 520-640; ACT composite between 25-30. 68% submitted SAT scores, 91% submitted ACT scores. **Characteristics:** 75% from in state, 98% live in college housing, 11% have minority backgrounds, 2% are foreign students. Average age is 18.

FALL-TERM APPLICATIONS. $40 fee, may be waived for applicants with need. No closing date; priority given to applications received by February 15; applicants notified on a rolling basis; must reply by May 1 or within 2 weeks if notified thereafter. Essay required. Interview recommended. CRDA. Deferred and early admission available.

STUDENT LIFE. Housing: Dormitories (coed); apartment, cooperative housing available. Japanese, Spanish, German, French language houses available. **Activities:** Student government, film, magazine, radio, student newspaper, yearbook, choral groups, concert band, dance, drama, jazz band, music ensembles, musical theater, symphony orchestra, Jewish and Christian interest groups, international student and black student organizations, College Forum, Women's Equity Coalition, volunteer bureau, environmental organization, film society, Habitat for Humanity, Amnesty International, Coalition on Racial Diversity.

ATHLETICS. NCAA. **Intercollegiate:** Baseball M, basketball, cross-country, diving, football M, golf, soccer, softball W, swimming, tennis, volleyball W. **Intramural:** Badminton, basketball, bowling, fencing, golf, handball, ice hockey M, racquetball M, skiing, softball, squash, swimming, table tennis, tennis, track and field, volleyball.

STUDENT SERVICES. Aptitude testing, career counseling, employment service for undergraduates, freshman orientation, health services, personal counseling, placement service for graduates.

ANNUAL EXPENSES. Tuition and fees: $15,135. **Room and board:** $4,839. **Books and supplies:** $450. **Other expenses:** $450.

FINANCIAL AID. 94% of freshmen, 79% of continuing students receive some form of aid. 66% of grants, 94% of loans, 85% of jobs based on need. Academic, music/drama, art, leadership, minority scholarships available. **Aid applications:** Closing date May 1; priority given to applications received by February 15; applicants notified on a rolling basis beginning on or about March 15; must reply by May 1. **Additional information:** Many students are paid for career development internship and senior project experiences. Earnings can be used for college expenses.

ADDRESS/TELEPHONE. Teresa M. Lahti, Dean of Admissions, Kalamazoo College, 1200 Academy Street, Kalamazoo, MI 49006-3295. (616) 337-7166. (800) 253-3602. Fax: (616) 337-7251.

Kalamazoo Valley Community College

Kalamazoo, Michigan CB code: 1378

2-year public community college, coed. Founded in 1966. **Accreditation:** Regional. **Undergraduate enrollment:** 1,449 men, 1,500 women full time; 2,910 men, 3,778 women part time. **Faculty:** 413 total (112 full time), 6 with doctorates or other terminal degrees. **Location:** Suburban campus in small city; 132 miles from Detroit. **Calendar:** Semester, limited summer session. Saturday and extensive evening/early morning classes. **Microcomputers:** 242 located in libraries, classrooms, computer centers. **Special facilities:** Museum.

DEGREES OFFERED. AA, AS, AAS. 612 associate degrees awarded in 1992. 23% in business/office and marketing/distribution, 10% engineering technologies, 9% health sciences, 58% letters/literature.

UNDERGRADUATE MAJORS. Accounting, air conditioning/heating/refrigeration technology, allied health, automotive technology, biological and physical sciences, business administration and management, business and office, business computer/console/peripheral equipment operation, business data processing and related programs, business data programming, chemical manufacturing technology, data processing, dental hygiene, drafting and design technology, education, electrical technology, electronic technology, English, humanities and social sciences, industrial technology, international studies, law enforcement and corrections technologies, legal assistant/paralegal, legal secretary, liberal/general studies, marketing and distribution, mechanical design technology, medical assistant, medical secretary, nursing, physical sciences, plastic technology, practical nursing, precision metal work, preengineering, respiratory therapy, respiratory therapy technology, secretarial and related programs, welding technology.

ACADEMIC PROGRAMS. 2-year transfer program, cooperative education, dual enrollment of high school students, honors program, independent study, internships, telecourses, weekend college, cross-registration. **Remedial services:** Learning center, reduced course load, remedial instruction, special counselor, tutoring. **Placement/credit:** AP, institutional tests; 32 credit hours maximum for associate degree.

ACADEMIC REQUIREMENTS. No policy requiring minimum GPA; records of students having academic difficulty are reviewed individually. 50% of freshmen return for sophomore year. **Graduation requirements:** 62 hours for associate. Most students required to take courses in English, mathematics.

FRESHMAN ADMISSIONS. Selection criteria: Open admissions.

1992 FRESHMAN CLASS PROFILE. 1,938 men applied, 1,938 accepted, 903 enrolled; 2,046 women applied, 2,046 accepted, 990 enrolled. **Characteristics:** 99% from in state, 100% commute, 15% have minority backgrounds, 1% are foreign students. Average age is 20.

FALL-TERM APPLICATIONS. No fee. No closing date; applicants notified on a rolling basis. Deferred and early admission available.

STUDENT LIFE. Activities: Student newspaper, choral groups, drama, Fellowship of Christian Athletes, International Student Club, Student American Dental Hygiene Association, Data Processing Association, African American Assoication, Latino Student Association, Native American Association.

ATHLETICS. NJCAA. **Intercollegiate:** Baseball M, basketball, golf M, softball W, tennis, volleyball W. **Intramural:** Basketball M, softball M, tennis W, volleyball W.

STUDENT SERVICES. Aptitude testing, career counseling, employment service for undergraduates, freshman orientation, on-campus day care, personal counseling, placement service for graduates, services/facilities for handicapped.

ANNUAL EXPENSES. Tuition and fees (1992-93): $868, $744 additional for out-of-district students, $1,488 additional for out-of-state students. **Books and supplies:** $384. **Other expenses:** $2,415.

FINANCIAL AID. 22% of continuing students receive some form of aid. 92% of grants, 65% of loans, all jobs based on need. Academic, athletic, leadership, minority scholarships available. **Aid applications:** No closing date; applicants notified on a rolling basis beginning on or about May 1; must reply immediately.

ADDRESS/TELEPHONE. Duncan Clarkson, Director of Admissions, Kalamazoo Valley Community College, 6767 West O Avenue, Kalamazoo, MI 49009. (616) 372-5346.

Kellogg Community College

Battle Creek, Michigan CB code: 1375

2-year public community college, coed. Founded in 1956. **Accreditation:** Regional. **Undergraduate enrollment:** 724 men, 1,133 women full time; 2,447 men, 3,828 women part time. **Faculty:** 341 total (150 full time), 16 with doctorates or other terminal degrees. **Location:** Suburban campus in small city; 20 miles from Kalamazoo, 130 miles from Detroit. **Calendar:**

Semester, limited summer session. Saturday and extensive evening/early morning classes. **Microcomputers:** 200 located in libraries, classrooms, computer centers. **Additional facts:** Regional Manufacturing Technical Center Uita open entry/open exit program in 7 different technical areas.

DEGREES OFFERED. AA, AS, AAS. 500 associate degrees awarded in 1992. 9% in business and management, 5% business/office and marketing/distribution, 22% allied health, 57% multi/interdisciplinary studies.

UNDERGRADUATE MAJORS. Accounting, automotive mechanics, automotive technology, biology, botany, business administration and management, business and management, business and office, business data entry equipment operation, business data processing and related programs, business data programming, chemical engineering, chemical manufacturing technology, chemistry, commercial art, communications, computer programming, criminal justice studies, criminal justice technology, data processing, dental hygiene, drafting and design technology, education, electrical installation, electrical technology, electronic technology, elementary education, emergency medical technologies, engineering, engineering and engineering-related technologies, English, fine arts, fire control and safety technology, food sciences, hazardous waste materials technology, history, industrial engineering, industrial technology, international and comparative education, law enforcement and corrections technologies, legal assistant/paralegal, legal secretary, liberal/general studies, machine tool operation/machine shop, manufacturing technology, mathematics, medical laboratory technologies, medical secretary, music, nursing, physical therapy assistant, physics, practical nursing, precision metal work, predentistry, prelaw, premedicine, prepharmacy, preveterinary, psychology, radio/television broadcasting, radiograph medical technology, robotics, secondary education, secretarial and related programs, social sciences, social work, sociology, studio art, systems analysis, visual and performing arts, water and wastewater technology, word processing.

ACADEMIC PROGRAMS. 2-year transfer program, cooperative education, dual enrollment of high school students, honors program, independent study, telecourses, weekend college, associate degree in fire science with Kalamazoo Valley Community College, 2-1 program in elementary education with Olivet College, 3-2 program in engineering with Flint General Motors Institute 3-1 program in business administration with Davenport College. **Remedial services:** Learning center, reduced course load, remedial instruction, special counselor, tutoring. **Placement/credit:** AP, CLEP General and Subject, institutional tests; 38 credit hours maximum for associate degree.

ACADEMIC REQUIREMENTS. No policy requiring minimum GPA; records of students having academic difficulty are reviewed individually. Students must declare major on application. **Graduation requirements:** 62 hours for associate (24 in major). Most students required to take courses in English, social sciences.

FRESHMAN ADMISSIONS. Selection criteria: Open admissions. Allied health applicants must supply high school record, ACT scores, any previous college record. Recommended units include biological science 1, English 3, foreign language 1, mathematics 1, physical science 1, social science 2 and science 2. College-preparatory program recommended. **Test requirements:** ACT required of health technology applicants. **Additional information:** Qualified high school students may take classes if they meet admissions guidelines.

1992 FRESHMAN CLASS PROFILE. 863 men, 981 women enrolled. **Characteristics:** 98% from in state, 100% commute, 9% have minority backgrounds, 1% are foreign students. Average age is 21.

FALL-TERM APPLICATIONS. No fee. No closing date; priority given to applications received by August 10; applicants notified on a rolling basis. Deferred and early admission available. Closing date for health technology applications: March 1.

STUDENT LIFE. Housing: Housing lists are continuously updated. **Activities:** Student government, magazine, student newspaper, choral groups, concert band, drama, jazz band, music ensembles, theater, Christian fellowship, Minority Student Association.

ATHLETICS. NJCAA. **Intercollegiate:** Baseball M, basketball, golf, softball W, volleyball W. **Intramural:** Basketball, bowling, golf, handball, racquetball, skiing, softball, tennis, volleyball.

STUDENT SERVICES. Career counseling, employment service for undergraduates, freshman orientation, on-campus day care, personal counseling, placement service for graduates, veterans counselor, services/facilities for handicapped.

ANNUAL EXPENSES. Tuition and fees: $1,095, $672 additional for out-of-district students, $1,737 additional for out-of-state students. **Books and supplies:** $380. **Other expenses:** $1,500.

FINANCIAL AID. 60% of freshmen, 60% of continuing students receive some form of aid. 85% of grants, 81% of loans, 35% of jobs based on need. Academic, music/drama, art, athletic, leadership, minority scholarships available. **Aid applications:** No closing date; priority given to applications received by June 1; applicants notified on a rolling basis beginning on or about July 1; must reply within 2 weeks.

ADDRESS/TELEPHONE. Connie Speers, Director of Admissions, Kellogg Community College, 450 North Avenue, Battle Creek, MI 49016-3397. (616) 965-3931 ext. 2622. (800) 955-4522. Fax: (616) 965-4133.

Kendall College of Art and Design
Grand Rapids, Michigan — CB code: 1376

Admissions: 80% of applicants accepted
Based on:
- ••• School record, special talents
- •• Test scores
- • Activities, essay, interview, recommendations

Completion: 85% of freshmen end year in good standing
50% graduate, 5% of these enter graduate study

4-year private art, liberal arts college, coed. Founded in 1928. **Accreditation:** Regional. **Undergraduate enrollment:** 232 men, 223 women full time; 61 men, 114 women part time. **Faculty:** 67 total (34 full time), 45 with doctorates or other terminal degrees. **Location:** Urban campus in small city; 175 miles from Detroit. **Calendar:** Semester, limited summer session. Saturday and extensive evening/early morning classes. **Microcomputers:** 30 located in libraries, computer centers. **Special facilities:** Kendall Gallery, 35,000 title slide collection.

DEGREES OFFERED. BFA. 3 associate degrees awarded in 1992. 100% in visual and performing arts. 126 bachelor's degrees awarded in 1992. 100% in visual and performing arts.

UNDERGRADUATE MAJORS. Advertising, fine arts, furniture design, graphic design, illustration design, industrial design, interior design, visual and performing arts.

ACADEMIC PROGRAMS. Dual enrollment of high school students, independent study, internships, visiting/exchange student program, New York semester, continuing education. **Remedial services:** Reduced course load, special counselor, tutoring. **Placement/credit:** AP, CLEP General, IB.

ACADEMIC REQUIREMENTS. Freshmen must earn minimum GPA of 2.0 to continue in good standing. 66% of freshmen return for sophomore year. Students must declare major by end of first year. **Graduation requirements:** 120 hours for bachelor's (48 in major). Most students required to take courses in arts/fine arts, English, history, humanities, mathematics, philosophy/religion, biological/physical sciences, social sciences. **Postgraduate studies:** 5% enter other graduate study.

FRESHMAN ADMISSIONS. Selection criteria: High school GPA, statement of purpose, test scores, and portfolio considered in admission process. Art courses or portfolio activities considered. **Test requirements:** SAT or ACT (ACT preferred); score report by August 1.

1992 FRESHMAN CLASS PROFILE. 126 men applied, 89 accepted, 57 enrolled; 104 women applied, 96 accepted, 31 enrolled. 10% had high school GPA of 3.0 or higher, 88% between 2.0 and 2.99. 2% were in top tenth and 12% were in top quarter of graduating class. **Academic background:** Mid 50% of enrolled freshmen had ACT composite between 19-20. 95% submitted ACT scores. **Characteristics:** 94% from in state, 100% commute, 20% have minority backgrounds, 1% are foreign students. Average age is 20.

FALL-TERM APPLICATIONS. $35 fee, may be waived for applicants with need. No closing date; priority given to applications received by August 1; applicants notified on a rolling basis beginning on or about August 1; must reply within 2 weeks. Portfolio required. Interview recommended. Essay recommended. Deferred and early admission available.

STUDENT LIFE. Housing: Referral service for roommates and apartments. **Activities:** Student government, student newspaper.

STUDENT SERVICES. Career counseling, employment service for undergraduates, freshman orientation, personal counseling, placement service for graduates, special adviser for adult students, veterans counselor, services/facilities for handicapped.

ANNUAL EXPENSES. Tuition and fees: $9,650. **Books and supplies:** $1,400. **Other expenses:** $990.

FINANCIAL AID. 73% of freshmen, 70% of continuing students receive some form of aid. 86% of grants, 90% of loans, all jobs based on need. 73 enrolled freshmen were judged to have need, all were offered aid. Academic, art scholarships available. **Aid applications:** No closing date; priority given to applications received by February 15; applicants notified on a rolling basis beginning on or about April 15; must reply within 30 days.

ADDRESS/TELEPHONE. Geoff Kehoe, Director of Enrollment Management, Kendall College of Art and Design, 111 Division Avenue North, Grand Rapids, MI 49503-3194. (616) 451-2787. (800) 676-2787. Fax: (616) 451-9867.

Kirtland Community College
Roscommon, Michigan — CB code: 1382

2-year public community college, coed. Founded in 1966. **Accreditation:** Regional. **Undergraduate enrollment:** 266 men, 340 women full time; 185 men, 518 women part time. **Faculty:** 95 total (39 full time). **Location:** Rural campus in rural community; 11 miles from Roscommon, 8 miles from St. Helen. **Calendar:** Semester, extensive summer session. **Microcomputers:** 65 located in libraries, classrooms, computer centers. **Special facilities:** Fitness and nature trail.

DEGREES OFFERED. AA, AS, AAS. 167 associate degrees awarded in 1992. 10% in business and management, 13% business/office and market-

ing/distribution, 18% health sciences, 27% multi/interdisciplinary studies, 16% parks/recreation, protective services, public affairs, 15% trade and industry.

UNDERGRADUATE MAJORS. Accounting, aircraft mechanics, automotive mechanics, automotive technology, business administration and management, business and office, computer and information sciences, cosmetology, criminal justice technology, drafting, drafting and design technology, drafting and design/manufacturing processes, education, engineering, finance, fire control and safety technology, law enforcement and corrections technologies, legal secretary, liberal/general studies, machine tool operation/machine shop, manufacturing technology, marketing management, medical secretary, multitechnology drafting and welding, nursing, physics, predentistry, prelaw, premedicine, prepharmacy, preveterinary, real estate, secretarial and related programs, word processing.

ACADEMIC PROGRAMS. 2-year transfer program, accelerated program, cooperative education, dual enrollment of high school students, internships. **Remedial services:** Learning center, reduced course load, remedial instruction, special counselor, tutoring, tutoring for dyslexic students. **Placement/credit:** AP, CLEP Subject, institutional tests; 45 credit hours maximum for associate degree.

ACADEMIC REQUIREMENTS. Freshmen must earn minimum GPA of 2.0 to continue in good standing. 50% of freshmen return for sophomore year. Students must declare major on enrollment. **Graduation requirements:** 60 hours for associate (45 in major). Most students required to take courses in English, humanities, mathematics, social sciences.

FRESHMAN ADMISSIONS. Selection criteria: Open admissions. Selective admission to nursing (levels I and II), and precorrections programs. Aviation Maintenance Technology, Criminal Justice Administation, Criminal Justice Pre-Service, and Corrections Administration; also have selective admission. **High school preparation:** 10 units recommended. Recommended units include biological science 1, English 4, mathematics 2, physical science 1 and social science 2.

1992 FRESHMAN CLASS PROFILE. 105 men, 161 women enrolled. **Characteristics:** 100% from in state, 100% commute, 1% have minority backgrounds. Average age is 29.

FALL-TERM APPLICATIONS. No fee. No closing date; applicants notified on a rolling basis beginning on or about May 1. Deferred and early admission available.

STUDENT LIFE. Housing: Privately-owned rental apartments available near campus. **Activities:** Student government, student newspaper, choral groups, drama, Student Senate, Phi Theta Kappa Honor Society, Christian Fellowship, Republican Club, Criminal Justice Club, Baseball Club, Archery Club.

STUDENT SERVICES. Aptitude testing, career counseling, employment service for undergraduates, freshman orientation, personal counseling, placement service for graduates, special adviser for adult students, veterans counselor, special needs counselor, services/facilities for handicapped.

ANNUAL EXPENSES. Tuition and fees: $1,380, $495 additional for out-of-district students, $1,200 additional for out-of-state students. **Books and supplies:** $415. **Other expenses:** $915.

FINANCIAL AID. 75% of freshmen, 74% of continuing students receive some form of aid. 94% of grants, 95% of loans, 71% of jobs based on need. Academic scholarships available. **Aid applications:** No closing date; priority given to applications received by May 15; applicants notified on a rolling basis beginning on or about April 1; must reply by May 1 or within 1 week if notified thereafter.

ADDRESS/TELEPHONE. Cary Vajda, Dean of Student Services, Kirtland Community College, 10775 North St. Helen Road, Roscommon, MI 48653. (517) 275-5121 ext. 284.

Lake Michigan College
Benton Harbor, Michigan — CB code: 1137

2-year public community college, coed. Founded in 1946. **Accreditation:** Regional. **Undergraduate enrollment:** 369 men, 588 women full time; 1,109 men, 1,750 women part time. **Faculty:** 267 total (67 full time), 20 with doctorates or other terminal degrees. **Location:** Rural campus in large town; 40 miles from South Bend, Indiana, 90 miles from Chicago. **Calendar:** Semester, limited summer session. Saturday and extensive evening/early morning classes. **Microcomputers:** 100 located in computer centers. **Special facilities:** Video production facility, nature area, art gallery, fitness center. **Additional facts:** Full service campus located in Niles, Michigan, with additional off-campus offerings at Van Buren Voc-Tech center, South Haven River Valley and Berren Springs high schools

DEGREES OFFERED. AA, AS, AAS. 270 associate degrees awarded in 1992.

UNDERGRADUATE MAJORS. Accounting, biological and physical sciences, biology, business administration and management, business and management, business and office, business data processing and related programs, business data programming, business education, chemistry, computer and information sciences, dental assistant, dental hygiene, drafting, drafting and design technology, education, electrical and electronics equipment repair, electromechanical technology, electronic technology, elementary education, engineering, engineering and engineering-related technologies, engineering and other disciplines, English, finance, fine arts, foreign languages (multiple emphasis), French, geography, German, hazardous materials technician, history, hospitality and recreation marketing, humanities and social sciences, industrial arts education, industrial technology, law enforcement and corrections, law enforcement and corrections technologies, legal secretary, liberal/general studies, machine tool operation/machine shop, manufacturing technology, marketing and distribution, mathematics, mechanical design technology, medical assistant, medical laboratory technologies, medical secretary, music, nursing, occupational therapy assistant, office supervision and management, physical education, physical sciences, physics, political science and government, practical nursing, predentistry, prelaw, premedicine, prepharmacy, preveterinary, psychology, radiograph medical technology, retailing, secondary education, secretarial and related programs, social sciences, sociology, Spanish, trade and industrial supervision and management, visual and performing arts, water and wastewater technology, word processing.

ACADEMIC PROGRAMS. 2-year transfer program, cooperative education, dual enrollment of high school students, honors program, telecourses, weekend college. **Remedial services:** Learning center, remedial instruction, special counselor, tutoring. **Placement/credit:** AP, CLEP General and Subject, institutional tests; 30 credit hours maximum for associate degree.

ACADEMIC REQUIREMENTS. Freshmen must earn minimum GPA of 2.0 to continue in good standing. 50% of freshmen return for sophomore year. Students must declare major on application. **Graduation requirements:** 61 hours for associate. Most students required to take courses in English, history.

FRESHMAN ADMISSIONS. Selection criteria: Open admissions. Selective admissions to health sciences programs based on 2.5 high school GPA in academic subjects. **Additional information:** LMC has adopted a mandatory Testing and Placement Testing (Asset).

1992 FRESHMAN CLASS PROFILE. 328 men, 455 women enrolled. **Characteristics:** 99% from in state, 100% commute, 18% have minority backgrounds, 1% are foreign students.

FALL-TERM APPLICATIONS. No fee. No closing date; applicants notified on a rolling basis. Interview required for dental assistant, radiologic technology, nursing applicants. Early admission available. ACT Asset required of all new students; mandatory placement based on test scores.

STUDENT LIFE. Activities: Student government, student newspaper, choral groups, concert band, drama, jazz band, music ensembles, fraternities, sororities.

ATHLETICS. NJCAA. **Intercollegiate:** Baseball M, basketball, golf M, softball W, volleyball W. **Intramural:** Badminton, baseball M, basketball, bowling, softball, table tennis, tennis, volleyball.

STUDENT SERVICES. Career counseling, employment service for undergraduates, health services, personal counseling, placement service for graduates, veterans counselor, services/facilities for handicapped.

ANNUAL EXPENSES. Tuition and fees (projected): $1,230, $300 additional for out-of-district students, $600 additional for out-of-state students. **Books and supplies:** $500. **Other expenses:** $950.

FINANCIAL AID. 30% of freshmen, 24% of continuing students receive some form of aid. 90% of grants, 58% of jobs based on need. Academic, music/drama, art, athletic, state/district residency, leadership, minority scholarships available. **Aid applications:** No closing date; priority given to applications received by June 1; applicants notified on a rolling basis; must reply within 2 weeks.

ADDRESS/TELEPHONE. Sherry Hoadley Pries, Director Enrollment Management, Lake Michigan College, 2755 East Napier, Benton Harbor, MI 49022-1899. (616) 927-3571 ext. 261. Fax: (616) 927-4491.

Lake Superior State University
Sault Ste. Marie, Michigan — CB code: 1421

Admissions:	77% of applicants accepted
Based on:	••• School record
	• Activities, essay, interview, recommendations, test scores
Completion:	62% of freshmen end year in good standing
	60% graduate, 10% of these enter graduate study

4-year public engineering, nursing college, coed. Founded in 1946. **Accreditation:** Regional. **Undergraduate enrollment:** 2,435 men and women full time; 619 men and women part time. **Graduate enrollment:** 312 men and women. **Faculty:** 179 total (116 full time), 51 with doctorates or other terminal degrees. **Location:** Suburban campus in large town; 280 miles from Lansing. **Calendar:** Semester, limited summer session. **Microcomputers:** 190 located in dormitories, libraries, classrooms, computer centers. **Special facilities:** Fish hatchery, aquatics research laboratory, planetarium, natural science museum, 200-acre biology station, 5 industrial robots, indoor rifle range, indoor ice arena. **Additional facts:** Michigan's smallest state university No teaching assistants.

DEGREES OFFERED. BA, BS, MBA. 155 associate degrees awarded in 1992. 14% in business/office and marketing/distribution, 6% computer sciences, 17% engineering technologies, 34% parks/recreation, protective services, public affairs, 19% social sciences. 420 bachelor's degrees awarded. 20% in business and management, 14% engineering technologies, 13% health sciences, 5% life sciences, 8% multi/interdisciplinary studies, 23% parks/recreation, protective services, public affairs, 6% social sciences. Graduate degrees offered in 1 major field of study.

UNDERGRADUATE MAJORS. Associate: Accounting, business and management, business and office, business data processing and related programs, chemistry, child development/care/guidance, computer and information sciences, computer technology, criminal justice studies, drafting and design technology, electrical technology, fire control and safety technology, law enforcement and corrections, legal assistant/paralegal, legal secretary, liberal/general studies, mechanical engineering technology, mental health/human services, office supervision and management, renewable natural resources, secretarial and related programs, water and wastewater technology. **Bachelor's:** Accounting, biology, business administration and management, business and management, business and office, business economics, computer mathematics, conservation and regulation, criminal justice studies, economics, electrical technology, English, English literature, environmental science, exercise science, finance, fire control and safety technology, fishing and fisheries, forensic studies, geology, history, hotel/motel and restaurant management, information sciences and systems, law enforcement and corrections, legal assistant/paralegal, management information systems, marketing and distribution, marketing management, mathematics, mechanical engineering technology, medical laboratory technologies, mental health/human services, nursing, office supervision and management, parks and recreation management, political science and government, predentistry, prelaw, premedicine, preveterinary, psychology, recreation therapy, robotics, social sciences, social work, sociology, tourism, wildlife management.

ACADEMIC PROGRAMS. 2-year transfer program, cooperative education, double major, dual enrollment of high school students, independent study, internships, telecourses, cross-registration; combined bachelor's/graduate program in business administration. **Remedial services:** Reduced course load, remedial instruction, special counselor, tutoring, study skills program, reading laboratory, writing laboratory, and mathematics laboratory. **Placement/credit:** AP, CLEP General and Subject, institutional tests; 30 credit hours maximum for associate degree; 30 credit hours maximum for bachelor's degree.

ACADEMIC REQUIREMENTS. Freshmen must earn minimum GPA of 1.81 to continue in good standing. 59% of freshmen return for sophomore year. Students must declare major on application. **Graduation requirements:** 62 hours for associate (20 in major), 124 hours for bachelor's (50 in major). Most students required to take courses in English, humanities, mathematics, biological/physical sciences, social sciences. **Postgraduate studies:** 20% from 2-year programs enter 4-year programs.

FRESHMAN ADMISSIONS. Selection criteria: School achievement most important. Test scores and recommendations considered when applicant's academic record is marginal. Academic courses only in GPA for high school students. **High school preparation:** 14 units recommended. Recommended units include biological science 1, English 4, foreign language 2, mathematics 3, physical science 1 and social science 3. Specific academic units required vary by college program. **Test requirements:** ACT for counseling; score report by August 16. **Additional information:** Each freshman applicant's high school GPA recalculated using academic subjects only.

1992 FRESHMAN CLASS PROFILE. 1,403 men and women applied, 1,086 accepted; 495 enrolled. 32% had high school GPA of 3.0 or higher, 68% between 2.0 and 2.99. 10% were in top tenth and 29% were in top quarter of graduating class. **Characteristics:** 92% from in state, 67% commute, 8% have minority backgrounds, 2% are foreign students, 4% join fraternities/sororities.

FALL-TERM APPLICATIONS. $20 fee, may be waived for applicants with need. Closing date August 2; applicants notified on a rolling basis; must reply immediately. Interview recommended. Deferred admission available. Applications may close early if capacity met.

STUDENT LIFE. Housing: Dormitories (men, women, coed); apartment, fraternity, sorority housing available. College mobile home park available. **Activities:** Student government, radio, student newspaper, television, yearbook, choral groups, concert band, drama, jazz band, music ensembles, musical theater, pep band, symphony orchestra, fraternities, sororities, Campus Crusade for Christ, HIS House Christian Fellowship, Newman Center, Anchor House Christian Fellowship, Native American Students' Council, political science club, BACCHUS, Student Senate, Environmental Awareness Club, Nordic Ski Club. **Additional information:** Outdoor activities important.

ATHLETICS. NCAA. **Intercollegiate:** Basketball, cross-country, golf M, ice hockey M, softball W, tennis, track and field, volleyball W, wrestling M. **Intramural:** Badminton, basketball, bowling, ice hockey M, racquetball, rifle, softball, tennis, track and field, volleyball, water polo, wrestling M.

STUDENT SERVICES. Aptitude testing, career counseling, employment service for undergraduates, freshman orientation, health services, on-campus day care, personal counseling, placement service for graduates.

ANNUAL EXPENSES. Tuition and fees (projected): $2,880, $2,730 additional for out-of-state students. **Room and board:** $4,080. **Books and supplies:** $500. **Other expenses:** $600.

FINANCIAL AID. 70% of freshmen, 67% of continuing students receive some form of aid. 76% of grants, 82% of loans, 37% of jobs based on need. 350 enrolled freshmen were judged to have need, 340 were offered aid. Academic, athletic, state/district residency, leadership, minority scholarships available. **Aid applications:** No closing date; priority given to applications received by April 1; applicants notified on a rolling basis beginning on or about April 15; must reply within 2 weeks.

ADDRESS/TELEPHONE. Bruce R. Johnson, Dean of Admissions, Lake Superior State University, 1000 College Drive, Sault Ste. Marie, MI 49783. (906) 635-2231. Fax: (906) 635-2111.

Lansing Community College
Lansing, Michigan — CB code: 1414

2-year public community college, coed. Founded in 1957. **Accreditation:** Regional. **Undergraduate enrollment:** 3,772 men, 5,078 women full time; 5,617 men, 7,137 women part time. **Faculty:** 1,050 total (204 full time). **Location:** Urban campus in small city; 90 miles from Detroit. Saturday and extensive evening/early morning classes. **Microcomputers:** Located in libraries, computer centers. **Special facilities:** Planetarium, observatory, science concepts laboratory, computer-integrated manufacturing institute, in-depth photography institute, truck driver training range, technical library. **Additional facts:** Largest single-campus community college in Michigan.

DEGREES OFFERED. AA, AS, AAS. 1,700 associate degrees awarded in 1992.

UNDERGRADUATE MAJORS. Accounting, advertising, aeronautical technology, Afro-American (black) studies, air conditioning/heating/refrigeration mechanics, air conditioning/heating/refrigeration technology, aircraft mechanics, airframe and power plant, airline piloting and navigation, American literature, anthropology, applied mathematics, art education, automotive mechanics, automotive technology, avionics technology, biological and physical sciences, biology, biomedical equipment technology, business administration and management, business and management, business and office, business computer/console/peripheral equipment operation, business data entry equipment operation, business data processing and related programs, business data programming, carpentry, chemistry, child development/care/guidance, cinematography/film, civil technology, commercial art, communications, computer and information sciences, computer graphics, computer programming, computer servicing technology, computer technology, construction, court reporting, criminal justice studies, dance, data processing, dental assistant, dental hygiene, diesel engine mechanics, digital electronics, drafting, drafting and design technology, dramatic arts, drawing, education, educational media technology, electrical and electronics equipment repair, electrical installation, electrical technology, electromechanical technology, electronic technology, elementary education, emergency medical technologies, energy conservation and use technology, engineering, engineering and engineering-related technologies, English, English education, environmental science, fashion merchandising, finance, fine arts, fire control and safety technology, food management, food production/management/services, foreign languages (multiple emphasis), foreign languages education, French, geographic resource and environmental technology, geography, geriatric aide, German, gerontology, graphic and printing production, graphic arts technology, graphic design, history, home economics, hospitality and recreation marketing, hotel/motel and restaurant management, humanities, illustration design, industrial equipment maintenance and repair, industrial supervision, industrial technology, insurance and risk management, insurance marketing, interior design, international business management, interpreter for the deaf, journalism, landscape architecture, law enforcement and corrections, law enforcement and corrections technologies, legal assistant/paralegal, legal secretary, liberal/general studies, machine tool operation/machine shop, management information systems, manufacturing technology, marketing and distribution, marketing management, masonry/tile setting, mathematics, mathematics education, mechanical design technology, media studies, medical assistant, medical laboratory technologies, medical records administration, medical secretary, mental health/human services, microcomputer software, millwright, motion picture technology, music, music education, music performance, music theory and composition, musical theater, numerical control programmer, nursing, occupational therapy, oceanographic technologies, office supervision and management, painting, personal services, personnel management, philosophy, photographic technology, photography, physical education, physical therapy, physician's assistant, physics, plastic technology, plumbing/pipefitting/steamfitting, political science and government, practical nursing, precision metal work, predentistry, prelaw, premedicine, prepharmacy, preveterinary, protective services, psychology, public affairs, quality control technology, radio/television broadcasting, radio/television technology, radiograph medical technology, real estate, recreation and community services technologies, religion, respiratory therapy, respiratory therapy technology, retailing, robotics, science education, science technologies, secondary education, secretarial and related programs, social science education, social sciences, social studies education, social work, sociology, solar heating and cooling technology, Spanish, special education, speech pathology/audiology, speech/communication/theater education, sports medicine, studio art, surgical technology, survey and mapping technology, systems analysis, telecommunications, tourism, trade and industrial education, transportation and travel marketing, transportation management, ultrasound technology, visual and performing arts, welding technology, word processing.

ACADEMIC PROGRAMS. 2-year transfer program, accelerated program, cooperative education, double major, dual enrollment of high school students, honors program, independent study, internships, study abroad, teacher preparation, telecourses, visiting/exchange student program, weekend college, cross-registration, external bachelor's degree with Northwood Institute. **Remedial services:** Learning center, preadmission summer program, reduced course load, remedial instruction, special counselor, tutoring, special programs for disadvantaged students. **ROTC:** Air Force, Army. **Placement/credit:** AP, CLEP General and Subject, institutional tests; 60 credit hours maximum for associate degree.

ACADEMIC REQUIREMENTS. Freshmen must earn minimum GPA of 1.9 to continue in good standing. 62% of freshmen return for sophomore year. **Graduation requirements:** 90 hours for associate (30 in major). Most students required to take courses in social sciences.

FRESHMAN ADMISSIONS. Selection criteria: Open admissions. Selective admission of foreign students, and for health program and aviation applicants. **Test requirements:** Michigan State University Test of English as a Second Language required of foreign students. TOEFL also accepted for foreign students.

1992 FRESHMAN CLASS PROFILE. 4,313 men and women enrolled. 31% had high school GPA of 3.0 or higher, 53% between 2.0 and 2.99. **Characteristics:** 99% from in state, 100% commute, 11% have minority backgrounds, 1% are foreign students. Average age is 25.

FALL-TERM APPLICATIONS. $10 fee. Closing date September 20; priority given to applications received by May 15; applicants notified on a rolling basis. Interview required for health program, foreign applicants. Audition recommended for music, dance, theater applicants. Portfolio recommended for art applicants. Deferred and early admission available.

STUDENT LIFE. Activities: Student government, film, radio, student newspaper, television, choral groups, concert band, dance, drama, jazz band, music ensembles, musical theater, symphony orchestra, Newman Club, Black Student Delegates, Hispanic Club, Campus Disciples, Baptist Student Union, International Club, Maranatha Christian Fellowship, OWLS, Student Adviser Club, Substance Abuse Association.

ATHLETICS. NJCAA. **Intercollegiate:** Basketball, cross-country, golf, track and field, volleyball W. **Intramural:** Basketball, bowling, boxing M.

STUDENT SERVICES. Aptitude testing, career counseling, employment service for undergraduates, freshman orientation, personal counseling, placement service for graduates, special adviser for adult students, veterans counselor, women's resource center, center for ageing education, center for student support, services/facilities for handicapped.

ANNUAL EXPENSES. Tuition and fees (projected): $1,260, $780 additional for out-of-district students, $1,590 additional for out-of-state students. **Books and supplies:** $650. **Other expenses:** $1,000.

FINANCIAL AID. 35% of freshmen, 35% of continuing students receive some form of aid. 93% of grants, 86% of loans, 31% of jobs based on need. 2,923 enrolled freshmen were judged to have need, all were offered aid. Academic, music/drama, art, athletic, state/district residency, leadership, minority scholarships available. **Aid applications:** No closing date; priority given to applications received by July 1; applicants notified on a rolling basis beginning on or about April 1; must reply within 2 weeks. **Additional information:** Short-term loans available on limited basis.

ADDRESS/TELEPHONE. Daniel LaFave, Director of Admissions, Lansing Community College, 422 North Washington Square, Lansing, MI 48901. (517) 483-1200.

Lawrence Technological University

Southfield, Michigan — CB code: 1399

4-year private university and business college, coed. Founded in 1932. **Accreditation:** Regional. **Undergraduate enrollment:** 1,809 men, 536 women full time; 1,723 men, 530 women part time. **Graduate enrollment:** 134 men, 5 women full time; 182 men, 88 women part time. **Faculty:** 307 total (112 full time), 68 with doctorates or other terminal degrees. **Location:** Suburban campus in small city; 20 miles from downtown Detroit. **Calendar:** Quarter, limited summer session. **Microcomputers:** 200 located in libraries, classrooms, computer centers. **Additional facts:** 5-year program leading to bachelor of architecture and 2-year bachelor of science in technology offered.

DEGREES OFFERED. AS, BS, BArch, MBA. 41 associate degrees awarded in 1992. 7% in computer sciences, 93% engineering technologies. 741 bachelor's degrees awarded. 13% in architecture and environmental design, 28% business and management, 47% engineering, 8% engineering technologies. Graduate degrees offered in 1 major field of study.

UNDERGRADUATE MAJORS. Associate: Chemical manufacturing technology, civil technology, computer and information sciences, electrical technology, industrial technology, mechanical design technology, mechanical engineering technology. **Bachelor's:** Accounting, architecture, business administration and management, business and management, chemistry, civil engineering, computer and information sciences, computer mathematics, electrical/electronics/communications engineering, engineering and engineering-related technologies, engineering and other disciplines, finance, human resources development, humanities, humanities and social sciences, information sciences and systems, insurance and risk management, interior design, management information systems, marketing management, mathematics, mechanical engineering, physics, prelaw, small business management and ownership, technology.

ACADEMIC PROGRAMS. Cooperative education, dual enrollment of high school students, independent study, internships, study abroad, combined associate/bachelor's degree programs in business administration and humanities. **Remedial services:** Preadmission summer program, reduced course load, remedial instruction, tutoring. **ROTC:** Air Force, Army. **Placement/credit:** AP, CLEP Subject, institutional tests.

ACADEMIC REQUIREMENTS. Freshmen must earn minimum GPA of 2.0 to continue in good standing. 88% of freshmen return for sophomore year. Students must declare major on application. **Graduation requirements:** 105 hours for associate, 199 hours for bachelor's. Most students required to take courses in computer science, English, humanities, mathematics, biological/physical sciences, social sciences. **Postgraduate studies:** 40% from 2-year programs enter 4-year programs.

FRESHMAN ADMISSIONS. Selection criteria: School achievement record. Minimum 2.0 GPA in English, mathematics, natural sciences, social studies. Minimum 2.5 GPA in 4 academic areas combined. Minimum school GPA 2.0 for business administration, industrial management, humanities (natural science courses excluded), and associate degree programs. **High school preparation:** 12.5 units required. Required units include English 4, mathematics 3.5, physical science 2 and social science 3. Programs in engineering, architecture, chemistry, computer science, and mathematics require 2 algebra, 1 geometry, .5 trigonometry, 1 physics. One chemistry required for all but architecture. Programs in business, industrial management, and humanities require 1.5 algebra, 1 laboratory science. Remedial courses available for any deficiencies. **Test requirements:** ACT for counseling; score report by August 1.

1992 FRESHMAN CLASS PROFILE. 575 men, 224 women enrolled. **Academic background:** Mid 50% of enrolled freshmen had ACT composite between 20-25. 67% submitted ACT scores. **Characteristics:** 90% from in state, 93% commute, 19% have minority backgrounds, 2% are foreign students. Average age is 18.

FALL-TERM APPLICATIONS. $30 fee. Closing date August 1; applicants notified on a rolling basis. Portfolio required for architecture applicants. Interview recommended. Essay recommended. CRDA. Deferred and early admission available. Institutional early decision plan.

STUDENT LIFE. Housing: Apartment, fraternity housing available. **Activities:** Student government, magazine, student newspaper, television, choral groups, drama, fraternities, sororities, Christian fellowship, Association of Black Students, Chess Club, Ski Club, 4 honor societies, 18 professional societies including Society of Women Engineers.

ATHLETICS. NCAA. **Intercollegiate:** Bowling. **Intramural:** Baseball, bowling, skiing, soccer M, softball W, table tennis.

STUDENT SERVICES. Aptitude testing, career counseling, employment service for undergraduates, freshman orientation, personal counseling, placement service for graduates, veterans counselor, services/facilities for handicapped.

ANNUAL EXPENSES. Tuition and fees: $6,975. **Room and board:** $2,400 room only. **Books and supplies:** $1,300. **Other expenses:** $800.

FINANCIAL AID. 60% of freshmen, 62% of continuing students receive some form of aid. 76% of grants, 95% of loans, 20% of jobs based on need. 378 enrolled freshmen were judged to have need, all were offered aid. Academic, minority scholarships available. **Aid applications:** Closing date September 1; priority given to applications received by June 1; applicants notified on a rolling basis beginning on or about April 1; must reply within 4 weeks.

ADDRESS/TELEPHONE. Timothy Kennedy, Director of Admissions, Lawrence Technological University, 21000 West Ten Mile Road, Southfield, MI 48075-1058. (313) 356-0200 ext. 3166. Fax: (313) 356-0200 ext. 4017.

Lewis College of Business

Detroit, Michigan — CB code: 1425

2-year private business, junior college, coed. Founded in 1874. **Accreditation:** Regional. **Undergraduate enrollment:** 45 men, 153 women full time; 28 men, 96 women part time. **Faculty:** 30 total (10 full time), 2 with doctorates or other terminal degrees. **Location:** Urban campus in very large city; 50 miles from Ann Arbor, 90 miles from Lansing. **Calendar:** Semester, extensive summer session. Saturday and extensive evening/early morning classes. **Microcomputers:** 50 located in libraries, classrooms. **Special facilities:** Slave trade special collections.

DEGREES OFFERED. AA. 26 associate degrees awarded in 1992. 53% in business and management, 21% computer sciences, 26% multi/interdisciplinary studies.

UNDERGRADUATE MAJORS. Accounting, business and office, business data processing and related programs, secretarial and related programs.

ACADEMIC PROGRAMS. Accelerated program, double major, honors program, independent study. **Remedial services:** Learning center, reduced course load, remedial instruction, special counselor, tutoring. **Placement/credit:** AP; 30 credit hours maximum for associate degree.

ACADEMIC REQUIREMENTS. Freshmen must earn minimum GPA of 2.0 to continue in good standing. 60% of freshmen return for sophomore year. Students must declare major on application. **Graduation requirements:** 62 hours for associate (62 in major). Most students required to take courses in computer science, English, mathematics, social sciences.

FRESHMAN ADMISSIONS. Selection criteria: Open admissions.

1992 FRESHMAN CLASS PROFILE. 214 men applied, 193 accepted, 49 enrolled; 643 women applied, 610 accepted, 146 enrolled. **Characteristics:** 98% from in state, 100% commute, 99% have minority backgrounds, 1% are foreign students, 1% join fraternities/sororities. Average age is 21.

FALL-TERM APPLICATIONS. $10 fee. No closing date; applicants notified on a rolling basis beginning on or about August 30. Interview required.

STUDENT LIFE. Activities: Student government, radio, student newspaper, choral groups, drama, sororities.

STUDENT SERVICES. Career counseling, employment service for undergraduates, freshman orientation, personal counseling, placement service for graduates, special adviser for adult students, veterans counselor.

ANNUAL EXPENSES. Tuition and fees (1992-93): $4,900. **Books and supplies:** $500.

FINANCIAL AID. 98% of freshmen, 98% of continuing students receive some form of aid.

ADDRESS/TELEPHONE. Frank DeShazor, Director of Admissions, Lewis College of Business, 17370 Meyers Road, Detroit, MI 48235. (313) 862-6300 ext. 230. Fax: (313) 862-1027.

Macomb Community College
Warren, Michigan CB code: 1722

2-year public community college, coed. Founded in 1954. **Accreditation:** Regional. **Undergraduate enrollment:** 28,465 men and women. **Faculty:** 784 total (338 full time), 37 with doctorates or other terminal degrees. **Location:** Suburban campus in small city; 20 miles from Detroit. **Calendar:** Semester, limited summer session. **Microcomputers:** 475 located in libraries, classrooms, computer centers. **Special facilities:** Nature preserves.

DEGREES OFFERED. AA, AAS. 2,900 associate degrees awarded in 1992.

UNDERGRADUATE MAJORS. Accounting, aeronautical technology, air conditioning/heating/refrigeration mechanics, air conditioning/heating/refrigeration technology, aircraft mechanics, architectural technologies, automotive mechanics, automotive technology, business administration and management, business and management, business and office, business data processing and related programs, carpentry, child development/care/guidance, civil technology, commercial art, computer and information sciences, construction, criminal justice technology, diesel engine mechanics, drafting, drafting and design technology, electrical and electronics equipment repair, electromechanical technology, electronic technology, emergency medical technologies, engineering and engineering-related technologies, fashion merchandising, finance, fire control and safety technology, geriatric aide, graphic and printing production, graphic arts technology, industrial technology, instrumentation technology, labor/industrial relations, law enforcement and corrections technologies, legal assistant/paralegal, legal secretary, liberal/general studies, management science, manufacturing technology, marketing and distribution, masonry/tile setting, mechanical design technology, medical assistant, medical secretary, mental health/human services, metallurgy, nursing, photography, physical therapy assistant, plastic technology, plumbing/pipefitting/steamfitting, power plant operation and maintenance, predentistry, preengineering, prelaw, premedicine, prepharmacy, preveterinary, protective services, respiratory therapy, respiratory therapy technology, robotics, secretarial and related programs, trade and industrial supervision and management, veterinarian's assistant, welding technology, word processing.

ACADEMIC PROGRAMS. 2-year transfer program, cooperative education, dual enrollment of high school students, independent study, internships, study abroad, weekend college, cross-registration. **Remedial services:** Learning center, reduced course load, remedial instruction, special counselor, tutoring, computer-assisted instruction. **Placement/credit:** AP, CLEP General and Subject, institutional tests; 47 credit hours maximum for associate degree.

ACADEMIC REQUIREMENTS. No policy requiring minimum GPA; records of students having academic difficulty are reviewed individually. 61% of freshmen return for sophomore year. Students must declare major by end of first year. **Graduation requirements:** 62 hours for associate. Most students required to take courses in English, humanities, mathematics, biological/physical sciences, social sciences. **Additional information:** Courses toward bachelor's degrees offered on campus by University of Detroit, Walsh College of Accountancy and Business Administration, Wayne State University, Central Michigan University, and Oakland University.

FRESHMAN ADMISSIONS. Selection criteria: Open admissions. Selective admissions to nursing and physical therapy assistant programs. Combination of GPA and test scores considered. **Test requirements:** Asset Form B required for placement for nursing and physical therapy assistant.

1992 FRESHMAN CLASS PROFILE. 3,500 men and women enrolled. **Characteristics:** 99% from in state, 100% commute, 5% have minority backgrounds, 1% are foreign students. Average age is 19.

FALL-TERM APPLICATIONS. No fee. Closing date August 12; applicants notified on a rolling basis. Deferred and early admission available. February 28 closing date for nursing and physical therapy assistant programs.

STUDENT LIFE. Activities: Student government, choral groups, concert band, dance, drama, jazz band, music ensembles, musical theater, symphony orchestra, educational and cultural series, religious organizations, Student Activities Council.

ATHLETICS. NJCAA. **Intercollegiate:** Baseball M, basketball M, cross-country, golf M, soccer M, softball W, tennis, track and field, volleyball W. **Intramural:** Basketball, racquetball, volleyball.

STUDENT SERVICES. Aptitude testing, career counseling, employment service for undergraduates, freshman orientation, health services, personal counseling, placement service for graduates, barrier-free campus, special career development program for handicapped and disadvantaged students, displaced homemakers program, services/facilities for handicapped.

ANNUAL EXPENSES. Tuition and fees (1992-93): $1,380, $750 additional for out-of-district students, $1,200 additional for out-of-state students. **Books and supplies:** $440. **Other expenses:** $700.

FINANCIAL AID. 15% of freshmen, 11% of continuing students receive some form of aid. 98% of grants, all loans, all jobs based on need. Academic, music/drama, athletic, leadership, minority scholarships available. **Aid applications:** No closing date; priority given to applications received by May 1; applicants notified on a rolling basis.

ADDRESS/TELEPHONE. James W. Varty, Dean of Academic Services, Macomb Community College, 14500 Twelve Mile Road, Warren, MI 48093-3896. (313) 445-7999. Fax: (313) 445-7157.

Madonna University
Livonia, Michigan CB code: 1437

Admissions:	87% of applicants accepted
Based on:	••• School record
	•• Test scores
	• Activities, essay, interview, recommendations
Completion:	83% of freshmen end year in good standing
	56% graduate, 48% of these enter graduate study

4-year private liberal arts college, coed, affiliated with Roman Catholic Church. Founded in 1947. **Accreditation:** Regional. **Undergraduate enrollment:** 278 men, 1,089 women full time; 656 men, 2,006 women part time. **Graduate enrollment:** 16 men, 8 women full time; 98 men, 268 women part time. **Faculty:** 266 total (107 full time), 117 with doctorates or other terminal degrees. **Location:** Suburban campus in small city; 18 miles from downtown Detroit. **Calendar:** Semester, limited summer session. **Microcomputers:** 63 located in libraries, classrooms, computer centers.

DEGREES OFFERED. AA, AS, AAS, BA, MS. 43 associate degrees awarded in 1992. 42% in business and management, 22% law, 20% social sciences. 544 bachelor's degrees awarded. 10% in business and management, 11% business/office and marketing/distribution, 19% health sciences, 7% allied health, 14% law, 6% letters/literature, 5% psychology, 10% social sciences. Graduate degrees offered in 8 major fields of study.

UNDERGRADUATE MAJORS. Associate: Biological and physical sciences, biology, business and management, child development/care/guidance, communications, computer and information sciences, criminal justice studies, education, emergency medical technologies, English, fine arts, fire protection, gerontology, graphic arts technology, history, home economics education, interpreter for the deaf, journalism, law enforcement and corrections, law enforcement and corrections technologies, legal assistant/paralegal, mathematics, occupational safety and health technology, physical sciences, protective services, public administration, religion, science technologies, social sciences, sociology, trade and industrial education, video, vocational trade. **Bachelor's:** Accounting, allied health, art education, biochemistry, biological and physical sciences, biology, business administration and management, business and management, chemistry, child development/care/guidance, clinical pastoral care, communications, computer and information sciences, computer programming, criminal justice studies, early childhood education, education, elementary education, English, English education, family/consumer resource management, fashion merchandising, finance, fine arts, fire protection, food production/management/services, food science and nutrition, foreign languages education, French, gerontology, graphic arts technology, health care administration, history, home economics, home economics education, hospitality and recreation marketing, information sciences and systems, international business management, interpreter for the deaf, journalism, junior high education, law enforcement and corrections, legal assistant/paralegal, management science, marketing and distribution, mathematics, mathematics education, medical laboratory technologies, music, music business management, music education, music performance, nursing, occupational safety and health technology, physical sciences, predentistry, prelaw, premedicine, prepharmacy, preveterinary, protective services, psychology, public administration, radiograph medical technology, religion, religious music, remedial education, science education, science technologies, secondary education, social science education, social sciences, social work, sociology, Spanish, special education, specific learning disabilities, technical and business writing, telecommunications, trade and industrial education, video, vocational trade.

ACADEMIC PROGRAMS. Accelerated program, cooperative education, double major, independent study, internships, study abroad, teacher preparation, cross-registration; liberal arts/career combination in engineering. **Remedial services:** Learning center, preadmission summer program, reduced course load, remedial instruction, special counselor, tutoring. **Placement/credit:** AP, CLEP General and Subject, institutional tests; 60 credit hours maximum for bachelor's degree.

ACADEMIC REQUIREMENTS. Freshmen must earn minimum GPA of 2.0 to continue in good standing. 65% of freshmen return for sophomore year. Students must declare major by end of first year. **Graduation requirements:** 60 hours for associate (30 in major), 120 hours for bachelor's (44 in major). Most students required to take courses in computer science, English, history, humanities, mathematics, philosophy/religion, biological/physical sciences, social sciences. **Postgraduate studies:** 98% from 2-year programs enter 4-year programs.

FRESHMAN ADMISSIONS. Selection criteria: Primarily concerned with cumulative high school GPA and curriculum. Majors in sciences, allied health and nursing, and mathematics require specific high school subjects. ACT test results important. Some majors require letters of recommendation. Additional placement tests may be requested. **High school preparation:** 19 units required. Required and recommended units include biological science 1, English 3, mathematics 2, social science 3 and science 2. Foreign language 2 recommended. One biology, 1 chemistry, 1 algebra required for nursing applicants. Biology, 1 chemistry, 2 algebra required for medical and radiologic technology program applicants. **Test requirements:** ACT; score report by August 15. **Additional information:** The college may request additional information and evidence of academic proficiency.

1992 FRESHMAN CLASS PROFILE. 84 men applied, 70 accepted, 53 enrolled; 365 women applied, 319 accepted, 205 enrolled. 51% had high school GPA of 3.0 or higher, 49% between 2.0 and 2.99. **Academic background:** Mid 50% of enrolled freshmen had ACT composite between 18-21. 99% submitted ACT scores. **Characteristics:** 97% from in state, 96% commute, 13% have minority backgrounds, 2% are foreign students. Average age is 20.

FALL-TERM APPLICATIONS. $25 fee. Closing date August 15; applicants notified on a rolling basis beginning on or about October 15; must reply within 4 weeks for basic nursing program. Interview recommended. Audition recommended. Portfolio recommended. Essay recommended. Deferred and early admission available.

STUDENT LIFE. Housing: Dormitories (men, women). **Activities:** Student government, student newspaper, television, choral groups, pep band, symphony orchestra, campus ministry, social work student association, gerontology association, student-faculty academic clubs, athletic club, computer club, nursing student association, multicultural student association, business professional association.

ATHLETICS. NAIA. **Intercollegiate:** Baseball M, basketball W, softball W, volleyball W. **Intramural:** Baseball, basketball W, bowling, golf, gymnastics, skiing, soccer, softball, table tennis, tennis, volleyball.

STUDENT SERVICES. Aptitude testing, career counseling, employment service for undergraduates, freshman orientation, health services, personal counseling, placement service for graduates, services/facilities for handicapped.

ANNUAL EXPENSES. Tuition and fees: $4,770. **Room and board:** $3,700. **Books and supplies:** $396. **Other expenses:** $638.

FINANCIAL AID. 24% of freshmen, 24% of continuing students receive some form of aid. 99% of grants, 80% of loans, all jobs based on need. 40 enrolled freshmen were judged to have need, all were offered aid. Academic, music/drama, art, athletic, alumni affiliation, minority scholarships available. **Aid applications:** No closing date; priority given to applications received by February 15; applicants notified on a rolling basis beginning on or about July 1; mustreply by July 15.

ADDRESS/TELEPHONE. Louis E. Brohl III, Director of Admissions and Marketing, Madonna University, 36600 Schoolcraft Road, Livonia, MI 48150-1173. (313) 591-5052. Fax: (313) 591-0156.

Marygrove College
Detroit, Michigan — CB code: 1452

Admissions: 51% of applicants accepted
Based on:
- ••• School record
- •• Interview, recommendations
- • Activities, special talents, test scores

Completion: 75% of freshmen end year in good standing
12% enter graduate study

4-year private liberal arts college, coed, affiliated with Roman Catholic Church. Founded in 1910. **Accreditation:** Regional. **Undergraduate enrollment:** 105 men, 537 women full time; 75 men, 422 women part time. **Graduate enrollment:** 2 men, 9 women full time; 44 men, 106 women part time. **Faculty:** 54 total (47 full time), 27 with doctorates or other terminal degrees. **Location:** Urban campus in very large city; 6 miles from downtown. **Calendar:** Semester, extensive summer session. **Microcomputers:** 25 located in computer centers. **Special facilities:** Gallery, theater, conference center.

DEGREES OFFERED. AA, AS, BA, BS, MA, MEd. 16 associate degrees awarded in 1992. 6% in business and management, 19% computer sciences, 56% allied health, 15% multi/interdisciplinary studies. 104 bachelor's degrees awarded. 22% in business and management, 8% education, 6% letters/literature, 5% psychology, 37% social sciences, 8% visual and performing arts. Graduate degrees offered in 9 major fields of study.

UNDERGRADUATE MAJORS. Associate: Accounting, allied health, business and management, business and office, business data processing and related programs, business data programming, cardiovascular technology, computer and information sciences, computer technology, diagnostic medical sonography, industrial technology, law enforcement and corrections technologies, liberal/general studies, medical assistant, psychology, radiograph medical technology, respiratory therapy, respiratory therapy technology, secretarial and related programs, ultrasound technology. **Bachelor's:** Accounting, allied health, art education, art history, art therapy, biology, business administration and management, business and management, business education, ceramics, chemistry, child development/care/guidance, clothing and textiles management/production/services, communications, computer and information sciences, computer graphics, computer programming, dance, dramatic arts, drawing, early childhood education, economics, education of the emotionally handicapped, education of the mentally handicapped, elementary education, English, English education, family and community services, family/consumer resource management, fashion design, fashion merchandising, food science and nutrition, foreign languages (multiple emphasis), foreign languages education, French, German, graphic arts technology, graphic design, history, home economics, home economics education, humanities and social sciences, individual and family development, institutional/home management/supporting programs, liberal/general studies, marketing and distribution, mathematics, mathematics education, music, music education, music performance, music theory and composition, nutritional education, painting, philosophy, physics, political science and government, predentistry, prelaw, premedicine, printmaking, psychology, reading education, religion, science education, secondary education, secretarial and related programs, social science education, social sciences, social studies education, social work, sociology, Spanish, systems analysis, textiles and clothing.

ACADEMIC PROGRAMS. Cooperative education, double major, independent study, internships, student-designed major, study abroad, teacher preparation, Washington semester, cross-registration, dual bachelor's/master's program with University of Michigan; liberal arts/career combination in health sciences. **Remedial services:** Learning center, preadmission summer program, reduced course load, remedial instruction, special counselor, tutoring. **Placement/credit:** AP, CLEP General and Subject, institutional tests; 16 credit hours maximum for associate degree; 32 credit hours maximum for bachelor's degree.

ACADEMIC REQUIREMENTS. Freshmen must earn minimum GPA of 2.0 to continue in good standing. 60% of freshmen return for sophomore year. Students must declare major by end of second year. **Graduation requirements:** 64 hours for associate (24 in major), 128 hours for bachelor's (36 in major). Most students required to take courses in arts/fine arts, computer science, English, history, humanities, mathematics, philosophy/religion, biological/physical sciences, social sciences. **Postgraduate studies:** 70% from 2-year programs enter 4-year programs. 1% enter law school, 1% enter medical school, 1% enter MBA programs, 9% enter other graduate study.

FRESHMAN ADMISSIONS. Selection criteria: School achievement record and test scores. **High school preparation:** 16 units recommended. Recommended units include English 4, foreign language 2, mathematics 2, social science 2 and science 2. One computer science recommended. **Test requirements:** SAT or ACT (ACT preferred); score report by August 15.

1992 FRESHMAN CLASS PROFILE. 58 men applied, 18 accepted, 16 enrolled; 302 women applied, 164 accepted, 121 enrolled. **Characteristics:** 95% from in state, 82% commute. Average age is 25.

FALL-TERM APPLICATIONS. $15 fee, may be waived for applicants with need. Closing date August 1; priority given to applications received by May 1; applicants notified on a rolling basis. Interview required for academically weak, older applicants. Audition required for music, theater, dance applicants. Portfolio required for art applicants. CRDA. Deferred and early admission available.

STUDENT LIFE. Housing: Dormitories (coed). All rooms single occupancy. **Activities:** Student government, student newspaper, choral groups, dance, drama, music ensembles, musical theater, International Club, Business Club, Computer Club, Black Social Worker Club, Council for Exceptional Children.

STUDENT SERVICES. Aptitude testing, career counseling, employment service for undergraduates, freshman orientation, health services, personal counseling, placement service for graduates, services/facilities for handicapped.

ANNUAL EXPENSES. Tuition and fees (1992-93): $7,140. **Room and board:** $3,700. **Books and supplies:** $460. **Other expenses:** $1,304.

FINANCIAL AID. 92% of freshmen, 98% of continuing students receive some form of aid. 91% of grants, 78% of loans, all jobs based on need. Academic, music/drama, art, leadership, alumni affiliation scholarships available. **Aid applications:** No closing date; priority given to applications received by March 15; applicants notified on a rolling basis beginning on or about May 15; must reply within 2 weeks.

ADDRESS/TELEPHONE. Karin Harabedian Jahn, Director of Admissions, Marygrove College, 8425 West McNichols Road, Detroit, MI 48221. (313) 862-5200. Fax: (313) 864-6670.

Michigan Christian College
Rochester Hills, Michigan — CB code: 1516

4-year private liberal arts college, coed, affiliated with Church of Christ. Founded in 1959. **Accreditation:** Regional. **Undergraduate enrollment:** 122 men, 132 women full time; 32 men, 19 women part time. **Faculty:** 35 total (20 full time), 8 with doctorates or other terminal degrees. **Location:** Suburban campus in small city; 25 miles from Detroit. **Calendar:** Semester. **Microcomputers:** 14 located in computer centers.

DEGREES OFFERED. AA, AS, AAS, B. 54 associate degrees awarded in 1992. 4 bachelor's degrees awarded.

UNDERGRADUATE MAJORS. Accounting, biological and physical sciences, business and management, business and office, business data processing and related programs, child development/care/guidance, computer and information sciences, computer programming, criminal justice studies, liberal/general studies, word processing. Bible studies, Christian ministry, counseling psychology, missionary studies.

ACADEMIC PROGRAMS. 2-year transfer program, honors program, independent study, internships, cross-registration. **Remedial services:** Reduced course load, remedial instruction, special counselor. **Placement/credit:** AP, CLEP Subject, institutional tests; 32 credit hours maximum for associate degree; 32 credit hours maximum for bachelor's degree.

ACADEMIC REQUIREMENTS. Freshmen must earn minimum GPA of 1.5 to continue in good standing. Students must declare major by end of second year. **Graduation requirements:** 64 hours for associate, 128 hours for bachelor's. Most students required to take courses in English, mathematics, philosophy/religion.

FRESHMAN ADMISSIONS. Selection criteria: Open admissions. **Test requirements:** SAT or ACT (ACT preferred) for placement and counseling only; score report by September 1. **Additional information:** Selective admissions after August 1 based on minimum 2.5 high school GPA or ACT composite score of 18.

1992 FRESHMAN CLASS PROFILE. 136 men and women enrolled. **Characteristics:** Average age is 19.

FALL-TERM APPLICATIONS. $15 fee. No closing date; applicants notified on a rolling basis. CRDA. Deferred and early admission available.

STUDENT LIFE. Housing: Dormitories (men, women); apartment housing available. **Activities:** Student government, yearbook, choral groups, drama, music ensembles, musical theater, service organizations, Mission Emphasis Club, social clubs.

ATHLETICS. NSCAA. **Intercollegiate:** Baseball M, basketball, cross-country, soccer M, softball W, track and field, volleyball W. **Intramural:** Basketball, softball, table tennis, volleyball.

STUDENT SERVICES. Aptitude testing, career counseling, employment service for undergraduates, freshman orientation, on-campus day care, personal counseling, veterans counselor, services/facilities for handicapped.

ANNUAL EXPENSES. Tuition and fees (1992-93): $4,812. **Room and board:** $2,800. **Books and supplies:** $300. **Other expenses:** $640.

FINANCIAL AID. 86% of continuing students receive some form of aid. Grants, loans, jobs available. Academic, music/drama, athletic, leadership, alumni affiliation scholarships available. **Aid applications:** No closing date; priority given to applications received by August 1; applicants notified on a rolling basis beginning on or about June 1; must reply within 2 weeks.

ADDRESS/TELEPHONE. Toby Osburn, Dean of Enrollment Services, Michigan Christian College, 800 West Avon Road, Rochester Hills, MI 48307-2764. (313) 651-5800 ext. 6017. (800) 521-6010. Fax: (313) 650-6060.

Michigan State University
East Lansing, Michigan — CB code: 1465

4-year public university, coed. Founded in 1855. **Accreditation:** Regional. **Undergraduate enrollment:** 12,902 men, 14,049 women full time; 2,177 men, 2,120 women part time. **Graduate enrollment:** 2,753 men, 2,292 women full time; 1,673 men, 2,081 women part time. **Faculty:** 2,670 total (2,520 full time), 2,521 with doctorates or other terminal degrees. **Location:** Suburban campus in small city; 3 miles from Lansing, 80 miles from Detroit. **Calendar:** Semester, extensive summer session. Extensive evening/early morning classes. **Microcomputers:** 2,500 located in dormitories, libraries, classrooms, computer centers, campus-wide network. **Special facilities:** Abrams Planetarium, Beal Botanical Garden, Center for Environmental Toxicology, Kellogg Center for Continuing Education, Kresge Art Museum, national superconducting cyclotron laboratory, pesticide research center, language labs, experimental farms, Wharton Center for Performing Arts, museum. **Additional facts:** Honors college and 2 residential colleges: James Madison (international relations political theory and prelaw) and Lyman Briggs School (mathematics and natural science).

DEGREES OFFERED. BA, BS, BFA, MA, MS, MBA, MFA, MSW, PhD, MD, DO, DVM. 7,706 bachelor's degrees awarded in 1992. 8% in agriculture, 19% business and management, 12% communications, 9% engineering, 5% home economics, 5% psychology, 15% social sciences. Graduate degrees offered in 147 major fields of study.

UNDERGRADUATE MAJORS. Accounting, advertising, agribusiness, agricultural education, agricultural engineering, agricultural production, agronomy, American studies, animal sciences, anthropology, art education, art history, astronomy, astrophysics, biochemistry, biological and physical sciences, biology, botany, business and management, chemical engineering, chemistry, Chinese, city/community/regional planning, civil engineering, classics, clinical laboratory science, communications, computer and information sciences, computer engineering, contract management and procurement/purchasing, criminal justice studies, criminology, dramatic arts, earth sciences, economics, education of the deaf and hearing impaired, education of the emotionally handicapped, education of the mentally handicapped, education of the visually handicapped, electrical/electronics/communications engineering, elementary education, engineering and other disciplines, engineering mechanics, English, English education, entomology, environmental science, family and community services, family/consumer resource management, finance, fine arts, fishing and fisheries, food science and nutrition, food sciences, foreign languages education, forensic studies, forestry and related sciences, French, geography, geology, German, health education, history, home economics education, horticultural science, horticulture, hotel/motel and restaurant management, human environment and housing, humanities and social sciences, individual and family development, interior design, journalism, landscape architecture, Latin, liberal/general studies, linguistics, marketing and distribution, marketing management, materials engineering, mathematics, mathematics education, mechanical engineering, medical laboratory technologies, microbiology, music, music education, music performance, music theory and composition, music therapy, musical theater, nursing, ornamental horticulture, parks and recreation management, personnel management, philosophy, physical chemistry, physical education, physical sciences, physics, physiology, human and animal, political science and government, predentistry, prelaw, premedicine, preveterinary, psychology, public administration, public affairs, radio/television broadcasting, recreation and community services technologies, religion, renewable natural resources, retailing, Russian, science education, science technologies, secondary education, social science education, social sciences, social studies education, social work, sociology, soil sciences, Spanish, special education, speech pathology/audiology, speech/communication/theater education, statistics, studio art, telecommunications, textiles and clothing, tourism, transportation management, urban studies, wildlife management, zoology.

ACADEMIC PROGRAMS. Accelerated program, cooperative education, double major, dual enrollment of high school students, education specialist degree, honors program, independent study, internships, student-designed major, study abroad, teacher preparation, telecourses, visiting/exchange student program; liberal arts/career combination in engineering; combined bachelor's/graduate program in medicine. **Remedial services:** Learning center, preadmission summer program, reduced course load, remedial instruction, tutoring. **ROTC:** Air Force, Army. **Placement/credit:** AP, CLEP General and Subject, institutional tests.

ACADEMIC REQUIREMENTS. Freshmen must earn minimum GPA of 1.5 to continue in good standing. Sliding scale determined by GPA and credits earned. 87% of freshmen return for sophomore year. Students must declare major by end of second year. **Graduation requirements:** 120 hours for bachelor's (30 in major). Most students required to take courses in English, foreign languages, humanities, mathematics, biological/physical sciences, social sciences. **Postgraduate studies:** 5% enter law school, 3% enter medical school, 3% enter MBA programs, 7% enter other graduate study.

FRESHMAN ADMISSIONS. Selection criteria: Emphasis on grades and test scores, supplemented by class rank, principal and counselor recommendations, leadership qualities. Requirements for out-of-state applicants slightly more restrictive. Recommended units include biological science 1,

English 4, foreign language 2, mathematics 3, physical science 2, social science 3 and science 2. **Test requirements:** SAT or ACT.

1992 FRESHMAN CLASS PROFILE. 2,820 men, 3,399 women enrolled. **Characteristics:** 92% from in state, 96% live in college housing, 15% have minority backgrounds, 1% are foreign students, 4% join fraternities/sororities. Average age is 18.

FALL-TERM APPLICATIONS. $30 fee, may be waived for applicants with need. Closing date July 30; applicants notified on a rolling basis; must reply within 4 weeks. Audition required for music applicants. Deferred admission available.

STUDENT LIFE. Housing: Dormitories (women, coed); apartment, fraternity, sorority, handicapped housing available. Freshmen must live in college housing unless aged 21, married, veterans, residing with parents or legal guardian, or registered for under 7 credits. Sophomore housing requirement currently being waived. **Activities:** Student government, film, radio, student newspaper, television, yearbook, choral groups, concert band, dance, drama, jazz band, marching band, music ensembles, musical theater, pep band, symphony orchestra, fraternities, sororities, over 400 academic, athletic, social, religious, and political organizations.

ATHLETICS. NCAA. **Intercollegiate:** Baseball M, basketball, cross-country, diving, fencing M, field hockey W, football M, golf, gymnastics, ice hockey M, lacrosse M, soccer M, softball W, swimming, tennis, track and field, volleyball W, wrestling M. **Intramural:** Archery, badminton, baseball M, basketball, cross-country, diving, fencing, golf, gymnastics, ice hockey, racquetball, rowing (crew), rugby, sailing, skiing, soccer, softball W, squash, swimming, table tennis, tennis, track and field, volleyball, water polo, wrestling M.

STUDENT SERVICES. Aptitude testing, career counseling, employment service for undergraduates, freshman orientation, health services, on-campus day care, personal counseling, placement service for graduates, special adviser for adult students, veterans counselor, services/facilities for handicapped.

ANNUAL EXPENSES. Tuition and fees (1992-93): $4,277, $5,798 additional for out-of-state students. **Room and board:** $3,568. **Books and supplies:** $480. **Other expenses:** $1,221.

FINANCIAL AID. 50% of freshmen, 50% of continuing students receive some form of aid. All grants, 88% of loans, all jobs based on need. 2,970 enrolled freshmen were judged to have need, all were offered aid. Academic, music/drama, art, athletic, minority scholarships available. **Aid applications:** No closing date; applicants notified on a rolling basis beginning on or about March 31; must reply within 3 weeks.

ADDRESS/TELEPHONE. William H. Turner, PhD, Director of Admissions, Michigan State University, 250 Administration Building, East Lansing, MI 48824-1046. (517) 355-8332.

Michigan Technological University

Houghton, Michigan — CB code: 1464

Admissions: 93% of applicants accepted
Based on: ••• School record, test scores
•• Recommendations
• Activities, essay, interview, special talents
Completion: 94% of freshmen end year in good standing
56% graduate, 16% of these enter graduate study

4-year public university, coed. Founded in 1885. **Accreditation:** Regional. **Undergraduate enrollment:** 4,428 men, 1,460 women full time; 337 men, 135 women part time. **Graduate enrollment:** 437 men, 132 women full time; 23 men, 9 women part time. **Faculty:** 365 total (340 full time), 281 with doctorates or other terminal degrees. **Location:** Rural campus in small town; 325 miles from Milwaukee, Wisconsin, 350 miles from Detroit. **Calendar:** Quarter, limited summer session. **Microcomputers:** 400 located in dormitories, libraries, classrooms, computer centers, campus-wide network. **Special facilities:** Mineral museum, Ford Forestry Center, university copper mine.

DEGREES OFFERED. AA, AAS, BA, BS, MS, PhD. 104 associate degrees awarded in 1992. 5% in agriculture, 93% engineering technologies. 931 bachelor's degrees awarded. 9% in business and management, 72% engineering. Graduate degrees offered in 17 major fields of study.

UNDERGRADUATE MAJORS. Associate: Civil technology, electrical technology, electromechanical technology, forestry and related sciences, liberal/general studies, mechanical design technology. **Bachelor's:** Applied geophysics, applied physics, biology, business administration and management, business economics, chemical engineering, chemistry, civil engineering, computer and information sciences, electrical/electronics/communications engineering, engineering, engineering management, environmental engineering, forestry and related sciences, geological engineering, geology, liberal/general studies, mathematics, mechanical engineering, medical laboratory technologies, metallurgical engineering, mining and mineral engineering, physics, scientific and technical communications, social sciences, surveying and mapping sciences, wood and fiber utilization.

ACADEMIC PROGRAMS. Cooperative education, double major, dual enrollment of high school students, independent study, internships, student-designed major, study abroad, teacher preparation, engineering program with Central Michigan University, Northwestern Michigan College, Adrian College, Albion College, Augsburg College (MN), College of St. Scholastica (MN), Mount Senario College (WI), Northland College (WI), University of Wisconsin-Superior (WI). **Remedial services:** Reduced course load, remedial instruction, tutoring. **ROTC:** Air Force, Army. **Placement/credit:** AP, CLEP Subject, institutional tests.

ACADEMIC REQUIREMENTS. Freshmen must earn minimum GPA of 2.0 to continue in good standing. 83% of freshmen return for sophomore year. Students must declare major by end of second year. **Graduation requirements:** 98 hours for associate (50 in major), 196 hours for bachelor's (70 in major). Most students required to take courses in computer science, English, humanities, mathematics, biological/physical sciences, social sciences. **Postgraduate studies:** 16% enter other graduate study.

FRESHMAN ADMISSIONS. Selection criteria: School record, class rank, and test scores considered. Rank in top quarter of class preferred for applicants to engineering and computer science programs. Rank in top third of class preferred for applicants to bachelor's degree programs. **High school preparation:** 15 units required; 21 recommended. Required and recommended units include English 3-4, mathematics 3-4 and physical science 1-2. Biological science 2, foreign language 3 and social science 3 recommended. Course requirements vary depending on curriculum.

1992 FRESHMAN CLASS PROFILE. 2,303 men applied, 2,110 accepted, 946 enrolled; 726 women applied, 693 accepted, 326 enrolled. 38% were in top tenth and 72% were in top quarter of graduating class. **Academic background:** Mid 50% of enrolled freshmen had SAT-V between 420-550, SAT-M between 550-670; ACT composite between 23-28. 21% submitted SAT scores, 92% submitted ACT scores. **Characteristics:** 76% from in state, 4% have minority backgrounds, 5% are foreign students. Average age is 19.

FALL-TERM APPLICATIONS. $20 fee, may be waived for applicants with need. Closing date August 1; priority given to applications received by February 1; applicants notified on a rolling basis; must reply immediately. Interview recommended for borderline applicants. Essay recommended. CRDA. Deferred admission available. SAT of ACT strongly recommended.

STUDENT LIFE. Housing: Dormitories (coed); apartment, fraternity, sorority housing available. **Activities:** Student government, film, magazine, radio, student newspaper, choral groups, concert band, drama, jazz band, music ensembles, musical theater, pep band, fraternities, sororities, International Club, Black Student's Association, Campus Crusade for Christ, APO service organization, College Republicans India Students Association, Chinese Student Association, Michigan Tech Student Foundation, Native American Association.

ATHLETICS. NCAA. **Intercollegiate:** Basketball, cross-country, football M, ice hockey M, skiing, tennis, track and field, volleyball W. **Intramural:** Archery, badminton, basketball, bowling, golf, handball, ice hockey, racquetball, rifle, soccer, softball, squash, swimming, table tennis, tennis, track and field, volleyball, water polo, wrestling.

STUDENT SERVICES. Aptitude testing, career counseling, employment service for undergraduates, freshman orientation, health services, personal counseling, placement service for graduates, veterans counselor, services/facilities for handicapped.

ANNUAL EXPENSES. Tuition and fees (1992-93): $3,249, $4,077 additional for out-of-state students. **Room and board:** $3,604. **Books and supplies:** $600. **Other expenses:** $550.

FINANCIAL AID. 70% of freshmen, 72% of continuing students receive some form of aid. 53% of grants, 93% of loans, 17% of jobs based on need. 457 enrolled freshmen were judged to have need, 398 were offered aid. Academic, athletic, leadership, minority scholarships available. **Aid applications:** Closing date March 1; applicants notified on or about May 1; must reply within 2 weeks. **Additional information:** In-state tuition granted to qualifying high school students, college transfer students, and children of active alumni.

ADDRESS/TELEPHONE. Joseph A. Galetto, Director of Enrollment Management, Michigan Technological University, 1400 Townsend Drive, Houghton, MI 49931-1295. (906) 487-2335. Fax: (906) 487-3343.

Mid Michigan Community College

Harrison, Michigan — CB code: 1523

2-year public community college, coed. Founded in 1965. **Accreditation:** Regional. **Undergraduate enrollment:** 341 men, 608 women full time; 460 men, 872 women part time. **Faculty:** 139 total (36 full time), 1 with doctorate or other terminal degree. **Location:** Rural campus in small town; 30 miles from Mount Pleasant. **Calendar:** Semester, limited summer session. **Microcomputers:** 140 located in computer centers.

DEGREES OFFERED. AA, AS, AAS. 165 associate degrees awarded in 1992. 6% in business and management, 13% business/office and marketing/distribution, 15% health sciences, 23% allied health, 17% multi/interdisciplinary studies, 22% trade and industry.

UNDERGRADUATE MAJORS. Accounting, air conditioning/heating/refrigeration mechanics, air conditioning/heating/refrigeration technology, automotive mechanics, automotive technology, biological and physical sciences, business administration and management, business and management, business and office, business data processing and related programs, business data programming, chemistry, computer and information sciences, computer programming, criminal justice studies, drafting, drafting and design technology, elementary education, engineering and engineering-related technologies, fashion merchandising, finance, fire control and safety technology, forestry and related sciences, graphic and printing production, hospitality and recreation marketing, humanities and social sciences, industrial technology, law enforcement and corrections, liberal/general studies, machine tool operation/machine shop, marketing and distribution, mechanical design technology, mechanical engineering, nursing, practical nursing, preengineering, radiograph medical technology, secondary education, secretarial and related programs, small business management and ownership, special education, wildlife management, word processing.

ACADEMIC PROGRAMS. 2-year transfer program, dual enrollment of high school students, honors program, independent study, internships. **Remedial services:** Learning center, reduced course load, remedial instruction, special counselor, tutoring. **Placement/credit:** CLEP General and Subject, institutional tests.

ACADEMIC REQUIREMENTS. Freshmen must earn minimum GPA of 2.0 to continue in good standing. 34% of freshmen return for sophomore year. Students must declare major on enrollment. **Graduation requirements:** 62 hours for associate. Most students required to take courses in English, mathematics, social sciences.

FRESHMAN ADMISSIONS. Selection criteria: Open admissions. Selective admissions for health occupations majors based on prerequisite course completion. One unit chemistry, 1 algebra, 1 biology required for health occupations majors. **Additional information:** High school diploma or GED recommended.

1992 FRESHMAN CLASS PROFILE. 334 men, 642 women enrolled. **Characteristics:** 100% from in state, 100% commute, 3% have minority backgrounds. Average age is 26.

FALL-TERM APPLICATIONS. No fee. No closing date; applicants notified on a rolling basis. Interview required for health program applicants. Early admission available.

STUDENT LIFE. Housing: Community-wide housing bulletin available on request. **Activities:** Student government, student newspaper, choral groups, drama, musical theater.

STUDENT SERVICES. Aptitude testing, career counseling, employment service for undergraduates, freshman orientation, personal counseling, placement service for graduates, veterans counselor, services/facilities for handicapped.

ANNUAL EXPENSES. Tuition and fees (1992-93): $1,220, $600 additional for out-of-district students, $1,080 additional for out-of-state students. **Books and supplies:** $400. **Other expenses:** $941.

FINANCIAL AID. 55% of freshmen, 54% of continuing students receive some form of aid. 92% of grants, 94% of loans, all jobs based on need. 343 enrolled freshmen were judged to have need, all were offered aid. Academic scholarships available. **Aid applications:** No closing date; priority given to applications received by May 1; applicants notified on a rolling basis beginning on or about July 1; must reply within 2 weeks.

ADDRESS/TELEPHONE. Gerald Hand, Admissions Director, Mid Michigan Community College, 1375 South Clare Avenue, Harrison, MI 48625. (517) 386-7792 ext. 290.

Monroe County Community College
Monroe, Michigan — CB code: 1514

2-year public community college, coed. Founded in 1964. **Accreditation:** Regional. **Undergraduate enrollment:** 499 men, 585 women full time; 1,001 men, 1,839 women part time. **Faculty:** 190 total (66 full time), 27 with doctorates or other terminal degrees. **Location:** Rural campus in large town; 45 miles from Detroit, 20 miles from Toledo, Ohio. **Calendar:** 4-4-1, limited summer session. Saturday and extensive evening/early morning classes. **Microcomputers:** 90 located in classrooms, computer centers. **Additional facts:** Off-campus sites at Whitman Center and Jefferson Center.

DEGREES OFFERED. AA, AS, AAS. 308 associate degrees awarded in 1992.

UNDERGRADUATE MAJORS. Accounting, architectural technologies, automotive technology, business and management, business and office, business computer/console/peripheral equipment operation, business data entry equipment operation, business data processing and related programs, business data programming, computer and information sciences, drafting, drafting and design technology, electronic technology, engineering and engineering-related technologies, finance, fine arts, industrial technology, legal secretary, liberal/general studies, marketing and distribution, mechanical design technology, medical secretary, nursing, office supervision and management, precision metal work, radiograph medical technology, respiratory therapy technology, retailing, science technologies, secretarial and related programs, welding technology.

ACADEMIC PROGRAMS. 2-year transfer program, accelerated program, dual enrollment of high school students, independent study. **Remedial services:** Learning center, reduced course load, remedial instruction, special counselor, tutoring. **Placement/credit:** AP, CLEP General and Subject, institutional tests; 30 credit hours maximum for associate degree.

ACADEMIC REQUIREMENTS. Freshmen must earn minimum GPA of 1.8 to continue in good standing. 55% of freshmen return for sophomore year. Students must declare major on application. **Graduation requirements:** 60 hours for associate (32 in major). Most students required to take courses in social sciences.

FRESHMAN ADMISSIONS. Selection criteria: Open admissions. Selective admissions for nursing and respiratory therapy applicants based on 2.5 high school GPA, ACT composite score of 21 preferred, and 2 recommendations. Completion of biological and chemistry courses, and completion of college mathematics required. Nursing and respiratory therapy applicants must have 1 unit chemistry and 1 biology. Strong science background highly recommended. **Test requirements:** ACT required for nursing and respiratory therapy applicants; score report by March 31.

1992 FRESHMAN CLASS PROFILE. 393 men, 574 women enrolled. **Characteristics:** 99% from in state, 100% commute, 3% have minority backgrounds. Average age is 26.

FALL-TERM APPLICATIONS. No fee. No closing date; priority given to applications received by May 1; applicants notified on a rolling basis. Interview required for nursing, respiratory therapy applicants. Deferred admission available. Closing date for nursing applications March 31, respiratory therapy April 30. All applicants must take ASSET for placement purposes.

STUDENT LIFE. Activities: Student government, student newspaper, choral groups, concert band, drama.

STUDENT SERVICES. Aptitude testing, career counseling, employment service for undergraduates, freshman orientation, on-campus day care, personal counseling, placement service for graduates, services/facilities for handicapped.

ANNUAL EXPENSES. Tuition and fees (1992-93): $900, $420 additional for out-of-district students, $420 additional for out-of-state students. **Books and supplies:** $700. **Other expenses:** $650.

FINANCIAL AID. 43% of freshmen, 57% of continuing students receive some form of aid. 93% of grants, all loans based on need. Academic, music/drama, art, state/district residency, leadership scholarships available. **Aid applications:** No closing date; priority given to applications received by June 1; applicants notified on a rolling basis beginning on or about July 1; must reply within 10 days.

ADDRESS/TELEPHONE. Admissions Office, Monroe County Community College, 1555 South Raisinville Road, Monroe, MI 48161. (313) 242-7300. Fax: (313) 242-9711.

Montcalm Community College
Sidney, Michigan — CB code: 1522

2-year public community college, coed. Founded in 1965. **Accreditation:** Regional. **Undergraduate enrollment:** 183 men, 399 women full time; 622 men, 814 women part time. **Faculty:** 106 total (29 full time), 7 with doctorates or other terminal degrees. **Location:** Rural campus in rural community; 50 miles from Grand Rapids, 65 miles from Lansing. **Calendar:** Semester, limited summer session. Saturday and extensive evening/early morning classes. **Microcomputers:** 400 located in classrooms, computer centers. **Special facilities:** Marked nature preserves and trails, Heritage Village. **Additional facts:** Off-campus centers in Ionia and Greenville.

DEGREES OFFERED. AA, AAS. 147 associate degrees awarded in 1992. 14% in business and management, 35% allied health, 25% multi/interdisciplinary studies, 11% trade and industry.

UNDERGRADUATE MAJORS. Accounting, automotive mechanics, automotive technology, business administration and management, business data processing and related programs, criminal justice studies, data processing, drafting, drafting and design technology, electronic technology, food production/management/services, industrial technology, law enforcement and corrections, legal assistant/paralegal, legal secretary, liberal/general studies, medical secretary, nursing, radiograph medical technology, secretarial and related programs, small business management and ownership, word processing.

ACADEMIC PROGRAMS. 2-year transfer program, cooperative education, dual enrollment of high school students, independent study, internships. **Remedial services:** Learning center, reduced course load, remedial instruction, special counselor, tutoring. **Placement/credit:** Institutional tests.

ACADEMIC REQUIREMENTS. Freshmen must earn minimum GPA of 2.0 to continue in good standing. 32% of freshmen return for sophomore year. Students must declare major on application. **Graduation requirements:** 60 hours for associate. Most students required to take courses in English, social sciences.

FRESHMAN ADMISSIONS. Selection criteria: Open admissions. Applicants to nursing program must have completed 1 semester of college biology with 2.0 GPA or higher. ASSET scores important. **Additional information:** ACT recommended. ASSET test required of most students.

1992 FRESHMAN CLASS PROFILE. Characteristics: 99% from in state, 100% commute, 14% have minority backgrounds.

FALL-TERM APPLICATIONS. No fee. No closing date; applicants notified on a rolling basis. CRDA. Deferred admission available.

STUDENT LIFE. Activities: Student government, student newspaper, choral groups, drama, jazz band, music ensembles, Phi Theta Kappa honor society.

ATHLETICS. Intramural: Archery, basketball, bowling, handball, racquetball, skiing, skin diving, soccer, softball, swimming, table tennis, tennis, volleyball.

STUDENT SERVICES. Aptitude testing, career counseling, employment service for undergraduates, freshman orientation, personal counseling, placement service for graduates, services/facilities for handicapped.

ANNUAL EXPENSES. Tuition and fees (projected): $1,284, $660 additional for out-of-district students, $990 additional for out-of-state students. **Books and supplies:** $500. **Other expenses:** $826.

FINANCIAL AID. 64% of freshmen, 73% of continuing students receive some form of aid. 96% of grants, 96% of loans, all jobs based on need. Academic, music/drama scholarships available. **Aid applications:** No closing date; priority given to applications received by April 1; applicants notified on a rolling basis beginning on or about May 1; must reply within 2 weeks.

ADDRESS/TELEPHONE. Carol Krumbach, Director of Admissions, Montcalm Community College, 2800 College Drive, P.O. Box 300, Sidney, MI 48885-0300. (517) 328-2111 ext. 224. Fax: (517) 328-2950.

Muskegon Community College
Muskegon, Michigan CB code: 1495

2-year public community college, coed. Founded in 1926. **Accreditation:** Regional. **Undergraduate enrollment:** 4,810 men and women. **Faculty:** 220 total (100 full time), 25 with doctorates or other terminal degrees. **Location:** Urban campus in small city; 45 miles from Grand Rapids. **Calendar:** Two 16-week terms followed by two 8-week terms. **Microcomputers:** Located in libraries, classrooms, computer centers. **Special facilities:** Planetarium, nature preserve, art gallery. **Additional facts:** Award-winning campus architecture enables students to traverse campus without going outside; convenient for handicapped.

DEGREES OFFERED. AA, AS, AAS. 490 associate degrees awarded in 1992.

UNDERGRADUATE MAJORS. Accounting, automotive technology, biomedical equipment technology, business and management, business data processing and related programs, business data programming, chemical manufacturing technology, computer and information sciences, data processing, drafting, drafting and design technology, electronic technology, elementary education, engineering and engineering-related technologies, finance, graphic and printing production, graphic arts technology, industrial technology, instrumentation technology, insurance marketing, law enforcement and corrections technologies, liberal/general studies, management science, marketing and distribution, marketing management, medical records technology, nursing, practical nursing, precision metal work, public affairs, recreation and community services technologies, respiratory therapy technology, science technologies, secretarial and related programs, teacher aide.

ACADEMIC PROGRAMS. 2-year transfer program, cooperative education, double major, dual enrollment of high school students, honors program, independent study, internships, teacher preparation, telecourses, cross-registration. **Remedial services:** Learning center, remedial instruction, tutoring. **Placement/credit:** AP, CLEP General and Subject, institutional tests; 30 credit hours maximum for associate degree.

ACADEMIC REQUIREMENTS. Freshmen must earn minimum GPA of 2.0 to continue in good standing. 50% of freshmen return for sophomore year. **Graduation requirements:** 62 hours for associate. Most students required to take courses in English, humanities, biological/physical sciences, social sciences.

FRESHMAN ADMISSIONS. Selection criteria: Open admissions. Nursing applicants must have mathematics (level 35) and basic college chemistry.

1992 FRESHMAN CLASS PROFILE. 1,813 men and women enrolled. **Characteristics:** 99% from in state, 90% commute, 10% have minority backgrounds. Average age is 25.

FALL-TERM APPLICATIONS. No fee. No closing date; applicants notified on a rolling basis. Deferred and early admission available.

STUDENT LIFE. Activities: Student government, student newspaper, television, choral groups, concert band, dance, drama, jazz band, music ensembles, musical theater, interdenominational religious group, Black Student Alliance, Students Again Gaining Enlightenment, Study Opportunities for Adults and Mature Citizens.

ATHLETICS. NJCAA. **Intercollegiate:** Basketball, golf, tennis W, volleyball W. **Intramural:** Basketball, golf.

STUDENT SERVICES. Aptitude testing, career counseling, employment service for undergraduates, freshman orientation, health services, personal counseling, placement service for graduates, veterans counselor, services/facilities for handicapped.

ANNUAL EXPENSES. Tuition and fees (1992-93): $1,060, $465 additional for out-of-district students, $855 additional for out-of-state students. **Books and supplies:** $400. **Other expenses:** $750.

FINANCIAL AID. 60% of freshmen, 60% of continuing students receive some form of aid. 92% of grants, 94% of loans, 62% of jobs based on need. Academic, music/drama, art, athletic, state/district residency, minority scholarships available. **Aid applications:** No closing date; priority given to applications received by June 1; applicants notified on a rolling basis beginning on or about May 1; must reply within 2 weeks.

ADDRESS/TELEPHONE. John Bamfield, Director of Admissions Services, Muskegon Community College, 221 South Quarterline Road, Muskegon, MI 49442. (616) 777-0363.

North Central Michigan College
Petoskey, Michigan CB code: 1569

2-year public community college, coed. Founded in 1958. **Accreditation:** Regional. **Undergraduate enrollment:** 2,230 men and women. **Location:** Suburban campus in small town; 40 miles from Mackinaw City. **Calendar:** Semester. **Additional facts:** Evening courses available at local high schools in Gaylord and Cheboygan.

FRESHMAN ADMISSIONS. Selection criteria: Open admissions. Applicants to nursing program required to have taken high school algebra, chemistry, English composition 1 and 2, political science, and speech.

ANNUAL EXPENSES. Tuition and fees: $1,268, $420 additional for out-of-district students, $810 additional for out-of-state students. **Room and board:** $3,046. **Books and supplies:** $1,050. **Other expenses:** $400.

ADDRESS/TELEPHONE. David Munger, Registrar, North Central Michigan College, 1515 Howard Street, Petoskey, MI 49770. (616) 348-6600.

Northern Michigan University
Marquette, Michigan CB code: 1560

Admissions:	85% of applicants accepted
Based on:	••• School record, test scores
	•• Interview, recommendations, special talents
	• Activities, essay
Completion:	63% of freshmen end year in good standing
	46% graduate, 15% of these enter graduate study

4-year public university, coed. Founded in 1899. **Accreditation:** Regional. **Undergraduate enrollment:** 3,051 men, 3,210 women full time; 737 men, 897 women part time. **Graduate enrollment:** 118 men, 144 women full time; 238 men, 502 women part time. **Faculty:** 374 total (335 full time), 215 with doctorates or other terminal degrees. **Location:** Urban campus in large town; 300 miles from Milwaukee, Wisconsin, 400 miles from Lansing, Grand Rapids, Chicago, and Minneapolis-St.Paul, Minnesota. **Calendar:** Semester, limited summer session. **Microcomputers:** 435 located in dormitories, libraries, computer centers. **Special facilities:** Observatory with 12.5 F:6 Newtonian telescope, field station, forest, art gallery.

DEGREES OFFERED. AS, BA, BS, BFA, MA, MS. 90 associate degrees awarded in 1992. 13% in business and management, 40% business/office and marketing/distribution, 7% allied health, 7% home economics, 13% parks/recreation, protective services, public affairs, 8% trade and industry. 800 bachelor's degrees awarded. 14% in business and management, 5% communications, 5% computer sciences, 12% education, 9% health sciences, 9% letters/literature, 5% life sciences, 10% parks/recreation, protective services, public affairs, 10% social sciences. Graduate degrees offered in 44 major fields of study.

UNDERGRADUATE MAJORS. Associate: Aeronautical technology, air conditioning/heating/refrigeration mechanics, air conditioning/heating/refrigeration technology, aircraft mechanics, automotive mechanics, automotive technology, biology, biomedical equipment technology, business and management, business and office, business data processing and related programs, chemistry, child development/care/guidance, clinical laboratory science, clothing and textiles management/production/services, computer and information sciences, computer servicing technology, computer technology, construction, crafts, criminal justice studies, data processing, diesel engine mechanics, drafting, drafting and design technology, earth sciences, economics, electrical and electronics equipment repair, electrical technology, electromechanical technology, electronic technology, English, food production/management/services, food science and nutrition, geography, graphic and printing production, graphic arts technology, history, illustration design, industrial technology, law enforcement and corrections, legal secretary, liberal/general studies, medical laboratory technologies, medical secretary, nursing, philosophy, photographic technology, physics, political science and government, psychology, recreation and community services technologies, rehabilitation counseling/services, secretarial and related programs, sociology, water and wastewater technology, woodworking, word processing. **Bachelor's:** Accounting, art education, automotive technology, biochemistry, biological and physical sciences, biology, botany, business administration and management, business data processing and related programs, business education, business systems analysis, ceramics, chemistry, child development/care/guidance, cinematography/film, city/community/regional planning, clinical laboratory science, clothing and textiles management/production/services, communications, computer and information sciences, computer graphics, computer mathematics, computer programming, conservation and regulation, construction, creative writing, criminal justice studies, cytotechnology, data processing, drafting and design technology, dramatic arts, drawing, early childhood education, earth sciences, ecology, economics, education, education of the mentally handicapped, electrical technology, electronic technology, elementary education, English, English education, English literature, environmental design, environmental science, environmental-occupational hygiene, fashion merchandising, film arts, finance, food management, food production/management/services, food science and nutrition, foreign languages education, French, geography, geriatric services, German, gerontology, graphic and printing production, graphic design, health education, health sciences, history, home economics, home economics education, humanities and social sciences, illustration design, industrial arts education, industrial design, industrial technology, information sciences and systems, interior design, international studies, journalism, junior high education, law enforcement and corrections, management information systems, management science, manufacturing technology, marketing and distribution, marketing management, mathematics, mathematics education, medical laboratory technologies, metal/jewelry, microbiology, music, music education, nursing, office supervision and management, painting, parks and recreation management, philosophy, photography, physical education, physics, physiology, human and animal, political science and government, predentistry, prelaw, premedicine, printmaking, psychology, public administration, public relations, radio/television broadcasting, radio/television technology, science education, sculpture, secondary education, secretarial and related programs, social science education, social sciences, social studies education, social work, sociology, Spanish, speech, speech correction, speech pathology/audiology, speech/communication/theater education, sports medicine, sports science, textiles and clothing, trade and industrial education, water resources, wildlife management, word processing, zoology.

ACADEMIC PROGRAMS. 2-year transfer program, double major, education specialist degree, internships, student-designed major, study abroad, teacher preparation, telecourses, weekend college. **Remedial services:** Learning center, reduced course load, remedial instruction, special counselor, tutoring. **ROTC:** Army. **Placement/credit:** AP, CLEP General and Subject, institutional tests; 32 credit hours maximum for bachelor's degree.

ACADEMIC REQUIREMENTS. Freshmen must earn minimum GPA of 2.0 to continue in good standing. 71% of freshmen return for sophomore year. Students must declare major on application. **Graduation requirements:** 64 hours for associate (24 in major), 128 hours for bachelor's (36 in major). Most students required to take courses in arts/fine arts, computer science, English, history, humanities, mathematics, biological/physical sciences, social sciences. **Postgraduate studies:** 1% enter law school, 1% enter medical school, 4% enter MBA programs, 9% enter other graduate study.

FRESHMAN ADMISSIONS. Selection criteria: Minimum high school 2.25 GPA, ACT composite 19 or combined SAT 800, plus 12 to 16 academic units by end of senior year. **High school preparation:** 13 units required; 19 recommended. Required and recommended units include English 4, mathematics 3-4, social science 3 and science 3. Foreign language 2 recommended. 2 fine arts and 1 computer literacy also recommended. **Test requirements:** SAT or ACT (ACT preferred); score report by August 1.

1992 FRESHMAN CLASS PROFILE. 2,233 men applied, 1,861 accepted, 731 enrolled; 2,286 women applied, 1,983 accepted, 701 enrolled. **Academic background:** Mid 50% of enrolled freshmen had ACT composite between 18-24. 71% submitted ACT scores. **Characteristics:** 88% from in state, 66% live in college housing, 5% have minority backgrounds, 2% are foreign students, 1% join fraternities/sororities. Average age is 19.

FALL-TERM APPLICATIONS. $25 fee. Closing date August 1; priority given to applications received by February 1; applicants notified on a rolling basis. Deferred admission available.

STUDENT LIFE. Housing: Dormitories (women, coed); apartment, fraternity housing available. **Activities:** Student government, film, magazine, radio, student newspaper, television, yearbook, choral groups, concert band, dance, drama, jazz band, marching band, music ensembles, musical theater, opera, pep band, symphony orchestra, fraternities, sororities, campus ministries, Young Democrats, College Republicans, Student Social Work Organization, Gonzo Media, Amnesty International. **Additional information:** Extracurricular activities oriented toward outdoor sports, with emphasis on winter and wilderness activities.

ATHLETICS. NCAA. **Intercollegiate:** Basketball, cross-country, diving W, football M, golf M, ice hockey M, skiing, swimming W, tennis W, volleyball W. **Intramural:** Basketball, bowling, handball, ice hockey, racquetball, skiing, soccer, softball, squash, table tennis, tennis, volleyball, water polo.

STUDENT SERVICES. Aptitude testing, career counseling, employment service for undergraduates, freshman orientation, health services, personal counseling, placement service for graduates, special adviser for adult students, veterans counselor, services/facilities for handicapped.

ANNUAL EXPENSES. Tuition and fees: $2,528, $2,111 additional for out-of-state students. **Room and board:** $3,811. **Books and supplies:** $400. **Other expenses:** $765.

FINANCIAL AID. 70% of freshmen, 71% of continuing students receive some form of aid. Grants, loans, jobs available. 720 enrolled freshmen were judged to have need, all were offered aid. Academic scholarships available. **Aid applications:** No closing date; priority given to applications received by February 1; applicants notified on a rolling basis beginning on or about May 1; must reply within 2 weeks. **Additional information:** Audition or portfolio required for music, drama, and art scholarship applicants.

ADDRESS/TELEPHONE. Nancy Rehling, Director of Admissions, Northern Michigan University, Marquette, MI 49855. (906) 227-2650. Fax: (906) 227-2204.

Northwestern Michigan College
Traverse City, Michigan — CB code: 1564

2-year public community college, coed. Founded in 1951. **Accreditation:** Regional. **Undergraduate enrollment:** 826 men, 1,141 women full time; 969 men, 1,339 women part time. **Faculty:** 200 total (102 full time), 10 with doctorates or other terminal degrees. **Location:** Suburban campus in large town; 180 miles from Lansing, 265 miles from Detroit, 140 miles from Grand Rapids. **Calendar:** Quarter, extensive summer session. Saturday and extensive evening/early morning classes. **Microcomputers:** 230 located in dormitories, libraries, classrooms, computer centers. **Special facilities:** Great Lakes Maritime Academy, pilot training center, observatory. **Additional facts:** Satellite campus in Cadillac.

DEGREES OFFERED. AA, AS, AAS. 489 associate degrees awarded in 1992. 22% in business and management, 15% allied health, 40% multi/interdisciplinary studies, 10% trade and industry.

UNDERGRADUATE MAJORS. Accounting, airline piloting and navigation, automotive mechanics, automotive technology, business administration and management, business and management, business and office, business computer/console/peripheral equipment operation, business data processing and related programs, business data programming, commercial art, computer programming, criminal justice studies, dental assistant, design engineering, digital electronics, drafting, drafting and design technology, education, electrical and electronics equipment repair, electronic technology, engineering and engineering-related technologies, food management, food production/management/services, graphic arts technology, hotel/motel and restaurant management, industrial technology, information sciences and systems, law enforcement and corrections, law enforcement and corrections technologies, legal secretary, liberal/general studies, mechanical design technology, medical assistant, medical secretary, nursing, preengineering, prelaw, secretarial and related programs, trade and industrial supervision and management.

ACADEMIC PROGRAMS. 2-year transfer program, accelerated program, cooperative education, dual enrollment of high school students, honors program, independent study, internships, telecourses, weekend college, cross-registration. **Remedial services:** Learning center, preadmission summer program, reduced course load, remedial instruction, special counselor, tutoring. **Placement/credit:** AP, CLEP Subject, institutional tests; 45 credit hours maximum for associate degree.

ACADEMIC REQUIREMENTS. Freshmen must earn minimum GPA of 2.0 to continue in good standing. 59% of freshmen return for sophomore year. Students must declare major by end of first year. **Graduation requirements:** 96 hours for associate (40 in major). Most students required to take courses in computer science, English, history, humanities, mathematics, biological/physical sciences, social sciences. **Additional information:** Great Lakes Maritime Academy (3-year deck officer and maritime engineer training program) for service in shipping industry on campus. 9 months spent aboard commercial vessels. Associate of applied science degree awarded to maritime academy graduates.

FRESHMAN ADMISSIONS. Selection criteria: Open admissions. Selective admissions for maritime, nursing, and out-of-district applicants based on school GPA, recommendation, career objective, and test scores. ACT required for maritime program. One year of algebra and chemistry required for nursing and maritime programs. Nursing applicants also need 1 year biology.

1992 FRESHMAN CLASS PROFILE. 535 men, 685 women enrolled. 34% had high school GPA of 3.0 or higher, 62% between 2.0 and 2.99. **Characteristics:** 98% from in state, 87% commute, 4% have minority backgrounds, 1% are foreign students. Average age is 20.

FALL-TERM APPLICATIONS. $15 fee, may be waived for applicants with need. No closing date; applicants notified on a rolling basis. Interview recommended for nursing and out-of-district applicants with GPA below 2.0. Deferred and early admission available.

STUDENT LIFE. Housing: Dormitories (coed); apartment housing available. **Activities:** Student government, magazine, radio, student newspaper, television, choral groups, concert band, dance, drama, jazz band, music ensembles, musical theater, symphony orchestra, residence hall council, propeller club, campus ministry.

ATHLETICS. Intramural: Basketball, cross-country, skiing, soccer, softball, volleyball.

STUDENT SERVICES. Aptitude testing, career counseling, employment service for undergraduates, freshman orientation, health services, on-campus day care, personal counseling, placement service for graduates, special adviser for adult students, veterans counselor, services/facilities for handicapped.

ANNUAL EXPENSES. Tuition and fees (projected): $1,620, $996 additional for out-of-district students, $1,296 additional for out-of-state students. **Room and board:** $3,344. **Books and supplies:** $450. **Other expenses:** $750.

FINANCIAL AID. 30% of freshmen, 42% of continuing students receive some form of aid. 89% of grants, 74% of loans, 17% of jobs based on need. 392 enrolled freshmen were judged to have need, 337 were offered aid. Academic, music/drama, art, state/district residency, leadership scholarships available. **Aid applications:** No closing date; priority given to applications received by April 1; applicants notified on a rolling basis beginning on or about August 1; must reply within 2 weeks.

ADDRESS/TELEPHONE. Robert D. Warner, Director of Admissions and Financial Aid, Northwestern Michigan College, 1701 East Front Street, Traverse City, MI 49684. (616) 922-1054. (800) 748-0566. Fax: (616) 922-1570.

Northwood University
Midland, Michigan — CB code: 1568

Admissions: 95% of applicants accepted
Based on: ••• School record
• Activities, interview, recommendations, test scores
Completion: 90% of freshmen end year in good standing
35% graduate

4-year private business college, coed. Founded in 1959. **Accreditation:** Regional. **Undergraduate enrollment:** 975 men, 726 women full time; 13 men, 16 women part time. **Faculty:** 57 total (33 full time), 12 with doctorates or other terminal degrees. **Location:** Suburban campus in large town; 135 miles from Detroit, 25 miles from Saginaw. **Calendar:** Quarter, limited summer session. **Microcomputers:** 85 located in computer centers. **Special facilities:** Art gallery, creativity center, college-operated hotel. **Additional facts:** Additional campuses in West Palm Beach, Florida, and Cedar Hills, Texas. Margaret Chase Smith Library Center in Skowhegan, Maine. Extension center in Paris, France.

DEGREES OFFERED. AA, B, MBA. 190 associate degrees awarded in 1992. 96% in business and management. 190 bachelor's degrees awarded. 100% in business and management.

UNDERGRADUATE MAJORS. Accounting, advertising, apparel and accessories marketing, automotive aftermarket management, automotive marketing, automotive service management, business administration and management, business and management, business data programming, computer and information sciences, computer programming, data processing, fashion merchandising, finance, food management, hotel/motel and restaurant management, information sciences and systems, liberal/general studies, management information systems. accounting, automotive marketing, business administration and management, business and management, business economics, computer and information sciences, computer programming, data processing, economics, marketing and distribution, marketing management.

ACADEMIC PROGRAMS. 2-year transfer program, accelerated program, double major, dual enrollment of high school students, external degree, independent study, internships, study abroad. **Remedial services:** Preadmission summer program, reduced course load, remedial instruction, tutoring. **ROTC:** Army. **Placement/credit:** AP, CLEP General and Subject, institutional tests.

ACADEMIC REQUIREMENTS. Freshmen must earn minimum GPA of 2.0 to continue in good standing. 70% of freshmen return for sophomore year. Students must declare major by end of second year. **Graduation requirements:** 90 hours for associate (36 in major), 180 hours for bachelor's (36 in major). Most students required to take courses in computer science, English, humanities, mathematics, philosophy/religion, biological/physical sciences, social sciences. **Postgraduate studies:** 85% from 2-year programs enter 4-year programs.

FRESHMAN ADMISSIONS. Selection criteria: Minimum GPA of 2.0 and strong interest in business or related field. Test scores considered. Students with lower GPA admitted on probation. Recommended units include English 3, foreign language 1, mathematics 2 and social science 2. **Test requirements:** SAT or ACT (ACT preferred) for placement and counseling only; score report by September 10.

1992 FRESHMAN CLASS PROFILE. 844 men and women applied, 800 accepted; 203 men enrolled, 139 women enrolled. **Characteristics:** 64% from in state, 98% live in college housing, 23% have minority backgrounds, 2% are foreign students, 5% join fraternities/sororities. Average age is 18.

FALL-TERM APPLICATIONS. $15 fee, may be waived for applicants with need. Closing date September 10; priority given to applications received by April 15; applicants notified on a rolling basis; must reply within 4 weeks. Interview recommended. Deferred and early admission available.

STUDENT LIFE. Housing: Dormitories (men, women); apartment, fraternity, sorority housing available. Unmarried freshmen under age 20 not living within commuting area required to live on campus. **Activities:** Student government, radio, student newspaper, yearbook, drama, jazz band, pep band, fraternities, sororities, Distributive Education Clubs of America, Business Professionals of America, Advertising Federation, Adcraft, Data Processing Management Association, Christian Fellowship, Investment Club, Nowman Club, Student Economic Leadership Forum, Black Leadership Awareness Coalition.

ATHLETICS. NAIA, NCAA. **Intercollegiate:** Baseball M, basketball, cross-country, football M, golf M, lacrosse M, softball W, tennis, track and field, volleyball W. **Intramural:** Basketball, bowling, ice hockey M, rugby M, skiing, soccer M, softball, swimming, volleyball.

STUDENT SERVICES. Career counseling, employment service for undergraduates, freshman orientation, health services, personal counseling, placement service for graduates, services/facilities for handicapped.

ANNUAL EXPENSES. Tuition and fees: $9,065. **Room and board:** $4,266. **Books and supplies:** $575. **Other expenses:** $582.

FINANCIAL AID. 89% of freshmen, 70% of continuing students receive some form of aid. 81% of grants, 74% of loans, 52% of jobs based on need. Academic, athletic, state/district residency scholarships available. **Aid applications:** No closing date; priority given to applications received by March 15; applicants notified on a rolling basis beginning on or about April 1; must reply within 2 weeks.

ADDRESS/TELEPHONE. Agostino DiMaggio/Daniel Toland, Director of Admissions, Northwood University, 3225 Cook Road, Midland, MI 48640. (517) 837-4200. (800) 457-7878. Fax: (517) 832-9590.

Oakland Community College
Bloomfield Hills, Michigan — CB code: 1607

2-year public community college, coed. Founded in 1964. **Accreditation:** Regional. **Undergraduate enrollment:** 3,020 men, 3,063 women full time; 9,097 men, 14,153 women part time. **Faculty:** 788 total (290 full time), 53 with doctorates or other terminal degrees. **Location:** Suburban campus in large city; 30 miles from downtown Detroit. **Calendar:** Semester, limited summer session. Saturday and extensive evening/early morning classes. **Additional facts:** Multicampus institution with locations in Auburn Hills, Farmington Hills, Southfield, Royal Oak, and Union Lake.

DEGREES OFFERED. AA, AS, AAS. 2,051 associate degrees awarded in 1992.

UNDERGRADUATE MAJORS. Accounting, air conditioning/heating/refrigeration mechanics, air conditioning/heating/refrigeration technology, architectural technologies, automotive technology, aviation management, business administration and management, business and office, business data processing and related programs, business data programming, ceramics, child development/care/guidance, clinical laboratory science, computer programming, court reporting, criminal justice studies, data processing, dental hygiene, drafting, drafting and design technology, electrical technology, electromechanical technology, electronic technology, emergency medical technologies, engineering and engineering-related technologies, fashion merchandising, finance, fine arts, food management, food production/management/services, gerontology, graphic and printing production, graphic arts technology, health care administration, hospitality and recreation marketing, hotel/motel and restaurant management, industrial technology, international business management, landscape architecture, law enforcement and corrections, law enforcement and corrections technologies, legal assistant/paralegal, liberal/general studies, library assistant, marketing and distribution, mechanical design technology, medical assistant, medical laboratory technologies, mental health/human services, noninvasive cardiovascular technology, nursing, personal services, photographic technology, practical nursing, precision metal work, preengineering, quality control technology, radio/television broadcasting, radio/television technology, radiograph medical technology, respiratory therapy technology, robotics, science technologies, secretarial and related programs, solar heating and cooling technology, systems analysis, ultrasound technology, welding technology.

ACADEMIC PROGRAMS. 2-year transfer program, dual enrollment of high school students, internships, telecourses. **Remedial services:** Learning center, reduced course load, remedial instruction, tutoring. **Placement/credit:** AP, CLEP General and Subject, institutional tests.

ACADEMIC REQUIREMENTS. No policy requiring minimum GPA; records of students having academic difficulty are reviewed individually. 20% of freshmen return for sophomore year. Students must declare major on application. **Graduation requirements:** 62 hours for associate. Most students required to take courses in arts/fine arts, English, humanities, mathematics, biological/physical sciences, social sciences.

FRESHMAN ADMISSIONS. Selection criteria: Open admissions.

1992 FRESHMAN CLASS PROFILE. 1,611 men and women enrolled. **Characteristics:** 99% from in state, 100% commute, 16% have minority backgrounds.

FALL-TERM APPLICATIONS. No fee. No closing date; priority given to applications received by September 1; applicants notified on a rolling basis. Interview recommended. Deferred admission available. ASSET exam required of new college students for placement in English.

STUDENT LIFE. Activities: Student government, radio, student newspaper, yearbook, choral groups, concert band, dance, drama, music ensembles, fraternities, Association of Black Students, gourmet club, debate squad, film club.

ATHLETICS. NJCAA. **Intercollegiate:** Basketball, cross-country, golf M, softball W, tennis, volleyball W. **Intramural:** Badminton, basketball, bowling, golf, handball, racquetball, softball, swimming, table tennis, tennis, volleyball.

STUDENT SERVICES. Aptitude testing, career counseling, employment service for undergraduates, freshman orientation, health services, on-campus day care, personal counseling, placement service for graduates, veterans counselor, services/facilities for handicapped.

ANNUAL EXPENSES. Tuition and fees (projected): $1,425, $885 additional for out-of-district students, $1,815 additional for out-of-state students. **Books and supplies:** $700. **Other expenses:** $360.

FINANCIAL AID. 99% of grants, 69% of loans, 63% of jobs based on need. Academic, athletic, minority scholarships available. **Aid applications:** No closing date; priority given to applications received by July 1; applicants notified on a rolling basis beginning on or about June 1; must reply within 2 weeks.

ADDRESS/TELEPHONE. Dr. Maurice H. McCall, Director of Enrollment Services, Oakland Community College, 2480 Opdyke Road, Bloomfield Hills, MI 48304-2266. (313) 540-1549. Fax: (313) 540-1841.

Oakland University
Rochester, Michigan CB code: 1497

4-year public university, coed. Founded in 1957. **Accreditation:** Regional. **Undergraduate enrollment:** 2,300 men, 4,061 women full time; 1,482 men, 2,708 women part time. **Graduate enrollment:** 237 men, 365 women full time; 672 men, 1,243 women part time. **Faculty:** 616 total (376 full time), 403 with doctorates or other terminal degrees. **Location:** Suburban campus in small city; 30 miles from Detroit. **Calendar:** Semester, limited summer session. **Microcomputers:** 300 located in libraries, classrooms, computer centers. **Special facilities:** Meadowbrook conference hall, museum, theater, art gallery, music pavilion, engineering and science research laboratories, robotics laboratory, CAD-CAM laboratory. **Additional facts:** Technological park adjacent to campus provides internship and cooperative education opportunities.

DEGREES OFFERED. BA, BS, MA, MS, MBA, MEd, PhD. 1,572 bachelor's degrees awarded in 1992. 21% in business and management, 10% communications, 8% teacher education, 8% engineering, 11% health sciences, 5% life sciences, 6% psychology, 9% social sciences. Graduate degrees offered in 37 major fields of study.

UNDERGRADUATE MAJORS. Accounting, African studies, Afro-American (black) studies, anthropology, art history, biochemistry, biological and physical sciences, biology, business administration and management, business and management, business economics, chemistry, Chinese, clinical laboratory science, communications, computer and information sciences, computer engineering, East Asian studies, economics, electrical/electronics/communications engineering, elementary education, engineering, engineering and other disciplines, engineering chemistry, engineering physics, English, English literature, environmental science, finance, French, German, history, human resources development, humanities and social sciences, industrial health and safety, journalism, Latin American studies, liberal/general studies, linguistics, management information systems, marketing management, mathematics, mathematics education, mechanical engineering, medical physics, music, music education, music performance, nursing, perfusion technology, personnel management, philosophy, physical sciences, physical therapy, physics, political science and government, psychology, public administration, public policy studies, secondary education, sociology, South Asian studies, Spanish, systems engineering.

ACADEMIC PROGRAMS. Accelerated program, cooperative education, double major, dual enrollment of high school students, education specialist degree, honors program, independent study, internships, student-designed major, study abroad, teacher preparation, visiting/exchange student program; liberal arts/career combination in engineering, health sciences; combined bachelor's/graduate program in business administration. **Remedial services:** Learning center, preadmission summer program, reduced course load, remedial instruction, special counselor, tutoring. **Placement/credit:** AP, CLEP General and Subject, institutional tests; 60 credit hours maximum for bachelor's degree.

ACADEMIC REQUIREMENTS. Freshmen must earn minimum GPA of 2.0 to continue in good standing. 75% of freshmen return for sophomore year. Students must declare major by end of second year. **Graduation requirements:** 124 hours for bachelor's (40 in major). Most students required to take courses in arts/fine arts, computer science, English, foreign languages, history, humanities, mathematics, philosophy/religion, biological/physical sciences, social sciences.

FRESHMAN ADMISSIONS. Selection criteria: Admissions based on high school GPA of 2.7, school and community activities, recommendations. Applicants with minimum GPA of 2.0 may be admitted to summer program. Engineering, business, education, nursing, and physical therapy programs require higher GPA. **High school preparation:** 12 units required. Required and recommended units include biological science 1, English 4, mathematics 3-4, physical science 1-2 and social science 3. Foreign language 3 recommended. Additional courses required for health sciences, engineering, and computer and information sciences. **Test requirements:** ACT; score report by August 1.

1992 FRESHMAN CLASS PROFILE. 410 men, 807 women enrolled. 63% had high school GPA of 3.0 or higher, 37% between 2.0 and 2.99. **Academic background:** Mid 50% of enrolled freshmen had ACT composite between 19-25. 86% submitted ACT scores. **Characteristics:** 95% from in state, 17% live in college housing, 15% have minority backgrounds, 1% are foreign students, 10% join fraternities/sororities. Average age is 18.

FALL-TERM APPLICATIONS. $25 fee, may be waived for applicants with need. Closing date July 15; priority given to applications received by April 1; applicants notified on a rolling basis; must reply by May 15 or within 2 weeks if notified thereafter. Audition required for music applicants. Interview recommended. CRDA. Early admission available. High school students who enroll early can only take those courses not available at their high school. They must complete those courses with B+ or better, and obtain principal's permission to enroll.

STUDENT LIFE. Housing: Dormitories (coed); apartment housing available. Residence halls easily accessible to handicapped persons. Freshmen must live on campus unless living with family. Honors Residence Hall and Wellness Hall on campus. **Activities:** Student government, radio, student newspaper, yearbook, choral groups, concert band, dance, drama, jazz band, music ensembles, musical theater, opera, pep band, symphony orchestra, fraternities, sororities, over 120 student organizations, extracurricular clubs, and activities.

ATHLETICS. NCAA. **Intercollegiate:** Baseball M, basketball, cross-country M, diving, golf, soccer M, swimming, tennis, volleyball W. **Intramural:** Basketball, cross-country M, fencing M, handball, racquetball, soccer, softball, swimming, tennis, volleyball.

STUDENT SERVICES. Aptitude testing, career counseling, employment service for undergraduates, freshman orientation, health services, on-campus day care, personal counseling, placement service for graduates, special adviser for adult students, veterans counselor, services/facilities for handicapped.

ANNUAL EXPENSES. Tuition and fees (1992-93): $2,499, $4,718 additional for out-of-state students. **Room and board:** $3,890. **Books and supplies:** $400. **Other expenses:** $650.

FINANCIAL AID. 35% of freshmen, 35% of continuing students receive some form of aid. 72% of grants, 86% of loans, 12% of jobs based on need. 420 enrolled freshmen were judged to have need, 393 were offered aid. Academic, music/drama, athletic, leadership scholarships available. **Aid applications:** No closing date; priority given to applications received by March 1; applicants notified on a rolling basis beginning on or about April 1; must reply by May 1 or within 1 week if notified thereafter.

ADDRESS/TELEPHONE. Jerry W. Rose, Director of Admissions, Oakland University, 205 Wilson Hall, Rochester, MI 48309-4401. (313) 370-3360.

Olivet College
Olivet, Michigan CB code: 1595

4-year private liberal arts college, coed, affiliated with Congregational Christian Churches and United Church of Christ. Founded in 1844. **Accreditation:** Regional. **Undergraduate enrollment:** 676 men and women. **Faculty:** 77 total (41 full time), 26 with doctorates or other terminal degrees. **Location:** Rural campus in rural community; 30 miles from Lansing. **Calendar:** Semester. **Microcomputers:** 20 located in libraries, classrooms, computer centers. **Special facilities:** Observatory/planetarium, Kirkelldel Dynamic Ecology Laboratory.

DEGREES OFFERED. BA. 102 bachelor's degrees awarded in 1992. 26% in business and management, 5% communications, 42% teacher education, 7% psychology, 6% visual and performing arts.

UNDERGRADUATE MAJORS. Accounting, American studies, anthropology, applied mathematics, art history, biochemistry, biology, business administration and management, business and management, business economics, chemistry, communications, comparative literature, computer and information sciences, computer mathematics, computer programming, creative writing, dramatic arts, economics, education, elementary education, English, English literature, French, history, humanities and social sciences, insurance and risk management, journalism, junior high education, liberal/general studies, marketing management, mathematics, music, music history and appreciation, music performance, music theory and composition, painting, personnel management, physical education, predentistry, prelaw, premedicine, prepharmacy, preveterinary, psychology, radio/television broadcasting, religious education, religious music, sculpture, secondary education, sociology, Spanish, speech, visual and performing arts.

ACADEMIC PROGRAMS. Accelerated program, cooperative education, double major, dual enrollment of high school students, honors program, independent study, internships, student-designed major, study abroad, teacher preparation, visiting/exchange student program. **Remedial services:** Learning center, reduced course load, remedial instruction, special counselor, tutoring. **Placement/credit:** AP, CLEP General and Subject, institutional tests.

ACADEMIC REQUIREMENTS. Freshmen must earn minimum GPA

of 1.67 to continue in good standing. 60% of freshmen return for sophomore year. Students must declare major by end of second year. **Graduation requirements:** 120 hours for bachelor's (42 in major). Most students required to take courses in arts/fine arts, English, history, humanities, mathematics, biological/physical sciences.

FRESHMAN ADMISSIONS. Selection criteria: Minimum 2.6 high school GPA, test scores, school achievement record. **High school preparation:** 16 units recommended. Recommended units include English 4, foreign language 1, mathematics 2, social science 3 and science 2. **Test requirements:** SAT or ACT (ACT preferred); score report by August 15.

1992 FRESHMAN CLASS PROFILE. 104 men, 54 women enrolled. 23% had high school GPA of 3.0 or higher, 73% between 2.0 and 2.99. **Characteristics:** 97% from in state, 94% live in college housing, 8% have minority backgrounds, 18% join fraternities/sororities. Average age is 18.

FALL-TERM APPLICATIONS. $10 fee, may be waived for applicants with need. Closing date August 1; priority given to applications received by May 15; applicants notified on a rolling basis; Must reply by August 1 or within 1 week if notified thereafter. Interview recommended. Audition recommended for music, drama applicants. Portfolio recommended for art applicants. CRDA. Deferred and early admission available. EDP-F.

STUDENT LIFE. Housing: Dormitories (men, women, coed); fraternity, sorority housing available. **Activities:** Student government, radio, student newspaper, yearbook, choral groups, concert band, dance, drama, jazz band, marching band, music ensembles, musical theater, opera, symphony orchestra, fraternities, sororities, Inter-Varsity Christian Fellowship, United Black Organization, Music Educators National Conference, Pi Kappa Delta.

ATHLETICS. NCAA. **Intercollegiate:** Baseball M, basketball, cross-country, field hockey W, football M, golf M, soccer M, softball W, swimming, tennis, track and field, volleyball W, wrestling M. **Intramural:** Badminton, basketball M, handball, racquetball, softball, swimming, tennis, volleyball.

STUDENT SERVICES. Career counseling, employment service for undergraduates, health services, personal counseling, placement service for graduates, special adviser for adult students, services/facilities for handicapped.

ANNUAL EXPENSES. Tuition and fees (1992-93): $8,291. **Room and board:** $2,890. **Books and supplies:** $500. **Other expenses:** $490.

FINANCIAL AID. 98% of freshmen, 98% of continuing students receive some form of aid. Grants, loans, jobs available. Academic, music/drama scholarships available. **Aid applications:** Closing date August 1; priority given to applications received by April 15; applicants notified on a rolling basis beginning on or about February 15; must reply by May 1 or within 3 weeks if notified thereafter. **Additional information:** Each enrolled student guaranteed job on campus.

ADDRESS/TELEPHONE. Timothy J. Nelson, Vice President for Enrollment/Strategic Management, Olivet College, Olivet, MI 49076. (616) 749-7635. (800) 456-7189. Fax: (616) 749-7121.

Reformed Bible College
Grand Rapids, Michigan — CB code: 1672

4-year private Bible college, coed, affiliated with Christian Reformed Church, Reformed Church in America, Reformed Presbyterian Church of North America. Founded in 1939. **Undergraduate enrollment:** 74 men, 70 women full time; 18 men, 24 women part time. **Faculty:** 20 total (14 full time), 10 with doctorates or other terminal degrees. **Location:** Suburban campus in large city; 6.5 miles from downtown. **Calendar:** Semester. **Microcomputers:** 6 located in libraries. **Additional facts:** Calvinist institution.

DEGREES OFFERED. AA, B. 15 associate degrees awarded in 1992. 100% in philosophy, religion, theology. 24 bachelor's degrees awarded. 100% in philosophy, religion, theology.

UNDERGRADUATE MAJORS. Bible studies, liberal/general studies. religious education.

ACADEMIC PROGRAMS. 2-year transfer program, accelerated program, double major, independent study, internships, study abroad. **Remedial services:** Reduced course load, remedial instruction. **Placement/credit:** AP, CLEP General and Subject, institutional tests; 6 credit hours maximum for associate degree; 6 credit hours maximum for bachelor's degree.

ACADEMIC REQUIREMENTS. Freshmen must earn minimum GPA of 1.75 to continue in good standing. 85% of freshmen return for sophomore year. Students must declare major by end of first year. **Graduation requirements:** 66 hours for associate (30 in major), 129 hours for bachelor's (30 in major). Most students required to take courses in arts/fine arts, English, history, philosophy/religion, social sciences. **Postgraduate studies:** 25% from 2-year programs enter 4-year programs. 22% enter other graduate study.

FRESHMAN ADMISSIONS. Selection criteria: Open admissions. Applicants with GPA below 2.0 admitted on probation and evaluated individually. **Test requirements:** SAT or ACT.

1992 FRESHMAN CLASS PROFILE. 19 men applied, 19 accepted, 19 enrolled; 33 women applied, 31 accepted, 21 enrolled. 37% had high school GPA of 3.0 or higher, 49% between 2.0 and 2.99. **Characteristics:** 63% from in state, 68% live in college housing, 2% have minority backgrounds, 20% are foreign students. Average age is 19.

FALL-TERM APPLICATIONS. $10 fee. No closing date; applicants notified on a rolling basis. Interview recommended for borderline applicants. Deferred admission available.

STUDENT LIFE. Housing: Dormitories (coed); apartment housing available. **Activities:** Student government, student newspaper, yearbook, choral groups, drama, music ensembles.

ATHLETICS. Intercollegiate: Basketball M, soccer M. **Intramural:** Ice hockey M, volleyball W.

STUDENT SERVICES. Aptitude testing, career counseling, employment service for undergraduates, freshman orientation, personal counseling, placement service for graduates, services/facilities for handicapped.

ANNUAL EXPENSES. Tuition and fees (1992-93): $5,670. **Room and board:** $3,100. **Books and supplies:** $375. **Other expenses:** $635.

FINANCIAL AID. 88% of freshmen, 84% of continuing students receive some form of aid. 89% of grants, 82% of loans, all jobs based on need. **Aid applications:** No closing date; applicants notified on a rolling basis beginning on or about April 20.

ADDRESS/TELEPHONE. Dorothy Hostetter, Director of Admissions and Financial Aid, Reformed Bible College, 3333 East Beltline NE, Grand Rapids, MI 49505-9749. (616) 363-2050 ext. 134. Fax: (616) 363-9771.

Sacred Heart Major Seminary
Detroit, Michigan — CB code: 1686

Admissions: 83% of applicants accepted
Based on: ••• Interview, recommendations, school record
•• Activities
• Test scores
Completion: 90% of freshmen end year in good standing
50% enter graduate study

4-year private seminary college, coed, affiliated with Roman Catholic Church. Founded in 1919. **Accreditation:** Regional. **Undergraduate enrollment:** 28 men, 1 woman full time; 4 men, 6 women part time. **Graduate enrollment:** 32 men full time; 9 men, 9 women part time. **Faculty:** 48 total (24 full time), 23 with doctorates or other terminal degrees. **Location:** Urban campus in very large city; within Detroit City limits. **Calendar:** Semester. Saturday and extensive evening/early morning classes. **Microcomputers:** Located in computer centers. **Additional facts:** Most B.A. candidates for priesthood. 2-year programs leading to ordination as deacon or certification in pastoral-liturgical ministry offered. Pastoral ministry courses and degree programs open to men and women. Master level courses designed for laity who wish to minister in Church.

DEGREES OFFERED. AA, BA, MA, M.Div. 4 bachelor's degrees awarded. 50% in philosophy, religion, theology, 50% social sciences. Graduate degrees offered in 2 major fields of study.

UNDERGRADUATE MAJORS. Associate: Theological studies. **Bachelor's:** Liberal/general studies, philosophy.

ACADEMIC PROGRAMS. Telecourses, cross-registration, program requiring 3 minors in interdisciplinary studies. **Remedial services:** Reduced course load, tutoring. **Placement/credit:** AP, institutional tests; 6 credit hours maximum for associate degree; 12 credit hours maximum for bachelor's degree.

ACADEMIC REQUIREMENTS. Freshmen must earn minimum GPA of 2.0 to continue in good standing. 90% of freshmen return for sophomore year. Students must declare major by end of second year. **Graduation requirements:** 64 hours for associate (16 in major), 128 hours for bachelor's (30 in major). Most students required to take courses in arts/fine arts, computer science, English, foreign languages, history, humanities, philosophy/religion, biological/physical sciences, social sciences. **Postgraduate studies:** 50% enter other graduate study. **Additional information:** 30% to 40% of undergraduate course work taken at other consortium colleges.

FRESHMAN ADMISSIONS. Selection criteria: Recommendations of parish pastor and high school principal or high school or college counselor vital. School, community, and church-related activities viewed as important formative experiences. Minimum high school involvement in college preparatory program. **Test requirements:** SAT or ACT (ACT preferred); score report by August 1.

1992 FRESHMAN CLASS PROFILE. 12 men applied, 10 accepted, 9 enrolled. 50% had high school GPA of 3.0 or higher, 38% between 2.0 and 2.99. **Characteristics:** 100% from in state, 100% live in college housing. Average age is 22.

FALL-TERM APPLICATIONS. $30 fee, may be waived for applicants with need. No closing date; priority given to applications received by March 1; applicants notified on a rolling basis beginning on or about March 1. Interview required for priesthood candidates applicants. Deferred admission available.

STUDENT LIFE. Housing: Dormitories (men). Graduate student housing for men only. **Activities:** Student government, student newspaper, yearbook, choral groups, Christian ministry program. **Additional information:** Religious observance required.

ATHLETICS. Intercollegiate: Basketball M. **Intramural:** Handball M, racquetball M, softball M, volleyball M.

STUDENT SERVICES. Freshman orientation, health services, personal counseling, services/facilities for handicapped.

ANNUAL EXPENSES. Tuition and fees: $4,030. **Room and board:** $4,100. **Books and supplies:** $750. **Other expenses:** $750.

FINANCIAL AID. 100% of freshmen, 100% of continuing students receive some form of aid. 76% of grants, all loans, all jobs based on need. 4 enrolled freshmen were judged to have need, 3 were offered aid. **Aid applications:** No closing date; priority given to applications received by April 1; applicants notified on a rolling basis beginning on or about May 1; must reply within 3 weeks.

ADDRESS/TELEPHONE. Rev. William Easton, Vice Rector, Sacred Heart Major Seminary, 2701 West Chicago Boulevard, Detroit, MI 48206. (313) 883-8500. Fax: (313) 868-6440.

Saginaw Valley State University
University Center, Michigan CB code: 1766

4-year public university and college of arts and sciences and business, engineering, health science, nursing, teachers college, coed. Founded in 1963. **Accreditation:** Regional. **Undergraduate enrollment:** 1,534 men, 2,000 women full time; 821 men, 1,220 women part time. **Graduate enrollment:** 16 men, 16 women full time; 194 men, 438 women part time. **Faculty:** 386 total (170 full time), 136 with doctorates or other terminal degrees. **Location:** Suburban campus in small city; 10 miles from Bay City, Saginaw. **Calendar:** Semester, limited summer session. **Microcomputers:** 160 located in classrooms, computer centers. **Special facilities:** Aubury Fine Arts Center, Marshall M. Fredericks Sculpture Gallery.

DEGREES OFFERED. BA, BS, MA, MS, MBA, MEd. 705 bachelor's degrees awarded in 1992. 24% in business and management, 5% computer sciences, 13% education, 6% engineering, 7% health sciences, 17% parks/recreation, protective services, public affairs, 5% psychology, 7% social sciences. Graduate degrees offered in 18 major fields of study.

UNDERGRADUATE MAJORS. Accounting, art education, bilingual/bicultural education, biochemistry, biological and physical sciences, biology, business administration and management, business and management, business chemistry, business economics, chemistry, communications, computer and information sciences, computer mathematics, computer programming, criminal justice studies, dramatic arts, economics, education of the emotionally handicapped, electrical/electronics/communications engineering, elementary education, English, English education, finance, fine arts, foreign languages education, French, history, industrial technology, information sciences and systems, law enforcement and corrections, marketing management, mathematics, mathematics education, mechanical engineering, medical laboratory technologies, music, music education, nursing, occupational therapy, optical physics, physical education, physics, political science and government, prelaw, psychology, public administration, science education, secondary education, social studies education, social work, sociology, Spanish, special education, specific learning disabilities, speech.

ACADEMIC PROGRAMS. Accelerated program, cooperative education, double major, dual enrollment of high school students, honors program, independent study, student-designed major, study abroad, teacher preparation. **Remedial services:** Learning center, preadmission summer program, reduced course load, remedial instruction, tutoring, writing laboratory, reading specialist. **Placement/credit:** AP, CLEP General and Subject, institutional tests. Maximum of 62 semester hours of credit by CLEP examinations may be counted toward degree.

ACADEMIC REQUIREMENTS. Freshmen must earn minimum GPA of 1.7 to continue in good standing. 64% of freshmen return for sophomore year. Students must declare major by end of second year. **Graduation requirements:** 124 hours for bachelor's (36 in major). Most students required to take courses in English, humanities, mathematics, biological/physical sciences, social sciences. **Postgraduate studies:** 3% enter law school, 1% enter medical school, 6% enter MBA programs, 16% enter other graduate study.

FRESHMAN ADMISSIONS. Selection criteria: Minimum high school GPA of 2.5 in academic subjects preferred. Recommendations, test scores, and interview considered for applicants with minimum 2.0 GPA. **High school preparation:** 16 units recommended. Recommended units include English 4, foreign language 2, mathematics 4, physical science 3 and social science 3. Computer science also recommended. **Test requirements:** SAT or ACT (ACT preferred); score report by September 1.

1992 FRESHMAN CLASS PROFILE. 320 men, 399 women enrolled. 53% had high school GPA of 3.0 or higher, 46% between 2.0 and 2.99. **Academic background:** Mid 50% of enrolled freshmen had ACT composite between 21-22. 90% submitted ACT scores. **Characteristics:** 99% from in state, 65% commute, 10% have minority backgrounds. Average age is 19.

FALL-TERM APPLICATIONS. $20 fee, may be waived for applicants with need. No closing date; priority given to applications received by July 30; applicants notified on a rolling basis. Interview recommended. CRDA. Early admission available.

STUDENT LIFE. Housing: Dormitories (coed); apartment housing available. Dormitory suites with facilities designed for the physically handicapped. **Activities:** Student government, magazine, student newspaper, literary newsletter, choral groups, concert band, drama, jazz band, marching band, music ensembles, pep band, stage band, fraternities, sororities, 44 campus organizations including ministry, Institute of Polish Studies, student volunteer organization, Non-Traditional Students Organization.

ATHLETICS. NCAA. **Intercollegiate:** Baseball M, basketball, bowling M, cross-country, football M, golf M, softball W, tennis W, track and field, volleyball W. **Intramural:** Badminton, basketball, bowling, field hockey W, golf, handball, horseback riding, racquetball, skiing, soccer M, softball, swimming, table tennis, tennis, track and field, volleyball, water polo.

STUDENT SERVICES. Career counseling, employment service for undergraduates, freshman orientation, health services, on-campus day care, personal counseling, placement service for graduates, special adviser for adult students, services/facilities for handicapped.

ANNUAL EXPENSES. Tuition and fees (projected): $2,883, $2,826 additional for out-of-state students. **Room and board:** $3,729. **Books and supplies:** $550. **Other expenses:** $918.

FINANCIAL AID. 70% of freshmen, 51% of continuing students receive some form of aid. 76% of grants, 91% of loans, 45% of jobs based on need. 429 enrolled freshmen were judged to have need, all were offered aid. Academic, music/drama, athletic, leadership, minority scholarships available. **Aid applications:** No closing date; priority given to applications received by April 1; applicants notified on a rolling basis beginning on or about May 15; must reply within 10 days. **Additional information:** Students should submit need analysis application after January 1, since all awards are made on first-come first-served basis.

ADDRESS/TELEPHONE. James P. Dwyer, Director of Admissions, Saginaw Valley State University, 2250 Pierce Road, University Center, MI 48710-0001. (517) 790-4200. Fax: (517) 790-0180.

St. Clair County Community College
Port Huron, Michigan CB code: 1628

2-year public community college, coed. Founded in 1923. **Accreditation:** Regional. **Undergraduate enrollment:** 633 men, 922 women full time; 1,254 men, 2,105 women part time. **Faculty:** 241 total (91 full time), 6 with doctorates or other terminal degrees. **Location:** Urban campus in large town; 55 miles from Detroit. **Calendar:** Semester, limited summer session. **Microcomputers:** 250 located in classrooms, computer centers.

DEGREES OFFERED. AA, AS, AAS. 409 associate degrees awarded in 1992.

UNDERGRADUATE MAJORS. Accounting, advertising design, architecture, business and management, business and office, business data processing and related programs, business data programming, communications, computer programming, data processing, dietetic aide/assistant, drafting, drafting and design technology, electronic technology, fine arts, fire control and safety technology, horticulture, industrial technology, journalism, law enforcement and corrections technologies, legal secretary, liberal/general studies, machine tool operation/machine shop, manufacturing technology, marketing and distribution, medical secretary, mental health/human services, microcomputer software, nursing, plastic technology, quality control technology, radio/television broadcasting, robotics, secretarial and related programs, welding technology, word processing.

ACADEMIC PROGRAMS. 2-year transfer program, double major, dual enrollment of high school students, internships. **Remedial services:** Learning center, reduced course load, remedial instruction, special counselor, tutoring. **Placement/credit:** AP, CLEP General and Subject, institutional tests; 45 credit hours maximum for associate degree.

ACADEMIC REQUIREMENTS. Freshmen must earn minimum GPA of 2.0 to continue in good standing. 81% of freshmen return for sophomore year. **Graduation requirements:** 62 hours for associate. Most students required to take courses in English, biological/physical sciences, social sciences.

FRESHMAN ADMISSIONS. Selection criteria: Open admissions.

1992 FRESHMAN CLASS PROFILE. 472 men, 597 women enrolled. **Characteristics:** 100% commute, 4% have minority backgrounds. Average age is 23.

FALL-TERM APPLICATIONS. $10 fee. No closing date; applicants notified on a rolling basis; must reply immediately. Deferred and early admission available.

STUDENT LIFE. Activities: Student government, radio, student newspaper, television, choral groups, concert band, drama, jazz band, music ensembles, symphony orchestra.

ATHLETICS. NJCAA. **Intercollegiate:** Baseball M, basketball, golf, softball W **Intramural:** Volleyball.

STUDENT SERVICES. Aptitude testing, career counseling, employment service for undergraduates, freshman orientation, on-campus day care, personal counseling, placement service for graduates, veterans counselor, services/facilities for handicapped.

ANNUAL EXPENSES. Tuition and fees (projected): $1,530, $750 additional for out-of-district students, $1,650 additional for out-of-state students. **Books and supplies:** $450. **Other expenses:** $800.

FINANCIAL AID. 45% of freshmen, 25% of continuing students receive some form of aid. 98% of grants, 86% of loans, 94% of jobs based on need. 375 enrolled freshmen were judged to have need, all were offered aid.

Academic, music/drama, art, athletic, state/district residency, leadership scholarships available. **Aid applications:** No closing date; priority given to applications received by June 1; applicants notified on a rolling basis beginning on or about May 15; must reply within 2 weeks.

ADDRESS/TELEPHONE. Michelle K. Mueller, Director of Admissions, St. Clair County Community College, PO PO Box 5015, 323 Erie Street, Port Huron, MI 48061-5015. (313) 984-3881 ext. 236. Fax: (313) 984-4730.

St. Mary's College
Orchard Lake, Michigan — CB code: 1753

4-year private liberal arts college, coed, affiliated with Roman Catholic Church. Founded in 1885. **Accreditation:** Regional. **Undergraduate enrollment:** 83 men, 117 women full time; 74 men, 133 women part time. **Faculty:** 42 total (18 full time), 19 with doctorates or other terminal degrees. **Location:** Suburban campus in small town; 25 miles from downtown Detroit. **Calendar:** Semester, limited summer session. **Microcomputers:** 12 located in computer centers. **Special facilities:** Large collection of Polish language research books, Center of Polish Studies, Polish-American Sports Hall of Fame.

DEGREES OFFERED. BA, BS. 50 bachelor's degrees awarded in 1992. 20% in business and management, 10% communications, 8% computer sciences, 10% allied health, 7% letters/literature, 10% life sciences, 15% philosophy, religion, theology, 5% physical sciences, 5% psychology, 10% social sciences.

UNDERGRADUATE MAJORS. Biology, business administration and management, business and management, chemistry, communications, computer and information sciences, English, foreign languages (multiple emphasis), liberal/general studies, mental health/human services, philosophy, psychology, radiograph medical technology, religious education, social sciences, theological studies.

ACADEMIC PROGRAMS. Accelerated program, cooperative education, double major, dual enrollment of high school students, independent study, internships, student-designed major, study abroad, cross-registration, priestly formation program prepares men for Roman Catholic priesthood; liberal arts/career combination in health sciences. **Remedial services:** Learning center, reduced course load, tutoring. **Placement/credit:** AP, CLEP General and Subject, institutional tests; 30 credit hours maximum for bachelor's degree.

ACADEMIC REQUIREMENTS. Freshmen must earn minimum GPA of 2.0 to continue in good standing. 75% of freshmen return for sophomore year. Students must declare major by end of second year. **Graduation requirements:** 120 hours for bachelor's (30 in major). Most students required to take courses in arts/fine arts, computer science, English, foreign languages, history, humanities, mathematics, philosophy/religion, biological/physical sciences, social sciences. **Postgraduate studies:** 5% enter law school, 1% enter medical school, 5% enter MBA programs, 40% enter other graduate study.

FRESHMAN ADMISSIONS. Selection criteria: 2.5 high school GPA, SAT combined scores of 900 or ACT composite score of 19, and counselor's or teacher's recommendation. **High school preparation:** 16 units recommended. Recommended units include biological science 1, English 4, foreign language 1, mathematics 2, physical science 1 and social science 4. **Test requirements:** SAT or ACT (ACT preferred); score report by September 1.

1992 FRESHMAN CLASS PROFILE. 38 men, 73 women enrolled. 60% had high school GPA of 3.0 or higher, 36% between 2.0 and 2.99. **Academic background:** Mid 50% of enrolled freshmen had ACT composite between 14-23. 96% submitted ACT scores. **Characteristics:** 94% from in state, 50% commute, 10% have minority backgrounds, 3% are foreign students, 30% join fraternities/sororities. Average age is 19.

FALL-TERM APPLICATIONS. $20 fee, may be waived for applicants with need. Closing date September 1; applicants notified on a rolling basis. Interview required for applicants with GPA below 2.5 o. Deferred admission available.

STUDENT LIFE. Housing: Dormitories (men, women). **Activities:** Student government, magazine, radio, student newspaper, choral groups, dance, drama, fraternities, sororities.

ATHLETICS. NAIA. **Intramural:** Baseball M, basketball, softball, tennis, volleyball.

STUDENT SERVICES. Aptitude testing, career counseling, employment service for undergraduates, freshman orientation, health services, personal counseling, placement service for graduates, services/facilities for handicapped.

ANNUAL EXPENSES. Tuition and fees: $5,250. **Room and board:** $3,200. **Books and supplies:** $500.

FINANCIAL AID. 60% of freshmen, 40% of continuing students receive some form of aid. 96% of grants, all jobs based on need. Academic, athletic, state/district residency, leadership scholarships available. **Aid applications:** Closing date March 15; applicants notified on a rolling basis beginning on or about June 1; must reply by August 1 or within 2 weeks if notified thereafter.

ADDRESS/TELEPHONE. Darrell Brockway, Dean of Enrollment Services, St. Mary's College, Commerce and Orchard Lake Roads, Orchard Lake, MI 48324. (313) 683-0523. Fax: (313) 683-0402.

Schoolcraft College
Livonia, Michigan — CB code: 1764

2-year public community college, coed. Founded in 1961. **Accreditation:** Regional. **Undergraduate enrollment:** 1,006 men, 1,448 women full time; 3,117 men, 4,485 women part time. **Faculty:** 441 total (125 full time), 15 with doctorates or other terminal degrees. **Location:** Suburban campus in small city; 8 miles from Detroit. **Calendar:** Semester, limited summer session. Saturday and extensive evening/early morning classes. **Microcomputers:** 321 located in classrooms.

DEGREES OFFERED. AA, AS, AAS. 747 associate degrees awarded in 1992. 15% in business and management, 5% business/office and marketing/distribution, 5% communications, 5% computer sciences, 10% education, 5% engineering, 5% health sciences, 15% allied health, 5% life sciences, 5% mathematics, 5% philosophy, religion, theology, 5% physical sciences, 5% psychology, 5% social sciences.

UNDERGRADUATE MAJORS. Accounting, architectural technologies, automation/electro mechanical technician, biomedical equipment technology, business and management, child development/care/guidance, computer programming, computer servicing technology, construction drawing technology, cosmetology management, criminal justice studies, drafting and design technology, electronic technology, engineering and engineering-related technologies, engineering and other disciplines, food production/management/services, graphic arts technology, laser electro-optic technology, law enforcement and corrections, liberal/general studies, manufacturing technology, marketing management, medical records technology, metallurgical engineering, nursing, occupational therapy assistant, office supervision and management, physical sciences, protective services, quality control technology, radio/television broadcasting, science technologies, secretarial and related programs, small business management and ownership.

ACADEMIC PROGRAMS. 2-year transfer program, cooperative education, dual enrollment of high school students, honors program, independent study, internships, telecourses, weekend college. **Remedial services:** Learning center, remedial instruction, special counselor, tutoring. **Placement/credit:** AP, CLEP General and Subject; 15 credit hours maximum for associate degree.

ACADEMIC REQUIREMENTS. Freshmen must earn minimum GPA of 2.0 to continue in good standing. 44% of freshmen return for sophomore year. Students must declare major by end of first year. **Graduation requirements:** 64 hours for associate (25 in major). Most students required to take courses in arts/fine arts, computer science, English, history, humanities, mathematics, biological/physical sciences, social sciences.

FRESHMAN ADMISSIONS. Selection criteria: Open admissions. School achievement record, test scores, completion of developmental courses considered for admission to allied health and culinary arts programs.

1992 FRESHMAN CLASS PROFILE. 663 men, 862 women enrolled. **Characteristics:** 99% from in state, 100% commute, 1% have minority backgrounds, 1% are foreign students. Average age is 18.

FALL-TERM APPLICATIONS. $10 fee. No closing date; applicants notified on a rolling basis. Early admission available.

STUDENT LIFE. Activities: Student government, student newspaper, choral groups, drama, jazz band, music ensembles, symphony orchestra, fraternities, Student Programming Board, music club, beekeepers club, chess club, electronics club, Euchre Club, international students club, quilting club.

ATHLETICS. NJCAA. **Intercollegiate:** Basketball, cross-country W, golf M, soccer, volleyball W. **Intramural:** Basketball, cross-country, golf, soccer, volleyball. **Clubs:** Skiing.

STUDENT SERVICES. Aptitude testing, career counseling, employment service for undergraduates, freshman orientation, health services, on-campus day care, personal counseling, placement service for graduates, veterans counselor, services/facilities for handicapped.

ANNUAL EXPENSES. Tuition and fees (1992-93): $1,285, $600 additional for out-of-district students, $1,425 additional for out-of-state students. **Books and supplies:** $400. **Other expenses:** $800.

FINANCIAL AID. 25% of freshmen, 20% of continuing students receive some form of aid. 95% of grants, 94% of loans, 27% of jobs based on need. Academic, music/drama, art, athletic, state/district residency scholarships available. **Aid applications:** No closing date; priority given to applications received by March 31; applicants notified on a rolling basis beginning on or about June 1; must reply within 2 weeks.

ADDRESS/TELEPHONE. John B. Tomey, Director of Admissions and Financial Aid, Schoolcraft College, 18600 Haggerty Road, Livonia, MI 48152-2696. (313) 462-4426. Fax: (313) 462-4506.

Siena Heights College
Adrian, Michigan — CB code: 1719

4-year private liberal arts college, coed, affiliated with Roman Catholic

Church. Founded in 1919. **Accreditation:** Regional. **Undergraduate enrollment:** 287 men, 474 women full time. **Graduate enrollment:** 8 men, 16 women full time; 14 men, 85 women part time. **Faculty:** 156 total (78 full time), 45 with doctorates or other terminal degrees. **Location:** Rural campus in large town; 30 miles from Toledo, Ohio, 60 miles from Detroit. **Calendar:** Semester, limited summer session. **Microcomputers:** 35 located in libraries, classrooms, computer centers. **Special facilities:** Art gallery. **Additional facts:** Monroe County Community College, Lake Michigan College, and Southfield Community Center provide off-campus upper-division completion.

DEGREES OFFERED. AA, AS, BA, BS, BFA, MA. 65 associate degrees awarded in 1992. 310 bachelor's degrees awarded. Graduate degrees offered in 3 major fields of study.

UNDERGRADUATE MAJORS. Associate: Accounting, biology, business administration and management, chemistry, computer and information sciences, criminal justice studies, fashion merchandising, fine arts, hotel/motel and restaurant management, liberal/general studies, mathematics, preengineering, psychology, public administration, social work. **Bachelor's:** Accounting, American studies, biology, business administration and management, business education, chemistry, clinical laboratory science, computer and information sciences, criminal justice studies, dramatic arts, elementary education, English, fashion merchandising, fine arts, history, hotel/motel and restaurant management, humanities, liberal/general studies, mathematics, music, philosophy, predentistry, prelaw, premedicine, prepharmacy, preveterinary, psychology, public administration, religion, social sciences, social work, Spanish, studio art.

ACADEMIC PROGRAMS. 2-year transfer program, accelerated program, cooperative education, double major, dual enrollment of high school students, external degree, honors program, independent study, internships, student-designed major, study abroad, teacher preparation, 3-1 field experience/liberal arts in technical and nursing programs; liberal arts/career combination in health sciences. **Remedial services:** Learning center, preadmission summer program, reduced course load, remedial instruction, special counselor, tutoring. **Placement/credit:** AP, CLEP General and Subject; 36 credit hours maximum for bachelor's degree.

ACADEMIC REQUIREMENTS. Freshmen must earn minimum GPA of 2.0 to continue in good standing. 68% of freshmen return for sophomore year. Students must declare major by end of second year. **Graduation requirements:** 60 hours for associate (30 in major), 120 hours for bachelor's (60 in major). Most students required to take courses in arts/fine arts, English, history, humanities, mathematics, philosophy/religion, biological/physical sciences, social sciences. **Postgraduate studies:** 3% enter law school, 2% enter medical school, 3% enter MBA programs, 10% enter other graduate study.

FRESHMAN ADMISSIONS. Selection criteria: School achievement record, test scores, self-motivation, and ability to benefit from available resources. **Test requirements:** SAT or ACT (ACT preferred); score report by August 15.

1992 FRESHMAN CLASS PROFILE. 208 men and women enrolled. 35% had high school GPA of 3.0 or higher, 63% between 2.0 and 2.99. **Academic background:** Mid 50% of enrolled freshmen had ACT composite between 17-22. 98% submitted ACT scores. **Characteristics:** 85% from in state, 60% live in college housing, 21% have minority backgrounds, 2% are foreign students. Average age is 18.

FALL-TERM APPLICATIONS. $15 fee, may be waived for applicants with need. Closing date August 15; applicants notified on a rolling basis; must reply within 4 weeks. Essay required. Interview recommended. Audition recommended for music applicants. Portfolio recommended for art applicants. Deferred and early admission available.

STUDENT LIFE. Housing: Dormitories (men, women, coed). **Activities:** Student government, film, student newspaper, choral groups, dance, drama, jazz band, music ensembles, musical theater, fraternities, sororities, campus ministry, Hispanics for Education, College Republicans, human services club, International Association, Student Talk about Narcotics and Drugs, counseling support group.

ATHLETICS. NAIA. **Intercollegiate:** Baseball M, basketball, cross-country, soccer, softball W, tennis, track and field, volleyball W. **Intramural:** Basketball, golf, softball, volleyball W.

STUDENT SERVICES. Career counseling, employment service for undergraduates, freshman orientation, health services, personal counseling, placement service for graduates, special adviser for adult students, veterans counselor, services/facilities for handicapped.

ANNUAL EXPENSES. Tuition and fees: $8,820. **Room and board:** $3,700. **Books and supplies:** $475. **Other expenses:** $575.

FINANCIAL AID. 91% of freshmen, 88% of continuing students receive some form of aid. 73% of grants, 93% of loans, all jobs based on need. 177 enrolled freshmen were judged to have need, all were offered aid. Academic, music/drama, art scholarships available. **Aid applications:** No closing date; priority given to applications received by April 1; applicants notified on a rolling basis beginning on or about March 1.

ADDRESS/TELEPHONE. Norman Bukwaz, Dean of Admissions and External Programs, Siena Heights College, 1247 East Siena Heights Drive, Adrian, MI 49221-9937. (517) 263-0731 ext. 214.

Southwestern Michigan College
Dowagiac, Michigan

CB code: 1783

2-year public community college, coed. Founded in 1964. **Accreditation:** Regional. **Undergraduate enrollment:** 534 men, 660 women full time; 563 men, 1,116 women part time. **Faculty:** 170 total (45 full time), 17 with doctorates or other terminal degrees. **Location:** Rural campus in small town; 30 miles from South Bend, Indiana. **Calendar:** Semester, extensive summer session. Saturday and extensive evening/early morning classes. **Microcomputers:** Located in libraries, classrooms, computer centers. **Special facilities:** Museum.

DEGREES OFFERED. AA, AS, AAS. 319 associate degrees awarded in 1992.

UNDERGRADUATE MAJORS. Accounting, agribusiness, agricultural business and management, agricultural sciences, allied health, automotive mechanics, automotive technology, business administration and management, business data entry equipment operation, business data processing and related programs, business data programming, chemical manufacturing technology, computer programming, drafting, electronic technology, engineering, engineering and engineering-related technologies, fire control and safety technology, graphic and printing production, graphic arts technology, horticultural science, industrial technology, legal secretary, liberal/general studies, marketing and distribution, mechanical design technology, medical secretary, nursing, office supervision and management, practical nursing, precision metal work, secretarial and related programs, social work, word processing.

ACADEMIC PROGRAMS. 2-year transfer program, cooperative education, double major, dual enrollment of high school students, independent study, internships, telecourses, cross-registration. **Remedial services:** Learning center, preadmission summer program, reduced course load, remedial instruction, special counselor, tutoring. **Placement/credit:** AP, CLEP Subject, institutional tests; 30 credit hours maximum for associate degree.

ACADEMIC REQUIREMENTS. Freshmen must earn minimum GPA of 1.70 to continue in good standing. Students must declare major on application. **Graduation requirements:** 62 hours for associate. Most students required to take courses in arts/fine arts, computer science, English, humanities, mathematics, biological/physical sciences, social sciences.

FRESHMAN ADMISSIONS. Selection criteria: Open admissions. Selective admission to nursing programs. **Test requirements:** SAT or ACT for placement; score report by September 5. ACT scores used for admission of nursing applicants.

1992 FRESHMAN CLASS PROFILE. 984 men, 1,065 women enrolled.

FALL-TERM APPLICATIONS. No fee. No closing date; applicants notified on a rolling basis. Interview required for nursing applicants. Deferred and early admission available. SAT or ACT recommended for all students for placement and counseling.

STUDENT LIFE. Activities: Student newspaper, choral groups, concert band, drama, jazz band, music ensembles, musical theater, Phi Theta Kappa.

ATHLETICS. NJCAA. **Intercollegiate:** Baseball M, basketball, cross-country, softball W, track and field, volleyball W. **Intramural:** Archery, badminton, basketball, bowling, cross-country, field hockey, golf, handball, racquetball, skiing, soccer, softball, table tennis, tennis, track and field, volleyball, wrestling M.

STUDENT SERVICES. Aptitude testing, career counseling, employment service for undergraduates, freshman orientation, personal counseling, placement service for graduates, veterans counselor, special needs counselor, services/facilities for handicapped.

ANNUAL EXPENSES. Tuition and fees (1992-93): $1,200, $300 additional for out-of-district students, $600 additional for out-of-state students. **Books and supplies:** $500. **Other expenses:** $2,400.

FINANCIAL AID. 45% of freshmen, 45% of continuing students receive some form of aid. 80% of grants, all loans, 62% of jobs based on need. 900 enrolled freshmen were judged to have need, all were offered aid. Academic, music/drama, art, athletic, leadership, minority scholarships available. **Aid applications:** No closing date; priority given to applications received by June 1; applicants notified on a rolling basis beginning on or about April 1; must reply within 2 weeks.

ADDRESS/TELEPHONE. James D. Kensinger, Associate Dean of Admissions and Counseling, Southwestern Michigan College, 58900 Cherry Grove Road, Dowagiac, MI 49047. (616) 782-5113. (800) 456-8675. Fax: (616) 782-8414.

Spring Arbor College
Spring Arbor, Michigan CB code: 1732

Admissions: 86% of applicants accepted
Based on: ••• School record, test scores
• Activities, essay, interview, recommendations, religious affiliation/commitment, special talents
Completion: 41% graduate, 9% of these enter graduate study

4-year private liberal arts college, coed, affiliated with Free Methodist Church of North America. Founded in 1873. **Accreditation:** Regional. **Undergraduate enrollment:** 310 men, 380 women full time; 68 men, 126 women part time. **Faculty:** 98 total (67 full time), 33 with doctorates or other terminal degrees. **Location:** Rural campus in rural community; 45 miles from Ann Arbor and Lansing. **Calendar:** 4-1-4, limited summer session. **Microcomputers:** 30 located in computer centers.

DEGREES OFFERED. AA, BA. 2 associate degrees awarded in 1992. 186 bachelor's degrees awarded. 21% in business and management, 6% communications, 18% teacher education, 5% letters/literature, 5% life sciences, 7% philosophy, religion, theology, 8% psychology, 17% social sciences, 5% visual and performing arts.

UNDERGRADUATE MAJORS. Associate: Liberal/general studies. **Bachelor's:** Accounting, biology, business administration and management, business economics, chemistry, Christian ministries, communications, computer and information sciences, contemporary music ministries, early childhood education, elementary education, English, English/speech, fine arts, French, history, mathematics, music, philosophy, physical education, physics/mathematics, psychology, religion, religious music, secondary education, social sciences, social work, sociology, Spanish.

ACADEMIC PROGRAMS. Double major, dual enrollment of high school students, external degree, honors program, independent study, internships, student-designed major, study abroad, teacher preparation, weekend college, Washington semester, cross-registration, environmental study semester at AuSable Trails Institute in northern Michigan. **Remedial services:** Learning center, reduced course load, special counselor, tutoring. **Placement/credit:** AP, CLEP General and Subject, institutional tests; 60 credit hours maximum for bachelor's degree.

ACADEMIC REQUIREMENTS. Freshmen must earn minimum GPA of 1.6 to continue in good standing. 65% of freshmen return for sophomore year. Students must declare major by end of second year. **Graduation requirements:** 62 hours for associate, 124 hours for bachelor's (30 in major). Most students required to take courses in arts/fine arts, computer science, English, foreign languages, history, humanities, mathematics, philosophy/religion, biological/physical sciences, social sciences. **Postgraduate studies:** 9% enter other graduate study.

FRESHMAN ADMISSIONS. Selection criteria: Enhanced ACT composite score of 20 and 2.6 high school GPA preferred. Recommended units include English 4, foreign language 2, mathematics 2, social science 2 and science 2. College-preparatory courses recommended. **Test requirements:** SAT or ACT (ACT preferred).

1992 FRESHMAN CLASS PROFILE. 155 men applied, 126 accepted, 67 enrolled; 205 women applied, 185 accepted, 88 enrolled. 52% had high school GPA of 3.0 or higher, 48% between 2.0 and 2.99. 17% were in top tenth and 39% were in top quarter of graduating class. **Academic background:** Mid 50% of enrolled freshmen had ACT composite between 18-24. 98% submitted ACT scores. **Characteristics:** 86% from in state, 92% live in college housing, 6% have minority backgrounds, 1% are foreign students.

FALL-TERM APPLICATIONS. $15 fee, may be waived for applicants with need. No closing date; priority given to applications received by March 1; applicants notified on a rolling basis. Interview recommended for borderline applicants. Deferred and early admission available.

STUDENT LIFE. Housing: Dormitories (men, women); apartment housing available. **Activities:** Student government, radio, student newspaper, yearbook, choral groups, concert band, drama, jazz band, music ensembles, musical theater, religious and community organizations. **Additional information:** Emphasis on active commitment to person and teachings of Jesus Christ. Chapel required twice weekly. Religious observance required.

ATHLETICS. NAIA. **Intercollegiate:** Baseball M, basketball, cross-country, golf M, soccer, softball W, tennis, track and field, volleyball W. **Intramural:** Basketball, soccer, softball, table tennis, tennis, volleyball, water polo.

STUDENT SERVICES. Aptitude testing, career counseling, employment service for undergraduates, freshman orientation, health services, personal counseling, placement service for graduates, special adviser for adult students, veterans counselor, services/facilities for handicapped.

ANNUAL EXPENSES. Tuition and fees: $8,706. **Room and board:** $3,550. **Books and supplies:** $385. **Other expenses:** $665.

FINANCIAL AID. 90% of freshmen, 90% of continuing students receive some form of aid. 62% of grants, 81% of loans, 43% of jobs based on need. Academic, music/drama, art, athletic, state/district residency, religious affiliation, minority scholarships available. **Aid applications:** No closing date; priority given to applications received by February 15; applicants notified on a rolling basis beginning on or about April 1; must reply within 2 weeks.

ADDRESS/TELEPHONE. Steve W. Schippers, Director of Admissions, Spring Arbor College, Spring Arbor, MI 49283. (517) 750-1200 ext. 590. (800) 968-0011. Fax: (517) 750-2108.

Suomi College
Hancock, Michigan CB code: 1743

Admissions: 74% of applicants accepted
Based on: ••• School record, test scores
•• Interview, recommendations
• Activities, essay
Completion: 75% of freshmen end year in good standing
55% enter 4-year programs

2-year private junior, liberal arts college, coed, affiliated with Evangelical Lutheran Church in America. Founded in 1896. **Accreditation:** Regional. **Undergraduate enrollment:** 171 men, 359 women full time; 10 men, 47 women part time. **Faculty:** 55 total (23 full time), 2 with doctorates or other terminal degrees. **Location:** Rural campus in small town; 100 miles from Marquette, 220 miles from Green Bay, Wisconsin. **Calendar:** Semester, limited summer session. **Microcomputers:** Located in classrooms, computer centers. **Special facilities:** Finnish archives. **Additional facts:** Program focuses on completion of general requirements with goal of transfer to 4-year college.

DEGREES OFFERED. AA, AAS. 90 associate degrees awarded in 1992. 14% in business and management, 17% business/office and marketing/distribution, 24% health sciences, 8% multi/interdisciplinary studies, 19% parks/recreation, protective services, public affairs.

UNDERGRADUATE MAJORS. Allied health, business administration and management, business and management, business and office, criminal justice studies, early childhood education, education, elementary education, English, fine arts, Finnish studies, health sciences, history, human services, law enforcement and corrections, liberal/general studies, music, nursing, philosophy, preengineering, prelaw, religion, Scandinavian languages, secondary education, social sciences, social work, teacher aide, transportation and travel marketing.

ACADEMIC PROGRAMS. 2-year transfer program, double major, dual enrollment of high school students, honors program, independent study, internships, study abroad, teacher preparation. **Remedial services:** Learning center, preadmission summer program, remedial instruction, special counselor, tutoring. **Placement/credit:** AP, CLEP General and Subject, institutional tests; 16 credit hours maximum for associate degree.

ACADEMIC REQUIREMENTS. Freshmen must earn minimum GPA of 2.0 to continue in good standing. 58% of freshmen return for sophomore year. Students must declare major by end of first year. **Graduation requirements:** 60 hours for associate (20 in major). Most students required to take courses in arts/fine arts, English, humanities, mathematics, philosophy/religion, biological/physical sciences, social sciences.

FRESHMAN ADMISSIONS. Selection criteria: Selective admissions for nursing program. Minimum 2.5 high school GPA for nursing applicants. Recommended units include English 4 and mathematics 2. One algebra and 1 chemistry with minimum grade of 2.0 required of nursing applicants. **Additional information:** If GPA is below 2.0, special consideration given in determining admission.

1992 FRESHMAN CLASS PROFILE. 246 men applied, 182 accepted, 96 enrolled; 547 women applied, 405 accepted, 189 enrolled. 14% had high school GPA of 3.0 or higher, 62% between 2.0 and 2.99. **Characteristics:** 80% from in state, 57% live in college housing, 16% have minority backgrounds, 5% are foreign students. Average age is 19.

FALL-TERM APPLICATIONS. $35 fee, may be waived for applicants with need. Closing date September 1; priority given to applications received by May 1; applicants notified on a rolling basis; must reply within 4 weeks. Interview recommended. Essay recommended. Deferred and early admission available. February 15 closing date for nursing applicants.

STUDENT LIFE. Housing: Dormitories (men, women). Houses available for single students. **Activities:** Student government, magazine, choral groups, drama, music ensembles, musical theater, Religious Life Committee, Commuters Club, Finnish Club.

ATHLETICS. NJCAA. **Intramural:** Badminton, basketball, bowling, golf, horseback riding, ice hockey M, racquetball, skiing, softball, swimming, table tennis, tennis, volleyball, water polo. **Clubs:** Hockey.

STUDENT SERVICES. Aptitude testing, career counseling, employment service for undergraduates, freshman orientation, health services, personal counseling, placement service for graduates, services/facilities for handicapped.

ANNUAL EXPENSES. Tuition and fees: $8,990. **Room and board:** $3,700. **Books and supplies:** $500. **Other expenses:** $800.

FINANCIAL AID. 94% of freshmen, 87% of continuing students receive some form of aid. 63% of grants, 98% of loans, all jobs based on need. 559 enrolled freshmen were judged to have need, all were offered aid. Academic, music/drama, art, state/district residency, alumni affiliation, religious affiliation, minority scholarships available. **Aid applications:** No closing date;

priority given to applications received by May 1; applicants notified on a rolling basis beginning on or about March 1; must reply within 4 weeks.

ADDRESS/TELEPHONE. Sue Forbes, Dean of Enrollment, Suomi College, Quincy Street, Hancock, MI 49930. (906) 487-7274. (800) 682-7604. Fax: (906) 487-7383.

University of Detroit Mercy

Detroit, Michigan — CB code: 1835

Admissions: 69% of applicants accepted
Based on: •• School record, test scores
• Activities, interview, recommendations
Completion: 87% of freshmen end year in good standing
60% graduate, 22% of these enter graduate study

4-year private university, coed, affiliated with Roman Catholic Church. Founded in 1991. **Accreditation:** Regional. **Undergraduate enrollment:** 1,017 men, 1,253 women full time; 605 men, 1,753 women part time. **Graduate enrollment:** 843 men, 657 women full time; 838 men, 808 women part time. **Faculty:** 450 total (330 full time), 304 with doctorates or other terminal degrees. **Location:** Urban campus in very large city. **Calendar:** Trimester, extensive summer session. **Microcomputers:** Located in dormitories, libraries, classrooms, computer centers. **Special facilities:** CAD/CAM, Polymer Institute. **Additional facts:** Society of Jesus and Sisters of Mercy University. Merger of University of Detroit and Mercy College.

DEGREES OFFERED. BA, BS, MA, MS, MBA, D, DMD. 76 associate degrees awarded in 1992. 12% in health sciences, 68% allied health, 18% law. 792 bachelor's degrees awarded. 20% in business and management, 5% communications, 11% engineering, 22% health sciences, 7% allied health, 9% social sciences. Graduate degrees offered in 43 major fields of study.

UNDERGRADUATE MAJORS. Associate: Legal assistant/paralegal. **Bachelor's:** Accounting, advertising, applied mathematics, architecture, art history, biochemistry, biology, business administration and management, business and management, business economics, chemical engineering, chemistry, civil engineering, clinical laboratory science, communications, community services, computer and information sciences, computer engineering, criminal justice studies, cytotechnology, dental hygiene, developmental psychology, dramatic arts, economics, education, education of the emotionally handicapped, education of the mentally handicapped, electrical/electronics/communications engineering, elementary education, engineering, English, finance, foreign languages (multiple emphasis), French, German, history, humanities and social sciences, industrial and organizational psychology, journalism, law enforcement and corrections, legal assistant/paralegal, management information systems, marketing management, mathematics, mechanical engineering, medical laboratory technologies, nuclear medical technology, nursing, personnel management, philosophy, plastic technology, political science and government, predentistry, prelaw, premedicine, psychology, public relations, radio/television broadcasting, religion, secondary education, social work, sociology, Spanish, special education, specific learning disabilities, speech, sports medicine, statistics, systems analysis.

ACADEMIC PROGRAMS. Accelerated program, cooperative education, double major, education specialist degree, honors program, independent study, internships, student-designed major, study abroad, teacher preparation, visiting/exchange student program, cross-registration, bachelor's degree completion program for registered nurses; liberal arts/career combination in engineering, health sciences; combined bachelor's/graduate program in law. **Remedial services:** Learning center, preadmission summer program, reduced course load, remedial instruction, special counselor, tutoring. **Placement/credit:** AP, CLEP Subject, institutional tests; 30 credit hours maximum for bachelor's degree.

ACADEMIC REQUIREMENTS. Freshmen must earn minimum GPA of 2.0 to continue in good standing. 78% of freshmen return for sophomore year. Students must declare major by end of second year. **Graduation requirements:** 124 hours for bachelor's (35 in major). Most students required to take courses in computer science, English, history, mathematics, philosophy/religion, biological/physical sciences, social sciences. **Postgraduate studies:** 2% enter law school, 2% enter medical school, 8% enter MBA programs, 10% enter other graduate study.

FRESHMAN ADMISSIONS. Selection criteria: High school GPA in college-preparatory work, SAT or ACT scores, counselor's recommendation considered. **High school preparation:** 12 units required; 16 recommended. Required units include English 4, mathematics 2, social science 2 and science 2. **Test requirements:** SAT or ACT (ACT preferred); score report by August 1.

1992 FRESHMAN CLASS PROFILE. 1,330 men and women applied, 915 accepted; 165 men enrolled, 202 women enrolled. **Academic background:** Mid 50% of enrolled freshmen had SAT-V between 400-530, SAT-M between 470-610; ACT composite between 20-26. 34% submitted SAT scores, 88% submitted ACT scores. **Characteristics:** 87% from in state, 50% commute, 40% have minority backgrounds, 1% are foreign students, 8% join fraternities/sororities. Average age is 18.

FALL-TERM APPLICATIONS. $25 fee, may be waived for applicants with need. No closing date; priority given to applications received by August 15; applicants notified on a rolling basis. Interview recommended. Interview required for Project 100/Challenge applicants; recommended for all other applicants. CRDA. Early admission available.

STUDENT LIFE. Housing: Dormitories (men, women, coed); apartment, fraternity housing available. **Activities:** Student government, radio, student newspaper, yearbook, drama, fraternities, sororities, religious, political, ethnic, social organizations.

ATHLETICS. NCAA. **Intercollegiate:** Baseball M, basketball, cross-country, fencing, golf M, rifle, soccer M, softball W, tennis M. **Intramural:** Archery, badminton, baseball, basketball, bowling, golf, handball, racquetball, rugby M, sailing, skiing, soccer M, softball, table tennis, tennis, volleyball.

STUDENT SERVICES. Aptitude testing, career counseling, employment service for undergraduates, freshman orientation, health services, personal counseling, placement service for graduates, special adviser for minority students.

ANNUAL EXPENSES. Tuition and fees: $8,550. **Room and board:** $3,192. **Books and supplies:** $510. **Other expenses:** $1,370.

FINANCIAL AID. 70% of freshmen, 73% of continuing students receive some form of aid. Grants, loans, jobs available. Academic, athletic scholarships available. **Aid applications:** No closing date; priority given to applications received by June 1; applicants notified on a rolling basis beginning on or about March 1; must reply by May 1 or within 4 weeks if notified thereafter.

ADDRESS/TELEPHONE. Robert Johnson, Dean of Enrollment Management, University of Detroit Mercy, 4001 West McNichols, Detroit, MI 48221. (313) 993-1245.

University of Michigan

Ann Arbor, Michigan — CB code: 1839

Admissions: 69% of applicants accepted
Based on: ••• School record, test scores
•• Special talents
• Activities, essay, recommendations
Completion: 96% of freshmen end year in good standing
83% graduate

4-year public university, coed. Founded in 1817. **Accreditation:** Regional. **Undergraduate enrollment:** 11,681 men, 10,264 women full time; 621 men, 632 women part time. **Graduate enrollment:** 6,540 men, 4,557 women full time; 1,334 men, 997 women part time. **Faculty:** 3,374 total (2,723 full time), 2,590 with doctorates or other terminal degrees. **Location:** Suburban campus in small city; 50 miles from Detroit. **Calendar:** Trimester, limited summer session. **Microcomputers:** 4,200 located in dormitories, libraries, classrooms, computer centers. **Special facilities:** Botanical garden, many museums, biological station in northern Michigan.

DEGREES OFFERED. BA, BS, BFA, MA, MS, MBA, MFA, MSW, PhD, EdD, DDS, MD, B. Pharm, Pharm D. 5,341 bachelor's degrees awarded in 1992. 5% in business and management, 5% communications, 15% engineering, 10% letters/literature, 6% life sciences, 8% multi/interdisciplinary studies, 10% psychology, 19% social sciences, 5% visual and performing arts. Graduate degrees offered in 133 major fields of study.

UNDERGRADUATE MAJORS. Aerospace/aeronautical/astronautical engineering, African studies, Afro-American (black) studies, American studies, anthropological zoology, anthropology, applied mathematics, Arabic, architecture, art education, art history, arts and ideas, Asian studies, astronomy, atmospheric sciences and meteorology, Bible studies, biology, biomedical science, biophysics, botany, business administration and management, Caribbean studies, cell biology, ceramics, chemical engineering, chemical/materials science, chemistry, Chinese, Chinese studies, civil engineering, classical architecture, classical art and architecture, classics, communications, comparative literature, computer and information sciences, computer engineering, creative writing, dance, dramatic arts, drawing, Eastern European studies, economics, education, electrical/electronics/communications engineering, elementary education, engineering, engineering and other disciplines, engineering mathematics, engineering physics, engineering science, English, environmental advocacy, environmental design, environmental health engineering, environmental instruction, fiber/textiles/weaving, field biology/research naturalist, film arts, fishing and fisheries, food science and nutrition, forestry and related sciences, French, geography, geology, German, graphic design, Greek (classical), Hebrew, Hispanic American studies, history, humanities, humanities and social sciences, industrial design, industrial engineering, interior design, international studies, Iranian languages, Iranian studies, Islamic studies, Italian, Japanese, jazz, Jewish studies, journalism, kinesiology, landscape architecture, Latin, Latin American studies, liberal/general studies, linguistics, marine geology, materials engineering, mathematics, mechanical engineering, medical laboratory technologies, medicinal chemistry, medieval studies, metal/jewelry, metallurgical engineering, microbiology, molecular biology, music, music education, music history and appreciation, music performance, music theory and composition, musical theater, naval architecture and marine engineering, nuclear engineering, nursing, oceanography, painting, pharmacy, philosophy, photography, physical education, physics, political science and government, predentistry, premedicine, printmaking, psychology, psychology as a natural science, psychology: speech and hearing sciences, religion, renewable natural resources, resource ecology and management, resource policy and behavior, resources biometry, Russian, Russian and Slavic studies, Scandinavian studies, sculpture, secondary education, social sciences, sociology, South Asian studies, Southeast Asian studies, Spanish, special education, speech, sports management, statistics, Turkish, Western European studies, wildlife management, women's studies, zoology.

ACADEMIC PROGRAMS. Accelerated program, cooperative education, double major, education specialist degree, honors program, independent study, internships, student-designed major, study abroad, teacher preparation, telecourses, visiting/exchange student program, weekend college, Washington semester, cross-registration, several programs offer a small-scale learning environment within a large university; preferred admissions program to UM graduate/professional schools; graduate business program available through branch campus; liberal arts/career combination in engineering, forestry, health sciences; combined bachelor's/graduate program in medicine. **Remedial services:** Learning center, reduced course load, special counselor, tutoring, summer intensive program for qualified liberal arts undergraduates. **ROTC:** Air Force, Army, Naval. **Placement/credit:** AP, CLEP Subject, IB, institutional tests; 60 credit hours maximum for bachelor's degree.

ACADEMIC REQUIREMENTS. Freshmen must earn minimum GPA of 2.0 to continue in good standing. 94% of freshmen return for sophomore year. Students must declare major by end of second year. **Graduation requirements:** 120 hours for bachelor's (32 in major). Most students required to take courses in English, foreign languages, humanities, biological/physical sciences, social sciences. **Additional information:** Small-scale, interdisciplinary programs offering instruction in residence halls available through the College of Literature, Science, and the Arts/Residential College, Pilot Program, and Community College Program. Comprehensive StudiesProgram provides academic support in counseling, intensive course sections, tutorials and skills workshops, internships, and mentoring.

FRESHMAN ADMISSIONS. Selection criteria: Admissions based on school achievement record, including quality of school and courses elected, and test scores. Talents and extracurricular activities considered. Special consideration to educationally disadvantaged applicants. **High school preparation:** 20 units recommended. Recommended units include English 4, foreign language 4, mathematics 4, social science 4 and science 4. **Test requirements:** SAT or ACT; score report by February 1. 3 ACH required of applicants from schools that do not give grades or have less rigorous academic programs. French, German, or Spanish ACH required of all liberal arts applicants. Score report by February 1.

1992 FRESHMAN CLASS PROFILE. 9,961 men applied, 6,764 accepted, 2,601 enrolled; 8,157 women applied, 5,678 accepted, 2,269 enrolled. 95% had high school GPA of 3.0 or higher, 5% between 2.0 and 2.99. 64% were in top tenth and 92% were in top quarter of graduating class. **Academic background:** Mid 50% of enrolled freshmen had SAT-V between 490-600, SAT-M between 580-700; ACT composite between 25-29. 80% submitted SAT scores, 76% submitted ACT scores. **Characteristics:** 65% from in state, 99% live in college housing, 25% have minority backgrounds, 3% are foreign students. Average age is 18.

FALL-TERM APPLICATIONS. $40 fee, may be waived for applicants with need. Closing date February 1; applicants notified on a rolling basis beginning on or about October 15; must reply by May 1. Audition required for music applicants. Portfolio required for art applicants. Essay required. CRDA. Deferred and early admission available. Applications may be considered after February 1 for art, music, natural resources, and nursing programs on space availability basis.

STUDENT LIFE. Housing: Dormitories (men, women, coed); apartment, fraternity, sorority, cooperative housing available. **Activities:** Student government, film, magazine, radio, student newspaper, television, yearbook, choral groups, concert band, dance, drama, jazz band, marching band, music ensembles, musical theater, opera, pep band, symphony orchestra, fraternities, sororities, over 400 student organizations.

ATHLETICS. NCAA. **Intercollegiate:** Baseball M, basketball, cross-country, diving, field hockey W, football M, golf, gymnastics, ice hockey M, softball W, swimming, tennis, track and field, volleyball W, wrestling M. **Intramural:** Archery, badminton, baseball M, basketball, cross-country, diving, fencing M, golf, handball, ice hockey M, lacrosse, racquetball, rowing (crew), rugby, sailing, skiing, soccer, softball, squash, swimming, table tennis, tennis, track and field, volleyball, water polo.

STUDENT SERVICES. Aptitude testing, career counseling, employment service for undergraduates, freshman orientation, health services, personal counseling, placement service for graduates, special adviser for adult students, veterans counselor, minority student services, services/facilities for handicapped.

ANNUAL EXPENSES. Tuition and fees (1992-93): $4,365, $9,704 additional for out-of-state students. **Room and board:** $4,285. **Books and supplies:** $460. **Other expenses:** $1,207.

FINANCIAL AID. 35% of freshmen, 32% of continuing students receive some form of aid. 95% of grants, 91% of loans, all jobs based on need. 1,850 enrolled freshmen were judged to have need, all were offered aid. Academic, music/drama, art, athletic, state/district residency scholarships available. **Aid applications:** Closing date September 30; priority given to applications received by February 1; applicants notified on a rolling basis beginning on or about March 15; must reply by May 1 or within 4 weeks if notified thereafter.

ADDRESS/TELEPHONE. Theodore Spencer, Director of Undergraduate Admissions, University of Michigan, 1220 Student Activities Building, Ann Arbor, MI 48109-1316. (313) 764-7433.

University of Michigan: Dearborn

Dearborn, Michigan CB code: 1861

Admissions: 68% of applicants accepted
Based on: ••• School record, test scores
• Activities, essay, interview, recommendations, special talents
Completion: 87% of freshmen end year in good standing

4-year public university, coed. Founded in 1959. **Accreditation:** Regional. **Undergraduate enrollment:** 1,635 men, 1,824 women full time; 1,547 men, 1,843 women part time. **Graduate enrollment:** 22 men, 35 women full time; 749 men, 468 women part time. **Faculty:** 377 total (206 full time), 233 with doctorates or other terminal degrees. **Location:** Suburban campus in small city; 10 miles from Detroit. **Calendar:** Semester, limited summer session. Saturday and extensive evening/early morning classes. **Microcomputers:** 350 located in libraries, classrooms, computer centers. **Special facilities:** Henry Ford's Fair Lane estate, environmental study area, extensive rotating art collection in university library, engineering CAD-CAM robotics laboratory.

DEGREES OFFERED. BA, BS, MA, MBA. 956 bachelor's degrees awarded in 1992. 20% in business and management, 8% teacher education, 15% engineering, 16% letters/literature, 5% life sciences, 8% psychology, 16% social sciences. Graduate degrees offered in 9 major fields of study.

UNDERGRADUATE MAJORS. Accounting, American studies, anthropology, art history, arts management, behavioral sciences, biochemistry, biological and physical sciences, biology, business administration and management, business and management, business education, chemistry, computer and information sciences, computer engineering, early childhood education, economics, education, electrical/electronics/communications engineering, elementary education, engineering, engineering and other disciplines, engineering mathematics, English, English education, environmental science, finance, French, health policy studies, history, human resources development, humanities, industrial engineering, information sciences and systems, international business management, international studies, liberal/general studies, management information systems, management science, manufacturing engineering, marketing management, mathematics, mathematics education, mechanical engineering, microbiology, music, music history and appreciation, Operations management, organizational behavior, philosophy, physical sciences, physics, political science and government, psychology, public administration, science education, secondary education, social foundations, social science education, social studies education, sociology, systems engineering.

ACADEMIC PROGRAMS. Accelerated program, cooperative education, double major, dual enrollment of high school students, honors program, independent study, internships, student-designed major, study abroad, teacher preparation, Washington semester, cross-registration, professional development courses in education, engineering, liberal arts, and management. **Remedial services:** Learning center, preadmission summer program, reduced course load, remedial instruction, special counselor, tutoring, science learning laboratory, Pace. **ROTC:** Air Force, Army, Naval. **Placement/credit:** AP, institutional tests; 30 credit hours maximum for bachelor's degree.

ACADEMIC REQUIREMENTS. Freshmen must earn minimum GPA of 2.0 to continue in good standing. Admission to School of Management BBA or BSA program requires junior standing, 3.0 average. 82% of freshmen return for sophomore year. Students must declare major by end of second year. **Graduation requirements:** 120 hours for bachelor's (24 in major). Most students required to take courses in English, humanities, mathematics, biological/physical sciences, social sciences.

FRESHMAN ADMISSIONS. Selection criteria: Minimum 3.0 high school GPA with minimum SAT-verbal and mathematics scores of 500 or ACT composite score of 22 preferred. Class rank considered. **High school preparation:** 15 units required. Required and recommended units include English 4-4, mathematics 3-4, social science 3-3 and science 2-3. Foreign language 2 recommended. Computer Science .5 unit required, 1 unit recommended. Special recommendations for students in Computer Science, PreNursing, Engineering, Business Administration, Physical and Natural Science: required 2 units algebra, 1 unit geometry, and .5 unit of trigonometry, and 1 unit of trigonometry recommended. Also required is 1 unit of chemistry and at least 1 year of physics or biological science. **Test requirements:** SAT or ACT (ACT preferred); score report by August 15.

1992 FRESHMAN CLASS PROFILE. 917 men applied, 619 accepted, 366 enrolled; 992 women applied, 687 accepted, 396 enrolled. 78% had high school GPA of 3.0 or higher, 22% between 2.0 and 2.99. 37% were in top tenth and 72% were in top quarter of graduating class. **Academic background:** Mid 50% of enrolled freshmen had SAT-V between 420-520, SAT-M between 480-640; ACT composite between 21-27. 13% submitted SAT scores, 87% submitted ACT scores. **Characteristics:** 99% from in state, 100% commute, 15% have minority backgrounds, 1% are foreign students. Average age is 19.

FALL-TERM APPLICATIONS. $30 fee, may be waived for applicants with need. Closing date August 15; priority given to applications received by March 15; applicants notified on a rolling basis; must reply by May 1 or within 15 days if notified thereafter. Interview recommended. Essay recommended. Interview recommended for applicants with high school GPA of less than 3.0 or with ACT composite score of less than 20 or combined SAT score less than 1000. CRDA. Deferred and early admission available.

STUDENT LIFE. Housing: Housing bulletin board in University Mall. **Activities:** Student government, film, magazine, radio, student newspaper, television, choral groups, concert band, drama, jazz band, music ensembles, pep band, fraternities, sororities, Arab Student Association, Association of Black Students, Dearborn Campus Engineers, Alpha Kappa PSI, Panhellenic Council, Asian American Student Association, Hispanic Student Alliance, Student Activities Board.

ATHLETICS. NAIA. **Intercollegiate:** Basketball, volleyball W. **Intramural:** Basketball, ice hockey, softball, table tennis, tennis, volleyball.

STUDENT SERVICES. Aptitude testing, career counseling, employment service for undergraduates, freshman orientation, health services, on-campus day care, personal counseling, placement service for graduates, special adviser for adult students, veterans counselor, women's center, services/facilities for handicapped.

ANNUAL EXPENSES. Tuition and fees (1992-93): $2,954, $6,348 additional for out-of-state students. **Books and supplies:** $440. **Other expenses:** $1,040.

FINANCIAL AID. 46% of freshmen, 27% of continuing students receive some form of aid. 84% of grants, 77% of loans, all jobs based on need. 348 enrolled freshmen were judged to have need, 273 were offered aid. Academic, athletic, leadership, minority scholarships available. **Aid applications:** No closing date; priority given to applications received by April 1; applicants notified on a rolling basis beginning on or about June 15; must reply within 3 weeks.

ADDRESS/TELEPHONE. Carol Mack, Director of Admissions, University of Michigan: Dearborn, 4901 Evergreen, Dearborn, MI 48128-1491. (313) 593-5100. Fax: (313) 593-5452.

University of Michigan: Flint

Flint, Michigan — CB code: 1853

Admissions: 90% of applicants accepted
Based on:
••• School record, test scores
•• Activities, interview
• Recommendations
Completion: 84% of freshmen end year in good standing
31% graduate, 13% of these enter graduate study

4-year public university, coed. Founded in 1956. **Accreditation:** Regional. **Undergraduate enrollment:** 1,332 men, 1,861 women full time; 1,129 men, 1,889 women part time. **Graduate enrollment:** 19 men, 28 women full time; 231 men, 163 women part time. **Faculty:** 323 total (184 full time), 183 with doctorates or other terminal degrees. **Location:** Urban campus in small city; 60 miles from Detroit. **Calendar:** Semester, limited summer session. **Microcomputers:** 140 located in classrooms, computer centers. **Special facilities:** Public Broadcasting Service television station. **Additional facts:** Commuter campus in urban riverfront setting. Institution shares many resources of entire University of Michigan system.

DEGREES OFFERED. BA, BS, BFA, MA, MS, MBA. 913 bachelor's degrees awarded in 1992. 25% in business and management, 14% teacher education, 10% health sciences, 5% letters/literature, 5% life sciences, 8% parks/recreation, protective services, public affairs, 5% psychology, 10% social sciences. Graduate degrees offered in 5 major fields of study.

UNDERGRADUATE MAJORS. Accounting, actuarial sciences, anthropology, applied mathematics, art education, biological and physical sciences, biology, business and management, chemistry, clinical psychology, communications, computer and information sciences, criminal justice studies, dramatic arts, early childhood education, economics, education, elementary education, engineering science, English, finance, fine arts, French, geography, German, health care administration, health sciences, history, law enforcement and corrections, liberal/general studies, marketing management, mathematics, medical laboratory technologies, music, music education, nursing, philosophy, physical sciences, physics, political science and government, psychology, public administration, secondary education, social sciences, social work, sociology, Spanish, urban studies.

ACADEMIC PROGRAMS. Cooperative education, double major, dual enrollment of high school students, honors program, independent study, internships, student-designed major, study abroad, teacher preparation. **Remedial services:** Learning center, reduced course load, remedial instruction, special counselor, tutoring, college bound program. **Placement/credit:** AP, institutional tests; 9 credit hours maximum for bachelor's degree.

ACADEMIC REQUIREMENTS. Freshmen must earn minimum GPA of 2.0 to continue in good standing. 80% of freshmen return for sophomore year. Students must declare major by end of second year. **Graduation requirements:** 120 hours for bachelor's (30 in major). Most students required to take courses in arts/fine arts, English, foreign languages, history, humanities, mathematics, philosophy/religion, biological/physical sciences, social sciences.

FRESHMAN ADMISSIONS. Selection criteria: Minimum 2.7 academic high school GPA, test scores. **High school preparation:** 16 units recommended. Recommended units include English 4, foreign language 2, mathematics 4, social science 3 and science 3. **Test requirements:** SAT or ACT; score report by September 1.

1992 FRESHMAN CLASS PROFILE. 973 men and women applied, 879 accepted; 239 men enrolled, 343 women enrolled. 56% had high school GPA of 3.0 or higher, 44% between 2.0 and 2.99. 23% were in top tenth and 55% were in top quarter of graduating class. **Academic background:** Mid 50% of enrolled freshmen had SAT-V between 410-540, SAT-M between 450-600; ACT composite between 19-24. 6% submitted SAT scores, 98% submitted ACT scores. **Characteristics:** 100% from in state, 100% commute, 18% have minority backgrounds. Average age is 18.

FALL-TERM APPLICATIONS. $30 fee, may be waived for applicants with need. Closing date August 21; priority given to applications received by August 15; applicants notified on a rolling basis; must reply by May 1 or within 2 weeks if notified thereafter. Audition required for music applicants. Interview recommended. CRDA. Deferred and early admission available.

STUDENT LIFE. Activities: Student government, magazine, radio, student newspaper, television, choral groups, concert band, dance, drama, jazz band, music ensembles, symphony orchestra, fraternities, sororities, Inter-Varsity Christian Fellowship, Students for Black Achievement, Women's Work, Native American Indian Student Organization, The Student Coalition, Amnesty International, Asian American, Muslim Student Organization, Hispanic Student Organization.

ATHLETICS. Intramural: Basketball M, racquetball, softball, tennis, volleyball.

STUDENT SERVICES. Aptitude testing, career counseling, employment service for undergraduates, freshman orientation, health services, personal counseling, placement service for graduates, special adviser for adult students, services/facilities for handicapped.

ANNUAL EXPENSES. Tuition and fees (1992-93): $2,700, $6,100 additional for out-of-state students. **Books and supplies:** $470. **Other expenses:** $900.

FINANCIAL AID. 38% of freshmen, 29% of continuing students receive some form of aid. 93% of grants, all loans, all jobs based on need. 203 enrolled freshmen were judged to have need, all were offered aid. Academic, music/drama, state/district residency, leadership, alumni affiliation, minority scholarships available. **Aid applications:** Closing date April 15; applicants notified on a rolling basis beginning on or about May 1; must reply within 4 weeks. **Additional information:** Participatant in Michigan Education Trust (MET) program.

ADDRESS/TELEPHONE. David L. James, Director of Admissions, University of Michigan: Flint, Flint, MI 48502-2186. (313) 762-3300. Fax: (313) 762-3687.

Walsh College of Accountancy and Business Administration

Troy, Michigan — CB code: 0372

2-year upper-division private business college, coed. Founded in 1968. **Accreditation:** Regional. **Undergraduate enrollment:** 164 men, 174 women full time; 707 men, 1,001 women part time. **Graduate enrollment:** 1,411 men and women. **Faculty:** 134 total (10 full time), 13 with doctorates or other terminal degrees. **Location:** Suburban campus in large city; 17 miles from Detroit. **Calendar:** Trimester, extensive summer session. Saturday and extensive evening/early morning classes. **Microcomputers:** 72 located in computer centers. **Additional facts:** Bachelor degree partnership with Macomb Community College University Center. Three off-site campuses: Port Huron, University Center, Western Oakland County.

DEGREES OFFERED. B, MS. 390 bachelor's degrees awarded in 1992. 89% in business and management, 11% computer sciences. Graduate degrees offered in 4 major fields of study.

UNDERGRADUATE MAJORS. Accounting, business administration and management, business and management, computer and information sciences, finance, marketing management.

ACADEMIC PROGRAMS. Double major, honors program, internships. **Remedial services:** Reduced course load, tutoring. **Placement/credit:** Institutional tests.

ACADEMIC REQUIREMENTS. Students must declare major on application. **Graduation requirements:** 127 hours for bachelor's (15 in major). Most students required to take courses in computer science, English, mathematics. **Postgraduate studies:** 1% enter law school, 19% enter MBA programs.

STUDENT LIFE. Activities: Student government, American Marketing Association, Data Processing Management Association, Finance/Economics Club, National Black Accounting Association, Delta Mu Delta.

STUDENT SERVICES. Career counseling, employment service for

undergraduates, placement service for graduates, services/facilities for handicapped.

ANNUAL EXPENSES. Tuition and fees (1992-93): $4,500. **Other expenses:** $900.

FINANCIAL AID. 14% of continuing students receive some form of aid. 64% of grants, 91% of loans, 29% of jobs based on need. Academic, minority scholarships available. **Aid applications:** No closing date; priority given to applications received by August 1; applicants notified on a rolling basis; must reply within 4 weeks.

ADDRESS/TELEPHONE. Patrick D. Barrett, Director of Undergraduate Admissions, Walsh College of Accountancy and Business Administration, 3838 Livernois, Troy, MI 48007-7006. (313) 689-8282 ext. 215. Fax: (313) 524-2520.

Washtenaw Community College
Ann Arbor, Michigan CB code: 1935

2-year public community college, coed. Founded in 1965. **Accreditation:** Regional. **Undergraduate enrollment:** 1,162 men, 1,187 women full time; 3,691 men, 4,801 women part time. **Faculty:** 525 total (173 full time), 21 with doctorates or other terminal degrees. **Location:** Suburban campus in small city; 50 miles from Detroit. **Calendar:** Trimester, extensive summer session. Saturday and extensive evening/early morning classes. **Microcomputers:** 125 located in libraries, computer centers. **Special facilities:** Child care center. **Additional facts:** Classes taught in Brighton, Saline, Chelsea, and Ypsilanti.

DEGREES OFFERED. AA, AS, AAS. 635 associate degrees awarded in 1992.

UNDERGRADUATE MAJORS. Accounting, air conditioning/heating/refrigeration mechanics, air conditioning/heating/refrigeration technology, architectural technologies, automotive mechanics, automotive technology, biology, business administration and management, business and management, business and office, business computer/console/peripheral equipment operation, business data entry equipment operation, business data processing and related programs, business data programming, chemistry, child development/care/guidance, commercial art, computer and information sciences, computer programming, computer servicing technology, criminal justice technology, dental assistant, drafting, drafting and design technology, electrical and electronics equipment repair, electromechanical technology, electronic technology, engineering and engineering-related technologies, English, fire control and safety technology, fire protection, food management, food production/management/services, food science and nutrition, graphic and printing production, graphic arts technology, hospitality and recreation marketing, hotel/motel and restaurant management, humanities, information sciences and systems, law enforcement and corrections technologies, liberal/general studies, management science, manufacturing technology, marketing and distribution, marketing management, mathematics, mechanical design technology, medical secretary, nursing, photographic technology, photography, precision metal work, preengineering, premedicine, quality control technology, radiograph medical technology, respiratory therapy technology, robotics, secretarial and related programs, social sciences, technical and business writing, telecommunications, welding technology, word processing.

ACADEMIC PROGRAMS. 2-year transfer program, dual enrollment of high school students, internships, telecourses, cross-registration. **Remedial services:** Learning center, remedial instruction, tutoring. **Placement/credit:** AP, CLEP General and Subject, IB, institutional tests; 45 credit hours maximum for associate degree.

ACADEMIC REQUIREMENTS. No policy requiring minimum GPA; records of students having academic difficulty are reviewed individually. 68% of freshmen return for sophomore year. Students must declare major by end of first year. **Graduation requirements:** 60 hours for associate. Most students required to take courses in computer science, English, mathematics, social sciences.

FRESHMAN ADMISSIONS. Selection criteria: Open admissions. Selective admission to health service technologies programs and for international students. **Test requirements:** ASSET (basic skills) required of all first-time freshmen.

1992 FRESHMAN CLASS PROFILE. 1,329 men, 1,596 women enrolled. **Characteristics:** 98% from in state, 100% commute, 22% have minority backgrounds, 2% are foreign students. Average age is 27.

FALL-TERM APPLICATIONS. $15 fee. Closing date September 2; priority given to applications received by July 28; applicants notified on a rolling basis. Early admission available.

STUDENT LIFE. Housing: Students may seek to live in Eastern Michigan University housing. **Activities:** Student government, magazine, student newspaper, choral groups, dance, drama, jazz band.

STUDENT SERVICES. Aptitude testing, career counseling, employment service for undergraduates, freshman orientation, on-campus day care, personal counseling, placement service for graduates, special adviser for adult students, veterans counselor, services/facilities for handicapped.

ANNUAL EXPENSES. Tuition and fees (projected): $1,416, $600 additional for out-of-district students, $1,140 additional for out-of-state students. **Books and supplies:** $500. **Other expenses:** $600.

FINANCIAL AID. 50% of freshmen, 31% of continuing students receive some form of aid. All grants based on need. Academic, art, state/district residency, leadership scholarships available. **Aid applications:** No closing date; priority given to applications received by June 1; applicants notified on a rolling basis beginning on or about August 1.

ADDRESS/TELEPHONE. David Placey, Dir Admissions, Washtenaw Community College, PO Box D-1, 4800 E. Huron River Dr, Ann Arbor, MI 48106-0978. (313) 973-3543. Fax: (313) 677-5414.

Wayne County Community College
Detroit, Michigan CB code: 1937

2-year public community college, coed. Founded in 1967. **Accreditation:** Regional. **Undergraduate enrollment:** 530 men, 1,412 women full time; 2,030 men, 5,605 women part time. **Faculty:** 417 total (164 full time), 72 with doctorates or other terminal degrees. **Location:** Urban campus in very large city. **Calendar:** Semester, extensive summer session. Saturday and extensive evening/early morning classes. **Microcomputers:** 100 located in libraries, classrooms, computer centers. **Additional facts:** 5 campuses.

DEGREES OFFERED. AA, AS, AAS. 695 associate degrees awarded in 1992. 30% in business and management, 10% business/office and marketing/distribution, 30% computer sciences, 10% engineering technologies, 10% allied health, 10% multi/interdisciplinary studies.

UNDERGRADUATE MAJORS. Accounting, aeronautical technology, Afro-American (black) studies, air conditioning/heating/refrigeration mechanics, air conditioning/heating/refrigeration technology, automotive technology, business administration and management, business and management, business and office, business computer/console/peripheral equipment operation, business data entry equipment operation, business data processing and related programs, business data programming, child development/care/guidance, clinical laboratory science, computer and information sciences, computer technology, dental assistant, dental hygiene, dental laboratory technology, diesel engine mechanics, dietetic aide/assistant, drafting, drawing, electrical and electronics equipment repair, electrical technology, electromechanical technology, electronic technology, elementary education, finance, fine arts, fire control and safety technology, food management, food production/management/services, gerontology, home economics, hospitality and recreation marketing, hotel/motel and restaurant management, institutional/home management/supporting programs, interior design, law enforcement and corrections technologies, liberal/general studies, machine tool operation/machine shop, marketing and distribution, marketing management, medical assistant, medical laboratory technologies, medical records technology, mental health/human services, nursing, occupational therapy assistant, painting, preengineering, real estate, recreation and community services technologies, renewable natural resources, sculpture, secondary education, secretarial and related programs, telecommunications, veterinarian's assistant, visual and performing arts, welding technology, word processing.

ACADEMIC PROGRAMS. 2-year transfer program, cooperative education, dual enrollment of high school students, honors program, independent study, internships, telecourses. **Remedial services:** Learning center, reduced course load, remedial instruction, tutoring. **Placement/credit:** CLEP General, institutional tests; 18 credit hours maximum for associate degree.

ACADEMIC REQUIREMENTS. Freshmen must earn minimum GPA of 2.0 to continue in good standing. Students must declare major on application. **Graduation requirements:** 60 hours for associate (32 in major). Most students required to take courses in arts/fine arts, English, history, humanities, mathematics, biological/physical sciences, social sciences.

FRESHMAN ADMISSIONS. Selection criteria: Open admissions. Nursing applicants must have high school diploma or GED, 2.0 GPA or higher in prerequisite courses, and must take the Psychological Service Bureau Nursing School Aptitude Examination. High school diploma, or parent's approval, or age 18 required. **Additional information:** Applicants under 18 must have high school diploma.

1992 FRESHMAN CLASS PROFILE. 754 men, 1,523 women enrolled. **Characteristics:** 95% from in state, 100% commute, 3% are foreign students. Average age is 25.

FALL-TERM APPLICATIONS. $10 fee, may be waived for applicants with need. No closing date; priority given to applications received by August 1; applicants notified on a rolling basis. Deferred and early admission available.

STUDENT LIFE. Activities: Student government, film, magazine, student newspaper, choral groups, dance, drama, fraternities, sororities.

ATHLETICS. Intramural: Baseball M, basketball, bowling, soccer M, softball W, volleyball.

STUDENT SERVICES. Aptitude testing, career counseling, employment service for undergraduates, freshman orientation, on-campus day care, personal counseling, placement service for graduates, veterans counselor, services/facilities for handicapped.

ANNUAL EXPENSES. Tuition and fees (1992-93): $1,790, $480 additional for out-of-district students, $1,050 additional for out-of-state students. **Books and supplies:** $400. **Other expenses:** $1,000.

FINANCIAL AID. 42% of freshmen, 42% of continuing students receive some form of aid. All aid based on need. **Aid applications:** No closing date; priority given to applications received by August 1; applicants notified on a rolling basis beginning on or about July 1.

ADDRESS/TELEPHONE. Jacqueline Hodges, Admissions Administrator, Wayne County Community College, 801 West Fort Street, Detroit, MI 48226. (313) 496-2651. Fax: (313) 961-2791.

Wayne State University
Detroit, Michigan — CB code: 1898

Admissions: 73% of applicants accepted
Based on:
- ••• School record
- •• Test scores
- • Essay

Completion: 77% of freshmen end year in good standing
37% graduate

4-year public university, coed. Founded in 1868. **Accreditation:** Regional. **Undergraduate enrollment:** 4,236 men, 5,648 women full time; 4,686 men, 6,295 women part time. **Graduate enrollment:** 3,201 men, 2,677 women full time; 3,882 men, 4,320 women part time. **Faculty:** 2,533 total (1,403 full time). **Location:** Urban campus in very large city; 3 miles from downtown. **Calendar:** Semester, extensive summer session. Saturday and extensive evening/early morning classes. **Microcomputers:** 600 located in libraries, classrooms, computer centers. **Special facilities:** 3 theaters. **Additional facts:** Eight off-campus locations and University Center at local community college.

DEGREES OFFERED. BA, BS, BFA, MA, MS, MBA, MFA, MEd, MSW, PhD, EdD, MD, B. Pharm. 2,490 bachelor's degrees awarded in 1992. 17% in business and management, 10% teacher education, 9% engineering, 5% health sciences, 7% allied health, 5% letters/literature, 5% multi/interdisciplinary studies, 7% psychology, 8% social sciences, 10% visual and performing arts. Graduate degrees offered in 122 major fields of study.

UNDERGRADUATE MAJORS. Accounting, Afro-American (black) studies, American studies, anthropology, art education, art history, bilingual/bicultural education, biology, business and management, business economics, business education, chemical engineering, chemistry, Chicano-Boricua studies, city/community/regional planning, civil engineering, classics, communications, computer and information sciences, criminal justice studies, dance, developmental psychology, dramatic arts, early childhood education, East Asian studies, economics, education of exceptional children, education of the mentally handicapped, education of the multiple handicapped, education of the physically handicapped, electrical technology, electrical/electronics/communications engineering, electromechanical technology, electronic technology, elementary education, English, English education, English literature, fashion merchandising, film arts, finance, fine arts, food science and nutrition, foreign languages (multiple emphasis), foreign languages education, French, funeral services/mortuary science, geography, geology, German, Greek (classical), health occupations, Hebrew, history, humanities, individual and family development, industrial arts education, industrial engineering, industrial technology, information sciences and systems, interior design, Italian, jazz, journalism, labor/industrial relations, Latin, liberal/general studies, linguistics, management information systems, management science, manufacturing technology, marketing and distribution, marketing and distributive education, mathematics, mathematics education, mechanical design technology, mechanical engineering, medical laboratory technologies, medical radiation dosimetry, metallurgical engineering, music, music business management, music education, music performance, music theory and composition, music therapy, near Eastern languages, nursing, occupational therapy, parks and recreation management, peace studies, pharmacy, philosophy, photography, physical education, physical therapy, physics, Polish, political science and government, psychology, public affairs, public relations, quality control technology, radiation therapy technology, radio/television broadcasting, religious music, Russian, science education, secondary education, Slavic languages, social studies education, social work, sociology, Spanish, special education, speech, speech/communication/theater education, student counseling and personnel services, urban studies, women's studies.

ACADEMIC PROGRAMS. Accelerated program, cooperative education, double major, dual enrollment of high school students, education specialist degree, honors program, independent study, internships, study abroad, telecourses, visiting/exchange student program, weekend college, cross-registration, off-campus courses for credit, city-wide adult education program; combined bachelor's/graduate program in law. **Remedial services:** Learning center, preadmission summer program, special counselor, tutoring, Project 350 and Chicano-Boricua Program (minority programs) and Division of Community Education. **ROTC:** Air Force, Army. **Placement/credit:** AP, CLEP General and Subject, institutional tests; 32 credit hours maximum for bachelor's degree.

ACADEMIC REQUIREMENTS. Freshmen must earn minimum GPA of 2.0 to continue in good standing. 74% of freshmen return for sophomore year. Students must declare major by end of second year. **Graduation requirements:** 120 hours for bachelor's (30 in major). Most students required to take courses in arts/fine arts, computer science, English, foreign languages, history, humanities, mathematics, philosophy/religion, biological/physical sciences, social sciences.

FRESHMAN ADMISSIONS. Selection criteria: High school record, test scores. Minimum 2.75 GPA. A 2.0 GPA combined with ACT test score of 21 or greater also favorable. **High school preparation:** 18 units recommended. Recommended units include English 4, foreign language 2, mathematics 4, social science 3 and science 3. 2 units fine arts also recommended, and computer literacy. **Test requirements:** SAT or ACT (ACT preferred); score report by August 1.

1992 FRESHMAN CLASS PROFILE. 4,086 men and women applied, 2,996 accepted; 844 men enrolled, 1,392 women enrolled. **Academic background:** Mid 50% of enrolled freshmen had ACT composite between 15-23. 89% submitted ACT scores. **Characteristics:** 99% from in state, 95% commute, 53% have minority backgrounds, 2% are foreign students. Average age is 18.

FALL-TERM APPLICATIONS. $20 fee, may be waived for applicants with need. Closing date August 1; applicants notified on a rolling basis. Portfolio required for art applicants. Audition recommended. Audition required of music applicants, recommended for dance and theater applicants.

STUDENT LIFE. Housing: Apartment, fraternity, handicapped housing available. **Activities:** Student government, radio, student newspaper, yearbook, choral groups, concert band, dance, drama, jazz band, marching band, music ensembles, musical theater, symphony orchestra, fraternities, sororities.

ATHLETICS. NCAA. **Intercollegiate:** Baseball M, basketball, cross-country M, diving, fencing, football M, golf M, softball W, swimming, tennis, volleyball W. **Intramural:** Badminton, basketball, football M, handball, racquetball, soccer, softball, squash, tennis, volleyball.

STUDENT SERVICES. Aptitude testing, career counseling, employment service for undergraduates, freshman orientation, health services, on-campus day care, personal counseling, placement service for graduates, veterans counselor, educational rehabilitation services for disabled students, military services, international student services, services/facilities for handicapped.

ANNUAL EXPENSES. Tuition and fees: $2,403, $2,835 additional for out-of-state students. **Room and board:** $4,860. **Books and supplies:** $487. **Other expenses:** $791.

FINANCIAL AID. 50% of freshmen, 50% of continuing students receive some form of aid. 69% of grants, 81% of loans, all jobs based on need. 650 enrolled freshmen were judged to have need, all were offered aid. Academic, music/drama, art, athletic scholarships available. **Aid applications:** Closing date May 1; applicants notified on or about August 15; must reply within 2 weeks.

ADDRESS/TELEPHONE. Ronald Hughes, Director of Undergraduate Admissions, Wayne State University, HNJ, 3 East, Detroit, MI 48202. (313) 577-3577. Fax: (313) 577-7536.

West Shore Community College
Scottville, Michigan — CB code: 1941

2-year public community college, coed. Founded in 1967. **Accreditation:** Regional. **Undergraduate enrollment:** 237 men, 348 women full time; 286 men, 559 women part time. **Faculty:** 68 total (26 full time), 10 with doctorates or other terminal degrees. **Location:** Rural campus in rural community; 54 miles from Muskegon. **Calendar:** Semester, limited summer session. Saturday classes. **Microcomputers:** 45 located in libraries, computer centers. **Special facilities:** Nature course, cross-country running course.

DEGREES OFFERED. AA, AS, AAS. 137 associate degrees awarded in 1992.

UNDERGRADUATE MAJORS. Accounting, biology, business and office, business data processing and related programs, chemistry, computer-aided design, criminal justice studies, criminal justice technology, data processing, education, electrical and electronics equipment repair, electronic technology, fine arts, food management, history, law enforcement and corrections technologies, liberal/general studies, machine tool operation/machine shop, manufacturing technology, marketing and distribution, marketing management, microcomputer software, nursing, practical nursing, precision metal work, preengineering, psychology, science technologies, secretarial and related programs, social sciences, social work, sociology, studio art, teacher aide, welding technology, word processing.

ACADEMIC PROGRAMS. 2-year transfer program, dual enrollment of high school students, honors program, independent study, internships. **Remedial services:** Learning center, remedial instruction, special counselor, tutoring. **Placement/credit:** CLEP Subject, institutional tests; 10 credit hours maximum for associate degree.

ACADEMIC REQUIREMENTS. Freshmen must earn minimum GPA of 2.0 to continue in good standing. 76% of freshmen return for sophomore year. Students must declare major on application. **Graduation requirements:** 60 hours for associate. Most students required to take courses in English, humanities, mathematics, social sciences.

FRESHMAN ADMISSIONS. Selection criteria: Open admissions. Selective admission to nursing programs. **Test requirements:** ACT required of practical nursing applicants.

1992 FRESHMAN CLASS PROFILE. 310 men, 559 women enrolled. **Characteristics:** 93% from in state, 100% commute, 3% have minority backgrounds. Average age is 27.

FALL-TERM APPLICATIONS. $10 fee, may be waived for applicants with need. No closing date; applicants notified on a rolling basis. CRDA. Deferred and early admission available. Practical nursing program applicants must apply by June 1. Applicants for associate degree in nursing must apply by January 1.

STUDENT LIFE. Activities: Student government, student newspaper, choral groups, drama, jazz band, musical theater, Phi Theta Kappa.

ATHLETICS. Intramural: Basketball, racquetball, softball, table tennis, volleyball.

STUDENT SERVICES. Aptitude testing, career counseling, employment service for undergraduates, freshman orientation, personal counseling, placement service for graduates, veterans counselor, services/facilities for handicapped.

ANNUAL EXPENSES. Tuition and fees (1992-93): $1,134, $660 additional for out-of-district students, $1,110 additional for out-of-state students. **Books and supplies:** $600. **Other expenses:** $950.

FINANCIAL AID. 50% of freshmen, 50% of continuing students receive some form of aid. 93% of grants, 90% of loans, 93% of jobs based on need. 195 enrolled freshmen were judged to have need, all were offered aid. Academic, music/drama, leadership scholarships available. **Aid applications:** No closing date; priority given to applications received by May 1; applicants notified on a rolling basis beginning on or about May 15; must reply within 2 weeks.

ADDRESS/TELEPHONE. Thomas Hoiles, Director of Admissions, West Shore Community College, 3000 North Stiles Road, Scottville, MI 49454-0277. (616) 845-6211 ext. 133. Fax: (616) 845-0207.

Western Michigan University
Kalamazoo, Michigan

CB code: 1902

Admissions: 76% of applicants accepted
Based on:
••• School record
•• Test scores
• Activities, interview, recommendations, special talents
Completion: 84% of freshmen end year in good standing
42% graduate, 2% of these enter graduate study

4-year public university, coed. Founded in 1903. **Accreditation:** Regional. **Undergraduate enrollment:** 7,829 men, 8,512 women full time; 1,991 men, 2,343 women part time. **Graduate enrollment:** 532 men, 698 women full time; 2,205 men, 3,172 women part time. **Faculty:** 1,115 total (704 full time), 580 with doctorates or other terminal degrees. **Location:** Urban campus in small city; 140 miles from Detroit and Chicago. **Calendar:** Semester, extensive summer session. **Microcomputers:** 900 located in dormitories, libraries, classrooms, computer centers, campus-wide network. **Special facilities:** Van de Graaff particle accelerator, pilot plant for manufacturing and printing of paper and fiber recovery, Fetzer Business Center, theaters. **Additional facts:** Institution provides credit-bearing courses and programs at regional centers located in Grand Rapids, Kalamazoo, Lansing, Muskegon, Benton Harbor, and Battle Creek.

DEGREES OFFERED. BA, BS, BFA, MA, MS, MBA, MFA, MSW, PhD, EdD. 3,838 bachelor's degrees awarded in 1992. 30% in business and management, 7% communications, 14% teacher education, 5% health sciences, 5% parks/recreation, protective services, public affairs, 5% social sciences. Graduate degrees offered in 75 major fields of study.

UNDERGRADUATE MAJORS. Accounting, administrative systems, advertising, aeronautical technology, aerospace/aeronautical/astronautical engineering, African studies, airline piloting and navigation, American studies, anthropology, art education, Asian studies, automotive technology, biological and physical sciences, biology, biomedical science, broadcast and cable production, business administration and management, business and management, business communication, business communications, business economics, business education, business statistics, chemistry, clothing and textiles management/production/services, communications, community health work, computer and information sciences, computer engineering, contract management and procurement/purchasing, criminal justice studies, dance, drafting, drafting and design technology, dramatic arts, earth sciences, economics, education, education of the deaf and hearing impaired, education of the emotionally handicapped, education of the mentally handicapped, education of the physically handicapped, education of the visually handicapped, electrical/electronics/communications engineering, elementary education, engineering and other disciplines, engineering metallurgy, English, English education, environmental science, European studies, fashion merchandising, field hydrogeology, finance, fine arts, food marketing, food marketing, food science and nutrition, foreign languages education, French, geography, geology, geophysics and seismology, German, graphic and printing production, health education, health sciences, history, home economics education, human environment and housing, humanities and social sciences, hydrogeology, individual and family development, industrial arts education, industrial engineering, industrial marketing, industrial technology, information sciences and systems, insurance and risk management, integrated supply management, interior design, international business management, jazz, junior high education, Latin, Latin American studies, Latvian, law enforcement and corrections, liberal/general studies, management information systems, manufacturing technology, marketing and distribution, marketing and distributive education, mathematics, mathematics education, mechanical engineering, media studies, music, music education, music history and appreciation, music performance, music theory and composition, music therapy, musical theater, occupational therapy, organizational communication, paper engineering, parks and recreation management, philosophy, physical education, physical sciences, physician's assistant, physics, political science and government, precision metal work, predentistry, prelaw, premedicine, production technology, psychology, public administration, public relations, real estate, religion, retailing, science education, secondary education, social science education, social sciences, social studies education, social work, sociology, Spanish, speech correction, speech pathology/audiology, speech/communication/theater education, statistics, technical education, telecommunications, textile technology, textiles and clothing, tourism, trade and industrial education, trade and industrial supervision and management, woodworking.

ACADEMIC PROGRAMS. Accelerated program, cooperative education, double major, dual enrollment of high school students, education specialist degree, honors program, independent study, internships, student-designed major, study abroad, teacher preparation, weekend college, cross-registration. **Remedial services:** Learning center, preadmission summer program, reduced course load, remedial instruction, special counselor, tutoring. **ROTC:** Army. **Placement/credit:** AP, CLEP General and Subject, institutional tests. Maximum semester hours of credit by examination which may be counted toward degree varies by department. Credit by examination may not be used to satisfy minimum residency requirement of 30 semester hours.

ACADEMIC REQUIREMENTS. Freshmen must earn minimum GPA of 2.0 to continue in good standing. 79% of freshmen return for sophomore year. Students must declare major by end of second year. **Graduation requirements:** 122 hours for bachelor's (24 in major). Most students required to take courses in computer science, English, humanities, biological/physical sciences, social sciences. **Postgraduate studies:** 2% enter medical school.

FRESHMAN ADMISSIONS. Selection criteria: School achievement record, class rank, test scores, trend of grades, and number of solid high school academic subjects completed considered. **High school preparation:** 12 units recommended. Required and recommended units include English 4, mathematics 3-4, social science 3-3 and science 2-2. Foreign language 3 recommended. Students not meeting above requirements, but do meet other admissions requirements may still be admitted on a conditional basis. **Test requirements:** ACT; score report by September 1.

1992 FRESHMAN CLASS PROFILE. 4,358 men applied, 3,134 accepted, 1,229 enrolled; 5,343 women applied, 4,271 accepted, 1,590 enrolled. 58% had high school GPA of 3.0 or higher, 42% between 2.0 and 2.99. 22% were in top tenth and 47% were in top quarter of graduating class. **Academic background:** Mid 50% of enrolled freshmen had ACT composite between 20-25. 98% submitted ACT scores. **Characteristics:** 92% from in state, 90% live in college housing, 12% have minority backgrounds, 2% are foreign students. Average age is 18.

FALL-TERM APPLICATIONS. $25 fee, may be waived for applicants with need. No closing date; applicants notified on a rolling basis; must reply by May 1 or immediately if notified thereafter. Audition required for music and dance, theater applicants. Interview recommended.

STUDENT LIFE. Housing: Dormitories (men, women, coed); apartment, fraternity, sorority housing available. Special interest living arrangements available. **Activities:** Student government, film, magazine, radio, student newspaper, television, yearbook, choral groups, concert band, dance, drama, jazz band, marching band, music ensembles, musical theater, opera, pep band, symphony orchestra, fraternities, sororities, diverse professional/departmental, political, social, religious, special interest, sports and honorary organizations. **Additional information:** University will offer most intramural sports whenever there is sufficient student interest.

ATHLETICS. NCAA. **Intercollegiate:** Baseball M, basketball, cross-country, football M, gymnastics, ice hockey M, soccer M, softball W, tennis, track and field, volleyball W. **Intramural:** Archery, badminton, basketball, bowling, golf, ice hockey M, lacrosse, racquetball, rifle, sailing, skiing, soccer, softball, swimming, table tennis, tennis, track and field, volleyball, water polo, wrestling M.

STUDENT SERVICES. Aptitude testing, career counseling, employment service for undergraduates, freshman orientation, health services, on-campus day care, personal counseling, placement service for graduates, special adviser for adult students, veterans counselor, center for women's services, services/facilities for handicapped.

ANNUAL EXPENSES. Tuition and fees (1992-93): $2,685, $3,690 additional for out-of-state students. **Room and board:** $3,630. **Books and supplies:** $470. **Other expenses:** $1,160.

FINANCIAL AID. 68% of freshmen, 59% of continuing students receive some form of aid. 61% of grants, 86% of loans, 17% of jobs based on

need. 1,230 enrolled freshmen were judged to have need, all were offered aid. Academic, music/drama, art, athletic, leadership, minority scholarships available. **Aid applications:** No closing date; priority given to applications received by March 1; applicants notified on a rolling basis beginning on or about April 1; must reply within 4 weeks.

ADDRESS/TELEPHONE. Stanley E. Henderson, Director of Admissions, Western Michigan University, Kalamazoo, MI 49008. (616) 387-2000.

William Tyndale College
Farmington Hills, Michigan — CB code: 1167

4-year private Bible, liberal arts college, coed, affiliated with interdenominational/evangelical. Founded in 1945. **Accreditation:** Regional. **Undergraduate enrollment:** 471 men and women. **Faculty:** 49 total (13 full time), 15 with doctorates or other terminal degrees. **Location:** Suburban campus in small city; 15 miles from Detroit. **Calendar:** Semester, limited summer session. **Microcomputers:** 8 located in computer centers.

DEGREES OFFERED. AA, BA. 20 associate degrees awarded in 1992. 88% in multi/interdisciplinary studies, 12% social sciences. 40 bachelor's degrees awarded. 5% in communications, 17% education, 10% multi/interdisciplinary studies, 47% philosophy, religion, theology, 17% psychology.

UNDERGRADUATE MAJORS. Associate: Early childhood education, liberal/general studies. **Bachelor's:** Bible studies, business and management, communications, counseling psychology, humanities, humanities and social sciences, liberal/general studies, missionary studies, music, religious music, social sciences, theological studies, youth ministries.

ACADEMIC PROGRAMS. 2-year transfer program, accelerated program, double major, independent study, internships, weekend college. **Remedial services:** Learning center, reduced course load, remedial instruction, special counselor. **Placement/credit:** AP, CLEP Subject, institutional tests; 18 credit hours maximum for associate degree; 18 credit hours maximum for bachelor's degree.

ACADEMIC REQUIREMENTS. Freshmen must earn minimum GPA of 1.6 to continue in good standing. 65% of freshmen return for sophomore year. Students must declare major by end of second year. **Graduation requirements:** 63 hours for associate (24 in major), 126 hours for bachelor's (30 in major). Most students required to take courses in arts/fine arts, English, foreign languages, history, humanities, mathematics, philosophy/religion, biological/physical sciences, social sciences. **Postgraduate studies:** 50% from 2-year programs enter 4-year programs.

FRESHMAN ADMISSIONS. Selection criteria: School achievement record and test scores. Rank in top half of class. **Test requirements:** SAT or ACT (ACT preferred); score report by August 29.

1992 FRESHMAN CLASS PROFILE. 51 men, 47 women enrolled. **Characteristics:** 92% commute. Average age is 31.

FALL-TERM APPLICATIONS. $20 fee. No closing date; applicants notified on a rolling basis. Interview required for music applicants. Audition required for music applicants. Essay recommended. Deferred and early admission available.

STUDENT LIFE. Housing: Dormitories (coed). **Activities:** Student government, yearbook, choral groups, drama, music ensembles, World Missions Fellowship. **Additional information:** Religious observance required.

ATHLETICS. Intercollegiate: Basketball, soccer M. **Intramural:** Volleyball.

STUDENT SERVICES. Aptitude testing, career counseling, freshman orientation, personal counseling, services/facilities for handicapped.

ANNUAL EXPENSES. Tuition and fees (1992-93): $4,880. **Room and board:** $3,400. **Books and supplies:** $450. **Other expenses:** $480.

FINANCIAL AID. 60% of freshmen receive some form of aid. 96% of grants, 44% of jobs based on need. 72 enrolled freshmen were judged to have need, all were offered aid. Academic, music/drama, leadership, alumni affiliation scholarships available. **Aid applications:** Closing date May 1; priority given to applications received by February 15; applicants notified on or about August 15; must reply within 2 weeks.

ADDRESS/TELEPHONE. Tim Cocking, Director of Admissions, William Tyndale College, 35700 West 12 Mile Road, Farmington Hills, MI 48331-9985. (313) 553-7200. Fax: 553-5963.

Yeshiva Beth Yehuda-Yeshiva Gedolah of Greater Detroit
Oak Park, Michigan — CB code: 7010

4-year private rabbinical college, affiliated with Jewish faith. **Undergraduate enrollment:** 24 men full time. **Graduate enrollment:** 8 men full time; 4 men part time. **Location:** Suburban campus in large town; Detroit suburb. Saturday and extensive evening/early morning classes.

ADDRESS/TELEPHONE. Admissions, Yeshiva Beth Yehuda-Yeshiva Gedolah of Greater Detroit, 24600 Greenfield Road, Oak Park, MI 48237. (313) 968-3361. Fax: (313) 968-8613.

Minnesota

Alexandria Technical College
Alexandria, Minnesota CB code: 0771

2-year public technical college, coed. Founded in 1961. **Accreditation:** Regional. **Undergraduate enrollment:** 888 men, 536 women full time; 88 men, 40 women part time. **Faculty:** 108 total (85 full time). **Location:** Rural campus in large town; 135 miles from Minneapolis-St. Paul. **Calendar:** Quarter. **Microcomputers:** 310 located in libraries, classrooms.

DEGREES OFFERED. AAS. 259 associate degrees awarded in 1992. 9% in architecture and environmental design, 15% business and management, 10% business/office and marketing/distribution, 17% computer sciences, 19% engineering technologies, 26% parks/recreation, protective services, public affairs.

UNDERGRADUATE MAJORS. Accounting, aquaculture, business computer/console/peripheral equipment operation, business data programming, computer graphics, computer programming, electrical and electronics equipment repair, electronic technology, fashion merchandising, finance, fishing and fisheries, Fluid power technology, hotel/motel and restaurant management, information sciences and systems, interior design, law enforcement and corrections, manufacturing technology, marketing and distribution, marketing management, mechanical design technology, medical laboratory technologies, office supervision and management.

ACADEMIC PROGRAMS. Computer delivered (on-line) credit-bearing course offerings, independent study, internships, telecourses. **Remedial services:** Preadmission summer program, reduced course load, remedial instruction, tutoring. **Placement/credit:** AP, CLEP Subject, institutional tests.

ACADEMIC REQUIREMENTS. Freshmen must earn minimum GPA of 2.0 to continue in good standing. 56% of freshmen return for sophomore year. Students must declare major on application. **Graduation requirements:** 96 hours for associate (64 in major). Most students required to take courses in computer science, English, humanities, mathematics, social sciences.

FRESHMAN ADMISSIONS. Selection criteria: Open admissions. School achievement record, test scores and interview considered for placement. **Test requirements:** Minnesota Multiphasic Personality Inventory required. ACT and physical ability test required for law enforcement applicants. PSB-Aptitude for practical nursing examination required for practical nursing applicants. Mechanical reasoning tests required for marine and small engine mechanics and diesel mechanics applicants. **Additional information:** Applicants considered in order of applications received.

1992 FRESHMAN CLASS PROFILE. 601 men, 481 women enrolled. **Characteristics:** 96% from in state, 100% commute, 1% have minority backgrounds. Average age is 23.

FALL-TERM APPLICATIONS. No fee. No closing date; applicants notified on a rolling basis; must reply within 4 weeks. Portfolio required. Interview recommended. Deferred admission available. Early admission available for high school students ranked in top half of their class.

STUDENT LIFE. Activities: Student government, student newspaper, yearbook, choral groups, dance, pep band, Phi Theta Kappa, student senate, cheerleading, and several student organizations.

ATHLETICS. Intercollegiate: Basketball M, volleyball. **Intramural:** Basketball M, bowling M, golf M, gymnastics M, ice hockey M, softball M, tennis M, volleyball.

STUDENT SERVICES. Aptitude testing, career counseling, employment service for undergraduates, freshman orientation, health services, personal counseling, placement service for graduates, services/facilities for handicapped.

ANNUAL EXPENSES. Tuition and fees (1992-93): $1,677, $1,618 additional for out-of-state students. **Books and supplies:** $400. **Other expenses:** $900.

FINANCIAL AID. 95% of freshmen, 85% of continuing students receive some form of aid. 97% of grants, 78% of loans, all jobs based on need. Academic scholarships available. **Aid applications:** No closing date; priority given to applications received by May 1; applicants notified on a rolling basis beginning on or about July 15; must reply within 2 weeks.

ADDRESS/TELEPHONE. David Trites, Counselor, Alexandria Technical College, 1601 Jefferson Street, Alexandria, MN 56308-3799. (612) 762-4520. (800) 253-9884. Fax: (612) 762-4501.

Anoka-Ramsey Community College
Coon Rapids, Minnesota CB code: 6024

2-year public community college, coed. Founded in 1965. **Accreditation:** Regional. **Undergraduate enrollment:** 932 men, 1,216 women full time; 800 men, 2,267 women part time. **Faculty:** 225 total (95 full time), 9 with doctorates or other terminal degrees. **Location:** Suburban campus in small city; 20 miles from Minneapolis-St. Paul. **Calendar:** Quarter, limited summer session. Saturday and extensive evening/early morning classes. **Microcomputers:** 300 located in libraries, classrooms, computer centers, campus-wide network. **Special facilities:** Glass blowing studio, native prairie ground.

DEGREES OFFERED. AA, AS, AAS. 500 associate degrees awarded in 1992.

UNDERGRADUATE MAJORS. Accounting, air traffic control, business and office, diagnostic optic technician, electrodiagnostic technologies, engineering, legal secretary, liberal/general studies, marketing and distribution, marketing management, medical records technology, medical secretary, nursing, occupational therapy assistant, office supervision and management, physical therapy assistant, secretarial and related programs, small business management and ownership, word processing.

ACADEMIC PROGRAMS. 2-year transfer program, cooperative education, dual enrollment of high school students, honors program, independent study, internships, weekend college, cross-registration, joint admission with University of Minnesota and St. Cloud State University. **Remedial services:** Learning center, reduced course load, remedial instruction, tutoring. **Placement/credit:** AP, CLEP General and Subject, institutional tests; 15 credit hours maximum for associate degree.

ACADEMIC REQUIREMENTS. After accumulating 12 credits students must complete 60% of attempted courses with minimum 1.6 GPA, increasing to 2.0 as number of credits increases. 65% of freshmen return for sophomore year. **Graduation requirements:** 96 hours for associate. Most students required to take courses in arts/fine arts, English, humanities, mathematics, biological/physical sciences, social sciences.

FRESHMAN ADMISSIONS. Selection criteria: Open admissions. Selective admissions to nursing programs and for foreign students. Applicants to joint programs must also be accepted by Anoka Hennepin-Technical College. One unit chemistry or biology required for nursing applicants. **Test requirements:** Psychological Services Bureau Associate Degree Pre-admissions Test required for nursing applicants.

1992 FRESHMAN CLASS PROFILE. 2,552 men and women applied, 2,552 accepted; 2,125 enrolled. **Characteristics:** 97% from in state, 100% commute, 3% have minority backgrounds, 1% are foreign students. Average age is 25.

FALL-TERM APPLICATIONS. $15 fee. No closing date; priority given to applications received by August 3; applicants notified on a rolling basis. Deferred and early admission available.

STUDENT LIFE. Activities: Student government, magazine, student newspaper, fine arts publication, choral groups, concert band, drama, jazz band, music ensembles, musical theater, speech, art exhibits, Phi Theta Kappa.

ATHLETICS. NJCAA. **Intercollegiate:** Baseball M, basketball, softball W, volleyball W, wrestling M. **Intramural:** Baseball M, basketball, bowling, golf, ice hockey M, racquetball, skiing, soccer, softball, track and field, volleyball.

STUDENT SERVICES. Aptitude testing, career counseling, employment service for undergraduates, freshman orientation, personal counseling, placement service for graduates, special adviser for adult students, veterans counselor, interest and personality testing, freshmen year experience course, services/facilities for handicapped.

ANNUAL EXPENSES. Tuition and fees (1992-93): $1,687, $1,688 additional for out-of-state students. **Books and supplies:** $500. **Other expenses:** $650.

FINANCIAL AID. 40% of freshmen, 40% of continuing students receive some form of aid. Academic scholarships available. **Aid applications:** No closing date; priority given to applications received by May 15; applicants notified on a rolling basis beginning on or about June 15; must reply within 2 weeks.

ADDRESS/TELEPHONE. Irene K. Campanaro, Director of Admissions/ Registrar, Anoka-Ramsey Community College, 11200 Mississippi Boulevard Northwest, Coon Rapids, MN 55433. (612) 427-2600. Fax: (612) 422-3341.

Augsburg College
Minneapolis, Minnesota CB code: 6014

Admissions: 76% of applicants accepted
Based on:
- ••• School record
- •• Activities, essay, interview, recommendations, test scores
- • Religious affiliation/commitment, special talents

Completion: 85% of freshmen end year in good standing
11% enter graduate study

4-year private liberal arts college, coed, affiliated with Evangelical Lutheran Church in America. Founded in 1869. **Accreditation:** Regional. **Undergraduate enrollment:** 807 men, 1,253 women full time; 211 men, 514 women part time. **Graduate enrollment:** 18 men, 74 women full time; 19 men, 33 women part time. **Faculty:** 282 total (130 full time), 145 with doctorates or other terminal degrees. **Location:** Urban campus in large city; 2 miles from downtown. **Calendar:** 4-1-4, extensive summer session. Saturday classes. **Microcomputers:** 115 located in dormitories, libraries, classrooms, computer centers, campus-wide network. **Special facilities:** Center for atmospheric research.

DEGREES OFFERED. BA, BS, MA, MEd, MSW. 504 bachelor's degrees awarded in 1992. 35% in business and management, 10% communications, 12% teacher education, 7% health sciences, 5% letters/literature, 9% social sciences. Graduate degrees offered in 2 major fields of study.

UNDERGRADUATE MAJORS. Accounting, art history, biology, business administration and management, business and management, business economics, chemistry, Chinese, communications, computer and information sciences, dramatic arts, early childhood education, East Asian studies, Eastern European studies, economics, elementary education, engineering, English, finance, French, German, health education, history, humanities, international business management, international relations, Japanese, management information systems, marketing management, mathematics, music, music education, music performance, music therapy, nursing, philosophy, physical education, physics, political science and government, psychology, religion, Russian, Scandinavian languages, Scandinavian studies, secondary education, social sciences, social work, sociology, Spanish, speech, studio art, transdisciplinary studies, urban studies, women's studies.

ACADEMIC PROGRAMS. Cooperative education, double major, dual enrollment of high school students, honors program, independent study, internships, student-designed major, study abroad, teacher preparation, visiting/exchange student program, weekend college, cross-registration, Metro-Urban Studies internship program, Conservation of Human Resources extension program; liberal arts/career combination in engineering. **Remedial services:** Learning center, reduced course load, remedial instruction, special counselor, tutoring. **ROTC:** Air Force, Naval. **Placement/credit:** AP, CLEP General and Subject, institutional tests; 36 credit hours maximum for bachelor's degree.

ACADEMIC REQUIREMENTS. Freshmen must earn minimum GPA of 1.6 to continue in good standing. 80% of freshmen return for sophomore year. Students must declare major by end of second year. **Graduation requirements:** 140 hours for bachelor's (40 in major). Most students required to take courses in arts/fine arts, English, foreign languages, history, humanities, mathematics, philosophy/religion, biological/physical sciences, social sciences. **Postgraduate studies:** 1% enter law school, 1% enter medical school, 9% enter other graduate study.

FRESHMAN ADMISSIONS. Selection criteria: School achievement record, class rank in top half, test scores, recommendations, interviews, and extracurricular activities. **High school preparation:** 14 units recommended. Recommended units include English 4, foreign language 2, mathematics 3, social science 2 and science 3. **Test requirements:** SAT or ACT (ACT preferred); score report by August 1. PSAT may be submitted in place of SAT or ACT.

1992 FRESHMAN CLASS PROFILE. 46% had high school GPA of 3.0 or higher, 49% between 2.0 and 2.99. 12% were in top tenth and 48% were in top quarter of graduating class. **Academic background:** Mid 50% of enrolled freshmen had ACT composite between 18-23. 87% submitted ACT scores. **Characteristics:** 81% from in state, 81% live in college housing, 17% have minority backgrounds, 1% are foreign students. Average age is 21.

FALL-TERM APPLICATIONS. $15 fee, may be waived for applicants with need. Closing date August 1; priority given to applications received by June 1; applicants notified on a rolling basis. Essay required. Interview recommended. CRDA. Deferred and early admission available. EDP-F.

STUDENT LIFE. Housing: Dormitories (men, women, coed); apartment, handicapped housing available. Annex housing provides alternative opportunity for group living. Groups of upperclass men or women share living space, house responsibilities and cooking. **Activities:** Student government, film, magazine, radio, student newspaper, yearbook, choral groups, concert band, drama, jazz band, music ensembles, pep band, symphony orchestra, Religious Life Commission, Fellowship of Christian Athletes, cross-cultural, Black Student Union, Intertribal Student Union, Minnesota Public Interest Research Group, Global Awareness Community, International Association for Business Communication. **Additional information:** Statement of student rights and responsibilities provides for due process in matters of disciplinary action, grievances, and grade appeal.

ATHLETICS. NCAA. **Intercollegiate:** Baseball M, basketball, cross-country, football M, golf, ice hockey M, soccer, softball W, tennis, track and field, volleyball W, wrestling M. **Intramural:** Basketball, racquetball, softball, tennis, volleyball.

STUDENT SERVICES. Aptitude testing, career counseling, employment service for undergraduates, freshman orientation, health services, personal counseling, placement service for graduates, special adviser for adult students, services/facilities for handicapped.

ANNUAL EXPENSES. Tuition and fees: $11,404. **Room and board:** $4,204. **Books and supplies:** $500. **Other expenses:** $850.

FINANCIAL AID. 90% of freshmen, 83% of continuing students receive some form of aid. 89% of grants, 75% of loans, 33% of jobs based on need. 204 enrolled freshmen were judged to have need, all were offered aid. Academic, music/drama, leadership, religious affiliation scholarships available. **Aid applications:** No closing date; priority given to applications received by April 15; applicants notified on a rolling basis beginning on or about February 15; must reply by May 1 or within 3 weeks if notified thereafter.

ADDRESS/TELEPHONE. Sally Daniels, Director of Admissions, Augsburg College, 731 21st Avenue South, Minneapolis, MN 55454. (612) 330-1001. (800) 788-5678. Fax: (612) 330-1649.

Austin Community College
Austin, Minnesota — CB code: 6017

2-year public community college, coed. Founded in 1940. **Accreditation:** Regional. **Undergraduate enrollment:** 220 men, 321 women full time; 220 men, 596 women part time. **Faculty:** 70 total (30 full time), 1 with doctorate or other terminal degree. **Location:** Suburban campus in large town; 90 miles from Minneapolis-St. Paul. **Calendar:** Quarter, limited summer session. **Microcomputers:** 140 located in libraries, classrooms, computer centers.

DEGREES OFFERED. AA, AS, AAS. 275 associate degrees awarded in 1992.

UNDERGRADUATE MAJORS. Accounting, business administration and management, business and management, computer and information sciences, liberal/general studies, nursing, occupational therapy assistant, radio/television broadcasting.

ACADEMIC PROGRAMS. 2-year transfer program, dual enrollment of high school students, internships, weekend college, cross-registration. **Remedial services:** Learning center, reduced course load, remedial instruction, tutoring. **Placement/credit:** AP, CLEP General, institutional tests; 20 credit hours maximum for associate degree.

ACADEMIC REQUIREMENTS. Freshmen must earn minimum GPA of 1.75 to continue in good standing. 72% of freshmen return for sophomore year. **Graduation requirements:** 96 hours for associate. Most students required to take courses in arts/fine arts, English, history, humanities, mathematics, philosophy/religion, biological/physical sciences, social sciences.

FRESHMAN ADMISSIONS. Selection criteria: Open admissions. Selective admissions to human services, nursing, and occupational therapy assistant programs. High school chemistry required of nursing applicants.

1992 FRESHMAN CLASS PROFILE. 424 men and women enrolled. **Characteristics:** 91% from in state, 100% commute, 7% have minority backgrounds, 2% are foreign students. Average age is 24.

FALL-TERM APPLICATIONS. $15 fee. No closing date; applicants notified on a rolling basis. Interview required for occupational therapy and human services applicants, recommended for others. CRDA. Deferred and early admission available.

STUDENT LIFE. Activities: Student government, student newspaper, choral groups, concert band, drama, music ensembles, musical theater, symphony orchestra, Inter-varsity Club.

ATHLETICS. NJCAA. **Intercollegiate:** Baseball M, basketball, golf, softball W, tennis, volleyball W. **Intramural:** Basketball M, bowling, golf, skiing, softball, tennis, volleyball.

STUDENT SERVICES. Aptitude testing, career counseling, employment service for undergraduates, freshman orientation, on-campus day care, personal counseling, special adviser for adult students, veterans counselor, services/facilities for handicapped.

ANNUAL EXPENSES. Tuition and fees (projected): $1,893, $1,890 additional for out-of-state students. **Books and supplies:** $600. **Other expenses:** $675.

FINANCIAL AID. 67% of continuing students receive some form of aid. 97% of grants, 85% of loans, 84% of jobs based on need. Academic, music/drama, athletic, state/district residency, leadership, alumni affiliation scholarships available. **Aid applications:** No closing date; priority given to applications received by March 15; applicants notified on a rolling basis beginning on or about May 1; must reply within 2 weeks. **Additional information:** One class tuition-free for Minnesota residents over 25 who have not attended college for at least 7 years.

ADDRESS/TELEPHONE. Penny Reynen, Director of Admissions, Austin Community College, 1600 Eighth Avenue Northwest, Austin, MN 55912. (507) 433-0535. (800) 747-6941. Fax: (507) 433-0515.

Bemidji State University
Bemidji, Minnesota — CB code: 6676

Admissions:	69% of applicants accepted
Based on:	•• School record, test scores
	• Activities, interview, recommendations
Completion:	75% of freshmen end year in good standing
	29% graduate

4-year public university, coed. Founded in 1919. **Accreditation:** Regional. **Undergraduate enrollment:** 1,942 men, 2,002 women full time; 266 men, 561 women part time. **Graduate enrollment:** 22 men, 32 women full time; 100 men, 264 women part time. **Faculty:** 302 total (287 full time), 132 with doctorates or other terminal degrees. **Location:** Rural campus in large town; 150 miles from Duluth, 230 miles from Minneapolis-St. Paul. **Calendar:** Quarter, extensive summer session. **Microcomputers:** 190 located in dormitories, libraries, classrooms, computer centers, campus-wide network. **Special facilities:** Freshwater aquatics laboratory. **Additional facts:** Arrowhead University Center located on Minnesota's Mesabi Iron Range offers several degree programs.

DEGREES OFFERED. AA, BA, BS, BFA, MA, MS. 46 associate degrees awarded in 1992. 87% in multi/interdisciplinary studies, 9% parks/recreation, protective services, public affairs. 776 bachelor's degrees awarded. 20% in business and management, 32% teacher education, 10% parks/recreation, protective services, public affairs, 6% social sciences, 7% visual and performing arts. Graduate degrees offered in 15 major fields of study.

UNDERGRADUATE MAJORS. Associate: Early childhood education, liberal/general studies. **Bachelor's:** Accounting, American Indian studies, art education, biology, business administration and management, business and management, chemistry, city/community/regional planning, clinical laboratory science, community services, computer and information sciences, criminal justice studies, dramatic arts, earth sciences, economics, elementary education, engineering physics, English, English education, environmental science, fine arts, foreign languages education, French, geography, geology, German, health education, health sciences, history, humanities, illustration design, industrial arts education, industrial technology, information sciences and systems, journalism, marine biology, mathematics, mathematics education, medical laboratory technologies, music, music education, nursing, parks and recreation management, philosophy, physical education, physical sciences, physics, political science and government, premedicine, psychology, radio/television broadcasting, radio/television technology, science education, secondary education, social science education, social sciences, social studies education, social work, sociology, Spanish, speech, sports management, trade and industrial education, trade and industrial supervision and management.

ACADEMIC PROGRAMS. 2-year transfer program, accelerated program, cooperative education, double major, dual enrollment of high school students, external degree, honors program, independent study, internships, study abroad, teacher preparation, exchange program with other Minnesota state universities. **Remedial services:** Learning center, reduced course load, remedial instruction, special counselor, tutoring. **Placement/credit:** AP, CLEP General and Subject, IB, institutional tests. Unlimited number of hours of credit by examination may be counted towards degree.

ACADEMIC REQUIREMENTS. Freshmen must earn minimum GPA of 2.0 to continue in good standing. 68% of freshmen return for sophomore year. Students must declare major by end of second year. **Graduation requirements:** 96 hours for associate, 192 hours for bachelor's. Most students required to take courses in arts/fine arts, English, humanities, biological/physical sciences, social sciences.

FRESHMAN ADMISSIONS. Selection criteria: Rank in top half of class or test scores above 50th percentile preferred, ACT composite 21 or greater. **High school preparation:** 16 units required. Required units include biological science 1, English 4, foreign language 2, mathematics 3, physical science 1, social science 3 and science 1. **Test requirements:** ACT; score report by August 15. ACT used for admission of applicants in bottom half of class.

1992 FRESHMAN CLASS PROFILE. 635 men applied, 429 accepted, 275 enrolled; 591 women applied, 420 accepted, 295 enrolled. 8% were in top tenth and 34% were in top quarter of graduating class. **Academic background:** Mid 50% of enrolled freshmen had ACT composite between 19-23. 85% submitted ACT scores. **Characteristics:** 91% from in state, 81% live in college housing, 8% have minority backgrounds, 4% are foreign students, 1% join fraternities/sororities. Average age is 21.

FALL-TERM APPLICATIONS. $15 fee. Closing date August 15; priority given to applications received by May 15; applicants notified on a rolling basis; must reply by August 15 or within 10 days if notified thereafter. Interview recommended. Audition recommended for music applicants. Portfolio recommended for art applicants. Deferred and early admission available.

STUDENT LIFE. Housing: Dormitories (coed); apartment housing available. One resident hall specifically designed for single parents-with child care facilities. **Activities:** Student government, radio, student newspaper, television, choral groups, concert band, dance, drama, jazz band, marching band, music ensembles, musical theater, opera, pep band, symphony orchestra, fraternities, sororities, Newman Center, Lutheran Center, Young Republicans, Young Democrats, social service organizations, international students' club, veterans club, campus ministry, Council of Indian Students, Black Student Coalition.

ATHLETICS. NAIA, NCAA. **Intercollegiate:** Baseball M, basketball, football M, golf M, ice hockey M, softball W, tennis W, track and field, volleyball W. **Intramural:** Basketball, bowling, cross-country, golf M, ice hockey M, racquetball, skiing, soccer, softball, tennis, volleyball.

STUDENT SERVICES. Aptitude testing, career counseling, employment service for undergraduates, freshman orientation, health services, on-campus day care, personal counseling, placement service for graduates, special adviser for adult students, veterans counselor, Indian Student Services, services/facilities for handicapped.

ANNUAL EXPENSES. Tuition and fees (projected): $2,545, $2,000 additional for out-of-state students. North Dakota, South Dakota, Wisconsin, and Manitoba residents receive reciprocal tuition rates. **Room and board:** $2,800. **Books and supplies:** $660. **Other expenses:** $1,191.

FINANCIAL AID. 80% of freshmen, 79% of continuing students receive some form of aid. 86% of grants, 72% of loans, 37% of jobs based on need. 355 enrolled freshmen were judged to have need, all were offered aid. Academic, music/drama, art, athletic, alumni affiliation scholarships available. **Aid applications:** No closing date; priority given to applications received by August 15; applicants notified on a rolling basis beginning on or about August 1; must reply by registration.

ADDRESS/TELEPHONE. Paul Muller, Assoc Dir Admissions, Bemidji State University, 1500 Birchmont Drive Northeast, Bemidji, MN 56601. (218) 755-2040. (800) 475-2001. Fax: (218) 755-4048.

Bethany Lutheran College
Mankato, Minnesota — CB code: 6035

2-year private junior, liberal arts college, coed, affiliated with Evangelical Lutheran Synod. Founded in 1927. **Accreditation:** Regional. **Undergraduate enrollment:** 116 men, 183 women full time; 15 men, 3 women part time. **Faculty:** 40 total (19 full time), 3 with doctorates or other terminal degrees. **Location:** Urban campus in large town; 80 miles from Minneapolis-St. Paul. **Calendar:** Semester. **Microcomputers:** Located in libraries, classrooms, computer centers.

DEGREES OFFERED. AA. 107 associate degrees awarded in 1992. 100% in letters/literature.

UNDERGRADUATE MAJORS. Agricultural sciences, allied health, American studies, Bible studies, biblical languages, biological and physical sciences, biology, business and management, business and office, business computer/console/peripheral equipment operation, communications, community services, education, elementary education, engineering, engineering and other disciplines, English, fine arts, foreign languages (multiple emphasis), German, Greek (classical), health sciences, Hebrew, home economics, humanities and social sciences, liberal/general studies, library science, mathematics, physical sciences, preengineering, protective services, psychology, religious education, religious music, secretarial and related programs, social sciences, visual and performing arts.

ACADEMIC PROGRAMS. 2-year transfer program, dual enrollment of high school students, honors program, independent study, cross-registration. **Remedial services:** Reduced course load, remedial instruction, special counselor, tutoring. **ROTC:** Army. **Placement/credit:** AP, institutional tests.

ACADEMIC REQUIREMENTS. No policy requiring minimum GPA; records of students having academic difficulty are reviewed individually. 80% of freshmen return for sophomore year. **Graduation requirements:** 65 hours for associate (32 in major). Most students required to take courses in arts/fine arts, English, humanities, mathematics, biological/physical sciences, social sciences.

FRESHMAN ADMISSIONS. Selection criteria: School rank and test scores considered. **Test requirements:** SAT or ACT (ACT preferred); score report by August 15.

1992 FRESHMAN CLASS PROFILE. 184 men and women enrolled. 35% had high school GPA of 3.0 or higher, 60% between 2.0 and 2.99. 19% were in top tenth and 35% were in top quarter of graduating class. **Academic background:** Mid 50% of enrolled freshmen had ACT composite between 17-24. 92% submitted ACT scores. **Characteristics:** 72% from in state, 96% live in college housing, 4% have minority backgrounds. Average age is 18.

FALL-TERM APPLICATIONS. $20 fee. Closing date August 15; applicants notified on a rolling basis; must reply within 4 weeks. Interview recommended for all applicants applicants. Deferred and early admission available.

STUDENT LIFE. Housing: Dormitories (men, women). Freshman and sophomores not living with family required to live on campus. **Activities:** Student government, student newspaper, yearbook, choral groups, concert band, drama, jazz band, music ensembles, opera, pep band, Spiritual Life Committee, Lutherans for Life.

ATHLETICS. NJCAA. **Intercollegiate:** Baseball M, basketball, soccer M, softball W, tennis, volleyball W. **Intramural:** Baseball M, basketball, soccer, softball, table tennis, tennis, track and field, volleyball.

STUDENT SERVICES. Aptitude testing, career counseling, employment service for undergraduates, freshman orientation, personal counseling, veterans counselor, reading specialist.

ANNUAL EXPENSES. Tuition and fees (1992-93): $6,720. **Room and board:** $2,940. **Books and supplies:** $400. **Other expenses:** $800.

FINANCIAL AID. 88% of freshmen, 89% of continuing students receive some form of aid. 72% of grants, 83% of loans, all jobs based on need. 138 enrolled freshmen were judged to have need, 105 were offered aid. Academic, music/drama, art, athletic scholarships available. **Aid applications:** No closing date; priority given to applications received by May 1; applicants notified on a rolling basis beginning on or about March 1; must reply within 3 weeks.

ADDRESS/TELEPHONE. Steven C. Jaeger, Director of Admissions, Bethany Lutheran College, 734 Marsh Street, Mankato, MN 56001-4490. (507) 625-2977 ext. 330. Fax: (507) 625-1849.

Bethel College
St. Paul, Minnesota CB code: 6038

4-year private liberal arts college, coed, affiliated with Baptist General Conference. Founded in 1871. **Accreditation:** Regional. **Undergraduate enrollment:** 655 men, 962 women full time; 39 men, 63 women part time. **Location:** Suburban campus in large city; 10 miles from downtown Minneapolis-St. Paul. **Calendar:** 4-1-4.

FRESHMAN ADMISSIONS. Selection criteria: Rank in top half of class, PSAT of 80 combined, ACT composite score of 21, or SAT combined score of 800. Applicant must make personal statement regarding Christian commitment and agree to live in accordance with college's lifestyle. 2 recommendations are also required.

ANNUAL EXPENSES. Tuition and fees: $11,050. **Room and board:** $4,000. **Books and supplies:** $500. **Other expenses:** $1,450.

ADDRESS/TELEPHONE. John Lassen, Director of Admissions, Bethel College, 3900 Bethel Drive, St. Paul, MN 55112. (612) 638-6242. (800) 255-8706. Fax: (612) 638-6001.

Brainerd Community College
Brainerd, Minnesota CB code: 6045

2-year public community college, coed. Founded in 1938. **Accreditation:** Regional. **Undergraduate enrollment:** 437 men, 474 women full time; 209 men, 403 women part time. **Faculty:** 94 total (47 full time), 1 with doctorate or other terminal degree. **Location:** Rural campus in large town; 125 miles from Minneapolis-St. Paul. **Calendar:** Quarter, limited summer session. Saturday and extensive evening/early morning classes. **Microcomputers:** 40 located in computer centers. **Special facilities:** Art gallery, academic learning center. **Additional facts:** Access to 1.5 million book titles through participation in online catalog system with 28 other libraries.

DEGREES OFFERED. AA, AS, AAS. 405 associate degrees awarded in 1992.

UNDERGRADUATE MAJORS. Business and management, liberal/general studies, nursing, preengineering.

ACADEMIC PROGRAMS. 2-year transfer program, dual enrollment of high school students, telecourses, weekend college, 2+2 management program with College of St. Scholastica. **Remedial services:** Learning center, remedial instruction, tutoring, developmental classes. **Placement/credit:** AP, CLEP General and Subject.

ACADEMIC REQUIREMENTS. Freshmen must earn minimum GPA of 1.7 to continue in good standing. **Graduation requirements:** 96 hours for associate. Most students required to take courses in arts/fine arts, English, humanities, mathematics, biological/physical sciences, social sciences. **Additional information:** Credit given for faculty-guided summer travel in Great Britain.

FRESHMAN ADMISSIONS. Selection criteria: Open admissions. Applicants to mobility nursing program must have graduate license in practical nursing (LPN). Practical nurse program grades and college grades considered. Instructor and employer references, practical to registered nursing mobility profile, and mathematics test scores also considered. **Additional information:** Applications accepted until the start of each term.

1992 FRESHMAN CLASS PROFILE. 294 men, 339 women enrolled. **Characteristics:** 98% from in state, 100% commute, 7% have minority backgrounds. Average age is 18.

FALL-TERM APPLICATIONS. $15 fee. No closing date; applicants notified on a rolling basis. Deferred and early admission available.

STUDENT LIFE. Activities: Student government, student newspaper, choral groups, concert band, drama, jazz band, music ensembles, musical theater, Anishinabe Student Association, campus ambassadors, cheerleading, law enforcement club, mentoring, theater club, Phi Theta Kappa, student senate, spanish club, minority student forum.

ATHLETICS. NJCAA. **Intercollegiate:** Baseball M, basketball, football M, softball W, tennis, volleyball W, wrestling M. **Intramural:** Baseball M, basketball, bowling, golf, softball, tennis, volleyball.

STUDENT SERVICES. Aptitude testing, career counseling, freshman orientation, personal counseling, veterans counselor, services/facilities for handicapped.

ANNUAL EXPENSES. Tuition and fees (projected): $2,021, $1,920 additional for out-of-state students. **Books and supplies:** $510. **Other expenses:** $1,230.

FINANCIAL AID. 79% of freshmen, 75% of continuing students receive some form of aid. 97% of grants, 75% of loans, 92% of jobs based on need. Academic, music/drama, art, athletic, state/district residency, leadership, minority scholarships available. **Aid applications:** No closing date; priority given to applications received by June 1; applicants notified on a rolling basis beginning on or about July 1; must reply within 2 weeks.

ADDRESS/TELEPHONE. Marilynn Stoxen, Admissions and Records Officer/Registrar, Brainerd Community College, 501 West College Drive, Brainerd, MN 56401. (218) 828-2508. (800) 779-1112. Fax: (218) 828-2710.

Carleton College
Northfield, Minnesota CB code: 6081

Admissions: 54% of applicants accepted
Based on: ••• Recommendations, school record
•• Activities, essay, interview, special talents, test scores
Completion: 97% of freshmen end year in good standing
89% graduate, 29% of these enter graduate study

4-year private liberal arts college, coed. Founded in 1866. **Accreditation:** Regional. **Undergraduate enrollment:** 846 men, 816 women full time; 6 men, 5 women part time. **Faculty:** 163 total (150 full time), 156 with doctorates or other terminal degrees. **Location:** Rural campus in large town; 35 miles from Minneapolis-St. Paul. **Calendar:** Trimester. **Microcomputers:** 115 located in libraries, classrooms, computer centers. **Special facilities:** Observatory with 2 telescopes, 450-acre college-owned arboretum, 35-acre college-owned virgin prairie. **Additional facts:** More than 60% of Carleton students spend at least one term on an off-campus program (most of them abroad) for academic credit.

DEGREES OFFERED. BA. 453 bachelor's degrees awarded in 1992. 6% in languages, 13% letters/literature, 8% life sciences, 6% philosophy, religion, theology, 10% physical sciences, 7% psychology, 37% social sciences, 6% visual and performing arts.

UNDERGRADUATE MAJORS. Afro-American (black) studies, American studies, anthropology, art history, Asian studies, biology, chemistry, classics, computer and information sciences, economics, English, English literature, foreign languages (multiple emphasis), French, geology, German, Greek (classical), history, Latin, Latin American studies, mathematics, music, philosophy, physics, political science and government, psychology, religion, Russian, Russian and Slavic studies, sociology, Spanish, studio art.

ACADEMIC PROGRAMS. Double major, independent study, internships, student-designed major, study abroad, teacher preparation, Washington semester, cross-registration; liberal arts/career combination in engineering, health sciences; combined bachelor's/graduate program in law. **Remedial services:** Free tutoring, math skills center and writing skills center. **Placement/credit:** AP, institutional tests.

ACADEMIC REQUIREMENTS. Freshmen must earn minimum GPA of 1.6 to continue in good standing. 92% of freshmen return for sophomore year. Students must declare major by end of second year. **Graduation requirements:** 120 hours for bachelor's (48 in major). Most students required to take courses in English, foreign languages, humanities, mathematics, philosophy/religion, biological/physical sciences, social sciences. **Postgraduate studies:** 4% enter law school, 3% enter medical school, 1% enter MBA programs, 21% enter other graduate study. **Additional information:** 15-20 freshman seminars offered with enrollment limited to 15 students each.

FRESHMAN ADMISSIONS. Selection criteria: School achievement record and recommendations most important. Test scores, extracurricular school and community activities considered. **High school preparation:** 13 units recommended. Recommended units include English 4, foreign language 2, mathematics 3, social science 2 and science 2. **Test requirements:** SAT or ACT; score report by March 1.

1992 FRESHMAN CLASS PROFILE. 1,267 men applied, 688 accepted, 245 enrolled; 1,392 women applied, 737 accepted, 249 enrolled. 73% were in top tenth and 93% were in top quarter of graduating class. **Academic background:** Mid 50% of enrolled freshmen had SAT-V between 560-670, SAT-M between 610-700; ACT composite between 28-31. 89% submitted SAT scores, 46% submitted ACT scores. **Characteristics:** 22% from in state, 100% live in college housing, 18% have minority backgrounds, 1% are foreign students. Average age is 18.

FALL-TERM APPLICATIONS. $30 fee, may be waived for applicants with need. Closing date February 1; applicants notified on or about April 7; must reply by May 1. Essay required. Interview recommended. CRDA. Deferred and early admission available. EDP-F. 3 ACH recommended for admissions. Score reports due by March 1. Foreign language ACH used for placement.

STUDENT LIFE. Housing: Dormitories (coed). 25 college-owned houses within 2 blocks of campus, some coeducational, with varying board options. Several for special interest groups. **Activities:** Student government, film, magazine, radio, student newspaper, yearbook, choral groups, concert band, dance, drama, jazz band, music ensembles, musical theater, symphony orchestra, more than 100 religious, political, ethnic, and social service organizations.

ATHLETICS. NCAA. **Intercollegiate:** Baseball M, basketball, cross-country, diving, football M, golf M, skiing, soccer, softball W, swimming, tennis, track and field, volleyball W, wrestling M. **Intramural:** Badminton W, basketball, gymnastics W, handball, ice hockey M, racquetball, skiing, soccer, softball, swimming, table tennis, tennis, volleyball.

STUDENT SERVICES. Aptitude testing, career counseling, employment service for undergraduates, freshman orientation, health services, personal counseling, placement service for graduates, services/facilities for handicapped.

ANNUAL EXPENSES. Tuition and fees: $18,405. **Room and board:** $3,750. **Books and supplies:** $500.

FINANCIAL AID. 72% of freshmen, 88% of continuing students receive some form of aid. 94% of grants, 84% of loans, 77% of jobs based on need. 263 enrolled freshmen were judged to have need, all were offered aid. Academic scholarships available. **Aid applications:** Closing date March 1; applicants notified on or about April 7; must reply by May 1. **Additional information:** Full financial need of all admitted applicants met through combination of work, loans, grants.

ADDRESS/TELEPHONE. Paul Thiboutot, Dean of Admissions, Carleton College, 100 South College Street, Northfield, MN 55057. (507) 663-4190. (800) 955-2275. Fax: (507) 663-4526.

College of Associated Arts

St. Paul, Minnesota CB code: 0275

Admissions:	71% of applicants accepted
Based on:	••• Interview, school record, special talents
	•• Essay
	• Activities, recommendations, test scores
Completion:	90% of freshmen end year in good standing
	62% graduate, 5% of these enter graduate study

4-year private art college, coed. Founded in 1924. **Undergraduate enrollment:** 31 men, 20 women full time. **Faculty:** 26 total (6 full time). **Location:** Urban campus in large city; 1 mile from downtown. **Calendar:** Semester. **Microcomputers:** 12 located in computer centers.

DEGREES OFFERED. BFA. 32 bachelor's degrees awarded in 1992. 100% in visual and performing arts.

UNDERGRADUATE MAJORS. Drawing, fine arts, graphic design, illustration design, painting, photographic technology, photography, printmaking, sculpture, studio art.

ACADEMIC PROGRAMS. Double major, independent study, internships, student-designed major, study abroad. **Remedial services:** Tutoring.

ACADEMIC REQUIREMENTS. Freshmen must earn minimum GPA of 2.0 to continue in good standing. 90% of freshmen return for sophomore year. Students must declare major by end of second year. **Graduation requirements:** 125 hours for bachelor's (85 in major). Most students required to take courses in arts/fine arts, computer science, English, history, humanities, philosophy/religion, social sciences. **Postgraduate studies:** 5% enter other graduate study.

FRESHMAN ADMISSIONS. Selection criteria: School achievement record, essay, interview, portfolio, minority status considered. Minimum GPA 2.2 (on 4.0 scale) test scores considered, not required. 2 years high school art preferred. **Test requirements:** SAT or ACT (ACT preferred); score report by June 1.

1992 FRESHMAN CLASS PROFILE. 26 men applied, 18 accepted, 12 enrolled; 16 women applied, 12 accepted, 7 enrolled. 32% had high school GPA of 3.0 or higher, 63% between 2.0 and 2.99. **Characteristics:** 100% from in state, 100% commute, 16% have minority backgrounds, 11% are foreign students. Average age is 21.

FALL-TERM APPLICATIONS. $25 fee, may be waived for applicants with need. No closing date; priority given to applications received by May 1; applicants notified on a rolling basis; must reply within 4 weeks. Interview required. Portfolio required. Essay required. CRDA. Deferred admission available.

STUDENT LIFE. Housing: Housing notices distributed to students as requested. **Activities:** Student government.

STUDENT SERVICES. Career counseling, personal counseling, placement service for graduates, services/facilities for handicapped.

ANNUAL EXPENSES. Tuition and fees: $7,600. **Books and supplies:** $1,600. **Other expenses:** $1,200.

FINANCIAL AID. 80% of freshmen, 76% of continuing students receive some form of aid. 95% of grants, 69% of loans, 71% of jobs based on need. 19 enrolled freshmen were judged to have need, all were offered aid. Academic, art scholarships available. **Aid applications:** No closing date; applicants notified on a rolling basis.

ADDRESS/TELEPHONE. Sherry Essen, Director of Admissions, College of Associated Arts, 344 Summit Avenue, St. Paul, MN 55102-2199. (612) 224-3416. Fax: (612) 224-8854.

College of St. Benedict ⇎

St. Joseph, Minnesota CB code: 6104

Admissions:	93% of applicants accepted
Based on:	••• School record
	•• Activities, essay, interview, recommendations, special talents, test scores
Completion:	95% of freshmen end year in good standing
	74% graduate, 25% of these enter graduate study

4-year private liberal arts college, women only, affiliated with Roman Catholic Church. Founded in 1913. **Accreditation:** Regional. **Undergraduate enrollment:** 1,698 women full time; 2 men, 87 women part time. **Faculty:** 147 total (124 full time), 117 with doctorates or other terminal degrees. **Location:** Rural campus in small town; 5 miles from St. Cloud, 75 miles from Minneapolis-St. Paul. **Calendar:** 4-1-4. **Microcomputers:** 250 located in dormitories, libraries, classrooms, computer centers, campus-wide network. **Special facilities:** Fine arts complex, access to all St. John's University facilities. **Additional facts:** Coeducational academic and campus life shared with St. John's University.

DEGREES OFFERED. BA, BS. 412 bachelor's degrees awarded in 1992. 13% in business and management, 15% teacher education, 10% health sciences, 5% languages, 7% letters/literature, 10% multi/interdisciplinary studies, 9% psychology, 12% social sciences, 5% visual and performing arts.

UNDERGRADUATE MAJORS. Accounting, art history, biological and physical sciences, biology, business administration and management, chemistry, classics, communications, computer and information sciences, dramatic arts, early childhood education, economics, elementary education, English, fine arts, food science and nutrition, French, German, history, humanities, liberal/general studies, Math/computer science, mathematics, medical laboratory technologies, medieval studies, music, music performance, nursing, pastoral ministry, philosophy, physics, Physics/computer science, political science and government, predentistry, preengineering, preforestry, prelaw, premedicine, preoccupational therapy, prepharmacy, preveterinary, psychology, religious education, religious music, secondary education, social sciences, social work, sociology, Spanish, theological studies, visual and performing arts.

ACADEMIC PROGRAMS. Double major, dual enrollment of high school students, honors program, independent study, internships, student-designed major, study abroad, teacher preparation, Washington semester, cross-registration, 5 urban study programs through Higher Education Consortium for Urban Affairs (HECUA), January term overseas exchange program through the Upper Midwest Association for International Education (UNAIE), Tri-college with St. John's University and St. Cloud State University; liberal arts/career combination in engineering, health sciences. **Remedial services:** Learning center, reduced course load, special counselor, tutoring, Writing and math skills workshops. **ROTC:** Army. **Placement/credit:** AP, CLEP Subject, institutional tests.

ACADEMIC REQUIREMENTS. Freshmen must earn minimum GPA of 2.0 to continue in good standing. 85% of freshmen return for sophomore year. Students must declare major by end of second year. **Graduation requirements:** 124 hours for bachelor's (40 in major). Most students required to take courses in arts/fine arts, English, foreign languages, history, humanities, mathematics, philosophy/religion, biological/physical sciences, social sciences. **Postgraduate studies:** 5% enter law school, 5% enter medical school, 5% enter MBA programs, 10% enter other graduate study. **Additional information:** Special allied health programs in premedicine, predentistry, prephysical therapy, pre-occupational therapy, prepharmacy, and preveterinary offered. Professional programs in forestry, engineering, divinity, and law. Formalized 3-1-1 engineering program with University of Minnesota, Washington University-St. Louis.

FRESHMAN ADMISSIONS. Selection criteria: Scholastic achievement, GPA, and high school rank most important. Test scores, extracurricular involvement, and essay also important. **High school preparation:** 17 units recommended. Recommended units include English 4, foreign language 2, mathematics 3, social science 2 and science 2. **Test requirements:** SAT or ACT; score report by August 15. PSAT/NMSQT may be submitted in place of SAT or ACT.

1992 FRESHMAN CLASS PROFILE. 796 women applied, 742 accepted, 443 enrolled. 78% had high school GPA of 3.0 or higher, 22% between 2.0 and 2.99. 30% were in top tenth and 58% were in top quarter of graduating class. **Academic background:** Mid 50% of enrolled freshmen had SAT-V between 390-560, SAT-M between 440-580; ACT composite between 20-25. 14% submitted SAT scores, 98% submitted ACT scores. **Characteristics:** 85% from in state, 98% live in college housing, 5% have minority backgrounds, 1% are foreign students. Average age is 18.

FALL-TERM APPLICATIONS. $20 fee, may be waived for applicants with need. No closing date; priority given to applications received by February 15; applicants notified on a rolling basis; must reply by registration. Essay required. Interview recommended for conditionally accepted applicants. Audition recommended for music, theater applicants. Portfolio recommended for art applicants. Deferred and early admission available.

STUDENT LIFE. Housing: Dormitories (women); apartment housing available. **Activities:** Student government, magazine, radio, student newspaper, yearbook, literary journal, international student newspaper, choral groups, concert band, dance, drama, jazz band, music ensembles, musical theater, opera, pep band, symphony orchestra, Forum debate, Volunteers in Services to Others, international students organization, Social Action Coalition, Pax Christi, Amnesty International, Young Republicans, Young Democrats, AIESEC (International Association of Students in Economics and Commerce), Peer Resource Group, Campus Ministry. **Additional information:** Students encouraged to participate in extracurricular activites and provide leardership outside classroom.

ATHLETICS. NCAA. **Intercollegiate:** Basketball, cross-country, diving, golf, soccer, softball, swimming, tennis, track and field, volleyball. **Intramural:** Badminton, basketball, cross-country, lacrosse, racquetball, rifle, rowing (crew), rugby, sailing, skiing, soccer, softball, swimming, table tennis, tennis, volleyball, water polo.

STUDENT SERVICES. Aptitude testing, career counseling, employment service for undergraduates, freshman orientation, health services, personal counseling, placement service for graduates, special adviser for adult students, services/facilities for handicapped.

ANNUAL EXPENSES. Tuition and fees: $11,428. **Room and board:** $4,040. **Books and supplies:** $500. **Other expenses:** $500.

FINANCIAL AID. 85% of freshmen, 85% of continuing students receive some form of aid. 85% of grants, 83% of loans, all jobs based on need. 279 enrolled freshmen were judged to have need, all were offered aid. Academic, music/drama, art, leadership, minority scholarships available. **Aid applications:** No closing date; priority given to applications received by August 16; applicants notified on a rolling basis beginning on or about March 15; must reply within 2 weeks. **Additional information:** Special travel allowance for out-of-state students.

ADDRESS/TELEPHONE. Rick Smith, Vice President for Admission and Enrollment Management, College of St. Benedict, 37 South College Avenue, St. Joseph, MN 56374-2099. (612) 363-5308. (800) 544-1489. Fax: (612) 363-6099.

College of St. Catherine: St. Catherine Campus
St. Paul, Minnesota CB code: 6105

Admissions: 85% of applicants accepted
Based on: ••• School record
•• Activities, recommendations, test scores
• Essay, interview, special talents
Completion: 84% of freshmen end year in good standing
58% graduate, 16% of these enter graduate study

4-year private liberal arts college, women only, affiliated with Roman Catholic Church. Founded in 1905. **Accreditation:** Regional. **Undergraduate enrollment:** 5 men, 1,738 women full time; 12 men, 513 women part time. **Graduate enrollment:** 4 men, 77 women full time; 13 men, 113 women part time. **Faculty:** 176 total (132 full time), 85 with doctorates or other terminal degrees. **Location:** Suburban campus in large city; midway between St. Paul and Minneapolis, approximately 7 miles from each. **Calendar:** Semester, extensive summer session. **Microcomputers:** 63 located in libraries, classrooms, computer centers. **Special facilities:** Art gallery, Abigail Center for Women's Research, observatory, auditorium. **Additional facts:** Men may attend classes through cross-registration.

DEGREES OFFERED. BA, MA. 506 bachelor's degrees awarded in 1992. 14% in business and management, 6% communications, 14% education, 21% health sciences, 5% letters/literature, 5% life sciences, 8% parks/recreation, protective services, public affairs, 5% psychology, 5% social sciences. Graduate degrees offered in 6 major fields of study.

UNDERGRADUATE MAJORS. Accounting, art education, art history, biology, business administration and management, business and management, business education, chemistry, clinical laboratory science, communications, computer and information sciences, dramatic arts, early childhood education, East Asian studies, economics, education, elementary education, English, English education, fashion merchandising, finance, food science and nutrition, foreign languages education, French, German, history, home economics, home economics education, information management, information management, information sciences and systems, international business management, international relations, international studies, junior high education, Latin, mathematics, mathematics education, music, music education, music performance, musical theater, nursing, occupational therapy, philosophy, physical education, physical education/nutrition, physical education/social work, physics, political science and government, predentistry, preengineering, prelaw, premedicine, prepharmacy, preveterinary, psychology, Russian, Russian and Slavic studies, secondary education, social sciences, social work, sociology, Spanish, studio art, textiles and clothing, theological studies, visual and performing arts, women's studies.

ACADEMIC PROGRAMS. Double major, dual enrollment of high school students, honors program, independent study, internships, student-designed major, study abroad, teacher preparation, visiting/exchange student program, weekend college, cross-registration, cooperative program in home economics with Fashion Institute of Technology in New York City and Fashion Institute of Design in Los Angeles, academic year of study in New York City, exchange program with other Carondolet Colleges, internship program includes over 500 sites in Twin Cities area; liberal arts/career combination in health sciences. **Remedial services:** Learning center, reduced course load, special counselor, tutoring. **ROTC:** Air Force. **Placement/credit:** AP, CLEP General and Subject, institutional tests; 32 credit hours maximum for bachelor's degree.

ACADEMIC REQUIREMENTS. Freshmen must earn minimum GPA of 2.0 to continue in good standing. 67% of freshmen return for sophomore year. Students must declare major by end of second year. **Graduation requirements:** 128 hours for bachelor's. Most students required to take courses in arts/fine arts, computer science, English, foreign languages, history, mathematics, philosophy/religion, biological/physical sciences, social sciences. **Postgraduate studies:** 1% enter law school, 1% enter medical school, 2% enter MBA programs, 12% enter other graduate study.

FRESHMAN ADMISSIONS. Selection criteria: School achievement record with rank in top half of class and test scores. Extracurricular and community involvement also considered. Recommendations important. **High school preparation:** 16 units recommended. Recommended units include biological science 1, English 4, foreign language 2, mathematics 3, physical science 1 and social science 2. **Test requirements:** SAT or ACT; score report by August 15.

1992 FRESHMAN CLASS PROFILE. 507 women applied, 432 accepted, 212 enrolled. 69% had high school GPA of 3.0 or higher, 30% between 2.0 and 2.99. 24% were in top tenth and 52% were in top quarter of graduating class. **Academic background:** Mid 50% of enrolled freshmen had SAT-V between 390-560, SAT-M between 390-560; ACT composite between 19-25. 20% submitted SAT scores, 93% submitted ACT scores. **Characteristics:** 75% from in state, 84% live in college housing, 13% have minority backgrounds, 5% are foreign students. Average age is 18.

FALL-TERM APPLICATIONS. $20 fee, may be waived for applicants with need. No closing date; priority given to applications received by August 15; applicants notified on a rolling basis; must reply by May 1 or within 2 weeks if notified thereafter. Audition recommended. Portfolio recommended. Essay recommended for marginal applicants. Interview recommended for all applicants, required for marginal students. CRDA. Deferred and early admission available. Students must be accepted by Feb. 1 to be eligible to compete in merit scholarship competition based on high school achievement.

STUDENT LIFE. Housing: Dormitories (women); apartment housing available. **Activities:** Student government, magazine, radio, student newspaper, yearbook, choral groups, concert band, dance, drama, jazz band, music ensembles, musical theater, opera, symphony orchestra, Volunteers in Action, Campus Ministry, Young Republicans, Young Democrats, Angel Flight service group, League of Women Voters, Minnesota Public Interest Research Group, clubs for majors, women's issues. **Additional information:** Cooperative social activities offered through Associated Colleges of Twin Cities consortium.

ATHLETICS. NCAA. **Intercollegiate:** Basketball, cross-country, softball, swimming, tennis, track and field, volleyball. **Intramural:** Basketball, golf, soccer, softball, tennis, volleyball.

STUDENT SERVICES. Aptitude testing, career counseling, employment service for undergraduates, freshman orientation, health services, on-campus day care, personal counseling, placement service for graduates, special adviser for adult students, services/facilities for handicapped.

ANNUAL EXPENSES. Tuition and fees: $11,530. **Room and board:** $4,210. **Books and supplies:** $450. **Other expenses:** $800.

FINANCIAL AID. 90% of freshmen, 74% of continuing students receive some form of aid. 92% of grants, 74% of loans, 66% of jobs based on need. 184 enrolled freshmen were judged to have need, all were offered aid. Academic, music/drama, leadership scholarships available. **Aid applications:** No closing date; priority given to applications received by April 1; applicants notified on a rolling basis beginning on or about March 15; must reply by May 1 or within 2 weeks if notified thereafter. **Additional information:** Interview required for academic merit, audition required for music scholarships.

ADDRESS/TELEPHONE. Colleen Hegranes, Vice President of Enrollment Management/Dean of Students, College of St. Catherine: St. Catherine Campus, 2004 Randolph Avenue, St. Paul, MN 55105. (612) 690-6505. Fax: (612) 690-6024.

College of St. Scholastica
Duluth, Minnesota CB code: 6107

Admissions: 85% of applicants accepted
Based on: ••• School record, test scores
•• Activities, essay, interview, recommendations
• Special talents
Completion: 85% of freshmen end year in good standing
58% graduate, 10% of these enter graduate study

4-year private liberal arts college, coed, affiliated with Roman Catholic Church. Founded in 1912. **Accreditation:** Regional. **Undergraduate enrollment:** 404 men, 1,050 women full time; 76 men, 230 women part time. **Graduate enrollment:** 11 men, 35 women full time; 79 men, 103 women part time. **Faculty:** 162 total (122 full time), 83 with doctorates or other terminal degrees. **Location:** Suburban campus in small city; 2 miles from downtown. **Calendar:** Quarter, limited summer session. Extensive evening/early morning classes. **Microcomputers:** 300 located in libraries, classrooms, computer centers.

DEGREES OFFERED. BA, MA, MEd. 326 bachelor's degrees awarded in 1992. 14% in business and management, 5% communications, 12% education, 38% health sciences, 5% mathematics, 8% social sciences. Graduate degrees offered in 6 major fields of study.

UNDERGRADUATE MAJORS. Accounting, American Indian studies, biological and physical sciences, biology, business administration and management, business and management, chemistry, clinical laboratory science, communications, computer and information sciences, early childhood education, elementary education, English, English education, exercise physiology, family/consumer resource management, fashion management, food management, food science and nutrition, health care administration, health information administration, health sciences, history, home economics, home economics education, human resources development, humanities, individual and family development, information sciences and systems, institutional/home management/supporting programs, international business management, liberal/general studies, marketing management, mathematics, mathematics education, medical records administration, music, music business management, music education, music history and appreciation, music performance, nursing, pastoral ministry, physical therapy, prelaw, psychology, radio/television technology, religion, religious education, science education, secondary education, social science education, social sciences, social studies education, social work, sociology, sports management, textiles and clothing, youth ministry.

ACADEMIC PROGRAMS. Accelerated program, double major, dual enrollment of high school students, independent study, internships, student-designed major, study abroad, teacher preparation, cross-registration; liberal arts/career combination in engineering. **Remedial services:** Learning center, reduced course load, remedial instruction, special counselor, tutoring. **ROTC:** Air Force, Army. **Placement/credit:** AP, CLEP General and Subject, institutional tests.

ACADEMIC REQUIREMENTS. Freshmen must earn minimum GPA of 2.0 to continue in good standing. 91% of freshmen return for sophomore year. Students must declare major by end of second year. **Graduation requirements:** 192 hours for bachelor's. Most students required to take courses in arts/fine arts, computer science, English, foreign languages, history, humanities, mathematics, philosophy/religion, biological/physical sciences, social sciences. **Postgraduate studies:** 1% enter law school, 2% enter medical school, 2% enter MBA programs, 5% enter other graduate study. **Additional information:** One quarter internship in major-related work recommended.

FRESHMAN ADMISSIONS. Selection criteria: School achievement record and test scores most important. College preparatory courses recommended. Recommended units include biological science 2, English 4, foreign language 3, mathematics 3, physical science 1 and social science 4. **Test requirements:** SAT or ACT (ACT preferred); score report by August 20. PSAT/NMSQT may be submitted in place of SAT or ACT.

1992 FRESHMAN CLASS PROFILE. 190 men applied, 160 accepted, 127 enrolled; 554 women applied, 472 accepted, 332 enrolled. 30% were in top tenth and 63% were in top quarter of graduating class. **Characteristics:** 89% from in state, 50% commute, 2% have minority backgrounds, 1% are foreign students. Average age is 18.

FALL-TERM APPLICATIONS. $15 fee, may be waived for applicants with need. No closing date; priority given to applications received by June 1; applicants notified on a rolling basis; must reply by May 1 or within 4 weeks if notified thereafter. Audition required for music applicants. Interview recommended. Deferred and early admission available.

STUDENT LIFE. Housing: Dormitories (coed); apartment housing available. Quiet or study wing available. **Activities:** Student government, student newspaper, yearbook, choral groups, drama, music ensembles, musical theater, pep band, symphony orchestra, Circle-K, Inter-Varsity Christian Fellowship, international students organization, youth ministry club, liturgical committee.

ATHLETICS. NAIA, NCAA, NSCAA. **Intercollegiate:** Baseball M, basketball, cross-country, golf, ice hockey M, soccer, softball W, tennis, volleyball W. **Intramural:** Badminton, basketball, bowling, golf, racquetball, soccer, softball, tennis, volleyball.

STUDENT SERVICES. Aptitude testing, career counseling, employment service for undergraduates, freshman orientation, health services, on-campus day care, personal counseling, placement service for graduates, special adviser for adult students, veterans counselor, services/facilities for handicapped.

ANNUAL EXPENSES. Tuition and fees (1992-93): $10,659. **Room and board:** $3,498. **Books and supplies:** $450. **Other expenses:** $648.

FINANCIAL AID. 93% of freshmen, 93% of continuing students receive some form of aid. 83% of grants, 89% of loans, 61% of jobs based on need. 273 enrolled freshmen were judged to have need, all were offered aid. Academic, music/drama, leadership, alumni affiliation scholarships available. **Aid applications:** No closing date; priority given to applications received by March 1; applicants notified on a rolling basis beginning on or about February 20.

ADDRESS/TELEPHONE. Becky Urbanski-Junkert, Vice President for Admissions, College of St. Scholastica, 1200 Kenwood Avenue, Duluth, MN 55811-4199. (218) 723-6046. (800) 447-5444. Fax: (218) 723-6394.

Concordia College: Moorhead

Moorhead, Minnesota — CB code: 6113

Admissions: 90% of applicants accepted
Based on:
••• School record
•• Recommendations, test scores
• Activities, interview
Completion: 94% of freshmen end year in good standing
65% graduate, 29% of these enter graduate study

4-year private liberal arts college, coed, affiliated with Evangelical Lutheran Church in America. Founded in 1891. **Accreditation:** Regional. **Undergraduate enrollment:** 1,110 men, 1,728 women full time; 40 men, 64 women part time. **Faculty:** 259 total (186 full time), 117 with doctorates or other terminal degrees. **Location:** Suburban campus in small city; 240 miles northwest of Minneapolis-St. Paul. 1 mile from Fargo, North Dakota. **Calendar:** Semester, limited summer session. **Microcomputers:** 100 located in libraries, classrooms, computer centers. **Special facilities:** Observatory, microparticle accelerator, Concordia Language Villages, Cyrus Running Art Gallery, Institute of German Studies.

DEGREES OFFERED. BA, BS. 654 bachelor's degrees awarded in 1992. 16% in business and management, 9% communications, 7% teacher education, 5% health sciences, 9% languages, 11% letters/literature, 7% life sciences, 6% psychology, 10% social sciences, 5% visual and performing arts.

UNDERGRADUATE MAJORS. Accounting, advertising, art education, art history, biology, business administration and management, business and management, business and office, business economics, business education, chemistry, child development/care/guidance, classics, clinical laboratory science, communications, computer and information sciences, criminal justice studies, dramatic arts, early childhood education, economics, education, elementary education, English, English education, environmental science, fine arts, food science and nutrition, foreign languages education, French, German, health care administration, health education, history, home economics, home economics education, hospital finance, humanities, humanities and social sciences, individual and family development, international business management, international relations, international studies, journalism, junior high education, Latin, long-term health care administration, mathematics, mathematics education, medical laboratory technologies, music, music education, music history and appreciation, music performance, music theory and composition, nursing, nutritional education, philosophy, physical education, physical sciences, physics, political science and government, practical nursing, prearchitecture, predentistry, preengineering, prelaw, premedicine, prepharmacy, preveterinary, psychology, public relations, radio/television broadcasting, religion, religious education, Russian and Slavic studies, Scandinavian languages, Scandinavian studies, science education, secondary education, secretarial and related programs, social science education, social studies education, social work, sociology, Spanish, speech, studio art, technical and business writing, textiles and clothing.

ACADEMIC PROGRAMS. Accelerated program, cooperative education, double major, dual enrollment of high school students, honors program, independent study, internships, study abroad, teacher preparation, visiting/exchange student program, Washington semester, cross-registration, 1-year intensive German studies program resulting in a German major, urban studies program in Chicago, Lutheran Consortium w/Dar es Salaam University in Tanzania. **Remedial services:** Learning center, reduced course load, special counselor, tutoring, reading improvement program. **ROTC:** Air Force, Army. **Placement/credit:** AP, CLEP Subject, IB, institutional tests; 20 credit hours maximum for bachelor's degree.

ACADEMIC REQUIREMENTS. Freshmen must earn minimum GPA of 1.7 to continue in good standing. 80% of freshmen return for sophomore year. Students must declare major by end of second year. **Graduation requirements:** 126 hours for bachelor's (36 in major). Most students required to take courses in arts/fine arts, English, foreign languages, history, humanities, mathematics, philosophy/religion, biological/physical sciences, social sciences. **Postgraduate studies:** 2% enter law school, 3% enter medical school, 1% enter MBA programs, 23% enter other graduate study.

FRESHMAN ADMISSIONS. Selection criteria: School achievement record most important, followed by test scores, school and community activities, and recommendations. **High school preparation:** 14 units recommended. Recommended units include biological science 1, English 4, foreign language 2, mathematics 3, physical science 2 and social science 2. English, mathematics, science, foreign language, computer science, and exposure to fine arts recommended. **Test requirements:** SAT or ACT. PSAT/NMSQT may be submitted in place of SAT or ACT.

1992 FRESHMAN CLASS PROFILE. 675 men applied, 587 accepted, 278 enrolled; 1,149 women applied, 1,056 accepted, 468 enrolled. 30% were in top tenth and 57% were in top quarter of graduating class. **Academic background:** Mid 50% of enrolled freshmen had SAT-V between 430-570, SAT-M between 490-640; ACT composite between 21-27. 16% submitted SAT scores, 92% submitted ACT scores. **Characteristics:** 61% from in state, 95% live in college housing, 4% have minority backgrounds, 6% are foreign students. Average age is 18.

FALL-TERM APPLICATIONS. $20 fee, may be waived for applicants

with need. No closing date; applicants notified on a rolling basis. Interview recommended. CRDA. Deferred and early admission available.

STUDENT LIFE. Housing: Dormitories (men, women); apartment housing available. Students studying Spanish, French or German have opportunity to live with native of language in campus apartments. **Activities:** Student government, radio, student newspaper, television, yearbook, literary magazine, choral groups, concert band, dance, drama, jazz band, music ensembles, musical theater, pep band, symphony orchestra, clown ministry, Christian Mission Fellowship, Outreach teams, Fellowship of Christian Athletes, College Democrats, College Republicans, Chemical Awareness and Responsibility Committee (CARE), International Students Organization, Sons of Norway, Big Brother and Sister Program, Women's Center.

ATHLETICS. NCAA. **Intercollegiate:** Baseball M, basketball, cross-country, football M, golf, ice hockey M, soccer, softball W, tennis, track and field, volleyball W, wrestling M. **Intramural:** Badminton, basketball, bowling, cross-country, fencing, golf, ice hockey M, racquetball, rugby M, skiing, skin diving, soccer, softball, swimming, table tennis, tennis, track and field, volleyball, water polo.

STUDENT SERVICES. Aptitude testing, career counseling, employment service for undergraduates, freshman orientation, health services, on-campus day care, personal counseling, placement service for graduates, special adviser for adult students, services/facilities for handicapped.

ANNUAL EXPENSES. Tuition and fees: $9,700. **Room and board:** $3,050. **Books and supplies:** $450. **Other expenses:** $600.

FINANCIAL AID. 85% of freshmen, 86% of continuing students receive some form of aid. 94% of grants, all loans based on need. Academic, music/drama, leadership, religious affiliation, minority scholarships available. **Aid applications:** No closing date; applicants notified on a rolling basis; must reply by registration. **Additional information:** Foreign students from Hong Kong, Norway, and Canada eligible to receive special scholarships. Students in the ACCORD program (age 25 and older) may apply for tuition reductions.

ADDRESS/TELEPHONE. James Hausmann, Vice President for Admissions and Financial Aid, Concordia College: Moorhead, 901 South Eighth Street, Moorhead, MN 56562-9981. (218) 299-3004. Fax: (218) 299-3947.

Concordia College: St. Paul

St. Paul, Minnesota 55104-5494 — CB code: 6114

Admissions: 71% of applicants accepted
Based on: ••• Recommendations, religious affiliation/commitment, school record, test scores
•• Activities, interview
Completion: 72% of freshmen end year in good standing
38% graduate, 16% of these enter graduate study

4-year private liberal arts, teachers college, coed, affiliated with Lutheran Church—Missouri Synod. Founded in 1893. **Accreditation:** Regional. **Undergraduate enrollment:** 491 men, 631 women full time; 43 men, 93 women part time. **Graduate enrollment:** 2 men, 5 women part time. **Faculty:** 122 total (63 full time), 71 with doctorates or other terminal degrees. **Location:** Urban campus in large city; midway between Minneapolis and Saint Paul. **Calendar:** Quarter, limited summer session. **Microcomputers:** 33 located in libraries, classrooms, computer centers.

DEGREES OFFERED. AA, BA, MA. 4 associate degrees awarded in 1992. 100% in multi/interdisciplinary studies. 302 bachelor's degrees awarded. 57% in business and management, 21% teacher education, 8% psychology, 6% social sciences. Graduate degrees offered in 1 major field of study.

UNDERGRADUATE MAJORS. Associate: Liberal/general studies, protective services, religion, science technologies, teacher aide. **Bachelor's:** Accounting, art education, biblical languages, biological and physical sciences, biology, business administration and management, business and management, business economics, communications, early childhood education, economics, education, elementary education, English, English education, environmental science, finance, foreign languages (multiple emphasis), health education, history, humanities and social sciences, junior high education, liberal/general studies, mathematics, mathematics education, missionary studies, music, music education, organizational behavior, physical education, physical sciences, political science and government, psychology, religion, religious education, religious music, science education, secondary education, social science education, social sciences, social work, speech/communication/theater education, theological studies, visual and performing arts.

ACADEMIC PROGRAMS. 2-year transfer program, accelerated program, double major, dual enrollment of high school students, independent study, internships, student-designed major, study abroad, teacher preparation, cross-registration. **Remedial services:** Learning center, reduced course load, remedial instruction, special counselor, tutoring. **ROTC:** Air Force, Army, Naval. **Placement/credit:** AP, CLEP General and Subject, institutional tests.

ACADEMIC REQUIREMENTS. Freshmen must earn minimum GPA of 2.0 to continue in good standing. 65% of freshmen return for sophomore year. Students must declare major by end of second year. **Graduation requirements:** 96 hours for associate, 192 hours for bachelor's (54 in major). Most students required to take courses in arts/fine arts, English, history, humanities, mathematics, philosophy/religion, biological/physical sciences, social sciences. **Postgraduate studies:** 50% from 2-year programs enter 4-year programs. 1% enter law school, 1% enter medical school, 2% enter MBA programs, 12% enter other graduate study. **Additional information:** Credit bearing night courses available.

FRESHMAN ADMISSIONS. Selection criteria: School record, test scores, recommendations important. Recommended units include English 4, mathematics 2, social science 2 and science 2. One unit of fine arts also recommended. **Test requirements:** SAT or ACT (ACT preferred); score report by September 1.

1992 FRESHMAN CLASS PROFILE. 157 men applied, 109 accepted, 60 enrolled; 261 women applied, 186 accepted, 90 enrolled. 51% had high school GPA of 3.0 or higher, 43% between 2.0 and 2.99. 15% were in top tenth and 35% were in top quarter of graduating class. **Academic background:** Mid 50% of enrolled freshmen had ACT composite between 17-23. 99% submitted ACT scores. **Characteristics:** 77% from in state, 71% live in college housing, 21% have minority backgrounds, 1% are foreign students. Average age is 19.

FALL-TERM APPLICATIONS. $15 fee. No closing date; priority given to applications received by August 15; applicants notified on a rolling basis; must reply by May 1 or within 4 weeks if notified thereafter. Interview recommended. CRDA. Deferred and early admission available.

STUDENT LIFE. Housing: Dormitories (men, women, coed); apartment housing available. **Activities:** Student government, student newspaper, yearbook, choral groups, concert band, drama, jazz band, music ensembles, pep band, intercultural support, neighborhood tutors.

ATHLETICS. NAIA. **Intercollegiate:** Baseball M, basketball, cross-country, football M, soccer M, softball W, tennis, volleyball W. **Intramural:** Bowling, ice hockey, skiing, softball, volleyball.

STUDENT SERVICES. Aptitude testing, career counseling, employment service for undergraduates, freshman orientation, health services, on-campus day care, personal counseling, placement service for graduates, services/facilities for handicapped.

ANNUAL EXPENSES. Tuition and fees (1992-93): $9,000. **Room and board:** $3,180. **Books and supplies:** $450. **Other expenses:** $750.

FINANCIAL AID. 90% of freshmen, 70% of continuing students receive some form of aid. Academic, music/drama, leadership scholarships available. **Aid applications:** No closing date; priority given to applications received by May 1; applicants notified on a rolling basis beginning on or about March 1; must reply by May 1 or within 3 weeks if notified thereafter. **Additional information:** Church districts and local congregations major sources of aid for church-vocation students.

ADDRESS/TELEPHONE. Tim Utter, Director of Admissions, Concordia College: St. Paul, 275 North Syndicate Street, St. Paul, MN 55104-5494. (612) 641-8231. (800) 333-4705. Fax: (612) 659-0207.

Crown College

St. Bonifacius, Minnesota — CB code: 6639

Admissions: 78% of applicants accepted
Based on: ••• Recommendations, religious affiliation/commitment, school record
•• Essay, test scores
• Interview, special talents
Completion: 83% of freshmen end year in good standing
36% graduate, 12% of these enter graduate study

4-year private Bible college, coed, affiliated with Christian and Missionary Alliance. Founded in 1916. **Accreditation:** Regional. **Undergraduate enrollment:** 173 men, 210 women full time; 11 men, 101 women part time. **Faculty:** 54 total (24 full time), 14 with doctorates or other terminal degrees. **Location:** Suburban campus in large city; 10 miles from Minneapolis suburbs. **Calendar:** Semester, limited summer session. Saturday classes. **Microcomputers:** 28 located in libraries, computer centers.

DEGREES OFFERED. AA, BA, BS. 10 associate degrees awarded in 1992. 10% in business and management, 10% business/office and marketing/distribution, 13% teacher education, 17% philosophy, religion, theology, 10% physical sciences, 40% psychology. 80 bachelor's degrees awarded. 10% in business and management, 34% teacher education, 37% philosophy, religion, theology, 5% psychology, 7% social sciences, 6% visual and performing arts.

UNDERGRADUATE MAJORS. Associate: Anthropology, Bible studies, biological and physical sciences, biology, business administration and management, counseling psychology, early childhood education, English, history, humanities, liberal/general studies, literature, music, office supervision and management, psychology, sociology. **Bachelor's:** Business administration and management, elementary education, English, English education, history, history/pre-counseling, history/pre-seminary, human resources development, individual and family development, management science, missionary nursing, missionary studies, music, music education, music performance, physical education, psychology, religious education, religious music, secondary education, social science education, theological studies.

ACADEMIC PROGRAMS. 2-year transfer program, double major, dual enrollment of high school students, honors program, independent study, internships, teacher preparation, 2+2 cooperative program with nonaccredited Bible colleges(2 years at approved cooperative institution accepted for first 2 years at Crown College. **Remedial services:** Learning center, reduced course load, remedial instruction, tutoring. **Placement/credit:** AP, CLEP Subject, institutional tests; 36 credit hours maximum for associate degree; 90 credit hours maximum for bachelor's degree.

ACADEMIC REQUIREMENTS. Freshmen must earn minimum GPA of 1.5 to continue in good standing. 60% of freshmen return for sophomore year. Students must declare major by end of second year. **Graduation requirements:** 66 hours for associate (18 in major), 125 hours for bachelor's (30 in major). Most students required to take courses in computer science, English, history, mathematics, philosophy/religion, biological/physical sciences, social sciences.

FRESHMAN ADMISSIONS. Selection criteria: Applicants must profess personal faith in Jesus Christ. Pastor's recommendation very important, academic records considered. Recommended units include English 3, foreign language 3, mathematics 3, social science 3 and science 4. **Test requirements:** SAT or ACT (ACT preferred); score report by August 15.

1992 FRESHMAN CLASS PROFILE. 100 men applied, 70 accepted, 25 enrolled; 123 women applied, 105 accepted, 43 enrolled. **Academic background:** Mid 50% of enrolled freshmen had ACT composite between 17-23. 94% submitted ACT scores. **Characteristics:** 55% from in state, 2% are foreign students. Average age is 19.

FALL-TERM APPLICATIONS. $35 fee. No closing date; applicants notified on a rolling basis; must reply immediately. Essay required. Interview recommended. Deferred and early admission available.

STUDENT LIFE. Housing: Dormitories (men, women); apartment, handicapped housing available. **Activities:** Student government, student newspaper, yearbook, choral groups, concert band, drama, music ensembles, pep band, student ministry groups, mission support groups, student missionary society, student senate, residence hall council, ethnic clubs.

ATHLETICS. Intercollegiate: Baseball M, basketball, football M, softball W, volleyball W. **Intramural:** Basketball, table tennis, volleyball.

STUDENT SERVICES. Aptitude testing, career counseling, employment service for undergraduates, freshman orientation, health services, personal counseling, placement service for graduates, student ministry opportunities, services/facilities for handicapped.

ANNUAL EXPENSES. Tuition and fees: $7,640. **Room and board:** $3,590. **Books and supplies:** $500. **Other expenses:** $700.

FINANCIAL AID. 96% of freshmen, 93% of continuing students receive some form of aid. 76% of grants, 86% of loans, all jobs based on need. 69 enrolled freshmen were judged to have need, all were offered aid. Academic, music/drama, state/district residency, leadership, religious affiliation scholarships available. **Aid applications:** No closing date; priority given to applications received by April 1; applicants notified on a rolling basis beginning on or about April 1; must reply within 2 weeks.

ADDRESS/TELEPHONE. James Rightler, Vice President/Enrollment Services, Crown College, 6425 County Road 30, St. Bonifacius, MN 55375-9001. (612) 446-4100. (800) 682-7696. Fax: (612) 446-4149.

Dr. Martin Luther College
New Ulm, Minnesota CB code: 6435

4-year private teachers college, coed, affiliated with Wisconsin Evangelical Lutheran Synod. Founded in 1884. **Accreditation:** Regional. **Undergraduate enrollment:** 194 men, 369 women full time; 3 men, 2 women part time. **Faculty:** 63 total (60 full time), 10 with doctorates or other terminal degrees. **Location:** Rural campus in large town; 90 miles from Minneapolis-St. Paul. **Calendar:** Semester, limited summer session. **Microcomputers:** 46 located in dormitories, libraries, classrooms. **Special facilities:** Music programs and facilities (voice, choral, organ, piano). **Additional facts:** Prepares students to enter teaching ministry in elementary and secondary school system of Wisconsin Evangelical Lutheran Synod.

DEGREES OFFERED. BS. 75 bachelor's degrees awarded in 1992. 100% in teacher education.

UNDERGRADUATE MAJORS. Elementary education, secondary education.

ACADEMIC PROGRAMS. Double major, independent study, teacher preparation. **Remedial services:** Learning center, reduced course load, remedial instruction, special counselor, tutoring. **Placement/credit:** AP.

ACADEMIC REQUIREMENTS. Freshmen must earn minimum GPA of 1.7 to continue in good standing. 76% of freshmen return for sophomore year. Students must declare major on application. **Graduation requirements:** 138 hours for bachelor's (42 in major). Most students required to take courses in arts/fine arts, English, history, mathematics, philosophy/religion, biological/physical sciences, social sciences.

FRESHMAN ADMISSIONS. Selection criteria: Primarily pastor's letter of recommendation, high school transcript, and test scores required. Rating provided by student's high school considered. **High school preparation:** 12 units required. Required units include biological science 1, English 4, mathematics 2, physical science 1 and social science 2. 2 additional academic units in English, mathematics, science, or social studies also required. **Test requirements:** ACT; score report by August 21.

1992 FRESHMAN CLASS PROFILE. 52 men, 115 women enrolled. 59% had high school GPA of 3.0 or higher, 39% between 2.0 and 2.99. **Academic background:** Mid 50% of enrolled freshmen had ACT composite between 20-25. 99% submitted ACT scores. **Characteristics:** 7% from in state, 99% live in college housing, 1% have minority backgrounds, 1% are foreign students. Average age is 19.

FALL-TERM APPLICATIONS. $25 fee. Closing date July 20; applicants notified on a rolling basis. Deferred admission available.

STUDENT LIFE. Housing: Dormitories (men, women). **Activities:** Student government, student newspaper, yearbook, choral groups, concert band, drama, jazz band, marching band, music ensembles, musical theater, pep band. **Additional information:** Students, faculty, and staff recognize and appreciate a oneness in faith and life as a Christian campus family.

ATHLETICS. NAIA, NSCAA. **Intercollegiate:** Baseball M, basketball, cross-country, football M, golf M, softball W, tennis, track and field W, volleyball W. **Intramural:** Badminton, basketball, softball W, tennis, volleyball.

STUDENT SERVICES. Employment service for undergraduates, freshman orientation, health services, personal counseling.

ANNUAL EXPENSES. Tuition and fees: $3,600. **Room and board:** $1,790. **Books and supplies:** $555. **Other expenses:** $650.

FINANCIAL AID. 96% of freshmen, 95% of continuing students receive some form of aid. 97% of grants, 77% of loans, all jobs based on need. 85 enrolled freshmen were judged to have need, all were offered aid. Academic, music/drama, state/district residency, leadership scholarships available. **Aid applications:** No closing date; priority given to applications received by May 15; applicants notified on a rolling basis beginning on or about June 15; must reply by August 15 or within 2 weeks if notified thereafter.

ADDRESS/TELEPHONE. Rev. Lloyd O. Huebner, President and Chief Admissions Officer, Dr. Martin Luther College, 1884 College Heights, New Ulm, MN 56073-3300. (507) 354-8221. Fax: (507) 354-8225.

Fergus Falls Community College
Fergus Falls, Minnesota CB code: 2110

2-year public community college, coed. Founded in 1960. **Accreditation:** Regional. **Undergraduate enrollment:** 325 men, 396 women full time; 210 men, 414 women part time. **Faculty:** 73 total (31 full time), 2 with doctorates or other terminal degrees. **Location:** Rural campus in large town; 180 miles from Minneapolis-St. Paul, 60 miles from Moorhead and Fargo, North Dakota. **Calendar:** Quarter, limited summer session. **Microcomputers:** Located in libraries, classrooms, computer centers. **Special facilities:** 2,500 audiovisual titles.

DEGREES OFFERED. AA, AS, AAS. 170 associate degrees awarded in 1992.

UNDERGRADUATE MAJORS. Accounting, business and management, business and office, clinical laboratory science, legal secretary, liberal/general studies, medical laboratory technologies, medical secretary, nursing, office supervision and management, practical nursing, secretarial and related programs, small business management and ownership.

ACADEMIC PROGRAMS. 2-year transfer program, dual enrollment of high school students, internships, weekend college. **Remedial services:** Learning center, remedial instruction, special counselor, tutoring. **Placement/credit:** Institutional tests.

ACADEMIC REQUIREMENTS. Freshmen must earn minimum GPA of 2.00 to continue in good standing. Students must declare major by end of first year. **Graduation requirements:** 96 hours for associate. Most students required to take courses in English, humanities, biological/physical sciences, social sciences.

FRESHMAN ADMISSIONS. Selection criteria: Open admissions. Rank in top 2/3 of class, minimum ACT composite score of 19 for all-non-Minnesota residents, except for residents of Wisconsin, Iowa, South Dakota, and Ontario, Canada. These requirements do not apply to international students. Inquire for more information.

1992 FRESHMAN CLASS PROFILE. 315 men, 406 women enrolled. 25% had high school GPA of 3.0 or higher, 38% between 2.0 and 2.99. **Characteristics:** 97% from in state, 87% commute, 2% have minority backgrounds, 2% are foreign students. Average age is 20.

FALL-TERM APPLICATIONS. $15 fee. No closing date; applicants notified on a rolling basis. Early admission available.

STUDENT LIFE. Housing: Privately owned dormitory within walking distance of the college. **Activities:** Student government, radio, student newspaper, video for vcr, choral groups, concert band, drama, jazz band, music ensembles, musical theater.

ATHLETICS. NJCAA. **Intercollegiate:** Baseball M, basketball, football M, softball W, volleyball W, wrestling M. **Intramural:** Archery, basketball, bowling, football, golf, skiing, softball, table tennis, tennis, volleyball.

STUDENT SERVICES. Career counseling, employment service for

undergraduates, freshman orientation, personal counseling, placement service for graduates, special adviser for adult students, veterans counselor, services/facilities for handicapped.

ANNUAL EXPENSES. Tuition and fees (1992-93): $1,850, $1,750 additional for out-of-state students. **Books and supplies:** $550. **Other expenses:** $622.

FINANCIAL AID. 89% of freshmen, 86% of continuing students receive some form of aid. Grants, loans, jobs available. Academic, music/drama, art, athletic, state/district residency scholarships available. **Aid applications:** No closing date; priority given to applications received by June 1; applicants notified on a rolling basis; must reply within 2 weeks.

ADDRESS/TELEPHONE. Harold Leland, Director of Admissions, Fergus Falls Community College, 1414 College Way, Fergus Falls, MN 56537-1000. (218) 739-7500. Fax: (218) 739-7475.

Gustavus Adolphus College
St. Peter, Minnesota CB code: 6253

Admissions: 79% of applicants accepted
Based on: ••• Essay, interview, school record, test scores
•• Activities, recommendations, religious affiliation/commitment
• Special talents
Completion: 96% of freshmen end year in good standing
79% graduate, 35% of these enter graduate study

4-year private liberal arts college, coed, affiliated with Evangelical Lutheran Church in America. Founded in 1862. **Accreditation:** Regional. **Undergraduate enrollment:** 1,011 men, 1,209 women full time; 24 men, 27 women part time. **Faculty:** 223 total (166 full time), 126 with doctorates or other terminal degrees. **Location:** Suburban campus in small town; 65 miles from Minneapolis-St. Paul. **Calendar:** 4-1-4, limited summer session. **Microcomputers:** 200 located in libraries, classrooms, computer centers. **Special facilities:** Linnaeus Arboretum.

DEGREES OFFERED. BA. 533 bachelor's degrees awarded in 1992. 16% in business and management, 5% communications, 7% teacher education, 6% health sciences, 5% languages, 10% letters/literature, 7% life sciences, 5% physical sciences, 9% psychology, 18% social sciences, 5% visual and performing arts.

UNDERGRADUATE MAJORS. Accounting, anthropology, art education, art history, biochemistry, biological and physical sciences, biology, botany, business administration and management, business and management, business education, chemistry, classics, communications, computer and information sciences, criminal justice studies, dramatic arts, earth sciences, economics, elementary education, English, English education, English literature, foreign languages education, French, geography, geology, German, Greek (classical), health education, history, humanities and social sciences, international business management, Japanese, junior high education, Latin, mathematics, mathematics education, music, music education, music history and appreciation, nursing, philosophy, physical education, physics, political science and government, psychology, pure mathematics, religion, religious music, Russian, Russian and Slavic studies, Scandinavian languages, Scandinavian studies, science education, secondary education, secretarial and related programs, social sciences, social studies education, sociology, Spanish, speech, speech/communication/theater education, visual and performing arts, zoology.

ACADEMIC PROGRAMS. Cooperative education, double major, dual enrollment of high school students, honors program, independent study, internships, student-designed major, study abroad, teacher preparation, visiting/exchange student program, Washington semester, cross-registration; liberal arts/career combination in engineering. **Remedial services:** Tutoring. **ROTC:** Army. **Placement/credit:** AP, institutional tests.

ACADEMIC REQUIREMENTS. Freshmen must earn minimum GPA of 2.0 to continue in good standing. 91% of freshmen return for sophomore year. Students must declare major by end of second year. **Graduation requirements:** 140 hours for bachelor's (28 in major). Most students required to take courses in arts/fine arts, English, foreign languages, history, humanities, mathematics, philosophy/religion, biological/physical sciences, social sciences. **Postgraduate studies:** 5% enter law school, 3% enter medical school, 5% enter MBA programs, 22% enter other graduate study.

FRESHMAN ADMISSIONS. Selection criteria: School achievement record, test scores, recommendations, interview, essay or personal statement, school and community activities most important. Special consideration given to children of alumni and minority applicants. **High school preparation:** 13 units required. Required units include biological science 1, English 3, foreign language 2, mathematics 3, physical science 1 and social science 3. **Test requirements:** SAT or ACT; score report by April 1.

1992 FRESHMAN CLASS PROFILE. 707 men applied, 580 accepted, 289 enrolled; 994 women applied, 764 accepted, 330 enrolled. 96% had high school GPA of 3.0 or higher, 4% between 2.0 and 2.99. 36% were in top tenth and 75% were in top quarter of graduating class. **Academic background:** Mid 50% of enrolled freshmen had SAT-V between 460-580, SAT-M between 520-660; ACT composite between 22-28. 31% submitted SAT scores, 95% submitted ACT scores. **Characteristics:** 74% from in state, 99% live in college housing, 5% have minority backgrounds, 3% are foreign students. Average age is 18.

FALL-TERM APPLICATIONS. $20 fee, may be waived for applicants with need. Closing date April 15; priority given to applications received by March 15; applicants notified on a rolling basis beginning on or about January 10; must reply by May 1. Essay required. Interview recommended. CRDA. Deferred and early admission available. EDP-F.

STUDENT LIFE. Housing: Dormitories (coed); apartment housing available. **Activities:** Student government, magazine, radio, student newspaper, television, yearbook, literary magazine, choral groups, concert band, dance, drama, jazz band, music ensembles, musical theater, pep band, symphony orchestra, Fellowship of Christian Athletes, Gustavus Youth Outreach, black student organization, Greens (environmental group).

ATHLETICS. NCAA. **Intercollegiate:** Baseball M, basketball, cross-country, diving, football M, golf, gymnastics W, ice hockey M, soccer, softball W, swimming, tennis, track and field, volleyball W. **Intramural:** Badminton, basketball, bowling, golf, handball, ice hockey M, lacrosse M, racquetball, rugby, skiing, soccer, softball, swimming, table tennis, tennis, volleyball.

STUDENT SERVICES. Aptitude testing, career counseling, employment service for undergraduates, freshman orientation, health services, personal counseling, placement service for graduates, black student counselor.

ANNUAL EXPENSES. Tuition and fees: $13,400. **Room and board:** $3,500. **Books and supplies:** $400. **Other expenses:** $750.

FINANCIAL AID. 82% of freshmen, 77% of continuing students receive some form of aid. 96% of grants, 82% of loans, 94% of jobs based on need. 457 enrolled freshmen were judged to have need, all were offered aid. Academic, leadership scholarships available. **Aid applications:** Closing date May 1; priority given to applications received by March 1; applicants notified on a rolling basis beginning on or about March 1; must reply by May 1 or within 2 weeks if notified thereafter.

ADDRESS/TELEPHONE. Mark H. Anderson, Director of Admissions, Gustavus Adolphus College, 800 West College Avenue, St. Peter, MN 56082-1498. (507) 933-7676. (800) 487-8288. Fax: (507) 933-7041.

Hamline University
St. Paul, Minnesota CB code: 6265

Admissions: 83% of applicants accepted
Based on: ••• School record
•• Test scores
• Activities, essay, interview, recommendations, religious affiliation/commitment, special talents
Completion: 94% of freshmen end year in good standing
68% graduate, 25% of these enter graduate study

4-year private university, coed, affiliated with United Methodist Church. Founded in 1854. **Accreditation:** Regional. **Undergraduate enrollment:** 585 men, 761 women full time; 22 men, 64 women part time. **Graduate enrollment:** 357 men, 323 women full time; 113 men, 240 women part time. **Faculty:** 230 total (121 full time), 114 with doctorates or other terminal degrees. **Location:** Urban campus in large city; 5 miles from downtowns of Minneapolis and St. Paul. **Calendar:** 4-1-4, extensive summer session. **Microcomputers:** 100 located in dormitories, libraries, classrooms, computer centers. **Special facilities:** Sundin Music Hall, new natural science facility.

DEGREES OFFERED. BA, MA, JD. 348 bachelor's degrees awarded in 1992. 15% in business and management, 6% languages, 8% letters/literature, 5% physical sciences, 15% psychology, 30% social sciences. Graduate degrees offered in 2 major fields of study.

UNDERGRADUATE MAJORS. American studies, anthropology, art education, art history, biology, business administration and management, chemistry, communications, dramatic arts, East Asian studies, economics, elementary education, English, environmental science, French, German, history, international and comparative education, international business management, international relations, Latin American studies, legal assistant/paralegal, mathematics, music, music education, philosophy, physical education, physics, political science and government, preengineering, prelaw, psychology, religion, Russian and Slavic studies, science education, secondary education, sociology, Spanish, studio art, urban studies, women's studies.

ACADEMIC PROGRAMS. Double major, honors program, independent study, internships, semester at sea, student-designed major, study abroad, teacher preparation, visiting/exchange student program, New York semester, United Nations semester, Washington semester, cross-registration; liberal arts/career combination in engineering; combined bachelor's/graduate program in law. **Remedial services:** Special counselor, tutoring. **ROTC:** Air Force. **Placement/credit:** AP, CLEP General and Subject, IB, institutional tests; 30 credit hours maximum for bachelor's degree.

ACADEMIC REQUIREMENTS. Freshmen must earn minimum GPA of 2.0 to continue in good standing. 82% of freshmen return for sophomore year. Students must declare major by end of second year. **Graduation re-**

quirements: 128 hours for bachelor's. Most students required to take courses in arts/fine arts, computer science, English, history, humanities, mathematics, philosophy/religion, biological/physical sciences, social sciences. **Postgraduate studies:** 6% enter law school, 2% enter medical school, 2% enter MBA programs, 15% enter other graduate study.

FRESHMAN ADMISSIONS. Selection criteria: Class rank, high school GPA and selection of college preparatory courses of primary importance. Test scores, extracurricular activities, recommendations of teacher and guidance counselor are also considered. **High school preparation:** 16 units recommended. Recommended units include English 4, foreign language 2, mathematics 3, social science 4 and science 3. **Test requirements:** SAT or ACT; score report by April 1.

1992 FRESHMAN CLASS PROFILE. 415 men applied, 319 accepted, 122 enrolled; 512 women applied, 452 accepted, 178 enrolled. 36% were in top tenth and 70% were in top quarter of graduating class. **Academic background:** Mid 50% of enrolled freshmen had SAT-V between 470-580, SAT-M between 500-630; ACT composite between 22-28. 21% submitted SAT scores, 89% submitted ACT scores. **Characteristics:** 70% from in state, 90% live in college housing, 14% have minority backgrounds, 3% are foreign students, 8% join fraternities/sororities. Average age is 18.

FALL-TERM APPLICATIONS. $25 fee, may be waived for applicants with need. No closing date; priority given to applications received by March 1; applicants notified on a rolling basis beginning on or about January 15; must reply within 2 weeks. Essay required. Interview recommended for all applicants applicants. Interview recommended, may be requested by admission committee. Deferred admission available. Institutional early decision plan. Foreign students admitted only to fall term.

STUDENT LIFE. Housing: Dormitories (coed); fraternity, sorority housing available. **Activities:** Student government, student newspaper, yearbook, literary magazine, choral groups, concert band, dance, drama, jazz band, music ensembles, musical theater, symphony orchestra, fraternities, sororities, black student group, service organization, student congress, Young Republicans, Young Democratic-Farm-Labor, honor societies, Campus Crusade for Christ, Ham PIRG/MPIRG, International Students Association.

ATHLETICS. NCAA. **Intercollegiate:** Baseball M, basketball, cross-country, diving, football M, golf M, gymnastics W, ice hockey M, soccer, softball W, swimming, tennis, track and field, volleyball W. **Intramural:** Basketball, bowling, racquetball, skiing, softball, swimming W, table tennis, tennis, volleyball, water polo.

STUDENT SERVICES. Aptitude testing, career counseling, employment service for undergraduates, freshman orientation, health services, personal counseling, placement service for graduates, veterans counselor, services/facilities for handicapped.

ANNUAL EXPENSES. Tuition and fees (1992-93): $12,365. **Room and board:** $3,895. **Books and supplies:** $425. **Other expenses:** $675.

FINANCIAL AID. 84% of freshmen, 80% of continuing students receive some form of aid. All jobs based on need. Academic scholarships available. **Aid applications:** No closing date; priority given to applications received by March 15; applicants notified on a rolling basis beginning on or about March 1; must reply within 2 weeks.

ADDRESS/TELEPHONE. Calvin N. Mosley, Vice President for Student Affairs/University Admissions, Hamline University, 1536 Hewitt Avenue, St. Paul, MN 55104-1284. (612) 641-2207. (800) 753-9753. Fax: (612) 641-2458.

Hibbing Community College
Hibbing, Minnesota CB code: 6275

2-year public community college, coed. Founded in 1916. **Accreditation:** Regional. **Undergraduate enrollment:** 247 men, 331 women full time; 250 men, 345 women part time. **Faculty:** 60 total (37 full time), 3 with doctorates or other terminal degrees. **Location:** Rural campus in large town; 75 miles from Duluth. **Calendar:** Quarter, limited summer session. Extensive evening/early morning classes. **Microcomputers:** 100 located in libraries, classrooms, computer centers. **Special facilities:** Planetarium.

DEGREES OFFERED. AA, AS, AAS. 250 associate degrees awarded in 1992. 12% in business and management.

UNDERGRADUATE MAJORS. Accounting, business administration and management, business and management, business and office, business computer/console/peripheral equipment operation, business data entry equipment operation, business data processing and related programs, clinical laboratory science, computer and information sciences, dental hygiene, drafting, drafting and design technology, education, finance, food production/management/services, investments and securities, law enforcement and corrections, legal secretary, liberal/general studies, medical laboratory technologies, medical secretary, nursing, occupational therapy assistant, personal services, physical therapy assistant, radiograph medical technology, respiratory therapy, respiratory therapy technology, retailing, secretarial and related programs, special education.

ACADEMIC PROGRAMS. 2-year transfer program, dual enrollment of high school students, honors program, independent study, telecourses, cross-registration. **Remedial services:** Learning center, reduced course load, remedial instruction, special counselor, tutoring. **Placement/credit:** Institutional tests; 17 credit hours maximum for associate degree.

ACADEMIC REQUIREMENTS. Freshmen must earn minimum GPA of 2.0 to continue in good standing. 60% of freshmen return for sophomore year. Students must declare major by end of first year. **Graduation requirements:** 96 hours for associate (30 in major). Most students required to take courses in English, humanities, mathematics, biological/physical sciences, social sciences.

FRESHMAN ADMISSIONS. Selection criteria: Open admissions. Applicants to nursing and radiologic technology programs may need to meet additional criteria to be admitted to programs. **Test requirements:** SAT or ACT (ACT preferred) for counseling.

1992 FRESHMAN CLASS PROFILE. 511 men and women enrolled. 27% had high school GPA of 3.0 or higher, 48% between 2.0 and 2.99. **Characteristics:** 98% from in state, 100% commute, 6% have minority backgrounds. Average age is 24.

FALL-TERM APPLICATIONS. $15 fee. No closing date; priority given to applications received by April 15; applicants notified on a rolling basis. Deferred and early admission available. Academic placement test required, ACT recommended.

STUDENT LIFE. Activities: Student government, magazine, choral groups, concert band, drama, jazz band, music ensembles, musical theater.

ATHLETICS. NJCAA. **Intercollegiate:** Baseball M, basketball, football M, ice hockey M, softball W, volleyball W. **Intramural:** Archery, badminton, baseball M, bowling, cross-country, golf M, handball, racquetball, skiing, soccer, table tennis, volleyball.

STUDENT SERVICES. Career counseling, employment service for undergraduates, freshman orientation, personal counseling, placement service for graduates, special adviser for adult students, veterans counselor, services/facilities for handicapped.

ANNUAL EXPENSES. Tuition and fees: $1,800, $1,800 additional for out-of-state students. **Books and supplies:** $510.

FINANCIAL AID. 64% of freshmen, 58% of continuing students receive some form of aid. Grants, loans, jobs available. Academic scholarships available. **Aid applications:** No closing date; priority given to applications received by July 1; applicants notified on a rolling basis beginning on or about June 30; must reply within 2 weeks.

ADDRESS/TELEPHONE. Teri McKusky, Director of Student Services, Hibbing Community College, 1515 East 25th Street, Hibbing, MN 55746. (218) 262-6700 ext. 716. Fax: (218) 262-6717.

Inver Hills Community College
Inver Grove Heights, Minnesota CB code: 6300

2-year public community college, coed. Founded in 1967. **Accreditation:** Regional. **Undergraduate enrollment:** 699 men, 1,024 women full time; 1,210 men, 2,384 women part time. **Faculty:** 202 total (89 full time), 20 with doctorates or other terminal degrees. **Location:** Suburban campus in large town; 6 miles from Minneapolis-St. Paul. **Calendar:** Quarter, limited summer session. Saturday and extensive evening/early morning classes. **Microcomputers:** Located in libraries, classrooms, computer centers.

DEGREES OFFERED. AA, AS, AAS. 602 associate degrees awarded in 1992. 8% in business and management, 14% health sciences, 20% law, 37% multi/interdisciplinary studies, 12% parks/recreation, protective services, public affairs, 7% trade and industry.

UNDERGRADUATE MAJORS. Accounting, air traffic control, airline piloting and navigation, automotive mechanics, aviation management, building inspection, business administration and management, business and management, business and office, child development/care/guidance, computer programming, conservation and regulation, engineering, interpreter for the deaf, law enforcement and corrections technologies, legal assistant/paralegal, legal secretary, liberal/general studies, marketing management, medical secretary, mental health/human services, nursing, secretarial and related programs.

ACADEMIC PROGRAMS. 2-year transfer program, accelerated program, cooperative education, dual enrollment of high school students, independent study, internships, student-designed major, telecourses, weekend college. **Remedial services:** Learning center, preadmission summer program, reduced course load, remedial instruction, special counselor, tutoring. **Placement/credit:** AP, CLEP General, institutional tests; 45 credit hours maximum for associate degree.

ACADEMIC REQUIREMENTS. Freshmen must earn minimum GPA of 2.0 to continue in good standing. Students must declare major on enrollment. **Graduation requirements:** 90 hours for associate (50 in major). Most students required to take courses in arts/fine arts, English, humanities, mathematics, biological/physical sciences, social sciences.

FRESHMAN ADMISSIONS. Selection criteria: Open admissions. Selective admissions to nursing program.

1992 FRESHMAN CLASS PROFILE. 637 men, 1,040 women enrolled. **Characteristics:** 99% from in state, 97% commute, 2% have minority backgrounds, 1% are foreign students. Average age is 19.

FALL-TERM APPLICATIONS. $15 fee. No closing date; applicants notified on a rolling basis. Deferred and early admission available.

STUDENT LIFE. Housing: Dormitories (coed). Privately-owned apartments available on campus. **Activities:** Student government, student newspaper, choral groups, concert band, drama, jazz band, music ensembles, musical theater, asian student association.

ATHLETICS. Intramural: Basketball, field hockey, ice hockey, softball, table tennis, tennis, volleyball.

STUDENT SERVICES. Aptitude testing, career counseling, employment service for undergraduates, freshman orientation, health services, on-campus day care, personal counseling, placement service for graduates, services/facilities for handicapped.

ANNUAL EXPENSES. Tuition and fees (1992-93): $1,687, $1,688 additional for out-of-state students. **Books and supplies:** $500. **Other expenses:** $590.

FINANCIAL AID. 30% of freshmen receive some form of aid. 99% of grants, 80% of loans, 70% of jobs based on need. Academic, music/drama, art, athletic scholarships available. **Aid applications:** No closing date; priority given to applications received by June 1; applicants notified on a rolling basis.

ADDRESS/TELEPHONE. Darlene Kalbler, Admissions Officer, Inver Hills Community College, 8445 College Trail, Inver Grove Heights, MN 55076-3209. (612) 450-8500. Fax: (612) 450-8679.

Itasca Community College: Arrowhead Region
Grand Rapids, Minnesota — CB code: 6309

2-year public community college, coed. Founded in 1922. **Accreditation:** Regional. **Undergraduate enrollment:** 347 men, 455 women full time; 78 men, 289 women part time. **Faculty:** 85 total (45 full time), 1 with doctorate or other terminal degree. **Location:** Rural campus in large town; 78 miles from Duluth. **Calendar:** Quarter, limited summer session. **Microcomputers:** 97 located in libraries, classrooms, computer centers. **Additional facts:** Outreach classes held on Leech Lake Indian Reservation.

DEGREES OFFERED. AA, AS, AAS. 183 associate degrees awarded in 1992.

UNDERGRADUATE MAJORS. Accounting, American Indian studies, bilingual/bicultural education, conservation and regulation, data processing, education, education interpeter for the hearing Impaired, education of the deaf and hearing impaired, engineering, engineering and engineering-related technologies, forest products processing technology, forestry and related sciences, forestry production and processing, interpreter for the deaf, legal assistant/paralegal, legal secretary, liberal/general studies, marketing and distribution, marketing management, medical secretary, Ojibwe language, predentistry, premedicine, prepharmacy, preveterinary, renewable natural resources, retailing, secretarial and related programs, social work.

ACADEMIC PROGRAMS. 2-year transfer program, cooperative education, dual enrollment of high school students, honors program, independent study, internships, study abroad, telecourses. **Remedial services:** Learning center, preadmission summer program, remedial instruction, special counselor, tutoring. **Placement/credit:** AP, CLEP General and Subject, institutional tests.

ACADEMIC REQUIREMENTS. Freshmen must earn minimum GPA of 2.0 to continue in good standing. 60% of freshmen return for sophomore year. **Graduation requirements:** 96 hours for associate. Most students required to take courses in arts/fine arts, English, history, humanities, mathematics, biological/physical sciences, social sciences.

FRESHMAN ADMISSIONS. Selection criteria: Open admissions. Practical nursing students required to submit autobiography, 3 references, medical release form and college assessment test results. **High school preparation:** 12 units recommended. Recommended units include biological science 1, English 4, foreign language 2, mathematics 2, physical science 1 and social science 2.

1992 FRESHMAN CLASS PROFILE. 284 men, 320 women enrolled. 24% had high school GPA of 3.0 or higher, 54% between 2.0 and 2.99. **Characteristics:** 97% from in state, 91% commute. Average age is 20.

FALL-TERM APPLICATIONS. $15 fee. Closing date September 10; priority given to applications received by April 15; applicants notified on a rolling basis. Deferred and early admission available. Academic placement test required.

STUDENT LIFE. Housing: Apartment housing available. Privately owned apartments adjacent to campus for both single and married students. **Activities:** Student government, magazine, radio, student newspaper, choral groups, drama, symphony orchestra, Circle-K.

ATHLETICS. NJCAA. **Intercollegiate:** Baseball M, basketball W, football M, ice hockey M, softball W, volleyball W, wrestling M. **Intramural:** Basketball, softball, table tennis, volleyball.

STUDENT SERVICES. Aptitude testing, career counseling, employment service for undergraduates, freshman orientation, on-campus day care, personal counseling, services/facilities for handicapped.

ANNUAL EXPENSES. Tuition and fees (projected): $1,922, $1,920 additional for out-of-state students. **Books and supplies:** $510. **Other expenses:** $1,125.

FINANCIAL AID. 65% of freshmen, 65% of continuing students receive some form of aid. 93% of grants, 87% of loans, 79% of jobs based on need. 320 enrolled freshmen were judged to have need, all were offered aid. Academic, leadership, alumni affiliation scholarships available. **Aid applications:** No closing date; priority given to applications received by May 1; applicants notified on a rolling basis beginning on or about June 15.

ADDRESS/TELEPHONE. Candace Perry, Director of Enrollment Services, Itasca Community College: Arrowhead Region, 1851 Highway 169 East, Grand Rapids, MN 55744. (218) 327-4468.

Lakewood Community College
White Bear Lake, Minnesota — CB code: 6388

2-year public community college, coed. Founded in 1967. **Accreditation:** Regional. **Undergraduate enrollment:** 1,164 men, 1,196 women full time; 1,362 men, 2,692 women part time. **Faculty:** 215 total (97 full time). **Location:** Suburban campus in large town; 9 miles from Minneapolis-St. Paul. **Calendar:** Quarter, limited summer session. Saturday classes. **Microcomputers:** 108 located in libraries, classrooms, computer centers. **Special facilities:** Art gallery, 92-acre nature area, Center For Returning Adult Students. **Additional facts:** Courses are offered at a number of off-campus locations.

DEGREES OFFERED. AA, AS, AAS. 524 associate degrees awarded in 1992. 6% in business and management, 18% allied health, 64% multi/interdisciplinary studies, 11% parks/recreation, protective services, public affairs.

UNDERGRADUATE MAJORS. Accounting, apparel and accessories marketing, biomedical equipment technology, business and management, child development/care/guidance, clothing and textiles management/production/services, data processing, dietetic aide/assistant, fashion merchandising, home furnishings and equipment management/production/services, law enforcement and corrections, liberal/general studies, marketing and distribution, mental health/human services, nursing, orthotics technology, prosthetics technology, radiograph medical technology, secretarial and related programs, social work.

ACADEMIC PROGRAMS. 2-year transfer program, accelerated program, dual enrollment of high school students, honors program, independent study, internships, student-designed major, cross-registration. **Remedial services:** Learning center, reduced course load, remedial instruction, special counselor, tutoring. **Placement/credit:** AP, CLEP General, institutional tests; 45 credit hours maximum for associate degree.

ACADEMIC REQUIREMENTS. Freshmen must earn minimum GPA of 1.70 to continue in good standing. **Graduation requirements:** 90 hours for associate. Most students required to take courses in English, humanities, mathematics, biological/physical sciences, social sciences.

FRESHMAN ADMISSIONS. Selection criteria: Open admissions. Nursing and medical imaging programs have additional application and requirements. International students must submit international application.

1992 FRESHMAN CLASS PROFILE.
916 men enrolled, 1,145 women enrolled. **Characteristics:** 90% from in state, 100% commute, 9% have minority backgrounds, 1% are foreign students.

FALL-TERM APPLICATIONS. $15 fee. No closing date; applicants notified on a rolling basis beginning on or about January 15. Deferred and early admission available.

STUDENT LIFE. Activities: Student government, student newspaper, choral groups, concert band, dance, drama, jazz band, music ensembles, musical theater, symphony orchestra, Hmong Club, Counseling Club, Inter-Varsity Christian Fellowship, Alcoholics Anonymous, Alanon, Association of Children of Alcoholics, Student Support and Referral, Men's Support Group, Overeaters Support Group, Center for Returning Adult Students.

ATHLETICS. NJCAA. **Intramural:** Basketball, bowling, cross-country, golf, ice hockey M, skiing, soccer, softball, swimming, table tennis, tennis, volleyball.

STUDENT SERVICES. Aptitude testing, career counseling, employment service for undergraduates, freshman orientation, health services, on-campus day care, personal counseling, placement service for graduates, services/facilities for handicapped.

ANNUAL EXPENSES. Tuition and fees (1992-93): $1,687, $1,688 additional for out-of-state students. Tuition reciprocity agreement for students from bordering states. **Books and supplies:** $550. **Other expenses:** $750.

FINANCIAL AID. 40% of freshmen, 45% of continuing students receive some form of aid. 97% of grants, 90% of loans, 57% of jobs based on need. 560 enrolled freshmen were judged to have need, all were offered aid. Academic scholarships available. **Aid applications:** No closing date; applicants notified on a rolling basis beginning on or about July 15; must reply within 2 weeks. **Additional information:** Minnesota resident out of high school or not enrolled in college for 7 years without bachelor's or other higher degree offered cost of tuition and books for 1 course in 1 quarter up to maximum of 5 credits.

ADDRESS/TELEPHONE. Willie Nesbit, Registrar, Lakewood Community College, 3401 Century Avenue, White Bear Lake, MN 55110. (612) 779-3300. Fax: (612) 779-3417.

Macalester College

St. Paul, Minnesota CB code: 6390

Admissions: 53% of applicants accepted
Based on: ••• School record
•• Activities, essay, interview, recommendations, special talents, test scores
Completion: 97% of freshmen end year in good standing
70% graduate

4-year private liberal arts college, coed, affiliated with Presbyterian Church (USA). Founded in 1874. **Accreditation:** Regional. **Undergraduate enrollment:** 786 men, 943 women full time; 41 men, 68 women part time. **Faculty:** 187 total (126 full time), 157 with doctorates or other terminal degrees. **Location:** Urban campus in large city; 4 miles from downtown St. Paul, 6 miles from downtown Minneapolis. **Calendar:** 4-1-4. **Microcomputers:** 350 located in dormitories, libraries, computer centers. **Special facilities:** Observatory, planetarium, 250-acre nature preserve, nuclear accelerator, 2 electron microscopes, 500,000 book titles available through Clicnet which includes 8 libraries. **Additional facts:** Strong international program integrates symposia, foreign language study, and foreign student enrollment.

DEGREES OFFERED. BA. 437 bachelor's degrees awarded in 1992. 10% in languages, 12% letters/literature, 6% life sciences, 5% mathematics, 5% philosophy, religion, theology, 40% social sciences, 8% visual and performing arts.

UNDERGRADUATE MAJORS. Anthropology, art history, biology, chemistry, classics, computer and information sciences, creative writing, dramatic arts, East Asian studies, economics, English, environmental science, French, geography, geology, German, Greek (classical), history, humanities, international studies, Japan studies, Latin, Latin American studies, linguistics, mathematics, music, philosophy, physics, political science and government, psychology, religion, Russian, Russian and Slavic studies, science education, social science education, social sciences, sociology, Spanish, speech, teaching English as a second language/foreign language, urban studies, women's studies.

ACADEMIC PROGRAMS. Double major, honors program, independent study, internships, student-designed major, study abroad, teacher preparation, cross-registration; liberal arts/career combination in engineering, health sciences. **Remedial services:** Learning center, remedial instruction, special counselor, tutoring. **ROTC:** Air Force, Naval. **Placement/credit:** AP, IB, institutional tests.

ACADEMIC REQUIREMENTS. Freshmen must earn minimum GPA of 1.7 to continue in good standing. 93% of freshmen return for sophomore year. Students must declare major by end of second year. **Graduation requirements:** 136 hours for bachelor's (28 in major). Most students required to take courses in arts/fine arts, English, humanities, mathematics, biological/physical sciences, social sciences. **Additional information:** Grants from Howard Hughes Medical Institution and Pew Foundation provide undergraduates opportunity to engage in closely supervised, high-level research in natural sciences.

FRESHMAN ADMISSIONS. Selection criteria: Class rank, test scores, potential to succeed important. Social and ethical concerns, leadership potential, extracurricular involvements also important considerations. Special consideration given to African-American, Native American, Latino, and international applicants. Recommended units include English 4, foreign language 3, mathematics 3, social science 3 and science 3. **Test requirements:** SAT or ACT; score report by February 1.

1992 FRESHMAN CLASS PROFILE. 2,741 men and women applied, 1,456 accepted; 217 men enrolled, 259 women enrolled. 48% were in top tenth and 83% were in top quarter of graduating class. **Academic background:** Mid 50% of enrolled freshmen had SAT-V between 560-650, SAT-M between 560-680; ACT composite between 26-30. 82% submitted SAT scores, 39% submitted ACT scores. **Characteristics:** 19% from in state, 96% live in college housing, 17% have minority backgrounds, 8% are foreign students. Average age is 19.

FALL-TERM APPLICATIONS. $30 fee, may be waived for applicants with need. Closing date January 15; applicants notified on or about April 1; must reply by May 1. Essay required. Interview recommended. Audition recommended for music applicants. Portfolio recommended for art applicants. CRDA. Deferred and early admission available. EDP-S. Closing date for applications under first early decision planNovember 15, notification December 15, applicant must reply within 2 weeks. Second single choice early decision plan has January 1 closing date for February 7 notification.

STUDENT LIFE. Housing: Dormitories (coed). 5 language houses, (French, German, Russian, Spanish, Japanese) and Jewish cultural house offer opportunities to live in culturally enhanced environment. Campus housing may not be available to all entering transfer students. **Activities:** Student government, magazine, radio, student newspaper, yearbook, choral groups, concert band, dance, drama, jazz band, music ensembles, musical theater, pep band, symphony orchestra, pipe band and highland dancers, many religious, political, ethnic, and feminist groups, Public Interest Research Group, international clubs.

ATHLETICS. NCAA. **Intercollegiate:** Baseball M, basketball, cross-country, diving, football M, golf, soccer, softball W, swimming, tennis, track and field, volleyball W. **Intramural:** Badminton, basketball, bowling, fencing, football, golf, handball, lacrosse, racquetball, rowing (crew), rugby, skiing, skin diving, soccer, softball, squash, swimming, tennis, volleyball, water polo.

STUDENT SERVICES. Aptitude testing, career counseling, employment service for undergraduates, freshman orientation, health services, personal counseling, placement service for graduates, special adviser for adult students.

ANNUAL EXPENSES. Tuition and fees: $15,107. **Room and board:** $4,502. **Books and supplies:** $500. **Other expenses:** $700.

FINANCIAL AID. 70% of freshmen, 72% of continuing students receive some form of aid. 96% of grants, all loans, 96% of jobs based on need. 299 enrolled freshmen were judged to have need, all were offered aid. Academic, minority scholarships available. **Aid applications:** Closing date March 1; applicants notified on or about March 28; must reply by May 1. **Additional information:** Minnesota Self Loan available to qualified students. State residency not required. EXCEL Loan allows students to borrow amount up to price of college costs. College meets full need for all admitted students.

ADDRESS/TELEPHONE. William M. Shain, Dean of Admissions, Macalester College, 1600 Grand Avenue, St. Paul, MN 55105-1899. (612) 696-6357. (800) 231-7974. Fax: (612) 696-6724.

Mankato State University

Mankato, Minnesota CB code: 6677

4-year public university, coed. Founded in 1867. **Accreditation:** Regional. **Undergraduate enrollment:** 5,224 men, 5,335 women full time; 787 men, 992 women part time. **Graduate enrollment:** 667 men, 920 women full time. **Faculty:** 611 total (586 full time), 334 with doctorates or other terminal degrees. **Location:** Rural campus in large town; 85 miles from Minneapolis-St. Paul. **Calendar:** Quarter, extensive summer session. **Microcomputers:** 400 located in dormitories, libraries, classrooms, computer centers.

DEGREES OFFERED. AA, AS, BA, BS, BFA, MA, MS, MBA, MFA, MEd. 65 associate degrees awarded in 1992. 22% in allied health, 66% multi/interdisciplinary studies, 11% parks/recreation, protective services, public affairs. 1,950 bachelor's degrees awarded. 35% in business and management, 7% computer sciences, 21% teacher education, 8% parks/recreation, protective services, public affairs, 5% social sciences. Graduate degrees offered in 55 major fields of study.

UNDERGRADUATE MAJORS. Associate: Dance, dental hygiene, gerontology, law enforcement and corrections technologies, liberal/general studies, linguistics, secretarial and related programs. **Bachelor's:** Accounting, Afro-American (black) studies, American Indian studies, American studies, anthropology, art education, art history, astronomy, automotive technology, aviation management, biochemistry, biology, biotechnology, business administration and management, business and management, business economics, business education, cell biology, chemistry, city/community/regional planning, clinical laboratory science, clothing and textiles management/production/services, communications, community health work, community services, computer and information sciences, computer programming, creative writing, criminology, data processing, dramatic arts, early childhood education, earth sciences, economics, electrical technology, electrical/electronics/communications engineering, electronic technology, elementary education, engineering and engineering-related technologies, English, English education, environmental science, family/consumer resource management, finance, food science and nutrition, foreign languages education, French, geography, German, health education, health sciences, history, home economics, home economics education, human resources development, individual and family development, industrial arts education, information sciences and systems, insurance and risk management, interior design, international business management, international relations, investments and securities, journalism, junior high education, labor/industrial relations, law enforcement and corrections, legal assistant/paralegal, liberal/general studies, manufacturing technology, marketing and distributive education, marketing management, mathematics, mathematics education, mechanical engineering, microbiology, military science (Army), minority studies, music, music education, music history and appreciation, music performance, nursing, office supervision and management, parks and recreation management, personnel management, philosophy, physical education, physical sciences, physics, political science and government, prelaw, psychology, public administration, public health laboratory science, public relations, real estate, recreation therapy, religion, renewable natural resources, Scandinavian languages, Scandinavian studies, science education, secondary education, secretarial and related programs, social science education, social sciences, social studies education, social work, sociology, Spanish, speech, speech pathology/audiology, speech/communication/theater education, sports medicine, statistics, systems analysis, technical and business writing, technical education, textiles and clothing, theater design, toxicology, trade and industrial education, urban studies, wildlife management, women's studies.

ACADEMIC PROGRAMS. Accelerated program, double major, dual enrollment of high school students, education specialist degree, honors program, independent study, internships, student-designed major, study abroad, teacher preparation, weekend college, cross-registration; liberal arts/career combination in engineering, health sciences. **Remedial services:** Learning center, reduced course load, remedial instruction, special counselor, tutoring. **ROTC:** Army. **Placement/credit:** AP, CLEP General and Subject, institutional tests.

ACADEMIC REQUIREMENTS. Freshmen must earn minimum GPA of 2.0 to continue in good standing. 75% of freshmen return for sophomore year. Students must declare major by end of second year. **Graduation requirements:** 192 hours for bachelor's (80 in major). Most students required to take courses in arts/fine arts, English, history, humanities, mathematics, biological/physical sciences, social sciences.

FRESHMAN ADMISSIONS. Selection criteria: Rank in top half of high school class or equivalent ACT test score. **High school preparation:** 16 units recommended. Recommended units include English 4, foreign language 3, mathematics 3, social science 3 and science 3. 1 year world history/culture course or arts course. **Test requirements:** ACT; score report by September 1.

1992 FRESHMAN CLASS PROFILE. 1,589 men and women enrolled. 10% were in top tenth and 29% were in top quarter of graduating class. **Academic background:** Mid 50% of enrolled freshmen had ACT composite between 19-24. 99% submitted ACT scores. **Characteristics:** 88% from in state, 70% live in college housing, 4% have minority backgrounds, 1% are foreign students. Average age is 19.

FALL-TERM APPLICATIONS. $15 fee. No closing date; applicants notified on a rolling basis. Interview recommended. CRDA. Deferred and early admission available.

STUDENT LIFE. Housing: Dormitories (coed); fraternity, sorority housing available. **Activities:** Student government, magazine, radio, student newspaper, choral groups, concert band, dance, drama, jazz band, marching band, music ensembles, musical theater, opera, pep band, symphony orchestra, fraternities, sororities, various religious, political, ethnic, and social service organizations.

ATHLETICS. NCAA. **Intercollegiate:** Baseball M, basketball, cross-country, diving, football M, golf, ice hockey M, softball W, swimming, tennis, track and field, volleyball W, wrestling M. **Intramural:** Archery, badminton, basketball, bowling, diving, fencing, golf, gymnastics, ice hockey M, racquetball, rugby, skiing, soccer, softball, swimming, tennis, track and field, volleyball, wrestling M.

STUDENT SERVICES. Aptitude testing, career counseling, employment service for undergraduates, freshman orientation, health services, on-campus day care, personal counseling, placement service for graduates, special adviser for adult students, veterans counselor, services/facilities for handicapped.

ANNUAL EXPENSES. Tuition and fees (1992-93): $2,176, $1,865 additional for out-of-state students. **Room and board:** $2,535. **Books and supplies:** $450. **Other expenses:** $1,250.

FINANCIAL AID. 65% of freshmen, 70% of continuing students receive some form of aid. 92% of grants, 77% of loans, 31% of jobs based on need. 1,105 enrolled freshmen were judged to have need, 1,081 were offered aid. Academic, music/drama, art, athletic, leadership scholarships available. **Aid applications:** No closing date; priority given to applications received by July 1; applicants notified on a rolling basis beginning on or about April 1; must reply within 2 weeks.

ADDRESS/TELEPHONE. John M. Parkins, Director of Admissions, Mankato State University, PO MSU Box 55, MSU Box 55, P.O. Box 8400, Mankato, MN 56002-8400. (507) 389-1822. (800) 722-0544 (Minnesota only).

Mesabi Community College: Arrowhead Region
Virginia, Minnesota — CB code: 6432

2-year public community college, coed. Founded in 1918. **Accreditation:** Regional. **Undergraduate enrollment:** 602 men and women full time; 444 men and women part time. **Faculty:** 64 total (34 full time), 4 with doctorates or other terminal degrees. **Location:** Rural campus in large town; 70 miles from Duluth. **Calendar:** Quarter, limited summer session. **Microcomputers:** Located in libraries, computer centers. **Additional facts:** Located in historic area know as Iron Range. A short distance from a wide variety of outdoor recreational areas.

DEGREES OFFERED. AA, AS, AAS. 200 associate degrees awarded in 1992.

UNDERGRADUATE MAJORS. Computer technology, law enforcement and corrections technologies, liberal/general studies, marketing and distribution, mental health/human services, microprocessor technology, pre-engineering, protective services, secretarial and related programs.

ACADEMIC PROGRAMS. 2-year transfer program, dual enrollment of high school students, independent study, internships, study abroad, engineering with University of Minnesota: Duluth. **Remedial services:** Learning center, reduced course load, remedial instruction, special counselor, tutoring. **Placement/credit:** AP, CLEP General, institutional tests; 24 credit hours maximum for associate degree.

ACADEMIC REQUIREMENTS. Freshmen must earn minimum GPA of 1.7 to continue in good standing. 50% of freshmen return for sophomore year. Students must declare major on enrollment. **Graduation requirements:** 96 hours for associate. Most students required to take courses in English, humanities, mathematics, biological/physical sciences, social sciences.

FRESHMAN ADMISSIONS. Selection criteria: Open admissions. Recommended units include English 3, mathematics 2, social science 3 and science 2.

1992 FRESHMAN CLASS PROFILE. 401 men and women enrolled. 37% had high school GPA of 3.0 or higher, 43% between 2.0 and 2.99. **Characteristics:** 98% from in state, 100% commute, 8% have minority backgrounds. Average age is 23.

FALL-TERM APPLICATIONS. $15 fee. No closing date; applicants notified on a rolling basis beginning on or about January 1. Deferred and early admission available.

STUDENT LIFE. Housing: Low-cost housing based on student income available nearby. **Activities:** Student government, magazine, student newspaper, yearbook, choral groups, concert band, drama, jazz band, music ensembles, musical theater, pep band, symphony orchestra.

ATHLETICS. NJCAA. **Intercollegiate:** Basketball, football M, skiing, softball W, tennis, volleyball W. **Intramural:** Badminton, basketball, bowling, racquetball, softball, table tennis.

STUDENT SERVICES. Aptitude testing, career counseling, employment service for undergraduates, freshman orientation, on-campus day care, personal counseling, placement service for graduates, services/facilities for handicapped.

ANNUAL EXPENSES. Tuition and fees (1992-93): $1,687, $1,688 additional for out-of-state students. **Books and supplies:** $480. **Other expenses:** $1,000.

FINANCIAL AID. 82% of freshmen, 87% of continuing students receive some form of aid. Grants, loans, jobs available. Academic scholarships available. **Aid applications:** No closing date; priority given to applications received by April 22; applicants notified on a rolling basis beginning on or about May 1; must reply within 2 weeks.

ADDRESS/TELEPHONE. Richard N. Kohlhase, Provost, Mesabi Community College: Arrowhead Region, Ninth Avenue and Chestnut Street, Virginia, MN 55792. (218) 749-7700. Fax: (218) 749-9619.

Metropolitan State University
St. Paul, Minnesota — CB code: 1245

2-year upper-division public university, coed. Founded in 1971. **Accreditation:** Regional. **Undergraduate enrollment:** 429 men, 615 women full time; 1,640 men, 2,435 women part time. **Graduate enrollment:** 34 men, 31 women full time; 114 men, 92 women part time. **Faculty:** 522 total (67 full time), 39 with doctorates or other terminal degrees. **Location:** Urban campus in large city; located in downtown metropolitan area. **Calendar:** Quarter, extensive summer session. Saturday and extensive evening/early morning classes. **Microcomputers:** 100 located in computer centers. **Additional facts:** Community-based university designed for adults uses resources of metropolitan area libraries.

DEGREES OFFERED. BA, M. 773 bachelor's degrees awarded in 1992. Graduate degrees offered in 1 major field of study.

UNDERGRADUATE MAJORS. Accounting, business and management, communications, computer and information sciences, liberal/general studies, nursing.

ACADEMIC PROGRAMS. Independent study, internships, student-designed major, weekend college, cross-registration. **Remedial services:** Tutoring, programmed computer-assisted instruction in mathematics and reading. **Placement/credit:** CLEP General and Subject; 99 credit hours maximum for bachelor's degree.

ACADEMIC REQUIREMENTS. Graduation requirements: 188 hours for bachelor's (98 in major).

ADMISSIONS. Students must have completed 60 credit hours before acceptance into bachelor's program and must complete at least 12 competencies (equivalent to 48 credits) at University.

FALL-TERM APPLICATIONS. $15 fee. Applicants notified on a rolling basis.

STUDENT LIFE. Activities: Student government, student newspaper.

ATHLETICS. Intramural: Basketball, soccer, softball, volleyball.

STUDENT SERVICES. Career counseling, personal counseling, services/facilities for handicapped.

ANNUAL EXPENSES. Tuition and fees (1992-93): $1,959, $1,865 additional for out-of-state students. **Books and supplies:** $500. **Other expenses:** $1,800.

FINANCIAL AID. 18% of continuing students receive some form of aid. All grants, 82% of loans, 60% of jobs based on need. **Aid applications:** No closing date; applicants notified on a rolling basis beginning on or about July 1; must reply within 2 weeks.

ADDRESS/TELEPHONE. Janice Harring-Hendon, Admissions Director, Metropolitan State University, 700 East Seventh Street, St. Paul, MN 55106-5000. (612) 772-7600. Fax: (612) 772-7632.

Minneapolis College of Art and Design
Minneapolis, Minnesota CB code: 6411

Admissions: 81% of applicants accepted
Based on: ••• Essay, recommendations, school record, special talents
•• Interview
• Activities, test scores
Completion: 80% of freshmen end year in good standing
60% graduate, 5% of these enter graduate study

4-year private art college, coed. Founded in 1886. **Accreditation:** Regional. **Undergraduate enrollment:** 263 men, 245 women full time; 39 men, 38 women part time. **Faculty:** 63 total (45 full time), 4 with doctorates or other terminal degrees. **Location:** Urban campus in large city; 1 mile from downtown. **Calendar:** Semester, limited summer session. **Microcomputers:** 100 located in libraries, computer centers.

DEGREES OFFERED. BFA. 117 bachelor's degrees awarded in 1992. 100% in visual and performing arts.

UNDERGRADUATE MAJORS. Design, fine arts, media arts.

ACADEMIC PROGRAMS. Dual enrollment of high school students, honors program, independent study, internships, student-designed major, study abroad, visiting/exchange student program, New York semester, cross-registration, New York Studio Study Program, Florence Honors Program. **Remedial services:** Developmental reading and writing center. **Placement/credit:** AP, institutional tests.

ACADEMIC REQUIREMENTS. Freshmen must earn minimum GPA of 2.0 to continue in good standing. 80% of freshmen return for sophomore year. Students must declare major by end of first year. **Graduation requirements:** 120 hours for bachelor's (48 in major). Most students required to take courses in arts/fine arts, English, history, humanities.

FRESHMAN ADMISSIONS. Selection criteria: Applicants required to submit a portfolio of creative work. Academic record and test scores reviewed. Level of interest and motivation determined through personal statement of interest and letter of recommendation. **Test requirements:** SAT or ACT; score report by August 31.

1992 FRESHMAN CLASS PROFILE. 111 men applied, 88 accepted, 44 enrolled; 95 women applied, 79 accepted, 35 enrolled. 37% had high school GPA of 3.0 or higher, 56% between 2.0 and 2.99. **Academic background:** Mid 50% of enrolled freshmen had SAT-V between 430-520, SAT-M between 380-590; ACT composite between 17-23. 18% submitted SAT scores, 72% submitted ACT scores. **Characteristics:** 72% from in state, 60% commute, 12% have minority backgrounds, 2% are foreign students. Average age is 19.

FALL-TERM APPLICATIONS. $35 fee, may be waived for applicants with need. No closing date; priority given to applications received by March 1; applicants notified on a rolling basis; must reply by May 1. Portfolio required. Essay required. Interview recommended. CRDA. Deferred admission available.

STUDENT LIFE. Housing: Apartment housing available. About 155 students live in 6 on-campus apartment buildings. Resident asistant assigned to each building. **Activities:** Student government, film, magazine, student newspaper, television, art exhibitions, multi-cultural club, Afro-American student caucus, international students,Native American caucus, B-Glad (Bisexual, Gay and Lesbian artists and designers). **Additional information:** Art-related activities (competitions, exhibitions, and gallery events).

STUDENT SERVICES. Aptitude testing, career counseling, employment service for undergraduates, freshman orientation, personal counseling, placement service for graduates, transfer student adviser, services/facilities for handicapped.

ANNUAL EXPENSES. Tuition and fees: $12,014. **Room and board:** $2,000 room only. **Books and supplies:** $1,200. **Other expenses:** $500.

FINANCIAL AID. 72% of freshmen, 75% of continuing students receive some form of aid. 97% of grants, 73% of loans, all jobs based on need. 60 enrolled freshmen were judged to have need, all were offered aid. Academic, art scholarships available. **Aid applications:** No closing date; priority given to applications received by April 1; applicants notified on a rolling basis beginning on or about April 1; must reply by May 1 or within 2 weeks if notified thereafter.

ADDRESS/TELEPHONE. Rebecca Haas, Director of Admissions, Minneapolis College of Art and Design, 2501 Stevens Avenue South, Minneapolis, MN 55404. (612) 874-3760. (800) 874-6223. Fax: (612) 874-3704.

Minneapolis Community College
Minneapolis, Minnesota CB code: 6434

2-year public community college, coed. Founded in 1965. **Accreditation:** Regional. **Undergraduate enrollment:** 833 men, 1,105 women full time; 923 men, 1,449 women part time. **Faculty:** 189 total (87 full time), 16 with doctorates or other terminal degrees. **Location:** Urban campus in large city; downtown. **Calendar:** Quarter, limited summer session. **Microcomputers:** 121 located in classrooms.

DEGREES OFFERED. AA, AS, AAS. 340 associate degrees awarded in 1992. 25% in health sciences, 74% multi/interdisciplinary studies.

UNDERGRADUATE MAJORS. Accounting, business administration and management, business and management, cinematography/film, computer and information sciences, law enforcement and corrections technologies, liberal/general studies, marketing and distribution, nursing, video.

ACADEMIC PROGRAMS. 2-year transfer program, accelerated program, dual enrollment of high school students, honors program, independent study, internships, weekend college, cross-registration, human services career option program, law enforcement, film/video production. **Remedial services:** Learning center, remedial instruction, special counselor, tutoring. **Placement/credit:** AP, CLEP General and Subject, institutional tests.

ACADEMIC REQUIREMENTS. Freshmen must earn minimum GPA of 2.0 to continue in good standing. 46% of freshmen return for sophomore year. Students must declare major on application. **Graduation requirements:** 90 hours for associate. Most students required to take courses in arts/fine arts, English, humanities, biological/physical sciences, social sciences.

FRESHMAN ADMISSIONS. Selection criteria: Open admissions. Nursing Program applicants should request copy of Nursing Admission Requirements Packet. Nursing program admits accepted students only in fall quarter. Human Services applicants must pass fundamentals of English writing test and college level reading test.

1992 FRESHMAN CLASS PROFILE. 1,187 men, 1,649 women enrolled. **Characteristics:** 95% from in state, 100% commute. Average age is 27.

FALL-TERM APPLICATIONS. $15 fee. Closing date September 1; applicants notified on a rolling basis. Deferred and early admission available.

STUDENT LIFE. Activities: Student government, magazine, student newspaper, choral groups, drama, jazz band, musical theater, international student organization, studnet government, Phi Theta Kappa.

ATHLETICS. NJCAA. **Intercollegiate:** Basketball, cross-country, golf, softball W, track and field. **Intramural:** Badminton, basketball, bowling, cross-country, golf, handball M, racquetball, soccer M, tennis, volleyball.

STUDENT SERVICES. Aptitude testing, career counseling, freshman orientation, on-campus day care, personal counseling, veterans counselor, orientation and support program for American Indian, black, and handicapped students, services/facilities for handicapped.

ANNUAL EXPENSES. Tuition and fees (1992-93): $1,687, $1,586 additional for out-of-state students. **Books and supplies:** $525. **Other expenses:** $450.

FINANCIAL AID. 50% of freshmen, 60% of continuing students receive some form of aid. Grants, loans, jobs available. 600 enrolled freshmen were judged to have need, 500 were offered aid. Academic scholarships available. **Aid applications:** No closing date; priority given to applications received by June 1; applicants notified on a rolling basis beginning on or about July 15; must reply within 2 weeks.

ADDRESS/TELEPHONE. Bonnie Wiger, Registrar, Minneapolis Community College, 1501 Hennepin Avenue, Minneapolis, MN 55403-1779. (612) 341-7000. Fax: (612) 341-7075.

Minnesota Bible College
Rochester, Minnesota CB code: 6412

4-year private Bible college, coed, affiliated with Christian Church. Founded in 1913. **Undergraduate enrollment:** 54 men, 39 women full time; 12 men, 15 women part time. **Faculty:** 15 total (8 full time), 5 with doctorates or other terminal degrees. **Location:** Suburban campus in small city; 85 miles from Minneapolis-St. Paul. **Calendar:** Quarter. **Microcomputers:** 5 located in computer centers. **Special facilities:** 40-acre wooded area with nature trails. **Additional facts:** Education for leadership in church-related ministries.

DEGREES OFFERED. AA, BA, BS. 23 associate degrees awarded in 1992. 100% in philosophy, religion, theology. 15 bachelor's degrees awarded. 100% in philosophy, religion, theology.

UNDERGRADUATE MAJORS. Associate: Bible studies. **Bachelor's:** Religious education, theological studies.

ACADEMIC PROGRAMS. 2-year transfer program, double major, internships, cross-registration. **Remedial services:** Reduced course load, remedial instruction, special counselor. **Placement/credit:** AP, CLEP General and Subject, institutional tests; 30 credit hours maximum for bachelor's degree.

ACADEMIC REQUIREMENTS. Freshmen must earn minimum GPA of 1.8 to continue in good standing. 75% of freshmen return for sophomore year. Students must declare major by end of second year. **Graduation requirements:** 98 hours for associate, 194 hours for bachelor's (40 in major). Most students required to take courses in computer science, English, foreign languages, humanities, philosophy/religion, biological/physical sciences, social sciences. **Postgraduate studies:** 75% from 2-year programs enter 4-year programs.

FRESHMAN ADMISSIONS. Selection criteria: Open admissions. High school rank, experience, and aptitude for Christian ministry, character references, and personal statement of goals considered for placement purposes. **Test requirements:** SAT or ACT (ACT preferred); score report by August 28.

1992 FRESHMAN CLASS PROFILE. 20 men applied, 19 accepted, 15 enrolled; 20 women applied, 15 accepted, 13 enrolled. 63% had high school GPA of 3.0 or higher, 27% between 2.0 and 2.99. 11% were in top tenth and 30% were in top quarter of graduating class. **Characteristics:** 64% from in state, 96% live in college housing, 7% have minority backgrounds. Average age is 19.

FALL-TERM APPLICATIONS. $20 fee. Closing date August 15; applicants notified on a rolling basis beginning on or about April 1; must reply by August 15 or within two weeks if notified thereafter. Essay required. Interview recommended.

STUDENT LIFE. Housing: Dormitories (men, women); apartment housing available. **Activities:** Student government, yearbook, choral groups, drama, music ensembles, pep band, Christians Outdoors. **Additional information:** Religious observance required.

ATHLETICS. Intercollegiate: Baseball M, basketball M, golf M, softball W, tennis, volleyball. **Intramural:** Bowling, golf, ice hockey, skiing, swimming, table tennis, tennis, volleyball.

STUDENT SERVICES. Aptitude testing, career counseling, employment service for undergraduates, freshman orientation, personal counseling, placement service for graduates.

ANNUAL EXPENSES. Tuition and fees (1992-93): $4,286. **Room and board:** $1,530 room only. **Books and supplies:** $300. **Other expenses:** $1,650.

FINANCIAL AID. 84% of freshmen, 87% of continuing students receive some form of aid. Academic, music/drama, state/district residency, leadership, religious affiliation scholarships available. **Aid applications:** No closing date; priority given to applications received by June 1; applicants notified on a rolling basis.

ADDRESS/TELEPHONE. Tay J. Schield, Director of Recruitment, Minnesota Bible College, 920 Mayowood Road Southwest, Rochester, MN 55902. (507) 288-4563. (800) 456-7651. Fax: (507) 288-9046.

Moorhead State University
Moorhead, Minnesota CB code: 6678

4-year public university, coed. Founded in 1885. **Accreditation:** Regional. **Undergraduate enrollment:** 2,705 men, 3,890 women full time; 404 men, 872 women part time. **Graduate enrollment:** 52 men, 108 women full time; 77 men, 200 women part time. **Faculty:** 435 total (353 full time), 233 with doctorates or other terminal degrees. **Location:** Urban campus in large town; 240 miles from Minneapolis-St. Paul, across border from Fargo, North Dakota. **Calendar:** Quarter, extensive summer session. Saturday and extensive evening/early morning classes. **Microcomputers:** 250 located in dormitories, libraries, classrooms, computer centers. **Special facilities:** Art gallery, planetarium, biology museum, regional science center.

DEGREES OFFERED. AA, BA, BS, BFA, MA, MS, MBA. 45 associate degrees awarded in 1992. 1,383 bachelor's degrees awarded. 35% in business and management, 9% communications, 19% teacher education, 8% social sciences. Graduate degrees offered in 22 major fields of study.

UNDERGRADUATE MAJORS. Associate: Liberal/general studies, medical records administration, medical records technology. **Bachelor's:** Accounting, advertising, American studies, anthropology, art education, art history, biology, business administration and management, business education, ceramics, chemistry, chiropractic, clinical laboratory science, communications, computer and information sciences, criminal justice studies, cytotechnology, dramatic arts, early childhood education, economics, education of the emotionally handicapped, education of the mentally handicapped, elementary education, energy conservation and use technology, English, English education, finance, fine arts, foreign languages (multiple emphasis), foreign languages education, French, German, graphic design, health education, history, hotel/motel and restaurant management, illustration design, industrial arts education, industrial chemistry, industrial technology, information sciences and systems, international business management, journalism, junior high education, legal assistant/paralegal, marketing and distribution, marketing management, mathematics, mathematics education, medical laboratory technologies, music, music education, nursing, optometry, painting, personnel management, philosophy, photography, physical education, physical sciences, physics, political science and government, predentistry, prelaw, premedicine, preveterinary, printmaking, psychology, public relations, radio/television broadcasting, science education, sculpture, secondary education, social studies education, social work, sociology, Spanish, special education, speech, speech correction, speech pathology/audiology, trade and industrial education, vocational rehabilitation.

ACADEMIC PROGRAMS. 2-year transfer program, cooperative education, double major, dual enrollment of high school students, education specialist degree, external degree, honors program, independent study, internships, student-designed major, study abroad, teacher preparation, visiting/exchange student program, Washington semester, cross-registration, reciprocal bachelor's degree programs with North Dakota State University; combined bachelor's/graduate program in business administration. **Remedial services:** Preadmission summer program, reduced course load, remedial instruction, special counselor, tutoring. **ROTC:** Air Force, Army. **Placement/credit:** AP, CLEP Subject, IB, institutional tests; 24 credit hours maximum for bachelor's degree.

ACADEMIC REQUIREMENTS. Freshmen must earn minimum GPA of 2.0 to continue in good standing. 72% of freshmen return for sophomore year. Students must declare major by end of second year. **Graduation requirements:** 96 hours for associate, 192 hours for bachelor's. Most students required to take courses in English, humanities, mathematics, biological/physical sciences, social sciences. **Postgraduate studies:** 2% enter law school, 1% enter medical school, 1% enter MBA programs, 6% enter other graduate study.

FRESHMAN ADMISSIONS. Selection criteria: Applicants must rank in top half of class or have minimum ACT composite score of 21 or equivalent scores on SAT or PSAT/NMSQT. Some applicants not meeting requirements admitted to transitional college program. **High school preparation:** 15 units required. Required units include English 4, mathematics 3, social science 3 and science 3. One unit fine arts, .5 computer science recommended. **Test requirements:** SAT or ACT (ACT preferred); score report by August 15. PSAT/NMSQT may be submitted in place of SAT or ACT.

1992 FRESHMAN CLASS PROFILE. 617 men, 902 women enrolled. 14% were in top tenth and 39% were in top quarter of graduating class. **Academic background:** Mid 50% of enrolled freshmen had ACT composite between 18-25. 95% submitted ACT scores. **Characteristics:** 55% from in state, 86% live in college housing, 4% have minority backgrounds, 2% are foreign students. Average age is 19.

FALL-TERM APPLICATIONS. $15 fee. Closing date August 15; applicants notified on a rolling basis. Deferred and early admission available.

STUDENT LIFE. Housing: Dormitories (men, women, coed); fraternity, sorority housing available. Suites available accommodating 4 students each. **Activities:** Student government, radio, student newspaper, television, choral groups, concert band, dance, drama, jazz band, music ensembles, musical theater, opera, pep band, symphony orchestra, fraternities, sororities, Spurs, Circle-K, Newman Club, United Campus Ministry.

ATHLETICS. NCAA. **Intercollegiate:** Basketball, cross-country, field hockey W, football M, golf, softball W, tennis, track and field, volleyball W, wrestling M. **Intramural:** Archery, badminton, basketball, bowling, golf, ice hockey M, racquetball, soccer, softball, swimming, tennis, track and field, volleyball, wrestling M.

STUDENT SERVICES. Aptitude testing, career counseling, employment service for undergraduates, freshman orientation, health services, on-campus day care, personal counseling, placement service for graduates, special adviser for adult students, veterans counselor, minority student adviser, peer tutoring, services/facilities for handicapped.

ANNUAL EXPENSES. Tuition and fees (1992-93): $2,172, $1,865 additional for out-of-state students. **Room and board:** $2,535. **Books and supplies:** $600. **Other expenses:** $1,514.

FINANCIAL AID. 78% of freshmen, 69% of continuing students receive some form of aid. 94% of grants, 81% of loans, 38% of jobs based on need. 1,036 enrolled freshmen were judged to have need, all were offered aid. Academic, music/drama, art, athletic, leadership, minority scholarships available. **Aid applications:** No closing date; priority given to applications received by March 15; applicants notified on a rolling basis beginning on or about May 1; must reply within 2 weeks.

ADDRESS/TELEPHONE. Floyd W. Brown, Director of Admissions, Moorhead State University, Owens Hall, Moorhead, MN 56563. (218) 236-2161. Fax: (218) 236-2168.

National College
St. Paul, Minnesota CB code: 5358

4-year proprietary business college, coed. **Undergraduate enrollment:** 149 men and women. **Location:** Urban campus in large city. **Calendar:** Quarter.

FRESHMAN ADMISSIONS. Selection criteria: Open admissions.

ANNUAL EXPENSES. Tuition and fees (1992-93): $4,791. **Books and supplies:** $675.

ADDRESS/TELEPHONE. Ken Norman, Director of Admissions, National College, 1380 Energy Lane, St. Paul, MN 55108. (612) 644-1265.

National Education Center: Brown Institute Campus
Minneapolis, Minnesota CB code: 1210

2-year proprietary art, business, technical college, coed. Founded in 1946. **Undergraduate enrollment:** 1,500 men and women. **Location:** Urban campus in large city. **Calendar:** Quarter.

FRESHMAN ADMISSIONS. Selection criteria: Institutional examinations required.

ANNUAL EXPENSES. Tuition and fees (1992-93): $5,990. Tuition includes cost of books and supplies.

ADDRESS/TELEPHONE. Director of Admissions, National Education Center: Brown Institute Campus, 2225 East Lake Street, Minneapolis, MN 55407. (612) 721-2481.

NEI College of Technology
Minneapolis, Minnesota — CB code: 1387

Admissions: 67% of applicants accepted
Based on: ••• Interview, test scores
• School record
Completion: 75% of freshmen end year in good standing
67% graduate, 2% of these enter 4-year programs

2-year private junior, technical college, coed. Founded in 1930. **Undergraduate enrollment:** 236 men, 14 women full time; 107 men, 17 women part time. **Faculty:** 27 total (16 full time), 1 with doctorate or other terminal degree. **Location:** Suburban campus in large city; 3 miles from downtown. **Calendar:** Quarter, extensive summer session. Extensive evening/early morning classes. **Microcomputers:** 39 located in classrooms. **Additional facts:** Students attend 4 quarters to complete 1 academic year.

DEGREES OFFERED. 135 associate degrees awarded in 1992. 100% in engineering technologies.

UNDERGRADUATE MAJORS. Aeronautical technology, aviation computer technology, computer and information sciences, computer servicing technology, computer technology, electrical and electronics equipment repair, electrical/electronics/communications engineering, electromechanical technology, electronic technology, industrial equipment maintenance and repair, industrial technology, instrumentation technology, radio/television technology.

ACADEMIC PROGRAMS. Double major, honors program. **Remedial services:** Tutoring. **Placement/credit:** Institutional tests; 60 credit hours maximum for associate degree.

ACADEMIC REQUIREMENTS. Freshmen must earn minimum GPA of 2.0 to continue in good standing. 75% of freshmen return for sophomore year. Students must declare major on application. **Graduation requirements:** 121 hours for associate. Most students required to take courses in English, mathematics, biological/physical sciences.

FRESHMAN ADMISSIONS. Selection criteria: Basic reading and mathematics skills determined by use of Wonderlic examination. **High school preparation:** 3 units recommended. Recommended units include English 2 and mathematics 1. **Test requirements:** Wonderlic Form IV or V. **Additional information:** Admission not determined by SAT or ACT scores.

1992 FRESHMAN CLASS PROFILE. 109 men applied, 75 accepted, 75 enrolled; 17 women applied, 9 accepted, 9 enrolled. **Characteristics:** 99% from in state, 100% commute, 4% have minority backgrounds. Average age is 25.

FALL-TERM APPLICATIONS. $40 fee. No closing date; applicants notified on a rolling basis. Interview required. Deferred admission available.

STUDENT LIFE. Activities: Student government, student newspaper. **Additional information:** Student Council active in community service and social activities.

ATHLETICS. Intramural: Basketball, bowling, tennis, volleyball.

STUDENT SERVICES. Career counseling, employment service for undergraduates, freshman orientation, personal counseling, placement service for graduates, veterans counselor.

ANNUAL EXPENSES. Tuition and fees (projected): $4,335. **Books and supplies:** $600. **Other expenses:** $1,740.

FINANCIAL AID. 68% of freshmen, 82% of continuing students receive some form of aid. 80% of grants, 85% of loans, 89% of jobs based on need. 40 enrolled freshmen were judged to have need, all were offered aid. Academic scholarships available. **Aid applications:** No closing date; applicants notified on a rolling basis; must reply within 2 weeks.

ADDRESS/TELEPHONE. Richard Thomson, Director of Admissions, NEI College of Technology, 825 41st Avenue NE, Minneapolis, MN 55421-9990. (612) 781-4881. (800) 777-7634. Fax: (612) 781-4884.

Normandale Community College
Bloomington, Minnesota — CB code: 6501

2-year public community college, coed. Founded in 1968. **Accreditation:** Regional. **Undergraduate enrollment:** 1,970 men, 2,047 women full time; 1,850 men, 3,354 women part time. **Location:** Suburban campus in small city; 14 miles from Minneapolis-St. Paul. **Calendar:** Quarter, limited summer session. Saturday and extensive evening/early morning classes. **Microcomputers:** 225 located in libraries, classrooms, computer centers. **Special facilities:** Japanese gardens, marshland area, small business development center.

DEGREES OFFERED. AA, AS, AAS. 893 associate degrees awarded in 1992. 7% in business and management, 5% business/office and marketing/distribution, 18% health sciences, 52% multi/interdisciplinary studies, 12% parks/recreation, protective services, public affairs.

UNDERGRADUATE MAJORS. Accounting, business and office, business data programming, computer programming, computer technology, dietetic aide/assistant, drafting, drafting and design technology, engineering and engineering-related technologies, food production/management/services, hospitality and recreation marketing, hotel/motel and restaurant management, law enforcement and corrections, law enforcement and corrections technologies, liberal/general studies, marketing and distribution, marketing management, marketing research, mechanical design technology, medical laboratory technologies, nursing, office supervision and management, radiograph medical technology, secretarial and related programs, small business management and ownership.

ACADEMIC PROGRAMS. 2-year transfer program, cooperative education, dual enrollment of high school students, independent study, internships, study abroad, telecourses, weekend college. **Remedial services:** Learning center, reduced course load, remedial instruction, special counselor, tutoring. **ROTC:** Air Force, Army, Naval. **Placement/credit:** AP, CLEP General, institutional tests; 30 credit hours maximum for associate degree.

ACADEMIC REQUIREMENTS. Freshmen must earn minimum GPA of 1.7 to continue in good standing. 59% of freshmen return for sophomore year. **Graduation requirements:** 90 hours for associate. Most students required to take courses in arts/fine arts, English, humanities, biological/physical sciences, social sciences.

FRESHMAN ADMISSIONS. Selection criteria: Open admissions. Nonresidents must rank in top half of class or have ACT composite score of 15. Selective admission to health-related programs. Chemistry required for nursing and dental hygiene programs. **Test requirements:** ACT required of foreign, out-of-state, and health program applicants.

1992 FRESHMAN CLASS PROFILE. 4,088 men and women applied, 2,584 accepted; 1,070 men enrolled, 1,514 women enrolled. 30% had high school GPA of 3.0 or higher, 60% between 2.0 and 2.99. **Characteristics:** 100% commute, 5% have minority backgrounds.

FALL-TERM APPLICATIONS. $15 fee. Closing date September 1; applicants notified on a rolling basis. Deferred and early admission available. In-house placement tests in English, mathematics, reading administered before registration.

STUDENT LIFE. Activities: Student government, magazine, student newspaper, television, choral groups, concert band, drama, jazz band, music ensembles, musical theater, Christian Fellowship Club, International Student Organization.

ATHLETICS. NJCAA. **Intercollegiate:** Baseball M, basketball, football M, golf, softball W, volleyball W. **Intramural:** Baseball, basketball, bowling, field hockey, golf, handball, ice hockey, racquetball, soccer, table tennis, tennis, volleyball.

STUDENT SERVICES. Aptitude testing, career counseling, employment service for undergraduates, freshman orientation, on-campus day care, personal counseling, placement service for graduates, veterans counselor, services/facilities for handicapped.

ANNUAL EXPENSES. Tuition and fees (1992-93): $1,687, $1,688 additional for out-of-state students. **Books and supplies:** $550. **Other expenses:** $500.

FINANCIAL AID. 33% of freshmen, 33% of continuing students receive some form of aid. Grants, loans, jobs available. **Aid applications:** No closing date; priority given to applications received by May 1; applicants notified on a rolling basis beginning on or about June 1; must reply within 2 weeks.

ADDRESS/TELEPHONE. Pam Smith Mentz, Director of Admissions, Normandale Community College, 9700 France Avenue South, Bloomington, MN 55431. (612) 832-6320.

North Central Bible College
Minneapolis, Minnesota — CB code: 0051

4-year private Bible, liberal arts college, coed, affiliated with Assemblies of God. Founded in 1930. **Accreditation:** Regional. **Undergraduate enrollment:** 444 men, 383 women full time; 107 men, 108 women part time. **Faculty:** 76 total (49 full time), 10 with doctorates or other terminal degrees. **Location:** Urban campus in large city; 10 blocks from downtown Minneapolis, 10 miles from Saint Paul. **Calendar:** Semester, limited summer session. Saturday classes. **Microcomputers:** 25 located in computer centers. **Special facilities:** Children's literature library, most of campus connected by skyways.

DEGREES OFFERED. AA, BA, BS. 5 associate degrees awarded in 1992. 100% in philosophy, religion, theology. 160 bachelor's degrees awarded. 100% in philosophy, religion, theology.

UNDERGRADUATE MAJORS. Associate: Behavioral sciences, biblical languages, business and management, communications, comparative literature, early childhood education, Greek (classical), Hebrew, humanities, journalism, liberal/general studies, missionary studies, office supervision and management, philosophy, radio/television broadcasting, secretarial and related programs. **Bachelor's:** Behavioral sciences, biblical languages, Christian education, communications, deaf culture ministries for hearing students, elementary education, Greek (classical), Hebrew, journalism, missionary studies, music performance, pastorial studies for deaf students, radio/television broadcasting, religious education, religious music, theological studies.

ACADEMIC PROGRAMS. 2-year transfer program, double major, independent study, internships, study abroad, weekend college. **Remedial services:** Reduced course load, remedial instruction, tutoring. **Placement/credit:** AP, CLEP General and Subject.

ACADEMIC REQUIREMENTS. Freshmen must earn minimum GPA of 1.5 to continue in good standing. Students must declare major on enrollment. **Graduation requirements:** 62 hours for associate (15 in major), 126 hours for bachelor's (61 in major). Most students required to take courses in arts/fine arts, English, history, mathematics, philosophy/religion, biological/physical sciences, social sciences.

FRESHMAN ADMISSIONS. Selection criteria: School achievement record, essay, and pastor's recommendation most important. **Test requirements:** SAT or ACT (ACT preferred) for placement and counseling only; score report by September 1.

1992 FRESHMAN CLASS PROFILE. 773 men and women applied, 771 accepted; 222 men enrolled, 209 women enrolled. **Characteristics:** 58% live in college housing. Average age is 19.

FALL-TERM APPLICATIONS. No fee. No closing date; applicants notified on a rolling basis. Audition required for religious music applicants. Interview recommended. Deferred admission available.

STUDENT LIFE. Housing: Dormitories (men, women); apartment housing available. Honor dormitories available. **Activities:** Student government, magazine, radio, student newspaper, television, yearbook, choral groups, concert band, drama, jazz band, music ensembles, musical theater, pep band, No Cultural Barriers in Christ (NCBC), Christians for Social and Political Awareness, Persona (behavioral science club), Artists Guild. **Additional information:** College participates in Upper Midwest Athletic Conference. Religious observance required.

ATHLETICS. Intercollegiate: Basketball, soccer M, volleyball W. **Intramural:** Ice hockey M, volleyball, wrestling M.

STUDENT SERVICES. Career counseling, employment service for undergraduates, freshman orientation, health services, personal counseling, placement service for graduates, services/facilities for handicapped.

ANNUAL EXPENSES. Tuition and fees (1992-93): $5,040. **Room and board:** $3,080. **Books and supplies:** $300. **Other expenses:** $900.

FINANCIAL AID. 80% of continuing students receive some form of aid. 70% of grants, all loans, all jobs based on need. Academic, music/drama, art, religious affiliation scholarships available. **Aid applications:** No closing date; priority given to applications received by April 30; applicants notified on a rolling basis; must reply within 2 weeks.

ADDRESS/TELEPHONE. Dan Neary, Director of Admissions, North Central Bible College, 910 Elliot Avenue South, Minneapolis, MN 55404. (612) 332-1629. (800) 289-NCBC. Fax: (612) 343-4778.

North Hennepin Community College
Minneapolis, Minnesota — CB code: 6498

2-year public community college, coed. Founded in 1966. **Accreditation:** Regional. **Undergraduate enrollment:** 6,250 men and women. **Faculty:** 250 total (100 full time), 45 with doctorates or other terminal degrees. **Location:** Suburban campus in large city; 12 miles from downtown. **Calendar:** Quarter, limited summer session. Saturday and extensive evening/early morning classes. **Microcomputers:** 100 located in libraries, classrooms, computer centers. **Special facilities:** Art galleries, dark room and laboratory super circuit training course, pool designed for water aerobics.

DEGREES OFFERED. AA, AS, AAS. 700 associate degrees awarded in 1992.

UNDERGRADUATE MAJORS. Accounting, automotive technology, biology, business and management, business and office, cardiopulmonary technology, chemistry, commercial art, communications, computer and information sciences, economics, education, electrical technology, engineering and engineering-related technologies, English, finance, fire protection, German, graphic arts technology, health sciences, history, home economics, law enforcement and corrections technologies, legal assistant/paralegal, legal secretary, liberal/general studies, manufacturing technology, marketing and distribution, mathematics, medical records technology, medical secretary, music, noninvasive cardiology, nursing, office supervision and management, physical sciences, physics, plastic technology, political science and government, preengineering, psychology, radiograph medical technology, retailing, secretarial and related programs, small business management and ownership, social sciences, sociology, Spanish, transportation management, visual and performing arts.

ACADEMIC PROGRAMS. 2-year transfer program, dual enrollment of high school students, honors program, independent study, internships, study abroad, weekend college, cross-registration. **Remedial services:** Learning center, reduced course load, remedial instruction, special counselor, tutoring. **Placement/credit:** AP, CLEP General and Subject, IB, institutional tests.

ACADEMIC REQUIREMENTS. No policy requiring minimum GPA; records of students having academic difficulty are reviewed individually. 65% of freshmen return for sophomore year. Students must declare major by end of first year. **Graduation requirements:** 96 hours for associate. Most students required to take courses in arts/fine arts, English, humanities, mathematics, biological/physical sciences, social sciences.

FRESHMAN ADMISSIONS. Selection criteria: Open admissions. Competitive admissions for allied health programs. One unit of chemistry, algebra required for nursing program. **Additional information:** Must show proof of immunization to be admitted into college.

1992 FRESHMAN CLASS PROFILE. 2,700 men and women enrolled. **Characteristics:** 99% from in state, 100% commute, 5% have minority backgrounds, 1% are foreign students.

FALL-TERM APPLICATIONS. No fee. No closing date; applicants notified on a rolling basis. Deferred and early admission available.

STUDENT LIFE. Activities: Student government, magazine, student newspaper, choral groups, concert band, drama, jazz band, music ensembles, musical theater, symphony orchestra.

ATHLETICS. NJCAA. **Intercollegiate:** Baseball M, football M, golf M, softball W, tennis, volleyball W. **Intramural:** Archery, badminton, basketball, bowling, soccer, softball, volleyball, water polo.

STUDENT SERVICES. Aptitude testing, career counseling, employment service for undergraduates, health services, on-campus day care, personal counseling, placement service for graduates, services/facilities for handicapped.

ANNUAL EXPENSES. Tuition and fees (1992-93): $1,687, $1,688 additional for out-of-state students. **Books and supplies:** $500. **Other expenses:** $200.

FINANCIAL AID. 26% of freshmen, 29% of continuing students receive some form of aid. 89% of grants, 51% of loans, 87% of jobs based on need. 625 enrolled freshmen were judged to have need, all were offered aid. Music/drama, art, leadership scholarships available. **Aid applications:** No closing date; applicants notified on a rolling basis beginning on or about March 1; must reply within 2 weeks.

ADDRESS/TELEPHONE. Roberta Cramer, Student Service Assistant, North Hennepin Community College, 7411 85th Avenue North, Minneapolis, MN 55445. (612) 424-0811.

Northland Community College
Thief River Falls, Minnesota — CB code: 6500

2-year public community college, coed. Founded in 1965. **Accreditation:** Regional. **Undergraduate enrollment:** 875 men and women. **Location:** Rural campus in small town; 55 miles from Grand Forks, North Dakota. **Calendar:** Quarter.

FRESHMAN ADMISSIONS. Selection criteria: Open admissions.

ANNUAL EXPENSES. Tuition and fees (projected): $1,950, $1,950 additional for out-of-state students. **Books and supplies:** $540. **Other expenses:** $975.

ADDRESS/TELEPHONE. Katy Henke, Administrative Assistant, Northland Community College, Highway 1 East, Thief River Falls, MN 56701. (218) 681-2181. (800) 628-9918. Fax: (218) 681-6405.

Northwest Technical Institute
Eden Prairie, Minnesota — CB code: 1388

2-year proprietary technical college, coed. Founded in 1957. **Undergraduate enrollment:** 10 men, 140 women full time. **Faculty:** 10 total. **Location:** Suburban campus in large town; 10 miles from Minneapolis-St. Paul. **Calendar:** Semester. **Microcomputers:** Located in classrooms.

DEGREES OFFERED. AAS. 112 associate degrees awarded in 1992. 48% in architecture and environmental design, 52% engineering.

UNDERGRADUATE MAJORS. Architecture, drafting, mechanical engineering.

ACADEMIC REQUIREMENTS. Freshmen must earn minimum GPA of 2.0 to continue in good standing. 80% of freshmen return for sophomore year.

FRESHMAN ADMISSIONS. Selection criteria: Personal interview.

1992 FRESHMAN CLASS PROFILE. 60 men and women enrolled. **Characteristics:** 100% commute. Average age is 19.

FALL-TERM APPLICATIONS. $25 fee. No closing date; applicants notified on a rolling basis. Interview required.

STUDENT SERVICES. Career counseling, freshman orientation, placement service for graduates.

ANNUAL EXPENSES. Tuition and fees: $7,465. **Books and supplies:** $300.

FINANCIAL AID. 71% of continuing students receive some form of aid. Grants, loans available. **Aid applications:** No closing date; applicants notified on a rolling basis. **Additional information:** Variety of institutional payment plans available.

ADDRESS/TELEPHONE. Shelly Zakariasen, Sales Manager, Northwest Technical Institute, 11995 Singletree Lane, Eden Prairie, MN 55344-5351. (612) 944-0080. (800) 443-4223.

Northwestern College
Roseville, Minnesota CB code: 6489

Admissions: 81% of applicants accepted
Based on:
••• Essay, recommendations, religious affiliation/commitment
•• School record
• Activities, interview, test scores
Completion: 80% of freshmen end year in good standing
25% enter graduate study

4-year private college of arts and sciences and Bible college, coed, interdenominational. Founded in 1902. **Accreditation:** Regional. **Undergraduate enrollment:** 1,244 men and women. **Faculty:** 119 total (59 full time), 30 with doctorates or other terminal degrees. **Location:** Suburban campus in large town; 10 miles from Minneapolis-St. Paul. **Calendar:** Quarter, limited summer session. **Microcomputers:** Located in computer centers. **Additional facts:** All students required to major in Bible (45 credits) and another field.

DEGREES OFFERED. AS, BA, BS. 15 associate degrees awarded in 1992. 73% in business/office and marketing/distribution, 13% philosophy, religion, theology, 6% physical sciences, 8% visual and performing arts. 161 bachelor's degrees awarded. 23% in business and management, 7% business/office and marketing/distribution, 8% communications, 5% computer sciences, 29% teacher education, 15% philosophy, religion, theology, 6% psychology.

UNDERGRADUATE MAJORS. Associate: Accounting, Bible studies, business administration and management, business and management, business and office, business data processing and related programs, chemistry, graphic arts technology, legal secretary, liberal/general studies, marketing and distribution, physical sciences, physics, radio/television broadcasting, radio/television technology, secretarial and related programs, social sciences. **Bachelor's:** Accounting, art education, Bible studies, business administration and management, business and management, business and office, commercial art, communications, computer and information sciences, cross-cultural ministries, dramatic arts, education, elementary education, English, English education, finance, fine arts, graphic arts technology, human resources development, international business management, journalism, marketing and distribution, marketing management, mathematics, mathematics education, ministries, missionary studies, music, music education, music performance, office supervision and management, physical education, preengineering, psychology, radio/television broadcasting, radio/television technology, religion, religious education, social sciences, sports management, theological studies.

ACADEMIC PROGRAMS. 2-year transfer program, double major, internships. **Remedial services:** Reduced course load, remedial instruction, special counselor, tutoring. **ROTC:** Air Force. **Placement/credit:** AP, CLEP General and Subject, institutional tests; 32 credit hours maximum for bachelor's degree.

ACADEMIC REQUIREMENTS. Freshmen must earn minimum GPA of 1.75 to continue in good standing. 58% of freshmen return for sophomore year. Students must declare major by end of first year. **Graduation requirements:** 90 hours for associate (33 in major), 188 hours for bachelor's (70 in major). Most students required to take courses in computer science, English, history, humanities, mathematics, philosophy/religion, biological/physical sciences, social sciences. **Postgraduate studies:** 5% from 2-year programs enter 4-year programs.

FRESHMAN ADMISSIONS. Selection criteria: Evidence of Christian commitment major criterion. Recommended units include English 4, foreign language 2, mathematics 2, social science 1 and science 2. **Test requirements:** SAT or ACT (ACT preferred) for placement and counseling only; score report by September 15. PSAT/NMSQT may be submitted in place of SAT or ACT.

1992 FRESHMAN CLASS PROFILE. 500 men and women applied, 403 accepted; 172 men enrolled, 168 women enrolled. **Academic background:** Mid 50% of enrolled freshmen had ACT composite between 15-24. 90% submitted ACT scores. **Characteristics:** 63% from in state, 70% live in college housing, 6% have minority backgrounds. Average age is 18.

FALL-TERM APPLICATIONS. $15 fee, may be waived for applicants with need. No closing date; priority given to applications received by August 15; applicants notified on a rolling basis beginning on or about November 1. Audition required for music applicants. Essay required. Interview recommended for borderline applicants. Portfolio recommended for art applicants. Deferred admission available.

STUDENT LIFE. Housing: Dormitories (men, women). **Activities:** Student government, magazine, radio, television, yearbook, choral groups, concert band, drama, jazz band, music ensembles, musical theater, pep band, symphony orchestra, Student Missionary Fellowship, Rotaract.

ATHLETICS. Intercollegiate: Baseball M, basketball, cross-country, football M, golf M, soccer M, softball W, tennis, track and field, volleyball W, wrestling M. **Intramural:** Basketball, ice hockey M, softball, volleyball.

STUDENT SERVICES. Aptitude testing, career counseling, employment service for undergraduates, health services, personal counseling, placement service for graduates, special adviser for adult students, services/facilities for handicapped.

ANNUAL EXPENSES. Tuition and fees: $10,659. **Room and board:** $2,895. **Books and supplies:** $400. **Other expenses:** $1,186.

FINANCIAL AID. 87% of freshmen, 99% of continuing students receive some form of aid. 45% of grants, 87% of loans, 53% of jobs based on need. 261 enrolled freshmen were judged to have need, all were offered aid. Academic, music/drama, art, athletic, leadership scholarships available. **Aid applications:** Closing date August 1; priority given to applications received by March 1; applicants notified on or about August 1; must reply within 2 weeks.

ADDRESS/TELEPHONE. Ralph D. Anderson, Dean of Admissions, Northwestern College, 3003 North Snelling Avenue, Roseville, MN 55113. (612) 631-5111. (800) 827-6827.

Oak Hills Bible College
Bemidji, Minnesota CB code: 7247

Admissions: 56% of applicants accepted
Based on:
••• Essay, recommendations, religious affiliation/commitment, school record, test scores
Completion: 85% of freshmen end year in good standing
25% graduate, 22% of these enter graduate study

4-year private Bible college, coed, interdenominational. **Undergraduate enrollment:** 53 men, 59 women full time; 12 men, 13 women part time. **Faculty:** 21 total (11 full time). **Location:** Rural campus in large town; 4 miles from Bemidji. **Calendar:** Quarter. **Microcomputers:** 4 located in computer centers.

DEGREES OFFERED. BA. 11 associate degrees awarded in 1992. 100% in philosophy, religion, theology. 14 bachelor's degrees awarded. 100% in philosophy, religion, theology.

UNDERGRADUATE MAJORS. Associate: Bible studies. **Bachelor's:** Bible studies, missionary studies, religious education, religious music, theological studies.

ACADEMIC PROGRAMS. Cooperative education, honors program, independent study. **Remedial services:** Tutoring. **Placement/credit:** AP, CLEP Subject, institutional tests.

ACADEMIC REQUIREMENTS. Freshmen must earn minimum GPA of 2.0 to continue in good standing. 63% of freshmen return for sophomore year. Students must declare major by end of second year. **Graduation requirements:** 100 hours for associate (22 in major), 197 hours for bachelor's (54 in major). Most students required to take courses in arts/fine arts, English, history, humanities, philosophy/religion, social sciences. **Postgraduate studies:** 50% from 2-year programs enter 4-year programs. 22% enter other graduate study.

FRESHMAN ADMISSIONS. Test requirements: ACT; score report by September 10.

1992 FRESHMAN CLASS PROFILE. 25 men applied, 15 accepted, 10 enrolled; 43 women applied, 23 accepted, 17 enrolled. 37% had high school GPA of 3.0 or higher, 48% between 2.0 and 2.99. 7% were in top tenth and 26% were in top quarter of graduating class. **Academic background:** Mid 50% of enrolled freshmen had ACT composite between 17-26. 67% submitted ACT scores. **Characteristics:** 85% from in state, 92% live in college housing, 4% have minority backgrounds. Average age is 22.

FALL-TERM APPLICATIONS. $20 fee, may be waived for applicants with need. Applicants notified on or about August 30. Deferred admission available.

STUDENT LIFE. Housing: Dormitories (men, women); apartment housing available. **Activities:** Student government, yearbook, choral groups, drama, married students, students older than average, student council, native American students.

ATHLETICS. Intramural: Badminton, basketball M, racquetball, table tennis, volleyball.

STUDENT SERVICES. Career counseling, freshman orientation, health services, special adviser for adult students.

ANNUAL EXPENSES. Tuition and fees (1992-93): $4,335. **Room and board:** $2,400. **Books and supplies:** $500.

FINANCIAL AID. 80% of freshmen, 80% of continuing students receive some form of aid. 96% of grants, all loans, all jobs based on need. Alumni affiliation scholarships available. **Aid applications:** No closing date; priority given to applications received by July 1; applicants notified on a rolling basis beginning on or about July 1.

ADDRESS/TELEPHONE. Monica Bush, Admissions Director, Oak Hills Bible College, 1600 Oak Hills Road, SW, Bemidji, MN 56601. (218) 751-8670 ext. 230.

Pillsbury Baptist Bible College
Owatonna, Minnesota CB code: 0260

4-year private Bible college, coed, affiliated with Minnesota Baptist Association. Founded in 1957. **Accreditation:** Regional candidate. **Undergraduate enrollment:** 140 men, 167 women full time; 16 men, 15 women part time. **Faculty:** 48 total (24 full time), 4 with doctorates or other terminal degrees.

Location: Suburban campus in large town; 65 miles from Minneapolis-St. Paul. **Calendar:** Semester, limited summer session. **Microcomputers:** 18 located in computer centers. **Additional facts:** Separatist fundamental Baptist Bible college.

DEGREES OFFERED. AAS, BA, BS. 7 associate degrees awarded in 1992. 100% in business/office and marketing/distribution. 48 bachelor's degrees awarded. 10% in business and management, 38% teacher education, 6% mathematics, 40% philosophy, religion, theology.

UNDERGRADUATE MAJORS. Associate: Bible studies, secretarial and related programs. **Bachelor's:** Bible studies, biology, business administration and management, business and management, business education, education, elementary education, English, English education, history, home economics education, mathematics, mathematics education, missionary studies, music, music education, religious education, religious music, science education, secondary education, secretarial and related programs, special education, speech/communication/theater education.

ACADEMIC PROGRAMS. Double major, independent study, internships, teacher preparation. **Remedial services:** Remedial instruction. **Placement/credit:** Institutional tests; 8 credit hours maximum for bachelor's degree.

ACADEMIC REQUIREMENTS. Freshmen must earn minimum GPA of 1.7 to continue in good standing. 53% of freshmen return for sophomore year. Students must declare major by end of second year. **Graduation requirements:** 64 hours for associate (25 in major), 128 hours for bachelor's (30 in major). Most students required to take courses in English, history, humanities, mathematics, philosophy/religion, biological/physical sciences, social sciences. **Additional information:** Every student is required to fulfill a major in Bible in addition to another major or two minors.

FRESHMAN ADMISSIONS. Selection criteria: Recommendations, essay or personal statement, religious commitment very important. Test scores, school achievement record, other factors also considered. **Test requirements:** ACT for counseling; score report by August 27.

1992 FRESHMAN CLASS PROFILE. 71 men, 30 women enrolled. **Characteristics:** 95% live in college housing. Average age is 18.

FALL-TERM APPLICATIONS. $25 fee. No closing date; priority given to applications received by July 15; applicants notified on a rolling basis beginning on or about August 27. Essay required.

STUDENT LIFE. Housing: Dormitories (men, women). Campus housing required all 4 years unless living with parents, over age 25, or married. **Activities:** Student government, yearbook, choral groups, drama, music ensembles, pep band, handbell choir, mission prayer band. **Additional information:** Student Life office staff meets physical, social, mental, spiritual needs of student body. Person on call at all times. Religious observance required.

ATHLETICS. Intercollegiate: Baseball M, basketball, golf, soccer M, softball W, volleyball W, wrestling M. **Intramural:** Basketball, golf M, volleyball.

STUDENT SERVICES. Career counseling, freshman orientation, health services, personal counseling, placement service for graduates.

ANNUAL EXPENSES. Tuition and fees (projected): $4,606. **Room and board:** $3,024. **Books and supplies:** $935. **Other expenses:** $1,722.

FINANCIAL AID. 77% of freshmen, 80% of continuing students receive some form of aid. 83% of grants, 89% of loans based on need. All jobs based on criteria other than need. 69 enrolled freshmen were judged to have need, all were offered aid. Academic, music/drama, alumni affiliation, minority scholarships available. **Aid applications:** No closing date; priority given to applications received by July 15; applicants notified on a rolling basis beginning on or about March 15; must reply by registration.

ADDRESS/TELEPHONE. Mr. Larry Tindall, Dean of Enrollment Management, Pillsbury Baptist Bible College, 315 South Grove, Owatonna, MN 55060. (507) 451-2710 ext. 235. (800) 747-4537. Fax: (507) 451-6459.

Rainy River Community College
International Falls, Minnesota CB code: 1637

2-year public community college, coed. Founded in 1967. **Accreditation:** Regional. **Undergraduate enrollment:** 158 men, 253 women full time; 121 men, 256 women part time. **Faculty:** 38 total (28 full time). **Location:** Rural campus in small town; 300 miles from Minneapolis-St. Paul. **Calendar:** Quarter, limited summer session. **Microcomputers:** 60 located in libraries, classrooms, computer centers.

DEGREES OFFERED. AA, AS, AAS. 63 associate degrees awarded in 1992.

UNDERGRADUATE MAJORS. Accounting, advertising, agricultural education, agricultural sciences, anthropology, architecture, art education, art history, biological and physical sciences, biology, botany, business administration and management, business and management, business computer/console/peripheral equipment operation, business data entry equipment operation, business education, chemistry, chiropractic, computer and information sciences, criminal justice studies, dramatic arts, ecology, economics, education, education administration, electrical and electronics equipment repair, elementary education, engineering, engineering and engineering-related technologies, English, English education, finance, fine arts, foreign languages education, forestry and related sciences, forestry production and processing, geography, health education, health sciences, history, home economics, home economics education, human resources development, inorganic chemistry, journalism, junior high education, liberal/general studies, mathematics, mathematics education, mental health/human services, music, music education, music history and appreciation, Native American languages, occupational therapy, Ojibwe language, organic chemistry, parks and recreation management, pharmacy, physical education, physical sciences, physical therapy, physics, political science and government, psychology, radio/television broadcasting, radio/television technology, reading education, renewable natural resources, science education, secondary education, secretarial and related programs, social science education, social sciences, social studies education, social work, sociology, special education, speech/communication/theater education, teacher aide, visual and performing arts, wildlife management, zoology.

ACADEMIC PROGRAMS. 2-year transfer program, dual enrollment of high school students, honors program. **Remedial services:** Learning center, preadmission summer program, reduced course load, remedial instruction, special counselor, tutoring. **Placement/credit:** AP, CLEP Subject, institutional tests.

ACADEMIC REQUIREMENTS. Freshmen must earn minimum GPA of 2.0 to continue in good standing. **Graduation requirements:** 96 hours for associate. Most students required to take courses in English, humanities, mathematics, biological/physical sciences, social sciences.

FRESHMAN ADMISSIONS. Selection criteria: Open admissions. Non-residents need to be in the upper two-thirds of their graduating class, or have an ACT composite of 19 (SAT verbal 390, Math 420), or have completed at least 15 college credits with at least a 2.0 GPA. Selective admissions to nursing program determined by department.

1992 FRESHMAN CLASS PROFILE. 111 men, 154 women enrolled. **Characteristics:** 80% commute. Average age is 21.

FALL-TERM APPLICATIONS. $15 fee. No closing date; applicants notified on a rolling basis. Deferred and early admission available.

STUDENT LIFE. Housing: Apartment, handicapped housing available. **Activities:** Student government, magazine, student newspaper, choral groups, dance, drama, music ensembles, musical theater.

ATHLETICS. NJCAA. **Intercollegiate:** Basketball, ice hockey M, volleyball W. **Intramural:** Archery, badminton, bowling, golf, skiing, softball, table tennis, tennis, volleyball.

STUDENT SERVICES. Aptitude testing, career counseling, employment service for undergraduates, freshman orientation, personal counseling, placement service for graduates, special adviser for adult students, veterans counselor, services/facilities for handicapped.

ANNUAL EXPENSES. Tuition and fees (projected): $1,922, $1,920 additional for out-of-state students. **Room and board:** $1,795 room only. **Books and supplies:** $510. **Other expenses:** $1,200.

FINANCIAL AID. 82% of freshmen, 86% of continuing students receive some form of aid. 96% of grants, 91% of loans, 75% of jobs based on need. Academic, music/drama, art, athletic, leadership, minority scholarships available. **Aid applications:** No closing date; priority given to applications received by August 1; applicants notified on or about July 1; must reply by August 15. **Additional information:** Many scholarship and employment opportunities for applicants showing little or no need.

ADDRESS/TELEPHONE. Sue Collins, Director of Student Development, Rainy River Community College, Highway 11-71, International Falls, MN 56649. (218) 285-7722 ext. 212. (800) 456-3996. Fax: (218) 285-2239.

Rochester Community College
Rochester, Minnesota CB code: 6610

2-year public community college, coed. Founded in 1915. **Accreditation:** Regional. **Undergraduate enrollment:** 916 men, 1,215 women full time; 583 men, 1,287 women part time. **Faculty:** 202 total (97 full time), 9 with doctorates or other terminal degrees. **Location:** Urban campus in small city; 80 miles from Minneapolis-St. Paul. **Calendar:** Quarter, limited summer session. Saturday and extensive evening/early morning classes. **Microcomputers:** 90 located in computer centers. **Special facilities:** Art exhibits, observatory.

DEGREES OFFERED. AA, AS, AAS. 576 associate degrees awarded in 1992. 21% in business and management, 6% business/office and marketing/distribution, 23% allied health, 37% multi/interdisciplinary studies.

UNDERGRADUATE MAJORS. Agricultural sciences, business and management, business and office, business data processing and related programs, civil technology, computer and information sciences, dental hygiene, early childhood education, education, electronic technology, engineering, engineering and engineering-related technologies, fashion merchandising, forestry and related sciences, graphic design, home economics, journalism, law enforcement and corrections technologies, legal secretary, liberal/general studies, marketing and distribution, marketing management, mechanical design technology, medical laboratory technologies, medical secretary, nursing, predentistry, preengineering, prelaw, premedicine, prepharmacy, preveterinary, radiograph medical technology, respiratory therapy, respiratory therapy technology, secretarial and related programs.

ACADEMIC PROGRAMS. 2-year transfer program, dual enrollment of

high school students, independent study, internships, telecourses, weekend college. **Remedial services:** Learning center, reduced course load, remedial instruction, tutoring. **Placement/credit:** AP, CLEP General, institutional tests.

ACADEMIC REQUIREMENTS. Freshmen must earn minimum GPA of 1.85 to continue in good standing. 60% of freshmen return for sophomore year. Students must declare major on application. **Graduation requirements:** 96 hours for associate. Most students required to take courses in arts/fine arts, English, humanities, mathematics, biological/physical sciences, social sciences.

FRESHMAN ADMISSIONS. **Selection criteria:** Selective admissions to medical and other health programs based on course work, class rank, and institutional placement test scores. Open admissions for students from Minnesota, Iowa, Wisconsin, North Dakota, South Dakota, and Ontario, Canada. For specific programs high school biology, chemistry, algebra and/or english are required.

1992 FRESHMAN CLASS PROFILE. 580 men, 827 women enrolled. **Characteristics:** 95% from in state, 93% commute, 6% have minority backgrounds, 2% are foreign students. Average age is 23.

FALL-TERM APPLICATIONS. $15 fee. Closing date September 1; priority given to applications received by August 1; applicants notified on a rolling basis. Early admission available.

STUDENT LIFE. **Housing:** Apartment housing available. **Activities:** Student government, radio, student newspaper, choral groups, concert band, drama, jazz band, music ensembles, musical theater, International Student Association.

ATHLETICS. NJCAA. **Intercollegiate:** Baseball M, basketball, football M, golf, softball W, tennis, volleyball W, wrestling M. **Intramural:** Badminton, basketball, golf, softball, volleyball.

STUDENT SERVICES. Aptitude testing, career counseling, employment service for undergraduates, freshman orientation, health services, on-campus day care, personal counseling, placement service for graduates, services/facilities for handicapped.

ANNUAL EXPENSES. **Tuition and fees (1992-93):** $1,699, $1,688 additional for out-of-state students. **Books and supplies:** $500. **Other expenses:** $950.

FINANCIAL AID. 50% of freshmen, 55% of continuing students receive some form of aid. 93% of grants, 85% of loans, 81% of jobs based on need. 950 enrolled freshmen were judged to have need, 900 were offered aid. Academic, leadership scholarships available. **Aid applications:** No closing date; applicants notified on a rolling basis beginning on or about April 15; must reply by May 1 or within 2 weeks if notified thereafter.

ADDRESS/TELEPHONE. Enrollment Services Office, Rochester Community College, 851 30th Avenue SE, Rochester, MN 55904-4999. (507) 285-7265. Fax: (507) 285-7496.

St. Cloud State University

St. Cloud, Minnesota CB code: 6679

Admissions: 83% of applicants accepted
Based on: ••• School record
•• Test scores
Completion: 85% of freshmen end year in good standing
33% graduate, 7% of these enter graduate study

4-year public university, coed. Founded in 1869. **Accreditation:** Regional. **Undergraduate enrollment:** 6,019 men, 6,134 women full time; 1,019 men, 1,303 women part time. **Graduate enrollment:** 142 men, 196 women full time; 329 men, 905 women part time. **Faculty:** 761 total (627 full time), 458 with doctorates or other terminal degrees. **Location:** Urban campus in large town; 70 miles from Minneapolis-St. Paul. **Calendar:** Quarter, limited summer session. Extensive evening/early morning classes. **Microcomputers:** 400 located in dormitories, libraries, classrooms, computer centers. **Special facilities:** Art gallery, anthropology museum, greenhouse, aquarium, planetarium, nature preserve.

DEGREES OFFERED. AA, BA, BS, BFA, MA, MS, MBA, MFA. 95 associate degrees awarded in 1992. 100% in multi/interdisciplinary studies. 2,707 bachelor's degrees awarded. 24% in business and management, 5% communications, 24% teacher education, 7% letters/literature, 14% social sciences. Graduate degrees offered in 30 major fields of study.

UNDERGRADUATE MAJORS. **Associate:** Military science (Army), prepharmacy. **Bachelor's:** Accounting, advertising, American studies, anthropology, art education, art history, atmospheric sciences and meteorology, aviation management, biological and physical sciences, biology, biomedical science, biotechnology, business administration and management, business and management, business data processing and related programs, ceramics, chemistry, clinical laboratory science, communications, computer and information sciences, criminal justice studies, curriculum and instruction, dental assistant, dramatic arts, early childhood education, earth sciences, East Asian studies, economics, education, electrical/electronics/communications engineering, elementary education, engineering and engineering-related technologies, English, English education, finance, foreign languages education, French, geography, geology, German, graphic design, health education, history, industrial arts education, information sciences and systems, insurance and risk management, international business management, international relations, journalism, junior high education, Latin American studies, liberal/general studies, manufacturing engineering, manufacturing technology, marketing and distribution, marketing management, mathematics, mathematics education, music, music education, music performance, nuclear medical technology, oceanography, operations research, philosophy, photographic technology, physical education, physical sciences, physics, political science and government, predentistry, prelaw, premedicine, preveterinary, psychology, public administration, public health laboratory science, public relations, radio/television broadcasting, reading education, real estate, recreation and community services technologies, science education, science technologies, secondary education, social science education, social sciences, social studies education, social work, sociology, Spanish, special education, speech, speech correction, speech pathology/audiology, speech/communication/theater education, statistics, studio art, trade and industrial education, urban studies, zoology.

ACADEMIC PROGRAMS. Double major, dual enrollment of high school students, education specialist degree, honors program, independent study, internships, student-designed major, study abroad, teacher preparation, telecourses, visiting/exchange student program, cross-registration. **Remedial services:** Learning center, preadmission summer program, remedial instruction, special counselor, tutoring. **ROTC:** Army. **Placement/credit:** AP, CLEP General and Subject, institutional tests; 48 credit hours maximum for bachelor's degree.

ACADEMIC REQUIREMENTS. Freshmen must earn minimum GPA of 2.0 to continue in good standing. 75% of freshmen return for sophomore year. Students must declare major by end of second year. **Graduation requirements:** 96 hours for associate, 192 hours for bachelor's (84 in major). Most students required to take courses in arts/fine arts, computer science, English, humanities, mathematics, philosophy/religion, biological/physical sciences, social sciences. **Postgraduate studies:** 1% enter law school, 1% enter medical school, 1% enter MBA programs, 4% enter other graduate study. **Additional information:** Certificate programs offered in conjunction with bachelor's degree.

FRESHMAN ADMISSIONS. **Selection criteria:** Rank in top half of high school class or minimum ACT composite score of 25 or SAT combined score of 1000 or PSAT/NMSQT score of 100. Division of General Studies may accept applicants ranked between 33rd and 50th percentiles in high school class. ACT is required for students under 21 before registration for classes can take place. Recommended units include English 4, foreign language 2, mathematics 3, physical science 2 and social science 2. 1/2 unit Computer Science is recommended. **Test requirements:** ACT; score report by August 1. PSAT/NMSQT may be submitted in place of SAT or ACT.

1992 FRESHMAN CLASS PROFILE. 1,803 men applied, 1,494 accepted, 883 enrolled; 2,016 women applied, 1,670 accepted, 990 enrolled. 9% were in top tenth and 31% were in top quarter of graduating class. **Academic background:** Mid 50% of enrolled freshmen had ACT composite between 16-23. 95% submitted ACT scores. **Characteristics:** 91% from in state, 66% live in college housing, 4% have minority backgrounds, 1% are foreign students, 5% join fraternities/sororities. Average age is 18.

FALL-TERM APPLICATIONS. $15 fee, may be waived for applicants with need. Closing date August 15; priority given to applications received by May 1; applicants notified on a rolling basis. Audition recommended for music applicants. Portfolio recommended for art applicants. Deferred and early admission available.

STUDENT LIFE. **Housing:** Dormitories (men, women, coed); apartment, fraternity, sorority housing available. Early application recommended if on-campus housing desired. **Activities:** Student government, magazine, radio, student newspaper, television, choral groups, concert band, dance, drama, jazz band, marching band, music ensembles, musical theater, opera, pep band, symphony orchestra, fraternities, sororities.

ATHLETICS. NCAA. **Intercollegiate:** Baseball M, basketball, cross-country, diving, football M, golf, ice hockey, softball W, swimming, tennis, track and field, volleyball W, wrestling M. **Intramural:** Archery, badminton, baseball, basketball, bowling, cross-country, diving, fencing, field hockey M, golf, gymnastics, handball, ice hockey, racquetball, rifle, rowing (crew), rugby, skiing, skin diving, soccer, softball, swimming, table tennis, tennis, track and field, volleyball, water polo, wrestling M.

STUDENT SERVICES. Aptitude testing, career counseling, employment service for undergraduates, freshman orientation, health services, on-campus day care, personal counseling, placement service for graduates, special adviser for adult students, veterans counselor, legal services, services/facilities for handicapped.

ANNUAL EXPENSES. **Tuition and fees (projected):** $2,146, $1,865 additional for out-of-state students. **Room and board:** $2,535. **Books and supplies:** $600. **Other expenses:** $930.

FINANCIAL AID. 42% of freshmen, 55% of continuing students receive some form of aid. 82% of grants, 58% of loans, 31% of jobs based on need. 844 enrolled freshmen were judged to have need, all were offered aid. Academic, music/drama, art, athletic, state/district residency, leadership, alumni affiliation, minority scholarships available. **Aid applications:** No closing date; applicants notified on a rolling basis beginning on or about June 15; must reply within 3 weeks. **Additional information:** State loan program for students who do not qualify for other programs or who need additional aid.

ADDRESS/TELEPHONE. Sherwood Reid, Admissions Director, St. Cloud State University, 720 4th Avenue South, St. Cloud, MN 56301-4498. (612) 255-2244. (800) 369-4260. Fax: (612) 255-4223.

St. John's University
Collegeville, Minnesota CB code: 6624

Admissions: 88% of applicants accepted
Based on: ••• School record
•• Activities, essay, interview, special talents, test scores
Completion: 95% of freshmen end year in good standing
70% graduate, 25% of these enter graduate study

4-year private university and college of arts and sciences and liberal arts, seminary college, men only, affiliated with Roman Catholic Church. Founded in 1857. **Accreditation:** Regional. **Undergraduate enrollment:** 1,746 men full time; 42 men, 24 women part time. **Graduate enrollment:** 45 men, 25 women full time; 10 men, 10 women part time. **Faculty:** 173 total (146 full time), 144 with doctorates or other terminal degrees. **Location:** Rural campus in rural community; 75 miles from Minneapolis-St. Paul, 15 miles from St. Cloud. **Calendar:** 4-1-4. **Microcomputers:** 250 located in libraries, classrooms, computer centers, campus-wide network. **Special facilities:** Biology museum, observatory, art gallery, Ecumenical Center, Hill Monastic Microfilm Library, Liturgical Press, rare books collection, nature preserve. **Additional facts:** Coeducational academic and campus life shared with nearby College of St. Benedict. Affiliated with and operated by Benedictine Abbey of St. John's.

DEGREES OFFERED. BA, MA, M.Div. 418 bachelor's degrees awarded in 1992. 31% in business and management, 10% letters/literature, 8% life sciences, 5% multi/interdisciplinary studies, 7% psychology, 23% social sciences. Graduate degrees offered in 3 major fields of study.

UNDERGRADUATE MAJORS. Accounting, art history, biological and physical sciences, biology, business administration and management, chemistry, classics, communications, computer and information sciences, dramatic arts, early childhood education, economics, elementary education, English, fine arts, food science and nutrition, French, German, history, humanities, mathematics, mathematics/computer science, medical laboratory technologies, medieval studies, music, music performance, nursing, pastoral ministry, peace studies, philosophy, physics, physics/computer science, political science and government, predentistry, preengineering, preforestry, prelaw, premedicine, preoccupational therapy, prepharmacy, preveterinary, psychology, religious education, religious music, secondary education, social sciences, social work, sociology, Spanish, theological studies, visual and performing arts.

ACADEMIC PROGRAMS. Double major, dual enrollment of high school students, honors program, independent study, internships, student-designed major, study abroad, teacher preparation, Washington semester, cross-registration, 5 urban study programs through Higher Education Consortium for Urbab Affairs (HECUA), January term overseas exchange program through the Upper Midwest Association for International Education (UNAIE) Tri-college with St. Cloud State University; liberal arts/career combination in engineering, health sciences. **Remedial services:** Learning center, reduced course load, special counselor, tutoring, writing and mathematics workshops. **ROTC:** Army. **Placement/credit:** AP, IB, institutional tests.

ACADEMIC REQUIREMENTS. Freshmen must earn minimum GPA of 2.0 to continue in good standing. 85% of freshmen return for sophomore year. Students must declare major by end of second year. **Graduation requirements:** 124 hours for bachelor's (40 in major). Most students required to take courses in arts/fine arts, English, foreign languages, history, humanities, mathematics, philosophy/religion, biological/physical sciences, social sciences. **Postgraduate studies:** 5% enter law school, 5% enter medical school, 5% enter MBA programs, 10% enter other graduate study. **Additional information:** Endowed chairs of Jewish studies, humanities, creative thinking, economics and liberal education, management, writer-in-residence, artist-in-residence, rural social ministry.Pre-profession programs in premedicine, predentisty, prelaw, prephysical therapy, preoccupational therapy, preveternary medicine, preforesty, preengineering, predivinity. Formal 3-1-1 engineering program with University of Minnesota, Washington Univeristy-St. Louis, Missouri.

FRESHMAN ADMISSIONS. Selection criteria: Scholastic achievement, rank in class, recommendations, test scores, and personal qualities. Special consideration to minorities and children of alumni. **High school preparation:** 17 units recommended. Recommended units include English 4, foreign language 2, mathematics 3, social science 2 and science 2. **Test requirements:** SAT or ACT; score report by August 15. PSAT/NMSQT may be submitted in place of SAT or ACT.

1992 FRESHMAN CLASS PROFILE. 845 men applied, 745 accepted, 435 enrolled. 68% had high school GPA of 3.0 or higher, 31% between 2.0 and 2.99. 19% were in top tenth and 45% were in top quarter of graduating class. **Academic background:** Mid 50% of enrolled freshmen had SAT-V between 410-500, SAT-M between 440-600; ACT composite between 20-25. 24% submitted SAT scores, 96% submitted ACT scores. **Characteristics:** 80% from in state, 99% live in college housing, 7% have minority backgrounds, 1% are foreign students. Average age is 18.

FALL-TERM APPLICATIONS. $20 fee, may be waived for applicants with need. No closing date; priority given to applications received by February 15; applicants notified on a rolling basis; Must reply by registration. Essay required. Interview recommended for academically weak applicants. Audition recommended for music, theater applicants. Portfolio recommended for art applicants. Deferred and early admission available.

STUDENT LIFE. Housing: Dormitories (men); apartment, cooperative housing available. Earth-sheltered, solar-heated apartments available to upperclass students. **Activities:** Student government, magazine, radio, student newspaper, yearbook, foreign student publication, literary journal, choral groups, concert band, dance, drama, jazz band, music ensembles, musical theater, opera, pep band, symphony orchestra, forum debate society, Volunteers in Service to Others, Social Action Coalition, service fraternity, Amnesty International, campus ministry, Fellowship of Christian Athletes, College Republicans, Young Democrats, AIESEC Peer Resource Program, International Students Organization.

ATHLETICS. NCAA. **Intercollegiate:** Baseball, basketball, cross-country, diving, football, golf, ice hockey, soccer, swimming, tennis, track and field, wrestling. **Intramural:** Badminton, baseball, basketball, golf, handball, ice hockey, lacrosse, racquetball, rifle, rowing (crew), rugby, sailing, skiing, soccer, softball, swimming, table tennis, tennis, track and field, volleyball, water polo, wrestling.

STUDENT SERVICES. Aptitude testing, career counseling, employment service for undergraduates, freshman orientation, health services, personal counseling, placement service for graduates, services/facilities for handicapped.

ANNUAL EXPENSES. Tuition and fees: $11,428. **Room and board:** $3,936. **Books and supplies:** $500. **Other expenses:** $500.

FINANCIAL AID. 70% of freshmen, 70% of continuing students receive some form of aid. 95% of grants, 77% of loans, 79% of jobs based on need. 325 enrolled freshmen were judged to have need, all were offered aid. Academic, music/drama, art, leadership scholarships available. **Aid applications:** No closing date; priority given to applications received by March 1; applicants notified on a rolling basis beginning on or about March 1; must reply by May 1 or within 3 weeks if notified thereafter.

ADDRESS/TELEPHONE. Rick Smith, Dean of Admissions and Enrollment Management, St. John's University, PO Box 7155, Collegeville, MN 56321. (612) 363-2196. (800) 245-6467. Fax: (612) 363-2115.

St. Mary's Campus of the College of St. Catherine
Minneapolis, Minnesota CB code: 6701

Admissions: 79% of applicants accepted
Based on: ••• Essay
•• Recommendations, school record
• Activities, interview, test scores
Completion: 80% of freshmen end year in good standing
60% graduate, 15% of these enter 4-year programs

2-year private branch campus, health science college, coed, affiliated with Roman Catholic Church. Founded in 1964. **Accreditation:** Regional. **Undergraduate enrollment:** 45 men, 246 women full time; 93 men, 625 women part time. **Faculty:** 83 total (37 full time), 5 with doctorates or other terminal degrees. **Location:** Urban campus in very large city; 1 mile from downtown. **Calendar:** 4-1-4, extensive summer session. Saturday and extensive evening/early morning classes. **Microcomputers:** 30 located in computer centers. **Special facilities:** Experiential learning laboratories. **Additional facts:** Medical internships (clinicals) at over 150 sites in the Twin City's metropolitan area.

DEGREES OFFERED. AA, AAS. 215 associate degrees awarded in 1992. 49% in health sciences, 48% allied health. Graduate degrees offered in 1 major field of study.

UNDERGRADUATE MAJORS. Liberal/general studies, medical records technology, nursing, occupational therapy assistant, physical therapy assistant, radiograph medical technology, respiratory therapy, respiratory therapy technology, ultrasound technology.

ACADEMIC PROGRAMS. 2-year transfer program, internships, cross-registration. **Remedial services:** Learning center, preadmission summer program, reduced course load, remedial instruction, special counselor, tutoring. **Placement/credit:** Institutional tests.

ACADEMIC REQUIREMENTS. No policy requiring minimum GPA; records of students having academic difficulty are reviewed individually. 70% of freshmen return for sophomore year. Students must declare major on application. **Graduation requirements:** 65 hours for associate (36 in major). Most students required to take courses in arts/fine arts, English, philosophy/religion, biological/physical sciences, social sciences. **Additional information:** Associate of Arts transfer program offered.

FRESHMAN ADMISSIONS. Selection criteria: Essay, school record, recommendations important. Other factors considered. Special requirements for some programs. For nursing applicants, chemistry within last 7 years and minimum 2.0 high school GPA required. Algebra recommended for respiratory therapy applicants. Algebra required for radiography students.

1992 FRESHMAN CLASS PROFILE. 906 men and women applied, 712 accepted; 70 men enrolled, 400 women enrolled. **Characteristics:** 94% from in state, 90% commute, 6% have minority backgrounds. Average age is 28.

FALL-TERM APPLICATIONS. $20 fee, may be waived for applicants with need. No closing date; priority given to applications received by April 1; applicants notified on a rolling basis beginning on or about December 1; must reply within 3 weeks. Essay required. Interview recommended for chemical dependency family treatment, Montessori teacher training applicants. CRDA. Deferred admission available.

STUDENT LIFE. Housing: Dormitories (coed). Women's dormitory and women's apartments available at St. Catherine's campus. **Activities:** Student government, student newspaper, yearbook, campus ministry. **Additional information:** St. Mary's students may use the facilities at the St. Catherine Campus and participate in student organizations there.

STUDENT SERVICES. Aptitude testing, career counseling, employment service for undergraduates, freshman orientation, health services, personal counseling, placement service for graduates, special adviser for adult students, services/facilities for handicapped.

ANNUAL EXPENSES. Tuition and fees: $8,550. **Room and board:** $930 room only. **Books and supplies:** $500. **Other expenses:** $900.

FINANCIAL AID. 77% of freshmen, 78% of continuing students receive some form of aid. All grants, 67% of loans, 88% of jobs based on need. Academic scholarships available. **Aid applications:** No closing date; priority given to applications received by June 1; applicants notified on a rolling basis beginning on or about April 15; must reply within 15 days.

ADDRESS/TELEPHONE. Pamela A. Johnson, Director of Admission and Financial Aid, St. Mary's Campus of the College of St. Catherine, 2500 South Sixth Street, Minneapolis, MN 55454. (612) 690-7800. (800) 945-4599. Fax: (612) 690-7849.

St. Mary's College of Minnesota
Winona, Minnesota — CB code: 6632

Admissions: 97% of applicants accepted
Based on:
••• School record, test scores
•• Essay, interview
• Activities, recommendations, special talents
Completion: 81% of freshmen end year in good standing
61% graduate, 18% of these enter graduate study

4-year private liberal arts college, coed, affiliated with Roman Catholic Church. Founded in 1912. **Accreditation:** Regional. **Undergraduate enrollment:** 676 men, 553 women full time; 27 men, 56 women part time. **Graduate enrollment:** 66 men, 129 women full time; 1,375 men, 3,439 women part time. **Faculty:** 245 total (83 full time), 124 with doctorates or other terminal degrees. **Location:** Rural campus in large town; 110 miles from Minneapolis-St. Paul, 45 miles from Rochester. **Calendar:** Semester. **Microcomputers:** 300 located in computer centers. **Special facilities:** Woodland and stream nature preserve, observatory, art gallery.

DEGREES OFFERED. BA, BS, MA, MS. 280 bachelor's degrees awarded in 1992. 27% in business and management, 10% communications, 6% teacher education, 5% life sciences, 24% social sciences, 6% visual and performing arts. Graduate degrees offered in 10 major fields of study.

UNDERGRADUATE MAJORS. Accounting, biological and physical sciences, biology, business administration and management, business and management, business education, chemistry, communications, computer and information sciences, creative writing, criminal justice studies, cytotechnology, dramatic arts, early childhood education, economics, elementary education, English, English education, English literature, environmental science, fine arts, foreign languages (multiple emphasis), foreign languages education, French, graphic design, history, humanities and social sciences, international business management, junior high education, law enforcement and corrections, liberal/general studies, marketing and distribution, mathematics, mathematics education, medical laboratory technologies, music, music education, music performance, nuclear medical technology, philosophy, physical sciences, physical therapy, physics, political science and government, psychology, public administration, religious education, science education, secondary education, social sciences, social studies education, social work, sociology, Spanish, speech/communication/theater education, statistics, studio art, telecommunications, theological studies, visual and performing arts.

ACADEMIC PROGRAMS. Accelerated program, cooperative education, double major, dual enrollment of high school students, external degree, honors program, independent study, internships, student-designed major, study abroad, teacher preparation, cross-registration; liberal arts/career combination in engineering, health sciences. **Remedial services:** Learning center, preadmission summer program, reduced course load, remedial instruction, special counselor, tutoring. **Placement/credit:** AP, CLEP Subject, institutional tests; 30 credit hours maximum for bachelor's degree.

ACADEMIC REQUIREMENTS. Freshmen must earn minimum GPA of 1.6 to continue in good standing. 68% of freshmen return for sophomore year. Students must declare major by end of second year. **Graduation requirements:** 122 hours for bachelor's. Most students required to take courses in arts/fine arts, English, humanities, mathematics, philosophy/religion, biological/physical sciences, social sciences. **Postgraduate studies:** 1% enter law school, 1% enter medical school, 1% enter MBA programs, 15% enter other graduate study.

FRESHMAN ADMISSIONS. Selection criteria: Minimum 2.2 GPA, rank in top 50% of graduating class, ACT composite score of 18 required. Recommendations, school and community activities considered. **High school preparation:** 16 units required. Required and recommended units include biological science 1, English 4, mathematics 2-3 and science 2-3. Foreign language 2 and social science 2 recommended. **Test requirements:** SAT or ACT (ACT preferred); score report by July 1.

1992 FRESHMAN CLASS PROFILE. 831 men and women applied, 804 accepted; 206 men enrolled, 167 women enrolled. 26% had high school GPA of 3.0 or higher, 50% between 2.0 and 2.99. 14% were in top tenth and 30% were in top quarter of graduating class. **Academic background:** Mid 50% of enrolled freshmen had ACT composite between 18-23. 87% submitted ACT scores. **Characteristics:** 44% from in state, 98% live in college housing, 7% have minority backgrounds, 1% are foreign students. Average age is 18.

FALL-TERM APPLICATIONS. $20 fee, may be waived for applicants with need. Closing date June 1; priority given to applications received by April 1; applicants notified on a rolling basis; must reply by May 1 or within 3 weeks if notified thereafter. Essay required. Interview recommended for academically marginal applicants. Audition recommended. Portfolio recommended. CRDA. Deferred and early admission available.

STUDENT LIFE. Housing: Dormitories (men, women, coed); apartment housing available. Some residence spaces reserved for student-directed communities. **Activities:** Student government, film, magazine, radio, student newspaper, television, choral groups, concert band, dance, drama, jazz band, music ensembles, musical theater, symphony orchestra, chapel choir, fraternities, sororities, social justice coalition, peer ministry, volunteer services.

ATHLETICS. NCAA. **Intercollegiate:** Baseball M, basketball, cross-country, golf M, ice hockey M, skiing, soccer, softball W, tennis, track and field, volleyball W. **Intramural:** Badminton M, baseball M, basketball, bowling, golf, ice hockey M, racquetball, skiing, soccer, softball, tennis, volleyball.

STUDENT SERVICES. Aptitude testing, career counseling, employment service for undergraduates, freshman orientation, health services, personal counseling, placement service for graduates, services/facilities for handicapped.

ANNUAL EXPENSES. Tuition and fees: $10,380. **Room and board:** $3,470. **Books and supplies:** $350. **Other expenses:** $520.

FINANCIAL AID. 70% of freshmen, 60% of continuing students receive some form of aid. 90% of grants, 85% of loans, 79% of jobs based on need. 223 enrolled freshmen were judged to have need, all were offered aid. Academic, music/drama, art, leadership scholarships available. **Aid applications:** No closing date; priority given to applications received by March 15; applicants notified on a rolling basis beginning on or about February 15.

ADDRESS/TELEPHONE. Anthony Piscitiello, Vice President for Admissions, St. Mary's College of Minnesota, PO Campus Box 2, 700 Terrace Heights, Winona, MN 55987-1399. (507) 457-1700. (800) 635-5987. Fax: (507) 457-1633.

St. Olaf College
Northfield, Minnesota — CB code: 6638

Admissions: 69% of applicants accepted
Based on:
••• School record
•• Special talents, test scores
• Activities, essay, interview, recommendations, religious affiliation/commitment
Completion: 95% of freshmen end year in good standing
81% graduate, 24% of these enter graduate study

4-year private liberal arts college, coed, affiliated with Evangelical Lutheran Church in America. Founded in 1874. **Accreditation:** Regional. **Undergraduate enrollment:** 1,329 men, 1,574 women full time; 48 men, 64 women part time. **Faculty:** 329 total (260 full time), 251 with doctorates or other terminal degrees. **Location:** Rural campus in large town; 40 miles from Minneapolis-St. Paul. **Calendar:** 4-1-4, extensive summer session. **Microcomputers:** 321 located in dormitories, libraries, classrooms, computer centers. **Special facilities:** Norwegian-American Historical Society Archives, Kierkegaard library, 5 art galleries, music library, science library.

DEGREES OFFERED. BA. 729 bachelor's degrees awarded in 1992. 5% in area and ethnic studies, 5% health sciences, 7% languages, 11% letters/literature, 10% life sciences, 10% mathematics, 6% physical sciences, 8% psychology, 22% social sciences, 8% visual and performing arts.

UNDERGRADUATE MAJORS. Afro-American (black) studies, American literature, American studies, art education, art history, Asian studies, biology, chemistry, classics, comparative literature, dance, design in home economics, dramatic arts, economics, elementary education, elementary music education, English, English education, English literature, family/consumer resource management, fine arts, food science and nutrition, foreign languages education, French, German, Greek (classical), health education, health sciences, Hispanic American studies, history, home economics education, individual and family development, Latin, mathematics, mathematics education, music, music education, music history and appreciation, music performance, music theory and composition, nursing, nutritional education, philosophy, physical education, physics, political science and government, predentistry, preengineering, prelaw, premedicine, prepharmacy, preveterinary, psychology, religion, religious music, Russian, Russian and Slavic studies, Scandinavian languages, science education, secondary education, social studies education, social work, sociology, Spanish, speech, speech/communication/theater education, studio art, urban studies, women's studies.

ACADEMIC PROGRAMS. Accelerated program, double major, independent study, internships, student-designed major, study abroad, teacher preparation, Washington semester, cross-registration, 3-2 engineering program with Washington University in Missouri, elementary education program with Augsburg College; liberal arts/career combination in engineering; combined bachelor's/graduate program in law. **Remedial services:** Learning center, reduced course load, special counselor, tutoring. **Placement/credit:** AP, institutional tests; 20 credit hours maximum for bachelor's degree.

ACADEMIC REQUIREMENTS. Freshmen must earn minimum GPA of 2.0 to continue in good standing. 90% of freshmen return for sophomore year. Students must declare major by end of second year. **Graduation requirements:** 140 hours for bachelor's. Most students required to take courses in arts/fine arts, English, foreign languages, history, humanities, mathematics, philosophy/religion, biological/physical sciences, social sciences. **Postgraduate studies:** 2% enter law school, 3% enter medical school, 2% enter MBA programs, 17% enter other graduate study. **Additional information:** 50-60% of students participate in international studies program. Paracollege allows students to earn bachelor's degree through tutorials and individualized programs of study.

FRESHMAN ADMISSIONS. Selection criteria: School achievement record most important, followed by recommendations, activities, test scores. Special consideration given to Lutherans, children of alumni, minority applicants. **High school preparation:** 15 units required. Required and recommended units include English 3-4 and mathematics 2-4. Foreign language 2 and science 2 recommended. **Test requirements:** SAT or ACT; score report by February 15. PSAT/NMSQT may be submitted in place of SAT or ACT.

1992 FRESHMAN CLASS PROFILE. 917 men applied, 631 accepted, 293 enrolled; 1,288 women applied, 895 accepted, 412 enrolled. 95% had high school GPA of 3.0 or higher, 5% between 2.0 and 2.99. 37% were in top tenth and 70% were in top quarter of graduating class. **Academic background:** Mid 50% of enrolled freshmen had SAT-V between 460-590, SAT-M between 510-650; ACT composite between 23-28. 55% submitted SAT scores, 86% submitted ACT scores. **Characteristics:** 57% from in state, 100% live in college housing, 8% have minority backgrounds, 3% are foreign students. Average age is 18.

FALL-TERM APPLICATIONS. $25 fee. No closing date; priority given to applications received by February 1; applicants notified on a rolling basis beginning on or about January 10; must reply by April 1 or within 2 weeks if notified thereafter, unless applying to other CRDA schools. Audition required for music applicants. Essay required. Interview recommended. CRDA. Deferred and early admission available. EDP-S. Extension of reply date available upon written request to admissions office.

STUDENT LIFE. Housing: Dormitories (coed). College-owned honor houses near campus for students emphasizing service to college and/or community. **Activities:** Student government, magazine, radio, student newspaper, yearbook, choral groups, concert band, dance, drama, jazz band, music ensembles, musical theater, pep band, symphony orchestra, St. Olaf Christian Outreach, men's and women's service, political and ethnic groups, total of 94 organizations.

ATHLETICS. NCAA. **Intercollegiate:** Baseball M, basketball, cross-country, diving, football M, golf, ice hockey M, skiing, soccer, softball W, swimming, tennis, track and field, volleyball W, wrestling M. **Intramural:** Badminton, basketball, bowling, handball, racquetball, skiing, soccer, softball, swimming, table tennis, tennis, volleyball, water polo.

STUDENT SERVICES. Aptitude testing, career counseling, employment service for undergraduates, freshman orientation, health services, personal counseling, placement service for graduates, minority counseling, student affairs office, services/facilities for handicapped.

ANNUAL EXPENSES. Tuition and fees: $13,560. **Room and board:** $3,640. **Books and supplies:** $550. **Other expenses:** $550.

FINANCIAL AID. 67% of freshmen, 60% of continuing students receive some form of aid. 95% of grants, 89% of loans, 90% of jobs based on need. 482 enrolled freshmen were judged to have need, all were offered aid. **Aid applications:** No closing date; priority given to applications received by February 15; applicants notified on a rolling basis beginning on or about January 10; must reply within 2 weeks. **Additional information:** Limited number of music lesson fee waivers available for music majors, awarded on audition basis only.

ADDRESS/TELEPHONE. Bruce K. Moe, Vice President for Admissions and Financial Aid, St. Olaf College, 1520 St. Olaf Avenue, Northfield, MN 55057-1098. (507) 646-3025. Fax: (507) 646-3549.

St. Paul Technical College
St. Paul, Minnesota — CB code: 0534

2-year public technical college, coed. Founded in 1919. **Accreditation:** Regional. **Undergraduate enrollment:** 1,148 men, 1,144 women full time; 747 men, 741 women part time. **Faculty:** 565 total (115 full time), 4 with doctorates or other terminal degrees. **Location:** Urban campus in large city. **Calendar:** Quarter. **Microcomputers:** Located in classrooms, computer centers.

DEGREES OFFERED. AAS. 34 associate degrees awarded in 1992. 10% in business/office and marketing/distribution, 20% engineering technologies, 70% allied health.

UNDERGRADUATE MAJORS. Accounting, automated manufacturing technology, child development/care/guidance, interpreter for the deaf, manufacturing technology, medical laboratory technologies, microcomputer software, personnel management, respiratory therapy, word processing.

ACADEMIC PROGRAMS. Internships. **Remedial services:** Learning center, preadmission summer program, reduced course load, remedial instruction, special counselor, tutoring. **Placement/credit:** CLEP General, institutional tests.

ACADEMIC REQUIREMENTS. Students must declare major on application. **Graduation requirements:** 110 hours for associate (110 in major). Most students required to take courses in English, mathematics.

FRESHMAN ADMISSIONS. Selection criteria: Open admissions.

1992 FRESHMAN CLASS PROFILE. 860 men, 858 women enrolled. **Characteristics:** 95% from in state, 100% commute. Average age is 26.

FALL-TERM APPLICATIONS. No fee. No closing date; applicants notified on a rolling basis; must reply within 2 weeks. Interview recommended.

STUDENT LIFE. Activities: Student government, magazine, student newspaper, Business Professionals Of America, Vocational-Industrial Clubs of America, student senate.

STUDENT SERVICES. Aptitude testing, career counseling, employment service for undergraduates, freshman orientation, health services, on-campus day care, personal counseling, placement service for graduates, special adviser for adult students, veterans counselor, services/facilities for handicapped.

ANNUAL EXPENSES. Tuition and fees (1992-93): $1,663, $1,618 additional for out-of-state students. Residents of Wisconsin, and South Dakota pay in-state tuition rate. **Books and supplies:** $800.

FINANCIAL AID. 82% of continuing students receive some form of aid. All grants, 74% of loans, all jobs based on need. State/district residency, minority scholarships available. **Aid applications:** No closing date.

ADDRESS/TELEPHONE. Milo Loken, Vice President, St. Paul Technical College, 235 Marshall Avenue, St. Paul, MN 55102-9913. (612) 221-1300. (800) 227-6029. Fax: (612) 221-1416.

Saint Cloud Technical College
St. Cloud, Minnesota — CB code: 1986

2-year public technical college. **Accreditation:** Regional. **Undergraduate enrollment:** 950 men, 1,050 women full time; 450 men, 400 women part time. **Location:** Urban campus in large town; 65 miles from Minneapolis/St. Paul. **Microcomputers:** 225 located in classrooms, computer centers, campus-wide network. **Special facilities:** Interactive classrooms available for those pursuing AAS degree at Saint Cloud State University.

DEGREES OFFERED. AAS. 40 associate degrees awarded in 1992.

UNDERGRADUATE MAJORS. Accounting, advertising, architectural technologies, architecture, automotive mechanics, business and management, business and office, business computer/console/peripheral equipment operation, business data programming, computer and information sciences, computer graphics, computer programming, computer servicing technology, computer technology, drafting, drafting and design technology, electrical technology, electronic technology, finance, instrumentation technology, marketing and distribution, mechanical design technology, microcomputer software, public relations, respiratory therapy, retailing, taxation, telecommunications.

ACADEMIC PROGRAMS. Telecourses. **Remedial services:** Learning center, preadmission summer program, reduced course load, remedial instruction, special counselor, tutoring. **Placement/credit:** IB, institutional tests.

ACADEMIC REQUIREMENTS. Freshmen must earn minimum GPA of 2.0 to continue in good standing. 80% of freshmen return for sophomore year. Students must declare major on application. **Graduation requirements:** Most students required to take courses in computer science, English, mathematics, social sciences. **Additional information:** English language proficiency classes provided for foreign students.

FRESHMAN ADMISSIONS. Selection criteria: Open admissions. Math and science classes recommended for technical programs but not required.

1992 FRESHMAN CLASS PROFILE. 600 men, 650 women enrolled. 20% had high school GPA of 3.0 or higher, 60% between 2.0 and 2.99. **Characteristics:** 100% commute.

FALL-TERM APPLICATIONS. No fee. No closing date. Early admission available.

STUDENT LIFE. Housing: Have privately owned dormitory next to campus. **Activities:** Student government, film, student newspaper, television.

ATHLETICS. Intramural: Basketball, bowling, softball, track and field.

STUDENT SERVICES. Aptitude testing, career counseling, employment service for undergraduates, freshman orientation, on-campus day care, personal counseling, placement service for graduates, special adviser for adult students, veterans counselor, services/facilities for handicapped.

ANNUAL EXPENSES. Tuition and fees (1992-93):

ADDRESS/TELEPHONE. Rosa Rodriguez, Student Affairs Manager, Saint Cloud Technical College, 1540 Northway Drive, St. Cloud, MN 56303. (612)654-5089. Fax: (612)654-5981.

Southwest State University
Marshall, Minnesota CB code: 6703

Admissions: 88% of applicants accepted
Based on: ••• School record, test scores
Completion: 80% of freshmen end year in good standing
33% graduate, 12% of these enter graduate study

4-year public liberal arts, technical college, coed. Founded in 1963. **Accreditation:** Regional. **Undergraduate enrollment:** 1,124 men, 1,209 women full time; 142 men, 267 women part time. **Faculty:** 131 total (130 full time), 84 with doctorates or other terminal degrees. **Location:** Rural campus in large town; 150 miles from Minneapolis-St. Paul. **Calendar:** Quarter, limited summer session. **Microcomputers:** 460 located in dormitories, libraries, classrooms, computer centers. **Special facilities:** Natural history museum, anthropology museum, planetarium, William Whipple Gallery.

DEGREES OFFERED. AS, BA, BS. 8 associate degrees awarded in 1992. 63% in business and management, 37% business/office and marketing/distribution. 369 bachelor's degrees awarded. 35% in business and management, 5% business/office and marketing/distribution, 22% education, 5% engineering technologies, 12% social sciences.

UNDERGRADUATE MAJORS. Associate: Accounting, agribusiness, agricultural business and management, business administration and management, business and office, electrical technology, engineering and engineering-related technologies, manufacturing technology, marketing and distribution, marketing management, mechanical design technology, office supervision and management, secretarial and related programs. **Bachelor's:** Accounting, agribusiness, agricultural business and management, art education, biological and physical sciences, biology, business administration and management, business and management, business and office, business education, chemistry, clinical laboratory science, communications, computer and information sciences, creative writing, dramatic arts, early childhood behavior, early childhood education, education, electrical technology, elementary education, engineering and engineering-related technologies, English, English education, fine arts, food management, health education, history, hotel/motel and restaurant management, humanities and social sciences, information sciences and systems, junior high education, liberal/general studies, manufacturing technology, marketing and distribution, marketing management, mathematics, mathematics education, mechanical design technology, music, music education, office supervision and management, painting, physical education, physical sciences, physics, political science and government, prelaw, psychology, public relations, radio/television broadcasting, science education, sculpture, secondary education, secretarial and related programs, social science education, social sciences, social studies education, social work, sociology, speech, speech/communication/theater education.

ACADEMIC PROGRAMS. Accelerated program, cooperative education, double major, dual enrollment of high school students, honors program, independent study, internships, student-designed major, study abroad, teacher preparation, visiting/exchange student program, cross-registration, 2+2 bachelor's programs with Willmar Community College and Cooperative Nursing Program with Metro State. **Remedial services:** Learning center, reduced course load, remedial instruction, special counselor, tutoring. **Placement/credit:** AP, CLEP General and Subject, institutional tests; 30 credit hours maximum for associate degree; 30 credit hours maximum for bachelor's degree.

ACADEMIC REQUIREMENTS. Freshmen must earn minimum GPA of 2.0 to continue in good standing. 74% of freshmen return for sophomore year. **Graduation requirements:** 96 hours for associate, 192 hours for bachelor's. Most students required to take courses in English, mathematics, biological/physical sciences, social sciences. **Postgraduate studies:** 55% from 2-year programs enter 4-year programs.

FRESHMAN ADMISSIONS. Selection criteria: Class rank in top half of class or SAT combined score of 900 or ACT composite score of 21 or PSAT/NMSQT combined score of 90. **High school preparation:** 15 units recommended. Recommended units include English 4, foreign language 2, mathematics 3, social science 3 and science 3. **Test requirements:** SAT or ACT (ACT preferred); score report by September 9. PSAT/NMSQT may be submitted in place of SAT or ACT.

1992 FRESHMAN CLASS PROFILE. 1,508 men and women applied, 1,328 accepted; 781 enrolled. 45% had high school GPA of 3.0 or higher, 37% between 2.0 and 2.99. 14% were in top tenth and 23% were in top quarter of graduating class. **Academic background:** Mid 50% of enrolled freshmen had ACT composite between 17-22. 91% submitted ACT scores. **Characteristics:** 85% from in state, 67% live in college housing, 5% have minority backgrounds, 1% are foreign students. Average age is 19.

FALL-TERM APPLICATIONS. $15 fee. No closing date; applicants notified on a rolling basis. Interview recommended for academically weak applicants. Audition recommended for music applicants. Deferred and early admission available.

STUDENT LIFE. Housing: Dormitories (men, women, coed). **Activities:** Student government, film, magazine, radio, student newspaper, television, choral groups, concert band, dance, drama, jazz band, marching band, music ensembles, musical theater, pep band, symphony orchestra, Black Student Union, International Student Organization, Inter-Varsity Christian Fellowship, Lutheran Student Commission, Student Activities Committee, Republican Speakers Club, Young DFL, Non-Traditional Students Resource Center.

ATHLETICS. NAIA. **Intercollegiate:** Baseball M, basketball, football M, softball W, tennis W, volleyball W, wrestling M. **Intramural:** Badminton, basketball, ice hockey M, rugby, sailing, softball, tennis, track and field, volleyball, wrestling M.

STUDENT SERVICES. Aptitude testing, career counseling, employment service for undergraduates, freshman orientation, health services, on-campus day care, personal counseling, placement service for graduates, special adviser for adult students, veterans counselor, services/facilities for handicapped.

ANNUAL EXPENSES. Tuition and fees (projected): $2,650, $2,000 additional for out-of-state students. **Room and board:** $2,750. **Books and supplies:** $650. **Other expenses:** $1,500.

FINANCIAL AID. 82% of freshmen, 85% of continuing students receive some form of aid. 90% of grants, 83% of loans, 36% of jobs based on need. Academic, music/drama, athletic, state/district residency, leadership, alumni affiliation, minority scholarships available. **Aid applications:** No closing date; priority given to applications received by April 14; applicants notified on a rolling basis beginning on or about April 16; must reply within 15 days.

ADDRESS/TELEPHONE. Charles Richardson, Director of Admissions, Southwest State University, AS 108, Marshall, MN 56258-1598. (507) 537-6286. (800) 533-8605. Fax: (507) 537-7154.

University of Minnesota: Crookston
Crookston, Minnesota CB code: 6893

2-year public technical college, coed. Founded in 1965. **Accreditation:** Regional. **Undergraduate enrollment:** 424 men, 307 women full time; 233 men, 388 women part time. **Faculty:** 76 total (49 full time), 13 with doctorates or other terminal degrees. **Location:** Rural campus in small town; 160 miles from Winnipeg, Canada, 300 miles from Minneapolis-St. Paul. **Calendar:** Quarter, limited summer session. **Microcomputers:** 90 located in dormitories, libraries, classrooms. **Special facilities:** Natural history area near campus.

DEGREES OFFERED. AS, AAS. 137 associate degrees awarded in 1992. 41% in agriculture, 59% business and management, 20% business/office and marketing/distribution.

UNDERGRADUATE MAJORS. Accounting, agribusiness, agricultural business and management, agricultural economics, agricultural mechanics, agricultural production, agricultural sciences, agricultural/aviation technology, agronomy, animal sciences, biological laboratory technology, business and management, child development/care/guidance, court reporting, dairy, equestrian science, fashion merchandising, finance, food production/management/services, food science and nutrition, food sciences, forestry and related sciences, horticultural science, horticulture, hospitality and recreation marketing, hotel/motel and restaurant management, information sciences and systems, institutional management, legal secretary, marketing and distribution, office supervision and management, ornamental horticulture, parks and recreation management, real estate, renewable natural resources, science technologies, secretarial and related programs, soil sciences, word processing.

ACADEMIC PROGRAMS. 2-year transfer program, double major, dual enrollment of high school students, internships, study abroad, cross-registration. **Remedial services:** Learning center, remedial instruction, special counselor, tutoring. **Placement/credit:** AP, CLEP General; 12 credit hours maximum for associate degree.

ACADEMIC REQUIREMENTS. Freshmen must earn minimum GPA

of 2.0 to continue in good standing. 71% of freshmen return for sophomore year. Students must declare major by end of first year. **Graduation requirements:** 105 hours for associate (70 in major). Most students required to take courses in English, history, social sciences.

FRESHMAN ADMISSIONS. Selection criteria: Open admissions.

1992 FRESHMAN CLASS PROFILE. 382 men applied, 382 accepted, 255 enrolled; 347 women applied, 347 accepted, 170 enrolled. 4% were in top tenth and 15% were in top quarter of graduating class. **Characteristics:** 66% from in state, 55% commute, 4% have minority backgrounds. Average age is 18.

FALL-TERM APPLICATIONS. $25 fee. Closing date September 1; applicants notified on a rolling basis. CRDA. Deferred admission available.

STUDENT LIFE. Housing: Dormitories (men, coed); apartment housing available. **Activities:** Student government, radio, student newspaper, television, yearbook, choral groups, concert band, drama.

ATHLETICS. NJCAA. **Intercollegiate:** Baseball M, basketball, football M, ice hockey M, softball W, volleyball W. **Intramural:** Badminton, basketball, racquetball, table tennis, tennis, volleyball.

STUDENT SERVICES. Aptitude testing, career counseling, employment service for undergraduates, freshman orientation, health services, on-campus day care, personal counseling, placement service for graduates, veterans counselor, services/facilities for handicapped.

ANNUAL EXPENSES. Tuition and fees (1992-93): $2,678, $5,418 additional for out-of-state students. North Dakota and Wisconsin students pay less than other non-residents. **Room and board:** $3,355. **Books and supplies:** $450. **Other expenses:** $1,250.

FINANCIAL AID. 80% of freshmen, 80% of continuing students receive some form of aid. 88% of grants, 73% of loans, 75% of jobs based on need. Academic, leadership, alumni affiliation, minority scholarships available. **Aid applications:** No closing date; priority given to applications received by April 30; applicants notified on a rolling basis beginning on or about May 1; must reply within 2 weeks.

ADDRESS/TELEPHONE. John Bywater, Director of Admissions, University of Minnesota: Crookston, 4 Hill Hall, Crookston, MN 56716. (218) 281-6510. (800) 232-6466 ext. 369. Fax: (218) 281-5223 ext. 369.

University of Minnesota: Duluth
Duluth, Minnesota — CB code: 6873

Admissions: 77% of applicants accepted
Based on:
- ••• School record
- •• Test scores
- • Activities, recommendations, special talents

Completion: 77% of freshmen end year in good standing
37% graduate

4-year public university, coed. Founded in 1947. **Accreditation:** Regional. **Undergraduate enrollment:** 3,736 men, 3,285 women full time. **Graduate enrollment:** 239 men, 238 women full time. **Faculty:** 409 total (379 full time), 333 with doctorates or other terminal degrees. **Location:** Suburban campus in small city; 150 miles from Minneapolis-St. Paul. Extensive evening/early morning classes. **Microcomputers:** 180 located in dormitories, libraries, classrooms, computer centers, campus-wide network. **Special facilities:** Marshall Performing Arts Center, Tweed Museum and Art Gallery, Alworth Planetarium.

DEGREES OFFERED. BA, BS, BFA, MA, MS, MBA, MEd, MSW. 18 associate degrees awarded in 1992. 100% in allied health. 1,040 bachelor's degrees awarded in 1992. 23% in business and management, 9% communications, 10% education, 9% engineering, 5% life sciences, 8% psychology, 15% social sciences. Graduate degrees offered in 18 major fields of study.

UNDERGRADUATE MAJORS. Accounting, American studies, anthropology, art education, biology, business administration and management, chemical engineering, chemistry, child development/care/guidance, communications, community health work, computer and information sciences, computer engineering, criminology, dramatic arts, early childhood education, economics, elementary education, English, English education, foreign languages education, French, geography, geology, German, graphic design, health education, history, home economics education, industrial engineering, interdisciplinary studies, international studies, jazz, mathematics, mathematics education, music, music education, music history and appreciation, music performance, music theory and composition, philosophy, physical education, physics, political science and government, psychology, science education, social studies education, sociology, Spanish, speech pathology/audiology, studio art, theater design, urban studies, women's studies.

ACADEMIC PROGRAMS. Internships, study abroad, teacher preparation, cross-registration. **Remedial services:** Learning center, reduced course load, remedial instruction, special counselor, tutoring. **ROTC:** Air Force, Army. **Placement/credit:** AP, CLEP General and Subject, IB, institutional tests.

ACADEMIC REQUIREMENTS. Freshmen must earn minimum GPA of 1.8 to continue in good standing. 72% of freshmen return for sophomore year. Students must declare major by end of second year. **Graduation requirements:** 180 hours for bachelor's (90 in major). Most students required to take courses in arts/fine arts, English, biological/physical sciences, social sciences.

FRESHMAN ADMISSIONS. Selection criteria: Students in 65th percentile of high school class automatically admitted. ACT scores required.Students ranking between the 40th and 64th are selectively admitted based on ACT score and academic preparation. **High school preparation:** 14 units required. Required units include biological science 1, English 4, foreign language 2, mathematics 3, physical science 1, social science 2 and science 1. **Test requirements:** ACT; score report by February 1.

1992 FRESHMAN CLASS PROFILE. 2,004 men applied, 1,473 accepted, 831 enrolled; 1,898 women applied, 1,513 accepted, 737 enrolled. 17% were in top tenth and 45% were in top quarter of graduating class. **Academic background:** Mid 50% of enrolled freshmen had ACT composite between 20-25. 99% submitted ACT scores. **Characteristics:** 89% from in state, 93% live in college housing, 4% have minority backgrounds, 1% are foreign students. Average age is 18.

FALL-TERM APPLICATIONS. $25 fee. No closing date; priority given to applications received by February 1; applicants notified on a rolling basis; must reply within 2 weeks. Audition recommended for music applicants. Portfolio recommended. Freshman class limited to 1850. Applications accepted on space-available basis.

STUDENT LIFE. Housing: Dormitories (men, women, coed); apartment, handicapped housing available. Housing facilities fully accessible to handicapped persons. **Activities:** Student government, radio, student newspaper, choral groups, concert band, dance, drama, jazz band, marching band, music ensembles, musical theater, opera, pep band, symphony orchestra, fraternities, sororities, Intervarsity Christian Fellowship, MN Public Interest Research Group, Anishinabe Club (American Indian students), Black Students Association, Circle K, Hispanic Organization, International Club, Southeast Asia Organization. **Additional information:** Barrier-free access enables passage of handicapped persons from all residences to academic buildings.

ATHLETICS. NAIA, NCAA. **Intercollegiate:** Baseball M, basketball, cross-country, football M, ice hockey M, softball W, tennis, track and field, volleyball W, wrestling M. **Intramural:** Archery, basketball, bowling, cross-country, fencing, field hockey, golf, gymnastics, handball, ice hockey, lacrosse, racquetball, rowing (crew) M, rugby, sailing, skiing, soccer M, softball, swimming, tennis, track and field, volleyball.

STUDENT SERVICES. Aptitude testing, career counseling, employment service for undergraduates, freshman orientation, health services, personal counseling, placement service for graduates, veterans counselor, services/facilities for handicapped.

ANNUAL EXPENSES. Tuition and fees (1992-93): $3,061, $5,418 additional for out-of-state students. **Room and board:** $3,213. **Books and supplies:** $693. **Other expenses:** $1,401.

FINANCIAL AID. 79% of freshmen, 79% of continuing students receive some form of aid. 65% of grants, 82% of loans, all jobs based on need. Academic, music/drama, athletic, state/district residency, leadership, minority scholarships available. **Aid applications:** No closing date; priority given to applications received by March 31; applicants notified on a rolling basis beginning on or about May 15; must reply within 2 weeks.

ADDRESS/TELEPHONE. Gerald R. Allen, Director of Admissions/Registrar, University of Minnesota: Duluth, 10 University Drive, Duluth, MN 55812-2496. (218) 726-7171. (800) 232-1339.

University of Minnesota: Morris
Morris, Minnesota — CB code: 6890

Admissions: 46% of applicants accepted
Based on:
- ••• School record, test scores
- •• Activities, recommendations, special talents
- • Essay, interview

Completion: 96% of freshmen end year in good standing
64% graduate, 24% of these enter graduate study

4-year public university and branch campus, liberal arts college, coed. Founded in 1959. **Accreditation:** Regional. **Undergraduate enrollment:** 841 men, 1,082 women full time. **Faculty:** 142 total (128 full time), 102 with doctorates or other terminal degrees. **Location:** Rural campus in small town; 150 miles from Minneapolis-St. Paul. **Calendar:** Quarter, extensive summer session. **Microcomputers:** 120 located in dormitories, libraries, classrooms, computer centers. **Special facilities:** Art gallery, tropical conservatory, greenhouse, Prairie Gate Press, West Central Historical Center.

DEGREES OFFERED. BA. 426 bachelor's degrees awarded in 1992. 8% in business and management, 10% teacher education, 5% languages, 10% letters/literature, 10% life sciences, 12% multi/interdisciplinary studies, 7% physical sciences, 8% psychology, 20% social sciences.

UNDERGRADUATE MAJORS. Art history, biology, business economics, chemistry, communications, computer and information sciences, dramatic arts, economics, elementary education, English, European studies, French, geology, German, history, humanities and social sciences, junior high education, Latin American studies, mathematics, music, philosophy, physics, political science and government, prelaw, premedical technology, premedicine, prepharmacy, preveterinary, psychology, social sciences, sociology, Spanish, studio art.

ACADEMIC PROGRAMS. Accelerated program, double major, dual enrollment of high school students, external degree, honors program, independent study, internships, student-designed major, study abroad, teacher preparation, visiting/exchange student program. **Remedial services:** Learning center, preadmission summer program, reduced course load, special counselor, tutoring. **Placement/credit:** AP, CLEP General and Subject, institutional tests.

ACADEMIC REQUIREMENTS. Freshmen must earn minimum GPA of 1.4 to continue in good standing. 90% of freshmen return for sophomore year. Students must declare major by end of second year. **Graduation requirements:** 180 hours for bachelor's (60 in major). Most students required to take courses in arts/fine arts, computer science, English, foreign languages, history, humanities, mathematics, philosophy/religion, biological/physical sciences, social sciences. **Postgraduate studies:** 2% enter law school, 2% enter medical school, 4% enter MBA programs, 16% enter other graduate study.

FRESHMAN ADMISSIONS. Selection criteria: High school rank and test scores most important. High school course work, activities, letter of recommendation important. **High school preparation:** 14 units required. Required units include English 4, foreign language 2, mathematics 3, social science 2 and science 3. **Test requirements:** ACT; score report by March 15. PSAT/NMSQT may be submitted in place of SAT or ACT for admission, but students will still need to take ACT before registration.

1992 FRESHMAN CLASS PROFILE. 623 men applied, 274 accepted, 259 enrolled; 817 women applied, 385 accepted, 315 enrolled. **Academic background:** Mid 50% of enrolled freshmen had SAT-V between 400-600, SAT-M between 650-750; ACT composite between 23-29. 16% submitted SAT scores, 98% submitted ACT scores. **Characteristics:** 84% from in state, 96% live in college housing, 17% have minority backgrounds, 1% are foreign students, 1% join fraternities/sororities. Average age is 18.

FALL-TERM APPLICATIONS. $25 fee, may be waived for applicants with need. Closing date March 15; applicants notified on or about April 1; must reply within 30 days. Interview recommended. CRDA. Deferred and early admission available. EDP-S. December 1 deadline for early admission I, January 15 deadline for early admission II.

STUDENT LIFE. Housing: Dormitories (coed); apartment, handicapped housing available. **Activities:** Student government, film, magazine, radio, student newspaper, television, choral groups, concert band, dance, drama, jazz band, music ensembles, musical theater, pep band, symphony orchestra, fraternities, sororities, Saddle Club, International Students Club, Fellowship of Christian Athletes, campus ministry.

ATHLETICS. NAIA. **Intercollegiate:** Baseball M, basketball, football M, golf, softball W, tennis, track and field, volleyball W, wrestling M. **Intramural:** Basketball, field hockey, handball, racquetball, soccer, softball, swimming, tennis, volleyball.

STUDENT SERVICES. Aptitude testing, career counseling, employment service for undergraduates, freshman orientation, health services, personal counseling, placement service for graduates, special adviser for adult students, veterans counselor, services/facilities for handicapped.

ANNUAL EXPENSES. Tuition and fees (projected): $3,666, $6,189 additional for out-of-state students. **Room and board:** $3,927. **Books and supplies:** $654. **Other expenses:** $1,200.

FINANCIAL AID. 80% of freshmen, 86% of continuing students receive some form of aid. All grants, 99% of loans, all jobs based on need. 343 enrolled freshmen were judged to have need, all were offered aid. Academic, music/drama scholarships available. **Aid applications:** No closing date; priority given to applications received by April 1; applicants notified on a rolling basis beginning on or about March 15; must reply within 20 days. **Additional information:** Land-grant program waiving tuition for Native Americans.

ADDRESS/TELEPHONE. Robert J. Vikander, Director of Admissions and Financial Aid, University of Minnesota: Morris, Behmler Hall, Morris, MN 56267-2199. (612) 589-6035. (800) 992-8863. Fax: (612) 589-1673.

University of Minnesota: Twin Cities

Minneapolis-St. Paul, Minnesota CB code: 6874

Admissions: 58% of applicants accepted
Based on: ••• School record, test scores
• Activities, essay, interview, recommendations, special talents
Completion: 82% of freshmen end year in good standing
29% graduate

4-year public university, coed. Founded in 1851. **Accreditation:** Regional. **Undergraduate enrollment:** 19,972 men, 18,047 women full time; 7,856 men and women part time. **Graduate enrollment:** 6,791 men, 5,340 women full time; 5,775 men and women part time. **Faculty:** 2,953 total (2,663 full time), 76 with doctorates or other terminal degrees. **Location:** Urban campus in very large city; 1 mile from downtown. **Calendar:** Quarter, extensive summer session. Saturday and extensive evening/early morning classes. **Microcomputers:** 20,000 located in dormitories, libraries, classrooms, computer centers, campus-wide network. **Special facilities:** Humphrey Institute, Rarig Center, Bell Museum of Natural History, art museum, Goldstein Gallery, Katherine Nash Gallery, health science complex, computer center, Northrop Auditorium, Sports and Aquatic Center. **Additional facts:** One campus in Minneapolis, 1 in St. Paul, with easy transit between them. Certificate programs available at extension school.

DEGREES OFFERED. BA, BS, BFA, BArch, MA, MS, MBA, MFA, MEd, MSW, PhD, EdD, DDS, MD, B. Pharm, Pharm D, DVM, JD. 70 associate degrees awarded in 1992. 5,428 bachelor's degrees awarded in 1992. 9% in business and management, 6% education, 16% engineering, 6% health sciences, 5% home economics, 48% letters/literature. Graduate degrees offered in 146 major fields of study.

UNDERGRADUATE MAJORS. Accounting, aerospace/aeronautical/astronautical engineering, African studies, Afro-American (black) studies, agribusiness, agricultural business and management, agricultural education, agricultural engineering, agricultural industries/marketing, agricultural sciences, American Indian studies, American studies, ancient Near Eastern studies, animal sciences, anthropology, architecture, art education, art history, astronomy, astrophysics, biochemistry, biological and physical sciences, biology, biometrics and biostatistics, botany, business and management, business economics, business education, business statistics, chemical engineering, chemistry, Chicano studies, child psychology, Chinese, civil engineering, classics, clinical laboratory science, computer and information sciences, costume design, dance, dental hygiene, early childhood education, earth sciences, East Asian studies, economics, education, electrical/electronics/communications engineering, elementary education, engineering and other disciplines, English, English education, environmental design, Finnish, fishing and fisheries, food science and nutrition, food sciences, foreign languages education, forest products processing technology, forestry production and processing, French, French area studies, funeral services/mortuary science, genetics, human and animal, geography, geological engineering, geophysical engineering, geophysics and seismology, German, Greek (classical), health sciences, Hebrew, history, home economics, home economics education, human environment and housing, human relationships, humanities, humanities and social sciences, industrial arts education, industrial engineering, interior design, international relations, international studies, Italian, Italian area studies, Japanese, Jewish studies, journalism, junior high education, landscape architecture, Latin, Latin American studies, liberal/general studies, linguistics, marketing and distributive education, materials engineering, mathematics, mechanical engineering, medical laboratory technologies, microbiology, Middle Eastern studies, music, music education, music therapy, natural resources/environmental studies, nursing, nutritional sciences, occupational therapy, parks and recreation management, pharmacy, philosophy, physical education, physical sciences, physical therapy, physics, physiology, human and animal, plant genetics, plant sciences, political science and government, Portuguese, predentistry, prelaw, premedicine, prenursing, prepharmacy, preveterinary, psychology, recreation and community services technologies, religion, renewable natural resources, retailing, Russian, Russian and Slavic studies, Scandinavian languages, school psychology, science education, social studies education, sociology, South Asian studies, Spanish, speech, speech correction, sports and exercise science, statistics, studio art, teaching English as a second language/foreign language, technical communication, textiles and clothing, trade and industrial education, urban design, urban forestry, urban studies, visual and performing arts, water resources, women's studies.

ACADEMIC PROGRAMS. Cooperative education, double major, dual enrollment of high school students, honors program, independent study, internships, student-designed major, study abroad, telecourses, cross-registration; liberal arts/career combination in engineering, forestry, health sciences; combined bachelor's/graduate program in business administration, medicine, law. **Remedial services:** Learning center, preadmission summer program, reduced course load, remedial instruction, special counselor, tutoring. **ROTC:** Air Force, Army, Naval. **Placement/credit:** AP, CLEP General and Subject, IB, institutional tests.

ACADEMIC REQUIREMENTS. Freshmen must earn minimum GPA of 2.0 to continue in good standing. 82% of freshmen return for sophomore year. Students must declare major by end of second year. **Graduation requirements:** 180 hours for bachelor's (90 in major). Most students required to take courses in arts/fine arts, English, foreign languages, history, humanities, mathematics, philosophy/religion, biological/physical sciences, social sciences. **Additional information:** More than 4700 courses offered per year, in subjects covering the gamut of human experience, from asteroids to zygotes, from Jane Austen to Emile Zola, from Antarctica to Zanzibar, from anthropogenesis to Zen.

FRESHMAN ADMISSIONS. Selection criteria: School achievement record and test scores. High school rank is combined with PSAT/NMSQT, ACT, or SAT for an admission index. Some units also require certain mathematics and/or science courses. Special review for applicants not meeting admission indices considers minority status, course of study, grade trends, special schools, activities, and talents. **High school preparation:** 14 units required. Required units include English 4, foreign language 2, mathematics 3, physical science 3 and social science 2. Some departments require additional course preparation beyond these minimum requirements. **Test requirements:** ACT; score report by December 31.

1992 FRESHMAN CLASS PROFILE. 5,378 men applied, 3,026 accepted, 1,709 enrolled; 4,662 women applied, 2,752 accepted, 1,551 enrolled. 26% were in top tenth and 56% were in top quarter of graduating class. **Academic background:** Mid 50% of enrolled freshmen had SAT-V between 420-560, SAT-M between 500-660; ACT composite between 21-26. 24% submitted SAT scores, 89% submitted ACT scores. **Characteristics:** Average age is 19.

FALL-TERM APPLICATIONS. $25 fee. No closing date; priority given to applications received by December 15; applicants notified on a rolling basis; must reply by May 1 or within 2 weeks if notified thereafter. Audition required for performing arts applicants. Portfolio required for studio arts, architecture applicants. Interview recommended for academically weak, early admissions, special programs applicants. Deferred and early admission available. Rolling admission granted on a space available by unit basis. Applicants notified within 1 month of application. Tuition deposit required by May 1.

STUDENT LIFE. Housing: Dormitories (men, women, coed); apartment, fraternity, sorority, cooperative housing available. **Activities:** Student government, film, magazine, radio, student newspaper, yearbook, choral groups, concert band, dance, drama, jazz band, marching band, music ensembles, musical theater, opera, pep band, symphony orchestra, fraternities, sororities. **Additional information:** Concert, recital, film, art show, theater production, discussion group, presentation by visting poet or scholar, or spontaneous social or political gathering, all available, often simultaneously, on campus.

ATHLETICS. NCAA. **Intercollegiate:** Baseball, basketball, cross-country, diving, football M, golf, gymnastics, ice hockey M, rowing (crew) W, softball W, swimming, tennis, track and field, volleyball W, wrestling M. **Intramural:** Baseball, basketball, bowling, football, golf, ice hockey, rugby, skiing, soccer, softball W, tennis, volleyball, water polo, wrestling.

STUDENT SERVICES. Aptitude testing, career counseling, employment service for undergraduates, freshman orientation, health services, on-campus day care, personal counseling, placement service for graduates, veterans counselor, legal counseling, services/facilities for handicapped.

ANNUAL EXPENSES. Tuition and fees (projected): $3,492, $5,691 additional for out-of-state students. Graduate tuition varies by program. **Room and board:** $3,564. **Books and supplies:** $714. **Other expenses:** $2,118.

FINANCIAL AID. 41% of freshmen, 43% of continuing students receive some form of aid. Grants, loans, jobs available. 1,185 enrolled freshmen were judged to have need, 1,155 were offered aid. Academic, music/drama, art, athletic, state/district residency, leadership, alumni affiliation, religious affiliation, minority scholarships available. **Aid applications:** No closing date; priority given to applications received by April 1; applicants notified on a rolling basis.

ADDRESS/TELEPHONE. Wayne Sigler, Director of Admissions, University of Minnesota: Twin Cities, 240 Williamson Hall, 231 Pillsbury Drive S.E, Minneapolis, MN 55455-0213. (612) 625-2008. (800) 752-1000. Fax: (612) 626-1693.

University of St. Thomas
St. Paul, Minnesota CB code: 6110

Admissions: 92% of applicants accepted
Based on: ••• School record
•• Recommendations, test scores
• Activities, essay, religious affiliation/commitment, special talents
Completion: 94% of freshmen end year in good standing
65% graduate

4-year private university and liberal arts college, coed, affiliated with Roman Catholic Church. Founded in 1885. **Accreditation:** Regional. **Undergraduate enrollment:** 2,085 men, 2,147 women full time; 413 men, 543 women part time. **Graduate enrollment:** 167 men, 168 women full time; 2,560 men, 2,340 women part time. **Faculty:** 645 total (324 full time), 365 with doctorates or other terminal degrees. **Location:** Urban campus in large city; 5 miles from downtown. **Calendar:** 4-1-4, limited summer session. Saturday classes. **Microcomputers:** 316 located in dormitories, classrooms, computer centers. **Additional facts:** Largest private college in Minnesota.

DEGREES OFFERED. BA, MA, MS, MBA, MSW, EdD, M.Div. 1,063 bachelor's degrees awarded in 1992. 33% in business and management, 12% business/office and marketing/distribution, 10% communications, 15% social sciences. Graduate degrees offered in 34 major fields of study.

UNDERGRADUATE MAJORS. Accounting, advertising, anthropology, applied mathematics, art education, art history, biology, business administration and management, business home economics, chemistry, communications, computer and information sciences, criminology, dramatic arts, East Asian studies, Eastern European studies, economics, elementary education, English, English education, finance, food science and nutrition, foreign languages education, French, geography, geology, German, Greek (classical), health education, history, home economics, home economics education, human resources development, international business management, international relations, international studies, Japanese, journalism, Latin, liberal/general studies, management science, marketing and distribution, marketing management, mathematics, mathematics education, music, music education, music performance, nursing, occupational therapy, operations research, peace studies, personnel management, philosophy, physical education, physics, political science and government, psychology, public administration, public relations, radio/television broadcasting, religious music, Russian, Russian and Slavic studies, science education, small business management and ownership, social sciences, social studies education, social work, sociology, Spanish, speech/communication/theater education, studio art, telecommunications, textiles and clothing, theological studies, women's studies.

ACADEMIC PROGRAMS. Double major, dual enrollment of high school students, education specialist degree, honors program, independent study, internships, study abroad, teacher preparation, weekend college, Washington semester, cross-registration; liberal arts/career combination in engineering, business. **Remedial services:** Learning center, reduced course load, tutoring, Academic Development Program, Academic Preparation Program, Students with Learning Disabilities Program. **ROTC:** Air Force. **Placement/credit:** AP, CLEP General and Subject, IB, institutional tests.

ACADEMIC REQUIREMENTS. Freshmen must earn minimum GPA of 2.0 to continue in good standing. 82% of freshmen return for sophomore year. Students must declare major by end of second year. **Graduation requirements:** 132 hours for bachelor's (44 in major). Most students required to take courses in arts/fine arts, English, foreign languages, history, mathematics, philosophy/religion, biological/physical sciences, social sciences.

FRESHMAN ADMISSIONS. Selection criteria: School achievement record most important, followed by rank in top two-fifths of class and test scores. **High school preparation:** 16 units recommended. Required and recommended units include mathematics 3-4. English 4, foreign language 4, social science 2 and science 2 recommended. **Test requirements:** SAT or ACT (ACT preferred); score report by January 15. PSAT/NMSQT may be submitted in place of SAT or ACT.

1992 FRESHMAN CLASS PROFILE. 876 men applied, 796 accepted, 354 enrolled; 1,071 women applied, 990 accepted, 446 enrolled. 70% had high school GPA of 3.0 or higher, 29% between 2.0 and 2.99. 27% were in top tenth and 57% were in top quarter of graduating class. **Academic background:** Mid 50% of enrolled freshmen had SAT-V between 430-550, SAT-M between 480-610; ACT composite between 21-26. 27% submitted SAT scores, 94% submitted ACT scores. **Characteristics:** 84% from in state, 88% live in college housing, 8% have minority backgrounds, 1% are foreign students. Average age is 18.

FALL-TERM APPLICATIONS. $20 fee, may be waived for applicants with need. Closing date April 1; priority given to applications received by January 15; applicants notified on a rolling basis; must reply by May 1. Essay required. Interview recommended for academically weak applicants. Audition recommended for music applicants. CRDA. Deferred admission available.

STUDENT LIFE. Housing: Dormitories (men, women); apartment housing available. **Activities:** Student government, magazine, student newspaper, television, yearbook, choral groups, concert band, dance, drama, jazz band, music ensembles, musical theater, symphony orchestra, fraternities, sororities, International Student Association, campus ministry, Amnesty International, Volunteers in Action, Peace and Justice, Muslim Student Association, John Henry Newman Club, HANA, Best Buddies.

ATHLETICS. NCAA. **Intercollegiate:** Baseball M, basketball, cross-country, diving, football M, golf, ice hockey M, soccer, softball W, swimming, tennis, track and field, volleyball W, wrestling M. **Intramural:** Badminton, basketball, bowling, handball, racquetball, softball, squash, tennis, volleyball, wrestling M. **Clubs:** Lacrosse M, rowing M, rugby M.

STUDENT SERVICES. Aptitude testing, career counseling, employment service for undergraduates, freshman orientation, health services, personal counseling, placement service for graduates, special adviser for adult students, veterans counselor, services/facilities for handicapped.

ANNUAL EXPENSES. Tuition and fees: $11,200. **Room and board:** $4,000. **Books and supplies:** $500. **Other expenses:** $900.

FINANCIAL AID. 75% of freshmen, 70% of continuing students receive some form of aid. 78% of loans, 92% of jobs based on need. 480 enrolled freshmen were judged to have need, all were offered aid. Academic, music/drama, leadership scholarships available. **Aid applications:** No closing date; priority given to applications received by April 1; applicants notified on a rolling basis beginning on or about May 1; must reply within 2 weeks.

ADDRESS/TELEPHONE. Marla Friederichs, Director of Admissions, University of St. Thomas, 2115 Summit Avenue, Mail #32F-1, St. Paul, MN 55105-1096. (612) 962-6150. (800) 328-6819. Fax: (612) 962-6360.

Vermilion Community College
Ely, Minnesota CB code: 6194

2-year public community college, coed. Founded in 1922. **Accreditation:** Regional. **Undergraduate enrollment:** 950 men and women. **Faculty:** 36 total (32 full time), 2 with doctorates or other terminal degrees. **Location:**

Rural campus in small town; 100 miles from Duluth. **Calendar:** Quarter, limited summer session. **Microcomputers:** Located in libraries, computer centers. **Special facilities:** Museum, 40-acre outdoor learning center near Boundary Waters Canoe Area.

DEGREES OFFERED. AA, AS, AAS. 135 associate degrees awarded in 1992.

UNDERGRADUATE MAJORS. Accounting, advertising, agribusiness, agricultural business and management, air pollution control technology, airline piloting and navigation, anatomy, biology, botany, business and management, business and office, business data processing and related programs, chemistry, communications, computer and information sciences, computer programming, conservation and regulation, data processing, early childhood education, education, education administration, elementary education, engineering, engineering and engineering-related technologies, English, fishing and fisheries, forest products processing technology, forestry and related sciences, forestry production and processing, health education, health sciences, home economics, information sciences and systems, journalism, junior high education, law , law enforcement and corrections technologies, legal secretary, liberal/general studies, mathematics, mathematics education, medical records technology, medical secretary, music, occupational therapy assistant, parks and recreation management, physical sciences, physical therapy assistant, physics, prelaw, psychology, public relations, recreation and community services technologies, renewable natural resources, sanitation technology, science education, science technologies, secondary education, secretarial and related programs, social science education, social sciences, social studies education, water and wastewater technology, wildlife management, zoology.

ACADEMIC PROGRAMS. 2-year transfer program, cooperative education, dual enrollment of high school students, independent study, internships, cross-registration. **Remedial services:** Learning center, preadmission summer program, reduced course load, remedial instruction, special counselor, tutoring.

ACADEMIC REQUIREMENTS. Freshmen must earn minimum GPA of 1.4 to continue in good standing. 75% of freshmen return for sophomore year. **Graduation requirements:** 92 hours for associate. Most students required to take courses in English, humanities, mathematics, biological/physical sciences, social sciences.

FRESHMAN ADMISSIONS. Selection criteria: Open admissions.

1992 FRESHMAN CLASS PROFILE. 370 men and women enrolled. **Characteristics:** 95% from in state, 80% commute, 1% have minority backgrounds. Average age is 19.

FALL-TERM APPLICATIONS. $15 fee. No closing date; applicants notified on a rolling basis beginning on or about January 1. Interview recommended for natural resources, parks and recreation, law enforcement applicants. Early admission available.

STUDENT LIFE. Housing: Dormitories (coed). **Activities:** Student government, magazine, yearbook, choral groups, drama.

ATHLETICS. NJCAA. **Intercollegiate:** Baseball M, basketball, football M, softball W, volleyball W. **Intramural:** Basketball M, bowling, softball M, tennis.

STUDENT SERVICES. Career counseling, personal counseling, placement service for graduates.

ANNUAL EXPENSES. Tuition and fees (1992-93): $1,687, $1,688 additional for out-of-state students. **Room and board:** $2,980. **Books and supplies:** $480. **Other expenses:** $1,160.

FINANCIAL AID. 93% of freshmen, 93% of continuing students receive some form of aid. All grants, 91% of loans, all jobs based on need. Academic, leadership scholarships available. **Aid applications:** No closing date; applicants notified on a rolling basis beginning on or about March 1; must reply within 2 weeks.

ADDRESS/TELEPHONE. Doug Furnstahl, Director of Enrollment Services, Vermilion Community College, 1900 East Camp Street, Ely, MN 55731-9989. (218) 365-7200. (800) 657-3608. Fax: (218) 365-7207.

Willmar Community College
Willmar, Minnesota — CB code: 6949

2-year public community, liberal arts college, coed. Founded in 1961. **Accreditation:** Regional. **Undergraduate enrollment:** 461 men, 426 women full time; 125 men, 371 women part time. **Faculty:** 72 total (40 full time), 2 with doctorates or other terminal degrees. **Location:** Rural campus in large town; 100 miles from Minneapolis-St. Paul. **Calendar:** Quarter, limited summer session. Saturday classes. **Microcomputers:** 72 located in libraries, classrooms, computer centers. **Special facilities:** Natural wooded, prairie, and wetlands areas for biological study.

DEGREES OFFERED. AA, AS, AAS. 310 associate degrees awarded in 1992. 12% in business and management, 7% business/office and marketing/distribution, 12% teacher education, 11% allied health, 9% multi/interdisciplinary studies, 16% parks/recreation, protective services, public affairs, 7% psychology, 5% social sciences.

UNDERGRADUATE MAJORS. Accounting, aerospace/aeronautical/astronautical engineering, agribusiness, agricultural business and management, agricultural economics, agricultural education, agricultural engineering, agricultural production, agricultural sciences, agronomy, allied health, American literature, animal sciences, applied mathematics, art education, art history, art therapy, aviation management, behavioral sciences, biology, botany, business administration and management, business and management, business and office, business computer/console/peripheral equipment operation, business data processing and related programs, business data programming, business economics, business education, business statistics, chemical engineering, chemistry, child development/care/guidance, chiropractic, civil engineering, communications, computer and information sciences, computer engineering, computer programming, computer technology, conservation and regulation, counseling psychology, criminal justice studies, criminal justice technology, criminology, cytotechnology, dairy, data processing, dramatic arts, drawing, early childhood education, earth sciences, economics, education, education administration, electrical/electronics/communications engineering, electronic technology, elementary education, engineering, engineering physics, English, English education, English literature, environmental science, family and community services, finance, fine arts, fishing and fisheries, flight attendants, food sciences, foreign languages education, forestry and related sciences, forestry production and processing, funeral services/mortuary science, geography, geological engineering, German, gerontology, health care administration, health education, health sciences, history, home economics, home economics education, horticultural science, horticulture, hotel/motel and restaurant management, humanities, industrial arts education, industrial engineering, information sciences and systems, inorganic chemistry, institutional management, international business management, international relations, interpreter for the deaf, journalism, junior high education, landscape architecture, law enforcement and corrections, law enforcement and corrections technologies, legal secretary, liberal/general studies, library science, marine biology, marketing management, marriage and family counseling, mathematics, mathematics education, mechanical engineering, medical secretary, mental health/human services, microbiology, music, music education, music history and appreciation, music performance, music theory and composition, music therapy, musical theater, nursing, nursing education, nutritional education, occupational therapy, ocean engineering, oceanography, office supervision and management, organic chemistry, painting, parks and recreation management, personal services, personnel management, petroleum engineering, pharmaceutical chemistry, photography, physical education, physical sciences, physical therapy, physics, plant sciences, political science and government, predentistry, preengineering, prelaw, premedical technology, premedicine, prepharmacy, preveterinary, protective services, psychology, public affairs, public relations, pure mathematics, radio/television broadcasting, radiograph medical technology, reading education, recreation therapy, rehabilitation counseling/services, renewable natural resources, school psychology, science education, science technologies, secondary education, secretarial and related programs, small business management and ownership, social psychology, social science education, social sciences, social studies education, social work, sociology, soil sciences, Spanish, special education, speech, speech pathology/audiology, speech/communication/theater education, sports medicine, student counseling and personnel services, studio art, teacher aide, theological studies, tourism, urban studies, visual and performing arts, wildlife management, word processing, zoology.

ACADEMIC PROGRAMS. 2-year transfer program, dual enrollment of high school students, independent study, internships, telecourses, weekend college, cross-registration, business administration, psychology, sociology, speech communications programs with two 4-year state universities. **Remedial services:** Learning center, preadmission summer program, reduced course load, remedial instruction, special counselor, tutoring, group sessions for nontraditional students. **Placement/credit:** CLEP Subject, institutional tests; 30 credit hours maximum for associate degree.

ACADEMIC REQUIREMENTS. Freshmen must earn minimum GPA of 2.0 to continue in good standing. 67% of freshmen return for sophomore year. Students must declare major by end of first year. **Graduation requirements:** 96 hours for associate (30 in major). Most students required to take courses in arts/fine arts, computer science, English, humanities, mathematics, biological/physical sciences, social sciences. **Additional information:** Provides ten academic programs (AAS), in cooperation with Willmar Technical Institute. Four-year baccalaureate degrees available on campus, taught by state university system.

FRESHMAN ADMISSIONS. Selection criteria: Open admissions. Selective admissions for nursing program, chemical dependency counseling program. **High school preparation:** 13 units recommended. Recommended units include biological science 1, English 4, mathematics 3, physical science 1 and social science 4. Chemistry and mathematics recommended for mathematics, science, and health science majors. Computer science recommended for all. **Test requirements:** SAT or ACT (ACT preferred) for placement and counseling only; score report by September 15. PSAT/NMSQT may be submitted in place of SAT or ACT. **Additional information:** Applicants with neither high school diploma nor GED may enroll part-time and earn GED before completing 30 credits.

1992 FRESHMAN CLASS PROFILE. 612 men and women applied, 612 accepted; 251 men enrolled, 237 women enrolled. 24% had high school GPA of 3.0 or higher, 55% between 2.0 and 2.99. 5% were in top tenth and 15% were in top quarter of graduating class. **Characteristics:** 96% from in state, 100% commute, 3% have minority backgrounds, 1% are foreign students. Average age is 20.

FALL-TERM APPLICATIONS. $15 fee. Closing date September 6; applicants notified on a rolling basis. Interview recommended for nursing, law enforcement, chemical dependency counselor, and part-time applicants. Deferred and early admission available.

STUDENT LIFE. Housing: Subsidized apartment buildings adjacent to campus. **Activities:** Student government, student newspaper, choral groups, drama, jazz band, music ensembles, musical theater, symphony orchestra, theater, vocal ensemble, choir, fraternities, Religion and Life Center, Circle-K. **Additional information:** Monthly convocations held.

ATHLETICS. NJCAA. **Intercollegiate:** Baseball M, basketball, football M, softball W, tennis, volleyball W, wrestling M. **Intramural:** Basketball, bowling, golf, skiing, softball, tennis, volleyball.

STUDENT SERVICES. Aptitude testing, career counseling, employment service for undergraduates, freshman orientation, on-campus day care, personal counseling, placement service for graduates, special adviser for adult students, veterans counselor, counselor for adult women, chemical dependence, counseling program, services/facilities for handicapped.

ANNUAL EXPENSES. Tuition and fees (projected): $1,901, $1,803 additional for out-of-state students. **Books and supplies:** $600. **Other expenses:** $275.

FINANCIAL AID. 89% of freshmen, 76% of continuing students receive some form of aid. 98% of grants, 91% of loans, 97% of jobs based on need. 682 enrolled freshmen were judged to have need, all were offered aid. Academic, music/drama, art, state/district residency, leadership, minority scholarships available. **Aid applications:** Closing date May 1; priority given to applications received by April 23; applicants notified on or about June 15; must reply within 4 weeks. **Additional information:** Special funds (first 5 credits free) available for adult students returning or continuing education after 7-year absence from academic training.

ADDRESS/TELEPHONE. Arlen Sjerven, Director of Admissions, Willmar Community College, PO Box 797, Willmar, MN 56201. (612) 231-5116. Fax: (612) 231-6602.

Willmar Technical College
Willmar, Minnesota — CB code: 4924

2-year public technical college, coed. **Accreditation:** Regional. **Undergraduate enrollment:** 490 men, 256 women full time; 831 men, 401 women part time. **Faculty:** 95 total (85 full time). **Location:** Rural campus in large town; 100 miles from Minneapolis. **Calendar:** Quarter. **Microcomputers:** 180 located in libraries, classrooms, computer centers. **Additional facts:** On same campus as Willmar Community College.

DEGREES OFFERED. AAS. 30 associate degrees awarded in 1992. 10% in agriculture, 85% business and management, 5% trade and industry.

UNDERGRADUATE MAJORS. Accounting, agribusiness, agricultural business and management, agricultural production, drafting and design technology, human service technology, legal secretary, medical secretary, mobile communications, practical nursing, secretarial and related programs, trade and industrial supervision and management, veterinarian's assistant.

ACADEMIC PROGRAMS. Dual enrollment of high school students, independent study, internships, telecourses. **Remedial services:** Learning center, preadmission summer program, reduced course load, remedial instruction, special counselor, tutoring. **Placement/credit:** Institutional tests; 30 credit hours maximum for associate degree.

ACADEMIC REQUIREMENTS. Freshmen must earn minimum GPA of 2.0 to continue in good standing. 80% of freshmen return for sophomore year. Students must declare major on application. **Graduation requirements:** 90 hours for associate. Most students required to take courses in English, mathematics.

FRESHMAN ADMISSIONS. Selection criteria: Open admissions. Grade of 2.0 or higher in chemistry, biology, and algebra prerequisite for veterinary technology. Applicants not having all prerequisite courses must have overall 3.0 GPA to be accepted.

1992 FRESHMAN CLASS PROFILE. Characteristics: 97% from in state, 100% commute, 5% have minority backgrounds. Average age is 24.

FALL-TERM APPLICATIONS. $15 fee. Closing date September 1; priority given to applications received by July 15; applicants notified on a rolling basis beginning on or about July 1. Early admission available. Upon acceptance, students required to take Test of Adult Basic Education, for placement.

STUDENT LIFE. Activities: Student government, student newspaper, choral groups, drama, music ensembles.

ATHLETICS. NJCAA. **Intercollegiate:** Baseball M, basketball, football M, golf, softball W, volleyball W, wrestling M. **Intramural:** Basketball, softball, volleyball.

STUDENT SERVICES. Aptitude testing, career counseling, employment service for undergraduates, freshman orientation, health services, on-campus day care, personal counseling, placement service for graduates, special adviser for adult students, veterans counselor, services/facilities for handicapped.

ANNUAL EXPENSES. Tuition and fees (projected): $1,775, $1,740 additional for out-of-state students. Tuition reciprocity arrangements exist with North Dakota, South Dakota, and Wisconsin. **Books and supplies:** $400. **Other expenses:** $900.

FINANCIAL AID. 80% of freshmen, 80% of continuing students receive some form of aid. All grants, 82% of loans, all jobs based on need. **Aid applications:** No closing date; priority given to applications received by May 1; applicants notified on a rolling basis beginning on or about June 1; must reply within 2 weeks.

ADDRESS/TELEPHONE. Don Rinke, Admission Coordinator, Willmar Technical College, PO Box 1097, Willmar, MN 56201. (612) 235-5114 ext. 123. (800) 722-1151. Fax: (612) 235-0601.

Winona State University
Winona, Minnesota — CB code: 6680

Admissions: 66% of applicants accepted
Based on: ••• School record, test scores
• Activities, essay, interview, recommendations
Completion: 75% of freshmen end year in good standing
49% graduate, 10% of these enter graduate study

4-year public liberal arts college, coed. Founded in 1858. **Accreditation:** Regional. **Undergraduate enrollment:** 2,600 men, 3,400 women full time; 500 men, 500 women part time. **Graduate enrollment:** 25 men, 25 women full time; 175 men, 375 women part time. **Faculty:** 375 total (350 full time), 270 with doctorates or other terminal degrees. **Location:** Rural campus in large town; 110 miles from Minneapolis-St. Paul. **Calendar:** Quarter, extensive summer session. **Microcomputers:** 350 located in dormitories, libraries, classrooms, computer centers, campus-wide network.

DEGREES OFFERED. AA, AS, BA, BS, MA, MS, MBA, MEd. 50 associate degrees awarded in 1992. 850 bachelor's degrees awarded. 23% in business and management, 7% communications, 5% computer sciences, 12% teacher education, 6% engineering, 10% health sciences, 6% life sciences, 7% psychology, 9% social sciences. Graduate degrees offered in 21 major fields of study.

UNDERGRADUATE MAJORS. Associate: Airline piloting and navigation, aviation management, business and office, conservation and regulation, dance, fishing and fisheries, forestry and related sciences, gerontology, international studies, Japanese, liberal/general studies, nuclear technologies, philosophy, preengineering, science technologies, secretarial and related programs, wildlife management. **Bachelor's:** Accounting, administration of special education, advertising, art education, bilingual/bicultural education, biological and physical sciences, biology, business administration and management, business and management, business and office, business economics, business education, cell biology, chemical engineering, chemistry, city/community/regional planning, clinical laboratory science, communications, computer and information sciences, computer programming, criminal justice studies, criminology, cytotechnology, dramatic arts, drawing, early childhood education, earth sciences, ecology, economics, education, education of the emotionally handicapped, education of the gifted and talented, education of the mentally handicapped, elementary education, engineering and other disciplines, English, English education, environmental science, finance, fine arts, foreign languages education, French, geology, German, health care administration, health education, history, human resources development, humanities and social sciences, information sciences and systems, international public service, international relations, journalism, junior high education, labor/industrial relations, legal assistant/paralegal, liberal/general studies, management information systems, marketing management, materials engineering, mathematics, mathematics education, mechanical engineering, molecular biology, music, music education, music performance, music theory and composition, nursing, nursing education, office supervision and management, organizational behavior, painting, parks and recreation management, personnel management, physical education, physical sciences, physics, political science and government, predentistry, prelaw, premedicine, prepharmacy, preveterinary, psychology, public administration, public relations, radio/television broadcasting, reading education, recreation therapy, remedial education, science education, sculpture, secondary education, secretarial and related programs, social science education, social sciences, social studies education, social work, sociology, Spanish, special education, specific learning disabilities, speech, speech/communication/theater education, sports medicine, statistics, studio art, systems analysis, urban studies, visual and performing arts.

ACADEMIC PROGRAMS. 2-year transfer program, accelerated program, double major, dual enrollment of high school students, education specialist degree, external degree, honors program, independent study, internships, student-designed major, study abroad, teacher preparation, telecourses, visiting/exchange student program, cross-registration, adult program. **Remedial services:** Learning center, preadmission summer program, reduced course load, remedial instruction, special counselor, tutoring. **Placement/credit:** AP, CLEP General and Subject, IB, institutional tests.

ACADEMIC REQUIREMENTS. Freshmen must earn minimum GPA of 2.0 to continue in good standing. 75% of freshmen return for sophomore year. Students must declare major by end of second year. **Graduation re-**

quirements: 96 hours for associate, 192 hours for bachelor's (60 in major). Most students required to take courses in computer science, English, humanities, mathematics, biological/physical sciences, social sciences. **Postgraduate studies:** 2% enter law school, 2% enter medical school, 5% enter MBA programs, 1% enter other graduate study.

FRESHMAN ADMISSIONS. Selection criteria: Rank in top half of class or SAT combined score of 900 or ACT composite score of 21 required for regular admission. Provisional admission may be granted to applicants not meeting requirements. Required units include biological science 3, English 4, mathematics 3, physical science 3 and social science 3. One English unit may be speech. 3 elective units also required. In 1996, 2 units of foreign language will be required. **Test requirements:** SAT or ACT (ACT preferred); score report by August 1.

1992 FRESHMAN CLASS PROFILE. 1,200 men applied, 800 accepted, 500 enrolled; 1,700 women applied, 1,100 accepted, 800 enrolled. 50% had high school GPA of 3.0 or higher, 50% between 2.0 and 2.99. 15% were in top tenth and 40% were in top quarter of graduating class. **Academic background:** Mid 50% of enrolled freshmen had SAT-V between 400-520, SAT-M between 420-580; ACT composite between 21-26. 10% submitted SAT scores, 90% submitted ACT scores. **Characteristics:** 65% from in state, 90% live in college housing, 4% have minority backgrounds, 3% are foreign students. Average age is 18.

FALL-TERM APPLICATIONS. $15 fee. Closing date August 1; priority given to applications received by February 1; applicants notified on a rolling basis. Interview recommended for academically weak applicants. Deferred and early admission available.

STUDENT LIFE. Housing: Dormitories (men, women, coed); handicapped housing available. **Activities:** Student government, magazine, radio, student newspaper, television, choral groups, concert band, dance, drama, jazz band, music ensembles, musical theater, opera, pep band, symphony orchestra, fraternities, sororities.

ATHLETICS. NAIA, NCAA. **Intercollegiate:** Baseball M, basketball, cross-country, football M, golf, gymnastics W, softball W, tennis, track and field, volleyball W. **Intramural:** Archery, badminton, baseball M, basketball, bowling, cross-country, diving, fencing, field hockey, golf, gymnastics W, handball, horseback riding, ice hockey M, racquetball, rifle, skiing, soccer, softball, swimming, table tennis, tennis, track and field, volleyball, wrestling M.

STUDENT SERVICES. Aptitude testing, career counseling, employment service for undergraduates, freshman orientation, health services, on-campus day care, personal counseling, placement service for graduates, special adviser for adult students, veterans counselor, services/facilities for handicapped.

ANNUAL EXPENSES. Tuition and fees (1992-93): $2,214, $1,865 additional for out-of-state students. **Room and board:** $2,535. **Books and supplies:** $600. **Other expenses:** $600.

FINANCIAL AID. 70% of freshmen, 70% of continuing students receive some form of aid. Grants, loans, jobs available. 770 enrolled freshmen were judged to have need, all were offered aid. Academic, music/drama, art, athletic, alumni affiliation, minority scholarships available. **Aid applications:** No closing date; priority given to applications received by April 1; applicants notified on a rolling basis beginning on or about June 1; must reply within 2 weeks.

ADDRESS/TELEPHONE. Dr. J. A. Mootz, Director of Admissions, Winona State University, Winona, MN 55987. (507) 457-5100.

Worthington Community College
Worthington, Minnesota CB code: 6945

2-year public community college, coed. Founded in 1936. **Accreditation:** Regional. **Undergraduate enrollment:** 229 men, 269 women full time; 97 men, 311 women part time. **Faculty:** 39 total (25 full time), 5 with doctorates or other terminal degrees. **Location:** Rural campus in large town; 200 miles from Minneapolis-St. Paul, 60 miles from Sioux Falls, South Dakota. **Calendar:** Quarter, limited summer session. Extensive evening/early morning classes. **Microcomputers:** Located in libraries, computer centers.

DEGREES OFFERED. AA, AS, AAS. 160 associate degrees awarded in 1992. 10% in agriculture, 10% business and management, 5% business/office and marketing/distribution, 5% health sciences, 68% multi/interdisciplinary studies.

UNDERGRADUATE MAJORS. Agribusiness, agricultural business and management, agricultural sciences, aviation management, business administration and management, business and management, business and office, business data processing and related programs, communications, computer and information sciences, education, engineering, health sciences, liberal/general studies, marketing and distribution, preengineering, video.

ACADEMIC PROGRAMS. 2-year transfer program, cooperative education, dual enrollment of high school students, independent study, internships, student-designed major, study abroad, telecourses, cross-registration. **Remedial services:** Learning center, reduced course load, remedial instruction, special counselor, tutoring, preadmission summer program for nursing students. **Placement/credit:** AP, CLEP General and Subject, institutional tests; 60 credit hours maximum for associate degree.

ACADEMIC REQUIREMENTS. Freshmen must earn minimum GPA of 1.85 to continue in good standing. 50% of freshmen return for sophomore year. **Graduation requirements:** 96 hours for associate (45 in major). Most students required to take courses in computer science, English, humanities, biological/physical sciences, social sciences.

FRESHMAN ADMISSIONS. Selection criteria: Open admissions. Out-of-state applicants must have minimum ACT score or show other evidence of ability to do college work successfully. **Test requirements:** PSB-Aptitude for Practical Nursing Examination required of nursing applicants.

1992 FRESHMAN CLASS PROFILE. 146 men, 240 women enrolled. **Characteristics:** 88% from in state, 100% commute, 7% have minority backgrounds, 1% are foreign students. Average age is 24.

FALL-TERM APPLICATIONS. $15 fee. No closing date; applicants notified on a rolling basis. Interview recommended for practical nursing applicants. Deferred and early admission available. Priority deadline for practical nursing applicants January 15.

STUDENT LIFE. Housing: Subsidized apartments adjacent to campus. **Activities:** Student government, radio, student newspaper, television, yearbook, choral groups, drama, jazz band, music ensembles, musical theater, pep band.

ATHLETICS. NJCAA. **Intercollegiate:** Basketball, football M, volleyball W, wrestling M. **Intramural:** Basketball, bowling, golf, skiing, softball, tennis.

STUDENT SERVICES. Aptitude testing, career counseling, employment service for undergraduates, on-campus day care, personal counseling, special adviser for adult students, veterans counselor, services/facilities for handicapped.

ANNUAL EXPENSES. Tuition and fees (projected): $1,687, $1,688 additional for out-of-state students. **Books and supplies:** $500. **Other expenses:** $1,000.

FINANCIAL AID. 40% of freshmen, 45% of continuing students receive some form of aid. All grants, 90% of loans, 68% of jobs based on need. 200 enrolled freshmen were judged to have need, all were offered aid. Academic, music/drama, leadership scholarships available. **Aid applications:** No closing date; priority given to applications received by May 1; applicants notified on a rolling basis beginning on or about June 1.

ADDRESS/TELEPHONE. Student Services, Worthington Community College, 1450 College Way, Worthington, MN 56187. (507) 372-2107. (800) 652-9747. Fax: (507) 372-5801.

Mississippi

Alcorn State University

Lorman, Mississippi CB code: 1008

4-year public university, coed. Founded in 1871. **Accreditation:** Regional. **Undergraduate enrollment:** 2,741 men and women. **Graduate enrollment:** 178 men and women. **Faculty:** 184 total (173 full time), 81 with doctorates or other terminal degrees. **Location:** Rural campus in small town; 40 miles from Natchez and Vicksburg. **Calendar:** Semester, limited summer session. **Microcomputers:** 125 located in classrooms, computer centers. **Special facilities:** Nature trails, lakes.

DEGREES OFFERED. BA, BS, MS. 28 associate degrees awarded in 1992. 294 bachelor's degrees awarded. Graduate degrees offered in 16 major fields of study.

UNDERGRADUATE MAJORS. Associate: Nursing, preengineering. **Bachelor's:** Accounting, agricultural economics, agricultural education, agricultural sciences, agronomy, animal sciences, applied mathematics, biology, business administration and management, business education, chemistry, communications, computer and information sciences, criminal justice studies, criminology, drafting and design technology, economics, education of the emotionally handicapped, education of the mentally handicapped, electronic technology, elementary education, English, English education, food science and nutrition, health education, health sciences, history, home economics, home economics education, industrial arts education, industrial technology, institutional management, institutional/home management/supporting programs, journalism, mathematics, mathematics education, music, music education, nursing, nutritional education, nutritional sciences, physical education, political science and government, predentistry, prelaw, premedicine, prepharmacy, preveterinary, psychology, recreation and community services technologies, science education, secondary education, secretarial and related programs, social science education, social sciences, social studies education, social work, soil sciences, special education, technical education, textiles and clothing, trade and industrial education.

ACADEMIC PROGRAMS. Accelerated program, cooperative education, double major, honors program, independent study, internships, teacher preparation. **Remedial services:** Learning center, preadmission summer program, remedial instruction, special counselor, tutoring, special services program for disadvantaged students. **ROTC:** Army. **Placement/credit:** AP, CLEP General and Subject, institutional tests; 6 credit hours maximum for associate degree; 15 credit hours maximum for bachelor's degree.

ACADEMIC REQUIREMENTS. Freshmen must earn minimum GPA of 2.0 to continue in good standing. 68% of freshmen return for sophomore year. Students must declare major by end of second year. **Graduation requirements:** 70 hours for associate (34 in major), 128 hours for bachelor's (44 in major). Most students required to take courses in arts/fine arts, English, history, humanities, mathematics, biological/physical sciences, social sciences. **Postgraduate studies:** 2% enter law school, 2% enter medical school, 5% enter MBA programs, 16% enter other graduate study.

FRESHMAN ADMISSIONS. Selection criteria: Test scores, school achievement record, specific academic units considered. **High school preparation:** 14 units required. Required units include biological science 3, English 4, mathematics 3 and social science 3. One unit in foreign language, or additional unit in advanced mathematics or science required. **Test requirements:** SAT or ACT (ACT preferred); score report by July 21.

1992 FRESHMAN CLASS PROFILE. 502 men and women enrolled. 40% had high school GPA of 3.0 or higher, 60% between 2.0 and 2.99. **Academic background:** Mid 50% of enrolled freshmen had ACT composite between 14-23. 95% submitted ACT scores. **Characteristics:** 82% from in state, 94% live in college housing, 96% have minority backgrounds, 1% are foreign students, 20% join fraternities/sororities. Average age is 18.

FALL-TERM APPLICATIONS. No fee. No closing date; priority given to applications received by July 21; applicants notified on a rolling basis. Interview required for nursing applicants. Audition required for music applicants. Deferred and early admission available.

STUDENT LIFE. Housing: Dormitories (men, women). **Activities:** Student government, film, magazine, radio, student newspaper, television, yearbook, choral groups, concert band, dance, drama, jazz band, marching band, music ensembles, fraternities, sororities, Baptist Student Union.

ATHLETICS. NAIA, NCAA. **Intercollegiate:** Baseball M, basketball, cross-country, football M, gymnastics, tennis, track and field. **Intramural:** Basketball, bowling, golf, gymnastics, handball, softball, swimming, table tennis, tennis, track and field, volleyball, wrestling M.

STUDENT SERVICES. Aptitude testing, career counseling, employment service for undergraduates, freshman orientation, health services, on-campus day care, personal counseling, placement service for graduates, special adviser for adult students, veterans counselor.

ANNUAL EXPENSES. Tuition and fees (1992-93): $2,376, $1,960 additional for out-of-state students. **Room and board:** $2,098. **Books and supplies:** $400. **Other expenses:** $900.

FINANCIAL AID. 92% of freshmen, 90% of continuing students receive some form of aid. Grants, loans, jobs available. Academic, music/drama, athletic, alumni affiliation, minority scholarships available. **Aid applications:** No closing date; priority given to applications received by April 14; applicants notified on a rolling basis beginning on or about July 1; must reply within 30 days.

ADDRESS/TELEPHONE. Albert Z. Johnson, Director of Admissions, Alcorn State University, Box 300, Lorman, MS 39096. (601) 877-6147.

Belhaven College

Jackson, Mississippi CB code: 1055

4-year private liberal arts college, coed, affiliated with Presbyterian Church (USA). Founded in 1883. **Accreditation:** Regional. **Undergraduate enrollment:** 310 men, 413 women full time; 134 men, 199 women part time. **Faculty:** 77 total (34 full time), 27 with doctorates or other terminal degrees. **Location:** Urban campus in small city; 188 miles from New Orleans, Louisiana, 200 miles from Memphis, Tennessee. **Calendar:** Semester, extensive summer session. Saturday classes. **Microcomputers:** Located in libraries, classrooms, computer centers. **Special facilities:** Private lake.

DEGREES OFFERED. BFA. 156 bachelor's degrees awarded in 1992. 36% in business and management, 13% teacher education, 8% letters/literature, 7% life sciences, 5% mathematics, 5% philosophy, religion, theology, 7% psychology, 7% social sciences, 8% visual and performing arts.

UNDERGRADUATE MAJORS. Accounting, Bible studies, biology, business administration and management, chemistry, computer and information sciences, elementary education, English, fine arts, history, humanities and social sciences, mathematics, music, music performance, philosophy, physical sciences, prelaw, psychology.

ACADEMIC PROGRAMS. Double major, dual enrollment of high school students, honors program, independent study, internships, study abroad, teacher preparation, weekend college, cross-registration; liberal arts/career combination in health sciences. **Remedial services:** Preadmission summer program, reduced course load, remedial instruction, tutoring. **Placement/credit:** AP, institutional tests; 8 credit hours maximum for bachelor's degree.

ACADEMIC REQUIREMENTS. Freshmen must earn minimum GPA of 2.0 to continue in good standing. Students must declare major by end of second year. **Graduation requirements:** 124 hours for bachelor's (36 in major). Most students required to take courses in arts/fine arts, computer science, English, foreign languages, history, mathematics, philosophy/religion, biological/physical sciences, social sciences. **Postgraduate studies:** 2% enter law school, 1% enter medical school, 12% enter other graduate study.

FRESHMAN ADMISSIONS. Selection criteria: Test scores, school record, character. **High school preparation:** 16 units required. Required and recommended units include English 4, mathematics 2, social science 1 and science 1. Foreign language 2 recommended. Recommend a typing course and a computer course. **Test requirements:** SAT or ACT (ACT preferred); score report by August 15.

1992 FRESHMAN CLASS PROFILE. 71 men, 86 women enrolled. **Academic background:** Mid 50% of enrolled freshmen had ACT composite between 18-24. 92% submitted ACT scores. **Characteristics:** 8% from in state, 66% live in college housing, 14% have minority backgrounds, 1% are foreign students. Average age is 18.

FALL-TERM APPLICATIONS. $15 fee, may be waived for applicants with need. No closing date; priority given to applications received by May 1; applicants notified on a rolling basis. Audition required for music applicants. Interview recommended for art, music applicants. Portfolio recommended for art applicants. Deferred and early admission available.

STUDENT LIFE. Housing: Dormitories (men, women). **Activities:** Student government, student newspaper, yearbook, choral groups, drama, music ensembles, service clubs. **Additional information:** Soccer team ranked number one in the nation. Religious observance required.

ATHLETICS. NAIA. **Intercollegiate:** Baseball M, basketball, cross-country, soccer, tennis. **Intramural:** Basketball, football M, softball, swimming, tennis, volleyball.

STUDENT SERVICES. Aptitude testing, career counseling, employment service for undergraduates, freshman orientation, health services, personal counseling, placement service for graduates, services/facilities for handicapped.

ANNUAL EXPENSES. Tuition and fees: $7,140. **Room and board:** $2,580. **Books and supplies:** $1,400. **Other expenses:** $4,110.

FINANCIAL AID. 92% of freshmen, 90% of continuing students receive some form of aid. 43% of grants, 86% of loans, all jobs based on need. Academic, music/drama, art, athletic, leadership scholarships available. **Aid applications:** No closing date; priority given to applications received by April 1; applicants notified on a rolling basis beginning on or about April 15.

ADDRESS/TELEPHONE. Mary I. Word, Director of Admissions, Belhaven College, 1500 Peachtree Street, Jackson, MS 39202-1789. (601) 968-5940. Fax: (601) 968-9998.

Blue Mountain College
Blue Mountain, Mississippi CB code: 1066

4-year private liberal arts college, women only, affiliated with Southern Baptist Convention. Founded in 1873. **Accreditation:** Regional. **Undergraduate enrollment:** 48 men, 237 women full time; 19 men, 94 women part time. **Location:** Rural campus in rural community; 70 miles from Memphis, Tennessee. **Calendar:** Semester. **Additional facts:** Men admitted to church-related programs.

FRESHMAN ADMISSIONS. Selection criteria: High school record, test scores, and individual motivation considered.

ANNUAL EXPENSES. Tuition and fees: $3,718. **Room and board:** $2,090. **Books and supplies:** $500. **Other expenses:** $1,500.

ADDRESS/TELEPHONE. Glen Liebig, Director of Admissions, Blue Mountain College, PO Box 126, Route 1, Blue Mountain, MS 38610. (601) 685-4771 ext. 66. Fax: (601) 685-4776.

Coahoma Community College
Clarksdale, Mississippi CB code: 1126

2-year public community college, coed. Founded in 1949. **Accreditation:** Regional. **Undergraduate enrollment:** 851 men and women. **Location:** Rural campus in rural community. **Calendar:** Semester.

FRESHMAN ADMISSIONS. Selection criteria: High school record most important for admission to degree programs. Open admissions to vocational programs.

ANNUAL EXPENSES. Tuition and fees (projected): $910, $400 additional for out-of-district students, $1,900 additional for out-of-state students. **Room and board:** $2,037. **Books and supplies:** $500. **Other expenses:** $200.

ADDRESS/TELEPHONE. Rita S. Hanfor, Director of Admissions, Coahoma Community College, 3240 Friars Point Road, Clarksdale, MS 38614-9799. (601) 627-2571 ext. 154. (800) 844-1222. Fax: (601) 627-2571.

Copiah-Lincoln Community College
Wesson, Mississippi CB code: 1142

2-year public community college, coed. Founded in 1928. **Accreditation:** Regional. **Undergraduate enrollment:** 720 men, 930 women full time; 150 men, 385 women part time. **Faculty:** 122 total (88 full time), 7 with doctorates or other terminal degrees. **Location:** Rural campus in rural community; 45 miles from Jackson. **Calendar:** Semester, limited summer session. **Microcomputers:** 80 located in libraries, classrooms, computer centers. **Additional facts:** Natchez campus.

DEGREES OFFERED. AA, AS. 250 associate degrees awarded in 1992. 30% in business and management, 10% computer sciences, 10% education, 5% engineering, 5% health sciences, 10% allied health, 5% law, 25% trade and industry.

UNDERGRADUATE MAJORS. Accounting, architecture, automotive technology, business administration and management, business data entry equipment operation, business data processing and related programs, chemistry, clinical laboratory science, computer and information sciences, computer programming, computer technology, drafting, drafting and design technology, education, electrical and electronics equipment repair, electronic technology, elementary education, engineering, food production/management/services, laboratory technology, liberal/general studies, precision metal work, prelaw, radiograph medical technology, science technologies, secondary education, secretarial and related programs.

ACADEMIC PROGRAMS. 2-year transfer program, honors program. **Remedial services:** Learning center, remedial instruction, tutoring. **Placement/credit:** AP, CLEP General and Subject; 12 credit hours maximum for associate degree.

ACADEMIC REQUIREMENTS. No policy requiring minimum GPA; records of students having academic difficulty are reviewed individually. 60% of freshmen return for sophomore year. Students must declare major by end of first year. **Graduation requirements:** 64 hours for associate. Most students required to take courses in computer science, English, history, humanities, mathematics, biological/physical sciences.

FRESHMAN ADMISSIONS. Selection criteria: Open admissions. Prerequisites for admission to health occupation professions include minimum ACT composite score of 16. **Test requirements:** ACT for placement and counseling only; score report by August 1. ACT used for admissions for health occupation professions programs.

1992 FRESHMAN CLASS PROFILE. 611 men, 918 women enrolled. **Characteristics:** 95% from in state, 50% commute, 30% have minority backgrounds.

FALL-TERM APPLICATIONS. No fee. Closing date August 1; applicants notified on a rolling basis. Early admission available.

STUDENT LIFE. Housing: Dormitories (men, women); apartment housing available. **Activities:** Student government, radio, student newspaper, yearbook, choral groups, concert band, drama, marching band, music ensembles.

ATHLETICS. NJCAA. **Intercollegiate:** Baseball M, basketball, football M, golf, softball W, tennis, track and field M. **Intramural:** Basketball, softball, volleyball.

STUDENT SERVICES. Aptitude testing, career counseling, freshman orientation, health services, on-campus day care, personal counseling, veterans counselor.

ANNUAL EXPENSES. Tuition and fees: $1,000, $1,200 additional for out-of-state students. **Room and board:** $1,680. **Books and supplies:** $500.

FINANCIAL AID. 45% of freshmen, 52% of continuing students receive some form of aid. 78% of grants, 98% of loans, 66% of jobs based on need. 575 enrolled freshmen were judged to have need, all were offered aid. Academic, music/drama, art, athletic, leadership scholarships available. **Aid applications:** No closing date; priority given to applications received by April 1; applicants notified on a rolling basis beginning on or about July 15; must reply within 10 days.

ADDRESS/TELEPHONE. Ralph Frazier, Director of Admissions/Records, Copiah-Lincoln Community College, PO Box 371, Wesson, MS 39191. (601) 643-8307.

Delta State University
Cleveland, Mississippi CB code: 1163

4-year public university, coed. Founded in 1924. **Accreditation:** Regional. **Undergraduate enrollment:** 1,201 men, 1,606 women full time; 149 men, 269 women part time. **Graduate enrollment:** 59 men, 67 women full time; 125 men, 189 women part time. **Faculty:** 260 total (182 full time), 114 with doctorates or other terminal degrees. **Location:** Rural campus in large town; 110 miles from Memphis, Tennessee, 40 miles from Greenville, Mississippi. **Calendar:** Semester, extensive summer session. Extensive evening/early morning classes. **Microcomputers:** 270 located in libraries, classrooms, computer centers. **Special facilities:** Planetarium, art gallery, airport.

DEGREES OFFERED. BA, BS, BFA, MS, MBA, MEd, EdD. 646 bachelor's degrees awarded in 1992. 39% in business and management, 18% education, 5% life sciences, 13% social sciences, 5% trade and industry. Graduate degrees offered in 13 major fields of study.

UNDERGRADUATE MAJORS. Accounting, air traffic control, airline piloting and navigation, aviation management, biology, biomedical equipment technology, business and management, business education, chemistry, clinical laboratory science, criminal justice studies, elementary education, English, English education, environmental science, fashion merchandising, finance, fine arts, foreign languages education, history, home economics, home economics education, information sciences and systems, insurance and risk management, management science, marketing management, mathematics, mathematics education, music, music education, nursing, office supervision and management, physical education, political science and government, psychology, real estate, science education, social science education, social sciences, social work, Spanish, special education, speech pathology/audiology.

ACADEMIC PROGRAMS. Double major, dual enrollment of high school students, education specialist degree, honors program, independent study, internships, teacher preparation, visiting/exchange student program. **Remedial services:** Learning center, remedial instruction, special counselor, tutoring. **ROTC:** Air Force, Army. **Placement/credit:** AP, CLEP General and Subject, institutional tests; 30 credit hours maximum for bachelor's degree.

ACADEMIC REQUIREMENTS. Freshmen must earn minimum GPA of 2.0 to continue in good standing. 72% of freshmen return for sophomore year. Students must declare major by end of second year. **Graduation requirements:** 128 hours for bachelor's (45 in major). Most students required to take courses in arts/fine arts, English, history, humanities, mathematics, biological/physical sciences, social sciences. **Postgraduate studies:** 2% enter law school, 4% enter medical school, 10% enter MBA programs, 11% enter other graduate study.

FRESHMAN ADMISSIONS. Selection criteria: Academic record, test scores. **High school preparation:** 13.5 units required. Required units include English 4, foreign language 1, mathematics 3, social science 2.5 and science 3. Mathematics requirement includes algebra I and II and geometry. Social sciences must include US government and US history. Sciences to be chosen from introductory and advanced biology, physics, and chemistry. Additional science or mathematics may be substituted for a foreign language. **Test requirements:** SAT or ACT (ACT preferred); score report by September 1. Mississippi residents must take ACT for admission.

1992 FRESHMAN CLASS PROFILE. 196 men, 247 women enrolled. **Academic background:** Mid 50% of enrolled freshmen had ACT composite between 18-23. 99% submitted ACT scores. **Characteristics:** 91% from in state, 58% live in college housing, 27% have minority backgrounds, 1% are foreign students, 27% join fraternities/sororities. Average age is 18.

FALL-TERM APPLICATIONS. No fee. No closing date; priority given to applications received by May 1; applicants notified on a rolling basis. Interview recommended for art, music applicants. Audition recommended for music applicants. Portfolio recommended for art applicants. Deferred and early admission available.

STUDENT LIFE. Housing: Dormitories (men, women); apartment housing available. **Activities:** Student government, film, magazine, student newspaper, yearbook, choral groups, concert band, drama, jazz band, marching band, music ensembles, musical theater, opera, pep band, symphony orchestra, fraternities, sororities, several honorary, athletic, academic, professional, religious, ethnic, social, and political groups.

ATHLETICS. NCAA. **Intercollegiate:** Baseball M, basketball, cross-country W, diving, football M, golf M, softball W, swimming, tennis. **Intramural:** Archery, badminton, basketball, bowling, cross-country, diving, golf, handball, racquetball, rifle, softball, swimming, table tennis, tennis, track and field, volleyball.

STUDENT SERVICES. Aptitude testing, career counseling, employment service for undergraduates, freshman orientation, health services, on-campus day care, personal counseling, placement service for graduates, services/facilities for handicapped.

ANNUAL EXPENSES. Tuition and fees (1992-93): $2,194, $1,960 additional for out-of-state students. **Room and board:** $1,770. **Books and supplies:** $500. **Other expenses:** $3,090.

FINANCIAL AID. 68% of freshmen, 68% of continuing students receive some form of aid. 76% of grants, 84% of loans, 72% of jobs based on need. Academic, music/drama, art, athletic, state/district residency, leadership, alumni affiliation scholarships available. **Aid applications:** No closing date; priority given to applications received by June 1; applicants notified on a rolling basis beginning on or about July 1; must reply within 2 weeks.

ADDRESS/TELEPHONE. Betsy Bobo Elliot, Director of Admissions, Delta State University, PO Box 3151, Cleveland, MS 38733. (601) 846-4656. (800) 468-6378. Fax: (601) 846-4016.

East Central Community College
Decatur, Mississippi — CB code: 1196

2-year public community college, coed. Founded in 1928. **Accreditation:** Regional. **Undergraduate enrollment:** 490 men, 456 women full time; 111 men, 342 women part time. **Faculty:** 74 total (46 full time), 5 with doctorates or other terminal degrees. **Location:** Rural campus in rural community; 30 miles from Meridian. **Calendar:** Semester, limited summer session. Extensive evening/early morning classes. **Microcomputers:** Located in computer centers.

DEGREES OFFERED. AA, AS, AAS. 193 associate degrees awarded in 1992.

UNDERGRADUATE MAJORS. Biology, business administration and management, business and office, business data processing and related programs, business data programming, chemistry, computer and information sciences, drafting, education, engineering, fine arts, liberal/general studies, mathematics, music, nursing, precision metal work, predentistry, premedicine, prepharmacy, preveterinary, psychology, secretarial and related programs, word processing.

ACADEMIC PROGRAMS. 2-year transfer program, honors program. **Remedial services:** Remedial instruction, tutoring. **Placement/credit:** AP; 6 credit hours maximum for associate degree.

ACADEMIC REQUIREMENTS. Freshmen must earn minimum GPA of 2.0 to continue in good standing. 50% of freshmen return for sophomore year. Students must declare major on application. **Graduation requirements:** 64 hours for associate. Most students required to take courses in arts/fine arts, computer science, English, humanities, mathematics, biological/physical sciences.

FRESHMAN ADMISSIONS. Selection criteria: Open admissions. **Test requirements:** ACT for placement and counseling only; score report by August 30.

1992 FRESHMAN CLASS PROFILE. 675 men and women enrolled. **Characteristics:** 98% from in state, 55% commute, 46% have minority backgrounds. Average age is 19.

FALL-TERM APPLICATIONS. No fee. No closing date.

STUDENT LIFE. Housing: Dormitories (men, women); apartment housing available. **Activities:** Student government, student newspaper, yearbook, choral groups, concert band, drama, jazz band, marching band.

ATHLETICS. NJCAA. **Intercollegiate:** Baseball M, basketball, football M, golf, softball W, tennis. **Intramural:** Basketball, softball, table tennis.

STUDENT SERVICES. Career counseling, freshman orientation, health services, on-campus day care, personal counseling, veterans counselor, services/facilities for handicapped.

ANNUAL EXPENSES. Tuition and fees (projected): $1,000, $1,200 additional for out-of-state students. **Room and board:** $1,830. **Books and supplies:** $350.

FINANCIAL AID. 38% of freshmen, 43% of continuing students receive some form of aid. 74% of grants, 96% of loans, 76% of jobs based on need. 258 enrolled freshmen were judged to have need, all were offered aid. Academic, music/drama, art, athletic, state/district residency, leadership scholarships available. **Aid applications:** No closing date; priority given to applications received by June 1; applicants notified on a rolling basis beginning on or about July 31; must reply within 2 weeks.

ADDRESS/TELEPHONE. Raymond McMullan, Director of Admissions, East Central Community College, Decatur, MS 39327. (601) 635-2111 ext. 206.

East Mississippi Community College
Scooba, Mississippi — CB code: 1197

2-year public community college, coed. Founded in 1927. **Accreditation:** Regional. **Undergraduate enrollment:** 1,381 men and women. **Faculty:** 86 total (51 full time), 4 with doctorates or other terminal degrees. **Location:** Rural campus in rural community; 37 miles from Meridian. **Calendar:** Semester. Saturday and extensive evening/early morning classes. **Microcomputers:** 30 located in libraries, classrooms, computer centers.

DEGREES OFFERED. AA, AS, AAS. 85 associate degrees awarded in 1992.

UNDERGRADUATE MAJORS. Accounting, aeronautical technology, air conditioning/heating/refrigeration technology, allied health, automotive technology, biological and physical sciences, business and office, business education, drafting, drafting and design technology, education, electrical technology, elementary education, engineering and engineering-related technologies, finance, forest products processing technology, forestry production and processing, funeral services/mortuary science, graphic arts technology, health education, humanities, liberal/general studies, marketing and distribution, mathematics, mathematics education, music, music education, nursing, occupational therapy assistant, ophthalmic services, optical technology, physical education, physical therapy assistant, predentistry, prelaw, premedicine, prepharmacy, preveterinary, recreation and community services technologies, science education, science technologies, secondary education, social sciences, social studies education, welding technology, wildlife management.

ACADEMIC PROGRAMS. 2-year transfer program. **Remedial services:** Learning center, reduced course load, remedial instruction. **Placement/credit:** AP, CLEP General, institutional tests; 30 credit hours maximum for associate degree.

ACADEMIC REQUIREMENTS. Freshmen must earn minimum GPA of 2.0 to continue in good standing. Students must declare major on enrollment. **Graduation requirements:** 64 hours for associate. Most students required to take courses in English, humanities, mathematics, biological/physical sciences.

FRESHMAN ADMISSIONS. Selection criteria: Open admissions. **Test requirements:** ACT for placement and counseling only; score report by August 22.

1992 FRESHMAN CLASS PROFILE. 996 men and women enrolled. **Academic background:** Mid 50% of enrolled freshmen had ACT composite between 10-20. 90% submitted ACT scores. **Characteristics:** 80% from in state, 90% live in college housing, 40% have minority backgrounds, 1% are foreign students. Average age is 19.

FALL-TERM APPLICATIONS. No fee. No closing date; applicants notified on a rolling basis. Early admission available.

STUDENT LIFE. Housing: Dormitories (men, women). **Activities:** Student government, film, student newspaper, yearbook, choral groups, music ensembles, musical theater, pep band, Baptist Student Union, Wesley Foundation, Blacks Unlimited.

ATHLETICS. NJCAA. **Intercollegiate:** Baseball M, basketball, football M. **Intramural:** Basketball, softball, tennis, volleyball.

STUDENT SERVICES. Aptitude testing, career counseling, freshman orientation, personal counseling, placement service for graduates, services/facilities for handicapped.

ANNUAL EXPENSES. Tuition and fees (projected): $1,000, $1,000 additional for out-of-state students. **Room and board:** $1,960. **Books and supplies:** $300. **Other expenses:** $400.

FINANCIAL AID. 76% of freshmen, 73% of continuing students receive some form of aid. 72% of grants, 93% of loans, all jobs based on need. Academic, music/drama, athletic scholarships available. **Aid applications:** Closing date June 30; priority given to applications received by April 30; applicants notified on or about July 1; must reply by August 15.

ADDRESS/TELEPHONE. Melinda Sciple, Director of Admissions, East Mississippi Community College, PO Box 158, Scooba, MS 39358. (601) 476-8442. Fax: (601) 476-5618.

Hinds Community College
Raymond, Mississippi — CB code: 1296

2-year public community, junior college, coed. Founded in 1917. **Accreditation:** Regional. **Undergraduate enrollment:** 2,700 men, 3,852 women full time; 882 men, 1,853 women part time. **Faculty:** 725 total (392 full time), 30 with doctorates or other terminal degrees. **Location:** Suburban campus in small town; 6 miles from Jackson. **Calendar:** Semester, extensive summer session. Saturday and extensive evening/early morning classes. **Microcomputers:** 55 located in libraries.

DEGREES OFFERED. AA, AAS. 884 associate degrees awarded in 1992. 20% in business/office and marketing/distribution, 5% engineering technologies, 21% health sciences, 47% multi/interdisciplinary studies.

UNDERGRADUATE MAJORS. Aeronautical technology, agribusiness, agricultural mechanics, automotive technology, business and office, business data processing and related programs, business data programming, child development/care/guidance, commercial art, computer-aided manufacturing, dental assistant, diesel engine mechanics, drafting, drafting and design technology, educational media technology, electronic technology, emergency medical technologies, engineering and engineering-related technologies, fashion merchandising, finance, graphic and printing production, graphic arts technology, hospitality and recreation marketing, hotel/motel and restaurant management, landscape management, law enforcement and corrections technologies, liberal/general studies, marketing and distribution, mechanical design technology, medical laboratory technologies, medical records technology, mental health/human services, nuclear technologies, nursing, personal services, precision metal work, real estate, respiratory therapy technology, secretarial and related programs, surgical technology, veterinarian's assistant.

ACADEMIC PROGRAMS. 2-year transfer program, cooperative education, honors program, independent study, study abroad. **Remedial services:** Preadmission summer program, remedial instruction, special counselor, tutoring. **ROTC:** Army. **Placement/credit:** AP, CLEP Subject, institutional tests; 18 credit hours maximum for associate degree.

ACADEMIC REQUIREMENTS. Freshmen must earn minimum GPA of 1.75 to continue in good standing. Students must declare major on application. **Graduation requirements:** 64 hours for associate (32 in major). Most students required to take courses in English, history, mathematics, biological/physical sciences, social sciences.

FRESHMAN ADMISSIONS. Selection criteria: Open admissions. Selective admissions to allied health, data processing programs. **High school preparation:** 17 units recommended. Recommended units include English 4, mathematics 2, social science 2 and science 2. 17 high school units and ACT composite score of 18 may be substituted for diploma. **Test requirements:** ACT for placement and counseling only; score report by August 18. ACT not required of students enrolling in vocational programs.

1992 FRESHMAN CLASS PROFILE. 1,281 men, 1,598 women enrolled. **Characteristics:** 99% from in state, 81% commute, 41% have minority backgrounds.

FALL-TERM APPLICATIONS. No fee. Closing date August 18; applicants notified on a rolling basis beginning on or about March 1. Interview required for vocational, allied health applicants.

STUDENT LIFE. Housing: Dormitories (men, women). **Activities:** Student government, student newspaper, yearbook, choral groups, concert band, drama, jazz band, marching band, music ensembles, musical theater, pep band, Baptist Student Union, Afro-American Cultural Society.

ATHLETICS. NJCAA. **Intercollegiate:** Baseball M, basketball, football M, golf M, soccer M, softball W, tennis, track and field M. **Intramural:** Basketball, softball M, volleyball.

STUDENT SERVICES. Career counseling, employment service for undergraduates, freshman orientation, personal counseling, placement service for graduates, services/facilities for handicapped.

ANNUAL EXPENSES. Tuition and fees (projected): $1,120, $1,186 additional for out-of-state students. **Room and board:** $1,648. **Books and supplies:** $400. **Other expenses:** $1,309.

FINANCIAL AID. 40% of freshmen, 59% of continuing students receive some form of aid. 16% of grants, 79% of loans, 58% of jobs based on need. Academic, music/drama, art, athletic, state/district residency, leadership, minority scholarships available. **Aid applications:** No closing date; priority given to applications received by April 1; applicants notified on a rolling basis beginning on or about May 15; must reply within 2 weeks.

ADDRESS/TELEPHONE. Billy T. Irby, Director of Admissions and Records, Hinds Community College, Raymond, MS 39154-9799. (601) 857-5261.

Holmes Community College
Goodman, Mississippi — CB code: 1299

2-year public community college, coed. Founded in 1925. **Accreditation:** Regional. **Undergraduate enrollment:** 569 men, 619 women full time; 405 men, 724 women part time. **Faculty:** 141 total (105 full time), 3 with doctorates or other terminal degrees. **Location:** Rural campus in rural community; 45 miles from Jackson. **Calendar:** Semester. **Microcomputers:** Located in libraries. **Special facilities:** Observatory, planetarium.

DEGREES OFFERED. AA, AAS. 170 associate degrees awarded in 1992.

UNDERGRADUATE MAJORS. Allied health, architectural technologies, biological and physical sciences, business administration and management, child development/care/guidance, computer and information sciences, computer mathematics, computer programming, drafting and design technology, electronic technology, elementary education, engineering, engineering and engineering-related technologies, fashion merchandising, forestry and related sciences, liberal/general studies, marketing and distribution, mathematics, microcomputer software, music, nursing, predentistry, premedicine, prepharmacy, preveterinary, robotics, secondary education, secretarial and related programs.

ACADEMIC PROGRAMS. 2-year transfer program, cooperative education, dual enrollment of high school students, internships. **Remedial services:** Learning center, reduced course load, remedial instruction, special counselor, tutoring. **Placement/credit:** AP, institutional tests.

ACADEMIC REQUIREMENTS. Freshmen must earn minimum GPA of 1.5 to continue in good standing. 60% of freshmen return for sophomore year. Students must declare major on enrollment. **Graduation requirements:** 64 hours for associate. Most students required to take courses in English, mathematics, biological/physical sciences, social sciences.

FRESHMAN ADMISSIONS. Selection criteria: Test scores most important; school record considered. **High school preparation:** 18 units recommended. Recommended units include English 4, mathematics 2, social science 2 and science 2. **Test requirements:** SAT or ACT (ACT preferred); score report by January 10.

1992 FRESHMAN CLASS PROFILE. 261 men, 249 women enrolled.

FALL-TERM APPLICATIONS. No fee. No closing date; applicants notified on a rolling basis. Applicants accepted until registration closes.

STUDENT LIFE. Housing: Dormitories (men, women). **Activities:** Student government, radio, student newspaper, yearbook, creative writing publications, choral groups, concert band, dance, drama, jazz band, marching band, music ensembles, musical theater, pep band, Baptist Student Union, Wesley Foundation, College Republican Club, Fellowship of Christian Athletes, collegiate service club.

ATHLETICS. NJCAA. **Intercollegiate:** Baseball M, basketball, football M, golf, tennis. **Intramural:** Basketball W, football M, softball, volleyball.

STUDENT SERVICES. Aptitude testing, career counseling, freshman orientation, on-campus day care, personal counseling, special adviser for adult students, veterans counselor, services/facilities for handicapped.

ANNUAL EXPENSES. Tuition and fees (1992-93): $804, $1,000 additional for out-of-state students. **Room and board:** $1,400. **Books and supplies:** $400.

FINANCIAL AID. 78% of grants, 92% of loans, all jobs based on need. Academic, music/drama, art, athletic scholarships available. **Aid applications:** No closing date; applicants notified on a rolling basis.

ADDRESS/TELEPHONE. Gene Richardson, Director of Admissions and Records, Holmes Community College, PO Box 369, Goodman, MS 39079. (601) 472-2312 ext. 23. Fax: (601) 472-2566.

Itawamba Community College
Fulton, Mississippi — CB code: 1326

2-year public community college, coed. Founded in 1948. **Accreditation:** Regional. **Undergraduate enrollment:** 3,450 men and women. **Location:** Rural campus in small town. **Calendar:** Semester. **Additional facts:** Campuses in Fulton and Tupelo.

FRESHMAN ADMISSIONS. Selection criteria: Open admissions.

ANNUAL EXPENSES. Tuition and fees: $905, $850 additional for out-of-state students. **Room and board:** $1,775. **Books and supplies:** $600. **Other expenses:** $800.

ADDRESS/TELEPHONE. Carl Comer, Director of Admissions, Itawamba Community College, 602 W. Hill Street, Fulton, MS 38843. (601) 862-3101. Fax: (601) 842-6883.

Jackson State University
Jackson, Mississippi — CB code: 1341

4-year public university, coed. Founded in 1877. **Accreditation:** Regional. **Undergraduate enrollment:** 2,109 men, 2,744 women full time; 222 men, 381 women part time. **Graduate enrollment:** 114 men, 189 women full time; 147 men, 297 women part time. **Faculty:** 492 total (420 full time), 265 with doctorates or other terminal degrees. **Location:** Urban campus in small city; 210 miles from Memphis, Tennessee, 190 miles from New Orleans, Louisiana. **Calendar:** Semester, extensive summer session. **Microcomputers:** Located in libraries, classrooms, computer centers. **Special facilities:** University archives, Margaret Walker Alexander National Research Center, Just Hall Science Observatory, Academic Research and Computing Center.

DEGREES OFFERED. BA, BS, MA, MS, MBA, MEd, MSW, PhD, EdD. 641 bachelor's degrees awarded in 1992. 32% in business and management, 5% business/office and marketing/distribution, 7% communications, 7% computer sciences, 6% education, 5% engineering technologies, 5% life sciences, 13% parks/recreation, protective services, public affairs, 5% psychology, 5% social sciences. Graduate degrees offered in 28 major fields of study.

UNDERGRADUATE MAJORS. Accounting, atmospheric sciences and meteorology, biology, business administration and management, business and management, business economics, chemistry, city/community/regional planning, communications, computer and information sciences, computer programming, computer technology, criminal justice studies, data processing, dramatic arts, early childhood education, economics, education, education of exceptional children, education of the deaf and hearing impaired, education of the gifted and talented, education of the mentally handicapped, education of the physically handicapped, education of the visually handicapped, electronic technology, English, English literature, finance, health education, health sciences, history, industrial technology, information sciences and systems, journalism, law enforcement and corrections, marine biology, marketing and distribution, marketing management, mathematics, music, music performance, nursing, office supervision and management, pathology, human and animal, pharmacy, physical education, physics, political science and government, predentistry, prelaw, premedicine, prepharmacy, preveterinary, psychology, public relations, radio/television broadcasting, radio/television technology, remedial education, school psychology, secondary education, secretarial and related programs, social science education, social sciences, social work, sociology, Spanish, special education, speech, speech correction, urban studies.

ACADEMIC PROGRAMS. Cooperative education, double major, education specialist degree, honors program, independent study, internships, teacher preparation, visiting/exchange student program, weekend college, cross-registration; combined bachelor's/graduate program in business administration. **Remedial services:** Learning center, preadmission summer program, reduced course load, remedial instruction, special counselor, tutoring. **ROTC:** Army. **Placement/credit:** AP, CLEP General and Subject; 30 credit hours maximum for bachelor's degree.

ACADEMIC REQUIREMENTS. Freshmen must earn minimum GPA of 2.0 to continue in good standing. 65% of freshmen return for sophomore year. Students must declare major by end of second year. **Graduation requirements:** 128 hours for bachelor's (30 in major). Most students required to take courses in English, history, mathematics, biological/physical sciences, social sciences.

FRESHMAN ADMISSIONS. Selection criteria: Test scores and high school transcript important. **High school preparation:** 13.5 units required. Required units include English 4, foreign language 1, mathematics 3, social science 2.5 and science 3. **Test requirements:** SAT or ACT (ACT preferred); score report by August 1.

1992 FRESHMAN CLASS PROFILE. 784 men, 874 women enrolled. 43% had high school GPA of 3.0 or higher, 49% between 2.0 and 2.99. **Academic background:** Mid 50% of enrolled freshmen had ACT composite between 15-20. 84% submitted ACT scores. **Characteristics:** 63% from in state, 59% commute, 99% have minority backgrounds, 2% are foreign students. Average age is 18.

FALL-TERM APPLICATIONS. No fee. Closing date August 15; applicants notified on a rolling basis beginning on or about January 1. Audition recommended for music applicants. Deferred and early admission available. EDP-F.

STUDENT LIFE. Housing: Dormitories (men, women). **Activities:** Student government, film, magazine, radio, student newspaper, television, yearbook, choral groups, concert band, dance, drama, jazz band, marching band, music ensembles, opera, symphony orchestra, fraternities, sororities, COGIC, NAACP, Alpha Phi Omega.

ATHLETICS. NCAA. **Intercollegiate:** Baseball M, basketball, cross-country M, football M, golf, rifle, tennis, track and field, volleyball W. **Intramural:** Basketball, rifle, swimming, tennis, volleyball.

STUDENT SERVICES. Aptitude testing, career counseling, employment service for undergraduates, freshman orientation, health services, on-campus day care, personal counseling, placement service for graduates, special adviser for adult students, veterans counselor, services/facilities for handicapped.

ANNUAL EXPENSES. Tuition and fees (1992-93): $2,223, $1,960 additional for out-of-state students. **Room and board:** $2,413. **Books and supplies:** $500. **Other expenses:** $1,018.

FINANCIAL AID. 76% of freshmen, 74% of continuing students receive some form of aid. Grants, loans, jobs available. Academic, music/drama, art, athletic, state/district residency, leadership, alumni affiliation, minority scholarships available. **Aid applications:** Closing date April 1; applicants notified on or about June 30; must reply within 2 weeks.

ADDRESS/TELEPHONE. Barbara Luckett, Director of Admissions and Recruitment, Jackson State University, 1400 J. R. Lynch Street, Jackson, MS 39217. (601) 968-2100. (800) 848-6817.

Jones County Junior College
Ellisville, Mississippi CB code: 1347

2-year public junior college, coed. Founded in 1927. **Accreditation:** Regional. **Undergraduate enrollment:** 4,005 men and women. **Location:** Rural campus in small town; 7 miles from Laurel, 20 miles from Hattiesburg. **Calendar:** Semester.

FRESHMAN ADMISSIONS. Selection criteria: Open admissions. Selective admissions to health programs. Minimum ACT composite score of 16 required for practical nursing program, 17 for x-ray technology program, and 18 for AP nursing program.

ANNUAL EXPENSES. Tuition and fees (1992-93): $792, $1,400 additional for out-of-state students. **Room and board:** $1,780. **Books and supplies:** $300. **Other expenses:** $300.

ADDRESS/TELEPHONE. Emmett Harvey, Dean of Guidance and Admissions, Jones County Junior College, 900 South Court Street, Ellisville, MS 39437. (601) 477-4025. Fax: (601) 477-4017.

Magnolia Bible College
Kosciusko, Mississippi CB code: 0162

4-year private Bible college, coed, affiliated with Church of Christ. Founded in 1976. **Accreditation:** Regional. **Undergraduate enrollment:** 15 men, 4 women full time; 10 men, 6 women part time. **Faculty:** 10 total (6 full time), 3 with doctorates or other terminal degrees. **Location:** Suburban campus in small town; 70 miles from Jackson. **Calendar:** Semester, limited summer session. Extensive evening/early morning classes.

DEGREES OFFERED. BA. 2 bachelor's degrees awarded in 1992. 100% in philosophy, religion, theology.

UNDERGRADUATE MAJORS. Bible studies.

ACADEMIC PROGRAMS. Remedial services: Remedial instruction. **Placement/credit:** Institutional tests.

ACADEMIC REQUIREMENTS. No policy requiring minimum GPA; records of students having academic difficulty are reviewed individually. **Graduation requirements:** 128 hours for bachelor's. Most students required to take courses in English, history, humanities, mathematics, philosophy/religion, biological/physical sciences.

FRESHMAN ADMISSIONS. Selection criteria: Open admissions. **Test requirements:** SAT or ACT (ACT preferred).

1992 FRESHMAN CLASS PROFILE. 7 men, 3 women enrolled. **Characteristics:** 90% live in college housing.

FALL-TERM APPLICATIONS. No fee. No closing date; applicants notified on a rolling basis. Essay required. Early admission available.

STUDENT LIFE. Housing: Dormitories (men). Women students housed with families in the area. **Activities:** Student government. **Additional information:** Religious observance required.

STUDENT SERVICES. Freshman orientation, health services, personal counseling, placement service for graduates, services/facilities for handicapped.

ANNUAL EXPENSES. Tuition and fees: $2,560. **Room and board:** $1,441. **Books and supplies:** $400. **Other expenses:** $3,549.

FINANCIAL AID. 100% of freshmen, 94% of continuing students receive some form of aid. 84% of grants, all loans, all jobs based on need. 5 enrolled freshmen were judged to have need, all were offered aid. Academic, leadership, religious affiliation scholarships available. **Aid applications:** No closing date; priority given to applications received by August 1; applicants notified on a rolling basis beginning on or about April 15; must reply by registration.

ADDRESS/TELEPHONE. Cecil May III, Director of Admissions, Magnolia Bible College, PO PO Box 1109, PO Box 1109, Kosciusko, MS 39090. (601) 289-2896. (800) 748-8655.

Mary Holmes College
West Point, Mississippi CB code: 1450

2-year private junior, liberal arts college, coed, affiliated with Presbyterian Church (USA). Founded in 1892. **Accreditation:** Regional. **Undergraduate enrollment:** 790 men and women. **Location:** Rural campus in large town; 75 miles from Tuscalrosa, Alabama. **Calendar:** Semester.

FRESHMAN ADMISSIONS. Selection criteria: Open admissions.

ANNUAL EXPENSES. Tuition and fees: $4,100. **Room and board:** $3,800. **Books and supplies:** $700. **Other expenses:** $700.

ADDRESS/TELEPHONE. James Stewart, Enrollment Marketing Manager, Mary Holmes College, PO Drawer 1257, Highway 50 West, West Point, MS 39773-1257. (601) 494-6820 ext. 139. (800) 634-2749. Fax: (601) 494-5319.

Meridian Community College
Meridian, Mississippi CB code: 1461

2-year public community college, coed. Founded in 1937. **Accreditation:** Regional. **Undergraduate enrollment:** 580 men, 1,239 women full time; 465 men, 797 women part time. **Faculty:** 199 total (125 full time), 9 with doctorates or other terminal degrees. **Location:** Urban campus in large town; 90 miles from Jackson, 90 miles from Tuscaloosa, Alabama. **Calendar:** Semester, limited summer session. **Microcomputers:** 197 located in classrooms, computer centers. **Special facilities:** Art gallery.

DEGREES OFFERED. AA. 329 associate degrees awarded in 1992. 10% in business/office and marketing/distribution, 30% health sciences, 12% allied health, 41% multi/interdisciplinary studies.

UNDERGRADUATE MAJORS. Business data processing and related programs, dental hygiene, drafting and design technology, electronic technology, hotel/motel and restaurant management, law enforcement and corrections technologies, liberal/general studies, marketing and distribution, medical laboratory technologies, medical records technology, nursing, ornamental horticulture, practical nursing, radiograph medical technology, secretarial and related programs.

ACADEMIC PROGRAMS. 2-year transfer program, independent study, study abroad. **Remedial services:** Remedial instruction, tutoring, Learning to

Learn course. **Placement/credit:** CLEP General and Subject; 30 credit hours maximum for associate degree.

ACADEMIC REQUIREMENTS. Freshmen must earn minimum GPA of 2.0 to continue in good standing. 45% of freshmen return for sophomore year. Students must declare major by end of first year. **Graduation requirements:** 64 hours for associate. Most students required to take courses in English, foreign languages, history, humanities, mathematics, biological/physical sciences, social sciences.

FRESHMAN ADMISSIONS. Selection criteria: Open admissions. Test scores, interview, recommendations considered for health education applicants. **Test requirements:** SAT or ACT (ACT preferred) for placement and counseling only; score report by August 18.

1992 FRESHMAN CLASS PROFILE. 376 men, 749 women enrolled. **Characteristics:** 99% from in state, 95% commute, 13% have minority backgrounds. Average age is 19.

FALL-TERM APPLICATIONS. No fee. No closing date; applicants notified on a rolling basis beginning on or about March 1. Interview required for health programs, data processing applicants. Early admission available.

STUDENT LIFE. Housing: Dormitories (women, coed). **Activities:** Student newspaper, literary magazine, choral groups, concert band, drama, jazz band, music ensembles, musical theater, Baptist Student Union, T. J. Harris Organization.

ATHLETICS. NJCAA. **Intercollegiate:** Baseball M, basketball, golf M, softball W, tennis. **Intramural:** Basketball M, bowling, softball W, volleyball.

STUDENT SERVICES. Aptitude testing, career counseling, freshman orientation, personal counseling, veterans counselor, services/facilities for handicapped.

ANNUAL EXPENSES. Tuition and fees (1992-93): $960, $2,000 additional for out-of-state students. **Room and board:** $1,050. **Books and supplies:** $500.

FINANCIAL AID. 45% of freshmen, 49% of continuing students receive some form of aid. 87% of grants, 84% of loans, all jobs based on need. 260 enrolled freshmen were judged to have need, 257 were offered aid. Academic, music/drama, art, athletic, leadership, minority scholarships available. **Aid applications:** No closing date; priority given to applications received by March 1; applicants notified on a rolling basis beginning on or about May 15; must reply within 1 week.

ADDRESS/TELEPHONE. Tommy McDonald, Dean of Student Services, Meridian Community College, 910 Highway 19, North, Meridian, MS 39307. (601) 483-8241.

Millsaps College
Jackson, Mississippi — CB code: 1471

Admissions: 87% of applicants accepted
Based on: ••• Essay, school record, test scores
•• Activities, recommendations
• Interview, special talents
Completion: 90% of freshmen end year in good standing
60% graduate, 42% of these enter graduate study

4-year private liberal arts college, coed, affiliated with United Methodist Church. Founded in 1890. **Accreditation:** Regional. **Undergraduate enrollment:** 523 men, 517 women full time; 63 men, 109 women part time. **Graduate enrollment:** 15 men, 14 women full time; 59 men, 29 women part time. **Faculty:** 106 total (85 full time), 72 with doctorates or other terminal degrees. **Location:** Urban campus in small city. **Calendar:** Semester, limited summer session. **Microcomputers:** 124 located in dormitories, libraries, classrooms.

DEGREES OFFERED. BA, BS, MBA. 240 bachelor's degrees awarded in 1992. 31% in business and management, 6% teacher education, 16% letters/literature, 9% life sciences, 9% physical sciences, 6% psychology, 11% social sciences. Graduate degrees offered in 1 major field of study.

UNDERGRADUATE MAJORS. Accounting, biology, business administration and management, chemistry, classics, clinical laboratory science, computer and information sciences, dramatic arts, economics, elementary education, English, French, geology, German, Greek (classical), history, liberal/general studies, mathematics, music, music performance, philosophy, physics, political science and government, predentistry, prelaw, premedicine, preveterinary, psychology, religion, religious music, secondary education, sociology, Spanish.

ACADEMIC PROGRAMS. Double major, honors program, independent study, internships, study abroad, teacher preparation, United Nations semester, Washington semester; liberal arts/career combination in engineering; combined bachelor's/graduate program in business administration. **ROTC:** Army. **Placement/credit:** AP, CLEP Subject; 16 credit hours maximum for bachelor's degree.

ACADEMIC REQUIREMENTS. Freshmen must earn minimum GPA of 1.5 to continue in good standing. 82% of freshmen return for sophomore year. Students must declare major by end of second year. **Graduation requirements:** 128 hours for bachelor's. Most students required to take courses in arts/fine arts, English, history, mathematics, philosophy/religion, biological/physical sciences, social sciences. **Postgraduate studies:** 9% enter law school, 10% enter medical school, 7% enter MBA programs, 16% enter other graduate study. **Additional information:** Undergraduate research available in most academic departments. Montoring program for students considering college teaching.

FRESHMAN ADMISSIONS. Selection criteria: Test scores and 2.0 academic course GPA. **High school preparation:** 16 units required. Required and recommended units include English 4. Foreign language 2, mathematics 2, social science 2 and science 2 recommended. 10 additional academic units required from combination of science, social sciences, mathematics, foreign language. **Test requirements:** SAT or ACT; score report by July 1.

1992 FRESHMAN CLASS PROFILE. 406 men applied, 344 accepted, 139 enrolled; 414 women applied, 372 accepted, 124 enrolled. 86% had high school GPA of 3.0 or higher, 14% between 2.0 and 2.99. 57% were in top tenth and 88% were in top quarter of graduating class. **Academic background:** Mid 50% of enrolled freshmen had SAT-V between 450-580, SAT-M between 490-630; ACT composite between 23-29. 48% submitted SAT scores, 85% submitted ACT scores. **Characteristics:** 58% from in state, 89% live in college housing, 6% have minority backgrounds, 1% are foreign students, 75% join fraternities/sororities. Average age is 18.

FALL-TERM APPLICATIONS. $25 fee, may be waived for applicants with need. Closing date May 1; priority given to applications received by April 1; applicants notified on a rolling basis beginning on or about April 1; must reply by May 1. Essay required. Interview recommended. Audition recommended. Portfolio recommended. CRDA. Deferred and early admission available. Four notification dates: December 1, January 15, March 1, April 1; rolling admissions thereafter if vacancy exists.

STUDENT LIFE. Housing: Dormitories (men, women, coed); fraternity housing available. **Activities:** Student government, magazine, student newspaper, yearbook, choral groups, dance, drama, music ensembles, musical theater, opera, symphony orchestra, fraternities, sororities, Black Student Association, Circle-K, campus ministry team, Berean Fellowship, Newman Club, Methodist Student Association.

ATHLETICS. NCAA. **Intercollegiate:** Baseball M, basketball, cross-country, football M, golf M, soccer, tennis. **Intramural:** Basketball, bowling, handball, soccer, softball, volleyball.

STUDENT SERVICES. Aptitude testing, career counseling, employment service for undergraduates, freshman orientation, health services, personal counseling, placement service for graduates, special adviser for adult students, services/facilities for handicapped.

ANNUAL EXPENSES. Tuition and fees: $11,236. **Room and board:** $4,250. **Books and supplies:** $550. **Other expenses:** $900.

FINANCIAL AID. 75% of freshmen, 72% of continuing students receive some form of aid. Grants, loans, jobs available. 215 enrolled freshmen were judged to have need, all were offered aid. Academic, music/drama, art, minority scholarships available. **Aid applications:** No closing date; priority given to applications received by March 1; applicants notified on a rolling basis beginning on or about April 15; must reply by May 1 or within 2 weeks if notified thereafter.

ADDRESS/TELEPHONE. Gary Fretwell, Vice President of Enrollment and Student Affairs, Millsaps College, PO Box 150556, Jackson, MS 39210. (601) 974-1050. (800) 352-1050. Fax: (601) 974-1059.

Mississippi College
Clinton, Mississippi — CB code: 1477

4-year private liberal arts college, coed, affiliated with Southern Baptist Convention. Founded in 1826. **Accreditation:** Regional. **Undergraduate enrollment:** 2,795 men and women. **Graduate enrollment:** 1,051 men and women. **Faculty:** 207 total (133 full time), 82 with doctorates or other terminal degrees. **Location:** Suburban campus in large town; 10 miles from Jackson. **Calendar:** Semester, limited summer session. **Microcomputers:** 30 located in classrooms, computer centers. **Special facilities:** Communication laboratories.

DEGREES OFFERED. BA, BS, MA, MS, MBA, MEd. 467 bachelor's degrees awarded in 1992. Graduate degrees offered in 33 major fields of study.

UNDERGRADUATE MAJORS. Accounting, aerospace/aeronautical/astronautical engineering, art education, biology, business administration and management, business and management, business data processing and related programs, business economics, business education, chemical engineering, chemistry, child development/care/guidance, civil engineering, clinical laboratory science, communications, computer and information sciences, computer programming, criminal justice studies, cytotechnology, data processing, early childhood education, education of the deaf and hearing impaired, electrical/electronics/communications engineering, elementary education, English, English education, fashion design, fashion merchandising, foreign languages (multiple emphasis), foreign languages education, French, German, graphic design, Greek (classical), health education, history, home economics, home economics education, industrial engineering, institutional/home management/supporting programs, interior design, journalism, junior high education, Latin, legal assistant/paralegal, materials engineering, mathematics, mathematics education, mechanical engineering, medical laboratory technologies, medical radiation dosimetry, music, music education, music theory and composition, nursing, nutritional education, office supervision and management, physical education, physics, political science and government, predentistry, prelaw, premedicine, prepharmacy, preveterinary, psychology, public administration, public relations, religion, religious education, religious music, respiratory therapy technology, science education, secondary education, secretarial and related programs, social science education, social sciences, social studies education, social work, sociology, Spanish, special education, speech correction, speech pathology/audiology, textile engineering.

ACADEMIC PROGRAMS. Cooperative education, double major, dual enrollment of high school students, education specialist degree, honors program, independent study, internships, study abroad, teacher preparation, visiting/exchange student program; liberal arts/career combination in engineering, health sciences. **Remedial services:** Preadmission summer program, reduced course load, remedial instruction, special counselor, tutoring. **ROTC:** Army. **Placement/credit:** AP, CLEP Subject; 30 credit hours maximum for bachelor's degree.

ACADEMIC REQUIREMENTS. Freshmen must earn minimum GPA of 2.0 to continue in good standing. 90% of freshmen return for sophomore year. Students must declare major by end of second year. **Graduation requirements:** 130 hours for bachelor's. Most students required to take courses in arts/fine arts, computer science, English, foreign languages, history, humanities, mathematics, philosophy/religion, biological/physical sciences, social sciences.

FRESHMAN ADMISSIONS. Selection criteria: ACT/SAT scores most important, followed by high school record. Recommendations considered in marginal cases. **Test requirements:** SAT or ACT (ACT preferred); score report by August 15.

1992 FRESHMAN CLASS PROFILE. 132 men, 161 women enrolled. **Academic background:** Mid 50% of enrolled freshmen had ACT composite between 18-23. 90% submitted ACT scores. **Characteristics:** 83% from in state, 50% commute, 25% have minority backgrounds, 1% are foreign students. Average age is 20.

FALL-TERM APPLICATIONS. $15 fee. Closing date August 15; priority given to applications received by August 1; applicants notified on a rolling basis. Audition recommended for music applicants. Portfolio recommended for art applicants. Early admission available. Either SAT or ACT may be substituted for TOEFL scores for foreign students.

STUDENT LIFE. Housing: Dormitories (men, women); apartment housing available. Apartments for married ministerial students. **Activities:** Student government, magazine, radio, student newspaper, television, yearbook, choral groups, concert band, drama, jazz band, marching band, music ensembles, musical theater, opera, pep band, Baptist Student Union, Civitan, Circle-K, Rotorac, Young Democrats, Young Republicans, Black Student Association.

ATHLETICS. NCAA. **Intercollegiate:** Baseball M, basketball, cross-country M, football M, golf M, soccer M, softball W, tennis, track and field M, volleyball W. **Intramural:** Basketball M, football M, softball M.

STUDENT SERVICES. Aptitude testing, career counseling, employment service for undergraduates, freshman orientation, health services, on-campus day care, personal counseling, placement service for graduates, veterans counselor, services/facilities for handicapped.

ANNUAL EXPENSES. Tuition and fees (1992-93): $5,316. **Room and board:** $2,620. **Books and supplies:** $600. **Other expenses:** $1,500.

FINANCIAL AID. 75% of freshmen, 65% of continuing students receive some form of aid. 49% of grants, 82% of loans, 48% of jobs based on need. 182 enrolled freshmen were judged to have need, all were offered aid. Academic, music/drama, art, athletic, state/district residency, leadership, religious affiliation scholarships available. **Aid applications:** No closing date; priority given to applications received by April 1; applicants notified on a rolling basis beginning on or about April 1; must reply within 2 weeks.

ADDRESS/TELEPHONE. Jennifer Trussell, Director of Admissions, Mississippi College, PO Box 4203, Clinton, MS 39058. (601) 925-3240.

Mississippi Delta Community College
Moorhead, Mississippi — CB code: 1742

2-year public community college, coed. Founded in 1926. **Accreditation:** Regional. **Undergraduate enrollment:** 760 men, 945 women full time; 531 men, 347 women part time. **Faculty:** 137 total (121 full time), 14 with doctorates or other terminal degrees. **Location:** Rural campus in rural community; 20 miles from Greenwood. **Calendar:** Semester, limited summer session. Extensive evening/early morning classes. **Microcomputers:** Located in libraries, computer centers.

DEGREES OFFERED. AA, AS. 231 associate degrees awarded in 1992. 10% in agriculture, 30% business and management, 30% teacher education, 10% engineering, 12% allied health.

UNDERGRADUATE MAJORS. Agricultural business and management, agricultural sciences, architectural technologies, architecture, art education, biology, business and management, business and office, business data programming, business education, communications, computer programming, computer technology, construction, drafting, drafting and design technology, education, electronic technology, elementary education, engineering, engineering and engineering-related technologies, fine arts, forestry and related sciences, graphic arts technology, home economics, horticulture, liberal/general studies, mathematics, medical laboratory technologies, nursing, physical sciences, predentistry, prelaw, prepharmacy, preveterinary, psychology, radiograph medical technology, secondary education, secretarial and related programs, social sciences, special education, speech pathology/audiology, speech/communication/theater education.

ACADEMIC PROGRAMS. 2-year transfer program. **Remedial services:** Reduced course load. **Placement/credit:** AP; 15 credit hours maximum for associate degree.

ACADEMIC REQUIREMENTS. Freshmen must earn minimum GPA of 2.0 to continue in good standing. Students must declare major on application. **Graduation requirements:** 64 hours for associate. Most students required to take courses in English, history, mathematics, biological/physical sciences, social sciences.

FRESHMAN ADMISSIONS. Selection criteria: Test scores most important. Open admissions to vocational programs. Selective admissions to health occupations and computer technology curriculum. **Test requirements:** ACT; score report by August 28.

1992 FRESHMAN CLASS PROFILE. 1,037 men, 1,019 women enrolled. **Academic background:** Mid 50% of enrolled freshmen had ACT composite between 16-19. 60% submitted ACT scores. **Characteristics:** 97% from in state, 75% commute, 40% have minority backgrounds. Average age is 19.

FALL-TERM APPLICATIONS. No fee. Closing date August 31; priority given to applications received by August 1; applicants notified on a rolling basis beginning on or about May 30.

STUDENT LIFE. Housing: Dormitories (men, women). **Activities:** Student government, student newspaper, yearbook, choral groups, concert band, dance, drama, jazz band, marching band, Baptist Student Union, Wesley Foundation, Vocational Industrial Clubs of America.

ATHLETICS. NJCAA. **Intercollegiate:** Baseball M, basketball, football M, golf M, softball W, tennis, track and field M. **Intramural:** Basketball, softball, tennis, track and field, volleyball.

STUDENT SERVICES. Career counseling, employment service for undergraduates, freshman orientation, personal counseling, placement service for graduates, veterans counselor, services/facilities for handicapped.

ANNUAL EXPENSES. Tuition and fees (1992-93): $770, $90 additional for out-of-district students, $1,000 additional for out-of-state students. **Room and board:** $1,450. **Books and supplies:** $400. **Other expenses:** $400.

FINANCIAL AID. 90% of freshmen receive some form of aid. All jobs based on need. Academic, music/drama, art, athletic, state/district residency scholarships available. **Aid applications:** No closing date; applicants notified on a rolling basis beginning on or about August 12; must reply within 2 weeks.

ADDRESS/TELEPHONE. Joe Ray, Chief Admissions Officer, Mississippi Delta Community College, P.O. Box 668, Moorhead, MS 38761. (601) 246-5631 ext.106. Fax: (601) 246-8627.

Mississippi Gulf Coast Community College: Jackson County Campus
Gautier, Mississippi — CB code: 1354

2-year public community college, coed. Founded in 1965. **Accreditation:** Regional. **Undergraduate enrollment:** 724 men, 1,230 women full time; 452 men, 762 women part time. **Faculty:** 138 total (96 full time), 7 with doctorates or other terminal degrees. **Location:** Suburban campus in large town; 5 miles from Pascagoula, 45 miles from Mobile, Alabama. **Calendar:** Semester, extensive summer session. **Microcomputers:** Located in libraries, computer centers.

DEGREES OFFERED. AA, AAS. 372 associate degrees awarded in 1992.

UNDERGRADUATE MAJORS. Accounting, automated manufacturing, automotive mechanics, business administration and management, business and management, business data processing and related programs, clinical laboratory science, drafting and design technology, electronic technology, elementary education, engineering, fashion merchandising, legal assistant/paralegal, liberal/general studies, machine tool operation/machine shop, marine maintenance, marketing and distribution, marketing management, mathematics, medical laboratory technologies, mental health/human services, nursing, radiograph medical technology, secondary education, secretarial and related programs, word processing.

ACADEMIC PROGRAMS. 2-year transfer program, cooperative education, dual enrollment of high school students, honors program. **Remedial services:** Learning center, reduced course load, remedial instruction, special counselor, tutoring. **Placement/credit:** AP, CLEP General and Subject; 30 credit hours maximum for associate degree.

ACADEMIC REQUIREMENTS. Freshmen must earn minimum GPA of 1.0 to continue in good standing. 50% of freshmen return for sophomore year. Students must declare major by end of first year. **Graduation requirements:** 64 hours for associate. Most students required to take courses in arts/fine arts, English, humanities, mathematics, biological/physical sciences, social sciences.

FRESHMAN ADMISSIONS. Selection criteria: Open admissions. Selective admissions to health occupation programs. **Test requirements:** SAT accepted from out-of-state applicants. Test scores used for admissions to health programs.

1992 FRESHMAN CLASS PROFILE. 908 men, 1,447 women enrolled. **Characteristics:** 97% from in state, 100% commute, 19% have minority backgrounds. Average age is 25.

FALL-TERM APPLICATIONS. No fee. No closing date; applicants notified on a rolling basis. Application and other admission requirements should be submitted by June 1 for priority placement. Students not having an ACT score take Asset Assessment test.

STUDENT LIFE. Activities: Student government, student newspaper, yearbook, choral groups, concert band, dance, drama, marching band, music ensembles, musical theater, Baptist Student Union, United Ministries for Higher Education.

ATHLETICS. NJCAA. **Intercollegiate:** Golf, tennis. **Intramural:** Basketball, softball, table tennis, volleyball.

STUDENT SERVICES. Aptitude testing, career counseling, employment service for undergraduates, freshman orientation, health services, on-campus day care, personal counseling, placement service for graduates, special adviser for adult students, veterans counselor, services/facilities for handicapped.

ANNUAL EXPENSES. Tuition and fees: $860, $900 additional for out-of-state students. Required fees include book rental fee of $60. **Books and supplies:** $150.

FINANCIAL AID. 50% of freshmen, 55% of continuing students receive some form of aid. 77% of grants, 98% of loans, 51% of jobs based on need. Academic, leadership scholarships available. **Aid applications:** No closing date; priority given to applications received by June 1; applicants notified on a rolling basis; must reply by registration.

ADDRESS/TELEPHONE. Mary Spring-Graham, Director of Admissions/Registrar, Mississippi Gulf Coast Community College: Jackson County Campus, PO Box 100, Gautier, MS 39553. (601) 497-9602. Fax: (601) 497-9604.

Mississippi Gulf Coast Community College: Jefferson Davis Campus
Gulfport, Mississippi — CB code: 1353

2-year public community college, coed. Founded in 1965. **Accreditation:** Regional. **Undergraduate enrollment:** 811 men, 1,458 women full time; 596 men, 1,184 women part time. **Faculty:** 206 total (125 full time), 11 with doctorates or other terminal degrees. **Location:** Suburban campus in small city; 3 miles from Biloxi, 60 miles from New Orleans. **Calendar:** Semester, limited summer session. Saturday and extensive evening/early morning classes. **Microcomputers:** 139 located in classrooms, computer centers. **Special facilities:** Fitness trail, art gallery.

DEGREES OFFERED. AA, AAS. 385 associate degrees awarded in 1992. 13% in business and management, 14% business/office and marketing/distribution, 13% teacher education, 17% health sciences, 26% multi/interdisciplinary studies, 5% trade and industry.

UNDERGRADUATE MAJORS. Accounting, biology, business administration and management, business and management, business and office, business data processing and related programs, chemistry, communications, computer and information sciences, court reporting, criminal justice studies, drafting and design technology, education, electronic technology, elementary education, emergency medical technologies, engineering, English, fashion merchandising, finance, fine arts, health sciences, hotel/motel and restaurant management, legal assistant/paralegal, liberal/general studies, marketing and distribution, mathematics, nursing, office supervision and management, physics, predentistry, prelaw, premedicine, prepharmacy, preveterinary, psychology, science technologies, secondary education, secretarial and related programs, social sciences, word processing.

ACADEMIC PROGRAMS. 2-year transfer program, cooperative education, dual enrollment of high school students, honors program, internships, weekend college, cross-registration. **Remedial services:** Learning center, preadmission summer program, remedial instruction, tutoring. **Placement/credit:** AP, CLEP General and Subject, institutional tests; 32 credit hours maximum for associate degree.

ACADEMIC REQUIREMENTS. Freshmen must earn minimum GPA of 2.0 to continue in good standing. 42% of freshmen return for sophomore year. Students must declare major on enrollment. **Graduation requirements:** 64 hours for associate (27 in major). Most students required to take courses in arts/fine arts, English, humanities, mathematics, biological/physical sciences, social sciences.

FRESHMAN ADMISSIONS. Selection criteria: Open admissions. Selective admissions to nursing and computer science programs. **High school preparation:** 18 units recommended. Recommended units include biological science 3, English 4, foreign language 2, mathematics 3, social science 3 and science 3. 1 unit computer science elective recommended. **Test requirements:** ACT for placement and counseling only; score report by August 27.

1992 FRESHMAN CLASS PROFILE. 822 men, 1,376 women enrolled. 35% had high school GPA of 3.0 or higher, 55% between 2.0 and 2.99. **Academic background:** Mid 50% of enrolled freshmen had ACT composite between 17-18. 21% submitted ACT scores. **Characteristics:** 99% from in state, 100% commute, 17% have minority backgrounds, 1% are foreign students. Average age is 20.

FALL-TERM APPLICATIONS. No fee. No closing date; priority given to applications received by July 1; applicants notified on a rolling basis beginning on or about June 1; 0827. Interview required for foreign, nursing applicants. Deferred admission available. Dual enrollment available to high school seniors enrolled for no more than 6 semester hours each term while completing Carnegie units. Students who have not provided their ACT scores prior to registration must complete the ACT/ASSET evaluation for placement and counseling purposes.

STUDENT LIFE. Activities: Student government, magazine, student newspaper, yearbook, choral groups, concert band, drama, marching band, music ensembles, musical theater, Young Democrats, Young Republicans, Baptist Student Union, Reflections, New Horizions.

ATHLETICS. NJCAA. **Intercollegiate:** Golf, tennis. **Intramural:** Basketball, softball, volleyball.

STUDENT SERVICES. Aptitude testing, career counseling, freshman orientation, personal counseling, placement service for graduates, veterans counselor, counselor for displaced homemakers/single parents, services/facilities for handicapped.

ANNUAL EXPENSES. Tuition and fees (1992-93): $860, $900 additional for out-of-state students. Required fees include $60 book service fee. **Books and supplies:** $150. **Other expenses:** $260.

FINANCIAL AID. 70% of freshmen, 60% of continuing students receive some form of aid. Academic, music/drama, athletic, alumni affiliation scholarships available. **Aid applications:** Closing date September 1; priority given to applications received by June 1; applicants notified on a rolling basis beginning on or about June 1; must reply within 2 weeks.

ADDRESS/TELEPHONE. Patricia L. Holloway, Director of Admissions, Mississippi Gulf Coast Community College: Jefferson Davis Campus, 2226 Switzer Road, Gulfport, MS 39507-3894. (601) 896-2500. Fax: (601) 896-2520.

Mississippi Gulf Coast Community College: Perkinston
Perkinston, Mississippi — CB code: 1623

2-year public community college, coed. Founded in 1912. **Accreditation:** Regional. **Undergraduate enrollment:** 3,135 men, 3,420 women full time; 1,370 men, 2,196 women part time. **Faculty:** 68 total (57 full time), 9 with doctorates or other terminal degrees. **Location:** Rural campus in rural community; 28 miles from Gulfport. **Calendar:** Semester.

DEGREES OFFERED. AA, AAS. 145 associate degrees awarded in 1992. 31% in business/office and marketing/distribution, 10% computer sciences, 14% teacher education, 6% engineering, 9% health sciences, 11% multi/interdisciplinary studies.

UNDERGRADUATE MAJORS. Actuarial sciences, advertising, agricultural education, American literature, anatomy, art education, automotive mechanics, biological and physical sciences, biology, botany, business computer/console/peripheral equipment operation, business education, child development/care/guidance, commercial art, communications, computer and information sciences, computer programming, computer servicing technology, court reporting, drafting, drafting and design technology, economics, education, elementary education, engineering, engineering and other disciplines, English, English education, English literature, foreign languages education, French, health education, health sciences, history, home economics education, humanities and social sciences, industrial arts education, international relations, international studies, journalism, junior high education, law ., legal assistant/paralegal, legal secretary, library science, marine biology, marketing and distributive education, mathematics, mathematics education, microbiology, music education, ornamental horticulture, physical education, physiology, human and animal, political science and government, prelaw, psychology, public relations, radio/television broadcasting, reading education, science education, secondary education, secretarial and related programs, social science education, social sciences, social studies education, sociology, Spanish, speech, speech/communication/theater education, technical and business writing, trade and industrial education, welding technology, word processing.

ACADEMIC PROGRAMS. 2-year transfer program, cooperative education, dual enrollment of high school students, honors program, independent study. **Remedial services:** Learning center, remedial instruction, special counselor. **Placement/credit:** Institutional tests; 30 credit hours maximum for associate degree.

ACADEMIC REQUIREMENTS. 40% of freshmen return for sophomore year. Students must declare major by end of first year. **Graduation requirements:** 64 hours for associate. Most students required to take courses in arts/fine arts, English, history, humanities, mathematics, biological/physical sciences, social sciences.

FRESHMAN ADMISSIONS. Selection criteria: Open admissions. Selective admissions to health occupation programs. **Test requirements:** SAT or ACT (ACT preferred) for placement; score report by August 15. ACH required.

1992 FRESHMAN CLASS PROFILE. 253 men, 241 women enrolled. **Characteristics:** 85% live in college housing. Average age is 18.

FALL-TERM APPLICATIONS. No fee. No closing date; applicants notified on a rolling basis; must reply within 30 days. ACT no longer mandatory. Asset placement test administered if ACT scores not available.

STUDENT LIFE. Housing: Dormitories (men, women); apartment, handicapped housing available. **Activities:** Student government, student newspaper, yearbook, choral groups, concert band, dance, drama, marching band, music ensembles, musical theater.

ATHLETICS. NJCAA. **Intercollegiate:** Baseball M, basketball, football M, golf M, softball W, tennis, track and field M. **Intramural:** Basketball M, soccer M, softball M, table tennis, volleyball.

STUDENT SERVICES. Aptitude testing, career counseling, employment service for undergraduates, freshman orientation, personal counseling, placement service for graduates, special adviser for adult students, veterans counselor, services/facilities for handicapped.

ANNUAL EXPENSES. Tuition and fees: $860, $900 additional for out-of-state students. Required fees include $60 book rental fee. **Room and board:** $1,326.

FINANCIAL AID. 58% of freshmen, 93% of continuing students receive some form of aid. 68% of grants, 81% of loans, 39% of jobs based on need. Academic, music/drama, art, athletic, state/district residency, leadership, alumni affiliation scholarships available. **Aid applications:** No closing date; priority given to applications received by June 1; applicants notified on a rolling basis beginning on or about July 1; must reply within 2 weeks.

ADDRESS/TELEPHONE. Charles Cooper, Director of Admissions, Mississippi Gulf Coast Community College: Perkinston, PO Box 47, Perkinston, MS 39573. (601) 928-5211 ext. 264. Fax: (601) 928-6386.

Mississippi State University
Mississippi State, Mississippi — CB code: 1480

Admissions: 49% of applicants accepted
Based on:
••• Test scores
• Activities, recommendations, school record, special talents
Completion: 42% graduate

4-year public university, coed. Founded in 1878. **Accreditation:** Regional. **Undergraduate enrollment:** 6,072 men, 4,332 women full time; 862 men, 640 women part time. **Graduate enrollment:** 992 men, 550 women full time; 574 men, 597 women part time. **Faculty:** 816 total (740 full time), 620 with doctorates or other terminal degrees. **Location:** Rural campus in large town; 120 miles from Jackson, Mississippi. **Calendar:** Semester, extensive summer session. **Microcomputers:** 850 located in dormitories, libraries, classrooms, computer centers. **Special facilities:** Creative arts complex, observatory, physical fitness complex, solar energy laboratory, only student-operated florist in nation, second largest collegiate baseball facility in nation. **Additional facts:** Branches at Vicksburg Center for Graduate Studies in Engineering, the Meridian Degree-Granting Center, and the Stennis Center on Gulf Coast.

DEGREES OFFERED. BA, BS, BFA, BArch, MA, MS, MBA, MEd, PhD, EdD, DVM. 2,141 bachelor's degrees awarded in 1992. 7% in agriculture, 24% business and management, 8% business/office and marketing/distribution, 22% education, 14% engineering. Graduate degrees offered in 62 major fields of study.

UNDERGRADUATE MAJORS. Accounting, aerospace/aeronautical/astronautical engineering, agribusiness, agricommunication, agricultural economics, agricultural education, agricultural engineering, agricultural engineering technology and business, agricultural sciences, agronomy, animal sciences, anthropology, architecture, biochemistry, bioengineering and biomedical engineering, biological and physical sciences, biology, business administration and management, business data processing and related programs, business economics, business education, chemical engineering, chemistry, civil engineering, communications, computer and information sciences, computer engineering, dairy, economics, electrical/electronics/communications engineering, elementary education, English, entomology, finance, fishing and fisheries, food sciences, foreign languages (multiple emphasis), forest products processing technology, forestry and related sciences, geology, history, home economics, horticultural science, industrial arts education, industrial engineering, industrial technology, insurance and risk management, landscape architecture, landscape contracting, liberal/general studies, marketing and distributive education, marketing management, mathematics, mechanical engineering, medical laboratory technologies, microbiology, music education, philosophy, physical education, physics, plant protection, plant sciences, political science and government, poultry, psychology, real estate, school psychology, secondary education, social work, sociology, special education, trade and industrial education, transportation management, visual and performing arts.

ACADEMIC PROGRAMS. Accelerated program, cooperative education, double major, dual enrollment of high school students, education specialist degree, honors program, independent study, internships, study abroad, teacher preparation. **Remedial services:** Learning center, remedial instruction, special counselor, tutoring. **ROTC:** Air Force, Army. **Placement/credit:** AP, CLEP Subject, institutional tests; 32 credit hours maximum for bachelor's degree. Maximum of 25% of any curriculum may be earned by examination.

ACADEMIC REQUIREMENTS. Freshmen must earn minimum GPA of 2.0 to continue in good standing. Freshmen may not be more than 12 grade points deficient from 2.0 average to continue in good academic standing. 77% of freshmen return for sophomore year. Students must declare major on enrollment. **Graduation requirements:** 128 hours for bachelor's (32 in major). Most students required to take courses in arts/fine arts, computer science, English, foreign languages, humanities, mathematics, philosophy/religion, biological/physical sciences, social sciences.

FRESHMAN ADMISSIONS. High school preparation: 15 units required. Required units include English 4, mathematics 3, social science 2.5 and science 3. Mathematics requirement includes algebra I and II and geometry. Social sciences must include US government and US history. Sciences must be chosen from introductory and advanced biology, physics, and chemistry. Additional courses in mathematics, science, or foreign languages may be chosen as required elective; and 1.5 units of free electives may be chosen from any of those accepted toward graduation by applicant's high school. **Test requirements:** SAT or ACT (ACT preferred); score report by July 29. **Additional information:** $15 application fee for out-of-state students.

1992 FRESHMAN CLASS PROFILE. 4,109 men and women applied, 2,004 accepted; 938 men enrolled, 787 women enrolled. **Academic background:** Mid 50% of enrolled freshmen had ACT composite between 19-27. 99% submitted ACT scores. **Characteristics:** 80% live in college housing, 22% have minority backgrounds. Average age is 19.

FALL-TERM APPLICATIONS. No fee. Closing date August 1; applicants notified on a rolling basis; accepted architecture applicants must reply by March 1. Interview recommended for architecture, veterinary medicine applicants. Deferred and early admission available.

STUDENT LIFE. Housing: Dormitories (men, women); apartment, fraternity, sorority, handicapped housing available. One coed dormitory available for honors students. **Activities:** Student government, radio, student newspaper, television, yearbook, choral groups, concert band, drama, jazz band, marching band, music ensembles, pep band, symphony orchestra, fraternities, sororities, more than 2 dozen religious, ethnic, and special-interest groups.

ATHLETICS. NCAA. **Intercollegiate:** Baseball M, basketball, cross-country, football M, golf, tennis, track and field, volleyball W. **Intramural:** Archery, badminton, basketball, bowling, cross-country, golf, racquetball, rifle, rugby M, soccer, softball, swimming, table tennis, tennis, track and field, volleyball.

STUDENT SERVICES. Aptitude testing, career counseling, employment service for undergraduates, freshman orientation, health services, on-campus day care, personal counseling, placement service for graduates, special adviser for adult students, veterans counselor, services/facilities for handicapped.

ANNUAL EXPENSES. Tuition and fees (1992-93): $2,473, $1,960 additional for out-of-state students. **Room and board:** $2,969. **Books and supplies:** $480. **Other expenses:** $1,429.

FINANCIAL AID. 84% of freshmen, 78% of continuing students receive some form of aid. 56% of grants, 79% of loans, 27% of jobs based on need. 1,233 enrolled freshmen were judged to have need, all were offered aid. Academic, music/drama, athletic, state/district residency, leadership, alumni affiliation, minority scholarships available. **Aid applications:** No closing date; priority given to applications received by April 1; applicants notified on a rolling basis beginning on or about May 1; must reply within 2 weeks.

ADDRESS/TELEPHONE. Jerry Inmon, Director of Admissions, Mississippi State University, 111 Allen Hall, Mississippi State, MS 39762. (601) 325-2224. Fax: (601) 325-3299.

Mississippi University for Women
Columbus, Mississippi — CB code: 1481

Admissions: 87% of applicants accepted
Based on:
••• Test scores
•• School record
• Interview
Completion: 91% of freshmen end year in good standing
42% graduate

4-year public university, coed. Founded in 1884. **Accreditation:** Regional. **Undergraduate enrollment:** 319 men, 1,348 women full time; 206 men, 618 women part time. **Graduate enrollment:** 5 men, 37 women full time; 27 men, 92 women part time. **Faculty:** 161 total (111 full time), 67 with doctorates or other terminal degrees. **Location:** Suburban campus in large town; 120 miles from Birmingham, Alabama, 160 miles from Memphis, Tennessee. **Calendar:** Semester, limited summer session. Saturday and extensive evening/early morning classes. **Microcomputers:** 132 located in dormitories, libraries, classrooms, computer centers. **Special facilities:** Museum/gallery, environmental education center.

DEGREES OFFERED. AS, BA, BS, BFA, MS, MEd. 36 associate degrees awarded in 1992. 100% in health sciences. 330 bachelor's degrees awarded. 22% in business and management, 6% communications, 20% teacher education, 18% health sciences, 9% law, 5% letters/literature, 7% life sciences. Graduate degrees offered in 2 major fields of study.

UNDERGRADUATE MAJORS. Associate: Nursing. **Bachelor's:** Accounting, art education, biology, business administration and management, business and management, chemistry, communications, dramatic arts, drawing, early childhood education, elementary education, English, English education, fashion merchandising, fine arts, health education, history, home economics, home economics education, individual and family development, interior design, journalism, legal assistant/paralegal, management information systems, mathematics, mathematics education, microbiology, music, music education, music performance, nursing, painting, physical education, physical sciences, predentistry, prelaw, premedicine, prepharmacy, preveterinary, radio/television broadcasting, science education, secondary education, social science education, social sciences, Spanish, special education, speech pathology/audiology, speech/communication/theater education, studio art, textiles and clothing, visual and performing arts.

ACADEMIC PROGRAMS. Cooperative education, double major, dual enrollment of high school students, honors program, independent study, internships, study abroad, teacher preparation, telecourses, weekend college, cross-registration; liberal arts/career combination in engineering. **Remedial services:** Learning center, remedial instruction, special counselor, tutoring. **ROTC:** Air Force, Army. **Placement/credit:** AP, CLEP General and Subject, institutional tests; 60 credit hours maximum for bachelor's degree.

ACADEMIC REQUIREMENTS. Freshmen must earn minimum GPA of 2.0 to continue in good standing. 72% of freshmen return for sophomore year. Students must declare major by end of first year. **Graduation requirements:** 64 hours for associate, 128 hours for bachelor's (36 in major). Most students required to take courses in arts/fine arts, computer science, English, history, mathematics, philosophy/religion, biological/physical sciences, social sciences.

FRESHMAN ADMISSIONS. Selection criteria: Test scores, high school GPA, and academic achievement considered in that order. **High school preparation:** 13 units required; 16 recommended. Required and recommended units include English 4, foreign language 1-2, mathematics 3-4, social science 2 and science 3-4. **Test requirements:** SAT or ACT; score report by August 15.

1992 FRESHMAN CLASS PROFILE. 83 men applied, 72 accepted, 60 enrolled; 435 women applied, 381 accepted, 274 enrolled. 52% had high school GPA of 3.0 or higher, 39% between 2.0 and 2.99. 19% were in top tenth and 46% were in top quarter of graduating class. **Academic background:** Mid 50% of enrolled freshmen had ACT composite between 19-27. 94% submitted ACT scores. **Characteristics:** 86% from in state, 49% live in college housing, 19% have minority backgrounds, 25% join fraternities/sororities. Average age is 19.

FALL-TERM APPLICATIONS. $20 fee, may be waived for applicants with need. Closing date August 30; applicants notified on a rolling basis; must reply by August 30. Interview recommended. Deferred and early admission available.

STUDENT LIFE. Housing: Dormitories (men, women); apartment housing available. **Activities:** Student government, radio, student newspaper, television, yearbook, choral groups, concert band, dance, drama, jazz band, music ensembles, musical theater, symphony orchestra, fraternities, sororities, Methodist, Presbyterian, Episcopal, Baptist, Catholic, Student Interfaith Association, Black Students club.

ATHLETICS. NCAA. **Intercollegiate:** Basketball W, softball W, tennis W, volleyball W. **Intramural:** Badminton W, basketball, football M, racquetball, softball, swimming, table tennis, tennis, volleyball.

STUDENT SERVICES. Aptitude testing, career counseling, employment service for undergraduates, freshman orientation, health services, on-campus day care, personal counseling, placement service for graduates, special adviser for adult students, veterans counselor, services/facilities for handicapped.

ANNUAL EXPENSES. Tuition and fees (projected): $2,239, $1,960 additional for out-of-state students. **Room and board:** $2,217. **Books and supplies:** $600. **Other expenses:** $1,200.

FINANCIAL AID. 89% of freshmen, 87% of continuing students receive some form of aid. 49% of grants, 97% of loans, 42% of jobs based on need. Academic, music/drama, art, athletic, state/district residency, leadership, alumni affiliation, minority scholarships available. **Aid applications:** No closing date; priority given to applications received by June 1; applicants notified on a rolling basis beginning on or about April 15; must reply within 2 weeks.

ADDRESS/TELEPHONE. Teresa E. Thompson, Director of Enrollment Management, Mississippi University for Women, PO Box W-1613, Columbus, MS 39701. (601) 329-7106. Fax: (601) 329-7348.

Mississippi Valley State University
Itta Bena, Mississippi

CB code: 1482

Admissions: 41% of applicants accepted
Based on: ••• School record, test scores
•• Special talents
• Activities, interview, recommendations
Completion: 87% of freshmen end year in good standing
41% graduate, 10% of these enter graduate study

4-year public university, coed. Founded in 1946. **Accreditation:** Regional. **Undergraduate enrollment:** 908 men, 1,096 women full time; 33 men, 170 women part time. **Graduate enrollment:** 2 men, 5 women full time; 3 men, 5 women part time. **Faculty:** 137 total (96 full time), 44 with doctorates or other terminal degrees. **Location:** Rural campus in small town; 120 miles from Jackson, 50 miles from Greenville. **Calendar:** Semester, extensive summer session. **Microcomputers:** Located in libraries, classrooms, computer centers. **Special facilities:** Learning resource center with media collection.

DEGREES OFFERED. BA, BS, MS. 209 bachelor's degrees awarded in 1992. 15% in business and management, 5% computer sciences, 13% teacher education, 6% life sciences, 28% parks/recreation, protective services, public affairs, 17% social sciences. Graduate degrees offered in 1 major field of study.

UNDERGRADUATE MAJORS. Biology, business administration and management, computer and information sciences, criminal justice studies, elementary education, English, English education, industrial technology, mathematics, mathematics education, music, music education, office supervision and management, painting, physical education, political science and government, public relations, sanitation technology, secondary education, social science education, social work, sociology, speech.

ACADEMIC PROGRAMS. Cooperative education, dual enrollment of high school students, honors program, independent study, internships. **Remedial services:** Learning center, reduced course load, remedial instruction, special counselor, tutoring. **ROTC:** Air Force, Army. **Placement/credit:** Institutional tests; 30 credit hours maximum for bachelor's degree.

ACADEMIC REQUIREMENTS. Freshmen must earn minimum GPA of 2.0 to continue in good standing. 83% of freshmen return for sophomore year. Students must declare major by end of second year. **Graduation requirements:** 124 hours for bachelor's. Most students required to take courses in arts/fine arts, English, history, humanities, mathematics, biological/physical sciences, social sciences. **Postgraduate studies:** 2% enter law school, 1% enter medical school, 7% enter other graduate study.

FRESHMAN ADMISSIONS. Selection criteria: High school curriculum and SAT or ACT scores. **High school preparation:** 13.5 units required. Required units include English 4, foreign language 1, mathematics 3, social science 2.5 and science 3. Mathematics requirement includes algebra I and II and geometry. Social sciences must include US government and US history. Sciences must be chosen from introductory and advanced biology, physics, and chemistry. Advanced science or mathematics may be substituted for a foreign language. **Test requirements:** SAT or ACT (ACT preferred); score report by August 22. Stanford Test of Academic Skills and Kuder Preference Record for placement.

1992 FRESHMAN CLASS PROFILE. 2,600 men and women applied, 1,064 accepted; 571 enrolled. **Characteristics:** 93% from in state, 92% live in college housing, 99% have minority backgrounds. Average age is 18.

FALL-TERM APPLICATIONS. No fee. No closing date; priority given to applications received by August 1; applicants notified on a rolling basis beginning on or about February 1; must reply within 3 weeks. Audition required for music education applicants. Interview recommended. Deferred and early admission available. Students who have completed the 11th grade with 15 academic units and composite ACT score of 20 or better may enter college with letter of recommendation from high school principal.

STUDENT LIFE. Housing: Dormitories (men, women); apartment housing available. **Activities:** Student government, radio, student newspaper, yearbook, choral groups, concert band, dance, drama, jazz band, marching band, music ensembles, musical theater, symphony orchestra, fraternities, sororities, numerous honor societies, political, social, religious organizations, prelaw club.

ATHLETICS. NCAA. **Intercollegiate:** Baseball M, basketball, football M, golf M, tennis M, track and field. **Intramural:** Baseball M, basketball, bowling, cross-country, racquetball, softball, swimming, volleyball.

STUDENT SERVICES. Career counseling, freshman orientation, health services, personal counseling, placement service for graduates, special adviser for adult students, services/facilities for handicapped.

ANNUAL EXPENSES. Tuition and fees (1992-93): $2,164, $1,960 additional for out-of-state students. **Room and board:** $2,025. **Books and supplies:** $450. **Other expenses:** $800.

FINANCIAL AID. 93% of freshmen, 89% of continuing students receive some form of aid. Grants, loans, jobs available. 350 enrolled freshmen were judged to have need, 339 were offered aid. Academic, music/drama, athletic scholarships available. **Aid applications:** No closing date; priority given to applications received by April 1; applicants notified on a rolling basis beginning on or about August 15; must reply within 2 weeks.

ADDRESS/TELEPHONE. Maxine Rush, Director of Admissions, Mississippi Valley State University, PO Box 61, Itta Bena, MS 38941. (601) 254-9041 ext. 6393. Fax: (601) 254-6704.

Northeast Mississippi Community College
Booneville, Mississippi CB code: 1557

2-year public community college, coed. Founded in 1948. **Accreditation:** Regional. **Undergraduate enrollment:** 1,134 men, 1,557 women full time; 136 men, 247 women part time. **Location:** Suburban campus in small town; 30 miles from Tupelo, 110 miles from Memphis, Tennessee. **Calendar:** Semester.

FRESHMAN ADMISSIONS. Selection criteria: Open admissions. Selective admissions to nursing, dental hygiene, and medical laboratory programs based on test scores.

ANNUAL EXPENSES. Tuition and fees (1992-93): $850, $20 additional for out-of-district students, $840 additional for out-of-state students. **Room and board:** $1,720. **Books and supplies:** $400. **Other expenses:** $600.

ADDRESS/TELEPHONE. Ronald M. Sweeney, Director of Admissions, Northeast Mississippi Community College, Booneville, MS 38829. (601) 728-7751.

Northwest Mississippi Community College
Senatobia, Mississippi CB code: 1562

2-year public community college, coed. Founded in 1927. **Accreditation:** Regional. **Undergraduate enrollment:** 1,275 men, 1,505 women full time; 358 men, 783 women part time. **Faculty:** 175 total (161 full time), 13 with doctorates or other terminal degrees. **Location:** Suburban campus in small town; 30 miles from Memphis, Tennessee. **Calendar:** Semester, extensive summer session. **Microcomputers:** Located in computer centers.

DEGREES OFFERED. AA, AAS. 331 associate degrees awarded in 1992.

UNDERGRADUATE MAJORS. Accounting, agribusiness, agricultural economics, agricultural education, agricultural mechanics, air conditioning/heating/refrigeration mechanics, air conditioning/heating/refrigeration technology, animal sciences, architecture, art education, business administration and management, business and management, business and office, business data processing and related programs, business data programming, business education, civil technology, commercial art, computer and information sciences, computer programming, court reporting, dairy, data processing, drafting and design technology, education, electronic technology, elementary education, fashion merchandising, food sciences, graphic arts technology, home economics education, horticulture, hospitality and recreation marketing, hotel/motel and restaurant management, journalism, legal assistant/paralegal, liberal/general studies, machine tool operation/machine shop, marketing and distribution, marketing and distributive education, mathematics education, medical secretary, music education, nursing, office supervision and management, physical education, plant sciences, poultry, practical nursing, public relations, radio/television broadcasting, radio/television technology, respiratory therapy, science education, secondary education, social science education, social studies education, special education, speech/communication/theater education, telecommunications, word processing.

ACADEMIC PROGRAMS. 2-year transfer program. **Remedial services:** Reduced course load, remedial instruction, tutoring. **ROTC:** Air Force. **Placement/credit:** Institutional tests.

ACADEMIC REQUIREMENTS. Freshmen must earn minimum GPA of 1.5 to continue in good standing. 60% of freshmen return for sophomore year. Students must declare major on enrollment. **Graduation requirements:** 64 hours for associate (36 in major). Most students required to take courses in arts/fine arts, computer science, English, history, humanities, mathematics, biological/physical sciences, social sciences.

FRESHMAN ADMISSIONS. Selection criteria: Open admissions. **High school preparation:** 17 units recommended. Recommended units include biological science 2, English 4, mathematics 3 and social science 4. **Test requirements:** ACT; score report by August 22.

1992 FRESHMAN CLASS PROFILE. 572 men, 796 women enrolled.

FALL-TERM APPLICATIONS. No fee. Closing date August 28; applicants notified on a rolling basis beginning on or about July 1.

STUDENT LIFE. Housing: Dormitories (men, women); apartment housing available. **Activities:** Student government, student newspaper, yearbook, choral groups, concert band, drama, jazz band, marching band, music ensembles, musical theater.

ATHLETICS. NJCAA. **Intercollegiate:** Baseball M, basketball M, softball W, tennis, track and field M. **Intramural:** Archery, badminton.

STUDENT SERVICES. Aptitude testing, career counseling, health services, personal counseling, veterans counselor, services/facilities for handicapped.

ANNUAL EXPENSES. Tuition and fees (projected): $1,000, $90 additional for out-of-district students, $1,000 additional for out-of-state students. **Room and board:** $1,690. **Books and supplies:** $200. **Other expenses:** $375.

FINANCIAL AID. 80% of freshmen, 80% of continuing students receive some form of aid. Grants, loans, jobs available. **Aid applications:** Closing date March 15; priority given to applications received by April 15; applicants notified on or about August 16; must reply within 2 weeks.

ADDRESS/TELEPHONE. Gary Spears, Registrar, Northwest Mississippi Community College, Highway 51 North, Senatobia, MS 38668. (601) 562-3200 ext. 3205. (800) 748-8538 ext. 3219. Fax: (601) 562-3911.

Pearl River Community College
Poplarville, Mississippi CB code: 1622

2-year public community college, coed. Founded in 1921. **Accreditation:** Regional. **Undergraduate enrollment:** 850 men, 1,241 women full time; 198 men, 510 women part time. **Faculty:** 141 total (113 full time), 19 with doctorates or other terminal degrees. **Location:** Rural campus in small town; 70 miles from New Orleans, Louisiana, 35 miles from Hattiesburg. **Calendar:** Semester, limited summer session. Extensive evening/early morning classes. **Microcomputers:** 40 located in libraries, computer centers.

DEGREES OFFERED. AA, AAS. 281 associate degrees awarded in 1992. 17% in business/office and marketing/distribution, 5% computer sciences, 8% teacher education, 5% engineering technologies, 17% allied health, 48% multi/interdisciplinary studies.

UNDERGRADUATE MAJORS. Air conditioning/heating/refrigeration mechanics, air conditioning/heating/refrigeration technology, automotive mechanics, automotive technology, business and office, business computer/console/peripheral equipment operation, business data entry equipment operation, business data processing and related programs, business data programming, carpentry, data processing, diesel engine mechanics, drafting, drafting and design technology, electrical installation, electronic technology, liberal/general studies, marketing and distribution, masonry/tile setting, medical secretary, nursing, personal services, practical nursing, precision metal work, respiratory therapy technology, secretarial and related programs, teacher education, welding technology.

ACADEMIC PROGRAMS. 2-year transfer program, cooperative education, dual enrollment of high school students. **Remedial services:** Learning center, reduced course load, remedial instruction, special counselor, tutoring. **Placement/credit:** AP, CLEP General and Subject; 30 credit hours maximum for associate degree.

ACADEMIC REQUIREMENTS. Freshmen must earn minimum GPA of 1.5 to continue in good standing. 50% of freshmen return for sophomore year. **Graduation requirements:** 64 hours for associate. Most students required to take courses in English, history, humanities, mathematics, biological/physical sciences, social sciences.

FRESHMAN ADMISSIONS. Selection criteria: Open admissions. Selective admission to health occupation programs. **Test requirements:** ACT for placement and counseling only; score report by August 20.

1992 FRESHMAN CLASS PROFILE. 471 men, 607 women enrolled. **Characteristics:** 90% from in state, 80% commute, 21% have minority backgrounds. Average age is 20.

FALL-TERM APPLICATIONS. No fee. No closing date; priority given to applications received by May 1; applicants notified on a rolling basis. Interview recommended for nursing applicants. Deferred and early admission available.

STUDENT LIFE. Housing: Dormitories (men, women). **Activities:** Student government, film, student newspaper, yearbook, choral groups, concert band, drama, jazz band, marching band, music ensembles, pep band, Black Student Union, Wesley and Newman Clubs, Phi Theta Kappa, Afro-American Club, Baptist Student Union.

ATHLETICS. NJCAA. **Intercollegiate:** Baseball M, basketball, football M, golf M, softball W, tennis. **Intramural:** Badminton, basketball, softball, table tennis, tennis, volleyball.

STUDENT SERVICES. Aptitude testing, career counseling, employment service for undergraduates, health services, personal counseling, placement service for graduates, veterans counselor, services/facilities for handicapped.

ANNUAL EXPENSES. Tuition and fees (1992-93): $910, $1,000 additional for out-of-state students. **Room and board:** $1,648. **Books and supplies:** $200. **Other expenses:** $1,085.

FINANCIAL AID. 70% of freshmen, 65% of continuing students receive some form of aid. 95% of grants, 96% of loans, 66% of jobs based on need. 825 enrolled freshmen were judged to have need, all were offered aid. Academic, music/drama, athletic, state/district residency, leadership scholarships available. **Aid applications:** No closing date; priority given to applications received by May 1; applicants notified on a rolling basis beginning on or about July 1; must reply within 2 weeks.

ADDRESS/TELEPHONE. J. Dow Ford, Director of Admissions and Records, Pearl River Community College, Station A, Poplarville, MS 39470. (601) 795-6801.

Phillips Junior College of Jackson
Jackson, Mississippi CB code: 0367

2-year proprietary junior college, coed. Founded in 1973. **Accreditation:**

Regional. **Undergraduate enrollment:** 452 men and women. **Location:** Urban campus in small city; 3 miles from downtown. **Calendar:** Quarter, students attend year round.

FRESHMAN ADMISSIONS. Selection criteria: Test score, school achievement record, interview considered.

ANNUAL EXPENSES. Tuition and fees (1992-93): $4,125. Books and supplies included in tuition. **Other expenses:** $1,612.

ADDRESS/TELEPHONE. Bill Miltead, Director of Admissions, Phillips Junior College of Jackson, 2680 Insurance Center Drive, Jackson, MS 39216. (601) 362-6341. Fax: (601) 366-9407.

Phillips Junior College of the Mississippi Gulf Coast
Gulfport, Mississippi — CB code: 0361

2-year proprietary junior college, coed. Founded in 1927. **Accreditation:** Regional. **Undergraduate enrollment:** 480 men and women full time; 120 men and women part time. **Location:** Suburban campus in small city; 75 miles east of New Orleans, Louisiana. **Calendar:** Quarter.

FRESHMAN ADMISSIONS. Selection criteria: Interview important, test scores considered.

ANNUAL EXPENSES. Tuition and fees: $4,868. **Books and supplies:** $200.

ADDRESS/TELEPHONE. Michael King, Director of Admissions, Phillips Junior College of the Mississippi Gulf Coast, 942 Beach Drive, Gulfport, MS 39507-9905. (601) 896-6465. Fax: (601) 896-6501.

Rust College
Holly Springs, Mississippi — CB code: 1669

Admissions:	50% of applicants accepted
Based on:	••• Recommendations, school record
	•• Activities, test scores
	• Religious affiliation/commitment, special talents
Completion:	90% of freshmen end year in good standing
	38% graduate, 30% of these enter graduate study

4-year private liberal arts college, coed, affiliated with United Methodist Church. Founded in 1866. **Accreditation:** Regional. **Undergraduate enrollment:** 373 men, 636 women full time; 26 men, 94 women part time. **Faculty:** 61 total (55 full time), 27 with doctorates or other terminal degrees. **Location:** Rural campus in small town; 45 miles from Memphis, Tennessee. **Calendar:** Semester, limited summer session. **Microcomputers:** 250 located in dormitories, libraries, classrooms, computer centers, campus-wide network. **Additional facts:** Competency-based program. Upperclassmen attend 4 8-week sessions per year.

DEGREES OFFERED. AS, BA, BS. 142 bachelor's degrees awarded. 32% in business and management, 9% communications, 7% computer sciences, 17% teacher education, 8% letters/literature, 8% physical sciences, 18% social sciences.

UNDERGRADUATE MAJORS. Associate: Business and office, early childhood education, secretarial and related programs. **Bachelor's:** Biological and physical sciences, biology, business administration and management, business education, chemistry, communications, computer and information sciences, early childhood education, economics, elementary education, English, English education, history, humanities and social sciences, journalism, liberal/general studies, mathematics, mathematics education, medical records technology, music, music education, physical education, physics, political science and government, predentistry, prelaw, premedicine, prepharmacy, radio/television broadcasting, science education, secondary education, secretarial and related programs, social science education, social sciences, social work, sociology.

ACADEMIC PROGRAMS. Cooperative education, double major, honors program, independent study, internships, teacher preparation; liberal arts/career combination in engineering, health sciences. **Remedial services:** Learning center, preadmission summer program, reduced course load, remedial instruction, special counselor, tutoring, basic skills laboratories. **ROTC:** Air Force, Army. **Placement/credit:** Institutional tests; 18 credit hours maximum for bachelor's degree.

ACADEMIC REQUIREMENTS. Freshmen must earn minimum GPA of 2.0 to continue in good standing. 85% of freshmen return for sophomore year. Students must declare major by end of second year. **Graduation requirements:** 65 hours for associate, 124 hours for bachelor's (36 in major). Most students required to take courses in computer science, English, foreign languages, history, humanities, mathematics, philosophy/religion, biological/physical sciences, social sciences. **Postgraduate studies:** 2% enter law school, 1% enter medical school, 1% enter MBA programs, 26% enter other graduate study.

FRESHMAN ADMISSIONS. Selection criteria: School achievement record and recommendations most important. Test scores also considered. **High school preparation:** 15 units required. Required units include English 3, mathematics 2, social science 2 and science 2. 6 academic electives required. **Test requirements:** SAT or ACT (ACT preferred); score report by August 15.

1992 FRESHMAN CLASS PROFILE. 1,113 men and women applied, 559 accepted; 115 men enrolled, 173 women enrolled. 29% had high school GPA of 3.0 or higher, 58% between 2.0 and 2.99. **Characteristics:** 80% from in state, 88% live in college housing, 96% have minority backgrounds, 4% are foreign students. Average age is 17.

FALL-TERM APPLICATIONS. $10 fee, may be waived for applicants with need. Closing date June 15; priority given to applications received by May 15; applicants notified on a rolling basis; must reply by May 1 or within 2 weeks if notified thereafter. Early admission available. EDP-S.

STUDENT LIFE. Housing: Dormitories (men, women). **Activities:** Student government, radio, student newspaper, television, yearbook, choral groups, concert band, dance, drama, jazz band, marching band, music ensembles, fraternities, sororities, Methodist Student Movement, Baptist Student Union, Catholic Student Association, Pre-Law, NAACP, Social Work Club, Rust College Sunday School Association, International Student Association, All Saints Student Movement.

ATHLETICS. NCAA. **Intercollegiate:** Baseball M, basketball, cross-country, tennis, track and field. **Intramural:** Archery, badminton, basketball, bowling, cross-country, softball, swimming, table tennis, tennis, track and field, volleyball.

STUDENT SERVICES. Career counseling, freshman orientation, health services, on-campus day care, personal counseling, placement service for graduates, special adviser for adult students, veterans counselor, services/facilities for handicapped.

ANNUAL EXPENSES. Tuition and fees (1992-93): $4,152. Required fees includes cost of books. **Room and board:** $1,948. **Books and supplies:** $225. **Other expenses:** $150.

FINANCIAL AID. 98% of freshmen, 97% of continuing students receive some form of aid. All jobs based on need. Academic, music/drama, athletic, state/district residency, alumni affiliation, religious affiliation, minority scholarships available. **Aid applications:** Closing date July 15; priority given to applications received by May 1; applicants notified on a rolling basis beginning on or about June 1; must reply within 2 weeks.

ADDRESS/TELEPHONE. JoAnn Scott, Director of Admissions and Recruitment, Rust College, 150 Rust Avenue, Holly Springs, MS 38635-2328. (601) 252-8000. Fax: (601) 252-6107.

Southeastern Baptist College
Laurel, Mississippi — CB code: 1781

4-year private Bible college, coed, affiliated with Baptist Missionary Association of America. Founded in 1949. **Undergraduate enrollment:** 24 men, 11 women full time; 25 men, 23 women part time. **Faculty:** 11 total (5 full time), 4 with doctorates or other terminal degrees. **Location:** Suburban campus in large town; 90 miles from Jackson. **Calendar:** Semester, limited summer session.

DEGREES OFFERED. AA, BA, BS. 9 associate degrees awarded in 1992. 25% in business/office and marketing/distribution, 75% philosophy, religion, theology. 3 bachelor's degrees awarded. 100% in philosophy, religion, theology.

UNDERGRADUATE MAJORS. Associate: Bible studies, business and office, religious music, secretarial and related programs. **Bachelor's:** Bible studies, religion, religious education, religious music, theological studies.

ACADEMIC PROGRAMS. 2-year transfer program, double major, independent study. **Remedial services:** Remedial instruction. **Placement/credit:** CLEP General and Subject; 12 credit hours maximum for associate degree; 12 credit hours maximum for bachelor's degree.

ACADEMIC REQUIREMENTS. Freshmen must earn minimum GPA of 1.5 to continue in good standing. 71% of freshmen return for sophomore year. Students must declare major by end of first year. **Graduation requirements:** 66 hours for associate (15 in major), 129 hours for bachelor's (40 in major). Most students required to take courses in English, history, mathematics, philosophy/religion, social sciences. **Postgraduate studies:** 63% from 2-year programs enter 4-year programs. 35% enter other graduate study.

FRESHMAN ADMISSIONS. Selection criteria: Recommendations considered. Only professed Christians admitted to degree programs; others may enroll in some courses as special students. In place of high school diploma or GED, high school principal's recommendation and 15 high school units including 1 biological science, 3 English, 1 mathematics, 2 social sciences accepted.

1992 FRESHMAN CLASS PROFILE. 6 men applied, 6 accepted, 6 enrolled; 3 women applied, 3 accepted, 3 enrolled. **Characteristics:** 88% from in state, 56% live in college housing, 11% have minority backgrounds, 11% are foreign students. Average age is 29.

FALL-TERM APPLICATIONS. $15 fee. Closing date September 2; applicants notified on a rolling basis beginning on or about January 1; must reply by registration. Interview recommended. Audition recommended for religious music applicants. Essay recommended. Deferred and early admission available.

STUDENT LIFE. Housing: Dormitories (men, women); apartment housing available. **Activities:** Student government, yearbook, choral groups, music ensembles, Association of Baptist Students, Ministerial Alliance. **Additional information:** Religious observance required.

ATHLETICS. Intramural: Badminton, basketball, bowling, handball, softball, table tennis, tennis, volleyball.

STUDENT SERVICES. Employment service for undergraduates, personal counseling, placement service for graduates, veterans counselor, services/facilities for handicapped.

ANNUAL EXPENSES. Tuition and fees: $2,220. **Room and board:** $1,700. **Books and supplies:** $250. **Other expenses:** $325.

FINANCIAL AID. 90% of freshmen, 90% of continuing students receive some form of aid. All grants, all loans based on need. **Aid applications:** No closing date; priority given to applications received by July 1; applicants notified on a rolling basis beginning on or about July 15; must reply within 4 weeks.

ADDRESS/TELEPHONE. Medrick H. Savell, Academic Dean, Southeastern Baptist College, 4229 Highway 15 North, Laurel, MS 39440. (601) 426-6346.

Southwest Mississippi Community College
Summit, Mississippi CB code: 1729

2-year public community college, coed. Founded in 1918. **Accreditation:** Regional. **Undergraduate enrollment:** 506 men, 719 women full time; 80 men, 153 women part time. **Faculty:** 89 total (68 full time), 4 with doctorates or other terminal degrees. **Location:** Rural campus in rural community; 76 miles from Jackson, 100 miles from New Orleans, Louisiana. **Calendar:** Semester, limited summer session. **Microcomputers:** Located in libraries, classrooms, computer centers.

DEGREES OFFERED. AA, AS. 250 associate degrees awarded in 1992.

UNDERGRADUATE MAJORS. Automotive technology, business and office, business data processing and related programs, electromechanical technology, finance, law enforcement and corrections technologies, liberal/general studies, marketing and distribution, nursing, robotics, secretarial and related programs.

ACADEMIC PROGRAMS. 2-year transfer program, dual enrollment of high school students. **Remedial services:** Learning center, reduced course load, remedial instruction, tutoring. **Placement/credit:** AP, CLEP General; 12 credit hours maximum for associate degree.

ACADEMIC REQUIREMENTS. Freshmen must earn minimum GPA of 2.0 to continue in good standing. 55% of freshmen return for sophomore year. Students must declare major on enrollment. **Graduation requirements:** 64 hours for associate. Most students required to take courses in arts/fine arts, English, history, humanities, mathematics, biological/physical sciences.

FRESHMAN ADMISSIONS. Selection criteria: Open admissions. For ability to benefit from vocational programs high school graduation or GED preferred. **Test requirements:** ACT for placement and counseling only; score report by August 1.

1992 FRESHMAN CLASS PROFILE. 207 men, 299 women enrolled. **Characteristics:** 91% from in state, 60% live in college housing, 27% have minority backgrounds.

FALL-TERM APPLICATIONS. No fee. No closing date; priority given to applications received by August 5; applicants notified on a rolling basis.

STUDENT LIFE. Housing: Dormitories (men, women); apartment housing available. **Activities:** Student government, student newspaper, yearbook, choral groups, concert band, jazz band, marching band.

ATHLETICS. NJCAA. **Intercollegiate:** Baseball M, basketball, football M, golf M, tennis. **Intramural:** Basketball, tennis, volleyball.

STUDENT SERVICES. Aptitude testing, career counseling, health services, personal counseling, placement service for graduates, veterans counselor.

ANNUAL EXPENSES. Tuition and fees (1992-93): $850, $1,050 additional for out-of-state students. **Room and board:** $1,650. **Books and supplies:** $400. **Other expenses:** $1,300.

FINANCIAL AID. 45% of freshmen, 45% of continuing students receive some form of aid. Grants, loans, jobs available. **Aid applications:** No closing date; priority given to applications received by August 5; applicants notified on a rolling basis.

ADDRESS/TELEPHONE. R. Glenn Shoemake, Registrar, Southwest Mississippi Community College, Summit, MS 39666. (601) 276-2001.

Tougaloo College
Tougaloo, Mississippi CB code: 1807

Admissions: 59% of applicants accepted
Based on: •• Special talents
• Recommendations, school record, test scores
Completion: 75% of freshmen end year in good standing
37% graduate, 85% of these enter graduate study

4-year private liberal arts college, coed, affiliated with United Christian Mission Society and United Church of Christ. Founded in 1869. **Accreditation:** Regional. **Undergraduate enrollment:** 352 men, 709 women full time; 10 men, 60 women part time. **Faculty:** 102 total (74 full time), 43 with doctorates or other terminal degrees. **Location:** Suburban campus in rural community; within Jackson city limits. **Calendar:** Semester. **Microcomputers:** Located in libraries, classrooms, computer centers. **Special facilities:** Art galleries, largest collection of civil rights legal documents in state, East and West African art and artifacts, Tracy Sugarmon collection of original prints (Mississippi Civil Rights).

DEGREES OFFERED. AA, BA, BS. 5 associate degrees awarded in 1992. 100% in teacher education. 87 bachelor's degrees awarded. 15% in business and management, 11% teacher education, 7% letters/literature, 9% life sciences, 5% mathematics, 9% physical sciences, 12% psychology, 31% social sciences.

UNDERGRADUATE MAJORS. Associate: Early childhood education, teacher aide. **Bachelor's:** Accounting, biology, business economics, chemistry, computer programming, economics, elementary education, English, history, mathematics, music, physics, political science and government, psychology, secondary education, sociology, visual and performing arts.

ACADEMIC PROGRAMS. Accelerated program, cooperative education, double major, honors program, independent study, internships, student-designed major, study abroad, teacher preparation, visiting/exchange student program, Washington semester, cross-registration; liberal arts/career combination in engineering. **Remedial services:** Learning center, reduced course load, remedial instruction, special counselor, tutoring. **ROTC:** Army. **Placement/credit:** AP, CLEP General and Subject; 12 credit hours maximum for bachelor's degree.

ACADEMIC REQUIREMENTS. Freshmen must earn minimum GPA of 2.0 to continue in good standing. 75% of freshmen return for sophomore year. Students must declare major by end of second year. **Graduation requirements:** 64 hours for associate, 124 hours for bachelor's. Most students required to take courses in computer science, English, foreign languages, history, humanities, mathematics, biological/physical sciences, social sciences. **Postgraduate studies:** 10% enter law school, 30% enter medical school, 10% enter MBA programs, 35% enter other graduate study.

FRESHMAN ADMISSIONS. Selection criteria: School achievement record and recommendations. **High school preparation:** 16 units required. Required and recommended units include English 3, mathematics 2-3, social science 2 and science 2. Biological science 1 and foreign language 2 recommended. **Test requirements:** SAT or ACT; score report by August 24. **Additional information:** Minimum 3.0 GPA and ACT composite score of 18 required of applicants in junior year of high school.

1992 FRESHMAN CLASS PROFILE. 281 men applied, 177 accepted, 110 enrolled; 635 women applied, 364 accepted, 215 enrolled. 49% had high school GPA of 3.0 or higher, 51% between 2.0 and 2.99. **Characteristics:** 86% from in state, 67% live in college housing, 100% have minority backgrounds. Average age is 17.

FALL-TERM APPLICATIONS. No fee. No closing date; applicants notified on a rolling basis; must reply within 2 weeks. Audition required for music applicants. Portfolio recommended for art applicants. Early admission available.

STUDENT LIFE. Housing: Dormitories (men, women). **Activities:** Student government, radio, student newspaper, yearbook, choral groups, dance, drama, music ensembles, fraternities, sororities.

ATHLETICS. NAIA. **Intercollegiate:** Basketball, cross-country M. **Intramural:** Archery, badminton, baseball M, basketball, bowling, cross-country M, golf M, soccer M, softball, table tennis, tennis, track and field, volleyball.

STUDENT SERVICES. Career counseling, employment service for undergraduates, freshman orientation, health services, personal counseling, placement service for graduates, veterans counselor, services/facilities for handicapped.

ANNUAL EXPENSES. Tuition and fees: $5,275. **Room and board:** $2,185. **Books and supplies:** $500. **Other expenses:** $500.

FINANCIAL AID. 92% of freshmen, 86% of continuing students receive some form of aid. Academic, music/drama, athletic scholarships available. **Aid applications:** No closing date; priority given to applications received by April 15; applicants notified on a rolling basis beginning on or about May 1; must reply within 2 weeks.

ADDRESS/TELEPHONE. Washington Cole, IV, Director of Admissions and Recruiting, Tougaloo College, 500 W. CountyLine Road, Tougaloo, MS 39174. (601) 977-7700 ext. 7770.

University of Mississippi

University, Mississippi CB code: 1840

Admissions: 86% of applicants accepted
Based on: ••• School record, test scores
• Activities, interview, recommendations, special talents
Completion: 70% of freshmen end year in good standing
53% graduate

4-year public university, coed. Founded in 1844. **Accreditation:** Regional. **Undergraduate enrollment:** 4,995 men, 4,599 women full time; 498 men, 592 women part time. **Graduate enrollment:** 985 men, 693 women full time; 254 men, 292 women part time. **Faculty:** 558 total (463 full time), 478 with doctorates or other terminal degrees. **Location:** Rural campus in large town; 75 miles from Memphis, Tennessee. **Calendar:** Semester, extensive summer session. **Microcomputers:** 1,200 located in dormitories, libraries, classrooms, computer centers, campus-wide network. **Special facilities:** Accredited teaching museum, William Faulkner home and grounds, Center for Study of Southern Culture, National Center for Physical Acoustics, 2 super computers.

DEGREES OFFERED. BA, BS, BFA, MA, MS, MBA, MFA, MEd, PhD, EdD, MD, Pharm D, JD. 1,610 bachelor's degrees awarded in 1992. 27% in business and management, 7% business/office and marketing/distribution, 5% communications, 10% teacher education, 5% engineering, 7% health sciences, 5% letters/literature, 5% life sciences, 7% parks/recreation, protective services, public affairs, 5% psychology, 6% social sciences. Graduate degrees offered in 44 major fields of study.

UNDERGRADUATE MAJORS. Accounting, advertising, anthropology, art history, biology, business administration and management, business and management, business economics, chemical engineering, chemistry, civil engineering, classics, computer and information sciences, computer engineering, court reporting, criminal justice studies, dramatic arts, economics, electrical/electronics/communications engineering, elementary education, engineering, English, exercise science, finance, fine arts, forensic studies, French, geological engineering, geology, German, history, home economics, insurance and risk management, interior design, journalism, law enforcement and corrections, leisure management, liberal/general studies, linguistics, management information systems, managerial finance, marketing and distribution, marketing management, mathematics, mechanical engineering, medical laboratory technologies, music, pharmacy, philosophy, physics, political science and government, predentistry, premedicine, psychology, public administration, radio/television broadcasting, real estate, social work, sociology, southern studies, Spanish, special education, speech pathology/audiology.

ACADEMIC PROGRAMS. Accelerated program, double major, education specialist degree, honors program, independent study, internships, study abroad, teacher preparation. **Remedial services:** Learning center, reduced course load, remedial instruction, special counselor, tutoring. **ROTC:** Air Force, Army, Naval. **Placement/credit:** AP, CLEP General and Subject, institutional tests; 30 credit hours maximum for bachelor's degree.

ACADEMIC REQUIREMENTS. Freshmen must earn minimum GPA of 2.0 to continue in good standing. 78% of freshmen return for sophomore year. Students must declare major by end of second year. **Graduation requirements:** 126 hours for bachelor's (30 in major). Most students required to take courses in arts/fine arts, English, history, mathematics, biological/physical sciences, social sciences.

FRESHMAN ADMISSIONS. Selection criteria: School achievement record and test scores. **High school preparation:** 14 units required; 18 recommended. Required and recommended units include English 4-4, foreign language 1-2, mathematics 3-4, social science 3-4 and science 3-4. Mathematics units must include algebra and 2 higher courses. Social sciences units must include US history and US government. Physical science not acceptable. **Test requirements:** SAT or ACT; score report by August 6.

1992 FRESHMAN CLASS PROFILE. 3,516 men and women applied, 3,021 accepted; 841 men enrolled, 851 women enrolled. 60% had high school GPA of 3.0 or higher, 37% between 2.0 and 2.99. 47% were in top quarter of graduating class. **Academic background:** Mid 50% of enrolled freshmen had ACT composite between 21-25. 80% submitted ACT scores. **Characteristics:** 50% from in state, 95% live in college housing, 9% have minority backgrounds, 2% are foreign students, 50% join fraternities/sororities. Average age is 18.

FALL-TERM APPLICATIONS. No fee. $25 fee for out-of-state applicants. Closing date July 30; priority given to applications received by April 1; applicants notified on a rolling basis. Audition required for theater applicants. Portfolio recommended for art applicants. Deferred and early admission available. Audition recommended for music applicants.

STUDENT LIFE. Housing: Dormitories (men, women); apartment, fraternity, sorority housing available. Intensive study floors available to honors and other students. **Activities:** Student government, film, magazine, radio, student newspaper, television, yearbook, choral groups, concert band, dance, drama, jazz band, marching band, music ensembles, musical theater, opera, pep band, symphony orchestra, fraternities, sororities, Black Student Union, 20 religious organizations, Students for Environmental Awareness.

ATHLETICS. NCAA. **Intercollegiate:** Baseball M, basketball, bowling M, cross-country, football M, golf, lacrosse M, racquetball M, rugby M, skiing M, soccer M, swimming, tennis, track and field, volleyball W. **Intramural:** Archery, badminton, basketball, bowling, cross-country, diving, golf, gymnastics, handball, racquetball, rifle, soccer, softball, swimming, table tennis, tennis, track and field M, volleyball, water polo.

STUDENT SERVICES. Aptitude testing, career counseling, employment service for undergraduates, freshman orientation, health services, on-campus day care, personal counseling, placement service for graduates, special adviser for adult students, veterans counselor, services/facilities for handicapped.

ANNUAL EXPENSES. Tuition and fees (1992-93): $2,435, $1,960 additional for out-of-state students. **Room and board:** $2,660. **Books and supplies:** $460. **Other expenses:** $1,019.

FINANCIAL AID. 56% of freshmen, 58% of continuing students receive some form of aid. 39% of grants, 61% of loans, 29% of jobs based on need. Academic, music/drama, art, athletic, state/district residency, leadership, alumni affiliation, minority scholarships available. **Aid applications:** No closing date; priority given to applications received by April 1; applicants notified on a rolling basis beginning on or about May 1; must reply within 3 weeks. **Additional information:** Out-of-state portion of tuition waived for children of out-of-state alumni.

ADDRESS/TELEPHONE. Beckett Howorth, Director of Admission/Records, University of Mississippi, University, MS 38677. (601) 232-7226. Fax: (601) 232-5869.

University of Mississippi Medical Center

Jackson, Mississippi CB code: 0358

2-year upper-division public health science college, coed. Founded in 1955. **Accreditation:** Regional. **Undergraduate enrollment:** 123 men, 448 women full time; 2 men, 31 women part time. **Graduate enrollment:** 698 men, 272 women full time; 3 men, 54 women part time. **Faculty:** 572 total (415 full time). **Location:** Urban campus in small city. **Calendar:** Quarter, limited summer session. **Microcomputers:** 40 located in libraries, computer centers. **Special facilities:** Teaching laboratory. **Additional facts:** Health sciences campus for state. Includes schools of medicine, nursing, health-related professions, and dentistry; graduate programs in the health sciences; and a 593-bed teaching hospital.

DEGREES OFFERED. BS, MS, PhD, DMD, MD. 227 bachelor's degrees awarded in 1992. 54% in health sciences, 46% allied health. Graduate degrees offered in 13 major fields of study.

UNDERGRADUATE MAJORS. Cytotechnology, dental hygiene, medical laboratory technologies, medical records administration, nursing, occupational therapy, physical therapy.

ACADEMIC PROGRAMS. Remedial services: Preadmission summer program.

ACADEMIC REQUIREMENTS. Students must declare major on application. **Graduation requirements:** 132 hours for bachelor's (67 in major). Most students required to take courses in arts/fine arts, computer science, English, history, humanities, mathematics, biological/physical sciences. **Postgraduate studies:** 90% enter other graduate study. **Additional information:** Certificate programs in emergency medical technology and radiologic technology, clinical nuclear medicine, respiratory therapy (technician training), and radiation therapy offered.

STUDENT LIFE. Housing: Dormitories (women); apartment housing available. **Activities:** Student government, student newspaper, yearbook, University Christian Fellowship.

ATHLETICS. Intramural: Baseball, basketball, golf, soccer, softball, table tennis.

STUDENT SERVICES. Career counseling, health services, personal counseling, services/facilities for handicapped.

ANNUAL EXPENSES. Tuition and fees (projected): $2,101, $1,959 additional for out-of-state students. **Room and board:** $1,140 room only. **Books and supplies:** $660. **Other expenses:** $4,950.

FINANCIAL AID. 80% of continuing students receive some form of aid. 46% of grants, 89% of loans, all jobs based on need. Academic, state/district residency, alumni affiliation, minority scholarships available. **Aid applications:** No closing date; priority given to applications received by April 1; applicants notified on a rolling basis beginning on or about July 15; must reply within 2 weeks.

ADDRESS/TELEPHONE. Billy M. Bishop, EdD, Director of Student Services and Records/Registrar, University of Mississippi Medical Center, 2500 North State Street, Jackson, MS 39216. (601) 984-1080.

University of Southern Mississippi
Hattiesburg, Mississippi CB code: 1479

Admissions: 77% of applicants accepted
Based on: ••• School record, test scores
• Special talents
Completion: 39% enter graduate study

4-year public university, coed. Founded in 1910. **Accreditation:** Regional. **Undergraduate enrollment:** 3,836 men, 4,844 women full time; 450 men, 711 women part time. **Graduate enrollment:** 500 men, 544 women full time; 269 men, 526 women part time. **Faculty:** 646 total (556 full time). **Location:** Urban campus in large town; 85 miles from Jackson, 120 miles from New Orleans, Louisiana. **Calendar:** Semester, extensive summer session. **Microcomputers:** Located in dormitories, libraries, classrooms, computer centers. **Special facilities:** Woods Art Gallery, natural science museum, equestrian center. **Additional facts:** Branch campuses at Jackson and Long Beach.

DEGREES OFFERED. BA, BS, BFA, MA, MS, MBA, MFA, MEd, PhD, EdD. 2,425 bachelor's degrees awarded in 1992. 26% in business and management, 6% communications, 6% computer sciences, 19% teacher education, 5% engineering technologies, 7% health sciences, 5% psychology, 5% social sciences. Graduate degrees offered in 54 major fields of study.

UNDERGRADUATE MAJORS. Accounting, advertising, American studies, anthropology, architectural technologies, biology, business administration and management, business economics, business education, chemistry, city/community/regional planning, communications, computer and information sciences, computer technology, criminal justice studies, dance, dramatic arts, education of the deaf and hearing impaired, elementary education, engineering and engineering-related technologies, English, fashion merchandising, finance, fine arts, food science and nutrition, foreign languages (multiple emphasis), geography, geology, health education, history, home economics, hotel/motel and restaurant management, human environment and housing, individual and family development, industrial arts education, industrial technology, insurance and risk management, interior design, international studies, journalism, legal assistant/paralegal, library science, marketing management, mathematics, mechanical design technology, medical laboratory technologies, music, music education, nursing, parks and recreation management, personnel management, philosophy, physical education, physics, political science and government, polymer science, predentistry, prelaw, premedicine, prepharmacy, preveterinary, psychology, radio/television broadcasting, real estate, rehabilitation counseling/services, science education, secondary education, social sciences, sociology, special education, speech, speech pathology/audiology, technical education, textiles and clothing, trade and industrial education, trade and industrial supervision and management.

ACADEMIC PROGRAMS. Accelerated program, cooperative education, double major, dual enrollment of high school students, education specialist degree, honors program, independent study, internships, study abroad, teacher preparation, visiting/exchange student program. **Remedial services:** Learning center, preadmission summer program, reduced course load, remedial instruction, special counselor, tutoring. **ROTC:** Air Force, Army. **Placement/credit:** AP, CLEP General and Subject, institutional tests; 30 credit hours maximum for bachelor's degree.

ACADEMIC REQUIREMENTS. Freshmen must earn minimum GPA of 1.75 to continue in good standing. 79% of freshmen return for sophomore year. Students must declare major by end of second year. **Graduation requirements:** 128 hours for bachelor's (32 in major). Most students required to take courses in arts/fine arts, English, history, humanities, mathematics, philosophy/religion, biological/physical sciences, social sciences.

FRESHMAN ADMISSIONS. Selection criteria: School achievement record and test scores considered. **High school preparation:** 14 units required. Required and recommended units include English 4, foreign language 1-2, mathematics 3-4, social science 2.5-3 and science 3-4. Mathematics must include algebra I and II and geometry or a higher math. Social sciences must include US government and US history. Sciences must be chosen from introductory and advanced biology, physics, and chemistry, 1 must be laboratory based. Additional science or mathematics may be substituted for foreign language. **Test requirements:** ACT; score report by August 8. Out-of-state applicants may submit SAT instead of ACT.

1992 FRESHMAN CLASS PROFILE. 1,158 men applied, 891 accepted, 659 enrolled; 1,644 women applied, 1,261 accepted, 891 enrolled. **Academic background:** Mid 50% of enrolled freshmen had ACT composite between 16-23. 90% submitted ACT scores. **Characteristics:** 83% from in state, 62% commute, 21% have minority backgrounds, 7% join fraternities/sororities. Average age is 20.

FALL-TERM APPLICATIONS. No fee. No closing date; priority given to applications received by August 8; applicants notified on a rolling basis. Deferred and early admission available.

STUDENT LIFE. Housing: Dormitories (men, women); apartment, fraternity, sorority, handicapped housing available. Housing available for physically handicapped students. Freshmen who reside in area may live at home. All freshman who request campus housing required to live in freshman dorms. **Activities:** Student government, film, radio, student newspaper, television, yearbook, choral groups, concert band, dance, drama, jazz band, marching band, music ensembles, musical theater, opera, pep band, symphony orchestra, fraternities, sororities, numerous honor societies, service and religious organizations, Young Republicans, Young Democrats.

ATHLETICS. NCAA. **Intercollegiate:** Baseball M, basketball, cross-country, football M, golf, softball W, tennis, track and field, volleyball W. **Intramural:** Archery, badminton, baseball M, basketball, bowling, diving, golf, gymnastics, handball, horseback riding, racquetball, rifle, soccer, softball, swimming, tennis, track and field, volleyball.

STUDENT SERVICES. Aptitude testing, career counseling, employment service for undergraduates, freshman orientation, health services, personal counseling, placement service for graduates, special adviser for adult students, veterans counselor, services/facilities for handicapped.

ANNUAL EXPENSES. Tuition and fees (projected): $2,404, $1,960 additional for out-of-state students. **Room and board:** $2,335. **Books and supplies:** $500. **Other expenses:** $1,380.

FINANCIAL AID. 60% of freshmen, 60% of continuing students receive some form of aid. Grants, loans, jobs available. Academic, music/drama, art, athletic, state/district residency, leadership, alumni affiliation scholarships available. **Aid applications:** No closing date; priority given to applications received by March 15; applicants notified on a rolling basis beginning on or about June 1; must reply within 2 weeks.

ADDRESS/TELEPHONE. R. Wayne Pyle, Director of Admissions, University of Southern Mississippi, Southern Station, Box 5167, Hattiesburg, MS 39406-5167. (601) 266-4059. Fax: (601) 266-5735.

Wesley College
Florence, Mississippi CB code: 1923

4-year private Bible college, coed, affiliated with Congregational Methodist Church. Founded in 1972. **Undergraduate enrollment:** 31 men, 27 women full time; 18 men, 14 women part time. **Location:** Rural campus in small town; 12 miles from Jackson. **Calendar:** Semester.

FRESHMAN ADMISSIONS. Selection criteria: Test scores, school achievement record, interview important.

ANNUAL EXPENSES. Tuition and fees: $1,800. **Room and board:** $2,200. **Books and supplies:** $350. **Other expenses:** $650.

ADDRESS/TELEPHONE. Chris Lahrstarser, Director of Admissions, Wesley College, PO 1070, Florence, MS 39073-0070. (601) 845-2265. (800) 748-9972.

William Carey College
Hattiesburg, Mississippi CB code: 1907

4-year private liberal arts college, coed, affiliated with Southern Baptist Convention. Founded in 1906. **Accreditation:** Regional. **Undergraduate enrollment:** 448 men, 964 women full time; 123 men, 285 women part time. **Faculty:** 156 total (91 full time), 69 with doctorates or other terminal degrees. **Location:** Suburban campus in large town; 98 miles from New Orleans, Louisiana. **Calendar:** Trimester, extensive summer session. Saturday and extensive evening/early morning classes. **Microcomputers:** Located in computer centers. **Special facilities:** Art galleries on Gulfport and Hattiesburg campuses.

DEGREES OFFERED. BA, BS, BFA, MBA, MEd. 241 bachelor's degrees awarded in 1992. 31% in business and management, 30% teacher education, 10% allied health, 7% psychology. Graduate degrees offered in 4 major fields of study.

UNDERGRADUATE MAJORS. Biological and physical sciences, biology, business administration and management, business and management, business economics, chemistry, clinical laboratory science, communications, data processing, dramatic arts, education, elementary education, English, history, liberal/general studies, management information systems, mathematics, medical radiation dosimetry, music, nursing, psychology, religious education, religious music, secretarial and related programs, social sciences, Spanish, theological studies, visual and performing arts.

ACADEMIC PROGRAMS. Accelerated program, double major, dual enrollment of high school students, education specialist degree, honors program, independent study, internships, study abroad, teacher preparation, cross-registration; combined bachelor's/graduate program in business administration. **Remedial services:** Reduced course load, remedial instruction, special counselor, tutoring. **ROTC:** Air Force, Army. **Placement/credit:** AP, CLEP General and Subject, institutional tests; 32 credit hours maximum for bachelor's degree.

ACADEMIC REQUIREMENTS. Freshmen must earn minimum GPA of 1.4 to continue in good standing. 60% of freshmen return for sophomore year. Students must declare major by end of second year. **Graduation requirements:** 128 hours for bachelor's (30 in major). Most students required to take courses in English, history, mathematics, philosophy/religion, biological/physical sciences, social sciences. **Postgraduate studies:** 4% enter law school, 4% enter medical school, 11% enter MBA programs, 19% enter other graduate study.

FRESHMAN ADMISSIONS. Selection criteria: School record most important, followed by ACT or SAT scores. Recommendations considered. **High school preparation:** 15 units recommended. Recommended units include biological science 2, English 4, mathematics 2, physical science 1 and social science 2. **Test requirements:** SAT or ACT (ACT preferred); score report by August 15.

1992 FRESHMAN CLASS PROFILE. 83 men, 146 women enrolled. **Characteristics:** 80% from in state, 57% live in college housing, 29% have minority backgrounds, 4% are foreign students. Average age is 18.

FALL-TERM APPLICATIONS. $10 fee. Closing date August 15; priority given to applications received by May 1; applicants notified on a rolling basis beginning on or about May 15. Deferred and early admission available.

STUDENT LIFE. Housing: Dormitories (men, women); apartment housing available. **Activities:** Student government, student newspaper, yearbook, choral groups, dance, drama, music ensembles, musical theater, sororities, Baptist Student Union, Afro-American club, psychology club, Young Democrats, Fellowship of Christian Athletes, International Students Club, several honorary organizations, Church Related Vocations Fellowship, Science Society, Carey Student Nurses Association. **Additional information:** Religious observance required.

ATHLETICS. NAIA. **Intercollegiate:** Baseball M, basketball, soccer, tennis. **Intramural:** Badminton, basketball, football M, softball, tennis, volleyball.

STUDENT SERVICES. Career counseling, employment service for undergraduates, freshman orientation, personal counseling, placement service for graduates, veterans counselor, services/facilities for handicapped.

ANNUAL EXPENSES. Tuition and fees: $4,450. **Room and board:** $2,110. **Books and supplies:** $500. **Other expenses:** $1,200.

FINANCIAL AID. 90% of freshmen, 80% of continuing students receive some form of aid. 57% of grants based on need. Academic, music/drama, athletic, religious affiliation scholarships available. **Aid applications:** Closing date April 1; applicants notified on a rolling basis beginning on or about June 1; must reply within 2 weeks.

ADDRESS/TELEPHONE. Tim C. Bailey, Director of Marketing and College Relations, William Carey College, 498 Tuscan Avenue, Hattiesburg, MS 39401-5499. (601) 582-6103. (800) 962-5991. Fax: (601) 582-6454.

Wood Junior College
Mathiston, Mississippi

CB code: 1924

2-year private junior college, coed, affiliated with United Methodist Church. Founded in 1886. **Accreditation:** Regional. **Undergraduate enrollment:** 129 men, 228 women full time; 71 men, 109 women part time. **Faculty:** 36 total (26 full time), 9 with doctorates or other terminal degrees. **Location:** Rural campus in rural community; 17 miles from Starkville. **Calendar:** Modular (10 sessions of 3 or 4 weeks each). **Microcomputers:** 40 located in classrooms, computer centers.

DEGREES OFFERED. AA, AAS. 58 associate degrees awarded in 1992.

UNDERGRADUATE MAJORS. Equestrian science, liberal/general studies, office supervision and management.

ACADEMIC PROGRAMS. 2-year transfer program, dual enrollment of high school students, weekend pastor's program. **Remedial services:** Learning center, remedial instruction, special counselor, tutoring. **Placement/credit:** CLEP Subject, institutional tests; 15 credit hours maximum for associate degree.

ACADEMIC REQUIREMENTS. Freshmen must earn minimum GPA of 2.0 to continue in good standing. 50% of freshmen return for sophomore year. **Graduation requirements:** 64 hours for associate. Most students required to take courses in arts/fine arts, English, history, humanities, mathematics, philosophy/religion, biological/physical sciences, social sciences.

FRESHMAN ADMISSIONS. Selection criteria: Test scores very important. **Test requirements:** SAT or ACT; score report by August 20.

1992 FRESHMAN CLASS PROFILE. 64 men, 112 women enrolled. **Academic background:** Mid 50% of enrolled freshmen had ACT composite between 17-20. 100% submitted ACT scores. **Characteristics:** 97% from in state, 90% commute, 5% are foreign students. Average age is 27.

FALL-TERM APPLICATIONS. $15 fee. No closing date; priority given to applications received by June 1; applicants notified on a rolling basis beginning on or about March 15. Essay required. Deferred and early admission available. Modular calendar allows students to enter at start of any one of ten sessions.

STUDENT LIFE. Housing: Dormitories (men, women). **Activities:** Student government, student newspaper, yearbook, choral groups, drama.

ATHLETICS. Intramural: Basketball, horseback riding, softball, table tennis, tennis, volleyball.

STUDENT SERVICES. Aptitude testing, career counseling, freshman orientation, personal counseling, veterans counselor, services/facilities for handicapped.

ANNUAL EXPENSES. Tuition and fees: $2,750. **Room and board:** $2,560. **Books and supplies:** $400. **Other expenses:** $1,000.

FINANCIAL AID. 85% of freshmen, 85% of continuing students receive some form of aid. Academic, music/drama scholarships available. **Aid applications:** No closing date; priority given to applications received by June 1; applicants notified on a rolling basis beginning on or about July 15; must reply by August 1 or within 2 weeks if notified thereafter.

ADDRESS/TELEPHONE. Bobbie Shaw, Admissions Coordinator, Wood Junior College, PO Drawer C, Mathiston, MS 39752. (601) 263-5352. Fax: (601) 263-4964.

Missouri

Avila College
Kansas City, Missouri CB code: 6109

Admissions: 78% of applicants accepted
Based on: ••• School record, test scores
•• Recommendations
• Activities, interview, special talents
Completion: 89% of freshmen end year in good standing
48% graduate, 25% of these enter graduate study

4-year private liberal arts college, coed, affiliated with Roman Catholic Church. Founded in 1916. **Accreditation:** Regional. **Undergraduate enrollment:** 201 men, 429 women full time; 136 men, 439 women part time. **Graduate enrollment:** 12 men, 11 women full time; 78 men, 103 women part time. **Faculty:** 207 total (60 full time), 108 with doctorates or other terminal degrees. **Location:** Suburban campus in large city; 10 miles from downtown. **Calendar:** Semester, extensive summer session. Saturday and extensive evening/early morning classes. **Microcomputers:** 40 located in libraries, classrooms, computer centers. **Special facilities:** 2 theaters, Montessori laboratory classrooms, art gallery, radiological laboratory, 30 off-campus medical-clinical learning sites. **Additional facts:** Graduate programs in business, education, and psychology.

DEGREES OFFERED. BA, BS, BFA, MS, MBA. 183 bachelor's degrees awarded. 12% in business and management, 6% business/office and marketing/distribution, 5% communications, 14% education, 12% health sciences, 6% allied health, 8% parks/recreation, protective services, public affairs, 8% psychology, 7% social sciences, 6% visual and performing arts. Graduate degrees offered in 9 major fields of study.

UNDERGRADUATE MAJORS. Associate: Liberal/general studies. **Bachelor's:** Accounting, art education, biology, business administration and management, chemistry, communications, computer mathematics, cytotechnology, dramatic arts, education of the emotionally handicapped, education of the mentally handicapped, elementary education, English, finance, fine arts, history, human resources development, international business management, legal assistant/paralegal, liberal/general studies, management information systems, marketing and distribution, mathematics, medical laboratory technologies, Montessori education, music education, music performance, musical theater, nursing, political science and government, premedicine, psychology, public administration, radiograph medical technology, respiratory therapy technology, social work, sociology, specific learning disabilities, studio art, theological studies, visual and performing arts.

ACADEMIC PROGRAMS. Double major, dual enrollment of high school students, independent study, internships, teacher preparation, visiting/exchange student program, weekend college, Washington semester; liberal arts/career combination in health sciences. **Remedial services:** Learning center, preadmission summer program, reduced course load, special counselor, tutoring, study skill courses. **Placement/credit:** AP, CLEP General and Subject, IB, institutional tests; 16 credit hours maximum for associate degree; 32 credit hours maximum for bachelor's degree.

ACADEMIC REQUIREMENTS. Freshmen must earn minimum GPA of 2.0 to continue in good standing. 66% of freshmen return for sophomore year. Students must declare major by end of second year. **Graduation requirements:** 64 hours for associate, 128 hours for bachelor's (30 in major). Most students required to take courses in arts/fine arts, computer science, English, foreign languages, history, humanities, mathematics, philosophy/religion, biological/physical sciences, social sciences. **Postgraduate studies:** 100% from 2-year programs enter 4-year programs. 1% enter law school, 3% enter medical school, 8% enter MBA programs, 13% enter other graduate study.

FRESHMAN ADMISSIONS. Selection criteria: Unconditional acceptance for applicants who rank in top half of graduating class, with minimum SAT or ACT scores and GPA of 2.5. Others may be considered. **High school preparation:** 16 units recommended. Recommended units include English 4, foreign language 2, mathematics 3, social science 3 and science 3. One fine arts also recommended. **Test requirements:** SAT or ACT (ACT preferred); score report by August 15.

1992 FRESHMAN CLASS PROFILE. 136 men applied, 108 accepted, 41 enrolled; 245 women applied, 191 accepted, 54 enrolled. 56% had high school GPA of 3.0 or higher, 43% between 2.0 and 2.99. 17% were in top tenth and 30% were in top quarter of graduating class. **Academic background:** Mid 50% of enrolled freshmen had ACT composite between 16-21. 85% submitted ACT scores. **Characteristics:** 72% from in state, 51% commute, 6% have minority backgrounds. Average age is 19.

FALL-TERM APPLICATIONS. No application fee before June 30. $20 fee after June 30; maybe waived for applicants with financial need. No closing date; applicants notified on a rolling basis; must reply within 2 weeks. Interview recommended. Audition recommended for music, musical theater, drama applicants. Portfolio recommended for fine arts applicants. Essay required of applicants not meeting usual admissions criteria, recommended for all.

STUDENT LIFE. Housing: Dormitories (coed). Laundry and kitchen facilities on each floor in residence halls. **Activities:** Student government, student newspaper, television, choral groups, concert band, dance, drama, musical theater, Neuman Club, Avila Student Nurses Association, Psychology Club, Students in Free Enterprise, International Students Club, Afro-American Students for College Education, Prelaw, History Club, Premed Club.

ATHLETICS. NAIA. **Intercollegiate:** Baseball M, basketball, soccer M, softball W, volleyball W. **Intramural:** Basketball, bowling, skiing, soccer W, softball, swimming, table tennis, volleyball.

STUDENT SERVICES. Aptitude testing, career counseling, employment service for undergraduates, freshman orientation, health services, on-campus day care, personal counseling, placement service for graduates, veterans counselor, services/facilities for handicapped.

ANNUAL EXPENSES. Tuition and fees: $8,530. **Room and board:** $3,600. **Books and supplies:** $600. **Other expenses:** $1,600.

FINANCIAL AID. 95% of freshmen, 80% of continuing students receive some form of aid. 66% of grants, 86% of loans, all jobs based on need. 74 enrolled freshmen were judged to have need, all were offered aid. Academic, music/drama, art, athletic, leadership, alumni affiliation, religious affiliation scholarships available. **Aid applications:** No closing date; priority given to applications received by July 1; applicants notified on a rolling basis beginning on or about January 15; must reply by May 1 or within 2 weeks if notified thereafter. **Additional information:** Guaranteed tuition plan freezes tuition at first year level when student pays one-time premium of 10% at first year tuition rate.

ADDRESS/TELEPHONE. James E. Millard, Director of Admissions, Avila College, 11901 Wornall Road, Kansas City, MO 64145-1698. (816) 942-8400. Fax: (816) 942-3362.

Baptist Bible College
Springfield, Missouri CB code: 0991

4-year private Bible college, coed, affiliated with Baptist Bible Fellowship. Founded in 1950. **Undergraduate enrollment:** 902 men and women. **Graduate enrollment:** 66 men and women. **Location:** Urban campus in small city; 180 miles from Kansas City, 225 miles from St. Louis. **Calendar:** Semester.

FRESHMAN ADMISSIONS. Selection criteria: Open admissions.

ANNUAL EXPENSES. Tuition and fees (1992-93): $1,884. **Room and board:** $2,600. **Books and supplies:** $300. **Other expenses:** $1,300.

ADDRESS/TELEPHONE. Dr. Joseph K. Gleason, Director of Admissions and Records, Baptist Bible College, 628 East Kearney, Springfield, MO 65803. (417) 869-6000 ext. 2219.

Berean College
Springfield, Missouri CB code: 4916

4-year private Bible college, coed, affiliated with Assemblies of God. Founded in 1948. **Undergraduate enrollment:** 575 men and women. **Faculty:** 9 total (6 full time), 3 with doctorates or other terminal degrees. **Location:** Urban campus in small city. **Calendar:** No set calendar. **Additional facts:** Correspondence institution. All course work completed via distance education.

DEGREES OFFERED. AA, BA. 100% in philosophy, religion, theology. 4 bachelor's degrees awarded. 100% in philosophy, religion, theology.

UNDERGRADUATE MAJORS. Associate: Bible studies. **Bachelor's:** Bible studies, religious education.

ACADEMIC PROGRAMS. External degree, independent study. **Placement/credit:** 16 credit hours maximum for associate degree; 32 credit hours maximum for bachelor's degree.

ACADEMIC REQUIREMENTS. Freshmen must earn minimum GPA of 1.7 to continue in good standing. **Graduation requirements:** 64 hours for associate, 128 hours for bachelor's. Most students required to take courses in English, humanities, philosophy/religion, biological/physical sciences.

FRESHMAN ADMISSIONS. Selection criteria: Open admissions.

1992 FRESHMAN CLASS PROFILE. Characteristics: 100% commute.

FALL-TERM APPLICATIONS. $25 fee. No closing date; applicants notified on a rolling basis.

ANNUAL EXPENSES. Tuition and fees (1992-93): $2,095. **Books and supplies:** $500.

FINANCIAL AID. Aid applications: No closing date; applicants notified on a rolling basis.

ADDRESS/TELEPHONE. Admissions Office, Berean College, 1445 Boonville Avenue, Springfield, MO 65802. (417) 862-2781.

Calvary Bible College
Kansas City, Missouri CB code: 6331

4-year private Bible college, coed, affiliated with Independent Fundamental Churches of America. Founded in 1932. **Undergraduate enrollment:** 279 men and women. **Faculty:** 30 total (12 full time), 11 with doctorates or other terminal degrees. **Location:** Suburban campus in large city; 20 miles from downtown. **Calendar:** 4-4-1-1. **Microcomputers:** 12 located in computer centers.

DEGREES OFFERED. AA, BA, BS, MA, M.Div. 13 associate degrees awarded in 1992. 100% in philosophy, religion, theology. 55 bachelor's degrees awarded. 44% in education, 52% philosophy, religion, theology. Graduate degrees offered in 3 major fields of study.

UNDERGRADUATE MAJORS. Associate: Bible studies, biblical languages, camping/outdoor education, local church education, missionary studies, radio/television broadcasting, religious education, religious music, theological studies. **Bachelor's:** Bible studies, Biblical counseling, biblical languages, camping/outdoor education, elementary education, local church education, missionary aviation, missionary studies, music, music education, music performance, pastoral studies, physical education, radio/television broadcasting, religious education, religious music, secondary education, social studies education, theological studies.

ACADEMIC PROGRAMS. Double major, dual enrollment of high school students, independent study, internships, teacher preparation. **Remedial services:** Reduced course load, remedial instruction, special counselor. **Placement/credit:** AP, CLEP General and Subject, institutional tests.

ACADEMIC REQUIREMENTS. Freshmen must earn minimum GPA of 2.0 to continue in good standing. 63% of freshmen return for sophomore year. Students must declare major on enrollment. **Graduation requirements:** 68 hours for associate (18 in major), 131 hours for bachelor's (41 in major). Most students required to take courses in arts/fine arts, computer science, English, history, humanities, mathematics, philosophy/religion, biological/physical sciences, social sciences. **Additional information:** Each student carries major in Bible and theology and second major in a professional area. These majors are to prepare students for vocational and/or volunteer involvement in Christian Ministry.

FRESHMAN ADMISSIONS. Selection criteria: Christian character stressed above academic preparation. Pastor's and personal reference forms required. School achievement record and test scores considered. **Test requirements:** SAT or ACT (ACT preferred); score report by August 15.

1992 FRESHMAN CLASS PROFILE. 58 men and women enrolled. **Characteristics:** 18% from in state, 84% live in college housing, 6% have minority backgrounds, 2% are foreign students. Average age is 20.

FALL-TERM APPLICATIONS. $15 fee, may be waived for applicants with need. No closing date; priority given to applications received by July 15; applicants notified on a rolling basis. Audition required for music applicants. Deferred and early admission available.

STUDENT LIFE. Housing: Dormitories (men, women); apartment housing available. Single students required to live in college housing unless living with parents or aged at least 23 years. Duplexes for married students available. **Activities:** Student government, radio, yearbook, choral groups, music ensembles, drama team, Missionary Prayer Fellowship, Christian Ministry. **Additional information:** Weekly Christian ministry, chapel attendance, and church attendance required. Religious observance required.

ATHLETICS. Intercollegiate: Basketball, golf, soccer M, tennis, volleyball W. **Intramural:** Badminton, basketball, bowling, golf, racquetball, softball M, swimming, table tennis, tennis, volleyball.

STUDENT SERVICES. Employment service for undergraduates, freshman orientation, health services, personal counseling, placement service for graduates, veterans counselor, counseling for married students.

ANNUAL EXPENSES. Tuition and fees: $3,600. **Room and board:** $2,730. **Books and supplies:** $400. **Other expenses:** $350.

FINANCIAL AID. 77% of freshmen, 61% of continuing students receive some form of aid. All grants, all loans based on need. Academic, alumni affiliation scholarships available. **Aid applications:** Closing date August 15; priority given to applications received by July 15; applicants notified on a rolling basis; must reply within 3 weeks.

ADDRESS/TELEPHONE. Craig Wells, Director of Admissions, Calvary Bible College, 15800 Calvary Road, Kansas City, MO 64147-1341. (816) 322-0110. (800) 326-3960.

Central Bible College
Springfield, Missouri CB code: 6085

4-year private Bible college, coed, affiliated with Assemblies of God. Founded in 1922. **Undergraduate enrollment:** 553 men, 304 women full time; 35 men, 43 women part time. **Location:** Urban campus in small city; 210 miles southwest of St. Louis. **Calendar:** Semester.

FRESHMAN ADMISSIONS. Selection criteria: Special consideration given to members of Assemblies of God and all applicants who rank in top half of graduating class.

ANNUAL EXPENSES. Tuition and fees: $3,970. **Room and board:** $2,850. **Books and supplies:** $450. **Other expenses:** $800.

ADDRESS/TELEPHONE. Eunice Bruegman, Director of Admissions and Records, Central Bible College, 3000 North Grant Avenue, Springfield, MO 65803. (417) 833-2551 ext. 1184. (800) 358-3092 ext. 1184. Fax: (417) 833-5141.

Central Christian College of the Bible
Moberly, Missouri CB code: 6145

4-year private Bible college, coed, affiliated with Christian Church. Founded in 1957. **Undergraduate enrollment:** 37 men, 35 women full time; 9 men, 5 women part time. **Faculty:** 14 total (6 full time), 1 with doctorate or other terminal degree. **Location:** Suburban campus in large town; 35 miles from Columbia, equidistant from St. Louis and Kansas City. **Calendar:** Semester. **Microcomputers:** 9 located in libraries, classrooms.

DEGREES OFFERED. AA, AS, BA, BS. 2 associate degrees awarded in 1992. 100% in philosophy, religion, theology. 6 bachelor's degrees awarded. 100% in philosophy, religion, theology.

UNDERGRADUATE MAJORS. Associate: Bible studies. **Bachelor's:** Music, religion, religious education, religious music, theological studies.

ACADEMIC PROGRAMS. Double major, internships, cross-registration. **Remedial services:** Reduced course load, special counselor, tutoring. **Placement/credit:** CLEP General; 6 credit hours maximum for bachelor's degree.

ACADEMIC REQUIREMENTS. Freshmen must earn minimum GPA of 1.4 to continue in good standing. 54% of freshmen return for sophomore year. Students must declare major by end of second year. **Graduation requirements:** 64 hours for associate (16 in major), 130 hours for bachelor's (32 in major). Most students required to take courses in English, history, humanities, philosophy/religion, biological/physical sciences, social sciences. **Postgraduate studies:** 50% from 2-year programs enter 4-year programs. 6% enter other graduate study.

FRESHMAN ADMISSIONS. Selection criteria: References very important. **High school preparation:** 15 units recommended. Recommended units include biological science 1, English 2, mathematics 2, physical science 1 and social science 1. **Test requirements:** ACT for placement and counseling only. **Additional information:** Students with GPA below 2.0 assigned reduced course load.

1992 FRESHMAN CLASS PROFILE. 19 men applied, 19 accepted, 19 enrolled; 21 women applied, 21 accepted, 21 enrolled. **Characteristics:** 71% from in state, 89% live in college housing, 2% are foreign students. Average age is 19.

FALL-TERM APPLICATIONS. $30 fee. No closing date; priority given to applications received by July 1; applicants notified on a rolling basis. Deferred and early admission available.

STUDENT LIFE. Housing: Dormitories (men, women). **Activities:** Student government, student newspaper, yearbook, choral groups, music ensembles, Harvesters missions group. **Additional information:** Religious observance required.

ATHLETICS. Intercollegiate: Basketball M, volleyball W. **Intramural:** Basketball, bowling, softball, table tennis, tennis, volleyball.

STUDENT SERVICES. Career counseling, freshman orientation, personal counseling, placement service for graduates, services/facilities for handicapped.

ANNUAL EXPENSES. Tuition and fees (1992-93): $3,323. **Room and board:** $2,390. **Books and supplies:** $340. **Other expenses:** $1,300.

FINANCIAL AID. 82% of freshmen, 86% of continuing students receive some form of aid. 66% of grants, all loans, all jobs based on need. 18 enrolled freshmen were judged to have need, all were offered aid. Academic, music/drama scholarships available. **Aid applications:** Closing date April 1; applicants notified on or about June 30; must reply within 2 weeks. **Additional information:** April 1 closing date for loan applications; August 1 closing date for work-study applications.

ADDRESS/TELEPHONE. Cheryl L. Ratzlaff, Registrar, Central Christian College of the Bible, 911 Urbandale Drive East, Moberly, MO 65270-1997. (816) 263-3900.

Central Methodist College
Fayette, Missouri CB code: 6089

4-year private liberal arts college, coed, affiliated with United Methodist Church. Founded in 1853. **Accreditation:** Regional. **Faculty:** 70 total (58 full time), 26 with doctorates or other terminal degrees. **Location:** Rural campus in small town; 150 miles from St. Louis, 125 miles from Kansas City. **Calendar:** 4-1-4, limited summer session. **Microcomputers:** Located in dormitories, libraries, computer centers. **Special facilities:** Observatory and laboratory, natural history museum, 190-seat theater.

DEGREES OFFERED. AA, AS, BA, BS. 22 associate degrees awarded in 1992. 85% in health sciences. 99 bachelor's degrees awarded. 22% in business and management, 5% computer sciences, 26% teacher education, 5% health sciences, 6% life sciences, 5% psychology.

UNDERGRADUATE MAJORS. Associate: Nursing. **Bachelor's:** Accounting, biology, business administration and management, business and management, chemistry, communications, computer and information sciences, dramatic arts, economics, elementary education, English, English literature, foreign languages (multiple emphasis), French, German, history, mathematics, music, music history and appreciation, music performance, nursing, philosophy, physics, political science and government, predentistry, premedicine, prepharmacy, preveterinary, psychology, religion, secondary education, Spanish, visual and performing arts.

ACADEMIC PROGRAMS. 2-year transfer program, accelerated program, double major, dual enrollment of high school students, honors program, independent study, internships, student-designed major, study abroad, teacher preparation, 3-year bachelor's degree, 2-week January travel program; liberal arts/career combination in engineering, health sciences. **Remedial services:** Learning center, preadmission summer program, reduced course load, remedial instruction, special counselor, tutoring. **ROTC:** Army. **Placement/credit:** AP, CLEP General and Subject, institutional tests; 32 credit hours maximum for associate degree; 32 credit hours maximum for bachelor's degree.

ACADEMIC REQUIREMENTS. Freshmen must earn minimum GPA of 1.8 to continue in good standing. 65% of freshmen return for sophomore year. Students must declare major by end of second year. **Graduation requirements:** 62 hours for associate, 124 hours for bachelor's (35 in major). Most students required to take courses in arts/fine arts, computer science, English, history, humanities, mathematics, philosophy/religion, biological/physical sciences, social sciences. **Postgraduate studies:** 83% from 2-year programs enter 4-year programs. 3% enter law school, 3% enter medical school, 1% enter MBA programs, 5% enter other graduate study.

FRESHMAN ADMISSIONS. **Selection criteria:** Rank in upper half of class or above-average test scores. Must rank in top 20% for 3-year bachelor's degree program. Minimum high school cumulative GPA of 2.0. **High school preparation:** 20 units recommended. Recommended units include biological science 1, English 4, mathematics 3, physical science 2 and social science 3. **Test requirements:** SAT or ACT (ACT preferred); score report by August 15. **Additional information:** Admissions based on academic preparation, aptitude, character, and motivation.

1992 FRESHMAN CLASS PROFILE. 134 men, 76 women enrolled. 55% had high school GPA of 3.0 or higher, 41% between 2.0 and 2.99. 11% were in top tenth and 32% were in top quarter of graduating class. **Academic background:** Mid 50% of enrolled freshmen had ACT composite between 15-27. 86% submitted ACT scores. **Characteristics:** 90% from in state, 85% live in college housing, 12% have minority backgrounds, 1% are foreign students, 50% join fraternities/sororities. Average age is 18.

FALL-TERM APPLICATIONS. $10 fee. Closing date August 1; applicants notified on a rolling basis; must reply by May 1 or within 4 weeks if notified thereafter. Interview recommended. Audition recommended for music, drama applicants. Interview required for nursing applicants, recommended for all. CRDA. Deferred and early admission available. Institutional early decision plan. ACT recommended, GPA and class rank used to determine eligibility.

STUDENT LIFE. **Housing:** Dormitories (men, women); apartment housing available. **Activities:** Student government, magazine, radio, student newspaper, yearbook, choral groups, concert band, drama, jazz band, marching band, music ensembles, musical theater, pep band, symphony orchestra, fraternities, sororities, Alpha Phi Omega, prelaw club, drama club, religious service, business, and music organizations.

ATHLETICS. NAIA. **Intercollegiate:** Baseball M, basketball, cross-country, football M, golf, soccer, softball W, tennis, track and field, volleyball W. **Intramural:** Archery, badminton, basketball, bowling, field hockey M, golf, handball, racquetball, rugby, skiing, soccer, softball, swimming, table tennis, tennis, track and field, volleyball, water polo.

STUDENT SERVICES. Aptitude testing, career counseling, employment service for undergraduates, freshman orientation, health services, personal counseling, placement service for graduates, services/facilities for handicapped.

ANNUAL EXPENSES. **Tuition and fees:** $8,050. **Room and board:** $3,370. **Books and supplies:** $600. **Other expenses:** $1,800.

FINANCIAL AID. 82% of freshmen, 90% of continuing students receive some form of aid. 53% of grants, 89% of loans, 69% of jobs based on need. Academic, music/drama, athletic, leadership, alumni affiliation, religious affiliation, minority scholarships available. **Aid applications:** No closing date; priority given to applications received by April 1; applicants notified on a rolling basis beginning on or about March 1; must reply by May 1 or within 2 weeks if notified thereafter.

ADDRESS/TELEPHONE. Tony Boes, Dean of Students, Central Methodist College, 411 Central Methodist Square, Fayette, MO 65248-1198. (816) 248-3391. Fax: (816) 248-2287.

Central Missouri State University
Warrensburg, Missouri — CB code: 6090

Admissions: 91% of applicants accepted
Based on:
- ••• School record
- •• Test scores
- • Recommendations

Completion: 40% graduate, 9% of these enter graduate study

4-year public university, coed. Founded in 1871. **Accreditation:** Regional. **Undergraduate enrollment:** 4,203 men, 4,472 women full time; 734 men, 830 women part time. **Graduate enrollment:** 266 men, 199 women full time; 359 men, 568 women part time. **Faculty:** 524 total (444 full time), 319 with doctorates or other terminal degrees. **Location:** Suburban campus in large town; 50 miles from Kansas City. **Calendar:** Semester, extensive summer session. **Microcomputers:** 617 located in dormitories, libraries, classrooms, computer centers. **Special facilities:** Airport, 200-acre farm, art gallery, museum, Pertle Springs recreational area, automobile/driving safety range, Safety and Health Hall of Fame, children's literature collection, musical instruments collection, child development lab.

DEGREES OFFERED. AA, AS, BA, BS, BFA, MA, MS, MBA, MEd. 42 associate degrees awarded in 1992. 27% in business/office and marketing/distribution, 33% engineering technologies, 19% home economics, 17% trade and industry. 1,593 bachelor's degrees awarded. 23% in business and management, 6% communications, 17% education, 14% engineering technologies, 11% parks/recreation, protective services, public affairs, 5% psychology. Graduate degrees offered in 61 major fields of study.

UNDERGRADUATE MAJORS. **Associate:** Aeronautical technology, air conditioning/heating/refrigeration technology, airline piloting and navigation, automotive technology, child development/care/guidance, construction, drafting and design technology, electrical technology, electronic technology, engineering and engineering-related technologies, fashion merchandising, graphic and printing production, graphic arts technology, industrial design, legal secretary, manufacturing technology, secretarial and related programs, stenography. **Bachelor's:** Accounting, actuarial sciences, aeronautical technology, agribusiness, agricultural business and management, agricultural economics, agricultural education, airline piloting and navigation, art education, art history, biology, business administration and management, business education, chemistry, commercial art, communications, computer and information sciences, conservation and regulation, construction, criminal justice studies, dietetic aide/assistant, drafting and design technology, dramatic arts, driver and safety education, early childhood education, earth sciences, economics, education, electrical technology, elementary education, engineering and engineering-related technologies, engineering and other disciplines, English, English education, finance, fire control and safety technology, foreign languages education, French, geography, geology, German, graphic and printing production, graphic arts technology, history, home economics, home economics education, hotel/motel and restaurant management, industrial arts education, industrial technology, information sciences and systems, interior design, journalism, junior high education, law enforcement and corrections, management information systems, marketing and distributive education, marketing management, mathematics, mathematics education, mechanical design technology, medical laboratory technologies, music, music education, music performance, nursing, occupational safety and health technology, office supervision and management, personnel management, physical education, physics, political science and government, psychology, public relations, radio/television broadcasting, recreation and community services technologies, rehabilitation psychology, safety management, science education, secondary education, social studies education, social work, sociology, Spanish, special education, speech, speech pathology/audiology, speech/communication/theater education, studio art, textiles and clothing, trade and industrial education.

ACADEMIC PROGRAMS. Accelerated program, cooperative education, double major, dual enrollment of high school students, education specialist degree, honors program, independent study, internships, student-designed major, study abroad, teacher preparation, telecourses, visiting/exchange student program, weekend college, cross-registration, cooperative fire science program with Southwest Missouri State University, engineering program with University of Missouri (Columbia, Rolla) and University of Kansas; liberal arts/career combination in engineering. **Remedial services:** Learning center, preadmission summer program, reduced course load, remedial instruction, special counselor, tutoring. **ROTC:** Army. **Placement/credit:** AP, CLEP General and Subject, institutional tests; 30 credit hours maximum for bachelor's degree.

ACADEMIC REQUIREMENTS. Freshmen must earn minimum GPA of 2.0 to continue in good standing. 60% of freshmen return for sophomore year. **Graduation requirements:** 60 hours for associate, 124 hours for bachelor's (30 in major). Most students required to take courses in arts/fine arts, computer science, English, history, humanities, mathematics, philosophy/religion, biological/physical sciences, social sciences.

FRESHMAN ADMISSIONS. **Selection criteria:** Applicants in top two-thirds of high school class granted early admission. Academic preparation, achievement, test scores, counselor recommendations reviewed for those in bottom third. ACT composite score of 18 recommended. Recommended units include English 3, mathematics 2, social science 2 and science 2. **Test requirements:** SAT or ACT (ACT preferred); score report by August 20.

1992 FRESHMAN CLASS PROFILE. 2,211 men applied, 1,924 accepted, 938 enrolled; 2,462 women applied, 2,312 accepted, 1,005 enrolled. 10% were in top tenth and 39% were in top quarter of graduating class. **Academic background:** Mid 50% of enrolled freshmen had ACT composite between 16-23. 92% submitted ACT scores. **Characteristics:** 93% from in state, 65% live in college housing, 11% have minority backgrounds, 1% are foreign students. Average age is 18.

FALL-TERM APPLICATIONS. No fee. Closing date August 15; applicants notified on a rolling basis. Deferred and early admission available. Institutional early decision plan.

STUDENT LIFE. Housing: Dormitories (men, women, coed); apartment, fraternity, sorority housing available. Housing for handicapped students available. **Activities:** Student government, radio, student newspaper, television, yearbook, choral groups, concert band, dance, drama, jazz band, marching band, music ensembles, musical theater, opera, pep band, symphony orchestra, fraternities, sororities, Association of Black Collegiates, international student organizations, Nontraditional Student Association, student ambassadors, several religious organizations.

ATHLETICS. NCAA. **Intercollegiate:** Baseball M, basketball, cross-country, football M, golf M, softball W, tennis, track and field, volleyball W, wrestling M. **Intramural:** Archery M, badminton M, basketball, bowling, cross-country, diving, golf, handball M, racquetball, rifle, soccer, softball, swimming, table tennis, tennis, track and field, volleyball, wrestling M.

STUDENT SERVICES. Aptitude testing, career counseling, employment service for undergraduates, freshman orientation, health services, on-campus day care, personal counseling, placement service for graduates, special adviser for adult students, veterans counselor, services/facilities for handicapped.

ANNUAL EXPENSES. Tuition and fees (1992-93): $2,040, $1,950 additional for out-of-state students. **Room and board:** $2,986. **Books and supplies:** $250. **Other expenses:** $630.

FINANCIAL AID. 55% of freshmen, 55% of continuing students receive some form of aid. 70% of grants, 92% of loans, 10% of jobs based on need. Academic, music/drama, art, athletic, state/district residency, alumni affiliation, minority scholarships available. **Aid applications:** Closing date May 1; priority given to applications received by March 1; applicants notified on a rolling basis beginning on or about March 30; must reply within 2 weeks.

ADDRESS/TELEPHONE. Delores Hudson, Director of Admissions, Central Missouri State University, Warrensburg, MO 64093. (816) 543-4290.

College of the Ozarks
Point Lookout, Missouri — CB code: 6713

Admissions: 16% of applicants accepted
Based on:
- ••• Recommendations, school record
- •• Activities, essay, interview, test scores
- • Special talents

Completion: 85% of freshmen end year in good standing
66% graduate, 16% of these enter graduate study

4-year private liberal arts college, coed, affiliated with Presbyterian Church (USA). Founded in 1906. **Accreditation:** Regional. **Undergraduate enrollment:** 640 men, 710 women full time; 77 men, 97 women part time. **Faculty:** 109 total (91 full time), 46 with doctorates or other terminal degrees. **Location:** Rural campus in small town; 40 miles from Springfield. **Calendar:** Two 16-week terms. **Microcomputers:** 65 located in libraries, classrooms, computer centers. **Special facilities:** Art gallery, theater, museum, historic mill, glade (nature preserve), herbarium. **Additional facts:** Students pay no tuition but work to help defray expenses. Numerous room, board, and incidental scholarships available.

DEGREES OFFERED. BA, BS. 165 bachelor's degrees awarded in 1992. 16% in business and management, 17% teacher education, 6% physical sciences, 10% psychology, 10% social sciences, 8% trade and industry, 7% visual and performing arts.

UNDERGRADUATE MAJORS. Agribusiness, agricultural education, art education, biology, business and management, business education, chemistry, child development/care/guidance, clothing and textiles management/production/services, computer and information sciences, criminal justice studies, criminology, dramatic arts, elementary education, English, English education, family/consumer resource management, food science and nutrition, foreign languages (multiple emphasis), foreign languages education, forensic studies, French, German, graphic and printing production, graphic design, history, home economics, home economics education, individual and family development, industrial arts education, journalism, junior high education, law enforcement and corrections, liberal/general studies, mathematics, mathematics education, music, music education, music performance, nursing, philosophy, physical education, political science and government, predentistry, preengineering, prelaw, premedicine, prepharmacy, preveterinary, psychology, radio/television broadcasting, religion, science education, secondary education, social science education, social work, sociology, Spanish, studio art, technical education, textiles and clothing.

ACADEMIC PROGRAMS. Cooperative education, double major, dual enrollment of high school students, honors program, independent study, internships, student-designed major, teacher preparation; liberal arts/career combination in engineering, health sciences. **Remedial services:** Learning center, reduced course load, special counselor, tutoring. **Placement/credit:** CLEP General and Subject, institutional tests; 30 credit hours maximum for bachelor's degree.

ACADEMIC REQUIREMENTS. Freshmen must earn minimum GPA of 1.75 to continue in good standing. Sophomores must earn minimum 1.85 GPA; juniors and seniors, 2.0 GPA. 80% of freshmen return for sophomore year. Students must declare major by end of first year. **Graduation requirements:** 124 hours for bachelor's (36 in major). Most students required to take courses in English, history, mathematics, philosophy/religion, biological/physical sciences. **Postgraduate studies:** 2% enter law school, 1% enter medical school, 8% enter MBA programs, 5% enter other graduate study.

FRESHMAN ADMISSIONS. Selection criteria: High school record, financial need, test scores, rank in class, recommendations, activities, essay considered. **High school preparation:** 20 units recommended. Recommended units include biological science 2, English 4, mathematics 2, physical science 1 and social science 2. Public speaking also recommended. **Test requirements:** SAT or ACT (ACT preferred); score report by February 2. **Additional information:** Financial need a top priority since there are no tuition charges.

1992 FRESHMAN CLASS PROFILE. 1,622 men applied, 223 accepted, 223 enrolled; 1,783 women applied, 318 accepted, 318 enrolled. 45% had high school GPA of 3.0 or higher, 50% between 2.0 and 2.99. **Academic background:** Mid 50% of enrolled freshmen had ACT composite between 18-25. 99% submitted ACT scores. **Characteristics:** 46% from in state, 58% commute, 3% are foreign students. Average age is 18.

FALL-TERM APPLICATIONS. No fee. Closing date August 15; priority given to applications received by January 1; applicants notified on a rolling basis beginning on or about February 1; must reply by May 1 or within 2 weeks if notified thereafter. Interview recommended for aviation science applicants. Audition recommended for music applicants. Portfolio recommended for art applicants. Deferred admission available.

STUDENT LIFE. Housing: Dormitories (men, women). **Activities:** Student government, magazine, radio, student newspaper, television, yearbook, choral groups, concert band, drama, jazz band, music ensembles, musical theater, pep band, Baptist Student Union, Newman Club, Circle K Service Club, Young Democrats, Fire Department, Inter-Varsity Christian Fellowship, Wilderness Activities Club, Women's Auxiliary, Young Republicans. **Additional information:** Religious observance required.

ATHLETICS. NAIA. **Intercollegiate:** Baseball M, basketball, volleyball W. **Intramural:** Basketball, racquetball, softball, tennis, volleyball, water polo.

STUDENT SERVICES. Aptitude testing, career counseling, employment service for undergraduates, freshman orientation, health services, on-campus day care, personal counseling, placement service for graduates, special adviser for adult students, veterans counselor, services/facilities for handicapped.

ANNUAL EXPENSES. Tuition and fees (projected): $100. Resident students required to work 560 hours during academic year to contribute to cost of education. Part time commuting students pay $85 per hour. Full-time commuters work 15 hours per week. **Room and board:** $1,900. **Books and supplies:** $400. **Other expenses:** $1,200.

FINANCIAL AID. 100% of freshmen, 100% of continuing students receive some form of aid. All aid based on need. 600 enrolled freshmen were judged to have need, all were offered aid. Academic, athletic, state/district residency, alumni affiliation scholarships available. **Aid applications:** No closing date; applicants notified on a rolling basis beginning on or about March 15. **Additional information:** Room and board scholarships available. Qualified students may take summer jobs to pay for room and board.

ADDRESS/TELEPHONE. Glen Cameron, EdD, Dean of Admissions, College of the Ozarks, Point Lookout, MO 65726-0017. (417) 334-6411. (800) 222-0525. Fax: (417) 335-2618.

Columbia College
Columbia, Missouri — CB code: 6095

4-year private liberal arts college, coed, affiliated with Christian Church (Disciples of Christ). Founded in 1851. **Accreditation:** Regional. **Location:** Urban campus in small city; 120 miles from Kansas City, 120 miles from St. Louis. **Calendar:** Semester.

FRESHMAN ADMISSIONS. Selection criteria: School achievement record, recommendation, interview, ACT scores.

ANNUAL EXPENSES. Tuition and fees: $7,900. **Room and board:** $3,524. **Books and supplies:** $800. **Other expenses:** $900.

ADDRESS/TELEPHONE. Ron Kronacker, Director of Admissions, Columbia College, 1001 Rogers Street, Columbia, MO 65216. (314) 875-7352. (800) 231-2391. Fax: (314) 875-8765.

Conception Seminary College
Conception, Missouri CB code: 6112

4-year private seminary college, men only, affiliated with Roman Catholic Church. Founded in 1883. **Accreditation:** Regional. **Undergraduate enrollment:** 72 men full time; 8 men, 4 women part time. **Faculty:** 36 total (21 full time), 15 with doctorates or other terminal degrees. **Location:** Rural campus in rural community; 100 miles from Kansas City, 45 miles from St. Joseph, 17 miles from Maryville. **Calendar:** Semester. **Microcomputers:** Located in classrooms. **Additional facts:** Operated by Benedictines of Conception Abbey for both independent seminary students and candidates affiliated with sponsoring diocese. Special emphasis on character development, liturgical and spiritual formation, and field education. Women may enroll on part-time basis.

DEGREES OFFERED. BA. 9 bachelor's degrees awarded in 1992. 80% in philosophy, religion, theology, 15% psychology, 5% social sciences.

UNDERGRADUATE MAJORS. Philosophy, psychology, religion, social sciences.

ACADEMIC PROGRAMS. Double major, independent study. **Remedial services:** Learning center, reduced course load, remedial instruction, special counselor, tutoring. **Placement/credit:** AP, CLEP General and Subject, institutional tests; 12 credit hours maximum for bachelor's degree.

ACADEMIC REQUIREMENTS. Freshmen must earn minimum GPA of 2.0 to continue in good standing. 95% of freshmen return for sophomore year. Students must declare major by end of second year. **Graduation requirements:** 126 hours for bachelor's (30 in major). Most students required to take courses in arts/fine arts, English, foreign languages, history, mathematics, philosophy/religion, biological/physical sciences, social sciences. **Additional information:** Curriculum combines liberal arts and predivinity training to accommodate varying degrees of vocational commitment.

FRESHMAN ADMISSIONS. Selection criteria: ACT composite scores tend to count more heavily than high school grades or class rank. **High school preparation:** 16 units required. Required units include biological science 2, English 4, mathematics 4, physical science 2 and social science 4. **Test requirements:** SAT or ACT (ACT preferred); score report by July 31. **Additional information:** College graduates accepted as special students for preprofessional studies (2-year program) in philosophy and religion, and for spiritual and character formation work preparatory to entering a school of theology.

1992 FRESHMAN CLASS PROFILE. 19 men enrolled. 45% had high school GPA of 3.0 or higher, 55% between 2.0 and 2.99. 10% were in top tenth and 25% were in top quarter of graduating class. **Academic background:** Mid 50% of enrolled freshmen had ACT composite between 15-25. 100% submitted ACT scores. **Characteristics:** 45% from in state, 100% live in college housing, 21% have minority backgrounds. Average age is 20.

FALL-TERM APPLICATIONS. No fee. Closing date July 31; priority given to applications received by June 1; applicants notified on a rolling basis beginning on or about February 1; must reply by August 10. Essay required. Interview recommended. Interview recommended for all, required for applicants who have special difficulties or who wish admission without fulfilling all ordinary requirements. CRDA. Deferred and early admission available. EDP-F. Foreign applications require written certification of financial, ecclesiastical sponsorship.

STUDENT LIFE. Housing: Dormitories (men). **Activities:** Student government, student newspaper, yearbook, choral groups, drama, musical theater, Apostolic Work, Mission Club, Social Concerns, Community Council, Inner-Life. **Additional information:** Student life integrated into comprehensive personal and religious program to determine capacity and desire for Catholic priesthood. Religious observance required.

ATHLETICS. Intercollegiate: Basketball, soccer. **Intramural:** Bowling, cross-country, handball, racquetball, softball, swimming, table tennis, tennis, volleyball.

STUDENT SERVICES. Career counseling, health services, personal counseling, special adviser for adult students, religious counseling.

ANNUAL EXPENSES. Tuition and fees: $5,542. **Room and board:** $2,974. **Books and supplies:** $350. **Other expenses:** $800.

FINANCIAL AID. 100% of freshmen, 95% of continuing students receive some form of aid. 91% of grants, all loans based on need. 15 enrolled freshmen were judged to have need, all were offered aid. Academic, state/district residency, religious affiliation scholarships available. **Aid applications:** Closing date May 1; priority given to applications received by July 31; applicants notified on a rolling basis beginning on or about July 1. **Additional information:** All new students receive institutional aid of at least $1000.

ADDRESS/TELEPHONE. Fr. Albert Bruecken, OSB, Director of Admissions, Conception Seminary College, PO P.O. Box 502, Conception, MO 64433. (816) 944-2218.

Cottey College
Nevada, Missouri CB code: 6120

Admissions:	87% of applicants accepted
Based on:	••• Activities, essay, school record
	•• Interview, test scores
	• Recommendations, special talents
Completion:	85% of freshmen end year in good standing
	60% graduate, 94% of these enter 4-year programs

2-year private junior college, women only. Founded in 1884. **Accreditation:** Regional. **Undergraduate enrollment:** 405 women full time; 12 women part time. **Faculty:** 39 total (33 full time), 29 with doctorates or other terminal degrees. **Location:** Rural campus in small town; 100 miles from Kansas City. **Calendar:** Semester. **Microcomputers:** 38 located in dormitories, libraries, computer centers. **Special facilities:** 33-acre wooded area with lodge for outings and nature laboratory. **Additional facts:** Sponsored and supported by P.E.O. Sisterhood, nonsectarian philanthropic educational organization. Only college in the United States owned and supported by women for women.

DEGREES OFFERED. AA. 120 associate degrees awarded in 1992. 100% in multi/interdisciplinary studies.

UNDERGRADUATE MAJORS. Liberal/general studies.

ACADEMIC PROGRAMS. 2-year transfer program, dual enrollment of high school students, independent study. **Remedial services:** Reduced course load. **Placement/credit:** AP, IB, institutional tests.

ACADEMIC REQUIREMENTS. Freshmen must earn minimum GPA of 2.0 to continue in good standing. 65% of freshmen return for sophomore year. **Graduation requirements:** 62 hours for associate. Most students required to take courses in arts/fine arts, English, humanities, mathematics, biological/physical sciences, social sciences.

FRESHMAN ADMISSIONS. Selection criteria: High school course of study most important in accordance with grades received. Rank in top half of graduating class. SAT or ACT scores important. Essay required. Recommendations and interviews considered when other criteria not met. Recommended units include English 4, foreign language 2, mathematics 3, social science 3 and science 2. 2 units laboratory science also recommended. **Test requirements:** SAT or ACT; score report by June 1.

1992 FRESHMAN CLASS PROFILE. 439 women applied, 381 accepted, 243 enrolled. 78% had high school GPA of 3.0 or higher, 22% between 2.0 and 2.99. 56% were in top quarter of graduating class. **Characteristics:** 10% from in state, 98% live in college housing, 7% have minority backgrounds, 8% are foreign students. Average age is 18.

FALL-TERM APPLICATIONS. $20 fee, may be waived for applicants with need. Closing date June 1; applicants notified on a rolling basis. Essay required. Interview recommended. Audition recommended for music applicants. Portfolio recommended for art applicants. Deferred and early admission available.

STUDENT LIFE. Housing: Dormitories (women). European-style suites accommodate 8 to 10 students. **Activities:** Student government, student newspaper, yearbook, choral groups, dance, drama, music ensembles, recitals, choral, dance, and drama tours, 32 campus service and social organizations, including international students club, Christian fellowship, art and language clubs.

ATHLETICS. Intramural: Archery, badminton, basketball, field hockey, golf, soccer, tennis, volleyball, water polo, wrestling.

STUDENT SERVICES. Aptitude testing, career counseling, employment service for undergraduates, freshman orientation, health services, personal counseling, college transfer assistance.

ANNUAL EXPENSES. Tuition and fees: $5,700. **Room and board:** $2,800. **Books and supplies:** $425. **Other expenses:** $755.

FINANCIAL AID. 92% of continuing students receive some form of aid. 73% of grants, 90% of loans, 89% of jobs based on need. Academic, music/drama, art, athletic, state/district residency, leadership, alumni affiliation, minority scholarships available. **Aid applications:** No closing date; priority given to applications received by April 15; applicants notified on a rolling basis beginning on or about February 15; must reply within 3 weeks. **Additional information:** College guarantees to meet 100% of established need for all students who have been accepted, paid comprehensive fee deposit, and applied for aid by April 15.

ADDRESS/TELEPHONE. Judy Held, Director of Admission/Financial Aid, Cottey College, 1000 West Austin Boulevard, Nevada, MO 64772. (417) 667-8181. Fax: (417) 667-8103.

Crowder College
Neosho, Missouri CB code: 6138

2-year public community college, coed. Founded in 1963. **Accreditation:** Regional. **Undergraduate enrollment:** 1,750 men and women. **Faculty:** 120 total (60 full time), 4 with doctorates or other terminal degrees. **Location:** Rural campus in small town; 70 miles from Springfield, 28 miles from Joplin. **Calendar:** Semester, limited summer session. **Microcomputers:** Located in libraries, computer centers. **Special facilities:** Art museum.

DEGREES OFFERED. AA, AS, AAS. 275 associate degrees awarded in 1992.

UNDERGRADUATE MAJORS. Agribusiness, agricultural business and management, automotive technology, business administration and management, business and office, communications, computer and information sciences, construction, diesel engine mechanics, drafting and design technology, education, electronic technology, elementary education, hospitality and recreation marketing, hotel/motel and restaurant management, industrial technology, liberal/general studies, marketing and distribution, nursing, premedicine, public relations, secondary education, secretarial and related programs, water and wastewater technology.

ACADEMIC PROGRAMS. 2-year transfer program, internships. **Remedial services:** Learning center, reduced course load, remedial instruction, special counselor, tutoring. **Placement/credit:** AP, CLEP Subject; 30 credit hours maximum for associate degree.

ACADEMIC REQUIREMENTS. Freshmen must earn minimum GPA of 1.5 to continue in good standing. Students must declare major on enrollment. **Graduation requirements:** 60 hours for associate. Most students required to take courses in English, history, humanities, mathematics, biological/physical sciences, social sciences.

FRESHMAN ADMISSIONS. Selection criteria: Open admissions. **Test requirements:** ACT for placement; score report by August 19.

1992 FRESHMAN CLASS PROFILE. 625 men and women enrolled. **Characteristics:** 79% from in state, 85% commute, 7% have minority backgrounds, 1% are foreign students.

FALL-TERM APPLICATIONS. No fee. No closing date; applicants notified on a rolling basis; must reply by August 30 or within 1 week if notified thereafter. Interview recommended.

STUDENT LIFE. Housing: Dormitories (men, women). **Activities:** Student government, student newspaper, literary publication, choral groups, concert band, drama, jazz band, music ensembles, musical theater.

ATHLETICS. Intercollegiate: Baseball M, basketball W, softball W. **Intramural:** Bowling, tennis, volleyball.

STUDENT SERVICES. Career counseling, employment service for undergraduates, personal counseling, placement service for graduates.

ANNUAL EXPENSES. Tuition and fees (projected): $990, $330 additional for out-of-district students, $1,080 additional for out-of-state students. **Room and board:** $2,400. **Books and supplies:** $500. **Other expenses:** $1,000.

FINANCIAL AID. 60% of freshmen, 50% of continuing students receive some form of aid. 71% of grants, all loans, all jobs based on need. 208 enrolled freshmen were judged to have need, 187 were offered aid. Academic, music/drama, art, athletic, state/district residency, leadership scholarships available. **Aid applications:** No closing date; priority given to applications received by August 1; applicants notified on a rolling basis beginning on or about May 15.

ADDRESS/TELEPHONE. Cecilia Morris, Registrar, Crowder College, Neosho, MO 64850. (417) 451-3223.

Culver-Stockton College

Canton, Missouri — CB code: 6123

Admissions:	30% of applicants accepted
Based on:	••• School record, test scores
	•• Activities, interview, recommendations, special talents
	• Essay
Completion:	94% of freshmen end year in good standing
	45% graduate, 9% of these enter graduate study

4-year private liberal arts college, coed, affiliated with Christian Church (Disciples of Christ). Founded in 1853. **Accreditation:** Regional. **Undergraduate enrollment:** 375 men, 623 women full time; 42 men, 105 women part time. **Faculty:** 66 total (49 full time), 36 with doctorates or other terminal degrees. **Location:** Rural campus in rural community; 20 miles from Quincy, Illinois, 130 miles from St. Louis. **Calendar:** Semester, limited summer session. Extensive evening/early morning classes. **Microcomputers:** 50 located in computer centers. **Special facilities:** Art gallery, performing arts center. **Additional facts:** Academic life characterized by close faculty/student relationship. Students have voting representation on faculty committees.

DEGREES OFFERED. BA, BS, BFA. 212 bachelor's degrees awarded in 1992. 39% in business and management, 20% teacher education, 9% health sciences, 6% psychology, 10% social sciences, 5% visual and performing arts.

UNDERGRADUATE MAJORS. Accounting, art education, arts management, biology, business administration and management, chemistry, communications, criminal justice studies, dramatic arts, elementary education, engineering and engineering-related technologies, English, English education, fine arts, history, mathematics, mathematics education, medical laboratory technologies, music, music education, nursing, parks and recreation management, physical education, psychology, religion, science education, social studies education, sociology, speech, speech/communication/theater education, studio art, visual and performing arts.

ACADEMIC PROGRAMS. Accelerated program, double major, honors program, independent study, internships, student-designed major, study abroad, teacher preparation, combined bachelor's/graduate degree program in business with Washington University; liberal arts/career combination in engineering, health sciences; combined bachelor's/graduate program in business administration. **Remedial services:** Reduced course load, remedial instruction, special counselor, tutoring. **Placement/credit:** AP, CLEP General and Subject, institutional tests.

ACADEMIC REQUIREMENTS. Freshmen must earn minimum GPA of 1.75 to continue in good standing. 71% of freshmen return for sophomore year. Students must declare major by end of second year. **Graduation requirements:** 124 hours for bachelor's (30 in major). Most students required to take courses in arts/fine arts, computer science, English, humanities, mathematics, philosophy/religion, biological/physical sciences, social sciences. **Postgraduate studies:** 2% enter law school, 1% enter medical school, 1% enter MBA programs, 5% enter other graduate study. **Additional information:** Honors Program available to qualified students wishing to undertake in-depth study project directed by faculty members. Participation may be especially beneficial for those considering graduate study.

FRESHMAN ADMISSIONS. Selection criteria: Admissions based on school achievement record, test scores. Recommended units include English 4, mathematics 2, social science 3 and science 2. **Test requirements:** SAT or ACT (ACT preferred); score report by September 1.

1992 FRESHMAN CLASS PROFILE. 67% had high school GPA of 3.0 or higher, 33% between 2.0 and 2.99. 23% were in top tenth and 53% were in top quarter of graduating class. **Academic background:** Mid 50% of enrolled freshmen had ACT composite between 19-25. 95% submitted ACT scores. **Characteristics:** 52% from in state, 83% live in college housing, 7% have minority backgrounds, 1% are foreign students, 31% join fraternities/sororities. Average age is 18.

FALL-TERM APPLICATIONS. No fee. Closing date June 1; priority given to applications received by April 1; applicants notified on a rolling basis; must reply within 8 weeks. Interview recommended. Audition recommended for music, drama applicants. Portfolio recommended for art applicants. Essay recommended. Deferred admission available.

STUDENT LIFE. Housing: Dormitories (men, women, coed); fraternity, sorority housing available. Coordinate housing available with upperclass men and women in same building but different wings. **Activities:** Student government, magazine, student newspaper, yearbook, choral groups, concert band, drama, jazz band, music ensembles, pep band, fraternities, sororities, United Campus Fellowship, Fellowship of Christian Athletes. **Additional information:** Students have active, voting representation on faculty committees that deal with academic and student life.

ATHLETICS. NAIA. **Intercollegiate:** Baseball M, basketball, football M, golf M, soccer M, softball W, tennis, volleyball W. **Intramural:** Basketball, racquetball M, soccer M, softball, swimming W, table tennis, tennis, volleyball, wrestling M.

STUDENT SERVICES. Aptitude testing, career counseling, employment service for undergraduates, freshman orientation, health services, personal counseling, placement service for graduates, special adviser for adult students, veterans counselor.

ANNUAL EXPENSES. Tuition and fees: $7,650. **Room and board:** $3,500. **Books and supplies:** $400. **Other expenses:** $1,200.

FINANCIAL AID. 85% of freshmen, 85% of continuing students receive some form of aid. 26% of grants, 97% of loans, 37% of jobs based on need. Academic, music/drama, art, athletic, state/district residency, religious affiliation scholarships available. **Aid applications:** No closing date; priority given to applications received by March 15; applicants notified on a rolling basis beginning on or about February 15; must reply within 2 to 4 weeks.

ADDRESS/TELEPHONE. Betty Smith, Director of Admissions, Culver-Stockton College, One College Hill, Canton, MO 63435-1299. (314) 288-5221 ext. 331. (800) 537-1883. Fax: (314) 288-3984.

Deaconess College of Nursing

St. Louis, Missouri — CB code: 3139

4-year private nursing college, coed, affiliated with United Church of Christ. Founded in 1889. **Accreditation:** Regional. **Undergraduate enrollment:** 338 men and women. **Faculty:** 22 total, 2 with doctorates or other terminal degrees. **Location:** Urban campus in large city. **Calendar:** Semester, limited summer session. Saturday and extensive evening/early morning classes. **Microcomputers:** 7 located in libraries. **Special facilities:** Deaconess Hospital. **Additional facts:** Affiliated with Fontbonne College. General education requirements offered on both campuses.

DEGREES OFFERED. AS, BS. 14 associate degrees awarded in 1992. 100% in health sciences. 31 bachelor's degrees awarded. 100% in health sciences.

UNDERGRADUATE MAJORS. Associate: Nursing. **Bachelor's:** Nursing.

ACADEMIC PROGRAMS. Accelerated program, cross-registration; liberal arts/career combination in health sciences. **Remedial services:** Learning center, reduced course load, remedial instruction, tutoring. **Placement/credit:** CLEP General and Subject, institutional tests; 30 credit hours maximum for bachelor's degree.

ACADEMIC REQUIREMENTS. Freshmen must earn minimum GPA of 2.0 to continue in good standing. 87% of freshmen return for sophomore year. Students must declare major on application. **Graduation requirements:** 68 hours for associate (34 in major), 128 hours for bachelor's (60 in major). Most students required to take courses in computer science, English, history, humanities, mathematics, philosophy/religion, biological/physical sciences, social sciences. **Postgraduate studies:** 13% enter other graduate study.

FRESHMAN ADMISSIONS. Selection criteria: High school GPA of 2.5, class rank in top third, ACT or SAT test required. Interview and reference may be considered. Required units include English 4, mathematics 3 and science 3. **Test requirements:** SAT or ACT (ACT preferred); score report by June 1.

1992 FRESHMAN CLASS PROFILE. 100 men and women enrolled. 10% were in top tenth and 35% were in top quarter of graduating class. **Academic background:** Mid 50% of enrolled freshmen had ACT composite between 19-24. 100% submitted ACT scores. **Characteristics:** 70% from in state, 64% commute, 12% have minority backgrounds, 0% are foreign students. Average age is 20.

FALL-TERM APPLICATIONS. $20 fee. Closing date June 1; priority given to applications received by May 1; applicants notified on a rolling basis; must reply within 3 weeks. Interview recommended. Personal statement required. CRDA. Deferred admission available.

STUDENT LIFE. Housing: Dormitories (men, women). **Activities:** Student government, student newspaper, yearbook, National Student Nurse Association, Nurse's Christian Fellowship, Ambassadors.

ATHLETICS. Intramural: Basketball, soccer, volleyball.

STUDENT SERVICES. Aptitude testing, employment service for undergraduates, freshman orientation, health services, on-campus day care, personal counseling.

ANNUAL EXPENSES. Tuition and fees: $6,020. **Room and board:** $2,184. **Books and supplies:** $600. **Other expenses:** $300.

FINANCIAL AID. 85% of freshmen, 85% of continuing students receive some form of aid. Grants, loans, jobs available. Academic, religious affiliation, minority scholarships available. **Aid applications:** Closing date July 1; priority given to applications received by April 15; applicants notified on a rolling basis beginning on or about July 1; must reply by registration. **Additional information:** Long-term, no-interest loans available. Working scholarships available to students who wish to make commitment to work at Deaconess Hospital after graduation.

ADDRESS/TELEPHONE. Barbara Bizer, Admissions Coordinator, Deaconess College of Nursing, 6150 Oakland Avenue, St. Louis, MO 63139. (314) 768-3044. Fax: (314) 768-3136.

DeVry Institute of Technology: Kansas City

Kansas City, Missouri — CB code: 6092

Admissions: 92% of applicants accepted
Based on: ••• Test scores
Completion: 39% graduate

4-year proprietary business, technical college, coed. Founded in 1931. **Accreditation:** Regional. **Undergraduate enrollment:** 1,107 men, 252 women full time; 331 men, 91 women part time. **Faculty:** 76 total (59 full time). **Location:** Suburban campus in large city; 15 miles from downtown Kansas City. **Calendar:** 3 continuous calendar terms. Extensive evening/early morning classes. **Microcomputers:** 150 located in computer centers.

DEGREES OFFERED. AAS, BS. 138 associate degrees awarded in 1992. 100% in engineering technologies. 257 bachelor's degrees awarded. 13% in business and management, 39% communications, 27% computer sciences, 21% engineering technologies.

UNDERGRADUATE MAJORS. Associate: Electronic technology. **Bachelor's:** Accounting, business administration and management, electronic technology, information sciences and systems, telecommunications.

ACADEMIC PROGRAMS. Accelerated program. **Remedial services:** Learning center, reduced course load, special counselor, tutoring, developmental coursework. **Placement/credit:** Institutional tests; 30 credit hours maximum for associate degree; 47 credit hours maximum for bachelor's degree.

ACADEMIC REQUIREMENTS. Freshmen must earn minimum GPA of 2.0 to continue in good standing. 47% of freshmen return for sophomore year. Students must declare major on enrollment. **Graduation requirements:** 87 hours for associate, 132 hours for bachelor's. Most students required to take courses in computer science, English, history, humanities, mathematics, social sciences.

FRESHMAN ADMISSIONS. Selection criteria: Applicants must have high school diploma or equivalant, pass institutional entrance examination or submit acceptable ACT/SAT/WPCT scores, and be 17 years of age. **Test requirements:** SAT or ACT. **Additional information:** New students may enter at beginning of any semester.

1992 FRESHMAN CLASS PROFILE. 928 men and women applied, 856 accepted; 350 men enrolled, 75 women enrolled. **Characteristics:** 61% from in state, 100% commute, 20% have minority backgrounds.

FALL-TERM APPLICATIONS. $25 fee. Closing date November 4; applicants notified on a rolling basis. Deferred admission available.

STUDENT LIFE. Housing: School-contracted furnished apartments available for single students. **Activities:** Student government, student newspaper, Data Processing Management Association, Institute of Electrical and Electronic Engineers.

ATHLETICS. Intramural: Basketball, bowling, soccer, softball, volleyball.

STUDENT SERVICES. Career counseling, employment service for undergraduates, freshman orientation, placement service for graduates, veterans counselor, services/facilities for handicapped.

ANNUAL EXPENSES. Tuition and fees: $5,609. **Books and supplies:** $525.

FINANCIAL AID. 77% of freshmen, 84% of continuing students receive some form of aid. All grants, 68% of loans, all jobs based on need. Academic scholarships available. **Aid applications:** No closing date; applicants notified on a rolling basis; must reply immediately. **Additional information:** Approximately 80% of students work part-time at jobs found through Institute.

ADDRESS/TELEPHONE. Gayle Dykes-Grimmett, Director of Admissions, DeVry Institute of Technology: Kansas City, 11224 Holmes Road, Kansas City, MO 64131-3626. (816) 941-2810. (800) 821-3766. Fax: (816) 941-0896.

Drury College

Springfield, Missouri — CB code: 6169

4-year private liberal arts college, coed, affiliated with United Church of Christ and Christian Church (Disciples of Christ). Founded in 1873. **Accreditation:** Regional. **Undergraduate enrollment:** 485 men, 551 women full time; 28 men, 19 women part time. **Graduate enrollment:** 15 men, 17 women full time; 66 men, 232 women part time. **Faculty:** 119 total (84 full time), 83 with doctorates or other terminal degrees. **Location:** Urban campus in small city; 170 miles from Kansas City, 212 miles from St. Louis. **Calendar:** 4-4-1, limited summer session. **Microcomputers:** 56 located in libraries, classrooms, computer centers. **Special facilities:** Art gallery, writing laboratory center.

DEGREES OFFERED. BA, BS, BArch, MBA, MEd. 195 bachelor's degrees awarded in 1992. 20% in business and management, 10% communications, 12% teacher education, 5% languages, 7% letters/literature, 9% life sciences, 8% psychology, 13% social sciences, 7% visual and performing arts. Graduate degrees offered in 2 major fields of study.

UNDERGRADUATE MAJORS. Accounting, architecture, art history, biology, business administration and management, business and management, chemistry, communications, criminology, dramatic arts, economics, education, education of the mentally handicapped, elementary education, English, French, German, history, mathematics, music, music history and appreciation, nursing, philosophy, physics, political science and government, psychology, religion, secondary education, social sciences, sociology, Spanish, special education.

ACADEMIC PROGRAMS. Accelerated program, double major, honors program, independent study, internships, study abroad, teacher preparation, weekend college, Washington semester, cross-registration; liberal arts/career combination in engineering, health sciences. **Remedial services:** Preadmission summer program, reduced course load, remedial instruction, academic contract featuring more regimented schedule and specialized attention. **Placement/credit:** AP, CLEP General and Subject, institutional tests.

ACADEMIC REQUIREMENTS. Freshmen must earn minimum GPA of 1.6 to continue in good standing. 77% of freshmen return for sophomore year. Students must declare major by end of second year. **Graduation requirements:** 124 hours for bachelor's (35 in major). Most students required to take courses in arts/fine arts, English, foreign languages, history, humanities, mathematics, philosophy/religion, biological/physical sciences, social sciences. **Postgraduate studies:** 6% enter law school, 6% enter medical school, 5% enter MBA programs, 6% enter other graduate study.

FRESHMAN ADMISSIONS. Selection criteria: School achievement record, test scores, personality form, interview required for admission. **High school preparation:** 18 units recommended. Recommended units include biological science 1, English 4, foreign language 2, mathematics 4, social science 3 and science 1. **Test requirements:** SAT or ACT; score report by August 15.

1992 FRESHMAN CLASS PROFILE. 112 men, 148 women enrolled. 75% had high school GPA of 3.0 or higher, 25% between 2.0 and 2.99. **Academic background:** Mid 50% of enrolled freshmen had ACT composite between 22-27. 96% submitted ACT scores. **Characteristics:** 85% from in state, 65% live in college housing, 5% have minority backgrounds, 1% are foreign students, 40% join fraternities/sororities. Average age is 18.

FALL-TERM APPLICATIONS. $20 fee, may be waived for applicants with need. Closing date August 1; priority given to applications received by March 1; applicants notified on a rolling basis; must reply by May 1 or within 3 weeks if notified thereafter. Essay required. Interview recommended. Audition recommended for music, theater applicants. Portfolio recommended for art, architecture applicants. CRDA. Deferred and early admission available. EDP-F.

STUDENT LIFE. Housing: Dormitories (men, women); fraternity housing available. **Activities:** Student government, film, radio, student newspaper, television, yearbook, choral groups, concert band, dance, drama, jazz band, music ensembles, musical theater, opera, pep band, symphony orchestra, fraternities, sororities, Black student organization, Logos (religious group), Young Republicans, Young Democrats, WO/MEN women's organization.

ATHLETICS. NAIA, NCAA. **Intercollegiate:** Basketball M, diving, golf M, soccer, swimming, tennis, volleyball W. **Intramural:** Basketball, bowling, racquetball, soccer, softball, table tennis, tennis, volleyball, water polo M.

STUDENT SERVICES. Aptitude testing, career counseling, employment service for undergraduates, freshman orientation, health services, personal counseling, placement service for graduates, special adviser for adult students, veterans counselor.

ANNUAL EXPENSES. Tuition and fees: $8,760. Tuition for master in education program is $140 per credit hour. **Room and board:** $3,380. **Books and supplies:** $700. **Other expenses:** $750.

FINANCIAL AID. 79% of freshmen, 83% of continuing students receive some form of aid. 49% of grants, 88% of loans, 48% of jobs based on need. Academic, music/drama, art, athletic, leadership, alumni affiliation, religious affiliation scholarships available. **Aid applications:** Closing date June 15; priority given to applications received by April 1; applicants notified on a rolling basis; must reply by May 1 or within 2 weeks if notified thereafter.

ADDRESS/TELEPHONE. Michael G. Thomas, Director of Admissions, Drury College, 900 North Benton, Springfield, MO 65802-9977. (417) 865-8731. (800) 922-2274.

East Central College
Union, Missouri — CB code: 0845

2-year public community college, coed. Founded in 1968. **Accreditation:** Regional. **Undergraduate enrollment:** 574 men, 882 women full time; 650 men, 1,110 women part time. **Faculty:** 113 total (60 full time), 22 with doctorates or other terminal degrees. **Location:** Rural campus in small town; 45 miles from St. Louis. **Calendar:** Fall, spring, and summer semesters. Saturday and extensive evening/early morning classes. **Microcomputers:** 45 located in classrooms, computer centers.

DEGREES OFFERED. AA, AS, AAS. 295 associate degrees awarded in 1992. 22% in business and management, 8% business/office and marketing/distribution, 10% teacher education, 10% engineering, 11% engineering technologies, 6% allied health, 5% multi/interdisciplinary studies, 5% trade and industry.

UNDERGRADUATE MAJORS. Accounting, air conditioning/heating/refrigeration mechanics, air conditioning/heating/refrigeration technology, allied health, anthropology, architectural engineering, architecture, automotive mechanics, biology, botany, business administration and management, business and management, business and office, business data processing and related programs, business data programming, carpentry, chemical engineering, chemistry, chiropractic, civil engineering, communications, computer and information sciences, computer programming, construction, criminal justice studies, criminal justice technology, dental assistant, drafting, drafting and design technology, early childhood education, economics, education, electrical and electronics equipment repair, electronic technology, elementary education, emergency medical technologies, engineering, engineering mechanics, engineering physics, English, fine arts, fire control and safety technology, fishing and fisheries, forestry and related sciences, French, geography, geological engineering, geophysical engineering, health sciences, history, home economics, horticulture, hospitality and recreation marketing, industrial engineering, journalism, junior high education, legal secretary, liberal/general studies, library science, mathematics, medical secretary, metallurgical engineering, music, nuclear engineering, nursing, ocean engineering, optometry, petroleum engineering, philosophy, physical sciences, physics, political science and government, predentistry, prelaw, premedicine, prepharmacy, preveterinary, psychology, public administration, public affairs, public health laboratory science, public relations, radio/television broadcasting, radio/television technology, religion, retailing, secondary education, secretarial and related programs, social sciences, social work, sociology, Spanish, special education, speech, speech pathology/audiology, surveying and mapping sciences, teacher aide, transportation and travel marketing, welding technology, wildlife management, word processing, zoology.

ACADEMIC PROGRAMS. 2-year transfer program, dual enrollment of high school students, honors program, independent study, internships, study abroad, telecourses, weekend college. **Remedial services:** Learning center, reduced course load, remedial instruction, tutoring, adult basic education (ABE), adult literacy program. **Placement/credit:** CLEP General and Subject, institutional tests.

ACADEMIC REQUIREMENTS. Freshmen must earn minimum GPA of 1.6 to continue in good standing. 65% of freshmen return for sophomore year. Students must declare major on application. **Graduation requirements:** 64 hours for associate (23 in major). Most students required to take courses in arts/fine arts, English, foreign languages, history, humanities, mathematics, philosophy/religion, biological/physical sciences, social sciences.

FRESHMAN ADMISSIONS. Selection criteria: Open admissions. Selective admissions to certain programs. **Test requirements:** ACT for placement and counseling only; score report by August 15.

1992 FRESHMAN CLASS PROFILE. 350 men applied, 350 accepted, 248 enrolled; 340 women applied, 340 accepted, 322 enrolled. 14% had high school GPA of 3.0 or higher, 54% between 2.0 and 2.99. **Academic background:** Mid 50% of enrolled freshmen had ACT composite between 14-22. 70% submitted ACT scores. **Characteristics:** 99% from in state, 100% commute, 1% have minority backgrounds. Average age is 23.

FALL-TERM APPLICATIONS. No fee. No closing date; applicants notified on a rolling basis. Interview recommended. Deferred and early admission available.

STUDENT LIFE. Activities: Student government, student newspaper, television, yearbook, choral groups, drama, jazz band, music ensembles, musical theater, Phi Theta Kappa honor society, department clubs.

ATHLETICS. NJCAA. **Intercollegiate:** Baseball M, basketball, soccer M, softball W, volleyball W. **Intramural:** Basketball, table tennis, volleyball.

STUDENT SERVICES. Aptitude testing, career counseling, employment service for undergraduates, freshman orientation, on-campus day care, personal counseling, placement service for graduates, special adviser for adult students, veterans counselor, services/facilities for handicapped.

ANNUAL EXPENSES. Tuition and fees: $1,080, $420 additional for out-of-district students, $1,230 additional for out-of-state students. **Books and supplies:** $600. **Other expenses:** $500.

FINANCIAL AID. 50% of freshmen, 60% of continuing students receive some form of aid. 95% of grants, 95% of loans, 60% of jobs based on need. 483 enrolled freshmen were judged to have need, all were offered aid. Academic, music/drama, art, athletic, state/district residency, leadership scholarships available. **Aid applications:** No closing date; priority given to applications received by July 1; applicants notified on a rolling basis beginning on or about May 1; must reply within 2 weeks.

ADDRESS/TELEPHONE. Colleen Himmelberg, Director of Admissions, East Central College, Highway 50 and Prairie Dell Road, Union, MO 63084. (314) 583-5193. Fax: (314) 583-5195 ext. 2432.

Evangel College
Springfield, Missouri — CB code: 6198

Admissions:	97% of applicants accepted
Based on:	••• Recommendations, religious affiliation/commitment, school record, test scores
	•• Essay
Completion:	91% of freshmen end year in good standing
	51% graduate, 25% of these enter graduate study

4-year private college of arts and sciences, coed, affiliated with Assemblies of God. Founded in 1955. **Accreditation:** Regional. **Undergraduate enrollment:** 641 men, 678 women full time; 45 men, 56 women part time. **Faculty:** 115 total (84 full time), 46 with doctorates or other terminal degrees. **Location:** Urban campus in small city; 170 miles from Kansas City, 212 miles from St. Louis. **Calendar:** Semester, limited summer session. **Microcomputers:** Located in libraries, computer centers.

DEGREES OFFERED. AA, BA, BS. 7 associate degrees awarded in 1992. 57% in business and management, 14% business/office and marketing/distribution, 28% communications. 295 bachelor's degrees awarded. 30% in business and management, 14% communications, 29% teacher education, 12% letters/literature.

UNDERGRADUATE MAJORS. Associate: Accounting, business and office, communications, dramatic arts, early childhood education, education, graphic arts technology, journalism, liberal/general studies, medical laboratory technologies, music, radio/television broadcasting, secretarial and related programs, social sciences, social work. **Bachelor's:** Accounting, art education, Bible studies, biology, business administration and management, business and management, business education, chemistry, clinical laboratory science, communications, computer and information sciences, dramatic arts, early childhood education, education, education of the mentally handicapped, elementary education, English, English education, foreign languages education, French, history, journalism, junior high education, marketing management, mathematics, mathematics education, music, music education, music performance, physical education, political science and government, predentistry, prelaw, premedicine, preveterinary, psychology, public administration, radio/television broadcasting, radio/television technology, recreation and community services technologies, religious music, science education, secondary education, secretarial and related programs, social sciences, social studies education, social work, sociology, Spanish, special education, speech.

ACADEMIC PROGRAMS. Double major, dual enrollment of high school students, internships, study abroad, teacher preparation, Washington semester, cross-registration. **Remedial services:** Learning center, reduced course load, remedial instruction, special counselor. **ROTC:** Army. **Placement/credit:** AP, CLEP General and Subject.

ACADEMIC REQUIREMENTS. Freshmen must earn minimum GPA of 1.5 to continue in good standing. 49% of freshmen return for sophomore year. Students must declare major by end of second year. **Graduation requirements:** 60 hours for associate, 124 hours for bachelor's. Most students required to take courses in arts/fine arts, computer science, English, history, humanities, philosophy/religion, biological/physical sciences, social sciences. **Postgraduate studies:** 60% from 2-year programs enter 4-year programs.

FRESHMAN ADMISSIONS. Selection criteria: Minimum 2.0 high school GPA, acceptance of college's moral and religious standards, acceptable ACT or SAT scores, rank in top half of graduating class. Recommended units include English 3, mathematics 2, social science 2 and science 1. **Test requirements:** SAT or ACT (ACT preferred); score report by August 15.

1992 FRESHMAN CLASS PROFILE. 422 men and women applied, 408 accepted; 351 enrolled. 19% had high school GPA of 3.0 or higher, 75% between 2.0 and 2.99. **Characteristics:** 22% from in state, 80% live in college housing, 6% have minority backgrounds, 2% are foreign students. Average age is 18.

FALL-TERM APPLICATIONS. $25 fee. No closing date; applicants notified on a rolling basis; August 15. Audition recommended for music applicants. Essay recommended. Statement of Christian faith required. CRDA. Early admission available.

STUDENT LIFE. Housing: Dormitories (men, women, coed); apartment housing available. **Activities:** Student government, radio, student newspaper, television, yearbook, choral groups, concert band, drama, music ensembles, pep band, symphony orchestra, international students club, honor fraternities, student ministries.

ATHLETICS. NAIA. **Intercollegiate:** Baseball M, basketball, cross-country, football M, softball W, track and field, volleyball W. **Intramural:** Basketball, soccer M, softball, volleyball W.

STUDENT SERVICES. Career counseling, employment service for undergraduates, freshman orientation, health services, on-campus day care, personal counseling, placement service for graduates, veterans counselor, services/facilities for handicapped.

ANNUAL EXPENSES. Tuition and fees: $6,730. **Room and board:** $3,090. **Books and supplies:** $500. **Other expenses:** $1,500.

FINANCIAL AID. 90% of freshmen, 86% of continuing students receive some form of aid. 38% of grants, 97% of loans, 82% of jobs based on need. Academic, music/drama, art, athletic, leadership, alumni affiliation scholarships available. **Aid applications:** No closing date; applicants notified on a rolling basis beginning on or about April 1.

ADDRESS/TELEPHONE. David I. Schoolfield, Executive Director of Enrollment, Evangel College, 1111 North Glenstone, Springfield, MO 65802. (417) 865-2811. Fax: (417) 865-9599.

Fontbonne College

St. Louis, Missouri — CB code: 6216

Admissions:	89% of applicants accepted
Based on:	••• School record
	•• Test scores
	• Activities, essay, interview, recommendations, special talents
Completion:	80% of freshmen end year in good standing

4-year private liberal arts college, coed, affiliated with Roman Catholic Church. Founded in 1923. **Accreditation:** Regional. **Undergraduate enrollment:** 157 men, 480 women full time; 69 men, 169 women part time. **Graduate enrollment:** 16 men, 20 women full time; 130 men, 168 women part time. **Faculty:** 131 total (55 full time), 73 with doctorates or other terminal degrees. **Location:** Suburban campus in large city; 6 miles from downtown. **Calendar:** Semester, limited summer session. **Microcomputers:** 20 located in libraries, classrooms, computer centers. **Special facilities:** Speech and hearing clinic, art gallery.

DEGREES OFFERED. BA, BS, BFA, MA, MS, MBA, MFA. 177 bachelor's degrees awarded in 1992. 23% in business and management, 24% business/office and marketing/distribution, 8% education, 10% teacher education, 8% home economics, 8% mathematics, 7% social sciences, 12% visual and performing arts. Graduate degrees offered in 4 major fields of study.

UNDERGRADUATE MAJORS. Accounting, art education, biological chemistry, biology, business administration and management, business and management, computer and information sciences, computer programming, dramatic arts, early childhood education, early childhood music, education, education of the deaf and hearing impaired, education of the emotionally handicapped, education of the mentally handicapped, education of the multiple handicapped, elementary education, English, English education, English literature, environmental science, fashion merchandising, finance, fine arts, food science and nutrition, gerontology, health education, health sciences, history, history education, home economics, home economics education, information sciences and systems, international business management, junior high education, liberal/general studies, management science, marketing management, mathematics, medical laboratory technologies, mental health/human services, music, music business management, music performance, music/theater, prelaw, premedicine, professional writing, public relations, radio/television broadcasting, retailing, science education, secondary education, social science education, social sciences, social work, specific learning disabilities, speech correction, speech pathology/audiology, speech/communication/theater education, theater design.

ACADEMIC PROGRAMS. Accelerated program, cooperative education, double major, dual enrollment of high school students, independent study, internships, student-designed major, study abroad, teacher preparation, visiting/exchange student program, weekend college, cross-registration, 3-2 program in social work with washington University. **Remedial services:** Learning center, reduced course load, remedial instruction, special counselor, tutoring. **ROTC:** Army. **Placement/credit:** AP, CLEP General and Subject, institutional tests; 27 credit hours maximum for bachelor's degree.

ACADEMIC REQUIREMENTS. Freshmen must earn minimum GPA of 2.0 to continue in good standing. 70% of freshmen return for sophomore year. Students must declare major by end of second year. **Graduation requirements:** 128 hours for bachelor's (60 in major). Most students required to take courses in arts/fine arts, English, history, mathematics, philosophy/religion, biological/physical sciences, social sciences.

FRESHMAN ADMISSIONS. Selection criteria: High school GPA, class rank, test scores considered. Recommendations may be requested. **High school preparation:** 16 units required. **Test requirements:** SAT or ACT (ACT preferred); score report by May 1.

1992 FRESHMAN CLASS PROFILE. 59 men applied, 54 accepted, 33 enrolled; 216 women applied, 191 accepted, 110 enrolled. 18% were in top tenth and 50% were in top quarter of graduating class. **Academic background:** Mid 50% of enrolled freshmen had ACT composite between 20-25. 98% submitted ACT scores. **Characteristics:** 88% from in state, 57% live in college housing, 27% have minority backgrounds, 15% are foreign students. Average age is 18.

FALL-TERM APPLICATIONS. $20 fee, may be waived for applicants with need. Closing date August 1; priority given to applications received by January 15; applicants notified on a rolling basis; must reply by May 1 or within 2 weeks if notified thereafter. Audition required for music, theater applicants. Portfolio required for art applicants. Interview recommended. Essay recommended. CRDA. Deferred and early admission available.

STUDENT LIFE. Housing: Dormitories (women, coed). **Activities:** Student government, magazine, student newspaper, department newsletters, choral groups, concert band, dance, drama, music ensembles, musical theater, pep band, fraternities, Association of Black Collegiates, Campus Ministry, Ass. of International Students.

ATHLETICS. NCAA. **Intercollegiate:** Basketball, cross-country, golf, soccer M, volleyball W. **Intramural:** Basketball, soccer, softball, table tennis, tennis, volleyball.

STUDENT SERVICES. Aptitude testing, career counseling, employment service for undergraduates, freshman orientation, health services, personal counseling, placement service for graduates, special adviser for adult students, campus ministry, services/facilities for handicapped.

ANNUAL EXPENSES. Tuition and fees: $8,140. **Room and board:** $4,020. **Books and supplies:** $590. **Other expenses:** $980.

FINANCIAL AID. 82% of freshmen, 65% of continuing students receive some form of aid. 79% of grants, 87% of loans, 82% of jobs based on need. Academic, music/drama, art, leadership, religious affiliation, minority scholarships available. **Aid applications:** No closing date; priority given to applications received by April 1; applicants notified on a rolling basis beginning on or about April 1; must reply within 15 days.

ADDRESS/TELEPHONE. Peggy Musen, Director, Fontbonne College, 6800 Wydown Boulevard, St. Louis, MO 63105. (314) 889-1400. Fax: (314) 889-1451.

Hannibal-LaGrange College

Hannibal, Missouri — CB code: 6266

4-year private liberal arts college, coed, affiliated with Southern Baptist Convention. Founded in 1858. **Accreditation:** Regional. **Undergraduate enrollment:** 203 men, 322 women full time; 97 men, 180 women part time. **Graduate enrollment:** 172 men and women. **Faculty:** 82 total (39 full time), 18 with doctorates or other terminal degrees. **Location:** Suburban campus in large town; 100 miles from St. Louis. **Calendar:** Semester, limited summer session. **Microcomputers:** 50 located in libraries, computer centers.

DEGREES OFFERED. AA, AS, AAS, BA, BS. 42 associate degrees awarded in 1992. 130 bachelor's degrees awarded.

UNDERGRADUATE MAJORS. Associate: Allied health, Bible studies, engineering, engineering and engineering-related technologies, fine arts, graphic arts technology, law enforcement and corrections technologies, liberal/general studies, nursing, recreation and community services technologies, science technologies, secretarial and related programs, teacher aide. **Bachelor's:** Accounting, biology, business administration and management, business and management, communications, computer and information sciences, criminal justice studies, data processing, early childhood education, elementary education, English, information sciences and systems, marketing management, music education, nursing, religion, religious education, religious music, secondary education, theological studies.

ACADEMIC PROGRAMS. 2-year transfer program, accelerated program, double major, dual enrollment of high school students, external degree, honors program, independent study, internships, student-designed major, study abroad, teacher preparation. **Remedial services:** Reduced course load, remedial instruction, tutoring, video supplements to some courses. **Placement/credit:** AP, CLEP General and Subject; 30 credit hours maximum for bachelor's degree.

ACADEMIC REQUIREMENTS. Freshmen must earn minimum GPA of 2.0 to continue in good standing. 58% of freshmen return for sophomore year. **Graduation requirements:** 64 hours for associate, 124 hours for bachelor's. Most students required to take courses in arts/fine arts, English, history, mathematics, philosophy/religion, biological/physical sciences, social sciences. **Postgraduate studies:** 65% from 2-year programs enter 4-year programs.

FRESHMAN ADMISSIONS. Selection criteria: Open admissions. **Test requirements:** SAT or ACT (ACT preferred) for placement and counseling only; score report by October 1.

1992 FRESHMAN CLASS PROFILE. 48 men, 63 women enrolled. **Characteristics:** 82% from in state, 68% commute, 2% have minority backgrounds, 6% are foreign students. Average age is 19.

FALL-TERM APPLICATIONS. $25 fee. No closing date; applicants notified on a rolling basis. Early admission available.

STUDENT LIFE. Housing: Dormitories (men, women); apartment housing available. **Activities:** Student government, magazine, student newspaper, television, yearbook, choral groups, concert band, drama, music ensembles, musical theater, pep band, Baptist Student Union. **Additional information:** Liberal arts education provided in distinctively Christian environment. Religious observance required.

ATHLETICS. NAIA. **Intercollegiate:** Baseball M, basketball M, cross-country, softball W, volleyball W. **Intramural:** Baseball, basketball, softball, table tennis, tennis, volleyball.

STUDENT SERVICES. Career counseling, employment service for undergraduates, freshman orientation, health services, personal counseling, placement service for graduates, veterans counselor, services/facilities for handicapped.

ANNUAL EXPENSES. Tuition and fees (1992-93): $5,456. **Room and board:** $2,300. **Books and supplies:** $500. **Other expenses:** $1,300.

FINANCIAL AID. 89% of freshmen, 91% of continuing students receive some form of aid. Grants, loans, jobs available. **Aid applications:** No closing date; priority given to applications received by June 1; applicants notified on a rolling basis.

ADDRESS/TELEPHONE. Bill Creech, Dean of Admissions, Hannibal-LaGrange College, 2800 Palmyra Road, Hannibal, MO 63401. (314) 221-3113.

Harris Stowe State College
St. Louis, Missouri — CB code: 6269

4-year public teachers college, coed. Founded in 1857. **Accreditation:** Regional. **Undergraduate enrollment:** 180 men, 499 women full time; 293 men, 1,006 women part time. **Faculty:** 92 total (37 full time), 45 with doctorates or other terminal degrees. **Location:** Urban campus in large city. **Calendar:** Semester, limited summer session. **Microcomputers:** 89 located in computer centers. **Additional facts:** Experience-oriented education courses. Urban education specialist degree offered.

DEGREES OFFERED. BS. 42 bachelor's degrees awarded in 1992. 10% in education, 90% teacher education.

UNDERGRADUATE MAJORS. Early childhood education, elementary education, junior high education.

ACADEMIC PROGRAMS. Double major, dual enrollment of high school students, internships, teacher preparation, cross-registration. **Remedial services:** Learning center, preadmission summer program, reduced course load, remedial instruction, tutoring. **ROTC:** Air Force, Army.

ACADEMIC REQUIREMENTS. Freshmen must earn minimum GPA of 2.1 to continue in good standing. To continue in good academic standing, freshmen must successfully complete 8 hours or 67% of hours attempted, whichever is less. Students must declare major by end of second year. **Graduation requirements:** 128 hours for bachelor's (64 in major). Most students required to take courses in arts/fine arts, computer science, English, history, humanities, mathematics, philosophy/religion, biological/physical sciences, social sciences. **Postgraduate studies:** 17% enter other graduate study.

FRESHMAN ADMISSIONS. Selection criteria: Applicants who score 18 on ACT or 800 on combined SAT admitted unconditionally. High school GPA, test scores, curriculum, recommendations considered. Those not meeting requirements admitted conditionally. Required units include English 4, mathematics 3, social science 2 and science 2. **Test requirements:** SAT or ACT (ACT preferred).

1992 FRESHMAN CLASS PROFILE. 29 men, 97 women enrolled. **Characteristics:** 93% from in state, 100% commute, 81% have minority backgrounds, 3% are foreign students.

FALL-TERM APPLICATIONS. $15 fee. No closing date; priority given to applications received by August 15; applicants notified on a rolling basis. Interview required. CRDA. Deferred admission available.

STUDENT LIFE. Activities: Student government, magazine, student newspaper, yearbook, choral groups, drama, music ensembles, fraternities, sororities.

ATHLETICS. NAIA. **Intercollegiate:** Baseball M, basketball, soccer M, track and field W, volleyball W. **Intramural:** Basketball, table tennis, tennis, volleyball.

STUDENT SERVICES. Career counseling, employment service for undergraduates, freshman orientation, health services, personal counseling, placement service for graduates, veterans counselor, services/facilities for handicapped.

ANNUAL EXPENSES. Tuition and fees (1992-93): $1,635, $1,572 additional for out-of-state students. **Books and supplies:** $500. **Other expenses:** $1,200.

FINANCIAL AID. 78% of grants, 97% of loans, 79% of jobs based on need. Academic, athletic scholarships available. **Aid applications:** No closing date; applicants notified on a rolling basis.

ADDRESS/TELEPHONE. Valerie Beeson, Director of Admissions, Harris Stowe State College, 3026 Laclede Avenue, St. Louis, MO 63103. (314) 340-3000. Fax: (314) 340-3322.

ITT Technical Institute: St. Louis
Earth City, Missouri — CB code: 1216

Admissions: 48% of applicants accepted
Based on: ••• Interview, test scores
•• School record
• Recommendations
Completion: 65% of freshmen end year in good standing

2-year proprietary technical college, coed. Founded in 1936. **Undergraduate enrollment:** 580 men, 36 women full time. **Faculty:** 22 total. **Location:** Suburban campus in large city. **Calendar:** Quarter, extensive summer session. **Microcomputers:** 68 located in classrooms.

DEGREES OFFERED. AAS, BS. 191 associate degrees awarded in 1992. 100% in engineering technologies.

UNDERGRADUATE MAJORS. Associate: Computer-aided drafting, drafting and design technology, electronic technology.

ACADEMIC PROGRAMS. Double major, honors program. **Remedial services:** Learning center, remedial instruction, tutoring. **Placement/credit:** Institutional tests; 60 credit hours maximum for associate degree.

ACADEMIC REQUIREMENTS. Freshmen must earn minimum GPA of 2.0 to continue in good standing. 60% of freshmen return for sophomore year. Students must declare major on application. **Graduation requirements:** 120 hours for associate. Most students required to take courses in mathematics, biological/physical sciences. **Additional information:** Qualified graduates of associate degree program automatically admitted to ITT Technical Institute's bachelor of applied science program.

FRESHMAN ADMISSIONS. Selection criteria: Institutional tests, school record, interview. **Test requirements:** Institutional tests in reading, mathematics, English, algebra required.

1992 FRESHMAN CLASS PROFILE. Characteristics: 70% from in state, 100% commute, 17% have minority backgrounds. Average age is 22.

FALL-TERM APPLICATIONS. $100 fee. Application fee refunded if student not accepted. No closing date; applicants notified on a rolling basis. Interview recommended. Deferred admission available.

ATHLETICS. Intramural: Soccer M, softball. **Clubs:** Various club sports.

STUDENT SERVICES. Aptitude testing, career counseling, employment service for undergraduates, freshman orientation, placement service for graduates, veterans counselor, substance abuse program, services/facilities for handicapped.

ANNUAL EXPENSES. Tuition and fees (1992-93): Tuition for 18-month computer-aided drafting program $12,817; books and supplies $1,300. Tuition for 2-year electronics program $14,405; books and supplies $1,500. Tuition for bachelor's electronics program $7,253; books and supplies $850.

FINANCIAL AID. 98% of grants, 31% of loans, all jobs based on need. 205 enrolled freshmen were judged to have need, all were offered aid. Academic, leadership scholarships available. **Aid applications:** No closing date; applicants notified on a rolling basis.

ADDRESS/TELEPHONE. Jerome S. Padak, Director of Education, ITT Technical Institute: St. Louis, 13505 Lakefront Drive, Earth City, MO 63045. (314) 298-7800.

Jefferson College
Hillsboro, Missouri — CB code: 6320

2-year public community college, coed. Founded in 1963. **Accreditation:** Regional. **Undergraduate enrollment:** 854 men, 997 women full time; 863 men, 1,496 women part time. **Faculty:** 199 total (105 full time), 6 with doctorates or other terminal degrees. **Location:** Rural campus in rural community; 25 miles from St. Louis. **Calendar:** Semester, limited summer session. Saturday and extensive evening/early morning classes. **Microcomput-**

ers: Located in libraries, computer centers. **Special facilities:** Outdoor theater, facility for computer-related technologies, large animal facilities. **Additional facts:** College also serves as area vocational school.

DEGREES OFFERED. AA, AS, AAS. 423 associate degrees awarded in 1992. 11% in business/office and marketing/distribution, 16% engineering technologies, 18% health sciences, 44% multi/interdisciplinary studies.

UNDERGRADUATE MAJORS. Accounting, air conditioning/heating/refrigeration mechanics, air conditioning/heating/refrigeration technology, architectural technologies, art history, automotive technology, biology, business data processing and related programs, business data programming, child development/care/guidance, civil technology, communications, computer and information sciences, data processing, drafting, drafting and design technology, electronic technology, elementary education, emergency/disaster science, engineering, English, fine arts, fire control and safety technology, French, history, hospitality and recreation marketing, hotel/motel and restaurant management, laser electro-optic technology, law enforcement and corrections technologies, legal secretary, liberal/general studies, machine tool operation/machine shop, mathematics, mechanical design technology, medical secretary, music, music performance, nursing, physical sciences, political science and government, practical nursing, precision metal work, prelaw, premedicine, preveterinary, psychology, retailing, robotics, secondary education, secretarial and related programs, social sciences, sociology, Spanish, telecommunications, veterinarian's assistant, word processing.

ACADEMIC PROGRAMS. 2-year transfer program, double major, dual enrollment of high school students, honors program, independent study, internships, teacher preparation, telecourses, weekend college, cooperative agreement with 2 neighboring community colleges, special programs taught in local industries. **Remedial services:** Learning center, reduced course load, remedial instruction, special counselor, tutoring. **Placement/credit:** AP, CLEP General and Subject, institutional tests; 30 credit hours maximum for associate degree.

ACADEMIC REQUIREMENTS. Freshmen must earn minimum GPA of 1.8 to continue in good standing. 63% of freshmen return for sophomore year. Students must declare major by end of first year. **Graduation requirements:** 62 hours for associate. Most students required to take courses in English, history, mathematics, biological/physical sciences.

FRESHMAN ADMISSIONS. Selection criteria: Open admissions. Selective admissions to nursing, animal health technology, and electronics programs. Elementary algebra required for electronics, chemistry required for nursing and veterinarian's assistant programs. **Test requirements:** ACT for placement and counseling only; score report by August 1. School and College Ability Tests required if SAT or ACT scores not available.

1992 FRESHMAN CLASS PROFILE. 846 men, 1,167 women enrolled. **Academic background:** Mid 50% of enrolled freshmen had ACT composite between 16-22. 30% submitted ACT scores. **Characteristics:** 99% from in state, 100% commute, 1% have minority backgrounds.

FALL-TERM APPLICATIONS. $15 fee. No closing date; priority given to applications received by July 1; applicants notified on a rolling basis beginning on or about May 1. Interview required for health services technologies applicants. All students are required to take ASSET test before enrolling in classes.

STUDENT LIFE. Activities: Student government, student newspaper, television, yearbook, choral groups, concert band, drama, jazz band, music ensembles, musical theater, Phi Theta Kappa, Phi Beta Lambda, Jefferson College Ambassadors.

ATHLETICS. NJCAA. **Intercollegiate:** Baseball M, basketball W, tennis M, volleyball W. **Intramural:** Basketball, softball, tennis, volleyball.

STUDENT SERVICES. Aptitude testing, career counseling, employment service for undergraduates, freshman orientation, on-campus day care, personal counseling, placement service for graduates, veterans counselor, counselor for handicapped single parents, nontraditional students, homemakers, and displaced homemakers, services/facilities for handicapped.

ANNUAL EXPENSES. Tuition and fees (1992-93): $960, $360 additional for out-of-district students, $720 additional for out-of-state students. **Books and supplies:** $300. **Other expenses:** $1,070.

FINANCIAL AID. 37% of freshmen, 30% of continuing students receive some form of aid. Grants, loans, jobs available. Academic, music/drama, art, athletic, state/district residency scholarships available. **Aid applications:** No closing date; applicants notified on a rolling basis beginning on or about April 15; must reply within 2 weeks.

ADDRESS/TELEPHONE. Director of Admissions, Jefferson College, PO Box 1000, 1000 Viking Drive, Hillsboro, MO 63050-2441. (314) 789-3951 ext. 217. Fax: (314) 789-4012.

Kansas City Art Institute
Kansas City, Missouri — CB code: 6330

4-year private art college, coed. Founded in 1885. **Accreditation:** Regional. **Undergraduate enrollment:** 564 men and women. **Faculty:** 71 total (42 full time). **Location:** Urban campus in large city. **Calendar:** Semester, limited summer session. Extensive evening/early morning classes. **Microcomputers:** Located in computer centers. **Special facilities:** Professional and student art gallery, foundry, new generation computer graphic system for animation, arboretum, slide library of 60,000 works of art.

DEGREES OFFERED. BFA. 100 bachelor's degrees awarded in 1992. 100% in visual and performing arts.

UNDERGRADUATE MAJORS. Ceramics, crafts, drawing, fiber/textiles/weaving, film arts, fine arts, graphic design, illustration design, painting, photography, printmaking, sculpture, studio art, video.

ACADEMIC PROGRAMS. Independent study, internships, study abroad, visiting/exchange student program, New York semester, cross-registration, New York studio study and internship. **Remedial services:** Learning center, preadmission summer program, remedial instruction, tutoring. **Placement/credit:** AP, CLEP General, institutional tests; 15 credit hours maximum for bachelor's degree.

ACADEMIC REQUIREMENTS. Freshmen must earn minimum GPA of 2.0 to continue in good standing. 77% of freshmen return for sophomore year. Students must declare major by end of first year. **Graduation requirements:** 138 hours for bachelor's. Most students required to take courses in arts/fine arts, English, history, philosophy/religion.

FRESHMAN ADMISSIONS. Selection criteria: Portfolio, academic record, recommendations most important. Test scores, personal interview considered. **Test requirements:** SAT or ACT; score report by June 1. **Additional information:** Acceptable level of studio proficiency required prior to consideration of other credentials.

1992 FRESHMAN CLASS PROFILE. 126 men and women enrolled. **Characteristics:** 32% from in state, 63% live in college housing, 25% have minority backgrounds, 2% are foreign students. Average age is 18.

FALL-TERM APPLICATIONS. $25 fee. No closing date; priority given to applications received by February 15; applicants notified on a rolling basis; must reply by May 1 or within 2 weeks if notified thereafter. Portfolio required. Interview recommended. Essay recommended. CRDA. Deferred and early admission available. February 15 deadline for priority admissions. March 1 scholarship deadline; applicant must have been accepted prior to that date to be eligible for consideration. Test scores required before March 1 if student to be considered for priority admission or scholarship.

STUDENT LIFE. Housing: Dormitories (men, women, coed). **Activities:** Student film series, visiting artists program, student-operated gallery.

STUDENT SERVICES. Career counseling, employment service for undergraduates, personal counseling, placement service for graduates.

ANNUAL EXPENSES. Tuition and fees: $12,810. **Room and board:** $4,090. **Books and supplies:** $1,470. **Other expenses:** $735.

FINANCIAL AID. 68% of freshmen, 68% of continuing students receive some form of aid. 86% of grants, 83% of loans, 58% of jobs based on need. 84 enrolled freshmen were judged to have need, all were offered aid. Art scholarships available. **Aid applications:** No closing date; priority given to applications received by February 15; applicants notified on a rolling basis beginning on or about April 15; must reply within 2 weeks.

ADDRESS/TELEPHONE. Charles Van Gilder, Director of Admissions, Kansas City Art Institute, 4415 Warwick Boulevard, Kansas City, MO 64111. (816) 931-5224. (800) 522-5224. Fax: (816) 561-6404.

Kemper Military School and College
Boonville, Missouri — CB code: 6338

2-year private junior, liberal arts, military college, coed. Founded in 1844. **Accreditation:** Regional. **Undergraduate enrollment:** 136 men, 43 women full time; 10 men, 17 women part time. **Faculty:** 14 total (9 full time), 2 with doctorates or other terminal degrees. **Location:** Rural campus in small town; 100 miles from Kansas City, 150 miles from St. Louis. **Calendar:** Semester. **Microcomputers:** Located in classrooms. **Special facilities:** Military history book collection.

DEGREES OFFERED. AA. 52 associate degrees awarded in 1992. 100% in multi/interdisciplinary studies.

UNDERGRADUATE MAJORS. Liberal/general studies.

ACADEMIC PROGRAMS. 2-year transfer program, dual enrollment of high school students, cross-registration, 2-year ROTC commissioning program. **Remedial services:** Remedial instruction, tutoring. **ROTC:** Army. **Placement/credit:** AP, CLEP General and Subject, institutional tests; 15 credit hours maximum for associate degree.

ACADEMIC REQUIREMENTS. Freshmen must earn minimum GPA of 1.85 to continue in good standing. 95% of freshmen return for sophomore year. **Graduation requirements:** 62 hours for associate. Most students required to take courses in English, history, humanities, mathematics, biological/physical sciences, social sciences.

FRESHMAN ADMISSIONS. Selection criteria: Open admissions. Open admissions to liberal/general studies program. School achievement record, recommendations, and test scores considered for military science program. Children of alumni generally accepted without recommendations or interview. Graduates of our high school eligible without application. Army ROTC applicants must have ACT score of 19. Recommended units include biological science 1, English 3, mathematics 2, social science 3 and science 2. **Test requirements:** SAT or ACT required for admission to 2-year commissioning program; score report by May 15.

1992 FRESHMAN CLASS PROFILE. 71 men, 23 women enrolled.

Characteristics: 37% from in state, 91% live in college housing, 39% have minority backgrounds, 1% are foreign students. Average age is 18.

FALL-TERM APPLICATIONS. $25 fee. $500 reservation fee also required. No closing date; applicants notified on a rolling basis beginning on or about January 1. Interview recommended. Deferred and early admission available.

STUDENT LIFE. Housing: Dormitories (men, women). **Activities:** Student government, yearbook, choral groups, marching band, Phi Beta Kappa, Standard of Honor. **Additional information:** Boarding students required to participate in Corps of Cadets.

ATHLETICS. NJCAA. **Intercollegiate:** Baseball M, basketball M, football M, golf, rifle, tennis, track and field, volleyball W. **Intramural:** Basketball, golf, rifle, softball, swimming, tennis, track and field W, volleyball M.

STUDENT SERVICES. Career counseling, health services, personal counseling, placement service for graduates, veterans counselor.

ANNUAL EXPENSES. Tuition and fees (1992-93): $8,300. **Room and board:** $2,600. **Books and supplies:** $1,800. **Other expenses:** $1,080.

FINANCIAL AID. 99% of freshmen, 99% of continuing students receive some form of aid. 24% of grants, 94% of loans, all jobs based on need. Academic, music/drama, athletic scholarships available. **Aid applications:** No closing date; priority given to applications received by July 1; applicants notified on a rolling basis beginning on or about October 4; must reply within 8 weeks. **Additional information:** Army ROTC Commission Program, Simultaneous Membership Program through Army Reserve and National Guard.

ADDRESS/TELEPHONE. Mary Almond, Director of Admissions, Kemper Military School and College, 701 Third Street, Boonville, MO 65233. (816) 882-5623. (800) 553-6737. Fax: (816) 882-3332.

Lincoln University
Jefferson City, Missouri — CB code: 6366

4-year public university and college of arts and sciences and agricultural and technical, business college, coed. Founded in 1866. **Accreditation:** Regional. **Undergraduate enrollment:** 987 men, 1,157 women full time; 536 men, 940 women part time. **Graduate enrollment:** 17 men, 30 women full time; 102 men, 262 women part time. **Faculty:** 246 total (154 full time). **Location:** Suburban campus in large town; 132 miles from St. Louis, 152 miles from Kansas City. **Calendar:** Semester, limited summer session. **Microcomputers:** Located in computer centers. **Special facilities:** Ethnic studies center.

DEGREES OFFERED. AA, AAS, BA, BS, MA, MBA, MEd. 60 associate degrees awarded in 1992. 13% in computer sciences, 77% health sciences, 5% multi/interdisciplinary studies. 225 bachelor's degrees awarded. 5% in agriculture, 35% business and management, 6% business/office and marketing/distribution, 15% education, 15% social sciences. Graduate degrees offered in 8 major fields of study.

UNDERGRADUATE MAJORS. Associate: Computer and information sciences, drafting, drafting and design technology, electronic technology, graphic and printing production, law enforcement and corrections technologies, nursing, secretarial and related programs. **Bachelor's:** Accounting, agricultural sciences, biology, business administration and management, business economics, chemistry, computer and information sciences, criminal justice studies, elementary education, English, fashion merchandising, French, history, journalism, mathematics, nursing, philosophy, physics, political science and government, psychology, public administration, radio/television broadcasting, secretarial and related programs, social sciences, sociology, special education.

ACADEMIC PROGRAMS. Accelerated program, cooperative education, double major, dual enrollment of high school students, honors program, independent study, internships, teacher preparation. **Remedial services:** Preadmission summer program, reduced course load, remedial instruction, special counselor, tutoring. **ROTC:** Army. **Placement/credit:** CLEP General and Subject, institutional tests; 30 credit hours maximum for bachelor's degree.

ACADEMIC REQUIREMENTS. Freshmen must earn minimum GPA of 2.0 to continue in good standing. Students must declare major by end of second year. **Graduation requirements:** 64 hours for associate, 124 hours for bachelor's. Most students required to take courses in English, history, mathematics, biological/physical sciences, social sciences.

FRESHMAN ADMISSIONS. Selection criteria: Open admissions. Out-of-state applicants must have 2.0 high school GPA. **Test requirements:** ACT for placement and counseling only; score report by July 15. School and College Ability Tests also required for placement and counseling.

1992 FRESHMAN CLASS PROFILE. 349 men, 387 women enrolled. 4% were in top tenth of graduating class. **Characteristics:** 11% live in college housing. Average age is 23.

FALL-TERM APPLICATIONS. $17 fee. No closing date; priority given to applications received by July 15; applicants notified on a rolling basis; must reply as soon as possible. Audition required for music education applicants. Deferred admission available.

STUDENT LIFE. Housing: Dormitories (men, women). **Activities:** Student government, radio, student newspaper, television, yearbook, choral groups, concert band, dance, drama, jazz band, marching band, music ensembles, musical theater, opera, pep band, fraternities, sororities.

ATHLETICS. NCAA. **Intercollegiate:** Baseball M, basketball, cross-country M, golf M, soccer M, softball W, tennis W, track and field. **Intramural:** Bowling, boxing.

STUDENT SERVICES. Aptitude testing, career counseling, employment service for undergraduates, freshman orientation, health services, personal counseling, placement service for graduates, veterans counselor, services/facilities for handicapped.

ANNUAL EXPENSES. Tuition and fees (1992-93): $1,498, $1,478 additional for out-of-state students. **Room and board:** $2,728. **Books and supplies:** $480. **Other expenses:** $1,496.

FINANCIAL AID. 48% of continuing students receive some form of aid. 75% of grants, 92% of loans, 80% of jobs based on need. Academic, music/drama, art, athletic scholarships available. **Aid applications:** No closing date; priority given to applications received by March 1; applicants notified on a rolling basis beginning on or about April 1; must reply within 10 days.

ADDRESS/TELEPHONE. Charles E. Glasper, Director of Admissions, Lincoln University, 820 Chestnut, Jefferson City, MO 65102-0029. (314) 681-5000. Fax: (314) 681-5566.

Lindenwood College
St. Charles, Missouri — CB code: 6367

Admissions:	61% of applicants accepted
Based on:	••• Interview, school record, test scores
	•• Activities, special talents
	• Essay, recommendations
Completion:	87% of freshmen end year in good standing
	65% graduate, 43% of these enter graduate study

4-year private liberal arts college, coed, affiliated with Presbyterian Church (USA). Founded in 1827. **Accreditation:** Regional. **Undergraduate enrollment:** 779 men, 873 women full time; 179 men, 312 women part time. **Graduate enrollment:** 232 men, 184 women full time; 136 men, 130 women part time. **Faculty:** 162 total (80 full time), 107 with doctorates or other terminal degrees. **Location:** Suburban campus in large town; 20 miles from St. Louis. **Calendar:** Semester, limited summer session. **Microcomputers:** 65 located in libraries, classrooms, computer centers. **Special facilities:** Art gallery, arboretum, greenhouse, 5000-seat stadium, 40-acre nature trail. **Additional facts:** Evening school students attend in quarter term.

DEGREES OFFERED. BA, BS, BFA, MA, MS, MBA, MFA, MEd. 344 bachelor's degrees awarded in 1992. 50% in business and management, 10% communications, 20% teacher education. Graduate degrees offered in 21 major fields of study.

UNDERGRADUATE MAJORS. Art history, biology, business administration and management, chemistry, communications, computer and information sciences, corporate and industrial communication, creative writing, criminal justice studies, dramatic arts, education, elementary education, English, French, gerontology, health care administration, history, human resources development, international studies, journalism, mathematics, medical laboratory technologies, music, music education, music performance, political science and government, psychology, sociology, Spanish, special education, studio art, valuation science, visual and performing arts.

ACADEMIC PROGRAMS. Accelerated program, cooperative education, double major, dual enrollment of high school students, external degree, independent study, internships, student-designed major, study abroad, teacher preparation, visiting/exchange student program, Washington semester, cross-registration; liberal arts/career combination in engineering, health sciences; combined bachelor's/graduate program in business administration. **Remedial services:** Learning center, reduced course load, special counselor, tutoring, placement testing, refresher courses in reading, writing, mathematics. **Placement/credit:** AP, CLEP General and Subject, institutional tests; 60 credit hours maximum for bachelor's degree.

ACADEMIC REQUIREMENTS. Freshmen must earn minimum GPA of 1.8 to continue in good standing. 75% of freshmen return for sophomore year. Students must declare major by end of second year. **Graduation requirements:** 120 hours for bachelor's (40 in major). Most students required to take courses in arts/fine arts, English, foreign languages, history, humanities, mathematics, philosophy/religion, biological/physical sciences, social sciences. **Postgraduate studies:** 3% enter law school, 2% enter medical school, 18% enter MBA programs, 20% enter other graduate study. **Additional information:** Internships available in St. Louis area corporations and social service organizations. Special program for working adults offers 9 credit hours per term. Freshmen seminars also available.

FRESHMAN ADMISSIONS. Selection criteria: Admissions based on test scores and high school school record. Writing sample may be required for those below normal admission standards. **High school preparation:** 15 units recommended. Recommended units include biological science 1, English 4, foreign language 2, mathematics 3, physical science 1 and social science 4. **Test requirements:** SAT or ACT; score report by August 31.

1992 FRESHMAN CLASS PROFILE. 637 men applied, 378 accepted,

183 enrolled; 589 women applied, 367 accepted, 176 enrolled. 64% had high school GPA of 3.0 or higher, 34% between 2.0 and 2.99. 9% were in top tenth and 51% were in top quarter of graduating class. **Academic background:** Mid 50% of enrolled freshmen had SAT-V between 370-480, SAT-M between 370-480; ACT composite between 18-23. 5% submitted SAT scores, 95% submitted ACT scores. **Characteristics:** 80% from in state, 74% live in college housing, 9% have minority backgrounds, 25% join fraternities/sororities. Average age is 19.

FALL-TERM APPLICATIONS. $25 fee, may be waived for applicants with need. No closing date; priority given to applications received by November 30; applicants notified on a rolling basis beginning on or about December 1; must reply within 2 weeks. Interview recommended for scholarship applicants applicants. Audition recommended for music, theater applicants. Portfolio recommended for art applicants. Essay recommended. CRDA. Deferred and early admission available. EDP-F.

STUDENT LIFE. Housing: Dormitories (men, women); apartment, fraternity, sorority housing available. **Activities:** Student government, film, magazine, radio, student newspaper, television, yearbook, literary magazine, choral groups, concert band, dance, drama, jazz band, marching band, music ensembles, musical theater, pep band, symphony orchestra, fraternities, sororities, Christian Student Union, Lindenwood Student Government, international student group, Circle-K, Student Association of Fine Arts, Association of Collegiate Entrepreneurs, American Humantics Student Association.

ATHLETICS. NAIA. **Intercollegiate:** Baseball M, basketball, cross-country, football M, golf, soccer, softball W, swimming, track and field, volleyball, wrestling M. **Intramural:** Basketball, bowling, cross-country, soccer M, softball, tennis, volleyball, water polo.

STUDENT SERVICES. Aptitude testing, career counseling, employment service for undergraduates, freshman orientation, health services, personal counseling, placement service for graduates, special adviser for adult students, veterans counselor.

ANNUAL EXPENSES. Tuition and fees: $8,950. **Room and board:** $4,600. **Books and supplies:** $1,000. **Other expenses:** $2,625.

FINANCIAL AID. 89% of freshmen, 87% of continuing students receive some form of aid. 83% of grants, 93% of loans, 74% of jobs based on need. Academic, music/drama, art, athletic, leadership, alumni affiliation scholarships available. **Aid applications:** No closing date; priority given to applications received by April 30; applicants notified on a rolling basis; must reply within 2 weeks.

ADDRESS/TELEPHONE. John Guffey, Dean of Admissions/Financial Aid, Lindenwood College, 209 South Kingshighway, St. Charles, MO 63301-1695. (314) 949-4949. Fax: (314) 949-4910.

Longview Community College
Lee's Summit, Missouri — CB code: 6359

2-year public community college, coed. Founded in 1968. **Accreditation:** Regional. **Undergraduate enrollment:** 1,395 men, 1,560 women full time; 2,398 men, 4,061 women part time. **Faculty:** 386 total (95 full time), 21 with doctorates or other terminal degrees. **Location:** Suburban campus in large town; 10 miles from Kansas City. **Calendar:** Semester, extensive summer session. Saturday and extensive evening/early morning classes. **Microcomputers:** 500 located in libraries, classrooms, computer centers, campus-wide network. **Special facilities:** Longview Lake recreational area. **Additional facts:** Additional campus at Blue Springs.

DEGREES OFFERED. AA, AS, AAS. 710 associate degrees awarded in 1992. 13% in business/office and marketing/distribution, 6% engineering technologies, 73% multi/interdisciplinary studies.

UNDERGRADUATE MAJORS. Accounting, automotive technology, biology, business administration and management, business and management, business and office, business computer/console/peripheral equipment operation, business data processing and related programs, business data programming, chemistry, computer programming, criminal justice technology, data processing, diesel engine mechanics, drafting, drafting and design technology, electrical/electronics/communications engineering, electronic technology, engineering, law enforcement and corrections technologies, legal secretary, liberal/general studies, marketing and distribution, medical secretary, mental health/human services, office supervision and management, quality control technology, secretarial and related programs, word processing.

ACADEMIC PROGRAMS. 2-year transfer program, cooperative education, dual enrollment of high school students, honors program, independent study, internships, cross-registration. **Remedial services:** Learning center, remedial instruction, special counselor, tutoring. **Placement/credit:** AP, CLEP General and Subject, institutional tests; 30 credit hours maximum for associate degree.

ACADEMIC REQUIREMENTS. No policy requiring minimum GPA; records of students having academic difficulty are reviewed individually. 40% of freshmen return for sophomore year. Students must declare major on enrollment. **Graduation requirements:** 62 hours for associate. Most students required to take courses in English, history, mathematics, social sciences.

FRESHMAN ADMISSIONS. Selection criteria: Open admissions. **High school preparation:** 16 units recommended. Recommended units include English 4, foreign language 2, mathematics 3, social science 3 and science 3. 1 unit in visual/performing arts recommended. **Test requirements:** ACT required for placement and counseling.

1992 FRESHMAN CLASS PROFILE. 1,980 men and women enrolled. **Characteristics:** 100% commute.

FALL-TERM APPLICATIONS. No fee. No closing date; applicants notified on a rolling basis.

STUDENT LIFE. Activities: Student government, magazine, student newspaper, choral groups, drama.

ATHLETICS. NJCAA. **Intercollegiate:** Baseball M, volleyball W. **Intramural:** Basketball, swimming, volleyball.

STUDENT SERVICES. Aptitude testing, career counseling, employment service for undergraduates, freshman orientation, on-campus day care, personal counseling, placement service for graduates, special adviser for adult students, veterans counselor, services/facilities for handicapped.

ANNUAL EXPENSES. Tuition and fees: $1,230, $780 additional for out-of-district students, $1,680 additional for out-of-state students. **Books and supplies:** $550. **Other expenses:** $1,306.

FINANCIAL AID. 17% of freshmen, 17% of continuing students receive some form of aid. 86% of grants, 86% of loans, 32% of jobs based on need. Academic, music/drama, art, athletic, state/district residency, leadership scholarships available. **Aid applications:** No closing date; priority given to applications received by May 31; applicants notified on a rolling basis beginning on or about July 15; must reply immediately.

ADDRESS/TELEPHONE. College Relations Office, Longview Community College, 500 Longview Road, Lee's Summit, MO 64081. (816) 763-7777. Fax: (816) 761-4457.

Maple Woods Community College
Kansas City, Missouri — CB code: 6436

2-year public community college, coed. Founded in 1968. **Accreditation:** Regional. **Undergraduate enrollment:** 752 men, 835 women full time; 1,464 men, 2,116 women part time. **Faculty:** 185 total (54 full time), 10 with doctorates or other terminal degrees. **Location:** Suburban campus in large city; 15 miles from downtown. **Calendar:** Semester, limited summer session. Saturday and extensive evening/early morning classes. **Microcomputers:** 125 located in computer centers, campus-wide network.

DEGREES OFFERED. AA, AS, AAS. 299 associate degrees awarded in 1992. 22% in business/office and marketing/distribution, 5% allied health, 36% multi/interdisciplinary studies, 28% trade and industry.

UNDERGRADUATE MAJORS. Accounting, aircraft mechanics, biology, business and management, business and office, chemistry, computer and information sciences, criminal justice technology, data processing, electronic technology, engineering, engineering and engineering-related technologies, liberal/general studies, machine tool operation/machine shop, marketing and distribution, office supervision and management, secretarial and related programs, veterinarian's assistant, word processing.

ACADEMIC PROGRAMS. 2-year transfer program, dual enrollment of high school students, honors program, internships, visiting/exchange student program, cross-registration. **Remedial services:** Learning center, reduced course load, remedial instruction, tutoring. **Placement/credit:** AP, CLEP General and Subject, institutional tests; 30 credit hours maximum for associate degree.

ACADEMIC REQUIREMENTS. 42% of freshmen return for sophomore year. Students must declare major on enrollment. **Graduation requirements:** 62 hours for associate. Most students required to take courses in English, history, mathematics, social sciences.

FRESHMAN ADMISSIONS. Selection criteria: Open admissions. **High school preparation:** 16 units recommended. Recommended units include English 4, foreign language 2, mathematics 3, social science 3 and science 3. 1 unit in visual/performing arts recommended. **Test requirements:** ACT ASSET required for placement and counseling.

1992 FRESHMAN CLASS PROFILE. 943 men and women enrolled. **Characteristics:** 100% commute.

FALL-TERM APPLICATIONS. No fee. Closing date August 16; applicants notified on a rolling basis. Early admission available. Separate application required for animal health technology and aviation maintenance technology. Animal health application deadline March 1.

STUDENT LIFE. Activities: Student government, student newspaper, choral groups.

ATHLETICS. NJCAA. **Intercollegiate:** Baseball M. **Intramural:** Softball, volleyball.

STUDENT SERVICES. Career counseling, employment service for undergraduates, freshman orientation, personal counseling, placement service for graduates, special adviser for adult students, veterans counselor, services/facilities for handicapped.

ANNUAL EXPENSES. Tuition and fees: $1,230, $780 additional for out-of-district students, $1,680 additional for out-of-state students. **Books and supplies:** $550. **Other expenses:** $1,972.

FINANCIAL AID. 19% of freshmen, 19% of continuing students receive some form of aid. 85% of grants, 70% of loans, 28% of jobs based on need. Academic, music/drama, art, athletic, state/district residency, leadership scholarships available. **Aid applications:** No closing date; priority given to applications received by May 31; applicants notified on a rolling basis beginning on or about July 30; must reply immediately.

ADDRESS/TELEPHONE. Office of Admissions, Maple Woods Community College, 2601 Northeast Barry Road, Kansas City, MO 64156-1299. (816) 437-3100. Fax: (816) 437-3049.

Maryville University
St. Louis, Missouri — CB code: 6399

Admissions: 39% of applicants accepted
Based on: ••• School record, test scores
•• Interview
• Activities, recommendations
Completion: 95% of freshmen end year in good standing
50% graduate

4-year private liberal arts college, coed. Founded in 1872. **Accreditation:** Regional. **Undergraduate enrollment:** 405 men, 739 women full time; 571 men, 1,323 women part time. **Graduate enrollment:** 7 men, 20 women full time; 217 men, 440 women part time. **Faculty:** 280 total (82 full time), 84 with doctorates or other terminal degrees. **Location:** Suburban campus in large city; 20 miles from downtown. **Calendar:** 4-4-1, extensive summer session. Saturday classes. **Microcomputers:** Located in libraries, computer centers. **Special facilities:** Art galleries, observatory.

DEGREES OFFERED. BA, BS, BFA, MA, MS, MBA. 467 bachelor's degrees awarded in 1992. 31% in business and management, 6% communications, 9% computer sciences, 15% education, 26% allied health, 5% psychology. Graduate degrees offered in 3 major fields of study.

UNDERGRADUATE MAJORS. Accounting, actuarial sciences, American studies, art education, biological and physical sciences, biology, business administration and management, business and management, chemistry, clinical laboratory science, communications, computer programming, drawing, early childhood education, education, elementary education, English, English education, English literature, fine arts, health care administration, history, humanities, humanities and social sciences, information sciences and systems, institutional management, interior design, journalism, junior high education, liberal/general studies, management information systems, marketing management, mathematics, mathematics education, music history and appreciation, music performance, music theory and composition, music therapy, nursing, occupational therapy, philosophy, physical sciences, physical therapy, political science and government, prelaw, psychology, religion, science education, secondary education, social science education, sociology, studio art.

ACADEMIC PROGRAMS. Accelerated program, cooperative education, double major, dual enrollment of high school students, education specialist degree, honors program, independent study, internships, study abroad, teacher preparation, weekend college, Washington semester, cross-registration, bridge program for psychology majors with St. Louis University; liberal arts/career combination in engineering, health sciences. **Remedial services:** Learning center, reduced course load, remedial instruction, special counselor, tutoring. **ROTC:** Army. **Placement/credit:** AP, CLEP General and Subject, institutional tests; 30 credit hours maximum for bachelor's degree.

ACADEMIC REQUIREMENTS. Freshmen must earn minimum GPA of 2.0 to continue in good standing. 79% of freshmen return for sophomore year. Students must declare major by end of second year. **Graduation requirements:** 128 hours for bachelor's. Most students required to take courses in arts/fine arts, English, history, humanities, mathematics, philosophy/religion, biological/physical sciences, social sciences.

FRESHMAN ADMISSIONS. Selection criteria: School record most important. Recommendations and extracurricular activities considered. ACT or SAT weigh heavily. **High school preparation:** 22 units required. Required units include English 4, mathematics 3, social science 2 and science 2. **Test requirements:** SAT or ACT (ACT preferred); score report by September 1.

1992 FRESHMAN CLASS PROFILE. 421 men and women applied, 166 accepted; 38 men enrolled, 93 women enrolled. 73% had high school GPA of 3.0 or higher, 26% between 2.0 and 2.99. 32% were in top tenth and 72% were in top quarter of graduating class. **Academic background:** Mid 50% of enrolled freshmen had ACT composite between 21-28. 97% submitted ACT scores. **Characteristics:** 85% from in state, 58% live in college housing, 13% have minority backgrounds, 2% are foreign students. Average age is 19.

FALL-TERM APPLICATIONS. $20 fee, may be waived for applicants with need. No closing date; priority given to applications received by May 1; applicants notified on a rolling basis; must reply within 4 weeks. Interview required for physical therapy, nursing applicants. Audition required for music applicants. Portfolio required for studio art, interior design applicants. Deferred and early admission available. EDP-F. Nursing candidates, physical therapy applicants should apply in fall of senior year.

STUDENT LIFE. Housing: Dormitories (coed). **Activities:** Student government, magazine, radio, student newspaper, television, yearbook, choral groups, drama, music ensembles, Band, Black Student Union, campus ministry, Community Service Club, Student-Alumni Relations Committee, International Club, Fellowship of Christian Athletes.

ATHLETICS. NCAA. **Intercollegiate:** Baseball M, basketball, cross-country, golf, soccer, softball W, tennis, volleyball W. **Intramural:** Baseball M, basketball, soccer, softball W, table tennis, tennis, volleyball.

STUDENT SERVICES. Aptitude testing, career counseling, employment service for undergraduates, freshman orientation, health services, personal counseling, placement service for graduates, special adviser for adult students, veterans counselor, campus ministry, services/facilities for handicapped.

ANNUAL EXPENSES. Tuition and fees: $8,700. **Room and board:** $4,200. **Books and supplies:** $400. **Other expenses:** $780.

FINANCIAL AID. 69% of freshmen, 74% of continuing students receive some form of aid. 56% of grants, 75% of loans, 48% of jobs based on need. 80 enrolled freshmen were judged to have need, all were offered aid. Academic, leadership, alumni affiliation, religious affiliation scholarships available. **Aid applications:** No closing date; priority given to applications received by April 15; applicants notified on a rolling basis beginning on or about March 1; must reply within 2 weeks.

ADDRESS/TELEPHONE. Martha Wade, Dean of Admissions/Enrollment Management, Maryville University, 13550 Conway Road, St. Louis, MO 63141. (314) 576-9350. (800) 627-9855. Fax: (314) 542-9085.

Mineral Area College
Flat River, Missouri — CB code: 6323

2-year public community college, coed. Founded in 1965. **Accreditation:** Regional. **Undergraduate enrollment:** 643 men, 771 women full time; 534 men, 1,116 women part time. **Faculty:** 180 total (59 full time), 11 with doctorates or other terminal degrees. **Location:** Rural campus in small town; 60 miles from St. Louis. **Calendar:** Semester, limited summer session. Saturday and extensive evening/early morning classes. **Microcomputers:** 30 located in computer centers.

DEGREES OFFERED. AA, AS, AAS. 321 associate degrees awarded in 1992.

UNDERGRADUATE MAJORS. Agricultural sciences, biology, business administration and management, business and management, business and office, chemistry, civil technology, communications, computer and information sciences, construction, criminal justice technology, drafting and design technology, early childhood education, education, electronic technology, elementary education, engineering, engineering and engineering-related technologies, English, fashion merchandising, finance, fine arts, foreign languages (multiple emphasis), home economics, industrial technology, information sciences and systems, junior high education, law enforcement and corrections technologies, liberal/general studies, manufacturing technology, marketing and distribution, mathematics, music, nursing, office supervision and management, physical sciences, prelaw, psychology, secondary education, secretarial and related programs, social sciences.

ACADEMIC PROGRAMS. 2-year transfer program, dual enrollment of high school students, honors program, independent study, internships, weekend college, cross-registration. **Remedial services:** Learning center, preadmission summer program, reduced course load, remedial instruction, special counselor, tutoring. **Placement/credit:** CLEP General and Subject, institutional tests; 30 credit hours maximum for associate degree.

ACADEMIC REQUIREMENTS. No policy requiring minimum GPA; records of students having academic difficulty are reviewed individually. 40% of freshmen return for sophomore year. Students must declare major by end of first year. **Graduation requirements:** 62 hours for associate (20 in major). Most students required to take courses in computer science, English, history, humanities, mathematics, biological/physical sciences, social sciences.

FRESHMAN ADMISSIONS. Selection criteria: Open admissions. Selective admissions to allied health programs. **Test requirements:** SAT/ACT required of nursing applicants. ACT strongly encouraged for others.

1992 FRESHMAN CLASS PROFILE. 463 men, 571 women enrolled. 2% were in top tenth and 29% were in top quarter of graduating class. **Academic background:** Mid 50% of enrolled freshmen had ACT composite between 15-20. 55% submitted ACT scores. **Characteristics:** 99% from in state, 100% commute. Average age is 22.

FALL-TERM APPLICATIONS. No fee. No closing date; applicants notified on a rolling basis beginning on or about February 15. Interview required for allied health applicants. Early admission available.

STUDENT LIFE. Activities: Student government, student newspaper, choral groups, concert band, drama, jazz band, music ensembles, musical theater, pep band, Young Democrats, Young Republicans, Baptist youth.

ATHLETICS. NJCAA. **Intercollegiate:** Baseball M, basketball, volleyball W.

STUDENT SERVICES. Aptitude testing, career counseling, employment service for undergraduates, freshman orientation, on-campus day care, personal counseling, placement service for graduates, special adviser for adult students, veterans counselor, services/facilities for handicapped.

ANNUAL EXPENSES. Tuition and fees: $990, $450 additional for out-of-district students, $510 additional for out-of-state students. **Books and supplies:** $550. **Other expenses:** $1,365.

FINANCIAL AID. 50% of freshmen, 45% of continuing students receive some form of aid. 87% of grants, all loans, all jobs based on need. 768 enrolled freshmen were judged to have need, all were offered aid. Academic, music/drama, art, athletic, leadership scholarships available. **Aid applications:** No closing date; priority given to applications received by April 15; applicants notified on a rolling basis beginning on or about April 1; must reply within 4 weeks.

ADDRESS/TELEPHONE. Barbara Bockenkamp, Registrar/Counselor, Mineral Area College, P.O. Box 1000, Flat River, MO 63601. (314) 431-4593.

Missouri Baptist College
St. Louis, Missouri CB code: 2258

4-year private liberal arts college, coed, affiliated with Southern Baptist Convention. Founded in 1963. **Accreditation:** Regional. **Undergraduate enrollment:** 234 men, 295 women full time; 316 men, 553 women part time. **Faculty:** 79 total (26 full time), 27 with doctorates or other terminal degrees. **Location:** Suburban campus in large city; 15 miles from downtown. **Calendar:** 4-4-1, limited summer session. Saturday and extensive evening/early morning classes. **Microcomputers:** 15 located in classrooms, computer centers. **Special facilities:** 65-acre wooded area with flora and fauna. **Additional facts:** Extension centers in Troy, Wentzville, Union, Jefferson County

DEGREES OFFERED. AS, BA, BS. 6 associate degrees awarded in 1992. 107 bachelor's degrees awarded. 31% in business and management, 14% education, 11% teacher education, 9% philosophy, religion, theology, 7% physical sciences, 10% social sciences.

UNDERGRADUATE MAJORS. Associate: Business and management, religion. **Bachelor's:** Accounting, behavioral sciences, biological and physical sciences, biology, business administration and management, business and management, chemistry, child development/care/guidance, communications, computer and information sciences, early childhood education, education, elementary education, English, English education, health education, history, humanities, humanities and social sciences, mathematics, mathematics education, music, music education, music performance, nursing, physical education, psychology, religion, religious education, religious music, science education, secondary education, social science education, social sciences, sociology, theological studies.

ACADEMIC PROGRAMS. Double major, honors program, independent study, internships, student-designed major, study abroad, teacher preparation, cross-registration; liberal arts/career combination in engineering. **ROTC:** Army. **Placement/credit:** AP, institutional tests; 30 credit hours maximum for bachelor's degree.

ACADEMIC REQUIREMENTS. Freshmen must earn minimum GPA of 2.0 to continue in good standing. 60% of freshmen return for sophomore year. Students must declare major by end of second year. **Graduation requirements:** 64 hours for associate (33 in major), 128 hours for bachelor's (30 in major). Most students required to take courses in arts/fine arts, computer science, English, foreign languages, history, humanities, mathematics, philosophy/religion, biological/physical sciences, social sciences. **Postgraduate studies:** 1% enter law school, 2% enter MBA programs, 4% enter other graduate study.

FRESHMAN ADMISSIONS. Selection criteria: Open admissions. **High school preparation:** 13 units recommended. Recommended units include biological science 2, English 4, foreign language 1, mathematics 2, physical science 2 and social science 2. **Test requirements:** SAT or ACT (ACT preferred) for placement and counseling only; score report by August 30. **Additional information:** Applicants with high school GPA below 2.0 admitted on probation.

1992 FRESHMAN CLASS PROFILE. 51 men, 48 women enrolled. 34% had high school GPA of 3.0 or higher, 64% between 2.0 and 2.99. **Academic background:** Mid 50% of enrolled freshmen had ACT composite between 16-21. 68% submitted ACT scores. **Characteristics:** 99% from in state, 85% commute, 11% have minority backgrounds, 1% are foreign students. Average age is 18.

FALL-TERM APPLICATIONS. $20 fee, may be waived for applicants with need. No closing date; applicants notified on a rolling basis. Interview required for academically weak applicants. Audition required for music applicants. CRDA. Deferred admission available.

STUDENT LIFE. Housing: Dormitories (men, women). **Activities:** Student government, student newspaper, yearbook, choral groups, drama, music ensembles, pep band, campus ministry, SGA, Phi Beta Lamda (Honor), BSU, ministerial alliance. **Additional information:** Religious observance required.

ATHLETICS. NAIA. **Intercollegiate:** Baseball M, basketball, golf, soccer, softball W, volleyball W.

STUDENT SERVICES. Career counseling, employment service for undergraduates, freshman orientation, health services, personal counseling, placement service for graduates, special adviser for adult students.

ANNUAL EXPENSES. Tuition and fees (1992-93): $6,220. **Room and board:** $2,800. **Books and supplies:** $600. **Other expenses:** $1,500.

FINANCIAL AID. 77% of freshmen, 80% of continuing students receive some form of aid. 37% of grants, 86% of loans, all jobs based on need. Academic, music/drama, athletic, leadership, alumni affiliation, religious affiliation scholarships available. **Aid applications:** No closing date; priority given to applications received by April 1; applicants notified on a rolling basis beginning on or about April 15; must reply within 2 weeks.

ADDRESS/TELEPHONE. Gloria Vertrees, Director of Admissions, Missouri Baptist College, 12542 Conway Road, St. Louis, MO 63141. (314) 434-1115 ext. 232. Fax: (314) 434-7596.

Missouri Southern State College
Joplin, Missouri CB code: 6322

4-year public business, teachers college, coed. Founded in 1965. **Accreditation:** Regional. **Undergraduate enrollment:** 1,692 men, 1,997 women full time; 858 men, 1,342 women part time. **Faculty:** 305 total (231 full time), 116 with doctorates or other terminal degrees. **Location:** Rural campus in large town; 138 miles from Kansas City, 70 miles from Springfield. **Calendar:** Semester, extensive summer session. Extensive evening/early morning classes. **Microcomputers:** 300 located in dormitories, libraries, classrooms, computer centers. **Special facilities:** Art museum, biological pond, nature trail, greenhouse. **Additional facts:** Extension courses offered in Lamar, Monett and Nevada (evening only).

DEGREES OFFERED. AA, AS, AAS, BA, BS. 136 associate degrees awarded in 1992. 9% in architecture and environmental design, 18% business/office and marketing/distribution, 7% computer sciences, 5% engineering technologies, 28% health sciences, 18% allied health, 7% multi/interdisciplinary studies. 463 bachelor's degrees awarded. 35% in business and management, 33% teacher education, 5% mathematics.

UNDERGRADUATE MAJORS. Associate: Accounting, business and management, business and office, business computer/console/peripheral equipment operation, business data entry equipment operation, business data processing and related programs, business data programming, computer programming, dental hygiene, drafting, drafting and design technology, environmental science, law enforcement and corrections technologies, legal assistant/paralegal, liberal/general studies, machine tool operation/machine shop, nursing, radiograph medical technology, secretarial and related programs, systems analysis. **Bachelor's:** Accounting, biology, business administration and management, business and management, business economics, chemistry, communications, computer and information sciences, computer programming, criminal justice studies, dramatic arts, education, education of the mentally handicapped, elementary education, English, environmental science, finance, fine arts, graphic design, history, information sciences and systems, journalism, junior high education, liberal/general studies, marketing management, mathematics, medical laboratory technologies, military science (Army), music, nursing, philosophy, physical sciences, physics, political science and government, prelaw, psychology, radio/television technology, secondary education, sociology, Spanish, special education, specific learning disabilities, speech.

ACADEMIC PROGRAMS. Accelerated program, double major, dual enrollment of high school students, honors program, independent study, internships, study abroad, teacher preparation, cross-registration; liberal arts/career combination in engineering. **Remedial services:** Learning center, preadmission summer program, reduced course load, remedial instruction, special counselor, tutoring. **ROTC:** Army. **Placement/credit:** AP, CLEP General and Subject, institutional tests.

ACADEMIC REQUIREMENTS. Freshmen must earn minimum GPA of 1.6 to continue in good standing. 56% of freshmen return for sophomore year. Students must declare major by end of first year. **Graduation requirements:** 64 hours for associate (38 in major), 128 hours for bachelor's (50 in major). Most students required to take courses in arts/fine arts, computer science, English, history, humanities, mathematics, biological/physical sciences, social sciences. **Postgraduate studies:** 30% from 2-year programs enter 4-year programs. 1% enter law school, 1% enter medical school, 2% enter MBA programs, 9% enter other graduate study.

FRESHMAN ADMISSIONS. Selection criteria: Minimum ACT composite score of 17 or rank in top two-thirds of class. **High school preparation:** 15 units recommended. Required and recommended units include English 3-4, mathematics 2-3, social science 2-2 and science 1-3. 3 units selected from foreign language, mathematics, physical or biological science, or social science also recommended. **Test requirements:** SAT or ACT (ACT preferred); score report by August 16.

1992 FRESHMAN CLASS PROFILE. 1,097 men applied, 1,097 accepted, 1,097 enrolled; 1,306 women applied, 1,306 accepted, 1,306 enrolled. 35% had high school GPA of 3.0 or higher, 46% between 2.0 and 2.99. 15% were in top tenth and 25% were in top quarter of graduating class. **Academic background:** Mid 50% of enrolled freshmen had ACT composite between 21-23. 94% submitted ACT scores. **Characteristics:** 95% from in state, 94% commute, 3% have minority backgrounds, 1% are foreign students, 2% join fraternities/sororities. Average age is 20.

FALL-TERM APPLICATIONS. $10 fee. Closing date August 16; priority given to applications received by August 8; applicants notified on a rolling basis. Interview required for allied health applicants. Audition required for music applicants. Portfolio recommended for art applicants. Deferred and early admission available. EDP-F.

STUDENT LIFE. Housing: Dormitories (men, women, coed); apartment, handicapped housing available. **Activities:** Student government, film, magazine, radio, student newspaper, television, yearbook, choral groups, concert band, drama, jazz band, marching band, music ensembles, musical theater, pep band, string orchestra, fraternities, sororities.

ATHLETICS. NCAA. **Intercollegiate:** Baseball M, basketball, cross-country, football M, golf M, soccer M, softball W, tennis W, track and field, volleyball W. **Intramural:** Basketball, golf M, racquetball, rifle, rugby M, softball, swimming, table tennis, tennis, volleyball.

STUDENT SERVICES. Aptitude testing, career counseling, employment service for undergraduates, freshman orientation, health services, on-campus day care, personal counseling, placement service for graduates, special adviser for adult students, veterans counselor, services/facilities for handicapped.

ANNUAL EXPENSES. Tuition and fees (1992-93): $1,598, $1,392 additional for out-of-state students. **Room and board:** $2,490. **Books and supplies:** $400. **Other expenses:** $900.

FINANCIAL AID. 75% of freshmen, 76% of continuing students receive some form of aid. 69% of grants, 93% of loans, 25% of jobs based on need. 634 enrolled freshmen were judged to have need, all were offered aid. Academic, music/drama, art, athletic scholarships available. **Aid applications:** No closing date; priority given to applications received by February 15; applicants notified on a rolling basis beginning on or about February 15; must reply within 2 weeks.

ADDRESS/TELEPHONE. Richard D. Humphrey, Director of Admissions, Missouri Southern State College, Newman and Duquesne Roads, Joplin, MO 64801-1595. (417) 625-9300 ext. 537.

Missouri Valley College
Marshall, Missouri — CB code: 6413

Admissions: 67% of applicants accepted
Based on: ••• Activities, essay, interview, recommendations
•• School record, special talents, test scores
Completion: 87% of freshmen end year in good standing
12% enter graduate study

4-year private liberal arts college, coed, affiliated with Presbyterian Church (USA). Founded in 1888. **Accreditation:** Regional. **Undergraduate enrollment:** 700 men, 398 women full time; 10 men, 45 women part time. **Faculty:** 67 total (60 full time), 39 with doctorates or other terminal degrees. **Location:** Rural campus in large town; 85 miles from Kansas City. **Calendar:** 4-1-4, limited summer session. **Microcomputers:** Located in libraries, computer centers. **Special facilities:** Burns Multipurpose Athletic Complex.

DEGREES OFFERED. AA, BA, BS. 1 associate degree awarded in 1992. 100% in business and management. 92 bachelor's degrees awarded. 17% in business and management, 29% communications, 6% education, 11% teacher education, 6% mathematics, 14% psychology.

UNDERGRADUATE MAJORS. Associate: Small business management and ownership. **Bachelor's:** Accounting, actuarial sciences, agribusiness, alcohol and drug studies counseling, applied mathematics, biological and physical sciences, biology, business administration and management, business economics, communications, computer and information sciences, dramatic arts, economics, education, elementary education, English, fine arts, history, humanities and social sciences, journalism, junior high education, liberal/general studies, marketing management, mathematics, mathematics education, parks and recreation management, philosophy, physical education, political science and government, prelaw, psychology, public administration, radio/television broadcasting, religion, religious education, science education, secondary education, social sciences, social studies education, sociology, special education, speech/communication/theater education.

ACADEMIC PROGRAMS. Accelerated program, cooperative education, double major, dual enrollment of high school students, honors program, independent study, internships, student-designed major, teacher preparation. **Remedial services:** Learning center, preadmission summer program, reduced course load, remedial instruction, special counselor, tutoring. **Placement/credit:** AP, CLEP General and Subject, institutional tests; 30 credit hours maximum for bachelor's degree.

ACADEMIC REQUIREMENTS. 82% of freshmen return for sophomore year. Students must declare major by end of second year. **Graduation requirements:** 128 hours for bachelor's. Most students required to take courses in arts/fine arts, computer science, English, history, humanities, mathematics, philosophy/religion, biological/physical sciences, social sciences.

FRESHMAN ADMISSIONS. Selection criteria: Admissions based on high school record, class rank, SAT or ACT scores, extracurricular activities, personal attributes, interview, and recommendations. **High school preparation:** 16 units recommended. Recommended units include English 4, mathematics 2, social science 3 and science 2. **Test requirements:** SAT or ACT (ACT preferred). Institutional ability-to-benefit test required of incoming students.

1992 FRESHMAN CLASS PROFILE. 900 men applied, 600 accepted, 258 enrolled; 600 women applied, 400 accepted, 118 enrolled. 30% had high school GPA of 3.0 or higher, 65% between 2.0 and 2.99. **Academic background:** Mid 50% of enrolled freshmen had ACT composite between 16-20. 85% submitted ACT scores. **Characteristics:** 65% from in state, 82% live in college housing, 32% have minority backgrounds, 1% are foreign students. Average age is 18.

FALL-TERM APPLICATIONS. $10 fee, may be waived for applicants with need. No closing date; applicants notified on a rolling basis. Interview recommended. Audition recommended for drama applicants. Portfolio recommended for fine arts applicants. Essay recommended for academically weak applicants. Deferred and early admission available.

STUDENT LIFE. Housing: Dormitories (men, women); apartment, fraternity, sorority housing available. Honors dormitories; separate housing facilities available for students in alcohol and drug studies. **Activities:** Student government, film, radio, student newspaper, television, yearbook, choral groups, dance, drama, jazz band, music ensembles, musical theater, pep band, symphony orchestra, fraternities, sororities, Fellowship of Christian Athletes, minority and service organizations.

ATHLETICS. NAIA. **Intercollegiate:** Baseball M, basketball, cross-country, football M, soccer, softball W, tennis, track and field, volleyball W, wrestling M. **Intramural:** Baseball M, basketball, bowling M, cross-country, soccer, softball, table tennis, track and field, volleyball.

STUDENT SERVICES. Aptitude testing, career counseling, employment service for undergraduates, freshman orientation, personal counseling, placement service for graduates.

ANNUAL EXPENSES. Tuition and fees: $8,650. **Room and board:** $4,950. **Books and supplies:** $1,000. **Other expenses:** $1,880.

FINANCIAL AID. 97% of freshmen, 97% of continuing students receive some form of aid. 88% of grants, all jobs based on need. 280 enrolled freshmen were judged to have need, all were offered aid. Academic, music/drama, art, athletic, leadership, alumni affiliation scholarships available. **Aid applications:** Closing date September 1; priority given to applications received by April 15; applicants notified on or about September 1; must reply by May 1 or within 4 weeks if notified thereafter.

ADDRESS/TELEPHONE. Chadwick B. Freeman, VP Admis/Fin Aid, Missouri Valley College, 500 East College Street, Marshall, MO 65340. (816) 886-6924 ext. 117. Fax: (816) 886-9818.

Missouri Western State College
St. Joseph, Missouri — CB code: 6625

4-year public college of arts and sciences and business college, coed. Founded in 1915. **Accreditation:** Regional. **Undergraduate enrollment:** 1,532 men, 2,131 women full time; 469 men, 961 women part time. **Faculty:** 296 total (162 full time), 96 with doctorates or other terminal degrees. **Location:** Suburban campus in small city; 48 miles from Kansas City. **Calendar:** Semester, extensive summer session. Saturday and extensive evening/early morning classes. **Microcomputers:** 200 located in dormitories, libraries, classrooms, computer centers. **Special facilities:** Biology nature study area, planetarium.

DEGREES OFFERED. AS, BA, BS. 72 associate degrees awarded in 1992. 31% in business/office and marketing/distribution, 23% law, 45% parks/recreation, protective services, public affairs. 501 bachelor's degrees awarded. 23% in business and management, 14% teacher education, 13% health sciences, 17% parks/recreation, protective services, public affairs, 7% psychology.

UNDERGRADUATE MAJORS. Associate: Accounting, business data processing and related programs, civil technology, criminal justice technology, electronic technology, finance, legal assistant/paralegal, retailing. **Bachelor's:** Accounting, art education, biological and physical sciences, biology, business administration and management, chemistry, civil technology, commercial art, communications, computer programming, criminal justice studies, economics, electronic technology, elementary education, English, English education, fine arts, foreign languages education, French, history, information sciences and systems, marketing management, mathematics, medical laboratory technologies, music, music education, nursing, parks and recreation management, political science and government, psychology, secondary education, social work, Spanish, special education, speech, speech/communication/theater education.

ACADEMIC PROGRAMS. Double major, dual enrollment of high school students, honors program, internships, teacher preparation. **Remedial services:** Learning center, preadmission summer program, reduced course load, remedial instruction, special counselor, tutoring. **ROTC:** Army. **Placement/credit:** CLEP General and Subject, institutional tests; 30 credit hours maximum for associate degree; 30 credit hours maximum for bachelor's degree.

ACADEMIC REQUIREMENTS. Freshmen must earn minimum GPA of 2.0 to continue in good standing. 57% of freshmen return for sophomore year. Students must declare major by end of second year. **Graduation requirements:** 62 hours for associate (42 in major), 124 hours for bachelor's (60 in major). Most students required to take courses in English, history, humanities, mathematics, biological/physical sciences, social sciences. **Post-**

graduate studies: 60% from 2-year programs enter 4-year programs. 1% enter law school, 4% enter medical school, 5% enter MBA programs, 10% enter other graduate study.

FRESHMAN ADMISSIONS. Selection criteria: Open admissions. School record, test scores, interview, and recommendations important for nursing, mathematics, computer science, and social work applicants. Special talents important for music and art applicants. **High school preparation:** 14 units recommended. Recommended units include biological science 1, English 4, foreign language 2, mathematics 3, physical science 1 and social science 3. **Test requirements:** ACT for placement and counseling only; score report by August 1.

1992 FRESHMAN CLASS PROFILE. 382 men, 510 women enrolled. 7% were in top tenth and 29% were in top quarter of graduating class. **Academic background:** Mid 50% of enrolled freshmen had ACT composite between 17-21. 100% submitted ACT scores. **Characteristics:** 84% from in state, 75% commute, 12% have minority backgrounds. Average age is 21.

FALL-TERM APPLICATIONS. $30 fee. Closing date July 30; priority given to applications received by June 30; applicants notified on a rolling basis. Interview required for nursing, education, social work applicants. Audition recommended for music applicants. Portfolio recommended for art applicants. Early admission available.

STUDENT LIFE. Housing: Dormitories (coed); apartment, fraternity housing available. **Activities:** Student government, student newspaper, yearbook, choral groups, concert band, dance, drama, marching band, music ensembles, musical theater, pep band, symphony orchestra, fraternities, sororities, black and international student associations.

ATHLETICS. NCAA. **Intercollegiate:** Baseball M, basketball, football M, golf M, softball W, tennis W, volleyball W. **Intramural:** Archery, badminton, baseball, basketball, bowling, golf, handball, racquetball, rugby M, soccer M, softball, table tennis, tennis, volleyball.

STUDENT SERVICES. Aptitude testing, career counseling, employment service for undergraduates, freshman orientation, health services, on-campus day care, personal counseling, placement service for graduates, veterans counselor, services/facilities for handicapped.

ANNUAL EXPENSES. Tuition and fees (1992-93): $1,822, $1,638 additional for out-of-state students. **Room and board:** $2,480. **Books and supplies:** $500. **Other expenses:** $1,500.

FINANCIAL AID. 73% of continuing students receive some form of aid. 72% of grants, 89% of loans, 46% of jobs based on need. Academic, music/drama, athletic, leadership, minority scholarships available. **Aid applications:** No closing date; priority given to applications received by April 1; applicants notified on a rolling basis beginning on or about May 15; must reply within 2 weeks.

ADDRESS/TELEPHONE. Howard McCauley, Director of Admissions, Missouri Western State College, 4525 Downs Drive, St. Joseph, MO 64507-2294. (816) 271-4200.

Moberly Area Community College
Moberly, Missouri — CB code: 6414

2-year public community college, coed. Founded in 1927. **Accreditation:** Regional. **Undergraduate enrollment:** 396 men, 638 women full time; 274 men, 538 women part time. **Faculty:** 86 total (48 full time), 2 with doctorates or other terminal degrees. **Location:** Rural campus in large town; 35 miles from Columbia. **Calendar:** Semester, limited summer session. Saturday and extensive evening/early morning classes. **Microcomputers:** 48 located in libraries, classrooms, computer centers.

DEGREES OFFERED. AA, AAS. 214 associate degrees awarded in 1992. 13% in business/office and marketing/distribution, 18% health sciences, 59% multi/interdisciplinary studies.

UNDERGRADUATE MAJORS. Accounting, agribusiness, agricultural business and management, agricultural sciences, automotive technology, biology, botany, business administration and management, business and management, business and office, business data processing and related programs, chemistry, child development/care/guidance, data processing, dramatic arts, early childhood education, education, electronic technology, elementary education, emergency medical technologies, English, fine arts, industrial technology, junior high education, law enforcement and corrections, legal secretary, liberal/general studies, marketing and distribution, marketing management, mathematics, medical secretary, music, nursing, office supervision and management, parks and recreation management, physical sciences, physics, practical nursing, psychology, secondary education, secretarial and related programs, small business management and ownership, social sciences, visual and performing arts, word processing, zoology.

ACADEMIC PROGRAMS. 2-year transfer program, cooperative education, dual enrollment of high school students, internships. **Remedial services:** Learning center, remedial instruction, special counselor, tutoring. **Placement/credit:** CLEP General and Subject, institutional tests; 30 credit hours maximum for associate degree.

ACADEMIC REQUIREMENTS. Freshmen must earn minimum GPA of 2.0 to continue in good standing. 65% of freshmen return for sophomore year. Students must declare major on enrollment. **Graduation requirements:** 64 hours for associate (46 in major). Most students required to take courses in computer science, English, history, humanities, mathematics, biological/physical sciences, social sciences.

FRESHMAN ADMISSIONS. Selection criteria: Open admissions. Applicants to nursing or allied health programs subject to selection by admission committee. **Test requirements:** SAT or ACT (ACT preferred) for placement and counseling only; score report by September 9.

1992 FRESHMAN CLASS PROFILE. 356 men, 595 women enrolled. 3% were in top tenth and 17% were in top quarter of graduating class. **Characteristics:** 95% from in state, 98% commute, 11% have minority backgrounds, 1% are foreign students. Average age is 24.

FALL-TERM APPLICATIONS. No fee. No closing date; applicants notified on a rolling basis.

STUDENT LIFE. Housing: Dormitories (men, women). Housing for 10 male students and 30 female students only. **Activities:** Student government, student newspaper, yearbook, choral groups, drama, jazz band, music ensembles, pep band, NGN Brothers Ox, Phi Theta Kappa, marketing association, Student Nurses Association, Practical Nurses Assoication.

ATHLETICS. NJCAA. **Intercollegiate:** Basketball. **Intramural:** Baseball, basketball, volleyball.

STUDENT SERVICES. Aptitude testing, career counseling, employment service for undergraduates, on-campus day care, personal counseling, placement service for graduates, veterans counselor, services/facilities for handicapped.

ANNUAL EXPENSES. Tuition and fees (1992-93): $790, $750 additional for out-of-district students, $2,130 additional for out-of-state students. **Books and supplies:** $400. **Other expenses:** $1,025.

FINANCIAL AID. 30% of freshmen, 41% of continuing students receive some form of aid. Grants, loans, jobs available. 251 enrolled freshmen were judged to have need, all were offered aid. Academic, music/drama, athletic, leadership scholarships available. **Aid applications:** Closing date June 30; applicants notified on or about July 1; must reply by July 15.

ADDRESS/TELEPHONE. Donald Vangsnes, Dean of Student Services, Moberly Area Community College, College and Rollins Streets, Moberly, MO 65270. (816) 263-4110. Fax: (816) 263-6252.

National College
Kansas City, Missouri — CB code: 5357

4-year proprietary business college, coed. **Accreditation:** Regional candidate. **Undergraduate enrollment:** 225 men and women. **Faculty:** 18 total (2 full time). **Location:** Urban campus in large city. **Calendar:** Quarter. **Microcomputers:** 16 located in computer centers.

DEGREES OFFERED. AAS, BS. 24 associate degrees awarded in 1992. 70% in business and management, 30% computer sciences. 41 bachelor's degrees awarded. 70% in business and management, 30% computer sciences.

UNDERGRADUATE MAJORS. Associate: Business administration and management, business and management, computer and information sciences, tourism, transportation and travel marketing. **Bachelor's:** Business administration and management, business and management, computer and information sciences.

ACADEMIC PROGRAMS. Double major, independent study. **Remedial services:** Tutoring. **Placement/credit:** CLEP General and Subject, institutional tests; 62 credit hours maximum for associate degree; 144 credit hours maximum for bachelor's degree.

ACADEMIC REQUIREMENTS. Freshmen must earn minimum GPA of 2.0 to continue in good standing. 90% of freshmen return for sophomore year. Students must declare major on enrollment. **Graduation requirements:** 98 hours for associate (98 in major), 194 hours for bachelor's. Most students required to take courses in computer science, English, foreign languages, humanities, mathematics, biological/physical sciences, social sciences. **Post-graduate studies:** 75% from 2-year programs enter 4-year programs. 5% enter law school, 10% enter MBA programs.

FRESHMAN ADMISSIONS. Selection criteria: Open admissions.

1992 FRESHMAN CLASS PROFILE. 79 men and women enrolled. 20% had high school GPA of 3.0 or higher, 60% between 2.0 and 2.99. **Characteristics:** 60% from in state, 100% commute, 52% have minority backgrounds, 5% are foreign students. Average age is 25.

FALL-TERM APPLICATIONS. $25 fee. Closing date August 31; applicants notified on a rolling basis. Interview required. Early admission available.

STUDENT LIFE. Activities: Student government, student newspaper.

STUDENT SERVICES. Aptitude testing, career counseling, employment service for undergraduates, freshman orientation, personal counseling, placement service for graduates, special adviser for adult students.

ANNUAL EXPENSES. Tuition and fees (1992-93): $6,363. **Books and supplies:** $600.

FINANCIAL AID. 100% of freshmen, 98% of continuing students receive some form of aid. 93% of grants, 64% of loans, all jobs based on need. Academic scholarships available. **Aid applications:** No closing date; applicants notified on a rolling basis beginning on or about June 4; must reply by registration.

ADDRESS/TELEPHONE. Lawrence Smith, Senior Admissions Representative, National College, 600 West 39th Street, Kansas City, MO 64111. (816) 753-4554. Fax: (816) 753-5707.

North Central Missouri College
Trenton, Missouri — CB code: 6830

2-year public community college, coed. Founded in 1925. **Accreditation:** Regional. **Undergraduate enrollment:** 1,044 men and women. **Location:** Rural campus in small town; 90 miles from Kansas City. **Calendar:** Semester. **Additional facts:** Evening classes offered at sites in many area communities.

FRESHMAN ADMISSIONS. Selection criteria: Open admissions. Selective admissions for nursing applicants.

ANNUAL EXPENSES. Tuition and fees: $1,020, $450 additional for out-of-district students, $1,380 additional for out-of-state students. **Room and board:** $900 room only. **Books and supplies:** $460. **Other expenses:** $976.

ADDRESS/TELEPHONE. Gloria Carpenter, Dean of Student Services, North Central Missouri College, 1301 Main Street, Trenton, MO 64683. (816) 359-3948 ext.401.

Northeast Missouri State University
Kirksville, Missouri — CB code: 6483

Admissions: 77% of applicants accepted
Based on:
••• School record, test scores
•• Activities, essay
• Interview, recommendations, special talents
Completion: 92% of freshmen end year in good standing
57% graduate, 33% of these enter graduate study

4-year public liberal arts and sciences university, coed. Founded in 1867. **Accreditation:** Regional. **Undergraduate enrollment:** 2,446 men, 3,038 women full time; 112 men, 146 women part time. **Graduate enrollment:** 44 men, 122 women full time; 3 men, 14 women part time. **Faculty:** 470 total (337 full time), 264 with doctorates or other terminal degrees. **Location:** Rural campus in large town; 220 miles from St. Louis, 150 miles from Kansas City and from Des Moines, Iowa. **Calendar:** Semester, extensive summer session. **Microcomputers:** 860 located in dormitories, libraries, classrooms, computer centers. **Special facilities:** Observatory, art gallery, greenhouse, residential colleges, university museum specializing in local history and artifacts, university farm, human performance laboratory, newly expanded library, foreign language laboratory, speech and hearing clinic, biofeedback laboratory. **Additional facts:** Designated Missouri's public liberal arts and sciences institution.

DEGREES OFFERED. BA, BS, BFA, MA, MS. 1,065 bachelor's degrees awarded in 1992. 26% in business and management, 5% communications, 9% health sciences, 9% letters/literature, 6% life sciences, 8% psychology, 13% social sciences, 5% visual and performing arts. Graduate degrees offered in 24 major fields of study.

UNDERGRADUATE MAJORS. Accounting, agricultural economics, agricultural sciences, agronomy, animal sciences, applied mathematics, biology, business administration and management, chemistry, commercial art, computer and information sciences, criminal justice studies, dramatic arts, economics, English, equestrian science, finance, fine arts, French, German, health sciences, history, industrial science, journalism, marketing management, mathematics, music, music performance, nursing, philosophy, physics, political science and government, predentistry, prelaw, premedical technology, premedicine, prepharmacy, preveterinary, psychology, religion, sociology, Spanish, speech, speech correction, speech pathology/audiology, studio art.

ACADEMIC PROGRAMS. Accelerated program, dual enrollment of high school students, honors program, independent study, internships, study abroad, teacher preparation, visiting/exchange student program. **Remedial services:** Learning center, reduced course load, tutoring, writing and study skills center, math labs. **ROTC:** Army. **Placement/credit:** AP, CLEP General and Subject, IB, institutional tests.

ACADEMIC REQUIREMENTS. Freshmen must earn minimum GPA of 2.0 to continue in good standing. 83% of freshmen return for sophomore year. Students must declare major by end of second year. **Graduation requirements:** 124 hours for bachelor's (30 in major). Most students required to take courses in arts/fine arts, computer science, English, foreign languages, history, humanities, mathematics, philosophy/religion, biological/physical sciences, social sciences. **Postgraduate studies:** 2% enter law school, 2% enter medical school, 3% enter MBA programs, 26% enter other graduate study. **Additional information:** Offers interdisciplinary approach to education while emphasizing active learning and undergraduate research and writing.

FRESHMAN ADMISSIONS. Selection criteria: High school performance (class rank, GPA, college preparatory curriculum), test scores (SAT, ACT or PSAT/NMSQT), essay, special ability, talent, or achievement all considered. Required and recommended units include English 4-4, foreign language 2-2, mathematics 3-3, social science 2-3 and science 2-3. College-preparatory program recommended. One fine arts and 1 computer science recommended. **Test requirements:** SAT or ACT (ACT preferred); score report by June 1. **Additional information:** Admission for out-of-state students is competitive.

1992 FRESHMAN CLASS PROFILE. 2,096 men applied, 1,588 accepted, 600 enrolled; 2,892 women applied, 2,251 accepted, 801 enrolled. 77% had high school GPA of 3.0 or higher, 23% between 2.0 and 2.99. **Academic background:** Mid 50% of enrolled freshmen had SAT-V between 420-550, SAT-M between 460-610; ACT composite between 23-28. 1% submitted SAT scores, 98% submitted ACT scores. **Characteristics:** 69% from in state, 97% live in college housing, 7% have minority backgrounds, 4% are foreign students, 17% join fraternities/sororities. Average age is 18.

FALL-TERM APPLICATIONS. No fee. Closing date March 1; priority given to applications received by November 15; applicants notified on a rolling basis beginning on or about January 1; must reply by May 1. Essay required. Audition recommended. Portfolio recommended. CRDA. Deferred and early admission available. Early admission application must be received by November 15.

STUDENT LIFE. Housing: Dormitories (men, women, coed); apartment, sorority, handicapped housing available. Study wings, no-smoking floors, international roommate options, quiet floors, faculty advisers in residence halls, weight equipment (Nautilus), and computer laboratories in the residence halls. **Activities:** Student government, magazine, radio, student newspaper, television, yearbook, choral groups, concert band, dance, drama, jazz band, marching band, music ensembles, musical theater, opera, pep band, symphony orchestra, fraternities, sororities, religious organizations, Association of Black Collegians, Young Democrats, College Republicans, NOW, United Campus Ministry, Amnesty International, Blue Key, Cardinal Key, Circle K. **Additional information:** All students encouraged to affiliate with at least 1 organization, with over 150 organizations providing leadership development opportunities. Low-cost entertainment available.

ATHLETICS. NCAA. **Intercollegiate:** Baseball M, basketball, cross-country, football M, golf, rifle, soccer, softball W, swimming, tennis, track and field, volleyball W, wrestling M. **Intramural:** Archery, badminton, basketball, bowling, cross-country, diving, football M, golf, handball, racquetball, soccer, softball, swimming, table tennis, tennis, track and field, volleyball, wrestling M.

STUDENT SERVICES. Aptitude testing, career counseling, employment service for undergraduates, freshman orientation, health services, on-campus day care, personal counseling, placement service for graduates, veterans counselor, Disabled student services, services/facilities for handicapped.

ANNUAL EXPENSES. Tuition and fees: $2,456, $1,880 additional for out-of-state students. **Room and board:** $3,080. **Books and supplies:** $400. **Other expenses:** $1,690.

FINANCIAL AID. 88% of freshmen, 75% of continuing students receive some form of aid. 31% of grants, 97% of loans, 14% of jobs based on need. 691 enrolled freshmen were judged to have need, all were offered aid. Academic, music/drama, art, athletic, state/district residency, leadership, alumni affiliation scholarships available. **Aid applications:** No closing date; priority given to applications received by April 1; applicants notified on a rolling basis beginning on or about April 15; must reply within 2 weeks. **Additional information:** Out-of-state students whose parents work in Missouri may deduct $1 for every dollar paid in Missouri income taxes from the out-of-state tuition.

ADDRESS/TELEPHONE. Kathy Rieck, Dean of Admission and Records, Northeast Missouri State University, MC 205, Kirksville, MO 63501-9980. (816) 785-4114. Fax: (816) 785-4181.

Northwest Missouri Community College
St. Joseph, Missouri — CB code: 0376

2-year proprietary community, technical college, coed. Founded in 1879. **Accreditation:** Regional. **Undergraduate enrollment:** 565 men and women. **Faculty:** 39 total (35 full time). **Location:** Suburban campus in small city; 32 miles from Kansas City International Airport. **Calendar:** Semester. Extensive evening/early morning classes. **Microcomputers:** Located in classrooms, computer centers.

DEGREES OFFERED. AA, AAS. 48 associate degrees awarded in 1992. 14% in business and management, 44% business/office and marketing/distribution, 19% law, 23% trade and industry.

UNDERGRADUATE MAJORS. Accounting, advertising, agribusiness, agricultural business and management, architecture, business administration and management, business and management, business and office, business computer/console/peripheral equipment operation, business economics, communications, computer and information sciences, computer programming, criminal justice studies, criminal justice technology, criminology, data processing, drafting, drafting and design technology, engineering and engineering-related technologies, fashion merchandising, finance, gerontology, health care administration, legal assistant/paralegal, legal secretary, management science, mathematics, medical laboratory technologies, nursing, office supervision and management, personnel management, prelaw, premedicine, prepharmacy, psychology, public administration, public relations, secretarial and related programs, small business management and ownership, sociology, sports medicine, tourism.

ACADEMIC PROGRAMS. 2-year transfer program, double major, dual enrollment of high school students, independent study, internships, student-designed major. **Remedial services:** Learning center, remedial instruction, tutoring.

ACADEMIC REQUIREMENTS. Freshmen must earn minimum GPA of 2.0 to continue in good standing. 85% of freshmen return for sophomore year. Students must declare major on application. **Graduation requirements:** 64 hours for associate. Most students required to take courses in arts/fine arts, computer science, English, history, mathematics, biological/physical sciences, social sciences.

FRESHMAN ADMISSIONS. Selection criteria: GPA and entrance test considered. Letters of reference considered for nursing program. **Test requirements:** ACT for placement and counseling only.

1992 FRESHMAN CLASS PROFILE. 146 men and women enrolled. **Characteristics:** 80% from in state, 100% commute, 18% have minority backgrounds. Average age is 19.

FALL-TERM APPLICATIONS. $130 fee. No closing date; applicants notified on a rolling basis. Deferred admission available. Classes start every 6 weeks. Application may be made anytime by scheduling interview with representative.

STUDENT LIFE. Activities: Student government, student newspaper, television, yearbook.

ATHLETICS. NJCAA. **Intramural:** Softball, volleyball.

STUDENT SERVICES. Aptitude testing, career counseling, employment service for undergraduates, freshman orientation, personal counseling, placement service for graduates, veterans counselor, services/facilities for handicapped.

ANNUAL EXPENSES. Tuition and fees (1992-93): $7,680.

FINANCIAL AID. 90% of freshmen, 90% of continuing students receive some form of aid. **Aid applications:** Closing date May 1; applicants notified on a rolling basis beginning on or about May 30.

ADDRESS/TELEPHONE. Dana Davis, Director of Admissions, Northwest Missouri Community College, 4315 Pickett Road, St. Joseph, MO 64503-2911. (816) 233-9563. (800) 748-1415. Fax: (816) 364-0413.

Northwest Missouri State University
Maryville, Missouri CB code: 6488

Admissions: 81% of applicants accepted
Based on: ••• School record
•• Test scores
• Activities, essay, interview, recommendations
Completion: 79% of freshmen end year in good standing
46% graduate

4-year public university, coed. Founded in 1905. **Accreditation:** Regional. **Undergraduate enrollment:** 2,163 men, 2,623 women full time; 226 men, 240 women part time. **Graduate enrollment:** 71 men, 72 women full time; 120 men, 348 women part time. **Faculty:** 271 total (244 full time), 139 with doctorates or other terminal degrees. **Location:** Rural campus in large town; 90 miles from Kansas City. **Calendar:** Semester, extensive summer session. **Microcomputers:** 1,560 located in dormitories, libraries, classrooms, computer centers, campus-wide network. **Special facilities:** Elementary laboratory school and preschool facilities, 750-acre farm. **Additional facts:** Nation's first public electronic campus.

DEGREES OFFERED. BA, BS, BFA, MA, MS, MBA, MEd. 834 bachelor's degrees awarded in 1992. 22% in business and management, 8% communications, 26% teacher education, 7% psychology, 8% social sciences. Graduate degrees offered in 29 major fields of study.

UNDERGRADUATE MAJORS. Accounting, agribusiness, agricultural computer science, agricultural economics, agricultural education, agricultural sciences, agriculture computer science, agronomy, animal sciences, art education, biology, botany, business administration and management, business and management, business economics, business education, chemistry, clinical laboratory science, computer and information sciences, dairy, dietetic aide/assistant, dramatic arts, early childhood education, ecology, economics, education of the mentally handicapped, elementary education, English, English education, family/consumer resource management, fashion merchandising, finance, fine arts, food science and nutrition, foreign languages education, French, geography, geology, health education, history, home economics education, horticultural science, horticulture, human environment and housing, humanities, industrial arts education, industrial technology, international business management, journalism, junior high education, management data processing, management information systems, marketing and distribution, marketing management, mathematics, mathematics education, molecular biology, music, music education, office supervision and management, organizational communication, personnel management, philosophy, physical education, physics, political science and government, predentistry, prelaw, premedicine, preveterinary, psychobiology, psychology, psychology/sociology, public administration, public relations, radio/television broadcasting, recreation and community services technologies, remedial education, science education, secondary education, small business management and ownership, social science education, social sciences, sociology, Spanish, special education, specific learning disabilities, speech, speech/communication/theater education, studio art, textiles and clothing, trade and industrial education, trade and industrial supervision and management, wildlife management, zoology.

ACADEMIC PROGRAMS. Double major, dual enrollment of high school students, education specialist degree, independent study, internships, study abroad, teacher preparation, Washington semester, cross-registration. **Remedial services:** Learning center, reduced course load, remedial instruction, special counselor, tutoring. **ROTC:** Army. **Placement/credit:** AP, CLEP General and Subject, institutional tests; 30 credit hours maximum for bachelor's degree.

ACADEMIC REQUIREMENTS. Freshmen must earn minimum GPA of 1.75 to continue in good standing. 69% of freshmen return for sophomore year. Students must declare major by end of second year. **Graduation requirements:** 124 hours for bachelor's (60 in major). Most students required to take courses in arts/fine arts, computer science, English, history, humanities, mathematics, philosophy/religion, biological/physical sciences, social sciences.

FRESHMAN ADMISSIONS. Selection criteria: In-state applicants should rank in top two-thirds of class or have ACT composite score of 20; out-of-state applicants, top half of classtop half of class or ACT composite score of 21 or higher. Recommended units include English 4, foreign language 2, mathematics 3, social science 3 and science 2. **Test requirements:** SAT or ACT (ACT preferred); score report by August 1.

1992 FRESHMAN CLASS PROFILE. 1,083 men applied, 862 accepted, 506 enrolled; 1,633 women applied, 1,326 accepted, 739 enrolled. **Academic background:** Mid 50% of enrolled freshmen had ACT composite between 19-23. 97% submitted ACT scores. **Characteristics:** 52% from in state, 90% live in college housing, 6% have minority backgrounds, 1% are foreign students, 21% join fraternities/sororities. Average age is 18.

FALL-TERM APPLICATIONS. $15 fee, may be waived for applicants with need. No closing date; applicants notified on a rolling basis. Interview recommended. Audition recommended for dramatic arts, music applicants. Portfolio recommended for art applicants. Essay recommended. CRDA. Deferred and early admission available.

STUDENT LIFE. Housing: Dormitories (men, women, coed); fraternity, sorority housing available. Every room in dormitories has computer terminal. **Activities:** Student government, film, radio, student newspaper, television, yearbook, choral groups, concert band, dance, drama, jazz band, marching band, music ensembles, musical theater, pep band, fraternities, sororities, Cardinal Key, Circle K, International Student Organization, Alliance of Black Collegians, Kaleidoscope Peace, KIDS, Sigma Society, Young Democrats, Young Republicans.

ATHLETICS. NCAA. **Intercollegiate:** Baseball M, basketball, cross-country, football M, softball W, tennis, track and field, volleyball W. **Intramural:** Badminton, basketball, bowling, cross-country, golf, racquetball, skiing, softball, swimming, table tennis, tennis, track and field, volleyball.

STUDENT SERVICES. Aptitude testing, career counseling, freshman orientation, health services, on-campus day care, personal counseling, placement service for graduates, veterans counselor, services/facilities for handicapped.

ANNUAL EXPENSES. Tuition and fees: $2,010, $1,560 additional for out-of-state students. **Room and board:** $3,000. **Books and supplies:** $250. **Other expenses:** $1,000.

FINANCIAL AID. 79% of freshmen, 79% of continuing students receive some form of aid. 50% of grants, 96% of loans, 42% of jobs based on need. Academic, leadership scholarships available. **Aid applications:** No closing date; priority given to applications received by April 1; applicants notified on a rolling basis beginning on or about May 1; must reply within 2 weeks.

ADDRESS/TELEPHONE. Michael Walsh, Executive Director of Enrollment Management, Northwest Missouri State University, 800 University Drive, Maryville, MO 64468-6001. (816) 562-1148. (800) 633 1175. Fax: (816) 562-1900.

Ozark Christian College
Joplin, Missouri CB code: 6542

4-year private Bible college, coed, affiliated with nondenominational Christian Churches/Churches of Christ. Founded in 1942. **Undergraduate enrollment:** 282 men, 177 women full time; 40 men, 59 women part time. **Faculty:** 44 total (24 full time). **Location:** Urban campus in large town; 70 miles from Springfield, 100 miles from Tulsa, Oklahoma. **Calendar:** Semester. **Microcomputers:** 12 located in classrooms, computer centers. **Additional facts:** Ministerial, missionary, education, and music training.

DEGREES OFFERED. B. 16 associate degrees awarded in 1992. 100% in philosophy, religion, theology. 105 bachelor's degrees awarded. 100% in philosophy, religion, theology.

UNDERGRADUATE MAJORS. Bible studies, elementary education, secondary education, theological studies. Bible studies, missionary studies, religious education, religious music, theological studies.

ACADEMIC PROGRAMS. Double major, internships, 5-year bachelor's degree program in theology, cooperative program with Pittsburgh State University and Missouri Southern State College for certification in elementary education. **Remedial services:** Learning center.

ACADEMIC REQUIREMENTS. Freshmen must earn minimum GPA of 2.0 to continue in good standing. 65% of freshmen return for sophomore year. Students must declare major by end of second year. **Graduation requirements:** 96 hours for associate (29 in major), 128 hours for bachelor's (32 in major). Most students required to take courses in English, history, humanities, philosophy/religion, social sciences.

FRESHMAN ADMISSIONS. Selection criteria: Open admissions. **High school preparation:** 15 units recommended. Recommended units include English 3, mathematics 2, social science 1 and science 2. 7 units of electives recommended. **Test requirements:** ACT for placement and counseling only; score report by August 1. **Additional information:** Recommendations, student's personal data and stated goals on application form most important. School record and test scores considered.

1992 FRESHMAN CLASS PROFILE. 137 men and women enrolled. **Characteristics:** 90% live in college housing. Average age is 19.

FALL-TERM APPLICATIONS. $30 fee. Closing date August 1; applicants notified on a rolling basis. Essay required. Deferred admission available. ACT required for placement and counseling.

STUDENT LIFE. Housing: Dormitories (men, women). **Activities:** Student government, radio, yearbook, choral groups, concert band, music ensembles, pep band.

ATHLETICS. Intercollegiate: Basketball M, volleyball W. **Intramural:** Basketball, racquetball, soccer M, softball, volleyball.

STUDENT SERVICES. Career counseling, freshman orientation, health services, personal counseling, special adviser for adult students.

ANNUAL EXPENSES. Tuition and fees (1992-93): $2,971. **Room and board:** $2,740. **Books and supplies:** $450.

FINANCIAL AID. 68% of freshmen, 65% of continuing students receive some form of aid. 90% of grants, 98% of loans, 57% of jobs based on need. Academic, music/drama, leadership scholarships available. **Aid applications:** No closing date; priority given to applications received by May 1; applicants notified on a rolling basis beginning on or about June 1.

ADDRESS/TELEPHONE. James R. Marcum, Director of Enrollment Growth, Ozark Christian College, 1111 North Main Street, Joplin, MO 64801. (417) 624-2518. Fax: (417)624-0090.

Park College
Parkville, Missouri — CB code: 6574

Admissions: 63% of applicants accepted
Based on: ••• School record
•• Essay, interview, test scores
• Activities, recommendations, special talents
Completion: 85% of freshmen end year in good standing
33% graduate, 28% of these enter graduate study

4-year private liberal arts college, coed, affiliated with Reorganized Church of Jesus Christ of Latter-day Saints. Founded in 1875. **Accreditation:** Regional. **Undergraduate enrollment:** 275 men, 275 women full time; 100 men, 200 women part time. **Graduate enrollment:** 85 men and women. **Faculty:** 80 total (41 full time), 27 with doctorates or other terminal degrees. **Location:** Suburban campus in small town; 12 miles from downtown Kansas City. **Calendar:** Semester, limited summer session. Saturday classes. **Microcomputers:** 30 located in libraries, classrooms, computer centers. **Special facilities:** 800 acres of woodland, equine center, 250,000 square foot underground library complex. **Additional facts:** MetroPark School for continuing education in Kansas City offers bachelor's degree. 34 military sites nationwide serve 10,000 students.

DEGREES OFFERED. AA, BA, MA. 20 associate degrees awarded in 1992. 75 bachelor's degrees awarded. 30% in business and management, 20% communications, 15% education, 5% teacher education, 6% psychology, 5% social sciences. Graduate degrees offered in 4 major fields of study.

UNDERGRADUATE MAJORS. Associate: Business and management, interior design, nursing. **Bachelor's:** Accounting, advertising, art education, biology, business administration and management, business and management, business economics, chemistry, communications, computer and information sciences, creative writing, criminal justice studies, criminology, dramatic arts, early childhood education, economics, elementary education, English, English education, English literature, equestrian science, finance, fine arts, graphic design, history, information sciences and systems, interior design, international business management, journalism, junior high education, law enforcement and corrections, legal assistant/paralegal, management information systems, marketing management, mathematics, mathematics education, military science (Army), political science and government, predentistry, prelaw, premedicine, prepharmacy, preveterinary, psychology, public administration, public relations, radio/television broadcasting, science education, secondary education, social studies education, social work, sociology, sports medicine.

ACADEMIC PROGRAMS. Accelerated program, double major, dual enrollment of high school students, honors program, independent study, internships, student-designed major, teacher preparation, telecourses, weekend college, United Nations semester, Washington semester, cross-registration. **Remedial services:** Learning center, preadmission summer program, reduced course load, remedial instruction, special counselor, tutoring. **ROTC:** Army. **Placement/credit:** AP, CLEP General and Subject, IB, institutional tests; 30 credit hours maximum for associate degree; 60 credit hours maximum for bachelor's degree.

ACADEMIC REQUIREMENTS. Freshmen must earn minimum GPA of 2.0 to continue in good standing. 60% of freshmen return for sophomore year. Students must declare major by end of second year. **Graduation requirements:** 60 hours for associate (18 in major), 120 hours for bachelor's (36 in major). Most students required to take courses in arts/fine arts, computer science, English, foreign languages, humanities, mathematics, biological/physical sciences, social sciences. **Postgraduate studies:** 5% enter law school, 2% enter medical school, 6% enter MBA programs, 15% enter other graduate study. **Additional information:** Degree programs offered through Corporate Education System and at 34 military resident centers in United States, using adjunct Park College faculty.

FRESHMAN ADMISSIONS. Selection criteria: Most important is GPA (minimum 2.0), followed by test scores and rank in top half of class. Exceptions considered on individual merit. **High school preparation:** 15 units recommended. Recommended units include English 3, foreign language 1, mathematics 3, social science 3 and science 3. **Test requirements:** SAT or ACT; score report by August 1. **Additional information:** Students must meet 2 of 3: Top 1/2 of class; 2.0 GPA; 20 ACT (780 SAT).

1992 FRESHMAN CLASS PROFILE. 100 men applied, 70 accepted, 47 enrolled; 200 women applied, 120 accepted, 50 enrolled. 50% had high school GPA of 3.0 or higher, 45% between 2.0 and 2.99. 12% were in top tenth and 35% were in top quarter of graduating class. **Academic background:** Mid 50% of enrolled freshmen had SAT-V between 310-470, SAT-M between 300-450; ACT composite between 14-23. 20% submitted SAT scores, 80% submitted ACT scores. **Characteristics:** 40% from in state, 70% live in college housing, 47% have minority backgrounds, 15% are foreign students. Average age is 20.

FALL-TERM APPLICATIONS. $25 fee, may be waived for applicants with need. No closing date; priority given to applications received by April 15; applicants notified on a rolling basis. Interview recommended for academically weak applicants. Audition recommended for theater applicants. Portfolio recommended for art applicants. Essay recommended. CRDA. Deferred and early admission available.

STUDENT LIFE. Housing: Dormitories (men, women, coed); apartment housing available. **Activities:** Student government, magazine, radio, student newspaper, television, yearbook, poetry journal, choral groups, drama, symphony orchestra, service organizations, Christian Fellowship, International Club, Black Student Union, accounting society, Latin American Club.

ATHLETICS. NAIA. **Intercollegiate:** Basketball, cross-country, horseback riding, soccer, track and field, volleyball. **Intramural:** Basketball, cross-country, horseback riding, soccer, softball, table tennis, tennis, track and field, volleyball.

STUDENT SERVICES. Aptitude testing, career counseling, employment service for undergraduates, freshman orientation, health services, personal counseling, placement service for graduates, veterans counselor, special services for disadvantaged, services/facilities for handicapped.

ANNUAL EXPENSES. Tuition and fees: $3,540. **Room and board:** $3,780. **Books and supplies:** $800. **Other expenses:** $3,620.

FINANCIAL AID. 97% of freshmen, 93% of continuing students receive some form of aid. 90% of grants, 71% of loans, all jobs based on need. Academic, music/drama, art, athletic, alumni affiliation, religious affiliation scholarships available. **Aid applications:** Closing date August 1; priority given to applications received by April 1; applicants notified on a rolling basis beginning on or about April 1; must reply by May 1 or within 3 weeks if notified thereafter.

ADDRESS/TELEPHONE. Randy Condit, Director of Admissions, Park College, 8700 River Park Drive, Parkville, MO 64152-9970. (816) 741-2000 ext. 215. (800) 745-7275. Fax: (816) 746-6423.

Penn Valley Community College
Kansas City, Missouri — CB code: 6324

2-year public community college, coed. Founded in 1915. **Accreditation:** Regional. **Undergraduate enrollment:** 640 men, 1,059 women full time; 1,386 men, 2,737 women part time. **Faculty:** 314 total (87 full time), 18 with doctorates or other terminal degrees. **Location:** Urban campus in large city; 2 miles from downtown. **Calendar:** Semester, extensive summer session. Saturday and extensive evening/early morning classes. **Microcomputers:** 311 located in libraries, computer centers, campus-wide network.

DEGREES OFFERED. AA, AS, AAS. 530 associate degrees awarded in 1992. 10% in business/office and marketing/distribution, 18% health sciences, 12% allied health, 8% home economics, 11% law, 25% multi/interdisciplinary studies.

UNDERGRADUATE MAJORS. Accounting, air conditioning/heating/refrigeration mechanics, air conditioning/heating/refrigeration technology, biology, business and management, business and office, chemistry, child development/care/guidance, computer programming, criminal justice technology, data processing, electronic technology, emergency medical technologies, engineering, engineering and engineering-related technologies, fashion design, fashion merchandising, fire control and safety technology, home economics, hotel/motel and restaurant management, journalism, law enforcement and corrections technologies, legal assistant/paralegal, liberal/general studies, marketing and distribution, medical records technology, music, nursing, occupational therapy assistant, office supervision and management, physical therapy assistant, physics, radiograph medical technology, respiratory therapy, respiratory therapy technology, secretarial and related programs, word processing.

ACADEMIC PROGRAMS. 2-year transfer program, dual enrollment of high school students, honors program, internships, weekend college, cross-registration, cooperative programs in allied health with Johnson County Community College. **Remedial services:** Learning center, reduced course load, remedial instruction, tutoring. **Placement/credit:** AP, CLEP General and Subject, institutional tests; 30 credit hours maximum for associate degree.

ACADEMIC REQUIREMENTS. No policy requiring minimum GPA; records of students having academic difficulty are reviewed individually. 31% of freshmen return for sophomore year. Students must declare major by end of first year. **Graduation requirements:** 62 hours for associate. Most students required to take courses in English, history, mathematics, social sciences.

FRESHMAN ADMISSIONS. Selection criteria: Open admissions. **High school preparation:** 16 units recommended. Recommended units include English 4, foreign language 2, mathematics 3, social science 3 and science 3. 1 unit in visual/performing arts recommended. **Test requirements:** ACT asset required for placement and counseling.

1992 FRESHMAN CLASS PROFILE. 1,090 men and women enrolled. **Characteristics:** 100% commute.

FALL-TERM APPLICATIONS. No fee. No closing date; applicants notified on a rolling basis. Early admission available.

STUDENT LIFE. Activities: Student government, student newspaper, drama, jazz band, music ensembles, opera, Black Student Association, Los Americanos.

ATHLETICS. NJCAA. **Intercollegiate:** Basketball M, golf M.

STUDENT SERVICES. Aptitude testing, career counseling, employment service for undergraduates, freshman orientation, on-campus day care, personal counseling, placement service for graduates, veterans counselor, services/facilities for handicapped.

ANNUAL EXPENSES. Tuition and fees: $1,230, $780 additional for out-of-district students, $1,680 additional for out-of-state students. **Books and supplies:** $550. **Other expenses:** $1,972.

FINANCIAL AID. 29% of freshmen, 29% of continuing students receive some form of aid. 92% of grants, all loans, 28% of jobs based on need. Academic, athletic, state/district residency, leadership scholarships available. **Aid applications:** No closing date; priority given to applications received by May 31; applicants notified on a rolling basis beginning on or about April 25; must reply immediately.

ADDRESS/TELEPHONE. Office of Admissions, Penn Valley Community College, 3201 Southwest Trafficway, Kansas City, MO 64111. (816) 759-4100. Fax: (816) 759-4161.

Phillips Junior College
Springfield, Missouri — CB code: 1478

2-year proprietary junior college, coed. Founded in 1979. **Undergraduate enrollment:** 750 men and women. **Faculty:** 40 total (15 full time). **Location:** Urban campus in small city; 250 miles from St. Louis, 190 miles from Kansas City. **Calendar:** 4 12-week sessions per year. Extensive evening/early morning classes. **Microcomputers:** 65 located in libraries, classrooms.

DEGREES OFFERED. AAS. 70 associate degrees awarded in 1992. 20% in business and management, 10% business/office and marketing/distribution, 20% computer sciences, 40% allied health, 10% law.

UNDERGRADUATE MAJORS. Accounting, business administration and management, business and management, data processing, legal assistant/paralegal, medical assistant, secretarial and related programs.

ACADEMIC PROGRAMS. Accelerated program, internships. **Remedial services:** Learning center, remedial instruction, tutoring. **Placement/credit:** AP, institutional tests; 12 credit hours maximum for associate degree.

ACADEMIC REQUIREMENTS. Freshmen must earn minimum GPA of 1.5 to continue in good standing. 76% of freshmen return for sophomore year. Students must declare major on application. **Graduation requirements:** 96 hours for associate (80 in major). Most students required to take courses in English, mathematics, social sciences.

FRESHMAN ADMISSIONS. Selection criteria: Institution's own examination and interview considered. **Test requirements:** SAT or ACT.

1992 FRESHMAN CLASS PROFILE. 125 men and women enrolled. **Characteristics:** 100% from in state, 100% commute, 2% have minority backgrounds. Average age is 21.

FALL-TERM APPLICATIONS. $25 fee. No closing date; applicants notified on a rolling basis. Interview required.

STUDENT LIFE. Activities: Student government, student newspaper, Phi Beta Lambda.

ATHLETICS. Intramural: Softball.

STUDENT SERVICES. Aptitude testing, career counseling, employment service for undergraduates, personal counseling, placement service for graduates, special adviser for adult students, veterans counselor, services/facilities for handicapped.

ANNUAL EXPENSES. Tuition and fees (projected): $3,498. Tuition includes book fee. **Books and supplies:** $305. **Other expenses:** $1,260.

FINANCIAL AID. 90% of freshmen, 90% of continuing students receive some form of aid. All grants, 97% of loans, all jobs based on need. **Aid applications:** No closing date; applicants notified on a rolling basis.

ADDRESS/TELEPHONE. Marilyn Smith, Director of Admissions, Phillips Junior College, 1010 W. Sunshine Avenue, Springfield, MO 65807. (417) 864-7220. (800) 475-2669. Fax: (417) 864-5697.

Ranken Technical College
St. Louis, Missouri — CB code: 7028

2-year private technical college, coed. **Accreditation:** Regional. **Undergraduate enrollment:** 710 men, 12 women full time; 693 men, 13 women part time. **Faculty:** 250 total (125 full time). **Location:** Urban campus in large city. **Calendar:** Trimester. **Microcomputers:** Located in libraries, classrooms, computer centers.

DEGREES OFFERED. AAS. 193 associate degrees awarded in 1992. 8% in architecture and environmental design, 8% communications, 8% computer sciences, 76% trade and industry.

UNDERGRADUATE MAJORS. Accounting, advertising, aerospace/aeronautical/astronautical engineering, air conditioning/heating/refrigeration mechanics, air conditioning/heating/refrigeration technology, air pollution control technology, architectural drafting, architectural engineering, architecture, automotive mechanics, automotive technology, business and management, business and office, business computer/console/peripheral equipment operation, business data entry equipment operation, business data processing and related programs, business data programming, business economics, business statistics, business systems analysis, carpentry, civil technology, communications, communications electronics, computer and information sciences, computer graphics, computer mathematics, computer programming, computer technology, contract management and procurement/purchasing, court reporting, data processing, drafting and design technology, electrical technology, electronic technology, engineering mechanics, engineering physics, engineering science, environmental design, finance, historic preservation, human resources development, information sciences and systems, instrumentation technology, interior design, labor/industrial relations, landscape architecture, legal secretary, machine tool operation/machine shop, management information systems, marketing management, marketing research, masonry/tile setting, medical secretary, microcomputer software, office supervision and management, personnel management, robotics, secretarial and related programs, survey and mapping technology, systems analysis, trade and industrial supervision and management, urban design, welding technology, word processing.

ACADEMIC PROGRAMS. Remedial services: Learning center, preadmission summer program, reduced course load, remedial instruction, special counselor, tutoring.

ACADEMIC REQUIREMENTS. 80% of freshmen return for sophomore year. Students must declare major on enrollment. **Graduation requirements:** 95 hours for associate (54 in major). Most students required to take courses in computer science, English, mathematics.

FRESHMAN ADMISSIONS. Selection criteria: Institutional admissions test and counseling session required.

1992 FRESHMAN CLASS PROFILE. 355 men and women enrolled. 20% had high school GPA of 3.0 or higher, 70% between 2.0 and 2.99. 10% were in top tenth and 20% were in top quarter of graduating class. **Characteristics:** 80% from in state, 100% commute, 33% have minority backgrounds, 1% are foreign students, 25% join fraternities/sororities. Average age is 19.

FALL-TERM APPLICATIONS. No fee. Closing date May 30; priority given to applications received by January 30; applicants notified on or about May 30; must reply by June 15. Interview and tour recommended for new applicants.

STUDENT LIFE. Activities: Student government, radio, student newspaper, fraternities.

STUDENT SERVICES. Aptitude testing, career counseling, employment service for undergraduates, freshman orientation, personal counseling, placement service for graduates, special adviser for adult students, veterans counselor, services/facilities for handicapped.

ANNUAL EXPENSES. Tuition and fees: $4,650. **Books and supplies:** $1,648.

FINANCIAL AID. 95% of grants, all loans, all jobs based on need. 600 enrolled freshmen were judged to have need, 550 were offered aid. Academic, leadership scholarships available. **Aid applications:** No closing date; applicants notified on a rolling basis beginning on or about June 1.

ADDRESS/TELEPHONE. Debra McPeak, Dean of Students, Ranken Technical College, 4431 Finney Avenue, St. Louis, MO 63113. (314) 371-0233 ext. 1070. (800) 535-2683.

Research College of Nursing
Kansas City, Missouri CB code: 6612

Admissions: 82% of applicants accepted
Based on: ••• School record
•• Activities, interview, recommendations, test scores
• Essay, special talents
Completion: 80% of freshmen end year in good standing
70% graduate

4-year private nursing college, coed, in the Jesuit tradition. Founded in 1905. **Accreditation:** Regional. **Undergraduate enrollment:** 17 men, 182 women full time; 52 women part time. **Faculty:** 42 total (31 full time), 8 with doctorates or other terminal degrees. **Location:** Urban campus in large city; 5 miles from downtown. **Calendar:** Semester, limited summer session. **Microcomputers:** 270 located in dormitories, libraries, classrooms, computer centers. **Special facilities:** Medical library, 532-bed Research Medical Center. **Additional facts:** Natural science, social science, and liberal arts courses taken at Rockhurst College. Students have access to facilities, organizations, sports, and activities on both campuses.

DEGREES OFFERED. BS. 14 bachelor's degrees awarded in 1992. 100% in health sciences.

UNDERGRADUATE MAJORS. Nursing.

ACADEMIC PROGRAMS. Accelerated program, double major, dual enrollment of high school students, honors program, independent study, study abroad, visiting/exchange student program, Washington semester, cross-registration. **Remedial services:** Learning center, reduced course load, special counselor, tutoring. **ROTC:** Army. **Placement/credit:** AP, CLEP Subject, institutional tests; 32 credit hours maximum for bachelor's degree.

ACADEMIC REQUIREMENTS. Freshmen must earn minimum GPA of 2.25 to continue in good standing. 79% of freshmen return for sophomore year. Students must declare major by end of first year. **Graduation requirements:** 128 hours for bachelor's (59 in major). Most students required to take courses in English, history, humanities, philosophy/religion, biological/physical sciences, social sciences. **Additional information:** Students admitted into nursing program in freshman year. Guaranteed a place in upper division nursing courses if academic requirements are maintained.

FRESHMAN ADMISSIONS. Selection criteria: Academic record, high school GPA, rank in top half of class, counselor's recommendation, and test scores strongly considered. Interview and high school activities also considered. **High school preparation:** 16 units recommended. Recommended units include biological science 2, English 4, foreign language 2, mathematics 3, physical science 2 and social science 3. Visual or performing arts also recommended. Mathematics should include algebra II.Biological science should include chemistry. **Test requirements:** SAT or ACT; score report by June 30.

1992 FRESHMAN CLASS PROFILE. 6 men applied, 3 accepted, 1 enrolled; 93 women applied, 78 accepted, 34 enrolled. **Academic background:** Mid 50% of enrolled freshmen had SAT-V between 400-500, SAT-M between 400-500; ACT composite between 21-26. 21% submitted SAT scores, 96% submitted ACT scores. **Characteristics:** 75% from in state, 70% live in college housing, 26% have minority backgrounds. Average age is 19.

FALL-TERM APPLICATIONS. $20 fee, may be waived for applicants with need. Closing date June 30; applicants notified on a rolling basis; must reply by May 1 or within 2 weeks if notified thereafter. Interview recommended. Interview recommended for all, strongly recommended for applicants with ACT scores below 20. CRDA. Deferred admission available.

STUDENT LIFE. Housing: Dormitories (men, women, coed); apartment, fraternity housing available. Freshmen nursing students not living at home must live on Rockhurst College campus. All other undergraduates may choose to live on Research College campus or Rockhurst College. **Activities:** Student government, radio, student newspaper, yearbook, choral groups, drama, music ensembles, musical theater, pep band, Rockhurst College Chamber Singers, fraternities, Alpha Phi Omega, Black Student Union, campus ministry, Young Republicans, Young Democrats, Missouri Student Nurses Association, National Student Nurses Association, Rockhurst Organization of Collegiate Women. **Additional information:** Students in joint nursing program have access to all services and student activities on both Research College of Nursing and Rockhurst College campuses.

ATHLETICS. NAIA. **Intercollegiate:** Baseball M, basketball, cross-country, soccer, tennis, volleyball W. **Intramural:** Basketball, golf, gymnastics M, handball W, racquetball, soccer, table tennis, volleyball.

STUDENT SERVICES. Aptitude testing, career counseling, employment service for undergraduates, freshman orientation, health services, on-campus day care, personal counseling, placement service for graduates, veterans counselor, Multicultural Affairs, services/facilities for handicapped.

ANNUAL EXPENSES. Tuition and fees: $9,430. **Room and board:** $4,440. **Books and supplies:** $675. **Other expenses:** $850.

FINANCIAL AID. 88% of continuing students receive some form of aid. 91% of grants, 58% of loans, 22% of jobs based on need. Academic, leadership, alumni affiliation scholarships available. **Aid applications:** No closing date; priority given to applications received by March 15; applicants notified on a rolling basis beginning on or about June 15; must reply by May 1 or within 3 weeks if notified thereafter. **Additional information:** Financial aid handled by Rockhurst College for freshmen and sophomores.

ADDRESS/TELEPHONE. Leslie A. Mendenhall, Assistant Director of Admission, Research College of Nursing, 1100 Rockhurst Road, Kansas City, MO 64110-2508. (816) 926-4100. (800) 842-6776. Fax: (816) 926-4588.

Rockhurst College
Kansas City, Missouri CB code: 6611

Admissions: 86% of applicants accepted
Based on: ••• School record
•• Activities, interview, recommendations, test scores
• Essay, special talents
Completion: 85% of freshmen end year in good standing
61% graduate, 21% of these enter graduate study

4-year private college of arts and sciences and business, nursing college, coed, affiliated with Roman Catholic Church. Founded in 1910. **Accreditation:** Regional. **Undergraduate enrollment:** 470 men, 714 women full time; 350 men, 510 women part time. **Graduate enrollment:** 72 men, 32 women full time; 235 men, 223 women part time. **Faculty:** 161 total (96 full time), 76 with doctorates or other terminal degrees. **Location:** Urban campus in very large city; 5 miles from downtown. **Calendar:** Semester, extensive summer session. Saturday and extensive evening/early morning classes. **Microcomputers:** 115 located in dormitories, libraries, classrooms, computer centers. **Special facilities:** Van Ackeren Gallery of Religious Art, Massman Art Gallery, Linda Hall Science Library, Nelson-Atkins Museum of Art. **Additional facts:** Institution in the Jesuit tradition. New South Campus offers undergraduate and accelerated MBA degrees.

DEGREES OFFERED. BA, BS, MS, MBA. 330 bachelor's degrees awarded in 1992. 44% in business and management, 10% health sciences, 10% allied health, 5% psychology, 8% social sciences. Graduate degrees offered in 4 major fields of study.

UNDERGRADUATE MAJORS. Accounting, biology, business administration and management, business and management, business economics, business education, chemistry, communications, computer and information sciences, computer programming, contract management and procurement/purchasing, cytotechnology, economics, education, elementary education, English, English education, finance, foreign languages education, French, history, human resources development, humanities and social sciences, information sciences and systems, international relations, international studies, junior high education, labor/industrial relations, marketing and distribution, marketing management, mathematics, mathematics education, medical laboratory technologies, nursing, personnel management, philosophy, physics, political science and government, preengineering, psychology, science education, secondary education, social sciences, social studies education, sociology, Spanish, systems analysis, theological studies.

ACADEMIC PROGRAMS. Accelerated program, cooperative education, double major, dual enrollment of high school students, honors program, independent study, internships, student-designed major, study abroad, teacher preparation, visiting/exchange student program, Washington semester, cross-registration, 3+3 physical therapy masters program; liberal arts/career combination in engineering, health sciences; combined bachelor's/graduate program in business administration. **Remedial services:** Learning center, special counselor, tutoring, Freshman Incentive Program. **Placement/credit:** AP, CLEP Subject, IB, institutional tests; 32 credit hours maximum for bachelor's degree.

ACADEMIC REQUIREMENTS. Freshmen must earn minimum GPA of 2.0 to continue in good standing. 86% of freshmen return for sophomore year. Students must declare major by end of second year. **Graduation requirements:** 128 hours for bachelor's (30 in major). Most students required to take courses in English, foreign languages, history, humanities, mathematics, philosophy/religion, biological/physical sciences, social sciences. **Postgraduate studies:** 3% enter law school, 3% enter medical school, 4% enter MBA programs, 11% enter other graduate study.

FRESHMAN ADMISSIONS. Selection criteria: Class rank, SAT or ACT scores, high school GPA, school and community service activities, interview, recommendations considered. **High school preparation:** 15 units required; 18 recommended. Required and recommended units include English 4, foreign language 2-4, mathematics 3, physical science 4 and social science 2. Biological science 1 recommended. Visual or performing arts also recommended. **Test requirements:** SAT or ACT (ACT preferred); score report by June 30.

1992 FRESHMAN CLASS PROFILE. 309 men applied, 254 accepted, 78 enrolled; 521 women applied, 462 accepted, 124 enrolled. 30% were in top tenth and 45% were in top quarter of graduating class. **Academic background:** Mid 50% of enrolled freshmen had SAT-V between 400-500, SAT-M between 400-500; ACT composite between 20-25. 25% submitted SAT scores, 95% submitted ACT scores. **Characteristics:** 66% from in state, 75% live in college housing, 18% have minority backgrounds, 2% are foreign students, 17% join fraternities/sororities. Average age is 18.

FALL-TERM APPLICATIONS. $20 fee, may be waived for applicants with need. Closing date June 30; priority given to applications received by February 1; applicants notified on a rolling basis; must reply by May 1 or within 2 weeks if notified thereafter. Interview recommended. Essay recommended. CRDA. Deferred and early admission available.

STUDENT LIFE. Housing: Dormitories (men, women, coed); fraternity, cooperative housing available. Student townhouse and theme housing available. **Activities:** Student government, magazine, radio, student newspaper, yearbook, choral groups, drama, music ensembles, musical theater, pep band, fraternities, Alpha Phi Omega, Black Student Union, campus ministry, Multicultural Affairs Office, American Humanics, Appalachian Service Project, Peace of the World, Amnesty International. **Additional information:** Professional student activities staff, including a Multicultural Affairs Specialist, available to advise and assist students in pursuing cocurricular activities and interests.

ATHLETICS. NAIA. **Intercollegiate:** Baseball M, basketball, soccer, volleyball W. **Intramural:** Baseball M, basketball, cross-country, football M, golf, handball M, racquetball, soccer, softball, table tennis, volleyball, wrestling M.

STUDENT SERVICES. Aptitude testing, career counseling, employment service for undergraduates, freshman orientation, health services, personal counseling, placement service for graduates, special adviser for adult students, veterans counselor, multicultural affairs, services/facilities for handicapped.

ANNUAL EXPENSES. Tuition and fees (1992-93): $8,810. **Room and board:** $3,718. **Books and supplies:** $525. **Other expenses:** $1,373.

FINANCIAL AID. 87% of freshmen, 80% of continuing students receive some form of aid. 55% of grants, 88% of loans, all jobs based on need. Academic, athletic, leadership, alumni affiliation, religious affiliation, minority scholarships available. **Aid applications:** No closing date; priority given to applications received by April 1; applicants notified on a rolling basis beginning on or about March 1; must reply by May 1 or within 3 weeks if notified thereafter.

ADDRESS/TELEPHONE. Barbara K. O'Connell, Director of Enrollment Services, Rockhurst College, 1100 Rockhurst Road, Kansas City, MO 64110-2508. (816) 926-4100. (800) 842-6776. Fax: (816) 926-4588.

St. Charles County Community College
St. Peters, Missouri — CB code: 0168

2-year public community college, coed. **Accreditation:** Regional. **Undergraduate enrollment:** 548 men, 768 women full time; 974 men, 2,341 women part time. **Faculty:** 201 total (55 full time), 8 with doctorates or other terminal degrees. **Location:** Suburban campus in large town; Forty miles from St. Louis. **Calendar:** Semester. Saturday and extensive evening/early morning classes. **Microcomputers:** 150 located in classrooms, computer centers.

DEGREES OFFERED. AA, AS, AAS. 173 associate degrees awarded in 1992. 25% in business/office and marketing/distribution, 44% allied health, 30% multi/interdisciplinary studies.

UNDERGRADUATE MAJORS. Accounting, business administration and management, business and management, criminal justice technology, electronic technology, finance, medical records technology, nursing, word processing.

ACADEMIC PROGRAMS. 2-year transfer program, dual enrollment of high school students, independent study, internships, telecourses. **Remedial services:** Learning center, remedial instruction, special counselor, tutoring. **Placement/credit:** CLEP Subject; 49 credit hours maximum for associate degree.

ACADEMIC REQUIREMENTS. Freshmen must earn minimum GPA of 2.0 to continue in good standing. 84% of freshmen return for sophomore year. **Graduation requirements:** 64 hours for associate. Most students required to take courses in computer science, English, humanities, mathematics, biological/physical sciences, social sciences.

FRESHMAN ADMISSIONS. Selection criteria: Open admissions. Selective admission to nursing and allied health programs. **High school preparation:** 16 units recommended. Recommended units include biological science 2, English 4, foreign language 2, mathematics 3 and social science 3. One unit in visual arts, music, or dance and theatre and 1 elective unit. **Test requirements:** ACT for placement; score report by August 15. ACT scores required for admission to nursing and allied health programs. Deadline: August 15. **Additional information:** ACT scores required from all full-time entering freshmen and all part-time freshmen when they accumulate 15 credit hours.

1992 FRESHMAN CLASS PROFILE. 448 men, 707 women enrolled. 2% were in top tenth and 14% were in top quarter of graduating class. **Characteristics:** 25% from in state, 100% commute. Average age is 20.

FALL-TERM APPLICATIONS. No fee. No closing date; applicants notified on a rolling basis. Essay required. 5-year waiting list for associate degree program in nursing. Only 200 nursing applicants admitted every year; in-state applicants preferred.

STUDENT LIFE. Housing: Students must make their own arrangements for housing. **Activities:** Student government, student newspaper, dance.

ATHLETICS. Intramural: Basketball, volleyball.

STUDENT SERVICES. Aptitude testing, career counseling, employment service for undergraduates, freshman orientation, personal counseling, veterans counselor, services/facilities for handicapped.

ANNUAL EXPENSES. Tuition and fees: $1,177, $600 additional for out-of-district students, $1,620 additional for out-of-state students. **Books and supplies:** $550. **Other expenses:** $1,000.

FINANCIAL AID. 20% of freshmen, 20% of continuing students receive some form of aid. Grants, loans, jobs available. Academic, music/drama, state/district residency, leadership scholarships available. **Aid applications:** No closing date; priority given to applications received by April 30; applicants notified on a rolling basis.

ADDRESS/TELEPHONE. James Benedict, Associate Dean of Students, St. Charles County Community College, 4601 Mid Rivers Mall Drive, St. Peters, MO 63376. (314) 922-8000. Fax: (314) 922-8352.

St. Louis Christian College
Florissant, Missouri — CB code: 0334

4-year private Bible college, coed, affiliated with Christian Churches/Churches of Christ. Founded in 1956. **Undergraduate enrollment:** 69 men, 35 women full time; 18 men, 15 women part time. **Faculty:** 20 total (16 full time), 4 with doctorates or other terminal degrees. **Location:** Suburban campus in small city; 15 miles from St. Louis. **Calendar:** Semester. **Microcomputers:** 6 located in libraries, computer centers. **Additional facts:** Personalized student/faculty interaction. Students highly involved in service and field education.

DEGREES OFFERED. AA, BA, BS. 7 associate degrees awarded in 1992. 14% in business and management, 72% education, 14% philosophy, religion, theology. 18 bachelor's degrees awarded. 100% in philosophy, religion, theology.

UNDERGRADUATE MAJORS. Associate: Bible studies, business and office, education, humanities, religion, secretarial and related programs. **Bachelor's:** Missionary studies, religion, religious education, religious music, theological studies.

ACADEMIC PROGRAMS. 2-year transfer program, double major, dual enrollment of high school students, internships, cross-registration. **Remedial services:** Remedial instruction. **Placement/credit:** AP, CLEP General and Subject, institutional tests.

ACADEMIC REQUIREMENTS. Freshmen must earn minimum GPA of 2.0 to continue in good standing. 66% of freshmen return for sophomore year. Students must declare major on enrollment. **Graduation requirements:** 64 hours for associate (20 in major), 130 hours for bachelor's (40 in major). Most students required to take courses in arts/fine arts, English, foreign languages, history, humanities, mathematics, philosophy/religion, biological/physical sciences, social sciences. **Postgraduate studies:** 50% from 2-year programs enter 4-year programs. **Additional information:** Preparation for ministries in preaching, Christian education, mission fields, Christian music, church secretary, youth work, and urban ministry.

FRESHMAN ADMISSIONS. Selection criteria: Essay or personal statement and recommendations considered, as well as high school GPA, class rank, and test scores. Recommended units include biological science .5, English 3, foreign language 2, mathematics 2, physical science .5, social science 2 and science .5. **Test requirements:** SAT or ACT (ACT preferred); score report by July 1.

1992 FRESHMAN CLASS PROFILE. 20 men, 8 women enrolled. 13% were in top tenth and 42% were in top quarter of graduating class. **Academic background:** Mid 50% of enrolled freshmen had ACT composite between 15-24. 80% submitted ACT scores. **Characteristics:** 37% from in state, 78% live in college housing, 4% have minority backgrounds. Average age is 21.

FALL-TERM APPLICATIONS. $30 fee. Closing date July 1; priority given to applications received by July 1; applicants notified on a rolling basis. Audition required for religious music applicants. Essay required. Interview recommended. Deferred and early admission available.

STUDENT LIFE. Housing: Dormitories (men, women); apartment housing available. **Activities:** Student government, radio, student newspaper, yearbook, choral groups, drama, music ensembles, pep band, missions interest group, ministry team. **Additional information:** Students involved in evangelistic activities of area churches. College aims to spread the Gospel. Religious observance required.

ATHLETICS. Intercollegiate: Baseball M, basketball, soccer M, tennis, volleyball W. **Intramural:** Baseball M, basketball, softball, table tennis, tennis, volleyball.

STUDENT SERVICES. Career counseling, employment service for undergraduates, freshman orientation, health services, personal counseling, Christian Service guidance and internship.

ANNUAL EXPENSES. Tuition and fees (1992-93): $3,400. **Room and board:** $2,420. **Books and supplies:** $300. **Other expenses:** $600.

FINANCIAL AID. 85% of freshmen, 90% of continuing students receive some form of aid. 46% of grants, 93% of loans, 17% of jobs based on need. 35 enrolled freshmen were judged to have need, all were offered aid. Academic, music/drama, leadership, alumni affiliation scholarships available. **Aid applications:** No closing date; priority given to applications received by July 1; applicants notified on a rolling basis beginning on or about July 20; must reply within 2 weeks.

ADDRESS/TELEPHONE. Pamela Ralls, Director of Admissions, St. Louis Christian College, 1360 Grandview Drive, Florissant, MO 63033. (314) 837-6777.

St. Louis College of Pharmacy
St. Louis, Missouri CB code: 6626

Admissions:	72% of applicants accepted
Based on:	••• School record, test scores
	•• Essay
	• Activities, interview, recommendations, special talents
Completion:	78% of freshmen end year in good standing
	76% graduate, 12% of these enter graduate study

5-year private pharmacy college, coed. Founded in 1864. **Accreditation:** Regional. **Undergraduate enrollment:** 250 men, 521 women full time. **Graduate enrollment:** 17 men, 15 women full time; 6 men, 4 women part time. **Faculty:** 82 total (52 full time), 65 with doctorates or other terminal degrees. **Location:** Urban campus in large city; 5 miles from downtown. **Calendar:** Semester, limited summer session. **Microcomputers:** 51 located in libraries, computer centers. **Additional facts:** Washington University Medical Center and other regional hospitals available to students for employment/clinical and practical experience.

DEGREES OFFERED. BS, MS, EdD, B. Pharm. 146 bachelor's degrees awarded in 1992. 100% in health sciences. Graduate degrees offered in 2 major fields of study.

UNDERGRADUATE MAJORS. Pharmacy.

ACADEMIC PROGRAMS. Honors program, internships. **Remedial services:** Reduced course load, special counselor, tutoring. **Placement/credit:** AP, CLEP Subject, institutional tests; 28 credit hours maximum for bachelor's degree.

ACADEMIC REQUIREMENTS. Freshmen must earn minimum GPA of 2.0 to continue in good standing. 80% of freshmen return for sophomore year. Students must declare major on application. **Graduation requirements:** 163 hours for bachelor's. Most students required to take courses in arts/fine arts, English, history, humanities, mathematics, philosophy/religion, biological/physical sciences, social sciences. **Postgraduate studies:** 2% enter law school, 2% enter medical school, 8% enter other graduate study.

FRESHMAN ADMISSIONS. Selection criteria: Rank in top half of class and in top two-thirds on test scores. **High school preparation:** 20 units required. Required and recommended units include biological science 1-2, English 4, mathematics 2-4 and physical science 1-2. Biology, chemistry, and physics preferred, as well as alegbra I, geometry, and algebra II and/or pre-calculus-trigonometry. **Test requirements:** SAT or ACT (ACT preferred); score report by July 15.

1992 FRESHMAN CLASS PROFILE. 112 men applied, 76 accepted, 53 enrolled; 189 women applied, 142 accepted, 94 enrolled. 73% had high school GPA of 3.0 or higher, 27% between 2.0 and 2.99. **Academic background:** Mid 50% of enrolled freshmen had ACT composite between 20-26. 98% submitted ACT scores. **Characteristics:** 35% from in state, 59% live in college housing, 7% have minority backgrounds, 40% join fraternities/sororities. Average age is 18.

FALL-TERM APPLICATIONS. $25 fee, may be waived for applicants with need. Closing date August 1; priority given to applications received by April 1; applicants notified on a rolling basis; must reply by May 1 or within 30 days if notified thereafter. Interview recommended. CRDA. Eligibility placement can also be determined based on either P-CAT test scores or college's own test given in December.

STUDENT LIFE. Housing: Dormitories (coed); apartment, fraternity, sorority housing available. **Activities:** Student government, student newspaper, yearbook, choral groups, concert band, drama, music ensembles, musical theater, fraternities, sororities, Student American Pharmaceutical Association, Student National Pharmaceutical Association, Rho Chi (pharmaceutical honor society), SCODAE (Student Committee on Drug Abuse Education); SCOPE Student Ambassadors, Gateway Association of Student Pharmacists (GASP). **Additional information:** Small student body encourages extracurricular participation.

ATHLETICS. NSCAA. **Intercollegiate:** Baseball M, volleyball. **Intramural:** Basketball, bowling, soccer, softball, tennis, volleyball.

STUDENT SERVICES. Career counseling, employment service for undergraduates, freshman orientation, personal counseling, placement service for graduates, services/facilities for handicapped.

ANNUAL EXPENSES. Tuition and fees (1992-93): Tuition and fees for incoming freshmen, $6360; for upperclassmen, $8010. Room and board, $2390. **Books and supplies:** $300. **Other expenses:** $1,350.

FINANCIAL AID. 76% of freshmen, 83% of continuing students receive some form of aid. 69% of grants, 93% of loans, 35% of jobs based on need. 85 enrolled freshmen were judged to have need, all were offered aid. Academic, state/district residency, leadership scholarships available. **Aid applications:** No closing date; priority given to applications received by May 31; applicants notified on a rolling basis beginning on or about April 1; must reply by May 1 or within 2 weeks if notified thereafter.

ADDRESS/TELEPHONE. Office of Admissions, St. Louis College of Pharmacy, 4588 Parkview Place, St. Louis, MO 63110. (314) 367-8700 ext. 264. Fax: (314) 367-2784.

St. Louis Community College at Florissant Valley
St. Louis, Missouri CB code: 6225

2-year public branch campus, community college, coed. Founded in 1962. **Accreditation:** Regional. **Undergraduate enrollment:** 1,207 men, 1,494 women full time; 2,659 men, 4,563 women part time. **Faculty:** 513 total (134 full time), 32 with doctorates or other terminal degrees. **Location:** Suburban campus in large city; 17 miles from downtown. **Calendar:** Semester, extensive summer session. Saturday and extensive evening/early morning classes. **Microcomputers:** Located in libraries, computer centers. **Special facilities:** Art gallery, observatory, Child Development Center.

DEGREES OFFERED. AA, AAS. 625 associate degrees awarded in 1992. 17% in business and management, 9% communications, 6% engineering technologies, 53% multi/interdisciplinary studies.

UNDERGRADUATE MAJORS. Advertising, biology, business administration and management, business and office, business computer/console/peripheral equipment operation, business data processing and related programs, business data programming, chemical manufacturing technology, chemistry, child development/care/guidance, civil technology, commercial art, communications, communications research, computer and information sciences, computer programming, computer servicing technology, data processing, drafting, dramatic arts, early childhood education, electrical technology, electronic technology, engineering, engineering and engineering-related technologies, fashion merchandising, finance, fine arts, fire control and safety technology, food production/management/services, graphic arts technology, home economics, illustration design, industrial technology, interpreter for the deaf, journalism, law enforcement and corrections technologies, liberal/general studies, marketing and distribution, mathematics, mechanical design technology, music, nursing, physics, predentistry, premedicine, prepharmacy, psychology, public relations, quality control technology, radio/television broadcasting, secretarial and related programs, social sciences, speech, systems analysis, teacher aide, technical and business writing, telecommunications, visual and performing arts, word processing.

ACADEMIC PROGRAMS. 2-year transfer program, cooperative education, dual enrollment of high school students, honors program, independent study, internships, study abroad, teacher preparation, telecourses, visiting/exchange student program, weekend college, cross-registration. **Remedial services:** Learning center, remedial instruction, special counselor, tutoring. **ROTC:** Air Force, Army. **Placement/credit:** AP, CLEP General and Subject, institutional tests; 49 credit hours maximum for associate degree.

ACADEMIC REQUIREMENTS. Freshmen must earn minimum GPA of 2.0 to continue in good standing. 46% of freshmen return for sophomore year. **Graduation requirements:** 64 hours for associate (12 in major). Most students required to take courses in English, history, humanities, mathematics, biological/physical sciences, social sciences.

FRESHMAN ADMISSIONS. Selection criteria: Open admissions. Nursing program applicants required to pass institutional test. **Test requirements:** Asset required for placement and counseling. Deadline: Aug. 18.

1992 FRESHMAN CLASS PROFILE. 6,618 men and women enrolled. **Characteristics:** 98% from in state, 100% commute, 20% have minority backgrounds.

FALL-TERM APPLICATIONS. No fee. No closing date; applicants notified on a rolling basis.

STUDENT LIFE. Activities: Student government, radio, student newspaper, television, concert band, drama, musical theater, Black Student Association.

ATHLETICS. NJCAA. **Intercollegiate:** Baseball M, basketball, cross-country, soccer, softball W, track and field, volleyball W.

STUDENT SERVICES. Aptitude testing, career counseling, employment service for undergraduates, health services, on-campus day care, personal counseling, placement service for graduates, services/facilities for handicapped.

ANNUAL EXPENSES. Tuition and fees: $1,148, $280 additional for out-of-district students, $588 additional for out-of-state students. **Books and supplies:** $500. **Other expenses:** $1,500.

FINANCIAL AID. 18% of freshmen, 25% of continuing students receive some form of aid. Grants, loans, jobs available. Academic, music/drama, art, athletic, leadership scholarships available. **Aid applications:** No closing date; priority given to applications received by August 1; applicants notified on a rolling basis beginning on or about May 1.

ADDRESS/TELEPHONE. Mr. Milton F. Woody, Dir of Admissions/Registrar, St. Louis Community College at Florissant Valley, 3400 Pershall Road, St. Louis, MO 63135. (314) 595-4244. Fax: (314) 595-4544.

St. Louis Community College at Forest Park
St. Louis, Missouri CB code: 6226

2-year public community college, coed. Founded in 1962. **Accreditation:** Regional. **Undergraduate enrollment:** 1,763 men and women full time; 5,812 men and women part time. **Faculty:** 311 total (119 full time), 17 with doctorates or other terminal degrees. **Location:** Urban campus in large city. **Calendar:** Semester, extensive summer session. **Microcomputers:** Located in libraries, classrooms, computer centers.

DEGREES OFFERED. AA, AAS. 802 associate degrees awarded in 1992. 15% in business and management, 5% business/office and marketing/distribution, 11% computer sciences, 12% engineering technologies, 21% health sciences, 15% allied health, 5% home economics, 6% multi/interdisciplinary studies.

UNDERGRADUATE MAJORS. Accounting, automotive technology, biology, biomedical equipment technology, business and management, business data processing and related programs, chemistry, child development/care/guidance, communications, computer and information sciences, computer programming, data processing, dental assistant, dental hygiene, drafting, electrical technology, electronic technology, emergency medical technologies, engineering, engineering and engineering-related technologies, finance, fine arts, fire control and safety technology, food production/management/services, funeral services/mortuary science, general life sciences, graphic arts technology, hotel/motel and restaurant management, industrial technology, international business management, law enforcement and corrections technologies, liberal/general studies, mathematics, mechanical design technology, medical laboratory technologies, music, nursing, photography, physical sciences, physics, psychology, radiograph medical technology, respiratory therapy, respiratory therapy technology, science technologies, secretarial and related programs, social sciences, surgical technology, systems analysis, teacher aide, tourism, ultrasound technology.

ACADEMIC PROGRAMS. 2-year transfer program, double major, dual enrollment of high school students, honors program, independent study, cross-registration. **Remedial services:** Learning center, remedial instruction, special counselor, tutoring. **Placement/credit:** AP, CLEP General and Subject, institutional tests; 30 credit hours maximum for associate degree.

ACADEMIC REQUIREMENTS. Freshmen must earn minimum GPA of 1.6 to continue in good standing. 53% of freshmen return for sophomore year. Students must declare major on application. **Graduation requirements:** 64 hours for associate. Most students required to take courses in English, history, mathematics, biological/physical sciences, social sciences.

FRESHMAN ADMISSIONS. Selection criteria: Open admissions.

1992 FRESHMAN CLASS PROFILE. 6,002 men and women enrolled. **Characteristics:** 96% from in state, 100% commute, 43% have minority backgrounds. Average age is 28.

FALL-TERM APPLICATIONS. No fee. No closing date; applicants notified on a rolling basis beginning on or about April 1.

STUDENT LIFE. Activities: Student government, magazine, student newspaper, choral groups, drama, jazz band, musical theater.

ATHLETICS. NJCAA. **Intercollegiate:** Baseball M, basketball, soccer M, softball W, tennis M, volleyball W, wrestling M.

STUDENT SERVICES. Aptitude testing, career counseling, employment service for undergraduates, health services, on-campus day care, personal counseling, placement service for graduates, veterans counselor, services/facilities for handicapped.

ANNUAL EXPENSES. Tuition and fees (1992-93): $1,170, $300 additional for out-of-district students, $630 additional for out-of-state students. **Books and supplies:** $500. **Other expenses:** $1,440.

FINANCIAL AID. 39% of freshmen, 34% of continuing students receive some form of aid. 97% of grants, 80% of loans, all jobs based on need. 1,782 enrolled freshmen were judged to have need, 384 were offered aid. Academic, music/drama, art, athletic, leadership scholarships available. **Aid applications:** No closing date; priority given to applications received by March 19; applicants notified on a rolling basis beginning on or about March 15.

ADDRESS/TELEPHONE. Bart Devoti, Director of Admissions and Registrar, St. Louis Community College at Forest Park, 5600 Oakland, St. Louis, MO 63110. (314) 644-9127.

St. Louis Community College at Meramec
St. Louis, Missouri CB code: 6430

2-year public community college, coed. Founded in 1963. **Accreditation:** Regional. **Undergraduate enrollment:** 2,441 men, 2,401 women full time; 3,750 men, 6,909 women part time. **Faculty:** 577 total (177 full time), 31 with doctorates or other terminal degrees. **Location:** Suburban campus in large city; 15 miles from St. Louis. **Calendar:** Semester, extensive summer session. Saturday and extensive evening/early morning classes. **Microcomputers:** 300 located in classrooms, computer centers. **Additional facts:** Two off-campus sites at South County Education Center and West County Education Center.

DEGREES OFFERED. AA, AS, AAS. 987 associate degrees awarded in 1992. 17% in business and management, 16% health sciences, 26% multi/interdisciplinary studies, 5% visual and performing arts.

UNDERGRADUATE MAJORS. Accounting, architectural technologies, architecture, biological and physical sciences, biology, business and management, business and office, business computer/console/peripheral equipment operation, business data processing and related programs, business data programming, business systems analysis, commercial art, communications, computer and information sciences, court reporting, criminal justice studies, data processing, education, electronic technology, elementary education, emergency medical technologies, engineering, finance, fine arts, graphic arts technology, horticultural science, horticulture, humanities and social sciences, illustration design, interior design, law enforcement and corrections, legal assistant/paralegal, legal secretary, liberal/general studies, management science, marketing and distribution, mathematics, music, nursing, occupational therapy assistant, ornamental horticulture, photography, physical sciences, physical therapy assistant, real estate, secondary education, secretarial and related programs, social sciences, social work, word processing.

ACADEMIC PROGRAMS. 2-year transfer program, accelerated program, computer delivered (on-line) credit-bearing course offerings, dual enrollment of high school students, honors program, independent study, internships, study abroad, telecourses, cross-registration. **Remedial services:** Learning center, preadmission summer program, reduced course load, remedial instruction, special counselor, tutoring. **Placement/credit:** AP, CLEP General and Subject, institutional tests; 49 credit hours maximum for associate degree.

ACADEMIC REQUIREMENTS. Freshmen must earn minimum GPA of 2.0 to continue in good standing. 56% of freshmen return for sophomore year. Students must declare major on enrollment. **Graduation requirements:** 64 hours for associate. Most students required to take courses in English, history, humanities, mathematics, biological/physical sciences, social sciences.

FRESHMAN ADMISSIONS. Selection criteria: Open admissions. Nursing, occupational therapy assistant, and physical therapist assistant and paramedic technology programs have admissions requirements. **High school preparation:** 22 units recommended. Recommended units include English 4, mathematics 2, social science 3 and science 2. 7 elective units, 2 physical education/health, 1 practical art, 1 fine art. **Test requirements:** College Assessment Test Battery required.

1992 FRESHMAN CLASS PROFILE. 992 men, 1,488 women enrolled. **Characteristics:** 99% from in state, 100% commute, 13% have minority backgrounds, 1% are foreign students. Average age is 22.

FALL-TERM APPLICATIONS. No fee. No closing date; priority given to applications received by August 1; applicants notified on a rolling basis beginning on or about March 1. Interview required for some allied health programs applicants. Early admission available.

STUDENT LIFE. Activities: Student government, magazine, student newspaper, choral groups, concert band, drama, jazz band, musical theater, symphony orchestra.

ATHLETICS. NJCAA. **Intercollegiate:** Baseball M, basketball M, ice hockey M, soccer, softball W, volleyball W, wrestling M. **Intramural:** Basketball, volleyball.

STUDENT SERVICES. Aptitude testing, career counseling, employment service for undergraduates, freshman orientation, health services, personal counseling, placement service for graduates, veterans counselor, special adviser for adult returning women, services/facilities for handicapped.

ANNUAL EXPENSES. Tuition and fees: $1,200, $300 additional for out-of-district students, $600 additional for out-of-state students. **Books and supplies:** $500. **Other expenses:** $1,600.

FINANCIAL AID. 25% of freshmen, 25% of continuing students receive some form of aid. 93% of grants, 89% of loans, all jobs based on need. 1,952 enrolled freshmen were judged to have need, all were offered aid. Academic, music/drama, art, athletic, minority scholarships available. **Aid applications:** No closing date; priority given to applications received by May 1; applicants notified on a rolling basis beginning on or about February 1; must reply immediately.

ADDRESS/TELEPHONE. Jean DeGrand Belt, Director of Admissions and Registrar, St. Louis Community College at Meramec, 11333 Big Bend Boulevard, Kirkwood, MO 63122-5799. (314) 984-7601. Fax: (314) 984-7117.

St. Louis University
St. Louis, Missouri CB code: 6629

Admissions: 86% of applicants accepted
Based on: ••• School record
•• Test scores
• Activities, special talents
Completion: 92% of freshmen end year in good standing
61% graduate, 21% of these enter graduate study

4-year private university, coed, affiliated with Roman Catholic Church. Founded in 1818. **Accreditation:** Regional. **Undergraduate enrollment:** 3,423 men, 2,756 women full time; 477 men, 682 women part time. **Graduate enrollment:** 234 men, 273 women full time; 446 men, 881 women part time. **Faculty:** 1,733 total (1,135 full time), 1,217 with doctorates or other terminal degrees. **Location:** Urban campus in large city; 3 miles from downtown St. Louis. **Calendar:** Semester, extensive summer session. **Microcomputers:** 300 located in dormitories, classrooms, computer centers. **Special facilities:** Vatican Manuscripts Microfilm Library, Cupples House Museum, Reis Biological Station.

DEGREES OFFERED. AA, AS, BA, BS, MA, MS, MBA, MSW, PhD, EdD, MD, OD, JD. 100 associate degrees awarded in 1992. 50% in engineering technologies, 50% philosophy, religion, theology. 1,406 bachelor's degrees awarded. 34% in business and management, 7% communications, 10% engineering, 7% health sciences, 7% allied health, 6% psychology, 6% social sciences, 6% trade and industry. Graduate degrees offered in 58 major fields of study.

UNDERGRADUATE MAJORS. Bachelor's: Accounting, aerospace/aeronautical/astronautical engineering, air traffic control, airline piloting and navigation, American studies, applied computer science, atmospheric sciences and meteorology, aviation computer technology, aviation management, avionics, biological and physical sciences, biology, business administration and management, business economics, cardiovascular perfusion technology, chemistry, classics, clinical laboratory science, communications, computer mathematics, computer software systems, criminal justice studies, decision sciences, early childhood education, earth sciences, economics, electrical/electronics/communications engineering, elementary education, engineering and other disciplines, English, finance, fine arts, French, geology, geophysics and seismology, German, Greek (classical), history, humanities, humanities and social sciences, international business management, junior high education, labor/industrial relations, Latin, liberal/general studies, logistics, management information systems, management science, marketing management, mathematics, medical laboratory technologies, medical records administration, medical records technology, nuclear medical technology, nursing, occupational therapy, personnel management, philosophy, physical therapy, physician's assistant, physics, political science and government, Portuguese, psychology, Russian, secondary education, social work, sociology, Spanish, specific learning disabilities, speech correction, speech pathology/audiology, theological studies, tourism, urban studies, visual and performing arts.

ACADEMIC PROGRAMS. Accelerated program, double major, dual enrollment of high school students, education specialist degree, honors program, independent study, internships, student-designed major, study abroad, teacher preparation, cross-registration; liberal arts/career combination in engineering. **Remedial services:** Preadmission summer program, reduced course load, remedial instruction, special counselor, tutoring. **ROTC:** Air Force, Army. **Placement/credit:** AP, CLEP Subject, institutional tests; 30 credit hours maximum for bachelor's degree.

ACADEMIC REQUIREMENTS. Freshmen must earn minimum GPA of 2.0 to continue in good standing. 2.5 minimum GPA required for good standing in nursing nd allied health programs. 81% of freshmen return for sophomore year. Students must declare major by end of first year. **Graduation requirements:** 60 hours for associate (12 in major), 120 hours for bachelor's (30 in major). Most students required to take courses in arts/fine arts, English, foreign languages, history, humanities, mathematics, philosophy/religion, biological/physical sciences, social sciences. **Postgraduate studies:** 3% enter law school, 3% enter medical school, 4% enter MBA programs, 11% enter other graduate study. **Additional information:** Aerospace courses offered on Parks College campus in Illinois.

FRESHMAN ADMISSIONS. Selection criteria: School achievement record most important. Test scores, extracurricular activities considered. **High school preparation:** 16 units recommended. Recommended units include biological science 1, English 4, foreign language 2, mathematics 3, physical science 1 and social science 2. Nursing and allied health programs require 1 chemistry, 1 algebra, 1 biology. **Test requirements:** SAT or ACT; score report by August 1.

1992 FRESHMAN CLASS PROFILE. 1,621 men applied, 1,373 accepted, 389 enrolled; 1,643 women applied, 1,443 accepted, 524 enrolled. 71% had high school GPA of 3.0 or higher, 29% between 2.0 and 2.99. 19% were in top tenth and 55% were in top quarter of graduating class. **Academic background:** Mid 50% of enrolled freshmen had ACT composite between 21-27. 92% submitted ACT scores. **Characteristics:** 73% from in state, 56% live in college housing, 20% have minority backgrounds, 3% are foreign students, 8% join fraternities/sororities. Average age is 18.

FALL-TERM APPLICATIONS. $25 fee, may be waived for applicants with need. No closing date; applicants notified on a rolling basis. CRDA. Deferred and early admission available. For physical therapy scholarship candidates, application deadlines apply. They are December 15 for incoming freshmen and Febuary 1 for transfer students. Occupational therapy students should apply early. Both should take the ACT.

STUDENT LIFE. Housing: Dormitories (men, women, coed); fraternity, sorority housing available. Limited fraternity sorority housing available. Housing available all 4 years as undergraduate. **Activities:** Student government, magazine, radio, student newspaper, yearbook, choral groups, drama, jazz band, music ensembles, musical theater, pep band, fraternities, sororities, service organizations, Black Student Alliance, sports clubs.

ATHLETICS. NCAA. **Intercollegiate:** Baseball M, basketball, cross-country, diving, field hockey W, golf M, rifle, soccer M, softball W, swimming, tennis, volleyball W. **Intramural:** Badminton, basketball, bowling, handball, racquetball, rugby M, soccer, softball, swimming, table tennis, tennis, volleyball, water polo.

STUDENT SERVICES. Aptitude testing, career counseling, employment service for undergraduates, freshman orientation, health services, personal counseling, placement service for graduates, special adviser for adult students, veterans counselor, services/facilities for handicapped.

ANNUAL EXPENSES. Tuition and fees: $10,820. **Room and board:** $4,610. **Books and supplies:** $750. **Other expenses:** $3,470.

FINANCIAL AID. 85% of freshmen, 80% of continuing students receive some form of aid. 88% of grants, 89% of loans, all jobs based on need. Academic, music/drama, art, athletic, minority scholarships available. **Aid applications:** No closing date; priority given to applications received by January 1; applicants notified on a rolling basis beginning on or about February 15. **Additional information:** Physical therapy scholarship candidates must apply by December 15; February 1 for transfer students. Occupational therapy students should apply earlier. ACT required.

ADDRESS/TELEPHONE. Kent R. Hopkins, Director of Undergraduate Admission, St. Louis University, 221 North Grand Boulevard, St. Louis, MO 63103-2097. (314) 658-2500. (800) 325-6666. Fax: (314) 658-3874.

Southeast Missouri State University
Cape Girardeau, Missouri CB code: 6655

4-year public university, coed. Founded in 1873. **Accreditation:** Regional. **Undergraduate enrollment:** 2,967 men, 3,586 women full time; 494 men, 756 women part time. **Graduate enrollment:** 29 men, 64 women full time; 140 men, 408 women part time. **Faculty:** 442 total (407 full time), 243 with doctorates or other terminal degrees. **Location:** Rural campus in large town; 120 miles from St. Louis. **Microcomputers:** 1,000 located in dormitories, libraries, classrooms, computer centers.

DEGREES OFFERED. AA, AAS, BA, BS, MA, MS. 40 associate degrees awarded in 1992. 86% in health sciences, 14% home economics. 1,240 bachelor's degrees awarded. 22% in business and management, 5% communications, 24% education, 6% home economics, 8% letters/literature, 11% social sciences. Graduate degrees offered in 27 major fields of study.

UNDERGRADUATE MAJORS. Associate: Child development/care/guidance, nursing. **Bachelor's:** Accounting, advertising, agribusiness, agricultural sciences, agronomy, American studies, animal sciences, anthropology, art education, biological and physical sciences, biology, business administration and management, business economics, business education, chemistry, classics, clothing and textiles management/production/services, computer and information sciences, criminal justice studies, dramatic arts, early childhood education, earth sciences, economics, education of the emotionally handicapped, education of the mentally handicapped, education of the physically handicapped, electronic technology, elementary education, engineering physics, English, English education, family/consumer resource management, fashion merchandising, finance, food science and nutrition, foreign languages education, French, geography, geology, historic preservation, history, home economics education, home furnishings and equipment management/production/services, horticultural science, human environment and housing, humanities and social sciences, individual and family development, industrial arts education, interior design, journalism, law enforcement and corrections, liberal/general studies, marketing and distribution, marketing management, mathematics, mathematics education, music, music education, music performance, music theory and composition, nursing, office supervision and management, parks and recreation management, personnel management, philosophy, physical education, physics, political science and government, productions/operations management, psychology, public relations, radio/television broadcasting, science education, secondary education, secretarial and related programs, social science education, social work, sociology, Spanish, special education, specific learning disabilities, speech pathology/audiology, speech/communication/theater education, textiles and clothing.

ACADEMIC PROGRAMS. 2-year transfer program, accelerated program, cooperative education, double major, dual enrollment of high school students, education specialist degree, honors program, independent study, internships, study abroad, teacher preparation, visiting/exchange student program, cross-registration, eligible biology and chemistry students may attend Gulf Coast Research Laboratory at Ocean Springs, Mississippi; combined bachelor's/graduate program in law. **Remedial services:** Reduced course load, remedial instruction, tutoring, writing center. **ROTC:** Air Force, Army. **Placement/credit:** AP, CLEP Subject, institutional tests; 30 credit hours maximum for bachelor's degree.

ACADEMIC REQUIREMENTS. Freshmen must earn minimum GPA of 2.0 to continue in good standing. 65% of freshmen return for sophomore year. Students must declare major by end of first year. **Graduation requirements:** 64 hours for associate, 124 hours for bachelor's (30 in major). Most students required to take courses in arts/fine arts, English, history, humanities, mathematics, biological/physical sciences, social sciences. **Postgraduate studies:** 50% from 2-year programs enter 4-year programs.

FRESHMAN ADMISSIONS. Selection criteria: Enhanced ACT composite score of 18 for in-state and out-of-state applicants, and high school GPA of 2.0. Must not need any remedial courses. **High school preparation:** 11 units required. Required and recommended units include English 4, mathematics 2, social science 3 and science 2. Biological science 1, foreign language 2 and physical science 1 recommended. Four additional units required from foreign language, speech, and fine arts. **Test requirements:** ACT; score report by August 1.

1992 FRESHMAN CLASS PROFILE. 629 men, 845 women enrolled. 47% had high school GPA of 3.0 or higher, 47% between 2.0 and 2.99. **Academic background:** Mid 50% of enrolled freshmen had ACT composite between 18-23. 95% submitted ACT scores. **Characteristics:** 92% from in state, 55% live in college housing, 8% have minority backgrounds, 1% are foreign students, 9% join fraternities/sororities. Average age is 19.

FALL-TERM APPLICATIONS. $20 fee, may be waived for applicants with need. No closing date; priority given to applications received by June 1; applicants notified on a rolling basis beginning on or about October 1. Audition required for music applicants. Deferred and early admission available.

STUDENT LIFE. Housing: Dormitories (men, women, coed); fraternity, sorority housing available. **Activities:** Student government, magazine, radio, student newspaper, television, yearbook, choral groups, concert band, dance, drama, jazz band, marching band, music ensembles, musical theater, opera, pep band, symphony orchestra, fraternities, sororities, Baptist Student Union, Marquette-Newman, Wesley Foundation, Lutheran Center, Young Democrats, Young Republicans, Association of Black Collegians. **Additional information:** Automobiles permitted.

ATHLETICS. NCAA. **Intercollegiate:** Baseball M, basketball, cross-country, football M, golf M, gymnastics W, softball W, tennis, track and field, volleyball W. **Intramural:** Archery, badminton, basketball, bowling, cross-country, fencing, field hockey W, golf, gymnastics, handball, racquetball, rugby M, soccer, softball, swimming, tennis, track and field, volleyball, water polo.

STUDENT SERVICES. Aptitude testing, career counseling, employment service for undergraduates, freshman orientation, health services, personal counseling, placement service for graduates, special adviser for adult students, veterans counselor, services/facilities for handicapped.

ANNUAL EXPENSES. Tuition and fees (1992-93): $2,158, $1,664 additional for out-of-state students. **Room and board:** $3,085. **Books and supplies:** $210. **Other expenses:** $1,350.

FINANCIAL AID. 45% of freshmen, 54% of continuing students receive some form of aid. 75% of grants, 97% of loans, 31% of jobs based on need. Academic, music/drama, art, athletic, state/district residency, leadership, alumni affiliation, religious affiliation, minority scholarships available. **Aid applications:** No closing date; priority given to applications received by March 31; applicants notified on a rolling basis beginning on or about March 31; must reply within 2 weeks.

ADDRESS/TELEPHONE. Dr. Fred Snider, Dean of Admissions and Records, Southeast Missouri State University, One University Plaza, Cape Girardeau, MO 63701. (314) 651-2255.

Southwest Baptist University

Bolivar, Missouri — CB code: 6664

4-year private university and liberal arts college, coed, affiliated with Southern Baptist Convention. Founded in 1878. **Accreditation:** Regional. **Undergraduate enrollment:** 815 men, 1,042 women full time; 255 men, 976 women part time. **Graduate enrollment:** 18 men, 11 women full time; 43 men, 164 women part time. **Faculty:** 208 total (100 full time), 49 with doctorates or other terminal degrees. **Location:** Rural campus in small town; 30 miles from Springfield, 120 miles from Kansas City. **Calendar:** 4-1-4, extensive summer session. **Microcomputers:** 40 located in libraries, classrooms, computer centers. **Additional facts:** Classes scheduled at six off-campus locations.

DEGREES OFFERED. AA, AS, AAS, BA, BS, MS. 10 associate degrees awarded in 1992. 30% in business/office and marketing/distribution, 10% computer sciences, 20% home economics, 50% letters/literature, 10% philosophy, religion, theology. 390 bachelor's degrees awarded. 12% in business and management, 10% education, 11% teacher education, 6% mathematics, 13% philosophy, religion, theology, 8% psychology, 11% social sciences, 5% visual and performing arts. Graduate degrees offered in 2 major fields of study.

UNDERGRADUATE MAJORS. Associate: Computer and information sciences, emergency medical technologies, emergency/disaster science, liberal/general studies, secretarial and related programs. **Bachelor's:** Accounting, art education, Bible studies, biology, business administration and management, business and management, business education, chemistry, clinical laboratory science, communications, computer and information sciences, dramatic arts, elementary education, English, fine arts, health care administration, history, liberal/general studies, marketing management, mathematics, music, music education, nursing, physical education, physical therapy, political science and government, psychology, recreation and community services technologies, religion, religious education, religious music, social science education, social work, sociology, Spanish, speech, sports management, sports medicine, telecommunications, theological studies.

ACADEMIC PROGRAMS. Cooperative education, double major, dual enrollment of high school students, honors program, independent study, internships, study abroad, teacher preparation; liberal arts/career combination in engineering, health sciences. **Remedial services:** Learning center, preadmission summer program, reduced course load, remedial instruction, special counselor, tutoring. **ROTC:** Army. **Placement/credit:** AP, CLEP General and Subject, IB, institutional tests; 25 credit hours maximum for associate degree; 25 credit hours maximum for bachelor's degree.

ACADEMIC REQUIREMENTS. Freshmen must earn minimum GPA of 1.66 to continue in good standing. 70% of freshmen return for sophomore year. Students must declare major by end of second year. **Graduation requirements:** 64 hours for associate, 128 hours for bachelor's (30 in major). Most students required to take courses in arts/fine arts, computer science, English, history, humanities, mathematics, philosophy/religion, biological/physical sciences, social sciences. **Postgraduate studies:** 97% from 2-year programs enter 4-year programs. 5% enter law school, 3% enter medical school, 10% enter MBA programs, 30% enter other graduate study.

FRESHMAN ADMISSIONS. Selection criteria: Admission based on school achievement record (2.0 high school GPA). **High school preparation:** 14 units recommended. Recommended units include biological science 1, English 4, foreign language 2, mathematics 3, physical science 1 and social science 3. **Test requirements:** SAT or ACT (ACT preferred); score report by September 15.

1992 FRESHMAN CLASS PROFILE. 647 men applied, 647 accepted, 242 enrolled; 775 women applied, 775 accepted, 443 enrolled. 59% had high school GPA of 3.0 or higher, 36% between 2.0 and 2.99. 6% were in top tenth and 19% were in top quarter of graduating class. **Academic background:** Mid 50% of enrolled freshmen had ACT composite between 17-25. 56% submitted ACT scores. **Characteristics:** 76% from in state, 78% live in college housing, 17% have minority backgrounds, 1% are foreign students. Average age is 18.

FALL-TERM APPLICATIONS. $25 fee, may be waived for applicants with need. Closing date September 15; priority given to applications received by August 1; applicants notified on a rolling basis. Audition required for music applicants. Portfolio required for art applicants. Interview required for academically weak applicants, recommended for all. Deferred and early admission available.

STUDENT LIFE. Housing: Dormitories (men, women); apartment housing available. **Activities:** Student government, student newspaper, television, yearbook, choral groups, concert band, drama, jazz band, marching band, music ensembles, musical theater, opera, pep band, symphony orchestra, campus ministries, Young Democrats, Young Republicans. **Additional information:** Religious observance required.

ATHLETICS. NCAA. **Intercollegiate:** Baseball M, basketball, cross-country, football M, golf M, softball W, tennis, track and field, volleyball W. **Intramural:** Baseball M, basketball, bowling, football M, golf M, soccer, softball W, table tennis, volleyball.

STUDENT SERVICES. Career counseling, employment service for undergraduates, freshman orientation, health services, personal counseling, placement service for graduates, veterans counselor, services/facilities for handicapped.

ANNUAL EXPENSES. Tuition and fees (1992-93): $6,401. **Room and board:** $2,380. **Books and supplies:** $450. **Other expenses:** $600.

FINANCIAL AID. 90% of freshmen, 85% of continuing students receive some form of aid. 78% of grants, 86% of loans, 66% of jobs based on need. Academic, music/drama, athletic, religious affiliation scholarships available. **Aid applications:** No closing date; priority given to applications received by April 30; applicants notified on a rolling basis beginning on or about March 1; must reply within 2 weeks.

ADDRESS/TELEPHONE. Ben Sells, V.P. for Adm/Student Life, Southwest Baptist University, 1601 South Springfield, Bolivar, MO 65613-2496. (417) 326-1810. (800) 526-5859. Fax: (417) 326-1514.

Southwest Missouri State University

Springfield, Missouri CB code: 6665

Admissions: 91% of applicants accepted
Based on: ••• School record, test scores
• Activities, essay, interview, recommendations, special talents
Completion: 80% of freshmen end year in good standing
31% graduate

4-year public university, coed. Founded in 1906. **Accreditation:** Regional. **Undergraduate enrollment:** 6,734 men, 7,609 women full time; 1,717 men, 2,341 women part time. **Graduate enrollment:** 158 men, 194 women full time; 358 men, 862 women part time. **Faculty:** 903 total (680 full time), 530 with doctorates or other terminal degrees. **Location:** Urban campus in small city; 170 miles from Kansas City. **Calendar:** Semester, extensive summer session. **Microcomputers:** 250 located in dormitories, libraries, classrooms, computer centers. **Special facilities:** Observatory, student exhibition center, 125-acre agriculture research and demonstration center.

DEGREES OFFERED. AA, AS, BA, BS, BFA, MA, MS, MBA, MEd. 99 associate degrees awarded in 1992. 11% in business/office and marketing/distribution, 36% health sciences, 53% multi/interdisciplinary studies. 2,515 bachelor's degrees awarded. 32% in business and management, 10% communications, 17% teacher education, 7% psychology, 7% social sciences. Graduate degrees offered in 21 major fields of study.

UNDERGRADUATE MAJORS. **Associate:** Liberal/general studies, medical secretary, nursing. **Bachelor's:** Accounting, agribusiness, agricultural education, agricultural sciences, agronomy, animal sciences, architectural technologies, art education, automotive technology, biology, business administration and management, business and management, business education, chemistry, city/community/regional planning, communications, computer and information sciences, creative writing, dance, design general, drafting and design technology, dramatic arts, economics, education of the mentally handicapped, electromechanical technology, electronic technology, elementary education, English, English education, finance, fine arts, food production/management/services, food science and nutrition, foreign languages education, French, geography, geology, German, gerontology, graphic design, history, home economics, home economics education, horticultural science, human environment and housing, humanities and social sciences, individual and family development, industrial arts education, industrial technology, Latin, Latin American studies, management information systems, manufacturing technology, marketing management, mathematics, mathematics education, medical laboratory technologies, music education, music performance, music theory and composition, nursing, office supervision and management, parks and recreation management, philosophy, physical education, physical science technology, physics, political science and government, psychology, public administration, public relations, radio/television broadcasting, radiograph medical technology, religion, respiratory therapy technology, science education, social science education, social studies education, social work, sociology, Spanish, specific learning disabilities, speech pathology/audiology, survey and mapping technology, textiles and clothing, wildlife management.

ACADEMIC PROGRAMS. 2-year transfer program, cooperative education, double major, dual enrollment of high school students, education specialist degree, honors program, internships, student-designed major, study abroad, teacher preparation, telecourses, visiting/exchange student program; liberal arts/career combination in health sciences. **Remedial services:** Learning center, preadmission summer program, reduced course load, remedial instruction, tutoring. **ROTC:** Army. **Placement/credit:** AP, CLEP Subject, institutional tests; 30 credit hours maximum for bachelor's degree.

ACADEMIC REQUIREMENTS. Freshmen must earn minimum GPA of 1.75 to continue in good standing. 69% of freshmen return for sophomore year. Students must declare major by end of second year. **Graduation requirements:** 62 hours for associate, 124 hours for bachelor's. Most students required to take courses in English, history, humanities, mathematics, biological/physical sciences, social sciences.

FRESHMAN ADMISSIONS. **Selection criteria:** Admissions based on sliding scale of class rank and minimum ACT composite score of 17. **High school preparation:** 14 units recommended. Recommended units include English 4, foreign language 2, mathematics 3, social science 2 and science 2. One speech recommended. **Test requirements:** ACT; score report by August 15. **Additional information:** Priority for housing and class registration based admission date.

1992 FRESHMAN CLASS PROFILE. 6,791 men and women applied, 6,197 accepted; 1,458 men enrolled, 1,855 women enrolled. 15% were in top tenth of graduating class. **Academic background:** Mid 50% of enrolled freshmen had ACT composite between 19-24. 100% submitted ACT scores. **Characteristics:** 93% from in state, 63% live in college housing, 6% have minority backgrounds, 10% join fraternities/sororities. Average age is 19.

FALL-TERM APPLICATIONS. $15 fee, may be waived for applicants with need. Closing date August 1; priority given to applications received by February 1; applicants notified on a rolling basis beginning on or about October 1. Interview recommended for academically weak applicants. Essay recommended.

STUDENT LIFE. **Housing:** Dormitories (men, women, coed); apartment, fraternity, sorority, handicapped housing available. Honors House for students in University Honors Program. **Activities:** Student government, magazine, radio, student newspaper, yearbook, choral groups, concert band, dance, drama, jazz band, marching band, music ensembles, musical theater, opera, pep band, symphony orchestra, fraternities, sororities, Association of Black Collegians, Association of International Students, College Young Democrats, College Young Republicans, University Christian Fellowship, Gamma Sigma Sigma, Alpha Phi Omega, BACCHUS Bears, Missouri Scholars Academy, World Affairs Council. **Additional information:** Approximately 240 student organizations supplement academic work and provide opportunities for socializing.

ATHLETICS. NCAA. **Intercollegiate:** Baseball M, basketball, cross-country, diving M, field hockey W, football M, golf, rifle M, soccer M, softball W, swimming M, tennis, track and field, volleyball W, wrestling M. **Intramural:** Badminton, baseball M, basketball, bowling, cross-country, golf, handball, racquetball, rugby M, soccer, softball, swimming, table tennis, tennis, track and field, volleyball, wrestling.

STUDENT SERVICES. Aptitude testing, career counseling, employment service for undergraduates, freshman orientation, health services, personal counseling, placement service for graduates, special adviser for adult students, veterans counselor, services/facilities for handicapped.

ANNUAL EXPENSES. **Tuition and fees:** $2,386, $2,250 additional for out-of-state students. **Room and board:** $3,024. **Books and supplies:** $600. **Other expenses:** $2,000.

FINANCIAL AID. 50% of freshmen, 50% of continuing students receive some form of aid. 53% of grants, 94% of loans, 13% of jobs based on need. 1,440 enrolled freshmen were judged to have need, 1,334 were offered aid. Academic, music/drama, art, athletic, leadership, minority scholarships available. **Aid applications:** No closing date; priority given to applications received by March 31; applicants notified on a rolling basis beginning on or about July 1; must reply within 4 weeks.

ADDRESS/TELEPHONE. Donald E. Simpson, Director of Admissions and Records, Southwest Missouri State University, 901 South National, Springfield, MO 65804-0094. (417) 836-5517. (800) 492-7900. Fax: (417) 836-6334.

State Fair Community College

Sedalia, Missouri CB code: 6709

2-year public community college, coed. Founded in 1966. **Accreditation:** Regional. **Undergraduate enrollment:** 463 men, 633 women full time; 595 men, 730 women part time. **Faculty:** 142 total (67 full time). **Location:** Rural campus in large town; 78 miles from Kansas City. **Calendar:** Semester, limited summer session. **Microcomputers:** Located in classrooms, computer centers.

DEGREES OFFERED. AA, AS, AAS. 261 associate degrees awarded in 1992. 8% in business and management, 15% business/office and marketing/distribution, 14% health sciences, 53% multi/interdisciplinary studies, 7% trade and industry.

UNDERGRADUATE MAJORS. Accounting, agribusiness, agricultural business and management, automotive technology, business and management, business and office, business data processing and related programs, computer and information sciences, court reporting, electrical and electronics equipment repair, electronic technology, finance, food production/management/services, law enforcement and corrections technologies, legal secretary, liberal/general studies, machine tool operation/machine shop, marketing and distribution, medical records technology, medical secretary, nursing, precision metal work, secretarial and related programs, trade and industrial supervision and management, word processing.

ACADEMIC PROGRAMS. 2-year transfer program, dual enrollment of high school students, internships. **Remedial services:** Remedial instruction, Tech Prep Semester. **Placement/credit:** AP, CLEP General and Subject, institutional tests; 30 credit hours maximum for associate degree.

ACADEMIC REQUIREMENTS. Freshmen must earn minimum GPA of 1.6 to continue in good standing. 55% of freshmen return for sophomore year. Students must declare major by end of second year. **Graduation requirements:** 64 hours for associate. Most students required to take courses in English, history, humanities, mathematics, biological/physical sciences, social sciences.

FRESHMAN ADMISSIONS. **Selection criteria:** Open admissions. Health occupations and court reporting programs have selective admissions. **Test requirements:** ACT for placement and counseling only; score report by August 19.

1992 FRESHMAN CLASS PROFILE. 230 men applied, 230 accepted, 218 enrolled; 272 women applied, 272 accepted, 236 enrolled. **Characteristics:** 98% from in state, 100% commute, 6% have minority backgrounds. Average age is 27.

FALL-TERM APPLICATIONS. No fee. No closing date; applicants notified on a rolling basis. Interview recommended for vocational-technical applicants. Deferred and early admission available.

STUDENT LIFE. **Activities:** Student government, student newspaper, yearbook, choral groups, drama, pep band.

ATHLETICS. NJCAA. **Intercollegiate:** Basketball, soccer M. **Intramural:** Bowling.

STUDENT SERVICES. Aptitude testing, career counseling, employment service for undergraduates, freshman orientation, personal counseling, placement service for graduates, veterans counselor, services/facilities for handicapped.

ANNUAL EXPENSES. Tuition and fees (1992-93): $795, $441 additional for out-of-district students, $1,619 additional for out-of-state students. **Books and supplies:** $300. **Other expenses:** $500.

FINANCIAL AID. 63% of freshmen, 41% of continuing students receive some form of aid. 86% of grants, 91% of loans, 74% of jobs based on need. Academic, music/drama, art, athletic scholarships available. **Aid applications:** No closing date; priority given to applications received by July 1; applicants notified on a rolling basis beginning on or about July 15; must reply within 3 weeks.

ADDRESS/TELEPHONE. Marina Kroenke, Admissions Counselor, State Fair Community College, 3201 West 16th Street, Sedalia, MO 65301-2199. (816) 530-5800. Fax: (816) 530-5820.

Stephens College
Columbia, Missouri — CB code: 6683

4-year private liberal arts college, women only. Founded in 1833. **Accreditation:** Regional. **Undergraduate enrollment:** 667 women. **Faculty:** 94 total (69 full time), 41 with doctorates or other terminal degrees. **Location:** Urban campus in small city; 125 miles from St. Louis and Kansas City. **Calendar:** Semester, limited summer session. **Microcomputers:** 51 located in libraries, computer centers. **Special facilities:** Professional-level theater, private preschool and elementary school, stables. **Additional facts:** Bachelor of fine arts in theater program open to limited number of men with associate degree.

DEGREES OFFERED. AA, BA, BS, BFA. 13 associate degrees awarded in 1992. 100% in multi/interdisciplinary studies. 204 bachelor's degrees awarded. 27% in business and management, 14% communications, 7% teacher education, 11% multi/interdisciplinary studies, 5% psychology, 20% visual and performing arts.

UNDERGRADUATE MAJORS. Associate: Liberal/general studies. **Bachelor's:** American studies, biology, business administration and management, communications, computer and information sciences, counseling psychology, dance, dramatic arts, early childhood education, education, elementary education, English, equestrian science, European studies, fashion design, fashion merchandising, fine arts, foreign languages (multiple emphasis), French, health sciences, history, journalism, liberal/general studies, mathematics, medical records administration, musical theater, philosophy, political science and government, psychology, public relations, radio/television broadcasting, religion, social sciences, Spanish, studio art.

ACADEMIC PROGRAMS. Accelerated program, double major, dual enrollment of high school students, external degree, independent study, internships, student-designed major, study abroad, teacher preparation, Washington semester, cross-registration, Oxford-Cambridge program; liberal arts/career combination in engineering, health sciences. **Remedial services:** Reduced course load, remedial instruction, special counselor, tutoring, learning skills course. **ROTC:** Air Force, Army, Naval. **Placement/credit:** AP, CLEP General and Subject, institutional tests.

ACADEMIC REQUIREMENTS. Freshmen must earn minimum GPA of 2.0 to continue in good standing. 63% of freshmen return for sophomore year. Students must declare major by end of second year. **Graduation requirements:** 60 hours for associate, 120 hours for bachelor's (36 in major). Most students required to take courses in arts/fine arts, English, history, mathematics, philosophy/religion, biological/physical sciences, social sciences. **Postgraduate studies:** 95% from 2-year programs enter 4-year programs. 5% enter law school, 5% enter medical school, 3% enter MBA programs, 10% enter other graduate study.

FRESHMAN ADMISSIONS. Selection criteria: School achievement record given more weight than test scores. Campus visit very important. **High school preparation:** 12 units required; 13 recommended. Recommended units include English 4, foreign language 1, mathematics 3, social science 2 and science 2. **Test requirements:** SAT or ACT; score report by August 1. **Additional information:** Male students admitted by audition in dance, theater, and musical theater.

1992 FRESHMAN CLASS PROFILE. 187 men and women enrolled. 64% had high school GPA of 3.0 or higher, 34% between 2.0 and 2.99. **Academic background:** Mid 50% of enrolled freshmen had SAT-V between 380-560, SAT-M between 380-530; ACT composite between 18-25. 60% submitted SAT scores, 67% submitted ACT scores. **Characteristics:** 27% from in state, 95% live in college housing, 9% have minority backgrounds, 1% are foreign students, 20% join fraternities/sororities. Average age is 18.

FALL-TERM APPLICATIONS. $25 fee, may be waived for applicants with need. Closing date August 14; priority given to applications received by May 1; applicants notified on a rolling basis; must reply by May 1 or within 2 weeks if notified thereafter. Interview recommended. Audition recommended for theater, musical theater applicants. Portfolio recommended for art applicants. Essay recommended. Deferred admission available.

STUDENT LIFE. Housing: Dormitories (women). Seniors may live off-campus with permission from Dean of Students. Freshman academic residence hall available. **Activities:** Student government, magazine, radio, student newspaper, television, yearbook, choral groups, dance, drama, musical theater, opera, sororities, Burrall Cabinet, Martin Luther King, Jr., Scholarship Committee, People Projects, Model United Nations, Fine Arts House, honor societies.

ATHLETICS. Intramural: Archery, badminton, basketball, fencing, golf, horseback riding, sailing, softball, swimming, table tennis, tennis, volleyball.

STUDENT SERVICES. Aptitude testing, career counseling, employment service for undergraduates, freshman orientation, health services, personal counseling, placement service for graduates, special adviser for adult students, services/facilities for handicapped.

ANNUAL EXPENSES. Tuition and fees: $13,410. **Room and board:** $5,040. **Books and supplies:** $450. **Other expenses:** $1,450.

FINANCIAL AID. 65% of freshmen, 60% of continuing students receive some form of aid. 68% of grants, 94% of loans, all jobs based on need. 117 enrolled freshmen were judged to have need, all were offered aid. Academic, music/drama, state/district residency, leadership scholarships available. **Aid applications:** No closing date; priority given to applications received by March 15; applicants notified on a rolling basis beginning on or about March 15; must reply by May 1 or within 2 weeks if notified thereafter.

ADDRESS/TELEPHONE. Colleen Bevins, Director of Admission, Stephens College, PO Box 2121, 1200 East Broadway, Columbia, MO 65215-9986. (314) 876-7207 ext. 207. (800) 876-7207. Fax: (314) 876-7248.

Three Rivers Community College
Poplar Bluff, Missouri — CB code: 6836

2-year public community college, coed. Founded in 1966. **Accreditation:** Regional. **Undergraduate enrollment:** 484 men, 861 women full time; 448 men, 1,468 women part time. **Faculty:** 99 total (58 full time), 2 with doctorates or other terminal degrees. **Location:** Rural campus in large town; 160 miles from St. Louis. **Calendar:** Semester, limited summer session. Extensive evening/early morning classes. **Additional facts:** Selected courses offered at Bootheel Education Center at Malden.

DEGREES OFFERED. AA, AS, AAS. 212 associate degrees awarded in 1992. 9% in business and management, 6% business/office and marketing/distribution, 5% computer sciences, 20% allied health, 51% multi/interdisciplinary studies, 5% parks/recreation, protective services, public affairs.

UNDERGRADUATE MAJORS. Accounting, agricultural business and management, agricultural sciences, architectural technologies, business and management, business and office, civil technology, clinical laboratory science, computer and information sciences, criminal justice technology, drafting, finance, hospitality and recreation marketing, law enforcement and corrections technologies, liberal/general studies, manufacturing technology, marketing management, mechanical design technology, medical laboratory technologies, nursing, secretarial and related programs.

ACADEMIC PROGRAMS. 2-year transfer program, dual enrollment of high school students, independent study, internships. **Remedial services:** Learning center, remedial instruction, tutoring. **Placement/credit:** CLEP General and Subject, institutional tests; 30 credit hours maximum for associate degree.

ACADEMIC REQUIREMENTS. Freshmen must earn minimum GPA of 1.5 to continue in good standing. 52% of freshmen return for sophomore year. Students must declare major on application. **Graduation requirements:** 64 hours for associate. Most students required to take courses in English, history, humanities, mathematics, biological/physical sciences, social sciences.

FRESHMAN ADMISSIONS. Selection criteria: Open admissions. **Test requirements:** ACT for placement and counseling only; score report by August 1.

1992 FRESHMAN CLASS PROFILE. 601 men, 1,144 women enrolled. **Characteristics:** 96% from in state, 100% commute.

FALL-TERM APPLICATIONS. $10 fee. No closing date; applicants notified on a rolling basis.

STUDENT LIFE. Activities: Student government, student newspaper, choral groups, concert band, drama, jazz band, music ensembles, pep band.

ATHLETICS. NJCAA. **Intercollegiate:** Baseball M, basketball, golf M, volleyball W. **Intramural:** Basketball, table tennis, volleyball.

STUDENT SERVICES. Career counseling, employment service for undergraduates, personal counseling, placement service for graduates, veterans counselor, services/facilities for handicapped.

ANNUAL EXPENSES. Tuition and fees (1992-93): $840, $300 additional for out-of-district students, $960 additional for out-of-state students. **Books and supplies:** $256. **Other expenses:** $900.

FINANCIAL AID. 75% of freshmen, 75% of continuing students receive some form of aid. Grants, loans, jobs available. Academic scholarships available. **Aid applications:** No closing date; applicants notified on a rolling basis; must reply within 4 weeks.

ADDRESS/TELEPHONE. Vida Stanard, Coordinator of Admissions, 2080 Three Rivers Community College, Three Rivers Boulevard, Poplar Bluff, MO 63901-1308. (314) 686-4101 ext. 232. Fax: (314) 686-9604.

University of Missouri: Columbia
Columbia, Missouri CB code: 6875

Admissions: 77% of applicants accepted
Based on: ••• School record, test scores
Completion: 50% graduate

4-year public university, coed. Founded in 1839. **Accreditation:** Regional. **Undergraduate enrollment:** 7,768 men, 7,965 women full time; 789 men, 864 women part time. **Graduate enrollment:** 1,880 men, 1,521 women full time; 1,214 men, 1,345 women part time. **Faculty:** 1,517 total (1,479 full time), 1,275 with doctorates or other terminal degrees. **Location:** Rural campus in small city; 125 miles from Kansas City and St. Louis. **Calendar:** Semester, limited summer session. **Microcomputers:** 700 located in dormitories, libraries, classrooms, computer centers, campus-wide network. **Special facilities:** Museum of art and archaeology, museum of anthropology, observatory, research nuclear reactor, Freedom of Information Center, university forest, geology museum, food for 21st century program, engineering experiment station, center for research in social behavior. **Additional facts:** Correspondence courses offered.

DEGREES OFFERED. BA, BS, BFA, MA, MS, MBA, MFA, MEd, MSW, PhD, EdD, MD, DVM, JD. 3,680 bachelor's degrees awarded in 1992. 5% in agriculture, 18% business and management, 11% communications, 9% education, 9% engineering, 6% health sciences, 5% home economics, 5% letters/literature, 10% social sciences. Graduate degrees offered in 134 major fields of study.

UNDERGRADUATE MAJORS. Accounting, advertising, Afro-American (black) studies, agricultural economics, agricultural education, agricultural engineering, agricultural mechanics, agricultural sciences, agronomy, animal sciences, anthropology, apparel and accessories marketing, archeology, art education, art history, atmospheric sciences and meteorology, biochemistry, biology, business administration and management, business and management, business education, chemical engineering, chemistry, civil engineering, classics, communications, computer and information sciences, computer engineering, crafts, curriculum and instruction, cytotechnology, dramatic arts, early childhood education, East Asian studies, economics, education, education of the mentally handicapped, education of the physically handicapped, electrical/electronics/communications engineering, elementary education, English, English education, environmental design, environmental health engineering, family/consumer resource management, fashion merchandising, finance, fine arts, fishing and fisheries, food management, food science and nutrition, food sciences, foreign languages education, forestry and related sciences, French, geography, geology, German, graphic design, Greek (classical), health physics, history, home economics, home economics education, horticulture, hospitality and recreation marketing, hotel/motel and restaurant management, human environment and housing, individual and family development, industrial arts education, industrial engineering, insurance and risk management, international agriculture, international business management, international studies, journalism, Latin, Latin American studies, liberal/general studies, linguistics, marketing and distribution, marketing and distributive education, mathematics, mathematics education, mechanical engineering, medical laboratory technologies, microbiology, music, music education, nuclear medical technology, nursing, occupational therapy, operations research, parks and recreation management, personnel management, philosophy, physical therapy, physics, political science and government, psychology, radio/television broadcasting, radiograph medical technology, real estate, religion, respiratory therapy, respiratory therapy technology, rural sociology, Russian, Russian and Slavic studies, science education, secondary education, social sciences, social studies education, social work, sociology, South American studies, South Asian studies, Spanish, specific learning disabilities, speech, speech correction, speech pathology/audiology, speech/communication/theater education, statistics, textiles and clothing, tourism, trade and industrial education, wildlife management, women's studies.

ACADEMIC PROGRAMS. Accelerated program, computer delivered (on-line) credit-bearing course offerings, cooperative education, double major, dual enrollment of high school students, education specialist degree, honors program, independent study, internships, student-designed major, study abroad, teacher preparation, telecourses, visiting/exchange student program, Washington semester, cross-registration, freshman early admission with 30 ACT score and required interview to law school and school of medicine. **Remedial services:** Learning center, preadmission summer program, remedial instruction, special counselor, tutoring. **ROTC:** Air Force, Army. **Placement/credit:** AP, CLEP Subject, IB, institutional tests; 15 credit hours maximum for bachelor's degree.

ACADEMIC REQUIREMENTS. Freshmen must earn minimum GPA of 2.0 to continue in good standing. 81% of freshmen return for sophomore year. Students must declare major by end of second year. **Graduation requirements:** 120 hours for bachelor's (30 in major). Most students required to take courses in computer science, English, foreign languages, humanities, mathematics, biological/physical sciences, social sciences. **Additional information:** Honors college for high ability students. Guaranteed admission to School of Law with ACT composite 30 or higher, and must maintain 3.3 GPA. Early admission to School of Medicine with ACT composite 30 or higher and required interview.

FRESHMAN ADMISSIONS. Selection criteria: Selective admissions based on required core courses, and combination of high school rank and test scores. **High school preparation:** 15 units required. Required and recommended units include English 4, mathematics 3-4, social science 2-3 and science 2-3. Foreign language 2 recommended. Mathematics units only count algebra I and higher. One unit fine arts. **Test requirements:** ACT; score report by May 15. **Additional information:** Trial summer admission open to Missouri residents. Student must complete English with C or better to continue enrollment on probation in fall.

1992 FRESHMAN CLASS PROFILE. 3,200 men applied, 2,415 accepted, 1,327 enrolled; 3,783 women applied, 2,970 accepted, 1,624 enrolled. 32% were in top tenth and 63% were in top quarter of graduating class. **Academic background:** Mid 50% of enrolled freshmen had ACT composite between 23-27. 93% submitted ACT scores. **Characteristics:** 87% from in state, 76% live in college housing, 8% have minority backgrounds, 1% are foreign students, 25% join fraternities/sororities. Average age is 18.

FALL-TERM APPLICATIONS. $25 fee, may be waived for applicants with need. $50 fee for foreign applicants. Closing date May 15; priority given to applications received by February 1; applicants notified on a rolling basis. Interview required for School of Medicine applicants applicants. Deferred and early admission available. High school students must meet freshmen admission criteria to qualify for early admission.

STUDENT LIFE. Housing: Dormitories (men, women, coed); apartment, fraternity, sorority, handicapped housing available. Cable television in each residence hall room. Access to university's computer mainframe in each room; students provide own computers. Honors/international houses available through honors college. **Activities:** Student government, film, magazine, radio, student newspaper, television, yearbook, daily community newspaper, choral groups, concert band, dance, drama, jazz band, marching band, music ensembles, musical theater, opera, pep band, symphony orchestra, fraternities, sororities, wide variety of religious, political, ethnic, and social service organizations.

ATHLETICS. NCAA. **Intercollegiate:** Baseball M, basketball, cross-country, diving, football M, golf, gymnastics W, softball W, swimming, tennis, track and field, volleyball W, wrestling M. **Intramural:** Badminton, basketball, bowling, cross-country, diving, fencing, football M, golf, gymnastics W, handball M, horseback riding, lacrosse, racquetball, rugby, soccer, softball, swimming, table tennis, tennis, track and field, volleyball, wrestling M.

STUDENT SERVICES. Aptitude testing, career counseling, employment service for undergraduates, freshman orientation, health services, on-campus day care, personal counseling, placement service for graduates, veterans counselor, services/facilities for handicapped.

ANNUAL EXPENSES. Tuition and fees: $3,125, $5,076 additional for out-of-state students. **Room and board:** $3,168. **Books and supplies:** $540. **Other expenses:** $1,706.

FINANCIAL AID. 62% of freshmen, 57% of continuing students receive some form of aid. 47% of grants, 88% of loans, 12% of jobs based on need. 1,115 enrolled freshmen were judged to have need, 1,095 were offered aid. Academic, music/drama, art, athletic, leadership scholarships available. **Aid applications:** No closing date; priority given to applications received by March 1; applicants notified on a rolling basis beginning on or about April 15; must reply within 3 weeks. **Additional information:** George C. Brooks scholarship provides up to $6,000 (in-state) or $9,000 (out-State) for students of color with top 10% rank and high ACT scores.

ADDRESS/TELEPHONE. Gary L. Smith, Director of Admissions and Registrar, University of Missouri: Columbia, 228 Jesse Hall, Columbia, MO 65211. (314) 882-7651. Fax: (314) 882-7887.

University of Missouri: Kansas City
Kansas City, Missouri CB code: 6872

Admissions: 62% of applicants accepted
Based on: ••• School record, test scores
Completion: 82% of freshmen end year in good standing
26% graduate

4-year public university, coed. Founded in 1929. **Accreditation:** Regional. **Undergraduate enrollment:** 1,688 men, 2,038 women full time; 968 men, 1,202 women part time. **Graduate enrollment:** 978 men, 995 women full time; 891 men, 1,729 women part time. **Faculty:** 622 total (436 full time), 416 with doctorates or other terminal degrees. **Location:** Urban campus in very large city. **Calendar:** Semester, extensive summer session. Saturday and extensive evening/early morning classes. **Microcomputers:** 300 located in dormitories, libraries, classrooms, computer centers. **Special facilities:** Art gallery, observatory, Linda Hall Library of Science and Technology, recital series.

DEGREES OFFERED. BA, BS, BFA, MA, MS, MBA, MFA, PhD, DDS, MD, B. Pharm, Pharm D, JD. 1,091 bachelor's degrees awarded in 1992. 19% in business and management, 5% communications, 20% teacher education, 5% health sciences, 10% life sciences, 9% multi/interdisciplinary studies, 5% psychology, 8% social sciences, 5% visual and performing arts. Graduate degrees offered in 74 major fields of study.

UNDERGRADUATE MAJORS. Accounting, American studies, art history, biology, business and management, chemistry, civil engineering, communications, computer and information sciences, criminal justice studies, dance, dental hygiene, direct marketing, dramatic arts, earth sciences, economics, electrical/electronics/communications engineering, elementary education, English, English education, fine arts, French, geography, geology, German, health education, history, Jewish studies, liberal/general studies, mathematics, mathematics education, mechanical engineering, medical laboratory technologies, music, music education, music performance, music theory and composition, nursing, pharmacy, philosophy, physical education, physics, political science and government, psychology, science education, secondary education, social science education, social studies education, sociology, Spanish, studio art, urban studies.

ACADEMIC PROGRAMS. Accelerated program, cooperative education, double major, dual enrollment of high school students, education specialist degree, honors program, independent study, internships, student-designed major, study abroad, teacher preparation, visiting/exchange student program, weekend college, cross-registration, cooperative engineering program with University of Missouri: Columbia, cooperative architecture program with Kansas State University; combined bachelor's/graduate program in business administration, medicine, law. **Remedial services:** Learning center, reduced course load. **ROTC:** Army. **Placement/credit:** AP, CLEP Subject, institutional tests; 30 credit hours maximum for bachelor's degree.

ACADEMIC REQUIREMENTS. Freshmen must earn minimum GPA of 2.0 to continue in good standing. 63% of freshmen return for sophomore year. Students must declare major by end of second year. **Graduation requirements:** 120 hours for bachelor's (30 in major). Most students required to take courses in arts/fine arts, English, foreign languages, history, humanities, mathematics, philosophy/religion, biological/physical sciences, social sciences.

FRESHMAN ADMISSIONS. Selection criteria: Admissions based on class rank, test scores, and high school course requirements. Admission very selective to combined arts and sciences/medical, dental programs; moderately selective to pharmacy program. **High school preparation:** 14 units required. Required and recommended units include English 4, mathematics 3, social science 2-3 and science 2. Biological science 1, foreign language 2 and physical science 1 recommended. Science must include 1 unit with laboratory. Mathematics units must be algebra I and above. Required: 3 more units in either foreign language, social science, mathematics, English or science plus 1 unit of fine arts. **Test requirements:** SAT or ACT (ACT preferred); score report by July 1.

1992 FRESHMAN CLASS PROFILE. 1,506 men and women applied, 930 accepted; 233 men enrolled, 271 women enrolled. **Academic background:** Mid 50% of enrolled freshmen had ACT composite between 22-27. 92% submitted ACT scores. **Characteristics:** 81% from in state, 95% commute, 30% have minority backgrounds, 5% are foreign students, 4% join fraternities/sororities.

FALL-TERM APPLICATIONS. $25 fee. Closing date July 1; priority given to applications received by May 1; applicants notified on a rolling basis. Interview required for medicine, dentistry and pharmacy applicants applicants. Audition required for music applicants. Portfolio recommended for art applicants. Deferred and early admission available. Architecture, dentistry, medicine programs have different deadlines and admissions requirements.

STUDENT LIFE. Housing: Dormitories (coed); fraternity, sorority housing available. Off-campus housing plentiful in immediate area of campus. **Activities:** Student government, film, magazine, radio, student newspaper, television, choral groups, concert band, dance, drama, jazz band, music ensembles, musical theater, opera, pep band, symphony orchestra, repertory theater, fraternities, sororities, various religious, political, ethnic, and social service organizations.

ATHLETICS. NCAA. **Intercollegiate:** Basketball, cross-country, golf, rifle, soccer M, softball W, tennis, track and field, volleyball W. **Intramural:** Archery, badminton, basketball, fencing, football, golf, handball, horseback riding, racquetball, skiing, soccer, softball, squash, swimming, table tennis, tennis, track and field, volleyball, water polo.

STUDENT SERVICES. Aptitude testing, career counseling, employment service for undergraduates, freshman orientation, on-campus day care, personal counseling, placement service for graduates, veterans counselor, women's center, ethnic awareness center, services/facilities for handicapped.

ANNUAL EXPENSES. Tuition and fees (1992-93): $2,841, $4,860 additional for out-of-state students. **Room and board:** $3,355. **Books and supplies:** $568. **Other expenses:** $5,850.

FINANCIAL AID. 40% of freshmen, 38% of continuing students receive some form of aid. 48% of grants, 87% of loans, 27% of jobs based on need. Academic, music/drama, art, athletic, state/district residency, leadership, minority scholarships available. **Aid applications:** No closing date; priority given to applications received by March 15; applicants notified on a rolling basis beginning on or about April 15; must reply within 2 weeks.

ADDRESS/TELEPHONE. Nancy Mead, Director of Admissions, University of Missouri: Kansas City, Student Srvcs Bldg, 4825 Troost Avenue, Kansas City, MO 64110-2944. (816) 235-1111. Fax: (816) 235-1717.

University of Missouri: Rolla
Rolla, Missouri

CB code: 6876

Admissions: 81% of applicants accepted
Based on: ••• School record, test scores
Completion: 80% of freshmen end year in good standing
36% graduate, 30% of these enter graduate study

4-year public university and engineering college, coed. Founded in 1870. **Accreditation:** Regional. **Undergraduate enrollment:** 3,012 men, 829 women full time; 387 men, 206 women part time. **Graduate enrollment:** 364 men, 76 women full time; 661 men, 122 women part time. **Faculty:** 434 total (342 full time), 397 with doctorates or other terminal degrees. **Location:** Rural campus in large town; 90 miles from St. Louis. **Calendar:** Semester, extensive summer session. **Microcomputers:** 480 located in dormitories, libraries, classrooms, computer centers, campus-wide network. **Special facilities:** Computerized manufacturing system, nuclear reactor, observatory, experimental mine.

DEGREES OFFERED. BA, BS, MS, PhD. 697 bachelor's degrees awarded in 1992. 6% in computer sciences, 81% engineering. Graduate degrees offered in 23 major fields of study.

UNDERGRADUATE MAJORS. Premedicine. aerospace/aeronautical/astronautical engineering, applied mathematics, biology, ceramic engineering, chemical engineering, chemistry, civil engineering, computer and information sciences, economics, electrical/electronics/communications engineering, engineering management, English, geological engineering, geology, geophysics and seismology, history, industrial engineering, management systems, mechanical engineering, metallurgical engineering, mining and mineral engineering, nuclear engineering, petroleum engineering, philosophy, physics, psychology.

ACADEMIC PROGRAMS. Cooperative education, double major, dual enrollment of high school students, honors program, independent study, study abroad, teacher preparation. **Remedial services:** Learning center, preadmission summer program, reduced course load, special counselor, tutoring. **ROTC:** Air Force, Army. **Placement/credit:** AP, CLEP Subject, institutional tests.

ACADEMIC REQUIREMENTS. Freshmen must earn minimum GPA of 2.0 to continue in good standing. 75% of freshmen return for sophomore year. Students must declare major by end of first year. **Graduation requirements:** 132 hours for bachelor's. Most students required to take courses in arts/fine arts, English, history, mathematics, biological/physical sciences.

FRESHMAN ADMISSIONS. Selection criteria: Admissions based on high school class rank and test scores. **High school preparation:** 15 units required. Required and recommended units include English 4, mathematics 3-4, social science 2 and science 2. Foreign language 2 recommended. 4 units mathematics recommended for engineering applicants. 1 unit fine arts. 3 additional units selected from foreign language, English, mathematics, science, or social studies. **Test requirements:** SAT or ACT (ACT preferred). Preferred date for SAT or ACT score reports July 1.

1992 FRESHMAN CLASS PROFILE. 1,948 men and women applied, 1,579 accepted; 643 men enrolled, 178 women enrolled. 48% were in top tenth of graduating class. **Academic background:** Mid 50% of enrolled freshmen had SAT-V between 460-590, SAT-M between 570-690; ACT composite between 25-31. 32% submitted SAT scores, 94% submitted ACT scores. **Characteristics:** 73% from in state, 90% live in college housing, 9% have minority backgrounds, 1% are foreign students, 30% join fraternities/sororities. Average age is 18.

FALL-TERM APPLICATIONS. $20 fee. $50 fee for non-U.S. citizens. No closing date; priority given to applications received by July 1; applicants notified on a rolling basis. Deferred and early admission available.

STUDENT LIFE. Housing: Dormitories (men, women, coed); apartment, fraternity, sorority, handicapped housing available. **Activities:** Student government, radio, student newspaper, yearbook, choral groups, concert band, jazz band, marching band, music ensembles, musical theater, pep band, symphony orchestra, fraternities, sororities, student union board, student council, St. Pat's Board, international students club, Association for Black Students, Society of Women Engineers.

ATHLETICS. NCAA. **Intercollegiate:** Basketball, cross-country, diving M, football M, golf M, rifle, soccer M, softball W, swimming M, tennis M, track and field. **Intramural:** Badminton, baseball M, basketball, bowling, cross-country M, diving, football M, golf M, handball M, racquetball, rugby M, soccer M, softball, swimming, table tennis, tennis, track and field, volleyball, water polo M, wrestling M.

STUDENT SERVICES. Aptitude testing, career counseling, employment service for undergraduates, freshman orientation, health services, personal counseling, placement service for graduates, special adviser for adult students, services/facilities for handicapped.

ANNUAL EXPENSES. Tuition and fees: $3,254, $5,016 additional for

out-of-state students. **Room and board:** $3,498. **Books and supplies:** $600. **Other expenses:** $862.

FINANCIAL AID. 62% of freshmen, 65% of continuing students receive some form of aid. 27% of grants, 91% of loans, 8% of jobs based on need. 545 enrolled freshmen were judged to have need, 500 were offered aid. Academic, music/drama, athletic, state/district residency, alumni affiliation, minority scholarships available. **Aid applications:** No closing date; priority given to applications received by March 31; applicants notified on a rolling basis beginning on or about May 1; must reply within 3 weeks.

ADDRESS/TELEPHONE. Dave Allen, Director of Admissions/Student Financial Aid, University of Missouri: Rolla, 102 Parker Hall, Rolla, MO 65401. (314) 341-4164. (800) 522-0938. Fax: (314) 341-4082.

University of Missouri: St. Louis

St. Louis, Missouri — CB code: 6889

4-year public university, coed. Founded in 1963. **Accreditation:** Regional. **Undergraduate enrollment:** 2,177 men, 2,611 women full time; 1,981 men, 2,570 women part time. **Graduate enrollment:** 172 men, 191 women full time; 680 men, 1,235 women part time. **Faculty:** 635 total (390 full time). **Location:** Urban campus in large city; 5 miles from downtown. **Calendar:** Semester, extensive summer session. **Microcomputers:** Located in computer centers.

DEGREES OFFERED. BA, BS, MA, MS, MBA, MEd, PhD, EdD, OD. 1,758 bachelor's degrees awarded in 1992. 42% in business and management, 18% teacher education, 6% physical sciences, 6% psychology, 6% social sciences. Graduate degrees offered in 29 major fields of study.

UNDERGRADUATE MAJORS. Anthropology, applied mathematics, art history, biology, business and management, chemistry, communications, computer and information sciences, computer programming, early childhood education, economics, elementary education, English, French, German, history, industrial and organizational psychology, information sciences and systems, law enforcement and corrections, liberal/general studies, mathematics, music, nursing, philosophy, physics, political science and government, psychology, social psychology, social work, sociology, Spanish, special education, speech.

ACADEMIC PROGRAMS. Cooperative education, double major, dual enrollment of high school students, honors program, independent study, internships, student-designed major, study abroad, teacher preparation, cross-registration. **Remedial services:** Learning center, remedial instruction, special counselor, tutoring. **ROTC:** Air Force, Army. **Placement/credit:** AP, CLEP General and Subject, institutional tests; 30 credit hours maximum for bachelor's degree.

ACADEMIC REQUIREMENTS. Freshmen must earn minimum GPA of 1.75 to continue in good standing. 63% of freshmen return for sophomore year. Students must declare major by end of second year. **Graduation requirements:** 120 hours for bachelor's. Most students required to take courses in English, history, humanities, mathematics, biological/physical sciences, social sciences.

FRESHMAN ADMISSIONS. Selection criteria: Admissions based on class rank and test scores. **High school preparation:** 15 units required. Required units include English 4, mathematics 3, social science 2 and science 2. 3 additional units in English, mathematics, or sciences with 2 foreign language recommended; 1 fine art required. **Test requirements:** SAT or ACT; score report by July 1. School and College Ability Tests may be submitted in place of SAT or ACT.

1992 FRESHMAN CLASS PROFILE. 529 men and women enrolled. **Academic background:** Mid 50% of enrolled freshmen had ACT composite between 19-25. 89% submitted ACT scores. **Characteristics:** 99% from in state, 17% have minority backgrounds, 1% are foreign students. Average age is 19.

FALL-TERM APPLICATIONS. No fee. No closing date; priority given to applications received by July 1; applicants notified on a rolling basis. Audition required for music applicants. Portfolio required for art applicants. Early admission available.

STUDENT LIFE. Activities: Student government, film, radio, student newspaper, choral groups, music ensembles, fraternities, sororities.

ATHLETICS. NAIA, NCAA. **Intercollegiate:** Baseball M, basketball, soccer, softball W, swimming, tennis, volleyball W. **Intramural:** Baseball, basketball, golf, handball, racquetball, soccer, softball, swimming, table tennis, tennis, volleyball.

STUDENT SERVICES. Career counseling, employment service for undergraduates, freshman orientation, health services, on-campus day care, personal counseling, placement service for graduates, veterans counselor, services/facilities for handicapped.

ANNUAL EXPENSES. Tuition and fees: $3,171, $5,439 additional for out-of-state students. **Room and board:** $3,964. **Books and supplies:** $500. **Other expenses:** $855.

FINANCIAL AID. 54% of freshmen, 37% of continuing students receive some form of aid. 69% of grants, 85% of loans, 10% of jobs based on need. 288 enrolled freshmen were judged to have need, 218 were offered aid. Academic, athletic, leadership scholarships available. **Aid applications:** Closing date October 31; priority given to applications received by April 1; applicants notified on a rolling basis beginning on or about May 15; must reply within 2 weeks.

ADDRESS/TELEPHONE. Mimi LaMarca, Director of Admissions/Registrar, University of Missouri: St. Louis, 8001 Natural Bridge Road, St. Louis, MO 63121. (314) 553-5454.

Washington University

St. Louis, Missouri — CB code: 6929

Admissions:	65% of applicants accepted
Based on:	••• School record
	•• Essay, recommendations, special talents, test scores
	• Activities
Completion:	97% of freshmen end year in good standing
	84% graduate, 84% of these enter graduate study

4-year private university, coed. Founded in 1853. **Accreditation:** Regional. **Undergraduate enrollment:** 2,511 men, 2,303 women full time; 638 men, 622 women part time. **Graduate enrollment:** 1,852 men, 1,497 women full time; 1,330 men, 819 women part time. **Faculty:** 3,284 total (1,847 full time), 3,218 with doctorates or other terminal degrees. **Location:** Suburban campus in large city; 7 miles from downtown. **Calendar:** Semester, extensive summer session. Extensive evening/early morning classes. **Microcomputers:** 1,500 located in dormitories, libraries, classrooms, computer centers. **Special facilities:** University Gallery of Art, Tyson Research Center, 59-acre medical campus.

DEGREES OFFERED. BA, BS, BFA, BArch, MA, MS, MBA, MFA, MEd, MSW, PhD, EdD, MD, JD. 1,423 bachelor's degrees awarded in 1992. 9% in business and management, 5% computer sciences, 13% engineering, 6% allied health, 5% languages, 5% letters/literature, 7% life sciences, 8% psychology, 22% social sciences, 8% visual and performing arts. Graduate degrees offered in 98 major fields of study.

UNDERGRADUATE MAJORS. African studies, Afro-American (black) studies, American literature, anthropology, Arabic, archeology, architecture, art education, art history, arts management, Asian studies, biochemistry, biological and physical sciences, biology, business administration and management, ceramics, chemical engineering, chemistry, Chinese, civil engineering, classics, comparative literature, computer and information sciences, computer engineering, design (general), dramatic arts, drawing, early childhood, early childhood education, earth sciences, East Asian studies, economics, education, education of the deaf and hearing impaired, electrical/electronics/communications engineering, elementary education, engineering and other disciplines, engineering mechanics, engineering physics, English, English education, English literature, European studies, fashion design, fine arts, foreign languages education, French, geology, German, glass, graphic design, Greek (classical), Hebrew, history, illustration design, information sciences and systems, international studies, Islamic studies, Italian, Japanese, Jewish studies, junior high education, Latin, Latin American studies, linguistics, mathematics, mathematics education, mechanical engineering, medieval studies, multimedia, music, music education, music history and appreciation, music performance, music theory and composition, occupational therapy, painting, philosophy, photography, physics, planetary science, political economy, political science and government, printmaking, psychology, religion, Russian, science education, sculpture, secondary education, social foundations, social science education, social studies education, Spanish, special education, speech/communication/theater education, studio art, systems analysis, systems engineering, visual and performing arts, Western European studies, women's studies.

ACADEMIC PROGRAMS. Accelerated program, cooperative education, double major, dual enrollment of high school students, honors program, independent study, internships, student-designed major, study abroad, teacher preparation, visiting/exchange student program, Washington semester, cross-registration; liberal arts/career combination in engineering; combined bachelor's/graduate program in business administration. **Remedial services:** Learning center, reduced course load, remedial instruction, special counselor, tutoring. **ROTC:** Air Force, Army. **Placement/credit:** AP, IB, institutional tests.

ACADEMIC REQUIREMENTS. No policy requiring minimum GPA; records of students having academic difficulty are reviewed individually. 94% of freshmen return for sophomore year. Students must declare major by end of second year. **Graduation requirements:** 120 hours for bachelor's (21 in major). Most students required to take courses in arts/fine arts, English, history, humanities, mathematics, biological/physical sciences, social sciences. **Postgraduate studies:** 13% enter law school, 12% enter medical school, 13% enter MBA programs, 46% enter other graduate study.

FRESHMAN ADMISSIONS. Selection criteria: Rigor of high school curriculum very important, as well as high school achievement measured by class rank and GPA. Test scores next in order of importance. **High school preparation:** 15 units required; 20 recommended. Required and recommended units include English 4, foreign language 2-4, mathematics 3-4, social science 3-4 and science 3-4. **Test requirements:** SAT or ACT; score report by February 1. Achievement tests recommended for placement. **Additional in-**

formation: Statement from student's guidance counselor supporting early admission decision required. Counselor and teacher recommendations required of all applicants.

1992 FRESHMAN CLASS PROFILE. 4,356 men applied, 2,820 accepted, 574 enrolled; 3,974 women applied, 2,617 accepted, 530 enrolled. 65% were in top tenth and 92% were in top quarter of graduating class. **Academic background:** Mid 50% of enrolled freshmen had SAT-V between 520-620, SAT-M between 600-700; ACT composite between 26-31. 92% submitted SAT scores, 49% submitted ACT scores. **Characteristics:** 12% from in state, 98% live in college housing, 24% have minority backgrounds, 3% are foreign students, 30% join fraternities/sororities. Average age is 18.

FALL-TERM APPLICATIONS. $50 fee, may be waived for applicants with need. Closing date January 15; applicants notified on or about April 1; must reply by May 1. Essay required. Portfolio recommended for fine arts applicants. CRDA. Deferred and early admission available. EDP-F.

STUDENT LIFE. Housing: Dormitories (coed); apartment, fraternity, handicapped housing available. Suites common living space shared by up to 6 students (2 doubles, 2 singles) available. **Activities:** Student government, magazine, radio, student newspaper, yearbook, choral groups, concert band, dance, drama, jazz band, music ensembles, musical theater, pep band, symphony orchestra, fraternities, sororities, religious, political, community service, and ethnic organizations.

ATHLETICS. NCAA. **Intercollegiate:** Baseball M, basketball, cross-country, diving, fencing, football M, golf M, ice hockey M, lacrosse M, rowing (crew), rugby M, soccer, swimming, tennis, track and field, volleyball W. **Intramural:** Badminton, basketball, bowling, cross-country, golf, racquetball, soccer, squash, swimming, table tennis, tennis, track and field, volleyball, wrestling M.

STUDENT SERVICES. Aptitude testing, career counseling, employment service for undergraduates, freshman orientation, health services, personal counseling, placement service for graduates, special adviser for adult students, veterans counselor, services/facilities for handicapped.

ANNUAL EXPENSES. Tuition and fees: $17,776. **Room and board:** $5,639. **Books and supplies:** $746. **Other expenses:** $1,512.

FINANCIAL AID. 61% of freshmen, 60% of continuing students receive some form of aid. 87% of grants, 98% of loans, all jobs based on need. 521 enrolled freshmen were judged to have need, all were offered aid. Academic, art scholarships available. **Aid applications:** Closing date February 15; applicants notified on a rolling basis beginning on or about April 1; must reply by May 1 or within 2 weeks if notified thereafter.

ADDRESS/TELEPHONE. Harold Wingood, Dean of Undergraduate Admission, Washington University, Campus Box 1089 One Brookings Drive, St. Louis, MO 63130-4899. (314) 935-6000. (800) 638-0700. Fax: (314) 935-4290.

Webster University

Webster Groves, Missouri — CB code: 6933

Admissions:	66% of applicants accepted
Based on:	••• School record
	•• Essay, recommendations, special talents, test scores
	• Activities, interview
Completion:	85% of freshmen end year in good standing
	45% graduate, 25% of these enter graduate study

4-year private university, coed. Founded in 1915. **Accreditation:** Regional. **Undergraduate enrollment:** 616 men, 1,037 women full time; 439 men, 1,147 women part time. **Graduate enrollment:** 1,025 men, 577 women full time; 2,561 men, 2,297 women part time. **Faculty:** 414 total (114 full time), 110 with doctorates or other terminal degrees. **Location:** Suburban campus in large city; 12 miles from downtown St. Louis. **Calendar:** Semester, limited summer session. Saturday and extensive evening/early morning classes. **Microcomputers:** 125 located in computer centers. **Special facilities:** Repertory Theater of St. Louis, Opera Theater of St. Louis, Dance St. Louis, community symphony, Webster Wind Quintet, 2 art galleries. **Additional facts:** European campuses in Geneva, Switzerland; Vienna, Austria; Leiden, The Netherlands; and London, England, offer bachelor's and master's programs in business and management, computer studies, and international studies.

DEGREES OFFERED. BA, BFA, MA, MS, MBA, D. 891 bachelor's degrees awarded in 1992. 43% in business and management, 11% communications, 8% computer sciences, 8% health sciences, 5% psychology, 10% social sciences, 7% visual and performing arts. Graduate degrees offered in 28 major fields of study.

UNDERGRADUATE MAJORS. Accounting, advertising, anthropology, art education, biology, business administration and management, business and management, business economics, ceramics, cinematography/film, communications, comparative literature, computer and information sciences, creative writing, dance, dramatic arts, drawing, early childhood education, education, education of the emotionally handicapped, education of the mentally handicapped, elementary education, English, English education, fine arts, foreign languages (multiple emphasis), foreign languages education, French, graphic design, health care administration, history, human resources development, international relations, international studies, jazz, journalism, junior high education, legal assistant/paralegal, liberal/general studies, management information systems, management science, marketing management, mathematics, mathematics education, music, music business management, music education, music history and appreciation, music performance, music theory and composition, musical theater, nursing, painting, personnel management, philosophy, photography, political science and government, pre-architecture, predentistry, preengineering, prelaw, premedicine, printmaking, psychology, public relations, radio/television broadcasting, radio/television technology, real estate, religion, science education, science technologies, sculpture, secondary education, social sciences, social studies education, sociology, Spanish, special education, specific learning disabilities, studio art, technical and business writing, technical theater, theater design, video, visual and performing arts.

ACADEMIC PROGRAMS. Accelerated program, double major, honors program, independent study, internships, student-designed major, study abroad, teacher preparation, visiting/exchange student program, cross-registration, combination bachelor's/master's degree in many subject areas; liberal arts/career combination in engineering. **Remedial services:** Learning center, reduced course load, remedial instruction, special counselor, tutoring. **Placement/credit:** AP, CLEP General and Subject, institutional tests; 64 credit hours maximum for bachelor's degree.

ACADEMIC REQUIREMENTS. Freshmen must earn minimum GPA of 2.0 to continue in good standing. 72% of freshmen return for sophomore year. Students must declare major by end of second year. **Graduation requirements:** 128 hours for bachelor's (36 in major). **Additional information:** Professional Actors Equity theater company in residence for theater program. Internships and practicums available in most areas.

FRESHMAN ADMISSIONS. Selection criteria: School achievement record, test scores. Rank in top half of class recommended. Recommendation and autobiographical statement required. **High school preparation:** 16 units recommended. Recommended units include English 4, foreign language 2, mathematics 2, social science 4 and science 2. Must have 1 unit fine arts, and 3 units in electives. **Test requirements:** SAT or ACT; score report by June 1. **Additional information:** RN required for nursing major.

1992 FRESHMAN CLASS PROFILE. 256 men applied, 170 accepted, 84 enrolled; 399 women applied, 261 accepted, 124 enrolled. 54% had high school GPA of 3.0 or higher, 45% between 2.0 and 2.99. 22% were in top tenth and 42% were in top quarter of graduating class. **Academic background:** Mid 50% of enrolled freshmen had SAT-V between 420-560, SAT-M between 420-570; ACT composite between 20-26. 37% submitted SAT scores, 77% submitted ACT scores. **Characteristics:** 68% from in state, 50% commute, 15% have minority backgrounds, 2% are foreign students. Average age is 19.

FALL-TERM APPLICATIONS. $20 fee, may be waived for applicants with need. Closing date June 1; priority given to applications received by April 1; applicants notified on a rolling basis; must reply by May 1 or within 4 weeks if notified thereafter. Audition required for dance, music, theater arts, musical theater applicants. Portfolio required for art applicants. Essay required. Interview recommended. CRDA. Deferred and early admission available.

STUDENT LIFE. Housing: Dormitories (coed). **Activities:** Student government, film, magazine, radio, student newspaper, choral groups, dance, drama, jazz band, music ensembles, musical theater, opera, symphony orchestra, Association for African-American Collegians, multi-cultural resource office, Social Action Collective, International Club, Council on Student Activities, Women's Resource Center, Business Fraternity, Education Club, Media Association, Campus Ministry Council.

ATHLETICS. NCAA. **Intercollegiate:** Baseball M, basketball, cross-country, soccer, softball W, tennis, track and field, volleyball.

STUDENT SERVICES. Aptitude testing, career counseling, employment service for undergraduates, freshman orientation, health services, personal counseling, services/facilities for handicapped.

ANNUAL EXPENSES. Tuition and fees: $8,560. **Room and board:** $4,004. **Books and supplies:** $800. **Other expenses:** $1,500.

FINANCIAL AID. 83% of freshmen, 58% of continuing students receive some form of aid. 78% of grants, 84% of loans, 93% of jobs based on need. 164 enrolled freshmen were judged to have need, all were offered aid. Academic, music/drama, art, leadership scholarships available. **Aid applications:** No closing date; priority given to applications received by April 1; applicants notified on a rolling basis beginning on or about March 15; must reply by May 1 or within 2 weeks if notified thereafter.

ADDRESS/TELEPHONE. Charles E. Beech, Director of Admission, Webster University, 470 East Lockwood Avenue, St. Louis, MO 63119-3194. (314) 968-7000. (800) 75-ENROL.

Wentworth Military Academy and Junior College

Lexington, Missouri — CB code: 6934

2-year private junior, military college, coed. Founded in 1880. **Accreditation:** Regional. **Undergraduate enrollment:** 308 men and women. **Location:**

Rural campus in small town; 45 miles from Kansas City. **Calendar:** Semester. **Additional facts:** Adult evening program open to both men and women.

FRESHMAN ADMISSIONS. Selection criteria: 2.5 GPA, test scores, recommendations important.

ANNUAL EXPENSES. Tuition and fees: Comprehensive fee: $14,880.

ADDRESS/TELEPHONE. Maj. Michael Lierman, Director of Admissions, Wentworth Military Academy and Junior College, 1880 Washington Avenue, Lexington, MO 64067-1799. (816) 259-2221. (800) WMA-1880. Fax: (816) 259-2677.

Westminster College

Fulton, Missouri CB code: 6937

Admissions: 87% of applicants accepted
Based on: ••• School record, test scores
•• Essay, recommendations
• Activities, interview, special talents
Completion: 85% of freshmen end year in good standing
67% graduate, 29% of these enter graduate study

4-year private liberal arts college, coed, affiliated with Presbyterian Church (USA). Founded in 1851. **Accreditation:** Regional. **Undergraduate enrollment:** 434 men, 273 women full time; 9 men, 16 women part time. **Faculty:** 63 total (50 full time), 34 with doctorates or other terminal degrees. **Location:** Rural campus in large town; 100 miles from St. Louis, 22 miles from Jefferson City. **Calendar:** Semester. **Microcomputers:** 65 located in libraries, computer centers. **Special facilities:** Winston Churchill Memorial and Library, Church of St. Mary Aldermanbury. **Additional facts:** Site of Sir Winston Churchill's prophetic "Iron Curtain" speech in 1946. College annually invites social, economic, and political authorities of world-wide prominence to provide students access to leaders.

DEGREES OFFERED. BA, BFA. 110 bachelor's degrees awarded in 1992. 28% in business and management, 14% letters/literature, 5% life sciences, 8% multi/interdisciplinary studies, 8% psychology, 25% social sciences.

UNDERGRADUATE MAJORS. Accounting, anthropology, art education, Asian studies, biology, business administration and management, business economics, chemistry, creative writing, Eastern European studies, economics, elementary education, engineering, English, English education, European studies, fine arts, foreign languages education, French, German, history, international business management, international relations, international studies, mathematics, mathematics education, music, musical theater, philosophy, physical education, physics, political science and government, predentistry, prelaw, premedicine, preveterinary, psychology, religion, science education, secondary education, social studies education, sociology, Spanish, special education, studio art, visual and performing arts.

ACADEMIC PROGRAMS. Double major, dual enrollment of high school students, honors program, independent study, internships, semester at sea, student-designed major, study abroad, New York semester, United Nations semester, Washington semester, cross-registration, learning disabilities program; liberal arts/career combination in engineering. **Remedial services:** Reduced course load, special counselor, tutoring, reading and study skills program. **ROTC:** Air Force, Army. **Placement/credit:** AP, CLEP Subject, institutional tests; 30 credit hours maximum for bachelor's degree.

ACADEMIC REQUIREMENTS. Freshmen must earn minimum GPA of 1.7 to continue in good standing. 75% of freshmen return for sophomore year. Students must declare major by end of second year. **Graduation requirements:** 122 hours for bachelor's (30 in major). Most students required to take courses in English, history, mathematics, philosophy/religion, biological/physical sciences, social sciences. **Postgraduate studies:** 12% enter law school, 3% enter medical school, 5% enter MBA programs, 9% enter other graduate study. **Additional information:** Students (15 chosen annually) with learning handicaps offered faculty/student tutoring, counseling, and special facilities.

FRESHMAN ADMISSIONS. Selection criteria: Admissions based on high school achievement (including class rank, involvement, curriculum, GPA) and recommendations from school. **High school preparation:** 12 units required. Required units include biological science 2, English 4, mathematics 3, physical science 1 and social science 2. **Test requirements:** SAT or ACT (ACT preferred); score report by August 1. **Additional information:** Admission to Learning Disabilities Program requires additional credentials and interview. Deadline is April 1.

1992 FRESHMAN CLASS PROFILE. 359 men applied, 302 accepted, 113 enrolled; 314 women applied, 283 accepted, 92 enrolled. 54% had high school GPA of 3.0 or higher, 35% between 2.0 and 2.99. **Academic background:** Mid 50% of enrolled freshmen had SAT-V between 400-600, SAT-M between 400-640; ACT composite between 20-30. 20% submitted SAT scores, 90% submitted ACT scores. **Characteristics:** 49% from in state, 96% live in college housing, 8% have minority backgrounds, 1% are foreign students, 80% join fraternities/sororities. Average age is 18.

FALL-TERM APPLICATIONS. $20 fee, may be waived for applicants with need. No closing date; priority given to applications received by June 1; applicants notified on a rolling basis; must reply by May 1 or within 3 weeks if notified thereafter. Essay required. Interview recommended for borderline applicants. CRDA. Deferred and early admission available. Learning Disabilities Program applicants must have completed applications credentials and personal interview prior to April 1, including untimed SAT or ACT results.

STUDENT LIFE. Housing: Dormitories (men, women, coed); fraternity housing available. Students may request quiet house living option or honors suite. **Activities:** Student government, magazine, student newspaper, yearbook, choral groups, dance, drama, jazz band, music ensembles, musical theater, pep band, fraternities, sororities, Young Democrats, Young Republicans, Fellowship of Christian Athletes, Chaplains Associates, Big Brother-Big Sister Program, Youth Escorting Seniors, Amnesty International, Outdoor Club, Jesters, Model United Nations.

ATHLETICS. NCAA. **Intercollegiate:** Baseball M, basketball, cross-country, golf, rifle, soccer, softball W, tennis, volleyball W. **Intramural:** Badminton, basketball, bowling, racquetball, rifle, softball, swimming, table tennis, tennis, track and field M, volleyball, wrestling M.

STUDENT SERVICES. Aptitude testing, career counseling, employment service for undergraduates, freshman orientation, health services, personal counseling, placement service for graduates, services/facilities for handicapped.

ANNUAL EXPENSES. Tuition and fees: $9,950. **Room and board:** $3,800. **Books and supplies:** $600. **Other expenses:** $1,200.

FINANCIAL AID. 75% of freshmen, 75% of continuing students receive some form of aid. 42% of grants, all loans, 52% of jobs based on need. Academic, music/drama, art, athletic, leadership scholarships available. **Aid applications:** No closing date; priority given to applications received by March 31; applicants notified on a rolling basis beginning on or about January 15; must reply within 3 weeks.

ADDRESS/TELEPHONE. Dean of Admissions, Office of Admissions, Westminster College, 501 Westminster Avenues, Fulton, MO 65251-1299. (314) 642-3361. Fax: (314) 642-6356.

William Jewell College

Liberty, Missouri CB code: 6941

Admissions: 83% of applicants accepted
Based on: ••• Activities, recommendations, school record
•• Interview, test scores
• Essay, special talents
Completion: 98% of freshmen end year in good standing
30% enter graduate study

4-year private liberal arts college, coed, affiliated with American Baptist Churches in the USA and Missouri Baptists. Founded in 1849. **Accreditation:** Regional. **Undergraduate enrollment:** 583 men, 729 women full time; 23 men, 31 women part time. **Faculty:** 153 total (100 full time), 71 with doctorates or other terminal degrees. **Location:** Suburban campus in large town; 14 miles from Kansas City. **Calendar:** 4-1-4, limited summer session. Saturday and extensive evening/early morning classes. **Microcomputers:** 50 located in libraries, classrooms, computer centers. **Special facilities:** Stocksdale Art Gallery, Spurgeon Library, Pillsbury Observatory.

DEGREES OFFERED. BA, BS. 352 bachelor's degrees awarded in 1992. 27% in business and management, 9% communications, 6% computer sciences, 9% teacher education, 5% health sciences, 6% letters/literature, 5% multi/interdisciplinary studies, 8% psychology, 8% social sciences, 6% visual and performing arts.

UNDERGRADUATE MAJORS. Accounting, biology, British studies, business administration and management, business and management, chemistry, computer and information sciences, economics, elementary education, English, French, German, history, information sciences and systems, international relations, Japanese studies, mathematics, medical laboratory technologies, molecular biology, music, music education, music performance, music theory and composition, nursing, Oxbridge institutions and policy, philosophy, physics, political science and government, psychology, public relations, religion, rhetoric, secondary education, sociology, Spanish, speech, studio art.

ACADEMIC PROGRAMS. Double major, dual enrollment of high school students, honors program, independent study, internships, student-designed major, study abroad, teacher preparation, visiting/exchange student program, United Nations semester, Washington semester, 1 semester's study option at college's campus in Harlaxton, England; liberal arts/career combination in engineering, forestry, health sciences. **Remedial services:** Learning center, reduced course load, remedial instruction, tutoring. **Placement/credit:** AP, CLEP General and Subject, IB, institutional tests; 30 credit hours maximum for bachelor's degree.

ACADEMIC REQUIREMENTS. Freshmen must earn minimum GPA of 2.0 to continue in good standing. 87% of freshmen return for sophomore year. Students must declare major by end of second year. **Graduation requirements:** 124 hours for bachelor's (24 in major). Most students required to take courses in computer science, English, foreign languages, history, humanities, mathematics, philosophy/religion, biological/physical sciences, social sciences. **Postgraduate studies:** 3% enter law school, 2% enter medical school, 5% enter MBA programs, 20% enter other graduate study. **Additional information:** Oxbridge honors program allows students to study their major subject using tutorial mode of instruction used at Oxford and Cambridge. Interdisciplinary core curriculum offered.

FRESHMAN ADMISSIONS. Selection criteria: Class rank, recommendations, personal statement, interview, courses taken, and test scores considered. **High school preparation:** 20 units recommended. Recommended units include English 4, foreign language 2, mathematics 3, social science 2 and science 2. **Test requirements:** SAT or ACT; score report by August 15.

1992 FRESHMAN CLASS PROFILE. 326 men applied, 261 accepted, 160 enrolled; 385 women applied, 331 accepted, 197 enrolled. 80% had high school GPA of 3.0 or higher, 19% between 2.0 and 2.99. 35% were in top tenth and 63% were in top quarter of graduating class. **Academic background:** Mid 50% of enrolled freshmen had SAT-V between 420-560, SAT-M between 460-600; ACT composite between 20-27. 20% submitted SAT scores, 97% submitted ACT scores. **Characteristics:** 75% from in state, 87% live in college housing, 7% have minority backgrounds, 1% are foreign students, 40% join fraternities/sororities. Average age is 18.

FALL-TERM APPLICATIONS. $25 fee, may be waived for applicants with need. No closing date; applicants notified on a rolling basis; must reply by May 1 or within 4 weeks if notified thereafter. Interview required. Audition required for music applicants. Essay required. CRDA. Deferred and early admission available.

STUDENT LIFE. Housing: Dormitories (men, women); apartment, fraternity housing available. **Activities:** Student government, radio, student newspaper, television, yearbook, choral groups, concert band, drama, jazz band, music ensembles, musical theater, opera, pep band, symphony orchestra, fraternities, sororities, Young Democrats, Young Republicans, Christian Student Union, Alpha Phi Omega.

ATHLETICS. NAIA. **Intercollegiate:** Baseball M, basketball, cross-country, diving W, football M, golf, soccer, softball W, swimming W, tennis, track and field, volleyball W, wrestling M. **Intramural:** Badminton, basketball, bowling, cross-country, football, golf, racquetball, softball, swimming, table tennis, tennis, track and field, volleyball, wrestling M.

STUDENT SERVICES. Aptitude testing, career counseling, employment service for undergraduates, freshman orientation, health services, personal counseling, placement service for graduates, special adviser for adult students, veterans counselor, services/facilities for handicapped.

ANNUAL EXPENSES. Tuition and fees: $9,720. **Room and board:** $2,780. **Books and supplies:** $500. **Other expenses:** $1,800.

FINANCIAL AID. 88% of freshmen, 89% of continuing students receive some form of aid. 37% of grants, 89% of loans, 77% of jobs based on need. Academic, music/drama, art, athletic, leadership, alumni affiliation, religious affiliation scholarships available. **Aid applications:** No closing date; priority given to applications received by March 15; applicants notified on a rolling basis beginning on or about March 15; must reply by May 1 or within 15 days if notified thereafter.

ADDRESS/TELEPHONE. T. Edwin Norris, Director of Admission, William Jewell College, 500 College Hill, Liberty, MO 64068. (816) 781-7700 ext. 5137. (800) 753-7009. Fax: (816) 781-3164.

William Woods College ⇎
Fulton, Missouri — CB code: 6944

Admissions:	91% of applicants accepted
Based on:	••• School record, test scores
	•• Essay, interview
	• Activities, recommendations, special talents
Completion:	90% of freshmen end year in good standing
	60% graduate, 20% of these enter graduate study

4-year private liberal arts college, women only, affiliated with Christian Church/Disciples of Christ. Founded in 1870. **Accreditation:** Regional. **Undergraduate enrollment:** 766 women full time; 67 women part time. **Faculty:** 73 total (48 full time), 26 with doctorates or other terminal degrees. **Location:** Rural campus in large town; 100 miles from St. Louis, 30 miles from Jefferson City. **Calendar:** Semester. **Microcomputers:** 61 located in dormitories, libraries, classrooms, computer centers. **Special facilities:** Equestrian science facilities, art gallery, observatory, preschool, broadcasting lab.

DEGREES OFFERED. AA, BA, BFA. 150 bachelor's degrees awarded. 17% in agriculture, 24% business and management, 16% teacher education, 5% psychology, 9% visual and performing arts.

UNDERGRADUATE MAJORS. Associate: Interpreter for the deaf. **Bachelor's:** Accounting, art education, biology, business administration and management, business and management, business economics, chemistry, commercial art, communications, dramatic arts, early childhood education, economics, elementary education, English, English education, equestrian science, fashion merchandising, fine arts, foreign languages (multiple emphasis), foreign languages education, French, German, graphic design, history, illustration design, information sciences and systems, interior design, international studies, junior high education, legal assistant/paralegal, marketing management, mathematics, mathematics education, philosophy, physical education, physics, political science and government, prelaw, premedicine, preveterinary, psychology, radio/television broadcasting, science education, secondary education, social science education, social work, sociology, Spanish, special education, studio art.

ACADEMIC PROGRAMS. Accelerated program, double major, dual enrollment of high school students, independent study, internships, semester at sea, student-designed major, study abroad, teacher preparation, visiting/exchange student program, New York semester, United Nations semester, Washington semester, cross-registration, St. Louis Broadcasting Center for radio/television, Broadway semester, fashion merchandising internship in Paris, Hollywood semester. **Remedial services:** Reduced course load, special counselor, tutoring, special 1-semester course. **Placement/credit:** AP, CLEP General and Subject, IB, institutional tests; 30 credit hours maximum for bachelor's degree.

ACADEMIC REQUIREMENTS. Freshmen must earn minimum GPA of 2.0 to continue in good standing. 66% of freshmen return for sophomore year. Students must declare major by end of second year. **Graduation requirements:** 65 hours for associate (50 in major), 122 hours for bachelor's (35 in major). Most students required to take courses in arts/fine arts, English, history, humanities, mathematics, biological/physical sciences, social sciences. **Postgraduate studies:** 2% enter law school, 1% enter medical school, 13% enter MBA programs, 4% enter other graduate study.

FRESHMAN ADMISSIONS. High school preparation: 16 units required. 11 of 16 required units must be in English, foreign lanquage, mathematics, natural sciences, social sciences, or history. **Test requirements:** SAT or ACT; score report by August 1.

1992 FRESHMAN CLASS PROFILE. 498 women applied, 452 accepted, 267 enrolled. 57% had high school GPA of 3.0 or higher, 40% between 2.0 and 2.99. **Characteristics:** 56% from in state, 95% live in college housing, 4% have minority backgrounds, 50% join fraternities/sororities. Average age is 18.

FALL-TERM APPLICATIONS. $25 fee. No closing date; applicants notified on a rolling basis; must reply within 30 days. Audition required for performing arts, equestrian science, broadcast, art applicants. Portfolio required for visual arts applicants. Essay required. Interview recommended. Deferred admission available.

STUDENT LIFE. Housing: Dormitories (women); apartment, sorority housing available. On-campus apartments available to upperclassmen. **Activities:** Student government, magazine, radio, student newspaper, yearbook, choral groups, dance, drama, music ensembles, musical theater, sororities, Campus Christian Fellowship, YWCA, Young Democrats, College Republicans, BASIC (Brothers and Sisters in Christ), SADD, Students for Social Work, Epsilon Sigma Alpha. **Additional information:** Non-denominational services held every Sunday evening in campus chapel.

ATHLETICS. NAIA. **Intercollegiate:** Basketball, diving, soccer, softball, swimming, tennis, volleyball. **Intramural:** Basketball, bowling, soccer, softball, swimming, table tennis, tennis, volleyball.

STUDENT SERVICES. Aptitude testing, career counseling, employment service for undergraduates, freshman orientation, health services, personal counseling, placement service for graduates, services/facilities for handicapped.

ANNUAL EXPENSES. Tuition and fees: $9,965. **Room and board:** $4,200. **Books and supplies:** $550. **Other expenses:** $2,700.

FINANCIAL AID. 80% of freshmen, 85% of continuing students receive some form of aid. 45% of grants, 90% of loans, 75% of jobs based on need. Academic, music/drama, art, athletic, leadership, alumni affiliation, religious affiliation, minority scholarships available. **Aid applications:** Closing date June 1; priority given to applications received by April 30; applicants notified on a rolling basis beginning on or about April 1; must reply by May 1 or within 4 weeks if notified thereafter.

ADDRESS/TELEPHONE. Leslie K. Krieger, Director of Admission, William Woods College, 200 West Twelfth, Fulton, MO 65251-1098. (314) 592-4221. (800) 995-3159. Fax: (314) 592-1146.

Montana

Billings Vocational-Technical Center
Billings, Montana CB code: 1990

2-year public technical college. **Accreditation:** Regional. **Undergraduate enrollment:** 422 men and women. **Location:** Suburban campus in small city.

DEGREES OFFERED. AAS. 40 associate degrees awarded in 1992.

UNDERGRADUATE MAJORS. Accounting, air conditioning/heating/refrigeration mechanics, automotive mechanics, drafting and design technology, legal secretary, medical secretary, microcomputer software, secretarial and related programs.

ACADEMIC REQUIREMENTS. Students must declare major on application. **Graduation requirements:** 60 hours for associate.

FRESHMAN ADMISSIONS. Selection criteria: Open admissions.

1992 FRESHMAN CLASS PROFILE. 100 men and women enrolled. **Characteristics:** 100% commute.

FALL-TERM APPLICATIONS. No closing date; applicants notified on a rolling basis.

ANNUAL EXPENSES. Tuition and fees (1992-93):

ADDRESS/TELEPHONE. William Barr, Admissions Officer, Billings Vocational-Technical Center, 3803 Central Avenue, Billings, MT 59102.

Blackfeet Community College
Browning, Montana CB code: 0379

2-year public community college, coed. Founded in 1976. **Accreditation:** Regional. **Undergraduate enrollment:** 500 men and women. **Location:** Rural campus in small town. **Calendar:** Quarter. **Additional facts:** Tribally controlled college located on the Blackfeet Indian reservation.

DEGREES OFFERED. AA, AS, AAS. 53 associate degrees awarded in 1992.

UNDERGRADUATE MAJORS. Bilingual/bicultural education, Blackfeet bilingual education, Blackfeet studies, business and office, construction, human services, liberal/general studies, protective services, secretarial and related programs, social work, teacher aide.

ACADEMIC PROGRAMS. Internships, 2-2 teacher training program with University of Montana. **Remedial services:** Preadmission summer program, remedial instruction, special counselor, tutoring, tutoring.

ACADEMIC REQUIREMENTS. Freshmen must earn minimum GPA of 1.75 to continue in good standing.

FRESHMAN ADMISSIONS. Selection criteria: Open admissions.

1992 FRESHMAN CLASS PROFILE. 60 men and women enrolled. **Characteristics:** 98% from in state, 100% commute, 98% have minority backgrounds.

FALL-TERM APPLICATIONS. $5 fee. No closing date. Deferred and early admission available.

STUDENT LIFE. Activities: Student government, student newspaper.

STUDENT SERVICES. Aptitude testing, career counseling, employment service for undergraduates, personal counseling, placement service for graduates.

ANNUAL EXPENSES. Tuition and fees (1992-93): $1,371. **Books and supplies:** $200. **Other expenses:** $450.

FINANCIAL AID. 90% of freshmen, 95% of continuing students receive some form of aid.

ADDRESS/TELEPHONE. Carol Murray, Dean of Student Services, Blackfeet Community College, PO Box 819, Browning, MT 59417. (406) 338-5421.

Butte Vocational-Technical Center
Butte, Montana CB code: 2085

2-year public technical college, coed. **Accreditation:** Regional. **Undergraduate enrollment:** 95 men, 164 women full time; 21 men, 31 women part time. **Faculty:** 26 total (23 full time). **Location:** Suburban campus in large town; 8 miles from downtown Butte, 66 miles from Helena. **Calendar:** Semester. **Microcomputers:** 91 located in classrooms.

DEGREES OFFERED. AAS. 26 associate degrees awarded in 1992. 100% in engineering technologies.

UNDERGRADUATE MAJORS. Automotive mechanics, automotive technology, business data processing and related programs, civil technology, data processing, drafting and design technology, electrical and electronics equipment repair, word processing.

ACADEMIC PROGRAMS. Cooperative education. **Remedial services:** Learning center, reduced course load, tutoring.

ACADEMIC REQUIREMENTS. Freshmen must earn minimum GPA of 2.0 to continue in good standing. Students must declare major on application. **Graduation requirements:** 60 hours for associate. Most students required to take courses in English, mathematics.

FRESHMAN ADMISSIONS. Selection criteria: Open admissions. Special admissions for nursing program.

1992 FRESHMAN CLASS PROFILE. 75 men and women enrolled. **Characteristics:** 100% from in state, 100% commute, 12% have minority backgrounds.

FALL-TERM APPLICATIONS. $20 fee. No closing date; applicants notified on a rolling basis.

STUDENT LIFE. Activities: Student government, student newspaper.

STUDENT SERVICES. Career counseling, freshman orientation, placement service for graduates, services/facilities for handicapped.

ANNUAL EXPENSES. Tuition and fees (projected): $1,250, $1,344 additional for out-of-state students. **Books and supplies:** $450. **Other expenses:** $1,000.

FINANCIAL AID. 65% of freshmen, 75% of continuing students receive some form of aid. All grants, 98% of loans, all jobs based on need. **Aid applications:** No closing date; priority given to applications received by April 1; applicants notified on a rolling basis beginning on or about June 15.

ADDRESS/TELEPHONE. Danetta Lee, Registrar, Butte Vocational-Technical Center, 25 Basin Creek Road, Butte, MT 59701. (406) 494-2894. Fax: (406) 494-2977.

Carroll College ⇹
Helena, Montana CB code: 4041

Admissions: 95% of applicants accepted
Based on: ••• School record
•• Essay, recommendations, special talents, test scores
• Activities, interview
Completion: 87% of freshmen end year in good standing
52% graduate, 47% of these enter graduate study

4-year private college of arts and sciences, coed, affiliated with Roman Catholic Church. Founded in 1909. **Accreditation:** Regional. **Undergraduate enrollment:** 412 men, 632 women full time; 100 men, 240 women part time. **Faculty:** 114 total (74 full time), 32 with doctorates or other terminal degrees. **Location:** Suburban campus in large town; 90 miles from Great Falls, 240 miles from Billings. **Calendar:** Semester, limited summer session. **Microcomputers:** 125 located in dormitories, libraries, computer centers.

DEGREES OFFERED. AA, BA. 2 associate degrees awarded in 1992. 100% in letters/literature. 183 bachelor's degrees awarded. 18% in business and management, 11% teacher education, 20% health sciences, 7% allied health, 6% letters/literature, 9% life sciences, 5% parks/recreation, protective services, public affairs, 5% psychology, 6% social sciences.

UNDERGRADUATE MAJORS. Associate: Business administration and management, communications, computer and information sciences, creative writing, English, visual and performing arts. **Bachelor's:** Accounting, applied mathematics, biology, business administration and management, business and management, business economics, communications, computer and information sciences, creative writing, dramatic arts, economics, elementary education, English, English education, foreign languages education, French, Greek (classical), history, international relations, Latin, liberal/general studies, mathematics, mathematics education, medical laboratory technologies, medical records technology, medical technician, nursing, pastoral ministry, philosophy, physical education, political science and government, practical nursing, prelaw, psychology, public administration, public affairs, public relations, religion, religious education, science education, social science education, social sciences, social work, sociology, Spanish, speech, speech/communication/theater education, technical and business writing, theological studies.

ACADEMIC PROGRAMS. Cooperative education, double major, dual enrollment of high school students, honors program, independent study, internships, student-designed major, study abroad, visiting/exchange student program; liberal arts/career combination in engineering, health sciences. **Remedial services:** Learning center, preadmission summer program, reduced course load, special counselor, tutoring, writing center. **Placement/credit:** AP, CLEP General and Subject, institutional tests; 15 credit hours maximum for associate degree; 30 credit hours maximum for bachelor's degree.

ACADEMIC REQUIREMENTS. Freshmen must earn minimum GPA of 1.7 to continue in good standing. 69% of freshmen return for sophomore year. Students must declare major by end of second year. **Graduation requirements:** 66 hours for associate (18 in major), 122 hours for bachelor's (36 in major). Most students required to take courses in arts/fine arts, English, history, mathematics, philosophy/religion, biological/physical sciences, social sciences. **Postgraduate studies:** 75% from 2-year programs enter 4-year programs. 8% enter law school, 14% enter medical school, 5% enter MBA programs, 20% enter other graduate study.

FRESHMAN ADMISSIONS. Selection criteria: School achievement record and test scores most important. **High school preparation:** 15 units recommended. Recommended units include English 4, foreign language 2, mathematics 3 and science 3. 2 American history and government also recommended. **Test requirements:** SAT or ACT (ACT preferred); score report by August 15. ASSET test required for non-traditional first-time freshmen.

1992 FRESHMAN CLASS PROFILE. 509 men and women applied, 486 accepted; 259 enrolled. 62% had high school GPA of 3.0 or higher, 36% between 2.0 and 2.99. **Academic background:** Mid 50% of enrolled freshmen had SAT-V between 380-510, SAT-M between 440-580; ACT composite between 20-26. 47% submitted SAT scores, 53% submitted ACT scores. **Characteristics:** 70% from in state, 90% live in college housing, 4% have minority backgrounds, 5% are foreign students. Average age is 22.

FALL-TERM APPLICATIONS. $25 fee, may be waived for applicants with need. Closing date July 31; priority given to applications received by March 1; applicants notified on a rolling basis. Essay required. Interview recommended for academically weak applicants. CRDA. Deferred and early admission available. EDP-F.

STUDENT LIFE. Housing: Dormitories (men, women, coed). Freshmen and sophomores required to live on campus. **Activities:** Student government, student newspaper, yearbook, literary magazine, choral groups, dance, drama, jazz band, musical theater, pep band, symphony orchestra, Spur, Circle-K, CARE, Life Science Club, debate club, Cultural Exchange Club.

ATHLETICS. NAIA. **Intercollegiate:** Basketball, football M, swimming, volleyball W. **Intramural:** Badminton, basketball, bowling, football M, golf, handball, racquetball, skiing, soccer, softball, swimming, table tennis, tennis, volleyball.

STUDENT SERVICES. Aptitude testing, career counseling, employment service for undergraduates, freshman orientation, health services, personal counseling, placement service for graduates, special adviser for adult students, veterans counselor, learning assistance center, services/facilities for handicapped.

ANNUAL EXPENSES. Tuition and fees: $7,760. **Room and board:** $3,650. **Books and supplies:** $390. **Other expenses:** $700.

FINANCIAL AID. 85% of freshmen, 80% of continuing students receive some form of aid. 47% of grants, 73% of loans, 66% of jobs based on need. Academic, music/drama, athletic, state/district residency, leadership, alumni affiliation, religious affiliation, minority scholarships available. **Aid applications:** No closing date; priority given to applications received by March 1; applicants notified on a rolling basis beginning on or about April 15; must reply within 2 weeks.

ADDRESS/TELEPHONE. Candace Cain, Director of Admission, Carroll College, North Benton Avenue, Helena, MT 59625. (406) 442-3450. (800) 992-3648.

College of Great Falls
Great Falls, Montana — CB code: 4058

4-year private liberal arts college, coed, affiliated with Roman Catholic Church. Founded in 1932. **Accreditation:** Regional. **Undergraduate enrollment:** 257 men, 443 women full time; 197 men, 340 women part time. **Graduate enrollment:** 7 men, 17 women full time; 19 men, 48 women part time. **Faculty:** 139 total (42 full time), 33 with doctorates or other terminal degrees. **Location:** Urban campus in small city; 600 miles from Seattle, 400 miles from Spokane, Washington. **Calendar:** Semester, limited summer session. **Microcomputers:** 30 located in computer centers. **Additional facts:** Servicemen's Opportunity College.

DEGREES OFFERED. AA, AS, BA, BS, M. 52 associate degrees awarded in 1992. 11% in business and management, 13% computer sciences, 6% teacher education, 10% allied health, 25% law, 31% parks/recreation, protective services, public affairs. 127 bachelor's degrees awarded. 22% in business and management, 15% teacher education, 14% law, 20% parks/recreation, protective services, public affairs, 15% social sciences. Graduate degrees offered in 2 major fields of study.

UNDERGRADUATE MAJORS. Associate: Accounting, business administration and management, community services, computer and information sciences, criminal justice studies, early childhood education, health sciences, human services, legal assistant/paralegal, mathematics, microcomputer management, recreation and community services technologies, rehabilitation counseling/services, religion, respiratory therapy. **Bachelor's:** Accounting, biology, business administration and management, chemistry, communications, computer and information sciences, criminal justice studies, elementary education, English, health care administration, history, legal assistant/paralegal, liberal/general studies, marketing and distribution, mathematics, microcomputer management, physical education, religion, science education, secondary education, social sciences, sociology.

ACADEMIC PROGRAMS. Cooperative education, double major, independent study, internships, teacher preparation. **Remedial services:** Learning center, remedial instruction, special counselor, tutoring, study skills. **Placement/credit:** AP, CLEP General and Subject, institutional tests; 9 credit hours maximum for associate degree; 30 credit hours maximum for bachelor's degree.

ACADEMIC REQUIREMENTS. Freshmen must earn minimum GPA of 2.0 to continue in good standing. **Graduation requirements:** 64 hours for associate (30 in major), 128 hours for bachelor's (42 in major). Most students required to take courses in arts/fine arts, English, mathematics, philosophy/religion, biological/physical sciences, social sciences. **Postgraduate studies:** 28% from 2-year programs enter 4-year programs. 2% enter law school, 3% enter medical school, 2% enter MBA programs, 1% enter other graduate study.

FRESHMAN ADMISSIONS. Selection criteria: Open admissions. **High school preparation:** 20 units recommended. Recommended units include biological science 2, English 4, mathematics 3 and social science 3.

1992 FRESHMAN CLASS PROFILE. 82 men, 120 women enrolled. **Characteristics:** 89% from in state, 90% commute, 4% have minority backgrounds, 2% are foreign students, 90% join fraternities/sororities. Average age is 25.

FALL-TERM APPLICATIONS. $25 fee. No closing date; priority given to applications received by August 15; applicants notified on a rolling basis. Early admission available.

STUDENT LIFE. Housing: Apartment housing available. **Activities:** Student government, literary magazine, choral groups, drama, music ensembles, symphony orchestra, campus ministry, Advocates.

ATHLETICS. Intramural: Basketball, bowling, cross-country, golf, skiing, softball, volleyball.

STUDENT SERVICES. Aptitude testing, career counseling, employment service for undergraduates, freshman orientation, health services, on-campus day care, personal counseling, placement service for graduates, veterans counselor, services/facilities for handicapped.

ANNUAL EXPENSES. Tuition and fees: $5,240. **Room and board:** $990 room only. **Books and supplies:** $520. **Other expenses:** $640.

FINANCIAL AID. 95% of freshmen, 85% of continuing students receive some form of aid. 88% of grants, 93% of loans, 85% of jobs based on need. Academic, state/district residency, leadership, religious affiliation, minority scholarships available. **Aid applications:** No closing date; priority given to applications received by April 1; applicants notified on a rolling basis beginning on or about May 1; must reply within 15 days.

ADDRESS/TELEPHONE. Audrey Thompson, Director of Admissions and Records, College of Great Falls, 1301 20th Street South, Great Falls, MT 59405. (406) 761-8210 ext. 260.

Dawson Community College
Glendive, Montana — CB code: 4280

2-year public community college, coed. Founded in 1940. **Accreditation:** Regional. **Undergraduate enrollment:** 176 men, 210 women full time; 45 men, 122 women part time. **Faculty:** 70 total (19 full time), 2 with doctorates or other terminal degrees. **Location:** Rural campus in small town; 220 miles from Billings, 100 miles from Dickinson, North Dakota. **Calendar:** Semester, limited summer session. Extensive evening/early morning classes. **Microcomputers:** 45 located in libraries, computer centers. **Additional facts:** Extension site located at Sidney.

DEGREES OFFERED. AA, AAS. 107 associate degrees awarded in 1992. 10% in agriculture, 5% business and management, 5% business/office and marketing/distribution, 54% multi/interdisciplinary studies, 26% parks/recreation, protective services, public affairs.

UNDERGRADUATE MAJORS. Agribusiness, automotive mechanics, business and management, business and office, computer servicing technology, equestrian science, law enforcement and corrections, law enforcement and corrections technologies, liberal/general studies, mental health/human services, microcomputer software, nursing, secretarial and related programs.

ACADEMIC PROGRAMS. 2-year transfer program, double major, dual enrollment of high school students, independent study, internships, telecourses. **Remedial services:** Learning center, reduced course load, remedial instruction, special counselor, tutoring. **Placement/credit:** CLEP Subject, institutional tests.

ACADEMIC REQUIREMENTS. Freshmen must earn minimum GPA of 1.75 to continue in good standing. 40% of freshmen return for sophomore year. **Graduation requirements:** 60 hours for associate (45 in major). Most students required to take courses in computer science, English, humanities, mathematics, biological/physical sciences, social sciences.

FRESHMAN ADMISSIONS. Selection criteria: Open admissions. **Test requirements:** SAT or ACT (ACT preferred) for placement and counseling only; score report by September 15.

1992 FRESHMAN CLASS PROFILE. 91 men, 76 women enrolled. **Characteristics:** 95% from in state, 1% are foreign students.

FALL-TERM APPLICATIONS. $20 fee. No closing date; applicants notified on a rolling basis. Early admission available.

STUDENT LIFE. Housing: Dormitories (coed). **Activities:** Student government, choral groups, concert band, drama, jazz band, music ensembles, pep band, Indian club, Inter-Varsity Christian Fellowship, Human Services Club, Law Enforcement Club, music club.

ATHLETICS. NJCAA. **Intercollegiate:** Basketball. **Intramural:** Basketball, bowling, golf, racquetball, softball, tennis, volleyball. **Clubs:** Rodeo.

STUDENT SERVICES. Aptitude testing, career counseling, freshman orientation, personal counseling, placement service for graduates, special adviser for adult students, veterans counselor, services/facilities for handicapped.

ANNUAL EXPENSES. Tuition and fees: $1,239, $336 additional for out-of-district students, $2,653 additional for out-of-state students. **Room**

and board: $1,080 room only. **Books and supplies:** $550. **Other expenses:** $1,097.

FINANCIAL AID. 52% of freshmen, 47% of continuing students receive some form of aid. 87% of grants, all loans, all jobs based on need. 133 enrolled freshmen were judged to have need, all were offered aid. Academic, music/drama, art, athletic scholarships available. **Aid applications:** No closing date; priority given to applications received by March 1; applicants notified on a rolling basis beginning on or about May 1; must reply within 2 weeks.

ADDRESS/TELEPHONE. Jolene Myers, Director of Admissions, Dawson Community College, PO Box 421, Glendive, MT 59330. (406) 365-3396. Fax: (406) 365-8132.

Dull Knife Memorial College
Lame Deer, Montana CB code: 5938

2-year private junior college, coed. **Accreditation:** Regional candidate. **Undergraduate enrollment:** 19 men, 35 women full time; 112 men, 202 women part time. **Faculty:** 21 total (6 full time). **Location:** Rural campus in rural community; 110 miles from Billings. **Calendar:** Semester, limited summer session. Extensive evening/early morning classes. **Microcomputers:** 25 located in computer centers.

DEGREES OFFERED. AA, AS, AAS. 23 associate degrees awarded in 1992. 8% in business/office and marketing/distribution, 26% allied health, 66% multi/interdisciplinary studies.

UNDERGRADUATE MAJORS. Liberal/general studies, mental health/human services, office supervision and management, rehabilitation counseling/services.

ACADEMIC PROGRAMS. 2-year transfer program, cooperative education, double major, internships. **Remedial services:** Learning center, remedial instruction, special counselor. **Placement/credit:** Institutional tests; 9 credit hours maximum for associate degree.

ACADEMIC REQUIREMENTS. Freshmen must earn minimum GPA of 2.0 to continue in good standing. 40% of freshmen return for sophomore year. Students must declare major by end of first year. **Graduation requirements:** 60 hours for associate (30 in major). Most students required to take courses in arts/fine arts, English, history, humanities, mathematics, biological/physical sciences, social sciences.

FRESHMAN ADMISSIONS. Selection criteria: Open admissions. **Test requirements:** SAT or ACT for placement.

1992 FRESHMAN CLASS PROFILE. 23 men, 41 women enrolled. **Characteristics:** 100% from in state, 100% commute, 86% have minority backgrounds. Average age is 23.

FALL-TERM APPLICATIONS. No fee. No closing date; applicants notified on a rolling basis.

STUDENT LIFE. Activities: Student government, student newspaper.

ATHLETICS. Intramural: Basketball.

STUDENT SERVICES. Aptitude testing, career counseling, freshman orientation, on-campus day care, personal counseling, veterans counselor, services/facilities for handicapped.

ANNUAL EXPENSES. Tuition and fees (1992-93): $894.

FINANCIAL AID. 65% of freshmen, 55% of continuing students receive some form of aid. 97% of grants based on need. 17 enrolled freshmen were judged to have need, all were offered aid. Academic scholarships available. **Aid applications:** No closing date.

ADDRESS/TELEPHONE. William L. Wertman, Director of Admissions, Dull Knife Memorial College, PO Box 98, Lame Deer, MT 59043. (406) 477-6215. Fax: (406) 477-6219.

Eastern Montana College
Billings, Montana CB code: 4298

4-year public college of arts and sciences and business, teachers college, coed. Founded in 1927. **Accreditation:** Regional. **Undergraduate enrollment:** 891 men, 1,609 women full time; 288 men, 590 women part time. **Graduate enrollment:** 49 men, 87 women full time; 66 men, 181 women part time. **Faculty:** 192 total (146 full time), 122 with doctorates or other terminal degrees. **Location:** Urban campus in small city; 224 miles from Helena, 560 miles from Denver. **Calendar:** Semester, limited summer session. Extensive evening/early morning classes. **Microcomputers:** 166 located in dormitories, classrooms, computer centers. **Special facilities:** Biological station, center for business enterprise, Montana Center for Handicapped Children, special education learning center, center for gerontological studies.

DEGREES OFFERED. AA, AS, BA, BS, MS, MEd. 18 associate degrees awarded in 1992. 39% in business/office and marketing/distribution, 55% multi/interdisciplinary studies, 6% psychology. 432 bachelor's degrees awarded. 33% in business and management, 5% communications, 7% education, 30% teacher education, 9% allied health. Graduate degrees offered in 13 major fields of study.

UNDERGRADUATE MAJORS. Associate: Business data processing and related programs, chemistry, elementary education, liberal/general studies, psychology, rehabilitation counseling/services, sociology, special education, word processing. **Bachelor's:** Accounting, art education, biology, business administration and management, business and management, business economics, chemistry, communications, early childhood education, economics, education, elementary education, English, English education, finance, fine arts, foreign languages education, German, health education, history, information sciences and systems, management information systems, marketing management, mathematics, mathematics education, mental health/human services, music, music education, music therapy, physical education, psychology, rehabilitation counseling/services, science education, secondary education, social science education, sociology, Spanish, special education.

ACADEMIC PROGRAMS. 2-year transfer program, accelerated program, double major, dual enrollment of high school students, independent study, internships, teacher preparation, cross-registration. **Remedial services:** Reduced course load, remedial instruction, special counselor, tutoring. **ROTC:** Army. **Placement/credit:** AP, CLEP General and Subject, institutional tests.

ACADEMIC REQUIREMENTS. Freshmen must earn minimum GPA of 2.0 to continue in good standing. 47% of freshmen return for sophomore year. Students must declare major by end of second year. **Graduation requirements:** 64 hours for associate, 128 hours for bachelor's. Most students required to take courses in arts/fine arts, English, foreign languages, history, humanities, mathematics, philosophy/religion, biological/physical sciences, social sciences. **Postgraduate studies:** 45% from 2-year programs enter 4-year programs. 4% enter MBA programs, 8% enter other graduate study.

FRESHMAN ADMISSIONS. Selection criteria: In-state and out-of-state applicants must meet admission and/or college preparatory requirements unless out of high school 3 or more years. **High school preparation:** 14 units recommended. Recommended units include biological science 1, English 4, foreign language 2, mathematics 3, physical science 1 and social science 3. **Test requirements:** SAT or ACT (ACT preferred); score report by August 1.

1992 FRESHMAN CLASS PROFILE. 208 men, 385 women enrolled. 40% had high school GPA of 3.0 or higher, 48% between 2.0 and 2.99. 7% were in top tenth and 23% were in top quarter of graduating class. **Academic background:** Mid 50% of enrolled freshmen had SAT-V between 360-410, SAT-M between 390-470; ACT composite between 17-22. 18% submitted SAT scores, 82% submitted ACT scores. **Characteristics:** 94% from in state, 81% commute, 9% have minority backgrounds, 1% are foreign students. Average age is 21.

FALL-TERM APPLICATIONS. $20 fee. No closing date; applicants notified on a rolling basis beginning on or about June 15. Deferred and early admission available.

STUDENT LIFE. Housing: Dormitories (men, women, coed). **Activities:** Student government, radio, student newspaper, choral groups, concert band, dance, drama, jazz band, music ensembles, musical theater, fraternities, sororities, Hispanic and Native American clubs, service, religious and political organizations, forensic club.

ATHLETICS. NCAA. **Intercollegiate:** Basketball, cross-country, tennis, volleyball. **Intramural:** Archery, basketball, cross-country, golf, racquetball, skiing, softball, swimming, table tennis, tennis, volleyball.

STUDENT SERVICES. Aptitude testing, career counseling, employment service for undergraduates, freshman orientation, health services, personal counseling, placement service for graduates, special adviser for adult students, veterans counselor, services/facilities for handicapped.

ANNUAL EXPENSES. Tuition and fees (projected): $1,905, $3,556 additional for out-of-state students. **Room and board:** $3,804. **Books and supplies:** $550. **Other expenses:** $1,200.

FINANCIAL AID. 67% of freshmen, 55% of continuing students receive some form of aid. 85% of grants, 89% of loans, 23% of jobs based on need. Academic, music/drama, art, athletic, state/district residency, leadership, alumni affiliation, minority scholarships available. **Aid applications:** No closing date; priority given to applications received by March 1; applicants notified on a rolling basis beginning on or about June 1; must reply within 3 weeks.

ADDRESS/TELEPHONE. Karen Everett, Director of Admissions, Eastern Montana College, 1500 North 30th Street, Billings, MT 59101-0298. (406) 657-2211. Fax: (406) 657-2299.

Flathead Valley Community College
Kalispell, Montana CB code: 4317

2-year public community college, coed. Founded in 1967. **Accreditation:** Regional. **Undergraduate enrollment:** 332 men, 544 women full time; 254 men, 589 women part time. **Faculty:** 105 total (31 full time), 8 with doctorates or other terminal degrees. **Location:** Urban campus in large town; 250 miles from Spokane, Washington. **Calendar:** Semester, extensive summer session. Extensive evening/early morning classes. **Microcomputers:** 112 located on campus.

DEGREES OFFERED. AA, AS, AAS. 174 associate degrees awarded in 1992.

UNDERGRADUATE MAJORS. Accounting, business and management, business management with computer application, child development/care/guidance, forestry and related sciences, hotel/motel and restaurant management, liberal/general studies, medical secretary, mental health/human services, science technologies, secretarial and related programs, surveying and mapping sciences, word processing.

ACADEMIC PROGRAMS. 2-year transfer program, independent study, internships, student-designed major. **Remedial services:** Learning center, reduced course load, remedial instruction, special counselor, tutoring, special services project for additional assistance to students outside classroom. **Placement/credit:** CLEP General and Subject, institutional tests.

ACADEMIC REQUIREMENTS. No policy requiring minimum GPA; records of students having academic difficulty are reviewed individually. **Graduation requirements:** 64 hours for associate. Most students required to take courses in computer science, English, humanities, mathematics, biological/physical sciences, social sciences.

FRESHMAN ADMISSIONS. Selection criteria: Open admissions.

1992 FRESHMAN CLASS PROFILE. 128 men, 157 women enrolled. **Characteristics:** 95% from in state, 100% commute, 5% have minority backgrounds.

FALL-TERM APPLICATIONS. No fee. No closing date; priority given to applications received by August 1; applicants notified on a rolling basis.

STUDENT LIFE. Activities: Student government, student newspaper, drama, Phi Theta Kappa honor society, veterans organization, forestry club, campus ministry group, Bitta Club (native American), Human Service Club, International Student Association. **Additional information:** Scholarships available for intercollegiate loggering team.

ATHLETICS. Intramural: Badminton, basketball, football M, softball, table tennis, tennis, volleyball.

STUDENT SERVICES. Aptitude testing, career counseling, employment service for undergraduates, personal counseling, special adviser for adult students, veterans counselor, services/facilities for handicapped.

ANNUAL EXPENSES. Tuition and fees (1992-93): $1,080, $432 additional for out-of-district students, $1,080 additional for out-of-state students. **Books and supplies:** $500. **Other expenses:** $600.

FINANCIAL AID. 50% of continuing students receive some form of aid. 80% of grants, all loans, all jobs based on need. Academic, athletic, state/district residency, leadership scholarships available. **Aid applications:** No closing date; priority given to applications received by May 1; applicants notified on a rolling basis beginning on or about July 1; must reply within 2 weeks.

ADDRESS/TELEPHONE. Loraine K. Bundrock, Director of Student Services, Flathead Valley Community College, 777 Grandview Drive, Kalispell, MT 59901. (406) 756-3846. Fax: (406) 756-3815.

Fort Belknap College
Harlem, Montana — CB code: 5971

2-year public community college, coed. **Accreditation:** Regional candidate. **Undergraduate enrollment:** 232 men and women. **Location:** Rural campus in small town. Extensive evening/early morning classes.

DEGREES OFFERED. AA, AAS. 26 associate degrees awarded in 1992.

UNDERGRADUATE MAJORS. Business and management, liberal/general studies.

ACADEMIC PROGRAMS. 2-year transfer program.

FRESHMAN ADMISSIONS. Selection criteria: Open admissions.

1992 FRESHMAN CLASS PROFILE. 26 men and women enrolled. **Characteristics:** 100% commute.

FALL-TERM APPLICATIONS. No closing date; applicants notified on a rolling basis.

ANNUAL EXPENSES. Tuition and fees (1992-93): $1,485. **Books and supplies:** $909. **Other expenses:** $1,431.

FINANCIAL AID. Aid applications: No closing date; applicants notified on a rolling basis.

ADDRESS/TELEPHONE. Michelle Lewis, Registrar, Fort Belknap College, PO Box 159, Harlem, MT 59526-0159. (406) 353-2607. Fax: (406) 353-2841.

Fort Peck Community College
Poplar, Montana — CB code: 5972

2-year public community college, coed. **Accreditation:** Regional. **Undergraduate enrollment:** 125 men, 162 women full time; 32 men, 93 women part time. **Faculty:** 45 total (15 full time). **Location:** Rural campus in rural community; 300 miles from Billings. **Calendar:** Semester. Extensive evening/early morning classes. **Microcomputers:** 25 located in classrooms, computer centers. **Additional facts:** Tribally controlled college.

DEGREES OFFERED. AA, AS, AAS. 20 associate degrees awarded in 1992.

UNDERGRADUATE MAJORS. American Indian studies, automotive mechanics, business administration and management, business and office, business computer/console/peripheral equipment operation, carpentry, computer graphics, criminal justice studies, early childhood education, education, environmental science, liberal/general studies, social sciences.

ACADEMIC PROGRAMS. 2-year transfer program, computer delivered (on-line) credit-bearing course offerings, double major, dual enrollment of high school students, independent study, internships. **Remedial services:** Learning center, remedial instruction, special counselor, tutoring.

ACADEMIC REQUIREMENTS. 75% of freshmen return for sophomore year. Students must declare major by end of first year. **Graduation requirements:** 60 hours for associate (29 in major). Most students required to take courses in arts/fine arts, computer science, English, history, humanities, mathematics, biological/physical sciences, social sciences.

FRESHMAN ADMISSIONS. Selection criteria: Open admissions.

1992 FRESHMAN CLASS PROFILE. 60 men applied, 60 accepted, 60 enrolled; 68 women applied, 68 accepted, 68 enrolled. **Characteristics:** 95% from in state, 100% commute, 91% have minority backgrounds. Average age is 28.

FALL-TERM APPLICATIONS. $15 fee. Closing date September 16; applicants notified on a rolling basis. Early admission available.

STUDENT LIFE. Activities: Student government, student newspaper, Indian language club.

STUDENT SERVICES. Aptitude testing, career counseling, employment service for undergraduates, freshman orientation, on-campus day care, personal counseling, placement service for graduates, special adviser for adult students, services/facilities for handicapped.

ANNUAL EXPENSES. Tuition and fees: $990. **Books and supplies:** $440. **Other expenses:** $700.

FINANCIAL AID. 67% of freshmen, 68% of continuing students receive some form of aid. 96% of grants, all jobs based on need. 171 enrolled freshmen were judged to have need, all were offered aid. Academic, leadership, minority scholarships available. **Aid applications:** No closing date; applicants notified on a rolling basis; must reply within 3 weeks.

ADDRESS/TELEPHONE. Terri DeLong, Director of Admissions, Fort Peck Community College, P.O. Box 398, Poplar, MT 59255-0398. (406) 768-5551. Fax: (406) 768-5552.

Great Falls Vocational-Technical Center
Great Falls, Montana — CB code: 2000

2-year public technical college, coed. **Accreditation:** Regional. **Undergraduate enrollment:** 836 men and women. **Location:** Small city. **Calendar:** Semester.

ADDRESS/TELEPHONE. Great Falls Vocational-Technical Center, 2100 16th Avenue South, Great Falls, MT 59401. (406) 771-1240. Fax: (406) 453-6789.

Helena Vocational-Technical Center
Helena, Montana — CB code: 2022

2-year public technical college. **Accreditation:** Regional. **Undergraduate enrollment:** 207 men, 128 women full time; 78 men, 156 women part time. **Faculty:** 28 total (26 full time). **Location:** Suburban campus in large town; 90 miles from Great Falls. **Calendar:** Semester. **Microcomputers:** Located in libraries, classrooms.

DEGREES OFFERED. AAS. 20 associate degrees awarded in 1992. 25% in business and management, 25% computer sciences, 25% allied health, 25% trade and industry.

UNDERGRADUATE MAJORS. Accounting, automotive mechanics, aviation maintenance technician, business data processing and related programs, computer programming, electrical and electronics equipment repair, legal secretary, medical secretary, word processing.

ACADEMIC PROGRAMS. Remedial services: Remedial instruction, tutoring.

ACADEMIC REQUIREMENTS. Freshmen must earn minimum GPA of 2.0 to continue in good standing. Students must declare major on application. **Graduation requirements:** 67 hours for associate. Most students required to take courses in mathematics.

FRESHMAN ADMISSIONS. Selection criteria: Open admissions. Recommended units include English 3 and mathematics 3.

1992 FRESHMAN CLASS PROFILE. 40 men and women enrolled. **Characteristics:** 100% from in state, 100% commute, 4% have minority backgrounds.

FALL-TERM APPLICATIONS. $20 fee. No closing date; applicants notified on a rolling basis. Interview recommended.

STUDENT LIFE. Activities: Student government.

ATHLETICS. Intramural: Volleyball.

STUDENT SERVICES. Career counseling, employment service for undergraduates, freshman orientation, placement service for graduates, special adviser for adult students, services/facilities for handicapped.

ANNUAL EXPENSES. Tuition and fees (projected): $1,250, $1,344 additional for out-of-state students. **Books and supplies:** $350.

FINANCIAL AID. 75% of freshmen, 75% of continuing students receive some form of aid. All grants, 83% of loans, all jobs based on need. 185 enrolled freshmen were judged to have need, all were offered aid. Academic scholarships available. **Aid applications:** No closing date; priority given to applications received by March 15; applicants notified on a rolling basis beginning on or about May 5; must reply by registration.

ADDRESS/TELEPHONE. Paul Justice, Admissions Officer, Helena Vocational-Technical Center, 1115 North Roberts Street, Helena, MT 59601. (406) 444-6800. Fax: (406) 444-6892. (800) 241-4882 (in-state only).

Little Big Horn College
Crow Agency, Montana CB code: 0536

2-year private community college, coed. Founded in 1980. **Accreditation:** Regional candidate. **Undergraduate enrollment:** 66 men, 118 women full time; 31 men, 73 women part time. **Faculty:** 6 total. **Location:** Rural campus in rural community; 60 miles from Billings. **Calendar:** Quarter. Extensive evening/early morning classes. **Microcomputers:** Located in classrooms, computer centers. **Additional facts:** Provides education for Crow Indian community. Crow lifeways, economic environment, history, language, and culture emphasied with standard curriculum.

DEGREES OFFERED. AA, AAS. 20 associate degrees awarded in 1992. 10% in business/office and marketing/distribution, 90% multi/interdisciplinary studies.

UNDERGRADUATE MAJORS. American Indian studies, biology, business administration and management, business and management, business and office, business data processing and related programs, home economics, information sciences and systems, liberal/general studies, mathematics, Native American languages, physical sciences, psychology, secretarial and related programs.

ACADEMIC PROGRAMS. 2-year transfer program, internships, visiting/exchange student program. **Remedial services:** Remedial instruction, tutoring. **Placement/credit:** Institutional tests.

ACADEMIC REQUIREMENTS. Freshmen must earn minimum GPA of 2.0 to continue in good standing. 50% of freshmen return for sophomore year. Students must declare major on enrollment. **Graduation requirements:** 90 hours for associate (45 in major). Most students required to take courses in English, history, mathematics, biological/physical sciences, social sciences. **Additional information:** Bilingual methodologies approach in some course work.

FRESHMAN ADMISSIONS. Selection criteria: Open admissions.

1992 FRESHMAN CLASS PROFILE. 33 men and women enrolled. **Characteristics:** 99% from in state, 100% commute, 99% have minority backgrounds. Average age is 27.

FALL-TERM APPLICATIONS. $10 fee. No closing date; applicants notified on a rolling basis. Deferred admission available.

STUDENT LIFE. Activities: Student government, Native American cultural activities.

ATHLETICS. Intercollegiate: Basketball, bowling, cross-country, volleyball.

STUDENT SERVICES. Career counseling, employment service for undergraduates, personal counseling.

ANNUAL EXPENSES. Tuition and fees (1992-93): $1,165. **Books and supplies:** $400. **Other expenses:** $450.

FINANCIAL AID. Grants available. **Aid applications:** No closing date; applicants notified on a rolling basis.

ADDRESS/TELEPHONE. Ethyl Big Medicine, Admissions Clerk, Little Big Horn College, PO Box 370, Crow Agency, MT 59022. (406) 638-2228. Fax: (406) 638-7213.

Miles Community College
Miles City, Montana CB code: 4081

2-year public community college, coed. Founded in 1939. **Accreditation:** Regional. **Undergraduate enrollment:** 192 men, 308 women full time; 32 men, 166 women part time. **Faculty:** 72 total (35 full time), 9 with doctorates or other terminal degrees. **Location:** Rural campus in large town; 150 miles from Billings. **Calendar:** Semester, limited summer session. Extensive evening/early morning classes. **Microcomputers:** 80 located in libraries, classrooms, computer centers, campus-wide network.

DEGREES OFFERED. AA, AAS. 122 associate degrees awarded in 1992. 14% in business/office and marketing/distribution, 6% computer sciences, 20% teacher education, 9% engineering technologies, 24% health sciences, 27% multi/interdisciplinary studies.

UNDERGRADUATE MAJORS. Accounting, agricultural sciences, automotive mechanics, automotive technology, biology, business administration and management, business and management, business and office, business computer/console/peripheral equipment operation, business data processing and related programs, business data programming, communications, computer graphics, computer programming, data processing, electrical and electronics equipment repair, electronic technology, elementary education, engineering, English, fine arts, graphic and printing production, graphic design, home economics, information sciences and systems, journalism, junior high education, legal secretary, liberal/general studies, marketing and distribution, mathematics, medical secretary, microcomputer software, music, nursing, physical sciences, physiology, human and animal, prelaw, psychology, secondary education, secretarial and related programs, social sciences, social work, Spanish, telecommunications, visual and performing arts.

ACADEMIC PROGRAMS. 2-year transfer program, cooperative education, dual enrollment of high school students, independent study, internships, telecourses. **Remedial services:** Learning center, preadmission summer program, reduced course load, remedial instruction, tutoring. **Placement/credit:** CLEP General and Subject, institutional tests; 30 credit hours maximum for associate degree.

ACADEMIC REQUIREMENTS. No policy requiring minimum GPA; records of students having academic difficulty are reviewed individually. 72% of freshmen return for sophomore year. Students must declare major by end of first year. **Graduation requirements:** 60 hours for associate (24 in major). Most students required to take courses in arts/fine arts, computer science, English, history, humanities, mathematics, biological/physical sciences, social sciences.

FRESHMAN ADMISSIONS. Selection criteria: Open admissions. Selective admissions to nursing program. **Test requirements:** SAT or ACT for placement and counseling only; score report by August 15. NLN test required of nursing applicants.

1992 FRESHMAN CLASS PROFILE. 72 men, 78 women enrolled. **Characteristics:** 94% from in state, 90% commute, 6% have minority backgrounds, 6% are foreign students. Average age is 22.

FALL-TERM APPLICATIONS. $10 fee. No closing date; applicants notified on a rolling basis beginning on or about February 1. Deferred and early admission available.

STUDENT LIFE. Housing: Dormitories (coed). **Activities:** Student government, choral groups, Student Nurses Association, campus ministry, psychology club, multicultural club.

ATHLETICS. NJCAA. **Intercollegiate:** Basketball, volleyball W. **Intramural:** Badminton, basketball, bowling, cross-country, golf, gymnastics, handball, ice hockey, racquetball, skiing, soccer, swimming, table tennis, tennis, track and field, volleyball. **Clubs:** Rodeo.

STUDENT SERVICES. Career counseling, employment service for undergraduates, freshman orientation, personal counseling, placement service for graduates, veterans counselor, services/facilities for handicapped.

ANNUAL EXPENSES. Tuition and fees: $1,288, $658 additional for out-of-district students, $2,604 additional for out-of-state students. **Room and board:** $2,300. **Books and supplies:** $600. **Other expenses:** $630.

FINANCIAL AID. 93% of freshmen, 87% of continuing students receive some form of aid. 81% of grants, 83% of loans, 66% of jobs based on need. Academic, music/drama, athletic scholarships available. **Aid applications:** No closing date; priority given to applications received by March 1; applicants notified on a rolling basis beginning on or about May 15; must reply within 4 weeks.

ADDRESS/TELEPHONE. Dale Oberlander, Dean of Student Services, Miles Community College, 2715 Dickinson Street, Miles City, MT 59301. (406) 232-3031 ext. 22. (800) 541-9281. Fax: (406) 232-5705.

Missoula Vocational-Technical Center
Missoula, Montana CB code: 2041

2-year public technical college. **Accreditation:** Regional. **Undergraduate enrollment:** 189 men, 290 women full time; 36 men, 97 women part time. **Faculty:** 58 total (36 full time), 23 with doctorates or other terminal degrees. **Location:** Suburban campus in small city; 200 miles from Spokane, Washington. **Microcomputers:** Located in libraries, classrooms, computer centers, campus-wide network.

DEGREES OFFERED. AAS. 80 associate degrees awarded in 1992. 7% in business and management, 29% business/office and marketing/distribution, 15% computer sciences, 10% home economics, 25% law, 14% trade and industry.

UNDERGRADUATE MAJORS. Accounting, computer programming, diesel engine mechanics, electronic technology, food management, food production/management/services, information sciences and systems, legal assistant/paralegal, legal secretary, marketing management, medical secretary, office supervision and management.

ACADEMIC PROGRAMS. Internships. **Remedial services:** Learning center, preadmission summer program, reduced course load, remedial instruction, special counselor, tutoring. **Placement/credit:** Institutional tests.

ACADEMIC REQUIREMENTS. Students must declare major on enrollment. **Graduation requirements:** 72 hours for associate. Most students required to take courses in computer science, English, mathematics.

FRESHMAN ADMISSIONS. Selection criteria: Open admissions.

1992 FRESHMAN CLASS PROFILE. 65 men and women enrolled. **Characteristics:** 100% from in state, 100% commute, 6% have minority backgrounds, 1% are foreign students.

FALL-TERM APPLICATIONS. $20 fee. No closing date; applicants notified on a rolling basis.

STUDENT LIFE. Activities: Student government.

STUDENT SERVICES. Aptitude testing, career counseling, employment service for undergraduates, freshman orientation, personal counseling, placement service for graduates, special adviser for adult students, veterans counselor, ethnic minority advising, services/facilities for handicapped.

ANNUAL EXPENSES. Tuition and fees (1992-93):

ADDRESS/TELEPHONE. Charles Couture, Admissions Officer, Missoula Vocational-Technical Center, 909 South Avenue West, Missoula, MT 59801. (406) 542-6811.

Montana College of Mineral Science and Technology

Butte, Montana — CB code: 4487

Admissions: 94% of applicants accepted
Based on: ••• School record
•• Test scores
• Recommendations
Completion: 75% of freshmen end year in good standing
40% graduate, 26% of these enter graduate study

4-year public engineering college, coed. Founded in 1893. **Accreditation:** Regional. **Undergraduate enrollment:** 912 men, 532 women full time; 168 men, 259 women part time. **Graduate enrollment:** 25 men, 8 women full time; 55 men, 16 women part time. **Faculty:** 119 total (89 full time), 57 with doctorates or other terminal degrees. **Location:** Urban campus in large town; 82 miles from Bozeman. **Calendar:** Semester, limited summer session. Extensive evening/early morning classes. **Microcomputers:** 500 located in dormitories, libraries, classrooms, computer centers, campus-wide network. **Special facilities:** Mineral museum, Montana Technical Research Center, map collection, neutron acceleration laboratory, patent depository library, rare book collection, Montana Bureau of Mines and Geology, Earthquake Studies Office.

DEGREES OFFERED. AA, AS, BS, MS. 17 associate degrees awarded in 1992. 25% in engineering, 75% multi/interdisciplinary studies. 227 bachelor's degrees awarded. 13% in business and management, 26% computer sciences, 47% engineering, 5% multi/interdisciplinary studies, 5% physical sciences. Graduate degrees offered in 9 major fields of study.

UNDERGRADUATE MAJORS. Associate: Communications, engineering, engineering and engineering-related technologies, engineering and other disciplines, liberal/general studies, technical and business writing. **Bachelor's:** Accounting, applied mathematics, business administration and management, business and management, chemistry, communications, computer and information sciences, computer programming, engineering science, environmental health engineering, finance, geological engineering, geophysical engineering, information sciences and systems, mathematics, metallurgical engineering, mining and mineral engineering, occupational safety and health technology, petroleum engineering, prelaw, pure mathematics, society and technology, technical and business writing.

ACADEMIC PROGRAMS. 2-year transfer program, cooperative education, double major, dual enrollment of high school students, independent study, internships, 3-2 liberal arts-engineering program with Carroll College; liberal arts/career combination in engineering, health sciences. **Remedial services:** Learning center, special counselor, tutoring, writing center. **Placement/credit:** AP, CLEP General and Subject, institutional tests; 30 credit hours maximum for bachelor's degree.

ACADEMIC REQUIREMENTS. Freshmen must earn minimum GPA of 1.7 to continue in good standing. 54% of freshmen return for sophomore year. Students must declare major on application. **Graduation requirements:** 63 hours for associate, 128 hours for bachelor's. Most students required to take courses in English, history, humanities, mathematics, biological/physical sciences, social sciences. **Postgraduate studies:** 80% from 2-year programs enter 4-year programs. 1% enter law school, 1% enter medical school, 12% enter MBA programs, 12% enter other graduate study. **Additional information:** Environmental Engineering Program combines engineering and science courses with specialized environmental courses; emphasis on "hands on" experience in laboratory and field.

FRESHMAN ADMISSIONS. Selection criteria: High school GPA, class rank, and ACT or SAT scores are important. **High school preparation:** 14 units required. Required and recommended units include English 4, mathematics 3-4, physical science 2-3 and social science 3. Biological science 1 recommended. 2 additional units from foreign language, computer science, visual or performing arts, or vocational instruction which meets office of public instruction guidelines required. **Test requirements:** SAT or ACT (ACT preferred); score report by August 1.

1992 FRESHMAN CLASS PROFILE. 259 men applied, 245 accepted, 213 enrolled; 162 women applied, 150 accepted, 140 enrolled. 54% had high school GPA of 3.0 or higher, 46% between 2.0 and 2.99. **Academic background:** Mid 50% of enrolled freshmen had ACT composite between 19-25. 90% submitted ACT scores. **Characteristics:** 86% from in state, 50% commute, 3% have minority backgrounds, 1% are foreign students. Average age is 20.

FALL-TERM APPLICATIONS. $20 fee. No closing date; priority given to applications received by August 1; applicants notified on a rolling basis. Deferred and early admission available.

STUDENT LIFE. Housing: Dormitories (coed); apartment housing available. Rooms for handicapped students available. **Activities:** Student government, radio, student newspaper, yearbook, choral groups, pep band, Baptist Student Union, Newman Club, International Club, Circle-K, Baha'i Club, Chi Alpha.

ATHLETICS. NAIA. **Intercollegiate:** Basketball, football M, swimming, volleyball W, wrestling M. **Intramural:** Badminton, basketball, bowling, cross-country, handball, ice hockey M, racquetball, rugby M, skiing, soccer M, softball, swimming, tennis, volleyball, water polo, wrestling M.

STUDENT SERVICES. Aptitude testing, career counseling, employment service for undergraduates, freshman orientation, health services, on-campus day care, personal counseling, placement service for graduates, special adviser for adult students, veterans counselor, services/facilities for handicapped.

ANNUAL EXPENSES. Tuition and fees (projected): $1,767, $3,892 additional for out-of-state students. **Room and board:** $3,250. **Books and supplies:** $500. **Other expenses:** $1,100.

FINANCIAL AID. 58% of freshmen, 62% of continuing students receive some form of aid. 58% of grants, 83% of loans, 20% of jobs based on need. 182 enrolled freshmen were judged to have need, all were offered aid. Academic, athletic, leadership, alumni affiliation, minority scholarships available. **Aid applications:** No closing date; priority given to applications received by April 1; applicants notified on a rolling basis beginning on or about June 15; must reply within 2 weeks.

ADDRESS/TELEPHONE. Office of Admissions, Montana College of Mineral Science and Technology, West Park Street, Butte, MT 59701. (406) 496-4178. (800) 445-8324. Fax: (406) 496-4133.

Montana State University

Bozeman, Montana — CB code: 4488

Admissions: 86% of applicants accepted
Based on: ••• School record, test scores
• Essay, interview, recommendations, special talents
Completion: 80% of freshmen end year in good standing
40% graduate, 13% of these enter graduate study

4-year public university, coed. Founded in 1893. **Accreditation:** Regional. **Undergraduate enrollment:** 4,885 men, 3,711 women full time; 500 men, 601 women part time. **Graduate enrollment:** 353 men, 188 women full time; 149 men, 153 women part time. **Faculty:** 798 total (650 full time), 453 with doctorates or other terminal degrees. **Location:** Rural campus in large town; 139 miles from Billings. **Calendar:** Semester, limited summer session. **Microcomputers:** 750 located in dormitories, libraries, classrooms, computer centers. **Special facilities:** Museum of the Rockies and Planetarium, Foothills Nature Area, Bridger Bowl ski area.

DEGREES OFFERED. BA, BS, BArch, MA, MS, MFA, MEd, PhD, EdD. 1,411 bachelor's degrees awarded in 1992. 7% in agriculture, 15% business and management, 12% education, 13% engineering, 5% engineering technologies, 9% health sciences, 7% life sciences, 6% social sciences, 7% visual and performing arts. Graduate degrees offered in 45 major fields of study.

UNDERGRADUATE MAJORS. Accounting, agribusiness, agricultural economics, agricultural education, agricultural engineering, agricultural mechanics, agronomy, animal sciences, anthropology, architecture, art education, biology, business and management, chemical engineering, chemistry, cinematography/film, civil engineering, civil technology, communications, computer and information sciences, criminal justice studies, dramatic arts, early childhood education, earth sciences, economics, electrical technology, electrical/electronics/communications engineering, electronic technology, elementary education, English, English education, English literature, film arts, finance, fine arts, fishing and fisheries, food science and nutrition, foreign languages education, French, geography, geology, geophysics and seismology, German, graphic design, health education, history, home economics, home economics education, horticulture, individual and family development, industrial arts education, industrial engineering, interior design, junior high education, landscape architecture, marketing management, mathematics, mathematics education, mechanical design technology, mechanical engineering, microbiology, motion picture technology, music, music education, nursing, philosophy, photographic technology, photography, physical education, physics, plant protection, plant sciences, political science and government, psychology, range management, renewable natural resources, science education, secondary education, social studies education, sociology, soil sciences, Spanish, statistics, textiles and clothing, video, visual and performing arts, wildlife management.

ACADEMIC PROGRAMS. Double major, dual enrollment of high school students, education specialist degree, honors program, independent study, internships, student-designed major, study abroad, teacher preparation, visiting/exchange student program. **Remedial services:** Learning center, remedial instruction, special counselor, tutoring. **ROTC:** Air Force, Army. **Placement/credit:** AP, CLEP Subject, institutional tests.

ACADEMIC REQUIREMENTS. Freshmen must earn minimum GPA of 2.5 to continue in good standing. 69% of freshmen return for sophomore year. Students must declare major by end of second year. **Graduation requirements:** 128 hours for bachelor's (36 in major). Most students required

to take courses in arts/fine arts, English, history, humanities, mathematics, biological/physical sciences, social sciences. **Additional information:** Honors program offered to all students who seek challenging and innovative college experience. Admission to program not based on academic standing.

FRESHMAN ADMISSIONS. Selection criteria: Minimum GPA of 2.5 or minimum ACT composite score of 20 or SAT combined score of 800 or rank in top half of graduating class; completion of state college-preparatory requirements important. **High school preparation:** 12 units required. Required and recommended units include English 4, mathematics 3, social science 3 and science 2. Foreign language 2 recommended. 4 mathematics recommended for science majors. Substitutions for foreign language requirement possible. **Test requirements:** SAT or ACT; score report by September 4.

1992 FRESHMAN CLASS PROFILE. 1,689 men applied, 1,425 accepted, 935 enrolled; 1,257 women applied, 1,094 accepted, 678 enrolled. 61% had high school GPA of 3.0 or higher, 36% between 2.0 and 2.99. 17% were in top tenth and 42% were in top quarter of graduating class. **Academic background:** Mid 50% of enrolled freshmen had SAT-V between 390-510, SAT-M between 450-600; ACT composite between 20-25. 38% submitted SAT scores, 70% submitted ACT scores. **Characteristics:** 68% from in state, 78% live in college housing, 4% have minority backgrounds, 1% are foreign students. Average age is 19.

FALL-TERM APPLICATIONS. $20 fee. No closing date; priority given to applications received by July 1; applicants notified on a rolling basis. Interview recommended. Deferred and early admission available.

STUDENT LIFE. Housing: Dormitories (men, women, coed); apartment, fraternity, sorority, handicapped housing available. Wellness Hall with programs geared toward personal wellness; older student housing available. **Activities:** Student government, radio, student newspaper, television, choral groups, concert band, dance, drama, jazz band, marching band, music ensembles, musical theater, opera, pep band, symphony orchestra, fraternities, sororities, Spurs, FANGS (campus service organization), campus ministry, Circle-K, Native American Club, International Coordinating Council. **Additional information:** Rodeo scholarships available.

ATHLETICS. NCAA. **Intercollegiate:** Basketball, cross-country, football M, tennis, track and field, volleyball W. **Intramural:** Archery, badminton, baseball M, basketball, bowling, cross-country, diving, fencing, golf, handball, racquetball, skiing, soccer, softball, squash, swimming, table tennis, tennis, track and field, volleyball, wrestling M. **Clubs:** Rodeo.

STUDENT SERVICES. Career counseling, freshman orientation, health services, on-campus day care, personal counseling, placement service for graduates, special adviser for adult students, veterans counselor, study skills program, interest inventory, services/facilities for handicapped.

ANNUAL EXPENSES. Tuition and fees (projected): $1,909, $3,892 additional for out-of-state students. **Room and board:** $3,462. **Books and supplies:** $550. **Other expenses:** $1,800.

FINANCIAL AID. 83% of freshmen, 70% of continuing students receive some form of aid. 85% of grants, 83% of loans, 42% of jobs based on need. 790 enrolled freshmen were judged to have need, all were offered aid. Academic, music/drama, art, athletic, state/district residency, minority scholarships available. **Aid applications:** No closing date; priority given to applications received by March 1; applicants notified on a rolling basis beginning on or about May 1; must reply within 3 weeks.

ADDRESS/TELEPHONE. Charles A. Nelson, Director of Admissions, Montana State University, 120 Hamilton Hall, Bozeman, MT 59717-0016. (406) 994-2452.

Northern Montana College
Havre, Montana — CB code: 4538

4-year public college of arts and sciences and business, nursing, teachers, technical college, coed. Founded in 1929. **Accreditation:** Regional. **Undergraduate enrollment:** 482 men, 562 women full time; 163 men, 230 women part time. **Graduate enrollment:** 37 men, 37 women full time; 112 men, 184 women part time. **Faculty:** 121 total (84 full time), 35 with doctorates or other terminal degrees. **Location:** Rural campus in large town; 100 miles from Great Falls. **Calendar:** Semester, extensive summer session. Extensive evening/early morning classes. **Microcomputers:** Located in libraries, classrooms, computer centers. **Additional facts:** Classes for military personnel available at resident center at Malmstrom Air Force Base, Great Falls. Extended campus in Great Falls.

DEGREES OFFERED. AA, AS, BA, BS, MEd. 151 associate degrees awarded in 1992. 23% in business and management, 39% health sciences, 6% life sciences, 23% trade and industry. 239 bachelor's degrees awarded. 27% in business and management, 43% teacher education, 25% trade and industry. Graduate degrees offered in 2 major fields of study.

UNDERGRADUATE MAJORS. Associate: Agribusiness, agricultural sciences, American Indian studies, automotive mechanics, automotive technology, biology, business and management, business and office, business computer/console/peripheral equipment operation, business data programming, chemistry, computer programming, computer technology, construction, diesel engine mechanics, drafting, drafting and design technology, ecology, electrical and electronics equipment repair, electronic technology, humanities and social sciences, industrial technology, liberal/general studies, mechanical design technology, nursing, practical nursing, precision metal work, secretarial and related programs, water and wastewater technology. **Bachelor's:** American Indian studies, automotive mechanics, automotive technology, biology, business and management, chemistry, communications, construction, diesel engine mechanics, drafting, drafting and design technology, dramatic arts, ecology, education, electrical and electronics equipment repair, electronic technology, elementary education, English, English education, French, humanities and social sciences, industrial arts education, liberal/general studies, mathematics, mathematics education, mechanical design technology, music, nursing, physical education, practical nursing, science education, secondary education, social science education, technical education, trade and industrial education.

ACADEMIC PROGRAMS. 2-year transfer program, accelerated program, cooperative education, double major, dual enrollment of high school students, independent study, internships, teacher preparation. **Remedial services:** Learning center, preadmission summer program, reduced course load, remedial instruction, special counselor, tutoring. **Placement/credit:** AP, CLEP General and Subject, institutional tests.

ACADEMIC REQUIREMENTS. Freshmen must earn minimum GPA of 2.0 to continue in good standing. 55% of freshmen return for sophomore year. Students must declare major by end of second year. **Graduation requirements:** 64 hours for associate, 128 hours for bachelor's. Most students required to take courses in computer science, English, humanities, mathematics, biological/physical sciences, social sciences. **Postgraduate studies:** 60% from 2-year programs enter 4-year programs.

FRESHMAN ADMISSIONS. Selection criteria: Test scores, minimum high school GPA of 2.5 or upper half of class, in conjunction with college preparatory program important. **High school preparation:** 14 units required. Required units include English 4, mathematics 3, social science 3 and science 2. Science units must be laboratory sciences. 2 additional academic units required. **Test requirements:** SAT or ACT (ACT preferred); score report by August 18.

1992 FRESHMAN CLASS PROFILE. 168 men and women enrolled. 25% had high school GPA of 3.0 or higher, 75% between 2.0 and 2.99. **Academic background:** Mid 50% of enrolled freshmen had ACT composite between 14-22. 48% submitted ACT scores. **Characteristics:** 96% from in state, 69% commute, 11% have minority backgrounds, 1% are foreign students. Average age is 22.

FALL-TERM APPLICATIONS. $20 fee. No closing date; applicants notified on a rolling basis. Deferred and early admission available.

STUDENT LIFE. Housing: Dormitories (men, women, coed); apartment housing available. **Activities:** Student government, radio, student newspaper, television, yearbook, choral groups, concert band, drama, musical theater, pep band, North Star Ambassadors, Inter-Christian fellowship, Delta Alpha Theta, Sweetgrass Society.

ATHLETICS. NAIA. **Intercollegiate:** Basketball, volleyball W, wrestling M. **Intramural:** Basketball, bowling, skiing, softball, tennis, volleyball.

STUDENT SERVICES. Aptitude testing, career counseling, employment service for undergraduates, freshman orientation, health services, on-campus day care, personal counseling, placement service for graduates, special adviser for adult students, veterans counselor, services/facilities for handicapped.

ANNUAL EXPENSES. Tuition and fees (projected): $1,802, $3,556 additional for out-of-state students. **Room and board:** $3,216. **Books and supplies:** $473. **Other expenses:** $465.

FINANCIAL AID. 49% of freshmen, 50% of continuing students receive some form of aid. Grants, loans, jobs available. Academic, music/drama, athletic, state/district residency, leadership, alumni affiliation, minority scholarships available. **Aid applications:** No closing date; priority given to applications received by March 1; applicants notified on a rolling basis beginning on or about May 1; must reply within 2 weeks.

ADDRESS/TELEPHONE. Mr. Kelly Palmer, Director of Admissions, Northern Montana College, PO Box 7751, Havre, MT 59501. (406) 265-3700. Fax: (406) 265-3777.

Rocky Mountain College
Billings, Montana — CB code: 4660

4-year private liberal arts college, coed, affiliated with United Church of Christ, United Methodist Church, and United Presbyterian Church. Founded in 1878. **Accreditation:** Regional. **Undergraduate enrollment:** 304 men, 313 women full time; 38 men, 93 women part time. **Faculty:** 63 total (38 full time), 23 with doctorates or other terminal degrees. **Location:** Suburban campus in small city. **Calendar:** 4-4-1, limited summer session. Extensive evening/early morning classes. **Microcomputers:** Located in libraries, computer centers. **Special facilities:** Geology library, theater, J. K. Ralston Art Museum and Studio, rock climbing wall, outdoor recreation center.

DEGREES OFFERED. AA, BA, BS. 15 associate degrees awarded in 1992. 100% in multi/interdisciplinary studies. 120 bachelor's degrees awarded. 37% in business and management, 20% teacher education, 5% letters/literature, 5% life sciences, 10% psychology, 10% social sciences.

UNDERGRADUATE MAJORS. Associate: Data processing, equestrian science, legal assistant/paralegal, liberal/general studies. **Bachelor's:** Accounting, airline piloting and navigation, American literature, anthropology, art education, aviation management, aviation studies, biological and physical sciences, biology, business administration and management, business and management, business economics, chemistry, computer and information sciences, computer mathematics, computer sciences/mathematics, dramatic arts, economics, elementary education, engineering, English, English education, English literature, equestrian science, fine arts, French, geology, history, humanities and social sciences, liberal/general studies, mathematics, mathematics education, music, music education, occupational therapy, petroleum management, philosophy, physical education, physical therapy, political science and government, predentistry, prelaw, premedicine, prepharmacy, preveterinary, psychology, religion, secondary education, social science education, social sciences, sociology, Spanish, visual and performing arts.

ACADEMIC PROGRAMS. Accelerated program, cooperative education, double major, dual enrollment of high school students, honors program, independent study, internships, student-designed major, study abroad, teacher preparation, weekend college; liberal arts/career combination in engineering, health sciences. **Remedial services:** Preadmission summer program, reduced course load, remedial instruction, tutoring. **ROTC:** Army. **Placement/credit:** AP, CLEP General and Subject, institutional tests; 30 credit hours maximum for bachelor's degree.

ACADEMIC REQUIREMENTS. Freshmen must earn minimum GPA of 2.0 to continue in good standing. 70% of freshmen return for sophomore year. Students must declare major by end of second year. **Graduation requirements:** 62 hours for associate, 124 hours for bachelor's (24 in major). Most students required to take courses in arts/fine arts, English, foreign languages, humanities, mathematics, philosophy/religion, biological/physical sciences, social sciences.

FRESHMAN ADMISSIONS. Selection criteria: 2.0 GPA required. Recommendations and secondary school record important. Class rank, ACT, SAT scores and essay considered. **High school preparation:** 13 units recommended. Recommended units include English 4, foreign language 2, mathematics 3, social science 2 and science 2. One US history or government and 2 units each in the following: foreign language, mathematics, natural sciences. Social sciences also recommended. **Test requirements:** SAT or ACT (ACT preferred); score report by August 15.

1992 FRESHMAN CLASS PROFILE. 89 men, 89 women enrolled. **Academic background:** Mid 50% of enrolled freshmen had ACT composite between 15-24. 65% submitted ACT scores. **Characteristics:** 67% from in state, 59% live in college housing, 7% have minority backgrounds, 5% are foreign students. Average age is 19.

FALL-TERM APPLICATIONS. $25 fee, may be waived for applicants with need. Closing date August 1; applicants notified on a rolling basis. Interview recommended for academically weak applicants. Audition recommended for music applicants. Portfolio recommended for art applicants. Essay recommended. CRDA. Deferred and early admission available.

STUDENT LIFE. Housing: Dormitories (men, women, coed). **Activities:** Student government, magazine, student newspaper, yearbook, choral groups, concert band, dance, drama, jazz band, marching band, music ensembles, musical theater, pep band, Fellowship of Christian Athletes, Circle-K, Spurs, Intervarsity.

ATHLETICS. NAIA. **Intercollegiate:** Basketball, football M, skiing, volleyball W. **Intramural:** Baseball, basketball, football M, golf, handball, horseback riding, racquetball, skiing, soccer, softball, swimming, table tennis, tennis, track and field, volleyball, water polo, wrestling M.

STUDENT SERVICES. Aptitude testing, career counseling, employment service for undergraduates, freshman orientation, health services, on-campus day care, personal counseling, placement service for graduates, services/facilities for handicapped.

ANNUAL EXPENSES. Tuition and fees (projected): $8,818. **Room and board:** $3,327. **Books and supplies:** $600. **Other expenses:** $630.

FINANCIAL AID. 80% of freshmen, 80% of continuing students receive some form of aid. 43% of grants, 87% of loans, all jobs based on need. 109 enrolled freshmen were judged to have need, all were offered aid. Academic, music/drama, art, athletic, leadership, religious affiliation scholarships available. **Aid applications:** No closing date; priority given to applications received by April 1; applicants notified on a rolling basis; must reply within 4 weeks.

ADDRESS/TELEPHONE. David Heringer, Director of Admissions, Rocky Mountain College, 1511 Poly Drive, Billings, MT 59102-1796. (406) 657-1026. (800) 877-6259. Fax: (406) 259-9751.

Salish Kootenai College
Pablo, Montana CB code: 0898

2-year private community college, coed. Founded in 1977. **Accreditation:** Regional. **Undergraduate enrollment:** 715 men and women. **Faculty:** 64 total (37 full time), 6 with doctorates or other terminal degrees. **Location:** Rural campus in rural community; 60 miles from Missoula. **Calendar:** Quarter, limited summer session. Extensive evening/early morning classes. **Additional facts:** Located on Flathead Indian Reservation area in midst of Indian communities.

DEGREES OFFERED. AA, AS, AAS. 57 associate degrees awarded in 1992.

UNDERGRADUATE MAJORS. American Indian studies, computer and information sciences, dental assistant, elementary education, forestry and related sciences, liberal/general studies, nursing, renewable natural resources, secretarial and related programs, social work.

ACADEMIC PROGRAMS. 2-year transfer program, cooperative education, double major, dual enrollment of high school students. **Remedial services:** Learning center, special counselor, tutoring. **Placement/credit:** Institutional tests.

ACADEMIC REQUIREMENTS. Freshmen must earn minimum GPA of 2.0 to continue in good standing. 70% of freshmen return for sophomore year. Students must declare major on enrollment. **Graduation requirements:** 90 hours for associate. Most students required to take courses in arts/fine arts, computer science, English, history, humanities, mathematics, biological/physical sciences, social sciences.

FRESHMAN ADMISSIONS. Selection criteria: Open admissions. **Additional information:** Students without high school diploma or GED must earn GED in first 2 quarters.

1992 FRESHMAN CLASS PROFILE. 26 men and women enrolled. **Characteristics:** 100% from in state, 100% commute. Average age is 21.

FALL-TERM APPLICATIONS. No fee. No closing date; applicants notified on a rolling basis. Deferred and early admission available.

STUDENT LIFE. Activities: Student government, film, student newspaper, television, yearbook, drama.

ATHLETICS. Intramural: Bowling, skiing, softball, tennis, volleyball.

STUDENT SERVICES. Aptitude testing, career counseling, employment service for undergraduates, freshman orientation, on-campus day care, personal counseling, placement service for graduates, veterans counselor, services/facilities for handicapped.

ANNUAL EXPENSES. Tuition and fees (1992-93): $1,440, $576 additional for out-of-district students, $576 additional for out-of-state students. **Books and supplies:** $525. **Other expenses:** $1,350.

FINANCIAL AID. 65% of freshmen, 85% of continuing students receive some form of aid. 94% of grants, all loans, all jobs based on need. **Aid applications:** No closing date; priority given to applications received by March 31; applicants notified on a rolling basis beginning on or about August 10.

ADDRESS/TELEPHONE. Cleo Kenmille, Registrar/Assistant Director, Student Services, Salish Kootenai College, PO Box 117, Pablo, MT 59855. (406) 675-4800. Fax: (406) 675-4801.

Stone Child College
Box Elder, Montana CB code: 7044

2-year public community college, coed. **Accreditation:** Regional candidate. **Undergraduate enrollment:** 60 men, 80 women full time; 6 men, 15 women part time. **Faculty:** 19 total (10 full time). **Location:** Rural campus in rural community; 26 miles from Havre, 100 miles from Great Falls. **Calendar:** Semester. Extensive evening/early morning classes. **Microcomputers:** 12 located in computer centers. **Additional facts:** Tribally controlled college located on the Rocky Boys Indian Reservation.

DEGREES OFFERED. AA, AS. 17 associate degrees awarded in 1992. 29% in business and management, 6% computer sciences, 41% multi/interdisciplinary studies, 24% trade and industry.

UNDERGRADUATE MAJORS. Biological and physical sciences, building maintenance, business and management, business and office, computer and information sciences, computer graphics, elementary education, engineering and other disciplines, information sciences and systems, liberal/general studies, mental health/human services.

ACADEMIC PROGRAMS. 2-year transfer program, dual enrollment of high school students. **Remedial services:** Remedial instruction, special counselor, tutoring.

ACADEMIC REQUIREMENTS. Students must declare major on application. **Graduation requirements:** 64 hours for associate (33 in major). Most students required to take courses in arts/fine arts, computer science, English, foreign languages, history, humanities, mathematics, philosophy/religion, biological/physical sciences, social sciences.

FRESHMAN ADMISSIONS. Selection criteria: Open admissions.

1992 FRESHMAN CLASS PROFILE. 25 men, 15 women enrolled. **Characteristics:** 98% from in state, 100% commute, 99% have minority backgrounds. Average age is 25.

FALL-TERM APPLICATIONS. $10 fee. No closing date; applicants notified on a rolling basis. Essay recommended. Tests for placement and counseling required.

STUDENT LIFE. Activities: Student government.

ATHLETICS. Intramural: Basketball.

STUDENT SERVICES. Freshman orientation, on-campus day care, personal counseling, services/facilities for handicapped.

ANNUAL EXPENSES. Tuition and fees (1992-93): $1,630, $300 additional for out-of-state students. **Books and supplies:** $150.

FINANCIAL AID. All grants, all jobs based on need. 4 enrolled freshmen were judged to have need, all were offered aid. Academic, religious affiliation, minority scholarships available. **Aid applications:** No closing date; priority given to applications received by March 27; applicants notified on a rolling basis. **Additional information:** Freshman fee waiver and a GED fee waiver available.

ADDRESS/TELEPHONE. Admissions Office, Stone Child College, PO Box 1082, Box Elder, MT 59521-9796. (406) 395-4313. Fax: (406) 395-4836.

University of Montana
Missoula, Montana — CB code: 4489

Admissions: 91% of applicants accepted
Based on: ••• School record
•• Test scores
• Recommendations, special talents
Completion: 82% of freshmen end year in good standing
23% enter graduate study

4-year public university, coed. Founded in 1893. **Accreditation:** Regional. **Undergraduate enrollment:** 3,685 men, 3,740 women full time; 511 men, 640 women part time. **Graduate enrollment:** 444 men, 357 women full time; 286 men, 227 women part time. **Faculty:** 601 total (438 full time), 376 with doctorates or other terminal degrees. **Location:** Suburban campus in small city; 210 miles from Spokane, Washington. **Calendar:** Semester, extensive summer session. Extensive evening/early morning classes. **Microcomputers:** 217 located in dormitories, libraries, classrooms, computer centers. **Special facilities:** Performing arts, radio and television building, 3 art galleries, wildlife museum, 29,000-acre experimental forest, Yellow Bay biological research station on Flathead Lake, bureau of business and economic research, geology field camp, wood chemistry laboratory, environmental studies laboratory, Montana forest and conservation experiment station, Boone & Crockett Ranch.

DEGREES OFFERED. AA, BA, BS, BFA, MA, MS, MBA, MFA, MEd, PhD, EdD, B. Pharm, Pharm D, JD. 3 associate degrees awarded in 1992. 100% in multi/interdisciplinary studies. 1,350 bachelor's degrees awarded. 28% in business and management, 12% education, 11% letters/literature, 8% parks/recreation, protective services, public affairs, 5% psychology, 14% social sciences. Graduate degrees offered in 58 major fields of study.

UNDERGRADUATE MAJORS. Associate: Liberal/general studies. **Bachelor's:** Accounting, anthropology, art education, astronomy, biology, botany, business administration and management, business and management, business and office, business economics, business education, ceramics, chemistry, classics, communications, computer and information sciences, conservation and regulation, dance, dramatic arts, drawing, early childhood education, economics, education, elementary education, English, English education, finance, fine arts, foreign languages education, forestry and related sciences, French, geography, geology, German, Greek (classical), health education, history, information sciences and systems, journalism, junior high education, Latin, liberal/general studies, management information systems, marketing and distribution, marketing management, mathematics, mathematics education, medical laboratory technologies, microbiology, music, music education, music performance, music theory and composition, painting, parks and recreation management, pharmacy, philosophy, physical education, physical therapy, physics, physics/astronomy, political science and government, predentistry, prelaw, premedicine, preveterinary, psychology, radio/television broadcasting, radio/television technology, Russian, Russian and Slavic studies, science education, secondary education, social science education, social studies education, social work, sociology, Spanish, speech pathology/audiology, speech/communication/theater education, sports medicine, studio art, theater design, wildlife biology, wildlife management, zoology.

ACADEMIC PROGRAMS. 2-year transfer program, accelerated program, cooperative education, double major, dual enrollment of high school students, honors program, independent study, internships, study abroad, teacher preparation, telecourses, visiting/exchange student program; liberal arts/career combination in forestry. **Remedial services:** Learning center, reduced course load, remedial instruction, special counselor, tutoring. **ROTC:** Army. **Placement/credit:** AP, CLEP General and Subject, institutional tests.

ACADEMIC REQUIREMENTS. Freshmen must earn minimum GPA of 1.75 to continue in good standing. 60% of freshmen return for sophomore year. Students must declare major by end of second year. **Graduation requirements:** 65 hours for associate, 130 hours for bachelor's (38 in major). Most students required to take courses in arts/fine arts, English, foreign languages, history, mathematics, philosophy/religion, biological/physical sciences, social sciences. **Additional information:** University Transition program introduces incoming freshman to basic college study skills, effective writing, and use of word processing systems.

FRESHMAN ADMISSIONS. Selection criteria: Minimum 2.5 GPA, or minimum ACT composite score of 20 or combined SAT score of 800, or rank in top half of graduating class required. **High school preparation:** 14 units required. Required units include English 4, mathematics 3, social science 3 and science 2. 2 additional units from foreign language, computer science, visual and performing arts, or vocational education that meet office of public instruction requirements required. **Test requirements:** SAT or ACT (ACT preferred); score report by July 1.

1992 FRESHMAN CLASS PROFILE. 1,364 men applied, 1,223 accepted, 651 enrolled; 1,321 women applied, 1,216 accepted, 679 enrolled. **Academic background:** Mid 50% of enrolled freshmen had ACT composite between 18-25. 75% submitted ACT scores. **Characteristics:** 66% from in state, 88% live in college housing, 1% are foreign students, 15% join fraternities/sororities. Average age is 19.

FALL-TERM APPLICATIONS. $20 fee. Closing date July 1; applicants notified on a rolling basis. Interview required for physical therapy applicants. Audition required for music applicants. Portfolio required for art applicants. Deferred and early admission available.

STUDENT LIFE. Housing: Dormitories (men, women, coed); apartment, fraternity, sorority, handicapped housing available. Honors floors, international floors, quiet floors, activity dorms, personal development housing available. **Activities:** Student government, radio, student newspaper, yearbook, student publications in poetry, creative writing, choral groups, concert band, dance, drama, jazz band, marching band, music ensembles, musical theater, pep band, symphony orchestra, fraternities, sororities, Associated Students of University of Montana, University of Montana Advocates, Mortar Board, Spurs, Circle- K.

ATHLETICS. NCAA. **Intercollegiate:** Basketball, cross-country, football M, tennis, track and field, volleyball W. **Intramural:** Archery, badminton, baseball M, basketball, golf, gymnastics, handball, ice hockey M, rugby, skiing, soccer, softball, swimming, tennis, track and field, volleyball, water polo, wrestling M.

STUDENT SERVICES. Aptitude testing, career counseling, employment service for undergraduates, freshman orientation, health services, on-campus day care, personal counseling, placement service for graduates, special adviser for adult students, veterans counselor, services/facilities for handicapped.

ANNUAL EXPENSES. Tuition and fees (projected): $1,962, $3,892 additional for out-of-state students. **Room and board:** $3,600. **Books and supplies:** $550. **Other expenses:** $2,200.

FINANCIAL AID. 60% of freshmen, 66% of continuing students receive some form of aid. Grants, loans, jobs available. Academic, music/drama, art, athletic, state/district residency, leadership scholarships available. **Aid applications:** No closing date; priority given to applications received by March 1; applicants notified on a rolling basis beginning on or about June 1; must reply within 2 weeks.

ADDRESS/TELEPHONE. Mr. Michael L. Akin, Director of Admissions, University of Montana, Lodge 101, Missoula, MT 59812. (406) 243-6266. (800) 462-8636. Fax: (406) 243-2327.

Western Montana College of the University of Montana
Dillon, Montana — CB code: 4945

4-year public teachers college, coed. Founded in 1893. **Accreditation:** Regional. **Undergraduate enrollment:** 465 men, 508 women full time; 68 men, 110 women part time. **Faculty:** 42 total (36 full time), 20 with doctorates or other terminal degrees. **Location:** Rural campus in small town; 75 miles from Yellowstone National Park, 65 miles from Butte. **Calendar:** Semester, extensive summer session. Saturday and extensive evening/early morning classes. **Microcomputers:** 113 located in dormitories, libraries, classrooms, computer centers. **Special facilities:** Outdoor education center in Pioneer Mountains, Siedensticker Wildlife Exhibit, student art gallery.

DEGREES OFFERED. AA, AS, BS. 65 associate degrees awarded in 1992. 110 bachelor's degrees awarded.

UNDERGRADUATE MAJORS. Associate: Advertising Design, business and management, business and office, business data processing and related programs, computer and information sciences, education, human resources development, legal secretary, management information systems, medical secretary, office supervision and management, secretarial and related programs, tourism, word processing. **Bachelor's:** Art education, business education, education, elementary education, English education, industrial arts education, junior high education, mathematics education, music education, physical education, science education, secondary education, social science education.

ACADEMIC PROGRAMS. 2-year transfer program, cooperative education, double major, internships, teacher preparation, visiting/exchange student program, weekend college. **Remedial services:** Learning center, preadmission summer program, reduced course load, remedial instruction, tutoring. **Placement/credit:** AP, CLEP General and Subject, institutional tests.

ACADEMIC REQUIREMENTS. Freshmen must earn minimum GPA of 2.0 to continue in good standing. 60% of freshmen return for sophomore year. Students must declare major by end of first year. **Graduation requirements:** 64 hours for associate (28 in major), 128 hours for bachelor's (39 in major). Most students required to take courses in English, history, mathematics, philosophy/religion, biological/physical sciences, social sciences.

FRESHMAN ADMISSIONS. Selection criteria: Nonresidents must rank in top half of graduating class. **High school preparation:** 12 units required. Required units include English 4, foreign language 2, mathematics 3 and social science 3. **Test requirements:** SAT or ACT (ACT preferred); score report by August 24.

1992 FRESHMAN CLASS PROFILE. 200 men and women enrolled. **Academic background:** Mid 50% of enrolled freshmen had ACT composite between 13-20. 100% submitted ACT scores. **Characteristics:** 90% from in state, 93% live in college housing, 1% have minority backgrounds, 1% are foreign students.

FALL-TERM APPLICATIONS. $20 fee. No closing date; priority given to applications received by July 26; applicants notified on a rolling basis. Interview recommended. CRDA. Deferred and early admission available.

STUDENT LIFE. Housing: Dormitories (men, women, coed); apartment housing available. Students under 20 not living with family required to live in dormitory. **Activities:** Student government, student newspaper, yearbook, choral groups, concert band, dance, drama, jazz band, music ensembles, musical theater, pep band, Circle-K, women's service organizations, Spurs, Inter-Varsity Christian Fellowship, Student Ambassadors, Presidential Scholars, Activities Board, M-Club. **Additional information:** Rodeo scholarships available.

ATHLETICS. NAIA. **Intercollegiate:** Basketball, football M, volleyball W, wrestling M. **Intramural:** Badminton, basketball, golf, handball, racquetball, skiing, soccer, softball, table tennis, tennis, volleyball.

STUDENT SERVICES. Aptitude testing, career counseling, employment service for undergraduates, freshman orientation, health services, on-campus day care, personal counseling, placement service for graduates, veterans counselor.

ANNUAL EXPENSES. Tuition and fees (projected): $1,780, $3,556 additional for out-of-state students. **Room and board:** $3,000. **Books and supplies:** $550. **Other expenses:** $1,100.

FINANCIAL AID. 62% of freshmen, 73% of continuing students receive some form of aid. 92% of grants, 93% of loans, 93% of jobs based on need. 140 enrolled freshmen were judged to have need, all were offered aid. Academic, music/drama, art, athletic, state/district residency, leadership, alumni affiliation scholarships available. **Aid applications:** No closing date; priority given to applications received by March 1; applicants notified on a rolling basis beginning on or about June 1; must reply by July 15 or immediately if notified thereafter. **Additional information:** Tuition and/or fee waiver for veterans and Native Americans.

ADDRESS/TELEPHONE. Michele F. O'Neill, Director of Admissions, Western Montana College of the University of Montana, Dillon, MT 59725. (406) 683-7331. (800) WMC-MONT. Fax: (406) 683-7493.

Nebraska

Bellevue College

Bellevue, Nebraska — CB code: 6053

4-year private business, liberal arts college, coed. Founded in 1965. **Accreditation:** Regional. **Undergraduate enrollment:** 483 men, 490 women full time; 435 men, 647 women part time. **Graduate enrollment:** 59 men, 43 women full time. **Faculty:** 83 total (40 full time), 25 with doctorates or other terminal degrees. **Location:** Suburban campus in large town; adjacent to Omaha. **Calendar:** Semester, extensive summer session. **Microcomputers:** 35 located in computer centers. **Additional facts:** Evening classes offered on trimester calendar.

DEGREES OFFERED. BA, BS, BFA, MA. 415 bachelor's degrees awarded in 1992. 88% in business and management. Graduate degrees offered in 1 major field of study.

UNDERGRADUATE MAJORS. Accounting, business administration and management, communications, criminal justice studies, English, fine arts, geography, history, human resources development, management information systems, marketing management, mathematics, philosophy, physical education, political science and government, psychology, social sciences, sociology, Spanish, urban studies.

ACADEMIC PROGRAMS. Accelerated program, double major, dual enrollment of high school students, external degree, independent study, internships, cross-registration. **Remedial services:** Learning center, remedial instruction, tutoring. **ROTC:** Air Force, Army. **Placement/credit:** AP, CLEP General and Subject, institutional tests; 30 credit hours maximum for bachelor's degree.

ACADEMIC REQUIREMENTS. Freshmen must earn minimum GPA of 2.0 to continue in good standing. 54% of freshmen return for sophomore year. Students must declare major by end of second year. **Graduation requirements:** 127 hours for bachelor's (30 in major). Most students required to take courses in English, foreign languages, mathematics, biological/physical sciences, social sciences. **Postgraduate studies:** 6% enter MBA programs, 4% enter other graduate study. **Additional information:** All degree programs also available through attendance in evening division.

FRESHMAN ADMISSIONS. Selection criteria: Rank in top two-thirds of class and minimum ACT composite score of 19 preferred. Provisional acceptance possible for those not meeting these standards. **Test requirements:** SAT or ACT (ACT preferred) for placement and counseling only.

1992 FRESHMAN CLASS PROFILE. 36 men, 49 women enrolled. **Characteristics:** 100% commute, 9% have minority backgrounds, 5% are foreign students. Average age is 25.

FALL-TERM APPLICATIONS. $10 fee. No closing date; applicants notified on a rolling basis beginning on or about April 15. CRDA. Deferred and early admission available. EDP-F.

STUDENT LIFE. Activities: Student government, magazine, student newspaper, drama, history club, behavioral and social sciences club, accounting club, foreign student club.

ATHLETICS. NAIA. **Intercollegiate:** Baseball M, basketball M, golf, volleyball W. **Intramural:** Archery, badminton, bowling, golf, racquetball, softball, table tennis.

STUDENT SERVICES. Career counseling, employment service for undergraduates, freshman orientation, personal counseling, placement service for graduates, veterans counselor, continuous academic advising, services/facilities for handicapped.

ANNUAL EXPENSES. Tuition and fees: $3,100. **Books and supplies:** $455. **Other expenses:** $1,800.

FINANCIAL AID. 61% of freshmen, 65% of continuing students receive some form of aid. All grants, 72% of loans, all jobs based on need. 85 enrolled freshmen were judged to have need, all were offered aid. Academic, athletic, leadership scholarships available. **Aid applications:** Closing date June 15; priority given to applications received by April 15; applicants notified on or about April 15; must reply within 2 weeks.

ADDRESS/TELEPHONE. Jon VanMetck, Director of Marketing and Enrollment, Bellevue College, 1000 Galvin Road South, Bellevue, NE 68005-3098. (402) 293-3766.

Central Community College

Grand Island, Nebraska — CB code: 6136

2-year public community, technical college, coed. Founded in 1966. **Accreditation:** Regional. **Undergraduate enrollment:** 714 men, 937 women full time; 4,216 men, 5,147 women part time. **Faculty:** 764 total (126 full time), 14 with doctorates or other terminal degrees. **Location:** Rural campus in large town; 100 miles from Lincoln. **Calendar:** Semester, extensive summer session. Saturday and extensive evening/early morning classes. **Microcomputers:** Located in dormitories, classrooms, computer centers. **Additional facts:** Multilocation institution with campuses at Columbus, Grand Island, and Hastings. Multiple starting dates for most programs and courses.

DEGREES OFFERED. AA, AS, AAS. 336 associate degrees awarded in 1992. 8% in business and management, 21% business/office and marketing/distribution, 7% computer sciences, 5% health sciences, 12% allied health, 6% multi/interdisciplinary studies, 28% trade and industry.

UNDERGRADUATE MAJORS. Accounting, agribusiness, agricultural production, air conditioning/heating/refrigeration mechanics, air conditioning/heating/refrigeration technology, allied health, animal sciences, architecture, automotive mechanics, automotive technology, biology, biomedical equipment technology, biotechnology, business administration and management, business and management, business and office, business data processing and related programs, child development/care/guidance, commercial art, communications, computer programming, construction, data processing, dental assistant, dental hygiene, dental laboratory technology, diesel engine mechanics, drafting, economics, education, electrical and electronics equipment repair, electrical installation, electromechanical technology, engineering and engineering-related technologies, fine arts, food production/management/services, graphic and printing production, graphic arts technology, health care administration, history, home economics, horticultural science, horticulture, hotel/motel and restaurant management, industrial technology, interior design, landscape architecture, legal assistant/paralegal, legal secretary, liberal/general studies, manufacturing technology, marketing and distribution, mathematics, medical assistant, medical secretary, mental health/human services, nursing, physical sciences, plastic technology, political science and government, practical nursing, precision metal work, psychology, radio/television broadcasting, radio/television technology, secretarial and related programs, social sciences, sociology, teacher aide, welding technology.

ACADEMIC PROGRAMS. 2-year transfer program, accelerated program, cooperative education, double major, dual enrollment of high school students, honors program, independent study, internships, telecourses. **Remedial services:** Learning center, reduced course load, remedial instruction, tutoring. **Placement/credit:** AP, CLEP General and Subject, institutional tests; 32 credit hours maximum for associate degree.

ACADEMIC REQUIREMENTS. Freshmen must earn minimum GPA of 2.0 to continue in good standing. Records of students having academic difficulty reviewed individually. 55% of freshmen return for sophomore year. Students must declare major by end of first year. **Graduation requirements:** 64 hours for associate (37 in major). Most students required to take courses in English, mathematics, biological/physical sciences, social sciences. **Additional information:** Open entry/open exit, self-paced, flexible scheduling for most programs.

FRESHMAN ADMISSIONS. Selection criteria: Open admissions. Selective admissions and space limitations in dental hygiene, dental laboratory technology, dental assisting, medical assisting, and practical nursing programs based on test scores, school achievement record and state residency. **Test requirements:** ASSET required for placement of all students enrolled in six or more credits. ACT or Dental Hygiene Aptitude Test required for dental hygiene program. Score report by September 2.

1992 FRESHMAN CLASS PROFILE. 398 men, 361 women enrolled. **Characteristics:** 98% from in state, 80% commute, 4% have minority backgrounds. Average age is 21.

FALL-TERM APPLICATIONS. No fee. No closing date; applicants notified on a rolling basis. Interview recommended for allied health, dental hygiene, practical nursing applicants. Deferred and early admission available. Institutional early decision plan. Closing dates for dental hygiene, practical nursing programs 2 weeks before start of classes.

STUDENT LIFE. Housing: Dormitories (men, women, coed). **Activities:** Student government, radio, student newspaper, choral groups, dance, drama, jazz band, music ensembles, musical theater.

ATHLETICS. NJCAA. **Intercollegiate:** Basketball, golf, soccer M, volleyball W. **Intramural:** Archery, basketball, bowling, racquetball, softball, table tennis, tennis, volleyball.

STUDENT SERVICES. Aptitude testing, career counseling, employment service for undergraduates, freshman orientation, health services, on-campus day care, personal counseling, placement service for graduates, special adviser for adult students, veterans counselor, services/facilities for handicapped.

ANNUAL EXPENSES. Tuition and fees: $1,050, $450 additional for out-of-state students. **Room and board:** $1,824. **Books and supplies:** $400. **Other expenses:** $1,444.

FINANCIAL AID. 75% of freshmen, 75% of continuing students receive some form of aid. 97% of grants, 85% of loans, all jobs based on need. Academic, music/drama, art, athletic, state/district residency, leadership scholarships available. **Aid applications:** No closing date; priority given to applications received by July 1; applicants notified on a rolling basis; must reply within 2 weeks. **Additional information:** Personalized service offered to applicants who contact campus financial aid office for assistance.

ADDRESS/TELEPHONE. Dr. Dennis Tyson, Vice President of Educational Services, Central Community College, PO Box 4903, 3134 West Highway 34, Grand Island, NE 68802-4903. (308) 389-6305. Fax: (308) 389-6399.

Chadron State College
Chadron, Nebraska CB code: 6466

4-year public liberal arts, teachers college, coed. Founded in 1911. **Accreditation:** Regional. **Undergraduate enrollment:** 813 men, 962 women full time; 177 men, 419 women part time. **Graduate enrollment:** 10 men, 19 women full time; 330 men, 963 women part time. **Faculty:** 130 total (90 full time), 57 with doctorates or other terminal degrees. **Location:** Rural campus in small town; 100 miles from Scottsbluff, 100 miles from Rapid City, South Dakota. **Calendar:** Semester, limited summer session. **Microcomputers:** 65 located in dormitories, libraries, classrooms, computer centers. **Special facilities:** Art gallery, planetarium, classroom instruction offered via audio/visual T1/satellite system network for 30 classes, library automation with connections provided by MIDNET and INTERNET.

DEGREES OFFERED. AA, BA, BS, MA, MS, MBA, MEd. 4 associate degrees awarded in 1992. 33% in agriculture, 67% home economics. 289 bachelor's degrees awarded. 28% in business and management, 21% teacher education, 6% engineering technologies, 6% law, 5% life sciences, 5% social sciences. Graduate degrees offered in 7 major fields of study.

UNDERGRADUATE MAJORS. Associate: Agribusiness, child development/care/guidance, early childhood education. **Bachelor's:** Accounting, agribusiness, allied health, art education, aviation management, biological and physical sciences, biology, business administration and management, business and management, business and office, business economics, business education, carpentry, chemistry, child development/care/guidance, clinical laboratory science, computer and information sciences, construction, counseling psychology, criminal justice studies, drafting, dramatic arts, early childhood education, earth sciences, economics, education, education of the mentally handicapped, electrical and electronics equipment repair, electrical installation, elementary education, English, English education, fashion merchandising, finance, fine arts, graphic and printing production, graphic arts technology, health education, health sciences, history, home economics, home economics education, humanities and social sciences, industrial arts education, industrial technology, interior design, journalism, junior high education, law enforcement and corrections, liberal/general studies, library science, machine tool operation/machine shop, manufacturing technology, marketing and distribution, marketing and distributive education, masonry/tile setting, mathematics, mathematics education, medical laboratory technologies, music, music education, office supervision and management, physical education, physical sciences, physics, political science and government, predentistry, prelaw, premedicine, prepharmacy, preveterinary, psychology, public health laboratory science, real estate, science education, secondary education, social psychology, social science education, social sciences, social studies education, social work, sociology, special education, specific learning disabilities, speech, speech/communication/theater education, woodworking.

ACADEMIC PROGRAMS. Accelerated program, cooperative education, dual enrollment of high school students, education specialist degree, external degree, honors program, independent study, internships, study abroad, teacher preparation, telecourses. **Remedial services:** Learning center, preadmission summer program, reduced course load, remedial instruction, special counselor, tutoring. **Placement/credit:** AP, CLEP General and Subject, institutional tests; 65 credit hours maximum for bachelor's degree.

ACADEMIC REQUIREMENTS. Freshmen must earn minimum GPA of 2.0 to continue in good standing. 83% of freshmen return for sophomore year. Students must declare major on enrollment. **Graduation requirements:** 60 hours for associate (33 in major), 125 hours for bachelor's (60 in major). Most students required to take courses in arts/fine arts, English, history, humanities, mathematics, biological/physical sciences, social sciences. **Postgraduate studies:** 41% from 2-year programs enter 4-year programs.

FRESHMAN ADMISSIONS. Selection criteria: Open admissions. For out-of-state applicants, test scores, class rank, recommendation of school counselor considered. **High school preparation:** 10 units recommended. Recommended units include English 4, foreign language 2, mathematics 3, social science 3 and science 2. One unit of visual or performing arts, one-half unit of computer literacy. **Test requirements:** SAT or ACT for placement and counseling only; score report by August 22.

1992 FRESHMAN CLASS PROFILE. Academic background: Mid 50% of enrolled freshmen had ACT composite between 16-24. 64% submitted ACT scores. **Characteristics:** 83% from in state, 65% live in college housing, 2% have minority backgrounds.

FALL-TERM APPLICATIONS. $10 fee. No closing date; priority given to applications received by May 1; applicants notified on a rolling basis. Interview recommended. Audition recommended for music applicants. Deferred admission available.

STUDENT LIFE. Housing: Dormitories (men, women, coed); apartment, handicapped housing available. Telephone and cable television service is provided in rooms. **Activities:** Student government, student newspaper, yearbook, choral groups, concert band, drama, jazz band, music ensembles, musical theater, pep band, symphony orchestra, forensics, United Campus Ministries, Circle-K, Fellowship of Christian Athletes, Young Democrats, Young Republicans, International Club, Criminal Justice Club, Student Education Association, club rodeo team.

ATHLETICS. NCAA. **Intercollegiate:** Basketball, football M, golf W, track and field, volleyball W, wrestling M. **Intramural:** Badminton, basketball, bowling, golf, handball, racquetball, softball, table tennis, tennis, track and field, volleyball, water polo, wrestling M.

STUDENT SERVICES. Aptitude testing, career counseling, employment service for undergraduates, freshman orientation, health services, on-campus day care, personal counseling, placement service for graduates, special adviser for adult students, veterans counselor, services/facilities for handicapped.

ANNUAL EXPENSES. Tuition and fees (projected): $1,708, $1,170 additional for out-of-state students. **Room and board:** $2,591. **Books and supplies:** $600. **Other expenses:** $450.

FINANCIAL AID. 90% of freshmen, 85% of continuing students receive some form of aid. 95% of grants, 90% of loans, 71% of jobs based on need. 290 enrolled freshmen were judged to have need, all were offered aid. Academic, music/drama, art, athletic, alumni affiliation scholarships available. **Aid applications:** No closing date; priority given to applications received by July 1; applicants notified on a rolling basis beginning on or about August 5; must reply within 4 weeks.

ADDRESS/TELEPHONE. Dale Williamson, Director of Admissions and Records, Chadron State College, 1000 Main, Chadron, NE 69337. (308) 432-6000. (800) 242-3766. Fax: (308) 432-6464.

Clarkson College
Omaha, Nebraska CB code: 2250

Admissions:	67% of applicants accepted
Based on:	••• School record, test scores
	• Activities, essay, special talents
Completion:	89% of freshmen end year in good standing
	85% graduate, 3% of these enter graduate study

4-year private health science college, coed, affiliated with Episcopal Church. Founded in 1888. **Accreditation:** Regional. **Undergraduate enrollment:** 5 men, 87 women full time; 31 men, 327 women part time. **Graduate enrollment:** 10 women full time; 3 men, 52 women part time. **Faculty:** 30 total (26 full time), 6 with doctorates or other terminal degrees. **Location:** Urban campus in large city; 200 miles from Kansas City, 150 miles from Des Moines. **Calendar:** Semester, extensive summer session. Extensive evening/early morning classes. **Microcomputers:** 10 located in dormitories, libraries, computer centers. **Special facilities:** Health care clinical facilities for professional education. **Additional facts:** Graduate studies available 4 weekends per semester. Distance education alternatives available for RNs.

DEGREES OFFERED. AS, BS, MS. 77 bachelor's degrees awarded. 100% in health sciences. Graduate degrees offered in 2 major fields of study.

UNDERGRADUATE MAJORS. Associate: Physical therapy assistant, radiograph medical technology. **Bachelor's:** Nursing, radiograph medical technology.

ACADEMIC PROGRAMS. Accelerated program, external degree, independent study, student-designed major, weekend college, general education courses through Bellevue College. **Remedial services:** Learning center, reduced course load, tutoring. **ROTC:** Army. **Placement/credit:** AP, CLEP General and Subject, institutional tests; 50 credit hours maximum for associate degree; 88 credit hours maximum for bachelor's degree. Unlimited number of hours of credit by examination may be counted toward degree if residency requirement of 40 hours is met.

ACADEMIC REQUIREMENTS. Freshmen must earn minimum GPA of 2.0 to continue in good standing. 90% of freshmen return for sophomore year. Students must declare major on application. **Graduation requirements:** 70 hours for associate (40 in major), 128 hours for bachelor's (68 in major). Most students required to take courses in English, humanities, mathematics, biological/physical sciences, social sciences. **Postgraduate studies:** 50% from 2-year programs enter 4-year programs.

FRESHMAN ADMISSIONS. Selection criteria: Academic performance, test scores, class rank considered. **High school preparation:** 5 units recommended. Recommended units include biological science 1, English 2, mathematics 1 and social science 1. **Test requirements:** SAT or ACT (ACT preferred).

1992 FRESHMAN CLASS PROFILE. 50% had high school GPA of 3.0 or higher, 40% between 2.0 and 2.99. **Academic background:** Mid 50% of enrolled freshmen had ACT composite between 17-22. 100% submitted ACT scores. **Characteristics:** 40% from in state, 80% commute, 5% have minority backgrounds. Average age is 23.

FALL-TERM APPLICATIONS. $15 fee. No closing date; priority given to applications received by March 15; applicants notified on a rolling basis; must reply within 2 weeks. Essay required. Deferred admission available.

STUDENT LIFE. Housing: Dormitories (coed). Board plan not available, kitchens located on each floor. **Activities:** Student government, student newspaper, yearbook, Christian Fellowship, Red Cross, National Student Nurses Association.

ATHLETICS. Intramural: Golf, softball, track and field W.

STUDENT SERVICES. Aptitude testing, career counseling, employment service for undergraduates, freshman orientation, health services, on-campus day care, personal counseling, services/facilities for handicapped.

ANNUAL EXPENSES. Tuition and fees (1992-93): $6,350. **Room and board:** $1,670 room only. **Books and supplies:** $330. **Other expenses:** $1,206.

FINANCIAL AID. 75% of freshmen, 85% of continuing students receive some form of aid. 87% of grants based on need. Academic scholarships available. **Aid applications:** No closing date; priority given to applications received by May 30; applicants notified on a rolling basis; must reply within 10 days. **Additional information:** CARES loans available. Opportunity to have large portion of tuition paid in return for employment at Bishop Clarkson Memorial Hospital.

ADDRESS/TELEPHONE. D. Lynn Taylor, Director of Enrollment Services, Clarkson College, 101 South 42nd Street, Omaha, NE 68131-2739. (402) 552-3036. (800) 647-5500 ext. 3297. Fax: (402) 552-2899.

College of St. Mary
Omaha, Nebraska — CB code: 6106

Admissions: 78% of applicants accepted
Based on: ••• Interview, recommendations, school record, test scores
•• Special talents
• Activities, essay
Completion: 85% of freshmen end year in good standing
40% graduate, 10% of these enter graduate study

4-year private liberal arts college, women only, affiliated with Roman Catholic Church. Founded in 1923. **Accreditation:** Regional. **Undergraduate enrollment:** 19 men, 520 women full time; 116 men, 667 women part time. **Faculty:** 134 total (60 full time), 31 with doctorates or other terminal degrees. **Location:** Suburban campus in large city. **Calendar:** Semester, limited summer session. Saturday classes. **Microcomputers:** Located in computer centers. **Special facilities:** Hillmer Art Gallery. **Additional facts:** Men admitted to evening and weekend programs only.

DEGREES OFFERED. AA, AS, BA, BS. 75 associate degrees awarded in 1992. 5% in business and management, 85% health sciences, 6% law. 98 bachelor's degrees awarded. 16% in business and management, 10% computer sciences, 10% education, 24% health sciences, 18% law, 6% visual and performing arts.

UNDERGRADUATE MAJORS. Associate: Accounting, business administration and management, business data programming, computer programming, legal assistant/paralegal, liberal/general studies, medical records administration, medical records technology, nursing, prelaw. **Bachelor's:** Accounting, art education, biology, business administration and management, business education, chemistry, communications, computer and information sciences, computer graphics, computer programming, early childhood education, education, elementary education, English, English education, fine arts, history, human resources development, humanities, legal assistant/paralegal, mathematics, mathematics education, medical laboratory technologies, medical records administration, music, music education, nursing, predentistry, prelaw, premedicine, prepharmacy, preveterinary, science education, secondary education, social science education, social sciences, social work, special education.

ACADEMIC PROGRAMS. Double major, independent study, internships, study abroad, teacher preparation, weekend college. **Remedial services:** Learning center, reduced course load, remedial instruction, special counselor, tutoring. **ROTC:** Air Force, Army. **Placement/credit:** AP, CLEP Subject, institutional tests. Unlimited number of hours of credit by examination may be counted toward degree if 30 of last 45 hours are taken at College of Saint Mary.

ACADEMIC REQUIREMENTS. Freshmen must earn minimum GPA of 2.0 to continue in good standing. 61% of freshmen return for sophomore year. Students must declare major by end of second year. **Graduation requirements:** 64 hours for associate, 128 hours for bachelor's (30 in major). Most students required to take courses in arts/fine arts, computer science, English, history, mathematics, philosophy/religion, biological/physical sciences, social sciences. **Postgraduate studies:** 20% from 2-year programs enter 4-year programs. 2% enter law school, 2% enter medical school, 4% enter MBA programs, 2% enter other graduate study.

FRESHMAN ADMISSIONS. Selection criteria: Class rank, high school record (2.0 GPA), recommendations considered. **High school preparation:** 16 units required. Required units include English 4, mathematics 2, social science 2 and science 2. Chemistry and biology required of nursing applicants. **Test requirements:** SAT or ACT (ACT preferred); score report by August 22.

1992 FRESHMAN CLASS PROFILE. Characteristics: 89% from in state, 54% commute, 3% have minority backgrounds. Average age is 22.

FALL-TERM APPLICATIONS. $20 fee, may be waived for applicants with need. No closing date; applicants notified on a rolling basis; must reply within 4 weeks. Interview recommended. Audition recommended. Portfolio recommended. Essay recommended. Deferred admission available.

STUDENT LIFE. Housing: Dormitories (women). **Activities:** Student government, student newspaper, yearbook, choral groups.

ATHLETICS. NAIA. **Intercollegiate:** Softball, tennis, volleyball. **Intramural:** Archery, badminton, basketball, bowling, golf, racquetball, softball, table tennis, volleyball.

STUDENT SERVICES. Aptitude testing, career counseling, employment service for undergraduates, freshman orientation, health services, personal counseling, placement service for graduates, special adviser for adult students, veterans counselor, services/facilities for handicapped.

ANNUAL EXPENSES. Tuition and fees: $9,300. **Room and board:** $3,500. **Books and supplies:** $400. **Other expenses:** $1,794.

FINANCIAL AID. 96% of freshmen, 63% of continuing students receive some form of aid. Grants, loans, jobs available. 87 enrolled freshmen were judged to have need, all were offered aid. Academic, music/drama, art, athletic, religious affiliation, minority scholarships available. **Aid applications:** No closing date; priority given to applications received by April 15; applicants notified on a rolling basis beginning on or about February 15; must reply within 2 weeks.

ADDRESS/TELEPHONE. Sheila K. Haggas, Director of Enrollment Services, College of St. Mary, 1901 South 72nd Street, Omaha, NE 68124. (402) 399-2405. (800) 926-5534. Fax: (402) 399-2341.

Concordia College
Seward, Nebraska — CB code: 6116

Admissions: 92% of applicants accepted
Based on: ••• School record, test scores
• Activities, interview, recommendations
Completion: 92% of freshmen end year in good standing
10% enter graduate study

4-year private college of arts and sciences and liberal arts, teachers college, coed, affiliated with Lutheran Church—Missouri Synod. Founded in 1894. **Accreditation:** Regional. **Undergraduate enrollment:** 783 men and women full time; 34 men and women part time. **Faculty:** 114 total (95 full time), 55 with doctorates or other terminal degrees. **Location:** Rural campus in small town; 25 miles from Lincoln. **Calendar:** 4-4-1, limited summer session. **Microcomputers:** 40 located in dormitories, classrooms, computer centers. **Special facilities:** Natural history museum, observatory, art galleries. **Additional facts:** Dedicated to education of whole person for effective Christian living in church and world.

DEGREES OFFERED. BA, BS, BFA, MEd. 144 bachelor's degrees awarded in 1992. 12% in business and management, 75% teacher education. Graduate degrees offered in 7 major fields of study.

UNDERGRADUATE MAJORS. Accounting, allied health, art education, biology, business administration and management, business education, chemistry, commercial art, communications, computer and information sciences, dramatic arts, early childhood education, education of the mentally handicapped, elementary education, English, English education, English literature, exercise science, fitness, and sports management, fine arts, health education, history, junior high education, mathematics, mathematics education, medical laboratory technologies, music, music education, physical education, physical sciences, pre-nursing, pre-physician's assistant, predentistry, prelaw, premedicine, prepharmacy, psychology, reading education, religious education, religious music, science education, secondary education, social science education, social sciences, social studies education, sociology, Spanish, special education, speech, sports communication, sports medicine, studio art, theological studies.

ACADEMIC PROGRAMS. Double major, honors program, independent study, internships, student-designed major, study abroad, teacher preparation. **Remedial services:** Learning center, reduced course load, remedial instruction, special counselor, tutoring. **ROTC:** Air Force, Army. **Placement/credit:** AP, CLEP Subject, institutional tests.

ACADEMIC REQUIREMENTS. Freshmen must earn minimum GPA of 2.0 to continue in good standing. 70% of freshmen return for sophomore year. Students must declare major by end of second year. **Graduation requirements:** 128 hours for bachelor's (30 in major). Most students required to take courses in arts/fine arts, computer science, English, history, humanities, mathematics, philosophy/religion, biological/physical sciences, social sciences. **Postgraduate studies:** 1% enter medical school, 4% enter MBA programs, 5% enter other graduate study.

FRESHMAN ADMISSIONS. Selection criteria: 2.5 high school GPA and rank in top half of class very important. Students with GPA below 2.5 or ACT scores between 15-18 remanded to admission committee for decision. **High school preparation:** 16 units required. Required and recommended units include biological science 1, English 4, mathematics 2, physical science 1 and social science 3. Foreign language 1 recommended. One unit each in music, art, and physical education recommended. **Test requirements:** SAT or ACT (ACT preferred); score report by August 1.

1992 FRESHMAN CLASS PROFILE. 624 men and women applied, 574 accepted; 86 men enrolled, 111 women enrolled. **Academic background:** Mid 50% of enrolled freshmen had ACT composite between 18-24. 100% submitted ACT scores. **Characteristics:** 31% from in state, 90% live in college housing, 4% have minority backgrounds, 1% are foreign students. Average age is 18.

FALL-TERM APPLICATIONS. $25 fee, may be waived for applicants

with need. Closing date August 1; priority given to applications received by July 1; applicants notified on a rolling basis; must reply by May 1 or within 4 weeks if notified thereafter. Interview recommended. Audition recommended for music, speech, drama applicants. Portfolio recommended for art applicants. CRDA. Deferred and early admission available. Early application encouraged owing to limited housing availability. Campus visit required for conditionally admitted students.

STUDENT LIFE. Housing: Dormitories (men, women); apartment housing available. **Activities:** Student government, student newspaper, yearbook, choral groups, concert band, drama, jazz band, marching band, music ensembles, pep band, symphony orchestra, religious organizations, volunteer organization, Black Student Association.

ATHLETICS. NAIA, NSCAA. **Intercollegiate:** Baseball M, basketball, cross-country, football M, golf, soccer M, softball W, tennis, track and field, volleyball W. **Intramural:** Badminton, basketball, bowling, soccer, softball, table tennis, tennis, volleyball.

STUDENT SERVICES. Aptitude testing, career counseling, employment service for undergraduates, freshman orientation, health services, on-campus day care, personal counseling, placement service for graduates, special adviser for adult students, services/facilities for handicapped.

ANNUAL EXPENSES. Tuition and fees (1992-93): $8,090. **Room and board:** $3,030. **Books and supplies:** $450. **Other expenses:** $1,200.

FINANCIAL AID. 99% of freshmen, 98% of continuing students receive some form of aid. 42% of grants, 88% of loans, 40% of jobs based on need. Academic, music/drama, art, athletic, state/district residency, leadership, alumni affiliation, religious affiliation, minority scholarships available. **Aid applications:** No closing date; priority given to applications received by May 1; applicants notified on a rolling basis beginning on or about March 1; must reply by May 1 or within 4 weeks if notified thereafter. **Additional information:** Numerous private donor restricted and endowment scholarships, many special grant sources.

ADDRESS/TELEPHONE. Judy J. Williams, Dean of Admission and Financial Aid, Concordia College, 800 North Columbia Avenue, Seward, NE 68434-9989. (402) 643-7233. (800) 535-5494. Fax: (402) 643-4073.

Creighton University
Omaha, Nebraska — CB code: 6121

Admissions:	92% of applicants accepted
Based on:	••• School record, test scores
	•• Recommendations
	• Activities, essay, interview, special talents
Completion:	90% of freshmen end year in good standing
	64% graduate, 35% of these enter graduate study

4-year private university, coed, affiliated with Roman Catholic Church. Founded in 1878. **Accreditation:** Regional. **Undergraduate enrollment:** 1,375 men, 1,885 women full time; 205 men, 418 women part time. **Graduate enrollment:** 1,177 men, 729 women full time; 212 men, 224 women part time. **Faculty:** 1,227 total (602 full time), 1,064 with doctorates or other terminal degrees. **Location:** Urban campus in large city; 60 miles from Lincoln, 120 miles from Des Moines, Iowa. **Calendar:** Semester, limited summer session. Saturday and extensive evening/early morning classes. **Microcomputers:** 175 located in libraries, classrooms, computer centers. **Special facilities:** Satellite station, observatory, art gallery, dental clinic. **Additional facts:** Institution in the Jesuit tradition.

DEGREES OFFERED. AA, AS, BA, BS, BFA, MA, MS, MBA, PhD, DDS, MD, Pharm D. 3 associate degrees awarded in 1992. 33% in allied health, 33% mathematics, 34% philosophy, religion, theology. 731 bachelor's degrees awarded. 23% in business and management, 5% communications, 10% health sciences, 6% allied health, 10% life sciences, 7% psychology, 11% social sciences. Graduate degrees offered in 23 major fields of study.

UNDERGRADUATE MAJORS. Associate: Computer and information sciences, journalism, mathematics, public relations, statistics, theological studies. **Bachelor's:** Accounting, advertising, American studies, applied mathematics, art education, art history, atmospheric sciences and meteorology, biology, business administration and management, business economics, business education, business/law, chemistry, classics, computer and information sciences, dance, dramatic arts, economics, elementary education, English, English education, exercise science, finance, fine arts, foreign languages education, French, German, Greek (classical), history, journalism, junior high education, Latin, management information systems, management science, marketing management, mathematics, mathematics education, nursing, occupational therapy, pharmacy, philosophy, physical education, physics, political science and government, psychology, public relations, radio/television broadcasting, science education, secondary education, social science education, social studies education, social work, sociology, Spanish, special education, speech, speech/communication/theater education, statistics, studio art, theological studies, visual and performing arts.

ACADEMIC PROGRAMS. Accelerated program, double major, honors program, independent study, internships, study abroad, teacher preparation, Washington semester, 3/2 program in engineering with University of Detroit Mercy; combined bachelor's/graduate program in law. **Remedial services:** Preadmission summer program, reduced course load, remedial instruction, special counselor, tutoring. **ROTC:** Air Force, Army. **Placement/credit:** AP, CLEP Subject, institutional tests.

ACADEMIC REQUIREMENTS. Freshmen must earn minimum GPA of 2.0 to continue in good standing. 84% of freshmen return for sophomore year. Students must declare major by end of second year. **Graduation requirements:** 64 hours for associate, 128 hours for bachelor's (24 in major). Most students required to take courses in arts/fine arts, computer science, English, foreign languages, history, humanities, mathematics, philosophy/religion, biological/physical sciences, social sciences. **Postgraduate studies:** 10% enter law school, 10% enter medical school, 2% enter MBA programs, 13% enter other graduate study. **Additional information:** Sequences of courses offered in preengineering, predentistry, prelaw, premedicine, preoptometry, prepharmacy, prephysical therapy, preveterinary. Arabic offered.

FRESHMAN ADMISSIONS. Selection criteria: School record, class rank, type of school, test scores, letters of recommendation important. **High school preparation:** 15 units required; 16 recommended. Required and recommended units include biological science 1-2, English 3-4, mathematics 2-3, physical science 1 and social science 2-2. Foreign language 2 recommended. Applicants to nursing programs should have 1 year of chemistry. **Test requirements:** SAT or ACT; score report by August 1.

1992 FRESHMAN CLASS PROFILE. 1,264 men applied, 1,148 accepted, 328 enrolled; 1,609 women applied, 1,491 accepted, 517 enrolled. 80% had high school GPA of 3.0 or higher, 19% between 2.0 and 2.99. 30% were in top tenth and 67% were in top quarter of graduating class. **Academic background:** Mid 50% of enrolled freshmen had ACT composite between 20-26. 84% submitted ACT scores. **Characteristics:** 39% from in state, 88% live in college housing, 12% have minority backgrounds, 1% are foreign students, 23% join fraternities/sororities. Average age is 19.

FALL-TERM APPLICATIONS. $30 fee, may be waived for applicants with need. Closing date August 1; applicants notified on a rolling basis; must reply within 2 weeks. Interview recommended. CRDA. Deferred admission available.

STUDENT LIFE. Housing: Dormitories (women, coed); apartment housing available. Guaranteed housing for freshmen and sophomores. Creighton House allows undergraduates to combine independent study projects with community living. **Activities:** Student government, magazine, radio, student newspaper, television, yearbook, choral groups, dance, drama, music ensembles, musical theater, pep band, fraternities, sororities, campus ministry, World Hunger Awareness Group, Afro-American Students Association, international relations club, Women's Resource Center, community service center, Christian Life Community, Young Democrats, Young Republicans.

ATHLETICS. NCAA. **Intercollegiate:** Baseball M, basketball, cross-country, golf, soccer, softball W, tennis. **Intramural:** Basketball, bowling, golf, racquetball, soccer, softball, tennis, volleyball W. **Clubs:** Lacrosse M, rowing, rugby, ice hockey, sailing, judo, Kendo, Taekwondo.

STUDENT SERVICES. Aptitude testing, career counseling, employment service for undergraduates, freshman orientation, health services, on-campus day care, personal counseling, placement service for graduates, special adviser for adult students, veterans counselor, services/facilities for handicapped.

ANNUAL EXPENSES. Tuition and fees: $10,252. **Room and board:** $4,178. **Books and supplies:** $625. **Other expenses:** $1,480.

FINANCIAL AID. 80% of freshmen, 75% of continuing students receive some form of aid. 60% of grants, 94% of loans, 47% of jobs based on need. 517 enrolled freshmen were judged to have need, all were offered aid. Academic, athletic, leadership, alumni affiliation, minority scholarships available. **Aid applications:** No closing date; priority given to applications received by April 1; applicants notified on a rolling basis beginning on or about April 1; must reply within 4 weeks.

ADDRESS/TELEPHONE. Howard J. Bachman, Director of Admissions, Creighton University, 2500 California Plaza, Omaha, NE 68178. (402) 280-2703. Fax: (402) 280-2685.

Dana College
Blair, Nebraska — CB code: 6157

Admissions:	83% of applicants accepted
Based on:	••• School record
	•• Test scores
	• Activities, essay, interview, recommendations
Completion:	90% of freshmen end year in good standing
	33% graduate, 21% of these enter graduate study

4-year private liberal arts college, coed, affiliated with Evangelical Lutheran Church in America. Founded in 1884. **Accreditation:** Regional. **Undergraduate enrollment:** 224 men, 258 women full time; 25 men, 65 women part time. **Faculty:** 54 total (37 full time), 19 with doctorates or other terminal degrees. **Location:** Rural campus in small town; 20 miles from Omaha. **Calendar:** 4-1-4, limited summer session. Saturday classes. **Microcomputers:** 37 located in dormitories, libraries, classrooms, computer centers. **Special**

facilities: Madsen Fine Arts Center, C.A. Dana Life Library, Danish Heritage Room, Danish Immigrant Archives.

DEGREES OFFERED. BA, BS. 77 bachelor's degrees awarded in 1992. 44% in business and management, 19% teacher education, 6% life sciences, 10% social sciences, 5% visual and performing arts.

UNDERGRADUATE MAJORS. Accounting, allied health, art education, biology, business administration and management, business and management, business economics, business education, chemistry, clinical laboratory science, commercial art, communications, computer and information sciences/business administration, computer and information sciences/economics, computer and information sciences/mathematics, Danish, economics, education, elementary education, English, English education, environmental science, finance, fine arts, foreign languages education, German, graphic design, health care administration, health sciences, history, humanities, humanities and social sciences, institutional management, international studies, journalism, liberal/general studies, management information systems, marketing management, mathematics, mathematics education, medical laboratory technologies, music, music education, nuclear medical technology, organizational behavior, physical education, predentistry, prelaw, premedicine, prepharmacy, preveterinary, psychology, radio/television broadcasting, radiograph medical technology, religion, science education, secondary education, social science education, social sciences, social studies education, social work, sociology, Spanish, special education, speech, speech/communication/theater education, studio art.

ACADEMIC PROGRAMS. Accelerated program, double major, dual enrollment of high school students, independent study, internships, study abroad, teacher preparation, weekend college, cross-registration, Danish language certificate program. **Remedial services:** Learning center, reduced course load, remedial instruction, special counselor, tutoring. **ROTC:** Army. **Placement/credit:** AP, CLEP General and Subject, institutional tests; 30 credit hours maximum for bachelor's degree.

ACADEMIC REQUIREMENTS. Freshmen must earn minimum GPA of 1.75 to continue in good standing. 65% of freshmen return for sophomore year. Students must declare major by end of second year. **Graduation requirements:** 128 hours for bachelor's (30 in major). Most students required to take courses in arts/fine arts, computer science, English, foreign languages, history, humanities, mathematics, philosophy/religion, biological/physical sciences, social sciences. **Postgraduate studies:** 2% enter law school, 6% enter medical school, 2% enter MBA programs, 11% enter other graduate study.

FRESHMAN ADMISSIONS. Selection criteria: Applicants should rank in top half of graduating class, have a 2.0 cumulative GPA and provide test scores (ACT minimum 19, SAT combined 860). School and community activities, recommendations by school officials and interview considered. TOEFL not required for entry into English as a Second Language program. **High school preparation:** 16 units recommended. Recommended units include English 4, foreign language 2, mathematics 3, social science 4 and science 3. **Test requirements:** SAT or ACT (ACT preferred); score report by August 25.

1992 FRESHMAN CLASS PROFILE. 252 men applied, 194 accepted, 62 enrolled; 236 women applied, 211 accepted, 69 enrolled. 50% had high school GPA of 3.0 or higher, 45% between 2.0 and 2.99. 10% were in top tenth and 34% were in top quarter of graduating class. **Academic background:** Mid 50% of enrolled freshmen had ACT composite between 19-24. 86% submitted ACT scores. **Characteristics:** 47% from in state, 95% live in college housing, 10% have minority backgrounds, 6% are foreign students. Average age is 18.

FALL-TERM APPLICATIONS. $15 fee, may be waived for applicants with need. Closing date August 25; applicants notified on a rolling basis; must reply within 4 weeks. Interview recommended. CRDA. Deferred and early admission available.

STUDENT LIFE. Housing: Dormitories (women, coed); apartment, handicapped housing available. **Activities:** Student government, magazine, radio, student newspaper, television, yearbook, choral groups, concert band, drama, jazz band, music ensembles, musical theater, opera, pep band, folk dance, Fellowship of Christian Athletes, social awareness organization, campus ministry, social service organizations, student activities board, health sciences club, radio club, German club, student education association, environmental awareness organization, HOPE (Help Our People Expand), BACCHUS.

ATHLETICS. NAIA. **Intercollegiate:** Baseball M, basketball, football M, golf, softball W, tennis, track and field, volleyball W, wrestling M. **Intramural:** Basketball, bowling, football, golf, handball, racquetball, soccer, softball, swimming, table tennis, tennis, track and field, volleyball. **Clubs:** Soccer.

STUDENT SERVICES. Aptitude testing, career counseling, employment service for undergraduates, freshman orientation, health services, personal counseling, placement service for graduates, services/facilities for handicapped.

ANNUAL EXPENSES. Tuition and fees (1992-93): $8,050. **Room and board:** $2,930. **Books and supplies:** $450. **Other expenses:** $1,000.

FINANCIAL AID. 97% of freshmen, 91% of continuing students receive some form of aid. 51% of grants, all loans, 88% of jobs based on need. 115 enrolled freshmen were judged to have need, all were offered aid. Academic, athletic, religious affiliation scholarships available. **Aid applications:** No closing date; priority given to applications received by April 1; applicants notified on a rolling basis beginning on or about February 20; must reply within 2 weeks. **Additional information:** Auditions recommended for music, drama, and forensics scholarship applicants. Portfolios recommended for art and commercial art scholarship applicants.

ADDRESS/TELEPHONE. John Schueth, Director of Admissions, Dana College, 2848 College Drive, Blair, NE 68008-1099. (402) 426-7222. (800) 444-3262. Fax: (402) 426-7386.

Doane College
Crete, Nebraska — CB code: 6165

Admissions: 89% of applicants accepted
Based on:
••• School record, test scores
•• Recommendations
• Activities, essay, interview, special talents
Completion: 99% of freshmen end year in good standing
46% graduate, 40% of these enter graduate study

4-year private liberal arts college, coed, affiliated with United Church of Christ. Founded in 1872. **Accreditation:** Regional. **Undergraduate enrollment:** 457 men, 554 women full time; 171 men, 246 women part time. **Graduate enrollment:** 4 men, 4 women full time; 68 men, 224 women part time. **Faculty:** 89 total (55 full time), 39 with doctorates or other terminal degrees. **Location:** Rural campus in small town; 25 miles from Lincoln, 75 miles from Omaha. **Calendar:** 4-1-4, limited summer session. Extensive evening/early morning classes. **Microcomputers:** 140 located in dormitories, libraries, classrooms, computer centers, campus-wide network. **Special facilities:** Art gallery, arboretum, open air theater, extensive rose garden. **Additional facts:** Degree-offering courses at off-campus adult education center in Lincoln.

DEGREES OFFERED. BA, BS, MA, MEd. 267 bachelor's degrees awarded in 1992. 55% in business and management, 6% communications, 10% education, 7% social sciences.

UNDERGRADUATE MAJORS. Accounting, allied health, art education, biological and physical sciences, biology, business administration and management, business education, chemistry, communications, computer and information sciences, dramatic arts, economics, elementary education, English, English education, environmental science, fine arts, German, history, human resources development, humanities and social sciences, international and comparative education, international studies, journalism, liberal/general studies, mathematics, mathematics education, mental health/human services, music, music education, philosophy, philosophy/religion, physical education, physical sciences, physics/mathematics, political science and government, psychology, public administration, religion, science education, social science education, social sciences, social work, sociology, Spanish, special education, speech/communication/theater education, trade and industrial supervision and management.

ACADEMIC PROGRAMS. Accelerated program, double major, dual enrollment of high school students, honors program, independent study, internships, student-designed major, study abroad, teacher preparation, visiting/exchange student program, Washington semester, preprofessional programs in medical fields, law and ministry; liberal arts/career combination in engineering, forestry, health sciences. **Remedial services:** Learning center, reduced course load, remedial instruction, special counselor, tutoring. **ROTC:** Air Force, Army. **Placement/credit:** AP, CLEP Subject, institutional tests; 36 credit hours maximum for bachelor's degree.

ACADEMIC REQUIREMENTS. Freshmen must earn minimum GPA of 1.7 to continue in good standing. 70% of freshmen return for sophomore year. Students must declare major by end of second year. **Graduation requirements:** 132 hours for bachelor's (48 in major). Most students required to take courses in arts/fine arts, computer science, English, history, mathematics, philosophy/religion, biological/physical sciences, social sciences. **Postgraduate studies:** 1% enter law school, 3% enter medical school, 1% enter MBA programs, 35% enter other graduate study. **Additional information:** Midwest Institute for International Students prepares international students to meet the English language requirement for admission for Doane and other American Colleges.

FRESHMAN ADMISSIONS. Selection criteria: Academic and personal record, class rank, test scores, recommendations are important. Recommended units include English 4, mathematics 3, social science 4 and science 3. Recommended units include 4 communication (English and speech) and distribution of courses from fine arts, foreign languages, humanities, mathematics, natural sciences, and social sciences. **Test requirements:** SAT or ACT (ACT preferred); score report by August 20.

1992 FRESHMAN CLASS PROFILE. 364 men applied, 313 accepted, 117 enrolled; 352 women applied, 325 accepted, 126 enrolled. 71% had high school GPA of 3.0 or higher, 29% between 2.0 and 2.99. **Academic background:** Mid 50% of enrolled freshmen had ACT composite between 20-25. 97% submitted ACT scores. **Characteristics:** 80% from in state, 97% live in college housing, 5% have minority backgrounds, 2% are foreign students, 40% join fraternities/sororities. Average age is 18.

FALL-TERM APPLICATIONS. $15 fee, may be waived for applicants with need. No closing date; priority given to applications received by August 15; applicants notified on a rolling basis; must reply by May 1 or within 4 weeks if notified thereafter. Interview required for academically marginal applicants. Audition required for music, drama applicants. Portfolio required for art applicants. CRDA. Deferred and early admission available.

STUDENT LIFE. Housing: Dormitories (men, women, coed); apartment housing available. Unmarried students under 22 not living with parents expected to live on campus. **Activities:** Student government, magazine, radio, student newspaper, television, yearbook, literary publication of student works, choral groups, concert band, drama, jazz band, marching band, music ensembles, musical theater, pep band, fraternities, sororities, Student Education Association, Doane Speakers, Club Internationale, Doane Players, Fellowship of Christian Athletes, C-Pals (big brother/sister program), Campus Ministry, American Minority Student Alliance, BAR (Building Alchol Responsibility), Student Government.

ATHLETICS. NAIA. **Intercollegiate:** Baseball M, basketball, cross-country, football M, golf, softball W, tennis, track and field, volleyball W. **Intramural:** Basketball, swimming, track and field, volleyball.

STUDENT SERVICES. Aptitude testing, career counseling, employment service for undergraduates, freshman orientation, health services, personal counseling, placement service for graduates, special adviser for adult students, veterans counselor.

ANNUAL EXPENSES. Tuition and fees: $9,390. **Room and board:** $2,830. **Books and supplies:** $350. **Other expenses:** $1,000.

FINANCIAL AID. 99% of freshmen, 95% of continuing students receive some form of aid. 42% of grants, 97% of loans, 85% of jobs based on need. 195 enrolled freshmen were judged to have need, all were offered aid. Academic, music/drama, art, athletic, leadership scholarships available. **Aid applications:** No closing date; priority given to applications received by March 15; applicants notified on a rolling basis beginning on or about March 15; must reply by May 1 or within 2 weeks if notified thereafter.

ADDRESS/TELEPHONE. Dan Kunzman, Dean of Admissions, Doane College, 1014 Boswell Ave, Crete, NE 68333. (402) 826-8222. (800) 333-6263. Fax: (402) 826-8600.

Grace College of the Bible
Omaha, Nebraska CB code: 6248

4-year private Bible college, coed, interdenominational. Founded in 1943. **Undergraduate enrollment:** 123 men, 99 women full time; 43 men, 28 women part time. **Faculty:** 27 total (20 full time), 7 with doctorates or other terminal degrees. **Location:** Urban campus in large city. **Calendar:** Semester, limited summer session. **Microcomputers:** 7 located in libraries, computer centers.

DEGREES OFFERED. AA, BA, BS. 16 associate degrees awarded in 1992. 100% in philosophy, religion, theology. 26 bachelor's degrees awarded. 96% in philosophy, religion, theology.

UNDERGRADUATE MAJORS. Associate: Bible studies, elementary education. **Bachelor's:** Airline piloting and navigation, counseling psychology, music education, nursing, radio/television broadcasting, rehabilitation counseling/services, religious education, religious music, theological studies.

ACADEMIC PROGRAMS. Independent study, internships. **Remedial services:** Reduced course load, tutoring. **Placement/credit:** AP, CLEP Subject; 15 credit hours maximum for bachelor's degree.

ACADEMIC REQUIREMENTS. Freshmen must earn minimum GPA of 1.75 to continue in good standing. 82% of freshmen return for sophomore year. Students must declare major by end of second year. **Graduation requirements:** 90 hours for associate (30 in major), 127 hours for bachelor's (36 in major). Most students required to take courses in arts/fine arts, computer science, English, history, humanities, philosophy/religion, biological/physical sciences, social sciences.

FRESHMAN ADMISSIONS. Selection criteria: School achievement record, test scores, recommendations and student profile important. Those admitted to teacher education program must have 4 units of language arts, 2 units of mathematics, 2 units of sciences, 2 units of social sciences. **Test requirements:** ACT.

1992 FRESHMAN CLASS PROFILE. 37 men, 41 women enrolled. **Characteristics:** 60% live in college housing, 1% are foreign students.

FALL-TERM APPLICATIONS. $20 fee. No closing date; applicants notified on a rolling basis; must reply within 2 weeks. Audition required for music applicants. Interview recommended for academically weak applicants.

STUDENT LIFE. Housing: Dormitories (men, women); apartment housing available. **Activities:** Student government, radio, yearbook, choral groups, music ensembles. **Additional information:** Religious observance required.

ATHLETICS. Intercollegiate: Basketball, golf, tennis, volleyball W. **Intramural:** Basketball, bowling, volleyball.

STUDENT SERVICES. Career counseling, employment service for undergraduates, freshman orientation, health services, personal counseling, placement service for graduates, services/facilities for handicapped.

ANNUAL EXPENSES. Tuition and fees: $4,492, $2,630 additional for out-of-state students. **Room and board:** $2,630. **Books and supplies:** $400. **Other expenses:** $1,400.

FINANCIAL AID. 62% of freshmen, 65% of continuing students receive some form of aid. 86% of grants, 83% of loans based on need. All jobs based on criteria other than need. 73 enrolled freshmen were judged to have need, 69 were offered aid. Academic, music/drama, leadership, alumni affiliation, minority scholarships available. **Aid applications:** No closing date; priority given to applications received by March 15; applicants notified on a rolling basis beginning on or about April 1; must reply within 30 days.

ADDRESS/TELEPHONE. Deborah Howe, Director of Admissions, Grace College of the Bible, 1515 South 10th Street, Omaha, NE 68108. (402) 449-2831.

Hastings College
Hastings, Nebraska CB code: 6270

4-year private liberal arts college, coed, affiliated with Presbyterian Church (USA). Founded in 1882. **Accreditation:** Regional. **Undergraduate enrollment:** 1,016 men and women. **Graduate enrollment:** 30 men and women. **Location:** Rural campus in large town; 150 miles from Omaha, 385 miles from Denver, Colorado. **Calendar:** 4-1-4.

FRESHMAN ADMISSIONS. Selection criteria: School achievement record, recommendation from high school counselor, rank in top half of class, test scores, 2 instructor references important.

ANNUAL EXPENSES. Tuition and fees: $9,296. **Room and board:** $3,130. **Books and supplies:** $600. **Other expenses:** $700.

ADDRESS/TELEPHONE. Sam Rennick, Director of Admissions, Hastings College, Seventh and Turner, Hastings, NE 68901. (402) 463-2402. Fax: (402) 463-3002.

Lincoln School of Commerce
Lincoln, Nebraska CB code: 3385

Admissions: 95% of applicants accepted
Based on: ••• School record, test scores
•• Interview
• Activities, recommendations
Completion: 85% of freshmen end year in good standing
72% go on to graduate

2-year proprietary junior college, coed. Founded in 1884. **Undergraduate enrollment:** 97 men, 545 women full time. **Faculty:** 47 total (19 full time), 10 with doctorates or other terminal degrees. **Location:** Urban campus in small city; 50 miles from Omaha. **Calendar:** Quarter. **Microcomputers:** 60 located in libraries, classrooms, computer centers.

DEGREES OFFERED. AAS. 190 associate degrees awarded in 1992.

UNDERGRADUATE MAJORS. Accounting, business and management, business and office, computer and information sciences, computer programming, court reporting, data processing, legal assistant/paralegal, office supervision and management, secretarial and related programs, word processing.

ACADEMIC PROGRAMS. 2-year transfer program, honors program, internships. **Remedial services:** Learning center, remedial instruction, special counselor, tutoring. **Placement/credit:** Institutional tests; 50 credit hours maximum for associate degree.

ACADEMIC REQUIREMENTS. Freshmen must earn minimum GPA of 2.0 to continue in good standing. 80% of freshmen return for sophomore year. Students must declare major on application. **Graduation requirements:** 96 hours for associate (30 in major). Most students required to take courses in computer science, English, mathematics, social sciences.

FRESHMAN ADMISSIONS. Selection criteria: School achievement record most important. Recommended units include English 4, mathematics 3 and social science 3. **Test requirements:** Career Placement and Assessment Test required for admission.

1992 FRESHMAN CLASS PROFILE. 64 men applied, 60 accepted, 53 enrolled; 326 women applied, 312 accepted, 272 enrolled. **Characteristics:** 75% commute. Average age is 19.

FALL-TERM APPLICATIONS. $75 fee. No closing date; applicants notified on a rolling basis. Interview required. Early admission available.

STUDENT LIFE. Housing: Dormitories (coed). **Activities:** Student government, student newspaper, business club, speech club, computer club, court reporting club, tour and travel club.

ATHLETICS. Intramural: Basketball, softball, volleyball W.

STUDENT SERVICES. Aptitude testing, career counseling, employment service for undergraduates, freshman orientation, personal counseling, placement service for graduates.

ANNUAL EXPENSES. Tuition and fees: $4,725. **Room and board:** $1,350 room only. **Books and supplies:** $450. **Other expenses:** $800.

FINANCIAL AID. 95% of freshmen, 95% of continuing students receive some form of aid. Grants, loans, jobs available. Academic, leadership scholarships available. **Aid applications:** No closing date; applicants notified on a rolling basis.

ADDRESS/TELEPHONE. Brad Blodersen, Assisatant Director of Admissions, Lincoln School of Commerce, 1821 K Street, P.O.Box 82826, Lincoln, NE 68501-2826. (402) 474-5315. Fax: (402) 474-5302.

McCook Community College
McCook, Nebraska CB code: 6401

2-year public community college, coed. Founded in 1926. **Accreditation:** Regional. **Undergraduate enrollment:** 205 men, 272 women full time; 257 men, 392 women part time. **Faculty:** 64 total (27 full time), 4 with doctorates or other terminal degrees. **Location:** Rural campus in small town; 230 miles from Lincoln, 240 miles from Denver. **Calendar:** Semester, limited summer session. **Microcomputers:** Located in libraries, classrooms, computer centers.

DEGREES OFFERED. AA, AS, AAS. 125 associate degrees awarded in 1992. 12% in business and management, 7% business/office and marketing/distribution, 13% education, 6% engineering, 8% health sciences, 8% home economics, 16% multi/interdisciplinary studies, 11% social sciences, 5% visual and performing arts. 3,189 bachelor's degrees awarded. 18% in business and management, 5% communications, 9% engineering, 6% letters/literature, 11% multi/interdisciplinary studies, 7% psychology, 10% social sciences. Graduate degrees offered in 1 major field of study.

UNDERGRADUATE MAJORS. Accounting, agribusiness, agricultural production, agronomy, allied health, animal sciences, architecture, arts management, biology, business administration and management, business and management, business and office, business computer/console/peripheral equipment operation, business data processing and related programs, business data programming, business home economics, chemistry, child development/care/guidance, communications, computer and information sciences, criminal justice studies, dietetic aide/assistant, drawing, education, elementary education, engineering, engineering and engineering-related technologies, English, family/consumer resource management, fashion merchandising, food production/management/services, information sciences and systems, junior high education, legal secretary, liberal/general studies, mathematics, medical records administration, medical secretary, music, office supervision and management, physical sciences, predentistry, prelaw, premedicine, prepharmacy, preveterinary, psychology, science technologies, secondary education, secretarial and related programs, social sciences, special education, speech.

ACADEMIC PROGRAMS. Independent study, student-designed major, teacher preparation, external degree program with University of Nebraska at Kearney. **Remedial services:** Learning center, remedial instruction, tutoring. **Placement/credit:** AP, CLEP Subject; 15 credit hours maximum for associate degree.

ACADEMIC REQUIREMENTS. Freshmen must earn minimum GPA of 2.0 to continue in good standing. 76% of freshmen return for sophomore year. Students must declare major by end of first year. **Graduation requirements:** 60 hours for associate. Most students required to take courses in English, humanities, mathematics, biological/physical sciences, social sciences.

FRESHMAN ADMISSIONS. Selection criteria: Open admissions. **Test requirements:** SAT or ACT for placement and counseling only; score report by August 20. ASSET test for placement required of all students. **Additional information:** Applicants working toward GED and graduates of non-accredited high schools may be admitted provisionally for 1 semester.

1992 FRESHMAN CLASS PROFILE. 235 men, 340 women enrolled. 26% were in top tenth and 54% were in top quarter of graduating class. **Characteristics:** 84% from in state, 52% commute, 3% have minority backgrounds, 2% are foreign students. Average age is 18.

FALL-TERM APPLICATIONS. $10 fee, may be waived for applicants with need. No closing date; applicants notified on a rolling basis.

STUDENT LIFE. Housing: Dormitories (men, women). **Activities:** Student government, student newspaper, choral groups, concert band, drama, jazz band, music ensembles, pep band.

ATHLETICS. NJCAA. **Intercollegiate:** Basketball, football M, golf M, volleyball W. **Intramural:** Basketball, bowling, softball, table tennis, tennis, volleyball.

STUDENT SERVICES. Aptitude testing, career counseling, employment service for undergraduates, freshman orientation, on-campus day care, personal counseling, placement service for graduates, services/facilities for handicapped.

ANNUAL EXPENSES. Tuition and fees (1992-93): $870, $135 additional for out-of-state students. **Room and board:** $2,450. **Books and supplies:** $500. **Other expenses:** $550.

FINANCIAL AID. 64% of freshmen, 91% of continuing students receive some form of aid. 65% of grants, 95% of loans, 69% of jobs based on need. 179 enrolled freshmen were judged to have need, all were offered aid. Academic, music/drama, art, athletic, leadership scholarships available. **Aid applications:** Closing date May 1; priority given to applications received by April 1; applicants notified on or about June 20; must reply by July 1.

ADDRESS/TELEPHONE. Rick Michaelsen, Counselor, McCook Community College, 1205 East Third, McCook, NE 69001. (308) 345-6303. (800) 348-5343. Fax: (308) 345-3305.

Metropolitan Community College
Omaha, Nebraska CB code: 5755

2-year public community, technical college, coed. Founded in 1974. **Accreditation:** Regional. **Undergraduate enrollment:** 1,086 men, 1,467 women full time; 3,033 men, 4,715 women part time. **Faculty:** 524 total (122 full time), 6 with doctorates or other terminal degrees. **Location:** Urban campus in large city. **Calendar:** Quarter, extensive summer session. Saturday and extensive evening/early morning classes. **Microcomputers:** 750 located in classrooms, computer centers. **Special facilities:** Extensive CAD/CAM and electronic graphics facilities. **Additional facts:** Multilocation institution: Fort Omaha campus and Southcampus in Omaha, Elkhorn Valley campus 6 miles west of Omaha, Fremont site 35 miles northwest of Omaha.

DEGREES OFFERED. AA, AS, AAS. 430 associate degrees awarded in 1992. 20% in business and management, 10% computer sciences, 8% engineering technologies, 8% allied health, 9% law, 7% multi/interdisciplinary studies, 10% parks/recreation, protective services, public affairs, 17% trade and industry.

UNDERGRADUATE MAJORS. Accounting, air conditioning/heating/refrigeration mechanics, air conditioning/heating/refrigeration technology, automotive mechanics, business and management, child development/care/guidance, civil technology, commercial art, computer graphics, computer programming, construction, contract management and procurement/purchasing, drafting, drafting and design technology, early childhood education, electronic technology, fashion merchandising, finance, food production/management/services, graphic and printing production, graphic arts technology, health care administration, hotel/motel and restaurant management, human services, industrial design, industrial equipment maintenance and repair, insurance and risk management, interior design, law enforcement and corrections technologies, legal assistant/paralegal, legal secretary, liberal/general studies, marketing and distribution, medical secretary, nursing, ophthalmic services, ornamental horticulture, photographic technology, photography, physician's assistant, preengineering, preveterinary, protective services, public utilities, real estate, rehabilitation counseling/services, respiratory therapy, respiratory therapy technology, secretarial and related programs.

ACADEMIC PROGRAMS. 2-year transfer program, cooperative education, double major, dual enrollment of high school students, independent study, internships, telecourses, weekend college. **Remedial services:** Learning center, remedial instruction, special counselor, tutoring. **Placement/credit:** AP, CLEP General, institutional tests; 81 credit hours maximum for associate degree.

ACADEMIC REQUIREMENTS. Freshmen must earn minimum GPA of 1.99 to continue in good standing. 50% of freshmen return for sophomore year. Students must declare major on enrollment. **Graduation requirements:** 96 hours for associate (60 in major). Most students required to take courses in computer science, English, foreign languages, history, humanities, mathematics, biological/physical sciences, social sciences. **Additional information:** Individualized, self-paced instruction. Degree through telecourses available.

FRESHMAN ADMISSIONS. Selection criteria: Open admissions. Selective admissions to nursing and allied health programs based on test scores and references. High school diploma or GED required of nursing and allied health applicants. **Test requirements:** Assessment testing and standardized RN extrance examination required for nursing associate degree applicants. **Additional information:** Admission to college does not mean admission to all programs. Students may be required to take preparatory work before attending classes.

1992 FRESHMAN CLASS PROFILE. 1,279 men applied, 1,279 accepted, 1,279 enrolled; 1,648 women applied, 1,648 accepted, 1,648 enrolled. **Characteristics:** 98% from in state, 100% commute, 13% have minority backgrounds, 1% are foreign students. Average age is 29.

FALL-TERM APPLICATIONS. No fee. No closing date; applicants notified on a rolling basis. Interview required for nursing and allied health applicants. Early admission available.

STUDENT LIFE. Activities: Student government, student newsletter, Phi Theta Kappa Scholastic Honorary, student clubs, business club, food club, welding club. **Additional information:** Student activity program sponsors varied activities including social, educational, cultural, athletic, and community service programs for both students and their families.

ATHLETICS. Intramural: Basketball, bowling, softball, volleyball.

STUDENT SERVICES. Aptitude testing, career counseling, employment service for undergraduates, freshman orientation, on-campus day care, personal counseling, placement service for graduates, veterans counselor, services/facilities for handicapped.

ANNUAL EXPENSES. Tuition and fees: $990, $990 additional for out-of-state students. **Books and supplies:** $450. **Other expenses:** $270.

FINANCIAL AID. 31% of freshmen, 26% of continuing students receive some form of aid. 94% of grants, all loans, 14% of jobs based on need. Academic, state/district residency scholarships available. **Aid applications:** No closing date; priority given to applications received by March 30; applicants notified on a rolling basis beginning on or about June 1; must reply within 2 weeks. **Additional information:** Grants or scholarships usually available until August each year.

ADDRESS/TELEPHONE. Randy Schmailzl, Director of Enrollment Management, Metropolitan Community College, PO Box 3777, Omaha, NE 68103-3777. (402) 449-8418. Fax: (402) 449-8334.

Mid Plains Community College
North Platte, Nebraska CB code: 6497

2-year public community college, coed. Founded in 1964. **Accreditation:** Regional. **Undergraduate enrollment:** 294 men, 422 women full time; 586 men, 725 women part time. **Faculty:** 84 total (56 full time), 3 with doctorates or other terminal degrees. **Location:** Suburban campus in large town; 230 miles from Lincoln, 270 miles from Denver. **Calendar:** Semester, limited summer session. Extensive evening/early morning classes. **Microcomputers:** Located in libraries, classrooms, computer centers.

DEGREES OFFERED. AA, AAS. 85 associate degrees awarded in 1992.

UNDERGRADUATE MAJORS. Accounting, air conditioning/heating/refrigeration mechanics, air conditioning/heating/refrigeration technology, automotive mechanics, automotive technology, biology, business administration and management, business and management, business and office, business computer/console/peripheral equipment operation, business data entry equipment operation, business data processing and related programs, business data programming, carpentry, chemistry, communications, computer and information sciences, computer programming, construction, criminal justice studies, data processing, dental assistant, diesel engine mechanics, drafting, drafting and design technology, education, electrical and electronics equipment repair, electrical installation, electromechanical technology, elementary education, engineering, industrial equipment maintenance and repair, law enforcement and corrections technologies, liberal/general studies, marketing and distribution, mathematics, medical laboratory technologies, ophthalmic services, physical sciences, practical nursing, precision metal work, premedicine, prepharmacy, preveterinary, psychology, real estate, secretarial and related programs, social sciences, word processing.

ACADEMIC PROGRAMS. 2-year transfer program, dual enrollment of high school students, independent study, internships, external degree program with Kearney State College. **Remedial services:** Learning center, remedial instruction, special counselor, tutoring. **Placement/credit:** CLEP Subject; 20 credit hours maximum for associate degree.

ACADEMIC REQUIREMENTS. Freshmen must earn minimum GPA of 2.0 to continue in good standing. 77% of freshmen return for sophomore year. **Graduation requirements:** 60 hours for associate. Most students required to take courses in English, humanities, mathematics, social sciences.

FRESHMAN ADMISSIONS. Selection criteria: Open admissions. Selective admissions to nursing program. **Test requirements:** ACT for placement and counseling only; score report by August 1. General Aptitude Test Battery required of applicants to technical programs. Psychological Services Bureau test required of applicants to nursing program.

1992 FRESHMAN CLASS PROFILE. 165 men, 268 women enrolled. **Characteristics:** 99% from in state, 90% commute, 6% have minority backgrounds.

FALL-TERM APPLICATIONS. $20 fee. No closing date; applicants notified on a rolling basis. Deferred admission available.

STUDENT LIFE. Housing: Dormitories (coed); handicapped housing available. **Activities:** Student government, choral groups, dance, drama, jazz band, music ensembles, pep band.

ATHLETICS. NJCAA. **Intercollegiate:** Basketball, volleyball W. **Intramural:** Basketball, volleyball.

STUDENT SERVICES. Aptitude testing, career counseling, employment service for undergraduates, freshman orientation, personal counseling, placement service for graduates, services/facilities for handicapped.

ANNUAL EXPENSES. Tuition and fees (projected): $1,048, $162 additional for out-of-state students. **Room and board:** $800 room only. **Books and supplies:** $450. **Other expenses:** $500.

FINANCIAL AID. 67% of freshmen, 72% of continuing students receive some form of aid. All aid based on need. Academic, music/drama, art, athletic scholarships available. **Aid applications:** No closing date; priority given to applications received by April 15; applicants notified on a rolling basis beginning on or about April 15; must reply within 2 weeks.

ADDRESS/TELEPHONE. Kenneth L. Aten, Voc-Tech Campus President, Mid Plains Community College, 1101 Halligan Drive, North Platte, NE 69101-0001. (308) 532-8740. (800) 658-4308.

Midland Lutheran College
Fremont, Nebraska CB code: 6406

Admissions: 94% of applicants accepted
Based on: ••• School record, test scores
•• Activities, interview
• Recommendations
Completion: 86% of freshmen end year in good standing
55% graduate, 16% of these enter graduate study

4-year private college of arts and sciences, coed, affiliated with Evangelical Lutheran Church in America. Founded in 1883. **Accreditation:** Regional. **Undergraduate enrollment:** 372 men, 509 women full time; 14 men, 67 women part time. **Faculty:** 70 total (55 full time), 32 with doctorates or other terminal degrees. **Location:** Suburban campus in large town; 35 miles from Omaha, 52 miles from Lincoln. **Calendar:** 4-1-4, limited summer session. **Microcomputers:** 100 located in libraries, classrooms, computer centers, campus-wide network. **Special facilities:** Planetarium/observatory.

DEGREES OFFERED. AA, BA, BS. 11 associate degrees awarded in 1992. 40% in business/office and marketing/distribution, 40% computer sciences, 20% social sciences. 201 bachelor's degrees awarded. 30% in business and management, 5% communications, 5% computer sciences, 26% teacher education, 25% health sciences.

UNDERGRADUATE MAJORS. Associate: Accounting, Bible studies, business data processing and related programs, business data programming, community services, computer programming, data processing, legal assistant/paralegal, legal secretary, marketing and distribution, recreation and community services technologies, respiratory therapy technology, secretarial and related programs, social sciences, teacher aide. **Bachelor's:** Accounting, advertising, American studies, behavioral sciences, biological and physical sciences, biology, business administration and management, business and management, business economics, chemistry, clinical laboratory science, communications, computer and information sciences, computer programming, data processing, dramatic arts, earth sciences, economics, education, elementary education, English, finance, fine arts, German, health sciences, history, humanities and social sciences, journalism, junior high education, legal assistant/paralegal, liberal/general studies, marketing management, mathematics, music, nursing, physical sciences, predentistry, prelaw, premedicine, prepharmacy, preveterinary, psychology, religion, respiratory therapy, respiratory therapy technology, secondary education, secretarial and related programs, social sciences, social work, sociology, Spanish, speech.

ACADEMIC PROGRAMS. Accelerated program, double major, dual enrollment of high school students, independent study, internships, student-designed major, study abroad, teacher preparation; liberal arts/career combination in health sciences, business. **Remedial services:** Learning center, reduced course load, special counselor, tutoring. **ROTC:** Army. **Placement/credit:** AP, CLEP General and Subject, institutional tests; 32 credit hours maximum for associate degree; 32 credit hours maximum for bachelor's degree.

ACADEMIC REQUIREMENTS. Freshmen must earn minimum GPA of 1.5 to continue in good standing. 82% of freshmen return for sophomore year. Students must declare major by end of first year. **Graduation requirements:** 64 hours for associate (33 in major), 128 hours for bachelor's (36 in major). Most students required to take courses in English. **Postgraduate studies:** 50% from 2-year programs enter 4-year programs.

FRESHMAN ADMISSIONS. Selection criteria: School achievement record, test scores, recommendation by school official, rank in top half of class reviewed. Applicants with lesser qualifications considered by review of test scores and personal educational objectives. **High school preparation:** 10 units recommended. Recommended units include biological science 1, English 3, mathematics 2 and social science 2. **Test requirements:** ACT; score report by September 5.

1992 FRESHMAN CLASS PROFILE. 311 men applied, 290 accepted, 133 enrolled; 350 women applied, 334 accepted, 192 enrolled. 22% were in top tenth and 46% were in top quarter of graduating class. **Characteristics:** 70% from in state, 80% live in college housing, 5% have minority backgrounds, 1% are foreign students, 10% join fraternities/sororities. Average age is 18.

FALL-TERM APPLICATIONS. $20 fee, may be waived for applicants with need. Closing date September 1; applicants notified on a rolling basis. Interview recommended. Audition recommended for music, drama applicants. Portfolio recommended for art applicants. Early admission available.

STUDENT LIFE. Housing: Dormitories (men, women, coed). **Activities:** Student government, magazine, student newspaper, yearbook, choral groups, concert band, dance, drama, jazz band, music ensembles, musical theater, pep band, fraternities, sororities, Fellowship of Christian Athletes.

ATHLETICS. NAIA. **Intercollegiate:** Baseball M, basketball, cross-country, football M, golf, softball W, tennis, track and field, volleyball W. **Intramural:** Basketball, bowling, field hockey W, handball, racquetball, soccer M, softball, swimming, tennis, track and field, volleyball.

STUDENT SERVICES. Career counseling, employment service for undergraduates, freshman orientation, health services, personal counseling, placement service for graduates, services/facilities for handicapped.

ANNUAL EXPENSES. Tuition and fees (1992-93): $8,800. **Room and board:** $2,700. **Books and supplies:** $350. **Other expenses:** $900.

FINANCIAL AID. 93% of freshmen, 86% of continuing students receive some form of aid. Grants, loans, jobs available. Academic, music/drama, art, athletic, leadership, religious affiliation scholarships available. **Aid applications:** Closing date August 1; priority given to applications received by May 1; applicants notified on a rolling basis beginning on or about March 15; must reply within 2 weeks.

ADDRESS/TELEPHONE. Roland R. Kahnk, Vice President for Admissions/Financial Aid, Midland Lutheran College, 900 North Clarkson, Fremont, NE 68025. (402) 721-5480.

Nebraska Christian College
Norfolk, Nebraska CB code: 1332

4-year private Bible college, coed, affiliated with Christian Churches/Churches of Christ. Founded in 1944. **Undergraduate enrollment:** 63 men, 56 women full time; 9 men, 6 women part time. **Faculty:** 19 total (12 full time), 3 with doctorates or other terminal degrees. **Location:** Suburban campus in large town; 110 miles from Omaha. **Calendar:** Semester. **Microcomputers:** Located in computer centers.

DEGREES OFFERED. AA, BA, BS. 12 associate degrees awarded in 1992. 50% in education, 50% philosophy, religion, theology. 21 bachelor's degrees awarded. 29% in education, 71% philosophy, religion, theology.

UNDERGRADUATE MAJORS. Associate: Christian education, education of the deaf and hearing impaired, missionary studies, religious education, religious music, secretarial and related programs, theological studies. **Bachelor's:** Bible studies, Christian education, elementary education, junior high education, missionary studies, religion, religious education, religious music, secondary education, theological studies.

ACADEMIC PROGRAMS. Double major, independent study, internships, teacher preparation, cross-registration.

ACADEMIC REQUIREMENTS. Freshmen must earn minimum GPA of 1.7 to continue in good standing. 58% of freshmen return for sophomore year. Students must declare major by end of second year. **Graduation requirements:** 64 hours for associate (25 in major), 130 hours for bachelor's (40 in major). Most students required to take courses in English, history, philosophy/religion, biological/physical sciences. **Additional information:** Bachelor's degree in Bible studies awarded jointly with bachelor's degree in education from Wayne State College.

FRESHMAN ADMISSIONS. Selection criteria: Christian commitment and references very important, school achievement record, ACT test scores considered. **Test requirements:** ACT; score report by August 15.

1992 FRESHMAN CLASS PROFILE. 31 men, 34 women enrolled. 14% were in top tenth and 24% were in top quarter of graduating class. **Characteristics:** 33% from in state, 100% live in college housing, 1% have minority backgrounds. Average age is 19.

FALL-TERM APPLICATIONS. $10 fee. Closing date August 15; applicants notified on a rolling basis. Essay required. Deferred admission available.

STUDENT LIFE. Housing: Dormitories (men, women); apartment housing available. **Activities:** Student government, choral groups, drama, music ensembles, pep band. **Additional information:** Religious observance required.

ATHLETICS. Intercollegiate: Basketball, volleyball W. **Intramural:** Basketball M, golf, softball M.

STUDENT SERVICES. Career counseling, employment service for undergraduates, health services, personal counseling, placement service for graduates, special adviser for adult students, services/facilities for handicapped.

ANNUAL EXPENSES. Tuition and fees: $3,470. **Room and board:** $2,440. **Books and supplies:** $300. **Other expenses:** $1,623.

FINANCIAL AID. 97% of freshmen, 89% of continuing students receive some form of aid. 64% of grants, 90% of loans, 45% of jobs based on need. 62 enrolled freshmen were judged to have need, all were offered aid. Academic, leadership scholarships available. **Aid applications:** No closing date; priority given to applications received by June 1; applicants notified on a rolling basis beginning on or about May 1; must reply within 15 days.

ADDRESS/TELEPHONE. Jerry Hopkins, Director of Admissions and Student Development, Nebraska Christian College, 1800 Syracuse, Norfolk, NE 68701. (402) 371-5960.

Nebraska College of Technical Agriculture
Curtis, Nebraska CB code: 1305

2-year public agricultural and technical college, coed. Founded in 1965. **Accreditation:** Regional. **Undergraduate enrollment:** 96 men, 81 women full time; 10 men, 15 women part time. **Faculty:** 19 total (17 full time). **Location:** Rural campus in rural community; 47 miles from North Platte and McCook. **Calendar:** Semester. **Microcomputers:** 23 located in libraries, computer centers. **Special facilities:** College farm and campus on site of arboretum.

DEGREES OFFERED. AAS. 51 associate degrees awarded in 1992. 100% in agriculture.

UNDERGRADUATE MAJORS. Agricultural business and management, agricultural mechanics, agricultural production, conservation and regulation, horticulture, renewable natural resources, veterinarian's assistant.

ACADEMIC PROGRAMS. Internships.

ACADEMIC REQUIREMENTS. Freshmen must earn minimum GPA of 1.0 to continue in good standing. 85% of freshmen return for sophomore year. Students must declare major on enrollment. **Graduation requirements:** Most students required to take courses in computer science, English, humanities, mathematics, biological/physical sciences, social sciences.

FRESHMAN ADMISSIONS. Selection criteria: Open admissions. **High school preparation:** 11 units recommended. Recommended units include biological science 2, English 3, mathematics 3, physical science 2 and social science 1. **Test requirements:** ACT for counseling; score report by August 1.

1992 FRESHMAN CLASS PROFILE. 75 men applied, 75 accepted, 66 enrolled; 80 women applied, 80 accepted, 67 enrolled. 15% had high school GPA of 3.0 or higher, 40% between 2.0 and 2.99. 2% were in top tenth and 17% were in top quarter of graduating class. **Academic background:** Mid 50% of enrolled freshmen had ACT composite between 10-20. 95% submitted ACT scores. **Characteristics:** 50% commute, 1% have minority backgrounds, 1% are foreign students. Average age is 19.

FALL-TERM APPLICATIONS. $10 fee. Closing date August 15; priority given to applications received by July 1; applicants notified on a rolling basis.

STUDENT LIFE. Housing: Dormitories (men, women). **Activities:** Student government, student newspaper, yearbook, fraternities.

ATHLETICS. Intramural: Basketball, cross-country, softball, volleyball.

STUDENT SERVICES. Employment service for undergraduates, freshman orientation, health services, placement service for graduates, veterans counselor.

ANNUAL EXPENSES. Tuition and fees (projected): $1,586, $1,456 additional for out-of-state students. **Room and board:** $2,550. **Books and supplies:** $500. **Other expenses:** $1,100.

FINANCIAL AID. 85% of freshmen, 75% of continuing students receive some form of aid. 92% of grants, 91% of loans, all jobs based on need. 85 enrolled freshmen were judged to have need, all were offered aid. Academic, leadership scholarships available. **Aid applications:** No closing date; priority given to applications received by April 1; applicants notified on a rolling basis beginning on or about May 1; must reply within 2 weeks.

ADDRESS/TELEPHONE. Gerald J. Huntwork, Assistant Dean, Nebraska College of Technical Agriculture, PO Box 69, Curtis, NE 69025-0069. (308) 367-4124 ext. 247. (800) 328-7847. Fax: (308) 367-4203.

Nebraska Indian Community College
Winnebago, Nebraska CB code: 1431

2-year public community college, coed. Founded in 1979. **Accreditation:** Regional. **Undergraduate enrollment:** 62 men, 61 women full time; 39 men, 60 women part time. **Faculty:** 38 total (12 full time), 4 with doctorates or other terminal degrees. **Location:** Rural campus in rural community; 20 miles from Sioux City, Iowa. **Calendar:** Semester, limited summer session. Extensive evening/early morning classes. **Microcomputers:** 20 located in computer centers.

DEGREES OFFERED. AA, AS, AAS. 39 associate degrees awarded in 1992.

UNDERGRADUATE MAJORS. American Indian studies, carpentry, computer and information sciences, counseling psychology, electrical installation, graphic arts technology, liberal/general studies, masonry/tile setting, plumbing/pipefitting/steamfitting, secretarial and related programs.

ACADEMIC PROGRAMS. 2-year transfer program, cooperative education, double major, independent study, internships. **Remedial services:** Remedial instruction, tutoring.

ACADEMIC REQUIREMENTS. Freshmen must earn minimum GPA of 2.0 to continue in good standing. 30% of freshmen return for sophomore year. Students must declare major on enrollment. **Graduation requirements:** 60 hours for associate (30 in major). Most students required to take courses in English, history, humanities, mathematics, biological/physical sciences, social sciences. **Additional information:** Certificate programs offered.

FRESHMAN ADMISSIONS. Selection criteria: Open admissions. Strong background in English, mathematics, and science recommended.

1992 FRESHMAN CLASS PROFILE. 44 men, 62 women enrolled. **Characteristics:** 99% from in state, 100% commute, 95% have minority backgrounds. Average age is 27.

FALL-TERM APPLICATIONS. $10 fee. No closing date; applicants notified on a rolling basis.

STUDENT LIFE. Activities: Student government, student newspaper.

ATHLETICS. Intercollegiate: Basketball M, cross-country M, volleyball W. **Intramural:** Basketball, bowling, softball, volleyball.

STUDENT SERVICES. Aptitude testing, career counseling, personal counseling, special adviser for adult students.

ANNUAL EXPENSES. Tuition and fees (1992-93): $2,000. **Books and supplies:** $420. **Other expenses:** $800.

FINANCIAL AID. 90% of freshmen, 70% of continuing students receive some form of aid. All grants, all jobs based on need. 97 enrolled freshmen were judged to have need, all were offered aid. **Aid applications:** No closing date; priority given to applications received by July 15; applicants notified on a rolling basis beginning on or about July 15; must reply within 2 weeks.

ADDRESS/TELEPHONE. Karen Kemling, Admissions Officer/Registrar, Nebraska Indian Community College, PO Box 752, Winnebago, NE 68071. (402) 878-2414. Fax: (402) 878-2522.

Nebraska Methodist College of Nursing and Allied Health

Omaha, Nebraska — CB code: 6510

Admissions: 81% of applicants accepted
Based on: ••• Interview
•• Essay, school record, test scores
• Activities, recommendations
Completion: 98% of freshmen end year in good standing
65% graduate

4-year private health science college, coed, affiliated with United Methodist Church. Founded in 1891. **Accreditation:** Regional. **Undergraduate enrollment:** 27 men, 291 women full time; 13 men, 136 women part time. **Faculty:** 33 total (25 full time), 3 with doctorates or other terminal degrees. **Location:** Suburban campus in large city. **Calendar:** Semester, limited summer session. **Microcomputers:** 20 located in libraries, computer centers. **Additional facts:** Affiliated with University of Nebraska at Omaha.

DEGREES OFFERED. AS, BS. 11 associate degrees awarded in 1992. 100% in allied health. 40 bachelor's degrees awarded. 100% in health sciences.

UNDERGRADUATE MAJORS. Associate: Rehabilitation counseling/services, respiratory therapy technology, ultrasound technology. **Bachelor's:** Medical radiation dosimetry, nursing, respiratory therapy technology, ultrasound technology.

ACADEMIC PROGRAMS. Independent study, internships; liberal arts/career combination in health sciences. **Remedial services:** Learning center, preadmission summer program, reduced course load, remedial instruction, special counselor, tutoring. **Placement/credit:** Institutional tests.

ACADEMIC REQUIREMENTS. Freshmen must earn minimum GPA of 2.0 to continue in good standing. Must earn minimum grades of 2.0 in major. 81% of freshmen return for sophomore year. Students must declare major on enrollment. **Graduation requirements:** 60 hours for associate (36 in major), 120 hours for bachelor's (55 in major). Most students required to take courses in English, humanities, mathematics, philosophy/religion, biological/physical sciences, social sciences. **Postgraduate studies:** 70% from 2-year programs enter 4-year programs.

FRESHMAN ADMISSIONS. Selection criteria: Interview, school achievement, test scores, personal statement, recommendations important. Recommended units include biological science 1, English 4, mathematics 2, physical science 1 and social science 2. **Test requirements:** ACT; score report by August 1. **Additional information:** Application deadlines vary by program.

1992 FRESHMAN CLASS PROFILE. 3 men applied, 3 accepted, 3 enrolled; 50 women applied, 40 accepted, 30 enrolled. 28% had high school GPA of 3.0 or higher, 61% between 2.0 and 2.99. **Academic background:** Mid 50% of enrolled freshmen had ACT composite between 12-18. 100% submitted ACT scores. **Characteristics:** 98% from in state, 75% commute. Average age is 18.

FALL-TERM APPLICATIONS. $20 fee. Applicants notified on a rolling basis; must reply within 30 days. Interview required for all applicants applicants. Essay required. Deferred admission available.

STUDENT LIFE. Housing: Dormitories (coed). **Activities:** Student government.

STUDENT SERVICES. Career counseling, employment service for undergraduates, freshman orientation, personal counseling, placement service for graduates, special adviser for adult students, services/facilities for handicapped.

ANNUAL EXPENSES. Tuition and fees (1992-93): $5,485. **Room and board:** $1,200 room only. **Books and supplies:** $500. **Other expenses:** $900.

FINANCIAL AID. 64% of grants, 80% of loans based on need. All jobs based on criteria other than need. Academic, leadership scholarships available. **Aid applications:** No closing date; priority given to applications received by April 1; applicants notified on a rolling basis beginning on or about June 1; must reply within 4 weeks.

ADDRESS/TELEPHONE. Deann Clyde, Coordinator of Admissions, Nebraska Methodist College of Nursing and Allied Health, 8501 West Dodge Road, Omaha, NE 68114. (402) 390-4879.

Nebraska Wesleyan University

Lincoln, Nebraska — CB code: 6470

Admissions: 93% of applicants accepted
Based on: ••• School record, test scores
•• Interview, special talents
• Activities, essay, recommendations
Completion: 93% of freshmen end year in good standing
65% graduate

4-year private liberal arts college, coed, affiliated with United Methodist Church. Founded in 1887. **Accreditation:** Regional. **Undergraduate enrollment:** 648 men, 762 women full time; 64 men, 220 women part time. **Faculty:** 151 total (86 full time), 68 with doctorates or other terminal degrees. **Location:** Suburban campus in small city; 55 miles from Omaha. **Calendar:** Semester, limited summer session. Extensive evening/early morning classes. **Microcomputers:** 170 located in dormitories, libraries, computer centers, campus-wide network. **Special facilities:** Art and art laboratory galleries, planetarium, carbon-dating laboratory, theater, laboratory theater.

DEGREES OFFERED. 298 bachelor's degrees awarded in 1992. 22% in business and management, 11% teacher education, 5% letters/literature, 19% life sciences, 10% psychology, 6% social sciences, 7% visual and performing arts.

UNDERGRADUATE MAJORS. Art education, biology, biophysics, business and management, business education, chemistry, communications, computer and information sciences, dramatic arts, economics, elementary education, English, English education, fine arts, foreign languages education, French, German, history, information sciences and systems, international studies, junior high education, mathematics, mathematics education, music, music education, music performance, nursing, philosophy, physical education, physics, political science and government, psychology, religion, science education, secondary education, social science education, social work, sociology, Spanish, special education, speech, speech/communication/theater education.

ACADEMIC PROGRAMS. Double major, dual enrollment of high school students, independent study, internships, study abroad, teacher preparation, visiting/exchange student program, United Nations semester, Washington semester, cross-registration, Rocky Ridge Music Camp, Cooperative Urban Teacher Education, 3/2 program in engineering with Washington University, Missouri. **Remedial services:** Reduced course load, tutoring. **ROTC:** Air Force, Army, Naval. **Placement/credit:** AP, CLEP General and Subject, institutional tests. Unlimited number of hours of credit by examination may be counted toward degree.

ACADEMIC REQUIREMENTS. Freshmen must earn minimum GPA of 1.6 to continue in good standing. 86% of freshmen return for sophomore year. Students must declare major by end of second year. **Graduation requirements:** 126 hours for bachelor's (30 in major). Most students required to take courses in arts/fine arts, computer science, English, humanities, mathematics, philosophy/religion, biological/physical sciences, social sciences.

FRESHMAN ADMISSIONS. Selection criteria: Good school achievement record and rank in top half of class, or combined SAT score of 800 or ACT composite score of 18 or enhanced ACT composite score of 20 required. **Test requirements:** SAT or ACT; score report by August 1.

1992 FRESHMAN CLASS PROFILE. 979 men and women applied, 911 accepted; 154 men enrolled; 213 women enrolled. 31% were in top tenth of graduating class. **Characteristics:** 95% from in state, 83% live in college housing, 5% have minority backgrounds, 52% join fraternities/sororities. Average age is 18.

FALL-TERM APPLICATIONS. $20 fee, may be waived for applicants with need. Closing date August 15; priority given to applications received by May 1; applicants notified on a rolling basis; must reply by May 1 or within 4 weeks if notified thereafter. Interview recommended. Audition recommended for music, drama applicants. Portfolio recommended for art applicants. Essay recommended. Deferred and early admission available.

STUDENT LIFE. Housing: Dormitories (men, women, coed); fraternity, sorority housing available. **Activities:** Student government, student newspaper, yearbook, choral groups, concert band, dance, drama, jazz band, marching band, music ensembles, musical theater, opera, pep band, symphony orchestra, fraternities, sororities, Circle-K, pretheology organization, Fellowship of Christian Athletes, Religion and Life Fellowship, international student association.

ATHLETICS. NAIA, NCAA. **Intercollegiate:** Baseball M, basketball, cross-country, football M, golf, softball W, tennis, track and field, volleyball W. **Intramural:** Basketball, bowling, golf, soccer M, softball, tennis, track and field, volleyball.

STUDENT SERVICES. Aptitude testing, career counseling, employment service for undergraduates, freshman orientation, health services, personal counseling, placement service for graduates, special adviser for adult students, leadership training, services/facilities for handicapped.

ANNUAL EXPENSES. Tuition and fees: $9,186. **Room and board:** $3,200. **Books and supplies:** $450. **Other expenses:** $1,800.

FINANCIAL AID. 93% of freshmen, 93% of continuing students receive some form of aid. 73% of grants, 98% of loans, 79% of jobs based on

need. 250 enrolled freshmen were judged to have need, all were offered aid. Academic, music/drama, art, religious affiliation scholarships available. **Aid applications:** No closing date; applicants notified on a rolling basis beginning on or about February 15; must reply within 3 weeks.

ADDRESS/TELEPHONE. Ken Sieg, Director of Admissions, Nebraska Wesleyan University, 5000 St. Paul Avenue, Lincoln, NE 68504. (402) 465-2218. (800) 541-3818. Fax: (402) 465-2179.

Northeast Community College
Norfolk, Nebraska CB code: 6473

2-year public community college, coed. Founded in 1973. **Accreditation:** Regional. **Undergraduate enrollment:** 734 men, 614 women full time; 1,060 men, 849 women part time. **Faculty:** 127 total (86 full time), 1 with doctorate or other terminal degree. **Location:** Rural campus in large town; 110 miles from Omaha. **Calendar:** Semester, limited summer session. **Microcomputers:** 150 located in classrooms, computer centers. **Special facilities:** Fitness center. **Additional facts:** Off-campus credit classes available at O'Neill and other surrounding towns.

DEGREES OFFERED. AA, AS, AAS. 333 associate degrees awarded in 1992. 7% in agriculture, 6% business and management, 10% business/office and marketing/distribution, 5% computer sciences, 5% teacher education, 60% trade and industry.

UNDERGRADUATE MAJORS. Accounting, agribusiness, agricultural business and management, agricultural products and processing, agricultural sciences, agronomy, air conditioning/heating/refrigeration mechanics, animal sciences, art history, automotive mechanics, automotive technology, biological and physical sciences, biology, business administration and management, business and management, business and office, business data entry equipment operation, business data processing and related programs, business data programming, business education, carpentry, chemistry, communications, computer programming, criminal justice studies, diesel engine mechanics, drafting, dramatic arts, education, electrical and electronics equipment repair, electrical installation, elementary education, English, humanities and social sciences, industrial equipment maintenance and repair, industrial maintenance, industrial technology, journalism, law enforcement and corrections technologies, legal secretary, liberal/general studies, marketing and distribution, marketing management, mathematics, medical secretary, music, music education, music history and appreciation, music performance, nursing, photographic technology, photography, physical education, physical sciences, physics, psychology, public affairs, radio/television broadcasting, range management, real estate, science technologies, secondary education, secretarial and related programs, social sciences, soil sciences, speech, teacher aide, visual and performing arts.

ACADEMIC PROGRAMS. 2-year transfer program, dual enrollment of high school students, cross-registration. **Remedial services:** Learning center, remedial instruction, tutoring, developmental mathematics, developmental reading. **Placement/credit:** CLEP Subject, institutional tests; 16 credit hours maximum for associate degree.

ACADEMIC REQUIREMENTS. Freshmen must earn minimum GPA of 2.0 to continue in good standing. 75% of freshmen return for sophomore year. Students must declare major on application. **Graduation requirements:** 60 hours for associate. Most students required to take courses in English, mathematics.

FRESHMAN ADMISSIONS. Selection criteria: Open admissions. Selective admissions to nursing programs. **Test requirements:** Pre-Admissions and Classification examination required for practical nursing program applicants and degree nursing applicants. **Additional information:** Non-high school graduates may be accepted under special admission policy.

1992 FRESHMAN CLASS PROFILE. 714 men applied, 714 accepted, 361 enrolled; 573 women applied, 573 accepted, 262 enrolled. **Characteristics:** 93% from in state, 85% commute, 2% have minority backgrounds, 1% are foreign students. Average age is 19.

FALL-TERM APPLICATIONS. No fee. No closing date; applicants notified on a rolling basis.

STUDENT LIFE. Housing: Dormitories (coed); apartment housing available. **Activities:** Student government, radio, student newspaper, choral groups, concert band, drama, jazz band, music ensembles, musical theater, pep band.

ATHLETICS. NJCAA. **Intercollegiate:** Basketball, golf, volleyball W. **Intramural:** Archery, badminton, basketball, bowling, cross-country, skiing, softball, volleyball, wrestling M.

STUDENT SERVICES. Aptitude testing, career counseling, employment service for undergraduates, freshman orientation, health services, on-campus day care, personal counseling, placement service for graduates, veterans counselor, services/facilities for handicapped.

ANNUAL EXPENSES. Tuition and fees: $966, $258 additional for out-of-state students. **Room and board:** $1,188 room only. **Books and supplies:** $500. **Other expenses:** $700.

FINANCIAL AID. 71% of freshmen, 58% of continuing students receive some form of aid. 91% of grants, 78% of loans, 86% of jobs based on need. Academic, music/drama, art, athletic, state/district residency, leadership scholarships available. **Aid applications:** No closing date; priority given to applications received by May 1; applicants notified on a rolling basis beginning on or about June 1; must reply within 2 weeks. **Additional information:** Resident and nonresident assistance for single parents, displaced homemakers, farmers in transition.

ADDRESS/TELEPHONE. Eugene C. Hart, Director of Admissions, Northeast Community College, PO Box 469, 801 East Benjamin Avenue, Norfolk, NE 68702-0469. (402) 371-2020. (800) 348-9033. Fax: (402) 644-0650.

Peru State College
Peru, Nebraska CB code: 6468

4-year public liberal arts, teachers college, coed. Founded in 1867. **Accreditation:** Regional. **Undergraduate enrollment:** 456 men, 501 women full time; 219 men, 221 women part time. **Graduate enrollment:** 63 men, 122 women part time. **Faculty:** 77 total (49 full time), 27 with doctorates or other terminal degrees. **Location:** Rural campus in rural community; 65 miles from Omaha. **Calendar:** Semester, limited summer session. **Microcomputers:** 120 located in dormitories, libraries, classrooms, computer centers. **Special facilities:** Wildlife habitat, art gallery.

DEGREES OFFERED. AA, BA, BS, MEd. 202 bachelor's degrees awarded. Graduate degrees offered in 1 major field of study.

UNDERGRADUATE MAJORS. Associate: Teacher aide. **Bachelor's:** Accounting, art education, biology, business administration and management, chemistry, clinical laboratory science, computer and information sciences, computer science education, dramatic arts, driver and safety education, early childhood education, electronic technology, elementary education, English, English education, health education, history, industrial arts education, industrial technology, information sciences and systems, junior high education, language arts, marketing management, mathematics, mathematics education, music, music education, nuclear technologies, physical education, physical sciences, predentistry, prelaw, premedicine, prepharmacy, preveterinary, psychology, robotics, science education, secondary education, social science education, social sciences, social studies education, sociology, special education, speech, speech/communication/theater education, trade and industrial supervision and management, wildlife management.

ACADEMIC PROGRAMS. 2-year transfer program, cooperative education, double major, dual enrollment of high school students, honors program, independent study, internships, teacher preparation; liberal arts/career combination in health sciences. **Remedial services:** Learning center, preadmission summer program, remedial instruction, special counselor, tutoring. **ROTC:** Army. **Placement/credit:** CLEP Subject; 16 credit hours maximum for bachelor's degree.

ACADEMIC REQUIREMENTS. Freshmen must earn minimum GPA of 2.0 to continue in good standing. 80% of freshmen return for sophomore year. Students must declare major by end of second year. **Graduation requirements:** 125 hours for bachelor's (60 in major). Most students required to take courses in arts/fine arts, computer science, English, history, humanities, mathematics, biological/physical sciences, social sciences. **Postgraduate studies:** 90% from 2-year programs enter 4-year programs.

FRESHMAN ADMISSIONS. Selection criteria: Open admissions. Out-of-state applicants must rank in top half of graduating class or have ACT composite score of 14 or SAT combined of 560. **High school preparation:** 16 units recommended. Recommended units include English 3, foreign language 1, mathematics 2, social science 3 and science 2. **Test requirements:** SAT or ACT (ACT preferred); score report by September 1.

1992 FRESHMAN CLASS PROFILE. 253 men and women enrolled. **Academic background:** Mid 50% of enrolled freshmen had ACT composite between 16-23. 90% submitted ACT scores. **Characteristics:** 92% from in state, 85% live in college housing, 5% have minority backgrounds, 1% are foreign students. Average age is 18.

FALL-TERM APPLICATIONS. $10 fee. No closing date; priority given to applications received by July 1; applicants notified on a rolling basis. Interview recommended. Audition recommended for music applicants. Early admission available.

STUDENT LIFE. Housing: Dormitories (men, women, coed); apartment, fraternity, sorority housing available. **Activities:** Student government, student newspaper, yearbook, choral groups, concert band, drama, jazz band, marching band, music ensembles, musical theater, pep band, fraternities, sororities, Fellowship of Christian Athletes, Multicultural Committee, Phi Beta Lambda, Peru Players, Women's Athletic Association.

ATHLETICS. NAIA. **Intercollegiate:** Baseball M, basketball, football M, softball W, volleyball W. **Intramural:** Basketball, soccer, softball, swimming, tennis, volleyball.

STUDENT SERVICES. Aptitude testing, career counseling, employment service for undergraduates, freshman orientation, health services, on-campus day care, personal counseling, placement service for graduates, special adviser for adult students, veterans counselor, services/facilities for handicapped.

ANNUAL EXPENSES. Tuition and fees (projected): $1,704, $1,140 additional for out-of-state students. **Room and board:** $2,600. **Books and supplies:** $520. **Other expenses:** $951.

FINANCIAL AID. 89% of freshmen, 83% of continuing students receive some form of aid. 82% of grants, 71% of loans, 80% of jobs based on need. Academic, music/drama, art, athletic, leadership, minority scholarships available. **Aid applications:** No closing date; priority given to applications received by April 1; applicants notified on a rolling basis beginning on or about April 1; must reply within 4 weeks.

ADDRESS/TELEPHONE. Pam Sherwood-Cosgrove, Director of Admissions, Peru State College, Peru, NE 68421. (402) 872-3815 ext. 2221. (800) 742-4412. Fax: (402) 872-2375.

Southeast Community College: Beatrice Campus
Beatrice, Nebraska CB code: 6795

2-year public community, liberal arts college, coed. Founded in 1941. **Accreditation:** Regional. **Undergraduate enrollment:** 232 men, 281 women full time; 109 men, 329 women part time. **Faculty:** 46 total (36 full time), 3 with doctorates or other terminal degrees. **Location:** Rural campus in large town; 40 miles from Lincoln. **Calendar:** Semester, limited summer session. Extensive evening/early morning classes. **Microcomputers:** Located in computer centers. **Special facilities:** 2 agricultural centers with 640-acre farm and 80 acres of pasture and grassland. **Additional facts:** Satellite programs available in 7 locations.

DEGREES OFFERED. AA, AS, AAS. 100 associate degrees awarded in 1992. 30% in agriculture, 16% business and management, 30% business/office and marketing/distribution.

UNDERGRADUATE MAJORS. Accounting, agricultural business and management, agricultural mechanics, agricultural production, agricultural sciences, animal sciences, biology, botany, broadcast journalism, business administration and management, business and management, business and office, chemistry, computer and information sciences, crop production, diversified agriculture, early childhood education, education, elementary education, English, finance, fine arts, history, international studies, journalism, legal secretary, liberal/general studies, marketing management, mathematics, medical secretary, music, nursing, office supervision and management, photography, physical sciences, physics, political science and government, practical nursing, prearchitecture, prechiropractic, preengineering, prelaw, premedical technology, premedicine, prepharmacy, preradiology, preveterinary, psychology, radio/television broadcasting, secondary education, secretarial and related programs, social sciences, sociology, zoology.

ACADEMIC PROGRAMS. 2-year transfer program, cooperative education, double major, dual enrollment of high school students, independent study, internships. **Remedial services:** Learning center, reduced course load, remedial instruction, special counselor, tutoring. **Placement/credit:** Institutional tests.

ACADEMIC REQUIREMENTS. Freshmen must earn minimum GPA of 2.0 to continue in good standing. 85% of freshmen return for sophomore year. Students must declare major by end of first year. **Graduation requirements:** 60 hours for associate. Most students required to take courses in English, humanities, mathematics, biological/physical sciences, social sciences.

FRESHMAN ADMISSIONS. Selection criteria: Open admissions. Selective admissions to practical nursing program. **High school preparation:** 16 units recommended. Recommended units include biological science 1, English 3, foreign language 1, mathematics 2, physical science 2, social science 2 and science 1. Four electives recommended. **Test requirements:** SAT or ACT (ACT preferred) for placement and counseling only; score report by August 15. ACT/ASSET required for practical nursing program applicants. ASSET administered to all incoming freshmen.

1992 FRESHMAN CLASS PROFILE. 265 men applied, 265 accepted, 176 enrolled; 398 women applied, 398 accepted, 396 enrolled. **Characteristics:** 81% from in state, 65% commute, 1% have minority backgrounds, 2% are foreign students. Average age is 21.

FALL-TERM APPLICATIONS. $10 fee, may be waived for applicants with need. No closing date; applicants notified on a rolling basis. Interview required for practical nursing applicants. Deferred admission available. High school seniors permitted to enroll for limited number of hours if recommended by school adminstration.

STUDENT LIFE. Housing: Dormitories (women, coed); apartment housing available. Apartment-style dormitories and sleeping rooms available. **Activities:** Student government, radio, student newspaper, choral groups, drama, music ensembles, musical theater, pep band, Nebraska Young Farmers, health occupations student association, agri-business association, history club, drama club, business fraternities, honorary society, spirit groups, broadcasting club, Fellowship of Christian Athletes.

ATHLETICS. NJCAA. **Intercollegiate:** Basketball, golf M, volleyball W. **Intramural:** Basketball.

STUDENT SERVICES. Aptitude testing, career counseling, employment service for undergraduates, freshman orientation, health services, personal counseling, placement service for graduates, special adviser for adult students, veterans counselor, placement testing, services/facilities for handicapped.

ANNUAL EXPENSES. Tuition and fees (projected): $1,064, $270 additional for out-of-state students. Students from Iowa, Kansas, Missouri, South Dakota, Wyoming, and Colorado pay same tuition as in-state students. **Room and board:** $996 room only. **Books and supplies:** $450. **Other expenses:** $500.

FINANCIAL AID. 58% of freshmen, 37% of continuing students receive some form of aid. 82% of grants, 92% of loans, all jobs based on need. 176 enrolled freshmen were judged to have need, 171 were offered aid. Academic, music/drama, art, athletic, state/district residency, leadership, minority scholarships available. **Aid applications:** No closing date; priority given to applications received by April 1; applicants notified on a rolling basis; must reply within 2 weeks.

ADDRESS/TELEPHONE. Joe R. Renteria, Dean of Student Services, Southeast Community College: Beatrice Campus, Route 2, Box 35A, Beatrice, NE 68310. (402) 228-3468. Fax: (402) 228-3468.

Southeast Community College: Lincoln Campus
Lincoln, Nebraska CB code: 1189

2-year public community college, coed. Founded in 1973. **Accreditation:** Regional. **Undergraduate enrollment:** 528 men, 852 women full time; 1,180 men, 1,608 women part time. **Faculty:** 539 total (139 full time), 8 with doctorates or other terminal degrees. **Location:** Suburban campus in small city; 50 miles from Omaha. **Calendar:** Quarter, extensive summer session. Saturday and extensive evening/early morning classes. **Microcomputers:** 200 located in libraries, classrooms, computer centers. **Additional facts:** Extensive adult and continuing education programs, both credit and noncredit.

DEGREES OFFERED. AAS. 413 associate degrees awarded in 1992. 30% in business and management, 15% business/office and marketing/distribution, 20% allied health, 15% home economics, 20% trade and industry.

UNDERGRADUATE MAJORS. Automotive mechanics, automotive technology, business administration and management, child development/care/guidance, dietetic aide/assistant, drafting, drafting and design technology, electrical and electronics equipment repair, electronic technology, fashion merchandising, fire control and safety technology, food production/management/services, legal secretary, machine tool operation/machine shop, manufacturing technology, medical laboratory technologies, medical secretary, mental health/human services, nursing, radiograph medical technology, rehabilitation counseling/services, respiratory therapy, respiratory therapy technology, science technologies, secretarial and related programs, welding technology, word processing.

ACADEMIC PROGRAMS. Cooperative education, dual enrollment of high school students, independent study, internships. **Remedial services:** Learning center, remedial instruction, tutoring. **Placement/credit:** Institutional tests; 32 credit hours maximum for associate degree.

ACADEMIC REQUIREMENTS. Freshmen must earn minimum GPA of 1.5 to continue in good standing. Students must declare major on application. **Graduation requirements:** 96 hours for associate. Most students required to take courses in mathematics.

FRESHMAN ADMISSIONS. Selection criteria: Open admissions. All applicants reviewed for placement. ACT or SAT scores recommended. **Test requirements:** ASSET test required for placement. **Additional information:** Applicants screened for basic mathematics and reading skills. Some required to take diagnostic tests before admission.

1992 FRESHMAN CLASS PROFILE. 357 men, 490 women enrolled. **Characteristics:** 99% from in state, 100% commute, 4% have minority backgrounds, 1% are foreign students. Average age is 21.

FALL-TERM APPLICATIONS. $10 fee, may be waived for applicants with need. No closing date; applicants notified on a rolling basis; must reply within 15 days. Deferred admission available.

STUDENT LIFE. Activities: Student government, student newspaper, multi-cultural student advisory board.

ATHLETICS. Intramural: Basketball, softball, table tennis, tennis, volleyball.

STUDENT SERVICES. Aptitude testing, career counseling, employment service for undergraduates, freshman orientation, on-campus day care, personal counseling, placement service for graduates, veterans counselor, wellness/fitness center/programs, services/facilities for handicapped.

ANNUAL EXPENSES. Tuition and fees (1992-93): $1,049, $315 additional for out-of-state students. Students from Kansas, Iowa, Missouri, South Dakota, Wyoming, and Colorado pay same tuition as in-state students. **Books and supplies:** $450. **Other expenses:** $900.

FINANCIAL AID. 50% of freshmen, 30% of continuing students receive some form of aid. 94% of grants, 78% of loans, 65% of jobs based on need. Academic, state/district residency, leadership, minority scholarships available. **Aid applications:** No closing date; applicants notified on a rolling basis; must reply within 2 weeks.

ADDRESS/TELEPHONE. Robin Moore, Enrollment Management Specialist, Southeast Community College: Lincoln Campus, 8800 O Street, Lincoln, NE 68520. (402) 437-2600. Fax: (402) 437-2404.

Southeast Community College: Milford Campus
Milford, Nebraska CB code: 6502

2-year public community, technical college, coed. Founded in 1941. **Accreditation:** Regional. **Undergraduate enrollment:** 850 men, 57 women full time; 22 men, 4 women part time. **Faculty:** 90 total. **Location:** Rural campus in rural community; 25 miles from Lincoln. **Calendar:** Quarter, extensive summer session. **Microcomputers:** 50 located in libraries, classrooms, computer centers. **Special facilities:** High-tech laboratories. **Additional facts:** Selected by General Motors and John Deere as training facility. Autocad training center for Nebraska. John Deere agricultural and technical programs.

DEGREES OFFERED. AAS. 513 associate degrees awarded in 1992. 100% in trade and industry.

UNDERGRADUATE MAJORS. Air conditioning/heating/refrigeration mechanics, air conditioning/heating/refrigeration technology, architectural engineering, architectural technologies, architecture, auto body, automotive mechanics, automotive technology, business data processing and related programs, business data programming, carpentry, civil engineering, civil technology, commercial art, computer graphics, computer programming, computer servicing technology, construction, diesel engine mechanics, drafting, drafting and design technology, electrical and electronics equipment repair, electrical installation, electrical technology, electrical/electronics/communications engineering, electromechanical technology, electronic technology, engineering and engineering-related technologies, graphic arts technology, industrial equipment maintenance and repair, industrial technology, machine tool operation/machine shop, manufacturing technology, masonry/tile setting, mechanical design technology, mechanical engineering, microcomputer software, nondestructive testing (welds), plastic technology, plumbing/pipefitting/steamfitting, precision metal work, quality control technology, robotics, solar heating and cooling technology, survey and mapping technology, surveying and mapping sciences, systems analysis, welding technology, woodworking.

ACADEMIC PROGRAMS. Cooperative education, internships. **Remedial services:** Reduced course load, remedial instruction, special counselor, tutoring. **Placement/credit:** Institutional tests.

ACADEMIC REQUIREMENTS. Freshmen must earn minimum GPA of 1.5 to continue in good standing. Students must declare major on application. **Graduation requirements:** Most students required to take courses in computer science, English, mathematics. **Additional information:** Programs start 4 times annually.

FRESHMAN ADMISSIONS. Selection criteria: Open admissions. Selective admissions to commercial art program. **Additional information:** High School diploma recommended.

1992 FRESHMAN CLASS PROFILE. 155 men, 8 women enrolled. **Characteristics:** 90% from in state, 60% live in college housing, 2% have minority backgrounds, 1% are foreign students. Average age is 20.

FALL-TERM APPLICATIONS. $10 fee. No closing date; applicants notified on a rolling basis. Interview, portfolio required of commercial art applicants.

STUDENT LIFE. Housing: Dormitories (men, women); apartment housing available. **Activities:** Student government.

ATHLETICS. Intramural: Basketball, bowling, cross-country, golf, racquetball, softball, table tennis, tennis, volleyball, wrestling M.

STUDENT SERVICES. Aptitude testing, career counseling, employment service for undergraduates, personal counseling, placement service for graduates, veterans counselor, services/facilities for handicapped.

ANNUAL EXPENSES. Tuition and fees: $1,115, $270 additional for out-of-state students. Students from Iowa, Kansas, Missouri, South Dakota, Wyoming, and Colorado pay same tuition as in-state students. **Room and board:** $1,805. **Books and supplies:** $450. **Other expenses:** $900.

FINANCIAL AID. 60% of freshmen, 60% of continuing students receive some form of aid. 86% of grants, 86% of loans, 28% of jobs based on need. Academic, leadership, minority scholarships available. **Aid applications:** No closing date; priority given to applications received by April 1; applicants notified on a rolling basis; must reply within 2 weeks.

ADDRESS/TELEPHONE. Larry E. Meyer, Dean of Students, Chief Admissions Officer, Southeast Community College: Milford Campus, Route 2 Box D, Milford, NE 68405. (402) 761-2131. (800) 933-7223. Fax: (402) 761-2324.

Union College
Lincoln, Nebraska CB code: 6865

4-year private liberal arts college, coed, affiliated with Seventh-day Adventists. Founded in 1889. **Accreditation:** Regional. **Undergraduate enrollment:** 196 men, 251 women full time; 52 men, 59 women part time. **Faculty:** 48 total (41 full time), 19 with doctorates or other terminal degrees. **Location:** Suburban campus in small city. **Calendar:** Semester, limited summer session. **Microcomputers:** 520 located in dormitories, libraries, classrooms, computer centers.

DEGREES OFFERED. AA, AS, BA, BS. 21 associate degrees awarded in 1992. 21% in business/office and marketing/distribution, 36% computer sciences, 31% allied health, 8% visual and performing arts. 95 bachelor's degrees awarded. 37% in business and management, 7% communications, 6% computer sciences, 14% teacher education, 12% health sciences, 5% philosophy, religion, theology, 5% physical sciences, 6% social sciences.

UNDERGRADUATE MAJORS. Associate: Allied health, business administration and management, engineering, information sciences and systems, legal assistant/paralegal, liberal/general studies, office supervision and management, studio art. **Bachelor's:** Accounting, art education, behavioral sciences, biology, business administration and management, business education, chemistry, clinical laboratory science, commercial art, elementary education, English, English education, history, information sciences and systems, journalism, management science, marketing management, mathematics, mathematics education, music, music education, music performance, nursing, office supervision and management, physical education, physician's assistant, physics, psychology, public relations, religion, religious education, religious music, science education, secondary education, social science education, social sciences, social work, Spanish, sports management, studio art, theological studies.

ACADEMIC PROGRAMS. 2-year transfer program, double major, dual enrollment of high school students, independent study, internships, student-designed major, study abroad, teacher preparation, cross-registration. **Remedial services:** Learning center, reduced course load, remedial instruction, special counselor, tutoring. **Placement/credit:** AP, CLEP General and Subject, institutional tests.

ACADEMIC REQUIREMENTS. Freshmen must earn minimum GPA of 2.0 to continue in good standing. 73% of freshmen return for sophomore year. **Graduation requirements:** 62 hours for associate (25 in major), 124 hours for bachelor's (42 in major). Most students required to take courses in arts/fine arts, computer science, English, history, mathematics, philosophy/religion, biological/physical sciences.

FRESHMAN ADMISSIONS. Selection criteria: 3 references, including 1 from pastor required. **High school preparation:** 18 units required. Required units include English 3, mathematics 1, social science 1 and science 1. 2 algebra, 1 geometry, trigonometry recommended for mathematics and science-related programs. Physics and chemistry recommended for nursing, biology, chemistry, physics, engineering, medical technology, premedicine, and predental programs. **Test requirements:** SAT or ACT (ACT preferred) for placement and counseling only; score report by August 10.

1992 FRESHMAN CLASS PROFILE. 106 men and women applied, 106 accepted; 48 men enrolled, 58 women enrolled. **Characteristics:** 90% live in college housing, 8% are foreign students. Average age is 19.

FALL-TERM APPLICATIONS. $10 fee, may be waived for applicants with need. Closing date July 15; applicants notified on a rolling basis beginning on or about January 1; must reply by August 1. Audition recommended for music applicants. Deferred and early admission available. Institutional early decision plan.

STUDENT LIFE. Housing: Dormitories (men, women); apartment housing available. **Activities:** Student government, magazine, student newspaper, yearbook, choral groups, concert band, drama, music ensembles, symphony orchestra, Collegiate Adventists for Better Living, Union for Christ, service organizations, Union for Kids. **Additional information:** Religious observance required.

ATHLETICS. Intercollegiate: Basketball. **Intramural:** Badminton, baseball, basketball, soccer, softball, tennis, volleyball.

STUDENT SERVICES. Aptitude testing, career counseling, employment service for undergraduates, freshman orientation, health services, on-campus day care, personal counseling, placement service for graduates, veterans counselor, services/facilities for handicapped.

ANNUAL EXPENSES. Tuition and fees (1992-93): $8,100. **Room and board:** $2,510. **Books and supplies:** $500.

FINANCIAL AID. 71% of freshmen, 79% of continuing students receive some form of aid. 55% of grants, 79% of loans, 85% of jobs based on need. Academic, music/drama, state/district residency, leadership, minority scholarships available. **Aid applications:** No closing date; applicants notified on a rolling basis beginning on or about January 1. **Additional information:** Special institutional grants offered to all freshmen and sophomores demonstrating exceptional financial need.

ADDRESS/TELEPHONE. Mrs. Leona Murray, Vice President for Enrollment Services, Union College, 3800 South 48th Street, Lincoln, NE 68506-4300. (402) 486-2504. (800) 228-4600. Fax: (402) 486-2895.

University of Nebraska Medical Center
Omaha, Nebraska CB code: 6896

3-year public university and health science college, coed. Founded in 1869. **Accreditation:** Regional. **Undergraduate enrollment:** 128 men, 686 women full time; 19 men, 265 women part time. **Graduate enrollment:** 840 men, 579 women full time; 56 men, 184 women part time. **Faculty:** 708 total (558 full time), 500 with doctorates or other terminal degrees. **Location:** Urban campus in large city. **Calendar:** Semester, limited summer session. **Microcomputers:** Located in libraries, classrooms, computer centers. **Additional facts:** Students admitted at sophomore level or higher.

DEGREES OFFERED. BS, MS, PhD, DMD, MD, B. Pharm. 380

bachelor's degrees awarded in 1992. 65% in health sciences, 35% allied health. Graduate degrees offered in 16 major fields of study.

UNDERGRADUATE MAJORS. Clinical laboratory science, dental hygiene, medical laboratory technologies, nuclear medical technology, nursing, physician's assistant, radiograph medical technology, ultrasound technology.

ACADEMIC PROGRAMS. Honors program. **Remedial services:** Tutoring. **Placement/credit:** AP, CLEP General and Subject, institutional tests; 24 credit hours maximum for bachelor's degree.

ACADEMIC REQUIREMENTS. Students must earn minimum GPA of 2.0 to continue in good academic standing. Students must declare major on application. **Graduation requirements:** 125 hours for bachelor's.

STUDENT LIFE. Activities: Student government, fraternities, Committee on Minority Concerns, American Academy of Physician Assistants, Religious Life Council, Christian Fellowship, Student Association for Rural Health, student services council, student professional organizations.

STUDENT SERVICES. Career counseling, employment service for undergraduates, health services, personal counseling, placement service for graduates, veterans counselor, services/facilities for handicapped.

ANNUAL EXPENSES. Tuition and fees (projected): $2,077, $3,339 additional for out-of-state students. **Books and supplies:** $450. **Other expenses:** $1,500.

FINANCIAL AID. 60% of continuing students receive some form of aid. 67% of grants, 81% of loans, all jobs based on need. Academic, state/district residency, minority scholarships available. **Aid applications:** No closing date; applicants notified on a rolling basis. **Additional information:** Parental data collected from applicants for certain types of aid.

ADDRESS/TELEPHONE. M. Jo Wagner, Associate Director of Academic Records, University of Nebraska Medical Center, 600 South 42nd Street, Omaha, NE 68198-4230. (402) 559-4206. (800) 626-8431. Fax: (402) 559-5844.

University of Nebraska—Kearney
Kearney, Nebraska — CB code: 6467

4-year public university, coed. Founded in 1903. **Accreditation:** Regional. **Undergraduate enrollment:** 2,756 men, 3,171 women full time; 487 men, 788 women part time. **Graduate enrollment:** 99 men, 132 women full time; 404 men, 942 women part time. **Faculty:** 409 total (296 full time), 179 with doctorates or other terminal degrees. **Location:** Rural campus in large town; 180 miles from Omaha. **Calendar:** Semester. **Microcomputers:** Located in dormitories, libraries, computer centers. **Special facilities:** Nebraska State Art Collection, state arboretum, planetarium.

DEGREES OFFERED. BA, BS, BFA, MA, MS, MBA, MEd. 1,008 bachelor's degrees awarded in 1992. 38% in business and management, 19% education, 6% parks/recreation, protective services, public affairs, 6% social sciences. Graduate degrees offered in 39 major fields of study.

UNDERGRADUATE MAJORS. Actuarial sciences, advertising, agribusiness, art education, art history, aviation computer technology, aviation management, biology, business administration and management, business and management, business and office, business education, business home economics, chemistry, clinical laboratory science, communications, computer and information sciences, crafts, criminal justice studies, dramatic arts, early childhood education, earth sciences, economics, education, education of the mentally handicapped, education of the multiple handicapped, education of the physically handicapped, elementary education, English, English education, fine arts, food science and nutrition, foreign languages education, French, geography, German, graphic design, health education, history, home economics, home economics education, human environment and housing, individual and family development, industrial arts education, information sciences and systems, international studies, journalism, junior high education, language interpretation and translation, law enforcement and corrections, mathematics, mathematics education, medical radiation dosimetry, music, music education, music performance, musical theater, office supervision and management, parks and recreation management, physical education, physical sciences, physics, political science and government, psychobiology, psychology, radio/television broadcasting, radiograph medical technology, respiratory therapy technology, science education, secondary education, social science education, social sciences, social work, sociology, Spanish, special education, specific learning disabilities, speech, speech correction, speech pathology/audiology, speech/communication/theater education, sports management, statistics, teaching English as a second language/foreign language, telecommunications, tourism, visual and performing arts.

ACADEMIC PROGRAMS. Accelerated program, double major, education specialist degree, honors program, independent study, internships, study abroad, teacher preparation, telecourses, visiting/exchange student program, cross-registration, International Student Exchange Program, exchange with Sapporo University (Japan). **Remedial services:** Learning center, tutoring. **ROTC:** Army. **Placement/credit:** AP, CLEP Subject, institutional tests.

ACADEMIC REQUIREMENTS. Freshmen must earn minimum GPA of 2.0 to continue in good standing. 56% of freshmen return for sophomore year. **Graduation requirements:** 125 hours for bachelor's (32 in major). Most students required to take courses in arts/fine arts, English, history, humanities, mathematics, biological/physical sciences, social sciences.

FRESHMAN ADMISSIONS. Selection criteria: Test scores, school achievement record most important. **High school preparation:** 10 units required. Required units include English 4, mathematics 2, social science 2 and science 2. 4 English units must include 1 unit from composition and 1 unit from speech or journalism. Elective courses recommended from foreign language, fine arts and/or humanities. **Test requirements:** SAT or ACT (ACT preferred); score report by August 1. **Additional information:** Applicants who show promise of academic success, but don't meet admissions requirements, may be admitted on conditional basis.

1992 FRESHMAN CLASS PROFILE. 2,761 men and women applied, 2,611 accepted; 660 men enrolled, 818 women enrolled. 58% had high school GPA of 3.0 or higher, 37% between 2.0 and 2.99. **Academic background:** Mid 50% of enrolled freshmen had ACT composite between 18-24. 86% submitted ACT scores. **Characteristics:** 93% from in state, 70% commute, 1% have minority backgrounds, 1% are foreign students. Average age is 19.

FALL-TERM APPLICATIONS. $10 fee. Closing date August 1; applicants notified on a rolling basis beginning on or about January 1. Early admission available.

STUDENT LIFE. Housing: Dormitories (men, women, coed); apartment, fraternity, sorority housing available. **Activities:** Student government, magazine, radio, student newspaper, television, yearbook, choral groups, concert band, dance, drama, jazz band, marching band, music ensembles, musical theater, pep band, symphony orchestra, fraternities, sororities, Young Republicans, Young Democrats, Alpha Phi Omega, Fellowship of Christian Athletes, International Student Association.

ATHLETICS. NCAA. **Intercollegiate:** Baseball M, basketball, cross-country, football M, golf M, softball W, swimming W, tennis, track and field, volleyball W, wrestling M. **Intramural:** Basketball, bowling, golf, softball, swimming, table tennis, tennis, track and field, volleyball, wrestling M.

STUDENT SERVICES. Aptitude testing, career counseling, employment service for undergraduates, freshman orientation, health services, personal counseling, placement service for graduates, veterans counselor, services/facilities for handicapped.

ANNUAL EXPENSES. Tuition and fees (1992-93): $1,721, $1,050 additional for out-of-state students. **Room and board:** $2,400. **Books and supplies:** $450. **Other expenses:** $1,200.

FINANCIAL AID. 76% of freshmen, 65% of continuing students receive some form of aid. 79% of grants, 93% of loans, 83% of jobs based on need. 876 enrolled freshmen were judged to have need, all were offered aid. Academic, music/drama, art, athletic, state/district residency, leadership scholarships available. **Aid applications:** No closing date; priority given to applications received by March 1; applicants notified on a rolling basis beginning on or about May 1; must reply within 3 weeks.

ADDRESS/TELEPHONE. Dr. Wayne Samuelson, Director of Admissions, University of Nebraska—Kearney, 905 West 25th, Kearney, NE 68849. (308) 234-8526. (800) 445-3434. Fax: (308) 234-8157.

University of Nebraska—Lincoln
Lincoln, Nebraska — CB code: 6877

Admissions: 96% of applicants accepted
Based on: ••• School record, test scores
Completion: 92% of freshmen end year in good standing
44% graduate

4-year public university, coed. Founded in 1869. **Accreditation:** Regional. **Undergraduate enrollment:** 9,102 men, 7,612 women full time; 1,580 men, 1,452 women part time. **Graduate enrollment:** 1,542 men, 1,022 women full time; 993 men, 1,270 women part time. **Faculty:** 1,516 total (1,261 full time), 1,038 with doctorates or other terminal degrees. **Location:** Urban campus in small city; 50 miles from Omaha. **Calendar:** Semester, extensive summer session. Extensive evening/early morning classes. **Microcomputers:** 500 located in dormitories, libraries, classrooms, computer centers, campus-wide network. **Special facilities:** Sheldon Memorial Art Gallery, state museum, planetarium, campus recreation facilities. Lied Center for performing arts, arboretum. Lentz Center for Asian Culture, Center for Great Plains Studies Art Collection.

DEGREES OFFERED. AS, BA, BS, BFA, BArch, MA, MS, MBA, MFA, MEd, PhD, EdD. 16 associate degrees awarded in 1992. 100% in engineering technologies. 2,965 bachelor's degrees awarded. 7% in agriculture, 18% business and management, 9% communications, 5% education, 13% teacher education, 10% engineering, 7% home economics, 5% life sciences, 5% psychology, 5% social sciences. Graduate degrees offered in 96 major fields of study.

UNDERGRADUATE MAJORS. Associate: Construction, drafting and design technology, electronic technology, fire protection, manufacturing technology. **Bachelor's:** Accounting, actuarial sciences, advertising, agribusiness, agricultural business and management, agricultural economics, agricultural education, agricultural engineering, agricultural journalism, agricultural mechanics, agricultural sciences, agronomy, animal sciences, anthropology,

anthropology education, architecture, art education, art history, athletic training, atmospheric sciences and meteorology, biochemistry, bioengineering and biomedical engineering, biology, biology education, business administration and management, business and management, business economics, business education, chemical engineering, chemistry, civil engineering, classics, communications, community health work, computer and information sciences, computer engineering, conservation and regulation, construction, construction management, dance, dentistry, drafting and design technology, dramatic arts, early childhood education, economics, education, education administration, education of the deaf and hearing impaired, education of the mentally handicapped, education of the multiple handicapped, education of the physically handicapped, electrical/electronics/communications engineering, electronic technology, elementary education, engineering mechanics, English, English education, environmental science, family/consumer resource management, finance, fine arts, fishing and fisheries, food science and nutrition, food sciences, foreign languages (multiple emphasis), foreign languages education, French, geography, geology, German, Great Plains studies, Greek (classical), Greek (modern), health education, health, physical education and recreation, history, history education, horticulture, individual and family development, industrial arts education, industrial engineering, industrial technology, interdisciplinary engineering, international business management, international relations, international studies, journalism, junior high education, language arts education, Latin, Latin American studies, law, liberal/general studies, life science, management science, manufacturing technology, marketing and distributive education, marketing management, mathematics, mathematics education, mechanical engineering, medicine, music, music education, musical theater, office supervision and management, pharmacy, philosophy, physical education, physical sciences, physics, plant protection, political science and government, prelaw, psychology, radio/television broadcasting, range management, reading education, recreation and community services technologies, renewable natural resources, Russian, science education, secondary education, social science education, social studies education, sociology, soil sciences, Spanish, special education, speech, speech correction, speech pathology/audiology, speech/communication/theater education, teaching English as a second language/foreign language, technical education, textiles and clothing, trade and industrial education, university studies, veterinary science, visual and performing arts, Western European studies, wildlife management, women's studies.

ACADEMIC PROGRAMS. Accelerated program, cooperative education, double major, dual enrollment of high school students, education specialist degree, honors program, independent study, internships, student-designed major, study abroad, teacher preparation, telecourses, visiting/exchange student program, cross-registration, tuition reciprocity agreement for selected programs with University of Missouri-Columbia, Kansas State University and University of South Dakota; combined bachelor's/graduate program in law. **Remedial services:** Learning center, reduced course load, remedial instruction, special counselor, tutoring, Accent on Developing Abstract Processes program. **ROTC:** Air Force, Army, Naval. **Placement/credit:** AP, CLEP General and Subject, institutional tests.

ACADEMIC REQUIREMENTS. Freshmen must earn minimum GPA of 2.0 to continue in good standing. 74% of freshmen return for sophomore year. Students must declare major by end of second year. **Graduation requirements:** 128 hours for bachelor's (30 in major). Most students required to take courses in English, biological/physical sciences, social sciences. **Additional information:** General liberal education courses being integrated into curriculum.

FRESHMAN ADMISSIONS. Selection criteria: College preparatory program or rank in top half of class or ACT composite score of 20 required. Some programs require higher test scores and no core deficiencies. **High school preparation:** 16 units recommended. Recommended units include English 4, foreign language 2, mathematics 2, social science 2 and science 2. English must include 1 composition. Mathematics must include 1 algebra. Individual colleges have specific requirements. College preparatory program not required, but highly recommended, for applicants who meet test score or class rank criteria. **Test requirements:** SAT or ACT (ACT preferred); score report by July 25.

1992 FRESHMAN CLASS PROFILE. 6,353 men and women applied, 6,106 accepted; 1,791 men enrolled, 1,689 women enrolled. 16% were in top tenth and 45% were in top quarter of graduating class. **Academic background:** Mid 50% of enrolled freshmen had ACT composite between 18-26. 97% submitted ACT scores. **Characteristics:** 90% from in state, 56% live in college housing, 6% have minority backgrounds, 2% are foreign students, 18% join fraternities/sororities. Average age is 19.

FALL-TERM APPLICATIONS. $10 fee, may be waived for applicants with need. $25 fee for out-of-state aplicants. Closing date August 1; applicants notified on a rolling basis beginning on or about October 1. Audition required for music applicants. Deferred admission available.

STUDENT LIFE. Housing: Dormitories (men, women, coed); apartment, fraternity, sorority, cooperative housing available. Special floors for students sharing specific interests available. **Activities:** Student government, film, magazine, radio, student newspaper, television, choral groups, concert band, dance, drama, jazz band, marching band, music ensembles, musical theater, opera, pep band, symphony orchestra, fraternities, sororities, Afrikan People's Union, University of Nebraska Inter-Tribal Exchange, Mexican-American Student Association, Adult Student Network, Ecology Now, Student Foundation, Student Alumni Association, UNL Entrepreneurial Society. **Additional information:** Active Greek life system on campus defines social life of many students. Increasing multi-ethnic and multi-cultural opportunities also available.

ATHLETICS. NCAA. **Intercollegiate:** Baseball M, basketball, cross-country, diving, football M, golf, gymnastics, softball W, swimming, tennis, track and field, volleyball W, wrestling M. **Intramural:** Archery, badminton, basketball, bowling, cross-country, golf, racquetball, rifle, soccer, softball, squash, swimming, table tennis, tennis, track and field, volleyball, water polo, wrestling.

STUDENT SERVICES. Aptitude testing, career counseling, employment service for undergraduates, freshman orientation, health services, on-campus day care, personal counseling, placement service for graduates, special adviser for adult students, veterans counselor, Campus recreation facilities, services/facilities for handicapped.

ANNUAL EXPENSES. Tuition and fees (1992-93): $2,188, $3,180 additional for out-of-state students. **Room and board:** $2,980. **Books and supplies:** $450. **Other expenses:** $1,940.

FINANCIAL AID. 48% of freshmen, 66% of continuing students receive some form of aid. 56% of grants, 92% of loans, 28% of jobs based on need. Academic, music/drama, athletic, state/district residency, leadership, minority scholarships available. **Aid applications:** No closing date; priority given to applications received by March 1; applicants notified on a rolling basis beginning on or about May 15; must reply within 3 weeks.

ADDRESS/TELEPHONE. John Beacon, Director of Admissions, University of Nebraska—Lincoln, Room 106 Administration Bldg, Lincoln, NE 68588-0417. (402) 472-2023. (800) 742-8800. Fax: (402) 472-8189.

University of Nebraska—Omaha
Omaha, Nebraska

CB code: 6420

4-year public university, coed. Founded in 1908. **Accreditation:** Regional. **Undergraduate enrollment:** 3,976 men, 3,922 women full time; 2,560 men, 3,077 women part time. **Graduate enrollment:** 189 men, 308 women full time; 795 men, 1,400 women part time. **Faculty:** 820 total (420 full time), 480 with doctorates or other terminal degrees. **Location:** Urban campus in large city; 550 miles from Denver, Colorado; 500 miles from Chicago, Illinois. **Calendar:** Semester, extensive summer session. Extensive evening/early morning classes. **Microcomputers:** 371 located in classrooms, computer centers. **Special facilities:** Planetarium, outdoor venture center.

DEGREES OFFERED. AS, BA, BS, BFA, MA, MS, MBA, MFA, MEd, MSW. 1,363 bachelor's degrees awarded. Graduate degrees offered in 39 major fields of study.

UNDERGRADUATE MAJORS. Associate: Construction, drafting and design technology, electronic technology, fire control and safety technology, fire protection, manufacturing technology, parks and recreation management. **Bachelor's:** Accounting, Afro-American (black) studies, applied mathematics, art history, aviation management, biological and physical sciences, biology, business administration and management, business and management, business economics, business education, chemistry, civil engineering, communications, computer and information sciences, construction, creative writing, criminal justice studies, drafting and design technology, dramatic arts, early childhood education, economics, education of the deaf and hearing impaired, education of the mentally handicapped, electronic technology, elementary education, English, English education, family/consumer resource management, fashion merchandising, finance, food science and nutrition, foreign languages education, French, geography, geology, German, health education, history, home economics, home economics education, hotel/motel and restaurant management, human resources development, humanities and social sciences, individual and family development, industrial technology, information sciences and systems, institutional/home management/supporting programs, insurance and risk management, interior design, international relations, journalism, junior high education, labor/industrial relations, liberal/general studies, library science, management information systems, management science, manufacturing technology, marketing management, marketing research, mathematics, mathematics education, music, music education, music performance, organizational behavior, personnel management, philosophy, physical education, physical sciences, physics, political science and government, prelaw, psychology, public relations, radio/television broadcasting, real estate, recreation and community services technologies, religion, science education, secondary education, social science education, social work, sociology, Spanish, speech, speech correction, speech/communication/theater education, studio art, systems analysis, textiles and clothing, trade and industrial education, urban studies.

ACADEMIC PROGRAMS. 2-year transfer program, accelerated program, cooperative education, double major, dual enrollment of high school students, education specialist degree, honors program, independent study, internships, student-designed major, study abroad, teacher preparation, visiting/exchange student program, cross-registration, doctoral degree course in psychology from University of Nebraska-Lincoln given at Omaha campus. **Remedial services:** Learning center, reduced course load, special counselor, tutoring. **ROTC:** Air Force, Army. **Placement/credit:** AP, CLEP General and Subject, institutional tests; 30 credit hours maximum for bachelor's degree.

ACADEMIC REQUIREMENTS. Freshmen must earn minimum GPA of 2.0 to continue in good standing. Students must declare major by end of first year. **Graduation requirements:** 125 hours for bachelor's (30 in major). Most students required to take courses in English, humanities, mathematics, biological/physical sciences, social sciences.

FRESHMAN ADMISSIONS. Selection criteria: School achievement record and test scores important. **High school preparation:** 16 units required. Required units include English 4, mathematics 2, social science 2 and science 2. Specific course requirements for programs in business administration and home economics, and for College of Engineering and Technology. **Test requirements:** SAT or ACT (ACT preferred); score report by August 1.

1992 FRESHMAN CLASS PROFILE. 2,808 men and women applied, 2,598 accepted; 1,740 enrolled. **Academic background:** Mid 50% of enrolled freshmen had ACT composite between 17-22. 98% submitted ACT scores. **Characteristics:** 96% from in state, 100% commute, 12% have minority backgrounds, 1% are foreign students, 4% join fraternities/sororities.

FALL-TERM APPLICATIONS. $10 fee. $25 fee for out-of-state applicants. Closing date August 1; applicants notified on a rolling basis. Audition required for music applicants. Deferred and early admission available.

STUDENT LIFE. Activities: Student government, film, magazine, radio, student newspaper, television, choral groups, concert band, dance, drama, jazz band, marching band, music ensembles, musical theater, opera, pep band, symphony orchestra, fraternities, sororities, College republicans, UNO Democrats, Students for Choice, Students for Life, American multi-cultural students, international student services, Catholic campus ministry, chapter summary Bible Study, Lutherans in Fellowship Together, Latter Day Saints Student Association.

ATHLETICS. NCAA. **Intercollegiate:** Baseball M, basketball, cross-country W, football M, softball W, volleyball W, wrestling M. **Intramural:** Badminton, basketball, bowling, golf, gymnastics, handball, racquetball, soccer, softball, squash, swimming, tennis, volleyball, wrestling M.

STUDENT SERVICES. Aptitude testing, career counseling, employment service for undergraduates, freshman orientation, health services, on-campus day care, personal counseling, placement service for graduates, special adviser for adult students, women's, minority, veterans, and foreign students programs, services/facilities for handicapped.

ANNUAL EXPENSES. Tuition and fees (1992-93): $1,805, $2,873 additional for out-of-state students. **Books and supplies:** $600. **Other expenses:** $650.

FINANCIAL AID. 55% of freshmen, 45% of continuing students receive some form of aid. 91% of grants, 84% of loans, 41% of jobs based on need. 850 enrolled freshmen were judged to have need, 750 were offered aid. Academic, music/drama, art, athletic, state/district residency, leadership, alumni affiliation, minority scholarships available. **Aid applications:** No closing date; priority given to applications received by March 1; applicants notified on a rolling basis beginning on or about April 1; must reply within 2 weeks.

ADDRESS/TELEPHONE. John Flemming, Director of Admissions, University of Nebraska—Omaha, 60th and Dodge Streets, Omaha, NE 68182-0005. (402) 554-2393. Fax: (402) 554-2244.

Wayne State College
Wayne, Nebraska — CB code: 6469

4-year public liberal arts, teachers college, coed. Founded in 1909. **Accreditation:** Regional. **Undergraduate enrollment:** 1,173 men, 1,446 women full time; 144 men, 255 women part time. **Graduate enrollment:** 25 men, 24 women full time; 211 men, 493 women part time. **Faculty:** 209 total (116 full time), 70 with doctorates or other terminal degrees. **Location:** Rural campus in small town; 45 miles from Sioux City, Iowa. **Calendar:** Semester, extensive summer session. Extensive evening/early morning classes. **Microcomputers:** 200 located in libraries, classrooms, computer centers, campus-wide network. **Special facilities:** Planetarium, outdoor amphitheater. **Additional facts:** Campus is state arboretum.

DEGREES OFFERED. BA, BS, BFA, MBA, MEd. 375 bachelor's degrees awarded in 1992. 24% in business and management, 31% teacher education, 5% parks/recreation, protective services, public affairs, 10% psychology, 11% social sciences. Graduate degrees offered in 12 major fields of study.

UNDERGRADUATE MAJORS. Art education, biology, business administration and management, business education, chemistry, commercial art, communications, computer and information sciences, criminal justice studies, dramatic arts, economics, elementary education, English, English education, fashion merchandising, fine arts, foreign languages education, French, funeral services/mortuary science, geography, geology, German, health education, health sciences, history, home economics, home economics education, industrial arts education, industrial technology, interior design, international studies, mathematics, mathematics education, medical laboratory technologies, mental health/human services, music education, music performance, music theory and composition, physical education, political science and government, prelaw, psychology, public administration, recreation and community services technologies, science education, social science education, social sciences, sociology, Spanish, special education, speech, speech/communication/theater education, trade and industrial education, trade and industrial supervision and management.

ACADEMIC PROGRAMS. Accelerated program, cooperative education, double major, dual enrollment of high school students, education specialist degree, external degree, honors program, independent study, internships, student-designed major, study abroad, teacher preparation. **Remedial services:** Learning center, reduced course load, special counselor, tutoring. **Placement/credit:** AP, CLEP General and Subject, institutional tests.

ACADEMIC REQUIREMENTS. Freshmen must earn minimum GPA of 2.0 to continue in good standing. 64% of freshmen return for sophomore year. Students must declare major by end of second year. **Graduation requirements:** 125 hours for bachelor's (40 in major). Most students required to take courses in arts/fine arts, computer science, English, history, mathematics, philosophy/religion, biological/physical sciences, social sciences.

FRESHMAN ADMISSIONS. Selection criteria: Open admissions. Selective admissions for out-of-state applicants and student athletes based on test scores and high school record. **High school preparation:** 18 units recommended. Recommended units include English 4, foreign language 3, mathematics 3, social science 3 and science 3. 2 electives recommended. **Test requirements:** SAT or ACT (ACT preferred) for placement and counseling only; score report by September 1.

1992 FRESHMAN CLASS PROFILE. 288 men, 358 women enrolled. 11% were in top tenth and 29% were in top quarter of graduating class. **Academic background:** Mid 50% of enrolled freshmen had ACT composite between 18-23. 90% submitted ACT scores. **Characteristics:** 76% from in state, 89% live in college housing, 4% have minority backgrounds. Average age is 18.

FALL-TERM APPLICATIONS. $10 fee. No closing date; applicants notified on a rolling basis. Interview recommended. Deferred and early admission available.

STUDENT LIFE. Housing: Dormitories (coed); apartment, fraternity, sorority housing available. **Activities:** Student government, film, radio, student newspaper, television, choral groups, concert band, drama, jazz band, marching band, music ensembles, musical theater, pep band, symphony orchestra, fraternities, sororities, religious and political organizations.

ATHLETICS. NAIA, NCAA. **Intercollegiate:** Baseball M, basketball, cross-country, football M, golf, softball W, track and field, volleyball W. **Intramural:** Archery, badminton, basketball, bowling, cross-country, diving, golf, gymnastics, handball, racquetball, soccer, softball, swimming, table tennis, tennis, track and field, volleyball, water polo, wrestling M.

STUDENT SERVICES. Career counseling, freshman orientation, health services, personal counseling, placement service for graduates, veterans counselor, services/facilities for handicapped.

ANNUAL EXPENSES. Tuition and fees (1992-93): $1,557, $1,095 additional for out-of-state students. Projected room and board $2590 **Books and supplies:** $600. **Other expenses:** $2,500.

FINANCIAL AID. 70% of freshmen, 70% of continuing students receive some form of aid. 56% of grants, all loans, 50% of jobs based on need. 500 enrolled freshmen were judged to have need, all were offered aid. Academic, music/drama, art, athletic, state/district residency, leadership scholarships available. **Aid applications:** No closing date; priority given to applications received by May 1; applicants notified on a rolling basis beginning on or about June 1; must reply within 3 weeks.

ADDRESS/TELEPHONE. Robert Zetocha, Director of Admissions, Wayne State College, 200 East Tenth Street, Wayne, NE 68787. (402) 375-7234. (800) 228-9972.

Western Nebraska Community College: Scottsbluff Campus
Scottsbluff, Nebraska — CB code: 6648

2-year public community college, coed. Founded in 1926. **Accreditation:** Regional. **Undergraduate enrollment:** 327 men, 475 women full time; 540 men, 906 women part time. **Faculty:** 69 total (68 full time), 4 with doctorates or other terminal degrees. **Location:** Rural campus in large town; 100 miles from Cheyenne, Wyoming, 200 miles from Denver, Colorado. **Calendar:** Semester, limited summer session. Saturday and extensive evening/early morning classes. **Microcomputers:** 90 located in libraries, classrooms, computer centers. **Additional facts:** Additional campus at Sidney.

DEGREES OFFERED. AA, AS, AAS. 126 associate degrees awarded in 1992. 12% in agriculture, 23% business and management, 8% business/office and marketing/distribution, 14% education, 5% health sciences, 5% allied health, 5% multi/interdisciplinary studies, 14% trade and industry.

UNDERGRADUATE MAJORS. Accounting, agribusiness, agricultural sciences, automotive mechanics, automotive technology, biological and physical sciences, biology, business and management, business and office, business computer/console/peripheral equipment operation, business data entry equipment operation, business data processing and related programs, business data programming, chemistry, computer and information sciences, data processing, early childhood education, education, elementary education, engineering, English, French, German, health sciences, journalism, liberal/general studies, marketing management, mathematics, mental health/human services, music, physical sciences, practical nursing, precision metal work, prelaw, psychology, radiograph medical technology, real estate, secondary education, secretarial and related programs, social sciences, Spanish, video, visual and performing arts, welding technology, wildlife management.

ACADEMIC PROGRAMS. 2-year transfer program, computer delivered (on-line) credit-bearing course offerings, cooperative education, double major, dual enrollment of high school students, independent study, internships, student-designed major, telecourses, cross-registration, 1-1 RN nursing program with Region West Medical Center. **Remedial services:** Learning center, preadmission summer program, reduced course load, remedial instruction, special counselor, tutoring. **Placement/credit:** AP, CLEP General and Subject, institutional tests; 12 credit hours maximum for associate degree.

ACADEMIC REQUIREMENTS. Freshmen must earn minimum GPA of 1.5 to continue in good standing. 45% of freshmen return for sophomore year. Students must declare major by end of first year. **Graduation requirements:** 60 hours for associate (30 in major). Most students required to take courses in English, mathematics, biological/physical sciences, social sciences.

FRESHMAN ADMISSIONS. Selection criteria: Open admissions. Selective admissions to practical nursing and radiologic technologies programs. **Test requirements:** SAT or ACT (ACT preferred) for placement and counseling only; score report by August 15. **Additional information:** ACT/ASSET test required of all applicants for placement.

1992 FRESHMAN CLASS PROFILE. 270 men applied, 270 accepted, 248 enrolled; 236 women applied, 236 accepted, 193 enrolled. **Academic background:** Mid 50% of enrolled freshmen had ACT composite between 17-22. 55% submitted ACT scores. **Characteristics:** 95% from in state, 90% commute, 9% have minority backgrounds. Average age is 26.

FALL-TERM APPLICATIONS. No fee. No closing date; applicants notified on a rolling basis beginning on or about May 15. Interview required for radiologic technologies, practical nursing applicants. Deferred and early admission available.

STUDENT LIFE. Housing: Dormitories (coed). **Activities:** Student government, student newspaper, choral groups, drama, jazz band, music ensembles, musical theater, pep band.

ATHLETICS. NJCAA. **Intercollegiate:** Basketball, golf, volleyball W. **Intramural:** Basketball, handball M, racquetball, softball, tennis, volleyball.

STUDENT SERVICES. Aptitude testing, career counseling, employment service for undergraduates, freshman orientation, on-campus day care, personal counseling, placement service for graduates, special adviser for adult students, veterans counselor, services/facilities for handicapped.

ANNUAL EXPENSES. Tuition and fees: $1,110, $60 additional for out-of-state students. **Room and board:** $2,330. **Books and supplies:** $480. **Other expenses:** $660.

FINANCIAL AID. 75% of freshmen, 75% of continuing students receive some form of aid. 91% of loans, 87% of jobs based on need. 295 enrolled freshmen were judged to have need, all were offered aid. Academic, music/drama, art, athletic, leadership, minority scholarships available. **Aid applications:** No closing date; priority given to applications received by April 1; applicants notified on a rolling basis beginning on or about May 1; must reply within 2 weeks.

ADDRESS/TELEPHONE. Roger Hovey, Enrollment Director, Western Nebraska Community College: Scottsbluff Campus, 1601 East 27 St, Scottsbluff, NE 69361. (308) 635-3606. Fax: (308) 635-6100.

Western Nebraska Community College: Sidney Campus
Sidney, Nebraska — CB code: 6957

2-year public community, junior, technical college, coed. **Accreditation:** Regional. **Undergraduate enrollment:** 596 men and women. **Location:** Rural campus in small town; 90 miles east of Cheyenne, Wyoming. **Calendar:** Semester.

FRESHMAN ADMISSIONS. Selection criteria: Open admissions. Selective admissions to practical nursing, radiologic technologies, and cosmetology programs.

ANNUAL EXPENSES. Tuition and fees (1992-93): $1,065, $30 additional for out-of-state students. **Room and board:** $2,180. **Books and supplies:** $480. **Other expenses:** $660.

ADDRESS/TELEPHONE. John Marrin, Assistant Dean of Student Services, Western Nebraska Community College: Sidney Campus, RR 1 Box 300, Sidney, NE 69162. (308) 254-5450. (800) 221-9682. Fax: (308) 254-5033.

York College
York, Nebraska — CB code: 6984

2-year private Bible, liberal arts college, coed, affiliated with Church of Christ. Founded in 1956. **Accreditation:** Regional. **Undergraduate enrollment:** 189 men, 182 women full time; 15 men, 24 women part time. **Faculty:** 30 total (15 full time), 9 with doctorates or other terminal degrees. **Location:** Rural campus in small town; 50 miles from Lincoln. **Calendar:** Semester, limited summer session. **Microcomputers:** 16 located in classrooms, computer centers.

DEGREES OFFERED. AA, AS, AAS. 68 associate degrees awarded in 1992.

UNDERGRADUATE MAJORS. Allied health, American literature, anatomy, Bible studies, biblical languages, biological and physical sciences, biology, biometrics and biostatistics, business data programming, chemistry, drawing, earth sciences, economics, English, English literature, fine arts, geochemistry, geological engineering, health sciences, history, home economics, home economics education, humanities, humanities and social sciences, information sciences and systems, investments and securities, liberal/general studies, marine biology, mathematics, microbiology, music, music history and appreciation, music performance, music theory and composition, optometry, organic chemistry, painting, physical sciences, physics, political science and government, psychology, recreation and community services technologies, secretarial and related programs, social sciences, sociology, solar heating and cooling technology, Spanish, special education, telecommunications, theological studies.

ACADEMIC PROGRAMS. 2-year transfer program, dual enrollment of high school students, honors program, independent study, internships, study abroad. **Remedial services:** Learning center, reduced course load, remedial instruction, tutoring, study skills classes. **Placement/credit:** AP, CLEP General and Subject, institutional tests; 12 credit hours maximum for associate degree.

ACADEMIC REQUIREMENTS. Freshmen must earn minimum GPA of 1.75 to continue in good standing. 76% of freshmen return for sophomore year. **Graduation requirements:** 64 hours for associate. Most students required to take courses in arts/fine arts, English, history, humanities, mathematics, philosophy/religion, biological/physical sciences, social sciences. **Additional information:** Four year degrees in Bible, business, and education.

FRESHMAN ADMISSIONS. Selection criteria: Test scores, school achievement and recommendations most important. **High school preparation:** 15 units required. Required units include English 3. **Test requirements:** ACT; score report by August 29.

1992 FRESHMAN CLASS PROFILE. 107 men, 100 women enrolled. **Academic background:** Mid 50% of enrolled freshmen had ACT composite between 16-23. 90% submitted ACT scores. **Characteristics:** 35% from in state, 86% live in college housing, 6% have minority backgrounds, 2% are foreign students. Average age is 19.

FALL-TERM APPLICATIONS. $25 fee, may be waived for applicants with need. No closing date; priority given to applications received by July 15; applicants notified on a rolling basis. Essay recommended. Deferred and early admission available.

STUDENT LIFE. Housing: Dormitories (men, women); apartment housing available. **Activities:** Student government, student newspaper, yearbook, choral groups, drama, music ensembles, musical theater, pep band, service clubs.

ATHLETICS. NJCAA, NSCAA. **Intercollegiate:** Baseball M, basketball, soccer, softball W, tennis, volleyball W. **Intramural:** Basketball, bowling, cross-country, football M, golf, soccer M, softball, swimming, table tennis, track and field, volleyball.

STUDENT SERVICES. Aptitude testing, career counseling, employment service for undergraduates, freshman orientation, on-campus day care, personal counseling, special adviser for adult students.

ANNUAL EXPENSES. Tuition and fees: $4,760. **Room and board:** $2,850. **Books and supplies:** $600. **Other expenses:** $1,600.

FINANCIAL AID. 91% of freshmen, 97% of continuing students receive some form of aid. 52% of grants, 88% of loans, 86% of jobs based on need. 117 enrolled freshmen were judged to have need, all were offered aid. Academic, music/drama, art, athletic, state/district residency, leadership, alumni affiliation scholarships available. **Aid applications:** No closing date; priority given to applications received by July 15; applicants notified on a rolling basis beginning on or about March 1; must reply within 2 weeks.

ADDRESS/TELEPHONE. Steddon Sikes, Director of Admissions, York College, York, NE 68467-2699. (402) 362-4441 ext. 222. Fax: (402) 362-6841.

Nevada

Community College of Southern Nevada
North Las Vegas, Nevada CB code: 4136

2-year public community college, coed. Founded in 1971. **Accreditation:** Regional. **Undergraduate enrollment:** 17,747 men and women. **Location:** Urban campus in small city; 6 miles from Las Vegas. **Calendar:** Semester. **Additional facts:** College serves Southern Nevada. Branch campus at Henderson. Health Science Center in West Las Vegas.

FRESHMAN ADMISSIONS. Selection criteria: Open admissions. Selective admissions for some programs (nursing, dental hygiene) based on courses taken and GPA.

ANNUAL EXPENSES. Tuition and fees: $882, $3,000 additional for out-of-state students. **Books and supplies:** $600. **Other expenses:** $1,665.

ADDRESS/TELEPHONE. Arlie J. Stops, Director of Admissions and Records, Community College of Southern Nevada, 3200 East Cheyenne Avenue, North Las Vegas, NV 89030. (702) 643-0830. Fax: (702) 643-6427.

Deep Springs College
Dyer, Nevada CB code: 4281

Admissions:	7% of applicants accepted
Based on:	••• Essay, interview, school record
	•• Activities, recommendations
	• Special talents, test scores
Completion:	100% of freshmen end year in good standing
	100% enter 4-year programs

2-year private liberal arts college, men only. Founded in 1917. **Accreditation:** Regional. **Undergraduate enrollment:** 25 men full time. **Faculty:** 5 total, 4 with doctorates or other terminal degrees. **Location:** Rural campus in rural community; 45 miles from Bishop, California. **Calendar:** 6 terms of 7 weeks each. **Microcomputers:** Located in dormitories, computer centers. **Special facilities:** Student-operated cattle-and-alfalfa ranch, dairy, dining hall, bookstore, and library. **Additional facts:** Rigorous liberal arts seminars, laboratory and field studies, community governance, and responsibility for a 2600 acre alfalfa farm and cattle ranch. Curriculum is intended to prepare students for lives and careers in public service.

DEGREES OFFERED. AA. 100% in multi/interdisciplinary studies.

UNDERGRADUATE MAJORS. Liberal/general studies.

ACADEMIC PROGRAMS. 2-year transfer program, independent study.

ACADEMIC REQUIREMENTS. Freshmen must earn minimum GPA of 2.0 to continue in good standing. Student's over-all performance evaluated by student-faculty reinvitation committee. 90% of freshmen return for sophomore year. **Graduation requirements:** 60 hours for associate. Most students required to take courses in English, humanities. **Additional information:** Small classes, some tutorials. Flexible curriculum includes English composition and literature, language study, mathematics, physics and chemistry, geology, biology, philosophy, political science, fine arts.

FRESHMAN ADMISSIONS. Selection criteria: School achievement record, interview, and essay most important. Community activities and recommendations also considered. Must have completed at least junior year of high school. **Test requirements:** SAT or ACT (SAT preferred); score report by January 15. **Additional information:** Student body plays active role in admission decisions.

1992 FRESHMAN CLASS PROFILE. 178 men applied, 13 accepted, 13 enrolled. 100% had high school GPA of 3.0 or higher. **Academic background:** Mid 50% of enrolled freshmen had SAT-V between 640-730, SAT-M between 640-760; ACT composite between 28-30. 100% submitted SAT scores, 20% submitted ACT scores. **Characteristics:** 100% live in college housing. Average age is 19.

FALL-TERM APPLICATIONS. Closing date November 15; applicants notified on or about April 15; must reply by May 1. Interview required. Essay required. CRDA. Early admission available.

STUDENT LIFE. Housing: Dormitories (men). All students required to live in dormitory. **Activities:** Student government, magazine, newsletter, photography, choral groups, drama, music ensembles, talent show. **Additional information:** All students required to work at least 20 hours per week on jobs related to operation of college and ranch. Student committees organize all community events. Alcohol and drugs forbidden. Students may not leave campus during term.

ATHLETICS. Intramural: Archery, cross-country, football, horseback riding, skiing, swimming, table tennis, track and field, volleyball.

STUDENT SERVICES. Career counseling, freshman orientation, health services, personal counseling.

ANNUAL EXPENSES. Tuition and fees: All students receive full scholarship to cover all costs of tuition and fees, room and board. **Other expenses:** $350.

ADDRESS/TELEPHONE. Sherwin W. Howard, President, Deep Springs College, HC 72, Box 45001, Dyer, NV 89010-9803. (619) 872-2000.

Northern Nevada Community College
Elko, Nevada CB code: 4293

2-year public community college, coed. Founded in 1967. **Accreditation:** Regional. **Undergraduate enrollment:** 153 men, 178 women full time; 1,018 men, 1,583 women part time. **Faculty:** 228 total (28 full time). **Location:** Rural campus in large town; 280 miles from Reno, 220 miles from Salt Lake City, Utah. **Calendar:** Semester, limited summer session. **Microcomputers:** 30 located in computer centers.

DEGREES OFFERED. AA, AS, AAS. 50 associate degrees awarded in 1992. 11% in business and management, 7% teacher education, 28% health sciences, 50% multi/interdisciplinary studies.

UNDERGRADUATE MAJORS. Automotive mechanics, automotive technology, business administration and management, business and office, business data entry equipment operation, business data processing and related programs, business data programming, computer and information sciences, criminal justice studies, data processing, diesel engine mechanics, early childhood education, law enforcement and corrections technologies, liberal/general studies, marketing and distribution, mining and petroleum technologies, nursing, precision metal work, protective services, secretarial and related programs, teacher aide.

ACADEMIC PROGRAMS. 2-year transfer program, cooperative education, dual enrollment of high school students, independent study. **Remedial services:** Learning center, reduced course load, remedial instruction, special counselor, tutoring. **Placement/credit:** CLEP General and Subject, institutional tests; 30 credit hours maximum for associate degree.

ACADEMIC REQUIREMENTS. No policy requiring minimum GPA; records of students having academic difficulty are reviewed individually. Students must declare major on application. **Graduation requirements:** 60 hours for associate (24 in major). Most students required to take courses in English, history, humanities, mathematics, biological/physical sciences, social sciences.

FRESHMAN ADMISSIONS. Selection criteria: Open admissions. Selective admissions to certain programs.

1992 FRESHMAN CLASS PROFILE. 442 men, 927 women enrolled. **Characteristics:** 95% from in state, 100% commute, 8% have minority backgrounds. Average age is 21.

FALL-TERM APPLICATIONS. $5 fee. No closing date; applicants notified on a rolling basis. Early admission available.

STUDENT LIFE. Activities: Student government, student newspaper, choral groups, drama, vocational clubs, nursing club.

ATHLETICS. Intramural: Basketball, skiing, tennis, volleyball.

STUDENT SERVICES. Aptitude testing, career counseling, employment service for undergraduates, freshman orientation, personal counseling, placement service for graduates, special adviser for adult students, veterans counselor, services/facilities for handicapped.

ANNUAL EXPENSES. Tuition and fees (1992-93): $840, $3,000 additional for out-of-state students. **Books and supplies:** $500. **Other expenses:** $1,195.

FINANCIAL AID. 20% of freshmen, 15% of continuing students receive some form of aid. 57% of grants, 97% of loans, 16% of jobs based on need. Academic, state/district residency, leadership scholarships available. **Aid applications:** No closing date; priority given to applications received by April 1; applicants notified on a rolling basis; must reply within 10 days.

ADDRESS/TELEPHONE. Stan Aiazzi, Dean of Student Services, Northern Nevada Community College, 901 Elm Street, Elko, NV 89801. (702) 738-8493. (800) 343-2724. Fax: (702) 738-8771.

Sierra Nevada College
Incline Village, Nevada CB code: 4757

4-year private business, liberal arts college, coed. Founded in 1969. **Accreditation:** Regional. **Undergraduate enrollment:** 150 men, 90 women full time; 150 men, 150 women part time. **Faculty:** 38 total (8 full time), 11 with doctorates or other terminal degrees. **Location:** Rural campus in small town; 35 miles from Reno. **Calendar:** Semester, limited summer session. **Microcomputers:** 30 located in libraries, classrooms, computer centers. **Special facilities:** Observatory, art gallery. **Additional facts:** On north shore of Lake Tahoe.

DEGREES OFFERED. BA, BS, BFA. 80 bachelor's degrees awarded in 1992. 75% in business and management, 7% letters/literature, 6% life sciences, 8% multi/interdisciplinary studies.

UNDERGRADUATE MAJORS. Business administration and management, English, English literature, environmental science, fine arts, hospitality and recreation marketing, hotel/motel and restaurant management, humanities, humanities and social sciences, liberal/general studies, music, predentistry, premedicine, preveterinary, ski business management, small business management and ownership.

ACADEMIC PROGRAMS. Double major, independent study, internships, student-designed major, teacher preparation. **Remedial services:** Pre-admission summer program, remedial instruction, special counselor, tutoring. **ROTC:** Army. **Placement/credit:** AP, CLEP General and Subject; 30 credit hours maximum for bachelor's degree.

ACADEMIC REQUIREMENTS. Freshmen must earn minimum GPA of 2.5 to continue in good standing. 75% of freshmen return for sophomore year. Students must declare major by end of second year. **Graduation requirements:** 120 hours for bachelor's (40 in major). Most students required to take courses in arts/fine arts, computer science, English, history, humanities, mathematics, philosophy/religion, biological/physical sciences, social sciences.

FRESHMAN ADMISSIONS. Selection criteria: Motivation as evidenced in personal interview and/or autobiographical statement very important. Few applicants refused on basis of academic performance. College-preparatory courses recommended. **Test requirements:** SAT or ACT; score report by August 15.

1992 FRESHMAN CLASS PROFILE. 55 men, 35 women enrolled. **Characteristics:** 15% from in state, 35% live in college housing, 2% have minority backgrounds, 4% are foreign students. Average age is 19.

FALL-TERM APPLICATIONS. $25 fee, may be waived for applicants with need. No closing date; applicants notified on a rolling basis beginning on or about January 1; must reply by May 1 or within 4 weeks if notified thereafter. Essay required. Interview recommended. Audition recommended. Portfolio recommended. CRDA. Deferred and early admission available.

STUDENT LIFE. Housing: Apartment housing available. **Activities:** Student government, student newspaper, television, choral groups, jazz band, music ensembles, symphony orchestra.

ATHLETICS. Intercollegiate: Skiing. **Intramural:** Fencing, sailing, skiing, soccer, softball, volleyball.

STUDENT SERVICES. Career counseling, employment service for undergraduates, freshman orientation, personal counseling, veterans counselor.

ANNUAL EXPENSES. Tuition and fees (1992-93): $7,500. **Room and board:** $2,400 room only. **Books and supplies:** $500. **Other expenses:** $2,820.

FINANCIAL AID. 53% of freshmen, 45% of continuing students receive some form of aid. 63% of grants based on need. Academic, music/drama, art, athletic scholarships available. **Aid applications:** No closing date; applicants notified on a rolling basis beginning on or about August 15; must reply within 4 weeks.

ADDRESS/TELEPHONE. Lane Murray, Director of Admissions, Sierra Nevada College, PO Box 4269-CB, Incline Village, NV 89450-4269. (702) 831-1314. (800) 332-8666. Fax: (702) 831-1347.

Truckee Meadows Community College
Reno, Nevada — CB code: 1096

2-year public community college, coed. Founded in 1971. **Accreditation:** Regional. **Undergraduate enrollment:** 749 men, 830 women full time; 3,188 men, 4,652 women part time. **Faculty:** 495 total (91 full time), 9 with doctorates or other terminal degrees. **Location:** Suburban campus in large city; 120 miles from Sacramento, California. **Calendar:** Semester, limited summer session. Saturday and extensive evening/early morning classes. **Microcomputers:** 100 located in libraries, classrooms.

DEGREES OFFERED. AA, AAS. 240 associate degrees awarded in 1992. 33% in business and management, 12% engineering technologies, 27% allied health, 21% trade and industry.

UNDERGRADUATE MAJORS. Accounting, air conditioning/heating/refrigeration mechanics, air conditioning/heating/refrigeration technology, architectural technologies, architecture, auto body service, automotive mechanics, automotive technology, business administration and management, business and management, business and office, business data processing and related programs, business data programming, carpentry, child development/care/guidance, computer and information sciences, computer technology, construction, counseling psychology, criminal justice studies, data processing, dental assistant, diesel engine mechanics, drafting, drafting and design technology, early childhood education, electrical and electronics equipment repair, electrical installation, electronic technology, engineering and engineering-related technologies, finance, fire control and safety technology, food management, food production/management/services, landscape architecture, law enforcement and corrections technologies, legal assistant/paralegal, legal secretary, liberal/general studies, marketing and distribution, marketing management, masonry/tile setting, medical secretary, microcomputer software, military occupations, nursing, office supervision and management, plumbing/pipefitting/steamfitting, power plant operation and maintenance, precision metal work, radiograph medical technology, real estate, secretarial and related programs, small business management and ownership, solar heating and cooling technology, word processing.

ACADEMIC PROGRAMS. 2-year transfer program, cooperative education, dual enrollment of high school students, independent study, internships, telecourses. **Remedial services:** Learning center, reduced course load, remedial instruction, special counselor, tutoring. **Placement/credit:** AP, CLEP General and Subject, institutional tests; 30 credit hours maximum for associate degree.

ACADEMIC REQUIREMENTS. No policy requiring minimum GPA; records of students having academic difficulty are reviewed individually. 60% of freshmen return for sophomore year. Students must declare major by end of first year. **Graduation requirements:** 60 hours for associate. Most students required to take courses in English, history, humanities, mathematics, biological/physical sciences, social sciences. **Additional information:** Many courses articulated with and transfer to University of Nevada: Reno, and University of Nevada: Las Vegas.

FRESHMAN ADMISSIONS. Selection criteria: Open admissions. High school diploma required if student under 18 years of age. Special requirements for allied health programs.

1992 FRESHMAN CLASS PROFILE. 1,233 men, 1,472 women enrolled. **Characteristics:** 97% from in state, 100% commute, 14% have minority backgrounds, 2% are foreign students. Average age is 30.

FALL-TERM APPLICATIONS. $5 fee. No closing date; applicants notified on a rolling basis; must reply by registration.

STUDENT LIFE. Housing: Housing available 2 miles away at University of Nevada: Reno, for students enrolled for 12 or more credits. **Activities:** Student government, student newspaper, social organization for handicapped students.

STUDENT SERVICES. Aptitude testing, career counseling, employment service for undergraduates, freshman orientation, health services, personal counseling, placement service for graduates, veterans counselor, services/facilities for handicapped.

ANNUAL EXPENSES. Tuition and fees (1992-93): $840, $3,000 additional for out-of-state students. Students from 11 counties bordering Nevada pay $400 additional tuition. **Books and supplies:** $440. **Other expenses:** $470.

FINANCIAL AID. 18% of freshmen, 30% of continuing students receive some form of aid. All grants, 95% of loans, 33% of jobs based on need. **Aid applications:** No closing date; priority given to applications received by April 10; applicants notified on a rolling basis beginning on or about July 1; must reply within 2 weeks. **Additional information:** Institutional grants to state residents are available as well as short-term emergency loans.

ADDRESS/TELEPHONE. Ken Johnson, Director of Admissions and Records, Truckee Meadows Community College, 7000 Dandini Boulevard, Reno, NV 89512. (702) 673-7042. Fax: (702) 673-7108.

University of Nevada: Las Vegas
Las Vegas, Nevada — CB code: 4861

4-year public university, coed. Founded in 1957. **Accreditation:** Regional. **Undergraduate enrollment:** 4,225 men, 4,376 women full time; 3,369 men, 3,897 women part time. **Graduate enrollment:** 273 men, 302 women full time; 1,131 men, 1,636 women part time. **Faculty:** 1,040 total (622 full time), 526 with doctorates or other terminal degrees. **Location:** Urban campus in very large city; 300 miles from Los Angeles, 300 miles from Phoenix. **Calendar:** Semester, limited summer session. **Microcomputers:** 300 located in dormitories, libraries, classrooms, computer centers. **Special facilities:** National supercomputing center for energy and environment, natural history museum, arboretum, art gallery, 3 theaters, concert hall. **Additional facts:** Credit courses available at Nellis Air Force Base.

DEGREES OFFERED. BA, BS, BFA, BArch, MA, MS, MBA, MFA, MEd, MSW, PhD, EdD. 1,493 bachelor's degrees awarded in 1992. 46% in business and management, 5% communications, 16% education, 6% health sciences, 12% social sciences. Graduate degrees offered in 45 major fields of study.

UNDERGRADUATE MAJORS. Accounting, anthropology, applied mathematics, applied physics, architecture, biology, business administration and management, business economics, chemistry, civil engineering, clinical laboratory science, communications, computer and information sciences, computer engineering, criminal justice studies, criminology, dance, dramatic arts, earth sciences, electrical/electronics/communications engineering, elementary education, English, environmental science, finance, fine arts, foreign languages (multiple emphasis), French, geology, German, health care administration, history, hotel/motel and restaurant management, humanities and social sciences, information sciences and systems, liberal/general studies, management information systems, marketing management, mathematics, mechanical design technology, mechanical engineering, music, nursing, philosophy, physics, political science and government, psychology, radiograph medical technology, real estate, secondary education, secondary/postsecondary/vocational education, social sciences, social work, sociology, Spanish, special education.

ACADEMIC PROGRAMS. Double major, dual enrollment of high school students, education specialist degree, honors program, independent study, internships, student-designed major, study abroad, teacher preparation, visiting/exchange student program, Washington semester. **Remedial services:** Learning center, remedial instruction, special counselor, tutoring. **Placement/credit:** AP, CLEP General and Subject, institutional tests; 30 credit hours maximum for bachelor's degree.

ACADEMIC REQUIREMENTS. Freshmen must earn minimum GPA

of 2.3 to continue in good standing. 75% of freshmen return for sophomore year. Students must declare major by end of second year. **Graduation requirements:** 124 hours for bachelor's (36 in major). Most students required to take courses in arts/fine arts, computer science, English, history, humanities, mathematics, biological/physical sciences, social sciences.

FRESHMAN ADMISSIONS. Selection criteria: 2.3 high school GPA required. State residents admitted on probationary basis with minimum 2.0 high school GPA. **High school preparation:** 13.5 units required. Required units include English 4, mathematics 3, social science 3 and science 3. 3 sciences should include 2 laboratory. 0.5 unit computer science required. **Test requirements:** SAT or ACT for placement and counseling only; score report by August 15.

1992 FRESHMAN CLASS PROFILE. 646 men, 737 women enrolled. **Characteristics:** 87% from in state, 95% commute, 24% have minority backgrounds. Average age is 20.

FALL-TERM APPLICATIONS. $20 fee. Closing date August 17; priority given to applications received by July 15; applicants notified on a rolling basis beginning on or about February 6; must reply by registration. Essay required for academically marginal applicants. Interview recommended for GED, alternate criteria applicants. Audition recommended for music, theater arts applicants. Portfolio recommended for art applicants. Deferred and early admission available.

STUDENT LIFE. Housing: Dormitories (coed); fraternity, sorority, handicapped housing available. All rooms have jimmy-proof latch locks or deadbolts. Exterior doors equipped with electro-magnetic locks requiring passcard to enter. **Activities:** Student government, film, magazine, radio, student newspaper, television, choral groups, concert band, dance, drama, jazz band, marching band, music ensembles, musical theater, opera, pep band, symphony orchestra, fraternities, sororities, 40 clubs, 30 boards and committees, 22 Greek societies, 12 music groups, several religious and ethnic groups.

ATHLETICS. NCAA. **Intercollegiate:** Baseball M, basketball, cross-country W, diving, football M, golf M, soccer M, softball W, swimming, tennis, track and field W. **Intramural:** Badminton, basketball, bowling, football, golf, racquetball, soccer, softball, swimming, tennis, track and field, volleyball, wrestling M.

STUDENT SERVICES. Aptitude testing, career counseling, employment service for undergraduates, freshman orientation, health services, on-campus day care, personal counseling, placement service for graduates, special adviser for adult students, veterans counselor, services/facilities for handicapped.

ANNUAL EXPENSES. Tuition and fees (1992-93): $1,680, $4,050 additional for out-of-state students. **Room and board:** $4,930. **Books and supplies:** $600. **Other expenses:** $900.

FINANCIAL AID. 46% of grants, 86% of loans, 12% of jobs based on need. Academic, music/drama, art, athletic, state/district residency, leadership, alumni affiliation, minority scholarships available. **Aid applications:** No closing date; priority given to applications received by February 15; applicants notified on a rolling basis beginning on or about May 1; must reply within 2 weeks.

ADDRESS/TELEPHONE. Larry P. Mason, Director of Admissions, University of Nevada: Las Vegas, 4505 Maryland Parkway, Las Vegas, NV 89154-1021. (702) 895-3443. (800) 334-UNLV. Fax: (702) 895-1118.

University of Nevada: Reno

Reno, Nevada CB code: 4844

Admissions:	96% of applicants accepted
Based on:	••• School record
	• Test scores
Completion:	80% of freshmen end year in good standing

4-year public university, coed. Founded in 1864. **Accreditation:** Regional. **Undergraduate enrollment:** 2,900 men, 2,821 women full time; 1,314 men, 1,717 women part time. **Graduate enrollment:** 539 men, 579 women full time; 942 men, 1,097 women part time. **Faculty:** 991 total (880 full time). **Location:** Urban campus in small city; 225 miles from San Francisco, 450 miles from Las Vegas and Los Angeles. **Calendar:** Semester, extensive summer session. **Microcomputers:** 425 located in libraries, classrooms, computer centers. **Special facilities:** Planetarium. **Additional facts:** Constitutionally established land grant university.

DEGREES OFFERED. BA, BS, BFA, MA, MS, MBA, MEd, MSW, PhD, EdD, MD, B. Pharm. 1,170 bachelor's degrees awarded in 1992. 11% in business and management, 11% education, 9% engineering, 10% health sciences, 7% parks/recreation, protective services, public affairs, 5% psychology, 17% social sciences. Graduate degrees offered in 54 major fields of study.

UNDERGRADUATE MAJORS. Accounting, agribusiness, agricultural education, animal sciences, anthropology, biochemistry, biology, business economics, chemical engineering, chemistry, civil engineering, clinical laboratory science, computer and information sciences, criminal justice studies, dramatic arts, economics, electrical/electronics/communications engineering, elementary education, engineering physics, English, finance, fine arts, food science and nutrition, French, geography, geological engineering, geology, geophysics and seismology, German, health education, health sciences, history, home economics, individual and family development, interior design, international studies, journalism, liberal/general studies, logistics management, management information systems, management science, marketing management, materials engineering, mathematics, mechanical engineering, metallurgical engineering, mining and mineral engineering, music, music education, music performance, nursing, philosophy, physical education, physics, political science and government, predentistry, premedicine, preveterinary, psychology, recreation and community services technologies, resource management, secondary education, social psychology, social work, sociology, Spanish, special education, speech, speech pathology/audiology, visual and performing arts.

ACADEMIC PROGRAMS. Double major, dual enrollment of high school students, education specialist degree, honors program, independent study, internships, study abroad, teacher preparation, visiting/exchange student program; combined bachelor's/graduate program in business administration, medicine. **Remedial services:** Remedial instruction, special counselor, tutoring, writing specialist. **ROTC:** Army. **Placement/credit:** AP, CLEP General and Subject, institutional tests; 60 credit hours maximum for bachelor's degree.

ACADEMIC REQUIREMENTS. Freshmen must earn minimum GPA of 2.0 to continue in good standing. 67% of freshmen return for sophomore year. Students must declare major by end of second year. **Graduation requirements:** 128 hours for bachelor's (32 in major). Most students required to take courses in arts/fine arts, English, history, mathematics, biological/physical sciences, social sciences.

FRESHMAN ADMISSIONS. Selection criteria: Minimum 2.5 high school GPA required. Applicants not meeting these requirements may apply for "special admission". High test scores may favorably influence admission decisions. **High school preparation:** 13.5 units required. Required units include English 4, mathematics 3, social science 3 and science 3. .5 computer science also required. Science units should include laboratory work. **Test requirements:** SAT or ACT (ACT preferred) for placement; score report by August 18.

1992 FRESHMAN CLASS PROFILE. 1,294 men applied, 1,241 accepted, 617 enrolled; 1,295 women applied, 1,242 accepted, 609 enrolled. 59% had high school GPA of 3.0 or higher, 41% between 2.0 and 2.99. **Characteristics:** 80% from in state, 90% commute, 10% have minority backgrounds, 3% are foreign students. Average age is 19.

FALL-TERM APPLICATIONS. $20 fee. Closing date July 1; priority given to applications received by June 1; applicants notified on a rolling basis; must reply by registration. Interview recommended for nursing applicants. Audition recommended for music applicants. Portfolio recommended for fine arts applicants. Deferred and early admission available.

STUDENT LIFE. Housing: Dormitories (men, women, coed); apartment, fraternity, sorority housing available. Special interest floors available include fitness, arts and culture, stereo limitation, alcohol prohibition, honors. **Activities:** Student government, magazine, radio, student newspaper, television, yearbook, choral groups, concert band, dance, drama, jazz band, marching band, music ensembles, musical theater, opera, pep band, symphony orchestra, fraternities, sororities, Social service organizations, Inter-Varsity Christian Fellowship, Black Student Union, Mexican-American Organization, American Indian Organization, Asian-American Alliance, Chinese Students Association, Young Republicans, Young Democrats, Jewish Students Organization.

ATHLETICS. NCAA. **Intercollegiate:** Baseball M, basketball, cross-country, football M, golf M, skiing, swimming W, tennis, track and field, volleyball W. **Intramural:** Basketball, cross-country, diving, golf, handball M, skiing, soccer, swimming, tennis, track and field, volleyball, water polo.

STUDENT SERVICES. Aptitude testing, career counseling, employment service for undergraduates, freshman orientation, health services, on-campus day care, personal counseling, placement service for graduates, special adviser for adult students, veterans counselor, services/facilities for handicapped.

ANNUAL EXPENSES. Tuition and fees: $1,665, $4,300 additional for out-of-state students. **Room and board:** $4,858. **Books and supplies:** $600. **Other expenses:** $1,856.

FINANCIAL AID. 65% of freshmen, 65% of continuing students receive some form of aid. 83% of loans, 8% of jobs based on need. Academic, music/drama, athletic, state/district residency, leadership, alumni affiliation, minority scholarships available. **Aid applications:** No closing date; priority given to applications received by April 15; applicants notified on a rolling basis beginning on or about May 15; must reply within 2 weeks.

ADDRESS/TELEPHONE. Melisa N. Choroszy, Associate Dean of Records/Enrollment Services, University of Nevada: Reno, Reno, NV 89557-0002. (702) 784-6865. Fax: (702) 784-4015.

Western Nevada Community College

Carson City, Nevada CB code: 1141

2-year public community college, coed. Founded in 1971. **Accreditation:** Regional. **Undergraduate enrollment:** 271 men, 371 women full time; 1,598 men, 2,468 women part time. **Faculty:** 334 total (69 full time), 11 with doctorates or other terminal degrees. **Location:** Suburban campus in large town; 30 miles from Reno. **Calendar:** Semester, limited summer session. Saturday and extensive evening/early morning classes. **Microcomputers:** 88 located in classrooms. **Additional facts:** College maintains 7 teaching centers in western Nevada.

DEGREES OFFERED. AA, AS, AAS. 206 associate degrees awarded in 1992. 12% in business and management, 10% health sciences, 66% multi/interdisciplinary studies, 6% parks/recreation, protective services, public affairs.

UNDERGRADUATE MAJORS. Accounting, automotive mechanics, automotive technology, biological and physical sciences, biology, business administration and management, business and office, business data processing and related programs, computer and information sciences, computer programming, criminal justice studies, drafting, electronic technology, fire control and safety technology, law enforcement and corrections technologies, liberal/general studies, machine tool operation/machine shop, marketing and distribution, mathematics, nursing, physical sciences, precision metal work, real estate, word processing.

ACADEMIC PROGRAMS. 2-year transfer program, cooperative education, double major, dual enrollment of high school students, internships, telecourses. **Remedial services:** Learning center, remedial instruction, tutoring. **Placement/credit:** AP, CLEP General and Subject, institutional tests; 30 credit hours maximum for associate degree.

ACADEMIC REQUIREMENTS. No policy requiring minimum GPA; records of students having academic difficulty are reviewed individually. 65% of freshmen return for sophomore year. Students must declare major by end of first year. **Graduation requirements:** 60 hours for associate (36 in major). Most students required to take courses in arts/fine arts, English, humanities, mathematics, biological/physical sciences, social sciences.

FRESHMAN ADMISSIONS. Selection criteria: Open admissions. Selective admissions to nursing program.

1992 FRESHMAN CLASS PROFILE. 1,752 men, 2,604 women enrolled. **Characteristics:** 96% from in state, 100% commute, 10% have minority backgrounds. Average age is 26.

FALL-TERM APPLICATIONS. $5 fee. No closing date; applicants notified on a rolling basis; must reply by registration. Early admission available.

STUDENT LIFE. Activities: Student government, choral groups, musical theater.

STUDENT SERVICES. Aptitude testing, career counseling, employment service for undergraduates, freshman orientation, personal counseling, placement service for graduates, veterans counselor, services/facilities for handicapped.

ANNUAL EXPENSES. Tuition and fees: $882, $3,000 additional for out-of-state students. **Books and supplies:** $450. **Other expenses:** $1,230.

FINANCIAL AID. 32% of freshmen, 22% of continuing students receive some form of aid. 96% of grants, 70% of loans based on need. Academic, state/district residency scholarships available. **Aid applications:** No closing date; priority given to applications received by June 1; applicants notified on a rolling basis beginning on or about June 1; must reply within 2 weeks.

ADDRESS/TELEPHONE. Robert Johnston, Director Admissions/Records, Western Nevada Community College, 2201 West Nye Lane, Carson City, NV 89703. (702) 887-3138. Fax: (702) 885-0642.

New Hampshire

Castle College
Windham, New Hampshire CB code: 0884

Admissions: 86% of applicants accepted
Based on: ••• Recommendations, school record
•• Interview
• Activities
Completion: 80% of freshmen end year in good standing
85% graduate, 90% of these enter 4-year programs

2-year private business, junior college, coed, affiliated with Roman Catholic Church. Founded in 1963. **Accreditation:** Regional. **Undergraduate enrollment:** 14 men, 257 women full time; 1 man, 10 women part time. **Faculty:** 36 total (9 full time), 3 with doctorates or other terminal degrees. **Location:** Rural campus in small town; 35 miles from Boston. **Calendar:** Four 8-week terms, one 5-week term in day division; four 9-week terms in night division. Extensive evening/early morning classes. **Microcomputers:** 36 located in classrooms, computer centers. **Special facilities:** Stanton-Harcourt Castle, built in 1912, on campus.

DEGREES OFFERED. AA, AS. 95 associate degrees awarded in 1992. 35% in business and management, 33% business/office and marketing/distribution, 32% allied health.

UNDERGRADUATE MAJORS. Accounting, business administration and management, business and management, business and office, early childhood education, legal secretary, mental health/human services, office supervision and management, secretarial and related programs, word processing.

ACADEMIC PROGRAMS. 2-year transfer program, computer delivered (on-line) credit-bearing course offerings, cooperative education, double major, dual enrollment of high school students, independent study, internships, student-designed major. **Remedial services:** Reduced course load, tutoring, study skill course. **Placement/credit:** Institutional tests; 12 credit hours maximum for associate degree.

ACADEMIC REQUIREMENTS. Freshmen must earn minimum GPA of 2.0 to continue in good standing. 85% of freshmen return for sophomore year. Students must declare major by end of first year. **Graduation requirements:** 60 hours for associate (27 in major). Most students required to take courses in computer science, English, humanities.

FRESHMAN ADMISSIONS. Selection criteria: 2.0 GPA required; English grades weighed heavily. Interview, counselor's and/or teacher's recommendation considered. 2.0 or better in high school English classes recommended. **Test requirements:** Stanford Achievement Test and Otis-Lennon School Ability Test required for placement. **Additional information:** Some academically unprepared applicants admitted on probation.

1992 FRESHMAN CLASS PROFILE. 17 men applied, 15 accepted, 12 enrolled; 198 women applied, 169 accepted, 153 enrolled. 8% had high school GPA of 3.0 or higher, 92% between 2.0 and 2.99. **Characteristics:** 50% from in state, 100% commute, 5% have minority backgrounds. Average age is 19.

FALL-TERM APPLICATIONS. $25 fee, may be waived for applicants with need. No closing date; applicants notified on a rolling basis; must reply by May 1 or within 4 weeks if notified thereafter. Interview required. CRDA. Deferred admission available.

STUDENT LIFE. Housing: Area families offer housing to students at reduced rates. **Activities:** Student government, yearbook, Student Government Newsletter, student activities board. **Additional information:** Group trips available every spring. Student government very active.

STUDENT SERVICES. Aptitude testing, career counseling, employment service for undergraduates, freshman orientation, personal counseling, placement service for graduates, academic counseling, services/facilities for handicapped.

ANNUAL EXPENSES. Tuition and fees (projected): $4,550. **Books and supplies:** $400. **Other expenses:** $1,541.

FINANCIAL AID. 75% of freshmen, 82% of continuing students receive some form of aid. 25% of grants, 86% of loans, 78% of jobs based on need. 92 enrolled freshmen were judged to have need, all were offered aid. Academic, leadership scholarships available. **Aid applications:** No closing date; priority given to applications received by April 15; applicants notified on a rolling basis beginning on or about April 16; must reply within 2 weeks.

ADDRESS/TELEPHONE. Andrea Bard, Admissions Director, Castle College, Searles Road, Windham, NH 03087-1297. (603) 893-6111.

Colby-Sawyer College
New London, New Hampshire CB code: 3281

4-year private liberal arts college, coed. Founded in 1837. **Accreditation:** Regional. **Undergraduate enrollment:** 611 men and women. **Faculty:** 67 total (42 full time). **Location:** Rural campus in small town; 100 miles from Boston, 25 miles from Hanover. **Calendar:** Semester. **Microcomputers:** 57 located in libraries, classrooms, computer centers. **Special facilities:** Fine arts center, preschool, kindergarten, and 3 primary grades of instruction.

DEGREES OFFERED. BA, BS, BFA. 90 bachelor's degrees awarded in 1992.

UNDERGRADUATE MAJORS. Liberal/general studies. American studies, art education, arts management, biology, business administration and management, communications, early childhood education, elementary education, fine arts, graphic design, humanities, nursing, predentistry, prelaw, premedicine, preveterinary, psychology, science education, secondary education, social studies education, sports management, sports medicine.

ACADEMIC PROGRAMS. 2-year transfer program, accelerated program, independent study, internships, semester at sea, student-designed major, study abroad, teacher preparation, visiting/exchange student program, Washington semester, cross-registration. **Remedial services:** Learning center, reduced course load, tutoring. **ROTC:** Air Force, Army. **Placement/credit:** AP, CLEP General and Subject, institutional tests; 64 credit hours maximum for bachelor's degree.

ACADEMIC REQUIREMENTS. Freshmen must earn minimum GPA of 1.75 to continue in good standing. 86% of freshmen return for sophomore year. Students must declare major by end of second year. **Graduation requirements:** 60 hours for associate, 120 hours for bachelor's (60 in major). Most students required to take courses in arts/fine arts, English, history, humanities, mathematics, philosophy/religion, biological/physical sciences, social sciences. **Postgraduate studies:** 85% from 2-year programs enter 4-year programs. **Additional information:** 3-month internship required for bachelor of science degree.

FRESHMAN ADMISSIONS. Selection criteria: School achievement record, school and community activities, recommendations, test scores, and interview important. **High school preparation:** 15 units recommended. Recommended units include English 4, foreign language 2, mathematics 3, social science 2 and science 2. One biology, 1 chemistry recommended for nursing applicants. **Test requirements:** SAT or ACT; score report by May 15.

1992 FRESHMAN CLASS PROFILE. 203 men and women enrolled. **Academic background:** Mid 50% of enrolled freshmen had SAT-V between 390-460, SAT-M between 420-480. 100% submitted SAT scores. **Characteristics:** 23% from in state, 98% live in college housing, 2% have minority backgrounds, 2% are foreign students. Average age is 18.

FALL-TERM APPLICATIONS. $40 fee, may be waived for applicants with need. No closing date; priority given to applications received by April 15; applicants notified on a rolling basis beginning on or about January 15; must reply by May 1 or within 3 weeks if notified thereafter. Essay required. Interview recommended. Portfolio recommended for art applicants. CRDA. Deferred admission available.

STUDENT LIFE. Housing: Dormitories (women, coed); cooperative housing available. **Activities:** Student government, film, student newspaper, yearbook, choral groups, dance, drama, music ensembles.

ATHLETICS. NCAA. **Intercollegiate:** Basketball, gymnastics W, horseback riding, lacrosse W, skiing, soccer, tennis W, volleyball W. **Intramural:** Archery, badminton, basketball, horseback riding, lacrosse M, racquetball, skiing, soccer, softball W, swimming, table tennis, tennis, volleyball, water polo.

STUDENT SERVICES. Aptitude testing, career counseling, employment service for undergraduates, freshman orientation, health services, on-campus day care, personal counseling, placement service for graduates, services/facilities for handicapped.

ANNUAL EXPENSES. Tuition and fees (1992-93): $12,775. **Room and board:** $5,120. **Books and supplies:** $400. **Other expenses:** $1,000.

FINANCIAL AID. 43% of freshmen, 50% of continuing students receive some form of aid. 88% of grants, 92% of loans, 73% of jobs based on need. 138 enrolled freshmen were judged to have need, all were offered aid. Academic, music/drama scholarships available. **Aid applications:** No closing date; priority given to applications received by February 15; applicants notified on a rolling basis beginning on or about February 15; must reply by May 1 or within 2 weeks if notified thereafter.

ADDRESS/TELEPHONE. Joanna Henderson, Dean of Admission/Financial Aid, Colby-Sawyer College, 100 Main Street, New London, NH 03257. (603) 526-2010 ext. 700. (800) 272-1015. Fax: (603) 526-2135.

Daniel Webster College
Nashua, New Hampshire CB code: 3648

Admissions: 83% of applicants accepted
Based on: ••• Recommendations, school record
•• Activities, interview
• Essay, special talents, test scores
Completion: 77% of freshmen end year in good standing
83% graduate, 10% of these enter graduate study

4-year private college of aviation, business, computer science, and engineering, coed. Founded in 1965. **Accreditation:** Regional. **Undergraduate enrollment:** 382 men, 85 women full time; 19 men, 3 women part time. **Faculty:**

47 total (24 full time), 11 with doctorates or other terminal degrees. **Location:** Suburban campus in small city; 45 miles from Boston. **Calendar:** Semester, limited summer session. **Microcomputers:** 45 located in libraries, computer centers. **Special facilities:** On-campus flight center, 27 aircraft including powered gliders, aerobatic planes, 3 flight simulators, air traffic control simulation system.

DEGREES OFFERED. AS, BS. 56 associate degrees awarded in 1992. 52% in business and management, 5% engineering, 38% trade and industry. 114 bachelor's degrees awarded. 26% in business and management, 14% computer sciences, 60% trade and industry.

UNDERGRADUATE MAJORS. Associate: Accounting, aerospace/aeronautical/astronautical engineering, airline piloting and navigation, aviation management, business and management, computer and information sciences, computer programming, engineering, engineering and other disciplines, information sciences and systems, liberal/general studies, management information systems, marketing and distribution, marketing management, systems analysis, transportation and travel marketing, transportation management, travel management. **Bachelor's:** Air traffic control, airline piloting and navigation, aviation management, business administration and management, business and management, computer and information sciences, computer engineering, computer programming, information sciences and systems, management information systems, systems analysis.

ACADEMIC PROGRAMS. 2-year transfer program, accelerated program, cooperative education, double major, dual enrollment of high school students, independent study, internships, study abroad, cross-registration. **Remedial services:** Reduced course load, special counselor, tutoring. **ROTC:** Air Force, Army, Naval. **Placement/credit:** AP, CLEP General and Subject, institutional tests; 30 credit hours maximum for associate degree; 30 credit hours maximum for bachelor's degree.

ACADEMIC REQUIREMENTS. Freshmen must earn minimum GPA of 2.0 to continue in good standing. 65% of freshmen return for sophomore year. Students must declare major on enrollment. **Graduation requirements:** 60 hours for associate (12 in major), 120 hours for bachelor's (18 in major). Most students required to take courses in computer science, English, history, humanities, mathematics, biological/physical sciences, social sciences. **Postgraduate studies:** 75% from 2-year programs enter 4-year programs. **Additional information:** Credit granted for pilot licenses. Flight students must have an FAA Class II physical examination. Flight operations majors must pass FAA written examinations and flight tests to earn pilot ratings.

FRESHMAN ADMISSIONS. Selection criteria: High school transcript, interview, recommendations, test scores considered. School and community activities, minority status, and alumni relation also considered. **High school preparation:** 16 units required. Required and recommended units include biological science 1, English 4, mathematics 3-4, physical science 2-3 and social science 2. One computer science also recommended. **Test requirements:** SAT or ACT (SAT preferred); score report by September 1.

1992 FRESHMAN CLASS PROFILE. 627 men applied, 531 accepted, 146 enrolled; 134 women applied, 104 accepted, 34 enrolled. 7% were in top tenth and 25% were in top quarter of graduating class. **Characteristics:** 75% from in state, 84% live in college housing, 6% have minority backgrounds, 3% are foreign students. Average age is 18.

FALL-TERM APPLICATIONS. $30 fee, may be waived for applicants with need. No closing date; applicants notified on a rolling basis; must reply by May 1 or within 2 weeks if notified thereafter. Interview recommended. Essay recommended. CRDA. Deferred and early admission available.

STUDENT LIFE. Housing: Dormitories (men, women); apartment housing available. **Activities:** Student government, student newspaper, yearbook, jazz band, Arnold Air Society, professional pilots organization, Entrepreneurial Assembly, Alpha Eta Rho.

ATHLETICS. NCAA. **Intercollegiate:** Baseball M, basketball M, cross-country, soccer M, softball W, volleyball W. **Intramural:** Basketball, cross-country, ice hockey M, skiing, soccer M, softball, tennis, volleyball.

STUDENT SERVICES. Aptitude testing, career counseling, employment service for undergraduates, freshman orientation, health services, personal counseling, placement service for graduates, special adviser for adult students, veterans counselor, services/facilities for handicapped.

ANNUAL EXPENSES. Tuition and fees (projected): $11,852. **Room and board:** $4,656. **Books and supplies:** $500. **Other expenses:** $500.

FINANCIAL AID. 65% of freshmen, 63% of continuing students receive some form of aid. All grants, 59% of loans, 67% of jobs based on need. 124 enrolled freshmen were judged to have need, 118 were offered aid. Academic, state/district residency scholarships available. **Aid applications:** No closing date; priority given to applications received by March 12; applicants notified on a rolling basis beginning on or about March 12; must reply by May 1 or within 2 weeks if notified thereafter.

ADDRESS/TELEPHONE. Terry Whittum, Director of Admissions, Daniel Webster College, 20 University Drive, Nashua, NH 03063-1300. (603) 883-3556 ext. 224. Fax: (603) 882-8505.

Dartmouth College
Hanover, New Hampshire

CB code: 3351

Admissions: 26% of applicants accepted
Based on: ••• Activities, essay, school record, special talents, test scores
•• Recommendations
• Interview
Completion: 94% of freshmen end year in good standing
94% graduate, 21% of these enter graduate study

4-year private liberal arts college, coed. Founded in 1769. **Accreditation:** Regional. **Undergraduate enrollment:** 2,118 men, 1,732 women full time; 15 men, 18 women part time. **Graduate enrollment:** 718 men, 389 women full time; 33 men, 67 women part time. **Faculty:** 523 total (330 full time), 310 with doctorates or other terminal degrees. **Location:** Rural campus in small town; 130 miles from Boston. **Calendar:** Quarter, extensive summer session. **Microcomputers:** Located in dormitories, libraries, classrooms, computer centers, campus-wide network. Lease or purchase required**Special facilities:** Hopkins Center for the Performing Arts, Hood Museum of Art, Nelson Rockefeller Center for the Social Sciences, Sherman Fairchild Physical Science Center, Gilman Life Science Center, Kiewit Computation Center, Shattuck Observatory, Burke Laboratory.

DEGREES OFFERED. BA, MA, MS, MBA, PhD, MD. 1,071 bachelor's degrees awarded in 1992. 5% in engineering, 5% languages, 12% letters/literature, 7% life sciences, 7% psychology, 39% social sciences, 6% visual and performing arts. Graduate degrees offered in 19 major fields of study.

UNDERGRADUATE MAJORS. African studies, Afro-American (black) studies, American Indian studies, anthropology, art history, Asian studies, biochemistry, biology, chemistry, Chinese, cinematography/film, classics, comparative literature, computer and information sciences, dramatic arts, earth sciences, economics, education, engineering, English, fine arts, foreign languages (multiple emphasis), French, geography, German, Greek (classical), history, Italian, Latin, linguistics, mathematics, music, philosophy, physics, political science and government, psychology, religion, Russian, Russian and Slavic studies, sociology, Spanish, studio art, visual and performing arts.

ACADEMIC PROGRAMS. Accelerated program, double major, dual enrollment of high school students, honors program, independent study, internships, semester at sea, student-designed major, study abroad, teacher preparation, visiting/exchange student program, Washington semester, Twelve College Exchange Program, University of California: San Diego Exchange Program, McGill University Exchange Program, exchange program with Germany, Hungary, Japan, Peoples Republic of China; liberal arts/career combination in engineering; combined bachelor's/graduate program in business administration. **Remedial services:** Learning center, special counselor, tutoring, intensive academic support program, study skills workshops. **Placement/credit:** AP, institutional tests. Unlimited number of hours of credit by examination may be counted toward bachelor's degree.

ACADEMIC REQUIREMENTS. No policy requiring minimum GPA; records of students having academic difficulty are reviewed individually. 97% of freshmen return for sophomore year. Students must declare major by end of second year. **Graduation requirements:** 116 hours for bachelor's (27 in major). Most students required to take courses in English, foreign languages, humanities, biological/physical sciences, social sciences. **Postgraduate studies:** 4% enter law school, 5% enter medical school, 1% enter MBA programs, 11% enter other graduate study.

FRESHMAN ADMISSIONS. Selection criteria: Evidence of intellectual capability, motivation, and personal integrity of primary importance. Talent, accomplishment, and involvement in nonacademic areas also evaluated. Applicants whose records suggest ability to complete academic work and add to quality of campus life sought. Recommended units include English 4, foreign language 3, mathematics 4, social science 2 and science 3. Strongest academic program available to applicant recommended. **Test requirements:** SAT or ACT; score report by March 1. 3 ACH required. Score report by March 1.

1992 FRESHMAN CLASS PROFILE. 4,907 men applied, 1,148 accepted, 593 enrolled; 3,169 women applied, 959 accepted, 482 enrolled. 85% were in top tenth and 97% were in top quarter of graduating class. **Academic background:** Mid 50% of enrolled freshmen had SAT-V between 580-680, SAT-M between 650-730. 100% submitted SAT scores. **Characteristics:** 3% from in state, 100% live in college housing, 24% have minority backgrounds, 4% are foreign students. Average age is 19.

FALL-TERM APPLICATIONS. $60 fee, may be waived for applicants with need. Closing date January 1; applicants notified on or about April 15; must reply by May 1. Interview required. Essay required. CRDA. Deferred and early admission available. EDP-F.

STUDENT LIFE. Housing: Dormitories (coed); apartment, fraternity, sorority, cooperative housing available. Special interest or affinity houses (language or academic subjects) available. Handicapped facilities available. **Activities:** Student government, film, magazine, radio, student newspaper, yearbook, video, choral groups, concert band, dance, drama, jazz band, marching band, music ensembles, musical theater, opera, pep band, symphony orchestra, fraternities, sororities, Tucker Foundation coordinates community and other service programs, more than 35 religious, political, ethnic organizations.

ATHLETICS. NCAA. **Intercollegiate:** Baseball M, basketball, cross-country, diving, fencing, field hockey W, football M, golf, gymnastics M, horseback riding, ice hockey, lacrosse, rowing (crew), rugby, sailing, skiing, soccer, softball W, squash, swimming, tennis, track and field, volleyball, water polo, wrestling M. **Intramural:** Basketball, bowling, cross-country, diving, football, golf, handball, ice hockey, lacrosse, racquetball, rifle, rugby, skiing, soccer, softball, squash, swimming, table tennis, tennis, track and field, volleyball, water polo, wrestling M.

STUDENT SERVICES. Aptitude testing, career counseling, employment service for undergraduates, freshman orientation, health services, on-campus day care, personal counseling, placement service for graduates, services/facilities for handicapped.

ANNUAL EXPENSES. Tuition and fees: $18,375. **Room and board:** $5,874. **Books and supplies:** $1,590.

FINANCIAL AID. 37% of freshmen, 50% of continuing students receive some form of aid. All grants, 99% of loans, all jobs based on need. 553 enrolled freshmen were judged to have need, all were offered aid. **Aid applications:** Closing date February 1; applicants notified on or about April 15; must reply by May 1. **Additional information:** Full demonstrated need of all admitted students met.

ADDRESS/TELEPHONE. Karl M. Furstenberg, Dean of Admissions and Financial Aid, Dartmouth College, McNutt Hall, Hanover, NH 03755. (603) 646-2875. Fax: (603) 646-1216.

Franklin Pierce College
Rindge, New Hampshire — CB code: 3395

Admissions:	86% of applicants accepted
Based on:	••• School record
	•• Activities, interview, recommendations, test scores
	• Essay, special talents
Completion:	90% of freshmen end year in good standing
	38% graduate, 21% of these enter graduate study

4-year private business, liberal arts college, coed. Founded in 1962. **Accreditation:** Regional. **Undergraduate enrollment:** 617 men, 578 women full time; 20 men, 20 women part time. **Faculty:** 106 total (76 full time), 51 with doctorates or other terminal degrees. **Location:** Rural campus in rural community; 20 miles from Keene, 60 miles from Boston. **Calendar:** Semester, extensive summer session. Saturday and extensive evening/early morning classes. **Microcomputers:** 80 located in classrooms, computer centers. **Special facilities:** Thoreau Art Gallery, graphics workshop, lakeside waterfront. **Additional facts:** 5 satellite campuses offer continuing education sequence of 8-week sessions.

DEGREES OFFERED. BA, BS. 244 bachelor's degrees awarded in 1992. 23% in business and management, 8% business/office and marketing/distribution, 14% communications, 9% education, 6% letters/literature, 5% psychology, 8% social sciences, 14% visual and performing arts.

UNDERGRADUATE MAJORS. Computer and information sciences, marketing and distribution. accounting, advertising, anthropology, archeology, art education, art history, biological and physical sciences, biology, business administration and management, business and management, business economics, clinical psychology, communications, computer and information sciences, computer mathematics, computer programming, counseling psychology, creative writing, dramatic arts, early childhood education, ecology, economics, education, elementary education, English, English education, English literature, environmental science, experimental psychology, finance, fine arts, foreign languages education, French, graphic arts technology, graphic design, history, humanities and social sciences, international business management, journalism, junior high education, liberal/general studies, management information systems, management science, marketing and distribution, marketing management, marketing research, mathematics, mathematics education, music, music history and appreciation, music performance, music theory and composition, parks and recreation management, political science and government, predentistry, prelaw, premedicine, preveterinary, psychology, radio/television broadcasting, science education, secondary education, small business management and ownership, social science education, social sciences, social studies education, social work, sociology, Spanish, student counseling and personnel services, studio art, theater design, video, visual and performing arts.

ACADEMIC PROGRAMS. Accelerated program, double major, dual enrollment of high school students, honors program, independent study, internships, student-designed major, study abroad, teacher preparation, visiting/exchange student program, cross-registration. **Remedial services:** Learning center, preadmission summer program, reduced course load, special counselor, tutoring, special help program in writing skills and mathematics. **ROTC:** Air Force. **Placement/credit:** AP, CLEP General and Subject, institutional tests; 30 credit hours maximum for bachelor's degree.

ACADEMIC REQUIREMENTS. Freshmen must earn minimum GPA of 2.0 to continue in good standing. 66% of freshmen return for sophomore year. Students must declare major by end of second year. **Graduation requirements:** 64 hours for associate, 128 hours for bachelor's. Most students required to take courses in arts/fine arts, computer science, English, history, humanities, mathematics, biological/physical sciences, social sciences. **Postgraduate studies:** 1% enter law school, 1% enter medical school, 4% enter MBA programs, 15% enter other graduate study.

FRESHMAN ADMISSIONS. Selection criteria: School achievement record, difficulty of course work, and school involvement primary considerations. Recommendations considered. Test scores less important. **High school preparation:** 16 units required. Required and recommended units include English 4, mathematics 2-3, social science 2-3 and science 2. Biological science 1 and physical science 2 recommended. **Test requirements:** SAT or ACT.

1992 FRESHMAN CLASS PROFILE. 2,256 men applied, 1,908 accepted, 233 enrolled; 2,560 women applied, 2,246 accepted, 234 enrolled. 16% had high school GPA of 3.0 or higher, 65% between 2.0 and 2.99. 4% were in top tenth and 13% were in top quarter of graduating class. **Academic background:** Mid 50% of enrolled freshmen had SAT-V between 350-450, SAT-M between 360-480. 91% submitted SAT scores. **Characteristics:** 9% from in state, 100% live in college housing, 5% have minority backgrounds, 3% are foreign students. Average age is 18.

FALL-TERM APPLICATIONS. No fee. No closing date; priority given to applications received by April 1; applicants notified on a rolling basis; must reply by May 1 or within 4 weeks if notified thereafter. Interview recommended. Audition recommended. Portfolio recommended. Essay recommended. Interview required for borderline applicants, recommended for all. CRDA. Deferred and early admission available.

STUDENT LIFE. Housing: Dormitories (men, women, coed); apartment housing available. College-owned townhouses within 1 mile of campus. **Activities:** Student government, magazine, radio, student newspaper, television, yearbook, choral groups, dance, drama, music ensembles, musical theater.

ATHLETICS. NCAA. **Intercollegiate:** Baseball M, basketball, golf M, ice hockey M, sailing, skiing, soccer, softball W, tennis, volleyball W. **Intramural:** Baseball M, basketball, cross-country, field hockey W, golf, gymnastics, ice hockey M, sailing, skiing, soccer, softball, table tennis, tennis, volleyball.

STUDENT SERVICES. Aptitude testing, career counseling, employment service for undergraduates, freshman orientation, health services, personal counseling, placement service for graduates, services/facilities for handicapped.

ANNUAL EXPENSES. Tuition and fees (1992-93): $12,160. **Room and board:** $4,250. **Books and supplies:** $450. **Other expenses:** $700.

FINANCIAL AID. 69% of freshmen, 64% of continuing students receive some form of aid. 69% of grants, all loans, 66% of jobs based on need. 342 enrolled freshmen were judged to have need, all were offered aid. Academic, athletic, leadership scholarships available. **Aid applications:** No closing date; priority given to applications received by February 28; applicants notified on a rolling basis beginning on or about February 15; must reply by May 1 or within 2 weeks if notified thereafter.

ADDRESS/TELEPHONE. Thomas E. Desrosiers, Dir of Admissions, Franklin Pierce College, College Road PO Box 60, Rindge, NH 03461-0060. (603) 899-4050. Fax: (603) 889-6448.

Hesser College
Manchester, New Hampshire — CB code: 3452

Admissions:	95% of applicants accepted
Based on:	••• Recommendations, school record
	•• Interview
	• Activities
Completion:	72% of freshmen end year in good standing
	35% enter 4-year programs

2-year proprietary business, junior college, coed. Founded in 1900. **Accreditation:** Regional. **Undergraduate enrollment:** 3,500 men and women. **Faculty:** 123 total (18 full time), 5 with doctorates or other terminal degrees. **Location:** Urban campus in small city; 50 miles from Boston. **Calendar:** Semester, limited summer session. **Microcomputers:** 75 located in libraries, classrooms, computer centers. **Additional facts:** Courses also available at centers in Nashua, Salem, and Portsmouth.

DEGREES OFFERED. AA, AS. 460 associate degrees awarded in 1992. 50% in business and management, 30% business/office and marketing/distribution, 10% computer sciences, 10% teacher education.

UNDERGRADUATE MAJORS. Accounting, business administration and management, business and management, business data processing and related programs, business data programming, communications, computer programming, court reporting, criminal justice studies, early childhood education, fashion merchandising, hotel/motel and restaurant management, interior design, law enforcement and corrections, legal assistant/paralegal, legal secretary, liberal/general studies, management information systems, marketing and distribution, marketing communications, marketing research, medical assistant, office supervision and management, retailing, secretarial and related programs, small business management and ownership, tourism.

ACADEMIC PROGRAMS. 2-year transfer program, accelerated program, cooperative education, double major, dual enrollment of high school students, external degree, honors program, independent study, internships, student-designed major. **Remedial services:** Learning center, reduced course load, tutoring. **Placement/credit:** CLEP General and Subject; 30 credit hours maximum for associate degree.

ACADEMIC REQUIREMENTS. Freshmen must earn minimum GPA of 2.0 to continue in good standing. 67% of freshmen return for sophomore year. Students must declare major on application. **Graduation requirements:** 60 hours for associate. Most students required to take courses in English, humanities, mathematics, social sciences.

FRESHMAN ADMISSIONS. Selection criteria: School achievement record most important. Admission granted to applicants in top 70% of graduating class with 2.0 high school GPA. References and interview considered for all others.

1992 FRESHMAN CLASS PROFILE. 500 men applied, 465 accepted, 195 enrolled; 1,200 women applied, 1,150 accepted, 280 enrolled. 30% had high school GPA of 3.0 or higher, 60% between 2.0 and 2.99. 10% were in top tenth and 40% were in top quarter of graduating class. **Characteristics:** 68% from in state, 52% commute, 1% have minority backgrounds, 1% are foreign students. Average age is 19.

FALL-TERM APPLICATIONS. $10 fee, may be waived for applicants with need. No closing date; applicants notified on a rolling basis; must reply within 4 weeks. Interview recommended. Portfolio recommended for interior design, fashion design applicants. Deferred and early admission available.

STUDENT LIFE. Housing: Dormitories (men, women, coed); apartment housing available. **Activities:** Student government, student newspaper, yearbook, special interest organizations relating to data processing, secretarial, engineering, accounting, business, travel, retailing.

ATHLETICS. NJCAA. **Intercollegiate:** Basketball, soccer, softball W, volleyball. **Intramural:** Basketball, soccer, volleyball.

STUDENT SERVICES. Career counseling, employment service for undergraduates, freshman orientation, health services, personal counseling, placement service for graduates, veterans counselor, services/facilities for handicapped.

ANNUAL EXPENSES. Tuition and fees (1992-93): $6,285. **Room and board:** $4,300. **Books and supplies:** $500. **Other expenses:** $1,000.

FINANCIAL AID. 70% of freshmen, 65% of continuing students receive some form of aid. 97% of grants, 72% of loans, 94% of jobs based on need. Academic, athletic, state/district residency scholarships available. **Aid applications:** No closing date; priority given to applications received by March 1; applicants notified on a rolling basis beginning on or about April 1; must reply within 3 weeks.

ADDRESS/TELEPHONE. David Boisvert, Senior Vice President of Enrollment, Hesser College, 3 Sundial Avenue, Manchester, NH 03103-9969. (603) 668-6660. (800) 526-9231. Fax: (603) 666-4722.

Keene State College
Keene, New Hampshire — CB code: 3472

Admissions:	78% of applicants accepted
Based on:	••• School record
	•• Recommendations, test scores
	• Activities, essay, interview, special talents
Completion:	91% of freshmen end year in good standing
	52% graduate, 15% of these enter graduate study

4-year public liberal arts college, coed. Founded in 1909. **Accreditation:** Regional. **Undergraduate enrollment:** 1,505 men, 1,945 women full time; 148 men, 240 women part time. **Graduate enrollment:** 12 men, 19 women full time; 29 men, 89 women part time. **Faculty:** 340 total (169 full time), 119 with doctorates or other terminal degrees. **Location:** Suburban campus in large town; 52 miles from Concord, 85 miles from Boston. **Calendar:** Semester, extensive summer session. Extensive evening/early morning classes. **Microcomputers:** 75 located in dormitories, libraries, computer centers. **Special facilities:** Art gallery, theater complex, child development center, laboratory elementary school.

DEGREES OFFERED. AA, AS, BA, BS, MA. 231 associate degrees awarded in 1992. 14% in engineering technologies, 8% allied health, 71% multi/interdisciplinary studies. 637 bachelor's degrees awarded. 22% in business and management, 20% teacher education, 8% engineering technologies, 9% psychology, 8% social sciences, 7% visual and performing arts. Graduate degrees offered in 5 major fields of study.

UNDERGRADUATE MAJORS. Associate: Chemistry, child development/care/guidance, computer and information sciences, drafting and design technology, driver and safety education, drug and alcohol abuse counseling, electronic technology, industrial technology, liberal/general studies, manufacturing technology, occupational safety and health technology, preengineering. **Bachelor's:** American studies, biological and physical sciences, biology, business administration and management, chemistry, child development/care/guidance, computer and information sciences, computer mathematics, drafting and design technology, early childhood education, economics, education, electronic technology, elementary education, English, English education, environmental science, film arts, fine arts, food science and nutrition, foreign languages education, French, geography, geology, graphic design, health education, history, home economics, home economics education, humanities and social sciences, industrial arts education, industrial technology, journalism, liberal/general studies, manufacturing technology, mathematics, mathematics education, music, music education, music performance, occupational safety and health technology, physical education, physics, political science and government, psychology, science education, secondary education, social science education, social sciences, sociology, Spanish, special education, sports management, sports medicine, visual and performing arts.

ACADEMIC PROGRAMS. 2-year transfer program, accelerated program, cooperative education, double major, honors program, independent study, internships, student-designed major, study abroad, teacher preparation, telecourses, visiting/exchange student program, weekend college, cross-registration. **Remedial services:** Learning center, preadmission summer program, reduced course load, mathematics center, reading center, writing process center. **ROTC:** Air Force, Army. **Placement/credit:** AP, CLEP General and Subject; 30 credit hours maximum for associate degree; 60 credit hours maximum for bachelor's degree.

ACADEMIC REQUIREMENTS. Freshmen must earn minimum GPA of 1.8 to continue in good standing. 74% of freshmen return for sophomore year. Students must declare major by end of second year. **Graduation requirements:** 60 hours for associate (30 in major), 126 hours for bachelor's (36 in major). Most students required to take courses in arts/fine arts, English, history, humanities, mathematics, biological/physical sciences, social sciences. **Postgraduate studies:** 78% from 2-year programs enter 4-year programs. 1% enter MBA programs, 14% enter other graduate study.

FRESHMAN ADMISSIONS. Selection criteria: High school record, class rank, recommendations, SAT scores. Preference to state residents. **High school preparation:** 10 units required. Required and recommended units include biological science 1, English 4, mathematics 2-3, physical science 1 and social science 2. **Test requirements:** SAT; score report by April 1.

1992 FRESHMAN CLASS PROFILE. 3,150 men and women applied, 2,443 accepted; 310 men enrolled, 452 women enrolled. **Characteristics:** 50% from in state, 75% live in college housing, 2% have minority backgrounds, 30% join fraternities/sororities. Average age is 19.

FALL-TERM APPLICATIONS. $20 fee, may be waived for applicants with need. $30 fee for out-of-state applicants. Closing date April 1; applicants notified on a rolling basis; must reply by May 1 or within 2 weeks if notified thereafter. Audition required for music education, music performance applicants. Portfolio required for art applicants. Essay required. Interview recommended. Deferred and early admission available.

STUDENT LIFE. Housing: Dormitories (women, coed); apartment, fraternity, sorority housing available. Special interest housing available. **Activities:** Student government, radio, student newspaper, television, yearbook, choral groups, concert band, dance, drama, jazz band, music ensembles, musical theater, symphony orchestra, guitar orchestra, saxophone quartet, fraternities, sororities, Newman Center, social activities council, Students Opposed to Arms Race (SOAR), public affairs forum, Concerned Students Coalition.

ATHLETICS. NCAA. **Intercollegiate:** Baseball M, basketball, cross-country, diving, field hockey W, skiing, soccer, softball W, swimming, track and field M, volleyball W. **Intramural:** Badminton, basketball, handball, ice hockey M, lacrosse, racquetball, rugby, soccer, softball, squash, swimming, tennis, volleyball, water polo.

STUDENT SERVICES. Aptitude testing, career counseling, employment service for undergraduates, freshman orientation, health services, on-campus day care, personal counseling, placement service for graduates, special adviser for adult students, veterans counselor, Student Academic Support Services, Developmental Studies, services/facilities for handicapped.

ANNUAL EXPENSES. Tuition and fees (1992-93): $2,856, $4,480 additional for out-of-state students. **Room and board:** $3,772. **Books and supplies:** $500. **Other expenses:** $800.

FINANCIAL AID. 54% of freshmen, 43% of continuing students receive some form of aid. 86% of grants, 79% of loans, 73% of jobs based on need. 321 enrolled freshmen were judged to have need, 310 were offered aid. Academic, music/drama, art, athletic scholarships available. **Aid applications:** No closing date; priority given to applications received by March 1; applicants notified on a rolling basis beginning on or about March 1.

ADDRESS/TELEPHONE. Kathryn Dodge, Director of Admissions, Keene State College, 229 Main Street, Keene, NH 03431. (603) 358-2276. (800) 833-4800.

McIntosh College
Dover, New Hampshire — CB code: 3553

2-year proprietary business college, coed. Founded in 1896. **Undergraduate enrollment:** 528 men and women full time; 413 men and women part time. **Faculty:** 21 total (10 full time), 7 with doctorates or other terminal degrees.

Location: Urban campus in large town; 5 miles from Durham, 75 miles from Boston. **Calendar:** Modular system of 6 8-week terms per year. **Microcomputers:** 71 located in libraries, classrooms.

DEGREES OFFERED. AS. 200 associate degrees awarded in 1992. 40% in business and management, 40% computer sciences, 20% allied health.

UNDERGRADUATE MAJORS. Accounting, business and management, business and office, business data programming, business systems analysis, computer and information sciences, information sciences and systems, legal secretary, marketing and distribution, medical assistant, medical secretary, microcomputer software, office supervision and management, secretarial and related programs, systems analysis.

ACADEMIC PROGRAMS. Double major, internships. **Remedial services:** Tutoring. **Placement/credit:** CLEP General and Subject; 15 credit hours maximum for associate degree.

ACADEMIC REQUIREMENTS. Freshmen must earn minimum GPA of 1.7 to continue in good standing.

FRESHMAN ADMISSIONS. Selection criteria: Open admissions.

1992 FRESHMAN CLASS PROFILE. 102 men and women enrolled. **Characteristics:** 78% from in state, 100% commute, 5% have minority backgrounds. Average age is 22.

FALL-TERM APPLICATIONS. $15 fee, may be waived for applicants with need. No closing date; applicants notified on a rolling basis. Interview recommended. Deferred and early admission available.

STUDENT LIFE. Activities: Student government, student newspaper, yearbook, drama.

ATHLETICS. Intercollegiate: Softball.

STUDENT SERVICES. Career counseling, employment service for undergraduates, freshman orientation, personal counseling, placement service for graduates.

ANNUAL EXPENSES. Tuition and fees (1992-93): $3,480. Tuition for 12-month period is $3,480, or $305 per course. Travel course tuition is $440 per course. **Books and supplies:** $363. **Other expenses:** $100.

FINANCIAL AID. 30% of freshmen, 35% of continuing students receive some form of aid. **Aid applications:** No closing date.

ADDRESS/TELEPHONE. Dorothy Johnsen, Director of Admissions, McIntosh College, 23 Cataract Avenue, Dover, NH 03820. (603) 742-1234. (800) MCINTOSH. Fax: (603) 742-7292.

New England College
Henniker, New Hampshire — CB code: 3657

4-year private business, liberal arts college, coed. Founded in 1946. **Accreditation:** Regional. **Undergraduate enrollment:** 523 men, 309 women full time; 97 men, 175 women part time. **Graduate enrollment:** 3 men, 24 women part time. **Faculty:** 108 total (88 full time), 29 with doctorates or other terminal degrees. **Location:** Rural campus in small town; 18 miles from Concord. **Calendar:** Semester, limited summer session. **Microcomputers:** 50 located in libraries, classrooms, computer centers. **Special facilities:** Electron microscope, art gallery, indoor hockey arena. **Additional facts:** Full-time study available at branch campus in Arundel, Sussex, England in 3 majors: business, international studies, British and European humanities.

DEGREES OFFERED. AA, BA, BS, MS. 6 associate degrees awarded in 1992. 100% in multi/interdisciplinary studies. 245 bachelor's degrees awarded. 25% in business and management, 14% communications, 11% teacher education, 5% letters/literature, 21% psychology, 8% social sciences, 8% visual and performing arts.

UNDERGRADUATE MAJORS. Associate: Liberal/general studies. **Bachelor's:** Accounting, advertising, biology, biology education, business administration and management, business and management, business economics, civil engineering, communications, dramatic arts, drawing, economics, elementary education, engineering and other disciplines, English, English education, environmental science, finance, history, international business management, international relations, journalism, liberal/general studies, management engineering, marketing and distribution, mathematics, mathematics education, painting, philosophy, photography, physical education, political science and government, prelaw, psychology, public relations, radio/television broadcasting, secondary education, social studies education, sociology, sports management.

ACADEMIC PROGRAMS. Double major, dual enrollment of high school students, honors program, independent study, internships, student-designed major, study abroad, teacher preparation, visiting/exchange student program, cross-registration, exchange program with Aichi Gakusen University, Japan; Quebec exchange program; liberal arts/career combination in engineering, business. **Remedial services:** Learning center, preadmission summer program, reduced course load, remedial instruction, special counselor, tutoring. **ROTC:** Air Force, Army. **Placement/credit:** AP, CLEP General and Subject, IB, institutional tests; 21 credit hours maximum for bachelor's degree.

ACADEMIC REQUIREMENTS. Freshmen must earn minimum GPA of 2.0 to continue in good standing. 75% of freshmen return for sophomore year. Students must declare major by end of second year. **Graduation requirements:** 60 hours for associate, 120 hours for bachelor's (45 in major). Most students required to take courses in arts/fine arts, English, history, humanities, mathematics, philosophy/religion, biological/physical sciences, social sciences. **Postgraduate studies:** 2% enter law school, 1% enter medical school, 10% enter MBA programs, 8% enter other graduate study.

FRESHMAN ADMISSIONS. Selection criteria: School achievement record most important, followed by recommendations, essay or personal statement, test scores, evidence of leadership, extracurricular activities. **High school preparation:** 12 units required. Required and recommended units include English 4, mathematics 2-3, social science 2 and science 2. Foreign language 2 recommended. **Test requirements:** SAT or ACT (SAT preferred); score report by August 15.

1992 FRESHMAN CLASS PROFILE. 7% had high school GPA of 3.0 or higher, 80% between 2.0 and 2.99. **Academic background:** Mid 50% of enrolled freshmen had SAT-V between 340-450, SAT-M between 370-490. 90% submitted SAT scores. **Characteristics:** 10% from in state, 95% live in college housing, 1% have minority backgrounds, 8% join fraternities/sororities. Average age is 18.

FALL-TERM APPLICATIONS. $30 fee, may be waived for applicants with need. No fee for in-state applicants. No closing date; priority given to applications received by April 1; applicants notified on a rolling basis; must reply by May 1 or within 5 weeks if notified thereafter. Essay required. Interview recommended. Portfolio recommended for art applicants. CRDA. Deferred and early admission available.

STUDENT LIFE. Housing: Dormitories (coed); apartment, fraternity, sorority housing available. 12 person suites, 4 person suites, and apartments available. Freshmen and sophomores required to live in college housing. Substance free residence hall available. **Activities:** Student government, magazine, radio, student newspaper, television, yearbook, dance, drama, music ensembles, musical theater, fraternities, sororities, International Student Association, Students Against Drunk Driving, Jewish Student Organization, Political Action Committee, Young Republicans, Literary Society, Environmental Action Committee, Womens' Network, Film Society, International Diplomacy Council, Student Outreach.

ATHLETICS. NCAA. **Intercollegiate:** Baseball M, basketball, field hockey W, horseback riding, ice hockey M, lacrosse, skiing, soccer, softball W. **Intramural:** Badminton, baseball M, basketball, cross-country, field hockey W, golf, gymnastics, horseback riding, lacrosse, rugby, skiing, skin diving, soccer, softball, table tennis, tennis, volleyball.

STUDENT SERVICES. Aptitude testing, career counseling, employment service for undergraduates, freshman orientation, health services, personal counseling, placement service for graduates, skills center, services/facilities for handicapped.

ANNUAL EXPENSES. Tuition and fees (1992-93): $11,990. **Room and board:** $4,970. **Books and supplies:** $400. **Other expenses:** $1,000.

FINANCIAL AID. 44% of freshmen, 32% of continuing students receive some form of aid. 99% of grants, 83% of loans, 86% of jobs based on need. 150 enrolled freshmen were judged to have need, all were offered aid. Academic, leadership scholarships available. **Aid applications:** No closing date; priority given to applications received by March 1; applicants notified on a rolling basis beginning on or about April 15; must reply by May 1 or within 2 weeks if notified thereafter.

ADDRESS/TELEPHONE. John Spaulding, Director of Admissions, New England College, 26 Bridge Street, Henniker, NH 03242-0792. (603) 428-2223. (800) 521-7642. Fax: (603) 428-7230.

New Hampshire College
Manchester, New Hampshire — CB code: 3649

Admissions: 86% of applicants accepted
Based on:
••• School record
•• Interview, recommendations, test scores
• Activities, essay, special talents
Completion: 75% of freshmen end year in good standing
10% enter graduate study

4-year private business, liberal arts college, coed. Founded in 1932. **Accreditation:** Regional. **Undergraduate enrollment:** 1,182 men and women full time. **Graduate enrollment:** 154 men, 66 women full time; 730 men, 483 women part time. **Faculty:** 184 total (96 full time), 53 with doctorates or other terminal degrees. **Location:** Suburban campus in small city; 60 miles from Boston. **Calendar:** Semester, limited summer session. Saturday and extensive evening/early morning classes. **Microcomputers:** 150 located in computer centers. **Special facilities:** Art gallery, video recording studio, on-campus hockey rink. **Additional facts:** Campuses in Manchester and Hooksett total 700 acres, Continuing Education Centers in Manchester, Nashua, Salem, Concord, Portsmouth and Laconia, Brunswick (ME), and Puerto Rico. Graduate School of Business located on North Campus, Concord, Laconia, Nashua, Portsmouth, Salem, Brunswick (ME), Celba, Puerto Rico.

DEGREES OFFERED. AS, AAS, BS, MS, MBA. 168 associate degrees awarded in 1992. 100% in business/office and marketing/distribution. 734 bachelor's degrees awarded. 75% in business and management, 18% business/office and marketing/distribution. Graduate degrees offered in 6 major fields of study.

UNDERGRADUATE MAJORS. Associate: Accounting, business administration and management, business and management, business and office, computer and information sciences, culinary arts, fashion merchandising, food production/management/services, liberal/general studies. **Bachelor's:** Accounting, business administration and management, business and management, business and office, business communication, business economics, business education, communications, computer and information sciences, English, English education, English literature, finance, hotel/motel and restaurant management, humanities, information sciences and systems, international business management, marketing and distribution, marketing and distributive education, marketing management, mathematics education, retailing, social sciences, sports management, systems analysis, technical management advisory services, tourism, transportation and travel marketing.

ACADEMIC PROGRAMS. 2-year transfer program, accelerated program, double major, honors program, independent study, internships, study abroad, teacher preparation, weekend college, cross-registration. **Remedial services:** Learning center, reduced course load, remedial instruction, special counselor, tutoring. **ROTC:** Air Force, Army. **Placement/credit:** AP, CLEP General and Subject, IB, institutional tests; 32 credit hours maximum for associate degree; 64 credit hours maximum for bachelor's degree.

ACADEMIC REQUIREMENTS. Freshmen must earn minimum GPA of 2.0 to continue in good standing. 65% of freshmen return for sophomore year. Students must declare major by end of first year. **Graduation requirements:** 60 hours for associate (18 in major), 120 hours for bachelor's (36 in major). Most students required to take courses in computer science, English, history, humanities, mathematics, social sciences. **Postgraduate studies:** 35% from 2-year programs enter 4-year programs.

FRESHMAN ADMISSIONS. Selection criteria: Academic success in high school, rank in class, SAT scores, recommendations, extracurricular activities, personal interview and essay considered. Required and recommended units include English 4 and mathematics 2-4. Social science 2 and science 2 recommended. Although the majority of applicants have a college preparatory background, those with a combination of business and college preparatory background will be considered. **Test requirements:** SAT; score report by August 1.

1992 FRESHMAN CLASS PROFILE. 938 men applied, 806 accepted, 203 enrolled; 734 women applied, 631 accepted, 128 enrolled. 23% had high school GPA of 3.0 or higher, 65% between 2.0 and 2.99. **Academic background:** Mid 50% of enrolled freshmen had SAT-V between 320-480, SAT-M between 360-530. 92% submitted SAT scores. **Characteristics:** 25% from in state, 89% live in college housing, 4% have minority backgrounds, 12% are foreign students, 10% join fraternities/sororities. Average age is 18.

FALL-TERM APPLICATIONS. No fee. No closing date; applicants notified on a rolling basis; must reply within 4 weeks. Essay required. Interview recommended. Deferred and early admission available. Institutional early decision plan. Applicants to undergraduate school of business encouraged to apply as early as possible.

STUDENT LIFE. Housing: Dormitories (coed); apartment, sorority housing available. Townhouses available on campus. **Activities:** Student government, radio, student newspaper, television, yearbook, drama, fraternities, sororities, over 40 clubs and organizations including Organization of International Students, Jewish Student Association, Catholic Student Association, Student Alumni Relations Council, Delta Mu Delta, Protestant Student Association, Muslim Student Association, Commuter Club, Student Activities Council.

ATHLETICS. NCAA. **Intercollegiate:** Baseball M, basketball, ice hockey M, lacrosse M, soccer, softball W, volleyball W. **Intramural:** Basketball, football M, ice hockey M, racquetball, soccer W, softball, tennis, volleyball. **Clubs:** Outing, ski clubs.

STUDENT SERVICES. Aptitude testing, career counseling, employment service for undergraduates, freshman orientation, health services, personal counseling, special adviser for adult students, services/facilities for handicapped.

ANNUAL EXPENSES. Tuition and fees (1992-93): $10,008. **Room and board:** $5,004. **Books and supplies:** $400. **Other expenses:** $900.

FINANCIAL AID. 73% of freshmen, 72% of continuing students receive some form of aid. 66% of grants, 93% of loans, 25% of jobs based on need. 170 enrolled freshmen were judged to have need, all were offered aid. Academic, athletic scholarships available. **Aid applications:** No closing date; priority given to applications received by March 15; applicants notified on a rolling basis beginning on or about February 15; must reply within 2 weeks.

ADDRESS/TELEPHONE. Brad Poznanski, Director of Admission, New Hampshire College, 2500 North River Road, Manchester, NH 03106-1045. (603) 645-9611. (800) NHC-4YOU. Fax: (603) 645-9665.

New Hampshire Technical College: Berlin

Berlin, New Hampshire CB code: 3646

2-year public technical college, coed. Founded in 1966. **Accreditation:** Regional. **Undergraduate enrollment:** 178 men, 202 women full time; 51 men, 154 women part time. **Faculty:** 44 total (32 full time), 2 with doctorates or other terminal degrees. **Location:** Suburban campus in large town; 110 miles from Concord, 100 miles from Portland, Maine. **Calendar:** Semester, limited summer session. **Microcomputers:** 45 located in libraries, classrooms, computer centers.

DEGREES OFFERED. AS, AAS. 120 associate degrees awarded in 1992.

UNDERGRADUATE MAJORS. Accounting, automotive technology, business and management, computer and information sciences, drafting, education, electromechanical technology, food production/management/services, forestry and related sciences, industrial equipment maintenance and repair, machine tool operation/machine shop, mental health/human services, nursing, renewable natural resources, secretarial and related programs.

ACADEMIC PROGRAMS. Double major, independent study, internships. **Remedial services:** Learning center, reduced course load, tutoring. **Placement/credit:** AP, CLEP General and Subject, institutional tests; 32 credit hours maximum for associate degree.

ACADEMIC REQUIREMENTS. Freshmen must earn minimum GPA of 1.6 to continue in good standing. 60% of freshmen return for sophomore year. Students must declare major on application. **Graduation requirements:** 64 hours for associate (25 in major). Most students required to take courses in computer science, English, mathematics, biological/physical sciences, social sciences.

FRESHMAN ADMISSIONS. Selection criteria: School record, class rank, counselor recommendations, test results, interview considered. **High school preparation:** 9 units required. Required and recommended units include science 1-2. Biological science 1, English 4 and mathematics 2 recommended. Other high school course requirements vary according to major field of study. **Test requirements:** ACT. NLN PreAdmission Exam-RN required for nursing students. All others participate in a campus-designed placement test battery.

1992 FRESHMAN CLASS PROFILE. 145 men, 261 women enrolled. 15% had high school GPA of 3.0 or higher, 70% between 2.0 and 2.99. **Characteristics:** 80% from in state, 99% commute, 1% have minority backgrounds. Average age is 23.

FALL-TERM APPLICATIONS. $10 fee, may be waived for applicants with need. No closing date; priority given to applications received by May 1; applicants notified on a rolling basis beginning on or about December 1; must reply within 4 weeks. Interview recommended. Deferred admission available. Closing date for nursing applications is February 1.

STUDENT LIFE. Housing: Dormitories (women, coed). **Activities:** Student government, student newspaper, yearbook, drama.

ATHLETICS. Intercollegiate: Basketball, skiing, soccer. **Intramural:** Basketball, bowling, golf, skiing, softball, volleyball.

STUDENT SERVICES. Career counseling, employment service for undergraduates, freshman orientation, on-campus day care, personal counseling, placement service for graduates, special adviser for adult students, veterans counselor, financial adviser, services/facilities for handicapped.

ANNUAL EXPENSES. Tuition and fees (1992-93): $2,125, $1,038 additional for out-of-district students, $2,854 additional for out-of-state students. **Room and board:** $2,030 room only. **Books and supplies:** $450. **Other expenses:** $1,800.

FINANCIAL AID. 80% of freshmen, 80% of continuing students receive some form of aid. All grants, 87% of loans, all jobs based on need. 152 enrolled freshmen were judged to have need, all were offered aid. **Aid applications:** No closing date; priority given to applications received by May 1; applicants notified on a rolling basis beginning on or about June 1; must reply within 2 weeks. **Additional information:** Students from other New England states may qualify for special out-of-state tuition rate through New England Regional Student Progam.

ADDRESS/TELEPHONE. Kathleen Tremblay, Dean of Student Affairs, New Hampshire Technical College: Berlin, 2020 Riverside Drive, Berlin, NH 03570. (603) 752-1113. (800) 445-4525. Fax: (603) 752-6335.

New Hampshire Technical College: Claremont

Claremont, New Hampshire CB code: 3684

2-year public technical college, coed. Founded in 1967. **Accreditation:** Regional. **Undergraduate enrollment:** 81 men, 170 women full time; 153 men, 316 women part time. **Faculty:** 48 total (36 full time). **Location:** Rural campus in large town; 50 miles from Concord. **Calendar:** Semester, limited summer session. **Microcomputers:** 45 located in libraries, computer centers.

DEGREES OFFERED. AS, AAS. 83 associate degrees awarded in 1992. 5% in business and management, 8% engineering technologies, 87% allied health.

UNDERGRADUATE MAJORS. Accounting, business and management, computer technology, electrical and electronics equipment repair, manufacturing technology, medical laboratory technologies, microcomputer software, nursing, occupational therapy assistant, physical therapy assistant, respiratory therapy.

ACADEMIC PROGRAMS. Accelerated program, cooperative education, double major, independent study, internships. **Remedial services:** Learning center, reduced course load, tutoring. **Placement/credit:** CLEP General and Subject, institutional tests; 16 credit hours maximum for associate degree.

ACADEMIC REQUIREMENTS. Freshmen must earn minimum GPA

of 1.9 to continue in good standing. 75% of freshmen return for sophomore year. Students must declare major on enrollment. **Graduation requirements:** 64 hours for associate (32 in major). Most students required to take courses in English, mathematics, biological/physical sciences, social sciences.

FRESHMAN ADMISSIONS. Selection criteria: School achievement record, interview, test scores, recommendations, previous work experience considered. Preference to those in top 50% of class and to state residents. Typing required for medical assistant, chemistry required for nursing and medical laboratory programs. Algebra recommended for all applicants.

1992 FRESHMAN CLASS PROFILE. 60 men, 156 women enrolled. **Characteristics:** 80% from in state, 100% commute. Average age is 28.

FALL-TERM APPLICATIONS. $10 fee. Closing date August 1; priority given to applications received by May 1; applicants notified on a rolling basis; must reply within 4 weeks. Interview required.

STUDENT LIFE. Activities: Student government.

STUDENT SERVICES. Employment service for undergraduates, freshman orientation, health services, on-campus day care, personal counseling, placement service for graduates, veterans counselor, services/facilities for handicapped.

ANNUAL EXPENSES. Tuition and fees (1992-93): $2,135, $2,854 additional for out-of-state students. **Books and supplies:** $550. **Other expenses:** $1,100.

FINANCIAL AID. 76% of freshmen, 80% of continuing students receive some form of aid. 79% of grants, 88% of loans, all jobs based on need. 128 enrolled freshmen were judged to have need, all were offered aid. Academic, state/district residency scholarships available. **Aid applications:** No closing date; priority given to applications received by May 1; applicants notified on a rolling basis beginning on or about June 1; must reply within 2 weeks.

ADDRESS/TELEPHONE. Marie T. Bender, Dean of Student Affairs, New Hampshire Technical College: Claremont, One College Drive, Claremont, NH 03743-9707. (603) 542-7744. Fax: (603) 543-1844.

New Hampshire Technical College: Laconia
Laconia, New Hampshire CB code: 3850

2-year public technical college, coed. Founded in 1967. **Accreditation:** Regional. **Undergraduate enrollment:** 216 men, 82 women full time; 94 men, 60 women part time. **Faculty:** 43 total (27 full time). **Location:** Suburban campus in large town; 95 miles from Boston, 25 miles from Concord. **Calendar:** Semester, limited summer session. Extensive evening/early morning classes. **Microcomputers:** 80 located in libraries, classrooms, computer centers. **Additional facts:** Off-campus site.

DEGREES OFFERED. AAS. 110 associate degrees awarded in 1992. 5% in business and management, 5% business/office and marketing/distribution, 20% engineering technologies, 13% parks/recreation, protective services, public affairs, 57% trade and industry.

UNDERGRADUATE MAJORS. Accounting, airline piloting and navigation, automotive mechanics, automotive technology, aviation management, business and management, business and office, electrical installation, electrical technology, fire control and safety technology, fire protection, graphic and printing production, graphic arts technology, hotel/motel and restaurant management, marine maintenance, office supervision and management, power plant operation and maintenance, secretarial and related programs.

ACADEMIC PROGRAMS. Accelerated program, cooperative education, double major, independent study, internships. **Remedial services:** Learning center, reduced course load, remedial instruction, special counselor, tutoring. **Placement/credit:** AP, CLEP Subject, institutional tests; 12 credit hours maximum for associate degree.

ACADEMIC REQUIREMENTS. Freshmen must earn minimum GPA of 1.5 to continue in good standing. 80% of freshmen return for sophomore year. Students must declare major on application. **Graduation requirements:** 65 hours for associate (45 in major). Most students required to take courses in English, mathematics, biological/physical sciences, social sciences. **Additional information:** Cooperative programs in graphic arts, automotive technology, hospitality management, electrical programs and marine technology.

FRESHMAN ADMISSIONS. Selection criteria: School achievement record, class rank, test scores, and recommendations important. Interview, extracurricular and work experience also considered. Recommended units include biological science 2, English 4, mathematics 3, physical science 2 and social science 2. One algebra and 1 geometry required for electrical programs, 2 algebra recommended. Algebra recommended for automotive degree. **Test requirements:** ACT ASSET required except of students with prior degrees or with test scores above certain point.

1992 FRESHMAN CLASS PROFILE. 193 men, 94 women enrolled. 10% had high school GPA of 3.0 or higher, 70% between 2.0 and 2.99. **Characteristics:** 75% from in state, 50% commute, 1% have minority backgrounds. Average age is 23.

FALL-TERM APPLICATIONS. $10 fee, may be waived for applicants with need. No closing date; priority given to applications received by March 1; applicants notified on a rolling basis; must reply within 4 weeks. Interview recommended.

STUDENT LIFE. Housing: Some fire science majors may reside in local fire stations; room and board in exchange for volunteer firefighter status. Dormitory option available at New Hampshire Technical Institute, 25 miles away. **Activities:** Student government, student newspaper, yearbook.

ATHLETICS. Intercollegiate: Baseball M, basketball, golf, soccer M, softball W, volleyball. **Intramural:** Ice hockey M, skiing, table tennis.

STUDENT SERVICES. Aptitude testing, career counseling, employment service for undergraduates, freshman orientation, personal counseling, placement service for graduates, veterans counselor, learning disabled counseling and advocacy, services/facilities for handicapped.

ANNUAL EXPENSES. Tuition and fees (1992-93): $2,135, $2,854 additional for out-of-state students. **Books and supplies:** $500. **Other expenses:** $800.

FINANCIAL AID. 41% of freshmen, 35% of continuing students receive some form of aid. 72% of grants, 82% of loans, all jobs based on need. 129 enrolled freshmen were judged to have need, all were offered aid. Academic, state/district residency scholarships available. **Aid applications:** No closing date; priority given to applications received by May 1; applicants notified on a rolling basis beginning on or about June 15; must reply within 2 weeks.

ADDRESS/TELEPHONE. Donald E. Morrissey, Dean of Students, New Hampshire Technical College: Laconia, Route 106, Prescott Hill, Laconia, NH 03246. (603) 524-3207 ext. 40. Fax: (603) 524-8084.

New Hampshire Technical College: Manchester
Manchester, New Hampshire CB code: 3660

2-year public technical college, coed. Founded in 1945. **Accreditation:** Regional. **Undergraduate enrollment:** 302 men, 289 women full time; 530 men, 578 women part time. **Faculty:** 200 total (50 full time), 11 with doctorates or other terminal degrees. **Location:** Suburban campus in small city; 50 miles from Boston. **Calendar:** Semester, limited summer session. **Microcomputers:** 75 located in libraries, classrooms, computer centers.

DEGREES OFFERED. AS, AAS. 192 associate degrees awarded in 1992. 5% in business/office and marketing/distribution, 23% engineering technologies, 29% health sciences, 18% allied health, 25% trade and industry.

UNDERGRADUATE MAJORS. Advertising, air conditioning/heating/refrigeration mechanics, air conditioning/heating/refrigeration technology, automotive mechanics, automotive technology, biomedical equipment technology, business and office, commercial art, community services, construction, drafting, drafting and design technology, early childhood education, electrical and electronics equipment repair, electrical technology, electrical/electronics/communications engineering, electromechanical technology, electronic technology, exercise science technician, family and community services, health unit clerk/coordinator, illustration design, marriage and family counseling, mechanical design technology, medical records administration, medical secretary, mental health/human services, nursing, office supervision and management, power plant operation and maintenance, rehabilitation counseling/services, secretarial and related programs, sports medicine, welding technology.

ACADEMIC PROGRAMS. Cooperative education, independent study, internships, student-designed major. **Remedial services:** Learning center, preadmission summer program, reduced course load, special counselor, tutoring, pretechnology curriculum. **Placement/credit:** AP, CLEP General and Subject, institutional tests; 32 credit hours maximum for associate degree.

ACADEMIC REQUIREMENTS. Freshmen must earn minimum GPA of 1.5 to continue in good standing. 63% of freshmen return for sophomore year. Students must declare major on application. **Graduation requirements:** 64 hours for associate (32 in major). Most students required to take courses in computer science, English, mathematics, biological/physical sciences, social sciences.

FRESHMAN ADMISSIONS. Selection criteria: Academic achievement record, recommendations, interview considered. Required units include English 4 and mathematics 1. Algebra required. Geometry and biology required for some programs. **Test requirements:** SAT or ACT required for nursing applicants; score report by July 31.

1992 FRESHMAN CLASS PROFILE. 155 men, 225 women enrolled. **Academic background:** Mid 50% of enrolled freshmen had ACT composite between 15-20. 15% submitted ACT scores. **Characteristics:** 85% from in state, 100% commute, 4% have minority backgrounds. Average age is 21.

FALL-TERM APPLICATIONS. $10 fee, may be waived for applicants with need. No closing date; applicants notified on a rolling basis; must reply within 2 weeks. Interview required. Essay required for nursing applicants. Portfolio recommended for Commercial design and illustration applicants. Deferred admission available. Early application (by March 1) recommended for nursing, commercial design and illustration.

STUDENT LIFE. Activities: Student government, student newspaper, yearbook.

ATHLETICS. Intercollegiate: Basketball M, golf, ice hockey, skiing, volleyball. **Intramural:** Basketball, skiing, skin diving, volleyball.

STUDENT SERVICES. Aptitude testing, career counseling, employment service for undergraduates, freshman orientation, personal counsel-

ing, placement service for graduates, veterans counselor, services/facilities for handicapped.

ANNUAL EXPENSES. Tuition and fees (1992-93): $2,145, $2,854 additional for out-of-state students. **Books and supplies:** $500. **Other expenses:** $1,770.

FINANCIAL AID. 32% of freshmen, 21% of continuing students receive some form of aid. 88% of loans, all jobs based on need. **Aid applications:** No closing date; priority given to applications received by May 1; applicants notified on a rolling basis beginning on or about April 15; must reply within 2 weeks.

ADDRESS/TELEPHONE. Kenneth R. McCann, Dean of Student Affairs and Admissions Officer, New Hampshire Technical College: Manchester, 1066 Front Street, Manchester, NH 03102-8518. (603) 668-6706 ext. 202. Fax: (603) 668 5354.

New Hampshire Technical College: Nashua
Nashua, New Hampshire CB code: 3643

2-year public technical college, coed. Founded in 1967. **Accreditation:** Regional. **Undergraduate enrollment:** 322 men, 136 women full time; 397 men, 270 women part time. **Faculty:** 86 total (36 full time), 2 with doctorates or other terminal degrees. **Location:** Suburban campus in small city; 20 miles from Lowell, Massachusetts. **Calendar:** Semester, limited summer session. Extensive evening/early morning classes. **Microcomputers:** 85 located in libraries, classrooms, computer centers.

DEGREES OFFERED. AAS. 165 associate degrees awarded in 1992. 35% in business and management, 10% business/office and marketing/distribution, 30% engineering technologies, 25% trade and industry.

UNDERGRADUATE MAJORS. Accounting, aeronautical technology, aircraft mechanics, auto body repair technology, automotive mechanics, automotive technology, business and management, business computer applications, business computer/console/peripheral equipment operation, computer servicing technology, computer technology, drafting, drafting and design technology, electrical and electronics equipment repair, electromechanical technology, electronic technology, industrial equipment maintenance and repair, industrial technology, legal assistant/paralegal, machine tool operation/machine shop, manufacturing technology, marketing and distribution, marketing management, mechanical design technology, microcomputer software, optical technology, quality control technology, robotics, telecommunications, trade and industrial supervision and management.

ACADEMIC PROGRAMS. Internships. **Remedial services:** Learning center, preadmission summer program, reduced course load, remedial instruction, tutoring, college skills course. **Placement/credit:** AP, CLEP Subject, institutional tests; 48 credit hours maximum for associate degree.

ACADEMIC REQUIREMENTS. Freshmen must earn minimum GPA of 1.8 to continue in good standing. 75% of freshmen return for sophomore year. Students must declare major on application. **Graduation requirements:** 64 hours for associate (32 in major). Most students required to take courses in English, humanities, mathematics, biological/physical sciences, social sciences.

FRESHMAN ADMISSIONS. Selection criteria: Open admissions. One unit algebra required for business and technical programs, 2 for computer technology. **Test requirements:** ACT/ASSET required.

1992 FRESHMAN CLASS PROFILE. 163 men, 159 women enrolled. **Characteristics:** 85% from in state, 100% commute, 3% have minority backgrounds, 1% are foreign students. Average age is 23.

FALL-TERM APPLICATIONS. $10 fee, may be waived for applicants with need. No closing date; applicants notified on a rolling basis; must reply within 4 weeks. Interview required. Deferred and early admission available. Priority given to applicants for full-time study.

STUDENT LIFE. Activities: Student government, student newspaper, yearbook.

ATHLETICS. Intercollegiate: Baseball M, basketball M, ice hockey M, softball W. **Intramural:** Golf. **Clubs:** Outing.

STUDENT SERVICES. Career counseling, employment service for undergraduates, freshman orientation, on-campus day care, personal counseling, placement service for graduates, special adviser for adult students, veterans counselor, services/facilities for handicapped.

ANNUAL EXPENSES. Tuition and fees (1992-93): $2,155, $1,038 additional for out-of-district students, $2,854 additional for out-of-state students. **Books and supplies:** $500. **Other expenses:** $500.

FINANCIAL AID. All grants, 77% of loans, 79% of jobs based on need. **Aid applications:** No closing date; priority given to applications received by May 1; applicants notified on a rolling basis beginning on or about June 1; must reply within 2 weeks.

ADDRESS/TELEPHONE. John T. Fischer, Dean of Student Affairs, New Hampshire Technical College: Nashua, 505 Amherst Street, Nashua, NH 03061-2052. (603) 882-6923. Fax: (603) 882-8690.

New Hampshire Technical College: Stratham
Stratham, New Hampshire CB code: 3661

2-year public technical college, coed. Founded in 1945. **Accreditation:** Regional. **Undergraduate enrollment:** 156 men, 161 women full time; 69 men, 130 women part time. **Faculty:** 46 total (31 full time), 7 with doctorates or other terminal degrees. **Location:** Rural campus in small town; 45 miles from Boston. **Calendar:** Semester, limited summer session. **Microcomputers:** 100 located in classrooms, computer centers. **Additional facts:** Proximity to University of New Hampshire provides for extended resources.

DEGREES OFFERED. AS, AAS. 122 associate degrees awarded in 1992. 28% in business and management, 9% engineering technologies, 33% allied health, 30% trade and industry.

UNDERGRADUATE MAJORS. Accounting, automotive mechanics, automotive technology, business administration and management, business and management, business computer/console/peripheral equipment operation, drafting, drafting and design technology, electromechanical technology, electronic technology, human resources development, liberal/general studies, machine tool operation/machine shop, mechanical design technology, microcomputer software, nursing, secretarial and related programs, surgical technology.

ACADEMIC PROGRAMS. Accelerated program, double major, dual enrollment of high school students, independent study, internships. **Remedial services:** Preadmission summer program, reduced course load, remedial instruction, tutoring. **Placement/credit:** AP, CLEP General and Subject, institutional tests.

ACADEMIC REQUIREMENTS. Freshmen must earn minimum GPA of 1.7 to continue in good standing. 70% of freshmen return for sophomore year. Students must declare major on enrollment. **Graduation requirements:** 72 hours for associate (40 in major). Most students required to take courses in English, mathematics, biological/physical sciences, social sciences. **Additional information:** Part-time day study available to matriculated and nonmatriculated students.

FRESHMAN ADMISSIONS. Selection criteria: Rank in top three-fifths of class preferred. Out-of-state applicants must rank in top half. State residents given priority. Recommended units include biological science 1, English 4, mathematics 2, physical science 1 and social science 2. High school vocational and college-preparatory courses recommended. For mechanical-technical majors, algebra I and II and geometry recommended. For associate nursing applicants, biology, chemistry, algebra I required. For business management, typing or keyboarding skills required. **Test requirements:** National League for Nursing Pre-Admission Assessment for Registered Nursing required for registered nursing applicants. ACT-PEP Nursing Fundamentals Test required for admissions to associate degree nursing program as advanced standing students. Career Guidance Placement Test given to technical majors on selected basis.

1992 FRESHMAN CLASS PROFILE. 149 men, 217 women enrolled. 10% had high school GPA of 3.0 or higher, 80% between 2.0 and 2.99. **Characteristics:** 86% from in state, 100% commute, 4% have minority backgrounds, 1% are foreign students. Average age is 23.

FALL-TERM APPLICATIONS. $10 fee, may be waived for applicants with need. Closing date July 15; priority given to applications received by April 1; applicants notified on a rolling basis beginning on or about February 1; must reply within 4 weeks. Interview recommended. Interview required for allied health applicants, recommended for all technical applicants. Early admission available. Out-of-state students encouraged to apply in early fall of senior year but not before completion of one marking period.

STUDENT LIFE. Housing: Housing at off-season prices along New Hampshire-Maine seacoast is 15-minute commute from campus. **Activities:** Student government, student newspaper, student senate, Phi Theta Kappa.

ATHLETICS. Intercollegiate: Baseball, basketball, golf, skiing, soccer, softball, volleyball. **Intramural:** Table tennis.

STUDENT SERVICES. Aptitude testing, career counseling, employment service for undergraduates, freshman orientation, placement service for graduates, veterans counselor, financial aid counselor, services/facilities for handicapped.

ANNUAL EXPENSES. Tuition and fees (1992-93): $2,135, $2,854 additional for out-of-state students. **Books and supplies:** $750. **Other expenses:** $2,000.

FINANCIAL AID. 57% of freshmen, 43% of continuing students receive some form of aid. All grants, 73% of loans, all jobs based on need. 101 enrolled freshmen were judged to have need, all were offered aid. **Aid applications:** No closing date; priority given to applications received by May 1; applicants notified on a rolling basis; must reply within 2 weeks.

ADDRESS/TELEPHONE. Karen Blanchard, Admissions Counselor, New Hampshire Technical College: Stratham, 277 Portsmouth Avenue, Stratham, NH 03885-2297. (603) 772-1194. Fax: (603) 772-1198. (800) 522-1194.

New Hampshire Technical Institute
Concord, New Hampshire CB code: 3647

Admissions: 58% of applicants accepted
Based on: ••• School record
•• Interview, recommendations, test scores
Completion: 60% of freshmen end year in good standing
70% graduate, 20% of these enter 4-year programs

2-year public technical college, coed. Founded in 1965. **Accreditation:** Regional. **Undergraduate enrollment:** 565 men, 443 women full time; 119 men, 293 women part time. **Faculty:** 135 total (110 full time), 2 with doctorates or other terminal degrees. **Location:** Suburban campus in large town; 75 miles from Boston. **Calendar:** Semester, extensive summer session. Saturday and extensive evening/early morning classes. **Microcomputers:** 125 located in dormitories, libraries, computer centers. **Special facilities:** Christa McAuliffe Planetarium.

DEGREES OFFERED. AS. 432 associate degrees awarded in 1992. 20% in business and management, 6% computer sciences, 25% engineering technologies, 49% allied health.

UNDERGRADUATE MAJORS. Accounting, architectural technologies, business administration and management, business and management, computer and information sciences, computer programming, computer technology, criminal justice studies, dental hygiene, early childhood education, electronic technology, emergency medical technologies, engineering and engineering-related technologies, finance, health sciences, industrial technology, manufacturing technology, mechanical design technology, mental health/human services, nursing, radiograph medical technology, ultrasound technology.

ACADEMIC PROGRAMS. Remedial services: Learning center, preadmission summer program, reduced course load, remedial instruction, special counselor, tutoring. **Placement/credit:** AP, CLEP General and Subject, institutional tests.

ACADEMIC REQUIREMENTS. Freshmen must earn minimum GPA of 1.5 to continue in good standing. Students must declare major on application. **Graduation requirements:** 64 hours for associate. Most students required to take courses in English, social sciences.

FRESHMAN ADMISSIONS. Selection criteria: School grade average, class rank, interview considered. Test scores important for health program applicants. Recommended units include English 4, mathematics 3 and science 2. High school academic subject requirements vary according to program. Strong background in mathematics and natural sciences recommended. **Test requirements:** Allied Health Aptitude Test, National League for Nursing Pre-Nursing Test, special challenge test for practical nursing required.

1992 FRESHMAN CLASS PROFILE. 1,985 men and women applied, 1,144 accepted; 446 men enrolled, 452 women enrolled. 56% had high school GPA of 3.0 or higher, 38% between 2.0 and 2.99. **Academic background:** Mid 50% of enrolled freshmen had SAT-V between 400-600, SAT-M between 400-600. 70% submitted SAT scores. **Characteristics:** 90% from in state, 75% commute, 9% have minority backgrounds, 5% join fraternities/sororities. Average age is 22.

FALL-TERM APPLICATIONS. $10 fee. No closing date; applicants notified on a rolling basis; must reply within 30 days. Essay required for dental hygiene, radiograph techology applicants. Interview recommended. Interview required for health program applicants, recommended for others. Deferred admission available.

STUDENT LIFE. Housing: Dormitories (men, women, coed). **Activities:** Student government, student newspaper, yearbook, fraternities, sororities.

ATHLETICS. NJCAA, NSCAA. **Intercollegiate:** Baseball M, basketball, golf, ice hockey M, skiing, soccer, softball W, track and field, volleyball W. **Intramural:** Basketball, golf, ice hockey M, volleyball.

STUDENT SERVICES. Aptitude testing, career counseling, freshman orientation, health services, personal counseling, placement service for graduates, special adviser for adult students, veterans counselor, tutoring service, services/facilities for handicapped.

ANNUAL EXPENSES. Tuition and fees (1992-93): $2,241, $2,852 additional for out-of-state students. **Room and board:** $2,990. **Books and supplies:** $400. **Other expenses:** $1,600.

FINANCIAL AID. 45% of freshmen, 65% of continuing students receive some form of aid. 71% of grants, 71% of loans, all jobs based on need. 187 enrolled freshmen were judged to have need, all were offered aid. Academic, state/district residency, leadership scholarships available. **Aid applications:** No closing date; priority given to applications received by May 1; applicants notified on a rolling basis beginning on or about June 1; must reply within 2 weeks.

ADDRESS/TELEPHONE. Francis P. Meyer, Coordinator of Admissions, New Hampshire Technical Institute, 11 Institute Drive, Concord, NH 03301. (603) 225-1800 ext. 863. Fax: (603) 225-1895.

Notre Dame College
Manchester, New Hampshire CB code: 3670

Admissions: 79% of applicants accepted
Based on: ••• School record
•• Recommendations, test scores
• Activities, essay, interview, religious affiliation/commitment, special talents
Completion: 92% of freshmen end year in good standing
40% graduate, 15% of these enter graduate study

4-year private liberal arts college, coed, affiliated with Roman Catholic Church. Founded in 1950. **Accreditation:** Regional. **Undergraduate enrollment:** 127 men, 349 women full time; 52 men, 275 women part time. **Graduate enrollment:** 35 men, 133 women full time; 64 men, 302 women part time. **Faculty:** 120 total (45 full time), 24 with doctorates or other terminal degrees. **Location:** Suburban campus in small city; 50 miles from Boston. **Calendar:** Semester. **Microcomputers:** 26 located in libraries, computer centers. **Additional facts:** Graduate education courses offered at off-campus sites in Nashua, Newport, and Manchester.

DEGREES OFFERED. AA, AS, BA, BS, MA, MEd. 7 associate degrees awarded in 1992. 57% in teacher education, 43% multi/interdisciplinary studies. 106 bachelor's degrees awarded. 17% in business and management, 31% teacher education, 7% law, 19% psychology, 6% social sciences, 11% visual and performing arts. Graduate degrees offered in 11 major fields of study.

UNDERGRADUATE MAJORS. Associate: Early childhood education, liberal/general studies, prepharmacy, teacher aide. **Bachelor's:** Art education, biology, biology education, business and management, business education, commercial art, communications, early childhood education, education, elementary education, English, English education, fine arts, history, junior high education, legal assistant/paralegal, psychology, religion, secondary education, social studies education, special education, visual and performing arts.

ACADEMIC PROGRAMS. Accelerated program, double major, education specialist degree, independent study, internships, study abroad, teacher preparation, visiting/exchange student program, cross-registration. **Remedial services:** Learning center, reduced course load, remedial instruction, special counselor, tutoring. **Placement/credit:** AP, CLEP General and Subject, institutional tests; 30 credit hours maximum for bachelor's degree.

ACADEMIC REQUIREMENTS. Freshmen must earn minimum GPA of 1.5 to continue in good standing. 67% of freshmen return for sophomore year. Students must declare major by end of first year. **Graduation requirements:** 60 hours for associate (30 in major), 123 hours for bachelor's (45 in major). Most students required to take courses in arts/fine arts, English, history, humanities, mathematics, philosophy/religion, biological/physical sciences, social sciences. **Postgraduate studies:** 1% from 2-year programs enter 4-year programs.

FRESHMAN ADMISSIONS. Selection criteria: High school achievement record is most important. Test scores, recommendations, activities, essay, and interview considered. **High school preparation:** 16 units required. Required and recommended units include English 4, foreign language 2, mathematics 2-3, social science 2-3 and science 2-3. Art applicants may substitute vocational subjects for academic requirements. **Test requirements:** SAT or ACT (SAT preferred); score report by May 31.

1992 FRESHMAN CLASS PROFILE. 89 men applied, 65 accepted, 26 enrolled; 298 women applied, 241 accepted, 83 enrolled. 42% had high school GPA of 3.0 or higher, 54% between 2.0 and 2.99. 15% were in top tenth and 35% were in top quarter of graduating class. **Academic background:** Mid 50% of enrolled freshmen had SAT-V between 390-450, SAT-M between 400-460. 90% submitted SAT scores. **Characteristics:** 61% from in state, 65% live in college housing, 4% have minority backgrounds, 2% are foreign students. Average age is 20.

FALL-TERM APPLICATIONS. $25 fee, may be waived for applicants with need. Closing date August 1; priority given to applications received by May 1; applicants notified on a rolling basis beginning on or about January 1; must reply by May 1 or within 3 weeks if notified thereafter. Portfolio required for art applicants. Essay required. Interview recommended. CRDA. Deferred and early admission available. EDP-F.

STUDENT LIFE. Housing: Dormitories (men, women, coed). Residences are large Victorian homes housing 10 to 40 students each. **Activities:** Student government, magazine, radio, student newspaper, yearbook, choral groups, drama, music ensembles, musical theater, choir, handbells, New Thalian Players, Psychology Club, peer counseling program, Campus Ministry Council, student orientation committee, Students Against Drunk Drivers, Amnesty International, Habitat for Humanity, commuter club.

ATHLETICS. NAIA. **Intercollegiate:** Basketball, rowing (crew), soccer. **Intramural:** Basketball, swimming, tennis, volleyball.

STUDENT SERVICES. Career counseling, employment service for undergraduates, freshman orientation, health services, personal counseling, placement service for graduates, special adviser for adult students, services/facilities for handicapped.

ANNUAL EXPENSES. Tuition and fees (1992-93): $8,966. **Room and board:** $4,635. **Books and supplies:** $650. **Other expenses:** $925.

FINANCIAL AID. 90% of freshmen, 70% of continuing students receive some form of aid. 85% of grants, 82% of loans, 65% of jobs based on need. 95 enrolled freshmen were judged to have need, all were offered aid. Academic, leadership scholarships available. **Aid applications:** No closing date; priority given to applications received by March 15; applicants notified on a rolling basis beginning on or about April 1; must reply by May 1 or within 2 weeks if notified thereafter.

ADDRESS/TELEPHONE. Joseph P. Wagner, Dean of Admissions, Notre Dame College, 2321 Elm Street, Manchester, NH 03104-2299. (603) 669-4298 ext. 163. Fax: (603) 644-8316.

Plymouth State College of the University System of New Hampshire

Plymouth, New Hampshire — CB code: 3690

Admissions: 69% of applicants accepted
Based on:
••• School record
•• Activities, special talents, test scores
• Essay, interview, recommendations
Completion: 85% of freshmen end year in good standing
60% graduate, 20% of these enter graduate study

4-year public college of arts and sciences and business, teachers college, coed. Founded in 1871. **Accreditation:** Regional. **Undergraduate enrollment:** 3,600 men and women. **Graduate enrollment:** 400 men and women. **Faculty:** 264 total (162 full time), 216 with doctorates or other terminal degrees. **Location:** Suburban campus in small town; 40 miles from Concord, 100 miles from Boston. **Calendar:** Semester, limited summer session. **Microcomputers:** 185 located in dormitories, libraries, classrooms, computer centers, campus-wide network. **Special facilities:** Institute for New Hampshire Studies, art gallery, planetarium, cultural arts center.

DEGREES OFFERED. AA, AS, BA, BS, BFA, MBA, MEd. 35 associate degrees awarded in 1992. 589 bachelor's degrees awarded. Graduate degrees offered in 8 major fields of study.

UNDERGRADUATE MAJORS. Associate: Liberal/general studies, public affairs, teacher aide. **Bachelor's:** Accounting, actuarial sciences, American studies, anthropology, applied mathematics, art education, art history, atmospheric sciences and meteorology, biochemistry, biological and physical sciences, biology, business and management, business economics, chemistry, community health work, comparative literature, computer and information sciences, creative writing, dramatic arts, drawing, early childhood education, education, elementary education, English, English education, English literature, environmental science, European studies, fine arts, foreign languages education, French, geography, graphic design, health education, health sciences, history, humanities and social sciences, information sciences and systems, junior high education, liberal/general studies, marketing and distribution, marketing management, mathematics, mathematics education, medieval studies, music, music education, painting, philosophy, physical education, physical sciences, political science and government, printmaking, psychology, public administration, science education, sculpture, secondary education, social science education, social sciences, social studies education, social work, sociology, Spanish, special education, sports medicine, studio art, tourism, visual and performing arts.

ACADEMIC PROGRAMS. Double major, honors program, independent study, internships, student-designed major, study abroad, teacher preparation, telecourses, cross-registration. **Remedial services:** Reduced course load, special counselor, tutoring, reading laboratory, discussion/support group. **ROTC:** Air Force, Army. **Placement/credit:** AP, CLEP General and Subject, institutional tests; 30 credit hours maximum for bachelor's degree.

ACADEMIC REQUIREMENTS. Freshmen must earn minimum GPA of 2.0 to continue in good standing. 80% of freshmen return for sophomore year. Students must declare major by end of second year. **Graduation requirements:** 60 hours for associate (24 in major), 122 hours for bachelor's (48 in major). Most students required to take courses in arts/fine arts, computer science, English, foreign languages, history, mathematics, philosophy/religion, biological/physical sciences, social sciences. **Postgraduate studies:** 26% from 2-year programs enter 4-year programs.

FRESHMAN ADMISSIONS. Selection criteria: School achievement record most important followed by test scores, extracurricular activities, and recommendations. Recommended units include English 4, foreign language 2, mathematics 3, social science 3 and science 3. College preparatory program recommended. Mathematics units preferred algebra I and II and geometry. **Test requirements:** SAT or ACT (SAT preferred); score report by April 1.

1992 FRESHMAN CLASS PROFILE. 3,481 men and women applied, 2,400 accepted; 383 men enrolled, 395 women enrolled. **Academic background:** Mid 50% of enrolled freshmen had SAT-V between 430-480, SAT-M between 430-500. 95% submitted SAT scores. **Characteristics:** 50% from in state, 90% live in college housing, 2% have minority backgrounds, 8% join fraternities/sororities. Average age is 18.

FALL-TERM APPLICATIONS. $20 fee, may be waived for applicants with need. $30 fee for out-of-state applicants. Closing date April 1; applicants notified on a rolling basis beginning on or about November 1; must reply by May 1 or within 10 days if notified thereafter. Audition required for music applicants. Interview recommended. Essay recommended. CRDA. Early admission available.

STUDENT LIFE. Housing: Dormitories (men, women, coed); apartment, fraternity, sorority, cooperative housing available. **Activities:** Student government, film, magazine, radio, student newspaper, television, yearbook, choral groups, concert band, dance, drama, jazz band, music ensembles, musical theater, pep band, handbell ringers, fraternities, sororities, campus ministry, Big Brothers, Big Sisters, International Student Organization.

ATHLETICS. NCAA. **Intercollegiate:** Baseball M, basketball, diving W, field hockey W, football M, ice hockey M, lacrosse, skiing, soccer, softball W, swimming W, tennis, wrestling M. **Intramural:** Badminton, basketball, gymnastics, racquetball, rowing (crew), rugby, skiing, softball, squash, swimming, table tennis, track and field, volleyball.

STUDENT SERVICES. Career counseling, employment service for undergraduates, freshman orientation, health services, on-campus day care, personal counseling, placement service for graduates, veterans counselor, women's center, services/facilities for handicapped.

ANNUAL EXPENSES. Tuition and fees (projected): $3,281, $4,840 additional for out-of-state students. **Room and board:** $3,884. **Books and supplies:** $600. **Other expenses:** $850.

FINANCIAL AID. 60% of freshmen, 70% of continuing students receive some form of aid. 92% of grants, 84% of loans, 48% of jobs based on need. 426 enrolled freshmen were judged to have need, 423 were offered aid. Academic, music/drama scholarships available. **Aid applications:** No closing date; priority given to applications received by March 1; applicants notified on a rolling basis beginning on or about March 1; must reply by May 1 or within 4 weeks if notified thereafter. **Additional information:** Fifty scholarships based on academic achievement and potential and eight grants in recognition of music or theatre talent annually awarded.

ADDRESS/TELEPHONE. Eugene Fahey, Director of Admissions, Plymouth State College of the University System of New Hampshire, 15 Holderness Road, Plymouth, NH 03264. (603) 535-2237. (800) 842-6900. Fax: (603) 535-2714.

Rivier College

Nashua, New Hampshire — CB code: 3728

Admissions: 77% of applicants accepted
Based on:
••• School record
•• Activities, essay, interview, recommendations, test scores
Completion: 85% of freshmen end year in good standing
70% graduate

4-year private liberal arts college, coed, affiliated with Roman Catholic Church. Founded in 1933. **Accreditation:** Regional. **Undergraduate enrollment:** 71 men, 527 women full time; 28 men, 328 women part time. **Graduate enrollment:** 34 men, 49 women full time; 319 men, 613 women part time. **Faculty:** 202 total (64 full time), 26 with doctorates or other terminal degrees. **Location:** Suburban campus in small city; 19 miles from Manchester, 45 miles from Boston. **Calendar:** Semester, limited summer session. Saturday classes. **Microcomputers:** 88 located in dormitories, classrooms, computer centers. **Special facilities:** Multilevel studio art complex including art gallery, paralegal/law library.

DEGREES OFFERED. AA, AS, BA, BS, BFA, MA, MS, MBA, MEd. 79 associate degrees awarded in 1992. 17% in business and management, 6% computer sciences, 65% health sciences, 6% multi/interdisciplinary studies. 152 bachelor's degrees awarded. 17% in business and management, 10% business/office and marketing/distribution, 7% computer sciences, 15% teacher education, 12% law, 7% psychology, 7% social sciences, 7% visual and performing arts. Graduate degrees offered in 18 major fields of study.

UNDERGRADUATE MAJORS. Associate: Accounting, business data processing and related programs, computer and information sciences, early childhood education, liberal/general studies, nursing, studio art. **Bachelor's:** Accounting, art education, biological and physical sciences, biology, business administration and management, business and management, business and office, business data processing and related programs, business education, chemistry, communications, computer and information sciences, early childhood education, education, elementary education, English, English education, foreign languages education, French, graphic design, history, illustration design, legal assistant/paralegal, liberal/general studies, marketing and distribution, mathematics, mathematics education, mathematics/computer science, mathematics/computer science education, multimedia design, nursing, political science and government, predentistry, prelaw, premedicine, preveterinary, psychology, science education, secondary education, social science education, sociology, Spanish, special education, studio art.

ACADEMIC PROGRAMS. Double major, independent study, internships, student-designed major, teacher preparation, cross-registration. **Remedial services:** Learning center, reduced course load, special counselor, tutoring. **ROTC:** Air Force. **Placement/credit:** AP, CLEP General and Subject, institutional tests; 45 credit hours maximum for associate degree; 90 credit hours maximum for bachelor's degree.

ACADEMIC REQUIREMENTS. Freshmen must earn minimum GPA of 2.0 to continue in good standing. 65% of freshmen return for sophomore year. Students must declare major on enrollment. **Graduation requirements:** 60 hours for associate (45 in major), 120 hours for bachelor's (54 in major). Most students required to take courses in arts/fine arts, English, foreign languages, history, humanities, mathematics, philosophy/religion, biological/physical sciences, social sciences. **Additional information:** Graduates offered fifth year of tuition-free study in liberal arts.

FRESHMAN ADMISSIONS. Selection criteria: High school academic record most important. Activities and work, SAT scores, recommendations, and interviews also considered. Slide portfolio required for art and design applicants. **High school preparation:** 16 units required. Required and recommended units include English 4, foreign language 2, mathematics 2, social science 2 and science 1. Biological science 1 and physical science 1 recommended. 5 electives required in academic areas. Algebra I and chemistry required for nursing applicants. **Test requirements:** SAT or ACT (SAT preferred). **Additional information:** Applications submitted through spring and summer will be considered.

1992 FRESHMAN CLASS PROFILE. 107 men applied, 80 accepted, 46 enrolled; 349 women applied, 270 accepted, 156 enrolled. 50% had high school GPA of 3.0 or higher, 48% between 2.0 and 2.99. **Academic background:** Mid 50% of enrolled freshmen had SAT-V between 380-470, SAT-M between 380-520. 93% submitted SAT scores. **Characteristics:** 44% from in state, 70% commute, 3% have minority backgrounds, 1% are foreign students. Average age is 18.

FALL-TERM APPLICATIONS. $25 fee, may be waived for applicants with need. No closing date; applicants notified on a rolling basis; must reply by May 1 or within 4 weeks if notified thereafter. Portfolio required for art and design applicants. Essay required. Interview recommended. Interview required of nursing applicants, recommended for all. CRDA. Deferred admission available. Institutional early decision plan. early action applicants received by November 15 are given early action consideration automatically. Decision (by December 1) is based on academic record through junior year.

STUDENT LIFE. Housing: Dormitories (coed). Housing availability guaranteed. **Activities:** Student government, magazine, student newspaper, yearbook, choral groups, campus ministry, model United Nations, interest clubs, preprofessional clubs, Project HUG, recycling committee, social committee, nontraditional studentcommittee, Pax Christi.

ATHLETICS. Intercollegiate: Basketball, cross-country, softball W, volleyball W. **Intramural:** Basketball, skiing, soccer, softball, tennis, volleyball.

STUDENT SERVICES. Career counseling, employment service for undergraduates, freshman orientation, health services, on-campus day care, personal counseling, placement service for graduates, special adviser for adult students, veterans counselor, services/facilities for handicapped.

ANNUAL EXPENSES. Tuition and fees: $9,870. **Room and board:** $4,600. **Books and supplies:** $600. **Other expenses:** $900.

FINANCIAL AID. 80% of freshmen, 83% of continuing students receive some form of aid. 82% of grants, 80% of loans, 70% of jobs based on need. 65 enrolled freshmen were judged to have need, 60 were offered aid. Academic, leadership, alumni affiliation scholarships available. **Aid applications:** Closing date April 1; priority given to applications received by March 16; applicants notified on a rolling basis beginning on or about March 15; must reply by May 1 or within 2 weeks if notified thereafter.

ADDRESS/TELEPHONE. Maureen Karr, Director of Admissions, Rivier College, 420 South Main Street, Nashua, NH 03060-5086. (603) 888-1311 ext.8507. Fax: (603) 888-6447.

St. Anselm College
Manchester, New Hampshire — CB code: 3748

Admissions: 69% of applicants accepted
Based on: ••• Essay, school record
•• Recommendations, test scores
• Activities, interview, special talents
Completion: 88% of freshmen end year in good standing
78% graduate, 22% of these enter graduate study

4-year private liberal arts college, coed, affiliated with Roman Catholic Church. Founded in 1889. **Accreditation:** Regional. **Undergraduate enrollment:** 809 men, 1,048 women full time; 41 men, 95 women part time. **Faculty:** 160 total (120 full time), 104 with doctorates or other terminal degrees. **Location:** Suburban campus in small city; 50 miles from Boston. **Calendar:** Semester, limited summer session. **Microcomputers:** 200 located in dormitories, libraries, classrooms, computer centers. **Special facilities:** 670-seat theater, observatory, chapel, art center. **Additional facts:** Administered by Order of St. Benedict.

DEGREES OFFERED. AS, BA, BS. 100% in parks/recreation, protective services, public affairs. 457 bachelor's degrees awarded. 21% in business and management, 8% health sciences, 9% letters/literature, 7% life sciences, 10% parks/recreation, protective services, public affairs, 9% psychology, 23% social sciences.

UNDERGRADUATE MAJORS. Associate: Law enforcement and corrections. **Bachelor's:** Biochemistry, biological and physical sciences, biology, business and management, business economics, chemistry, classics, computer and information sciences, computer science/business, computer science/mathematics, criminal justice studies, economics, engineering and other disciplines, English, English literature, financial economics, fine arts, foreign languages (multiple emphasis), French, history, Latin, liberal/general studies, mathematics, nursing, philosophy, political science and government, predentistry, prelaw, premedicine, prepharmacy, psychology, secondary education, sociology, Spanish, theological studies.

ACADEMIC PROGRAMS. Independent study, internships, study abroad, teacher preparation, visiting/exchange student program, Washington semester, cross-registration; liberal arts/career combination in engineering. **Remedial services:** Learning center, reduced course load, special counselor, tutoring. **ROTC:** Air Force, Army. **Placement/credit:** AP, CLEP General and Subject, institutional tests; 30 credit hours maximum for bachelor's degree.

ACADEMIC REQUIREMENTS. Freshmen must earn minimum GPA of 1.8 to continue in good standing. 87% of freshmen return for sophomore year. Students must declare major by end of second year. **Graduation requirements:** 132 hours for bachelor's (30 in major). Most students required to take courses in English, foreign languages, humanities, philosophy/religion, biological/physical sciences. **Postgraduate studies:** 4% enter law school, 2% enter medical school, 6% enter MBA programs, 10% enter other graduate study. **Additional information:** 4-semester humanities program required of all students.

FRESHMAN ADMISSIONS. Selection criteria: School achievement record most important, followed by test scores, recommendations, character. Special consideration to disadvantaged students and children of alumni. Geographical distribution and special talents also considered. **High school preparation:** 16 units required. Required units include biological science 1, English 4, foreign language 2, mathematics 3, physical science 2 and social science 2. Chemistry required for nursing applicants. **Test requirements:** SAT or ACT (SAT preferred); score report by March 1.

1992 FRESHMAN CLASS PROFILE. 1,028 men applied, 722 accepted, 234 enrolled; 1,303 women applied, 896 accepted, 279 enrolled. 55% had high school GPA of 3.0 or higher, 45% between 2.0 and 2.99. 17% were in top tenth and 43% were in top quarter of graduating class. **Academic background:** Mid 50% of enrolled freshmen had SAT-V between 430-540, SAT-M between 450-570. 99% submitted SAT scores. **Characteristics:** 19% from in state, 88% live in college housing, 2% have minority backgrounds. Average age is 18.

FALL-TERM APPLICATIONS. $25 fee, may be waived for applicants with need. Closing date April 15; priority given to applications received by March 1; applicants notified on a rolling basis beginning on or about January 15; must reply by May 1. Essay required. Interview recommended. CRDA. Deferred and early admission available. EDP-F.

STUDENT LIFE. Housing: Dormitories (men, women); apartment housing available. **Activities:** Student government, magazine, student newspaper, yearbook, choral groups, drama, jazz band, pep band, Knights of Columbus, Oblates of St. Benedict, Big Brothers and Big Sisters, political union, King Edward Society, Red Key Society, Pax Christi, Center for Volunteers.

ATHLETICS. NCAA. **Intercollegiate:** Baseball M, basketball, cross-country, golf M, ice hockey M, skiing, soccer, softball W, tennis. **Intramural:** Basketball, bowling, field hockey W, handball, ice hockey M, racquetball, rowing (crew) M, rugby, skiing, soccer, softball, swimming, table tennis, tennis, volleyball.

STUDENT SERVICES. Aptitude testing, career counseling, employment service for undergraduates, freshman orientation, health services, personal counseling, placement service for graduates, veterans counselor, services/facilities for handicapped.

ANNUAL EXPENSES. Tuition and fees (1992-93): $10,870. **Room and board:** $5,200. **Books and supplies:** $400. **Other expenses:** $1,000.

FINANCIAL AID. 54% of freshmen, 50% of continuing students receive some form of aid. 79% of grants, 98% of loans, 64% of jobs based on need. 345 enrolled freshmen were judged to have need, 310 were offered aid. Athletic scholarships available. **Aid applications:** Closing date April 15; priority given to applications received by March 1; applicants notified on a rolling basis beginning on or about March 1; must reply by May 1.

ADDRESS/TELEPHONE. Donald E. Healy, Director of Admissions, St. Anselm College, St. Anselm Drive, Manchester, NH 03102-1310. (603) 641-7500. Fax: (603) 641-7116.

School for Lifelong Learning
Durham, New Hampshire — CB code: 0458

4-year public nontraditional college for adults, coed. Founded in 1972. **Accreditation:** Regional. **Undergraduate enrollment:** 70 men, 158 women full time; 347 men, 1,074 women part time. **Graduate enrollment:** 2 women full time; 73 men, 188 women part time. **Faculty:** 216 total. **Location:** Suburban campus in small town. **Calendar:** 10-, 12-, and 15-week terms, semester hour system. **Microcomputers:** 100 located in classrooms. **Additional facts:** 6 regions statewide. Calendar varies according to region. Academic resources of state university system available to all students. Classes held in local communities at 40 different sites. Master's courses provided at 5 sites for continuing education of teachers and nursing professionals.

DEGREES OFFERED. B. 133 associate degrees awarded in 1992. 100% in multi/interdisciplinary studies. 117 bachelor's degrees awarded. 50% in business and management, 11% multi/interdisciplinary studies, 39% social sciences.

UNDERGRADUATE MAJORS. Behavioral sciences, business and management, computer and information sciences, early childhood education, liberal/general studies. behavioral sciences, business administration and management, early childhood education, humanities and social sciences, liberal/general studies.

ACADEMIC PROGRAMS. 2-year transfer program, accelerated program, double major, independent study, internships, student-designed major, telecourses. **Remedial services:** Remedial instruction. **Placement/credit:** AP, CLEP General and Subject, institutional tests; 32 credit hours maximum for associate degree; 64 credit hours maximum for bachelor's degree.

ACADEMIC REQUIREMENTS. To continue in good academic standing, students must earn a 2.0 minimum GPA. Students must declare major on application. **Graduation requirements:** 64 hours for associate (28 in major), 124 hours for bachelor's (32 in major). Most students required to take courses in computer science, English, humanities, mathematics, biological/physical sciences, social sciences. **Postgraduate studies:** 26% from 2-year programs enter 4-year programs.

FRESHMAN ADMISSIONS. Selection criteria: Open admissions. 2 years work experience, or 2 years out of formal education, plus 60 credits required for admission to the Bachelor of General Studies program.

1992 FRESHMAN CLASS PROFILE. Characteristics: 100% commute.

FALL-TERM APPLICATIONS. $20 fee for applicants to associate degree program; $35 fee to bachelor's degree program. No closing date; applicants notified on a rolling basis. Essay required. Interview recommended.

STUDENT LIFE. Activities: Alumni/Learner Association.

STUDENT SERVICES. Career counseling, employment service for undergraduates, special adviser for adult students, veterans counselor, services/facilities for handicapped.

ANNUAL EXPENSES. Tuition and fees (projected): $3,540. **Books and supplies:** $550.

FINANCIAL AID. 16% of continuing students receive some form of aid. All grants, all loans based on need. 93 enrolled freshmen were judged to have need, 65 were offered aid. **Aid applications:** No closing date; applicants notified on a rolling basis.

ADDRESS/TELEPHONE. Tessa McDonnell, Assistant Dean for Learner Services, School for Lifelong Learning, USNH, Dunlap Center, Durham, NH 03824-3545. (603) 862-1692. Fax: (603) 868-3021.

University of New Hampshire
Durham, New Hampshire CB code: 3918

Admissions: 74% of applicants accepted
Based on: ••• School record
•• Activities, essay, recommendations, special talents, test scores
• Interview
Completion: 90% of freshmen end year in good standing
70% graduate, 15% of these enter graduate study

4-year public university, coed. Founded in 1866. **Accreditation:** Regional. **Undergraduate enrollment:** 4,570 men, 5,525 women full time; 201 men, 408 women part time. **Graduate enrollment:** 441 men, 399 women full time; 326 men, 387 women part time. **Faculty:** 904 total (647 full time), 584 with doctorates or other terminal degrees. **Location:** Rural campus in small town; 65 miles from Boston. **Calendar:** Semester, extensive summer session. Extensive evening/early morning classes. **Microcomputers:** 300 located in dormitories, libraries, computer centers, campus-wide network. **Special facilities:** Observatory, art gallery, natural area, estuary, shoals marine research laboratory, animal nutrition and exercise physiology laboratories, hyperbaric chamber.

DEGREES OFFERED. AA, AS, AAS, BA, BS, BFA, MA, MS, MBA, MEd, PhD. 226 associate degrees awarded in 1992. 28% in agriculture, 33% business and management, 8% engineering technologies, 31% multi/interdisciplinary studies. 2,304 bachelor's degrees awarded. 6% in agriculture, 15% business and management, 7% communications, 7% engineering, 11% letters/literature, 5% psychology, 18% social sciences. Graduate degrees offered in 70 major fields of study.

UNDERGRADUATE MAJORS. Associate: Animal sciences, business and management, civil technology, computer and information sciences, construction, food management, food production/management/services, forest products processing technology, horticultural science, hotel/motel and restaurant management, liberal/general studies, marketing and distribution, small business management and ownership, veterinarian's assistant. **Bachelor's:** Agricultural sciences, agronomy, animal sciences, anthropology, applied mathematics, art education, art history, biochemistry, biology, botany, business administration and management, cell biology, chemical engineering, chemistry, city/community/regional planning, civil engineering, classics, clinical laboratory science, communications, computer and information sciences, conservation and regulation, dairy, dramatic arts, earth sciences, ecology, economics, electrical technology, electrical/electronics/communications engineering, elementary education, English, English education, entomology, environmental science, family/consumer resource management, fine arts, food science and nutrition, forestry and related sciences, French, geography, geology, German, Greek (classical), health care administration, health sciences, history, horticulture, hotel/motel and restaurant management, humanities, individual and family development, international studies, journalism, Latin, liberal/general studies, linguistics, marine biology, mathematics, mathematics education, mechanical engineering, medical laboratory technologies, microbiology, molecular biology, music, music education, music history and appreciation, music performance, music theory and composition, nursing, nutritional sciences, occupational therapy, parks and recreation management, philosophy, physical education, physics, plant physiology, plant sciences, political science and government, practical nursing, preveterinary, psychology, recreation therapy, renewable natural resources, Russian, social work, sociology, soil sciences, Spanish, speech pathology/audiology, statistics, studio art, trade and industrial education, water resources, wildlife management, zoology.

ACADEMIC PROGRAMS. Accelerated program, double major, external degree, honors program, independent study, internships, semester at sea, student-designed major, study abroad, teacher preparation, telecourses, visiting/exchange student program, Washington semester, cross-registration, Undergraduate Research Opportunities Program; combined bachelor's/graduate program in business administration. **Remedial services:** Learning center, reduced course load, remedial instruction, special counselor, tutoring. **ROTC:** Air Force, Army. **Placement/credit:** AP, CLEP General and Subject, IB; 48 credit hours maximum for associate degree; 64 credit hours maximum for bachelor's degree.

ACADEMIC REQUIREMENTS. Freshmen must earn minimum GPA of 2.0 to continue in good standing. 84% of freshmen return for sophomore year. Students must declare major by end of second year. **Graduation requirements:** 64 hours for associate, 128 hours for bachelor's (32 in major). Most students required to take courses in arts/fine arts, English, foreign languages, history, humanities, mathematics, philosophy/religion, biological/physical sciences, social sciences. **Postgraduate studies:** 65% from 2-year programs enter 4-year programs.

FRESHMAN ADMISSIONS. Selection criteria: School achievement record, course selection, class rank, recommendations, test scores, cocurricular activities, character/leadership. Special consideration to children of alumni. Out-of-state students typically rank in the top 20% of their class. **High school preparation:** 17 units recommended. Recommended units include English 4, foreign language 3, mathematics 4, social science 2 and science 4. Additional requirements determined by intended major. **Test requirements:** SAT; score report by February 1.

1992 FRESHMAN CLASS PROFILE. 4,536 men applied, 3,217 accepted, 1,093 enrolled; 5,556 women applied, 4,299 accepted, 1,348 enrolled. 26% were in top tenth and 49% were in top quarter of graduating class. **Academic background:** Mid 50% of enrolled freshmen had SAT-V between 440-540, SAT-M between 490-610. 100% submitted SAT scores. **Characteristics:** 52% from in state, 81% live in college housing, 1% have minority backgrounds, 1% are foreign students, 10% join fraternities/sororities. Average age is 18.

FALL-TERM APPLICATIONS. $20 fee, may be waived for applicants with need. $40 fee for out-of-state applicants. Closing date February 1; applicants notified on or about April 15; must reply by May 1. Audition required for music applicants. Portfolio required for studio art applicants. Essay required. Interview recommended. CRDA. Deferred admission available. Institutional early decision plan. Early notification program is nonbinding early decision. Students need not respond until May 1.

STUDENT LIFE. Housing: Dormitories (men, women, coed); apartment, fraternity, sorority housing available. Special interest residence halls (environmental awareness, physical fitness) available. Undergraduate and graduate student apartments available on campus. **Activities:** Student government, magazine, radio, student newspaper, television, yearbook, choral groups, concert band, dance, drama, jazz band, marching band, music ensembles, musical theater, pep band, symphony orchestra, fraternities, sororities, Hillel, Progressive Student Network, Black Student Union, Catholic Student Organization, Democratic Student Organization, Great Bay Food Co-op, Handicapped Student Organization, Health Services Consumer Board, Young Republicans, Women's Center.

ATHLETICS. NCAA. **Intercollegiate:** Baseball M, basketball, cross-country, diving, field hockey W, football M, golf, gymnastics W, horseback riding, ice hockey, lacrosse, rowing (crew), skiing, soccer, swimming, tennis, track and field. **Intramural:** Basketball, bowling, cross-country, ice hockey M, sailing, soccer, softball, swimming, tennis, track and field, volleyball, water polo.

STUDENT SERVICES. Career counseling, freshman orientation, health services, on-campus day care, personal counseling, placement service for graduates, special adviser for adult students, veterans counselor, services/facilities for handicapped.

ANNUAL EXPENSES. Tuition and fees (1992-93): $3,941, $7,060 additional for out-of-state students. **Room and board:** $3,728. **Books and supplies:** $500. **Other expenses:** $1,100.

FINANCIAL AID. 49% of freshmen, 42% of continuing students receive some form of aid. All grants, 88% of loans, 50% of jobs based on need. 1,173 enrolled freshmen were judged to have need, 1,150 were offered aid. Academic, music/drama, art, athletic, leadership scholarships available. **Aid applications:** No closing date; priority given to applications received by February 15; applicants notified on a rolling basis beginning on or about February 15; must reply by July 1 or within 2 weeks if notified thereafter.

ADDRESS/TELEPHONE. Stanwood C. Fish, Dean of Admissions and Financial Aid, University of New Hampshire, 4 Garrison Avenue, Durham, NH 03824. (603) 862-1360.

University of New Hampshire at Manchester

Manchester, New Hampshire CB code: 2094

4-year public branch campus, liberal arts college, coed. **Accreditation:** Regional. **Undergraduate enrollment:** 140 men, 190 women full time; 63 men, 150 women part time. **Faculty:** 96 total (24 full time), 48 with doctorates or other terminal degrees. **Location:** Urban campus in small city; 50 miles from Boston. **Calendar:** Semester, limited summer session. Extensive evening/early morning classes. **Microcomputers:** Located in computer centers. **Additional facts:** Master of arts in teaching and master of education degrees may be completed at Manchester campus, but applicants must apply through Durham campus.

DEGREES OFFERED. AA, AS, BA, BS, MEd. 58 associate degrees awarded in 1992. 9% in business and management, 82% multi/interdisciplinary studies, 6% social sciences. 21 bachelor's degrees awarded. 43% in letters/literature, 57% psychology. Graduate degrees offered in 4 major fields of study.

UNDERGRADUATE MAJORS. Associate: Biology, business administration and management, liberal/general studies, studio art. **Bachelor's:** Business administration and management, communications, English, history, humanities, interpreter for the deaf, psychology.

ACADEMIC PROGRAMS. 2-year transfer program, independent study, internships, student-designed major, teacher preparation, telecourses, cross-registration. **Remedial services:** Learning center, reduced course load, remedial instruction, special counselor, tutoring, alternative freshman year. **Placement/credit:** AP, CLEP General and Subject, institutional tests; 48 credit hours maximum for associate degree; 64 credit hours maximum for bachelor's degree.

ACADEMIC REQUIREMENTS. Freshmen must earn minimum GPA of 2.0 to continue in good standing. 60% of freshmen return for sophomore year. Students must declare major by end of second year. **Graduation requirements:** 64 hours for associate (16 in major), 128 hours for bachelor's (36 in major). Most students required to take courses in arts/fine arts, computer science, English, foreign languages, history, humanities, mathematics, philosophy/religion, biological/physical sciences, social sciences. **Postgraduate studies:** 60% from 2-year programs enter 4-year programs.

FRESHMAN ADMISSIONS. Selection criteria: Achievement in high school college preparatory program most important. SAT scores should be consistent with achievement. Recommendation, essay, interview very helpful for students of moderate achievement or in nontraditional cases. **High school preparation:** 13 units required. Required and recommended units include English 4, foreign language 2-3, mathematics 3-4, social science 2 and science 2-3. **Test requirements:** SAT or ACT (SAT preferred); score report by June 15.

1992 FRESHMAN CLASS PROFILE. 247 men and women applied, 134 accepted; 89 enrolled. **Characteristics:** 99% from in state, 100% commute, 10% have minority backgrounds, 1% are foreign students. Average age is 21.

FALL-TERM APPLICATIONS. $20 fee, may be waived for applicants with need. Closing date June 15; priority given to applications received by April 1; applicants notified on a rolling basis; must reply by May 1. Interview required for alternative freshman year applicants. Essay required. CRDA. Deferred admission available.

STUDENT LIFE. Activities: Student government, student newspaper.

STUDENT SERVICES. Career counseling, freshman orientation, services/facilities for handicapped.

ANNUAL EXPENSES. Tuition and fees (1992-93): $2,820, $5,480 additional for out-of-state students. **Books and supplies:** $500. **Other expenses:** $1,000.

FINANCIAL AID. 26% of freshmen, 25% of continuing students receive some form of aid. All grants, 91% of loans, all jobs based on need. 21 enrolled freshmen were judged to have need, all were offered aid. Academic scholarships available. **Aid applications:** No closing date; priority given to applications received by May 1; applicants notified on a rolling basis beginning on or about May 1; must reply within 2 weeks.

ADDRESS/TELEPHONE. James Washington, Jr, Director of Admissions, University of New Hampshire at Manchester, 220 Hackett Hill Road, Manchester, NH 03102. (603) 668-0700 ext. 250. Fax: (603) 623-2745.

White Pines College

Chester, New Hampshire CB code: 3977

Admissions: 97% of applicants accepted
Based on: ••• Recommendations, school record
•• Essay, interview
• Activities, special talents, test scores
Completion: 75% of freshmen end year in good standing
64% graduate, 46% of these enter 4-year programs

2-year private junior, liberal arts college, coed. Founded in 1965. **Accreditation:** Regional. **Undergraduate enrollment:** 24 men, 41 women full time; 4 men, 6 women part time. **Faculty:** 20 total (8 full time), 8 with doctorates or other terminal degrees. **Location:** Rural campus in rural community; 10 miles from Manchester. **Calendar:** Semester. **Microcomputers:** 14 located in libraries, classrooms.

DEGREES OFFERED. AA. 24 associate degrees awarded in 1992. 8% in business and management, 17% communications, 20% multi/interdisciplinary studies, 13% parks/recreation, protective services, public affairs, 42% visual and performing arts.

UNDERGRADUATE MAJORS. Advertising, business and management, communications, fine arts, graphic design, illustration design, journalism, liberal/general studies, photography, radio/television broadcasting, small business management and ownership, social work.

ACADEMIC PROGRAMS. 2-year transfer program, double major, independent study, internships, student-designed major. **Remedial services:** Reduced course load, remedial instruction, special counselor, tutoring. **Placement/credit:** CLEP General, institutional tests; 12 credit hours maximum for associate degree.

ACADEMIC REQUIREMENTS. Freshmen must earn minimum GPA of 2.0 to continue in good standing. 65% of freshmen return for sophomore year. Students must declare major on application. **Graduation requirements:** 61 hours for associate (21 in major). Most students required to take courses in arts/fine arts, English, history, mathematics, biological/physical sciences, social sciences.

FRESHMAN ADMISSIONS. Selection criteria: School achievement record, interview, recommendations considered, and test scores if submitted. Recommended units include biological science 1, English 4, mathematics 2, physical science 1 and social science 1.

1992 FRESHMAN CLASS PROFILE. 29 men applied, 28 accepted, 18 enrolled; 42 women applied, 41 accepted, 25 enrolled. 50% had high school GPA of 3.0 or higher, 43% between 2.0 and 2.99. 23% were in top tenth and 57% were in top quarter of graduating class. **Academic background:** Mid 50% of enrolled freshmen had SAT-V between 350-480, SAT-M between 350-450. 30% submitted SAT scores. **Characteristics:** 67% from in state, 54% live in college housing, 1% have minority backgrounds, 14% are foreign students. Average age is 20.

FALL-TERM APPLICATIONS. $20 fee, may be waived for applicants with need. No closing date; applicants notified on a rolling basis; must reply by April 15 or within 2 weeks if notified after April 1. Interview recommended. Portfolio recommended for art applicants. Essay recommended. Deferred admission available.

STUDENT LIFE. Housing: Dormitories (men, women, coed). **Activities:** Student government, yearbook, choral groups, drama.

ATHLETICS. Intramural: Badminton, basketball, softball, swimming, table tennis, tennis, volleyball.

STUDENT SERVICES. Career counseling, freshman orientation, health services, personal counseling, placement service for graduates, services/facilities for handicapped.

ANNUAL EXPENSES. Tuition and fees (1992-93): $6,500. **Room and board:** $3,800. **Books and supplies:** $440. **Other expenses:** $900.

FINANCIAL AID. 50% of freshmen, 60% of continuing students receive some form of aid. All grants, 71% of loans, all jobs based on need. 18 enrolled freshmen were judged to have need, all were offered aid. Academic, state/district residency scholarships available. **Aid applications:** Closing date May 1; priority given to applications received by March 15; applicants notified on or about May 1; must reply within 4 weeks.

ADDRESS/TELEPHONE. Robert Fouquette, Director of Admissions, White Pines College, 40 Chester Street, Chester, NH 03036. (603) 887-4401.

New Jersey

Assumption College for Sisters
Mendham, New Jersey CB code: 2009

2-year private liberal arts college, women only, affiliated with Roman Catholic Church. Founded in 1953. **Accreditation:** Regional. **Undergraduate enrollment:** 13 women full time; 19 women part time. **Faculty:** 17 total (6 full time), 23 with doctorates or other terminal degrees. **Location:** Rural campus in small town; 35 miles from New York City. **Calendar:** Semester, limited summer session. **Microcomputers:** 11 located in libraries, classrooms, computer centers. **Special facilities:** Museum. **Additional facts:** Sister Formation College accepting only women belonging to Roman Catholic religious congregations. Conducted by Sisters of Christian Charity.

DEGREES OFFERED. AA. 100% in multi/interdisciplinary studies.

UNDERGRADUATE MAJORS. Liberal/general studies, theological studies.

ACADEMIC PROGRAMS. 2-year transfer program, independent study. **Remedial services:** Reduced course load, remedial instruction, tutoring. **Placement/credit:** AP, institutional tests.

ACADEMIC REQUIREMENTS. Freshmen must earn minimum GPA of 2.0 to continue in good standing. 100% of freshmen return for sophomore year. **Graduation requirements:** Most students required to take courses in arts/fine arts, computer science, English, foreign languages, history, humanities, mathematics, philosophy/religion, biological/physical sciences. **Additional information:** Students do not declare major. 66 credits required for associate degree in liberal arts, 60 credits for associate degree in religious arts. Those with degree receive certificate in theological studies with 24 semester hours in theology and 6 in philosophy.

FRESHMAN ADMISSIONS. Selection criteria: Interview, recommendations, school achievement record, test scores, commitment to obligations of religious vocation as well as acceptance of applicant by a religious community required. **High school preparation:** 16 units required. Required units include English 4, foreign language 2, mathematics 2, social science 2 and science 1. **Test requirements:** SAT or ACT for placement and counseling only; score report by June 30. Older applicants out of high school for several years need not submit SAT/ACT scores. Strong-Campbell Psychological Test required for admission.

1992 FRESHMAN CLASS PROFILE. 8 women applied, 8 accepted, 8 enrolled. 100% had high school GPA of 3.0 or higher. **Characteristics:** 13% from in state, 38% have minority backgrounds, 38% are foreign students. Average age is 30.

FALL-TERM APPLICATIONS. No fee. No closing date; applicants notified on a rolling basis; must reply by registration. Interview required.

STUDENT LIFE. Housing: Dormitories (women). All students reside in motherhouse of Sisters of Christian Charity or another religious congregation. **Activities:** Choral groups, drama, music ensembles. **Additional information:** Students comply with activities of their religious congregations. Religious observance required.

STUDENT SERVICES. Freshman orientation, health services, personal counseling, veterans counselor, services/facilities for handicapped.

ANNUAL EXPENSES. Tuition and fees (1992-93): $1,200. **Room and board:** $1,100. **Books and supplies:** $400.

FINANCIAL AID. Grants available. **Aid applications:** No closing date; applicants notified on a rolling basis; must reply by registration. **Additional information:** All students receive half of tuition as scholarship.

ADDRESS/TELEPHONE. Sr. Mary Renee Nelson, SCC, Registrar/Admissions Officer, Assumption College for Sisters, 350 Bernardsville Road, Mendham, NJ 07945-0800. (201) 543-6528. Fax: (201) 543-9459.

Atlantic Community College
Mays Landing, New Jersey CB code: 2024

2-year public community college, coed. Founded in 1964. **Accreditation:** Regional. **Undergraduate enrollment:** 684 men, 1,073 women full time; 928 men, 1,737 women part time. **Faculty:** 278 total (78 full time), 15 with doctorates or other terminal degrees. **Location:** Rural campus in small town; 15 miles from Atlantic City. **Calendar:** Semester, limited summer session. Saturday and extensive evening/early morning classes. **Microcomputers:** 200 located in computer centers. **Special facilities:** Student-run restaurant.

DEGREES OFFERED. AA, AS, AAS. 357 associate degrees awarded in 1992. 32% in business and management, 10% business/office and marketing/distribution, 9% computer sciences, 5% education, 22% allied health, 12% home economics.

UNDERGRADUATE MAJORS. Accounting, biological and physical sciences, biology, business administration and management, business and management, business and office, business data processing and related programs, chemistry, comparative literature, computer and information sciences, computer servicing technology, computer technology, construction code enforcement, criminal justice studies, education, electronic technology, finance, food management, food production/management/services, history, hospitality and recreation marketing, hotel/motel and restaurant management, humanities, humanities and social sciences, law enforcement and corrections technologies, legal assistant/paralegal, liberal/general studies, marine biology, marketing and distribution, marketing management, mathematics, medical laboratory technologies, music, nursing, occupational therapy assistant, oceanography, physical therapy assistant, prelaw, psychology, respiratory therapy, retailing, robotics, science technologies, secretarial and related programs, social sciences, sociology, studio art, tourism, visual and performing arts.

ACADEMIC PROGRAMS. 2-year transfer program, cooperative education, double major, dual enrollment of high school students, honors program, independent study, internships, telecourses, weekend college. **Remedial services:** Learning center, preadmission summer program, reduced course load, remedial instruction, special counselor, tutoring. **Placement/credit:** CLEP General and Subject, institutional tests; 32 credit hours maximum for associate degree.

ACADEMIC REQUIREMENTS. Freshmen must earn minimum GPA of 2.0 to continue in good standing. 50% of freshmen return for sophomore year. Students must declare major by end of first year. **Graduation requirements:** 64 hours for associate. Most students required to take courses in arts/fine arts, English, humanities, mathematics, biological/physical sciences, social sciences.

FRESHMAN ADMISSIONS. Selection criteria: Open admissions. Selected admissions to allied health and nursing programs.

1992 FRESHMAN CLASS PROFILE. 405 men, 613 women enrolled. **Characteristics:** 99% from in state, 100% commute, 24% have minority backgrounds, 1% are foreign students. Average age is 23.

FALL-TERM APPLICATIONS. $10 fee, may be waived for applicants with need. Closing date August 1; applicants notified on a rolling basis; must reply by registration. Deferred and early admission available.

STUDENT LIFE. Housing: Reserved housing program available. **Activities:** Student government, magazine, radio, student newspaper, choral groups, drama, music ensembles, Spanish-American Club, Minority Student Union, International Club, Jewish Club, Phi Beta Lambda, Phi Beta Kappa, special interest clubs.

ATHLETICS. NJCAA. **Intercollegiate:** Archery, basketball M, softball W, tennis. **Intramural:** Soccer M, softball W, volleyball M.

STUDENT SERVICES. Aptitude testing, career counseling, employment service for undergraduates, freshman orientation, health services, on-campus day care, personal counseling, placement service for graduates, special adviser for adult students, veterans counselor, services/facilities for handicapped.

ANNUAL EXPENSES. Tuition and fees (1992-93): $1,308, $1,128 additional for out-of-district students, $2,808 additional for out-of-state students. **Books and supplies:** $500. **Other expenses:** $360.

FINANCIAL AID. 99% of grants, 90% of loans, all jobs based on need. **Aid applications:** No closing date; priority given to applications received by May 1; applicants notified on a rolling basis beginning on or about July 1; must reply within 15 days. **Additional information:** Installment plan available for culinary arts majors.

ADDRESS/TELEPHONE. Bobby Royal, Director of College Recruitment, Atlantic Community College, 5100 Black Horse Pike, Mays Landing, NJ 08330-2699. (609) 343-5000. Fax: (609) 343-4917.

Bergen Community College ⇎
Paramus, New Jersey CB code: 2032

2-year public community college, coed. Founded in 1965. **Accreditation:** Regional. **Undergraduate enrollment:** 2,018 men, 2,141 women full time; 1,737 men, 2,737 women part time. **Faculty:** 655 total (253 full time), 129 with doctorates or other terminal degrees. **Location:** Suburban campus in large town; 12 miles from New York City. **Calendar:** Semester, extensive summer session. Saturday and extensive evening/early morning classes. **Microcomputers:** Located in classrooms, computer centers. **Special facilities:** Collegiate Center for Deaf Education, with counselors and specialized equipment.

DEGREES OFFERED. AA, AS, AAS. 1,005 associate degrees awarded in 1992. 20% in business and management, 17% business/office and marketing/distribution, 19% allied health, 22% multi/interdisciplinary studies.

UNDERGRADUATE MAJORS. Accounting, automotive technology, behavioral sciences, biology, business administration and management, business data programming, chemistry, commercial art, communications, comparative literature, computer and information sciences, computer graphics, computer integrated manufacturing technology, criminal justice studies, dance, dental hygiene, drafting, drafting and design technology, dramatic arts, drawing, economics, electrical technology, engineering, engineering and other disciplines, finance, foreign languages (multiple emphasis), history, hotel/motel and restaurant management, humanities, labor/industrial relations, law enforcement and corrections technologies, legal assistant/paralegal, liberal/general studies, marketing management, mathematics, medical assistant, medical laboratory technologies, music, nursing, ornamental horticulture, philosophy, physics, political science and government, psychology, radio/television broadcasting, radiograph medical technology, real estate, recreation and community services technologies, religion, respiratory therapy technology, retailing, secretarial and related programs, social sciences, sociology, speech, teacher aide, theater design, ultrasound technology, women's studies, word processing.

ACADEMIC PROGRAMS. 2-year transfer program, cooperative education, honors program, internships, study abroad, telecourses, semester at Disney World for selected students, semester in England (hotel restaurant program). **Remedial services:** Learning center, reduced course load, remedial instruction, special counselor, tutoring, Educational Opportunity Fund Program. **Placement/credit:** CLEP General and Subject, institutional tests; 45 credit hours maximum for associate degree.

ACADEMIC REQUIREMENTS. Freshmen must earn minimum GPA of 1.8 to continue in good standing. 55% of freshmen return for sophomore year. Students must declare major on application. **Graduation requirements:** 64 hours for associate (21 in major). Most students required to take courses in arts/fine arts, English, humanities, mathematics, biological/physical sciences, social sciences. **Additional information:** All new students must complete an algebra requirement regardless of program pursued.

FRESHMAN ADMISSIONS. Selection criteria: Open admissions. Selective admissions to allied health programs based on academic record and specific courses taken. Priority given to county residents. Mathematics, biology, and chemistry required for most allied health programs.

1992 FRESHMAN CLASS PROFILE. 905 men, 975 women enrolled. **Characteristics:** 100% from in state, 100% commute, 30% have minority backgrounds, 1% are foreign students. Average age is 20.

FALL-TERM APPLICATIONS. $20 fee, may be waived for applicants with need. Closing date July 30; applicants notified on a rolling basis; must reply within 4 weeks. Deferred admission available. Application closing date for nursing and dental hygiene is April 1.

STUDENT LIFE. Activities: Student government, magazine, student newspaper, choral groups, dance, drama, music ensembles, musical theater, Christian fellowship, Black Student Union, Social Awareness Club.

ATHLETICS. NJCAA. **Intercollegiate:** Baseball M, basketball, cross-country, golf M, soccer M, softball W, tennis M, track and field, volleyball W, wrestling M.

STUDENT SERVICES. Career counseling, employment service for undergraduates, freshman orientation, health services, on-campus day care, personal counseling, placement service for graduates, veterans counselor, services/facilities for handicapped.

ANNUAL EXPENSES. Tuition and fees (1992-93): $1,500, $1,320 additional for out-of-district students, $3,960 additional for out-of-state students. **Books and supplies:** $850.

FINANCIAL AID. 25% of freshmen, 20% of continuing students receive some form of aid. 99% of grants, 88% of loans, 61% of jobs based on need. Academic, athletic, leadership scholarships available. **Aid applications:** No closing date; priority given to applications received by June 15; applicants notified on a rolling basis beginning on or about April 1; must reply within 2 weeks.

ADDRESS/TELEPHONE. Josephine Figueras, Director of Admissions and Registration, Bergen Community College, 400 Paramus Road, Paramus, NJ 07652-1595. (201) 447-7857. Fax: (201) 670-7973.

Berkeley College of Business
West Paterson, New Jersey CB code: 2061

Admissions:	96% of applicants accepted
Based on:	••• School record
	•• Interview, test scores
	• Essay, recommendations
Completion:	80% of freshmen end year in good standing
	70% graduate, 25% of these enter 4-year programs

2-year proprietary business, junior college, coed. Founded in 1931. **Accreditation:** Regional. **Undergraduate enrollment:** 111 men, 896 women full time; 69 men, 518 women part time. **Faculty:** 110 total (29 full time), 11 with doctorates or other terminal degrees. **Location:** Suburban campus in large town; 20 miles from New York City. **Calendar:** Quarter, extensive summer session. **Microcomputers:** 225 located in libraries, classrooms, computer centers. **Additional facts:** Branch campuses located in Waldwick and Woodbridge.

DEGREES OFFERED. AAS. 375 associate degrees awarded in 1992. 7% in architecture and environmental design, 36% business and management, 57% business/office and marketing/distribution.

UNDERGRADUATE MAJORS. Accounting, business administration and management, fashion merchandising, interior design, legal assistant/paralegal, legal secretary, marketing and distribution, office supervision and management, retailing, secretarial and related programs, tourism, word processing.

ACADEMIC PROGRAMS. Cooperative education, double major, independent study, internships, study abroad. **Remedial services:** Learning center, remedial instruction, tutoring. **Placement/credit:** CLEP General and Subject, institutional tests.

ACADEMIC REQUIREMENTS. Students must maintain progressively higher GPA as they complete more credits. 80% of freshmen return for sophomore year. Students must declare major on application. **Graduation requirements:** 90 hours for associate. Most students required to take courses in English, humanities, mathematics, social sciences.

FRESHMAN ADMISSIONS. Selection criteria: Class rank, high school record, and interview considered.

1992 FRESHMAN CLASS PROFILE. 1,664 men and women applied, 1,592 accepted; 110 men enrolled, 721 women enrolled. 3% were in top tenth and 10% were in top quarter of graduating class. **Characteristics:** 93% from in state, 97% commute, 36% have minority backgrounds, 1% are foreign students, 5% join fraternities/sororities. Average age is 18.

FALL-TERM APPLICATIONS. $35 fee. No closing date; applicants notified on a rolling basis; must reply within 4 weeks. Interview required. Early admission available.

STUDENT LIFE. Housing: Apartment housing available. Outside contract based housing available in apartments within walking distance of main campus in West Paterson. **Activities:** Student government, student newspaper, fraternities, sororities, activity club, DELA, Phi Beta Lambda.

STUDENT SERVICES. Career counseling, employment service for undergraduates, freshman orientation, personal counseling, placement service for graduates, graduates entitled to free life-time placement service and refresher courses.

ANNUAL EXPENSES. Tuition and fees: $9,255. **Room and board:** $1,530. **Books and supplies:** $763. **Other expenses:** $1,044.

FINANCIAL AID. 85% of freshmen, 85% of continuing students receive some form of aid. 97% of grants, 75% of loans, 79% of jobs based on need. 489 enrolled freshmen were judged to have need, all were offered aid. Academic scholarships available. **Aid applications:** No closing date; applicants notified on a rolling basis; must reply within 4 weeks. **Additional information:** Alumni scholarship examination given in November and December. Full and partial scholarships awarded.

ADDRESS/TELEPHONE. Teri Duda, Director of Admissions, Berkeley College of Business, 44 Rifle Camp Road, West Paterson, NJ 07424-0440. (201) 278-5400. (800) 446-5400. Fax: (201) 278-2242.

Beth Medrash Govoha
Lakewood, New Jersey CB code: 0612

5-year private rabbinical college, men only, affiliated with Jewish faith. Founded in 1943. **Undergraduate enrollment:** 323 men full time; 3 men part time. **Graduate enrollment:** 1,010 men full time; 100 men part time. **Location:** Suburban campus in large town. **Calendar:** Semester. **Additional facts:** Ordination available.

FRESHMAN ADMISSIONS. Selection criteria: Institutional examination.

ANNUAL EXPENSES. Tuition and fees (1992-93): $3,150. **Room and board:** $3,800. **Books and supplies:** $450.

ADDRESS/TELEPHONE. Rabbi Yehuda Jacobs, Director of Admissions, Beth Medrash Govoha, 617 Sixth Street, Lakewood, NJ 08701. (908) 367-1060.

Bloomfield College
Bloomfield, New Jersey CB code: 2044

Admissions:	66% of applicants accepted
Based on:	••• School record, test scores
	•• Activities, essay, interview, recommendations
Completion:	80% of freshmen end year in good standing
	17% enter graduate study

4-year private liberal arts college, coed, affiliated with Presbyterian Church (USA). Founded in 1868. **Accreditation:** Regional. **Undergraduate enrollment:** 399 men, 839 women full time; 285 men, 478 women part time. **Faculty:** 180 total (47 full time), 46 with doctorates or other terminal degrees. **Location:** Suburban campus in small city; 20 miles from New York City. **Calendar:** Semester, limited summer session. Saturday and extensive evening/early morning classes. **Microcomputers:** 80 located in libraries, computer centers. **Special facilities:** Westminster Gallery. Robert V. Van Fossan Theater. **Additional facts:** Campus in Wroxton, England.

DEGREES OFFERED. BA, BS. 165 bachelor's degrees awarded in 1992. 47% in business and management, 8% communications, 10% computer sciences, 6% life sciences, 6% psychology, 14% social sciences.

UNDERGRADUATE MAJORS. Accounting, Afro-American (black) studies, basic clinical health sciences, biochemistry, biological and physical sciences, biological laboratory technology, biology, biomedical science, business administration and management, business and management, business economics, chemistry, chiropractic, clinical laboratory science, communications, comparative literature, computer and information sciences, contract management and procurement/purchasing, criminal justice studies, cytotechnology, dramatic arts, economics, English, environmental science, finance, fine arts, French, history, marketing management, medical laboratory technologies, medical social work, nursing, personality psychology, personnel management, philosophy, political science and government, predentistry, premedicine, prepharmacy, preveterinary, psychology, public policy studies, religion, retailing, sociology, Spanish, toxicology, visual and performing arts.

ACADEMIC PROGRAMS. Double major, dual enrollment of high school students, honors program, independent study, internships, student-designed major, study abroad, visiting/exchange student program, weekend college, 5-year clinical laboratory science program in conjunction with University of Medicine and Dentistry of New Jersey, combined bachelor's/DC degree programs with 9 chiropractic colleges. **Remedial services:** Learning center, preadmission summer program, reduced course load, remedial instruction, special counselor, tutoring. **Placement/credit:** AP, CLEP General and Subject, institutional tests; 64 credit hours maximum for bachelor's degree.

ACADEMIC REQUIREMENTS. Freshmen must earn minimum GPA of 2.0 to continue in good standing. 80% of freshmen return for sophomore year. Students must declare major by end of second year. **Graduation requirements:** 132 hours for bachelor's (48 in major). Most students required to take courses in arts/fine arts, computer science, English, history, humanities, mathematics, philosophy/religion, biological/physical sciences, social sciences. **Postgraduate studies:** 2% enter law school, 4% enter MBA programs, 11% enter other graduate study.

FRESHMAN ADMISSIONS. Selection criteria: High school record, class rank, SAT scores, interview, extracurricular activities, and recommendations considered. Students selected based on motivation, potential, and seriousness of purpose. **High school preparation:** 14 units required. Required and recommended units include English 4, mathematics 2-3, social science 2-4 and science 2-3. Biology and chemistry required for science, nursing, and prechiropractic applicants. **Test requirements:** SAT or ACT (SAT preferred); score report by August 30.

1992 FRESHMAN CLASS PROFILE. 549 men applied, 385 accepted, 124 enrolled; 1,132 women applied, 719 accepted, 230 enrolled. **Characteristics:** 97% from in state, 65% commute, 67% have minority backgrounds, 10% join fraternities/sororities. Average age is 19.

FALL-TERM APPLICATIONS. $20 fee, may be waived for applicants with need. No closing date; priority given to applications received by June 15; applicants notified on a rolling basis; must reply by May 1 or within 2 weeks if notified thereafter. Interview recommended for all students applicants. Essay recommended. CRDA. Deferred and early admission available. EDP-F.

STUDENT LIFE. Housing: Dormitories (men, women, coed); fraternity, sorority housing available. Nursing house, honors house for upper-level students, special scholastic communities available. **Activities:** Student government, magazine, student newspaper, yearbook, choral groups, drama, Circus troupe, Controversy, musical instrument instruction, fraternities, sororities.

ATHLETICS. NAIA. **Intercollegiate:** Baseball M, basketball, lacrosse M, soccer M, softball W, volleyball W. **Intramural:** Basketball, volleyball.

STUDENT SERVICES. Aptitude testing, career counseling, employment service for undergraduates, freshman orientation, health services, personal counseling, placement service for graduates, special adviser for adult students, veterans counselor, free tutors, services/facilities for handicapped.

ANNUAL EXPENSES. Tuition and fees: $8,050. **Room and board:** $4,100. **Books and supplies:** $400. **Other expenses:** $1,415.

FINANCIAL AID. 82% of freshmen, 82% of continuing students receive some form of aid. 92% of grants, 93% of loans, 73% of jobs based on need. 278 enrolled freshmen were judged to have need, all were offered aid. Academic, athletic, leadership, alumni affiliation, religious affiliation scholarships available. **Aid applications:** No closing date; priority given to applications received by June 1; applicants notified on a rolling basis beginning on or about April 1; must reply within 2 weeks.

ADDRESS/TELEPHONE. Andrew G. Nelson, Vice President of Admissions, Bloomfield College, One Park Place, Bloomfield, NJ 07003. (201) 748-9000 ext. 230. Fax: (201) 743-3998.

Brookdale Community College
Lincroft, New Jersey — CB code: 2181

2-year public community college, coed. Founded in 1967. **Accreditation:** Regional. **Undergraduate enrollment:** 2,304 men, 2,230 women full time; 3,145 men, 5,053 women part time. **Faculty:** 443 total (193 full time). **Location:** Suburban campus in large town; 5 miles from Red Bank. **Calendar:** 2 terms averaging 15 weeks each plus 2 terms averaging 6 weeks, with an optional concurrent 12 week summer term available. **Microcomputers:** 500 located in libraries, classrooms, computer centers.

DEGREES OFFERED. AA, AS, AAS. 1,287 associate degrees awarded in 1992. 19% in business and management, 9% business/office and marketing/distribution, 5% computer sciences, 5% education, 9% allied health, 8% letters/literature, 9% social sciences, 22% trade and industry.

UNDERGRADUATE MAJORS. Accounting, automotive mechanics, automotive technology, biology, business administration and management, business and office, business data processing and related programs, business data programming, chemistry, communications, computer and information sciences, computer programming, criminal justice studies, drafting, drafting and design technology, dramatic arts, early childhood education, education, electronic technology, engineering, engineering and engineering-related technologies, English, fashion merchandising, fine arts, food management, food production/management/services, foreign languages (multiple emphasis), French, German, graphic arts technology, hospitality and recreation marketing, humanities, insurance adjusting, insurance and risk management, interior design, international business management, journalism, law enforcement and corrections technologies, legal assistant/paralegal, liberal/general studies, library assistant, library science, marketing and distribution, mathematics, medical laboratory technologies, mental health/human services, music, nursing, personnel management, photographic technology, physics, political science and government, psychology, public relations, radio/television broadcasting, respiratory therapy technology, robotics, secretarial and related programs, small business management and ownership, social sciences, sociology, Spanish, speech, teacher aide, telecommunications, visual and performing arts.

ACADEMIC PROGRAMS. 2-year transfer program, cooperative education, dual enrollment of high school students, honors program, independent study, internships, study abroad, telecourses, weekend college. **Remedial services:** Learning center, preadmission summer program, reduced course load, remedial instruction, tutoring. **ROTC:** Air Force, Army. **Placement/credit:** AP, CLEP General and Subject; 30 credit hours maximum for associate degree.

ACADEMIC REQUIREMENTS. To continue in good academic standing, freshmen must successfully complete 50% of credit hours attempted. 50% of freshmen return for sophomore year. Students must declare major on application. **Graduation requirements:** 60 hours for associate (30 in major). Most students required to take courses in English, humanities, mathematics, biological/physical sciences, social sciences.

FRESHMAN ADMISSIONS. Selection criteria: Open admissions. Selective admissions to allied health programs. One unit high school or college algebra, 1 chemistry, 1 biology required for allied health programs. **Additional information:** Applicants without high school diploma or GED may be admitted. After specific number of credits in specific distribution must take equivalent of GED.

1992 FRESHMAN CLASS PROFILE. 4,702 men and women enrolled. **Characteristics:** 99% from in state, 100% commute, 14% have minority backgrounds, 1% are foreign students.

FALL-TERM APPLICATIONS. $25 fee. No closing date; applicants notified on a rolling basis; must reply by registration. Group interview required for nursing, medical laboratory technology, respiratory therapy applicants. Deferred admission available.

STUDENT LIFE. Activities: Student government, film, magazine, radio, student newspaper, television, choral groups, concert band, dance, drama, musical theater, opera, symphony orchestra.

ATHLETICS. NJCAA. **Intercollegiate:** Baseball M, basketball M, cross-country, soccer, softball W, tennis, track and field. **Intramural:** Badminton, basketball, bowling, cross-country, golf M, softball, volleyball.

STUDENT SERVICES. Aptitude testing, career counseling, employment service for undergraduates, freshman orientation, health services, on-campus day care, personal counseling, placement service for graduates, veterans counselor, services/facilities for handicapped.

ANNUAL EXPENSES. Tuition and fees: $1,628, $1,416 additional for out-of-district students, $2,832 additional for out-of-state students. **Books and supplies:** $550. **Other expenses:** $941.

FINANCIAL AID. 43% of freshmen, 20% of continuing students receive some form of aid. 98% of grants, 85% of loans, 42% of jobs based on need. 489 enrolled freshmen were judged to have need, 467 were offered aid. Academic, athletic scholarships available. **Aid applications:** No closing date; priority given to applications received by June 1; applicants notified on a rolling basis beginning on or about May 1; must reply within 2 weeks.

ADDRESS/TELEPHONE. Richard Pfeffer, Director of Enrollment Management, Brookdale Community College, Newman Springs Road, Lincroft, NJ 07738. (908) 224-2375. Fax: (908) 576-1643.

Burlington County College
Pemberton, New Jersey — CB code: 2180

2-year public community college, coed. Founded in 1966. **Accreditation:** Regional. **Undergraduate enrollment:** 936 men, 1,138 women full time; 1,762 men, 3,199 women part time. **Faculty:** 314 total (84 full time), 21 with doctorates or other terminal degrees. **Location:** Rural campus in rural community; 30 miles from Philadelphia, 80 miles from New York City. **Calendar:** Fall and spring semesters of 15 weeks each, 3 terms of 6 weeks each. Saturday and extensive evening/early morning classes. **Microcomputers:** 465 located in libraries, classrooms, computer centers. **Additional facts:** Credit courses offered at 6 high schools, 2 military bases, 2 prisons and 2 off-campus centers in Cinnaminson and Willingboro.

DEGREES OFFERED. AA, AS, AAS. 589 associate degrees awarded in 1992. 11% in business and management, 15% business/office and market-

ing/distribution, 6% computer sciences, 13% allied health, 46% multi/interdisciplinary studies, 5% social sciences.

UNDERGRADUATE MAJORS. Accounting, architectural technologies, architecture, biology, business administration and management, business and management, business and office, business data processing and related programs, business data programming, chemical engineering, chemistry, civil technology, communications, computer and information sciences, computer programming, criminal justice studies, data processing, drafting and design technology, education, electronic technology, engineering, engineering and engineering-related technologies, English, finance, fine arts, food management, graphic arts technology, history, hotel/motel and restaurant management, institutional management, journalism, liberal/general studies, marketing and distribution, marketing management, mathematics, medical records technology, music, music performance, office supervision and management, personnel management, philosophy, photography, physical sciences, physics, political science and government, practical nursing, psychology, radiograph medical technology, real estate, science technologies, secondary education, secretarial and related programs, social sciences, sociology, teacher aide, telecommunications, transportation management, visual and performing arts, word processing.

ACADEMIC PROGRAMS. 2-year transfer program, cooperative education, double major, dual enrollment of high school students, honors program, independent study, internships, student-designed major, telecourses, weekend college. **Remedial services:** Learning center, preadmission summer program, reduced course load, remedial instruction, special counselor, tutoring. **Placement/credit:** AP, CLEP General and Subject, institutional tests; 30 credit hours maximum for associate degree.

ACADEMIC REQUIREMENTS. Freshmen must earn minimum GPA of 1.6 to continue in good standing. Students must declare major by end of first year. **Graduation requirements:** 64 hours for associate (40 in major). Most students required to take courses in arts/fine arts, English, history, humanities, mathematics, biological/physical sciences, social sciences.

FRESHMAN ADMISSIONS. Selection criteria: Open admissions. Academic high school background required of nursing program applicants. **Test requirements:** New Jersey Basic Skills test required for placement.

1992 FRESHMAN CLASS PROFILE. 630 men, 779 women enrolled. **Characteristics:** 100% from in state, 100% commute, 20% have minority backgrounds. Average age is 19.

FALL-TERM APPLICATIONS. $15 fee, may be waived for applicants with need. No closing date; applicants notified on a rolling basis beginning on or about February 10; must reply by registration. Deferred and early admission available.

STUDENT LIFE. Activities: Student government, student newspaper, television, music ensembles, Minority Student Union, Veterans Club.

ATHLETICS. NJCAA. **Intercollegiate:** Baseball M, basketball, golf, soccer, softball W, swimming, tennis. **Intramural:** Basketball, soccer, softball, table tennis, tennis, volleyball.

STUDENT SERVICES. Aptitude testing, career counseling, employment service for undergraduates, freshman orientation, health services, personal counseling, placement service for graduates, veterans counselor, services/facilities for handicapped.

ANNUAL EXPENSES. Tuition and fees (1992-93): $1,325, $250 additional for out-of-district students, $2,170 additional for out-of-state students. **Books and supplies:** $762. **Other expenses:** $1,350.

FINANCIAL AID. 50% of freshmen, 50% of continuing students receive some form of aid. 99% of grants, 88% of loans, 19% of jobs based on need. Academic, athletic, state/district residency, leadership scholarships available. **Aid applications:** No closing date; applicants notified on a rolling basis beginning on or about July 1; must reply within 3 weeks.

ADDRESS/TELEPHONE. Earl Teasley, Director Admissions, Burlington County College, Route 530, Pemberton, NJ 08068-1599. (609) 894-9311 ext. 288. Fax: (609) 894-0183.

Caldwell College
Caldwell, New Jersey — CB code: 2072

Admissions: 69% of applicants accepted
Based on:
- ••• Recommendations, school record, test scores
- •• Activities, interview
- • Special talents

Completion: 94% of freshmen end year in good standing
41% graduate, 36% of these enter graduate study

4-year private liberal arts college, coed, affiliated with Roman Catholic Church. Founded in 1939. **Accreditation:** Regional. **Undergraduate enrollment:** 222 men, 402 women full time; 164 men, 551 women part time. **Faculty:** 96 total (48 full time), 28 with doctorates or other terminal degrees. **Location:** Suburban campus in large town; 20 miles from New York City. **Calendar:** Semester, limited summer session. Saturday classes. **Microcomputers:** 106 located in libraries, computer centers. **Special facilities:** Art gallery, cancer research facilities.

DEGREES OFFERED. BA, BS, BFA. 190 bachelor's degrees awarded in 1992. 33% in business and management, 10% education, 13% letters/literature, 17% psychology, 14% social sciences, 5% visual and performing arts.

UNDERGRADUATE MAJORS. Art education, biology, business administration and management, chemistry, computer and information sciences, education, elementary education, English, English education, fine arts, foreign languages education, French, history, information sciences and systems, management information systems, mathematics, mathematics education, medical laboratory technologies, music, psychology, religion, science education, social sciences, social studies education, sociology, Spanish.

ACADEMIC PROGRAMS. Accelerated program, cooperative education, double major, dual enrollment of high school students, external degree, honors program, independent study, internships, study abroad, teacher preparation; liberal arts/career combination in health sciences. **Remedial services:** Learning center, preadmission summer program, reduced course load, remedial instruction, tutoring. **ROTC:** Army. **Placement/credit:** AP, CLEP General and Subject, institutional tests; 30 credit hours maximum for bachelor's degree.

ACADEMIC REQUIREMENTS. Freshmen must earn minimum GPA of 1.8 to continue in good standing. 69% of freshmen return for sophomore year. Students must declare major by end of second year. **Graduation requirements:** 120 hours for bachelor's (30 in major). Most students required to take courses in arts/fine arts, computer science, English, foreign languages, history, humanities, mathematics, philosophy/religion, biological/physical sciences, social sciences.

FRESHMAN ADMISSIONS. Selection criteria: Class rank in top half, school achievement record, test scores, counselor's recommendation most important. Interview strongly recommended. **High school preparation:** 16 units required; 18 recommended. Required and recommended units include English 4, foreign language 2, mathematics 2-3, social science 1-2 and science 2. One science unit must be laboratory science. **Test requirements:** SAT or ACT (SAT preferred); score report by August 25. **Additional information:** Admissions policies designed to be flexible, to accept only students who have academic potential to succeed.

1992 FRESHMAN CLASS PROFILE. 286 men applied, 193 accepted, 84 enrolled; 583 women applied, 403 accepted, 149 enrolled. 34% had high school GPA of 3.0 or higher, 61% between 2.0 and 2.99. 3% were in top tenth and 21% were in top quarter of graduating class. **Academic background:** Mid 50% of enrolled freshmen had SAT-V between 410-500, SAT-M between 430-510. 92% submitted SAT scores. **Characteristics:** 83% from in state, 59% live in college housing, 37% have minority backgrounds, 14% are foreign students. Average age is 18.

FALL-TERM APPLICATIONS. $25 fee, may be waived for applicants with need. No closing date; priority given to applications received by March 15; applicants notified on a rolling basis; must reply by May 1 or within 4 weeks if notified thereafter. Audition required. Portfolio required for art, music applicants. Interview recommended. CRDA. Deferred and early admission available.

STUDENT LIFE. Housing: Dormitories (coed). **Activities:** Student government, magazine, student newspaper, yearbook, student-written foreign language paper, choral groups, drama, musical theater, Circle-K, service sororities, campus ministry, Black Students Cooperative Union, Association of Latin American Students.

ATHLETICS. NAIA. **Intercollegiate:** Basketball, soccer M, softball W. **Intramural:** Basketball, soccer, softball, tennis.

STUDENT SERVICES. Aptitude testing, career counseling, employment service for undergraduates, freshman orientation, health services, personal counseling, placement service for graduates, special adviser for adult students, substance abuse assistance, services/facilities for handicapped.

ANNUAL EXPENSES. Tuition and fees: $8,400. **Room and board:** $4,400. **Books and supplies:** $425. **Other expenses:** $900.

FINANCIAL AID. 63% of freshmen, 62% of continuing students receive some form of aid. 86% of grants, 92% of loans, all jobs based on need. Academic, art, athletic, leadership, alumni affiliation, minority scholarships available. **Aid applications:** Closing date July 15; priority given to applications received by April 15; applicants notified on a rolling basis; must reply within 4 weeks.

ADDRESS/TELEPHONE. J. Raymond Sheenan, Dean of Admissions, Caldwell College, 9 Ryerson Avenue, Caldwell, NJ 07006-6195. (201) 228-4424 ext. 301. (800) 831-9178. Fax: (201) 228-2897.

Camden County College
Blackwood, New Jersey — CB code: 2121

2-year public community college, coed. Founded in 1966. **Accreditation:** Regional. **Undergraduate enrollment:** 2,092 men, 2,695 women full time; 2,174 men, 3,627 women part time. **Faculty:** 667 total (129 full time), 97 with doctorates or other terminal degrees. **Location:** Suburban campus in large town; 15 miles from Philadelphia, 13 miles from Camden. **Calendar:** Semester, extensive summer session. **Microcomputers:** 600 located in libraries, classrooms. **Special facilities:** Art gallery.

DEGREES OFFERED. AA, AS, AAS. 784 associate degrees awarded in 1992.

UNDERGRADUATE MAJORS. Accounting, animal sciences, automotive technology, biological and physical sciences, business administration and management, business and office, business data processing and related programs, business data programming, communications, computer integrated manufacturing, computer servicing technology, computer technology, dance, dental hygiene, drafting and design technology, electrical/electronics/communications engineering, electromechanical technology, electronic technology, engineering, engineering and engineering-related technologies, engineering and other disciplines, engineering science, finance, fine arts, fire control and safety technology, food production/management/services, food science and nutrition, laser electro-optic technology, law enforcement and corrections technologies, legal secretary, liberal/general studies, marketing and distribution, mechanical design technology, medical laboratory technologies, mental health/human services, music, nursing, ophthalmic services, photography, protective services, public affairs, recreation and community services technologies, respiratory therapy, respiratory therapy technology, retailing, science technologies, secretarial and related programs, small business management and ownership, social work, veterinarian's assistant, visual and performing arts, word processing.

ACADEMIC PROGRAMS. 2-year transfer program, computer delivered (on-line) credit-bearing course offerings, cooperative education, dual enrollment of high school students, honors program, internships, weekend college, General Motors' Automotive Service Education Program. **Remedial services:** Learning center, preadmission summer program, reduced course load, remedial instruction, special counselor, tutoring. **Placement/credit:** AP, CLEP General and Subject, institutional tests; 30 credit hours maximum for associate degree.

ACADEMIC REQUIREMENTS. No policy requiring minimum GPA; records of students having academic difficulty are reviewed individually. 60% of freshmen return for sophomore year. Students must declare major on application. **Graduation requirements:** 64 hours for associate. Most students required to take courses in English.

FRESHMAN ADMISSIONS. Selection criteria: Open admissions. Selective admissions to certain programs. **Test requirements:** SAT or ACT required for admission to certain selective programs. New Jersey College Basic Skills Placement Test required of all applicants. Psychological Corporation Pre-Nursing Examination, Entrance Examination for School of Nursing or National League for Nursing Pre-Nursing and Guidance Examination required of nursing applicants. Mechanical aptitude test required for General Motors' Automotive Service Education Program applicants. Dental Hygiene Aptitude Test required.

1992 FRESHMAN CLASS PROFILE. 985 men, 1,313 women enrolled. **Characteristics:** 99% from in state, 100% commute, 30% have minority backgrounds, 1% are foreign students. Average age is 19.

FALL-TERM APPLICATIONS. $15 fee. Closing date August 1; applicants notified on a rolling basis beginning on or about February 1; must reply within 2 weeks. Interview recommended for dental hygiene, nursing, respiratory therapy, medical laboratory technician, General Motors and Nissan programs applicants. Early admission available.

STUDENT LIFE. Activities: Student government, magazine, radio, student newspaper, yearbook, choral groups, concert band, drama.

ATHLETICS. NJCAA. **Intercollegiate:** Baseball M, basketball, soccer, softball W. **Intramural:** Racquetball W.

STUDENT SERVICES. Career counseling, employment service for undergraduates, freshman orientation, health services, on-campus day care, personal counseling, placement service for graduates, veterans counselor, services/facilities for handicapped.

ANNUAL EXPENSES. Tuition and fees (1992-93): $1,350, $60 additional for out-of-district students, $60 additional for out-of-state students. **Books and supplies:** $500. **Other expenses:** $825.

FINANCIAL AID. 10% of freshmen, 10% of continuing students receive some form of aid. 98% of grants, 77% of loans, all jobs based on need. Academic scholarships available. **Aid applications:** Closing date December 21; priority given to applications received by July 1; applicants notified on a rolling basis beginning on or about July 15; must reply within 2 weeks.

ADDRESS/TELEPHONE. Dennis Ferry, Director of Admissions, Camden County College, PO Box 200, Blackwood, NJ 08012. (609) 227-7200.

Centenary College ⇋
Hackettstown, New Jersey — CB code: 2080

Admissions:	61% of applicants accepted
Based on:	••• School record
	•• Activities, interview, test scores
	• Essay, recommendations, special talents
Completion:	80% of freshmen end year in good standing
	75% graduate, 3% of these enter graduate study

4-year private liberal arts college, coed, affiliated with United Methodist Church. Founded in 1867. **Accreditation:** Regional. **Undergraduate enrollment:** 105 men, 310 women full time; 164 men, 399 women part time. **Faculty:** 103 total (37 full time), 48 with doctorates or other terminal degrees. **Location:** Suburban campus in large town; 55 miles from New York City. **Calendar:** Semester, limited summer session. Extensive evening/early morning classes. **Microcomputers:** 18 located in computer centers. **Special facilities:** Daycare center for education majors, textile laboratory, equestrian center, art gallery, theater.

DEGREES OFFERED. AA, AS, BA, BS, BFA. 23 associate degrees awarded in 1992. 16% in agriculture, 5% communications, 17% home economics, 59% multi/interdisciplinary studies. 115 bachelor's degrees awarded. 8% in agriculture, 38% business and management, 17% home economics, 17% multi/interdisciplinary studies, 7% psychology.

UNDERGRADUATE MAJORS. Associate: Early childhood education, equestrian science, interior design, liberal/general studies, textiles and clothing. **Bachelor's:** Accounting, applied mathematics, business administration and management, communications, computer and information sciences, elementary education, English, equestrian science, fashion design, fashion merchandising, fine arts, graphic design, history, interior design, international studies, junior high education, liberal/general studies, marketing management, psychology, pure mathematics, secondary education, textiles and clothing.

ACADEMIC PROGRAMS. Independent study, internships, student-designed major, study abroad, teacher preparation. **Remedial services:** Learning center, preadmission summer program, reduced course load, remedial instruction, special counselor, tutoring, learning differences program. **Placement/credit:** AP, CLEP General and Subject, IB; 15 credit hours maximum for associate degree; 30 credit hours maximum for bachelor's degree.

ACADEMIC REQUIREMENTS. Freshmen must earn minimum GPA of 2.0 to continue in good standing. 75% of freshmen return for sophomore year. Students must declare major by end of second year. **Graduation requirements:** 64 hours for associate (24 in major), 128 hours for bachelor's (48 in major). Most students required to take courses in arts/fine arts, English, history, humanities, mathematics, philosophy/religion, biological/physical sciences, social sciences. **Postgraduate studies:** 70% from 2-year programs enter 4-year programs. 1% enter law school, 1% enter MBA programs, 1% enter other graduate study.

FRESHMAN ADMISSIONS. Selection criteria: School achievement record (program and high school GPA) most important. Class rank, test scores , interview, and school and community activities secondary. Recommendations and essay also considered. **High school preparation:** 16 units required. Required and recommended units include biological science 1-2, English 4, mathematics 3-4, physical science 1-2 and social science 4. Foreign language 2 recommended. **Test requirements:** SAT or ACT (SAT preferred); score report by August 15.

1992 FRESHMAN CLASS PROFILE. 58 men applied, 52 accepted, 32 enrolled; 359 women applied, 201 accepted, 86 enrolled. 29% had high school GPA of 3.0 or higher, 61% between 2.0 and 2.99. 10% were in top tenth and 27% were in top quarter of graduating class. **Academic background:** Mid 50% of enrolled freshmen had SAT-V between 400-450, SAT-M between 400-450. 97% submitted SAT scores. **Characteristics:** 75% from in state, 60% live in college housing, 17% have minority backgrounds, 9% are foreign students, 60% join fraternities/sororities. Average age is 18.

FALL-TERM APPLICATIONS. $25 fee, may be waived for applicants with need. No closing date; applicants notified on a rolling basis; must reply by May 1 or within 4 weeks if notified thereafter. Portfolio required for art, interior design applicants. Interview recommended. Essay recommended. CRDA. Deferred admission available.

STUDENT LIFE. Housing: Dormitories (men, women, coed). **Activities:** Student government, magazine, radio, student newspaper, yearbook, choral groups, dance, drama, music ensembles, musical theater, fraternities, sororities, art guild, student activities committee, American Society of Interior Design.

ATHLETICS. NAIA. **Intercollegiate:** Basketball, cross-country, horseback riding, soccer, softball W, tennis W, volleyball W. **Intramural:** Badminton, baseball M, basketball, cross-country, horseback riding, lacrosse W, skiing W, softball W, tennis W, volleyball, wrestling M.

STUDENT SERVICES. Aptitude testing, career counseling, employment service for undergraduates, freshman orientation, health services, on-campus day care, personal counseling, placement service for graduates, services/facilities for handicapped.

ANNUAL EXPENSES. Tuition and fees (projected): $11,500. **Room and board:** $5,400. **Books and supplies:** $600. **Other expenses:** $600.

FINANCIAL AID. 80% of freshmen, 78% of continuing students receive some form of aid. 86% of grants, 63% of loans, 57% of jobs based on need. 64 enrolled freshmen were judged to have need, all were offered aid. Academic, athletic scholarships available. **Aid applications:** No closing date; priority given to applications received by May 1; applicants notified on a rolling basis beginning on or about April 15; must reply within 15 days.

ADDRESS/TELEPHONE. Michael McGraw, Vice President of Enrollment Management, Centenary College, 400 Jefferson Street, Hackettstown, NJ 07840-9989. (908) 852-1400 ext. 273. Fax: (908) 852-3454.

College of St. Elizabeth
Morristown, New Jersey CB code: 2090

Admissions: 80% of applicants accepted
Based on: ••• Recommendations, school record
•• Interview, test scores
• Activities, essay, special talents
Completion: 88% of freshmen end year in good standing
58% graduate, 17% of these enter graduate study

4-year private liberal arts college, women only, affiliated with Roman Catholic Church. Founded in 1899. **Accreditation:** Regional. **Undergraduate enrollment:** 5 men, 468 women full time; 121 men, 704 women part time. **Graduate enrollment:** 3 men, 14 women part time. **Faculty:** 156 total (74 full time), 62 with doctorates or other terminal degrees. **Location:** Suburban campus in large town; 40 miles from New York City. **Calendar:** Semester, limited summer session. **Microcomputers:** 136 located in dormitories, libraries, computer centers. **Special facilities:** Phillips Library of Rare Books and Manuscripts, Greek theater, Shakespeare garden. **Additional facts:** Men admitted to Weekend College and Center of Life-Long Learning.

DEGREES OFFERED. BA, BS. 156 bachelor's degrees awarded in 1992. 33% in business and management, 8% computer sciences, 10% teacher education, 6% home economics, 7% letters/literature, 5% life sciences, 12% psychology, 9% social sciences.

UNDERGRADUATE MAJORS. Accounting, biochemistry, biology, business administration and management, chemistry, clinical laboratory science, computer and information sciences, economics, education, elementary education, English, fashion design, fine arts, food science and nutrition, French, history, home economics, home economics education, human resources development, marketing management, mathematics, music, nursing, philosophy, psychology, sociology, Spanish, special education, toxicology.

ACADEMIC PROGRAMS. Accelerated program, double major, dual enrollment of high school students, honors program, independent study, internships, study abroad, teacher preparation, weekend college, United Nations semester, Washington semester, cross-registration, upper-level nursing for registered nurses; liberal arts/career combination in health sciences. **Remedial services:** Learning center, preadmission summer program, reduced course load, remedial instruction, special counselor, tutoring, academic skills program. **Placement/credit:** AP, CLEP Subject; 30 credit hours maximum for bachelor's degree.

ACADEMIC REQUIREMENTS. Freshmen must earn minimum GPA of 1.8 to continue in good standing. 72% of freshmen return for sophomore year. Students must declare major by end of second year. **Graduation requirements:** 128 hours for bachelor's (32 in major). Most students required to take courses in arts/fine arts, English, history, humanities, mathematics, philosophy/religion, biological/physical sciences, social sciences. **Postgraduate studies:** 3% enter law school, 2% enter medical school, 5% enter MBA programs, 7% enter other graduate study.

FRESHMAN ADMISSIONS. Selection criteria: School achievement record and recommendations most important, followed by interview, test scores, and class rank. **High school preparation:** 16 units required. Required and recommended units include English 3-4 and foreign language 2. Biological science 1, mathematics 2, physical science 1 and social science 2 recommended. 3 mathematics and/or science, 1 U.S. history also required. **Test requirements:** SAT or ACT (SAT preferred); score report by August 15. Mathematics Level I or II required of mathematics majors and those taking Calculus 1 freshman year. Score report by August 15.

1992 FRESHMAN CLASS PROFILE. 55% had high school GPA of 3.0 or higher, 44% between 2.0 and 2.99. 35% were in top tenth and 52% were in top quarter of graduating class. **Academic background:** Mid 50% of enrolled freshmen had SAT-V between 380-490, SAT-M between 410-520. 95% submitted SAT scores. **Characteristics:** 88% from in state, 81% live in college housing, 40% have minority backgrounds, 8% are foreign students. Average age is 18.

FALL-TERM APPLICATIONS. $25 fee, may be waived for applicants with need. Closing date August 15; priority given to applications received by May 1; applicants notified on a rolling basis; must reply by May 1 or within 2 weeks if notified thereafter. Essay required. Interview recommended. CRDA. Deferred and early admission available. EDP-F.

STUDENT LIFE. Housing: Dormitories (women). **Activities:** Student government, magazine, student newspaper, television, yearbook, choral groups, drama, music ensembles, campus ministry, Geraldine Riordan Center for Volunteer Services, International Intercultural Club, Women United in Color, Amnesty International.

ATHLETICS. NCAA. **Intercollegiate:** Basketball, horseback riding, softball, swimming, tennis, volleyball. **Intramural:** Badminton, softball, volleyball.

STUDENT SERVICES. Aptitude testing, career counseling, employment service for undergraduates, freshman orientation, health services, personal counseling, placement service for graduates, special adviser for adult students, services/facilities for handicapped.

ANNUAL EXPENSES. Tuition and fees: $10,900. **Room and board:** $5,000. **Books and supplies:** $380. **Other expenses:** $650.

FINANCIAL AID. 87% of freshmen, 80% of continuing students receive some form of aid. 77% of grants, 95% of loans, all jobs based on need. 97 enrolled freshmen were judged to have need, all were offered aid. Academic, art, leadership, alumni affiliation scholarships available. **Aid applications:** No closing date; priority given to applications received by April 1; applicants notified on a rolling basis beginning on or about March 1; must reply by May 1 or within 2 weeks if notified thereafter.

ADDRESS/TELEPHONE. George P. Lynes III, Dean of Admissions and Financial Aid, College of St. Elizabeth, 2 Convent Road, Morristown, NJ 07960-6989. (201) 292-6351. Fax: (201) 292-6777.

County College of Morris
Randolph, New Jersey CB code: 2124

2-year public community college, coed. Founded in 1965. **Accreditation:** Regional. **Undergraduate enrollment:** 2,367 men, 2,043 women full time; 1,465 men, 2,064 women part time. **Faculty:** 560 total (194 full time), 78 with doctorates or other terminal degrees. **Location:** Suburban campus in large town; 40 miles from New York City. **Calendar:** Semester, limited summer session. **Microcomputers:** Located in libraries, computer centers. **Special facilities:** Planetarium. **Additional facts:** Courses available at off-campus sites.

DEGREES OFFERED. AA, AS, AAS. 1,243 associate degrees awarded in 1992. 35% in business and management, 5% computer sciences, 5% engineering, 11% health sciences, 32% multi/interdisciplinary studies, 7% parks/recreation, protective services, public affairs.

UNDERGRADUATE MAJORS. Accounting, agricultural business and management, biological laboratory technology, biology, biomedical equipment technology, business administration and management, business and management, business data processing and related programs, business data programming, chemical manufacturing technology, chemistry, communications, computer and information sciences, criminal justice studies, dance, dramatic arts, electronic technology, engineering and engineering-related technologies, engineering science, environmental science, finance, fine arts, graphic design, hotel/motel and restaurant management, humanities, humanities and social sciences, information sciences and systems, insurance marketing, international studies, journalism, law enforcement and corrections, liberal/general studies, marketing and distribution, mathematics, mechanical design technology, medical laboratory technologies, music, nursing, photographic technology, photography, plant protection, public administration, public affairs, radio/television broadcasting, retailing, secretarial and related programs, social science education, social sciences, social work, telecommunications, visual and performing arts.

ACADEMIC PROGRAMS. 2-year transfer program, cooperative education, double major, dual enrollment of high school students, honors program, internships, telecourses. **Remedial services:** Learning center, preadmission summer program, reduced course load, remedial instruction, tutoring. **Placement/credit:** AP, CLEP Subject, institutional tests; 14 credit hours maximum for associate degree.

ACADEMIC REQUIREMENTS. Freshmen must earn minimum GPA of 1.6 to continue in good standing. 66% of freshmen return for sophomore year. Students must declare major on application. **Graduation requirements:** 64 hours for associate. Most students required to take courses in English, humanities, mathematics, social sciences.

FRESHMAN ADMISSIONS. Selection criteria: Open admissions. Selective admissions to some programs. **High school preparation:** 16 units recommended. Some programs require college preparatory courses, such as 2 to 4 units mathematics and 1 to 2 units laboratory science. **Test requirements:** SAT required of engineering science applicants and for honors programs.

1992 FRESHMAN CLASS PROFILE. 931 men, 857 women enrolled. 2% were in top tenth and 15% were in top quarter of graduating class. **Characteristics:** 100% from in state, 100% commute, 11% have minority backgrounds.

FALL-TERM APPLICATIONS. $15 fee, may be waived for applicants with need. No closing date; applicants notified on a rolling basis; must reply within 6 weeks. Interview required for selective program applicants. Audition required for music applicants. Early admission available.

STUDENT LIFE. Activities: Student government, magazine, radio, student newspaper, yearbook, choral groups, concert band, dance, drama, jazz band, music ensembles, symphony orchestra, fraternities, sororities.

ATHLETICS. NJCAA. **Intercollegiate:** Baseball M, basketball, golf, ice hockey M, soccer M, softball W, tennis M. **Intramural:** Badminton, basketball, bowling, softball W, tennis, volleyball.

STUDENT SERVICES. Career counseling, employment service for undergraduates, freshman orientation, health services, on-campus day care, personal counseling, placement service for graduates, veterans counselor, women's counselor, services/facilities for handicapped.

ANNUAL EXPENSES. Tuition and fees (1992-93): $1,530, $1,320 additional for out-of-district students, $2,328 additional for out-of-state students. Tuition reciprocity agreements with neighboring counties allow some out-of-county residents to pay in-county rates. **Books and supplies:** $500. **Other expenses:** $900.

FINANCIAL AID. 25% of freshmen, 20% of continuing students re-

ceive some form of aid. 91% of grants, 89% of loans, 34% of jobs based on need. 600 enrolled freshmen were judged to have need, 550 were offered aid. Academic, athletic, minority scholarships available. **Aid applications:** No closing date; priority given to applications received by April 15; applicants notified on a rolling basis beginning on or about June 5; must reply within 2 weeks.

ADDRESS/TELEPHONE. Carolyn Holmfelt, Coordinator of Admissions, County College of Morris, 214 Center Grove Road, Randolph, NJ 07869-2086. (201) 328-5100. Fax: (201) 328-1282.

Cumberland County College
Vineland, New Jersey CB code: 2118

2-year public community college, coed. Founded in 1963. **Accreditation:** Regional. **Undergraduate enrollment:** 444 men, 738 women full time; 543 men, 1,014 women part time. **Faculty:** 113 total (56 full time), 4 with doctorates or other terminal degrees. **Location:** Rural campus in small city; 35 miles from Philadelphia. **Calendar:** Semester, limited summer session. **Microcomputers:** 60 located in libraries, classrooms, computer centers. **Additional facts:** Member Marine Sciences Consortium with access to oceanographic research facilities in Seagirt.

DEGREES OFFERED. AA, AS, AAS. 273 associate degrees awarded in 1992. 8% in business and management, 22% business/office and marketing/distribution, 21% health sciences, 5% law, 21% multi/interdisciplinary studies, 6% parks/recreation, protective services, public affairs.

UNDERGRADUATE MAJORS. Accounting, agricultural sciences, aircraft mechanics, business administration and management, business and office, business data processing and related programs, community services, computer and information sciences, early childhood education, engineering, fine arts, industrial technology, law enforcement and corrections technologies, legal assistant/paralegal, legal secretary, liberal/general studies, marketing and distribution, mathematics, nursing, ornamental horticulture, personnel management, philosophy, plastic technology, radiograph medical technology, religion, secretarial and related programs, social sciences, trade and industrial supervision and management, word processing.

ACADEMIC PROGRAMS. 2-year transfer program, accelerated program, double major, dual enrollment of high school students, honors program, independent study, telecourses. **Remedial services:** Learning center, preadmission summer program, reduced course load, remedial instruction, special counselor, tutoring, special services program for educationally and economically disadvantaged students. **Placement/credit:** AP, CLEP General and Subject, institutional tests; 32 credit hours maximum for associate degree.

ACADEMIC REQUIREMENTS. Freshmen must earn minimum GPA of 1.6 to continue in good standing. Students must declare major by end of first year. **Graduation requirements:** 64 hours for associate. Most students required to take courses in English, humanities, mathematics, social sciences.

FRESHMAN ADMISSIONS. Selection criteria: Open admissions. Special requirements for nursing program. **Test requirements:** New Jersey College Basic Skills Test used for placing all students. National League for Nursing Pre-Entrance Examination required of nursing applicants.

1992 FRESHMAN CLASS PROFILE. 544 men and women enrolled. **Characteristics:** 99% from in state, 100% commute, 35% have minority backgrounds. Average age is 25.

FALL-TERM APPLICATIONS. $15 fee. No closing date; applicants notified on a rolling basis beginning on or about March 1; must reply by registration. Deferred and early admission available.

STUDENT LIFE. Activities: Student government, student newspaper, choral groups, symphony orchestra, Multi-Cultural Club, Latin-American Club, African-American Club. **Additional information:** Comprehensive support center for learning disabled students.

STUDENT SERVICES. Aptitude testing, career counseling, employment service for undergraduates, freshman orientation, personal counseling, placement service for graduates, veterans counselor, services/facilities for handicapped.

ANNUAL EXPENSES. Tuition and fees (projected): $1,584, $1,404 additional for out-of-district students, $4,212 additional for out-of-state students. **Books and supplies:** $450. **Other expenses:** $1,429.

FINANCIAL AID. 33% of freshmen, 37% of continuing students receive some form of aid. 97% of grants, 88% of loans, 36% of jobs based on need. State/district residency scholarships available. **Aid applications:** No closing date; priority given to applications received by June 1; applicants notified on a rolling basis beginning on or about May 1; must reply within 3 weeks.

ADDRESS/TELEPHONE. Maud Fried-Goodnight, Director of Enrollment Services, Cumberland County College, PO Box 517, College Drive, Vineland, NJ 08360. (609) 691-8600. Fax: (609) 691-6157.

Drew University
Madison, New Jersey CB code: 2193

Admissions: 77% of applicants accepted
Based on: ••• School record
•• Special talents, test scores
• Activities, essay, interview, recommendations
Completion: 94% of freshmen end year in good standing
78% graduate, 24% of these enter graduate study

4-year private university, coed, affiliated with United Methodist Church. Founded in 1867. **Accreditation:** Regional. **Undergraduate enrollment:** 506 men, 703 women full time; 15 men, 51 women part time. **Graduate enrollment:** 123 men, 87 women full time; 362 men, 245 women part time. **Faculty:** 220 total (116 full time), 160 with doctorates or other terminal degrees. **Location:** Suburban campus in large town; 30 miles west of New York City. **Calendar:** Semester, limited summer session. **Microcomputers:** 2,000 located in dormitories, libraries, classrooms, computer centers, campus-wide network. **Special facilities:** New Jersey Shakespeare Equity Theatre, 80-acre forest preserve and Zuck Arboretum, Korn Art Gallery, photography gallery, observatory, US Olympic field hockey field, research greenhouse, laser holography laboratory.

DEGREES OFFERED. BA, MA, PhD, M.Div. 311 bachelor's degrees awarded in 1992. 7% in languages, 15% letters/literature, 12% psychology, 42% social sciences, 6% visual and performing arts. Graduate degrees offered in 8 major fields of study.

UNDERGRADUATE MAJORS. American studies, anthropology, art history, behavioral sciences, biological and physical sciences, biology, chemistry, classics, computer and information sciences, dramatic arts, economics, English, English literature, French, German, Greek (classical), history, humanities, humanities and social sciences, Latin, liberal/general studies, mathematics, music, philosophy, physics, political science and government, psychobiology, psychology, religion, Russian, Russian and Slavic studies, sociology, Spanish, studio art.

ACADEMIC PROGRAMS. Double major, honors program, independent study, internships, semester at sea, student-designed major, study abroad, teacher preparation, visiting/exchange student program, New York semester, United Nations semester, Washington semester, cross-registration, university-sponsored semesters in Brussels, Chile, London; art and theater semester in New York City; summer semester in South Africa; liberal arts/career combination in engineering, forestry; combined bachelor's/graduate program in medicine. **Remedial services:** Preadmission summer program, reduced course load, special counselor, tutoring, Educational Opportunity Fund. **Placement/credit:** AP, CLEP General and Subject, IB, institutional tests; 30 credit hours maximum for bachelor's degree.

ACADEMIC REQUIREMENTS. Freshmen must earn minimum GPA of 2.0 to continue in good standing. 85% of freshmen return for sophomore year. Students must declare major by end of second year. **Graduation requirements:** 120 hours for bachelor's (33 in major). Most students required to take courses in arts/fine arts, English, foreign languages, history, humanities, mathematics, philosophy/religion, biological/physical sciences, social sciences. **Postgraduate studies:** 4% enter law school, 3% enter medical school, 1% enter MBA programs, 16% enter other graduate study. **Additional information:** RISE (Research Institute Scientists Emeritii) program enables students to conduct scientific research with retired scientists.

FRESHMAN ADMISSIONS. Selection criteria: School achievement record most important, followed by test scores and special talents. Recommendations, interview, essay, and school and community activities are also considered. Rank in top quarter of class preferred. **High school preparation:** 16 units recommended. Recommended units include English 4, foreign language 2, mathematics 3, social science 2 and science 2. Mathematics, chemistry and physics majors should have 4 years college-preparatory mathematics. **Test requirements:** SAT or ACT (SAT preferred); score report by March 1. 3 ACH (including English Composition) recommended. Score report by March 1.

1992 FRESHMAN CLASS PROFILE. 688 men applied, 505 accepted, 129 enrolled; 1,097 women applied, 873 accepted, 203 enrolled. 56% were in top tenth of graduating class. **Academic background:** Mid 50% of enrolled freshmen had SAT-V between 500-630, SAT-M between 530-670. 98% submitted SAT scores. **Characteristics:** 54% from in state, 95% live in college housing, 16% have minority backgrounds, 1% are foreign students. Average age is 18.

FALL-TERM APPLICATIONS. $35 fee, may be waived for applicants with need. Closing date February 15; applicants notified on or about March 15; must reply by May 1. Essay required. Interview recommended. CRDA. Deferred admission available. EDP-F. Early Decision Plan application deadlines, December 1 or January 15, admission notification by December 24 or February 15.

STUDENT LIFE. Housing: Dormitories (men, women, coed); apartment housing available. theme house options available. **Activities:** Student government, film, magazine, radio, student newspaper, television, yearbook, 4 literary publications, choral groups, concert band, dance, drama, music ensembles, musical theater, community orchestras, madrigal singers, 11 religious organizations, 11 minority and foreign student issue groups, 9 academic related clubs. Social service and political organizations include Amnesty International, Environmental Action League, Animal Rights Coalition, College Democrats, College Republicans, Center for Social Outreach, Social Democrats. **Additional information:** All entering freshmen are given a personal computer, a printer, and software.

ATHLETICS. NCAA. **Intercollegiate:** Baseball M, basketball, cross-country, fencing W, field hockey W, horseback riding, lacrosse, soccer, softball W, tennis, track and field. **Intramural:** Badminton, basketball, bowling, football M, racquetball, soccer, softball, tennis, volleyball.

STUDENT SERVICES. Aptitude testing, career counseling, employment service for undergraduates, freshman orientation, health services, on-campus day care, personal counseling, placement service for graduates, special adviser for adult students, services/facilities for handicapped.

ANNUAL EXPENSES. Tuition and fees: $18,058. **Room and board:** $5,348. **Books and supplies:** $520. **Other expenses:** $370.

FINANCIAL AID. 65% of freshmen, 58% of continuing students receive some form of aid. 68% of grants, 77% of loans, 37% of jobs based on need. 223 enrolled freshmen were judged to have need, all were offered aid. Academic, minority scholarships available. **Aid applications:** Closing date March 1; applicants notified on or about April 15; must reply by May 1.

ADDRESS/TELEPHONE. Roberto Noya, Director of College Admissions, Drew University, 36 Madison Avenue, Madison, NJ 07940. (201) 408-3739. Fax: (201) 408-3068.

Essex County College
Newark, New Jersey CB code: 2237

2-year public community college, coed. Founded in 1966. **Accreditation:** Regional. **Undergraduate enrollment:** 1,720 men, 2,512 women full time; 1,749 men, 2,424 women part time. **Faculty:** 303 total (153 full time), 57 with doctorates or other terminal degrees. **Location:** Urban campus in large city; 12 miles from New York City. **Calendar:** Semester, limited summer session. Extensive evening/early morning classes. **Microcomputers:** Located in computer centers. **Special facilities:** Mary B. Burch Theater. **Additional facts:** Classes given at several locations in Essex County, Newark, and at West Caldwell campus.

DEGREES OFFERED. AA, AS, AAS. 403 associate degrees awarded in 1992. 9% in computer sciences, 7% engineering technologies, 18% allied health, 7% letters/literature, 7% parks/recreation, protective services, public affairs, 7% social sciences.

UNDERGRADUATE MAJORS. Accounting, architectural technologies, biology, business administration and management, business and management, business computer/console/peripheral equipment operation, business data entry equipment operation, business data processing and related programs, business data programming, business education, chemical manufacturing technology, chemistry, civil technology, computer and information sciences, computer integrated manufacturing, computer programming, criminal justice studies, dental hygiene, early childhood education, education, electronic technology, elementary education, emergency medical technologies, engineering, engineering and engineering-related technologies, fine arts, fire control and safety technology, health care administration, humanities, humanities and social sciences, journalism, law enforcement and corrections technologies, liberal/general studies, mathematics, medical secretary, music, music education, nursing, ophthalmic services, optical technology, physical education, physical therapy assistant, premedicine, radio/television technology, radiograph medical technology, secondary education, secretarial and related programs, social sciences, social work, technical and business writing.

ACADEMIC PROGRAMS. 2-year transfer program, cooperative education, double major, dual enrollment of high school students, honors program, independent study, internships, study abroad, teacher preparation, cross-registration, civil construction engineering program with New Jersey Institute of Technology; criminal justice program with Rutgers. **Remedial services:** Learning center, reduced course load, remedial instruction, special counselor, tutoring. **Placement/credit:** AP, CLEP General and Subject, institutional tests; 30 credit hours maximum for associate degree.

ACADEMIC REQUIREMENTS. Freshmen must earn minimum GPA of 2.0 to continue in good standing. 60% of freshmen return for sophomore year. Students must declare major on application. **Graduation requirements:** 64 hours for associate (39 in major). Most students required to take courses in English, history, humanities, mathematics, biological/physical sciences, social sciences. **Additional information:** Cross-registration with other institutions in Council of Higher Education in Newark. Civil construction engineering program with New Jersey Institute of Technology and criminal justice program with Rutgers—The State University of New Jersey.

FRESHMAN ADMISSIONS. Selection criteria: Open admissions. Selective admissions to allied health programs. **Test requirements:** NLN test for nursing students.

1992 FRESHMAN CLASS PROFILE. 1,005 men, 1,273 women enrolled. **Characteristics:** 95% from in state, 100% commute, 77% have minority backgrounds, 7% are foreign students. Average age is 23.

FALL-TERM APPLICATIONS. $10 fee. No closing date; priority given to applications received by August 15; applicants notified on a rolling basis; must reply by registration. Interview recommended for physical therapy, nursing, and ophthalmic science applicants. Deferred and early admission available. Priority given to allied health program applications received by April 15.

STUDENT LIFE. Activities: Student government, student newspaper, yearbook, choral groups, dance, drama, jazz band, music ensembles, musical theater, gospel choir, Cercle Francophone (French club), Islamic student organization, Latin student union, DECA (Distributive Education Club of America), criminal justice organization.

ATHLETICS. NJCAA. **Intercollegiate:** Basketball, cross-country, soccer M, softball W, track and field. **Intramural:** Basketball, racquetball, table tennis, volleyball.

STUDENT SERVICES. Aptitude testing, career counseling, employment service for undergraduates, freshman orientation, health services, on-campus day care, personal counseling, placement service for graduates, veterans counselor, services/facilities for handicapped.

ANNUAL EXPENSES. Tuition and fees (1992-93): $1,848, $1,650 additional for out-of-district students, $3,300 additional for out-of-state students. **Books and supplies:** $600. **Other expenses:** $1,061.

FINANCIAL AID. 65% of freshmen, 65% of continuing students receive some form of aid. 99% of grants, 90% of loans, all jobs based on need. Academic, athletic, state/district residency, leadership, minority scholarships available. **Aid applications:** No closing date; priority given to applications received by June 30; applicants notified on a rolling basis beginning on or about June 15; must reply within 3 weeks.

ADDRESS/TELEPHONE. Vivian McCollough, Associate Director of Admissions, Essex County College, 303 University Avenue, Newark, NJ 07102. (201) 877-3100.

Fairleigh Dickinson University
Madison, New Jersey CB code: 2262

Admissions:	57% of applicants accepted
Based on:	••• School record
	•• Interview, test scores
	• Activities, essay, recommendations, special talents
Completion:	66% of freshmen end year in good standing
	49% graduate

4-year private university, coed. Founded in 1942. **Accreditation:** Regional. **Undergraduate enrollment:** 1,462 men, 1,402 women full time; 777 men, 999 women part time. **Graduate enrollment:** 402 men, 377 women full time; 1,550 men, 1,431 women part time. **Faculty:** 603 total (277 full time), 229 with doctorates or other terminal degrees. **Location:** Suburban campus in large town; Madison campus 25 miles from New York City, Rutherford campus 11 miles, Teaneck campus 5 miles. **Calendar:** Semester, extensive summer session. Saturday and extensive evening/early morning classes. **Microcomputers:** 300 located in dormitories, libraries, computer centers, campus-wide network. **Special facilities:** Food science laboratory, Institute for Entrepreneurial Studies, photonics laboratory, art galleries. **Additional facts:** Campuses located at Madison, Teaneck-Hackensack, and Rutherford. Teacher certification available at Teaneck. Rutherford campus dedicated to business studies, offering upper-division undergraduate and graduate programs. 2-year degree programs offered at Edward Williams College, Teaneck, and Rutherford campus.

DEGREES OFFERED. AS, BA, BS, MA, MS, MBA, PhD. 1 associate degree awarded in 1992. 100% in allied health. 978 bachelor's degrees awarded. 46% in business and management, 6% communications, 6% engineering technologies, 5% health sciences, 6% letters/literature, 10% psychology, 8% social sciences. Graduate degrees offered in 42 major fields of study.

UNDERGRADUATE MAJORS. Associate: Physical therapy assistant, radiograph medical technology, respiratory therapy. **Bachelor's:** Accounting, biochemistry, biological and physical sciences, biology, business administration and management, business economics, chemistry, civil technology, clinical laboratory science, communications, computer and information sciences, construction, cytotechnology, economics, electrical technology, electrical/electronics/communications engineering, English literature, environmental science, finance, fine arts, French, history, hotel/motel and restaurant management, humanities, international relations, international studies, marine biology, marketing management, mathematics, mechanical design technology, medical laboratory technologies, nursing, philosophy, political science and government, prepharmacy, psychology, radiograph medical technology, sociology, Spanish, studio art.

ACADEMIC PROGRAMS. Accelerated program, cooperative education, double major, dual enrollment of high school students, education specialist degree, honors program, independent study, internships, student-designed major, study abroad, teacher preparation, visiting/exchange student program, weekend college, Washington semester, cross-registration, semester abroad at Wroxton College, England; combined bachelor's/graduate program in business administration. **Remedial services:** Learning center, preadmission summer program, reduced course load, remedial instruction, special counselor, tutoring, freshman intensive studies program. **ROTC:** Air Force,

Army. **Placement/credit:** AP, CLEP General and Subject, IB, institutional tests; 30 credit hours maximum for associate degree; 60 credit hours maximum for bachelor's degree. Maximum of 32 semester hours of credit by examination may be counted toward degree from business administration college.

ACADEMIC REQUIREMENTS. Freshmen must earn minimum GPA of 2.0 to continue in good standing. 71% of freshmen return for sophomore year. Students must declare major by end of second year. **Graduation requirements:** 72 hours for associate, 128 hours for bachelor's (42 in major). Most students required to take courses in arts/fine arts, computer science, English, foreign languages, history, humanities, mathematics, philosophy/religion, biological/physical sciences, social sciences. **Additional information:** All students encouraged to study abroad at Wroxton, England campus. Marine biology majors spend 1 semester in Hilo, Hawaii, or Schoals laboratory, Maine.

FRESHMAN ADMISSIONS. High school preparation: 16 units required. Required units include English 4, foreign language 2 and mathematics 2. 2 history, 1 laboratory science required. Additional mathematics and science requirements for science and health applicants. **Test requirements:** SAT or ACT (SAT preferred); score report by August 1. PAA or SAT required from students applying from Puerto Rico. **Additional information:** Separate application procedures apply for Learning Disabled College Students Program.

1992 FRESHMAN CLASS PROFILE. 3,045 men and women applied, 1,743 accepted; 295 men enrolled, 271 women enrolled. 9% were in top tenth and 21% were in top quarter of graduating class. **Academic background:** Mid 50% of enrolled freshmen had SAT-V between 380-490, SAT-M between 430-540. 82% submitted SAT scores. **Characteristics:** 68% from in state, 51% live in college housing, 10% have minority backgrounds, 13% are foreign students. Average age is 21.

FALL-TERM APPLICATIONS. $35 fee, may be waived for applicants with need. No closing date; applicants notified on a rolling basis; must reply by May 1 or within 2 weeks if notified thereafter. Portfolio required for art applicants. Essay required. Interview recommended. CRDA. Deferred and early admission available. EDP-F.

STUDENT LIFE. Housing: Dormitories (coed); apartment, fraternity, sorority housing available. 24-hour quiet housing, honors student housing, theme housing. **Activities:** Student government, radio, student newspaper, television, yearbook, literary magazine, psychology journal, choral groups, dance, drama, jazz band, music ensembles, musical theater, pep band, jazz ensemble, fraternities, sororities, several religious, ethnic, and cultural organizations, Student Volunteer Program, Big Brothers/Big Sisters, Progressive Forum, Politics Plus. **Additional information:** NCAA division I teams at Teaneck and Rutherford campuses, division III teams at Madison campus.

ATHLETICS. NCAA. **Intercollegiate:** Baseball M, basketball, cross-country, fencing W, field hockey W, football M, golf, horseback riding, lacrosse M, soccer M, softball W, tennis, track and field, volleyball W. **Intramural:** Archery M, basketball, bowling, cross-country, field hockey W, football M, golf, horseback riding, racquetball, rugby M, soccer, softball, table tennis, tennis, track and field, volleyball, water polo M.

STUDENT SERVICES. Aptitude testing, career counseling, employment service for undergraduates, freshman orientation, health services, personal counseling, placement service for graduates, special adviser for adult students, veterans counselor, services/facilities for handicapped.

ANNUAL EXPENSES. Tuition and fees: $10,988. **Room and board:** $5,336. **Books and supplies:** $570. **Other expenses:** $1,273.

FINANCIAL AID. 85% of freshmen, 63% of continuing students receive some form of aid. Academic, athletic, state/district residency, leadership scholarships available. **Aid applications:** No closing date; priority given to applications received by March 15; applicants notified on a rolling basis beginning on or about March 1; must reply by May 1 or within 2 weeks if notified thereafter.

ADDRESS/TELEPHONE. Dale Herold, Director of Admissions and Financial Aid, Fairleigh Dickinson University, 270 Montross Avenue, Rutherford, NJ 07070. (201) 460-5267. (800) 338-8803. Fax: (201) 460-5010.

Fairleigh Dickinson University: Edward Williams College

Hackensack, New Jersey — CB code: 2232

Admissions:	96% of applicants accepted
Based on:	••• School record
	•• Interview, recommendations, test scores
	• Activities, essay
Completion:	57% of freshmen end year in good standing
	90% enter 4-year programs

2-year private junior college, coed. Founded in 1964. **Accreditation:** Regional. **Undergraduate enrollment:** 414 men, 444 women full time; 112 men, 188 women part time. **Faculty:** 71 total (35 full time), 14 with doctorates or other terminal degrees. **Location:** Suburban campus in large town; 5 miles from New York City. **Calendar:** Semester, extensive summer session. Saturday classes. **Microcomputers:** 300 located in dormitories, libraries, computer centers. **Special facilities:** Art gallery. **Additional facts:** Located on university's 4-year campus. Students have full access to all university facilities.

DEGREES OFFERED. AA. 224 associate degrees awarded in 1992. 100% in multi/interdisciplinary studies.

UNDERGRADUATE MAJORS. Liberal/general studies.

ACADEMIC PROGRAMS. 2-year transfer program, cooperative education, dual enrollment of high school students, honors program, independent study, study abroad, weekend college, cross-registration. **Remedial services:** Learning center, preadmission summer program, reduced course load, remedial instruction, special counselor, tutoring. **ROTC:** Air Force, Army. **Placement/credit:** AP, CLEP General; 30 credit hours maximum for associate degree.

ACADEMIC REQUIREMENTS. Freshmen must earn minimum GPA of 2.0 to continue in good standing. 67% of freshmen return for sophomore year. Students must declare major by end of second year. **Graduation requirements:** 60 hours for associate. Most students required to take courses in English, history, mathematics, philosophy/religion, biological/physical sciences, social sciences.

FRESHMAN ADMISSIONS. Selection criteria: School achievement record most important, followed by test scores, counselor recommendation, interview, school and community activities. **High school preparation:** 16 units required. Required and recommended units include English 4, mathematics 2, social science 2 and science 1. Foreign language 2 recommended. **Test requirements:** SAT or ACT (SAT preferred); score report by September 1.

1992 FRESHMAN CLASS PROFILE. 1,393 men and women applied, 1,331 accepted; 232 men enrolled, 264 women enrolled. 2% were in top tenth and 9% were in top quarter of graduating class. **Academic background:** Mid 50% of enrolled freshmen had SAT-V between 260-350, SAT-M between 300-380. 83% submitted SAT scores. **Characteristics:** 83% from in state, 52% live in college housing, 64% have minority backgrounds, 3% are foreign students. Average age is 19.

FALL-TERM APPLICATIONS. $35 fee, may be waived for applicants with need. No closing date; applicants notified on a rolling basis beginning on or about December 15; must reply within 4 weeks. Interview required. Essay recommended. Deferred and early admission available. EDP-F.

STUDENT LIFE. Housing: Dormitories (coed); fraternity, sorority housing available. **Activities:** Student government, magazine, radio, student newspaper, yearbook, choral groups, concert band, dance, drama, jazz band, fraternities, sororities.

ATHLETICS. NCAA. **Intercollegiate:** Baseball M, basketball, cross-country, fencing W, golf M, horseback riding, soccer M, tennis, track and field, volleyball W. **Intramural:** Archery M, basketball, bowling, cross-country, football M, golf, racquetball, softball, table tennis, track and field, volleyball.

STUDENT SERVICES. Aptitude testing, career counseling, employment service for undergraduates, freshman orientation, health services, personal counseling, services/facilities for handicapped.

ANNUAL EXPENSES. Tuition and fees: $10,295. **Room and board:** $5,336. **Books and supplies:** $473. **Other expenses:** $1,050.

FINANCIAL AID. 90% of freshmen, 63% of continuing students receive some form of aid. Academic, state/district residency, leadership scholarships available. **Aid applications:** No closing date; priority given to applications received by March 15; applicants notified on a rolling basis beginning on or about March 1; must reply within 2 weeks.

ADDRESS/TELEPHONE. Dr. Phillip E. Lyon, Assoc Dean at Rutherford, Fairleigh Dickinson University: Edward Williams College, 150 Kotte Place, Hackensack, NJ 07601. (201) 692-2675.

Felician College

Lodi, New Jersey — CB code: 2321

4-year private liberal arts college, coed, affiliated with Roman Catholic Church. Founded in 1942. **Accreditation:** Regional. **Undergraduate enrollment:** 51 men, 371 women full time; 59 men, 510 women part time. **Faculty:** 99 total (50 full time), 35 with doctorates or other terminal degrees. **Location:** Suburban campus in large town; 15 miles from New York City. **Calendar:** Semester, limited summer session. Saturday classes. **Microcomputers:** 50 located in computer centers. **Special facilities:** Felician School for Exceptional Children, nursing skills laboratory, performance and theater facilities.

DEGREES OFFERED. AA, AAS, BA, BS. 43 associate degrees awarded in 1992. 7% in business and management, 89% allied health. 56 bachelor's degrees awarded. 5% in business and management, 5% computer sciences, 29% teacher education, 14% health sciences, 9% letters/literature, 5% life sciences, 18% psychology, 9% social sciences.

UNDERGRADUATE MAJORS. Associate: Biology, business and management, business/computer science, business/liberal arts, computer and information sciences, English, fine arts, history, humanities, liberal/general studies, mathematics, medical laboratory technologies, natural science and mathematics, nursing, psychology, religion. **Bachelor's:** Biology, business and management, business/computer science, computer and information sciences, cytotechnology, elementary education, English, fine arts, history, humanities, liberal/general studies, mathematics, medical laboratory technologies, natural science and mathematics, nursing, psychology, religion, social sciences, special education.

ACADEMIC PROGRAMS. 2-year transfer program, accelerated program, double major, dual enrollment of high school students, honors program, independent study, internships, student-designed major, teacher preparation, weekend college, joint degree in clinical laboratory sciences with University of Medicine and Dentistry of New Jersey. **Remedial services:** Learning center, preadmission summer program, reduced course load, remedial instruction, tutoring, program for academically and/or economically disadvantaged students. **Placement/credit:** AP, CLEP General and Subject, institutional tests; 15 credit hours maximum for associate degree; 30 credit hours maximum for bachelor's degree.

ACADEMIC REQUIREMENTS. Freshmen must earn minimum GPA of 1.8 to continue in good standing. Freshmen must earn minimum GPA of 2.5 for education and nursing programs. 65% of freshmen return for sophomore year. Students must declare major by end of second year. **Graduation requirements:** 64 hours for associate (18 in major), 120 hours for bachelor's (39 in major). Most students required to take courses in arts/fine arts, English, history, humanities, mathematics, philosophy/religion, biological/physical sciences, social sciences.

FRESHMAN ADMISSIONS. Selection criteria: School achievement record and test scores are most important. Interview recommendation of high school counselor, school and community activities are also considered. **High school preparation:** 8 units required. 8 high school units required: 4 english, 2 mathematics, 2 social studies/history, 2 foreign language, 1 additional mathematics and social studies/history, and 3 sciences recommended. Biology, chemistry, and mathematics required for nursing and medical laboratory technology applicants. **Test requirements:** SAT or ACT (SAT preferred).

1992 FRESHMAN CLASS PROFILE. 17 men, 147 women enrolled. 26% had high school GPA of 3.0 or higher, 59% between 2.0 and 2.99. 4% were in top tenth and 14% were in top quarter of graduating class. **Academic background:** Mid 50% of enrolled freshmen had SAT-V between 320-430, SAT-M between 350-420. 44% submitted SAT scores. **Characteristics:** 99% from in state, 100% commute, 32% have minority backgrounds, 1% are foreign students, 3% join fraternities/sororities. Average age is 27.

FALL-TERM APPLICATIONS. $25 fee, may be waived for applicants with need. No closing date; applicants notified on a rolling basis; must reply within 4 weeks. Interview required. Essay required for nontraditional applicants. Deferred admission available.

STUDENT LIFE. Activities: Student government, magazine, drama, fraternities, sororities, Campus Ministry Team, Mendel Science Club, Education Club, New Jersey Nursing Students, American Nurses' Association, American Society of Medical Technology, Student National Education Association, business club, psychology club, drama club.

STUDENT SERVICES. Aptitude testing, career counseling, employment service for undergraduates, freshman orientation, health services, on-campus day care, personal counseling, special adviser for adult students, peer tutoring, spiritual counseling, services/facilities for handicapped.

ANNUAL EXPENSES. Tuition and fees: $7,925. **Books and supplies:** $450.

FINANCIAL AID. 45% of freshmen, 32% of continuing students receive some form of aid. 89% of grants, 71% of loans, all jobs based on need. Academic scholarships available. **Aid applications:** No closing date; priority given to applications received by June 1; applicants notified on a rolling basis beginning on or about April 1; must reply within 3 weeks.

ADDRESS/TELEPHONE. Sr. Mary Austin Blank, O.S.B, Director of Admissions, Felician College, 262 South Main Street, Lodi, NJ 07644-2198. (201) 778-1029. Fax: (201) 778-4111.

Georgian Court College
Lakewood, New Jersey

CB code: 2274

Admissions:	85% of applicants accepted
Based on:	••• School record
	•• Interview, test scores
	• Activities, essay, recommendations, special talents
Completion:	91% of freshmen end year in good standing
	58% graduate, 20% of these enter graduate study

4-year private liberal arts college, women only, affiliated with Roman Catholic Church. Founded in 1908. **Accreditation:** Regional. **Undergraduate enrollment:** 49 men, 985 women full time; 129 men, 670 women part time. **Graduate enrollment:** 2 men, 24 women full time; 85 men, 559 women part time. **Faculty:** 198 total (96 full time), 68 with doctorates or other terminal degrees. **Location:** Suburban campus in large town; 60 miles from New York City, 60 miles from Philadelphia. **Calendar:** Semester, limited summer session. **Microcomputers:** 90 located in libraries, campus-wide network. **Special facilities:** Sister Mary Grace Burns Arboretum, M. Christina Geis Art Gallery. **Additional facts:** Evening and graduate divisions coeducational. Campus is national historic landmark.

DEGREES OFFERED. BA, BS, MA, MS. 299 bachelor's degrees awarded in 1992. 30% in business and management, 8% education, 7% letters/literature, 6% life sciences, 13% multi/interdisciplinary studies, 14% psychology, 12% social sciences. Graduate degrees offered in 5 major fields of study.

UNDERGRADUATE MAJORS. Accounting, art education, art history, biochemistry, biology, business administration and management, chemistry, English, fine arts, French, history, humanities, mathematics, music, music performance, nuclear medical technology, physics, predentistry, prelaw, premedicine, preveterinary, psychology, religion, social work, sociology, Spanish, special education, studio art.

ACADEMIC PROGRAMS. Double major, dual enrollment of high school students, education specialist degree, independent study, internships, study abroad, teacher preparation, 5-year joint liberal arts/engineering or computer science programs with George Washington University(DC), gerontology certificate program open to applicants with associate's degree or 2 years clinical experience; liberal arts/career combination in engineering. **Remedial services:** Learning center, preadmission summer program, reduced course load, remedial instruction, special counselor, tutoring. **Placement/credit:** AP, CLEP General and Subject, institutional tests; 30 credit hours maximum for bachelor's degree.

ACADEMIC REQUIREMENTS. Freshmen must earn minimum GPA of 1.8 to continue in good standing. 78% of freshmen return for sophomore year. Students must declare major by end of second year. **Graduation requirements:** 132 hours for bachelor's (30 in major). Most students required to take courses in arts/fine arts, English, foreign languages, history, humanities, mathematics, philosophy/religion, biological/physical sciences, social sciences.

FRESHMAN ADMISSIONS. Selection criteria: School achievement record very important. Interview and test scores also considered. Applicant should rank in top half of class. **High school preparation:** 16 units required. Required units include English 4, foreign language 2, mathematics 2, social science 1 and science 1. One unit laboratory science, 6 electives in areas listed are required. **Test requirements:** SAT; score report by August 1.

1992 FRESHMAN CLASS PROFILE. 349 men and women applied, 295 accepted; 1 man enrolled, 136 women enrolled. **Academic background:** Mid 50% of enrolled freshmen had SAT-V between 360-450, SAT-M between 370-480. 77% submitted SAT scores. **Characteristics:** 98% from in state, 67% commute, 15% have minority backgrounds. Average age is 22.

FALL-TERM APPLICATIONS. $20 fee, may be waived for applicants with need. Closing date July 1; priority given to applications received by November 15; applicants notified on a rolling basis; must reply by May 1 or within 2 weeks if notified thereafter. Audition required for music applicants. Portfolio recommended for art applicants. Essay recommended. Interviews required when distance permits. CRDA. Early admission available. EDP-F.

STUDENT LIFE. Housing: Dormitories (women). Housing guaranteed for 4 years. **Activities:** Student government, magazine, student newspaper, yearbook, choral groups, concert band, drama, Council for Exceptional Children, Black Women's League, Re-Entry Women's Club, Latin American Women's League, campus ministry, Alliance Francaisede Georgian Court College, Amnesty International.

ATHLETICS. NAIA. **Intercollegiate:** Basketball, cross-country, soccer, softball.

STUDENT SERVICES. Aptitude testing, career counseling, freshman orientation, health services, personal counseling, special adviser for adult students, services/facilities for handicapped.

ANNUAL EXPENSES. Tuition and fees: $8,750. **Room and board:** $3,850. **Books and supplies:** $500. **Other expenses:** $800.

FINANCIAL AID. 64% of freshmen, 60% of continuing students receive some form of aid. 95% of grants, 93% of loans, 95% of jobs based on need. Academic, music/drama, art, athletic, state/district residency, leadership, alumni affiliation scholarships available. **Aid applications:** Closing date October 1; priority given to applications received by March 1; applicants notified on a rolling basis beginning on or about March 15; must reply by May 1 or within 2 weeks if notified thereafter. **Additional information:** FAF also required of applicants for no-need scholarships and jobs.

ADDRESS/TELEPHONE. John P. Burke, Director of Admissions, Georgian Court College, 900 Lakewood Avenue, Lakewood, NJ 08701-2697. (908) 367-4440.

Gloucester County College
Sewell, New Jersey

CB code: 2281

2-year public community college, coed. Founded in 1966. **Accreditation:** Regional. **Undergraduate enrollment:** 877 men, 1,069 women full time; 1,154 men, 2,166 women part time. **Faculty:** 264 total (74 full time), 13 with doctorates or other terminal degrees. **Location:** Rural campus in rural community; 12 miles from Camden and 16 miles from Philadelphia. **Calendar:** Semester, limited summer session. Saturday and extensive evening/early morning classes. **Microcomputers:** 150 located in libraries, classrooms, computer centers. **Special facilities:** 5 CD-ROM machines in library, satellite downlink dish, monthly art exhibits, production studio. **Additional facts:** Off-campus institutional site for automotive technology at Williamstown high school.

DEGREES OFFERED. AA, AS, AAS. 580 associate degrees awarded in 1992. 13% in business and management, 16% education, 30% health sciences, 20% multi/interdisciplinary studies, 7% parks/recreation, protective services, public affairs.

UNDERGRADUATE MAJORS. Accounting, automotive mechanics, biology, business administration and management, business data processing and related programs, chemical manufacturing technology, chemistry, civil technology, computer and information sciences, drafting and design technology, education, electronic technology, engineering science, finance, information sciences and systems, law enforcement and corrections technologies, legal secretary, liberal/general studies, manufacturing technology, marketing and distribution, marketing management, medical secretary, nuclear medical technology, nursing, parks and recreation management, physical education, physical sciences, respiratory therapy technology, retailing, secretarial and related programs, small business management and ownership, special education, survey and mapping technology, ultrasound technology, water and wastewater technology, word processing.

ACADEMIC PROGRAMS. 2-year transfer program, cooperative education, dual enrollment of high school students, telecourses. **Remedial services:** Learning center, reduced course load, remedial instruction, tutoring, basic skills program. **Placement/credit:** CLEP Subject, institutional tests; 16 credit hours maximum for associate degree.

ACADEMIC REQUIREMENTS. Freshmen must earn minimum GPA of 2.0 to continue in good standing. 23% of freshmen return for sophomore year. Students must declare major on application. **Graduation requirements:** 65 hours for associate. Most students required to take courses in computer science, English, humanities, mathematics, biological/physical sciences, social sciences. **Additional information:** Weekend and evening nursing and LPN mobility programs available.

FRESHMAN ADMISSIONS. Selection criteria: Open admissions. Selective admissions to nursing, respiratory therapy, nuclear medicine technology, and diagnostic medical sonography programs. Special-need students, hearing impaired, or deaf can apply and are evaluated for the support our college can offer. Biology and chemistry required for nursing applicants. Algebra also required for respiratory therapy, nuclear medicine, and diagnostic medical sonography applicants. **Test requirements:** Minimum SAT combined score of 640 or ACT composite score of 17 required for nursing, respiratory therapy, nuclear medicine, and diagnostic medical sonography applicants. **Additional information:** Admission to nursing and respiratory therapy, nuclear medicine, and diagnostic medical sonography begins October. Each program has different closing date. Contact Admissions Office for details.

1992 FRESHMAN CLASS PROFILE. 772 men, 1,041 women enrolled. **Characteristics:** 99% from in state, 100% commute, 1% are foreign students. Average age is 25.

FALL-TERM APPLICATIONS. $10 fee, may be waived for applicants with need. No closing date; applicants notified on a rolling basis; must reply within 2 weeks.

STUDENT LIFE. Activities: Student government, radio, student newspaper, choral groups, concert band, drama, gospel choir, student activities board, minority student union, silent club.

ATHLETICS. NJCAA. **Intercollegiate:** Baseball M, basketball M, cross-country, soccer M, tennis, track and field, wrestling M. **Intramural:** Volleyball.

STUDENT SERVICES. Aptitude testing, career counseling, employment service for undergraduates, freshman orientation, health services, on-campus day care, personal counseling, placement service for graduates, veterans counselor, special adviser and handicapped students orientation, services/facilities for handicapped.

ANNUAL EXPENSES. Tuition and fees (1992-93): $1,590, $30 additional for out-of-district students, $4,320 additional for out-of-state students. **Books and supplies:** $400. **Other expenses:** $800.

FINANCIAL AID. 25% of freshmen, 19% of continuing students receive some form of aid. All grants, 97% of loans, all jobs based on need. Academic scholarships available. **Aid applications:** No closing date; priority given to applications received by May 1; applicants notified on a rolling basis beginning on or about June 1; must reply within 2 weeks.

ADDRESS/TELEPHONE. Office of Admissions and Financial Aid, Gloucester County College, Tanyard Road, Deptford Township, RR #4, Box 203, Sewell Post Office, NJ 08080. (609) 468-5000 ext. 341. Fax: (609) 468-8498.

Hudson County Community College
Jersey City, New Jersey — CB code: 2291

2-year public community college, coed. Founded in 1975. **Accreditation:** Regional. **Undergraduate enrollment:** 809 men, 1,026 women full time; 554 men, 687 women part time. **Faculty:** 196 total (41 full time), 35 with doctorates or other terminal degrees. **Location:** Urban campus in small city; 10 miles from New York City. **Calendar:** Semester, limited summer session. Saturday and extensive evening/early morning classes. **Microcomputers:** 175 located in libraries, classrooms, computer centers. **Additional facts:** College has contractual relationships with St. Peter's College and Jersey City State College for facilities and services, including library facilities, and maintains educational centers throughout Hudson County.

DEGREES OFFERED. AA, AS, AAS. 150 associate degrees awarded in 1992. 28% in business and management, 8% business/office and marketing/distribution, 7% engineering, 36% home economics, 9% parks/recreation, protective services, public affairs.

UNDERGRADUATE MAJORS. Accounting, business and management, business and office, business data processing and related programs, child development/care/guidance, computer and information sciences, computer integrated manufacturing, computer technology, criminal justice studies, electronic technology, engineering, engineering and engineering-related technologies, engineering science, food production/management/services, human services, legal assistant/paralegal, liberal/general studies, medical assistant, medical records technology, public administration, secretarial and related programs, social work.

ACADEMIC PROGRAMS. 2-year transfer program, dual enrollment of high school students, internships, weekend college, cross-registration. **Remedial services:** Learning center, preadmission summer program, reduced course load, remedial instruction, special counselor, tutoring, computer-assisted instruction. **Placement/credit:** CLEP General and Subject, institutional tests; 6 credit hours maximum for associate degree.

ACADEMIC REQUIREMENTS. Freshmen must earn minimum GPA of 1.7 to continue in good standing. 45% of freshmen return for sophomore year. Students must declare major on application. **Graduation requirements:** 63 hours for associate (30 in major). Most students required to take courses in computer science, English, history, humanities, mathematics, biological/physical sciences, social sciences. **Additional information:** Students may attain a second degree by completing 24 additional credits, including all requirements for second major.

FRESHMAN ADMISSIONS. Selection criteria: Open admissions. **Test requirements:** New Jersey College Basic Skills Test required for all applicants for placement.

1992 FRESHMAN CLASS PROFILE. 463 men, 524 women enrolled. **Characteristics:** 99% from in state, 100% commute, 75% have minority backgrounds, 2% are foreign students. Average age is 23.

FALL-TERM APPLICATIONS. $10 fee, may be waived for applicants with need. Closing date September 1; applicants notified on a rolling basis.

STUDENT LIFE. Activities: Student government, student newspaper, yearbook, choral groups, drama, musical theater, fraternities, sororities, medical assisting club, ice sculpture club, black awareness club, creative writing club, electronics club, multicultural club, photography club, health club, sophisticated diners club, chemistry club.

ATHLETICS. NJCAA. **Intercollegiate:** Baseball M, basketball, soccer M, softball W, volleyball W. **Intramural:** Basketball, bowling, football M, sailing, skiing, soccer M, volleyball.

STUDENT SERVICES. Aptitude testing, career counseling, employment service for undergraduates, freshman orientation, personal counseling, placement service for graduates, special adviser for adult students, veterans counselor, services/facilities for handicapped.

ANNUAL EXPENSES. Tuition and fees (1992-93): $1,386, $1,128 additional for out-of-district students, $1,128 additional for out-of-state students. **Books and supplies:** $681. **Other expenses:** $941.

FINANCIAL AID. 48% of freshmen, 57% of continuing students receive some form of aid. 71% of loans, all jobs based on need. Academic, leadership scholarships available. **Aid applications:** No closing date; applicants notified on a rolling basis; must reply within 1 week.

ADDRESS/TELEPHONE. Juan Harris, Asst Dean Enrollment Services, Hudson County Community College, 168 Sip Avenue, Jersey City, NJ 07306. (201) 714-2127 ext. 2128. Fax: (201) 656-8961.

Jersey City State College
Jersey City, New Jersey — CB code: 2516

Admissions: 58% of applicants accepted
Based on:
••• School record, test scores
•• Essay
• Activities, interview, recommendations, special talents
Completion: 85% of freshmen end year in good standing
40% graduate, 17% of these enter graduate study

4-year public college of arts and sciences, coed. Founded in 1927. **Accreditation:** Regional. **Undergraduate enrollment:** 1,693 men, 1,947 women full time; 961 men, 1,287 women part time. **Graduate enrollment:** 1 man, 14 women full time; 328 men, 961 women part time. **Faculty:** 434 total (241 full time), 325 with doctorates or other terminal degrees. **Location:** Urban campus in small city; within New York metropolitan area. **Calendar:** Semester, extensive summer session. Saturday classes. **Microcomputers:** 1,400 located in libraries, classrooms, computer centers. **Special facilities:** School for multihandicapped children, performing arts center, computer technology center, 3 art galleries, cooperative education center, catalyst teaching center.

DEGREES OFFERED. BA, BS, BFA, MA, MS. 622 bachelor's degrees awarded in 1992. 29% in business and management, 6% communications, 7% computer sciences, 9% education, 9% health sciences, 10% parks/recreation, protective services, public affairs, 12% social sciences, 6% visual and performing arts. Graduate degrees offered in 10 major fields of study.

UNDERGRADUATE MAJORS. Accounting, art education, art history, art therapy, astronomy, biology, business administration and management, business and management, business economics, chemistry, cinematography/film, computer and information sciences, crafts, creative writing, criminal justice studies, cytotechnology, early childhood education, economics, elementary education, English, English education, fashion merchandising, film arts, finance, fine arts, fire control and safety technology, geography, geology, graphic design, health education, health sciences, history, jazz, management science, marketing and distribution, mathematics, mathematics education, medical laboratory technologies, motion picture technology, music, music education, music history and appreciation, music performance, music theory and composition, nuclear medical technology, nursing, philosophy, photographic technology, photography, political science and government, predentistry, prelaw, premedicine, prepharmacy, preveterinary, psychology, radio/television broadcasting, radio/television technology, science education, secondary education, social studies education, sociology, Spanish, special education, sports management, studio art, visual and performing arts.

ACADEMIC PROGRAMS. Accelerated program, cooperative education, double major, dual enrollment of high school students, honors program, independent study, internships, study abroad, teacher preparation, visiting/exchange student program, weekend college, Washington semester, cross-registration. **Remedial services:** Learning center, preadmission summer program, reduced course load, remedial instruction, special counselor, tutoring. **Placement/credit:** AP, CLEP General and Subject, institutional tests; 30 credit hours maximum for bachelor's degree.

ACADEMIC REQUIREMENTS. Freshmen must earn minimum GPA of 2.0 to continue in good standing. 70% of freshmen return for sophomore year. Students must declare major by end of second year. **Graduation requirements:** 128 hours for bachelor's (36 in major). Most students required to take courses in arts/fine arts, computer science, English, foreign languages, history, humanities, mathematics, philosophy/religion, biological/physical sciences, social sciences. **Postgraduate studies:** 2% enter law school, 2% enter medical school, 5% enter MBA programs, 8% enter other graduate study. **Additional information:** Cooperative education placements offered in all majors.

FRESHMAN ADMISSIONS. Selection criteria: High school courses, grades, class rank, and test scores most important, followed by essay or personal statement. Special program for educationally disadvantaged applicants is available with the above criteria. **High school preparation:** 16 units required. Required and recommended units include English 4, mathematics 3, social science 2 and science 2. Foreign language 2 recommended. At least 5 additional academic elective units required. **Test requirements:** SAT or ACT (SAT preferred); score report by June 1.

1992 FRESHMAN CLASS PROFILE. 1,449 men applied, 850 accepted, 451 enrolled; 1,710 women applied, 987 accepted, 464 enrolled. 7% were in top tenth and 24% were in top quarter of graduating class. **Characteristics:** 95% from in state, 95% commute, 56% have minority backgrounds, 5% are foreign students, 1% join fraternities/sororities. Average age is 18.

FALL-TERM APPLICATIONS. $20 fee, may be waived for applicants with need. Closing date June 1; priority given to applications received by April 15; applicants notified on a rolling basis; must reply by May 1 or within 3 weeks if notified thereafter. Audition required for music applicants. Essay required. Interview recommended. Portfolio recommended for art applicants. CRDA. Deferred and early admission available.

STUDENT LIFE. Housing: Dormitories (coed); apartment, cooperative housing available. **Activities:** Student government, magazine, radio, student newspaper, yearbook, choral groups, dance, drama, jazz band, music ensembles, musical theater, symphony orchestra, fraternities, sororities, Campus Christian Fellowship, Black Freedom Society, Latin Power Association, International Students Association, Africana Journal.

ATHLETICS. NCAA. **Intercollegiate:** Baseball M, basketball, cross-country W, football M, soccer, softball W, tennis M, volleyball. **Intramural:** Basketball, bowling, football M, soccer, softball, swimming, table tennis, tennis, volleyball.

STUDENT SERVICES. Aptitude testing, career counseling, employment service for undergraduates, freshman orientation, health services, on-campus day care, personal counseling, placement service for graduates, special adviser for adult students, veterans counselor, services/facilities for handicapped.

ANNUAL EXPENSES. Tuition and fees (1992-93): $2,653, $960 additional for out-of-state students. **Room and board:** $5,000. **Books and supplies:** $427. **Other expenses:** $1,400.

FINANCIAL AID. 58% of freshmen, 38% of continuing students receive some form of aid. 99% of grants, 89% of loans, all jobs based on need. 407 enrolled freshmen were judged to have need, all were offered aid. Academic, music/drama, leadership scholarships available. **Aid applications:** No closing date; priority given to applications received by April 15; applicants notified on a rolling basis beginning on or about May 1; must reply within 2 weeks.

ADDRESS/TELEPHONE. Samuel T. McGhee, Director of Admissions, Jersey City State College, 2039 Kennedy Boulevard, Jersey City, NJ 07305-1597. (201) 200-3234. (800) 441-JCSC. Fax: (201) 200-2044.

Katharine Gibbs School
Montclair, New Jersey — CB code: 4914

2-year proprietary business, junior college, coed. **Undergraduate enrollment:** 600 men and women. **Location:** Suburban campus in large town. **Calendar:** Quarter. **Microcomputers:** Located in libraries, computer centers.

DEGREES OFFERED. AAS. 45 associate degrees awarded in 1992.

UNDERGRADUATE MAJORS. Secretarial and related programs.

ACADEMIC PROGRAMS. Study abroad, weekend college.

FRESHMAN ADMISSIONS. Selection criteria: Interview, high school transcript, institutional test most important. SAT scores considered.

1992 FRESHMAN CLASS PROFILE. 100 men and women enrolled. **Characteristics:** 100% commute, 27% have minority backgrounds, 1% are foreign students. Average age is 20.

FALL-TERM APPLICATIONS. $25 fee. No closing date; applicants notified on a rolling basis; must reply by registration.

STUDENT LIFE. Activities: Student government, yearbook.

STUDENT SERVICES. Aptitude testing, career counseling, employment service for undergraduates, freshman orientation, health services, personal counseling, placement service for graduates, special adviser for adult students.

ANNUAL EXPENSES. Tuition and fees: $7,545. **Books and supplies:** $500.

FINANCIAL AID. 75% of continuing students receive some form of aid. 94% of grants, 68% of loans, all jobs based on need. **Aid applications:** No closing date; applicants notified on a rolling basis.

ADDRESS/TELEPHONE. John F. Walsh, Admissions Director, Katharine Gibbs School, 33 Plymouth Street, Montclair, NJ 07042. (201) 744-6967. Fax: (201) 744-2298.

Kean College of New Jersey
Union, New Jersey — CB code: 2517

Admissions:	69% of applicants accepted
Based on:	••• School record, test scores
	•• Recommendations, special talents
	• Activities, essay, interview
Completion:	88% of freshmen end year in good standing
	47% graduate

4-year public college of arts and sciences, coed. Founded in 1855. **Accreditation:** Regional. **Undergraduate enrollment:** 2,793 men, 4,011 women full time; 1,304 men, 2,629 women part time. **Graduate enrollment:** 65 men, 181 women full time; 327 men, 1,191 women part time. **Faculty:** 799 total (329 full time), 279 with doctorates or other terminal degrees. **Location:** Suburban campus in small city; 18 miles from New York City. **Calendar:** 4-1-4, limited summer session. Saturday and extensive evening/early morning classes. **Microcomputers:** 528 located in libraries, classrooms, computer centers. **Special facilities:** Planetarium, art gallery.

DEGREES OFFERED. BA, BS, BFA, MA, MS, MFA. 1,468 bachelor's degrees awarded in 1992. 38% in business and management, 13% teacher education, 5% parks/recreation, protective services, public affairs, 5% psychology, 8% social sciences. Graduate degrees offered in 29 major fields of study.

UNDERGRADUATE MAJORS. Accounting, applied mathematics, art education, art history, atmospheric sciences and meteorology, bilingual/bicultural education, biology, business and management, chemistry, clinical laboratory science, communications, computer and information sciences, construction, crafts, data processing, drafting and design technology, dramatic arts, early childhood education, earth sciences, economics, education of the deaf and hearing impaired, education of the emotionally handicapped, education of the mentally handicapped, education of the physically handicapped, electronic technology, elementary education, English, English education, English literature, environmental science, foreign languages education, French, geology, graphic arts technology, health education, history, industrial arts education, industrial technology, interior design, manufacturing technology, mathematics, mathematics education, mechanical design technology, medical records administration, music, music education, nursing, occupational therapy, parks and recreation management, philosophy, physical education, physical therapy, physics, political science and government, psychology, public administration, science education, secondary education, social studies education, social work, sociology, Spanish, special education, speech, speech correction, studio art, teaching English as a second language/foreign language, trade and industrial education, visual and performing arts.

ACADEMIC PROGRAMS. Cooperative education, double major, honors program, independent study, internships, study abroad, teacher preparation, Washington semester, cross-registration, 2-year bachelor's degree program for RNs, foreign transfer program with various foreign universities. **Remedial services:** Learning center, preadmission summer program, reduced course load, remedial instruction, tutoring, Learning-to-Learn Program. **ROTC:** Air Force, Army. **Placement/credit:** AP, CLEP General and Subject, institutional tests; 46 credit hours maximum for bachelor's degree.

ACADEMIC REQUIREMENTS. Freshmen must earn minimum GPA of 2.0 to continue in good standing. 79% of freshmen return for sophomore year. Students must declare major by end of second year. **Graduation requirements:** 124 hours for bachelor's (40 in major). Most students required to take courses in arts/fine arts, computer science, English, humanities, mathematics, biological/physical sciences, social sciences. **Additional information:** Cross-registration with New Jersey Institute of Technology.

FRESHMAN ADMISSIONS. Selection criteria: High school class rank at or above 50th percentile, test scores, counselor recommendations important. Consideration given to military service, work, and personal life experiences. **High school preparation:** 16 units required. Required units include English 4, foreign language 2, mathematics 3, social science 2 and science 2. **Test requirements:** SAT or ACT (SAT preferred); score report by July 15. Prueba de Aptitud Academica for Spanish speaking applicants.

1992 FRESHMAN CLASS PROFILE. 3,344 men and women applied, 2,320 accepted; 526 men enrolled, 696 women enrolled. 28% had high school GPA of 3.0 or higher, 62% between 2.0 and 2.99. **Characteristics:** 96% from in state, 79% commute, 41% have minority backgrounds, 3% are foreign students. Average age is 18.

FALL-TERM APPLICATIONS. $20 fee, may be waived for applicants with need. Closing date June 30; applicants notified on a rolling basis beginning on or about November 1; must reply by May 1 or within 2 weeks if notified thereafter. Interview recommended for elementary education, fine arts, social work, special education, speech and hearing applicants. Audition recommended for music applicants. Portfolio recommended for art applicants. Essay recommended. CRDA.

STUDENT LIFE. Housing: Dormitories (men, women, coed); apartment housing available. Small off-campus housing program jointly administered by college and private owner. **Activities:** Student government, film, radio, student newspaper, yearbook, literary magazine, choral groups, concert band, dance, drama, jazz band, music ensembles, musical theater, fraternities, sororities, several honor societies, social service and special interest organizations.

ATHLETICS. NCAA. **Intercollegiate:** Baseball M, basketball, field hockey W, football M, ice hockey M, lacrosse M, soccer, softball W, swimming W, tennis, volleyball W, wrestling M. **Intramural:** Basketball, ice hockey M, racquetball W, skiing, softball, swimming, tennis, volleyball.

STUDENT SERVICES. Aptitude testing, career counseling, employment service for undergraduates, freshman orientation, health services, on-campus day care, personal counseling, placement service for graduates, special adviser for adult students, veterans counselor, services/facilities for handicapped.

ANNUAL EXPENSES. Tuition and fees (1992-93): $2,613, $780 additional for out-of-state students. **Room and board:** $3,690. **Books and supplies:** $500. **Other expenses:** $800.

FINANCIAL AID. 55% of freshmen, 45% of continuing students receive some form of aid. 97% of grants, 66% of loans, 27% of jobs based on need. 627 enrolled freshmen were judged to have need, all were offered aid. Academic scholarships available. **Aid applications:** No closing date; priority given to applications received by April 1; applicants notified on a rolling basis beginning on or about May 1; must reply by May 1 or within 2 weeks if notified thereafter.

ADDRESS/TELEPHONE. Audley Bridges, Director of Admissions, Kean College of New Jersey, PO Box 411, 1000 Morris Avenue, Union, NJ 07083-7131. (908) 527-2195. Fax: (908) 527-2243.

Mercer County Community College
Trenton, New Jersey CB code: 2444

2-year public community college, coed. Founded in 1966. **Accreditation:** Regional. **Undergraduate enrollment:** 1,488 men, 1,358 women full time; 1,814 men, 2,763 women part time. **Faculty:** 356 total (121 full time), 47 with doctorates or other terminal degrees. **Location:** Suburban campus in small city; 8 miles from Trenton, 35 miles from Philadelphia, 60 miles from New York City. **Calendar:** Semester, extensive summer session. Saturday and extensive evening/early morning classes. **Microcomputers:** 350 located in libraries, classrooms. **Special facilities:** Art gallery, CAD laboratory, computer graphics laboratory. **Additional facts:** Courses also available at downtown Trenton location. External degree program for military service members.

DEGREES OFFERED. AA, AS, AAS. 807 associate degrees awarded in 1992. 26% in business and management, 5% engineering technologies, 18% health sciences, 21% multi/interdisciplinary studies, 9% parks/recreation, protective services, public affairs, 5% trade and industry, 6% visual and performing arts.

UNDERGRADUATE MAJORS. Accounting, air conditioning/heating/refrigeration technology, airline piloting and navigation, architectural technologies, architecture, automotive technology, aviation customer relations, aviation management, biological laboratory technology, biology, business administration and management, business and office, ceramics, chemistry, civil technology, communications, community services, computer and information sciences, computer graphics, computer integrated manufacturing, dance, data processing, drafting and design technology, dramatic arts, electrical technology, electrical/electronics/communications engineering, electronic technology, engineering science, finance, fine arts, fire control and safety technology, funeral services/mortuary science, graphic design, hotel/motel and restaurant management, humanities and social sciences, law enforcement and corrections, legal assistant/paralegal, liberal/general studies, mathematics, mechanical engineering, medical laboratory technologies, music, nursing, office supervision and management, ornamental horticulture, photography, physics, plant sciences, radio/television technology, radiograph medical technology, sculpture, special education, teacher aide.

ACADEMIC PROGRAMS. 2-year transfer program, cooperative education, double major, dual enrollment of high school students, external degree, independent study, internships, study abroad, telecourses, cross-registration. **Remedial services:** Learning center, remedial instruction, special counselor, tutoring. **ROTC:** Air Force, Army. **Placement/credit:** CLEP General and Subject, institutional tests; 45 credit hours maximum for associate degree.

ACADEMIC REQUIREMENTS. Freshmen must earn minimum GPA of 1.4 to continue in good standing. 63% of freshmen return for sophomore year. **Graduation requirements:** 63 hours for associate. Most students required to take courses in English, humanities, mathematics, biological/physical sciences, social sciences. **Additional information:** Cross-registration with area hospitals for nursing.

FRESHMAN ADMISSIONS. Selection criteria: Open admissions. Selective admission to certain programs. **Test requirements:** New Jersey Basic Skills Placement Test required. **Additional information:** Applicants without high school diploma or GED must be 18 or older and have completed the New Jersey Basic Skills Placement Examination.

1992 FRESHMAN CLASS PROFILE. 730 men, 717 women enrolled. **Characteristics:** 97% from in state, 100% commute, 26% have minority backgrounds, 2% are foreign students. Average age is 19.

FALL-TERM APPLICATIONS. $15 fee, may be waived for applicants with need. No closing date; applicants notified on a rolling basis; must reply by registration. Early admission available.

STUDENT LIFE. Activities: Student government, film, magazine, radio, student newspaper, television, choral groups, concert band, dance, drama, jazz band, music ensembles, musical theater, Christian Fellowship, Bilingual Club, African-American Student Organization, EOF Club, Hispanic organization, international student organization, Fuerza Latina, Caribbean Club, Ecology Club, Inter/ACT (multi-cultural club).

ATHLETICS. NJCAA. **Intercollegiate:** Baseball M, basketball, soccer, softball W, tennis, track and field. **Intramural:** Basketball, softball, volleyball.

STUDENT SERVICES. Aptitude testing, career counseling, employment service for undergraduates, freshman orientation, health services, on-campus day care, personal counseling, placement service for graduates, special adviser for adult students, veterans counselor, counselor for handicapped, services/facilities for handicapped.

ANNUAL EXPENSES. Tuition and fees (1992-93): $1,590, $1,500 additional for out-of-district students, $3,450 additional for out-of-state students. **Books and supplies:** $700. **Other expenses:** $941.

FINANCIAL AID. 96% of grants, all loans, 88% of jobs based on need. Academic, music/drama, athletic, state/district residency, leadership, minority scholarships available. **Aid applications:** No closing date; priority given to applications received by May 1; applicants notified on a rolling basis beginning on or about June 1.

ADDRESS/TELEPHONE. Michael Glass, Director of Admissions, Mercer County Community College, 1200 Old Trenton Road, Trenton, NJ 08690-1099. (609) 586-0505. Fax: (609) 586-6944.

Middlesex County College
Edison, New Jersey CB code: 2441

2-year public community college, coed. Founded in 1964. **Accreditation:** Regional. **Undergraduate enrollment:** 2,543 men, 2,502 women full time; 3,102 men, 4,282 women part time. **Location:** Suburban campus in small city; 5 miles from New Brunswick. **Calendar:** Semester.

FRESHMAN ADMISSIONS. Selection criteria: Open admissions. Selective admissions to dental hygiene, nursing automotive technology, and radiography.

ANNUAL EXPENSES. Tuition and fees (1992-93): $1,556, $1,272 additional for out-of-district students, $1,272 additional for out-of-state students. **Books and supplies:** $655. **Other expenses:** $1,319.

ADDRESS/TELEPHONE. Diane Lemko, Director of Admissions and Recruitment, Middlesex County College, PO Box 3050, 155 Mill Road, Edison, NJ 08818-3050. (908) 548-6000. Fax: (908) 494-8244.

Monmouth College
West Long Branch, New Jersey CB code: 2416

Admissions: 81% of applicants accepted
Based on: ••• School record
•• Activities, interview, recommendations, test scores
• Essay, special talents
Completion: 87% of freshmen end year in good standing
45% graduate, 25% of these enter graduate study

4-year private comprehensive college, coed. Founded in 1933. **Accreditation:** Regional. **Undergraduate enrollment:** 830 men, 965 women full time; 336 men, 626 women part time. **Graduate enrollment:** 80 men, 105 women full time; 684 men, 575 women part time. **Faculty:** 321 total (155 full time), 131 with doctorates or other terminal degrees. **Location:** Suburban campus in small town; 50 miles from New York City, 75 miles from Philadelphia. **Calendar:** Semester, extensive summer session. Saturday and extensive evening/early morning classes. **Microcomputers:** 150 located in dormitories, libraries, classrooms, computer centers. **Special facilities:** Art gallery, theater.

DEGREES OFFERED. AA, BA, BS, MA, MS, MBA, MEd. 7 associate degrees awarded in 1992. 100% in multi/interdisciplinary studies. 546 bachelor's degrees awarded. 40% in business and management, 11% communications, 6% computer sciences, 6% teacher education, 5% parks/recreation, protective services, public affairs, 7% psychology, 6% social sciences. Graduate degrees offered in 15 major fields of study.

UNDERGRADUATE MAJORS. Associate: Liberal/general studies. **Bachelor's:** Anthropology, art education, biological and physical sciences, biology, business administration and management, business and management, chemistry, clinical laboratory science, communications, computer and information sciences, criminal justice studies, cytotechnology, early childhood education, ecology, electrical/electronics/communications engineering, elementary education, English, English education, environmental science, fine arts, foreign languages (multiple emphasis), foreign languages education, history, liberal/general studies, mathematics, mathematics education, medical laboratory technologies, music, music education, nursing, philosophy, physics, political science and government, predentistry, prelaw, premedicine, preveterinary, psychology, science education, secondary education, social work, sociology, special education, speech/communication/theater education.

ACADEMIC PROGRAMS. Cooperative education, double major, dual enrollment of high school students, honors program, independent study, internships, student-designed major, study abroad, teacher preparation, weekend college, Washington semester, upper-division program for BS in nursing; combined bachelor's/graduate program in business administration. **Remedial services:** Learning center, preadmission summer program, reduced course load, remedial instruction, special counselor, tutoring. **Placement/credit:** AP, CLEP General and Subject, IB, institutional tests; 30 credit hours maximum for bachelor's degree. AP credit awarded only for institutional course equivalents.

ACADEMIC REQUIREMENTS. Freshmen must earn minimum GPA of 2.0 to continue in good standing. 70% of freshmen return for sophomore year. Students must declare major by end of second year. **Graduation requirements:** 63 hours for associate, 128 hours for bachelor's (30 in major). Most students required to take courses in computer science, English, history, humanities, mathematics, biological/physical sciences, social sciences.

FRESHMAN ADMISSIONS. Selection criteria: School achievement record most important. Class rank, test scores, interview, activities, and personal statement considered. **High school preparation:** 12 units required; 16 recommended. Required and recommended units include English 4 and mathematics 2-3. Foreign language 2, social science 4 and science 3 recommended. **Test requirements:** SAT or ACT (SAT preferred); score report by August 1.

1992 FRESHMAN CLASS PROFILE. 994 men applied, 758 accepted, 220 enrolled; 1,227 women applied, 1,039 accepted, 319 enrolled. 15% had high school GPA of 3.0 or higher, 67% between 2.0 and 2.99. **Academic background:** Mid 50% of enrolled freshmen had SAT-V between 450-650, SAT-M between 480-650. 98% submitted SAT scores. **Characteristics:** 89% from in state, 78% live in college housing, 14% have minority backgrounds, 6% are foreign students. Average age is 18.

FALL-TERM APPLICATIONS. $30 fee, may be waived for applicants with need. Closing date March 1; applicants notified on or about March 1; must reply by May 1. Interview recommended. Audition recommended for music applicants. Portfolio recommended for art applicants. Essay recommended. CRDA. Deferred and early admission available.

STUDENT LIFE. Housing: Dormitories (men, women, coed); apartment housing available. Garden apartments available primarily for graduate students. Quiet sections, honors, International House, Wellness House offered to all, dependent on space available. **Activities:** Student government, magazine, radio, student newspaper, television, yearbook, choral groups, concert band, dance, drama, jazz band, music ensembles, musical theater, fraternities, sororities, Hillel, Christian Fellowship, African-American Student Union, Young Democrats, Young Republicans, Veterans Club, Alpha Phi Alpha, Latin American Club, International Club, Omicron Delta Kappa. **Additional information:** Departmental honor societies.

ATHLETICS. NCAA. **Intercollegiate:** Baseball M, basketball, cross-country, golf M, soccer, softball W, tennis, track and field. **Intramural:** Badminton W, basketball, softball, volleyball.

STUDENT SERVICES. Aptitude testing, career counseling, employment service for undergraduates, freshman orientation, health services, personal counseling, placement service for graduates, special adviser for adult students, veterans counselor, day care services available near campus, services/facilities for handicapped.

ANNUAL EXPENSES. Tuition and fees: $11,820. **Room and board:** $5,160. **Books and supplies:** $520. **Other expenses:** $1,330.

FINANCIAL AID. 68% of freshmen, 59% of continuing students receive some form of aid. 76% of grants, 93% of loans, 24% of jobs based on need. 271 enrolled freshmen were judged to have need, all were offered aid. Academic, athletic, leadership, alumni affiliation scholarships available. **Aid applications:** No closing date; priority given to applications received by March 1; applicants notified on a rolling basis beginning on or about March 15; must reply by May 1 or within 4 weeks if notified thereafter. **Additional information:** 15 full-tuition scholarships available each year; half-tuition scholarships available for students that meet specific requirements.

ADDRESS/TELEPHONE. Barry Ward, Director of Undergraduate Admissions, Monmouth College, Cedar Avenue, West Long Branch, NJ 07764-1898. (908) 571-3456. (800) 543-9671. Fax: (908) 571-3629.

Montclair State College
Upper Montclair, New Jersey CB code: 2520

Admissions: 40% of applicants accepted
Based on: ••• School record
•• Activities, special talents, test scores
• Essay, recommendations
Completion: 44% graduate

4-year public multi-purpose institution offering liberal arts and professional programs, coed. Founded in 1908. **Accreditation:** Regional. **Undergraduate enrollment:** 2,697 men, 3,966 women full time; 1,096 men, 2,306 women part time. **Graduate enrollment:** 147 men, 305 women full time; 593 men, 1,280 women part time. **Faculty:** 808 total (420 full time), 357 with doctorates or other terminal degrees. **Location:** Suburban campus in large town; 14 miles from New York City. **Calendar:** Semester, limited summer session. Saturday and extensive evening/early morning classes. **Microcomputers:** 1,500 located in computer centers. **Special facilities:** Art galleries. **Additional facts:** Includes Institute for the Humanities; Institute for the Advancement of Philosophy for Children; Institute for Critical Thinking; New Jersey School of Conservation in Stokes State Forest, Branchville; and Center for Continuing Education.

DEGREES OFFERED. BA, BS, BFA, MA, MS, MBA, MEd. 1,460 bachelor's degrees awarded in 1992. 28% in business and management, 7% teacher education, 6% home economics, 10% letters/literature, 12% psychology, 12% social sciences, 11% visual and performing arts. Graduate degrees offered in 29 major fields of study.

UNDERGRADUATE MAJORS. Allied health, anthropology, biochemistry, biology, business administration and management, business education, chemistry, classics, computer and information sciences, dance, dramatic arts, economics, English, fine arts, French, geography, geology, German, health education, history, home economics, humanities and social sciences, industrial arts education, Italian, Latin, linguistics, mathematics, molecular biology, music, music performance, music therapy, parks and recreation management, philosophy, physical education, physics, political science and government, psychology, religion, sociology, Spanish, studio art.

ACADEMIC PROGRAMS. Accelerated program, cooperative education, double major, honors program, independent study, internships, study abroad, teacher preparation, visiting/exchange student program, weekend college, Washington semester. **Remedial services:** Learning center, preadmission summer program, reduced course load, remedial instruction, special counselor, tutoring. **ROTC:** Air Force, Army. **Placement/credit:** AP, CLEP General and Subject, institutional tests; 60 credit hours maximum for bachelor's degree.

ACADEMIC REQUIREMENTS. Freshmen must earn minimum GPA of 1.6 to continue in good standing. 80% of freshmen return for sophomore year. Students must declare major by end of second year. **Graduation requirements:** 128 hours for bachelor's (33 in major). Most students required to take courses in arts/fine arts, computer science, English, foreign languages, history, humanities, mathematics, biological/physical sciences, social sciences.

FRESHMAN ADMISSIONS. Selection criteria: School achievement record most important. Extracurricular activities, test scores, community activities also considered. Consideration given to disadvantaged applicants. **High school preparation:** 16 units required. Required units include English 4, foreign language 2, mathematics 3, social science 2 and science 2. Science units must include laboratory. 4 mathematics (including trigonometry) required of computer science majors. Algebra II required for business administration majors. **Test requirements:** SAT; score report by January 15.

1992 FRESHMAN CLASS PROFILE. 5,681 men and women applied, 2,268 accepted; 1,120 enrolled. 21% were in top tenth and 61% were in top quarter of graduating class. **Academic background:** Mid 50% of enrolled freshmen had SAT-V between 380-490, SAT-M between 430-550. 98% submitted SAT scores. **Characteristics:** 97% from in state, 52% live in college housing, 34% have minority backgrounds, 2% are foreign students. Average age is 18.

FALL-TERM APPLICATIONS. $30 fee, may be waived for applicants with need. Closing date March 1; applicants notified on a rolling basis; must reply by May 1. Interview required for art, music, music therapy, speech, theater, dance applicants. Audition required for music, speech, theater, dance applicants. Portfolio required for art applicants. Essay recommended. CRDA. Deferred admission available. Immediate-decision process available to seniors at some local high schools.

STUDENT LIFE. Housing: Dormitories (men, women, coed); apartment housing available. International students may request assignment to the international cluster apartments. **Activities:** Student government, magazine, radio, student newspaper, yearbook, choral groups, concert band, dance, drama, jazz band, marching band, music ensembles, musical theater, symphony orchestra, fraternities, sororities, Newman Community Club; African-American, Latin American, Jewish, and Arab student organizations; Council for National and International Affairs; Conservation Club; Players; College Life Union Board; and Student Intramural and Leisure Council.

ATHLETICS. NCAA. **Intercollegiate:** Baseball M, basketball, cross-country, diving, field hockey W, football M, golf M, lacrosse M, soccer, softball W, swimming, tennis, track and field, volleyball W, wrestling M. **Intramural:** Baseball M, basketball, bowling, ice hockey M, skiing, soccer, softball, tennis, volleyball.

STUDENT SERVICES. Career counseling, employment service for undergraduates, freshman orientation, health services, on-campus day care, personal counseling, placement service for graduates, special adviser for adult students, veterans counselor, services/facilities for handicapped.

ANNUAL EXPENSES. Tuition and fees (1992-93): $2,550, $1,050 additional for out-of-state students. **Room and board:** $4,542. **Books and supplies:** $600. **Other expenses:** $700.

FINANCIAL AID. 50% of freshmen, 50% of continuing students receive some form of aid. 91% of grants, 85% of loans, 64% of jobs based on need. **Aid applications:** Closing date March 1; applicants notified on or about June 1; must reply within 2 weeks.

ADDRESS/TELEPHONE. Dr. Alan L. Buechler, Director of Admissions, Montclair State College, Normal Avenue and Valley Road, Upper Montclair, NJ 07043-1624. (201) 893-4444. (800) 331-9205. Fax: (201) 893-5455.

New Jersey Institute of Technology
Newark, New Jersey — CB code: 2513

Admissions: 67% of applicants accepted
Based on:
••• School record
•• Test scores
• Activities, recommendations, special talents
Completion: 75% of freshmen end year in good standing
70% graduate, 10% of these enter graduate study

4-year public university and technical college, coed. Founded in 1881. **Accreditation:** Regional. **Undergraduate enrollment:** 2,865 men, 527 women full time; 1,431 men, 240 women part time. **Graduate enrollment:** 593 men, 185 women full time; 1,429 men, 427 women part time. **Faculty:** 459 total (327 full time), 416 with doctorates or other terminal degrees. **Location:** Urban campus in large city; 10 miles from New York City. **Calendar:** Semester, limited summer session. Saturday and extensive evening/early morning classes. **Microcomputers:** 400 located in dormitories, libraries, computer centers.

DEGREES OFFERED. BA, BS, BArch, MS, PhD. 605 bachelor's degrees awarded in 1992. 12% in architecture and environmental design, 7% business and management, 8% computer sciences, 51% engineering, 19% engineering technologies. Graduate degrees offered in 15 major fields of study.

UNDERGRADUATE MAJORS. Actuarial sciences, applied chemistry, applied mathematics, applied physics, architecture, business administration and management, chemical engineering, civil engineering, civil technology, computer and information sciences, computer engineering, computer technology, electrical technology, electrical/electronics/communications engineering, engineering and other disciplines, engineering science, industrial engineering, information sciences and systems, manufacturing engineering, manufacturing technology, materials engineering, mechanical design technology, mechanical engineering, statistics.

ACADEMIC PROGRAMS. Accelerated program, computer delivered (on-line) credit-bearing course offerings, cooperative education, double major, honors program, independent study, internships, student-designed major, telecourses, weekend college, cross-registration; liberal arts/career combination in engineering. **Remedial services:** Learning center, preadmission summer program, reduced course load, remedial instruction, special counselor, tutoring, Educational Opportunity Program for economically and educationally disadvantaged students. **ROTC:** Air Force. **Placement/credit:** AP, CLEP Subject, institutional tests.

ACADEMIC REQUIREMENTS. Freshmen must earn minimum GPA of 2.0 to continue in good standing. 80% of freshmen return for sophomore year. Students must declare major on enrollment. **Graduation requirements:** 124 hours for bachelor's (50 in major). Most students required to take courses in computer science, English, history, humanities, mathematics, biological/physical sciences, social sciences. **Additional information:** Computing-intensive campus, leader in integrating computer education into curricula.

FRESHMAN ADMISSIONS. Selection criteria: Class rank, SAT and ACH scores, and high school grades in mathematics and science (especially for engineering, engineering science, and computer science applicants) most important. **High school preparation:** 16 units required. Required and recommended units include English 4, mathematics 4 and science 2. Biological science 1, foreign language 2 and physical science 2 recommended. 3 mathematics required of management, science technology and society majors. Science units should be laboratory. One laboratory science required for management majors. **Test requirements:** SAT or ACT (SAT preferred); score report by May 1. Mathematics Level I or II ACH required. Score report by June 15.

1992 FRESHMAN CLASS PROFILE. 1,235 men applied, 830 accepted, 439 enrolled; 271 women applied, 177 accepted, 79 enrolled. 80% had high school GPA of 3.0 or higher, 20% between 2.0 and 2.99. 23% were in top tenth and 57% were in top quarter of graduating class. **Academic background:** Mid 50% of enrolled freshmen had SAT-V between 430-530, SAT-M between 530-680. 100% submitted SAT scores. **Characteristics:** 90% from in state, 70% commute, 46% have minority backgrounds, 4% are foreign students, 15% join fraternities/sororities. Average age is 18.

FALL-TERM APPLICATIONS. $25 fee, may be waived for applicants with need. No closing date; priority given to applications received by April 1; applicants notified on a rolling basis; must reply by May 1 or within 2 weeks if notified thereafter. Portfolio required for architecture applicants. CRDA. Early admission available. Institutional early decision plan.

STUDENT LIFE. Housing: Dormitories (coed); fraternity housing available. **Activities:** Student government, radio, student newspaper, yearbook, drama, musical theater, fraternities, sororities, broad range of professional, cultural, social, and service organizations. **Additional information:** Entering freshmen given microcomputer for personal use. Available for purchase for nominal fee upon graduation.

ATHLETICS. NCAA. **Intercollegiate:** Baseball M, basketball, bowling, cross-country, fencing, golf, skiing, soccer M, softball W, tennis, volleyball. **Intramural:** Archery, badminton, baseball, basketball, bowling, cross-country, fencing, golf, skiing, soccer M, softball, swimming, tennis, track and field, volleyball, wrestling M.

STUDENT SERVICES. Aptitude testing, career counseling, employment service for undergraduates, freshman orientation, health services, on-campus day care, personal counseling, placement service for graduates, veterans counselor, services/facilities for handicapped.

ANNUAL EXPENSES. Tuition and fees (projected): $4,714, $4,323 additional for out-of-state students. **Room and board:** $5,119. **Books and supplies:** $700. **Other expenses:** $750.

FINANCIAL AID. 71% of freshmen, 60% of continuing students receive some form of aid. 89% of grants, 97% of loans, all jobs based on need. 298 enrolled freshmen were judged to have need, 278 were offered aid. Academic scholarships available. **Aid applications:** No closing date; priority given to applications received by March 15; applicants notified on a rolling basis beginning on or about March 1; must reply by May 1 or within 2 weeks if notified thereafter.

ADDRESS/TELEPHONE. Mr. William Anderson, Asst VP Enrollment Planning, New Jersey Institute of Technology, University Heights, Newark, NJ 07102-9938. (201) 596-3300. Fax: (201) 802-1854.

Ocean County College
Toms River, New Jersey — CB code: 2630

2-year public community college, coed. Founded in 1964. **Accreditation:** Regional. **Undergraduate enrollment:** 1,759 men, 1,945 women full time; 1,622 men, 3,027 women part time. **Faculty:** 409 total (127 full time), 90 with doctorates or other terminal degrees. **Location:** Suburban campus in small city; 60 miles from Philadelphia, 80 miles from New York City. **Calendar:** Semester, extensive summer session. Saturday and extensive evening/early morning classes. **Microcomputers:** 200 located in libraries, computer centers. **Special facilities:** Planetarium, arboretum, fine arts theater. **Additional facts:** Off-campus sites at 13 locations in Ocean County.

DEGREES OFFERED. AA, AS, AAS. 1,045 associate degrees awarded in 1992. 17% in business and management, 13% health sciences, 55% multi/interdisciplinary studies, 6% parks/recreation, protective services, public affairs.

UNDERGRADUATE MAJORS. Accounting, biological and physical

sciences, business administration and management, business and management, chemistry, civil engineering, clinical laboratory science, computer and information sciences, computer engineering, computer programming, computer technology, construction, criminal justice studies, electrical/electronics/communications engineering, electronic technology, elementary education, engineering, English, finance, fine arts, fire control and safety technology, gerontology, graphic arts technology, history, journalism, legal assistant/paralegal, liberal/general studies, manufacturing technology, marketing and distribution, mathematics, modern language, music education, nursing, photographic technology, physical sciences, physics, political science and government, psychology, real estate, secretarial and related programs, social studies education, social work, sociology, speech, survey and mapping technology.

ACADEMIC PROGRAMS. 2-year transfer program, dual enrollment of high school students, honors program, independent study, study abroad, telecourses. **Remedial services:** Learning center, reduced course load, remedial instruction, special counselor, tutoring, basic studies program. **Placement/credit:** AP, CLEP General and Subject, institutional tests; 30 credit hours maximum for associate degree.

ACADEMIC REQUIREMENTS. Freshmen must earn minimum GPA of 2.0 to continue in good standing. 66% of freshmen return for sophomore year. Students must declare major on application. **Graduation requirements:** 64 hours for associate. Most students required to take courses in English, history, humanities, mathematics, biological/physical sciences, social sciences.

FRESHMAN ADMISSIONS. Selection criteria: Open admissions. Selective admissions to nursing and medical laboratory technology programs based on test scores and academic record. Algebra, chemistry, and biology required of nursing applicants. **Test requirements:** SAT or ACT required of nursing and honors program applicants. Score report by May 30.

1992 FRESHMAN CLASS PROFILE. 927 men, 1,138 women enrolled. **Characteristics:** 99% from in state, 100% commute, 8% have minority backgrounds. Average age is 20.

FALL-TERM APPLICATIONS. $15 fee, may be waived for applicants with need. No closing date; applicants notified on a rolling basis beginning on or about November 1; must reply within 2 weeks. Deferred and early admission available.

STUDENT LIFE. Activities: Student government, magazine, radio, student newspaper, yearbook, choral groups, concert band, dance, drama, musical theater, Circle-K, special interest clubs, Student Life Program Board, Phi Theta Kappa, Silver Edge club (for adults aged 62 and over), veterans club, Sojourners, student health organization, disabled students service club.

ATHLETICS. NJCAA. **Intercollegiate:** Baseball M, basketball, cross-country, diving, field hockey W, golf, ice hockey M, soccer M, softball W, swimming, tennis, volleyball W. **Intramural:** Basketball, bowling, cross-country, swimming, track and field, volleyball. **Clubs:** Several sports clubs.

STUDENT SERVICES. Aptitude testing, career counseling, employment service for undergraduates, freshman orientation, health services, personal counseling, placement service for graduates, veterans counselor, services/facilities for handicapped.

ANNUAL EXPENSES. Tuition and fees (1992-93): $1,622, $130 additional for out-of-district students, $1,410 additional for out-of-state students. **Books and supplies:** $500. **Other expenses:** $900.

FINANCIAL AID. All grants, 90% of loans, all jobs based on need. Academic scholarships available. **Aid applications:** No closing date; priority given to applications received by May 31; applicants notified on a rolling basis beginning on or about July 15; must reply within 1 week.

ADDRESS/TELEPHONE. Carey Trevisan, Director of Admissions and Records, Ocean County College, College Drive, CN 2001, Toms River, NJ 08753-2001. (908) 255-0304. Fax: (908) 255-0444.

Passaic County Community College
Paterson, New Jersey — CB code: 2694

2-year public community college, coed. Founded in 1968. **Accreditation:** Regional. **Undergraduate enrollment:** 435 men, 592 women full time; 1,127 men, 1,622 women part time. **Faculty:** 208 total (61 full time), 8 with doctorates or other terminal degrees. **Location:** Urban campus in small city; approximately 15 miles from New York City. **Calendar:** Semester, limited summer session. **Microcomputers:** 150 located in computer centers. **Special facilities:** 2 art galleries, playhouse (home of Now Theater Company, professional black theater group), poetry center (open poetry forum receiving material from poets across country). **Additional facts:** 3 extension centers throughout Passaic County.

DEGREES OFFERED. AA, AS, AAS. 114 associate degrees awarded in 1992. 18% in business and management, 15% business/office and marketing/distribution, 10% computer sciences, 31% allied health, 14% multi/interdisciplinary studies, 8% parks/recreation, protective services, public affairs.

UNDERGRADUATE MAJORS. Accounting, Afro-American (black) studies, biological and physical sciences, business administration and management, computer and information sciences, computer integrated manufacturing, criminal justice studies, early childhood education, engineering and other disciplines, finance, fire control and safety technology, humanities, law enforcement and corrections technologies, liberal/general studies, machine tool operation/machine shop, manufacturing technology, marketing and distribution, mathematics, nursing, practical nursing, radiograph medical technology, registered nurse mobility, retailing.

ACADEMIC PROGRAMS. 2-year transfer program, cooperative education, double major, internships, weekend college. **Remedial services:** Learning center, reduced course load, remedial instruction, tutoring, bilingual remedial mathematics, English as a second language. **Placement/credit:** CLEP General and Subject, institutional tests; 12 credit hours maximum for associate degree.

ACADEMIC REQUIREMENTS. Freshmen must earn minimum GPA of 1.6 to continue in good standing. 35% of freshmen return for sophomore year. Students must declare major by end of first year. **Graduation requirements:** 64 hours for associate (30 in major). Most students required to take courses in English, humanities, social sciences. **Additional information:** Articulation agreements ensure transfer to selected 4-year institutions.

FRESHMAN ADMISSIONS. Selection criteria: Open admissions. Selective admissions to some programs such as nursing and other allied health programs. **Test requirements:** New Jersey Basic Skills test required for placement.

1992 FRESHMAN CLASS PROFILE. 457 men, 645 women enrolled. **Characteristics:** 100% from in state, 100% commute, 75% have minority backgrounds, 1% are foreign students. Average age is 27.

FALL-TERM APPLICATIONS. $10 fee. No closing date; applicants notified on a rolling basis; must reply by registration. Interview required for allied health applicants. Deferred and early admission available. Early admissions are available to high school students based on decisions made by high school guidance counselor and the college's director of admissions.

STUDENT LIFE. Activities: Student government, choral groups, Latin American club, Newman club, international club, Organization of African Ancestry, Earth Awareness, Fashion Awareness, chess club, veterans club, PhiTheta Kappa, cheerleading club, photography club, Arabic club, bicycle club, writing club.

ATHLETICS. NJCAA. **Intercollegiate:** Basketball. **Clubs:** Volleyball.

STUDENT SERVICES. Career counseling, employment service for undergraduates, freshman orientation, personal counseling, placement service for graduates, veterans counselor, bilingual counselors, services/facilities for handicapped.

ANNUAL EXPENSES. Tuition and fees (projected): $2,017, $1,708 additional for out-of-state students. **Books and supplies:** $735. **Other expenses:** $945.

FINANCIAL AID. 50% of freshmen, 45% of continuing students receive some form of aid. All grants, 90% of loans, all jobs based on need. Academic, leadership, alumni affiliation scholarships available. **Aid applications:** No closing date; priority given to applications received by August 1; applicants notified on a rolling basis; must reply by registration.

ADDRESS/TELEPHONE. Steven Rose, Dean of Admissions and Enrollment Management, Passaic County Community College, One College Boulevard, Paterson, NJ 07509. (201) 684-6868. Fax: (201) 684-6778.

Princeton University
Princeton, New Jersey — CB code: 2672

4-year private university, coed. Founded in 1746. **Accreditation:** Regional. **Undergraduate enrollment:** 2,549 men, 1,976 women full time. **Graduate enrollment:** 1,259 men, 654 women full time. **Faculty:** 950 total (743 full time), 798 with doctorates or other terminal degrees. **Location:** Suburban campus in large town; 50 miles from New York City, 45 miles from Philadelphia. **Calendar:** Semester. **Microcomputers:** 438 located in dormitories, libraries, classrooms, computer centers. **Special facilities:** Art museum with permanent collection, museum of natural history, center for energy and environmental studies, Lake Carnegie, plasma physics laboratory.

DEGREES OFFERED. BA, BS, MA, PhD. 1,079 bachelor's degrees awarded in 1992. 14% in engineering, 13% letters/literature, 7% parks/recreation, protective services, public affairs, 5% philosophy, religion, theology, 36% social sciences. Graduate degrees offered in 47 major fields of study.

UNDERGRADUATE MAJORS. Aerospace/aeronautical/astronautical engineering, anthropology, archeology, architecture, art history, astrophysics, biology, chemical engineering, chemistry, civil engineering, classics, comparative literature, computer and information sciences, computer engineering, East Asian studies, economics, electrical/electronics/communications engineering, English, foreign languages (multiple emphasis), geology, geophysics and seismology, German, history, international public service, international relations, international studies, mathematics, mechanical engineering, Middle Eastern studies, molecular biology, music, philosophy, physics, political science and government, psychology, public administration, religion, Russian, Russian and Slavic studies, sociology, statistics.

ACADEMIC PROGRAMS. Accelerated program, independent study, internships, student-designed major, study abroad, teacher preparation, cross-registration, field study opportunities. **ROTC:** Air Force, Army. **Placement/credit:** AP, institutional tests.

ACADEMIC REQUIREMENTS. No policy requiring minimum GPA; records of students having academic difficulty are reviewed individually.

Required withdrawals based on patterns of unsatisfactory performance. 98% of freshmen return for sophomore year. Students must declare major by end of second year. **Graduation requirements:** Most students required to take courses in English, foreign languages, humanities, philosophy/religion, biological/physical sciences, social sciences. **Additional information:** Independent project in junior year and senior thesis required for graduation.

FRESHMAN ADMISSIONS. Selection criteria: School achievement record and recommendations of guidance counselor and 2 teachers very important. Test scores and essay also requested of each applicant reviewed. Recommended units include English 4, foreign language 4, mathematics 4 and science 2. 2 history also recommended. One unit physics or chemistry (preferably both) and 4 mathematics required for engineering majors. Diversity of high school programs recognized, quality and breadth of individual study program evaluated. **Test requirements:** SAT or ACT (SAT preferred); score report by March 1. ACH recommended for all applicants. Used for admissions, placement, and counseling. Score report by March 1. **Additional information:** Alumni interview recommended for all candidates.

1992 FRESHMAN CLASS PROFILE. 7,393 men applied, 1,085 accepted, 624 enrolled; 5,464 women applied, 956 accepted, 516 enrolled. 90% were in top tenth and 100% were in top quarter of graduating class. **Academic background:** Mid 50% of enrolled freshmen had SAT-V between 600-700, SAT-M between 660-750. 100% submitted SAT scores. **Characteristics:** 14% from in state, 100% live in college housing, 21% have minority backgrounds, 6% are foreign students. Average age is 18.

FALL-TERM APPLICATIONS. $50 fee, may be waived for applicants with need. Closing date January 2; applicants notified on or about April 3; must reply by May 1. Essay required. Interview recommended. Audition recommended for music applicants. Portfolio recommended for visual arts, creative writing applicants. CRDA. Deferred and early admission available. Early action program available. Application closing date November 1, notification in mid-December. No commitment to matriculate if admitted.

STUDENT LIFE. Housing: Dormitories (men, women, coed); apartment, cooperative housing available. Residential colleges for freshmen and sophomores Kosher dining facilities available. **Activities:** Student government, film, magazine, radio, student newspaper, yearbook, press club, choral groups, concert band, dance, drama, jazz band, marching band, music ensembles, musical theater, opera, pep band, symphony orchestra, Whig-Clio (politics and debate), Student Volunteers Council, Third World Center, Chapel Fellowship, Hillel Foundation, Women's Center, Community House, International Center. **Additional information:** Over 200 student organizations available. Student employment office supervises 39 student agencies.

ATHLETICS. NCAA. **Intercollegiate:** Baseball M, basketball, cross-country, diving, fencing, field hockey W, football M, golf, ice hockey, lacrosse, rowing (crew), rugby, sailing, skiing, soccer, softball W, squash, swimming, table tennis, tennis, track and field, volleyball, water polo, wrestling M. **Intramural:** Basketball, field hockey W, ice hockey, racquetball, rifle, soccer, softball, squash, table tennis, tennis, volleyball.

STUDENT SERVICES. Career counseling, employment service for undergraduates, freshman orientation, health services, personal counseling, placement service for graduates, services/facilities for handicapped.

ANNUAL EXPENSES. Tuition and fees: $18,940. **Room and board:** $5,710. **Books and supplies:** $665. **Other expenses:** $1,500.

FINANCIAL AID. 70% of freshmen, 70% of continuing students receive some form of aid. All grants, 90% of loans, 73% of jobs based on need. 485 enrolled freshmen were judged to have need, all were offered aid. **Aid applications:** Closing date February 1; applicants notified on or about April 3; must reply by May 1.

ADDRESS/TELEPHONE. Fred Hargadon, Dean of Admissions, Princeton University, Box 430, Princeton, NJ 08544-0430. (609) 258-3060. Fax: (609) 258-6743.

Rabbinical College of America
Morristown, New Jersey — CB code: 1546

4-year private college of Jewish studies, men only, affiliated with Jewish faith. Founded in 1956. **Undergraduate enrollment:** 235 men full time. **Location:** Suburban campus in large town; 1 mile from downtown. **Calendar:** Semester. **Additional facts:** Affiliate of world-wide Lubavitch movement.

FRESHMAN ADMISSIONS. Selection criteria: Applicants must demonstrate interest, ability, and perseverance necessary for successful completion of required courses. Recommendation required, preferably from local rabbi.

ADDRESS/TELEPHONE. Israel Teitelbaum, Registrar, Rabbinical College of America, 226 Sussex Avenue, CN 1996, Morristown, NJ 07960. (201) 267-9404.

Ramapo College of New Jersey
Mahwah, New Jersey — CB code: 2884

Admissions: 44% of applicants accepted
Based on:
••• School record
•• Test scores
• Activities, essay, interview, recommendations, special talents
Completion: 80% of freshmen end year in good standing
7% enter graduate study

4-year public college of arts and sciences, coed. Founded in 1969. **Accreditation:** Regional. **Undergraduate enrollment:** 1,461 men, 1,314 women full time; 801 men, 1,060 women part time. **Faculty:** 238 total (130 full time), 162 with doctorates or other terminal degrees. **Location:** Suburban campus in large town; 35 miles from New York City. **Calendar:** Semester, limited summer session. Saturday classes. **Microcomputers:** 200 located in dormitories, computer centers. **Special facilities:** Art gallery, alternate energy center, International Telecommunications Center.

DEGREES OFFERED. BA, BS. 621 bachelor's degrees awarded in 1992. 47% in business and management, 11% communications, 8% physical sciences, 11% psychology, 11% social sciences.

UNDERGRADUATE MAJORS. Accounting, American literature, American studies, biology, business administration and management, chemistry, communications, computer and information sciences, contemporary arts, economics, English literature, environmental science, environmental studies, fine arts, history, international business management, international studies, law , management information systems, mathematics, metropolitan studies, philosophy, physics/mathematics, political science and government, psychology, social work, sociology.

ACADEMIC PROGRAMS. Accelerated program, cooperative education, double major, dual enrollment of high school students, honors program, independent study, internships, student-designed major, study abroad, teacher preparation, visiting/exchange student program, weekend college. **Remedial services:** Learning center, reduced course load, remedial instruction, special counselor, tutoring, academic counselors for learning disabled. **Placement/credit:** AP, CLEP General and Subject; 75 credit hours maximum for bachelor's degree.

ACADEMIC REQUIREMENTS. Freshmen must earn minimum GPA of 2.0 to continue in good standing. 75% of freshmen return for sophomore year. Students must declare major by end of second year. **Graduation requirements:** 128 hours for bachelor's (30 in major). Most students required to take courses in English, history, humanities, mathematics, biological/physical sciences, social sciences. **Postgraduate studies:** 2% enter law school, 1% enter medical school, 3% enter MBA programs, 1% enter other graduate study.

FRESHMAN ADMISSIONS. Selection criteria: School achievement record, test scores most important. Applicants should rank in top 40% of high school class. **High school preparation:** 16 units required. Required and recommended units include English 4, mathematics 3, social science 2 and science 2. Biological science 1, foreign language 2 and physical science 1 recommended. **Test requirements:** SAT or ACT (SAT preferred); score report by March 15.

1992 FRESHMAN CLASS PROFILE. 1,114 men applied, 501 accepted, 218 enrolled; 1,186 women applied, 506 accepted, 239 enrolled. 65% had high school GPA of 3.0 or higher, 35% between 2.0 and 2.99. 6% were in top tenth and 25% were in top quarter of graduating class. **Academic background:** Mid 50% of enrolled freshmen had SAT-V between 420-500, SAT-M between 440-540. 98% submitted SAT scores. **Characteristics:** 92% from in state, 60% commute, 29% have minority backgrounds, 5% are foreign students. Average age is 18.

FALL-TERM APPLICATIONS. $25 fee, may be waived for applicants with need. Closing date March 15; applicants notified on a rolling basis beginning on or about December 1; must reply by May 1 or within 2 weeks if notified thereafter. Essay required. Interview recommended. CRDA. Deferred and early admission available.

STUDENT LIFE. Housing: Dormitories (coed); apartment, handicapped housing available. Garden apartments and traditional suite-style facilities available. **Activities:** Student government, film, radio, student newspaper, yearbook, choral groups, drama, jazz band, music ensembles, musical theater, fraternities, sororities, Organization for African Unity, Organization of Latin Unity, emergency squad, Hear and Now Drop-In Center, Ramapo Political Forum, women's center, veterans' association, international students organization, Returning Adult Students Organization, Commuters at Ramapo (CAR).

ATHLETICS. NCAA. **Intercollegiate:** Baseball M, basketball, cross-country, golf M, soccer, softball W, tennis, track and field, volleyball. **Intramural:** Basketball, cross-country, football M, soccer, softball, swimming, tennis, volleyball, water polo M.

STUDENT SERVICES. Career counseling, employment service for undergraduates, freshman orientation, health services, on-campus day care, personal counseling, placement service for graduates, special adviser for adult students, veterans counselor, services/facilities for handicapped.

ANNUAL EXPENSES. Tuition and fees (1992-93): $3,024, $1,887

additional for out-of-state students. **Room and board:** $4,626. **Books and supplies:** $600. **Other expenses:** $855.

FINANCIAL AID. 45% of freshmen, 43% of continuing students receive some form of aid. 89% of grants, 96% of loans, 62% of jobs based on need. Academic, state/district residency, leadership scholarships available. **Aid applications:** Closing date May 1; priority given to applications received by March 15; applicants notified on or about June 15; must reply within 3 weeks.

ADDRESS/TELEPHONE. Nancy E. Jaeger, Director of Admissions, Ramapo College of New Jersey, 505 Ramapo Valley Road, Mahwah, NJ 07430-1680. (201) 529-7600. Fax: (201) 529-7508.

Raritan Valley Community College
Somerville, New Jersey CB code: 2867

2-year public community college, coed. Founded in 1966. **Accreditation:** Regional. **Undergraduate enrollment:** 891 men, 921 women full time; 1,502 men, 2,568 women part time. **Faculty:** 290 total (90 full time), 25 with doctorates or other terminal degrees. **Location:** Rural campus in large town; 36 miles from New York City. **Calendar:** Semester, extensive summer session. Saturday and extensive evening/early morning classes. **Microcomputers:** 100 located in libraries, classrooms, computer centers. **Special facilities:** Planetarium, professional theater.

DEGREES OFFERED. AA, AS, AAS. 495 associate degrees awarded in 1992. 29% in business and management, 12% business/office and marketing/distribution, 5% computer sciences, 5% engineering technologies, 14% health sciences, 5% life sciences, 10% multi/interdisciplinary studies, 6% social sciences.

UNDERGRADUATE MAJORS. Accounting, air conditioning/heating/refrigeration mechanics, air conditioning/heating/refrigeration technology, automotive mechanics, automotive technology, biology, business administration and management, business and management, business computer/console/peripheral equipment operation, business data entry equipment operation, business data processing and related programs, business data programming, chemistry, child development/care/guidance, commercial art, communications, computer and information sciences, computer graphics, computer programming, construction, criminal justice studies, data processing, diesel engine mechanics, drafting, drafting and design technology, dramatic arts, early childhood education, electromechanical technology, electronic technology, engineering, engineering and engineering-related technologies, environmental science, finance, fine arts, hotel/motel and restaurant management, humanities and social sciences, information sciences and systems, law enforcement and corrections, liberal/general studies, management information systems, marketing and distribution, marketing management, mathematics, mechanical design technology, music, nursing, office supervision and management, ophthalmic services, real estate, retailing, robotics, science technologies, science/mathematics, secretarial and related programs, social sciences, studio art, teacher aide, telecommunications, word processing.

ACADEMIC PROGRAMS. 2-year transfer program, cooperative education, double major, dual enrollment of high school students, telecourses. **Remedial services:** Learning center, preadmission summer program, remedial instruction, special counselor, tutoring. **ROTC:** Air Force. **Placement/credit:** AP, CLEP General and Subject, institutional tests; 45 credit hours maximum for associate degree.

ACADEMIC REQUIREMENTS. Freshmen must earn minimum GPA of 2.0 to continue in good standing. 56% of freshmen return for sophomore year. Students must declare major on application. **Graduation requirements:** 62 hours for associate (32 in major). Most students required to take courses in English, humanities, mathematics, biological/physical sciences, social sciences.

FRESHMAN ADMISSIONS. Selection criteria: Open admissions. **High school preparation:** 16 units recommended. Recommended units include English 4, mathematics 2 and science 2. **Test requirements:** Matriculated students required to take New Jersey Basic Skills Placement Test prior to registration unless exempt.

1992 FRESHMAN CLASS PROFILE. 480 men, 720 women enrolled. **Characteristics:** 100% from in state, 100% commute, 11% have minority backgrounds, 1% are foreign students. Average age is 22.

FALL-TERM APPLICATIONS. $20 fee, may be waived for applicants with need. No closing date; applicants notified on a rolling basis; must reply within 10 days. Interview recommended for nursing applicants.

STUDENT LIFE. Activities: Student government, radio, student newspaper, choral groups, dance, drama, music ensembles, symphony orchestra, Black Student Union, International Club, Students for Environmental Awareness.

ATHLETICS. NJCAA. **Intercollegiate:** Baseball M, basketball, cross-country M, soccer, softball W, tennis, volleyball W. **Intramural:** Archery, basketball M, bowling, football M, racquetball, soccer, softball, tennis, volleyball.

STUDENT SERVICES. Aptitude testing, career counseling, employment service for undergraduates, freshman orientation, health services, on-campus day care, personal counseling, placement service for graduates, special adviser for adult students, veterans counselor, services/facilities for handicapped.

ANNUAL EXPENSES. Tuition and fees: $1,513, $1,317 additional for out-of-district students, $3,951 additional for out-of-state students. **Books and supplies:** $600. **Other expenses:** $900.

FINANCIAL AID. 20% of freshmen, 10% of continuing students receive some form of aid. All grants, 75% of loans, all jobs based on need. Alumni affiliation scholarships available. **Aid applications:** No closing date; priority given to applications received by July 15; applicants notified on a rolling basis beginning on or about June 1; must reply within 2 weeks.

ADDRESS/TELEPHONE. Thomas R. Bridegum, Director of Admissions, Raritan Valley Community College, PO Box 3300, Somerville, NJ 08876-1265. (908) 218-8861.

Rider College
Lawrenceville, New Jersey CB code: 2758

Admissions:	69% of applicants accepted
Based on:	••• School record
	•• Test scores
	• Activities, essay, interview, recommendations, special talents
Completion:	57% graduate

4-year private college of arts and sciences and business college, coed. Founded in 1865. **Accreditation:** Regional. **Undergraduate enrollment:** 1,338 men, 1,532 women full time; 479 men, 882 women part time. **Graduate enrollment:** 39 men, 77 women full time; 383 men, 754 women part time. **Faculty:** 299 total (239 full time), 220 with doctorates or other terminal degrees. **Location:** Suburban campus in large town; 5 miles from Princeton, 3 miles from Trenton. **Calendar:** Semester, extensive summer session. **Microcomputers:** 100 located in classrooms, computer centers. **Special facilities:** Art gallery, cross-country trail, holocaust/genocide center, multicultural center.

DEGREES OFFERED. BA, BS, MA, MBA. 16 associate degrees awarded in 1992. 818 bachelor's degrees awarded in 1992. Graduate degrees offered in 6 major fields of study.

UNDERGRADUATE MAJORS. Accounting, actuarial sciences, American studies, biochemistry, biology, business administration and management, business and management, business economics, chemistry, communications, computer and information sciences, creative writing, early childhood education, economics, elementary education, English education, English literature, finance, fine arts, foreign languages education, French, geology, German, history, journalism, marine biology, marketing and distribution, marketing and distributive education, mathematics, mathematics education, organizational behavior, personnel management, philosophy, physics, political science and government, predentistry, prelaw, premedicine, preveterinary, psychology, public relations, radio/television broadcasting, Russian, science education, secondary education, social studies education, sociology, Spanish.

ACADEMIC PROGRAMS. Accelerated program, double major, dual enrollment of high school students, honors program, independent study, internships, study abroad, teacher preparation, cross-registration. **Remedial services:** Learning center, preadmission summer program, reduced course load, remedial instruction, special counselor, tutoring. **ROTC:** Air Force, Army. **Placement/credit:** AP, CLEP General and Subject, institutional tests. Varies by major. 30 hours of general credit by examination may be counted toward degree. No limit for subject examinations. Not acceptable for last 30 credits of degree program.

ACADEMIC REQUIREMENTS. Freshmen must earn minimum GPA of 1.67 to continue in good standing. 71% of freshmen return for sophomore year. Students must declare major by end of second year. **Graduation requirements:** 120 hours for bachelor's. Most students required to take courses in English, history, humanities, mathematics, biological/physical sciences, social sciences. **Additional information:** School of Education offers bachelor's and master's degrees. Teaching certificates available in teaching English as a Second Language, elementary education, secondary education, business education, marketing and distributive education, psychology teacher preparation.

FRESHMAN ADMISSIONS. Selection criteria: High school curriculum most important, followed by class rank and test scores. Extracurricular activities and interview considered. **High school preparation:** 16 units required. Required and recommended units include English 4. Foreign language 2, mathematics 3, social science 4 and science 3 recommended. Algebra I and II and geometry required for business administration, science, and math majors. **Test requirements:** SAT or ACT (SAT preferred).

1992 FRESHMAN CLASS PROFILE. 3,603 men and women applied, 2,499 accepted; 330 men enrolled, 402 women enrolled. **Academic background:** Mid 50% of enrolled freshmen had SAT-V between 370-470, SAT-M between 420-550. 99% submitted SAT scores. **Characteristics:** 75% from in state, 86% live in college housing, 16% have minority backgrounds, 1% are foreign students. Average age is 18.

FALL-TERM APPLICATIONS. $30 fee, may be waived for applicants with need. No closing date; applicants notified on a rolling basis; must reply by May 1 or within 3 weeks if notified thereafter. Interview recommended. Essay recommended. Deferred and early admission available.

STUDENT LIFE. Housing: Dormitories (women, coed); fraternity, sorority housing available. **Activities:** Student government, magazine, radio, student newspaper, yearbook, choral groups, concert band, drama, jazz band, music ensembles, musical theater, pep band, fraternities, sororities, Hillel, Canterbury Club, Catholic campus ministry, Protestant campus ministry, Alpha Phi Omega, Asian Students at Rider, Black Student Union, Aegis Justice.

ATHLETICS. NCAA. **Intercollegiate:** Baseball M, basketball, cross-country, diving, field hockey W, golf M, soccer M, softball W, swimming, tennis, track and field, volleyball W, wrestling M. **Intramural:** Basketball, bowling, cross-country, football M, golf, horseback riding, lacrosse M, soccer, softball, swimming, tennis, volleyball, water polo.

STUDENT SERVICES. Aptitude testing, career counseling, employment service for undergraduates, freshman orientation, health services, on-campus day care, personal counseling, placement service for graduates, special adviser for adult students, services/facilities for handicapped.

ANNUAL EXPENSES. Tuition and fees: $12,950. **Room and board:** $5,210. **Books and supplies:** $700. **Other expenses:** $1,200.

FINANCIAL AID. 70% of freshmen, 70% of continuing students receive some form of aid. 81% of grants, 85% of loans, 37% of jobs based on need. Academic, music/drama, athletic, state/district residency, leadership, minority scholarships available. **Aid applications:** No closing date; priority given to applications received by April 1; applicants notified on a rolling basis beginning on or about April 1; must reply within 15 days.

ADDRESS/TELEPHONE. James F. Reilly, Dean of Admissions and Financial Aid, Rider College, 2083 Lawrenceville Road, Lawrenceville, NJ 08648-3099. (609) 896-5042. (800) 257-9026. Fax: (609) 895-6645.

Rowan College of New Jersey

Glassboro, New Jersey — CB code: 2515

Admissions: 40% of applicants accepted
Based on: ••• School record, test scores
•• Essay, recommendations, special talents
• Activities, interview
Completion: 85% of freshmen end year in good standing
41% graduate, 35% of these enter graduate study

4-year public liberal arts college, coed. Founded in 1923. **Accreditation:** Regional. **Undergraduate enrollment:** 3,712 men, 6,143 women full time; 660 men, 1,200 women part time. **Graduate enrollment:** 119 men and women full time; 1,387 men and women part time. **Faculty:** 323 total (278 full time), 246 with doctorates or other terminal degrees. **Location:** Rural campus in large town; 20 miles from Philadelphia. **Calendar:** Semester, extensive summer session. **Microcomputers:** 180 located in dormitories, libraries, classrooms, computer centers. **Special facilities:** Observatory, glass-blowing museum. **Additional facts:** Camden campus offers general education courses and major programs in elementary education, business administration, law/justice, and sociology.

DEGREES OFFERED. BA, BS, MA, MS, MBA. 1,364 bachelor's degrees awarded in 1992. 14% in business and management, 8% business/office and marketing/distribution, 17% communications, 27% teacher education, 5% law, 5% psychology, 8% social sciences, 5% visual and performing arts. Graduate degrees offered in 26 major fields of study.

UNDERGRADUATE MAJORS. Accounting, advertising, art education, biology, business administration and management, chemistry, communications, computer and information sciences, criminal justice studies, criminology, dramatic arts, drawing, early childhood education, economics, education of the mentally handicapped, elementary education, English education, English literature, fiber/textiles/weaving, finance, foreign languages education, geography, history, human resources development, illustration design, industrial arts education, information sciences and systems, journalism, law enforcement and corrections, management information systems, marketing and distribution, marketing management, mathematics, mathematics education, metal/jewelry, music, music education, music performance, music theory and composition, painting, physical education, physical sciences, political science and government, predentistry, prelaw, premedicine, prepharmacy, preveterinary, psychology, public relations, radio/television broadcasting, reading education, science education, sculpture, social science education, sociology, Spanish, special education, speech, speech/communication/theater education.

ACADEMIC PROGRAMS. Accelerated program, cooperative education, double major, dual enrollment of high school students, education specialist degree, honors program, independent study, internships, study abroad, teacher preparation, visiting/exchange student program, cross-registration; liberal arts/career combination in engineering. **Remedial services:** Learning center, preadmission summer program, reduced course load, remedial instruction, special counselor, tutoring. **ROTC:** Army. **Placement/credit:** AP, CLEP General and Subject, institutional tests; 30 credit hours maximum for bachelor's degree.

ACADEMIC REQUIREMENTS. Freshmen must earn minimum GPA of 1.6 to continue in good standing. 76% of freshmen return for sophomore year. Students must declare major by end of second year. **Graduation requirements:** 122 hours for bachelor's (30 in major). Most students required to take courses in arts/fine arts, computer science, English, history, humanities, mathematics, philosophy/religion, biological/physical sciences, social sciences. **Postgraduate studies:** 1% enter law school, 3% enter medical school, 8% enter MBA programs, 23% enter other graduate study. **Additional information:** Cross-registration with Drexel University (PA), Temple University (PA), Rutgers—The State University of New Jersey, and New Jersey Institute of Technology. Combination programs with University of Medicine and Dentistry of New Jersey, Philadelphia College of Pharmacy and Science (PA), and others.

FRESHMAN ADMISSIONS. Selection criteria: School achievement record and test scores most important, followed by recommendations. Special admissions program for in-state disadvantaged and minority students. **High school preparation:** 16 units required. Required and recommended units include biological science 1, English 4, mathematics 3, physical science 1 and social science 2. Foreign language 2 recommended. 5 additional units in academic course work, including foreign languages. **Test requirements:** SAT or ACT; score report by March 15.

1992 FRESHMAN CLASS PROFILE. 1,642 men applied, 654 accepted, 331 enrolled; 2,370 women applied, 942 accepted, 462 enrolled. **Academic background:** Mid 50% of enrolled freshmen had SAT-V between 410-500, SAT-M between 460-550; ACT composite between 21-26. 97% submitted SAT scores, 2% submitted ACT scores. **Characteristics:** 97% from in state, 65% live in college housing, 24% have minority backgrounds, 1% are foreign students, 18% join fraternities/sororities. Average age is 20.

FALL-TERM APPLICATIONS. $30 fee, may be waived for applicants with need. Closing date March 15; applicants notified on or about April 15; must reply by May 1. Audition required for music, theater applicants. Portfolio required for art applicants. Essay required. CRDA. Deferred and early admission available.

STUDENT LIFE. Housing: Dormitories (women, coed); apartment, handicapped housing available. Limited housing available for single parents. Students under age 21 not married or living with parent/guardian required to live in college housing for freshman and sophomore years. **Activities:** Student government, magazine, radio, student newspaper, yearbook, choral groups, concert band, dance, drama, jazz band, marching band, music ensembles, musical theater, opera, pep band, symphony orchestra, fraternities, sororities, over 150 clubs and student organizations including Hillel, Newman Club, Inter-Varsity Club, Muslim Association.

ATHLETICS. NCAA. **Intercollegiate:** Baseball M, basketball, cross-country, diving, field hockey W, football M, lacrosse W, soccer M, softball W, swimming, tennis, track and field, wrestling M. **Intramural:** Archery, basketball, bowling, fencing, handball, soccer W, softball, volleyball.

STUDENT SERVICES. Aptitude testing, career counseling, employment service for undergraduates, freshman orientation, health services, on-campus day care, personal counseling, placement service for graduates, special adviser for adult students, veterans counselor, services/facilities for handicapped.

ANNUAL EXPENSES. Tuition and fees (1992-93): $2,703, $1,050 additional for out-of-state students. **Room and board:** $4,565. **Books and supplies:** $600. **Other expenses:** $1,000.

FINANCIAL AID. 69% of freshmen, 63% of continuing students receive some form of aid. All grants, 63% of loans, all jobs based on need. Academic, music/drama, art, state/district residency, leadership, minority scholarships available. **Aid applications:** Closing date April 15; applicants notified on a rolling basis beginning on or about June 15; by August 1 or within 2 weeks.

ADDRESS/TELEPHONE. Marvin G. Sills, Director of Admissions, Rowan College of New Jersey, Oak Hall, Glassboro, NJ 08028. (609) 863-5346. Fax: (609) 863-6553.

Rutgers—The State University of New Jersey: Camden College of Arts and Sciences

Camden, New Jersey — CB code: 2092

Admissions: 51% of applicants accepted
Based on: ••• School record, test scores
• Activities, essay, recommendations, special talents
Completion: 44% graduate

4-year public college of arts and sciences, coed. Founded in 1927. **Accreditation:** Regional. **Undergraduate enrollment:** 1,011 men, 1,179 women full time; 201 men, 281 women part time. **Faculty:** 139 total, 125 with doctorates or other terminal degrees. **Location:** Urban campus in small city; 1 mile from Philadelphia. **Calendar:** Semester, extensive summer session. **Microcomputers:** 156 located in dormitories, libraries, classrooms, computer centers, campus-wide network. **Special facilities:** Fine arts center including theater and art gallery. **Additional facts:** Camden College of Arts and Sciences and University College Camden share faculty. Rutgers-Camden offers graduate studies in biology, English, history, physical therapy, and public administration as well as graduate professional schools of law, business, and social work.

DEGREES OFFERED. BA, BS. 671 bachelor's degrees awarded in 1992. 34% in business and management, 6% health sciences, 9% letters/literature, 10% psychology, 23% social sciences, 5% visual and performing arts.

UNDERGRADUATE MAJORS. Accounting, Afro-American (black) studies, art education, art history, biochemistry, biological and physical sciences, biology, botany, business administration and management, business and management, cell biology, chemistry, clinical laboratory science, computer and information sciences, dramatic arts, early childhood education, ecology, economics, elementary education, English, English education, entomology, fine arts, foreign languages education, French, general science, genetics, human and animal, German, history, junior high education, Latin American studies, liberal/general studies, management science, marketing management, mathematics, mathematics education, microbiology, molecular biology, music, music education, music history and appreciation, nursing, philosophy, physics, physiology, human and animal, political science and government, psychology, science education, secondary education, social studies education, social work, sociology, Spanish, speech/communication/theater education, urban studies, women's studies, zoology.

ACADEMIC PROGRAMS. Accelerated program, double major, dual enrollment of high school students, honors program, independent study, internships, student-designed major, study abroad, teacher preparation, visiting/exchange student program, cross-registration, 2-3 degree program with School of Engineering, 2-2 program with College of Engineering, 2-3 program with College of Pharmacy, 8-year bachelor's/MD program with University of Medicine and Dentistry of New Jersey; liberal arts/career combination in engineering; combined bachelor's/graduate program in medicine. **Remedial services:** Learning center, preadmission summer program, reduced course load, remedial instruction, special counselor, tutoring. **ROTC:** Air Force, Army, Naval. **Placement/credit:** AP, CLEP Subject, institutional tests.

ACADEMIC REQUIREMENTS. Freshmen must earn minimum GPA of 2.0 to continue in good standing. 75% of freshmen return for sophomore year. Students must declare major by end of second year. **Graduation requirements:** 126 hours for bachelor's. Most students required to take courses in arts/fine arts, English, foreign languages, history, humanities, mathematics, philosophy/religion, biological/physical sciences, social sciences. **Additional information:** Teacher certification programs (K-12) available. Students complete major in field other than education and take teacher certification curriculum.

FRESHMAN ADMISSIONS. Selection criteria: School achievement record (including grades, rank, strength of program, honors) and test scores most important. Extracurricular activities, talent, disadvantaged status considered. **High school preparation:** 16 units required. Required and recommended units include English 4, foreign language 2, mathematics 3-4 and science 2. Mathematics requirement includes algebra I and II and geometry. 4 mathematics, 1 chemistry, 1 physics required for engineering applicants. **Test requirements:** SAT or ACT; score report by May 1. 3 ACH required of applicants for admission by examination (non-high school graduates, graduates of nonaccredited high schools, those without required academic courses, or applicants with GED). ACH required: English, Mathematics Level I or II, and third subject of the student's choice. Score report by May 1. **Additional information:** State residents with educationally and economically disadvantaged backgrounds given consideration through state Educational Opportunity Fund (EOF) program.

1992 FRESHMAN CLASS PROFILE. 1,672 men applied, 902 accepted, 134 enrolled; 1,473 women applied, 694 accepted, 111 enrolled. 17% were in top tenth and 54% were in top quarter of graduating class. **Academic background:** Mid 50% of enrolled freshmen had SAT-V between 450-540, SAT-M between 510-610. 97% submitted SAT scores. **Characteristics:** 96% from in state, 27% live in college housing, 36% have minority backgrounds. Average age is 18.

FALL-TERM APPLICATIONS. $40 fee, may be waived for applicants with need. Closing date May 1; applicants notified on a rolling basis; must reply by May 1 or within 2 weeks if notified thereafter. CRDA. Deferred and early admission available. May apply to up to 3 colleges with 1 application.

STUDENT LIFE. Housing: Dormitories (coed); apartment, fraternity housing available. **Activities:** Student government, magazine, radio, student newspaper, yearbook, choral groups, dance, drama, musical theater, fraternities, sororities, accounting society, forensics society, political science association, Black Student Union, Latin American Students' Organization, physics society, Jewish Student Union, marketing association, psychology club, student theater, computer science association.

ATHLETICS. NCAA. **Intercollegiate:** Baseball M, basketball, cross-country W, diving, golf M, soccer M, softball W, swimming, tennis, track and field, wrestling M. **Intramural:** Badminton, basketball, handball, racquetball, softball W, squash, volleyball.

STUDENT SERVICES. Aptitude testing, career counseling, employment service for undergraduates, freshman orientation, health services, on-campus day care, personal counseling, placement service for graduates, veterans counselor, services/facilities for handicapped.

ANNUAL EXPENSES. Tuition and fees: $4,082, $3,538 additional for out-of-state students. **Room and board:** $4,604. **Books and supplies:** $650.

FINANCIAL AID. 63% of freshmen, 50% of continuing students receive some form of aid. All grants, 82% of loans, all jobs based on need. 293 enrolled freshmen were judged to have need, 265 were offered aid. Academic, state/district residency, leadership, alumni affiliation, minority scholarships available. **Aid applications:** No closing date; priority given to applications received by March 1; applicants notified on a rolling basis beginning on or about April 1.

ADDRESS/TELEPHONE. Elizabeth Mitchell, Assistant Vice President for University Undergraduate Admissions, Rutgers—The State University of New Jersey: Camden College of Arts and Sciences, 406 Penn Street, Camden, NJ 08102. (609) 225-6104. Fax: (609) 225-6498.

Rutgers—The State University of New Jersey: College of Engineering

New Brunswick, New Jersey — CB code: 2838

Admissions: 74% of applicants accepted
Based on: ••• School record, test scores
• Activities, essay, recommendations, special talents
Completion: 71% graduate

4-year public engineering college, coed. Founded in 1864. **Accreditation:** Regional. **Undergraduate enrollment:** 1,978 men, 418 women full time; 53 men, 5 women part time. **Faculty:** 124 total, 112 with doctorates or other terminal degrees. **Location:** Suburban campus in large town; 33 miles from New York City. **Calendar:** Semester, extensive summer session. **Microcomputers:** Located in dormitories, libraries, classrooms, computer centers. **Special facilities:** Center for ceramics research, fiber optic materials research program, center for plastics recycling research, center for packaging engineering, manufacturing automation and robotics laboratories, wireless information networks laboratory, bioprocessing pilot facility, computer-aided design laboratory, geology museum, 4 art galleries, Hutcheson Memorial Forest Ecological Preserve, agricultural museum, large black box theater. **Additional facts:** University has graduate programs in over 60 fields in addition to graduate professional schools of law, education, business, library/information studies, criminal justice, psychology, social work, the arts.

DEGREES OFFERED. BS. 444 bachelor's degrees awarded in 1992. 100% in engineering.

UNDERGRADUATE MAJORS. Aerospace/aeronautical/astronautical engineering, agricultural engineering, applied sciences in engineering, bioengineering and biomedical engineering, ceramic engineering, chemical engineering, civil engineering, computer engineering, electrical/electronics/communications engineering, industrial engineering, mechanical engineering.

ACADEMIC PROGRAMS. Double major, honors program, independent study, internships, student-designed major, study abroad, visiting/exchange student program, 5-year dual bachelor programs with Douglass, Rutgers, Livingston, Camden College of Arts and Sciences, Newark College of Arts and Sciences, 5-year bachelor of science program with Cook College, 5-year bachelor's program with Graduate school of Management, 8-year bachelor's/MD program with University of Medicine and Dentistry of New Jersey; liberal arts/career combination in engineering; combined bachelor's/graduate program in business administration, medicine. **Remedial services:** Learning center, preadmission summer program, reduced course load, remedial instruction, special counselor, tutoring, writing laboratory. **ROTC:** Air Force, Army. **Placement/credit:** AP, IB, institutional tests; 30 credit hours maximum for bachelor's degree.

ACADEMIC REQUIREMENTS. Freshmen must earn minimum GPA of 1.8 to continue in good standing. 90% of freshmen return for sophomore year. Students must declare major by end of first year. **Graduation requirements:** 138 hours for bachelor's (113 in major). Most students required to take courses in computer science, English, humanities, mathematics, biological/physical sciences, social sciences.

FRESHMAN ADMISSIONS. Selection criteria: School achievement record (including grades, rank, strength of program, honors, AP) and test scores most important. Mathematical aptitude very important. Extracurricular activities, leadership talent, minority and disadvantaged status considered. Minorities and women encouraged to apply. **High school preparation:** 16 units required. Required units include English 4, mathematics 4 and physical science 2. Mathematics requirement includes precalculus. One chemistry, 1 physics also required. Computer programming recommended. **Test requirements:** SAT or ACT; score report by January 15. 3 ACH required of applicants for admission by examination (non-high school graduates, graduates of nonaccredited high schools, those without required academic courses, and some applicants with GED). Score report by January 15. **Additional information:** State residents with educationally and economically disadvantaged backgrounds given consideration through state Educational Opportunity Fund (EOF) program.

1992 FRESHMAN CLASS PROFILE. 2,533 men applied, 1,821 accepted, 469 enrolled; 671 women applied, 547 accepted, 125 enrolled. 42%

were in top tenth and 80% were in top quarter of graduating class. **Academic background:** Mid 50% of enrolled freshmen had SAT-V between 450-570, SAT-M between 610-700. 99% submitted SAT scores. **Characteristics:** 89% from in state, 92% live in college housing, 42% have minority backgrounds, 3% are foreign students. Average age is 18.

FALL-TERM APPLICATIONS. $40 fee, may be waived for applicants with need. Closing date January 15; must reply by May 1. CRDA. Deferred and early admission available. May apply to up to 3 colleges with 1 application. Students notified by April 15.

STUDENT LIFE. Housing: Dormitories (men, women, coed); apartment, fraternity housing available. Housing guaranteed for freshmen and sophomores. Special interest, language and cultural houses, math-science dormitory for women, and substance free housing available. **Activities:** Student government, film, magazine, radio, student newspaper, television, yearbook, choral groups, concert band, dance, drama, jazz band, marching band, music ensembles, musical theater, pep band, symphony orchestra, fraternities, sororities, over 100 organizations including technical engineering societies, honor society, Minority Engineering Educational Task organization, women's center and various religious, political, and ethnic organizations. **Additional information:** Students affiliate with 1 of university's New Brunswick residential colleges (Douglass, Livingston, Rutgers, or Cook) for housing and student life services and facilities.

ATHLETICS. NCAA. **Intercollegiate:** Baseball M, basketball, cross-country, diving, fencing, field hockey W, football M, golf, gymnastics W, lacrosse, rowing (crew), soccer, softball W, swimming, tennis, track and field, volleyball W, wrestling M. **Intramural:** Badminton, basketball, bowling, field hockey, golf, horseback riding, ice hockey M, lacrosse, racquetball, rugby, sailing, skiing, skin diving, soccer, softball, squash, table tennis, tennis, volleyball, water polo, wrestling M.

STUDENT SERVICES. Career counseling, employment service for undergraduates, freshman orientation, health services, on-campus day care, personal counseling, placement service for graduates, veterans counselor, services/facilities for handicapped.

ANNUAL EXPENSES. Tuition and fees: $4,638, $3,924 additional for out-of-state students. Students pay fees of residential college with which they affiliate. Fees range from $808 to 890 per year. **Room and board:** $4,454. **Books and supplies:** $650.

FINANCIAL AID. 62% of freshmen, 62% of continuing students receive some form of aid. 98% of grants, 84% of loans, all jobs based on need. 329 enrolled freshmen were judged to have need, 274 were offered aid. Academic, athletic, state/district residency, alumni affiliation, minority scholarships available. **Aid applications:** No closing date; priority given to applications received by March 1; applicants notified on a rolling basis beginning on or about April 1.

ADDRESS/TELEPHONE. Elizabeth Mitchell, Assistant Vice President for University Undergraduate Admissions, Rutgers: The State University of New Jersey: College of Engineering, PO Box 2101, New Brunswick, NJ 08903-2101. (908) 932-3770. Fax: (908) 932-0237.

Rutgers—The State University of New Jersey: College of Nursing ⇎

Newark, New Jersey CB code: 2789

Admissions: 23% of applicants accepted
Based on: ••• School record, test scores
• Activities, essay, interview, recommendations, special talents
Completion: 56% graduate

4-year public nursing college, coed. Founded in 1956. **Accreditation:** Regional. **Undergraduate enrollment:** 27 men, 320 women full time; 10 men, 34 women part time. **Faculty:** 40 total, 36 with doctorates or other terminal degrees. **Location:** Urban campus in large city; 10 miles from New York City. **Calendar:** Semester, limited summer session. **Microcomputers:** 440 located in dormitories, libraries, computer centers, campus-wide network. **Special facilities:** Biology learning center, jazz institute, animal behavior institute, center for molecular and behavioral neuroscience. **Additional facts:** University has graduate programs in over 60 fields in addition to graduate professional schools of law, education, business, library/information studies, criminal justice, psychology, social work, the arts.

DEGREES OFFERED. BS. 88 bachelor's degrees awarded in 1992. 100% in health sciences. Graduate degrees offered in 1 major field of study.

UNDERGRADUATE MAJORS. Nursing.

ACADEMIC PROGRAMS. Honors program, internships, study abroad, cross-registration, New Brunswick nursing program for limited number of students. **Remedial services:** Learning center, preadmission summer program, reduced course load, remedial instruction, special counselor, tutoring. **ROTC:** Air Force, Army. **Placement/credit:** AP, CLEP General and Subject, institutional tests.

ACADEMIC REQUIREMENTS. Freshmen must earn minimum GPA of 1.4 to continue in good standing. 91% of freshmen return for sophomore year. Students must declare major on application. **Graduation requirements:** 125 hours for bachelor's. Most students required to take courses in English, history, biological/physical sciences, social sciences. **Additional information:** Program includes clinical experience in New Jersey hospitals and health agencies. Students who are registered nurses may be exempt from certain courses.

FRESHMAN ADMISSIONS. Selection criteria: School achievement record (including grades, rank, strength of program, honors, AP) and test scores most important. Competency in mathematics and science very important. Extracurricular activities, leadership talent, minority, disadvantaged status considered. **High school preparation:** 16 units required. Required and recommended units include biological science 1, English 4, mathematics 3-4 and physical science 1. Mathematics requirement includes algebra I and II and geometry. Chemistry I also required. **Test requirements:** SAT or ACT; score report by March 15. 3 ACH required of applicants for admission by examination (non-high school graduates, graduates of nonaccredited high schools, those without required academic courses, or applicants with GED). Score report by March 15. **Additional information:** State residents with educationally and economically disadvantaged backgrounds given consideration through state Educational Opportunity Fund (EOF) program.

1992 FRESHMAN CLASS PROFILE. 80 men applied, 14 accepted, 6 enrolled; 622 women applied, 150 accepted, 36 enrolled. 38% were in top tenth and 71% were in top quarter of graduating class. **Academic background:** Mid 50% of enrolled freshmen had SAT-V between 460-560, SAT-M between 510-620. 98% submitted SAT scores. **Characteristics:** 100% from in state, 63% commute, 64% have minority backgrounds. Average age is 18.

FALL-TERM APPLICATIONS. $40 fee, may be waived for applicants with need. Closing date March 15; applicants notified on a rolling basis; must reply by May 1 or within 2 weeks if notified thereafter. Interview recommended for borderline applicants. CRDA. Deferred and early admission available. May apply to up to 3 colleges with 1 application.

STUDENT LIFE. Housing: Dormitories (coed); apartment housing available. **Activities:** Student government, magazine, radio, student newspaper, television, yearbook, choral groups, concert band, drama, jazz band, music ensembles, musical theater, symphony orchestra, string orchestra, summer theater, fraternities, sororities, over 60 clubs and organizations including registered nurses organization. **Additional information:** Students participate in activities at Newark College of Arts and Sciences.

ATHLETICS. Intercollegiate: Baseball M, basketball, soccer M, softball W, tennis, volleyball, wrestling M. **Intramural:** Basketball, fencing, handball, racquetball, skiing, soccer, softball, squash, swimming, tennis, track and field, volleyball, water polo.

STUDENT SERVICES. Aptitude testing, career counseling, employment service for undergraduates, freshman orientation, health services, personal counseling, placement service for graduates, veterans counselor, daycare available adjacent to campus, services/facilities for handicapped.

ANNUAL EXPENSES. Tuition and fees: $4,068, $3,538 additional for out-of-state students. **Room and board:** $4,624. **Books and supplies:** $650.

FINANCIAL AID. 60% of freshmen, 53% of continuing students receive some form of aid. All grants, 85% of loans, all jobs based on need. 30 enrolled freshmen were judged to have need, 27 were offered aid. Academic, state/district residency, leadership, alumni affiliation, minority scholarships available. **Aid applications:** No closing date; priority given to applications received by March 1; applicants notified on a rolling basis beginning on or about April 1.

ADDRESS/TELEPHONE. Elizabeth Mitchell, Assistant Vice President for University Undergraduate Admissions, Rutgers—The State University of New Jersey: College of Nursing, 249 University Avenue, Newark, NJ 07102-1896. (201) 648-5205. Fax: (201) 648-1440.

Rutgers—The State University of New Jersey: College of Pharmacy ⇎

New Brunswick, New Jersey CB code: 2839

Admissions: 40% of applicants accepted
Based on: ••• School record, test scores
• Activities, essay, recommendations, special talents
Completion: 63% graduate

5-year public pharmacy college, coed. Founded in 1892. **Accreditation:** Regional. **Undergraduate enrollment:** 273 men, 535 women full time; 3 men, 11 women part time. **Graduate enrollment:** 3 men, 23 women full time; 3 men, 7 women part time. **Faculty:** 54 total, 49 with doctorates or other terminal degrees. **Location:** Suburban campus in large town; 33 miles from New York City. **Calendar:** Semester, extensive summer session. **Microcomputers:** 677 located in dormitories, libraries, classrooms, computer centers, campus-wide network. **Special facilities:** Agricultural museum, geology museum, 4 art galleries, Hutcheson Memorial Forest Ecological Preserve, large black box theater (university-wide), laboratory for cancer research. **Additional facts:** University has graduate programs in over 60 fields in addition to graduate professional schools of law, education, business, library/information studies, criminal justice, psychology, social work, the arts. Library and other facilities shared by New Brunswick colleges.

DEGREES OFFERED. BS, B. Pharm, Pharm D. 138 bachelor's degrees awarded in 1992. 100% in health sciences. Graduate degrees offered in 1 major field of study.

UNDERGRADUATE MAJORS. Pharmacy.

ACADEMIC PROGRAMS. Honors program, independent study, internships, study abroad, visiting/exchange student program, externship programs in community, hospital, and industrial pharmacy. **Remedial services:** Learning center, preadmission summer program, reduced course load, remedial instruction, special counselor, tutoring, writing laboratory. **ROTC:** Air Force, Army. **Placement/credit:** AP, CLEP General and Subject, IB, institutional tests; 6 credit hours maximum for bachelor's degree.

ACADEMIC REQUIREMENTS. Freshmen must earn minimum GPA of 2.0 to continue in good standing. 95% of freshmen return for sophomore year. Students must declare major on application. **Graduation requirements:** 173 hours for bachelor's. Most students required to take courses in English, humanities, mathematics, biological/physical sciences, social sciences. **Additional information:** Program of study comprises pharmacy, pharmacy administration, pharmaceutical chemistry, pharmacognosy, and pharmacology as well as natural and social sciences and humanities.

FRESHMAN ADMISSIONS. Selection criteria: School achievement record (including grades, rank, strength of program, honors, test scores) most important. Record in mathematics and science very important. Extracurricular activities, leadership talent, minority, disadvantaged status considered. **High school preparation:** 16 units required. Required units include biological science 1, English 4, foreign language 2, mathematics 3 and physical science 1. Mathematics requirement includes algebra I and II and geometry. One chemistry, 1 biology required, physics recommended. Fourth unit of college preparatory mathematics strongly recommended. **Test requirements:** SAT or ACT; score report by January 15. 3 ACH required of applicants for admission by examination (non-high school graduates, graduates of nonaccredited high schools, those without required academic courses, and some applicants with GED). Score report by January 15. **Additional information:** State residents with educationally and economically disadvantaged backgrounds given consideration through state Educational Opportunity Fund (EOF) program.

1992 FRESHMAN CLASS PROFILE. 517 men applied, 215 accepted, 67 enrolled; 707 women applied, 277 accepted, 114 enrolled. 70% were in top tenth and 98% were in top quarter of graduating class. **Academic background:** Mid 50% of enrolled freshmen had SAT-V between 470-580, SAT-M between 590-690. 99% submitted SAT scores. **Characteristics:** 88% from in state, 95% live in college housing, 56% have minority backgrounds, 1% are foreign students. Average age is 18.

FALL-TERM APPLICATIONS. $40 fee, may be waived for applicants with need. Closing date January 15; must reply by May 1. CRDA. Deferred and early admission available. May apply to up to 3 colleges with 1 application. Students notified by April 15.

STUDENT LIFE. Housing: Dormitories (men, women, coed); apartment, fraternity housing available. Housing guaranteed for freshmen and sophomores. Substance free housing, language and cultural houses, and math-science dormitory for women available. **Activities:** Student government, film, magazine, radio, student newspaper, television, yearbook, choral groups, concert band, dance, drama, jazz band, marching band, music ensembles, musical theater, pep band, symphony orchestra, fraternities, sororities, over 100 organizations including professional pharmacy associations, pharmacy fraternities and sorority, honor society, and various religious, political, and ethnic organizations, women's center. **Additional information:** Students affiliate with 1 of university's New Brunswick residential colleges (Douglass, Livingston, or Rutgers) for housing and student life services and facilities. Some students spend first 2 years in Newark or Camden College of Arts and Science.

ATHLETICS. Intercollegiate: Baseball M, basketball, cross-country, diving, fencing, field hockey W, football M, golf, gymnastics W, lacrosse, rowing (crew), soccer, softball W, swimming, tennis, track and field, volleyball W, wrestling M. **Intramural:** Badminton, basketball, bowling, field hockey, golf, horseback riding, ice hockey M, lacrosse, racquetball, rugby, sailing, skiing, skin diving, soccer, softball, squash, table tennis, tennis, volleyball, water polo, wrestling M.

STUDENT SERVICES. Career counseling, employment service for undergraduates, freshman orientation, health services, on-campus day care, personal counseling, placement service for graduates, veterans counselor, services/facilities for handicapped.

ANNUAL EXPENSES. Tuition and fees: $4,638, $3,924 additional for out-of-state students. Students pay fees of residential college with which they affiliate. Fees range from $808 to 890. **Room and board:** $4,454. **Books and supplies:** $650.

FINANCIAL AID. 73% of freshmen, 69% of continuing students receive some form of aid. All grants, 76% of loans, all jobs based on need. 180 enrolled freshmen were judged to have need, 168 were offered aid. Academic, athletic, state/district residency, leadership, alumni affiliation, minority scholarships available. **Aid applications:** No closing date; priority given to applications received by March 1; applicants notified on a rolling basis beginning on or about April 1.

ADDRESS/TELEPHONE. Elizabeth Mitchell, Assistant Vice President Undergraduate Admissions, Rutgers—The State University of New Jersey: College of Pharmacy, PO Box 2101, New Brunswick, NJ 08903-2101. (908) 932-3770. Fax: (908) 932-0237.

Rutgers—The State University of New Jersey: Cook College

New Brunswick, New Jersey — CB code: 2170

Admissions: 58% of applicants accepted
Based on:
- ••• School record, test scores
- •• Special talents
- • Activities, essay, recommendations

Completion: 65% graduate

4-year public college of agricultural, life, and environmental sciences, coed. Founded in 1864. **Accreditation:** Regional. **Undergraduate enrollment:** 1,430 men, 1,136 women full time; 153 men, 189 women part time. **Faculty:** 92 total, 83 with doctorates or other terminal degrees. **Location:** Suburban campus in large town; 33 miles from New York City. **Calendar:** Semester, extensive summer session. **Microcomputers:** 677 located in libraries, computer centers, campus-wide network. **Special facilities:** Geology museum, 4 art galleries, Hutcheson Memorial Forest Ecological Preserve, center for advanced food technology, large black box theater, marine and coastal sciences institute, center for agricultural molecular biology, Helyar Woods, log cabin, agricultural museum, environmental and occupational health sciences institution. **Additional facts:** University has graduate programs in over 60 fields in addition to graduate professional schools of law, education, business, library/information studies, criminal justice, psychology, social work and the arts. Library, other facilities, and faculty shared with all New Brunswick colleges.

DEGREES OFFERED. BA, BS. 637 bachelor's degrees awarded in 1992. 11% in agriculture, 11% architecture and environmental design, 23% life sciences, 20% physical sciences, 16% social sciences.

UNDERGRADUATE MAJORS. Agribusiness, agricultural economics, agricultural education, agricultural engineering, agricultural sciences, agronomy, animal sciences, atmospheric sciences and meteorology, biochemistry, biological and physical sciences, biology, biomedical science, biometrics and biostatistics, biotechnology, botany, cell biology, chemistry, communications, computer and information sciences, earth sciences, ecology, entomology, environmental and business economics, environmental design, environmental science, environmental science education, exercise science and sports studies, fishing and fisheries, food science and nutrition, food sciences, forestry and related sciences, geography, geology, health care education and supervision, horticultural science, international agriculture, journalism, landscape architecture, microbiology, molecular biology, nutritional sciences, oceanography, physical education, physiology, human and animal, plant sciences, professional/occupational education, public health laboratory science, radiobiology, renewable natural resources, science education, soil sciences, technical education, turfgrass management, wildlife management.

ACADEMIC PROGRAMS. Cooperative education, double major, dual enrollment of high school students, honors program, independent study, internships, student-designed major, study abroad, teacher preparation, visiting/exchange student program, 5-year dual bachelor's degree program with College of Engineering in bioresource engineering and agricultural science or environmental studies, 8-year bachelor's/MD program with University of Medicine and Dentistry of New Jersey; liberal arts/career combination in engineering; combined bachelor's/graduate program in medicine. **Remedial services:** Learning center, preadmission summer program, reduced course load, remedial instruction, special counselor, tutoring, writing laboratory. **ROTC:** Air Force, Army. **Placement/credit:** AP, institutional tests.

ACADEMIC REQUIREMENTS. Freshmen must earn minimum GPA of 2.0 to continue in good standing. 86% of freshmen return for sophomore year. Students must declare major by end of second year. **Graduation requirements:** 128 hours for bachelor's (30 in major). Most students required to take courses in arts/fine arts, computer science, English, humanities, mathematics, biological/physical sciences, social sciences. **Additional information:** Teacher certification programs (K-12) available. Students complete major in field other than education and take teacher certification curriculum.

FRESHMAN ADMISSIONS. Selection criteria: School achievement record (including grades, rank, strength of program, honors, AP) and test scores most important. Extracurricular activities, leadership talent, minority, disadvantaged status considered. **High school preparation:** 16 units required. Required and recommended units include English 4 and mathematics 3-4. Mathematics requirement includes algebra I and II and geometry. 4 mathematics, including 1 precalculus, and 1 chemistry, 1 physics required for engineering program. **Test requirements:** SAT or ACT; score report by January 15. 3 ACH required of applicants for admission by examination (non-high school graduates, graduates of nonaccredited high schools, those without required academic courses, and some applicants with GED). Score report by January 15. **Additional information:** State residents with educationally and economically disadvantaged backgrouds given consideration through state Educational Opportunity Fund (EOF) program.

1992 FRESHMAN CLASS PROFILE. 3,064 men applied, 1,663 accepted, 245 enrolled; 2,358 women applied, 1,496 accepted, 249 enrolled. 33% were in top tenth and 81% were in top quarter of graduating class. **Academic background:** Mid 50% of enrolled freshmen had SAT-V between 460-560, SAT-M between 530-640. 99% submitted SAT scores. **Characteristics:** 87% from in state, 80% live in college housing, 21% have minority backgrounds. Average age is 18.

FALL-TERM APPLICATIONS. $40 fee, may be waived for applicants with need. Closing date January 15; must reply by May 1. CRDA. Deferred and early admission available. May apply to up to 3 colleges with 1 application. Students notified by April 15.

STUDENT LIFE. Housing: Dormitories (coed); apartment, fraternity, cooperative housing available. Reduced-cost housing for students with financial need. All freshmen, sophomores, and transfer students guaranteed housing. Substance free housing available. **Activities:** Student government, film, magazine, radio, student newspaper, television, yearbook, choral groups, concert band, dance, drama, jazz band, marching band, musical theater, pep band, symphony orchestra, fraternities, sororities, over 100 organizations including environmental clubs, Amanea Society, Latin American organization, women's center and various religious, political, and ethnic organizations. **Additional information:** Students may participate in organizations and activities and use facilities at other undergraduate colleges of Rutgers University in New Brunswick.

ATHLETICS. NCAA. **Intercollegiate:** Baseball M, basketball, cross-country, diving, fencing, field hockey W, football M, golf, gymnastics W, lacrosse, rowing (crew), soccer, softball W, swimming, tennis, track and field, volleyball W, wrestling M. **Intramural:** Badminton, basketball, bowling, field hockey, golf, horseback riding, ice hockey M, lacrosse, racquetball, rugby, sailing, skiing, skin diving, soccer, softball, squash, table tennis, tennis, volleyball, water polo, wrestling M.

STUDENT SERVICES. Career counseling, employment service for undergraduates, freshman orientation, health services, on-campus day care, personal counseling, placement service for graduates, veterans counselor, services/facilities for handicapped.

ANNUAL EXPENSES. Tuition and fees: $4,625, $3,924 additional for out-of-state students. **Room and board:** $4,596. **Books and supplies:** $650.

FINANCIAL AID. 64% of freshmen, 55% of continuing students receive some form of aid. 90% of grants, 87% of loans, all jobs based on need. 281 enrolled freshmen were judged to have need, 233 were offered aid. Academic, athletic, state/district residency, leadership, alumni affiliation, minority scholarships available. **Aid applications:** No closing date; priority given to applications received by March 1; applicants notified on a rolling basis beginning on or about April 1.

ADDRESS/TELEPHONE. Elizabeth Mitchell, Assistant Vice President for University Undergraduate Admissions, Rutgers—The State University of New Jersey: Cook College, PO Box 2101, New Brunswick, NJ 08903-2101. (908) 932-3770. Fax: (908) 932-0237.

Rutgers—The State University of New Jersey: Douglass College

New Brunswick, New Jersey CB code: 2192

Admissions: 65% of applicants accepted
Based on: ••• School record, test scores
•• Special talents
• Activities, essay, recommendations
Completion: 81% graduate

4-year public college of arts and sciences, women only. Founded in 1918. **Accreditation:** Regional. **Undergraduate enrollment:** 2,998 women full time; 183 women part time. **Faculty:** 771 total, 694 with doctorates or other terminal degrees. **Location:** Suburban campus in large town; 33 miles from New York City. **Calendar:** Semester, extensive summer session. Extensive evening/early morning classes. **Microcomputers:** 626 located in dormitories, libraries, computer centers, campus-wide network. **Special facilities:** Geology museum, 4 art galleries, Hutcheson Memorial Forest Ecological Preserve, large black box theater, agricultural museum, Eagleton Institute of Politics, Institute of Management and Labor Relations, Institute for Research on Women, Waksman Institute of Microbiology, Center for Mathematical Sciences Research. **Additional facts:** University has graduate programs in over 60 fields in addition to graduate professional schools of law, education, business, library/information studies, criminal justice, psychology, social work, the arts. Library, other facilities, and faculty shared by all New Brunswick colleges.

DEGREES OFFERED. BA, BS. 870 bachelor's degrees awarded in 1992. 8% in business and management, 13% communications, 6% languages, 14% letters/literature, 13% psychology, 26% social sciences. Graduate degrees offered in 9 major fields of study.

UNDERGRADUATE MAJORS. Accounting, African studies, Afro-American (black) studies, American studies, anthropology, art history, Asian studies, atmospheric sciences and meteorology, biochemistry, biological and physical sciences, biology, biomedical science, biometrics and biostatistics, biotechnology, botany, business and management, cell biology, chemistry, Chinese, classics, clinical laboratory science, communications, comparative literature, computer and information sciences, dance, dramatic arts, earth sciences, Eastern European studies, ecology, economics, English, entomology, exercise science and sports studies, finance, fine arts, food science and nutrition, French, genetics, human and animal, geography, geology, German, Greek (classical), Hispanic American studies, history, humanities, humanities and social sciences, Italian, Jewish studies, journalism, labor/industrial relations, Latin, Latin American studies, liberal/general studies, linguistics, management science, marketing management, mathematics, medical laboratory technologies, microbiology, Middle Eastern studies, molecular biology, music, music history and appreciation, nutritional sciences, oceanography, philosophy, physical education, physics, physiology, human and animal, political science and government, Portuguese, psychology, public health laboratory science, Puerto Rican and Hispanic/Caribbean studies, religion, Russian, Russian and Slavic studies, sociology, Spanish, special education, statistics, urban studies, visual and performing arts, women's studies.

ACADEMIC PROGRAMS. Accelerated program, double major, dual enrollment of high school students, honors program, independent study, internships, student-designed major, study abroad, teacher preparation, visiting/exchange student program, Washington semester, science management internship, junior-year program for women's studies, 5-year dual bachelor's degree program with Rutgers College of Engineering, bachelors/master's program with Graduate School of Management, 8-year bachelor's/master's program with University of Medicine and Dentistry of New Jersey, 5-year bachelor's/M.Ed program with Graduate School of Education; liberal arts/career combination in engineering; combined bachelor's/graduate program in business administration, medicine. **Remedial services:** Learning center, preadmission summer program, remedial instruction, special counselor, tutoring, writing laboratory. **ROTC:** Air Force, Army. **Placement/credit:** AP, CLEP Subject, IB, institutional tests.

ACADEMIC REQUIREMENTS. Freshmen must earn minimum GPA of 1.8 to continue in good standing. 91% of freshmen return for sophomore year. Students must declare major by end of second year. **Graduation requirements:** 120 hours for bachelor's. Most students required to take courses in English, foreign languages, history, humanities, mathematics, biological/physical sciences, social sciences.

FRESHMAN ADMISSIONS. Selection criteria: School achievement record (including grades, rank, strength of program, honors, AP) and test scores most important. Extracurricular activities, leadership talent, minority, disadvantaged status considered. **High school preparation:** 16 units required. Required and recommended units include English 4, foreign language 2, mathematics 3-4 and science 2. Mathematics requirement includes algebra I and II and geometry. 4 mathematics, 1 chemistry, 1 physics required for engineering program. **Test requirements:** SAT or ACT; score report by January 15. 3 ACH required of applicants for admission by examination (non-high school graduates, graduates of nonaccredited high schools, those without required academic courses, and some applicants with GED). Score report by January 15. **Additional information:** State residents with educationally and economically disadvantaged backgrounds given consideration through state Educational Opportunity Fund (EOF) program.

1992 FRESHMAN CLASS PROFILE. 6,237 women applied, 4,032 accepted, 658 enrolled. 25% were in top tenth and 78% were in top quarter of graduating class. **Academic background:** Mid 50% of enrolled freshmen had SAT-V between 460-550, SAT-M between 500-600. 99% submitted SAT scores. **Characteristics:** 92% from in state, 86% live in college housing, 30% have minority backgrounds, 1% are foreign students. Average age is 18.

FALL-TERM APPLICATIONS. $40 fee, may be waived for applicants with need. Closing date January 15; must reply by May 1. Auditions/portfolios optional for all applicants in art, music, theater arts, dance. CRDA. Deferred and early admission available. May apply to up to 3 colleges with 1 application. Students notified by April 15.

STUDENT LIFE. Housing: Dormitories (women); apartment housing available. 7 cultural and language houses, music house available. Housing guaranteed for all students. Special housing for 100 women majoring in mathematics and science fields with 10 women graduate students serving as mentors in-residence. Substance free housing available. **Activities:** Student government, film, magazine, radio, student newspaper, television, yearbook, choral groups, concert band, dance, drama, jazz band, marching band, music ensembles, musical theater, pep band, symphony orchestra, sororities, over 100 organizations including women's center and religious and political organizations. **Additional information:** Students may participate in organizations and activities and use facilities at other undergraduate colleges of Rutgers University in New Brunswick.

ATHLETICS. NCAA. **Intercollegiate:** Basketball, cross-country, diving, fencing, field hockey, golf, gymnastics, lacrosse, rowing (crew), soccer, softball, swimming, tennis, track and field, volleyball. **Intramural:** Badminton, basketball, bowling, field hockey, golf, horseback riding, lacrosse, racquetball, rugby, sailing, skiing, skin diving, soccer, softball, squash, table tennis, tennis, volleyball, water polo.

STUDENT SERVICES. Career counseling, employment service for undergraduates, freshman orientation, health services, on-campus day care, personal counseling, placement service for graduates, special adviser for adult students, veterans counselor, services/facilities for handicapped.

ANNUAL EXPENSES. Tuition and fees: $4,225, $3,538 additional for out-of-state students. **Room and board:** $4,614. **Books and supplies:** $650.

FINANCIAL AID. 61% of freshmen, 57% of continuing students receive some form of aid. 98% of grants, 84% of loans, all jobs based on need. 389 enrolled freshmen were judged to have need, 322 were offered aid. Academic, music/drama, athletic, state/district residency, leadership, alumni affiliation, minority scholarships available. **Aid applications:** No closing date; priority given to applications received by March 1; applicants notified on a rolling basis beginning on or about April 1.

ADDRESS/TELEPHONE. Elizabeth Mitchell, Assistant Vice President of University Undergraduate Admissions, Rutgers—The State University of New Jersey: Douglass College, PO Box 2101, New Brunswick, NJ 08903-2101. (908) 932-3770.

Rutgers—The State University of New Jersey: Livingston College

New Brunswick, New Jersey CB code: 2384

Admissions: 59% of applicants accepted
Based on: ••• School record, test scores
•• Special talents
• Activities, essay, recommendations
Completion: 56% graduate

4-year public college of arts and sciences, coed. Founded in 1965. **Accreditation:** Regional. **Undergraduate enrollment:** 2,026 men, 1,390 women full time; 136 men, 93 women part time. **Faculty:** 771 total, 694 with doctorates or other terminal degrees. **Location:** Suburban campus in large town; 33 miles from New York City. **Calendar:** Semester, extensive summer session. Extensive evening/early morning classes. **Microcomputers:** 626 located in libraries, computer centers, campus-wide network. **Special facilities:** Agricultural museum; geology museum; 4 art galleries; Hutcheson Memorial Forest Ecological Preserve; large black box theater; Livingston Theater; center for urban policy research; institute for health, health care policy and aging research; journalism resources institute; laboratory for computer science research; center for mathematics, science and computer education. **Additional facts:** University has graduate programs in over 60 fields in addition to graduate professional schools of law, education, business, library/information studies, criminal justice, psychology, social work, the arts. Library, other facilities, and faculty shared by New Brunswick colleges. Students can cross-register at Newark or Camden campuses.

DEGREES OFFERED. BA, BS. 932 bachelor's degrees awarded in 1992. 8% in business and management, 14% communications, 8% letters/literature, 9% parks/recreation, protective services, public affairs, 9% psychology, 32% social sciences. Graduate degrees offered in 9 major fields of study.

UNDERGRADUATE MAJORS. Accounting, African studies, Afro-American (black) studies, American studies, anthropology, art history, Asian studies, biochemistry, biological and physical sciences, biology, biomedical science, biometrics and biostatistics, botany, business administration and management, cell biology, chemistry, chemistry, foods, and nutrition, Chinese, classics, clinical laboratory science, communications, comparative literature, computer and information sciences, criminal justice studies, dance, dramatic arts, Eastern European studies, ecology, economics, English, entomology, exercise science and sports studies, finance, fine arts, French, genetics, human and animal, geography, geology, German, Greek (classical), Hispanic American studies, history, humanities and social sciences, Italian, Jewish studies, journalism, labor/industrial relations, Latin, Latin American studies, liberal/general studies, linguistics, management science, marketing management, mathematics, medical laboratory technologies, microbiology, Middle Eastern studies, molecular biology, music, music history and appreciation, nutritional sciences, philosophy, physical education, physician's assistant, physics, physiology, human and animal, political science and government, Portuguese, psychology, public health laboratory science, Puerto Rican and Hispanic/Caribbean studies, religion, Russian, Russian and Slavic studies, social work, sociology, Spanish, special education, statistics, urban studies, visual and performing arts, women's studies.

ACADEMIC PROGRAMS. Double major, dual enrollment of high school students, honors program, independent study, internships, student-designed major, study abroad, teacher preparation, visiting/exchange student program, Washington semester, 5-year dual bachelor's degree program with College of Engineering, 5-year bachelor's/MBA program with Graduate School of Management, 8-year bachelor's/MD program with University of Medicine and Dentistry of New Jersey. 5-year bachelor's/M.Ed program with Graduate School of Education; liberal arts/career combination in engineering; combined bachelor's/graduate program in business administration, medicine. **Remedial services:** Learning center, preadmission summer program, reduced course load, remedial instruction, special counselor, tutoring, writing laboratory. **ROTC:** Air Force, Army. **Placement/credit:** AP, CLEP General, institutional tests; 30 credit hours maximum for bachelor's degree.

ACADEMIC REQUIREMENTS. Freshmen must have minimum 12 credits and higher than 1.6 GPA to remain in good academic standing. 84% of freshmen return for sophomore year. Students must declare major by end of second year. **Graduation requirements:** 120 hours for bachelor's. Most students required to take courses in arts/fine arts, English, humanities, mathematics, biological/physical sciences, social sciences.

FRESHMAN ADMISSIONS. Selection criteria: School achievement record (including grades, rank, strength of program, honors, AP) and test scores most important. Extracurricular activities, leadership talent, minority, disadvantaged status considered. **High school preparation:** 16 units required. Required and recommended units include English 4, foreign language 2, mathematics 3-4 and science 2. Mathematics requirements includes algebra I and II and geometry. 4 mathematics, 1 chemistry, 1 physics required for engineering program. **Test requirements:** SAT or ACT; score report by January 15. 3 ACH required of applicants for admission by examination (non-high school graduates, graduates of nonaccredited high schools, those without required academic courses, and some applicants with GED). Score report by January 15. **Additional information:** State residents with educationally and economically disadvantaged backgrounds given consideration through state Educational Opportunity Fund (EOF) program.

1992 FRESHMAN CLASS PROFILE. 5,563 men applied, 3,168 accepted, 356 enrolled; 6,165 women applied, 3,696 accepted, 249 enrolled. 12% were in top tenth and 62% were in top quarter of graduating class. **Academic background:** Mid 50% of enrolled freshmen had SAT-V between 430-530, SAT-M between 510-610. 99% submitted SAT scores. **Characteristics:** 89% from in state, 59% live in college housing, 37% have minority backgrounds, 2% are foreign students. Average age is 18.

FALL-TERM APPLICATIONS. $40 fee, may be waived for applicants with need. Closing date January 15; must reply by May 1. Audition/portfolio optional for all applicants in art, music, theater arts, dance. CRDA. Deferred and early admission available. May apply to up to 3 colleges with 1 application. Students notified by April 15.

STUDENT LIFE. Housing: Dormitories (coed); apartment, fraternity housing available. Freshmen and sophomores guaranteed housing. Substance-free housing available. **Activities:** Student government, film, magazine, radio, student newspaper, television, yearbook, choral groups, concert band, dance, drama, jazz band, marching band, music ensembles, musical theater, pep band, symphony orchestra, fraternities, sororities, over 100 organizations including black, Puerto Rican, and various service, religious, and political organizations, women's center. **Additional information:** Students may participate in organizations and activities and use facilities at other undergraduate colleges of Rutgers University in New Brunswick.

ATHLETICS. NCAA. **Intercollegiate:** Baseball M, basketball, cross-country, diving, fencing, field hockey W, football M, golf, gymnastics W, lacrosse, rowing (crew), soccer, softball W, swimming, tennis, track and field, volleyball W, wrestling M. **Intramural:** Badminton, basketball, bowling, field hockey, golf, horseback riding, ice hockey M, lacrosse, racquetball, rugby, sailing, skiing, skin diving, soccer, softball, squash, table tennis, tennis, volleyball, water polo, wrestling M.

STUDENT SERVICES. Career counseling, employment service for undergraduates, freshman orientation, health services, on-campus day care, personal counseling, placement service for graduates, special adviser for adult students, veterans counselor, services/facilities for handicapped.

ANNUAL EXPENSES. Tuition and fees: $4,307, $3,538 additional for out-of-state students. **Room and board:** $4,610. **Books and supplies:** $650.

FINANCIAL AID. 59% of freshmen, 50% of continuing students receive some form of aid. 91% of grants, 83% of loans, all jobs based on need. 511 enrolled freshmen were judged to have need, 440 were offered aid. Academic, music/drama, athletic, state/district residency, leadership, alumni affiliation, minority scholarships available. **Aid applications:** No closing date; priority given to applications received by March 1; applicants notified on a rolling basis beginning on or about April 1.

ADDRESS/TELEPHONE. Elizabeth Mitchell, Assistant Vice President for University Undergraduate Admissions, Rutgers—The State University of New Jersey: Livingston College, PO Box 2101, New Brunswick, NJ 08903-2101. (908) 932-3770. Fax: (908) 932-0237.

Rutgers—The State University of New Jersey: Mason Gross School of the Arts

New Brunswick, New Jersey CB code: 2736

Admissions: 27% of applicants accepted
Based on: ••• Interview, special talents
•• School record
• Activities, essay, recommendations, test scores
Completion: 55% graduate

4-year public school of the arts, coed. Founded in 1976. **Accreditation:** Regional. **Undergraduate enrollment:** 178 men, 229 women full time; 11 men, 18 women part time. **Graduate enrollment:** 66 men, 72 women full time; 30 men, 26 women part time. **Faculty:** 78 total, 70 with doctorates or other terminal degrees. **Location:** Suburban campus in large town; 33 miles from New York City. **Calendar:** Semester, extensive summer session. **Microcomputers:** 677 located in dormitories, libraries, computer centers, campus-wide network. **Special facilities:** 4 dance studios, 4 theaters, visual arts studios, fine arts complex, concert hall seating 800 people, small recital halls, proscenium theater. **Additional facts:** University has graduate programs in over 60 fields in addition to graduate professional schools of law, education, business, library/information studies, criminal justice, psychology, social work, the arts. Library and other facilities shared by New Brunswick colleges.

DEGREES OFFERED. BFA, MFA, D. 73 bachelor's degrees awarded in 1992. 100% in visual and performing arts. Graduate degrees offered in 9 major fields of study.

UNDERGRADUATE MAJORS. Dance, dramatic arts, drawing, film arts, graphic design, jazz, music education, music performance, painting, photography, printmaking, sculpture, studio art, theater design, video, visual and performing arts.

ACADEMIC PROGRAMS. Independent study, internships, study abroad, teacher preparation, visiting/exchange student program. **Remedial services:** Learning center, preadmission summer program, reduced course load, remedial instruction, special counselor, tutoring, writing laboratory. **ROTC:** Air Force, Army. **Placement/credit:** AP, CLEP General and Subject, institutional tests; 30 credit hours maximum for bachelor's degree.

ACADEMIC REQUIREMENTS. Freshmen must earn minimum GPA of 1.8 to continue in good standing. 81% of freshmen return for sophomore year. Students must declare major on application. **Graduation requirements:** 126 hours for bachelor's. Most students required to take courses in arts/fine arts, English, history, humanities, mathematics, biological/physical sciences, social sciences. **Additional information:** Teacher certification program (K-12) in music available. Students complete major in music and take teacher certification curriculum.

FRESHMAN ADMISSIONS. Selection criteria: Artistic talent and ability most important. **High school preparation:** 16 units required. Required and recommended units include English 4 and mathematics 3-4. Mathematics requirement includes algebra I and II and geometry. 2 years of one foreign language recommended. **Test requirements:** SAT or ACT. 3 ACH required of applicants for admission by examination (non-high school graduates, graduates of nonaccredited high schools, those without required academic courses, and some applicants with GED). SAT or ACT and ACH score report dates: January 15 for visual arts, March 15 for theater arts, dance, and music. **Additional information:** State residents with educationally and economically disadvantaged backgrounds given consideration through state Educational Opportunity Fund (EOF) program.

1992 FRESHMAN CLASS PROFILE. 409 men applied, 112 accepted, 43 enrolled; 565 women applied, 151 accepted, 54 enrolled. 14% were in top tenth and 33% were in top quarter of graduating class. **Academic background:** Mid 50% of enrolled freshmen had SAT-V between 420-550, SAT-M between 470-600. 99% submitted SAT scores. **Characteristics:** 88% from in state, 95% live in college housing, 19% have minority backgrounds. Average age is 18.

FALL-TERM APPLICATIONS. $40 fee, may be waived for applicants with need. Interview required for theater arts/production design applicants. Audition required for theater arts/acting, dance, music applicants. Portfolio required for visual arts applicants. CRDA. Deferred and early admission available. May apply to up to 3 colleges with 1 application. Application closing date of January 15 for visual arts and March 15 for theater arts, dance, and music. Students notified by April 15 and must reply by May 1.

STUDENT LIFE. Housing: Dormitories (men, women, coed); apartment, fraternity housing available. Freshmen and sophomores guaranteed housing. Special Interest, language and cultural houses, music house, and substances-free housing available. **Activities:** Student government, film, magazine, radio, student newspaper, television, yearbook, choral groups, concert band, dance, drama, jazz band, marching band, music ensembles, musical theater, opera, pep band, symphony orchestra, fraternities, sororities, various religious, political, and ethnic organizations, women's center. **Additional information:** Students affiliate with 1 of university's residential colleges in New Brunswick (Cook, Douglass, Livingston, Rutgers) for housing and student life services and facilities.

ATHLETICS. NCAA. **Intercollegiate:** Baseball M, basketball, cross-country, diving, fencing, field hockey W, football M, golf, gymnastics W, lacrosse, rowing (crew), soccer, softball W, swimming, tennis, track and field, volleyball W, wrestling M. **Intramural:** Badminton, basketball, bowling, field hockey, golf, horseback riding, ice hockey M, lacrosse, racquetball, rugby, sailing, skiing, skin diving, soccer, softball, squash, table tennis, tennis, volleyball, water polo, wrestling M.

STUDENT SERVICES. Career counseling, employment service for undergraduates, freshman orientation, health services, on-campus day care, personal counseling, placement service for graduates, veterans counselor, services/facilities for handicapped.

ANNUAL EXPENSES. Tuition and fees: $4,263, $3,538 additional for out-of-state students. Students pay fees of residential college with which they affiliate. Fees range from $808 to 890 per year. **Room and board:** $4,454. **Books and supplies:** $650.

FINANCIAL AID. 56% of freshmen, 54% of continuing students receive some form of aid. 99% of grants, 88% of loans, all jobs based on need. 54 enrolled freshmen were judged to have need, 43 were offered aid. Academic, music/drama, art, athletic, state/district residency, leadership, alumni affiliation, minority scholarships available. **Aid applications:** No closing date; priority given to applications received by March 1; applicants notified on a rolling basis beginning on or about April 1.

ADDRESS/TELEPHONE. Elizabeth Mitchell, Assistant Vice President for University Undergraduate Admissions, Rutgers—The State University of New Jersey: Mason Gross School of the Arts, PO Box 2101, New Brunswick, NJ 08903-2101. (908) 932-3770. Fax: (908) 932-8794.

Rutgers—The State University of New Jersey: Newark College of Arts and Sciences

Newark, New Jersey — CB code: 2512

Admissions:	51% of applicants accepted
Based on:	••• School record, test scores
	• Activities, essay, interview, recommendations, special talents
Completion:	46% graduate

4-year public college of arts and sciences, coed. Founded in 1930. **Accreditation:** Regional. **Undergraduate enrollment:** 1,575 men, 1,699 women full time; 275 men, 233 women part time. **Faculty:** 210 total, 189 with doctorates or other terminal degrees. **Location:** Urban campus in large city; 10 miles from New York City. **Calendar:** Semester, extensive summer session. **Microcomputers:** 440 located in dormitories, libraries, computer centers, campus-wide network. **Special facilities:** Biology learning center, jazz institute, animal behavior institute, center for molecular and behavioral neuroscience, center for negotiation and conflict resolution. **Additional facts:** Newark College of Arts and Science and University College Newark share faculty. University has graduate programs in over 60 fields in addition to graduate professional schools of law, education, business, library/information studies, criminal justice, psychology, social work, the arts.

DEGREES OFFERED. BA, BS. 697 bachelor's degrees awarded in 1992. 49% in business and management, 8% life sciences, 9% psychology, 12% social sciences.

UNDERGRADUATE MAJORS. Accounting, African studies, Afro-American (black) studies, American studies, anthropology, applied mathematics, applied physics, art education, art history, biochemistry, biological and physical sciences, biology, botany, chemistry, classics, clinical laboratory science, clinical laboratory sciences, communications, computer and information sciences, criminal justice studies, dramatic arts, early childhood education, economics, elementary education, English, English education, finance, fine arts, foreign languages education, French, geology, German, graphic design, Hebrew, Hispanic American studies, history, humanities and social sciences, information sciences and systems, Italian, Jewish studies, journalism, junior high education, liberal/general studies, management science, marketing management, mathematics, mathematics education, microbiology, music, music education, music history and appreciation, philosophy, physics, physiology, human and animal, political science and government, psychology, Puerto Rican studies, Russian, Russian and Slavic studies, science education, science, technology, and society, secondary education, Slavic languages, social studies education, social work, sociology, Spanish, zoology.

ACADEMIC PROGRAMS. Accelerated program, double major, dual enrollment of high school students, honors program, independent study, internships, student-designed major, study abroad, teacher preparation, Washington semester, cross-registration, dual bachelor's degree program with Rutgers College of Engineering, joint degree with University of Medicine and Dentistry of New Jersey in medical technology, 8-year bachelor's/MD degree program with University of Medicine and Dentistry of New Jersey; liberal arts/career combination in engineering; combined bachelor's/graduate program in business administration. **Remedial services:** Learning center, preadmission summer program, reduced course load, remedial instruction, special counselor, tutoring. **ROTC:** Air Force, Army. **Placement/credit:** AP, CLEP General and Subject, institutional tests; 24 credit hours maximum for bachelor's degree.

ACADEMIC REQUIREMENTS. Freshmen must earn minimum GPA of 2.0 to continue in good standing. 83% of freshmen return for sophomore year. Students must declare major by end of second year. **Graduation requirements:** 124 hours for bachelor's. Most students required to take courses in arts/fine arts, English, history, humanities, mathematics, biological/physical sciences, social sciences. **Additional information:** Teacher certification programs (K-12) available. Students complete major in field other than education and take teacher certification curriculum. Cross-registration with New Jersey Institute of Technology, University of Medicine and Dentistry of New Jersey, and Essex County College.

FRESHMAN ADMISSIONS. Selection criteria: School achievement record (including grades, rank, strength of program, honors, AP) and test scores most important. Extracurricular activities, leadership talent, minority, disadvantaged status considered. **High school preparation:** 16 units required. Required and recommended units include English 4, foreign language 2, mathematics 3-4 and science 2. Mathematics requirement includes algebra I and II and geometry. 4 mathematics, 2 chemistry, 1 physics required for engineering applicants. **Test requirements:** SAT or ACT; score report by May 1. 3 ACH required of applicants for admission by examination (non-high school graduates, graduates of nonaccredited high schools, those without required academic courses, or applicants with GED). Score report by May 1. **Additional information:** State residents with educationally and economically disadvantaged backgrounds given consideration through state Educational Opportunity Fund (EOF) program.

1992 FRESHMAN CLASS PROFILE. 2,546 men applied, 1,331 accepted, 225 enrolled; 2,131 women applied, 1,048 accepted, 276 enrolled. 22% were in top tenth and 60% were in top quarter of graduating class. **Academic background:** Mid 50% of enrolled freshmen had SAT-V between 400-490, SAT-M between 450-550. 97% submitted SAT scores. **Characteristics:** 93% from in state, 87% commute, 58% have minority backgrounds, 4% are foreign students. Average age is 18.

FALL-TERM APPLICATIONS. $40 fee, may be waived for applicants with need. Closing date May 1; applicants notified on a rolling basis; must reply by May 1 or within 2 weeks if notified thereafter. CRDA. Deferred and early admission available. May apply to up to 3 colleges with 1 application.

STUDENT LIFE. Housing: Dormitories (coed); apartment housing available. **Activities:** Student government, film, magazine, radio, student newspaper, television, yearbook, choral groups, concert band, drama, jazz band, music ensembles, musical theater, symphony orchestra, summer theater, fraternities, sororities, Black Organization of Students, Puerto Rican and Latin American student organizations, political, religious, and service organizations.

ATHLETICS. NCAA. **Intercollegiate:** Baseball M, basketball, soccer M, softball W, tennis, volleyball, wrestling M. **Intramural:** Basketball, fencing, handball, racquetball, skiing, soccer, softball, squash, swimming, tennis, track and field, volleyball, water polo.

STUDENT SERVICES. Aptitude testing, career counseling, employment service for undergraduates, freshman orientation, health services, personal counseling, placement service for graduates, veterans counselor, telecollege (home/classroom telephone hookup for immobilized students), daycare adjacent to campus, services/facilities for handicapped.

ANNUAL EXPENSES. Tuition and fees: $4,075, $3,538 additional for out-of-state students. **Room and board:** $4,624. **Books and supplies:** $650.

FINANCIAL AID. 54% of freshmen, 52% of continuing students receive some form of aid. All grants, 88% of loans, all jobs based on need. 574 enrolled freshmen were judged to have need, 495 were offered aid. Academic, state/district residency, leadership, alumni affiliation, minority scholarships available. **Aid applications:** No closing date; priority given to applications received by March 1; applicants notified on a rolling basis beginning on or about April 1.

ADDRESS/TELEPHONE. Elizabeth Mitchell, Assistant Vice President for University Undergraduate Admissions, Rutgers—The State University of New Jersey: Newark College of Arts and Sciences, 249 University Avenue, Newark, NJ 07102-1896. (201) 648-5205.

Rutgers—The State University of New Jersey: Rutgers College ⇎

New Brunswick, New Jersey CB code: 2765

Admissions: 45% of applicants accepted
Based on: ••• School record, test scores
•• Special talents
• Activities, essay, recommendations
Completion: 76% graduate

4-year public college of arts and sciences, coed. Founded in 1766. **Accreditation:** Regional. **Undergraduate enrollment:** 4,141 men, 4,041 women full time; 213 men, 155 women part time. **Faculty:** 771 total, 694 with doctorates or other terminal degrees. **Location:** Suburban campus in large town; 33 miles from New York City. **Calendar:** Semester, extensive summer session. Extensive evening/early morning classes. **Microcomputers:** 626 located in dormitories, libraries, computer centers, campus-wide network. **Special facilities:** Agricultural museum, geology museum, 4 art galleries, Hutcheson Memorial Forest Ecological Preserve, large black box theater, center for discrete mathematics and theoretical computer science, center of alcohol studies, center for critical analysis of contemporary culture, Eagleton institute of politics. **Additional facts:** University has graduate programs in over 60 fields in addition to graduate professional schools of law, education, business, library/information studies, criminal justice, psychology, social work, the arts. Library, other facilities, and faculty shared by New Brunswick colleges.

DEGREES OFFERED. BA, BS. 2,328 bachelor's degrees awarded in 1992. 8% in business and management, 7% communications, 5% languages, 13% letters/literature, 6% life sciences, 11% psychology, 33% social sciences. Graduate degrees offered in 9 major fields of study.

UNDERGRADUATE MAJORS. Accounting, African studies, Afro-American (black) studies, American studies, anthropology, art history, Asian studies, biochemistry, biological and physical sciences, biology, biomedical science, biometrics and biostatistics, botany, cell biology, chemistry, Chinese, classics, communications, comparative literature, computer and information sciences, criminal justice studies, dance, dramatic arts, Eastern European studies, ecology, economics, English, entomology, exercise science and sports studies, finance, fine arts, food science and nutrition, French, genetics, human and animal, geography, geology, German, Greek (classical), Hispanic American studies, history, humanities and social sciences, Italian, Jewish studies, journalism, labor/industrial relations, Latin, Latin American studies, liberal/general studies, linguistics, management science, marketing management, mathematics, microbiology, Middle Eastern studies, molecular biology, music, music history and appreciation, nutritional sciences, philosophy, physical education, physics, physiology, human and animal, political science and government, Portuguese, psychology, public health laboratory science, Puerto Rican and Hispanic/Caribbean studies, religion, Russian, Russian and Slavic studies, sociology, Spanish, special education, statistics, urban studies, visual and performing arts, women's studies.

ACADEMIC PROGRAMS. Double major, dual enrollment of high school students, honors program, independent study, internships, student-designed major, study abroad, teacher preparation, visiting/exchange student program, Washington semester, 5-year dual bachelor's degree program with College of Engineering, bachelor's/MBA degree program with Graduate School of Management, 8-year bachelor's/MD degree program with University of Medicine and Dentistry of New Jersey, 5-year bachelor's/M.Ed program with Graduate School of Education; liberal arts/career combination in engineering; combined bachelor's/graduate program in business administration, medicine. **Remedial services:** Learning center, preadmission summer program, reduced course load, remedial instruction, special counselor, tutoring, writing laboratory, mathematics and science learning center. **ROTC:** Air Force, Army. **Placement/credit:** AP, CLEP Subject, IB, institutional tests.

ACADEMIC REQUIREMENTS. Freshmen must earn minimum GPA of 2.0 to continue in good standing. 91% of freshmen return for sophomore year. Students must declare major by end of second year. **Graduation requirements:** 120 hours for bachelor's. Most students required to take courses in English, humanities, mathematics, biological/physical sciences, social sciences.

FRESHMAN ADMISSIONS. Selection criteria: School achievement record (including grades, rank, strength of program, honors, AP) and test scores most important. Extracurricular activities, leadership talent, minority, disadvantaged status considered. **High school preparation:** 16 units required. Required and recommended units include English 4, foreign language 2, mathematics 3-4 and science 2. Mathematics requirement includes algebra I and II and geometry. 4 mathematics, 1 chemistry, 1 physics required for engineering program. **Test requirements:** SAT or ACT; score report by January 15. 3 ACH required of applicants for admission by examination (non-high school graduates, graduates of nonaccredited high schools, those without required academic courses, and some applicants with GED). Score report by January 15. **Additional information:** State residents with educationally and economically disadvantaged backgrounds given consideration through state Educational Opportunity Fund (EOF) program.

1992 FRESHMAN CLASS PROFILE. 7,709 men applied, 3,302 accepted, 746 enrolled; 8,663 women applied, 4,052 accepted, 839 enrolled. 51% were in top tenth and 89% were in top quarter of graduating class. **Academic background:** Mid 50% of enrolled freshmen had SAT-V between 490-590, SAT-M between 560-680. 99% submitted SAT scores. **Characteristics:** 87% from in state, 83% live in college housing, 41% have minority backgrounds, 2% are foreign students. Average age is 18.

FALL-TERM APPLICATIONS. $40 fee, may be waived for applicants with need. Closing date January 15; must reply by May 1. Audition/portfolio optional for all applicants in art, music, theater arts, dance. CRDA. Deferred and early admission available. May apply to up to 3 colleges with 1 application. Students notified by April 15.

STUDENT LIFE. Housing: Dormitories (men, women, coed); apartment, fraternity housing available. Special interest housing, substance free housing available. Housing guaranteed for freshmen and sophomores. **Activities:** Student government, film, magazine, radio, student newspaper, television, yearbook, choral groups, concert band, dance, drama, jazz band, marching band, music ensembles, musical theater, opera, pep band, symphony orchestra, fraternities, sororities, over 100 religious, political, and ethnic organizations including community action group, commuter council, Afro-American society, Puerto Rican organization, and Public Interest Research Group. **Additional information:** Students may participate in organizations and activities and use facilities at other undergraduate colleges of Rutgers University in New Brunswick.

ATHLETICS. NCAA. **Intercollegiate:** Baseball M, basketball, cross-country, diving, fencing, field hockey W, football M, golf, gymnastics W, lacrosse, rowing (crew), soccer, softball W, swimming, tennis, track and field, volleyball W, wrestling M. **Intramural:** Badminton, basketball, bowling, cross-country, field hockey, golf, horseback riding, ice hockey M, lacrosse, racquetball, rugby, sailing, skiing, skin diving, soccer, softball, squash, table tennis, tennis, track and field, volleyball, water polo M, wrestling M.

STUDENT SERVICES. Career counseling, employment service for undergraduates, freshman orientation, health services, on-campus day care, personal counseling, placement service for graduates, veterans counselor, services/facilities for handicapped.

ANNUAL EXPENSES. Tuition and fees: $4,271, $3,538 additional for out-of-state students. **Room and board:** $4,596. **Books and supplies:** $650.

FINANCIAL AID. 69% of freshmen, 66% of continuing students receive some form of aid. 95% of grants, 86% of loans, all jobs based on need. 846 enrolled freshmen were judged to have need, 715 were offered aid. Academic, music/drama, athletic, state/district residency, leadership, alumni affiliation, minority scholarships available. **Aid applications:** No closing date; priority given to applications received by March 1; applicants notified on a rolling basis beginning on or about April 1.

ADDRESS/TELEPHONE. Elizabeth Mitchell, Assistant Vice President for University Undergraduate Admissions, Rutgers—The State University of New Jersey: Rutgers College, PO Box 2101, New Brunswick, NJ 08903-2101. (908) 932-3770. Fax: (908) 932-0237.

Rutgers—The State University of New Jersey: University College Camden

Camden, New Jersey CB code: 2742

4-year public college of arts and sciences, coed. Founded in 1934. **Accreditation:** Regional. **Undergraduate enrollment:** 152 men, 123 women full time; 261 men, 315 women part time. **Faculty:** 139 total, 125 with doctorates or other terminal degrees. **Location:** Urban campus in small city; One mile from Philadelphia. **Calendar:** Semester, extensive summer session. Extensive evening/early morning classes. **Microcomputers:** 156 located in libraries, classrooms, computer centers, campus-wide network. **Special facilities:** Fine arts center including theater, art gallery. **Additional facts:** Evening school providing programs of study designed for part-time, adult students. Camden College of Arts and Sciences and University College Camden share 9 faculty. Rutgers-Camden offers graduate studies in biology, English, history, physical therapy, and public administration as well as graduate professional schools of law, business, and social work.

DEGREES OFFERED. BA, BS. 29 bachelor's degrees awarded in 1992. 48% in computer sciences, 7% letters/literature, 8% physical sciences, 24% psychology, 10% social sciences.

UNDERGRADUATE MAJORS. Accounting, Afro-American (black) studies, art history, biochemistry, biological and physical sciences, biology, business administration and management, business and management, chemistry, clinical laboratory science, computer and information sciences, dramatic arts, economics, English, fine arts, French, general science, German, history, liberal/general studies, management science, marketing management, mathematics, music, nursing, philosophy, physics, political science and government, psychology, social work, sociology, Spanish, urban studies.

ACADEMIC PROGRAMS. Double major, honors program, independent study, student-designed major, study abroad, cross-registration. **Remedial services:** Learning center, preadmission summer program, reduced course load, remedial instruction, special counselor, tutoring. **ROTC:** Air Force, Army, Naval. **Placement/credit:** AP, CLEP Subject, institutional tests.

ACADEMIC REQUIREMENTS. Freshmen must earn minimum GPA of 2.0 to continue in good standing. Students must declare major by end of second year. **Graduation requirements:** 126 hours for bachelor's. Most students required to take courses in arts/fine arts, English, foreign languages, history, humanities, mathematics, philosophy/religion, biological/physical sciences, social sciences.

FRESHMAN ADMISSIONS. Selection criteria: Academic record most important. Experience, motivation, personal strength considered. **High school preparation:** 16 units required. Required and recommended units include English 4, foreign language 2 and mathematics 3-4. Mathematics requirement includes algebra I and II and geometry. **Test requirements:** SAT or ACT; score report by May 1. 3 ACH required of applicants for admission by examination (non-high school graduates, graduates of nonaccredited high schools, those without required academic courses, and some applicants with GED). Score report by May 1 New Jersey Basic Skills Examination required.

1992 FRESHMAN CLASS PROFILE. 245 men applied, 191 accepted, 51 enrolled; 245 women applied, 198 accepted, 57 enrolled. **Characteristics:** 96% from in state, 100% commute, 14% have minority backgrounds. Average age is 20.

FALL-TERM APPLICATIONS. $40 fee, may be waived for applicants with need. Closing date May 1; applicants notified on a rolling basis; must reply by May 1 or within 2 weeks if notified thereafter. Deferred admission available. May apply to up to 3 colleges with 1 application.

STUDENT LIFE. Activities: Student government, magazine, student newspaper, yearbook, fraternities, sororities.

ATHLETICS. NCAA.

STUDENT SERVICES. Aptitude testing, career counseling, employment service for undergraduates, freshman orientation, health services, personal counseling, placement service for graduates, special adviser for adult students, veterans counselor, services/facilities for handicapped.

ANNUAL EXPENSES. Tuition and fees: Tuition on per-credit-hour basis: $110/hour for in-state students, $226/hour for out-of-state students. Required fees: $176. ($88 per semester) **Books and supplies:** $650.

FINANCIAL AID. All grants, 74% of loans, all jobs based on need. 59 enrolled freshmen were judged to have need, 50 were offered aid. **Aid applications:** No closing date; priority given to applications received by March 1; applicants notified on a rolling basis. **Additional information:** Very limited funds available.

ADDRESS/TELEPHONE. Dr Elizabeth Mitchell, Assistant Vice President for University Undergraduate Admissions, Rutgers: The State University of New Jersey: University College Camden, 406 Penn Street, Camden, NJ 08102. (609) 225-6104.

Rutgers—The State University of New Jersey: University College New Brunswick

New Brunswick, New Jersey CB code: 2777

4-year public college of arts and sciences, coed. Founded in 1934. **Accreditation:** Regional. **Undergraduate enrollment:** 335 men, 345 women full time; 1,148 men, 1,421 women part time. **Faculty:** 771 total, 694 with doctorates or other terminal degrees. **Location:** Suburban campus in large town; 33 miles from New York City. **Calendar:** Semester, extensive summer session. Extensive evening/early morning classes. **Microcomputers:** 677 located in libraries, computer centers, campus-wide network. **Special facilities:** Geology museum, 4 art galleries, Hutcheson Memorial Forest Ecological Preserve, large black box theater, agricultural museum bureau of government research, center for critical analysis of contemporary culture, center for discrete mathematics and theoretical computer science. **Additional facts:** College provides undergraduate programs of study especially for adult, part-time day and evening students. University has graduate programs in over 60 fields in addition to graduate professional schools of law, education, business, library/information studies, criminal justice, psychology, social work, the arts. Library, other facilities, and faculty shared by New Brunswick colleges.

DEGREES OFFERED. BA, BS. 397 bachelor's degrees awarded in 1992. 16% in business and management, 8% communications, 6% computer sciences, 11% letters/literature, 11% psychology, 27% social sciences. Graduate degrees offered in 9 major fields of study.

UNDERGRADUATE MAJORS. Accounting, African studies, Afro-American (black) studies, American studies, anthropology, art history, Asian studies, biochemistry, biological and physical sciences, biology, biomedical science, biometrics and biostatistics, botany, cell biology, chemistry, Chinese, classics, communications, comparative literature, computer and information sciences, criminal justice studies, dance, dramatic arts, Eastern European studies, ecology, economics, English, entomology, finance, fine arts, food science and nutrition, food sciences, French, genetics, human and animal, geography, geology, German, Greek (classical), history, humanities and social sciences, Italian, Jewish studies, journalism, labor/industrial relations, Latin, Latin American studies, liberal/general studies, linguistics, management science, marketing management, mathematics, microbiology, Middle Eastern studies, molecular biology, music, music history and appreciation, nutritional sciences, philosophy, physical education, physics, physiology, human and animal, political science and government, Portuguese, professional-occupational education, psychology, public health laboratory science, Puerto Rican and Hispanic/Caribbean studies, religion, Russian, Russian and Slavic studies, sociology, Spanish, special education, statistics, technical education, urban studies, visual and performing arts, women's studies.

ACADEMIC PROGRAMS. Double major, honors program, independent study, internships, student-designed major, study abroad, teacher preparation, visiting/exchange student program, Washington semester, 5-year bachelor's/MBA program with Graduate School of Management. 5-year bachelor's/M.Ed program with Graduate School of Education; combined bachelor's/graduate program in business administration. **Remedial services:** Learning center, reduced course load, remedial instruction, special counselor, tutoring, writing laboratory. **ROTC:** Air Force, Army. **Placement/credit:** AP, CLEP General and Subject, institutional tests; 45 credit hours maximum for bachelor's degree.

ACADEMIC REQUIREMENTS. Freshmen must earn minimum GPA of 2.0 to continue in good standing. Students must declare major by end of second year. **Graduation requirements:** 120 hours for bachelor's. Most students required to take courses in English, humanities, mathematics, biological/physical sciences, social sciences.

FRESHMAN ADMISSIONS. Selection criteria: Academic record most important. Experience, motivation, personal strengths considered. Applicants applying within two years of high school graduation not considered for admission unless they have completed minimum of 24 transferable credits with 2.5 cumulative average. **High school preparation:** 16 units required. Required units include English 4, foreign language 2 and mathematics 3. Mathematics requirement includes algebra I and II and geometry. **Test requirements:** SAT or ACT; score report by June 1. School and College Ability Tests required of applicants who do not have high school diploma or who have marginal academic qualifications.

1992 FRESHMAN CLASS PROFILE. 253 men and women applied, 157 accepted; 101 enrolled. **Characteristics:** 100% from in state, 100% commute, 20% have minority backgrounds. Average age is 28.

FALL-TERM APPLICATIONS. $40 fee, may be waived for applicants with need. Closing date June 1; priority given to applications received by

May 1; applicants notified on a rolling basis beginning on or about May 1; must reply by August 1. Deferred admission available.

STUDENT LIFE. Activities: Student government, magazine, student newspaper, yearbook. **Additional information:** Full-time students may participate in sports offered through Rutgers undergraduate colleges in New Brunswick.

ATHLETICS. NCAA.

STUDENT SERVICES. Aptitude testing, career counseling, employment service for undergraduates, health services, personal counseling, placement service for graduates, special adviser for adult students, orientation program, nearby evening child care, services/facilities for handicapped.

ANNUAL EXPENSES. Tuition and fees: Tuition on per-credit-hour basis: $110/hour for in-state students, $226/hour for out-of-state students. Required fees: $158. ($79 per semester) **Books and supplies:** $650.

FINANCIAL AID. 4% of continuing students receive some form of aid. All grants, 76% of loans, all jobs based on need. 56 enrolled freshmen were judged to have need, 35 were offered aid. **Aid applications:** No closing date; priority given to applications received by April 1; applicants notified on a rolling basis. **Additional information:** Very limited funds available.

ADDRESS/TELEPHONE. S. Loretta Daniels, Director of Admissions, Rutgers—The State University of New Jersey: University College New Brunswick, 14 College Avenue, New Brunswick, NJ 08903. (908) 932-7346.

Rutgers—The State University of New Jersey: University College Newark

Newark, New Jersey — CB code: 2753

4-year public college of arts and sciences, coed. Founded in 1934. **Accreditation:** Regional. **Undergraduate enrollment:** 244 men, 261 women full time; 732 men, 763 women part time. **Faculty:** 210 total, 189 with doctorates or other terminal degrees. **Location:** Urban campus in large city; 10 miles from New York City. **Calendar:** Semester, extensive summer session. Extensive evening/early morning classes. **Microcomputers:** 440 located in libraries, computer centers, campus-wide network. **Special facilities:** Biology learning center, jazz institute, animal behavior institute, center for molecular and behavioral neuroscience, center for negotiation and conflict resolution. **Additional facts:** Evening college primarily serves adult, part-time students. Newark College of Arts and Sciences and University College Newark share faculty. University has graduate programs in over 60 fields in addition to graduate professional schools of law, education, business, library/information studies, criminal justice, psychology, social work, the arts.

DEGREES OFFERED. BA, BS. 174 bachelor's degrees awarded in 1992. 59% in business and management, 5% letters/literature, 10% parks/recreation, protective services, public affairs, 6% psychology, 17% social sciences.

UNDERGRADUATE MAJORS. Accounting, art education, computer and information sciences, criminal justice studies, early childhood education, economics, elementary education, English, English education, finance, foreign languages education, history, information sciences and systems, junior high education, management science, marketing management, mathematics, mathematics education, music education, philosophy, political science and government, psychology, science education, secondary education, social studies education, social work, sociology, Spanish.

ACADEMIC PROGRAMS. Double major, honors program, independent study, student-designed major, study abroad, teacher preparation, cross-registration, bachelor's/MBA program with Graduate School of Management; combined bachelor's/graduate program in business administration. **Remedial services:** Learning center, preadmission summer program, remedial instruction, special counselor, tutoring. **ROTC:** Air Force, Army. **Placement/credit:** AP, CLEP General and Subject, institutional tests; 45 credit hours maximum for bachelor's degree.

ACADEMIC REQUIREMENTS. Freshmen must earn minimum GPA of 2.0 to continue in good standing. Students must declare major by end of second year. **Graduation requirements:** 124 hours for bachelor's. Most students required to take courses in arts/fine arts, English, history, humanities, mathematics, biological/physical sciences, social sciences. **Additional information:** Teacher certification programs (K-12) available. Students complete major in field other than education and take teacher certification curriculum.

FRESHMAN ADMISSIONS. Selection criteria: Experience, motivation, other personal qualifications considered. **High school preparation:** 16 units required. Required and recommended units include English 4, foreign language 2 and mathematics 3-4. Mathematics requirement includes algebra I and II and geometry. **Test requirements:** SAT or ACT; score report by August 1. ACH required of applicants applying for admission by examination. Score report by August 1.

1992 FRESHMAN CLASS PROFILE. 216 men applied, 96 accepted, 46 enrolled; 304 women applied, 144 accepted, 59 enrolled. **Characteristics:** 94% from in state, 100% commute, 2% are foreign students. Average age is 22.

FALL-TERM APPLICATIONS. $40 fee, may be waived for applicants with need. Closing date August 1; priority given to applications received by May 1; applicants notified on a rolling basis beginning on or about June 1; must reply within 2 weeks. Deferred admission available. May apply to up to 3 colleges with 1 application.

STUDENT LIFE. Activities: Student government, magazine, student newspaper, yearbook, choral groups, concert band, drama, jazz band, music ensembles, symphony orchestra, honor societies.

ATHLETICS. NCAA.

STUDENT SERVICES. Aptitude testing, career counseling, employment service for undergraduates, freshman orientation, health services, personal counseling, placement service for graduates, special adviser for adult students, veterans counselor, daycare adjacent to campus, services/facilities for handicapped.

ANNUAL EXPENSES. Tuition and fees: Tuition on per-credit-hour basis: $110/hour for in-state students, $226/hour for out-of-state students. Required fees: $168. ($84 per semester) **Books and supplies:** $650.

FINANCIAL AID. All grants, 87% of loans, all jobs based on need. 166 enrolled freshmen were judged to have need, 145 were offered aid. **Aid applications:** No closing date; priority given to applications received by March 1; applicants notified on a rolling basis.

ADDRESS/TELEPHONE. Elizabeth Mitchell, Assistant Vice President for University Undergraduate Admissions, Rutgers—The State University of New Jersey: University College Newark, 249 University Avenue, Newark, NJ 07102-1896. (201) 648-5205. Fax: (201) 648-1440.

St. Peter's College

Jersey City, New Jersey — CB code: 2806

4-year private liberal arts college, coed, affiliated with Roman Catholic Church. Founded in 1872. **Accreditation:** Regional. **Undergraduate enrollment:** 925 men, 1,056 women full time; 354 men, 854 women part time. **Graduate enrollment:** 23 men, 28 women full time; 169 men, 129 women part time. **Faculty:** 420 total (120 full time), 90 with doctorates or other terminal degrees. **Location:** Urban campus in small city; 3 miles from New York City. **Calendar:** Semester, extensive summer session. Saturday and extensive evening/early morning classes. **Microcomputers:** 108 located in computer centers. **Additional facts:** Affiliated with Jesuit order. Branch location at Englewood Cliffs for adult learners.

DEGREES OFFERED. AA, AAS, BA, BS, MA, MBA, MEd. 36 associate degrees awarded in 1992. 52% in business and management, 14% business/office and marketing/distribution, 5% computer sciences, 28% social sciences. 432 bachelor's degrees awarded. 47% in business and management, 11% business/office and marketing/distribution, 6% computer sciences, 6% health sciences, 14% social sciences. Graduate degrees offered in 6 major fields of study.

UNDERGRADUATE MAJORS. Associate: Business and management, business data processing and related programs, computer and information sciences, finance, marketing management, public affairs, social sciences. **Bachelor's:** Accounting, American studies, art history, biochemistry, biology, business administration and management, business and management, chemistry, classics, computer and information sciences, cytotechnology, economics, elementary education, English, foreign languages (multiple emphasis), French, health care administration, history, humanities, liberal/general studies, marketing and distribution, marketing management, mathematics, medical laboratory technologies, nursing, philosophy, physics, political science and government, psychology, secondary education, social sciences, sociology, Spanish, special education, theological studies, toxicology, urban studies.

ACADEMIC PROGRAMS. 2-year transfer program, accelerated program, cooperative education, double major, dual enrollment of high school students, honors program, independent study, internships, student-designed major, study abroad, teacher preparation, visiting/exchange student program, Washington semester; liberal arts/career combination in health sciences. **Remedial services:** Learning center, preadmission summer program, reduced course load, remedial instruction, special counselor, tutoring. **Placement/credit:** AP, CLEP General and Subject, institutional tests; 30 credit hours maximum for bachelor's degree.

ACADEMIC REQUIREMENTS. Freshmen must earn minimum GPA of 1.8 to continue in good standing. 85% of freshmen return for sophomore year. Students must declare major by end of second year. **Graduation requirements:** 69 hours for associate (18 in major), 129 hours for bachelor's (30 in major). Most students required to take courses in arts/fine arts, English, foreign languages, history, mathematics, philosophy/religion, biological/physical sciences, social sciences. **Postgraduate studies:** 20% from 2-year programs enter 4-year programs. **Additional information:** Offers a 7-year B.S./D.D.S. program in affiliation with New York University and also a 2-year upper-division bachelor's program in nursing for registered nurses with nursing diploma or associate degree.

FRESHMAN ADMISSIONS. Selection criteria: School achievement record 80% of admissions decision, test scores 20%. Special consideration given to children of alumni. **High school preparation:** 16 units required; 18 recommended. Required and recommended units include English 4, foreign language 2, mathematics 3-4, social science 2 and science 2-3. **Test requirements:** SAT or ACT (SAT preferred); score report by August 1.

1992 FRESHMAN CLASS PROFILE. 280 men, 252 women enrolled.

17% were in top tenth and 47% were in top quarter of graduating class. **Academic background:** Mid 50% of enrolled freshmen had SAT-V between 330-450, SAT-M between 350-500. 95% submitted SAT scores. **Characteristics:** 90% from in state, 78% commute, 41% have minority backgrounds, 1% are foreign students, 1% join fraternities/sororities. Average age is 18.

FALL-TERM APPLICATIONS. $30 fee, may be waived for applicants with need. $40 fee for transfer applicants. No closing date; priority given to applications received by May 1; applicants notified on a rolling basis; must reply by May 1 or within 2 weeks if notified thereafter. Essay required. Interview recommended. CRDA. Deferred and early admission available. EDP-F.

STUDENT LIFE. Housing: Dormitories (coed). **Activities:** Student government, magazine, radio, student newspaper, yearbook, choral groups, drama, pep band, fraternities, sororities, Knights of Columbus, numerous ethnic organizations, Alpha Phi Omega, Emmaus Spiritual Retreats, circle K.

ATHLETICS. NCAA. **Intercollegiate:** Baseball M, basketball, bowling M, cross-country, diving, football M, golf, soccer, softball W, swimming, tennis, track and field, volleyball W, water polo M. **Intramural:** Basketball, bowling, boxing M, cross-country, golf, ice hockey, racquetball, soccer, softball, swimming, table tennis, tennis, volleyball, water polo.

STUDENT SERVICES. Aptitude testing, career counseling, employment service for undergraduates, freshman orientation, health services, personal counseling, placement service for graduates, special adviser for adult students, services/facilities for handicapped.

ANNUAL EXPENSES. Tuition and fees: $8,835. **Room and board:** $2,680 room only. **Books and supplies:** $600. **Other expenses:** $600.

FINANCIAL AID. 80% of freshmen, 75% of continuing students receive some form of aid. 66% of grants, 73% of loans, 61% of jobs based on need. 335 enrolled freshmen were judged to have need, 325 were offered aid. Academic, athletic, leadership scholarships available. **Aid applications:** No closing date; priority given to applications received by February 15; applicants notified on a rolling basis beginning on or about April 1. **Additional information:** Cooperative education internships available in all majors with average salaries exceeding $5,200. Maximum of 3 interships may be utilized.

ADDRESS/TELEPHONE. Mary Beth Carey, Director of Admissions, St. Peter's College, 2641 Kennedy Boulevard, Jersey City, NJ 07306-5944. (201) 915-9213. Fax: (201) 915-9458.

Salem Community College
Carneys Point, New Jersey — CB code: 2868

2-year public community college, coed. Founded in 1972. **Accreditation:** Regional. **Undergraduate enrollment:** 227 men, 366 women full time; 366 men, 594 women part time. **Faculty:** 75 total (27 full time), 6 with doctorates or other terminal degrees. **Location:** Rural campus in rural community; 25 miles from Philadelphia. **Calendar:** Semester, limited summer session. Extensive evening/early morning classes. **Microcomputers:** 125 located in libraries, classrooms, computer centers. **Special facilities:** Computer integrated manufacturing laboratory for simulations, open technology laboratory for environmental control monitoring and computer simulations.

DEGREES OFFERED. AA, AS, AAS. 111 associate degrees awarded in 1992. 17% in business and management, 25% business/office and marketing/distribution, 7% computer sciences, 16% engineering technologies, 19% allied health, 7% trade and industry.

UNDERGRADUATE MAJORS. Accounting, air conditioning/heating/refrigeration mechanics, air conditioning/heating/refrigeration technology, biology, business administration and management, business and management, business and office, chemistry, communications, community services, computer and information sciences, computer programming, computer servicing technology, computer technology, criminal justice studies, drafting, drafting and design technology, early childhood education, education, electrical and electronics equipment repair, electromechanical technology, electronic technology, engineering and engineering-related technologies, English, humanities, information sciences and systems, instrumentation technology, journalism, legal secretary, liberal/general studies, management information systems, manufacturing technology, marketing and distribution, mathematics, medical assistant, medical secretary, nuclear technologies, occupational safety and health technology, personnel management, physics, psychology, public administration, science technologies, secretarial and related programs, social sciences, sociology, word processing.

ACADEMIC PROGRAMS. 2-year transfer program, cooperative education, dual enrollment of high school students, honors program, independent study, internships, telecourses. **Remedial services:** Learning center, preadmission summer program, reduced course load, remedial instruction, special counselor, tutoring. **Placement/credit:** AP, CLEP General and Subject, institutional tests; 30 credit hours maximum for associate degree.

ACADEMIC REQUIREMENTS. No policy requiring minimum GPA; records of students having academic difficulty are reviewed individually. 45% of freshmen return for sophomore year. Students must declare major on enrollment. **Graduation requirements:** 66 hours for associate (30 in major). Most students required to take courses in computer science, English, history, humanities, mathematics, biological/physical sciences, social sciences.

FRESHMAN ADMISSIONS. Selection criteria: Open admissions. Nursing applicants must take ACT and satisfy academic prerequisites. Scientific glass technology applicants must take physical/digital coordination test.

1992 FRESHMAN CLASS PROFILE. 178 men, 289 women enrolled. **Characteristics:** 88% from in state, 100% commute, 17% have minority backgrounds, 2% are foreign students. Average age is 28.

FALL-TERM APPLICATIONS. $15 fee, may be waived for applicants with need. Closing date September 20. Interview required for scientific glassblowing, nursing applicants. Deferred and early admission available.

STUDENT LIFE. Activities: Student government, student newspaper, choral groups.

ATHLETICS. NJCAA. **Intercollegiate:** Baseball M, basketball, field hockey W, softball W, tennis. **Intramural:** Volleyball.

STUDENT SERVICES. Aptitude testing, career counseling, employment service for undergraduates, freshman orientation, health services, personal counseling, placement service for graduates, veterans counselor, services/facilities for handicapped.

ANNUAL EXPENSES. Tuition and fees (1992-93): $1,458, $300 additional for out-of-district students, $300 additional for out-of-state students. **Books and supplies:** $600. **Other expenses:** $775.

FINANCIAL AID. 94% of grants, 96% of loans, all jobs based on need. Academic, athletic scholarships available. **Aid applications:** No closing date; priority given to applications received by March 1; applicants notified on a rolling basis beginning on or about May 1.

ADDRESS/TELEPHONE. Teresa Haman, Coordinator of Admissions, Salem Community College, 460 Hollywood Avenue, Carneys Point, NJ 08069-2799. (609) 299-2100 ext. 309. Fax: (609) 299-6740.

Seton Hall University
South Orange, New Jersey — CB code: 2811

Admissions: 77% of applicants accepted
Based on: ••• School record, test scores
•• Essay, interview, recommendations
• Activities, special talents
Completion: 86% of freshmen end year in good standing
62% graduate, 25% of these enter graduate study

4-year private university, coed, affiliated with Roman Catholic Church. Founded in 1856. **Accreditation:** Regional. **Undergraduate enrollment:** 2,196 men, 2,238 women full time; 361 men, 651 women part time. **Graduate enrollment:** 761 men, 731 women full time; 1,239 men, 1,693 women part time. **Faculty:** 640 total (336 full time). **Location:** Suburban campus in large town; 14 miles from New York City. **Calendar:** Semester, extensive summer session. **Microcomputers:** 350 located in dormitories, libraries, classrooms, computer centers. **Special facilities:** Museum, computer graphics and communications laboratories, educational media center, nursing demonstration room, art center, recreation center, music laboratories. **Additional facts:** Immaculate Conception seminary and school of theology located on campus. Off-campus sites for nursing and education.

DEGREES OFFERED. BA, BS, MA, MS, MBA, PhD, EdD, JD, M.Div. 1,011 bachelor's degrees awarded in 1992. 38% in business and management, 13% communications, 6% education, 5% health sciences, 5% letters/literature, 7% psychology, 16% social sciences. Graduate degrees offered in 39 major fields of study.

UNDERGRADUATE MAJORS. Accounting, advertising, Afro-American (black) studies, anthropology, art education, Asian studies, biology, business administration and management, business economics, chemistry, Chinese, classics, communications, computer and information sciences, computer graphics, criminal justice studies, economics, education, education of the deaf and hearing impaired, education of the emotionally handicapped, education of the gifted and talented, education of the mentally handicapped, education of the multiple handicapped, education of the physically handicapped, education of the visually handicapped, elementary education, English, English education, finance, fine arts, foreign languages (multiple emphasis), foreign languages education, French, health education, history, Italian, Japanese, journalism, liberal/general studies, management information systems, marketing and distribution, marketing management, mathematics, mathematics education, music, music education, music history and appreciation, nursing, philosophy, physical education, physics, political science and government, psychology, radio/television broadcasting, religion, religious education, science education, secondary education, social science education, social studies education, social work, sociology, Spanish, special education, visual and performing arts.

ACADEMIC PROGRAMS. Accelerated program, cooperative education, double major, education specialist degree, honors program, independent study, internships, study abroad, teacher preparation, visiting/exchange student program, Washington semester, cross-registration, Plus Program for disadvantaged students; liberal arts/career combination in engineering; combined bachelor's/graduate program in business administration. **Remedial services:** Learning center, preadmission summer program, reduced course load, remedial instruction, special counselor, tutoring, educational opportunity programs for disadvantaged students. **ROTC:** Air Force, Army. **Placement/**

credit: AP, CLEP General and Subject, institutional tests; 30 credit hours maximum for bachelor's degree.

ACADEMIC REQUIREMENTS. Freshmen must earn minimum GPA of 1.75 to continue in good standing. 86% of freshmen return for sophomore year. Students must declare major by end of second year. **Graduation requirements:** 130 hours for bachelor's (45 in major). Most students required to take courses in arts/fine arts, computer science, English, foreign languages, history, humanities, mathematics, philosophy/religion, biological/physical sciences, social sciences. **Postgraduate studies:** 4% enter law school, 2% enter medical school, 19% enter other graduate study.

FRESHMAN ADMISSIONS. Selection criteria: School achievement record and test scores most important. Teacher and counselor recommendations and interview recommended. Special consideration given to children of alumni. School and community activities significant. SAT: 500 math and 450 verbal recommended scores. **High school preparation:** 16 units required. Required and recommended units include English 4, foreign language 2, mathematics 3, physical science 1-2, social science 2 and science 1. One laboratory science also required. **Test requirements:** SAT or ACT; score report by April 1.

1992 FRESHMAN CLASS PROFILE. 2,142 men applied, 1,680 accepted, 508 enrolled; 2,503 women applied, 1,894 accepted, 492 enrolled. 13% were in top tenth and 44% were in top quarter of graduating class. **Academic background:** Mid 50% of enrolled freshmen had SAT-V between 400-490, SAT-M between 440-550. 99% submitted SAT scores. **Characteristics:** 82% from in state, 60% live in college housing, 26% have minority backgrounds. Average age is 18.

FALL-TERM APPLICATIONS. $25 fee, may be waived for applicants with need. No closing date; priority given to applications received by March 1; applicants notified on a rolling basis beginning on or about February 1; must reply by May 1 or within 4 weeks if notified thereafter. Interview recommended. Essay recommended. CRDA. Deferred admission available. Students who reside in Puerto Rico may submit the SAT or the TOEFL with their PAA scores.

STUDENT LIFE. Housing: Dormitories (women, coed); apartment, handicapped housing available. Quiet floors and Modern Languages floor available. **Activities:** Student government, magazine, radio, student newspaper, yearbook, choral groups, drama, musical theater, pep band, fraternities, sororities, Adelante, Black Students Union, international students organization, community service organizations, campus ministry, Puerto Rican Institute, Amnesty International, Student Ambassadors.

ATHLETICS. NCAA. **Intercollegiate:** Baseball M, basketball, cross-country, diving, golf M, gymnastics W, soccer M, softball W, swimming, tennis, track and field, volleyball W, wrestling M. **Intramural:** Badminton, basketball, bowling, diving, handball, ice hockey M, lacrosse M, racquetball, rifle, rugby M, soccer, softball, squash, swimming, table tennis, tennis, volleyball, water polo.

STUDENT SERVICES. Aptitude testing, career counseling, employment service for undergraduates, freshman orientation, health services, personal counseling, placement service for graduates, special adviser for adult students, services/facilities for handicapped.

ANNUAL EXPENSES. Tuition and fees: $11,485. **Room and board:** $6,254. **Books and supplies:** $650. **Other expenses:** $1,147.

FINANCIAL AID. 75% of freshmen, 70% of continuing students receive some form of aid. 60% of grants, 95% of loans, 35% of jobs based on need. 740 enrolled freshmen were judged to have need, 730 were offered aid. Academic, athletic, alumni affiliation, religious affiliation, minority scholarships available. **Aid applications:** No closing date; priority given to applications received by April 1; applicants notified on a rolling basis beginning on or about April 15; must reply by May 1 or within 2 weeks if notified thereafter.

ADDRESS/TELEPHONE. Patricia Burgh, Dean of Enrollment Services, Seton Hall University, 400 South Orange Avenue, South Orange, NJ 07079-2689. (201) 761-9332. (800) THE-HALL. Fax: (201) 761-9452.

Stevens Institute of Technology

Hoboken, New Jersey CB code: 2819

Admissions: 73% of applicants accepted
Based on:
- ••• School record
- •• Activities, recommendations, test scores
- • Essay, interview, special talents

Completion: 73% graduate, 15% of these enter graduate study

4-year private university and engineering college, coed. Founded in 1870. **Accreditation:** Regional. **Undergraduate enrollment:** 1,016 men, 260 women full time. **Graduate enrollment:** 452 men, 108 women full time; 1,041 men, 319 women part time. **Faculty:** 240 total (150 full time), 140 with doctorates or other terminal degrees. **Location:** Urban campus in large town; One mile from New York City. **Calendar:** Semester, limited summer session. **Microcomputers:** 1,600 located in dormitories, libraries, classrooms, computer centers, campus-wide network. Lease or purchase required**Special facilities:** Davidson Laboratory-coastal and ocean engineering, Nicoll Environmental Laboratory, Design and Manufacturing Institute. **Additional facts:** Concentrations available in premed, prelaw, co-op education. Graduate level courses available for undergraduates, accelerated premed and prelaw programs.

DEGREES OFFERED. BA, BS, MS, PhD. 215 bachelor's degrees awarded in 1992. 75% in engineering, 22% physical sciences. Graduate degrees offered in 55 major fields of study.

UNDERGRADUATE MAJORS. American literature, analytical chemistry, applied mathematics, atomic/molecular physics, biochemistry, bioengineering and biomedical engineering, biological and physical sciences, biophysics, business administration and management, business and management, cell biology, chemical engineering, chemistry, city/community/regional planning, civil engineering, computer and information sciences, computer engineering, computer mathematics, economics, electrical/electronics/communications engineering, electron physics, elementary particle physics, engineering, engineering and other disciplines, engineering management, engineering physics, English, English literature, environmental design, environmental health engineering, environmental science, fluids and plasmas, genetics, human and animal, history, humanities, humanities and social sciences, industrial and organizational psychology, information sciences and systems, inorganic chemistry, management information systems, management science, materials engineering, mathematics, mechanical engineering, metallurgical engineering, metallurgy, microbiology, molecular biology, nuclear engineering, nuclear physics, ocean engineering, optics, organic chemistry, philosophy, physical chemistry, physics, Polymer engineering, predentistry, prelaw, premedicine, psychology, pure mathematics, robotics, social sciences, sociology, solid state physics, statistics, systems analysis, urban design.

ACADEMIC PROGRAMS. Accelerated program, cooperative education, double major, honors program, independent study, internships, study abroad, visiting/exchange student program, cross-registration, 4-year bachelor's/master's programs in all disciplines; liberal arts/career combination in engineering; combined bachelor's/graduate program in business administration, medicine, law. **Remedial services:** Reduced course load, remedial instruction, special counselor, tutoring. **ROTC:** Air Force, Army. **Placement/credit:** AP, institutional tests; 21 credit hours maximum for bachelor's degree.

ACADEMIC REQUIREMENTS. Freshmen must earn minimum GPA of 2.0 to continue in good standing. 85% of freshmen return for sophomore year. Students must declare major by end of second year. **Graduation requirements:** 154 hours for bachelor's (48 in major). Most students required to take courses in computer science, English, humanities, mathematics, biological/physical sciences, social sciences. **Postgraduate studies:** 1% enter law school, 2% enter medical school, 3% enter MBA programs, 9% enter other graduate study. **Additional information:** Freshman intersession is available for course grade improvements before spring.

FRESHMAN ADMISSIONS. Selection criteria: School achievement record and test scores most important. School and community activities, recommendations considered. **High school preparation:** 16 units required. Required and recommended units include biological science 1, English 4, foreign language 2, mathematics 4 and physical science 2. Social science 2 recommended. Engineering, computer science, and science programs require 4 mathematics, 1 chemistry, 1 physics, 1 other science. **Test requirements:** SAT or ACT (SAT preferred); score report by April 1. ACH required as requested by admissions counselor. Score report by April 1.

1992 FRESHMAN CLASS PROFILE. 1,054 men applied, 773 accepted, 272 enrolled; 316 women applied, 222 accepted, 68 enrolled. 88% had high school GPA of 3.0 or higher, 12% between 2.0 and 2.99. 51% were in top tenth and 73% were in top quarter of graduating class. **Academic background:** Mid 50% of enrolled freshmen had SAT-V between 460-570, SAT-M between 560-690. 96% submitted SAT scores. **Characteristics:** 63% from in state, 80% live in college housing, 42% have minority backgrounds, 6% are foreign students, 45% join fraternities/sororities. Average age is 18.

FALL-TERM APPLICATIONS. $35 fee, may be waived for applicants with need. Closing date March 1; applicants notified on a rolling basis; must reply by May 1 or within 3 weeks if notified thereafter. Interview required. Essay recommended. CRDA. Deferred and early admission available. EDP-S. Additional interview with departmental committee for applicants to accelerated premed, predentistry, and prelaw programs.

STUDENT LIFE. Housing: Dormitories (men, women, coed); apartment, fraternity, sorority housing available. Housing guaranteed all four years for undergraduates. Freshmen not living at home must live on campus. **Activities:** Student government, magazine, radio, student newspaper, television, yearbook, literary publications, freshman handbook, senior booklet, choral groups, concert band, drama, jazz band, music ensembles, musical theater, pep band, fraternities, sororities, foreign student clubs, Newman Club, Jewish and Protestant fellowships, Black Student Union, Latin American Association. **Additional information:** Honor system observed.

ATHLETICS. NCAA. **Intercollegiate:** Baseball M, basketball M, cross-country M, fencing, ice hockey M, lacrosse M, sailing, skiing, soccer M, squash M, tennis, volleyball, wrestling M. **Intramural:** Archery, basketball, football, golf, gymnastics, horseback riding, ice hockey M, racquetball, rugby, skiing, soccer, softball, squash, tennis, track and field M, volleyball.

STUDENT SERVICES. Aptitude testing, career counseling, employment service for undergraduates, freshman orientation, health services,

personal counseling, placement service for graduates, faculty advisers for all students, services/facilities for handicapped.

ANNUAL EXPENSES. Tuition and fees: $16,740. Freshmen must purchase computer for $1,890 or lease computer at $55 **Room and board:** $5,680. **Books and supplies:** $450. **Other expenses:** $570.

FINANCIAL AID. 70% of freshmen, 75% of continuing students receive some form of aid. 66% of grants, 82% of loans, all jobs based on need. 277 enrolled freshmen were judged to have need, all were offered aid. Academic, leadership, alumni affiliation scholarships available. **Aid applications:** No closing date; priority given to applications received by February 1; applicants notified on a rolling basis beginning on or about March 15; must reply by May 1. **Additional information:** Early financial aid estimate form available for applicants.

ADDRESS/TELEPHONE. Maureen Weatherall, Dean of Admissions and Financial Aid, Stevens Institute of Technology, Castle Point on the Hudson, Hoboken, NJ 07030. (201) 216-5194. (800) 458-LEAD. Fax: (201) 216-1606.

Stockton State College
Pomona, New Jersey CB code: 2889

Admissions: 43% of applicants accepted
Based on: ••• School record, test scores
•• Activities, essay
• Interview, recommendations, special talents
Completion: 94% of freshmen end year in good standing
56% graduate, 39% of these enter graduate study

4-year public liberal arts college, coed. Founded in 1969. **Accreditation:** Regional. **Undergraduate enrollment:** 2,104 men, 2,220 women full time; 293 men, 437 women part time. **Faculty:** 293 total (190 full time), 173 with doctorates or other terminal degrees. **Location:** Suburban campus in small town; 12 miles from Atlantic City, 50 miles from Philadelphia. **Calendar:** Semester, extensive summer session. Saturday and extensive evening/early morning classes. **Microcomputers:** 750 located in dormitories, libraries, classrooms, computer centers. **Special facilities:** Natural environmental laboratory, marina, art gallery, observatory, performing arts center, holocaust center.

DEGREES OFFERED. BA, BS. 1,030 bachelor's degrees awarded in 1992. 39% in business and management, 5% computer sciences, 7% allied health, 9% life sciences, 7% psychology, 22% social sciences.

UNDERGRADUATE MAJORS. Accounting, actuarial sciences, advertising, anthropology, biological and physical sciences, biology, business administration and management, business and management, chemistry, computer and information sciences, computer graphics, criminal justice studies, criminology, dance, drawing, economics, engineering and other disciplines, English, English education, English literature, environmental science, fine arts, foreign languages (multiple emphasis), French, geology, health care administration, health sciences, history, humanities and social sciences, information sciences and systems, journalism, Latin, law enforcement and corrections, liberal/general studies, management information systems, marine biology, marketing and distribution, mathematics, mathematics education, medical social work, music, music performance, music theory and composition, nursing, oceanography, philosophy, photography, physical therapy, physics, political science and government, preengineering, prelaw, premedicine, psychology, public health laboratory science, public relations, radio/television broadcasting, religion, renewable natural resources, science education, secondary education, social science education, social studies education, social work, sociology, Spanish, speech pathology/audiology, statistics, systems analysis, video, visual and performing arts.

ACADEMIC PROGRAMS. Accelerated program, cooperative education, double major, dual enrollment of high school students, honors program, independent study, internships, student-designed major, study abroad, teacher preparation, weekend college, Washington semester, joint bachelor's/master's degree program in engineering with New Jersey Institute of Technology; joint bachelor's/first professional degree programs in medicine with UMDNJ-New Jersey School of Osteopathic Medicine, UMDNJ-New Jersey Dental School, UMDNJ-New Jersey Medical School, UMDNJ-Robert Wood Johnson Medical School, Pennsylvania College of Podiatric Medicine, New York College of Podiatric Medicine, and in veterinary medicine with Cornell University; liberal arts/career combination in engineering, health sciences. **Remedial services:** Learning center, preadmission summer program, remedial instruction, tutoring, basic skills courses. **Placement/credit:** AP, CLEP Subject, IB, institutional tests; 32 credit hours maximum for bachelor's degree.

ACADEMIC REQUIREMENTS. Freshmen must earn minimum GPA of 2.0 to continue in good standing. 84% of freshmen return for sophomore year. Students must declare major by end of second year. **Graduation requirements:** 128 hours for bachelor's (64 in major). Most students required to take courses in computer science, English, biological/physical sciences, social sciences. **Postgraduate studies:** 2% enter law school, 3% enter medical school, 16% enter MBA programs, 18% enter other graduate study.

FRESHMAN ADMISSIONS. Selection criteria: Rank in top 25% of class, recommendations, and test scores most important. Essay, extracurricular activities, and work experience also considered. **High school preparation:** 16 units required. Required units include English 4, mathematics 3 and social science 2. 2 laboratory sciences required. **Test requirements:** SAT or ACT (SAT preferred); score report by May 1. English, Mathematics Level I or II, Chemistry or Physics required for premed applicants. **Additional information:** Generally, accepted students who do not enroll must reapply and be reconsidered for admission, deferred admission on case-by-case basis.

1992 FRESHMAN CLASS PROFILE. 1,772 men applied, 757 accepted, 325 enrolled; 1,920 women applied, 821 accepted, 416 enrolled. 17% were in top tenth and 55% were in top quarter of graduating class. **Academic background:** Mid 50% of enrolled freshmen had SAT-V between 450-530, SAT-M between 520-580. 95% submitted SAT scores. **Characteristics:** 97% from in state, 90% live in college housing, 18% have minority backgrounds, 1% are foreign students, 6% join fraternities/sororities. Average age is 18.

FALL-TERM APPLICATIONS. $25 fee, may be waived for applicants with need. Closing date May 1; applicants notified on a rolling basis beginning on or about January 1; must reply by June 30. Essay required. Interview recommended for academically underprepared applicants. Audition recommended for visual and performing arts (dance) applicants. CRDA. Early admission available.

STUDENT LIFE. Housing: Dormitories (coed); apartment housing available. **Activities:** Student government, film, magazine, radio, student newspaper, television, yearbook, poetry book, choral groups, dance, drama, music ensembles, musical theater, fraternities, sororities, Christian Fellowship, Hillel, women's union, Jewish Activities Club, Unified Black Students Society, Los Latinos Unidos, 70 clubs.

ATHLETICS. NCAA. **Intercollegiate:** Basketball, cross-country, lacrosse M, rowing (crew), soccer, softball W, track and field, volleyball W. **Intramural:** Baseball M, basketball M, bowling, diving, fencing, gymnastics, horseback riding, ice hockey M, lacrosse M, racquetball, skiing, soccer W, softball, swimming, tennis, volleyball, wrestling M.

STUDENT SERVICES. Aptitude testing, career counseling, employment service for undergraduates, freshman orientation, health services, on-campus day care, personal counseling, placement service for graduates, veterans counselor, services/facilities for handicapped.

ANNUAL EXPENSES. Tuition and fees (projected): $2,648, $600 additional for out-of-state students. No additional charges for out-of-state and foreign students during summer session. **Room and board:** $4,288. **Books and supplies:** $725. **Other expenses:** $1,125.

FINANCIAL AID. 76% of freshmen, 78% of continuing students receive some form of aid. 91% of grants, 77% of loans, 25% of jobs based on need. Academic, state/district residency, leadership scholarships available. **Aid applications:** No closing date; priority given to applications received by March 1; applicants notified on a rolling basis beginning on or about June 1; must reply within 2 weeks.

ADDRESS/TELEPHONE. Sal Catalfamo, Dean of Admissions and Freshman Scholarship Programs, Stockton State College, Jim Leeds Road, Pomona, NJ 08240-9988. (609) 652-4261. Fax: (608) 652-4958.

Sussex County Community College
Newton, New Jersey CB code: 2711

2-year public community college, coed. Founded in 1981. **Accreditation:** Regional candidate. **Undergraduate enrollment:** 339 men, 415 women full time; 554 men, 1,112 women part time. **Faculty:** 103 total (28 full time), 22 with doctorates or other terminal degrees. **Location:** Suburban campus in small town; Approximately 70 miles from New York City. **Calendar:** Semester, limited summer session. Saturday and extensive evening/early morning classes. **Microcomputers:** 95 located in classrooms, computer centers. **Special facilities:** Art gallery. **Additional facts:** Extension sites at Sussex County Vocational Technical School, Lenape Valley High School, and Newton High School.

DEGREES OFFERED. AA, AS, AAS. 41 associate degrees awarded in 1992. 49% in business and management, 49% multi/interdisciplinary studies.

UNDERGRADUATE MAJORS. Business administration and management, liberal/general studies, secretarial and related programs.

ACADEMIC PROGRAMS. 2-year transfer program, double major, dual enrollment of high school students, honors program, independent study, internships, telecourses. **Remedial services:** Learning center, reduced course load, remedial instruction, special counselor, tutoring, extended course completion time for learning disabled students. **Placement/credit:** AP, CLEP General and Subject, institutional tests; 30 credit hours maximum for associate degree.

ACADEMIC REQUIREMENTS. Freshmen must earn minimum GPA of 1.4 to continue in good standing. Second semester freshmen must earn minimum GPA of 1.6. 50% of freshmen return for sophomore year. Students must declare major by end of first year. **Graduation requirements:** 61 hours for associate (15 in major). Most students required to take courses in arts/fine arts, computer science, English, foreign languages, history, humanities, mathematics, philosophy/religion, biological/physical sciences, social sciences.

FRESHMAN ADMISSIONS. Selection criteria: Open admissions.

Applicants to all programs required to pass New Jersey Basic Skills test. Those failing any part of test must satisfactorily complete remedial study in appropriate area(s) before advancing to any program of study.

1992 FRESHMAN CLASS PROFILE. 202 men, 302 women enrolled. **Characteristics:** 99% from in state, 100% commute, 4% have minority backgrounds. Average age is 19.

FALL-TERM APPLICATIONS. $15 fee. No closing date; applicants notified on a rolling basis; must reply by registration.

STUDENT LIFE. Activities: Student government, magazine, student newspaper, choral groups, Student Ambassadors, business club, humanities club, environmental studies club.

ATHLETICS. NJCAA. **Intercollegiate:** Baseball M, basketball M, soccer M, softball W. **Intramural:** Archery, badminton, basketball, softball, table tennis, volleyball. **Clubs:** Flag football, floor hockey.

STUDENT SERVICES. Aptitude testing, career counseling, employment service for undergraduates, freshman orientation, personal counseling, placement service for graduates, veterans counselor, learning disabled counseling, services/facilities for handicapped.

ANNUAL EXPENSES. Tuition and fees (projected): $1,584, $1,392 additional for out-of-district students, $2,784 additional for out-of-state students. **Books and supplies:** $600. **Other expenses:** $966.

FINANCIAL AID. 40% of freshmen, 40% of continuing students receive some form of aid. 68% of grants, 88% of loans, all jobs based on need. Academic, leadership scholarships available. **Aid applications:** Closing date August 1; priority given to applications received by March 1; applicants notified on a rolling basis; must reply within 2 weeks.

ADDRESS/TELEPHONE. Harold Damato, Director Admissions/Registration, Sussex County Community College, College Hill, Newton, NJ 07860. (201) 579-5400 ext. 218. Fax: (201) 579-1620.

Talmudical Academy of New Jersey
Adelphia, New Jersey CB code: 0686

4-year private rabbinical college, men only, affiliated with Jewish faith. Founded in 1967. **Undergraduate enrollment:** 30 men full time. **Location:** Suburban campus in large town; near Freehold. **Calendar:** Semester. **Additional facts:** Ordination available.

FRESHMAN ADMISSIONS. Selection criteria: Personal interview most important.

ANNUAL EXPENSES. Tuition and fees (1992-93): Comprehensive fee: $6,500.

ADDRESS/TELEPHONE. Rabbi G. Finkel, Registrar and Admissions Director, Talmudical Academy of New Jersey, Route 524, PO Box 7, Adelphia, NJ 07710. (908) 431-1600.

Thomas Edison State College
Trenton, New Jersey CB code: 0682

4-year public business, liberal arts college, coed. Founded in 1972. **Accreditation:** Regional. **Undergraduate enrollment:** 5,250 men, 3,362 women part time. **Location:** Urban campus in small city; 60 miles from New York City, 40 miles from Philadelphia. **Calendar:** Students may enroll at any time. Degrees conferred bi-monthly. **Additional facts:** College offers instruction through guided independent study. College credits earned elsewhere accepted in transfer. Entire degree may be obtained based on demonstration of knowledge from previous experiences, as long as degree requirements are met. No residency requirement. Out-of-state students need not travel to New Jersey to earn degree.

DEGREES OFFERED. AA, AS, AAS, BA, BS. 283 associate degrees awarded in 1992. 22% in business and management, 32% engineering technologies, 43% multi/interdisciplinary studies. 516 bachelor's degrees awarded. 23% in business and management, 35% engineering technologies, 16% letters/literature, 8% life sciences, 13% social sciences.

UNDERGRADUATE MAJORS. Associate: Accounting, agricultural mechanics, air traffic control, aircraft mechanics, airline piloting and navigation, architectural technologies, biology, business and management, business data processing and related programs, business data programming, chemistry, child development/care/guidance, civil technology, community services, computer and information sciences, computer technology, construction, contract management and procurement/purchasing, criminal justice studies, data processing, drafting and design technology, electrical technology, electronic technology, engineering and engineering-related technologies, family and community services, finance, fire protection, food science and nutrition, forestry and related sciences, health care administration, histotechnology, horticultural science, hotel/motel and restaurant management, human resources development, industrial technology, insurance and risk management, international business management, liberal/general studies, marketing and distribution, marketing management, mathematics, nuclear technologies, office supervision and management, operations research, physical sciences, physics, public administration, real estate, recreation and community services technologies, rehabilitation counseling/services, retailing, social sciences, survey and mapping technology, transportation management, water and wastewater technology, water resources. **Bachelor's:** Accounting, Afro-American (black) studies, agricultural mechanics, air traffic control, aircraft mechanics, airline piloting and navigation, American studies, anthropology, archeology, architectural technologies, art therapy, Asian studies, biological and physical sciences, biological laboratory technology, biology, biomedical equipment technology, business administration and management, business and management, business data processing and related programs, chemistry, child development/care/guidance, civil technology, clinical laboratory science, communications, community services, computer and information sciences, computer technology, construction, contract management and procurement/purchasing, criminal justice studies, dance, data processing, dental hygiene, drafting and design technology, economics, electrical technology, electronic technology, engineering and engineering-related technologies, English, English literature, family and community services, finance, fine arts, fire protection, food science and nutrition, foreign languages (multiple emphasis), forestry and related sciences, geography, geriatric services, health care administration, history, horticultural science, hotel/motel and restaurant management, human resources development, humanities, industrial technology, information sciences and systems, insurance and risk management, international business management, journalism, labor/industrial relations, marketing and distribution, marketing management, mathematics, medical laboratory technologies, mental health/human services, music, nuclear medical technology, nuclear technologies, nursing, office supervision and management, operations research, personnel management, philosophy, photography, physical sciences, physics, political science and government, psychology, public administration, radiograph medical technology, real estate, recreation and community services technologies, rehabilitation counseling/services, religion, respiratory therapy, respiratory therapy technology, retailing, social sciences, sociology, survey and mapping technology, transportation management, urban studies, water and wastewater technology, water resources, women's studies.

ACADEMIC PROGRAMS. 2-year transfer program, computer delivered (on-line) credit-bearing course offerings, external degree, independent study, telecourses, cross-registration. **Placement/credit:** AP, CLEP General and Subject, institutional tests; 60 credit hours maximum for associate degree; 120 credit hours maximum for bachelor's degree.

ACADEMIC REQUIREMENTS. Freshmen must earn minimum GPA of 2.0 to continue in good standing. Students must declare major on enrollment. **Graduation requirements:** 60 hours for associate (18 in major), 120 hours for bachelor's (33 in major). Most students required to take courses in computer science, English, humanities, mathematics, biological/physical sciences, social sciences. **Postgraduate studies:** 60% from 2-year programs enter 4-year programs. **Additional information:** No time limit on degree completion. 10-year limit for credits transferred into business administration. 5-year limit for technical services, radiology technology degrees.

FRESHMAN ADMISSIONS. Selection criteria: Open admissions. Certain programs in health professions limited to persons holding appropriate certification. Admission to bachelor's degree nursing program limited to registered nurses who live or work in New Jersey. Applicants should be at least 21 years old. Applicants without high school diploma accepted on case-by-case basis.

FALL-TERM APPLICATIONS. $75 fee. No closing date; applicants notified on a rolling basis; must reply within 1 year of date of application. Deferred admission available.

STUDENT SERVICES. Special adviser for adult students, veterans counselor, computer predictive tests, services/facilities for handicapped.

ANNUAL EXPENSES. Tuition and fees (projected): Annual enrollment fee: $375 for state residents, $665 for out-of-state, $850 for international students. Credit transfer fee charged on sliding scale. Fees for credit by college examination, $30 per test for state residents, $45 per test for out-of-state. Portfolio assessment: $12 per credit for state residents, $18 per credit for out-of-state.

FINANCIAL AID. 1% of continuing students receive some form of aid. All grants, all loans based on need. **Aid applications:** Closing date August 1; applicants notified on a rolling basis; must reply within 30 days.

ADDRESS/TELEPHONE. Janice Toliver, Director of Admissions Services, Thomas Edison State College, 101 West State Street, Trenton, NJ 08608-1176. (609) 984-1150. Fax: (609) 984-8447.

Trenton State College
Trenton, New Jersey CB code: 2519

Admissions: 42% of applicants accepted
Based on: ••• School record, test scores
•• Activities, special talents
• Essay, interview, recommendations
Completion: 94% of freshmen end year in good standing
67% graduate, 13% of these enter graduate study

4-year public liberal arts college, coed. Founded in 1855. **Accreditation:** Regional. **Undergraduate enrollment:** 1,900 men, 3,246 women full time; 356 men, 647 women part time. **Graduate enrollment:** 18 men, 66 women full time; 167 men, 717 women part time. **Faculty:** 526 total (316 full time), 271 with doctorates or other terminal degrees. **Location:** Suburban campus in large town; 6 miles from Trenton, 10 miles from Princeton. **Calendar:** Semester, limited summer session. Extensive evening/early morning classes. **Microcomputers:** 420 located in libraries, classrooms, computer centers. **Special facilities:** Art gallery, observatory, oceanographic center, comprehensive microscopy facility, 16 computer laboratories. **Additional facts:** College comprised of 5 academic schools: arts and sciences, business, education, nursing, and engineering.

DEGREES OFFERED. BA, BS, BFA, MA, MS, MEd. 1,199 bachelor's degrees awarded in 1992. 14% in business and management, 7% communications, 34% teacher education, 6% engineering technologies, 7% letters/literature, 7% parks/recreation, protective services, public affairs, 5% psychology, 5% social sciences, 5% visual and performing arts. Graduate degrees offered in 14 major fields of study.

UNDERGRADUATE MAJORS. Accounting, art education, art therapy, biology, business administration and management, business and management, business economics, chemistry, communications, computer and information sciences, criminal justice studies, early childhood education, economics, education of the deaf and hearing impaired, elementary education, engineering science, English, English education, finance, fine arts, graphic design, health education, history, interior design, journalism, management science, marketing management, mathematics, mathematics education, music, music education, nursing, office supervision and management, philosophy, physical education, physics, political science and government, prelaw, premedicine, psychology, public administration, science education, social studies education, sociology, special education, speech, speech correction, speech pathology/audiology, statistics, studio art, technical and business writing, technology education, television and theather production.

ACADEMIC PROGRAMS. Double major, honors program, independent study, internships, study abroad, teacher preparation, visiting/exchange student program, joint BS/MD program with UMDNJ-New Jersey Medical School, joint BS/OD degree with State University of New York College of Optometry, agreement with Philadelphia College of Pharmacy and Science for pharmacy and physical therapy students. **Remedial services:** Learning center, preadmission summer program, reduced course load, remedial instruction, special counselor, tutoring. **ROTC:** Air Force, Army. **Placement/credit:** AP, CLEP General and Subject, institutional tests; 30 credit hours maximum for bachelor's degree.

ACADEMIC REQUIREMENTS. Freshmen must earn minimum GPA of 1.6 to continue in good standing. 96% of freshmen return for sophomore year. Students must declare major by end of first year. **Graduation requirements:** 128 hours for bachelor's (47 in major). Most students required to take courses in arts/fine arts, English, history, humanities, mathematics, philosophy/religion, biological/physical sciences, social sciences. **Postgraduate studies:** 3% enter law school, 1% enter medical school, 2% enter MBA programs, 7% enter other graduate study.

FRESHMAN ADMISSIONS. Selection criteria: Class rank, high school academic record, and test scores most important. School and community activities, and special talents and abilities are also important. Minority status, essay, recommendation, interview considered. **High school preparation:** 16 units required. Required and recommended units include English 4, mathematics 3, social science 2 and science 2. Foreign language 2 recommended. 5 additional units of academic electives required. **Test requirements:** SAT or ACT (SAT preferred); score report by March 1. Mathematics Level I or II ACH required of engineering science applicants. Score report by March 1.

1992 FRESHMAN CLASS PROFILE. 2,068 men applied, 759 accepted, 285 enrolled; 3,188 women applied, 1,432 accepted, 606 enrolled. 95% had high school GPA of 3.0 or higher, 5% between 2.0 and 2.99. 58% were in top tenth and 99% were in top quarter of graduating class. **Academic background:** Mid 50% of enrolled freshmen had SAT-V between 480-560, SAT-M between 540-630. 100% submitted SAT scores. **Characteristics:** 90% from in state, 92% live in college housing, 17% have minority backgrounds, 1% are foreign students. Average age is 19.

FALL-TERM APPLICATIONS. $50 fee, may be waived for applicants with need. Closing date March 1; applicants notified on or about April 1; must reply by May 1. Audition required for music, television and theatre production applicants. Portfolio required for art applicants. Essay required. Interview used only in marginal cases. CRDA. Deferred and early admission available. EDP-S.

STUDENT LIFE. Housing: Dormitories (women, coed); handicapped housing available. Housing guaranteed for first 2 years for incoming freshmen. Honors housing, study floors, single sex (female) residence hall available. First-year student housing offered, core class taught in-house. **Activities:** Student government, magazine, radio, student newspaper, television, yearbook, choral groups, concert band, dance, drama, jazz band, music ensembles, musical theater, opera, pep band, symphony orchestra, fraternities, sororities, more than 120 special interest groups, clubs, and societies, including social service, honors, professional, political, religious, ethnic, social, performing arts, athletic/recreational. **Additional information:** Emphasis on self-government and developing a sense of community on campus.

ATHLETICS. NCAA. **Intercollegiate:** Baseball M, basketball, cross-country, diving, field hockey W, football M, golf M, lacrosse W, soccer, softball W, swimming, tennis, track and field, wrestling M. **Intramural:** Archery, baseball M, basketball, bowling, golf M, ice hockey M, lacrosse M, racquetball, skiing, skin diving, soccer, softball, swimming, tennis, volleyball, wrestling M.

STUDENT SERVICES. Aptitude testing, career counseling, employment service for undergraduates, freshman orientation, health services, on-campus day care, personal counseling, placement service for graduates, special adviser for adult students, veterans counselor, services/facilities for handicapped.

ANNUAL EXPENSES. Tuition and fees (projected): $3,810, $1,650 additional for out-of-state students. **Room and board:** $5,325. **Books and supplies:** $700. **Other expenses:** $1,000.

FINANCIAL AID. 50% of freshmen, 46% of continuing students receive some form of aid. 67% of grants, 56% of loans, 4% of jobs based on need. Academic, music/drama, minority scholarships available. **Aid applications:** Closing date May 1; applicants notified on a rolling basis beginning on or about April 15; must reply by May 1 or within 2 weeks if notified thereafter.

ADDRESS/TELEPHONE. Mr. Alfred Bridges, Vice President for College Advancement, Trenton State College, Hillwood Lakes CN 4700, Trenton, NJ 08650-4700. (609) 771-2131. (800) 345-7354. Fax: (609) 771-3067.

Union County College ⇎
Cranford, New Jersey — CB code: 2921

2-year public community college, coed. Founded in 1933. **Accreditation:** Regional. **Undergraduate enrollment:** 1,973 men, 2,355 women full time; 1,920 men, 4,228 women part time. **Faculty:** 424 total (169 full time), 68 with doctorates or other terminal degrees. **Location:** Suburban campus in large town; 20 miles from New York City. **Calendar:** Semester, limited summer session. Saturday and extensive evening/early morning classes. **Microcomputers:** 629 located in libraries, classrooms, computer centers. **Special facilities:** Observatory, art gallery.

DEGREES OFFERED. AA, AS, AAS. 709 associate degrees awarded in 1992. 16% in business and management, 30% health sciences, 11% allied health, 23% multi/interdisciplinary studies.

UNDERGRADUATE MAJORS. Accounting, architectural engineering, biology, business and management, business and office, business data programming, civil technology, communications, computer and information sciences, criminal justice studies, education of the deaf and hearing impaired, electromechanical technology, electronic technology, elementary education, engineering, engineering and engineering-related technologies, engineering management, environmental science, finance, fine arts, fire control and safety technology, gerontology, graphic arts technology, illustration design, international studies, interpreter for the deaf, laser electro-optic technology, law enforcement and corrections technologies, liberal/general studies, mechanical design technology, music, nursing, occupational therapy assistant, physical sciences, physical therapy assistant, radiograph medical technology, respiratory therapy, respiratory therapy technology, secretarial and related programs, teacher aide, urban studies, visual and performing arts.

ACADEMIC PROGRAMS. 2-year transfer program, dual enrollment of high school students, honors program, internships, telecourses, weekend college, cross-registration. **Remedial services:** Learning center, reduced course load, remedial instruction, special counselor, tutoring. **ROTC:** Air Force. **Placement/credit:** AP, CLEP General and Subject, institutional tests; 32 credit hours maximum for associate degree.

ACADEMIC REQUIREMENTS. Freshmen must earn minimum GPA of 2.0 to continue in good standing. 62% of freshmen return for sophomore year. Students must declare major by end of first year. **Graduation requirements:** 64 hours for associate. Most students required to take courses in English, mathematics, biological/physical sciences.

FRESHMAN ADMISSIONS. Selection criteria: Open admissions. Selective admissions to physical therapy, occupational therapy, respiratory therapy, and nursing programs. **High school preparation:** 19 units recommended. Recommended units include English 4, foreign language 2, mathematics 3, physical science 2, social science 3 and science 5. Chemistry and algebra II required of nursing applicants. Trigonometry, physics, and chemistry required of engineering and biology applicants. Level 3 proficiency in American Sign Language required of interpreter for the deaf program applicants. **Test requirements:** SAT required of dental hygiene program applicants; score report by April.

1992 FRESHMAN CLASS PROFILE. 810 men, 1,095 women enrolled. **Characteristics:** 99% from in state, 100% commute, 40% have minority backgrounds, 29% are foreign students. Average age is 21.

FALL-TERM APPLICATIONS. $20 fee, may be waived for applicants with need. No closing date; applicants notified on a rolling basis; must reply by May 1 or within 3 weeks if notified thereafter. Interview recommended for interpreters for the deaf, nursing applicants. CRDA. Deferred admission available. EDP-F.

STUDENT LIFE. Activities: Student government, radio, student newspaper, television, drama.

ATHLETICS. NJCAA. **Intercollegiate:** Baseball M, basketball, golf, soccer M, softball W. **Intramural:** Badminton, basketball, softball, table tennis, tennis, volleyball.

STUDENT SERVICES. Aptitude testing, career counseling, employment service for undergraduates, freshman orientation, health services, personal counseling, placement service for graduates, services/facilities for handicapped.

ANNUAL EXPENSES. Tuition and fees (1992-93): $1,564, $1,320 additional for out-of-district students, $3,960 additional for out-of-state students. **Books and supplies:** $585. **Other expenses:** $2,573.

FINANCIAL AID. 17% of freshmen, 13% of continuing students receive some form of aid. 99% of grants, 99% of loans, 25% of jobs based on need. Academic, art, athletic, leadership scholarships available. **Aid applications:** No closing date; priority given to applications received by March 15; applicants notified on a rolling basis beginning on or about May 15; must reply within 2 weeks.

ADDRESS/TELEPHONE. Joseph T. Ragusa, Director of Admissions and Records, Union County College, 1033 Springfield Avenue, Cranford, NJ 07016-1599. (908) 709-7000. Fax: (908) 709-0527.

University of Medicine and Dentistry of New Jersey: School of Health Related Professions

Newark, New Jersey — CB code: 0598

4-year public health science college, coed. Founded in 1976. **Accreditation:** Regional. **Undergraduate enrollment:** 100 men, 170 women full time; 77 men, 90 women part time. **Graduate enrollment:** 9 men, 63 women full time; 4 men, 24 women part time. **Faculty:** 78 total (57 full time), 14 with doctorates or other terminal degrees. **Location:** Urban campus in large city. **Calendar:** Semester, limited summer session. **Microcomputers:** 25 located in libraries, computer centers. **Special facilities:** Accelerators, lithotripsy facilities.

DEGREES OFFERED. AAS, BS, MA, MS. 18 associate degrees awarded in 1992. 15% in health sciences, 85% allied health. 12 bachelor's degrees awarded. 100% in allied health. Graduate degrees offered in 1 major field of study.

UNDERGRADUATE MAJORS. Associate: Dental hygiene, emergency medical technologies, respiratory therapy. **Bachelor's:** Cytotechnology, medical laboratory technologies, physical therapy, physician's assistant, toxicology.

ACADEMIC PROGRAMS. Dual enrollment of high school students, independent study, internships, retraining of cytotechnologists, specialty tracks in medical technology; liberal arts/career combination in health sciences. **Remedial services:** Preadmission summer program, special counselor, tutoring, college survival skills seminars. **Placement/credit:** CLEP General and Subject, institutional tests.

ACADEMIC REQUIREMENTS. Freshmen must earn minimum GPA of 2.0 to continue in good standing. 70% of freshmen return for sophomore year. Students must declare major on application. **Graduation requirements:** 60 hours for associate, 120 hours for bachelor's. Most students required to take courses in English, history, humanities, mathematics, biological/physical sciences, social sciences.

FRESHMAN ADMISSIONS. Selection criteria: Each program has established criteria for admissions. Minimum GPA and interview most important. Health related experiences and letters of recommendation also important. Specific high school course requirements vary by program. **Additional information:** Qualified minority, handicapped, and disadvantaged students encouraged to apply.

1992 FRESHMAN CLASS PROFILE. Characteristics: 86% from in state, 100% commute, 33% have minority backgrounds.

FALL-TERM APPLICATIONS. $25 fee, may be waived for applicants with need. Applicants notified on a rolling basis; must reply within 10 days. Interview required. Essay required. Deferred admission available. Closing date varies for each program.

STUDENT LIFE. Activities: Student government, student newspaper, Student professional organizations (by allied health specialty).

STUDENT SERVICES. Career counseling, employment service for undergraduates, freshman orientation, health services, on-campus day care, personal counseling, placement service for graduates, tutorial services, services/facilities for handicapped.

ANNUAL EXPENSES. Tuition and fees (1992-93): Tuition varies between $1,334 and $3,278 depending on program. Out-of-state and foreign students pay one-third more tuition. **Books and supplies:** $666.

FINANCIAL AID. 60% of freshmen, 40% of continuing students receive some form of aid. 81% of grants, 93% of loans, all jobs based on need. Academic, state/district residency, minority scholarships available. **Aid applications:** No closing date; applicants notified on a rolling basis; must reply within 2 weeks.

ADDRESS/TELEPHONE. Dr. Laura Nelson, Associate Dean for Academic and Student Services, University of Medicine and Dentistry of New Jersey: School of Health Related Professions, 65 Bergen Street, Newark, NJ 07107-3001. (201) 982-5454. Fax: (201) 982-7596.

University of Medicine and Dentistry of New Jersey: School of Nursing

Newark, NJ — CB code: 0769

4-year public nursing college, coed. **Accreditation:** Regional. **Undergraduate enrollment:** 8 men, 53 women full time; 13 men, 88 women part time. **Faculty:** 32 total (30 full time), 7 with doctorates or other terminal degrees. **Location:** Urban campus in large city. **Calendar:** Semester, extensive summer session. Saturday and extensive evening/early morning classes. **Microcomputers:** 7 located in computer centers.

DEGREES OFFERED. AS, BS, MS. Graduate degrees offered in 1 major field of study.

UNDERGRADUATE MAJORS. Associate: Nursing. **Bachelor's:** Nursing.

ACADEMIC PROGRAMS. Accelerated program, double major, independent study, MS in nursing bridge for registered nurses, double master's degree program in nursing and in public health with UMDNJ: Robert Wood Johnson Medical School. **Remedial services:** Reduced course load, special counselor, tutoring.

ACADEMIC REQUIREMENTS. Freshmen must earn minimum GPA of 2.0 to continue in good standing. Students must declare major on application. **Graduation requirements:** 69 hours for associate, 128 hours for bachelor's. Most students required to take courses in computer science, English, history, humanities, mathematics, biological/physical sciences, social sciences.

FRESHMAN ADMISSIONS. Selection criteria: Each program has established criteria for admissions. Minimum GPA and interview most important. Nursing and health related experiences and letters of recommendation also important. Specific high school course requirements vary by program. **Additional information:** Qualified minority, handicapped, and disadvantaged students encouraged to apply. (PG) Transfer applicants evaluated by faculty and associate dean.

FALL-TERM APPLICATIONS. $30 fee. Applicants notified on a rolling basis; must reply within 10 days. Interview recommended. Essay recommended. Closing date varies for each program.

STUDENT LIFE. Activities: Student government, student newspaper, Student professional organizations by nursing specialty.

STUDENT SERVICES. Career counseling, employment service for undergraduates, freshman orientation, health services, on-campus day care, personal counseling, placement service for graduates, special adviser for adult students, services/facilities for handicapped.

ANNUAL EXPENSES. Tuition and fees (1992-93):

ADDRESS/TELEPHONE. Manager Enrollment and Student Services, University of Medicine and Dentistry of New Jersey: School of Nursing, 65 Bergen Street, Room 901, Newark, NJ 07107-3006. (201) 982-5447. Fax: (201) 982-7543.

Upsala College

East Orange, New Jersey — CB code: 2930

Admissions:	43% of applicants accepted
Based on:	••• School record
	•• Activities, interview, recommendations, special talents, test scores
	• Essay
Completion:	75% of freshmen end year in good standing
	40% graduate, 33% of these enter graduate study

4-year private liberal arts college, coed, affiliated with Evangelical Lutheran Church in America. Founded in 1893. **Accreditation:** Regional. **Undergraduate enrollment:** 480 men, 405 women full time; 76 men, 183 women part time. **Graduate enrollment:** 3 men and women full time; 40 men and women part time. **Faculty:** 104 total (58 full time), 52 with doctorates or other terminal degrees. **Location:** Urban campus in small city; 15 miles from New York City. **Calendar:** Semester, limited summer session. **Microcomputers:** 60 located in libraries, computer centers. **Special facilities:** Open access microcomputer laboratory. **Additional facts:** Courses offered at Wirths Campus in Sussex County.

DEGREES OFFERED. BA, BS, MS. 19 associate degrees awarded in 1992. 217 bachelor's degrees awarded in 1992. 53% in business and management, 5% computer sciences, 10% life sciences, 7% physical sciences, 5% psychology, 12% social sciences. Graduate degrees offered in 2 major fields of study.

UNDERGRADUATE MAJORS. Accounting, anthropology, biochemistry, biological and physical sciences, biology, business administration and management, business and management, chemistry, communications, computer and information sciences, dramatic arts, economics, English literature, fine arts, history, human resources development, humanities and social sciences, information sciences and systems, international business management, liberal/general studies, mathematics, multinational corporate studies, music, philosophy, political science and government, psychology, public administration, religion, social work, sociology, Spanish, visual and performing arts.

ACADEMIC PROGRAMS. 2-year transfer program, double major, dual enrollment of high school students, honors program, independent study, internships, student-designed major, study abroad, weekend college, Washington semester, cross-registration, liberal arts and career combination programs in engineering with New Jersey Institute of Technology and Washington University (St. Louis, Missouri), in forestry with Duke University, and in health sciences with University of Medicine and Dentistry of New Jersey. **Remedial services:** Learning center, preadmission summer program, reduced course load, remedial instruction, special counselor, tutoring, writing center. **Placement/credit:** AP, CLEP General and Subject, institutional tests; 32 credit hours maximum for bachelor's degree.

ACADEMIC REQUIREMENTS. Freshmen must earn minimum GPA of 2.0 to continue in good standing. 65% of freshmen return for sophomore year. Students must declare major by end of second year. **Graduation requirements:** 128 hours for bachelor's (24 in major). Most students required to take courses in arts/fine arts, computer science, English, foreign languages, history, humanities, mathematics, philosophy/religion, biological/physical sciences, social sciences. **Postgraduate studies:** 3% enter law school, 7% enter medical school, 13% enter MBA programs, 10% enter other graduate study. **Additional information:** Required courses emphasizing writing skills integrated into all fields of study. Cross-registration with New Jersey Institute of Technology and Seton Hall University.

FRESHMAN ADMISSIONS. Selection criteria: High school curriculum and achievement most important. Motivation, extracurricular activities, talents, counselor recommendation, test scores, interview considered. **High school preparation:** 16 units required. Required units include biological science 1, English 4, foreign language 2, mathematics 3, physical science 1 and social science 2. **Test requirements:** SAT or ACT (SAT preferred); score report by July 1.

1992 FRESHMAN CLASS PROFILE. 1,341 men and women applied, 582 accepted; 383 enrolled. **Academic background:** Mid 50% of enrolled freshmen had SAT-V between 300-500, SAT-M between 300-500. 84% submitted SAT scores. **Characteristics:** 85% from in state, 50% commute, 65% have minority backgrounds, 10% are foreign students, 35% join fraternities/sororities. Average age is 18.

FALL-TERM APPLICATIONS. $30 fee, may be waived for applicants with need. Closing date August 15; priority given to applications received by March 1; applicants notified on a rolling basis; must reply by May 1 or within 2 weeks if notified thereafter. Essay required for full-time applicants. Interview required for honors candidates and candidates for special admissions programs, recommended for all. CRDA. Deferred and early admission available. EDP-F.

STUDENT LIFE. Housing: Dormitories (men, women, coed). **Activities:** Student government, film, magazine, radio, student newspaper, yearbook, choral groups, drama, musical theater, orchestra for musicals, fraternities, sororities, Christian fellowship, Circle-K, Alpha Phi Omega, Jewish and Roman Catholic organizations, foreign student and Third World associations, political science and business clubs.

ATHLETICS. NCAA. **Intercollegiate:** Baseball M, basketball, cross-country, football M, golf, ice hockey M, lacrosse M, soccer M, softball W, tennis, track and field, volleyball W, wrestling M. **Intramural:** Baseball M, basketball, fencing, golf, horseback riding, racquetball, rifle, skiing, soccer M, softball W, tennis, track and field, volleyball, wrestling M.

STUDENT SERVICES. Aptitude testing, career counseling, employment service for undergraduates, freshman orientation, health services, personal counseling, placement service for graduates, special adviser for adult students, services/facilities for handicapped.

ANNUAL EXPENSES. Tuition and fees (1992-93): $11,500. **Room and board:** $4,580. **Books and supplies:** $600. **Other expenses:** $6,072.

FINANCIAL AID. 98% of freshmen, 94% of continuing students receive some form of aid. All aid based on need. Academic, state/district residency, alumni affiliation, religious affiliation scholarships available. **Aid applications:** No closing date; priority given to applications received by March 1; applicants notified on a rolling basis beginning on or about February 15; must reply by May 1 or within 4 weeks if notified thereafter.

ADDRESS/TELEPHONE. Susan Chalfin, Director of Admissions, Upsala College, Prospect Street, East Orange, NJ 07019. (201) 266-7191. Fax: (201) 678-8837.

Warren County Community College

Washington, New Jersey CB code: 2722

2-year public community college, coed. Founded in 1981. **Accreditation:** Regional candidate. **Faculty:** 60 total (12 full time), 5 with doctorates or other terminal degrees. **Location:** Rural campus in small town; 12 miles from Easton, Pennsylvania. **Calendar:** Semester, limited summer session. **Microcomputers:** 62 located in libraries, classrooms, computer centers. **Special facilities:** Audio-visual tutorial laboratory, small business collection, extensive video tape collection.

DEGREES OFFERED. AA, AAS. 37 associate degrees awarded in 1992.

UNDERGRADUATE MAJORS. Accounting, business and management, liberal/general studies.

ACADEMIC PROGRAMS. 2-year transfer program, dual enrollment of high school students, internships, cross-registration. **Remedial services:** Learning center, reduced course load, remedial instruction, tutoring. **Placement/credit:** AP, CLEP General and Subject, institutional tests; 45 credit hours maximum for associate degree.

ACADEMIC REQUIREMENTS. Freshmen must earn minimum GPA of 1.6 to continue in good standing. 59% of freshmen return for sophomore year. **Graduation requirements:** 65 hours for associate (15 in major). Most students required to take courses in English, humanities, mathematics, biological/physical sciences, social sciences.

FRESHMAN ADMISSIONS. Selection criteria: Open admissions. Selective admissions for some programs. High school diploma or GED strongly recommended.

1992 FRESHMAN CLASS PROFILE. 95 men, 132 women enrolled. **Characteristics:** 100% from in state, 100% commute, 6% have minority backgrounds. Average age is 21.

FALL-TERM APPLICATIONS. $10 fee. No closing date; applicants notified on a rolling basis. Interview recommended. Deferred and early admission available. Early admission students below age 18 must provide written permission from parent/guardian and high school official.

STUDENT LIFE. Activities: Student government, student newspaper, drama.

ATHLETICS. Intramural: Basketball, bowling, tennis, volleyball.

STUDENT SERVICES. Aptitude testing, career counseling, employment service for undergraduates, freshman orientation, personal counseling, placement service for graduates, veterans counselor, off-campus day care for children of evening students, services/facilities for handicapped.

ANNUAL EXPENSES. Tuition and fees (1992-93): $1,680, $1,560 additional for out-of-district students, $3,120 additional for out-of-state students. **Books and supplies:** $500. **Other expenses:** $900.

FINANCIAL AID. 8% of freshmen, 6% of continuing students receive some form of aid. All aid based on need. 55 enrolled freshmen were judged to have need, 41 were offered aid. Academic, state/district residency scholarships available. **Aid applications:** No closing date; priority given to applications received by November 1; applicants notified on a rolling basis. **Additional information:** Several national, local and institutional scholarship programs available to students who meet scholarship eligibility requirements.

ADDRESS/TELEPHONE. Peggy Heim, Director of Admissions and Counseling, Warren County Community College, Route #57 West, Box 55A, Washington, NJ 07882-9605. (908) 689-1090 ext. 520. Fax: (908) 689-7488.

Westminster Choir College School of Music of Rider College

Princeton, New Jersey CB code: 2974

Admissions: 58% of applicants accepted
Based on: ••• Special talents
•• Recommendations, school record, test scores
• Activities, essay, interview
Completion: 80% of freshmen end year in good standing
51% graduate, 30% of these enter graduate study

4-year private music college, coed. Founded in 1926. **Accreditation:** Regional. **Undergraduate enrollment:** 72 men, 137 women full time; 9 men, 24 women part time. **Graduate enrollment:** 101 men and women. **Faculty:** 64 total (38 full time), 19 with doctorates or other terminal degrees. **Location:** Suburban campus in large town; 50 miles from New York City and Philadelphia. **Calendar:** Semester, limited summer session. **Microcomputers:** 58 located in libraries, computer centers. **Special facilities:** 26 pipe organs, 114 pianos, 400,000-volume choral library, archives of Organ Historical Society, 8,000 recordings, Voice Resource Center. **Additional facts:** All students perform for 3 years in Symphonic Choir with major orchestras such as New York Philharmonic and Philadelphia Orchestra. Most students receive Bachelor of Music degree.

DEGREES OFFERED. B, M. 41 bachelor's degrees awarded in 1992. 48% in teacher education, 52% visual and performing arts. Graduate degrees offered in 4 major fields of study.

UNDERGRADUATE MAJORS. Music, music education, music performance, music theory and composition, religious music.

ACADEMIC PROGRAMS. Double major, dual enrollment of high school students, independent study, internships, study abroad, teacher preparation, cooperative program with Princeton University. **Remedial services:** Learning center, preadmission summer program, reduced course load, remedial instruction, tutoring. **Placement/credit:** AP, institutional tests.

ACADEMIC REQUIREMENTS. Freshmen must earn minimum GPA of 2.0 to continue in good standing. 82% of freshmen return for sophomore year. Students must declare major by end of first year. **Graduation requirements:** 124 hours for bachelor's (91 in major). Most students required to take courses in English, foreign languages, history, mathematics, philosophy/religion, biological/physical sciences, social sciences. **Additional information:** 75% music, 25% liberal arts required for Bachelor of Music. All students study voice and keyboard and sing in choirs. Bachelor of Arts students study 50% music, 50% liberal arts.Master's of Music degree awarded.

Air Force ROTC offered at Rutgers University, Army ROTC through Rider College.

FRESHMAN ADMISSIONS. Selection criteria: Music audition and music test primary. School achievement record and test scores also considered. **High school preparation:** 16 units required. Required and recommended units include English 4, mathematics 1 and social science 2. Biological science 1, foreign language 2, physical science 1 and science 3 recommended. 2 music units required. Background in choral music expected and music theory recommended. **Test requirements:** SAT or ACT; score report by August 1. Examination of basic music theory and skills required.

1992 FRESHMAN CLASS PROFILE. 51 men applied, 31 accepted, 20 enrolled; 108 women applied, 62 accepted, 27 enrolled. **Academic background:** Mid 50% of enrolled freshmen had SAT-V between 360-530, SAT-M between 380-560. 96% submitted SAT scores. **Characteristics:** 48% from in state, 98% live in college housing, 29% have minority backgrounds, 4% are foreign students. Average age is 19.

FALL-TERM APPLICATIONS. $30 fee, may be waived for applicants with need. Closing date August 1; priority given to applications received by May 1; applicants notified on a rolling basis. Audition required. Essay required. Interview recommended. CRDA. Deferred and early admission available. EDP-F.

STUDENT LIFE. Housing: Dormitories (men, women, coed). Practice rooms available in all residence halls. **Activities:** Student government, radio, student newspaper, yearbook, choral groups, drama, music ensembles, musical theater, opera, composers' guild, Music Educator's National Conference, Black and Hispanic Alliance, Christian Fellowship. **Additional information:** Counseling and health service offered through Princeton University, intercollegiate sports through Rider College.

ATHLETICS. Intramural: Basketball, volleyball.

STUDENT SERVICES. Career counseling, employment service for undergraduates, freshman orientation, health services, personal counseling, placement service for graduates.

ANNUAL EXPENSES. Tuition and fees (1992-93): $12,200. **Room and board:** $5,250. **Books and supplies:** $500. **Other expenses:** $700.

FINANCIAL AID. 87% of freshmen, 87% of continuing students receive some form of aid. 79% of grants, 95% of loans, 50% of jobs based on need. 31 enrolled freshmen were judged to have need, 30 were offered aid. Academic, music/drama, leadership scholarships available. **Aid applications:** No closing date; priority given to applications received by March 15; applicants notified on a rolling basis beginning on or about April 1; must reply by May 1 or within 2 weeks if notified after April 7. **Additional information:** Approximately 130 churches employ students for weekend positions as organists, directors, and soloists. Average earnings are $2,000 to $3,000 per year.

ADDRESS/TELEPHONE. Deborah J. Erie, Director of Admissions, Westminster Choir College School of Music of Rider College, 101 Walnut Lane, Princeton, NJ 08540-3899. (609) 921-7144. (800) 962-4647. Fax: (609) 921-8829.

William Paterson College of New Jersey ⇎
Wayne, New Jersey CB code: 2518

Admissions:	47% of applicants accepted
Based on:	••• School record
	•• Test scores
	• Activities, essay, interview, recommendations, special talents
Completion:	80% of freshmen end year in good standing
	15% graduate, 6% of these enter graduate study

4-year public college of arts and sciences, coed. Founded in 1855. **Accreditation:** Regional. **Undergraduate enrollment:** 2,478 men, 3,183 women full time; 715 men, 1,296 women part time. **Graduate enrollment:** 36 men, 90 women full time; 162 men, 644 women part time. **Faculty:** 320 total (307 full time), 247 with doctorates or other terminal degrees. **Location:** Suburban campus in large town; 20 miles from New York City. **Calendar:** Semester, limited summer session. **Microcomputers:** 184 located in classrooms, computer centers. **Special facilities:** State-of-the-art scientific instrumentation (FTNMR, FTIR, ESR, ICP, AA and UU-visible spectrometers, HPLC's, SEM and TEM), 5 silicon graphics iris workstations, satellite uplink and downlink capabilities, 3 art galleries, 2 theaters.

DEGREES OFFERED. BA, BS, BFA, MA, MS, MBA, MEd. 1,187 bachelor's degrees awarded in 1992. 25% in business and management, 14% communications, 18% teacher education, 9% health sciences, 13% social sciences. Graduate degrees offered in 25 major fields of study.

UNDERGRADUATE MAJORS. Accounting, African studies, Afro-American (black) studies, anthropology, art history, biological and physical sciences, biology, biotechnology, business administration and management, business economics, chemistry, communications, computer and information sciences, dramatic arts, economics, elementary education, English, English literature, environmental science, environmental studies, fine arts, French, geography, graphic design, health education, health sciences, history, humanities and social sciences, international business management, jazz, mathematics, music, music business management, music education, music performance, music theory and composition, nursing, philosophy, physical education, political science and government, psychology, public administration, secondary education, social sciences, sociology, Spanish, special education, speech correction, speech pathology/audiology, visual and performing arts.

ACADEMIC PROGRAMS. Accelerated program, double major, honors program, independent study, internships, study abroad, teacher preparation, visiting/exchange student program. **Remedial services:** Learning center, pre-admission summer program, reduced course load, remedial instruction, special counselor, tutoring. **ROTC:** Air Force. **Placement/credit:** AP, CLEP General and Subject, institutional tests; 60 credit hours maximum for bachelor's degree.

ACADEMIC REQUIREMENTS. Freshmen must earn minimum GPA of 2.0 to continue in good standing. 78% of freshmen return for sophomore year. Students must declare major by end of second year. **Graduation requirements:** 128 hours for bachelor's. Most students required to take courses in English, foreign languages, history, humanities, mathematics, philosophy/religion, biological/physical sciences, social sciences. **Postgraduate studies:** 1% enter law school, 1% enter medical school, 1% enter MBA programs, 3% enter other graduate study. **Additional information:** Honors programs available in biopsychology, humanities, and international management.

FRESHMAN ADMISSIONS. Selection criteria: High school academic program, rank in class, and SAT or ACT test scores are evaluated. Consideration also given to extracurricular and community activities. **High school preparation:** 16 units required. Required and recommended units include English 4, foreign language 1-2, mathematics 3, social science 2-3 and science 2. Biological science 1 and physical science 2 recommended. Biology and laboratory chemistry required for nursing. Academic electives to make up the balance for 16 units. **Test requirements:** SAT or ACT (SAT preferred); score report by May 30.

1992 FRESHMAN CLASS PROFILE. 5,329 men and women applied, 2,504 accepted; 1,044 enrolled. 33% were in top quarter of graduating class. **Academic background:** Mid 50% of enrolled freshmen had SAT-V between 370-460, SAT-M between 410-520. 98% submitted SAT scores. **Characteristics:** 98% from in state, 57% commute, 28% have minority backgrounds, 1% are foreign students. Average age is 19.

FALL-TERM APPLICATIONS. $20 fee, may be waived for applicants with need. Closing date June 30; priority given to applications received by April 15; applicants notified on a rolling basis; must reply by May 1 or within 2 weeks if notified thereafter. Audition required for music applicants. Portfolio required for art applicants. Essay recommended for academically marginal applicants. CRDA. Deferred and early admission available.

STUDENT LIFE. Housing: Dormitories (coed); apartment housing available. **Activities:** Student government, film, magazine, radio, student newspaper, television, yearbook, choral groups, concert band, dance, drama, jazz band, music ensembles, musical theater, symphony orchestra, gospel choir, fraternities, sororities, Black Student Union, Christian Fellowship Club, Jewish Student Association, Women's Collective, other language and cultural clubs, Organization of Latin American Students, Catholic Campus Ministry.

ATHLETICS. NCAA. **Intercollegiate:** Baseball M, basketball, cross-country, diving, fencing, field hockey W, football M, ice hockey M, soccer M, softball W, swimming, track and field, volleyball W. **Intramural:** Basketball, field hockey W, racquetball, soccer W, softball, tennis, volleyball. **Clubs:** Bowling, horseback riding W.

STUDENT SERVICES. Aptitude testing, career counseling, employment service for undergraduates, health services, on-campus day care, personal counseling, placement service for graduates, special adviser for adult students, veterans counselor, free legal services, services/facilities for handicapped.

ANNUAL EXPENSES. Tuition and fees (1992-93): $2,644, $840 additional for out-of-state students. **Room and board:** $4,595. **Books and supplies:** $450. **Other expenses:** $1,500.

FINANCIAL AID. 31% of freshmen, 31% of continuing students receive some form of aid. 90% of grants, 79% of loans, 44% of jobs based on need. Academic, music/drama scholarships available. **Aid applications:** No closing date; priority given to applications received by April 15; applicants notified on a rolling basis beginning on or about May 1; must reply by May 1 or within 1 week if notified thereafter.

ADDRESS/TELEPHONE. Leo DeBartolo, Director of Admissions, William Paterson College of New Jersey, 300 Pompton Road, Wayne, NJ 07470. (201) 595-2125. Fax: (201) 595-3593.

New Mexico

Albuquerque Technical-Vocational Institute

Albuquerque, New Mexico CB code: 3387

2-year public community, technical college, coed. **Accreditation:** Regional. **Undergraduate enrollment:** 1,736 men, 2,019 women full time; 3,936 men, 5,924 women part time. **Faculty:** 807 total (240 full time). **Location:** Urban campus in large city. **Calendar:** Trimester. Extensive evening/early morning classes. **Microcomputers:** Located in libraries, computer centers.

DEGREES OFFERED. AA, AS, AAS. 480 associate degrees awarded in 1992. 50% in business and management, 22% engineering technologies, 12% allied health, 16% parks/recreation, protective services, public affairs.

UNDERGRADUATE MAJORS. Accounting, architectural technologies, business administration and management, court reporting, electronic technology, engineering and engineering-related technologies, environmental science, fire control and safety technology, laser electro-optic technology, law enforcement and corrections, legal assistant/paralegal, medical laboratory technologies, nursing, respiratory therapy technology, secretarial and related programs.

ACADEMIC PROGRAMS. 2-year transfer program, dual enrollment of high school students, internships. **Remedial services:** Learning center, remedial instruction, special counselor, tutoring. **Placement/credit:** AP, CLEP Subject, institutional tests; 30 credit hours maximum for associate degree.

ACADEMIC REQUIREMENTS. Freshmen must earn minimum GPA of 2.0 to continue in good standing. Students must declare major on enrollment. **Graduation requirements:** 60 hours for associate. **Additional information:** 2-year programs without class levels.

FRESHMAN ADMISSIONS. Selection criteria: Interview required for all applicants. For nursing applicants, ACT minimum score of 18 required, recommendation required, school achievement record and test scores important for placement.

1992 FRESHMAN CLASS PROFILE. 959 men, 1,979 women enrolled. **Academic background:** Mid 50% of enrolled freshmen had SAT-V between 370-600, SAT-M between 400-650; ACT composite between 12-19. 1% submitted SAT scores, 22% submitted ACT scores. **Characteristics:** 100% commute, 45% have minority backgrounds. Average age is 27.

FALL-TERM APPLICATIONS. No fee. Closing date September 7; priority given to applications received by August 31; applicants notified on a rolling basis. Interview required.

STUDENT LIFE. Activities: Student government.

STUDENT SERVICES. Aptitude testing, career counseling, employment service for undergraduates, health services, placement service for graduates, services/facilities for handicapped.

ANNUAL EXPENSES. Tuition and fees (projected): $924, $1,548 additional for out-of-state students. In-state students do not pay tuition for technical courses, only arts and sciences courses. **Books and supplies:** $497. **Other expenses:** $1,691.

FINANCIAL AID. All grants, 95% of loans, 50% of jobs based on need. **Aid applications:** No closing date; priority given to applications received by March 1; applicants notified on a rolling basis beginning on or about August 1.

ADDRESS/TELEPHONE. Jane Campbell, Registrar, Albuquerque Technical-Vocational Institute, 525 Buena Vista Southeast, Albuquerque, NM 87106. (505) 224-3160.

Clovis Community College

Clovis, New Mexico CB code: 4921

2-year public community college, coed. Founded in 1990. **Accreditation:** Regional. **Undergraduate enrollment:** 3,851 men and women. **Faculty:** 171 total (41 full time). **Location:** Rural campus in large town; 200 miles from Albuquerque, 100 miles from Lubbock, Texas. **Calendar:** Semester, limited summer session. **Microcomputers:** 100 located in computer centers. **Special facilities:** Museum, gallery, large art collection representing the multiple cultures of New Mexico.

DEGREES OFFERED. AA, AS, AAS. 202 associate degrees awarded in 1992.

UNDERGRADUATE MAJORS. Accounting, air conditioning/heating/refrigeration mechanics, automotive mechanics, aviation science, business and management, computer and information sciences, computer programming, construction, criminal justice studies, drafting, finance, fine arts, fire protection, graphic design, legal studies, nursing, office supervision and management, psychology, radiograph medical technology, real estate, retailing, secretarial and related programs, systems analysis, word processing.

ACADEMIC PROGRAMS. Dual enrollment of high school students, honors program, internships, telecourses. **Remedial services:** Learning center, remedial instruction, tutoring. **Placement/credit:** CLEP General and Subject; 32 credit hours maximum for associate degree.

ACADEMIC REQUIREMENTS. Freshmen must earn minimum GPA of 2.0 to continue in good standing. **Graduation requirements:** 64 hours for associate (22 in major). Most students required to take courses in English, mathematics, biological/physical sciences, social sciences.

FRESHMAN ADMISSIONS. Selection criteria: Open admissions. **Test requirements:** Test of Adult Basic Education (TABE) required for vocational programs.

1992 FRESHMAN CLASS PROFILE. 583 men and women enrolled. **Characteristics:** 100% commute, 32% have minority backgrounds.

FALL-TERM APPLICATIONS. No closing date; applicants notified on a rolling basis; must reply by registration.

STUDENT LIFE. Activities: Student government, magazine, Hispanic Advisory Council, Black Advisory Council.

STUDENT SERVICES. Career counseling, employment service for undergraduates, freshman orientation, on-campus day care, personal counseling, placement service for graduates, special adviser for adult students, veterans counselor, Skills Development Center, services/facilities for handicapped.

ANNUAL EXPENSES. Tuition and fees (projected): $536, $24 additional for out-of-district students, $992 additional for out-of-state students. **Books and supplies:** $500. **Other expenses:** $850.

FINANCIAL AID. 30% of freshmen, 66% of continuing students receive some form of aid. 96% of grants, 98% of loans, 19% of jobs based on need. Academic, state/district residency, minority scholarships available. **Aid applications:** No closing date; applicants notified on a rolling basis beginning on or about August 1.

ADDRESS/TELEPHONE. Victoria Quintela, Director of Enrollment Management, Clovis Community College, 417 Schepps Boulevard, Clovis, NM 88101-8345. (505) 769-4025. Fax: (505) 769-4190.

College of Santa Fe

Santa Fe, New Mexico CB code: 4676

Admissions:	81% of applicants accepted
Based on:	••• School record
	•• Activities, essay, interview, test scores
	• Recommendations, special talents
Completion:	85% of freshmen end year in good standing
	20% enter graduate study

4-year private liberal arts college, coed, affiliated with Roman Catholic Church. Founded in 1947. **Accreditation:** Regional. **Undergraduate enrollment:** 361 men, 420 women full time; 180 men, 377 women part time. **Graduate enrollment:** 9 men, 10 women full time; 36 men, 81 women part time. **Faculty:** 127 total (46 full time), 83 with doctorates or other terminal degrees. **Location:** Urban campus in small city; 60 miles from Albuquerque. **Calendar:** Semester, limited summer session. **Microcomputers:** Located in libraries, classrooms, computer centers. **Special facilities:** Art gallery, Greer Garson Theater, Garson Communications Center. **Additional facts:** Christian Brothers institution. Additional campus in Albuquerque offers night and weekend courses for graduate and external programs.

DEGREES OFFERED. AA, AS, BA, BS, BFA, MBA, MEd. 9 associate degrees awarded in 1992. 78% in business and management, 22% social sciences. 171 bachelor's degrees awarded. 28% in business and management, 30% education, 5% letters/literature, 6% life sciences, 8% psychology, 14% visual and performing arts. Graduate degrees offered in 3 major fields of study.

UNDERGRADUATE MAJORS. Associate: Accounting, biology, business administration and management, business and management, business and office, chemistry, English, liberal/general studies, mathematics, physical sciences, public administration, secretarial and related programs, social sciences, theater design. **Bachelor's:** Accounting, applied mathematics, bilingual/bicultural education, biology, business administration and management, business and management, chemistry, communications, computer and information sciences, counseling psychology, creative writing, dramatic arts, education, education of the culturally disadvantaged, elementary education, English, English literature, environmental science, fine arts, humanities, humanities and social sciences, liberal/general studies, management information systems, managerial psychology, marketing and distribution, mathematics, motion picture technology, music, musical theater, performing arts management, premedicine, preveterinary, psychology, public administration, radio/television broadcasting, religion, secondary education, social sciences, technical and business writing, theological studies, visual and performing arts.

ACADEMIC PROGRAMS. Cooperative education, double major, dual enrollment of high school students, external degree, honors program, independent study, internships, student-designed major, study abroad, teacher preparation, weekend college, New York semester, cross-registration, evening curriculum for adults, London semester. **Remedial services:** Learning center, reduced course load, remedial instruction, special counselor, tutoring. **Placement/credit:** AP, CLEP General and Subject, institutional tests; 24 credit hours maximum for associate degree; 48 credit hours maximum for bachelor's degree.

ACADEMIC REQUIREMENTS. Freshmen must earn minimum GPA

of 2.0 to continue in good standing. 60% of freshmen return for sophomore year. Students must declare major by end of second year. **Graduation requirements:** 64 hours for associate (24 in major), 128 hours for bachelor's (69 in major). Most students required to take courses in English, history, humanities, mathematics, philosophy/religion, biological/physical sciences, social sciences. **Postgraduate studies:** 12% from 2-year programs enter 4-year programs. 1% enter law school, 1% enter medical school, 8% enter MBA programs, 10% enter other graduate study. **Additional information:** London semester offered, minor in Spanish available.

FRESHMAN ADMISSIONS. Selection criteria: School achievement record and test scores. Applicants not meeting requirements may be asked to submit two letters of recommendation and personal statement. **High school preparation:** 16 units required; 21 recommended. Required and recommended units include biological science 2-3, English 3-4, mathematics 2-3 and social science 2-3. Foreign language 2 and physical science 1 recommended. **Test requirements:** SAT or ACT; score report by August 1.

1992 FRESHMAN CLASS PROFILE. 208 men applied, 184 accepted, 94 enrolled; 265 women applied, 200 accepted, 83 enrolled. 31% had high school GPA of 3.0 or higher, 64% between 2.0 and 2.99. 17% were in top tenth and 29% were in top quarter of graduating class. **Academic background:** Mid 50% of enrolled freshmen had SAT-V between 470-540, SAT-M between 440-530; ACT composite between 19-24. 51% submitted SAT scores, 39% submitted ACT scores. **Characteristics:** 62% from in state, 89% live in college housing, 16% have minority backgrounds, 2% are foreign students. Average age is 20.

FALL-TERM APPLICATIONS. $25 fee, may be waived for applicants with need. No closing date; priority given to applications received by May 1; applicants notified on a rolling basis beginning on or about November 1; must reply by May 1 or within 3 weeks if notified thereafter. Interview required for design/technical theater, arts administration, contemporary music applicants. Audition required for music theater, dramatic arts applicants. Portfolio recommended for visual arts applicants. Essay recommended. CRDA. Deferred and early admission available.

STUDENT LIFE. Housing: Dormitories (men, women, coed). Separate floors for honor and older students; substance-free floors. **Activities:** Student government, film, magazine, student newspaper, yearbook, dance, drama, music ensembles, musical theater, campus ministries, Hispanic, drama, art, business, science, and international students clubs, student alumni association, council of Presidential Scholars, Black Student Union, Executive Leadership Council.

ATHLETICS. Intramural: Baseball, basketball, racquetball, skiing, soccer, softball, squash, table tennis, tennis, volleyball.

STUDENT SERVICES. Aptitude testing, career counseling, employment service for undergraduates, freshman orientation, health services, personal counseling, placement service for graduates, special adviser for adult students, veterans counselor, services/facilities for handicapped.

ANNUAL EXPENSES. Tuition and fees: $9,830. **Room and board:** $3,958. **Books and supplies:** $400. **Other expenses:** $1,200.

FINANCIAL AID. 90% of freshmen, 80% of continuing students receive some form of aid. 60% of grants, 93% of loans, 85% of jobs based on need. 95 enrolled freshmen were judged to have need, all were offered aid. Academic, music/drama, art, state/district residency, leadership, religious affiliation, minority scholarships available. **Aid applications:** No closing date; priority given to applications received by March 1; applicants notified on a rolling basis.

ADDRESS/TELEPHONE. Monica Martinez, Director of Admissions, College of Santa Fe, 1600 St Michael's Drive, Santa Fe, NM 87501-5634. (505) 473-6131. (800) 456-2673. Fax: (505) 473-6127.

College of the Southwest
Hobbs, New Mexico — CB code: 4116

Admissions: 36% of applicants accepted
Based on: •• School record, test scores
• Essay, recommendations, special talents
Completion: 80% of freshmen end year in good standing
13% graduate, 30% of these enter graduate study

4-year private college of arts and sciences and business, teachers college, coed. Founded in 1956. **Accreditation:** Regional. **Undergraduate enrollment:** 85 men, 120 women full time; 50 men, 92 women part time. **Faculty:** 52 total (18 full time), 8 with doctorates or other terminal degrees. **Location:** Suburban campus in large town; 110 miles from Lubbock, Texas. **Calendar:** Semester, extensive summer session. Saturday and extensive evening/early morning classes. **Microcomputers:** Located in libraries, classrooms.

DEGREES OFFERED. BS. 60 bachelor's degrees awarded in 1992. 29% in business and management, 47% teacher education, 19% psychology.

UNDERGRADUATE MAJORS. Accounting, business administration and management, business and management, business education, elementary education, English education, language arts education, liberal/general studies, marketing management, mathematics education, petroleum land management, physical education, prelaw, psychology, psychology education, science education, secondary education, social science education, special education.

ACADEMIC PROGRAMS. Internships, student-designed major, teacher preparation. **Remedial services:** Reduced course load, tutoring. **Placement/credit:** AP, CLEP General and Subject, institutional tests; 45 credit hours maximum for bachelor's degree.

ACADEMIC REQUIREMENTS. Freshmen must earn minimum GPA of 1.75 to continue in good standing. 20% of freshmen return for sophomore year. Students must declare major by end of second year. **Graduation requirements:** 128 hours for bachelor's (48 in major). Most students required to take courses in arts/fine arts, computer science, English, history, humanities, mathematics, philosophy/religion, biological/physical sciences, social sciences. **Additional information:** 6 hours religious studies and 3 hours economics required of all students.

FRESHMAN ADMISSIONS. Selection criteria: Applicants must meet 2 of 3 criteria: ACT composite score of 18 or SAT combined score of 700; cumulative high school GPA of 2.0; top half of graduating class. **Test requirements:** SAT or ACT (ACT preferred); score report by August 1.

1992 FRESHMAN CLASS PROFILE. 32 men applied, 14 accepted, 14 enrolled; 56 women applied, 18 accepted, 18 enrolled. 47% had high school GPA of 3.0 or higher, 53% between 2.0 and 2.99. 7% were in top tenth and 38% were in top quarter of graduating class. **Characteristics:** 65% from in state, 65% live in college housing, 28% have minority backgrounds, 6% are foreign students. Average age is 19.

FALL-TERM APPLICATIONS. $25 fee. Closing date July 1; priority given to applications received by April 1; applicants notified on a rolling basis beginning on or about July 1; must reply by August 15. Deferred admission available.

STUDENT LIFE. Housing: Apartment housing available. Organized food service available. **Activities:** Student government, student newspaper, drama, music ensembles, accounting, teaching, and game clubs, Students in Free Enterprise, Alpha Phi Omega service organization.

ATHLETICS. NAIA. **Intercollegiate:** Baseball M, soccer. **Intramural:** Badminton, basketball, cross-country, football M, racquetball, soccer W, table tennis, volleyball.

STUDENT SERVICES. Freshman orientation, personal counseling, placement service for graduates, services/facilities for handicapped.

ANNUAL EXPENSES. Tuition and fees (1992-93): $3,800. **Room and board:** $2,550. **Books and supplies:** $400. **Other expenses:** $590.

FINANCIAL AID. 83% of freshmen, 97% of continuing students receive some form of aid. 71% of grants, 96% of loans, 74% of jobs based on need. 10 enrolled freshmen were judged to have need, all were offered aid. Academic, music/drama, athletic, leadership scholarships available. **Aid applications:** Closing date June 1; priority given to applications received by April 1; applicants notified on or about July 1; must reply within 2 weeks.

ADDRESS/TELEPHONE. Rhonda Tyler, Director of Admissions, College of the Southwest, 6610 Lovington Highway, Hobbs, NM 88240-9987. (505) 392-6561 ext. 320. (800) 530-4400. Fax: (505) 392-6006.

Dona Ana Branch Community College of New Mexico State University
Las Cruces, New Mexico — CB code: 6296

2-year public branch campus, community college, coed. **Accreditation:** Regional. **Undergraduate enrollment:** 409 men, 341 women full time; 1,418 men, 1,447 women part time. **Faculty:** 134 total (58 full time), 13 with doctorates or other terminal degrees. **Location:** Suburban campus in small city; 42 miles from El Paso, Texas. **Calendar:** Semester, limited summer session. Saturday and extensive evening/early morning classes. **Microcomputers:** 100 located in classrooms, computer centers. **Additional facts:** Access to New Mexico State University facilities and activities, i.e., dormitories, health services, concerts, intercollegiate sports.

DEGREES OFFERED. AAS. 175 associate degrees awarded in 1992. 14% in business and management, 15% business/office and marketing/distribution, 17% computer sciences, 10% engineering technologies, 12% allied health, 28% trade and industry.

UNDERGRADUATE MAJORS. Accounting, air conditioning/heating/refrigeration mechanics, air conditioning/heating/refrigeration technology, airline piloting and navigation, architectural technologies, architecture, automotive mechanics, automotive technology, aviation management, business administration and management, business and management, business and office, business computer/console/peripheral equipment operation, computer programming, computer servicing technology, drafting, electrical and electronics equipment repair, electronic technology, emergency medical technologies, fashion design, fashion merchandising, fire control and safety technology, hospitality and recreation marketing, hotel/motel and restaurant management, legal assistant/paralegal, legal secretary, marketing management, medical secretary, microcomputer software, office supervision and management, radiograph medical technology, respiratory therapy technology, secretarial and related programs, trade and industrial supervision and management, water and wastewater technology, water resources, welding technology, word processing.

ACADEMIC PROGRAMS. Cooperative education, dual enrollment of high school students, internships, cross-registration. **Remedial services:** Learning center, preadmission summer program, remedial instruction, special counselor, tutoring. **ROTC:** Air Force, Army. **Placement/credit:** Institutional tests; 30 credit hours maximum for associate degree.

ACADEMIC REQUIREMENTS. Freshmen must earn minimum GPA of 2.0 to continue in good standing. 74% of freshmen return for sophomore year. Students must declare major by end of first year. **Graduation requirements:** 66 hours for associate (48 in major). Most students required to take courses in English, mathematics.

FRESHMAN ADMISSIONS. Selection criteria: Open admissions. Students in the radiology technology EMT-paramedic, and respiratory care programs are selected on the basis of ACT/ASSET scores, Health Occupations Aptiude Test scores, resume, three letters of recommendation, clinical observation, and interview. **Test requirements:** ACT-ASSET required for placement.

1992 FRESHMAN CLASS PROFILE. 1,024 men, 1,059 women enrolled. **Characteristics:** 98% from in state, 90% commute, 57% have minority backgrounds, 1% are foreign students. Average age is 24.

FALL-TERM APPLICATIONS. $10 fee, may be waived for applicants with need. No closing date; applicants notified on a rolling basis. February 15th application deadline for radiology technology, EMT-paramedic, and respiratory care programs.

STUDENT LIFE. Housing: Dormitories (men, women, coed); apartment, fraternity, sorority, handicapped housing available. Housing available on adjacent New Mexico State University campus. **Activities:** Student government, student newspaper, Vocational Industrial Clubs of America, Distributive Education Clubs of America, Phi Beta Lamda, fraternities and sororities available to students through New Mexico State University.

STUDENT SERVICES. Aptitude testing, career counseling, employment service for undergraduates, freshman orientation, health services, personal counseling, placement service for graduates, special adviser for adult students, veterans counselor, services/facilities for handicapped.

ANNUAL EXPENSES. Tuition and fees (1992-93): $696, $120 additional for out-of-district students, $1,224 additional for out-of-state students. **Books and supplies:** $300.

FINANCIAL AID. 21% of freshmen, 46% of continuing students receive some form of aid. Grants, loans, jobs available. 450 enrolled freshmen were judged to have need, all were offered aid. **Aid applications:** No closing date; priority given to applications received by March 1; applicants notified on a rolling basis beginning on or about May 1. **Additional information:** Financial aid services provided through New Mexico State University.

ADDRESS/TELEPHONE. Joan Pharr, Student Development Coordinator, Dona Ana Branch Community College of New Mexico State University, Box 30001, Department 3DA, Las Cruces, NM 88003-0001. (505) 527-7500. Fax: (505) 527-7515.

Eastern New Mexico University
Portales, New Mexico — CB code: 4299

4-year public university, coed. Founded in 1927. **Accreditation:** Regional. **Undergraduate enrollment:** 1,245 men, 1,625 women full time; 196 men, 294 women part time. **Graduate enrollment:** 34 men, 26 women full time; 183 men, 313 women part time. **Faculty:** 224 total (147 full time), 80 with doctorates or other terminal degrees. **Location:** Rural campus in large town; 120 miles from Lubbock, Texas, 225 miles from Albuquerque. **Calendar:** Semester, extensive summer session. Extensive evening/early morning classes. **Microcomputers:** 83 located in dormitories, classrooms, computer centers. **Special facilities:** Natural history museum, mineral museum, scanning and transmission electron microscopes.

DEGREES OFFERED. AA, AS, BA, BS, BFA, MA, MS, MBA, MEd. 4 associate degrees awarded in 1992. 10% in business and management, 17% business/office and marketing/distribution, 7% engineering technologies, 14% home economics, 52% multi/interdisciplinary studies. 416 bachelor's degrees awarded. 20% in business and management, 8% communications, 6% computer sciences, 24% teacher education, 5% life sciences, 7% multi/interdisciplinary studies, 7% psychology, 6% social sciences, 6% visual and performing arts. Graduate degrees offered in 29 major fields of study.

UNDERGRADUATE MAJORS. Associate: Business and office, child development/care/guidance, civil engineering, civil technology, drafting, early childhood education, electronic technology, engineering and engineering-related technologies, liberal/general studies, medical assistant, psychology, secretarial and related programs, teacher aide, trade and industrial education. **Bachelor's:** Accounting, agribusiness, agricultural business and management, agricultural education, agricultural sciences, allied health, American studies, anthropology, art education, bilingual/bicultural education, biological and physical sciences, biology, business administration and management, business and management, business data processing and related programs, business economics, business education, business home economics, chemistry, clinical laboratory science, communications, computer and information sciences, computer programming, dramatic arts, earth sciences, education, elementary education, English, English education, environmental science, family and community services, finance, fine arts, French, geology, graphic design, health education, history, home economics, home economics education, humanities and social sciences, individual and family development, industrial arts education, information sciences and systems, junior high education, liberal/general studies, marketing and distribution, marketing management, mathematics, mathematics education, medical records technology, music, music business management, music education, music therapy, personnel management, physical education, physical sciences, physics, political science and government, predentistry, premedicine, prepharmacy, preveterinary, psychology, radio/television broadcasting, radio/television technology, reading education, religion, secondary education, social sciences, social studies education, sociology, Spanish, special education, speech, speech correction, speech pathology/audiology, speech/communication/theater education, statistics, telecommunications, theological studies, wildlife management.

ACADEMIC PROGRAMS. Accelerated program, cooperative education, double major, dual enrollment of high school students, honors program, independent study, internships, student-designed major, study abroad, teacher preparation, telecourses, visiting/exchange student program, United Nations semester; combined bachelor's/graduate program in business administration. **Remedial services:** Learning center, preadmission summer program, remedial instruction, special counselor, tutoring. **ROTC:** Army. **Placement/credit:** AP, CLEP General and Subject, institutional tests; 32 credit hours maximum for associate degree; 50 credit hours maximum for bachelor's degree.

ACADEMIC REQUIREMENTS. Freshmen must earn minimum GPA of 2.0 to continue in good standing. 54% of freshmen return for sophomore year. Students must declare major by end of second year. **Graduation requirements:** 64 hours for associate, 128 hours for bachelor's. Most students required to take courses in arts/fine arts, English, history, humanities, mathematics, philosophy/religion, biological/physical sciences, social sciences. **Postgraduate studies:** 2% enter law school, 3% enter medical school, 23% enter MBA programs, 24% enter other graduate study.

FRESHMAN ADMISSIONS. Selection criteria: Test scores, school record, recommendations important. **High school preparation:** 14 units recommended. Recommended units include English 4, foreign language 1, mathematics 3, social science 2 and science 4. **Test requirements:** SAT or ACT (ACT preferred); score report by August 20.

1992 FRESHMAN CLASS PROFILE. 247 men, 325 women enrolled. **Characteristics:** 79% from in state, 91% live in college housing, 28% have minority backgrounds, 4% are foreign students. Average age is 18.

FALL-TERM APPLICATIONS. $15 fee. Closing date August 31; priority given to applications received by August 20; applicants notified on a rolling basis. CRDA. Deferred and early admission available.

STUDENT LIFE. Housing: Dormitories (men, women, coed); apartment, fraternity, sorority housing available. **Activities:** Student government, radio, student newspaper, television, yearbook, choral groups, concert band, dance, drama, jazz band, marching band, music ensembles, musical theater, pep band, symphony orchestra, fraternities, sororities, several religious, political, honorary, and service organizations, American Indian club.

ATHLETICS. NCAA. **Intercollegiate:** Baseball M, basketball, football M, rifle, tennis W, volleyball W. **Intramural:** Badminton, basketball, bowling, cross-country, golf, handball, racquetball, soccer, softball, swimming, table tennis, tennis, track and field, volleyball, wrestling M.

STUDENT SERVICES. Aptitude testing, career counseling, employment service for undergraduates, freshman orientation, health services, on-campus day care, personal counseling, placement service for graduates, special adviser for adult students, veterans counselor, services/facilities for handicapped.

ANNUAL EXPENSES. Tuition and fees (1992-93): $1,356, $3,558 additional for out-of-state students. **Room and board:** $2,410. **Books and supplies:** $500. **Other expenses:** $1,200.

FINANCIAL AID. 80% of freshmen, 75% of continuing students receive some form of aid. 75% of grants, 95% of loans, 95% of jobs based on need. Academic, music/drama, art, athletic, state/district residency, leadership, minority scholarships available. **Aid applications:** No closing date; priority given to applications received by March 1; applicants notified on a rolling basis beginning on or about May 15; must reply within 2 weeks.

ADDRESS/TELEPHONE. Larry Fuqua, Director of Admissions, Eastern New Mexico University, Station 7, Portales, NM 88130. (505) 562-2178. (800) 367-3668. Fax: (505) 562-2566.

Eastern New Mexico University: Roswell Campus
Roswell, New Mexico — CB code: 4662

2-year public branch campus, community college, coed. Founded in 1958. **Accreditation:** Regional. **Undergraduate enrollment:** 385 men, 574 women full time; 360 men, 766 women part time. **Faculty:** 165 total (65 full time), 3 with doctorates or other terminal degrees. **Location:** Suburban campus in large town; 200 miles from Albuquerque. **Calendar:** Semester, limited summer session. Saturday and extensive evening/early morning classes. **Microcomputers:** 50 located in libraries, classrooms.

DEGREES OFFERED. AA, AS, AAS. 139 associate degrees awarded in 1992.

UNDERGRADUATE MAJORS. Aircraft mechanics, airline piloting and navigation, automotive mechanics, business and management, child development/care/guidance, computer and information sciences, criminal justice studies, drafting, electrical and electronics equipment repair, emergency medical technologies, finance, fire control and safety technology, legal assistant/paralegal, liberal/general studies, mining and petroleum technologies, nursing, secretarial and related programs, social work, teacher aide.

ACADEMIC PROGRAMS. 2-year transfer program, dual enrollment of high school students, independent study, internships. **Remedial services:** Learning center, remedial instruction, tutoring. **Placement/credit:** CLEP General and Subject, institutional tests; 20 credit hours maximum for associate degree.

ACADEMIC REQUIREMENTS. Freshmen must earn minimum GPA of 2.0 to continue in good standing. 64% of freshmen return for sophomore year. Students must declare major on application. **Graduation requirements:** 64 hours for associate. Most students required to take courses in English, mathematics.

FRESHMAN ADMISSIONS. Selection criteria: Open admissions.

1992 FRESHMAN CLASS PROFILE. 96 men, 111 women enrolled. **Characteristics:** 90% from in state, 40% have minority backgrounds. Average age is 27.

FALL-TERM APPLICATIONS. No fee. No closing date; applicants notified on a rolling basis beginning on or about July 1. Interview recommended for nursing applicants.

STUDENT LIFE. Housing: Dormitories (coed). **Activities:** Student government, drama, Spanish club, Christian fellowship.

ATHLETICS. Intramural: Baseball M, basketball M, racquetball, softball W, tennis, volleyball.

STUDENT SERVICES. Aptitude testing, career counseling, employment service for undergraduates, on-campus day care, personal counseling, placement service for graduates, veterans counselor, services/facilities for handicapped.

ANNUAL EXPENSES. Tuition and fees (1992-93): $612, $24 additional for out-of-district students, $1,328 additional for out-of-state students. **Room and board:** $2,700. **Books and supplies:** $552. **Other expenses:** $600.

FINANCIAL AID. 70% of freshmen, 70% of continuing students receive some form of aid. 96% of grants, 78% of loans, all jobs based on need. Academic, state/district residency, leadership scholarships available. **Aid applications:** No closing date; priority given to applications received by May 1; applicants notified on a rolling basis beginning on or about June 1; must reply within 2 weeks.

ADDRESS/TELEPHONE. Tim Raftery, Director of Admissions and Records, Eastern New Mexico University: Roswell Campus, PO Box 6000, Roswell, NM 88202-6000. (505) 624-7145. (800) 243-6687. Fax: (505) 624-7119.

Institute of American Indian Arts
Santa Fe, New Mexico — CB code: 0180

Admissions:	37% of applicants accepted
Based on:	••• Essay, school record
	•• Activities, interview, recommendations, special talents
Completion:	46% of freshmen end year in good standing
	40% graduate, 50% of these enter 4-year programs

2-year public art, junior college, coed. Founded in 1962. **Accreditation:** Regional. **Undergraduate enrollment:** 112 men, 74 women full time; 20 men, 38 women part time. **Faculty:** 36 total (30 full time), 2 with doctorates or other terminal degrees. **Location:** Suburban campus in small city; 60 miles from Albuquerque. **Calendar:** Semester. **Microcomputers:** Located in libraries, computer centers. **Special facilities:** Art gallery, museum. **Additional facts:** Dedicated to providing education in the fine arts to Native Americans and Alaska Natives.

DEGREES OFFERED. AA. 43 associate degrees awarded in 1992. 96% in visual and performing arts.

UNDERGRADUATE MAJORS. Art conservation, ceramics, crafts, creative writing, fiber/textiles/weaving, fine arts, graphic arts technology, graphic design, metal/jewelry, museum studies, painting, photography, printmaking, sculpture, studio art.

ACADEMIC PROGRAMS. Double major, independent study, internships, cross-registration. **Remedial services:** Learning center, remedial instruction, special counselor, tutoring. **Placement/credit:** Institutional tests.

ACADEMIC REQUIREMENTS. Freshmen must earn minimum GPA of 2.0 to continue in good standing. 46% of freshmen return for sophomore year. Students must declare major on enrollment. **Graduation requirements:** 64 hours for associate (12 in major). Most students required to take courses in arts/fine arts, English, mathematics, social sciences. **Additional information:** Most courses emphasize Native American perpective.

FRESHMAN ADMISSIONS. Selection criteria: Academic achievement, 2.0 high school GPA, art interest. Art portfolio evaluated for potential. Handwritten statement of educational intention. **Additional information:** Quality of art portfolio most important.

1992 FRESHMAN CLASS PROFILE. 125 men applied, 42 accepted, 36 enrolled; 73 women applied, 32 accepted, 32 enrolled. 24% had high school GPA of 3.0 or higher, 76% between 2.0 and 2.99. **Characteristics:** 90% live in college housing, 88% have minority backgrounds, 1% are foreign students. Average age is 23.

FALL-TERM APPLICATIONS. No fee. Closing date April 15; applicants notified on a rolling basis; must reply by July 1. Portfolio required. Essay required. Interview recommended. Deferred admission available.

STUDENT LIFE. Housing: Dormitories (men, women, coed). Student housing provided on College of Santa Fe campus. **Activities:** Student government, magazine, student newspaper, dance, drama, student senate, Pow-Wow Club, traditional dance club, ski club. **Additional information:** Age range of students from 17 to 74, representing 76 Tribes.

ATHLETICS. Intramural: Badminton, basketball, bowling, skiing, softball, swimming, table tennis, tennis, volleyball.

STUDENT SERVICES. Career counseling, freshman orientation, personal counseling, placement service for graduates.

ANNUAL EXPENSES. Tuition and fees: $9,135. **Room and board:** $3,166. **Books and supplies:** $1,350. **Other expenses:** $1,042.

FINANCIAL AID. 85% of freshmen, 92% of continuing students receive some form of aid. 30% of grants, all loans, 38% of jobs based on need. Minority scholarships available. **Aid applications:** Closing date April 15; applicants notified on or about June 1; must reply by July 1. **Additional information:** For American Indian and Alaskan natives, financial aid available through Tribe or Native Corporation in which student is enrolled.

ADDRESS/TELEPHONE. Jerry Zollars, Director of Admissions, Institute of American Indian Arts, PO Box 20007, Santa Fe, NM 87504. (505) 988-6495. Fax: (505) 988-6446.

National College
Albuquerque, New Mexico — CB code: 5360

4-year proprietary business college, coed. **Accreditation:** Regional. **Undergraduate enrollment:** 153 men and women. **Faculty:** 20 total, 3 with doctorates or other terminal degrees. **Location:** Urban campus in large city. **Calendar:** Quarter. Saturday and extensive evening/early morning classes. **Microcomputers:** 14 located in computer centers.

DEGREES OFFERED. AS, AAS, BS. 9 associate degrees awarded in 1992. 98% in business and management. 10 bachelor's degrees awarded. 82% in business and management, 18% computer sciences.

UNDERGRADUATE MAJORS. Associate: Accounting, business administration and management, business and management, computer and information sciences, tourism. **Bachelor's:** Accounting, business administration and management, business and management, computer and information sciences.

ACADEMIC PROGRAMS. 2-year transfer program, double major, independent study. **Remedial services:** Tutoring. **Placement/credit:** CLEP General and Subject.

ACADEMIC REQUIREMENTS. Freshmen must earn minimum GPA of 2.0 to continue in good standing. 76% of freshmen return for sophomore year. **Graduation requirements:** 98 hours for associate (24 in major), 194 hours for bachelor's (48 in major). Most students required to take courses in computer science, English, foreign languages, history, humanities, mathematics, biological/physical sciences, social sciences. **Postgraduate studies:** 51% from 2-year programs enter 4-year programs.

FRESHMAN ADMISSIONS. Selection criteria: Open admissions.

1992 FRESHMAN CLASS PROFILE. 26 men, 17 women enrolled. **Characteristics:** 100% commute, 49% have minority backgrounds. Average age is 25.

FALL-TERM APPLICATIONS. $25 fee. No closing date; applicants notified on a rolling basis.

STUDENT LIFE. Activities: Student government.

STUDENT SERVICES. Employment service for undergraduates, freshman orientation, special adviser for adult students, veterans counselor, services/facilities for handicapped.

ANNUAL EXPENSES. Tuition and fees (1992-93): $6,288. **Books and supplies:** $800.

FINANCIAL AID. 75% of freshmen, 70% of continuing students receive some form of aid. 95% of grants, 96% of loans, all jobs based on need. Academic scholarships available. **Aid applications:** No closing date; applicants notified on a rolling basis.

ADDRESS/TELEPHONE. Dottie Flint, Director of Admissions, National College, 1202 Pennsylvania, NE, Albuquerque, NM 87110-3156. (505) 265-7518. Fax: (505) 265-7542.

New Mexico Highlands University

Las Vegas, New Mexico CB code: 4532

Admissions: 84% of applicants accepted
Based on: •• School record
• Activities, recommendations, special talents, test scores
Completion: 72% of freshmen end year in good standing
55% enter graduate study

4-year public university, coed. Founded in 1893. **Accreditation:** Regional. **Undergraduate enrollment:** 791 men, 894 women full time; 73 men, 152 women part time. **Graduate enrollment:** 135 men, 161 women full time; 208 men, 375 women part time. **Faculty:** 142 total (109 full time), 74 with doctorates or other terminal degrees. **Location:** Rural campus in large town; 68 miles from Santa Fe. **Calendar:** Semester, limited summer session. **Microcomputers:** 250 located in libraries, classrooms, computer centers.

DEGREES OFFERED. AA, BA, BS, BFA, MA, MS, MBA, MSW. 1 associate degree awarded in 1992. 100% in education. 206 bachelor's degrees awarded. 17% in business and management, 23% education, 5% engineering technologies, 8% allied health, 9% parks/recreation, protective services, public affairs, 7% psychology, 13% social sciences. Graduate degrees offered in 11 major fields of study.

UNDERGRADUATE MAJORS. Associate: Computer and information sciences, elementary education, information sciences and systems, teacher aide. **Bachelor's:** Art education, biology, business administration and management, chemistry, communications, computer and information sciences, computer technology, electrical technology, electronic technology, elementary education, engineering, English, English education, environmental science, fine arts, foreign languages education, graphic design, history, industrial arts education, information sciences and systems, mathematics, mathematics education, medical social work, music, music education, office supervision and management, physical education, political science and government, prelaw, psychology, science education, secondary education, social studies education, sociology/anthropology, Spanish, special education, technical education, visual and performing arts.

ACADEMIC PROGRAMS. 2-year transfer program, cooperative education, double major, dual enrollment of high school students, honors program, independent study, internships, teacher preparation; combined bachelor's/graduate program in business administration. **Remedial services:** Learning center, reduced course load, remedial instruction, special counselor, tutoring. **Placement/credit:** AP, CLEP General and Subject, IB.

ACADEMIC REQUIREMENTS. Freshmen must earn minimum GPA of 1.75 to continue in good standing. 52% of freshmen return for sophomore year. Students must declare major by end of second year. **Graduation requirements:** 64 hours for associate (40 in major), 128 hours for bachelor's (30 in major). Most students required to take courses in arts/fine arts, English, history, humanities, mathematics, biological/physical sciences, social sciences. **Additional information:** Teacher preparatory program in elementary and secondary education available for students with bachelors degree for licensure or education certification.

FRESHMAN ADMISSIONS. Selection criteria: 2.0 high school GPA. **High school preparation:** 15 units recommended. **Test requirements:** SAT or ACT (ACT preferred) for placement and counseling only; score report by August 15.

1992 FRESHMAN CLASS PROFILE. 343 men applied, 299 accepted, 187 enrolled; 419 women applied, 342 accepted, 187 enrolled. 35% had high school GPA of 3.0 or higher, 60% between 2.0 and 2.99. **Characteristics:** 80% from in state, 54% commute, 84% have minority backgrounds. Average age is 18.

FALL-TERM APPLICATIONS. $15 fee, may be waived for applicants with need. Closing date August 1; applicants notified on a rolling basis. Deferred and early admission available.

STUDENT LIFE. Housing: Dormitories (men, women, coed); apartment housing available. **Activities:** Student government, film, radio, student newspaper, television, choral groups, concert band, drama, marching band, music ensembles, Spanish theater, social work club, international student club, several ethnic and religious groups.

ATHLETICS. NCAA. **Intercollegiate:** Baseball M, basketball, cross-country, football M, softball W, volleyball W. **Intramural:** Baseball M, basketball, bowling, golf, racquetball, rifle, skiing, softball, swimming, table tennis, tennis, track and field.

STUDENT SERVICES. Aptitude testing, career counseling, employment service for undergraduates, freshman orientation, health services, on-campus day care, personal counseling, placement service for graduates, special adviser for adult students, veterans counselor, services/facilities for handicapped.

ANNUAL EXPENSES. Tuition and fees (projected): $1,480, $3,754 additional for out-of-state students. Charges for over 18 semester hours are $39/hour for state residents, $149/hour additional for out-of-state students per semester. **Room and board:** $2,780. **Books and supplies:** $600. **Other expenses:** $800.

FINANCIAL AID. 73% of freshmen, 80% of continuing students receive some form of aid. 98% of grants, 97% of loans, 89% of jobs based on need. 313 enrolled freshmen were judged to have need, 298 were offered aid. Academic, music/drama, art, athletic, state/district residency, leadership, minority scholarships available. **Aid applications:** No closing date; priority given to applications received by March 1; applicants notified on a rolling basis beginning on or about April 15; must reply within 2 weeks. **Additional information:** Work study funds available on no-need basis to New Mexico residents.

ADDRESS/TELEPHONE. John Coca, Director of Admissions, New Mexico Highlands University, Las Vegas, NM 87701. (505) 454-3439. Fax: (505) 454-0026.

New Mexico Institute of Mining and Technology

Socorro, New Mexico CB code: 4533

Admissions: 79% of applicants accepted
Based on: ••• School record, test scores
• Essay, interview, recommendations
Completion: 70% of freshmen end year in good standing
29% graduate, 25% of these enter graduate study

4-year public university and engineering college, coed. Founded in 1889. **Accreditation:** Regional. **Undergraduate enrollment:** 638 men, 301 women full time; 100 men, 225 women part time. **Graduate enrollment:** 186 men, 53 women full time; 55 men, 34 women part time. **Faculty:** 103 total (101 full time), 97 with doctorates or other terminal degrees. **Location:** Suburban campus in small town; 75 miles from Albuquerque. **Calendar:** Semester, limited summer session. Extensive evening/early morning classes. **Microcomputers:** 50 located in computer centers. **Special facilities:** Experimental mine, mineral museum, laboratory for atmospheric physics and chemistry, center for explosives technology research, seismic research network, scanning electron microscope, scanning transmission electron microscope, transmission electron microscope, joint observatory for cometary research, New Mexico Bureau of Mines.

DEGREES OFFERED. AS, BS, MS, PhD. 3 associate degrees awarded in 1992. 115 bachelor's degrees awarded. 5% in computer sciences, 32% engineering, 11% life sciences, 10% mathematics, 7% multi/interdisciplinary studies, 28% physical sciences. Graduate degrees offered in 24 major fields of study.

UNDERGRADUATE MAJORS. Associate: Biological and physical sciences, liberal/general studies. **Bachelor's:** Applied mathematics, astrophysics, biological and physical sciences, biology, business and management, chemical engineering, chemistry, clinical laboratory science, computer and information sciences, computer programming, electrical/electronics/communications engineering, engineering, engineering and other disciplines, engineering mechanics, engineering science, environmental health engineering, environmental science, experimental psychology, geological engineering, geology, geophysics and seismology, liberal/general studies, materials engineering, mathematics, mathematics education, medical laboratory technologies, mining and mineral engineering, petroleum engineering, physical sciences, physics, predentistry, prelaw, premedicine, prepharmacy, preveterinary, psychology, science education, secondary education, systems analysis, technical and business writing, technical communications.

ACADEMIC PROGRAMS. Cooperative education, double major, dual enrollment of high school students, honors program, independent study, internships, study abroad, teacher preparation, telecourses, visiting/exchange student program, Waste Energy Resources Consortium certificate awarded with bachelor's degree; liberal arts/career combination in engineering. **Remedial services:** Preadmission summer program, tutoring. **Placement/credit:** AP, institutional tests.

ACADEMIC REQUIREMENTS. Freshmen must earn minimum GPA of 2.0 to continue in good standing. To continue in good academic standing, students must successfully complete 12 credits each semester. 75% of freshmen return for sophomore year. Students must declare major on application. **Graduation requirements:** 65 hours for associate, 130 hours for bachelor's (50 in major). Most students required to take courses in computer science, English, humanities, mathematics, biological/physical sciences, social sciences. **Postgraduate studies:** 2% enter law school, 2% enter medical school, 3% enter MBA programs, 18% enter other graduate study.

FRESHMAN ADMISSIONS. Selection criteria: Test scores and high school GPA. Interview considered. 2.0 minimum GPA in high school required. Minimum test scores on ACT (21) or SAT (880) also required. **High school preparation:** 15 units required. Required and recommended units include English 4, mathematics 3-4 and science 2. Biological science 1, foreign language 2 and physical science 2 recommended. Science units must include 1 laboratory science. **Test requirements:** SAT or ACT (ACT preferred); score report by August 1. Students may receive freshman credit for minimum ACT English score of 27.

1992 FRESHMAN CLASS PROFILE. 497 men applied, 396 accepted, 172 enrolled; 278 women applied, 218 accepted, 114 enrolled. 70% had high school GPA of 3.0 or higher, 30% between 2.0 and 2.99. **Academic background:** Mid 50% of enrolled freshmen had ACT composite between 24-30. 100% submitted ACT scores. **Characteristics:** 55% from in state, 85% live in college housing, 28% have minority backgrounds, 7% are foreign students. Average age is 20.

FALL-TERM APPLICATIONS. $15 fee, may be waived for applicants with need. Closing date August 1; priority given to applications received by March 1; applicants notified on a rolling basis; must reply by August 1. Interview recommended. CRDA. Deferred and early admission available.

STUDENT LIFE. Housing: Dormitories (men, women, coed); apartment housing available. **Activities:** Student government, radio, student newspaper, choral groups, concert band, drama, jazz band, music ensembles, musical theater, symphony orchestra, college orchestra, Baptist Student Union, Black Awareness Association, Muslim Student Association, Newman Association, Society for Hispanic Professional Engineers, American Indians in Science and Engineering Society.

ATHLETICS. Intramural: Badminton, baseball, basketball, cross-country, fencing, golf, handball, lacrosse, racquetball, rugby, skiing, soccer, softball, squash, swimming, table tennis, tennis, track and field, volleyball. **Clubs:** Yachting.

STUDENT SERVICES. Aptitude testing, career counseling, employment service for undergraduates, freshman orientation, on-campus day care, personal counseling, placement service for graduates, special adviser for adult students, veterans counselor, services/facilities for handicapped.

ANNUAL EXPENSES. Tuition and fees: $1,784, $3,862 additional for out-of-state students. **Room and board:** $3,440. **Books and supplies:** $600. **Other expenses:** $1,000.

FINANCIAL AID. 74% of freshmen, 63% of continuing students receive some form of aid. 61% of grants, 94% of loans, 34% of jobs based on need. 132 enrolled freshmen were judged to have need, all were offered aid. Academic, state/district residency, minority scholarships available. **Aid applications:** No closing date; priority given to applications received by March 1; applicants notified on a rolling basis beginning on or about April 1; must reply within 2 weeks. **Additional information:** Campus research projects offer student employment based on merit.

ADDRESS/TELEPHONE. Louise E. Chamberlin, Director of Admissions, New Mexico Institute of Mining and Technology, Campus Station, Socorro, NM 87801. (505) 835-5424 ext. 1. (800) 428-8324. Fax: (505) 835-6329.

New Mexico Junior College
Hobbs, New Mexico

CB code: 4553

2-year public community, junior, technical college, coed. Founded in 1965. **Accreditation:** Regional. **Undergraduate enrollment:** 432 men, 642 women full time; 622 men, 1,116 women part time. **Faculty:** 124 total (75 full time), 15 with doctorates or other terminal degrees. **Location:** Rural campus in large town; 110 miles from Roswell, 100 miles from Lubbock, Texas. **Calendar:** Semester, extensive summer session. Saturday and extensive evening/early morning classes. **Microcomputers:** 150 located in libraries, classrooms, computer centers. **Special facilities:** Cowboy Hall of Fame.

DEGREES OFFERED. AA, AS, AAS. 225 associate degrees awarded in 1992. 8% in business and management, 5% business/office and marketing/distribution, 13% computer sciences, 7% teacher education, 26% health sciences, 7% mathematics, 5% multi/interdisciplinary studies, 14% trade and industry.

UNDERGRADUATE MAJORS. Accounting, agricultural sciences, architecture, automotive mechanics, automotive technology, biology, business administration and management, business and management, business and office, business computer/console/peripheral equipment operation, business data entry equipment operation, business data processing and related programs, business data programming, chemistry, clinical laboratory science, communications, computer and information sciences, computer graphics, computer programming, drafting, drafting and design technology, education, elementary education, emergency medical technologies, engineering, finance, fine arts, fire protection, graphic and printing production, graphic arts technology, law enforcement and corrections technologies, liberal/general studies, machine tool operation/machine shop, marketing and distribution, mathematics, mechanical design technology, medical laboratory technologies, mining and petroleum technologies, music, nursing, office supervision and management, physical education, physics, practical nursing, precision metal work, predentistry, preengineering, prelaw, premedicine, prepharmacy, psychology, radiograph medical technology, real estate, secondary education, secretarial and related programs, small business management and ownership, social sciences, Spanish, sports medicine, word processing.

ACADEMIC PROGRAMS. 2-year transfer program, computer delivered (on-line) credit-bearing course offerings, dual enrollment of high school students, honors program, internships, weekend college, cross-registration. **Remedial services:** Learning center, preadmission summer program, reduced course load, remedial instruction, tutoring. **Placement/credit:** AP, CLEP Subject, institutional tests; 30 credit hours maximum for associate degree.

ACADEMIC REQUIREMENTS. Freshmen must earn minimum GPA of 1.75 to continue in good standing. 60% of freshmen return for sophomore year. Students must declare major by end of first year. **Graduation requirements:** 64 hours for associate. Most students required to take courses in arts/fine arts, English, history, humanities, mathematics, biological/physical sciences, social sciences.

FRESHMAN ADMISSIONS. Selection criteria: Open admissions. **High school preparation:** 18 units recommended. Recommended units include biological science 1, English 4, mathematics 3, physical science 1 and social science 4. **Additional information:** Applicants admitted without high school diploma or GED must pass GED before completion of degree program.

1992 FRESHMAN CLASS PROFILE. 434 men, 625 women enrolled. 32% had high school GPA of 3.0 or higher, 49% between 2.0 and 2.99. 5% were in top tenth and 20% were in top quarter of graduating class. **Characteristics:** 87% from in state, 80% commute, 30% have minority backgrounds, 1% are foreign students. Average age is 26.

FALL-TERM APPLICATIONS. No fee. No closing date; applicants notified on a rolling basis. Interview required for nursing, medical laboratory technician, automotive service education program (ASEP)(ASSET) applicants. Deferred and early admission available.

STUDENT LIFE. Housing: Dormitories (men, women); handicapped housing available. **Activities:** Student government, student newspaper, choral groups, drama, jazz band, music ensembles, musical theater, pep band, Young Republicans, Young Democrats.

ATHLETICS. NJCAA. **Intercollegiate:** Baseball M, basketball, cross-country M, golf M. **Intramural:** Badminton, basketball, bowling, golf, handball, racquetball, skiing, softball, swimming, table tennis, tennis, volleyball.

STUDENT SERVICES. Aptitude testing, career counseling, employment service for undergraduates, freshman orientation, personal counseling, placement service for graduates, veterans counselor, services/facilities for handicapped.

ANNUAL EXPENSES. Tuition and fees (1992-93): $385, $360 additional for out-of-district students, $480 additional for out-of-state students. **Room and board:** $3,000. **Books and supplies:** $450. **Other expenses:** $1,050.

FINANCIAL AID. 37% of freshmen, 37% of continuing students receive some form of aid. 78% of grants, 96% of loans, 40% of jobs based on need. 353 enrolled freshmen were judged to have need, all were offered aid. Academic, music/drama, athletic, state/district residency, leadership scholarships available. **Aid applications:** No closing date; priority given to applications received by April 1; applicants notified on a rolling basis beginning on or about May 1; must reply within 2 weeks.

ADDRESS/TELEPHONE. Robert Snow, Dean of Admissions and Records, New Mexico Junior College, Lovington Highway, Hobbs, NM 88240. (505) 392-5092. (800) 657-6260. Fax: (505) 392-2526.

New Mexico Military Institute
Roswell, New Mexico

CB code: 4534

2-year public military college, coed. Founded in 1891. **Accreditation:** Regional. **Undergraduate enrollment:** 424 men, 58 women full time. **Faculty:** 65 total, 7 with doctorates or other terminal degrees. **Location:** Suburban campus in large town; 200 miles from Albuquerque and El Paso, and Midland, Texas. **Calendar:** Semester. **Microcomputers:** 60 located in libraries, classrooms, computer centers. **Special facilities:** General McBride Museum specializing in history of Institute.

DEGREES OFFERED. AA. 119 associate degrees awarded in 1992. 100% in multi/interdisciplinary studies.

UNDERGRADUATE MAJORS. Liberal/general studies.

ACADEMIC PROGRAMS. 2-year transfer program, dual enrollment of high school students. **Remedial services:** Learning center, remedial instruction, tutoring. **ROTC:** Army. **Placement/credit:** AP, CLEP General and Subject, institutional tests; 30 credit hours maximum for associate degree.

ACADEMIC REQUIREMENTS. Freshmen must earn minimum GPA of 2.0 to continue in good standing. 66% of freshmen return for sophomore year. Students must declare major on enrollment. **Graduation requirements:** 68 hours for associate. Most students required to take courses in English, foreign languages, history, mathematics, biological/physical sciences, social sciences.

FRESHMAN ADMISSIONS. Selection criteria: 2.0 minimum high school GPA, ACT composite score of 19 or SAT combined score of 850 for Advanced Army ROTC. Minimum ACT composite score of 15 or SAT combined score of 700 for Basic Army ROTC program. Preference given to in-state applicants. **High school preparation:** 21 units recommended. Recommended units include biological science 2, English 4, foreign language 2, mathematics 3 and social science 3. **Test requirements:** SAT or ACT (ACT preferred); score report by August 1.

1992 FRESHMAN CLASS PROFILE. 236 men, 28 women enrolled. 42% had high school GPA of 3.0 or higher, 55% between 2.0 and 2.99. **Academic background:** Mid 50% of enrolled freshmen had ACT composite between 19-21. 77% submitted ACT scores. **Characteristics:** 30% from in state, 100% live in college housing, 30% have minority backgrounds, 2% are foreign students. Average age is 18.

FALL-TERM APPLICATIONS. $60 fee, may be waived for applicants with need. No closing date; applicants notified on a rolling basis beginning on or about February 1. Interview recommended for all applicants, required of those who do not meet admission requirements. Deferred admission available. Advanced Army ROTC applicants must pass Army physical examination.

STUDENT LIFE. Housing: Dormitories (men, women). All students must live in college housing. **Activities:** Student government, film, student newspaper, television, yearbook, choral groups, concert band, marching band, music ensembles, pep band, symphony orchestra. **Additional information:** Maximum age of 23 for enrollment. Students cannot be married or have children.

ATHLETICS. NJCAA. **Intercollegiate:** Baseball M, basketball M, bowling, cross-country, football M, golf, rifle, soccer, tennis, track and field. **Intramural:** Archery, baseball, basketball, bowling, diving, fencing, field hockey, gymnastics, handball, horseback riding, racquetball, skiing, skin diving, soccer, softball, swimming, tennis, track and field, volleyball, water polo, wrestling.

STUDENT SERVICES. Aptitude testing, career counseling, health services, personal counseling.

ANNUAL EXPENSES. Tuition and fees (1992-93): $1,495, $1,425 additional for out-of-state students. Uniforms, book, supplies $1500. **Room and board:** $2,300. **Other expenses:** $1,000.

FINANCIAL AID. 90% of freshmen, 77% of continuing students receive some form of aid. 49% of grants, all loans, 70% of jobs based on need. 110 enrolled freshmen were judged to have need, all were offered aid. Academic, athletic, state/district residency, leadership, alumni affiliation scholarships available. **Aid applications:** No closing date; priority given to applications received by May 1; applicants notified on a rolling basis beginning on or about May 1.

ADDRESS/TELEPHONE. Col. James H. Matchin, Director of Admissions, New Mexico Military Institute, 101 West College Boulevard, Roswell, NM 88201-5173. (505) 624-8050. (800) 421-5376. Fax: (505) 624-8107.

New Mexico State University

Las Cruces, New Mexico — CB code: 4531

Admissions: 79% of applicants accepted
Based on: ••• School record, test scores
Completion: 38% graduate

4-year public university, coed. Founded in 1888. **Accreditation:** Regional. **Undergraduate enrollment:** 4,926 men, 4,557 women full time; 1,526 men, 1,948 women part time. **Graduate enrollment:** 890 men, 625 women full time; 508 men, 520 women part time. **Faculty:** 794 total (650 full time), 513 with doctorates or other terminal degrees. **Location:** Suburban campus in small city; 42 miles from El Paso, Texas. **Calendar:** 4-4-1, extensive summer session. **Microcomputers:** 3,683 located in dormitories, computer centers. **Special facilities:** Museum, observatory, horsefarm, rodeo grounds, art gallery.

DEGREES OFFERED. AA, AS, AAS, BA, BS, BFA, MA, MS, MBA, MFA, MEd, MSW, PhD, EdD. 188 associate degrees awarded in 1992. 19% in business and management, 30% teacher education, 5% engineering technologies, 35% health sciences, 7% parks/recreation, protective services, public affairs. 1,782 bachelor's degrees awarded. 6% in agriculture, 19% business and management, 6% business/office and marketing/distribution, 10% education, 15% engineering, 13% social sciences. Graduate degrees offered in 68 major fields of study.

UNDERGRADUATE MAJORS. Associate: Air conditioning/heating/refrigeration mechanics, automotive mechanics, business and management, business and office, business computer/console/peripheral equipment operation, business data entry equipment operation, civil technology, construction, criminal justice studies, drafting, education paraprofessional, electrical and electronics equipment repair, electronic technology, engineering and engineering-related technologies, exercise technology, fire protection, law enforcement and corrections technologies, legal assistant/paralegal, liberal/general studies, marketing and distribution, mechanical technology, medical laboratory technologies, nursing, occupational business, practical nursing, radiograph medical technology, secretarial and related programs, water utility operation, word processing. **Bachelor's:** Accounting, advertising, agribusiness, agricultural biology, agricultural business and management, agricultural economics, agricultural education, agricultural engineering, agricultural extension education, agricultural sciences, agronomy, animal sciences, anthropology, art education, art history, athletic training education, aviation management, biochemistry, biology, botany, business administration and management, business and management, business computer systems, business data programming, business economics, business education, ceramics, chemical engineering, chemistry, city/community/regional planning, civil engineering, civil technology, communication disorders, communications, community health work, computer and information sciences, computer engineering, criminal justice studies, dramatic arts, earth sciences, ecology, economics, education, electrical/electronics/communications engineering, electronic technology, elementary education, engineering, engineering and engineering-related technologies, English, English education, entomology, environmental health engineering, family/consumer resource management, fashion merchandising, finance, fine arts, fishing and fisheries, food science and nutrition, food sciences, foreign languages education, French, geography, geological engineering, geological sciences, geology, geophysics and seismology, German, graphic design, health education, health sciences, history, home economics, home economics education, horticultural science, horticulture, hospitality and recreation marketing, hospitality and tourism, hotel/motel and restaurant management, industrial engineering, international business management, journalism, Latin American studies, law enforcement and corrections, law enforcement and corrections technologies, liberal/general studies, marketing and distribution, marketing management, mathematics, mathematics education, mechanical engineering, mechanical technology, medical laboratory technologies, metal/jewelry, microbiology, music, music education, music performance, nursing, operations research, optics, organizational behavior, painting, parks and recreation management, personnel management, philosophy, photography, physical education, physical sciences, physics, plant protection, plant sciences, political science and government, practical nursing, predentistry, prelaw, premedicine, prepharmacy, preveterinary, printmaking, pro golf management, psychology, public relations, radio/television broadcasting, range management, real estate, renewable natural resources, retailing, Russian, science education, sculpture, secondary education, social science education, social sciences, social studies education, social work, sociology, soil sciences, Spanish, special education, speech pathology/audiology, speech/communication/theater education, sports medicine, studio art, textiles and clothing, transportation and travel marketing, transportation management, wildlife management, zoology.

ACADEMIC PROGRAMS. Accelerated program, cooperative education, double major, dual enrollment of high school students, education specialist degree, honors program, independent study, internships, student-designed major, study abroad, teacher preparation, visiting/exchange student program, weekend college, cross-registration. **Remedial services:** Learning center, reduced course load, remedial instruction, special counselor, tutoring. **ROTC:** Air Force, Army. **Placement/credit:** AP, CLEP General and Subject, institutional tests; 30 credit hours maximum for bachelor's degree.

ACADEMIC REQUIREMENTS. Freshmen must earn minimum GPA of 2.0 to continue in good standing. 74% of freshmen return for sophomore year. Students must declare major by end of second year. **Graduation requirements:** 66 hours for associate, 128 hours for bachelor's (24 in major). Most students required to take courses in arts/fine arts, computer science, English, history, humanities, mathematics, biological/physical sciences, social sciences.

FRESHMAN ADMISSIONS. Selection criteria: School achievement record, test scores most important. **High school preparation:** 10 units required. Required units include English 4, foreign language 1, mathematics 3 and science 2. English: must include at least 2 units of composition, 1 which must be at junior or senior level. Mathematics: from algebra I, algebra II, geometry, trigonometry or advanced mathematics. Will accept 1 unit of foreign language or fine arts. 2 science must be laboratory sciences. **Test requirements:** SAT or ACT (ACT preferred); score report by August 15.

1992 FRESHMAN CLASS PROFILE. 3,763 men and women applied, 2,990 accepted; 778 men enrolled, 852 women enrolled. 41% had high school GPA of 3.0 or higher, 33% between 2.0 and 2.99. **Characteristics:** 59% commute, 22% have minority backgrounds. Average age is 20.

FALL-TERM APPLICATIONS. $10 fee. No closing date; priority given to applications received by August 15; applicants notified on a rolling basis. Deferred and early admission available.

STUDENT LIFE. Housing: Dormitories (men, women, coed); apartment, fraternity, sorority housing available. **Activities:** Student government, magazine, radio, student newspaper, television, choral groups, concert band, dance, drama, jazz band, marching band, music ensembles, musical theater, pep band, symphony orchestra, fraternities, sororities.

ATHLETICS. NCAA. **Intercollegiate:** Baseball M, basketball, cross-country, diving, football M, golf, softball W, swimming, tennis, track and field, volleyball W. **Intramural:** Archery, badminton, basketball, fencing, golf, racquetball, rugby M, skiing, soccer, softball, swimming, table tennis, tennis, track and field, volleyball, water polo.

STUDENT SERVICES. Aptitude testing, career counseling, employment service for undergraduates, freshman orientation, health services, on-campus day care, personal counseling, placement service for graduates, special adviser for adult students, veterans counselor, services/facilities for handicapped.

ANNUAL EXPENSES. Tuition and fees: $1,872, $4,200 additional for out-of-state students. **Room and board:** $3,998. **Books and supplies:** $550. **Other expenses:** $1,066.

FINANCIAL AID. 65% of continuing students receive some form of aid. 71% of grants, 91% of loans, 75% of jobs based on need. Academic, music/drama, athletic, state/district residency, leadership, minority scholarships available. **Aid applications:** No closing date; priority given to applications received by March 1; applicants notified on a rolling basis beginning on or about May 1; must reply within 2 weeks.

ADDRESS/TELEPHONE. Bill Bruner, Director of Admissions and Records, New Mexico State University, PO Box 30001 Department 3A, Las Cruces, NM 88003-0001. (505) 646-3121. Fax: (505) 646-6330.

New Mexico State University at Alamogordo
Alamogordo, New Mexico CB code: 4012

2-year public branch campus college, coed. Founded in 1958. **Accreditation:** Regional. **Undergraduate enrollment:** 231 men, 385 women full time; 561 men, 830 women part time. **Faculty:** 124 total (41 full time), 10 with doctorates or other terminal degrees. **Location:** Urban campus in large town; 85 miles from El Paso, Texas, 65 miles from Las Cruces. **Calendar:** Semester, limited summer session. Saturday and extensive evening/early morning classes. **Microcomputers:** 59 located in libraries, classrooms, computer centers, campus-wide network. **Special facilities:** Planetarium.

DEGREES OFFERED. AA, AAS. 159 associate degrees awarded in 1992.

UNDERGRADUATE MAJORS. Business and management, business and office, clinical laboratory science, criminal justice technology, data processing, electronic technology, fire control and safety technology, information sciences and systems, liberal/general studies, medical laboratory technologies, nursing, secretarial and related programs.

ACADEMIC PROGRAMS. 2-year transfer program, cooperative education, double major, dual enrollment of high school students, independent study, weekend college, cross-registration. **Remedial services:** Learning center, reduced course load, remedial instruction, special counselor, tutoring. **Placement/credit:** AP, CLEP General and Subject, institutional tests; 30 credit hours maximum for associate degree.

ACADEMIC REQUIREMENTS. Freshmen must earn minimum GPA of 2.0 to continue in good standing. 45% of freshmen return for sophomore year. **Graduation requirements:** 66 hours for associate. Most students required to take courses in English.

FRESHMAN ADMISSIONS. Selection criteria: Open admissions. Recommended units include English 3, mathematics 3, social science 1 and science 1.

1992 FRESHMAN CLASS PROFILE. 286 men, 486 women enrolled. **Characteristics:** 94% from in state, 100% commute, 20% have minority backgrounds.

FALL-TERM APPLICATIONS. $10 fee. No closing date; applicants notified on a rolling basis. Interview required for nursing, medical laboratory technology applicants. Essay required for nursing, medical laboratory technology applicants. Early admission available.

STUDENT LIFE. Activities: Student government, choral groups, drama, jazz band, music ensembles.

ATHLETICS. Intramural: Softball, table tennis, volleyball.

STUDENT SERVICES. Aptitude testing, career counseling, employment service for undergraduates, freshman orientation, personal counseling, placement service for graduates, veterans counselor, services/facilities for handicapped.

ANNUAL EXPENSES. Tuition and fees (1992-93): $682, $120 additional for out-of-district students, $1,224 additional for out-of-state students. **Books and supplies:** $310.

FINANCIAL AID. All grants, all loans, 83% of jobs based on need. **Aid applications:** Closing date March 1; applicants notified on or about June 1; must reply within 30 days.

ADDRESS/TELEPHONE. Eltima Mobley, Admissions Coordinator, New Mexico State University at Alamogordo, PO Box 477, Alamogordo, NM 88310. (505) 439-3700.

New Mexico State University at Carlsbad
Carlsbad, New Mexico CB code: 4547

2-year public branch campus, community college, coed. Founded in 1950. **Accreditation:** Regional. **Undergraduate enrollment:** 154 men, 344 women full time; 295 men, 421 women part time. **Faculty:** 72 total (23 full time), 6 with doctorates or other terminal degrees. **Location:** Rural campus in large town; 165 miles from of El Paso, Texas. **Calendar:** Semester, limited summer session. **Microcomputers:** 85 located in libraries, classrooms, computer centers.

DEGREES OFFERED. AA, AAS. 87 associate degrees awarded in 1992.

UNDERGRADUATE MAJORS. Business and management, business and office, computer and information sciences, criminal justice studies, electronic technology, health physics technician, law enforcement and corrections technologies, liberal/general studies, nursing, Radioactive and hazardous materials technology, radiograph medical technology, secretarial and related programs, welding technology.

ACADEMIC PROGRAMS. 2-year transfer program, double major, dual enrollment of high school students, internships, student-designed major, weekend college. **Remedial services:** Learning center, remedial instruction, tutoring, GED preparation, English as a second language. **Placement/credit:** AP, CLEP General, institutional tests; 30 credit hours maximum for associate degree.

ACADEMIC REQUIREMENTS. Freshmen must earn minimum GPA of 2.0 to continue in good standing. 50% of freshmen return for sophomore year. Students must declare major by end of first year. **Graduation requirements:** 66 hours for associate (32 in major). Most students required to take courses in arts/fine arts, English, history, humanities, mathematics, biological/physical sciences, social sciences.

FRESHMAN ADMISSIONS. Selection criteria: Open admissions. One semester provisional admission if high school or previous college GPA is below 2.0, or GED score is below 50. Special admissions requirements for nursing, radiological technology, and health physics applicants. **Test requirements:** SAT or ACT (ACT preferred) for placement and counseling only; score report by August 31. ACT required for admission for nursing applicants.

1992 FRESHMAN CLASS PROFILE. 201 men, 353 women enrolled. **Characteristics:** 95% from in state, 100% commute, 9% have minority backgrounds. Average age is 22.

FALL-TERM APPLICATIONS. $10 fee, may be waived for applicants with need. Closing date August 31; priority given to applications received by August 1; applicants notified on a rolling basis; must reply by registration. Interview required for nursing, radiological technology applicants. Deferred admission available.

STUDENT LIFE. Activities: Student government, student newspaper, choral groups, drama, business club, Student Nursing Association, Vocational Trade Association, NMSU-C Ambassadors, Phi Theta Kappa, Computer Science Club.

ATHLETICS. Intramural: Basketball, racquetball, table tennis, tennis, volleyball.

STUDENT SERVICES. Aptitude testing, career counseling, employment service for undergraduates, freshman orientation, personal counseling, placement service for graduates, veterans counselor, services/facilities for handicapped.

ANNUAL EXPENSES. Tuition and fees: $750, $120 additional for out-of-district students, $1,950 additional for out-of-state students. **Books and supplies:** $600. **Other expenses:** $1,100.

FINANCIAL AID. 37% of continuing students receive some form of aid. All grants, 98% of loans, 99% of jobs based on need. Academic scholarships available. **Aid applications:** No closing date; priority given to applications received by March 1; applicants notified on a rolling basis beginning on or about May 30; must reply within 30 days.

ADDRESS/TELEPHONE. Michael J. Cleary, Assistant Provost for Student Services, New Mexico State University at Carlsbad, 1500 University Drive, Carlsbad, NM 88220. (505) 885-8831. Fax: (505) 885-4951.

New Mexico State University at Grants
Grants, New Mexico CB code: 0461

2-year public community college, coed. Founded in 1968. **Accreditation:** Regional. **Undergraduate enrollment:** 70 men, 151 women full time; 109 men, 251 women part time. **Location:** Rural campus in large town; 75 miles from Albuquerque. **Calendar:** Semester.

FRESHMAN ADMISSIONS. Selection criteria: Open admissions.

ANNUAL EXPENSES. Tuition and fees (1992-93): $750, $90 additional for out-of-district students, $1,530 additional for out-of-state students. **Books and supplies:** $400.

ADDRESS/TELEPHONE. Richard Danek, Assistant Provost, New Mexico State University at Grants, 1500 North Third Street, Grants, NM 87020. (505) 287-7981.

Northern New Mexico Community College
Espanola, New Mexico CB code: 0425

2-year public community college, coed. Founded in 1909. **Accreditation:** Regional. **Undergraduate enrollment:** 318 men, 570 women full time; 271 men, 673 women part time. **Faculty:** 163 total (40 full time), 11 with doctorates or other terminal degrees. **Location:** Rural campus in small town; 24 miles from Santa Fe. **Calendar:** Semester, limited summer session. Extensive evening/early morning classes. **Microcomputers:** 12 located in computer centers. **Additional facts:** Campus at El Rito, attendance center in Taos.

DEGREES OFFERED. AA, AS, AAS. 157 associate degrees awarded in 1992. 34% in business/office and marketing/distribution, 9% computer sciences, 10% health sciences, 17% allied health, 5% multi/interdisciplinary studies, 5% parks/recreation, protective services, public affairs, 6% trade and industry.

UNDERGRADUATE MAJORS. Accounting, automotive mechanics, biological and physical sciences, business administration and management, business and management, business and office, business data processing and related programs, computer and information sciences, criminal justice technology, drafting, drafting and design technology, early childhood education, electrical installation, electronic technology, fine arts, forestry and related sciences, liberal/general studies, library assistant, machine tool operation/machine shop, management information systems, mental health/human services, nursing, plumbing/pipefitting/steamfitting, radiograph medical technology, renewable natural resources, science technologies, secretarial and related programs, small business management and ownership, social work, substance abuse counseling, woodworking, word processing.

ACADEMIC PROGRAMS. 2-year transfer program, dual enrollment of

high school students, internships. **Remedial services:** Learning center, remedial instruction, special counselor, tutoring. **Placement/credit:** CLEP General and Subject, institutional tests; 15 credit hours maximum for associate degree.

ACADEMIC REQUIREMENTS. Freshmen must earn minimum GPA of 2.0 to continue in good standing. 52% of freshmen return for sophomore year. Students must declare major on application. **Graduation requirements:** 64 hours for associate (36 in major). Most students required to take courses in computer science, English, humanities, mathematics, social sciences.

FRESHMAN ADMISSIONS. Selection criteria: Open admissions. Nursing, radiography, and cosmetology programs require separate applications subsequent to admission. 2-year nursing program requires 2.5 GPA and NLN Pre-Admission Test; work experience needed for the second year.

1992 FRESHMAN CLASS PROFILE. 97 men, 142 women enrolled. **Characteristics:** 99% from in state, 99% commute, 92% have minority backgrounds, 1% are foreign students.

FALL-TERM APPLICATIONS. No fee. No closing date; applicants notified on a rolling basis. Deferred and early admission available.

STUDENT LIFE. Housing: Dormitories (coed). **Activities:** Student government, choral groups, drama, music ensembles, Phi Theta Kappa.

ATHLETICS. Intramural: Basketball, softball.

STUDENT SERVICES. Aptitude testing, career counseling, employment service for undergraduates, freshman orientation, personal counseling, placement service for graduates, veterans counselor, services/facilities for handicapped.

ANNUAL EXPENSES. Tuition and fees (1992-93): $528, $900 additional for out-of-state students. **Room and board:** $2,768. **Books and supplies:** $460. **Other expenses:** $1,300.

FINANCIAL AID. 85% of freshmen, 85% of continuing students receive some form of aid. 99% of grants, all loans, 88% of jobs based on need. Academic scholarships available. **Aid applications:** No closing date; priority given to applications received by March 1; applicants notified on a rolling basis beginning on or about June 1; must reply within 2 weeks.

ADDRESS/TELEPHONE. Michael L. Costello, Director of Admissions, Recruiting, and Records, Northern New Mexico Community College, 1002 North Onate Street, Espanola, NM 87532. (505) 747-2115. Fax: (505) 747-2180.

Parks College
Albuquerque, New Mexico — CB code: 3389

2-year proprietary junior college, coed. **Undergraduate enrollment:** 30 men, 105 women full time. **Faculty:** 13 total (12 full time), 1 with doctorate or other terminal degree. **Location:** Suburban campus in large city. **Calendar:** Quarter. Extensive evening/early morning classes. **Microcomputers:** 18 located in libraries, classrooms, computer centers.

DEGREES OFFERED. AS, AAS. 75 associate degrees awarded in 1992. 50% in business and management, 35% business/office and marketing/distribution, 5% computer sciences, 8% engineering technologies.

UNDERGRADUATE MAJORS. Accounting, business administration and management, business and management, business and office, computer and information sciences, court reporting, drafting, drafting and design technology, trade and industrial supervision and management.

ACADEMIC PROGRAMS. Independent study, internships. **Remedial services:** Remedial instruction. **Placement/credit:** Institutional tests.

ACADEMIC REQUIREMENTS. Freshmen must earn minimum GPA of 2.0 to continue in good standing. 93% of freshmen return for sophomore year. Students must declare major on enrollment. **Graduation requirements:** 96 hours for associate. Most students required to take courses in computer science, English, humanities, mathematics, social sciences. **Additional information:** Contractual agreements for vocational and associate degree programs in various fields. Programs range from 6 months to 2 years.

FRESHMAN ADMISSIONS. Selection criteria: Applicants must score at least 142 on CPAT. Applicants to court reporter program must score 150. **Test requirements:** CPAT test required of all applicants.

1992 FRESHMAN CLASS PROFILE. 15 men applied, 10 accepted, 10 enrolled; 35 women applied, 29 accepted, 29 enrolled. **Characteristics:** 100% from in state. Average age is 22.

FALL-TERM APPLICATIONS. $395 fee. No closing date; applicants notified on a rolling basis. Interview required.

STUDENT LIFE. Housing: Apartment housing available.

STUDENT SERVICES. Career counseling, employment service for undergraduates, freshman orientation, personal counseling, placement service for graduates, special adviser for adult students, veterans counselor, services/facilities for handicapped.

ANNUAL EXPENSES. Tuition and fees (1992-93): $4,320. Tuition varies by program. Book costs are included in tuition.

FINANCIAL AID. All jobs based on need. Academic scholarships available. **Aid applications:** Closing date May 31; applicants notified on a rolling basis.

ADDRESS/TELEPHONE. Robert Paper, Director of Admissions, Parks College, 1023 Tijeras Northwest, Albuquerque, NM 87102. (505) 843-7500.

St. John's College
Santa Fe, New Mexico — CB code: 4737

Admissions: 84% of applicants accepted
Based on:
- ••• Essay, interview, school record
- •• Recommendations
- • Activities, special talents, test scores

Completion: 60% graduate, 20% of these enter graduate study

4-year private liberal arts college, coed. Founded in 1964. **Accreditation:** Regional. **Undergraduate enrollment:** 219 men, 168 women full time; 2 men, 2 women part time. **Graduate enrollment:** 38 men, 39 women full time; 3 men, 3 women part time. **Faculty:** 49 total (45 full time), 39 with doctorates or other terminal degrees. **Location:** Rural campus in small city; 60 miles from Albuquerque. **Calendar:** Semester, limited summer session. **Microcomputers:** 10 located in computer centers. **Special facilities:** Art gallery, music library, search and rescue center. **Additional facts:** Interdisciplinary education based on great books of Western intellectual heritage stressing connections among different branches of knowledge. All classes are small discussion groups. Second campus in Annapolis, Maryland. Students may transfer between campuses.

DEGREES OFFERED. BA, MA. 90 bachelor's degrees awarded in 1992. 100% in multi/interdisciplinary studies. Graduate degrees offered in 3 major fields of study.

UNDERGRADUATE MAJORS. European studies, great books, humanities, liberal/general studies.

ACADEMIC PROGRAMS. Teacher preparation, cross-registration. **Remedial services:** Tutoring.

ACADEMIC REQUIREMENTS. No policy requiring minimum GPA; records of students having academic difficulty are reviewed individually. 81% of freshmen return for sophomore year. **Graduation requirements:** 137 hours for bachelor's. Most students required to take courses in arts/fine arts, English, foreign languages, history, humanities, mathematics, philosophy/religion, biological/physical sciences, social sciences. **Postgraduate studies:** 5% enter law school, 2% enter medical school, 2% enter MBA programs, 11% enter other graduate study.

FRESHMAN ADMISSIONS. Selection criteria: Three essays describing educational and personal background and goals most important along with 2 letters of reference. Interview and 3-day campus visit strongly recommended. High school achievement record considered. **High school preparation:** 16 units required. Required and recommended units include English 4, mathematics 3-4 and science 3-4. Foreign language 2 recommended. Mathematics requirement includes 2 algebra, 1 geometry. Precalculus or trigonometry recommended. **Additional information:** 1/4 of freshmen have attended college elsewhere, but all start at beginning of 4-year program.

1992 FRESHMAN CLASS PROFILE. 146 men applied, 121 accepted, 63 enrolled; 129 women applied, 109 accepted, 52 enrolled. **Academic background:** Mid 50% of enrolled freshmen had SAT-V between 550-650, SAT-M between 520-650; ACT composite between 26-29. 80% submitted SAT scores, 20% submitted ACT scores. **Characteristics:** 6% from in state, 97% live in college housing, 7% have minority backgrounds, 2% are foreign students. Average age is 19.

FALL-TERM APPLICATIONS. No fee. No closing date; priority given to applications received by March 1; applicants notified on a rolling basis; must reply by May 1 or within 2 weeks if notified thereafter. Essay required. Interview recommended. CRDA. Deferred and early admission available. Self-selectivity is a large part of application process. Consequently, yield on acceptance is unusually high. Early application encouraged.

STUDENT LIFE. Housing: Dormitories (women, coed). Most undergraduates live in single rooms. Graduate housing for single students available but limited. **Activities:** Student government, film, magazine, student newspaper, photography, choral groups, dance, drama, jazz band, music ensembles, search and rescue team, Amnesty International, adult literacy, historic church restoration, Koran study group, women's literature group, peer counseling.

ATHLETICS. Intercollegiate: Fencing, soccer. **Intramural:** Baseball, basketball, cross-country, fencing, gymnastics, skiing, soccer, softball, swimming, table tennis, tennis, track and field, volleyball.

STUDENT SERVICES. Career counseling, employment service for undergraduates, freshman orientation, health services, personal counseling, placement service for graduates.

ANNUAL EXPENSES. Tuition and fees: $16,300. **Room and board:** $5,450. **Books and supplies:** $275. **Other expenses:** $900.

FINANCIAL AID. 64% of freshmen, 60% of continuing students receive some form of aid. All grants, 98% of loans, 88% of jobs based on need. 73 enrolled freshmen were judged to have need, all were offered aid. **Aid applications:** No closing date; priority given to applications received by March 1; applicants notified on a rolling basis beginning on or about April 15; must reply by May 1 or within 2 weeks if notified thereafter. **Additional information:** 100% of need met for those qualified to receive aid. Families receive individual attention in determining need fairly. Independent students must submit parental data. Financial aid information also required of noncustodial parent in cases of separation or divorce.

ADDRESS/TELEPHONE. Larry Clendenin, Director of Admission, St. John's College, 1160 Camino Cruz Blanca, Santa Fe, NM 87501-4599. (505) 982-3691 ext. 267. (800) 331-5232. Fax: (505) 989-9269.

San Juan College

Farmington, New Mexico — CB code: 4732

2-year public community college, coed. Founded in 1956. **Accreditation:** Regional. **Undergraduate enrollment:** 497 men, 767 women full time; 742 men, 1,531 women part time. **Faculty:** 195 total (63 full time), 22 with doctorates or other terminal degrees. **Location:** Rural campus in large town; 180 miles from Albuquerque. **Calendar:** Semester, limited summer session. Saturday and extensive evening/early morning classes. **Microcomputers:** Located in libraries, classrooms, computer centers. **Special facilities:** Planetarium, art gallery, special collection of Southwestern books and materials, geographic information system for computer analysis of satellite images.

DEGREES OFFERED. AA, AS, AAS. 231 associate degrees awarded in 1992. 16% in business and management, 24% health sciences, 37% multi/interdisciplinary studies, 13% trade and industry.

UNDERGRADUATE MAJORS. Accounting, airline piloting and navigation, automotive mechanics, business and management, criminal justice technology, data processing, diesel engine mechanics, drafting, drafting and design technology, electronic technology, finance, industrial technology, instrumentation technology, law enforcement and corrections technologies, legal assistant/paralegal, liberal/general studies, machine tool operation/machine shop, microcomputer software, nursing, physical therapy assistant, public administration, radio/television broadcasting, real estate, secretarial and related programs, welding technology.

ACADEMIC PROGRAMS. 2-year transfer program, cooperative education, dual enrollment of high school students, independent study, internships. **Remedial services:** Learning center, reduced course load, remedial instruction, special counselor, tutoring. **Placement/credit:** CLEP General and Subject, institutional tests; 30 credit hours maximum for associate degree.

ACADEMIC REQUIREMENTS. Freshmen must earn minimum GPA of 2.0 to continue in good standing. 47% of freshmen return for sophomore year. Students must declare major by end of first year. **Graduation requirements:** 62 hours for associate. Most students required to take courses in English, mathematics.

FRESHMAN ADMISSIONS. Selection criteria: Open admissions. **High school preparation:** 13 units recommended. Recommended units include English 4, foreign language 1, mathematics 3, social science 3 and science 2.

1992 FRESHMAN CLASS PROFILE. 223 men, 289 women enrolled. **Characteristics:** 93% from in state, 100% commute, 45% have minority backgrounds. Average age is 28.

FALL-TERM APPLICATIONS. $10 fee. Closing date August 25; applicants notified on a rolling basis.

STUDENT LIFE. Activities: Student government, film, radio, student newspaper, television, choral groups, dance, drama, jazz band, music ensembles, musical theater, Indian club, Student Ambassadors, Phi Theta Kappa (honor society).

ATHLETICS. Intramural: Archery, badminton, baseball, basketball, bowling, cross-country, golf, handball, racquetball, skiing, softball, table tennis, tennis, volleyball.

STUDENT SERVICES. Aptitude testing, career counseling, employment service for undergraduates, freshman orientation, on-campus day care, personal counseling, placement service for graduates, veterans counselor, Native American programs, services/facilities for handicapped.

ANNUAL EXPENSES. Tuition and fees (1992-93): $360, $240 additional for out-of-state students. **Books and supplies:** $400. **Other expenses:** $600.

FINANCIAL AID. 60% of freshmen, 61% of continuing students receive some form of aid. 91% of grants, 96% of loans, 94% of jobs based on need. 275 enrolled freshmen were judged to have need, all were offered aid. Academic, music/drama, leadership, minority scholarships available. **Aid applications:** No closing date; priority given to applications received by May 1; applicants notified on a rolling basis beginning on or about June 1; must reply within 2 weeks.

ADDRESS/TELEPHONE. Jim Ratliff, Director of Admissions, San Juan College, 4601 College Boulevard, Farmington, NM 87402. (505) 326-3311. (800) 232-6327. Fax: (505) 599-0385.

Santa Fe Community College

Santa Fe, New Mexico — CB code: 4816

2-year public community college, coed. Founded in 1983. **Accreditation:** Regional. **Undergraduate enrollment:** 773 men and women. **Faculty:** 294 total (38 full time), 46 with doctorates or other terminal degrees. **Location:** Urban campus in small city; 60 miles from of Albuquerque. **Calendar:** Semester, limited summer session. **Microcomputers:** 200 located in classrooms, computer centers.

DEGREES OFFERED. AA, AS, AAS. 86 associate degrees awarded in 1992. 13% in business and management, 10% business/office and marketing/distribution, 6% computer sciences, 5% engineering technologies, 22% health sciences, 7% law, 25% multi/interdisciplinary studies, 7% trade and industry.

UNDERGRADUATE MAJORS. Accounting, biological and physical sciences, biology, business administration and management, business and management, business and office, computer and information sciences, construction, criminal justice studies, drafting, drafting and design technology, early childhood education, electronic technology, finance, hotel/motel and restaurant management, legal assistant/paralegal, liberal/general studies, nursing, office technology, preengineering, real estate, secretarial and related programs, small business management and ownership, Southwest studies, survey and mapping technology, telecommunications, word processing.

ACADEMIC PROGRAMS. 2-year transfer program, cooperative education, dual enrollment of high school students, honors program, independent study, internships. **Remedial services:** Learning center, remedial instruction, special counselor, tutoring. **Placement/credit:** CLEP General and Subject, institutional tests; 30 credit hours maximum for associate degree.

ACADEMIC REQUIREMENTS. Freshmen must earn minimum GPA of 2.0 to continue in good standing. **Graduation requirements:** 64 hours for associate (32 in major). Most students required to take courses in computer science, English, humanities, mathematics, biological/physical sciences, social sciences.

FRESHMAN ADMISSIONS. Selection criteria: Open admissions. Admission to degree-seeking status granted to applicants with high school diploma or GED. Admission to non-degree-seeking status is granted to persons with or without high school diploma or GED.

1992 FRESHMAN CLASS PROFILE. Characteristics: 95% from in state, 100% commute, 68% have minority backgrounds. Average age is 31.

FALL-TERM APPLICATIONS. No fee. Interview required for concurrent high school/college, foreign applicants. Essay required for foreign applicants. Deferred admission available.

STUDENT LIFE. Activities: Student government, radio, television, choral groups, drama, music ensembles.

STUDENT SERVICES. Aptitude testing, career counseling, employment service for undergraduates, freshman orientation, personal counseling, placement service for graduates, veterans counselor, services/facilities for handicapped.

ANNUAL EXPENSES. Tuition and fees: $434, $72 additional for out-of-district students, $672 additional for out-of-state students. **Books and supplies:** $500. **Other expenses:** $440.

FINANCIAL AID. 20% of freshmen, 15% of continuing students receive some form of aid. 98% of grants, 90% of loans, 60% of jobs based on need. 200 enrolled freshmen were judged to have need, 150 were offered aid. Academic, music/drama scholarships available. **Aid applications:** No closing date; priority given to applications received by March 1; applicants notified on a rolling basis beginning on or about May 15; must reply within 30 days.

ADDRESS/TELEPHONE. Anita J. Shields, Director of Admissions and Records, Santa Fe Community College, PO Box 4187, South Richards Avenue, Santa Fe, NM 87502-4187. (505) 471-8200 ext. 267. Fax: (505) 438-1237.

Southwestern Indian Polytechnic Institute

Albuquerque, New Mexico — CB code: 7047

2-year public technical college, coed. **Accreditation:** Regional. **Undergraduate enrollment:** 494 men and women. **Location:** Urban campus in large city. **Calendar:** Trimester.

FRESHMAN ADMISSIONS. Selection criteria: Students must have certificate verifying American Indian status and high school transcript or GED scores. Also require physical examination and copy of immunization record.

ANNUAL EXPENSES. Tuition and fees: $50. Native American students may attend tuition-free. **Room and board:** $3,450. **Books and supplies:** $250. **Other expenses:** $1,000.

ADDRESS/TELEPHONE. Dr. Michael Immerman, Director of Admissions, Southwestern Indian Polytechnic Institute, 9169 Coors NW, Box 10146, Albuquerque, NM 87184. (505) 897-5346. Fax: (505) 897-5343.

University of New Mexico

Albuquerque, New Mexico — CB code: 4845

4-year public university, coed. Founded in 1889. **Accreditation:** Regional. **Undergraduate enrollment:** 5,847 men, 6,570 women full time; 3,218 men, 4,302 women part time. **Graduate enrollment:** 1,387 men, 1,410 women full time; 1,107 men, 1,294 women part time. **Faculty:** 1,780 total (1,315 full time). **Location:** Urban campus in large city; 2 miles from downtown, 450 miles from of Denver, Colorado. **Calendar:** Semester, limited summer session. Saturday and extensive evening/early morning classes. **Microcomputers:** 338 located in dormitories, classrooms, computer centers. **Special facilities:** 5 museums, fine arts center, observatory, Meteoritics Institute, arboretum, teaching hospital for nursing students, major research facilities in ceramics, optoelectronics, space nuclear power and high power devices and systems. **Additional facts:** Branch campuses in Valencia County, Los Alamos, and Gallup.

DEGREES OFFERED. AA, AS, AAS, BA, BS, BFA, MA, MS, MBA, MFA, PhD, EdD, MD, JD. 78 associate degrees awarded in 1992. 21% in business/office and marketing/distribution, 15% computer sciences, 58% allied health. 2,310 bachelor's degrees awarded. 14% in business and management, 11% education, 7% engineering, 8% health sciences, 7% letters/literature, 12% multi/interdisciplinary studies, 5% psychology, 11% social sciences, 5% visual and performing arts. Graduate degrees offered in 83 major fields of study.

UNDERGRADUATE MAJORS. Associate: Business and office, community services, computer programming, dental hygiene, elementary education, preengineering, radiograph medical technology, respiratory therapy technology, teacher aide. **Bachelor's:** Accounting, American studies, anthropology, architecture, art education, art history, Asian studies, astrophysics, bilingual/bicultural education, biochemistry, bioengineering and biomedical engineering, biology, biophysics, business administration and management, business and management, business education, chemical engineering, chemistry, civil engineering, classics, communications, comparative literature, computer and information sciences, computer engineering, construction engineering, construction management, creative writing, criminal justice studies, dance, dental hygiene, dramatic arts, economics, economics/philosophy, electrical/electronics/communications engineering, elementary education, energy and power systems, engineering, English, English/philosophy, entrepreneurial studies, environmental design, family/consumer resource management, finance, fine arts, foreign languages education, French, geography, geology, German, health education, history, home economics, human resources development, individual and family development, industrial arts education, international business management, interpreter for the deaf, journalism, Latin American studies, liberal/general studies, linguistics, management science, manufacturing and robotics, marketing and distribution, marketing management, mathematics, mathematics education, mechanical engineering, medical laboratory technologies, microtelectronics processing, music, music education, music performance, nuclear engineering, nursing, nutritional education, operations research, pharmacy, philosophy, philosophy/prelaw, physical education, physical therapy, physics, political science and government, Portuguese, predentistry, prelaw, premedicine, preveterinary, psychology, recreation and community services technologies, religion, Russian and Slavic studies, science education, social studies education, sociology, Spanish, special education, speech, speech pathology/audiology, studio art, teaching English as a second language/foreign language, technical and business writing, technical education, tourism, transportation and travel marketing, ultrasound technology.

ACADEMIC PROGRAMS. Cooperative education, double major, dual enrollment of high school students, education specialist degree, honors program, independent study, internships, student-designed major, study abroad, teacher preparation, telecourses, visiting/exchange student program, weekend college, Washington semester; combined bachelor's/graduate program in business administration, law. **Remedial services:** Learning center, reduced course load, remedial instruction, special counselor, tutoring. **ROTC:** Air Force, Army. **Placement/credit:** AP, CLEP General and Subject, institutional tests; 30 credit hours maximum for bachelor's degree.

ACADEMIC REQUIREMENTS. Freshmen must earn minimum GPA of 2.0 to continue in good standing. 72% of freshmen return for sophomore year. Students must declare major by end of second year. **Graduation requirements:** 60 hours for associate, 128 hours for bachelor's. Most students required to take courses in English.

FRESHMAN ADMISSIONS. Selection criteria: School achievement record (high school GPA of 2.0 required in college-preparatory units). Test scores, class rank, essays, recommendations considered. **High school preparation:** 14 units required. Required units include English 4, foreign language 2, mathematics 3, social science 2 and science 3. Social sciences must include 1 US history. Foreign language requirements must be in same language. One science must be laboratory. **Test requirements:** SAT or ACT (ACT preferred); score report by July 24.

1992 FRESHMAN CLASS PROFILE. 3,653 men and women applied, 3,066 accepted; 778 men enrolled, 966 women enrolled. 60% had high school GPA of 3.0 or higher, 40% between 2.0 and 2.99. 22% were in top tenth and 51% were in top quarter of graduating class. **Academic background:** Mid 50% of enrolled freshmen had ACT composite between 19-24. 82% submitted ACT scores. **Characteristics:** 81% from in state, 44% have minority backgrounds, 2% are foreign students. Average age is 18.

FALL-TERM APPLICATIONS. $15 fee, may be waived for applicants with need. Closing date July 22; applicants notified on a rolling basis. Interview recommended. Essay recommended. Deferred and early admission available.

STUDENT LIFE. Housing: Dormitories (men, women, coed); apartment, fraternity, sorority housing available. **Activities:** Student government, magazine, radio, student newspaper, television, yearbook, choral groups, concert band, dance, drama, jazz band, marching band, music ensembles, musical theater, opera, pep band, symphony orchestra, fraternities, sororities.

ATHLETICS. NCAA. **Intercollegiate:** Baseball M, basketball, cross-country, diving, football M, golf, gymnastics M, skiing, soccer, softball W, swimming, tennis, track and field, volleyball W, wrestling M. **Intramural:** Archery, badminton, basketball, bowling, cross-country, diving, fencing, football, golf, gymnastics, handball, lacrosse M, racquetball, rugby M, sailing, skiing, soccer, softball, swimming, table tennis, tennis, track and field, volleyball, water polo, wrestling M.

STUDENT SERVICES. Aptitude testing, career counseling, employment service for undergraduates, freshman orientation, health services, on-campus day care, personal counseling, placement service for graduates, veterans counselor, services/facilities for handicapped.

ANNUAL EXPENSES. Tuition and fees: $1,788, $4,680 additional for out-of-state students. **Room and board:** $4,726. **Books and supplies:** $546. **Other expenses:** $1,816.

FINANCIAL AID. 60% of freshmen, 54% of continuing students receive some form of aid. 80% of grants, 96% of loans, 79% of jobs based on need. 800 enrolled freshmen were judged to have need, all were offered aid. Academic, music/drama, athletic, minority scholarships available. **Aid applications:** No closing date; priority given to applications received by March 1; applicants notified on a rolling basis beginning on or about May 17; must reply within 3 weeks. **Additional information:** Scholarship financial aid has priority date of February 1.

ADDRESS/TELEPHONE. Cynthia Stuart, Director of Admissions, University of New Mexico, Albuquerque, NM 87131. (505) 277-2446.

Western New Mexico University

Silver City, New Mexico — CB code: 4535

4-year public university, coed. Founded in 1893. **Accreditation:** Regional. **Undergraduate enrollment:** 603 men, 683 women full time; 334 men, 617 women part time. **Graduate enrollment:** 6 men, 17 women full time; 157 men, 373 women part time. **Faculty:** 107 total (78 full time), 58 with doctorates or other terminal degrees. **Location:** Rural campus in large town; 155 miles from El Paso, Texas, 210 miles from Tucson Arizona. **Calendar:** Semester, extensive summer session. Extensive evening/early morning classes. **Microcomputers:** 110 located in libraries, classrooms, computer centers. **Special facilities:** Museum specializing in technology and Native American cultures, fine arts center and gallery, theater, amphitheater.

DEGREES OFFERED. AA, AS, AAS, BA, BS, MA, MBA, MD, B. Pharm. 26 associate degrees awarded in 1992. 36% in business/office and marketing/distribution, 7% parks/recreation, protective services, public affairs, 57% trade and industry. 149 bachelor's degrees awarded. 10% in area and ethnic studies, 21% business and management, 37% teacher education, 7% life sciences, 5% parks/recreation, protective services, public affairs, 12% social sciences. Graduate degrees offered in 13 major fields of study.

UNDERGRADUATE MAJORS. Associate: Automotive mechanics, automotive technology, business and office, carpentry, construction, drafting, drafting and design technology, law enforcement and corrections technologies, legal secretary, machine tool operation/machine shop, medical secretary, nursing, office supervision and management, precision metal work, predentistry, prelaw, premedicine, prepharmacy, preveterinary, public affairs, secretarial and related programs, welding technology. **Bachelor's:** Accounting, art education, biology, botany, business administration and management, business and management, business economics, chemistry, child development/care/guidance, computer and information sciences, criminal justice studies, criminology, early childhood education, earth sciences, economics, education, elementary education, English, fine arts, geology, health education, Hispanic American studies, history, humanities, humanities and social sciences, international business management, junior high education, law enforcement and corrections, liberal/general studies, management information systems, marketing management, mathematics, music, music education, personnel management, physical education, physical sciences, psychology, public administration, reading education, secondary education, social sciences, social work, sociology, Spanish, special education, zoology.

ACADEMIC PROGRAMS. 2-year transfer program, cooperative education, double major, dual enrollment of high school students, honors program, independent study, internships, student-designed major, teacher preparation; liberal arts/career combination in health sciences; combined bachelor's/graduate program in business administration. **Remedial services:** Learning center, remedial instruction, special counselor, tutoring. **Placement/credit:** CLEP General and Subject; 12 credit hours maximum for associate degree; 30 credit hours maximum for bachelor's degree.

ACADEMIC REQUIREMENTS. Freshmen must earn minimum GPA of 2.0 to continue in good standing. 46% of freshmen return for sophomore year. Students must declare major by end of second year. **Graduation requirements:** 64 hours for associate, 128 hours for bachelor's (30 in major). Most students required to take courses in arts/fine arts, computer science, English, foreign languages, history, humanities, mathematics, biological/physical sciences, social sciences. **Postgraduate studies:** 60% from 2-year programs enter 4-year programs.

FRESHMAN ADMISSIONS. Selection criteria: All applicants with minimum high school GPA of 2.0 accepted. All others considered individually. Good ACT or SAT test scores warrant strong consideration. Recommended units include English 3, mathematics 2, social science 2 and science

2. **Test requirements:** SAT or ACT (ACT preferred); score report by August 15.

1992 FRESHMAN CLASS PROFILE. 638 men applied, 638 accepted, 264 enrolled; 674 women applied, 674 accepted, 277 enrolled. 29% had high school GPA of 3.0 or higher, 59% between 2.0 and 2.99. **Characteristics:** 84% from in state, 80% live in college housing, 49% have minority backgrounds, 1% are foreign students. Average age is 19.

FALL-TERM APPLICATIONS. $10 fee, may be waived for applicants with need. Closing date September 3; priority given to applications received by August 10; applicants notified on a rolling basis. Deferred and early admission available.

STUDENT LIFE. Housing: Dormitories (men, women, coed); apartment housing available. All first-time full-time freshmen from outside Grant County area required to live in residence halls. **Activities:** Student government, student newspaper, yearbook, choral groups, concert band, drama, jazz band, music ensembles, musical theater, pep band, symphony orchestra, instrumental-vocal music center, Baptist Student Union, Society for the Advancement of Management, St. Francis Newman Club, Chicano student organization, United Campus Ministry, Criminal Justice, Native American Club.

ATHLETICS. NAIA. **Intercollegiate:** Baseball M, basketball, football M, golf M, softball W, volleyball W. **Intramural:** Baseball M, basketball, racquetball, softball, swimming, tennis, volleyball, wrestling.

STUDENT SERVICES. Aptitude testing, career counseling, employment service for undergraduates, freshman orientation, health services, on-campus day care, personal counseling, placement service for graduates, services/facilities for handicapped.

ANNUAL EXPENSES. Tuition and fees (1992-93): $1,214, $3,180 additional for out-of-state students. **Room and board:** $2,110. **Books and supplies:** $400. **Other expenses:** $1,000.

FINANCIAL AID. 43% of freshmen, 83% of continuing students receive some form of aid. 88% of grants, 99% of loans, 47% of jobs based on need. 175 enrolled freshmen were judged to have need, 167 were offered aid. Academic, music/drama, art, athletic, state/district residency, leadership, alumni affiliation scholarships available. **Aid applications:** No closing date; priority given to applications received by April 1; applicants notified on a rolling basis; must reply within 2 weeks.

ADDRESS/TELEPHONE. Michael Alecksen, Director of Admissions/Registrar, Western New Mexico University, 100 College Avenue, Box 680, Silver City, NM 88062. (505) 538-6106. (800) 222-9668. Fax: (505) 538-6155.

New York

Adelphi University
Garden City, New York CB code: 2003

Admissions: 86% of applicants accepted
Based on: ••• Essay, school record, test scores
•• Activities, interview, recommendations
• Special talents
Completion: 97% of freshmen end year in good standing
61% graduate

4-year private university, coed. Founded in 1896. **Accreditation:** Regional. **Undergraduate enrollment:** 1,054 men, 1,840 women full time; 332 men, 927 women part time. **Graduate enrollment:** 178 men, 659 women full time; 918 men, 2,353 women part time. **Faculty:** 669 total (269 full time), 189 with doctorates or other terminal degrees. **Location:** Suburban campus in large town; 20 miles from New York City. **Calendar:** Semester, limited summer session. **Microcomputers:** 450 located in libraries, classrooms, computer centers, campus-wide network. **Special facilities:** Theater, speech and hearing center, art gallery.

DEGREES OFFERED. AS, BA, BS, BFA, MA, MS, MBA, MSW, PhD. 19 associate degrees awarded in 1992. 95% in multi/interdisciplinary studies, 5% social sciences. 1,019 bachelor's degrees awarded. 40% in business and management, 9% teacher education, 8% health sciences, 5% psychology, 20% social sciences. Graduate degrees offered in 31 major fields of study.

UNDERGRADUATE MAJORS. Associate: Court administration, liberal/general studies. **Bachelor's:** Accounting, American studies, anthropology, art education, art history, biochemistry, biology, business administration and management, chemistry, communications, communicative disorders, computer and information sciences, dance, dramatic arts, earth sciences, economics, elementary education, English, English education, exercise physiology, finance, foreign languages (multiple emphasis), foreign languages education, French, graphic design, history, humanities, Latin American studies, mathematics, mathematics education, modern foreign language, music, music education, nursing, painting, philosophy, physical education, physics, political science and government, psychology, science education, secondary education, social sciences, social studies education, social work, sociology, Spanish, speech pathology/audiology, speech/communication/theater education, theater design.

ACADEMIC PROGRAMS. 2-year transfer program, double major, dual enrollment of high school students, honors program, independent study, internships, study abroad, teacher preparation, cross-registration, learning disabled program combining matriculation with support services, and ABLE (Adult Better Learning Experience) for adults 21 and over; liberal arts/career combination in engineering; combined bachelor's/graduate program in business administration. **Remedial services:** Learning center, special counselor, tutoring. **ROTC:** Air Force, Army. **Placement/credit:** AP, CLEP General and Subject, IB; 30 credit hours maximum for bachelor's degree.

ACADEMIC REQUIREMENTS. Freshmen must earn minimum GPA of 2.0 to continue in good standing. 62% of freshmen return for sophomore year. Students must declare major by end of second year. **Graduation requirements:** 64 hours for associate, 120 hours for bachelor's. Most students required to take courses in English, humanities, biological/physical sciences, social sciences.

FRESHMAN ADMISSIONS. Selection criteria: 3.0 cumulative high school GPA, rank in top third of class, and SAT combined score of 950 or higher very important. School and community activities considered. References and interview strongly recommended. **High school preparation:** 16 units recommended. Recommended units include English 4, foreign language 2, mathematics 3, social science 4 and science 3. **Test requirements:** SAT or ACT; score report by August 31.

1992 FRESHMAN CLASS PROFILE. 2,831 men and women applied, 2,448 accepted; 232 men enrolled, 356 women enrolled. 51% had high school GPA of 3.0 or higher, 45% between 2.0 and 2.99. 11% were in top tenth and 32% were in top quarter of graduating class. **Academic background:** Mid 50% of enrolled freshmen had SAT-V between 400-500, SAT-M between 430-560. 87% submitted SAT scores. **Characteristics:** 80% from in state, 55% live in college housing, 30% have minority backgrounds, 4% are foreign students. Average age is 20.

FALL-TERM APPLICATIONS. $35 fee, may be waived for applicants with need. No closing date; priority given to applications received by March 1; applicants notified on a rolling basis; must reply by May 1 or within 3 weeks if notified thereafter. Audition required for dance, theater, music applicants. Portfolio required for art, technical theater applicants. Essay required. Interview recommended. CRDA. Deferred and early admission available. November 30 priority date for spring-term applications.

STUDENT LIFE. Housing: Dormitories (women, coed); apartment housing available. **Activities:** Student government, film, magazine, radio, student newspaper, yearbook, choral groups, dance, drama, music ensembles, musical theater, pep band, symphony orchestra, fraternities, sororities, over 70 clubs, including political and social interest groups, cultural organizations, religious groups, international societies, course-related interest clubs, honor societies, service groups.

ATHLETICS. NCAA. **Intercollegiate:** Baseball M, basketball, cross-country, golf M, lacrosse M, soccer, softball W, swimming, tennis, volleyball W. **Intramural:** Badminton, basketball, bowling, football M, golf W, handball, racquetball, soccer, softball, squash, swimming, table tennis, tennis, track and field, volleyball.

STUDENT SERVICES. Aptitude testing, career counseling, employment service for undergraduates, freshman orientation, health services, on-campus day care, personal counseling, placement service for graduates, special adviser for adult students, veterans counselor, services/facilities for handicapped.

ANNUAL EXPENSES. Tuition and fees: $12,300. **Room and board:** $6,000. **Books and supplies:** $700. **Other expenses:** $1,500.

FINANCIAL AID. 74% of freshmen, 66% of continuing students receive some form of aid. 59% of grants, all loans, all jobs based on need. 405 enrolled freshmen were judged to have need, all were offered aid. Academic, music/drama, art, athletic scholarships available. **Aid applications:** No closing date; priority given to applications received by February 15; applicants notified on a rolling basis beginning on or about April 1; must reply by May 1 or within 2 weeks if notified thereafter.

ADDRESS/TELEPHONE. Scott Healy, VP Enrollment Planning and Management, Adelphi University, South Avenue, Levermore 114, Garden City, NY 11530. (516) 877-3050. In-state toll-free number (800) 233-5744.

Adirondack Community College
Queensbury, New York CB code: 2017

2-year public community college, coed. Founded in 1960. **Accreditation:** Regional. **Undergraduate enrollment:** 627 men, 1,024 women full time; 797 men, 1,340 women part time. **Faculty:** 251 total (124 full time), 28 with doctorates or other terminal degrees. **Location:** Rural campus in large town; 50 miles from Albany. **Calendar:** Semester, extensive summer session. **Microcomputers:** 125 located in libraries, classrooms, computer centers. **Special facilities:** Comprehensive learning center, art gallery, solar botany laboratory, fitness trail. **Additional facts:** Off-campus evening classes available in Saratoga Springs.

DEGREES OFFERED. AA, AS, AAS. 559 associate degrees awarded in 1992. 25% in business and management, 5% business/office and marketing/distribution, 5% computer sciences, 11% health sciences, 29% multi/interdisciplinary studies, 7% parks/recreation, protective services, public affairs, 8% physical sciences.

UNDERGRADUATE MAJORS. Accounting, biological and physical sciences, biology, business administration and management, business and management, business and office, business computer/console/peripheral equipment operation, business data processing and related programs, business data programming, chemistry, computer and information sciences, computer programming, computer technology, criminal justice studies, criminal justice technology, data processing, drafting, drafting and design technology, engineering, engineering and engineering-related technologies, English, finance, fine arts, food management, food production/management/services, food science and nutrition, forestry and related sciences, geology, history, humanities, humanities and social sciences, law enforcement and corrections, law enforcement and corrections technologies, liberal/general studies, marketing and distribution, marketing management, mathematics, mechanical design technology, medical records administration, medical records technology, medical secretary, music, nursing, photography, physical sciences, physics, political science and government, prelaw, protective services, psychology, radio/television broadcasting, radio/television technology, retailing, science technologies, secretarial and related programs, social sciences, sociology, tourism, transportation and travel marketing, visual and performing arts, word processing.

ACADEMIC PROGRAMS. 2-year transfer program, dual enrollment of high school students, honors program, independent study, internships, cross-registration. **Remedial services:** Learning center, reduced course load, remedial instruction, special counselor, tutoring. **Placement/credit:** AP, CLEP General and Subject, institutional tests; 34 credit hours maximum for associate degree.

ACADEMIC REQUIREMENTS. Freshmen must earn minimum GPA of 2.0 to continue in good standing. 82% of freshmen return for sophomore year. Students must declare major on application. **Graduation requirements:** 64 hours for associate (20 in major). Most students required to take courses in English, humanities, mathematics, biological/physical sciences, social sciences.

FRESHMAN ADMISSIONS. Selection criteria: Open admissions. **High school preparation:** 19 units recommended. Recommended units include biological science 1, English 4, foreign language 1, mathematics 3, physical science 2 and social science 4. Nursing and medical records technology programs require Regents biology and chemistry examinations. Engineering program requires biology, chemistry and mathematics through advanced algebra. Computer science program requires mathematics through advanced algebra. Forestry requires Regents biology, chemistry and mathematics through intermediate algebra. Mechanical technology program requires mathematics through elementary algebra.

1992 FRESHMAN CLASS PROFILE. 407 men, 560 women enrolled. 25% had high school GPA of 3.0 or higher, 45% between 2.0 and 2.99. **Characteristics:** 99% from in state, 100% commute, 2% have minority backgrounds, 1% are foreign students. Average age is 21.

FALL-TERM APPLICATIONS. $25 fee, may be waived for applicants with need. Closing date August 1; priority given to applications received by April 15; applicants notified on a rolling basis beginning on or about January 15; must reply by May 1 or within 2 weeks if notified thereafter. Interview recommended. CRDA. Deferred and early admission available. SAT or ACT recommended.

STUDENT LIFE. Housing: Privately owned, dormitory-style housing adjacent to campus. **Activities:** Student government, radio, student newspaper, television, choral groups, concert band, dance, drama, jazz band, music ensembles, musical theater, symphony orchestra.

ATHLETICS. NJCAA. **Intercollegiate:** Basketball, bowling, golf M, skiing, soccer, softball W, tennis, volleyball W. **Intramural:** Basketball, bowling, softball, volleyball.

STUDENT SERVICES. Career counseling, employment service for undergraduates, freshman orientation, on-campus day care, personal counseling, placement service for graduates, special adviser for adult students, veterans counselor, services/facilities for handicapped.

ANNUAL EXPENSES. Tuition and fees (projected): $1,873, $1,750 additional for out-of-state students. **Books and supplies:** $530. **Other expenses:** $1,697.

FINANCIAL AID. 60% of freshmen, 60% of continuing students receive some form of aid. 64% of grants, 78% of loans, 55% of jobs based on need. Academic, state/district residency, leadership scholarships available. **Aid applications:** No closing date; priority given to applications received by April 15; applicants notified on a rolling basis beginning on or about May 1.

ADDRESS/TELEPHONE. Lee Brown, Director of Admissions, Adirondack Community College, Bay Road, Queensbury, NY 12804-1498. (518) 793-4491 ext. 264. Fax: (518) 745-1433.

Albany College of Pharmacy
Albany, New York CB code: 2013

Admissions: 78% of applicants accepted
Based on: ••• School record
•• Essay, test scores
• Activities, interview, recommendations
Completion: 88% of freshmen end year in good standing
77% graduate, 13% of these enter graduate study

5-year private pharmacy college, coed. Founded in 1881. **Accreditation:** Regional. **Undergraduate enrollment:** 236 men, 382 women full time; 5 men, 21 women part time. **Graduate enrollment:** 3 men, 14 women full time; 1 woman part time. **Faculty:** 48 total (35 full time), 27 with doctorates or other terminal degrees. **Location:** Urban campus in small city; 200 miles from New York City. **Calendar:** Semester. **Microcomputers:** 100 located in libraries, classrooms, computer centers. **Special facilities:** Turn-of-the-century antique pharmacy.

DEGREES OFFERED. BS, Pharm D. 137 bachelor's degrees awarded in 1992. 100% in health sciences. Graduate degrees offered in 1 major field of study.

UNDERGRADUATE MAJORS. Pharmacy.

ACADEMIC PROGRAMS. Independent study, cross-registration, externships. **Remedial services:** Special counselor, tutoring. **Placement/credit:** AP, CLEP General and Subject, IB.

ACADEMIC REQUIREMENTS. Freshmen must earn minimum GPA of 2.0 to continue in good standing. 78% of freshmen return for sophomore year. Students must declare major on application. **Graduation requirements:** 160 hours for bachelor's (100 in major). Most students required to take courses in English, humanities, mathematics, biological/physical sciences.

FRESHMAN ADMISSIONS. Selection criteria: High school record, SAT or ACT scores, essay, letters of recommendation, New York State Regents Examinations. Special emphasis on science and mathematics grades. **High school preparation:** 16 units required. Required units include English 4, mathematics 4 and science 3. Chemistry and precalculus required. **Test requirements:** SAT or ACT (SAT preferred); score report by August 15.

1992 FRESHMAN CLASS PROFILE. 122 men applied, 99 accepted, 56 enrolled; 197 women applied, 150 accepted, 74 enrolled. 85% had high school GPA of 3.0 or higher, 15% between 2.0 and 2.99. 24% were in top tenth and 65% were in top quarter of graduating class. **Characteristics:** 90% from in state, 95% live in college housing, 14% have minority backgrounds, 1% are foreign students, 67% join fraternities/sororities. Average age is 18.

FALL-TERM APPLICATIONS. $25 fee, may be waived for applicants with need. No closing date; priority given to applications received by January 1; applicants notified on a rolling basis; must reply by January 15 or within 4 weeks if notified thereafter. Essay required. Interview recommended. Early admission available.

STUDENT LIFE. Housing: Dormitories (coed); handicapped housing available. **Activities:** Student government, student newspaper, yearbook, fraternities, sororities, Student American Pharmaceutical Association, American Chemical Society, International Club.

ATHLETICS. Intercollegiate: Basketball, bowling, golf, soccer. **Intramural:** Cross-country, skiing, volleyball.

STUDENT SERVICES. Aptitude testing, career counseling, employment service for undergraduates, freshman orientation, health services, personal counseling, placement service for graduates, services/facilities for handicapped.

ANNUAL EXPENSES. Tuition and fees (1992-93): $8,000. **Room and board:** $4,200 room only. **Books and supplies:** $500. **Other expenses:** $700.

FINANCIAL AID. 79% of freshmen, 77% of continuing students receive some form of aid. All grants, 93% of loans, 54% of jobs based on need. 91 enrolled freshmen were judged to have need, all were offered aid. **Aid applications:** Closing date April 15; priority given to applications received by February 15; applicants notified on or about April 15; must reply by May 1 or within 2 weeks if notified thereafter.

ADDRESS/TELEPHONE. Janis L. Fisher, Director of Admissions/Registrar, Albany College of Pharmacy, 106 New Scotland Avenue, Albany, NY 12208. (518) 445-7221. Fax: (518) 445-7202.

Alfred University ⇎
Alfred, New York CB code: 2005

Admissions: 78% of applicants accepted
Based on: ••• School record
•• Activities, essay, recommendations
• Interview, special talents, test scores
Completion: 90% of freshmen end year in good standing
73% graduate, 30% of these enter graduate study

4-year private university, coed. Founded in 1836. **Accreditation:** Regional. **Undergraduate enrollment:** 1,071 men, 797 women full time; 45 men, 74 women part time. **Graduate enrollment:** 106 men, 89 women full time; 77 men, 68 women part time. **Faculty:** 197 total (160 full time), 157 with doctorates or other terminal degrees. **Location:** Rural campus in rural community; 70 miles from Rochester. **Calendar:** Semester, extensive summer session. **Microcomputers:** 400 located in dormitories, libraries, classrooms, computer centers. **Special facilities:** Observatory, 2 art galleries, Scholes Library of Ceramics, carillon (oldest bells in Western hemisphere), Brentwood stables. **Additional facts:** New York State College of Ceramics integral part of university (Ceramic Engineering and School of Art and Design).

DEGREES OFFERED. BA, BS, BFA, MA, MS, MFA, PhD. 517 bachelor's degrees awarded in 1992. 16% in business and management, 20% engineering, 12% health sciences, 7% physical sciences, 6% psychology, 10% social sciences, 14% visual and performing arts. Graduate degrees offered in 19 major fields of study.

UNDERGRADUATE MAJORS. Accounting, applied mathematics, art education, biological and physical sciences, biology, business administration and management, business economics, business education, ceramic engineering, ceramics, chemistry, clinical laboratory science, clinical psychology, communications, computer and information sciences, criminal justice studies, dramatic arts, drawing, economics, electrical/electronics/communications engineering, elementary education, English, English education, environmental science, experimental psychology, finance, fine arts, foreign languages (multiple emphasis), foreign languages education, French, geology, gerontology, glass, graphic design, health care administration, health planning and management, history, humanities and social sciences, illustration design, international business management, junior high education, liberal/general studies, management information systems, management science, marketing management, mathematics, mathematics education, mechanical engineering, painting, philosophy, photography, physics, political science and government, predentistry, prelaw, premedicine, preveterinary, printmaking, psychology, public administration, science education, sculpture, secondary education, social science education, sociology, Spanish, video.

ACADEMIC PROGRAMS. Accelerated program, cooperative education, double major, dual enrollment of high school students, honors program, independent study, internships, student-designed major, study abroad, teacher preparation, visiting/exchange student program, New York semester, United Nations semester, Washington semester, cross-registration, combined bachelor's/graduate degree programs in business administration with Clarkson University and in forestry with Duke University, North Carolina; liberal arts/career combination in engineering. **Remedial services:** Preadmission summer program, reduced course load, remedial instruction, special counselor, tutoring, writing and mathematics laboratories. **ROTC:** Army. **Placement/credit:** AP, CLEP Subject, institutional tests.

ACADEMIC REQUIREMENTS. Freshmen must earn minimum GPA of 1.75 to continue in good standing. 89% of freshmen return for sophomore year. Students must declare major by end of second year. **Graduation requirements:** 124 hours for bachelor's (60 in major). Most students required to take courses in arts/fine arts, computer science, English, history, humanities, mathematics, philosophy/religion, biological/physical sciences, social sciences. **Postgraduate studies:** 3% enter medical school.

FRESHMAN ADMISSIONS. Selection criteria: Rigor of high school curriculum, grades, extracurricular activities, recommenditions, and test scores, considered. **High school preparation:** 16 units required. Required units include English 4, mathematics 2, social science 2 and science 2. 3 mathematics required for business and engineering programs. 2 science required for engineering program. **Test requirements:** SAT or ACT; score report by February 15.

1992 FRESHMAN CLASS PROFILE. 1,198 men applied, 917 accepted, 279 enrolled; 1,006 women applied, 792 accepted, 208 enrolled. 39% were in top tenth and 70% were in top quarter of graduating class. **Academic background:** Mid 50% of enrolled freshmen had SAT-V between 480-580, SAT-M between 510-650; ACT composite between 23-28. 75% submitted SAT scores, 25% submitted ACT scores. **Characteristics:** 66% from in state, 96% live in college housing, 10% have minority backgrounds, 2% are foreign students, 30% join fraternities/sororities. Average age is 18.

FALL-TERM APPLICATIONS. $25 fee, may be waived for applicants with need. Closing date February 15; applicants notified on or about April 1; must reply by May 1 or within 2 weeks if notified thereafter. Portfolio required for art applicants. Essay required. Interview recommended. CRDA. Deferred and early admission available. EDP-F.

STUDENT LIFE. Housing: Dormitories (coed); apartment, fraternity, sorority housing available. Apartments, suites, singles, and corridor style living arrangements available. All students required to live in residence halls for 4 semesters. **Activities:** Student government, film, magazine, radio, student newspaper, yearbook, choral groups, concert band, dance, drama, jazz band, music ensembles, musical theater, fraternities, sororities, student tutorial and volunteer organizations, Hillel, World Friends, Brothers and Sisters in Christ, World Awareness Coalition, APO (service fraternity), student volunteers for Community Action, Ibero American Student Union, Minorities Educating, Growing, and Achieving. **Additional information:** Of undergraduates not residing in college housing, 4% live in their own apartments off campus, 11% commute from home.

ATHLETICS. NCAA. **Intercollegiate:** Basketball, diving, football M, golf, horseback riding, lacrosse M, skiing, soccer, swimming, tennis, track and field M, volleyball W. **Intramural:** Badminton, basketball, bowling, football M, handball, lacrosse M, racquetball, skiing, soccer, softball, swimming, table tennis, tennis, volleyball, water polo.

STUDENT SERVICES. Aptitude testing, career counseling, employment service for undergraduates, freshman orientation, health services, personal counseling, placement service for graduates, special adviser for adult students, services/facilities for handicapped.

ANNUAL EXPENSES. Tuition and fees (1992-93): $14,998. **Room and board:** $4,735. **Books and supplies:** $500. **Other expenses:** $525.

FINANCIAL AID. 90% of freshmen, 80% of continuing students receive some form of aid. 88% of grants, 88% of loans, 54% of jobs based on need. 214 enrolled freshmen were judged to have need, all were offered aid. Academic, art, state/district residency scholarships available. **Aid applications:** No closing date; applicants notified on a rolling basis beginning on or about January 25; must reply by May 1 or within 2 weeks if notified thereafter.

ADDRESS/TELEPHONE. Daniel L. Meyer, Assistant Vice President/Dean of Admissions, Alfred University, PO Alumni Hall, Alumni Hall, Alfred, NY 14802-9987. (607) 871-2115. (800) 541-9229. Fax: (607) 871-2198.

American Academy of Dramatic Arts
New York, New York — CB code: 2603

Admissions: 86% of applicants accepted
Based on:
- ••• Special talents
- •• Interview, recommendations, school record
- • Activities, test scores

Completion: 85% of freshmen end year in good standing

2-year private school of dramatic arts, coed. Founded in 1884. **Accreditation:** Regional. **Undergraduate enrollment:** 90 men, 117 women full time. **Faculty:** 37 total (24 full time). **Location:** Urban campus in very large city. **Calendar:** 28-week program. **Special facilities:** 3 theaters, dance studio, costume department, prop/production areas, audio/visual center. **Additional facts:** Oldest school of professional actor training in English-speaking world. West coast facility in Pasadena. Certificate program available for evening and Saturday part-time students.

DEGREES OFFERED. 58 associate degrees awarded in 1992. 100% in visual and performing arts.

UNDERGRADUATE MAJORS. Dramatic arts.

ACADEMIC PROGRAMS. Students may study 1 year at each of 2 campuses. **Remedial services:** Tutoring.

ACADEMIC REQUIREMENTS. Freshmen must earn minimum GPA of 2.0 to continue in good standing. Faculty invitation required to continue into second year of program. 48% of freshmen return for sophomore year. Students must declare major on application. **Graduation requirements:** 60 hours for associate. Most students required to take courses in arts/fine arts, English, history, humanities. **Additional information:** 2-year professional actor training program offered with associate of occupational studies degree. Third year, available by faculty invitation, forms showcase Academy Company.

FRESHMAN ADMISSIONS. Selection criteria: Audition/interview results take priority. Serious consideration given academic record, letters of recommendation. **Test requirements:** SAT or ACT. **Additional information:** Health certificate also required.

1992 FRESHMAN CLASS PROFILE. 160 men applied, 140 accepted, 59 enrolled; 190 women applied, 160 accepted, 68 enrolled. **Characteristics:** 15% from in state, 100% commute, 11% have minority backgrounds, 16% are foreign students. Average age is 21.

FALL-TERM APPLICATIONS. $35 fee. No closing date; applicants notified on a rolling basis beginning on or about December 1; must reply within 4 weeks. Interview required. Audition required. Regional audition/interviews may be arranged. Deferred admission available. Notification of acceptance within 2 weeks of completing application/audition.

STUDENT LIFE. Over 50% of freshmen have previous college study, over 30% hold bachelor's or master's degrees from other institutions.

STUDENT SERVICES. Career counseling, employment service for undergraduates, freshman orientation, personal counseling, placement service for graduates.

ANNUAL EXPENSES. Tuition and fees: $7,975. **Books and supplies:** $400. **Other expenses:** $875.

FINANCIAL AID. 65% of freshmen, 78% of continuing students receive some form of aid. All grants, 78% of loans, all jobs based on need. **Aid applications:** No closing date; priority given to applications received by July 1; applicants notified on a rolling basis; must reply within 3 weeks. **Additional information:** Need-based incentive grants of $200-$500 for first-year students available.

ADDRESS/TELEPHONE. Jeanne Gosselin, Director of Admissions, American Academy of Dramatic Arts, 120 Madison Avenue, New York, NY 10016. (212) 686-9244.

American Academy McAllister Institute of Funeral Service
New York, New York — CB code: 0774

2-year private college of mortuary science, coed. Founded in 1926. **Undergraduate enrollment:** 115 men, 45 women full time. **Faculty:** 18 total (4 full time). **Location:** Urban campus in very large city. **Calendar:** Three 15-week semesters.

DEGREES OFFERED. 34 associate degrees awarded in 1992.

UNDERGRADUATE MAJORS. Funeral services/mortuary science.

ACADEMIC PROGRAMS. Cross-registration.

ACADEMIC REQUIREMENTS. Freshmen must earn minimum GPA of 2.0 to continue in good standing. 65% of freshmen return for sophomore year. Students must declare major on application. **Graduation requirements:** 70 hours for associate.

FRESHMAN ADMISSIONS. Selection criteria: Open admissions.

1992 FRESHMAN CLASS PROFILE. 50 men and women enrolled. **Characteristics:** 100% commute, 45% have minority backgrounds. Average age is 24.

FALL-TERM APPLICATIONS. $25 fee. Closing date August 25; priority given to applications received by June 15; applicants notified on a rolling basis beginning on or about June 15. Interview recommended.

STUDENT LIFE. Activities: Student government.

STUDENT SERVICES. Freshman orientation, personal counseling, placement service for graduates, services/facilities for handicapped.

ANNUAL EXPENSES. Tuition and fees (1992-93): $5,185. **Books and supplies:** $700.

FINANCIAL AID. 65% of freshmen, 65% of continuing students receive some form of aid. 99% of grants, 71% of loans based on need. 35 enrolled freshmen were judged to have need, all were offered aid. Academic scholarships available. **Aid applications:** No closing date; applicants notified on a rolling basis.

ADDRESS/TELEPHONE. Saundra Honig, Director of Admissions and Financial Aid, American Academy McAllister Institute of Funeral Service, 450 West 56th Street, New York, NY 10019. (212) 757-1190.

Audrey Cohen College
New York, New York CB code: 4802

Admissions: 72% of applicants accepted
Based on: ••• Interview, recommendations, school record
•• Activities, essay, test scores
• Special talents
Completion: 75% of freshmen end year in good standing
62% graduate, 63% of these enter graduate study

4-year private professional college, coed. Founded in 1964. **Accreditation:** Regional. **Undergraduate enrollment:** 276 men, 680 women full time; 10 men, 15 women part time. **Graduate enrollment:** 10 men, 30 women full time; 1 woman part time. **Faculty:** 66 total (17 full time), 27 with doctorates or other terminal degrees. **Location:** Urban campus in very large city. **Calendar:** Trimester, extensive summer session. Saturday and extensive evening/early morning classes. **Microcomputers:** 32 located in libraries, computer centers. **Additional facts:** Off-site extensions for human services program in the Bronx and Staten Island. Students receive credit for applying their studies to jobs or internship sites.

DEGREES OFFERED. B, MS. 154 bachelor's degrees awarded in 1992. 25% in business and management, 75% social sciences. Graduate degrees offered in 1 major field of study.

UNDERGRADUATE MAJORS. Business and management, human resources development, human services professions.

ACADEMIC PROGRAMS. Accelerated program, cooperative education, internships, study abroad, weekend college. **Remedial services:** Learning center, remedial instruction, special counselor, tutoring, professional preparation courses. **Placement/credit:** 32 credit hours maximum for bachelor's degree.

ACADEMIC REQUIREMENTS. Freshmen must earn minimum GPA of 2.0 to continue in good standing. 75% of freshmen return for sophomore year. Students must declare major on application. **Graduation requirements:** 128 hours for bachelor's. Most students required to take courses in computer science, English, history, humanities, mathematics, philosophy/religion, biological/physical sciences, social sciences. **Postgraduate studies:** 5% enter law school, 8% enter MBA programs, 50% enter other graduate study. **Additional information:** All programs involve application of course work to career, community or internship site.

FRESHMAN ADMISSIONS. Selection criteria: Academic record, test scores, previous volunteer experience, school and community activities, interviews, professional recommendations, motivation and communication skills as demonstrated in interviews. **High school preparation:** 16 units required. Required and recommended units include biological science 1, English 4, mathematics 2-3 and social science 4. Foreign language 2 recommended. **Test requirements:** Combined SAT score of 900 or higher can be substituted for institution-administered Stanford TASK examination, required for admission.

1992 FRESHMAN CLASS PROFILE. 367 men applied, 252 accepted, 62 enrolled; 573 women applied, 428 accepted, 96 enrolled. **Characteristics:** 95% from in state, 100% commute, 79% have minority backgrounds. Average age is 27.

FALL-TERM APPLICATIONS. $20 fee, may be waived for applicants with need. No closing date; priority given to applications received by May 1; applicants notified on a rolling basis beginning on or about March 15; 0810. Interview required. Essay required. Deferred admission available.

STUDENT LIFE. Activities: Student government, student newspaper, yearbook, drama, dance committee, honor society.

STUDENT SERVICES. Career counseling, employment service for undergraduates, freshman orientation, personal counseling, placement service for graduates, special adviser for adult students, veterans counselor, services/facilities for handicapped.

ANNUAL EXPENSES. Tuition and fees (1992-93): $9,900. **Books and supplies:** $300. **Other expenses:** $640.

FINANCIAL AID. 85% of freshmen, 85% of continuing students receive some form of aid. 92% of grants, 62% of loans, all jobs based on need. **Aid applications:** No closing date; applicants notified on a rolling basis. **Additional information:** Grant-in-aid also available. Limited merit schlorships.

ADDRESS/TELEPHONE. Steven K. Lenhart, Director of Admissions, Audrey Cohen College, 345 Hudson Street, New York, NY 10014-9931. (212) 989-2002 ext. 501. Fax: (212) 627-5104.

Bard College
Annandale-on-Hudson, New York CB code: 2037

Admissions: 49% of applicants accepted
Based on: ••• Essay, school record
•• Activities, interview, recommendations, special talents
• Test scores
Completion: 90% of freshmen end year in good standing
77% graduate, 50% of these enter graduate study

4-year private college of arts and sciences, coed, affiliated with Episcopal Church. Founded in 1860. **Accreditation:** Regional. **Undergraduate enrollment:** 501 men, 522 women full time; 22 men, 23 women part time. **Faculty:** 135 total (92 full time), 128 with doctorates or other terminal degrees. **Location:** Rural campus in small town; 100 miles from New York City, 50 miles from Albany. **Calendar:** 4-1-4. **Microcomputers:** 75 located in libraries, classrooms, computer centers. **Special facilities:** Edith Blum Art Institute and Gallery, Olin Humanities Building, ecology field station (contiguous to Hudson River Estuary Preserves), center for curatorial studies and art in contemporary culture, Rivendell Collection of late 20th century art, archaeological field school.

DEGREES OFFERED. BA, MS, MFA. 240 bachelor's degrees awarded in 1992. 22% in letters/literature, 8% life sciences, 33% social sciences, 36% visual and performing arts. Graduate degrees offered in 12 major fields of study.

UNDERGRADUATE MAJORS. African studies, American literature, American studies, anthropology, archeology, art history, Asian studies, biological and physical sciences, biology, chemistry, Chinese, cinematography/film, classics, community and regional studies, comparative literature, creative writing, dance, dramatic arts, drawing, Eastern European studies, economics, English, English literature, environmental science, European studies, film arts, fine arts, French, gender studies, German, Greek (classical), history, history and philosophy of science, humanities, humanities and social sciences, international relations, international studies, language interpretation and translation, Latin, Latin American studies, mathematics, multicultural and ethnic studies, music, music history and appreciation, music performance, music theory and composition, painting, philosophy, photography, physical sciences, physics, political science and government, predentistry, prelaw, premedicine, preveterinary, psychology, religion, Russian, Russian and Slavic studies, sculpture, social sciences, sociology, Spanish, visual and performing arts, Western European studies.

ACADEMIC PROGRAMS. Accelerated program, double major, independent study, internships, semester at sea, student-designed major, study abroad, visiting/exchange student program, Washington semester, cross-registration, combined degree programs in engineering with Columbia University and Washington University (Missouri), in forestry or environmental management with Duke University (North Carolina), and in public health with Yale University. Combined bachelor's/graduate degree programs in architecture or city and regional planning with Pratt Institute, in business administration with University of Rochester, in law with Benjamin N. Cardozo School of Law, in public administration with Syracuse University, and in social work with Hunter College and University of Pennsylvania. **Remedial services:** Tutoring, New York State/Higher Education Opportunity Program. **Placement/credit:** AP, IB, institutional tests.

ACADEMIC REQUIREMENTS. Freshmen must earn minimum GPA of 2.0 to continue in good standing. 89% of freshmen return for sophomore year. Students must declare major by end of second year. **Graduation requirements:** 124 hours for bachelor's. Most students required to take courses in arts/fine arts, humanities, mathematics, biological/physical sciences, social sciences. **Postgraduate studies:** 6% enter law school, 2% enter medical school, 1% enter MBA programs, 41% enter other graduate study. **Additional information:** Strong tradition of independent study and tutorial work with faculty member.

FRESHMAN ADMISSIONS. Selection criteria: School achievement record, essays important. Recommendations, independent study, school and community activities, performance, creative work considered. **High school preparation:** 20 units recommended. Recommended units include English 4, foreign language 4, mathematics 4, social science 4 and science 4.

1992 FRESHMAN CLASS PROFILE. 1,857 men and women applied, 910 accepted; 153 men enrolled, 160 women enrolled. **Academic background:** Mid 50% of enrolled freshmen had SAT-V between 550-670, SAT-M between 550-690. 74% submitted SAT scores. **Characteristics:** 23% from in state, 99% live in college housing, 10% have minority backgrounds, 10% are foreign students. Average age is 18.

FALL-TERM APPLICATIONS. $40 fee, may be waived for applicants with need. Closing date February 15; applicants notified on or about April 1; must reply by May 1. Essay required. Interview recommended. Portfolio recommended. CRDA. Deferred and early admission available. EDP-F. Applicants may be admitted either by regular procedure or under Immediate Decision Plan which gives same-day decision after day-long program and individual interview.

STUDENT LIFE. Housing: Dormitories (women, coed). Housing includes small houses and restored Hudson River mansions. 60% of rooms are singles. **Activities:** Student government, film, magazine, radio, student newspaper, literary and art publications, choral groups, dance, drama, jazz band, music ensembles, opera, symphony orchestra, recording studio, black and Latin American groups, Asian student organization, religious organizations, political action coalition, women's center, language clubs, academic clubs, Amnesty International, community outreach groups, outing club, student operated garage. **Additional information:** All students are members of the student government. Students serve on academic and policy making committees.

ATHLETICS. NAIA, NCAA. **Intercollegiate:** Basketball M, cross-country, fencing, soccer, tennis, volleyball. **Intramural:** Badminton, basketball, diving, fencing, skiing, softball, squash, swimming, tennis, volleyball, water polo. **Clubs:** Squash.

STUDENT SERVICES. Aptitude testing, career counseling, employment service for undergraduates, freshman orientation, health services, personal counseling, placement service for graduates, special adviser for adult students, on-campus nursery school, services/facilities for handicapped.

ANNUAL EXPENSES. Tuition and fees (1992-93): $17,700. All graduate students also pay independent study fee of $925. **Room and board:** $5,830. **Books and supplies:** $550. **Other expenses:** $450.

FINANCIAL AID. 65% of freshmen, 63% of continuing students receive some form of aid. 55% of grants, 79% of loans, 69% of jobs based on need. 140 enrolled freshmen were judged to have need, all were offered aid. Academic, music/drama, art, leadership scholarships available. **Aid applications:** No closing date; priority given to applications received by February 15; applicants notified on a rolling basis beginning on or about April 1; must reply by May 1 or within 2 weeks if notified thereafter. **Additional information:** Excellence and Equal Cost Program for students who graduated in top ten of their public high school class lowers fees to levels equivalent to attendence at home state university or college. Distinguished Scientist Scholars Program for students who will major in science or mathematics.

ADDRESS/TELEPHONE. Mary Backlund, Director of Admissions, Bard College, P.O. Box 5000, Annandale-on-Hudson, NY 12504. (914) 758-7472. Fax: (914) 758-9654.

Barnard College
New York, New York — CB code: 2038

Admissions:	55% of applicants accepted
Based on:	••• Essay, recommendations, school record, test scores
	•• Activities, special talents
	• Interview
Completion:	98% of freshmen end year in good standing
	82% graduate, 25% of these enter graduate study

4-year private liberal arts college, women only. Founded in 1889. **Accreditation:** Regional. **Undergraduate enrollment:** 2,114 women full time; 67 women part time. **Faculty:** 249 total (165 full time), 154 with doctorates or other terminal degrees. **Location:** Urban campus in very large city. **Calendar:** Semester. **Microcomputers:** 108 located in dormitories, libraries, classrooms, computer centers, campus-wide network. **Special facilities:** Center for toddler development, center for research on women, theater, greenhouse, 3600 acre nature preserve. **Additional facts:** Affiliate of Columbia University, with full cross-registration and access to all facilities and resources, including 6-million-volume library and Lamont-Doherty Geological Observatory. Students receive Columbia University degrees.

DEGREES OFFERED. BA. 567 bachelor's degrees awarded in 1992. 20% in letters/literature, 7% life sciences, 5% physical sciences, 11% psychology, 36% social sciences, 5% visual and performing arts.

UNDERGRADUATE MAJORS. African studies, American studies, anthropology, applied mathematics, architecture, art history, Asian studies, astronomy, biochemistry, biology, biophysics, chemistry, classics, computer and information sciences, creative writing, dance, dramatic arts, East Asian studies, economics, English, environmental science, European studies, French, German, Greek (classical), history, Italian, Latin, Latin American studies, linguistics, mathematics, Medieval and Renaissance studies, medieval studies, Middle Eastern studies, music, philosophy, physics, political science and government, psychobiology, psychology, religion, Russian, Russian and Slavic studies, sociology, Spanish, statistics, urban studies, visual and performing arts, Western European studies, women's studies.

ACADEMIC PROGRAMS. Accelerated program, double major, honors program, independent study, internships, student-designed major, study abroad, teacher preparation, visiting/exchange student program, cross-registration, independent scholars program; liberal arts/career combination in engineering; combined bachelor's/graduate program in law. **Placement/credit:** AP, IB, institutional tests; 30 credit hours maximum for bachelor's degree.

ACADEMIC REQUIREMENTS. Freshmen must earn minimum GPA of 2.0 to continue in good standing. 95% of freshmen return for sophomore year. Students must declare major by end of second year. **Graduation requirements:** 120 hours for bachelor's (34 in major). Most students required to take courses in English, foreign languages, humanities, mathematics, biological/physical sciences, social sciences. **Postgraduate studies:** 7% enter law school, 6% enter medical school, 2% enter MBA programs, 10% enter other graduate study. **Additional information:** Interdisciplinary first year seminar mandatory. Quantitative reasoning may be substituted for core curricular mathematics requirement.

FRESHMAN ADMISSIONS. Selection criteria: High school record most important. Depth and difficulty of high school program taken into account. SAT and 3 ACH, or ACT, recommendations, involvement in school and community activities, special talents, skills considered. Recommended units include English 4, foreign language 4, mathematics 3, social science 1 and science 2. Additional units in social sciences, art, music also recommended. **Test requirements:** SAT or ACT; score report by February 15. 3 ACH required (including English Composition or Literature) of applicants who take SAT. Score report by February 15.

1992 FRESHMAN CLASS PROFILE. 2,116 women applied, 1,155 accepted, 555 enrolled. 97% had high school GPA of 3.0 or higher, 3% between 2.0 and 2.99. 54% were in top tenth and 83% were in top quarter of graduating class. **Academic background:** Mid 50% of enrolled freshmen had SAT-V between 560-640, SAT-M between 580-660. 98% submitted SAT scores. **Characteristics:** 39% from in state, 95% live in college housing, 38% have minority backgrounds, 3% are foreign students. Average age is 18.

FALL-TERM APPLICATIONS. $40 fee, may be waived for applicants with need. Closing date January 15; applicants notified on or about April 2; must reply by May 1. Essay required. Interview recommended. CRDA. Deferred and early admission available. EDP-F.

STUDENT LIFE. Housing: Dormitories (women, coed); apartment, handicapped housing available. Rooms modified to accommodate disabled students. **Activities:** Student government, film, magazine, radio, student newspaper, yearbook, choral groups, concert band, dance, drama, marching band, music ensembles, musical theater, opera, pep band, symphony orchestra, Gilbert and Sullivan Society, chamber orchestra, sororities, religious organizations representing all faiths, Asian women's coalition, Organization of Black Women, Latin American students' organizations, Amnesty International, Earth Coalition, Community Impact, Students Helping Students (tutoring), and more than 80 extracurricular groups.

ATHLETICS. NCAA. **Intercollegiate:** Basketball, cross-country, diving, fencing, rowing (crew), soccer, swimming, tennis, track and field, volleyball. **Intramural:** Archery, badminton, basketball, bowling, cross-country, fencing, ice hockey, lacrosse, racquetball, rifle, sailing, soccer, softball, swimming, tennis, volleyball.

STUDENT SERVICES. Career counseling, employment service for undergraduates, freshman orientation, health services, personal counseling, placement service for graduates, services/facilities for handicapped.

ANNUAL EXPENSES. Tuition and fees: $17,756. **Room and board:** $7,736. **Books and supplies:** $520. **Other expenses:** $850.

FINANCIAL AID. 60% of freshmen, 60% of continuing students receive some form of aid. All grants, 99% of loans, 91% of jobs based on need. 310 enrolled freshmen were judged to have need, all were offered aid. **Aid applications:** Closing date February 1; applicants notified on or about April 1; must reply by May 1.

ADDRESS/TELEPHONE. Doris Davis, Director of Admissions, Barnard College, 3009 Broadway, New York, NY 10027-6598. (212) 854-2014. Fax: (212) 749-6531.

Berkeley College
White Plains, New York — CB code: 2064

2-year proprietary business, junior college, coed. Founded in 1945. **Accreditation:** Regional. **Undergraduate enrollment:** 548 men and women. **Faculty:** 48 total (12 full time), 8 with doctorates or other terminal degrees. **Location:** Suburban campus in small city; 18 miles from New York City. **Calendar:** Quarter, extensive summer session. **Microcomputers:** 99 located in libraries, classrooms, computer centers.

DEGREES OFFERED. AAS. 187 associate degrees awarded in 1992. 60% in business and management, 40% business/office and marketing/distribution.

UNDERGRADUATE MAJORS. Accounting, business administration and management, business and management, business and office, fashion merchandising, information sciences and systems, legal assistant/paralegal, marketing management, microcomputer software, office supervision and management, secretarial and related programs, tourism.

ACADEMIC PROGRAMS. 2-year transfer program, accelerated program, cooperative education, honors program, internships, study abroad. **Remedial services:** Learning center, preadmission summer program, remedial instruction, special counselor, tutoring. **Placement/credit:** 30 credit hours maximum for associate degree.

ACADEMIC REQUIREMENTS. Freshmen must earn minimum GPA of 2.0 to continue in good standing. 85% of freshmen return for sophomore year. Students must declare major on enrollment. **Graduation requirements:** 92 hours for associate (60 in major). Most students required to take courses in computer science, English, humanities, social sciences.

FRESHMAN ADMISSIONS. Selection criteria: High school average, rank in class, courses studied and personal interview all considered. **High**

school preparation: 16 units recommended. **Test requirements:** ASSET test given to students after admission to determine who needs remedial work. **Additional information:** Submission of SAT or ACT highly encouraged.

1992 FRESHMAN CLASS PROFILE. 256 men and women enrolled. 25% had high school GPA of 3.0 or higher, 55% between 2.0 and 2.99. **Characteristics:** 95% from in state, 90% commute, 21% have minority backgrounds, 2% are foreign students. Average age is 19.

FALL-TERM APPLICATIONS. $35 fee, may be waived for applicants with need. No closing date; applicants notified on a rolling basis; must reply within 4 weeks. Interview required. Deferred and early admission available.

STUDENT LIFE. Housing: Dormitories (men, women, coed). **Activities:** Student government, student newspaper, yearbook, Distributive Education Clubs of America, accounting club, Berkeley club, Phi Beta Lambda, men's club.

ATHLETICS. Intramural: Softball, volleyball.

STUDENT SERVICES. Career counseling, employment service for undergraduates, freshman orientation, personal counseling, placement service for graduates, special adviser for adult students, services/facilities for handicapped.

ANNUAL EXPENSES. Tuition and fees (1992-93): $8,625. **Room and board:** $4,225. **Books and supplies:** $630. **Other expenses:** $1,010.

FINANCIAL AID. 80% of freshmen, 80% of continuing students receive some form of aid. Grants, loans, jobs available. 170 enrolled freshmen were judged to have need, all were offered aid. Academic scholarships available. **Aid applications:** No closing date; applicants notified on a rolling basis beginning on or about March 1; must reply within 2 weeks. **Additional information:** Matching scholarships, merit scholarships, and work aid programs available.

ADDRESS/TELEPHONE. Lori Merante, Director of Admissions, Berkeley College, West Red Oak Lane, White Plains, NY 10604-9990. (914) 694-1122. Fax: (914) 684-5832.

Berkeley School: New York City
New York, New York CB code: 0954

2-year proprietary business, junior college, coed. Founded in 1936. **Accreditation:** Regional candidate. **Undergraduate enrollment:** 696 men and women. **Faculty:** 32 total (19 full time). **Location:** Urban campus in very large city; in midtown Manhattan. **Calendar:** Quarter, extensive summer session. **Microcomputers:** Located in computer centers.

DEGREES OFFERED. AAS. 220 associate degrees awarded in 1992. 10% in business and management, 90% business/office and marketing/distribution.

UNDERGRADUATE MAJORS. Accounting, business and management, customer relations, fashion merchandising, legal secretary, marketing and distribution, secretarial and related programs, transportation and travel marketing, word processing.

ACADEMIC PROGRAMS. 2-year transfer program, cooperative education, internships, study abroad. **Remedial services:** Learning center, remedial instruction, tutoring. **Placement/credit:** AP, institutional tests.

ACADEMIC REQUIREMENTS. Freshmen must earn minimum GPA of 2.0 to continue in good standing. 85% of freshmen return for sophomore year. Students must declare major on application. **Graduation requirements:** 96 hours for associate (32 in major). Most students required to take courses in English.

FRESHMAN ADMISSIONS. Selection criteria: Class rank or test scores, interview most important. **Test requirements:** Institutional entrance tests required of applicants not in top half of graduating class.

1992 FRESHMAN CLASS PROFILE. 218 men and women enrolled. 10% had high school GPA of 3.0 or higher, 60% between 2.0 and 2.99. **Characteristics:** 80% from in state, 100% commute, 60% have minority backgrounds. Average age is 18.

FALL-TERM APPLICATIONS. $35 fee. No closing date; applicants notified on a rolling basis; must reply within 2 weeks. Interview required. Deferred and early admission available.

STUDENT LIFE. Activities: Student government.

STUDENT SERVICES. Career counseling, employment service for undergraduates, personal counseling, placement service for graduates.

ANNUAL EXPENSES. Tuition and fees (1992-93): $9,195. **Books and supplies:** $700.

FINANCIAL AID. 86% of freshmen, 86% of continuing students receive some form of aid. All grants, 95% of loans based on need. 149 enrolled freshmen were judged to have need, all were offered aid. Academic scholarships available. **Aid applications:** No closing date; applicants notified on a rolling basis.

ADDRESS/TELEPHONE. Tracy Dicostanzo, Director of Admissions, Berkeley School: New York City, 3 East 43rd Street, New York, NY 10017. (212) 986-4343.

Beth Hamedrash Shaarei Yosher Institute
Brooklyn, New York CB code: 0731

5-year private rabbinical college, men only, affiliated with Jewish faith. Founded in 1962. **Undergraduate enrollment:** 100 men full time. **Location:** Urban campus in very large city. **Calendar:** Semester. **Additional facts:** First Talmudic degree and ordination available.

FRESHMAN ADMISSIONS. Selection criteria: Test scores most important. High school record considered.

ADDRESS/TELEPHONE. Rabbi Steinberg, Director of Student Financial Aid, Beth Hamedrash Shaarei Yosher Institute, 4102-10 16th Avenue, Brooklyn, NY 11204. (718) 854-2290.

Beth Hatalmud Rabbinical College
Brooklyn, New York CB code: 7317

4-year private rabbinical college, men only, affiliated with Jewish faith. Founded in 1950. **Undergraduate enrollment:** 150 men full time. **Graduate enrollment:** 80 men full time. **Location:** Urban campus in very large city. **Calendar:** Semester. **Additional facts:** Ordination and First Rabbinic degree available.

FRESHMAN ADMISSIONS. Selection criteria: Institutional examination.

ADDRESS/TELEPHONE. Rabbi Perkowski, Director of Admissions, Beth Hatalmud Rabbinical College, 2127 82nd Street, Brooklyn, NY 11214. (718) 259-2525.

Boricua College
New York, New York CB code: 2901

4-year private liberal arts college, coed. Founded in 1974. **Accreditation:** Regional. **Undergraduate enrollment:** 1,200 men and women full time. **Faculty:** 131 total (49 full time), 18 with doctorates or other terminal degrees. **Location:** Urban campus in very large city. **Calendar:** Trimester, limited summer session. **Microcomputers:** Located in computer centers. **Special facilities:** Art galleries. **Additional facts:** 2 additional campuses in Brooklyn.

DEGREES OFFERED. AA, BA, BS. 120 associate degrees awarded in 1992. 180 bachelor's degrees awarded.

UNDERGRADUATE MAJORS. Associate: Liberal/general studies. **Bachelor's:** Business administration and management, elementary education, human services, Latin American studies, liberal/general studies, social work.

ACADEMIC PROGRAMS. 2-year transfer program, accelerated program, independent study, internships. **Remedial services:** Special counselor, tutoring. **Placement/credit:** CLEP General and Subject, institutional tests; 30 credit hours maximum for bachelor's degree.

ACADEMIC REQUIREMENTS. Freshmen must earn minimum GPA of 2.0 to continue in good standing. 72% of freshmen return for sophomore year. Students must declare major by end of second year. **Graduation requirements:** 60 hours for associate, 124 hours for bachelor's (40 in major). Most students required to take courses in English, foreign languages, mathematics, biological/physical sciences, social sciences. **Postgraduate studies:** 46% from 2-year programs enter 4-year programs. **Additional information:** Curriculum comprised of 5 courses per semester: 3 applied studies courses (individualized instruction, colloquium, experiential), 1 theoretical, and 1 cultural class.

FRESHMAN ADMISSIONS. Selection criteria: Entrance examination, academic record, interview, 2 letters of recommendation, working knowledge of English and Spanish. **Test requirements:** Institutional tests required for admissions and placement.

1992 FRESHMAN CLASS PROFILE. 150 men and women enrolled. **Characteristics:** 100% from in state, 100% commute, 94% have minority backgrounds. Average age is 27.

FALL-TERM APPLICATIONS. $20 fee. No closing date; applicants notified on a rolling basis. Interview required. Essay required. Deferred admission available.

STUDENT LIFE. Activities: Student government, student newspaper, choral groups, dance, drama, opera. **Additional information:** National Puerto Rican Cultural Center periodically exhibits at Manhattan and Brooklyn campuses.

STUDENT SERVICES. Career counseling, employment service for undergraduates, personal counseling, placement service for graduates.

ANNUAL EXPENSES. Tuition and fees (1992-93): $5,229. **Books and supplies:** $450. **Other expenses:** $844.

FINANCIAL AID. 87% of freshmen, 90% of continuing students receive some form of aid. All aid based on need. Academic, leadership, minority scholarships available. **Aid applications:** Closing date July 15; priority given to applications received by May 2; applicants notified on a rolling basis; must reply within 3 weeks.

ADDRESS/TELEPHONE. Miriam Santiago Pagan, General Director of Admissions, Boricua College, 3755 Broadway, New York, NY 10032. (212) 694-1000.

Bramson ORT Technical Institute
Forest Hills, New York CB code: 0944

2-year private junior, technical college, coed, affiliated with Jewish faith. Founded in 1977. **Undergraduate enrollment:** 1,300 men and women. **Faculty:** 102 total (25 full time), 16 with doctorates or other terminal degrees. **Location:** Urban campus in very large city. **Calendar:** Semester, extensive summer session. **Microcomputers:** 35 located in libraries, classrooms, computer centers. **Additional facts:** Extensions in Brooklyn and Manhattan.

DEGREES OFFERED. AAS. 30 associate degrees awarded in 1992. 30% in business and management, 40% computer sciences, 30% engineering technologies.

UNDERGRADUATE MAJORS. Accounting, business administration and management, business and management, business computer/console/peripheral equipment operation, business data entry equipment operation, business data processing and related programs, business data programming, computer and information sciences, computer programming, computer technology, data processing, electrical and electronics equipment repair, electrical technology, electromechanical technology, electronic technology, engineering and engineering-related technologies, Jewish studies, management information systems, marketing and distribution, marketing management, robotics, secretarial and related programs, technical and business writing, word processing.

ACADEMIC PROGRAMS. Accelerated program, double major, internships. **Remedial services:** Learning center, preadmission summer program, reduced course load, remedial instruction, special counselor, tutoring, English as a Second Language, Fundamentals of Mathematics. **Placement/credit:** AP, CLEP General and Subject, institutional tests. 50% of total hours needed for degree may be earned by examination.

ACADEMIC REQUIREMENTS. No policy requiring minimum GPA; records of students having academic difficulty are reviewed individually. 85% of freshmen return for sophomore year. Students must declare major on enrollment. **Graduation requirements:** 65 hours for associate (54 in major). Most students required to take courses in computer science, English, history, humanities, mathematics, philosophy/religion.

FRESHMAN ADMISSIONS. Selection criteria: Open admissions. **Test requirements:** Mathematics placement examination required.

1992 FRESHMAN CLASS PROFILE. 500 men and women enrolled. **Characteristics:** 100% from in state, 100% commute, 2% have minority backgrounds, 1% are foreign students. Average age is 30.

FALL-TERM APPLICATIONS. $50 fee, may be waived for applicants with need. No closing date; applicants notified on a rolling basis; must reply by registration. Interview recommended. Deferred admission available.

STUDENT LIFE. Activities: Student government, student newspaper.

STUDENT SERVICES. Career counseling, employment service for undergraduates, freshman orientation, personal counseling, placement service for graduates, special adviser for adult students, veterans counselor, services/facilities for handicapped.

ANNUAL EXPENSES. Tuition and fees (1992-93): $5,635. **Books and supplies:** $240. **Other expenses:** $1,300.

FINANCIAL AID. 95% of freshmen, 90% of continuing students receive some form of aid. All jobs based on need. 240 enrolled freshmen were judged to have need, all were offered aid. Academic scholarships available. **Aid applications:** No closing date; applicants notified on a rolling basis; must reply within 3 weeks.

ADDRESS/TELEPHONE. Lois Shallit, Director of Admissions, Bramson ORT Technical Institute, 6930 Austin Street, Forest Hills, NY 11375. (718) 261-5800. Fax: (718) 575-5118.

Briarcliffe: The College for Business/Data System Institute
Woodbury, New York CB code: 3108

2-year proprietary business, technical college, coed. Founded in 1966. **Accreditation:** Regional candidate. **Undergraduate enrollment:** 500 men, 500 women full time; 200 men, 100 women part time. **Location:** Suburban campus in large town; 20 miles from New York City. **Calendar:** Semester. **Additional facts:** Branch campuses at Lynbrook and Patchogue. Institution also offers programs of recently acquired Grumman Data Systems Institute.

FRESHMAN ADMISSIONS. Selection criteria: School achievement record, interview required, recommendations suggested.

ANNUAL EXPENSES. Tuition and fees: $6,500. **Books and supplies:** $500. **Other expenses:** $1,500.

ADDRESS/TELEPHONE. Jack Turan, Director of Admissions, Briarcliffe: The College for Business/Data System Institute, 250 Crossways Park Drive, Woodbury, NY 11797. (516) 364-2055 ext. 221.

Broome Community College
Binghamton, New York CB code: 2048

2-year public community college, coed. Founded in 1946. **Accreditation:** Regional. **Undergraduate enrollment:** 1,743 men, 2,130 women full time; 1,163 men, 1,749 women part time. **Faculty:** 467 total (202 full time), 24 with doctorates or other terminal degrees. **Location:** Suburban campus in small city; 3 miles from downtown. **Calendar:** Semester, limited summer session. **Microcomputers:** Located in libraries, computer centers. **Special facilities:** Computer-aided design and computer-aided manufacturing laboratory. **Additional facts:** SUNY institution.

DEGREES OFFERED. AA, AS, AAS. 1,082 associate degrees awarded in 1992. 28% in business/office and marketing/distribution, 5% engineering, 10% engineering technologies, 17% health sciences, 37% multi/interdisciplinary studies.

UNDERGRADUATE MAJORS. Accounting, business administration and management, business and management, business data processing and related programs, chemical manufacturing technology, child development/care/guidance, civil technology, communications, computer and information sciences, criminal justice studies, data processing, dental hygiene, electrical technology, electromechanical technology, engineering and engineering-related technologies, engineering science, fire control and safety technology, hospitality and recreation marketing, hotel/motel and restaurant management, industrial technology, legal assistant/paralegal, liberal/general studies, marketing management, mechanical design technology, medical assistant, medical laboratory technologies, medical records technology, nursing, physical therapy assistant, radiograph medical technology, secretarial and related programs, small business management and ownership, tool and die making, tourism, word processing.

ACADEMIC PROGRAMS. 2-year transfer program, cooperative education, double major, dual enrollment of high school students, honors program, independent study, internships, student-designed major, study abroad, weekend college, cross-registration. **Remedial services:** Learning center, preadmission summer program, reduced course load, remedial instruction, special counselor, tutoring. **Placement/credit:** AP, CLEP Subject, institutional tests.

ACADEMIC REQUIREMENTS. Freshmen must earn minimum GPA 1.25. After accumulating 20 credits, they must earn 1.5. 70% of freshmen return for sophomore year. Students must declare major on application. **Graduation requirements:** 62 hours for associate (45 in major). Most students required to take courses in English, mathematics, social sciences.

FRESHMAN ADMISSIONS. Selection criteria: Open admissions. County residents given priority in health services, engineering science, and computer studies programs. High school subject requirements vary with each program.

1992 FRESHMAN CLASS PROFILE. 976 men, 1,150 women enrolled. **Characteristics:** 95% from in state, 100% commute, 7% have minority backgrounds, 2% are foreign students. Average age is 23.

FALL-TERM APPLICATIONS. $10 fee, may be waived for applicants with need. Closing date August 27; applicants notified on a rolling basis; must reply within 4 weeks. Interview recommended for health science, computer science applicants. Early admission available.

STUDENT LIFE. Activities: Student government, radio, student newspaper, yearbook, choral groups, concert band, dance, drama, jazz band, music ensembles, musical theater, Circle-K, minority student and international student organizations.

ATHLETICS. NJCAA. **Intercollegiate:** Baseball M, basketball, cross-country, golf, ice hockey M, soccer M, softball W, tennis, volleyball W, wrestling M. **Intramural:** Basketball, cross-country, volleyball.

STUDENT SERVICES. Aptitude testing, career counseling, employment service for undergraduates, freshman orientation, health services, on-campus day care, personal counseling, placement service for graduates, special adviser for adult students, veterans counselor, services/facilities for handicapped.

ANNUAL EXPENSES. Tuition and fees (projected): $1,938, $1,830 additional for out-of-state students. **Books and supplies:** $500. **Other expenses:** $750.

FINANCIAL AID. 60% of freshmen, 55% of continuing students receive some form of aid. 99% of grants, 76% of loans, 59% of jobs based on need. Academic, athletic, state/district residency, leadership, alumni affiliation, minority scholarships available. **Aid applications:** No closing date; priority given to applications received by April 1; applicants notified on a rolling basis beginning on or about May 1; must reply within 2 weeks.

ADDRESS/TELEPHONE. Anthony Fiorelli, Director of Admissions, Broome Community College, PO Box 1017, Binghamton, NY 13902. (607) 778-5001.

Bryant & Stratton Business Institute: Albany
Albany, New York CB code: 2018

2-year proprietary business college, coed. Founded in 1854. **Undergraduate enrollment:** 527 men and women. **Faculty:** 35 total (10 full time), 3 with doctorates or other terminal degrees. **Location:** Urban campus in small city; 5 miles from downtown, Albany 150 miles from New York City. **Calendar:** Quarter. **Microcomputers:** 82 located in classrooms, computer centers. **Additional facts:** No fee Lifetime Placement provided to all graduates. Part-time placement provided for current students.

DEGREES OFFERED. 11 associate degrees awarded in 1992. 85% in business and management, 15% computer sciences.

UNDERGRADUATE MAJORS. Accounting, business administration and management, business data programming, computer programming, electronic technology, fashion merchandising, legal assistant/paralegal, legal secretary, microcomputer software, secretarial and related programs, tourism, transportation and travel marketing, word processing.

ACADEMIC PROGRAMS. Accelerated program, double major, independent study, internships. **Remedial services:** Reduced course load, remedial instruction, special counselor, tutoring. **Placement/credit:** CLEP Subject; 45 credit hours maximum for associate degree.

ACADEMIC REQUIREMENTS. Freshmen must earn minimum GPA of 1.65 to continue in good standing. 69% of freshmen return for sophomore year. Students must declare major on enrollment. **Graduation requirements:** 90 hours for associate (60 in major). Most students required to take courses in computer science, English, mathematics.

FRESHMAN ADMISSIONS. Selection criteria: Admissions committee considers high school record, entrance exam score, SAT/ACT scores, personal interview and personal essay. Business courses recommended. Mathematics concentration preferred. **Test requirements:** SAT or ACT (ACT preferred); score report by October 1. Career Placement Achievement Test required.

1992 FRESHMAN CLASS PROFILE. 95 men and women enrolled. 30% had high school GPA of 3.0 or higher, 60% between 2.0 and 2.99. **Characteristics:** 90% from in state, 100% commute, 50% have minority backgrounds, 3% are foreign students. Average age is 20.

FALL-TERM APPLICATIONS. $25 fee, may be waived for applicants with need. No closing date; priority given to applications received by August 1; applicants notified on a rolling basis; must reply by May 1 or within 4 weeks if notified thereafter. Interview required. Essay required. Deferred admission available.

STUDENT LIFE. Activities: Student government, student newspaper, yearbook.

ATHLETICS. Intramural: Bowling, volleyball.

STUDENT SERVICES. Aptitude testing, career counseling, employment service for undergraduates, freshman orientation, personal counseling, placement service for graduates, veterans counselor.

ANNUAL EXPENSES. Tuition and fees (1992-93): $5,310. **Books and supplies:** $675. **Other expenses:** $1,100.

FINANCIAL AID. 75% of freshmen, 75% of continuing students receive some form of aid. Grants, loans, jobs available. 160 enrolled freshmen were judged to have need, all were offered aid. **Aid applications:** Closing date September 20; applicants notified on or about September 27; must reply within 10 days.

ADDRESS/TELEPHONE. Mark Diduch, Director of Admissions, Bryant & Stratton Business Institute: Albany, 1259 Central Avenue, Albany, NY 12205. (518) 437-1802 ext. 230. Fax: (518) 437-1048.

Bryant & Stratton Business Institute: Buffalo
Buffalo, New York CB code: 2058

2-year proprietary business college, coed. Founded in 1854. **Undergraduate enrollment:** 237 men, 520 women full time; 9 men, 29 women part time. **Location:** Urban campus in large city. **Calendar:** Quarter. **Additional facts:** Branch campus in Clarence and Lackawanna.

FRESHMAN ADMISSIONS. Selection criteria: High school transcript or GED, personal interview, recommendation of guidance counselor, 50-word writing sample.

ANNUAL EXPENSES. Tuition and fees (projected): $5,760. **Room and board:** $2,241. **Books and supplies:** $750.

ADDRESS/TELEPHONE. Kathleen Galla, Director of Admissions, Bryant & Stratton Business Institute: Buffalo, 1028 Main Street, Buffalo, NY 14202. (716) 884-9120. Fax: (716) 884-0091.

Bryant & Stratton Business Institute: Rochester
Rochester, New York CB code: 7327

2-year proprietary college of business and technology, coed. Founded in 1973. **Undergraduate enrollment:** 530 men and women. **Faculty:** 60 total (30 full time). **Location:** Urban campus in large city. **Calendar:** Quarter, extensive summer session. **Additional facts:** Second campus in suburban Rochester. Degree program runs 6 consecutive quarters (18 months).

DEGREES OFFERED. 160 associate degrees awarded in 1992.

UNDERGRADUATE MAJORS. Accounting, business and office, business computer/console/peripheral equipment operation, business data entry equipment operation, business data processing and related programs, business data programming, fashion merchandising, medical assistant, professional sales, secretarial and related programs, small business management and ownership.

ACADEMIC PROGRAMS. Internships. **Remedial services:** Reduced course load, tutoring.

ACADEMIC REQUIREMENTS. Freshmen must earn minimum GPA of 1.75 to continue in good standing. 64% of freshmen return for sophomore year. Students must declare major on application. **Graduation requirements:** 96 hours for associate.

FRESHMAN ADMISSIONS. Selection criteria: Character, previous scholastic record, and counselor recommendation. **Test requirements:** CPAT required for admission.

1992 FRESHMAN CLASS PROFILE. 190 men and women enrolled. **Characteristics:** 96% from in state, 100% commute, 15% have minority backgrounds. Average age is 20.

FALL-TERM APPLICATIONS. $25 fee, may be waived for applicants with need. No closing date; applicants notified on a rolling basis; must reply by registration. Interview required. Deferred admission available.

STUDENT LIFE. Activities: Student government, student newspaper, professional interest clubs.

STUDENT SERVICES. Employment service for undergraduates, personal counseling, placement service for graduates.

ANNUAL EXPENSES. Tuition and fees (1992-93): $5,442. **Books and supplies:** $450.

FINANCIAL AID. Aid applications: No closing date; applicants notified on a rolling basis.

ADDRESS/TELEPHONE. William Bernys, Director of Admissions, Bryant & Stratton Business Institute: Rochester, 82 St. Paul Street, Rochester, NY 14604-1381. (716) 325-6010.

Bryant & Stratton Business Institute: Syracuse
Syracuse, New York CB code: 0654

Admissions:	88% of applicants accepted
Based on:	••• Essay, interview, test scores
	•• Recommendations
	• School record
Completion:	70% of freshmen end year in good standing
	35% graduate, 5% of these enter 4-year programs

2-year proprietary business college, coed. Founded in 1919. **Undergraduate enrollment:** 135 men, 521 women full time; 4 men, 37 women part time. **Faculty:** 44 total (14 full time). **Location:** Urban campus in small city. **Calendar:** Quarter, extensive summer session. Extensive evening/early morning classes. **Microcomputers:** 100 located in classrooms, computer centers.

DEGREES OFFERED. 261 associate degrees awarded in 1992.

UNDERGRADUATE MAJORS. Accounting, business and management, business data processing and related programs, business data programming, computer programming, fashion merchandising, hospitality and recreation marketing, hotel/motel and restaurant management, legal secretary, marketing and distribution, medical assistant, microcomputer software, office supervision and management, secretarial and related programs, word processing.

ACADEMIC PROGRAMS. Accelerated program, internships. **Remedial services:** Reduced course load, remedial instruction, special counselor, tutoring.

ACADEMIC REQUIREMENTS. Freshmen must earn minimum GPA of 1.75 to continue in good standing. 92% of freshmen return for sophomore year. Students must declare major on application. **Graduation requirements:** 92 hours for associate (46 in major). Most students required to take courses in computer science, English, mathematics.

FRESHMAN ADMISSIONS. Selection criteria: High school record, interview, guidance counselor recommendation, admissions evaluation test, and essay required.

1992 FRESHMAN CLASS PROFILE. 58 men applied, 56 accepted, 56 enrolled; 210 women applied, 179 accepted, 179 enrolled. **Characteristics:** 98% from in state, 70% commute, 41% have minority backgrounds.

FALL-TERM APPLICATIONS. $25 fee, may be waived for applicants with need. No closing date; applicants notified on a rolling basis. Interview required. Essay required.

STUDENT LIFE. Housing: Dormitories (coed). **Activities:** Student government, student newspaper, American Management Society, Distributive Education Clubs of America, Future Secretaries Association.

STUDENT SERVICES. Career counseling, employment service for undergraduates, freshman orientation, personal counseling, placement service for graduates, services/facilities for handicapped.

ANNUAL EXPENSES. Tuition and fees (1992-93): $5,310. **Room and board:** $2,400 room only. **Books and supplies:** $550. **Other expenses:** $360.

FINANCIAL AID. 62% of continuing students receive some form of aid. Grants, loans available. **Aid applications:** No closing date; applicants notified on a rolling basis beginning on or about August 15.

ADDRESS/TELEPHONE. Susan Cumulatti, Director of Admissions, Bryant & Stratton Business Institute: Syracuse, 400 Montgomery Street, Syracuse, NY 13202. (315) 472-6603. Fax: (315) 474-4383.

Canisius College

Buffalo, New York CB code: 2073

Admissions: 77% of applicants accepted
Based on: ••• School record
•• Test scores
• Activities, essay, interview, recommendations, special talents
Completion: 95% of freshmen end year in good standing
59% graduate, 29% of these enter graduate study

4-year private liberal arts college, coed, affiliated with Roman Catholic Church. Founded in 1870. **Accreditation:** Regional. **Undergraduate enrollment:** 1,685 men, 1,363 women full time; 262 men, 223 women part time. **Graduate enrollment:** 144 men, 265 women full time; 431 men, 486 women part time. **Faculty:** 348 total (198 full time), 230 with doctorates or other terminal degrees. **Location:** Urban campus in large city; 70 miles from Rochester, 185 miles from Cleveland, Ohio. **Calendar:** Semester, extensive summer session. Extensive evening/early morning classes. **Microcomputers:** 129 located in libraries, classrooms, computer centers. **Special facilities:** Campus connected by underground tunnel system; planetarium, seismograph.

DEGREES OFFERED. AA, BA, BS, MS, MBA, MEd. 37 associate degrees awarded in 1992. 100% in multi/interdisciplinary studies. 732 bachelor's degrees awarded. 39% in business and management, 10% communications, 6% computer sciences, 10% teacher education, 8% letters/literature, 10% psychology, 10% social sciences. Graduate degrees offered in 10 major fields of study.

UNDERGRADUATE MAJORS. Associate: Humanities, social sciences. **Bachelor's:** Accounting, anthropology, art history, biochemistry, biology, business administration and management, business economics, business education, chemistry, communications, computer and information sciences, economics, elementary education, English, English education, finance, foreign languages education, French, German, history, information sciences and systems, international relations, management information systems, marketing management, mathematics, mathematics education, medical laboratory technologies, philosophy, physical education, physics, political science and government, predentistry, prelaw, premedicine, preveterinary, psychology, religion, science education, secondary education, social studies education, sociology, Spanish, urban studies.

ACADEMIC PROGRAMS. 2-year transfer program, double major, honors program, independent study, internships, student-designed major, study abroad, teacher preparation, telecourses, Washington semester, cross-registration, Early Assurance Program for pre-med students with SUNY Buffalo Medical School, joint degree program with SUNY Buffalo Dental School; combined bachelor's/graduate program in business administration. **Remedial services:** Learning center, preadmission summer program, reduced course load, remedial instruction, special counselor, tutoring. **ROTC:** Army. **Placement/credit:** AP, CLEP Subject, institutional tests; 30 credit hours maximum for bachelor's degree.

ACADEMIC REQUIREMENTS. Freshmen must earn minimum GPA of 1.5 to continue in good standing. 93% of freshmen return for sophomore year. Students must declare major by end of second year. **Graduation requirements:** 120 hours for bachelor's. Most students required to take courses in English, foreign languages, history, mathematics, philosophy/religion, biological/physical sciences, social sciences. **Postgraduate studies:** 2% enter law school, 2% enter medical school, 7% enter MBA programs, 18% enter other graduate study.

FRESHMAN ADMISSIONS. Selection criteria: Admissions decisions reached by reviewing applicants' high school record and test scores from either SAT or ACT. **High school preparation:** 16 units required. Required units include English 4, foreign language 2, mathematics 3, social science 2 and science 1. 3.5 mathematics and 2 sciences required of mathematics majors. 2 sciences required of science majors. **Test requirements:** SAT or ACT; score report by August 31.

1992 FRESHMAN CLASS PROFILE. 1,576 men applied, 1,181 accepted, 412 enrolled; 1,277 women applied, 1,012 accepted, 341 enrolled. **Academic background:** Mid 50% of enrolled freshmen had SAT-V between 390-500, SAT-M between 440-560; ACT composite between 18-21. 77% submitted SAT scores, 14% submitted ACT scores. **Characteristics:** 93% from in state, 51% commute, 12% have minority backgrounds, 1% are foreign students, 4% join fraternities/sororities. Average age is 18.

FALL-TERM APPLICATIONS. $20 fee, may be waived for applicants with need. No closing date; applicants notified on a rolling basis; Prefer applicants reply by May 1. Interview recommended. Essay recommended. CRDA. Deferred and early admission available. Early admission applicants must submit recommendation from high school counselor or principal and SAT or ACT results. Must also have completed 3 years of high school, and turn 16 by end of first semester of college.

STUDENT LIFE. Housing: Dormitories (coed); apartment, fraternity, handicapped housing available. Upperclassmen may choose to live in college-owned and supervised residences off campus. **Activities:** Student government, film, magazine, radio, student newspaper, television, yearbook, choral groups, drama, jazz band, music ensembles, musical theater, private instrumental instruction, fraternities, sororities, campus ministry, political science association, ethnic and social service organizations, international affairs society, social justice club.

ATHLETICS. NAIA, NCAA. **Intercollegiate:** Baseball M, basketball, cross-country, diving M, football M, golf, ice hockey M, lacrosse, rifle, rowing (crew), soccer, softball W, swimming, tennis, track and field, volleyball W. **Intramural:** Basketball, racquetball, soccer, softball, tennis, volleyball, water polo. **Clubs:** Rugby M.

STUDENT SERVICES. Aptitude testing, career counseling, employment service for undergraduates, freshman orientation, health services, personal counseling, placement service for graduates, special adviser for adult students, veterans counselor, services/facilities for handicapped.

ANNUAL EXPENSES. Tuition and fees: $10,270. **Room and board:** $5,240. **Books and supplies:** $400. **Other expenses:** $700.

FINANCIAL AID. 90% of freshmen, 83% of continuing students receive some form of aid. 98% of grants, 90% of loans, 84% of jobs based on need. 464 enrolled freshmen were judged to have need, all were offered aid. Academic, athletic, alumni affiliation, minority scholarships available. **Aid applications:** No closing date; priority given to applications received by February 1; applicants notified on a rolling basis beginning on or about March 15; must reply by May 1 or within 2 weeks if notified thereafter.

ADDRESS/TELEPHONE. Penelope H. Lips, Director of Admissions, Canisius College, 2001 Main Street, Buffalo, NY 14208-9989. (716) 888-2200. (800) 843-1517. Fax: (716) 888-2525.

Catholic Medical Center of Brooklyn and Queens School of Nursing

Woodhaven, New York CB code: 3400

2-year private nursing college, coed, affiliated with Roman Catholic Church. Founded in 1969. **Undergraduate enrollment:** 6 men, 40 women full time; 12 men, 55 women part time. **Faculty:** 16 total (13 full time). **Location:** Urban campus in very large city; 10 miles from Manhattan. **Calendar:** Semester.

DEGREES OFFERED. AAS. 28 associate degrees awarded in 1992. 100% in health sciences.

UNDERGRADUATE MAJORS. Nursing.

ACADEMIC PROGRAMS. Placement/credit: CLEP Subject.

ACADEMIC REQUIREMENTS. Freshmen must earn minimum GPA of 2.5 to continue in good standing. Students must declare major on application. **Graduation requirements:** 64 hours for associate. Most students required to take courses in English, mathematics, philosophy/religion, biological/physical sciences, social sciences.

FRESHMAN ADMISSIONS. Selection criteria: Test scores, high school achievement, interview, and personal essay considered. **High school preparation:** 11 units required. Required units include English 4, mathematics 2, social science 3 and science 2. **Test requirements:** National League for Nursing test required.

1992 FRESHMAN CLASS PROFILE. 2 men, 4 women enrolled. 10% had high school GPA of 3.0 or higher, 90% between 2.0 and 2.99. **Characteristics:** 100% commute, 17% have minority backgrounds. Average age is 26.

FALL-TERM APPLICATIONS. $20 fee. No closing date; applicants notified on a rolling basis; must reply by May 1 or within 2 weeks if notified thereafter. Interview required. Essay required. CRDA. Deferred admission available. SAT or ACT used for admissions, placement, counseling, credit if available.

STUDENT SERVICES. Health services, personal counseling.

ANNUAL EXPENSES. Tuition and fees (1992-93): $3,625. **Room and board:** $1,200 room only. **Books and supplies:** $500. **Other expenses:** $1,000.

FINANCIAL AID. 60% of continuing students receive some form of aid. Grants, loans available. 30 enrolled freshmen were judged to have need, all were offered aid. **Aid applications:** No closing date; applicants notified on a rolling basis; must reply within 2 weeks.

ADDRESS/TELEPHONE. Mary Rohan, Admissions Officer, Catholic Medical Center of Brooklyn and Queens School of Nursing, 89-15 Woodhaven Boulevard, Woodhaven, NY 11421. (718) 849-1200.

Cayuga County Community College

Auburn, New York CB code: 2010

2-year public community college, coed. Founded in 1953. **Accreditation:** Regional. **Undergraduate enrollment:** 723 men, 658 women full time; 532 men, 1,011 women part time. **Faculty:** 223 total (73 full time), 9 with doctorates or other terminal degrees. **Location:** Rural campus in large town; 20 miles from Syracuse. **Calendar:** Semester, limited summer session. **Microcomputers:** 140 located in libraries, computer centers. **Special facilities:** Solar building, nature trail.

DEGREES OFFERED. AA, AS, AAS. 486 associate degrees awarded in 1992.

UNDERGRADUATE MAJORS. Accounting, biological and physical sciences, biology, business administration and management, business and management, business and office, business computer/console/peripheral equipment operation, business data entry equipment operation, business data processing and related programs, business data programming, chemistry, computer and information sciences, computer programming, computer technology, criminology, data processing, drafting, education, electrical technology, elementary education, engineering, engineering and other disciplines, engineering science, English, English literature, history, humanities and social sciences, law enforcement and corrections, liberal/general studies, mathematics, mechanical design technology, nursing, physical sciences, political science and government, psychology, radio/television broadcasting, retailing, secretarial and related programs, social sciences, sociology, teacher aide, telecommunications.

ACADEMIC PROGRAMS. 2-year transfer program, accelerated program, double major, dual enrollment of high school students, honors program, study abroad. **Remedial services:** Learning center, preadmission summer program, reduced course load, remedial instruction, special counselor, tutoring. **Placement/credit:** AP, CLEP General and Subject, institutional tests; 32 credit hours maximum for associate degree.

ACADEMIC REQUIREMENTS. Freshmen must earn minimum GPA of 1.5 to continue in good standing. 80% of freshmen return for sophomore year. Students must declare major on application. **Graduation requirements:** 62 hours for associate. Most students required to take courses in English, mathematics, biological/physical sciences, social sciences.

FRESHMAN ADMISSIONS. Selection criteria: Open admissions. Selective admissions to nursing and computer science programs based on school achievement record and recommendations first, then test scores. School and community activities, minority status, and interview also considered.

1992 FRESHMAN CLASS PROFILE. 414 men and women enrolled. **Characteristics:** 90% from in state, 100% commute, 25% have minority backgrounds. Average age is 21.

FALL-TERM APPLICATIONS. No fee. No closing date; applicants notified on a rolling basis beginning on or about February 15. Interview required. Interview required for nursing applicants, recommended for all. CRDA. Deferred and early admission available.

STUDENT LIFE. Activities: Student government, film, magazine, radio, student newspaper, television, yearbook, choral groups, drama, Model United Nations.

ATHLETICS. NJCAA. **Intercollegiate:** Basketball, cross-country, golf, softball W, tennis, track and field, volleyball W. **Intramural:** Basketball M, racquetball, volleyball.

STUDENT SERVICES. Aptitude testing, career counseling, employment service for undergraduates, freshman orientation, health services, on-campus day care, personal counseling, placement service for graduates, veterans counselor, services/facilities for handicapped.

ANNUAL EXPENSES. Tuition and fees (projected): $2,039, $1,880 additional for out-of-state students. **Books and supplies:** $750. **Other expenses:** $500.

FINANCIAL AID. 75% of freshmen, 75% of continuing students receive some form of aid. 99% of grants, 67% of loans, 73% of jobs based on need. Academic, state/district residency, leadership, minority scholarships available. **Aid applications:** No closing date; priority given to applications received by May 1; applicants notified on a rolling basis beginning on or about June 1; must reply within 2 weeks.

ADDRESS/TELEPHONE. Patricia Powers-Burdick, Director of Admissions, Cayuga County Community College, 197 Franklin Street, Auburn, NY 13021. (315) 255-1743 ext. 241. Fax: (315) 255-2050.

Cazenovia College
Cazenovia, New York — CB code: 2078

Admissions: 91% of applicants accepted
Based on: ••• Activities, school record
•• Interview, recommendations, test scores
• Essay, special talents
Completion: 85% of freshmen end year in good standing

4-year private junior, liberal arts college, coed. Founded in 1824. **Accreditation:** Regional. **Undergraduate enrollment:** 294 men, 730 women full time; 1 man, 3 women part time. **Faculty:** 110 total (40 full time), 42 with doctorates or other terminal degrees. **Location:** Suburban campus in small town; 20 miles from Syracuse. **Calendar:** Modified trimester (fall 12 weeks, winter 12, spring 6). **Microcomputers:** 50 located in libraries, computer centers. **Special facilities:** 20-acre farm and equine center, art galleries, cultural center, interior architecture design center, theater.

DEGREES OFFERED. AA, AS, AAS, BS. 301 associate degrees awarded in 1992. 11% in architecture and environmental design, 28% business and management, 12% business/office and marketing/distribution, 10% education, 8% home economics, 16% multi/interdisciplinary studies, 10% visual and performing arts. 28 bachelor's degrees awarded.

UNDERGRADUATE MAJORS. Associate: Accounting, advertising, architecture, business and management, business and office, early childhood education, equestrian science, family and community services, fashion design, fashion merchandising, graphic design, illustration design, interior design, liberal/general studies, secretarial and related programs, social work, special education, studio art. **Bachelor's:** Fashion merchandising, liberal/general studies.

ACADEMIC PROGRAMS. 2-year transfer program, double major, dual enrollment of high school students, honors program, independent study, internships, student-designed major, study abroad, fall term of sophomore year offered in London, Geneva, Puerto Rico; spring term in Ireland for equine studies. **Remedial services:** Learning center, preadmission summer program, reduced course load, remedial instruction, special counselor, tutoring. **Placement/credit:** AP, CLEP General and Subject, institutional tests; 30 credit hours maximum for associate degree; 30 credit hours maximum for bachelor's degree.

ACADEMIC REQUIREMENTS. Freshmen must earn minimum GPA of 1.7 to continue in good standing. 70% of freshmen return for sophomore year. Students must declare major on application. **Graduation requirements:** 61 hours for associate, 127 hours for bachelor's. Most students required to take courses in English. **Postgraduate studies:** 64% from 2-year programs enter 4-year programs.

FRESHMAN ADMISSIONS. Selection criteria: School achievement record, SAT or ACT scores, recommendation, school activities considered. Minimum 2.0 high school GPA. **High school preparation:** 16 units recommended. Recommended units include English 4, mathematics 2, social science 2 and science 2. Art courses recommended for admission into design majors. **Test requirements:** SAT or ACT (SAT preferred); score report by September 1.

1992 FRESHMAN CLASS PROFILE. 1,028 men applied, 912 accepted, 175 enrolled; 2,606 women applied, 2,386 accepted, 383 enrolled. 10% had high school GPA of 3.0 or higher, 85% between 2.0 and 2.99. **Academic background:** Mid 50% of enrolled freshmen had SAT-V between 400-450, SAT-M between 400-450; ACT composite between 17-19. 82% submitted SAT scores, 34% submitted ACT scores. **Characteristics:** 85% from in state, 98% live in college housing. Average age is 18.

FALL-TERM APPLICATIONS. $25 fee, may be waived for applicants with need. Closing date September 1; applicants notified on a rolling basis; must reply within 30 days. Interview recommended. Portfolio recommended for studio art, advertising design, commercial illustration, interior design applicants. Essay recommended. Deferred and early admission available.

STUDENT LIFE. Housing: Dormitories (women, coed); apartment housing available. Apartment-style housing available for juniors and seniors. **Activities:** Student government, magazine, radio, student newspaper, yearbook, choral groups, drama, Brothers and Sisters United, Cazenovia Alcohol Resistance Efforts, Students for Social Responsibility, campus ministry.

ATHLETICS. NJCAA. **Intercollegiate:** Basketball, golf M, soccer, softball W, tennis, volleyball W. **Intramural:** Basketball, racquetball, soccer, softball, swimming, table tennis, tennis, volleyball. **Clubs:** Horseback riding, skiing.

STUDENT SERVICES. Career counseling, employment service for undergraduates, freshman orientation, health services, on-campus day care, personal counseling, placement service for graduates, special adviser for adult students, student advocacy program, services/facilities for handicapped.

ANNUAL EXPENSES. Tuition and fees: $9,445. **Room and board:** $4,608. **Books and supplies:** $400. **Other expenses:** $350.

FINANCIAL AID. 87% of freshmen, 87% of continuing students receive some form of aid. 87% of grants, 74% of loans, 73% of jobs based on need. Academic, art, athletic, state/district residency, leadership, minority scholarships available. **Aid applications:** No closing date; priority given to applications received by March 1; applicants notified on a rolling basis beginning on or about March 1; must reply within 2 weeks.

ADDRESS/TELEPHONE. Dr. James T. Parker, Vice President of Enrollment Management, Cazenovia College, Joy Hall, Cazenovia, NY 13035-9989. (315) 655-8005. (800) 654-3210. Fax: (315) 655-2190.

Central City Business Institute
Syracuse, New York — CB code: 2601

Admissions: 87% of applicants accepted
Based on: ••• Interview, school record
•• Recommendations
• Activities, essay, test scores
Completion: 65% of freshmen end year in good standing
52% graduate, 15% of these enter 4-year programs

2-year proprietary business college, coed. Founded in 1904. **Undergraduate enrollment:** 63 men, 355 women full time; 9 men, 28 women part time. **Faculty:** 33 total (21 full time). **Location:** Urban campus in small city; 250 miles from Buffalo; 150 miles from Albany. **Calendar:** Semester, limited summer session. **Microcomputers:** 40 located in libraries, computer centers. **Additional facts:** Court reporting program approved by National Court Reporters Association.

DEGREES OFFERED. 204 associate degrees awarded in 1992. 20% in business and management, 80% business/office and marketing/distribution.

UNDERGRADUATE MAJORS. Accounting, business administration and management, business and office, business computer/console/peripheral equipment operation, business data entry equipment operation, business data processing and related programs, business data programming, court reporting, fashion merchandising, legal secretary, marketing and distribution, medical secretary, office supervision and management, retailing, secretarial and related programs.

ACADEMIC PROGRAMS. 2-year transfer program, internships. **Remedial services:** Reduced course load, remedial instruction, tutoring. **Placement/credit:** AP; 12 credit hours maximum for associate degree.

ACADEMIC REQUIREMENTS. Freshmen must earn minimum GPA of 2.0 to continue in good standing. 71% of freshmen return for sophomore year. Students must declare major on application. **Graduation requirements:** 64 hours for associate (64 in major). Most students required to take courses in English.

FRESHMAN ADMISSIONS. Selection criteria: School achievement record, test scores, interview, recommendation of guidance counselor, school and community activities. Candidates evaluated on skills, accomplishments, character, prior education, and interview with member of admissions staff or department chairperson. **Test requirements:** Applicants with weak grades, and all adult students, must take Career Programs Assessment Test.

1992 FRESHMAN CLASS PROFILE. 101 men applied, 75 accepted, 40 enrolled; 417 women applied, 377 accepted, 182 enrolled. 8% had high school GPA of 3.0 or higher, 92% between 2.0 and 2.99. 5% were in top quarter of graduating class. **Characteristics:** 99% from in state, 65% commute, 36% have minority backgrounds, 1% join fraternities/sororities. Average age is 20.

FALL-TERM APPLICATIONS. $25 fee, may be waived for applicants with need. No closing date; applicants notified on a rolling basis; must reply within 4 weeks. Interview required. Essay recommended. Deferred admission available.

STUDENT LIFE. Housing: Dormitories (coed). Off-campus housing provided at Syracuse University. **Activities:** Student government, student newspaper, yearbook, fraternities, sororities, student services club, Phi Beta Lambda, student team of admissions representatives.

ATHLETICS. Intramural: Bowling, volleyball. **Clubs:** Skiing.

STUDENT SERVICES. Aptitude testing, career counseling, employment service for undergraduates, freshman orientation, health services, placement service for graduates, special adviser for adult students, veterans counselor, services/facilities for handicapped.

ANNUAL EXPENSES. Tuition and fees (1992-93): $4,770. **Room and board:** $3,000. **Books and supplies:** $500. **Other expenses:** $700.

FINANCIAL AID. 90% of freshmen, 90% of continuing students receive some form of aid. 98% of grants, 92% of loans, 91% of jobs based on need. Academic, state/district residency scholarships available. **Aid applications:** No closing date; priority given to applications received by June 1; applicants notified on a rolling basis beginning on or about July 1; must reply within 4 weeks.

ADDRESS/TELEPHONE. Robert F. Flynn, Director of Admissions, Central City Business Institute, 224 Harrison Street, Syracuse, NY 13202. (315) 472-6233. (800) 666-2224. Fax: (315) 472-6201.

Central Yeshiva Tomchei Tmimim Lubavitz

Brooklyn, New York CB code: 0549

5-year private rabbinical college, men only, affiliated with Jewish faith. Founded in 1941. **Undergraduate enrollment:** 370 men full time. **Graduate enrollment:** 54 men full time. **Location:** Urban campus in very large city. **Calendar:** Semester. **Additional facts:** Talmudic jurisprudence degree and ordination available.

FRESHMAN ADMISSIONS. Selection criteria: Rabbinical high school background, rigorous interview with dean most important.

ADDRESS/TELEPHONE. Rabbi A. Sharfstein, Registrar, Central Yeshiva Tomchei Tmimim Lubavitz, 841-853 Ocean Parkway, Brooklyn, NY 11230. (718) 434-0784.

City University of New York: Baruch College

New York, New York CB code: 2034

4-year public college of arts and sciences and business college, coed. Founded in 1919. **Accreditation:** Regional. **Undergraduate enrollment:** 3,474 men, 4,902 women full time; 1,594 men, 2,469 women part time. **Graduate enrollment:** 404 men, 263 women full time; 1,054 men, 895 women part time. **Faculty:** 860 total (480 full time), 425 with doctorates or other terminal degrees. **Location:** Urban campus in very large city; the Gramercy Park area of Manhattan. **Calendar:** Semester, limited summer session. Extensive evening/early morning classes. **Microcomputers:** 265 located in libraries, classrooms, computer centers. **Special facilities:** Sidney Mishkin Gallery, several performing groups in residence: Jean Cocttau Repertory Theater group, Milt Hinton Jazz Workshop, and Alexander String Quartet. **Additional facts:** Students have access to institution's library and 4.5 million-volume CUNY library. Business programs approved by American Assembly of Collegiate Schools of Business.

DEGREES OFFERED. BA, BS, MS, MBA, MEd, PhD. 1,848 bachelor's degrees awarded in 1992. 80% in business and management, 6% computer sciences. Graduate degrees offered in 34 major fields of study.

UNDERGRADUATE MAJORS. Accounting, actuarial sciences, advertising, American literature, arts management, biological and physical sciences, business administration and management, business and management, business economics, business education, business statistics, comparative literature, creative writing, early childhood education, economics, education of the emotionally handicapped, education of the mentally handicapped, elementary education, English, English literature, finance, Hebrew, history, human resources development, humanities and social sciences, industrial and organizational psychology, information sciences and systems, journalism, liberal/general studies, management information systems, marketing and distributive education, marketing management, marketing research, mathematics, music, music business management, office supervision and management, operations research, personnel management, philosophy, political science and government, psychology, psychometrics, public administration, religion, retailing, sociology, sociometrics, Spanish, special education, specific learning disabilities, statistics, systems analysis.

ACADEMIC PROGRAMS. Honors program, independent study, student-designed major, study abroad, teacher preparation, visiting/exchange student program, exchange program with institutions in England, France, Israel, Germany, and Mexico. **Remedial services:** Preadmission summer program, remedial instruction, special counselor, tutoring. **Placement/credit:** AP, CLEP General and Subject, institutional tests; 32 credit hours maximum for bachelor's degree.

ACADEMIC REQUIREMENTS. Freshmen must earn minimum GPA of 1.75 to continue in good standing. Students must declare major by end of second year. **Graduation requirements:** 128 hours for bachelor's (24 in major). Most students required to take courses in arts/fine arts, computer science, English, foreign languages, history, humanities, mathematics, philosophy/religion, biological/physical sciences, social sciences. **Additional information:** Optional humanities seminar offered, examining two or more disciplines in arts and sciences.

FRESHMAN ADMISSIONS. Selection criteria: Minimum high school average in academic subjects of 80% or above 66th percentile. Other applicants with SAT combined score above 900 or ACT composite score of 19 or better accepted on space-available basis. Special consideration given to educationally disadvantaged students from low-income families. **High school preparation:** 11 units required; 17.5 recommended. Recommended units include English 4.0, foreign language 3.5, mathematics 3.0, social science 4 and science 2. College prepatory program strongly advised, but not required.

1992 FRESHMAN CLASS PROFILE. 5,209 men and women applied, 3,027 accepted; 1,423 enrolled. **Characteristics:** 96% from in state, 100% commute, 72% have minority backgrounds, 2% are foreign students. Average age is 18.

FALL-TERM APPLICATIONS. $35 fee, may be waived for applicants with need. Closing date January 15; applicants notified on a rolling basis beginning on or about March 15. Interview recommended. SAT or ACT optional. Applicants with high school average below 80 may substitute combined test score of 900 on SAT or 19 on ACT.

STUDENT LIFE. Activities: Student government, magazine, radio, student newspaper, yearbook, drama, jazz band, musical theater, gospel chorus, over 100 student groups including ethnic associations, religious organizations, academic clubs and organizations, peer counseling organizations. **Additional information:** Three student government represent graduate students and day and evening students. Students also represented on boards approving all student activity for expenditures.

ATHLETICS. NCAA. **Intercollegiate:** Baseball M, basketball, cross-country W, fencing, soccer M, tennis, volleyball. **Intramural:** Badminton, basketball, table tennis, volleyball. **Clubs:** Intercollegiate archery.

STUDENT SERVICES. Aptitude testing, career counseling, employment service for undergraduates, freshman orientation, health services, on-campus day care, personal counseling, placement service for graduates, services/facilities for handicapped.

ANNUAL EXPENSES. Tuition and fees (1992-93): $2,552, $2,600 additional for out-of-state students. **Books and supplies:** $500. **Other expenses:** $2,100.

FINANCIAL AID. 70% of freshmen, 72% of continuing students receive some form of aid. 99% of grants, 57% of loans, 80% of jobs based on need. Academic scholarships available. **Aid applications:** Closing date May 30; priority given to applications received by April 15; applicants notified on or about August 1; must reply within 3 weeks.

ADDRESS/TELEPHONE. Ellen Washington, Director of Undrgraduate Admissions, City University of New York: Baruch College, PO Box 279, 17 Lexington Avenue, New York, NY 10010. (212) 447-3750.

City University of New York: Borough of Manhattan Community College

New York, New York CB code: 2063

2-year public community college, coed. Founded in 1963. **Accreditation:** Regional. **Undergraduate enrollment:** 3,001 men, 5,665 women full time; 2,244 men, 4,767 women part time. **Faculty:** 980 total (298 full time), 235 with doctorates or other terminal degrees. **Location:** Urban campus in very large city; in lower Manhattan near the World Trade Center. **Calendar:** Semester, limited summer session. Saturday and extensive evening/early morning classes. **Microcomputers:** 400 located in libraries, classrooms, computer centers. **Special facilities:** Theaters.

DEGREES OFFERED. AA, AS, AAS. 1,264 associate degrees awarded in 1992. 34% in business and management, 5% business/office and marketing/distribution, 9% computer sciences, 8% teacher education, 8% health sciences, 7% allied health, 24% multi/interdisciplinary studies.

UNDERGRADUATE MAJORS. Accounting, business administration and management, computer and information sciences, computer programming, early childhood education, emergency medical technologies, engineering and engineering-related technologies, engineering science, information sciences and systems, liberal/general studies, marketing and distribution, medical records technology, mental health/human services, nursing, office automation, office supervision and management, real estate, respiratory therapy technology, telecommunications, tourism.

ACADEMIC PROGRAMS. 2-year transfer program, cooperative education, dual enrollment of high school students, independent study, internships, study abroad, visiting/exchange student program, weekend college, cross-registration. **Remedial services:** Learning center, preadmission summer program, remedial instruction, special counselor, tutoring, prefreshman summer immersion program. **Placement/credit:** AP, CLEP Subject, institutional tests; 34 credit hours maximum for associate degree.

ACADEMIC REQUIREMENTS. Freshmen must earn minimum GPA of 1.5 to continue in good standing. 1.75 minmum GPA required after accumulating 12 credits, 2.0 minimum GPA after 25 or more credits. 59% of freshmen return for sophomore year. Students must declare major on application. **Graduation requirements:** 66 hours for associate (38 in major). Most students required to take courses in computer science, English, foreign languages, humanities, mathematics, biological/physical sciences, social sciences.

FRESHMAN ADMISSIONS. Selection criteria: Open admissions. Applicants to associate degree program in nursing must complete all remedial courses in addition to prenursing courses of 13 credits and score in 40th percentile on National League for Nursing examination. 2.0 GPA must be maintained. **High school preparation:** 9 units recommended. Recommended units include English 3, mathematics 2 and science 1. **Additional information:** Units recommended for admission must be acquired before graduation from any CUNY community college.

1992 FRESHMAN CLASS PROFILE. 1,036 men, 1,779 women enrolled. 9% had high school GPA of 3.0 or higher, 68% between 2.0 and 2.99. **Characteristics:** 98% from in state, 100% commute, 91% have minority backgrounds, 1% are foreign students. Average age is 20.

FALL-TERM APPLICATIONS. $35 fee, may be waived for applicants with need. Closing date August 1; priority given to applications received by February 6; applicants notified on a rolling basis beginning on or about March 1. Deferred admission available.

STUDENT LIFE. Activities: Student government, magazine, radio, student newspaper, television, yearbook, choral groups, dance, drama, jazz band, music ensembles, musical theater, fraternities, sororities, numerous religious, political, ethnic, social service, and special interest organizations.

ATHLETICS. Intercollegiate: Baseball M, basketball, diving, fencing W, gymnastics, soccer M, softball W, swimming, tennis, track and field, volleyball, water polo M. **Intramural:** Basketball, diving, gymnastics, skiing, swimming, tennis, volleyball, wrestling M.

STUDENT SERVICES. Career counseling, employment service for undergraduates, freshman orientation, health services, on-campus day care, personal counseling, placement service for graduates, special adviser for adult students, veterans counselor, services/facilities for handicapped.

ANNUAL EXPENSES. Tuition and fees (1992-93): $2,182, $576 additional for out-of-state students. **Books and supplies:** $500. **Other expenses:** $2,100.

FINANCIAL AID. 85% of freshmen, 80% of continuing students receive some form of aid. All grants, all loans based on need. **Aid applications:** No closing date; applicants notified on a rolling basis beginning on or about August 1; must reply within 2 weeks.

ADDRESS/TELEPHONE. Dennis Bonner, Director of Admissions and Enrollment Management, City University of New York: Borough of Manhattan Community College, 199 Chambers Street, New York, NY 10007-1097. (212) 346-8100. Fax: (212) 346-8886.

City University of New York: Bronx Community College

New York, New York CB code: 2051

2-year public community college, coed. Founded in 1957. **Accreditation:** Regional. **Undergraduate enrollment:** 8,000 men and women. **Faculty:** 690 total (360 full time), 113 with doctorates or other terminal degrees. **Location:** Urban campus in very large city. **Calendar:** Semester, limited summer session. **Microcomputers:** Located in libraries, classrooms. **Special facilities:** Hall of fame for great Americans.

DEGREES OFFERED. AA, AS, AAS. 700 associate degrees awarded in 1992.

UNDERGRADUATE MAJORS. Accounting, automotive technology, business and office, business data processing and related programs, business data programming, chemical manufacturing technology, data processing, electrical technology, engineering and engineering-related technologies, lay advocate, legal assistant/paralegal, liberal/general studies, marketing and distribution, medical assistant, medical laboratory technologies, music performance, nuclear medical technology, nuclear technologies, nursing, ornamental horticulture, secretarial and related programs, teacher aide. radiograph medical technology.

ACADEMIC PROGRAMS. 2-year transfer program, cooperative education, dual enrollment of high school students, external degree, independent study, internships, cross-registration. **Remedial services:** Learning center, preadmission summer program, reduced course load, remedial instruction, tutoring. **Placement/credit:** CLEP Subject, institutional tests; 30 credit hours maximum for associate degree.

ACADEMIC REQUIREMENTS. Freshmen must earn minimum GPA of 1.75 to continue in good standing. Students must declare major on enrollment. **Graduation requirements:** Most students required to take courses in English, foreign languages, history, mathematics, biological/physical sciences, social sciences.

FRESHMAN ADMISSIONS. Selection criteria: Open admissions. **High school preparation:** 9 units recommended. Recommended units include English 3, mathematics 2 and science 1. **Additional information:** Units recommended for admission must be acquired before graduation from any CUNY community college.

1992 FRESHMAN CLASS PROFILE. 4,000 men and women enrolled. **Characteristics:** 98% from in state, 100% commute, 95% have minority backgrounds. Average age is 21.

FALL-TERM APPLICATIONS. $35 fee, may be waived for applicants with need. Closing date August 20; priority given to applications received by January 15; applicants notified on a rolling basis beginning on or about June 1. Audition required for music applicants. Interview recommended for paralegal studies applicants.

STUDENT LIFE. Activities: Student government, magazine, radio, student newspaper, yearbook, choral groups, dance, drama, music ensembles.

ATHLETICS. Intercollegiate: Baseball M, basketball, soccer M, track and field.

STUDENT SERVICES. Career counseling, employment service for undergraduates, health services, personal counseling, placement service for graduates, services/facilities for handicapped.

ANNUAL EXPENSES. Tuition and fees (1992-93): $2,204, $576 additional for out-of-state students. **Books and supplies:** $500. **Other expenses:** $2,100.

FINANCIAL AID. 90% of freshmen, 90% of continuing students receive some form of aid. **Aid applications:** No closing date; applicants notified on a rolling basis beginning on or about August 1.

ADDRESS/TELEPHONE. Alba Concetta Cummings, Director of Admissions, City University of New York: Bronx Community College, West 181st Street and University Avenue, New York, NY 10453. (718) 220-6284.

City University of New York: Brooklyn College

Brooklyn, New York CB code: 2046

Admissions: 64% of applicants accepted
Based on: ••• School record
•• Test scores
• Recommendations
Completion: 50% enter graduate study

4-year public liberal arts college, coed. Founded in 1930. **Accreditation:** Regional. **Undergraduate enrollment:** 3,529 men, 4,490 women full time; 1,394 men, 2,208 women part time. **Graduate enrollment:** 3,097 men and women. **Faculty:** 850 total (594 full time). **Location:** Urban campus in very large city; 10 miles from Manhattan. **Calendar:** Semester, extensive summer session. **Microcomputers:** 250 located in libraries, classrooms, computer centers. **Special facilities:** 2 art galleries, astronomical observatory, greenhouse. **Additional facts:** College has conservatory of music.

DEGREES OFFERED. BA, BS, BFA, MA, MS, MFA, MEd. 1,370 bachelor's degrees awarded in 1992. Graduate degrees offered in 84 major fields of study.

UNDERGRADUATE MAJORS. Accounting, African studies, Afro-

American (black) studies, allied health, American literature, American studies, anthropology, applied mathematics, archeology, art education, art history, Asian studies, basic clinical health sciences, behavioral sciences, bilingual/bicultural education, biological and physical sciences, biology, biomedical science, business and management, business economics, Caribbean studies, chemistry, cinematography/film, classics, clinical psychology, communications, community health work, comparative literature, computer and information sciences, computer mathematics, computer programming, creative writing, dramatic arts, early childhood education, East Asian studies, Eastern European studies, economics, education, education of the deaf and hearing impaired, education of the emotionally handicapped, education of the mentally handicapped, education of the multiple handicapped, education of the physically handicapped, elementary education, English, English education, English literature, European studies, film arts, fine arts, food science and nutrition, foreign languages education, French, geology, German, Greek (classical), health and nutrition sciences, health education, health sciences, Hebrew, Hispanic American studies, history, home economics, home economics education, information sciences and systems, Italian, Jewish studies, journalism, junior high education, language interpretation and translation, Latin, Latin American studies, linguistics, management information systems, mathematics, mathematics education, Middle Eastern studies, music, music education, music performance, music theory and composition, musical theater, nutritional education, nutritional sciences, philosophy, physical education, physical sciences, physics, political science and government, predentistry, prelaw, premedicine, prepharmacy, preveterinary, psychology, pure mathematics, radio/television broadcasting, reading education, religion, remedial education, Russian, Russian and Slavic studies, science education, secondary education, social science education, social studies education, sociology, Spanish, special education, specific learning disabilities, speech, speech correction, speech pathology/audiology, speech/communication/theater education, teaching English as a second language/foreign language, theater design, urban studies, video, visual and performing arts, Western European studies, women's studies.

ACADEMIC PROGRAMS. Accelerated program, double major, dual enrollment of high school students, education specialist degree, honors program, independent study, internships, study abroad, teacher preparation, visiting/exchange student program, weekend college, Washington semester, cross-registration; liberal arts/career combination in engineering, health sciences; combined bachelor's/graduate program in medicine, law. **Remedial services:** Learning center, preadmission summer program, reduced course load, remedial instruction, special counselor, tutoring, SEEK program. **Placement/credit:** AP, CLEP Subject, institutional tests; 35 credit hours maximum for bachelor's degree.

ACADEMIC REQUIREMENTS. To continue in good academic standing, students with up to 12 credits must maintain 1.5 GPA, those with 13-24. Students must declare major by end of second year. **Graduation requirements:** 128 hours for bachelor's (30 in major). Most students required to take courses in arts/fine arts, computer science, English, foreign languages, history, humanities, mathematics, philosophy/religion, biological/physical sciences, social sciences. **Additional information:** Students must pass CUNY Assessment Test by the completion of 60 credits. Consists of diagnostic reading, writing, mathematics skills examination.

FRESHMAN ADMISSIONS. Selection criteria: Students must meet any 1 of the following criteria: 2.7 high school GPA in academic subjects, rank in top third of class, or SAT combined score of 900 or better or ACT composite score of 20 or better. **High school preparation:** 15 units recommended. Recommended units include English 4, foreign language 3, mathematics 3, social science 4 and science 1. **Test requirements:** CUNY skills assessment test required in mathematics and English for placement. **Additional information:** 11 of 15 units recommended for admission (including 4 English, 2 mathematics, and 1 laboratory science) must be acquired before graduation from any CUNY senior college.

1992 FRESHMAN CLASS PROFILE. 3,914 men and women applied, 2,505 accepted; 1,428 enrolled. **Characteristics:** 90% from in state, 100% commute, 40% have minority backgrounds, 2% are foreign students, 5% join fraternities/sororities. Average age is 18.

FALL-TERM APPLICATIONS. $35 fee, may be waived for applicants with need. $40 application fee for transfer students. Closing date May 15; priority given to applications received by May 1; applicants notified on a rolling basis beginning on or about March 1. Audition required for music conservatory, theater applicants. Portfolio required for fine arts applicants. Essay required for scholars' program applicants. Interview recommended for scholars' program applicants. Deferred and early admission available.

STUDENT LIFE. Activities: Student government, film, magazine, radio, student newspaper, yearbook, literary and scientific publications, choral groups, concert band, drama, jazz band, music ensembles, musical theater, opera, symphony orchestra, fraternities, sororities, Hillel, Newman Club, Student Christian Association, Alpha Phi Omega, more than 100 other clubs.

ATHLETICS. Intramural: Badminton W, basketball, fencing W, football M, racquetball, soccer M, softball, table tennis, tennis, volleyball.

STUDENT SERVICES. Aptitude testing, career counseling, employment service for undergraduates, freshman orientation, health services, on-campus day care, personal counseling, placement service for graduates, special adviser for adult students, veterans counselor, handicapped student adviser, services/facilities for handicapped.

ANNUAL EXPENSES. Tuition and fees (1992-93): $2,605, $2,600 additional for out-of-state students. **Books and supplies:** $500. **Other expenses:** $2,100.

FINANCIAL AID. 50% of freshmen, 53% of continuing students receive some form of aid. All grants, 94% of loans, all jobs based on need. 810 enrolled freshmen were judged to have need, 720 were offered aid. Academic, music/drama, art scholarships available. **Aid applications:** No closing date; priority given to applications received by May 1; applicants notified on a rolling basis beginning on or about August 15; must reply within 2 weeks.

ADDRESS/TELEPHONE. Glenn N. Sklarin, Director of Enrollment Management, City University of New York: Brooklyn College, 2900 Bedford Avenue/ 1602 William James Hall, Brooklyn, NY 11210. (718) 951-5611. Fax: (718) 951-4506.

City University of New York: City College

New York, New York — CB code: 2083

Admissions:	76% of applicants accepted
Based on:	••• School record
	• Test scores
Completion:	60% of freshmen end year in good standing
	41% enter graduate study

4-year public university, coed. Founded in 1847. **Accreditation:** Regional. **Undergraduate enrollment:** 4,472 men, 3,426 women full time; 1,839 men, 1,804 women part time. **Graduate enrollment:** 235 men, 143 women full time; 1,418 men, 1,446 women part time. **Faculty:** 1,110 total (588 full time), 463 with doctorates or other terminal degrees. **Location:** Urban campus in very large city. **Calendar:** Semester, extensive summer session. **Microcomputers:** 3,000 located in libraries, computer centers. **Special facilities:** Planetarium, weather station, ultra-fast laser spectroscopy laboratory, microwave laboratory, computer-aided design facilities, slide library, darkroom facilities.

DEGREES OFFERED. BA, BS, BFA, BArch, MA, MS, MBA, MFA, MEd, PhD. 1,218 bachelor's degrees awarded in 1992. 9% in architecture and environmental design, 10% area and ethnic studies, 5% computer sciences, 8% education, 30% engineering, 12% health sciences, 12% letters/literature. Graduate degrees offered in 55 major fields of study.

UNDERGRADUATE MAJORS. Aerospace/aeronautical/astronautical engineering, African languages, African studies, Afro-American (black) studies, American literature, American studies, anthropology, architecture, art history, Asian studies, atmospheric sciences and meteorology, bilingual/bicultural education, biochemistry, biology, business and management, Caribbean studies, chemical engineering, chemistry, cinematography/film, civil engineering, classics, communications, comparative literature, computer and information sciences, creative writing, dance, dance research and reconstruction, dramatic arts, economics, education of the emotionally handicapped, education of the mentally handicapped, electrical/electronics/communications engineering, elementary education, English, English literature, European studies, foreign languages (multiple emphasis), French, geography, geology, German, Greek (classical), Hebrew, Hispanic American studies, history, industrial arts education, interior design, international relations, Italian, Jewish studies, journalism, landscape architecture, Latin, Latin American studies, linguistics, mathematics, mathematics education, mechanical engineering, music, music history and appreciation, nursing, oceanography, philosophy, photography, physical education, physical sciences, physician's assistant, physics, political science and government, predentistry, prelaw, premedicine, preveterinary, psychology, Puerto Rican studies, Russian, Russian and Slavic studies, science education, secondary education, social studies education, sociology, Spanish, special education, speech, speech correction, studio art, video, visual and performing arts.

ACADEMIC PROGRAMS. Accelerated program, cooperative education, dual enrollment of high school students, honors program, independent study, internships, study abroad, teacher preparation, visiting/exchange student program, cross-registration, Center for Worker Education, doctoral degrees through CUNY Graduate center, combined bachelor's/graduate degree programs in law with CUNY Law School and in medicine with Albany Medical College, Mount Sinai School of Medicine, SUNY at Buffalo, New York Medical College, New York University School of Medicine. **Remedial services:** Learning center, preadmission summer program, reduced course load, remedial instruction, special counselor, tutoring. **Placement/credit:** AP, institutional tests; 32 credit hours maximum for bachelor's degree.

ACADEMIC REQUIREMENTS. Freshmen must earn minimum GPA of 1.75 to continue in good standing. 70% of freshmen return for sophomore year. Students must declare major by end of second year. **Graduation requirements:** 128 hours for bachelor's (27 in major). Most students required to take courses in English, foreign languages, mathematics, biological/physical sciences, social sciences. **Postgraduate studies:** 3% enter law school, 15% enter medical school, 2% enter MBA programs, 21% enter other graduate study.

FRESHMAN ADMISSIONS. Selection criteria: Minimum high school academic average of 80 or rank in top third of class, or minimum combined SAT score of 900 or minimum ACT composite score of 20 important. **High school preparation:** 11 units recommended. Recommended units include English 4, mathematics 2 and science 1. **Additional information:** Units recommended for admission must be required before graduatuion from any CUNY senior college.

1992 FRESHMAN CLASS PROFILE. 3,396 men and women applied, 2,582 accepted; 662 men enrolled, 498 women enrolled. **Characteristics:** 85% from in state, 100% commute, 89% have minority backgrounds, 10% are foreign students. Average age is 20.

FALL-TERM APPLICATIONS. $35 fee, may be waived for applicants with need. No closing date; priority given to applications received by January 15; applicants notified on a rolling basis beginning on or about March 1. Interview required for biomedical education, urban legal studies applicants. Audition required for theater, dance, music applicants. Deferred and early admission available. SAT or ACT recommended for all applicants.

STUDENT LIFE. Activities: Student government, film, radio, student newspaper, television, yearbook, choral groups, dance, drama, jazz band, marching band, music ensembles, musical theater, symphony orchestra, fraternities, numerous religious, political, ethnic, and social service organizations.

ATHLETICS. NCAA. **Intercollegiate:** Baseball M, basketball, cross-country, diving, fencing, gymnastics M, lacrosse M, soccer M, softball W, swimming, tennis, track and field, volleyball W. **Intramural:** Badminton, baseball, basketball, fencing, gymnastics, handball W, soccer M, softball W, swimming, tennis, track and field, volleyball.

STUDENT SERVICES. Career counseling, employment service for undergraduates, health services, on-campus day care, personal counseling, placement service for graduates, veterans counselor, services/facilities for handicapped.

ANNUAL EXPENSES. Tuition and fees (projected): $2,547, $2,600 additional for out-of-state students. **Books and supplies:** $500. **Other expenses:** $2,100.

FINANCIAL AID. 86% of freshmen, 70% of continuing students receive some form of aid. 99% of grants, 82% of loans, all jobs based on need. 1,050 enrolled freshmen were judged to have need, all were offered aid. Academic scholarships available. **Aid applications:** No closing date; priority given to applications received by May 1; applicants notified on a rolling basis beginning on or about August 1; must reply by registration.

ADDRESS/TELEPHONE. Nancy P. Campbell, Director of Enrollment Management, City University of New York: City College, Convent Avenue at 138th Street, New York, NY 10031. (212) 650-6977. Fax: (212) 650-6417.

City University of New York: College of Staten Island

Staten Island, New York CB code: 2778

4-year public college of arts and sciences, coed. Founded in 1955. **Accreditation:** Regional. **Undergraduate enrollment:** 2,669 men, 2,181 women full time; 1,877 men, 3,245 women part time. **Graduate enrollment:** 26 men, 37 women full time; 249 men, 839 women part time. **Faculty:** 751 total (301 full time), 205 with doctorates or other terminal degrees. **Location:** Urban campus in very large city; 5 miles from downtown Manhattan. **Calendar:** Semester, extensive summer session. Saturday and extensive evening/early morning classes. **Microcomputers:** 300 located in classrooms, computer centers. **Additional facts:** Most classes at new 204-acre campus. Performing and creative arts, health and physical education departments remaining temporarily at Sunnyside and St. George campuses.

DEGREES OFFERED. AA, AS, AAS, BA, BS, MA, MS, PhD. 424 associate degrees awarded in 1992. 20% in business and management, 5% computer sciences, 5% engineering technologies, 34% health sciences, 36% multi/interdisciplinary studies. 813 bachelor's degrees awarded. 28% in business and management, 5% health sciences, 9% letters/literature, 7% multi/interdisciplinary studies, 19% psychology, 15% social sciences. Graduate degrees offered in 13 major fields of study.

UNDERGRADUATE MAJORS. Associate: Architecture, business and management, business and office, child development/care/guidance, civil technology, computer technology, electrical technology, electromechanical technology, engineering and engineering-related technologies, industrial technology, liberal/general studies, mechanical design technology, medical laboratory technologies, nursing. **Bachelor's:** Accounting, Afro-American (black) studies, American studies, biochemistry, biology, business and management, chemistry, cinematography/film, communications, computer and information sciences, computer mathematics, dramatic arts, economics, education, engineering science, English, foreign languages (multiple emphasis), history, international studies, mathematics, medical laboratory technologies, music, nursing, philosophy, physics, political science and government, psychology, science, letters and society, sociology-anthropology, Spanish, studio art, women's studies.

ACADEMIC PROGRAMS. 2-year transfer program, double major, dual enrollment of high school students, honors program, independent study, internships, student-designed major, study abroad, teacher preparation, weekend college, cross-registration. **Remedial services:** Learning center, preadmission summer program, remedial instruction, special counselor, tutoring. **Placement/credit:** AP, CLEP General and Subject, institutional tests; 30 credit hours maximum for bachelor's degree.

ACADEMIC REQUIREMENTS. Freshmen must earn minimum GPA of 1.5 to continue in good standing. 67% of freshmen return for sophomore year. Students must declare major by end of second year. **Graduation requirements:** 64 hours for associate (30 in major), 128 hours for bachelor's (32 in major). Most students required to take courses in arts/fine arts, computer science, English, foreign languages, history, humanities, mathematics, philosophy/religion, biological/physical sciences, social sciences. **Postgraduate studies:** 42% from 2-year programs enter 4-year programs. **Additional information:** Credits from associate degree fully transferable to bachelor's degree program in same or related field.

FRESHMAN ADMISSIONS. Selection criteria: Open admissions. Applicants must have average of 80 or rank in upper two-thirds of their class to be eligible for admission to 4-year programs. Applicants with lower average or class rank eligible for admission to 2-year programs. **High school preparation:** 9 units recommended. Recommended units include English 3, mathematics 2 and science 1. 11 units including 4 English recommended for bachelor's programs. **Additional information:** Units recommended for admission must be acquired before graduation from CUNY.

1992 FRESHMAN CLASS PROFILE. 701 men, 831 women enrolled. **Characteristics:** 96% from in state, 100% commute, 26% have minority backgrounds, 4% are foreign students. Average age is 21.

FALL-TERM APPLICATIONS. $35 fee. $40 application fee for transfer students. Closing date July 1; priority given to applications received by January 15; applicants notified on a rolling basis beginning on or about March 1. Audition required for music applicants. Portfolio recommended for art applicants. Deferred admission available.

STUDENT LIFE. Activities: Student government, film, magazine, radio, student newspaper, yearbook, choral groups, drama, music ensembles, ethnic clubs, International Club, Christian Fellowship Club, Hillel Club, Newman Club, Gay, Lesbian and Bisexual Alliance, Women's Network.

ATHLETICS. NCAA. **Intercollegiate:** Baseball M, basketball, soccer M, softball W, tennis, volleyball W. **Intramural:** Badminton, basketball, bowling, fencing, golf, gymnastics, racquetball, skiing, softball, swimming, table tennis, tennis, track and field, volleyball.

STUDENT SERVICES. Aptitude testing, career counseling, employment service for undergraduates, freshman orientation, health services, on-campus day care, personal counseling, placement service for graduates, special adviser for adult students, veterans counselor, services/facilities for handicapped.

ANNUAL EXPENSES. Tuition and fees (1992-93): $2,556, $2,600 additional for out-of-state students. **Books and supplies:** $500. **Other expenses:** $2,100.

FINANCIAL AID. 33% of freshmen, 33% of continuing students receive some form of aid. 98% of grants, 85% of loans, all jobs based on need. Leadership scholarships available. **Aid applications:** Closing date September 30; priority given to applications received by May 25; applicants notified on a rolling basis beginning on or about July 1; must reply within 30 days.

ADDRESS/TELEPHONE. Ramon H. Hulsey, Director of Admissions, City University of New York: College of Staten Island, 2800 Victory Boulevard, Staten Island, NY 10314. (718) 390-7557. Fax: (718) 273-5052.

City University of New York: Hostos Community College

Bronx, New York CB code: 2303

2-year public community college, coed. Founded in 1970. **Accreditation:** Regional. **Undergraduate enrollment:** 893 men, 2,691 women full time; 255 men, 651 women part time. **Faculty:** 403 total (229 full time), 66 with doctorates or other terminal degrees. **Location:** Urban campus in very large city. **Calendar:** Semester, limited summer session. **Microcomputers:** 150 located in libraries, classrooms, computer centers. **Special facilities:** Art gallery. **Additional facts:** Bilingual Spanish/English liberal arts program.

DEGREES OFFERED. AA, AS, AAS. 386 associate degrees awarded in 1992. 7% in business and management, 6% communications, 7% education, 15% allied health, 34% multi/interdisciplinary studies, 25% parks/recreation, protective services, public affairs.

UNDERGRADUATE MAJORS. Accounting, business administration and management, civil and public administration, data processing, dental hygiene, early childhood education, gerontology, liberal/general studies, medical laboratory technologies, practical nursing, public administration, radiograph medical technology, secretarial and related programs.

ACADEMIC PROGRAMS. 2-year transfer program, dual enrollment of high school students, internships. **Remedial services:** Learning center, preadmission summer program, remedial instruction, special counselor, tutoring, Intersession Program. **Placement/credit:** Institutional tests.

ACADEMIC REQUIREMENTS. Freshmen must earn minimum GPA of 1.75 to continue in good standing. 58% of freshmen return for sophomore year. Students must declare major by end of first year. **Graduation requirements:** 66 hours for associate (40 in major). Most students required to take courses in arts/fine arts, English, foreign languages, humanities, mathematics, biological/physical sciences, social sciences. **Additional information:** Extensive ESL program.

FRESHMAN ADMISSIONS. Selection criteria: Open admissions. Selective admissions to allied health programs based on Freshman Skills Assessment. **High school preparation:** 9 units recommended. Recommended units include English 3, mathematics 2 and science 1. High school biology, chemistry, mathematics required of allied health applicants. **Additional information:** Units recommended for admission must be acquired before graduation from CUNY. January 15 closing date for spring term applications.

1992 FRESHMAN CLASS PROFILE. 268 men, 597 women enrolled. **Characteristics:** 90% from in state, 100% commute, 99% have minority backgrounds, 7% are foreign students. Average age is 30.

FALL-TERM APPLICATIONS. $35 fee. $40 fee for transfer applications. Closing date August 15; applicants notified on a rolling basis; must reply immediately.

STUDENT LIFE. Activities: Student government, student newspaper, yearbook, choral groups, drama, Puerto Rican club, Christian club, Black Student Union, Dominican Association, South American Student Union, Equadorian Student Association, Career Association.

ATHLETICS. Intramural: Baseball, basketball, bowling, swimming, table tennis, tennis, volleyball.

STUDENT SERVICES. Aptitude testing, career counseling, employment service for undergraduates, freshman orientation, health services, on-campus day care, personal counseling, placement service for graduates, veterans counselor, women's center, immigrants' center, services/facilities for handicapped.

ANNUAL EXPENSES. Tuition and fees (1992-93): $2,174, $576 additional for out-of-state students. **Books and supplies:** $500. **Other expenses:** $2,100.

FINANCIAL AID. 95% of freshmen, 95% of continuing students receive some form of aid. All aid based on need. **Aid applications:** No closing date; applicants notified on a rolling basis; must reply immediately.

ADDRESS/TELEPHONE. Nydia R. Edgecombe, Director of Admissions, City University of New York: Hostos Community College, 500 Grand Concourse, B435, Bronx, NY 10451. (718) 518-6633. Fax: (718) 518-6809.

City University of New York: Hunter College

New York, New York CB code: 2301

4-year public college of arts and sciences and health science college, coed. Founded in 1870. **Accreditation:** Regional. **Undergraduate enrollment:** 2,116 men, 5,601 women full time; 1,858 men, 4,502 women part time. **Graduate enrollment:** 181 men, 545 women full time; 884 men, 2,833 women part time. **Faculty:** 1,341 total (696 full time). **Location:** Urban campus in very large city. **Calendar:** Semester, limited summer session. Extensive evening/early morning classes. **Microcomputers:** 200 located in computer centers. **Special facilities:** Art gallery, mathematics learning center.

DEGREES OFFERED. BA, BS, BFA, MA, MS, MFA, MEd, MSW. 1,580 bachelor's degrees awarded in 1992. 10% in business and management, 9% communications, 6% computer sciences, 14% health sciences, 9% letters/literature, 14% psychology, 16% social sciences, 8% visual and performing arts. Graduate degrees offered in 53 major fields of study.

UNDERGRADUATE MAJORS. Accounting, Afro-American (black) studies, American literature, anthropology, archeology, art education, art history, biology, Black and Puerto Rican studies, chemistry, Chinese, cinematography/film, classics, clinical laboratory science, communications, community health work, comparative literature, computer and information sciences, dance, dance education, dramatic arts, economics, elementary education, English education, English language arts, English literature, fine arts, food science and nutrition, foreign languages (multiple emphasis), foreign languages education, French, geography, geology, German, Greek (classical), health education, Hebrew, history, international relations, international studies, Italian, Jewish studies, Latin, mathematics, mathematics education, music, music education, music history and appreciation, music performance, music theory and composition, nursing, philosophy, physical education, physical therapy, physics, political science and government, predentistry, prelaw, premedicine, prepharmacy, preveterinary, psychology, religion, Russian, science education, secondary education, social science education, social studies education, sociology, Spanish, statistics, studio art, urban studies, women's studies.

ACADEMIC PROGRAMS. Accelerated program, double major, dual enrollment of high school students, education specialist degree, honors program, independent study, internships, student-designed major, study abroad, teacher preparation, visiting/exchange student program, cross-registration; liberal arts/career combination in health sciences. **Remedial services:** Learning center, reduced course load, remedial instruction, special counselor, tutoring, SEEK educational opportunity program. **Placement/credit:** AP, CLEP Subject, institutional tests; 24 credit hours maximum for bachelor's degree.

ACADEMIC REQUIREMENTS. Freshmen must earn minimum GPA of 2.0 to continue in good standing. 77% of freshmen return for sophomore year. Students must declare major by end of second year. **Graduation requirements:** 125 hours for bachelor's (24 in major). Most students required to take courses in English, foreign languages, humanities, mathematics, biological/physical sciences, social sciences.

FRESHMAN ADMISSIONS. Selection criteria: Minimum high school GPA of 80 or rank in top third of class or SAT combined score of 900. **High school preparation:** 11 units recommended. Recommended units include English 4, mathematics 2 and science 1. **Additional information:** Units recommended for admission must be acquired before graduation from CUNY.

1992 FRESHMAN CLASS PROFILE. 248 men, 773 women enrolled. 54% had high school GPA of 3.0 or higher, 36% between 2.0 and 2.99. **Characteristics:** 95% from in state, 96% commute, 54% have minority backgrounds, 2% are foreign students. Average age is 19.

FALL-TERM APPLICATIONS. $35 fee, may be waived for applicants with need. No closing date; priority given to applications received by January 15; applicants notified on a rolling basis beginning on or about March 1. Deferred admission available. SAT test scores recommended but not required.

STUDENT LIFE. Housing: Dormitories (coed). **Activities:** Student government, film, magazine, radio, student newspaper, television, yearbook, choral groups, concert band, dance, drama, jazz band, music ensembles, musical theater, symphony orchestra, fraternities, sororities, over 100 political, ethnic, social, and religious organizations.

ATHLETICS. NCAA. **Intercollegiate:** Baseball M, basketball, cross-country, fencing, gymnastics W, soccer M, softball W, swimming W, tennis, track and field, volleyball, wrestling M. **Intramural:** Basketball, bowling, gymnastics, racquetball, rugby, soccer M, softball W, swimming, table tennis, tennis, volleyball.

STUDENT SERVICES. Career counseling, employment service for undergraduates, freshman orientation, health services, on-campus day care, personal counseling, placement service for graduates, veterans counselor, Disabled students services, women's center, services/facilities for handicapped.

ANNUAL EXPENSES. Tuition and fees (1992-93): $2,553, $2,600 additional for out-of-state students. **Room and board:** $1,600 room only. **Books and supplies:** $500. **Other expenses:** $2,188.

FINANCIAL AID. 72% of freshmen, 72% of continuing students receive some form of aid. All grants, 93% of loans, all jobs based on need. Academic scholarships available. **Aid applications:** No closing date; priority given to applications received by May 1; applicants notified on a rolling basis beginning on or about July 24; must reply within 2 weeks. **Additional information:** Tuition fund grants available.

ADDRESS/TELEPHONE. William Zlata, Director of Admissions, City University of New York: Hunter College, 695 Park Avenue, Room 203 North, New York, NY 10021. (212) 772-4490.

City University of New York: John Jay College of Criminal Justice

New York, New York CB code: 2115

4-year public liberal arts college, coed. Founded in 1964. **Accreditation:** Regional. **Undergraduate enrollment:** 2,449 men, 2,797 women full time; 1,483 men, 1,211 women part time. **Graduate enrollment:** 36 men, 53 women full time; 336 men, 254 women part time. **Faculty:** 503 total (287 full time), 245 with doctorates or other terminal degrees. **Location:** Urban campus in very large city. **Calendar:** Semester, limited summer session. **Microcomputers:** 160 located in libraries, computer centers. **Special facilities:** Security laboratory, fire science laboratory, explosion proof toxicology research laboratory.

DEGREES OFFERED. AS, BA, BS, MA, MS, PhD. 30 associate degrees awarded in 1992. 100% in social sciences. 592 bachelor's degrees awarded. 9% in psychology, 88% social sciences. Graduate degrees offered in 6 major fields of study.

UNDERGRADUATE MAJORS. Associate: Law enforcement and corrections, protective services, public administration. **Bachelor's:** Behavioral sciences, computer and information sciences, criminal justice studies, criminology, deviant behavior and social control, fire control and safety technology, fire protection, forensic psychology, forensic studies, law , law enforcement and corrections, political science and government, prelaw, protective services, psychology, public administration.

ACADEMIC PROGRAMS. 2-year transfer program, cooperative education, dual enrollment of high school students, honors program, independent study, internships, study abroad, visiting/exchange student program, cross-registration. **Remedial services:** Learning center, preadmission summer program, reduced course load, remedial instruction, special counselor, tutoring, peer counseling. **ROTC:** Army. **Placement/credit:** AP, CLEP Subject, institutional tests; 32 credit hours maximum for associate degree; 32 credit hours maximum for bachelor's degree.

ACADEMIC REQUIREMENTS. Freshmen must earn minimum GPA of 2.0 to continue in good standing. Students must declare major on application. **Graduation requirements:** 67 hours for associate (24 in major), 128 hours for bachelor's (36 in major). Most students required to take courses in arts/fine arts, English, foreign languages, history, humanities, mathematics, philosophy/religion, biological/physical sciences, social sciences. **Postgrad-**

uate studies: 90% from 2-year programs enter 4-year programs. **Additional information:** Degree requirements and curriculum combine professional education with the liberal arts. All students must pass CUNY proficiency examinations in reading, writing, mathematics.

FRESHMAN ADMISSIONS. Selection criteria: Open admissions. Open admissions to associate degree programs only. Minimum high school GPA of 2.5 or rank in top half of class for admission to bachelor's programs. Applicants with SAT combined score above 900 or ACT composite score above 20 admitted on space-available basis.'. **High school preparation:** 9 units recommended. Recommended units include English 3, mathematics 2 and science 1. 11 units, including 4 English, recommended for admission to bachelors programs. **Additional information:** Units recommended for admission must be acquired before graduation from CUNY.

1992 FRESHMAN CLASS PROFILE. 666 men, 701 women enrolled. 20% had high school GPA of 3.0 or higher, 40% between 2.0 and 2.99. **Characteristics:** 98% from in state, 100% commute, 65% have minority backgrounds, 1% are foreign students. Average age is 18.

FALL-TERM APPLICATIONS. $35 fee, may be waived for applicants with need. No closing date; priority given to applications received by March 15; applicants notified on a rolling basis beginning on or about February 15. Deferred and early admission available. Centralized application processing allows students to apply to 6 schoolswithin CUNY system at same time. Admissions to John Jay on space-available basis.

STUDENT LIFE. Housing: Limited dormitory space available at Long Island University. **Activities:** Student government, radio, student newspaper, yearbook, choral groups, dance, drama, musical theater, Law Society, Irish club, Students against War and Racism, Haitian club, Christian Seekers Fellowship Club, Jewish Students Society, Newman Club, Betances Society, Black Student Society, ethnic organizations. **Additional information:** Students represented on all faculty committees.

ATHLETICS. NCAA. **Intercollegiate:** Baseball M, basketball, cross-country, soccer M, softball W, tennis, volleyball W, wrestling M. **Intramural:** Basketball, bowling, cross-country, diving, handball, racquetball, skiing, skin diving, soccer, swimming, table tennis, tennis, track and field, volleyball.

STUDENT SERVICES. Aptitude testing, career counseling, employment service for undergraduates, freshman orientation, health services, on-campus day care, personal counseling, placement service for graduates, special adviser for adult students, veterans counselor, services/facilities for handicapped.

ANNUAL EXPENSES. Tuition and fees (1992-93): $2,554, $2,600 additional for out-of-state students. **Books and supplies:** $500. **Other expenses:** $2,100.

FINANCIAL AID. 70% of freshmen, 70% of continuing students receive some form of aid. Grants, loans, jobs available. 900 enrolled freshmen were judged to have need, all were offered aid. Academic scholarships available. **Aid applications:** No closing date; priority given to applications received by June 1; applicants notified on a rolling basis beginning on or about July 15; must reply within 2 weeks.

ADDRESS/TELEPHONE. Francis M. McHugh, Dean of Admissions and Registration, City University of New York: John Jay College of Criminal Justice, 445 West 59th Street, New York, NY 10019. (212) 564-6529. Fax: (212) 237-8777.

City University of New York: Kingsborough Community College

Brooklyn, New York — CB code: 2358

2-year public community college, coed. Founded in 1963. **Accreditation:** Regional. **Undergraduate enrollment:** 2,610 men, 4,165 women full time; 2,642 men, 4,914 women part time. **Faculty:** 818 total (326 full time). **Location:** Urban campus in very large city; 10 miles from midtown Manhattan. **Calendar:** 4 terms (12-6-12-6). Saturday and extensive evening/early morning classes. **Microcomputers:** 300 located in libraries, computer centers, campus-wide network. **Special facilities:** Art galleries.

DEGREES OFFERED. AA, AS, AAS. 1,532 associate degrees awarded in 1992. 30% in business and management, 16% business/office and marketing/distribution, 5% computer sciences, 9% teacher education, 5% health sciences, 20% multi/interdisciplinary studies.

UNDERGRADUATE MAJORS. Accounting, biological and physical sciences, biology, business administration and management, business and office, business data processing and related programs, business data programming, chemistry, community health work, computer and information sciences, computer programming, data processing, dramatic arts, early childhood education, engineering and engineering-related technologies, engineering science, environmental science, fashion merchandising, fine arts, fishing and fisheries, graphic arts technology, journalism, liberal/general studies, marketing and distribution, marketing management, mathematics, medical records administration, medical records technology, mental health/human services, music, nursing, personnel management, physical sciences, physical therapy assistant, physics, radio/television broadcasting, recreation and community services technologies, secretarial and related programs, teacher aide, tourism, transportation and travel marketing.

ACADEMIC PROGRAMS. 2-year transfer program, accelerated program, dual enrollment of high school students, honors program, independent study, cross-registration, College Now Program for high school seniors, My Turn Program for senior citizens, New Start Program for students academically dismissed from 4-year institutions. **Remedial services:** Learning center, preadmission summer program, reduced course load, remedial instruction, special counselor, tutoring, College Discovery program for low-income and minority students, bilingual program. **Placement/credit:** AP, CLEP Subject, institutional tests; 16 credit hours maximum for associate degree.

ACADEMIC REQUIREMENTS. Freshmen must earn minimum GPA of 1.5 to continue in good standing. 65% of freshmen return for sophomore year. Students must declare major on enrollment. **Graduation requirements:** 64 hours for associate. Most students required to take courses in arts/fine arts, English, humanities, social sciences.

FRESHMAN ADMISSIONS. Selection criteria: Open admissions. **High school preparation:** 9 units recommended. Recommended units include English 3, mathematics 2 and science 1. **Additional information:** Units recommended for admission must be acquired before graduation from any CUNY community college.

1992 FRESHMAN CLASS PROFILE. 995 men, 1,504 women enrolled. 7% had high school GPA of 3.0 or higher, 45% between 2.0 and 2.99. **Characteristics:** 96% from in state, 100% commute, 39% have minority backgrounds, 1% are foreign students. Average age is 19.

FALL-TERM APPLICATIONS. $35 fee, may be waived for applicants with need. Closing date August 15; priority given to applications received by July 15; applicants notified on a rolling basis beginning on or about March 31; must reply within 10 days. Audition required for music applicants.

STUDENT LIFE. Activities: Student government, film, magazine, radio, student newspaper, yearbook, choral groups, concert band, dance, drama, jazz band, music ensembles, musical theater, opera, symphony orchestra, over 60 ethnic, academic, religious, and political groups.

ATHLETICS. NJCAA. **Intercollegiate:** Baseball M, basketball, bowling W, golf M, soccer M, softball W, tennis, track and field, volleyball W. **Intramural:** Archery, basketball, cross-country, football M, handball, racquetball, skiing, soccer M, softball, swimming, table tennis, tennis, track and field, volleyball.

STUDENT SERVICES. Aptitude testing, career counseling, employment service for undergraduates, health services, on-campus day care, personal counseling, placement service for graduates, special adviser for adult students, veterans counselor, services/facilities for handicapped.

ANNUAL EXPENSES. Tuition and fees (1992-93): $2,190, $576 additional for out-of-state students. **Books and supplies:** $500. **Other expenses:** $2,100.

FINANCIAL AID. 90% of freshmen, 80% of continuing students receive some form of aid. Grants, loans, jobs available. **Aid applications:** No closing date; priority given to applications received by August 1; applicants notified on a rolling basis beginning on or about August 15; must reply within 2 weeks.

ADDRESS/TELEPHONE. Morton Tanenbaum, Director of Admissions, City University of New York: Kingsborough Community College, 2001 Oriental Boulevard, Brooklyn, NY 11235. (718) 368-5800. Fax: (718) 368-5357.

City University of New York: La Guardia Community College

Long Island City, New York — CB code: 2246

2-year public community college, coed. Founded in 1970. **Accreditation:** Regional. **Undergraduate enrollment:** 2,775 men, 621 women full time; 4,987 men, 1,319 women part time. **Faculty:** 761 total (411 full time), 129 with doctorates or other terminal degrees. **Location:** Urban campus in very large city. **Calendar:** Enhanced semester alternating terms of 12 weeks and 6 weeks. **Microcomputers:** 200 located in libraries, classrooms, computer centers. **Special facilities:** Mayor Fiorello H. LaGuardia Archives, Mayor Robert F. Wagner Jr. Archives, Senator Robert Wagner Archives.

DEGREES OFFERED. AA, AS, AAS. 1,084 associate degrees awarded in 1992. 27% in business and management, 10% business/office and marketing/distribution, 24% computer sciences, 14% allied health, 23% multi/interdisciplinary studies.

UNDERGRADUATE MAJORS. Accounting, bilingual/bicultural education, business administration and management, business and management, business and office, business computer/console/peripheral equipment operation, business data entry equipment operation, business data processing and related programs, business data programming, child development/care/guidance, computer and information sciences, computer programming, computer technology, data processing, early childhood education, education, elementary education, emergency medical technologies, finance, food management, food production/management/services, food science and nutrition, funeral services/mortuary science, geriatric services, gerontology, information sciences and systems, junior high education, legal assistant/paralegal, legal secretary, liberal/general studies, mental health/human services, microcomputer software, nursing, occupational therapy assistant, photography, physical therapy assistant, science technologies, secondary education, secretarial and related programs, teacher aide, telecommunications, tourism, transportation and travel marketing, veterinarian's assistant.

ACADEMIC PROGRAMS. 2-year transfer program, cooperative education, dual enrollment of high school students, independent study, internships, student-designed major, teacher preparation, cross-registration, summer program with Vassar College. **Remedial services:** Learning center, preadmission summer program, reduced course load, remedial instruction, special counselor, tutoring. **Placement/credit:** AP, CLEP Subject, institutional tests; 10 credit hours maximum for associate degree.

ACADEMIC REQUIREMENTS. Freshmen must earn minimum GPA of 1.75 to continue in good standing. Students must declare major on application. **Graduation requirements:** 66 hours for associate (35 in major). Most students required to take courses in English, humanities, mathematics, social sciences.

FRESHMAN ADMISSIONS. Selection criteria: Open admissions. **High school preparation:** 9 units recommended. Recommended units include English 3, mathematics 2 and science 1. **Additional information:** November 15 priority for spring term applications. Units recommended for admission must be acquired before graduation from any CUNY community college.

1992 FRESHMAN CLASS PROFILE. 2,207 men and women enrolled. **Characteristics:** 100% commute, 78% have minority backgrounds. Average age is 23.

FALL-TERM APPLICATIONS. $35 fee, may be waived for applicants with need. No closing date; priority given to applications received by January 15; applicants notified on a rolling basis. Deferred admission available.

STUDENT LIFE. Activities: Student government, radio, student newspaper, television, yearbook, newsletter, choral groups, concert band, dance, drama, jazz band, music ensembles.

ATHLETICS. Intramural: Badminton, basketball, bowling, handball, soccer, softball, swimming, table tennis, volleyball.

STUDENT SERVICES. Career counseling, employment service for undergraduates, freshman orientation, health services, on-campus day care, personal counseling, placement service for graduates, special adviser for adult students, veterans counselor, services/facilities for handicapped.

ANNUAL EXPENSES. Tuition and fees (1992-93): $2,200, $576 additional for out-of-state students. **Books and supplies:** $500. **Other expenses:** $2,100.

FINANCIAL AID. 83% of freshmen, 83% of continuing students receive some form of aid. All grants, 91% of loans, all jobs based on need. **Aid applications:** No closing date; priority given to applications received by July 1; applicants notified on a rolling basis beginning on or about August 15; must reply within 4 weeks.

ADDRESS/TELEPHONE. Linda Tobash, Director of Admissions, City University of New York: La Guardia Community College, 31-10 Thomson Avenue, Long Island City, NY 11101. (718) 482-5106. Fax: (718) 482-5599.

City University of New York: Lehman College

Bronx, New York — CB code: 2312

4-year public liberal arts college, coed. Founded in 1931. **Accreditation:** Regional. **Undergraduate enrollment:** 8,300 men and women. **Graduate enrollment:** 1,520 men and women. **Faculty:** 565 total (365 full time). **Location:** Urban campus in very large city; 8 miles from midtown Manhattan. **Calendar:** Semester, limited summer session. **Microcomputers:** 500 located in libraries, classrooms, computer centers. **Special facilities:** Art gallery, 2,500-seat performing arts center theater.

DEGREES OFFERED. BA, BS, BFA, MA, MS, MFA, MEd. 850 bachelor's degrees awarded in 1992. 5% in communications, 7% computer sciences, 20% health sciences, 6% multi/interdisciplinary studies, 11% psychology, 33% social sciences. Graduate degrees offered in 34 major fields of study.

UNDERGRADUATE MAJORS. Accounting, Afro-American (black) studies, American studies, anthropology, art history, arts management, biochemistry, biological and physical sciences, biology, business administration and management, business education, Caribbean studies, chemistry, classics, communications, comparative literature, computer and information sciences, dance, dramatic arts, early childhood education, economics, elementary education, English, fine arts, food science and nutrition, French, geography, geology, German, Greek (classical), health care administration, health education, Hebrew, Hispanic American studies, history, humanities and social sciences, Italian, Jewish studies, journalism, junior high education, Latin, Latin American studies, liberal/general studies, linguistics, mathematics, music, music performance, music theory and composition, nursing, philosophy, physics, political science and government, psychology, Russian, Russian and Slavic studies, secondary education, secretarial and related programs, social work, sociology, Spanish, speech, speech correction, speech pathology/audiology, studio art.

ACADEMIC PROGRAMS. Accelerated program, cooperative education, double major, dual enrollment of high school students, honors program, independent study, internships, student-designed major, study abroad, teacher preparation, visiting/exchange student program, weekend college, Washington semester, cross-registration, 4-year bachelor's/master's programs, 2-year transfer program in engineering, bilingual liberal arts (first 2 years may be taken in Spanish), professional writing concentration. **Remedial services:** Learning center, preadmission summer program, reduced course load, remedial instruction, special counselor, tutoring, SEEK program. **ROTC:** Army. **Placement/credit:** AP, CLEP General and Subject, institutional tests; 30 credit hours maximum for bachelor's degree.

ACADEMIC REQUIREMENTS. Freshmen must earn minimum GPA of 2.0 to continue in good standing. 65% of freshmen return for sophomore year. Students must declare major by end of second year. **Graduation requirements:** 128 hours for bachelor's. Most students required to take courses in English, foreign languages, humanities, mathematics, biological/physical sciences, social sciences.

FRESHMAN ADMISSIONS. Selection criteria: Minimum GPA of 2.7 (80% in academic subjects), or rank in top third of class, or achieve 900 or above on SAT, or ACT composite score above 20, or 300 or above on GED, most important. Recommended units include English 4, foreign language 3, mathematics 3, social science 4 and science 3. **Additional information:** 11 units recommended for admission, including 1 laboratory science, 2 mathematics, and 4 English, must be acquired before graduation from any CUNY senior college.

1992 FRESHMAN CLASS PROFILE. 861 men and women enrolled. 32% had high school GPA of 3.0 or higher, 45% between 2.0 and 2.99. **Characteristics:** 98% from in state, 100% commute, 75% have minority backgrounds, 1% are foreign students, 1% join fraternities/sororities. Average age is 20.

FALL-TERM APPLICATIONS. $35 fee, may be waived for applicants with need. No closing date; priority given to applications received by January 15; applicants notified on a rolling basis beginning on or about March 1. Deferred and early admission available.

STUDENT LIFE. Activities: Student government, magazine, radio, student newspaper, yearbook, choral groups, concert band, dance, drama, music ensembles, musical theater, symphony orchestra, fraternities, sororities, various religious, political, ethnic, and social service organizations.

ATHLETICS. NCAA. **Intercollegiate:** Baseball M, basketball M, cross-country, diving, soccer M, softball W, swimming, tennis, track and field, volleyball. **Intramural:** Badminton, basketball, soccer M, softball, swimming, tennis, volleyball.

STUDENT SERVICES. Career counseling, employment service for undergraduates, freshman orientation, on-campus day care, personal counseling, placement service for graduates, special adviser for adult students, veterans counselor, services/facilities for handicapped.

ANNUAL EXPENSES. Tuition and fees (1992-93): $2,560, $2,600 additional for out-of-state students. **Books and supplies:** $500. **Other expenses:** $2,100.

FINANCIAL AID. 90% of freshmen, 80% of continuing students receive some form of aid. Grants, loans, jobs available. Academic scholarships available. **Aid applications:** No closing date; priority given to applications received by May 30; applicants notified on a rolling basis beginning on or about August 15.

ADDRESS/TELEPHONE. Jane Herbert, Director of Enrollment Management, City University of New York: Lehman College, Bedford Park Boulevard West, Bronx, NY 10468. (718) 960-8131.

City University of New York: Medgar Evers College

Brooklyn, New York — CB code: 2460

4-year public liberal arts college, coed. Founded in 1969. **Accreditation:** Regional. **Undergraduate enrollment:** 620 men, 1,614 women full time; 340 men, 1,252 women part time. **Faculty:** 375 total (203 full time). **Location:** Urban campus in very large city. **Calendar:** Semester, extensive summer session. Saturday and extensive evening/early morning classes. **Microcomputers:** 250 located in classrooms, computer centers.

DEGREES OFFERED. AA, AS, AAS, BA, BS. 48 associate degrees awarded in 1992. 38% in business and management, 48% computer sciences, 5% education, 5% multi/interdisciplinary studies, 5% social sciences. 169 bachelor's degrees awarded. 46% in business and management, 18% teacher education, 21% health sciences, 6% life sciences, 7% parks/recreation, protective services, public affairs.

UNDERGRADUATE MAJORS. Associate: Biology, business and management, business data programming, computer and information sciences, education, liberal/general studies, nursing, physical sciences, public administration, science technologies, secretarial and related programs, social sciences. **Bachelor's:** Accounting, biology, business and management, elementary education, nursing, psychology, public administration, special education.

ACADEMIC PROGRAMS. 2-year transfer program, cooperative education, dual enrollment of high school students, honors program, independent study, internships, study abroad, teacher preparation, weekend college, cross-registration, 2-year bachelor's program in nursing for RNs. **Remedial services:** Learning center, preadmission summer program, reduced course load, remedial instruction, special counselor, tutoring, computer-based instruction. **Placement/credit:** CLEP Subject, institutional tests; 15 credit hours maximum for associate degree; 30 credit hours maximum for bachelor's degree.

ACADEMIC REQUIREMENTS. Freshmen must earn minimum GPA of 1.5 to continue in good standing. Graduated GPA requirements. 60% of freshmen return for sophomore year. Students must declare major by end of second year. **Graduation requirements:** 64 hours for associate (36 in major), 120 hours for bachelor's (65 in major). Most students required to take courses in arts/fine arts, computer science, English, foreign languages, history, humanities, mathematics, philosophy/religion, biological/physical sciences, social sciences. **Postgraduate studies:** 80% from 2-year programs enter 4-year programs. 3% enter law school, 2% enter medical school, 9% enter MBA programs, 10% enter other graduate study.

FRESHMAN ADMISSIONS. Selection criteria: Open admissions. Selective admission to nursing program. **High school preparation:** 9 units recommended. Recommended units include English 3, mathematics 2 and science 1. 11 units (including 4 English) recommended for admission to bachelor's program. **Additional information:** Discretionary policy admits 25 students each semester without high school diplomas. Must be 21 years old, legal residents of New York City. Units recommended for admission must be acquired before graduation from our institution.

1992 FRESHMAN CLASS PROFILE. 208 men, 478 women enrolled. 8% had high school GPA of 3.0 or higher, 19% between 2.0 and 2.99. **Characteristics:** 98% from in state, 100% commute, 90% have minority backgrounds, 3% are foreign students. Average age is 22.

FALL-TERM APPLICATIONS. $35 fee, may be waived for applicants with need. Closing date August 23; applicants notified on a rolling basis. Admission may be deferred for 1 semester.

STUDENT LIFE. Activities: Student government, radio, student newspaper, television, yearbook, choral groups, dance, drama, numerous religious, political, ethnic, and social service clubs.

ATHLETICS. NCAA. **Intercollegiate:** Basketball M, cross-country, soccer M, track and field, volleyball W. **Intramural:** Basketball, bowling, swimming.

STUDENT SERVICES. Career counseling, employment service for undergraduates, freshman orientation, health services, on-campus day care, personal counseling, placement service for graduates, veterans counselor, Head Start for children of faculty, students, and community, services/facilities for handicapped.

ANNUAL EXPENSES. Tuition and fees (1992-93): $2,150, $576 additional for out-of-state students. **Books and supplies:** $500. **Other expenses:** $2,100.

FINANCIAL AID. 90% of freshmen, 67% of continuing students receive some form of aid. All grants, 96% of loans, all jobs based on need. **Aid applications:** Closing date August 31; priority given to applications received by June 1; applicants notified on a rolling basis; must reply within 2 weeks.

ADDRESS/TELEPHONE. Lincoln Sessons, Assistant Dean of Enrollment Services, City University of New York: Medgar Evers College, 1650 Bedford Avenue, Brooklyn, NY 11225-2201. (718) 270-4900. Fax: (718) 270-5126.

City University of New York: New York City Technical College

Brooklyn, New York — CB code: 2550

4-year public technical college, coed. Founded in 1946. **Accreditation:** Regional. **Undergraduate enrollment:** 10,604 men and women. **Faculty:** 750 total (300 full time). **Location:** Urban campus in very large city; in downtown area. **Calendar:** Semester, extensive summer session. **Microcomputers:** Located in computer centers. **Special facilities:** Ophthalmic dispensing and dental clinics, laboratory kitchens and dining room, data processing laboratories, art gallery.

DEGREES OFFERED. AA, AS, AAS, B. 1,105 associate degrees awarded in 1992. 20% in business and management, 14% business/office and marketing/distribution, 8% computer sciences, 19% engineering technologies, 21% allied health, 11% multi/interdisciplinary studies, 7% parks/recreation, protective services, public affairs. 33 bachelor's degrees awarded.

UNDERGRADUATE MAJORS. Accounting, advertising, air conditioning/heating/refrigeration technology, air pollution control technology, architectural technologies, business data processing and related programs, chemical technology, civil technology, clinical laboratory science, community services, computer and information sciences, computer servicing technology, construction, data processing, dental hygiene, dental laboratory technology, drafting and design technology, electrical and electronics equipment repair, electrical technology, electromechanical technology, engineering and engineering-related technologies, environmental control technology, fashion merchandising, geriatric services, graphic and printing production, graphic arts technology, hotel/motel and restaurant management, human services, information sciences and systems, legal assistant/paralegal, legal secretary, liberal/general studies, lithographic offset technology, machine tool operation/machine shop, marketing and distribution, marketing management, mechanical design technology, medical laboratory technologies, nursing, ophthalmic services, radiograph medical technology, secretarial and related programs, telecommunications. graphic and printing production, hotel/motel and restaurant management, legal assistant/paralegal, telecommunications.

ACADEMIC PROGRAMS. 2-year transfer program, dual enrollment of high school students, independent study, internships, study abroad, weekend college, cross-registration, bridge programs to higher education or careers in engineering technology, alternate format program for those out of high school 5 years with or without diploma. **Remedial services:** Learning center, preadmission summer program, remedial instruction, special counselor, tutoring, English as second language program, Freshman Year Experience, academic access course, SEEK. **Placement/credit:** AP, CLEP Subject, institutional tests; 30 credit hours maximum for associate degree.

ACADEMIC REQUIREMENTS. Freshmen must earn minimum GPA of 1.5 to continue in good standing. Students must declare major on application. **Graduation requirements:** 64 hours for associate (40 in major), 128 hours for bachelor's (76 in major). Most students required to take courses in English, history, humanities, mathematics, philosophy/religion, social sciences. **Additional information:** Students in health science programs work under supervision with patients in clinical settings. Industry standard facilities used in hotel and restaurant management program.

FRESHMAN ADMISSIONS. Selection criteria: Open admissions. Admission to some programs on first-come basis. **High school preparation:** 9 units recommended. Recommended units include English 4, mathematics 2 and science 1. 2 additional units, including 1 in English, recommended for applicants to bachelor's programs. **Test requirements:** CUNY skills assessment tests in reading, writing, and mathematics for placement.

1992 FRESHMAN CLASS PROFILE. 2,108 men and women enrolled. 12% had high school GPA of 3.0 or higher, 24% between 2.0 and 2.99. **Characteristics:** 97% from in state, 100% commute, 85% have minority backgrounds, 2% are foreign students. Average age is 19.

FALL-TERM APPLICATIONS. $35 fee. No closing date; priority given to applications received by January 15; applicants notified on a rolling basis beginning on or about March 1.

STUDENT LIFE. Housing: Some housing available at nearby university. **Activities:** Student government, magazine, student newspaper, yearbook, choral groups, dance, drama, musical theater, full range of student clubs.

ATHLETICS. NJCAA. **Intercollegiate:** Baseball M, basketball, bowling, soccer M, softball W, volleyball W. **Intramural:** Badminton, basketball, cross-country, softball, table tennis, track and field, volleyball.

STUDENT SERVICES. Career counseling, employment service for undergraduates, freshman orientation, on-campus day care, personal counseling, placement service for graduates, veterans counselor, Special services for disabled and ESL students, services/facilities for handicapped.

ANNUAL EXPENSES. Tuition and fees (1992-93): $2,499, $2,600 additional for out-of-state students. **Books and supplies:** $500. **Other expenses:** $2,100.

FINANCIAL AID. 83% of freshmen, 85% of continuing students receive some form of aid. 92% of loans, all jobs based on need. **Aid applications:** Closing date October 15; priority given to applications received by June 30; applicants notified on or about July 15; must reply within 2 weeks. **Additional information:** Foreign students applying for aid must have resided in New York for at least a year.

ADDRESS/TELEPHONE. Arlene Floyd, Director of Admissions, City Univ of New York: New York City Technical College, 300 Jay Street, Brooklyn, NY 11201-2983. (718) 260-5500.

City University of New York: Queens College

Flushing, New York — CB code: 2750

Admissions:	64% of applicants accepted
Based on:	••• School record
	•• Special talents, test scores
	• Essay, recommendations
Completion:	80% of freshmen end year in good standing
	41% graduate, 32% of these enter graduate study

4-year public liberal arts college, coed. Founded in 1937. **Accreditation:** Regional. **Undergraduate enrollment:** 14,478 men and women. **Graduate enrollment:** 3,443 men and women. **Faculty:** 1,274 total (628 full time). **Location:** Urban campus in very large city; 15 miles from Manhattan. **Calendar:** Semester, limited summer session. **Microcomputers:** 450 located in libraries, classrooms, computer centers. **Special facilities:** Specialized libraries in art, education, music, and science, Godwin-Ternbach Museum, Caumsett Center for Environmental Teaching and Research.

DEGREES OFFERED. BA, BS, BFA, MA, MFA, MEd. 1,800 bachelor's degrees awarded in 1992. 13% in business and management, 9% communications, 9% computer sciences, 9% education, 10% letters/literature, 7% psychology, 23% social sciences, 5% visual and performing arts. Graduate degrees offered in 52 major fields of study.

UNDERGRADUATE MAJORS. Accounting, African studies, American literature, American studies, anthropology, applied mathematics, art education, art history, biochemistry, biological and physical sciences, biology, Byzantine studies, Caribbean studies, chemistry, classics, communications, comparative literature, computer and information sciences, creative writing, dance, dramatic arts, drawing, early childhood education, earth sciences, East Asian studies, economics, elementary education, English, English education, English literature, environmental science, family/consumer resource management, film arts, fine arts, food science and nutrition, foreign languages education, French, geology, German, Greek (classical), Greek (modern), health education, Hebrew, history, home economics, home economics education, humanities and social sciences, Italian, Jewish studies, junior high education, labor/industrial relations, Latin, Latin American studies, linguistics, mathematics, mathematics education, music, music education, music performance, music theory and composition, painting, philosophy, physical education, physics, political science and government, Portuguese, predentistry, premedicine, psychology, pure mathematics, radio/television broadcasting, radio/television technology, religion, Russian, science education, sculpture, secondary education, social studies education, sociology, Spanish, speech, speech pathology/audiology, studio art, teaching English as a second language/foreign language, telecommunications, textiles and clothing, urban studies, visual and performing arts, women's studies, Yiddish.

ACADEMIC PROGRAMS. Accelerated program, cooperative education, double major, dual enrollment of high school students, honors program, independent study, internships, student-designed major, study abroad, teacher preparation, New York semester, cross-registration, Albany semester, mayor's semester; liberal arts/career combination in engineering, business. **Remedial services:** Learning center, preadmission summer program, remedial instruction, special counselor, tutoring, SEEK program for academically and economically disadvantaged students. **Placement/credit:** AP, CLEP Subject, institutional tests.

ACADEMIC REQUIREMENTS. Freshmen must earn minimum GPA of 2.0 to continue in good standing. 70% of freshmen return for sophomore year. Students must declare major by end of second year. **Graduation requirements:** 128 hours for bachelor's (36 in major). Most students required to take courses in arts/fine arts, English, foreign languages, history, humanities, mathematics, philosophy/religion, biological/physical sciences, social sciences. **Postgraduate studies:** 6% enter law school, 5% enter medical school, 7% enter MBA programs, 14% enter other graduate study.

FRESHMAN ADMISSIONS. Selection criteria: Minimum high school GPA of 3.0 or rank in top third of class, or SAT combined score over of 900, or ACT composite score over 20 required. Recommended units include English 4, foreign language 3, mathematics 3, social science 3 and science 3. English, science, foreign language, mathematics, and social science recommended. **Test requirements:** SAT/ACT required for scholarship applicants. Score report by February 15. **Additional information:** Scholarship and honors program applicants must provide SAT and ACH test results, write essay, and have personal interview.

1992 FRESHMAN CLASS PROFILE. 5,500 men and women applied, 3,522 accepted; 1,647 enrolled. 70% had high school GPA of 3.0 or higher, 30% between 2.0 and 2.99. **Characteristics:** 100% commute. Average age is 18.

FALL-TERM APPLICATIONS. $35 fee, may be waived for applicants with need. Closing date May 1; priority given to applications received by January 15; applicants notified on a rolling basis beginning on or about January 15. Interview required for scholar program, some honors programs applicants. Audition required for music, performance applicants. Essay recommended. Deferred and early admission available. SAT may substitute, on appeal, for other admissions criteria.

STUDENT LIFE. Activities: Student government, film, magazine, student newspaper, yearbook, choral groups, concert band, dance, drama, jazz band, music ensembles, musical theater, symphony orchestra, fraternities, sororities, Catholic, Protestant, Jewish, Greek Orthodox, and Black student organizations, academic honorary societies, Union Estudiantil Pedro Albizu Compos, Haitian Club.

ATHLETICS. NAIA, NCAA. **Intercollegiate:** Baseball M, basketball, bowling, cross-country M, golf M, gymnastics, lacrosse M, soccer M, softball, swimming, tennis, track and field, volleyball, water polo M. **Intramural:** Baseball M, basketball, fencing M, ice hockey M, racquetball, softball, tennis, volleyball, water polo.

STUDENT SERVICES. Career counseling, employment service for undergraduates, freshman orientation, health services, on-campus day care, personal counseling, placement service for graduates, special adviser for adult students, veterans counselor, peer advisement, services/facilities for handicapped.

ANNUAL EXPENSES. Tuition and fees (1992-93): $2,631, $2,600 additional for out-of-state students. **Books and supplies:** $500. **Other expenses:** $2,100.

FINANCIAL AID. 60% of freshmen, 60% of continuing students receive some form of aid. 98% of grants, 88% of loans, all jobs based on need. Academic scholarships available. **Aid applications:** Closing date August 1; priority given to applications received by May 31; applicants notified on a rolling basis beginning on or about August 15; must reply within 2 weeks. **Additional information:** SAT/ACH required for scholarship applicants.

ADDRESS/TELEPHONE. Susan Reantillo, Executive Director of Admissions, City University of New York: Queens College, 65-30 Kissena Boulevard, Kiely Hall 206, Flushing, NY 11367. (718) 997-5600.

City University of New York: Queensborough Community College
Bayside, New York — CB code: 2751

2-year public community college, coed. Founded in 1958. **Accreditation:** Regional. **Undergraduate enrollment:** 2,732 men, 3,095 women full time; 2,543 men, 3,726 women part time. **Faculty:** 638 total (299 full time), 220 with doctorates or other terminal degrees. **Location:** Suburban campus in very large city; 10 miles from midtown Manhattan. **Calendar:** Semester, limited summer session. Saturday and extensive evening/early morning classes. **Microcomputers:** 500 located in libraries, classrooms, computer centers. **Special facilities:** Art gallery, resource center for Holocaust studies, observatory.

DEGREES OFFERED. AA, AS, AAS. 956 associate degrees awarded in 1992. 33% in business and management, 6% business/office and marketing/distribution, 7% computer sciences, 13% engineering technologies, 13% health sciences, 24% multi/interdisciplinary studies.

UNDERGRADUATE MAJORS. Accounting, biology, business administration and management, business and management, business data processing and related programs, chemistry, clinical laboratory science, computer and information sciences, computer technology, dance, drafting and design technology, dramatic arts, electrical technology, electronic technology, environmental health, fine arts, history, information sciences and systems, laser electro-optic technology, liberal/general studies, manufacturing technology, mechanical design technology, medical laboratory technologies, music electronic technology, music history and appreciation, nursing, office supervision and management, photography, political science and government, preengineering, preoccupational therapy, psychology, real estate, secretarial and related programs, sociology, transportation management.

ACADEMIC PROGRAMS. 2-year transfer program, cooperative education, dual enrollment of high school students, independent study, internships, study abroad, external education for homebound students, honors program for high school seniors. **Remedial services:** Learning center, preadmission summer program, remedial instruction, special counselor, tutoring, writing center. **Placement/credit:** AP, CLEP Subject, institutional tests. AP policy varies by department.

ACADEMIC REQUIREMENTS. Freshmen must earn minimum GPA of 1.75 to continue in good standing. 50% of freshmen return for sophomore year. Students must declare major on application. **Graduation requirements:** 64 hours for associate (24 in major). Most students required to take courses in arts/fine arts, English, history, mathematics, biological/physical sciences, social sciences.

FRESHMAN ADMISSIONS. Selection criteria: Open admissions. **High school preparation:** 9 units recommended. Recommended units include English 3, mathematics 2 and science 1. **Additional information:** Units recommended for admission must be acquired before graduation from CUNY.

1992 FRESHMAN CLASS PROFILE. 1,196 men, 1,274 women enrolled. **Characteristics:** 99% from in state, 100% commute, 52% have minority backgrounds, 1% are foreign students. Average age is 19.

FALL-TERM APPLICATIONS. $35 fee. No closing date; priority given to applications received by January 4; applicants notified on a rolling basis. Deferred admission available.

STUDENT LIFE. Activities: Student government, film, radio, student newspaper, yearbook, Electrical and Computer Technology Review, choral groups, concert band, dance, drama, jazz band, music ensembles, musical theater, symphony orchestra, numerous ethnic, religious, social, political, and special interest clubs.

ATHLETICS. NJCAA. **Intercollegiate:** Baseball M, basketball, cross-country, soccer M, softball W, tennis, track and field, volleyball. **Intramural:** Archery, basketball, bowling, cross-country, fencing, skiing, soccer, softball, swimming, table tennis, tennis, track and field, volleyball.

STUDENT SERVICES. Aptitude testing, career counseling, employment service for undergraduates, freshman orientation, health services, on-campus day care, personal counseling, placement service for graduates, special adviser for adult students, veterans counselor, services/facilities for handicapped.

ANNUAL EXPENSES. Tuition and fees (1992-93): $2,200, $576 additional for out-of-state students. **Books and supplies:** $500. **Other expenses:** $2,100.

FINANCIAL AID. 92% of freshmen, 92% of continuing students receive some form of aid. All grants, 94% of loans, all jobs based on need. **Aid applications:** No closing date; priority given to applications received by May 1; applicants notified on a rolling basis beginning on or about August 15; must reply within 2 weeks.

ADDRESS/TELEPHONE. Mary Bryce, Director of Admissions, City University of New York: Queensborough Community College, Springfield Boulevard and 56th Avenue, Bayside, NY 11364-1497. (718) 631-6236.

City University of New York: York College
Jamaica, New York — CB code: 2992

4-year public college of arts and sciences, coed. Founded in 1966. **Accredi-**

tation: Regional. **Undergraduate enrollment:** 1,416 men, 2,125 women full time; 842 men, 2,097 women part time. **Faculty:** 267 total (138 full time), 110 with doctorates or other terminal degrees. **Location:** Urban campus in very large city. **Calendar:** Semester, limited summer session. Saturday and extensive evening/early morning classes. **Microcomputers:** 528 located in libraries, classrooms, computer centers.

DEGREES OFFERED. BA, BS. 488 bachelor's degrees awarded in 1992. 48% in business and management, 6% education, 16% teacher education, 7% health sciences, 7% parks/recreation, protective services, public affairs, 5% psychology, 7% social sciences.

UNDERGRADUATE MAJORS. Accounting, Afro-American (black) studies, anthropology, bilingual/bicultural education, biology, business administration and management, chemistry, community health work, economics, elementary education, English, English literature, environmental science, fine arts, French, geology, gerontology, health education, health promotion, history, Italian, management information systems, marketing and distribution, mathematics, medical laboratory technologies, music, music education, nursing, occupational therapy, philosophy, physical education, physics, political science and government, psychology, social work, sociology, Spanish, special education, speech, visual and performing arts.

ACADEMIC PROGRAMS. Cooperative education, dual enrollment of high school students, honors program, independent study, internships, study abroad, teacher preparation, weekend college, cross-registration. **Remedial services:** Learning center, preadmission summer program, remedial instruction, special counselor, tutoring, SEEK program. **Placement/credit:** AP, CLEP Subject, institutional tests; 32 credit hours maximum for bachelor's degree.

ACADEMIC REQUIREMENTS. Freshmen must earn minimum GPA of 2.0 to continue in good standing. Students must declare major on enrollment. **Graduation requirements:** 128 hours for bachelor's. Most students required to take courses in English, humanities, mathematics, biological/physical sciences, social sciences.

FRESHMAN ADMISSIONS. Selection criteria: High school GPA of 75 or rank in top third of class required. Other applicants with SAT combined score over 900 or ACT composite score over 20 admitted on space available basis. **High school preparation:** 11 units recommended. Recommended units include English 4, mathematics 2 and science 1. **Additional information:** Units recommended for admission must be acquired before graduation from any CUNY senior college. Admission requirements for CUNY senior colleges will be automatically satisfied with completion of our core requirement.

1992 FRESHMAN CLASS PROFILE. 284 men, 458 women enrolled. 18% had high school GPA of 3.0 or higher, 72% between 2.0 and 2.99. **Characteristics:** 86% from in state, 100% commute, 92% have minority backgrounds, 12% are foreign students. Average age is 20.

FALL-TERM APPLICATIONS. $30 fee. No closing date; applicants notified on a rolling basis. Early admission available. Centralized application processing allows students to apply to 6 schools within CUNY system at same time.

STUDENT LIFE. Activities: Student government, radio, student newspaper, television, yearbook, choral groups, dance, drama, jazz band, music ensembles, symphony orchestra.

ATHLETICS. NCAA. **Intercollegiate:** Baseball M, basketball, cross-country, lacrosse M, soccer M, tennis, track and field, volleyball. **Intramural:** Badminton, basketball, soccer, softball, swimming, table tennis, tennis, track and field, volleyball.

STUDENT SERVICES. Career counseling, employment service for undergraduates, health services, on-campus day care, personal counseling, placement service for graduates, veterans counselor, services/facilities for handicapped.

ANNUAL EXPENSES. Tuition and fees (1992-93): $2,534, $2,600 additional for out-of-state students. **Books and supplies:** $500. **Other expenses:** $2,100.

FINANCIAL AID. 70% of freshmen, 42% of continuing students receive some form of aid. Grants, loans, jobs available. 390 enrolled freshmen were judged to have need, 350 were offered aid. **Aid applications:** Closing date August 1; priority given to applications received by April 1; applicants notified on a rolling basis beginning on or about July 5; must reply within 3 weeks. **Additional information:** Closing date for campus-based aid, College Work Study, Supplemental Education Opportunity Grant, and Perkins Loan only.

ADDRESS/TELEPHONE. Sally Nelson, Director of Admissions, City University of New York: York College, 94-20 Guy R. Brewer Boulevard, Jamaica, NY 11451-9989. (718) 262-2165.

Clarkson University
Potsdam, New York

CB code: 2084

Admissions:	98% of applicants accepted
Based on:	••• School record
	•• Recommendations, test scores
	• Activities, essay, interview, special talents
Completion:	90% of freshmen end year in good standing
	75% graduate, 15% of these enter graduate study

4-year private university, coed. Founded in 1896. **Accreditation:** Regional. **Undergraduate enrollment:** 1,982 men, 562 women full time; 34 men, 27 women part time. **Graduate enrollment:** 257 men, 83 women full time; 19 men, 14 women part time. **Faculty:** 203 total (184 full time), 169 with doctorates or other terminal degrees. **Location:** Rural campus in large town; 140 miles from Syracuse. **Calendar:** Semester, extensive summer session. **Microcomputers:** 2,805 located in dormitories, libraries, classrooms, computer centers. **Special facilities:** Laboratories for study of robotics, artificial intelligence, acid rain, high voltage power, hydraulics, automated manufacturing, and management information systems.

DEGREES OFFERED. BS, MS, MBA, PhD. 783 bachelor's degrees awarded in 1992. 20% in business and management, 56% engineering, 12% multi/interdisciplinary studies. Graduate degrees offered in 17 major fields of study.

UNDERGRADUATE MAJORS. Accounting, aerospace/aeronautical/astronautical engineering, biology, business administration and management, business and management, business economics, business studies, chemical engineering, chemistry, civil engineering, computer and information sciences, computer engineering, electrical/electronics/communications engineering, engineering, engineering and other disciplines, engineering management, finance, humanities and social sciences, management information systems, management science, marketing management, mathematics, mechanical engineering, physics, psychology, social sciences, technical and business writing, technical communications, toxicology.

ACADEMIC PROGRAMS. Cooperative education, double major, independent study, student-designed major, study abroad, cross-registration; liberal arts/career combination in engineering; combined bachelor's/graduate program in business administration. **Remedial services:** Preadmission summer program, special counselor, tutoring. **ROTC:** Air Force, Army. **Placement/credit:** AP, CLEP Subject.

ACADEMIC REQUIREMENTS. Freshmen must earn minimum GPA of 2.0 to continue in good standing. 85% of freshmen return for sophomore year. Students must declare major by end of second year. **Graduation requirements:** 120 hours for bachelor's. Most students required to take courses in computer science, English, humanities, mathematics, biological/physical sciences, social sciences.

FRESHMAN ADMISSIONS. Selection criteria: School achievement record, test scores, recommendations, school and community involvement important. **High school preparation:** 10 units required. Required units include English 4, mathematics 4 and physical science 2. For business administration, 3 mathematics, 1 science required. **Test requirements:** SAT or ACT; score report by February 1.

1992 FRESHMAN CLASS PROFILE. 2,694 men and women applied, 2,647 accepted; 413 men enrolled, 136 women enrolled. 90% had high school GPA of 3.0 or higher, 10% between 2.0 and 2.99. **Academic background:** Mid 50% of enrolled freshmen had SAT-V between 470-590, SAT-M between 560-660. 97% submitted SAT scores. **Characteristics:** 62% from in state, 96% live in college housing, 8% have minority backgrounds, 4% are foreign students. Average age is 18.

FALL-TERM APPLICATIONS. $25 fee, may be waived for applicants with need. No closing date; priority given to applications received by February 1; applicants notified on a rolling basis beginning on or about February 1; must reply by May 1 or within 2 weeks if notified thereafter. Interview recommended. Essay recommended. CRDA. Deferred and early admission available. EDP-F. ACH recommended.

STUDENT LIFE. Housing: Dormitories (men, women, coed); apartment, fraternity, sorority, handicapped housing available. **Activities:** Student government, magazine, radio, student newspaper, television, yearbook, choral groups, drama, jazz band, musical theater, pep band, fraternities, sororities. **Additional information:** Each freshman issued personal computer upon matriculation.

ATHLETICS. NCAA. **Intercollegiate:** Baseball M, basketball, cross-country, diving, golf, ice hockey M, lacrosse, skiing, soccer, swimming, tennis, volleyball W. **Intramural:** Basketball, ice hockey, lacrosse, racquetball, soccer, softball, volleyball, water polo.

STUDENT SERVICES. Career counseling, employment service for undergraduates, freshman orientation, health services, personal counseling, placement service for graduates, services/facilities for handicapped.

ANNUAL EXPENSES. Tuition and fees: $15,383. **Room and board:** $5,326. **Books and supplies:** $700. **Other expenses:** $691.

FINANCIAL AID. 87% of freshmen, 90% of continuing students receive some form of aid. 88% of grants, all loans, all jobs based on need. 457 enrolled freshmen were judged to have need, all were offered aid. Academic, music/drama, art, athletic, state/district residency, leadership, alumni affiliation, minority scholarships available. **Aid applications:** Closing date February 15; priority given to applications received by February 1; applicants notified on or about April 1. **Additional information:** Supplemental financing available.

ADDRESS/TELEPHONE. Robert A. Croot, Exec Dir/Admissions, Clarkson University, Holcroft House, Potsdam, NY 13699. (315) 268-6479. (800) 527-6577. Fax: (315) 268-7647.

Clinton Community College
Plattsburgh, New York CB code: 2135

2-year public community college, coed. Founded in 1966. **Accreditation:** Regional. **Undergraduate enrollment:** 611 men, 588 women full time; 385 men, 556 women part time. **Faculty:** 184 total (59 full time), 8 with doctorates or other terminal degrees. **Location:** Rural campus in large town; 60 miles from Montreal, Canada. **Calendar:** Semester, limited summer session. Saturday and extensive evening/early morning classes. **Microcomputers:** 70 located in libraries, classrooms, computer centers. **Additional facts:** SUNY institution.

DEGREES OFFERED. AA, AS, AAS. 325 associate degrees awarded in 1992. 25% in business and management, 5% business/office and marketing/distribution, 19% allied health, 34% multi/interdisciplinary studies, 14% parks/recreation, protective services, public affairs.

UNDERGRADUATE MAJORS. Accounting, business administration and management, business and management, business and office, clinical laboratory science, community services, hotel/motel and restaurant management, humanities and social sciences, law enforcement and corrections, liberal/general studies, mathematics, medical laboratory technologies, nursing, office supervision and management, secretarial and related programs.

ACADEMIC PROGRAMS. 2-year transfer program, dual enrollment of high school students, honors program, independent study, internships, student-designed major, telecourses, cross-registration. **Remedial services:** Learning center, remedial instruction, tutoring. **Placement/credit:** AP, CLEP General and Subject, institutional tests; 30 credit hours maximum for associate degree.

ACADEMIC REQUIREMENTS. Freshmen must earn minimum GPA of 1.25 to continue in good standing. 55% of freshmen return for sophomore year. Students must declare major on enrollment. **Graduation requirements:** 64 hours for associate (30 in major). Most students required to take courses in English, mathematics, biological/physical sciences, social sciences.

FRESHMAN ADMISSIONS. Selection criteria: Open admissions. Selective admissions to nursing program and medical laboratory technology program.

1992 FRESHMAN CLASS PROFILE. 340 men, 339 women enrolled. 10% had high school GPA of 3.0 or higher, 70% between 2.0 and 2.99. **Characteristics:** 99% from in state, 100% commute, 10% have minority backgrounds. Average age is 24.

FALL-TERM APPLICATIONS. $25 fee, may be waived for applicants with need. No closing date; applicants notified on a rolling basis beginning on or about February 1; must reply within 4 weeks. Interview recommended for nursing, medical laboratory technician applicants. Early admission available.

STUDENT LIFE. Housing: Residence Halls available at SUNY Plattsburgh, space permitting. **Activities:** Student government, yearbook, choral groups, returning students, nursing, laboratory technology, and art clubs.

ATHLETICS. NJCAA. **Intercollegiate:** Baseball M, basketball, ice hockey M, soccer, softball W. **Intramural:** Bowling, racquetball, skiing, soccer, volleyball. **Clubs:** Skiing, bowling, tennis.

STUDENT SERVICES. Aptitude testing, career counseling, employment service for undergraduates, freshman orientation, health services, on-campus day care, personal counseling, placement service for graduates, veterans counselor, services/facilities for handicapped.

ANNUAL EXPENSES. Tuition and fees (projected): $1,810, $1,700 additional for out-of-state students. **Books and supplies:** $500. **Other expenses:** $739.

FINANCIAL AID. 80% of freshmen, 82% of continuing students receive some form of aid. All grants, 91% of loans, all jobs based on need. 275 enrolled freshmen were judged to have need, all were offered aid. Academic scholarships available. **Aid applications:** No closing date; priority given to applications received by April 15; applicants notified on a rolling basis beginning on or about July 1; must reply within 20 days.

ADDRESS/TELEPHONE. Debra J. Luff, Associate Dean for Enrollment Management/Retention, Clinton Community College, Plattsburgh, NY 12901-4297. (518) 561-4170 ext. 371. Fax: (518) 561-8621.

Cochran School of Nursing-St. John's Riverside Hospital
Yonkers, New York CB code: 2894

2-year private nursing college, coed. Founded in 1894. **Undergraduate enrollment:** 6 men, 68 women full time; 5 men, 64 women part time. **Faculty:** 16 total (12 full time). **Location:** Urban campus in small city; 20 miles from New York City. **Calendar:** Semester. **Microcomputers:** 4 located in libraries. **Additional facts:** Access to all clinical facilities at St. John's Riverside Hospital.

DEGREES OFFERED. AAS. 30 associate degrees awarded in 1992. 100% in health sciences.

UNDERGRADUATE MAJORS. Applied science, nursing.

ACADEMIC PROGRAMS. 2-year transfer program. **Remedial services:** Learning center, reduced course load, special counselor, tutoring. **Placement/credit:** AP, CLEP General and Subject, institutional tests; 24 credit hours maximum for associate degree.

ACADEMIC REQUIREMENTS. Freshmen must earn minimum GPA of 2.0 to continue in good standing. 70% of freshmen return for sophomore year. Students must declare major on application. **Graduation requirements:** 74 hours for associate (47 in major). Most students required to take courses in English, biological/physical sciences, social sciences. **Additional information:** Special testing program facilitates career goals of LPNs who want to become RNs. Program with College of New Rochelle for BS in nursing.

FRESHMAN ADMISSIONS. Selection criteria: School achievement record, test scores, interview most important. **High school preparation:** 16 units required. Required units include biological science 1, English 4, mathematics 2, physical science 1 and social science 3. Mathematics units should include 1 algebra, science units should include 1 biology and 1 chemistry. **Test requirements:** SAT; score report by August 1.

1992 FRESHMAN CLASS PROFILE. 5 men, 77 women enrolled. **Characteristics:** 99% from in state, 100% commute, 10% have minority backgrounds. Average age is 26.

FALL-TERM APPLICATIONS. $25 fee. Closing date July 31; applicants notified on a rolling basis; must reply within 2 weeks. Interview required. Essay required. Deferred admission available.

STUDENT LIFE. Activities: Student government.

STUDENT SERVICES. Aptitude testing, career counseling, employment service for undergraduates, health services, personal counseling, placement service for graduates, special adviser for adult students, services/facilities for handicapped.

ANNUAL EXPENSES. Tuition and fees (1992-93): $7,970. **Books and supplies:** $650. **Other expenses:** $2,050.

FINANCIAL AID. 90% of freshmen, 85% of continuing students receive some form of aid. All grants, 64% of loans based on need. 66 enrolled freshmen were judged to have need, all were offered aid. **Aid applications:** No closing date; applicants notified on a rolling basis.

ADDRESS/TELEPHONE. Lucetta Ganley, Director, Cochran School of Nursing-St. John's Riverside Hospital, 967 North Broadway, Yonkers, NY 10701. (914) 964-4283.

Colgate University
Hamilton, New York CB code: 2086

Admissions:	45% of applicants accepted
Based on:	••• Recommendations, school record
	•• Special talents, test scores
	• Activities, essay, interview
Completion:	96% of freshmen end year in good standing
	89% graduate, 27% of these enter graduate study

4-year private liberal arts college, coed. Founded in 1819. **Accreditation:** Regional. **Undergraduate enrollment:** 1,361 men, 1,287 women full time; 8 men, 14 women part time. **Graduate enrollment:** 12 men, 9 women full time. **Faculty:** 315 total (239 full time), 235 with doctorates or other terminal degrees. **Location:** Rural campus in rural community; 38 miles from Syracuse. **Calendar:** Semester. **Microcomputers:** 260 located in libraries, classrooms, computer centers. **Special facilities:** Automated observatory, Picker Art Gallery, Longyear Museum of Anthropology.

DEGREES OFFERED. BA, MA. 677 bachelor's degrees awarded in 1992. 5% in area and ethnic studies, 14% letters/literature, 6% life sciences, 8% philosophy, religion, theology, 8% physical sciences, 41% social sciences. Graduate degrees offered in 3 major fields of study.

UNDERGRADUATE MAJORS. African studies, Afro-American (black) studies, American Indian studies, anthropology, Asian studies, astrogeophysics, astronomy, astrophysics, biochemistry, biological and physical sciences, biology, chemistry, Chinese, classics, computer and information sciences, computer mathematics, economics, education, elementary education, English, experimental psychology, fine arts, foreign languages (multiple emphasis), French, geochemistry, geography, geology, German, Greek (classical), Hispanic American studies, history, humanities, humanities and social sciences, international relations, international studies, Japanese, Latin, Latin American studies, marine biology, mathematics, molecular biology, music, neurosciences, peace studies, philosophy, philosophy/religion, physical sciences, physics, political science and government, predentistry, prelaw, premedicine, prepharmacy, preveterinary, psychology, pure mathematics, religion, Russian, Russian and Slavic studies, secondary education, social sciences, sociology, Spanish, women's studies.

ACADEMIC PROGRAMS. Accelerated program, double major, independent study, internships, semester at sea, student-designed major, study abroad, teacher preparation, visiting/exchange student program, Washington semester, cross-registration, 3+2 programs in architecture with Washington University in St. Louis and in engineering with Columbia University, Rensselaer Polytechnic Institute, and Washington University. **Remedial services:** Learning center, preadmission summer program, reduced course load, remedial instruction, special counselor, tutoring. **Placement/credit:** AP, CLEP General and Subject, IB, institutional tests; 24 credit hours maximum for bachelor's degree.

ACADEMIC REQUIREMENTS. Freshmen must earn minimum GPA of 1.35 to continue in good standing. 96% of freshmen return for sophomore year. Students must declare major by end of second year. **Graduation requirements:** 120 hours for bachelor's (32 in major). Most students required to take courses in foreign languages, humanities, biological/physical sciences, social sciences. **Postgraduate studies:** 9% enter law school, 3% enter medical school, 2% enter MBA programs, 13% enter other graduate study.

FRESHMAN ADMISSIONS. Selection criteria: School achievement record of primary importance. Teacher/counselor recommendations, test scores, and major talent or personal accomplishment considered. Disadvantaged, nontraditional, and minority applicants given special consideration. **High school preparation:** 16 units recommended. Recommended units include English 4, foreign language 3, mathematics 4, social science 2 and science 3. Science units should include 1 laboratory science, 3 recommended. Foreign language requirement should be met in 1 language. **Test requirements:** SAT or ACT; score report by February 1. 3 ACH required (including English Composition, preferably with essay) of students submitting SAT scores. Score report by February 1 ACT accepted in place of ACH. 5 ACH including English and Mathematics accepted in place of SAT or ACT.

1992 FRESHMAN CLASS PROFILE. 2,544 men applied, 1,129 accepted, 322 enrolled; 2,498 women applied, 1,133 accepted, 369 enrolled. 56% were in top tenth and 85% were in top quarter of graduating class. **Academic background:** Mid 50% of enrolled freshmen had SAT-V between 550-640, SAT-M between 600-700; ACT composite between 27-31. 98% submitted SAT scores, 24% submitted ACT scores. **Characteristics:** 37% from in state, 100% live in college housing, 15% have minority backgrounds, 3% are foreign students, 43% join fraternities/sororities. Average age is 18.

FALL-TERM APPLICATIONS. $50 fee, may be waived for applicants with need. Closing date January 1; applicants notified on or about April 1; must reply by May 1. Essay required. Interview recommended. CRDA. Deferred and early admission available. EDP-F.

STUDENT LIFE. Housing: Dormitories (coed); apartment, fraternity, sorority housing available. Coeducational cooperative housing available. **Activities:** Student government, film, magazine, radio, student newspaper, television, yearbook, scientific and literary journals, choral groups, dance, drama, jazz band, marching band, music ensembles, musical theater, pep band, symphony orchestra, fraternities, sororities, over 90 campus organizations, including Colgate Volunteer Bureau, Women's Coalition, Newman Club, Jewish Union and other religious associations, coffee houses, Black Student Union, UNIDAD, Asian Society, Volunteer Colgate, political groups. **Additional information:** Undergraduates not residing in college housing live in their own apartments off campus.

ATHLETICS. NCAA. **Intercollegiate:** Basketball, cross-country, diving, field hockey W, football M, golf M, ice hockey M, lacrosse, rowing (crew), skiing, soccer, softball W, swimming, tennis, track and field, volleyball, water polo M. **Intramural:** Basketball, bowling, cross-country, golf, gymnastics W, ice hockey, lacrosse, racquetball, rifle, soccer, softball, squash, swimming, table tennis, tennis, track and field, volleyball. **Clubs:** Rugby, sailing, squash, ice hockey.

STUDENT SERVICES. Aptitude testing, career counseling, employment service for undergraduates, freshman orientation, health services, personal counseling, placement service for graduates, services/facilities for handicapped.

ANNUAL EXPENSES. Tuition and fees: $18,620. **Room and board:** $5,400. **Books and supplies:** $500. **Other expenses:** $750.

FINANCIAL AID. 61% of freshmen, 79% of continuing students receive some form of aid. All grants, 96% of loans, 59% of jobs based on need. 292 enrolled freshmen were judged to have need, all were offered aid. **Aid applications:** Closing date February 1; applicants notified on or about April 1; must reply by May 1.

ADDRESS/TELEPHONE. Thomas S. Anthony, Dean of Admissions, Colgate University, 13 Oak Drive, Hamilton, NY 13346-1383. (315) 824-7401.

College of Aeronautics
Flushing, New York

CB code: 2001

4-year private technical college, coed. Founded in 1932. **Accreditation:** Regional. **Undergraduate enrollment:** 1,125 men, 41 women full time; 87 men, 9 women part time. **Faculty:** 80 total (64 full time), 28 with doctorates or other terminal degrees. **Location:** Suburban campus in very large city; 5 miles from Manhattan. **Calendar:** Trimester, extensive summer session. Saturday classes. **Microcomputers:** 30 located in libraries, computer centers. **Special facilities:** Computerized engine test-cell, Boeing 737 flight systems simulator.

DEGREES OFFERED. AAS, B. 100 associate degrees awarded in 1992. 45 bachelor's degrees awarded.

UNDERGRADUATE MAJORS. Aeronautical technology, aerospace/aeronautical/astronautical engineering, aircraft mechanics, aviation computer technology, electrical and electronics equipment repair, electrical/electronics/communications engineering, electronic technology, engineering and engineering-related technologies, power plant operation and maintenance. aeronautical technology, aeronautics maintenance technology, aerospace/aeronautical/astronautical engineering, aircraft mechanics, manufacturing technology.

ACADEMIC PROGRAMS. 2-year transfer program, accelerated program, cooperative education. **Remedial services:** Learning center, remedial instruction, special counselor, tutoring. **ROTC:** Air Force. **Placement/credit:** AP, CLEP Subject, IB, institutional tests.

ACADEMIC REQUIREMENTS. Freshmen must earn minimum GPA of 2.0 to continue in good standing. Students must declare major on application. **Graduation requirements:** 75 hours for associate, 135 hours for bachelor's. Most students required to take courses in computer science, English, mathematics, biological/physical sciences. **Postgraduate studies:** 20% from 2-year programs enter 4-year programs.

FRESHMAN ADMISSIONS. Selection criteria: Open admissions. **High school preparation:** 14 units required; 18 recommended. Required and recommended units include English 4, mathematics 3-4, physical science 2-4 and social science 1-4. Mathematics and physics recommended. **Test requirements:** SAT; score report by August 1.

1992 FRESHMAN CLASS PROFILE. 285 men, 10 women enrolled. 10% had high school GPA of 3.0 or higher, 65% between 2.0 and 2.99. 10% were in top tenth and 25% were in top quarter of graduating class. **Academic background:** Mid 50% of enrolled freshmen had SAT-V between 310-340, SAT-M between 390-420. 40% submitted SAT scores. **Characteristics:** 95% from in state, 100% commute, 69% have minority backgrounds, 4% are foreign students. Average age is 21.

FALL-TERM APPLICATIONS. $25 fee, may be waived for applicants with need. No closing date; priority given to applications received by July 1; applicants notified on a rolling basis; must reply by registration. Interview recommended. Essay recommended. Deferred and early admission available. Examinations and interviews may be required to assist in course placement.

STUDENT LIFE. Activities: Student government, yearbook, Hellenic club, American Institute of Aeronautics and Astronautics, Society of Automotive Engineers, Institute of Electrical and Electronics Engineers, flying, model airplane, and chess clubs.

ATHLETICS. Intramural: Basketball, soccer, softball, volleyball.

STUDENT SERVICES. Aptitude testing, career counseling, employment service for undergraduates, freshman orientation, personal counseling, placement service for graduates, veterans counselor, services/facilities for handicapped.

ANNUAL EXPENSES. Tuition and fees (projected): $6,070. **Books and supplies:** $950. **Other expenses:** $265.

FINANCIAL AID. 82% of freshmen, 78% of continuing students receive some form of aid. All grants, 85% of loans, all jobs based on need. 260 enrolled freshmen were judged to have need, all were offered aid. Academic scholarships available. **Aid applications:** No closing date; priority given to applications received by May 1; applicants notified on a rolling basis; must reply within 30 days.

ADDRESS/TELEPHONE. John Fitzpatrick, Vice President/Dean of Enrollment, College of Aeronautics, La Guardia Airport, Flushing, NY 11371. (718) 429-6600. (800) 776-2376. Fax: (718) 429-0256.

College of Insurance
New York, New York

CB code: 2112

5-year private business college, coed. Founded in 1962. **Accreditation:** Regional. **Undergraduate enrollment:** 90 men, 49 women full time; 253 men, 350 women part time. **Graduate enrollment:** 60 men, 31 women full time; 50 men, 40 women part time. **Faculty:** 115 total (22 full time), 35 with doctorates or other terminal degrees. **Location:** Urban campus in very large city; in lower Manhattan near Wall Street. **Calendar:** 2 semesters and two summer terms (alternating work and study periods). **Microcomputers:** 15 located in computer centers. **Additional facts:** Full-time undergraduates may participate, if accepted, in a 5-year cooperative education program. Curriculum emphasizes insurance, business, financial, and actuarial services.

DEGREES OFFERED. BS, MBA. 3 associate degrees awarded in 1992. 100% in business and management. 41 bachelor's degrees awarded. 100% in business and management. Graduate degrees offered in 4 major fields of study.

UNDERGRADUATE MAJORS. Associate: Insurance and risk management. **Bachelor's:** Actuarial sciences, business administration and management, business and management, insurance and risk management.

ACADEMIC PROGRAMS. 2-year transfer program, accelerated program, cooperative education, dual enrollment of high school students, internships, study abroad; combined bachelor's/graduate program in business administration. **Remedial services:** Reduced course load, tutoring. **Placement/credit:** AP, CLEP Subject, institutional tests.

ACADEMIC REQUIREMENTS. Freshmen must earn minimum GPA of 2.0 to continue in good standing. 85% of freshmen return for sophomore year. Students must declare major on application. **Graduation requirements:** 60 hours for associate, 126 hours for bachelor's. Most students required to take courses in computer science, English, foreign languages, history, humanities, mathematics, philosophy/religion, social sciences. **Postgraduate studies:** 40% from 2-year programs enter 4-year programs. 1% enter law school, 15% enter MBA programs, 2% enter other graduate study. **Additional information:** Full-time undergraduate curriculum is 50% liberal arts, 25% business administration, and 25% insurance.

FRESHMAN ADMISSIONS. Selection criteria: High school GPA, class rank, test scores, activities, recommendations, interview very important. Maturity, interest, and commitment important. **High school preparation:** 19 units required. Required units include English 4 and mathematics 3. **Test requirements:** SAT or ACT (SAT preferred); score report by August 1.

1992 FRESHMAN CLASS PROFILE. 50 men, 105 women enrolled. 86% had high school GPA of 3.0 or higher, 14% between 2.0 and 2.99. **Academic background:** Mid 50% of enrolled freshmen had SAT-V between 480-570, SAT-M between 540-650; ACT composite between 25-27. 90% submitted SAT scores, 10% submitted ACT scores. **Characteristics:** 48% from in state, 50% commute, 28% have minority backgrounds. Average age is 20.

FALL-TERM APPLICATIONS. $25 fee, may be waived for applicants with need. Closing date May 1; applicants notified on a rolling basis beginning on or about April 15; must reply by May 1 or within 2 weeks if notified thereafter. Interview required. Essay recommended. Deferred and early admission available. EDP-S.

STUDENT LIFE. Housing: Dormitories (coed). **Activities:** Student government, student newspaper, yearbook, drama, music ensembles, fraternities, Circle-K.

ATHLETICS. Intercollegiate: Bowling, volleyball. **Intramural:** Basketball M.

STUDENT SERVICES. Career counseling, employment service for undergraduates, freshman orientation, personal counseling, special adviser for adult students, veterans counselor, services/facilities for handicapped.

ANNUAL EXPENSES. Tuition and fees: $10,500. **Room and board:** $6,888. **Books and supplies:** $500. **Other expenses:** $1,016.

FINANCIAL AID. 88% of freshmen, 91% of continuing students receive some form of aid. 34% of grants, 13% of loans, 19% of jobs based on need. 12 enrolled freshmen were judged to have need, all were offered aid. Academic, leadership, minority scholarships available. **Aid applications:** No closing date; applicants notified on a rolling basis; must reply within 4 weeks. **Additional information:** 5-year cooperative education program enables some students to earn up to 2.5 years work experience and salary while working toward degree. Up to two-thirds to 100% of college costs sponsored.

ADDRESS/TELEPHONE. Theresa Marro, Director of Admissions, College of Insurance, 101 Murray Street, New York, NY 10007-2132. (212) 962-4111 ext. 332. (800) 356-5146. Fax: (212) 964-3381.

College of Mount St. Vincent

Riverdale, New York — CB code: 2088

Admissions: 72% of applicants accepted
Based on:
- ••• School record
- •• Recommendations, test scores
- • Activities, essay, interview, special talents

Completion: 95% of freshmen end year in good standing
64% graduate, 19% of these enter graduate study

4-year private liberal arts college, coed, affiliated with Roman Catholic Church. Founded in 1847. **Accreditation:** Regional. **Undergraduate enrollment:** 126 men, 573 women full time; 37 men, 289 women part time. **Graduate enrollment:** 15 women full time; 20 women part time. **Faculty:** 97 total (59 full time), 55 with doctorates or other terminal degrees. **Location:** Suburban campus in very large city; 10 miles from downtown Manhattan. **Calendar:** Semester, limited summer session. Saturday classes. **Microcomputers:** 60 located in classrooms, computer centers. **Special facilities:** 2 electron microscopes, computer graphics and animation center. **Additional facts:** Facilities, programs, and faculty shared with nearby Manhattan College.

DEGREES OFFERED. AA, AAS, BA, BS, MS. 2 associate degrees awarded in 1992. 34% in business and management, 66% letters/literature. 182 bachelor's degrees awarded. 20% in business and management, 13% communications, 8% teacher education, 23% health sciences, 11% letters/literature, 6% life sciences, 10% psychology, 7% social sciences. Graduate degrees offered in 2 major fields of study.

UNDERGRADUATE MAJORS. Associate: Business and management, liberal/general studies, psychology, social sciences. **Bachelor's:** Allied health, biochemistry, biology, business and management, chemistry, communications, computer and information sciences, economics, English, English education, foreign languages (multiple emphasis), foreign languages education, French, health education, history, international business management, international relations, liberal/general studies, mathematics, mathematics education, nursing, philosophy, physical education, physics, predentistry, premedicine, psychology, religion, science education, social studies education, sociology, Spanish, special education, sports medicine, urban studies.

ACADEMIC PROGRAMS. Accelerated program, double major, dual enrollment of high school students, education specialist degree, honors program, independent study, internships, student-designed major, study abroad, teacher preparation, visiting/exchange student program, weekend college, cross-registration, 3-2 engineering program with Manhattan College. **Remedial services:** Learning center, preadmission summer program, reduced course load, remedial instruction, special counselor, tutoring, New York State Higher Education Opportunity Program. **ROTC:** Air Force. **Placement/credit:** AP, CLEP General and Subject, institutional tests; 18 credit hours maximum for bachelor's degree.

ACADEMIC REQUIREMENTS. Freshmen must earn minimum GPA of 1.7 to continue in good standing. 80% of freshmen return for sophomore year. Students must declare major by end of second year. **Graduation requirements:** 62 hours for associate (30 in major), 126 hours for bachelor's (30 in major). Most students required to take courses in arts/fine arts, computer science, English, foreign languages, history, humanities, mathematics, philosophy/religion, biological/physical sciences, social sciences. **Postgraduate studies:** 80% from 2-year programs enter 4-year programs. 3% enter law school, 3% enter medical school, 8% enter MBA programs, 5% enter other graduate study. **Additional information:** Dual teaching certification offered in elementary and special education. Certification in elementary and secondary education available in many fields.

FRESHMAN ADMISSIONS. Selection criteria: School achievement record (rank in top half of class, 3.0 high school GPA), test scores, recommendations, and school and community activities. **High school preparation:** 16 units required. Required and recommended units include English 4, foreign language 2, mathematics 2-3, social science 2-3 and science 2-3. One American history required of all students, 3 mathematics for nursing, science, and mathematics majors, 3 science for nursing and science majors. **Test requirements:** SAT or ACT; score report by July 30.

1992 FRESHMAN CLASS PROFILE. 124 men applied, 95 accepted, 32 enrolled; 627 women applied, 442 accepted, 145 enrolled. 65% had high school GPA of 3.0 or higher, 34% between 2.0 and 2.99. **Academic background:** Mid 50% of enrolled freshmen had SAT-V between 400-480, SAT-M between 410-560. 96% submitted SAT scores. **Characteristics:** 89% from in state, 55% live in college housing, 46% have minority backgrounds, 1% are foreign students. Average age is 18.

FALL-TERM APPLICATIONS. $25 fee, may be waived for applicants with need. Closing date August 15; priority given to applications received by February 1; must reply by May 1 or within 4 weeks if notified thereafter. Interview recommended. Essay recommended. Interview recommended for all applicants, required for applicants to BRIDGE Program (modified 4.5-year program). CRDA. Deferred and early admission available. EDP-S.

STUDENT LIFE. Housing: Dormitories (men, women, coed). Students guaranteed on-campus housing for 4 years. **Activities:** Student government, magazine, radio, student newspaper, television, yearbook, choral groups, dance, drama, Culturally Aware students of today, international students club, Gaelic Society, campus ministry team, community volunteers, pep club, dance club, and student nurses association.

ATHLETICS. NCAA. **Intercollegiate:** Basketball, cross-country, soccer, softball W, tennis, track and field W, volleyball. **Intramural:** Basketball, soccer, softball, volleyball, water polo M. **Clubs:** Skiing.

STUDENT SERVICES. Aptitude testing, career counseling, employment service for undergraduates, freshman orientation, health services, personal counseling, placement service for graduates, special adviser for adult students, services/facilities for handicapped.

ANNUAL EXPENSES. Tuition and fees: $11,330. **Room and board:** $5,600. **Books and supplies:** $500. **Other expenses:** $850.

FINANCIAL AID. 80% of freshmen, 75% of continuing students receive some form of aid. 70% of grants, 94% of loans, 65% of jobs based on need. 127 enrolled freshmen were judged to have need, all were offered aid. Academic, leadership, alumni affiliation scholarships available. **Aid applications:** Closing date March 15; applicants notified on a rolling basis beginning on or about March 26; must reply by May 1 or within 4 weeks if notified thereafter. **Additional information:** Essay required for WNYW academic scholarship.

ADDRESS/TELEPHONE. Lenore Mott, Dean of Admissions and Financial Aid, College of Mount St. Vincent, 6301 Riverdale Avenue, Riverdale, NY 10471. (718) 405-3400. Fax: (718) 601-6392.

College of New Rochelle
New Rochelle, New York CB code: 2089

Admissions: 71% of applicants accepted
Based on: ••• School record
•• Recommendations, test scores
• Activities, essay, interview, special talents
Completion: 86% of freshmen end year in good standing
54% graduate, 21% of these enter graduate study

4-year private college of arts and sciences and nursing college, women only, affiliated with Roman Catholic Church. Founded in 1904. **Accreditation:** Regional. **Undergraduate enrollment:** 7 men, 504 women full time; 5 men, 271 women part time. **Graduate enrollment:** 3 men, 66 women full time; 160 men, 1,393 women part time. **Faculty:** 212 total (87 full time), 82 with doctorates or other terminal degrees. **Location:** Suburban campus in small city; 14 miles from New York City. **Calendar:** Semester, limited summer session. **Microcomputers:** 69 located in computer centers. **Special facilities:** Art galleries, 2 learning skills centers (including 1 for nursing), electron microscope. Institute for Entrepreneurial Studies, computer graphics laboratory, model classroom, rare book collections of James Joyce, Thomas More, and Ursuline Order. **Additional facts:** Independent institution in Roman Catholic tradition. Coeducational school of nursing and graduate school. School of nursing also accredited by National League For Nursing.

DEGREES OFFERED. BA, BS, BFA, MA, MS. 161 bachelor's degrees awarded in 1992. 9% in business and management, 8% communications, 51% health sciences, 14% psychology, 6% social sciences. Graduate degrees offered in 21 major fields of study.

UNDERGRADUATE MAJORS. Advertising, American studies, art education, art history, art therapy, biology, business and management, business economics, chemistry, classics, communications, early childhood education, economics, education of the emotionally handicapped, education of the mentally handicapped, elementary education, English, fine arts, foreign languages education, French, history, humanities and social sciences, international relations, international studies, journalism, junior high education, Latin, mathematics, mathematics education, nursing, philosophy, physics, political science and government, psychology, radio/television broadcasting, religion, science education, secondary education, social studies education, social work, sociology, Spanish, special education, specific learning disabilities, visual and performing arts, women's studies.

ACADEMIC PROGRAMS. Accelerated program, cooperative education, double major, education specialist degree, honors program, independent study, internships, student-designed major, study abroad, teacher preparation, telecourses, visiting/exchange student program, United Nations semester, Washington semester, cross-registration, preprofessional programs in law, medicine, and health; liberal arts/career combination in business. **Remedial services:** Learning center, preadmission summer program, reduced course load, remedial instruction, special counselor, tutoring, Higher Education Opportunity Program for New York State residents. **Placement/credit:** AP, CLEP General and Subject, institutional tests; 15 credit hours maximum for bachelor's degree.

ACADEMIC REQUIREMENTS. Freshmen must earn minimum GPA of 2.0 to continue in good standing. 87% of freshmen return for sophomore year. Students must declare major by end of second year. **Graduation requirements:** 120 hours for bachelor's (30 in major). Most students required to take courses in English, history, mathematics, philosophy/religion, biological/physical sciences, social sciences. **Postgraduate studies:** 2% enter law school, 2% enter medical school, 6% enter MBA programs, 11% enter other graduate study. **Additional information:** Honors program offers one-to-one learning with mentor, independent study, special seminars, academic internships and flexibility in college requirements. Director and students actively involved in National Collegiate Honors Council.

FRESHMAN ADMISSIONS. Selection criteria: High school performance most important, as well as test scores, class rank, recommendations, and activities in school and community. **High school preparation:** 21 units required. Required units include biological science 1, English 4, foreign language 2, mathematics 3, physical science 2, social science 3 and science 3. Biology, chemistry, and 3 mathematics required for school of nursing. **Test requirements:** SAT or ACT (SAT preferred); score report by August 15.

1992 FRESHMAN CLASS PROFILE. 20% were in top tenth and 49% were in top quarter of graduating class. **Academic background:** Mid 50% of enrolled freshmen had SAT-V between 420-460, SAT-M between 390-450. 98% submitted SAT scores. **Characteristics:** 75% from in state, 60% live in college housing, 57% have minority backgrounds, 2% are foreign students. Average age is 18.

FALL-TERM APPLICATIONS. $20 fee, may be waived for applicants with need. No closing date; priority given to applications received by April 1; applicants notified on a rolling basis; must reply by May 1 or within 3 weeks if notified thereafter. Portfolio required for art applicants. Interview recommended. Essay recommended. CRDA. Deferred and early admission available. EDP-F.

STUDENT LIFE. Housing: Dormitories (women). **Activities:** Student government, film, magazine, student newspaper, television, yearbook, choral groups, drama, musical theater, community services, campus ministry, international and ethnic student organizations.

ATHLETICS. NCAA. **Intercollegiate:** Basketball, softball, swimming, tennis, volleyball. **Intramural:** Soccer.

STUDENT SERVICES. Aptitude testing, career counseling, employment service for undergraduates, freshman orientation, health services, personal counseling, placement service for graduates, services/facilities for handicapped.

ANNUAL EXPENSES. Tuition and fees: $10,680. **Room and board:** $4,750. **Books and supplies:** $500. **Other expenses:** $250.

FINANCIAL AID. 95% of freshmen, 74% of continuing students receive some form of aid. 81% of grants, 86% of loans, 76% of jobs based on need. 100 enrolled freshmen were judged to have need, all were offered aid. Academic, music/drama, art, leadership, alumni affiliation scholarships available. **Aid applications:** No closing date; applicants notified on a rolling basis beginning on or about February 25; must reply by May 1 or within 2 weeks if notified thereafter. **Additional information:** Gift aid guaranteed for 4 years. New York Regents Scholarships matched with equal amount of institutional aid.

ADDRESS/TELEPHONE. John Hine, Director of Admissions, College of New Rochelle, Castle Place, New Rochelle, NY 10805-2308. (914) 654-5452. Fax: (914) 654-5554.

College of New Rochelle: School of New Resources
New Rochelle, New York CB code: 1236

4-year private liberal arts college, coed. Founded in 1972. **Accreditation:** Regional. **Undergraduate enrollment:** 432 men, 2,306 women full time; 65 men, 424 women part time. **Faculty:** 491 total (21 full time), 103 with doctorates or other terminal degrees. **Location:** Suburban campus in small city; 12 miles from New York City. **Calendar:** Semester, extensive summer session. Extensive evening/early morning classes. **Microcomputers:** 69 located in classrooms, computer centers. **Special facilities:** Art gallery, 2 learning skills center, Institute for Entrepreneurial Studies. **Additional facts:** 7 branch campuses, including locations in Manhattan, Bronx, Brooklyn, and New Rochelle. School designed for adult students.

DEGREES OFFERED. BA. 431 bachelor's degrees awarded in 1992. 100% in multi/interdisciplinary studies.

UNDERGRADUATE MAJORS. Liberal/general studies.

ACADEMIC PROGRAMS. Accelerated program, independent study, internships, student-designed major. **Remedial services:** Reduced course load, remedial instruction, special counselor, tutoring, preparatory program. **Placement/credit:** CLEP General, institutional tests; 30 credit hours maximum for bachelor's degree.

ACADEMIC REQUIREMENTS. Freshmen must earn minimum GPA of 1.8 to continue in good standing. 75% of freshmen return for sophomore year. Students must declare major by end of second year. **Graduation requirements:** 120 hours for bachelor's (24 in major). Most students required to take courses in English, humanities, mathematics. **Postgraduate studies:** 1% enter law school, 10% enter MBA programs, 25% enter other graduate study. **Additional information:** Semesterly course development process gives students direct involvement in designing their own program.

FRESHMAN ADMISSIONS. Selection criteria: Interview and school administered tests important. **Test requirements:** Institutional Language Arts test required for admissions and placement. **Additional information:** Applicants must be over 21 years old.

1992 FRESHMAN CLASS PROFILE. 123 men, 543 women enrolled. **Characteristics:** 98% from in state, 100% commute, 84% have minority backgrounds, 2% are foreign students. Average age is 34.

FALL-TERM APPLICATIONS. No fee. No closing date; applicants notified on a rolling basis. Interview required. Essay required. Deferred admission available.

STUDENT LIFE. Activities: Student government, student newspaper, yearbook, women's center, campus ministry, community service organizations, and social work oriented clubs.

STUDENT SERVICES. Aptitude testing, career counseling, employment service for undergraduates, health services, personal counseling, special adviser for adult students, veterans counselor.

ANNUAL EXPENSES. Tuition and fees: $4,960. Full-time students normally take only 24 credit hours per year. **Room and board:** $4,760. **Books and supplies:** $500. **Other expenses:** $100.

FINANCIAL AID. 96% of freshmen, 96% of continuing students receive some form of aid. All aid based on need. **Aid applications:** No closing date; applicants notified on a rolling basis.

ADDRESS/TELEPHONE. Patricia A. Furman, Assistant Dean for Support Services, College of New Rochelle: School of New Resources, Newman Hall, Castle Place, New Rochelle, NY 10805-2308. (914) 632-5300.

College of St. Rose
Albany, New York CB code: 2091

4-year private liberal arts college, coed, affiliated with Roman Catholic Church. Founded in 1920. **Accreditation:** Regional. **Undergraduate enrollment:** 2,588 men and women. **Graduate enrollment:** 1,302 men and women. **Faculty:** 231 total (120 full time), 65 with doctorates or other terminal degrees. **Location:** Urban campus in small city; 140 miles from New York City. **Calendar:** Semester, limited summer session. **Microcomputers:** 70 located in dormitories, computer centers. **Special facilities:** Art gallery, music studio, observatory, communications studio. **Additional facts:** Independent institution with Roman Catholic heritage.

DEGREES OFFERED. BA, BS, MA, MS, MBA. 471 bachelor's degrees awarded in 1992. 21% in business and management, 8% communications, 10% education, 30% teacher education, 5% letters/literature, 7% social sciences, 8% visual and performing arts. Graduate degrees offered in 20 major fields of study.

UNDERGRADUATE MAJORS. Accounting, American studies, art education, biochemistry, biology, business administration and management, business and management, chemistry, communications, computer and information sciences, cytotechnology, education of the mentally handicapped, elementary education, English, graphic design, history, mathematics, medical laboratory technologies, music, music education, music performance, political science and government, psychology, religion, secondary education, social work, sociology, Spanish, special education, speech correction, studio art.

ACADEMIC PROGRAMS. Accelerated program, double major, dual enrollment of high school students, independent study, internships, student-designed major, study abroad, teacher preparation, telecourses, visiting/exchange student program, cross-registration, 3+2 program in engineering with Alfred University, Clarkson University, and Union College, combined bachelor's/graduate degree program in law with Albany Law School. **Remedial services:** Preadmission summer program, remedial instruction, special counselor, tutoring, New York State Higher Education Opportunity Program. **ROTC:** Air Force, Army, Naval. **Placement/credit:** AP, CLEP Subject; 15 credit hours maximum for bachelor's degree.

ACADEMIC REQUIREMENTS. Freshmen must earn minimum GPA of 2.0 to continue in good standing. 80% of freshmen return for sophomore year. Students must declare major by end of second year. **Graduation requirements:** 122 hours for bachelor's (45 in major). Most students required to take courses in arts/fine arts, English, history, mathematics, biological/physical sciences, social sciences.

FRESHMAN ADMISSIONS. Selection criteria: School achievement record, test scores, recommendations most important. School and community involvement and interview also considered. **High school preparation:** 16 units required. Required units include English 4, mathematics 2 and social science 2. Music applicants must read music and play at least 1 instrument. **Test requirements:** SAT or ACT; score report by March 15. California Achievement Test, comprehensive mathematics and writing tests required of students entering Higher Education Opportunity Program for admissions and placement.

1992 FRESHMAN CLASS PROFILE. 244 men and women enrolled. **Characteristics:** 97% from in state, 75% commute, 2% have minority backgrounds, 1% are foreign students. Average age is 18.

FALL-TERM APPLICATIONS. $25 fee, may be waived for applicants with need. Closing date August 15; applicants notified on a rolling basis beginning on or about November 1; must reply by May 1 or within 2 weeks if notified thereafter. Audition required for music applicants. Portfolio required for art applicants. Essay required. Interview recommended. CRDA. Deferred and early admission available.

STUDENT LIFE. Housing: Dormitories (men, women, coed). **Activities:** Student government, film, magazine, radio, student newspaper, television, yearbook, choral groups, concert band, drama, jazz band, music ensembles, opera, many religious, ethnic, political, and social service organizations.

ATHLETICS. NCAA. **Intercollegiate:** Baseball M, basketball, cross-country, soccer, softball W, swimming, tennis, volleyball W. **Intramural:** Basketball, bowling, soccer, table tennis, volleyball.

STUDENT SERVICES. Aptitude testing, career counseling, employment service for undergraduates, freshman orientation, health services, personal counseling, placement service for graduates, special adviser for adult students, services/facilities for handicapped.

ANNUAL EXPENSES. Tuition and fees (1992-93): $9,026. **Room and board:** $5,260. **Books and supplies:** $550. **Other expenses:** $1,439.

FINANCIAL AID. 85% of freshmen, 82% of continuing students receive some form of aid. 63% of grants, 88% of loans, 56% of jobs based on need. Academic, music/drama, art, alumni affiliation scholarships available. **Aid applications:** Closing date March 1; applicants notified on or about April 15; must reply within 2 weeks.

ADDRESS/TELEPHONE. Mary M. O'Donnell, Dean of Admissions, College of St. Rose, 432 Western Avenue, Albany, NY 12203. (518) 454-5150. (800) 637-8556. Fax: (518) 438-3293.

Columbia University: Columbia College
New York, New York CB code: 2116

Admissions: 30% of applicants accepted
Based on: ••• Activities, recommendations, school record, special talents
•• Essay, test scores
• Interview
Completion: 96% of freshmen end year in good standing
90% graduate, 55% of these enter graduate study

4-year private liberal arts college, coed. Founded in 1754. **Accreditation:** Regional. **Undergraduate enrollment:** 1,766 men, 1,656 women full time. **Faculty:** 478 total, 478 with doctorates or other terminal degrees. **Location:** Urban campus in very large city. **Calendar:** Semester, extensive summer session. **Microcomputers:** Located in dormitories, libraries, classrooms, computer centers, campus-wide network. **Special facilities:** Lamont-Doherty Geological Observatory, art galleries, theaters.

DEGREES OFFERED. BA. 831 bachelor's degrees awarded in 1992. 8% in computer sciences, 20% letters/literature, 16% life sciences, 6% multi/interdisciplinary studies, 5% physical sciences, 8% psychology, 22% social sciences.

UNDERGRADUATE MAJORS. African studies, Afro-American (black) studies, anthropology, applied mathematics, Arabic, archeology, architecture, art history, astronomy, astrophysics, biochemistry, biology, biophysics, chemistry, Chinese, classics, comparative literature, computer and information sciences, dramatic arts, earth sciences, East Asian studies, Eastern European studies, economics, engineering and other disciplines, English, environmental science, film arts, French, geochemistry, geology, geophysics and seismology, German, German studies, Greek (classical), Hebrew, history, Indic languages, Italian, Japanese, Latin, Latin American studies, mathematics, medieval studies, Middle Eastern studies, music, oceanography, philosophy, physical chemistry, physics, political science and government, Portuguese, psychology, religion, Russian, Russian and Slavic studies, Scandinavian languages, sociology, South Asian studies, Spanish, statistics, urban studies, visual and performing arts, women's studies.

ACADEMIC PROGRAMS. Double major, independent study, internships, student-designed major, study abroad, teacher preparation, visiting/exchange student program, cross-registration, study abroad in Paris, and at Cambridge, Oxford, and Kyoto Universities; five-year joint degree program with Juilliard School; liberal arts/career combination in engineering; combined bachelor's/graduate program in law. **Remedial services:** Preadmission summer program, special counselor, tutoring. **Placement/credit:** AP, IB, institutional tests.

ACADEMIC REQUIREMENTS. No policy requiring minimum GPA; records of students having academic difficulty are reviewed individually. 95% of freshmen return for sophomore year. Students must declare major by end of second year. **Graduation requirements:** 124 hours for bachelor's (27 in major). Most students required to take courses in arts/fine arts, English, foreign languages, history, humanities, philosophy/religion, biological/physical sciences, social sciences.

FRESHMAN ADMISSIONS. Selection criteria: School achievement record, school and community activities, recommendations, and special talents most important. Test scores and essay also considered. **High school preparation:** 20 units recommended. Recommended units include English 4, foreign language 4, mathematics 4, social science 4 and science 4. **Test requirements:** SAT or ACT; score report by March 1. 3 ACH required (including English Composition). Score report by March 1.

1992 FRESHMAN CLASS PROFILE. 3,467 men applied, 1,020 accepted, 448 enrolled; 3,117 women applied, 933 accepted, 414 enrolled. 96% had high school GPA of 3.0 or higher, 4% between 2.0 and 2.99. 78% were in top tenth and 93% were in top quarter of graduating class. **Academic background:** Mid 50% of enrolled freshmen had SAT-V between 560-680, SAT-M between 610-720. 98% submitted SAT scores. **Characteristics:** 19% from in state, 99% live in college housing, 38% have minority backgrounds, 3% are foreign students, 4% join fraternities/sororities. Average age is 18.

FALL-TERM APPLICATIONS. $55 fee, may be waived for applicants with need. Closing date January 1; applicants notified on or about April 1; must reply by May 1. Audition required for Juilliard Program applicants. Essay required. Interview recommended. CRDA. Deferred and early admission available. EDP-F.

STUDENT LIFE. Housing: Dormitories (coed); apartment, fraternity, sorority housing available. Language houses available. Housing for upper-division students includes suites and kitchens. Students selecting housing as freshmen or sophomores guaranteed housing for entire career as long as they maintain good standing. New Schapiro Residence Hall includes housing for 400 students, new theater and practice rooms. **Activities:** Student government, film, magazine, radio, student newspaper, television, yearbook, humor magazine, political journals, literary magazine, women's magazine, video yearbook, choral groups, concert band, dance, drama, jazz band, marching band, music ensembles, musical theater, pep band, symphony orchestra, improvisational comedy troupe, fraternities, sororities, black, Latin American, Asian, and Chicano student organizations, community service groups, religious groups of all major denominations, gay students group.

ATHLETICS. NCAA. **Intercollegiate:** Baseball M, basketball, cross-country, diving, fencing, football M, golf M, rowing (crew), soccer, swimming, tennis, track and field, volleyball W, wrestling M. **Intramural:** Badminton, basketball, handball, racquetball, soccer, softball, squash, swimming, tennis, volleyball. **Clubs:** Intercollegiate archery W, intramural flag football, and 28 clubs, including archery, field hockey, ice hockey, lacrosse, riflery, sailing, skiing, table tennis, and water polo.

STUDENT SERVICES. Aptitude testing, career counseling, employment service for undergraduates, freshman orientation, health services, personal counseling, placement service for graduates, services/facilities for handicapped.

ANNUAL EXPENSES. Tuition and fees (projected): $17,948. **Room and board:** $6,610. **Books and supplies:** $550. **Other expenses:** $990.

FINANCIAL AID. 46% of freshmen, 41% of continuing students receive some form of aid. All aid based on need. 360 enrolled freshmen were judged to have need, all were offered aid. **Aid applications:** Closing date February 1; applicants notified on or about April 15; must reply by May 1.

ADDRESS/TELEPHONE. Lawrence J. Momo, Director of Undergraduate Admissions, Columbia University: Columbia College, 212 Hamilton Hall, Columbia University, New York, NY 10027. (212) 854-2521. Fax: (212) 854-1209.

Columbia University: School of Engineering and Applied Science

New York, New York — CB code: 2111

Admissions:	42% of applicants accepted
Based on:	••• School record
	•• Activities, essay, interview, recommendations, test scores
	• Special talents
Completion:	90% of freshmen end year in good standing
	70% enter graduate study

4-year private engineering college, coed. Founded in 1864. **Accreditation:** Regional. **Graduate enrollment:** 410 men, 68 women full time; 280 men, 54 women part time. **Faculty:** 120 total (100 full time), 120 with doctorates or other terminal degrees. **Location:** Urban campus in very large city. **Calendar:** Semester, limited summer session. **Microcomputers:** Located in dormitories, libraries, classrooms, computer centers, campus-wide network. **Special facilities:** Interactive graphics laboratory, telecommunications research center, plasma laboratory, materials laboratory, observatory, geological observatory, Columbia Presbyterian Hospital.

DEGREES OFFERED. BS, MS, PhD. 242 bachelor's degrees awarded in 1992. 20% in computer sciences, 80% engineering. Graduate degrees offered in 24 major fields of study.

UNDERGRADUATE MAJORS. Applied chemistry, applied mathematics, applied physics, bioengineering and biomedical engineering, chemical engineering, civil engineering, computer and information sciences, computer engineering, electrical/electronics/communications engineering, engineering, engineering mechanics, engineering physics, geological engineering, geophysical engineering, geophysics and seismology, industrial engineering, information sciences and systems, materials engineering, mechanical engineering, metallurgical engineering, metallurgy, mining and mineral engineering, operations research.

ACADEMIC PROGRAMS. Accelerated program, honors program, internships, telecourses, IBM graduate cooperative program, MS/MBA program in operations research; liberal arts/career combination in engineering; combined bachelor's/graduate program in business administration, law. **Remedial services:** Preadmission summer program, reduced course load, special counselor, tutoring, New York State Higher Education Opportunity Program. **Placement/credit:** AP, institutional tests.

ACADEMIC REQUIREMENTS. Freshmen must earn overall minimum GPA of 2.0 with satisfactory completion of certain courses. 98% of freshmen return for sophomore year. Students must declare major by end of second year. **Graduation requirements:** 124 hours for bachelor's (66 in major). Most students required to take courses in computer science, English, humanities, mathematics, biological/physical sciences, social sciences. **Additional information:** Specialized engineering study generally begins in third year; however, entering students usually have defined interests.

FRESHMAN ADMISSIONS. Selection criteria: Strong school achievement record and class rank in top 15% preferred. Mathematics teacher's recommendation, scores on SATs and 3 ACH important. Personal qualities considered, with attention given to personal essay and interview. Preference given to applicants who have taken advanced high school courses when available, and those demonstrating verbal skill and success in nonquantitative courses. **High school preparation:** 16 units required. Required units include biological science 1, English 4, foreign language 2, mathematics 4, physical science 1, social science 3 and science 1. Mathematics units should include calculus. Additional social studies unit recommended. **Test requirements:** SAT or ACT (SAT preferred); score report by March 1. 3 ACH required (including English Composition, Mathematics Level I or II, and Physics or Chemistry). Score report by March 1 Recommend tests be taken by end of junior year or December of senior year.

1992 FRESHMAN CLASS PROFILE. 95% had high school GPA of 3.0 or higher, 5% between 2.0 and 2.99. **Academic background:** Mid 50% of enrolled freshmen had SAT-V between 540-620, SAT-M between 680-770. 98% submitted SAT scores. **Characteristics:** 50% from in state, 97% live in college housing, 58% have minority backgrounds, 12% are foreign students, 10% join fraternities/sororities. Average age is 18.

FALL-TERM APPLICATIONS. $55 fee, may be waived for applicants with need. Closing date January 1; applicants notified on or about April 1; must reply by May 1. Essay required. Interview recommended. CRDA. Deferred and early admission available. EDP-F.

STUDENT LIFE. Housing: Dormitories (coed); fraternity housing available. Apartments available near campus. **Activities:** Student government, film, magazine, radio, student newspaper, television, yearbook, choral groups, concert band, drama, jazz band, marching band, music ensembles, musical theater, symphony orchestra, fraternities, sororities, 40 religious, political, ethnic, social service, and professional organizations, 100 student organizations, 25 sports clubs.

ATHLETICS. NCAA. **Intercollegiate:** Baseball M, basketball, cross-country, diving, fencing, football M, golf, gymnastics W, rowing (crew), soccer M, softball W, swimming, tennis, track and field, volleyball W, wrestling M. **Intramural:** Badminton, basketball, cross-country, diving, fencing, gymnastics, handball, racquetball, rowing (crew) M, soccer, softball, squash, swimming, tennis, track and field, volleyball, wrestling M. **Clubs:** Archery W, ice hockey M, squash M, water polo, lacrosse, sailing, skiing, table tennis, rugby M.

STUDENT SERVICES. Career counseling, employment service for undergraduates, health services, personal counseling, placement service for graduates.

ANNUAL EXPENSES. Tuition and fees (projected): $17,902. **Room and board:** $6,610. **Books and supplies:** $550. **Other expenses:** $990.

FINANCIAL AID. 59% of freshmen, 53% of continuing students receive some form of aid. All grants, 91% of loans, all jobs based on need. 136 enrolled freshmen were judged to have need, all were offered aid. Academic scholarships available. **Aid applications:** Closing date February 1; applicants notified on or about April 15; must reply by May 1 or within 2 weeks if notified thereafter.

ADDRESS/TELEPHONE. Lawrence J. Momo, Director of Undergraduate Admissions, Columbia University: School of Engineering and Applied Science, 212 Hamilton Hall, Columbia University, New York, NY 10027. (212) 854-2521. Fax: (212) 854-1209.

Columbia University: School of General Studies

New York, New York — CB code: 2095

4-year private university and liberal arts college, coed. Founded in 1947. **Accreditation:** Regional. **Undergraduate enrollment:** 1,200 men and women. **Graduate enrollment:** 125 men and women. **Faculty:** 450 total, 450 with doctorates or other terminal degrees. **Location:** Urban campus in very large city. **Calendar:** Semester, extensive summer session. **Microcomputers:** 230 located in dormitories, libraries, computer centers. **Special facilities:** Rare book collection, 24 million manuscripts and over 350 online data bases. **Additional facts:** Liberal arts division of university for adult men and women and for younger students who have completed at least 2 full years of undergraduate study elsewhere or have jobs or professional activities that prevent them from attending college on full-time basis.

DEGREES OFFERED. BA, BS, MA. 260 bachelor's degrees awarded in 1992. 5% in computer sciences, 6% languages, 24% letters/literature, 6% philosophy, religion, theology, 5% psychology, 41% social sciences. Graduate degrees offered in 5 major fields of study.

UNDERGRADUATE MAJORS. Anthropology, applied mathematics, architecture, art history, biology, chemistry, cinematography/film, classics, comparative literature, computer and information sciences, creative writing, dramatic arts, East Asian studies, economics, English literature, French, geochemistry, geology, geophysics and seismology, German, Greek (classical), Hispanic American studies, history, Italian, Latin, mathematics, Middle Eastern studies, music, painting, philosophy, physics, political science and government, psychobiology, psychology, religion, Russian, Russian and Slavic studies, sculpture, Slavic languages, sociology, Spanish, statistics, terrestrial geology, urban studies, visual and performing arts, women's studies.

ACADEMIC PROGRAMS. Accelerated program, double major, honors program, independent study, internships, student-designed major, study abroad, teacher preparation, visiting/exchange student program, cross-registration, combined degree program with Jewish Theological Seminary, Juilliard School; liberal arts/career combination in engineering; combined bachelor's/graduate program in business administration, medicine, law. **Remedial services:** Learning center, preadmission summer program, reduced course load, remedial instruction, special counselor, tutoring, New York State Higher Education Opportunity Program. **Placement/credit:** AP, institutional tests; 30 credit hours maximum for bachelor's degree.

ACADEMIC REQUIREMENTS. Freshmen must earn minimum GPA of 2.0 to continue in good standing. Students must declare major by end of second year. **Graduation requirements:** 124 hours for bachelor's (30 in major). Most students required to take courses in arts/fine arts, English, foreign languages, humanities, mathematics, philosophy/religion, biological/physical sciences, social sciences.

FRESHMAN ADMISSIONS. Selection criteria: Essay, high school transcript, college transcript, test scores are most important. Applicants under 21 with less than 2 years of college must submit certification of number of hours a week involved in job or professional activity. Interviews encouraged. **High school preparation:** 13 units recommended. Recommended units include biological science 1, English 4, foreign language 2, mathematics 3, physical science 1 and social science 2. **Test requirements:** SAT or ACT; score report by September 1. Applicants under 21 must submit SAT or ACT scores. Applicants over 21 may take General Studies Aptitude Examination administered by University. English as a Second Language students must take American Language Program Placement Test, administered by institution. **Additional information:** Maturity and varied backgrounds of students considered. Aptitude and motivation important together with academic performance, test scores, and employment history.

1992 FRESHMAN CLASS PROFILE. 180 men and women enrolled. **Characteristics:** 85% from in state, 11% have minority backgrounds, 14% are foreign students. Average age is 25.

FALL-TERM APPLICATIONS. $35 fee, may be waived for applicants with need. Closing date July 15; applicants notified on a rolling basis; must reply by registration. Essay required. Interview recommended. Deferred admission available.

STUDENT LIFE. Housing: Dormitories (coed); apartment housing available. Limited on-campus housing available. Off-campus housing registry provides listings of Columbia affiliated apartments. **Activities:** Student government, magazine, radio, student newspaper, choral groups, dance, drama, music ensembles, musical theater, symphony orchestra, many religious, political, and ethnic organizations.

ATHLETICS. Intercollegiate: Baseball, basketball, cross-country, diving, fencing, field hockey W, football M, golf M, rowing (crew), soccer M, softball W, swimming, tennis, track and field, volleyball W, wrestling M. **Intramural:** Baseball M, basketball M, lacrosse M, racquetball, softball, squash.

STUDENT SERVICES. Aptitude testing, career counseling, employment service for undergraduates, freshman orientation, health services, personal counseling, placement service for graduates, special adviser for adult students, services/facilities for handicapped.

ANNUAL EXPENSES. Tuition and fees (1992-93): $14,972. **Books and supplies:** $900. **Other expenses:** $400.

FINANCIAL AID. 50% of freshmen, 50% of continuing students receive some form of aid. Grants, loans, jobs available. **Aid applications:** Closing date July 1; applicants notified on a rolling basis; must reply within 2 weeks.

ADDRESS/TELEPHONE. Barbara Tischler, Director of Admissions and Financial Aid, Columbia University: School of General Studies, 303 Lewisohn Hall, New York, NY 10027. (212) 854-3331.

Columbia University: School of Nursing
New York, New York

2-year upper-division private nursing college, coed. Founded in 1892. **Accreditation:** Regional. **Undergraduate enrollment:** 110 men and women. **Graduate enrollment:** 400 men and women. **Faculty:** 115 total (35 full time), 16 with doctorates or other terminal degrees. **Location:** Urban campus in very large city; in uptown Manhattan. **Calendar:** Semester, limited summer session. **Microcomputers:** Located in libraries, computer centers. **Additional facts:** Located on health sciences campus at Columbia Presbyterian Medical Center. Access to major university library system. Combined bachelor's/master's program offered in nursing.

DEGREES OFFERED. BS, MS, D. 50 bachelor's degrees awarded in 1992. 100% in health sciences. Graduate degrees offered in 3 major fields of study.

UNDERGRADUATE MAJORS. Nursing.

ACADEMIC PROGRAMS. Accelerated program, double major, independent study, cross-registration, combined MS/MPH with School of Public Health; liberal arts/nursing combination programs with Fordham University, Middlebury College, Nyack College, St. Lawrence University, and Stern College of Yeshiva University. **Remedial services:** Learning center, reduced course load, special counselor, tutoring. **ROTC:** Army. **Placement/credit:** Institutional tests; 30 credit hours maximum for bachelor's degree.

ACADEMIC REQUIREMENTS. Students must declare major on application. **Graduation requirements:** 120 hours for bachelor's (60 in major). Most students required to take courses in English, humanities, biological/physical sciences, social sciences. **Postgraduate studies:** 10% enter other graduate study. **Additional information:** Liberal arts courses available through Barnard College, School of General Studies, and Columbia College.

STUDENT LIFE. Housing: Dormitories (coed); apartment housing available. **Activities:** Student government, student newspaper, yearbook, choral groups, dance, drama, musical theater, various religious, political, ethnic, social service organizations. **Additional information:** Students guaranteed either on-site housing or parking.

STUDENT SERVICES. Career counseling, employment service for undergraduates, health services, personal counseling, placement service for graduates, special adviser for adult students, veterans counselor, services/facilities for handicapped.

ANNUAL EXPENSES. Tuition and fees (projected): $17,492. No annual meal plan; students buy meal cards in $50 increments. **Room and board:** $3,555 room only. **Books and supplies:** $1,400. **Other expenses:** $1,200.

FINANCIAL AID. 80% of continuing students receive some form of aid. Grants, loans, jobs available. Academic scholarships available. **Aid applications:** No closing date; priority given to applications received by April 15; applicants notified on a rolling basis beginning on or about May 1; must reply within 2 weeks.

ADDRESS/TELEPHONE. Dr. Cheryl Holly, Associate Dean of Student Affairs, Columbia University: School of Nursing, 617 West 168th Street, New York, NY 10032. (212) 305-5756.

Columbia-Greene Community College
Hudson, New York — CB code: 2138

2-year public community college, coed. Founded in 1966. **Accreditation:** Regional. **Undergraduate enrollment:** 431 men, 488 women full time; 286 men, 573 women part time. **Faculty:** 115 total (48 full time), 15 with doctorates or other terminal degrees. **Location:** Rural campus in small town; 30 miles from Albany. **Calendar:** Semester, limited summer session. **Microcomputers:** 53 located in classrooms, computer centers. **Special facilities:** 4 art galleries, Hudson River biological field station. **Additional facts:** SUNY institution.

DEGREES OFFERED. AA, AS, AAS. 281 associate degrees awarded in 1992. 25% in business/office and marketing/distribution, 15% computer sciences, 45% allied health, 13% social sciences.

UNDERGRADUATE MAJORS. Accounting, automotive mechanics, automotive technology, biological and physical sciences, business administration and management, business and office, business data entry equipment operation, business data processing and related programs, business data programming, computer and information sciences, criminal justice studies, data processing, English, finance, fine arts, funeral services/mortuary science, humanities, humanities and social sciences, insurance and risk management, law enforcement and corrections technologies, liberal/general studies, mathematics, nursing, real estate, science technologies, secretarial and related programs, social sciences, visual and performing arts, word processing.

ACADEMIC PROGRAMS. 2-year transfer program, cooperative education, dual enrollment of high school students, independent study, internships, student-designed major, cross-registration. **Remedial services:** Learning center, remedial instruction, special counselor, tutoring. **Placement/credit:** AP, CLEP General and Subject, institutional tests; 30 credit hours maximum for associate degree.

ACADEMIC REQUIREMENTS. No policy requiring minimum GPA; records of students having academic difficulty are reviewed individually. 60% of freshmen return for sophomore year. Students must declare major on application. **Graduation requirements:** 62 hours for associate. Most students required to take courses in English, humanities, mathematics, biological/physical sciences, social sciences.

FRESHMAN ADMISSIONS. Selection criteria: Open admissions. Selective admission to some programs based on school achievement record, test scores, and recommendations. Recommended units include English 3, foreign language 3, mathematics 3 and science 3.

1992 FRESHMAN CLASS PROFILE. 219 men, 252 women enrolled. **Characteristics:** 95% from in state, 100% commute, 7% have minority backgrounds, 1% are foreign students. Average age is 22.

FALL-TERM APPLICATIONS. $25 fee, may be waived for applicants with need. No closing date; applicants notified on a rolling basis; must reply within 4 weeks. Interview recommended. Deferred and early admission available.

STUDENT LIFE. Housing: College maintains regular communication with local realtors to assist students with housing needs. **Activities:** Student government, radio, student newspaper, yearbook, choral groups, drama, International Rotaract Club, minority alliance group, community theater troupe, College Union Board.

ATHLETICS. NJCAA. **Intercollegiate:** Baseball M, basketball, bowling, cross-country, soccer, softball W, volleyball. **Intramural:** Basketball, bowling, skiing, volleyball.

STUDENT SERVICES. Aptitude testing, career counseling, employment service for undergraduates, freshman orientation, on-campus day care, personal counseling, placement service for graduates, special adviser for adult students, veterans counselor, transfer counseling, services/facilities for handicapped.

ANNUAL EXPENSES. Tuition and fees (projected): $1,786, $1,680 additional for out-of-district students, $1,680 additional for out-of-state students. **Books and supplies:** $450. **Other expenses:** $950.

FINANCIAL AID. 75% of freshmen, 60% of continuing students re-

ceive some form of aid. 99% of grants, 67% of loans, all jobs based on need. Academic scholarships available. **Aid applications:** No closing date; priority given to applications received by May 1; applicants notified on a rolling basis beginning on or about June 15; must reply within 2 weeks.

ADDRESS/TELEPHONE. Patricia Hallenbeck, Director of Admissions/Registrar, Columbia-Greene Community College, PO Box 1000, Hudson, NY 12534. (518) 828-4181 ext. 364. Fax: (518) 828-8543.

Concordia College
Bronxville, New York — CB code: 2096

4-year private liberal arts college, coed, affiliated with Lutheran Church—Missouri Synod. Founded in 1881. **Accreditation:** Regional. **Undergraduate enrollment:** 197 men, 249 women full time; 35 men, 133 women part time. **Faculty:** 68 total (42 full time), 22 with doctorates or other terminal degrees. **Location:** Suburban campus in small town; 17 miles from New York City. **Calendar:** Semester, limited summer session. **Microcomputers:** Located in libraries, computer centers. **Special facilities:** 650-seat Sommer Center, electric-piano laboratory, art gallery. **Additional facts:** Christian principles central to program of study.

DEGREES OFFERED. AA, AS, BA, BS. 7 associate degrees awarded in 1992. 72 bachelor's degrees awarded.

UNDERGRADUATE MAJORS. Associate: Business and management, business and office, legal secretary, liberal/general studies, medical secretary, secretarial and related programs. **Bachelor's:** Behavioral sciences, biological and physical sciences, biology, business and management, business education, early childhood education, education, elementary education, English, English education, environmental science, history, humanities and social sciences, international studies, junior high education, liberal/general studies, mathematics, mathematics education, music, music education, music history and appreciation, music performance, music theory and composition, religion, religious music, science education, secondary education, social studies education, social work, theological studies.

ACADEMIC PROGRAMS. 2-year transfer program, accelerated program, double major, honors program, independent study, internships, student-designed major, study abroad, teacher preparation, cross-registration. **Remedial services:** Learning center, reduced course load, remedial instruction, tutoring, 7-credit Achiever's Program during first fall semester. **Placement/credit:** AP, CLEP General and Subject, institutional tests; 30 credit hours maximum for bachelor's degree.

ACADEMIC REQUIREMENTS. Freshmen must earn minimum GPA of 1.25 to continue in good standing. 75% of freshmen return for sophomore year. Students must declare major by end of second year. **Graduation requirements:** 66 hours for associate, 122 hours for bachelor's (30 in major). Most students required to take courses in English, history, mathematics, philosophy/religion, biological/physical sciences, social sciences.

FRESHMAN ADMISSIONS. Selection criteria: Test scores, school achievement record, interview, community and church involvement considered. **High school preparation:** 16 units required. Required and recommended units include English 4, mathematics 2, social science 2 and science 3-4. Foreign language 2 recommended. **Test requirements:** SAT or ACT; score report by August 1.

1992 FRESHMAN CLASS PROFILE. 44 men, 62 women enrolled. **Characteristics:** 70% from in state, 75% live in college housing, 11% have minority backgrounds, 10% are foreign students. Average age is 18.

FALL-TERM APPLICATIONS. $15 fee, may be waived for applicants with need. No closing date; applicants notified on a rolling basis; must reply by May 1 or within 4 weeks if notified thereafter. Interview required. Audition required for music applicants. Essay required for honors program applicants. CRDA. Deferred and early admission available.

STUDENT LIFE. Housing: Dormitories (men, women). **Activities:** Student government, magazine, student newspaper, television, yearbook, choral groups, concert band, drama, jazz band, music ensembles, musical theater, children's theater, touring choir, mime troupe, Student Religious Activities Committee, Christian service organizations, World Hunger Committee.

ATHLETICS. NCAA. **Intercollegiate:** Baseball M, basketball, cross-country, soccer M, softball W, tennis, volleyball. **Intramural:** Badminton, baseball M, basketball, bowling, handball, racquetball, soccer M, softball W, squash, table tennis, tennis, volleyball.

STUDENT SERVICES. Aptitude testing, career counseling, employment service for undergraduates, health services, personal counseling, placement service for graduates, special adviser for adult students, services/facilities for handicapped.

ANNUAL EXPENSES. Tuition and fees (1992-93): $9,370. **Room and board:** $4,330. **Books and supplies:** $400. **Other expenses:** $850.

FINANCIAL AID. 82% of freshmen, 72% of continuing students receive some form of aid. Grants, loans, jobs available. Academic, music/drama, athletic, alumni affiliation, religious affiliation, minority scholarships available. **Aid applications:** Closing date March 31; applicants notified on a rolling basis beginning on or about April 1; must reply by May 15.

ADDRESS/TELEPHONE. John Bahr, Director of Admissions, Concordia College, 171 White Plains Road, Bronxville, NY 10708. (914) 337-9300. Fax: (914) 395-4500.

Cooper Union
New York, New York — CB code: 2097

Admissions:	14% of applicants accepted
Based on:	••• School record, special talents, test scores
	• Activities, essay, recommendations
Completion:	90% of freshmen end year in good standing
	80% graduate, 61% of these enter graduate study

4-year private college of engineering, art, and architecture, coed. Founded in 1859. **Accreditation:** Regional. **Undergraduate enrollment:** 644 men, 302 women full time; 20 men, 17 women part time. **Graduate enrollment:** 34 men, 1 woman full time; 27 men, 5 women part time. **Faculty:** 188 total (60 full time), 88 with doctorates or other terminal degrees. **Location:** Urban campus in very large city. **Calendar:** Semester, limited summer session. **Microcomputers:** 90 located in computer centers. **Additional facts:** 5-year architecture program offers strong design orientation. Member of library consortium with New School for Social Research and New York University. Historical Great Hall has hosted lectures by notables since Abraham Lincoln

DEGREES OFFERED. BS, BFA, BArch, M. 192 bachelor's degrees awarded in 1992. 15% in architecture and environmental design, 55% engineering, 30% visual and performing arts. Graduate degrees offered in 4 major fields of study.

UNDERGRADUATE MAJORS. Architecture, chemical engineering, civil engineering, electrical/electronics/communications engineering, engineering, fine arts, graphic design, mechanical engineering.

ACADEMIC PROGRAMS. Honors program, independent study, internships, student-designed major, study abroad, visiting/exchange student program, cross-registration. **Remedial services:** Speech and writing. **Placement/credit:** AP, CLEP Subject, institutional tests.

ACADEMIC REQUIREMENTS. Freshmen must earn minimum 2.5 GPA in architecture and studio art courses and 2.2 minimum cumulative GPA in engineering. 94% of freshmen return for sophomore year. Students must declare major by end of first year. **Graduation requirements:** Most students required to take courses in English, history, humanities, mathematics, social sciences. **Postgraduate studies:** 3% enter law school, 3% enter medical school, 15% enter MBA programs, 40% enter other graduate study. **Additional information:** Engineering tutorials and engineering mentor program available. All freshman engineering majors required to prove or acquire computer literacy. 128 credit hours required for graduation in art program, 135 in engineering, and 169 in architecture.

FRESHMAN ADMISSIONS. Selection criteria: High school record, SAT and ACH scores for engineering applicants required. Art and architecture applicants selected on basis of design aptitude and/or artistic talent. SAT scores and high school GPA for latter also considered. **High school preparation:** 16 units required. Required units include English 4 and social science 2. One science required for architecture and art, 2 science and 3.5 mathematics for engineering including physics, chemistry, and pre-calculus, 1 mathematics for art, 3 mathematics for architecture including trigonometry. **Test requirements:** SAT or ACT (SAT preferred); score report by March 5. 2 ACH (including Mathematics Level I or II, and Chemistry or Physics) required of engineering applicants. Score report by March 5 Institutional examinations of art talent and/or design aptitude for architecture and art applicants. **Additional information:** SAT score ranges for middle 50% of fall 1992 freshman class: for art program, 380-550 verbal and 390-600 mathematics, for engineering program, 580-640 verbal and 690-750 mathematics, and for architecture program, 360-580 verbal and 490-650 mathematics.

1992 FRESHMAN CLASS PROFILE. 1,390 men applied, 219 accepted, 142 enrolled; 816 women applied, 98 accepted, 71 enrolled. 95% had high school GPA of 3.0 or higher, 5% between 2.0 and 2.99. 75% were in top tenth and 100% were in top quarter of graduating class. **Academic background:** Mid 50% of enrolled freshmen had SAT-V between 580-640, SAT-M between 690-750. 98% submitted SAT scores. **Characteristics:** 63% from in state, 62% live in college housing, 43% have minority backgrounds, 10% are foreign students. Average age is 18.

FALL-TERM APPLICATIONS. $25 fee, may be waived for applicants with need. Applicants notified on or about April 1; must reply by May 1. Portfolio required for art, architecture applicants. Essay required. CRDA. Deferred and early admission available. EDP-F. Application closing date for art January 10, for architecture January 1, for engineering February 1. Foreign students must apply from a domestic address.

STUDENT LIFE. Housing: Dormitories (coed); apartment housing available. Limited shared studio-type apartments available via lottery. **Activities:** Student government, film, magazine, student newspaper, yearbook, choral groups, music ensembles, fraternities, sororities, Catholic Culture Society, Chinese Students Association, Concerned Cooper Community, Hispanic, black, and Jewish organizations, Cooper Troopers, Habitat for Humanity.

ATHLETICS. Intercollegiate: Basketball, bowling, tennis. **Intramural:** Baseball, basketball, bowling, fencing, golf, soccer, softball, table tennis, tennis, volleyball.

STUDENT SERVICES. Career counseling, employment service for undergraduates, freshman orientation, health services, personal counseling, placement service for graduates, services/facilities for handicapped.

ANNUAL EXPENSES. Tuition and fees: $300. Every student admitted receives full tuition scholarship for duration of stay. **Room and board:** $8,415. **Books and supplies:** $1,255. **Other expenses:** $1,260.

FINANCIAL AID. 42% of freshmen, 40% of continuing students receive some form of aid. 97% of grants, 92% of loans, 22% of jobs based on need. 93 enrolled freshmen were judged to have need, all were offered aid. Academic scholarships available. **Aid applications:** Closing date May 1; priority given to applications received by February 15; applicants notified on or about May 1; must reply by June 1 or within 2 weeks. **Additional information:** All students receive a full-tution scholarship. Students able to document need receive financial aid package that may include combination of grants, loans, work-study, internships.

ADDRESS/TELEPHONE. Richard Bory, Dean of Admissions and Records, Cooper Union, 41 Cooper Square, New York, NY 10003-7183. (212) 353-4120. Fax: (212) 353-4343.

Cornell University

Ithaca, New York

CB code: 2098

Admissions: 32% of applicants accepted
Based on: ••• School record
•• Activities, essay, recommendations, test scores
• Interview, special talents
Completion: 95% of freshmen end year in good standing
88% graduate, 32% of these enter graduate study

4-year private university, coed. Founded in 1865. **Accreditation:** Regional. **Undergraduate enrollment:** 6,802 men, 5,761 women full time. **Graduate enrollment:** 3,456 men, 2,153 women full time. **Faculty:** 1,592 total (1,533 full time), 1,530 with doctorates or other terminal degrees. **Location:** Rural campus in large town; 60 miles from Syracuse. **Calendar:** Semester, extensive summer session. **Microcomputers:** Located in dormitories, libraries, classrooms, computer centers, campus-wide network. **Special facilities:** Art museum, plantations, ornithology laboratory, particle accelerator, biotechnology institute, supercomputer, 6 national research centers, 5 national resource centers, center for performing arts, observatory. **Additional facts:** 7 undergraduate colleges: agriculture and life sciences; architecture, art, and planning; arts and sciences; engineering; hotel administration; human ecology; industrial and labor relations. 6 graduate/professional colleges: Graduate School; Johnson Graduate School of Management; Law School; Veterinary Medicine. Medical College and Graduate School of Medicine in New York City.

DEGREES OFFERED. BA, BS, BFA, BArch, MA, MS, MBA, MFA, PhD, EdD, MD, DVM, JD. 3,442 bachelor's degrees awarded in 1992. 15% in agriculture, 11% business and management, 17% engineering, 7% home economics, 10% life sciences, 12% social sciences. Graduate degrees offered in 194 major fields of study.

UNDERGRADUATE MAJORS. African studies, agribusiness, agricultural business and management, agricultural economics, agricultural education, agricultural engineering, agricultural sciences, agronomy, American Indian studies, American studies, anatomy, animal sciences, anthropology, aquatic science, Arabic, archeology, architecture, art history, Asian studies, astronomy, atmospheric sciences and meteorology, behavioral sciences, biochemistry, biological and physical sciences, biology, biometrics and biostatistics, botany, business and management, business home economics, cell biology, chemical engineering, chemistry, Chinese, cinematography/film, city/community/regional planning, civil engineering, classics, communications, community services, comparative literature, computer and information sciences, crop science, dairy, dance, design communication, dramatic arts, ecology, economics, education, electrical/electronics/communications engineering, engineering, engineering and other disciplines, engineering physics, English, English education, entomology, environmental design, environmental health engineering, environmental science, European studies, family and community services, family/consumer resource management, fiber/textiles/weaving, fine arts, fishing and fisheries, food management, food science and nutrition, food sciences, foreign languages (multiple emphasis), foreign languages education, forestry and related sciences, French, genetics, human and animal, geological engineering, geology, German, German studies, Greek (modern), history, history of architecture and urban development, home economics, home economics education, horticultural science, hotel/motel and restaurant management, human environment and housing, humanities and social sciences, Indic languages, individual and family development, industrial engineering, interior design, international agriculture, international development, Islamic studies, Italian, Japanese, Jewish studies, Korean, labor/industrial relations, landscape architecture, Latin, Latin American studies, liberal/general studies, linguistics, livestock management, materials engineering, mathematics, mathematics education, mechanical engineering, medieval studies, microbiology, music, Near Eastern studies, neurosciences, nutritional sciences, operations research, ornamental horticulture, painting, philosophy, photography, physics, physiology, human and animal, plant genetics, plant pathology, plant protection, plant sciences, political science and government, pomology, Portuguese, poultry, prelaw, premedicine, preveterinary, printmaking, psychology, public affairs, religion, renewable natural resources, rural sociology, Russian, Russian and Slavic studies, Scandinavian languages, science education, sculpture, social sciences, social work, sociology, soil sciences, South Asian studies, Southeast Asian studies, Spanish, statistics, textiles and clothing, urban design, urban studies, Western European studies, wildlife management, women's studies, Yiddish.

ACADEMIC PROGRAMS. Accelerated program, cooperative education, double major, honors program, independent study, internships, semester at sea, student-designed major, study abroad, teacher preparation, visiting/exchange student program, New York semester, Washington semester, cross-registration, undergraduate research program; liberal arts/career combination in engineering; combined bachelor's/graduate program in business administration, medicine, law. **Remedial services:** Learning center, preadmission summer program, reduced course load, special counselor, tutoring. **ROTC:** Air Force, Army, Naval. **Placement/credit:** AP, IB, institutional tests. AP policy varies by department.

ACADEMIC REQUIREMENTS. Policies vary by division. 95% of freshmen return for sophomore year. Students must declare major by end of second year. **Graduation requirements:** 120 hours for bachelor's. Most students required to take courses in English. **Postgraduate studies:** 6% enter law school, 7% enter medical school, 1% enter MBA programs, 18% enter other graduate study. **Additional information:** Cornell/Hughes Scholars program for independent research in neurobiology, physiology, genetics and development, and biochemistry (molecular and cell biology); Cornell in Rome program for studies in architecture and fine arts; undergraduate research opportunities in traditional majors as well as in many interdisciplinary fields including American Indian studies, cognitive studies, and agriculture, food and society.

FRESHMAN ADMISSIONS. Selection criteria: Reviews both quantitative and qualitative information. School achievement record (difficulty of courses as well as grades earned), test scores, preparation and background for specific programs especially important. Some specialized programs have additional requirements. Essays, recommendations considered. Committed to enrolling underrepresented minority students. **High school preparation:** 16 units required. Required and recommended units include English 4 and mathematics 3. Foreign language 3 and science 3 recommended. Requirements vary by college. **Test requirements:** SAT or ACT; score report by February 1. 3 ACH required (including English Composition) for arts and sciences applicants; Mathematics I or II, English Composition, and a science ACH for engineering; Mathematics I or II and English Composition for industrial and labor relations if SAT submitted; English Composition, and Mathematics I or II for human ecology; Mathematics I or II for architecture. Score report by February 1. **Additional information:** Equality of educational opportunity vigorously supported. Affirmative action programs include Committee on Special Education Projects, Higher Education Opportunity Program, Educational Opportunity Program.

1992 FRESHMAN CLASS PROFILE. 11,270 men applied, 3,492 accepted, 1,551 enrolled; 9,054 women applied, 2,936 accepted, 1,408 enrolled. 84% were in top tenth and 95% were in top quarter of graduating class. **Academic background:** Mid 50% of enrolled freshmen had SAT-V between 540-650, SAT-M between 630-730. 99% submitted SAT scores. **Characteristics:** 91% live in college housing, 29% have minority backgrounds, 7% are foreign students. Average age is 18.

FALL-TERM APPLICATIONS. $60 fee, may be waived for applicants with need. Closing date January 1; applicants notified on or about April 5; must reply by May 1. Interview required for architecture, art, industrial and labor relations, hotel administration applicants. Portfolio required for art, architecture applicants. Essay required. CRDA. Deferred and early admission available. EDP-F. Agriculture and life sciences, industrial and labor relations, and hotel administration on rolling notifications with applicants notified between March 1 and April 15. Accepted applicants must reply by May 1.

STUDENT LIFE. Housing: Dormitories (men, women, coed); apartment, fraternity, sorority, cooperative housing available. Ecology house, JAM (Just About Music), Language House, International Living Center, Ujamaa Residential College (Third World house), Risley Residential College (theater and expresessive arts). **Activities:** Student government, magazine, radio, student newspaper, television, yearbook, choral groups, concert band, dance, drama, jazz band, marching band, music ensembles, musical theater, pep band, symphony orchestra, gospel choir, fraternities, sororities, over 500 campus organizations. **Additional information:** Of those undergraduates who do not reside in college housing, approximately one-third live in fraternity or sorority housing. Another 19%, including 9% of freshmen, live in their own apartments off campus.

ATHLETICS. NCAA. **Intercollegiate:** Baseball M, basketball, cross-country, diving, field hockey W, football M, golf M, ice hockey M, lacrosse, rifle M, rowing (crew), skiing, soccer, swimming, tennis, track and field, volleyball W, water polo M, wrestling M. **Intramural:** Badminton, basketball, bowling, cross-country, fencing, golf, ice hockey, lacrosse, sailing, skiing, soccer, softball, squash, swimming, tennis, track and field, volleyball, water polo M, wrestling M. **Clubs:** Ice hockey W, sailing, squash M.

STUDENT SERVICES. Aptitude testing, career counseling, employment service for undergraduates, freshman orientation, health services, personal counseling, placement service for graduates, veterans counselor,

counselor for the disabled, women's services, services/facilities for handicapped.

ANNUAL EXPENSES. Tuition and fees: $18,226. Tuition and fees for statutory divisions (Agriculture and Life Science, Human Ecology, and Industrial and Labor Relations): $7,426 for in-state residents, $14,106 for out-of-state. **Room and board:** $6,044. **Books and supplies:** $500. **Other expenses:** $1,030.

FINANCIAL AID. 70% of freshmen, 70% of continuing students receive some form of aid. All grants, 92% of loans, 74% of jobs based on need. 1,471 enrolled freshmen were judged to have need, all were offered aid. **Aid applications:** Closing date March 15; applicants notified on or about April 15; must reply by May 1.

ADDRESS/TELEPHONE. Susan H. Murphy, Dean of Admissions and Financial Aid, Cornell University, 410 Thurston Avenue, Ithaca, NY 14850. (607) 255-5241.

Corning Community College
Corning, New York CB code: 2106

2-year public community college, coed. Founded in 1956. **Accreditation:** Regional. **Undergraduate enrollment:** 944 men, 1,015 women full time; 826 men, 1,112 women part time. **Faculty:** 183 total (101 full time), 15 with doctorates or other terminal degrees. **Location:** Rural campus in large town; 20 miles from Elmira, 3 miles from Corning. **Calendar:** Semester, limited summer session. **Microcomputers:** 250 located in classrooms, computer centers. **Special facilities:** Nature center with alternate energy dwelling, astronomical observatory. **Additional facts:** SUNY institution.

DEGREES OFFERED. AA, AS, AAS. 617 associate degrees awarded in 1992. 16% in business and management, 8% engineering technologies, 10% health sciences, 5% allied health, 6% mathematics, 15% multi/interdisciplinary studies, 18% social sciences.

UNDERGRADUATE MAJORS. Accounting, automotive mechanics, automotive technology, business administration and management, business and management, business and office, business data processing and related programs, business data programming, chemical manufacturing technology, computer and information sciences, computer graphics, computer programming, computing graphics technology (CAD/CAM), criminal justice studies, data processing, electrical technology, electronic technology, engineering, engineering and engineering-related technologies, fine arts, fire control and safety technology, human services, humanities and social sciences, industrial technology, information sciences and systems, legal assistant/paralegal, liberal/general studies, mathematics, mathematics/science, mechanical design technology, nursing, secretarial and related programs, social sciences, word processing.

ACADEMIC PROGRAMS. 2-year transfer program, double major, dual enrollment of high school students, honors program, independent study, internships. **Remedial services:** Learning center, reduced course load, remedial instruction, special counselor, tutoring. **Placement/credit:** AP, CLEP General and Subject, institutional tests; 30 credit hours maximum for associate degree.

ACADEMIC REQUIREMENTS. Freshmen must earn minimum GPA of .75 to continue in good standing. 62% of freshmen return for sophomore year. Students must declare major on enrollment. **Graduation requirements:** 60 hours for associate (30 in major). Most students required to take courses in English, mathematics, biological/physical sciences, social sciences.

FRESHMAN ADMISSIONS. Selection criteria: Open admissions. Selective admissions to some programs. 4 mathematics and 4 science required of engineering science applicants; 1 algebra and 1 biology required of nursing applicants. **Additional information:** Applicants without diploma or GED evaluated on individual basis.

1992 FRESHMAN CLASS PROFILE. 520 men, 514 women enrolled. 4% had high school GPA of 3.0 or higher, 44% between 2.0 and 2.99. 3% were in top tenth and 18% were in top quarter of graduating class. **Characteristics:** 95% from in state, 100% commute, 4% have minority backgrounds, 1% are foreign students. Average age is 23.

FALL-TERM APPLICATIONS. $25 fee, may be waived for applicants with need. No closing date; applicants notified on a rolling basis; must reply immediately. Early admission available.

STUDENT LIFE. Activities: Student government, radio, student newspaper, choral groups, dance, drama, music ensembles, Human Services Club, Law Society, REACH, International Club, Nursing Society, African-American Cultural Awareness Club, Christian Club, College Republicans.

ATHLETICS. NJCAA. **Intercollegiate:** Baseball M, basketball, lacrosse M, soccer M, softball W, volleyball W, wrestling M. **Intramural:** Archery, badminton, basketball, bowling, cross-country, golf, skiing, swimming, table tennis, tennis, volleyball.

STUDENT SERVICES. Career counseling, employment service for undergraduates, freshman orientation, health services, personal counseling, placement service for graduates, off-campus day care center, services/facilities for handicapped.

ANNUAL EXPENSES. Tuition and fees (projected): $2,146, $2,000 additional for out-of-state students. **Books and supplies:** $520. **Other expenses:** $400.

FINANCIAL AID. 85% of freshmen, 85% of continuing students receive some form of aid. All grants, 93% of loans, 92% of jobs based on need. 800 enrolled freshmen were judged to have need, all were offered aid. **Aid applications:** No closing date; priority given to applications received by July 1; applicants notified on a rolling basis beginning on or about June 1; must reply within 2 weeks.

ADDRESS/TELEPHONE. David N. Biviano, Director of Admissions, Corning Community College, Spencer Hill, Corning, NY 14830. (607) 962-9220. (800) 358-7171. Fax: (607) 962-9456.

Culinary Institute of America
Hyde Park, New York CB code: 3301

Admissions: 79% of applicants accepted
Based on:
••• Special talents
•• Essay, interview, recommendations, school record
• Test scores
Completion: 87% of freshmen end year in good standing

2-year private technical college, coed. Founded in 1946. **Undergraduate enrollment:** 1,511 men, 412 women full time. **Faculty:** 101 total (99 full time). **Location:** Suburban campus in large town; 80 miles from New York City. **Calendar:** 4 terms of 15 weeks and externship term of 21 weeks. **Microcomputers:** Located in classrooms, computer centers. **Special facilities:** Audiovisual library on food service industry. **Additional facts:** Curriculum devoted exclusively to culinary training. Terms 1, 2, 4, and 5 in residence. Term 3 is externship-work program. Students may enroll at any of 16 starting dates throughout year. Enrollment at each entry limited to 72 .

DEGREES OFFERED. 950 associate degrees awarded in 1992. 10% in business/office and marketing/distribution, 90% home economics.

UNDERGRADUATE MAJORS. Baking and pastry arts, food production/management/services, hospitality and recreation marketing.

ACADEMIC PROGRAMS. Internships, cross-registration. **Remedial services:** Learning center, remedial instruction, special counselor, tutoring.

ACADEMIC REQUIREMENTS. Freshmen must earn minimum GPA of 2.0 to continue in good standing. 92% of freshmen return for sophomore year. Students must declare major on application. **Graduation requirements:** 81 hours for associate. **Additional information:** Two-thirds of class time involves cooking, baking, table service, and dining room operations management in nutrition, cafe, and haute cuisine restaurants.

FRESHMAN ADMISSIONS. Selection criteria: School achievement record, work experience, particularly in food preparation, and interview. **High school preparation:** 6 units recommended. Recommended units include English 4 and mathematics 2.

1992 FRESHMAN CLASS PROFILE. 1,478 men applied, 1,152 accepted, 891 enrolled; 325 women applied, 280 accepted, 234 enrolled. **Characteristics:** 31% from in state, 75% live in college housing, 18% have minority backgrounds, 2% are foreign students. Average age is 22.

FALL-TERM APPLICATIONS. $30 fee. No closing date; applicants notified on a rolling basis; must reply within 8 weeks. Essay required. Interview recommended. Deferred admission available. Applicants should apply 4-6 months prior to desired starting date.

STUDENT LIFE. Housing: Dormitories (coed). **Activities:** Student government, film, radio, student newspaper, television, Gourmet Society, Barmen's Society, Maitre d'Hotel, Epicures of Wine, Women in Industry, Bakers Club, Sauciers Club, and Dormitory Council. **Additional information:** 45% of enrolled students have had prior college experience, including other degrees.

ATHLETICS. Intercollegiate: Ice hockey M. **Intramural:** Soccer M, softball, tennis, volleyball.

STUDENT SERVICES. Career counseling, employment service for undergraduates, health services, personal counseling, placement service for graduates, special adviser for adult students, veterans counselor, services/facilities for handicapped.

ANNUAL EXPENSES. Tuition and fees (1992-93): $11,615. Board included in tuition. **Room and board:** $3,450 room only. **Other expenses:** $1,300.

FINANCIAL AID. 75% of freshmen, 75% of continuing students receive some form of aid. Grants, loans, jobs available. Academic, leadership scholarships available. **Aid applications:** No closing date; applicants notified on a rolling basis; must reply within 2 weeks.

ADDRESS/TELEPHONE. Janis Wertz, Associate Vice President of Administration, Culinary Institute of America, 433 Albany Post Road, Hyde Park, NY 12538-1499. (914) 452-9430. (800) CULINARY. Fax: (914) 452-8629.

Daemen College
Amherst, New York CB code: 2762

4-year private liberal arts college, coed. Founded in 1947. **Accreditation:** Regional. **Undergraduate enrollment:** 404 men, 787 women full time; 85

men, 431 women part time. **Faculty:** 152 total (68 full time). **Location:** Suburban campus in large town; 5 miles from Buffalo. **Calendar:** Semester, limited summer session. **Microcomputers:** 80 located in computer centers. **Special facilities:** Art gallery.

DEGREES OFFERED. BA, BS, BFA, MS. 247 bachelor's degrees awarded in 1992.

UNDERGRADUATE MAJORS. Accounting, allied health, art education, biology, business administration and management, business and management, business economics, business education, chemistry, clinical laboratory science, drawing, education, elementary education, English, English education, fine arts, foreign languages education, French, graphic design, history, humanities and social sciences, illustration design, junior high education, management information systems, marketing management, mathematics, mathematics education, medical laboratory technologies, nursing, painting, physical therapy, predentistry, prelaw, premedicine, preveterinary, printmaking, psychology, public relations, religion, science education, sculpture, secondary education, social science education, social studies education, social work, Spanish, special education, tourism, transportation and travel marketing.

ACADEMIC PROGRAMS. Cooperative education, double major, dual enrollment of high school students, independent study, internships, study abroad, teacher preparation, cross-registration, 2-year bachelor's program in nursing for RN's (upper division only). **Remedial services:** Learning center, preadmission summer program, reduced course load, remedial instruction, tutoring. **ROTC:** Army. **Placement/credit:** AP, CLEP General and Subject, institutional tests.

ACADEMIC REQUIREMENTS. Freshmen must earn minimum GPA of 2.0 to continue in good standing. Students must declare major by end of second year. **Graduation requirements:** 123 hours for bachelor's (60 in major). Most students required to take courses in arts/fine arts, English, history, mathematics, philosophy/religion, biological/physical sciences, social sciences.

FRESHMAN ADMISSIONS. Selection criteria: Emphasis on academic achievement and test scores with secondary consideration given to school activities and recommendations. **High school preparation:** 9 units recommended. Recommended units include English 3, mathematics 3 and science 3. Most science and medical programs require 3 mathematics and 3 science. Business program requires 3 mathematics. **Test requirements:** SAT or ACT (SAT preferred); score report by September 2. **Additional information:** Applications reviewed individually by admissions committee.

1992 FRESHMAN CLASS PROFILE. 98 men, 214 women enrolled. **Characteristics:** 85% from in state, 63% live in college housing, 22% have minority backgrounds, 2% are foreign students. Average age is 18.

FALL-TERM APPLICATIONS. $15 fee, may be waived for applicants with need. No closing date; priority given to applications received by January 1; applicants notified on a rolling basis; must reply within 4 weeks. Portfolio required for art applicants. Interview recommended. Deferred and early admission available.

STUDENT LIFE. Housing: Dormitories (men, women); apartment housing available. **Activities:** Student government, magazine, student newspaper, yearbook, drama, musical theater, fraternities, sororities, campus ministry and veterans affairs, United Student Caucus.

ATHLETICS. NAIA. **Intercollegiate:** Basketball. **Intramural:** Basketball, football M, golf, lacrosse, racquetball, skiing, softball, table tennis, volleyball.

STUDENT SERVICES. Aptitude testing, career counseling, employment service for undergraduates, freshman orientation, personal counseling, placement service for graduates, veterans counselor, services/facilities for handicapped.

ANNUAL EXPENSES. Tuition and fees: $8,730. **Room and board:** $4,350. **Books and supplies:** $700. **Other expenses:** $800.

FINANCIAL AID. 93% of freshmen, 96% of continuing students receive some form of aid. 91% of grants, 84% of loans, 91% of jobs based on need. 223 enrolled freshmen were judged to have need, all were offered aid. Academic, athletic scholarships available. **Aid applications:** No closing date; priority given to applications received by February 15; applicants notified on a rolling basis beginning on or about March 1; must reply within 2 weeks.

ADDRESS/TELEPHONE. Maria P. Dillard, Director of Admissions/Enrollment Management, Daemen College, 4380 Main Street, Amherst, NY 14226-3592. (716) 839-8225. Fax: (716) 839-8516.

Darkei No'Am Rabbinical College
Brooklyn, New York — CB code: 1270

5-year private rabbinical college, men only, affiliated with Jewish faith. Founded in 1977. **Undergraduate enrollment:** 45 men full time. **Graduate enrollment:** 6 men full time. **Location:** Urban campus in very large city. **Calendar:** Semester. **Additional facts:** First and second Talmudic degrees offered.

FRESHMAN ADMISSIONS. Selection criteria: Precollege rabbinical requirements, entrance examination, interview important.

ADDRESS/TELEPHONE. Rabbi Horowitz, Director of Admissions, Darkei No'Am Rabbinical College, 2822 Avenue J, Brooklyn, NY 11210. (718) 338-6464.

Dominican College of Blauvelt
Orangeburg, New York — CB code: 2190

4-year private liberal arts college, coed, affiliated with Roman Catholic Church. Founded in 1952. **Accreditation:** Regional. **Undergraduate enrollment:** 253 men, 500 women full time; 210 men, 580 women part time. **Faculty:** 132 total (52 full time), 27 with doctorates or other terminal degrees. **Location:** Suburban campus in small town; 17 miles from New York City. **Calendar:** Semester, limited summer session. **Microcomputers:** 86 located in dormitories, classrooms, computer centers.

DEGREES OFFERED. AA, BA, BS. 10 associate degrees awarded in 1992. 100% in multi/interdisciplinary studies. 200 bachelor's degrees awarded. 43% in business and management, 34% health sciences, 5% multi/interdisciplinary studies, 6% psychology, 7% social sciences.

UNDERGRADUATE MAJORS. Associate: Liberal/general studies. **Bachelor's:** Accounting, actuarial sciences, American studies, business administration and management, business and management, business economics, computer and information sciences, computer programming, early childhood education, economics, education, education of the mentally handicapped, education of the visually handicapped, elementary education, English, English education, English literature, finance, foreign languages (multiple emphasis), health care administration, history, human resources development, humanities and social sciences, information sciences and systems, international business management, liberal/general studies, management information systems, marketing management, mathematics, mathematics education, nursing, occupational therapy, political science and government, prelaw, psychology, public administration, science education, secondary education, social science education, social sciences, social studies education, social work, sociology, Spanish, special education.

ACADEMIC PROGRAMS. Accelerated program, cooperative education, dual enrollment of high school students, honors program, independent study, internships, teacher preparation, weekend college, cross-registration, upper-division occupational therapy program; liberal arts/career combination in engineering. **Remedial services:** Learning center, reduced course load, remedial instruction, special counselor, tutoring. **ROTC:** Army. **Placement/credit:** AP, CLEP General and Subject, institutional tests; 30 credit hours maximum for associate degree; 60 credit hours maximum for bachelor's degree.

ACADEMIC REQUIREMENTS. Freshmen must earn minimum GPA of 2.0 to continue in good standing. 70% of freshmen return for sophomore year. Students must declare major by end of second year. **Graduation requirements:** 60 hours for associate, 120 hours for bachelor's. Most students required to take courses in English, history, humanities, mathematics, biological/physical sciences.

FRESHMAN ADMISSIONS. Selection criteria: High school GPA, class rank, SAT or ACT scores, interview, recommendations, and school and community activities important. **High school preparation:** 16 units recommended. Recommended units include English 4, foreign language 2, mathematics 2 and science 2. **Test requirements:** SAT or ACT (SAT preferred); score report by August 15.

1992 FRESHMAN CLASS PROFILE. 104 men and women enrolled. 14% had high school GPA of 3.0 or higher, 66% between 2.0 and 2.99. **Academic background:** Mid 50% of enrolled freshmen had SAT-V between 270-390, SAT-M between 310-400. 91% submitted SAT scores. **Characteristics:** 70% from in state, 85% commute, 30% have minority backgrounds. Average age is 19.

FALL-TERM APPLICATIONS. $25 fee, may be waived for applicants with need. Closing date September 1; applicants notified on a rolling basis; must reply by May 15 or within 30 days if notified thereafter. Interview recommended. Essay recommended. CRDA. Deferred and early admission available. EDP-F.

STUDENT LIFE. Housing: Dormitories (coed). **Activities:** Student government, magazine, student newspaper, yearbook, choral groups, drama, Alpha Club, Council for Exceptional Children, Association for Education of the Visually Handicapped, National Honor Society, nursing association, psychology club, business club, social work club, campus ministry.

ATHLETICS. NAIA. **Intercollegiate:** Baseball M, basketball, cross-country, golf M, soccer, softball W, volleyball W. **Intramural:** Basketball, softball, volleyball.

STUDENT SERVICES. Career counseling, employment service for undergraduates, freshman orientation, personal counseling, placement service for graduates, special adviser for adult students, services/facilities for handicapped.

ANNUAL EXPENSES. Tuition and fees (projected): $8,060. **Room and board:** $5,540. **Books and supplies:** $500. **Other expenses:** $900.

FINANCIAL AID. 75% of freshmen, 41% of continuing students receive some form of aid. 97% of grants, all loans, 68% of jobs based on need. 56 enrolled freshmen were judged to have need, all were offered aid. Academic, athletic, leadership, religious affiliation scholarships available. **Aid**

applications: No closing date; priority given to applications received by March 1; applicants notified on a rolling basis beginning on or about April 15; must reply by May 1 or within 2 weeks if notified thereafter.

ADDRESS/TELEPHONE. Harry White, Director of Admissions, Dominican College of Blauvelt, 470 Western Highway, Orangeburg, NY 10962. (914) 359-7800. Fax: (914) 359-2313.

Dowling College
Oakdale, New York CB code: 2011

Admissions:	68% of applicants accepted
Based on:	••• School record
	•• Test scores
	• Activities, interview, recommendations, special talents
Completion:	70% of freshmen end year in good standing
	30% graduate, 25% of these enter graduate study

4-year private college of arts and sciences and business college, coed. Founded in 1959. **Accreditation:** Regional. **Undergraduate enrollment:** 483 men, 696 women full time; 950 men, 1,344 women part time. **Graduate enrollment:** 6 men, 8 women full time; 579 men, 973 women part time. **Faculty:** 377 total (93 full time), 134 with doctorates or other terminal degrees. **Location:** Suburban campus in large town; 50 miles from New York City. **Calendar:** Semester, extensive summer session. **Microcomputers:** 77 located in libraries, computer centers. **Special facilities:** Dowling College/Anthony Giordano Art Gallery.

DEGREES OFFERED. BA, BS, MBA, MEd. 790 bachelor's degrees awarded in 1992. 50% in business and management, 18% education, 8% physical sciences, 8% social sciences. Graduate degrees offered in 6 major fields of study.

UNDERGRADUATE MAJORS. Accounting, air traffic control, airline piloting and navigation, anthropology, applied mathematics, art education, aviation computer technology, aviation management, biological and physical sciences, biology, business administration and management, business and management, business education, computer and information sciences, dramatic arts, economics, education, elementary education, English, English education, foreign languages (multiple emphasis), foreign languages education, history, humanities and social sciences, liberal/general studies, management information systems, marine biology, marketing management, mathematics, mathematics education, music education, physical sciences, psychology, science education, secondary education, social sciences, social studies education, sociology, special education, speech, visual and performing arts.

ACADEMIC PROGRAMS. Accelerated program, cooperative education, double major, dual enrollment of high school students, independent study, internships, teacher preparation, weekend college, cross-registration, Federal Aviation Agency cooperative program; combined bachelor's/graduate program in business administration. **Remedial services:** Learning center, preadmission summer program, reduced course load, tutoring, writing laboratory, New York State Higher Education Opportunity Program. **ROTC:** Air Force. **Placement/credit:** AP, CLEP General and Subject, institutional tests; 30 credit hours maximum for bachelor's degree.

ACADEMIC REQUIREMENTS. Freshmen must earn minimum GPA of 2.0 to continue in good standing. 67% of freshmen return for sophomore year. Students must declare major by end of second year. **Graduation requirements:** 120 hours for bachelor's (36 in major). Most students required to take courses in arts/fine arts, English, mathematics, biological/physical sciences, social sciences. **Additional information:** Optional winter term enables students to take 2 additional courses.

FRESHMAN ADMISSIONS. Selection criteria: Program of study, recent achievement, academic rank, school record, interview, standardized test scores, counselor's recommendation. **High school preparation:** 16 units required. Required units include English 4. Minimum of 8 units from mathematics (including intermediate algebra), science, history, foreign language recommended. **Test requirements:** SAT or ACT; score report by September 1.

1992 FRESHMAN CLASS PROFILE. 330 men applied, 225 accepted, 151 enrolled; 456 women applied, 310 accepted, 206 enrolled. 28% had high school GPA of 3.0 or higher, 67% between 2.0 and 2.99. **Academic background:** Mid 50% of enrolled freshmen had SAT-V between 330-430, SAT-M between 380-530; ACT composite between 15-20. 61% submitted SAT scores, 19% submitted ACT scores. **Characteristics:** 96% from in state, 92% commute, 8% have minority backgrounds. Average age is 19.

FALL-TERM APPLICATIONS. $25 fee, may be waived for applicants with need. No closing date; applicants notified on a rolling basis; must reply within 3 weeks. Interview recommended. Deferred and early admission available.

STUDENT LIFE. Housing: Apartment housing available. **Activities:** Student government, magazine, radio, student newspaper, yearbook, choral groups, dance, drama, jazz band, music ensembles, musical theater, symphony orchestra, 23 clubs and organizations related to academics, honor societies in business, education, economics, and psychology, Circle-K, computer science, national dean's list, Who's Who, Scholarship Society.

ATHLETICS. NCAA. **Intercollegiate:** Baseball M, basketball, golf M, lacrosse M, rowing (crew), soccer M, softball W, tennis, volleyball W. **Intramural:** Basketball, bowling, sailing.

STUDENT SERVICES. Career counseling, employment service for undergraduates, freshman orientation, health services, personal counseling, placement service for graduates, special adviser for adult students, services/facilities for handicapped.

ANNUAL EXPENSES. Tuition and fees (1992-93): $8,690. **Room and board:** $2,700 room only. **Books and supplies:** $450. **Other expenses:** $1,413.

FINANCIAL AID. 70% of freshmen, 75% of continuing students receive some form of aid. 80% of grants, 92% of loans, 72% of jobs based on need. Academic, athletic scholarships available. **Aid applications:** Closing date August 1; applicants notified on a rolling basis beginning on or about March 1; must reply within 4 weeks.

ADDRESS/TELEPHONE. Stephen Dougherty, Assistant Provost of Enrollment Services, Dowling College, Idle Hour Boulevard, Oakdale, NY 11769-1999. (516) 244-3030. (800) 258-1112. Fax: (516) 563-3827.

Dutchess Community College
Poughkeepsie, New York CB code: 2198

2-year public community college, coed. Founded in 1957. **Accreditation:** Regional. **Undergraduate enrollment:** 7,693 men and women. **Faculty:** 429 total (149 full time). **Location:** Suburban campus in large town; 70 miles from New York City. **Calendar:** Semester, limited summer session. **Microcomputers:** 135 located in classrooms, computer centers. **Special facilities:** Biological experimentation site on Hudson River. **Additional facts:** SUNY institution. Extension programs at 6 sites.

DEGREES OFFERED. AA, AS, AAS. 910 associate degrees awarded in 1992. 32% in business and management, 5% business/office and marketing/distribution, 14% health sciences, 18% multi/interdisciplinary studies, 6% social sciences.

UNDERGRADUATE MAJORS. Accounting, architectural technologies, biological and physical sciences, business administration and management, business data processing and related programs, child development/care/guidance, clinical laboratory science, communications, computer and information sciences, computer programming, criminal justice studies, criminology, drafting, drafting and design technology, early childhood education, earth sciences, electrical technology, electromechanical technology, engineering, engineering and engineering-related technologies, food production/management/services, food science and nutrition, graphic arts technology, humanities and social sciences, liberal/general studies, mathematics, mechanical design technology, medical laboratory technologies, nursing, orthotics technology, recreation and community services technologies, renewable natural resources, retailing, secretarial and related programs.

ACADEMIC PROGRAMS. 2-year transfer program, cooperative education, dual enrollment of high school students, honors program, independent study, internships, study abroad, cross-registration, combined degree in elementary education with SUNY at New Paltz. **Remedial services:** Learning center, preadmission summer program, reduced course load, remedial instruction, special counselor, tutoring. **Placement/credit:** AP, CLEP General and Subject, institutional tests; 40 credit hours maximum for associate degree.

ACADEMIC REQUIREMENTS. Freshmen must earn minimum GPA of 1.75 to continue in good standing. 50% of freshmen return for sophomore year. Students must declare major on application. **Graduation requirements:** 64 hours for associate (30 in major). Most students required to take courses in English, history, biological/physical sciences, social sciences.

FRESHMAN ADMISSIONS. Selection criteria: Open admissions. Selective admission to nursing and engineering programs.

1992 FRESHMAN CLASS PROFILE. 1,488 men and women enrolled. **Characteristics:** 100% commute, 16% have minority backgrounds. Average age is 18.

FALL-TERM APPLICATIONS. $25 fee, may be waived for applicants with need. No closing date; applicants notified on a rolling basis. Portfolio required for art applicants. Early admission available.

STUDENT LIFE. Activities: Student government, film, radio, student newspaper, television, choral groups, dance, drama, jazz band, special interest clubs, foreign student organization.

ATHLETICS. NJCAA. **Intercollegiate:** Baseball M, basketball, bowling, cross-country, golf, soccer, softball W, tennis, volleyball W. **Intramural:** Archery, basketball, bowling, fencing, racquetball, softball, tennis, volleyball.

STUDENT SERVICES. Aptitude testing, career counseling, employment service for undergraduates, freshman orientation, health services, on-campus day care, personal counseling, placement service for graduates, special adviser for adult students, veterans counselor, services/facilities for handicapped.

ANNUAL EXPENSES. Tuition and fees (projected): $1,845, $1,750 additional for out-of-state students. **Books and supplies:** $560. **Other expenses:** $750.

FINANCIAL AID. 50% of freshmen, 50% of continuing students receive some form of aid. 99% of grants, 64% of loans based on need. Academic scholarships available. **Aid applications:** No closing date; priority given to applications received by May 1; applicants notified on a rolling basis beginning on or about May 15; must reply within 2 weeks.

ADDRESS/TELEPHONE. Alexander Cutonilli, Director of Admissions, Dutchess Community College, Pendell Road, Poughkeepsie, NY 12601-1595. (914) 471-4500. Fax: (914) 471-8467.

D'Youville College
Buffalo, New York CB code: 2197

Admissions: 73% of applicants accepted
Based on:
••• School record
•• Test scores
• Activities, essay, interview, recommendations, special talents
Completion: 76% of freshmen end year in good standing
43% graduate, 24% of these enter graduate study

4-year private liberal arts college, coed. Founded in 1908. **Accreditation:** Regional. **Undergraduate enrollment:** 244 men, 767 women full time; 59 men, 267 women part time. **Graduate enrollment:** 23 men, 119 women full time; 24 men, 218 women part time. **Faculty:** 128 total (81 full time), 57 with doctorates or other terminal degrees. **Location:** Urban campus in large city; 2 miles from downtown. **Calendar:** Semester, extensive summer session. Extensive evening/early morning classes. **Microcomputers:** Located in dormitories, libraries, classrooms, computer centers. **Special facilities:** Equipment for blind and visually impaired including computer system with speech synthesizer, Braille printer, versabraille, and print enhancer.

DEGREES OFFERED. BA, BS, MS, MEd. 225 bachelor's degrees awarded in 1992. 15% in business and management, 14% education, 61% health sciences. Graduate degrees offered in 6 major fields of study.

UNDERGRADUATE MAJORS. Accounting, American literature, bilingual/bicultural education, biology, business administration and management, business and management, business education, computer and information sciences, computer science education, creative writing, education, education of the emotionally handicapped, education of the mentally handicapped, education of the multiple handicapped, education of the physically handicapped, education of the visually handicapped, elementary education, English, English education, food science and nutrition, history, human resources development, humanities and social sciences, management information systems, marketing management, mathematics, mathematics education, nursing, occupational therapy, personnel management, philosophy, physical therapy, physician's assistant, predentistry, prelaw, premedicine, preveterinary, science education, secondary education, social sciences, social studies education, social work, sociology, special education, specific learning disabilities.

ACADEMIC PROGRAMS. Accelerated program, double major, honors program, independent study, internships, study abroad, teacher preparation, visiting/exchange student program, weekend college, cross-registration. **Remedial services:** Learning center, preadmission summer program, reduced course load, remedial instruction, special counselor, tutoring, summer skills building program. **ROTC:** Army. **Placement/credit:** AP, CLEP General and Subject, institutional tests; 30 credit hours maximum for bachelor's degree.

ACADEMIC REQUIREMENTS. Freshmen must earn minimum GPA of 1.8 to continue in good standing. 70% of freshmen return for sophomore year. Students must declare major by end of second year. **Graduation requirements:** 120 hours for bachelor's (68 in major). Most students required to take courses in computer science, English, history, humanities, mathematics, philosophy/religion, biological/physical sciences, social sciences. **Postgraduate studies:** 3% enter law school, 3% enter medical school, 6% enter MBA programs, 12% enter other graduate study.

FRESHMAN ADMISSIONS. Selection criteria: High school GPA, class rank, SAT or ACT scores important. Interview, essay, letters of recommendation optional. Three recommendations required for physician assistant's program. **High school preparation:** 16 units required. Required and recommended units include English 4, mathematics 1-3 and science 1-3. Biological science 1, physical science 1 and social science 2 recommended. Biology and chemistry required for nursing, occupational therapy, physical therapy, dietetics, and physician's assistant programs. 3 years mathematics for accounting. **Test requirements:** SAT or ACT; score report by August 31. **Additional information:** Students admitted to major at freshman year.

1992 FRESHMAN CLASS PROFILE. 88% had high school GPA of 3.0 or higher, 11% between 2.0 and 2.99. **Academic background:** Mid 50% of enrolled freshmen had SAT-V between 400-500, SAT-M between 450-550; ACT composite between 22-23. 95% submitted SAT scores, 30% submitted ACT scores. **Characteristics:** 85% from in state, 55% live in college housing, 16% have minority backgrounds, 1% are foreign students. Average age is 18.

FALL-TERM APPLICATIONS. $20 fee, may be waived for applicants with need. No closing date; applicants notified on a rolling basis; must reply by May 1 or within 2 weeks if notified thereafter. Essay recommended for academically marginal applicants. Interview required for physician assistant program, recommended for all. CRDA. Deferred admission available.

STUDENT LIFE. Housing: Dormitories (coed). Quiet floors for third through fifth-year students. **Activities:** Student government, student newspaper, yearbook, literary journal, Black Student Union, Latin American Club, campus ministry, Lambda Sigma, writers club, and Student Nurses Association.

ATHLETICS. NSCAA. **Intercollegiate:** Basketball, volleyball W. **Intramural:** Basketball, skiing, soccer M, softball, swimming, table tennis, volleyball.

STUDENT SERVICES. Aptitude testing, career counseling, employment service for undergraduates, freshman orientation, health services, personal counseling, placement service for graduates, special adviser for adult students, veterans counselor, services/facilities for handicapped.

ANNUAL EXPENSES. Tuition and fees: $8,720. **Room and board:** $4,130. **Books and supplies:** $650. **Other expenses:** $680.

FINANCIAL AID. 95% of freshmen, 89% of continuing students receive some form of aid. 69% of grants, all loans, 71% of jobs based on need. Academic, athletic, leadership scholarships available. **Aid applications:** No closing date; priority given to applications received by April 15; applicants notified on a rolling basis beginning on or about April 15; must reply within 30 days.

ADDRESS/TELEPHONE. Ronald H. Dannecker, Director of Admissions/Financial Aid, D'Youville College, 320 Porter Avenue, Buffalo, NY 14201-1084. (716) 881-7600. (800) 777-3921. Fax: (716) 881-7790.

Eastman School of Music of the University of Rochester
Rochester, New York CB code: 2224

Admissions: 38% of applicants accepted
Based on:
••• Special talents
•• Interview, recommendations, school record, test scores
• Essay
Completion: 96% of freshmen end year in good standing
80% graduate, 60% of these enter graduate study

4-year private music college, coed. Founded in 1921. **Accreditation:** Regional. **Undergraduate enrollment:** 220 men, 238 women full time. **Graduate enrollment:** 105 men, 132 women full time; 31 men, 42 women part time. **Faculty:** 105 total (88 full time), 49 with doctorates or other terminal degrees. **Location:** Urban campus in large city. **Calendar:** Semester, limited summer session. **Microcomputers:** 15 located in dormitories, libraries, computer centers, campus-wide network. **Special facilities:** Professional recording studios, Sibley Music Library (largest collegiate music library in the country).

DEGREES OFFERED. BA, MA, PhD. 91 bachelor's degrees awarded in 1992. 13% in teacher education, 87% visual and performing arts. Graduate degrees offered in 5 major fields of study.

UNDERGRADUATE MAJORS. Music, music education, music performance, music theory and composition.

ACADEMIC PROGRAMS. Double major, teacher preparation. **Placement/credit:** AP, institutional tests.

ACADEMIC REQUIREMENTS. Freshmen must earn minimum GPA of 2.0 to continue in good standing. 90% of freshmen return for sophomore year. Students must declare major on application. **Graduation requirements:** 131 hours for bachelor's (107 in major). Most students required to take courses in English, humanities.

FRESHMAN ADMISSIONS. Selection criteria: Proficiency on instrument most important, followed by academic record, test scores, interview, recommendations. **High school preparation:** 16 units recommended. Recommended units include English 4. **Test requirements:** Institution's theory test required.

1992 FRESHMAN CLASS PROFILE. 295 men applied, 113 accepted, 51 enrolled; 407 women applied, 156 accepted, 70 enrolled. **Academic background:** Mid 50% of enrolled freshmen had SAT-V between 450-590, SAT-M between 500-660; ACT composite between 22-28. 77% submitted SAT scores, 19% submitted ACT scores. **Characteristics:** 17% from in state, 98% live in college housing, 14% have minority backgrounds, 11% are foreign students. Average age is 18.

FALL-TERM APPLICATIONS. $50 fee, may be waived for applicants with need. No closing date; priority given to applications received by February 1; applicants notified on a rolling basis beginning on or about March 15; must reply within 4 weeks. Audition required. Interview recommended. Early admission available. SAT or ACT recommended; score report by February 1.

STUDENT LIFE. Housing: Dormitories (men, women, coed); fraternity, handicapped housing available. Undergraduates required to live in college housing unless living with family or released by Dean of Students. **Activities:** Student government, magazine, student newspaper, yearbook, choral groups, concert band, jazz band, music ensembles, musical theater, opera, symphony orchestra, fraternities, sororities.

STUDENT SERVICES. Career counseling, employment service for

undergraduates, freshman orientation, health services, personal counseling, placement service for graduates, services/facilities for handicapped.

ANNUAL EXPENSES. Tuition and fees: $15,779. **Room and board:** $6,286. **Books and supplies:** $600. **Other expenses:** $850.

FINANCIAL AID. 88% of freshmen, 87% of continuing students receive some form of aid. 86% of grants, 98% of loans, 51% of jobs based on need. 82 enrolled freshmen were judged to have need, all were offered aid. Academic, music/drama scholarships available. **Aid applications:** No closing date; priority given to applications received by February 1; applicants notified on a rolling basis beginning on or about March 15; must reply within 4 weeks.

ADDRESS/TELEPHONE. Charles Krusenstjerna, Director of Admissions, Eastman School of Music of the University of Rochester, 26 Gibbs Street, Rochester, NY 14604-2599. (716) 274-1060. Fax: (716) 263-2807.

Elmira College
Elmira, New York — CB code: 2226

Admissions: 74% of applicants accepted
Based on: ••• School record
•• Activities, essay, recommendations
• Interview, special talents, test scores
Completion: 85% of freshmen end year in good standing
75% graduate, 49% of these enter graduate study

4-year private liberal arts college, coed. Founded in 1855. **Accreditation:** Regional. **Undergraduate enrollment:** 452 men, 624 women full time. **Faculty:** 80 total (70 full time), 69 with doctorates or other terminal degrees. **Location:** Suburban campus in large town; 90 miles from Syracuse, 50 miles from Binghamton. **Calendar:** 4-4-1, limited summer session. **Microcomputers:** 81 located in libraries, classrooms, computer centers. **Special facilities:** Center for Mark Twain Studies. **Additional facts:** Master of science in education available through continuing education office.

DEGREES OFFERED. BA, BS. 190 bachelor's degrees awarded in 1992. 32% in business and management, 16% teacher education, 16% multi/interdisciplinary studies, 6% psychology, 14% social sciences.

UNDERGRADUATE MAJORS. Accounting, American studies, anthropology, art education, biochemistry, biological and physical sciences, biology, business administration and management, business economics, chemistry, classics, clinical laboratory science, computer and information sciences, criminal justice studies, dramatic arts, economics, education, education of the deaf and hearing impaired, elementary education, English, English education, English literature, environmental science, foreign languages (multiple emphasis), foreign languages education, French, German, Greek (classical), history, humanities and social sciences, international business management, international relations, Latin, law enforcement and corrections, liberal/general studies, marketing and distribution, marketing management, mathematics, mathematics education, music, nursing, philosophy, political science and government, predentistry, prelaw, premedicine, psychology, science education, secondary education, social sciences, social studies education, social work, sociology, Spanish, speech correction, speech pathology/audiology, studio art, systems analysis.

ACADEMIC PROGRAMS. Accelerated program, double major, dual enrollment of high school students, honors program, independent study, internships, student-designed major, study abroad, teacher preparation, visiting/exchange student program, United Nations semester, Washington semester, cross-registration, critical languages programs; liberal arts/career combination in health sciences. **Remedial services:** Learning center, reduced course load, tutoring. **ROTC:** Air Force, Army. **Placement/credit:** AP, CLEP General and Subject, institutional tests; 30 credit hours maximum for bachelor's degree.

ACADEMIC REQUIREMENTS. Freshmen must earn minimum GPA of 2.0 to continue in good standing. 90% of freshmen return for sophomore year. Students must declare major by end of second year. **Graduation requirements:** 120 hours for bachelor's (36 in major). Most students required to take courses in arts/fine arts, computer science, English, humanities, mathematics, biological/physical sciences, social sciences. **Postgraduate studies:** 5% enter law school, 2% enter medical school, 12% enter MBA programs, 30% enter other graduate study. **Additional information:** Mandatory writing program for all freshmen. 6-credit internship/community service, often done during 6-week spring term, required of all students. Off-campus study emphasized.

FRESHMAN ADMISSIONS. Selection criteria: School academic record primary. Test scores, recommendations, essay and extracurricular activities considered. Interview highly recommended. **High school preparation:** 16 units recommended. Recommended units include English 4, foreign language 2, mathematics 3, social science 4 and science 3. One additional unit of foreign language recommended for foreign language and international business programs. **Test requirements:** SAT or ACT; score report by March 1.

1992 FRESHMAN CLASS PROFILE. 457 men applied, 347 accepted, 127 enrolled; 880 women applied, 644 accepted, 233 enrolled. 59% had high school GPA of 3.0 or higher, 41% between 2.0 and 2.99. 22% were in top tenth and 48% were in top quarter of graduating class. **Academic background:** Mid 50% of enrolled freshmen had SAT-V between 420-540, SAT-M between 450-590; ACT composite between 20-26. 95% submitted SAT scores, 33% submitted ACT scores. **Characteristics:** 56% from in state, 96% live in college housing, 8% have minority backgrounds, 8% are foreign students. Average age is 19.

FALL-TERM APPLICATIONS. $40 fee, may be waived for applicants with need. Closing date June 15; priority given to applications received by April 15; applicants notified on a rolling basis beginning on or about December 1; must reply by May 1 or within 2 weeks if notified thereafter. Essay required. Interview recommended. CRDA. Deferred and early admission available.

STUDENT LIFE. Housing: Dormitories (men, women, coed); apartment housing available. Honors floor available. All undergraduates required to live in college housing unless living with family. **Activities:** Student government, magazine, radio, student newspaper, yearbook, choral groups, dance, drama, music ensembles, musical theater, over 30 student interest groups, including campus ministry, PAL program, international students club, League of Intern Speech Pathologists, political union. **Additional information:** Special co-curricular emphasis placed on student activities and college athletics.

ATHLETICS. NCAA. **Intercollegiate:** Basketball, field hockey W, golf M, ice hockey M, lacrosse M, soccer, softball W, tennis, volleyball W. **Intramural:** Badminton, baseball M, basketball, bowling, golf, horseback riding, ice hockey, racquetball, skiing, skin diving, soccer, softball, squash, swimming, table tennis, tennis, volleyball.

STUDENT SERVICES. Aptitude testing, career counseling, employment service for undergraduates, freshman orientation, health services, personal counseling, placement service for graduates, veterans counselor, services/facilities for handicapped.

ANNUAL EXPENSES. Tuition and fees: $13,900. **Room and board:** $4,550. **Books and supplies:** $450. **Other expenses:** $550.

FINANCIAL AID. 80% of freshmen, 80% of continuing students receive some form of aid. 73% of grants, 82% of loans, 84% of jobs based on need. 250 enrolled freshmen were judged to have need, all were offered aid. Academic, music/drama, art, leadership scholarships available. **Aid applications:** No closing date; priority given to applications received by March 1; applicants notified on a rolling basis beginning on or about March 15; must reply by May 1 or within 3 weeks if notified thereafter. **Additional information:** Sibling Scholarship program provides 50% discounts on second family member's room and board, regardless of need.

ADDRESS/TELEPHONE. William S. Neal, Dean of Admissions, Elmira College, Park Place, Elmira, NY 14901-2345. (607) 735-1800.

Erie Community College: City Campus
Buffalo, New York — CB code: 2213

2-year public community college, coed. Founded in 1971. **Accreditation:** Regional. **Undergraduate enrollment:** 820 men, 1,616 women full time; 554 men, 1,044 women part time. **Faculty:** 256 total (132 full time), 20 with doctorates or other terminal degrees. **Location:** Urban campus in large city. **Calendar:** Semester, limited summer session. Saturday and extensive evening/early morning classes. **Microcomputers:** 150 located in libraries, classrooms, computer centers. **Additional facts:** SUNY institution.

DEGREES OFFERED. AA, AS, AAS. 352 associate degrees awarded in 1992. 14% in business and management, 31% business/office and marketing/distribution, 7% engineering technologies, 17% allied health, 8% home economics, 13% law, 7% multi/interdisciplinary studies, 19% parks/recreation, protective services, public affairs, 12% social sciences.

UNDERGRADUATE MAJORS. Building management and maintenance, business and management, business and office, child development/care/guidance, criminal justice studies, engineering science, fashion merchandising, food management, hospitality and recreation marketing, hotel/motel and restaurant management, humanities and social sciences, information sciences and systems, insurance and risk management, international business management, legal assistant/paralegal, manufacturing technology, nursing, radiograph medical technology, real estate, retailing, robotics, science lab technology, science technologies, secretarial and related programs, social sciences, word processing.

ACADEMIC PROGRAMS. 2-year transfer program, double major, honors program, independent study, internships, study abroad, teacher preparation, telecourses, weekend college, cross-registration, dual admissions with 4-year institutions. **Remedial services:** Learning center, preadmission summer program, reduced course load, remedial instruction, special counselor, tutoring. **ROTC:** Army. **Placement/credit:** AP, CLEP General and Subject, institutional tests.

ACADEMIC REQUIREMENTS. Freshmen must earn minimum GPA of 1.75 to continue in good standing. 62% of freshmen return for sophomore year. **Graduation requirements:** 64 hours for associate (40 in major). Most students required to take courses in English, mathematics.

FRESHMAN ADMISSIONS. Selection criteria: Open admissions. Selective admissions for nursing, hotel technology, and radiologic technology programs.

1992 FRESHMAN CLASS PROFILE. 349 men, 546 women enrolled. **Characteristics:** 99% from in state, 100% commute, 36% have minority backgrounds.

FALL-TERM APPLICATIONS. $25 fee, may be waived for applicants with need. Closing date August 14; applicants notified on a rolling basis; must reply within 4 weeks. Interview required for nursing, hotel technology, radiologic technology applicants.

STUDENT LIFE. Activities: Student government, student newspaper, yearbook, choral groups.

ATHLETICS. NJCAA. **Intercollegiate:** Baseball M, basketball, bowling, cross-country, golf, ice hockey M, soccer M, softball W, tennis, track and field, volleyball W, wrestling M. **Intramural:** Badminton, basketball, bowling, ice hockey, softball W, swimming, tennis.

STUDENT SERVICES. Aptitude testing, career counseling, employment service for undergraduates, freshman orientation, health services, on-campus day care, personal counseling, placement service for graduates, special adviser for adult students, veterans counselor, disabled student resource center, services/facilities for handicapped.

ANNUAL EXPENSES. Tuition and fees (1992-93): $1,908, $1,830 additional for out-of-district students, $1,830 additional for out-of-state students. **Books and supplies:** $500. **Other expenses:** $750.

FINANCIAL AID. 82% of freshmen, 75% of continuing students receive some form of aid. Grants, loans, jobs available. **Aid applications:** No closing date; priority given to applications received by April 30; applicants notified on a rolling basis beginning on or about May 1; must reply within 2 weeks.

ADDRESS/TELEPHONE. B. Paul Hodan, Director of Student Services, Erie Community College: City Campus, 121 Ellicott Street, Buffalo, NY 14203-2601. (716) 851-1155.

Erie Community College: North Campus
Williamsville, New York CB code: 2228

2-year public community college, coed. Founded in 1946. **Accreditation:** Regional. **Undergraduate enrollment:** 1,969 men, 1,750 women full time; 1,620 men, 1,792 women part time. **Faculty:** 391 total (238 full time), 21 with doctorates or other terminal degrees. **Location:** Suburban campus in large town; 10 miles from Buffalo. **Calendar:** Semester, limited summer session. Saturday and extensive evening/early morning classes. **Microcomputers:** 100 located in libraries, classrooms, computer centers. **Special facilities:** Vehicle Training Technological Center, IBM-Computer Integrated Management Center. **Additional facts:** SUNY institution.

DEGREES OFFERED. AA, AS, AAS. 894 associate degrees awarded in 1992. 14% in business and management, 13% engineering technologies, 13% health sciences, 17% allied health, 16% multi/interdisciplinary studies, 12% parks/recreation, protective services, public affairs, 5% social sciences.

UNDERGRADUATE MAJORS. Automotive technology, business administration and management, business and office, business data processing and related programs, chemical engineering, chemical manufacturing technology, civil engineering, computer and information sciences, computer servicing technology, computer technology, contract management and procurement/purchasing, criminal justice studies, criminal justice technology, dental hygiene, dietetic aide/assistant, electrical technology, electrical/electronics/communications engineering, electromechanical technology, engineering, engineering and engineering-related technologies, engineering science, food management, food production/management/services, humanities and social sciences, industrial technology, liberal/general studies, manufacturing technology, mathematics, mechanical design technology, mechanical engineering, medical assistant, medical laboratory technologies, nursing, occupational therapy assistant, ophthalmic services, respiratory therapy, secretarial and related programs, social sciences, word processing.

ACADEMIC PROGRAMS. 2-year transfer program, cooperative education, double major, honors program, independent study, internships, student-designed major, study abroad, teacher preparation, telecourses, weekend college, cross-registration, dual admissions with 4-year institutions. **Remedial services:** Learning center, preadmission summer program, reduced course load, remedial instruction, special counselor, tutoring. **ROTC:** Army. **Placement/credit:** AP, CLEP General and Subject, institutional tests.

ACADEMIC REQUIREMENTS. Freshmen must earn minimum GPA of 1.75 to continue in good standing. 71% of freshmen return for sophomore year. **Graduation requirements:** 60 hours for associate (40 in major). Most students required to take courses in computer science, English, mathematics, biological/physical sciences.

FRESHMAN ADMISSIONS. Selection criteria: Open admissions. Selective admissions for nursing and occupational therapy programs.

1992 FRESHMAN CLASS PROFILE. 982 men, 834 women enrolled. **Characteristics:** 97% from in state, 100% commute, 8% have minority backgrounds.

FALL-TERM APPLICATIONS. $25 fee, may be waived for applicants with need. Closing date August 14; applicants notified on a rolling basis; must reply within 4 weeks. Interview required for nursing, occupational therapy assistant applicants.

STUDENT LIFE. Activities: Student government, magazine, radio, student newspaper, yearbook, choral groups, concert band, drama, Phi Theta Kappa (honor society).

ATHLETICS. NJCAA. **Intercollegiate:** Baseball M, basketball, bowling, cross-country, golf, ice hockey M, rifle, soccer, softball W, swimming, tennis, track and field, volleyball, wrestling M. **Intramural:** Badminton, basketball, bowling, ice hockey, soccer, softball W, swimming, tennis, volleyball.

STUDENT SERVICES. Aptitude testing, career counseling, employment service for undergraduates, freshman orientation, health services, personal counseling, placement service for graduates, special adviser for adult students, veterans counselor, services/facilities for handicapped.

ANNUAL EXPENSES. Tuition and fees (projected): $1,908, $1,830 additional for out-of-district students, $1,830 additional for out-of-state students. **Books and supplies:** $500. **Other expenses:** $750.

FINANCIAL AID. Grants, loans, jobs available. **Aid applications:** No closing date; priority given to applications received by April 30; applicants notified on a rolling basis beginning on or about June 15; must reply within 2 weeks.

ADDRESS/TELEPHONE. B. Paul Hodan, Director of Student Services, Erie Community College: North Campus, 6205 Main Street, Williamsville, NY 14221. (716) 851-1455. Fax: (716) 634-3802.

Erie Community College: South Campus
Orchard Park, New York CB code: 2211

2-year public community college, coed. Founded in 1974. **Accreditation:** Regional. **Undergraduate enrollment:** 1,001 men, 843 women full time; 804 men, 897 women part time. **Faculty:** 292 total (119 full time), 14 with doctorates or other terminal degrees. **Location:** Suburban campus in large town; 10 miles from Buffalo. **Calendar:** Semester, limited summer session. Saturday and extensive evening/early morning classes. **Microcomputers:** 136 located in computer centers. **Additional facts:** SUNY institution.

DEGREES OFFERED. AA, AS, AAS. 352 associate degrees awarded in 1992. 28% in business and management, 6% business/office and marketing/distribution, 21% engineering technologies, 27% multi/interdisciplinary studies, 5% parks/recreation, protective services, public affairs, 11% social sciences.

UNDERGRADUATE MAJORS. Architectural technologies, architecture, automotive technology, biological and physical sciences, biomedical equipment technology, business administration and management, business and office, communications equipment technology, computer servicing technology, computer technology, construction, data processing, dental laboratory technology, finance, fire control and safety technology, graphic and printing production, humanities, humanities and social sciences, industrial technology, information sciences and systems, insurance and risk management, insurance marketing, liberal/general studies, marketing and distribution, mathematics, mechanical design technology, mechanical drafting, recreation and community services technologies, recreation leadership-bowling management, secretarial and related programs, social sciences, solar heating and cooling technology, word processing.

ACADEMIC PROGRAMS. 2-year transfer program, double major, honors program, independent study, internships, study abroad, teacher preparation, telecourses, weekend college, cross-registration, dual admissions with 4-year institutions. **Remedial services:** Learning center, preadmission summer program, reduced course load, remedial instruction, special counselor, tutoring. **ROTC:** Army. **Placement/credit:** AP, CLEP General and Subject, institutional tests.

ACADEMIC REQUIREMENTS. Freshmen must earn minimum GPA of 1.75 to continue in good standing. 65% of freshmen return for sophomore year. **Graduation requirements:** 60 hours for associate (40 in major). Most students required to take courses in English, mathematics.

FRESHMAN ADMISSIONS. Selection criteria: Open admissions. Selective admissions for dental laboratory technician program.

1992 FRESHMAN CLASS PROFILE. 574 men, 495 women enrolled. **Characteristics:** 97% from in state, 100% commute, 5% have minority backgrounds.

FALL-TERM APPLICATIONS. $25 fee, may be waived for applicants with need. Closing date August 14; applicants notified on a rolling basis; must reply within 4 weeks. Interview required for dental laboratory technician applicants.

STUDENT LIFE. Activities: Student government, magazine, radio, student newspaper, yearbook, choral groups, drama, pep band.

ATHLETICS. NJCAA. **Intercollegiate:** Baseball M, basketball, bowling, cross-country, golf M, ice hockey M, soccer M, softball W, swimming, tennis, track and field, volleyball, wrestling M. **Intramural:** Badminton, baseball M, basketball, softball W, swimming, tennis, volleyball.

STUDENT SERVICES. Aptitude testing, career counseling, employment service for undergraduates, freshman orientation, health services, on-campus day care, personal counseling, placement service for graduates, veterans counselor, coordinator of handicapped services, mentoring, disabled student resource center, services/facilities for handicapped.

ANNUAL EXPENSES. Tuition and fees (1992-93): $1,908, $1,830 additional for out-of-district students, $1,830 additional for out-of-state students. **Books and supplies:** $500. **Other expenses:** $750.

FINANCIAL AID. 53% of freshmen, 53% of continuing students receive some form of aid. Grants, loans, jobs available. **Aid applications:** No closing date; priority given to applications received by April 30; applicants notified on a rolling basis beginning on or about June 15; must reply within 2 weeks.

ADDRESS/TELEPHONE. B. Paul Hodan, Assistant Director of Student Services, Erie Community College: South Campus, 4140 Southwestern Boulevard, Orchard Park, NY 14127-2199. (716) 85116550.

Eugene Lang College/New School for Social Research

New York, New York CB code: 2521

Admissions: 73% of applicants accepted
Based on: ••• Essay, school record
•• Interview, recommendations
• Activities, special talents, test scores
Completion: 90% of freshmen end year in good standing
75% graduate, 40% of these enter graduate study

4-year private liberal arts college, coed. Founded in 1976. **Accreditation:** Regional. **Undergraduate enrollment:** 150 men, 200 women full time. **Faculty:** 80 total (15 full time), 65 with doctorates or other terminal degrees. **Location:** Urban campus in very large city. **Calendar:** Semester. **Microcomputers:** 25 located in computer centers. **Special facilities:** Photography laboratories, film theaters, screening rooms, 500-seat auditorium, art galleries, studios, environmental simulation center. **Additional facts:** Students design own academic programs with advisers. Access to New York University and Cooper Union libraries, ability to select courses within New School for Social Research, Cooper Union, and Brooklyn Polytechnic.

DEGREES OFFERED. BA. 50 bachelor's degrees awarded in 1992. 8% in communications, 5% letters/literature, 49% multi/interdisciplinary studies, 7% philosophy, religion, theology, 8% psychology, 19% social sciences.

UNDERGRADUATE MAJORS. American literature, American studies, anthropology, behavioral sciences, biological and physical sciences, cinematography/film, classics, comparative literature, creative writing, dramatic arts, economics, English, English literature, European studies, film arts, foreign languages (multiple emphasis), history, humanities, humanities and social sciences, international relations, international studies, liberal/general studies, mathematics, music, music history and appreciation, music theory and composition, philosophy, physical sciences, political science and government, psychology, public administration, public affairs, public policy studies, religion, social sciences, sociology, urban studies, visual and performing arts, Western European studies, women's studies.

ACADEMIC PROGRAMS. Accelerated program, double major, dual enrollment of high school students, independent study, internships, student-designed major, study abroad, visiting/exchange student program, cross-registration, 5-year BA/BFA with Parsons School of Design, 5-year BA/MS with Bank Street School of Education. **Remedial services:** Tutoring, English as a second language, writing center, New York State Higher Education Opportunity Program. **Placement/credit:** AP, IB; 18 credit hours maximum for bachelor's degree.

ACADEMIC REQUIREMENTS. Freshmen must earn minimum GPA of 2.0 to continue in good standing. 75% of freshmen return for sophomore year. Students must declare major by end of second year. **Graduation requirements:** 120 hours for bachelor's (32 in major). Most students required to take courses in English. **Postgraduate studies:** 10% enter law school, 30% enter other graduate study. **Additional information:** Student maps out individual program of study within 5 broad areas of concentration. Seminars rather than lecture classes emphasized.

FRESHMAN ADMISSIONS. Selection criteria: Success in college preparatory studies most important supplemented by writing ability, intellectual curiosity, and interview. Extracurricular/community activities, evidence of special talents, and recommendations important. Each candidate judged individually. **High school preparation:** 16 units required; 18 recommended. **Test requirements:** SAT or ACT; score report by February 15. Students may opt to take 4 ACH in lieu of SAT or ACT. Score report by February 15. **Additional information:** Telephone interviews available to students who cannot travel to New York.

1992 FRESHMAN CLASS PROFILE. 292 men and women applied, 213 accepted; 90 enrolled. 85% had high school GPA of 3.0 or higher, 15% between 2.0 and 2.99. 19% were in top tenth and 58% were in top quarter of graduating class. **Academic background:** Mid 50% of enrolled freshmen had SAT-V between 570-700, SAT-M between 520-600; ACT composite between 22-27. 90% submitted SAT scores, 3% submitted ACT scores. **Characteristics:** 35% from in state, 75% live in college housing, 14% have minority backgrounds, 5% are foreign students. Average age is 18.

FALL-TERM APPLICATIONS. $30 fee, may be waived for applicants with need. Closing date February 1; applicants notified on or about April 1; must reply by May 1. Interview required. Audition required for jazz applicants. Portfolio required for art applicants. Essay required. CRDA. Deferred and early admission available. EDP-F. Early admissions deadline July 1.

STUDENT LIFE. Housing: Dormitories (coed). Preference given to first-year and new transfer students. **Activities:** Magazine, student newspaper, choral groups, drama, Amnesty International, women's group, outdoors group, student union. **Additional information:** Of undergraduates who do not reside in college housing, approximately 40-50% live in their own apartments off campus, 20-30% commute from home.

ATHLETICS. Intramural: Basketball, bowling, fencing, golf, racquetball, skiing, softball, table tennis, tennis, volleyball.

STUDENT SERVICES. Freshman orientation, personal counseling, services/facilities for handicapped.

ANNUAL EXPENSES. Tuition and fees (1992-93): $12,940. **Room and board:** $8,426. **Books and supplies:** $680. **Other expenses:** $975.

FINANCIAL AID. 60% of freshmen, 65% of continuing students receive some form of aid. 99% of grants, 82% of loans, 93% of jobs based on need. Academic, state/district residency, minority scholarships available. **Aid applications:** No closing date; priority given to applications received by March 1; applicants notified on a rolling basis beginning on or about March 15; must reply by May 1 or within 30 days if notified thereafter.

ADDRESS/TELEPHONE. Laura A. Bruno, Director of Admissions: Eugene Lang College, Eugene Lang College/New School for Social Research, 65 West 11th Street (3rd floor), New York, NY 10114-0059. (212) 229-5665.

Fashion Institute of Technology

New York, New York CB code: 2257

Admissions: 36% of applicants accepted
Based on: ••• School record, special talents
•• Activities, essay, interview
• Recommendations, test scores
Completion: 85% of freshmen end year in good standing

4-year public college of art and design, business, and technology, coed. Founded in 1944. **Accreditation:** Regional. **Undergraduate enrollment:** 743 men, 3,459 women full time; 1,575 men, 6,346 women part time. **Faculty:** 820 total (225 full time). **Location:** Urban campus in very large city. **Calendar:** 4-1-4, limited summer session. **Microcomputers:** 200 located in classrooms. **Special facilities:** Galleries, textile and costume collection, lighting lab. **Additional facts:** Specialized 2-year and 4-year programs provide professional preparation for fashion and related industries. SUNY institution.

DEGREES OFFERED. AAS, BS, BFA, MA. 1,740 associate degrees awarded in 1992. 690 bachelor's degrees awarded.

UNDERGRADUATE MAJORS. Associate: Accessories design, advertising, advertising design, communications, display and exhibit design, fashion design, fashion merchandising, fine arts, fur design, graphic arts technology, illustration design, interior design, menswear, metal/jewelry, patternmaking, photographic technology, production management/apparel, textile technology, textile/surface design. **Bachelor's:** Advertising design, fabric styling, fashion design, fashion merchandising, graphic arts technology, illustration design, interior design, marketing and distribution, packaging design, production management/apparel, production management/textiles, restoration, textile technology, textile/surface design, toy design.

ACADEMIC PROGRAMS. 2-year transfer program, cooperative education, internships, study abroad, weekend college, 1-year visiting student program with colleges and universities throughout United States. **Remedial services:** Learning center, reduced course load, remedial instruction, special counselor, tutoring. **Placement/credit:** AP, CLEP General and Subject.

ACADEMIC REQUIREMENTS. Freshmen must earn minimum GPA of 2.0 to continue in good standing. 80% of freshmen return for sophomore year. Students must declare major on application. **Graduation requirements:** 69 hours for associate (24 in major), 63 hours for bachelor's (22 in major). Most students required to take courses in English, history, mathematics, biological/physical sciences, social sciences. **Postgraduate studies:** 45% from 2-year programs enter 4-year programs.

FRESHMAN ADMISSIONS. Selection criteria: Rank in class, portfolio, test scores, community service, work experience, and awards and honors. **High school preparation:** 16 units recommended. Recommended units include English 4, mathematics 2 and social science 3. College preparatory program recommended. **Test requirements:** SAT or ACT for placement; score report by April 1.

1992 FRESHMAN CLASS PROFILE. 4,202 men and women applied, 1,517 accepted; 1,517 enrolled. **Characteristics:** 50% from in state, 21% live in college housing, 38% have minority backgrounds, 10% are foreign students. Average age is 19.

FALL-TERM APPLICATIONS. $25 fee. No closing date; applicants notified on a rolling basis; must reply by May 1 or within 3 weeks if notified thereafter. Portfolio required for art and design applicants. Essay required. CRDA.

STUDENT LIFE. Housing: Dormitories (women, coed). **Activities:** Student government, magazine, radio, student newspaper, television, yearbook, dance, drama, musical theater, more than 60 groups and organizations. **Additional information:** Of undergraduates who do not live in college housing, 10% of freshmen, 15% of all undergraduates live in their own apartments off campus, 69% of freshmen, 52% of all undergraduates commute from home.

ATHLETICS. NJCAA. **Intercollegiate:** Basketball M, tennis, volleyball W. **Intramural:** Basketball, tennis, volleyball.

STUDENT SERVICES. Career counseling, employment service for undergraduates, health services, personal counseling, placement service for graduates, services/facilities for handicapped.

ANNUAL EXPENSES. Tuition and fees (1992-93): $2,210, $2,650 additional for out-of-state students. **Room and board:** $4,655. **Books and supplies:** $1,200. **Other expenses:** $1,050.

FINANCIAL AID. 51% of freshmen, 48% of continuing students receive some form of aid. All grants, 88% of loans based on need. 730 enrolled freshmen were judged to have need, 674 were offered aid. **Aid applications:** Closing date March 15; applicants notified on or about June 1; must reply within 2 weeks.

ADDRESS/TELEPHONE. James C. Pidgeon, Director of Admissions, Fashion Institute of Technology, Seventh Avenue at 27 Street, New York, NY 10001-5992. (212) 760-7675. Fax: (212) 594-9413.

Finger Lakes Community College
Canandaigua, New York

CB code: 2134

2-year public community college, coed. Founded in 1965. **Accreditation:** Regional. **Undergraduate enrollment:** 1,065 men, 1,124 women full time; 684 men, 1,129 women part time. **Faculty:** 240 total (97 full time), 7 with doctorates or other terminal degrees. **Location:** Rural campus in large town; 20 miles from Rochester. **Calendar:** Semester, extensive summer session. Saturday and extensive evening/early morning classes. **Microcomputers:** 300 located in libraries, computer centers. **Special facilities:** Outdoor classrooms, art gallery, nature trails. **Additional facts:** SUNY institution.

DEGREES OFFERED. AA, AS, AAS. 631 associate degrees awarded in 1992.

UNDERGRADUATE MAJORS. Accounting, biology, business administration and management, business and office, business data processing and related programs, business data programming, chemistry, communications, computer programming, computer servicing technology, conservation and regulation, criminal justice studies, drafting, dramatic arts, electrical and electronics equipment repair, electrical technology, electrical/electronics/communications engineering, engineering, engineering and engineering-related technologies, fine arts, graphic arts technology, hotel/motel and restaurant management, humanities, humanities and social sciences, information sciences and systems, instrumentation technology, landscape architecture, law enforcement and corrections technologies, legal secretary, liberal/general studies, mathematics, mechanical design technology, medical secretary, music, nursing, office supervision and management, ornamental horticulture, physics, renewable natural resources, retailing, science technologies, secretarial and related programs, social sciences, studio art, tourism, wildlife management, word processing.

ACADEMIC PROGRAMS. 2-year transfer program, double major, dual enrollment of high school students, honors program, internships, weekend college, cross-registration, credit-bearing travel opportunities. **Remedial services:** Learning center, preadmission summer program, reduced course load, remedial instruction, special counselor, tutoring, educational opportunity program, developmental studies program, learning laboratory. **Placement/credit:** AP, CLEP General and Subject, institutional tests; 32 credit hours maximum for associate degree.

ACADEMIC REQUIREMENTS. No policy requiring minimum GPA; records of students having academic difficulty are reviewed individually. 55% of freshmen return for sophomore year. Students must declare major on application. **Graduation requirements:** 64 hours for associate. Most students required to take courses in English, social sciences.

FRESHMAN ADMISSIONS. Selection criteria: Open admissions. Selective admissions to nursing program based on high school GPA. Previous health services experience also considered. One unit each biology, chemistry, and mathematics required of nursing applicants. Mathematics through trigonometry and physics recommended for electrical technology program. Students without high school diploma or GED must pass federally approved Ability to Benefit test prior to acceptance.

1992 FRESHMAN CLASS PROFILE. 651 men, 811 women enrolled. **Characteristics:** 99% from in state, 2% have minority backgrounds. Average age is 20.

FALL-TERM APPLICATIONS. $25 fee, may be waived for applicants with need. Closing date August 1; priority given to applications received by May 1; applicants notified on a rolling basis beginning on or about December 15; must reply within 4 weeks. Portfolio recommended for graphic arts applicants. Deferred and early admission available. Interview required following acceptance.

STUDENT LIFE. Housing: Privately owned apartments for students adjacent to campus. **Activities:** Student government, film, radio, student newspaper, choral groups, drama, jazz band, music ensembles, musical theater, fraternities, sororities, Newman Club, Brothers and Sisters in Christ, Human Services Club, Afro-Latin club, Circle-K, Phi Theta Kappa.

ATHLETICS. NJCAA. **Intercollegiate:** Baseball M, basketball, cross-country, soccer, softball W. **Intramural:** Basketball M, tennis, volleyball.

STUDENT SERVICES. Aptitude testing, career counseling, employment service for undergraduates, freshman orientation, health services, on-campus day care, personal counseling, placement service for graduates, special adviser for adult students, veterans counselor, services/facilities for handicapped.

ANNUAL EXPENSES. Tuition and fees (projected): $1,910, $1,780 additional for out-of-state students. **Books and supplies:** $500. **Other expenses:** $480.

FINANCIAL AID. 75% of freshmen, 75% of continuing students receive some form of aid. 99% of grants, 76% of loans, 74% of jobs based on need. Academic, music/drama, art, athletic, leadership, alumni affiliation scholarships available. **Aid applications:** No closing date; priority given to applications received by May 1; applicants notified on a rolling basis beginning on or about May 15; must reply within 2 weeks.

ADDRESS/TELEPHONE. John M. Meuser, Director of Admissions, Finger Lakes Community College, 4355 Lake Shore Drive, Canandaigua, NY 14424-8399. (716) 394-3500 ext. 278. Fax: (716) 394-5005.

Five Towns College
Dix Hills, New York

CB code: 3142

Admissions: 90% of applicants accepted
Based on:
••• School record
•• Special talents, test scores
• Activities, essay, interview, recommendations
Completion: 80% of freshmen end year in good standing

4-year proprietary music, liberal arts college, coed. Founded in 1972. **Accreditation:** Regional. **Undergraduate enrollment:** 463 men, 186 women full time; 26 men, 9 women part time. **Faculty:** 67 total (34 full time), 17 with doctorates or other terminal degrees. **Location:** Suburban campus in large town; 18 miles from New York City. **Calendar:** Semester, limited summer session. **Microcomputers:** 25 located in classrooms, computer centers. **Special facilities:** 24-track and 48-track recording studios, professional video arts studio, MIDI technology studio. **Additional facts:** New location on 34-acre campus

DEGREES OFFERED. AA, AS, AAS, B. 105 associate degrees awarded in 1992. 55% in business and management, 40% visual and performing arts. 2 bachelor's degrees awarded. 100% in visual and performing arts.

UNDERGRADUATE MAJORS. Accounting, audio recording technology, business administration and management, business and management, business and office, computer and information sciences, data processing, jazz, liberal/general studies, marketing and distribution, marketing management, microcomputer software, music, music business management, music performance, real estate, retailing, secretarial and related programs, video. audio recording technology, jazz, music, music business management, music education, music performance, music theory and composition, video.

ACADEMIC PROGRAMS. 2-year transfer program, double major, dual enrollment of high school students, independent study, internships, teacher preparation, cross-registration. **Remedial services:** Learning center, preadmission summer program, reduced course load, remedial instruction, special counselor, tutoring. **Placement/credit:** AP, CLEP General and Subject, institutional tests; 30 credit hours maximum for associate degree.

ACADEMIC REQUIREMENTS. Freshmen must earn minimum GPA of 2.0 to continue in good standing. 55% of freshmen return for sophomore year. Students must declare major on enrollment. **Graduation requirements:** 60 hours for associate (24 in major), 128 hours for bachelor's (45 in major). Most students required to take courses in English, history, humanities, mathematics, social sciences. **Postgraduate studies:** 25% from 2-year programs enter 4-year programs. **Additional information:** Number of credit hours required for students in major field of study varies depending on program.

FRESHMAN ADMISSIONS. Selection criteria: Minimum 2.5 GPA recommended. Applicants for 4-year music programs must pass audition and demonstrate competency in music, mathematics, and English. **High school preparation:** 21 units recommended. Recommended units include biological science 2, English 4, foreign language 2, mathematics 3, physical science 1 and social science 3. Music harmony and other applied music classes recommended for music students.

1992 FRESHMAN CLASS PROFILE. 298 men applied, 260 accepted, 224 enrolled; 117 women applied, 113 accepted, 83 enrolled. 6% had high school GPA of 3.0 or higher, 80% between 2.0 and 2.99. **Academic background:** Mid 50% of enrolled freshmen had SAT-V between 350-470, SAT-M between 330-470. 60% submitted SAT scores. **Characteristics:** 90% from in state, 100% commute, 29% have minority backgrounds, 2% are foreign students. Average age is 18.

FALL-TERM APPLICATIONS. $20 fee, may be waived for applicants with need. No closing date; priority given to applications received by July 1; applicants notified on a rolling basis; must reply within 2 weeks. Interview required. Audition required for music bachelor's degree applicants; recommended for music associate degree applicants applicants. Deferred and early admission available.

STUDENT LIFE. Housing: Housing accommodations available at an off-campus hotel for all students, on space available basis. **Activities:** Student government, radio, yearbook, choral groups, jazz band, music ensembles, musical theater.

STUDENT SERVICES. Aptitude testing, career counseling, employment service for undergraduates, freshman orientation, personal counseling, placement service for graduates.

ANNUAL EXPENSES. Tuition and fees: $6,750. $350 fee per semester for music students' private instruction. **Books and supplies:** $600. **Other expenses:** $2,000.

FINANCIAL AID. 67% of freshmen, 60% of continuing students receive some form of aid. 97% of grants, 93% of loans, 63% of jobs based on need. 192 enrolled freshmen were judged to have need, 185 were offered aid. Academic, music/drama, leadership scholarships available. **Aid applications:** Closing date August 21; priority given to applications received by May 15; applicants notified on a rolling basis; must reply within 2 weeks.

ADDRESS/TELEPHONE. Robert Goldschlager, Admissions Coordinator, Five Towns College, 305 North Service Road, Dix Hills, NY 11746-6055. (516) 424-7000.

Fordham University
Bronx, New York — CB code: 2259

Admissions: 68% of applicants accepted
Based on: ••• School record, test scores
•• Activities, essay, interview, recommendations, special talents
Completion: 95% of freshmen end year in good standing
80% graduate, 24% of these enter graduate study

4-year private university, coed, affiliated with Roman Catholic Church. Founded in 1841. **Accreditation:** Regional. **Undergraduate enrollment:** 2,330 men, 2,426 women full time; 524 men, 1,113 women part time. **Graduate enrollment:** 1,874 men, 3,058 women full time; 1,249 men, 2,038 women part time. **Faculty:** 759 total (522 full time), 736 with doctorates or other terminal degrees. **Location:** Urban campus in very large city; in metropolitan New York. Saturday and extensive evening/early morning classes. **Microcomputers:** 221 located in dormitories, classrooms, computer centers, campus-wide network. **Special facilities:** Calder Environmental Center in Armonk, seismic station, Fordham Hispanic Research Third Age Center addressing issues of older population. **Additional facts:** Independent institution in Jesuit tradition. Rose Hill campus in Bronx, Lincoln Center campus in Manhattan.

DEGREES OFFERED. BA, BS, MA, MS, MBA, MEd, MSW, PhD, EdD, JD. 1,394 bachelor's degrees awarded in 1992. 24% in business and management, 7% communications, 12% letters/literature, 7% multi/interdisciplinary studies, 6% physical sciences, 9% psychology, 23% social sciences. Graduate degrees offered in 56 major fields of study.

UNDERGRADUATE MAJORS. Accounting, African studies, Afro-American (black) studies, American literature, American studies, anthropology, art history, bilingual bicultural studies, biological and physical sciences, biology, business administration and management, business and management, business economics, chemistry, classics, communications, comparative literature, computational mathematics, computer and information sciences, creative writing, criminal justice studies, dramatic arts, economics, education, elementary education, English, English literature, film arts, finance, fine arts, foreign languages (multiple emphasis), French, German, Greek (classical), history, humanities, humanities and social sciences, information sciences and systems, international development, international relations, international studies, Italian, journalism, junior high education, Latin, Latin American studies, management information systems, management science, marketing management, mathematics, media studies, medieval studies, Middle Eastern studies, music history and appreciation, philosophy, photography and graphic arts, physical sciences, physics, political science and government, predentistry, prelaw, premedicine, preveterinary, psychology, radio/television broadcasting, radio/television technology, religion, Russian, Russian and Slavic studies, secondary education, social sciences, sociology, Spanish, studio art, theological studies, urban studies, visual and performing arts, women's studies.

ACADEMIC PROGRAMS. Double major, honors program, independent study, internships, student-designed major, study abroad, teacher preparation, visiting/exchange student program, United Nations semester, 3-2 engineering program with Columbia University and Case Western Reserve University, 3-2 pharmacy program with Long Island University Globe Program in international Business; combined bachelor's/graduate program in law. **Remedial services:** Preadmission summer program, tutoring, New York State Higher Education Opportunity Program. **ROTC:** Air Force, Army, Naval. **Placement/credit:** AP, CLEP Subject, institutional tests; 36 credit hours maximum for bachelor's degree.

ACADEMIC REQUIREMENTS. Freshmen must earn minimum GPA of 1.6 to continue in good standing. 87% of freshmen return for sophomore year. Students must declare major by end of second year. **Graduation requirements:** 124 hours for bachelor's (36 in major). Most students required to take courses in arts/fine arts, English, foreign languages, history, humanities, mathematics, philosophy/religion, biological/physical sciences, social sciences. **Postgraduate studies:** 10% enter law school, 1% enter medical school, 5% enter MBA programs, 8% enter other graduate study.

FRESHMAN ADMISSIONS. Selection criteria: School achievement record, test scores, class rank, extracurricular activities, personal characteristics. Special consideration given to children of alumni. **High school preparation:** 18 units required; 20 recommended. Required and recommended units include English 4-4, foreign language 2-4, mathematics 3-4, social science 2-4 and science 1-1. Biological science 1 and physical science 2 recommended. Science units must include 1 laboratory science. **Test requirements:** SAT or ACT; score report by February 1.

1992 FRESHMAN CLASS PROFILE. 82% had high school GPA of 3.0 or higher, 18% between 2.0 and 2.99. 32% were in top tenth and 53% were in top quarter of graduating class. **Characteristics:** 68% from in state, 67% live in college housing, 27% have minority backgrounds, 2% are foreign students. Average age is 18.

FALL-TERM APPLICATIONS. $40 fee, may be waived for applicants with need. No closing date; priority given to applications received by February 1; applicants notified on a rolling basis beginning on or about February 1; must reply by May 1 or within 2 weeks if notified thereafter. Audition required for theater applicants. Essay required. Interview recommended. CRDA. Deferred and early admission available. EDP-S. To live on campus apply by February 1. No closing date for commuters.

STUDENT LIFE. Housing: Dormitories (coed); apartment, handicapped housing available. Undergraduate housing guaranteed for 4 years. **Activities:** Student government, film, magazine, radio, student newspaper, yearbook, choral groups, concert band, dance, drama, marching band, musical theater, pep band, early music ensemble, Maroon Key, political clubs, Pro-Life Alliance, Hunger Action Committee, campus ministries, Big Brothers and Big Sisters, El Grito, Gaelic Society, RoseHill Ambassadors, International Black Student Union. **Additional information:** Fordham has 130 registered campus organizations as well as extensive campus ministry and community service programs.

ATHLETICS. NCAA. **Intercollegiate:** Baseball M, basketball, cross-country, diving, football M, golf M, ice hockey M, lacrosse, soccer, softball W, squash M, swimming, tennis, track and field, volleyball W, water polo M, wrestling M. **Intramural:** Badminton, baseball M, basketball, field hockey, golf W, handball, horseback riding, racquetball, rifle, rowing (crew), skiing, softball, squash, swimming, tennis, volleyball, water polo M, wrestling M. **Clubs:** Rugby, horseback riding.

STUDENT SERVICES. Career counseling, employment service for undergraduates, freshman orientation, health services, personal counseling, placement service for graduates, special adviser for adult students, services/facilities for handicapped.

ANNUAL EXPENSES. Tuition and fees (1992-93): $12,175. College at Lincoln Center per credit hour charge $337. **Room and board:** $6,725. **Books and supplies:** $300. **Other expenses:** $1,800.

FINANCIAL AID. 80% of freshmen, 80% of continuing students receive some form of aid. 93% of grants, 80% of loans, all jobs based on need. 486 enrolled freshmen were judged to have need, all were offered aid. Academic, music/drama, athletic, alumni affiliation scholarships available. **Aid applications:** Closing date February 1; applicants notified on or about April 1; must reply by May 1.

ADDRESS/TELEPHONE. John Buckley, Director of Admissions, Fordham University, East Fordham Road, Bronx, NY 10458. (718) 579-2133. Fax: (718) 367-9404.

Fulton-Montgomery Community College
Johnstown, New York — CB code: 2254

2-year public community college, coed. Founded in 1963. **Accreditation:** Regional. **Undergraduate enrollment:** 1,950 men and women. **Faculty:** 129 total (69 full time), 9 with doctorates or other terminal degrees. **Location:** Rural campus in large town; 40 miles from Albany. **Calendar:** 4-1-4, extensive summer session. **Microcomputers:** 90 located in libraries, classrooms, computer centers. **Special facilities:** Island on Great Sacandaga Lake for study in Natural Resourses Conservation degree program. **Additional facts:** SUNY institution.

DEGREES OFFERED. AA, AS, AAS. 400 associate degrees awarded in 1992. 26% in business and management, 10% business/office and marketing/distribution, 6% computer sciences, 5% engineering, 9% health sciences, 16% letters/literature, 18% trade and industry.

UNDERGRADUATE MAJORS. Accounting, airline piloting and navigation, American studies, automotive mechanics, automotive technology, biological and physical sciences, biology, business administration and management, business and management, business and office, business data processing and related programs, business data programming, communications, computer and information sciences, computer programming, computer technology, conservation and regulation, construction, crafts, crafts management, criminal justice studies, data processing, early childhood education, electrical technology, elementary education, engineering, engineering and engineering-related technologies, engineering and other disciplines, English, finance, fine arts, food management, food production/management/services, forestry and related sciences, funeral services/mortuary science, graphic and printing production, graphic arts technology, health education, health sciences, history, humanities, humanities and social sciences, industrial technology, leather technology, legal secretary, liberal/general studies, mathematics, medical laboratory technologies, medical records technology, medical secretary, nursing, physical education, physical sciences, political science and government, psychology, science technologies, secondary education, secretarial and related programs, small business management and ownership, social sciences, social work, sociology, textile technology, visual and performing arts, word processing.

ACADEMIC PROGRAMS. 2-year transfer program, cooperative education, dual enrollment of high school students, honors program, independent study, internships, student-designed major, study abroad, weekend college, cross-registration, 1+1 programs with SUNY Agricultural and Technical Colleges at Canton and Cobleskill. **Remedial services:** Learning center, reduced course load, remedial instruction, special counselor, tutoring. **ROTC:** Air Force, Army, Naval. **Placement/credit:** AP, CLEP General and Subject, institutional tests; 30 credit hours maximum for associate degree.

ACADEMIC REQUIREMENTS. No policy requiring minimum GPA; records of students having academic difficulty are reviewed individually. 75% of freshmen return for sophomore year. Students must declare major on application. **Graduation requirements:** 62 hours for associate (42 in major). Most students required to take courses in English, humanities, mathematics, biological/physical sciences, social sciences. **Additional information:** Career-oriented individual studies program offered.

FRESHMAN ADMISSIONS. Selection criteria: Open admissions. Selective admissions for nursing program based on SAT scores, high school GPA, class rank, and any college experience. Biology required for nursing program.

1992 FRESHMAN CLASS PROFILE. 674 men and women enrolled. 30% had high school GPA of 3.0 or higher, 60% between 2.0 and 2.99. **Characteristics:** 92% from in state, 100% commute, 6% have minority backgrounds, 3% are foreign students. Average age is 20.

FALL-TERM APPLICATIONS. $25 fee, may be waived for applicants with need. No closing date; applicants notified on a rolling basis. Interview recommended. Deferred and early admission available. For nursing program, priority given to applications received by first Friday in January.

STUDENT LIFE. Housing: Private dormitory-style housing available adjacent to campus. **Activities:** Student government, student newspaper, television, photography, art publication, drama, musical theater, Circle-K, Phitheta Kappa Alpha Omega, ski club, chess club, outing club, International Student Union, business club, criminal justice club. **Additional information:** Shuttle bus service from campus to 3 neighboring cities. Approximately 15% of undergraduates live in their own apartments off campus, approximately 85% commute from home.

ATHLETICS. NJCAA. **Intercollegiate:** Baseball M, basketball M, bowling, cross-country, golf, soccer M, softball W, track and field, volleyball W, wrestling M. **Intramural:** Basketball M, racquetball, volleyball.

STUDENT SERVICES. Aptitude testing, career counseling, employment service for undergraduates, freshman orientation, on-campus day care, personal counseling, placement service for graduates, special adviser for adult students, veterans counselor, adult learner support group, services/facilities for handicapped.

ANNUAL EXPENSES. Tuition and fees (projected): $2,014, $1,900 additional for out-of-state students. **Books and supplies:** $500. **Other expenses:** $500.

FINANCIAL AID. 75% of freshmen, 75% of continuing students receive some form of aid. 49% of jobs based on need. Academic, state/district residency scholarships available. **Aid applications:** No closing date; priority given to applications received by April 1; applicants notified on a rolling basis; must reply within 2 weeks.

ADDRESS/TELEPHONE. C. Campbell Baker, Director of Admissions, Fulton-Montgomery Community College, Route 67, Johnstown, NY 12095-9609. (518) 762-4651 ext. 201. Fax: (516) 762-4334.

Genesee Community College
Batavia, New York — CB code: 2272

2-year public community college, coed. Founded in 1966. **Accreditation:** Regional. **Undergraduate enrollment:** 1,019 men, 1,313 women full time; 637 men, 1,306 women part time. **Faculty:** 214 total (76 full time), 23 with doctorates or other terminal degrees. **Location:** Rural campus in large town; 30 miles from Buffalo, 30 miles from Rochester. **Calendar:** Semester, limited summer session. **Microcomputers:** 300 located in classrooms, computer centers. **Special facilities:** Academic/arts center. **Additional facts:** SUNY institution. Mall-type campus, suited to handicapped. Off-campus sites in Orleans, Wyoming, and Livingston Counties.

DEGREES OFFERED. AA, AS, AAS. 587 associate degrees awarded in 1992. 21% in business and management, 7% business/office and marketing/distribution, 8% teacher education, 10% allied health, 12% parks/recreation, protective services, public affairs, 20% social sciences, 11% trade and industry.

UNDERGRADUATE MAJORS. Accounting, biological and physical sciences, biology, business administration and management, business and management, business and office, business computer/console/peripheral equipment operation, commercial art, communications, computer and information sciences, computer servicing technology, criminal justice studies, criminal justice technology, drafting, drafting and design technology, dramatic arts, education, electrical and electronics equipment repair, electrical technology, elementary education, engineering, engineering and engineering-related technologies, engineering and other disciplines, environmental science, fashion merchandising, hospitality and recreation marketing, hotel/motel and restaurant management, humanities, humanities and social sciences, industrial modelmaking, information sciences and systems, legal assistant/paralegal, liberal/general studies, marketing and distribution, marketing management, mathematics, medical laboratory technologies, nursing, occupational therapy assistant, physical therapy assistant, psychology, respiratory therapy technology, retailing, secretarial and related programs, social sciences, tourism, visual and performing arts.

ACADEMIC PROGRAMS. 2-year transfer program, cooperative education, double major, dual enrollment of high school students, honors program, independent study, internships, teacher preparation, telecourses, bachelor's programs with SUNY College at Brockport, SUNY College at Geneseo, and in commercial art and communicational media arts with Rochester Institute of Technology. **Remedial services:** Learning center, preadmission summer program, reduced course load, remedial instruction, special counselor, tutoring, Intermediate Studies Program providing transition to regular freshman program. **Placement/credit:** AP, CLEP General and Subject; 30 credit hours maximum for associate degree.

ACADEMIC REQUIREMENTS. Freshmen must earn minimum GPA of 1.67 to continue in good standing. 48% of freshmen return for sophomore year. Students must declare major on application. **Graduation requirements:** 62 hours for associate (36 in major). Most students required to take courses in English, mathematics, biological/physical sciences, social sciences.

FRESHMAN ADMISSIONS. Selection criteria: Open admissions. Special consideration given in-county applicants to nursing program. Selective admissions to nursing, physical therapist assistant, paralegal, and occupational therapy assistant programs based on academic achievement, test scores, and school and community activities. **High school preparation:** 20 units recommended. Recommended units include English 4, foreign language 2, mathematics 1, social science 4 and science 1. Additional units of mathematics and science recommended for students planning to transfer to 4-year programs. 18 units, including biology and chemistry, required for nursing applicants. 18 units, including biology and physics, required for physical therapist assistant applicants. Biology and chemistry required for occupational therapy applicants. **Test requirements:** ACT for placement and counseling only; score report by August 15. ACT required of nursing, paralegal and occupational therapy assistant physical therapist assistant applicants; score report by March 31.

1992 FRESHMAN CLASS PROFILE. 564 men, 769 women enrolled. **Characteristics:** 97% from in state, 100% commute, 1% have minority backgrounds. Average age is 22.

FALL-TERM APPLICATIONS. No fee. Closing date August 16; applicants notified on a rolling basis beginning on or about January 15; must reply within 4 weeks. Portfolio recommended for commercial art applicants. Interview required for nursing and physical therapist assistant applicants, recommended for others. Deferred and early admission available.

STUDENT LIFE. Housing: Privately operated apartments, located within short walk to campus, house 10% of students. **Activities:** Student government, radio, student newspaper, television, choral groups, drama, musical theater, Delta Epsilon Chi (Distributive Education Clubs of America).

ATHLETICS. NJCAA. **Intercollegiate:** Baseball M, basketball, soccer, softball W, volleyball. **Intramural:** Archery, badminton, baseball M, basketball, golf, skiing, soccer, softball, table tennis, tennis, volleyball.

STUDENT SERVICES. Aptitude testing, career counseling, employment service for undergraduates, freshman orientation, health services, on-campus day care, personal counseling, placement service for graduates, special adviser for adult students, veterans counselor, services/facilities for handicapped.

ANNUAL EXPENSES. Tuition and fees (1992-93): $1,950, $1,800 additional for out-of-state students. **Books and supplies:** $520. **Other expenses:** $550.

FINANCIAL AID. 75% of freshmen, 75% of continuing students receive some form of aid. 99% of grants, 80% of loans, all jobs based on need. 350 enrolled freshmen were judged to have need, all were offered aid. Academic, music/drama, art scholarships available. **Aid applications:** Closing date June 1; applicants notified on a rolling basis beginning on or about April 15; must reply within 2 weeks.

ADDRESS/TELEPHONE. Malcolm Wormley, Director of Admissions, Genesee Community College, College Road, Batavia, NY 14020. (716) 343-0055 ext. 215.

Hamilton College
Clinton, New York

CB code: 2286

Admissions: 49% of applicants accepted
Based on: ••• Recommendations, school record
•• Activities, essay
• Interview, special talents, test scores
Completion: 96% of freshmen end year in good standing
89% graduate, 20% of these enter graduate study

4-year private liberal arts college, coed. Founded in 1812. **Accreditation:** Regional. **Undergraduate enrollment:** 914 men, 767 women full time; 9 men, 20 women part time. **Faculty:** 192 total (165 full time), 172 with doctorates or other terminal degrees. **Location:** Rural campus in small town; 10 miles from Utica, 50 miles from Syracuse. **Calendar:** Semester. **Microcomputers:** 300 located in libraries, classrooms, computer centers. **Special facilities:** Art museum, observatory, nature preserve.

DEGREES OFFERED. BA. 463 bachelor's degrees awarded in 1992. 6% in languages, 17% letters/literature, 5% life sciences, 5% mathematics, 5% philosophy, religion, theology, 6% physical sciences, 7% psychology, 40% social sciences, 7% visual and performing arts.

UNDERGRADUATE MAJORS. American studies, ancient Mediterranean civilization, anthropology, art history, Asian studies, biochemistry, biology, chemistry, Chinese, classics, comparative literature, computer and information sciences, creative writing, dance, dramatic arts, economics, English, English literature, foreign languages (multiple emphasis), French, geology, German, Greek (classical), history, international relations, Japanese, Latin, liberal/general studies, linguistics, mathematics, molecular biology, music, philosophy, physics, political science and government, psychobiology, psychology, public policy studies, religion, Russian, Russian and Slavic studies, sociology, Spanish, studio art, women's studies.

ACADEMIC PROGRAMS. Double major, honors program, independent study, student-designed major, study abroad, visiting/exchange student program, Washington semester, cross-registration, 3-2 program in engineering with Columbia University, Rensselaer Polytechnic Institute, and University of Rochester; 3-3 program in law with Columbia University, study abroad programs in France, Spain, former Soviet Union, Sweden, Greece, and Italy. **Remedial services:** Learning center, preadmission summer program, reduced course load, special counselor, tutoring. **Placement/credit:** AP, institutional tests.

ACADEMIC REQUIREMENTS. Freshmen must earn minimum GPA of 2.0 to continue in good standing. 96% of freshmen return for sophomore year. Students must declare major by end of second year. **Graduation requirements:** 128 hours for bachelor's (36 in major). Most students required to take courses in arts/fine arts, English, humanities, biological/physical sciences, social sciences. **Postgraduate studies:** 6% enter law school, 4% enter medical school, 1% enter MBA programs, 9% enter other graduate study. **Additional information:** Sophomores may attain guaranteed early admission to one of 6 participating medical schools. Students must complete Senior Program or Project in their concentration. May participate in Williams College Mystic Seaport Program.

FRESHMAN ADMISSIONS. Selection criteria: School achievement record, rank in high school class, school and community activities, test scores, interview, application essay, graded example of expository writing, recommendations considered. Some preference given children of alumni. Special consideration given students from minority groups, disadvantaged backgrounds, and certain geographic regions. **High school preparation:** 16 units recommended. Recommended units include English 4, foreign language 3, mathematics 3 and science 2. **Test requirements:** SAT or ACT; score report by February 1.

1992 FRESHMAN CLASS PROFILE. 1,963 men applied, 876 accepted, 241 enrolled; 1,586 women applied, 868 accepted, 222 enrolled. 41% were in top tenth and 78% were in top quarter of graduating class. **Academic background:** Mid 50% of enrolled freshmen had SAT-V between 500-600, SAT-M between 560-660. 99% submitted SAT scores. **Characteristics:** 40% from in state, 100% live in college housing, 10% have minority backgrounds, 6% are foreign students, 29% join fraternities/sororities. Average age is 18.

FALL-TERM APPLICATIONS. $50 fee, may be waived for applicants with need. Closing date January 15; applicants notified on or about April 1; must reply by May 1. Essay required. Interview recommended. Portfolio recommended for studio art applicants. Audition tape recommended for music applicants. CRDA. Deferred and early admission available. EDP-F. 2 Early Decision Plans offered. Plan 1 application deadline November 15, notification December 15; Plan 2, application deadline January 15, notification February 15.

STUDENT LIFE. Housing: Dormitories (coed); apartment, fraternity, cooperative housing available. Special interest housing available including language houses and international house, quiet areas, substance-free areas. **Activities:** Student government, film, magazine, radio, student newspaper, yearbook, debate, choral groups, dance, drama, jazz band, music ensembles, musical theater, pep band, chamber orchestra, fraternities, sororities, service organizations, Newman Club, Jewish students organization, Black and Latin Student Union, Women's Center, international student association, La Vanguardia, Amnesty International, Muslim Student Organization, Asian Cultural Society. **Additional information:** Honor code covers all examinations, papers, research, and use of library. Campus partially accessible to students in wheelchairs. Of those undergraduates who do not reside in college housing, approximately 12% live in fraternity or sorority housing, 1-2% live in their own apartments off campus.

ATHLETICS. NCAA. **Intercollegiate:** Baseball M, basketball, cross-country, diving, field hockey W, football M, golf M, ice hockey, lacrosse, rowing (crew), rugby, soccer, softball W, squash, swimming, tennis, track and field, volleyball W. **Intramural:** Badminton, basketball, cross-country, diving, fencing, football M, golf, handball, ice hockey, lacrosse M, racquetball, sailing, skiing, soccer, softball, squash, swimming, tennis, track and field, volleyball, water polo.

STUDENT SERVICES. Career counseling, employment service for undergraduates, freshman orientation, health services, on-campus day care, personal counseling, placement service for graduates, special adviser for adult students.

ANNUAL EXPENSES. Tuition and fees (1992-93): $17,650. **Room and board:** $4,750. **Books and supplies:** $400. **Other expenses:** $600.

FINANCIAL AID. 57% of freshmen, 61% of continuing students receive some form of aid. All aid based on need. 207 enrolled freshmen were judged to have need, all were offered aid. **Aid applications:** Closing date February 1; applicants notified on or about April 10; must reply by May 1. **Additional information:** All accepted students with need will have that need met.

ADDRESS/TELEPHONE. Douglas C. Thompson, Dean of Admission, Hamilton College, 198 College Hill Road, Clinton, NY 13323-1293. (315) 859-4421. (800) 843-2655. Fax: (315) 859-4457.

Hartwick College
Oneonta, New York

CB code: 2288

Admissions: 79% of applicants accepted
Based on: ••• School record
•• Activities, essay, recommendations, test scores
• Interview, special talents
Completion: 93% of freshmen end year in good standing
71% graduate, 20% of these enter graduate study

4-year private liberal arts college, coed. Founded in 1797. **Accreditation:** Regional. **Undergraduate enrollment:** 651 men, 814 women full time; 3 men, 24 women part time. **Faculty:** 139 total (117 full time), 98 with doctorates or other terminal degrees. **Location:** Rural campus in large town; 68 miles from Binghamton, 75 miles from Albany. **Calendar:** 4-1-4. **Microcomputers:** 145 located in libraries, classrooms, computer centers, campus-wide network. **Special facilities:** 900-acre ecological preserve, art gallery, museum, Native American artifact and library collections, tissue culture laboratory, electron microscope, 16-inch telescope, observatory, nuclear magnetic resonance spectrometer, all-weather lighted playing field, fine and performing arts center.

DEGREES OFFERED. BA, BS. 313 bachelor's degrees awarded in 1992. 19% in business and management, 8% letters/literature, 7% life sciences, 11% psychology, 31% social sciences, 8% visual and performing arts.

UNDERGRADUATE MAJORS. Accounting, anthropology, art history, biochemistry, biology, business administration and management, chemistry, clinical laboratory science, computer and information sciences, dramatic arts, economics, English, fine arts, French, geology, German, history, information sciences and systems, liberal/general studies, mathematics, music, music education, nursing, philosophy, physics, political science and government, psychology, religion, sociology, Spanish.

ACADEMIC PROGRAMS. Accelerated program, double major, honors program, independent study, internships, student-designed major, study abroad, teacher preparation, visiting/exchange student program, Washington semester, cross-registration, January thematic term, Philadelphia Urban Semester, Boston Semester, Outward Bound, NOLS programs in nursing with SUNY College of Technology at Delhi, in law with Albany Law School, and in engineering with Clarkson University and Columbia University, study abroad programs in 15 countries including Kenya, China, Japan and India. **Remedial services:** Tutoring, writing center, mathematics clinic. **Placement/credit:** AP, CLEP General and Subject, IB, institutional tests; 30 credit hours maximum for bachelor's degree.

ACADEMIC REQUIREMENTS. Freshmen must earn minimum GPA of 2.0 to continue in good standing. 83% of freshmen return for sophomore year. Students must declare major by end of second year. **Graduation requirements:** 120 hours for bachelor's (40 in major). Most students required to take courses in arts/fine arts, computer science, English, foreign languages, history, humanities, mathematics, philosophy/religion, biological/physical sciences, social sciences. **Postgraduate studies:** 4% enter law school, 3% enter medical school, 10% enter MBA programs, 3% enter other graduate study. **Additional information:** Curriculum XXI includes freshman seminar and core requirements.

FRESHMAN ADMISSIONS. Selection criteria: School achievement record, class rank, test scores, personal qualities, extracurricular activities, and recommendations. **High school preparation:** 15 units required; 19 recommended. Required and recommended units include English 4-4, foreign language 2-3, mathematics 3-4, social science 3-4 and science 3-4. **Test requirements:** SAT or ACT; score report by February 15.

1992 FRESHMAN CLASS PROFILE. 1,119 men applied, 839 accepted, 218 enrolled; 1,118 women applied, 923 accepted, 228 enrolled. 17% were in top tenth and 43% were in top quarter of graduating class. **Academic background:** Mid 50% of enrolled freshmen had SAT-V between 410-510, SAT-M between 460-570; ACT composite between 21-24. 99% submitted SAT scores, 25% submitted ACT scores. **Characteristics:** 57% from in state, 99% live in college housing, 7% have minority backgrounds, 1% are foreign students. Average age is 18.

FALL-TERM APPLICATIONS. $35 fee, may be waived for applicants with need. Closing date February 15; applicants notified on or about March 15; must reply by May 1. Audition required for music applicants. Essay required. Interview recommended. Portfolio recommended for art applicants. CRDA. Deferred and early admission available. EDP-F. 2 achievement tests recommended including 1 English. Early notification plan available.

STUDENT LIFE. Housing: Dormitories (men, women, coed); apartment, fraternity, sorority housing available. Self-governing, self-maintenance residence hall for upperclassmen. Townhouse-style residence halls and special interest housing also available. **Activities:** Student government, magazine, radio, student newspaper, yearbook, choral groups, dance, drama, jazz band, music ensembles, musical theater, pep band, symphony orchestra, wind ensemble, fraternities, sororities, over 60 academic and social organizations including ethnic coalition, Hillel, SADD, environmental club, philosophy forum, all-Greek council, management association. **Additional information:** 75% of students participate in athletic activities. As of September 1993 every first-year student receives own notebook-sized personal computer, printer, modem, and basic word processing, spread sheet, and telecommunications software. Each dorm room outfitted with computer network hook-up, free telephone with voice mail, and free video cable service.

ATHLETICS. NCAA. **Intercollegiate:** Baseball M, basketball, cross-country, diving, field hockey W, football M, lacrosse, soccer, softball W, swimming, tennis, track and field, volleyball W. **Intramural:** Archery, badminton, baseball M, basketball, cross-country, football M, golf M, ice hockey M, racquetball, rugby M, soccer, softball W, squash, swimming, table tennis, tennis, track and field, volleyball, water polo M. **Clubs:** Golf, water polo.

STUDENT SERVICES. Aptitude testing, career counseling, employment service for undergraduates, freshman orientation, health services, personal counseling, placement service for graduates, academic early warning system for freshmen, resident peer counseling, services/facilities for handicapped.

ANNUAL EXPENSES. Tuition and fees (1992-93): $14,450. **Room and board:** $4,450. **Books and supplies:** $600. **Other expenses:** $250.

FINANCIAL AID. 69% of freshmen, 64% of continuing students receive some form of aid. 76% of grants, 99% of loans, 52% of jobs based on need. 234 enrolled freshmen were judged to have need, all were offered aid. Academic, music/drama, athletic scholarships available. **Aid applications:** Closing date April 1; applicants notified on a rolling basis beginning on or about March 15; must reply by May 1 or within 2 weeks if notified thereafter. **Additional information:** Need-based parent loan program available.

ADDRESS/TELEPHONE. Karyl B. Clemens, Dean of Admissions, Hartwick College, Oneonta, NY 13820-9989. (607) 431-4150. (800) 828-2200. Fax: (607) 431-4154.

Helene Fuld School of Nursing
New York, New York CB code: 2327

1-year private nursing college, coed. Founded in 1964. **Accreditation:** Regional. **Undergraduate enrollment:** 183 men and women. **Faculty:** 16 total (13 full time), 2 with doctorates or other terminal degrees. **Location:** Urban campus in very large city; in midtown. **Calendar:** Quarter, limited summer session. **Microcomputers:** Located in libraries. **Additional facts:** One year, full-time program accredited by National League for Nursing. Part-time acredited study also offered.

DEGREES OFFERED. AAS. 101 associate degrees awarded in 1992. 100% in health sciences.

UNDERGRADUATE MAJORS. Nursing, practical nursing.

ACADEMIC PROGRAMS. 2-year transfer program. **Remedial services:** Learning center, reduced course load, remedial instruction, tutoring. **Placement/credit:** CLEP Subject, institutional tests.

ACADEMIC REQUIREMENTS. Freshmen must earn minimum GPA of 1.5 to continue in good standing. Students must declare major on application. **Graduation requirements:** 68 hours for associate (40 in major). Most students required to take courses in English, mathematics, biological/physical sciences, social sciences.

FRESHMAN ADMISSIONS. Selection criteria: All must be LPN with 1 year work experience. Exceptions for graduates of cooperating New York City Board of Education Schools of Adult Learning, who must rank in top 5% of their class and be recommended by their School's Director. Criteria for all applicants include satisfactory performance on preentrance testing and 4 credits of introductory chemistry, or successful performance on challenge tests and satisfactory employment references. **Test requirements:** Nelson-Denny Reading Comprehension Test; McGraw Hill's California Arithmetic Achievement Test required.

1992 FRESHMAN CLASS PROFILE. 1 man, 18 women enrolled. **Characteristics:** 100% commute, 90% have minority backgrounds. Average age is 32.

FALL-TERM APPLICATIONS. $50 fee. No closing date; applicants notified on a rolling basis; must reply by registration. Interview required. Deferred admission available.

STUDENT LIFE. Activities: Student government, magazine, radio, television.

STUDENT SERVICES. Career counseling, employment service for undergraduates, health services, personal counseling, special adviser for adult students.

ANNUAL EXPENSES. Tuition and fees (1992-93): $6,091. **Books and supplies:** $900. **Other expenses:** $1,524.

FINANCIAL AID. 84% of freshmen, 80% of continuing students receive some form of aid. 94% of grants based on need. Academic scholarships available. **Aid applications:** No closing date; applicants notified on a rolling basis beginning on or about May 15; must reply within 2 weeks.

ADDRESS/TELEPHONE. Gladys Pineda, Assistant Director of Student Administrative Services, Helene Fuld School of Nursing, 1879 Madison Avenue, New York, NY 10035. (212) 423-1000. Fax: (212) 427-2453.

Herkimer County Community College
Herkimer, New York CB code: 2316

2-year public community college, coed. Founded in 1966. **Accreditation:** Regional. **Undergraduate enrollment:** 783 men, 1,041 women full time; 192 men, 375 women part time. **Faculty:** 145 total (110 full time), 14 with doctorates or other terminal degrees. **Location:** Rural campus in small town; 15 miles from Utica. **Calendar:** Semester, limited summer session. **Microcomputers:** 130 located in libraries, classrooms, computer centers. **Special facilities:** 50-acre nature center, natural history museum, archeology museum, art gallery.

DEGREES OFFERED. AA, AS, AAS. 542 associate degrees awarded in 1992.

UNDERGRADUATE MAJORS. Accounting, allied health, biological and physical sciences, biology, business administration and management, business and management, business and office, business data processing and related programs, business data programming, chemical manufacturing technology, chemistry, clinical laboratory science, computer and information sciences, computer programming, conservation and regulation, construction, court reporting, criminal justice studies, data processing, drafting, early childhood education, engineering, engineering and engineering-related technologies, engineering and other disciplines, engineering science, fashion merchandising, finance, fine arts, flight attendants, food management, food production/management/services, food sciences, forestry and related sciences, funeral services/mortuary science, geriatric aide, gerontology, health care administration, hospitality and recreation marketing, humanities, humanities and social sciences, industrial technology, institutional/home management/supporting programs, insurance and risk management, insurance marketing, journalism, landscape architecture, law enforcement and corrections technologies, legal assistant/paralegal, legal secretary, liberal/general studies, marketing and distribution, marketing management, marketing research, mathematics, medical assistant, medical laboratory technologies, medical secretary, mental health/human services, occupational therapy assistant, office supervision and management, parks and recreation management, personal services, photographic technology, physical education, physical sciences, physical therapy, physical therapy assistant, physics, prepharmacy, psychology, public administration, public relations, radio/television broadcasting, radio/television technology, real estate, recreation and community services technologies, robotics, science technologies, secretarial and related programs, small business management and ownership, social sciences, social work, sociology, special education, sports management, sports medicine, telecommunications, tourism, word processing.

ACADEMIC PROGRAMS. 2-year transfer program, dual enrollment of high school students, honors program, internships. **Remedial services:** Learning center, reduced course load, remedial instruction, special counselor, tutoring. **Placement/credit:** AP, CLEP General and Subject, institutional tests; 32 credit hours maximum for associate degree.

ACADEMIC REQUIREMENTS. Freshmen must earn minimum GPA of 1.4 to continue in good standing. Students must declare major on enrollment. **Graduation requirements:** 62 hours for associate. Most students required to take courses in English, humanities, mathematics, biological/physical sciences, social sciences.

FRESHMAN ADMISSIONS. Selection criteria: Open admissions. Selective admissions for engineering science program and physical/occupational therapist assistant programs. Intermediate algebra and trigonometry, or Mathematics Level III required for engineering science applicants.

1992 FRESHMAN CLASS PROFILE. 479 men, 639 women enrolled. **Characteristics:** 99% from in state, 40% commute, 3% have minority backgrounds. Average age is 21.

FALL-TERM APPLICATIONS. $25 fee, may be waived for applicants with need. No closing date; applicants notified on a rolling basis; must reply within 4 weeks. Interview recommended for occupational/physical therapy assistant applicants. Early admission available.

STUDENT LIFE. Housing: Privately owned apartments in area available to students, with some shuttle bus service. Housing near campus available for 724 students. Approximately 60% of students live in this housing, another 40% commute from home. **Activities:** Student government, magazine, radio, student newspaper, television, dance, drama, musical theater, Students for a Better World, Social Issues Club, Students Against Drunk Driving, Campus Christian Fellowship.

ATHLETICS. NJCAA. **Intercollegiate:** Baseball M, basketball, bowling, field hockey W, lacrosse M, soccer, softball W, tennis W, track and field, volleyball W. **Intramural:** Basketball, bowling, lacrosse M, skiing, soccer, softball, tennis M, volleyball W.

STUDENT SERVICES. Career counseling, employment service for undergraduates, freshman orientation, health services, on-campus day care, personal counseling, placement service for graduates, special adviser for adult students, veterans counselor, services/facilities for handicapped.

ANNUAL EXPENSES. Tuition and fees (projected): $2,040, $1,900 additional for out-of-state students. **Books and supplies:** $500. **Other expenses:** $660.

FINANCIAL AID. 84% of freshmen, 76% of continuing students receive some form of aid. All grants, 92% of loans, 56% of jobs based on need. 690 enrolled freshmen were judged to have need, all were offered aid. Academic, athletic scholarships available. **Aid applications:** Closing date April 1; applicants notified on a rolling basis beginning on or about April 1; must reply within 2 weeks.

ADDRESS/TELEPHONE. Janet L. Tamburrino, Director of Admissions, Herkimer County Community College, Reservoir Road, Herkimer, NY 13350-1598. (315) 866-0300 ext. 278. (800) 947-4432 ext. 278. Fax: (315) 866-7253 ext. 278.

Hilbert College
Hamburg, New York — CB code: 2334

Admissions: 95% of applicants accepted
Based on: ••• School record
•• Activities, interview, recommendations
• Essay, special talents, test scores
Completion: 75% of freshmen end year in good standing

4-year private liberal arts college, coed. Founded in 1957. **Accreditation:** Regional. **Undergraduate enrollment:** 181 men, 313 women full time; 74 men, 241 women part time. **Faculty:** 53 total (23 full time), 14 with doctorates or other terminal degrees. **Location:** Suburban campus in large town; 10 miles from Buffalo. **Calendar:** Semester, limited summer session. Extensive evening/early morning classes. **Microcomputers:** 53 located in libraries, classrooms, computer centers. **Special facilities:** Comprehensive law library. **Additional facts:** Legal assistant program approved by American Bar Association.

DEGREES OFFERED. AA, AS, AAS, BA, BS. 140 associate degrees awarded in 1992. 24% in business and management, 26% law, 48% social sciences.

UNDERGRADUATE MAJORS. Associate: Accounting, business administration and management, business and management, business and office, business data processing and related programs, business economics, criminal justice studies, data processing, finance, humanities and social sciences, law enforcement and corrections technologies, legal assistant/paralegal, legal secretary, liberal/general studies, marketing and distribution, medical secretary, mental health/human services, secretarial and related programs, social sciences, social work, word processing. **Bachelor's:** Business administration and management, business and management, business economics, criminal justice studies, English, human services, humanities and social sciences, law enforcement and corrections technologies, legal assistant/paralegal.

ACADEMIC PROGRAMS. 2-year transfer program, cooperative education, double major, dual enrollment of high school students, independent study, internships, cross-registration. **Remedial services:** Reduced course load, remedial instruction, special counselor, tutoring. **Placement/credit:** AP, CLEP General and Subject, IB, institutional tests; 18 credit hours maximum for associate degree; 32 credit hours maximum for bachelor's degree.

ACADEMIC REQUIREMENTS. Freshmen must earn minimum GPA of 2.0 to continue in good standing. 85% of freshmen return for sophomore year. Students must declare major by end of first year. **Graduation requirements:** 64 hours for associate (24 in major), 120 hours for bachelor's (36 in major). Most students required to take courses in computer science, English, humanities, mathematics, philosophy/religion, biological/physical sciences, social sciences. **Postgraduate studies:** 65% from 2-year programs enter 4-year programs.

FRESHMAN ADMISSIONS. Selection criteria: Modified open admissions policy requires interview to determine if candidate meets minimum standards or should be referred for remedial assistance prior to acceptance. **High school preparation:** 9 units required; 10 recommended. Required and recommended units include English 4-4, mathematics 1-1 and social science 2-2. Biological science 1, physical science 1 and science 1 recommended. **Additional information:** GED preparation and fundamental skills programs available to prepare students for college-level study.

1992 FRESHMAN CLASS PROFILE. 78 men applied, 73 accepted, 63 enrolled; 167 women applied, 160 accepted, 107 enrolled. 8% had high school GPA of 3.0 or higher, 54% between 2.0 and 2.99. 5% were in top tenth and 20% were in top quarter of graduating class. **Academic background:** Mid 50% of enrolled freshmen had SAT-V between 360-490, SAT-M between 370-430; ACT composite between 14-17. 34% submitted SAT scores, 8% submitted ACT scores. **Characteristics:** 94% from in state, 92% commute, 6% have minority backgrounds, 1% are foreign students. Average age is 18.

FALL-TERM APPLICATIONS. $20 fee, may be waived for applicants with need. Closing date August 1; applicants notified on a rolling basis; must reply within 4 weeks. Interview recommended. Essay recommended. Deferred and early admission available.

STUDENT LIFE. Housing: Dormitories (coed). **Activities:** Student government, magazine, student newspaper, drama, Phi Beta Lambda, English club, Wanderers, paralegal club, ski club, Alpha Beta Gamma business honor fraternity, Comeback Club for Adults, accounting club, Criminal Justice Student Association, Business Administration Student Association.

ATHLETICS. NCAA. **Intercollegiate:** Baseball M, basketball, cross-country M, soccer, softball W, volleyball W. **Intramural:** Badminton, baseball, basketball, skiing, soccer, softball, table tennis, tennis, volleyball.

STUDENT SERVICES. Aptitude testing, career counseling, employment service for undergraduates, freshman orientation, personal counseling, placement service for graduates, special adviser for adult students, veterans counselor, services/facilities for handicapped.

ANNUAL EXPENSES. Tuition and fees: $7,200. **Room and board:** $4,250. **Books and supplies:** $500. **Other expenses:** $660.

FINANCIAL AID. 76% of freshmen, 78% of continuing students receive some form of aid. 92% of grants, 86% of loans, all jobs based on need. Academic, leadership, minority scholarships available. **Aid applications:** No closing date; priority given to applications received by February 28; applicants notified on a rolling basis beginning on or about April 15; must reply within 2 weeks.

ADDRESS/TELEPHONE. Bea Slick, Director of Admissions, Hilbert College, 5200 South Park Avenue, Hamburg, NY 14075. (716) 649-7900 ext. 211. Fax: (716) 649-0702.

Hobart College
Geneva, New York — CB code: 2294

Admissions: 72% of applicants accepted
Based on: ••• Activities, school record
•• Essay, recommendations, test scores
• Interview, special talents
Completion: 92% of freshmen end year in good standing
80% graduate, 26% of these enter graduate study

4-year private liberal arts college, men only, affiliated with Episcopal Church. Founded in 1822. **Accreditation:** Regional. **Undergraduate enrollment:** 1,061 men full time. **Faculty:** 154 total (141 full time), 148 with doctorates or other terminal degrees. **Location:** Rural campus in large town; 50 miles from Syracuse and Ithaca, 40 miles from Rochester. **Calendar:** Trimester. **Microcomputers:** 180 located in libraries, classrooms, computer centers, campus-wide network. **Special facilities:** 70-foot research vessel, 100-acre nature preserve, art gallery. **Additional facts:** Coordinate institution with William Smith College. All classes coeducational. All facilities and faculty shared.

DEGREES OFFERED. BA, BS. 239 bachelor's degrees awarded in 1992. 6% in area and ethnic studies, 20% letters/literature, 5% mathematics, 13% multi/interdisciplinary studies, 5% physical sciences, 39% social sciences.

UNDERGRADUATE MAJORS. Afro-American (black) studies, American studies, anthropology, architecture, art history, Asian studies, biology, chemistry, Chinese, classics, comparative literature, computer and information sciences, dance, dramatic arts, economics, English, environmental science, foreign languages (multiple emphasis), French, geoscience, geoscience, German, Greek (classical), history, Japanese, Latin, mathematics, music, philosophy, physics, political science and government, psychology, religion, Russian, Russian and Slavic studies, sociology, Spanish, studio art, third world studies, urban studies, women's studies.

ACADEMIC PROGRAMS. Accelerated program, double major, honors program, independent study, internships, semester at sea, student-designed major, study abroad, teacher preparation, visiting/exchange student program, New York semester, United Nations semester, Washington semester, cross-registration, Urban Semester, architecture and urban studies program in New York City, Intercollegiate Sri Lanka Educational Program, New York Visiting Students Program, combined degree program in architecture with Washington University, Missouri, and in engineering with Dartmouth College,

New Hampshire, Rensselaer Polytechnic Institute, and Rochester Institute of Technology, combined bachelor's/graduate degree program in business administration with Clarkson University, study abroad programs in China and India. **Remedial services:** Learning center, preadmission summer program, reduced course load, special counselor, tutoring, New York State Higher Education Opportunity Program. **Placement/credit:** AP, IB, institutional tests. Credit by examination counted toward degree is limited to equivalent of 7 courses.

ACADEMIC REQUIREMENTS. Freshmen must earn minimum GPA of 2.0 to continue in good standing. 85% of freshmen return for sophomore year. Students must declare major by end of second year. **Graduation requirements:** Most students required to take courses in arts/fine arts, humanities, biological/physical sciences, social sciences. **Postgraduate studies:** 4% enter law school, 3% enter medical school, 4% enter MBA programs, 15% enter other graduate study. **Additional information:** First-year seminar and sophomore bidisciplinary course required as part of general curriculum. Total of 36 courses required for graduation.

FRESHMAN ADMISSIONS. Selection criteria: Secondary school record, school and community activites, and test scores important. Recommendations, interview, and talent considered. Economically and educationally disadvantaged New York State students may apply through HEOP (Higher Education Opportunity Program). **High school preparation:** 18 units required. Required and recommended units include English 4, foreign language 2-3, mathematics 3, social science 2-3 and science 2. 2 history and 1 laboratory science required. Mathematics must include algebra, geometry, and trigonometry sequence. **Test requirements:** SAT or ACT; score report by March 1. Will review ACH tests if submitted by March 1.

1992 FRESHMAN CLASS PROFILE. 1,394 men applied, 1,004 accepted, 305 enrolled. **Academic background:** Mid 50% of enrolled freshmen had SAT-V between 500-550, SAT-M between 530-610; ACT composite between 23-27. 94% submitted SAT scores, 6% submitted ACT scores. **Characteristics:** 43% from in state, 100% live in college housing, 10% have minority backgrounds, 3% are foreign students. Average age is 18.

FALL-TERM APPLICATIONS. $40 fee, may be waived for applicants with need. Closing date February 15; applicants notified on or about April 1; must reply by May 1. Essay required. Interview recommended. Audition recommended. Portfolio recommended. CRDA. Deferred and early admission available. EDP-F. Early decision plan available. Application deadlines: November 15 and January 1. Notification within 30 days, must reply within 2 weeks.

STUDENT LIFE. Housing: Dormitories (men, coed); fraternity, cooperative housing available. Theme residences available. Coed dormitories available with William Smith College. **Activities:** Student government, film, magazine, radio, student newspaper, yearbook, choral groups, concert band, dance, drama, jazz band, music ensembles, musical theater, symphony orchestra, fraternities, Service Network, International Students Club, Big Brother, denominational clubs, African-American Student Coalition, political educational network, Latin-American Organization, Pan-African-Latin Organization, Gay, Lesbian, Bisexual, and Friends Network. **Additional information:** Undergraduates not residing in college housing live in their own apartments off campus.

ATHLETICS. NCAA. **Intercollegiate:** Baseball, basketball, cross-country, diving, football, golf, ice hockey, lacrosse, rowing (crew), skiing, soccer, squash, swimming, tennis, track and field. **Intramural:** Archery, badminton, basketball, bowling, cross-country, diving, fencing, golf, gymnastics, horseback riding, ice hockey, lacrosse, racquetball, rowing (crew), rugby, sailing, skiing, soccer, softball, squash, swimming, table tennis, tennis, track and field, volleyball, water polo. **Clubs:** Sailing.

STUDENT SERVICES. Career counseling, employment service for undergraduates, freshman orientation, health services, personal counseling, placement service for graduates, special adviser for adult students, services/facilities for handicapped.

ANNUAL EXPENSES. Tuition and fees: $18,309. **Room and board:** $5,616. **Books and supplies:** $650. **Other expenses:** $600.

FINANCIAL AID. 54% of freshmen, 48% of continuing students receive some form of aid. 89% of grants, 99% of loans, 69% of jobs based on need. 166 enrolled freshmen were judged to have need, 163 were offered aid. **Aid applications:** Closing date February 15; applicants notified on or about April 1; must reply by May 1.

ADDRESS/TELEPHONE. Mara O'Laughlin, Director of Admissions, Hobart College, 639 South Main Street, Geneva, NY 14456-3385. (315) 781-3622. (800) 852-2256. Fax: (315) 781-3914.

Hofstra University

Hempstead, New York — CB code: 2295

Admissions: 70% of applicants accepted
Based on:
- ••• School record, test scores
- •• Interview, recommendations
- • Activities, essay, special talents

Completion: 98% of freshmen end year in good standing
56% graduate, 36% of these enter graduate study

4-year private university, coed. Founded in 1935. **Accreditation:** Regional. **Undergraduate enrollment:** 3,113 men, 3,664 women full time; 641 men, 752 women part time. **Graduate enrollment:** 676 men, 631 women full time; 920 men, 1,601 women part time. **Faculty:** 904 total (433 full time), 513 with doctorates or other terminal degrees. **Location:** Suburban campus in large town; 25 miles from New York City. **Calendar:** Semester, limited summer session. Extensive evening/early morning classes. **Microcomputers:** 300 located in computer centers. **Special facilities:** Art gallery, animal tissue library, cell and tissue culture laboratory, arboretum, Kurzweil reading machines, electron microscopes, comprehensive child care and family center, arts-technology complex.

DEGREES OFFERED. BA, BS, BFA, MA, MS, MBA, MEd, PhD, EdD. 1,846 bachelor's degrees awarded in 1992. 46% in business and management, 7% communications, 5% letters/literature, 5% multi/interdisciplinary studies, 9% psychology, 11% social sciences. Graduate degrees offered in 61 major fields of study.

UNDERGRADUATE MAJORS. Accounting, African studies, American literature, American studies, anthropology, applied social science, aquaculture/mariculture, art education, art history, Asian studies, biochemistry, biological and physical sciences, biology, business administration and management, business and management, business economics, business education, ceramics, chemistry, cinematography/film, classics, communications, community health work, computer and information sciences, creative writing, dance, dramatic arts, earth sciences, economics, electrical/electronics/communications engineering, elementary education, engineering, engineering and other disciplines, engineering science, English, English education, English literature, finance, fine arts, foreign languages (multiple emphasis), foreign languages education, French, geography, geology, German, health education, Hebrew, Hispanic American studies, history, humanities and social sciences, Ibero-American studies, industrial engineering, information sciences and systems, international business management, Italian, jazz, Jewish studies, journalism, liberal/general studies, management information systems, management science, marketing management, mathematics, mathematics education, mechanical engineering, metal/jewelry, music, music education, music history and appreciation, music performance, painting, philosophy, photography, physical education, physics, political science and government, predentistry, prelaw, premedicine, preveterinary, psychology, publishing studies and literature, radio/television broadcasting, Russian, science education, sculpture, secondary education, secretarial and related programs, social sciences, social studies education, sociology, Spanish, speech, speech correction, speech pathology/audiology, speech/communication/theater education, technology and public policy, technology and public policy and economics, visual and performing arts.

ACADEMIC PROGRAMS. Accelerated program, double major, honors program, independent study, internships, student-designed major, study abroad, teacher preparation, Washington semester; liberal arts/career combination in engineering; combined bachelor's/graduate program in law. **Remedial services:** Preadmission summer program, reduced course load, special counselor, tutoring, basic studies program. **ROTC:** Army. **Placement/credit:** AP, CLEP General and Subject, institutional tests; 30 credit hours maximum for bachelor's degree.

ACADEMIC REQUIREMENTS. Freshmen must earn minimum GPA of 1.7 to continue in good standing. 87% of freshmen return for sophomore year. Students must declare major by end of second year. **Graduation requirements:** 124 hours for bachelor's (30 in major). Most students required to take courses in English, humanities, mathematics, biological/physical sciences, social sciences. **Postgraduate studies:** 6% enter law school, 4% enter medical school, 20% enter MBA programs, 6% enter other graduate study. **Additional information:** New College offers independent study, off-campus internships, and study abroad in addition to classroom work.

FRESHMAN ADMISSIONS. Selection criteria: Class rank most important, followed by SAT or ACT scores. Rank in top third of class and SAT combined score of 1000 usually result in acceptance. **High school preparation:** 16 units required. Required and recommended units include English 4, foreign language 2, mathematics 2-3, social science 3 and science 2. Physical science 1 recommended. Social sciences should include history. 4 mathematics, 1 chemistry, and 1 physics required for engineering. **Test requirements:** SAT or ACT; score report by April 15.

1992 FRESHMAN CLASS PROFILE. 6,890 men and women applied, 4,809 accepted; 1,485 enrolled. 50% had high school GPA of 3.0 or higher, 50% between 2.0 and 2.99. 25% were in top tenth and 65% were in top quarter of graduating class. **Academic background:** Mid 50% of enrolled freshmen had SAT-V between 430-560, SAT-M between 480-590; ACT composite between 23-27. 79% submitted SAT scores, 21% submitted ACT scores. **Characteristics:** 70% from in state, 50% commute, 13% have minority backgrounds, 1% are foreign students, 22% join fraternities/sororities. Average age is 19.

FALL-TERM APPLICATIONS. $25 fee, may be waived for applicants with need. No closing date; priority given to applications received by February 15; applicants notified on a rolling basis; must reply by May 1 or within 10 days if notified thereafter; special programs may have other deadlines. Interview recommended. Portfolio recommended for fine arts applicants. Essay recommended. Interview required of HEOP, special studies, and academic learning skills applicants, recommended for others. CRDA. Deferred and early admission available. EDP-S.

STUDENT LIFE. Housing: Dormitories (women, coed); apartment, handicapped housing available. Special interest housing available. **Activities:** Student government, film, magazine, radio, student newspaper, television, yearbook, choral groups, concert band, dance, drama, jazz band, music ensembles, musical theater, opera, pep band, symphony orchestra, fraternities, sororities, Over 117 political, religious, ethnic, academic, athletic, and social service organizations.

ATHLETICS. NCAA. **Intercollegiate:** Baseball M, basketball, cross-country, field hockey W, football M, golf M, lacrosse, soccer M, softball W, tennis, volleyball W, wrestling M. **Intramural:** Badminton, basketball, bowling, football M, rugby, soccer M, softball W, swimming, volleyball, water polo M, wrestling M.

STUDENT SERVICES. Aptitude testing, career counseling, employment service for undergraduates, freshman orientation, health services, on-campus day care, personal counseling, placement service for graduates, special adviser for adult students, veterans counselor, tutoring, services/facilities for handicapped.

ANNUAL EXPENSES. Tuition and fees (projected): $11,240. **Room and board:** $6,100. **Books and supplies:** $660. **Other expenses:** $1,000.

FINANCIAL AID. 80% of freshmen, 70% of continuing students receive some form of aid. 89% of grants, 79% of loans, 20% of jobs based on need. 1,393 enrolled freshmen were judged to have need, 1,044 were offered aid. Academic scholarships available. **Aid applications:** No closing date; priority given to applications received by March 1; applicants notified on a rolling basis beginning on or about March 1; must reply by May 1 or within 2 weeks if notified thereafter. **Additional information:** Special financial aid funds may be available for minority and low-income applicants.

ADDRESS/TELEPHONE. Joan Isaac Mohr, Dean of Admissions, Hofstra University, Holland House 100 Hofstra University, Hempstead, NY 11550-1090. (516) 463-6700. Fax: (516) 560-7660.

Holy Trinity Orthodox Seminary
Jordanville, New York — CB code: 2298

4-year private seminary college, men only, affiliated with Russian Orthodox Church. Founded in 1948. **Undergraduate enrollment:** 37 men full time. **Location:** Rural campus in rural community. **Calendar:** Semester.

FRESHMAN ADMISSIONS. Selection criteria: Orthodoxy, knowledge of Russian, entrance exam required. Recommendation from spiritual Father important.

ANNUAL EXPENSES. Tuition and fees: $1,000. **Room and board:** $1,000. **Books and supplies:** $100.

ADDRESS/TELEPHONE. Rev. George Skrinniko, Chief of Administration, Holy Trinity Orthodox Seminary, Jordanville, NY 13361. (315) 858-0940.

Houghton College ⇎
Houghton, New York — CB code: 2299

Admissions:	84% of applicants accepted
Based on:	••• Religious affiliation/commitment, school record
	•• Essay, recommendations, test scores
	• Activities, interview, special talents
Completion:	95% of freshmen end year in good standing
	63% graduate, 21% of these enter graduate study

4-year private liberal arts college, coed, affiliated with Wesleyan Church. Founded in 1883. **Accreditation:** Regional. **Undergraduate enrollment:** 429 men, 697 women full time; 17 men, 20 women part time. **Faculty:** 121 total (82 full time), 84 with doctorates or other terminal degrees. **Location:** Rural campus in rural community; 55 miles from Buffalo. **Calendar:** Semester, limited summer session. **Microcomputers:** 110 located in dormitories, libraries, classrooms, computer centers. **Special facilities:** Equestrian farm with indoor riding ring, initiatives course, downhill and cross-country skiing facilities. **Additional facts:** Extension campus in suburban Buffalo.

DEGREES OFFERED. AA, AAS, BA, BS. 5 associate degrees awarded in 1992. 67% in multi/interdisciplinary studies, 33% philosophy, religion, theology. 214 bachelor's degrees awarded. 18% in business and management, 7% communications, 18% teacher education, 6% life sciences, 8% mathematics, 7% philosophy, religion, theology, 17% psychology, 6% social sciences.

UNDERGRADUATE MAJORS. Associate: Bible studies, liberal/general studies. **Bachelor's:** Accounting, art education, Bible studies, biological and physical sciences, biology, business administration and management, chemistry, communications, creative writing, elementary education, English, English education, English literature, fine arts, foreign languages education, French, history, humanities, humanities and social sciences, international studies, junior high education, mathematics, mathematics education, medical laboratory technologies, music, music education, music performance, music theory and composition, philosophy, physical education, physics, political science and government, predentistry, preengineering, prelaw, premedicine, preveterinary, psychology, recreation and community services technologies, recreation therapy, religion, religious education, science education, secondary education, social sciences, social studies education, sociology, Spanish.

ACADEMIC PROGRAMS. 2-year transfer program, accelerated program, double major, dual enrollment of high school students, honors program, independent study, internships, study abroad, teacher preparation, visiting/exchange student program, Washington semester, cross-registration, 3-2 combined degree program with Clarkson University. **Remedial services:** Learning center, reduced course load, remedial instruction, special counselor, tutoring. **ROTC:** Army. **Placement/credit:** AP, CLEP Subject, institutional tests; 30 credit hours maximum for associate degree; 30 credit hours maximum for bachelor's degree.

ACADEMIC REQUIREMENTS. Freshmen must earn minimum GPA of 2.0 to continue in good standing. 88% of freshmen return for sophomore year. Students must declare major by end of second year. **Graduation requirements:** 65 hours for associate (17 in major), 125 hours for bachelor's (25 in major). Most students required to take courses in arts/fine arts, English, foreign languages, history, mathematics, philosophy/religion, biological/physical sciences, social sciences. **Postgraduate studies:** 61% from 2-year programs enter 4-year programs. 2% enter law school, 5% enter medical school, 1% enter MBA programs, 13% enter other graduate study. **Additional information:** School of Music accredited by National Association of Schools of Music.

FRESHMAN ADMISSIONS. Selection criteria: Class rank, GPA, test scores, pastor's recommendation, personal letter required. **High school preparation:** 13 units recommended. Recommended units include English 4, foreign language 2, mathematics 2, social science 3 and science 2. Mathematics recommendation includes 1 algebra, 1 geometry. **Test requirements:** SAT or ACT; score report by June 30.

1992 FRESHMAN CLASS PROFILE. 265 men applied, 212 accepted, 99 enrolled; 516 women applied, 443 accepted, 195 enrolled. 74% had high school GPA of 3.0 or higher, 26% between 2.0 and 2.99. 29% were in top tenth and 57% were in top quarter of graduating class. **Academic background:** Mid 50% of enrolled freshmen had SAT-V between 440-570, SAT-M between 470-590; ACT composite between 19-27. 91% submitted SAT scores, 32% submitted ACT scores. **Characteristics:** 62% from in state, 95% live in college housing, 6% have minority backgrounds, 3% are foreign students. Average age is 18.

FALL-TERM APPLICATIONS. $25 fee, may be waived for applicants with need. Closing date June 1; priority given to applications received by March 1; applicants notified on a rolling basis; must reply by May 1 or within 4 weeks if notified thereafter. Audition required for music applicants. Essay required. Interview recommended. Portfolio recommended for art applicants. CRDA. Deferred and early admission available.

STUDENT LIFE. Housing: Dormitories (men, women); apartment, cooperative housing available. **Activities:** Student government, magazine, radio, student newspaper, television, yearbook, choral groups, concert band, drama, jazz band, music ensembles, opera, symphony orchestra, Christian Student Outreach, Allegany County Outreach, campus prayer meetings, Bible studies, international student association, World Missions Fellowship, Afro-American Culture Exchange, Evangelicals for Social Action, Habitat for Humanity. **Additional information:** Compulsory chapel attendance. Smoking, social dancing, and drinking of alcoholic beverages on or off campus prohibited. Most students live either in dormitories or in residences approved by institution. Approximately 5% commute from home. Religious observance required.

ATHLETICS. NAIA. **Intercollegiate:** Basketball, cross-country, field hockey W, soccer, track and field, volleyball W. **Intramural:** Basketball, horseback riding, racquetball, skiing, soccer, softball, swimming, tennis, volleyball.

STUDENT SERVICES. Aptitude testing, career counseling, employment service for undergraduates, freshman orientation, health services, personal counseling, placement service for graduates, services/facilities for handicapped.

ANNUAL EXPENSES. Tuition and fees (1992-93): $9,230. **Room and board:** $3,260. **Books and supplies:** $500. **Other expenses:** $600.

FINANCIAL AID. 94% of freshmen, 90% of continuing students receive some form of aid. 88% of grants, 99% of loans, 53% of jobs based on need. 224 enrolled freshmen were judged to have need, all were offered aid. Academic, music/drama, art, athletic, state/district residency, leadership, alumni affiliation, religious affiliation, minority scholarships available. **Aid applications:** No closing date; priority given to applications received by March 15; applicants notified on a rolling basis beginning on or about March 1; must reply by May 1 or within 4 weeks if notified thereafter.

ADDRESS/TELEPHONE. Tim Fuller, Executive Director of Admissions, Houghton College, 1 Willard Avenue, Houghton, NY 14744-9989. (716) 567-9353. (800) 777-2556. Fax: (716) 567-9522.

Hudson Valley Community College
Troy, New York CB code: 2300

2-year public community college, coed. Founded in 1953. **Accreditation:** Regional. **Undergraduate enrollment:** 3,673 men, 2,371 women full time; 1,934 men, 2,669 women part time. **Faculty:** 540 total (269 full time), 19 with doctorates or other terminal degrees. **Location:** Suburban campus in small city; 10 miles from Albany. **Calendar:** Semester, limited summer session. Saturday and extensive evening/early morning classes. **Microcomputers:** 300 located in libraries, classrooms, computer centers. **Special facilities:** Language laboratory. **Additional facts:** SUNY institution.

DEGREES OFFERED. AA, AS, AAS. 1,543 associate degrees awarded in 1992. 30% in business/office and marketing/distribution, 30% engineering technologies, 20% life sciences, 10% mathematics, 10% parks/recreation, protective services, public affairs.

UNDERGRADUATE MAJORS. Accounting, air conditioning/heating/refrigeration mechanics, air conditioning/heating/refrigeration technology, automotive mechanics, biological and physical sciences, biology, business administration and management, business and office, business data processing and related programs, carpentry, chemical manufacturing technology, chemistry, child development/care/guidance, civil technology, community services, construction, criminal justice technology, data processing, dental hygiene, drafting, electrical installation, electrical technology, engineering, engineering and engineering-related technologies, engineering and other disciplines, engineering science, environmental science, finance, forestry and related sciences, funeral services/mortuary science, humanities and social sciences, industrial technology, insurance and risk management, international business management, laser electro-optic technology, law enforcement and corrections technologies, liberal/general studies, machine tool operation/machine shop, marketing and distribution, marketing management, mathematics, mechanical design technology, medical laboratory technologies, medical secretary, nursing, physical education, physical sciences, physician's assistant, protective services, public affairs, radiograph medical technology, real estate, respiratory therapy, respiratory therapy technology, secretarial and related programs, social sciences, social work, telecommunications, ultrasound technology.

ACADEMIC PROGRAMS. 2-year transfer program, accelerated program, computer delivered (on-line) credit-bearing course offerings, cooperative education, dual enrollment of high school students, internships, student-designed major, cross-registration. **Remedial services:** Learning center, pre-admission summer program, reduced course load, remedial instruction, special counselor, tutoring, reading, writing, mathematics laboratories. **ROTC:** Army. **Placement/credit:** AP, CLEP General and Subject; 30 credit hours maximum for associate degree.

ACADEMIC REQUIREMENTS. Freshmen must earn minimum GPA of 1.7 to continue in good standing. 50% of freshmen return for sophomore year. Students must declare major on application. **Graduation requirements:** 65 hours for associate (50 in major). Most students required to take courses in English, mathematics.

FRESHMAN ADMISSIONS. Selection criteria: Open admissions. Selective admissions to some programs, based on school achievement record and test scores. Interview also considered for some programs. Requirements vary for selective programs. **Test requirements:** SAT or ACT required for admission to some programs.

1992 FRESHMAN CLASS PROFILE. 2,271 men, 1,792 women enrolled. **Characteristics:** 97% from in state, 100% commute, 7% have minority backgrounds, 1% are foreign students. Average age is 19.

FALL-TERM APPLICATIONS. $25 fee, may be waived for applicants with need. No closing date; applicants notified on a rolling basis; must reply within 4 weeks. Interview recommended for mortuary science, human services, environmental science, individual studies applicants. Deferred and early admission available.

STUDENT LIFE. Activities: Student government, radio, student newspaper, television, yearbook, concert band, drama, jazz band, musical theater.

ATHLETICS. NJCAA. **Intercollegiate:** Baseball M, basketball, bowling, cross-country, football M, golf, ice hockey M, lacrosse M, soccer, softball W, tennis, track and field, volleyball W. **Intramural:** Baseball M, basketball, bowling, cross-country, field hockey, golf, ice hockey, lacrosse, racquetball, skiing, soccer, softball, table tennis, tennis, track and field, volleyball, wrestling M.

STUDENT SERVICES. Aptitude testing, career counseling, employment service for undergraduates, freshman orientation, health services, on-campus day care, personal counseling, placement service for graduates, special adviser for adult students, veterans counselor, services/facilities for handicapped.

ANNUAL EXPENSES. Tuition and fees (1992-93): $1,584, $1,650 additional for out-of-state students. **Books and supplies:** $550. **Other expenses:** $800.

FINANCIAL AID. 60% of freshmen receive some form of aid. All grants, 75% of loans, all jobs based on need. **Aid applications:** No closing date; priority given to applications received by May 30; applicants notified on a rolling basis beginning on or about May 1; must reply within 2 weeks.

ADDRESS/TELEPHONE. Linda Sweetman, Director of Admissions, Hudson Valley Community College, 80 Vandenburgh Avenue, Troy, NY 12180. (518) 283-1100. Fax: (518) 270-1576.

Institute of Design and Construction
Brooklyn, New York CB code: 0677

2-year private junior, technical college, coed. Founded in 1947. **Undergraduate enrollment:** 75 men, 8 women full time; 128 men, 21 women part time. **Faculty:** 40 total. **Location:** Urban campus in very large city. **Calendar:** Semester. Saturday and extensive evening/early morning classes. **Additional facts:** Classes and seminars available for candidates preparing for Architects Registration Exam (ARE).

DEGREES OFFERED. 15 associate degrees awarded in 1992. 100% in architecture and environmental design.

UNDERGRADUATE MAJORS. Architectural technologies, architecture, construction, drafting.

ACADEMIC PROGRAMS. 2-year transfer program, double major. **Remedial services:** Remedial instruction.

ACADEMIC REQUIREMENTS. Freshmen must earn minimum GPA of 1.00 to continue in good standing. Students must declare major by end of first year. **Graduation requirements:** 66 hours for associate (24 in major). Most students required to take courses in mathematics. **Additional information:** Work and study plan available. Students can spend 2 full-time semesters in accelerated study, then complete degree through post-time evening study while working during day as junior drafters. Credits transferable to Pratt Institute and New York Institute of Technology.

FRESHMAN ADMISSIONS. Selection criteria: Open admissions.

1992 FRESHMAN CLASS PROFILE. 93 men and women enrolled. **Characteristics:** 95% from in state, 100% commute, 80% have minority backgrounds, 5% are foreign students. Average age is 22.

FALL-TERM APPLICATIONS. $20 fee, may be waived for applicants with need. No closing date; applicants notified on a rolling basis; must reply within 6 weeks. Interview recommended. Deferred and early admission available.

STUDENT SERVICES. Career counseling, employment service for undergraduates, freshman orientation, personal counseling, placement service for graduates.

ANNUAL EXPENSES. Tuition and fees: $3,650. **Books and supplies:** $600. **Other expenses:** $400.

FINANCIAL AID. 60% of freshmen, 50% of continuing students receive some form of aid. All loans based on need. **Aid applications:** No closing date; applicants notified on a rolling basis beginning on or about March 1; must reply within 4 weeks.

ADDRESS/TELEPHONE. Kevin Giannetti, Director of Admissions, Institute of Design and Construction, 141 Willoughby Street, Brooklyn, NY 11201-5380. (718) 855-3661. Fax: (718) 852-5889.

Interboro Institute
New York, New York CB code: 1675

2-year proprietary business college, coed. Founded in 1888. **Undergraduate enrollment:** 290 men, 578 women full time; 23 men, 28 women part time. **Location:** Urban campus in very large city. **Calendar:** Trimester. **Additional facts:** Articulation agreements with several 4-year colleges. Ophthalmic dispensing program offered.

FRESHMAN ADMISSIONS. Selection criteria: Open admissions.

ANNUAL EXPENSES. Tuition and fees: $7,878. **Books and supplies:** $450. **Other expenses:** $1,000.

ADDRESS/TELEPHONE. Alvin Morrison, Director of Admissions, Interboro Institute, 450 West 56th Street, New York, NY 10019. (212) 399-0091.

Iona College
New Rochelle, New York CB code: 2324

Admissions: 70% of applicants accepted
Based on:
- ••• School record
- •• Interview
- • Activities, essay, recommendations, special talents, test scores

Completion: 85% of freshmen end year in good standing
60% graduate, 10% of these enter graduate study

4-year private liberal arts college, coed, nondenominational. Founded in 1940. **Accreditation:** Regional. **Undergraduate enrollment:** 1,958 men, 2,207 women full time; 629 men, 1,245 women part time. **Graduate enrollment:** 55 men, 83 women full time; 591 men, 834 women part time. **Faculty:** 511

total (204 full time), 275 with doctorates or other terminal degrees. **Location:** Suburban campus in small city; 20 miles from New York City. **Calendar:** 4-1-4, extensive summer session. **Microcomputers:** 350 located in dormitories, libraries, classrooms, computer centers, campus-wide network. **Special facilities:** Extensive Irish and rare books collection, community arts center. **Additional facts:** Independent institution in Roman Catholic Christian Brothers tradition.

DEGREES OFFERED. AA, AAS, BA, BS, MA, MS, MBA, MEd. 261 associate degrees awarded in 1992. 23% in business and management, 5% teacher education, 41% health sciences, 5% law, 23% multi/interdisciplinary studies. 897 bachelor's degrees awarded. 44% in business and management, 11% communications, 7% computer sciences, 7% psychology, 7% social sciences. Graduate degrees offered in 34 major fields of study.

UNDERGRADUATE MAJORS. Associate: Business administration and management, business and office, data processing, early childhood education, fine arts, illustration design, legal assistant/paralegal, liberal/general studies, marketing and distribution, nursing, practical nursing, radio/television broadcasting, retailing. **Bachelor's:** Accounting, advertising, American studies, behavioral sciences, biochemistry, biological and physical sciences, biology, business administration and management, business and management, business economics, business education, chemistry, classics, clinical laboratory science, communications, computer and information sciences, criminal justice studies, criminology, demography, dramatic arts, ecology, economics, education, elementary education, English, English education, English literature, finance, foreign languages education, French, health care administration, history, humanities, humanities and social sciences, information sciences and systems, institutional management, international relations, international studies, Italian, journalism, junior high education, law enforcement and corrections, liberal/general studies, management information systems, management science, marketing and distribution, marketing management, mathematics, mathematics education, medical laboratory technologies, philosophy, physics, political science and government, predentistry, prelaw, premedicine, psychology, public relations, radio/television broadcasting, radio/television technology, religion, science education, secondary education, social sciences, social studies education, social work, sociology, Spanish, special education, speech, speech pathology/audiology, speech/communication/theater education, trade and industrial supervision and management, urban studies.

ACADEMIC PROGRAMS. 2-year transfer program, accelerated program, cooperative education, double major, education specialist degree, honors program, independent study, internships, study abroad, teacher preparation, weekend college, cross-registration; liberal arts/career combination in engineering; combined bachelor's/graduate program in business administration. **Remedial services:** Learning center, preadmission summer program, reduced course load, remedial instruction, special counselor, tutoring. **ROTC:** Air Force, Army. **Placement/credit:** AP, CLEP General and Subject, institutional tests; 60 credit hours maximum for bachelor's degree.

ACADEMIC REQUIREMENTS. Freshmen must earn minimum GPA of 2.0 to continue in good standing. 80% of freshmen return for sophomore year. Students must declare major by end of second year. **Graduation requirements:** 60 hours for associate (20 in major), 120 hours for bachelor's (65 in major). Most students required to take courses in arts/fine arts, computer science, English, foreign languages, history, humanities, mathematics, philosophy/religion, biological/physical sciences, social sciences.

FRESHMAN ADMISSIONS. Selection criteria: High school achievement record and interview most important, followed by test scores, recommendations, and extracurricular activities. **High school preparation:** 16 units required. Required units include English 4, foreign language 2, mathematics 3, social science 2 and science 2. Social science should include 1 American history. **Test requirements:** SAT or ACT (SAT preferred); score report by July 15. ACH required. Score report by July 15.

1992 FRESHMAN CLASS PROFILE. 4,652 men and women applied, 3,264 accepted; 553 men enrolled, 570 women enrolled. 13% were in top tenth and 33% were in top quarter of graduating class. **Academic background:** Mid 50% of enrolled freshmen had SAT-V between 350-470, SAT-M between 390-520. 96% submitted SAT scores. **Characteristics:** 100% from in state, 92% commute, 34% have minority backgrounds, 31% join fraternities/sororities. Average age is 19.

FALL-TERM APPLICATIONS. $25 fee, may be waived for applicants with need. No closing date; priority given to applications received by March 15; applicants notified on a rolling basis beginning on or about February 15; must reply by May 1 or within 4 weeks if notified thereafter. Interview recommended. Essay recommended. CRDA. Deferred and early admission available. EDP-F.

STUDENT LIFE. Housing: Dormitories (men, women, coed). Women's housing at nearby College of New Rochelle. Coed housing available at Concordia College. New 320-bed dormitory. **Activities:** Student government, film, magazine, radio, student newspaper, television, yearbook, choral groups, dance, drama, musical theater, pep band, bagpipe band, fraternities, sororities, Big Brothers, Big Sisters, Special Olympics, Circle-K, People's Club, Gaelic Society, and campus ministry. **Additional information:** Active campus ministry.

ATHLETICS. NAIA, NCAA. **Intercollegiate:** Baseball M, basketball, cross-country M, diving, football M, golf, ice hockey M, lacrosse M, rowing (crew), soccer M, softball W, swimming, tennis, track and field M, volleyball W, water polo M. **Intramural:** Badminton M, basketball M, bowling, lacrosse M, rugby M, softball, tennis M, volleyball.

STUDENT SERVICES. Aptitude testing, career counseling, employment service for undergraduates, freshman orientation, health services, personal counseling, placement service for graduates, special adviser for adult students, tutorial center, services/facilities for handicapped.

ANNUAL EXPENSES. Tuition and fees (1992-93): $9,540. **Room and board:** $6,000. **Books and supplies:** $500. **Other expenses:** $1,050.

FINANCIAL AID. 89% of freshmen, 89% of continuing students receive some form of aid. Grants, loans, jobs available. 960 enrolled freshmen were judged to have need, all were offered aid. Academic, art, athletic, leadership, alumni affiliation scholarships available. **Aid applications:** No closing date; priority given to applications received by April 1; applicants notified on a rolling basis beginning on or about February 1; must reply by May 1 or within 2 weeks if notified thereafter.

ADDRESS/TELEPHONE. Laurie Austin, Director of Admissions, Iona College, 715 North Avenue, New Rochelle, NY 10801-1890. (914) 633-2000. (800) 231-IONA (New York State).

Ithaca College

Ithaca, New York — CB code: 2325

Admissions:	78% of applicants accepted
Based on:	••• School record
	•• Activities, essay, recommendations, special talents, test scores
	• Interview
Completion:	95% of freshmen end year in good standing
	68% graduate, 26% of these enter graduate study

4-year private college of arts and sciences and health science college, coed. Founded in 1892. **Accreditation:** Regional. **Undergraduate enrollment:** 2,769 men, 3,084 women full time; 41 men, 47 women part time. **Graduate enrollment:** 31 men, 71 women full time; 4 men, 11 women part time. **Faculty:** 597 total (470 full time), 458 with doctorates or other terminal degrees. **Location:** Suburban campus in large town; 250 miles from New York City. **Calendar:** Semester, extensive summer session. **Microcomputers:** 300 located in libraries, classrooms, computer centers, campus-wide network. **Special facilities:** Multi-image and interactive video labs, nuclear magnetic resonance equipment, new science complex.

DEGREES OFFERED. BA, BS, BFA, MS. 1,534 bachelor's degrees awarded in 1992. 19% in business and management, 16% communications, 5% education, 8% teacher education, 9% health sciences, 5% allied health, 8% letters/literature, 6% psychology, 8% social sciences, 5% visual and performing arts. Graduate degrees offered in 9 major fields of study.

UNDERGRADUATE MAJORS. Accounting, anthropology, art history, basic clinical health sciences, biochemistry, biology, business administration and management, chemistry, cinematography/film, communications, community health work, computer and information sciences, computer mathematics, dance, dramatic arts, economics, education of the deaf and hearing impaired, educational media technology, English, English education, film arts, finance, foreign languages education, French, German, health care administration, health education, health sciences, history, information sciences and systems, international business management, jazz, journalism, labor/industrial relations, liberal/general studies, marketing research, mathematics, mathematics education, medical records administration, music, music education, music performance, music theory and composition, musical theater, parks and recreation management, personnel management, philosophy, photography, physical education, physical therapy, physics, political science and government, predentistry, prelaw, premedicine, psychology, radio/television broadcasting, religion, science education, social sciences, social studies education, sociology, Spanish, speech, speech correction, speech pathology/audiology, speech/communication/theater education, studio art, telecommunications, theater design.

ACADEMIC PROGRAMS. Double major, dual enrollment of high school students, honors program, independent study, internships, student-designed major, study abroad, teacher preparation, cross-registration, London Center; liberal arts/career combination in engineering. **Remedial services:** Learning center, tutoring. **ROTC:** Air Force, Army. **Placement/credit:** AP, CLEP General and Subject, IB, institutional tests; 90 credit hours maximum for bachelor's degree.

ACADEMIC REQUIREMENTS. Freshmen must earn minimum GPA of 2.0 to continue in good standing. 87% of freshmen return for sophomore year. Students must declare major by end of second year. **Graduation requirements:** 120 hours for bachelor's (40 in major). Most students required to take courses in computer science, English, humanities, social sciences. **Postgraduate studies:** 3% enter law school, 1% enter medical school, 2% enter MBA programs, 20% enter other graduate study.

FRESHMAN ADMISSIONS. Selection criteria: School achievement record most important. School and community activities, accomplishments, special talents, interview, test scores also considered. **High school preparation:** 16 units required. Required units include biological science 1, English

4, foreign language 2, mathematics 3, physical science 2 and social science 2. **Test requirements:** SAT or ACT (SAT preferred); score report by March 1.

1992 FRESHMAN CLASS PROFILE. 7,113 men and women applied, 5,572 accepted; 735 men enrolled, 833 women enrolled. 21% were in top tenth and 52% were in top quarter of graduating class. **Academic background:** Mid 50% of enrolled freshmen had SAT-V between 440-530, SAT-M between 490-590. 95% submitted SAT scores. **Characteristics:** 46% from in state, 99% live in college housing, 6% have minority backgrounds, 1% are foreign students. Average age is 18.

FALL-TERM APPLICATIONS. $40 fee, may be waived for applicants with need. No closing date; priority given to applications received by March 1; applicants notified on a rolling basis beginning on or about December 15; must reply by May 1 or within 2 weeks if notified thereafter. Audition required for music, theater arts applicants. Essay required. Interview recommended. Portfolio recommended for BFA program applicants. CRDA. Deferred and early admission available. EDP-F.

STUDENT LIFE. Housing: Dormitories (men, women, coed); apartment, fraternity, sorority housing available. Housing guaranteed for undergraduates. **Activities:** Student government, film, magazine, radio, student newspaper, television, yearbook, forensics, choral groups, concert band, dance, drama, jazz band, music ensembles, musical theater, opera, pep band, symphony orchestra, fraternities, sororities, Jewish, Christian, Catholic, and Christian Science organizations, Afro-Latin Society, Fellowship for Human Awareness, social service organizations, Young Republicans, International Club.

ATHLETICS. NCAA. **Intercollegiate:** Baseball M, basketball, cross-country, diving, field hockey W, football M, golf M, gymnastics W, lacrosse, rowing (crew), soccer, softball W, swimming, tennis, track and field, volleyball W, wrestling M. **Intramural:** Badminton, basketball, cross-country, golf, soccer, softball, table tennis, tennis, volleyball. **Clubs:** Ice hockey M.

STUDENT SERVICES. Aptitude testing, career counseling, employment service for undergraduates, freshman orientation, health services, personal counseling, placement service for graduates, special adviser for adult students, veterans counselor.

ANNUAL EXPENSES. Tuition and fees (1992-93): $12,870. **Room and board:** $5,512. **Books and supplies:** $500. **Other expenses:** $910.

FINANCIAL AID. 55% of freshmen, 51% of continuing students receive some form of aid. All grants, 89% of loans, all jobs based on need. 868 enrolled freshmen were judged to have need, all were offered aid. Music/drama scholarships available. **Aid applications:** Closing date March 1; applicants notified on a rolling basis beginning on or about March 1; must reply by May 1.

ADDRESS/TELEPHONE. Paula J. Mitchell, Director of Admissions, Ithaca College, Job Hall, Ithaca, NY 14850. (607) 274-3124. Fax: (607) 274-3474.

Jamestown Business College
Jamestown, New York — CB code: 2346

Admissions: 95% of applicants accepted
Based on:
- ••• School record
- •• Interview, test scores
- • Activities

Completion: 81% of freshmen end year in good standing
3% enter 4-year programs

2-year proprietary business college, coed. Founded in 1886. **Undergraduate enrollment:** 21 men, 276 women full time; 10 women part time. **Faculty:** 14 total (7 full time). **Location:** Suburban campus in large town; 80 miles from Buffalo, 60 miles from Erie, Pennsylvania. **Calendar:** Semester. **Microcomputers:** 45 located in classrooms, computer centers.

DEGREES OFFERED. 76 associate degrees awarded in 1992. 29% in business and management, 71% business/office and marketing/distribution.

UNDERGRADUATE MAJORS. Accounting, business and office, business data processing and related programs, legal secretary, marketing and distribution, marketing management, medical assistant, medical secretary, secretarial and related programs, word processing.

ACADEMIC PROGRAMS. Cross-registration. **Remedial services:** Reduced course load, remedial instruction, special counselor, tutoring. **Placement/credit:** Institutional tests.

ACADEMIC REQUIREMENTS. Freshmen must earn minimum GPA of 1.75 to continue in good standing. 74% of freshmen return for sophomore year. Students must declare major on enrollment. **Graduation requirements:** 60 hours for associate. Most students required to take courses in computer science, English, mathematics.

FRESHMAN ADMISSIONS. Selection criteria: Class rank and academic record important. School and community activities considered. **Test requirements:** Institutionally designed tests required for academically weak applicants.

1992 FRESHMAN CLASS PROFILE. 9 men applied, 7 accepted, 6 enrolled; 173 women applied, 165 accepted, 117 enrolled. **Characteristics:** 74% from in state, 85% commute, 1% have minority backgrounds. Average age is 23.

FALL-TERM APPLICATIONS. $25 fee. No closing date; applicants notified on a rolling basis. Interview recommended.

STUDENT LIFE. Activities: Student government, student newspaper, yearbook, business club, secretarial club. **Additional information:** Approximately 15% of undergraduates live in privately owned housing available to students, remaining 85% commute from home.

ATHLETICS. Intramural: Baseball M, softball W, volleyball.

STUDENT SERVICES. Career counseling, employment service for undergraduates, freshman orientation, personal counseling, placement service for graduates, special adviser for adult students, services/facilities for handicapped.

ANNUAL EXPENSES. Tuition and fees (1992-93): $4,925. **Books and supplies:** $450. **Other expenses:** $725.

FINANCIAL AID. 89% of freshmen, 89% of continuing students receive some form of aid. 94% of grants, 93% of loans based on need. Academic, minority scholarships available. **Aid applications:** No closing date; applicants notified on a rolling basis beginning on or about February 15; must reply by July 31 or within 2 weeks if notified thereafter.

ADDRESS/TELEPHONE. Sherrie L. Benson, Director of Admissions, Jamestown Business College, 7 Fairmount Avenue, Jamestown, NY 14701. (716) 664-5100. Fax: (716) 664-3144.

Jamestown Community College
Jamestown, New York — CB code: 2335

2-year public community college, coed. Founded in 1950. **Accreditation:** Regional. **Undergraduate enrollment:** 1,036 men, 1,305 women full time; 772 men, 1,551 women part time. **Faculty:** 316 total (129 full time), 21 with doctorates or other terminal degrees. **Location:** Rural campus in large town; 70 miles from Buffalo, New York and Erie, Pennsylvania. **Calendar:** Semester, extensive summer session. **Microcomputers:** 130 located in libraries, classrooms, computer centers. **Special facilities:** Forum art gallery, local history special collections, Roger Tory Peterson Institute for Natural History. **Additional facts:** SUNY institution. Branch campus at Olean for Cattaraugus County. Extensions in Dunkirk, Warren, and Ripley.

DEGREES OFFERED. AA, AS, AAS. 773 associate degrees awarded in 1992. 21% in business and management, 10% health sciences, 11% letters/literature, 7% life sciences, 7% mathematics, 9% parks/recreation, protective services, public affairs, 28% social sciences.

UNDERGRADUATE MAJORS. Accounting, air conditioning/heating/refrigeration mechanics, air conditioning/heating/refrigeration technology, anthropology, biological and physical sciences, biology, business administration and management, business and management, business data processing and related programs, business data programming, chemistry, communications, community services, computer and information sciences, computer programming, computer servicing technology, computer technology, criminal justice studies, economics, electrical technology, engineering, engineering and engineering-related technologies, English, environmental science, fine arts, French, geology, history, humanities, humanities and social sciences, information sciences and systems, law enforcement and corrections technologies, liberal/general studies, marketing and distribution, marketing management, mathematics, mechanical design technology, mechanical technology, medical laboratory technologies, music, nursing, philosophy, physical sciences, physics, political science and government, psychology, retailing, social sciences, social work, sociology, Spanish, visual and performing arts.

ACADEMIC PROGRAMS. 2-year transfer program, dual enrollment of high school students, honors program, independent study, internships, study abroad, telecourses, weekend college, Washington semester, cross-registration, nursing in cooperation with Daemen College. **Remedial services:** Learning center, preadmission summer program, reduced course load, remedial instruction, special counselor, tutoring. **Placement/credit:** AP, CLEP General and Subject, institutional tests; 36 credit hours maximum for associate degree.

ACADEMIC REQUIREMENTS. Freshmen must earn minimum GPA of 1.5 to continue in good standing. 60% of freshmen return for sophomore year. Students must declare major by end of first year. **Graduation requirements:** 60 hours for associate (30 in major). Most students required to take courses in English, humanities, mathematics, biological/physical sciences, social sciences. **Additional information:** Strong liberal arts tradition, with a balance between transfer and career-oriented programs.

FRESHMAN ADMISSIONS. Selection criteria: Open admissions. Preference given area students in highly subscribed programs. Selective admission to technology, nursing, engineering, and computer science courses, with school achievement record very important.

1992 FRESHMAN CLASS PROFILE. 647 men, 886 women enrolled. **Characteristics:** 95% from in state, 90% commute, 4% have minority backgrounds, 1% are foreign students. Average age is 28.

FALL-TERM APPLICATIONS. $25 fee, may be waived for applicants with need. No closing date; priority given to applications received by August 15; applicants notified on a rolling basis; must reply by May 1 or within

2 weeks if notified thereafter. CRDA. Deferred and early admission available.

STUDENT LIFE. Activities: Student government, film, radio, student newspaper, television, choral groups, concert band, dance, drama, jazz band, music ensembles, musical theater, Theater groups, Minority Students, Chi Alpha Ministries, Earth Awareness, Intervarsity Christian Fellowship, Early Childhood Educators, Political Awareness, Psychology Club, Nursing Club, Humanities Club, Criminal Justice Club. **Additional information:** Approximately 10% of undergraduates live in private apartments off campus, remaining 90% commute from home.

ATHLETICS. NJCAA. **Intercollegiate:** Baseball M, basketball, golf, soccer M, softball W, volleyball W. **Intramural:** Basketball, bowling, racquetball, softball, swimming, table tennis, tennis, track and field, volleyball, water polo.

STUDENT SERVICES. Aptitude testing, career counseling, employment service for undergraduates, freshman orientation, health services, on-campus day care, personal counseling, placement service for graduates, special adviser for adult students, veterans counselor, services/facilities for handicapped.

ANNUAL EXPENSES. Tuition and fees (projected): $2,000, $1,800 additional for out-of-state students. **Books and supplies:** $500. **Other expenses:** $400.

FINANCIAL AID. 80% of freshmen, 81% of continuing students receive some form of aid. 96% of grants, all loans, all jobs based on need. Academic, music/drama, athletic scholarships available. **Aid applications:** No closing date; priority given to applications received by March 1; applicants notified on a rolling basis beginning on or about May 1; must reply within 15 days. **Additional information:** Tuition waived for students in top 20% of high school graduating class, with Regents diploma, if residents of Chautauqua, Cattaraugus, or Allegany counties. In Pennsylvania, guaranteed in-state tuition rate for students in Warren, Potter, and McKean countires if they graduate in top 20% of their graduating clas with an academic diploma.

ADDRESS/TELEPHONE. James A. Gallagher, Director of Admissions, Jamestown Community College, 525 Falconer Street, Jamestown, NY 14701. (716) 665-5220 ext. 239. (800) 388-8557. Fax: (716) 664-3498.

Jefferson Community College

Watertown, New York — CB code: 2345

2-year public community college, coed. Founded in 1961. **Accreditation:** Regional. **Undergraduate enrollment:** 620 men, 772 women full time; 546 men, 780 women part time. **Faculty:** 180 total (80 full time), 8 with doctorates or other terminal degrees. **Location:** Suburban campus in large town; 70 miles from Syracuse. **Calendar:** Semester, limited summer session. Saturday and extensive evening/early morning classes. **Microcomputers:** Located in libraries, classrooms, computer centers. Lease or purchase required**Special facilities:** Madison Barracks Restaurant facility for culinary arts program.

DEGREES OFFERED. AA, AS, AAS. 424 associate degrees awarded in 1992.

UNDERGRADUATE MAJORS. Accounting, behavioral sciences, biological and physical sciences, biological laboratory technology, biology, business administration and management, business and management, business and office, business data processing and related programs, business data programming, chemistry, computer and information sciences, criminal justice studies, cytotechnology, data processing, engineering, engineering and other disciplines, engineering science, family and community services, fashion design, fashion merchandising, finance, food production/management/services, forestry and related sciences, geology, hospitality and recreation marketing, hotel/motel and restaurant management, humanities, humanities and social sciences, industrial technology, journalism, law enforcement and corrections technologies, liberal/general studies, mathematics, medical laboratory technologies, medical secretary, nursing, physics, public affairs, radio/television broadcasting, respiratory therapy, retailing, science technologies, secretarial and related programs, social sciences, tourism, transportation and travel marketing, word processing.

ACADEMIC PROGRAMS. 2-year transfer program, dual enrollment of high school students, honors program, independent study, internships, weekend college. **Remedial services:** Learning center, reduced course load, remedial instruction, tutoring. **Placement/credit:** AP, CLEP General and Subject, institutional tests; 30 credit hours maximum for associate degree.

ACADEMIC REQUIREMENTS. Freshmen must earn minimum GPA of 1.0 to continue in good standing. Nursing students must maintain 2.0 average in courses in their major. 70% of freshmen return for sophomore year. Students must declare major on application. **Graduation requirements:** 60 hours for associate (28 in major). Most students required to take courses in English, humanities, mathematics, biological/physical sciences, social sciences. **Additional information:** Students in engineering science, computer science, and computer information systems programs required to purchase or lease microcomputers.

FRESHMAN ADMISSIONS. Selection criteria: Open admissions. Selective admissions to some programs based on grades, class rank, test scores, school recommendation, and sometimes personal interview. Strong background in mathematics and science required for engineering science, computer science, nursing, science, and medical laboratory technologies programs. **Test requirements:** SAT or ACT (ACT preferred) for placement and counseling only; score report by August 25.

1992 FRESHMAN CLASS PROFILE. 438 men, 412 women enrolled. **Characteristics:** 99% from in state, 100% commute, 7% have minority backgrounds. Average age is 19.

FALL-TERM APPLICATIONS. $25 fee. No closing date; applicants notified on a rolling basis; must reply by April 30 or within 4 weeks if notified thereafter. Interview recommended for nursing, engineering science applicants. Early admission available.

STUDENT LIFE. Housing: Privately owned dorm/apts available for students. **Activities:** Student government, magazine, student newspaper, yearbook, choral groups, drama, Interfaith Club, veterans club, African/Latin Society, Human Services Club.

ATHLETICS. NJCAA. **Intercollegiate:** Baseball M, basketball, golf, soccer M, softball W, volleyball W. **Intramural:** Badminton, baseball M, basketball, bowling, field hockey W, softball, table tennis, tennis, volleyball.

STUDENT SERVICES. Career counseling, employment service for undergraduates, freshman orientation, health services, on-campus day care, personal counseling, placement service for graduates, special adviser for adult students, veterans counselor, services/facilities for handicapped.

ANNUAL EXPENSES. Tuition and fees (projected): $1,656, $1,464 additional for out-of-state students. **Books and supplies:** $600. **Other expenses:** $500.

FINANCIAL AID. 86% of freshmen, 85% of continuing students receive some form of aid. Grants, loans, jobs available. 700 enrolled freshmen were judged to have need, all were offered aid. Academic, athletic scholarships available. **Aid applications:** No closing date; priority given to applications received by April 1; applicants notified on a rolling basis beginning on or about April 15; must reply within 2 weeks.

ADDRESS/TELEPHONE. Rosanne N. Weir, Director of Admissions, Jefferson Community College, Outer Coffeen Street, Watertown, NY 13601. (315) 786-2408.

Jewish Theological Seminary of America

New York, New York — CB code: 2339

Admissions:	83% of applicants accepted
Based on:	••• School record, test scores
	•• Activities, essay, interview, recommendations
	• Religious affiliation/commitment, special talents
Completion:	90% of freshmen end year in good standing
	80% enter graduate study

4-year private university, coed, affiliated with Jewish faith. Founded in 1886. **Accreditation:** Regional. **Undergraduate enrollment:** 30 men, 32 women full time; 8 men, 17 women part time. **Graduate enrollment:** 96 men, 95 women full time; 68 men, 67 women part time. **Faculty:** 98 total (43 full time), 55 with doctorates or other terminal degrees. **Location:** Urban campus in very large city. **Calendar:** Semester, extensive summer session.

DEGREES OFFERED. BA, MA, PhD, Rab. 33 bachelor's degrees awarded in 1992. 100% in area and ethnic studies. Graduate degrees offered in 6 major fields of study.

UNDERGRADUATE MAJORS. Jewish studies, theological studies.

ACADEMIC PROGRAMS. Double major, honors program, independent study, student-designed major, study abroad, double bachelor's degree programs with Columbia University and Barnard College. **Remedial services:** Preadmission summer program, remedial instruction, special counselor, tutoring. **Placement/credit:** Institutional tests; 6 credit hours maximum for bachelor's degree.

ACADEMIC REQUIREMENTS. No policy requiring minimum GPA; records of students having academic difficulty are reviewed individually. 95% of freshmen return for sophomore year. Students must declare major by end of second year. **Graduation requirements:** 156 hours for bachelor's (21 in major). Most students required to take courses in foreign languages, history, humanities, philosophy/religion. **Additional information:** Students enrolled in combined programs with Columbia University and Barnard College earn 2 degrees simultaneously.

FRESHMAN ADMISSIONS. Selection criteria: School achievement record, interest in Jewish studies, test scores, recommendations, leadership potential considered. **High school preparation:** 14 units required. Required units include English 4, foreign language 3, mathematics 3, physical science 1 and social science 3. **Test requirements:** SAT or ACT; score report by July 15. English Composition ACH required of all native English speakers. Score report by August 15.

1992 FRESHMAN CLASS PROFILE. 60 men and women applied, 50 accepted; 6 men enrolled, 11 women enrolled. 85% had high school GPA of 3.0 or higher, 15% between 2.0 and 2.99. **Academic background:** Mid 50% of enrolled freshmen had SAT-V between 540-650, SAT-M between 550-

660. 98% submitted SAT scores. **Characteristics:** 20% from in state, 95% live in college housing, 1% are foreign students. Average age is 18.

FALL-TERM APPLICATIONS. $45 fee, may be waived for applicants with need. Closing date February 1; applicants notified on a rolling basis beginning on or about February 16; must reply by May 1. Essay required. Interview recommended for Recommended for applicants who live within 100 mile radius. applicants. interviews recommended for applicants who live within 10 mile radius. CRDA. Deferred and early admission available. EDP-F.

STUDENT LIFE. Housing: Dormitories (coed); apartment housing available. Women undergraduates enrolled in double degree program with Barnard may live in Barnard dorms. **Activities:** Student government, magazine, radio, student newspaper, television, yearbook, choral groups, concert band, dance, drama, jazz band, music ensembles, musical theater, symphony orchestra, Door L' Door, Vaad Gemilut Hasidim. **Additional information:** Student life centers around supportive Jewish community. Undergraduates enrolled in joint degree programs with Barnard and Columbia may also join their fraternities and sororities.

ATHLETICS. Intramural: Basketball, bowling, field hockey W, lacrosse M, softball, volleyball.

STUDENT SERVICES. Career counseling, employment service for undergraduates, freshman orientation, health services, personal counseling, placement service for graduates, services/facilities for handicapped.

ANNUAL EXPENSES. Tuition and fees: $6,870. **Room and board:** $3,465 room only. **Books and supplies:** $500. **Other expenses:** $2,500.

FINANCIAL AID. 60% of freshmen, 60% of continuing students receive some form of aid. 91% of grants, 99% of loans based on need. 9 enrolled freshmen were judged to have need, all were offered aid. Academic scholarships available. **Aid applications:** Closing date March 1; applicants notified on a rolling basis beginning on or about April 1; must reply within 2 weeks.

ADDRESS/TELEPHONE. Marci Blumenthal, Director of Admissions, Jewish Theological Seminary of America, 3080 Broadway, New York, NY 10027. (212) 678-8832.

Juilliard School
New York, New York — CB code: 2340

Admissions:	18% of applicants accepted
Based on:	••• Special talents
	• Activities, essay, school record
Completion:	90% of freshmen end year in good standing
	75% graduate

4-year private college of performing arts: dance, drama, music, coed. Founded in 1905. **Accreditation:** Regional. **Undergraduate enrollment:** 221 men, 284 women full time. **Graduate enrollment:** 180 men, 187 women full time; 13 men, 13 women part time. **Faculty:** 233 total (52 full time). **Location:** Urban campus in very large city. **Calendar:** Semester. **Microcomputers:** Located in dormitories. **Special facilities:** Listening library, media center, 47,000 musical scores, 210 video cassettes, over 100 practice rooms with over 200 pianos, scenery and costume shops, 15 2-story rehearsal studios, 5 theaters, 2 recital halls, part of Lincoln Center.

DEGREES OFFERED. BFA, M, D. 89 bachelor's degrees awarded in 1992. 100% in visual and performing arts. Graduate degrees offered in 3 major fields of study.

UNDERGRADUATE MAJORS. Dance, dramatic arts, music performance, music theory and composition, visual and performing arts.

ACADEMIC PROGRAMS. Accelerated program, double major, honors program, study abroad, visiting/exchange student program, cross-registration, 5 year BA/MM with Barnard and Columbia. **Remedial services:** Remedial English instruction for foreign students. **Placement/credit:** Institutional tests.

ACADEMIC REQUIREMENTS. No policy requiring minimum GPA; records of students having academic difficulty are reviewed individually. 95% of freshmen return for sophomore year. Students must declare major on application. **Graduation requirements:** 146 hours for bachelor's (40 in major). Most students required to take courses in humanities. **Additional information:** Three-year certificate program available in performing arts.

FRESHMAN ADMISSIONS. Selection criteria: Quality of performance at personal audition most important. SAT or ACT scores or high school profile not required. Extensive previous study in major field of dance, drama, or music required. **Additional information:** Foreign students given English proficiency examination at time of audition or may present TOEFL.

1992 FRESHMAN CLASS PROFILE. 292 men applied, 62 accepted, 45 enrolled; 547 women applied, 92 accepted, 65 enrolled. **Characteristics:** 18% from in state, 100% live in college housing, 23% have minority backgrounds, 37% are foreign students. Average age is 18.

FALL-TERM APPLICATIONS. $75 fee, may be waived for applicants with need. Closing date January 8; applicants notified on or about April 6; must reply by May 1. Audition required. Essay recommended. CRDA. Early admissions available in Dance Division. Dance, music auditions held in March, May. Application closing dates, respectively, January 8 and March 15. Applicants notified within 4 weeks after audition; must reply by May 1 or July 1. Drama auditions in February, application closing date January 8, notification by April 6 or 1 month after audition. Auditions in all 3 divisions held in New York City and regionally. Contact Office of Admissions for specific locations.

STUDENT LIFE. Housing: Dormitories (coed); apartment housing available. Single sex floor, quiet floor, graduate student floor, non-smoking floors available. **Activities:** Student government, film, student newspaper, yearbook, choral groups, dance, drama, music ensembles, opera, symphony orchestra, Juilliard Symphony Orchestra, Laboratory Orchestra, Dance Troupe, Drama, Repertory Troupe, string quartets, Brass Quintets, Intervarsity Christian Fellowship, Minority Student Organization. **Additional information:** Ongoing orientation for first-time college students.

ATHLETICS. Intramural: Cross-country, ice hockey, tennis.

STUDENT SERVICES. Career counseling, employment service for undergraduates, freshman orientation, health services, personal counseling, placement service for graduates, housing referral, services/facilities for handicapped.

ANNUAL EXPENSES. Tuition and fees (1992-93): $11,250. **Room and board:** $5,900. **Books and supplies:** $2,400. **Other expenses:** $6,500.

FINANCIAL AID. 87% of freshmen, 86% of continuing students receive some form of aid. All grants, 97% of loans, 98% of jobs based on need. 76 enrolled freshmen were judged to have need, all were offered aid. Academic, music/drama, minority scholarships available. **Aid applications:** Closing date February 15; applicants notified on or about April 1; must reply by May 1.

ADDRESS/TELEPHONE. Carole Everett, Director of Admissions, Juilliard School, 60 Lincoln Center Plaza, New York, NY 10023-6590. (212) 799-5000 ext. 223. Fax: (212) 724-0263.

Katharine Gibbs School: Melville
Melville, New York — CB code: 1039

2-year proprietary junior college, coed. Founded in 1911. **Undergraduate enrollment:** 620 men and women. **Faculty:** 35 total (14 full time), 3 with doctorates or other terminal degrees. **Location:** Suburban campus in small town; 40 miles from New York City. **Calendar:** Quarter. **Microcomputers:** Located in computer centers.

DEGREES OFFERED. AAS. 100 associate degrees awarded in 1992. 100% in business/office and marketing/distribution.

UNDERGRADUATE MAJORS. Secretarial and related programs.

ACADEMIC PROGRAMS. Study abroad. **Remedial services:** Preadmission summer program, remedial instruction, tutoring.

ACADEMIC REQUIREMENTS. Freshmen must earn minimum GPA of 2.0 to continue in good standing. Students must declare major on application. **Graduation requirements:** 65 hours for associate. Most students required to take courses in English, mathematics.

FRESHMAN ADMISSIONS. Selection criteria: All applicants must take CPAT admission test. Academic record, interview important. **Test requirements:** Institutional entrance test required for admission.

1992 FRESHMAN CLASS PROFILE. 110 men and women enrolled. 10% had high school GPA of 3.0 or higher, 60% between 2.0 and 2.99. **Characteristics:** 95% from in state, 100% commute, 14% have minority backgrounds. Average age is 19.

FALL-TERM APPLICATIONS. $25 fee. No closing date; applicants notified on a rolling basis; must reply by registration. Interview required. Essay required.

STUDENT LIFE. Activities: Student government, yearbook.

STUDENT SERVICES. Career counseling, freshman orientation, placement service for graduates.

ANNUAL EXPENSES. Tuition and fees (1992-93): $7,445. **Books and supplies:** $550. **Other expenses:** $1,053.

FINANCIAL AID. 70% of freshmen, 73% of continuing students receive some form of aid. All grants, all loans based on need. **Aid applications:** No closing date; applicants notified on a rolling basis; must reply within 3 weeks.

ADDRESS/TELEPHONE. Patricia A. Martin, Director of Admissions, Katharine Gibbs School: Melville, 535 Broad Hollow Road, Melville, NY 11747. (516) 293-2460. Fax: (516) 293-2709.

Katharine Gibbs School: New York
New York, New York — CB code: 2355

2-year proprietary business college, coed. Founded in 1918. **Undergraduate enrollment:** 300 men and women. **Faculty:** 42 total (17 full time). **Location:** Urban campus in very large city. **Calendar:** Quarter, limited summer session. **Microcomputers:** Located in computer centers.

DEGREES OFFERED. 200 associate degrees awarded in 1992. 100% in business/office and marketing/distribution.

UNDERGRADUATE MAJORS. Microcomputer accounting, secretarial and related programs, word processing.

ACADEMIC PROGRAMS. Accelerated program, cooperative education, internships. **Remedial services:** Remedial instruction.

ACADEMIC REQUIREMENTS. Freshmen must earn minimum GPA of 1.7 to continue in good standing. 85% of freshmen return for sophomore year. Students must declare major on application. **Graduation requirements:** 65 hours for associate. Most students required to take courses in English, mathematics.

FRESHMAN ADMISSIONS. Selection criteria: School achievement record, test scores, interview, essay or personal statement important. **Test requirements:** Institution-administered CPAT test required for admission.

1992 FRESHMAN CLASS PROFILE. 150 men and women enrolled. **Characteristics:** 85% from in state, 100% commute, 33% have minority backgrounds, 2% are foreign students. Average age is 18.

FALL-TERM APPLICATIONS. $25 fee. No closing date; priority given to applications received by September 30; must reply by registration. Interview required. Essay required for paralegal applicants. Deferred admission available.

STUDENT SERVICES. Career counseling, employment service for undergraduates, personal counseling, placement service for graduates.

ANNUAL EXPENSES. Tuition and fees (1992-93): $7,350. **Books and supplies:** $600.

FINANCIAL AID. 75% of continuing students receive some form of aid. 66% of grants, 94% of loans, all jobs based on need. **Aid applications:** No closing date; applicants notified on a rolling basis; must reply within 3 weeks.

ADDRESS/TELEPHONE. Elizabeth Brannen, Director of Admissions, Katharine Gibbs School: New York, 200 Park Avenue, New York, NY 10166. (212) 973-4956.

Kehilath Yakov Rabbinical Seminary
Brooklyn, New York CB code: 0619

5-year private rabbinical college, men only, affiliated with Jewish faith. Founded in 1948. **Undergraduate enrollment:** 120 men full time. **Graduate enrollment:** 25 men full time. **Location:** Urban campus in very large city. **Additional facts:** First Talmudic degree and ordination available.

FRESHMAN ADMISSIONS. Selection criteria: Institutional examination considered.

ADDRESS/TELEPHONE. Sandor Schwartz, President, Kehilath Yakov Rabbinical Seminary, 206 Wilson Street, Brooklyn, NY 11211. (718) 963-3940.

Keuka College
Keuka Park, New York CB code: 2350

Admissions: 83% of applicants accepted
Based on: ••• Essay, school record
•• Activities, interview, special talents, test scores
• Recommendations
Completion: 81% of freshmen end year in good standing
54% graduate, 12% of these enter graduate study

4-year private liberal arts college, coed, affiliated with American Baptist Churches in the USA. Founded in 1890. **Accreditation:** Regional. **Undergraduate enrollment:** 204 men, 523 women full time; 81 men and women part time. **Faculty:** 80 total (45 full time), 32 with doctorates or other terminal degrees. **Location:** Rural campus in small town; 50 miles from Rochester. **Calendar:** 4-1-4, limited summer session. **Microcomputers:** 30 located in computer centers. **Special facilities:** 2 student art galleries, Keuka challenge ropes course. **Additional facts:** Emphasis on experiential learning outside classroom.

DEGREES OFFERED. BA, BS. 126 bachelor's degrees awarded in 1992. 22% in business and management, 8% education, 16% teacher education, 7% health sciences, 33% allied health, 6% parks/recreation, protective services, public affairs.

UNDERGRADUATE MAJORS. Biochemistry, biology, business administration and management, business and management, chemistry, clinical laboratory science, early childhood education, education, elementary education, English, history, hotel/motel and restaurant management, human resources development, journalism, marketing management, mathematics, nursing, occupational therapy, political science and government, predentistry, prelaw, premedicine, preveterinary, psychology, public administration, secondary education, social work, sociology, special education.

ACADEMIC PROGRAMS. Internships, study abroad, teacher preparation, visiting/exchange student program, cross-registration, combined degree program in engineering with Clarkson University; liberal arts/career combination in health sciences. **Remedial services:** Learning center, preadmission summer program, reduced course load, remedial instruction, special counselor, tutoring. **ROTC:** Army. **Placement/credit:** AP, CLEP General and Subject, institutional tests.

ACADEMIC REQUIREMENTS. Freshmen must earn minimum GPA of 2.0 to continue in good standing. 80% of freshmen return for sophomore year. Students must declare major by end of second year. **Graduation requirements:** 120 hours for bachelor's (40 in major). Most students required to take courses in arts/fine arts, computer science, English, history, humanities, mathematics, philosophy/religion, biological/physical sciences, social sciences.

FRESHMAN ADMISSIONS. Selection criteria: Academic achievement record most important, nature of program considered. Special interests, leadership qualities, talents, and test scores also significant. **High school preparation:** 15 units required; 16 recommended. Required and recommended units include biological science 1, English 4, foreign language 2, mathematics 3, physical science 2-3 and social science 3. **Test requirements:** SAT or ACT; score report by August 30.

1992 FRESHMAN CLASS PROFILE. 133 men applied, 101 accepted, 47 enrolled; 320 women applied, 273 accepted, 127 enrolled. 17% were in top tenth and 30% were in top quarter of graduating class. **Academic background:** Mid 50% of enrolled freshmen had SAT-V between 400-550, SAT-M between 450-550. 83% submitted SAT scores. **Characteristics:** 94% from in state, 93% live in college housing, 4% have minority backgrounds. Average age is 18.

FALL-TERM APPLICATIONS. $25 fee, may be waived for applicants with need. No closing date; applicants notified on a rolling basis; must reply within 30 days. Essay required. Interview recommended. CRDA. Deferred and early admission available.

STUDENT LIFE. Housing: Dormitories (women, coed). **Activities:** Student government, magazine, radio, student newspaper, yearbook, choral groups, dance, drama, music ensembles, campus ministries, campus activities board, Afro-American Club, International Club, social work club, Model United Nations. **Additional information:** Student participation in clubs and extracurricular activities strongly encouraged.

ATHLETICS. NCAA. **Intercollegiate:** Basketball, cross-country, lacrosse M, soccer, softball W, volleyball W. **Intramural:** Basketball, soccer, softball, volleyball, water polo.

STUDENT SERVICES. Career counseling, employment service for undergraduates, freshman orientation, health services, personal counseling, placement service for graduates.

ANNUAL EXPENSES. Tuition and fees: $9,310. **Room and board:** $4,350. **Books and supplies:** $600. **Other expenses:** $500.

FINANCIAL AID. 96% of freshmen, 91% of continuing students receive some form of aid. 97% of grants, 93% of loans, 87% of jobs based on need. 142 enrolled freshmen were judged to have need, all were offered aid. Academic, leadership scholarships available. **Aid applications:** No closing date; priority given to applications received by March 1; applicants notified on a rolling basis beginning on or about April 1; must reply within 3 weeks.

ADDRESS/TELEPHONE. Robert J. Iannuzzo, Dean of Admissions and Financial Aid, Keuka College, Keuka Park, NY 14478-0098. (315) 536-5254. (800) 54-KEUKA. Fax: (315) 536-5216.

King's College
Briarcliff Manor, New York CB code: 2352

Admissions: 78% of applicants accepted
Based on: ••• Religious affiliation/commitment, school record, test scores
•• Activities, recommendations, special talents
• Essay, interview
Completion: 80% of freshmen end year in good standing
45% graduate

4-year private liberal arts college, coed, nondenominational. Founded in 1938. **Accreditation:** Regional. **Undergraduate enrollment:** 157 men, 228 women full time; 7 men, 13 women part time. **Faculty:** 53 total (39 full time), 19 with doctorates or other terminal degrees. **Location:** Suburban campus in small town; 30 miles from New York City. **Calendar:** Semester, limited summer session. **Microcomputers:** 50 located in dormitories, libraries, computer centers.

DEGREES OFFERED. AA, BA, BS. 3 associate degrees awarded in 1992. 100% in multi/interdisciplinary studies. 93 bachelor's degrees awarded. 19% in business and management, 31% teacher education, 11% letters/literature, 6% life sciences, 8% psychology, 15% social sciences.

UNDERGRADUATE MAJORS. Associate: Liberal/general studies. **Bachelor's:** Accounting, biology, business administration and management, chemistry, comparative literature, computer and information sciences, creative writing, early childhood education, elementary education, English, foreign languages (multiple emphasis), history, mathematics, medical laboratory technologies, music, music education, music performance, nursing, physical education, psychology, religion, sociology, speech.

ACADEMIC PROGRAMS. 2-year transfer program, independent study, internships, study abroad, teacher preparation, Washington semester, cross-registration, combined bachelor's/graduate degree program in public accounting with Pace University. **Remedial services:** Learning center, reduced course load, remedial instruction, special counselor, tutoring. **Placement/credit:** AP, CLEP General and Subject, institutional tests; 32 credit hours maximum for associate degree; 32 credit hours maximum for bachelor's degree.

ACADEMIC REQUIREMENTS. Freshmen must earn minimum GPA of 1.8 to continue in good standing. 76% of freshmen return for sophomore year. Students must declare major by end of second year. **Graduation requirements:** 65 hours for associate (16 in major), 130 hours for bachelor's (30 in major). Most students required to take courses in English, foreign languages, history, mathematics, philosophy/religion, biological/physical sciences, social sciences.

FRESHMAN ADMISSIONS. Selection criteria: In order of importance: GPA and courses taken, class rank, SAT/ACT scores, extracurricular activities, recommendations. **High school preparation:** 16 units required. Required and recommended units include English 3-4. Biological science 2, foreign language 2, mathematics 3, physical science 1 and social science 3 recommended. 6 units of science/mathematics/language combination also required. **Test requirements:** SAT or ACT; score report by August 15.

1992 FRESHMAN CLASS PROFILE. 414 men and women applied, 321 accepted; 50 men enrolled, 60 women enrolled. 51% had high school GPA of 3.0 or higher, 44% between 2.0 and 2.99. 10% were in top tenth and 28% were in top quarter of graduating class. **Academic background:** Mid 50% of enrolled freshmen had SAT-V between 380-510, SAT-M between 410-550; ACT composite between 19-22. 86% submitted SAT scores, 6% submitted ACT scores. **Characteristics:** 44% from in state, 97% live in college housing, 23% have minority backgrounds, 2% are foreign students. Average age is 18.

FALL-TERM APPLICATIONS. $20 fee, may be waived for applicants with need. No closing date; applicants notified on a rolling basis; must reply by May 1 or within 2 weeks if notified thereafter. Audition required for music applicants. Interview recommended. Essay recommended. Deferred and early admission available.

STUDENT LIFE. Housing: Dormitories (men, women). **Activities:** Student government, student newspaper, yearbook, choral groups, drama, jazz band, music ensembles, musical theater, pep band, Christian service organization, prayer and Bible study groups, legal society. **Additional information:** Student life appeals to religiously oriented and socially conservative. No smoking or alcoholic beverages allowed. Religious observance required.

ATHLETICS. NAIA. **Intercollegiate:** Baseball M, basketball, cross-country, soccer, softball W, volleyball W. **Intramural:** Basketball, volleyball.

STUDENT SERVICES. Aptitude testing, career counseling, employment service for undergraduates, freshman orientation, health services, personal counseling, placement service for graduates, services/facilities for handicapped.

ANNUAL EXPENSES. Tuition and fees (1992-93): $8,310. **Room and board:** $3,920. **Books and supplies:** $500. **Other expenses:** $500.

FINANCIAL AID. 87% of freshmen, 85% of continuing students receive some form of aid. 76% of grants, 96% of loans, all jobs based on need. 94 enrolled freshmen were judged to have need, all were offered aid. Academic, music/drama, athletic, state/district residency, leadership scholarships available. **Aid applications:** No closing date; priority given to applications received by March 15; applicants notified on a rolling basis beginning on or about April 1; must reply within 2 weeks of notification.

ADDRESS/TELEPHONE. Miss Cheryl Burdick, Dean of Admissions, King's College, 150 Lodge Road, Briarcliff Manor, NY 10510-9985. (914) 941-7200. (800) 344-4926. Fax: (914) 944-5636.

Kol Yaakov Torah Center
Monsey, New York — CB code: 0541

4-year private seminary college, men only, affiliated with Jewish faith. Founded in 1981. **Undergraduate enrollment:** 25 men full time; 7 men part time. **Graduate enrollment:** 10 men full time. **Location:** Suburban campus in small town; 30 miles from New York City. **Calendar:** Semester. **Additional facts:** First Talmudic degree and ordination available.

FRESHMAN ADMISSIONS. Selection criteria: Interview, academic recommendations, religious commitment primary considerations.

ADDRESS/TELEPHONE. Rabbi Aaron Parry, Director of Admissions/Registrar, Kol Yaakov Torah Center, 29 West Maple Avenue, Monsey, NY 10952. (914) 425-3863.

Laboratory Institute of Merchandising
New York, New York — CB code: 2380

4-year proprietary 4-year college of business of fashion, coed. Founded in 1939. **Accreditation:** Regional. **Undergraduate enrollment:** 195 men and women. **Location:** Urban campus in very large city; in midtown Manhattan. **Calendar:** 4-1-4. **Additional facts:** All students participate in cooperative education program.

FRESHMAN ADMISSIONS. Selection criteria: Interview, recommendations, high school record, test scores required. For upper-division programs, 2 recommendations, interview, high school and college transcripts.

ANNUAL EXPENSES. Tuition and fees: $9,450. **Books and supplies:** $400. **Other expenses:** $1,000.

ADDRESS/TELEPHONE. Maryann M. Elberfeld, Director of Admissions, Laboratory Institute of Merchandising, 12 East 53rd Street, New York, NY 10022-5268. (212) 752-1530. (800) 677-1323. Fax: (212) 832-6708.

Le Moyne College
Syracuse, New York — CB code: 2366

Admissions:	78% of applicants accepted
Based on:	••• School record
	•• Activities, essay, interview, recommendations, special talents, test scores
Completion:	96% of freshmen end year in good standing
	76% graduate, 30% of these enter graduate study

4-year private liberal arts college, coed, affiliated with Roman Catholic Church. Founded in 1946. **Accreditation:** Regional. **Undergraduate enrollment:** 820 men, 1,006 women full time; 216 men, 358 women part time. **Faculty:** 205 total (119 full time), 139 with doctorates or other terminal degrees. **Location:** Suburban campus in small city; 2 miles from downtown. **Calendar:** Semester, extensive summer session. **Microcomputers:** 105 located in dormitories, libraries, classrooms, computer centers. **Special facilities:** Wilson Art Gallery. **Additional facts:** Jesuit institution.

DEGREES OFFERED. BA, BS. 552 bachelor's degrees awarded in 1992. 43% in business and management, 14% letters/literature, 9% life sciences, 8% psychology, 18% social sciences.

UNDERGRADUATE MAJORS. Accounting, biological and physical sciences, biology, business administration and management, business and management, business education, chemistry, computer and information sciences, criminology, economics, elementary education, English, English education, English/communications, English/drama, finance, foreign languages education, French, history, human resources development, labor/industrial relations, marketing management, mathematics, mathematics education, multiple science, personnel management, philosophy, physics, political science and government, psychology, religion, religious education, science education, secondary education, social studies education, sociology, sociology/human services, Spanish, special education, teaching English as a second language/foreign language.

ACADEMIC PROGRAMS. Accelerated program, double major, honors program, independent study, internships, study abroad, teacher preparation, visiting/exchange student program, Washington semester, 3-2 programs in engineering with Clarkson University, Detroit University, and Manhattan College, transfer program with SUNY College of Environmental Science and Forestry at Syracuse University, 3-4 programs with Pennsylvania College of Optometry, College of Dental Medicine at SUNY Buffalo, and New York College of Podiatric Medicine, early assurance programs with School of Dental Medicine and School of Medicine and Biomedical Sciences at SUNY Buffalo and SUNY Health Science Center at Syracuse. **Remedial services:** Learning center, preadmission summer program, reduced course load, remedial instruction, special counselor, tutoring, New York State Higher Education Opportunity Program. **ROTC:** Air Force, Army. **Placement/credit:** AP, CLEP General and Subject; 60 credit hours maximum for bachelor's degree.

ACADEMIC REQUIREMENTS. Freshmen must earn minimum GPA of 1.61 to continue in good standing. 89% of freshmen return for sophomore year. Students must declare major by end of second year. **Graduation requirements:** 120 hours for bachelor's (45 in major). Most students required to take courses in English, foreign languages, history, humanities, mathematics, philosophy/religion, biological/physical sciences, social sciences. **Postgraduate studies:** 4% enter law school, 3% enter medical school, 3% enter MBA programs, 20% enter other graduate study.

FRESHMAN ADMISSIONS. Selection criteria: School achievement record, school recommendation, test scores, motivation, extracurricular activities, leadership considered. Applicants from minority or low-income families given every possible consideration. Children of alumni, out-of-state applicants encouraged. **High school preparation:** 16 units required. Required and recommended units include English 4, mathematics 3, social science 2 and science 1. Foreign language 2 recommended. 4 mathematics required for science, mathematics, and computer science majors. **Test requirements:** SAT or ACT; score report by March 1.

1992 FRESHMAN CLASS PROFILE. 716 men applied, 534 accepted, 155 enrolled; 833 women applied, 671 accepted, 221 enrolled. 85% had high school GPA of 3.0 or higher, 15% between 2.0 and 2.99. 19% were in top tenth and 57% were in top quarter of graduating class. **Academic background:** Mid 50% of enrolled freshmen had SAT-V between 420-510, SAT-M between 460-560; ACT composite between 21-25. 98% submitted SAT scores, 45% submitted ACT scores. **Characteristics:** 90% from in state, 90% live in college housing, 12% have minority backgrounds, 1% are foreign students. Average age is 18.

FALL-TERM APPLICATIONS. $25 fee, may be waived for applicants with need. Closing date March 15; priority given to applications received by February 1; applicants notified on a rolling basis beginning on or about January 1; must reply by May 1. Essay required. Interview recommended. CRDA. Deferred and early admission available. EDP-F.

STUDENT LIFE. Housing: Dormitories (men, women, coed); apartment housing available. Supportive living arrangements for students in recovery from drug/alcohol dependency. **Activities:** Student government, film, magazine, radio, student newspaper, yearbook, choral groups, drama, opera, pep band, Amnesty International, POWER (Pride in Our Work, Ethnicity, and Race), Democratic and Republican Clubs, Project in the Community, Christian Fellowship, social action groups, International House, Le Moyne Women's Association, International Relations Association, Environmental Coalition.

ATHLETICS. NCAA. **Intercollegiate:** Baseball M, basketball, cross-country, diving, golf M, lacrosse M, soccer, softball W, swimming, tennis, volleyball W. **Intramural:** Basketball, handball, ice hockey M, lacrosse, racquetball, rugby M, skiing, soccer, softball, tennis, volleyball.

STUDENT SERVICES. Aptitude testing, career counseling, employment service for undergraduates, freshman orientation, health services, personal counseling, placement service for graduates, special adviser for adult students, services/facilities for handicapped.

ANNUAL EXPENSES. Tuition and fees: $10,660. **Room and board:** $4,540. **Books and supplies:** $250. **Other expenses:** $300.

FINANCIAL AID. 75% of freshmen, 75% of continuing students receive some form of aid. 89% of grants, 97% of loans, all jobs based on need. 330 enrolled freshmen were judged to have need, 325 were offered aid. Academic, athletic, leadership scholarships available. **Aid applications:** Closing date April 15; priority given to applications received by February 15; applicants notified on a rolling basis beginning on or about March 15; must reply by May 1 or within 4 weeks if notified thereafter. **Additional information:** Parent loan program with low interest and 15-year repayment available.

ADDRESS/TELEPHONE. Edwin B. Harris, PhD, Director of Admissions, Le Moyne College, Syracuse, NY 13214-1399. (315) 445-4300. (800) 333-4733. Fax: (315) 445-4540.

Long Island College Hospital School of Nursing
Brooklyn, New York — CB code: 2377

2-year private nursing college, coed. Founded in 1883. **Undergraduate enrollment:** 200 men and women. **Faculty:** 20 total (10 full time). **Location:** Urban campus in very large city. **Calendar:** Semester. **Microcomputers:** 15 located in classrooms. **Special facilities:** Computer-assisted learning laboratory featuring interactive videodisc technology. **Additional facts:** Affiliated with St. Francis College

DEGREES OFFERED. AAS. 60 associate degrees awarded in 1992. 100% in health sciences.

UNDERGRADUATE MAJORS. Nursing.

ACADEMIC PROGRAMS. Cooperative education, cross-registration. **Remedial services:** Learning center, remedial instruction, tutoring. **Placement/credit:** CLEP General.

ACADEMIC REQUIREMENTS. Freshmen must earn minimum GPA of 2.0 to continue in good standing. 83% of freshmen return for sophomore year. Students must declare major on application. **Graduation requirements:** 67 hours for associate (37 in major). Most students required to take courses in English, biological/physical sciences, social sciences.

FRESHMAN ADMISSIONS. Selection criteria: School achievement record, test scores, interview most important. 2 references also important. **High school preparation:** 16 units required. Required units include English 4, mathematics 2, social science 3 and science 2. **Test requirements:** National League for Nursing Pre-Admission Examinations for Registered Nursing.

1992 FRESHMAN CLASS PROFILE. 20 men and women enrolled. **Characteristics:** 99% from in state, 100% commute, 59% have minority backgrounds. Average age is 32.

FALL-TERM APPLICATIONS. $50 fee. Closing date March 31; applicants notified on or about May 1; must reply by May 15. Interview required. Essay required. Deferred admission available.

STUDENT LIFE. Activities: Student government, yearbook.

STUDENT SERVICES. Health services, on-campus day care, personal counseling, placement service for graduates.

ANNUAL EXPENSES. Tuition and fees: $6,810. **Books and supplies:** $1,150. **Other expenses:** $1,161.

FINANCIAL AID. 72% of freshmen, 75% of continuing students receive some form of aid. 96% of grants, 60% of loans, all jobs based on need. Academic scholarships available. **Aid applications:** No closing date; priority given to applications received by June 1; applicants notified on a rolling basis beginning on or about April 15; must reply within 2 weeks.

ADDRESS/TELEPHONE. Margaret Sogliuzzo, Registrar, Long Island College Hospital School of Nursing, 397 Hicks Street, Brooklyn, NY 11201. (718) 780-1898. Fax: (718) 780-2830.

Long Island University: Brooklyn Campus
Brooklyn, New York — CB code: 2369

Admissions:	80% of applicants accepted
Based on:	••• School record, test scores
	•• Activities, recommendations
	• Essay, interview, special talents
Completion:	75% of freshmen end year in good standing
	45% enter graduate study

4-year private university, coed. Founded in 1926. **Accreditation:** Regional. **Undergraduate enrollment:** 1,544 men, 2,903 women full time; 272 men, 472 women part time. **Graduate enrollment:** 254 men, 329 women full time; 416 men, 648 women part time. **Faculty:** 320 total (270 full time), 175 with doctorates or other terminal degrees. **Location:** Urban campus in very large city. **Calendar:** Semester, extensive summer session. **Microcomputers:** 200 located in dormitories, libraries, computer centers.

DEGREES OFFERED. BA, BS, BFA, MA, MS, MBA, PhD. 20 associate degrees awarded in 1992. 470 bachelor's degrees awarded. Graduate degrees offered in 45 major fields of study.

UNDERGRADUATE MAJORS. Associate: Business and office, legal assistant/paralegal. **Bachelor's:** Accounting, anthropology, biology, business administration and management, business and management, business and office, business education, chemistry, clinical laboratory science, computer and information sciences, cytotechnology, dance, dramatic arts, early childhood education, economics, education, elementary education, English, finance, foreign languages (multiple emphasis), health care administration, health sciences, history, humanities, information sciences and systems, jazz, journalism, junior high education, marketing and distributive education, marketing management, mathematics, medical laboratory technologies, molecular biology, music, music theory and composition, nursing, pharmacy, philosophy, physical education, physical therapy, physician's assistant, political science and government, predentistry, prelaw, premedicine, prepharmacy, psychology, public administration, radio/television technology, respiratory therapy, secondary education, social sciences, sociology, speech, speech pathology/audiology, sports medicine, visual and performing arts.

ACADEMIC PROGRAMS. Cooperative education, double major, dual enrollment of high school students, honors program, independent study, internships, student-designed major, teacher preparation, visiting/exchange student program, United Nations semester, cross-registration; liberal arts/career combination in health sciences; combined bachelor's/graduate program in business administration. **Remedial services:** Learning center, preadmission summer program, reduced course load, remedial instruction, special counselor, tutoring. **Placement/credit:** AP, CLEP General and Subject, institutional tests; 60 credit hours maximum for bachelor's degree.

ACADEMIC REQUIREMENTS. Freshmen must earn minimum GPA of 2.0 to continue in good standing. 68% of freshmen return for sophomore year. Students must declare major by end of second year. **Graduation requirements:** 64 hours for associate (24 in major), 128 hours for bachelor's (36 in major). Most students required to take courses in English, foreign languages, history, mathematics, biological/physical sciences, social sciences. **Postgraduate studies:** 40% from 2-year programs enter 4-year programs. 6% enter law school, 3% enter medical school, 21% enter MBA programs, 15% enter other graduate study.

FRESHMAN ADMISSIONS. Selection criteria: GPA, test scores, recommendations, class rank important. **High school preparation:** 16 units required. Required units include English 4, foreign language 3, mathematics 3, social science 3 and science 3.

1992 FRESHMAN CLASS PROFILE. 722 men applied, 554 accepted, 300 enrolled; 1,405 women applied, 1,143 accepted, 563 enrolled. 15% had high school GPA of 3.0 or higher, 35% between 2.0 and 2.99. **Characteristics:** 90% from in state, 95% commute, 59% have minority backgrounds, 4% are foreign students. Average age is 19.

FALL-TERM APPLICATIONS. $30 fee, may be waived for applicants with need. No closing date; applicants notified on a rolling basis; must reply by May 1 or within 2 weeks if notified thereafter. Essay recommended for physical therapy applicants. CRDA. Deferred and early admission available. EDP-S. SAT or ACT scores required for admission to computer science, nursing, pharmacy, and physical therepy programs, score report by September 15.

STUDENT LIFE. Housing: Dormitories (coed). **Activities:** Student government, magazine, radio, student newspaper, yearbook, choral groups, dance, drama, jazz band, music ensembles, musical theater, pep band.

ATHLETICS. NCAA. **Intercollegiate:** Baseball M, basketball, cross-country M, golf, soccer M, softball W, tennis, track and field. **Intramural:** Table tennis, volleyball.

STUDENT SERVICES. Career counseling, employment service for undergraduates, health services, personal counseling, placement service for graduates, services/facilities for handicapped.

ANNUAL EXPENSES. Tuition and fees (projected): $10,805. **Room and board:** $5,790. **Books and supplies:** $700. **Other expenses:** $800.

FINANCIAL AID. 90% of freshmen, 85% of continuing students receive some form of aid. 87% of grants, 64% of loans, 71% of jobs based on need. 680 enrolled freshmen were judged to have need, all were offered aid.

Academic, music/drama, art, athletic, alumni affiliation, minority scholarships available. **Aid applications:** No closing date; applicants notified on a rolling basis beginning on or about April 1; must reply by May 1 or within 2 weeks if notified thereafter.

ADDRESS/TELEPHONE. Alan B. Chaves, Dean of Admissions and Financial Aid, Long Island University: Brooklyn Campus, University Plaza, Brooklyn, NY 11201. (718) 488-1011. (800) 548-7526. Fax: (718) 797-2399.

Long Island University: C. W. Post Campus

Brookville, New York CB code: 2070

Admissions: 75% of applicants accepted
Based on: ••• School record, test scores
•• Interview, recommendations
• Activities, essay, special talents
Completion: 71% of freshmen end year in good standing
36% graduate, 35% of these enter graduate study

4-year private university, coed. Founded in 1954. **Accreditation:** Regional. **Undergraduate enrollment:** 1,735 men, 2,096 women full time; 346 men, 622 women part time. **Graduate enrollment:** 347 men, 459 women full time; 846 men, 1,769 women part time. **Faculty:** 649 total (313 full time), 265 with doctorates or other terminal degrees. **Location:** Suburban campus in small town; 25 miles from New York City. **Calendar:** Semester, extensive summer session. Saturday and extensive evening/early morning classes. **Microcomputers:** 350 located in dormitories, libraries, computer centers. **Special facilities:** Tilles Center for the Performing Arts, Hutchins Gallery, Hillwood Gallery.

DEGREES OFFERED. AA, BA, BS, BFA, MA, MS, MBA, MFA, D. 967 bachelor's degrees awarded. 44% in business and management, 8% communications, 16% education, 11% social sciences, 6% visual and performing arts. Graduate degrees offered in 50 major fields of study.

UNDERGRADUATE MAJORS. Associate: Liberal/general studies. **Bachelor's:** Accounting, American studies, applied mathematics/computer science, art education, art history, art therapy, arts management, biology, business administration and management, business and management, chemistry, cinematography/film, clinical laboratory science, commercial art, communications, computer and information sciences, computer mathematics, criminal justice studies, curriculum and instruction, economics, education of the deaf and hearing impaired, elementary education, English, English education, environmental studies, environmental studies, film arts, fine arts, food science and nutrition, foreign languages (multiple emphasis), foreign languages education, French, geography, geology, German, health care administration, health education, history, information sciences and systems, interdisciplinary studies, international studies, Italian, journalism, law enforcement and corrections, marketing and distribution, marketing management, mathematics, mathematics education, mathematics/physics, medical biology, medical laboratory technologies, medical records administration, medical records technology, music, music education, musical theater, nuclear medical technology, nursing, philosophy, photography, photojournalism, physical education, physics, political science and government, prelaw, production, psychology, public administration, public relations, radio/television broadcasting, radio/television technology, radiograph medical technology, secondary education, social studies education, sociology, Spanish, special education, speech, speech correction, studio art, teaching English as a second language/foreign language.

ACADEMIC PROGRAMS. 2-year transfer program, accelerated program, cooperative education, double major, dual enrollment of high school students, education specialist degree, honors program, independent study, internships, semester at sea, student-designed major, study abroad, teacher preparation, visiting/exchange student program, weekend college, United Nations semester, cross-registration, 3-2 preengineering program in cooperation with Polytechnic University and Pratt Institute; liberal arts/career combination in health sciences; combined bachelor's/graduate program in business administration. **Remedial services:** Learning center, preadmission summer program, reduced course load, remedial instruction, special counselor, tutoring, English for International Students. **ROTC:** Air Force, Army. **Placement/credit:** AP, CLEP General and Subject, institutional tests; 60 credit hours maximum for bachelor's degree.

ACADEMIC REQUIREMENTS. Freshmen must earn minimum GPA of 2.0 to continue in good standing. 96% of freshmen return for sophomore year. Students must declare major by end of second year. **Graduation requirements:** 64 hours for associate, 128 hours for bachelor's. Most students required to take courses in arts/fine arts, computer science, English, foreign languages, history, humanities, mathematics, philosophy/religion, biological/physical sciences, social sciences.

FRESHMAN ADMISSIONS. Selection criteria: High school curriculum, GPA, test scores, school recommendations, and interview important. **High school preparation:** 16 units required. Required units include English 4, foreign language 2, mathematics 2, social science 3 and science 1. **Test requirements:** SAT or ACT (SAT preferred); score report by September 11.

1992 FRESHMAN CLASS PROFILE. 1,330 men applied, 1,007 accepted, 381 enrolled; 1,948 women applied, 1,459 accepted, 410 enrolled. 71% had high school GPA of 3.0 or higher, 28% between 2.0 and 2.99. 19% were in top tenth and 41% were in top quarter of graduating class. **Academic background:** Mid 50% of enrolled freshmen had SAT-V between 400-500, SAT-M between 400-550. 86% submitted SAT scores. **Characteristics:** 84% from in state, 54% live in college housing, 22% have minority backgrounds, 5% are foreign students. Average age is 18.

FALL-TERM APPLICATIONS. $30 fee, may be waived for applicants with need. No closing date; applicants notified on a rolling basis; must reply by May 1 or within 2 weeks if notified thereafter. Interview required for communication arts, theater/film applicants. Audition required for music applicants. Portfolio required for art applicants. Essay recommended. CRDA. Deferred and early admission available.

STUDENT LIFE. Housing: Dormitories (women, coed). **Activities:** Student government, film, magazine, radio, student newspaper, television, yearbook, choral groups, concert band, dance, drama, jazz band, marching band, music ensembles, musical theater, pep band, symphony orchestra, fraternities, sororities, African Peoples Organization, Women's Center, commuter and resident student associations, foreign student associations, Newman Club.

ATHLETICS. NCAA. **Intercollegiate:** Baseball M, basketball, cross-country, field hockey W, football M, lacrosse M, soccer M, softball W, tennis W, track and field, volleyball W. **Intramural:** Basketball, ice hockey M, lacrosse W, rugby M, soccer W, softball M.

STUDENT SERVICES. Aptitude testing, career counseling, employment service for undergraduates, freshman orientation, health services, on-campus day care, personal counseling, placement service for graduates, special adviser for adult students, veterans counselor, services/facilities for handicapped.

ANNUAL EXPENSES. Tuition and fees (projected): $11,450. **Room and board:** $5,370. **Books and supplies:** $500. **Other expenses:** $1,150.

FINANCIAL AID. 77% of freshmen, 75% of continuing students receive some form of aid. 69% of grants, 75% of loans, 41% of jobs based on need. 490 enrolled freshmen were judged to have need, 475 were offered aid. Academic, music/drama, art, athletic scholarships available. **Aid applications:** No closing date; priority given to applications received by May 15; applicants notified on a rolling basis beginning on or about March 1; must reply by May 1 or within 3 weeks if notified thereafter. **Additional information:** Financial assistance available to qualified part-time students.

ADDRESS/TELEPHONE. Christine Natali, Director of Admissions, Long Island University: C. W. Post Campus, Northern Boulevard, Brookville, NY 11548. (516) 299-2413. (800) LIU-PLAN. Fax: (516) 625-4347.

Long Island University: Southampton Campus

Southampton, New York CB code: 2853

Admissions: 81% of applicants accepted
Based on: ••• School record, special talents, test scores
•• Interview, recommendations
• Activities, essay
Completion: 92% of freshmen end year in good standing
55% graduate, 40% of these enter graduate study

4-year private liberal arts college, coed. Founded in 1963. **Accreditation:** Regional. **Undergraduate enrollment:** 459 men, 692 women full time; 58 men, 85 women part time. **Graduate enrollment:** 6 men, 71 women part time. **Faculty:** 113 total (72 full time). **Location:** Rural campus in small town; 85 miles from New York City. **Calendar:** 4-1-4, extensive summer session. **Microcomputers:** 100 located in computer centers, campus-wide network. **Special facilities:** Marine science research station, art gallery, nursery school, fleet of research vessels, psychobiology lab. **Additional facts:** One of 6 campuses. Home to North American Center of Friends World Program.

DEGREES OFFERED. BA, BS, BFA, MS. 235 bachelor's degrees awarded in 1992. 21% in business and management, 18% teacher education, 29% life sciences, 9% psychology, 10% social sciences, 11% visual and performing arts. Graduate degrees offered in 3 major fields of study.

UNDERGRADUATE MAJORS. Accounting, advertising, art education, arts management, biological and physical sciences, biology, business administration and management, business and management, cell biology, chemistry, communications, computer and information sciences, creative writing, education, elementary education, English, English education, English literature, environmental science, fine arts, geology, graphic design, history, information sciences and systems, journalism, junior high education, management information systems, marine biology, marketing management, oceanography, political science and government, prelaw, premedicine, preveterinary, psychobiology, psychology, public relations, radio/television broadcasting, science education, secondary education, social science education, social sciences, social studies education, sociology, studio art, visual and performing arts.

ACADEMIC PROGRAMS. Accelerated program, cooperative education, double major, dual enrollment of high school students, honors program, independent study, internships, semester at sea, study abroad, teacher preparation, cross-registration, 5-week midwinter travel courses, International Study through Friends World Program. **Remedial services:** Learning center, preadmission summer program, reduced course load, remedial instruction, special counselor, tutoring. **Placement/credit:** AP, CLEP General and Subject, institutional tests; 60 credit hours maximum for bachelor's degree.

ACADEMIC REQUIREMENTS. Freshmen must earn minimum GPA of 1.8 to continue in good standing. 92% of freshmen return for sophomore year. Students must declare major by end of second year. **Graduation requirements:** 128 hours for bachelor's (83 in major). Most students required to take courses in arts/fine arts, computer science, English, humanities, biological/physical sciences, social sciences. **Postgraduate studies:** 1% enter law school, 1% enter medical school, 8% enter MBA programs, 30% enter other graduate study.

FRESHMAN ADMISSIONS. Selection criteria: School achievement record, test scores, and special talents are most important. Interview and recommendations also considered. **High school preparation:** 16 units required. Required and recommended units include English 4, mathematics 3, social science 2 and science 2. Biological science 2 and physical science 2 recommended. 3 units of laboratory science required for science applicants. **Test requirements:** SAT or ACT; score report by September 1.

1992 FRESHMAN CLASS PROFILE. 483 men applied, 361 accepted, 164 enrolled; 708 women applied, 607 accepted, 223 enrolled. 33% had high school GPA of 3.0 or higher, 51% between 2.0 and 2.99. **Academic background:** Mid 50% of enrolled freshmen had SAT-V between 400-590, SAT-M between 410-630. 95% submitted SAT scores. **Characteristics:** 70% from in state, 85% live in college housing, 13% have minority backgrounds, 2% are foreign students. Average age is 18.

FALL-TERM APPLICATIONS. $30 fee, may be waived for applicants with need. No closing date; applicants notified on a rolling basis; must reply by May 1 or within 4 weeks if notified thereafter. Interview recommended for academically weak applicants. Portfolio recommended for art applicants. Essay recommended for academically weak applicants. CRDA. Deferred and early admission available.

STUDENT LIFE. Housing: Dormitories (women, coed). On-campus housing guaranteed. **Activities:** Student government, magazine, radio, student newspaper, yearbook, choral groups, drama, music ensembles, Spectrum of Unity.

ATHLETICS. NCAA. **Intercollegiate:** Basketball, lacrosse M, soccer, softball W, volleyball. **Intramural:** Basketball, bowling, cross-country, golf, horseback riding, racquetball, sailing, skin diving, soccer, softball, tennis, volleyball.

STUDENT SERVICES. Aptitude testing, career counseling, employment service for undergraduates, freshman orientation, health services, personal counseling, placement service for graduates, special adviser for adult students, veterans counselor, career counseling prior to admission, services/facilities for handicapped.

ANNUAL EXPENSES. Tuition and fees (projected): $11,520. **Room and board:** $5,680. **Books and supplies:** $525. **Other expenses:** $550.

FINANCIAL AID. 85% of freshmen, 78% of continuing students receive some form of aid. 58% of grants, 94% of loans, all jobs based on need. 210 enrolled freshmen were judged to have need, 155 were offered aid. Academic, art, athletic scholarships available. **Aid applications:** No closing date; applicants notified on a rolling basis beginning on or about February 10; must reply by May 1 or within 4 weeks if notified thereafter.

ADDRESS/TELEPHONE. Carol Gilbert, Director of Admissions, Long Island University: Southampton Campus, Montauk Highway, Southampton, NY 11968. (516) 287-1273. (800) LIU-PLAN. Fax: (516) 283-4081.

Machzikei Hadath Rabbinical College
Brooklyn, New York — CB code: 0726

5-year private seminary college, men only, affiliated with Jewish faith. Founded in 1956. **Undergraduate enrollment:** 102 men full time. **Graduate enrollment:** 30 men full time. **Location:** Urban campus in very large city. **Calendar:** Semester. **Additional facts:** First Talmudic degree and ordination available.

FRESHMAN ADMISSIONS. Selection criteria: Interview most important.

ADDRESS/TELEPHONE. Rabbi A. M. Leizerowitz, Director of Admissions, Machzikei Hadath Rabbinical College, 5824 17th Avenue, Brooklyn, NY 11204. (718) 331-6613. Fax: (718) 331-4451.

Manhattan College
Riverdale, New York — CB code: 2395

Admissions: 72% of applicants accepted
Based on: ••• School record
•• Essay, interview, recommendations, test scores
• Activities, special talents
Completion: 90% of freshmen end year in good standing
70% graduate, 17% of these enter graduate study

4-year private college of arts and sciences and engineering college, coed, sponsored by De La Salle Christian Brothers. Founded in 1853. **Accreditation:** Regional. **Undergraduate enrollment:** 1,579 men, 1,105 women full time; 165 men, 89 women part time. **Graduate enrollment:** 65 men, 29 women full time; 354 men, 230 women part time. **Faculty:** 286 total (202 full time). **Location:** Urban campus in very large city; 15 miles from midtown Manhattan. **Calendar:** Semester, extensive summer session. **Microcomputers:** 320 located in libraries, classrooms, computer centers. **Special facilities:** Research and learning center, nuclear reactor, plant morphogenesis laboratory, engineering library. **Additional facts:** Independent institution in the Roman Catholic tradition.

DEGREES OFFERED. AAS, BA, BS, MA, MS, MBA. 6 associate degrees awarded in 1992. 50% in business and management, 50% health sciences. 670 bachelor's degrees awarded. 22% in business and management, 8% computer sciences, 8% teacher education, 28% engineering, 6% letters/literature, 6% psychology, 8% social sciences. Graduate degrees offered in 16 major fields of study.

UNDERGRADUATE MAJORS. Associate: Nuclear medical technology. **Bachelor's:** Accounting, administration of special education, advertising, American literature, applied mathematics, biochemistry, bioengineering and biomedical engineering, biological and physical sciences, biological laboratory technology, biology, biotechnology, business administration and management, business and management, business economics, chemical engineering, chemistry, civil engineering, communications, computer and information sciences, computer mathematics, computer programming, early childhood education, economics, education, education of the physically handicapped, electrical/electronics/communications engineering, elementary education, engineering, engineering and other disciplines, English, English education, English literature, environmental health engineering, environmental science, finance, fine arts, foreign languages (multiple emphasis), French, health education, history, humanities and social sciences, industrial engineering, information sciences and systems, international business management, international relations, international studies, journalism, junior high education, liberal/general studies, management information systems, management science, marketing and distribution, marketing management, mathematics, mechanical engineering, medical radiation dosimetry, nuclear engineering, nuclear medical technology, peace studies, philosophy, physical education, physical sciences, physics, political science and government, psychology, public relations, radio/television broadcasting, radio/television technology, religion, religious education, science education, secondary education, social science education, social sciences, social studies education, social work, sociology, Spanish, special education, sports medicine, statistics, theological studies, urban studies.

ACADEMIC PROGRAMS. Accelerated program, cooperative education, double major, honors program, independent study, internships, study abroad, teacher preparation, cross-registration. **Remedial services:** Reduced course load, special counselor, tutoring, New York State Higher Education Opportunity Program. **ROTC:** Air Force. **Placement/credit:** AP, CLEP General and Subject; 30 credit hours maximum for bachelor's degree.

ACADEMIC REQUIREMENTS. Freshmen must earn minimum GPA of 1.8 to continue in good standing. 86% of freshmen return for sophomore year. Students must declare major by end of second year. **Graduation requirements:** 66 hours for associate, 128 hours for bachelor's. Most students required to take courses in arts/fine arts, computer science, English, foreign languages, history, humanities, mathematics, philosophy/religion, biological/physical sciences, social sciences. **Postgraduate studies:** 2% enter law school, 2% enter medical school, 1% enter MBA programs, 12% enter other graduate study.

FRESHMAN ADMISSIONS. Selection criteria: School achievement record, curriculum, SAT scores most important. **High school preparation:** 16 units required. Required and recommended units include English 4, foreign language 2-3, mathematics 3-4, physical science 3 and social science 3. Science 3 recommended. 4 mathematics, 4 science (including precalculus, chemistry, and physics) recommended of engineering majors and most science majors. **Test requirements:** SAT or ACT (SAT preferred); score report by March 1.

1992 FRESHMAN CLASS PROFILE. 2,187 men and women applied, 1,566 accepted; 332 men enrolled, 254 women enrolled. 85% had high school GPA of 3.0 or higher, 15% between 2.0 and 2.99. 23% were in top tenth and 61% were in top quarter of graduating class. **Academic background:** Mid 50% of enrolled freshmen had SAT-V between 430-540, SAT-M between 510-590. 98% submitted SAT scores. **Characteristics:** 70% from in state, 60% live in college housing, 24% have minority backgrounds, 1% are foreign students, 3% join fraternities/sororities. Average age is 18.

FALL-TERM APPLICATIONS. $25 fee, may be waived for applicants with need. Closing date March 1; priority given to applications received by January 1; applicants notified on a rolling basis beginning on or about February 1; must reply by May 1. Essay required. Interview recommended. CRDA. Deferred and early admission available. EDP-S.

STUDENT LIFE. Housing: Dormitories (men, coed); apartment housing available. **Activities:** Student government, magazine, radio, student newspaper, yearbook, choral groups, drama, jazz band, marching band, musical theater, pep band, fraternities, sororities, campus ministry, African American Club, Caribbean Society, Chinese Student Association, Circle-K, Gaelic Society, Young Conservatives, Democrats, Republicans.

ATHLETICS. NCAA. **Intercollegiate:** Baseball M, basketball, cross-country, golf M, lacrosse M, rowing (crew), soccer, softball W, swimming, tennis, track and field, volleyball W, wrestling M. **Intramural:** Badminton, baseball M, basketball, cross-country, golf, gymnastics M, handball, skiing, soccer M, softball W, swimming, tennis, track and field, volleyball, water polo.

STUDENT SERVICES. Aptitude testing, career counseling, employment service for undergraduates, freshman orientation, health services, personal counseling, placement service for graduates, veterans counselor, services/facilities for handicapped.

ANNUAL EXPENSES. Tuition and fees: $12,600. **Room and board:** $6,600. **Books and supplies:** $500. **Other expenses:** $1,000.

FINANCIAL AID. 85% of freshmen, 65% of continuing students receive some form of aid. 54% of grants, 95% of loans, 70% of jobs based on need. 450 enrolled freshmen were judged to have need, all were offered aid. Academic, athletic scholarships available. **Aid applications:** No closing date; priority given to applications received by February 15; applicants notified on a rolling basis beginning on or about March 1; must reply by May 1 or within 2 weeks if notified thereafter.

ADDRESS/TELEPHONE. John J. Brennan, Jr, Dean of Admissions, Manhattan College, Manhattan College Parkway, Riverdale, NY 10471. (718) 920-0200. (800) MC2-XCEL. Fax: (718) 548-1008.

Manhattan School of Music
New York, New York — CB code: 2396

Admissions: 43% of applicants accepted
Based on:
••• Special talents
•• School record
• Activities, essay, recommendations, test scores
Completion: 95% of freshmen end year in good standing
65% graduate, 85% of these enter graduate study

4-year private music college, coed. Founded in 1917. **Accreditation:** Regional. **Undergraduate enrollment:** 217 men, 210 women full time; 20 men, 11 women part time. **Graduate enrollment:** 139 men, 201 women full time; 38 men, 49 women part time. **Faculty:** 250 total (20 full time). **Location:** Urban campus in very large city. **Calendar:** Semester, limited summer session. **Special facilities:** 1000-seat concert hall, 3 recital halls, 2 electronic music studios, recording studio.

DEGREES OFFERED. B, M, D. 74 bachelor's degrees awarded in 1992. 100% in visual and performing arts. Graduate degrees offered in 3 major fields of study.

UNDERGRADUATE MAJORS. Jazz, music performance, music theory and composition.

ACADEMIC PROGRAMS. Cross-registration. **Remedial services:** Remedial instruction, tutoring. **Placement/credit:** AP, CLEP General and Subject, institutional tests; 60 credit hours maximum for bachelor's degree.

ACADEMIC REQUIREMENTS. Freshmen must earn minimum GPA of 2.0 to continue in good standing. 90% of freshmen return for sophomore year. Students must declare major on application. **Graduation requirements:** 122 hours for bachelor's (90 in major). Most students required to take courses in arts/fine arts, English, humanities.

FRESHMAN ADMISSIONS. Selection criteria: Audition, availability of space in specific performance area, and academic record are considered. Recommended units include biological science 2, English 4, foreign language 2, mathematics 2, physical science 2 and social science 3. Extensive music training required.

1992 FRESHMAN CLASS PROFILE. 181 men applied, 82 accepted, 35 enrolled; 185 women applied, 76 accepted, 46 enrolled. **Characteristics:** 34% from in state, 50% commute, 15% have minority backgrounds, 30% are foreign students. Average age is 19.

FALL-TERM APPLICATIONS. $85 fee, may be waived for applicants with need. Closing date April 15; priority given to applications received by January 15; applicants notified on a rolling basis; must reply by May 1. Audition required. Essay required. CRDA. SAT or ACT recommended.

STUDENT LIFE. Housing: Dormitories (coed). Housing available in conjunction with nearby International House. **Activities:** Student newspaper, choral groups, concert band, jazz band, music ensembles, opera, symphony orchestra, Pan-African Student Association, Chinese Students Association, Chess Club, Composers Now, Gay Lesbian and Bisexual Student Association.

STUDENT SERVICES. Career counseling, employment service for undergraduates, freshman orientation, health services, personal counseling, placement service for graduates.

ANNUAL EXPENSES. Tuition and fees (1992-93): $11,000. **Room and board:** $3,500 room only. **Books and supplies:** $525. **Other expenses:** $900.

FINANCIAL AID. 69% of freshmen, 61% of continuing students receive some form of aid. 28% of grants, 94% of loans, all jobs based on need. 57 enrolled freshmen were judged to have need, all were offered aid. Academic, music/drama scholarships available. **Aid applications:** Closing date April 15; priority given to applications received by March 1; applicants notified on a rolling basis; must reply by May 1. **Additional information:** Performance-based scholarships available.

ADDRESS/TELEPHONE. James Gandre, Dean of Admission and Alumni, Manhattan School of Music, 120 Claremont Avenue, New York, NY 10027-4698. (212) 749-3025. Fax: (212) 749-5471.

Manhattanville College
Purchase, New York — CB code: 2397

Admissions: 79% of applicants accepted
Based on:
••• Activities, recommendations, school record
•• Essay, special talents
• Interview, test scores
Completion: 95% of freshmen end year in good standing
72% graduate, 28% of these enter graduate study

4-year private liberal arts college, coed. Founded in 1841. **Accreditation:** Regional. **Undergraduate enrollment:** 286 men, 579 women full time; 44 men, 143 women part time. **Graduate enrollment:** 9 men, 89 women full time; 13 men, 147 women part time. **Faculty:** 207 total (76 full time), 65 with doctorates or other terminal degrees. **Location:** Suburban campus in large town; 25 miles from New York City. **Calendar:** Semester, limited summer session. **Microcomputers:** 43 located in libraries, computer centers. **Special facilities:** Art gallery, photography laboratory, observatory, greenhouse.

DEGREES OFFERED. BA, BFA, MA. 202 bachelor's degrees awarded in 1992. 20% in business and management, 11% languages, 8% multi/interdisciplinary studies, 5% physical sciences, 9% psychology, 26% social sciences, 13% visual and performing arts. Graduate degrees offered in 21 major fields of study.

UNDERGRADUATE MAJORS. Accounting, American literature, American studies, art history, Asian studies, biochemistry, biological and physical sciences, biology, business administration and management, chemistry, classics, computer and information sciences, dance, dramatic arts, economics, English, English literature, finance, fine arts, foreign languages (multiple emphasis), French, history, humanities, humanities and social sciences, international relations, international studies, mathematics, medieval studies, music, music business management, music history and appreciation, music performance, music theory and composition, philosophy, physics, political science and government, psychology, religion, Russian and Slavic studies, sociology, Spanish, studio art.

ACADEMIC PROGRAMS. Accelerated program, double major, honors program, independent study, internships, student-designed major, study abroad, teacher preparation, visiting/exchange student program, Washington semester, cross-registration, combined degree programs in engineering with Clarkson University and in nursing with New York University, combined bachelor's/graduate degree program in business administration with New York University. Exchange programs in Bath and Oxford, Great Britain, Paris, Tokyo, Madrid, and Florence. Summer program in Crete. **Remedial services:** Learning center, reduced course load, remedial instruction, tutoring, Higher Education Opportunity Program for New York State residents. **Placement/credit:** AP, CLEP General and Subject, institutional tests.

ACADEMIC REQUIREMENTS. Freshmen must earn minimum GPA of 2.0 to continue in good standing. 90% of freshmen return for sophomore year. Students must declare major by end of second year. **Graduation requirements:** 120 hours for bachelor's (36 in major). Most students required to take courses in arts/fine arts, computer science, English, history, humanities, mathematics, biological/physical sciences, social sciences. **Postgraduate studies:** 7% enter law school, 7% enter medical school, 10% enter MBA programs, 4% enter other graduate study.

FRESHMAN ADMISSIONS. Selection criteria: School achievement record, recommendations, test scores or samples of academic work most important. Essay, school and community activities and geographic distribution also considered. Interview strongly recommended. **High school preparation:** 14 units required. Required and recommended units include English 4-4, foreign language 2-3, mathematics 3-3, social science 3-3 and science 2-3. **Test requirements:** SAT or ACT (SAT preferred); score report by March 15. English Composition and Mathematics Level I or II ACH required for those applying through alternate admissions plan. Score report by March 15

Applicants with high class rank may submit academic work and English Composition and Mathematics Level I or II ACH in place of SAT scores.

1992 FRESHMAN CLASS PROFILE. 306 men applied, 235 accepted, 57 enrolled; 604 women applied, 480 accepted, 164 enrolled. 77% had high school GPA of 3.0 or higher, 23% between 2.0 and 2.99. 33% were in top tenth and 65% were in top quarter of graduating class. **Academic background:** Mid 50% of enrolled freshmen had SAT-V between 470-590, SAT-M between 490-590. 85% submitted SAT scores. **Characteristics:** 48% from in state, 86% live in college housing, 33% have minority backgrounds, 14% are foreign students. Average age is 18.

FALL-TERM APPLICATIONS. $30 fee, may be waived for applicants with need. Closing date March 1; applicants notified on a rolling basis; must reply by May 1. Audition required for Bachelor of Music degree applicants. Portfolio required for Bachelor of Fine Arts applicants. Essay required. Interview recommended. CRDA. Deferred and early admission available. EDP-F. December 1 deadline for Early Decision applications.

STUDENT LIFE. Housing: Dormitories (coed); apartment housing available. Intercultural dormitories available. **Activities:** Student government, magazine, radio, student newspaper, yearbook, prelaw review, choral groups, concert band, dance, drama, jazz band, music ensembles, musical theater, symphony orchestra, campus ministry, language and culture clubs, international students club, student organization for political awareness, Recognition of Women in Society, Amnesty International, Project Earth, Intercultural House, Students Organized Against Racism, Model UN.

ATHLETICS. NCAA. **Intercollegiate:** Baseball M, basketball, diving W, field hockey W, lacrosse M, soccer, softball W, swimming W, tennis, volleyball W. **Intramural:** Basketball, cross-country, horseback riding W, lacrosse W, soccer M, softball, swimming M, volleyball, water polo.

STUDENT SERVICES. Aptitude testing, career counseling, employment service for undergraduates, freshman orientation, health services, personal counseling, placement service for graduates, special adviser for adult students, services/facilities for handicapped.

ANNUAL EXPENSES. Tuition and fees: $14,290. **Room and board:** $6,250. **Books and supplies:** $450. **Other expenses:** $800.

FINANCIAL AID. 67% of freshmen, 68% of continuing students receive some form of aid. 99% of loans, all jobs based on need. Academic, music/drama, art, leadership scholarships available. **Aid applications:** No closing date; priority given to applications received by March 1; applicants notified on a rolling basis beginning on or about March 1; must reply by May 1 or within 2 weeks if notified thereafter. **Additional information:** Upper level students may earn additional money and academic credit through internship program.

ADDRESS/TELEPHONE. Priscilla Hambrick-Dixon, Assistant Provost, Manhattanville College, 2900 Purchase Street, Purchase, NY 10577. (914) 694-2200 ext. 464. (800) 328-4553. Fax: (914) 694-1732.

Mannes College of Music
New York, New York CB code: 2398

Admissions:	38% of applicants accepted
Based on:	••• Special talents
	•• Interview, recommendations, school record
	• Essay, test scores
Completion:	80% of freshmen end year in good standing
	70% graduate, 35% of these enter graduate study

4-year private music college, coed. Founded in 1916. **Accreditation:** Regional. **Undergraduate enrollment:** 37 men, 60 women full time; 1 man, 1 woman part time. **Graduate enrollment:** 52 men, 71 women full time; 3 men, 5 women part time. **Faculty:** 150 total (30 full time), 29 with doctorates or other terminal degrees. **Location:** Urban campus in very large city; located in mid-Manhattan. **Calendar:** Semester, limited summer session. **Special facilities:** 2 concert halls.

DEGREES OFFERED. BS, M. 23 bachelor's degrees awarded in 1992. 100% in visual and performing arts. Graduate degrees offered in 2 major fields of study.

UNDERGRADUATE MAJORS. Music performance, music theory and composition.

ACADEMIC PROGRAMS. Double major, cross-registration. **Remedial services:** Remedial instruction, tutoring. **Placement/credit:** Institutional tests.

ACADEMIC REQUIREMENTS. Freshmen must earn minimum GPA of 2.3 to continue in good standing. Minimum GPA of 3.0 in major (instrumental, vocal, composition, conducting, or theory) required to continue in good academic standing. 75% of freshmen return for sophomore year. Students must declare major on application. **Graduation requirements:** 150 hours for bachelor's (36 in major). Most students required to take courses in arts/fine arts, English, foreign languages, history, humanities. **Postgraduate studies:** 35% enter other graduate study.

FRESHMAN ADMISSIONS. Selection criteria: In order of importance, specific talent for major as evidenced by audition in major instrument or evaluation of previous accomplishment for composers and theory majors, general musicianship skills (ear, theory, etc.), academic record. **High school preparation:** 16 units required. Required units include English 4, foreign language 2, mathematics 2 and science 1. **Test requirements:** Institutionally-designed entrance examination, including major audition. Written examinations in music theory, dictation, ear training, and English usage.

1992 FRESHMAN CLASS PROFILE. 56 men applied, 22 accepted, 7 enrolled; 76 women applied, 28 accepted, 11 enrolled. **Characteristics:** 50% from in state, 97% commute, 21% have minority backgrounds, 13% are foreign students. Average age is 19.

FALL-TERM APPLICATIONS. $60 fee, may be waived for applicants with need. Closing date July 15; applicants notified on a rolling basis; must reply within 5 weeks. Interview required. Audition required. Essay recommended. Tapes may be sumitted for advisory opinion. Deferred admission available. Closing date for applications 30 days before winter, March, May, or August auditions.

STUDENT LIFE. Housing: Dormitories (coed). **Activities:** Choral groups, jazz band, music ensembles, opera, symphony orchestra.

STUDENT SERVICES. Career counseling, employment service for undergraduates, placement service for graduates, services/facilities for handicapped.

ANNUAL EXPENSES. Tuition and fees: $12,000. **Room and board:** $5,400 room only. **Books and supplies:** $1,200. **Other expenses:** $1,000.

FINANCIAL AID. 81% of freshmen, 76% of continuing students receive some form of aid. Grants, loans, jobs available. Music/drama scholarships available. **Aid applications:** No closing date; priority given to applications received by May 15; applicants notified on a rolling basis beginning on or about May 15; must reply within 2 weeks. **Additional information:** Closing date for scholarship applications 2 weeks prior to audition date.

ADDRESS/TELEPHONE. Marilyn Groves, Director of Admissions, Mannes College of Music, 150 West 85th Street, New York, NY 10024. (212) 580-0210 ext. 46. (800) 292-3040. Fax: (212) 580-1738.

Maria College
Albany, New York CB code: 2434

2-year private junior college, coed. Founded in 1958. **Accreditation:** Regional. **Undergraduate enrollment:** 881 men and women. **Faculty:** 57 total (33 full time), 5 with doctorates or other terminal degrees. **Location:** Urban campus in small city; 150 miles from New York City and Boston. **Calendar:** Semester, limited summer session. **Microcomputers:** 15 located in computer centers.

DEGREES OFFERED. AA, AS, AAS. 231 associate degrees awarded in 1992. 23% in business and management, 21% teacher education, 45% allied health, 11% multi/interdisciplinary studies.

UNDERGRADUATE MAJORS. Accounting, business and management, business and office, early childhood education, liberal/general studies, nursing, occupational therapy assistant, office supervision and management, physical therapy assistant, teacher aide, tourism.

ACADEMIC PROGRAMS. 2-year transfer program, dual enrollment of high school students, independent study, internships, teacher preparation, weekend college, cross-registration. **Remedial services:** Learning center, preadmission summer program, reduced course load, remedial instruction, tutoring. **Placement/credit:** AP, CLEP General and Subject, institutional tests; 16 credit hours maximum for associate degree.

ACADEMIC REQUIREMENTS. Freshmen must earn minimum GPA of 2.0 to continue in good standing. Special requirements for continuance in some programs. 76% of freshmen return for sophomore year. Students must declare major on application. **Graduation requirements:** 64 hours for associate. Most students required to take courses in English, philosophy/religion, social sciences.

FRESHMAN ADMISSIONS. Selection criteria: School achievement record, test scores, interviews, recommendations important. **High school preparation:** 18 units required. Required units include biological science 1, English 4, mathematics 2, physical science 1, social science 3 and science 2. Requirements vary with program. **Test requirements:** SAT or ACT (SAT preferred); score report by August 1.

1992 FRESHMAN CLASS PROFILE. Academic background: Mid 50% of enrolled freshmen had SAT-V between 400-450, SAT-M between 420-460; ACT composite between 14-22. 63% submitted SAT scores, 15% submitted ACT scores. **Characteristics:** 99% from in state, 6% have minority backgrounds. Average age is 20.

FALL-TERM APPLICATIONS. $20 fee, may be waived for applicants with need. Closing date August 15; priority given to applications received by June 15; applicants notified on a rolling basis; must reply within 4 weeks. Interview required. Essay required. CRDA. Early admission available.

STUDENT LIFE. Approximately 15% of all undergraduates, including freshmen, live in their own apartments off campus, 85% commute from home.

STUDENT SERVICES. Career counseling, employment service for undergraduates, freshman orientation, health services, personal counseling, placement service for graduates, special adviser for adult students, services/facilities for handicapped.

ANNUAL EXPENSES. Tuition and fees (1992-93): $4,275. **Books and supplies:** $550. **Other expenses:** $500.

FINANCIAL AID. 60% of freshmen, 65% of continuing students receive some form of aid. 99% of grants, 86% of loans, 67% of jobs based on need. **Aid applications:** No closing date; priority given to applications received by August 1; applicants notified on a rolling basis.

ADDRESS/TELEPHONE. Laurie A. Gilmore, Director of Admissions, Maria College, 700 New Scotland Avenue, Albany, NY 12208. (518) 438-3111 ext. 17.

Marist College
Poughkeepsie, New York CB code: 2400

Admissions: 69% of applicants accepted
Based on:
••• School record
•• Activities, test scores
• Essay, interview, recommendations, special talents
Completion: 90% of freshmen end year in good standing
62% graduate, 21% of these enter graduate study

4-year private branch campus college, coed, In Roman Catholic tradition. Founded in 1929. **Accreditation:** Regional. **Undergraduate enrollment:** 1,474 men, 1,670 women full time; 303 men, 331 women part time. **Graduate enrollment:** 61 men, 27 women full time; 261 men, 254 women part time. **Faculty:** 357 total (156 full time), 93 with doctorates or other terminal degrees. **Location:** Suburban campus in small city; 75 miles from New York City, 75 miles from Albany. **Calendar:** Semester, extensive summer session. **Microcomputers:** 350 located in dormitories, libraries, classrooms, computer centers, campus-wide network. **Special facilities:** Lowell Thomas Gallery, communications center, on-line journalism laboratory, Margaret M. & Charles H. Dyson Management Studies Center for estuarine and environmental studies, Marist Institute for Public Opinion.

DEGREES OFFERED. BA, BS, MA, MS, MBA. 710 bachelor's degrees awarded in 1992. 25% in business and management, 30% communications, 8% computer sciences, 8% letters/literature, 7% physical sciences, 10% psychology, 9% social sciences. Graduate degrees offered in 6 major fields of study.

UNDERGRADUATE MAJORS. Accounting, adult and continuing education administration, American studies, biochemistry, biology, business administration and management, business economics, chemistry, clinical laboratory science, communications, computer and information sciences, computer mathematics, criminal justice studies, economics, elementary education, English, environmental science, fashion design, fine arts, French, history, information sciences and systems, mathematics, medical laboratory technologies, political science and government, prelaw, psychology, Russian, social work, Spanish, special education.

ACADEMIC PROGRAMS. Accelerated program, cooperative education, double major, dual enrollment of high school students, honors program, independent study, internships, study abroad, teacher preparation, Washington semester, cross-registration. **Remedial services:** Learning center, preadmission summer program, reduced course load, remedial instruction, special counselor, tutoring, New York State Higher Education Opportunity Program. **Placement/credit:** AP, CLEP General and Subject, institutional tests.

ACADEMIC REQUIREMENTS. Freshmen must earn minimum GPA of 2.0 to continue in good standing. 89% of freshmen return for sophomore year. Students must declare major by end of second year. **Graduation requirements:** 120 hours for bachelor's (36 in major). Most students required to take courses in computer science, English, history, mathematics, philosophy/religion, biological/physical sciences, social sciences. **Postgraduate studies:** 9% enter law school, 1% enter medical school, 3% enter MBA programs, 8% enter other graduate study.

FRESHMAN ADMISSIONS. Selection criteria: School achievement record, rank in top half of class primary consideration. SAT scores, recommendations, activities, personal qualities also considered. **High school preparation:** 16 units required. Required and recommended units include English 4, foreign language 2, mathematics 3-4, social science 3 and science 2-4. One American history required. 4 units mathematics recommended for computer science and physical science majors. **Test requirements:** SAT or ACT; score report by May 1. **Additional information:** About 15-20 students enter each year in a Special Services program for the learning disabled. Candidates selected from a pool of 200 or more applicants.

1992 FRESHMAN CLASS PROFILE. 1,969 men applied, 1,268 accepted, 374 enrolled; 2,427 women applied, 1,756 accepted, 459 enrolled. 66% had high school GPA of 3.0 or higher, 34% between 2.0 and 2.99. 12% were in top tenth and 31% were in top quarter of graduating class. **Academic background:** Mid 50% of enrolled freshmen had SAT-V between 420-540, SAT-M between 460-580; ACT composite between 18-23. 96% submitted SAT scores, 8% submitted ACT scores. **Characteristics:** 49% from in state, 84% live in college housing, 11% have minority backgrounds, 1% are foreign students, 4% join fraternities/sororities. Average age is 18.

FALL-TERM APPLICATIONS. $30 fee, may be waived for applicants with need. No closing date; priority given to applications received by March 1; applicants notified on a rolling basis beginning on or about February 1; must reply by May 1 or within 3 weeks if notified thereafter. Portfolio required for fashion design majors applicants. Interview recommended. Essay recommended. CRDA. Deferred and early admission available. Institutional early decision plan. Deadline for Early Decision applicants is December 1, with notification by December 15. Candidates not limited to a single choice and have until May 1 to finalize their decision.

STUDENT LIFE. Housing: Dormitories (coed); apartment, fraternity housing available. 33 town house units and 52 garden apartments available on campus for upperclass students. **Activities:** Student government, film, magazine, radio, student newspaper, television, yearbook, choral groups, dance, drama, musical theater, pep band, debate team, fraternities, sororities, campus ministry, Black Student Union, Circle-K, Hispanic club, literary club, International Student Association, polital science club, many volunteer activities and social action clubs. **Additional information:** Of those undergraduates who do not reside in college housing, approximately 6% live in their own apartments off campus, 23% commute from home.

ATHLETICS. NAIA, NCAA. **Intercollegiate:** Baseball M, basketball, cross-country, diving, football M, horseback riding W, ice hockey M, lacrosse M, racquetball, rowing (crew), rugby M, sailing, skiing, soccer, softball, swimming, tennis, track and field, volleyball, wrestling M. **Intramural:** Basketball M, bowling, football M, golf, handball, racquetball, sailing, skiing, soccer, softball, table tennis, tennis, volleyball, water polo, wrestling M.

STUDENT SERVICES. Aptitude testing, career counseling, employment service for undergraduates, freshman orientation, health services, personal counseling, placement service for graduates, special adviser for adult students, veterans counselor, commuting population counselor, services/facilities for handicapped.

ANNUAL EXPENSES. Tuition and fees (projected): $10,545. **Room and board:** $5,817. **Books and supplies:** $500. **Other expenses:** $548.

FINANCIAL AID. 75% of freshmen, 75% of continuing students receive some form of aid. 60% of grants, 99% of loans, 32% of jobs based on need. 581 enrolled freshmen were judged to have need, all were offered aid. Academic, music/drama, athletic, leadership, minority scholarships available. **Aid applications:** No closing date; priority given to applications received by March 15; applicants notified on a rolling basis beginning on or about March 15; must reply by May 1 or within 2 weeks if notified thereafter. **Additional information:** 3 independent agencies arrange college financing on monthly payment basis.

ADDRESS/TELEPHONE. Harry W. Wood, Vice President of Admissions of Enrollment Planning, Marist College, North Road, Poughkeepsie, NY 12601-1387. (914) 575-3226. Fax: (914) 471-6213.

Marymount College
Tarrytown, New York CB code: 2406

Admissions: 69% of applicants accepted
Based on:
••• Interview, school record, test scores
•• Activities, essay, recommendations, special talents
Completion: 95% of freshmen end year in good standing
60% graduate, 16% of these enter graduate study

4-year private liberal arts college, coed. Founded in 1907. **Accreditation:** Regional. **Undergraduate enrollment:** 43 men, 645 women full time; 85 men, 342 women part time. **Faculty:** 129 total (59 full time), 102 with doctorates or other terminal degrees. **Location:** Suburban campus in large town; 25 miles from New York City. **Calendar:** Semester, limited summer session. **Microcomputers:** 45 located in classrooms, computer centers. **Special facilities:** Equestrian stables located on adjacent Rockefeller estate, office and residence in London for study abroad. **Additional facts:** Independent institution in Roman Catholic tradition. Weekend college sessions for working men and women. Women only in day session.

DEGREES OFFERED. BA, BS. 201 bachelor's degrees awarded in 1992. 40% in business and management, 7% business/office and marketing/distribution, 6% education, 7% home economics, 10% letters/literature, 6% psychology, 12% social sciences.

UNDERGRADUATE MAJORS. American studies, art education, art history, biological and physical sciences, biology, business administration and management, business and management, business economics, chemistry, communications, dramatic arts, early childhood education, economics, education, education of the emotionally handicapped, education of the mentally handicapped, elementary education, English, English education, fashion design, fashion merchandising, fine arts, food production/management/services, food science and nutrition, foreign languages education, French, history, home economics, home economics education, humanities and social sciences, information sciences and systems, interior design, international business management, international relations, international studies, journalism, junior high education, liberal/general studies, mathematics, mathematics education, philosophy, political science and government, psychology, religion, science education, secondary education, social studies education, social work, sociology, Spanish, special education, specific learning disabilities, studio art, textiles and clothing.

ACADEMIC PROGRAMS. Double major, dual enrollment of high school students, honors program, independent study, internships, student-designed major, study abroad, teacher preparation, visiting/exchange student program, weekend college, Washington semester, cross-registration, combined bachelor's/graduate degree programs in occupational therapy and speech-hearing-language pathology with New York University and in business administration with Fordham University. **Remedial services:** Learning center, preadmission summer program, reduced course load, remedial instruction, special counselor, tutoring, writing center, mathematics center, New York State Higher Education Opportunity Program, Center for English Language studies. **Placement/credit:** AP, CLEP Subject, institutional tests; 30 credit hours maximum for bachelor's degree.

ACADEMIC REQUIREMENTS. Freshmen must earn minimum GPA of 2.0 to continue in good standing. 80% of freshmen return for sophomore year. Students must declare major by end of second year. **Graduation requirements:** 120 hours for bachelor's (33 in major). Most students required to take courses in arts/fine arts, computer science, English, foreign languages, history, humanities, mathematics, philosophy/religion, biological/physical sciences, social sciences. **Postgraduate studies:** 2% enter law school, 1% enter medical school, 8% enter MBA programs, 5% enter other graduate study. **Additional information:** Mentorship program with Chase Bank. Extensive internship program in metropolitan area and abroad open to qualified juniors, seniors in any major.

FRESHMAN ADMISSIONS. Selection criteria: School achievement record most important. 3.0 high school GPA desired. SAT or ACT scores important. Recommendations from guidance counselors also weigh heavily. Special consideration given to foreign applicants. Interviews are required of academically weak applicants. **High school preparation:** 16 units recommended. Recommended units include English 4, foreign language 3, mathematics 3, social science 3 and science 3. **Test requirements:** SAT or ACT; score report by August 15. **Additional information:** College seeking a diverse student body and does not specify a required pattern of distribution for courses taken in high school.

1992 FRESHMAN CLASS PROFILE. 488 women applied, 335 accepted, 108 enrolled. 30% had high school GPA of 3.0 or higher, 67% between 2.0 and 2.99. **Academic background:** Mid 50% of enrolled freshmen had SAT-V between 380-490, SAT-M between 380-500. 99% submitted SAT scores. **Characteristics:** 52% from in state, 86% live in college housing, 17% have minority backgrounds, 1% are foreign students. Average age is 18.

FALL-TERM APPLICATIONS. $25 fee, may be waived for applicants with need. Closing date August 15; priority given to applications received by April 15; applicants notified on a rolling basis; must reply by May 1 or within 2 weeks if notified thereafter. Essay required. Interview recommended. CRDA. Deferred and early admission available.

STUDENT LIFE. Housing: Dormitories (women). Single rooms available on limited basis. Limited on-campus housing available for male and female weekend college students. **Activities:** Student government, magazine, student newspaper, yearbook, choral groups, dance, drama, music ensembles, musical theater, campus ministry, international students club, women's center, Amnesty International, Special Olympics, students against multiple sclerosis, community service, Alcohol and Drug Task Force, Committee on Cultural and Racial Diversity, SADD. **Additional information:** Proximity to New York City enables students to attend numerous cultural events. Musicians in residence give individual lessons to interested students.

ATHLETICS. Intercollegiate: Basketball W, diving W, softball W, swimming W, tennis W, volleyball W. **Intramural:** Archery W, badminton W, basketball W, bowling W, cross-country W, field hockey W, softball W, swimming W, table tennis W, tennis W, volleyball W. **Clubs:** Horseback riding.

STUDENT SERVICES. Aptitude testing, career counseling, employment service for undergraduates, freshman orientation, health services, on-campus day care, personal counseling, placement service for graduates, special adviser for adult students, services/facilities for handicapped.

ANNUAL EXPENSES. Tuition and fees: $11,150. **Room and board:** $6,200. **Books and supplies:** $500. **Other expenses:** $600.

FINANCIAL AID. 63% of freshmen, 57% of continuing students receive some form of aid. All grants, 97% of loans, all jobs based on need. 74 enrolled freshmen were judged to have need, all were offered aid. Academic, music/drama, art, leadership scholarships available. **Aid applications:** No closing date; priority given to applications received by March 1; applicants notified on a rolling basis beginning on or about March 30; must reply by May 1 or within 2 weeks if notified thereafter. **Additional information:** Comprehensive financial assistance program offered. Variety of merit scholarships range in value from $500 to $5,000.

ADDRESS/TELEPHONE. Gina R. Campbell, Director of Admissions, Marymount College, 100 Marymount Avenue, Tarrytown, NY 10591-3796. (914) 332-8295. (800) 724-4312. Fax: (914) 332-4956.

Marymount Manhattan College

New York, New York CB code: 2405

Admissions: 81% of applicants accepted
Based on:
- ••• School record, test scores
- •• Activities, interview, recommendations, special talents
- • Essay

Completion: 68% of freshmen end year in good standing
27% enter graduate study

4-year private liberal arts college, coed. Founded in 1936. **Accreditation:** Regional. **Undergraduate enrollment:** 168 men, 709 women full time; 40 men, 519 women part time. **Faculty:** 132 total (45 full time), 67 with doctorates or other terminal degrees. **Location:** Urban campus in very large city. **Calendar:** 4-1-4, limited summer session. Saturday and extensive evening/early morning classes. **Microcomputers:** Located in libraries, computer centers. **Special facilities:** Theater, communications and learning center, clinical facilities for speech pathology and audiology majors, art gallery, dance studio.

DEGREES OFFERED. BA, BS, BFA. 150 bachelor's degrees awarded in 1992. 30% in business and management, 13% communications, 12% letters/literature, 5% multi/interdisciplinary studies, 10% psychology, 14% social sciences, 13% visual and performing arts.

UNDERGRADUATE MAJORS. Accounting, biology, business administration and management, communications, dance, dramatic arts, elementary education, English, history, international relations, liberal/general studies, political science and government, psychology, secondary education, sociology, speech pathology/audiology, studio art.

ACADEMIC PROGRAMS. Accelerated program, dual enrollment of high school students, honors program, independent study, internships, study abroad, teacher preparation, visiting/exchange student program, weekend college, Washington semester, cooperative programs with international consortium leading to degree in international business communications, Mannes College of Music, Laboratory Institute of Merchandising, New York School of Interior Design, Cornell University School of Industrial and Labor Relations, Deutsches Haus at New York University, China Institute, New York Institute of Finance, Columbia University: School of Nursing. **Remedial services:** Learning center, preadmission summer program, reduced course load, remedial instruction, special counselor, tutoring, New York State Higher Education Opportunity Program, Education Enrichment Program. **Placement/credit:** AP, CLEP General and Subject, institutional tests; 30 credit hours maximum for bachelor's degree.

ACADEMIC REQUIREMENTS. Freshmen must earn minimum GPA of 2.0 to continue in good standing. 64% of freshmen return for sophomore year. Students must declare major by end of second year. **Graduation requirements:** 120 hours for bachelor's. Most students required to take courses in arts/fine arts, English, foreign languages, history, humanities, mathematics, biological/physical sciences, social sciences. **Postgraduate studies:** 6% enter law school, 3% enter medical school, 8% enter MBA programs, 10% enter other graduate study. **Additional information:** Teacher certification programs available.

FRESHMAN ADMISSIONS. Selection criteria: Rank in top half of class, recommended high school GPA of 3.0, SAT verbal and mathematical scores of 450 each, letters of recommendation from teachers and administrators, extracurricular and community activities. **High school preparation:** 16 units required. Required and recommended units include English 4, foreign language 2-3, mathematics 2-3, social science 2-3 and science 2-3. **Test requirements:** SAT or ACT; score report by July 1. If ACH submitted, will review for placement.

1992 FRESHMAN CLASS PROFILE. 133 men applied, 107 accepted, 60 enrolled; 525 women applied, 428 accepted, 230 enrolled. **Academic background:** Mid 50% of enrolled freshmen had SAT-V between 360-530, SAT-M between 360-530. 75% submitted SAT scores. **Characteristics:** 55% from in state, 50% commute, 44% have minority backgrounds, 12% are foreign students. Average age is 22.

FALL-TERM APPLICATIONS. $30 fee, may be waived for applicants with need. No closing date; priority given to applications received by March 15; applicants notified on a rolling basis; must reply by May 1 or within 4 weeks if notified thereafter. Audition required for fine arts, drama, dance applicants. Interview recommended. Portfolio recommended for art applicants. Essay recommended. CRDA. Deferred and early admission available.

STUDENT LIFE. Housing: Apartment housing available. 2% of student body accommodated in college housing. Alternative residence program places students in off-campus housing. **Activities:** Student government, film, magazine, radio, student newspaper, yearbook, choral groups, dance, drama, musical theater, many ethnic, religious, political, women's, environmental, and cultural groups, student professional organizations, and honor societies.

ATHLETICS. Intramural: Volleyball.

STUDENT SERVICES. Aptitude testing, career counseling, employment service for undergraduates, freshman orientation, health services, personal counseling, placement service for graduates, special adviser for adult students, services/facilities for handicapped.

ANNUAL EXPENSES. Tuition and fees (1992-93): $9,820. **Room and board:** $6,000. **Books and supplies:** $300. **Other expenses:** $1,000.

FINANCIAL AID. 93% of freshmen, 78% of continuing students receive some form of aid. 39% of grants, 69% of loans, all jobs based on need. 250 enrolled freshmen were judged to have need, all were offered aid. Academic, music/drama, art, state/district residency, leadership, alumni affiliation scholarships available. **Aid applications:** Closing date April 1; priority given to applications received by March 1; applicants notified on a rolling basis beginning on or about April 1; must reply within 3 weeks. **Additional information:** Financial Planning and Debt Management Program and variety of low-interest loan programs available.

ADDRESS/TELEPHONE. Suzanne Murphy, Director of Admissions, Marymount Manhattan College, 221 East 71st Street, New York, NY 10021-4597. (212) 517-0555. Fax: (212) 517-0413.

Mater Dei College
Ogdensburg, New York CB code: 2436

Admissions: 96% of applicants accepted
Based on: ••• School record
• Activities, interview, test scores
Completion: 70% of freshmen end year in good standing
40% graduate, 40% of these enter 4-year programs

2-year private junior college, coed, affiliated with Roman Catholic Church. Founded in 1960. **Accreditation:** Regional. **Undergraduate enrollment:** 124 men, 317 women full time; 15 men, 48 women part time. **Faculty:** 61 total (31 full time), 6 with doctorates or other terminal degrees. **Location:** Rural campus in large town; 6 miles from town. **Calendar:** Semester, limited summer session. Extensive evening/early morning classes. **Microcomputers:** 50 located in classrooms, computer centers. **Additional facts:** Branch campus at St. Regis Mohawk reservation. Extension centers in Massena and Gouverneur.

DEGREES OFFERED. AA, AS, AAS. 132 associate degrees awarded in 1992. 29% in business and management, 22% teacher education, 11% allied health, 11% multi/interdisciplinary studies, 27% parks/recreation, protective services, public affairs.

UNDERGRADUATE MAJORS. Alcohol and chemical dependence counseling, business administration and management, court reporting, criminal justice studies, early childhood education, legal secretary, liberal/general studies, medical secretary, ophthalmic services, religious education, secretarial and related programs, social work, teacher aide.

ACADEMIC PROGRAMS. 2-year transfer program, double major, dual enrollment of high school students, independent study, internships. **Remedial services:** Learning center, reduced course load, remedial instruction, special counselor, tutoring, developmental semester. **Placement/credit:** AP, CLEP General and Subject, institutional tests; 30 credit hours maximum for associate degree.

ACADEMIC REQUIREMENTS. Freshmen must earn minimum GPA of 2.0 to continue in good standing. 50% of freshmen return for sophomore year. Students must declare major on application. **Graduation requirements:** 60 hours for associate (30 in major). Most students required to take courses in English, mathematics, philosophy/religion, biological/physical sciences, social sciences.

FRESHMAN ADMISSIONS. Selection criteria: Academic record, extra-curricular activities, and test scores important. **High school preparation:** 12 units recommended. Recommended units include English 4, mathematics 2, social science 4 and science 2.

1992 FRESHMAN CLASS PROFILE. 59 men applied, 58 accepted, 47 enrolled; 161 women applied, 154 accepted, 99 enrolled. **Characteristics:** 99% from in state, 75% commute, 15% have minority backgrounds, 1% are foreign students. Average age is 23.

FALL-TERM APPLICATIONS. $25 fee. Closing date August 20; priority given to applications received by August 13; applicants notified on a rolling basis. Interview recommended. Deferred and early admission available. SAT or ACT recommended for placement and counseling; submit scores by August 1. Institutional English and mathematics tests required for all applicants.

STUDENT LIFE. Housing: Dormitories (men, women). **Activities:** Student government, student newspaper, yearbook, Concern Community World Action Group.

ATHLETICS. NJCAA. **Intercollegiate:** Basketball W, soccer W. **Intramural:** Badminton, basketball, bowling, skiing, soccer, volleyball.

STUDENT SERVICES. Career counseling, employment service for undergraduates, freshman orientation, health services, personal counseling, placement service for graduates, veterans counselor, services/facilities for handicapped.

ANNUAL EXPENSES. Tuition and fees (1992-93): $5,153. **Room and board:** $3,416. **Books and supplies:** $550. **Other expenses:** $600.

FINANCIAL AID. 90% of freshmen, 85% of continuing students receive some form of aid. 98% of grants, 91% of loans, all jobs based on need. Academic, athletic, state/district residency, leadership scholarships available. **Aid applications:** No closing date; priority given to applications received by April 15; applicants notified on a rolling basis beginning on or about May 1; must reply within 2 weeks.

ADDRESS/TELEPHONE. Mark Dougherty, Director of Admission Services, Mater Dei College, Riverside Drive, Ogdensburg, NY 13669. (315) 393-5930 ext. 409. Fax: (315) 393-5930 ext. 440.

Medaille College
Buffalo, New York CB code: 2422

Admissions: 60% of applicants accepted
Based on: ••• Interview, school record
•• Activities, essay, recommendations, test scores
• Special talents
Completion: 65% of freshmen end year in good standing
30% graduate, 21% of these enter graduate study

4-year private liberal arts college, coed. Founded in 1875. **Accreditation:** Regional. **Undergraduate enrollment:** 338 men, 408 women full time; 131 men, 338 women part time. **Faculty:** 88 total (40 full time), 26 with doctorates or other terminal degrees. **Location:** Urban campus in large city; 15 miles from downtown. **Calendar:** Semester, extensive summer session. Saturday and extensive evening/early morning classes. **Microcomputers:** 45 located in libraries, classrooms, computer centers. **Special facilities:** Art gallery, conference center. **Additional facts:** All preprofessional programs require participation in at least 1 internship.

DEGREES OFFERED. AS, BA, BS. 80 associate degrees awarded in 1992. 35% in allied health, 65% multi/interdisciplinary studies. 170 bachelor's degrees awarded. 19% in business and management, 5% communications, 7% computer sciences, 20% teacher education, 17% multi/interdisciplinary studies, 14% parks/recreation, protective services, public affairs, 19% social sciences.

UNDERGRADUATE MAJORS. Associate: Liberal/general studies, political science and government, veterinarian's assistant. **Bachelor's:** Advertising, business administration and management, business and management, child development/care/guidance, communications, computer and information sciences, criminal justice studies, early childhood education, education in nonschool settings, elementary education, finance, human resources development, humanities, humanities and social sciences, information sciences and systems, journalism, liberal/general studies, management of nonprofit agencies, political science and government, prelaw, public administration, public relations, radio/television broadcasting, reading education, small business management and ownership, social sciences, social work, sports management.

ACADEMIC PROGRAMS. 2-year transfer program, accelerated program, double major, honors program, independent study, internships, student-designed major, study abroad, teacher preparation, cross-registration. **Remedial services:** Learning center, preadmission summer program, reduced course load, remedial instruction, special counselor, tutoring, Higher Education Opportunity Program for New York State residents. **ROTC:** Army. **Placement/credit:** AP, CLEP General and Subject, institutional tests; 30 credit hours maximum for associate degree; 60 credit hours maximum for bachelor's degree.

ACADEMIC REQUIREMENTS. Freshmen must earn minimum GPA of 2.0 to continue in good standing. 70% of freshmen return for sophomore year. Students must declare major by end of second year. **Graduation requirements:** 60 hours for associate (30 in major), 120 hours for bachelor's (35 in major). Most students required to take courses in arts/fine arts, English, history, humanities, mathematics, philosophy/religion, biological/physical sciences, social sciences. **Postgraduate studies:** 90% from 2-year programs enter 4-year programs. 1% enter law school, 5% enter MBA programs, 15% enter other graduate study. **Additional information:** Evening module system enables students to have full-time status by attending two nights per week.

FRESHMAN ADMISSIONS. Selection criteria: Academic background and interview are important. Life experience and test scores are considered. **High school preparation:** 12 units recommended. Recommended units include biological science 1, English 4, foreign language 1, mathematics 3, physical science 2 and social science 2. **Test requirements:** SAT or ACT.

1992 FRESHMAN CLASS PROFILE. 321 men and women applied, 191 accepted; 114 enrolled. 5% had high school GPA of 3.0 or higher, 33% between 2.0 and 2.99. **Characteristics:** 98% from in state, 99% commute, 30% have minority backgrounds. Average age is 20.

FALL-TERM APPLICATIONS. $15 fee, may be waived for applicants with need. No closing date; applicants notified on a rolling basis; must reply within 4 weeks. Interview required. Essay recommended. Deferred admission available. SAT or ACT recommended for placement.

STUDENT LIFE. Housing: Dormitories (women, coed). **Activities:** Student government, magazine, radio, student newspaper, television, yearbook, choral groups, drama, music ensembles, Black Student Union, human services club, child and youth services club, riding club, returning adults students club, Big Brother-Big Sister.

ATHLETICS. Intramural: Basketball, bowling, field hockey, golf, soccer, softball, table tennis, tennis, volleyball.

STUDENT SERVICES. Career counseling, employment service for undergraduates, freshman orientation, personal counseling, placement service for graduates, special adviser for adult students, veterans counselor, services/facilities for handicapped.

ANNUAL EXPENSES. Tuition and fees (1992-93): $7,750. **Room and board:** $4,100. **Books and supplies:** $500. **Other expenses:** $600.

FINANCIAL AID. 99% of grants, 77% of loans, all jobs based on need. Academic scholarships available. **Aid applications:** No closing date; priority given to applications received by May 1; applicants notified on a rolling basis beginning on or about April 1; must reply within 2 weeks.

ADDRESS/TELEPHONE. Jacqueline S. Matheny, Director of Enrollment Management, Medaille College, 18 Agassiz Circle, Buffalo, NY 14214. (716) 884-3281. Fax: (716) 884-0291.

Mercy College

Dobbs Ferry, New York CB code: 2409

4-year private liberal arts college, coed. Founded in 1950. **Accreditation:** Regional. **Undergraduate enrollment:** 4,126 men and women full time; 2,085 men and women part time. **Graduate enrollment:** 149 women part time. **Faculty:** 480 total (139 full time), 120 with doctorates or other terminal degrees. **Location:** Suburban campus in large town; 17 miles from New York City, 3 miles from Yonkers. **Calendar:** Semester, extensive summer session. **Microcomputers:** 150 located in libraries, computer centers. **Additional facts:** 4 additional campuses in Westchester County and the Bronx.

DEGREES OFFERED. AA, AS, BA, BS, BFA, MS. 125 associate degrees awarded in 1992. 672 bachelor's degrees awarded. Graduate degrees offered in 3 major fields of study.

UNDERGRADUATE MAJORS. Associate: Liberal/general studies. **Bachelor's:** Accounting, behavioral sciences, biology, business administration and management, clinical laboratory science, computer and information sciences, criminal justice studies, education of the deaf and hearing impaired, education of the emotionally handicapped, education of the mentally handicapped, English, English literature, French, graphic design, history, humanities and social sciences, information sciences and systems, Italian, journalism, law enforcement and corrections, legal assistant/paralegal, liberal/general studies, mathematics, music, nursing, pharmacy, political science and government, protective services, psychology, radio/television broadcasting, recreation therapy, social work, sociology, Spanish, special education, specific learning disabilities, speech, speech correction, speech pathology/audiology, teaching English as a second language/foreign language, veterinarian's assistant.

ACADEMIC PROGRAMS. 2-year transfer program, accelerated program, cooperative education, double major, honors program, independent study, internships, student-designed major, study abroad, teacher preparation, weekend college, cross-registration; combined bachelor's/graduate program in business administration. **Remedial services:** Preadmission summer program, reduced course load, remedial instruction, special counselor, tutoring, writing centers, mathematics laboratory. **ROTC:** Air Force, Army. **Placement/credit:** AP, CLEP General and Subject, institutional tests; 30 credit hours maximum for associate degree; 30 credit hours maximum for bachelor's degree.

ACADEMIC REQUIREMENTS. Freshmen must earn minimum GPA of 2.0 to continue in good standing. Students must declare major by end of second year. **Graduation requirements:** 60 hours for associate, 120 hours for bachelor's (36 in major). Most students required to take courses in arts/fine arts, computer science, English, foreign languages, history, mathematics, philosophy/religion, biological/physical sciences, social sciences. **Postgraduate studies:** 1% enter law school, 10% enter MBA programs, 17% enter other graduate study. **Additional information:** Programs leading to provisional state certification offered in elementary, special and speech and hearing handicapped education.

FRESHMAN ADMISSIONS. Selection criteria: All applicants must pass a placement exam determining their writing and mathematics skills.

1992 FRESHMAN CLASS PROFILE. 2,102 men and women enrolled. **Characteristics:** 95% from in state, 97% commute, 40% have minority backgrounds, 4% are foreign students. Average age is 20.

FALL-TERM APPLICATIONS. $20 fee, may be waived for applicants with need. No closing date; priority given to applications received by March 1; applicants notified on a rolling basis; must reply by May 1 or within 3 weeks if notified thereafter. Audition required for music applicants. Portfolio required for graphic design applicants. Interview recommended. Deferred and early admission available. SAT recommended; score report by July 1.

STUDENT LIFE. Activities: Student government, film, magazine, radio, student newspaper, television, yearbook, choral groups, dance, drama, jazz band, music ensembles, musical theater, symphony orchestra, sororities, radio club, International Students Association, accounting club, Latin-American Club, Educational Volunteers Council, Student Activities Council, African Heritage Club, A.R.T.E.-Adults Returning to Education, Social Enterprise Council. **Additional information:** 60% of students are evening or adult students. Student services geared to commuter population with mid-day activities and programs.

ATHLETICS. NCAA. **Intercollegiate:** Baseball M, basketball, cross-country, golf, soccer M, softball W, tennis M, track and field, volleyball W. **Intramural:** Basketball M, table tennis.

STUDENT SERVICES. Aptitude testing, career counseling, employment service for undergraduates, freshman orientation, health services, on-campus day care, personal counseling, placement service for graduates, special adviser for adult students, veterans counselor, services/facilities for handicapped.

ANNUAL EXPENSES. Tuition and fees (1992-93): $7,200. **Room and board:** $6,380. **Books and supplies:** $500. **Other expenses:** $800.

FINANCIAL AID. 80% of freshmen, 75% of continuing students receive some form of aid. 46% of grants, all loans, 35% of jobs based on need. 470 enrolled freshmen were judged to have need, 432 were offered aid. Academic, athletic scholarships available. **Aid applications:** No closing date; priority given to applications received by March 1; applicants notified on a rolling basis beginning on or about March 1; must reply within 4 weeks.

ADDRESS/TELEPHONE. William Rothenberg, Dean for Admissions, Mercy College, 555 Broadway, Dobbs Ferry, NY 10522. (914) 693-7600. (800) MERCY-NY. Fax: (914) 693-9455.

Mesivta Eastern Parkway Rabbinical Seminary

Brooklyn, New York CB code: 1590

4-year private rabbinical college, men only, affiliated with Jewish faith. Founded in 1947. **Undergraduate enrollment:** 33 men full time. **Graduate enrollment:** 15 men full time. **Location:** Urban campus in very large city. **Calendar:** Semester. **Additional facts:** First Talmudic degree and ordination available.

FRESHMAN ADMISSIONS. Selection criteria: Ability to benefit from study most important.

ADDRESS/TELEPHONE. Rabbi C.L. Epstein, Dean of Students, Mesivta Eastern Parkway Rabbinical Seminary, 510 Dahill, Brooklyn, NY 11218. (718) 438-1002.

Mesivta Tifereth Jerusalem of America

New York, New York CB code: 0632

5-year private rabbinical college, men only, affiliated with Jewish faith. Founded in 1907. **Undergraduate enrollment:** 65 men full time. **Graduate enrollment:** 30 men full time. **Location:** Urban campus in very large city. **Calendar:** Semester. **Additional facts:** Ordination available.

FRESHMAN ADMISSIONS. Selection criteria: Institutional examinations, recommendations, and academic record.

ADDRESS/TELEPHONE. Rabbi Michael Barenbaum, Admissions Officer, Mesivta Tifereth Jerusalem of America, 145 East Broadway, New York, NY 10002. (212) 964-2830.

Mesivta Torah Vodaath Seminary

Brooklyn, New York CB code: 0636

5-year private rabbinical college, men only, affiliated with Jewish faith. Founded in 1918. **Undergraduate enrollment:** 317 men full time; 53 men part time. **Graduate enrollment:** 83 men full time; 15 men part time. **Location:** Urban campus in very large city. **Calendar:** Semester. **Additional facts:** First Talmudic degree and ordination available.

FRESHMAN ADMISSIONS. Selection criteria: Religious affiliation or commitment very important. Test scores, interview, school and community activities, recommendations, alumni relation important. School achievement record considered.

ADDRESS/TELEPHONE. Rabbi A. Braun, Director of Admissions, Mesivta Torah Vodaath Seminary, 425 East Ninth Street, Brooklyn, NY 11218. (718) 941-8000.

Mirrer Yeshiva Central Institute

Brooklyn, New York CB code: 0661

4-year private rabbinical college, men only, affiliated with Jewish faith. Founded in 1926. **Undergraduate enrollment:** 125 men full time. **Graduate enrollment:** 100 men full time. **Location:** Urban campus in very large city. **Calendar:** Semester. **Additional facts:** Ordination available.

FRESHMAN ADMISSIONS. Selection criteria: Institutional examination and religious affiliation.

ADDRESS/TELEPHONE. Rabbi Mordechai Kirzner, Registrar, Mirrer Yeshiva Central Institute, 1791-5 Ocean Parkway, Brooklyn, NY 11223. (718) 645-0536.

Mohawk Valley Community College
Utica, New York CB code: 2414

2-year public community college, coed. Founded in 1946. **Accreditation:** Regional. **Undergraduate enrollment:** 2,017 men, 1,699 women full time; 1,050 men, 1,507 women part time. **Faculty:** 490 total (240 full time), 22 with doctorates or other terminal degrees. **Location:** Urban campus in small city; 50 miles from Syracuse. **Calendar:** Semester, limited summer session. **Microcomputers:** Located in classrooms, computer centers. **Additional facts:** SUNY institution. Branch campus in Rome, New York.

DEGREES OFFERED. AA, AS, AAS. 900 associate degrees awarded in 1992.

UNDERGRADUATE MAJORS. Accounting, advertising, air conditioning/heating/refrigeration mechanics, air conditioning/heating/refrigeration technology, art education, aviation management, biological and physical sciences, biology, business administration and management, business and office, business data processing and related programs, chemical dependency counseling, chemical manufacturing technology, chemistry, civil technology, commercial art, computer and information sciences, computer programming, computer servicing technology, computer technology, crafts, criminal justice studies, data processing, drafting, drafting and design technology, electrical and electronics equipment repair, electrical installation, electrical technology, electronic technology, engineering, engineering and engineering-related technologies, engineering and other disciplines, English, finance, fine arts, food production/management/services, food science and nutrition, foreign languages (multiple emphasis), foreign languages education, geology, graphic and printing production, graphic design, humanities, humanities and social sciences, illustration design, industrial equipment maintenance and repair, insurance and risk management, international relations, international studies, law enforcement and corrections, legal secretary, liberal/general studies, machine tool operation/machine shop, manufacturing technology, marketing management, mathematics, mathematics education, mechanical design technology, medical records administration, medical records technology, medical secretary, mental health/human services, nursing, nutritional sciences, photography, physical chemistry, physical education, physical sciences, physics, precision metal work, psychology, recreation and community services technologies, recreation therapy, respiratory therapy, respiratory therapy technology, retailing, science education, science technologies, secretarial and related programs, social science education, social sciences, social work, survey and mapping technology, welding technology, word processing.

ACADEMIC PROGRAMS. 2-year transfer program, dual enrollment of high school students, honors program, internships, study abroad, associate in fine arts cooperative program with Munson-Williams-Proctor Institute of Art. **Remedial services:** Learning center, reduced course load, remedial instruction, special counselor, tutoring. **Placement/credit:** AP, CLEP General, institutional tests; 45 credit hours maximum for associate degree.

ACADEMIC REQUIREMENTS. Freshmen must earn minimum GPA of 2.0 to continue in good standing. 45% of freshmen return for sophomore year. Students must declare major on application. **Graduation requirements:** 64 hours for associate (50 in major). Most students required to take courses in English, mathematics, social sciences.

FRESHMAN ADMISSIONS. Selection criteria: Open admissions. Applicant's record reviewed for completion of program-specific prerequisites to determine regular or under-prepared acceptance to program. Recommended units include English 4, mathematics 2, social science 1 and science 2. Requirements vary for admission to nursing and certain other programs.

1992 FRESHMAN CLASS PROFILE. 808 men, 642 women enrolled. **Characteristics:** 99% from in state, 90% commute, 10% have minority backgrounds, 2% are foreign students. Average age is 22.

FALL-TERM APPLICATIONS. $25 fee, may be waived for applicants with need. No closing date; applicants notified on a rolling basis; must reply within 4 weeks. Portfolio required for fine arts applicants. Interview recommended for all, required of respiratory therapy applicants. Deferred admission available.

STUDENT LIFE. Housing: Dormitories (men, women, coed). **Activities:** Student government, radio, student newspaper, yearbook, choral groups, concert band, drama, jazz band, musical theater, fraternities, sororities, Campus Christian Fellowship, Newman Club.

ATHLETICS. NJCAA. **Intercollegiate:** Baseball M, basketball, bowling, cross-country, golf, ice hockey M, lacrosse M, soccer, softball W, tennis, track and field, volleyball W, wrestling M. **Intramural:** Badminton, basketball, gymnastics, handball M, horseback riding, lacrosse M, racquetball, skiing, softball, swimming, table tennis, volleyball.

STUDENT SERVICES. Aptitude testing, career counseling, employment service for undergraduates, freshman orientation, health services, on-campus day care, personal counseling, placement service for graduates, veterans counselor, services/facilities for handicapped.

ANNUAL EXPENSES. Tuition and fees (projected): $2,150, $2,000 additional for out-of-state students. **Room and board:** $3,902. **Books and supplies:** $750. **Other expenses:** $1,262.

FINANCIAL AID. 85% of freshmen, 85% of continuing students receive some form of aid. All grants, 85% of loans, all jobs based on need. Academic, leadership scholarships available. **Aid applications:** No closing date; priority given to applications received by May 15; applicants notified on a rolling basis beginning on or about May 15; Must reply by July 15 or within 2 weeks if notified thereafter.

ADDRESS/TELEPHONE. Ian Lindsey, Director of Admissions, Mohawk Valley Community College, 1101 Sherman Drive, Utica, NY 13501-9979. (315) 792-5354. Fax: (315) 792-5666.

Molloy College
Rockville Centre, New York CB code: 2415

4-year private liberal arts college, coed, affiliated with Roman Catholic Church. Founded in 1955. **Accreditation:** Regional. **Undergraduate enrollment:** 304 men, 1,145 women full time; 75 men, 452 women part time. **Graduate enrollment:** 100 women part time. **Faculty:** 214 total (102 full time), 56 with doctorates or other terminal degrees. **Location:** Suburban campus in large town; 20 miles from New York City. **Calendar:** 4-1-4, limited summer session. **Microcomputers:** 60 located in computer centers. **Special facilities:** Hays Theater. **Additional facts:** Independent institution in Dominican tradition.

DEGREES OFFERED. AA, AAS, BA, BS, MS. 20 associate degrees awarded in 1992. 100% in multi/interdisciplinary studies. 260 bachelor's degrees awarded. 16% in business and management, 5% communications, 13% teacher education, 40% health sciences, 6% psychology, 6% social sciences. Graduate degrees offered in 1 major field of study.

UNDERGRADUATE MAJORS. Associate: Health information technology, liberal/general studies, nuclear medical technology. **Bachelor's:** Accounting, art history, biology, business administration and management, clinical psychology, communications, comparative literature, computer and information sciences, counseling psychology, drawing, education, elementary education, English, English literature, fine arts, French, gerontology, history, humanities and social sciences, interdisciplinary studies, international place justice, junior high education, mathematics, music, music history and appreciation, music performance, music therapy, nursing, peace studies, philosophy, physical sciences, political science and government, prelaw, psychology, religion, religious education, respiratory therapy technology, secondary education, social sciences, social work, sociology, Spanish, special education, speech, speech pathology/audiology, teaching English as a second language/foreign language, theological studies, visual and performing arts.

ACADEMIC PROGRAMS. 2-year transfer program, accelerated program, cooperative education, double major, independent study, internships, student-designed major, study abroad, teacher preparation, weekend college, Washington semester, cross-registration. **Remedial services:** Learning center, preadmission summer program, reduced course load, remedial instruction, special counselor, tutoring. **ROTC:** Air Force, Army. **Placement/credit:** AP, CLEP General and Subject, institutional tests; 42 credit hours maximum for bachelor's degree.

ACADEMIC REQUIREMENTS. Freshmen must earn minimum GPA of 1.8 to continue in good standing. 93% of freshmen return for sophomore year. Students must declare major by end of second year. **Graduation requirements:** 64 hours for associate, 128 hours for bachelor's (30 in major). Most students required to take courses in arts/fine arts, English, foreign languages, history, mathematics, philosophy/religion, biological/physical sciences, social sciences. **Postgraduate studies:** 75% from 2-year programs enter 4-year programs. 3% enter law school, 1% enter medical school, 3% enter MBA programs, 16% enter other graduate study.

FRESHMAN ADMISSIONS. Selection criteria: Secondary school achievement, with particular attention to grade 11 performance, test scores, recommendations, school and community activities, interview considered. **High school preparation:** 16 units required. Required units include English 4, foreign language 2, mathematics 2, social science 3 and science 2. Science, mathematics, and nursing majors must have 1 biology, 1 chemistry, and 3 mathematics. **Test requirements:** SAT or ACT (SAT preferred); score report by June 1.

1992 FRESHMAN CLASS PROFILE. 171 men and women enrolled. 42% had high school GPA of 3.0 or higher, 48% between 2.0 and 2.99. **Academic background:** Mid 50% of enrolled freshmen had SAT-V between 450-570, SAT-M between 450-580. 96% submitted SAT scores. **Characteristics:** 99% from in state, 100% commute, 5% have minority backgrounds, 1% are foreign students, 6% join fraternities/sororities. Average age is 18.

FALL-TERM APPLICATIONS. $25 fee, may be waived for applicants with need. No closing date; priority given to applications received by March 1; applicants notified on a rolling basis. Audition required for music applicants. Portfolio required for art applicants. Essay required. Interview recommended. CRDA. Deferred and early admission available. EDP-F.

STUDENT LIFE. Activities: Student government, magazine, student newspaper, television, yearbook, language club publications, weekly newsletter, choral groups, concert band, dance, drama, jazz band, music ensembles, musical theater, fraternities, sororities, Students at Molloy Interested in Life and Environment, Siena Women's Center, campus ministry, business club, community service organization.

ATHLETICS. NCAA. **Intercollegiate:** Basketball W, horseback riding W, softball W, tennis W, volleyball W. **Intramural:** Baseball M, basketball M, soccer M.

STUDENT SERVICES. Aptitude testing, career counseling, em-

ployment service for undergraduates, freshman orientation, health services, on-campus day care, personal counseling, placement service for graduates, special adviser for adult students, services/facilities for handicapped.

ANNUAL EXPENSES. Tuition and fees: $8,650. **Books and supplies:** $600. **Other expenses:** $1,200.

FINANCIAL AID. 70% of freshmen, 65% of continuing students receive some form of aid. 82% of grants, 83% of loans, all jobs based on need. 122 enrolled freshmen were judged to have need, all were offered aid. Academic, music/drama, art, athletic scholarships available. **Aid applications:** No closing date; priority given to applications received by April 15; applicants notified on a rolling basis beginning on or about April 1; must reply by May 1 or within 2 weeks if notified thereafter.

ADDRESS/TELEPHONE. Wayne James, MS, CAGS, Director of Admissions, Molloy College, 1000 Hempstead Avenue, Rockville Centre, NY 11570. (516) 678-5000 ext. 240. Fax: (516) 678-7295.

Monroe College
Bronx, New York — CB code: 2463

Admissions:	64% of applicants accepted
Based on:	••• Interview, test scores • Activities, essay, recommendations, school record
Completion:	65% of freshmen end year in good standing 37% graduate, 12% of these enter 4-year programs

2-year proprietary business, junior college, coed. Founded in 1933. **Accreditation:** Regional. **Undergraduate enrollment:** 567 men, 1,776 women full time; 41 men, 83 women part time. **Faculty:** 105 total (58 full time), 23 with doctorates or other terminal degrees. **Location:** Urban campus in very large city. **Calendar:** 3 terms of 15 weeks each. Saturday and extensive evening/early morning classes. **Microcomputers:** 167 located in classrooms, computer centers. **Additional facts:** Branch campus in New Rochelle.

DEGREES OFFERED. AAS. 584 associate degrees awarded in 1992. 70% in business and management, 30% computer sciences.

UNDERGRADUATE MAJORS. Accounting, business administration and management, business and office, business data processing and related programs, business data programming, computer and information sciences, hotel/motel and restaurant management, secretarial and related programs, word processing.

ACADEMIC PROGRAMS. Cooperative education, dual enrollment of high school students, internships. **Remedial services:** Learning center, preadmission summer program, remedial instruction, special counselor, tutoring. **Placement/credit:** CLEP General and Subject; 30 credit hours maximum for associate degree.

ACADEMIC REQUIREMENTS. Freshmen must earn minimum GPA of 2.0 to continue in good standing. 58% of freshmen return for sophomore year. Students must declare major on application. **Graduation requirements:** 60 hours for associate (30 in major). Most students required to take courses in English, humanities, mathematics, social sciences.

FRESHMAN ADMISSIONS. Selection criteria: Interview, school achievement record, test scores required. Modified open admissions for students who pass admissions test. **Test requirements:** ACT/ASSET required for admissions and placement. CPAT for non-high school graduate/non-GED holder.

1992 FRESHMAN CLASS PROFILE. 417 men applied, 263 accepted, 250 enrolled; 1,109 women applied, 709 accepted, 698 enrolled. **Characteristics:** 99% from in state, 100% commute, 94% have minority backgrounds, 1% are foreign students. Average age is 24.

FALL-TERM APPLICATIONS. No fee. No closing date; applicants notified on a rolling basis. Interview required. Essay required.

STUDENT LIFE. Activities: Student newspaper, yearbook.

ATHLETICS. NJCAA. **Intercollegiate:** Basketball M. **Intramural:** Basketball M, softball M, volleyball.

STUDENT SERVICES. Aptitude testing, career counseling, employment service for undergraduates, freshman orientation, personal counseling, placement service for graduates, veterans counselor, services/facilities for handicapped.

ANNUAL EXPENSES. Tuition and fees (1992-93): $5,040. **Books and supplies:** $555. **Other expenses:** $680.

FINANCIAL AID. 98% of freshmen, 98% of continuing students receive some form of aid. All aid based on need. 817 enrolled freshmen were judged to have need, 812 were offered aid. **Aid applications:** Closing date March 31; applicants notified on a rolling basis beginning on or about July 1.

ADDRESS/TELEPHONE. Anthony Allen, Dean of Admissions, Monroe College, 29 East Fordham Road, Bronx, NY 10468. (718) 933-6700 ext. 265. Fax: (718) 295-5861. Address branch campus applications to: Director, Monroe Business Institute, 434 Main Street, New Rochelle, New York 10801.

Monroe Community College
Rochester, New York — CB code: 2429

2-year public community college, coed. Founded in 1961. **Accreditation:** Regional. **Undergraduate enrollment:** 3,214 men, 3,625 women full time; 3,042 men, 3,431 women part time. **Faculty:** 699 total (298 full time). **Location:** Suburban campus in large city; 4 miles from downtown. **Calendar:** Semester, limited summer session. **Microcomputers:** Located in libraries. **Special facilities:** Art gallery, human ecology habitat. **Additional facts:** SUNY institution. Off-campus extension centers in 8 area high schools.

DEGREES OFFERED. AA, AS, AAS. 2,131 associate degrees awarded in 1992.

UNDERGRADUATE MAJORS. Accounting, air conditioning/heating/refrigeration technology, automotive technology, biological and physical sciences, business administration and management, chemical manufacturing technology, civil technology, communications, computer and information sciences, computer technology, criminal justice studies, data processing, dental hygiene, electronic technology, engineering, fashion merchandising, fire control and safety technology, food management, food production/management/services, graphic arts technology, hotel/motel and restaurant management, humanities and social sciences, instrumentation technology, law enforcement and corrections technologies, legal secretary, liberal/general studies, marketing and distribution, mechanical design technology, medical laboratory technologies, medical records technology, nursing, prepharmacy, quality control technology, radiograph medical technology, recreation and community services technologies, recreation therapy, respiratory therapy, science technologies, secretarial and related programs.

ACADEMIC PROGRAMS. 2-year transfer program, cooperative education, honors program, independent study, internships, study abroad, cross-registration, 2+2 cooperative degree programs with 12 4-year institutions. **Remedial services:** Learning center, reduced course load, remedial instruction, special counselor, tutoring. **ROTC:** Air Force, Naval. **Placement/credit:** CLEP General and Subject, institutional tests; 36 credit hours maximum for associate degree.

ACADEMIC REQUIREMENTS. Freshmen must earn minimum GPA of 1.9 to continue in good standing. 70% of freshmen return for sophomore year. Students must declare major on application. **Graduation requirements:** 64 hours for associate. Most students required to take courses in English, mathematics, biological/physical sciences, social sciences.

FRESHMAN ADMISSIONS. Selection criteria: Open admissions. Selective admissions to certain programs based on high school records, with preference given county residents. Individual programs have specific mathematics and science requirements.

1992 FRESHMAN CLASS PROFILE. 1,194 men, 1,346 women enrolled. **Characteristics:** 99% from in state, 100% commute, 14% have minority backgrounds, 1% are foreign students. Average age is 22.

FALL-TERM APPLICATIONS. $20 fee, may be waived for applicants with need. No closing date; priority given to applications received by March 1; applicants notified on a rolling basis; must reply within 2 weeks. Early admission available. Applicants to nursing program are encouraged to apply 1 year prior to registration. SAT or ACT not required, but will be wed for placment if submitted.

STUDENT LIFE. Activities: Student government, magazine, radio, student newspaper, choral groups, concert band, drama, symphony orchestra, jazz ensemble, free theater, Christian, Jewish, and Christian Science groups, Latin American, Italian-American, black, and international student organizations, veterans and handicapped student clubs.

ATHLETICS. NJCAA. **Intercollegiate:** Baseball M, basketball, cross-country M, golf M, ice hockey M, soccer, softball W, swimming, tennis, volleyball W, wrestling M. **Intramural:** Baseball M, basketball M, bowling, golf, lacrosse M, racquetball, softball, swimming, tennis, volleyball, water polo M.

STUDENT SERVICES. Career counseling, employment service for undergraduates, freshman orientation, health services, on-campus day care, personal counseling, placement service for graduates, veterans counselor, services/facilities for handicapped.

ANNUAL EXPENSES. Tuition and fees (projected): $2,130, $1,950 additional for out-of-state students. **Books and supplies:** $450. **Other expenses:** $1,475.

FINANCIAL AID. 70% of freshmen, 67% of continuing students receive some form of aid. 70% of loans, all jobs based on need. Academic, athletic scholarships available. **Aid applications:** No closing date; priority given to applications received by May 1; applicants notified on a rolling basis beginning on or about May 1; must reply within 2 weeks.

ADDRESS/TELEPHONE. Anthony J. Felicetti, Dean of Admissions and Financial Aid, Monroe Community College, PO Box 9892, 1000 East Henrietta Road, Rochester, NY 14623. (716) 292-2200. Fax: (716) 427-2749.

Mount St. Mary College
Newburgh, New York CB code: 2423

Admissions: 78% of applicants accepted
Based on: ••• School record
•• Interview, test scores
• Activities, essay, recommendations, special talents
Completion: 97% of freshmen end year in good standing
51% graduate, 14% of these enter graduate study

4-year private liberal arts college, coed. Founded in 1954. **Accreditation:** Regional. **Undergraduate enrollment:** 318 men, 737 women full time; 192 men, 290 women part time. **Graduate enrollment:** 5 women full time; 38 men, 141 women part time. **Faculty:** 147 total (53 full time), 57 with doctorates or other terminal degrees. **Location:** Suburban campus in small city; 58 miles from New York City. **Calendar:** Semester, limited summer session. **Microcomputers:** 89 located in libraries, computer centers. **Special facilities:** Elementary school on campus, arboretum. **Additional facts:** Independent institution in the Judeo-Christian tradition, founded by the Dominican Sisters of Newburgh.

DEGREES OFFERED. BA, BS, MBA, MEd. 247 bachelor's degrees awarded in 1992. 25% in business and management, 8% communications, 10% computer sciences, 5% teacher education, 15% health sciences, 9% letters/literature, 7% psychology, 12% social sciences. Graduate degrees offered in 2 major fields of study.

UNDERGRADUATE MAJORS. Accounting, biology, business administration and management, chemistry, communications, computer and information sciences, dramatic arts, elementary education, English, Hispanic American studies, history, history/political science, human services, humanities and social sciences, junior high education, liberal/general studies, mathematics, medical laboratory technologies, nursing, prelaw, psychology, public relations, radio/television broadcasting, science technologies, secondary education, social sciences, sociology, special education.

ACADEMIC PROGRAMS. Accelerated program, cooperative education, double major, dual enrollment of high school students, education specialist degree, honors program, independent study, internships, study abroad, visiting/exchange student program, cross-registration. **Remedial services:** Learning center, preadmission summer program, reduced course load, remedial instruction, special counselor, tutoring, New York State Higher Education Opportunity Program. **ROTC:** Army. **Placement/credit:** AP, CLEP General and Subject, institutional tests; 45 credit hours maximum for bachelor's degree.

ACADEMIC REQUIREMENTS. Freshmen must earn minimum GPA of 2.0 to continue in good standing. 74% of freshmen return for sophomore year. Students must declare major by end of first year. **Graduation requirements:** 120 hours for bachelor's (30 in major). Most students required to take courses in computer science, English, humanities, philosophy/religion, social sciences. **Postgraduate studies:** 2% enter medical school, 1% enter MBA programs, 11% enter other graduate study.

FRESHMAN ADMISSIONS. Selection criteria: Admissions decisions based on total admission score which assigns weights to high school average, class rank, and SAT or ACT scores as well as teacher/counselor recommendations. Interview recommended. **High school preparation:** 13 units required; 15 recommended. Required and recommended units include biological science 1, English 4-4, foreign language 2-3, mathematics 2-3, physical science 1 and social science 3-4. Biology and chemistry required for nursing majors. **Test requirements:** SAT or ACT (SAT preferred); score report by August 15.

1992 FRESHMAN CLASS PROFILE. 272 men applied, 187 accepted, 83 enrolled; 776 women applied, 630 accepted, 192 enrolled. 32% had high school GPA of 3.0 or higher, 65% between 2.0 and 2.99. 8% were in top tenth and 30% were in top quarter of graduating class. **Academic background:** Mid 50% of enrolled freshmen had SAT-V between 370-470, SAT-M between 390-510; ACT composite between 18-21. 90% submitted SAT scores, 7% submitted ACT scores. **Characteristics:** 78% from in state, 80% live in college housing, 15% have minority backgrounds. Average age is 18.

FALL-TERM APPLICATIONS. $20 fee, may be waived for applicants with need. Closing date August 15; applicants notified on a rolling basis; must reply within 6 weeks. Essay required for academically weak applicants. Interview recommended for academically weak applicants. CRDA. Deferred and early admission available. EDP-F.

STUDENT LIFE. Housing: Dormitories (men, women). **Activities:** Student government, magazine, student newspaper, yearbook, literary magazine, choral groups, drama, music ensembles, musical theater, Black Student Union, Latin American Club, campus ministry, Gaelic Society.

ATHLETICS. NCAA. **Intercollegiate:** Baseball M, basketball, soccer, softball W, tennis, volleyball W. **Intramural:** Badminton, baseball M, basketball, bowling, field hockey W, soccer, softball, swimming, table tennis, tennis, volleyball.

STUDENT SERVICES. Aptitude testing, career counseling, employment service for undergraduates, freshman orientation, health services, personal counseling, placement service for graduates, special adviser for adult students, skills center, services/facilities for handicapped.

ANNUAL EXPENSES. Tuition and fees (projected): $8,260. **Room and board:** $4,880. **Books and supplies:** $300. **Other expenses:** $700.

FINANCIAL AID. 70% of freshmen, 68% of continuing students receive some form of aid. 90% of grants, 92% of loans, 87% of jobs based on need. 150 enrolled freshmen were judged to have need, all were offered aid. Academic scholarships available. **Aid applications:** No closing date; priority given to applications received by March 15; applicants notified on a rolling basis; must reply within 2 weeks.

ADDRESS/TELEPHONE. J. Randall Ognibene, Director of Admissions, Mount St. Mary College, 330 Powell Avenue, Newburgh, NY 12550. (914) 561-0800. (800) 558-0942. Fax: (914) 562-6762.

Nassau Community College
Garden City, New York CB code: 2563

2-year public community college, coed. Founded in 1959. **Accreditation:** Regional. **Undergraduate enrollment:** 5,900 men, 5,984 women full time; 4,176 men, 6,461 women part time. **Faculty:** 1,803 total (636 full time), 315 with doctorates or other terminal degrees. **Location:** Suburban campus in large town; 20 miles from New York City. **Calendar:** Semester, extensive summer session. Saturday and extensive evening/early morning classes. **Microcomputers:** 600 located in libraries, classrooms, computer centers. **Additional facts:** SUNY institution.

DEGREES OFFERED. AA, AS, AAS. 3,050 associate degrees awarded in 1992. 18% in business and management, 17% business/office and marketing/distribution, 5% health sciences, 48% multi/interdisciplinary studies.

UNDERGRADUATE MAJORS. Accounting, Afro-American (black) studies, business administration and management, business data processing and related programs, civil technology, communications, computer and information sciences, dance, data processing, engineering, fashion merchandising, finance, fine arts, food management, funeral services/mortuary science, hotel/motel and restaurant management, humanities and social sciences, industrial technology, information sciences and systems, instrumentation technology, interpreter for the deaf, law enforcement and corrections technologies, legal assistant/paralegal, legal secretary, liberal/general studies, life science/mathematics/physical science, marketing and distribution, mathematics, medical laboratory technologies, medical radiation dosimetry, medical secretary, music performance, nursing, physical therapy assistant, radio/television broadcasting, radiograph medical technology, respiratory therapy technology, retailing, secretarial and related programs, surgical technology, teacher aide, transportation management, visual and performing arts, word processing.

ACADEMIC PROGRAMS. 2-year transfer program, cooperative education, honors program, internships, telecourses, cross-registration, cooperative programs with SUNY College of Technology at Utica-Rome and College at New Paltz, New York State Chiropractic College, Fashion Institute of Technology, Adelphi University; joint admissions with SUNY at Stony Brook and SUNY College at Old Westbury. **Remedial services:** Learning center, preadmission summer program, reduced course load, remedial instruction, special counselor, tutoring. **ROTC:** Army. **Placement/credit:** AP, CLEP General and Subject, institutional tests. No maximum, but 33 credit-hour residency requirement.

ACADEMIC REQUIREMENTS. Freshmen must earn minimum GPA of 1.8 to continue in good standing. 71% of freshmen return for sophomore year. Students must declare major on application. **Graduation requirements:** 64 hours for associate. Most students required to take courses in English, humanities, mathematics, biological/physical sciences, social sciences.

FRESHMAN ADMISSIONS. Selection criteria: Open admissions. Selective admission for business, engineering, nursing and allied health applicants based on class rank and fulfillment of mathematics and science requirements. Requirements vary by program. **Additional information:** Part-time students without high school diploma or equivalent may apply for GED after successful completion of 24 college credits.

1992 FRESHMAN CLASS PROFILE. 2,194 men, 2,682 women enrolled. 2% were in top tenth and 10% were in top quarter of graduating class. **Characteristics:** 100% from in state, 100% commute, 23% have minority backgrounds. Average age is 19.

FALL-TERM APPLICATIONS. $20 fee. Closing date August 23; applicants notified on a rolling basis; must reply within 3 weeks. Interview required for allied health program applicants. Audition required for music, theater applicants. Portfolio required for art applicants.

STUDENT LIFE. Activities: Student government, magazine, radio, student newspaper, television, yearbook, choral groups, concert band, dance, drama, jazz band, marching band, music ensembles, musical theater, pep band, symphony orchestra, fraternities, sororities.

ATHLETICS. NJCAA. **Intercollegiate:** Baseball M, basketball, bowling M, cross-country, diving W, football M, golf, gymnastics W, ice hockey M, lacrosse M, soccer, softball W, swimming M, tennis, volleyball W, wrestling M. **Intramural:** Badminton W, baseball M, basketball, bowling, cross-country, diving W, field hockey W, lacrosse M, racquetball, soccer, softball W, swimming M, table tennis, tennis, volleyball, wrestling M.

STUDENT SERVICES. Aptitude testing, career counseling, employment service for undergraduates, freshman orientation, health services,

on-campus day care, personal counseling, placement service for graduates, special adviser for adult students, transfer office, services/facilities for handicapped.

ANNUAL EXPENSES. Tuition and fees (1992-93): $1,940, $1,850 additional for out-of-state students. **Books and supplies:** $650. **Other expenses:** $950.

FINANCIAL AID. 99% of grants, 79% of loans, 37% of jobs based on need. Academic, music/drama, art, athletic, state/district residency, leadership, alumni affiliation, minority scholarships available. **Aid applications:** No closing date; priority given to applications received by May 1; applicants notified on a rolling basis beginning on or about July 15; must reply within 10 days.

ADDRESS/TELEPHONE. Bernard Iantosca, Director of Admissions, Nassau Community College, 1 Education Drive, Garden City, NY 11530-6793. (516) 222-7345.

Nazareth College of Rochester
Rochester, New York — CB code: 2511

Admissions: 80% of applicants accepted
Based on: ••• School record, test scores
•• Interview, recommendations
• Activities, essay, special talents
Completion: 80% of freshmen end year in good standing
57% graduate, 30% of these enter graduate study

4-year private liberal arts college, coed. Founded in 1924. **Accreditation:** Regional. **Undergraduate enrollment:** 341 men, 962 women full time; 91 men, 344 women part time. **Graduate enrollment:** 9 men, 62 women full time; 132 men, 732 women part time. **Faculty:** 185 total (111 full time), 136 with doctorates or other terminal degrees. **Location:** Suburban campus in large city; 7 miles from downtown. **Calendar:** Semester, extensive summer session. **Microcomputers:** 90 located in dormitories, libraries, classrooms, computer centers. **Special facilities:** Marie Callahan Reading Clinic, foreign language houses, arts center, psychology research facility, speech clinic.

DEGREES OFFERED. BA, BS, MS. 463 bachelor's degrees awarded in 1992. 25% in business and management, 12% teacher education, 7% languages, 11% letters/literature, 5% parks/recreation, protective services, public affairs, 14% psychology, 11% social sciences, 6% visual and performing arts. Graduate degrees offered in 13 major fields of study.

UNDERGRADUATE MAJORS. Accounting, American studies, anthropology, art education, art history, biochemistry, biological and physical sciences, biology, business administration and management, business education, chemistry, computer and information sciences, creative writing, dramatic arts, economics, education, elementary education, English, English literature, environmental science, foreign languages (multiple emphasis), French, German, history, humanities and social sciences, Italian, junior high education, mathematics, music, music education, music performance, music theory and composition, music therapy, nursing, philosophy, political science and government, psychology, religion, secondary education, social sciences, social work, sociology, Spanish, special education, specific learning disabilities, speech correction, speech pathology/audiology, studio art, visual and performing arts.

ACADEMIC PROGRAMS. Double major, honors program, independent study, internships, study abroad, teacher preparation, visiting/exchange student program, Washington semester, cross-registration, 2-2 bachelor's degree completion program for RNs and Monroe Community College graduates. **Remedial services:** Reduced course load, remedial instruction, tutoring, New York State Higher Education Opportunity Program. **Placement/credit:** AP, CLEP General and Subject, institutional tests; 30 credit hours maximum for bachelor's degree.

ACADEMIC REQUIREMENTS. Freshmen must earn minimum GPA of 1.8 to continue in good standing. 85% of freshmen return for sophomore year. Students must declare major by end of second year. **Graduation requirements:** 120 hours for bachelor's. Most students required to take courses in arts/fine arts, computer science, English, foreign languages, history, humanities, mathematics, philosophy/religion, biological/physical sciences, social sciences. **Postgraduate studies:** 2% enter law school, 1% enter medical school, 2% enter MBA programs, 25% enter other graduate study.

FRESHMAN ADMISSIONS. Selection criteria: School achievement record, strength of academic program, class rank, SAT or ACT scores, and recommendations considered. **High school preparation:** 17 units required. Required and recommended units include English 4, foreign language 3, mathematics 3, social science 4 and science 3. Physical science 2 recommended. **Test requirements:** SAT or ACT; score report by June 1.

1992 FRESHMAN CLASS PROFILE. 172 men applied, 135 accepted, 51 enrolled; 542 women applied, 433 accepted, 161 enrolled. 88% had high school GPA of 3.0 or higher, 12% between 2.0 and 2.99. 18% were in top tenth and 50% were in top quarter of graduating class. **Academic background:** Mid 50% of enrolled freshmen had SAT-V between 450-550, SAT-M between 490-590; ACT composite between 23-27. 95% submitted SAT scores, 5% submitted ACT scores. **Characteristics:** 95% from in state, 82% live in college housing, 8% have minority backgrounds, 1% are foreign students. Average age is 18.

FALL-TERM APPLICATIONS. $25 fee, may be waived for applicants with need. Closing date April 1; priority given to applications received by February 15; applicants notified on a rolling basis; must reply by May 1 or within 4 weeks if notified thereafter. Audition required for music, music therapy, music education, theatre arts applicants. Portfolio required for studio art, art education applicants. Essay required. Interview recommended. CRDA. Deferred and early admission available. Applications received after June 1 reviewed on per case basis.

STUDENT LIFE. Housing: Dormitories (women, coed). Foreign language houses and collective housing for students in various majors available. Special interest housing also available. **Activities:** Student government, magazine, radio, student newspaper, yearbook, choral groups, concert band, drama, jazz band, music ensembles, musical theater, opera, pep band, Circle-K, Pre-law Club, Social Work Club, Young in Spirit Club, Black Interest Group, Amnesty International, Rotaract, Music Therapy Club.

ATHLETICS. NCAA. **Intercollegiate:** Basketball, diving, golf, lacrosse, soccer, swimming, tennis, volleyball W. **Intramural:** Basketball, diving, soccer, softball, swimming, tennis, volleyball.

STUDENT SERVICES. Career counseling, employment service for undergraduates, freshman orientation, health services, on-campus day care, personal counseling, placement service for graduates, services/facilities for handicapped.

ANNUAL EXPENSES. Tuition and fees: $10,380. **Room and board:** $4,830. **Books and supplies:** $500. **Other expenses:** $800.

FINANCIAL AID. 79% of freshmen, 82% of continuing students receive some form of aid. 85% of grants, 87% of loans, 43% of jobs based on need. 156 enrolled freshmen were judged to have need, all were offered aid. Academic, music/drama, art, state/district residency, alumni affiliation scholarships available. **Aid applications:** No closing date; priority given to applications received by March 30; applicants notified on a rolling basis beginning on or about March 1; must reply by May 1 or within 2 weeks if notified thereafter.

ADDRESS/TELEPHONE. Thomas K. DaRin, Director of Admissions, Nazareth College of Rochester, 4245 East Avenue, Rochester, NY 14618-3790. (716) 586-2525 ext. 265. (800) 248-3939. Fax: (716) 586-2431.

New York Institute of Technology
Old Westbury, New York — CB code: 2561

4-year private college of arts and sciences, coed. Founded in 1955. **Accreditation:** Regional. **Undergraduate enrollment:** 3,557 men, 1,516 women full time; 1,585 men, 643 women part time. **Graduate enrollment:** 1,220 men, 279 women full time; 860 men, 561 women part time. **Faculty:** 1,456 total (271 full time), 293 with doctorates or other terminal degrees. **Location:** Suburban campus in large town; 22 miles from New York City. **Calendar:** Semester, extensive summer session. Saturday and extensive evening/early morning classes. **Microcomputers:** 300 located in dormitories, libraries, classrooms, computer centers. **Special facilities:** Art gallery, health clinic. **Additional facts:** 3-campus institution: main campus at Old Westbury, Manhattan campus in New York City, and Central Islip campus in Suffolk County.

DEGREES OFFERED. AAS, BA, BS, BFA, BArch, MA, MS, MBA, DO. 66 associate degrees awarded in 1992. 14% in architecture and environmental design, 15% business and management, 12% communications, 24% engineering technologies, 33% home economics. 1,528 bachelor's degrees awarded. 20% in architecture and environmental design, 25% business and management, 10% communications, 12% engineering, 6% engineering technologies, 9% multi/interdisciplinary studies. Graduate degrees offered in 8 major fields of study.

UNDERGRADUATE MAJORS. Associate: Accounting, architectural technologies, business administration and management, business and office, communications, data processing, electrical technology, food production/management/services, health education, insurance and risk management, insurance marketing, mechanical design technology, secretarial and related programs, technical education, toxicology, trade and industrial education. **Bachelor's:** Accounting, advertising, aeronautical technology, architectural technologies, architecture, art education, behavioral sciences, biology, biomedical science, business administration and management, business education, communications, computer and information sciences, economics, electrical/electronics/communications engineering, electromechanical technology, engineering and engineering-related technologies, engineering management, finance, fine arts, graphic design, health education, hotel/motel and restaurant management, industrial engineering, interior design, liberal/general studies, life sciences: chemistry, life sciences: industrial hygiene, life sciences: premedical and allied health professions, management information systems, mathematics education, mechanical design technology, mechanical engineering, medical laboratory technologies, physics, political science and government, science education, technical and business writing, technical education, toxicology, trade and industrial education, trade and industrial supervision and management.

ACADEMIC PROGRAMS. 2-year transfer program, accelerated program, computer delivered (on-line) credit-bearing course offerings, cooperative education, external degree, independent study, internships, study abroad, teacher preparation, weekend college, cross-registration, combined bachelor's/graduate degree program in life sciences/osteopathic medicine, architectural technology/energy management. **Remedial services:** Learning center, preadmission summer program, reduced course load, remedial instruction, special counselor, tutoring, GOLD program for students with learning disabilities. **ROTC:** Air Force. **Placement/credit:** AP, CLEP General and Subject, institutional tests; 30 credit hours maximum for associate degree; 60 credit hours maximum for bachelor's degree.

ACADEMIC REQUIREMENTS. Freshmen must earn minimum GPA of 1.7 to continue in good standing. 65% of freshmen return for sophomore year. Students must declare major by end of first year. **Graduation requirements:** 68 hours for associate, 120 hours for bachelor's. Most students required to take courses in English, history, mathematics, biological/physical sciences, social sciences. **Postgraduate studies:** 2% enter law school, 1% enter medical school, 6% enter MBA programs, 6% enter other graduate study. **Additional information:** Freshmen in selected majors required to prove or acquire computer literacy.

FRESHMAN ADMISSIONS. Selection criteria: Open admissions. Selective admissions to engineering and architecture programs. **High school preparation:** 16 units recommended. Recommended units include English 4, mathematics 2, social science 2 and science 1. **Test requirements:** SAT or ACT (SAT preferred) for placement and counseling only; score report by September 1. SAT or ACT scores (SAT preferred) required for admission to engineering and architecture programs. Combined score of 1100 on SAT or 27 on ACT required to be considered for freshman Honor and Challenge Scholarship.

1992 FRESHMAN CLASS PROFILE. 614 men, 234 women enrolled. **Characteristics:** 91% from in state, 10% live in college housing, 38% have minority backgrounds, 13% are foreign students. Average age is 18.

FALL-TERM APPLICATIONS. $30 fee, may be waived for applicants with need. No closing date; applicants notified on a rolling basis; must reply within 4 weeks. Portfolio required for fine arts applicants. Interview recommended. Interview required for medical applicants. Deferred and early admission available.

STUDENT LIFE. Housing: Dormitories (coed). Central Islip campus fully residential. **Activities:** Student government, film, magazine, radio, student newspaper, television, yearbook, choral groups, drama, fraternities, sororities, departmental clubs, honor societies, special interest clubs, community service clubs, religious organizations, Women's Association, international association.

ATHLETICS. NCAA. **Intercollegiate:** Baseball M, basketball M, cross-country, lacrosse M, soccer, softball W, tennis M, track and field, volleyball W. **Intramural:** Basketball, diving, softball, swimming, tennis, volleyball.

STUDENT SERVICES. Aptitude testing, career counseling, employment service for undergraduates, freshman orientation, health services, personal counseling, placement service for graduates, special adviser for adult students, veterans counselor, services/facilities for handicapped.

ANNUAL EXPENSES. Tuition and fees (projected): $8,225. Architecture and engineering undergraduate students pay $298 per credit hour. Tuition and fees for architecture and engineering is $9,790. **Room and board:** $5,480. **Books and supplies:** $500. **Other expenses:** $1,200.

FINANCIAL AID. 92% of freshmen, 65% of continuing students receive some form of aid. 62% of grants, 84% of loans, 31% of jobs based on need. Academic, athletic, alumni affiliation scholarships available. **Aid applications:** No closing date; priority given to applications received by June 1; applicants notified on a rolling basis beginning on or about May 15; must reply within 2 weeks.

ADDRESS/TELEPHONE. Arthur Lambert, Executive Director of Enrollment Services, New York Institute of Technology, Old Westbury, NY 11568-0170. (516) 686-7520. (800) 345-NYIT. Fax: (516) 626-6830.

New York School of Interior Design
New York, New York — CB code: 0333

4-year private college of interior design, coed. Founded in 1916. **Undergraduate enrollment:** 16 men, 106 women full time; 55 men, 428 women part time. **Faculty:** 105 total (4 full time), 5 with doctorates or other terminal degrees. **Location:** Urban campus in very large city. **Calendar:** 4-1-4, limited summer session. **Microcomputers:** 15 located in libraries, classrooms, computer centers. **Special facilities:** Gallery for architecture and interior design exhibits.

DEGREES OFFERED. AAS, BFA. 37 associate degrees awarded in 1992. 100% in architecture and environmental design. 30 bachelor's degrees awarded. 100% in architecture and environmental design.

UNDERGRADUATE MAJORS. Associate: Interior design. **Bachelor's:** Interior design.

ACADEMIC PROGRAMS. Accelerated program, study abroad. **Placement/credit:** CLEP General.

ACADEMIC REQUIREMENTS. Freshmen must earn minimum GPA of 2.0 to continue in good standing. 86% of freshmen return for sophomore year. Students must declare major on application. **Graduation requirements:** 66 hours for associate (43 in major), 132 hours for bachelor's (102 in major). Most students required to take courses in arts/fine arts, English, humanities, mathematics, social sciences. **Postgraduate studies:** 80% from 2-year programs enter 4-year programs.

FRESHMAN ADMISSIONS. Selection criteria: Admissions Committee reviews applicants, school transcripts, SAT/ACT scores, 2 letters of recommendation, and portfolio in art/design or home exam to determine student's acceptability. **High school preparation:** 16 units recommended. Recommended units include English 4, mathematics 1, social science 1 and science 2. 3 additional electives and 5 general electives (studio art or drafting recommended). **Test requirements:** SAT or ACT (SAT preferred); score report by August 30. **Additional information:** Home exam test may replace portfolio requirement.

1992 FRESHMAN CLASS PROFILE. 4 men, 17 women enrolled. **Characteristics:** 72% from in state, 100% commute, 21% have minority backgrounds, 6% are foreign students. Average age is 20.

FALL-TERM APPLICATIONS. $25 fee, may be waived for applicants with need. No closing date; applicants notified on a rolling basis; must reply upon receipt of acceptance letter. Portfolio required. Essay required. Interview recommended. Deferred admission available.

STUDENT LIFE. Activities: Student Chapter of American Society of Interior Designers.

STUDENT SERVICES. Career counseling, employment service for undergraduates, personal counseling, placement service for graduates, veterans counselor, services/facilities for handicapped.

ANNUAL EXPENSES. Tuition and fees: $9,950. **Books and supplies:** $1,000. **Other expenses:** $700.

FINANCIAL AID. 36% of freshmen, 23% of continuing students receive some form of aid. All grants, 76% of loans based on need. Academic, art, leadership scholarships available. **Aid applications:** No closing date; priority given to applications received by July 1; applicants notified on a rolling basis; must reply within 2 weeks.

ADDRESS/TELEPHONE. June Soyka, Director of Admissions, New York School of Interior Design, 155 East 56th Street, New York, NY 10022. (212) 753-5365. (800) 33 NYSID. Fax: (212) 753-2034.

New York University
New York, New York — CB code: 2562

Admissions:	61% of applicants accepted
Based on:	••• School record, test scores
	•• Activities, essay, interview, recommendations, special talents
Completion:	94% of freshmen end year in good standing
	66% graduate, 73% of these enter graduate study

4-year private university, coed. Founded in 1831. **Accreditation:** Regional. **Undergraduate enrollment:** 5,365 men, 6,887 women full time; 1,267 men, 1,894 women part time. **Graduate enrollment:** 4,664 men, 4,489 women full time; 4,320 men, 5,721 women part time. **Faculty:** 4,110 total (1,218 full time). **Location:** Urban campus in very large city. **Calendar:** Semester, extensive summer session. **Microcomputers:** 940 located in dormitories, libraries, classrooms, computer centers. **Special facilities:** Jerome S. Coles Sports and Recreation Center, Institute of Fine Arts, Grey Art Gallery, Courant Institute of Mathematical Sciences. **Additional facts:** School of Continuing Education also available for adult degree programs.

DEGREES OFFERED. AA, AAS, BA, BS, BFA, MA, MS, MBA, MFA, MSW, PhD, EdD, DDS, MD, JD. 340 associate degrees awarded in 1992. 2,834 bachelor's degrees awarded. 21% in business and management, 5% communications, 7% multi/interdisciplinary studies, 5% psychology, 17% social sciences, 21% visual and performing arts. Graduate degrees offered in 178 major fields of study.

UNDERGRADUATE MAJORS. Associate: Art history, business and management, business and office, business data processing and related programs, computer programming, dental hygiene, early childhood education, elementary education, liberal/general studies, medical assistant, physical therapy assistant, social work. **Bachelor's:** Accounting, actuarial sciences, American literature, anthropology, applied mathematics, Arabic, art education, behavioral sciences, biochemistry, biology, business administration and management, business and management, business economics, business education, business statistics, chemical engineering, chemistry, cinematography/film, civil engineering, classics, communications, comparative literature, computer and information sciences, computer engineering, creative writing, dance, dramatic arts, early childhood education, earth sciences, East Asian studies, economics, education, education of the deaf and hearing impaired, education of the emotionally handicapped, education of the mentally handicapped, education of the multiple handicapped, education of the physically handicapped, education of the visually handicapped, electrical/electronics/communications engineering, elementary education, engineering and other disciplines, engineering physics, English, English education, English literature, film animation, film arts, finance, fine arts, food management, food production/management/services, food science and nutrition, foreign languages (multiple emphasis), foreign languages education, French, German, graphic arts technology, Greek (classical), health education, Hebrew, history, hotel/motel and restaurant management, human resources development, humanities, humanities and social sciences, information sciences and systems, institutional/home management/supporting programs, international business management, international relations, international studies, Iranian languages, Islamic studies, Italian, jazz, Jewish studies, journalism, junior high education, Latin, Latin American studies, liberal/general studies, linguistics, management information systems, marketing management, mathematics, mathematics education, mechanical engineering, medieval studies, Middle Eastern studies, motion picture technology, museum studies, music, music business management, music education, music history and appreciation, music performance, music theory and composition, musical theater, nursing, nursing education, nutritional education, occupational therapy, operations research, organizational behavior, painting, parks and recreation management, philosophy, photography, physical sciences, physical therapy, physics, political science and government, Portuguese, predentistry, prelaw, premedicine, preveterinary, psychobiology, psychology, public administration, radio/television broadcasting, radio/television technology, rehabilitation counseling/services, religion, Russian, Russian and Slavic studies, science education, sculpture, secondary education, social sciences, social studies education, social work, sociology, Spanish, special education, speech, speech correction, speech pathology/audiology, speech/communication/theater education, statistics, studio art, theater design, urban design, urban studies, video, visual and performing arts, women's studies.

ACADEMIC PROGRAMS. 2-year transfer program, accelerated program, double major, honors program, independent study, internships, student-designed major, study abroad, teacher preparation, visiting/exchange student program, weekend college, New York semester, Washington semester, cross-registration; liberal arts/career combination in engineering; combined bachelor's/graduate program in business administration, medicine. **Remedial services:** Learning center, preadmission summer program, reduced course load, remedial instruction, special counselor, tutoring. **ROTC:** Air Force, Army. **Placement/credit:** AP, CLEP Subject, institutional tests; 32 credit hours maximum for bachelor's degree.

ACADEMIC REQUIREMENTS. Freshmen must earn minimum GPA of 2.0 to continue in good standing. 85% of freshmen return for sophomore year. Students must declare major by end of second year. **Graduation requirements:** 64 hours for associate, 128 hours for bachelor's (32 in major). Most students required to take courses in arts/fine arts, English, foreign languages, history, humanities, mathematics, philosophy/religion, biological/physical sciences, social sciences. **Postgraduate studies:** 13% enter law school, 14% enter medical school, 8% enter MBA programs, 38% enter other graduate study.

FRESHMAN ADMISSIONS. Selection criteria: School achievement record most important. Standardized test scores, activities, recommendations considered. Interviews required for those seeking early admission. Minority status, alumni relationship, creative talent given special consideration. Audition and/or submission of creative material required for applicants to either Tisch School of the Arts or art and music programs within the School of Education. **High school preparation:** 16 units required; 20 recommended. Required and recommended units include English 4, foreign language 2-3, mathematics 3-4, social science 3-4 and science 2-3. **Test requirements:** SAT or ACT; score report by February 1. 3 ACH (including English Composition) required of BA/MD joint degree applicants. Score report by February 1.

1992 FRESHMAN CLASS PROFILE. 4,534 men applied, 2,815 accepted, 1,159 enrolled; 6,303 women applied, 3,826 accepted, 1,447 enrolled. 77% had high school GPA of 3.0 or higher, 23% between 2.0 and 2.99. **Academic background:** Mid 50% of enrolled freshmen had SAT-V between 460-590, SAT-M between 530-650. 86% submitted SAT scores. **Characteristics:** 50% from in state, 60% live in college housing, 45% have minority backgrounds, 6% are foreign students, 7% join fraternities/sororities. Average age is 18.

FALL-TERM APPLICATIONS. $45 fee, may be waived for applicants with need. Closing date February 1; priority given to applications received by December 15; applicants notified on or about April 1; must reply by May 1. Audition required for dance, music, and drama applicants. Portfolio required for art, theater design, photography, cinema studies, film, television, radio applicants. Essay required. Interview recommended. Writing sample required for dramatic writing applicants. CRDA. Deferred and early admission available. EDP-F.

STUDENT LIFE. Housing: Dormitories (coed); apartment, fraternity, sorority, handicapped housing available. All freshmen who request housing on their application and meet all deadlines guaranteed 4 years of on-campus housing. **Activities:** Student government, film, magazine, radio, student newspaper, television, yearbook, choral groups, concert band, dance, drama, jazz band, music ensembles, musical theater, opera, pep band, symphony orchestra, fraternities, sororities, 230 clubs and organizations.

ATHLETICS. NCAA. **Intercollegiate:** Basketball, cross-country, diving, fencing, golf M, soccer M, swimming, tennis, track and field, volleyball, wrestling M. **Intramural:** Badminton, baseball M, basketball, cross-country, fencing, golf M, horseback riding, ice hockey M, lacrosse M, racquetball, rowing (crew), softball, squash, swimming, tennis, track and field, volleyball, water polo.

STUDENT SERVICES. Aptitude testing, career counseling, employment service for undergraduates, freshman orientation, health services, personal counseling, placement service for graduates, special adviser for adult students, veterans counselor, services/facilities for handicapped.

ANNUAL EXPENSES. Tuition and fees (1992-93): $16,590. **Room and board:** $6,700. **Books and supplies:** $450. **Other expenses:** $1,000.

FINANCIAL AID. 82% of freshmen, 68% of continuing students receive some form of aid. 98% of grants, 78% of loans, 38% of jobs based on need. 1,936 enrolled freshmen were judged to have need, all were offered aid. Academic, music/drama, state/district residency, leadership, minority scholarships available. **Aid applications:** Closing date February 15; applicants notified on a rolling basis beginning on or about April 1; must reply by May 1 or within 2 weeks if notified thereafter.

ADDRESS/TELEPHONE. David F. Finney, Associate Vice President of Enrollment Services, New York University, 22 Washington Square North, New York, NY 10011-9108. (212) 998-4500. Fax: (212) 995-4902.

Niagara County Community College

Sanborn, New York CB code: 2568

2-year public institution, coed. Founded in 1962. **Accreditation:** Regional. **Undergraduate enrollment:** 1,458 men, 1,795 women full time; 842 men, 1,515 women part time. **Faculty:** 455 total (223 full time), 17 with doctorates or other terminal degrees. **Location:** Rural campus in rural community; 10 miles from Niagara Falls. **Calendar:** Semester, extensive summer session. Saturday classes. **Microcomputers:** 300 located in libraries, classrooms, computer centers. **Special facilities:** Art gallery, planetarium, theater. **Additional facts:** SUNY institution.

DEGREES OFFERED. AA, AS, AAS. 761 associate degrees awarded in 1992. 13% in business and management, 10% business/office and marketing/distribution, 6% engineering technologies, 13% health sciences, 32% multi/interdisciplinary studies, 8% parks/recreation, protective services, public affairs, 5% visual and performing arts.

UNDERGRADUATE MAJORS. Accounting, animal management, animal sciences, business administration and management, business data processing and related programs, communications, computer and information sciences, criminal justice studies, data processing, drafting and design technology, dramatic arts, electrical technology, electrodiagnostic technologies, engineering and engineering-related technologies, fine arts, fitness center specialist, food management, human services, humanities and social sciences, liberal/general studies, mechanical design technology, mechanical engineering, medical assistant, mental health/human services, music performance, nursing, physical education, physical therapy assistant, radiograph medical technology, retailing, science technologies, secretarial and related programs.

ACADEMIC PROGRAMS. 2-year transfer program, cooperative education, honors program, independent study, internships, student-designed major, study abroad, cross-registration. **Remedial services:** Learning center, preadmission summer program, reduced course load, remedial instruction, special counselor, tutoring. **Placement/credit:** AP, CLEP General and Subject, institutional tests; 30 credit hours maximum for associate degree.

ACADEMIC REQUIREMENTS. Freshmen must earn minimum GPA of 2.0 to continue in good standing. 58% of freshmen return for sophomore year. Students must declare major on application. **Graduation requirements:** 62 hours for associate. Most students required to take courses in English.

FRESHMAN ADMISSIONS. Selection criteria: Open admissions. Selective admission to nursing program based on school achievement record and test scores. One drafting required for drafting applicants, 1 biology or chemistry required for nursing applicants, 3 mathematics for engineering technology, 1 biology, 1 chemistry and 2 mathematics for physical therapist assistant, 1 chemistry, 1 biology, 2 mathematics for radiologic technology. **Additional information:** Admission to programs on space-available basis.

1992 FRESHMAN CLASS PROFILE. 715 men, 870 women enrolled. 12% had high school GPA of 3.0 or higher, 62% between 2.0 and 2.99. 5% were in top tenth and 19% were in top quarter of graduating class. **Characteristics:** 99% from in state, 100% commute, 6% have minority backgrounds, 1% are foreign students. Average age is 23.

FALL-TERM APPLICATIONS. No fee. Closing date August 31; priority given to applications received by August 1; applicants notified on a rolling basis; must reply within 4 weeks. Interview recommended. Early admission available.

STUDENT LIFE. Activities: Student government, film, magazine, radio, student newspaper, television, yearbook, choral groups, concert band, dance, drama, jazz band, music ensembles, musical theater, veterans club, disabled student association, comeback club, outdoor adventure club, Black student union, Native American club, nursing.

ATHLETICS. NJCAA. **Intercollegiate:** Baseball M, basketball M, bowling, cross-country, soccer, softball W, volleyball W, wrestling M. **Intramural:** Basketball, bowling, racquetball, skiing, softball W, swimming, table tennis, tennis, volleyball.

STUDENT SERVICES. Aptitude testing, career counseling, employment service for undergraduates, freshman orientation, health services, on-campus day care, personal counseling, placement service for graduates, special adviser for adult students, veterans counselor, counselor for handicapped, minority outreach coordinator, Native American adviser, women in technology counselor, counselor for social service students, services/facilities for handicapped.

ANNUAL EXPENSES. Tuition and fees (1992-93): $1,800, $1,700 additional for out-of-state students. **Books and supplies:** $375. **Other expenses:** $600.

FINANCIAL AID. 70% of freshmen, 70% of continuing students receive some form of aid. 93% of grants, 78% of loans, 34% of jobs based on need. 880 enrolled freshmen were judged to have need, 720 were offered aid. Academic, state/district residency, leadership, alumni affiliation scholarships available. **Aid applications:** No closing date; priority given to applications received by April 1; applicants notified on a rolling basis beginning on or about May 1; must reply within 2 weeks. **Additional information:** Assistance offered placing students in part-time employment. Students can charge books, food coupons, or $100 advance against anticipated financial aid.

ADDRESS/TELEPHONE. Ronald Mirabelli, Dean of Enrollment/and Computer Services, Niagara County Community College, 3111 Saunders Settlement Road, Sanborn, NY 14132. (716) 731-3271 ext. 100. Fax: (716) 731-4053.

Niagara University
Niagara Falls, New York CB code: 2558

Admissions: 78% of applicants accepted
Based on:
••• School record
•• Interview, recommendations, test scores
• Activities, essay, special talents
Completion: 80% of freshmen end year in good standing
60% graduate, 12% of these enter graduate study

4-year private university, coed. Founded in 1856. **Accreditation:** Regional. **Undergraduate enrollment:** 2,057 men and women full time; 329 men and women part time. **Graduate enrollment:** 616 men and women. **Faculty:** 214 total (114 full time), 112 with doctorates or other terminal degrees. **Location:** Suburban campus in small city; 20 miles from Buffalo, New York; 90 miles from Toronto, Ontario, Canada. **Calendar:** Semester, extensive summer session. **Microcomputers:** 200 located in libraries, computer centers. **Special facilities:** Clet Theater, Kiernan Athletic And Recreation Complex, Castellani Fine Arts Museum. **Additional facts:** Independent institution in the Vincentian tradition.

DEGREES OFFERED. AA, AS, AAS, BA, BS, BFA, MBA, MEd. 4 associate degrees awarded in 1992. 100% in business and management. 512 bachelor's degrees awarded. 48% in business and management, 5% communications, 7% education, 6% health sciences, 5% physical sciences, 17% social sciences. Graduate degrees offered in 15 major fields of study.

UNDERGRADUATE MAJORS. Associate: Business and management, engineering, liberal/general studies. **Bachelor's:** Accounting, biochemistry, biology, biotechnology, business administration and management, business and management, business economics, business education, chemistry, communications, computer and information sciences, criminal justice studies, criminology, dramatic arts, education, elementary education, English, English education, food management, foreign languages education, French, history, hotel/motel and restaurant management, human resources development, information sciences and systems, international business management, international relations, international studies, junior high education, life sciences, management information systems, management science, marketing management, mathematics, mathematics education, nursing, peace studies, personnel management, philosophy, political science and government, predentistry, prelaw, premedicine, prepharmacy, preveterinary, psychology, religion, science education, secondary education, social sciences, social studies education, social work, sociology, Spanish, tourism, transportation management.

ACADEMIC PROGRAMS. 2-year transfer program, accelerated program, cooperative education, double major, dual enrollment of high school students, education specialist degree, honors program, independent study, internships, study abroad, teacher preparation, visiting/exchange student program, New York semester, Washington semester, cross-registration, visiting student program with participating colleges and universities in New York State. **Remedial services:** Learning center, preadmission summer program, reduced course load, remedial instruction, special counselor, tutoring, New York State Higher Education Opportunity Program. **ROTC:** Army. **Placement/credit:** AP, CLEP General and Subject, institutional tests; 15 credit hours maximum for associate degree; 15 credit hours maximum for bachelor's degree.

ACADEMIC REQUIREMENTS. Freshmen must earn minimum GPA of 2.0 to continue in good standing. Students must declare major by end of second year. **Graduation requirements:** 60 hours for associate (33 in major), 120 hours for bachelor's (60 in major). Most students required to take courses in English, history, humanities, mathematics, philosophy/religion, biological/physical sciences, social sciences. **Postgraduate studies:** 2% enter law school, 1% enter medical school, 1% enter MBA programs, 8% enter other graduate study. **Additional information:** Academic exploration program for students undecided about their choice of major.

FRESHMAN ADMISSIONS. Selection criteria: School achievement record, class rank, test scores required. School recommendation, character, personality, and extracurricular activities also important. Alumni relationship considered. **High school preparation:** 16 units required. Required units include English 4, foreign language 2, mathematics 2, social science 2 and science 2. 3 units science (biology, chemistry mandatory, physics recommended) for nursing applicants. 2 units foreign language required of all except business applicants. 3 units mathematics required for mathematics, biology, business, biochemistry, chemistry, computer and information sciences, natural sciences, and nursing applicants. 3 units social studies required for prospective social studies majors. **Test requirements:** SAT or ACT; score report by August 15.

1992 FRESHMAN CLASS PROFILE. 2,415 men and women applied, 1,888 accepted; 574 enrolled. 43% had high school GPA of 3.0 or higher, 55% between 2.0 and 2.99. **Academic background:** Mid 50% of enrolled freshmen had SAT-V between 400-500, SAT-M between 430-530; ACT composite between 19-24. 85% submitted SAT scores, 34% submitted ACT scores. **Characteristics:** 91% from in state, 60% live in college housing, 8% have minority backgrounds, 1% are foreign students. Average age is 18.

FALL-TERM APPLICATIONS. $15 fee, may be waived for applicants with need. Closing date August 1; applicants notified on a rolling basis; must reply by May 1 or within 4 weeks if notified thereafter. Interview recommended. Essay recommended. CRDA. Deferred and early admission available. Institutional early decision plan.

STUDENT LIFE. Housing: Dormitories (men, women, coed). Freshmen students who do not reside within reasonable commuting distance required to live on campus for two years. **Activities:** Student government, magazine, radio, student newspaper, television, yearbook, choral groups, dance, drama, musical theater, pep band, ethnic awareness association, Knights of Columbus, community action program, muscular dystrophy association, foreign student council, St. Vincent DePaul Society.

ATHLETICS. NCAA. **Intercollegiate:** Baseball M, basketball, cross-country, diving, golf M, soccer, softball W, swimming, tennis, volleyball W. **Intramural:** Baseball M, basketball, bowling, golf, ice hockey M, lacrosse, racquetball, rugby, skiing, softball, track and field M, volleyball, water polo.

STUDENT SERVICES. Aptitude testing, career counseling, employment service for undergraduates, freshman orientation, health services, personal counseling, placement service for graduates, special adviser for adult students, veterans counselor, services/facilities for handicapped.

ANNUAL EXPENSES. Tuition and fees: $10,070. **Room and board:** $4,482. **Books and supplies:** $450. **Other expenses:** $650.

FINANCIAL AID. 84% of freshmen, 84% of continuing students receive some form of aid. 45% of grants, 96% of loans, 80% of jobs based on need. 437 enrolled freshmen were judged to have need, all were offered aid. Academic, music/drama, athletic scholarships available. **Aid applications:** No closing date; priority given to applications received by February 15; applicants notified on a rolling basis beginning on or about March 15; must reply by May 1 or within 3 weeks if notified thereafter. **Additional information:** Niagara University Opportunity program available for academically and economically disadvantaged students.

ADDRESS/TELEPHONE. George C. Pachter, Dean of Admissions/Records, Niagara University, Niagara Falls, NY 14109. (716) 286-8700. (800) 462-2111. Fax: (716) 285-2971.

North Country Community College
Saranac Lake, New York CB code: 2571

2-year public community college, coed. Founded in 1967. **Accreditation:** Regional. **Undergraduate enrollment:** 454 men, 492 women full time; 160 men, 246 women part time. **Faculty:** 161 total (53 full time), 10 with doctorates or other terminal degrees. **Location:** Rural campus in small town; 150 miles from Albany, 50 miles from Plattsburgh. **Calendar:** Semester, limited summer session. **Microcomputers:** 70 located in libraries, classrooms, computer centers. **Additional facts:** SUNY institution. Branch campuses at Malone, Ticonderoga

DEGREES OFFERED. AA, AS, AAS. 209 associate degrees awarded in 1992. 11% in business and management, 5% business/office and marketing/distribution, 12% health sciences, 29% allied health, 10% mathematics, 21% multi/interdisciplinary studies, 12% parks/recreation, protective services, public affairs.

UNDERGRADUATE MAJORS. Business administration and management, business and management, business and office, criminal justice studies, humanities and social sciences, liberal/general studies, marketing and distribution, mathematics, mental health/human services, nursing, parks and recreation management, radiograph medical technology, recreation and community services technologies.

ACADEMIC PROGRAMS. 2-year transfer program, double major, dual enrollment of high school students, independent study, internships, student-designed major. **Remedial services:** Learning center, reduced course load, remedial instruction, special counselor, tutoring. **Placement/credit:** AP, CLEP General and Subject, institutional tests; 31 credit hours maximum for associate degree.

ACADEMIC REQUIREMENTS. Freshmen must earn minimum GPA

of 2.0 to continue in good standing. 48% of freshmen return for sophomore year. Students must declare major on application. **Graduation requirements:** 62 hours for associate (24 in major). Most students required to take courses in English, humanities, mathematics, philosophy/religion, biological/physical sciences, social sciences.

FRESHMAN ADMISSIONS. Selection criteria: Open admissions. Selective admissions to nursing and radiograph medical technology programs. One science, 1 mathematics and 1 English required for radiograph medical technology applicants.

1992 FRESHMAN CLASS PROFILE. 211 men, 183 women enrolled. 20% had high school GPA of 3.0 or higher, 70% between 2.0 and 2.99. 2% were in top tenth and 10% were in top quarter of graduating class. **Academic background:** Mid 50% of enrolled freshmen had SAT-V between 310-450, SAT-M between 340-500. 35% submitted SAT scores. **Characteristics:** 93% from in state, 100% commute, 8% have minority backgrounds, 1% are foreign students. Average age is 23.

FALL-TERM APPLICATIONS. No fee. No closing date; priority given to applications received by August 1; applicants notified on a rolling basis. Interview recommended for radiologic, X-ray technology, nursing applicants. Deferred admission available. SAT or ACT recommended for placement and counseling. Score report by July 15.

STUDENT LIFE. Activities: Student government, student newspaper, yearbook, drama.

ATHLETICS. NJCAA. **Intercollegiate:** Basketball, ice hockey M, skiing, soccer, softball W. **Intramural:** Archery, badminton, basketball, bowling, cross-country, golf, skiing, soccer, softball, swimming, tennis, volleyball.

STUDENT SERVICES. Aptitude testing, career counseling, employment service for undergraduates, freshman orientation, on-campus day care, personal counseling, placement service for graduates, services/facilities for handicapped.

ANNUAL EXPENSES. Tuition and fees (1992-93): $1,905, $1,800 additional for out-of-state students. **Books and supplies:** $500. **Other expenses:** $700.

FINANCIAL AID. 85% of freshmen, 85% of continuing students receive some form of aid. All grants, 94% of loans, 79% of jobs based on need. **Aid applications:** No closing date; priority given to applications received by April 30; applicants notified on a rolling basis beginning on or about June 15; must reply within 3 weeks.

ADDRESS/TELEPHONE. Tim Gerrish, Director of Admissions and Treasurer, North Country Community College, 20 Winona Avenue, Saranac Lake, NY 12983. (518) 891-2915 ext. 233. (800) 541-1021. Fax: (518) 891-2915 ext. 214.

Nyack College
Nyack, New York — CB code: 2560

4-year private liberal arts college, coed, affiliated with Christian and Missionary Alliance. Founded in 1882. **Accreditation:** Regional. **Graduate enrollment:** 239 men and women. **Faculty:** 74 total (61 full time), 21 with doctorates or other terminal degrees. **Location:** Suburban campus in large town; 25 miles from New York City. **Calendar:** 4-4-1, limited summer session. **Microcomputers:** 60 located in computer centers. **Additional facts:** Graduate division offering master's degree is Alliance Theological Seminary.

DEGREES OFFERED. AA, AS, BA, BS, MA, M.Div. 96 bachelor's degrees awarded. 5% in business and management, 31% teacher education, 20% letters/literature, 8% multi/interdisciplinary studies, 14% philosophy, religion, theology, 20% psychology. Graduate degrees offered in 3 major fields of study.

UNDERGRADUATE MAJORS. Associate: Bible studies, liberal/general studies. **Bachelor's:** Bible studies, business administration and management, business and management, communications, elementary education, English, history, human resources development, humanities, international studies, missionary studies, music, music education, music performance, music theory and composition, philosophy, psychology, religion, religious education, religious music, secondary education, social sciences, theological studies.

ACADEMIC PROGRAMS. 2-year transfer program, external degree, independent study, internships, study abroad, visiting/exchange student program, cross-registration. **Remedial services:** Preadmission summer program, reduced course load, remedial instruction, special counselor, tutoring. **Placement/credit:** AP, CLEP General and Subject, institutional tests; 30 credit hours maximum for bachelor's degree.

ACADEMIC REQUIREMENTS. Freshmen must earn minimum GPA of 1.70 to continue in good standing. 70% of freshmen return for sophomore year. Students must declare major by end of second year. **Graduation requirements:** 64 hours for associate, 128 hours for bachelor's (28 in major). Most students required to take courses in arts/fine arts, computer science, English, foreign languages, history, mathematics, philosophy/religion, biological/physical sciences, social sciences.

FRESHMAN ADMISSIONS. Selection criteria: Christian commitment required. Academic record, class rank, and test scores most important. 3 recommendations required. **High school preparation:** 16 units recommended. Recommended units include English 4, foreign language 2, physical science 2, social science 3 and science 2. **Test requirements:** SAT or ACT; score report by September 1. **Additional information:** Applicants must have Christian commitment and sign agreement to abide by community life standards.

1992 FRESHMAN CLASS PROFILE. 105 men and women enrolled. 22% had high school GPA of 3.0 or higher, 54% between 2.0 and 2.99. **Academic background:** Mid 50% of enrolled freshmen had SAT-V between 350-500, SAT-M between 350-510; ACT composite between 13-19. 68% submitted SAT scores, 27% submitted ACT scores. **Characteristics:** 63% from in state, 90% live in college housing, 40% have minority backgrounds, 1% are foreign students. Average age is 19.

FALL-TERM APPLICATIONS. $15 fee, may be waived for applicants with need. Closing date September 1; applicants notified on a rolling basis; must reply within 30 days. Audition required for music applicants. Essay required. Interview recommended for those with unsatisfactory recommendations or academic concerns. Deferred and early admission available.

STUDENT LIFE. Housing: Dormitories (men, women); apartment housing available. **Activities:** Student government, magazine, radio, student newspaper, yearbook, choral groups, drama, music ensembles, musical theater, chamber orchestra, brass ensemble, handbell choir, Afro-American Club, Brooklyn, Chinatown, and Nyack gospel teams, St. Dominic's Orphanage ministry. **Additional information:** Religious observance required.

ATHLETICS. NAIA. **Intercollegiate:** Baseball M, basketball, soccer M, softball W, volleyball. **Intramural:** Basketball, bowling, football M, soccer, softball, table tennis, tennis, volleyball.

STUDENT SERVICES. Career counseling, employment service for undergraduates, freshman orientation, health services, personal counseling, placement service for graduates, services/facilities for handicapped.

ANNUAL EXPENSES. Tuition and fees (1992-93): $7,860. **Room and board:** $3,610. **Books and supplies:** $500. **Other expenses:** $600.

FINANCIAL AID. 87% of freshmen, 87% of continuing students receive some form of aid. Grants, loans, jobs available. Academic, leadership, religious affiliation scholarships available. **Aid applications:** No closing date; priority given to applications received by March 1; applicants notified on a rolling basis beginning on or about March 1; must reply within 2 weeks.

ADDRESS/TELEPHONE. Dennis Whalen, Director of Admissions, Nyack College, Nyack, NY 10960. (914) 358-1710. (800) 336-9225.

Ohr Hameir Theological Seminary
Peekskill, New York — CB code: 0610

4-year private rabbinical college, men only, affiliated with Jewish faith. Founded in 1962. **Undergraduate enrollment:** 40 men full time. **Location:** Suburban campus in large town. **Calendar:** Semester. **Additional facts:** Ordination available.

ADDRESS/TELEPHONE. Naftoly Kemper, Chief Development Officer, Ohr Hameir Theological Seminary, PO Box 2130, Peekskill, NY 10566. (914) 736-1500.

Ohr Somayach Tanenbaum Education Center
Monsey, New York — CB code: 3357

5-year private rabbinical college, men only, affiliated with Jewish faith. Founded in 1979. **Undergraduate enrollment:** 58 men full time; 20 men part time. **Faculty:** 7 total (5 full time), 7 with doctorates or other terminal degrees. **Location:** Suburban campus in large town; one-half mile from Spring Valley. **Calendar:** Semester, extensive summer session. **Additional facts:** First and Second Talmudic degrees offered.

DEGREES OFFERED. Graduate degrees offered in 3 major fields of study.

UNDERGRADUATE MAJORS. Religious education, theological studies.

ACADEMIC PROGRAMS. Accelerated program, independent study, study abroad, teacher preparation, cross-registration. **Remedial services:** Preadmission summer program, reduced course load, tutoring. **Placement/credit:** Institutional tests.

ACADEMIC REQUIREMENTS. Freshmen must earn minimum GPA of 3.0 to continue in good standing. 70% of freshmen return for sophomore year. **Graduation requirements:** 120 hours for bachelor's. Most students required to take courses in foreign languages, philosophy/religion. **Postgraduate studies:** 10% enter law school, 10% enter medical school, 50% enter MBA programs, 10% enter other graduate study.

FRESHMAN ADMISSIONS. Selection criteria: Potential for scholastic and character achievement evaluated through personal interview, recommendations, departmental examinations, and prior religious and secular studies.

1992 FRESHMAN CLASS PROFILE. 70 men enrolled. **Characteristics:** 100% live in college housing. Average age is 22.

FALL-TERM APPLICATIONS. No closing date; applicants notified on a rolling basis; must reply by August 31 or within 2 weeks if notified thereafter. Interview required. Essay recommended. CRDA. Deferred admission available. EDP-F.

STUDENT LIFE. Housing: Dormitories (men); apartment housing available. Students above age 30 must arrange own housing off campus. Assistance provided in locating housing. **Activities:** Singing group, community volunteers. **Additional information:** Religious observance required.

ATHLETICS. Intramural: Baseball, basketball, skiing, swimming.

STUDENT SERVICES. Career counseling, employment service for undergraduates, personal counseling, placement service for graduates.

ANNUAL EXPENSES. Tuition and fees (1992-93): $3,600. **Room and board:** $3,600. **Books and supplies:** $300. **Other expenses:** $725.

FINANCIAL AID. 95% of continuing students receive some form of aid. Grants, jobs available. 15 enrolled freshmen were judged to have need, all were offered aid. **Aid applications:** No closing date; applicants notified on a rolling basis beginning on or about July 1; must reply within 4 weeks.

ADDRESS/TELEPHONE. Rabbi Avrohom Braun, Dean of Students, Ohr Somayach Tanenbaum Education Center, PO Box 334, 142 Route 306, Monsey, NY 10952. (914) 425-1370. Fax: (914) 425-8865.

Olean Business Institute
Olean, New York — CB code: 0630

2-year proprietary business college, coed. Founded in 1961. **Undergraduate enrollment:** 250 men and women. **Faculty:** 16 total (10 full time). **Location:** Suburban campus in large town; 90 miles from Buffalo, 90 miles from Erie, Pennsylvania. **Calendar:** Semester. **Microcomputers:** 30 located in classrooms, computer centers.

DEGREES OFFERED. 45 associate degrees awarded in 1992. 50% in business/office and marketing/distribution, 50% computer sciences.

UNDERGRADUATE MAJORS. Accounting, business administration and management, legal assistant/paralegal, medical secretary, secretarial and related programs, word processing.

ACADEMIC PROGRAMS. 2-year transfer program, internships. **Remedial services:** Learning center, reduced course load, remedial instruction, special counselor, tutoring.

ACADEMIC REQUIREMENTS. Freshmen must earn minimum GPA of 1.5 to continue in good standing. Students must declare major on enrollment. **Graduation requirements:** 65 hours for associate. Most students required to take courses in computer science.

FRESHMAN ADMISSIONS. Selection criteria: School achievement record most important.

1992 FRESHMAN CLASS PROFILE. 125 men and women enrolled. **Characteristics:** 88% commute, 5% have minority backgrounds.

FALL-TERM APPLICATIONS. $25 fee, may be waived for applicants with need. No closing date; applicants notified on a rolling basis.

STUDENT LIFE. Housing: Dormitories (women). **Activities:** Student government.

STUDENT SERVICES. Career counseling, employment service for undergraduates, freshman orientation, personal counseling, placement service for graduates, special adviser for adult students, services/facilities for handicapped.

ANNUAL EXPENSES. Tuition and fees (1992-93): $4,305. **Books and supplies:** $500.

FINANCIAL AID. Aid applications: No closing date; priority given to applications received by May 1; applicants notified on a rolling basis.

ADDRESS/TELEPHONE. Patrick McCarthy, Director of Admissions, Olean Business Institute, 301 North Union Street, Olean, NY 14760-2691. (716) 372-7978. Fax: (716) 372-2120.

Onondaga Community College
Syracuse, New York — CB code: 2627

2-year public community college, coed. Founded in 1962. **Accreditation:** Regional. **Undergraduate enrollment:** 2,125 men, 2,111 women full time; 1,632 men, 2,639 women part time. **Faculty:** 494 total (182 full time), 40 with doctorates or other terminal degrees. **Location:** Suburban campus in small city; 4 miles from downtown. **Calendar:** Semester, extensive summer session. **Microcomputers:** 90 located in libraries, classrooms, computer centers. **Special facilities:** Police academy, branch of New York State Employment Service, county library. **Additional facts:** SUNY institution.

DEGREES OFFERED. AA, AS, AAS. 1,123 associate degrees awarded in 1992. 19% in business and management, 11% health sciences, 5% allied health, 19% letters/literature, 5% life sciences, 9% parks/recreation, protective services, public affairs, 12% visual and performing arts.

UNDERGRADUATE MAJORS. Accounting, architectural technologies, architecture, automotive technology, business administration and management, business and management, business data processing and related programs, chemical technology, commercial art, computer and information sciences, computer servicing technology, computer technology, construction, criminal justice studies, data processing, dental hygiene, electrical technology, engineering science, finance, fine arts, fire control and safety technology, fire protection, food management, food production/management/services, graphic and printing production, graphic arts technology, hotel/motel and restaurant management, humanities, humanities and social sciences, insurance and risk management, interior design, labor/industrial relations, liberal/general studies, mathematics, mechanical design technology, medical records administration, medical records technology, music, nursing, parks and recreation management, photographic technology, photography, physical therapy assistant, quality control technology, radio/television broadcasting, radio/television technology, recreation and community services technologies, recreation therapy, respiratory therapy, respiratory therapy technology, science technologies, secretarial and related programs, telecommunications, textiles and clothing.

ACADEMIC PROGRAMS. 2-year transfer program, cooperative education, double major, dual enrollment of high school students, independent study, internships, telecourses, cross-registration. **Remedial services:** Learning center, reduced course load, remedial instruction, special counselor, tutoring. **ROTC:** Air Force. **Placement/credit:** AP, CLEP General and Subject, institutional tests; 30 credit hours maximum for associate degree.

ACADEMIC REQUIREMENTS. Freshmen must earn minimum GPA of 2.0 to continue in good standing. 66% of freshmen return for sophomore year. Students must declare major on enrollment. **Graduation requirements:** 62 hours for associate (30 in major). Most students required to take courses in arts/fine arts, computer science, English, humanities, mathematics, biological/physical sciences, social sciences.

FRESHMAN ADMISSIONS. Selection criteria: Open admissions. Selective admissions to some programs based on high school GPA, test scores, and specific course prerequisites. **High school preparation:** 12 units recommended. Recommended units include English 4, foreign language 2, mathematics 3 and science 3. Algebra, biology, chemistry required of dental hygiene, respiratory care, surgical technology, nursing applicants. 4 mathematics required for engineering, science, computer science applicants. **Test requirements:** SAT for placement; score report by August 15. SAT or ACT required for admission to some programs; score report by August 15. **Additional information:** Mandatory developmental skills courses required as condition of acceptance for students lacking adequate academic background. School achievement record, test scores, special talents considered after student admitted for placement. Interview, recommendations required for some programs.

1992 FRESHMAN CLASS PROFILE. 2,708 men, 3,435 women enrolled. 10% had high school GPA of 3.0 or higher, 80% between 2.0 and 2.99. **Characteristics:** 90% from in state, 100% commute, 10% have minority backgrounds, 5% are foreign students.

FALL-TERM APPLICATIONS. $25 fee, may be waived for applicants with need. Closing date August 10; applicants notified on a rolling basis. Interview required for dental hygiene, radio-television, graphic arts applicants. Audition required for music applicants. Portfolio required for art, photographic technology applicants. CRDA. Deferred admission available.

STUDENT LIFE. Housing: Privately owned student housing adjacent to campus. **Activities:** Student government, film, radio, student newspaper, choral groups, concert band, jazz band, music ensembles, musical theater, international students, minority, veterans, interreligious, and older/returning student clubs.

ATHLETICS. NJCAA. **Intercollegiate:** Baseball M, basketball, lacrosse M, softball W, tennis, volleyball W. **Intramural:** Archery, badminton, basketball, bowling, fencing, golf, horseback riding, lacrosse M, racquetball, skiing, skin diving, softball W, swimming, tennis, volleyball.

STUDENT SERVICES. Aptitude testing, career counseling, employment service for undergraduates, freshman orientation, health services, on-campus day care, personal counseling, placement service for graduates, veterans counselor, services/facilities for handicapped.

ANNUAL EXPENSES. Tuition and fees (projected): $2,088, $2,000 additional for out-of-district students, $4,000 additional for out-of-state students. **Books and supplies:** $540. **Other expenses:** $450.

FINANCIAL AID. 80% of freshmen, 80% of continuing students receive some form of aid. All grants, 84% of loans, all jobs based on need. Academic scholarships available. **Aid applications:** No closing date; priority given to applications received by March 1; applicants notified on a rolling basis beginning on or about April 1; must reply by April 15 or within 2 weeks if notified thereafter.

ADDRESS/TELEPHONE. Karen Bender, Director of Admissions, Onondaga Community College, Onondaga Road, Rte 173, Syracuse, NY 13215. (315) 469-2201. Fax: (315) 492-9208.

Orange County Community College
Middletown, New York — CB code: 2625

2-year public community college, coed. **Accreditation:** Regional. **Undergraduate enrollment:** 1,244 men, 1,410 women full time; 1,108 men, 2,265 women part time. **Faculty:** 349 total (149 full time), 17 with doctorates or other terminal degrees. **Location:** Suburban campus in large town; 25 miles from Newburgh, 60 miles from New York City. **Calendar:** Semester, limited summer session. Saturday and extensive evening/early morning classes. **Microcomputers:** Located in libraries, classrooms, computer centers. **Additional facts:** First community college founded as part of SUNY.

DEGREES OFFERED. AA, AS, AAS. 662 associate degrees awarded in 1992.

UNDERGRADUATE MAJORS. Accounting, architectural technologies, architecture, business administration and management, business and management, business data processing and related programs, child development/care/guidance, clinical laboratory science, communications, computer and information sciences, criminal justice studies, data processing, dental hygiene, electrical technology, electronic technology, engineering, exercise studies, finance, foreign languages (multiple emphasis), French, German, humanities and social sciences, law enforcement and corrections technologies, leisure services management, marketing management, math and science, mathematics, medical laboratory technologies, mental health/human services, nursing, occupational therapy assistant, physical therapy assistant, radiograph medical technology, real estate, recreation and community services technologies, retailing, secretarial and related programs, Spanish, word processing.

ACADEMIC PROGRAMS. 2-year transfer program, cooperative education, dual enrollment of high school students, independent study, internships, weekend college. **Remedial services:** Learning center, reduced course load, remedial instruction, special counselor, tutoring. **Placement/credit:** AP, CLEP Subject, institutional tests; 30 credit hours maximum for associate degree.

ACADEMIC REQUIREMENTS. Freshmen must earn minimum GPA of 2.0 to continue in good standing. 50% of freshmen return for sophomore year. Students must declare major by end of first year. **Graduation requirements:** 62 hours for associate (24 in major). Most students required to take courses in English, humanities, social sciences.

FRESHMAN ADMISSIONS. Selection criteria: Open admissions. Selective admissions for out-of-county residents. Admission to certain allied health and health science programs based on school achievement record. Test scores and recommendations considered.

1992 FRESHMAN CLASS PROFILE. 729 men, 1,014 women enrolled. **Characteristics:** 98% from in state, 100% commute, 17% have minority backgrounds, 1% are foreign students. Average age is 24.

FALL-TERM APPLICATIONS. $15 fee, may be waived for applicants with need. Closing date July 31; applicants notified on a rolling basis beginning on or about March 1. Interview recommended for dental hygiene, physical therapy assistant, occupational therapy assistant applicants. Deferred and early admission available. August 20 application closing date for all programs besides nursing and dental hygiene.

STUDENT LIFE. Activities: Student government, magazine, radio, student newspaper, television, yearbook, choral groups, concert band, dance, drama, jazz band, music ensembles, musical theater, Jewish Student Organization, Newman Club, Harvest Club, minority student club.

ATHLETICS. NJCAA. **Intercollegiate:** Baseball M, basketball, golf, soccer, softball W, swimming, tennis, volleyball W. **Intramural:** Racquetball, soccer M, softball, tennis, volleyball.

STUDENT SERVICES. Aptitude testing, career counseling, employment service for undergraduates, freshman orientation, health services, on-campus day care, personal counseling, placement service for graduates, special adviser for adult students, veterans counselor, services/facilities for handicapped.

ANNUAL EXPENSES. Tuition and fees (projected): $1,835, $1,750 additional for out-of-state students. **Books and supplies:** $525. **Other expenses:** $465.

FINANCIAL AID. 32% of continuing students receive some form of aid. Grants, loans, jobs available. Academic, music/drama, art, athletic, leadership scholarships available. **Aid applications:** No closing date; priority given to applications received by May 1; applicants notified on a rolling basis beginning on or about May 1; must reply within 2 weeks.

ADDRESS/TELEPHONE. Margot St. Lawrence, Director of Admissions, Orange County Community College, 115 South Street, Middletown, NY 10940. (914) 344-6222. Fax: (914) 343-1228.

Pace University

New York, New York CB code: 2635

Admissions:	68% of applicants accepted
Based on:	••• School record, test scores • Activities, essay, interview, recommendations, special talents
Completion:	90% of freshmen end year in good standing 55% graduate

4-year private university, coed. Founded in 1906. **Accreditation:** Regional. **Undergraduate enrollment:** 1,260 men, 1,914 women full time; 430 men, 768 women part time. **Graduate enrollment:** 138 men, 132 women full time; 1,103 men, 813 women part time. **Faculty:** 485 total (206 full time). **Location:** Urban campus in very large city. **Calendar:** Semester, limited summer session. Saturday classes. **Microcomputers:** Located in computer centers.

DEGREES OFFERED. AA, AS, AAS, BA, BS, MS, MBA, MFA, MEd, D. 56 associate degrees awarded in 1992. 769 bachelor's degrees awarded. Graduate degrees offered in 15 major fields of study.

UNDERGRADUATE MAJORS. Associate: Accounting, business and management, dramatic arts, early childhood education, finance, information sciences and systems, secretarial and related programs. **Bachelor's:** Accounting, anthropology, art history, biology, business administration and management, business and management, business economics, business education, chemical engineering, chemistry, clinical laboratory science, computer and information sciences, dramatic arts, early childhood education, economics, electrical/electronics/communications engineering, English, finance, French, history, humanities and social sciences, information sciences and systems, insurance and risk management, international business management, labor/industrial relations, liberal/general studies, management information systems, management science, marketing management, mathematics, medical records administration, nursing, office information systems, political science and government, predentistry, prelaw, premedicine, psychology, real estate, respiratory therapy technology, retailing, secretarial and related programs, social psychology, social sciences, sociology, Spanish, speech, speech pathology/audiology, technology theater, theater design, ultrasound technology.

ACADEMIC PROGRAMS. 2-year transfer program, cooperative education, dual enrollment of high school students, honors program, independent study, internships, study abroad, teacher preparation, weekend college, cross-registration; liberal arts/career combination in engineering; combined bachelor's/graduate program in business administration. **Remedial services:** Learning center, reduced course load, remedial instruction, tutoring. **ROTC:** Air Force. **Placement/credit:** AP, CLEP General and Subject, institutional tests; 30 credit hours maximum for associate degree; 90 credit hours maximum for bachelor's degree.

ACADEMIC REQUIREMENTS. Freshmen must earn minimum GPA of 2.0 to continue in good standing. 80% of freshmen return for sophomore year. Students must declare major by end of second year. **Graduation requirements:** 64 hours for associate (15 in major), 128 hours for bachelor's (24 in major). Most students required to take courses in arts/fine arts, computer science, English, foreign languages, history, humanities, mathematics, philosophy/religion, biological/physical sciences, social sciences. **Additional information:** Continuing education degrees in liberal/general studies available.

FRESHMAN ADMISSIONS. Selection criteria: 3.0 high school GPA, rank in top half of class, test scores, recommendations, personal statement important. Extracurricular activities also considered. **High school preparation:** 16 units required; 20 recommended. Required and recommended units include English 4, foreign language 2-3, mathematics 3-4, social science 4 and science 2-4. 2 required science units must be laboratory science. **Test requirements:** SAT or ACT; score report by August 15.

1992 FRESHMAN CLASS PROFILE. 1,800 men and women applied, 1,228 accepted; 392 enrolled. 67% had high school GPA of 3.0 or higher, 33% between 2.0 and 2.99. 27% were in top tenth and 60% were in top quarter of graduating class. **Academic background:** Mid 50% of enrolled freshmen had SAT-V between 350-550, SAT-M between 400-600. 90% submitted SAT scores. **Characteristics:** 88% from in state, 90% commute, 59% have minority backgrounds, 5% are foreign students. Average age is 19.

FALL-TERM APPLICATIONS. $25 fee, may be waived for applicants with need. Closing date August 15; priority given to applications received by February 1; applicants notified on a rolling basis; must reply by May 1 or within 3 weeks if notified thereafter. Interview recommended. Essay recommended. CRDA. Deferred and early admission available. EDP-F. English, mathematics, and science ACH recommended for nursing students; score report by August 15.

STUDENT LIFE. Housing: Dormitories (coed). **Activities:** Student government, magazine, radio, student newspaper, television, yearbook, dance, drama, music club, fraternities, sororities, Model United Nations team, debate team, ethnic and foreign student associations, honor societies, religious groups, American Humanics Students Association.

ATHLETICS. NCAA. **Intercollegiate:** Baseball M, basketball, cross-country, fencing W, football M, golf, lacrosse M, softball W, tennis, volleyball W. **Intramural:** Basketball, horseback riding, ice hockey M, rugby, skiing, softball, tennis, volleyball.

STUDENT SERVICES. Aptitude testing, career counseling, employment service for undergraduates, freshman orientation, health services, on-campus day care, personal counseling, placement service for graduates, special adviser for adult students, veterans counselor, services/facilities for handicapped.

ANNUAL EXPENSES. Tuition and fees (1992-93): $10,100. **Room and board:** $4,660. **Books and supplies:** $500. **Other expenses:** $850.

FINANCIAL AID. 76% of freshmen, 70% of continuing students receive some form of aid. 86% of grants, 88% of loans, 35% of jobs based on need. Academic, music/drama, athletic, leadership scholarships available. **Aid applications:** Closing date July 1; priority given to applications received by March 15; applicants notified on a rolling basis beginning on or about February 1; must reply by May 1 or within 3 weeks if notified thereafter.

ADDRESS/TELEPHONE. Leo Kornfeld, Vice President for Enrollment Planning, Pace University, Pace Plaza, New York, NY 10038. (212) 346-1323. Fax: (212) 346-1643.

Pace University: College of White Plains
White Plains, New York CB code: 2276

Admissions: 67% of applicants accepted
Based on: ••• School record, test scores
• Activities, essay, interview, recommendations, special talents
Completion: 90% of freshmen end year in good standing
50% graduate

4-year private university, coed. Founded in 1923. **Accreditation:** Regional. **Undergraduate enrollment:** 257 men, 489 women full time; 55 men, 116 women part time. **Graduate enrollment:** 91 men, 66 women full time; 775 men, 713 women part time. **Faculty:** 482 total (208 full time). **Location:** Suburban campus in small city; 25 miles from New York City. **Calendar:** Semester, limited summer session. **Microcomputers:** Located in computer centers. **Additional facts:** Branch campus including school of law and law library.

DEGREES OFFERED. AA, AS, AAS, BA, BS, MS, MBA, JD. 4 associate degrees awarded in 1992. 238 bachelor's degrees awarded. Graduate degrees offered in 12 major fields of study.

UNDERGRADUATE MAJORS. Associate: Accounting, business and management, information sciences and systems, secretarial and related programs. **Bachelor's:** Accounting, aerospace/aeronautical/astronautical engineering, anthropology, bioengineering and biomedical engineering, biology, business administration and management, business education, chemical engineering, chemistry, civil engineering, communications, computer and information sciences, computer engineering, economics, electrical/electronics/communications engineering, elementary education, English, finance, French, history, humanities and social sciences, industrial engineering, information sciences and systems, international business management, journalism, liberal/general studies, management information systems, marketing management, materials engineering, mathematics, nuclear engineering, office information systems, political science and government, prelaw, psychology, retailing, secondary education, secretarial and related programs, social psychology, sociology, sociology/anthropology, Spanish.

ACADEMIC PROGRAMS. 2-year transfer program, cooperative education, dual enrollment of high school students, honors program, independent study, internships, study abroad, teacher preparation, cross-registration; liberal arts/career combination in engineering; combined bachelor's/graduate program in business administration. **Remedial services:** Reduced course load, remedial instruction, tutoring, writing center. **ROTC:** Air Force. **Placement/credit:** AP, CLEP General and Subject, institutional tests; 30 credit hours maximum for associate degree; 90 credit hours maximum for bachelor's degree.

ACADEMIC REQUIREMENTS. Freshmen must earn minimum GPA of 2.0 to continue in good standing. 80% of freshmen return for sophomore year. Students must declare major by end of second year. **Graduation requirements:** 64 hours for associate (15 in major), 128 hours for bachelor's (24 in major). Most students required to take courses in arts/fine arts, computer science, English, foreign languages, history, humanities, mathematics, philosophy/religion, biological/physical sciences, social sciences. **Additional information:** Continuing education degree in liberal/general studies available.

FRESHMAN ADMISSIONS. Selection criteria: 3.0 high school GPA, rank in top half of class, test scores, recommendations, and personal statement important. Extracurricular activities considered. **High school preparation:** 16 units required; 20 recommended. Required and recommended units include English 4, foreign language 2-3, mathematics 3-4, social science 4 and science 2-4. 2 required science units must be laboratory science. **Test requirements:** SAT or ACT; score report by August 15.

1992 FRESHMAN CLASS PROFILE. 441 men and women applied, 296 accepted; 91 enrolled. 60% had high school GPA of 3.0 or higher, 40% between 2.0 and 2.99. 16% were in top tenth and 58% were in top quarter of graduating class. **Academic background:** Mid 50% of enrolled freshmen had SAT-V between 350-550, SAT-M between 400-600. 65% submitted SAT scores. **Characteristics:** 75% from in state, 70% commute, 40% have minority backgrounds, 8% are foreign students. Average age is 18.

FALL-TERM APPLICATIONS. $25 fee, may be waived for applicants with need. Closing date August 15; priority given to applications received by February 1; applicants notified on a rolling basis; must reply by May 1 or within 3 weeks if notified thereafter. Interview recommended. Essay recommended. CRDA. Deferred and early admission available. EDP-F.

STUDENT LIFE. Housing: Dormitories (coed). **Activities:** Student government, magazine, student newspaper, yearbook, dance, drama, Black Student Union, Spanish club, Caribbean Students Association, activities council, Circle-K, resident student association, Silver Gavel Society.

ATHLETICS. NCAA. **Intercollegiate:** Baseball M, basketball, cross-country, football M, golf, lacrosse M, softball W, tennis, volleyball W. **Intramural:** Basketball, horseback riding, ice hockey M, rugby, skiing, softball, tennis, volleyball.

STUDENT SERVICES. Aptitude testing, career counseling, employment service for undergraduates, freshman orientation, health services, on-campus day care, personal counseling, placement service for graduates, special adviser for adult students, services/facilities for handicapped.

ANNUAL EXPENSES. Tuition and fees (1992-93): $10,100. **Room and board:** $4,660. **Books and supplies:** $500. **Other expenses:** $850.

FINANCIAL AID. 61% of freshmen, 60% of continuing students receive some form of aid. 63% of grants, 90% of loans, 18% of jobs based on need. Academic, leadership scholarships available. **Aid applications:** Closing date July 1; priority given to applications received by March 15; applicants notified on a rolling basis beginning on or about March 1; must reply by May 1 or within 3 weeks if notified thereafter.

ADDRESS/TELEPHONE. Leo Kornfeld, Vice President of Enrollment Planning, Pace University: College of White Plains, 78 North Broadway, White Plains, NY 10603-3796. (914) 422-4070. Fax: (914) 422-4028.

Pace University: Pleasantville/Briarcliff
Pleasantville, New York CB code: 2685

Admissions: 80% of applicants accepted
Based on: ••• School record, test scores
• Activities, essay, interview, recommendations, special talents
Completion: 90% of freshmen end year in good standing
65% graduate

4-year private university, coed. Founded in 1963. **Accreditation:** Regional. **Undergraduate enrollment:** 1,256 men, 1,713 women full time; 114 men, 219 women part time. **Graduate enrollment:** 2 men, 8 women full time; 8 men, 180 women part time. **Faculty:** 524 total (225 full time). **Location:** Suburban campus in small town; 10 miles from White Plains. **Calendar:** Semester, limited summer session. **Microcomputers:** Located in computer centers. **Special facilities:** Environmental farm. **Additional facts:** Branch campus including school of nursing.

DEGREES OFFERED. AA, AS, AAS, BA, BS, BFA, MS, MBA. 35 associate degrees awarded in 1992. 888 bachelor's degrees awarded. Graduate degrees offered in 7 major fields of study.

UNDERGRADUATE MAJORS. Associate: Accounting, business and management, equestrian science, fine arts, information sciences and systems, interior design, nursing, visual and performing arts. **Bachelor's:** Accounting, aerospace/aeronautical/astronautical engineering, anthropology, biochemistry, bioengineering and biomedical engineering, biology, business administration and management, business education, chemical engineering, chemistry, civil engineering, clinical laboratory science, communications, computer and information sciences, computer engineering, criminal justice studies, economics, electrical/electronics/communications engineering, elementary education, finance, French, history, industrial engineering, information sciences and systems, international business management, international studies, journalism, liberal/general studies, literature and communications, management information systems, marketing management, materials engineering, mathematics, nuclear engineering, nursing, office information systems, political science and government, prelaw, psychology, retailing, secondary education, social psychology, social sciences, sociology, sociology/anthropology, Spanish, studio art, urban studies.

ACADEMIC PROGRAMS. 2-year transfer program, cooperative education, dual enrollment of high school students, honors program, independent study, study abroad; liberal arts/career combination in engineering; combined bachelor's/graduate program in business administration, law. **Remedial services:** Reduced course load, tutoring, writing center. **ROTC:** Air Force. **Placement/credit:** AP, CLEP General and Subject, institutional tests; 30 credit hours maximum for associate degree; 90 credit hours maximum for bachelor's degree.

ACADEMIC REQUIREMENTS. Freshmen must earn minimum GPA of 2.0 to continue in good standing. 80% of freshmen return for sophomore year. Students must declare major by end of second year. **Graduation requirements:** 64 hours for associate, 128 hours for bachelor's. Most students required to take courses in arts/fine arts, computer science, English, foreign languages, history, humanities, mathematics, philosophy/religion, biological/physical sciences, social sciences.

FRESHMAN ADMISSIONS. Selection criteria: 3.0 high school GPA, rank in top half of class, test scores, recommendations, personal statement important. Extracurricular activities also considered. **High school preparation:** 16 units required; 20 recommended. Required and recommended units include English 4, foreign language 2-3, mathematics 3-4 and science 2-4. 2 required science units must be in laboratory sciences. **Test requirements:** SAT or ACT; score report by August 15.

1992 FRESHMAN CLASS PROFILE. 1,672 men and women applied, 1,338 accepted; 397 enrolled. 70% had high school GPA of 3.0 or higher, 30% between 2.0 and 2.99. 16% were in top tenth and 44% were in top quarter of graduating class. **Academic background:** Mid 50% of enrolled freshmen had SAT-V between 350-550, SAT-M between 400-600. 90% submitted SAT scores. **Characteristics:** 78% from in state, 60% commute, 16% have minority backgrounds, 2% are foreign students. Average age is 18.

FALL-TERM APPLICATIONS. $25 fee, may be waived for applicants with need. Closing date August 15; priority given to applications received by February 1; applicants notified on a rolling basis; must reply by May 1 or within 3 weeks if notified thereafter. Portfolio required for art applicants.

Interview recommended. Essay recommended. CRDA. Deferred and early admission available. EDP-F. English, mathematics, and science ACH recommended for nursing students; score report by August 15.

STUDENT LIFE. Housing: Dormitories (men, women, coed). Achievement House available for select upperclassmen. **Activities:** Student government, magazine, radio, student newspaper, television, yearbook, choral groups, dance, drama, fraternities, sororities, Newman Club, Jewish Students Association, Interdenominational Church, debate team, ethnic associations, ecology club.

ATHLETICS. NCAA. **Intercollegiate:** Baseball M, basketball, cross-country, football M, golf, lacrosse M, softball W, tennis, volleyball W. **Intramural:** Basketball, horseback riding, ice hockey M, rugby, skiing, softball, tennis, volleyball.

STUDENT SERVICES. Aptitude testing, career counseling, employment service for undergraduates, freshman orientation, health services, on-campus day care, personal counseling, placement service for graduates, special adviser for adult students, services/facilities for handicapped.

ANNUAL EXPENSES. Tuition and fees (1992-93): $10,100. **Room and board:** $4,660. **Books and supplies:** $500. **Other expenses:** $800.

FINANCIAL AID. 58% of freshmen, 55% of continuing students receive some form of aid. 74% of grants, 94% of loans, 12% of jobs based on need. Academic, music/drama, athletic, leadership scholarships available. **Aid applications:** Closing date July 1; priority given to applications received by March 15; applicants notified on a rolling basis beginning on or about February 1; must reply by May 1 or within 3 weeks if notified thereafter.

ADDRESS/TELEPHONE. Leo Kornfeld, Vice President for Enrollment Planning, Pace University: Pleasantville/Briarcliff, Bedford Road, Pleasantville, NY 10570. (914) 773-3746. Fax: (914) 773-3541.

Parsons School of Design
New York, New York — CB code: 2638

Admissions:	33% of applicants accepted
Based on:	••• School record, special talents
	•• Essay, interview, test scores
	• Activities, recommendations
Completion:	88% of freshmen end year in good standing
	65% graduate, 12% of these enter graduate study

4-year private art college, coed. Founded in 1896. **Accreditation:** Regional. **Undergraduate enrollment:** 840 men, 1,000 women full time. **Graduate enrollment:** 75 men, 95 women full time. **Faculty:** 435 total (35 full time). **Location:** Urban campus in very large city. **Calendar:** Semester, extensive summer session. **Microcomputers:** 75 located in libraries, computer centers. **Special facilities:** 2 art galleries, with exhibitions rotated monthly. **Additional facts:** Division of New School for Social Research.

DEGREES OFFERED. AAS, BFA, MA, MFA. 145 associate degrees awarded in 1992. 100% in visual and performing arts. 419 bachelor's degrees awarded. 10% in architecture and environmental design, 87% visual and performing arts. Graduate degrees offered in 6 major fields of study.

UNDERGRADUATE MAJORS. Associate: Ceramics, crafts, fashion design, fiber/textiles/weaving, fine arts, graphic arts technology, graphic design, illustration design, interior design, metal/jewelry, painting, photography, sculpture, studio art. **Bachelor's:** Advertising, apparel and accessories marketing, architecture, art education, ceramics, drawing, environmental design, fashion design, fashion merchandising, fiber/textiles/weaving, fine arts, glass, graphic design, illustration design, industrial design, interior design, marketing and distribution, metal/jewelry, painting, photography, printmaking, sculpture, studio art, urban design.

ACADEMIC PROGRAMS. 2-year transfer program, study abroad, teacher preparation, visiting/exchange student program, cross-registration, five-year combined BA/BFA, New York Studio Program. **Remedial services:** Tutoring, Higher Education Opportunity Program for New York State residents. **Placement/credit:** AP, institutional tests.

ACADEMIC REQUIREMENTS. Freshmen must earn minimum GPA of 2.0 to continue in good standing. 84% of freshmen return for sophomore year. Students must declare major by end of first year. **Graduation requirements:** 65 hours for associate, 134 hours for bachelor's (79 in major). Most students required to take courses in arts/fine arts, English, history, humanities, philosophy/religion, biological/physical sciences, social sciences.

FRESHMAN ADMISSIONS. Selection criteria: Portfolio and home examination most important, followed by school achievement record and test scores. Activities, leadership, motivation considered. Recommended units include English 4, mathematics 3 and social science 4. As much art as possible also recommended. **Test requirements:** SAT or ACT (SAT preferred); score report by April 1. Applicants required to complete home examination of 4 specific art and design problems as supplement to portfolio.

1992 FRESHMAN CLASS PROFILE. 2,000 men and women applied, 657 accepted; 129 men enrolled, 228 women enrolled. 75% had high school GPA of 3.0 or higher, 25% between 2.0 and 2.99. **Academic background:** Mid 50% of enrolled freshmen had SAT-V between 490-590, SAT-M between 460-560. 90% submitted SAT scores. **Characteristics:** 29% from in state, 80% live in college housing, 19% have minority backgrounds, 19% are foreign students. Average age is 18.

FALL-TERM APPLICATIONS. $30 fee, may be waived for applicants with need. Closing date July 1; priority given to applications received by April 1; applicants notified on a rolling basis; must reply by May 1 or within 4 weeks if notified thereafter. Interview required for geographically close applicants. Portfolio required. Essay recommended. CRDA. Early admission available.

STUDENT LIFE. Housing: Dormitories (coed). **Activities:** Student government, student newspaper. **Additional information:** Of students who do not reside in college housing, most live in their own apartments off campus.

STUDENT SERVICES. Career counseling, employment service for undergraduates, freshman orientation, personal counseling, placement service for graduates, services/facilities for handicapped.

ANNUAL EXPENSES. Tuition and fees (1992-93): $13,216. **Room and board:** $6,700. **Books and supplies:** $1,200. **Other expenses:** $1,080.

FINANCIAL AID. 85% of freshmen, 85% of continuing students receive some form of aid. All aid based on need. **Aid applications:** Closing date July 1; priority given to applications received by March 1; applicants notified on a rolling basis beginning on or about April 1; must reply by May 1 or within 4 weeks if notified thereafter.

ADDRESS/TELEPHONE. Nadine M. Bourgeois, Director of Admissions, Parsons School of Design, 66 Fifth Avenue, New York, NY 10011. (212) 229-8910. (800) 252-0852. Fax: (212) 229-8975.

Paul Smith's College
Paul Smiths, New York — CB code: 2640

Admissions:	96% of applicants accepted
Based on:	••• School record
	•• Activities, essay, recommendations, special talents
	• Interview
Completion:	87% of freshmen end year in good standing
	57% graduate, 36% of these enter 4-year programs

2-year private college of arts and sciences and junior college, coed. Founded in 1937. **Accreditation:** Regional. **Undergraduate enrollment:** 531 men, 242 women full time; 16 men, 20 women part time. **Faculty:** 66 total (54 full time), 8 with doctorates or other terminal degrees. **Location:** Rural campus in rural community; 21 miles from Lake Placid, 150 miles from Albany. **Calendar:** Semester, limited summer session. **Microcomputers:** 60 located in libraries, classrooms, computer centers. **Special facilities:** Sugar maple plantation, sawmill, hotel, restaurant, and travel agency (student training facilities owned and operated by college), commercial tree seed processing operation, 13,000-acre forest, forest fire simulator, gas and ion chromatographs, computer-aided drafting and design laboratory. **Additional facts:** Hands-on experience in major, internship programs within college, and externships with leading companies.

DEGREES OFFERED. AA, AS, AAS. 175 associate degrees awarded in 1992. 21% in agriculture, 60% business and management, 7% parks/recreation, protective services, public affairs, 10% physical sciences.

UNDERGRADUATE MAJORS. American studies, biological and physical sciences, business and management, chef training, ecology, ecology and environmental technology, environmental science, environmental studies, food production/management/services, food science and nutrition, forestry and related sciences, franchise management, hospitality and recreation marketing, hotel/motel and restaurant management, liberal/general studies, mathematics, parks and recreation management, physical sciences, survey and mapping technology, surveying and mapping sciences, technical and business writing, technical communications, tourism, urban tree management, water and wastewater technology.

ACADEMIC PROGRAMS. 2-year transfer program, cooperative education, double major, independent study, internships, study abroad. **Remedial services:** Learning center, reduced course load, remedial instruction, special counselor, tutoring, New York State Higher Education Opportunity Program. **Placement/credit:** AP, CLEP Subject, institutional tests; 15 credit hours maximum for associate degree.

ACADEMIC REQUIREMENTS. Freshmen must earn minimum GPA of 1.5 to continue in good standing. 85% of freshmen return for sophomore year. Students must declare major on application. **Graduation requirements:** 72 hours for associate (34 in major). Most students required to take courses in English, mathematics, biological/physical sciences, social sciences. **Additional information:** Hotel and Resturant Management, Culinary Arts, and Travel and Tourism students spend semester in college's Hotel, Restaurant, and Travel Agency.

FRESHMAN ADMISSIONS. Selection criteria: High school GPA, interview, extracurricular activities, recommendations are important. **High school preparation:** 8 units required. Required units include English 4, mathematics 2 and science 2. High school subject requirements vary according to program. All programs require 1 algebra and 1 laboratory science.

1992 FRESHMAN CLASS PROFILE. Characteristics: 64% from in state, 97% live in college housing, 4% have minority backgrounds, 4% are foreign students. Average age is 19.

FALL-TERM APPLICATIONS. $20 fee, may be waived for applicants with need. No closing date; applicants notified on a rolling basis; must reply by May 1 or within 3 weeks if notified thereafter. Interview recommended. Essay recommended. CRDA. Deferred and early admission available. SAT/ACT scores optional. If submitted, will be used for placement.

STUDENT LIFE. Housing: Dormitories (men, women, coed). Campus housing guaranteed. Athletic scholarships also offered for men and women in alpine and nordic skiing and in woodsmen's teams. **Activities:** Student government, magazine, radio, student newspaper, yearbook, choral groups, drama, musical theater, Phi Theta Kappa, Students Against Driving Drunk, Cool It Environmental Club, International Students Club, Campus Fellowship Club.

ATHLETICS. NJCAA. **Intercollegiate:** Basketball, skiing, soccer. **Intramural:** Basketball, bowling, ice hockey M, skiing, soccer, softball, table tennis, tennis, volleyball.

STUDENT SERVICES. Career counseling, employment service for undergraduates, freshman orientation, health services, personal counseling, placement service for graduates, special adviser for adult students, veterans counselor, services/facilities for handicapped.

ANNUAL EXPENSES. Tuition and fees: $9,790. **Room and board:** $4,120. **Books and supplies:** $677. **Other expenses:** $1,000.

FINANCIAL AID. 82% of freshmen, 80% of continuing students receive some form of aid. All grants, 91% of loans, all jobs based on need. Academic, athletic, leadership, alumni affiliation scholarships available. **Aid applications:** No closing date; priority given to applications received by February 28; applicants notified on a rolling basis beginning on or about March 15; must reply within 2 weeks.

ADDRESS/TELEPHONE. Enrico Miller, Dean of Admissions, Paul Smith's College, Intersection of Routes 30 and 86, Paul Smiths, NY 12970-0265. (518) 327-6227. (800) 421-2605. Fax: (518) 327-3030.

Phillips Beth Israel School of Nursing
New York, New York — CB code: 2031

Admissions:	7% of applicants accepted
Based on:	••• Interview, school record, test scores
	•• Activities, essay, recommendations
	• Special talents
Completion:	85% of freshmen end year in good standing
	80% graduate, 70% of these enter 4-year programs

2-year private nursing college, coed. Founded in 1904. **Undergraduate enrollment:** 37 men, 131 women full time; 6 men, 18 women part time. **Faculty:** 37 total (23 full time), 11 with doctorates or other terminal degrees. **Location:** Urban campus in very large city. **Calendar:** Semester, limited summer session. **Microcomputers:** 11 located in libraries, computer centers.

DEGREES OFFERED. AAS. 68 associate degrees awarded in 1992. 100% in health sciences.

UNDERGRADUATE MAJORS. Nursing.

ACADEMIC PROGRAMS. 2-year transfer program. **Remedial services:** Learning center, preadmission summer program, reduced course load, remedial instruction, special counselor, tutoring. **Placement/credit:** Institutional tests.

ACADEMIC REQUIREMENTS. Freshmen must earn minimum GPA of 2.0 to continue in good standing. 85% of freshmen return for sophomore year. Students must declare major on enrollment. **Graduation requirements:** 67 hours for associate. Most students required to take courses in English, philosophy/religion, biological/physical sciences, social sciences.

FRESHMAN ADMISSIONS. Selection criteria: Academic achievement, aptitude test scores, personal interview, recommendations, and prior experience of primary consideration. 55th percentile score on National League for Nursing's Preadmission Examination-RN mandatory standing in top half of high school class recommended. **High school preparation:** 16 units required. Required units include biological science 1, English 4, mathematics 2, physical science 1 and social science 2. Chemistry and biology required.

1992 FRESHMAN CLASS PROFILE. 130 men applied, 10 accepted, 9 enrolled; 225 women applied, 15 accepted, 10 enrolled. 30% had high school GPA of 3.0 or higher, 70% between 2.0 and 2.99. 25% were in top tenth and 60% were in top quarter of graduating class. **Academic background:** Mid 50% of enrolled freshmen had SAT-V between 350-450, SAT-M between 370-470. 35% submitted SAT scores. **Characteristics:** 98% from in state, 100% commute, 90% have minority backgrounds, 8% are foreign students. Average age is 32.

FALL-TERM APPLICATIONS. $25 fee, may be waived for applicants with need. Closing date April 1; applicants notified on or about May 15; must reply within 3 weeks. Interview required. Essay required. Deferred admission available.

STUDENT LIFE. Activities: Student government, yearbook.

STUDENT SERVICES. Career counseling, freshman orientation, health services, personal counseling, services/facilities for handicapped.

ANNUAL EXPENSES. Tuition and fees: $6,710. **Books and supplies:** $910. **Other expenses:** $1,180.

FINANCIAL AID. 95% of freshmen, 95% of continuing students receive some form of aid. 40% of grants, 82% of loans based on need. Academic scholarships available. **Aid applications:** Closing date June 1; applicants notified on or about July 1; must reply within 3 weeks. **Additional information:** Full scholarship program available to qualified students based on academics.

ADDRESS/TELEPHONE. Bernice Pass-Stern, Coordinator of Student Services, Phillips Beth Israel School of Nursing, 310 East 22nd Street, New York, NY 10010. (212) 614-6108. Fax: (212) 614-6109.

Plaza Business Institute
Jackson Heights, New York — CB code: 0545

2-year proprietary business, junior college, coed. Founded in 1916. **Undergraduate enrollment:** 122 men, 638 women full time. **Location:** Urban campus in very large city. **Calendar:** Quarter.

FRESHMAN ADMISSIONS. Selection criteria: Essay, interview, and test scores most important.

ANNUAL EXPENSES. Tuition and fees: $4,925. **Books and supplies:** $600. **Other expenses:** $900.

ADDRESS/TELEPHONE. Sally Ann Weger, Director of Admissions, Plaza Business Institute, 74-09 37th Avenue, Jackson Heights, NY 11372. (718) 779-1430. Fax: (718) 779-1456.

Polytechnic University
Brooklyn, New York — CB code: 2668

Admissions:	75% of applicants accepted
Based on:	••• School record, test scores
	•• Recommendations
	• Activities, essay, interview
Completion:	78% of freshmen end year in good standing
	45% graduate, 5% of these enter graduate study

4-year private university, coed. Founded in 1854. **Accreditation:** Regional. **Undergraduate enrollment:** 873 men, 136 women full time; 112 men, 16 women part time. **Graduate enrollment:** 256 men, 29 women full time; 621 men, 96 women part time. **Faculty:** 393 total (195 full time), 369 with doctorates or other terminal degrees. **Location:** Urban campus in very large city. **Calendar:** Semester, extensive summer session. **Microcomputers:** 160 located in libraries, computer centers. **Additional facts:** Long Island campus in Farmingdale offers both undergraduate and graduate engineering programs. Graduate center in Hawthorne (Westchester county).

DEGREES OFFERED. BS, MS, PhD. 235 bachelor's degrees awarded in 1992. 5% in computer sciences, 87% engineering. Graduate degrees offered in 22 major fields of study.

UNDERGRADUATE MAJORS. Aerospace/aeronautical/astronautical engineering, applied mathematics, chemical engineering, chemistry, civil engineering, computer and information sciences, computer engineering, electrical/electronics/communications engineering, humanities and social sciences, industrial engineering, journalism, management information systems, materials engineering, mathematics, mechanical engineering, metallurgical engineering, operations research, physics, social sciences.

ACADEMIC PROGRAMS. Cooperative education, double major, honors program, joint master's degree program in dental materials science with New York University. **Remedial services:** Learning center, preadmission summer program, special counselor, tutoring. **ROTC:** Air Force, Army. **Placement/credit:** AP, institutional tests; 18 credit hours maximum for bachelor's degree.

ACADEMIC REQUIREMENTS. Freshmen must earn minimum GPA of 2.0 to continue in good standing. 75% of freshmen return for sophomore year. Students must declare major by end of first year. **Graduation requirements:** 136 hours for bachelor's. Most students required to take courses in computer science, English, humanities, mathematics, biological/physical sciences, social sciences.

FRESHMAN ADMISSIONS. Selection criteria: School achievement record, class rank, test scores, and recommendations required. Special emphasis on mathematics and science areas. **High school preparation:** 16 units required. Required and recommended units include English 4, mathematics 3-4 and physical science 2-3. Foreign language 2 and social science 3 recommended. Requirement includes 1 chemistry, 1 physics. Pre-calculus and advanced laboratory science strongly recommended. **Test requirements:** SAT or ACT (SAT preferred); score report by March 1.

1992 FRESHMAN CLASS PROFILE. 654 men applied, 489 accepted, 186 enrolled; 115 women applied, 86 accepted, 26 enrolled. 99% had high school GPA of 3.0 or higher, 1% between 2.0 and 2.99. 42% were in top tenth and 73% were in top quarter of graduating class. **Academic background:** Mid 50% of enrolled freshmen had SAT-V between 450-550, SAT-M between 550-650. 99% submitted SAT scores. **Characteristics:** 91% from in state, 95% commute, 68% have minority backgrounds, 9% are foreign students. Average age is 18.

FALL-TERM APPLICATIONS. $40 fee, may be waived for applicants with need. No closing date; priority given to applications received by February 1; applicants notified on a rolling basis beginning on or about February 1; must reply by May 1 or within 4 weeks if notified thereafter. Interview recommended. Essay recommended. CRDA. Deferred and early admission available. EDP-F.

STUDENT LIFE. Housing: Dormitories (coed); fraternity housing available. Housing available through Long Island University, Brooklyn Campus and Pratt Institute. **Activities:** Student government, student newspaper, yearbook, jazz band, fraternities, sororities, Society of Women Engineers, Society of Black Engineers, Ambassador Society, ethnic and service organizations.

ATHLETICS. NCAA. **Intercollegiate:** Baseball M, basketball M, cross-country M, lacrosse M, soccer M, tennis M, volleyball W, wrestling M. **Intramural:** Basketball, handball M, skiing, soccer, softball, table tennis.

STUDENT SERVICES. Career counseling, employment service for undergraduates, freshman orientation, placement service for graduates, services/facilities for handicapped.

ANNUAL EXPENSES. Tuition and fees (1992-93): $15,620. **Room and board:** $4,400. **Books and supplies:** $436. **Other expenses:** $1,225.

FINANCIAL AID. 93% of freshmen, 85% of continuing students receive some form of aid. 66% of grants, 83% of loans, all jobs based on need. 292 enrolled freshmen were judged to have need, all were offered aid. Academic scholarships available. **Aid applications:** No closing date; priority given to applications received by March 1; applicants notified on a rolling basis beginning on or about March 15; must reply by May 1 or within 4 weeks if notified thereafter.

ADDRESS/TELEPHONE. Ellen F. Hartigan, Dean of Admissions and Enrollment Planning, Polytechnic University, 6 Metrotech Center, Brooklyn, NY 11201-2999. (718) 260-3100. (800) POLYTEC. Fax: (718) 260-3136.

Polytechnic University: Long Island Campus
Farmingdale, New York — CB code: 2695

Admissions: 73% of applicants accepted
Based on: ••• School record, test scores
•• Recommendations
• Activities, essay, interview
Completion: 78% of freshmen end year in good standing
50% graduate, 5% of these enter graduate study

4-year private university, coed. Founded in 1961. **Accreditation:** Regional. **Undergraduate enrollment:** 311 men, 34 women full time; 46 men, 5 women part time. **Graduate enrollment:** 15 men, 6 women full time; 170 men, 24 women part time. **Faculty:** 393 total (195 full time), 369 with doctorates or other terminal degrees. **Location:** Suburban campus in large town; 40 miles from New York City. **Calendar:** Semester, extensive summer session. **Microcomputers:** 160 located in dormitories, libraries, classrooms, computer centers. **Additional facts:** Brooklyn campus offers engineering and science disciplines, humanities and social science programs. Graduate center in Hawthorne (Westchester county).

DEGREES OFFERED. BS, MS, PhD. 72 bachelor's degrees awarded in 1992. 7% in computer sciences, 92% engineering. Graduate degrees offered in 7 major fields of study.

UNDERGRADUATE MAJORS. Aerospace/aeronautical/astronautical engineering, chemical engineering, chemistry, civil engineering, computer and information sciences, computer engineering, electrical/electronics/communications engineering, industrial engineering, management information systems, mathematics, mechanical engineering, metallurgical engineering.

ACADEMIC PROGRAMS. Accelerated program, cooperative education, double major, honors program, cross-registration. **Remedial services:** Learning center, preadmission summer program, special counselor, tutoring. **ROTC:** Air Force, Army. **Placement/credit:** AP, institutional tests; 18 credit hours maximum for bachelor's degree.

ACADEMIC REQUIREMENTS. Freshmen must earn minimum GPA of 2.0 to continue in good standing. 80% of freshmen return for sophomore year. Students must declare major by end of first year. **Graduation requirements:** 136 hours for bachelor's. Most students required to take courses in computer science, English, humanities, mathematics, biological/physical sciences, social sciences.

FRESHMAN ADMISSIONS. Selection criteria: School achievement record, class rank, test scores, and recommendations. Special emphasis on mathematics and science areas. **High school preparation:** 16 units required. Required and recommended units include English 4, mathematics 3-4 and physical science 2-3. Foreign language 2 and social science 3 recommended. One chemistry, 1 physics also required. Pre-calculus and advanced laboratory science strongly recommended. **Test requirements:** SAT or ACT (SAT preferred); score report by September 1.

1992 FRESHMAN CLASS PROFILE. 357 men applied, 261 accepted, 77 enrolled; 63 women applied, 46 accepted, 10 enrolled. 99% had high school GPA of 3.0 or higher, 1% between 2.0 and 2.99. 69% were in top tenth and 80% were in top quarter of graduating class. **Academic background:** Mid 50% of enrolled freshmen had SAT-V between 450-550, SAT-M between 550-650. 99% submitted SAT scores. **Characteristics:** 94% from in state, 80% commute, 34% have minority backgrounds, 2% are foreign students, 15% join fraternities/sororities. Average age is 18.

FALL-TERM APPLICATIONS. $40 fee, may be waived for applicants with need. No closing date; priority given to applications received by February 1; applicants notified on a rolling basis beginning on or about February 1; must reply by May 1 or within 4 weeks if notified thereafter. Interview recommended. Essay recommended. CRDA. Deferred and early admission available. EDP-F.

STUDENT LIFE. Housing: Dormitories (coed). **Activities:** Student government, student newspaper, yearbook, jazz band, fraternities, Society of Women Engineers, Society of Black Engineers, ethnic organizations, service organization, Ambassador Society.

ATHLETICS. NCAA. **Intercollegiate:** Baseball M, basketball M, cross-country M, lacrosse M, soccer M, tennis M, volleyball W, wrestling M. **Intramural:** Baseball M, basketball, bowling, racquetball, rifle, skiing, soccer, softball, table tennis, tennis, volleyball M.

STUDENT SERVICES. Career counseling, employment service for undergraduates, freshman orientation, personal counseling, placement service for graduates, services/facilities for handicapped.

ANNUAL EXPENSES. Tuition and fees (1992-93): $15,620. **Room and board:** $4,400. **Books and supplies:** $436. **Other expenses:** $1,225.

FINANCIAL AID. 82% of freshmen, 80% of continuing students receive some form of aid. 61% of grants, 81% of loans, all jobs based on need. 292 enrolled freshmen were judged to have need, all were offered aid. Academic scholarships available. **Aid applications:** No closing date; priority given to applications received by March 1; applicants notified on a rolling basis beginning on or about March 15; must reply by May 1 or within 4 weeks if notified thereafter.

ADDRESS/TELEPHONE. Ellen F. Hartigan, Dean of Admissions, Polytechnic University: Long Island Campus, Route 110, Farmingdale, NY 11735-3995. (516) 755-4200. (800) POLYTEC. Fax: (516) 755-4404.

Pratt Institute
Brooklyn, New York — CB code: 2669

4-year private architecture, art and design, and information sciences college, coed. Founded in 1887. **Accreditation:** Regional. **Undergraduate enrollment:** 1,911 men and women. **Graduate enrollment:** 995 men and women. **Faculty:** 512 total (96 full time). **Location:** Urban campus in very large city; 1 mile from Manhattan. **Calendar:** 4-1-4, extensive summer session. **Microcomputers:** 210 located in dormitories, libraries, classrooms, computer centers. **Special facilities:** Computer graphics laboratory, printmaking workshop, fine arts center, telecommunications lab, Schaffler Art Gallery, Pratt Institute Center for Community and Environmental Development (PICCED), Pratt Center for Advanced Design Research (CADRE). **Additional facts:** Additional campus located in Manhattan with associate degree programs and various graduate programs.

DEGREES OFFERED. BS, BFA, BArch, MS, MFA. 21 associate degrees awarded in 1992. 100% in visual and performing arts. 455 bachelor's degrees awarded. 27% in architecture and environmental design, 22% engineering, 48% visual and performing arts. Graduate degrees offered in 17 major fields of study.

UNDERGRADUATE MAJORS. Associate: Constructional management, graphic arts technology, graphic design, illustration design. **Bachelor's:** Advertising, architecture, art education, ceramics, cinematography/film, computer graphics, constructional management, drawing, fashion design, fashion merchandising, film arts, fine arts, graphic design, illustration design, industrial design, interior design, metal/jewelry, painting, photography, printmaking, sculpture, studio art, video.

ACADEMIC PROGRAMS. Accelerated program, cooperative education, double major, independent study, internships, student-designed major, study abroad, teacher preparation, visiting/exchange student program, New York semester, School of Information and Library Science offers joint MS/JD with Brooklyn Law School. **Remedial services:** Learning center, preadmission summer program, reduced course load, special counselor, tutoring. **Placement/credit:** AP, CLEP General, institutional tests; 30 credit hours maximum for bachelor's degree.

ACADEMIC REQUIREMENTS. Freshmen must earn minimum GPA of 2.0 to continue in good standing. 80% of freshmen return for sophomore year. Students must declare major on application. **Graduation requirements:** 66 hours for associate, 132 hours for bachelor's. Most students required to take courses in English, history, humanities, philosophy/religion, biological/physical sciences, social sciences. **Postgraduate studies:** 1% enter law school, 6% enter MBA programs, 18% enter other graduate study.

FRESHMAN ADMISSIONS. Selection criteria: Admissions committee considers overall academic record which includes academic performance, curriculum, standardized test results, recommendation and essay. **High school preparation:** 16 units recommended. Recommended units include English 4, mathematics 3, social science 2 and science 2. 4 mathematics required for architecture and construction management applicants. **Test requirements:** SAT or ACT (SAT preferred); score report by April 1.

1992 FRESHMAN CLASS PROFILE. 326 men and women enrolled. 57% had high school GPA of 3.0 or higher, 38% between 2.0 and 2.99. **Academic background:** Mid 50% of enrolled freshmen had SAT-V between 340-490, SAT-M between 430-580. 75% submitted SAT scores. **Characteristics:** 55% from in state, 70% live in college housing, 45% have minority backgrounds, 10% are foreign students. Average age is 19.

FALL-TERM APPLICATIONS. $30 fee, may be waived for applicants with need. No closing date; priority given to applications received by February 1; applicants notified on a rolling basis; must reply by May 1 or within 2 weeks if notified thereafter. Portfolio required for architecture applicants. Interview recommended. Essay recommended. Interview required for architecture, art and design applicants living within 100 miles radius; Letter of recommendation required for all applicants. Home examination required of some art and design applicants. CRDA. Deferred admission available. EDP-F. Recommend architecture applicants submit 2 ACH tests: English composition and Mathematics (Level I or II). Submit scores by April 1.

STUDENT LIFE. Housing: Dormitories (women, coed); apartment, handicapped housing available. Caroline Ladd Pratt House, historic turn-of-the-century mansion, houses 17 upperclassmen and graduate students. **Activities:** Student government, magazine, radio, student newspaper, yearbook, dance, drama, jazz band, musical theater, fraternities, sororities, Christian Fellowship, Jewish Student Union, Muslim Student Association, Gay/Lesbians/Bi-Sexuals at Pratt.

ATHLETICS. NCAA. **Intercollegiate:** Basketball M, cross-country, soccer M, tennis, track and field, volleyball W. **Intramural:** Badminton, basketball, field hockey, football M, wrestling M.

STUDENT SERVICES. Career counseling, employment service for undergraduates, freshman orientation, health services, personal counseling, placement service for graduates, veterans counselor, services/facilities for handicapped.

ANNUAL EXPENSES. Tuition and fees: $13,298. **Room and board:** $6,456. **Books and supplies:** $1,400. **Other expenses:** $630.

FINANCIAL AID. 85% of freshmen, 73% of continuing students receive some form of aid. 77% of grants, 83% of loans, all jobs based on need. 240 enrolled freshmen were judged to have need, all were offered aid. Academic, art scholarships available. **Aid applications:** No closing date; priority given to applications received by March 1; applicants notified on a rolling basis beginning on or about April 15; must reply by May 1 or within 2 weeks if notified thereafter.

ADDRESS/TELEPHONE. Judith Arrow, Dean of Admissions, Pratt Institute, 200 Willoughby Avenue, Brooklyn, NY 11205. (718) 636-3669. (800) 331-0834. Fax: (718) 662-6174.

Rabbinical College Beth Shraga
Monsey, New York CB code: 0668

4-year private rabbinical college, men only, affiliated with Jewish faith. Founded in 1965. **Undergraduate enrollment:** 33 men full time. **Location:** Suburban campus in small town. **Calendar:** Semester. **Additional facts:** Ordination available.

FRESHMAN ADMISSIONS. Selection criteria: Applicants must take oral and written entrance examinations.

ADDRESS/TELEPHONE. Rabbi Sidney Schiff, President, Rabbinical College Beth Shraga, 28 Saddle River Road, Monsey, NY 10952. (914) 356-1980.

Rabbinical College Bobover Yeshiva B'nei Zion
Brooklyn, New York CB code: 7011

5-year private rabbinical college. **Undergraduate enrollment:** 260 men full time. **Location:** Urban campus in very large city.

FRESHMAN ADMISSIONS. Selection criteria: Approximately 150 folio pages of Talmud, courses on Pentateuch with commentaries, Orach Cham Codes of Jewish Law.

ADDRESS/TELEPHONE. Rabbi N. Halberstam, Director, Rabbinical College Bobover Yeshiva B'nei Zion, 1577 48th Street, Brooklyn, NY 11219. (718) 438-2018.

Rabbinical College Ch'san Sofer of New York
Brooklyn, New York CB code: 0714

4-year private rabbinical college, men only, affiliated with Jewish faith. Founded in 1940. **Undergraduate enrollment:** 83 men full time. **Location:** Urban campus in very large city. **Calendar:** Semester. **Additional facts:** Ordination and First Talmudic degree available.

FRESHMAN ADMISSIONS. Selection criteria: Religious commitment, school achievement record, and interview most important.

ADDRESS/TELEPHONE. Rabbi S. B. Erhenfeld, Dean of the College, Rabbinical College Ch'san Sofer of New York, 1876 50th Street, Brooklyn, NY 11204. (718) 236-1171.

Rabbinical College of Long Island
Long Beach, New York CB code: 0675

4-year private seminary, teachers college, men only, affiliated with Jewish faith. Founded in 1965. **Undergraduate enrollment:** 150 men full time. **Location:** Suburban campus in large town. **Calendar:** Trimester. **Additional facts:** Ordination and First Talmudic degree available.

FRESHMAN ADMISSIONS. Selection criteria: Religious commitment, interview, and recommendations most important.

ADDRESS/TELEPHONE. Rabbi C. Hoberman, Director of Admissions, Rabbinical College of Long Island, 201 Magnolia Boulevard, Long Beach, NY 11561. (516) 431-7414.

Rabbinical Seminary Adas Yereim
Brooklyn, New York CB code: 0666

4-year private rabbinical college, men only, affiliated with Jewish faith. Founded in 1961. **Undergraduate enrollment:** 75 men full time. **Location:** Urban campus in very large city. **Calendar:** Semester. **Additional facts:** First Talmudic degree offered.

FRESHMAN ADMISSIONS. Selection criteria: Interview and entrance examination considered.

ADDRESS/TELEPHONE. Rabbi Greenzweig, Director of Finances, Rabbinical Seminary Adas Yereim, 185 Wilson Street, Brooklyn, NY 11211. (718) 388-1751.

Rabbinical Seminary of America
Forest Hills, New York CB code: 2776

5-year private seminary college, men only, affiliated with Jewish faith. Founded in 1933. **Undergraduate enrollment:** 125 men full time. **Graduate enrollment:** 52 men full time. **Faculty:** 25 total (10 full time). **Location:** Urban campus in very large city. **Calendar:** Semester. **Additional facts:** Ordination available. 4-and 5-year undergraduate programs as well as graduate study. Campus in Jerusalem enrolls 50 students.

DEGREES OFFERED. B, PhD. Graduate degrees offered in 1 major field of study.

ACADEMIC PROGRAMS. Independent study, internships.

ACADEMIC REQUIREMENTS. Students must declare major on application. **Graduation requirements:** Most students required to take courses in history, philosophy/religion, social sciences.

FRESHMAN ADMISSIONS. Selection criteria: Interview most important. School record and test scores considered. Diploma from Hebrew high school required.

1992 FRESHMAN CLASS PROFILE. 50 men enrolled. **Characteristics:** 60% from in state, 70% live in college housing. Average age is 18.

FALL-TERM APPLICATIONS. No fee. Closing date July 1; applicants notified on a rolling basis. Interview required. Deferred and early admission available.

STUDENT LIFE. Housing: Dormitories (men).

FINANCIAL AID. 95% of freshmen, 90% of continuing students receive some form of aid. **Aid applications:** No closing date; applicants notified on a rolling basis.

ADDRESS/TELEPHONE. Rabbi Abraham Semmel, Registrar, Rabbinical Seminary of America, 92-15 69th Avenue, Forest Hills, NY 11375. (718) 268-4700.

Rabbinical Seminary M'Kor Chaim
Brooklyn, New York CB code: 0767

5-year private rabbinical college, men only, affiliated with Jewish faith. Founded in 1965. **Undergraduate enrollment:** 100 men full time. **Graduate enrollment:** 31 men full time. **Location:** Urban campus in very large city. **Calendar:** Semester. **Additional facts:** Ordination available.

ADDRESS/TELEPHONE. Rabbi Benjamin Paler, President, Rabbinical Seminary M'Kor Chaim, 1571 55th Street, Brooklyn, NY 11219. (718) 851-0183.

Rensselaer Polytechnic Institute
Troy, New York CB code: 2757

Admissions: 81% of applicants accepted
Based on: ••• School record
•• Activities, recommendations, test scores
• Essay, interview, special talents
Completion: 98% of freshmen end year in good standing
70% graduate, 35% of these enter graduate study

4-year private university, coed. Founded in 1824. **Accreditation:** Regional. **Undergraduate enrollment:** 3,508 men, 868 women full time; 10 men, 12 women part time. **Graduate enrollment:** 1,438 men, 374 women full time; 346 men, 101 women part time. **Faculty:** 470 total (400 full time), 445 with doctorates or other terminal degrees. **Location:** Suburban campus in small city; 10 miles from Albany, 165 miles from New York City. **Calendar:** Semester, extensive summer session. **Microcomputers:** 618 located in dormitories, libraries, classrooms, computer centers, campus-wide network. **Special facilities:** Manufacturing productivity, integrated electronics, computer graphics centers, Shelnutt Gallery, observatory, Rensselaer Technology Park, incubator center, IEAR studios, linear accelerator, class 100 clean room, Fresh-Water Institute, geology museum.

DEGREES OFFERED. BS, BArch, MS, MBA, MFA, PhD. 1,057 bachelor's degrees awarded in 1992. 6% in architecture and environmental design, 5% business and management, 13% computer sciences, 60% engineering, 5% life sciences, 8% physical sciences. Graduate degrees offered in 38 major fields of study.

UNDERGRADUATE MAJORS. Aerospace/aeronautical/astronautical engineering, architecture, biochemistry, bioengineering and biomedical engineering, biological and physical sciences, biology, biophysics, building sciences, business administration and management, chemical engineering, chemistry, civil engineering, communications, computer and information sciences, computer engineering, economics, electric power engineering, electrical/electronics/communications engineering, engineering, engineering and other disciplines, engineering management, engineering physics, engineering science, environmental health engineering, environmental science, geology, humanities and social sciences, industrial engineering, materials engineering, mathematics, mathematics education, mechanical engineering, nuclear engineering, philosophy, physics, prelaw, psychology, science education, social science and technology studies, systems engineering.

ACADEMIC PROGRAMS. Accelerated program, cooperative education, double major, dual enrollment of high school students, honors program, independent study, internships, study abroad, teacher preparation, telecourses, visiting/exchange student program, cross-registration, school in Rome for architecture majors, combined bachelor's/graduate degree programs in dentistry with University of Pennsylvania School of Dental Medicine, in law with Albany Law School, and in medicine with Albany Medical College; liberal arts/career combination in engineering; combined bachelor's/ graduate program in business administration. **Remedial services:** Learning center, preadmission summer program, reduced course load, tutoring, writing center, learning assistants in residence halls, services for students with learning disabilities. **ROTC:** Air Force, Army, Naval. **Placement/credit:** AP, institutional tests.

ACADEMIC REQUIREMENTS. Freshmen must earn minimum GPA of 1.8 to continue in good standing. 85% of freshmen return for sophomore year. Students must declare major by end of second year. **Graduation requirements:** 124 hours for bachelor's. Most students required to take courses in computer science, English, humanities, mathematics, biological/physical sciences, social sciences. **Postgraduate studies:** 1% enter law school, 3% enter medical school, 5% enter MBA programs, 26% enter other graduate study. **Additional information:** Teacher certification program in mathematics and science.

FRESHMAN ADMISSIONS. Selection criteria: School achievement record, test scores required, activities considered. **High school preparation:** 16 units required. Required units include English 4, mathematics 4 and physical science 2. Physical sciences should include 1 physics, 1 chemistry. Mathematics should include progression through trigonometry and preferably calculus. Additional units should include any combination of science, foreign language, social sciences. Advanced Placement or Honors courses preferred. **Test requirements:** SAT or ACT (SAT preferred); score report by February 15. 3 ACH (including English, Mathematics Level I or II, and Chemistry, Physics or Biology) required of biomedical and biodental program applicants. 2 ACH (English and Mathematics I or II) required for 6-year management students. Score report by January 31.

1992 FRESHMAN CLASS PROFILE. 3,943 men applied, 3,177 accepted, 1,084 enrolled; 1,167 women applied, 945 accepted, 216 enrolled. **Academic background:** Mid 50% of enrolled freshmen had SAT-V between 480-590, SAT-M between 620-710; ACT composite between 26-32. 95% submitted SAT scores, 5% submitted ACT scores. **Characteristics:** 37% from in state, 99% live in college housing, 26% have minority backgrounds, 7% are foreign students. Average age is 18.

FALL-TERM APPLICATIONS. $35 fee, may be waived for applicants with need. $40 fee for accelerated programs, no application fee for transfer students. Closing date January 15; applicants notified on or about March 1; must reply by May 1. Portfolio required for architecture applicants. Interview recommended. Essays required for architecture applicants and for accelerated program; recommended for all others. CRDA. Deferred and early admission available. EDP-F. Early decision plan with application closing date of January 1, notification on rolling basis. Mathematics, Chemistry, and Physics ACH strongly recommended; score report by January 31.

STUDENT LIFE. Housing: Dormitories (men, coed); apartment, fraternity, sorority housing available. College housing required for all freshmen unless student lives within 50-mile radius of campus with parent(s) or legal guardian(s). **Activities:** Student government, magazine, radio, student newspaper, yearbook, choral groups, concert band, dance, drama, jazz band, music ensembles, musical theater, pep band, symphony orchestra, fraternities, sororities, Over 120 groups including a variety of religious, cultural, special interest, and social service organizations. **Additional information:** Of undergraduates who do not reside in college housing, 45% live in their own apartments off campus connected by shuttle bus, 1% commute from home.

ATHLETICS. NCAA. **Intercollegiate:** Baseball M, basketball, cross-country, diving, field hockey W, football M, golf M, ice hockey M, lacrosse, skiing, soccer, softball W, swimming, tennis, track and field, water polo M. **Intramural:** Badminton, baseball M, basketball, bowling, diving, fencing, golf, gymnastics, handball, horseback riding, ice hockey, lacrosse M, racquetball, rifle, rowing (crew), rugby M, sailing, skiing, soccer, softball, squash, swimming, table tennis, tennis, track and field, volleyball, water polo, wrestling M. **Clubs:** Archery, badminton, cricket, cycling, judo, juggling and unicycling, Tae Kwan Do, scuba diving, weightlifting.

STUDENT SERVICES. Career counseling, employment service for undergraduates, freshman orientation, health services, on-campus day care, personal counseling, placement service for graduates, disabled students coordinator, services/facilities for handicapped.

ANNUAL EXPENSES. Tuition and fees: $17,325. **Room and board:** $5,742. **Books and supplies:** $525. **Other expenses:** $658.

FINANCIAL AID. 79% of freshmen, 79% of continuing students receive some form of aid. 94% of grants, 95% of loans, all jobs based on need. 745 enrolled freshmen were judged to have need, all were offered aid. Academic, athletic, alumni affiliation scholarships available. **Aid applications:** No closing date; priority given to applications received by February 15; applicants notified on a rolling basis beginning on or about April 10; must reply by May 1 or within 3 weeks if notified thereafter.

ADDRESS/TELEPHONE. Conrad Sharrow, Dean of Admissions, Rensselaer Polytechnic Institute, Admissions and Financial Aid Building, Troy, NY 12180-3590. (518) 276-6216. (800) 448-6562. Fax: (518) 276-4072.

Roberts Wesleyan College
Rochester, New York CB code: 2759

Admissions: 93% of applicants accepted
Based on: ••• Interview, religious affiliation/commitment, school record
•• Activities, recommendations, test scores
• Essay, special talents
Completion: 89% of freshmen end year in good standing
48% graduate, 30% of these enter graduate study

4-year private liberal arts college, coed, affiliated with Free Methodist Church of North America. Founded in 1866. **Accreditation:** Regional. **Undergraduate enrollment:** 333 men, 534 women full time; 26 men, 45 women part time. **Graduate enrollment:** 9 men, 13 women full time; 7 men, 33 women part time. **Faculty:** 117 total (64 full time), 31 with doctorates or other terminal degrees. **Location:** Suburban campus in large city; 8 miles from downtown. **Calendar:** Semester, limited summer session. **Microcomputers:** 23 located in libraries, computer centers. **Special facilities:** Davis mountain campus in Bristol Hills retreat center and site for study of ecology.

DEGREES OFFERED. AS, BA, BS, MEd. 225 bachelor's degrees awarded. 44% in business and management, 15% teacher education, 7% health sciences, 6% philosophy, religion, theology, 7% social sciences. Graduate degrees offered in 1 major field of study.

UNDERGRADUATE MAJORS. Associate: Liberal/general studies, science technologies. **Bachelor's:** Accounting, art education, biochemistry, biological and physical sciences, biology, business and management, chemistry, communications, computer and information sciences, contemporary ministries, criminal justice studies, elementary education, English, fine arts, gerontology, history, human resources development, humanities and social sciences, mathematics, music, music education, nursing, physics, psychology, Religion/Philosophy, social sciences, social work, sociology, studio art, visual and performing arts.

ACADEMIC PROGRAMS. Double major, dual enrollment of high school students, honors program, independent study, internships, study abroad, teacher preparation, Washington semester, cross-registration, 3+2 program in engineering with Clarkson University, Rensselaer Polytechnic Institute, and Rochester Institute of Technology. **Remedial services:** Learning center, reduced course load, remedial instruction, special counselor, tutoring. **ROTC:** Air Force, Army. **Placement/credit:** AP, CLEP Subject; 30 credit hours maximum for bachelor's degree.

ACADEMIC REQUIREMENTS. Freshmen must earn minimum GPA of 1.75 to continue in good standing. 78% of freshmen return for sophomore year. Students must declare major by end of second year. **Graduation requirements:** 62 hours for associate (30 in major), 124 hours for bachelor's (30 in major). Most students required to take courses in arts/fine arts, English, foreign languages, history, mathematics, philosophy/religion, biological/physical sciences, social sciences.

FRESHMAN ADMISSIONS. Selection criteria: Rank in top 60% of high school class, 2.5 GPA, recommendations, ACT or SAT scores. Student expected to recognize Christian perspectives and values college upholds. Interview important. **High school preparation:** 12 units required. Required and recommended units include English 4, mathematics 2 and social science 2. Foreign language 3 recommended. Biology and chemistry required of nursing applicants. **Test requirements:** SAT or ACT; score report by June 30. ACH may be required of some applicants at discretion of admissions committee. Score report by July 20 ACT score report must be received by July 30 for fall-term admissions.

1992 FRESHMAN CLASS PROFILE. 137 men applied, 125 accepted, 115 enrolled; 212 women applied, 198 accepted, 162 enrolled. 25% had high school GPA of 3.0 or higher, 73% between 2.0 and 2.99. **Academic background:** Mid 50% of enrolled freshmen had SAT-V between 390-510, SAT-M between 410-570; ACT composite between 17-26. 73% submitted SAT scores, 31% submitted ACT scores. **Characteristics:** 78% from in state, 85% live in college housing, 6% have minority backgrounds, 10% are foreign students. Average age is 18.

FALL-TERM APPLICATIONS. $25 fee, may be waived for applicants with need. Closing date August 15; priority given to applications received by May 1; applicants notified on a rolling basis; must reply by May 1 or within 3 weeks if notified thereafter. Audition required for music applicants. Essay required. Interview recommended. Portfolio recommended for studio art, art education applicants. CRDA. Deferred and early admission available.

STUDENT LIFE. Housing: Dormitories (men, women); apartment housing available. **Activities:** Student government, film, student newspaper, television, yearbook, choral groups, concert band, drama, jazz band, music ensembles, musical theater, opera, pep band, symphony orchestra, outreach service, committee on ministries, International Club, Rotoract. **Additional information:** Religious observance required.

ATHLETICS. Intercollegiate: Basketball, cross-country, soccer, track and field. **Intramural:** Basketball, bowling, cross-country, racquetball, softball, swimming, table tennis, tennis, track and field, volleyball.

STUDENT SERVICES. Aptitude testing, career counseling, employment service for undergraduates, freshman orientation, health services, personal counseling, placement service for graduates, special adviser for adult students, veterans counselor.

ANNUAL EXPENSES. Tuition and fees: $9,931. **Room and board:** $3,366. **Books and supplies:** $520. **Other expenses:** $950.

FINANCIAL AID. 97% of freshmen, 87% of continuing students receive some form of aid. 72% of grants, 94% of loans, 39% of jobs based on need. 151 enrolled freshmen were judged to have need, all were offered aid. Academic, music/drama, art, athletic, leadership, religious affiliation scholarships available. **Aid applications:** No closing date; priority given to applications received by May 15; applicants notified on a rolling basis beginning on or about March 1; must reply by May 1 or within 3 weeks if notified thereafter. **Additional information:** Invitational Scholarship Competition awards, Partnership Awards Sholarship provide additional aid to eligible applicants.

ADDRESS/TELEPHONE. Linda Kurtz, Director of Admissions, Roberts Wesleyan College, 2301 Westside Drive, Rochester, NY 14624-1997. (716) 594-9471. (800) 777-4792. Fax: (716) 594-9757.

Rochester Business Institute
Rochester, New York — CB code: 2770

2-year proprietary business college, coed. Founded in 1863. **Undergraduate enrollment:** 537 men and women. **Location:** Urban campus in large city. **Calendar:** Quarter.

FRESHMAN ADMISSIONS. Selection criteria: Interview, examination scores, transcripts.

ANNUAL EXPENSES. Tuition and fees: $5,100. **Books and supplies:** $600. **Other expenses:** $1,200.

ADDRESS/TELEPHONE. Terry A. Nichols, Director of Adult Admissions, Rochester Business Institute, 1850 East Ridge Road, Rochester, NY 14622. (716) 266-0430.

Rochester Institute of Technology
Rochester, New York — CB code: 2760

Admissions: 81% of applicants accepted
Based on:
••• School record
•• Test scores
• Activities, essay, interview, recommendations, special talents
Completion: 95% of freshmen end year in good standing
54% graduate

4-year private university, coed. Founded in 1829. **Accreditation:** Regional. **Undergraduate enrollment:** 5,632 men, 2,437 women full time; 1,872 men, 1,092 women part time. **Graduate enrollment:** 318 men, 221 women full time; 905 men, 527 women part time. **Faculty:** 1,126 total (713 full time), 554 with doctorates or other terminal degrees. **Location:** Suburban campus in large city; 5 miles from downtown. **Calendar:** Quarter, extensive summer session. Saturday and extensive evening/early morning classes. **Microcomputers:** 1,100 located in dormitories, libraries, classrooms, computer centers. **Special facilities:** Bevier Art Gallery, photographic arts gallery, lithography collection, imaging science center, packaging testing facility, student-operated restaurant, computer chip manufacturing facility,technical center for graphic arts. **Additional facts:** University comprises 9 colleges, including National Technical Institute for the deaf that enrolls approximately 900 deaf undergraduates. Many are cross-registered in other RIT academic programs.

DEGREES OFFERED. AA, AS, AAS, BS, BFA, MS, MBA, MFA, PhD. 345 associate degrees awarded in 1992. 17% in business/office and marketing/distribution, 12% engineering technologies, 16% multi/interdisciplinary studies, 6% trade and industry, 38% visual and performing arts. 1,780 bachelor's degrees awarded. 18% in business and management, 12% engineering, 15% engineering technologies, 5% trade and industry, 23% visual and performing arts. Graduate degrees offered in 55 major fields of study.

UNDERGRADUATE MAJORS. Associate: Accounting, applied arts and sciences, applied mathematics, architectural technologies, biochemistry, biology, biomedical photographic communications, biotechnology, business administration and management, business and management, business data entry equipment operation, business data processing and related programs, ceramics, chemistry, cinematography/film, civil technology, communications, computer and information sciences, computer programming, computer technology, crafts, education of the deaf and hearing impaired, electrical technology, electromechanical technology, fiber/textiles/weaving, film arts, finance, fine arts, food management, food production/management/services, food science and nutrition, glass, graphic and printing production, graphic design, health care administration, hospitality and recreation marketing, hotel/motel and restaurant management, illustration design, industrial design, information sciences and systems, interior design, interpreter for the deaf, liberal/general studies, management information systems, manufacturing technology, marketing and distribution, marketing management, mechanical design technology, medical laboratory technologies, medical records technology, metal/jewelry, motion picture technology, ophthalmic services, painting, personnel management, photographic systems management, photographic technology, photography, physics, printmaking, real estate, sculpture, small business management and ownership, studio art, telecommunications, tourism, trade and industrial supervision and management, travel management, video, woodworking. **Bachelor's:** Accounting, advertising, advertising photography, advertising photography, aerospace/aeronautical/astronautical engineering, applied arts and sciences, applied mathematics, biochemistry, biological laboratory technology, biology, biomedical computing, biomedical photographic communications, biotechnology, business administration and management, business and management, business information systems, ceramics, chemistry, chemistry-biochemistry, cinematography/film, civil technology, clinical laboratory science, communications, computational mathematics, computer and information sciences, computer engineering, computer mathematics, computer programming, computer technology, crafts, criminal justice studies, economics, electrical technology, electrical/electronics/communications engineering, engineering and other disciplines, environmental management, environmental science, fiber/textiles/weaving, film arts, finance, fine arts, fine arts photography, food management, food production/management/services, food science and nutrition, glass, graphic and printing production, graphic arts technology, graphic design, hospitality and recreation marketing, hotel/motel and restaurant management, illustration design, industrial design, industrial engineering, information sciences and systems, interior design, international business management, law enforcement and corrections, management information systems, manufacturing management, manufacturing technology, marketing and distribution, marketing management, mathematics, mechanical design technology, mechanical engineering, medical illustrating, medical laboratory technologies, metal/jewelry, microelectronic engineering, motion picture technology, newspaper operations management, nuclear medical technology, packaging science, painting, photographic marketing management, photographic systems management, photographic technology, photography, photojournalism, physician's assistant, physics, polymer chemistry, predentistry, prelaw, premedicine, prepharmacy, preveterinary, printmaking, professional and technical communication, sculpture, small business management and ownership, social work, statistics, studio art, systems analysis, telecommunications, tourism, trade and industrial supervision and management, travel management, ultrasound technology, video, woodworking.

ACADEMIC PROGRAMS. 2-year transfer program, accelerated program, cooperative education, dual enrollment of high school students, independent study, internships, student-designed major, study abroad, telecourses, visiting/exchange student program, weekend college, cross-registration; combined bachelor's/graduate program in business administration. **Remedial services:** Learning center, preadmission summer program, reduced course load, remedial instruction, special counselor, tutoring, New York State Higher Education Opportunity Program. **ROTC:** Air Force, Army, Naval. **Placement/credit:** AP, CLEP General and Subject, institutional tests; 45 credit hours maximum for associate degree; 135 credit hours maximum for bachelor's degree.

ACADEMIC REQUIREMENTS. Freshmen must earn minimum GPA of 2.0 to continue in good standing. 84% of freshmen return for sophomore year. Students must declare major by end of first year. **Graduation requirements:** 90 hours for associate (60 in major), 180 hours for bachelor's (120 in major). Most students required to take courses in arts/fine arts, English, history, humanities, biological/physical sciences, social sciences.

FRESHMAN ADMISSIONS. Selection criteria: High school record, class rank, counselor recommendation, test scores, optional interviews, extracurricular activities considered. Admission requirements vary by major. Minority applicants given special consideration. **High school preparation:** 19 units required; 25 recommended. Required and recommended units include English 4, mathematics 2-4 and science 2-3. Social science 3 recommended. Requirements vary with program. Engineering, science, engineering technology, and computer science programs require 4 units mathematics. **Test requirements:** SAT or ACT; score report by August 15. **Additional information:** Candidates allowed to apply for up to 3 majors and will receive counseling related to choices. Admissions requirements vary by major. Applications received after March 1 will be processed if space is available.

1992 FRESHMAN CLASS PROFILE. 3,531 men applied, 2,859 accepted, 1,060 enrolled; 1,306 women applied, 1,057 accepted, 470 enrolled. 90% had high school GPA of 3.0 or higher, 10% between 2.0 and 2.99. 25% were in top tenth and 55% were in top quarter of graduating class. **Academic background:** Mid 50% of enrolled freshmen had SAT-V between 430-540, SAT-M between 510-630; ACT composite between 22-27. 94% submitted SAT scores, 30% submitted ACT scores. **Characteristics:** 60% from in state, 90% live in college housing, 13% have minority backgrounds, 4% are foreign students, 10% join fraternities/sororities. Average age is 18.

FALL-TERM APPLICATIONS. $35 fee, may be waived for applicants with need. Closing date August 1; priority given to applications received by March 1; applicants notified on a rolling basis beginning on or about March 1; must reply by May 1 or within 2 weeks if notified thereafter. Portfolio required for art, design, crafts applicants. Essay required. Interview recommended. CRDA. Deferred and early admission available. EDP-F.

STUDENT LIFE. Housing: Dormitories (men, women, coed); apartment, fraternity, sorority, handicapped housing available. Special interest houses in art, business, computer science, engineering,photography, and community service available. International house for both foreign and American students, and Unity House emphasizing Black culture available. **Activities:** Student government, film, magazine, radio, student newspaper, television, yearbook, choral groups, drama, jazz band, music ensembles, pep band, sing/sign Choir, gospel ensemble, fraternities, sororities, Campus Parish, Hillel, Black Awareness Coordinating Committee, Hispanic Student Association, Jewish Student Coalition, Alpha Phi Omega, Phi Beta Sigma, Women's Concern Groups, Parents Council, Campus Crusade for Christ, InterVarsity Christian Fellowship.

ATHLETICS. NCAA. **Intercollegiate:** Baseball M, basketball, cross-country, diving, ice hockey, lacrosse M, soccer, softball W, swimming, tennis, track and field, volleyball W, wrestling M. **Intramural:** Basketball, bowling, diving, fencing, golf, ice hockey, lacrosse, racquetball, rugby M, skiing, soccer, softball, swimming, tennis, volleyball, water polo.

STUDENT SERVICES. Aptitude testing, career counseling, employment service for undergraduates, freshman orientation, health services, on-campus day care, personal counseling, placement service for graduates, special adviser for adult students, veterans counselor, international student counselors, services/facilities for handicapped.

ANNUAL EXPENSES. Tuition and fees: $13,515. **Room and board:** $5,511. **Books and supplies:** $500. **Other expenses:** $575.

FINANCIAL AID. 68% of freshmen, 67% of continuing students receive some form of aid. 95% of grants, 84% of loans, 24% of jobs based on need. 1,084 enrolled freshmen were judged to have need, all were offered aid. Academic, art, leadership scholarships available. **Aid applications:** No closing date; priority given to applications received by March 15; applicants notified on a rolling basis beginning on or about March 15; must reply by May 1 or within 2 weeks if notified thereafter. **Additional information:** Scholarship assistance for undergraduate foreign students extremely limited.

ADDRESS/TELEPHONE. Daniel R. Shelley, Director of Admissions, Rochester Institute of Technology, PO Box 9887, One Lomb Memorial Drive, Rochester, NY 14623-0887. (716) 475-6631. Fax: (716) 475-7424.

Rockland Community College
Suffern, New York — CB code: 2767

2-year public community college, coed. Founded in 1959. **Accreditation:** Regional. **Undergraduate enrollment:** 1,831 men, 2,039 women full time; 1,613 men, 2,561 women part time. **Faculty:** 807 total (192 full time), 37 with doctorates or other terminal degrees. **Location:** Suburban campus in large town; 35 miles from New York City. **Calendar:** Semester, extensive summer session. Saturday and extensive evening/early morning classes. **Microcomputers:** 177 located in computer centers. **Additional facts:** SUNY institution. Extension sites/centers located throughout county.

DEGREES OFFERED. AA, AS, AAS. 1,032 associate degrees awarded in 1992. 17% in business and management, 9% business/office and marketing/distribution, 10% health sciences, 50% multi/interdisciplinary studies.

UNDERGRADUATE MAJORS. Accounting, automotive technology, business administration and management, business and office, business data processing and related programs, commercial art, communications, criminal justice technology, data processing, dietetic aide/assistant, electrical technology, electromechanical technology, emergency medical technologies, finance, fire control and safety technology, food management, graphic arts technology, graphic design, humanities and social sciences, liberal/general studies, marketing and distribution, mechanical design technology, medical laboratory technologies, medical records technology, nursing, occupational therapy assistant, respiratory therapy, respiratory therapy technology, secretarial and related programs, tourism, visual and performing arts.

ACADEMIC PROGRAMS. 2-year transfer program, double major, dual enrollment of high school students, honors program, independent study, internships, student-designed major, study abroad, weekend college, cross-registration. **Remedial services:** Learning center, remedial instruction, special counselor, tutoring. **Placement/credit:** AP, CLEP General and Subject, institutional tests; 45 credit hours maximum for associate degree.

ACADEMIC REQUIREMENTS. Freshmen must earn minimum GPA of 1.5 to continue in good standing. 81% of freshmen return for sophomore year. Students must declare major on enrollment. **Graduation requirements:** 60 hours for associate (30 in major). Most students required to take courses in English, mathematics, biological/physical sciences, social sciences.

FRESHMAN ADMISSIONS. Selection criteria: Open admissions. **Additional information:** Students required to take assessment examination before enrolling full-time.

1992 FRESHMAN CLASS PROFILE. 832 men, 975 women enrolled. 46% had high school GPA of 3.0 or higher, 36% between 2.0 and 2.99. **Academic background:** Mid 50% of enrolled freshmen had SAT-V between 420-520, SAT-M between 440-540. 39% submitted SAT scores. **Characteristics:** 97% from in state, 100% commute, 27% have minority backgrounds, 2% are foreign students. Average age is 19.

FALL-TERM APPLICATIONS. $20 fee, may be waived for applicants with need. No closing date; priority given to applications received by August 1; applicants notified on a rolling basis. Deferred and early admission available.

STUDENT LIFE. Activities: Student government, magazine, radio, student newspaper, television, choral groups, dance, drama, jazz band, musical theater, symphony orchestra, special interest clubs.

ATHLETICS. NJCAA. **Intercollegiate:** Baseball M, basketball, bowling M, golf M, soccer, softball W, tennis, volleyball W. **Intramural:** Basketball, racquetball, soccer, softball, table tennis, volleyball.

STUDENT SERVICES. Career counseling, employment service for undergraduates, freshman orientation, health services, on-campus day care, personal counseling, placement service for graduates, special adviser for adult students, veterans counselor, services/facilities for handicapped.

ANNUAL EXPENSES. Tuition and fees (1992-93): $2,036, $1,950 additional for out-of-state students. **Books and supplies:** $600. **Other expenses:** $600.

FINANCIAL AID. 58% of freshmen, 58% of continuing students receive some form of aid. 98% of grants, 98% of loans, 30% of jobs based on need. Academic, minority scholarships available. **Aid applications:** No closing date; priority given to applications received by June 15; applicants notified on a rolling basis beginning on or about July 1; must reply within 3 weeks.

ADDRESS/TELEPHONE. Lawrence Gurney, Director of Admissions, Rockland Community College, 145 College Road, Suffern, NY 10901. (914) 574-4462. Fax: (914) 356-1529.

Russell Sage College
Troy, New York — CB code: 2764

4-year private college of arts and sciences, women only. Founded in 1916. **Accreditation:** Regional. **Undergraduate enrollment:** 1,008 women full time; 114 women part time. **Graduate enrollment:** 159 men and women full time; 908 men and women part time. **Faculty:** 170 total (120 full time), 82 with doctorates or other terminal degrees. **Location:** Urban campus in small city; 10 miles from Albany, 12 miles from Schenectady. **Calendar:** 4-1-4, limited summer session. **Microcomputers:** 38 located in libraries, computer centers.

Special facilities: Art gallery, theater, fine arts center, center for women's education. **Additional facts:** Coeducational at master's level.

DEGREES OFFERED. BA, BS, MA, MS, MBA, MEd. 330 bachelor's degrees awarded in 1992. 10% in business and management, 11% teacher education, 43% health sciences, 6% life sciences, 5% psychology, 8% social sciences. Graduate degrees offered in 14 major fields of study.

UNDERGRADUATE MAJORS. Accounting, art therapy, arts management, athletic training, biochemistry, biological and physical sciences, biology, business administration and management, business and management, business economics, chemistry, clinical laboratory science, computer and information sciences, criminal justice studies, criminology, early childhood education, economics, education, elementary education, English, English education, foreign languages education, French, health and fitness, history, humanities and social sciences, information sciences and systems, international studies, junior high education, law enforcement and corrections, liberal/general studies, marketing management, mathematics, mathematics education, medical laboratory technologies, music therapy, nursing, nutritional sciences, occupational therapy, physical therapy, political science and government, prelaw, premedicine, preveterinary, psychology, psychology/human services (presocial work), science education, secondary education, social science education, social studies education, sociology, Spanish, special education, speech/communication/theater education, technical education.

ACADEMIC PROGRAMS. Accelerated program, double major, dual enrollment of high school students, independent study, internships, student-designed major, study abroad, teacher preparation, visiting/exchange student program, Washington semester, cross-registration, 5-year BA/BS program in engineering with Rensselaer Polytechnic Institute, combined bachelor's/law degree program with Albany Law School; liberal arts/career combination in engineering; combined bachelor's/graduate program in business administration. **Remedial services:** Learning center, reduced course load, remedial instruction, special counselor, tutoring, New York State Higher Education Opportunity Program. **ROTC:** Air Force, Army, Naval. **Placement/credit:** AP, CLEP Subject, institutional tests; 60 credit hours maximum for bachelor's degree.

ACADEMIC REQUIREMENTS. Freshmen must earn minimum GPA of 2.0 to continue in good standing. 87% of freshmen return for sophomore year. Students must declare major by end of second year. **Graduation requirements:** 120 hours for bachelor's (33 in major). Most students required to take courses in arts/fine arts, English, history, humanities, mathematics, philosophy/religion, biological/physical sciences, social sciences. **Additional information:** Sage Study Program assists students who have ability and motivation, but have not yet fully realized their academic potential. Most students complete internship, field experience, or clinical experience.

FRESHMAN ADMISSIONS. Selection criteria: High school record, test scores, recommendations of school officials, intended major, interview, school and community activities considered. **High school preparation:** 16 units required. Required and recommended units include English 4, mathematics 3, social science 3 and science 3. Foreign language 2 recommended. Nursing program applicants must have 6 units in mathematics/science combination including chemistry. Physical therapy applicants must have 6 units in mathematics/science combination including biology, 3 chemistry and 3 physics, or advanced biology. **Test requirements:** SAT or ACT; score report by August 1.

1992 FRESHMAN CLASS PROFILE. Academic background: Mid 50% of enrolled freshmen had SAT-V between 420-520, SAT-M between 420-570; ACT composite between 20-26. 96% submitted SAT scores, 33% submitted ACT scores. **Characteristics:** 74% from in state, 90% live in college housing, 8% have minority backgrounds, 1% are foreign students. Average age is 18.

FALL-TERM APPLICATIONS. $20 fee, may be waived for applicants with need. Closing date August 1; priority given to applications received by March 1; applicants notified on a rolling basis beginning on or about December 15; must reply by May 1 or within 2 weeks if notified thereafter. Essay required. Interview recommended. CRDA. Deferred and early admission available. EDP-F. Early Decision must apply by November 1, decision by November 15.

STUDENT LIFE. Housing: Dormitories (women). Special houses available for students interested in language/international awareness activities. **Activities:** Student government, magazine, student newspaper, yearbook, choral groups, dance, drama, music ensembles, musical theater, Hillel, Big Brothers, Big Sisters, Black-Latin Alliance, Christian Association, Model United Nations club, international club.

ATHLETICS. Intercollegiate: Basketball, soccer, softball, tennis, volleyball. **Intramural:** Archery, badminton, basketball, bowling, field hockey, horseback riding, lacrosse, skiing, soccer, softball, swimming, tennis, track and field, volleyball.

STUDENT SERVICES. Aptitude testing, career counseling, employment service for undergraduates, freshman orientation, health services, on-campus day care, personal counseling, placement service for graduates, special adviser for adult students, services/facilities for handicapped.

ANNUAL EXPENSES. Tuition and fees (1992-93): $11,500. **Room and board:** $4,500. **Books and supplies:** $500. **Other expenses:** $650.

FINANCIAL AID. 85% of freshmen, 85% of continuing students receive some form of aid. 94% of grants, 95% of loans, 38% of jobs based on need. Academic, leadership scholarships available. **Aid applications:** No closing date; priority given to applications received by March 1; applicants notified on a rolling basis beginning on or about March 15; must reply within 2 weeks unless granted extension.

ADDRESS/TELEPHONE. Patrice M. Tate, Director of Admissions, Russell Sage College, 45 Ferry Street, Troy, NY 12180. (518) 270-2217. (800) 999-3772. Fax: (518) 271-4545.

Sage Junior College of Albany
Albany, New York CB code: 2343

2-year private junior college, coed. Founded in 1957. **Accreditation:** Regional. **Undergraduate enrollment:** 896 men and women full time; 100 men and women part time. **Faculty:** 91 total (49 full time), 6 with doctorates or other terminal degrees. **Location:** Urban campus in small city. **Calendar:** Semester, limited summer session. Extensive evening/early morning classes. **Microcomputers:** Located in classrooms, computer centers. **Special facilities:** Art gallery. **Additional facts:** One of Sage Colleges.

DEGREES OFFERED. AA, AS, AAS. 288 associate degrees awarded in 1992. 6% in architecture and environmental design, 11% business and management, 11% business/office and marketing/distribution, 9% health sciences, 20% military sciences, 29% visual and performing arts.

UNDERGRADUATE MAJORS. Accounting, biological and physical sciences, biology, business administration and management, business and management, chemistry, child development/care/guidance, communications, computer and information sciences, criminal justice studies, elementary education, fashion merchandising, fine arts, graphic design, history, information sciences and systems, interior design, legal assistant/paralegal, legal secretary, liberal/general studies, marketing and distribution, marketing management, mathematics, office supervision and management, photography, physical sciences, premedical records, premedicine, prenutrition, prepharmacy, preprofessional sciences, psychology, retailing, secretarial and related programs, social work, sociology.

ACADEMIC PROGRAMS. 2-year transfer program, dual enrollment of high school students, honors program, independent study, internships, student-designed major, study abroad, visiting/exchange student program, Washington semester, cross-registration. **Remedial services:** Learning center, preadmission summer program, reduced course load, remedial instruction, special counselor, tutoring. **Placement/credit:** AP, CLEP Subject, institutional tests; 30 credit hours maximum for associate degree.

ACADEMIC REQUIREMENTS. Freshmen must earn minimum GPA of 2.0 to continue in good standing. 75% of freshmen return for sophomore year. Students must declare major on enrollment. **Graduation requirements:** 60 hours for associate. Most students required to take courses in English. **Additional information:** Four programs in fine arts (photography, graphic design, interior design, and fine arts) are accredited by National Association of Schools of Art and Design.

FRESHMAN ADMISSIONS. Selection criteria: Recommendation of high school guidance counselor and academic record considered for all applicants. Applications reviewed and considered on an individual basis. **High school preparation:** 16 units recommended. Recommended units include English 4, foreign language 2, mathematics 3, social science 4 and science 3. Business administration and computer science applicants must have 3 mathematics, including algebra, geometry, trigonometry. Computer science applicants also need mathematics. Legal assistant majors need strong preparation in English, history. Pre-physical therapy applicants should have chemistry and algebra. **Test requirements:** SAT or ACT; score report by August 1. SAT or ACT required of liberal arts, accounting, mathematics, science, and legal assistant applicants.

1992 FRESHMAN CLASS PROFILE. 136 men, 284 women enrolled. 15% had high school GPA of 3.0 or higher, 85% between 2.0 and 2.99. **Academic background:** Mid 50% of enrolled freshmen had SAT-V between 500-680, SAT-M between 500-680. 66% submitted SAT scores. **Characteristics:** 97% from in state, 65% commute, 20% have minority backgrounds, 3% are foreign students. Average age is 19.

FALL-TERM APPLICATIONS. $10 fee, may be waived for applicants with need. Closing date August 1; priority given to applications received by March 1; applicants notified on a rolling basis; Must reply by May 1. After that date, must reply as indicated in acceptance letter. Interview recommended. Portfolio recommended. Essay recommended. CRDA. Deferred and early admission available.

STUDENT LIFE. Housing: Dormitories (women, coed). Women's dormitories located only on campus of Russell Sage College 10 miles away in Troy. College provides transportation. **Activities:** Student government, magazine, student newspaper, activities board, Distributive Education Club of America, Black and Latin Student Alliance, Phi Theta Kappa, student advisers, paralegal club.

ATHLETICS. NJCAA. **Intercollegiate:** Basketball M. **Intramural:** Basketball, volleyball.

STUDENT SERVICES. Aptitude testing, career counseling, employment service for undergraduates, freshman orientation, personal counseling, placement service for graduates, special adviser for adult students.

ANNUAL EXPENSES. Tuition and fees (1992-93): $6,620. **Room and board:** $4,500. **Books and supplies:** $500. **Other expenses:** $650.

FINANCIAL AID. 77% of freshmen, 65% of continuing students receive some form of aid. 99% of grants, 86% of loans, all jobs based on need. Academic, art, athletic, leadership scholarships available. **Aid applications:** No closing date; priority given to applications received by March 15; applicants notified on a rolling basis beginning on or about April 1; must reply within 2 weeks.

ADDRESS/TELEPHONE. Kristine Kokochak, Director of Admission, Sage Junior College of Albany, 140 New Scotland Avenue, Albany, NY 12208. (518) 445-1730. (800) 999-9522. Fax: (518) 436-0539.

St. Bonaventure University
St. Bonaventure, New York — CB code: 2793

Admissions: 86% of applicants accepted
Based on:
- ••• School record
- •• Activities, test scores
- • Essay, interview, recommendations, special talents

Completion: 82% of freshmen end year in good standing
72% graduate, 33% of these enter graduate study

4-year private university, coed, affiliated with Roman Catholic Church. Founded in 1858. **Accreditation:** Regional. **Undergraduate enrollment:** 1,004 men, 1,007 women full time; 58 men, 62 women part time. **Graduate enrollment:** 123 men, 134 women full time; 185 men, 224 women part time. **Faculty:** 231 total (176 full time), 126 with doctorates or other terminal degrees. **Location:** Suburban campus in large town; 75 miles from Buffalo, on Pennsylvania border. **Calendar:** Semester, limited summer session. **Microcomputers:** 140 located in libraries, classrooms, computer centers. **Special facilities:** Observatory. **Additional facts:** Independent institution in Franciscan tradition.

DEGREES OFFERED. BA, BS, MA, MS, MBA, MEd. 544 bachelor's degrees awarded in 1992. 22% in business and management, 6% business/office and marketing/distribution, 9% communications, 14% teacher education, 5% letters/literature, 7% psychology, 20% social sciences. Graduate degrees offered in 27 major fields of study.

UNDERGRADUATE MAJORS. Accounting, biological and physical sciences, biology, business administration and management, business and management, business economics, business education, chemistry, clinical laboratory science, communications, computer and information sciences, computer programming, economics, education, elementary education, engineering physics, English, English education, finance, foreign languages (multiple emphasis), foreign languages education, French, German, Greek (classical), history, humanities, humanities and social sciences, journalism, Latin, liberal/general studies, management science, marketing and distribution, marketing management, mathematics, mathematics education, medical laboratory technologies, military science (Army), philosophy, physical education, physics, political science and government, psychology, science education, secondary education, social science education, social sciences, sociology, Spanish, theological studies.

ACADEMIC PROGRAMS. Accelerated program, double major, dual enrollment of high school students, honors program, independent study, internships, student-designed major, study abroad, visiting/exchange student program, Washington semester; combined bachelor's/graduate program in business administration. **Remedial services:** Learning center, preadmission summer program, reduced course load, remedial instruction, special counselor, tutoring, New York State Higher Education Opportunity Program. **ROTC:** Army. **Placement/credit:** AP, CLEP General and Subject, institutional tests; 30 credit hours maximum for bachelor's degree.

ACADEMIC REQUIREMENTS. Freshmen must earn minimum GPA of 2.0 to continue in good standing. 85% of freshmen return for sophomore year. Students must declare major by end of second year. **Graduation requirements:** 129 hours for bachelor's (30 in major). Most students required to take courses in computer science, English, foreign languages, history, humanities, mathematics, philosophy/religion, biological/physical sciences, social sciences.

FRESHMAN ADMISSIONS. Selection criteria: High school GPA and curriculum most important. Recommendation, class rank, test scores, extracurricular activities also considered. **High school preparation:** 16 units required. Required units include English 4, foreign language 2, mathematics 3, social science 4 and science 3. Science majors must have 4 science, 4 mathematics. Business majors need 4 mathematics. **Test requirements:** SAT or ACT; score report by March 1.

1992 FRESHMAN CLASS PROFILE. 791 men applied, 652 accepted, 231 enrolled; 784 women applied, 704 accepted, 228 enrolled. 41% had high school GPA of 3.0 or higher, 55% between 2.0 and 2.99. 10% were in top tenth and 36% were in top quarter of graduating class. **Academic background:** Mid 50% of enrolled freshmen had SAT-V between 400-500, SAT-M between 450-570; ACT composite between 22-25. 97% submitted SAT scores, 41% submitted ACT scores. **Characteristics:** 72% from in state, 96% live in college housing, 4% have minority backgrounds, 2% are foreign students. Average age is 18.

FALL-TERM APPLICATIONS. $25 fee, may be waived for applicants with need. No closing date; priority given to applications received by March 1; applicants notified on a rolling basis; must reply by May 1 or date indicated in letter. Interview recommended. Essay recommended. CRDA. Deferred and early admission available. Applications considered until housing is closed.

STUDENT LIFE. Housing: Dormitories (coed); apartment, handicapped housing available. Students must live on campus until they are seniors or 21 years old, unless they live within commuting distance. **Activities:** Student government, magazine, radio, student newspaper, television, yearbook, choral groups, concert band, drama, jazz band, music ensembles, musical theater, pep band, campus ministry, drop-in center, Big Brother-Big Sister Youth Program, program to aid elderly, Knights of Columbus, Irish society, social action projects, World Hunger, Black Student Union.

ATHLETICS. NCAA. **Intercollegiate:** Baseball M, basketball, cross-country, diving, golf M, ice hockey M, lacrosse M, soccer, softball W, swimming, tennis, track and field, volleyball W. **Intramural:** Basketball, bowling, football M, golf, racquetball, rugby M, skiing, soccer, softball, swimming, table tennis, tennis, volleyball, water polo M.

STUDENT SERVICES. Aptitude testing, career counseling, employment service for undergraduates, freshman orientation, health services, personal counseling, placement service for graduates, veterans counselor, services/facilities for handicapped.

ANNUAL EXPENSES. Tuition and fees (1992-93): $9,584. **Room and board:** $4,824. **Books and supplies:** $450. **Other expenses:** $650.

FINANCIAL AID. 79% of freshmen, 85% of continuing students receive some form of aid. 62% of grants, 97% of loans, 30% of jobs based on need. 320 enrolled freshmen were judged to have need, all were offered aid. Academic, music/drama, athletic, minority scholarships available. **Aid applications:** Closing date March 1; applicants notified on or about April 1; must reply by May 1.

ADDRESS/TELEPHONE. June T. Solan, Director of Admissions, St. Bonaventure University, Route 417 P.O. Box D, St. Bonaventure, NY 14778-2284. (716) 375-2400. (800) 848-1181. Fax: (716) 375-2005. (800) 462-5050 (New York State only).

St. Francis College
Brooklyn Heights, New York — CB code: 2796

Admissions: 89% of applicants accepted
Based on:
- ••• School record
- •• Activities, essay, interview, recommendations, test scores
- • Special talents

Completion: 85% of freshmen end year in good standing
40% graduate

4-year private liberal arts college, coed. Founded in 1884. **Accreditation:** Regional. **Undergraduate enrollment:** 635 men, 826 women full time; 274 men, 364 women part time. **Faculty:** 132 total (55 full time), 51 with doctorates or other terminal degrees. **Location:** Urban campus in very large city. **Calendar:** Semester, limited summer session. Extensive evening/early morning classes. **Microcomputers:** 50 located in classrooms, computer centers.

DEGREES OFFERED. AS, AAS, BA, BS. 8 associate degrees awarded in 1992. 63% in business/office and marketing/distribution, 25% computer sciences, 12% parks/recreation, protective services, public affairs. 304 bachelor's degrees awarded. 48% in business and management, 5% communications, 7% teacher education, 8% allied health, 5% letters/literature, 12% multi/interdisciplinary studies, 9% social sciences.

UNDERGRADUATE MAJORS. Associate: Business and office, business data processing and related programs, criminal justice studies, data processing, law enforcement and corrections technologies. **Bachelor's:** Accounting, aviation management, biology, business administration and management, clinical laboratory science, communications, economics, elementary education, English, health care administration, history, international studies, liberal/general studies, mathematics, medical laboratory technologies, physical education, political science and government, prelaw, premedicine, psychology, secondary education, social sciences, sociology, special education.

ACADEMIC PROGRAMS. 2-year transfer program, accelerated program, double major, dual enrollment of high school students, honors program, independent study, internships, study abroad, teacher preparation, accelerated biomedical science program with New York College of Podiatric Medicine; medical technology program with 3 separate hospital clinical facilities; joint affiliation with SUNY Health Science Center at Brooklyn offering preprofessional education in the fields of nursing, occupational therapy, medical sonography, and medical records administration. **Remedial services:** Learning center, preadmission summer program, reduced course load, remedial instruction, special counselor, tutoring. **ROTC:** Air Force, Army. **Placement/credit:** AP, CLEP General and Subject, institutional tests; 30 credit hours maximum for associate degree; 96 credit hours maximum for bachelor's degree.

ACADEMIC REQUIREMENTS. Freshmen must earn minimum GPA of 1.5 to continue in good standing. 75% of freshmen return for sophomore year. Students must declare major by end of second year. **Graduation requirements:** 63 hours for associate (20 in major), 128 hours for bachelor's (35 in major). Most students required to take courses in arts/fine arts, English, foreign languages, history, humanities, mathematics, philosophy/religion, biological/physical sciences, social sciences. **Postgraduate studies:** 50% from 2-year programs enter 4-year programs.

FRESHMAN ADMISSIONS. Selection criteria: Academic achievement, test scores, counselor's recommendation, school and community activities, interview. 80% high school average required. **High school preparation:** 16 units required; 16 recommended. Required and recommended units include English 4-4, mathematics 2-2, social science 3-3 and science 1-2. Foreign language 2 recommended. **Test requirements:** SAT or ACT (SAT preferred); score report by September 1. **Additional information:** Degree-seeking students who do not meet criteria may be admitted after review and assessment of their educational background.

1992 FRESHMAN CLASS PROFILE. 432 men applied, 378 accepted, 200 enrolled; 589 women applied, 534 accepted, 270 enrolled. 38% had high school GPA of 3.0 or higher, 61% between 2.0 and 2.99. **Characteristics:** 99% from in state, 100% commute, 43% have minority backgrounds, 5% are foreign students, 10% join fraternities/sororities. Average age is 18.

FALL-TERM APPLICATIONS. $20 fee, may be waived for applicants with need. No closing date; applicants notified on a rolling basis; must reply within 8 weeks. Essay required. Interview required of academically weak applicants; recommended for all applicants. Deferred and early admission available.

STUDENT LIFE. Housing: Students may be accommodated at Long Island University residence halls located within 15 minute walk. **Activities:** Student government, magazine, student newspaper, yearbook, choral groups, drama, fraternities, sororities, 26 clubs and organizations, 10 honor societies, music club, foreign student association, black student association, Latin American Society, Flyers Club, Accounting Society, St. Thomas More Prelaw Society.

ATHLETICS. NCAA. **Intercollegiate:** Baseball M, basketball, cross-country, soccer M, softball W, swimming, tennis, track and field, volleyball W, water polo M. **Intramural:** Basketball, bowling, fencing, soccer, softball, table tennis, volleyball. **Clubs:** Bowling.

STUDENT SERVICES. Aptitude testing, career counseling, employment service for undergraduates, freshman orientation, health services, personal counseling, placement service for graduates, special adviser for adult students, veterans counselor, services/facilities for handicapped.

ANNUAL EXPENSES. Tuition and fees (1992-93): $6,150. **Books and supplies:** $450. **Other expenses:** $1,125.

FINANCIAL AID. 80% of freshmen, 73% of continuing students receive some form of aid. 92% of grants, 90% of loans, 95% of jobs based on need. 237 enrolled freshmen were judged to have need, all were offered aid. Academic, athletic scholarships available. **Aid applications:** No closing date; priority given to applications received by February 15; applicants notified on a rolling basis beginning on or about April 20; must reply within 30 days or if notified after June 1 must reply within 2 weeks.

ADDRESS/TELEPHONE. Brother George Larkin, O.S.F, Dean of Admissions, St. Francis College, 180 Remsen Street, Brooklyn Heights, NY 11201. (718) 522-2300. Fax: (718) 522-1274.

St. John Fisher College
Rochester, New York

CB code: 2798

Admissions: 73% of applicants accepted
Based on: ••• School record
•• Test scores
• Activities, essay, interview, recommendations, special talents
Completion: 92% of freshmen end year in good standing
57% graduate, 15% of these enter graduate study

4-year private college of arts and sciences and business college, coed, affiliated with Roman Catholic Church. Founded in 1948. **Accreditation:** Regional. **Undergraduate enrollment:** 774 men, 939 women full time; 138 men, 273 women part time. **Graduate enrollment:** 7 men, 1 woman full time; 119 men, 167 women part time. **Faculty:** 189 total (105 full time), 106 with doctorates or other terminal degrees. **Location:** Suburban campus in large city; 6 miles from downtown. **Calendar:** Semester, extensive summer session. Saturday and extensive evening/early morning classes. **Microcomputers:** 146 located in libraries, classrooms, computer centers. **Special facilities:** 2 electron microscopes, greenhouse, semiprofessional theater, Botsford Enid Knapp School of Dance, radiation and animal labs. **Additional facts:** Independent institution in the Roman Catholic tradition, taught by Basilian priests.

DEGREES OFFERED. BA, BS, MS, MBA. 475 bachelor's degrees awarded in 1992. 37% in business and management, 12% communications, 9% psychology, 23% social sciences. Graduate degrees offered in 2 major fields of study.

UNDERGRADUATE MAJORS. Elementary education, secondary education. accounting, anthropology, biochemistry, biology, business administration and management, business and management, chemistry, communications, computer and information sciences, economics, English, French, German, history, human resources development, international business management, international relations, international studies, Italian, journalism, liberal/general studies, management information systems, marketing management, mathematics, nursing, philosophy, physics, political science and government, predentistry, preengineering, prelaw, premedicine, prepharmacy, preveterinary, psychology, radio/television broadcasting, religion, sociology, Spanish.

ACADEMIC PROGRAMS. Accelerated program, double major, dual enrollment of high school students, honors program, independent study, internships, student-designed major, study abroad, teacher preparation, visiting/exchange student program, Washington semester, cross-registration, 3-4 optometry program, 2-2 environmental science and forestry program with SUNY; liberal arts/career combination in engineering; combined bachelor's/graduate program in business administration. **Remedial services:** Learning center, preadmission summer program, reduced course load, remedial instruction, special counselor, tutoring, writing center, mathematics help center. **ROTC:** Air Force, Army. **Placement/credit:** AP, CLEP Subject, institutional tests; 66 credit hours maximum for bachelor's degree.

ACADEMIC REQUIREMENTS. Freshmen must earn minimum GPA of 2.0 to continue in good standing. 81% of freshmen return for sophomore year. Students must declare major by end of second year. **Graduation requirements:** 120 hours for bachelor's (30 in major). Most students required to take courses in English, mathematics, philosophy/religion, biological/physical sciences, social sciences. **Postgraduate studies:** 3% enter law school, 1% enter medical school, 3% enter MBA programs, 8% enter other graduate study. **Additional information:** Institute for Polish Studies, concentration in urban studies available.

FRESHMAN ADMISSIONS. Selection criteria: Applicants should be in top half of class and have approximately 80% GPA. High school average most important factor. **High school preparation:** 16 units required. Recommended units include English 4, foreign language 2, mathematics 3, social science 4 and science 3. 4 mathematics courses required for programs needing college calculus. **Test requirements:** SAT or ACT; score report by August 15. **Additional information:** Those students not meeting regular admissions requirements will be considered if they demonstrate potential to successfully complete academic program.

1992 FRESHMAN CLASS PROFILE. 609 men applied, 406 accepted, 152 enrolled; 679 women applied, 540 accepted, 198 enrolled. 50% had high school GPA of 3.0 or higher, 50% between 2.0 and 2.99. 25% were in top tenth and 52% were in top quarter of graduating class. **Academic background:** Mid 50% of enrolled freshmen had SAT-V between 420-520, SAT-M between 480-580; ACT composite between 21-24. 98% submitted SAT scores, 36% submitted ACT scores. **Characteristics:** 95% from in state, 80% live in college housing, 10% have minority backgrounds. Average age is 18.

FALL-TERM APPLICATIONS. $25 fee, may be waived for applicants with need. No closing date; priority given to applications received by February 15; applicants notified on a rolling basis beginning on or about October 1; must reply by May 1 or within 2 weeks if notified thereafter. Essay required. Interview recommended. CRDA. Deferred and early admission available. EDP-S.

STUDENT LIFE. Housing: Dormitories (men, women, coed); handicapped housing available. Compatiblity forms used to assign new students to residence hall. **Activities:** Student government, film, magazine, radio, student newspaper, television, yearbook, choral groups, drama, musical theater, gospel choir, Young Republicans and Young Democrats, united culture club, social service organizations, Women in Communications, campus ministry, circle-K, independentstudent coalition, Teddi dance marathon project, Hispanic Coalition, International Studies Association. **Additional information:** Freshman wellness program available.

ATHLETICS. NCAA. **Intercollegiate:** Baseball M, basketball, cross-country, football M, golf, soccer, softball W, tennis, volleyball W. **Intramural:** Basketball, golf, racquetball, skiing, soccer, softball, tennis, volleyball. **Clubs:** Lacrosse M, rowing M, rugby M.

STUDENT SERVICES. Career counseling, employment service for undergraduates, freshman orientation, health services, on-campus day care, personal counseling, placement service for graduates, special adviser for adult students, veterans counselor, services/facilities for handicapped.

ANNUAL EXPENSES. Tuition and fees: $10,040. **Room and board:** $5,340. **Books and supplies:** $400. **Other expenses:** $600.

FINANCIAL AID. 82% of freshmen, 82% of continuing students receive some form of aid. 95% of grants, 90% of loans, 70% of jobs based on need. 308 enrolled freshmen were judged to have need, all were offered aid. Academic, leadership, minority scholarships available. **Aid applications:** No closing date; priority given to applications received by March 1; applicants notified on a rolling basis beginning on or about March 15; must reply by May 1 or within 2 weeks if notified thereafter.

ADDRESS/TELEPHONE. Peter E. Lindsey, Dean of Admissions, St. John Fisher College, 3690 East Avenue, Rochester, NY 14618-3597. (716) 385-8064. (800) 444-4640. Fax: (716) 385-8129.

St. John's University
Jamaica, New York — CB code: 2799

4-year private university, coed, affiliated with Roman Catholic Church. Founded in 1870. **Accreditation:** Regional. **Undergraduate enrollment:** 5,654 men, 6,131 women full time; 747 men, 1,005 women part time. **Graduate enrollment:** 936 men, 957 women full time; 1,512 men, 1,871 women part time. **Faculty:** 1,037 total (623 full time), 498 with doctorates or other terminal degrees. **Location:** Urban campus in very large city; 10 miles from Manhattan. **Calendar:** Semester, extensive summer session. Saturday and extensive evening/early morning classes. **Microcomputers:** 360 located in libraries, computer centers. **Special facilities:** Art gallery within Institute of Asian Studies, speech and hearing clinic, instructional media center, Hugh Carey collection of personal and gubernatorial documents. **Additional facts:** Branch campus on Staten Island.

DEGREES OFFERED. AA, AS, BA, BS, BFA, MA, MS, MBA, PhD, EdD, Pharm D, JD, M.Div. 587 associate degrees awarded in 1992. 43% in business and management, 6% languages, 40% letters/literature, 10% social sciences. 2,707 bachelor's degrees awarded. 27% in business and management, 9% business/office and marketing/distribution, 8% communications, 9% teacher education, 10% health sciences, 10% parks/recreation, protective services, public affairs, 5% psychology, 9% social sciences. Graduate degrees offered in 48 major fields of study.

UNDERGRADUATE MAJORS. Associate: Business and office, business data processing and related programs, law enforcement and corrections technologies, legal assistant/paralegal, liberal/general studies, photographic technology, teacher aide. **Bachelor's:** Accounting, American studies, anthropology, art education, Asian studies, biology, business administration and management, business economics, chemistry, clinical laboratory science, commercial art, communications, computer and information sciences, criminal justice studies, East Asian studies, ecology, economics, elementary education, English, English education, English literature, environmental science, finance, fine arts, foreign languages education, French, funeral services/mortuary science, German, graphic design, health care administration, history, Italian, journalism, legal assistant/paralegal, management information systems, marketing and distribution, marketing management, mathematics, mathematics education, operations research, pathologist's assistant, pharmacy, philosophy, photography, physical sciences, physician's assistant, physics, political science and government, protective services, psychology, public administration, reading education, religion, science education, secondary education, social sciences, social studies education, sociology, Spanish, special education, speech, speech pathology/audiology, statistics, theological studies, toxicology, transportation management.

ACADEMIC PROGRAMS. 2-year transfer program, accelerated program, double major, dual enrollment of high school students, honors program, internships, study abroad, teacher preparation, weekend college, cross-registration, combined bachelor's/graduate degree program in dentistry with Columbia University, College Europe study abroad program based in Hungary, study abroad program in Ireland, 3+2 program in engineering with Polytechnic University; combined bachelor's/graduate program in business administration, law. **Remedial services:** Preadmission summer program, reduced course load, remedial instruction, special counselor, tutoring, New York State Higher Education Opportunity Program, Options opportunity program for out-of-state residents, Self-Pace Program for pharmacy and other science majors, New York State Science and Technology Entry Program and Liberty Partnership Program. **ROTC:** Army. **Placement/credit:** AP, CLEP Subject, institutional tests.

ACADEMIC REQUIREMENTS. Freshmen must earn minimum GPA of 2.0 to continue in good standing. 83% of freshmen return for sophomore year. Students must declare major by end of second year. **Graduation requirements:** 60 hours for associate, 126 hours for bachelor's. Most students required to take courses in English, mathematics, philosophy/religion, biological/physical sciences, social sciences. **Postgraduate studies:** 94% from 2-year programs enter 4-year programs.

FRESHMAN ADMISSIONS. Selection criteria: School achievement record, standardized test scores, work experience, counselor recommendations, honors, and awards all considered. **High school preparation:** 16 units required. Required units include English 4, foreign language 2, mathematics 3, social science 1 and science 1. Elementary algebra, plane geometry, intermediate algebra, and trigonometry highly recommended or required for science, mathematics, physics, and computer science programs. Chemistry and physics strongly recommended for programs in sciences, pharmacy, and allied health professions. **Test requirements:** SAT or ACT (SAT preferred); score report by September 15. **Additional information:** Combined score of 1000 on SAT or cumulative high school average of 80% required for freshman admission to 4-year programs.

1992 FRESHMAN CLASS PROFILE. 1,140 men, 1,260 women enrolled. 89% had high school GPA of 3.0 or higher, 11% between 2.0 and 2.99. **Characteristics:** 90% from in state, 100% commute, 38% have minority backgrounds, 4% are foreign students. Average age is 18.

FALL-TERM APPLICATIONS. $20 fee, may be waived for applicants with need. No closing date; priority given to applications received by March 1; applicants notified on a rolling basis; must reply by May 1 or within 4 weeks if notified thereafter. Interview required for academically weak applicants. Portfolio required for fine art, creative photography, graphic design applicants. Deferred and early admission available.

STUDENT LIFE. Housing: Computerized off-campus housing and roommate lists available. **Activities:** Student government, magazine, radio, student newspaper, television, yearbook, literary and satirical publications, public speaking and debate, choral groups, dance, drama, marching band, pep band, gospel choir, fraternities, sororities, over 125 organizations, including CAUSE (Community and University Services in Education), Accounting Society, Harayal Black Student Union, St. Vincent de Paul Society, Golden Key Honor Society, and de Paul Social Action Group.

ATHLETICS. NCAA. **Intercollegiate:** Baseball M, basketball, cross-country, fencing, football M, golf M, lacrosse M, rifle, soccer, softball W, swimming, tennis, track and field. **Intramural:** Basketball, fencing, golf M, handball M, racquetball, softball M, swimming, tennis, track and field, volleyball M. **Clubs:** Bowling, horseback riding, rifle, rowing, table tennis, volleyball W, wrestling M.

STUDENT SERVICES. Aptitude testing, career counseling, employment service for undergraduates, freshman orientation, health services, personal counseling, placement service for graduates, special adviser for adult students, veterans counselor, multi-cultural student adviser, services/facilities for handicapped.

ANNUAL EXPENSES. Tuition and fees: $9,100. **Books and supplies:** $500. **Other expenses:** $1,350.

FINANCIAL AID. 75% of continuing students receive some form of aid. 89% of grants, 91% of loans, 30% of jobs based on need. 1,646 enrolled freshmen were judged to have need, 1,550 were offered aid. Academic, music/drama, art, athletic, state/district residency, leadership, alumni affiliation scholarships available. **Aid applications:** No closing date; priority given to applications received by April 1; applicants notified on a rolling basis beginning on or about May 1; must reply within 4 weeks.

ADDRESS/TELEPHONE. Vivian Liu, Director of Admissions, St. John's University, Grand Central and Utopia Parkways, Jamaica, NY 11439. (718) 990-6240. (800) 232-4SJU. Students may also write to Dean of Admissions, St. John's University, 300 Howard Avenue, Staten Island, NY 10301, or telephone (718) 447-4343.

St. Joseph's College
Brooklyn, New York — CB code: 2802

Admissions: 58% of applicants accepted
Based on: ••• School record, test scores
•• Activities, interview, recommendations
• Essay, special talents
Completion: 88% of freshmen end year in good standing
57% graduate, 40% of these enter graduate study

4-year private liberal arts college, coed. Founded in 1916. **Accreditation:** Regional. **Undergraduate enrollment:** 81 men, 297 women full time; 150 men, 434 women part time. **Faculty:** 109 total (50 full time), 35 with doctorates or other terminal degrees. **Location:** Urban campus in very large city; 8 miles from center of Manhattan. **Calendar:** Semester, limited summer session. **Microcomputers:** 20 located in computer centers. **Special facilities:** Laboratory preschool.

DEGREES OFFERED. BA, BS. 191 bachelor's degrees awarded in 1992. 13% in teacher education, 39% health sciences, 29% allied health, 5% social sciences.

UNDERGRADUATE MAJORS. Accounting, biology, business administration and management, business and management, chemistry, community health work, early childhood education, education, elementary education, English, English education, foreign languages education, French, health care administration, history, human relations, junior high education, liberal/general studies, mathematics, mathematics education, nursing, psychology, science education, secondary education, social sciences, social studies education, Spanish, special education, speech, speech/communication/theater education.

ACADEMIC PROGRAMS. Accelerated program, honors program, independent study, internships, teacher preparation, weekend college, accelerated biomedical program with New York College of Podiatric Medicine; liberal arts/career combination in business. **Remedial services:** Reduced course load, special counselor, tutoring, writing laboratory. **Placement/credit:** AP, CLEP General and Subject; 30 credit hours maximum for bachelor's degree.

ACADEMIC REQUIREMENTS. Freshmen must earn minimum GPA of 2.0 to continue in good standing. 79% of freshmen return for sophomore year. Students must declare major by end of second year. **Graduation requirements:** 128 hours for bachelor's (30 in major). Most students required to take courses in English, history, humanities, mathematics, biological/physical sciences, social sciences. **Postgraduate studies:** 4% enter law school,

4% enter medical school, 4% enter MBA programs, 28% enter other graduate study.

FRESHMAN ADMISSIONS. Selection criteria: School achievement record, SAT scores, class rank, activities, recommendations considered. Academic average of 80% required. **High school preparation:** 16 units required. Required units include English 4, foreign language 2, mathematics 2, social science 1 and science 1. 3 units mathematics recommended for mathematics, science, and business majors, 2 units science recommended for science majors. No specific course requirements for general studies applicants. **Test requirements:** SAT or ACT (SAT preferred); score report by August 15.

1992 FRESHMAN CLASS PROFILE. 60% had high school GPA of 3.0 or higher, 40% between 2.0 and 2.99. 42% were in top tenth and 65% were in top quarter of graduating class. **Academic background:** Mid 50% of enrolled freshmen had SAT-V between 400-500, SAT-M between 410-540. 99% submitted SAT scores. **Characteristics:** 99% from in state, 100% commute, 20% have minority backgrounds, 1% are foreign students. Average age is 18.

FALL-TERM APPLICATIONS. $25 fee, may be waived for applicants with need. Closing date August 15; priority given to applications received by March 15; applicants notified on a rolling basis; must reply by May 1 or within 2 weeks if notified thereafter. Interview recommended. Essay recommended. CRDA. Deferred and early admission available.

STUDENT LIFE. Activities: Student government, student newspaper, yearbook, dance, drama, musical theater, folk group, fraternities, sororities, campus ministry, Gaelic Society, Black Culture Club, Beta Upsilon Delta, Psi Psi Psi, Hispanic Awareness Club, The Heritage Gallery. **Additional information:** Undergraduate Association funds and monitors more than 20 clubs and organizations and students control much of extracurricular affairs.

ATHLETICS. Intercollegiate: Basketball M, softball W. **Intramural:** Badminton, basketball, bowling M, table tennis, volleyball.

STUDENT SERVICES. Career counseling, employment service for undergraduates, freshman orientation, personal counseling, placement service for graduates, special adviser for adult students.

ANNUAL EXPENSES. Tuition and fees: $7,122. **Books and supplies:** $500. **Other expenses:** $600.

FINANCIAL AID. 90% of freshmen, 75% of continuing students receive some form of aid. 57% of grants, 85% of loans, 57% of jobs based on need. 35 enrolled freshmen were judged to have need, all were offered aid. Academic, alumni affiliation scholarships available. **Aid applications:** No closing date; priority given to applications received by February 25; applicants notified on a rolling basis beginning on or about April 1; must reply by May 1 or within 2 weeks if notified thereafter.

ADDRESS/TELEPHONE. Angelo Araimo, Director of Admissions, St. Joseph's College, 245 Clinton Avenue, Brooklyn, NY 11205-3688. (718) 636-6868.

St. Joseph's College: Suffolk Campus
Patchogue, New York — CB code: 2841

Admissions: 82% of applicants accepted
Based on:
- ••• School record, test scores
- •• Recommendations
- • Activities, essay, interview

Completion: 85% of freshmen end year in good standing
55% graduate, 66% of these enter graduate study

4-year private branch campus, liberal arts college, coed. Founded in 1916. **Accreditation:** Regional. **Undergraduate enrollment:** 310 men, 817 women full time; 116 men, 690 women part time. **Faculty:** 168 total (55 full time), 29 with doctorates or other terminal degrees. **Location:** Suburban campus in large town; 50 miles from New York City. **Calendar:** 4-1-4, extensive summer session. Saturday and extensive evening/early morning classes. **Microcomputers:** 35 located in libraries, computer centers. **Special facilities:** Theater, Long Island history museum.

DEGREES OFFERED. BA, BS. 412 bachelor's degrees awarded in 1992. 16% in business and management, 38% teacher education, 27% health sciences, 7% multi/interdisciplinary studies, 5% psychology.

UNDERGRADUATE MAJORS. Accounting, biology, business administration and management, community health work, computer mathematics, early childhood education, education, elementary education, English, English education, health care administration, history, human relations, junior high education, mathematics, mathematics education, nursing, parks and recreation management, psychology, recreation and community services technologies, recreation therapy, secondary education, social sciences, social studies education, sociology, special education.

ACADEMIC PROGRAMS. Independent study, internships, teacher preparation, cross-registration. **Remedial services:** Reduced course load, special counselor, tutoring, English workshops, mathematics laboratory. **ROTC:** Air Force, Army. **Placement/credit:** AP, CLEP General and Subject, institutional tests; 30 credit hours maximum for bachelor's degree.

ACADEMIC REQUIREMENTS. Freshmen must earn minimum GPA of 2.0 to continue in good standing. 78% of freshmen return for sophomore year. Students must declare major by end of first year. **Graduation requirements:** 128 hours for bachelor's (30 in major). Most students required to take courses in arts/fine arts, English, foreign languages, history, humanities, mathematics, philosophy/religion, biological/physical sciences, social sciences. **Postgraduate studies:** 5% enter law school, 1% enter medical school, 10% enter MBA programs, 50% enter other graduate study. **Additional information:** 2-year upper-division general studies program for adults offers bachelor's degree in health administration, community health, general studies, and human resource management.

FRESHMAN ADMISSIONS. Selection criteria: Test scores, school achievement record, 3.0 GPA. **High school preparation:** 16 units required. Required units include English 4, foreign language 2, mathematics 2, social science 1 and science 1. Social science unit must be American history. **Test requirements:** SAT or ACT (SAT preferred); score report by August 15.

1992 FRESHMAN CLASS PROFILE. 113 men applied, 93 accepted, 36 enrolled; 284 women applied, 234 accepted, 113 enrolled. 76% had high school GPA of 3.0 or higher, 24% between 2.0 and 2.99. 32% were in top tenth and 40% were in top quarter of graduating class. **Academic background:** Mid 50% of enrolled freshmen had SAT-V between 450-590, SAT-M between 450-590. 99% submitted SAT scores. **Characteristics:** 100% from in state, 100% commute, 11% have minority backgrounds, 2% join fraternities/sororities. Average age is 18.

FALL-TERM APPLICATIONS. $25 fee, may be waived for applicants with need. Closing date August 15; priority given to applications received by May 15; applicants notified on a rolling basis; must reply by May 1 or immediately if notified thereafter. Interview recommended. Essay recommended. CRDA. Deferred and early admission available.

STUDENT LIFE. Activities: Student government, magazine, student newspaper, yearbook, choral groups, drama, musical theater, folk group, fraternities, sororities, Religious Affairs Committee, Student Volunteer Services, Human Relations Club.

ATHLETICS. NAIA. **Intercollegiate:** Baseball M, basketball M, bowling, horseback riding, soccer M, softball W, tennis, volleyball W. **Intramural:** Badminton, softball M, table tennis, tennis, volleyball. **Clubs:** Intercolligiate horseback riding.

STUDENT SERVICES. Aptitude testing, career counseling, employment service for undergraduates, freshman orientation, personal counseling, placement service for graduates, veterans counselor, services/facilities for handicapped.

ANNUAL EXPENSES. Tuition and fees: $7,332. **Books and supplies:** $500. **Other expenses:** $600.

FINANCIAL AID. 89% of freshmen, 72% of continuing students receive some form of aid. 53% of grants, 81% of loans, 48% of jobs based on need. 85 enrolled freshmen were judged to have need, all were offered aid. Academic scholarships available. **Aid applications:** No closing date; priority given to applications received by February 25; applicants notified on a rolling basis beginning on or about April 15; must reply by May 1 or within 2 weeks if notified thereafter.

ADDRESS/TELEPHONE. Marion E. Salgado, Director of Admissions, St. Joseph's College: Suffolk Campus, 155 Roe Boulevard, Patchogue, NY 11772-2603. (516) 447-3219. Fax: (516) 654-1782.

St. Joseph's School of Nursing
Syracuse, New York — CB code: 2825

2-year private nursing college, coed, affiliated with Roman Catholic Church. **Undergraduate enrollment:** 13 men, 95 women full time; 3 men, 58 women part time. **Faculty:** 24 total (13 full time). **Location:** Urban campus in small city. **Special facilities:** 462 bed teaching hospital.

DEGREES OFFERED. AAS. 70 associate degrees awarded in 1992. 100% in allied health.

UNDERGRADUATE MAJORS. Nursing.

ACADEMIC PROGRAMS. 2-year transfer program. **Remedial services:** Reduced course load, special counselor, tutoring. **Placement/credit:** AP, CLEP General.

ACADEMIC REQUIREMENTS. Freshmen must earn minimum GPA of 2.0 to continue in good standing. 85% of freshmen return for sophomore year. **Graduation requirements:** 70 hours for associate (70 in major). Most students required to take courses in English, humanities, philosophy/religion, biological/physical sciences, social sciences.

FRESHMAN ADMISSIONS. Selection criteria: High school record, SAT/ACT test scores or preentrance examination, and personal interview very important. **High school preparation:** 13 units required. Required and recommended units include biological science 1-2, English 4, mathematics 2-3, physical science 2 and social science 4. **Test requirements:** SAT or ACT.

1992 FRESHMAN CLASS PROFILE. 2 men, 2 women enrolled. 100% had high school GPA between 2.0 and 2.99. **Characteristics:** 99% from in state, 75% commute, 1% are foreign students. Average age is 27.

FALL-TERM APPLICATIONS. $20 fee. No closing date; priority given to applications received by December 31; applicants notified on a rolling basis. Interview required. Essay required. Deferred admission available.

STUDENT LIFE. Housing: Dormitories (coed). **Activities:** Student government.

STUDENT SERVICES. Career counseling, freshman orientation, health services, personal counseling, services/facilities for handicapped.

ANNUAL EXPENSES. Tuition and fees (1992-93): $4,316. **Room and board:** $1,650 room only. **Books and supplies:** $600. **Other expenses:** $780.

FINANCIAL AID. 85% of freshmen, 85% of continuing students receive some form of aid. 54% of grants, 90% of loans based on need. Academic, leadership scholarships available. **Aid applications:** No closing date; priority given to applications received by May 29; applicants notified on a rolling basis beginning on or about June 15. **Additional information:** Tuition scholorships awarded to students for 3-year work commitment with our hospital which commences upon graduation.

ADDRESS/TELEPHONE. JoAnne Kiggins, Director of Admissions, St. Joseph's School of Nursing, 206 Prospect Avenue, Syracuse, NY 13203. (315) 448-5040.

St. Lawrence University

Canton, New York — CB code: 2805

Admissions: 75% of applicants accepted
Based on:
••• School record, test scores
•• Activities, essay, interview, recommendations
• Special talents
Completion: 95% of freshmen end year in good standing
80% graduate, 60% of these enter graduate study

4-year private liberal arts college, coed. Founded in 1856. **Accreditation:** Regional. **Undergraduate enrollment:** 918 men, 880 women full time; 3 men, 9 women part time. **Graduate enrollment:** 8 men, 10 women full time; 36 men, 66 women part time. **Faculty:** 185 total (169 full time), 150 with doctorates or other terminal degrees. **Location:** Rural campus in small town; 150 miles from Syracuse, 70 miles from Ottawa, Ontario, Canada. **Calendar:** Semester, limited summer session. **Microcomputers:** 600 located in dormitories, libraries, classrooms, computer centers, campus-wide network. **Special facilities:** Art collection with 7,000 works. **Additional facts:** Environmental studies programs emphasize international understanding and provide practical applications of curricular offerings.

DEGREES OFFERED. BA, BS, MA, MS. 509 bachelor's degrees awarded in 1992. 14% in letters/literature, 6% life sciences, 7% multi/interdisciplinary studies, 11% psychology, 44% social sciences, 5% visual and performing arts. Graduate degrees offered in 4 major fields of study.

UNDERGRADUATE MAJORS. Anthropology, Asian studies, biology, biophysics, chemistry, computer mathematics, creative writing, dramatic arts, economics, economics/mathematics, English literature, environmental science, fine arts, foreign languages (multiple emphasis), French, geology, geophysics and seismology, German, history, mathematics, music, philosophy, physical education, physics, political science and government, psychology, religion, sociology, Spanish.

ACADEMIC PROGRAMS. Accelerated program, double major, independent study, internships, semester at sea, student-designed major, study abroad, teacher preparation, Washington semester, cross-registration, 3+2 program in engineering with Clarkson University, Columbia University, Rensselaer Polytechnic Institute, SUNY at Binghamton, University of Rochester, University of Southern California, Washington University in Missouri, and Worcester Polytechnic Institute in Massachusetts, early assurance programs in medicine with SUNY Health Science Center at Syracuse and in dentistry with Columbia University and SUNY at Buffalo, 3+2 program in nursing with University of Rochester, combined bachelor's/graduate degree program in business administration with Clarkson University, study abroad programs in Europe, Kenya, Japan, Costa Rica, India and Canada. **Remedial services:** Preadmission summer program, reduced course load, tutoring, writing center. **ROTC:** Air Force, Army. **Placement/credit:** AP, CLEP General and Subject, institutional tests; 60 credit hours maximum for bachelor's degree.

ACADEMIC REQUIREMENTS. Freshmen must earn minimum GPA of 2.0 to continue in good standing. 91% of freshmen return for sophomore year. Students must declare major by end of second year. **Graduation requirements:** 120 hours for bachelor's (30 in major). Most students required to take courses in humanities, biological/physical sciences, social sciences. **Additional information:** Required comprehensive freshman program combines required course, close advising, residential experience, and communication skill development.

FRESHMAN ADMISSIONS. Selection criteria: Primarily academic record, but extracurricular activities, intellectual curiosity, leadership, motivation, and creativity among critical nonobjective factors also considered. **High school preparation:** 18 units recommended. Recommended units include English 4, foreign language 3, mathematics 3, social science 3 and science 4. **Test requirements:** SAT or ACT; score report by February 1. English Composition ACH (with or without essay) required of applicants submitting SAT scores. Score report by February 1. **Additional information:** Diverse student body sought.

1992 FRESHMAN CLASS PROFILE. 1,291 men applied, 936 accepted, 311 enrolled; 1,182 women applied, 931 accepted, 293 enrolled. **Academic background:** Mid 50% of enrolled freshmen had SAT-V between 440-540, SAT-M between 500-610. 90% submitted SAT scores. **Characteristics:** 46% from in state, 100% live in college housing, 6% have minority backgrounds, 4% are foreign students. Average age is 18.

FALL-TERM APPLICATIONS. $40 fee, may be waived for applicants with need. Closing date February 1; applicants notified on or about March 15; must reply by May 1. Essay required. Interview recommended. CRDA. Deferred and early admission available. EDP-F.

STUDENT LIFE. Housing: Dormitories (coed); fraternity, sorority housing available. Some suites available. Housing for handicapped students may be arranged. Students can petition to have quiet or single-sex halls within a dormitory. **Activities:** Student government, magazine, radio, student newspaper, yearbook, choral groups, concert band, dance, drama, music ensembles, musical theater, pep band, singing saints and singing sinners accappella group, fraternities, sororities, Jewish student organization, Black Student Union, Environmental Awareness Organization, theme houses, Alpha Phi Omega, Forensic Society, Outing Club, academic honoraries, Thelomathesian Society. **Additional information:** Freshman Program integrates academic and residential life by requiring freshmen to reside in 1 of 12 colleges that have academic/administrative staff.

ATHLETICS. NCAA. **Intercollegiate:** Baseball M, basketball, cross-country, diving, field hockey W, football M, ice hockey, lacrosse, skiing, soccer, swimming, tennis, track and field, volleyball W, wrestling M. **Intramural:** Basketball, football M, golf, horseback riding, ice hockey M, racquetball M, rowing (crew) M, rugby, soccer, softball, squash, volleyball. **Clubs:** Intercollegiate horseback riding.

STUDENT SERVICES. Career counseling, employment service for undergraduates, freshman orientation, health services, personal counseling, placement service for graduates, veterans counselor, leadership counseling for residential assistants, services/facilities for handicapped.

ANNUAL EXPENSES. Tuition and fees: $17,895. **Room and board:** $5,530. **Books and supplies:** $650. **Other expenses:** $1,425.

FINANCIAL AID. 75% of freshmen, 70% of continuing students receive some form of aid. 99% of grants, all loans, all jobs based on need. 424 enrolled freshmen were judged to have need, all were offered aid. Academic scholarships available. **Aid applications:** Closing date February 15; priority given to applications received by February 1; applicants notified on or about March 15; must reply by May 1.

ADDRESS/TELEPHONE. Joel Wincowski, Dean of Admissions and Financial Aid, St. Lawrence University, Vilas Hall, Canton, NY 13617-1447. (315) 379-5261. Fax: (315) 379-5502.

St. Thomas Aquinas College

Sparkill, New York — CB code: 2807

Admissions: 71% of applicants accepted
Based on:
••• School record
•• Interview, test scores
• Activities, recommendations
Completion: 87% of freshmen end year in good standing
43% graduate, 50% of these enter graduate study

4-year private liberal arts college, coed. Founded in 1952. **Accreditation:** Regional. **Undergraduate enrollment:** 479 men, 639 women full time; 341 men, 556 women part time. **Graduate enrollment:** 5 men, 12 women full time; 18 men, 68 women part time. **Faculty:** 124 total (74 full time), 54 with doctorates or other terminal degrees. **Location:** Suburban campus in large town; 15 miles from New York City. **Calendar:** 4-1-4, extensive summer session. **Microcomputers:** 32 located in computer centers. **Special facilities:** United States government depository library.

DEGREES OFFERED. BA, BS, MEd. 354 bachelor's degrees awarded in 1992. 39% in business and management, 11% business/office and marketing/distribution, 5% communications, 12% education, 5% mathematics, 6% psychology, 10% social sciences. Graduate degrees offered in 1 major field of study.

UNDERGRADUATE MAJORS. Accounting, actuarial sciences, applied mathematics, art education, art therapy, biological and physical sciences, business administration and management, business and management, commercial design, communications, criminal justice studies, education, education of the emotionally handicapped, elementary education, engineering and other disciplines, English, English education, finance, foreign languages (multiple emphasis), foreign languages education, French, history, journalism, junior high education, liberal/general studies, marketing and distribution, mathematics, mathematics education, medical laboratory technologies, philosophy, psychology, pure mathematics, radio/television broadcasting, recreation and leisure, religion, secondary education, social sciences, social studies education, Spanish, special education, specific learning disabilities, studio art.

ACADEMIC PROGRAMS. Accelerated program, double major, dual enrollment of high school students, honors program, independent study, internships, study abroad, teacher preparation, comprehensive program for learning-disabled students, 3-2 program in engineering with George Washington University in Washington, D.C., and Manhattan College. **Remedial services:** Learning center, preadmission summer program, reduced course load, remedial instruction, tutoring, New York State Higher Education Opportunity Program. **ROTC:** Air Force. **Placement/credit:** AP, CLEP General and Subject, institutional tests; 30 credit hours maximum for bachelor's degree.

ACADEMIC REQUIREMENTS. Freshmen must earn minimum GPA of 1.8 to continue in good standing. 65% of freshmen return for sophomore year. Students must declare major by end of first year. **Graduation requirements:** 120 hours for bachelor's (48 in major). Most students required to take courses in arts/fine arts, computer science, English, foreign languages, history, humanities, mathematics, philosophy/religion, biological/physical sciences, social sciences.

FRESHMAN ADMISSIONS. Selection criteria: School achievement record, test scores, recommendation, and interview considered. Applicants should be in top half of class and have GPA above 2.7. **High school preparation:** 16 units required. Required units include biological science 1, English 4, foreign language 2, mathematics 2 and social science 1. **Test requirements:** SAT or ACT (SAT preferred); score report by May 1.

1992 FRESHMAN CLASS PROFILE. 837 men and women applied, 596 accepted; 93 men enrolled, 134 women enrolled. 65% had high school GPA of 3.0 or higher, 34% between 2.0 and 2.99. **Academic background:** Mid 50% of enrolled freshmen had SAT-V between 420-520, SAT-M between 410-500. 98% submitted SAT scores. **Characteristics:** 70% from in state, 80% commute, 2% have minority backgrounds, 1% are foreign students. Average age is 18.

FALL-TERM APPLICATIONS. $25 fee, may be waived for applicants with need. No closing date; applicants notified on a rolling basis; must reply by May 1 or within 4 weeks if notified thereafter. Interview recommended. CRDA. Deferred and early admission available.

STUDENT LIFE. Housing: Dormitories (men, women). Campus housing limited to 190 students. **Activities:** Student government, magazine, radio, student newspaper, television, yearbook, choral groups, drama, musical theater, political union, business association, community service organization.

ATHLETICS. NAIA. **Intercollegiate:** Baseball M, basketball, cross-country, golf, softball W, volleyball W. **Intramural:** Basketball, softball, tennis.

STUDENT SERVICES. Career counseling, employment service for undergraduates, freshman orientation, personal counseling, placement service for graduates, special adviser for adult students, extensive support services for learning-disabled students, services/facilities for handicapped.

ANNUAL EXPENSES. Tuition and fees: $8,150. **Room and board:** $5,400. **Books and supplies:** $500. **Other expenses:** $1,000.

FINANCIAL AID. 65% of freshmen, 60% of continuing students receive some form of aid. 83% of grants, 90% of loans, 44% of jobs based on need. 180 enrolled freshmen were judged to have need, all were offered aid. Academic, art, athletic, leadership scholarships available. **Aid applications:** No closing date; priority given to applications received by March 1; applicants notified on a rolling basis beginning on or about April 20; must reply within 15 days.

ADDRESS/TELEPHONE. Andrea Kraeft, Director of Admissions, St. Thomas Aquinas College, Route 340, Sparkill, NY 10976. (914) 359-9500. (800) 999-7822.

Sarah Lawrence College

Bronxville, New York — CB code: 2810

Admissions: 48% of applicants accepted
Based on: ••• Essay, recommendations, school record
•• Interview
• Activities, special talents, test scores
Completion: 80% graduate, 70% of these enter graduate study

4-year private liberal arts college, coed. Founded in 1926. **Accreditation:** Regional. **Undergraduate enrollment:** 1,050 men and women. **Graduate enrollment:** 194 men and women. **Faculty:** 211 total (161 full time), 190 with doctorates or other terminal degrees. **Location:** Suburban campus in small town; 15 miles from New York City. **Calendar:** Semester. **Microcomputers:** 20 located in computer centers. **Special facilities:** Performing arts center, drama and dance theaters, concert hall, film viewing room, music library, early childhood center, electronic sound studio, coral reef aquarium.

DEGREES OFFERED. BA, MA, MFA, MEd. 218 bachelor's degrees awarded in 1992. Graduate degrees offered in 7 major fields of study.

UNDERGRADUATE MAJORS. African studies, Afro-American (black) studies, American literature, American studies, analytical chemistry, anthropology, art history, Asian studies, behavioral sciences, biochemistry, biological and physical sciences, biology, ceramics, chemistry, cinematography/film, classics, cognitive psychology, comparative literature, comparative psychology, computer and information sciences, creative writing, dance, developmental psychology, dramatic arts, drawing, economics, English, English literature, European studies, experimental psychology, film arts, fine arts, folklore and mythology, foreign languages (multiple emphasis), French, geology, German, Greek (classical), history, humanities, humanities and social sciences, inorganic chemistry, international relations, international studies, Italian, Jewish studies, Latin, Latin American studies, liberal/general studies, marine biology, mathematics, medieval studies, music, music history and appreciation, music performance, music theory and composition, musical theater, organic chemistry, painting, personality psychology, philosophy, photography, physical sciences, physics, physiological psychology, political science and government, predentistry, prelaw, premedicine, printmaking, psychobiology, psycholinguistics, psychology, public policy studies, religion, rural sociology, Russian, Russian and Slavic studies, science and society, sculpture, social psychology, social sciences, sociology, Spanish, studio art, theater design, urban studies, video, visual and performing arts, women's studies.

ACADEMIC PROGRAMS. Double major, independent study, internships, semester at sea, student-designed major, study abroad, teacher preparation, visiting/exchange student program, art history courses at Museum of Modern Art and the Cloisters, academic year in Oxford, London, Moscow, Paris, and Florence, academic semester in St. Croix, joint summer sessions with University of Michigan in Florence and London, Laurence Hospital premedical health care program. **Placement/credit:** AP.

ACADEMIC REQUIREMENTS. No policy requiring minimum GPA; records of students having academic difficulty are reviewed individually. 96% of freshmen return for sophomore year. **Graduation requirements:** 120 hours for bachelor's. **Postgraduate studies:** 9% enter law school, 10% enter medical school, 14% enter MBA programs, 37% enter other graduate study. **Additional information:** 90% of classes are seminars with individual bi-weekly conferences in which students pursue self-designed independent study in addition to classwork.

FRESHMAN ADMISSIONS. Selection criteria: School record, application essays most important, followed by recommendations of counselors and teachers, test scores, and personal interview. **High school preparation:** 16 units recommended. Recommended units include English 4, foreign language 3, mathematics 3, social science 2 and science 3. **Test requirements:** SAT or ACT; score report by February 1. 3 ACH required of applicants who did not take SAT or ACT. English Composition with essay and Mathematics or science recommended. Score report by February 1.

1992 FRESHMAN CLASS PROFILE. 1,290 men and women applied, 620 accepted; 221 enrolled. 65% had high school GPA of 3.0 or higher, 34% between 2.0 and 2.99. **Academic background:** Mid 50% of enrolled freshmen had SAT-V between 540-650, SAT-M between 500-600. 93% submitted SAT scores. **Characteristics:** 15% from in state, 99% live in college housing, 15% have minority backgrounds, 6% are foreign students. Average age is 18.

FALL-TERM APPLICATIONS. $40 fee, may be waived for applicants with need. Closing date February 1; applicants notified on or about April 1; must reply by May 1. Essay required. Interview recommended. Portfolio recommended. CRDA. Deferred and early admission available. EDP-S. Applicants encouraged to include supplemental or creative materials with their application.

STUDENT LIFE. Housing: Dormitories (men, women, coed); apartment housing available. After freshman year most students who live on campus have their own room. **Activities:** Student government, film, magazine, student newspaper, yearbook, choral groups, dance, drama, music ensembles, symphony orchestra, Jewish Student Union, Feminist Alliance, Political Action Coalition, International Friends Association, SLC Task Force on Hunger and the Homeless, Amnesty International, Environmental Awareness, Animal Liberation Organization, Asian Students Union, Unidad, Harambe-African American Union, Lesbians, Gays, Bisexuals United.

ATHLETICS. Intercollegiate: Rowing (crew), soccer M, tennis, volleyball W. **Intramural:** Basketball M, bowling, fencing, racquetball, soccer, squash, swimming, volleyball. **Clubs:** Horseback riding.

STUDENT SERVICES. Career counseling, employment service for undergraduates, freshman orientation, health services, personal counseling, placement service for graduates, special adviser for adult students, field work placement for undergraduates.

ANNUAL EXPENSES. Tuition and fees: $18,584. **Room and board:** $7,016. **Books and supplies:** $500. **Other expenses:** $725.

FINANCIAL AID. 50% of freshmen, 50% of continuing students receive some form of aid. All grants, 99% of loans, 44% of jobs based on need. 122 enrolled freshmen were judged to have need, all were offered aid. **Aid applications:** Closing date February 1; applicants notified on or about April 1; must reply by May 1.

ADDRESS/TELEPHONE. Robin Mamlet, Dean of Admissions and Financial Aid, Sarah Lawrence College, One Meadway, Bronxville, NY 10708. (914) 395-2510. (800) 888-2858. Fax: (914) 395-2668.

Schenectady County Community College

Schenectady, New York — CB code: 2879

2-year public community college, coed. Founded in 1968. **Accreditation:** Regional. **Undergraduate enrollment:** 899 men, 908 women full time; 678 men, 1,266 women part time. **Faculty:** 263 total (83 full time), 16 with doctorates or other terminal degrees. **Location:** Urban campus in small city; 150 miles from New York City, 20 miles from Albany. **Calendar:** Semester, limited summer session. Saturday and extensive evening/early morning classes. **Microcomputers:** Located in libraries, classrooms, computer centers. **Additional facts:** SUNY institution.

DEGREES OFFERED. AA, AS, AAS. 361 associate degrees awarded in 1992. 27% in business and management, 20% computer sciences, 6% engineering technologies, 8% law, 6% parks/recreation, protective services, public affairs, 10% social sciences, 11% trade and industry.

UNDERGRADUATE MAJORS. Accounting, business administration and management, business and office, business data processing and related programs, business data programming, chemical manufacturing technology, computer and information sciences, criminal justice technology, data processing, dramatic arts, electrical technology, elementary education, fire control and safety technology, food production/management/services, hospitality and recreation marketing, hotel/motel and restaurant management, humanities and social sciences, legal assistant/paralegal, materials science technology, mathematics and science, music, music business management, plastic technology, secretarial and related programs, social work, telecommunications, tourism, word processing.

ACADEMIC PROGRAMS. 2-year transfer program, dual enrollment of high school students, honors program, independent study, internships, teacher preparation, cross-registration. **Remedial services:** Learning center, reduced course load, remedial instruction, special counselor, tutoring. **Placement/credit:** AP, CLEP General and Subject, institutional tests; 30 credit hours maximum for associate degree.

ACADEMIC REQUIREMENTS. Freshmen must earn minimum GPA of 1.5 to continue in good standing. 65% of freshmen return for sophomore year. Students must declare major by end of first year. **Graduation requirements:** 60 hours for associate (30 in major). Most students required to take courses in English, mathematics.

FRESHMAN ADMISSIONS. Selection criteria: Open admissions. Selective admissions to music program. Certain programs have specific mathematics and science prerequisites.

1992 FRESHMAN CLASS PROFILE. 1,236 men and women enrolled. **Characteristics:** 99% from in state, 100% commute, 11% have minority backgrounds. Average age is 25.

FALL-TERM APPLICATIONS. $25 fee, may be waived for applicants with need. No closing date; applicants notified on a rolling basis; must reply by registration. Audition required for music, music merchandising applicants. Interview recommended. Deferred and early admission available.

STUDENT LIFE. Activities: Student government, magazine, choral groups, concert band, drama, jazz band, music ensembles, Black and Latino Student Alliance, Christian Fellowship, Human Services Club, Disabled Student Awareness Committee, Culinary Club.

ATHLETICS. NJCAA. **Intercollegiate:** Baseball M, basketball M, bowling, softball W. **Intramural:** Soccer, volleyball.

STUDENT SERVICES. Aptitude testing, career counseling, employment service for undergraduates, freshman orientation, personal counseling, placement service for graduates, special adviser for adult students, veterans counselor, childcare subsidies, services/facilities for handicapped.

ANNUAL EXPENSES. Tuition and fees (projected): $1,853, $1,750 additional for out-of-state students. **Books and supplies:** $550. **Other expenses:** $900.

FINANCIAL AID. 70% of freshmen, 70% of continuing students receive some form of aid. All grants, 83% of loans, all jobs based on need. Academic, state/district residency, minority scholarships available. **Aid applications:** No closing date; priority given to applications received by May 1; applicants notified on a rolling basis beginning on or about April 15; must reply by May 1 or within 2 weeks if notified thereafter.

ADDRESS/TELEPHONE. Robert Dinello, Director of Admissions, Schenectady County Community College, 78 Washington Avenue, Schenectady, NY 12305. (518) 346-6211 ext. 166. Fax: (518) 346-0379.

School of Visual Arts

New York, New York — CB code: 2835

Admissions: 79% of applicants accepted
Based on:
••• Interview, school record, special talents
•• Activities, essay, recommendations, test scores
Completion: 85% of freshmen end year in good standing
45% graduate, 6% of these enter graduate study

4-year proprietary art college, coed. Founded in 1947. **Accreditation:** Regional. **Undergraduate enrollment:** 1,237 men, 819 women full time; 1,079 men, 1,468 women part time. **Graduate enrollment:** 116 men, 138 women full time; 7 men, 8 women part time. **Faculty:** 599 total (78 full time), 12 with doctorates or other terminal degrees. **Location:** Urban campus in very large city. **Calendar:** 4-1-4, extensive summer session. **Microcomputers:** 105 located in libraries, computer centers. **Special facilities:** Visual arts museum, 8 student galleries including gallery in New York City's SoHo district. **Additional facts:** Largest college of art and design in country. Member of National Association of Schools of Art and Design. Faculty composed entirely of working professionals.

DEGREES OFFERED. BFA, MFA. 370 bachelor's degrees awarded in 1992. 5% in teacher education, 95% visual and performing arts. Graduate degrees offered in 5 major fields of study.

UNDERGRADUATE MAJORS. Advertising, art education, cinematography/film, communications, computer graphics, drawing, film animation, film arts, fine arts, graphic arts technology, graphic design, illustration design, interior design, motion picture technology, painting, photographic technology, photography, printmaking, radio/television broadcasting, radio/television technology, sculpture, studio art, video, visual and performing arts.

ACADEMIC PROGRAMS. Double major, independent study, internships, study abroad, teacher preparation, summer programs in Italy, Spain, and Greece. **Remedial services:** Learning center, reduced course load, remedial instruction, special counselor, tutoring. **Placement/credit:** AP, CLEP Subject; 44 credit hours maximum for bachelor's degree.

ACADEMIC REQUIREMENTS. Freshmen must earn minimum GPA of 2.0 to continue in good standing. 86% of freshmen return for sophomore year. Students must declare major by end of first year. **Graduation requirements:** 128 hours for bachelor's (70 in major). Most students required to take courses in arts/fine arts, computer science, English, history, humanities, mathematics, biological/physical sciences. **Additional information:** Curriculum is designed to prepare students to graduate as working professionals in the arts.

FRESHMAN ADMISSIONS. Selection criteria: Portfolio, academic record, test scores, and interview important. Character and professional recommendations also considered. Art courses recommended. **Test requirements:** SAT or ACT; score report by August 1.

1992 FRESHMAN CLASS PROFILE. 616 men applied, 480 accepted, 213 enrolled; 398 women applied, 318 accepted, 109 enrolled. 33% had high school GPA of 3.0 or higher, 54% between 2.0 and 2.99. **Academic background:** Mid 50% of enrolled freshmen had SAT-V between 350-500, SAT-M between 360-490. 95% submitted SAT scores. **Characteristics:** 57% from in state, 78% commute, 32% have minority backgrounds, 11% are foreign students. Average age is 18.

FALL-TERM APPLICATIONS. $25 fee, may be waived for applicants with need. No closing date; applicants notified on a rolling basis; must reply by May 1 or within 3 weeks if notified thereafter. Portfolio required for art education, fine arts, media arts, photography, interior design applicants. Essay required for film applicants. Interview required but waived upon request for applicants who reside more than 250 miles from campus. CRDA. Deferred admission available.

STUDENT LIFE. Housing: Dormitories (coed). **Activities:** Student government, film, magazine, radio, student newspaper, television, yearbook, poster and professional competitions, drama, African-American artists, SV Gays, Servant (Christian Student group), Recycling group.

ATHLETICS. Intramural: Baseball M, basketball, fencing, skiing, soccer, softball W, tennis, volleyball.

STUDENT SERVICES. Career counseling, employment service for undergraduates, freshman orientation, health services, personal counseling, placement service for graduates, veterans counselor, services/facilities for handicapped.

ANNUAL EXPENSES. Tuition and fees: $11,900. **Room and board:** $4,700 room only. **Books and supplies:** $1,380. **Other expenses:** $1,745.

FINANCIAL AID. 85% of freshmen, 88% of continuing students receive some form of aid. 64% of grants, 79% of loans, 33% of jobs based on need. 472 enrolled freshmen were judged to have need, all were offered aid. Academic, art, leadership scholarships available. **Aid applications:** No closing date; priority given to applications received by February 28; applicants notified on a rolling basis beginning on or about April 23; must reply by May 1 or within 2 weeks if notified thereafter.

ADDRESS/TELEPHONE. Lawrence E. Wilson III, Director of Admissions, School of Visual Arts, 209 East 23rd Street, New York, NY 10010-3994. (212) 679-7350. Fax: (212) 725-3587.

Siena College

Loudonville, New York — CB code: 2814

Admissions: 64% of applicants accepted
Based on:
••• School record
•• Interview, test scores
• Activities, essay, recommendations, special talents
Completion: 93% of freshmen end year in good standing
80% graduate, 22% of these enter graduate study

4-year private liberal arts college, coed, Affilaited with Franciscan Friars. Founded in 1937. **Accreditation:** Regional. **Undergraduate enrollment:** 1,296 men, 1,374 women full time; 410 men, 412 women part time. **Faculty:** 272 total (188 full time), 302 with doctorates or other terminal degrees. **Location:** Suburban campus in large town; 2 miles from Albany. **Calendar:** Semester, limited summer session. **Microcomputers:** 208 located in computer centers.

DEGREES OFFERED. BA, BS. 814 bachelor's degrees awarded in 1992. 58% in business and management, 9% letters/literature, 6% life sciences, 7% psychology, 14% social sciences.

UNDERGRADUATE MAJORS. Accounting, American studies, biology, business education, chemistry, computer and information sciences, economics, English, English education, finance, foreign languages education, French, history, marketing management, mathematics, mathematics education, philosophy, physics, political science and government, predentistry, prelaw, premedicine, preveterinary, psychology, religion, religious education, science education, secondary education, social science education, social studies education, social work, sociology, Spanish.

ACADEMIC PROGRAMS. Honors program, internships, study abroad, teacher preparation, visiting/exchange student program, Washington semester, cross-registration, 3+2 program in engineering with Catholic University in Washington, D.C., Clarkson University, Manhattan College, and Rensselaer Polytechnic Institute, 2+2 program in forestry with SUNY College of Environmental Science and Forestry, combined bachelor's/graduate degree program in business administration eith Clarkson University, early assurance program in medicine with Albany Medical College. **Remedial services:** Reduced course load, special counselor, tutoring, New York State Higher Education Opportunity Program. **ROTC:** Air Force, Army. **Placement/credit:** AP, CLEP Subject, institutional tests; 18 credit hours maximum for bachelor's degree.

ACADEMIC REQUIREMENTS. Freshmen must earn minimum GPA of 2.0 to continue in good standing. 95% of freshmen return for sophomore year. Students must declare major by end of second year. **Graduation requirements:** 120 hours for bachelor's (36 in major). Most students required to take courses in arts/fine arts, English, history, mathematics, philosophy/religion, biological/physical sciences, social sciences. **Postgraduate studies:** 4% enter law school, 3% enter medical school, 2% enter MBA programs, 13% enter other graduate study. **Additional information:** Extensive internship program in capital district with state legislature, businesses, social agencies, libraries, museums.

FRESHMAN ADMISSIONS. Selection criteria: School achievement record is most important. Priority given to students with challenging courses; test scores, activities, recommendations considered. Special consideration given to minorities, foreign applicants, children of alumni. **High school preparation:** 18 units recommended. Recommended units include English 4, foreign language 3, mathematics 4, social science 4 and science 3. Three units mathematics required for business and liberal arts applicants, 4 units for science applicants. **Test requirements:** SAT or ACT; score report by February 1.

1992 FRESHMAN CLASS PROFILE. 1,268 men applied, 1,039 accepted, 245 enrolled; 1,614 women applied, 806 accepted, 333 enrolled. 86% had high school GPA of 3.0 or higher. 26% were in top tenth and 68% were in top quarter of graduating class. **Academic background:** Mid 50% of enrolled freshmen had SAT-V between 440-540, SAT-M between 540-640; ACT composite between 25-28. 95% submitted SAT scores, 25% submitted ACT scores. **Characteristics:** 77% from in state, 90% live in college housing, 8% have minority backgrounds, 5% are foreign students. Average age is 18.

FALL-TERM APPLICATIONS. $35 fee, may be waived for applicants with need. Closing date March 1; applicants notified on or about March 15; must reply by May 1. Essay required. Interview required for special medicine program finalists; recommended for all others. CRDA. Deferred and early admission available. Early action plan with January 1 notification.

STUDENT LIFE. Housing: Dormitories (coed); apartment housing available. **Activities:** Student government, film, radio, student newspaper, yearbook, literary magazine, choral groups, drama, musical theater, pep band, over 70 clubs and organizations including Big Brother, Big Sister, campus ministry, Black and Latin Student Union, Model United Nations.

ATHLETICS. NCAA. **Intercollegiate:** Baseball M, basketball, cross-country, field hockey W, football M, golf M, ice hockey M, lacrosse, skiing, soccer, softball W, tennis, track and field, volleyball W. **Intramural:** Basketball, fencing, football M, skiing, softball, volleyball. **Clubs:** Horseback riding, rugby.

STUDENT SERVICES. Aptitude testing, career counseling, employment service for undergraduates, freshman orientation, health services, personal counseling, placement service for graduates, special adviser for adult students, services/facilities for handicapped.

ANNUAL EXPENSES. Tuition and fees (1992-93): $9,810. **Room and board:** $4,680. **Books and supplies:** $550. **Other expenses:** $550.

FINANCIAL AID. 78% of freshmen, 74% of continuing students receive some form of aid. 89% of grants, 96% of loans, 42% of jobs based on need. 462 enrolled freshmen were judged to have need, all were offered aid. Academic, athletic, leadership, alumni affiliation scholarships available. **Aid applications:** Closing date February 1; applicants notified on or about April 15; must reply by May 1.

ADDRESS/TELEPHONE. Douglas Astolfi, Director of Admissions, Siena College, 515 Loudon Road, Loudonville, NY 11211-1462. (518) 783-2423.

Skidmore College
Saratoga Springs, New York

CB code: 2815

Admissions: 67% of applicants accepted
Based on: ••• Recommendations, school record
•• Activities, essay, interview, special talents, test scores
Completion: 98% of freshmen end year in good standing
80% graduate, 34% of these enter graduate study

4-year private liberal arts college, coed. Founded in 1903. **Accreditation:** Regional. **Undergraduate enrollment:** 879 men, 1,248 women full time; 10 men, 6 women part time. **Faculty:** 255 total (195 full time). **Location:** Suburban campus in large town; 30 miles from Albany. **Calendar:** 2 semesters followed by optional 6-week internship period. **Microcomputers:** 200 located in dormitories, libraries, classrooms, computer centers, campus-wide network. **Special facilities:** Art gallery, electron microscope, center for child study, quantitative reasoning laboratory, equestrian center, x-ray fluorescence spectrometer, nature and ski trails.

DEGREES OFFERED. BA, BS, M. 531 bachelor's degrees awarded in 1992. 14% in business and management, 13% letters/literature, 5% life sciences, 8% multi/interdisciplinary studies, 10% psychology, 23% social sciences, 14% visual and performing arts. Graduate degrees offered in 1 major field of study.

UNDERGRADUATE MAJORS. American studies, anthropology, art history, biochemistry, biological and physical sciences, biology, biology/philosophy, business and management, business economics, business/French, business/German, business/government, business/mathematics, business/physical education, business/Spanish, chemistry, classics, computer and information sciences, computer science/mathematics, dance, dance/theater, dramatic arts, economics, economics/French, economics/German, economics/mathematics, economics/philosophy, economics/sociology, economics/Spanish, elementary education, English, English/French, English/German, English/philosophy, English/Spanish, French, French area studies, geology, German, government/French, government/German, government/history, government/philosophy, government/sociology, government/Spanish, history, history/philosophy, humanities, humanities and social sciences, international studies, mathematics, music, philosophy, physics, political economy, political science and government, psychology, psychology/sociology, social work, sociology, sociology/anthropology, Spanish, studio art.

ACADEMIC PROGRAMS. Accelerated program, double major, external degree, independent study, internships, student-designed major, study abroad, teacher preparation, visiting/exchange student program, Washington semester, cross-registration, external degree program, Summer Six Arts Program, Judaic Studies Summer Program, summer school abroad in France and Italy, summer jazz institute. **Remedial services:** New York State Higher Education Opportunity Program. **ROTC:** Air Force, Army. **Placement/credit:** AP, CLEP Subject, IB, institutional tests; 12 credit hours maximum for bachelor's degree. Up to 60 hours of credit from non-Skidmore coursework may be counted toward degree.

ACADEMIC REQUIREMENTS. Freshmen must earn minimum GPA of 1.67 to continue in good standing. 91% of freshmen return for sophomore year. Students must declare major by end of second year. **Graduation requirements:** 120 hours for bachelor's (45 in major). Most students required to take courses in arts/fine arts, English, foreign languages, humanities, mathematics, biological/physical sciences, social sciences. **Postgraduate studies:** 7% enter law school, 2% enter medical school, 3% enter MBA programs, 22% enter other graduate study.

FRESHMAN ADMISSIONS. Selection criteria: High school achievement record, admission test scores, and counselor and teacher recommendations of critical importance. Personal interview, application essay, leadership, artistic, musical, athletic, and other special abilities and interests given careful consideration. Factors such as racial/ethnic/cultural/geographic diversity and family affiliation with college also considered. **High school preparation:** 16 units required; 18 recommended. Required and recommended units include English 4-4, foreign language 3-4, mathematics 3-4, social science 3-4 and science 3. Biological science 1 and physical science 1 recommended. **Test requirements:** SAT or ACT; score report by February 1.

1992 FRESHMAN CLASS PROFILE. 1,346 men applied, 981 accepted, 225 enrolled; 2,678 women applied, 1,719 accepted, 370 enrolled. **Academic background:** Mid 50% of enrolled freshmen had SAT-V between 470-570, SAT-M between 510-610; ACT composite between 21-26. 98% submitted SAT scores, 2% submitted ACT scores. **Characteristics:** 31% from in state, 99% live in college housing, 11% have minority backgrounds, 2% are foreign students. Average age is 18.

FALL-TERM APPLICATIONS. $40 fee, may be waived for applicants with need. Closing date February 1; applicants notified on or about April 1; must reply by May 1. Essay required. Interview recommended. CRDA. Deferred and early admission available. EDP-F. Round I, Round II early decision plan. Round I application deadline December 1, Round II deadline January 15. 3 ACH strongly recommended.

STUDENT LIFE. Housing: Dormitories (coed); apartment housing available. Theme housing available in variety of interest areas. 15 townhouse clusters available for upperclassmen. **Activities:** Student government, magazine, radio, student newspaper, television, yearbook, literary journal, journal of social science and philosophy, choral groups, dance, drama, jazz band, music ensembles, musical theater, symphony orchestra, 80 clubs and organizations, Phi Beta Kappa and 7 other national honor societies, 28 intercollegiate teams, Alliance multicultural group, FLIC, Student Speakers' Bureau, student entertainment committee, Benefaction community service organization, SOAR (Society Organizational Against Racism), Outing Club. **Additional information:** Students take initiative and responsibility for all aspects of cocurricular and residential life. Of those undergraduates who do not reside in college housing, approximately 18% live in their own apartments off campus, 1% commute from home.

ATHLETICS. NCAA. **Intercollegiate:** Baseball M, basketball, diving W, field hockey W, golf M, ice hockey M, lacrosse, rowing (crew), soccer, softball W, swimming W, tennis, volleyball W. **Intramural:** Badminton, baseball M, basketball, cross-country, diving, golf, horseback riding, lacrosse, racquetball, sailing, soccer, softball, squash, swimming, table tennis, tennis, volleyball, water polo M.

STUDENT SERVICES. Career counseling, employment service for undergraduates, freshman orientation, health services, on-campus day care, personal counseling, veterans counselor, services/facilities for handicapped.

ANNUAL EXPENSES. Tuition and fees: $17,775. **Room and board:** $5,455. **Books and supplies:** $550. **Other expenses:** $700.

FINANCIAL AID. 33% of freshmen, 47% of continuing students receive some form of aid. All grants, all loans, 61% of jobs based on need. 208 enrolled freshmen were judged to have need, 196 were offered aid. Music/drama scholarships available. **Aid applications:** Closing date February 1; applicants notified on or about April 1; must reply by May 1. **Additional information:** Annual Filene Music Competition awards four 4-year $24,000 scholarships ($6,000 per year) for musical ability, without regard to financial need. Additional financing plans available to families who do not qualify for need-based student aid.

ADDRESS/TELEPHONE. Mary Lou W. Bates, Director of Admissions, Skidmore College, Saratoga Springs, NY 12866. (518) 587-7569. Fax: (518) 584-3023.

State University of New York at Albany

Albany, New York — CB code: 2532

Admissions: 63% of applicants accepted
Based on:
••• School record, test scores
• Activities, recommendations, special talents
Completion: 90% of freshmen end year in good standing
69% graduate, 45% of these enter graduate study

4-year public university, coed. Founded in 1844. **Accreditation:** Regional. **Undergraduate enrollment:** 5,334 men, 5,020 women full time; 241 men, 310 women part time. **Graduate enrollment:** 1,014 men, 1,228 women full time; 776 men, 1,245 women part time. **Faculty:** 902 total (670 full time), 644 with doctorates or other terminal degrees. **Location:** Suburban campus in small city; 4 miles from downtown. **Calendar:** Semester, extensive summer session. Extensive evening/early morning classes. **Microcomputers:** 400 located in dormitories, libraries, classrooms, computer centers, campus-wide network. **Special facilities:** Art gallery, linear accelerator, East Coast lightning detection system, computerized weather data collection, graphics display system, performing arts center, 5000-seat fieldhouse.

DEGREES OFFERED. BA, BS, MA, MS, MBA, MFA, MSW, PhD, EdD. 2,709 bachelor's degrees awarded in 1992. 15% in business and management, 5% communications, 14% letters/literature, 5% life sciences, 15% psychology, 32% social sciences. Graduate degrees offered in 105 major fields of study.

UNDERGRADUATE MAJORS. Accounting, Afro-American (black) studies, anthropology, archeology, Asian studies, atmospheric sciences and meteorology, biology, business administration and management, business and management, Caribbean studies, chemistry, Chinese, city/community/regional planning, classics, communications, computer and information sciences, criminal justice studies, criminology, demography, dramatic arts, drawing, earth sciences, East Asian studies, Eastern European studies, economics, English, English education, finance, foreign languages education, French, geography, geology, German, Greek (classical), history, information sciences and systems, investments and securities, Italian, Japanese, Jewish studies, junior high education, Latin, Latin American studies, liberal/general studies, linguistics, management information systems, management science, marketing management, mathematics, mathematics education, medical laboratory technologies, molecular biology, music, music performance, music theory and composition, painting, philosophy, photography, physics, political science and government, psychology, public affairs, Puerto Rican studies, rhetoric, Russian, Russian and Slavic studies, science education, sculpture, secondary education, social studies education, social work, sociology, Spanish, speech, studio art, taxation, urban studies, women's studies.

ACADEMIC PROGRAMS. Accelerated program, double major, dual enrollment of high school students, education specialist degree, honors program, independent study, internships, student-designed major, study abroad, teacher preparation, visiting/exchange student program, cross-registration, combined bachelor's/master's programs in 40 fields, internships with New York state legislature, combined bachelor's/law degree with Albany Law School; liberal arts/career combination in health sciences; combined bachelor's/graduate program in business administration. **Remedial services:** Preadmission summer program, tutoring, New York State Higher Education Opportunity Program. **ROTC:** Air Force, Army, Naval. **Placement/credit:** AP, CLEP General and Subject, institutional tests; 90 credit hours maximum for bachelor's degree.

ACADEMIC REQUIREMENTS. Freshmen must successfully complete 24 semester hours of credits by end of freshman year to continue in good academic standing. 89% of freshmen return for sophomore year. Students must declare major by end of second year. **Graduation requirements:** 120 hours for bachelor's (30 in major). Most students required to take courses in arts/fine arts, English, humanities, biological/physical sciences, social sciences. **Postgraduate studies:** 11% enter law school, 2% enter medical school, 5% enter MBA programs, 27% enter other graduate study.

FRESHMAN ADMISSIONS. Selection criteria: High school GPA most important, followed by class rank, test scores, and end-of-year Regents examinations. Minority status considered. **High school preparation:** 18 units required. Required and recommended units include English 4, mathematics 2-4, social science 3-5 and science 2-3. Foreign language 3 recommended. 2 laboratory science preferred. **Test requirements:** SAT or ACT (SAT preferred); score report by February 15.

1992 FRESHMAN CLASS PROFILE. 7,021 men applied, 4,448 accepted, 1,004 enrolled; 7,376 women applied, 4,569 accepted, 921 enrolled. 37% had high school GPA of 3.0 or higher, 48% between 2.0 and 2.99. 17% were in top tenth and 67% were in top quarter of graduating class. **Academic background:** Mid 50% of enrolled freshmen had SAT-V between 470-550, SAT-M between 540-640. 99% submitted SAT scores. **Characteristics:** 97% from in state, 95% live in college housing, 27% have minority backgrounds, 1% are foreign students. Average age is 18.

FALL-TERM APPLICATIONS. $25 fee, may be waived for applicants with need. Closing date February 15; priority given to applications received by November 15; applicants notified on a rolling basis beginning on or about January 1; must reply by May 1. Interview required for social welfare applicants. Audition required for music applicants. Portfolio required for art applicants. CRDA. Deferred and early admission available. EDP-F.

STUDENT LIFE. Housing: Dormitories (men, women, coed); apartment housing available. Approximately 400 spaces available in aprtment-style dormitories on campus, in addition to regular dormitories. **Activities:** Student government, magazine, radio, student newspaper, yearbook, choral groups, concert band, dance, drama, jazz band, music ensembles, pep band, symphony orchestra, fraternities, sororities, over 160 student organizations. **Additional information:** Of undergraduates who do not reside in college housing, approximately 30% live in their own apartments off campus, 10% commute from home.

ATHLETICS. NCAA. **Intercollegiate:** Baseball M, basketball, cross-country, diving, football M, gymnastics W, lacrosse M, rowing (crew), soccer, softball W, swimming, tennis, track and field, volleyball W, wrestling M. **Intramural:** Baseball, basketball, bowling, field hockey, handball, ice hockey M, racquetball, soccer, softball, squash, tennis, track and field, volleyball, water polo.

STUDENT SERVICES. Aptitude testing, career counseling, freshman orientation, health services, on-campus day care, personal counseling, placement service for graduates, vocational testing, services/facilities for handicapped.

ANNUAL EXPENSES. Tuition and fees (1992-93): $2,877, $3,900 additional for out-of-state students. **Room and board:** $3,666. **Books and supplies:** $500. **Other expenses:** $900.

FINANCIAL AID. 76% of freshmen, 74% of continuing students receive some form of aid. 99% of grants, 94% of loans, all jobs based on need. 1,280 enrolled freshmen were judged to have need, 1,175 were offered aid. Academic, state/district residency, alumni affiliation scholarships available. **Aid applications:** No closing date; priority given to applications received by April 25; applicants notified on a rolling basis beginning on or about April 1; must reply by May 1 or within 2 weeks if notified thereafter.

ADDRESS/TELEPHONE. Micheileen Treadwell, Director of Admissions, State University of New York at Albany, 1400 Washington Avenue, Albany, NY 12222. (518) 442-5435.

State University of New York at Binghamton

Binghamton, New York — CB code: 2535

Admissions: 42% of applicants accepted
Based on:
••• School record, test scores
•• Activities, essay, recommendations
• Special talents
Completion: 77% graduate, 45% of these enter graduate study

4-year public university, coed. Founded in 1946. **Accreditation:** Regional. **Undergraduate enrollment:** 3,828 men, 4,561 women full time; 360 men, 383 women part time. **Graduate enrollment:** 647 men, 501 women full time; 872 men, 814 women part time. **Faculty:** 677 total (492 full time), 508 with doctorates or other terminal degrees. **Location:** Suburban campus in small city; 60 miles from Scranton, Pennsylvania, 180 miles from New York City. **Calendar:** Semester, limited summer session. **Microcomputers:** 335 located in dormitories, libraries, classrooms, computer centers. **Special facilities:** 117-acre nature preserve, indoor/outdoor theater, performing arts center, art gallery, multiclimate greenhouse.

DEGREES OFFERED. BA, BS, BFA, MA, MS, MBA, MFA, MEd, PhD, EdD. 2,249 bachelor's degrees awarded in 1992. 12% in business and management, 10% letters/literature, 10% life sciences, 6% philosophy, religion, theology, 8% psychology, 26% social sciences. Graduate degrees offered in 44 major fields of study.

UNDERGRADUATE MAJORS. Accounting, African studies, Afro-American (black) studies, American studies, anthropology, applied physics, Arabic, art history, biochemistry, biology, business administration and management, business and management, Caribbean studies, chemistry, classics, comparative literature, computer and information sciences, computer mathematics, dramatic arts, economics, electrical/electronics/communications engineering, English, environmental science, film arts, French, geography, geology, geophysics and seismology, German, Greek (classical), Hebrew, history, industrial technology, information sciences and systems, Italian, Jewish studies, Latin, Latin American studies, liberal/general studies, linguistics, mathematical physics, mathematics, mechanical engineering, medieval studies, music, music performance, near Eastern studies, nursing, philosophy, physics, political science and government, psychobiology, psychology, rhetoric, social sciences, sociology, Spanish, studio art, systems analysis.

ACADEMIC PROGRAMS. Double major, dual enrollment of high school students, honors program, independent study, internships, student-designed major, study abroad, visiting/exchange student program, cross-registration; liberal arts/career combination in engineering, health sciences, business; combined bachelor's/graduate program in business administration. **Remedial services:** Learning center, preadmission summer program, remedial instruction, special counselor, tutoring. **Placement/credit:** AP, CLEP Subject, IB, institutional tests; 90 credit hours maximum for bachelor's degree.

ACADEMIC REQUIREMENTS. Freshmen must earn minimum GPA of 2.0 to continue in good standing. 92% of freshmen return for sophomore year. Students must declare major by end of second year. **Graduation requirements:** 128 hours for bachelor's (32 in major). Most students required to take courses in arts/fine arts, humanities, biological/physical sciences, social sciences. **Postgraduate studies:** 11% enter law school, 5% enter medical school, 4% enter MBA programs, 25% enter other graduate study.

FRESHMAN ADMISSIONS. Selection criteria: Admission based on academic strength as measured by quality of courses, grades and grade trend, and test scores. Evidence of intellectual curiosity, interest in others, and nonacademic pursuits is sought through the application. Geographic and ethnic diversity are active goals of the campus. **High school preparation:** 16 units required. Required units include English 4, mathematics 2.5, social science 2 and science 2. 3 units of 1 foreign language or 2 each of 2 foreign languages required of liberal arts applicants. **Test requirements:** SAT or ACT (SAT preferred); score report by February 1.

1992 FRESHMAN CLASS PROFILE. 7,121 men applied, 2,806 accepted, 773 enrolled; 8,312 women applied, 3,711 accepted, 1,044 enrolled. 92% had high school GPA of 3.0 or higher, 8% between 2.0 and 2.99. 65% were in top tenth and 97% were in top quarter of graduating class. **Academic background:** Mid 50% of enrolled freshmen had SAT-V between 490-590, SAT-M between 560-670. 98% submitted SAT scores. **Characteristics:** 92% from in state, 96% live in college housing, 24% have minority backgrounds, 1% are foreign students. Average age is 18.

FALL-TERM APPLICATIONS. $25 fee, may be waived for applicants with need. No closing date; priority given to applications received by January 15; applicants notified on a rolling basis beginning on or about March 15; must reply by May 1 or within 4 weeks if notified thereafter. Essay required. Audition recommended for music applicants. Portfolio recommended for art applicants. CRDA. Deferred and early admission available. EDP-F. Closing dates vary with academic programs.

STUDENT LIFE. Housing: Dormitories (coed); apartment housing available. Special interest housing available. Off-campus, university-maintained housing for mature students. Extensive bus system, partly school operated, partly public transportation with free access. **Activities:** Student government, film, magazine, radio, student newspaper, television, yearbook, choral groups, concert band, dance, drama, jazz band, music ensembles, musical theater, opera, pep band, symphony orchestra, jazz workshop, collegium musicum, fraternities, sororities, religious organizations, ethnic, minority, women's, public interest, and voluntary service organizations. **Additional information:** Students participate extensively in campus governance. Of undergraduates who do not live in college housing, approximately 34% commute from their own apartments off campus, 15% commute from home.

ATHLETICS. NCAA. **Intercollegiate:** Baseball M, basketball, cross-country, diving, golf, soccer, softball W, swimming, tennis, track and field, volleyball W, wrestling M. **Intramural:** Badminton, basketball, bowling, cross-country, fencing, golf, horseback riding, lacrosse, racquetball, rowing (crew), rugby, skiing, soccer, softball, squash, table tennis, tennis, track and field, volleyball, water polo, wrestling M. **Clubs:** Over 20, including ski, karate, lacrosse, rugby, volleyball M, ice hockey, ultimate frisbee, crew, cycling, fencing, rollerblading, and snowboarding.

STUDENT SERVICES. Career counseling, employment service for undergraduates, freshman orientation, health services, on-campus day care, personal counseling, placement service for graduates, special adviser for adult students, veterans counselor, services/facilities for handicapped.

ANNUAL EXPENSES. Tuition and fees (1992-93): $2,987, $3,900 additional for out-of-state students. **Room and board:** $4,634. **Books and supplies:** $600. **Other expenses:** $704.

FINANCIAL AID. 60% of freshmen, 51% of continuing students receive some form of aid. All grants, 84% of loans, 50% of jobs based on need. 650 enrolled freshmen were judged to have need, all were offered aid. Academic, music/drama, art, minority scholarships available. **Aid applications:** No closing date; priority given to applications received by February 15; applicants notified on a rolling basis beginning on or about March 21; must reply by May 1 or within 2 weeks if notified thereafter.

ADDRESS/TELEPHONE. Fred R. Brooks, Jr, Assistant Vice President for Enrollment Services and Management, State University of New York at Binghamton, Vestal Parkway East, Binghamton, NY 13902-6001. (607) 777-2171.

State University of New York at Buffalo
Buffalo, New York

CB code: 2925

Admissions:	55% of applicants accepted
Based on:	••• School record, test scores
	• Activities, essay, recommendations, special talents
Completion:	95% of freshmen end year in good standing
	50% graduate, 35% of these enter graduate study

4-year public university, coed. Founded in 1846. **Accreditation:** Regional. **Undergraduate enrollment:** 7,587 men, 5,539 women full time; 1,087 men, 1,134 women part time. **Graduate enrollment:** 2,066 men, 1,630 women full time; 2,264 men, 2,116 women part time. **Faculty:** 1,947 total (1,292 full time). **Location:** Suburban campus in large city; 3 miles from downtown. **Calendar:** Semester, extensive summer session. Saturday and extensive evening/early morning classes. **Microcomputers:** 750 located in dormitories, libraries, classrooms, computer centers. **Special facilities:** Concert hall, theater, research museum of anthropology, nature preserve, observatory. **Additional facts:** Includes schools of law, pharmacy, and architecture.

DEGREES OFFERED. AA, AAS, BA, BS, BFA, MA, MS, MBA, MFA, MEd, MSW, PhD, EdD, DDS, MD, B. Pharm, Pharm D, JD. 116 associate degrees awarded in 1992. 3,403 bachelor's degrees awarded. 15% in business and management, 5% communications, 14% engineering, 8% health sciences, 5% letters/literature, 7% psychology, 24% social sciences. Graduate degrees offered in 111 major fields of study.

UNDERGRADUATE MAJORS. Associate: Liberal/general studies. **Bachelor's:** Accounting, aerospace/aeronautical/astronautical engineering, Afro-American (black) studies, American studies, anthropology, architecture, art education, art history, biochemical pharmacology, biochemistry, biology, biophysics, business administration and management, chemical engineering, chemistry, cinematography/film, civil engineering, classics, communications, computer and information sciences, dance, dramatic arts, economics, electrical/electronics/communications engineering, engineering physics, engineering science, English, English education, environmental design, fine arts, foreign languages education, French, geography, geology, German, history, industrial engineering, Italian, Latin, liberal/general studies, linguistics, mathematical physics, mathematics, mathematics education, mathematics/economics, mechanical engineering, medical laboratory technologies, medicinal chemistry, music, music education, music history and appreciation, music performance, nuclear medical technology, nursing, occupational therapy, pharmaceutical chemistry, pharmacy, philosophy, physical therapy, physics, political science and government, psychology, Russian, science education, social sciences, social studies education, sociology, Spanish, speech pathology/audiology, sports and exercise studies, statistics, studio art, visual and performing arts, women's studies.

ACADEMIC PROGRAMS. Accelerated program, double major, dual enrollment of high school students, honors program, independent study, internships, student-designed major, study abroad, teacher preparation, visiting/exchange student program, Washington semester, cross-registration, early admission to medical school; combined bachelor's/graduate program in business administration, law. **Remedial services:** Learning center, remedial instruction, special counselor, tutoring. **Placement/credit:** AP, CLEP General and Subject, IB, institutional tests.

ACADEMIC REQUIREMENTS. Freshmen must earn minimum GPA of 2.0 to continue in good standing. 88% of freshmen return for sophomore year. Students must declare major by end of second year. **Graduation requirements:** 128 hours for bachelor's. Most students required to take courses in English, foreign languages, history, humanities, mathematics, philosophy/religion, biological/physical sciences, social sciences.

FRESHMAN ADMISSIONS. Selection criteria: High school achievement record, class rank, SAT or ACT test scores. Recommendations required for early admissions, Educational Opportunity Program, invited individualized admission. **High school preparation:** 17 units recommended. Recommended units include English 4, foreign language 3, mathematics 3, social science 4 and science 3. **Test requirements:** SAT or ACT; score report by January 5. **Additional information:** Participates in SUNY common application process. Engineering, music, art applicants must note choice of major; others admitted to general undergraduate college.

1992 FRESHMAN CLASS PROFILE. 15,269 men and women applied, 8,382 accepted; 1,327 men enrolled, 1,072 women enrolled. 77% had high school GPA of 3.0 or higher, 23% between 2.0 and 2.99. 32% were in top tenth and 82% were in top quarter of graduating class. **Academic background:** Mid 50% of enrolled freshmen had SAT-V between 450-550, SAT-M between 550-650. 97% submitted SAT scores. **Characteristics:** 96% from in state, 70% live in college housing, 24% have minority backgrounds, 1% are foreign students. Average age is 18.

FALL-TERM APPLICATIONS. $25 fee, may be waived for applicants with need. No closing date; priority given to applications received by January 5; applicants notified on a rolling basis beginning on or about February 15; must reply by May 1 or within 4 weeks if notified thereafter. Audition required for music applicants. Portfolio required for art applicants. CRDA. Early admission available.

STUDENT LIFE. Housing: Dormitories (coed). Study dormitories, specially equipped rooms for handicapped students, special housing for freshmen only (by request). Freshman applicants who notfiy college of their acceptance by May 1 are guaranteed college housing for freshman year. **Activities:** Student government, film, magazine, radio, student newspaper, yearbook, choral groups, dance, drama, jazz band, music ensembles, musical theater, opera, pep band, symphony orchestra, fraternities, sororities, over 150 organizations in religion, ethnic background, international affairs, volunteer work, women, public interest.

ATHLETICS. NCAA. **Intercollegiate:** Basketball, cross-country, diving, football M, soccer, swimming, tennis, track and field, volleyball W, wrestling M. **Intramural:** Archery, badminton, basketball, bowling, cross-country, fencing, football M, golf M, gymnastics, handball, ice hockey M, lacrosse, racquetball, rowing (crew), rugby, skiing, skin diving, soccer, softball, squash, table tennis, tennis, volleyball, water polo.

STUDENT SERVICES. Aptitude testing, career counseling, employment service for undergraduates, freshman orientation, health services, on-campus day care, personal counseling, placement service for graduates, special adviser for adult students, veterans counselor, services/facilities for handicapped.

ANNUAL EXPENSES. Tuition and fees (1992-93): $3,020, $3,900 additional for out-of-state students. **Room and board:** $4,578. **Books and supplies:** $683. **Other expenses:** $924.

FINANCIAL AID. 65% of freshmen, 65% of continuing students receive some form of aid. 94% of grants, 90% of loans, all jobs based on need. 1,200 enrolled freshmen were judged to have need, all were offered aid. Academic, music/drama, art, state/district residency, leadership, religious affiliation, minority scholarships available. **Aid applications:** No closing date; priority given to applications received by March 16; applicants notified on a rolling basis beginning on or about April 15; must reply by May 1 or within 3 weeks if notified thereafter.

ADDRESS/TELEPHONE. Kevin M. Durkin, Director of Admissions, State University of New York at Buffalo, 3435 Main Street Hayes C, Buffalo, NY 14214. (716) 829-2111. Fax: (716) 829-3902.

State University of New York at Purchase
Purchase, New York — CB code: 2878

Admissions:	55% of applicants accepted
Based on:	••• School record
	•• Test scores
	• Essay, interview, recommendations, special talents
Completion:	84% of freshmen end year in good standing
	50% graduate, 22% of these enter graduate study

4-year public college of arts and sciences, coed. Founded in 1967. **Accreditation:** Regional. **Undergraduate enrollment:** 972 men, 1,206 women full time; 90 men, 207 women part time. **Graduate enrollment:** 16 men, 18 women full time; 4 men, 2 women part time. **Faculty:** 298 total (130 full time), 298 with doctorates or other terminal degrees. **Location:** Suburban campus in large town; 30 miles from New York City. **Calendar:** Semester, limited summer session. Extensive evening/early morning classes. **Microcomputers:** 55 located in libraries, computer centers. **Special facilities:** Art museum, performing arts center.

DEGREES OFFERED. BA, BS, BFA, MFA. 536 bachelor's degrees awarded in 1992. 19% in letters/literature, 6% life sciences, 14% multi/interdisciplinary studies, 6% psychology, 15% social sciences, 34% visual and performing arts. Graduate degrees offered in 5 major fields of study.

UNDERGRADUATE MAJORS. Anthropology, art history, biological and physical sciences, biology, chemistry, cinematography/film, dance, dramatic arts, drawing, economics, English literature, environmental science, foreign languages (multiple emphasis), French, graphic design, history, humanities and social sciences, liberal/general studies, mathematics, music performance, painting, philosophy, photography, physics, political science and government, prelaw, psychology, sculpture, sociology, Spanish, theater design, theater technology, video.

ACADEMIC PROGRAMS. Double major, dual enrollment of high school students, independent study, internships, student-designed major, study abroad, cross-registration, conservatory master-apprentice training in dance, music, acting, film, theater design technology, visual arts. **Remedial services:** Learning center, preadmission summer program, remedial instruction, special counselor, tutoring, New York State Higher Educational Opportunity Program. **Placement/credit:** AP, CLEP General and Subject, IB, institutional tests; 30 credit hours maximum for bachelor's degree.

ACADEMIC REQUIREMENTS. Freshmen must earn minimum GPA of 1.5 to continue in good standing. 73% of freshmen return for sophomore year. Students must declare major by end of second year. **Graduation requirements:** 120 hours for bachelor's. Most students required to take courses in arts/fine arts, English, humanities, social sciences. **Postgraduate studies:** 1% enter law school, 1% enter medical school, 20% enter other graduate study.

FRESHMAN ADMISSIONS. Selection criteria: High school achievement record, or test scores, class rank considered. For school of arts applicants, audition, interview, or portfolio most important. **High school preparation:** 16 units recommended. Recommended units include biological science 1, English 3, foreign language 2, mathematics 3, physical science 2 and social science 5. **Test requirements:** SAT or ACT; score report by February 1.

1992 FRESHMAN CLASS PROFILE. 839 men applied, 426 accepted, 150 enrolled; 1,313 women applied, 766 accepted, 191 enrolled. 63% had high school GPA of 3.0 or higher, 30% between 2.0 and 2.99. 13% were in top tenth and 37% were in top quarter of graduating class. **Academic background:** Mid 50% of enrolled freshmen had SAT-V between 410-550, SAT-M between 400-550. 84% submitted SAT scores. **Characteristics:** 84% from in state, 89% live in college housing, 29% have minority backgrounds, 1% are foreign students. Average age is 18.

FALL-TERM APPLICATIONS. $25 fee, may be waived for applicants with need. Closing date May 1; applicants notified on a rolling basis; must reply within 4 weeks if notified before May 1, within 2 weeks if notified after May 1. Interview required for film, theater design/technology applicants. Audition required for acting, dance, music applicants. Portfolio required for visual arts applicants. Essay required. CRDA. Early admission available. Application deadlines vary by program. March 1 application deadline for acting program.

STUDENT LIFE. Housing: Dormitories (coed); apartment, handicapped housing available. Freshman program, wellness program, nonsmoking hall, nontraditional age hall. **Activities:** Student government, magazine, radio, student newspaper, yearbook, choral groups, dance, drama, jazz band, music ensembles, opera, symphony orchestra, Black Students Association, Hillel, Newman Club, Women's Union.

ATHLETICS. Intercollegiate: Fencing, soccer M, tennis, volleyball W. **Intramural:** Badminton, basketball, handball, racquetball, soccer, softball, squash, swimming, table tennis, tennis, volleyball, water polo.

STUDENT SERVICES. Aptitude testing, career counseling, employment service for undergraduates, freshman orientation, health services, on-campus day care, personal counseling, placement service for graduates, special adviser for adult students, veterans counselor, services/facilities for handicapped.

ANNUAL EXPENSES. Tuition and fees (projected): $2,910, $3,900 additional for out-of-state students. **Room and board:** $4,374. **Books and supplies:** $400. **Other expenses:** $900.

FINANCIAL AID. 57% of freshmen, 40% of continuing students receive some form of aid. 97% of grants, 71% of loans, 88% of jobs based on need. 194 enrolled freshmen were judged to have need, all were offered aid. Academic, music/drama, art, state/district residency scholarships available. **Aid applications:** No closing date; priority given to applications received by February 15; applicants notified on a rolling basis beginning on or about April 15; must reply within 2 weeks. **Additional information:** Institutional scholarships offered to new freshmen, transfers, and returning students. Entering students should contact Divisional Dean's Office and returning students may pick up scholarship applications on-campus. An electronic library of outside agencies offering scholarships is also available in the Financial Aid Office.

ADDRESS/TELEPHONE. Betsy Immergut, Director of Admissions, State University of New York at Purchase, 735 Anderson Hill Road, Purchase, NY 10577-1400. (914) 251-6300. Fax: (914) 251-6314.

State University of New York at Stony Brook

Stony Brook, New York CB code: 2548

Admissions: 53% of applicants accepted
Based on: ••• School record
•• Test scores
• Activities, essay, interview, recommendations, special talents
Completion: 50% graduate, 44% of these enter graduate study

4-year public university, coed. Founded in 1957. **Accreditation:** Regional. **Undergraduate enrollment:** 4,866 men, 4,420 women full time; 392 men, 521 women part time. **Graduate enrollment:** 1,260 men, 796 women full time; 647 men, 965 women part time. **Faculty:** 911 total (726 full time), 690 with doctorates or other terminal degrees. **Location:** Suburban campus in large town; 60 miles from New York City. **Calendar:** Semester, limited summer session. **Microcomputers:** Located in libraries, computer centers. **Special facilities:** Van de Graaff nuclear accelerator, Museum of Long Island Natural Sciences, fine arts center with 3 theaters and art gallery, 26-acre nature preserve.

DEGREES OFFERED. BA, BS, MA, MS, MFA, MSW, PhD. 1,881 bachelor's degrees awarded in 1992. 7% in engineering, 6% letters/literature, 12% life sciences, 10% multi/interdisciplinary studies, 12% psychology, 34% social sciences. Graduate degrees offered in 42 major fields of study.

UNDERGRADUATE MAJORS. African studies, anthropology, applied mathematics, art history, astronomy, atmospheric sciences and meteorology, biochemistry, biology, business and management, chemistry, comparative literature, computer and information sciences, dramatic arts, economics, electrical/electronics/communications engineering, engineering, engineering chemistry, English, French, geology, German, history, humanities and social sciences, information sciences and systems, Italian, liberal/general studies, linguistics, mathematics, mechanical engineering, music, philosophy, physics, political science and government, psychology, religion, Russian, social sciences, sociology, Spanish, studio art, teaching English as a second language/foreign language.

ACADEMIC PROGRAMS. Double major, dual enrollment of high school students, honors program, independent study, internships, student-designed major, study abroad, teacher preparation, visiting/exchange student program, Washington semester, cross-registration. **Remedial services:** Learning center, reduced course load, remedial instruction, special counselor, tutoring. **Placement/credit:** AP, CLEP Subject, institutional tests; 30 credit hours maximum for bachelor's degree.

ACADEMIC REQUIREMENTS. Freshmen must earn total of 18 hours of credit in 2 semesters to continue in good academic standing. 83% of freshmen return for sophomore year. Students must declare major by end of second year. **Graduation requirements:** 120 hours for bachelor's. Most students required to take courses in arts/fine arts, computer science, English, foreign languages, history, humanities, mathematics, philosophy/religion, biological/physical sciences, social sciences.

FRESHMAN ADMISSIONS. Selection criteria: High school GPA, class rank, and standardized test scores most important factors. Interview, letters of recommendation, and extracurricular activities also taken into consideration. **High school preparation:** 17 units recommended. Recommended units include English 4, foreign language 3, mathematics 3, social science 3 and science 3. 4 units mathematics and chemistry or physics recommended for applicants to science, engineering, and mathematics programs. **Test requirements:** SAT or ACT; score report by August 28.

1992 FRESHMAN CLASS PROFILE. 12,785 men and women applied, 6,787 accepted; 805 men enrolled, 767 women enrolled. 85% had high school GPA of 3.0 or higher, 15% between 2.0 and 2.99. 28% were in top tenth and 70% were in top quarter of graduating class. **Academic background:** Mid 50% of enrolled freshmen had SAT-V between 410-510, SAT-M between 480-600. 93% submitted SAT scores. **Characteristics:** 96% from in state, 61% live in college housing, 36% have minority backgrounds, 1% are foreign students. Average age is 18.

FALL-TERM APPLICATIONS. $25 fee, may be waived for applicants with need. Closing date July 31; applicants notified on a rolling basis; must reply by May 1 or within 4 weeks if notified thereafter. Interview required for theater applicants. Audition required for music, theater applicants. Portfolio recommended for art applicants. Deferred and early admission available.

STUDENT LIFE. Housing: Dormitories (coed); apartment housing available. Some dormitories closed for renovation, resulting in increased percentage of students living in off-campus apartments. Fairly even balance normally exists between numbers of commuting and residential students. **Activities:** Student government, film, magazine, radio, student newspaper, yearbook, choral groups, concert band, drama, music ensembles, musical theater, opera, symphony orchestra, fraternities, sororities, Jewish, Protestant, Catholic, Baha'i religious organizations, Inter-Varsity Christian Fellowship, International Club, Chinese Association, Indian Student Association, Pakistan Club, African Students Association, Latin American Organization, Caribbean Association.

ATHLETICS. NCAA. **Intercollegiate:** Baseball M, basketball, cross-country, diving, football M, lacrosse M, soccer, softball W, swimming, tennis, track and field, volleyball W. **Intramural:** Badminton, basketball, cross-country, golf M, handball M, lacrosse, soccer, softball, squash M, tennis, volleyball. **Clubs:** Horseback riding, flag football M, squash M.

STUDENT SERVICES. Career counseling, employment service for undergraduates, freshman orientation, health services, on-campus day care, personal counseling, placement service for graduates, special adviser for adult students, veterans counselor, health care facilities, services/facilities for handicapped.

ANNUAL EXPENSES. Tuition and fees (projected): $2,942, $3,900 additional for out-of-state students. **Room and board:** $4,698. **Books and supplies:** $750. **Other expenses:** $1,120.

FINANCIAL AID. 35% of continuing students receive some form of aid. All grants, 90% of loans, 42% of jobs based on need. Academic scholarships available. **Aid applications:** No closing date; priority given to applications received by March 1; applicants notified on a rolling basis beginning on or about April 1; must reply within 2 weeks.

ADDRESS/TELEPHONE. Theresa LaRocca-Meyer, Assistant Vice President of Student Affairs, State University of New York at Stony Brook, Stony Brook, NY 11794-1901. (516) 632-6868.

State University of New York College of Agriculture and Technology at Cobleskill

Cobleskill, New York CB code: 2524

Admissions: 88% of applicants accepted
Based on: ••• Interview, school record
•• Activities, special talents, test scores
• Essay, recommendations
Completion: 65% of freshmen end year in good standing
60% graduate, 45% of these enter 4-year programs

2-year public agricultural and technical college, coed. Founded in 1911. **Accreditation:** Regional. **Undergraduate enrollment:** 1,328 men, 1,277 women full time; 87 men, 115 women part time. **Faculty:** 167 total (142 full time), 23 with doctorates or other terminal degrees. **Location:** Rural campus in small town; 35 miles from Albany, 39 miles from Oneonta. **Calendar:** Semester, limited summer session. **Microcomputers:** Located in libraries, classrooms, computer centers. **Special facilities:** Arboretum, 14 greenhouses, livestock pavilion, 350-acre farm, modern chemical and biological technology laboratories, art gallery, student-operated restaurant, fish hatchery. **Additional facts:** 4-year bachelor of technology degree in agriculture also offered.

DEGREES OFFERED. AA, AS, AAS. 624 associate degrees awarded in 1992. 32% in agriculture, 28% business and management, 12% teacher education, 14% home economics, 6% social sciences. 57 bachelor's degrees awarded.

UNDERGRADUATE MAJORS. Accounting, agribusiness, agricultural business and management, agricultural engineering, agricultural mechanics, agricultural sciences, agronomy, animal sciences, biological laboratory technology, biology, business administration and management, business data processing and related programs, chemical manufacturing technology, chemistry, child development/care/guidance, computer and information sciences, dairy, data processing, diesel engine mechanics, early childhood education, equestrian science, fishing and fisheries, food production/management/services, food science and nutrition, horticultural science, hospitality and recreation marketing, hotel/motel and restaurant management, liberal/general studies, mathematics, medical laboratory technologies, ornamental horticulture, parks and recreation management, plant sciences, public health technology/environmental health, science technologies, secretarial and related programs, social sciences, soil sciences, telecommunications, tourism, wildlife management, word processing. agricultural sciences.

ACADEMIC PROGRAMS. 2-year transfer program, honors program, independent study, internships, study abroad, cross-registration. **Remedial services:** Learning center, preadmission summer program, reduced course load, New York State Higher Education Opportunity Program. **Placement/credit:** AP, CLEP General, institutional tests; 33 credit hours maximum for associate degree.

ACADEMIC REQUIREMENTS. Freshmen must earn minimum GPA of 1.75 to continue in good standing. 70% of freshmen return for sophomore year. Students must declare major on application. **Graduation requirements:** 66 hours for associate (33 in major). Most students required to take courses in English, mathematics, biological/physical sciences, social sciences.

FRESHMAN ADMISSIONS. Selection criteria: Strength of high school curriculum most important. GPA, SAT and/or ACT scores, and extracurricular activities considered. Letters of recommendation and autobiographies welcome. **High school preparation:** 9 units recommended. Recommended units include biological science 1, English 4, mathematics 1 and social science 3. Additional recommendations for some programs.

1992 FRESHMAN CLASS PROFILE. 2,076 men applied, 1,834 accepted, 632 enrolled; 1,769 women applied, 1,563 accepted, 642 enrolled. 20% had high school GPA of 3.0 or higher, 67% between 2.0 and 2.99. **Academic background:** Mid 50% of enrolled freshmen had SAT-V between 370-470, SAT-M between 370-470; ACT composite between 14-22. 45%

submitted SAT scores, 14% submitted ACT scores. **Characteristics:** 88% live in college housing, 9% have minority backgrounds. Average age is 18.

FALL-TERM APPLICATIONS. $25 fee, may be waived for applicants with need. No closing date; priority given to applications received by March 1; applicants notified on a rolling basis; must reply within 4 weeks. Interview required. Deferred and early admission available. SAT or ACT recommended for admission and counseling.

STUDENT LIFE. Housing: Dormitories (men, women, coed). Privately owned apartments for students adjacent to campus. **Activities:** Student government, magazine, radio, student newspaper, yearbook, choral groups, drama, jazz band, music ensembles, musical theater, community orchestra, academic honorary society, Orange Key, Circle-K International, numerous special interest clubs.

ATHLETICS. NJCAA. **Intercollegiate:** Baseball M, basketball, cross-country, field hockey W, golf M, lacrosse M, skiing, soccer, softball W, tennis, track and field, volleyball W, wrestling M. **Intramural:** Archery, badminton, basketball, bowling, racquetball, softball, table tennis W, tennis, volleyball.

STUDENT SERVICES. Aptitude testing, career counseling, employment service for undergraduates, freshman orientation, health services, on-campus day care, personal counseling, placement service for graduates, special adviser for adult students, veterans counselor, services/facilities for handicapped.

ANNUAL EXPENSES. Tuition and fees (1992-93): $2,944, $3,900 additional for out-of-state students. **Room and board:** $4,470. **Books and supplies:** $500. **Other expenses:** $600.

FINANCIAL AID. 65% of freshmen, 65% of continuing students receive some form of aid. 96% of grants, 98% of loans, 40% of jobs based on need. 830 enrolled freshmen were judged to have need, all were offered aid. Academic, state/district residency, leadership, minority scholarships available. **Aid applications:** No closing date; priority given to applications received by April 1; applicants notified on a rolling basis beginning on or about April 15; must reply within 2 weeks.

ADDRESS/TELEPHONE. John Devney, Director of Admissions, State University of New York College of Agriculture and Technology at Cobleskill, Cobleskill, NY 12043. (518) 234-5525. Fax: (518) 234-5333.

State University of New York College of Agriculture and Technology at Morrisville

Morrisville, New York CB code: 2527

2-year public agricultural and technical college, coed. Founded in 1908. **Accreditation:** Regional. **Undergraduate enrollment:** 1,613 men, 1,294 women full time; 137 men, 391 women part time. **Faculty:** 194 total (124 full time), 15 with doctorates or other terminal degrees. **Location:** Rural campus in rural community; 30 miles from Syracuse and Utica. **Calendar:** Semester, limited summer session. Extensive evening/early morning classes. **Microcomputers:** 60 located in dormitories, libraries, computer centers. **Special facilities:** Horse arena, race track, dairy farm, aquaculture (fish rearing) ponds, observatory, wildlife museum. **Additional facts:** Evening extension centers at Norwich and Oneida offer liberal arts and some technical courses.

DEGREES OFFERED. AA, AS, AAS. 715 associate degrees awarded in 1992. 18% in agriculture, 15% business and management, 14% business/office and marketing/distribution, 5% communications, 17% engineering technologies, 15% health sciences, 7% multi/interdisciplinary studies.

UNDERGRADUATE MAJORS. Accounting, agribusiness, agricultural engineering, agricultural mechanics, agricultural products and processing, agricultural sciences, agronomy, animal sciences, automotive mechanics, automotive technology, biological laboratory technology, biology, biotechnology, business administration and management, business and management, business and office, business computer/console/peripheral equipment operation, business data entry equipment operation, business data processing and related programs, business data programming, chemistry, clinical laboratory science, computer and information sciences, computer servicing technology, conservation and regulation, construction, dairy, data processing, diesel engine mechanics, dietetic aide/assistant, drafting, drafting and design technology, electrical and electronics equipment repair, electrical technology, electromechanical technology, electronic technology, engineering and engineering-related technologies, engineering science, equestrian science, finance, fishing and fisheries, food management, food production/management/services, food sciences, forest products processing technology, forestry and related sciences, horticultural science, horticulture, hospitality and recreation marketing, hotel/motel and restaurant management, humanities, humanities and social sciences, industrial technology, information sciences and systems, journalism, landscape architecture, legal secretary, liberal/general studies, mathematics, mechanical design technology, mechanical engineering, medical laboratory technologies, medical secretary, nursing, office supervision and management, parks and recreation management, physics, plant sciences, preveterinary, science technologies, secretarial and related programs, social sciences, tourism, wildlife management, wood products technology.

ACADEMIC PROGRAMS. 2-year transfer program, double major, internships, student-designed major, joint program with SUNY Forest Technology School at Wanakena, 2-2 transfer program with SUNY College of Environmental Science and Forestry. **Remedial services:** Learning center, reduced course load, remedial instruction, tutoring, New York State Higher Educational Opportunity Program. **Placement/credit:** AP, CLEP General and Subject, institutional tests; 21 credit hours maximum for associate degree.

ACADEMIC REQUIREMENTS. Freshmen must earn minimum GPA of 1.5 to continue in good standing. 75% of freshmen return for sophomore year. Students must declare major on application. **Graduation requirements:** 64 hours for associate (24 in major). Most students required to take courses in English, mathematics, biological/physical sciences, social sciences.

FRESHMAN ADMISSIONS. Selection criteria: High school record most important. Requirements depend on program. Mathematics and science preparation important for technical majors.

1992 FRESHMAN CLASS PROFILE. 816 men, 730 women enrolled. **Characteristics:** 98% from in state, 95% live in college housing, 11% have minority backgrounds. Average age is 18.

FALL-TERM APPLICATIONS. $25 fee, may be waived for applicants with need. No closing date; applicants notified on a rolling basis; must reply within 4 weeks. Interview recommended. Deferred admission available. SAT or ACT strongly recommended, score report by August 23.

STUDENT LIFE. Housing: Dormitories (men, women, coed). **Activities:** Student government, magazine, radio, student newspaper, yearbook, choral groups, concert band, drama, jazz band, musical theater, fraternities, sororities.

ATHLETICS. NJCAA. **Intercollegiate:** Basketball, diving, horseback riding, lacrosse M, rifle, skiing, soccer, softball W, swimming, track and field, volleyball W, wrestling M. **Intramural:** Archery, badminton, basketball, bowling, cross-country, diving, golf, handball, horseback riding, lacrosse, racquetball, skin diving, soccer, swimming, table tennis, tennis, track and field, volleyball, wrestling M.

STUDENT SERVICES. Aptitude testing, career counseling, employment service for undergraduates, freshman orientation, health services, personal counseling, placement service for graduates, special adviser for adult students, veterans counselor, services/facilities for handicapped.

ANNUAL EXPENSES. Tuition and fees (1992-93): $2,900, $3,900 additional for out-of-state students. **Room and board:** $4,080. **Books and supplies:** $600. **Other expenses:** $770.

FINANCIAL AID. 85% of freshmen, 85% of continuing students receive some form of aid. 95% of grants, 92% of loans, 47% of jobs based on need. 1,110 enrolled freshmen were judged to have need, 810 were offered aid. Academic scholarships available. **Aid applications:** No closing date; priority given to applications received by March 1; applicants notified on a rolling basis beginning on or about May 1; must reply within 2 weeks.

ADDRESS/TELEPHONE. Joseph Insel, Director of Admissions, State University of New York College of Agriculture and Technology at Morrisville, Route 20, Morrisville, NY 13408. (315) 684-6046. Fax: (315) 684-6116.

State University of New York College at Brockport ⇆

Brockport, New York CB code: 2537

Admissions:	47% of applicants accepted
Based on:	••• School record
	•• Special talents, test scores
	• Activities, essay, interview, recommendations
Completion:	65% of freshmen end year in good standing
	43% graduate, 25% of these enter graduate study

4-year public college of arts and sciences, coed. Founded in 1867. **Accreditation:** Regional. **Undergraduate enrollment:** 2,686 men, 3,112 women full time; 564 men, 877 women part time. **Graduate enrollment:** 115 men, 185 women full time; 556 men, 1,132 women part time. **Faculty:** 620 total (350 full time), 267 with doctorates or other terminal degrees. **Location:** Rural campus in small town; 16 miles from Rochester. **Calendar:** Semester, limited summer session. Extensive evening/early morning classes. **Microcomputers:** 400 located in dormitories, libraries, classrooms, computer centers. **Special facilities:** Automated library system, art gallery, aquaculture ponds, unidata weather information system, weather radio receiver, nuclear lab, high resolution germanium detector, research vessel on Lake Ontario, electron microscope.

DEGREES OFFERED. BA, BS, BFA, MA, MS, MFA, MEd. 1,561 bachelor's degrees awarded in 1992. 18% in business and management, 7% communications, 8% teacher education, 8% health sciences, 5% letters/literature, 15% parks/recreation, protective services, public affairs, 10% psychology, 13% social sciences. Graduate degrees offered in 24 major fields of study.

UNDERGRADUATE MAJORS. Accounting, Afro-American (black) studies, American studies, anthropology, art history, atmospheric sciences and meteorology, biology, business administration and management, chemistry, communications, computer and information sciences, criminal justice studies, dance, dramatic arts, earth sciences, economics, elementary education, English, fine arts, French, geology, health sciences, history, interdisciplinary arts for children, international business management, international studies, liberal/general studies, mathematics, nursing, parks and recreation management, philosophy, physical education, physics, political science and government, psychology, social work, sociology, Spanish, studio art, water resources.

ACADEMIC PROGRAMS. Accelerated program, cooperative education, double major, dual enrollment of high school students, external degree, honors program, independent study, internships, student-designed major, study abroad, teacher preparation, telecourses, visiting/exchange student program, New York semester, Washington semester, cross-registration, 3+2 program in engineering with Case Western Reserve University, Ohio, Clarkson Univerity, SUNY Buffalo, SUNY at Binghamton, and Syracuse University; liberal arts/career combination in engineering. **Remedial services:** Learning center, preadmission summer program, reduced course load, remedial instruction, tutoring, auxiliary aids provided to students with documented disabilities. **ROTC:** Army. **Placement/credit:** AP, CLEP General and Subject, institutional tests; 60 credit hours maximum for bachelor's degree.

ACADEMIC REQUIREMENTS. Freshmen must earn minimum GPA of 2.0 to continue in good standing. 77% of freshmen return for sophomore year. Students must declare major by end of second year. **Graduation requirements:** 120 hours for bachelor's (36 in major). Most students required to take courses in arts/fine arts, computer science, English, humanities, mathematics, biological/physical sciences, social sciences. **Postgraduate studies:** 3% enter law school, 1% enter medical school, 5% enter MBA programs, 16% enter other graduate study. **Additional information:** Teacher Certification Programs in the following areas: adapted physical education (K-12), biology and general science, 7-12, chemistry and general science, 7-12, earth science and general science, 7-12, elementary teacher, n-6, elementary teacher and bilingual education, n-6, English, 7-12, French, 7-12, health, k-12, mathematics, 7-12, physical education, k-12, physics and general science, 7-12, social studies, 7-12, and Spanish, 7-12.

FRESHMAN ADMISSIONS. Selection criteria: High school academic record including number of academic units, GPA, class rank, test scores. Recommendations from counselors encouraged. Supplemental information form completed by applicants recommended and considered. **High school preparation:** 17 units required; 21 recommended. Required and recommended units include English 4, mathematics 2-3, physical science 1-2, social science 4 and science 3. Biological science 1 and foreign language 3 recommended. Laboratory science preferred. **Test requirements:** SAT or ACT; score report by February 1.

1992 FRESHMAN CLASS PROFILE. 3,644 men applied, 1,610 accepted, 390 enrolled; 4,255 women applied, 2,091 accepted, 487 enrolled. 89% had high school GPA of 3.0 or higher, 11% between 2.0 and 2.99. 9% were in top tenth and 43% were in top quarter of graduating class. **Academic background:** Mid 50% of enrolled freshmen had SAT-V between 390-480, SAT-M between 430-590; ACT composite between 21-23. 92% submitted SAT scores, 36% submitted ACT scores. **Characteristics:** 98% from in state, 85% live in college housing, 12% have minority backgrounds, 6% join fraternities/sororities. Average age is 18.

FALL-TERM APPLICATIONS. $25 fee, may be waived for applicants with need. Closing date May 1; priority given to applications received by January 1; applicants notified on a rolling basis beginning on or about January 15; must reply by May 1 or within 30 days if notified after April 15. Interview recommended. Audition recommended for dance applicants. Portfolio recommended for art applicants. Essay recommended. CRDA. Deferred and early admission available. EDP-F. Special admission requirements for early decision, transition and exceptional talent programs; accepted applicants must respond within 4 weeks of acceptance.

STUDENT LIFE. Housing: Dormitories (coed); handicapped housing available. Special living options include freshman first-year experience program, transfer student program, wellness program, single sex floors, 24-hour quiet, no smoking floors. **Activities:** Student government, radio, student newspaper, television, yearbook, choral groups, dance, drama, music ensembles, musical theater, symphony orchestra, fraternities, sororities, Organization for Students of African Descent, Association of Latin American Students, International Students Association, Hillel, Alpha Chi Honor Society, Caribbean Club, Women's Center, Adult Student Organization, peer counseling, student alumni association, Native American Students Organization. **Additional information:** Of undergraduates who do not reside in college housing, approximately 39% live in their own apartments off campus, 25% commute from home.

ATHLETICS. NCAA. **Intercollegiate:** Baseball M, basketball, cross-country, diving, field hockey W, football M, gymnastics W, ice hockey M, soccer, softball W, swimming, tennis W, track and field, volleyball W, wrestling M. **Intramural:** Badminton W, basketball, bowling, field hockey W, ice hockey M, lacrosse, racquetball, rugby, skiing, soccer, softball, squash, volleyball.

STUDENT SERVICES. Career counseling, employment service for undergraduates, freshman orientation, health services, on-campus day care, personal counseling, placement service for graduates, special adviser for adult students, veterans counselor, veterans outreach program, services/facilities for handicapped.

ANNUAL EXPENSES. Tuition and fees (projected): $2,940, $3,900 additional for out-of-state students. **Room and board:** $4,360. **Books and supplies:** $500. **Other expenses:** $730.

FINANCIAL AID. 75% of freshmen, 82% of continuing students receive some form of aid. 88% of grants, 67% of loans, 55% of jobs based on need. 657 enrolled freshmen were judged to have need, all were offered aid. Academic, music/drama, art, state/district residency, leadership, minority scholarships available. **Aid applications:** No closing date; priority given to applications received by May 1; applicants notified on a rolling basis beginning on or about February 15; must reply by May 1 or within 20 days if notified thereafter. **Additional information:** Brockport Foundation Scholarships administered by college.

ADDRESS/TELEPHONE. Marsha R. Gottovi, Director of Admissions, State University of New York College at Brockport, Brockport, NY 14420-2915. (716) 395-2751. Fax: (716) 395-5397.

State University of New York College at Buffalo

Buffalo, New York CB code: 2533

Admissions: 59% of applicants accepted
Based on: ••• School record
• Activities, essay, interview, recommendations, special talents, test scores
Completion: 74% of freshmen end year in good standing
31% graduate

4-year public college of arts and sciences, coed. Founded in 1867. **Accreditation:** Regional. **Undergraduate enrollment:** 3,367 men, 4,703 women full time; 1,084 men, 1,050 women part time. **Graduate enrollment:** 103 men, 238 women full time; 399 men, 1,165 women part time. **Faculty:** 577 total (429 full time). **Location:** Urban campus in large city. **Calendar:** Semester, limited summer session. Saturday and extensive evening/early morning classes. **Microcomputers:** 400 located in libraries, computer centers. **Special facilities:** Burchfield Art Gallery, planetarium, performing arts center.

DEGREES OFFERED. BA, BS, BFA, MA, MS, MEd. 1,851 bachelor's degrees awarded in 1992. 13% in business and management, 5% communications, 6% education, 24% teacher education, 6% engineering technologies, 12% parks/recreation, protective services, public affairs, 8% social sciences, 6% visual and performing arts. Graduate degrees offered in 30 major fields of study.

UNDERGRADUATE MAJORS. Anthropology, art education, art history, biology, business administration and management, business and management, business and office, business education, ceramics, chemistry, city/community/regional planning, communications, computer and information sciences, criminal justice studies, dramatic arts, early childhood education, earth sciences, economics, electrical technology, electromechanical technology, elementary education, English, fashion design, fiber/textiles/weaving, fine arts, food management, food science and nutrition, foreign languages education, forensic studies, French, geography, geology, graphic design, history, humanities and social sciences, industrial arts education, industrial technology, information sciences and systems, Italian, journalism, liberal/general studies, marketing and distributive education, mathematics, mathematics education, mechanical design technology, metal/jewelry, music, office supervision and management, painting, philosophy, photography, physics, physics/engineering, political science and government, printmaking, psychology, public relations, radio/television broadcasting, science education, sculpture, secondary education, social studies education, social work, sociology, Spanish, special education, speech correction, technical education, theater design, trade and industrial education, visual and performing arts.

ACADEMIC PROGRAMS. Cooperative education, double major, dual enrollment of high school students, honors program, independent study, internships, study abroad, teacher preparation, visiting/exchange student program, Washington semester, cross-registration; liberal arts/career combination in engineering. **Remedial services:** Learning center, preadmission summer program, remedial instruction, special counselor, tutoring. **Placement/credit:** AP, CLEP General and Subject, institutional tests; 30 credit hours maximum for bachelor's degree.

ACADEMIC REQUIREMENTS. Freshmen must earn minimum GPA of 2.0 to continue in good standing. 73% of freshmen return for sophomore year. Students must declare major by end of second year. **Graduation requirements:** 123 hours for bachelor's (36 in major). Most students required to take courses in arts/fine arts, English, humanities, mathematics, biological/physical sciences, social sciences.

FRESHMAN ADMISSIONS. Selection criteria: High school GPA, class rank important. Test scores, recommendations and extracurricular activities also considered. **High school preparation:** 16 units required; 18 recommended. Required and recommended units include English 4, foreign language 2-3, mathematics 2-3, social science 4 and science 3.

1992 FRESHMAN CLASS PROFILE. 2,625 men applied, 2,040 accepted, 459 enrolled; 3,220 women applied, 1,431 accepted, 621 enrolled. 8% were in top tenth and 38% were in top quarter of graduating class. **Characteristics:** 98% from in state, 58% commute, 26% have minority backgrounds, 1% are foreign students. Average age is 18.

FALL-TERM APPLICATIONS. $25 fee, may be waived for applicants with need. No closing date; priority given to applications received by December 15; applicants notified on a rolling basis beginning on or about December 15; must reply by May 1 or within 4 weeks if notified thereafter. Portfolio required for fine arts applicants. CRDA. Deferred and early admission available. EDP-F. SAT/ACT scores recommended.

STUDENT LIFE. Housing: Dormitories (coed). **Activities:** Student government, magazine, radio, student newspaper, yearbook, choral groups, concert band, dance, drama, jazz band, music ensembles, fraternities, sororities, Newman Club, Amnesty International, public interest groups, African American Student Organization, Adelante Estudiantes, International Student Organization, Native American Student Organization, Muslim Student Organization, Christian Fellowship groups.

ATHLETICS. NCAA. **Intercollegiate:** Baseball M, basketball, bowling, cross-country, diving, football M, ice hockey M, lacrosse M, rugby M, soccer, softball W, swimming, tennis, track and field, volleyball. **Intramural:** Basketball M, softball, volleyball.

STUDENT SERVICES. Career counseling, employment service for undergraduates, freshman orientation, health services, on-campus day care, personal counseling, placement service for graduates, special adviser for adult students, veterans counselor, services/facilities for handicapped.

ANNUAL EXPENSES. Tuition and fees (projected): $3,074, $3,900 additional for out-of-state students. **Room and board:** $4,731. **Books and supplies:** $708. **Other expenses:** $957.

FINANCIAL AID. 85% of freshmen, 80% of continuing students receive some form of aid. 97% of grants, 95% of loans, all jobs based on need. Academic, music/drama, art, athletic, state/district residency, leadership, minority scholarships available. **Aid applications:** No closing date; priority given to applications received by March 16; applicants notified on a rolling basis beginning on or about April 15; must reply by May 1 or within 3 weeks if notified thereafter.

ADDRESS/TELEPHONE. Deborah K. Renzi, Director of Admissions, State University of New York College at Buffalo, 1300 Elmwood Avenue, Buffalo, NY 14222-1095. (716) 878-4017. Fax: (716) 878-3039.

State University of New York College at Cortland

Cortland, New York — CB code: 2538

Admissions: 45% of applicants accepted
Based on:
••• School record
•• Activities, essay, recommendations, test scores
• Interview, special talents
Completion: 75% of freshmen end year in good standing
51% graduate, 24% of these enter graduate study

4-year public college of arts and sciences, coed. Founded in 1868. **Accreditation:** Regional. **Undergraduate enrollment:** 2,206 men, 2,977 women full time; 87 men, 135 women part time. **Graduate enrollment:** 53 men, 86 women full time; 161 men, 587 women part time. **Faculty:** 458 total (241 full time), 239 with doctorates or other terminal degrees. **Location:** Suburban campus in large town; 30 miles from Syracuse; 18 miles from Ithaca. **Calendar:** Semester, limited summer session. **Microcomputers:** 100 located in dormitories, libraries, classrooms, computer centers. **Special facilities:** Fine arts gallery, 3 outdoor education centers for field work, including 446-acre center at Raquette Lake in Adirondacks 70-acre Brauer geological field station outside Albany, and 173-acre nature preserve.

DEGREES OFFERED. BA, BS, MA, MS. 1,287 bachelor's degrees awarded in 1992. 59% in teacher education, 10% health sciences, 10% social sciences. Graduate degrees offered in 13 major fields of study.

UNDERGRADUATE MAJORS. Afro-American (black) studies, anthropology, biology, business and management, chemistry, dramatic arts, earth sciences, economics, education, education of the deaf and hearing impaired, elementary education, English, English education, fine arts, foreign languages education, French, geochemistry, geography, geology, German, health education, health sciences, history, international studies, junior high education, liberal/general studies, management science, mathematics, mathematics education, music, philosophy, physical education, physics, political science and government, psychology, radio/television broadcasting, recreation and community services technologies, science education, social studies education, sociology, Spanish, speech, speech correction, speech pathology/audiology, studio art.

ACADEMIC PROGRAMS. Cooperative education, double major, dual enrollment of high school students, honors program, independent study, internships, student-designed major, study abroad, teacher preparation, visiting/exchange student program, Washington semester, cross-registration, extensive study abroad program with 12 institutions in England, France, Germany, Switzerland, Mexico, China, and elsewhere, combined degree program in engineering with SUNY at Binghamton, SUNY at Buffalo, SUNY College of Ceramics at Alfred University, Case Western Reserve University in Ohio, Clarkson University, and SUNY at Stony Brook; liberal arts/career combination in forestry. **Remedial services:** Learning center, reduced course load, remedial instruction, tutoring. **ROTC:** Air Force, Army. **Placement/credit:** AP, CLEP Subject, IB, institutional tests; 30 credit hours maximum for bachelor's degree.

ACADEMIC REQUIREMENTS. Freshmen must earn minimum GPA of 2.0 to continue in good standing. 75% of freshmen return for sophomore year. Students must declare major by end of second year. **Graduation requirements:** 124 hours for bachelor's. Most students required to take courses in arts/fine arts, English, history, mathematics, biological/physical sciences, social sciences.

FRESHMAN ADMISSIONS. Selection criteria: Academic course selection and performance, test scores, class rank, recommendations, personal statement, and extracurricular involvement most important. Interview carefully considered. **High school preparation:** 16 units required. Required and recommended units include biological science 1, English 4, mathematics 2-3, physical science 1-2 and social science 4. Foreign language 3 recommended. **Test requirements:** SAT or ACT; score report by February 1. **Additional information:** At least one letter of recommendation and personal statement or essay required, interviews strongly encouraged.

1992 FRESHMAN CLASS PROFILE. 3,710 men applied, 1,471 accepted, 399 enrolled; 4,505 women applied, 2,235 accepted, 619 enrolled. 89% had high school GPA of 3.0 or higher, 11% between 2.0 and 2.99. 6% were in top tenth and 44% were in top quarter of graduating class. **Academic background:** Mid 50% of enrolled freshmen had SAT-V between 440-490, SAT-M between 470-550; ACT composite between 22-25. 89% submitted SAT scores, 30% submitted ACT scores. **Characteristics:** 96% from in state, 95% live in college housing, 9% have minority backgrounds. Average age is 18.

FALL-TERM APPLICATIONS. $25 fee, may be waived for applicants with need. Closing date March 30; priority given to applications received by February 1; applicants notified on a rolling basis beginning on or about January 30; must reply by May 1. Essay required. Interview recommended. Audition recommended. Portfolio recommended. CRDA. Deferred and early admission available. EDP-F.

STUDENT LIFE. Housing: Dormitories (coed); apartment, fraternity, sorority housing available. **Activities:** Student government, film, magazine, radio, student newspaper, television, yearbook, choral groups, concert band, dance, drama, jazz band, music ensembles, pep band, symphony orchestra, fraternities, sororities, Amnesty International, Hunger Homelessness Coalition, New York Public Interest Research Group, Black Student Union, Latin Student Union, Jewish Student Society, Community Service Council, Big Brothers/Big Sisters, Adopt-a-Grandparent program, Outing Club. **Additional information:** Of undergraduates who do not live in college housing, approximately 35% live in their own apartments off campus, 5% commute from home.

ATHLETICS. NCAA. **Intercollegiate:** Baseball M, basketball, cross-country, diving, field hockey W, football M, gymnastics, ice hockey M, lacrosse, soccer, softball W, swimming, tennis W, track and field, volleyball W, wrestling M. **Intramural:** Racquetball, softball, squash, volleyball.

STUDENT SERVICES. Aptitude testing, career counseling, employment service for undergraduates, freshman orientation, health services, personal counseling, placement service for graduates, special adviser for adult students, veterans counselor, services/facilities for handicapped.

ANNUAL EXPENSES. Tuition and fees (projected): $2,905, $3,900 additional for out-of-state students. **Room and board:** $4,400. **Books and supplies:** $650. **Other expenses:** $845.

FINANCIAL AID. 79% of freshmen, 85% of continuing students receive some form of aid. 99% of grants, 92% of loans, 73% of jobs based on need. 797 enrolled freshmen were judged to have need, 789 were offered aid. Academic, music/drama, leadership, minority scholarships available. **Aid applications:** Closing date May 1; applicants notified on a rolling basis beginning on or about April 15; must reply within 2 weeks.

ADDRESS/TELEPHONE. Michael K. McKeon, Director of Admissions, State University of New York College at Cortland, PO Box 2000, Cortland, NY 13045. (607) 753-4712. Fax: (607) 753-5999.

State University of New York College of Environmental Science and Forestry

Syracuse, New York — CB code: 2530

Admissions: 22% of applicants accepted
Based on:
••• School record
•• Essay, recommendations, test scores
• Activities, interview, special talents
Completion: 85% of freshmen end year in good standing
15% enter graduate study

4-year public college of environmental science and forestry, coed. Founded in 1911. **Accreditation:** Regional. **Undergraduate enrollment:** 716 men, 297 women full time; 110 men, 79 women part time. **Graduate enrollment:** 182 men, 110 women full time; 227 men, 123 women part time. **Faculty:** 131 total (119 full time), 90 with doctorates or other terminal degrees. **Location:** Urban campus in small city. **Calendar:** Semester. **Microcomputers:** 100 located in libraries, computer centers. **Special facilities:** 6 regional campuses and field stations used for field study and research, 25,000-acre multi-campus forest system, Adirondack Ecological Center, Roosevelt Wildlife Collection, semicommercial paper mill. **Additional facts:** Associate degree program in forestry technology offered through the New York State Ranger School, Wanakena campus in Adirondack Mountains. On-line access to Syracuse University library.

DEGREES OFFERED. AAS, BS, MS, PhD. 40 associate degrees awarded in 1992. 100% in agriculture. 212 bachelor's degrees awarded. 11% in agriculture, 17% architecture and environmental design, 19% engineering, 24% life sciences, 24% multi/interdisciplinary studies, 5% physical sciences. Graduate degrees offered in 48 major fields of study.

UNDERGRADUATE MAJORS. Associate: Forest products processing technology, forestry and related sciences, survey and mapping technology. **Bachelor's:** Analytical chemistry, biochemistry, biological and physical sciences, biology, biometrics and biostatistics, biotechnology, botany, cell biology, chemical engineering, chemistry, city/community/regional planning, civil engineering, conservation and regulation, construction, ecology, entomology, environmental design, environmental health engineering, environmental science, fishing and fisheries, forest products processing technology, forestry and related sciences, forestry production and processing, genetics, human and animal, landscape architecture, materials engineering, mechanical engineering, microbiology, molecular biology, mycology, organic chemistry, paper engineering, physical chemistry, physiology, human and animal, plant genetics, plant pathology, plant physiology, plant protection, plant sciences, predentistry, prelaw, premedicine, prepharmacy, preveterinary, renewable natural resources, science education, soil sciences, surveying and mapping sciences, toxicology, urban design, wildlife management, woodworking, zoology.

ACADEMIC PROGRAMS. Independent study, internships, study abroad, teacher preparation, cross-registration. **Remedial services:** Learning center, remedial instruction, tutoring. **ROTC:** Air Force, Army. **Placement/credit:** AP, CLEP General and Subject; 30 credit hours maximum for associate degree; 60 credit hours maximum for bachelor's degree.

ACADEMIC REQUIREMENTS. Freshmen must earn minimum GPA of 2.0 to continue in good standing. 85% of freshmen return for sophomore year. Students must declare major on enrollment. **Graduation requirements:** 75 hours for associate, 130 hours for bachelor's. Most students required to take courses in computer science, English, humanities, mathematics, biological/physical sciences, social sciences. **Postgraduate studies:** 10% from 2-year programs enter 4-year programs. 3% enter law school, 1% enter medical school, 1% enter MBA programs, 10% enter other graduate study.

FRESHMAN ADMISSIONS. Selection criteria: High school record most important, test scores and recommendations also important. **High school preparation:** 18 units required; 20 recommended. Required and recommended units include English 4, mathematics 4, social science 3 and science 4. Foreign language 2 recommended. 4 mathematics and 4 science essential, biology and chemistry preferred. **Test requirements:** SAT or ACT (SAT preferred); score report by January 1. **Additional information:** Advanced standing granted for any AP examination with score of 3 or higher which fulfills stated program requirements.

1992 FRESHMAN CLASS PROFILE. 426 men applied, 92 accepted, 44 enrolled; 284 women applied, 61 accepted, 23 enrolled. 100% had high school GPA of 3.0 or higher. 64% were in top tenth and 94% were in top quarter of graduating class. **Academic background:** Mid 50% of enrolled freshmen had SAT-V between 490-590, SAT-M between 540-650. 100% submitted SAT scores. **Characteristics:** 90% from in state, 95% live in college housing, 20% have minority backgrounds. Average age is 18.

FALL-TERM APPLICATIONS. $25 fee, may be waived for applicants with need. No closing date; priority given to applications received by February 1; applicants notified on a rolling basis beginning on or about February 1; must reply by May 1 or within 2 weeks if notified thereafter. Essay required. Interview recommended. CRDA. Deferred admission available. EDP-F. Application deadline for early decision is November 15.

STUDENT LIFE. Housing: Dormitories (men, women, coed); apartment, fraternity, sorority housing available. All on-campus college housing through Syracuse University. **Activities:** Student government, radio, student newspaper, yearbook, choral groups, concert band, drama, jazz band, marching band, music ensembles, pep band, symphony orchestra, fraternities, sororities, forestry club, woodsmen's team, zoology club, landscape architect club, botany club, Alpha Sigma Phi, Baobob. Over 300 organizations available through Syracuse University. **Additional information:** Our college and Syracuse University share campus life activities. Of students who do not live in college housing, approximately 70% live in their own apartments off campus, 5% commute from home.

ATHLETICS. Intramural: Baseball M, basketball, bowling, fencing, field hockey W, football M, golf, gymnastics W, ice hockey M, lacrosse, racquetball, rifle M, rugby M, sailing, skiing, soccer, softball W, squash, swimming, tennis, track and field, volleyball, wrestling M.

STUDENT SERVICES. Aptitude testing, career counseling, employment service for undergraduates, freshman orientation, health services, on-campus day care, personal counseling, placement service for graduates, special adviser for adult students, veterans counselor, services/facilities for handicapped.

ANNUAL EXPENSES. Tuition and fees (projected): $2,937, $3,900 additional for out-of-state students. **Room and board:** $6,320. **Books and supplies:** $600. **Other expenses:** $450.

FINANCIAL AID. 85% of freshmen, 85% of continuing students receive some form of aid. 64% of grants, 76% of jobs based on need. 57 enrolled freshmen were judged to have need, all were offered aid. Academic, leadership, minority scholarships available. **Aid applications:** No closing date; priority given to applications received by March 15; applicants notified on a rolling basis beginning on or about April 15; must reply within 2 weeks.

ADDRESS/TELEPHONE. Dennis O. Stratton, Director of Admissions, State University of New York Col Environ Sci and Forestry, 106 Bray Hall, 1 Forestry Drive, Syracuse, NY 13210-2779. (315) 470-6600. (800) 777-7373. Fax: (315) 470-6933.

State University of New York College at Fredonia
Fredonia, New York — CB code: 2539

Admissions: 56% of applicants accepted
Based on:
••• School record
•• Special talents, test scores
• Activities, essay, interview, recommendations
Completion: 93% of freshmen end year in good standing
58% graduate, 26% of these enter graduate study

4-year public college of arts and sciences, coed. Founded in 1826. **Accreditation:** Regional. **Undergraduate enrollment:** 1,817 men, 2,360 women full time; 90 men, 161 women part time. **Graduate enrollment:** 12 men, 64 women full time; 90 men, 295 women part time. **Faculty:** 271 total (243 full time). **Location:** Rural campus in large town; 45 miles from Buffalo. **Calendar:** Semester, limited summer session. **Microcomputers:** 350 located in dormitories, libraries, classrooms, computer centers, campus-wide network. **Special facilities:** Arts center, college lodge.

DEGREES OFFERED. BA, BS, BFA, MA, MS, MEd. 1,034 bachelor's degrees awarded in 1992. 20% in business and management, 5% communications, 15% teacher education, 8% letters/literature, 5% physical sciences, 6% psychology, 17% social sciences, 17% visual and performing arts. Graduate degrees offered in 16 major fields of study.

UNDERGRADUATE MAJORS. Accounting, art history, biological and physical sciences, biological laboratory technology, biology, biomedical science, business administration and management, chemistry, clinical laboratory science, communications, computer and information sciences, dramatic arts, early childhood education, earth sciences, economics, elementary education, engineering and other disciplines, English, French, geochemistry, geology, geophysics and seismology, health care administration, history, humanities, humanities and social sciences, international studies, junior high education, liberal/general studies, mathematics, music, music education, music history and appreciation, music performance, music theory and composition, music therapy, musical theater, philosophy, physics, political science and government, psychology, recombinant gene technology, secondary education, social studies education, sociology, Spanish, speech correction, speech pathology/audiology, studio art.

ACADEMIC PROGRAMS. Accelerated program, double major, dual enrollment of high school students, education specialist degree, honors program, independent study, internships, student-designed major, study abroad, teacher preparation, visiting/exchange student program, Washington semester, cross-registration, Albany semester, over 90 exchange programs within SUNY system, cooperative degree programs with Cornell University in agriculture and D'Youville College in special education; liberal arts/career combination in engineering; combined bachelor's/graduate program in business administration. **Placement/credit:** AP, CLEP General and Subject; 30 credit hours maximum for bachelor's degree.

ACADEMIC REQUIREMENTS. Freshmen must earn minimum GPA of 2.0 to continue in good standing. 86% of freshmen return for sophomore year. Students must declare major by end of second year. **Graduation requirements:** 120 hours for bachelor's (35 in major). Most students required to take courses in arts/fine arts, computer science, English, history, humanities, mathematics, philosophy/religion, biological/physical sciences, social sciences. **Additional information:** Extensive interdisciplinary special studies programs offered. Teacher certification and certificate of advanced study in educational administration available.

FRESHMAN ADMISSIONS. Selection criteria: Academic achievement, test results, and subjects taken given priority. Counselor recommendations, personal interview important when priority credentials marginal. **High school preparation:** 16 units required; 18 recommended. Required and recommended units include biological science 1, English 4, foreign language 2-3, mathematics 3-4, physical science 1, social science 4 and science 1. Special academic requirements for accounting, business, cooperative engineering, computer science, music, health sciences. **Test requirements:** SAT or ACT; score report by March 15.

1992 FRESHMAN CLASS PROFILE. 2,234 men applied, 1,167 accepted, 359 enrolled; 2,751 women applied, 1,647 accepted, 503 enrolled. 57% had high school GPA of 3.0 or higher, 43% between 2.0 and 2.99. 16% were in top tenth and 52% were in top quarter of graduating class. **Academic**

background: Mid 50% of enrolled freshmen had SAT-V between 420-520, SAT-M between 470-570; ACT composite between 21-24. 95% submitted SAT scores, 34% submitted ACT scores. **Characteristics:** 98% from in state, 91% live in college housing, 7% have minority backgrounds, 1% are foreign students, 2% join fraternities/sororities. Average age is 18.

FALL-TERM APPLICATIONS. $25 fee, may be waived for applicants with need. Closing date April 1; priority given to applications received by January 15; applicants notified on a rolling basis beginning on or about December 1; must reply by May 1 or within 4 weeks if notified thereafter. Audition required for music, musical theater applicants. Portfolio required for art applicants. Interview recommended. Essay recommended. CRDA. Deferred and early admission available.

STUDENT LIFE. Housing: Dormitories (men, women, coed); apartment, fraternity, sorority housing available. **Activities:** Student government, magazine, radio, student newspaper, television, yearbook, choral groups, concert band, dance, drama, jazz band, music ensembles, musical theater, opera, pep band, symphony orchestra, fraternities, sororities, campus ministry, Newman Club, Black Student Union, Young Republicans, service fraternities and sororities, Circle-K, Jewish Student Union, Native American Club, Hispanic Society, Young Democrats. **Additional information:** Of undergraduates who do not reside in college housing, approximately 30% live in their own apartments off campus, 20% commute from home.

ATHLETICS. NCAA. **Intercollegiate:** Baseball M, basketball, cross-country, ice hockey M, soccer, tennis, track and field, volleyball W. **Intramural:** Badminton, baseball, basketball, bowling, cross-country, handball, ice hockey, lacrosse M, racquetball, skiing, soccer, softball, volleyball, water polo.

STUDENT SERVICES. Aptitude testing, career counseling, employment service for undergraduates, freshman orientation, health services, on-campus day care, personal counseling, placement service for graduates, special adviser for adult students, veterans counselor, peer advisement program, services/facilities for handicapped.

ANNUAL EXPENSES. Tuition and fees (projected): $2,926, $3,900 additional for out-of-state students. **Room and board:** $4,200. **Books and supplies:** $620. **Other expenses:** $1,000.

FINANCIAL AID. 71% of freshmen, 64% of continuing students receive some form of aid. All grants, 95% of loans, 34% of jobs based on need. 634 enrolled freshmen were judged to have need, 603 were offered aid. **Aid applications:** No closing date; applicants notified on a rolling basis beginning on or about March 15.

ADDRESS/TELEPHONE. William S. Clark, Director of Admissions and Enrollment, State University of New York College at Fredonia, 178 Central Avenue, Fredonia, NY 14063. (716) 673-3251. Fax: (716) 673-3249.

State University of New York College at Geneseo

Geneseo, New York — CB code: 2540

Admissions: 48% of applicants accepted
Based on: ••• School record, test scores
•• Activities, essay, recommendations
• Interview, special talents
Completion: 97% of freshmen end year in good standing
70% graduate, 27% of these enter graduate study

4-year public college of arts and sciences, coed. Founded in 1867. **Accreditation:** Regional. **Undergraduate enrollment:** 1,672 men, 3,284 women full time; 68 men, 109 women part time. **Graduate enrollment:** 19 men, 93 women full time; 59 men, 274 women part time. **Faculty:** 323 total (237 full time), 230 with doctorates or other terminal degrees. **Location:** Rural campus in small town; 30 miles from Rochester. **Calendar:** Semester, limited summer session. **Microcomputers:** 300 located in dormitories, libraries, classrooms, computer centers. **Special facilities:** Nuclear accelerator, planetarium, art gallery, 3 theaters, ice arena.

DEGREES OFFERED. BA, BS, MA, MEd. 1,284 bachelor's degrees awarded in 1992. 16% in business and management, 8% communications, 18% education, 5% health sciences, 10% letters/literature, 7% life sciences, 5% mathematics, 5% physical sciences, 10% psychology, 14% social sciences. Graduate degrees offered in 18 major fields of study.

UNDERGRADUATE MAJORS. Accounting, Afro-American (black) studies, American studies, anthropology, art history, biochemistry, biology, biophysics, business administration and management, business and management, business economics, chemistry, clinical laboratory science, communications, comparative literature, computer and information sciences, creative writing, dramatic arts, early childhood education, earth sciences, economics, education of the emotionally handicapped, education of the mentally handicapped, education of the multiple handicapped, elementary education, engineering and other disciplines, English, English education, environmental science, foreign languages education, forestry and related sciences, French, geochemistry, geography, geology, geophysics and seismology, history, international business management, labor/industrial relations, management science, marketing management, mathematics, mathematics education, music, music history and appreciation, music performance, music theory and composition, personnel management, philosophy, physics, political science and government, predentistry, prelaw, premedicine, prepharmacy, preveterinary, psychology, radio/television broadcasting, science education, social science education, social studies education, sociology, Spanish, special education, specific learning disabilities, speech correction, speech pathology/audiology, studio art.

ACADEMIC PROGRAMS. Double major, honors program, independent study, internships, study abroad, teacher preparation, visiting/exchange student program, Washington semester, cross-registration, Albany semester, 3+2 program in engineering with Alfred University, Case Western Reserve University in Ohio, Clarkson University, Columbia University, Ohio State University, Syracuse University, SUNY at Binghamton, SUNY Buffalo, and University of Rochester, 3+3 program in engineering with Rochester Institute of Technology, combined bachelor's program in liberal arts and forestry with SUNY College of Environmental Science and Forestry, combined bachelor's/graduate degree in business administration with Clarkson University, Pace University, Rochester Institute of Technology, SUNY Buffalo, and Syracuse University. **Remedial services:** Learning center, preadmission summer program, reduced course load, tutoring. **ROTC:** Air Force, Army. **Placement/credit:** AP, CLEP General and Subject, institutional tests; 30 credit hours maximum for bachelor's degree.

ACADEMIC REQUIREMENTS. Freshmen must earn minimum GPA of 1.75 to continue in good standing. 92% of freshmen return for sophomore year. Students must declare major by end of second year. **Graduation requirements:** 120 hours for bachelor's (36 in major). Most students required to take courses in arts/fine arts, humanities, biological/physical sciences, social sciences.

FRESHMAN ADMISSIONS. Selection criteria: Rigor of high school preparation, high school GPA, class rank, test scores, school and community activities, special talent, leadership, personal essay. Special consideration given to minority applicants and children and grandchildren of alumni. **High school preparation:** 19 units recommended. Recommended units include English 4, foreign language 3, mathematics 4, social science 4 and science 4. Music, art also recommended. 4 mathematics required for computer science and business majors. **Test requirements:** SAT or ACT; score report by January 15.

1992 FRESHMAN CLASS PROFILE. 8,743 men and women applied, 4,174 accepted; 1,133 enrolled. 94% had high school GPA of 3.0 or higher, 6% between 2.0 and 2.99. 59% were in top tenth and 91% were in top quarter of graduating class. **Academic background:** Mid 50% of enrolled freshmen had SAT-V between 500-580, SAT-M between 550-650; ACT composite between 25-29. 80% submitted SAT scores, 20% submitted ACT scores. **Characteristics:** 97% from in state, 100% live in college housing, 19% have minority backgrounds, 1% are foreign students. Average age is 18.

FALL-TERM APPLICATIONS. $25 fee, may be waived for applicants with need. Closing date February 1; priority given to applications received by January 15; applicants notified on a rolling basis beginning on or about February 15; must reply by May 1. Audition required for music, dramatic arts applicants. Interview recommended. Portfolio recommended for art applicants. Essay recommended. CRDA. Deferred and early admission available. EDP-F.

STUDENT LIFE. Housing: Dormitories (coed); fraternity, sorority housing available. Special interest housing available. **Activities:** Student government, magazine, radio, student newspaper, television, yearbook, choral groups, concert band, dance, drama, jazz band, music ensembles, musical theater, symphony orchestra, fraternities, sororities, over 145 organizations and clubs, interfaith center. **Additional information:** Approximately 25% of undergraduates who do not reside in college housing, live in their own apartments off campus, 12% commute from home.

ATHLETICS. NCAA. **Intercollegiate:** Basketball, cross-country, diving, ice hockey M, lacrosse M, rugby, soccer, softball W, swimming, track and field, volleyball W. **Intramural:** Badminton W, baseball M, basketball, bowling, fencing, field hockey W, golf, gymnastics, handball, horseback riding, lacrosse, racquetball, rowing (crew), rugby, skiing, soccer, softball, squash, swimming, table tennis, tennis, volleyball.

STUDENT SERVICES. Aptitude testing, career counseling, employment service for undergraduates, freshman orientation, health services, personal counseling, placement service for graduates, veterans counselor, special minority student adviser, services/facilities for handicapped.

ANNUAL EXPENSES. Tuition and fees (projected): $3,075, $3,900 additional for out-of-state students. **Room and board:** $3,995. **Books and supplies:** $600. **Other expenses:** $650.

FINANCIAL AID. 70% of freshmen, 65% of continuing students receive some form of aid. 41% of grants, 95% of loans, 70% of jobs based on need. 765 enrolled freshmen were judged to have need, 750 were offered aid. Academic, music/drama, state/district residency, minority scholarships available. **Aid applications:** Closing date April 1; priority given to applications received by March 1; applicants notified on a rolling basis beginning on or about April 1; must reply by May 1 or within 3 weeks if notified thereafter.

ADDRESS/TELEPHONE. Jill E. Conlon, Director of Admissions, State University of New York College at Geneseo, 1 College Circle, Geneseo, NY 14454-1471. (716) 245-5571. Fax: (716) 245-5005.

State University of New York College at New Paltz

New Paltz, New York CB code: 2541

Admissions: 41% of applicants accepted
Based on: ••• School record
•• Recommendations, test scores
• Activities, essay, interview, special talents
Completion: 85% of freshmen end year in good standing
50% graduate, 35% of these enter graduate study

4-year public college of arts and sciences, coed. Founded in 1828. **Accreditation:** Regional. **Undergraduate enrollment:** 1,980 men, 2,894 women full time; 498 men, 937 women part time. **Graduate enrollment:** 106 men, 218 women full time; 350 men, 1,158 women part time. **Faculty:** 646 total (276 full time), 373 with doctorates or other terminal degrees. **Location:** Rural campus in small town; 95 miles from New York City, 75 miles from Albany. **Calendar:** Semester, extensive summer session. **Microcomputers:** 45 located in dormitories, libraries, classrooms, computer centers. **Special facilities:** 3 theaters, recital hall, speech and hearing center, music therapy training center, art gallery, planetarium, journalism laboratory, robotics laboratory, electron microscope.

DEGREES OFFERED. BA, BS, BFA, MA, MS, MFA, MEd. 1,336 bachelor's degrees awarded in 1992. 10% in business and management, 10% communications, 28% education, 9% letters/literature, 5% physical sciences, 9% psychology, 6% social sciences, 11% visual and performing arts. Graduate degrees offered in 38 major fields of study.

UNDERGRADUATE MAJORS. Accounting, Afro-American (black) studies, anthropology, applied mathematics, art education, art history, bilingual/bicultural education, biochemistry, biology, biophysics, business administration and management, business and management, business economics, ceramics, chemistry, communications, comparative literature, computer and information sciences, computer engineering, creative writing, dramatic arts, early childhood education, earth sciences, economics, electrical/electronics/communications engineering, elementary education, English, English education, finance, fine arts, foreign languages education, French, geography, geology, German, graphic design, history, international relations, journalism, junior high education, liberal/general studies, mathematics, mathematics education, metal/jewelry, music, music history and appreciation, music performance, music theory and composition, music therapy, musical theater, nursing, painting, philosophy, photography, physics, political science and government, predentistry, prelaw, premedicine, preveterinary, psychology, radio/television broadcasting, science education, sculpture, secondary education, social studies education, sociology, Spanish, speech, speech correction, speech pathology/audiology, theater design, visual and performing arts, women's studies.

ACADEMIC PROGRAMS. Cooperative education, double major, honors program, independent study, internships, student-designed major, study abroad, teacher preparation, visiting/exchange student program, cross-registration, 2+2 program in forestry with SUNY College of Environmental Science and Forestry, combined bachelor's/graduate program in optometry with SUNY College of Optometry; liberal arts/career combination in engineering, health sciences. **Remedial services:** Learning center, reduced course load, remedial instruction, special counselor, tutoring. **Placement/credit:** AP, CLEP Subject, institutional tests; 30 credit hours maximum for bachelor's degree.

ACADEMIC REQUIREMENTS. Freshmen must earn minimum GPA of 2.0 to continue in good standing. 80% of freshmen return for sophomore year. Students must declare major by end of second year. **Graduation requirements:** 120 hours for bachelor's (32 in major). Most students required to take courses in arts/fine arts, English, foreign languages, history, humanities, mathematics, philosophy/religion, biological/physical sciences, social sciences. **Additional information:** Bachelor's degree completion program for registered nurses.

FRESHMAN ADMISSIONS. Selection criteria: High school GPA, academic subjects and test scores important. Activities, recommendations, and interview may be considered. **High school preparation:** 14 units required; 17 recommended. Required and recommended units include English 4, foreign language 2-3, mathematics 2-3, social science 4 and science 2-3. **Test requirements:** SAT or ACT; score report by March 1. **Additional information:** Applicants, especially academically marginal, encouraged to send personal statements regarding academic work, recommendations from academic teachers, and any other pertinent information.

1992 FRESHMAN CLASS PROFILE. 3,527 men applied, 1,448 accepted, 265 enrolled; 5,291 women applied, 2,174 accepted, 399 enrolled. 58% had high school GPA of 3.0 or higher, 42% between 2.0 and 2.99. 21% were in top tenth and 42% were in top quarter of graduating class. **Academic background:** Mid 50% of enrolled freshmen had SAT-V between 430-540, SAT-M between 470-590. 97% submitted SAT scores. **Characteristics:** 85% from in state, 95% live in college housing, 30% have minority backgrounds, 3% are foreign students, 2% join fraternities/sororities. Average age is 18.

FALL-TERM APPLICATIONS. $25 fee, may be waived for applicants with need. Closing date May 1; priority given to applications received by March 1; applicants notified on a rolling basis beginning on or about December 15; must reply by May 1 or within 4 weeks if notified thereafter. Audition required for music, music therapy, theater arts applicants. Portfolio required for studio art, art education, visual arts, scenography applicants. Interview recommended for academically marginal applicants. Essay recommended. CRDA. Deferred and early admission available.

STUDENT LIFE. Housing: Dormitories (women, coed). Handicapped equipped rooms available. **Activities:** Student government, radio, student newspaper, television, yearbook, literary magazine, choral groups, concert band, dance, drama, jazz band, music ensembles, musical theater, symphony orchestra, gospel choir, fraternities, sororities, Newman Society, Hillel, student Christian center, residence hall student association, student ambassadors. **Additional information:** Of undergraduates who do not reside in college housing, approximately 41% live in their own apartments off campus, 25% commute from home.

ATHLETICS. NCAA. **Intercollegiate:** Baseball M, basketball, cross-country, diving, golf, soccer, softball W, swimming, tennis W, volleyball. **Intramural:** Archery, badminton M, basketball M, bowling, cross-country, fencing, golf M, handball M, lacrosse M, racquetball, softball, swimming, table tennis M, tennis, volleyball.

STUDENT SERVICES. Career counseling, employment service for undergraduates, freshman orientation, health services, on-campus day care, personal counseling, placement service for graduates, veterans counselor, services/facilities for handicapped.

ANNUAL EXPENSES. Tuition and fees (1992-93): $2,927, $3,900 additional for out-of-state students. **Room and board:** $4,240. **Books and supplies:** $550. **Other expenses:** $900.

FINANCIAL AID. 60% of freshmen, 55% of continuing students receive some form of aid. All grants, 89% of loans, 91% of jobs based on need. 384 enrolled freshmen were judged to have need, all were offered aid. **Aid applications:** Closing date April 1; priority given to applications received by March 15; applicants notified on or about April 1; must reply by May 1 or within 2 weeks if notified thereafter.

ADDRESS/TELEPHONE. Robert J. Seaman, Dean of Admissions, State University of New York College at New Paltz, 75 South Manheim Boulevard, New Paltz, NY 12561-2499. (914) 257-3200. Fax: (914) 257-3009.

State University of New York College at Old Westbury

Old Westbury, New York CB code: 2866

Admissions: 60% of applicants accepted
Based on: ••• School record
•• Activities, essay, recommendations, test scores
• Interview, special talents
Completion: 70% of freshmen end year in good standing
40% enter graduate study

4-year public college of arts and sciences, coed. Founded in 1968. **Accreditation:** Regional. **Undergraduate enrollment:** 1,271 men, 1,703 women full time; 461 men, 676 women part time. **Faculty:** 129 total (124 full time). **Location:** Suburban campus in large town; 25 miles from New York City. **Calendar:** Semester, limited summer session. **Microcomputers:** 208 located in libraries, classrooms, computer centers. **Special facilities:** Maguire Theater, Amalie Wallace Art Gallery, Duane Jones Recital Hall.

DEGREES OFFERED. BA, BS. 770 bachelor's degrees awarded in 1992. 5% in area and ethnic studies, 44% business and management, 6% computer sciences, 23% teacher education, 6% psychology, 6% social sciences.

UNDERGRADUATE MAJORS. Accounting, American studies, bilingual/bicultural education, biology, business and management, chemistry, computer and information sciences, economics, elementary education, finance, foreign languages education, humanities and social sciences, information sciences and systems, junior high education, labor/industrial relations, marketing management, mathematics, mathematics education, political science and government, psychology, religion and philosophy, science education, sociology, Spanish, special education, visual and performing arts, world cultures.

ACADEMIC PROGRAMS. Double major, independent study, internships, study abroad, teacher preparation, visiting/exchange student program, cross-registration, Minority Access to Research Careers, Minority Biomedical Research. **Remedial services:** Learning center, remedial instruction, special counselor, tutoring. **ROTC:** Air Force, Army. **Placement/credit:** AP, CLEP General and Subject; 72 credit hours maximum for bachelor's degree.

ACADEMIC REQUIREMENTS. Freshmen must earn minimum GPA of 2.0 to continue in good standing. 66% of freshmen return for sophomore year. Students must declare major by end of second year. **Graduation requirements:** 120 hours for bachelor's. Most students required to take courses in English, history, humanities, mathematics, biological/physical sciences, social sciences. **Additional information:** Majors in special and elementary education in a bilingual setting (Spanish-English) offered.

FRESHMAN ADMISSIONS. Selection criteria: Minimum high school average of 80%, letters of recommendation, personal essay, SAT scores. Recommended units include English 4, foreign language 2, mathematics 2 and science 2.

1992 FRESHMAN CLASS PROFILE. 1,062 men applied, 584 accepted, 184 enrolled; 1,439 women applied, 920 accepted, 262 enrolled. 10% had high school GPA of 3.0 or higher, 60% between 2.0 and 2.99. 3% were in top tenth and 17% were in top quarter of graduating class. **Academic background:** Mid 50% of enrolled freshmen had SAT-V between 280-410, SAT-M between 310-440. 51% submitted SAT scores. **Characteristics:** 97% from in state, 51% live in college housing, 77% have minority backgrounds, 3% are foreign students. Average age is 20.

FALL-TERM APPLICATIONS. $25 fee. Closing date March 15; priority given to applications received by December 1; applicants notified on a rolling basis beginning on or about February 15; must reply by May 1. Interview required for academically weak applicants. Essay required for academically weak applicants. Deferred admission available. SAT recommended.

STUDENT LIFE. Housing: Dormitories (coed); handicapped housing available. **Activities:** Student government, magazine, radio, student newspaper, yearbook, Video, dance, drama, fraternities, sororities, women's center, international student association, Alianza Latina, Afrikan People's Organization, Big Brother/Big Sister Club, Asian Club.

ATHLETICS. NCAA. **Intercollegiate:** Basketball, soccer M, softball W, tennis, volleyball W. **Intramural:** Basketball, boxing M, skiing, soccer, softball W, table tennis, tennis, volleyball.

STUDENT SERVICES. Career counseling, employment service for undergraduates, freshman orientation, health services, on-campus day care, personal counseling, placement service for graduates, veterans counselor, services/facilities for handicapped.

ANNUAL EXPENSES. Tuition and fees (1992-93): $2,898, $3,900 additional for out-of-state students. **Room and board:** $4,120. **Books and supplies:** $660. **Other expenses:** $1,210.

FINANCIAL AID. 43% of continuing students receive some form of aid. 98% of grants, 92% of loans, all jobs based on need. Minority scholarships available. **Aid applications:** No closing date; priority given to applications received by May 1; applicants notified on a rolling basis beginning on or about May 1; must reply within 2 weeks.

ADDRESS/TELEPHONE. Michael T. Sheehy, Director of Admissions, State University of New York College at Old Westbury, PO Box 307, Old Westbury, NY 11568-0307. (516) 876-3073. Fax: (516) 876-3209.

State University of New York College at Oneonta

Oneonta, New York — CB code: 2542

Admissions: 56% of applicants accepted
Based on: ••• School record, test scores
•• Activities, interview, recommendations
Completion: 92% of freshmen end year in good standing
56% graduate, 40% of these enter graduate study

4-year public college of arts and sciences, coed. Founded in 1887. **Accreditation:** Regional. **Undergraduate enrollment:** 1,914 men, 2,960 women full time; 164 men, 340 women part time. **Graduate enrollment:** 39 men, 84 women full time; 108 men, 318 women part time. **Faculty:** 363 total (294 full time), 203 with doctorates or other terminal degrees. **Location:** Rural campus in large town; 175 miles from New York City, 75 miles from Albany. **Calendar:** Semester, extensive summer session. **Microcomputers:** 200 located in libraries, classrooms, computer centers. **Special facilities:** 192-acre college camp, observatory, biological field station, wildlife preserve.

DEGREES OFFERED. BA, BS, MA, MS. 1,242 bachelor's degrees awarded in 1992. Graduate degrees offered in 15 major fields of study.

UNDERGRADUATE MAJORS. Accounting, anthropology, art history, biology, business economics, business education, chemistry, computer and information sciences, dramatic arts, early childhood education, earth sciences, economics, elementary education, English, English education, English literature, family/consumer resource management, food science and nutrition, foreign languages education, French, geography, geology, German, history, home economics, home economics education, human environment and housing, individual and family development, junior high education, liberal/general studies, mathematics, mathematics education, music, philosophy, physics, political science and government, prelaw, psychology, school nurse education, science education, secondary education, social science education, sociology, Spanish, speech, statistics, studio art, textiles and clothing.

ACADEMIC PROGRAMS. Double major, honors program, independent study, internships, study abroad, teacher preparation, telecourses, Washington semester, cross-registration, cooperative degree programs in fashion, art education, and music education, 3-2 program in engineering with Alfred University, Clarkson University, Georgia Insitute of Technology, Polytechnic Institute of New York, Rensselaer Polytechnic Institute, SUNY at Binghamton, SUNY Buffalo, and Syracuse University, 2-2 program in forestry with SUNY College of Environmental Science and Forestry, 2-2 program in nursing with Johns Hopkins University in Maryland and SUNY Health Science Center at Brooklyn, 2-2 programs in physical therapy, medical technology, respiratory care, and cytotechnology with SUNY Health Science Center at Syracuse, and combined bachelor's/graduate degree programs in accounting and management with SUNY Binghamton; liberal arts/career combination in engineering, forestry, health sciences. **Remedial services:** Learning center, reduced course load, remedial instruction, special counselor, tutoring, reading, writing, speech clinics. **Placement/credit:** AP, CLEP General and Subject; 36 credit hours maximum for bachelor's degree.

ACADEMIC REQUIREMENTS. Freshmen must earn minimum GPA of 2.0 to continue in good standing. 81% of freshmen return for sophomore year. Students must declare major by end of second year. **Graduation requirements:** 122 hours for bachelor's (36 in major). Most students required to take courses in arts/fine arts, English, humanities, mathematics, philosophy/religion, biological/physical sciences, social sciences.

FRESHMAN ADMISSIONS. Selection criteria: School achievement record, curriculum, test scores, personal experiences, motivations, awards and honors, and recommendations. **High school preparation:** 16 units required. Required units include English 4 and social science 3. 8 units from among mathematics, science, and foreign language (at least 2 each) also required. **Test requirements:** SAT or ACT; score report by February 1.

1992 FRESHMAN CLASS PROFILE. 8,603 men and women applied, 4,788 accepted; 336 men enrolled, 566 women enrolled. **Characteristics:** 99% from in state, 98% live in college housing, 9% have minority backgrounds. Average age is 18.

FALL-TERM APPLICATIONS. $25 fee, may be waived for applicants with need. Closing date April 1; priority given to applications received by January 5; applicants notified on a rolling basis beginning on or about December 1; must reply by May 1 or within 30 days if notified thereafter. Interview recommended. Audition recommended for music applicants. Portfolio recommended for art applicants. Deferred and early admission available.

STUDENT LIFE. Housing: Dormitories (women, coed); fraternity, sorority housing available. **Activities:** Student government, film, magazine, radio, student newspaper, yearbook, choral groups, concert band, dance, drama, music ensembles, musical theater, opera, pep band, symphony orchestra, fraternities, sororities, service organizations, Newman Association, Hillel. **Additional information:** Of undergraduates who do not reside in college housing, approximately 45% live in their own apartments off campus, 2% commute from home.

ATHLETICS. NCAA. **Intercollegiate:** Baseball M, basketball, cross-country, field hockey W, lacrosse, rugby M, soccer, softball W, swimming W, tennis, volleyball W, wrestling M. **Intramural:** Basketball, bowling, handball, ice hockey M, racquetball, skiing, soccer, softball, swimming, tennis, volleyball.

STUDENT SERVICES. Aptitude testing, career counseling, employment service for undergraduates, freshman orientation, health services, on-campus day care, personal counseling, placement service for graduates, veterans counselor, ombudsman, services/facilities for handicapped.

ANNUAL EXPENSES. Tuition and fees (projected): $2,916, $3,900 additional for out-of-state students. **Room and board:** $4,620. **Books and supplies:** $450. **Other expenses:** $1,000.

FINANCIAL AID. 69% of freshmen, 60% of continuing students receive some form of aid. 92% of loans, 34% of jobs based on need. 426 enrolled freshmen were judged to have need, all were offered aid. Academic, leadership, alumni affiliation, minority scholarships available. **Aid applications:** No closing date; priority given to applications received by May 1; applicants notified on a rolling basis beginning on or about April 1; must reply within 2 weeks.

ADDRESS/TELEPHONE. Richard Burr, Director of Admissions, State University of New York College at Oneonta, Oneonta, NY 13820-4016. (607) 436-2524.

State University of New York College at Plattsburgh

Plattsburgh, New York — CB code: 2544

Admissions: 57% of applicants accepted
Based on: ••• School record, test scores
•• Interview
• Activities, essay, recommendations, special talents
Completion: 73% of freshmen end year in good standing
55% graduate, 30% of these enter graduate study

4-year public college of arts and sciences and teachers college, coed. Founded in 1889. **Accreditation:** Regional. **Undergraduate enrollment:** 2,216 men, 2,790 women full time; 203 men, 273 women part time. **Graduate enrollment:** 73 men, 143 women full time; 140 men, 381 women part time. **Faculty:** 345 total (279 full time), 253 with doctorates or other terminal degrees. **Location:** Rural campus in large town; 60 miles from Montreal, Canada, 20 miles from Burlington, Vermont. **Calendar:** Semester, limited summer session. Saturday and extensive evening/early morning classes. **Microcomputers:** 160 located in libraries, classrooms, computer centers. **Special facilities:** Rockwell Kent gallery and collection, Nina Winkel sculpture courtyard and collection, part of SUNY Museum Without Walls, center for art, music, and theater, wilderness tract, planetarium, electron microscope, remote sensing lab, NMR oectrophotometer, computer operated infrared spectrophotometer, liquid scintillation counter. **Additional facts:** Residential satellite campus for biotechnology, in-vitro cell biology, and environmental science majors. Center for the Study of Canada.

DEGREES OFFERED. BA, BS, MA, MS, MEd. 1,239 bachelor's degrees awarded in 1992. 27% in business and management, 10% communications, 19% teacher education, 5% home economics, 8% psychology, 7% social sciences. Graduate degrees offered in 15 major fields of study.

UNDERGRADUATE MAJORS. Accounting, anthropology, art history, behavioral sciences, biochemistry, biological laboratory technology, biology, biophysics, business administration and management, business and management, business economics, cell biology, chemistry, clinical laboratory science, communications, computer and information sciences, computer programming, criminal justice studies, criminology, dramatic arts, earth sciences, ecology, economics, education, education of the deaf and hearing impaired, education of the emotionally handicapped, education of the mentally handicapped, elementary education, English, English education, environmental science, family and community services, finance, food production/management/services, food science and nutrition, foreign languages education, French, geography, geology, history, home economics, home economics education, hotel/motel and restaurant management, individual and family development, institutional/home management/supporting programs, international business management, journalism, junior high education, Latin American studies, liberal/general studies, management science, marketing and distribution, marketing management, mathematics, mathematics education, microbiology, microcomputer software, music, nursing, philosophy, physics, political science and government, psychology, radio/television broadcasting, radio/television technology, robotics, science education, secondary education, social science education, social work, sociology, Spanish, special education, specific learning disabilities, speech, speech correction, speech pathology/audiology, studio art, systems analysis, visual and performing arts.

ACADEMIC PROGRAMS. Double major, dual enrollment of high school students, education specialist degree, honors program, independent study, internships, student-designed major, study abroad, teacher preparation, visiting/exchange student program, cross-registration, combined degree program in engineering with Clarkson University. **Remedial services:** Learning center, preadmission summer program, reduced course load, remedial instruction, special counselor, tutoring, study skills laboratory. **Placement/credit:** AP, CLEP General and Subject, IB, institutional tests; 30 credit hours maximum for bachelor's degree.

ACADEMIC REQUIREMENTS. Freshmen must earn minimum GPA of 2.0 to continue in good standing. 73% of freshmen return for sophomore year. Students must declare major by end of second year. **Graduation requirements:** 125 hours for bachelor's. Most students required to take courses in arts/fine arts, English, foreign languages, history, humanities, mathematics, philosophy/religion, biological/physical sciences, social sciences.

FRESHMAN ADMISSIONS. Selection criteria: Curriculum, high school GPA, class rank, test scores most important. Trend of grades, school and community activities, personal interview, and recommendations also considered. Equal opportunity program for academically and financially disadvantaged students. **High school preparation:** 13 units required; 20 recommended. Required and recommended units include English 4-4, mathematics 2-4, social science 4-4 and science 2-3. Foreign language 4 recommended. Art and/or music also recommended. Minimum 5 mathematics/science required. Chemistry required for biochemistry, medical technology, nursing, food and nutrition programs. 3 mathematics required for programs in business, computer science, engineering, food and nutrition, hotel and restaurant management, science, and math. 3 sciences required for certain programs. **Test requirements:** SAT or ACT; score report by April 15.

1992 FRESHMAN CLASS PROFILE. 5,870 men and women applied, 3,354 accepted; 425 men enrolled, 571 women enrolled. 98% had high school GPA of 3.0 or higher, 2% between 2.0 and 2.99. **Academic background:** Mid 50% of enrolled freshmen had SAT-V between 420-500, SAT-M between 480-580; ACT composite between 20-25. 73% submitted SAT scores, 38% submitted ACT scores. **Characteristics:** 98% from in state, 90% live in college housing, 8% have minority backgrounds. Average age is 18.

FALL-TERM APPLICATIONS. $25 fee, may be waived for applicants with need. Closing date May 1; priority given to applications received by February 15; applicants notified on a rolling basis beginning on or about January 15; must reply by May 1 or within 4 weeks if notified thereafter. Interview recommended. Audition recommended for music, theater applicants. Portfolio recommended for art applicants. Essay recommended. CRDA. Deferred and early admission available.

STUDENT LIFE. Housing: Dormitories (coed); fraternity, sorority, handicapped housing available. Electric Access Systems installed in all 12 residence halls. **Activities:** Student government, film, magazine, radio, student newspaper, television, yearbook, choral groups, concert band, drama, jazz band, music ensembles, musical theater, pep band, symphony orchestra, fraternities, sororities, Akeba, El Pueblo, Akwekon, Omicron Delta Kappa, Environmental Action Committee, Students for a Recycled Tomorrow, Hillel, Inter-Varsity Christian Fellowship, Newman Association, International Relations Club.

ATHLETICS. NCAA. **Intercollegiate:** Basketball, cross-country, diving, ice hockey M, soccer, swimming, tennis W, track and field, volleyball W. **Intramural:** Basketball, bowling, lacrosse M, racquetball, rugby, soccer, softball, table tennis, tennis, volleyball.

STUDENT SERVICES. Aptitude testing, career counseling, employment service for undergraduates, freshman orientation, health services, on-campus day care, personal counseling, placement service for graduates, special adviser for adult students, veterans counselor, services/facilities for handicapped.

ANNUAL EXPENSES. Tuition and fees (projected): $2,925, $3,900 additional for out-of-state students. **Room and board:** $3,812. **Books and supplies:** $600. **Other expenses:** $857.

FINANCIAL AID. 57% of freshmen, 50% of continuing students receive some form of aid. 96% of grants, 86% of loans, 52% of jobs based on need. 411 enrolled freshmen were judged to have need, all were offered aid. Academic, music/drama, art, leadership, minority scholarships available. **Aid applications:** No closing date; priority given to applications received by April 15; applicants notified on a rolling basis beginning on or about April 1; must reply by May 1 or within 3 weeks if notified thereafter.

ADDRESS/TELEPHONE. Richard J. Higgins, Director of Admissions, State University of New York College at Plattsburgh, Kehoe Administration Building, Plattsburgh, NY 12901. (518) 564-2040. Fax: (518) 564-2094.

State University of New York College at Potsdam
Potsdam, New York — CB code: 2545

Admissions: 71% of applicants accepted
Based on:
- ••• School record
- •• Test scores
- • Activities, essay, interview, recommendations

Completion: 54% graduate, 22% of these enter graduate study

4-year public college of arts and sciences, coed. Founded in 1816. **Accreditation:** Regional. **Undergraduate enrollment:** 1,402 men, 2,260 women full time; 77 men, 95 women part time. **Graduate enrollment:** 45 men, 119 women full time; 55 men, 232 women part time. **Faculty:** 291 total (234 full time), 160 with doctorates or other terminal degrees. **Location:** Rural campus in large town; 80 miles from Montreal, Canada, 150 miles from Syracuse. **Calendar:** Semester, limited summer session. **Microcomputers:** 250 located in dormitories, libraries, classrooms, computer centers, campus-wide network. **Special facilities:** Art gallery, electronic music and recording studios, planetarium, seismographic laboratory, recreation facilities at Star Lake campus in Adirondack Mountains, 24-hour computer laboratory, concert hall, music theater, modern sports complex. **Additional facts:** Star Lake campus in Adirondack Mountains provides alternative environment for classes and workshops, such as for-credit cross-country skiing, canoeing, sailing, new games, and orienteering. Watertown extension offers undergraduate and graduate courses with emphasis on teacher education.

DEGREES OFFERED. BA, MA, MS, MEd. 817 bachelor's degrees awarded in 1992. 9% in business and management, 13% letters/literature, 5% life sciences, 9% mathematics, 17% psychology, 18% social sciences, 17% visual and performing arts. Graduate degrees offered in 17 major fields of study.

UNDERGRADUATE MAJORS. Anthropology, art history, biological and physical sciences, biology, ceramics, chemistry, communications, computer and information sciences, dance, dramatic arts, early childhood education, economics, elementary education, English, English education, foreign languages education, French, geology, history, junior high education, labor/industrial relations, liberal/general studies, literature, mathematics, mathematics education, music, music education, music performance, painting, philosophy, photography, physics, political science and government, printmaking, psychology, science education, sculpture, secondary education, social science education, social sciences, social studies education, sociology, Spanish, special education, studio art, writing.

ACADEMIC PROGRAMS. Cooperative education, double major, dual enrollment of high school students, honors program, independent study, internships, student-designed major, study abroad, teacher preparation, visiting/exchange student program, cross-registration, combined degreee programs in engineering with Clarkson University and in accounting, engineering or management with SUNY Institute of Technology at Utica/Rome, combined bachelor's/graduate degree programs in business administration with Clarkson University and in optometry with SUNY College of Optometry, program in secondary teaching certification for art with St. Lawrence University, exchange programs in Australia, England, and Mexico, and student teaching in England; liberal arts/career combination in business; combined bachelor's/graduate program in business administration. **Remedial services:** Learning center, preadmission summer program, special counselor, tutoring. **ROTC:** Air Force, Army. **Placement/credit:** AP, CLEP Subject, institutional tests.

ACADEMIC REQUIREMENTS. Freshmen must earn minimum GPA of 2.0 to continue in good standing. Freshmen must complete 12 hours per semester to remain in good standing. 87% of freshmen return for sophomore year. Students must declare major by end of second year. **Graduation re-**

quirements: 120 hours for bachelor's (30 in major). Most students required to take courses in arts/fine arts, English, foreign languages, history, humanities, mathematics, philosophy/religion, biological/physical sciences, social sciences. **Postgraduate studies:** 2% enter law school, 1% enter medical school, 2% enter MBA programs, 17% enter other graduate study. **Additional information:** Optional coordinating interdisciplinary seminar available for freshmen, as well as various interdisciplinary, team-taught programs at all undergraduate levels.

FRESHMAN ADMISSIONS. Selection criteria: Rank in top half of class and school achievement record most important. Test scores, interview, auditions or portfolio also considered. **High school preparation:** 16 units required; 23 recommended. Required and recommended units include biological science 1, English 4, mathematics 2-4, physical science 1-3 and social science 4. Foreign language 3 recommended. **Test requirements:** SAT or ACT; score report by May 1.

1992 FRESHMAN CLASS PROFILE. 3,550 men and women applied, 2,522 accepted; 304 men enrolled, 458 women enrolled. 41% had high school GPA of 3.0 or higher, 58% between 2.0 and 2.99. 16% were in top tenth and 51% were in top quarter of graduating class. **Academic background:** Mid 50% of enrolled freshmen had SAT-V between 410-500, SAT-M between 460-560; ACT composite between 20-24. 55% submitted SAT scores, 24% submitted ACT scores. **Characteristics:** 97% from in state, 94% live in college housing, 4% have minority backgrounds, 1% are foreign students, 10% join fraternities/sororities. Average age is 18.

FALL-TERM APPLICATIONS. $25 fee, may be waived for applicants with need. Closing date April 1; priority given to applications received by December 1; applicants notified on a rolling basis beginning on or about January 15; must reply by May 1 or within 30 days if notified thereafter. Audition required for music applicants. Interview recommended. Portfolio recommended for art applicants. Essay recommended. CRDA. Deferred and early admission available.

STUDENT LIFE. Housing: Dormitories (men, women, coed); apartment, fraternity, sorority housing available. Theme-oriented, living-learning residences available. **Activities:** Student government, magazine, radio, student newspaper, yearbook, choral groups, concert band, dance, drama, jazz band, music ensembles, musical theater, opera, pep band, symphony orchestra, fraternities, sororities, Circle-K, Harambee, International Student Organization, Inter-Varsity Christian Fellowship, Jewish Culture Club, Bible Club, Student Association for Gender Equality, Hispanics United for Progress, Black Student Alliance, Potsdam Association for Native Americans.

ATHLETICS. NCAA. **Intercollegiate:** Basketball, cross-country, diving, ice hockey M, lacrosse M, soccer, swimming, tennis W, track and field, volleyball W. **Intramural:** Badminton, basketball, football M, golf, horseback riding, racquetball, skiing, soccer W, squash, tennis, volleyball, water polo. **Clubs:** Intercollegiate horseback riding, rugby.

STUDENT SERVICES. Career counseling, employment service for undergraduates, freshman orientation, health services, on-campus day care, personal counseling, placement service for graduates, veterans counselor, services/facilities for handicapped.

ANNUAL EXPENSES. Tuition and fees (projected): $2,890, $3,900 additional for out-of-state students. **Room and board:** $4,560. **Books and supplies:** $500. **Other expenses:** $700.

FINANCIAL AID. 80% of freshmen, 80% of continuing students receive some form of aid. 90% of grants, 92% of loans, 24% of jobs based on need. 460 enrolled freshmen were judged to have need, all were offered aid. Academic, music/drama scholarships available. **Aid applications:** No closing date; priority given to applications received by March 1; applicants notified on a rolling basis beginning on or about March 15; must reply by May 1 or within 30 days if notified thereafter.

ADDRESS/TELEPHONE. Mary Lou Retelle, Director of Enrollment Management, State University of New York College at Potsdam, Pierrepont Avenue, Potsdam, NY 13676-2294. (315) 267-2180. (800) 433-3154. Fax: (315) 267-2170.

State University of New York College of Technology at Alfred

Alfred, New York

CB code: 2522

2-year public technical college, coed. Founded in 1908. **Accreditation:** Regional. **Undergraduate enrollment:** 2,065 men, 1,264 women full time; 74 men, 115 women part time. **Faculty:** 181 total (176 full time), 20 with doctorates or other terminal degrees. **Location:** Rural campus in rural community; 75 miles from Rochester. **Calendar:** Semester, limited summer session. **Microcomputers:** 1,000 located in dormitories, classrooms, computer centers. **Additional facts:** Bachelor of Technology degree also offered in several engineering technology majors.

DEGREES OFFERED. AA, AS, AAS, B. 1,036 associate degrees awarded in 1992. 5% in agriculture, 6% business and management, 11% business/office and marketing/distribution, 17% engineering technologies, 12% allied health, 7% letters/literature, 19% multi/interdisciplinary studies, 27% trade and industry.

UNDERGRADUATE MAJORS. Accounting, agribusiness, agricultural business and management, agricultural sciences, agronomy, air conditioning/heating/refrigeration technology, animal sciences, architectural technologies, auto body repair, automotive mechanics, baking production and management, biological and physical sciences, biological laboratory technology, biotechnology, business administration and management, business and office, business data processing and related programs, business data programming, chemical technology, civil technology, computer and information sciences, computer graphics, construction, court reporting, dairy, data processing, diesel engine mechanics, drafting, drafting and design technology, drafting/electromechanics, drafting/model building, electrical and electronics equipment repair, electrical installation, electrical technology, electromechanical technology, engineering and engineering-related technologies, engineering and other disciplines, engineering science, finance, food production/management/services, food sciences, horticulture, humanities and social sciences, liberal/general studies, marketing management, masonry/tile setting, mathematics/science, mechanical design technology, medical assistant, medical laboratory technologies, medical records technology, nursing, ornamental horticulture, plumbing/pipefitting/steamfitting, real estate, retailing, science technologies, secretarial and related programs, social sciences, survey and mapping technology, toxicology, word processing. electrical technology, electromechanical technology, mechanical design technology, survey and mapping technology.

ACADEMIC PROGRAMS. 2-year transfer program, honors program, independent study, internships, student-designed major, cross-registration. **Remedial services:** Learning center, reduced course load, remedial instruction, special counselor, tutoring. **Placement/credit:** AP, CLEP Subject, institutional tests; 30 credit hours maximum for associate degree.

ACADEMIC REQUIREMENTS. Freshmen must earn minimum GPA of 1.75 to continue in good standing. 85% of freshmen return for sophomore year. Students must declare major on application. **Graduation requirements:** 60 hours for associate. Most students required to take courses in English, mathematics, biological/physical sciences, social sciences.

FRESHMAN ADMISSIONS. Selection criteria: School achievement record, test scores, class rank, school and community service. Course requirements vary depending on program.

1992 FRESHMAN CLASS PROFILE. 1,097 men, 633 women enrolled. 15% had high school GPA of 3.0 or higher, 67% between 2.0 and 2.99. **Characteristics:** 97% from in state, 86% live in college housing, 5% have minority backgrounds, 1% are foreign students. Average age is 18.

FALL-TERM APPLICATIONS. $25 fee, may be waived for applicants with need. No closing date; priority given to applications received by November 1; applicants notified on a rolling basis beginning on or about November 1; must reply within 4 weeks. Interview recommended. Deferred admission available. SAT or ACT recommended. Early application recommended for vocational studies.

STUDENT LIFE. Housing: Dormitories (coed). **Activities:** Student government, film, magazine, radio, student newspaper, yearbook, choral groups, concert band, drama, jazz band, music ensembles, pep band, fraternities, sororities, community action group, environmental club. **Additional information:** Of students who commute, approximately 5% of freshmen, 10% of all undergraduates live in apartments off campus. Another 9% of freshmen, 29% of all undergraduates commute from home.

ATHLETICS. NJCAA. **Intercollegiate:** Basketball, cross-country, lacrosse M, soccer, softball W, track and field, volleyball W, wrestling M. **Intramural:** Baseball M, basketball, bowling, football M, golf, lacrosse, rifle, soccer, softball, table tennis, tennis, volleyball.

STUDENT SERVICES. Aptitude testing, career counseling, employment service for undergraduates, freshman orientation, health services, personal counseling, placement service for graduates, special adviser for adult students, services/facilities for handicapped.

ANNUAL EXPENSES. Tuition and fees (projected): $2,900, $3,900 additional for out-of-state students. **Room and board:** $4,310. **Books and supplies:** $600. **Other expenses:** $700.

FINANCIAL AID. 75% of freshmen, 80% of continuing students receive some form of aid. 94% of grants, 92% of loans, 95% of jobs based on need. Academic, music/drama, state/district residency, leadership, alumni affiliation, minority scholarships available. **Aid applications:** Closing date May 31; priority given to applications received by May 1; applicants notified on a rolling basis beginning on or about February 1; must reply within 2 weeks.

ADDRESS/TELEPHONE. Deborah J. Goodrich, Director of Admissions, State University of New York College of Technology at Alfred, Alfred, NY 14802-1196. (607) 587-4215. Fax: (607) 587-4209.

State University of New York College of Technology at Canton

Canton, New York

CB code: 2523

2-year public technical college, coed. Founded in 1906. **Accreditation:** Regional. **Undergraduate enrollment:** 1,144 men, 759 women full time; 114 men, 261 women part time. **Faculty:** 189 total (173 full time), 11 with doctorates or other terminal degrees. **Location:** Rural campus in small town; 135 miles from Syracuse, 120 miles from Montreal, Canada. **Calendar:** Semester. **Microcomputers:** 215 located in libraries, classrooms, computer centers. **Special facilities:** 425-acre farm.

DEGREES OFFERED. AA, AS, AAS. 578 associate degrees awarded in 1992. 20% in business and management, 20% engineering technologies, 7% health sciences, 27% multi/interdisciplinary studies, 14% parks/recreation, protective services, public affairs.

UNDERGRADUATE MAJORS. Accounting, air conditioning/heating/refrigeration technology, automotive technology, biological and physical sciences, biology, business administration and management, business and office, civil technology, computer and information sciences, criminal justice technology, electrical technology, electromechanical technology, electronic technology, engineering and engineering-related technologies, engineering science, forestry and related sciences, funeral services/mortuary science, humanities and social sciences, industrial technology, liberal/general studies, mechanical design technology, medical laboratory technologies, nursing, retailing, science technologies, secretarial and related programs, social sciences, veterinarian's assistant.

ACADEMIC PROGRAMS. 2-year transfer program, dual enrollment of high school students, independent study, internships, student-designed major, telecourses, cross-registration. **Remedial services:** Learning center, reduced course load, remedial instruction, special counselor, tutoring, nontraditional student remedial orientation. **ROTC:** Air Force, Army. **Placement/credit:** AP, CLEP Subject, institutional tests; 45 credit hours maximum for associate degree.

ACADEMIC REQUIREMENTS. Freshmen must earn minimum GPA of 1.5 to continue in good standing. 61% of freshmen return for sophomore year. Students must declare major on application. **Graduation requirements:** 61 hours for associate. Most students required to take courses in computer science, English, mathematics, biological/physical sciences, social sciences.

FRESHMAN ADMISSIONS. Selection criteria: High school record most important, test scores considered if available. **High school preparation:** 12 units recommended. Recommended units include English 4, mathematics 2, social science 4 and science 2. Required high school courses vary with major. Engineering science technologies and life sciences stress mathematics and science; business technologies stress algebra.

1992 FRESHMAN CLASS PROFILE. 514 men, 358 women enrolled. **Characteristics:** 99% from in state, 52% live in college housing, 14% have minority backgrounds, 3% join fraternities/sororities. Average age is 19.

FALL-TERM APPLICATIONS. $25 fee, may be waived for applicants with need. No closing date; priority given to applications received by December 1; applicants notified on a rolling basis beginning on or about November 1; must reply within 30 days. Interview required for nursing, veterinary science technology applicants. Essay recommended. Deferred and early admission available. Freshman applicants encouraged to submit ACT scores for placement and counseling purposes. Test administered periodically on campus for those admitted without ACT results.

STUDENT LIFE. Housing: Dormitories (coed); fraternity, sorority housing available. **Activities:** Student government, radio, student newspaper, yearbook, choral groups, dance, drama, pep band, fraternities, sororities, Afro-Latin Society, Native American Society, Inter-Varsity Christian Fellowship. **Additional information:** Of students who commute, approximately 22% live in apartments off campus. 26% of freshmen, 30% of all undergraduates commute from home.

ATHLETICS. NJCAA. **Intercollegiate:** Basketball, horseback riding, ice hockey M, lacrosse M, soccer, softball W. **Intramural:** Basketball, golf, soccer, softball, tennis, volleyball.

STUDENT SERVICES. Aptitude testing, career counseling, employment service for undergraduates, freshman orientation, health services, personal counseling, placement service for graduates, special adviser for adult students, veterans counselor, services/facilities for handicapped.

ANNUAL EXPENSES. Tuition and fees (1992-93): $2,914, $3,900 additional for out-of-state students. **Room and board:** $4,230. **Books and supplies:** $500. **Other expenses:** $700.

FINANCIAL AID. 80% of freshmen, 80% of continuing students receive some form of aid. 97% of grants, 83% of loans, 92% of jobs based on need. Academic, state/district residency, leadership, alumni affiliation scholarships available. **Aid applications:** No closing date; priority given to applications received by March 1; applicants notified on a rolling basis beginning on or about March 1; must reply within 2 weeks.

ADDRESS/TELEPHONE. Thomas Flatcher, Director of Enrollment Management, State University of New York College of Technology at Canton, Cornell Drive, Canton, NY 13617-1098. (315) 386-7123. Fax: (315) 386-7930. (800) 388-7123 New York State only.

State University of New York College of Technology at Delhi

Delhi, New York CB code: 2525

2-year public technical college, coed. Founded in 1913. **Accreditation:** Regional. **Undergraduate enrollment:** 2,286 men and women. **Faculty:** 138 total (115 full time), 18 with doctorates or other terminal degrees. **Location:** Rural campus in small town; 70 miles from Albany and Binghamton. **Calendar:** Semester. **Microcomputers:** 230 located in libraries, classrooms, computer centers. **Special facilities:** Demonstration forest and arboretum, student-operated restaurant, model office, veterinary science laboratory.

DEGREES OFFERED. AA, AS, AAS. 586 associate degrees awarded in 1992. 10% in agriculture, 27% business and management, 5% engineering technologies, 5% health sciences, 7% multi/interdisciplinary studies, 10% social sciences, 20% trade and industry.

UNDERGRADUATE MAJORS. Accounting, air conditioning/heating/refrigeration mechanics, air conditioning/heating/refrigeration technology, architectural technologies, architecture, automotive mechanics, automotive technology, biology, business administration and management, business and management, business and office, business data processing and related programs, business data programming, carpentry, chemistry, civil technology, computer and information sciences, construction, data processing, drafting, electrical installation, electrical technology, engineering and engineering-related technologies, engineering science, food management, food production/management/services, forestry and related sciences, forestry production and processing, golf course operations, history, horticultural science, horticulture, hospitality and recreation marketing, hotel/motel and restaurant management, humanities and social sciences, information sciences and systems, landscape architecture, legal secretary, liberal/general studies, marketing and distribution, marketing management, masonry/tile setting, mathematics, nursing, office supervision and management, parks and recreation management, physics, plant sciences, plumbing/pipefitting/steamfitting, practical nursing, psychology, secretarial and related programs, social sciences, sociology, tourism, veterinarian's assistant, water and wastewater technology, water resources, welding technology, word processing.

ACADEMIC PROGRAMS. 2-year transfer program, double major, dual enrollment of high school students, independent study, internships, student-designed major. **Remedial services:** Learning center, reduced course load, remedial instruction, tutoring. **Placement/credit:** AP, CLEP General and Subject, institutional tests; 30 credit hours maximum for associate degree.

ACADEMIC REQUIREMENTS. Freshmen must earn minimum GPA of 2.0 to continue in good standing. Students must declare major on application. **Graduation requirements:** 60 hours for associate (40 in major). Most students required to take courses in arts/fine arts, English, history, humanities, mathematics, philosophy/religion, biological/physical sciences, social sciences.

FRESHMAN ADMISSIONS. Selection criteria: High school record, test scores, followed by recommendations and interview. Requirements vary by program. College preparatory program required for some programs including liberal arts, computer science, engineering science, and engineering technologies.

1992 FRESHMAN CLASS PROFILE. 1,137 men and women enrolled. 6% had high school GPA of 3.0 or higher, 45% between 2.0 and 2.99. **Academic background:** Mid 50% of enrolled freshmen had SAT-V between 380-520, SAT-M between 400-540. 70% submitted SAT scores. **Characteristics:** 98% from in state, 84% live in college housing, 12% have minority backgrounds. Average age is 18.

FALL-TERM APPLICATIONS. $25 fee, may be waived for applicants with need. No closing date; applicants notified on a rolling basis; must reply within 4 weeks. Interview recommended. Deferred and early admission available. ACT highly recommended for placement, score report by time of entrance.

STUDENT LIFE. Housing: Dormitories (coed). **Activities:** Student government, magazine, radio, student newspaper, television, yearbook, choral groups, concert band, drama, jazz band, musical theater, University Christian Movement, Third World Caucus-Students Caring for Students. **Additional information:** Cocurricular organizations in over 14 academic areas. Over 66% of student body participates in intramural and recreation program.

ATHLETICS. NJCAA. **Intercollegiate:** Baseball M, basketball, cross-country, golf M, soccer, softball W, tennis M, track and field, wrestling M. **Intramural:** Badminton, baseball M, basketball, bowling, cross-country, golf, handball, horseback riding, racquetball, skiing, soccer, softball, swimming, table tennis, tennis, volleyball, wrestling M.

STUDENT SERVICES. Aptitude testing, career counseling, employment service for undergraduates, freshman orientation, health services, on-campus day care, personal counseling, placement service for graduates, special adviser for adult students, veterans counselor, services/facilities for handicapped.

ANNUAL EXPENSES. Tuition and fees (projected): $2,945, $3,900 additional for out-of-state students. **Room and board:** $4,544. **Books and supplies:** $500. **Other expenses:** $1,000.

FINANCIAL AID. 79% of freshmen, 60% of continuing students receive some form of aid. 99% of grants, 96% of loans, all jobs based on need. Academic, state/district residency, minority scholarships available. **Aid applications:** No closing date; priority given to applications received by April 1; applicants notified on a rolling basis beginning on or about April 15; must reply within 2 weeks.

ADDRESS/TELEPHONE. Richard A. Cardoza, Director of Admissions and Records, State University of New York College of Technology at Delhi, Main Street, Delhi, NY 13753-1190. (607) 746-4246.

State University of New York College of Technology at Farmingdale

Farmingdale, New York CB code: 2526

Admissions: 42% of applicants accepted
Based on: ••• School record
•• Recommendations
• Test scores
Completion: 88% of freshmen end year in good standing
45% enter 4-year programs

2-year public technical college, coed. Founded in 1912. **Accreditation:** Regional. **Undergraduate enrollment:** 2,618 men, 2,004 women full time; 2,078 men, 2,100 women part time. **Faculty:** 393 total (267 full time), 87 with doctorates or other terminal degrees. **Location:** Suburban campus in small town; 30 miles from New York City. **Calendar:** Semester, extensive summer session. **Microcomputers:** Located in libraries, classrooms, computer centers. **Special facilities:** CAD/CAM laboratory, fleet of single- and twin-engine aircraft, dental and health care laboratories. **Additional facts:** Bachelor of Technology degrees offered in electrical engineering technology and manufacturing engineering technology.

DEGREES OFFERED. AA, AS, AAS. 1,542 associate degrees awarded in 1992. 25% in business and management, 9% business/office and marketing/distribution, 9% computer sciences, 14% engineering technologies, 15% health sciences, 7% multi/interdisciplinary studies, 7% parks/recreation, protective services, public affairs, 6% visual and performing arts.

UNDERGRADUATE MAJORS. Accounting, advertising, aeronautical technology, aircraft mechanics, airline piloting and navigation, architectural technologies, automotive mechanics, automotive technology, biomedical equipment technology, biotechnology, business administration and management, business and office, business data processing and related programs, business data programming, civil technology, commercial art, computer and information sciences, criminal justice studies, data processing, dental hygiene, drafting, electrical technology, engineering, engineering and engineering-related technologies, engineering science, food science and nutrition, food sciences, graphic and printing production, graphic arts technology, graphic design, information sciences and systems, law enforcement and corrections technologies, legal secretary, liberal/general studies, marketing and distribution, mechanical design technology, medical laboratory technologies, medical secretary, nursing, office supervision and management, ornamental horticulture, secretarial and related programs, teacher aide, veterinarian's assistant. electrical technology, manufacturing technology.

ACADEMIC PROGRAMS. 2-year transfer program. **Remedial services:** Learning center, reduced course load, remedial instruction, special counselor, tutoring. **ROTC:** Air Force, Army. **Placement/credit:** AP, CLEP Subject, institutional tests; 30 credit hours maximum for associate degree.

ACADEMIC REQUIREMENTS. Freshmen must earn minimum GPA of 2.0 to continue in good standing. 61% of freshmen return for sophomore year. Students must declare major on application. **Graduation requirements:** 68 hours for associate (37 in major). Most students required to take courses in English, mathematics, social sciences.

FRESHMAN ADMISSIONS. Selection criteria: School achievement record. Required minimum school grade varies by curriculum. **High school preparation:** 16 units required. Required and recommended units include English 4, mathematics 2-4, social science 3-4 and science 2-4. Foreign language 2 recommended. High school subject requirements vary by curriculum.

1992 FRESHMAN CLASS PROFILE. 7,634 men and women applied, 3,239 accepted; 2,676 enrolled. **Characteristics:** 90% from in state, 83% commute, 9% have minority backgrounds, 1% join fraternities/sororities. Average age is 18.

FALL-TERM APPLICATIONS. $25 fee, may be waived for applicants with need. No closing date; applicants notified on a rolling basis. Interview required for advertising art and design applicants. Portfolio required for advertising art and design applicants. CRDA. Early admission available. Priority given to applications received by December 15 for dental hygiene program and January 15 for nursing program.

STUDENT LIFE. Housing: Dormitories (men, women, coed). **Activities:** Student government, radio, student newspaper, yearbook, drama, music ensembles, fraternities, sororities, Jewish Fellowship Club, Newman Club, numerous special interest clubs.

ATHLETICS. NJCAA. **Intercollegiate:** Baseball M, basketball, bowling, cross-country, diving, golf M, lacrosse M, soccer M, softball W, swimming, tennis, track and field, wrestling M. **Intramural:** Basketball, racquetball, softball W, squash, volleyball.

STUDENT SERVICES. Aptitude testing, career counseling, employment service for undergraduates, freshman orientation, health services, on-campus day care, personal counseling, placement service for graduates, special adviser for adult students, veterans counselor, services/facilities for handicapped.

ANNUAL EXPENSES. Tuition and fees (projected): $3,000, $3,900 additional for out-of-state students. **Room and board:** $4,320. **Books and supplies:** $600. **Other expenses:** $800.

FINANCIAL AID. 72% of freshmen, 65% of continuing students receive some form of aid. 98% of grants, 40% of loans, 57% of jobs based on need. 2,243 enrolled freshmen were judged to have need, all were offered aid. Academic, leadership scholarships available. **Aid applications:** No closing date; priority given to applications received by April 1; applicants notified on a rolling basis beginning on or about April 1; must reply within 2 weeks.

ADDRESS/TELEPHONE. Janet Snyder, Director of Admissions, State University of New York College of Technology at Farmingdale, Melville Road, Farmingdale, NY 11735. (516) 420-2200.

State University of New York Empire State College

Saratoga Springs, New York CB code: 2214

4-year public college of arts and sciences, coed. Founded in 1971. **Accreditation:** Regional. **Undergraduate enrollment:** 566 men, 906 women full time; 2,180 men, 2,411 women part time. **Graduate enrollment:** 7 men, 9 women full time; 114 men, 111 women part time. **Faculty:** 305 total (133 full time). **Calendar:** Continuous program with students enrolling anytime September through July. **Special facilities:** Library loan arrangements with other SUNY, CUNY, public, and private colleges across the state. **Additional facts:** No campus or classrooms; students meet with faculty and use facilities at regional centers and units throughout state. Centers in Genesee Valley (Rochester), Long Island (Old Westbury), Metropolitan New York, Hudson Valley (Nanuet), and Buffalo. Coordinating center at Saratoga Springs. Units in Binghamton, Glens Falls, Ithaca, Mid-Hudson (New Paltz), Mohawk Valley (Utica-Rome), North Country (Plattsburg), Onondaga (Syracuse), Saratoga Springs, Watertown, Israel (Jerusalem), Nicosai (Cyprus), and several other locations.

DEGREES OFFERED. AA, AS, BA, BS, MA. 509 associate degrees awarded in 1992. 23% in business and management, 27% multi/interdisciplinary studies, 13% parks/recreation, protective services, public affairs, 29% trade and industry. 1,215 bachelor's degrees awarded. 31% in business and management, 8% education, 7% letters/literature, 19% multi/interdisciplinary studies, 18% parks/recreation, protective services, public affairs, 5% psychology, 6% visual and performing arts. Graduate degrees offered in 1 major field of study.

UNDERGRADUATE MAJORS. Associate: Biological and physical sciences, business and management, community services, cultural studies, economics, education, fine arts, history, labor/industrial relations, liberal/general studies, psychology, social sciences. **Bachelor's:** Biological and physical sciences, business and management, community services, cultural studies, economics, education, fine arts, history, labor/industrial relations, liberal/general studies, psychology, social sciences.

ACADEMIC PROGRAMS. 2-year transfer program, accelerated program, double major, dual enrollment of high school students, external degree, independent study, internships, student-designed major, study abroad, cross-registration. **Placement/credit:** AP, CLEP General and Subject; 40 credit hours maximum for associate degree; 96 credit hours maximum for bachelor's degree.

ACADEMIC REQUIREMENTS. All students must show progress toward achievement of academic goals. No grades given. Students work on learning contract basis and written evaluation of learning is provided at conclusion of study. Maximum of 40 credit hours, granted on basis of experience, counted toward associate degree. **Graduation requirements:** 64 hours for associate, 128 hours for bachelor's. **Additional information:** Learning contracts between faculty mentors and students lead to program completion.

FRESHMAN ADMISSIONS. Selection criteria: Open admissions. High school diploma, its equivalent, or ability to do college-level work, as demonstrated by presentation of work or life experiences and responsibilities. Capability of center or unit to meet applicant's educational needs and objectives.

1992 FRESHMAN CLASS PROFILE. 38 men, 61 women enrolled. **Characteristics:** 98% from in state, 100% commute, 23% have minority backgrounds. Average age is 34.

FALL-TERM APPLICATIONS. No fee. No closing date; applicants notified on a rolling basis. Deferred and early admission available.

STUDENT SERVICES. Career counseling, personal counseling, special adviser for adult students, educational counseling, services/facilities for handicapped.

ANNUAL EXPENSES. Tuition and fees (1992-93): $2,887, $3,900 additional for out-of-state students. **Books and supplies:** $600. **Other expenses:** $1,500.

FINANCIAL AID. 50% of continuing students receive some form of aid. Grants, loans, jobs available. **Aid applications:** Closing date April 1; applicants notified on a rolling basis; must reply within 3 weeks.

ADDRESS/TELEPHONE. Martin Thorsland, Director of Admissions, State University of New York Empire State College, 2 Union Avenue, Saratoga Springs, NY 12866-4390. (518) 587-2100.

State University of New York Health Science Center at Brooklyn

Brooklyn, New York CB code: 2534

2-year upper-division public health science college, coed. Founded in 1858. **Accreditation:** Regional. **Undergraduate enrollment:** 860 men and women. **Graduate enrollment:** 850 men and women. **Faculty:** 688 total (533 full time), 121 with doctorates or other terminal degrees. **Location:** Urban campus in very large city; 6 miles from downtown Brooklyn, 10 miles from downtown Manhattan. **Calendar:** Semester, limited summer session. **Microcomputers:** Located in libraries, computer centers.

DEGREES OFFERED. BS, PhD, MD. 190 bachelor's degrees awarded in 1992. 50% in health sciences, 50% allied health. Graduate degrees offered in 12 major fields of study.

UNDERGRADUATE MAJORS. Medical radiation dosimetry, medical records administration, nursing, occupational therapy, physical therapy, physician's assistant.

ACADEMIC PROGRAMS. Combined bachelor's/graduate program in medicine. **Remedial services:** Reduced course load. **Placement/credit:** CLEP Subject.

ACADEMIC REQUIREMENTS. Students must declare major on enrollment. **Graduation requirements:** 125 hours for bachelor's (60 in major).

STUDENT LIFE. Housing: Dormitories (coed). **Activities:** Student government, student newspaper, yearbook. **Additional information:** Of undergraduates who do not live in college housing, approximately 40% commute from their own apartments off-campus, another 40% commute from home.

ATHLETICS. Intramural: Basketball M.

STUDENT SERVICES. Health services, services/facilities for handicapped.

ANNUAL EXPENSES. Tuition and fees (1992-93): $2,815, $3,900 additional for out-of-state students. **Room and board:** $2,760 room only. **Books and supplies:** $685. **Other expenses:** $820.

FINANCIAL AID. 81% of freshmen, 67% of continuing students receive some form of aid. 99% of grants, 81% of loans, all jobs based on need. **Aid applications:** Closing date April 30; priority given to applications received by April 10; applicants notified on or about June 30; must reply within 10 days.

ADDRESS/TELEPHONE. Anne Berg, Director of Admissions, State University of New York Health Science Center at Brooklyn, 450 Clarkson Avenue, Box 60A, Brooklyn, NY 11203-2098. (718) 270-2187.

State University of New York Health Science Center at Syracuse

Syracuse, New York CB code: 2547

Admissions: 14% of applicants accepted
Based on: ••• Interview, school record
•• Essay, recommendations
• Activities, test scores
Completion: 92% of freshmen end year in good standing

4-year public health science college, coed. Founded in 1834. **Accreditation:** Regional. **Undergraduate enrollment:** 78 men, 100 women full time; 23 men, 160 women part time. **Graduate enrollment:** 353 men, 258 women full time; 19 men, 33 women part time. **Faculty:** 443 total. **Location:** Urban campus in small city; 250 miles from New York City, 150 miles from Buffalo. **Calendar:** Semester, limited summer session. **Microcomputers:** 34 located in dormitories, libraries, classrooms, computer centers. **Special facilities:** Institutionally owned and operated 350-bed hospital. **Additional facts:** Undergraduate level consists of 2-year lower-division and 2-year upper-division programs. Affiliated with Crouse-Irving Memorial Hospital, Veteran's Administration Medical Center, Community General Hospital of Greater Syracuse, St. Joseph's Hospital Health Center, and Hutchings Psychiatric Center.

DEGREES OFFERED. AAS, BS, MS, PhD, MD. 49 associate degrees awarded in 1992. 100% in health sciences. 73 bachelor's degrees awarded. 100% in health sciences. Graduate degrees offered in 13 major fields of study.

UNDERGRADUATE MAJORS. Associate: Extracorporeal technology, radiation therapy technology, radiograph medical technology, respiratory therapy. **Bachelor's:** Clinical laboratory science, cytotechnology, medical laboratory technologies, nursing, physical therapy, respiratory therapy.

ACADEMIC PROGRAMS. Accelerated program, independent study. **Remedial services:** Reduced course load, special counselor, tutoring. **Placement/credit:** AP, CLEP General and Subject, institutional tests; 36 credit hours maximum for bachelor's degree.

ACADEMIC REQUIREMENTS. Freshmen must earn minimum GPA of 2.0 to continue in good standing. Clinical evaluation also required. 88% of freshmen return for sophomore year. Students must declare major on application. **Graduation requirements:** 72 hours for associate, 120 hours for bachelor's. Most students required to take courses in English, mathematics, biological/physical sciences, social sciences. **Postgraduate studies:** 35% from 2-year programs enter 4-year programs. **Additional information:** Undergraduate level consists of 2-year lower-division and 2-year upper-division programs.

FRESHMAN ADMISSIONS. Selection criteria: Academic performance in courses required for admission, overall academic performance, letters of recommendation, motivation, character, communication skills, volunteer or observational experience in chosen field, evaluation of personal interview, and standardized test scores. **High school preparation:** 13 units recommended. Recommended units include biological science 1, English 4, mathematics 3, physical science 2 and social science 3. Strong mathematics/science background required. Admission requirements, course recommendations vary by program.

1992 FRESHMAN CLASS PROFILE. 112 men applied, 15 accepted, 6 enrolled; 160 women applied, 24 accepted, 13 enrolled. 70% had high school GPA of 3.0 or higher, 30% between 2.0 and 2.99. **Characteristics:** 95% from in state, 75% live in college housing, 42% have minority backgrounds. Average age is 22.

FALL-TERM APPLICATIONS. $25 fee, may be waived for applicants with need. No closing date; applicants notified on a rolling basis beginning on or about November 15; must reply by May 1 or within 2 weeks if notified thereafter. Interview required. Essay required. CRDA. Deferred and early admission available. Submision of SAT or ACT test optional for admission. Application deadline for physical therapy program is mid-January. Extracorporeal technology program completes admissions review process by spring. Admissions preference given to stae residents. Appointments for pre-admissions advisement strongly recommended 1year prior to application to program. Observation or volunteer experience in a hospital recommended.

STUDENT LIFE. Housing: Dormitories (coed); apartment housing available. **Activities:** Student government, yearbook, campus activities governing board, Diversity in Allied Health. **Additional information:** Activities revolve around such projects as blood drives and humanistic approaches to medicine lectures. Of undergraduates who commute, approximately 38% live in apartments off campus, 6% commute from home.

ATHLETICS. Intramural: Basketball, handball, racquetball, softball, table tennis, tennis, volleyball, water polo.

STUDENT SERVICES. Career counseling, freshman orientation, health services, on-campus day care, personal counseling, placement service for graduates, veterans counselor, services/facilities for handicapped.

ANNUAL EXPENSES. Tuition and fees (projected): $2,865, $3,900 additional for out-of-state students. **Room and board:** $2,950 room only. **Books and supplies:** $515. **Other expenses:** $700.

FINANCIAL AID. 79% of freshmen, 63% of continuing students receive some form of aid. Grants, loans, jobs available. **Aid applications:** No closing date; priority given to applications received by April 1; applicants notified on a rolling basis beginning on or about June 1; must reply within 2 weeks.

ADDRESS/TELEPHONE. A. Geno Andreatta, Dean of Admissions and Student Affairs, State Univ of New York Health Sci Ctr Syracuse, 155 Elizabeth Blackwell Street, Syracuse, NY 13210. (315) 464-4570. Fax: (315) 464-8823.

State University of New York Health Sciences Center at Stony Brook

Stony Brook, New York

2-year upper-division public university, coed. Founded in 1970. **Accreditation:** Regional. **Undergraduate enrollment:** 74 men, 301 women full time; 7 men, 104 women part time. **Graduate enrollment:** 442 men, 549 women full time; 63 men, 387 women part time. **Faculty:** 619 total (544 full time). **Location:** Suburban campus in large town; 60 miles from New York City. **Calendar:** Mostly semester; some programs on modular calendar. **Microcomputers:** Located in libraries, classrooms, computer centers. **Special facilities:** University hospital.

DEGREES OFFERED. BS, MS, MSW, PhD, DDS, MD. 193 bachelor's degrees awarded in 1992. Graduate degrees offered in 9 major fields of study.

UNDERGRADUATE MAJORS. Medical laboratory technologies, nursing, physical therapy, physician's assistant, social work.

ACADEMIC PROGRAMS. Double major, independent study, internships; liberal arts/career combination in health sciences. **Remedial services:** Learning center, reduced course load, tutoring. **Placement/credit:** CLEP Subject.

ACADEMIC REQUIREMENTS. Students must declare major on application. **Graduation requirements:** 120 hours for bachelor's. Most students required to take courses in English, humanities, mathematics, biological/physical sciences, social sciences. **Additional information:** Some programs consist of nine five-week modules.

STUDENT LIFE. Housing: Dormitories (coed); apartment housing available. **Activities:** Student government, film, magazine, radio, student newspaper, yearbook, choral groups, concert band, drama, music ensembles, musical theater, opera, symphony orchestra, fraternities, sororities.

ATHLETICS. NCAA. **Intercollegiate:** Baseball M, basketball, cross-country, diving, football M, lacrosse M, soccer, softball W, swimming, tennis, track and field, volleyball W. **Intramural:** Badminton, basketball, cross-country, handball M, lacrosse, soccer, softball, squash, tennis, volleyball. **Clubs:** Horseback riding, squash.

STUDENT SERVICES. Career counseling, employment service for undergraduates, health services, on-campus day care, personal counseling, placement service for graduates, special adviser for adult students, veterans counselor, services/facilities for handicapped.

ANNUAL EXPENSES. Tuition and fees (projected): $2,928, $3,900 additional for out-of-state students. **Room and board:** $4,528. **Books and supplies:** $1,000. **Other expenses:** $1,730.

FINANCIAL AID. 45% of continuing students receive some form of aid. Grants, loans, jobs available. Academic, minority scholarships available. **Aid applications:** No closing date; priority given to applications received by March 15; applicants notified on a rolling basis beginning on or about June 1; must reply within 2 weeks.

ADDRESS/TELEPHONE. Ana Maria Torres, Director of Student Services, State University of New York Health Sciences Center at Stony Brook, Level 2, Room 271, Stony Brook, NY 11794-8276. (516) 444-2109. Fax: (516) 444-2771.

State University of New York Institute of Technology at Utica/Rome
Utica, New York — CB code: 0755

2-year upper-division public technical college, coed. Founded in 1966. **Accreditation:** Regional. **Undergraduate enrollment:** 817 men, 560 women full time; 241 men, 524 women part time. **Graduate enrollment:** 41 men, 21 women full time; 113 men, 104 women part time. **Faculty:** 135 total (89 full time). **Location:** Suburban campus in small city; 50 miles from Syracuse, 90 miles from Albany. **Calendar:** Semester, limited summer session. Extensive evening/early morning classes. **Microcomputers:** 222 located in libraries, classrooms, computer centers. **Special facilities:** Telecommunications institute, industrial robotic and computer-aided design laboratories, art gallery.

DEGREES OFFERED. BA, BS, MS. 668 bachelor's degrees awarded in 1992. 33% in business and management, 18% computer sciences, 22% engineering technologies, 18% health sciences, 5% social sciences. Graduate degrees offered in 4 major fields of study.

UNDERGRADUATE MAJORS. Accounting, business administration and management, business and management, computer and information sciences, computer technology, electrical technology, finance, health care administration, industrial technology, information sciences and systems, liberal/general studies, mechanical design technology, medical records administration, medical records technology, nursing, optical technology, psychology, sociology, technical communications, telecommunications.

ACADEMIC PROGRAMS. Accelerated program, double major, independent study, internships, cross-registration. **Remedial services:** Learning center, reduced course load, remedial instruction, special counselor, tutoring. **Placement/credit:** CLEP General and Subject.

ACADEMIC REQUIREMENTS. Students must declare major on application. **Graduation requirements:** 124 hours for bachelor's (40 in major). Most students required to take courses in computer science, English, history, humanities, mathematics, biological/physical sciences, social sciences.

STUDENT LIFE. Housing: Dormitories (coed); handicapped housing available. **Activities:** Student government, radio, student newspaper, yearbook, jazz band, fraternities, sororities, black student union, international student organization.

ATHLETICS. NCAA. **Intercollegiate:** Baseball M, basketball, golf M, soccer, softball W, volleyball W. **Intramural:** Badminton, basketball M, bowling, golf, racquetball, skiing, soccer, softball, table tennis, tennis, volleyball, water polo M.

STUDENT SERVICES. Aptitude testing, career counseling, employment service for undergraduates, health services, personal counseling, placement service for graduates, veterans counselor, services/facilities for handicapped.

ANNUAL EXPENSES. Tuition and fees (1992-93): $2,809, $3,900 additional for out-of-state students. **Room and board:** $4,660. **Books and supplies:** $480. **Other expenses:** $800.

FINANCIAL AID. 75% of continuing students receive some form of aid. 80% of grants, 57% of loans, 79% of jobs based on need. Academic, state/district residency, minority scholarships available. **Aid applications:** No closing date; priority given to applications received by May 1; applicants notified on a rolling basis beginning on or about March 1; must reply within 2 weeks.

ADDRESS/TELEPHONE. Eileen Collins, Director of Admissions, State University of New York Institute of Technology at Utica/Rome, Marcy Campus, PO Box 3050, Utica, NY 13504-3050. (315) 792-7208. Fax: (315) 792-7222.

State University of New York Maritime College
Throggs Neck, New York — CB code: 2536

Admissions: 65% of applicants accepted
Based on:
••• School record, test scores
•• Activities, interview, recommendations, special talents
• Essay
Completion: 80% of freshmen end year in good standing
63% graduate, 26% of these enter graduate study

4-year public maritime college: including college of science and engineering and college of business administration, coed. Founded in 1874. **Accreditation:** Regional. **Undergraduate enrollment:** 656 men, 65 women full time. **Graduate enrollment:** 10 men, 1 woman full time; 152 men, 21 women part time. **Faculty:** 108 total (93 full time), 46 with doctorates or other terminal degrees. **Location:** Suburban campus in very large city; 10 miles from Manhattan. **Calendar:** Semester plus required 2-month summer sea term. **Microcomputers:** 110 located in computer centers. **Special facilities:** 565-foot training ship, 110-foot training tug boat, sub-critical nuclear reactor, center for simulated marine operations, bridge and collision-avoidance simulators, model basin and towing tank, CAD-CAM facilities, diesel propulsion simulator, maritime museum, sailing center which includes several one-ton ocean racers. **Additional facts:** Prepares men and women for license as ship's officers for Merchant Marine (third mate or third assistant engineer). Graduates also eligible for commission as officers in Navy, Marine Corps, Coast Guard, Air Force and commissioned Corps of the National Oceanic and Atmospheric Administration. Three summer semesters at sea required.

DEGREES OFFERED. BS, MS. 131 bachelor's degrees awarded in 1992. 42% in business and management, 49% engineering, 8% physical sciences. Graduate degrees offered in 1 major field of study.

UNDERGRADUATE MAJORS. Atmospheric sciences and meteorology, business administration and management, business and management, electrical/electronics/communications engineering, facility engineering, humanities, marine engineering, mechanical engineering, Merchant Marine, naval architecture and marine engineering, naval science (Navy, Marines), oceanography, transportation management.

ACADEMIC PROGRAMS. Dual enrollment of high school students, internships, semester at sea. **Remedial services:** Learning center, preadmission summer program, reduced course load, special counselor, tutoring. **ROTC:** Air Force, Naval. **Placement/credit:** AP, CLEP Subject, institutional tests.

ACADEMIC REQUIREMENTS. Freshmen must earn minimum GPA of 2.0 to continue in good standing. 82% of freshmen return for sophomore year. Students must declare major on application. **Graduation requirements:** 158 hours for bachelor's (64 in major). Most students required to take courses in computer science, English, history, humanities, mathematics, biological/physical sciences, social sciences. **Postgraduate studies:** 3% enter law school, 12% enter MBA programs, 11% enter other graduate study. **Additional information:** Cadets acquire technical, leadership experience on training cruises to European and domestic ports during annual summer sea terms.

FRESHMAN ADMISSIONS. Selection criteria: Quality and strength of preparation, school achievement record, including first semester senior grades, class rank, test scores, extracurricular activities. **High school preparation:** 16 units required. Required and recommended units include English 4, mathematics 3-4, physical science 2-3 and social science 2. Foreign language 3 recommended. Mathematics requirement includes algebra, geometry, and trigonometry. Mathematics beyond trigonometry recommended. Chemistry or physics required, both strongly recommended. **Test requirements:** SAT or ACT; score report by April 1. ACH not required but will be used in evaluation if submitted.

1992 FRESHMAN CLASS PROFILE. 795 men applied, 522 accepted, 245 enrolled; 110 women applied, 69 accepted, 25 enrolled. 34% had high school GPA of 3.0 or higher, 66% between 2.0 and 2.99. 10% were in top tenth and 32% were in top quarter of graduating class. **Academic background:** Mid 50% of enrolled freshmen had SAT-V between 400-500, SAT-M between 480-580. 94% submitted SAT scores. **Characteristics:** 84% from in state, 97% live in college housing, 16% have minority backgrounds, 1% are foreign students. Average age is 18.

FALL-TERM APPLICATIONS. $25 fee, may be waived for applicants with need. No closing date; priority given to applications received by January 15; applicants notified on a rolling basis beginning on or about January 15; must reply by May 1 or within 4 weeks if notified thereafter. Essay required. Interview recommended. CRDA. Deferred and early admission available. EDP-F. Students who do not meet physical health requirements established by Coast Guard for license as officers for Merchant Marine may enroll if they can safely participate in all parts of the program, including sea terms.

STUDENT LIFE. Housing: Dormitories (coed). Most undergraduate students required to live in on-campus housing. **Activities:** Student government, magazine, radio, student newspaper, yearbook, choral groups, concert band, jazz band, marching band, music ensembles, Newman Club, Protestant Club, Jewish Society, Circle-K, Eagle Scout Fraternity, Multi-cultural Club,

Afro-Caribbean Club, International Club, Italian Club, Spanish Club. **Additional information:** Maritime students organized as a regiment of cadets to foster personal growth, development, leadership training, and experience. In this system of increasing responsibility and privilege, first-class cadets (seniors) are regimental officers ashore. Cadet officers are in charge of bridge and engine room of training ship during summer sea terms.

ATHLETICS. NCAA. **Intercollegiate:** Baseball M, basketball, cross-country, diving, ice hockey M, lacrosse M, rifle, rowing (crew), soccer M, softball W, swimming, tennis, wrestling M. **Intramural:** Basketball M, racquetball, sailing, soccer M, softball, squash M, swimming, table tennis, tennis, volleyball, water polo M, wrestling M. **Clubs:** Rugby M, sailing.

STUDENT SERVICES. Career counseling, freshman orientation, health services, personal counseling, placement service for graduates, veterans counselor.

ANNUAL EXPENSES. Tuition and fees (projected): $2,933, $3,900 additional for out-of-state students. $1,800 uniform charge for freshmen. **Room and board:** $4,344. **Books and supplies:** $500. **Other expenses:** $1,200.

FINANCIAL AID. 51% of freshmen, 60% of continuing students receive some form of aid. 70% of grants, 96% of loans, 42% of jobs based on need. Academic, state/district residency, minority scholarships available. **Aid applications:** No closing date; priority given to applications received by April 1; applicants notified on a rolling basis beginning on or about March 1; must reply by May 1 or within 4 weeks if notified thereafter. **Additional information:** All cadets who are United States citizens, physically qualified for Merchant Marine license, and not yet 25 at time of enrollment are eligible for Student Incentive Payment (SIP) of $1,200 per year from Maritime Administration of the Department of Transportation. Out-of-state students who elect to participate in SIP pay in-state tuition fees.

ADDRESS/TELEPHONE. Gerard Peter Cooney, Director of Admissions, State University of New York Maritime College, Fort Schuyler, Throggs Neck, NY 10465-4198. (718) 409-7220. (800) 642-1874. Fax: (718) 409-7392.

State University of New York at Oswego
Oswego, New York — CB code: 2543

Admissions:	54% of applicants accepted
Based on:	••• School record, test scores
	•• Activities
	• Essay, interview, recommendations, special talents
Completion:	90% of freshmen end year in good standing
	56% graduate, 23% of these enter graduate study

4-year public college of arts and sciences, coed. Founded in 1861. **Accreditation:** Regional. **Undergraduate enrollment:** 2,985 men, 3,513 women full time; 302 men, 353 women part time. **Graduate enrollment:** 73 men, 115 women full time; 277 men, 617 women part time. **Faculty:** 388 total (310 full time), 228 with doctorates or other terminal degrees. **Location:** Suburban campus in large town; 35 miles from Syracuse. **Calendar:** Semester, limited summer session. **Microcomputers:** 250 located in dormitories, libraries, classrooms, computer centers. **Special facilities:** 400-acre biological field station, weather facsimile machine, planetarium, cross-country ski facilities, Tyler art gallery, Waterman Theater.

DEGREES OFFERED. BA, BS, BFA, MA, MS, MFA. 1,598 bachelor's degrees awarded in 1992. 17% in business and management, 5% business/office and marketing/distribution, 8% communications, 27% teacher education, 5% letters/literature, 8% psychology, 14% social sciences. Graduate degrees offered in 17 major fields of study.

UNDERGRADUATE MAJORS. Accounting, American studies, anthropology, applied mathematical economics, applied mathematics, atmospheric sciences and meteorology, biology, business administration and management, business education, chemistry, communications, computer and information sciences, criminal justice studies, dramatic arts, economics, elementary education, English, English education, fine arts, foreign languages education, French, geochemistry, geology, German, history, industrial arts education, industrial training and development, information sciences and systems, linguistics, management science, marketing and distribution, marketing management, marketing research, mathematics, mathematics education, music, philosophy, philosophy/psychology, physics, political science and government, predentistry, premedicine, preveterinary, psychology, radio/television broadcasting, reading education, Russian, science education, secondary education, social studies education, sociology, Spanish, trade and industrial education, zoology.

ACADEMIC PROGRAMS. Double major, dual enrollment of high school students, honors program, independent study, internships, student-designed major, study abroad, visiting/exchange student program, Washington semester, 3+2 program in engineering with Case Western Reserve University in Ohio, Clarkson University, and SUNY Binghamton, 2+2 programs in forestry with SUNY College of Environmental Science and Forestry, cytotechnology and medical technology with SUNY Health Science Center at Syracuse, combined degree program in zoo technology with Santa Fe Community College in Florida, 3+4 program in optometry with SUNY College of Optometry; liberal arts/career combination in engineering, forestry, health sciences. **Remedial services:** Learning center, preadmission summer program, reduced course load, remedial instruction, special counselor, tutoring. **ROTC:** Army. **Placement/credit:** AP, CLEP General and Subject, institutional tests; 30 credit hours maximum for bachelor's degree.

ACADEMIC REQUIREMENTS. Freshmen must earn minimum GPA of 2.0 to continue in good standing. 87% of freshmen return for sophomore year. Students must declare major by end of second year. **Graduation requirements:** 122 hours for bachelor's. Most students required to take courses in English, humanities, mathematics, biological/physical sciences, social sciences. **Postgraduate studies:** 2% enter law school, 2% enter medical school, 5% enter MBA programs, 14% enter other graduate study.

FRESHMAN ADMISSIONS. Selection criteria: High school GPA and curriculum most important, followed by test scores, class rank, recommendations. Special talents considered. **High school preparation:** 16 units recommended. Recommended units include English 4, foreign language 3, mathematics 3, social science 3 and science 3. Combined minimum of 7 units mathematics and science recommended. 2-3 units of foreign language strongly recommended. **Test requirements:** SAT or ACT; score report by April 1.

1992 FRESHMAN CLASS PROFILE. 9,120 men and women applied, 4,960 accepted; 674 men enrolled, 775 women enrolled. 80% had high school GPA of 3.0 or higher, 15% between 2.0 and 2.99. 13% were in top tenth and 26% were in top quarter of graduating class. **Academic background:** Mid 50% of enrolled freshmen had SAT-V between 430-530, SAT-M between 510-590; ACT composite between 22-28. 70% submitted SAT scores, 30% submitted ACT scores. **Characteristics:** 98% from in state, 90% live in college housing, 12% have minority backgrounds. Average age is 18.

FALL-TERM APPLICATIONS. $25 fee, may be waived for applicants with need. No closing date; priority given to applications received by January 15; applicants notified on a rolling basis beginning on or about February 1; must reply by May 1 or within 4 weeks if notified thereafter. Interview recommended. Audition recommended for academically marginal music applicants. Portfolio recommended for academically marginal art applicants. Essay recommended. CRDA. Deferred and early admission available.

STUDENT LIFE. Housing: Dormitories (women, coed); fraternity, sorority housing available. **Activities:** Student government, film, magazine, radio, student newspaper, television, yearbook, choral groups, concert band, dance, drama, jazz band, music ensembles, musical theater, opera, symphony orchestra, fraternities, sororities, Christian, Jewish, Baha'i, and Baptist groups, Black Student Union, Native American Brotherhood, Latin Student Union.

ATHLETICS. NCAA. **Intercollegiate:** Baseball M, basketball, cross-country, diving, field hockey W, golf M, ice hockey M, lacrosse M, soccer, softball W, swimming, tennis, volleyball W, wrestling M. **Intramural:** Basketball, horseback riding, racquetball, rowing (crew), rugby, soccer, softball, squash, volleyball, wrestling M.

STUDENT SERVICES. Aptitude testing, career counseling, health services, on-campus day care, personal counseling, placement service for graduates, special adviser for adult students, veterans counselor, services/facilities for handicapped.

ANNUAL EXPENSES. Tuition and fees (projected): $2,975, $3,900 additional for out-of-state students. **Room and board:** $4,425. **Books and supplies:** $450. **Other expenses:** $900.

FINANCIAL AID. 80% of freshmen, 70% of continuing students receive some form of aid. All grants, 95% of loans, 21% of jobs based on need. 637 enrolled freshmen were judged to have need, 579 were offered aid. Academic, music/drama, leadership scholarships available. **Aid applications:** No closing date; priority given to applications received by March 1; applicants notified on a rolling basis beginning on or about April 1; must reply by May 1 or within 3 weeks if notified thereafter.

ADDRESS/TELEPHONE. Joseph F. Grant, Dean of Admissions, State University of New York at Oswego, Culkin Hall 211, Oswego, NY 13126-3599. (315) 341-2250.

Stenotype Academy
New York, New York — CB code: 5324

2-year proprietary college for paralegal studies and court reporting, coed. **Undergraduate enrollment:** 850 men and women. **Location:** Urban campus in very large city. **Calendar:** Trimester.

FRESHMAN ADMISSIONS. Selection criteria: Open admissions.

ANNUAL EXPENSES. Tuition and fees: $7,100. Full-time tuition for court reporting night program $4,300, part-time $3,300. Tuition for paralegal program $160 per credit hour. **Books and supplies:** $1,000. **Other expenses:** $4,000.

ADDRESS/TELEPHONE. Alice DeWalt, Director of Admissions, Stenotype Academy, 291 Broadway, New York, NY 10007. (212) 962-0002. Fax: (212) 608-8210.

Suffolk County Community College
Selden, New York CB code: 2827

2-year public community college, coed. Founded in 1959. **Accreditation:** Regional. **Undergraduate enrollment:** 12,870 men and women. **Faculty:** 773 total (245 full time), 56 with doctorates or other terminal degrees. **Location:** Suburban campus in large town; 40 miles from New York City. **Calendar:** Semester, extensive summer session. Saturday and extensive evening/early morning classes. **Microcomputers:** Located in libraries, classrooms, computer centers. **Special facilities:** Art gallery. **Additional facts:** Industry internships in New York City.

DEGREES OFFERED. AA, AS, AAS. 769 associate degrees awarded in 1992.

UNDERGRADUATE MAJORS. Accounting, automotive technology, biological and physical sciences, biology, business administration and management, business and management, business and office, business data processing and related programs, communications, computer and information sciences, construction, criminal justice studies, data processing, dietetic aide/assistant, drafting and design technology, early childhood education, electrical technology, engineering, engineering and engineering-related technologies, engineering and other disciplines, environmental design, finance, fine arts, food production/management/services, graphic design, horticultural science, hotel/motel and restaurant management, humanities, humanities and social sciences, insurance and risk management, interior design, interpreter for the deaf, legal assistant/paralegal, legal secretary, liberal/general studies, manufacturing technology, marketing and distribution, marketing research, mathematics, mechanical design technology, medical secretary, mental health/human services, music, music performance, nursing, office supervision and management, physical sciences, physical therapy assistant, real estate, recreation and community services technologies, recreation therapy, retailing, science technologies, secretarial and related programs, social sciences, telecommunications, visual and performing arts, women's studies.

ACADEMIC PROGRAMS. 2-year transfer program, cooperative education, dual enrollment of high school students, honors program, independent study, internships, telecourses, joint admissions with other SUNY units and private institutions. **Remedial services:** Learning center, reduced course load, remedial instruction, special counselor, tutoring. **Placement/credit:** AP, CLEP General and Subject, IB, institutional tests; 30 credit hours maximum for associate degree.

ACADEMIC REQUIREMENTS. Freshmen must earn minimum GPA of 1.6 to continue in good standing. 52% of freshmen return for sophomore year. Students must declare major on application. **Graduation requirements:** 64 hours for associate. Most students required to take courses in English, history, humanities, mathematics, philosophy/religion, biological/physical sciences, social sciences.

FRESHMAN ADMISSIONS. Selection criteria: Open admissions. Selective admissions to some programs including early childhood education, nursing and paralegal. Special course requirements vary by program. **Test requirements:** SAT or ACT required for admission into early childhood education, nursing and paralegal programs. SAT or ACT results submitted by other applicants will be reviewed for placement and counseling. **Additional information:** Institution-administered placement tests in English, math, and reading required of all first-time freshmen.

1992 FRESHMAN CLASS PROFILE. 1,651 men, 1,811 women enrolled. **Characteristics:** 100% from in state, 100% commute, 7% have minority backgrounds. Average age is 19.

FALL-TERM APPLICATIONS. $25 fee, may be waived for applicants with need. Closing date August 15; priority given to applications received by April 1; applicants notified on a rolling basis; must reply by May 1 or within 2 weeks if notified thereafter. Portfolio required for fine arts applicants. Interview recommended for health career, fine arts, performing arts, broadcast telecommunications, paralegal assistant applicants. Audition recommended for performing arts applicants. CRDA. Early admission available. Nursing applicants must apply by January 1. All other health career applicants must apply by February 1.

STUDENT LIFE. Activities: Student government, magazine, student newspaper, choral groups, concert band, dance, drama, jazz band, music ensembles, musical theater, African American Student Union, International Student Union, Suffolk Christian Fellowship, Club Outreach.

ATHLETICS. NJCAA. **Intercollegiate:** Baseball M, basketball, bowling, cross-country, golf M, horseback riding, soccer, softball W, tennis, track and field, volleyball W, wrestling M. **Intramural:** Badminton, baseball M, basketball, bowling, fencing, lacrosse M, racquetball, skiing, softball W, tennis, volleyball.

STUDENT SERVICES. Aptitude testing, career counseling, employment service for undergraduates, freshman orientation, health services, on-campus day care, personal counseling, placement service for graduates, special adviser for adult students, services/facilities for handicapped.

ANNUAL EXPENSES. Tuition and fees (projected): $1,968, $1,850 additional for out-of-state students. **Books and supplies:** $550. **Other expenses:** $1,048.

FINANCIAL AID. 65% of freshmen receive some form of aid. All aid based on need. Academic scholarships available. **Aid applications:** No closing date; priority given to applications received by June 1; applicants notified on a rolling basis beginning on or about July 1; must reply within 2 weeks.

ADDRESS/TELEPHONE. Douglas Steele, Director of Admissions, Suffolk County Community College, 533 College Road, Selden, NY 11784. (516) 451-4033.

Suffolk County Community College: Eastern Campus
Riverhead, New York CB code: 2846

2-year public community college, coed. Founded in 1977. **Accreditation:** Regional. **Undergraduate enrollment:** 2,615 men and women. **Faculty:** 242 total (32 full time), 2 with doctorates or other terminal degrees. **Location:** Rural campus in small town; 60 miles from New York City. **Calendar:** Semester, limited summer session. Saturday and extensive evening/early morning classes. **Microcomputers:** Located in classrooms, computer centers. **Special facilities:** Greenhouses, planetarium, marine sciences laboratory.

DEGREES OFFERED. AA, AS, AAS. 297 associate degrees awarded in 1992.

UNDERGRADUATE MAJORS. Accounting, biological laboratory technology, biology, business administration and management, business and management, business and office, chemistry, criminal justice studies, early childhood education, food management, food science and nutrition, graphic design, horticulture, hotel/motel and restaurant management, interior design, liberal/general studies, office supervision and management, ornamental horticulture, secretarial and related programs, tourism.

ACADEMIC PROGRAMS. 2-year transfer program, cooperative education, honors program, independent study, internships, telecourses, weekend college, joint admissions with other SUNY units and private institutions. **Remedial services:** Learning center, remedial instruction, special counselor, tutoring. **Placement/credit:** AP, CLEP Subject, institutional tests; 30 credit hours maximum for associate degree.

ACADEMIC REQUIREMENTS. Freshmen must earn minimum GPA of 1.6 to continue in good standing. 51% of freshmen return for sophomore year. Students must declare major on application. **Graduation requirements:** 64 hours for associate (20 in major). Most students required to take courses in English, foreign languages, history, humanities, mathematics, philosophy/religion, biological/physical sciences, social sciences.

FRESHMAN ADMISSIONS. Selection criteria: Open admissions. Selective admissions to some programs including early childhood education, nursing and paralegal. Special course requirements vary by programs. **Test requirements:** SAT or ACT required for admission into early childhood education, nursing, and paralegal programs. SAT or ACT results submitted by other applicants will be reviewed for placement and counseling. **Additional information:** Institution-administered placement tests in English, math, and reading required of all first-time freshmen.

1992 FRESHMAN CLASS PROFILE. 325 men, 414 women enrolled. **Characteristics:** 100% from in state, 100% commute, 7% have minority backgrounds.

FALL-TERM APPLICATIONS. $25 fee, may be waived for applicants with need. Closing date August 15; priority given to applications received by April 1; applicants notified on a rolling basis; must reply by registration. Some part-time students may be admitted without high school diploma or GED.

STUDENT LIFE. Activities: Student government, magazine, student newspaper, Peconic Campus Fellowship, ethnic student rainbow coalition.

ATHLETICS. Intramural: Basketball, bowling, softball.

STUDENT SERVICES. Aptitude testing, career counseling, employment service for undergraduates, freshman orientation, health services, personal counseling, placement service for graduates, special adviser for adult students, veterans counselor, services/facilities for handicapped.

ANNUAL EXPENSES. Tuition and fees (1992-93): $1,968, $1,850 additional for out-of-state students. **Books and supplies:** $550. **Other expenses:** $1,048.

FINANCIAL AID. Academic scholarships available. **Aid applications:** No closing date; priority given to applications received by June 1; applicants notified on a rolling basis beginning on or about July 1; must reply within 2 weeks.

ADDRESS/TELEPHONE. Charles Bartolotta, Assistant Director of Admissions and Financial Aid, Suffolk County Community College: Eastern Campus, Speonk-Riverhead Road, Riverhead, NY 11901. (516) 548-2500.

Suffolk County Community College: Western Campus
Brentwood, New York CB code: 2849

2-year public community college, coed. Founded in 1974. **Accreditation:** Regional. **Undergraduate enrollment:** 5,559 men and women. **Faculty:** 365 total (79 full time), 36 with doctorates or other terminal degrees. **Location:** Suburban campus in large town; 25 miles from New York City. **Calendar:** Semester, extensive summer session. Saturday and extensive evening/early morning classes. **Microcomputers:** Located in libraries, classrooms, computer centers.

DEGREES OFFERED. AA, AS, AAS. 642 associate degrees awarded in 1992.

UNDERGRADUATE MAJORS. Accounting, biology, business administration and management, business and management, business and office, business data processing and related programs, chemistry, criminal justice studies, data processing, early childhood education, earth sciences, elementary education, environmental science, finance, fine arts, insurance and risk management, law enforcement and corrections, legal assistant/paralegal, legal secretary, liberal/general studies, marketing and distribution, marketing research, medical assistant, office supervision and management, planetary science, real estate, retailing, secretarial and related programs, word processing.

ACADEMIC PROGRAMS. 2-year transfer program, cooperative education, dual enrollment of high school students, honors program, independent study, internships, telecourses, weekend college, joint admissions with other SUNY units and private institutions. **Remedial services:** Learning center, preadmission summer program, reduced course load, remedial instruction, special counselor, tutoring. **Placement/credit:** AP, CLEP Subject, IB, institutional tests; 30 credit hours maximum for associate degree.

ACADEMIC REQUIREMENTS. Freshmen must earn minimum GPA of 1.6 to continue in good standing. 47% of freshmen return for sophomore year. Students must declare major on application. **Graduation requirements:** 64 hours for associate. Most students required to take courses in English, history, humanities, mathematics, philosophy/religion, biological/physical sciences, social sciences.

FRESHMAN ADMISSIONS. Selection criteria: Open admissions. Selective admissions to some programs including early childhood education, nursing, and paralegal. Special course requirements vary by programs. **Test requirements:** SAT or ACT required for admission into early childhood education, nursing and paralegal programs. SAT or ACT results submitted by other applicants will be reviewed for placement and counseling. **Additional information:** Institution-administered placement tests in English, math, and reading required of all first-time freshmen.

1992 FRESHMAN CLASS PROFILE. 587 men, 899 women enrolled. **Characteristics:** 100% from in state, 100% commute, 18% have minority backgrounds. Average age is 19.

FALL-TERM APPLICATIONS. $25 fee, may be waived for applicants with need. Closing date August 15; priority given to applications received by April 1; applicants notified on a rolling basis; must reply by registration. Early admission available. Nursing applicants must apply by January 1. Other health career applicants must apply by February 1.

STUDENT LIFE. Activities: Student government, film, magazine, student newspaper, choral groups, drama, musical theater, African People's Association, Association of Latin American Students, Human Resource Club, Single Parents Support Group.

ATHLETICS. Intercollegiate: Baseball M, basketball M, bowling, golf M, soccer M, softball W.

STUDENT SERVICES. Aptitude testing, career counseling, employment service for undergraduates, freshman orientation, health services, on-campus day care, personal counseling, placement service for graduates, special adviser for adult students, veterans counselor, services/facilities for handicapped.

ANNUAL EXPENSES. Tuition and fees (1992-93): $1,968, $1,850 additional for out-of-state students. **Books and supplies:** $550. **Other expenses:** $1,048.

FINANCIAL AID. 65% of freshmen receive some form of aid. All aid based on need. Academic scholarships available. **Aid applications:** No closing date; priority given to applications received by June 1; applicants notified on a rolling basis beginning on or about July 1.

ADDRESS/TELEPHONE. Kathryn Reinauer, Assistant Director of Admissions, Suffolk County Community College: Western Campus, Crooked Hill Road, Brentwood, NY 11717. (516) 434-6719.

Sullivan County Community College
Loch Sheldrake, New York — CB code: 2855

2-year public community college, coed. Founded in 1962. **Accreditation:** Regional. **Undergraduate enrollment:** 759 men, 759 women full time; 330 men, 330 women part time. **Faculty:** 113 total (76 full time), 13 with doctorates or other terminal degrees. **Location:** Rural campus in small town; 100 miles from New York City, 90 miles from Binghamton. **Calendar:** 4-1-4, limited summer session. **Microcomputers:** 75 located in libraries, classrooms, computer centers. **Special facilities:** Complete kitchen, baking, production, and dining room for hotel technology program, mini-travel agency for travel and tourism program, color and black and white darkrooms, computer graphics system, child development center. **Additional facts:** SUNY institution. Campus in Japan.

DEGREES OFFERED. AA, AS, AAS. 287 associate degrees awarded in 1992. 17% in business and management, 7% communications, 8% computer sciences, 6% health sciences, 6% allied health, 43% trade and industry, 10% visual and performing arts.

UNDERGRADUATE MAJORS. Accounting, alcoholism and drug abuse, anthropology, biological and physical sciences, business administration and management, business and management, business and office, business computer/console/peripheral equipment operation, business data entry equipment operation, business data processing and related programs, business data programming, child development/care/guidance, commercial art, communications, computer and information sciences, criminal justice studies, data processing, early childhood education, economics, engineering, engineering science, environmental science, food management, food production/management/services, forestry and related sciences, graphic arts technology, graphic design, history, hospitality and recreation marketing, hotel/motel and restaurant management, humanities and social sciences, insurance and risk management, insurance marketing, law enforcement and corrections, legal assistant/paralegal, liberal/general studies, marketing and distribution, mathematics, nursing, office supervision and management, philosophy, photographic technology, photography, physical sciences, political science and government, predentistry, prelaw, premedicine, prepharmacy, preveterinary, psychology, radio/television broadcasting, radio/television technology, real estate, retailing, social sciences, sociology, sports management, survey and mapping technology, tourism, transportation and travel marketing, video, word processing.

ACADEMIC PROGRAMS. 2-year transfer program, dual enrollment of high school students, independent study, internships, study abroad, visiting/exchange student program. **Remedial services:** Learning center, reduced course load, remedial instruction, special counselor, tutoring, Project Success, intensive program for academically underprepared students. **Placement/credit:** AP, CLEP General and Subject, institutional tests; 31 credit hours maximum for associate degree.

ACADEMIC REQUIREMENTS. Freshmen must earn minimum GPA of 1.5 to continue in good standing. 41% of freshmen return for sophomore year. Students must declare major on application. **Graduation requirements:** 64 hours for associate (36 in major). Most students required to take courses in English, humanities, biological/physical sciences, social sciences. **Additional information:** Practical experience in class laboratory situations emphasized in technical programs.

FRESHMAN ADMISSIONS. Selection criteria: Open admissions. Special requirements for nursing programs. Liberal arts applicants entering science programs should have 3 units each in mathematics and sciences. Computer science applicants, 3 units mathematics and 1 chemistry or physics. Nursing applicants, 1 mathematics and 1 laboratory biology. Engineering science, 3.5 units mathematics and 1 unit chemistry or physics.

1992 FRESHMAN CLASS PROFILE. 588 men and women enrolled. **Characteristics:** 97% from in state, 40% commute, 22% have minority backgrounds. Average age is 18.

FALL-TERM APPLICATIONS. $25 fee, may be waived for applicants with need. No closing date; applicants notified on a rolling basis; must reply within 6 weeks. Interview recommended. Deferred and early admission available. SAT/ACT tests are recommended.

STUDENT LIFE. Activities: Student government, radio, yearbook, Black Student Union, Latin Student Union. **Additional information:** Only 45% of students are county residents. 60% of undergraduates live in their own apartments off campus including privately owned and operated housing available within walking distance, 40% commute from home.

ATHLETICS. NJCAA. **Intercollegiate:** Basketball M, cross-country, golf, softball W, volleyball W. **Intramural:** Archery, badminton, basketball, bowling, cross-country, fencing, golf, handball, horseback riding, lacrosse, racquetball, skiing, soccer, softball, swimming, table tennis, tennis, volleyball.

STUDENT SERVICES. Aptitude testing, career counseling, employment service for undergraduates, freshman orientation, health services, on-campus day care, personal counseling, placement service for graduates, special adviser for adult students, veterans counselor, services/facilities for handicapped.

ANNUAL EXPENSES. Tuition and fees (1992-93): $2,000, $1,850 additional for out-of-state students. **Books and supplies:** $600. **Other expenses:** $700.

FINANCIAL AID. 70% of freshmen, 70% of continuing students receive some form of aid. All grants, 94% of loans, all jobs based on need. Academic, art, leadership scholarships available. **Aid applications:** No closing date; priority given to applications received by May 15; applicants notified on a rolling basis beginning on or about May 15; must reply within 2 weeks. **Additional information:** 60% of students hold part-time jobs locally.

ADDRESS/TELEPHONE. Lawrence G. Appel, Director of Admissions, Sullivan County Community College, Box 4002, Loch Sheldrake, NY 12759. (914) 434-5750 ext. 287. Fax: (914) 434-4806.

Syracuse University

Syracuse, New York CB code: 2823

Admissions: 72% of applicants accepted
Based on: ••• School record, test scores
•• Essay
• Activities, interview, recommendations, special talents
Completion: 88% of freshmen end year in good standing
63% graduate, 20% of these enter graduate study

4-year private university, coed. Founded in 1870. **Accreditation:** Regional. **Undergraduate enrollment:** 5,435 men, 5,392 women full time; 60 men, 61 women part time. **Graduate enrollment:** 3,337 men and women full time; 1,136 men and women part time. **Faculty:** 1,579 total (924 full time), 679 with doctorates or other terminal degrees. **Location:** Urban campus in small city; 240 miles from New York City, 140 miles from Albany. **Calendar:** Semester, extensive summer session. **Microcomputers:** 400 located in dormitories, libraries, classrooms, computer centers. **Special facilities:** Lowe Art Gallery, Holden Observatory, audio archives with historic collection of audio materials, special library collections including rare books and manuscripts, laser spectroscopy laboratories, advanced technology center for computer applications, CAD studio.

DEGREES OFFERED. BA, BS, BFA, BArch, MA, MS, MBA, MFA, MSW, PhD, EdD, JD. 5 associate degrees awarded in 1992. 20% in engineering, 20% letters/literature, 60% social sciences. 2,940 bachelor's degrees awarded in 1992. 17% in business and management, 14% communications, 5% engineering, 6% letters/literature, 7% psychology, 16% social sciences, 16% visual and performing arts. Graduate degrees offered in 139 major fields of study.

UNDERGRADUATE MAJORS. Accounting, advertising, aerospace/aeronautical/astronautical engineering, Afro-American (black) studies, American studies, anthropology, architecture, art education, art history, bioengineering and biomedical engineering, biological and physical sciences, biology, business administration and management, business and management, business statistics, ceramics, chemical engineering, chemistry, child development/care/guidance, cinematography/film, civil engineering, classics, comparative literature, computer and information sciences, computer engineering, computer graphics, dramatic arts, early childhood education, economics, education of the deaf and hearing impaired, education of the multiple handicapped, electrical/electronics/communications engineering, elementary education, engineering and other disciplines, English, English education, environmental design, environmental health engineering, family/consumer resource management, fashion design, fiber/textiles/weaving, film arts, finance, fine arts, food management, food production/management/services, food science and nutrition, foreign languages (multiple emphasis), French, geography, geology, German, health education, history, human environment and housing, illustration design, individual and family development, industrial design, information sciences and systems, interior design, international relations, Italian, journalism, labor/industrial relations, Latin American studies, liberal/general studies, linguistics, management information systems, marketing management, mathematics, mathematics education, mechanical engineering, medieval studies, metal/jewelry, motion picture technology, music, music business management, music education, music performance, music theory and composition, musical theater, nursing, nutritional sciences, operations research, painting, personnel management, philosophy, photographic technology, photography, physical education, physics, political science and government, printmaking, psychology, public relations, radio/television broadcasting, radio/television technology, religion, retailing, Russian, Russian and Slavic studies, science education, sculpture, secondary education, social science education, social studies education, social work, sociology, Spanish, special education, speech, speech correction, speech pathology/audiology, speech/communication/theater education, telecommunications, textiles and clothing, transportation management, video, visual and performing arts, women's studies.

ACADEMIC PROGRAMS. Accelerated program, cooperative education, double major, education specialist degree, external degree, honors program, independent study, internships, student-designed major, study abroad, teacher preparation, visiting/exchange student program, Washington semester, cross-registration; liberal arts/career combination in engineering; combined bachelor's/graduate program in business administration, law. **Remedial services:** Learning center, preadmission summer program, reduced course load, remedial instruction, special counselor, tutoring, learning disability diagnosis, New York State Higher Education. **ROTC:** Air Force, Army. **Placement/credit:** AP, CLEP Subject, institutional tests; 30 credit hours maximum for bachelor's degree.

ACADEMIC REQUIREMENTS. Freshmen must earn minimum GPA of 2.0 to continue in good standing. 88% of freshmen return for sophomore year. Students must declare major by end of second year. **Graduation requirements:** 120 hours for bachelor's (30 in major). Most students required to take courses in English, humanities, mathematics, biological/physical sciences, social sciences. **Postgraduate studies:** 5% enter law school, 2% enter medical school, 7% enter MBA programs, 6% enter other graduate study.

FRESHMAN ADMISSIONS. Selection criteria: High school curriculum and performance most important, followed by SAT or ACT scores, essay, recommendations, portfolio or audition, extracurricular activities. Interviews and alumni relationship considered. **High school preparation:** 15 units required; 20 recommended. Required and recommended units include English 4-4, foreign language 2-4, mathematics 3-4, social science 3-4 and science 3-4. Additional requirements for some programs. **Test requirements:** SAT or ACT (SAT preferred); score report by February 1. **Additional information:** Applicants considered for alternate programs if not admitted to first choice school.

1992 FRESHMAN CLASS PROFILE. 5,068 men applied, 3,571 accepted, 1,258 enrolled; 5,373 women applied, 3,971 accepted, 1,337 enrolled. 28% were in top tenth and 67% were in top quarter of graduating class. **Academic background:** Mid 50% of enrolled freshmen had SAT-V between 470-560, SAT-M between 520-640. 95% submitted SAT scores. **Characteristics:** 36% from in state, 96% live in college housing, 18% have minority backgrounds, 2% are foreign students, 9% join fraternities/sororities. Average age is 18.

FALL-TERM APPLICATIONS. $40 fee, may be waived for applicants with need. Closing date February 1; applicants notified on or about March 15; must reply by May 1. Interview required for architecture, music, art, drama applicants. Audition required for music, drama applicants. Portfolio required for art, architecture applicants. Essay required. CRDA. Deferred and early admission available. EDP-F.

STUDENT LIFE. Housing: Dormitories (men, women, coed); apartment, fraternity, sorority housing available. International living center and language groups within residence halls available. **Activities:** Student government, film, magazine, radio, student newspaper, television, yearbook, choral groups, concert band, dance, drama, jazz band, marching band, music ensembles, musical theater, pep band, symphony orchestra, fraternities, sororities, over 200 religious, political, ethnic, sports, and social service organizations. **Additional information:** Freshmen and sophomores not permitted to keep cars on campus.

ATHLETICS. NCAA. **Intercollegiate:** Basketball, cross-country, diving, field hockey W, football M, gymnastics M, lacrosse M, rowing (crew), soccer M, swimming, tennis W, track and field, volleyball W, wrestling M. **Intramural:** Badminton, baseball M, basketball, bowling, cross-country, fencing, golf, gymnastics W, handball, lacrosse, racquetball, rifle, rugby, sailing, skiing, soccer, softball, squash, swimming, table tennis, tennis, track and field, volleyball, water polo M.

STUDENT SERVICES. Aptitude testing, career counseling, employment service for undergraduates, freshman orientation, health services, on-campus day care, personal counseling, placement service for graduates, special adviser for adult students, veterans counselor, legal counseling, minority student adviser, parents liaison office, athletic adviser, Greek adviser, services/facilities for handicapped.

ANNUAL EXPENSES. Tuition and fees: $14,705. **Room and board:** $6,600. **Books and supplies:** $580. **Other expenses:** $575.

FINANCIAL AID. 72% of freshmen, 62% of continuing students receive some form of aid. 86% of grants, 94% of loans, all jobs based on need. 1,500 enrolled freshmen were judged to have need, all were offered aid. Academic, music/drama, art, athletic scholarships available. **Aid applications:** Closing date January 31; applicants notified on or about March 15; must reply by May 1.

ADDRESS/TELEPHONE. David C. Smith, Dean of Admissions, Syracuse University, 201 Tolley Administration Building, Syracuse, NY 13244-1120. (315) 443-3611.

Talmudical Institute of Upstate New York

Rochester, New York CB code: 1426

4-year private rabbinical, seminary college, men only, affiliated with Jewish faith. Founded in 1974. **Undergraduate enrollment:** 6 men full time. **Graduate enrollment:** 14 men full time. **Faculty:** 6 total (3 full time). **Location:** Urban campus in large city. **Calendar:** Semester. **Microcomputers:** 2 located in computer centers. **Additional facts:** First Talmudic degree offered.

DEGREES OFFERED. B. 3 bachelor's degrees awarded in 1992.

UNDERGRADUATE MAJORS. Theological studies.

ACADEMIC PROGRAMS. Dual enrollment of high school students.

ACADEMIC REQUIREMENTS. No policy requiring minimum GPA; records of students having academic difficulty are reviewed individually. 95% of freshmen return for sophomore year. Students must declare major on application.

FRESHMAN ADMISSIONS. Selection criteria: Interview and school achievement record important.

1992 FRESHMAN CLASS PROFILE. 1 man enrolled. **Characteristics:** 65% from in state, 100% live in college housing. Average age is 20.

FALL-TERM APPLICATIONS. No fee. Closing date September 1; applicants notified on a rolling basis. Interview required.

STUDENT LIFE. Housing: Dormitories (men). **Activities:** Film, magazine.

ANNUAL EXPENSES. Tuition and fees (1992-93): $4,250. **Room and board:** $3,300.

FINANCIAL AID. 20% of freshmen receive some form of aid. **Aid applications:** No closing date; applicants notified on a rolling basis.

ADDRESS/TELEPHONE. Main Office, Talmudical Institute of Upstate New York, 769 Park Avenue, Rochester, NY 14607. (716) 473-2810.

Talmudical Seminary Oholei Torah
Brooklyn, New York CB code: 0712

4-year private rabbinical, seminary college, men only, affiliated with Jewish faith. Founded in 1956. **Undergraduate enrollment:** 190 men full time. **Faculty:** 14 total. **Location:** Urban campus in very large city. **Calendar:** Semester, limited summer session. **Additional facts:** First Talmudic degree offered.

DEGREES OFFERED. B, Talm, Rab. 50 bachelor's degrees awarded in 1992.

ACADEMIC PROGRAMS. Remedial services: Special counselor, tutoring. **Placement/credit:** Institutional tests.

ACADEMIC REQUIREMENTS. Freshmen must earn minimum GPA of 2.0 to continue in good standing. Students must declare major on application. **Graduation requirements:** 128 hours for bachelor's. Most students required to take courses in philosophy/religion. **Postgraduate studies:** 100% enter other graduate study.

FRESHMAN ADMISSIONS. Selection criteria: Interview and institutional entrance examinations.

1992 FRESHMAN CLASS PROFILE. 30 men enrolled. **Characteristics:** 90% commute. Average age is 16.

FALL-TERM APPLICATIONS. No fee. No closing date; applicants notified on a rolling basis. Interview required.

STUDENT LIFE. Housing: Dormitories (men). **Activities:** Magazine, marching band, Lubavitcher Youth Organization. **Additional information:** Religious observance required.

STUDENT SERVICES. Career counseling, personal counseling.

ANNUAL EXPENSES. Tuition and fees (1992-93): $5,700. **Room and board:** $5,400.

FINANCIAL AID. 80% of continuing students receive some form of aid. **Aid applications:** No closing date; applicants notified on a rolling basis beginning on or about May 21.

ADDRESS/TELEPHONE. Admissions Office, Talmudical Seminary Oholei Torah, 667 Eastern Parkway, Brooklyn, NY 11213-3397. (718) 774-5215.

Taylor Business Institute
New York, New York CB code: 0434

2-year proprietary business, technical college, coed. Founded in 1961. **Undergraduate enrollment:** 560 men and women. **Faculty:** 69 total (31 full time), 6 with doctorates or other terminal degrees. **Location:** Urban campus in very large city. **Calendar:** Quarter, extensive summer session. **Microcomputers:** Located in classrooms.

DEGREES OFFERED. 141 associate degrees awarded in 1992. 50% in business and management, 50% business/office and marketing/distribution.

UNDERGRADUATE MAJORS. Accounting, business and management, electronic technology, secretarial and related programs, transportation and travel marketing.

ACADEMIC PROGRAMS. 2-year transfer program. **Remedial services:** Remedial instruction. **Placement/credit:** Institutional tests.

ACADEMIC REQUIREMENTS. Freshmen must earn minimum GPA of 2.0 to continue in good standing. 70% of freshmen return for sophomore year. Students must declare major on enrollment. **Graduation requirements:** 97 hours for associate (60 in major). Most students required to take courses in computer science, English, humanities, mathematics, social sciences.

FRESHMAN ADMISSIONS. Selection criteria: Test scores most important.

1992 FRESHMAN CLASS PROFILE. 175 men and women enrolled. **Characteristics:** 97% from in state, 100% commute, 84% have minority backgrounds. Average age is 22.

FALL-TERM APPLICATIONS. $25 fee. No closing date; applicants notified on a rolling basis. Interview required. Deferred admission available.

STUDENT LIFE. Activities: Magazine, student newspaper, yearbook, dance.

STUDENT SERVICES. Career counseling, employment service for undergraduates, freshman orientation, personal counseling, placement service for graduates, services/facilities for handicapped.

ANNUAL EXPENSES. Tuition and fees (1992-93): $6,720. **Other expenses:** $210.

FINANCIAL AID. 100% of freshmen, 100% of continuing students receive some form of aid. All grants, all jobs based on need. **Aid applications:** No closing date; applicants notified on a rolling basis.

ADDRESS/TELEPHONE. Paul Goodman, Director of Admissions, Taylor Business Institute, 1 Penn Plaza, New York, NY 10119-0118. (212) 279-0510.

Technical Career Institutes
New York, New York CB code: 2755

Admissions: 90% of applicants accepted
Based on: ••• School record, test scores
•• Activities, recommendations
• Interview
Completion: 75% of freshmen end year in good standing
25% graduate, 12% of these enter 4-year programs

2-year proprietary technical college, coed. Founded in 1974. **Undergraduate enrollment:** 3,000 men, 1,150 women full time; 400 men, 50 women part time. **Faculty:** 193 total (93 full time), 49 with doctorates or other terminal degrees. **Location:** Urban campus in very large city; in downtown New York City. **Calendar:** Quarter, extensive summer session. Saturday and extensive evening/early morning classes. **Microcomputers:** 300 located in libraries, classrooms, computer centers.

DEGREES OFFERED. AAS. 450 associate degrees awarded in 1992. 20% in communications, 20% engineering technologies, 60% trade and industry.

UNDERGRADUATE MAJORS. Air conditioning/heating/refrigeration mechanics, electrical and electronics equipment repair, electronic technology, secretarial and related programs.

ACADEMIC PROGRAMS. Cooperative education, internships. **Remedial services:** Reduced course load, remedial instruction, tutoring. **Placement/credit:** Institutional tests.

ACADEMIC REQUIREMENTS. Freshmen must earn minimum GPA of 1.5 to continue in good standing. 45% of freshmen return for sophomore year. Students must declare major on enrollment. **Graduation requirements:** Most students required to take courses in computer science, English, humanities, mathematics.

FRESHMAN ADMISSIONS. Selection criteria: Admission based primarily on institution-administered placement test. Remediation and English as a Second Language programs available for students not meeting program requirements. High school algebra 1 unit, general science 1 required for engineering technology program. Geometry, trigonometry, physics preferred for engineering program.

1992 FRESHMAN CLASS PROFILE. 1,490 men applied, 1,380 accepted, 1,300 enrolled; 580 women applied, 480 accepted, 410 enrolled. **Characteristics:** 95% from in state, 100% commute, 89% have minority backgrounds, 1% are foreign students. Average age is 25.

FALL-TERM APPLICATIONS. $50 fee, may be waived for applicants with need. Closing date September 7; applicants notified on a rolling basis. Interview required.

STUDENT LIFE. Activities: Student government, student newspaper, choral groups, music ensembles, student chapter of Institute of Electrical and Electronics Engineering, Tau Alpha Pi honor fraternity, American Society of Heating, Refrigeration, and Air condition Engineers, chess club, Future Business Leaders, photography club.

STUDENT SERVICES. Career counseling, employment service for undergraduates, freshman orientation, personal counseling, placement service for graduates, sponsored-student adviser.

ANNUAL EXPENSES. Tuition and fees (1992-93): $5,700. **Books and supplies:** $450. **Other expenses:** $1,430.

FINANCIAL AID. 98% of freshmen, 98% of continuing students receive some form of aid. **Aid applications:** No closing date; applicants notified on a rolling basis.

ADDRESS/TELEPHONE. Michael Feder, Dean of Admissions, Technical Career Institutes, 320 West 31st Street, New York, NY 10001. (212) 594-4000. (800) 878-TCIN. Fax: (212) 629-3937.

Tompkins-Cortland Community College
Dryden, New York CB code: 2904

2-year public community college, coed. Founded in 1968. **Accreditation:** Regional. **Undergraduate enrollment:** 630 men, 901 women full time; 453 men, 915 women part time. **Faculty:** 183 total (83 full time), 20 with doctorates or other terminal degrees. **Location:** Rural campus in small town; 45 miles from Syracuse. **Calendar:** Semester, limited summer session. Saturday and extensive evening/early morning classes. **Additional facts:** SUNY institution.

DEGREES OFFERED. AA, AS, AAS. 405 associate degrees awarded in 1992. 35% in business and management, 13% health sciences, 9% parks/recreation, protective services, public affairs, 7% physical sciences, 12% social sciences, 7% trade and industry.

UNDERGRADUATE MAJORS. Accounting, business administration and management, business and office, business data processing and related programs, communications, computer and information sciences, computer graphics, data processing, electrical technology, engineering and engineering-related technologies, fire control and safety technology, food production/management/services, hospitality and recreation marketing, hotel/motel and restaurant management, humanities, humanities and social sciences, international business management, labor/industrial relations, law enforcement and corrections technologies, legal assistant/paralegal, liberal/general studies, marketing and distribution, medical laboratory technologies, nursing, physical sciences, protective services, radio/television technology, recreation and community services technologies, retailing, secretarial and related programs, social sciences, telecommunications, tourism, women's studies, word processing.

ACADEMIC PROGRAMS. 2-year transfer program, cooperative education, dual enrollment of high school students, honors program, cross-registration, 2-2 programs in business administration with Rochester Institute of Technology; communications with Ithaca College, Fredonia College, and Herbert Lehman College. **Remedial services:** Learning center, reduced course load, remedial instruction, special counselor, tutoring. **Placement/credit:** AP, CLEP General and Subject; 15 credit hours maximum for associate degree.

ACADEMIC REQUIREMENTS. Freshmen must earn minimum GPA of 2.0 to continue in good standing. 50% of freshmen return for sophomore year. Students must declare major by end of first year. **Graduation requirements:** 64 hours for associate. Most students required to take courses in English, mathematics, biological/physical sciences, social sciences.

FRESHMAN ADMISSIONS. Selection criteria: Open admissions. Selective admissions for nursing and engineering science applicants and foreign students. **Test requirements:** SAT or ACT for placement and counseling only; score report by September 1. ACT required for admission to nursing program.

1992 FRESHMAN CLASS PROFILE. 243 men, 381 women enrolled. **Academic background:** Mid 50% of enrolled freshmen had ACT composite between 11-26. 10% submitted ACT scores. **Characteristics:** 95% from in state, 100% commute, 9% have minority backgrounds, 1% are foreign students. Average age is 24.

FALL-TERM APPLICATIONS. $25 fee, may be waived for applicants with need. No closing date; applicants notified on a rolling basis; must reply within 4 weeks. Interview recommended for nursing applicants. Deferred and early admission available.

STUDENT LIFE. Housing: Privately owned student housing adjacent to campus. **Activities:** Student government, magazine, radio, student newspaper, television, yearbook.

ATHLETICS. NJCAA. **Intercollegiate:** Softball W, volleyball W, wrestling M. **Intramural:** Badminton, bowling, golf, handball, racquetball, skiing, soccer, squash, swimming, table tennis, tennis, water polo M, wrestling M.

STUDENT SERVICES. Aptitude testing, career counseling, employment service for undergraduates, freshman orientation, on-campus day care, personal counseling, placement service for graduates, veterans counselor, services/facilities for handicapped.

ANNUAL EXPENSES. Tuition and fees (1992-93): $2,064, $1,900 additional for out-of-state students. **Books and supplies:** $500. **Other expenses:** $900.

FINANCIAL AID. 75% of freshmen, 75% of continuing students receive some form of aid. All grants, 93% of loans, 71% of jobs based on need. 510 enrolled freshmen were judged to have need, all were offered aid. Academic scholarships available. **Aid applications:** No closing date; applicants notified on a rolling basis.

ADDRESS/TELEPHONE. Michael McGraw, Director of Admissions and Financial Aid, Tompkins-Cortland Community College, 170 North Street, Dryden, NY 13053-0139. (607) 844-8211. Fax: (607) 844-9665.

Touro College
New York, New York — CB code: 2902

Admissions: 66% of applicants accepted
Based on:
- ••• School record
- •• Essay, interview, recommendations, test scores
- • Activities

Completion: 85% of freshmen end year in good standing
40% enter graduate study

4-year private college of arts and sciences, coed. Founded in 1970. **Accreditation:** Regional. **Undergraduate enrollment:** 2,836 men, 4,493 women full time; 167 men, 207 women part time. **Graduate enrollment:** 430 men, 313 women full time; 218 men, 178 women part time. **Faculty:** 894 total (293 full time). **Location:** Urban campus in very large city; in midtown Manhattan. **Calendar:** Semester, limited summer session. **Microcomputers:** Located in computer centers. **Additional facts:** School of General Studies provides programs for part-time and adult students.

DEGREES OFFERED. AA, AS, BA, BS, MA. 245 associate degrees awarded in 1992. 361 bachelor's degrees awarded. Graduate degrees offered in 4 major fields of study.

UNDERGRADUATE MAJORS. Associate: Accounting, business administration and management, business and management, business and office, finance, liberal/general studies, management information systems. **Bachelor's:** Accounting, biological and physical sciences, biology, business administration and management, business and management, business economics, chemistry, communications, computer and information sciences, economics, English, English literature, finance, foreign languages (multiple emphasis), health sciences, Hebrew, history, humanities and social sciences, Jewish studies, liberal/general studies, management information systems, marketing management, mathematics, medical records administration, medical records technology, occupational therapy, philosophy, physical therapy, physician's assistant, political science and government, predentistry, premedicine, prepharmacy, preveterinary, psychology, religion, social sciences, sociology, speech.

ACADEMIC PROGRAMS. 2-year transfer program, accelerated program, double major, dual enrollment of high school students, honors program, independent study, internships, student-designed major, study abroad. **Remedial services:** Reduced course load, remedial instruction, tutoring. **Placement/credit:** AP, CLEP Subject, institutional tests.

ACADEMIC REQUIREMENTS. Freshmen must earn minimum GPA of 2.0 to continue in good standing. 70% of freshmen return for sophomore year. Students must declare major by end of second year. **Graduation requirements:** 60 hours for associate (30 in major), 120 hours for bachelor's (30 in major). Most students required to take courses in English, humanities. **Postgraduate studies:** 70% from 2-year programs enter 4-year programs. 10% enter law school, 5% enter medical school, 10% enter MBA programs, 15% enter other graduate study.

FRESHMAN ADMISSIONS. Selection criteria: For College of Liberal Arts and Sciences, 3.0 high school GPA, SAT-verbal and mathematical scores of 500 preferred. Recommendations from high school teachers and counselors and motivation considered. High school experience less important for applicants to School of Career and Urban Studies who take institutional admissions test. **High school preparation:** 16 units required; 17 recommended. Required and recommended units include English 4, foreign language 2-3, mathematics 2-3, social science 2-3 and science 2. Biological science 1 and physical science 2 recommended. **Test requirements:** SAT or ACT (SAT preferred); score report by July 1.

1992 FRESHMAN CLASS PROFILE. 5,083 men and women applied, 3,341 accepted; 2,228 enrolled. **Characteristics:** 92% commute.

FALL-TERM APPLICATIONS. $25 fee, may be waived for applicants with need. No closing date; applicants notified on a rolling basis; must reply by May 1 or within 2 weeks if notified thereafter. Interview recommended for College of Liberal Arts and Sciences applicants. Essay recommended for College of Liberal Arts and Sciences applicants. CRDA. Deferred and early admission available.

STUDENT LIFE. Housing: Dormitories (men, women). No board or meal plan available. Kitchen facilities in student housing. **Activities:** Student government, magazine, student newspaper, yearbook, student business review, literary review, humanities journal, accounting and business society, biology club, debating society, Jewish Affairs Committee, foreign students association, Omicron Delta.

STUDENT SERVICES. Aptitude testing, career counseling, employment service for undergraduates, freshman orientation, personal counseling, placement service for graduates, veterans counselor, services/facilities for handicapped.

ANNUAL EXPENSES. Tuition and fees (1992-93): $7,030. **Room and board:** $4,200 room only. **Books and supplies:** $575. **Other expenses:** $1,350.

FINANCIAL AID. 85% of freshmen, 80% of continuing students receive some form of aid. 90% of grants, 81% of jobs based on need. Academic, leadership scholarships available. **Aid applications:** No closing date; priority given to applications received by May 15; applicants notified on a rolling basis beginning on or about March 30; must reply by May 1 or within 4 weeks if notified thereafter.

ADDRESS/TELEPHONE. Jack Abramowitz, Associate Director of Admissions, Touro College, 27-33 West 23rd Street, New York, NY 10010. (212) 463-0400 ext. 401.

Trocaire College
Buffalo, New York — CB code: 2856

Admissions: 60% of applicants accepted
Based on:
- ••• School record
- •• Interview, recommendations, test scores
- • Activities, essay

Completion: 91% of freshmen end year in good standing
52% graduate, 13% of these enter 4-year programs

2-year private junior college, coed. Founded in 1958. **Accreditation:** Regional. **Undergraduate enrollment:** 85 men, 467 women full time; 60 men, 511 women part time. **Faculty:** 102 total (40 full time), 4 with doctorates or other terminal degrees. **Location:** Urban campus in large city. **Calendar:** Semester, limited summer session. **Microcomputers:** 55 located in classrooms, computer centers.

DEGREES OFFERED. AA, AS, AAS. 204 associate degrees awarded in 1992. 10% in business/office and marketing/distribution, 7% teacher education, 61% health sciences, 17% allied health.

UNDERGRADUATE MAJORS. Accounting, business administration and management, business and management, business and office, early childhood education, legal secretary, liberal/general studies, marketing and distribution, mathematics, medical assistant, medical laboratory technologies, medical records technology, medical secretary, nursing, office supervision and management, radiograph medical technology, science technologies, secretarial and related programs, surgical technology.

ACADEMIC PROGRAMS. 2-year transfer program, dual enrollment of high school students, independent study, internships, weekend college, cross-registration. **Remedial services:** Learning center, reduced course load, remedial instruction, tutoring. **Placement/credit:** AP, CLEP General and Subject, institutional tests; 30 credit hours maximum for associate degree.

ACADEMIC REQUIREMENTS. Freshmen must earn minimum GPA of 2.0 to continue in good standing. 79% of freshmen return for sophomore year. Students must declare major on application. **Graduation requirements:** 64 hours for associate (30 in major). Most students required to take courses in English, philosophy/religion, social sciences.

FRESHMAN ADMISSIONS. Selection criteria: GPA, test scores, recommendation, interview. Admissions standards slightly higher for health-related fields. **High school preparation:** 16 units required. Nursing, radiologic technology, and medical laboratory technology programs have specific high school mathematics and science requirements. Strong business background required for administrative assistant program. Medical record technology requires 1 unit of laboratory biology and keyboarding. **Test requirements:** SAT or ACT (SAT preferred); score report by September 1.

1992 FRESHMAN CLASS PROFILE. 114 men applied, 56 accepted, 12 enrolled; 664 women applied, 407 accepted, 122 enrolled. 10% had high school GPA of 3.0 or higher, 63% between 2.0 and 2.99. 6% were in top tenth and 20% were in top quarter of graduating class. **Academic background:** Mid 50% of enrolled freshmen had SAT-V between 300-380, SAT-M between 340-440; ACT composite between 13-21. 34% submitted SAT scores, 8% submitted ACT scores. **Characteristics:** 99% from in state, 100% commute, 9% have minority backgrounds, 1% are foreign students. Average age is 23.

FALL-TERM APPLICATIONS. $15 fee, may be waived for applicants with need. No closing date; applicants notified on a rolling basis; must reply within 4 weeks. Interview recommended. Deferred and early admission available.

STUDENT LIFE. Activities: Student government, magazine, student newspaper, yearbook, fraternities, Student Assembly, Christian community.

STUDENT SERVICES. Aptitude testing, career counseling, employment service for undergraduates, freshman orientation, health services, personal counseling, placement service for graduates, special adviser for adult students, veterans counselor, services/facilities for handicapped.

ANNUAL EXPENSES. Tuition and fees (1992-93): $5,300. **Books and supplies:** $700. **Other expenses:** $600.

FINANCIAL AID. 86% of freshmen, 90% of continuing students receive some form of aid. All grants, 70% of loans, all jobs based on need. 383 enrolled freshmen were judged to have need, all were offered aid. Academic, leadership scholarships available. **Aid applications:** No closing date; priority given to applications received by March 15; applicants notified on a rolling basis beginning on or about March 1; must reply within 2 weeks.

ADDRESS/TELEPHONE. Kathleen A. Hahn, Dean of Admissions, Trocaire College, 110 Red Jacket Parkway, Buffalo, NY 14220. (716) 826-1200.

Ulster County Community College
Stone Ridge, New York — CB code: 2938

2-year public community college, coed. Founded in 1963. **Accreditation:** Regional. **Undergraduate enrollment:** 830 men, 691 women full time; 491 men, 914 women part time. **Faculty:** 194 total (75 full time), 8 with doctorates or other terminal degrees. **Location:** Rural campus in small town; 8 miles from Kingston. **Calendar:** Semester, extensive summer session. **Microcomputers:** 195 located in classrooms, computer centers. **Special facilities:** Art gallery, word processing laboratories, computer art graphic laboratory. **Additional facts:** SUNY institution.

DEGREES OFFERED. AA, AS, AAS. 526 associate degrees awarded in 1992.

UNDERGRADUATE MAJORS. Biology, business administration and management, business and management, business and office, business data processing and related programs, commercial art, communications, community services, computer and information sciences, criminal justice technology, drafting, elementary education, engineering, engineering and engineering-related technologies, family and community services, finance, graphic arts technology, humanities, humanities and social sciences, journalism, law enforcement and corrections technologies, liberal/general studies, mathematics, nursing, protective services, radio/television broadcasting, recreation and community services technologies, retailing, science technologies, secretarial and related programs, social sciences, water and wastewater technology.

ACADEMIC PROGRAMS. 2-year transfer program, cooperative education, double major, dual enrollment of high school students, honors program, independent study, internships, student-designed major, teacher preparation, telecourses, cross-registration. **Remedial services:** Learning center, reduced course load, remedial instruction, special counselor, tutoring. **Placement/credit:** AP, CLEP General and Subject, institutional tests; 30 credit hours maximum for associate degree.

ACADEMIC REQUIREMENTS. Freshmen must earn minimum GPA of 1.5 to continue in good standing. 58% of freshmen return for sophomore year. Students must declare major on enrollment. **Graduation requirements:** 60 hours for associate (30 in major). Most students required to take courses in English, history, humanities, mathematics, biological/physical sciences, social sciences.

FRESHMAN ADMISSIONS. Selection criteria: Open admissions. Selective admissions to nursing and honors programs, with school achievement record very important, SAT recommended. **High school preparation:** 18 units recommended. Recommended units include English 4 and social science 4. 3 mathematics and 3 science, including chemistry and physics, required of engineering applicants. 4 English, 3 mathematics, 3 language required of honors program applicants.

1992 FRESHMAN CLASS PROFILE. 607 men and women enrolled. **Characteristics:** 98% from in state, 100% commute, 11% have minority backgrounds. Average age is 21.

FALL-TERM APPLICATIONS. $25 fee, may be waived for applicants with need. No closing date; priority given to applications received by June 1; applicants notified on a rolling basis. Portfolio recommended for graphic arts applicants. Interview required for nursing, honors program, early admissions applicants; recommended for others. Deferred and early admission available.

STUDENT LIFE. Activities: Student government, magazine, radio, student newspaper, television, choral groups, concert band, drama, music ensembles, musical theater.

ATHLETICS. NJCAA. **Intercollegiate:** Baseball M, basketball, bowling M, cross-country, golf, skiing, soccer M, softball W, tennis, track and field, volleyball W, wrestling M. **Intramural:** Badminton, basketball M, soccer M, softball, volleyball.

STUDENT SERVICES. Aptitude testing, career counseling, employment service for undergraduates, freshman orientation, health services, on-campus day care, personal counseling, placement service for graduates, special adviser for adult students, veterans counselor, services/facilities for handicapped.

ANNUAL EXPENSES. Tuition and fees (projected): $1,964, $1,850 additional for out-of-state students. **Books and supplies:** $500. **Other expenses:** $600.

FINANCIAL AID. 80% of freshmen, 65% of continuing students receive some form of aid. All grants, 84% of loans, 14% of jobs based on need. Academic scholarships available. **Aid applications:** No closing date; priority given to applications received by June 1; applicants notified on a rolling basis beginning on or about June 1; must reply within 2 weeks.

ADDRESS/TELEPHONE. Thomas Maiello, Director of Admissions, Ulster County Community College, Stone Ridge, NY 12484. (914) 687-5022. Fax: (914) 687-5083.

Union College
Schenectady, New York — CB code: 2920

Admissions: 52% of applicants accepted
Based on:
••• School record
•• Activities, essay, recommendations, special talents
• Interview, test scores
Completion: 95% of freshmen end year in good standing
83% graduate, 38% of these enter graduate study

4-year private engineering, liberal arts college, coed. Founded in 1795. **Accreditation:** Regional. **Undergraduate enrollment:** 1,074 men, 840 women full time; 117 men, 37 women part time. **Graduate enrollment:** 111 men, 83 women full time; 274 men, 116 women part time. **Faculty:** 170 total, 163 with doctorates or other terminal degrees. **Location:** Suburban campus in small city; 10 miles from Albany. **Calendar:** Three 10-week terms with 3 courses each term. **Microcomputers:** 175 located in libraries, computer centers. **Special facilities:** Tandem pelletron positive ion accelerator, superconducting nuclear magnetic resonance spectrometer, 2 electron microscopes.

DEGREES OFFERED. BA, BS, MS, MBA, PhD. 551 bachelor's degrees awarded in 1992. 16% in engineering, 8% letters/literature, 10% life sciences, 5% mathematics, 7% multi/interdisciplinary studies, 9% psychology, 27% social sciences. Graduate degrees offered in 14 major fields of study.

UNDERGRADUATE MAJORS. American studies, biological and physical sciences, biology, business economics, chemistry, civil engineering, classics, computer and information sciences, East Asian studies, economics, electrical/electronics/communications engineering, English, fine arts, foreign languages (multiple emphasis), geology, history, humanities, Latin American studies, mathematics, mechanical engineering, philosophy, physics, political science and government, psychology, social sciences, sociology, visual and performing arts, women's studies.

ACADEMIC PROGRAMS. Accelerated program, double major, independent study, internships, student-designed major, study abroad, teacher preparation, visiting/exchange student program, Washington semester, cross-registration, combined bachelor's/graduate degree program in law with Albany Law School and in medicine with Albany Medical College; liberal arts/career combination in engineering; combined bachelor's/graduate program in business administration. **Remedial services:** Preadmission summer program, reduced course load, remedial instruction, special counselor, tutoring, writing center. **ROTC:** Air Force, Army, Naval. **Placement/credit:** AP, institutional tests.

ACADEMIC REQUIREMENTS. Freshmen must earn minimum GPA of 2.0 to continue in good standing. 94% of freshmen return for sophomore year. **Graduation requirements:** 120 hours for bachelor's. Most students required to take courses in English, history, mathematics, biological/physical sciences, social sciences. **Postgraduate studies:** 10% enter law school, 9% enter medical school, 1% enter MBA programs, 18% enter other graduate study. **Additional information:** Several Educational Studies options available: certification to teach English, modern and classical languages, mathematics, sciences, and social studies in grades 7-12; 4-year undergraduate program combines education courses with regularmajor; 1-year graduate program leading to master of arts in teaching (MAT); 5-year combined degree (BA/MAT, BS/MAT) program.

FRESHMAN ADMISSIONS. Selection criteria: School achievement record, including course selection and grades most important. Essay, recommendations from teachers and counselor, special talents, skills, critical supporting materials, personal interview, and test scores considered. Ethnic and geographic diversity sought in student body. Special consideration given to economically disadvantaged students and children of alumni. **High school preparation:** 16 units recommended. Recommended units include English 4, foreign language 2, mathematics 3, social science 2 and science 2. Prefer 3.5 mathematics for engineering and science majors. **Test requirements:** ACT or 3 ACH (including English Composition), required for admission. Mathematics Level I or II and science preferred for engineering, science applicants; required of 7-year medical program applicants. Score report by March 1. **Additional information:** Submission of SAT optional.

1992 FRESHMAN CLASS PROFILE. 1,915 men applied, 953 accepted, 284 enrolled; 1,330 women applied, 749 accepted, 254 enrolled. 40% were in top tenth and 84% were in top quarter of graduating class. **Academic background:** Mid 50% of enrolled freshmen had ACT composite between 26-31. 25% submitted ACT scores. **Characteristics:** 51% from in state, 98% live in college housing, 11% have minority backgrounds, 3% are foreign students. Average age is 18.

FALL-TERM APPLICATIONS. $40 fee, may be waived for applicants with need. Closing date February 1; applicants notified on or about April 3; must reply by May 1. Essay required. Interview recommended. Portfolio recommended for art applicants. CRDA. Deferred and early admission available. EDP-F. Early decision application deadline February 1, notification on rolling basis.

STUDENT LIFE. Housing: Dormitories (men, women, coed); fraternity, sorority, cooperative housing available. 750 dormitory rooms have computer connections. **Activities:** Student government, magazine, radio, student newspaper, yearbook, choral groups, concert band, dance, drama, jazz band, music ensembles, musical theater, pep band, chamber orchestra, fraternities, sororities, Jewish Student Union, African/Latino Alliance of Students, Newman Club, campus Protestant ministry, Amnesty International, Big Brothers/Big Sisters, Asian Student Union, Students for Environmental Action, Students for Political Awareness, Women's Union. **Additional information:** Kosher cuisine available. Undergraduates not residing in college housing live in their own apartments off campus.

ATHLETICS. NCAA. **Intercollegiate:** Baseball M, basketball, cross-country, field hockey W, football M, golf M, ice hockey M, lacrosse, soccer, softball W, swimming, tennis, track and field, volleyball W. **Intramural:** Basketball, fencing, horseback riding, ice hockey, lacrosse, rowing (crew), rugby, sailing, skiing, soccer, softball, volleyball, water polo.

STUDENT SERVICES. Career counseling, freshman orientation, health services, personal counseling, placement service for graduates.

ANNUAL EXPENSES. Tuition and fees: $17,877. **Room and board:** $5,940. **Books and supplies:** $450. **Other expenses:** $783.

FINANCIAL AID. 50% of freshmen, 47% of continuing students receive some form of aid. All grants, 93% of loans, all jobs based on need. 246 enrolled freshmen were judged to have need, all were offered aid. **Aid applications:** Closing date February 1; applicants notified on or about March 30; must reply by May 1. **Additional information:** CAUSE Program: cancellable loans, given to eligible students who engage in public service work after graduation. Loans cancellable at rate of 20 percent for each year of service.

ADDRESS/TELEPHONE. Daniel Lundquist, Dean of Admissions and Financial Aid, Union College, Stanley R. Becker Hall, Schenectady, NY 12308-2311. (518) 370-6112.

United States Merchant Marine Academy
Kings Point, New York

CB code: 2923

Admissions: 25% of applicants accepted
Based on:
- ••• Activities, school record
- •• Recommendations, special talents, test scores
- • Essay

Completion: 75% of freshmen end year in good standing
69% graduate, 3% of these enter graduate study

4-year public engineering, military college, coed. Founded in 1943. **Accreditation:** Regional. **Undergraduate enrollment:** 911 men, 90 women full time. **Faculty:** 85 total (78 full time), 34 with doctorates or other terminal degrees. **Location:** Suburban campus in large town; 22 miles from New York City. **Calendar:** Quarter (students attend 4 quarters to complete 1 full academic year). **Microcomputers:** Located in libraries, classrooms. Lease or purchase required**Special facilities:** US Merchant Marine Museum. **Additional facts:** Accepted applicants appointed to academy as midshipmen, USNR.

DEGREES OFFERED. BS. 159 bachelor's degrees awarded in 1992. 100% in engineering.

UNDERGRADUATE MAJORS. Marine transportation, Merchant Marine, naval architecture and marine engineering.

ACADEMIC PROGRAMS. Double major, independent study, internships, dual-licensing program, sea training on merchant vessels, marine engineering systems program, ship's officer program. **Remedial services:** Tutoring. **Placement/credit:** Institutional tests.

ACADEMIC REQUIREMENTS. Freshmen must earn minimum GPA of 2.0 to continue in good standing. 75% of freshmen return for sophomore year. **Graduation requirements:** Most students required to take courses in computer science, English, history, mathematics, biological/physical sciences.

FRESHMAN ADMISSIONS. Selection criteria: Nomination by US representatives, congressmen, or senators. Competitive standing determined by test scores, high school GPA, class rank, motivation, interest in academy, industry, citizenship, recommendations from counselors, teachers, school principal, must also meet medical requirements. **High school preparation:** 15 units required. Required and recommended units include English 3, mathematics 3-4 and physical science 1-2. 8 units of elective courses. **Test requirements:** SAT or ACT; score report by March 15.

1992 FRESHMAN CLASS PROFILE. 1,464 men applied, 331 accepted, 248 enrolled; 118 women applied, 58 accepted, 33 enrolled. 45% were in top tenth and 82% were in top quarter of graduating class. **Academic background:** Mid 50% of enrolled freshmen had SAT-V between 470-580, SAT-M between 550-640. 83% submitted SAT scores. **Characteristics:** 12% from in state, 100% live in college housing, 6% have minority backgrounds, 4% are foreign students. Average age is 18.

FALL-TERM APPLICATIONS. No fee. Closing date March 1; applicants notified on or about May 1; must reply within 2 days of notification. Essay required. CRDA.

STUDENT LIFE. Housing: Dormitories (coed). **Activities:** Student government, student newspaper, yearbook, regimental broadcasting unit, regimental information service, choral groups, concert band, drama, marching band.

ATHLETICS. NCAA. **Intercollegiate:** Baseball M, basketball M, cross-country, football M, golf, lacrosse M, rifle, rowing (crew), soccer, swimming, tennis M, track and field, volleyball W, wrestling M. **Intramural:** Badminton M, basketball, bowling, racquetball, rifle M, soccer, softball, track and field M, volleyball M. **Clubs:** Intercollegiate sailing.

STUDENT SERVICES. Employment service for undergraduates, health services, personal counseling, placement service for graduates.

ANNUAL EXPENSES. Tuition and fees (1992-93): $3,450. All midshipmen receive full tuition, room and board, and dental expenses from federal government. Freshmen must purchase computer for $2,231.

FINANCIAL AID. 20% of freshmen, 11% of continuing students receive some form of aid. Loans available. **Aid applications:** Closing date January 30; priority given to applications received by January 15; applicants notified on or about May 1. **Additional information:** Students paid by steamship companies while at sea.

ADDRESS/TELEPHONE. Capt. James A. Skinner, Director of Admissions, United States Merchant Marine Academy, Kings Point, NY 11024. (516) 773-5000. (800) 732-6267. Fax: (516) 773-5390.

United States Military Academy
West Point, New York CB code: 2924

Admissions: 12% of applicants accepted
Based on: ••• School record, test scores
•• Activities, essay, interview, recommendations, special talents
Completion: 94% of freshmen end year in good standing
80% graduate, 2% of these enter graduate study

4-year public college of arts and sciences and military college, coed. Founded in 1802. **Accreditation:** Regional. **Undergraduate enrollment:** 3,788 men, 483 women full time. **Faculty:** 491 total, 181 with doctorates or other terminal degrees. **Location:** Rural campus in small town; 50 miles from New York City. **Calendar:** Semester, limited summer session. **Microcomputers:** 6,600 located in dormitories, libraries, classrooms, computer centers, campus-wide network. Lease or purchase required**Special facilities:** West Point Museum, Eisenhower Hall Theater and Gallery. **Additional facts:** Bachelor of science degree plus commission as second lieutenant in US Army. Obligated active duty commitment of 6 years commences immediately on graduation.

DEGREES OFFERED. BS. 961 bachelor's degrees awarded in 1992. 8% in business and management, 40% engineering, 8% mathematics, 22% social sciences.

UNDERGRADUATE MAJORS. Aerospace/aeronautical/astronautical engineering, American studies, applied mathematics, Arabic, astrophysics, automotive mechanics, behavioral sciences, biochemistry, business administration and management, chemical engineering, chemistry, Chinese, civil engineering, comparative literature, computer and information sciences, computer engineering, East Asian studies, economics, electrical/electronics/communications engineering, energy systems mechanical engineering, engineering and other disciplines, engineering management, engineering physics, environmental health engineering, foreign languages (multiple emphasis), French, geography, German, history, human resources development, humanities, humanities and social sciences, international relations, international studies, Latin American studies, law , leadership, management science, mathematics, mechanical engineering, Middle Eastern studies, military science (Army), nuclear engineering, nuclear physics, operations research, optics, philosophy, physical sciences, physics, political science and government, Portuguese, premedicine, psychology, quantitative analysis, Russian, Russian and Slavic studies, sociology, solid state physics, Spanish, systems engineering, Western European studies.

ACADEMIC PROGRAMS. Double major, independent study, visiting/exchange student program. **Remedial services:** Learning center, reduced course load, remedial instruction, special counselor, tutoring, individualized additional instruction. **Placement/credit:** AP, institutional tests.

ACADEMIC REQUIREMENTS. Freshmen must earn minimum GPA of 1.7 to continue in good standing. Records of students having academic difficulty reviewed individually. Cadets must obtain passing grades in every core course, meet specified standards of conduct and physical proficiency, and demonstrate aptitude for military service. 93% of freshmen return for sophomore year. Students must declare major by end of second year. **Graduation requirements:** 140 hours for bachelor's (30 in major). Most students required to take courses in computer science, English, foreign languages, history, humanities, mathematics, philosophy/religion, biological/physical sciences, social sciences. **Postgraduate studies:** 2% enter medical school. **Additional information:** Students must complete 40 academic courses, requirements of a major or field study, 4 military science courses, 4 physical education courses, and achieve 2.0 cumulative GPA at graduation.

FRESHMAN ADMISSIONS. Selection criteria: Candidate must be qualified academically, medically, physically. An equal opportunity admissions officer attempts to reach qualified minority group members who otherwise might not apply for admission. Candidate must be unmarried United States citizen at least 17 years of age but not yet 22 on July 1 of entering year. Candidate must not have a legal responsibility to support child or children and may not be pregnant. **High school preparation:** 14 units recommended. Recommended units include English 4, foreign language 2, mathematics 4, physical science 2 and social science 2. **Test requirements:** SAT or ACT; score report by March 21. Physical Aptitude Examination and Department of Defense Medical Examination. **Additional information:** To be considered for admission, applicant must secure nomination from authorized source: member of Congress, President, Vice President, or Department of the Army.

1992 FRESHMAN CLASS PROFILE. 11,802 men applied, 1,464 accepted, 987 enrolled; 1,934 women applied, 200 accepted, 123 enrolled. 59% were in top tenth and 85% were in top quarter of graduating class. **Academic background:** Mid 50% of enrolled freshmen had SAT-V between 520-620, SAT-M between 610-700. 59% submitted SAT scores. **Characteristics:** 8% from in state, 100% live in college housing, 15% have minority backgrounds, 1% are foreign students. Average age is 18.

FALL-TERM APPLICATIONS. No fee. Closing date March 21; applicants notified on a rolling basis; must reply by May 1. Essay required. Interview recommended. Institutional early decision plan. Candidates may apply for Early Action Program if West Point is their first choice. Notify West Point of intentions to apply by October 25. Complete application and physical aptitude exam by December 1. Will be notified of admissions decision by January 15.

STUDENT LIFE. Housing: Dormitories (coed). All students live in assigned housing. **Activities:** Student government, film, magazine, radio, television, yearbook, Bugle Notes calendar, choral groups, drama, music ensembles, musical theater, pep band, gospel choir, more than 100 sports and special interest clubs, including Contemporary Affairs Seminar, Student Conference on United States Affairs, and Cadet Scout. **Additional information:** Cultural opportunities include plays direct from Broadway and Cadet Fine Arts Forum with special interest seminars. Automobiles allowed on campus only during senior year. Military dress required. Cadets administer honor system with power to recommend dismissal.

ATHLETICS. NCAA. **Intercollegiate:** Baseball M, basketball, cross-country, diving, football M, golf M, gymnastics M, ice hockey M, lacrosse M, rifle, soccer, softball W, swimming, tennis, track and field, volleyball W, water polo M, wrestling M. **Intramural:** Archery, basketball, bowling, boxing M, cross-country, fencing, football M, golf, gymnastics, handball, horseback riding, lacrosse, racquetball, rowing (crew), rugby, sailing, skiing, skin diving, soccer, softball, squash, swimming, tennis, track and field, volleyball, water polo, wrestling M.

STUDENT SERVICES. Career counseling, health services, personal counseling, placement service for graduates, legal services.

ANNUAL EXPENSES. Tuition and fees (1992-93): $0. All cadets are members of United States Army and receive annual salary of more than $6,500. Tuition, room and board, medical, and dental care are provided at no cost to cadets. First-year students pay deposit of $1,500 for books, personal computer, and supplies.

FINANCIAL AID. Additional information: First-year students who cannot pay deposit of $1,500 for books, personal computer, and supplies, receive no-interest loan. Payments deducted from salary.

ADDRESS/TELEPHONE. Col. Pierce A. Rushton, Jr, Director of Admissions, United States Military Academy, 606 Thayer Road, West Point, NY 10996-1797. (914) 938-4041. Fax: (914) 938-3021.

United Talmudical Academy
Brooklyn, New York CB code: 0696

5-year private rabbinical college, men only, affiliated with Jewish faith. Founded in 1949. **Undergraduate enrollment:** 869 men full time. **Graduate enrollment:** 141 men full time. **Location:** Urban campus in very large city. **Calendar:** Semester. **Additional facts:** First Talmudic degree and ordination available.

FRESHMAN ADMISSIONS. Selection criteria: Institutional examination.

ADDRESS/TELEPHONE. Moses Greenfield, Director of Admissions, United Talmudical Academy, 82 Lee Avenue, Brooklyn, NY 11211. (718) 963-9260.

University of Rochester
Rochester, New York CB code: 2928

Admissions: 61% of applicants accepted
Based on: ••• Recommendations, school record
•• Activities, essay, interview, test scores
• Special talents
Completion: 98% of freshmen end year in good standing
75% graduate, 45% of these enter graduate study

4-year private university, coed. **Accreditation:** Regional. **Undergraduate enrollment:** 2,694 men, 2,291 women full time; 144 men, 300 women part time. **Graduate enrollment:** 1,722 men, 1,050 women full time; 601 men, 884 women part time. **Faculty:** 1,376 total (1,231 full time), 1,361 with doctorates or other terminal degrees. **Location:** Suburban campus in large city; 2 miles from downtown. **Calendar:** Semester, extensive summer session. **Microcomputers:** 275 located in dormitories, libraries, classrooms, computer centers. **Special facilities:** Memorial Art Gallery, nuclear structure research laboratory, laboratory for laser energetics, Frederick Douglass Institute for African and African-American Studies, C.E.K. Mees Observatory, Susan B. Anthony Center for Women's Studies, Strong Memorial Hospital, Center for Visual Science, Institute of Optics, Sage Art Center, 19 electron microscopes, Eastman School of Music.

DEGREES OFFERED. BA, BS, MA, MS, MBA, MEd, PhD, EdD, MD. 1,203 bachelor's degrees awarded in 1992. 13% in engineering, 6% letters/literature, 10% life sciences, 13% psychology, 30% social sciences, 10% visual and performing arts. Graduate degrees offered in 71 major fields of study.

UNDERGRADUATE MAJORS. Anthropology, applied mathematics, applied music, art history, biochemistry, biological and physical sciences, biology, biology/geology, cell biology, chemical engineering, chemistry, cinematography/film, classics, cognitive science, computer mathematics, ecology and evolutionary biology, economics, electrical/electronics/communications engineering, engineering and other disciplines, engineering science, English, environmental science, environmental studies, foreign literature, French, geology, geomechanics, German, health and society, history, integrated science, Japanese, linguistics, mathematics, mathematics/statistics, mechanical engineering, microbiology, molecular genetics, music, music education, music history and appreciation, music theory and composition, neurosciences, nursing, optics, philosophy, physics, physics/astronomy, political science and government, psychology, religion, Russian, Spanish, statistics, studio art, women's studies.

ACADEMIC PROGRAMS. Double major, dual enrollment of high school students, education specialist degree, independent study, internships, student-designed major, study abroad, teacher preparation, Washington semester, cross-registration, pre-freshman and sophomore selection to MD program, tuition-free fifth year option, Senior Scholars Program allows selected undergraduates to devote their entire senior year to a creative project; liberal arts/career combination in engineering; combined bachelor's/graduate program in business administration, medicine. **Remedial services:** Learning center, preadmission summer program, reduced course load, special counselor, tutoring, study skills center. **ROTC:** Air Force, Army, Naval. **Placement/credit:** AP, institutional tests.

ACADEMIC REQUIREMENTS. Freshmen must earn minimum GPA of 2.0 to continue in good standing. 92% of freshmen return for sophomore year. Students must declare major by end of second year. **Graduation requirements:** 128 hours for bachelor's (40 in major). Most students required to take courses in English, foreign languages, humanities, biological/physical sciences, social sciences. **Postgraduate studies:** 9% enter law school, 8% enter medical school, 2% enter MBA programs, 26% enter other graduate study.

FRESHMAN ADMISSIONS. Selection criteria: School achievement record and recommendations most important. Test scores, personal qualities, and extracurricular activities important. Alumni relationship, minority status, special talents considered. Recommended units include English 4, foreign language 2 and social science 4. 3-4 mathematics and 2-3 laboratory science also recommended. **Test requirements:** SAT or ACT; score report by March 1.

1992 FRESHMAN CLASS PROFILE. 4,680 men applied, 2,831 accepted, 688 enrolled; 4,012 women applied, 2,482 accepted, 582 enrolled. **Academic background:** Mid 50% of enrolled freshmen had SAT-V between 490-600, SAT-M between 570-680; ACT composite between 25-30. 93% submitted SAT scores, 24% submitted ACT scores. **Characteristics:** 41% from in state, 99% live in college housing, 19% have minority backgrounds, 10% are foreign students.

FALL-TERM APPLICATIONS. $50 fee, may be waived for applicants with need. Closing date January 15; applicants notified on or about April 15; must reply by May 1. Audition required for bachelor of music applicants. Essay required. Interview recommended. CRDA. Deferred and early admission available. EDP-F. February 1 application closing date for Eastman School of Music.

STUDENT LIFE. Housing: Dormitories (men, women, coed); apartment, fraternity, sorority, handicapped housing available. Drama House, Medieval House, and special interest floors available. **Activities:** Student government, magazine, radio, student newspaper, yearbook, amateur radio club, student guide to courses, minority newsletter, choral groups, concert band, dance, drama, jazz band, music ensembles, musical theater, opera, pep band, symphony orchestra, fraternities, sororities, more than 120 student organizations including Hillel, Newman Community, Protestant Community, Inter-Varsity Christian Fellowship, Black Students Union, Asian Cultural Exchange, Spanish and Latin Students Association, campus YMCA, Hindu Association, Amnesty International.

ATHLETICS. NCAA. **Intercollegiate:** Baseball M, basketball, cross-country, diving, field hockey W, football M, golf, ice hockey M, rowing (crew), skiing, soccer, softball W, swimming, tennis, track and field, volleyball. **Intramural:** Badminton, basketball, fencing, gymnastics, horseback riding, lacrosse, racquetball, sailing, soccer, softball, tennis, volleyball, water polo. **Clubs:** Intercollegiate rugby, squash.

STUDENT SERVICES. Aptitude testing, career counseling, employment service for undergraduates, freshman orientation, health services, on-campus day care, personal counseling, placement service for graduates, special adviser for adult students, preprofessional advising, services/facilities for handicapped.

ANNUAL EXPENSES. Tuition and fees (1992-93): $16,454. **Room and board:** $6,015. **Books and supplies:** $500. **Other expenses:** $831.

FINANCIAL AID. 71% of freshmen, 83% of continuing students receive some form of aid. 95% of grants, 99% of loans, 33% of jobs based on need. 804 enrolled freshmen were judged to have need, all were offered aid. Academic, music/drama, minority scholarships available. **Aid applications:** No closing date; priority given to applications received by February 1; applicants notified on a rolling basis beginning on or about April 2; must reply by May 1 or within 2 weeks if notified thereafter. **Additional information:** Supplemental loan program for parents and financing for tuition prepayment plan available.

ADDRESS/TELEPHONE. Wayne A. Locust, Director of Admissions, University of Rochester, Meliora Hall, Rochester, NY 14627-0251. (716) 275-3221. Fax: (716) 461-4595.

University of the State of New York: Regents College

Albany, New York — CB code: 0759

4-year private college of arts and sciences, coed. Founded in 1970. **Accreditation:** Regional. **Undergraduate enrollment:** 6,285 men, 8,179 women part time. **Faculty:** 54 total, 33 with doctorates or other terminal degrees. **Location:** Urban campus in small city. **Calendar:** Students enroll at any time and complete work at their own pace. **Additional facts:** Established to increase opportunities for adult learners. Assesses college-level learning and awards credit for that learning. College provides no instruction itself. Students may meet degree requirements entirely by proficiency examinations, but most students submit some work from conventional colleges or other approved sources. No residency requirement.

DEGREES OFFERED. AA, AS, AAS, BA, BS. 1,523 associate degrees awarded in 1992. 70% in health sciences, 28% multi/interdisciplinary studies. 2,481 bachelor's degrees awarded. 11% in business and management, 5% engineering technologies, 8% health sciences, 76% multi/interdisciplinary studies.

UNDERGRADUATE MAJORS. Associate: Business and management, computer and information sciences, computer technology, electronic technology, engineering and engineering-related technologies, liberal/general studies, nuclear technologies, nursing. **Bachelor's:** Accounting, area studies, biology, business and management, chemistry, computer and information sciences, computer technology, economics, electronic technology, engineering and engineering-related technologies, English literature, finance, French, geography, geology, German, history, human resources development, international business management, liberal/general studies, management information systems, marketing management, mathematics, music, nuclear technologies, nursing, operations management, operations research, philosophy, physics, political science and government, psychology, sociology, Spanish.

ACADEMIC PROGRAMS. 2-year transfer program, external degree, independent study. **Placement/credit:** AP, CLEP General and Subject.

ACADEMIC REQUIREMENTS. Freshmen must earn minimum GPA of 2.0 to continue in good standing. Students must declare major on enrollment. **Graduation requirements:** 60 hours for associate, 120 hours for bachelor's. Most students required to take courses in English. **Postgraduate studies:** 55% from 2-year programs enter 4-year programs. **Additional information:** Special assessment is an option in subject areas where proficiency or performance examinations are not available. Failing grades are not placed in student records or figured into GPA.

FRESHMAN ADMISSIONS. Selection criteria: Open admissions.

FALL-TERM APPLICATIONS. No fee. No closing date; applicants notified on a rolling basis. Students may enroll at any time and are not divided into traditional classifications such as freshmen or sophomores. Applicants without high school diploma admitted as special students.

STUDENT LIFE. Activities: Regents College Reports. **Additional information:** Since degrees are earned entirely through external program, involving proficiency examinations and other types of learning, students do not attend classes at institution. As a result, they neither commute nor live in college housing. Residing all over the world they are kept informed of program developments through mailings, correspondence, and program newsletters.

STUDENT SERVICES. Special adviser for adult students.

ANNUAL EXPENSES. Tuition and fees: $480. Examination fees vary.

FINANCIAL AID. 9% of continuing students receive some form of aid. All grants based on need. All loans based on criteria other than need. Leadership, minority scholarships available. **Aid applications:** Closing date July 1; applicants notified on a rolling basis; must reply within 2 weeks. **Additional information:** Institutional scholarships funded by alumni; deadline May 1. College is approved for all VA Educational benefit programs.

ADDRESS/TELEPHONE. Louise Koroluk, Dean of Enrollment Services and Records, University of the State of New York: Regents College, 1450 Western Ave, Albany, NY 12203. (518) 474-3703.

Utica College of Syracuse University

Utica, New York — CB code: 2932

Admissions: 79% of applicants accepted
Based on:
••• School record
•• Activities, interview, recommendations, test scores
• Essay, special talents
Completion: 68% of freshmen end year in good standing
10% enter graduate study

4-year private liberal arts college, coed. Founded in 1946. **Accreditation:** Regional. **Undergraduate enrollment:** 721 men, 899 women full time; 144 men, 251 women part time. **Faculty:** 222 total (111 full time), 100 with doctorates or other terminal degrees. **Location:** Suburban campus in small city; 50 miles from Syracuse. **Calendar:** Semester, limited summer session. **Microcomputers:** 348 located in classrooms, computer centers. **Special facilities:** Edith Barrett Art Gallery, Lake Julia wildlife sanctuary.

DEGREES OFFERED. BA, BS. 421 bachelor's degrees awarded in 1992. 31% in business and management, 12% communications, 9% allied health, 5% life sciences, 10% parks/recreation, protective services, public affairs, 10% psychology, 11% social sciences.

UNDERGRADUATE MAJORS. Accounting, actuarial sciences, biology, business administration and management, business economics, business education, chemistry, child development/care/guidance, computer and information sciences, construction management, criminal justice studies, dramatic arts, economic crime investigation, economics, electrical/electronics/communications engineering, English, English education, fine arts, gerontology, history, humanities, international studies, journalism, mathematics, mathematics education, nursing, occupational therapy, philosophy, physics, political science and government, psychology, public affairs, public relations, recreation therapy, science education, social sciences, social studies education, sociology, sociology/anthropology, speech.

ACADEMIC PROGRAMS. Accelerated program, cooperative education, double major, dual enrollment of high school students, external degree, honors program, independent study, internships, study abroad, teacher preparation, visiting/exchange student program, Washington semester, cross-registration; liberal arts/career combination in engineering, health sciences. **Remedial services:** Learning center, preadmission summer program, reduced course load, remedial instruction, special counselor, tutoring, New York State Higher Education Opportunity Program, Collegiate Science and Technology Entry Program. **ROTC:** Air Force, Army. **Placement/credit:** AP, CLEP General and Subject, institutional tests; 30 credit hours maximum for bachelor's degree.

ACADEMIC REQUIREMENTS. Freshmen must earn minimum GPA of 2.0 to continue in good standing. 66% of freshmen return for sophomore year. Students must declare major by end of second year. **Graduation requirements:** 120 hours for bachelor's (39 in major). Most students required to take courses in English, foreign languages, humanities, mathematics, biological/physical sciences, social sciences. **Postgraduate studies:** 1% enter law school, 1% enter medical school, 8% enter other graduate study.

FRESHMAN ADMISSIONS. Selection criteria: Academic record, high school course of study, and rank in class most important. Test scores, extracurricular activities, essay, interview, and recommendations also considered. **High school preparation:** 16 units recommended. Recommended units include biological science 2, English 4, foreign language 2, mathematics 3, physical science 1 and social science 3.

1992 FRESHMAN CLASS PROFILE. 652 men applied, 533 accepted, 141 enrolled; 859 women applied, 662 accepted, 185 enrolled. 60% had high school GPA of 3.0 or higher, 40% between 2.0 and 2.99. **Academic background:** Mid 50% of enrolled freshmen had SAT-V between 370-480, SAT-M between 390-530; ACT composite between 19-24. 85% submitted SAT scores, 8% submitted ACT scores. **Characteristics:** 79% from in state, 81% live in college housing, 20% have minority backgrounds. Average age is 18.

FALL-TERM APPLICATIONS. $25 fee, may be waived for applicants with need. No closing date; priority given to applications received by March 1; applicants notified on a rolling basis; must reply by May 1 or within 3 weeks if notified thereafter. Interview recommended. Essay recommended. Essay recommended for academically weak applicants and for those who cannot appear for interview. CRDA. Deferred and early admission available. EDP-F. SAT recommended, ACT may be substituted. Must be received by, May 1.

STUDENT LIFE. Housing: Dormitories (men, women, coed); apartment housing available. **Activities:** Student government, film, magazine, radio, student newspaper, television, yearbook, choral groups, dance, drama, music ensembles, musical theater, fraternities, sororities, black student union, black science students organization, Latin American student union, Jewish student union, Newman Society, Inter-Varsity Christian Fellowship, Alpha Phi Omega (coed service fraternity), social issues club, 28 academic-related clubs, Young Democrats, Young Republicans. **Additional information:** Students encouraged to participate in college governance committee.

ATHLETICS. NCAA. **Intercollegiate:** Baseball M, basketball, cross-country, diving, golf M, soccer, softball W, swimming, tennis. **Intramural:** Badminton, basketball, bowling, fencing, golf, lacrosse M, racquetball, soccer, softball, swimming, table tennis, tennis, volleyball, water polo.

STUDENT SERVICES. Career counseling, employment service for undergraduates, freshman orientation, health services, personal counseling, placement service for graduates, services/facilities for handicapped.

ANNUAL EXPENSES. Tuition and fees: $11,980. **Room and board:** $4,734. **Books and supplies:** $500. **Other expenses:** $625.

FINANCIAL AID. 84% of freshmen, 82% of continuing students receive some form of aid. 86% of grants, 87% of loans, 77% of jobs based on need. 271 enrolled freshmen were judged to have need, 266 were offered aid. Academic, leadership, minority scholarships available. **Aid applications:** No closing date; priority given to applications received by February 15; applicants notified on a rolling basis; must reply by May 1 or within 4 weeks if notified thereafter.

ADDRESS/TELEPHONE. Dominic Passalacqua, Director of Admissions, Utica College of Syracuse University, 1600 Burrstone Road, Utica, NY 13502-4892. (315) 792-3006. (800) 782-8884. Fax: (315) 792-3292.

Utica School of Commerce
Utica, New York — CB code: 0343

2-year proprietary business college, coed. Founded in 1896. **Undergraduate enrollment:** 108 men, 454 women full time; 25 men, 91 women part time. **Faculty:** 55 total (20 full time), 3 with doctorates or other terminal degrees. **Location:** Urban campus in small city; 50 miles from Syracuse. **Calendar:** Semester, extensive summer session. **Microcomputers:** 78 located in classrooms. **Additional facts:** Extension centers in Oneonta and in Canastota.

DEGREES OFFERED. 50 associate degrees awarded in 1992. 70% in business and management, 30% computer sciences.

UNDERGRADUATE MAJORS. Accounting, business administration and management, business and office, business data entry equipment operation, business data processing and related programs, data processing, legal secretary, marketing and distribution, medical records technology, medical secretary, retailing, secretarial and related programs, word processing.

ACADEMIC PROGRAMS. Accelerated program, dual enrollment of high school students, joint admissions with SUNY Institute of Technology. **Remedial services:** Learning center, reduced course load, remedial instruction, special counselor, tutoring. **Placement/credit:** Institutional tests; 30 credit hours maximum for associate degree.

ACADEMIC REQUIREMENTS. Freshmen must earn minimum GPA of 2.0 to continue in good standing. 80% of freshmen return for sophomore year. Students must declare major on enrollment. **Graduation requirements:** 112 hours for associate. Most students required to take courses in English, mathematics.

FRESHMAN ADMISSIONS. Selection criteria: Admissions interview highly recommended, 2.3 high school GPA preferred for students coming directly from high school.

1992 FRESHMAN CLASS PROFILE. 47 men, 221 women enrolled. **Characteristics:** 99% from in state, 100% commute, 10% have minority backgrounds. Average age is 20.

FALL-TERM APPLICATIONS. $20 fee, may be waived for applicants with need. No closing date; applicants notified on a rolling basis. Interview recommended. Essay recommended. Deferred and early admission available.

STUDENT LIFE. Activities: Student government, student newspaper, yearbook, Future Secretaries Association, Accounting Association.

STUDENT SERVICES. Aptitude testing, career counseling, employment service for undergraduates, freshman orientation, personal counseling, placement service for graduates, veterans counselor, services/facilities for handicapped.

ANNUAL EXPENSES. Tuition and fees: $4,325. **Books and supplies:** $650.

FINANCIAL AID. 85% of freshmen, 85% of continuing students receive some form of aid. 98% of grants, 89% of loans based on need. Academic, leadership, alumni affiliation scholarships available. **Aid applications:** No closing date; applicants notified on a rolling basis.

ADDRESS/TELEPHONE. Tracy M. Berie, Director of Admissions, Utica School of Commerce, 201 Bleecker Street, Utica, NY 13501. (315) 733-2307. (800) 321-4872. Fax: (315) 733-2446.

Vassar College ⇐⇒
Poughkeepsie, New York — CB code: 2956

Admissions:	47% of applicants accepted
Based on:	••• Activities, recommendations, school record
	•• Essay, interview, special talents, test scores
Completion:	92% of freshmen end year in good standing
	10% graduate, 30% of these enter graduate study

4-year private liberal arts college, coed. Founded in 1861. **Accreditation:** Regional. **Undergraduate enrollment:** 869 men, 1,299 women full time; 34 men, 70 women part time. **Faculty:** 263 total (217 full time), 304 with doctorates or other terminal degrees. **Location:** Suburban campus in small city; 75 miles from New York City. **Calendar:** Semester, limited summer session. **Microcomputers:** 296 located in dormitories, libraries, classrooms, computer centers. **Special facilities:** Farm and agricultural experiment station, observatory, electron microscope, art gallery, nursery school, experimental theater.

DEGREES OFFERED. BA, MA. 610 bachelor's degrees awarded in 1992. 6% in area and ethnic studies, 7% languages, 17% letters/literature, 5% life sciences, 11% multi/interdisciplinary studies, 6% philosophy, religion, theology, 8% psychology, 25% social sciences, 10% visual and performing arts. Graduate degrees offered in 6 major fields of study.

UNDERGRADUATE MAJORS. African studies, Afro-American (black) studies, American studies, anthropology, art history, Asian studies, astronomy, biochemistry, biology, chemistry, classics, computer and information sciences, computer mathematics, dramatic arts, economics, English, French, geography, geology, German, Greek (classical), history, international relations, international studies, Italian, Latin, Latin American studies, mathematics, medieval studies, music, philosophy, physics, political science and government, psychobiology, psychology, religion, Russian, sociology, Spanish, studio art, urban studies, women's studies.

ACADEMIC PROGRAMS. Accelerated program, double major, independent study, internships, student-designed major, study abroad, teacher preparation, visiting/exchange student program, cross-registration, independently designed junior year abroad programs, exchange programs with institutions in 12-college exchange as well as Fisk University, Hampton Institute, Howard University, Morehouse College, and Spelman College, 3-2 program in engineering with Dartmouth College; liberal arts/career combination in engineering. **Remedial services:** Learning center, special counselor, tutoring. **Placement/credit:** AP, CLEP General, institutional tests.

ACADEMIC REQUIREMENTS. Freshmen must earn minimum GPA of 2.0 to continue in good standing. 94% of freshmen return for sophomore year. Students must declare major by end of second year. **Graduation requirements:** 120 hours for bachelor's (39 in major). Most students required to take courses in foreign languages. **Postgraduate studies:** 9% enter law school, 5% enter medical school, 3% enter MBA programs, 13% enter other graduate study. **Additional information:** All freshmen are required to take an introductory-level college course that examines important cultures, themes and human activities in a multidisciplinary context.

FRESHMAN ADMISSIONS. Selection criteria: Academic experience most important factor, with school achievement record more important than test scores. Personal achievements, essay, and interview also considered carefully. Evidence that students have elected most demanding program available, or of special effort to overcome disadvantage given special recognition. **High school preparation:** 14 units recommended. Recommended units include English 4, foreign language 3, mathematics 3, social science 1 and science 3. Advanced and accelerated courses recommended whenever possible. 2 laboratory science recommended. **Test requirements:** SAT or ACT; score report by January 15. 3 ACH required. Score report by January 15.

1992 FRESHMAN CLASS PROFILE. 4,028 men and women applied, 1,892 accepted; 230 men enrolled, 375 women enrolled. 60% were in top tenth and 92% were in top quarter of graduating class. **Academic background:** Mid 50% of enrolled freshmen had SAT-V between 560-650, SAT-M between 580-680. 90% submitted SAT scores. **Characteristics:** 29% from in state, 99% live in college housing, 21% have minority backgrounds, 4% are foreign students. Average age is 18.

FALL-TERM APPLICATIONS. $60 fee, may be waived for applicants with need. Closing date January 15; applicants notified on or about April 7; must reply by May 1. Essay required. Interview recommended. CRDA. Deferred and early admission available. EDP-F. First choice early decision program available on a rolling system from November until January 15. Notification given within 1 month of completion of application.

STUDENT LIFE. Housing: Dormitories (women, coed); apartment, cooperative housing available. Ferry House, cooperative hall, accommodates 29 students who share common responsibility for house. **Activities:** Student government, film, magazine, radio, student newspaper, yearbook, video, choral groups, concert band, dance, drama, jazz band, music ensembles, musical theater, symphony orchestra, numerous and varied religious, political, ethnic, and social service organizations. **Additional information:** A Vassar administrator serves as Director of Religious Activities and Chaplaincy Services. Campus has limited wheelchair accessibility.

ATHLETICS. NCAA. **Intercollegiate:** Baseball M, basketball, cross-country, diving, fencing, field hockey W, lacrosse, soccer, squash, swimming, tennis, volleyball. **Intramural:** Basketball, racquetball, soccer, softball, squash, volleyball, water polo.

STUDENT SERVICES. Career counseling, employment service for undergraduates, freshman orientation, health services, on-campus day care, personal counseling, placement service for graduates, special adviser for adult students, minority adviser, services/facilities for handicapped.

ANNUAL EXPENSES. Tuition and fees: $18,456. **Room and board:** $5,750. **Books and supplies:** $600. **Other expenses:** $600.

FINANCIAL AID. 48% of freshmen, 58% of continuing students receive some form of aid. All grants, 99% of loans, 63% of jobs based on need. 260 enrolled freshmen were judged to have need, all were offered aid. **Aid applications:** Closing date January 15; applicants notified on or about April 12; must reply by May 1.

ADDRESS/TELEPHONE. Thomas A. Matos, Director of Admissions, Vassar College, Box 10, Poughkeepsie, NY 12601. (914) 437-7300. Fax: (914) 437-7187.

Villa Maria College of Buffalo
Buffalo, New York — CB code: 2962

Admissions:	73% of applicants accepted
Based on:	••• School record, test scores
	•• Interview
	• Activities, essay, recommendations, special talents
Completion:	82% of freshmen end year in good standing
	39% graduate, 45% of these enter 4-year programs

2-year private junior college, coed, affiliated with Roman Catholic Church. Founded in 1960. **Accreditation:** Regional. **Undergraduate enrollment:** 79 men, 251 women full time; 10 men, 98 women part time. **Faculty:** 48 total (18 full time), 2 with doctorates or other terminal degrees. **Location:** Suburban campus in large city; 10 miles from downtown. **Calendar:** Semester, limited summer session. **Microcomputers:** 57 located in libraries, classrooms, computer centers. **Special facilities:** Art gallery.

DEGREES OFFERED. AA, AS, AAS. 87 associate degrees awarded in 1992. 19% in architecture and environmental design, 11% business and management, 8% business/office and marketing/distribution, 6% computer sciences, 21% teacher education, 13% multi/interdisciplinary studies, 20% visual and performing arts.

UNDERGRADUATE MAJORS. Administrative assistant, business administration and management, business and management, early childhood education, elementary education, finance, fine arts, gerontology, graphic design, information sciences and systems, interior design, liberal/general studies, marketing and distribution, music, music business management, photographic technology, photography, religious education, retailing, word processing.

ACADEMIC PROGRAMS. 2-year transfer program, dual enrollment of high school students, internships, cross-registration, evening modules for adult students. **Remedial services:** Learning center, preadmission summer program, reduced course load, remedial instruction, special counselor, tutoring, reading, writing, mathematics laboratories, New York State Higher Education Opportunity Program. **Placement/credit:** AP, CLEP Subject, institutional tests; 30 credit hours maximum for associate degree.

ACADEMIC REQUIREMENTS. Freshmen must earn minimum GPA of 1.7 to continue in good standing. 58% of freshmen return for sophomore year. Students must declare major on application. **Graduation requirements:** 60 hours for associate (30 in major). Most students required to take courses in arts/fine arts, English, philosophy/religion, biological/physical sciences, social sciences. **Additional information:** Implemented Adviser Advisee Action Plan provides early identification of students encountering difficulty with scheduling, finances, academic skills, personal problems, and employment.

FRESHMAN ADMISSIONS. Selection criteria: High school academic achievement and scores demonstrated on the College Placement Test. Interview, recommendations also considered. **High school preparation:** 16 units recommended. Mathematics required for business administration and computer communication systems programs. **Test requirements:** SAT or ACT (SAT preferred). For non-traditional students, SAT or ACT scores are recommended, but not required. If scores are submitted by these applicants, SAT preferred. CGP, Nelson-Denny Reading Test, and institutional writing test required for course placement. Admission conditional, based on performance on these tests.

1992 FRESHMAN CLASS PROFILE. 233 men and women applied, 170 accepted; 24 men enrolled, 97 women enrolled. 22% had high school GPA of 3.0 or higher, 64% between 2.0 and 2.99. 3% were in top tenth and 14% were in top quarter of graduating class. **Academic background:** Mid 50% of enrolled freshmen had SAT-V between 300-430, SAT-M between 300-470. 47% submitted SAT scores. **Characteristics:** 98% from in state, 100% commute, 15% have minority backgrounds, 2% are foreign students.

FALL-TERM APPLICATIONS. $25 fee, may be waived for applicants with need. Closing date August 20; applicants notified on a rolling basis beginning on or about September 15; must reply by June 1 or within 3 weeks if notified thereafter. Interview recommended. Audition recommended for music applicants. Portfolio recommended for fine arts, graphic design, interior design, photography applicants. CRDA. Deferred admission available.

STUDENT LIFE. Activities: Student government, magazine, radio, student newspaper, choral groups, drama, jazz band, music ensembles, 18 organizations associated with programs and services.

ATHLETICS. NJCAA. **Intercollegiate:** Basketball M, volleyball W. **Intramural:** Bowling, soccer.

STUDENT SERVICES. Career counseling, employment service for undergraduates, freshman orientation, health services, on-campus day care, personal counseling, placement service for graduates, veterans counselor, support group for adult students, services/facilities for handicapped.

ANNUAL EXPENSES. Tuition and fees (projected): $5,830. **Books and supplies:** $400. **Other expenses:** $650.

FINANCIAL AID. 65% of freshmen, 70% of continuing students receive some form of aid. 89% of grants, 92% of loans, all jobs based on need. Academic, music/drama, art, athletic scholarships available. **Aid applications:** No closing date; priority given to applications received by May 1; applicants notified on a rolling basis beginning on or about April 1; must reply within 2 weeks.

ADDRESS/TELEPHONE. Gayle M Wiegand, Director of Enrollment Management, Villa Maria College of Buffalo, 240 Pine Ridge Road, Buffalo, NY 14225-3999. (716) 896-0704. Fax: (716) 896-0705.

Wadhams Hall Seminary-College
Ogdensburg, New York — CB code: 2965

4-year private liberal arts, seminary college, coed, affiliated with Roman Catholic Church. Founded in 1924. **Accreditation:** Regional. **Undergraduate enrollment:** 26 men, 3 women full time; 13 men, 16 women part time. **Fac-**

ulty: 18 total (10 full time), 5 with doctorates or other terminal degrees. **Location:** Rural campus in large town; 60 miles from Ottawa, Canada. **Calendar:** Semester. **Microcomputers:** 7 located in computer centers.

DEGREES OFFERED. BA. 3 bachelor's degrees awarded in 1992. 100% in philosophy, religion, theology.

UNDERGRADUATE MAJORS. Philosophy, religion.

ACADEMIC PROGRAMS. Double major, pretheology program for students with undergraduate degree but not philosophy credits and formation experience, Christian Leadership Program for students pursuing diaconate and others involved in Church leadership ministries. **Remedial services:** Reduced course load, remedial instruction, special counselor, tutoring. **Placement/credit:** AP, CLEP General and Subject, institutional tests; 30 credit hours maximum for bachelor's degree.

ACADEMIC REQUIREMENTS. Freshmen must earn minimum GPA of 2.0 to continue in good standing. 95% of freshmen return for sophomore year. Students must declare major on application. **Graduation requirements:** 125 hours for bachelor's (27 in major). Most students required to take courses in arts/fine arts, English, foreign languages, history, humanities, mathematics, philosophy/religion, biological/physical sciences, social sciences.

FRESHMAN ADMISSIONS. Selection criteria: 2.0 GPA, recommendations, desire to study for Roman Catholic priesthood, diaconate, or other Christian leadership ministry. On-campus personal interview very important. **High school preparation:** 18 units required. Required units include English 4, foreign language 2 and social science 3. 3 units mathematics/science also required. One Latin and 1 typing recommended. **Test requirements:** SAT or ACT (SAT preferred); score report by August 1.

1992 FRESHMAN CLASS PROFILE. 8 men applied, 8 accepted, 6 enrolled. 80% had high school GPA of 3.0 or higher, 20% between 2.0 and 2.99. 70% were in top tenth and 100% were in top quarter of graduating class. **Characteristics:** 50% from in state, 100% live in college housing, 16% have minority backgrounds, 30% are foreign students. Average age is 23.

FALL-TERM APPLICATIONS. $15 fee. Closing date August 15; priority given to applications received by May 15; applicants notified on a rolling basis; must reply by May 1 or within 4 weeks if notified thereafter. Interview required. Essay required. CRDA.

STUDENT LIFE. Housing: Dormitories (men). All priesthood candidates required to live in college housing as part of community formation experience. **Activities:** Student government, magazine, student newspaper, choral groups, drama, music ensembles, community service program. **Additional information:** Religious observance required.

ATHLETICS. Intramural: Baseball M, basketball, cross-country, handball, racquetball, skiing, softball, table tennis, volleyball.

STUDENT SERVICES. Career counseling, freshman orientation, health services, personal counseling, services/facilities for handicapped.

ANNUAL EXPENSES. Tuition and fees: $3,800. **Room and board:** $3,800. **Books and supplies:** $1,000. **Other expenses:** $700.

FINANCIAL AID. 100% of freshmen, 89% of continuing students receive some form of aid. 92% of grants, all loans, all jobs based on need. 6 enrolled freshmen were judged to have need, all were offered aid. Academic scholarships available. **Aid applications:** No closing date; priority given to applications received by August 1; applicants notified on a rolling basis beginning on or about August 29; must reply within 2 weeks.

ADDRESS/TELEPHONE. Rev. Donald Robinson, Director of Admissions, Wadhams Hall Seminary-College, RR 4, Box 80, Ogdensburg, NY 13669-9308. (315) 393-4231.

Wagner College
Staten Island, New York

CB code: 2966

Admissions: 74% of applicants accepted
Based on: ••• School record, test scores
•• Essay, interview, recommendations, special talents
• Activities
Completion: 86% of freshmen end year in good standing
65% graduate, 20% of these enter graduate study

4-year private liberal arts college, coed, historic association with Lutheran Church. Founded in 1883. **Accreditation:** Regional. **Undergraduate enrollment:** 525 men, 599 women full time; 40 men, 84 women part time. **Graduate enrollment:** 47 men, 55 women full time; 36 men, 115 women part time. **Faculty:** 151 total (66 full time), 132 with doctorates or other terminal degrees. **Location:** Suburban campus in very large city; 10 miles from midtown Manhattan. **Calendar:** Semester, limited summer session. **Microcomputers:** 140 located in libraries, classrooms, computer centers. **Special facilities:** Planetarium, art gallery, electron microscopes.

DEGREES OFFERED. BA, BS, MS, MBA. 262 bachelor's degrees awarded in 1992. 22% in business and management, 13% education, 16% health sciences, 5% letters/literature, 11% life sciences, 5% psychology, 8% social sciences, 14% visual and performing arts. Graduate degrees offered in 7 major fields of study.

UNDERGRADUATE MAJORS. Accounting, anthropology, arts management, biology, business administration and management, business and management, business economics, chemistry, clinical laboratory science, computer and information sciences, early childhood education, economics, education, elementary education, English, English literature, fine arts, foreign languages (multiple emphasis), French, German, gerontology, history, humanities, junior high education, marketing research, mathematics, medical laboratory technologies, microbiology, music, music education, music performance, music theory and composition, musical theater, nursing, philosophy, physician's assistant, physics, political science and government, predentistry, preengineering, prelaw, premedicine, prepharmacy, preveterinary, psychology, public administration, public health laboratory science, religion, secondary education, social work, sociology, Spanish, special education.

ACADEMIC PROGRAMS. Double major, honors program, independent study, internships, study abroad, visiting/exchange student program. **Remedial services:** Reduced course load, special counselor, tutoring. **ROTC:** Air Force, Army. **Placement/credit:** AP, CLEP General and Subject, IB, institutional tests; 32 credit hours maximum for bachelor's degree.

ACADEMIC REQUIREMENTS. Freshmen must earn minimum GPA of 2.0 to continue in good standing. 82% of freshmen return for sophomore year. Students must declare major by end of second year. **Graduation requirements:** 128 hours for bachelor's (55 in major). Most students required to take courses in arts/fine arts, English, foreign languages, history, mathematics, philosophy/religion, biological/physical sciences, social sciences. **Postgraduate studies:** 2% enter law school, 3% enter medical school, 10% enter MBA programs, 5% enter other graduate study.

FRESHMAN ADMISSIONS. Selection criteria: School achievement, test scores, recommendations, interview, special talents all considered. **High school preparation:** 16 units required; 19 recommended. Required and recommended units include English 4, foreign language 2-2, mathematics 2-3, social science 2-3 and science 2-3. 4 economics, arts, computers, or other elective areas of study required. **Test requirements:** SAT or ACT (SAT preferred); score report by August 1. Will accept PAA and 3 ACH in lieu of SAT for applicants from Puerto Rico.

1992 FRESHMAN CLASS PROFILE. 678 men applied, 431 accepted, 158 enrolled; 596 women applied, 510 accepted, 157 enrolled. 32% had high school GPA of 3.0 or higher, 65% between 2.0 and 2.99. **Academic background:** Mid 50% of enrolled freshmen had SAT-V between 430-540, SAT-M between 450-560. 92% submitted SAT scores. **Characteristics:** 68% from in state, 60% live in college housing, 6% have minority backgrounds, 4% are foreign students. Average age is 18.

FALL-TERM APPLICATIONS. $35 fee, may be waived for applicants with need. No closing date; priority given to applications received by March 15; applicants notified on a rolling basis; must reply by May 1 or within 2 weeks if notified thereafter. Audition required for music, theater applicants. Interview recommended. Portfolio recommended for art applicants. Essay recommended. CRDA. Deferred and early admission available. EDP-F.

STUDENT LIFE. Housing: Dormitories (coed); fraternity, sorority housing available. **Activities:** Student government, magazine, student newspaper, yearbook, choral groups, concert band, dance, drama, jazz band, music ensembles, musical theater, pep band, symphony orchestra, fraternities, sororities, Lutheran Student Club, Newman Society, Hillel, national honor societies. **Additional information:** Shuttle bus service links college with cultural and professional resources of NYC.

ATHLETICS. NCAA. **Intercollegiate:** Baseball M, basketball, football M, golf M, ice hockey M, lacrosse M, soccer W, softball W, tennis, track and field, volleyball W, wrestling M. **Intramural:** Basketball M, football M, golf, handball, racquetball, rugby M, soccer, softball, squash, volleyball, wrestling M.

STUDENT SERVICES. Aptitude testing, career counseling, employment service for undergraduates, freshman orientation, health services, personal counseling, placement service for graduates, services/facilities for handicapped.

ANNUAL EXPENSES. Tuition and fees (1992-93): $11,250. **Room and board:** $5,000. **Books and supplies:** $580. **Other expenses:** $1,080.

FINANCIAL AID. 70% of freshmen, 70% of continuing students receive some form of aid. 82% of grants, all loans based on need. 214 enrolled freshmen were judged to have need, all were offered aid. Academic, music/drama, athletic scholarships available. **Aid applications:** Closing date May 1; priority given to applications received by April 1; applicants notified on a rolling basis beginning on or about March 1; must reply by May 1 or within 4 weeks if notified thereafter.

ADDRESS/TELEPHONE. Marc M. Davis, Dean of Admissions and Financial Aid, Wagner College, 631 Howard Avenue, Staten Island, NY 10301-4495. (718) 390-3411. (800) 221-1010. Fax: (718) 390-3467.

Webb Institute of Naval Architecture
Glen Cove, New York CB code: 2970

Admissions: 33% of applicants accepted
Based on: ••• Interview, school record, test scores
•• Activities, recommendations
• Special talents
Completion: 90% of freshmen end year in good standing
75% graduate, 23% of these enter graduate study

4-year private college of naval architecture and marine engineering, coed. Founded in 1889. **Accreditation:** Regional. **Undergraduate enrollment:** 65 men, 16 women full time. **Faculty:** 15 total (9 full time), 7 with doctorates or other terminal degrees. **Location:** Suburban campus in large town; 30 miles from New York City. **Calendar:** Semester. **Microcomputers:** 22 located in classrooms, computer centers. **Special facilities:** Adjoining nature preserve, model testing tank. **Additional facts:** All students participate in 2-month paid winter work program in marine industry each year.

DEGREES OFFERED. BS. 16 bachelor's degrees awarded in 1992. 100% in engineering.

UNDERGRADUATE MAJORS. Naval architecture and marine engineering.

ACADEMIC PROGRAMS. Double major, internships.

ACADEMIC REQUIREMENTS. Freshmen must earn minimum GPA of 2.0 to continue in good standing. 90% of freshmen return for sophomore year. Students must declare major on application. **Graduation requirements:** 147 hours for bachelor's. **Additional information:** Intensive single curriculum program demands high career motivation.

FRESHMAN ADMISSIONS. Selection criteria: High school record, class rank, test scores, and interview most important. Character, motivation, and outside activities considered. **High school preparation:** 16 units required. Required units include English 4, mathematics 4, physical science 2 and social science 2. **Test requirements:** SAT; score report by March 1. 3 ACH required (including English Composition, Mathematics Level I or II, and Chemistry or Physics). Score report by March 1.

1992 FRESHMAN CLASS PROFILE. 77 men applied, 24 accepted, 19 enrolled; 11 women applied, 5 accepted, 4 enrolled. 100% had high school GPA of 3.0 or higher. 83% were in top tenth and 100% were in top quarter of graduating class. **Academic background:** Mid 50% of enrolled freshmen had SAT-V between 570-640, SAT-M between 680-740. 100% submitted SAT scores. **Characteristics:** 26% from in state, 100% live in college housing, 1% have minority backgrounds. Average age is 18.

FALL-TERM APPLICATIONS. $20 fee, may be waived for applicants with need. Closing date February 15; applicants notified on a rolling basis beginning on or about March 5; must reply by April 30. Interview required. EDP-F.

STUDENT LIFE. Housing: Dormitories (men, women). **Activities:** Student government, magazine, yearbook. **Additional information:** Honor code allows students 24-hour access to all facilities. Free membership available to local YMCA.

ATHLETICS. Intercollegiate: Basketball, soccer, tennis. **Intramural:** Basketball, soccer, softball, volleyball. **Clubs:** Intercollegiate sailing.

STUDENT SERVICES. Career counseling, employment service for undergraduates, freshman orientation, health services, personal counseling, placement service for graduates.

ANNUAL EXPENSES. Tuition and fees (1992-93): $0. All students admitted receive 4-year, full-tuition scholarships. **Room and board:** $4,800. **Books and supplies:** $600. **Other expenses:** $500.

FINANCIAL AID. 36% of freshmen, 18% of continuing students receive some form of aid. 19% of grants, all loans based on need. 1 enrolled freshman was judged to have need, all were offered aid. Academic, leadership scholarships available. **Aid applications:** Closing date July 1; applicants notified on or about August 1; must reply within 1 week.

ADDRESS/TELEPHONE. William G. Murray, Director of Admissions, Webb Institute of Naval Architecture, Crescent Beach Road, Glen Cove, NY 11542. (516) 671-2213. Fax: (516) 674-9838.

Wells College
Aurora, New York CB code: 2971

Admissions: 90% of applicants accepted
Based on: ••• Recommendations, school record
•• Activities, essay, interview, test scores
• Special talents
Completion: 98% of freshmen end year in good standing
65% graduate, 57% of these enter graduate study

4-year private liberal arts college, women only. Founded in 1868. **Accreditation:** Regional. **Undergraduate enrollment:** 360 women full time; 12 women part time. **Faculty:** 60 total (48 full time), 56 with doctorates or other terminal degrees. **Location:** Rural campus in rural community; 25 miles from Ithaca, 40 miles from Syracuse. **Calendar:** Semester. **Microcomputers:** 50 located in dormitories, classrooms, computer centers. **Special facilities:** String Room Art Gallery, golf course. **Additional facts:** Access to Cayuga Lake offers opportunity for special studies in biology and ecology based on actual observation. Students are provided with leadership transcript showing all cocurricular involvement and achievement.

DEGREES OFFERED. BA. 97 bachelor's degrees awarded in 1992. 11% in languages, 10% letters/literature, 7% life sciences, 6% multi/interdisciplinary studies, 10% psychology, 31% social sciences, 11% visual and performing arts.

UNDERGRADUATE MAJORS. American studies, art history, arts and performance, biology, chemistry, comparative literature, creative writing, economics, economics and management, economics and management, English, environmental policy, science and values, foreign languages (multiple emphasis), foreign languages, literatures and cultures, French, German, history, international studies, mathematics, mathematics, computer science and physics, philosophy, predentistry, preengineering, premedicine, preveterinary, psychology, public affairs, religion, religious studies and human values, sociology, Spanish, studio art, visual and performing arts, women's studies.

ACADEMIC PROGRAMS. Accelerated program, double major, dual enrollment of high school students, independent study, internships, student-designed major, study abroad, teacher preparation, visiting/exchange student program, Washington semester, cross-registration, 3+2 program in engineering with Clarkson University, Columbia University, Texas A&M University, and Washington University in St. Louis, combined bachelor's/graduate degree program in business administration with University of Rochester, study abroad and exchange programs in 13 locations including England, France, Spain, Italy, Germany, and Denmark. **Remedial services:** Reduced course load, tutoring. **Placement/credit:** AP, IB, institutional tests; 6 credit hours maximum for bachelor's degree.

ACADEMIC REQUIREMENTS. No policy requiring minimum GPA; records of students having academic difficulty are reviewed individually. 75% of freshmen return for sophomore year. Students must declare major by end of second year. **Graduation requirements:** 120 hours for bachelor's (33 in major). Most students required to take courses in arts/fine arts, computer science, English, foreign languages, history, humanities, mathematics, philosophy/religion, biological/physical sciences, social sciences. **Postgraduate studies:** 6% enter law school, 5% enter medical school, 1% enter MBA programs, 45% enter other graduate study. **Additional information:** Corporate affiliates program includes investment strategies course in which students manage actual portfolio, guest lecturers from major corporations, and month-long internship with member corporation.

FRESHMAN ADMISSIONS. Selection criteria: School achievement record most important. Test scores, school and community activities, recommendations also important. Interview strongly recommended. College looks for evidence of leadership ability and potential through academic and cocurricular involvement. **High school preparation:** 16 units required. Recommended units include biological science 1, English 4, foreign language 3, mathematics 3, social science 4 and science 3. **Test requirements:** SAT or ACT; score report by February 15.

1992 FRESHMAN CLASS PROFILE. 267 women applied, 240 accepted, 89 enrolled. 66% had high school GPA of 3.0 or higher, 34% between 2.0 and 2.99. 30% were in top tenth and 74% were in top quarter of graduating class. **Academic background:** Mid 50% of enrolled freshmen had SAT-V between 490-590, SAT-M between 490-580; ACT composite between 24-28. 85% submitted SAT scores, 27% submitted ACT scores. **Characteristics:** 67% from in state, 100% live in college housing, 17% have minority backgrounds. Average age is 18.

FALL-TERM APPLICATIONS. $25 fee, may be waived for applicants with need. Closing date March 1; priority given to applications received by February 1; applicants notified on or about April 1; must reply by May 1. Essay required. Interview recommended. CRDA. Deferred and early admission available. EDP-F. January 15 deadline for Wells early action plan, providing for immediate decision on application.

STUDENT LIFE. Housing: Dormitories (women). Facilities range from renovated 19th century home of Henry Wells to Modern dormitories. **Activities:** Student government, magazine, student newspaper, yearbook, choral groups, dance, drama, music ensembles, musical theater, social action clubs, Current Affairs Forum, Model United Nations, Minority Women's Association. **Additional information:** Honor Code governing academic and cocurricular life allows students 24-hour access to academic buildings, classrooms, and laboratories.

ATHLETICS. NCAA. **Intercollegiate:** Diving, field hockey, lacrosse, soccer, swimming, tennis. **Intramural:** Basketball, bowling, fencing, golf, horseback riding, sailing, skiing, soccer, softball, table tennis, volleyball.

STUDENT SERVICES. Aptitude testing, career counseling, employment service for undergraduates, freshman orientation, health services, personal counseling, placement service for graduates, special adviser for adult students, women's resource center.

ANNUAL EXPENSES. Tuition and fees: $14,160. **Room and board:** $5,300. **Books and supplies:** $600. **Other expenses:** $500.

FINANCIAL AID. 90% of freshmen, 84% of continuing students receive some form of aid. 95% of grants, 96% of loans, all jobs based on need. 83 enrolled freshmen were judged to have need, all were offered aid. Academic, leadership scholarships available. **Aid applications:** No closing date; priority given to applications received by February 15; applicants notified on a rolling basis beginning on or about March 1; must reply by May 1 or within 4 weeks if notified thereafter. **Additional information:** Independent loan programs for parents. College participates in Tuition Exchange.

ADDRESS/TELEPHONE. Mary Ann Kalbaugh, Dean of Admissions, Wells College, Route 90, Aurora, NY 13026. (315) 364-3264. (800) 952-9355. Fax: (315) 364-3227.

Westchester Business Institute
White Plains, New York CB code: 1023

2-year proprietary business college, coed. Founded in 1915. **Undergraduate enrollment:** 346 men, 753 women full time; 30 men, 60 women part time. **Faculty:** 55 total (34 full time), 2 with doctorates or other terminal degrees. **Location:** Suburban campus in small city; 30 miles from New York City. **Calendar:** Quarter, extensive summer session. Saturday and extensive evening/early morning classes. **Microcomputers:** 90 located in libraries, classrooms, computer centers. **Additional facts:** Evening and weekend college program also available on semester calendar.

DEGREES OFFERED. 320 associate degrees awarded in 1992.

UNDERGRADUATE MAJORS. Accounting, business administration and management, business and office, business data processing and related programs, business data programming, computer programming, data processing, investments and securities, legal secretary, management information systems, marketing and distribution, medical secretary, microcomputer software, office supervision and management, secretarial and related programs, small business management and ownership, systems analysis, tourism.

ACADEMIC PROGRAMS. Accelerated program, cooperative education, double major, internships, weekend college. **Remedial services:** Remedial instruction, special counselor, tutoring. **Placement/credit:** AP, CLEP General and Subject, institutional tests; 51 credit hours maximum for associate degree.

ACADEMIC REQUIREMENTS. Freshmen must earn minimum GPA of 2.0 to continue in good standing. 70% of freshmen return for sophomore year. Students must declare major on enrollment. **Graduation requirements:** Most students required to take courses in computer science, English, mathematics. **Additional information:** 102 credit hours required for graduation in day (quarterly) program, 66 in evening (semester) program.

FRESHMAN ADMISSIONS. Selection criteria: High school record, interview, and recommendations most important. Activities considered. Test scores considered when available. Institution administered entrance examinations used for both admissions and academic placement.

1992 FRESHMAN CLASS PROFILE. 366 men and women enrolled. **Characteristics:** 95% from in state, 100% commute, 49% have minority backgrounds. Average age is 18.

FALL-TERM APPLICATIONS. $25 fee, may be waived for applicants with need. No closing date; applicants notified on a rolling basis; must reply within 2 weeks. Interview required. EDP-F.

STUDENT LIFE. Activities: Student government, student newspaper, accounting society, secretarial club, management and marketing club, data processing club.

STUDENT SERVICES. Aptitude testing, career counseling, employment service for undergraduates, freshman orientation, personal counseling, placement service for graduates, special adviser for adult students, services/facilities for handicapped.

ANNUAL EXPENSES. Tuition and fees: $9,405. **Books and supplies:** $600. **Other expenses:** $1,281.

FINANCIAL AID. 91% of freshmen, 90% of continuing students receive some form of aid. Grants, loans, jobs available. Academic, alumni affiliation scholarships available. **Aid applications:** No closing date; applicants notified on a rolling basis beginning on or about February 1.

ADDRESS/TELEPHONE. Dale T. Smith, Dean of Admissions, The Westchester Business Institute, PO Box 710, White Plains, NY 10602. (914) 948-4442.

Westchester Community College
Valhalla, New York CB code: 2972

2-year public community college, coed. Founded in 1946. **Accreditation:** Regional. **Undergraduate enrollment:** 2,420 men, 2,390 women full time; 2,723 men, 4,254 women part time. **Faculty:** 725 total (225 full time), 50 with doctorates or other terminal degrees. **Location:** Suburban campus in large town; 30 miles from New York City, 3 miles from White Plains. **Calendar:** Semester, extensive summer session. **Microcomputers:** Located in libraries, classrooms, computer centers. **Special facilities:** Art gallery, computer-assisted drafting laboratory. **Additional facts:** SUNY institution.

DEGREES OFFERED. AA, AS, AAS. 833 associate degrees awarded in 1992. 33% in business and management, 7% engineering technologies, 5% health sciences, 9% allied health, 8% multi/interdisciplinary studies, 13% social sciences, 5% visual and performing arts.

UNDERGRADUATE MAJORS. Accounting, air pollution control technology, automotive technology, business administration and management, business and office, business data processing and related programs, chemical technology, chemistry, civil technology, communications, computer and information sciences, criminal justice studies, dance, dramatic arts, electrical technology, electromechanical technology, engineering, engineering and engineering-related technologies, engineering and other disciplines, engineering science, finance, fine arts, fire protection, food management, food production/management/services, food science and nutrition, forestry and related sciences, hotel/motel and restaurant management, humanities and social sciences, information sciences and systems, insurance and risk management, insurance marketing, law enforcement and corrections technologies, legal secretary, liberal/general studies, marketing and distribution, marketing management, mathematics, mechanical technoloy, medical laboratory technologies, mental health/human services, music, nursing, radiograph medical technology, real estate, respiratory therapy technology, retailing, secretarial and related programs, social sciences, tourism, transportation and travel marketing, visual and performing arts, word processing.

ACADEMIC PROGRAMS. 2-year transfer program, double major, honors program, internships, study abroad, telecourses. **Remedial services:** Learning center, reduced course load, remedial instruction, special counselor, tutoring. **Placement/credit:** AP, CLEP General and Subject, institutional tests; 32 credit hours maximum for associate degree.

ACADEMIC REQUIREMENTS. Freshmen must earn minimum GPA of 1.5 to continue in good standing. 20% of freshmen return for sophomore year. Students must declare major on application. **Graduation requirements:** 64 hours for associate (32 in major). Most students required to take courses in arts/fine arts, English, humanities, mathematics, biological/physical sciences, social sciences.

FRESHMAN ADMISSIONS. Selection criteria: Open admissions. Specific courses required for some programs.

1992 FRESHMAN CLASS PROFILE. 1,428 men, 1,737 women enrolled. **Characteristics:** 98% from in state, 100% commute, 30% have minority backgrounds, 1% are foreign students. Average age is 26.

FALL-TERM APPLICATIONS. $15 fee, may be waived for applicants with need. No closing date; priority given to applications received by September 12; applicants notified on a rolling basis. Deferred and early admission available. March 1 closing date for nursing applications.

STUDENT LIFE. Activities: Student government, magazine, radio, student newspaper, television, choral groups, dance, drama, music ensembles, musical theater, arts festival, Hillel, Newman Club, black, international, Spanish-American, and Middle Eastern student organizations, French and Italian language clubs, human services, communications clubs.

ATHLETICS. NJCAA. **Intercollegiate:** Baseball M, basketball, golf M, soccer M, softball W, tennis W, volleyball W. **Intramural:** Archery, badminton, basketball, boxing M, fencing, field hockey W, golf M, gymnastics W, softball, swimming, tennis, volleyball.

STUDENT SERVICES. Career counseling, employment service for undergraduates, freshman orientation, health services, on-campus day care, personal counseling, placement service for graduates, special adviser for adult students, veterans counselor, services/facilities for handicapped.

ANNUAL EXPENSES. Tuition and fees (projected): $2,168, $2,925 additional for out-of-state students. **Books and supplies:** $600. **Other expenses:** $500.

FINANCIAL AID. 30% of continuing students receive some form of aid. 97% of grants, 83% of loans, 45% of jobs based on need. Academic, music/drama, art, state/district residency scholarships available. **Aid applications:** No closing date; applicants notified on a rolling basis beginning on or about July 1; must reply within 2 weeks.

ADDRESS/TELEPHONE. Dr. Alan Seidman, Director of Admissions, Westchester Community College, 75 Grasslands Road, Valhalla, NY 10595-1698. (914) 285-6735. Fax: (914) 285-6540.

William Smith College
Geneva, New York CB code: 2978

Admissions: 78% of applicants accepted
Based on: ••• Activities, school record
•• Essay, recommendations, test scores
• Interview, special talents
Completion: 95% of freshmen end year in good standing
84% graduate, 26% of these enter graduate study

4-year private liberal arts college, women only. Founded in 1906. **Accreditation:** Regional. **Undergraduate enrollment:** 878 women full time. **Faculty:** 154 total (141 full time), 148 with doctorates or other terminal degrees. **Location:** Rural campus in large town; 40 miles from Rochester, 50 miles from Syracuse and Ithaca. **Calendar:** Trimester. **Microcomputers:** 180 located in libraries, classrooms, computer centers, campus-wide network. **Special facilities:** 70-foot research vessel, 100-acre nature preserve, art gallery. **Additional facts:** Coordinate institution with Hobart College. All classes coeducational. All facilities and faculty shared.

DEGREES OFFERED. BA, BS. 236 bachelor's degrees awarded in 1992. 6% in languages, 28% letters/literature, 5% life sciences, 13% multi/interdisciplinary studies, 10% psychology, 23% social sciences, 6% visual and performing arts.

UNDERGRADUATE MAJORS. Afro-American (black) studies, American studies, anthropology, architectural studies, art history, Asian studies, biology, chemistry, Chinese, classics, comparative literature, computer and information sciences, dance, dramatic arts, economics, English, environmental science, foreign languages (multiple emphasis), French, geoscience, German, Greek (classical), history, Japanese, Latin, mathematics, music, philosophy, physics, political science and government, psychology, religion, Russian, Russian and Slavic studies, sociology, Spanish, studio art, third world studies, urban studies, women's studies.

ACADEMIC PROGRAMS. Accelerated program, double major, honors program, independent study, internships, semester at sea, student-designed major, study abroad, teacher preparation, visiting/exchange student program, New York semester, United Nations semester, Washington semester, cross-registration, Urban Semester, architecture and urban studies program in New York City, Intercollegiate Sri Lanka Educational Program, New York Visiting Students Program, combined degree program in architecture with Washington University (MO), and in engineering with Dartmouth College (NH), Rensselaer Polytechnic Institute, and Rochester Institute of Technology, combined bachelor's/graduate degree program in business administration with Clarkson University, study abroad programs in China and India. **Remedial services:** Learning center, preadmission summer program, reduced course load, special counselor, tutoring, New York State Higher Education Opportunity Program. **Placement/credit:** AP, IB. Credit by examination counted toward degree limited to equivalent of 7 courses.

ACADEMIC REQUIREMENTS. Freshmen must earn minimum GPA of 2.0 to continue in good standing. 90% of freshmen return for sophomore year. Students must declare major by end of second year. **Graduation requirements:** Most students required to take courses in arts/fine arts, humanities, biological/physical sciences, social sciences. **Postgraduate studies:** 4% enter law school, 3% enter medical school, 4% enter MBA programs, 15% enter other graduate study. **Additional information:** First-year seminar and sophomore bidisciplinary course required as part of general curriculum. Total of 36 courses required for graduation.

FRESHMAN ADMISSIONS. Selection criteria: Secondary school record, school and community activities, and test scores important. Recommendations, interview, and talent considered. Economically and educationally disadvantaged New York State students may apply through HEOP (Higher Education Opportunity Program). **High school preparation:** 18 units required. Required and recommended units include English 4, foreign language 2-3, mathematics 3, social science 2-3 and science 2. 2 history and 1 laboratory science also required. Mathematics must include algebra, geometry, trigonometry sequence. **Test requirements:** SAT or ACT; score report by March 1. Will review ACH test if submitted.

1992 FRESHMAN CLASS PROFILE. 1,258 women applied, 978 accepted, 263 enrolled. **Academic background:** Mid 50% of enrolled freshmen had SAT-V between 500-580, SAT-M between 500-600; ACT composite between 24-27. 94% submitted SAT scores, 6% submitted ACT scores. **Characteristics:** 50% from in state, 100% live in college housing, 14% have minority backgrounds, 5% are foreign students. Average age is 18.

FALL-TERM APPLICATIONS. $40 fee, may be waived for applicants with need. Closing date February 15; applicants notified on or about April 1; must reply by May 1. Essay required. Interview recommended. CRDA. Deferred and early admission available. EDP-F. Early decision plan available. Application deadlines: November 15 and January 1. Notification within 30 days, must reply within 2 weeks.

STUDENT LIFE. Housing: Dormitories (women, coed); cooperative housing available. Theme residences available. Coed dorms available with Hobart College. **Activities:** Student government, film, radio, student newspaper, yearbook, choral groups, concert band, dance, drama, jazz band, music ensembles, musical theater, symphony orchestra, Service Network, denominational clubs, political education network, women's resource center, African-American Student Coalition, Latin American Organization, international students club, Big Brother/Big Sister, Pan African Latin Organization, William Smith Congress, Gay, Lesbian, Bisexual, and Friends Network. **Additional information:** Undergraduates not residing in college housing live in their own apartments off campus.

ATHLETICS. NCAA. **Intercollegiate:** Basketball, diving, field hockey, lacrosse, rowing (crew), skiing, soccer, swimming, tennis. **Intramural:** Archery, badminton, basketball, bowling, cross-country, fencing, golf, horseback riding, ice hockey, lacrosse, racquetball, rugby, sailing, skiing, skin diving, softball, squash, swimming, tennis, volleyball. **Clubs:** Sailing.

STUDENT SERVICES. Career counseling, employment service for undergraduates, freshman orientation, health services, personal counseling, placement service for graduates, special adviser for adult students, services/facilities for handicapped.

ANNUAL EXPENSES. Tuition and fees: $18,309. **Room and board:** $5,610. **Books and supplies:** $650. **Other expenses:** $600.

FINANCIAL AID. 67% of freshmen, 53% of continuing students receive some form of aid. 97% of grants, 98% of loans, all jobs based on need. 130 enrolled freshmen were judged to have need, 125 were offered aid. Academic scholarships available. **Aid applications:** Closing date February 15; applicants notified on or about April 1; must reply by May 1.

ADDRESS/TELEPHONE. Mara O'Laughlin, Director of Admissions, William Smith College, Geneva, NY 14456-3381. (315) 781-3472. (800) 245-0100. Fax: (315) 781-3471.

Wood Tobe-Coburn School
New York, New York — CB code: 3258

Admissions:	93% of applicants accepted
Based on:	••• School record
	•• Interview
	• Activities, recommendations
Completion:	82% of freshmen end year in good standing
	9% enter 4-year programs

2-year proprietary business, secretarial, and fashion merchandising college, coed. Founded in 1879. **Undergraduate enrollment:** 476 men and women. **Faculty:** 23 total (10 full time). **Location:** Urban campus in very large city. **Calendar:** Semester, extensive summer session.

DEGREES OFFERED. 135 associate degrees awarded in 1992. 100% in business/office and marketing/distribution.

UNDERGRADUATE MAJORS. Fashion design, fashion merchandising, secretarial and related programs.

ACADEMIC PROGRAMS. Cooperative education, internships. **Remedial services:** Remedial instruction, special counselor, tutoring. **Placement/credit:** CLEP Subject, institutional tests.

ACADEMIC REQUIREMENTS. Freshmen must earn minimum GPA of 2.0 to continue in good standing. Students must declare major on application. **Graduation requirements:** 60 hours for associate. Most students required to take courses in computer science, English, history, mathematics. **Additional information:** 16-month accelerated program available for fashion students, and 9 weeks of supervised on-the-job training each year.

FRESHMAN ADMISSIONS. Selection criteria: High school transcript necessary, personal interview required.

1992 FRESHMAN CLASS PROFILE. 1 man applied, 1 accepted, 1 enrolled; 845 women applied, 787 accepted, 312 enrolled. **Characteristics:** 97% from in state, 100% commute, 75% have minority backgrounds. Average age is 18.

FALL-TERM APPLICATIONS. $50 fee, may be waived for applicants with need. No closing date; applicants notified on a rolling basis; must reply within 8 weeks. Interview required.

STUDENT LIFE. Activities: Student government.

STUDENT SERVICES. Career counseling, employment service for undergraduates, freshman orientation, personal counseling, placement service for graduates.

ANNUAL EXPENSES. Tuition and fees (1992-93): $9,635. **Books and supplies:** $700. **Other expenses:** $2,800.

FINANCIAL AID. 86% of freshmen, 92% of continuing students receive some form of aid. 99% of grants, 80% of loans, all jobs based on need. 309 enrolled freshmen were judged to have need, all were offered aid. Academic scholarships available. **Aid applications:** No closing date; applicants notified on a rolling basis.

ADDRESS/TELEPHONE. Patricia Neimi, Director of Admissions, Wood Tobe-Coburn School, 8 East 40th Street, New York, NY 10016-0190. (212) 686-9040. (800) 344-4926. Fax: (212) 686-9171.

Yeshiva Derech Chaim
Brooklyn, New York — CB code: 0552

5-year private rabbinical college, men only, affiliated with Jewish faith. Founded in 1975. **Undergraduate enrollment:** 160 men full time. **Location:** Urban campus in very large city. **Calendar:** Semester. **Additional facts:** First and advanced Talmudic degrees available. Chaver Fellowship for more advanced scholars also available.

FRESHMAN ADMISSIONS. Selection criteria: Dean interviews each applicant. Recommendations very important.

ADDRESS/TELEPHONE. Rabbi Rennart, Menahel, Yeshiva Derech Chaim, 1573 39th Street, Brooklyn, NY 11218. (718) 438-3070.

Yeshiva Gedolah Zichron Moshe
South Fallsburg, New York — CB code: 0750

4-year private Talmudic seminary, men only, affiliated with Jewish faith. Founded in 1969. **Undergraduate enrollment:** 83 men full time. **Graduate enrollment:** 16 men full time; 5 men part time. **Location:** Rural campus in small town. **Calendar:** Semester. **Additional facts:** First Talmudic degree and ordination available.

FRESHMAN ADMISSIONS. Selection criteria: Institutional examination.

ADDRESS/TELEPHONE. Rabbi A. Gorelick, Dean of Admissions, Yeshiva Gedolah Zichron Moshe, PO Box 580, Laurel Park Road, South Fallsburg, NY 12779. (914) 434-5240. Fax: (914) 434-1009.

Yeshiva Karlin Stolin Beth Aron Y'Israel Rabbinical Institute
Brooklyn, New York CB code: 1582

5-year private rabbinical college, men only, affiliated with Jewish faith. Founded in 1948. **Undergraduate enrollment:** 60 men full time. **Graduate enrollment:** 20 men full time. **Location:** Urban campus in very large city. **Calendar:** Semester. **Additional facts:** Ordination available.

FRESHMAN ADMISSIONS. Selection criteria: Interview, institutional entrance examination, and recommendations considered.

ADDRESS/TELEPHONE. Dean of Men, Yeshiva Karlin Stolin Beth Aron Y'Israel Rab Inst, 1818 54th Street, Brooklyn, NY 11204-9961. (718) 232-7800. Fax: (718) 331-4833.

Yeshiva of Nitra Rabbinical College
Mt. Kisco, New York CB code: 0691

5-year private rabbinical college, men only, affiliated with Jewish faith. Founded in 1946. **Undergraduate enrollment:** 110 men full time. **Location:** Suburban campus in small town. **Calendar:** Semester. **Additional facts:** Ordination available. First and second rabbinical and Talmudic degrees offered.

FRESHMAN ADMISSIONS. Selection criteria: Institutional examination, references, Yeshiva high school background considered.

ADDRESS/TELEPHONE. Rabbi Sandor Sabel, Director of Admissions, Yeshiva of Nitra Rabbinical College, 194 Division Avenue, Brooklyn, NY 11211. (718) 384-5460.

Yeshiva Shaar Hatorah
Kew Gardens, New York CB code: 0743

4-year private rabbinical college, men only, affiliated with Jewish faith. Founded in 1976. **Undergraduate enrollment:** 60 men full time. **Graduate enrollment:** 27 men full time. **Faculty:** 7 total (6 full time), 2 with doctorates or other terminal degrees. **Location:** Urban campus in very large city. **Calendar:** Semester. Saturday and extensive evening/early morning classes. **Additional facts:** Ordination and first rabbinic degree available.

DEGREES OFFERED. B. Graduate degrees offered in 1 major field of study.

UNDERGRADUATE MAJORS. Talmudic studies.

ACADEMIC PROGRAMS. Double major.

ACADEMIC REQUIREMENTS. Freshmen must earn minimum GPA of 3.0 to continue in good standing. 60% of freshmen return for sophomore year. **Graduation requirements:** Most students required to take courses in philosophy/religion. **Postgraduate studies:** 80% enter other graduate study.

FRESHMAN ADMISSIONS. Selection criteria: Religious commitment, school achievement record, recommendations, and interview most important.

1992 FRESHMAN CLASS PROFILE. 25 men enrolled. 100% had high school GPA of 3.0 or higher. 100% were in top quarter of graduating class. **Characteristics:** 100% live in college housing. Average age is 17.

FALL-TERM APPLICATIONS. $100 fee. No closing date. Interview required.

STUDENT LIFE. Housing: Dormitories (men). **Additional information:** Religious observance required.

STUDENT SERVICES. Services/facilities for handicapped.

ANNUAL EXPENSES. Tuition and fees (1992-93):

ADDRESS/TELEPHONE. Rabbi Yoel Yankelewitz, Yeshiva Shaar Hatorah, 117-06 84th Avenue, Kew Gardens, NY 11418. (718) 846-1940.

Yeshiva University
New York, New York CB code: 2990

Admissions: 83% of applicants accepted
Based on: ••• School record, test scores
•• Activities, interview
• Essay, recommendations, special talents
Completion: 95% of freshmen end year in good standing
51% graduate, 52% of these enter graduate study

4-year private university, coed. Founded in 1886. **Accreditation:** Regional. **Undergraduate enrollment:** 1,021 men, 870 women full time; 33 men, 24 women part time. **Graduate enrollment:** 1,191 men, 1,196 women full time; 213 men, 351 women part time. **Faculty:** 445 total (253 full time). **Location:** Urban campus in very large city. **Calendar:** Semester. **Microcomputers:** 150 located in libraries, classrooms, computer centers. **Special facilities:** Museum. **Additional facts:** Undergraduate men attend Washington Heights Center (Yeshiva College of Liberal Arts and Sciences or Sy Syms School of Business). Women attend Midtown Center (Stern College of Liberal Arts and Sciences or Sy Syms School of Business). Some majors open only to men or to women. All undergraduates enroll in courses in Hebrew language and literature and Jewish culture and civilization.

DEGREES OFFERED. AA, BA, BS, MA, MS, MSW, PhD, EdD, MD. 146 associate degrees awarded in 1992. 100% in area and ethnic studies. 408 bachelor's degrees awarded. 21% in business and management, 7% communications, 6% health sciences, 7% letters/literature, 6% life sciences, 5% multi/interdisciplinary studies, 8% psychology, 24% social sciences. Graduate degrees offered in 23 major fields of study.

UNDERGRADUATE MAJORS. Associate: Jewish studies. **Bachelor's:** Accounting, biological and physical sciences, biology, chemistry, computer and information sciences, economics, elementary education, engineering, English, finance, French, Greek (classical), Hebrew, history, Jewish education, Jewish studies, Latin, management information systems, marketing management, mathematics, music, philosophy, physics, political science and government, predentistry, prehealth sciences, prelaw, premedicine, psychology, sociology, speech.

ACADEMIC PROGRAMS. Double major, dual enrollment of high school students, honors program, independent study, internships, student-designed major, study abroad, teacher preparation, visiting/exchange student program, cross-registration, 5-year engineering program with Columbia University. Cooperative programs with NYU and Columbia University in occupational therapy; liberal arts/career combination in engineering, health sciences. **Remedial services:** Tutoring, writing center. **Placement/credit:** AP, CLEP Subject, institutional tests; 70 credit hours maximum for bachelor's degree.

ACADEMIC REQUIREMENTS. Freshmen must earn minimum GPA of 2.0 to continue in good standing. 80% of freshmen return for sophomore year. Students must declare major by end of second year. **Graduation requirements:** 128 hours for bachelor's (36 in major). Most students required to take courses in arts/fine arts, English, foreign languages, humanities, biological/physical sciences, social sciences. **Postgraduate studies:** 17% enter law school, 13% enter medical school, 2% enter MBA programs, 20% enter other graduate study.

FRESHMAN ADMISSIONS. Selection criteria: In order of importance, high school GPA, SAT scores, ability and motivation as indicated in interview, school and community activities, recommendations of principal and guidance counselor. **High school preparation:** 16 units required; 18 recommended. Required and recommended units include English 4, foreign language 2-3, mathematics 2-3, social science 2-4 and science 2-3. One art and/or music also recommended. **Test requirements:** SAT or ACT (SAT preferred); score report by September 1. Hebrew ACH required for applicants with 2 or more years of high school Hebrew. Score report by July 1.

1992 FRESHMAN CLASS PROFILE. 697 men applied, 573 accepted, 313 enrolled; 636 women applied, 531 accepted, 264 enrolled. 60% had high school GPA of 3.0 or higher, 35% between 2.0 and 2.99. **Academic background:** Mid 50% of enrolled freshmen had SAT-V between 470-610, SAT-M between 520-660. 98% submitted SAT scores. **Characteristics:** 57% from in state, 93% live in college housing, 5% are foreign students. Average age is 18.

FALL-TERM APPLICATIONS. $35 fee, may be waived for applicants with need. No closing date; priority given to applications received by February 1; applicants notified on a rolling basis; must reply by May 1 or within 2 weeks if notified thereafter. Interview required. Essay required. CRDA. Deferred and early admission available.

STUDENT LIFE. Housing: Dormitories (men, women); apartment housing available. **Activities:** Student government, magazine, radio, student newspaper, yearbook, choral groups, drama, jazz band, music ensembles, musical theater, neighborhood social service, preprofessional, special interest, and political clubs. **Additional information:** Students participate in university governance through college senates.

ATHLETICS. NCAA. **Intercollegiate:** Basketball, cross-country M, fencing M, golf M, tennis M, wrestling M. **Intramural:** Basketball, tennis M, volleyball W.

STUDENT SERVICES. Aptitude testing, career counseling, employment service for undergraduates, freshman orientation, health services, personal counseling, placement service for graduates, services/facilities for handicapped.

ANNUAL EXPENSES. Tuition and fees (1992-93): $11,877. Mandatory $1,300 meal plan for full-time, first time on-campus students. **Room and board:** $2,650 room only. **Books and supplies:** $445. **Other expenses:** $600.

FINANCIAL AID. 75% of freshmen, 75% of continuing students receive some form of aid. 87% of grants, all loans, all jobs based on need. 251 enrolled freshmen were judged to have need, all were offered aid. Academic, leadership scholarships available. **Aid applications:** No closing date; priority given to applications received by April 15; applicants notified on a rolling basis beginning on or about June 1; must reply by July 15 or within 20 days if notified thereafter. **Additional information:** Essay required of Max Stern Scholarship applicants.

ADDRESS/TELEPHONE. Michael Kranzler, Associate Director of Undergraduate Admissions, Yeshiva University, 500 West 185th Street, New York, NY 10033-3299. (212) 960-5277. Fax: (212) 960-0087.

Yeshivat Mikdash Melech
Brooklyn, New York CB code: 1432

5-year private rabbinical college, men only, affiliated with Jewish faith. Founded in 1972. **Undergraduate enrollment:** 22 men full time; 1 man part time. **Graduate enrollment:** 18 men full time; 2 men part time. **Location:** Urban campus in very large city. **Calendar:** Semester. **Additional facts:** Ordination available. First and second rabbinic degrees offered.

FRESHMAN ADMISSIONS. Selection criteria: Religious commitment, school achievement record, and test scores important.

ADDRESS/TELEPHONE. Admissions Office, Yeshivat Mikdash Melech, 1326 Ocean Parkway, Brooklyn, NY 11230. (718) 339-1090.

North Carolina

Alamance Community College
Goraham, North Carolina CB code: 5790

2-year public community college, coed. Founded in 1958. **Accreditation:** Regional. **Undergraduate enrollment:** 1,349 men and women full time; 2,426 men and women part time. **Faculty:** 231 total (88 full time), 13 with doctorates or other terminal degrees. **Location:** Rural campus in small town; 4 miles from Burlington, 30 miles from Greensboro. **Calendar:** Quarter, extensive summer session. Saturday and extensive evening/early morning classes. **Microcomputers:** 110 located in libraries, classrooms, computer centers.

DEGREES OFFERED. AAS. 291 associate degrees awarded in 1992. 32% in business and management, 7% business/office and marketing/distribution, 5% engineering technologies, 17% health sciences, 10% parks/recreation, protective services, public affairs, 14% trade and industry.

UNDERGRADUATE MAJORS. Accounting, air conditioning/heating/refrigeration mechanics, air conditioning/heating/refrigeration technology, animal care and management, animal sciences, automotive mechanics, automotive technology, biomedical equipment technology, biomedical science, biotechnology, business administration and management, business and office, business computer/console/peripheral equipment operation, business data processing and related programs, business data programming, carpentry, child development/care/guidance, clinical laboratory science, commercial art, commercial art/audiovisual technology, computer programming, computer servicing technology, criminal justice technology, dental assistant, drafting, drafting and design technology, education, electrical and electronics equipment repair, electromechanical technology, electronic technology, engineering and engineering-related technologies, fashion merchandising, finance, fire control and safety technology, fire protection, food management, food production/management/services, horticultural science, industrial equipment maintenance and repair, law enforcement and corrections technologies, liberal/general studies, machine tool operation/machine shop, marketing and distribution, mechanical design technology, medical laboratory technologies, medical secretary, microcomputer software, nursing, office supervision and management, practical nursing, precision metal work, real estate, secretarial and related programs, teacher aide, trade and industrial supervision and management, welding technology.

ACADEMIC PROGRAMS. 2-year transfer program, cooperative education, double major, dual enrollment of high school students, independent study, internships, weekend college. **Remedial services:** Learning center, reduced course load, remedial instruction, tutoring. **Placement/credit:** Institutional tests. Maximum of 25% of hours needed for degree may be earned by examination.

ACADEMIC REQUIREMENTS. Freshmen must earn minimum GPA of 2.0 to continue in good standing. 60% of freshmen return for sophomore year. Students must declare major on application. **Graduation requirements:** 105 hours for associate. Most students required to take courses in English, mathematics.

FRESHMAN ADMISSIONS. Selection criteria: Open admissions. Selective admissions to allied health, engineering technology, and extension college transfer programs. Nursing applicants must have had biology and chemistry within 3 years with minimum grade of 2.0.

1992 FRESHMAN CLASS PROFILE. 481 men, 616 women enrolled. **Characteristics:** 99% from in state, 100% commute, 18% have minority backgrounds. Average age is 30.

FALL-TERM APPLICATIONS. No fee. No closing date; applicants notified on a rolling basis. Interview required for allied health applicants. Portfolio recommended for commercial art, advertising design applicants. Deferred admission available.

STUDENT LIFE. Activities: Student government, student newspaper, Ethnic Student Association, Fashion Awareness Club, Visual Arts Club, Student Nurses Association, Phi Beta Lambda (service organization), Criminal Justice Club, Peer Advisers Association, Early Childhood Education Club.

ATHLETICS. Intramural: Basketball, bowling, golf, softball, tennis, volleyball.

STUDENT SERVICES. Aptitude testing, career counseling, employment service for undergraduates, freshman orientation, health services, on-campus day care, personal counseling, placement service for graduates, veterans counselor, services/facilities for handicapped.

ANNUAL EXPENSES. Tuition and fees (1992-93): $578, $3,959 additional for out-of-state students. **Books and supplies:** $550. **Other expenses:** $650.

FINANCIAL AID. 18% of freshmen, 49% of continuing students receive some form of aid. 92% of grants, 93% of loans, all jobs based on need. 325 enrolled freshmen were judged to have need, all were offered aid. Academic, state/district residency scholarships available. **Aid applications:** No closing date; priority given to applications received by May 15; applicants notified on a rolling basis beginning on or about July 15; must reply within 2 weeks. **Additional information:** Work-stipend program available to provide tuition, fees, books, supplies.

ADDRESS/TELEPHONE. Suzanne Mintz, Coordinator, Admissions/Records, Alamance Community College, PO Box 8000, Graham, NC 27253. (919) 578-2002. Fax: (919) 578-1987.

Anson Community College
Polkton, North Carolina CB code: 0457

2-year public community college, coed. Founded in 1962. **Accreditation:** Regional. **Undergraduate enrollment:** 72 men, 173 women full time; 177 men, 332 women part time. **Faculty:** 64 total (21 full time), 3 with doctorates or other terminal degrees. **Location:** Rural campus in rural community; 55 miles from Charlotte. **Calendar:** Quarter, limited summer session. Extensive evening/early morning classes. **Microcomputers:** Located in libraries, classrooms.

DEGREES OFFERED. AAS. 46 associate degrees awarded in 1992. 33% in business and management, 16% business/office and marketing/distribution, 14% computer sciences, 25% education, 6% parks/recreation, protective services, public affairs.

UNDERGRADUATE MAJORS. Accounting, air conditioning/heating/refrigeration technology, business administration and management, business and office, business data processing and related programs, computer programming, construction, data processing, drafting, drafting and design technology, education, electronic technology, finance, graphic arts technology, legal secretary, liberal/general studies, marketing and distribution, medical secretary, photographic technology, secretarial and related programs, social science education, social work, teacher aide.

ACADEMIC PROGRAMS. 2-year transfer program, cooperative education, double major, dual enrollment of high school students, independent study, internships, telecourses, cross-registration. **Remedial services:** Learning center, reduced course load, remedial instruction, tutoring. **Placement/credit:** Institutional tests.

ACADEMIC REQUIREMENTS. Freshmen must earn minimum GPA of 1.50 to continue in good standing. 52% of freshmen return for sophomore year. Students must declare major by end of first year. **Graduation requirements:** Most students required to take courses in English, mathematics, social sciences.

FRESHMAN ADMISSIONS. Selection criteria: Open admissions. Selective admission to practical nursing program.

1992 FRESHMAN CLASS PROFILE. 254 men and women enrolled. **Characteristics:** 99% from in state, 100% commute, 40% have minority backgrounds. Average age is 27.

FALL-TERM APPLICATIONS. No fee. No closing date; applicants notified on a rolling basis. Interview required for practical nursing applicants. Deferred and early admission available.

STUDENT LIFE. Activities: Student government, student newspaper, Phi Beta Lambda business organization.

ATHLETICS. Intramural: Softball.

STUDENT SERVICES. Aptitude testing, career counseling, employment service for undergraduates, personal counseling, placement service for graduates, veterans counselor, services/facilities for handicapped.

ANNUAL EXPENSES. Tuition and fees (1992-93): $578, $3,959 additional for out-of-state students. **Books and supplies:** $650. **Other expenses:** $900.

FINANCIAL AID. 30% of freshmen, 45% of continuing students receive some form of aid. 99% of grants, all loans, all jobs based on need. 85 enrolled freshmen were judged to have need, all were offered aid. State/district residency, minority scholarships available. **Aid applications:** No closing date; applicants notified on a rolling basis. **Additional information:** Small amount of nonfederal scholarship aid available.

ADDRESS/TELEPHONE. Mark Ebersole, Counselor, Anson Community College, PO Box 126, Polkton, NC 28135. (704) 272-7635. Fax: (704) 826-8683.

Appalachian State University
Boone, North Carolina CB code: 5010

Admissions:	65% of applicants accepted
Based on:	••• School record, test scores
	• Special talents
Completion:	87% of freshmen end year in good standing
	60% graduate, 38% of these enter graduate study

4-year public university, coed. Founded in 1899. **Accreditation:** Regional. **Undergraduate enrollment:** 4,830 men, 5,121 women full time; 399 men, 376 women part time. **Graduate enrollment:** 240 men, 329 women full time; 116 men, 239 women part time. **Faculty:** 693 total (535 full time). **Location:** Rural campus in large town; 120 miles from Charlotte. **Calendar:** Semester, extensive summer session. **Microcomputers:** 450 located in computer centers. **Special facilities:** Observatory.

DEGREES OFFERED. BA, BS, BFA, MA, MS, MBA, MFA, MEd,

EdD. 2,052 bachelor's degrees awarded in 1992. 25% in business and management, 13% communications, 20% education, 8% parks/recreation, protective services, public affairs, 5% psychology, 8% social sciences. Graduate degrees offered in 50 major fields of study.

UNDERGRADUATE MAJORS. Accounting, administration of special education, anthropology, art education, biology, business administration and management, business and management, business and office, business economics, business education, chemistry, child development/care/guidance, city/community/regional planning, clinical laboratory science, clothing and textiles management/production/services, communications, counseling psychology, criminal justice studies, curriculum and instruction, drafting, dramatic arts, driver and safety education, economics, education, elementary education, English, English education, fashion design, finance, fine arts, food production/management/services, food science and nutrition, foreign languages education, French, geography, geology, graphic and printing production, health care administration, health education, history, home economics, home economics education, home furnishings and equipment management/production/services, hotel/motel and restaurant management, human environment and housing, industrial arts education, industrial technology, information sciences and systems, insurance and risk management, journalism, junior high education, liberal/general studies, management information systems, marketing and distribution, marketing and distributive education, marketing management, mathematics, mathematics education, medical laboratory technologies, music, music education, music performance, music theory and composition, parks and recreation management, philosophy, physical education, physics, political science and government, predentistry, prelaw, premedicine, prepharmacy, psychology, public relations, radio/television broadcasting, reading education, real estate, religion, science education, secondary education, social science education, social sciences, social work, sociology, Spanish, special education, speech, speech correction, speech pathology/audiology, sports medicine, statistics, textiles and clothing.

ACADEMIC PROGRAMS. Accelerated program, double major, dual enrollment of high school students, education specialist degree, honors program, independent study, internships, student-designed major, study abroad, teacher preparation, visiting/exchange student program; liberal arts/career combination in engineering, forestry, health sciences; combined bachelor's/graduate program in business administration. **Remedial services:** Learning center, remedial instruction, tutoring, federally funded special services program for disadvantaged students. **ROTC:** Army. **Placement/credit:** AP, CLEP Subject, institutional tests.

ACADEMIC REQUIREMENTS. Freshmen must earn minimum GPA of 1.5 to continue in good standing. 89% of freshmen return for sophomore year. Students must declare major by end of second year. **Graduation requirements:** 122 hours for bachelor's (40 in major). Most students required to take courses in English, history, mathematics, biological/physical sciences, social sciences.

FRESHMAN ADMISSIONS. Selection criteria: Satisfactory combination of grades and SAT, or class rank and SAT required. **High school preparation:** 19 units required; 20 recommended. Required and recommended units include biological science 2, English 4, mathematics 3, physical science 1 and social science 2. Foreign language 2 recommended. Mathematics units should include algebra I, algebra II, and geometry. **Test requirements:** SAT or ACT (SAT preferred); score report by February 15.

1992 FRESHMAN CLASS PROFILE. 3,653 men applied, 2,186 accepted, 916 enrolled; 4,107 women applied, 2,838 accepted, 1,138 enrolled. 75% had high school GPA of 3.0 or higher, 25% between 2.0 and 2.99. **Academic background:** Mid 50% of enrolled freshmen had SAT-V between 410-510, SAT-M between 470-560. 97% submitted SAT scores. **Characteristics:** 88% from in state, 97% live in college housing, 5% have minority backgrounds. Average age is 18.

FALL-TERM APPLICATIONS. $25 fee, may be waived for applicants with need. Closing date March 31; applicants notified on or about April 30; must reply within 3 weeks. Audition required for music applicants. Portfolio recommended for art applicants. Applicants notified 5 times per year. Contact school for exact dates.

STUDENT LIFE. Housing: Dormitories (men, women, coed); apartment housing available. **Activities:** Student government, radio, student newspaper, television, yearbook, choral groups, concert band, dance, drama, jazz band, marching band, music ensembles, pep band, symphony orchestra, fraternities, sororities.

ATHLETICS. NCAA. **Intercollegiate:** Baseball M, basketball, cross-country, field hockey W, football M, golf, soccer M, tennis, track and field, volleyball W, wrestling M. **Intramural:** Badminton, basketball, bowling, cross-country, fencing, golf, gymnastics, handball, racquetball, skiing, soccer, softball, squash, swimming, table tennis, tennis, track and field, volleyball, water polo, wrestling.

STUDENT SERVICES. Career counseling, employment service for undergraduates, health services, on-campus day care, personal counseling, placement service for graduates, veterans counselor, services/facilities for handicapped.

ANNUAL EXPENSES. Tuition and fees (1992-93): $1,405, $5,672 additional for out-of-state students. **Room and board:** $2,620. **Books and supplies:** $250. **Other expenses:** $1,000.

FINANCIAL AID. 44% of freshmen, 44% of continuing students receive some form of aid. 57% of grants, 82% of loans, 9% of jobs based on need. 701 enrolled freshmen were judged to have need, all were offered aid. Academic, music/drama, art, athletic, minority scholarships available. **Aid applications:** No closing date; priority given to applications received by February 1; applicants notified on a rolling basis beginning on or about May 1; must reply within 3 weeks.

ADDRESS/TELEPHONE. T. Joseph Watts, Director of Admissions, Appalachian State University, Administration Building, Boone, NC 28608. (704) 262-2120.

Asheville Buncombe Technical Community College
Asheville, North Carolina — CB code: 5033

2-year public community, technical college, coed. Founded in 1959. **Accreditation:** Regional. **Undergraduate enrollment:** 699 men, 811 women full time; 942 men, 1,563 women part time. **Faculty:** 273 total (91 full time), 14 with doctorates or other terminal degrees. **Location:** Urban campus in small city; 115 miles from Charlotte. **Calendar:** Quarter. Extensive evening/early morning classes. **Microcomputers:** 192 located in libraries, classrooms, computer centers. **Special facilities:** Smith McDowell House. **Additional facts:** Certain credit courses offered at the Madison Campus during evening hours.

DEGREES OFFERED. AA, AS, AAS. 280 associate degrees awarded in 1992. 30% in business and management, 25% business/office and marketing/distribution, 10% computer sciences, 6% engineering, 9% engineering technologies, 10% health sciences, 5% allied health, 5% parks/recreation, protective services, public affairs.

UNDERGRADUATE MAJORS. Accounting, business administration and management, business and management, business and office, business data entry equipment operation, business data programming, chemical engineering, civil engineering, civil technology, clinical laboratory science, computer programming, dental hygiene, drafting, drafting and design technology, electrical/electronics/communications engineering, electronic technology, emergency medical technologies, finance, food management, hospitality and recreation marketing, hotel/motel and restaurant management, law enforcement and corrections technologies, marketing and distribution, marketing management, mechanical engineering, medical laboratory technologies, nursing, radiograph medical technology, secretarial and related programs, survey and mapping technology, surveying and mapping sciences, tool design technology, word processing.

ACADEMIC PROGRAMS. 2-year transfer program, cooperative education, internships. **Remedial services:** Learning center, preadmission summer program, reduced course load, remedial instruction, special counselor, tutoring. **Placement/credit:** Institutional tests.

ACADEMIC REQUIREMENTS. Freshmen must earn minimum GPA of 2.0 to continue in good standing. 40% of freshmen return for sophomore year. Students must declare major on enrollment. **Graduation requirements:** 69 hours for associate. Most students required to take courses in computer science, English, mathematics, social sciences.

FRESHMAN ADMISSIONS. Selection criteria: Open admissions. Selective admissions to allied health programs based on academic record and state residency. Algebra 1 and algebra 2 or geometry for engineering; algebra 1, chemistry and biology for nursing, medical lab and dental programs; algebra 1 for radiologic technology; biology and 1 math for practical nursing. **Test requirements:** Computerized Placement Test (CPT) required for placement.

1992 FRESHMAN CLASS PROFILE. 999 men, 1,162 women enrolled. **Characteristics:** 99% from in state, 100% commute. Average age is 28.

FALL-TERM APPLICATIONS. No fee. No closing date; applicants notified on a rolling basis. Interview required for all medical programs applicants. Placement interview required of all entering students. Deferred admission available.

STUDENT LIFE. Activities: Student government, student newspaper.

STUDENT SERVICES. Career counseling, employment service for undergraduates, on-campus day care, personal counseling, placement service for graduates, veterans counselor, services/facilities for handicapped.

ANNUAL EXPENSES. Tuition and fees (1992-93): $578, $3,959 additional for out-of-state students. **Books and supplies:** $800. **Other expenses:** $1,750.

FINANCIAL AID. 32% of freshmen, 38% of continuing students receive some form of aid. 86% of grants, 88% of loans, 33% of jobs based on need. 295 enrolled freshmen were judged to have need, all were offered aid. Academic scholarships available. **Aid applications:** No closing date; priority given to applications received by March 1; applicants notified on a rolling basis beginning on or about June 1; must reply within 2 weeks.

ADDRESS/TELEPHONE. Connie S. Buckner, Director of Admissions, Asheville Buncombe Technical Community College, 340 Victoria Road, Asheville, NC 28801. (704) 254-1921 ext. 149.

Barber-Scotia College

Concord, North Carolina CB code: 5052

4-year private liberal arts college, coed, affiliated with Presbyterian Church (USA). Founded in 1867. **Accreditation:** Regional. **Undergraduate enrollment:** 352 men, 352 women full time. **Faculty:** 63 total (50 full time), 30 with doctorates or other terminal degrees. **Location:** Urban campus in large town; 20 miles from Charlotte. **Calendar:** Semester. **Microcomputers:** 93 located in dormitories, libraries, classrooms, computer centers.

DEGREES OFFERED. BA, BS. 57 bachelor's degrees awarded in 1992. 30% in business and management, 10% life sciences, 9% mathematics, 45% social sciences.

UNDERGRADUATE MAJORS. Accounting, anthropology, biology, business administration and management, business and management, computer and information sciences, computer mathematics, computer programming, criminal justice studies, elementary education, English, hotel/motel and restaurant management, journalism, management information systems, mathematics, mathematics education, parks and recreation management, physical education, political science and government, secondary education, sociology.

ACADEMIC PROGRAMS. Double major, honors program, internships, teacher preparation, cross-registration, dual degree program with St. John's Law School. **Remedial services:** Learning center, preadmission summer program, reduced course load, remedial instruction, special counselor, tutoring. **ROTC:** Air Force, Army. **Placement/credit:** AP, CLEP General and Subject, institutional tests.

ACADEMIC REQUIREMENTS. Freshmen must earn minimum GPA of 2.0 to continue in good standing. Students must declare major by end of second year. **Graduation requirements:** 125 hours for bachelor's (45 in major). Most students required to take courses in arts/fine arts, computer science, English, foreign languages, history, humanities, mathematics, philosophy/religion, biological/physical sciences, social sciences.

FRESHMAN ADMISSIONS. Selection criteria: Open admissions. Recommended units include English 4, mathematics 3, social science 2 and science 3. **Test requirements:** SAT or ACT (SAT preferred) for placement and counseling only; score report by August 17.

1992 FRESHMAN CLASS PROFILE. 247 men, 233 women enrolled. 2% had high school GPA of 3.0 or higher, 42% between 2.0 and 2.99. 1% were in top tenth and 3% were in top quarter of graduating class. **Academic background:** Mid 50% of enrolled freshmen had SAT-V between 280-330, SAT-M between 290-370. 78% submitted SAT scores. **Characteristics:** 53% from in state, 90% live in college housing, 100% have minority backgrounds. Average age is 19.

FALL-TERM APPLICATIONS. $10 fee, may be waived for applicants with need. No closing date; priority given to applications received by August 1; applicants notified on a rolling basis beginning on or about January 25. Interview recommended. Deferred admission available.

STUDENT LIFE. Housing: Dormitories (men, women); apartment housing available. **Activities:** Student government, magazine, student newspaper, yearbook, audio-visual center, choral groups, dance, drama, music ensembles, fraternities, sororities, NAACP.

ATHLETICS. NAIA. **Intercollegiate:** Basketball, cross-country, softball W, tennis, track and field, volleyball W. **Intramural:** Basketball, cross-country, football M, softball, swimming, table tennis M, tennis, track and field, volleyball.

STUDENT SERVICES. Aptitude testing, career counseling, employment service for undergraduates, freshman orientation, health services, personal counseling, placement service for graduates, services/facilities for handicapped.

ANNUAL EXPENSES. Tuition and fees: $4,494. **Room and board:** $2,795. **Books and supplies:** $700. **Other expenses:** $1,000.

FINANCIAL AID. 95% of freshmen, 95% of continuing students receive some form of aid. 88% of grants, all jobs based on need. Academic, athletic, state/district residency, religious affiliation scholarships available. **Aid applications:** No closing date; priority given to applications received by March 15; applicants notified on a rolling basis beginning on or about April 15; must reply within 2 weeks.

ADDRESS/TELEPHONE. Vivian Thompson, Director of Enrollment Management, Barber-Scotia College, 145 Cabarrus Avenue West, Concord, NC 28025. (704) 786-5171 ext.237. Fax: (704) 784-3817 ext. 237.

Barton College

Wilson, North Carolina CB code: 5016

Admissions: 74% of applicants accepted
Based on: ••• School record
•• Interview, recommendations, test scores
• Activities, essay
Completion: 87% of freshmen end year in good standing
65% graduate, 10% of these enter graduate study

4-year private liberal arts college, coed, affiliated with Christian Church (Disciples of Christ). Founded in 1902. **Accreditation:** Regional. **Undergraduate enrollment:** 396 men, 739 women full time; 162 men, 465 women part time. **Faculty:** 100 total (82 full time), 47 with doctorates or other terminal degrees. **Location:** Suburban campus in large town; 45 miles from Raleigh. **Calendar:** Semester, extensive summer session. Saturday classes. **Microcomputers:** 53 located in libraries, classrooms, computer centers. **Special facilities:** Art gallery, greenhouse.

DEGREES OFFERED. BA, BS, BFA. 262 bachelor's degrees awarded in 1992. 34% in business and management, 15% education, 18% health sciences, 11% social sciences.

UNDERGRADUATE MAJORS. Accounting, American studies, art education, biological and physical sciences, biology, business administration and management, business and management, cell biology, ceramics, chemistry, communications, early childhood education, education, education of the deaf and hearing impaired, elementary education, English, English education, environmental science, fine arts, foreign languages education, French, graphic design, history, humanities and social sciences, junior high education, liberal/general studies, mathematics, mathematics education, medical laboratory technologies, music, music education, music recording technology, nursing, painting, philosophy, photography, physical education, political science and government, predentistry, prelaw, premedicine, prepharmacy, preveterinary, printmaking, psychology, religion, science education, sculpture, secondary education, social sciences, social studies education, social work, sociology, Spanish, sports management, sports medicine, sports science, studio art, theological studies.

ACADEMIC PROGRAMS. Accelerated program, cooperative education, double major, dual enrollment of high school students, honors program, independent study, internships, study abroad, teacher preparation, weekend college; liberal arts/career combination in health sciences. **Remedial services:** Learning center, reduced course load, remedial instruction, special counselor, tutoring. **Placement/credit:** AP, CLEP General and Subject, institutional tests; 30 credit hours maximum for bachelor's degree.

ACADEMIC REQUIREMENTS. Freshmen must earn minimum GPA of 1.35 to continue in good standing. 87% of freshmen return for sophomore year. Students must declare major by end of first year. **Graduation requirements:** 126 hours for bachelor's (36 in major). Most students required to take courses in arts/fine arts, computer science, English, foreign languages, history, humanities, mathematics, philosophy/religion, biological/physical sciences, social sciences.

FRESHMAN ADMISSIONS. Selection criteria: Class rank, high school GPA, test scores important. **High school preparation:** 12 units required; 16 recommended. Required and recommended units include science 2. Foreign language 2 and physical science 3 recommended. Science units must include laboratory science. **Test requirements:** SAT or ACT (SAT preferred); score report by July 15.

1992 FRESHMAN CLASS PROFILE. 333 men applied, 240 accepted, 99 enrolled; 461 women applied, 350 accepted, 219 enrolled. **Academic background:** Mid 50% of enrolled freshmen had SAT-V between 340-440, SAT-M between 360-480. 85% submitted SAT scores. **Characteristics:** 77% from in state, 65% live in college housing, 11% have minority backgrounds, 1% are foreign students. Average age is 19.

FALL-TERM APPLICATIONS. $20 fee, may be waived for applicants with need. No closing date; priority given to applications received by May 1; applicants notified on a rolling basis beginning on or about October 1; must reply by May 1 or within 2 weeks if notified thereafter. Interview recommended for marginal applicants. Audition recommended for music applicants. Portfolio recommended for art applicants. CRDA. Deferred and early admission available.

STUDENT LIFE. Housing: Dormitories (men, women, coed); fraternity housing available. All full-time students who do not live with parents are required to live on campus. **Activities:** Student government, film, magazine, radio, student newspaper, television, yearbook, choral groups, concert band, dance, drama, jazz band, music ensembles, pep band, symphony orchestra, fraternities, sororities, campus Christian association, Young Democrats, SADD.

ATHLETICS. NAIA. **Intercollegiate:** Baseball M, basketball, golf M, soccer M, softball W, tennis, volleyball W. **Intramural:** Baseball M, basketball, football, soccer, softball, table tennis, tennis, track and field, volleyball.

STUDENT SERVICES. Career counseling, employment service for undergraduates, freshman orientation, health services, personal counseling, placement service for graduates, special adviser for adult students, veterans counselor, services/facilities for handicapped.

ANNUAL EXPENSES. Tuition and fees: $7,363. **Room and board:** $3,326. **Books and supplies:** $500. **Other expenses:** $1,200.

FINANCIAL AID. 80% of freshmen, 80% of continuing students receive some form of aid. Grants, loans, jobs available. Academic, music/drama, art, athletic, state/district residency, leadership, religious affiliation, minority scholarships available. **Aid applications:** No closing date; priority given to applications received by April 15; applicants notified on a rolling basis beginning on or about April 15; must reply within 15 days.

ADDRESS/TELEPHONE. Anthony C. Britt, Director of Admissions, Barton College, College Station, Wilson, NC 27893. (919) 399-6318. (800) 345-4973. Fax: (919) 399-1620.

Beaufort County Community College
Washington, North Carolina CB code: 7307

2-year public community college, coed. Founded in 1967. **Accreditation:** Regional. **Undergraduate enrollment:** 236 men, 478 women full time; 261 men, 408 women part time. **Faculty:** 107 total (47 full time), 3 with doctorates or other terminal degrees. **Location:** Rural campus in large town; 23 miles from Greenville. **Calendar:** Quarter, limited summer session. Extensive evening/early morning classes. **Microcomputers:** Located in libraries, classrooms, computer centers.

DEGREES OFFERED. AA, AS, AAS. 112 associate degrees awarded in 1992. 18% in business and management, 6% computer sciences, 5% education, 10% engineering technologies, 39% allied health, 9% parks/recreation, protective services, public affairs, 8% trade and industry.

UNDERGRADUATE MAJORS. Accounting, agricultural mechanics, automotive mechanics, business administration and management, business and office, business data programming, business education, clinical laboratory science, computer programming, drafting and design technology, education, electrical technology, electronic technology, elementary education, law enforcement and corrections technologies, liberal/general studies, medical laboratory technologies, microcomputer software, nursing, secondary education, secretarial and related programs, social work.

ACADEMIC PROGRAMS. 2-year transfer program, cooperative education, double major, dual enrollment of high school students, independent study, internships. **Remedial services:** Learning center, reduced course load, remedial instruction, special counselor, tutoring. **Placement/credit:** Institutional tests.

ACADEMIC REQUIREMENTS. Freshmen must earn minimum GPA of 2.0 to continue in good standing. 60% of freshmen return for sophomore year. Students must declare major on enrollment. **Graduation requirements:** 96 hours for associate. Most students required to take courses in computer science, English, mathematics, social sciences.

FRESHMAN ADMISSIONS. Selection criteria: Open admissions. Selective admissions to allied health programs. One unit chemistry required for nursing and medical technology applicants. **Test requirements:** CGP and TABE required for allied health applicants for admission and for placement in all other programs.

1992 FRESHMAN CLASS PROFILE. 184 men, 252 women enrolled. **Characteristics:** 98% from in state, 100% commute, 30% have minority backgrounds. Average age is 22.

FALL-TERM APPLICATIONS. No fee. No closing date; applicants notified on a rolling basis. Interview required for allied health programs applicants. Deferred admission available.

STUDENT LIFE. Activities: Student government.

STUDENT SERVICES. Aptitude testing, career counseling, employment service for undergraduates, freshman orientation, health services, personal counseling, placement service for graduates, veterans counselor, services/facilities for handicapped.

ANNUAL EXPENSES. Tuition and fees (1992-93): $575, $3,959 additional for out-of-state students. **Books and supplies:** $600. **Other expenses:** $400.

FINANCIAL AID. 26% of freshmen, 32% of continuing students receive some form of aid. 92% of grants, 98% of loans, all jobs based on need. Academic, state/district residency scholarships available. **Aid applications:** No closing date; priority given to applications received by July 1; applicants notified on a rolling basis beginning on or about August 1; must reply within 2 weeks.

ADDRESS/TELEPHONE. Gary R. Burbage, Director of Admissions and Recruiting, Beaufort County Community College, PO Box 1069, Washington, NC 27889. (919) 946-6194 ext. 233. Fax: (919) 946-0271.

Belmont Abbey College
Belmont, North Carolina CB code: 5055

Admissions:	59% of applicants accepted
Based on:	••• School record
	•• Essay, recommendations, test scores
	• Activities, interview
Completion:	75% of freshmen end year in good standing
	20% enter graduate study

4-year private liberal arts college, coed, affiliated with Roman Catholic Church. Founded in 1876. **Accreditation:** Regional. **Undergraduate enrollment:** 440 men, 440 women full time; 60 men, 80 women part time. **Faculty:** 84 total (49 full time), 40 with doctorates or other terminal degrees. **Location:** Suburban campus in small town; 12 miles from Charlotte. **Calendar:** Semester, limited summer session. **Microcomputers:** 46 located in libraries, computer centers. **Special facilities:** Observatory.

DEGREES OFFERED. BA, BS. 170 bachelor's degrees awarded in 1992. 52% in business and management, 5% computer sciences, 15% education, 6% parks/recreation, protective services, public affairs, 12% social sciences.

UNDERGRADUATE MAJORS. Accounting, biology, business administration and management, chemistry, distribution management, economics, elementary education, English, history, information sciences and systems, mathematics, medical laboratory technologies, philosophy, political science and government, psychology, recreation and community services technologies, secondary education, sociology, special education, sports management, theological studies.

ACADEMIC PROGRAMS. Accelerated program, cooperative education, double major, dual enrollment of high school students, honors program, independent study, internships, study abroad, teacher preparation, visiting/exchange student program, cross-registration; liberal arts/career combination in engineering, health sciences. **Remedial services:** Learning center, tutoring. **ROTC:** Air Force, Army. **Placement/credit:** AP, CLEP General and Subject, institutional tests; 30 credit hours maximum for bachelor's degree.

ACADEMIC REQUIREMENTS. Freshmen must earn minimum GPA of 1.5 to continue in good standing. 72% of freshmen return for sophomore year. Students must declare major by end of second year. **Graduation requirements:** 130 hours for bachelor's (30 in major). Most students required to take courses in English, foreign languages, history, mathematics, philosophy/religion, biological/physical sciences, social sciences.

FRESHMAN ADMISSIONS. Selection criteria: GPA, class rank, high school curriculum, and test scores most important. Personal accomplishments, extracurricular activities, and letters of recommendation strongly considered. **High school preparation:** 16 units required. Required units include English 4, foreign language 2, mathematics 3, social science 2 and science 2. One social science must be history. For science majors, 4 mathematics, 1 chemistry, 1 physics, 1 additional science recommended. **Test requirements:** SAT or ACT (SAT preferred); score report by August 15.

1992 FRESHMAN CLASS PROFILE. 520 men applied, 310 accepted, 85 enrolled; 510 women applied, 300 accepted, 95 enrolled. 38% had high school GPA of 3.0 or higher, 59% between 2.0 and 2.99. **Academic background:** Mid 50% of enrolled freshmen had SAT-V between 400-530, SAT-M between 430-580. 91% submitted SAT scores. **Characteristics:** 32% from in state, 80% live in college housing, 11% have minority backgrounds, 5% are foreign students, 35% join fraternities/sororities. Average age is 18.

FALL-TERM APPLICATIONS. $25 fee, may be waived for applicants with need. Closing date August 15; applicants notified on a rolling basis; must reply by May 1 or within 4 weeks if notified thereafter. Essay required for academically weak applicants. Interview recommended. CRDA. Deferred and early admission available. EDP-S.

STUDENT LIFE. Housing: Dormitories (coed); apartment housing available. **Activities:** Student government, magazine, radio, student newspaper, yearbook, drama, fraternities, sororities, campus ministry, Young Democrats, Young Republicans, Alpha Phi Omega, Circle-K.

ATHLETICS. NAIA. **Intercollegiate:** Baseball M, basketball, cross-country, golf M, soccer M, tennis, volleyball W. **Intramural:** Basketball, racquetball, soccer, softball, swimming, tennis, track and field, volleyball.

STUDENT SERVICES. Aptitude testing, career counseling, employment service for undergraduates, freshman orientation, health services, personal counseling, placement service for graduates, special adviser for adult students, veterans counselor.

ANNUAL EXPENSES. Tuition and fees: $9,084. **Room and board:** $4,506. **Books and supplies:** $500. **Other expenses:** $1,280.

FINANCIAL AID. 75% of freshmen, 80% of continuing students receive some form of aid. 60% of grants, 92% of loans, all jobs based on need. 120 enrolled freshmen were judged to have need, all were offered aid. Academic, athletic, state/district residency, leadership, alumni affiliation scholarships available. **Aid applications:** No closing date; priority given to applications received by April 1; applicants notified on a rolling basis beginning on or about March 15; must reply by May 1 or within 2 weeks if notified thereafter. **Additional information:** Many merit scholarships offered based solely on academic achievement, ranging from $1,000 to full tuition.

ADDRESS/TELEPHONE. Jeffery Miller, Director of Admissions, Belmont Abbey College, One Abbey Place, Belmont, NC 28012-2795. (704) 825-6665. (800) 523-2355. Fax: (704) 825-6670.

Bennett College
Greensboro, North Carolina CB code: 5058

Admissions:	57% of applicants accepted
Based on:	••• School record, test scores
	•• Essay, recommendations, special talents
	• Activities, interview
Completion:	80% of freshmen end year in good standing
	40% graduate, 40% of these enter graduate study

4-year private liberal arts college, women only, affiliated with United Methodist Church. Founded in 1873. **Accreditation:** Regional. **Undergraduate enrollment:** 617 women full time; 18 women part time. **Faculty:** 64 total (52 full time), 32 with doctorates or other terminal degrees. **Location:** Urban campus in small city; 295 miles from Washington, D.C. **Calendar:** Semester. **Microcomputers:** 73 located in libraries, classrooms, computer centers. **Special facilities:** Afro-American Women's Collection, Norris Wright Cuney Collection, Bennett College Archives, Palmer Memorial Institute Files.

DEGREES OFFERED. AA, BA, BS. 79 bachelor's degrees awarded. 24% in business and management, 16% teacher education, 5% letters/literature, 11% life sciences, 18% multi/interdisciplinary studies, 9% psychology, 6% social sciences.

UNDERGRADUATE MAJORS. Associate: Secretarial and related programs. **Bachelor's:** Accounting, arts management, biology, business and management, chemistry, communications, computer and information sciences, early childhood education, elementary education, English, English education, food science and nutrition, health sciences, home economics, journalism, junior high education, liberal/general studies, mathematics, mathematics education, medical laboratory technologies, music, music education, political science and government, psychology, science education, social work, sociology, special education, textiles and clothing, visual and performing arts.

ACADEMIC PROGRAMS. Accelerated program, double major, honors program, independent study, internships, student-designed major, teacher preparation, visiting/exchange student program, Washington semester, cross-registration; liberal arts/career combination in engineering. **Remedial services:** Learning center, preadmission summer program, reduced course load, remedial instruction, special counselor, tutoring. **ROTC:** Air Force, Army. **Placement/credit:** CLEP General and Subject, institutional tests.

ACADEMIC REQUIREMENTS. Freshmen must earn minimum GPA of 1.75 to continue in good standing. 75% of freshmen return for sophomore year. Students must declare major by end of second year. **Graduation requirements:** 124 hours for bachelor's (60 in major). Most students required to take courses in English, foreign languages, history, humanities, mathematics, philosophy/religion, biological/physical sciences, social sciences. **Postgraduate studies:** 3% enter law school, 11% enter medical school, 4% enter MBA programs, 22% enter other graduate study. **Additional information:** Accepted students who do not meet required SAT or ACT score admitted to Academic Enrichment Program which provides tutoring, counseling and other support services.

FRESHMAN ADMISSIONS. Selection criteria: School achievement record, test scores, recommendations of counselors, and applicant's personal statement important. **High school preparation:** 16 units required. Required and recommended units include English 4, mathematics 2, social science 1 and science 1. Foreign language 2 recommended. **Test requirements:** SAT or ACT (SAT preferred); score report by August 1.

1992 FRESHMAN CLASS PROFILE. 789 women applied, 450 accepted, 189 enrolled. 32% had high school GPA of 3.0 or higher, 61% between 2.0 and 2.99. **Characteristics:** 28% from in state, 95% live in college housing, 100% have minority backgrounds, 1% are foreign students. Average age is 19.

FALL-TERM APPLICATIONS. $20 fee, may be waived for applicants with need. Closing date August 1; priority given to applications received by July 1; applicants notified on a rolling basis; must reply within 4 weeks. Essay required. Interview recommended for borderline applicants. Deferred admission available.

STUDENT LIFE. Housing: Dormitories (women). Students with GPA of 3.0 may reside in honor residence hall. **Activities:** Student government, student newspaper, television, yearbook, choral groups, dance, drama, music ensembles, sororities, Student Christian Fellowship, NAACP, social work club, women in communications, student teachers association, psychology club, political science club.

ATHLETICS. NCAA. **Intercollegiate:** Basketball, cross-country, softball, tennis, track and field, volleyball. **Intramural:** Basketball, softball, swimming, tennis, volleyball.

STUDENT SERVICES. Aptitude testing, career counseling, employment service for undergraduates, freshman orientation, health services, on-campus day care, personal counseling, placement service for graduates.

ANNUAL EXPENSES. Tuition and fees: $6,011. **Room and board:** $2,909. **Books and supplies:** $600. **Other expenses:** $1,000.

FINANCIAL AID. 80% of freshmen, 79% of continuing students receive some form of aid. 49% of grants, 92% of loans, all jobs based on need. Academic, music/drama, state/district residency, leadership, alumni affiliation, religious affiliation scholarships available. **Aid applications:** Closing date April 15; applicants notified on or about July 15; must reply within 15 days.

ADDRESS/TELEPHONE. Susan Gibson, Director of Admissions, Bennett College, 900 East Washington Street, Greensboro, NC 27401-3239. (919) 273-4431. (800) 338-BENN. Fax: (919) 378-0511.

Bladen Community College
Dublin, North Carolina — CB code: 0478

2-year public community college, coed. Founded in 1967. **Accreditation:** Regional. **Undergraduate enrollment:** 125 men, 238 women full time; 105 men, 180 women part time. **Faculty:** 55 total (26 full time), 4 with doctorates or other terminal degrees. **Location:** Rural campus in rural community; 35 miles from Fayetteville. **Calendar:** Quarter, limited summer session. Saturday and extensive evening/early morning classes. **Microcomputers:** 100 located in classrooms, computer centers. **Special facilities:** High-technology center.

DEGREES OFFERED. AAS. 26 associate degrees awarded in 1992. 31% in business/office and marketing/distribution, 54% education, 11% parks/recreation, protective services, public affairs.

UNDERGRADUATE MAJORS. Business administration and management, business and office, business computer/console/peripheral equipment operation, business data programming, computer and information sciences, education, electrical and electronics equipment repair, law enforcement and corrections technologies, liberal/general studies, secretarial and related programs.

ACADEMIC PROGRAMS. 2-year transfer program, double major, dual enrollment of high school students, independent study, weekend college. **Remedial services:** Learning center, reduced course load, remedial instruction, special counselor, tutoring. **Placement/credit:** Institutional tests; 15 credit hours maximum for associate degree.

ACADEMIC REQUIREMENTS. Freshmen must earn minimum GPA of 1.5 to continue in good standing. 54% of freshmen return for sophomore year. Students must declare major on application. **Graduation requirements:** 96 hours for associate (84 in major). Most students required to take courses in English, history, mathematics, biological/physical sciences, social sciences.

FRESHMAN ADMISSIONS. Selection criteria: Open admissions. **High school preparation:** 20 units recommended. Recommended units include biological science 2, English 4, foreign language 2, mathematics 3, social science 1 and science 2.

1992 FRESHMAN CLASS PROFILE. 91 men, 178 women enrolled. 25% had high school GPA of 3.0 or higher, 70% between 2.0 and 2.99. 10% were in top tenth and 15% were in top quarter of graduating class. **Characteristics:** 99% from in state, 100% commute, 37% have minority backgrounds. Average age is 25.

FALL-TERM APPLICATIONS. No fee. No closing date; applicants notified on a rolling basis. Interview required. Deferred admission available.

STUDENT LIFE. Activities: Student government, student newspaper, yearbook.

ATHLETICS. Intercollegiate: Golf, softball, tennis, volleyball.

STUDENT SERVICES. Aptitude testing, career counseling, employment service for undergraduates, freshman orientation, personal counseling, placement service for graduates, veterans counselor, services/facilities for handicapped.

ANNUAL EXPENSES. Tuition and fees (1992-93): $587, $3,959 additional for out-of-state students. **Books and supplies:** $300. **Other expenses:** $1,550.

FINANCIAL AID. 37% of freshmen, 35% of continuing students receive some form of aid. All grants, all loans, 98% of jobs based on need. 258 enrolled freshmen were judged to have need, all were offered aid. **Aid applications:** No closing date; priority given to applications received by August 15; applicants notified on a rolling basis beginning on or about September 1; must reply within 2 weeks.

ADDRESS/TELEPHONE. James H. Oxendine, Dean of Student Services, Bladen Community College, PO Box 266, Dublin, NC 28332. (919) 862-2164 ext. 207. Fax: (919) 862-3484.

Blue Ridge Community College
Flat Rock, North Carolina — CB code: 5644

2-year public community college, coed. Founded in 1969. **Accreditation:** Regional. **Undergraduate enrollment:** 214 men, 382 women full time; 360 men, 558 women part time. **Faculty:** 120 total (46 full time), 4 with doctorates or other terminal degrees. **Location:** Rural campus in large town; 25 miles from Asheville. **Calendar:** Quarter, limited summer session. **Microcomputers:** Located in libraries, classrooms, computer centers.

DEGREES OFFERED. AA, AAS. 76 associate degrees awarded in 1992. 14% in business and management, 14% business/office and marketing/distribution, 13% computer sciences, 8% education, 17% engineering technologies, 31% health sciences.

UNDERGRADUATE MAJORS. Business administration and management, business and office, computer programming, drafting, drafting and design technology, education, electromechanical technology, electronic technology, horticulture, industrial technology, liberal/general studies, manufacturing technology, marketing and distribution, nursing, secretarial and related programs, tourism, transportation and travel marketing.

ACADEMIC PROGRAMS. 2-year transfer program, cooperative education, double major, dual enrollment of high school students, internships, telecourses. **Remedial services:** Learning center, reduced course load, remedial instruction, special counselor, tutoring. **Placement/credit:** Institutional tests. Maximum of 50% of credit hours by examination may be counted toward degree.

ACADEMIC REQUIREMENTS. Freshmen must earn minimum GPA of 2.0 to continue in good standing. Students must declare major on enrollment. **Graduation requirements:** 120 hours for associate. Most students required to take courses in English, humanities, mathematics, social sciences.

FRESHMAN ADMISSIONS. Selection criteria: Open admissions.

1992 FRESHMAN CLASS PROFILE. 215 men, 445 women enrolled.

Characteristics: 99% from in state, 100% commute, 4% have minority backgrounds. Average age is 23.

FALL-TERM APPLICATIONS. No fee. No closing date; applicants notified on a rolling basis.

STUDENT LIFE. Activities: Student government, yearbook, Circle-K, Rotaract, Phi Theta Kappa, National Vocational-Technical Honor Society, Students in Free Enterprise.

STUDENT SERVICES. Aptitude testing, career counseling, employment service for undergraduates, freshman orientation, on-campus day care, personal counseling, placement service for graduates, special adviser for adult students, veterans counselor, services/facilities for handicapped.

ANNUAL EXPENSES. Tuition and fees (1992-93): $587, $3,959 additional for out-of-state students. **Books and supplies:** $600. **Other expenses:** $787.

FINANCIAL AID. 15% of freshmen, 15% of continuing students receive some form of aid. 92% of grants, 58% of loans, 74% of jobs based on need. Academic, leadership scholarships available. **Aid applications:** No closing date; priority given to applications received by June 30; applicants notified on a rolling basis; must reply within 4 weeks.

ADDRESS/TELEPHONE. Donald Shoemaker, Dean Student/Admin Services, Blue Ridge Community College, Route 2, Box 133A, Flat Rock, NC 28731-9624. (704) 692-3572 ext. 221. Fax: (704) 692-2441.

Brevard College
Brevard, North Carolina — CB code: 5067

Admissions: 87% of applicants accepted
Based on: ••• School record, test scores
•• Activities, special talents
• Essay, interview, recommendations
Completion: 80% of freshmen end year in good standing
64% graduate, 94% of these enter 4-year programs

2-year private college of arts and sciences and junior college, coed, affiliated with United Methodist Church. Founded in 1853. **Accreditation:** Regional. **Undergraduate enrollment:** 394 men, 320 women full time; 15 men, 15 women part time. **Faculty:** 79 total (56 full time), 28 with doctorates or other terminal degrees. **Location:** Suburban campus in small town; 33 miles from Asheville. **Calendar:** Semester, limited summer session. **Microcomputers:** 68 located in libraries, classrooms, computer centers. **Special facilities:** Art gallery, barn theater, mountain climbing wall. **Additional facts:** Specifically designed for students who plan to go on for 4-year degree.

DEGREES OFFERED. AA, AS. 117 associate degrees awarded in 1992. 5% in architecture and environmental design, 15% business and management, 5% business/office and marketing/distribution, 5% communications, 5% computer sciences, 5% education, 10% engineering, 5% law, 5% parks/recreation, protective services, public affairs, 15% visual and performing arts.

UNDERGRADUATE MAJORS. Accounting, advertising, agricultural sciences, allied health, American literature, architecture, art education, art history, art therapy, Bible studies, biology, botany, business administration and management, business and management, business and office, business data programming, business economics, ceramics, chemical engineering, chemistry, communications, comparative literature, computer and information sciences, computer technology, crafts, creative writing, dramatic arts, drawing, earth sciences, ecology, economics, education, education administration, elementary education, engineering, engineering and engineering-related technologies, English, English literature, environmental science, finance, fine arts, forestry and related sciences, French, geology, German, health care administration, health sciences, history, humanities, information sciences and systems, jazz, journalism, liberal/general studies, marine biology, marketing and distribution, mathematics, mathematics education, music, music business management, music education, music history and appreciation, music performance, music theory and composition, music therapy, musical theater, nursing, painting, parks and recreation management, philosophy, photography, physical education, physical sciences, physical therapy, physics, political science and government, predentistry, prelaw, premedicine, prepharmacy, preveterinary, printmaking, psychology, public affairs, public relations, recreation and community services technologies, religion, religious education, religious music, rhetoric, science education, science technologies, sculpture, social sciences, social work, sociology, Spanish, special education, speech/communication/theater education, sports medicine, studio art, theater design, theological studies, visual and performing arts.

ACADEMIC PROGRAMS. 2-year transfer program, double major, honors program, independent study, study abroad. **Remedial services:** Learning center, reduced course load, remedial instruction, special counselor, tutoring, learning contract. **Placement/credit:** AP, CLEP General and Subject, institutional tests; 41 credit hours maximum for associate degree.

ACADEMIC REQUIREMENTS. Freshmen must earn minimum GPA of 1.75 to continue in good standing. 71% of freshmen return for sophomore year. Students must declare major by end of first year. **Graduation requirements:** 66 hours for associate. Most students required to take courses in English, foreign languages, history, mathematics, philosophy/religion, biological/physical sciences, social sciences.

FRESHMAN ADMISSIONS. Selection criteria: School achievement record most important, followed by test scores. **High school preparation:** 12 units recommended. Recommended units include biological science 1, English 4, foreign language 2, mathematics 3, physical science 1 and social science 1. US history also recommended. Mathematics units should include 2 algebra and 1 geometry. Science units should include laboratory. **Test requirements:** SAT or ACT (SAT preferred); score report by August 1.

1992 FRESHMAN CLASS PROFILE. 545 men applied, 471 accepted, 184 enrolled; 317 women applied, 282 accepted, 230 enrolled. 25% had high school GPA of 3.0 or higher, 65% between 2.0 and 2.99. **Academic background:** Mid 50% of enrolled freshmen had SAT-V between 330-520, SAT-M between 320-520; ACT composite between 15-19. 90% submitted SAT scores, 10% submitted ACT scores. **Characteristics:** 40% from in state, 88% live in college housing, 15% have minority backgrounds, 4% are foreign students. Average age is 18.

FALL-TERM APPLICATIONS. $15 fee, may be waived for applicants with need. Closing date June 15; priority given to applications received by May 1; applicants notified on a rolling basis; must reply by May 1 or within 3 weeks if notified thereafter. Audition required for music applicants. Interview recommended. Portfolio recommended for art applicants. Essay recommended. CRDA. Deferred and early admission available. Early admission contingent upon written approval of applicant's current school system.

STUDENT LIFE. Housing: Dormitories (men, women). All noncounty or nonadjacent county residents required to live on campus. **Activities:** Student government, magazine, student newspaper, yearbook, choral groups, concert band, dance, drama, jazz band, music ensembles, musical theater, college/community orchestra, honor society, Admissions Ambassadors, Christian Student Fellowship, environmental awareness.

ATHLETICS. NJCAA. **Intercollegiate:** Baseball M, basketball, cross-country, golf M, soccer, tennis W, track and field. **Intramural:** Badminton, basketball, bowling, horseback riding, skiing, softball, swimming, volleyball.

STUDENT SERVICES. Career counseling, employment service for undergraduates, freshman orientation, health services, personal counseling, services/facilities for handicapped.

ANNUAL EXPENSES. Tuition and fees: $6,445. **Room and board:** $3,650. **Books and supplies:** $550. **Other expenses:** $600.

FINANCIAL AID. 72% of freshmen, 74% of continuing students receive some form of aid. 57% of grants, 88% of loans, 76% of jobs based on need. 194 enrolled freshmen were judged to have need, all were offered aid. Academic, music/drama, art, athletic, leadership, religious affiliation scholarships available. **Aid applications:** No closing date; priority given to applications received by March 15; applicants notified on a rolling basis beginning on or about March 15; must reply within 4 weeks.

ADDRESS/TELEPHONE. Robert G. McLendon, Dean of Admissions, Brevard College, Brevard, NC 28712. (704) 884-8300. Fax: (704) 884-3790.

Brunswick Community College
Supply, North Carolina — CB code: 7314

2-year public community college, coed. Founded in 1979. **Accreditation:** Regional. **Undergraduate enrollment:** 131 men, 270 women full time; 192 men, 318 women part time. **Faculty:** 157 total (24 full time). **Location:** Rural campus in small town; 30 miles from Wilmington. **Calendar:** Quarter, limited summer session. Extensive evening/early morning classes. **Microcomputers:** 45 located in libraries, classrooms, computer centers.

DEGREES OFFERED. AS. 64 associate degrees awarded in 1992. 29% in business and management, 20% business/office and marketing/distribution, 20% computer sciences, 20% engineering technologies, 11% multi/interdisciplinary studies.

UNDERGRADUATE MAJORS. Business administration and management, business and office, business computer/console/peripheral equipment operation, business data programming, computer programming, electronic technology, liberal/general studies, medical assistant, medical records technology, parks and recreation management, real estate, respiratory therapy, secretarial and related programs.

ACADEMIC PROGRAMS. 2-year transfer program, accelerated program, double major, dual enrollment of high school students, internships, telecourses. **Remedial services:** Learning center, preadmission summer program, reduced course load, remedial instruction, special counselor, tutoring. **Placement/credit:** Institutional tests.

ACADEMIC REQUIREMENTS. Freshmen must earn minimum GPA of 2.0 to continue in good standing. 48% of freshmen return for sophomore year. Students must declare major on enrollment. **Graduation requirements:** 102 hours for associate (58 in major). Most students required to take courses in English, mathematics, social sciences.

FRESHMAN ADMISSIONS. Selection criteria: Open admissions. Selective admissions to nursing program.

1992 FRESHMAN CLASS PROFILE. 54 men, 97 women enrolled. **Characteristics:** 96% from in state, 100% commute, 22% have minority backgrounds. Average age is 32.

FALL-TERM APPLICATIONS. No fee. No closing date; applicants

notified on a rolling basis. Interview required for practical nursing applicants. ASSET scores used for placement.

STUDENT LIFE. Activities: Student government, student newspaper, yearbook, drama.

ATHLETICS. Intercollegiate: Volleyball. **Intramural:** Volleyball.

STUDENT SERVICES. Aptitude testing, career counseling, employment service for undergraduates, freshman orientation, personal counseling, placement service for graduates, special adviser for adult students, veterans counselor, services/facilities for handicapped.

ANNUAL EXPENSES. Tuition and fees (1992-93): $581, $3,959 additional for out-of-state students. **Books and supplies:** $390. **Other expenses:** $660.

FINANCIAL AID. 48% of continuing students receive some form of aid. 88% of grants, 97% of loans, all jobs based on need. Academic, leadership scholarships available. **Aid applications:** No closing date; priority given to applications received by August 1; applicants notified on a rolling basis; must reply within 2 weeks.

ADDRESS/TELEPHONE. H. Elizabeth McLean, Dean of Student Services, Brunswick Community College, PO Box 30, Supply, NC 28462. (919) 754-6900. Fax: (919) 754-7805.

Caldwell Community College and Technical Institute
Hudson, North Carolina — CB code: 5146

2-year public community, technical college, coed. Founded in 1964. **Accreditation:** Regional. **Undergraduate enrollment:** 357 men, 591 women full time; 644 men, 1,296 women part time. **Faculty:** 223 total (65 full time), 15 with doctorates or other terminal degrees. **Location:** Rural campus in small town; 65 miles from Charlotte. **Calendar:** Quarter, limited summer session. Saturday and extensive evening/early morning classes. **Microcomputers:** Located in libraries, classrooms, computer centers. **Special facilities:** Planetarium.

DEGREES OFFERED. AA, AS, AAS. 206 associate degrees awarded in 1992. 18% in business and management, 7% engineering technologies, 36% health sciences, 34% multi/interdisciplinary studies.

UNDERGRADUATE MAJORS. Accounting, biomedical equipment technology, business administration and management, business data processing and related programs, drafting, drafting and design technology, electronic technology, engineering and other disciplines, industrial equipment maintenance and repair, legal assistant/paralegal, liberal/general studies, machine tool operation/machine shop, medical secretary, microcomputer software, music, nursing, occupational therapy assistant, physical therapy assistant, radiograph medical technology, secretarial and related programs, ultrasound technology.

ACADEMIC PROGRAMS. 2-year transfer program, cooperative education, dual enrollment of high school students, honors program, independent study, internships, weekend college. **Remedial services:** Learning center, reduced course load, remedial instruction, special counselor, tutoring. **Placement/credit:** CLEP Subject, institutional tests; 32 credit hours maximum for associate degree.

ACADEMIC REQUIREMENTS. Freshmen must earn minimum GPA of 2.0 to continue in good standing. 44% of freshmen return for sophomore year. Students must declare major on enrollment. **Graduation requirements:** 96 hours for associate. Most students required to take courses in computer science, English, humanities, mathematics, biological/physical sciences, social sciences.

FRESHMAN ADMISSIONS. Selection criteria: Open admissions. Selective admissions to allied health programs. **High school preparation:** 21 units recommended. Recommended units include biological science 1, English 4, mathematics 2, physical science 1, social science 1 and science 1. **Test requirements:** College-administered examination used for placement and credit.

1992 FRESHMAN CLASS PROFILE. 371 men, 503 women enrolled. **Characteristics:** 99% from in state, 100% commute, 6% have minority backgrounds. Average age is 25.

FALL-TERM APPLICATIONS. No fee. No closing date; applicants notified on a rolling basis. Interview required for allied health program applicants.

STUDENT LIFE. Activities: Student government, magazine, television, literary magazine, choral groups, concert band, drama, jazz band, music ensembles, Ebony Kinship, Circle-K, special interest clubs, Phi Theta Kappa, Alpha Omega (non-denominational religious organization).

ATHLETICS. Intramural: Badminton, basketball M, table tennis, tennis, volleyball.

STUDENT SERVICES. Aptitude testing, career counseling, employment service for undergraduates, freshman orientation, health services, personal counseling, placement service for graduates, veterans counselor, services/facilities for handicapped.

ANNUAL EXPENSES. Tuition and fees (1992-93): $578, $3,959 additional for out-of-state students. **Books and supplies:** $450. **Other expenses:** $1,350.

FINANCIAL AID. 25% of freshmen, 25% of continuing students receive some form of aid. 94% of grants, 87% of loans, all jobs based on need. 437 enrolled freshmen were judged to have need, all were offered aid. Academic, state/district residency, leadership, minority scholarships available. **Aid applications:** No closing date; priority given to applications received by May 1; applicants notified on a rolling basis beginning on or about June 30; must reply within 2 weeks.

ADDRESS/TELEPHONE. Janice Van Osdol, Director of Enrollment Services, Caldwell Community College and Technical Institute, 1000 Hickory Boulevard, Hudson, NC 28638-2397. (704) 726-2200. Fax: (704) 726-2216.

Campbell University
Buies Creek, North Carolina — CB code: 5100

Admissions:	69% of applicants accepted
Based on:	••• School record
	•• Interview, test scores
	• Activities, essay, recommendations, special talents
Completion:	79% of freshmen end year in good standing
	66% graduate, 29% of these enter graduate study

4-year private university, coed, affiliated with Southern Baptist Convention. Founded in 1887. **Accreditation:** Regional. **Undergraduate enrollment:** 3,136 men and women full time; 821 men and women part time. **Graduate enrollment:** 511 men, 492 women full time; 47 men, 290 women part time. **Faculty:** 261 total (139 full time), 157 with doctorates or other terminal degrees. **Location:** Rural campus in rural community; 30 miles from Raleigh, 30 miles from Fayetteville. **Calendar:** Semester, extensive summer session. **Microcomputers:** 60 located in libraries, classrooms, computer centers. **Special facilities:** Geological collection, drug information center. **Additional facts:** Colleges of business, pharmacy, education, law, trust management, and arts and sciences.

DEGREES OFFERED. AA, AS, BA, BS, MS, MBA, MEd, EdD, Pharm D, JD. 91 associate degrees awarded in 1992. 426 bachelor's degrees awarded. 28% in business and management, 6% communications, 13% education, 5% philosophy, religion, theology, 5% physical sciences, 16% social sciences. Graduate degrees offered in 15 major fields of study.

UNDERGRADUATE MAJORS. Associate: Business and management, business data processing and related programs, business data programming, education. **Bachelor's:** Accounting, advertising, biology, business administration and management, business and management, business data processing and related programs, business economics, chemistry, clinical laboratory science, communications, computer and information sciences, data processing, dramatic arts, early childhood education, economics, education, elementary education, English, English education, fashion design, fashion merchandising, fine arts, food management, food production/management/services, food science and nutrition, foreign languages (multiple emphasis), foreign languages education, French, graphic design, health education, health sciences, history, home economics, home economics education, human environment and housing, institutional/home management/supporting programs, international business management, international studies, journalism, junior high education, mathematics, mathematics education, medical laboratory technologies, military science (Army), music, music education, music performance, nutritional education, philosophy, physical education, political science and government, predentistry, prelaw, premedicine, psychology, public administration, public relations, radio/television broadcasting, radio/television technology, reading education, religion, religious education, religious music, school psychology, science education, secondary education, social science education, social sciences, social studies education, social work, Spanish, sports management, textiles and clothing, theological studies, trust management.

ACADEMIC PROGRAMS. 2-year transfer program, accelerated program, cooperative education, double major, education specialist degree, honors program, independent study, internships, study abroad, teacher preparation, visiting/exchange student program, Washington semester; liberal arts/career combination in engineering; combined bachelor's/graduate program in business administration, law. **Remedial services:** Preadmission summer program, reduced course load, remedial instruction, special counselor, tutoring. **ROTC:** Army. **Placement/credit:** AP, CLEP General and Subject, institutional tests; 64 credit hours maximum for bachelor's degree.

ACADEMIC REQUIREMENTS. Freshmen must earn minimum GPA of 2.0 to continue in good standing. 75% of freshmen return for sophomore year. Students must declare major by end of second year. **Graduation requirements:** 64 hours for associate, 128 hours for bachelor's. Most students required to take courses in arts/fine arts, English, foreign languages, history, mathematics, philosophy/religion, biological/physical sciences, social sciences. **Postgraduate studies:** 1% from 2-year programs enter 4-year programs. 10% enter law school, 2% enter medical school, 10% enter MBA programs, 7% enter other graduate study.

FRESHMAN ADMISSIONS. Selection criteria: Minimum 2.5 GPA and rank in top half of class required. **High school preparation:** 13 units required. Required units include English 4, foreign language 2, mathematics 3, social science 2 and science 2. **Test requirements:** SAT or ACT (SAT preferred); score report by May 1.

1992 FRESHMAN CLASS PROFILE. 791 men applied, 545 accepted, 257 enrolled; 838 women applied, 586 accepted, 279 enrolled. 15% were in top tenth and 23% were in top quarter of graduating class. **Academic background:** Mid 50% of enrolled freshmen had SAT-V between 490-510, SAT-M between 540-550. 86% submitted SAT scores. **Characteristics:** 65% from in state, 82% live in college housing, 16% have minority backgrounds, 5% are foreign students. Average age is 19.

FALL-TERM APPLICATIONS. $15 fee. Closing date August 1; applicants notified on a rolling basis; must reply within 2 weeks. Interview recommended. Audition recommended for music applicants. Essay recommended. Deferred and early admission available.

STUDENT LIFE. Housing: Dormitories (men, women); apartment housing available. All off-campus housing must be approved by the Student Personnel Office. **Activities:** Student government, magazine, radio, student newspaper, television, yearbook, choral groups, concert band, drama, jazz band, music ensembles, musical theater, pep band, Baptist Student Union, Young Democrats/Republicans, Alpha Phi Omega, Inter-Varsity Christian Fellowship, Circle-K, Fellowship of Christian Athletes, North Carolina Student Legislature, Catholic Young Adults, Baptist Young Women, Gospel choir.

ATHLETICS. NCAA. **Intercollegiate:** Baseball M, basketball, cross-country, golf, soccer, softball W, tennis, track and field, volleyball W, wrestling M. **Intramural:** Basketball, football M, softball, swimming, table tennis, tennis, volleyball W.

STUDENT SERVICES. Aptitude testing, career counseling, employment service for undergraduates, freshman orientation, health services, personal counseling, placement service for graduates, special adviser for adult students, veterans counselor, services/facilities for handicapped.

ANNUAL EXPENSES. Tuition and fees (1992-93): $7,678. **Room and board:** $2,590. **Books and supplies:** $600. **Other expenses:** $1,927.

FINANCIAL AID. 86% of freshmen, 91% of continuing students receive some form of aid. 39% of grants, 81% of loans, 75% of jobs based on need. Academic, music/drama, athletic, leadership, religious affiliation scholarships available. **Aid applications:** No closing date; priority given to applications received by March 15; applicants notified on a rolling basis beginning on or about April 15; must reply within 2 weeks.

ADDRESS/TELEPHONE. Herbert V. Kerner, Dean of Admissions, Campbell University, PO Box 546, Buies Creek, NC 27506. (919) 893-1200 ext. 1320. (800) 334-4111 ext. 1320. Fax: (919) 893-9274.

Cape Fear Community College
Wilmington, North Carolina — CB code: 5094

2-year public community college, coed. Founded in 1959. **Accreditation:** Regional. **Undergraduate enrollment:** 812 men, 824 women full time; 642 men, 921 women part time. **Faculty:** 188 total (74 full time), 18 with doctorates or other terminal degrees. **Location:** Urban campus in small city; 125 miles from Raleigh. **Calendar:** Quarter, limited summer session. Saturday and extensive evening/early morning classes. **Microcomputers:** 10 located in libraries, classrooms. **Additional facts:** Branch campus at Burgaw, 20 miles from Wilmington campus.

DEGREES OFFERED. AA, AAS. 196 associate degrees awarded in 1992.

UNDERGRADUATE MAJORS. Accounting, business administration and management, chemical manufacturing technology, chemistry, computer servicing technology, computer technology, criminal justice technology, drafting and design technology, electrical and electronics equipment repair, electronic technology, instrumentation technology, legal assistant/paralegal, manufacturing technology, marine biology, mechanical design technology, medical records technology, nursing, oceanography, secretarial and related programs.

ACADEMIC PROGRAMS. 2-year transfer program, dual enrollment of high school students, internships, telecourses. **Remedial services:** Learning center, remedial instruction, special counselor, tutoring. **Placement/credit:** Institutional tests.

ACADEMIC REQUIREMENTS. Freshmen must earn minimum GPA of 1.75 to continue in good standing. 40% of freshmen return for sophomore year. Students must declare major on application. **Graduation requirements:** 106 hours for associate. Most students required to take courses in English, mathematics, social sciences.

FRESHMAN ADMISSIONS. Selection criteria: Open admissions. Selected admissions for allied health programs.

1992 FRESHMAN CLASS PROFILE. 401 men, 631 women enrolled. **Characteristics:** 92% from in state, 100% commute, 18% have minority backgrounds, 1% are foreign students. Average age is 23.

FALL-TERM APPLICATIONS. No fee. No closing date; applicants notified on a rolling basis; must reply within 2 weeks. Interview required for allied health programs applicants.

STUDENT LIFE. Activities: Student government, student newspaper, yearbook, choral groups, intramural chess team.

ATHLETICS. Intercollegiate: Basketball M, golf, softball, tennis, volleyball. **Intramural:** Swimming, volleyball. **Clubs:** Surfing.

STUDENT SERVICES. Aptitude testing, career counseling, employment service for undergraduates, freshman orientation, personal counseling, placement service for graduates, veterans counselor, special populations counselor, services/facilities for handicapped.

ANNUAL EXPENSES. Tuition and fees (1992-93): $576, $3,959 additional for out-of-state students. **Books and supplies:** $460. **Other expenses:** $770.

FINANCIAL AID. 45% of freshmen, 20% of continuing students receive some form of aid. All grants, 70% of loans based on need. Academic, state/district residency scholarships available. **Aid applications:** No closing date; priority given to applications received by March 15; applicants notified on a rolling basis beginning on or about May 1; must reply by registration.

ADDRESS/TELEPHONE. David J. Pate, Director of Admissions, Cape Fear Community College, 411 North Front Street, Wilmington, NC 28401. (919) 343-0481. Fax: (919) 763-2279.

Carteret Community College
Morehead City, North Carolina — CB code: 5092

2-year public community college, coed. Founded in 1963. **Accreditation:** Regional. **Undergraduate enrollment:** 238 men, 527 women full time; 269 men, 568 women part time. **Faculty:** 93 total (41 full time), 10 with doctorates or other terminal degrees. **Location:** Rural campus in small town; on the Atlantic Ocean, 150 miles from Raleigh. **Calendar:** Quarter, limited summer session. Extensive evening/early morning classes. **Microcomputers:** 40 located in libraries, classrooms. **Special facilities:** Crystal Coast Civic Center, county historical research headquarters. **Additional facts:** Health science programs and new library learning resources center on Bogue Sound.

DEGREES OFFERED. AAS. 95 associate degrees awarded in 1992. 35% in business and management, 35% business/office and marketing/distribution, 25% allied health, 5% parks/recreation, protective services, public affairs.

UNDERGRADUATE MAJORS. Automotive technology, business administration and management, business and office, criminal justice technology, education, interior design, law enforcement and corrections technologies, legal assistant/paralegal, legal secretary, liberal/general studies, medical assistant, medical secretary, photographic technology, radiograph medical technology, recreation and community services technologies, recreation therapy, respiratory therapy, respiratory therapy technology, secretarial and related programs.

ACADEMIC PROGRAMS. 2-year transfer program, double major, dual enrollment of high school students, internships, telecourses, cross-registration. **Remedial services:** Learning center, preadmission summer program, reduced course load, remedial instruction, tutoring. **Placement/credit:** Institutional tests.

ACADEMIC REQUIREMENTS. Freshmen must earn minimum GPA of 2.0 to continue in good standing. 40% of freshmen return for sophomore year. Students must declare major on enrollment. **Graduation requirements:** 108 hours for associate (80 in major). Most students required to take courses in English, mathematics, biological/physical sciences.

FRESHMAN ADMISSIONS. Selection criteria: Open admissions. Selective admissions to allied health programs based on test scores. Extensive science and mathematics recommended for allied health programs, particularly respiratory therapy, radiologic technology, and nursing. **Test requirements:** SAT required of radiologic technology and respiratory therapy applicants; score report due by August 30.

1992 FRESHMAN CLASS PROFILE. 275 men and women enrolled. **Characteristics:** 94% from in state, 100% commute, 9% have minority backgrounds. Average age is 26.

FALL-TERM APPLICATIONS. No fee. No closing date; applicants notified on a rolling basis beginning on or about April 1; accepted allied health program applicants must reply within 3 weeks. Interview required for allied health applicants. Deferred and early admission available.

STUDENT LIFE. Activities: Student government, student newspaper, Psi Beta (honorary society for psychology majors), Phi Beta Lambda (business organization).

ATHLETICS. Intercollegiate: Softball, volleyball.

STUDENT SERVICES. Aptitude testing, career counseling, employment service for undergraduates, freshman orientation, personal counseling, placement service for graduates, veterans counselor, services/facilities for handicapped.

ANNUAL EXPENSES. Tuition and fees (1992-93): $573, $3,959 additional for out-of-state students. **Books and supplies:** $500. **Other expenses:** $200.

FINANCIAL AID. 60% of freshmen, 20% of continuing students receive some form of aid. 97% of grants, all loans, all jobs based on need. Minority scholarships available. **Aid applications:** No closing date; priority given to applications received by August 1; applicants notified on a rolling basis beginning on or about August 1; must reply immediately. **Additional information:** Institutional student loan program administered by college. Student may charge up to $375 for books, supplies and tuition per quarter. Repayment due by end of quarter.

ADDRESS/TELEPHONE. Don Thompson, Director of Student Services, Carteret Community College, 3505 Arendell Street, Morehead City, NC 28557-2989. (919) 247-4142 ext. 152. Fax: (919) 247-3134.

Catawba College
Salisbury, North Carolina CB code: 5103

Admissions: 82% of applicants accepted
Based on: ••• School record, test scores
•• Essay, interview, recommendations, special talents
• Activities
Completion: 90% of freshmen end year in good standing
40% graduate, 24% of these enter graduate study

4-year private liberal arts college, coed, affiliated with United Church of Christ. Founded in 1851. **Accreditation:** Regional. **Undergraduate enrollment:** 473 men, 432 women full time; 20 men, 31 women part time. **Graduate enrollment:** 6 women part time. **Faculty:** 76 total (63 full time), 46 with doctorates or other terminal degrees. **Location:** Suburban campus in large town; 50 miles from Charlotte, Greensboro, 45 from Winston-Salem. **Calendar:** Semester, limited summer session. Extensive evening/early morning classes. **Microcomputers:** 50 located in libraries, computer centers. **Special facilities:** 60-acre nature study area.

DEGREES OFFERED. BA, MEd. 173 bachelor's degrees awarded in 1992. 34% in business and management, 6% communications, 10% teacher education, 8% parks/recreation, protective services, public affairs, 11% social sciences, 10% visual and performing arts. Graduate degrees offered in 3 major fields of study.

UNDERGRADUATE MAJORS. Accounting, arts management, biology, business administration and management, business and management, chemistry, communications, computer and information sciences, dramatic arts, early childhood education, education of the gifted and talented, education of the mentally handicapped, elementary education, English, English education, French, history, information sciences and systems, international business management, international relations, junior high education, mathematics, mathematics education, medical laboratory technologies, music, music education, musical theater, parks and recreation management, philosophy, physical education, physician's assistant, political science and government, predentistry, prelaw, premedicine, psychology, reading education, religion, religious music, science education, social science education, sociology, Spanish, special education, sports medicine.

ACADEMIC PROGRAMS. Double major, dual enrollment of high school students, honors program, independent study, internships, student-designed major, study abroad, teacher preparation, Washington semester, 3-2 program in forestry with Duke University; liberal arts/career combination in health sciences. **ROTC:** Army. **Placement/credit:** AP, CLEP General and Subject, institutional tests; 32 credit hours maximum for bachelor's degree.

ACADEMIC REQUIREMENTS. Freshmen must earn minimum GPA of 1.5 to continue in good standing. 71% of freshmen return for sophomore year. Students must declare major by end of second year. **Graduation requirements:** 128 hours for bachelor's (30 in major). Most students required to take courses in arts/fine arts, computer science, English, foreign languages, history, humanities, mathematics, philosophy/religion, biological/physical sciences, social sciences. **Postgraduate studies:** 1% enter law school, 2% enter medical school, 5% enter MBA programs, 16% enter other graduate study.

FRESHMAN ADMISSIONS. Selection criteria: School achievement record, class rank, standardized test scores, and school recommendations are important. **High school preparation:** 12 units required. Required and recommended units include English 4, mathematics 2-3, social science 2 and science 2. Foreign language 2 recommended. **Test requirements:** SAT or ACT (SAT preferred); score report by August 20.

1992 FRESHMAN CLASS PROFILE. 501 men applied, 386 accepted, 162 enrolled; 438 women applied, 384 accepted, 130 enrolled. 36% had high school GPA of 3.0 or higher, 53% between 2.0 and 2.99. **Academic background:** Mid 50% of enrolled freshmen had SAT-V between 370-480, SAT-M between 400-520. 90% submitted SAT scores. **Characteristics:** 37% from in state, 91% live in college housing, 11% have minority backgrounds, 1% are foreign students. Average age is 18.

FALL-TERM APPLICATIONS. $25 fee, may be waived for applicants with need. No closing date; applicants notified on a rolling basis. Interview recommended. Audition recommended for music, drama applicants. Essay recommended. Deferred and early admission available.

STUDENT LIFE. Housing: Dormitories (men, women, coed). **Activities:** Student government, magazine, student newspaper, choral groups, concert band, dance, drama, jazz band, music ensembles, musical theater, pep band, symphony orchestra, United in Service, Campus Crusade for Christ.

ATHLETICS. NAIA, NCAA. **Intercollegiate:** Baseball M, basketball, cross-country, field hockey W, football M, golf M, soccer, softball W, tennis, volleyball W. **Intramural:** Basketball, cross-country, football M, golf, handball, racquetball, soccer, softball, table tennis, tennis, volleyball.

STUDENT SERVICES. Aptitude testing, career counseling, employment service for undergraduates, freshman orientation, health services, personal counseling, placement service for graduates, special adviser for adult students, Alumni Career Resource Center.

ANNUAL EXPENSES. Tuition and fees: $9,000. **Room and board:** $3,950. **Books and supplies:** $600. **Other expenses:** $1,200.

FINANCIAL AID. 84% of freshmen, 81% of continuing students receive some form of aid. 25% of grants, 84% of loans, 36% of jobs based on need. 141 enrolled freshmen were judged to have need, all were offered aid. Academic, music/drama, athletic, state/district residency, leadership, religious affiliation scholarships available. **Aid applications:** No closing date; priority given to applications received by March 30; applicants notified on a rolling basis beginning on or about April 15; must reply within 2 weeks.

ADDRESS/TELEPHONE. Thomas C. Childress, Dean of Admissions, Catawba College, 2300 West Innes Street, Salisbury, NC 28144-2488. (704) 637-4402. (800) CATAWBA. Fax: (704) 637-4444.

Catawba Valley Community College
Hickory, North Carolina CB code: 5098

2-year public community college, coed. Founded in 1960. **Accreditation:** Regional. **Undergraduate enrollment:** 673 men, 757 women full time; 832 men, 1,304 women part time. **Faculty:** 245 total (95 full time). **Location:** Suburban campus in large town; 50 miles from Charlotte. **Calendar:** Quarter, limited summer session. Saturday and extensive evening/early morning classes. **Microcomputers:** Located in libraries, classrooms.

DEGREES OFFERED. AA, AS, AAS. 263 associate degrees awarded in 1992. 40% in business/office and marketing/distribution, 10% computer sciences, 25% engineering technologies, 15% allied health, 7% trade and industry.

UNDERGRADUATE MAJORS. Accounting, air conditioning/heating/refrigeration mechanics, architectural technologies, automotive mechanics, automotive technology, business and management, business and office, business data processing and related programs, commercial art, computer technology, data processing, drafting, early childhood education, education, electrical installation, electronic technology, elementary education, emergency medical technologies, engineering and engineering-related technologies, finance, food production/management/services, horticulture, industrial technology, junior high education, liberal/general studies, marketing and distribution, marketing management, mechanical design technology, nursing, ornamental horticulture, parks and recreation management, precision metal work, real estate, respiratory therapy technology, robotics, secondary education, secretarial and related programs, teacher aide, transportation management.

ACADEMIC PROGRAMS. 2-year transfer program, cooperative education, double major, dual enrollment of high school students, independent study, internships, telecourses, cross-registration. **Remedial services:** Learning center, preadmission summer program, reduced course load, remedial instruction, special counselor, tutoring. **Placement/credit:** Institutional tests. Maximum of half of total credit hours required for degree may be obtained by examination.

ACADEMIC REQUIREMENTS. Freshmen must earn minimum GPA of 2.0 to continue in good standing. 60% of freshmen return for sophomore year. Students must declare major on application. **Graduation requirements:** 118 hours for associate (97 in major). Most students required to take courses in English, mathematics, social sciences.

FRESHMAN ADMISSIONS. Selection criteria: Open admissions. Selective admissions to nursing, emergency medical technology, surgical technology, and respiratory care technology programs. 2 units algebra recommended for engineering technologies applicants. **Test requirements:** CGP Algebra I Test required of engineering technology applicants.

1992 FRESHMAN CLASS PROFILE. 548 men, 756 women enrolled. **Characteristics:** 97% from in state, 100% commute, 7% have minority backgrounds. Average age is 29.

FALL-TERM APPLICATIONS. No fee. No closing date; priority given to applications received by August 15; applicants notified on a rolling basis. Interview required for health program applicants, recommended for all others. Deferred and early admission available.

STUDENT LIFE. Activities: Student government, yearbook, Phi Beta Lambda, Future Secretaries, Data Processing Management Association, turf club, accounting club, radio club.

ATHLETICS. NJCAA. **Intercollegiate:** Golf M, tennis. **Intramural:** Volleyball.

STUDENT SERVICES. Aptitude testing, career counseling, employment service for undergraduates, freshman orientation, personal counseling, placement service for graduates, veterans counselor, services/facilities for handicapped.

ANNUAL EXPENSES. Tuition and fees (1992-93): $575, $3,959 additional for out-of-state students. **Books and supplies:** $800. **Other expenses:** $800.

FINANCIAL AID. 12% of freshmen, 14% of continuing students receive some form of aid. 95% of grants, 86% of loans, all jobs based on need. 400 enrolled freshmen were judged to have need, 275 were offered aid.

Academic, leadership scholarships available. **Aid applications:** No closing date; applicants notified on a rolling basis; must reply within 2 weeks.

ADDRESS/TELEPHONE. Louise M. Garrison, Director of Admissions and Records, Catawba Valley Community College, 2550 Highway 70 SE, Hickory, NC 28602. (704) 327-7000 ext. 221. Fax: (704) 327-7000 ext. 301.

Cecils College
Asheville, North Carolina CB code: 0508

2-year proprietary business, junior college, coed. Founded in 1905. **Accreditation:** Regional candidate. **Undergraduate enrollment:** 30 men, 200 women full time; 15 men, 10 women part time. **Location:** Suburban campus in small city; 4 miles from downtown. **Calendar:** Quarter.

FRESHMAN ADMISSIONS. Selection criteria: College-administered exam required of all applicants. Scores used for admission and placement.

ANNUAL EXPENSES. Tuition and fees (1992-93): $4,160. **Books and supplies:** $400. **Other expenses:** $1,080.

ADDRESS/TELEPHONE. Chip Culbertson, Director of Admissions, Cecils College, PO Box 6407, Asheville, NC 28816. (704) 252-2486.

Central Carolina Community College
Sanford, North Carolina CB code: 5147

2-year public community college, coed. Founded in 1958. **Accreditation:** Regional. **Undergraduate enrollment:** 681 men, 797 women full time; 586 men, 949 women part time. **Faculty:** 186 total (98 full time), 6 with doctorates or other terminal degrees. **Location:** Rural campus in large town; 45 miles from Raleigh. **Calendar:** Quarter. Extensive evening/early morning classes. **Microcomputers:** Located in classrooms.

DEGREES OFFERED. AAS. 233 associate degrees awarded in 1992. 17% in business and management, 9% business/office and marketing/distribution, 12% education, 14% engineering technologies, 13% health sciences, 13% allied health, 6% law, 7% trade and industry.

UNDERGRADUATE MAJORS. Accounting, automotive technology, business administration and management, business and office, business data processing and related programs, child development/care/guidance, computer programming, criminal justice technology, drafting, drafting and design technology, education, electronic technology, fashion merchandising, finance, instrumentation technology, laser electro-optic technology, law enforcement and corrections technologies, legal assistant/paralegal, legal secretary, liberal/general studies, medical secretary, nursing, quality control technology, radio/television broadcasting, secretarial and related programs, social work, trade and industrial supervision and management, veterinarian's assistant.

ACADEMIC PROGRAMS. 2-year transfer program, dual enrollment of high school students, honors program, independent study, internships, telecourses. **Remedial services:** Learning center, reduced course load, remedial instruction, tutoring. **Placement/credit:** CLEP General and Subject, institutional tests.

ACADEMIC REQUIREMENTS. Freshmen must earn minimum GPA of 2.0 to continue in good standing. 40% of freshmen return for sophomore year. Students must declare major on enrollment. **Graduation requirements:** Most students required to take courses in English, mathematics, social sciences.

FRESHMAN ADMISSIONS. Selection criteria: Open admissions. Selective admissions to animal laboratory, nursing education, radio-television broadcasting, laser electro-optic, electronics and instrumentation technology, and cosmetology programs. Strong background in mathematics, biology, and chemistry required for animal laboratory and nursing education option programs. **Additional information:** Placement interview required.

1992 FRESHMAN CLASS PROFILE. 299 men, 277 women enrolled. 1% had high school GPA of 3.0 or higher, 85% between 2.0 and 2.99. **Characteristics:** 98% from in state, 100% commute, 29% have minority backgrounds. Average age is 29.

FALL-TERM APPLICATIONS. No fee. No closing date; priority given to applications received by February 12; applicants notified on a rolling basis; must reply within 2 weeks. Interview required. Deferred admission available.

STUDENT LIFE. Activities: Student government, radio, Student Nurses Association, Student ambassador program.

ATHLETICS. Intramural: Basketball M, bowling, golf M, softball M, tennis M, volleyball.

STUDENT SERVICES. Aptitude testing, career counseling, employment service for undergraduates, freshman orientation, personal counseling, placement service for graduates, veterans counselor, services/facilities for handicapped.

ANNUAL EXPENSES. Tuition and fees (1992-93): $578, $3,959 additional for out-of-state students. **Books and supplies:** $450. **Other expenses:** $850.

FINANCIAL AID. 35% of freshmen, 40% of continuing students receive some form of aid. All jobs based on need. 225 enrolled freshmen were judged to have need, all were offered aid. **Aid applications:** No closing date; priority given to applications received by May 30; applicants notified on a rolling basis beginning on or about June 15; must reply within 2 weeks.

ADDRESS/TELEPHONE. Ron Miriello, Associate Dean of Student Development, Central Carolina Community College, 1105 Kelly Drive, Sanford, NC 27330. (919) 775-5401 ext. 300.

Central Piedmont Community College
Charlotte, North Carolina CB code: 5102

2-year public community college, coed. Founded in 1963. **Accreditation:** Regional. **Undergraduate enrollment:** 2,091 men, 2,350 women full time; 3,626 men, 4,805 women part time. **Faculty:** 1,800 total (600 full time), 17 with doctorates or other terminal degrees. **Location:** Urban campus in large city. **Calendar:** Quarter, extensive summer session. Saturday and extensive evening/early morning classes. **Microcomputers:** 1,300 located in libraries, classrooms. **Special facilities:** Audiovisual libraries.

DEGREES OFFERED. AA, AS. 755 associate degrees awarded in 1992.

UNDERGRADUATE MAJORS. Accounting, advertising, air conditioning/heating/refrigeration mechanics, air conditioning/heating/refrigeration technology, architectural technologies, architecture, automotive mechanics, automotive technology, business and management, business and office, business data processing and related programs, civil technology, commercial art, computer and information sciences, computer technology, data processing, dental hygiene, diesel engine mechanics, drafting, electrical and electronics equipment repair, electrical technology, electronic technology, engineering and engineering-related technologies, fashion merchandising, finance, fine arts, fire protection, food management, food production/management/services, graphic and printing production, graphic arts technology, horticultural science, horticulture, hotel/motel and restaurant management, industrial safety, insurance and risk management, insurance marketing, interior design, international business management, interpreter for the deaf, law enforcement and corrections technologies, legal secretary, liberal/general studies, manufacturing technology, marketing and distribution, mechanical design technology, mechanical engineering, medical assistant, medical records administration, medical records technology, medical secretary, music, nursing, physical therapy assistant, protective services, real estate, recreation and community services technologies, respiratory therapy technology, secretarial and related programs, surveying and mapping sciences, tourism, transportation management, visual and performing arts.

ACADEMIC PROGRAMS. 2-year transfer program, cooperative education, double major, dual enrollment of high school students, honors program, independent study, internships, student-designed major, telecourses, weekend college, cross-registration. **Remedial services:** Learning center, preadmission summer program, reduced course load, remedial instruction, special counselor, tutoring. **Placement/credit:** CLEP General and Subject, institutional tests; 64 credit hours maximum for associate degree.

ACADEMIC REQUIREMENTS. No policy requiring minimum GPA; records of students having academic difficulty are reviewed individually. 30% of freshmen return for sophomore year. Students must declare major on application. **Graduation requirements:** 96 hours for associate (45 in major). Most students required to take courses in English, biological/physical sciences, social sciences.

FRESHMAN ADMISSIONS. Selection criteria: Open admissions. Placement test scores used for admission to programs with specific requirements.

1992 FRESHMAN CLASS PROFILE. 642 men, 744 women enrolled. **Characteristics:** 97% from in state, 100% commute, 29% have minority backgrounds, 5% are foreign students.

FALL-TERM APPLICATIONS. No fee. Closing date September 2; applicants notified on a rolling basis. Interview required for allied health programs applicants. Deferred admission available.

STUDENT LIFE. Activities: Student government, film, magazine, radio, student newspaper, television, choral groups, concert band, dance, drama, jazz band, music ensembles, musical theater, opera, symphony orchestra, Afro-American Cultural Club, Baptist Student Union, International Students Club.

ATHLETICS. NJCAA. **Intercollegiate:** Basketball, golf M, softball, tennis, volleyball. **Intramural:** Basketball, golf, soccer, softball, tennis, volleyball.

STUDENT SERVICES. Aptitude testing, career counseling, employment service for undergraduates, health services, on-campus day care, personal counseling, placement service for graduates, veterans counselor, services/facilities for handicapped.

ANNUAL EXPENSES. Tuition and fees (1992-93): $572, $3,959 additional for out-of-state students. **Books and supplies:** $600. **Other expenses:** $1,125.

FINANCIAL AID. 15% of freshmen, 20% of continuing students receive some form of aid. All grants, 84% of loans, all jobs based on need. **Aid applications:** No closing date; priority given to applications received by April 1; applicants notified on a rolling basis; must reply within 2 weeks.

ADDRESS/TELEPHONE. Don Flowers, Director of Admissions, Central Piedmont Community College, PO Box 35009, Charlotte, NC 28235-5009. (704) 342-6687.

Chowan College
Murfreesboro, North Carolina CB code: 5107

Admissions:	74% of applicants accepted
Based on:	••• School record
	•• Test scores
	• Activities, essay, interview, recommendations, special talents
Completion:	60% of freshmen end year in good standing

4-year private liberal arts college, coed, affiliated with Southern Baptist Convention. Founded in 1848. **Accreditation:** Regional. **Undergraduate enrollment:** 403 men, 220 women full time; 11 men, 7 women part time. **Faculty:** 64 total (52 full time), 27 with doctorates or other terminal degrees. **Location:** Rural campus in small town; 60 miles from Norfolk, Virginia, 140 miles from Raleigh. **Calendar:** Semester, limited summer session. **Microcomputers:** 80 located in libraries, classrooms, computer centers. **Special facilities:** Horner Graphic Communications Center.

DEGREES OFFERED. AA, AS, AAS, BA, BS. 160 associate degrees awarded in 1992. 30% in business and management, 15% computer sciences, 9% education, 7% engineering, 6% life sciences, 7% psychology, 7% social sciences, 16% trade and industry.

UNDERGRADUATE MAJORS. Associate: Accounting, agricultural sciences, biology, business administration and management, business and management, business data entry equipment operation, business data processing and related programs, business data programming, chemistry, computer and information sciences, computer programming, education, engineering, engineering and engineering-related technologies, English, fashion merchandising, fine arts, forestry and related sciences, French, graphic arts technology, health sciences, law , liberal/general studies, mathematics, medical assistant, medical illustrating, medical records administration, medical records technology, music, nursing, pharmacy, photographic technology, photography, physical sciences, physical therapy, predentistry, premedicine, preveterinary, psychology, social sciences, sociology, Spanish, sports medicine. **Bachelor's:** Art education, business administration and management, business and management, commercial art, education, elementary education, English, English education, fine arts, graphic and printing production, graphic arts technology, liberal/general studies, mathematics, music, music education, physical education, physical sciences, religion, secondary education, studio art, theological studies.

ACADEMIC PROGRAMS. 2-year transfer program, dual enrollment of high school students, honors program, independent study, internships, teacher preparation, 4-year associate degree program in art. **Remedial services:** Learning center, preadmission summer program, reduced course load, remedial instruction, special counselor, tutoring, academic support department. **Placement/credit:** AP, CLEP General and Subject, institutional tests; 9 credit hours maximum for associate degree.

ACADEMIC REQUIREMENTS. Freshmen must earn minimum GPA of 1.5 to continue in good standing. 45% of freshmen return for sophomore year. Students must declare major by end of second year. **Graduation requirements:** 62 hours for associate (28 in major), 120 hours for bachelor's (30 in major). Most students required to take courses in arts/fine arts, computer science, English, foreign languages, history, humanities, mathematics, philosophy/religion, biological/physical sciences, social sciences. **Postgraduate studies:** 80% from 2-year programs enter 4-year programs.

FRESHMAN ADMISSIONS. Selection criteria: Primarily school achievement record. SAT or ACT required. **High school preparation:** 18 units required. Required units include biological science 2, English 4, mathematics 2, physical science 1 and social science 2. College-preparatory program recommended. **Test requirements:** SAT or ACT; score report by August 15.

1992 FRESHMAN CLASS PROFILE. 627 men applied, 445 accepted, 183 enrolled; 271 women applied, 219 accepted, 106 enrolled. 12% had high school GPA of 3.0 or higher, 65% between 2.0 and 2.99. **Characteristics:** 44% from in state, 92% live in college housing, 21% have minority backgrounds, 5% are foreign students. Average age is 18.

FALL-TERM APPLICATIONS. $20 fee, may be waived for applicants with need. No closing date; applicants notified on a rolling basis; must reply immediately. Audition required for performing arts in music applicants. Interview recommended. Portfolio recommended for commercial art applicants. CRDA. Deferred admission available.

STUDENT LIFE. Housing: Dormitories (men, women); apartment housing available. **Activities:** Student government, radio, student newspaper, yearbook, photography club, choral groups, concert band, dance, drama, jazz band, music ensembles, musical theater, pep band, Baptist Student Union, Circle-K, Student National Education Association, Fellowship of Christian Athletes, Rotaract, Black Student Association, International Student Association, outing club.

ATHLETICS. NCAA. **Intercollegiate:** Baseball M, basketball, football M, golf, soccer, softball W, tennis, volleyball W. **Intramural:** Badminton, basketball, football M, golf, handball, racquetball, skiing, soccer M, softball, swimming, table tennis, tennis, volleyball.

STUDENT SERVICES. Aptitude testing, career counseling, freshman orientation, health services, personal counseling, placement service for graduates, veterans counselor, services/facilities for handicapped.

ANNUAL EXPENSES. Tuition and fees: $6,730. **Room and board:** $3,250. **Books and supplies:** $450. **Other expenses:** $1,000.

FINANCIAL AID. 80% of freshmen, 86% of continuing students receive some form of aid. 50% of grants, 94% of loans, 82% of jobs based on need. Academic, music/drama, art, athletic, state/district residency, religious affiliation scholarships available. **Aid applications:** No closing date; priority given to applications received by March 1; applicants notified on a rolling basis beginning on or about April 15; must reply within 2 weeks.

ADDRESS/TELEPHONE. Mary Jo Byrd, Director of Admissions, Chowan College, PO Box 1848, Murfreesboro, NC 27855-9901. (919) 398-4101. (800) 488-4101. Fax: (919) 398-1190.

Cleveland Community College
Shelby, North Carolina CB code: 0488

2-year public community college, coed. Founded in 1965. **Accreditation:** Regional. **Undergraduate enrollment:** 240 men, 337 women full time; 454 men, 687 women part time. **Faculty:** 105 total (40 full time), 5 with doctorates or other terminal degrees. **Location:** Suburban campus in large town; 45 miles from Charlotte. **Calendar:** Quarter, extensive summer session. Extensive evening/early morning classes. **Microcomputers:** 100 located in computer centers. **Special facilities:** Art gallery, nature trail, amphitheater.

DEGREES OFFERED. AA, AS, AAS. 76 associate degrees awarded in 1992. 30% in business and management, 10% business/office and marketing/distribution, 15% computer sciences, 7% teacher education, 20% engineering technologies, 7% allied health, 10% parks/recreation, protective services, public affairs.

UNDERGRADUATE MAJORS. Accounting, business administration and management, business data processing and related programs, criminal justice studies, early childhood education, education, electronic technology, fashion merchandising, industrial technology, law enforcement and corrections technologies, liberal/general studies, medical secretary, microcomputer software, nursing, radio/television technology, radiograph medical technology, secretarial and related programs, trade and industrial supervision and management.

ACADEMIC PROGRAMS. 2-year transfer program, double major, dual enrollment of high school students, independent study, internships, telecourses. **Remedial services:** Learning center, reduced course load, remedial instruction, special counselor, tutoring. **Placement/credit:** AP, CLEP General and Subject, institutional tests.

ACADEMIC REQUIREMENTS. Freshmen must earn minimum GPA of 1.2 to continue in good standing. 60% of freshmen return for sophomore year. Students must declare major on enrollment. **Graduation requirements:** 115 hours for associate (60 in major). Most students required to take courses in computer science, English, humanities, mathematics, biological/physical sciences, social sciences. **Additional information:** Radiologic technology and electronics engineering technology students must attend 8 consecutive quarters.

FRESHMAN ADMISSIONS. Selection criteria: Open admissions. Selective admissions to health services programs.

1992 FRESHMAN CLASS PROFILE. 373 men, 571 women enrolled. **Characteristics:** 97% from in state, 100% commute, 24% have minority backgrounds. Average age is 23.

FALL-TERM APPLICATIONS. No fee. No closing date; applicants notified on a rolling basis. Interview required for nursing, radiologic technology applicants. Essay required for nursing, radiologic technology applicants. Deferred and early admission available.

STUDENT LIFE. Activities: Student government, magazine, student newspaper, television, drama, Afro-American Club, Gamma Beta Phi, Phi Beta Lambda, computer club, communications club, fashion club, photography club, criminal justice club, radiologic technology club, Student Government Association.

ATHLETICS. Intramural: Basketball, golf, softball, table tennis, tennis, volleyball.

STUDENT SERVICES. Aptitude testing, career counseling, employment service for undergraduates, freshman orientation, personal counseling, placement service for graduates, veterans counselor, services/facilities for handicapped.

ANNUAL EXPENSES. Tuition and fees (1992-93): $585, $3,959 additional for out-of-state students. **Books and supplies:** $490. **Other expenses:** $1,175.

FINANCIAL AID. 10% of freshmen, 10% of continuing students receive some form of aid. All grants, all jobs based on need. **Aid applications:** No closing date; applicants notified on a rolling basis beginning on or about August 15.

ADDRESS/TELEPHONE. LouAnn Bridges, Dean Enrollment Management, Cleveland Community College, 137 South Post Road, Shelby, NC 28150. (704) 484-4000. Fax: (704) 484-4036.

Coastal Carolina Community College
Jacksonville, North Carolina CB code: 5134

2-year public community college, coed. Founded in 1964. **Accreditation:** Regional. **Undergraduate enrollment:** 1,860 men and women full time; 1,730 men and women part time. **Faculty:** 159 total (94 full time), 14 with doctorates or other terminal degrees. **Location:** Suburban campus in large town; 100 miles from Raleigh. **Calendar:** Quarter, limited summer session. Extensive evening/early morning classes. **Microcomputers:** 100 located in libraries, computer centers. **Additional facts:** Off-campus classes available at Camp Lejeune Marine Corps Base and at New River Marine Corps Air Station.

DEGREES OFFERED. AA, AS, AAS. 320 associate degrees awarded in 1992. 10% in business and management, 19% business/office and marketing/distribution, 10% teacher education, 17% allied health, 20% multi/interdisciplinary studies, 11% parks/recreation, protective services, public affairs.

UNDERGRADUATE MAJORS. Accounting, architectural technologies, automotive technology, business administration and management, business and management, business and office, business data processing and related programs, clinical laboratory science, computer programming, criminal justice technology, dental hygiene, education, electronic technology, elementary education, fire protection, legal assistant/paralegal, legal secretary, liberal/general studies, marketing and distribution, medical laboratory technologies, medical secretary, music, nursing, secondary education, secretarial and related programs, social work, survey and mapping technology, visual and performing arts.

ACADEMIC PROGRAMS. 2-year transfer program, cooperative education, dual enrollment of high school students, independent study, internships. **Remedial services:** Learning center, reduced course load, remedial instruction, tutoring. **Placement/credit:** AP, CLEP General and Subject, institutional tests; 30 credit hours maximum for associate degree.

ACADEMIC REQUIREMENTS. Freshmen must earn minimum GPA of 1.85 to continue in good standing. 60% of freshmen return for sophomore year. Students must declare major on enrollment. **Graduation requirements:** 96 hours for associate. Most students required to take courses in arts/fine arts, English, history, humanities, mathematics, biological/physical sciences, social sciences.

FRESHMAN ADMISSIONS. Selection criteria: Open admissions. Exam-based selective admissions to medical technologies programs.

1992 FRESHMAN CLASS PROFILE. 298 men and women enrolled. **Characteristics:** 75% from in state, 100% commute, 22% have minority backgrounds. Average age is 25.

FALL-TERM APPLICATIONS. No fee. No closing date; applicants notified on a rolling basis beginning on or about February 15. Interview recommended. ASSET used for placement. Interview recommended for counseling and placement.

STUDENT LIFE. Activities: Student government, choral groups, dance, drama.

ATHLETICS. Intercollegiate: Golf, softball, tennis. **Intramural:** Archery, badminton, basketball, bowling, cross-country, soccer, table tennis, volleyball.

STUDENT SERVICES. Career counseling, employment service for undergraduates, freshman orientation, personal counseling, placement service for graduates, veterans counselor, services/facilities for handicapped.

ANNUAL EXPENSES. Tuition and fees (1992-93): $578, $3,959 additional for out-of-state students. **Books and supplies:** $450. **Other expenses:** $800.

FINANCIAL AID. 75% of freshmen, 75% of continuing students receive some form of aid. 87% of grants, 85% of jobs based on need. **Aid applications:** No closing date; priority given to applications received by May 15; applicants notified on a rolling basis beginning on or about May 15.

ADDRESS/TELEPHONE. Mr. Charles Lancaster, Director of Student Services, Coastal Carolina Community College, 444 Western Boulevard, Jacksonville, NC 28540-6877. (919) 455-1221. Fax: (919) 455-7027.

College of the Albemarle
Elizabeth City, North Carolina CB code: 5133

2-year public community college, coed. Founded in 1960. **Accreditation:** Regional. **Undergraduate enrollment:** 327 men, 648 women full time; 342 men, 721 women part time. **Faculty:** 117 total (55 full time), 13 with doctorates or other terminal degrees. **Location:** Rural campus in large town; 45 miles from Norfolk, Virginia Beach, and Portsmouth, Virginia. **Calendar:** Quarter, limited summer session. Extensive evening/early morning classes. **Microcomputers:** Located in libraries, computer centers. **Special facilities:** Community theater and civic auditorium. **Additional facts:** Dare County campus students can enroll full-time or part-time. Chowan center students can enroll in part-time curriculum credit bearing courses.

DEGREES OFFERED. AA, AS, AAS. 140 associate degrees awarded in 1992. 17% in business and management, 7% business/office and marketing/distribution, 5% computer sciences, 9% education, 9% engineering, 5% engineering technologies, 12% health sciences, 36% multi/interdisciplinary studies.

UNDERGRADUATE MAJORS. Agricultural sciences, business administration and management, business and management, business and office, business data programming, computer and information sciences, computer technology, drafting and design technology, dramatic arts, electronic technology, elementary education, engineering, finance, fine arts, forestry and related sciences, hotel/motel and restaurant management, liberal/general studies, mathematics, medical secretary, microcomputer software, music, nursing, office supervision and management, physical sciences, postal service technology, practical nursing, predentistry, prelaw, premedicine, prepharmacy, preveterinary, secondary education, secretarial and related programs.

ACADEMIC PROGRAMS. 2-year transfer program, cooperative education, double major, dual enrollment of high school students, independent study, cross-registration. **Remedial services:** Learning center, preadmission summer program, reduced course load, remedial instruction, special counselor, tutoring. **Placement/credit:** AP, CLEP Subject, institutional tests; 45 credit hours maximum for associate degree.

ACADEMIC REQUIREMENTS. Freshmen must earn minimum GPA of 2.0 to continue in good standing. 65% of freshmen return for sophomore year. Students must declare major on enrollment. **Graduation requirements:** 96 hours for associate. Most students required to take courses in English, history, humanities, mathematics, social sciences.

FRESHMAN ADMISSIONS. Selection criteria: Open admissions. Selective admission to allied health and cosmetology programs based on college administered exam, high school transcript and interview. Recommended units include biological science 2, English 4, foreign language 2, mathematics 3, physical science 1 and social science 2. **Test requirements:** Institutional placement test required for all matriculating applicants.

1992 FRESHMAN CLASS PROFILE. 927 men and women enrolled. **Characteristics:** 96% from in state, 100% commute, 18% have minority backgrounds.

FALL-TERM APPLICATIONS. No fee. No closing date; applicants notified on a rolling basis. Interview required for allied health applicants. Deferred admission available. Applicants to nursing programs advised to apply by January.

STUDENT LIFE. Activities: Student government, student newspaper, yearbook, choral groups, concert band, drama, musical theater, Phi Theta Kappa, Phi Beta Lambda, (Future Business Leaders of America).

ATHLETICS. Intramural: Basketball, softball, tennis, volleyball.

STUDENT SERVICES. Aptitude testing, career counseling, employment service for undergraduates, freshman orientation, personal counseling, placement service for graduates, veterans counselor, services/facilities for handicapped.

ANNUAL EXPENSES. Tuition and fees (1992-93): $585, $3,959 additional for out-of-state students. **Books and supplies:** $325. **Other expenses:** $750.

FINANCIAL AID. 35% of freshmen, 35% of continuing students receive some form of aid. All aid based on need. **Aid applications:** No closing date; priority given to applications received by June 1; applicants notified on a rolling basis beginning on or about March 1; must reply within 2 weeks.

ADDRESS/TELEPHONE. John M. Wells, Asst. Dean, Admissions/Testing, College of the Albemarle, PO Box 2327, Elizabeth City, NC 27906-2327. (919) 335-0821 ext. 220. Fax: (919) 335-2011.

Craven Community College
New Bern, North Carolina CB code: 5148

2-year public community college, coed. Founded in 1965. **Accreditation:** Regional. **Undergraduate enrollment:** 351 men, 729 women full time; 607 men, 731 women part time. **Faculty:** 294 total (62 full time), 8 with doctorates or other terminal degrees. **Location:** Rural campus in large town; 100 miles from Raleigh. **Calendar:** Quarter, limited summer session. Saturday and extensive evening/early morning classes. **Microcomputers:** 35 located in computer centers.

DEGREES OFFERED. AA, AS, AAS. 164 associate degrees awarded in 1992. 5% in business and management, 7% business/office and marketing/distribution, 9% engineering technologies, 25% health sciences, 40% multi/interdisciplinary studies, 13% trade and industry.

UNDERGRADUATE MAJORS. Accounting, air conditioning/heating/refrigeration mechanics, air conditioning/heating/refrigeration technology, business administration and management, business data programming, criminal justice technology, drafting, drafting and design technology, electrical and electronics equipment repair, electrical technology, electronic technology, industrial equipment maintenance and repair, legal secretary, liberal/general studies, marketing and distribution, medical secretary, microcomputer software, nursing, secretarial and related programs, teacher aide.

ACADEMIC PROGRAMS. 2-year transfer program, cooperative education, dual enrollment of high school students, internships, telecourses, weekend college, cross-registration. **Remedial services:** Learning center, reduced course load, remedial instruction, special counselor, tutoring. **Placement/credit:** AP, CLEP General and Subject, institutional tests.

ACADEMIC REQUIREMENTS. Freshmen must earn minimum GPA of 2.0 to continue in good standing. 40% of freshmen return for sophomore year. Students must declare major on application. **Graduation requirements:** 96 hours for associate. Most students required to take courses in English, mathematics, social sciences.

FRESHMAN ADMISSIONS. Selection criteria: Open admissions. Selective admissions to nursing program based on school achievement record and test scores. **Test requirements:** GPA required of all applicants unless SAT-verbal and mathematical scores of 400, or ACT composite score of 18 submitted.

1992 FRESHMAN CLASS PROFILE. 93 men, 180 women enrolled. 20% had high school GPA of 3.0 or higher, 60% between 2.0 and 2.99. **Characteristics:** 78% from in state, 100% commute, 28% have minority backgrounds.

FALL-TERM APPLICATIONS. No fee. No closing date; applicants notified on a rolling basis. Interview required. Deferred admission available. Nursing program applicants should apply before December 15 and must reply within 2 weeks of acceptance.

STUDENT LIFE. Activities: Student government, choral groups, Multi-Cultural Society, Data Processing Managers Association, Spanish club, cosmetology club, Forensics Society, Accounting Club, Phi Beta Lamda, Students in Free Enterprise.

ATHLETICS. NJCAA. **Intercollegiate:** Basketball M, golf, softball, tennis. **Intramural:** Basketball, golf, softball, tennis, volleyball.

STUDENT SERVICES. Aptitude testing, career counseling, employment service for undergraduates, freshman orientation, personal counseling, placement service for graduates, veterans counselor, services/facilities for handicapped.

ANNUAL EXPENSES. Tuition and fees (1992-93): $584, $3,959 additional for out-of-state students. **Books and supplies:** $519. **Other expenses:** $918.

FINANCIAL AID. 25% of continuing students receive some form of aid. 92% of grants, 98% of loans, all jobs based on need. 217 enrolled freshmen were judged to have need, all were offered aid. Academic scholarships available. **Aid applications:** No closing date; priority given to applications received by April 1; applicants notified on a rolling basis; must reply within 2 weeks.

ADDRESS/TELEPHONE. Matlynn Bryant, Dean of Students, Craven Community College, PO Box 885, Glenburnie Road & College Court, New Bern, NC 28560. (919) 638-4131. Fax: (919) 638-4232.

Davidson College ⇎
Davidson, North Carolina — CB code: 5150

Admissions: 48% of applicants accepted
Based on: ••• School record
•• Activities, essay, recommendations, special talents, test scores
Completion: 98% of freshmen end year in good standing
89% graduate, 40% of these enter graduate study

4-year private liberal arts college, coed, affiliated with Presbyterian Church (USA). Founded in 1837. **Accreditation:** Regional. **Undergraduate enrollment:** 819 men, 729 women full time; 1 man, 1 woman part time. **Faculty:** 144 total (127 full time), 135 with doctorates or other terminal degrees. **Location:** Suburban campus in small town; 19 miles from Charlotte. **Calendar:** Semester. **Microcomputers:** 104 located in libraries, classrooms, computer centers. **Special facilities:** Art gallery, laser facility, electron microscope, sports complex and arena, campus arboretum, lake campus.

DEGREES OFFERED. BA, BS. 342 bachelor's degrees awarded in 1992. 7% in languages, 14% letters/literature, 12% life sciences, 6% philosophy, religion, theology, 7% psychology, 40% social sciences, 5% visual and performing arts.

UNDERGRADUATE MAJORS. Anthropology, art history, biology, chemistry, classics, dramatic arts, economics, English, French, German, Greek (classical), history, Latin, liberal/general studies, mathematics, music, philosophy, physics, political science and government, psychology, religion, sociology, Spanish, studio art.

ACADEMIC PROGRAMS. Honors program, independent study, student-designed major, study abroad, teacher preparation, visiting/exchange student program, Washington semester, cross-registration, visiting student program with Howard University and Morehouse College; Dean Rusk Program in International Studies; liberal arts/career combination in engineering. **Remedial services:** Tutoring. **ROTC:** Army. **Placement/credit:** AP, IB, institutional tests.

ACADEMIC REQUIREMENTS. To continue in good academic standing, freshmen must pass 7 courses, earn minimum 12 grade points, and complete composition requirement. 95% of freshmen return for sophomore year. Students must declare major by end of second year. **Graduation requirements:** 136 hours for bachelor's (40 in major). Most students required to take courses in arts/fine arts, English, foreign languages, history, mathematics, philosophy/religion, biological/physical sciences, social sciences. **Postgraduate studies:** 12% enter law school, 10% enter medical school, 8% enter MBA programs, 10% enter other graduate study. **Additional information:** 2-year interdisciplinary course in humanities available for freshmen and sophomores. Center for Special Studies supervises student-designed majors. Dean Rusk Program encourages international studies.

FRESHMAN ADMISSIONS. Selection criteria: Seek students with high motivation, strong academic backgrounds, and strong personal qualities. School achievement record, test scores, recommendations, school, church, and community involvement, and personal statement considered. Special consideration for alumni children, minority students, international students, and some athletes. **High school preparation:** 16 units required. Required and recommended units include English 4, foreign language 2-4, mathematics 3-4, social science 1-2 and science 2-4. Foreign language units should be in same language. **Test requirements:** SAT or ACT; score report by February 1.

1992 FRESHMAN CLASS PROFILE. 933 men applied, 452 accepted, 193 enrolled; 912 women applied, 430 accepted, 221 enrolled. 76% were in top tenth and 98% were in top quarter of graduating class. **Academic background:** Mid 50% of enrolled freshmen had SAT-V between 520-630, SAT-M between 590-680; ACT composite between 29-33. 93% submitted SAT scores, 7% submitted ACT scores. **Characteristics:** 20% from in state, 100% live in college housing, 8% have minority backgrounds, 4% are foreign students, 65% join fraternities/sororities. Average age is 18.

FALL-TERM APPLICATIONS. $45 fee. Closing date February 1; priority given to applications received by January 15; applicants notified on or about April 1; must reply by May 1. Essay required. CRDA. Deferred and early admission available. EDP-S. 3 ACH recommended, score report by February 1.

STUDENT LIFE. Housing: Dormitories (men, women, coed). Suite/apartment-style housing available on campus. **Activities:** Student government, magazine, radio, student newspaper, television, yearbook, freshman handbook, video yearbook, choral groups, concert band, dance, drama, jazz band, music ensembles, musical theater, opera, pep band, chamber orchestra, string ensemble, wind ensemble, fraternities, black student coalition, service organizations, Public Interest Research Group, Amnesty International, Young Democrats, College Republicans, Women's Concerns Committee, CROP (hunger coalition), Habitat for Humanity, sports clubs. **Additional information:** Student life governed by honor code and code of responsibility.

ATHLETICS. NCAA. **Intercollegiate:** Baseball M, basketball, cross-country, diving, field hockey W, football M, golf M, soccer, swimming, tennis, track and field, volleyball W, wrestling M. **Intramural:** Basketball, cross-country, diving, football M, golf, handball, lacrosse, racquetball, soccer, softball, squash, swimming, tennis, track and field, volleyball.

STUDENT SERVICES. Aptitude testing, career counseling, employment service for undergraduates, freshman orientation, health services, personal counseling, placement service for graduates, services/facilities for handicapped.

ANNUAL EXPENSES. Tuition and fees: $16,263. **Room and board:** $4,774. **Books and supplies:** $550. **Other expenses:** $903.

FINANCIAL AID. 63% of freshmen, 62% of continuing students receive some form of aid. 32% of grants, 91% of loans, 53% of jobs based on need. 135 enrolled freshmen were judged to have need, all were offered aid. Academic, music/drama, art, athletic, state/district residency, leadership, minority scholarships available. **Aid applications:** Closing date February 15; applicants notified on or about April 15; must reply by May 1.

ADDRESS/TELEPHONE. Dr. Nancy Cable Wells, Dean of Admissions and Financial Aid, Davidson College, PO Box 1737, Box 1737, Davidson, NC 28036. (704) 892-2230. (800) 768-0380. Fax: (704) 892-2016.

Davidson County Community College
Lexington, North Carolina — CB code: 5170

2-year public community college, coed. Founded in 1958. **Accreditation:** Regional. **Undergraduate enrollment:** 399 men, 562 women full time; 566 men, 725 women part time. **Faculty:** 149 total (66 full time), 20 with doctorates or other terminal degrees. **Location:** Rural campus in large town; 30 miles from Greensboro. **Calendar:** Quarter, limited summer session. Saturday and extensive evening/early morning classes. **Microcomputers:** 200 located in libraries, classrooms, computer centers. **Special facilities:** Furniture design and decoration collection.

DEGREES OFFERED. AA, AS, AAS. 150 associate degrees awarded in 1992. 18% in business and management, 21% computer sciences, 11% engineering technologies, 8% health sciences, 8% law, 19% multi/interdisciplinary studies, 12% parks/recreation, protective services, public affairs.

UNDERGRADUATE MAJORS. Accounting, business administration and management, business data programming, child development/care/guidance, computer servicing technology, computer technology, data processing, electronic technology, law enforcement and corrections technologies, legal assistant/paralegal, liberal/general studies, medical records administration, nursing, personnel management, secretarial and related programs, teacher aide.

ACADEMIC PROGRAMS. 2-year transfer program, dual enrollment of high school students, independent study, telecourses. **Remedial services:** Learning center, preadmission summer program, reduced course load, remedial instruction, tutoring. **Placement/credit:** AP, CLEP Subject, institutional tests.

ACADEMIC REQUIREMENTS. Freshmen must earn minimum GPA of 1.65 to continue in good standing. Students must declare major on enrollment. **Graduation requirements:** 110 hours for associate (50 in major). Most students required to take courses in English, mathematics.

FRESHMAN ADMISSIONS. Selection criteria: Open admissions. Selective admissions to nursing, electronic engineering, business computer programming, and paralegal technology.

1992 FRESHMAN CLASS PROFILE. 181 men, 197 women enrolled. **Characteristics:** 99% from in state, 100% commute, 11% have minority backgrounds. Average age is 21.

FALL-TERM APPLICATIONS. No fee. No closing date; applicants notified on a rolling basis. Interview required for nursing applicants. Deferred admission available.

STUDENT LIFE. Activities: Student government, Alpha Beta Club, freshmen advisory council.

ATHLETICS. Intramural: Archery, badminton, basketball, fencing, golf, softball, table tennis, tennis, volleyball.

STUDENT SERVICES. Aptitude testing, career counseling, employment service for undergraduates, freshman orientation, on-campus day care, personal counseling, placement service for graduates, veterans counselor, services/facilities for handicapped.

ANNUAL EXPENSES. Tuition and fees (1992-93): $580, $3,959 additional for out-of-state students. **Books and supplies:** $500. **Other expenses:** $470.

FINANCIAL AID. 35% of freshmen, 42% of continuing students receive some form of aid. All grants, all loans, 33% of jobs based on need. 225 enrolled freshmen were judged to have need, all were offered aid. **Aid applications:** No closing date; priority given to applications received by May 30; applicants notified on a rolling basis beginning on or about July 15; must reply within 8 days.

ADDRESS/TELEPHONE. Judith Cottrell, Director, Admissions and Student Records, Davidson County Community College, PO Box 1287, Lexington, NC 27293-1287. (704) 249-8186 ext. 205. Fax: (704) 249-0379.

Duke University
Durham, North Carolina CB code: 5156

Admissions: 27% of applicants accepted
Based on:
- ••• School record
- •• Essay, recommendations, special talents, test scores
- • Activities, interview

Completion: 99% of freshmen end year in good standing
94% graduate, 38% of these enter graduate study

4-year private university, coed, affiliated with United Methodist Church. Founded in 1838. **Accreditation:** Regional. **Undergraduate enrollment:** 3,300 men, 2,767 women full time; 31 men, 32 women part time. **Graduate enrollment:** 2,939 men, 1,737 women full time; 285 men, 335 women part time. **Faculty:** 2,282 total (1,839 full time), 1,782 with doctorates or other terminal degrees. **Location:** Suburban campus in small city; 170 miles from Richmond, Virginia, 275 miles from Washington, D.C. **Calendar:** Semester, extensive summer session. **Microcomputers:** 800 located in dormitories, libraries, classrooms, computer centers. **Special facilities:** Art museum, phytotron, marine laboratory, primate center, Duke Forest, free electron laser, nuclear magnetic resonance machine, Triangle Universities Nuclear Laboratory. **Additional facts:** Duke University Marine Laboratory, located near Beaufort, offers semester and summer programs to qualified juniors, seniors, and graduate students from any college or university.

DEGREES OFFERED. BA, BS, MA, MS, MBA, PhD, MD, JD, M.Div. 1,510 bachelor's degrees awarded in 1992. 14% in engineering, 12% letters/literature, 10% life sciences, 8% psychology, 39% social sciences. Graduate degrees offered in 62 major fields of study.

UNDERGRADUATE MAJORS. Afro-American (black) studies, anatomy, anthropology, art history, bioengineering and biomedical engineering, biology, chemistry, civil engineering, classics, comparative area studies, comparative literature, computer and information sciences, design, dramatic arts, economics, electrical/electronics/communications engineering, English, environmental science, French, genetics, human and animal, geology, German, German studies, Greek (classical), history, Italian, Jewish studies, Latin, mathematics, mechanical engineering, medieval studies, music, neurosciences, philosophy, physics, political science and government, psychology, public policy studies, religion, Russian, Slavic languages, sociology, Spanish.

ACADEMIC PROGRAMS. Accelerated program, double major, honors program, independent study, internships, student-designed major, study abroad, teacher preparation, telecourses, visiting/exchange student program, New York semester, Washington semester, cross-registration, art program/internship in New York City, marine biology semester in Beaufort, NC; combined bachelor's/graduate program in business administration, law. **Remedial services:** Learning center, preadmission summer program, special counselor, tutoring, academic skills center. **ROTC:** Air Force, Army, Naval. **Placement/credit:** AP, IB.

ACADEMIC REQUIREMENTS. No policy requiring minimum GPA; records of students having academic difficulty are reviewed individually. 99% of freshmen return for sophomore year. Students must declare major by end of second year. **Graduation requirements:** 136 hours for bachelor's (24 in major). Most students required to take courses in English. **Postgraduate studies:** 11% enter law school, 12% enter medical school, 1% enter MBA programs, 14% enter other graduate study. **Additional information:** Comparative area studies with an emphasis in one or more areas available. Special focus groups for freshmen avaliable in Twentieth Century America; Evolution and Humankind; Science, Technology, and Modern Culture; and Contemporary Global Culture.

FRESHMAN ADMISSIONS. Selection criteria: Courses, school achievement record, school and community activities, essays, recommendations, test scores considered. Special consideration to alumni children and minority applicants. **High school preparation:** 15 units required. Required and recommended units include English 4. Foreign language 3, mathematics 3, social science 2 and science 3 recommended. 4 mathematics and 1 physics or chemistry required for engineering applicants. **Test requirements:** SAT or ACT; score report by March 1. 3 ACH required (including Mathematics Level I or II) for engineering students submitting SAT. 3 ACH required (including English Composition) for all other students submitting SAT. Score report by March 1 Most recent ACT scores used, highest individual SAT and Achievement scores used. **Additional information:** Applicants requesting alumni interview must submit Part I of application by October 1 for Early Decision or by December 1.

1992 FRESHMAN CLASS PROFILE. 7,591 men applied, 2,043 accepted, 886 enrolled; 6,937 women applied, 1,816 accepted, 740 enrolled. 100% had high school GPA of 3.0 or higher. 88% were in top tenth and 97% were in top quarter of graduating class. **Academic background:** Mid 50% of enrolled freshmen had SAT-V between 570-670, SAT-M between 650-740; ACT composite between 28-32. 99% submitted SAT scores, 26% submitted ACT scores. **Characteristics:** 14% from in state, 100% live in college housing, 24% have minority backgrounds, 2% are foreign students. Average age is 18.

FALL-TERM APPLICATIONS. $50 fee, may be waived for applicants with need. Closing date January 2; applicants notified on or about April 15; must reply by May 1. Essay required. Interview recommended. Audition recommended for drama, music applicants. Portfolio recommended for art applicants. CRDA. Deferred and early admission available. EDP-F. Achievement test used for placement in mathematics and foreign languages.

STUDENT LIFE. Housing: Dormitories (men, women, coed); apartment, fraternity, handicapped housing available. Special interest housing available for students in women's studies, the arts, languages, service (Alpha Phi Omega). **Activities:** Student government, film, magazine, radio, student newspaper, television, yearbook, humor, literary, photography, and science magazines, choral groups, concert band, dance, drama, jazz band, marching band, music ensembles, musical theater, opera, pep band, symphony orchestra, handbell choir, fraternities, sororities, Black Student Alliance, Hillel, Newman Club, Spanish American-Latin Student Association, Volunteers for Youth, Big Brother/Big Sister, Campus Crusade for Christ, Duke Democrats, College Republicans, Habitat for Humanity.

ATHLETICS. NCAA. **Intercollegiate:** Baseball M, basketball, cross-country, diving, fencing, field hockey W, football M, golf, lacrosse M, soccer, swimming, tennis, track and field, volleyball W, wrestling M. **Intramural:** Badminton, basketball, golf, racquetball, soccer M, softball, squash, swimming, table tennis, tennis, volleyball. **Clubs:** Badminton, horseback riding, ice hockey, lacrosse, racquetball, rowing (crew), rugby, sailing, skiing, softball, volleyball M, waterpolo.

STUDENT SERVICES. Aptitude testing, career counseling, employment service for undergraduates, freshman orientation, health services, on-campus day care, personal counseling, placement service for graduates, special adviser for adult students, veterans counselor, services/facilities for handicapped.

ANNUAL EXPENSES. Tuition and fees: $17,163. School of Engineering tuition is $17,810; tuition and fees $18,253. **Room and board:** $5,550. **Books and supplies:** $592. **Other expenses:** $1,045.

FINANCIAL AID. 38% of freshmen, 37% of continuing students receive some form of aid. 88% of grants, 99% of loans, all jobs based on need. 602 enrolled freshmen were judged to have need, all were offered aid. Academic, music/drama, art, athletic, state/district residency, leadership, alumni affiliation, religious affiliation, minority scholarships available. **Aid applications:** No closing date; priority given to applications received by February 1; applicants notified on a rolling basis beginning on or about April 15; must reply by May 1 or within 2 weeks if notified thereafter.

ADDRESS/TELEPHONE. Christoph Guttentag, Director of Undergraduate Admissions, Duke University, 2138 Campus Drive, Durham, NC 27706. (919) 684-3214. Fax: (919) 681-8941.

Durham Technical Community College
Durham, North Carolina CB code: 5172

2-year public community college, coed. Founded in 1958. **Accreditation:** Regional. **Undergraduate enrollment:** 597 men, 754 women full time; 1,381 men, 2,315 women part time. **Faculty:** 434 total (97 full time), 33 with doctorates or other terminal degrees. **Location:** Urban campus in small city; 20 miles from Raleigh, 50 miles from Greensboro. **Calendar:** Quarter, limited summer session. Saturday and extensive evening/early morning classes. **Microcomputers:** 600 located in libraries, classrooms, computer centers. **Additional facts:** Most programs structured to begin in fall and continue for 7 or 8 consecutive quarters. Off-campus sites in northern Durham and Orange Counties.

DEGREES OFFERED. AA, AS, AAS. 240 associate degrees awarded in 1992. 21% in business and management, 7% computer sciences, 9% engineering technologies, 9% health sciences, 14% allied health, 16% law, 15% multi/interdisciplinary studies, 7% parks/recreation, protective services, public affairs.

UNDERGRADUATE MAJORS. Accounting, business administration and management, business and management, business and office, business data processing and related programs, business data programming, computer programming, criminal justice studies, data processing, dental laboratory technology, early childhood education, electronic technology, fire control and safety technology, fire protection, legal assistant/paralegal, liberal/general studies, medical secretary, microcomputer software, military science (Army), nursing, ophthalmic services, respiratory therapy, respiratory therapy technology, secretarial and related programs.

ACADEMIC PROGRAMS. 2-year transfer program, dual enrollment of high school students, internships, telecourses, weekend college. **Remedial services:** Learning center, reduced course load, remedial instruction, special counselor, tutoring. **Placement/credit:** CLEP General and Subject, institutional tests. Maximum of 10% of total curriculum hours of credit by examination may be counted toward degree.

ACADEMIC REQUIREMENTS. No policy requiring minimum GPA; records of students having academic difficulty are reviewed individually. Students must declare major on application. **Graduation requirements:** 96 hours for associate. Most students required to take courses in computer science, English, humanities, mathematics, biological/physical sciences, social sciences.

FRESHMAN ADMISSIONS. Selection criteria: Open admissions. Selective admissions to some programs, including nursing and allied health, based on placement test scores, and completion of prerequisite courses. Algebra, chemistry, and biology required for nursing program. Algebra and science courses recommended for most associate degree programs. **Test requirements:** Descriptive Tests of Mathematic Skills (Basic Arithmetic, Elementary Algebra, Intermediate Algebra, and Graphs and Functions) for placement and admission to certain programs. Comparative Guidance and Placement Program tests used for reading and English course placement and admission to certain programs.

1992 FRESHMAN CLASS PROFILE. 765 men, 1,028 women enrolled. **Characteristics:** 99% from in state, 100% commute, 42% have minority backgrounds. Average age is 30.

FALL-TERM APPLICATIONS. No fee. Closing date August 17; applicants notified on a rolling basis. Interview recommended. Deferred admission available. Most freshman and undergraduate foreign applicants accepted quarterly throughout year. Contact school for application closing dates.

STUDENT LIFE. Activities: Student government, student newspaper, dental laboratory fraternity, student optician organization, Phi Beta Lambda, Gamma Beta Phi, literary club, science club, Nursing Student Organization, Students Concerned for Social Justice, Thespian Society.

ATHLETICS. Intramural: Basketball M, softball, tennis.

STUDENT SERVICES. Aptitude testing, career counseling, employment service for undergraduates, freshman orientation, personal counseling, placement service for graduates, veterans counselor, services for single parents/displaced homemakers, services/facilities for handicapped.

ANNUAL EXPENSES. Tuition and fees (1992-93): $575, $3,959 additional for out-of-state students. **Books and supplies:** $300. **Other expenses:** $562.

FINANCIAL AID. 50% of freshmen, 50% of continuing students receive some form of aid. 55% of loans, all jobs based on need. 483 enrolled freshmen were judged to have need, all were offered aid. **Aid applications:** No closing date; applicants notified on a rolling basis beginning on or about September 1; must reply within 2 weeks. **Additional information:** Special funds available to single parents or displaced homemakers for tuition, fees, books, supplies and child care expenses.

ADDRESS/TELEPHONE. Dr. Ellen Austin, Coordinator of Admissions, Durham Technical Community College, 1637 Lawson Street, Durham, NC 27703. (919) 598-9224. Fax: (919) 598-9412.

East Carolina University
Greenville, North Carolina CB code: 5180

Admissions: 75% of applicants accepted
Based on: ••• School record, test scores
• Activities, recommendations, special talents
Completion: 94% of freshmen end year in good standing
42% graduate, 22% of these enter graduate study

4-year public university, coed. Founded in 1907. **Accreditation:** Regional. **Undergraduate enrollment:** 6,038 men, 7,331 women full time; 628 men, 847 women part time. **Graduate enrollment:** 546 men, 776 women full time; 535 men, 1,056 women part time. **Faculty:** 1,188 total (1,144 full time), 937 with doctorates or other terminal degrees. **Location:** Suburban campus in large town; 90 miles from Raleigh. **Calendar:** Semester, extensive summer session. **Microcomputers:** 921 located in dormitories, libraries, classrooms, computer centers, campus-wide network. **Special facilities:** Gray Art Gallery, sports medicine facility. **Additional facts:** Credit-bearing courses offered at 16 sites, including educational institutions, business, industry and correctional facilities and hospitals, within 120 miles of home campus.

DEGREES OFFERED. BA, BS, BFA, MA, MS, MBA, MFA, MEd, MSW, PhD, EdD, MD. 2,303 bachelor's degrees awarded in 1992. 17% in business and management, 5% communications, 20% teacher education, 7% health sciences, 7% home economics, 8% parks/recreation, protective services, public affairs, 7% social sciences, 6% visual and performing arts. Graduate degrees offered in 69 major fields of study.

UNDERGRADUATE MAJORS. Accounting, anthropology, applied geography, applied physics, applied sociology, art education, art history, arts management, biochemistry, biology, business administration and management, business and management, business education, ceramics, chemistry, city/community/regional planning, clothing and textiles management/production/services, communication arts, communications, computer and information sciences, creative writing, criminal justice studies, cytotechnology, dance, dance education, decision science, dramatic arts, drawing, early childhood education, economics, elementary education, English, English education, environmental health, finance, food science and nutrition, foreign languages education, French, geography, geology, German, graphic design, health education, history, history education, home economics, home economics education, hospitality management, individual and family development, industrial arts education, industrial technology, interior design, junior high education, management science, marketing and distributive education, marketing management, mathematics, mathematics education, medical laboratory technologies, medical records administration, music, music education, music pedagogy, music performance, music theory and composition, music therapy, nursing, occupational therapy, painting, parks and recreation management, philosophy, physical education, physical therapy, physics, political science and government, printmaking, psychology, real estate, religious music, science education, sculpture, secondary education, secretarial and related programs, social work, sociology, Spanish, special education, speech pathology/audiology, technical education.

ACADEMIC PROGRAMS. Cooperative education, double major, dual enrollment of high school students, education specialist degree, honors program, independent study, internships, study abroad, teacher preparation, visiting/exchange student program, United Nations semester. **Remedial services:** Learning center, reduced course load, remedial instruction, tutoring. **ROTC:** Air Force, Army. **Placement/credit:** AP, CLEP General and Subject, institutional tests; 30 credit hours maximum for bachelor's degree.

ACADEMIC REQUIREMENTS. Freshmen must earn minimum GPA of 1.35 to continue in good standing. 78% of freshmen return for sophomore year. Students must declare major by end of second year. **Graduation requirements:** 120 hours for bachelor's (36 in major). Most students required to take courses in arts/fine arts, English, history, humanities, mathematics, biological/physical sciences, social sciences.

FRESHMAN ADMISSIONS. Selection criteria: School achievement record, test scores and recommendations reviewed. Out-of-state applicants must meet higher requirements as they are limited to 18% of freshman class. **High school preparation:** 20 units required. Required and recommended units include biological science 1, English 4, mathematics 3, physical science 1, social science 2 and science 1. Foreign language 2 recommended. One U.S. history required. Mathematics units must include 2 algebra and 1 geometry or 2 algebra and 1 advanced mathematics after algebra II. **Test requirements:** SAT or ACT; score report by March 15. **Additional information:** Non-traditional freshmen may be offered a performance-based admission.

1992 FRESHMAN CLASS PROFILE. 3,984 men applied, 2,829 accepted, 1,204 enrolled; 4,991 women applied, 3,865 accepted, 1,662 enrolled. 35% had high school GPA of 3.0 or higher, 65% between 2.0 and 2.99. 12% were in top tenth and 39% were in top quarter of graduating class. **Academic background:** Mid 50% of enrolled freshmen had SAT-V between 380-470, SAT-M between 420-520. 100% submitted SAT scores. **Characteristics:** 76% from in state, 88% live in college housing, 11% have minority backgrounds, 1% are foreign students, 10% join fraternities/sororities. Average age is 18.

FALL-TERM APPLICATIONS. $35 fee, may be waived for applicants

with need. Closing date March 15; priority given to applications received by December 31; applicants notified on a rolling basis beginning on or about November 15; must reply by May 1. Audition required for music applicants. Portfolio required for art applicants. CRDA. Early admission available. Out-of-state freshmen enrollment limited to 18% of incoming freshmen class. Out-of-state applicants processed on space available basis; applications received prior to December 31 receive priority.

STUDENT LIFE. Housing: Dormitories (men, women, coed); fraternity, sorority, handicapped housing available. Freshmen submitting housing applications and deposits by May 1 guaranteed space for 4 years. Roommates may be selected by submitting housing applications prior to April 1. International House for foreign students. Residence hall designated for honor students and North Carolina Teaching Fellows. **Activities:** Student government, film, magazine, radio, student newspaper, television, yearbook, choral groups, concert band, dance, drama, jazz band, marching band, music ensembles, musical theater, opera, pep band, symphony orchestra, fraternities, sororities, approximately 20 religious and ethnic organizations.

ATHLETICS. NCAA. **Intercollegiate:** Baseball M, basketball, cross-country, diving, football M, golf M, soccer M, softball W, swimming, tennis, track and field, volleyball W. **Intramural:** Basketball, bowling, cross-country, fencing, field hockey W, golf, lacrosse, racquetball, rugby M, soccer, softball, table tennis, tennis, volleyball, water polo M.

STUDENT SERVICES. Aptitude testing, career counseling, employment service for undergraduates, freshman orientation, health services, personal counseling, placement service for graduates, special adviser for adult students, veterans counselor, vocational interest testing, marriage and family counseling, pastoral counseling, commuter services, services/facilities for handicapped.

ANNUAL EXPENSES. Tuition and fees (1992-93): $1,246, $5,672 additional for out-of-state students. **Room and board:** $3,030. **Books and supplies:** $500. **Other expenses:** $1,007.

FINANCIAL AID. 48% of continuing students receive some form of aid. 85% of grants, 90% of loans, 18% of jobs based on need. 1,012 enrolled freshmen were judged to have need, all were offered aid. Academic, music/drama, art, athletic, leadership, minority scholarships available. **Aid applications:** No closing date; priority given to applications received by April 15; applicants notified on a rolling basis beginning on or about May 1; must reply within 2 weeks.

ADDRESS/TELEPHONE. Dr. Thomas E. Powell, Director of Admissions, East Carolina University, 106 Whichard Building, Greenville, NC 27858-4353. (919) 757-6640.

East Coast Bible College
Charlotte, North Carolina — CB code: 7308

4-year private Bible college, coed, affiliated with Church of God. Founded in 1976. **Accreditation:** Regional. **Undergraduate enrollment:** 107 men, 75 women full time; 57 men, 59 women part time. **Faculty:** 19 total (9 full time), 3 with doctorates or other terminal degrees. **Location:** Urban campus in large city. **Calendar:** Semester, limited summer session.

DEGREES OFFERED. AS, BA, BS. 13 associate degrees awarded in 1992. 54% in multi/interdisciplinary studies, 46% philosophy, religion, theology. 27 bachelor's degrees awarded. 11% in teacher education, 89% philosophy, religion, theology.

UNDERGRADUATE MAJORS. Associate: Bible studies, liberal/general studies, religious education, religious music. **Bachelor's:** Bible studies, elementary education, religious education, religious music.

ACADEMIC PROGRAMS. 2-year transfer program, double major, internships, teacher preparation. **Remedial services:** Reduced course load, remedial instruction. **Placement/credit:** AP, CLEP General and Subject, institutional tests; 23 credit hours maximum for bachelor's degree.

ACADEMIC REQUIREMENTS. Freshmen must earn minimum GPA of 1.5 to continue in good standing. 75% of freshmen return for sophomore year. Students must declare major by end of second year. **Graduation requirements:** 64 hours for associate (27 in major), 128 hours for bachelor's (50 in major). Most students required to take courses in English, history, humanities, mathematics, philosophy/religion, biological/physical sciences, social sciences. **Postgraduate studies:** 45% from 2-year programs enter 4-year programs. 25% enter other graduate study. **Additional information:** Each student graduates with major in Bible plus additional major.

FRESHMAN ADMISSIONS. Selection criteria: Open admissions. **Test requirements:** ACT for placement and counseling only. **Additional information:** Applicants who score minimum of 26 on each of 4 sections of ACT enter with 23 hours of credit.

1992 FRESHMAN CLASS PROFILE. 21 men, 23 women enrolled. **Academic background:** Mid 50% of enrolled freshmen had ACT composite between 10-30. 98% submitted ACT scores. **Characteristics:** 62% from in state, 70% live in college housing, 2% have minority backgrounds, 2% are foreign students, 25% join fraternities/sororities. Average age is 18.

FALL-TERM APPLICATIONS. $25 fee, may be waived for applicants with need. No closing date; applicants notified on a rolling basis.

STUDENT LIFE. Housing: Dormitories (men, women). **Activities:** Student government, student newspaper, yearbook, choral groups, drama, music ensembles, fraternities, sororities.

ATHLETICS. Intercollegiate: Basketball M, volleyball W. **Intramural:** Basketball, softball, volleyball.

STUDENT SERVICES. Career counseling, freshman orientation, personal counseling, veterans counselor, services/facilities for handicapped.

ANNUAL EXPENSES. Tuition and fees: $3,950. **Room and board:** $2,400. **Books and supplies:** $550.

FINANCIAL AID. 64% of freshmen, 63% of continuing students receive some form of aid. All grants, 93% of loans, all jobs based on need. scholarships available. **Aid applications:** Closing date May 15; applicants notified on or about June 15; must reply by July 1.

ADDRESS/TELEPHONE. Linda P. Allen, Registrar, East Coast Bible College, 6900 Wilkinson Boulevard, Charlotte, NC 28214. (704) 394-2307. Fax: (704) 393-3689 ext. 15.

Edgecombe Community College
Tarboro, North Carolina — CB code: 5199

2-year public community college, coed. Founded in 1967. **Accreditation:** Regional. **Undergraduate enrollment:** 179 men, 667 women full time; 381 men, 791 women part time. **Faculty:** 188 total (64 full time), 3 with doctorates or other terminal degrees. **Location:** Rural campus in large town; 75 miles from Raleigh. **Calendar:** Quarter, extensive summer session. Extensive evening/early morning classes. **Microcomputers:** 85 located in libraries, classrooms, computer centers. **Additional facts:** Branch campus in Rocky Mount.

DEGREES OFFERED. AA, AS, AAS. 110 associate degrees awarded in 1992. 14% in business/office and marketing/distribution, 12% computer sciences, 40% allied health, 16% multi/interdisciplinary studies, 6% parks/recreation, protective services, public affairs, 12% social sciences.

UNDERGRADUATE MAJORS. Accounting, business administration and management, business and office, business computer/console/peripheral equipment operation, business data entry equipment operation, computer programming, criminal justice technology, early childhood associate, early childhood education, electrical/electronics/communications engineering, engineering and engineering-related technologies, industrial engineering, industrial technology, law enforcement and corrections technologies, legal secretary, liberal/general studies, medical assistant, medical records administration, medical records technology, medical secretary, microcomputer software, nursing, practical nursing, protective services, radiograph medical technology, respiratory therapy, respiratory therapy technology, secretarial and related programs, social work, teacher aide, trade and industrial supervision and management.

ACADEMIC PROGRAMS. 2-year transfer program, cooperative education, double major, dual enrollment of high school students, independent study, telecourses. **Remedial services:** Learning center, reduced course load, remedial instruction, special counselor, tutoring. **Placement/credit:** CLEP Subject, institutional tests; 18 credit hours maximum for associate degree.

ACADEMIC REQUIREMENTS. Freshmen must earn minimum GPA of 2.0 to continue in good standing. 50% of freshmen return for sophomore year. Students must declare major on enrollment. **Graduation requirements:** 96 hours for associate (48 in major). Most students required to take courses in computer science, English, mathematics, social sciences.

FRESHMAN ADMISSIONS. Selection criteria: Open admissions. Selective admissions to nursing, radiologic technology, business computer programming and respiratory care programs based on college-administered exam. **Test requirements:** McGraw-Hill Comprehensive Tests of Basic Skills required for computer programming and radiologic technology applicants. Assessment and Placement Services for Community Colleges required for nursing applicants. Differential Aptitude Tests required for business computer programming applicants.

1992 FRESHMAN CLASS PROFILE. 51 men, 171 women enrolled. 5% had high school GPA of 3.0 or higher, 40% between 2.0 and 2.99. 2% were in top tenth and 6% were in top quarter of graduating class. **Characteristics:** 99% from in state, 100% commute, 60% have minority backgrounds. Average age is 26.

FALL-TERM APPLICATIONS. No fee. No closing date; applicants notified on a rolling basis. Interview required.

STUDENT LIFE. Activities: Student government, student newspaper.

ATHLETICS. Intercollegiate: Golf M, softball M, tennis M, volleyball. **Intramural:** Table tennis, volleyball.

STUDENT SERVICES. Aptitude testing, career counseling, employment service for undergraduates, freshman orientation, personal counseling, placement service for graduates, veterans counselor, services/facilities for handicapped.

ANNUAL EXPENSES. Tuition and fees (1992-93): $575, $3,959 additional for out-of-state students. **Books and supplies:** $500. **Other expenses:** $1,800.

FINANCIAL AID. 40% of freshmen, 43% of continuing students receive some form of aid. 99% of grants, all loans, all jobs based on need. Academic, athletic, state/district residency, leadership scholarships available.

Aid applications: Closing date July 15; applicants notified on a rolling basis beginning on or about August 15; must reply within 3 weeks.

ADDRESS/TELEPHONE. Thomas B. Anderson, Vice President of Student Services, Edgecombe Community College, 2009 West Wilson Street, Tarboro, NC 27886. (919) 823-5166. Fax: (919) 823-6817.

Elizabeth City State University
Elizabeth City, North Carolina — CB code: 5629

4-year public liberal arts college, coed. Founded in 1891. **Accreditation:** Regional. **Undergraduate enrollment:** 1,854 men and women full time; 165 men and women part time. **Faculty:** 133 total (111 full time), 79 with doctorates or other terminal degrees. **Location:** Rural campus in large town; 50 miles from Norfolk and Portsmouth, Virginia. **Calendar:** Semester, extensive summer session. Extensive evening/early morning classes. **Microcomputers:** Located in computer centers. **Special facilities:** Study carrels for honor students.

DEGREES OFFERED. BA, BS. 329 bachelor's degrees awarded in 1992. 34% in business and management, 7% computer sciences, 16% teacher education, 5% life sciences, 21% parks/recreation, protective services, public affairs.

UNDERGRADUATE MAJORS. Accounting, applied mathematics, biology, business administration and management, business education, chemistry, computer and information sciences, criminal justice studies, elementary education, English, English education, fine arts, geology, history, industrial arts education, industrial technology, junior high education, mathematics, mathematics education, music, music education, physical education, physics, political science and government, psychology, science education, social sciences, social studies education, social work, sociology, special education.

ACADEMIC PROGRAMS. Cooperative education, double major, honors program, independent study, internships, teacher preparation, weekend college. **Remedial services:** Learning center, preadmission summer program, reduced course load, remedial instruction, special counselor, tutoring. **ROTC:** Army. **Placement/credit:** AP, CLEP General and Subject.

ACADEMIC REQUIREMENTS. Freshmen must earn minimum GPA of 1.45 to continue in good standing. 74% of freshmen return for sophomore year. Students must declare major by end of second year. **Graduation requirements:** 126 hours for bachelor's (36 in major). Most students required to take courses in English, foreign languages, history, mathematics, biological/physical sciences, social sciences. **Postgraduate studies:** 1% enter law school, 1% enter medical school, 3% enter MBA programs, 25% enter other graduate study.

FRESHMAN ADMISSIONS. Selection criteria: GPA and test scores considered. Special consideration given to residents from 16 neighboring counties. **High school preparation:** 20 units required. Required units include biological science 1, English 4, foreign language 2, mathematics 3, physical science 1 and social science 2. One additional laboratory science also required. Mathematics must include 1 algebra and 1 geometry. Social science must include 1 history. **Test requirements:** SAT or ACT; score report by August 15.

1992 FRESHMAN CLASS PROFILE. 545 men and women enrolled. 23% had high school GPA of 3.0 or higher, 63% between 2.0 and 2.99. **Academic background:** Mid 50% of enrolled freshmen had SAT-V between 300-390, SAT-M between 330-430. 100% submitted SAT scores. **Characteristics:** 87% from in state, 60% live in college housing, 80% have minority backgrounds, 1% are foreign students. Average age is 19.

FALL-TERM APPLICATIONS. $15 fee. No closing date; priority given to applications received by August 15; applicants notified on a rolling basis; must reply as soon as possible. Deferred admission available.

STUDENT LIFE. Housing: Dormitories (men, women); apartment housing available. College-leased housing available. **Activities:** Student government, magazine, radio, student newspaper, yearbook, choral groups, concert band, dance, drama, jazz band, marching band, music ensembles, pep band, symphony orchestra, fraternities, sororities, United Campus Religious Fellowship, honor and recognition societies in education, science, dramatics, journalism, student union program.

ATHLETICS. NAIA, NCAA. **Intercollegiate:** Baseball M, basketball, football M, softball W, tennis M, track and field, volleyball W, wrestling M. **Intramural:** Baseball M, basketball, softball, volleyball.

STUDENT SERVICES. Aptitude testing, career counseling, employment service for undergraduates, health services, personal counseling, placement service for graduates, veterans counselor, services/facilities for handicapped.

ANNUAL EXPENSES. Tuition and fees (1992-93): $1,184, $5,018 additional for out-of-state students. **Room and board:** $2,648. **Books and supplies:** $300. **Other expenses:** $810.

FINANCIAL AID. 91% of freshmen, 81% of continuing students receive some form of aid. Grants, loans, jobs available. Academic, music/drama, athletic, minority scholarships available. **Aid applications:** No closing date; priority given to applications received by May 1; applicants notified on a rolling basis beginning on or about June 1; must reply within 3 weeks.

ADDRESS/TELEPHONE. Erthel Hines, Director of Admissions, Elizabeth City State University, Parkview Drive, Elizabeth City, NC 27909. (919) 335-3305. Fax: (919) 535-7408.

Elon College
Elon College, North Carolina — CB code: 5183

Admissions:	74% of applicants accepted
Based on:	••• School record, test scores
	• Activities, essay, interview, recommendations, special talents
Completion:	95% of freshmen end year in good standing
	55% graduate, 25% of these enter graduate study

4-year private liberal arts college, coed, affiliated with United Church of Christ. Founded in 1889. **Accreditation:** Regional. **Undergraduate enrollment:** 1,281 men, 1,571 women full time; 93 men, 137 women part time. **Graduate enrollment:** 8 men, 5 women full time; 65 men, 67 women part time. **Faculty:** 238 total (177 full time), 108 with doctorates or other terminal degrees. **Location:** Suburban campus in small town; adjacent to Burlington, 17 miles from Greensboro. **Calendar:** 4-1-4, extensive summer session. **Microcomputers:** 130 located in libraries, classrooms, computer centers. **Special facilities:** Fine arts center, tennis center, wellness center, writing center, greenhouse.

DEGREES OFFERED. BA, BS, MBA, MEd. 650 bachelor's degrees awarded in 1992. 26% in business and management, 14% communications, 10% teacher education, 9% parks/recreation, protective services, public affairs, 10% psychology, 18% social sciences. Graduate degrees offered in 3 major fields of study.

UNDERGRADUATE MAJORS. Accounting, biology, business administration and management, chemistry, computer and information sciences, corporate communications, dramatic arts, economics, elementary education, English, French, health education, history, information sciences and systems, journalism, junior high education, mathematics, medical laboratory technologies, music, music education, music performance, musical theater, parks and recreation management, philosophy, physical education, physics, political science and government, predentistry, preengineering, prelaw, premedicine, preveterinary, psychology, public administration, radio/television broadcasting, religion, science education, secondary education, social sciences, social work, sociology, Spanish, sports management, sports medicine.

ACADEMIC PROGRAMS. Accelerated program, cooperative education, double major, dual enrollment of high school students, honors program, independent study, internships, study abroad, teacher preparation, visiting/exchange student program, Washington semester, cross-registration, 3-2 program in engineering with North Carolina State University, University of North Carolina: Charlotte, North Carolina Agricultural and Technical State University. **Remedial services:** Learning center, reduced course load, remedial instruction, tutoring. **ROTC:** Army. **Placement/credit:** AP, CLEP General and Subject, institutional tests; 26 credit hours maximum for bachelor's degree.

ACADEMIC REQUIREMENTS. Freshmen must earn minimum GPA of 1.6 to continue in good standing. 75% of freshmen return for sophomore year. Students must declare major by end of second year. **Graduation requirements:** 126 hours for bachelor's (39 in major). Most students required to take courses in arts/fine arts, computer science, English, history, humanities, mathematics, philosophy/religion, biological/physical sciences, social sciences. **Postgraduate studies:** 2% enter law school, 1% enter medical school, 6% enter MBA programs, 16% enter other graduate study.

FRESHMAN ADMISSIONS. Selection criteria: School achievement record most important, followed by SAT scores. Class rank, interview, school and community activities, recommendations also considered. **High school preparation:** 16 units required. Required and recommended units include biological science 1, English 4, foreign language 2, mathematics 2-3, physical science 1 and social science 1-2. **Test requirements:** SAT or ACT (SAT preferred); score report by August 1.

1992 FRESHMAN CLASS PROFILE. 1,554 men applied, 1,046 accepted, 349 enrolled; 1,844 women applied, 1,467 accepted, 471 enrolled. 38% had high school GPA of 3.0 or higher, 61% between 2.0 and 2.99. 11% were in top tenth and 32% were in top quarter of graduating class. **Academic background:** Mid 50% of enrolled freshmen had SAT-V between 390-480, SAT-M between 430-530. 98% submitted SAT scores. **Characteristics:** 27% from in state, 96% live in college housing, 7% have minority backgrounds, 1% are foreign students, 18% join fraternities/sororities. Average age is 18.

FALL-TERM APPLICATIONS. $25 fee, may be waived for applicants with need. No closing date; priority given to applications received by June 1; applicants notified on a rolling basis; must reply by May 1 or within 4 weeks if notified thereafter. Interview recommended. CRDA. Deferred and early admission available. EDP-F.

STUDENT LIFE. Housing: Dormitories (men, women); apartment, fraternity, sorority housing available. **Activities:** Student government, magazine, radio, student newspaper, television, yearbook, choral groups, concert band, dance, drama, jazz band, music ensembles, musical theater, pep band, symphony orchestra, fraternities, sororities, religious organizations, discussion groups, social service fraternities, Inter-Varsity Christian Fellowship, Fellowship of Christian Atheletes, Young Republicans, Young Democrats, Habitat for Humanity, Black Cultural Society, Epsilon Sigma Alpha (service society).

ATHLETICS. NAIA, NCAA. **Intercollegiate:** Baseball M, basketball, cross-country, football M, golf M, soccer, softball W, tennis, track and field M, volleyball W. **Intramural:** Archery, badminton, basketball, football M, racquetball, soccer, softball, swimming, table tennis, tennis, track and field, volleyball, water polo.

STUDENT SERVICES. Aptitude testing, career counseling, employment service for undergraduates, freshman orientation, health services, personal counseling, placement service for graduates, special adviser for adult students, veterans counselor, peer tutorial program, services/facilities for handicapped.

ANNUAL EXPENSES. Tuition and fees: $8,630. **Room and board:** $3,660. **Books and supplies:** $425. **Other expenses:** $1,150.

FINANCIAL AID. 43% of freshmen, 41% of continuing students receive some form of aid. 43% of grants, 88% of loans, 52% of jobs based on need. 289 enrolled freshmen were judged to have need, all were offered aid. Academic, music/drama, athletic, state/district residency, leadership, religious affiliation scholarships available. **Aid applications:** No closing date; priority given to applications received by April 1; applicants notified on a rolling basis; must reply within 2 weeks.

ADDRESS/TELEPHONE. Nan P. Perkins, Dean of Admissions and Financial Planning, Elon College, PO 2700 Campus Box, Elon College, NC 27244-2010. (919) 584-2370. (800) 334-8448. Fax: (919) 538-3986.

Fayetteville State University
Fayetteville, North Carolina — CB code: 5212

Admissions: 65% of applicants accepted
Based on: ••• School record
•• Test scores
• Recommendations, special talents
Completion: 85% of freshmen end year in good standing
17% graduate, 15% of these enter graduate study

4-year public university, coed. Founded in 1867. **Accreditation:** Regional. **Undergraduate enrollment:** 958 men, 1,658 women full time; 125 men, 383 women part time. **Graduate enrollment:** 44 men, 83 women full time; 186 men, 465 women part time. **Faculty:** 185 total, 131 with doctorates or other terminal degrees. **Location:** Urban campus in small city; 60 miles from Raleigh. **Calendar:** Semester, extensive summer session. Extensive evening/early morning classes. **Microcomputers:** 125 located in dormitories, computer centers. **Special facilities:** Planetarium. **Additional facts:** Courses leading to bachelor's degree also available at Fort Bragg center.

DEGREES OFFERED. AA, BA, BS, MA, MS, MBA, MEd. 17 associate degrees awarded in 1992. 350 bachelor's degrees awarded. Graduate degrees offered in 5 major fields of study.

UNDERGRADUATE MAJORS. Associate: Business and office, liberal/general studies, secretarial and related programs. **Bachelor's:** Accounting, biology, business administration and management, business and office, business education, chemistry, clinical laboratory science, computer and information sciences, criminal justice studies, dramatic arts, economics, elementary education, English, English education, English literature, geography, health education, history, marketing and distribution, mathematics, mathematics education, music education, physical education, political science and government, psychology, public administration, science education, secondary education, social science education, social sciences, sociology, speech, visual and performing arts.

ACADEMIC PROGRAMS. Accelerated program, cooperative education, double major, honors program, independent study, internships, teacher preparation, weekend college. **Remedial services:** Learning center, preadmission summer program, remedial instruction, special counselor, tutoring. **ROTC:** Air Force. **Placement/credit:** AP, CLEP General and Subject, institutional tests; 36 credit hours maximum for bachelor's degree.

ACADEMIC REQUIREMENTS. Freshmen must earn minimum GPA of 2.0 to continue in good standing. 71% of freshmen return for sophomore year. Students must declare major by end of second year. **Graduation requirements:** 120 hours for bachelor's. Most students required to take courses in English, foreign languages, history, humanities, mathematics, biological/physical sciences, social sciences.

FRESHMAN ADMISSIONS. Selection criteria: 2.0 GPA, SAT scores, completion of 16 prescribed high school units required. **High school preparation:** 16 units required; 20 recommended. Required and recommended units include English 4, foreign language 1-2, mathematics 3, physical science 1, social science 2 and science 2. **Test requirements:** SAT or ACT (SAT preferred); score report by August 31.

1992 FRESHMAN CLASS PROFILE. 459 men applied, 296 accepted, 145 enrolled; 742 women applied, 488 accepted, 208 enrolled. 30% had high school GPA of 3.0 or higher, 63% between 2.0 and 2.99. **Academic background:** Mid 50% of enrolled freshmen had SAT-V between 250-450, SAT-M between 300-500. 100% submitted SAT scores. **Characteristics:** 87% from in state, 64% live in college housing, 79% have minority backgrounds. Average age is 18.

FALL-TERM APPLICATIONS. $15 fee. Closing date August 15; priority given to applications received by June 1; applicants notified on a rolling basis beginning on or about May 1; must reply within 1 week. Interview recommended for academically weak applicants. Deferred and early admission available.

STUDENT LIFE. Housing: Dormitories (men, women). **Activities:** Student government, film, radio, student newspaper, television, yearbook, choral groups, concert band, dance, drama, jazz band, marching band, music ensembles, fraternities, sororities, Baptist Student Union, Federation of Young Democrats.

ATHLETICS. NCAA. **Intercollegiate:** Basketball, cross-country, football M, golf, softball W, tennis, track and field, volleyball W. **Intramural:** Baseball M, basketball, bowling, football M, golf, gymnastics, swimming, tennis M, volleyball.

STUDENT SERVICES. Aptitude testing, career counseling, employment service for undergraduates, health services, on-campus day care, personal counseling, placement service for graduates, veterans counselor, services/facilities for handicapped.

ANNUAL EXPENSES. Tuition and fees (1992-93): $1,246, $5,672 additional for out-of-state students. **Room and board:** $2,250. **Books and supplies:** $350. **Other expenses:** $750.

FINANCIAL AID. 80% of freshmen, 70% of continuing students receive some form of aid. All grants, all jobs based on need. Academic, music/drama, athletic, alumni affiliation, religious affiliation, minority scholarships available. **Aid applications:** Closing date April 1; applicants notified on or about July 1; must reply within 8 weeks.

ADDRESS/TELEPHONE. Charles A. Darlington, Director of Enrollment Management, Fayetteville State University, 1200 Murchison Road, Fayetteville, NC 28301-4298. (919) 486-1371. (800) 222-2594. Fax: (919) 486-6024.

Fayetteville Technical Community College
Fayetteville, North Carolina — CB code: 5208

2-year public community, technical college, coed. Founded in 1961. **Accreditation:** Regional. **Undergraduate enrollment:** 1,145 men, 1,712 women full time; 1,748 men, 2,369 women part time. **Faculty:** 333 total (193 full time), 8 with doctorates or other terminal degrees. **Location:** Suburban campus in small city; 50 miles from Raleigh. **Calendar:** Quarter, limited summer session. Saturday and extensive evening/early morning classes. **Microcomputers:** 200 located in libraries. **Special facilities:** Center for Applied Technology. **Additional facts:** Offers the only funeral services curriculum in the North Carolina community college system.

DEGREES OFFERED. AA, AS, AAS. 480 associate degrees awarded in 1992.

UNDERGRADUATE MAJORS. Accounting, air conditioning/heating/refrigeration technology, architectural technologies, automotive mechanics, automotive technology, business administration and management, business and office, business computer/console/peripheral equipment operation, business data processing and related programs, civil technology, commercial art, computer and information sciences, criminal justice technology, dental hygiene, education, electronic technology, emergency medical technologies, finance, food management, food production/management/services, funeral services/mortuary science, historic preservation, horticultural science, horticulture, insurance and risk management, legal assistant/paralegal, liberal/general studies, machine tool operation/machine shop, marketing and distribution, nursing, physical therapy assistant, public administration, radiograph medical technology, real estate, recreation and community services technologies, respiratory therapy technology, secretarial and related programs, trade and industrial supervision and management, water and wastewater technology.

ACADEMIC PROGRAMS. 2-year transfer program, cooperative education, dual enrollment of high school students, weekend college. **Remedial services:** Learning center, preadmission summer program, reduced course load, remedial instruction, special counselor, tutoring. **Placement/credit:** CLEP General and Subject, institutional tests.

ACADEMIC REQUIREMENTS. Freshmen must earn minimum GPA of 1.85 to continue in good standing. 74% of freshmen return for sophomore year. Students must declare major on enrollment. **Graduation requirements:** 119 hours for associate (100 in major). Most students required to take courses in English, mathematics, social sciences.

FRESHMAN ADMISSIONS. Selection criteria: Open admissions. Selective admission of health applicants based on transcripts, school achievement record (to include prerequisites), institution placement tests, and interview. Engineering programs, 2 algebra; certain health programs, 2 algebra, 1 biology, and 1 chemistry.

1992 FRESHMAN CLASS PROFILE. 268 men, 330 women enrolled. **Characteristics:** 99% from in state, 100% commute, 37% have minority backgrounds. Average age is 28.

FALL-TERM APPLICATIONS. No fee. No closing date; applicants notified on a rolling basis; must reply immediately for health curriculums.

Interview required for health programs, funeral services, paralegal, auto service technology, architectural technology applicants.

STUDENT LIFE. Activities: Student government.

ATHLETICS. Intramural: Baseball, basketball, bowling, golf, softball, tennis, volleyball.

STUDENT SERVICES. Aptitude testing, career counseling, employment service for undergraduates, freshman orientation, health services, personal counseling, placement service for graduates, veterans counselor, services/facilities for handicapped.

ANNUAL EXPENSES. Tuition and fees (1992-93): $569, $3,959 additional for out-of-state students. **Books and supplies:** $600. **Other expenses:** $525.

FINANCIAL AID. 69% of freshmen, 70% of continuing students receive some form of aid. All grants, 91% of loans, all jobs based on need. Academic, alumni affiliation scholarships available. **Aid applications:** Closing date August 1; priority given to applications received by June 1; applicants notified on a rolling basis beginning on or about August 1; must reply within 2 weeks.

ADDRESS/TELEPHONE. Donald W. LaHuffman, Director of Admissions, Fayetteville Technical Community College, PO Box 35236, 2201 Hull Road, Fayetteville, NC 28303-0236. (919) 678-8473. Fax: (919) 484-6600.

Forsyth Technical Community College
Winston-Salem, North Carolina — CB code: 5234

2-year public community college, coed. Founded in 1964. **Accreditation:** Regional. **Undergraduate enrollment:** 758 men, 1,137 women full time; 990 men, 2,290 women part time. **Location:** Urban campus in small city; 32 miles west of Greensboro, 85 miles north of Charlotte. **Calendar:** Quarter.

FRESHMAN ADMISSIONS. Selection criteria: Open admissions. Selective admissions to health and developmental program based on school record, test scores, interview, and recommendations.

ANNUAL EXPENSES. Tuition and fees (1992-93): $577, $3,959 additional for out-of-state students. **Books and supplies:** $600. **Other expenses:** $750.

ADDRESS/TELEPHONE. George McLendon, Director of Admissions and Career Guidance, Forsyth Technical Community College, 2100 Silas Creek Parkway, Winston-Salem, NC 27103. (919) 723-0371 ext. 253. Fax: (919) 761-2399.

Gardner-Webb University
Boiling Springs, North Carolina — CB code: 5242

4-year private liberal arts college, coed, affiliated with Southern Baptist Convention. Founded in 1905. **Accreditation:** Regional. **Undergraduate enrollment:** 723 men, 791 women full time; 109 men, 314 women part time. **Graduate enrollment:** 2 women full time; 19 men, 85 women part time. **Faculty:** 155 total (78 full time), 61 with doctorates or other terminal degrees. **Location:** Rural campus in rural community; 50 miles from Charlotte. **Calendar:** Semester, limited summer session. **Microcomputers:** 20 located in libraries, computer centers. **Special facilities:** Observatory, convocation center with indoor track, state-of-the-art theater. **Additional facts:** Emphasis on Christian values.

DEGREES OFFERED. AA, BA, BS, MA, MBA, MEd. 21 associate degrees awarded in 1992. 430 bachelor's degrees awarded. 44% in business and management, 8% education, 8% teacher education, 8% health sciences, 5% philosophy, religion, theology, 16% social sciences. Graduate degrees offered in 9 major fields of study.

UNDERGRADUATE MAJORS. Associate: Interpreter for the deaf, nursing. **Bachelor's:** Accounting, biblical languages, biology, business administration and management, chemistry, clinical laboratory science, communications, computer and information sciences, criminal justice studies, data processing, elementary education, English, English education, foreign languages education, French, health education, history, labor/industrial relations, management information systems, mathematics, mathematics education, music, music education, nursing, physical education, physician's assistant, political science and government, psychology, religion, religious education, religious music, science education, secondary education, social science education, social sciences, social studies education, sociology, Spanish, theological studies.

ACADEMIC PROGRAMS. Double major, dual enrollment of high school students, honors program, independent study, internships, study abroad, spring break in New York, fall break in Washington; liberal arts/career combination in health sciences. **Remedial services:** Learning center, preadmission summer program, reduced course load, remedial instruction, tutoring. **Placement/credit:** AP, CLEP General and Subject; 30 credit hours maximum for bachelor's degree.

ACADEMIC REQUIREMENTS. Freshmen must earn minimum GPA of 1.5 to continue in good standing. 75% of freshmen return for sophomore year. Students must declare major by end of first year. **Graduation requirements:** 64 hours for associate, 128 hours for bachelor's. Most students required to take courses in arts/fine arts, computer science, English, foreign languages, history, mathematics, philosophy/religion, biological/physical sciences, social sciences. **Postgraduate studies:** 5% from 2-year programs enter 4-year programs.

FRESHMAN ADMISSIONS. Selection criteria: School achievement record most important, followed by test scores, recommendations, and school and community activities. Expected GPA 2.0. Recommended units include English 4, foreign language 2, mathematics 3, social science 2 and science 1. **Test requirements:** SAT or ACT; score report by August 1.

1992 FRESHMAN CLASS PROFILE. 159 men, 141 women enrolled. 10% were in top tenth and 25% were in top quarter of graduating class. **Academic background:** Mid 50% of enrolled freshmen had SAT-V between 320-430, SAT-M between 340-500. 89% submitted SAT scores. **Characteristics:** 64% from in state, 72% live in college housing, 10% have minority backgrounds, 1% are foreign students. Average age is 18.

FALL-TERM APPLICATIONS. $20 fee, may be waived for applicants with need. Closing date August 1; priority given to applications received by May 1; applicants notified on a rolling basis; must reply within 4 weeks. Audition required for music applicants. Interview recommended. Essay recommended. Deferred and early admission available. EDP-F.

STUDENT LIFE. Housing: Dormitories (men, women); apartment housing available. **Activities:** Student government, magazine, radio, student newspaper, yearbook, choral groups, concert band, drama, musical theater, pep band, symphony orchestra, Fellowship of Christian Athletes, Baptist Student Union, Ministerial Alliance, Outdoor Explorers club, several volunteer organizations.

ATHLETICS. NAIA, NCAA. **Intercollegiate:** Baseball M, basketball, football M, golf M, soccer, softball W, tennis, volleyball W, wrestling M. **Intramural:** Baseball M, basketball, racquetball, softball, swimming, tennis, volleyball.

STUDENT SERVICES. Aptitude testing, career counseling, employment service for undergraduates, freshman orientation, health services, personal counseling, placement service for graduates, services/facilities for handicapped.

ANNUAL EXPENSES. Tuition and fees: $7,680. **Room and board:** $4,070. **Books and supplies:** $500. **Other expenses:** $900.

FINANCIAL AID. 65% of freshmen, 66% of continuing students receive some form of aid. 47% of grants, 76% of loans, 43% of jobs based on need. 186 enrolled freshmen were judged to have need, all were offered aid. Academic, music/drama, athletic, state/district residency, leadership scholarships available. **Aid applications:** No closing date; priority given to applications received by April 1; applicants notified on a rolling basis beginning on or about April 1; must reply within 2 weeks.

ADDRESS/TELEPHONE. Ray M. Hardee, Dean of Admissions and Enrollment Planning, Gardner-Webb University, PO Box 817, Boiling Springs, NC 28017-9980. (704) 434-2361 ext. 230. (800) 222-2311. Fax: (704) 434-6246.

Gaston College
Dallas, North Carolina — CB code: 5262

2-year public community college, coed. Founded in 1963. **Accreditation:** Regional. **Undergraduate enrollment:** 760 men, 1,045 women full time; 830 men, 1,290 women part time. **Faculty:** 340 total (111 full time), 22 with doctorates or other terminal degrees. **Location:** Suburban campus in small town; 25 miles from Charlotte. **Calendar:** Quarter, limited summer session. Saturday and extensive evening/early morning classes. **Microcomputers:** 175 located in libraries, classrooms, computer centers. **Additional facts:** Branch campus at Lincolnton.

DEGREES OFFERED. AA, AS, AAS. 370 associate degrees awarded in 1992. 34% in business and management, 11% business/office and marketing/distribution, 10% engineering technologies, 22% health sciences, 14% parks/recreation, protective services, public affairs.

UNDERGRADUATE MAJORS. Accounting, automotive mechanics, automotive technology, biology, business administration and management, business and management, business and office, business data processing and related programs, business data programming, chemistry, civil technology, computer programming, criminal justice studies, early childhood education, electronic technology, elementary education, emergency medical technologies, engineering and engineering-related technologies, fashion merchandising, finance, fine arts, fire control and safety technology, humanities and social sciences, industrial technology, law enforcement and corrections technologies, legal secretary, liberal/general studies, marketing and distribution, marketing management, mathematics, mechanical design technology, medical assistant, medical secretary, music, nursing, practical nursing, predentistry, prelaw, premedicine, prepharmacy, preveterinary, psychology, radio/television technology, secretarial and related programs, social sciences, social work, visual and performing arts.

ACADEMIC PROGRAMS. 2-year transfer program, cooperative education, double major, dual enrollment of high school students, independent study, internships, telecourses, cross-registration. **Remedial services:** Learning center, reduced course load, remedial instruction, special counselor, tutoring. **Placement/credit:** AP, institutional tests; 18 credit hours maximum for associate degree.

ACADEMIC REQUIREMENTS. Freshmen must earn minimum GPA of 2.0 to continue in good standing. 35% of freshmen return for sophomore year. Students must declare major on enrollment. **Graduation requirements:** 101 hours for associate. Most students required to take courses in English, mathematics.

FRESHMAN ADMISSIONS. Selection criteria: Open admissions. Selective admissions to health services programs based on ACT scores and interview. **Test requirements:** ACT required for admission to health science programs, including nursing. ASSET used for placement only in all other programs.

1992 FRESHMAN CLASS PROFILE. 240 men, 340 women enrolled. **Academic background:** Mid 50% of enrolled freshmen had ACT composite between 15-25. 27% submitted ACT scores. **Characteristics:** 90% from in state, 100% commute, 10% have minority backgrounds, 1% are foreign students. Average age is 23.

FALL-TERM APPLICATIONS. No fee. No closing date; applicants notified on a rolling basis. Interview recommended for nursing, medical assistant, emergency medical technician applicants. Audition recommended for music applicants. Portfolio recommended for art applicants.

STUDENT LIFE. Activities: Student government, magazine, radio, choral groups, concert band, drama, music ensembles, symphony orchestra, Gamma Beta Phi, Phi Theta Kappa, Black Awareness Coalition, Baptist Student Union.

ATHLETICS. Intramural: Volleyball.

STUDENT SERVICES. Aptitude testing, career counseling, employment service for undergraduates, freshman orientation, on-campus day care, personal counseling, placement service for graduates, special adviser for adult students, veterans counselor, services/facilities for handicapped.

ANNUAL EXPENSES. Tuition and fees (1992-93): $587, $3,959 additional for out-of-state students. **Books and supplies:** $1,000. **Other expenses:** $1,000.

FINANCIAL AID. 42% of freshmen, 58% of continuing students receive some form of aid. 97% of grants, 89% of loans, 28% of jobs based on need. 76 enrolled freshmen were judged to have need, all were offered aid. Academic, minority scholarships available. **Aid applications:** No closing date; priority given to applications received by March 15; applicants notified on a rolling basis. **Additional information:** Grants/scholarships available for women pursuing nontraditional roles.

ADDRESS/TELEPHONE. Carol Harbers, Director of Admissions, Gaston College, 201 Highway 321 South, Dallas, NC 28034-1499. (704) 922-6214. Fax: (704) 922-6440.

Greensboro College

Greensboro, North Carolina — CB code: 5260

Admissions: 73% of applicants accepted
Based on:
- ••• School record
- •• Activities, essay, interview, special talents, test scores
- • Recommendations

Completion: 85% of freshmen end year in good standing
40% graduate, 13% of these enter graduate study

4-year private liberal arts college, coed, affiliated with United Methodist Church. Founded in 1838. **Accreditation:** Regional. **Undergraduate enrollment:** 304 men, 364 women full time; 103 men, 229 women part time. **Faculty:** 80 total (42 full time), 46 with doctorates or other terminal degrees. **Location:** Suburban campus in small city; 90 miles from Charlotte. **Calendar:** Semester, extensive summer session. Saturday and extensive evening/early morning classes. **Microcomputers:** 42 located in computer centers. **Special facilities:** Historical museum, art gallery, greenhouse, animal laboratory, computer laboratory, writing laboratory, computerized music laboratory.

DEGREES OFFERED. BA, BS. 135 bachelor's degrees awarded in 1992. 38% in business and management, 16% education, 6% letters/literature, 12% life sciences, 7% psychology, 12% social sciences.

UNDERGRADUATE MAJORS. Accounting, biology, business and management, chemistry, dramatic arts, education, education of the emotionally handicapped, education of the mentally handicapped, elementary education, English, fine arts, French, history, history/political science, junior high education, liberal/general studies, mathematics, medical laboratory technologies, medical radiation dosimetry, music, physical education, physician's assistant, political science and government, psychology, religion, religion/philosophy, religious education, religious music, secondary education, sociology, Spanish, special education, specific learning disabilities, studio art.

ACADEMIC PROGRAMS. Double major, dual enrollment of high school students, honors program, independent study, internships, student-designed major, study abroad, teacher preparation, visiting/exchange student program, weekend college, cross-registration, 2-year bachelor's degree program for registered nurses and other allied health professionals with registry. Academic Development Program; liberal arts/career combination in health sciences. **Remedial services:** Reduced course load, remedial instruction, special counselor, tutoring. **ROTC:** Air Force, Army. **Placement/credit:** AP, CLEP General and Subject, institutional tests; 45 credit hours maximum for bachelor's degree.

ACADEMIC REQUIREMENTS. Freshmen must earn minimum GPA of 1.6 to continue in good standing. 68% of freshmen return for sophomore year. Students must declare major by end of second year. **Graduation requirements:** 124 hours for bachelor's (30 in major). Most students required to take courses in arts/fine arts, English, foreign languages, history, mathematics, philosophy/religion, biological/physical sciences, social sciences. **Postgraduate studies:** 4% enter law school, 3% enter medical school, 2% enter MBA programs, 4% enter other graduate study.

FRESHMAN ADMISSIONS. Selection criteria: High school curriculum most important, followed by grades earned, class rank, standardized test scores, personal statement, school and community activities, and caliber of high school. Recommendations and campus interview also considered. **High school preparation:** 16 units recommended. Recommended units include English 4, foreign language 2, mathematics 3, social science 1 and science 2. Remaining units from foreign language, art, music, business, and physical education. **Test requirements:** SAT or ACT; score report by August 24.

1992 FRESHMAN CLASS PROFILE. 379 men applied, 250 accepted, 103 enrolled; 386 women applied, 306 accepted, 127 enrolled. 33% had high school GPA of 3.0 or higher, 64% between 2.0 and 2.99. **Academic background:** Mid 50% of enrolled freshmen had SAT-V between 370-480, SAT-M between 420-520. 97% submitted SAT scores. **Characteristics:** 43% from in state, 94% live in college housing, 18% have minority backgrounds. Average age is 18.

FALL-TERM APPLICATIONS. $20 fee, may be waived for applicants with need. No closing date; priority given to applications received by March 31; applicants notified on a rolling basis; must reply by May 1 or within 4 weeks if notified thereafter. Essay required. Interview recommended. Audition recommended for music applicants. Portfolio recommended for art applicants. CRDA. Deferred and early admission available. EDP-F.

STUDENT LIFE. Housing: Dormitories (men, women, coed). All students encouraged to live in college residence halls. All full-time students under 21 required to live in college housing unless married, veterans, or residing with parents. **Activities:** Student government, magazine, student newspaper, yearbook, choral groups, concert band, dance, drama, jazz band, music ensembles, musical theater, pep band, Student Christian Fellowship, United Afro-American Society, clown ministry, Jaycees, Alpha Kappa Omega (academic society for women), Beta Beta Beta (biology society), Student National Education Association, BACCHUS, North Carolina student legislature, GETHIP (Giving Everything To Help Important People).

ATHLETICS. NCAA. **Intercollegiate:** Baseball M, basketball, cross-country M, golf M, lacrosse, soccer, tennis, volleyball W. **Intramural:** Badminton, baseball M, basketball, bowling, golf, racquetball, skiing, soccer, softball, swimming, table tennis, tennis, volleyball, water polo.

STUDENT SERVICES. Aptitude testing, career counseling, employment service for undergraduates, freshman orientation, health services, personal counseling, placement service for graduates, special adviser for adult students, services/facilities for handicapped.

ANNUAL EXPENSES. Tuition and fees: $7,816. **Room and board:** $3,680. **Books and supplies:** $550. **Other expenses:** $970.

FINANCIAL AID. 67% of freshmen, 49% of continuing students receive some form of aid. 36% of grants, 90% of loans, 72% of jobs based on need. 118 enrolled freshmen were judged to have need, all were offered aid. Academic, music/drama, art, state/district residency, leadership, alumni affiliation, religious affiliation, minority scholarships available. **Aid applications:** No closing date; priority given to applications received by March 15; applicants notified on a rolling basis beginning on or about April 30; must reply within 15 days.

ADDRESS/TELEPHONE. Randy Doss, Dean of Enrollment Management, Greensboro College, 815 West Market Street, Greensboro, NC 27401-1875. (919) 272-7102. (800) 346-8226. Fax: (919) 271-2237.

Guilford College

Greensboro, North Carolina — CB code: 5261

Admissions: 80% of applicants accepted
Based on:
- ••• School record
- •• Essay, interview, recommendations, test scores
- • Activities, special talents

Completion: 95% of freshmen end year in good standing
71% graduate, 22% of these enter graduate study

4-year private liberal arts college, coed, affiliated with Religious Society of Friends (Quakers). Founded in 1837. **Accreditation:** Regional. **Undergraduate enrollment:** 656 men, 748 women full time; 133 men, 208 women part time. **Faculty:** 111 total (91 full time), 85 with doctorates or other terminal degrees. **Location:** Suburban campus in small city; 7 miles from downtown. **Calendar:** Semester, limited summer session. Extensive evening/early morning classes. **Microcomputers:** 120 located in dormitories, libraries, classrooms, computer centers. **Special facilities:** Observatory, telecommunications center.

DEGREES OFFERED. BA, BS, BFA. 363 bachelor's degrees awarded in 1992. 27% in business and management, 5% teacher education, 9% letters/literature, 5% life sciences, 9% parks/recreation, protective services, public affairs, 5% physical sciences, 8% psychology, 21% social sciences.

UNDERGRADUATE MAJORS. Accounting, anthropology, biology, business administration and management, business and management, chemistry, classics, criminal justice studies, dramatic arts, economics, education, elementary education, English, English literature, fine arts, French, geology, German, German area studies, history, humanities, international studies, mathematics, music, philosophy, physical education, physics, political science and government, prelaw, psychology, religion, secondary education, sociology, Spanish, sports management, sports medicine, studio art.

ACADEMIC PROGRAMS. Accelerated program, double major, dual enrollment of high school students, honors program, independent study, internships, student-designed major, study abroad, teacher preparation, visiting/exchange student program, United Nations semester, Washington semester, cross-registration; liberal arts/career combination in engineering, forestry, health sciences. **Remedial services:** Learning center, preadmission summer program, reduced course load, tutoring. **Placement/credit:** AP, CLEP General and Subject, IB, institutional tests; 32 credit hours maximum for bachelor's degree.

ACADEMIC REQUIREMENTS. Freshmen must earn minimum GPA of 2.0 to continue in good standing. 82% of freshmen return for sophomore year. Students must declare major by end of second year. **Graduation requirements:** 128 hours for bachelor's (32 in major). Most students required to take courses in arts/fine arts, English, foreign languages, history, humanities, mathematics, philosophy/religion, biological/physical sciences, social sciences. **Postgraduate studies:** 3% enter law school, 2% enter medical school, 1% enter MBA programs, 16% enter other graduate study.

FRESHMAN ADMISSIONS. Selection criteria: School achievement record, test scores, essay, interview, recommendations, interests, leadership ability important. **High school preparation:** 18 units required; 20 recommended. Required and recommended units include biological science 1-2, English 4, foreign language 2-3, mathematics 3-4, physical science 1-2, social science 2-3 and science 1. **Test requirements:** SAT or ACT; score report by February 1. **Additional information:** Applicants who show potential through the inerview or in other ways will be considered.

1992 FRESHMAN CLASS PROFILE. 639 men applied, 471 accepted, 151 enrolled; 607 women applied, 521 accepted, 189 enrolled. 72% had high school GPA of 3.0 or higher, 28% between 2.0 and 2.99. 22% were in top tenth and 50% were in top quarter of graduating class. **Academic background:** Mid 50% of enrolled freshmen had SAT-V between 460-570, SAT-M between 480-590; ACT composite between 22-27. 94% submitted SAT scores, 22% submitted ACT scores. **Characteristics:** 35% from in state, 99% live in college housing, 12% have minority backgrounds, 4% are foreign students. Average age is 18.

FALL-TERM APPLICATIONS. $25 fee, may be waived for applicants with need. Closing date February 1; priority given to applications received by January 10; applicants notified on or about March 15; must reply by May 1. Essay required. Interview recommended. CRDA. Deferred and early admission available. EDP-F; institutional early decision plan. Deadline for early decision application December 1.

STUDENT LIFE. Housing: Dormitories (men, women, coed); apartment, cooperative housing available. German, French and international issues housing available. **Activities:** Student government, film, magazine, radio, student newspaper, yearbook, choral groups, drama, jazz band, music ensembles, musical theater, pep band, Young Democrats, Young Republicans, International Relations Club, Hillel, African American Cultural Society, North Carolina Student Legislature.

ATHLETICS. NCAA. **Intercollegiate:** Baseball M, basketball, football M, golf M, lacrosse, soccer, tennis, volleyball W. **Intramural:** Basketball, diving, racquetball, soccer, softball, swimming, tennis, volleyball.

STUDENT SERVICES. Aptitude testing, career counseling, employment service for undergraduates, freshman orientation, health services, on-campus day care, personal counseling, placement service for graduates, special adviser for adult students, veterans counselor, services/facilities for handicapped.

ANNUAL EXPENSES. Tuition and fees: $12,610. **Room and board:** $5,070. **Books and supplies:** $475. **Other expenses:** $665.

FINANCIAL AID. 79% of freshmen, 72% of continuing students receive some form of aid. 66% of grants, 94% of loans, 68% of jobs based on need. 215 enrolled freshmen were judged to have need, all were offered aid. Academic, music/drama, art, state/district residency, leadership, minority scholarships available. **Aid applications:** Closing date March 1; applicants notified on or about April 1; must reply by May 1 or within 2 weeks if notified thereafter.

ADDRESS/TELEPHONE. Larry M. West, Director of Admissions, Guilford College, 5800 West Friendly Avenue, Greensboro, NC 27410. (919) 316-2100. (800) 992-7759. Fax: (919) 316-2951.

Guilford Technical Community College

Jamestown, North Carolina CB code: 5275

2-year public community college, coed. Founded in 1958. **Accreditation:** Regional. **Undergraduate enrollment:** 1,576 men, 1,626 women full time; 1,854 men, 2,160 women part time. **Location:** Suburban campus in small city; 2 miles from Greensboro, 5 miles from High Point. **Calendar:** Quarter. **Additional facts:** Campuses in Greensboro and High Point.

FRESHMAN ADMISSIONS. Selection criteria: Open admissions. Selective admissions to allied health programs based on school grade average, test scores, recommendations, interviews.

ANNUAL EXPENSES. Tuition and fees: $585, $3,959 additional for out-of-state students. **Books and supplies:** $750. **Other expenses:** $450.

ADDRESS/TELEPHONE. Mary Lockey, Coordinator of Admissions, Guilford Technical Community College, PO Box 309, Jamestown, NC 27282. (919) 334-4822 ext. 2311.

Halifax Community College

Weldon, North Carolina CB code: 0621

2-year public community college, coed. Founded in 1967. **Accreditation:** Regional. **Undergraduate enrollment:** 370 men, 565 women full time; 143 men, 345 women part time. **Faculty:** 89 total (44 full time), 4 with doctorates or other terminal degrees. **Location:** Rural campus in small town; 83 miles from Raleigh. **Calendar:** Quarter, extensive summer session. Extensive evening/early morning classes. **Microcomputers:** 50 located in computer centers.

DEGREES OFFERED. AA, AS, AAS. 96 associate degrees awarded in 1992. 15% in business/office and marketing/distribution, 29% allied health, 11% multi/interdisciplinary studies, 18% social sciences, 18% trade and industry.

UNDERGRADUATE MAJORS. Accounting, business administration and management, business and office, computer programming, criminology, education, electrical and electronics equipment repair, electromechanical technology, electronic technology, graphic arts technology, interior design, law enforcement and corrections technologies, liberal/general studies, marketing and distribution, medical laboratory technologies, medical secretary, nursing, office supervision and management, practical nursing, secretarial and related programs, social work, teacher aide.

ACADEMIC PROGRAMS. 2-year transfer program, dual enrollment of high school students, independent study, internships. **Remedial services:** Learning center, reduced course load, remedial instruction, special counselor, tutoring. **Placement/credit:** Institutional tests.

ACADEMIC REQUIREMENTS. Freshmen must earn minimum GPA of 2.0 to continue in good standing. 80% of freshmen return for sophomore year. Students must declare major on application. **Graduation requirements:** 96 hours for associate (47 in major). Most students required to take courses in English, mathematics, biological/physical sciences, social sciences.

FRESHMAN ADMISSIONS. Selection criteria: Open admissions. Selected admissions for nursing program. High school chemistry or equivalent and developmental mathematics required for nursing applicants.

1992 FRESHMAN CLASS PROFILE. 114 men, 93 women enrolled. **Characteristics:** 99% from in state, 100% commute, 56% have minority backgrounds. Average age is 25.

FALL-TERM APPLICATIONS. No fee. No closing date; applicants notified on a rolling basis. Interview recommended. Early admission available.

STUDENT LIFE. Activities: Student government, student newspaper.

STUDENT SERVICES. Career counseling, employment service for undergraduates, freshman orientation, personal counseling, placement service for graduates, veterans counselor, services/facilities for handicapped.

ANNUAL EXPENSES. Tuition and fees (1992-93): $575, $3,959 additional for out-of-state students. **Books and supplies:** $377. **Other expenses:** $896.

FINANCIAL AID. 43% of freshmen, 49% of continuing students receive some form of aid. 97% of grants, 51% of loans, 63% of jobs based on need. Academic, state/district residency, leadership scholarships available. **Aid applications:** No closing date; priority given to applications received by June 1; applicants notified on a rolling basis beginning on or about August 1; must reply within 2 weeks.

ADDRESS/TELEPHONE. Scottie Dickens, Director of Admissions, Halifax Community College, PO Drawer 809, Weldon, NC 27890. (919) 536-2551. Fax: (919) 536-4144.

Haywood Community College

Clyde, North Carolina CB code: 5289

2-year public community college, coed. Founded in 1965. **Accreditation:** Regional. **Undergraduate enrollment:** 398 men, 321 women full time; 200 men, 336 women part time. **Faculty:** 114 total (70 full time), 2 with doctorates or other terminal degrees. **Location:** Rural campus in rural community; 25 miles from Asheville. **Calendar:** Quarter, extensive summer session. Extensive evening/early morning classes. **Special facilities:** Thousands of acres of forest for use as field laboratories. **Additional facts:** Students attend 4 quarters to complete 1 full academic year.

DEGREES OFFERED. AAS. 161 associate degrees awarded in 1992. 28% in agriculture, 14% business and management, 6% business/office and marketing/distribution, 7% computer sciences, 9% engineering technologies, 9% health sciences, 16% multi/interdisciplinary studies, 6% parks/recreation, protective services, public affairs.

UNDERGRADUATE MAJORS. Business and office, business data processing and related programs, ceramics, computer programming, criminal justice technology, electromechanical technology, electronic technology, fiber/textiles/weaving, forestry and related sciences, forestry production and processing, horticulture, law enforcement and corrections technologies, liberal/general studies, manufacturing technology, medical assistant, metal/jewelry, nursing, secretarial and related programs, trade and industrial supervision and management, wildlife management.

ACADEMIC PROGRAMS. 2-year transfer program, dual enrollment of high school students, independent study, internships, telecourses. **Remedial services:** Learning center, reduced course load, remedial instruction, tutoring. **Placement/credit:** AP, institutional tests.

ACADEMIC REQUIREMENTS. Freshmen must earn minimum GPA of 2.0 to continue in good standing. 51% of freshmen return for sophomore year. Students must declare major on application. **Graduation requirements:** 120 hours for associate. Most students required to take courses in computer science, English, mathematics.

FRESHMAN ADMISSIONS. Selection criteria: Open admissions. Selective admissions to nursing program based on admission test scores, high school record, interview. Algebra, biology and chemistry required for nursing. Algebra recommended for electrical and manufacturing engineering, and microcomputer systems. **Test requirements:** Assessment and Placement Services for Community Colleges/The College Board.

1992 FRESHMAN CLASS PROFILE. 233 men, 199 women enrolled. **Characteristics:** 97% from in state, 100% commute, 3% have minority backgrounds. Average age is 27.

FALL-TERM APPLICATIONS. No fee. No closing date; applicants notified on a rolling basis. Interview required for nursing applicants. Placement interview required for criminal justice, electrical engineering technology, manufacturing engineering technology, horticulture and computer programming.

STUDENT LIFE. Activities: Student government, Christian fellowship group, Phi Theta Kappa, Phi Beta Lambda.

ATHLETICS. Intramural: Basketball, bowling, softball, volleyball.

STUDENT SERVICES. Career counseling, employment service for undergraduates, freshman orientation, personal counseling, placement service for graduates, veterans counselor, services/facilities for handicapped.

ANNUAL EXPENSES. Tuition and fees (1992-93): $577, $3,959 additional for out-of-state students. **Books and supplies:** $400. **Other expenses:** $870.

FINANCIAL AID. 27% of freshmen, 26% of continuing students receive some form of aid. All grants, 81% of loans, 38% of jobs based on need. **Aid applications:** No closing date; priority given to applications received by April 1; applicants notified on a rolling basis beginning on or about July 1; must reply within 2 weeks.

ADDRESS/TELEPHONE. Carol Smith, Director of Enrollment Management, Haywood Community College, Freelander Drive, Clyde, NC 28721. (704) 627-4500. Fax: (704) 627-3606.

High Point University
High Point, North Carolina — CB code: 5293

Admissions: 88% of applicants accepted
Based on: ••• Interview, school record, test scores
•• Recommendations
• Activities, essay
Completion: 80% of freshmen end year in good standing
43% graduate, 16% of these enter graduate study

4-year private liberal arts college, coed, affiliated with United Methodist Church. Founded in 1924. **Accreditation:** Regional. **Undergraduate enrollment:** 855 men, 1,111 women full time; 141 men, 219 women part time. **Faculty:** 147 total (94 full time), 64 with doctorates or other terminal degrees. **Location:** Suburban campus in small city; 15 miles from Greensboro, 20 miles from Winston-Salem. **Calendar:** Semester, limited summer session. **Microcomputers:** 110 located in libraries, classrooms, computer centers.

DEGREES OFFERED. BA, BS, MS. 525 bachelor's degrees awarded in 1992. 48% in business and management, 7% communications, 8% computer sciences, 6% multi/interdisciplinary studies, 8% psychology, 8% social sciences. Graduate degrees offered in 2 major fields of study.

UNDERGRADUATE MAJORS. Accounting, art education, biology, business administration and management, business and management, chemistry, chemistry/business, communications, computer and information sciences, creative writing, dramatic arts, early childhood education, education, elementary education, English, forestry and related sciences, French, history, home furnishings and equipment management/production/services, human resources development, humanities and social sciences, industrial and organizational psychology, information sciences and systems, international business management, international studies, junior high education, mathematics, medical laboratory technologies, philosophy, physical education, political science and government, psychology, religion, secondary education, social sciences, sociology, Spanish, special education, visual and performing arts.

ACADEMIC PROGRAMS. Double major, dual enrollment of high school students, honors program, independent study, internships, student-designed major, study abroad, teacher preparation, cross-registration, medical technology program with several other universities; liberal arts/career combination in forestry. **Remedial services:** Learning center, preadmission summer program, reduced course load, special counselor, tutoring. **Placement/credit:** AP, CLEP General and Subject, institutional tests; 31 credit hours maximum for bachelor's degree.

ACADEMIC REQUIREMENTS. Freshmen must earn minimum GPA of 2.0 to continue in good standing. 71% of freshmen return for sophomore year. Students must declare major by end of first year. **Graduation requirements:** 124 hours for bachelor's (48 in major). Most students required to take courses in arts/fine arts, English, foreign languages, history, humanities, mathematics, philosophy/religion, biological/physical sciences, social sciences. **Postgraduate studies:** 3% enter law school, 3% enter medical school, 5% enter MBA programs, 5% enter other graduate study.

FRESHMAN ADMISSIONS. Selection criteria: School achievement record, test scores, interview most important, followed by recommendations and school and community activities. **High school preparation:** 16 units required. Required and recommended units include biological science 1, English 4, foreign language 2, mathematics 2-3, social science 3 and science 1. Physical science 1 recommended. **Test requirements:** SAT or ACT (SAT preferred); score report by August 15.

1992 FRESHMAN CLASS PROFILE. 620 men applied, 533 accepted, 145 enrolled; 717 women applied, 644 accepted, 216 enrolled. 34% had high school GPA of 3.0 or higher, 56% between 2.0 and 2.99. 11% were in top tenth and 28% were in top quarter of graduating class. **Academic background:** Mid 50% of enrolled freshmen had SAT-V between 370-480, SAT-M between 390-530. 98% submitted SAT scores. **Characteristics:** 30% from in state, 77% live in college housing, 12% have minority backgrounds, 1% are foreign students, 29% join fraternities/sororities. Average age is 18.

FALL-TERM APPLICATIONS. $20 fee, may be waived for applicants with need. No closing date; priority given to applications received by March 1; applicants notified on a rolling basis; must reply within 4 weeks. Interview recommended. Essay recommended. Deferred and early admission available. ACH tests used for placement and counseling.

STUDENT LIFE. Housing: Dormitories (men, women, coed); fraternity, sorority housing available. All students living outside commuting distance must live in university housing. **Activities:** Student government, magazine, radio, student newspaper, television, yearbook, choral groups, drama, music ensembles, musical theater, pep band, fraternities, sororities, Alpha Phi Omega, Fellowship of Christian Athletes, Young Democrats, Young Republicans, Honors Club, International Trade and Commerce Club.

ATHLETICS. NAIA, NCAA. **Intercollegiate:** Baseball M, basketball, cross-country, field hockey W, golf M, soccer, tennis, track and field M, volleyball W. **Intramural:** Badminton, basketball, bowling, golf, racquetball, soccer, softball, swimming, table tennis, tennis, track and field M, volleyball.

STUDENT SERVICES. Aptitude testing, career counseling, employment service for undergraduates, freshman orientation, health services, personal counseling, placement service for graduates, special adviser for adult students, veterans counselor, services/facilities for handicapped.

ANNUAL EXPENSES. Tuition and fees: $7,760. **Room and board:** $3,700. **Books and supplies:** $570. **Other expenses:** $950.

FINANCIAL AID. 56% of freshmen, 66% of continuing students receive some form of aid. 64% of grants, 82% of loans, 31% of jobs based on need. 174 enrolled freshmen were judged to have need, 170 were offered aid. Academic, athletic, state/district residency, leadership, religious affiliation, minority scholarships available. **Aid applications:** No closing date; priority given to applications received by March 1; applicants notified on a rolling basis beginning on or about March 28; must reply within 2 weeks.

ADDRESS/TELEPHONE. Jim Schlimmer, Dean of Admissions, High Point University, PO University Station, Montlieu Avenue, High Point, NC 27262-3598. (919) 841-9216. (800) 345-6993. Fax: (919) 841-5123.

Isothermal Community College
Spindale, North Carolina — CB code: 5319

2-year public community college, coed. Founded in 1964. **Accreditation:** Regional. **Undergraduate enrollment:** 320 men, 457 women full time; 382 men, 613 women part time. **Faculty:** 85 total (48 full time). **Location:** Rural campus in small town; 65 miles from Charlotte, 30 from Spartanburg, South Carolina. **Calendar:** Quarter, extensive summer session. Extensive evening/early morning classes. **Microcomputers:** Located in classrooms, computer centers.

DEGREES OFFERED. AA, AS, AAS. 100 associate degrees awarded in 1992.

UNDERGRADUATE MAJORS. Automotive technology, business administration and management, business and management, business and office, business data entry equipment operation, business data processing and related programs, business data programming, business education, computer programming, criminal justice technology, early childhood education, education, electrical technology, elementary education, engineering and engineering-related technologies, fine arts, food management, graphic and printing production, health education, law enforcement and corrections technologies, liberal/general studies, machine tool operation/machine shop, marketing and distribution, mechanical design technology, music, practical nursing, prelaw, premedicine, prepharmacy, preveterinary, radio/television broadcasting, radio/television technology, recreation and community services technologies, science technologies, secondary education, secretarial and related programs, social sciences, teacher aide, textile technology.

ACADEMIC PROGRAMS. 2-year transfer program, cooperative education, dual enrollment of high school students, honors program, independent study. **Remedial services:** Learning center, preadmission summer program, reduced course load, remedial instruction, special counselor, tutoring. **Placement/credit:** AP, CLEP Subject, institutional tests; 12 credit hours maximum for associate degree.

ACADEMIC REQUIREMENTS. Freshmen must earn minimum GPA of 2.0 to continue in good standing. 71% of freshmen return for sophomore year. Students must declare major on application. **Graduation requirements:** 96 hours for associate (65 in major). Most students required to take courses in computer science, English, mathematics.

FRESHMAN ADMISSIONS. Selection criteria: Open admissions. **Test requirements:** ASSET test and high school transcript required of applicants.

1992 FRESHMAN CLASS PROFILE. 71 men, 114 women enrolled. **Characteristics:** 99% from in state, 100% commute, 15% have minority backgrounds. Average age is 20.

FALL-TERM APPLICATIONS. No fee. No closing date; applicants notified on a rolling basis. Interview recommended.

STUDENT LIFE. Activities: Student government, radio, student newspaper, television, yearbook, choral groups, drama, Afro-American Club, Phi Theta Kappa, Phi Beta Lambda.

ATHLETICS. Intramural: Badminton, basketball, softball, table tennis, volleyball.

STUDENT SERVICES. Aptitude testing, career counseling, employment service for undergraduates, freshman orientation, health services, personal counseling, placement service for graduates, veterans counselor, services/facilities for handicapped.

ANNUAL EXPENSES. Tuition and fees (1992-93): $585, $3,959 additional for out-of-state students. **Books and supplies:** $525. **Other expenses:** $1,137.

FINANCIAL AID. 33% of freshmen, 33% of continuing students receive some form of aid. 97% of grants, all loans, 74% of jobs based on need. Music/drama, state/district residency, leadership, minority scholarships available. **Aid applications:** No closing date; priority given to applications received by July 1; applicants notified on a rolling basis.

ADDRESS/TELEPHONE. Susan Monday, Admissions/Record Officer, Isothermal Community College, PO Box 804, Spindale, NC 28160. (704) 286-3636 ext. 288.

James Sprunt Community College
Kenansville, North Carolina — CB code: 6256

2-year public community college, coed. Founded in 1964. **Accreditation:** Regional. **Undergraduate enrollment:** 266 men, 371 women full time; 83 men, 312 women part time. **Faculty:** 71 total (41 full time), 2 with doctorates or other terminal degrees. **Location:** Rural campus in rural community; 75 miles from Raleigh, 45 miles from Wilmington. **Calendar:** Quarter, limited summer session. Extensive evening/early morning classes. **Microcomputers:** 90 located in classrooms, computer centers.

DEGREES OFFERED. AA, AS, AAS. 102 associate degrees awarded in 1992. 9% in agriculture, 19% business and management, 6% computer sciences, 26% education, 28% health sciences, 7% trade and industry.

UNDERGRADUATE MAJORS. Accounting, agribusiness, agricultural business and management, animal sciences, business and management, business and office, commercial art, early childhood education, education, elementary education, information sciences and systems, law enforcement and corrections technologies, liberal/general studies, medical assistant, medical records technology, nursing, secondary education, secretarial and related programs.

ACADEMIC PROGRAMS. 2-year transfer program, double major, dual enrollment of high school students, internships, telecourses. **Remedial services:** Learning center, preadmission summer program, reduced course load, remedial instruction, tutoring. **Placement/credit:** AP, CLEP General and Subject, institutional tests; 80 credit hours maximum for associate degree.

ACADEMIC REQUIREMENTS. Freshmen must earn minimum GPA of 1.75 to continue in good standing. 54% of freshmen return for sophomore year. Students must declare major on enrollment. **Graduation requirements:** 110 hours for associate (60 in major). Most students required to take courses in computer science, English, humanities, mathematics, social sciences.

FRESHMAN ADMISSIONS. Selection criteria: Open admissions. Selective admissions to nursing programs based on test scores and high school courses. 2.0 GPA in biology and chemistry courses required for nursing applicants. **Test requirements:** SAT required for placement.

1992 FRESHMAN CLASS PROFILE. 96 men, 244 women enrolled. **Characteristics:** 99% from in state, 100% commute, 31% have minority backgrounds. Average age is 21.

FALL-TERM APPLICATIONS. No fee. No closing date; applicants notified on a rolling basis. Interview required for nursing applicants. Closing date for nursing applicants is February 28.

STUDENT LIFE. Activities: Student government, student newspaper.

ATHLETICS. Intercollegiate: Softball, tennis M.

STUDENT SERVICES. Aptitude testing, career counseling, employment service for undergraduates, freshman orientation, personal counseling, placement service for graduates, veterans counselor, services/facilities for handicapped.

ANNUAL EXPENSES. Tuition and fees (1992-93): $581, $3,959 additional for out-of-state students. **Books and supplies:** $500. **Other expenses:** $600.

FINANCIAL AID. 45% of freshmen, 45% of continuing students receive some form of aid. 92% of grants, 97% of loans, 93% of jobs based on need. 150 enrolled freshmen were judged to have need, all were offered aid. Academic scholarships available. **Aid applications:** No closing date; priority given to applications received by July 1; applicants notified on a rolling basis beginning on or about July 15; must reply within 3 weeks.

ADDRESS/TELEPHONE. Rita B. Brown, Director of Admissions, James Sprunt Community College, PO Box 398, Kenansville, NC 28349-0398. (919) 296-2500. Fax: (919) 296-1636.

John Wesley College
High Point, North Carolina — CB code: 5348

4-year private Bible college, coed, interdenominational. **Undergraduate enrollment:** 77 men and women. **Faculty:** 14 total (8 full time), 1 with doctorate or other terminal degree. **Location:** Urban campus in small city; 15 miles from Greensboro, 60 miles from Charlotte. **Calendar:** Semester, limited summer session. Saturday and extensive evening/early morning classes. **Additional facts:** College's mission is educational development of students through balanced program of Biblical, general, and professional studies to equip them for service to God through church and society.

DEGREES OFFERED. AA, BA. 6 bachelor's degrees awarded. 100% in philosophy, religion, theology.

UNDERGRADUATE MAJORS. Associate: Education, liberal/general studies. **Bachelor's:** Bible studies, counseling psychology, elementary education, missionary studies, religion, religious education, theological studies.

ACADEMIC PROGRAMS. 2-year transfer program, accelerated program, double major, dual enrollment of high school students, independent study, internships, study abroad, teacher preparation, weekend college, elementary education cooperative program with High Point University. **Remedial services:** Reduced course load, remedial instruction. **Placement/credit:** AP, CLEP Subject, institutional tests; 18 credit hours maximum for bachelor's degree.

ACADEMIC REQUIREMENTS. Freshmen must earn minimum GPA of 2.0 to continue in good standing. 60% of freshmen return for sophomore year. Students must declare major by end of second year. **Graduation requirements:** 66 hours for associate, 128 hours for bachelor's (30 in major). Most students required to take courses in English, foreign languages, history, mathematics, philosophy/religion, biological/physical sciences, social sciences. **Postgraduate studies:** 95% from 2-year programs enter 4-year programs. **Additional information:** All students major in Bible; second major optional.

FRESHMAN ADMISSIONS. Selection criteria: Future career in church-related vocations and motivation; religious commitment and personal statement very important. **High school preparation:** 20 units recommended. Recommended units include English 4, mathematics 3, social science 2 and science 2. **Additional information:** Positive personal testimony required. Finding and following God's will foremost.

1992 FRESHMAN CLASS PROFILE. 9 men and women enrolled. **Characteristics:** 100% from in state, 50% commute, 22% have minority backgrounds. Average age is 24.

FALL-TERM APPLICATIONS. $25 fee, may be waived for applicants with need. Closing date August 1; applicants notified on a rolling basis. Interview required. Essay required. Deferred and early admission available. Inhouse testing is used in place of ACT or SAT because of large percentage of nontraditional students.

STUDENT LIFE. Housing: Apartment housing available. Housing limited to availability and/or payment of reservation fees. **Activities:** Student government, student newspaper, yearbook, choral groups, drama, music ensembles, evangelistic ministries, jail team, gospel music team, foreign missions involvement team, religious drama team. **Additional information:** Religious observance required.

ATHLETICS. Intramural: Basketball M, bowling, golf, horseback riding, racquetball, table tennis.

STUDENT SERVICES. Aptitude testing, career counseling, employment service for undergraduates, freshman orientation, personal counseling, placement service for graduates, veterans counselor, services/facilities for handicapped.

ANNUAL EXPENSES. Tuition and fees: $5,100. **Room and board:** $2,280. **Books and supplies:** $300. **Other expenses:** $1,500.

FINANCIAL AID. 67% of freshmen, 80% of continuing students receive some form of aid. 88% of grants, 95% of loans, all jobs based on need. 9 enrolled freshmen were judged to have need, all were offered aid. Academic, music/drama scholarships available. **Aid applications:** No closing date; priority given to applications received by May 1; applicants notified on a rolling basis beginning on or about June 1; must reply within 30 days. **Additional information:** Early Acceptance Scholarships, Academic Honor Scholarships, Married Student Credit and Minister/Missionary Dependent Scholarship available.

ADDRESS/TELEPHONE. Shirley Wagner, Admissions Officer, John Wesley College, 2314 North Centennial, High Point, NC 27265-3197. (919) 889-2262.

Johnson C. Smith University
Charlotte, North Carolina

CB code: 5333

Admissions:	69% of applicants accepted
Based on:	••• School record, test scores
	•• Interview, recommendations
	• Activities, essay, special talents
Completion:	75% of freshmen end year in good standing
	40% graduate, 19% of these enter graduate study

4-year private liberal arts college, coed. Founded in 1867. **Accreditation:** Regional. **Undergraduate enrollment:** 481 men, 744 women full time; 18 men, 29 women part time. **Faculty:** 95 total (82 full time), 58 with doctorates or other terminal degrees. **Location:** Urban campus in large city. **Calendar:** Semester, limited summer session. **Microcomputers:** 125 located in dormitories, libraries, classrooms, computer centers. **Special facilities:** Honors college, banking and finance center.

DEGREES OFFERED. BA, BS. 193 bachelor's degrees awarded in 1992. 33% in business and management, 14% communications, 7% computer sciences, 11% teacher education, 24% social sciences.

UNDERGRADUATE MAJORS. Accounting, biology, business administration and management, business and management, chemistry, communications, computer and information sciences, early childhood education, economics, elementary education, engineering and other disciplines, English, English education, finance, health education, history, marketing and distribution, mathematics, mathematics education, music, music education, physical education, physical sciences, physics, political science and government, prelaw, psychology, secondary education, social science education, social sciences, social work, sociology, urban studies.

ACADEMIC PROGRAMS. Accelerated program, cooperative education, double major, honors program, independent study, internships, study abroad, teacher preparation, visiting/exchange student program, Washington semester, cross-registration; liberal arts/career combination in engineering. **Remedial services:** Learning center, reduced course load, special counselor, tutoring, Freshman Mentoring program. **ROTC:** Air Force, Army. **Placement/credit:** AP, institutional tests.

ACADEMIC REQUIREMENTS. Freshmen must earn minimum GPA of 2.0 to continue in good standing. 70% of freshmen return for sophomore year. Students must declare major by end of second year. **Graduation requirements:** 122 hours for bachelor's (30 in major). Most students required to take courses in arts/fine arts, English, foreign languages, history, mathematics, philosophy/religion, biological/physical sciences, social sciences. **Postgraduate studies:** 1% enter law school, 1% enter medical school, 5% enter MBA programs, 12% enter other graduate study.

FRESHMAN ADMISSIONS. Selection criteria: Class rank, high school GPA, SAT scores important. **High school preparation:** 16 units required. Required units include English 4, mathematics 2, social science 2 and science 1. **Test requirements:** SAT or ACT (SAT preferred); score report by August 1.

1992 FRESHMAN CLASS PROFILE. 596 men applied, 365 accepted, 173 enrolled; 730 women applied, 546 accepted, 234 enrolled. **Academic background:** Mid 50% of enrolled freshmen had SAT-V between 260-350, SAT-M between 290-370. 92% submitted SAT scores. **Characteristics:** 24% from in state, 92% live in college housing, 99% have minority backgrounds, 10% join fraternities/sororities. Average age is 18.

FALL-TERM APPLICATIONS. $20 fee, may be waived for applicants with need. No closing date; priority given to applications received by August 1; applicants notified on a rolling basis beginning on or about October 1. Interview recommended. Essay recommended. Deferred and early admission available.

STUDENT LIFE. Housing: Dormitories (men, women, coed). Honors College Center houses 16 honors students in coed facility. **Activities:** Student government, film, radio, student newspaper, yearbook, choral groups, dance, drama, jazz band, marching band, music ensembles, pep band, fraternities, sororities, Student Christian Association.

ATHLETICS. NCAA. **Intercollegiate:** Basketball, football M, golf M, softball W, tennis M, track and field, volleyball W. **Intramural:** Badminton, basketball, softball, swimming, tennis, track and field, volleyball.

STUDENT SERVICES. Aptitude testing, career counseling, employment service for undergraduates, freshman orientation, health services, on-campus day care, personal counseling, placement service for graduates.

ANNUAL EXPENSES. Tuition and fees: $6,338. **Room and board:** $2,438. **Books and supplies:** $638. **Other expenses:** $1,608.

FINANCIAL AID. 90% of freshmen, 84% of continuing students receive some form of aid. 89% of grants, all loans, all jobs based on need. 342 enrolled freshmen were judged to have need, all were offered aid. Academic, music/drama, athletic, minority scholarships available. **Aid applications:** No closing date; priority given to applications received by May 15; applicants notified on a rolling basis beginning on or about May 15; must reply within 2 weeks.

ADDRESS/TELEPHONE. Marvin Dunlap, Director of Admissions, Johnson C. Smith University, 100 Beatties Ford Road, Charlotte, NC 28216-5398. (704) 378-1010. (800) 782-7303. Fax: (704) 372-5746.

Johnston Community College
Smithfield, North Carolina

CB code: 0727

2-year public technical college, coed. Founded in 1969. **Accreditation:** Regional. **Undergraduate enrollment:** 734 men, 664 women full time; 596 men, 856 women part time. **Faculty:** 235 total (110 full time), 3 with doctorates or other terminal degrees. **Location:** Rural campus in small town; 30 miles from Raleigh. **Calendar:** Quarter, extensive summer session. Extensive evening/early morning classes.

DEGREES OFFERED. AAS. 170 associate degrees awarded in 1992. 20% in business and management, 8% business/office and marketing/distribution, 5% computer sciences, 6% engineering technologies, 10% health sciences, 9% allied health, 6% home economics, 12% law, 10% multi/interdisciplinary studies, 11% visual and performing arts.

UNDERGRADUATE MAJORS. Accounting, business administration and management, business and office, child development/care/guidance, computer programming, electronic technology, graphic arts technology, law enforcement and corrections technologies, legal assistant/paralegal, liberal/general studies, medical secretary, nursing, radiograph medical technology, secretarial and related programs.

ACADEMIC PROGRAMS. 2-year transfer program, double major, dual enrollment of high school students, internships, cross-registration. **Remedial services:** Learning center, preadmission summer program, reduced course load, remedial instruction, special counselor. **Placement/credit:** AP, CLEP General, institutional tests.

ACADEMIC REQUIREMENTS. Freshmen must earn minimum GPA of 1.75 to continue in good standing. 55% of freshmen return for sophomore year. Students must declare major on application. **Graduation requirements:** 116 hours for associate (98 in major). Most students required to take courses in English, mathematics.

FRESHMAN ADMISSIONS. Selection criteria: Open admissions. Selective admission to health programs based on test scores, high school record and interview. **Test requirements:** CGP required for admission to nursing and radiologic technology programs.

1992 FRESHMAN CLASS PROFILE. 470 men, 610 women enrolled. **Characteristics:** 98% from in state, 100% commute, 22% have minority backgrounds. Average age is 24.

FALL-TERM APPLICATIONS. No fee. No closing date; applicants notified on a rolling basis. Interview required for health applicants applicants. Placement interview required for all applicants.

STUDENT LIFE. Activities: Student government, yearbook, jazz band.

STUDENT SERVICES. Aptitude testing, career counseling, employment service for undergraduates, freshman orientation, personal counseling, placement service for graduates, veterans counselor, services/facilities for handicapped.

ANNUAL EXPENSES. Tuition and fees (1992-93): $578, $3,959 additional for out-of-state students. **Books and supplies:** $450. **Other expenses:** $900.

FINANCIAL AID. 45% of freshmen, 55% of continuing students receive some form of aid. 73% of grants, 96% of loans, 52% of jobs based on need. Academic, state/district residency, minority scholarships available. **Aid applications:** No closing date; priority given to applications received by June 1; applicants notified on a rolling basis beginning on or about June 1; must reply within 2 weeks.

ADDRESS/TELEPHONE. Jimmy O'Neal, Director of Admissions, Johnston Community College, PO Box 2350, Smithfield, NC 27577-2350. (919) 934-3051. Fax: (919) 934-2823.

Lees-McRae College
Banner Elk, North Carolina CB code: 5364

4-year private liberal arts college, coed, affiliated with Presbyterian Church (USA). Founded in 1900. **Accreditation:** Regional. **Undergraduate enrollment:** 755 men and women. **Faculty:** 55 total (48 full time), 22 with doctorates or other terminal degrees. **Location:** Rural campus in rural community; 17 miles from Boone. **Calendar:** Semester, limited summer session. **Microcomputers:** Located in computer centers.

DEGREES OFFERED. AA, AS, BA, BS. 59 associate degrees awarded in 1992. 43 bachelor's degrees awarded. 32% in teacher education, 5% letters/literature, 9% life sciences, 14% multi/interdisciplinary studies, 18% social sciences, 22% visual and performing arts.

UNDERGRADUATE MAJORS. Associate: Biological and physical sciences, liberal/general studies, physical sciences. **Bachelor's:** Biology, business administration and management, communications, criminal justice studies, dance, dramatic arts, elementary education, English, English education, history, humanities, interdisciplinary studies, junior high education, mathematics, mathematics education, musical theater, naturalist, religion, science education, secondary education, social sciences, social studies education, speech/communication/theater education.

ACADEMIC PROGRAMS. 2-year transfer program, honors program, internships, student-designed major, study abroad, teacher preparation. **Remedial services:** Learning center, remedial instruction, tutoring. **Placement/credit:** AP, CLEP Subject, institutional tests; 16 credit hours maximum for associate degree; 16 credit hours maximum for bachelor's degree.

ACADEMIC REQUIREMENTS. Freshmen must earn minimum GPA of 1.4 to continue in good standing. 70% of freshmen return for sophomore year. Students must declare major by end of second year. **Graduation requirements:** 66 hours for associate, 126 hours for bachelor's (39 in major). Most students required to take courses in arts/fine arts, computer science, English, history, humanities, mathematics, philosophy/religion, biological/physical sciences, social sciences.

FRESHMAN ADMISSIONS. Selection criteria: High school record, test scores most important. Rank in top half of class preferred. Recommendations considered. **High school preparation:** 16 units required. Required and recommended units include biological science 1, English 4, mathematics 3, social science 2 and science 1. Foreign language 2 and physical science 1 recommended. **Test requirements:** SAT or ACT (SAT preferred); score report by June 1.

1992 FRESHMAN CLASS PROFILE. 284 men and women enrolled. **Academic background:** Mid 50% of enrolled freshmen had SAT-V between 290-390, SAT-M between 320-420; ACT composite between 13-18. 93% submitted SAT scores, 7% submitted ACT scores. **Characteristics:** 70% from in state, 92% live in college housing, 10% have minority backgrounds, 1% are foreign students. Average age is 18.

FALL-TERM APPLICATIONS. $15 fee, may be waived for applicants with need. No closing date; priority given to applications received by March 15; applicants notified on a rolling basis; must reply by March 15 or within 2 weeks if notified thereafter. Audition required for performing arts applicants. Essay required. Interview recommended. Early admission available.

STUDENT LIFE. Housing: Dormitories (men, women). Honors residence halls available. **Activities:** Student government, yearbook, choral groups, dance, drama, music ensembles, musical theater, pep band, Order of the Tower, Phi Theta Kappa.

ATHLETICS. NAIA. **Intercollegiate:** Baseball M, basketball, cross-country, football M, skiing, soccer, tennis, volleyball W. **Intramural:** Basketball, cross-country, golf, skiing, soccer, softball, table tennis, tennis, track and field, volleyball.

STUDENT SERVICES. Aptitude testing, career counseling, employment service for undergraduates, freshman orientation, health services, personal counseling, placement service for graduates, veterans counselor, services/facilities for handicapped.

ANNUAL EXPENSES. Tuition and fees: $8,200. **Room and board:** $3,050. **Books and supplies:** $450. **Other expenses:** $750.

FINANCIAL AID. 88% of freshmen, 78% of continuing students receive some form of aid. 31% of grants, 90% of loans, 43% of jobs based on need. 125 enrolled freshmen were judged to have need, all were offered aid. Academic, music/drama, athletic, state/district residency, leadership, religious affiliation scholarships available. **Aid applications:** No closing date; priority given to applications received by March 15; applicants notified on a rolling basis beginning on or about May 15; must reply within 2 weeks.

ADDRESS/TELEPHONE. Martha Dorage, Director of Admissions, Lees-McRae College, PO Box 128, Banner Elk, NC 28604. (704) 898-8723. Fax: (704) 898-8711.

Lenoir Community College
Kinston, North Carolina CB code: 5378

2-year public community college, coed. Founded in 1958. **Accreditation:** Regional. **Undergraduate enrollment:** 1,189 men and women full time; 1,067 men and women part time. **Faculty:** 126 total (71 full time), 7 with doctorates or other terminal degrees. **Location:** Rural campus in large town; 75 miles from Raleigh, 25 miles from Greenville. **Calendar:** Quarter, extensive summer session. Extensive evening/early morning classes. **Microcomputers:** Located in classrooms, computer centers.

DEGREES OFFERED. AA, AS, AAS. 157 associate degrees awarded in 1992.

UNDERGRADUATE MAJORS. Accounting, aeronautical technology, agribusiness, agricultural sciences, aviation management, business and office, business data processing and related programs, court reporting, drafting, education, electronic technology, engineering, finance, food production/management/services, graphic and printing production, graphic arts technology, health sciences, industrial technology, instrumentation technology, law enforcement and corrections technologies, legal secretary, liberal/general studies, library assistant, marketing and distribution, mechanical design technology, medical secretary, mental health/human services, nursing, ornamental horticulture, prelaw, radio/television broadcasting, secretarial and related programs.

ACADEMIC PROGRAMS. 2-year transfer program, cooperative education, dual enrollment of high school students. **Remedial services:** Learning center, reduced course load, remedial instruction, special counselor, tutoring. **Placement/credit:** AP, CLEP General and Subject, institutional tests.

ACADEMIC REQUIREMENTS. Freshmen must earn minimum GPA of 1.5 to continue in good standing.

FRESHMAN ADMISSIONS. Selection criteria: Open admissions. Selective admissions to allied health programs. One biology, 1 chemistry required for registered nursing program.

1992 FRESHMAN CLASS PROFILE. 356 men, 456 women enrolled. **Characteristics:** 97% from in state, 100% commute, 40% have minority backgrounds. Average age is 27.

FALL-TERM APPLICATIONS. No fee. No closing date; applicants notified on a rolling basis. Interview required for practical nursing, operating room, pharmacy technician, registered nursing applicants.

STUDENT LIFE. Activities: Student government, radio, student newspaper, Phi Theta Kappa, various clubs related to major fields of study.

ATHLETICS. NJCAA. **Intercollegiate:** Baseball M, basketball M, golf M. **Intramural:** Basketball, softball, tennis, volleyball.

STUDENT SERVICES. Career counseling, employment service for undergraduates, personal counseling, placement service for graduates, veterans counselor, services/facilities for handicapped.

ANNUAL EXPENSES. Tuition and fees (1992-93): $584, $3,959 additional for out-of-state students. **Books and supplies:** $450. **Other expenses:** $540.

FINANCIAL AID. Grants, loans, jobs available. **Aid applications:** No closing date; priority given to applications received by June 30; applicants notified on a rolling basis beginning on or about July 31; must reply within 2 weeks.

ADDRESS/TELEPHONE. Mark Hollar, Director of Admissions, Lenoir Community College, PO Box 188, Kinston, NC 28501. (919) 527-6223. Fax: (919) 527-6223 ext. 323.

Lenoir-Rhyne College
Hickory, North Carolina CB code: 5365

Admissions:	76% of applicants accepted
Based on:	••• School record
	•• Activities, recommendations, test scores
	• Essay, interview, religious affiliation/commitment, special talents
Completion:	90% of freshmen end year in good standing
	57% graduate, 35% of these enter graduate study

4-year private liberal arts college, coed, affiliated with Lutheran Church in America. Founded in 1891. **Accreditation:** Regional. **Undergraduate enrollment:** 527 men, 726 women full time; 66 men, 137 women part time. **Graduate enrollment:** 9 women full time; 8 men, 49 women part time. **Faculty:** 124 total (94 full time), 62 with doctorates or other terminal degrees. **Location:** Suburban campus in large town; 50 miles from Charlotte. **Calendar:** Semester, limited summer session. Extensive evening/early morning classes. **Microcomputers:** 120 located in libraries, classrooms, computer centers. **Special facilities:** Observatory.

DEGREES OFFERED. BA, BS, MA, MEd. 322 bachelor's degrees awarded in 1992. 34% in business and management, 23% teacher education, 7% health sciences, 6% psychology, 11% social sciences. Graduate degrees offered in 7 major fields of study.

UNDERGRADUATE MAJORS. Accounting, American studies, art education, biology, business administration and management, chemistry, classics, clinical laboratory science, communications, computer and information sciences, dramatic arts, early childhood education, economics, education, education of the deaf and hearing impaired, elementary education, English, environmental science, French, German, history, international business management, international relations, junior high education, liberal/general studies, mathematics, medical laboratory technologies, music, music education, music performance, nursing, philosophy, physician's assistant, physics, political science and government, predentistry, preengineering, prelaw, premedicine, prepharmacy, psychology, religion, religious education, secondary education, social sciences, sociology, Spanish, sports medicine.

ACADEMIC PROGRAMS. Double major, dual enrollment of high school students, honors program, independent study, internships, student-designed major, study abroad, teacher preparation, United Nations semester, Washington semester, special program for hearing impaired; liberal arts/career combination in engineering, forestry, health sciences. **Remedial services:** Learning center, preadmission summer program, remedial instruction, special counselor, tutoring. **ROTC:** Army. **Placement/credit:** AP, CLEP General and Subject, institutional tests.

ACADEMIC REQUIREMENTS. Freshmen must earn minimum GPA of 1.4 to continue in good standing. 81% of freshmen return for sophomore year. Students must declare major by end of second year. **Graduation requirements:** 128 hours for bachelor's (30 in major). Most students required to take courses in arts/fine arts, computer science, English, foreign languages, history, humanities, mathematics, philosophy/religion, biological/physical sciences, social sciences.

FRESHMAN ADMISSIONS. Selection criteria: School achievement record most important. Special consideration to children of alumni and minority applicants. **High school preparation:** 16 units required; 20 recommended. Required and recommended units include biological science 1, English 4, foreign language 2, mathematics 3, physical science 1 and social science 1-3. Science 1 recommended. Chemistry required for nursing program. **Test requirements:** SAT or ACT (SAT preferred); score report by August 15.

1992 FRESHMAN CLASS PROFILE. 451 men applied, 316 accepted, 95 enrolled; 542 women applied, 443 accepted, 164 enrolled. 50% had high school GPA of 3.0 or higher, 50% between 2.0 and 2.99. 20% were in top tenth and 54% were in top quarter of graduating class. **Academic background:** Mid 50% of enrolled freshmen had SAT-V between 400-500, SAT-M between 430-550; ACT composite between 21-23. 97% submitted SAT scores, 10% submitted ACT scores. **Characteristics:** 45% from in state, 85% live in college housing, 9% have minority backgrounds, 1% are foreign students, 28% join fraternities/sororities. Average age is 18.

FALL-TERM APPLICATIONS. $20 fee, may be waived for applicants with need. No closing date; applicants notified on a rolling basis; must reply by May 1 or within 4 weeks if notified thereafter. Audition required for music applicants. Essay required. Interview recommended. CRDA. Deferred and early admission available. EDP-F.

STUDENT LIFE. Housing: Dormitories (men, women, coed); apartment, handicapped housing available. **Activities:** Student government, magazine, radio, student newspaper, television, yearbook, choral groups, concert band, dance, drama, jazz band, marching band, music ensembles, musical theater, opera, pep band, symphony orchestra, fraternities, sororities, political, language, religious, debate, and service organizations.

ATHLETICS. NAIA, NCAA. **Intercollegiate:** Baseball M, basketball, cross-country, football M, golf M, soccer, softball W, tennis, track and field M, volleyball W. **Intramural:** Badminton, basketball, bowling, gymnastics, handball, racquetball, skiing, soccer, softball, swimming, table tennis, tennis, volleyball.

STUDENT SERVICES. Aptitude testing, career counseling, employment service for undergraduates, freshman orientation, health services, personal counseling, placement service for graduates, special adviser for adult students, veterans counselor, services/facilities for handicapped.

ANNUAL EXPENSES. Tuition and fees (1992-93): $9,500. **Room and board:** $3,665. **Books and supplies:** $500. **Other expenses:** $600.

FINANCIAL AID. 60% of freshmen, 71% of continuing students receive some form of aid. 85% of grants, 81% of loans, 37% of jobs based on need. 231 enrolled freshmen were judged to have need, all were offered aid. Academic, music/drama, athletic, state/district residency, leadership, minority scholarships available. **Aid applications:** No closing date; priority given to applications received by March 1; applicants notified on a rolling basis beginning on or about March 1; must reply within 4 weeks.

ADDRESS/TELEPHONE. Timothy L. Jackson, Director of Admissions, Lenoir-Rhyne College, PO Box 7227, Hickory, NC 28603. (704) 328-7300. (800) 277-5721. Fax: (704) 328-7338.

Livingstone College

Salisbury, North Carolina — CB code: 5367

Admissions: 81% of applicants accepted
Based on:
- ••• School record
- •• Recommendations, test scores
- • Activities, interview, special talents

Completion: 70% of freshmen end year in good standing
37% graduate, 24% of these enter graduate study

4-year private liberal arts college, coed, affiliated with African Methodist Episcopal Zion Church. Founded in 1879. **Accreditation:** Regional. **Undergraduate enrollment:** 332 men, 285 women full time; 4 men, 8 women part time. **Faculty:** 67 total (60 full time), 24 with doctorates or other terminal degrees. **Location:** Urban campus in large town; 44 miles from Charlotte. **Calendar:** Semester. **Microcomputers:** Located in libraries, computer centers. **Special facilities:** Walls Heritage House, center for Negro and African life and literature. **Additional facts:** Master's courses offered in conjunction with Hood Theological Seminary.

DEGREES OFFERED. BA, BS. 59 bachelor's degrees awarded in 1992. 50% in business and management, 5% computer sciences, 5% teacher education, 5% life sciences, 5% mathematics, 5% psychology, 18% social sciences. Graduate degrees offered in 1 major field of study.

UNDERGRADUATE MAJORS. Accounting, Bible studies, biology, business administration and management, business and management, chemistry, computer and information sciences, criminal justice studies, early childhood education, education, elementary education, engineering, English, English education, history, mathematics, mathematics education, music, music education, pharmacy, physical education, political science and government, predentistry, psychology, religious education, science education, social science education, social sciences, social studies education, social work, sociology, sports management.

ACADEMIC PROGRAMS. Double major, independent study, internships, teacher preparation; liberal arts/career combination in engineering, health sciences. **Remedial services:** Learning center, reduced course load, remedial instruction, special counselor, tutoring. **ROTC:** Army. **Placement/credit:** AP, CLEP General and Subject, institutional tests.

ACADEMIC REQUIREMENTS. Freshmen must earn minimum GPA of 1.25 to continue in good standing. 63% of freshmen return for sophomore year. Students must declare major by end of second year. **Graduation requirements:** 124 hours for bachelor's (30 in major). Most students required to take courses in English, foreign languages, history, humanities, mathematics, philosophy/religion, biological/physical sciences, social sciences. **Postgraduate studies:** 2% enter law school, 1% enter medical school, 6% enter MBA programs, 15% enter other graduate study.

FRESHMAN ADMISSIONS. Selection criteria: School achievement record, test scores, recommendations important. **High school preparation:** 16 units required. Required units include mathematics 2 and social science 1. **Test requirements:** SAT or ACT; score report by August 1.

1992 FRESHMAN CLASS PROFILE. 800 men and women applied, 650 accepted; 232 enrolled. **Academic background:** Mid 50% of enrolled freshmen had SAT-V between 250-400, SAT-M between 250-400. 90% submitted SAT scores. **Characteristics:** 36% from in state, 88% live in college housing, 100% have minority backgrounds. Average age is 18.

FALL-TERM APPLICATIONS. $10 fee, may be waived for applicants with need. Closing date August 1; priority given to applications received by June 30; applicants notified on a rolling basis beginning on or about May 15; must reply by July 15. Audition required for music applicants. Interview recommended for academically weak applicants. Deferred admission available.

STUDENT LIFE. Housing: Dormitories (men, women). **Activities:** Student government, student newspaper, yearbook, choral groups, concert band, jazz band, marching band, music ensembles, pep band, symphony orchestra, fraternities, sororities, Pre-Theological Union, Prayer Meeting Choir.

ATHLETICS. NCAA. **Intercollegiate:** Basketball, cross-country, football M, golf, softball W, tennis M, track and field, volleyball W. **Intramural:** Baseball M, basketball, softball, table tennis, volleyball.

STUDENT SERVICES. Aptitude testing, career counseling, employment service for undergraduates, freshman orientation, health services, personal counseling, placement service for graduates, veterans counselor.

ANNUAL EXPENSES. Tuition and fees (1992-93): $5,200. **Room and board:** $3,400. **Books and supplies:** $700. **Other expenses:** $800.

FINANCIAL AID. 84% of freshmen, 94% of continuing students receive some form of aid. 87% of grants, all loans, all jobs based on need. Academic, music/drama, athletic, state/district residency scholarships available. **Aid applications:** Closing date May 15; priority given to applications received by May 1; applicants notified on or about June 15; must reply by August 15.

ADDRESS/TELEPHONE. Grady Deese, Director of Admissions, Livingstone College, 701 West Monroe Street, Salisbury, NC 28144-5213. (704) 638-5500 ext. 5502. (800) 422-5430.

Louisburg College

Louisburg, North Carolina — CB code: 5369

Admissions: 90% of applicants accepted
Based on:
- ••• School record
- •• Test scores
- • Activities, essay, interview, recommendations, special talents

Completion: 70% of freshmen end year in good standing
90% enter 4-year programs

2-year private junior college, coed, affiliated with United Methodist Church. Founded in 1787. **Accreditation:** Regional. **Undergraduate enrollment:** 388 men, 318 women full time; 26 men, 72 women part time. **Faculty:** 49 total (36 full time), 7 with doctorates or other terminal degrees. **Location:** Rural campus in small town; 30 miles from Raleigh. **Calendar:** Semester. Saturday and extensive evening/early morning classes. **Microcomputers:** 30 located in computer centers.

DEGREES OFFERED. AA, AS. 151 associate degrees awarded in 1992.

UNDERGRADUATE MAJORS. Business and management, business and office, engineering, liberal/general studies.

ACADEMIC PROGRAMS. 2-year transfer program, cooperative education, independent study, weekend college. **Remedial services:** Preadmission summer program, reduced course load, remedial instruction, special counselor, tutoring, mathematics laboratory, writing center. **Placement/credit:** AP, CLEP General and Subject, institutional tests; 30 credit hours maximum for associate degree.

ACADEMIC REQUIREMENTS. Freshmen must earn minimum GPA of 1.7 to continue in good standing. 65% of freshmen return for sophomore year. **Graduation requirements:** 62 hours for associate. Most students required to take courses in arts/fine arts, English, foreign languages, history, humanities, mathematics, philosophy/religion, biological/physical sciences, social sciences.

FRESHMAN ADMISSIONS. Selection criteria: School achievement most important, followed by test scores and recommendations. Interview recommended for all applicants, required for some applicants. **High school preparation:** 20 units recommended. Recommended units include biological science 1, English 4, mathematics 2 and physical science 1. **Test requirements:** SAT or ACT; score report by June 1.

1992 FRESHMAN CLASS PROFILE. 466 men applied, 413 accepted, 231 enrolled; 310 women applied, 287 accepted, 170 enrolled. 16% had high school GPA of 3.0 or higher, 52% between 2.0 and 2.99. **Academic background:** Mid 50% of enrolled freshmen had SAT-V between 310-390, SAT-M between 330-440. 98% submitted SAT scores. **Characteristics:** 75% from in state, 85% live in college housing, 16% have minority backgrounds, 1% are foreign students. Average age is 18.

FALL-TERM APPLICATIONS. $15 fee, may be waived for applicants with need. No closing date; priority given to applications received by May 1; applicants notified on a rolling basis; must reply by May 1 or within 2 weeks if notified thereafter. Interview recommended. CRDA. Deferred admission available.

STUDENT LIFE. Housing: Dormitories (men, women, coed). **Activities:** Student government, magazine, radio, student newspaper, yearbook, choral groups, drama, music ensembles, musical theater, Christian Life Council, Young Democrats, Young Republicans, Spanish club, Workers Actively Volunteering Energetic Services, Peace group, French club.

ATHLETICS. NJCAA. **Intercollegiate:** Baseball M, basketball, golf M, softball W. **Intramural:** Basketball, soccer, softball, table tennis, tennis, volleyball.

STUDENT SERVICES. Aptitude testing, career counseling, employment service for undergraduates, freshman orientation, health services, personal counseling, special adviser for adult students, veterans counselor, services/facilities for handicapped.

ANNUAL EXPENSES. Tuition and fees: $6,249. **Room and board:** $3,035. **Books and supplies:** $450. **Other expenses:** $1,000.

FINANCIAL AID. 83% of freshmen, 88% of continuing students receive some form of aid. 55% of grants, 95% of loans, 91% of jobs based on need. 216 enrolled freshmen were judged to have need, all were offered aid. Academic, music/drama, athletic, state/district residency scholarships available. **Aid applications:** No closing date; priority given to applications received by April 1; applicants notified on a rolling basis beginning on or about April 1; must reply by May 1 or within 2 weeks if notified thereafter. **Additional information:** Job location and development program helps students obtain work in the community.

ADDRESS/TELEPHONE. Rick Lowe, Director of Admissions, Louisburg College, 501 North Main Street, Louisburg, NC 27549. (919) 496-2521 ext. 237. (800) 775-0208. Fax: (919) 496-1788.

Mars Hill College

Mars Hill, North Carolina — CB code: 5395

Admissions: 85% of applicants accepted
Based on:
- ••• Activities, recommendations, school record, test scores
- •• Interview
- • Essay, religious affiliation/commitment, special talents

Completion: 79% of freshmen end year in good standing
20% enter graduate study

4-year private liberal arts college, coed, affiliated with Southern Baptist Convention. Founded in 1856. **Accreditation:** Regional. **Undergraduate enrollment:** 554 men, 577 women full time; 52 men, 171 women part time. **Faculty:** 133 total (78 full time), 46 with doctorates or other terminal degrees. **Location:** Rural campus in rural community; 17 miles from Asheville. **Calendar:** Semester, extensive summer session. Extensive evening/early morning classes. **Microcomputers:** 60 located in libraries, classrooms, computer centers. **Special facilities:** Satellite receiver for foreign language study, Appalachian archives and artifacts museum, media center, Weizenblatt Art Gallery. **Additional facts:** Located in southern Appalachia. Continuing education programs available for adults on campus and at 2 off-campus sites.

DEGREES OFFERED. BA, BS, BFA. 251 bachelor's degrees awarded in 1992. 14% in business and management, 6% business/office and marketing/distribution, 31% teacher education, 5% letters/literature, 6% life sciences, 9% social sciences.

UNDERGRADUATE MAJORS. Accounting, allied health, art education, art history, biological and physical sciences, biology, botany, business administration and management, business and management, chemistry, communications, computer and information sciences, dramatic arts, education, elementary education, English, English education, fashion merchandising, finance, fine arts, foreign languages education, French, health sciences, history, home economics, humanities and social sciences, information sciences and systems, international business management, international studies, junior high education, liberal/general studies, marketing management, mathematics, mathematics education, medical laboratory technologies, music, music education, music performance, musical theater, parks and recreation management, physical education, political science and government, predentistry, prelaw, premedicine, prepharmacy, preveterinary, psychology, public relations, religion, religious education, religious music, science education, secondary education, social science education, social sciences, social studies education, social work, sociology, Spanish, studio art, visual and performing arts, zoology.

ACADEMIC PROGRAMS. Accelerated program, double major, dual enrollment of high school students, honors program, independent study, internships, student-designed major, study abroad, teacher preparation, visiting/exchange student program; liberal arts/career combination in health sciences. **Remedial services:** Learning center, preadmission summer program, reduced course load, remedial instruction, special counselor, tutoring. **Placement/credit:** AP, CLEP General and Subject, institutional tests; 32 credit hours maximum for bachelor's degree.

ACADEMIC REQUIREMENTS. Freshmen must earn minimum GPA of 2.0 to continue in good standing. 70% of freshmen return for sophomore year. Students must declare major by end of second year. **Graduation requirements:** 128 hours for bachelor's (42 in major). Most students required to take courses in arts/fine arts, computer science, English, foreign languages, history, humanities, mathematics, philosophy/religion, biological/physical sciences, social sciences. **Postgraduate studies:** 2% enter law school, 1% enter medical school, 3% enter MBA programs, 14% enter other graduate study.

FRESHMAN ADMISSIONS. Selection criteria: School achievement record, test scores, school and community activities, and recommendations from school officials all weighed equally. Minimum high school GPA 2.0. **High school preparation:** 18 units required. Required units include biological science 1, English 4, mathematics 2, physical science 1 and social science 2. 2 foreign language and/or 1 computer science recommended. **Test requirements:** SAT or ACT; score report by August 15. **Additional information:** Each application reviewed individually. Students will be contacted if further information is necessary in making admissions decision.

1992 FRESHMAN CLASS PROFILE. 570 men applied, 467 accepted, 115 enrolled; 511 women applied, 451 accepted, 150 enrolled. 29% had high school GPA of 3.0 or higher, 49% between 2.0 and 2.99. **Academic background:** Mid 50% of enrolled freshmen had SAT-V between 370-480, SAT-M between 380-520. 85% submitted SAT scores. **Characteristics:** 61% from in state, 78% live in college housing, 12% have minority backgrounds, 2% are foreign students, 8% join fraternities/sororities. Average age is 18.

FALL-TERM APPLICATIONS. $15 fee, may be waived for applicants with need. Closing date August 15; priority given to applications received by May 1; applicants notified on a rolling basis; must reply within 4 weeks. Interview required for selected applicants. Audition required for music, theater applicants. Essay required. Portfolio recommended. CRDA. Deferred and early admission available.

STUDENT LIFE. Housing: Dormitories (men, women); apartment housing available. College townhouses and apartments available to honor students and upperclassmen. **Activities:** Student government, magazine, radio, student newspaper, yearbook, choral groups, concert band, dance, drama, jazz band, marching band, music ensembles, musical theater, pep band, fraternities, sororities, Christian Student Movement, Fellowship of Christian Athletes. **Additional information:** Student activity revolves around college community. All students have opportunities to participate.

ATHLETICS. NAIA, NCAA. **Intercollegiate:** Baseball M, basketball, cross-country, football M, golf M, soccer, softball W, tennis, volleyball W. **Intramural:** Basketball, racquetball, softball, table tennis, tennis, volleyball.

STUDENT SERVICES. Aptitude testing, career counseling, employment service for undergraduates, freshman orientation, health services, personal counseling, placement service for graduates, special adviser for adult students, services/facilities for handicapped.

ANNUAL EXPENSES. Tuition and fees: $7,500. **Room and board:** $3,550. **Books and supplies:** $600. **Other expenses:** $800.

FINANCIAL AID. 72% of freshmen, 69% of continuing students receive some form of aid. 32% of grants, 88% of loans, 47% of jobs based on need. 198 enrolled freshmen were judged to have need, all were offered aid. Academic, music/drama, athletic, leadership scholarships available. **Aid ap-**

plications: No closing date; priority given to applications received by May 1; applicants notified on a rolling basis beginning on or about February 15; must reply within 10 days.

ADDRESS/TELEPHONE. Rick Hinshaw, Associate Dean of Admissions, Mars Hill College, PO Box 370, Mars Hill, NC 28754. (704) 689-1201. (800) 543-1514. Fax: (704) 689-1478.

Martin Community College
Williamston, North Carolina — CB code: 5445

2-year public community college, coed. Founded in 1967. **Accreditation:** Regional. **Undergraduate enrollment:** 146 men, 332 women full time; 114 men, 225 women part time. **Faculty:** 60 total (26 full time), 1 with doctorate or other terminal degree. **Location:** Rural campus in small town; 30 miles from Greenville. **Calendar:** Quarter, limited summer session. Saturday and extensive evening/early morning classes. **Microcomputers:** 45 located in computer centers.

DEGREES OFFERED. AA, AAS. 65 associate degrees awarded in 1992. 25% in agriculture, 26% business and management, 5% business/office and marketing/distribution, 10% teacher education, 23% allied health, 6% multi/interdisciplinary studies, 5% trade and industry.

UNDERGRADUATE MAJORS. Accounting, air conditioning/heating/refrigeration mechanics, air conditioning/heating/refrigeration technology, automotive mechanics, business administration and management, business data programming, elementary education, equestrian science, liberal/general studies, physical therapy assistant, secondary education, secretarial and related programs, social work.

ACADEMIC PROGRAMS. 2-year transfer program, cooperative education, dual enrollment of high school students, internships, telecourses. **Remedial services:** Learning center, reduced course load, remedial instruction, tutoring. **Placement/credit:** AP, CLEP General, institutional tests; 48 credit hours maximum for associate degree.

ACADEMIC REQUIREMENTS. Freshmen must earn minimum GPA of 2.0 to continue in good standing. 40% of freshmen return for sophomore year. Students must declare major on application. **Graduation requirements:** 96 hours for associate. Most students required to take courses in English, humanities, mathematics, social sciences.

FRESHMAN ADMISSIONS. Selection criteria: Open admissions. Limited enrollment in physical therapist assistant program. Selection based on high school record, placement, allied health test results, and interview. **Test requirements:** Assessment and placement Services test required of all applicants for placement; Health Occupations Aptitude Examination also required for physical therapist assistant applicants. **Additional information:** After earning 18 quarter hours, special credit students must meet regular admission requirements.

1992 FRESHMAN CLASS PROFILE. 48 men, 101 women enrolled. **Characteristics:** 99% from in state, 100% commute, 56% have minority backgrounds.

FALL-TERM APPLICATIONS. No fee. No closing date; applicants notified on a rolling basis. Interviews required for physical therapist assistant applicants; recommended for all others. Deferred admission available. Closing date for physical therapist assistant freshman applicants is April 1.

STUDENT LIFE. Activities: Student government.

STUDENT SERVICES. Career counseling, employment service for undergraduates, freshman orientation, on-campus day care, personal counseling, placement service for graduates, veterans counselor, services/facilities for handicapped.

ANNUAL EXPENSES. Tuition and fees (1992-93): $572, $3,959 additional for out-of-state students. **Books and supplies:** $400. **Other expenses:** $400.

FINANCIAL AID. 50% of freshmen, 55% of continuing students receive some form of aid. Grants, loans, jobs available. Academic scholarships available. **Aid applications:** No closing date; priority given to applications received by May 1; applicants notified on a rolling basis beginning on or about May 1.

ADDRESS/TELEPHONE. Carolyn H. Mills, Registrar/Admissions Officer, Martin Community College, Kehukee Park Road, Williamston, NC 27892-9988. (919) 792-1521 ext. 251. Fax: (919) 792-4425.

Mayland Community College
Spruce Pine, North Carolina — CB code: 0795

2-year public community college, coed. Founded in 1971. **Accreditation:** Regional. **Undergraduate enrollment:** 223 men, 268 women full time; 147 men, 263 women part time. **Faculty:** 78 total (25 full time), 3 with doctorates or other terminal degrees. **Location:** Rural campus in small town; 50 miles from Asheville. **Calendar:** Quarter, extensive summer session. Extensive evening/early morning classes. **Microcomputers:** 35 located in classrooms, computer centers.

DEGREES OFFERED. AAS. 88 associate degrees awarded in 1992. 21% in business and management, 18% business/office and marketing/distribution, 9% computer sciences, 6% engineering technologies, 5% home economics, 27% multi/interdisciplinary studies, 14% parks/recreation, protective services, public affairs.

UNDERGRADUATE MAJORS. Accounting, business administration and management, business and office, business data processing and related programs, child development/care/guidance, computer programming, electronic technology, liberal/general studies, medical secretary, public affairs, secretarial and related programs.

ACADEMIC PROGRAMS. Cooperative education, double major, dual enrollment of high school students, independent study, internships, telecourses, weekend college, cross-registration. **Remedial services:** Learning center, preadmission summer program, reduced course load, remedial instruction, special counselor, tutoring. **Placement/credit:** Institutional tests.

ACADEMIC REQUIREMENTS. No policy requiring minimum GPA; records of students having academic difficulty are reviewed individually. 70% of freshmen return for sophomore year. Students must declare major on enrollment. **Graduation requirements:** 105 hours for associate (92 in major). Most students required to take courses in English, mathematics, social sciences.

FRESHMAN ADMISSIONS. Selection criteria: Open admissions.

1992 FRESHMAN CLASS PROFILE. 303 men and women enrolled. **Characteristics:** 99% from in state, 100% commute, 5% have minority backgrounds. Average age is 24.

FALL-TERM APPLICATIONS. No fee. No closing date; applicants notified on a rolling basis beginning on or about March 1. Application by April 1 recommended for nursing program.

STUDENT LIFE. Activities: Student government, Phi Theta Kappa.

STUDENT SERVICES. Aptitude testing, career counseling, employment service for undergraduates, freshman orientation, personal counseling, placement service for graduates, veterans counselor, services/facilities for handicapped.

ANNUAL EXPENSES. Tuition and fees (1992-93): $581, $3,959 additional for out-of-state students. **Books and supplies:** $650. **Other expenses:** $1,087.

FINANCIAL AID. 52% of freshmen, 52% of continuing students receive some form of aid. 90% of grants, all loans, 34% of jobs based on need. 226 enrolled freshmen were judged to have need, 205 were offered aid. Academic, state/district residency, leadership scholarships available. **Aid applications:** No closing date; priority given to applications received by April 30; applicants notified on a rolling basis beginning on or about June 15.

ADDRESS/TELEPHONE. Dr. Loretta Church, Dean of Academic Services, Mayland Community College, PO Box 547, Spruce Pine, NC 28777. (704) 765-7351 ext. 230. Fax: (704) 765-0728.

McDowell Technical Community College
Marion, North Carolina — CB code: 0789

2-year public community, technical college, coed. Founded in 1964. **Accreditation:** Regional. **Undergraduate enrollment:** 103 men, 201 women full time; 175 men, 341 women part time. **Faculty:** 35 total (22 full time), 4 with doctorates or other terminal degrees. **Location:** Rural campus in small town; 35 miles from Asheville. **Calendar:** Quarter, extensive summer session. Extensive evening/early morning classes. **Microcomputers:** Located in libraries, classrooms, computer centers.

DEGREES OFFERED. AAS. 50 associate degrees awarded in 1992. 39% in business and management, 17% business/office and marketing/distribution, 15% engineering technologies, 7% multi/interdisciplinary studies, 22% visual and performing arts.

UNDERGRADUATE MAJORS. Accounting, business administration and management, business and office, business computer/console/peripheral equipment operation, business data processing and related programs, business data programming, commercial art, computer programming, electronic technology, graphic and printing production, graphic arts technology, health sciences, industrial technology, labor/industrial relations, law enforcement and corrections technologies, liberal/general studies, marketing and distribution, nursing, secretarial and related programs, teacher aide.

ACADEMIC PROGRAMS. 2-year transfer program, cooperative education, double major, dual enrollment of high school students, independent study, internships, telecourses. **Remedial services:** Learning center, reduced course load, remedial instruction, special counselor, tutoring. **Placement/credit:** AP, CLEP General and Subject, institutional tests; 30 credit hours maximum for associate degree.

ACADEMIC REQUIREMENTS. Freshmen must earn minimum GPA of 1.4 to continue in good standing. 60% of freshmen return for sophomore year. Students must declare major on enrollment. **Graduation requirements:** 108 hours for associate (82 in major). Most students required to take courses in computer science, English, humanities, mathematics.

FRESHMAN ADMISSIONS. Selection criteria: Open admissions. Selective admissions to industrial maintenance, business computer programming and nursing programs.

1992 FRESHMAN CLASS PROFILE. 152 men, 234 women enrolled. **Characteristics:** 99% from in state, 100% commute, 6% have minority backgrounds. Average age is 24.

FALL-TERM APPLICATIONS. No fee. No closing date; applicants notified on a rolling basis. Interview required for nursing applicants; recommended for all others.

STUDENT LIFE. Activities: Student government, student newspaper, yearbook.

ATHLETICS. Intercollegiate: Tennis M. **Intramural:** Basketball, golf, skiing, tennis, volleyball.

STUDENT SERVICES. Aptitude testing, career counseling, employment service for undergraduates, freshman orientation, on-campus day care, personal counseling, placement service for graduates, special adviser for adult students, veterans counselor, services/facilities for handicapped.

ANNUAL EXPENSES. Tuition and fees (1992-93): $575, $3,959 additional for out-of-state students. **Books and supplies:** $450. **Other expenses:** $675.

FINANCIAL AID. 34% of freshmen, 37% of continuing students receive some form of aid. 90% of grants, all loans, all jobs based on need. Academic scholarships available. **Aid applications:** No closing date; priority given to applications received by March 15; applicants notified on a rolling basis beginning on or about July 1.

ADDRESS/TELEPHONE. Mary L. Tate, Admissions Assistant, McDowell Technical Community College, Route 1, Box 170, Marion, NC 28752. (704) 652-6021. Fax: (704) 652-1014.

Meredith College
Raleigh, North Carolina CB code: 5410

Admissions: 86% of applicants accepted
Based on: ••• School record
•• Recommendations, test scores
• Activities, essay, interview, special talents
Completion: 93% of freshmen end year in good standing
68% graduate, 15% of these enter graduate study

4-year private liberal arts college, women only, affiliated with Southern Baptist Convention. Founded in 1891. **Accreditation:** Regional. **Undergraduate enrollment:** 1,642 women full time; 244 women part time. **Graduate enrollment:** 3 women full time; 160 women part time. **Faculty:** 220 total (121 full time), 94 with doctorates or other terminal degrees. **Location:** Urban campus in small city. **Calendar:** Semester, limited summer session. **Microcomputers:** 90 located in dormitories, libraries, classrooms, computer centers. **Special facilities:** Amphitheater, international house, Frankie G. Weems Art Gallery, child-care laboratory.

DEGREES OFFERED. BA, BS, MBA, MEd. 475 bachelor's degrees awarded in 1992. 5% in architecture and environmental design, 25% business and management, 13% home economics, 7% letters/literature, 6% life sciences, 5% parks/recreation, protective services, public affairs, 11% psychology, 11% social sciences, 7% visual and performing arts. Graduate degrees offered in 4 major fields of study.

UNDERGRADUATE MAJORS. American studies, biology, business administration and management, chemistry, child development/care/guidance, clinical laboratory science, computer mathematics, dance, dramatic arts, economics, English, fashion merchandising, fine arts, food science and nutrition, French, health sciences, history, home economics, interior design, international studies, mathematics, medical laboratory technologies, music, music education, music performance, political science and government, psychology, religion, social work, sociology, Spanish, speech.

ACADEMIC PROGRAMS. Cooperative education, double major, dual enrollment of high school students, honors program, independent study, internships, student-designed major, study abroad, teacher preparation, visiting/exchange student program, New York semester, United Nations semester, Washington semester, cross-registration, semester in Raleigh, study abroad in England, France, Spain, Italy, Japan, China and Switzerland; liberal arts/career combination in engineering, health sciences. **Remedial services:** Remedial instruction, tutoring, writing center. **ROTC:** Air Force, Army. **Placement/credit:** AP, CLEP General and Subject, institutional tests.

ACADEMIC REQUIREMENTS. Freshmen must earn minimum GPA of 1.35 to continue in good standing. 84% of freshmen return for sophomore year. Students must declare major by end of second year. **Graduation requirements:** 124 hours for bachelor's (36 in major). Most students required to take courses in arts/fine arts, English, foreign languages, history, humanities, mathematics, philosophy/religion, biological/physical sciences, social sciences. **Postgraduate studies:** 1% enter law school, 1% enter medical school, 2% enter MBA programs, 11% enter other graduate study. **Additional information:** Certification in school social work and graduate certificate in paralegal work available. Teacher certification in elementary, middle grades, secondary, occupational, and special subject areas.

FRESHMAN ADMISSIONS. Selection criteria: School record most important factor (includes courses taken, grades, and class rank). Test scores reviewed in relation to school record. Recommendations and other factors such as talent also considered. **High school preparation:** 16 units required. Required units include English 4, foreign language 1 and mathematics 3. At least 5 additional units from academic subjects. Up to 3 electives (such as arts, music, other) counted. **Test requirements:** SAT or ACT (SAT preferred); score report by March 1.

1992 FRESHMAN CLASS PROFILE. 855 women applied, 734 accepted, 383 enrolled. 25% were in top tenth and 57% were in top quarter of graduating class. **Academic background:** Mid 50% of enrolled freshmen had SAT-V between 380-490, SAT-M between 430-530. 99% submitted SAT scores. **Characteristics:** 78% from in state, 94% live in college housing, 6% have minority backgrounds, 2% are foreign students. Average age is 19.

FALL-TERM APPLICATIONS. $25 fee, may be waived for applicants with need. No closing date; priority given to applications received by February 15; applicants notified on a rolling basis; must reply by May 1 or within 2 weeks if notified thereafter. Interview recommended. Audition recommended for music applicants. Portfolio recommended for art applicants. Essay recommended. CRDA. Deferred and early admission available. EDP-S. October 15 application deadline for early decision candidates. Notification for early decision candidates begins on November 15. Early decision candidates must reply by December 15.

STUDENT LIFE. Housing: Dormitories (women). Students must live on campus or with parents/other relative. Campus housing is guarenteed for all 4 years. A limited number of juniors and seniors may have permission to live off campus. **Activities:** Student government, magazine, student newspaper, television, yearbook, choral groups, dance, drama, marching band, music ensembles, musical theater, symphony orchestra, handbell choir, synchronized swimming, Christian Association, Association for Black Awareness, 3 campus service societies, non-residents association, International Association, Entertainment Association, campus political organizations, clubs in most major fields. **Additional information:** Over 400 leadership positions and over 70 clubs, organizations, and honor societies provide opportunities for personal and leadership development. Leadership seminars.

ATHLETICS. NCAA. **Intercollegiate:** Basketball, golf, softball, tennis, volleyball. **Intramural:** Basketball, soccer, softball, volleyball.

STUDENT SERVICES. Aptitude testing, career counseling, employment service for undergraduates, freshman orientation, health services, personal counseling, placement service for graduates, special adviser for adult students, study skills/personal development seminars, career planning classes, health education programs, services/facilities for handicapped.

ANNUAL EXPENSES. Tuition and fees: $6,340. **Room and board:** $3,100. **Books and supplies:** $450. **Other expenses:** $1,200.

FINANCIAL AID. 61% of freshmen, 36% of continuing students receive some form of aid. 56% of grants, 85% of loans, 30% of jobs based on need. 154 enrolled freshmen were judged to have need, all were offered aid. Academic, music/drama, art, leadership scholarships available. **Aid applications:** No closing date; priority given to applications received by February 15; applicants notified on a rolling basis beginning on or about April 1; must reply by May 1 or within 2 weeks if notified thereafter. **Additional information:** Currently meets 100% of established need for entering freshmen and campus residents.

ADDRESS/TELEPHONE. Sue Kearney, Director of Admissions, Meredith College, 3800 Hillsborough Street, Raleigh, NC 27607-5298. (919) 829-8581. Fax: (919) 829-2828.

Methodist College
Fayetteville, North Carolina CB code: 5426

Admissions: 63% of applicants accepted
Based on: ••• School record
•• Interview, test scores
• Activities, essay, recommendations
Completion: 72% of freshmen end year in good standing
20% enter graduate study

4-year private liberal arts college, coed, affiliated with United Methodist Church. Founded in 1956. **Accreditation:** Regional. **Undergraduate enrollment:** 590 men, 524 women full time; 200 men, 194 women part time. **Faculty:** 85 total (53 full time), 36 with doctorates or other terminal degrees. **Location:** Suburban campus in small city; 5 miles from Fayetteville. **Calendar:** 4-1-4, limited summer session. Extensive evening/early morning classes. **Microcomputers:** 53 located in libraries, classrooms, computer centers. **Special facilities:** Computer-assisted English composition laboratory, psychology computer-experimental laboratory, nature trail, Rogers-Millet Art Gallery.

DEGREES OFFERED. AA, AS, AAS, BA, BS. 30 associate degrees awarded in 1992. 230 bachelor's degrees awarded.

UNDERGRADUATE MAJORS. Associate: Accounting, art education, arts management, biology, business administration and management, business and office, business data programming, business economics, chemistry, communications, computer and information sciences, creative writing, criminology, dramatic arts, economics, education, English, fine arts, foreign languages education, French, German, international studies, liberal/general studies, mathematics, mathematics education, military science (Army), music business management, music education, music performance, philosophy, physical education, physical sciences, political science and government, pre-engineering, prelaw, psychology, religion, religious education, social science education, social studies education, sociology, Spanish, special education, speech/communication/theater education. **Bachelor's:** Accounting, art education, arts management, biological and physical sciences, biology, business administration and management, chemistry, communications, computer and information sciences, creative writing, criminology, dramatic arts, early childhood education, education, elementary education, English, fine arts, foreign languages education, French, history, international studies, journalism, junior high education, mathematics, mathematics education, music, music business management, music education, music performance, personnel management, philosophy, physical education, physical sciences, political science and government, prelaw, premedicine, preveterinary, psychology, religion, secondary education, social science education, social studies education, social work, sociology, Spanish, special education, speech/communication/theater education.

ACADEMIC PROGRAMS. 2-year transfer program, accelerated program, double major, dual enrollment of high school students, honors program, independent study, internships, study abroad, visiting/exchange student program, Washington semester. **Remedial services:** Reduced course load, remedial instruction, tutoring. **ROTC:** Air Force, Army. **Placement/credit:** AP, CLEP General and Subject, institutional tests; 30 credit hours maximum for associate degree; 30 credit hours maximum for bachelor's degree.

ACADEMIC REQUIREMENTS. Freshmen must earn minimum GPA of 2.0 to continue in good standing. 60% of freshmen return for sophomore year. Students must declare major by end of second year. **Graduation requirements:** 62 hours for associate, 124 hours for bachelor's. Most students required to take courses in arts/fine arts, English, foreign languages, history, humanities, mathematics, philosophy/religion, biological/physical sciences, social sciences. **Postgraduate studies:** 2% enter law school, 3% enter medical school, 2% enter MBA programs, 13% enter other graduate study.

FRESHMAN ADMISSIONS. Selection criteria: High school record, test scores, interview, leadership, school and community activities are important. **High school preparation:** 18 units required. Required and recommended units include English 4, mathematics 2, social science 2 and science 2. Foreign language 2 recommended. **Test requirements:** SAT or ACT; score report by August 1.

1992 FRESHMAN CLASS PROFILE. 563 men applied, 312 accepted, 228 enrolled; 277 women applied, 216 accepted, 120 enrolled. 40% had high school GPA of 3.0 or higher, 60% between 2.0 and 2.99. **Academic background:** Mid 50% of enrolled freshmen had SAT-V between 340-450, SAT-M between 370-510; ACT composite between 17-21. 79% submitted SAT scores, 21% submitted ACT scores. **Characteristics:** 51% from in state, 65% live in college housing, 17% have minority backgrounds, 3% are foreign students, 10% join fraternities/sororities. Average age is 18.

FALL-TERM APPLICATIONS. $20 fee, may be waived for applicants with need. No closing date; priority given to applications received by August 25; applicants notified on a rolling basis; must reply within 4 weeks. Interview recommended. Audition recommended for music, drama applicants. Portfolio recommended for art applicants. Essay recommended. Deferred and early admission available.

STUDENT LIFE. Housing: Dormitories (men, women, coed); apartment, fraternity housing available. **Activities:** Student government, magazine, student newspaper, yearbook, choral groups, concert band, dance, drama, jazz band, music ensembles, musical theater, pep band, symphony orchestra, fraternities, sororities, Young Democrats, Young Republicans, behavioral sciences club, religious clubs, Spanish club, music club, black students club, Ethos Club, business/accounting club, outdoor adventure club, student activities council.

ATHLETICS. NCAA. **Intercollegiate:** Baseball M, basketball, cross-country, football M, golf, soccer, softball W, tennis, track and field, volleyball W. **Intramural:** Basketball, bowling, racquetball, soccer, softball, table tennis, tennis, volleyball.

STUDENT SERVICES. Aptitude testing, career counseling, employment service for undergraduates, freshman orientation, health services, personal counseling, placement service for graduates, veterans counselor, tutoring for all academic fields.

ANNUAL EXPENSES. Tuition and fees: $8,850. **Room and board:** $3,550. **Books and supplies:** $600. **Other expenses:** $1,360.

FINANCIAL AID. 85% of freshmen, 83% of continuing students receive some form of aid. 70% of grants, 83% of loans, 61% of jobs based on need. 195 enrolled freshmen were judged to have need, all were offered aid. Academic, music/drama, state/district residency, religious affiliation scholarships available. **Aid applications:** Closing date July 1; priority given to applications received by May 1; applicants notified on a rolling basis beginning on or about March 1; must reply within 2 weeks.

ADDRESS/TELEPHONE. J. Alan Coheley, Director of Enrollment Services, Methodist College, 5400 Ramsey Street, Fayetteville, NC 28311-1420. (919) 630-7027. (800) 488-7110. Fax: (919) 630-2123.

Mitchell Community College
Statesville, North Carolina — CB code: 5412

2-year public community college, coed. Founded in 1852. **Accreditation:** Regional. **Undergraduate enrollment:** 307 men, 462 women full time; 285 men, 472 women part time. **Faculty:** 90 total (47 full time), 2 with doctorates or other terminal degrees. **Location:** Suburban campus in large town; 40 miles from Charlotte and Winston-Salem. **Calendar:** Quarter, extensive summer session. Extensive evening/early morning classes. **Microcomputers:** Located in classrooms, computer centers. **Special facilities:** Louise Gilbert Memorial Art Gallery.

DEGREES OFFERED. AA, AS, AAS. 160 associate degrees awarded in 1992.

UNDERGRADUATE MAJORS. Accounting, business administration and management, business and management, business and office, business computer/console/peripheral equipment operation, business data entry equipment operation, business data processing and related programs, business data programming, computer programming, criminal justice studies, drafting, education, electrical and electronics equipment repair, electrical/electronics/communications engineering, engineering and engineering-related technologies, law enforcement and corrections technologies, liberal/general studies, mechanical design technology, nursing, protective services, public affairs, secretarial and related programs.

ACADEMIC PROGRAMS. 2-year transfer program, dual enrollment of high school students, independent study. **Remedial services:** Learning center, reduced course load, remedial instruction, tutoring. **Placement/credit:** AP, CLEP General and Subject, institutional tests.

ACADEMIC REQUIREMENTS. Freshmen must earn minimum GPA of 2.0 to continue in good standing. 55% of freshmen return for sophomore year. Students must declare major on application. **Graduation requirements:** 96 hours for associate (51 in major). Most students required to take courses in English, history, humanities, mathematics, biological/physical sciences, social sciences.

FRESHMAN ADMISSIONS. Selection criteria: Open admissions.

1992 FRESHMAN CLASS PROFILE. 118 men, 254 women enrolled. **Characteristics:** 98% from in state, 100% commute, 13% have minority backgrounds. Average age is 22.

FALL-TERM APPLICATIONS. No fee. No closing date; applicants notified on a rolling basis. Interview required for all applicants for placement applicants. Early admission available.

STUDENT LIFE. Activities: Student government, magazine, yearbook, choral groups, Circle-K, Christian Student Fellowship, Ebony Kinship.

ATHLETICS. NJCAA. **Intercollegiate:** Golf, tennis. **Intramural:** Archery, badminton, baseball, basketball, bowling, fencing, field hockey, golf, gymnastics, handball, soccer, softball, table tennis, tennis, volleyball.

STUDENT SERVICES. Career counseling, employment service for undergraduates, freshman orientation, health services, personal counseling, placement service for graduates, veterans counselor, services/facilities for handicapped.

ANNUAL EXPENSES. Tuition and fees (1992-93): $582, $3,959 additional for out-of-state students. **Books and supplies:** $425. **Other expenses:** $1,450.

FINANCIAL AID. 24% of freshmen, 13% of continuing students receive some form of aid. 44% of grants, 60% of loans, 71% of jobs based on need. 60 enrolled freshmen were judged to have need, 56 were offered aid. Academic, music/drama, art, state/district residency, leadership, alumni affiliation, minority scholarships available. **Aid applications:** No closing date; priority given to applications received by April 1; applicants notified on a rolling basis; must reply within 2 weeks.

ADDRESS/TELEPHONE. Phyllis Travis, Admissions Coordinator, Mitchell Community College, West Broad Street, Statesville, NC 28677. (704) 878-3266. Fax: (704) 878-0872.

Montgomery Community College
Troy, North Carolina — CB code: 0785

2-year public community college, coed. Founded in 1967. **Accreditation:** Regional. **Undergraduate enrollment:** 144 men, 101 women full time; 159 men, 130 women part time. **Faculty:** 71 total (26 full time), 1 with doctorate or other terminal degree. **Location:** Rural campus in small town; 50 miles from Greensboro, 62 miles from Charlotte. **Calendar:** Quarter, extensive summer session. Extensive evening/early morning classes. **Microcomputers:** Located in libraries, classrooms. **Special facilities:** Rifle/pistol firing range, archery range.

DEGREES OFFERED. AAS. 47 associate degrees awarded in 1992.

UNDERGRADUATE MAJORS. Accounting, business administration and management, computer and information sciences, criminal justice studies, early childhood education, education, secretarial and related programs.

ACADEMIC PROGRAMS. Double major, dual enrollment of high school students, independent study, telecourses, cross-registration. **Remedial services:** Learning center, reduced course load, remedial instruction, tutoring. **Placement/credit:** CLEP General and Subject, institutional tests.

ACADEMIC REQUIREMENTS. Freshmen must earn minimum GPA of 1.5 to continue in good standing. 60% of freshmen return for sophomore year. Students must declare major by end of first year. **Graduation requirements:** 96 hours for associate (76 in major). Most students required to take courses in English, history, mathematics, biological/physical sciences, social sciences. **Additional information:** Special programs in pottery production, metal engraving, gunsmithing, forestry skills, and taxidermy. Students required to attend 4 to 7 consecutive quarters.

FRESHMAN ADMISSIONS. Selection criteria: Open admissions. Selective admissions to nursing program primarily based on entrance test scores. **Test requirements:** California Achievement Tests required for nursing applicants; ACT, ASSET, Student Success System for placement of other applicants.

1992 FRESHMAN CLASS PROFILE. 41 men, 82 women enrolled. **Characteristics:** 99% from in state, 100% commute, 18% have minority backgrounds.

FALL-TERM APPLICATIONS. No fee. No closing date; applicants notified on a rolling basis beginning on or about February 1. Interview required for nursing appliciants; recommended for all others. Deferred and early admission available.

STUDENT LIFE. Activities: Student government, monthly newsletter.

ATHLETICS. Intramural: Basketball M, volleyball.

STUDENT SERVICES. Aptitude testing, career counseling, employment service for undergraduates, on-campus day care, personal counseling, placement service for graduates, veterans counselor, services/facilities for handicapped.

ANNUAL EXPENSES. Tuition and fees (1992-93): $573, $3,959 additional for out-of-state students. **Books and supplies:** $600. **Other expenses:** $1,885.

FINANCIAL AID. 52% of freshmen, 46% of continuing students receive some form of aid. Grants, jobs available. **Aid applications:** No closing date; priority given to applications received by July 15; applicants notified on a rolling basis beginning on or about June 1.

ADDRESS/TELEPHONE. Beth Smith, Admissions Officer, Montgomery Community College, PO Box 787, Troy, NC 27371-0787. (919) 572-3691 ext. 210. Fax: (919) 576-2176.

Montreat-Anderson College

Montreat, North Carolina — CB code: 5423

Admissions: 79% of applicants accepted
Based on: ••• School record
•• Recommendations, test scores
• Activities, essay, interview, special talents
Completion: 80% of freshmen end year in good standing
26% enter graduate study

4-year private liberal arts college, coed, affiliated with Presbyterian Church (USA). Founded in 1916. **Accreditation:** Regional. **Undergraduate enrollment:** 157 men, 138 women full time; 13 men, 10 women part time. **Faculty:** 35 total (24 full time), 21 with doctorates or other terminal degrees. **Location:** Rural campus in small town; 16 miles east of Asheville. **Calendar:** 4-4-1, limited summer session. **Microcomputers:** Located in libraries, computer centers. **Additional facts:** Christian faculty and campus life

DEGREES OFFERED. AA, AS, BA, BS. 14 associate degrees awarded in 1992. 45 bachelor's degrees awarded.

UNDERGRADUATE MAJORS. Associate: Liberal/general studies. **Bachelor's:** Accounting, American studies, Bible studies, business administration and management, business and management, business economics, English, environmental science, family science, history, human services and cultural studies, marketing management, mathematics, missionary studies, outdoor recreation, parks and recreation management, prelaw, premedicine, religion, secondary education.

ACADEMIC PROGRAMS. 2-year transfer program, accelerated program, dual enrollment of high school students, honors program, independent study, internships, study abroad, teacher preparation, Washington semester. **Remedial services:** Reduced course load, tutoring, reading. **Placement/credit:** AP, CLEP General and Subject.

ACADEMIC REQUIREMENTS. Freshmen must earn minimum GPA of 1.5 to continue in good standing. 68% of freshmen return for sophomore year. Students must declare major by end of second year. **Graduation requirements:** 64 hours for associate, 128 hours for bachelor's. Most students required to take courses in arts/fine arts, English, foreign languages, history, humanities, mathematics, philosophy/religion, biological/physical sciences, social sciences. **Postgraduate studies:** 98% from 2-year programs enter 4-year programs. 26% enter other graduate study. **Additional information:** Teacher certification on the secondary level in English, history, mathematics, social science, and science.

FRESHMAN ADMISSIONS. Selection criteria: School achievement record, class rank, GPA, 1 teacher or counselor recommendation. SAT or ACT scores and participation in school, community, church activities considered. **High school preparation:** 18 units required. Required and recommended units include biological science 1, English 4, mathematics 2-3 and social science 1-2. Foreign language 1 and physical science 1 recommended. College-preparatory program preferred. **Test requirements:** SAT or ACT (SAT preferred); score report by August 15.

1992 FRESHMAN CLASS PROFILE. 138 men applied, 108 accepted, 52 enrolled; 79 women applied, 64 accepted, 27 enrolled. 28% had high school GPA of 3.0 or higher, 60% between 2.0 and 2.99. **Academic background:** Mid 50% of enrolled freshmen had SAT-V between 400-460, SAT-M between 440-500. 91% submitted SAT scores. **Characteristics:** 62% from in state, 85% live in college housing, 20% have minority backgrounds. Average age is 18.

FALL-TERM APPLICATIONS. $15 fee, may be waived for applicants with need. No closing date; priority given to applications received by May 1; applicants notified on a rolling basis; must reply by May 1 or within 2 weeks if notified thereafter. Interview required for academically weak applicants. Essay required. CRDA. Deferred and early admission available.

STUDENT LIFE. Housing: Dormitories (men, women). **Activities:** Student government, magazine, student newspaper, yearbook, choral groups, drama, music ensembles, Student Christian Association, Alpha Chi, missions club, Spanish club, adventure club. **Additional information:** Alcoholic drinks not allowed on campus, first semester freshmen curfew. Religious observance required.

ATHLETICS. NAIA. **Intercollegiate:** Baseball M, basketball, soccer, tennis W, volleyball W. **Intramural:** Basketball, softball, volleyball.

STUDENT SERVICES. Career counseling, employment service for undergraduates, freshman orientation, health services, personal counseling, placement service for graduates, veterans counselor.

ANNUAL EXPENSES. Tuition and fees: $7,600. **Room and board:** $3,372. **Books and supplies:** $500. **Other expenses:** $2,358.

FINANCIAL AID. 85% of freshmen, 85% of continuing students receive some form of aid. 93% of grants, 93% of loans, 79% of jobs based on need. Academic, art, athletic, state/district residency, leadership, alumni affiliation scholarships available. **Aid applications:** No closing date; priority given to applications received by March 1; applicants notified on a rolling basis beginning on or about March 15; must reply within 2 weeks.

ADDRESS/TELEPHONE. Charles Lance, Director of Admissions, Montreat-Anderson College, PO Box 1267, Montreat, NC 28757-9987. (704) 669-8011. (800) 627-1750. Fax: (704) 669-9554.

Mount Olive College

Mount Olive, North Carolina — CB code: 5435

Admissions: 83% of applicants accepted
Based on: ••• School record
•• Test scores
• Activities, essay, interview, recommendations, religious affiliation/commitment, special talents
Completion: 75% of freshmen end year in good standing
18% graduate, 8% of these enter graduate study

4-year private liberal arts college, coed, affiliated with Free Will Baptists. Founded in 1951. **Accreditation:** Regional. **Undergraduate enrollment:** 291 men, 277 women full time; 132 men, 91 women part time. **Faculty:** 61 total (33 full time), 21 with doctorates or other terminal degrees. **Location:** Rural campus in small town; 13 miles from Goldsboro. **Calendar:** Semester, extensive summer session. Extensive evening/early morning classes. **Microcomputers:** 40 located in libraries, classrooms, computer centers. **Special facilities:** Historical collection, art collection.

DEGREES OFFERED. AA, AS, BA, BS. 21 associate degrees awarded in 1992. 43% in business and management, 57% letters/literature. 135 bachelor's degrees awarded. 58% in business and management, 13% parks/recreation, protective services, public affairs, 16% psychology.

UNDERGRADUATE MAJORS. Associate: Accounting, biology, business administration and management, business and office, computer and information sciences, education, English, fine arts, liberal/general studies, music, parks and recreation management, prelaw, public relations, recreation therapy, religion, religious education, science technologies, secretarial and related programs. **Bachelor's:** Accounting, biology, business administration and management, computer and information sciences, English, fine arts, graphic design, history, liberal/general studies, parks and recreation management, prelaw, psychology, public relations, recreation therapy, religion, religious education.

ACADEMIC PROGRAMS. 2-year transfer program, accelerated program, cooperative education, double major, dual enrollment of high school students, honors program, independent study, internships, cross-registration, accelerated extension program at Seymour Johnson Air Force Base in Goldsboro. **Remedial services:** Preadmission summer program, reduced course load, remedial instruction, special counselor, tutoring. **Placement/credit:** AP, CLEP Subject, institutional tests; 12 credit hours maximum for associate degree; 12 credit hours maximum for bachelor's degree.

ACADEMIC REQUIREMENTS. Freshmen must earn minimum GPA of 1.25 to continue in good standing. 60% of freshmen return for sophomore year. Students must declare major by end of second year. **Graduation requirements:** 64 hours for associate (22 in major), 126 hours for bachelor's (30 in major). Most students required to take courses in arts/fine arts, computer science, English, history, humanities, mathematics, philosophy/religion, biological/physical sciences, social sciences. **Postgraduate studies:** 75% from 2-year programs enter 4-year programs. 1% enter law school, 1% enter medical school, 1% enter MBA programs, 5% enter other graduate study.

FRESHMAN ADMISSIONS. Selection criteria: School record, test scores, class rank important. Personal recommendations considered. **High school preparation:** 10 units recommended. College-preparatory program recommended. **Test requirements:** SAT or ACT (SAT preferred); score report by August 31.

1992 FRESHMAN CLASS PROFILE. 229 men applied, 189 accepted, 94 enrolled; 128 women applied, 108 accepted, 68 enrolled. 27% had high school GPA of 3.0 or higher, 62% between 2.0 and 2.99. 6% were in top tenth and 31% were in top quarter of graduating class. **Academic background:** Mid 50% of enrolled freshmen had SAT-V between 350-450, SAT-M between 350-490. 67% submitted SAT scores. **Characteristics:** 94% from in state, 55% live in college housing, 23% have minority backgrounds. Average age is 18.

FALL-TERM APPLICATIONS. $15 fee. No closing date; priority given to applications received by January 15; applicants notified on a rolling basis beginning on or about October 1; must reply within 4 weeks. Audition required for music applicants. Interview recommended. Portfolio recommended for art applicants. Essay recommended. Deferred and early admission available.

STUDENT LIFE. Housing: Dormitories (men, women); apartment housing available. **Activities:** Student government, magazine, student newspaper, yearbook, choral groups, drama, Baptist Student Union, Free Will Baptist Fellowship, English society, science club, psychology club, political forum, recreation majors club, Fellowship of Christian Athletes. **Additional information:** Religious observance required.

ATHLETICS. NAIA, NCAA. **Intercollegiate:** Baseball M, basketball, golf M, soccer M, softball W, tennis, volleyball W. **Intramural:** Badminton, baseball M, basketball, football M, handball, racquetball, soccer, softball, table tennis, tennis, volleyball.

STUDENT SERVICES. Aptitude testing, career counseling, employment service for undergraduates, freshman orientation, health services, personal counseling, placement service for graduates, special adviser for adult students, veterans counselor, services/facilities for handicapped.

ANNUAL EXPENSES. Tuition and fees: $7,100. **Room and board:** $2,550. **Books and supplies:** $500. **Other expenses:** $900.

FINANCIAL AID. 95% of freshmen, 95% of continuing students receive some form of aid. 34% of grants, 93% of loans, 79% of jobs based on need. 82 enrolled freshmen were judged to have need, all were offered aid. Academic, music/drama, art, athletic, state/district residency, leadership, religious affiliation scholarships available. **Aid applications:** No closing date; priority given to applications received by March 1; applicants notified on a rolling basis beginning on or about April 1; must reply within 2 weeks.

ADDRESS/TELEPHONE. Dianne Riley, Director of Admissions, Mount Olive College, 514 Henderson Drive, Mount Olive, NC 28365. (919) 658-2502. Fax: (919) 658-8934.

Nash Community College
Rocky Mount, North Carolina CB code: 5881

2-year public community college, coed. Founded in 1967. **Accreditation:** Regional. **Undergraduate enrollment:** 260 men, 447 women full time; 447 men, 728 women part time. **Faculty:** 92 total (37 full time), 5 with doctorates or other terminal degrees. **Location:** Rural campus in large town; 55 miles from Raleigh. **Calendar:** Quarter, limited summer session. Saturday and extensive evening/early morning classes. **Microcomputers:** 87 located in computer centers.

DEGREES OFFERED. AA, AS, AAS. 120 associate degrees awarded in 1992.

UNDERGRADUATE MAJORS. Accounting, architectural technologies, business administration and management, business data programming, child development/care/guidance, computer programming, education, electronic technology, law enforcement and corrections technologies, legal secretary, liberal/general studies, marketing and distribution, medical secretary, nursing, physical therapy assistant, protective services, secretarial and related programs, teacher aide.

ACADEMIC PROGRAMS. 2-year transfer program, double major, dual enrollment of high school students, telecourses. **Remedial services:** Learning center, reduced course load, remedial instruction, special counselor, tutoring. **Placement/credit:** CLEP General and Subject, institutional tests.

ACADEMIC REQUIREMENTS. Freshmen must earn minimum GPA of 2.0 to continue in good standing. 38% of freshmen return for sophomore year. **Graduation requirements:** 120 hours for associate. Most students required to take courses in computer science, English, mathematics.

FRESHMAN ADMISSIONS. Selection criteria: Open admissions. Selective admissions to nursing, physical therapy assistant, phlebotomy, cosmetology, and college transfer programs. Chemistry required for nursing program. Biology required for physical therapy assistant program. For college transfer program, 4 English, 3 mathematics, 2 social sciences, and 3 natural sciences required.

1992 FRESHMAN CLASS PROFILE. 158 men, 407 women enrolled. **Characteristics:** 99% from in state, 100% commute. Average age is 25.

FALL-TERM APPLICATIONS. No fee. Closing date August 15; applicants notified on a rolling basis. Interview recommended. CRDA. Deferred admission available. Test scores used for placement and counseling.

STUDENT LIFE. Activities: Student government, information board, newsletter.

STUDENT SERVICES. Aptitude testing, career counseling, employment service for undergraduates, personal counseling, placement service for graduates, veterans counselor, services/facilities for handicapped.

ANNUAL EXPENSES. Tuition and fees (1992-93): $578, $3,959 additional for out-of-state students. **Books and supplies:** $750. **Other expenses:** $450.

FINANCIAL AID. 9% of freshmen, 16% of continuing students receive some form of aid. 99% of grants, all loans, 58% of jobs based on need. Academic, leadership, minority scholarships available. **Aid applications:** No closing date; priority given to applications received by March 15; applicants notified on a rolling basis beginning on or about July 15; must reply immediately.

ADDRESS/TELEPHONE. Mary R. Blount, Admissions Officer, Nash Community College, PO Box 7488, Rocky Mount, NC 27804-7488. (919) 443-4011 ext. 300. Fax: (919) 443-0828.

North Carolina Agricultural and Technical State University
Greensboro, North Carolina CB code: 5003

Admissions:	62% of applicants accepted
Based on:	••• School record
	•• Test scores
	• Activities, essay, recommendations, special talents
Completion:	90% of freshmen end year in good standing
	35% graduate

4-year public university and college of arts and sciences and agricultural and technical college, coed. Founded in 1891. **Accreditation:** Regional. **Undergraduate enrollment:** 2,908 men, 2,990 women full time; 420 men, 375 women part time. **Graduate enrollment:** 161 men, 114 women full time; 259 men, 353 women part time. **Faculty:** 409 total (338 full time), 243 with doctorates or other terminal degrees. **Location:** Urban campus in small city; 91 miles from Charlotte. **Calendar:** Semester, extensive summer session. Saturday classes. **Microcomputers:** 346 located in libraries, classrooms, computer centers. **Special facilities:** Taylor Art Gallery, Reed African Heritage Center, Microelectronics Center of North Carolina, planetarium, herbarium.

DEGREES OFFERED. BA, BS, BFA, MA, MS. 838 bachelor's degrees awarded in 1992. 28% in business and management, 5% communications, 5% computer sciences, 15% education, 18% engineering, 6% health sciences, 6% social sciences. Graduate degrees offered in 30 major fields of study.

UNDERGRADUATE MAJORS. Accounting, agribusiness, agricultural economics, agricultural education, agricultural engineering, agricultural sciences, animal sciences, architectural engineering, art education, biology, business administration and management, business economics, business education, chemical engineering, chemistry, civil engineering, communications, computer and information sciences, dramatic arts, drawing, driver and safety education, electrical/electronics/communications engineering, elementary education, engineering and other disciplines, engineering physics, English, English education, food science and nutrition, food sciences, foreign languages education, forest products processing technology, French, history, home economics, home economics education, individual and family development, industrial arts education, industrial engineering, industrial technology, landscape architecture, mathematics, mathematics education, mechanical engineering, music, music education, nursing, occupational safety and health technology, painting, parks and recreation management, physical education, physics, political science and government, psychology, secretarial and related programs, social science education, social sciences, social work, sociology, special education, speech, textiles and clothing, transportation management.

ACADEMIC PROGRAMS. Accelerated program, cooperative education, double major, honors program, independent study, internships, teacher preparation, weekend college, cross-registration. **Remedial services:** Learning center, preadmission summer program, reduced course load, remedial instruction, special counselor, tutoring. **ROTC:** Air Force, Army. **Placement/credit:** AP, CLEP General and Subject.

ACADEMIC REQUIREMENTS. Freshmen must earn minimum GPA of 1.2 to continue in good standing. 76% of freshmen return for sophomore year. Students must declare major by end of second year. **Graduation requirements:** 124 hours for bachelor's (62 in major). Most students required to take courses in English, foreign languages, history, humanities, mathematics, biological/physical sciences, social sciences.

FRESHMAN ADMISSIONS. Selection criteria: High school GPA, class rank, test scores, recommendations and course selection reviewed. **High school preparation:** 16 units required. Required and recommended units include biological science 1-2, English 4, foreign language 2, mathematics 3, physical science 1, social science 2 and science 1. **Test requirements:** SAT or ACT (SAT preferred); score report by July 1.

1992 FRESHMAN CLASS PROFILE. 2,442 men applied, 1,444 accepted, 709 enrolled; 2,632 women applied, 1,680 accepted, 786 enrolled. 34% had high school GPA of 3.0 or higher, 59% between 2.0 and 2.99. 11% were in top tenth and 31% were in top quarter of graduating class. **Academic background:** Mid 50% of enrolled freshmen had SAT-V between 450-500, SAT-M between 450-500. 95% submitted SAT scores. **Characteristics:** 78% from in state, 86% live in college housing, 97% have minority backgrounds. Average age is 18.

FALL-TERM APPLICATIONS. $25 fee. Closing date June 1; applicants notified on a rolling basis; must reply by May 1 or within 3 weeks if notified thereafter. Audition recommended for music applicants. Portfolio recommended for art applicants. CRDA.

STUDENT LIFE. Housing: Dormitories (men, women). Honors student housing available. **Activities:** Student government, film, radio, student newspaper, television, yearbook, choral groups, concert band, dance, drama, jazz band, marching band, pep band, fraternities, sororities.

ATHLETICS. NCAA. **Intercollegiate:** Baseball M, basketball, cross-country, football M, softball W, tennis, track and field, volleyball W. **Intramural:** Badminton, baseball M, basketball, bowling, field hockey, golf, gymnastics, handball, racquetball, soccer, softball, swimming, tennis, track and field, volleyball.

STUDENT SERVICES. Aptitude testing, career counseling, employment service for undergraduates, freshman orientation, health services, personal counseling, placement service for graduates, special adviser for adult students, veterans counselor, services/facilities for handicapped.

ANNUAL EXPENSES. Tuition and fees (1992-93): $1,270, $5,672 additional for out-of-state students. **Room and board:** $2,960. **Books and supplies:** $600. **Other expenses:** $1,147.

FINANCIAL AID. 64% of continuing students receive some form of aid. Grants, loans, jobs available. Academic, music/drama, art, athletic, state/district residency, leadership, alumni affiliation, minority scholarships available. **Aid applications:** No closing date; priority given to applications received by May 15; applicants notified on a rolling basis beginning on or about June 1; must reply within 2 weeks.

ADDRESS/TELEPHONE. John Smith, Director of Admissions, North Carolina Agricultural and Tec State Univ, 1601 East Market Street, Greensboro, NC 27411. (919) 334-7946. Fax: (919) 334-7013.

North Carolina Central University
Durham, North Carolina — CB code: 5495

Admissions: 69% of applicants accepted
Based on:
••• School record
•• Test scores
• Activities, essay, interview, recommendations, special talents
Completion: 98% of freshmen end year in good standing
24% graduate

4-year public university, coed. Founded in 1910. **Accreditation:** Regional. **Undergraduate enrollment:** 1,398 men, 2,133 women full time; 329 men, 479 women part time. **Graduate enrollment:** 225 men, 321 women full time; 219 men, 563 women part time. **Faculty:** 401 total (254 full time), 247 with doctorates or other terminal degrees. **Location:** Urban campus in small city; 23 miles from Raleigh. **Calendar:** Semester, extensive summer session. Extensive evening/early morning classes. **Microcomputers:** 20 located in computer centers. **Special facilities:** Treasury Room Collection of primary resources on black life and culture, art museum with works of Afro-American culture. **Additional facts:** Historically, the majority of constituents have been black. While the University will continue to educate its traditional clientele, it will be an educational resource for all people in its service area.

DEGREES OFFERED. BA, BS, BArch, MA, MS, MBA, MEd. 510 bachelor's degrees awarded in 1992. 22% in business and management, 8% teacher education, 7% life sciences, 8% parks/recreation, protective services, public affairs, 34% social sciences. Graduate degrees offered in 36 major fields of study.

UNDERGRADUATE MAJORS. Accounting, art education, biology, business administration and management, business and management, business economics, chemistry, computer and information sciences, dramatic arts, early childhood education, elementary education, English, English education, finance, fine arts, food science and nutrition, foreign languages education, French, geography, graphic design, health education, history, home economics, home economics education, junior high education, law enforcement and corrections, marketing and distribution, mathematics, mathematics education, music, music education, nursing, parks and recreation management, philosophy, physical education, physics, political science and government, psychology, sacred music, science education, secondary education, social sciences, social studies education, sociology, Spanish, speech/communication/theater education, textiles and clothing.

ACADEMIC PROGRAMS. Cooperative education, double major, education specialist degree, honors program, independent study, internships, teacher preparation; combined bachelor's/graduate program in law. **Remedial services:** Learning center, remedial instruction, special counselor, tutoring, Academic Support Program. **ROTC:** Air Force, Army. **Placement/credit:** AP, CLEP General and Subject, institutional tests; 30 credit hours maximum for bachelor's degree.

ACADEMIC REQUIREMENTS. Freshmen must earn minimum GPA of 2.0 to continue in good standing. 76% of freshmen return for sophomore year. Students must declare major by end of first year. **Graduation requirements:** 124 hours for bachelor's (30 in major). Most students required to take courses in arts/fine arts, English, foreign languages, history, humanities, mathematics, biological/physical sciences, social sciences.

FRESHMAN ADMISSIONS. Selection criteria: Academic achievement, class rank, test scores important. **High school preparation:** 11 units required. Required and recommended units include biological science 1, English 3, mathematics 3, physical science 1, social science 2 and science 1. Foreign language 2 recommended. Mathematics units must include algebra I and II, geometry. Science units must include 1 laboratory science. Social science units must include 1 US history. One foreign language, and 1 mathematics recommended during 12th grade. **Test requirements:** SAT or ACT; score report by August 1.

1992 FRESHMAN CLASS PROFILE. 971 men applied, 648 accepted, 317 enrolled; 1,455 women applied, 1,034 accepted, 467 enrolled. **Academic background:** Mid 50% of enrolled freshmen had SAT-V between 310-400, SAT-M between 340-430. 81% submitted SAT scores. **Characteristics:** 86% from in state, 85% live in college housing, 99% have minority backgrounds. Average age is 19.

FALL-TERM APPLICATIONS. $15 fee. Closing date August 1; priority given to applications received by July 1; applicants notified on a rolling basis; must reply by June 1 for college housing. Audition required for music applicants. Early admission available. Early admission available with permission from high school principle and University academic dean.

STUDENT LIFE. Housing: Dormitories (men, women, coed). Coed honors dormitory available. **Activities:** Student government, magazine, student newspaper, yearbook, choral groups, concert band, dance, drama, jazz band, marching band, fraternities, sororities.

ATHLETICS. NAIA, NCAA. **Intercollegiate:** Basketball, bowling, cross-country, football M, softball W, tennis, track and field, volleyball W. **Intramural:** Basketball M, racquetball M.

STUDENT SERVICES. Aptitude testing, career counseling, employment service for undergraduates, freshman orientation, health services, on-campus day care, personal counseling, placement service for graduates, veterans counselor, services/facilities for handicapped.

ANNUAL EXPENSES. Tuition and fees (1992-93): $1,211, $5,672 additional for out-of-state students. **Room and board:** $2,894. **Books and supplies:** $450. **Other expenses:** $1,250.

FINANCIAL AID. 69% of freshmen, 79% of continuing students receive some form of aid. Grants, loans, jobs available. Academic, leadership scholarships available. **Aid applications:** Closing date March 31; applicants notified on a rolling basis; must reply within 2 weeks. **Additional information:** Departmental grants based on need plus other criteria available.

ADDRESS/TELEPHONE. Nancy R. Rowland, Director of Admissions, North Carolina Central University, PO Box 19717, Durham, NC 27707. (919) 560-6298. Fax: (919) 560-5012.

North Carolina School of the Arts
Winston-Salem, North Carolina — CB code: 5512

4-year public college of performing arts, coed. Founded in 1963. **Accreditation:** Regional. **Undergraduate enrollment:** 223 men, 196 women full time; 11 men, 24 women part time. **Graduate enrollment:** 29 men, 25 women full time; 1 man, 1 woman part time. **Faculty:** 118 total (91 full time), 14 with doctorates or other terminal degrees. **Location:** Urban campus in small city; 90 miles from Charlotte, 350 miles from Washington, D.C. **Calendar:** Trimester, limited summer session. **Microcomputers:** 28 located in dormitories, classrooms, computer centers. **Special facilities:** Concert hall, stage production shop, art galleries. **Additional facts:** Trains exceptionally talented students professional careers in the performing arts.

DEGREES OFFERED. BFA, MFA. 74 bachelor's degrees awarded in 1992. 100% in visual and performing arts. Graduate degrees offered in 2 major fields of study.

UNDERGRADUATE MAJORS. Dance, dramatic arts, music performance, theater design.

ACADEMIC PROGRAMS. Dual enrollment of high school students, independent study, internships. **Remedial services:** Remedial instruction. **Placement/credit:** AP, CLEP General and Subject, institutional tests; 6 credit hours maximum for bachelor's degree.

ACADEMIC REQUIREMENTS. Freshmen must earn minimum GPA of 1.8 in general studies courses. For arts courses, no minimum GPA for School of Music. 3.0 for School of Dance, and 2.0 for Design and Production and School of Drama. 60% of freshmen return for sophomore year. Students must declare major on application. **Graduation requirements:** 185 hours for bachelor's (140 in major). Most students required to take courses in arts/fine arts, English, history, humanities, mathematics, philosophy/religion, biological/physical sciences, social sciences. **Postgraduate studies:** 1% enter law school, 1% enter medical school, 28% enter other graduate study.

Additional information: Professional training supplemented by strong general studies curriculum.

FRESHMAN ADMISSIONS. Selection criteria: Talent, achievement, career potential most important. Admission heavily dependent on audition. SAT combined score of 800 or ACT composite score of 19, school record, recommendations considered. **High school preparation:** 12 units required. Required units include biological science 1, English 4, mathematics 3, social science 2 and science 2. **Test requirements:** SAT or ACT (SAT preferred); score report by September 10.

1992 FRESHMAN CLASS PROFILE. 61 men, 61 women enrolled. **Characteristics:** 54% from in state, 84% live in college housing, 15% have minority backgrounds. Average age is 18.

FALL-TERM APPLICATIONS. $25 fee, may be waived for applicants with need. No closing date; applicants notified on a rolling basis beginning on or about April 1; must reply by May 1 or within 3 weeks if notified thereafter. Audition required for music, dance, drama applicants. Portfolio required for design, production, filmmaking applicants. Interview recommended. Application closing date dependent upon audition. Applications must be submitted at least 2 weeks before audition date. Dance and drama auditions begin in January and end in early March. Music and technical theater auditions begin in November and end early March. Decisions generally made by April 1, or about 2 weeks after audition if later than April 1. Auditions in April and May for all arts schools.

STUDENT LIFE. Housing: Dormitories (men, women, coed); apartment housing available. **Activities:** Student government, yearbook, choral groups, dance, drama, jazz band, music ensembles, musical theater, opera, symphony orchestra.

STUDENT SERVICES. Aptitude testing, career counseling, employment service for undergraduates, health services, personal counseling, services/facilities for handicapped.

ANNUAL EXPENSES. Tuition and fees (1992-93): $1,630, $6,459 additional for out-of-state students. **Room and board:** $3,163. **Books and supplies:** $595. **Other expenses:** $1,565.

FINANCIAL AID. 66% of freshmen, 75% of continuing students receive some form of aid. 60% of grants, 91% of loans, 46% of jobs based on need. 93 enrolled freshmen were judged to have need, 82 were offered aid. Academic, music/drama, art scholarships available. **Aid applications:** No closing date; priority given to applications received by March 15; applicants notified on a rolling basis beginning on or about April 1; must reply within 10 days.

ADDRESS/TELEPHONE. Carol Palm, Director of Admissions, North Carolina School of the Arts, 200 Waughtown Street, Winston-Salem, NC 27117-2189. (919) 770-3399. (800) 282-ARTS. Fax: (919) 770-3370.

North Carolina State University
Raleigh, North Carolina

CB code: 5496

Admissions: 63% of applicants accepted
Based on:
- ••• School record
- •• Test scores
- • Activities, essay, interview, recommendations, special talents

Completion: 98% of freshmen end year in good standing
55% graduate, 28% of these enter graduate study

4-year public university, coed. Founded in 1887. **Accreditation:** Regional. **Undergraduate enrollment:** 10,397 men, 6,147 women full time; 3,380 men, 2,559 women part time. **Graduate enrollment:** 1,076 men, 830 women full time; 1,662 men, 1,105 women part time. **Faculty:** 1,704 total (1,307 full time), 1,398 with doctorates or other terminal degrees. **Location:** Suburban campus in small city; 1 mile from downtown. **Calendar:** Semester, extensive summer session. Extensive evening/early morning classes. **Microcomputers:** 3,200 located in dormitories, libraries, classrooms, computer centers. **Special facilities:** 2 nuclear reactors, 3 electron microscopes, phytotron, art galleries, research farms, campus theater, craft center, stable isotope laboratory, teaching forest, wood products laboratory, fiber, fabric and garment manufacturing equipment, coastal marine science laboratory.

DEGREES OFFERED. AAS, BA, BS, BArch, MA, MS, MEd, PhD, EdD, DVM. 95 associate degrees awarded in 1992. 100% in agriculture. 3,652 bachelor's degrees awarded. 6% in agriculture, 17% business and management, 6% communications, 26% engineering, 5% life sciences, 13% social sciences. Graduate degrees offered in 85 major fields of study.

UNDERGRADUATE MAJORS. Associate: Agricultural mechanics, agricultural production, agricultural products and processing, agricultural sciences. **Bachelor's:** Accounting, aerospace/aeronautical/astronautical engineering, agribusiness, agricultural business and management, agricultural economics, agricultural education, agricultural engineering, agricultural systems technology, agronomy, animal sciences, anthropology, applied mathematics, applied sociology, architecture, atmospheric sciences and meteorology, biochemistry, biology, botany, business administration and management, business and management, business economics, chemical engineering, chemistry, civil engineering, clinical laboratory science, communications, computer and information sciences, computer engineering, conservation and regulation, creative writing, criminal justice studies, economics, education, electrical/electronics/communications engineering, English, English education, English literature, entomology, environmental design, fiber/textiles/weaving, fishing and fisheries, food sciences, foreign languages education, forest products processing technology, forestry and related sciences, French, geology, geophysics and seismology, graphic design, health education, history, horticultural science, horticulture, human resources development, humanities, humanities and social sciences, industrial arts education, industrial engineering, international business management, journalism, junior high education, landscape architecture, liberal/general studies, marketing and distributive education, materials engineering, mathematics, mathematics education, mechanical engineering, medical laboratory technologies, microbiology, nuclear engineering, nutritional sciences, ornamental horticulture, parks and recreation management, philosophy, physics, plant protection, political science and government, poultry, predentistry, prelaw, premedicine, preveterinary, product design, psychology, public relations, radio/television broadcasting, rural sociology, science education, secondary education, social sciences, social studies education, social work, sociology, soil sciences, Spanish, speech, statistics, technical education, textile chemistry, textile engineering, textile management, trade and industrial education, wildlife management, zoology.

ACADEMIC PROGRAMS. Accelerated program, cooperative education, double major, dual enrollment of high school students, honors program, independent study, internships, student-designed major, study abroad, teacher preparation, telecourses, visiting/exchange student program, cross-registration; liberal arts/career combination in engineering, forestry. **Remedial services:** Learning center, preadmission summer program, reduced course load, remedial instruction, special counselor, tutoring. **ROTC:** Air Force, Army, Naval. **Placement/credit:** AP, CLEP Subject, institutional tests.

ACADEMIC REQUIREMENTS. Freshmen must earn minimum GPA of 1.6 to continue in good standing. 89% of freshmen return for sophomore year. Students must declare major by end of first year. **Graduation requirements:** 60 hours for associate, 124 hours for bachelor's (60 in major). Most students required to take courses in English, history, humanities, mathematics, biological/physical sciences, social sciences. **Postgraduate studies:** 1% enter law school, 2% enter medical school, 3% enter MBA programs, 22% enter other graduate study.

FRESHMAN ADMISSIONS. Selection criteria: School achievement record and test scores are important. Counselor evaluations, extracurricular activities and work experience also considered. Preference given to students with strong high school record. Level and difficulty of courses considered. **High school preparation:** 20 units required. Required and recommended units include English 4, mathematics 3-4, social science 2 and science 3. Foreign language 2 recommended. Science units should include 1 life or biological science, 1 physical science, and 1 laboratory science. **Test requirements:** SAT or ACT (SAT preferred); score report by March 1. Mathematics Level I or II ACH required. Score report by June 15.

1992 FRESHMAN CLASS PROFILE. 6,319 men applied, 3,840 accepted, 1,849 enrolled; 4,363 women applied, 2,873 accepted, 1,216 enrolled. 89% had high school GPA of 3.0 or higher, 11% between 2.0 and 2.99. 38% were in top tenth and 78% were in top quarter of graduating class. **Academic background:** Mid 50% of enrolled freshmen had SAT-V between 430-540, SAT-M between 510-630. 100% submitted SAT scores. **Characteristics:** 82% from in state, 89% live in college housing, 18% have minority backgrounds, 1% are foreign students, 6% join fraternities/sororities. Average age is 18.

FALL-TERM APPLICATIONS. $35 fee, may be waived for applicants with need. Closing date February 1; priority given to applications received by November 1; applicants notified on a rolling basis beginning on or about October 1; must reply by May 1 or within 10 days if notified thereafter. Interview required for design applicants. Portfolio required for design applicants. Essay recommended. CRDA. Deferred and early admission available. Applications to School of Design should be submitted by January 1.

STUDENT LIFE. Housing: Dormitories (men, women, coed); apartment, fraternity, sorority housing available. Special residence hall programs include international student dormitory, Residential Scholars Program, Metcalf Living/Learning Program for freshmen, and residence hall for students interested in computers and visual and performing arts. **Activities:** Student government, magazine, radio, student newspaper, television, yearbook, choral groups, concert band, dance, drama, jazz band, marching band, music ensembles, musical theater, pep band, symphony orchestra, bagpipe band, fraternities, sororities, Alpha Phi Omega, Alpha Zeta, Baptist Student Union, Campus Crusade for Christ, Circle-K, International Student Board, Young Democrats, Young Republicans, Society of Afro-American Culture, YMCA.

ATHLETICS. NCAA. **Intercollegiate:** Baseball M, basketball, cross-country, diving, fencing, football M, golf, gymnastics, rifle, soccer, swimming, tennis, track and field, volleyball W, wrestling M. **Intramural:** Archery, badminton, baseball, basketball, bowling, cross-country, fencing, field hockey W, golf, gymnastics, handball, ice hockey M, lacrosse M, racquetball, rugby M, sailing, skiing, skin diving, soccer, softball, squash, swimming, table tennis, tennis, track and field, volleyball, wrestling M.

STUDENT SERVICES. Aptitude testing, career counseling, em-

ployment service for undergraduates, freshman orientation, health services, on-campus day care, personal counseling, placement service for graduates, special adviser for adult students, veterans counselor, services/facilities for handicapped.

ANNUAL EXPENSES. Tuition and fees (1992-93): $1,302, $6,584 additional for out-of-state students. **Room and board:** $3,350. **Books and supplies:** $600. **Other expenses:** $1,050.

FINANCIAL AID. 42% of freshmen, 40% of continuing students receive some form of aid. 50% of grants, 86% of loans, 12% of jobs based on need. 1,650 enrolled freshmen were judged to have need, 1,150 were offered aid. Academic, athletic, state/district residency, leadership, minority scholarships available. **Aid applications:** No closing date; priority given to applications received by March 15; applicants notified on a rolling basis beginning on or about June 1; must reply within 3 weeks.

ADDRESS/TELEPHONE. Dr. George R. Dixon, Director of Admissions, North Carolina State University, PO Box 7103, 112 Peele Hall, Raleigh, NC 27695-7103. (919) 515-2434. Fax: (919) 515-5039.

North Carolina Wesleyan College
Rocky Mount, North Carolina — CB code: 5501

Admissions: 82% of applicants accepted
Based on:
- ••• School record, test scores
- •• Activities, essay, recommendations, special talents
- • Interview

Completion: 55% of freshmen end year in good standing
35% graduate

4-year private liberal arts college, coed, affiliated with United Methodist Church. Founded in 1956. **Accreditation:** Regional. **Undergraduate enrollment:** 325 men, 306 women full time; 24 men, 42 women part time. **Faculty:** 66 total (47 full time), 35 with doctorates or other terminal degrees. **Location:** Suburban campus in small city; 57 miles from Raleigh. **Calendar:** 4-4-1, limited summer session. Extensive evening/early morning classes. **Microcomputers:** 41 located in dormitories, libraries, computer centers. **Special facilities:** Outsider art collection of Eastern North Carolina Artists, Black Mountain Collection (archival collection), Bellmonte House. **Additional facts:** Adult students, 22 and older, can attend classes at sites in Raleigh, Goldsboro, and New Bern.

DEGREES OFFERED. BA, BS. 106 bachelor's degrees awarded in 1992. 38% in business and management, 8% computer sciences, 11% teacher education, 9% law, 7% psychology, 12% social sciences.

UNDERGRADUATE MAJORS. Accounting, anthropology, biology, business administration and management, chemistry, computer and information sciences, criminal justice studies, elementary education, English, English education, environmental science, history, hotel/motel and restaurant management, journalism, junior high education, mathematics, mathematics education, music, philosophy, physical education, political science and government, prelaw, psychology, religion, science education, secondary education, social science education, social studies education, sociology, visual and performing arts.

ACADEMIC PROGRAMS. Cooperative education, double major, honors program, independent study, internships, study abroad, teacher preparation, summer program at University of Paris, Sorbonne. **Remedial services:** Learning center, preadmission summer program, reduced course load, remedial instruction, tutoring. **Placement/credit:** AP, CLEP General and Subject, institutional tests.

ACADEMIC REQUIREMENTS. Freshmen must earn minimum GPA of 2.0 to continue in good standing. 55% of freshmen return for sophomore year. Students must declare major by end of second year. **Graduation requirements:** 124 hours for bachelor's (30 in major). Most students required to take courses in arts/fine arts, English, history, humanities, mathematics, philosophy/religion, biological/physical sciences, social sciences.

FRESHMAN ADMISSIONS. Selection criteria: High school GPA most important, followed by SAT or ACT score, rigor of high school curriculum, class rank, and recommendations. School and community activities considered. **High school preparation:** 16 units required. Required and recommended units include English 4, mathematics 2-3, social science 2 and science 2-3. Foreign language 2 recommended. **Test requirements:** SAT or ACT; score report by July 15.

1992 FRESHMAN CLASS PROFILE. 473 men applied, 383 accepted, 118 enrolled; 385 women applied, 320 accepted, 93 enrolled. 9% had high school GPA of 3.0 or higher, 58% between 2.0 and 2.99. 5% were in top tenth and 25% were in top quarter of graduating class. **Academic background:** Mid 50% of enrolled freshmen had SAT-V between 350-440, SAT-M between 390-480. 99% submitted SAT scores. **Characteristics:** 23% from in state, 90% live in college housing, 18% have minority backgrounds, 1% are foreign students, 8% join fraternities/sororities. Average age is 18.

FALL-TERM APPLICATIONS. $25 fee, may be waived for applicants with need. Closing date July 15; priority given to applications received by March 1; applicants notified on a rolling basis; must reply 4 weeks after acceptance and if after May 1 within 2 weeks after notification. Interview recommended. Essay recommended. CRDA. Deferred and early admission available. Institutional early decision plan.

STUDENT LIFE. Housing: Dormitories (men, women, coed). **Activities:** Student government, radio, student newspaper, yearbook, choral groups, concert band, drama, jazz band, music ensembles, pep band, gospel choir, fraternities, sororities, Black Student Association, Fellowship of Christian Athletes, College Republicans, College Democrats.

ATHLETICS. NCAA. **Intercollegiate:** Baseball M, basketball, golf M, soccer, softball W, volleyball W. **Intramural:** Basketball, cross-country, softball, table tennis, tennis, volleyball.

STUDENT SERVICES. Aptitude testing, career counseling, employment service for undergraduates, freshman orientation, health services, personal counseling, placement service for graduates, special adviser for adult students, veterans counselor, services/facilities for handicapped.

ANNUAL EXPENSES. Tuition and fees (1992-93): $7,660. **Room and board:** $3,790. **Books and supplies:** $479. **Other expenses:** $863.

FINANCIAL AID. 70% of freshmen, 70% of continuing students receive some form of aid. Grants, loans, jobs available. Academic, state/district residency, leadership, religious affiliation scholarships available. **Aid applications:** No closing date; priority given to applications received by March 1; applicants notified on a rolling basis beginning on or about March 1; must reply by May 1 or within 2 weeks if notified thereafter. **Additional information:** Scholarships based on SAT scores and GPA. Various scholarship and leadership awards available.

ADDRESS/TELEPHONE. Steven W. Pochard, Vice President of Admissions and Financial Aid, North Carolina Wesleyan College, 3400 North Wesleyan Boulevard, Rocky Mount, NC 27804. (919) 985-5197. (800) 488-6292. Fax: (919) 977-3701.

Pamlico Community College
Grantsboro, North Carolina — CB code: 0864

2-year public community college, coed. Founded in 1962. **Accreditation:** Regional. **Undergraduate enrollment:** 173 men and women. **Faculty:** 17 total (11 full time). **Location:** Rural campus in rural community; 20 miles from New Bern. **Calendar:** Quarter, limited summer session. Extensive evening/early morning classes. **Microcomputers:** Located in libraries, classrooms. **Additional facts:** Community college works with students individually, providing each student with opportunity to learn on a one-on-one basis.

DEGREES OFFERED. AAS. 30 associate degrees awarded in 1992.

UNDERGRADUATE MAJORS. Accounting, automotive technology, business administration and management, business and office, education, electrical technology, liberal/general studies, medical assistant, medical secretary, secretarial and related programs.

ACADEMIC PROGRAMS. 2-year transfer program, dual enrollment of high school students, independent study, internships. **Remedial services:** Learning center, reduced course load, remedial instruction, special counselor, tutoring. **Placement/credit:** Institutional tests.

ACADEMIC REQUIREMENTS. Freshmen must earn minimum GPA of 2.0 to continue in good standing. 81% of freshmen return for sophomore year. Students must declare major on enrollment. **Graduation requirements:** 96 hours for associate.

FRESHMAN ADMISSIONS. Selection criteria: Open admissions.

1992 FRESHMAN CLASS PROFILE. 96 men and women enrolled. **Characteristics:** 99% from in state, 100% commute, 30% have minority backgrounds. Average age is 28.

FALL-TERM APPLICATIONS. No fee. No closing date; applicants notified on a rolling basis. Deferred admission available.

STUDENT LIFE. Activities: Student government, student newspaper.

ATHLETICS. Intramural: Basketball, softball, table tennis, tennis, volleyball.

STUDENT SERVICES. Career counseling, employment service for undergraduates, health services, personal counseling, placement service for graduates, veterans counselor, services/facilities for handicapped.

ANNUAL EXPENSES. Tuition and fees (1992-93): $572, $3,959 additional for out-of-state students. **Books and supplies:** $340. **Other expenses:** $1,623.

FINANCIAL AID. 80% of freshmen, 75% of continuing students receive some form of aid. All aid based on need. **Aid applications:** No closing date; applicants notified on a rolling basis.

ADDRESS/TELEPHONE. John Jones, Dean of Student Enrollment Services, Pamlico Community College, PO Box 185, Hwy 306S, Grantsboro, NC 28529. (919) 249-1851 ext. 28.

Peace College

Raleigh, North Carolina CB code: 5533

Admissions: 86% of applicants accepted
Based on: ••• School record
•• Interview, recommendations, test scores
• Activities, essay, special talents
Completion: 80% of freshmen end year in good standing

2-year private junior, liberal arts college, women only, affiliated with Presbyterian Church (USA). Founded in 1857. **Accreditation:** Regional. **Undergraduate enrollment:** 437 women full time; 29 women part time. **Faculty:** 43 total (26 full time), 18 with doctorates or other terminal degrees. **Location:** Urban campus in small city; 143 from Charlotte. **Calendar:** Semester. Extensive evening/early morning classes. **Microcomputers:** 20 located in classrooms, computer centers.

DEGREES OFFERED. AA, AS. 163 associate degrees awarded in 1992. 98% in multi/interdisciplinary studies.

UNDERGRADUATE MAJORS. Business and management, business data processing and related programs, fashion merchandising, fine arts, foreign languages (multiple emphasis), liberal/general studies, medical laboratory technologies, music, nursing, predentistry, premedicine, prepharmacy, secretarial and related programs.

ACADEMIC PROGRAMS. 2-year transfer program, double major, dual enrollment of high school students, honors program, independent study, internships, study abroad, cross-registration. **Remedial services:** Learning center, special counselor, tutoring, Summer writing institute. **Placement/credit:** AP, institutional tests.

ACADEMIC REQUIREMENTS. Freshmen must earn minimum GPA of 2.0 to continue in good standing. 75% of freshmen return for sophomore year. **Graduation requirements:** 63 hours for associate. Most students required to take courses in arts/fine arts, English, foreign languages, history, mathematics, philosophy/religion, biological/physical sciences, social sciences. **Additional information:** Summer writing institute for incoming freshmen provides intensive coursein language and writing.

FRESHMAN ADMISSIONS. Selection criteria: School achievement record, test scores, recommendations, rank in top half of class, 2.0 GPA on college preparatory courses required. SAT combined score of 800 and above preferred. **High school preparation:** 16 units required. Required and recommended units include English 4, foreign language 1-2, mathematics 3, social science 2 and science 2-3. Mathematics must include algebra I, algebra II and geometry. **Test requirements:** SAT or ACT; score report by August 1.

1992 FRESHMAN CLASS PROFILE. 483 women applied, 416 accepted, 253 enrolled. 39% had high school GPA of 3.0 or higher, 55% between 2.0 and 2.99. 23% were in top tenth and 40% were in top quarter of graduating class. **Academic background:** Mid 50% of enrolled freshmen had SAT-V between 350-480, SAT-M between 390-510. 100% submitted SAT scores. **Characteristics:** 90% from in state, 90% live in college housing, 2% have minority backgrounds, 1% are foreign students. Average age is 18.

FALL-TERM APPLICATIONS. $25 fee, may be waived for applicants with need. No closing date; priority given to applications received by December 1; applicants notified on a rolling basis. Audition required for music, drama applicants. Portfolio required for art applicants. Essay required. Interview recommended. Deferred and early admission available. Prefer early admission candidates score 1000 or above on SAT, have 3.0 GPA in college preparatory courses and rank in top 25% of class. On-campus interview required. Minimum 400 SAT verbal score required for international students.

STUDENT LIFE. Housing: Dormitories (women); handicapped housing available. Students required to live on campus unless living with relatives in area. **Activities:** Student government, magazine, student newspaper, yearbook, choral groups, dance, drama, music ensembles, musical theater, opera, Christian Association, honor societies, recreation association, Young Democrats/Republicans, Phi Theta Kappa, Sigma Delta Mu, Student Environmental Action Coalition. **Additional information:** Mandatory chapel attendance once a week. Religious observance required.

ATHLETICS. NJCAA. **Intercollegiate:** Soccer, tennis, volleyball. **Intramural:** Archery, badminton, basketball, bowling, golf, horseback riding, racquetball, softball, swimming, table tennis, tennis, volleyball.

STUDENT SERVICES. Career counseling, freshman orientation, health services, personal counseling, placement service for graduates, special adviser for adult students, services/facilities for handicapped.

ANNUAL EXPENSES. Tuition and fees: $5,220. **Room and board:** $4,440. **Books and supplies:** $500. **Other expenses:** $1,000.

FINANCIAL AID. 69% of freshmen, 64% of continuing students receive some form of aid. 51% of grants, all loans, 46% of jobs based on need. 90 enrolled freshmen were judged to have need, all were offered aid. Academic, music/drama, art, athletic, state/district residency, leadership, alumni affiliation, religious affiliation scholarships available. **Aid applications:** No closing date; priority given to applications received by April 1; applicants notified on a rolling basis beginning on or about January 21; must reply within 2 weeks.

ADDRESS/TELEPHONE. Cynthia G. Wyatt, Dean of Admissions, Peace College, 15 East Peace Street, Raleigh, NC 27604-1194. (919) 832-2881 ext. 214. Fax: (919) 834-6755.

Pembroke State University

Pembroke, North Carolina CB code: 5534

Admissions: 82% of applicants accepted
Based on: ••• School record
•• Activities, recommendations, test scores
• Essay, interview, special talents
Completion: 90% of freshmen end year in good standing
35% graduate, 17% of these enter graduate study

4-year public university and liberal arts college, coed. Founded in 1887. **Accreditation:** Regional. **Undergraduate enrollment:** 997 men, 1,168 women full time; 171 men, 366 women part time. **Graduate enrollment:** 3 men, 7 women full time; 81 men, 248 women part time. **Faculty:** 195 total (148 full time), 133 with doctorates or other terminal degrees. **Location:** Rural campus in small town; 38 miles from Fayetteville. **Calendar:** Semester, limited summer session. Extensive evening/early morning classes. **Microcomputers:** 255 located in libraries, classrooms, computer centers, campus-wide network. **Special facilities:** Native American Resource Center.

DEGREES OFFERED. BA, BS, MA, MS, MEd. 437 bachelor's degrees awarded in 1992. 18% in business and management, 28% education, 9% letters/literature, 7% life sciences, 6% parks/recreation, protective services, public affairs, 19% social sciences. Graduate degrees offered in 9 major fields of study.

UNDERGRADUATE MAJORS. Accounting, American Indian studies, art education, arts management, biology, business administration and management, business education, chemistry, clinical laboratory science, computer and information sciences, computer mathematics, criminal justice studies, education of the mentally handicapped, elementary education, English, fine arts, history, journalism, junior high education, mathematics, music, music education, music performance, nursing, office supervision and management, philosophy, physical education, political science and government, prelaw, psychology, public administration, public relations, radio/television broadcasting, religion, science education, social work, sociology, special education, specific learning disabilities.

ACADEMIC PROGRAMS. Double major, honors program, internships, teacher preparation. **Remedial services:** Learning center, preadmission summer program, reduced course load, remedial instruction, special counselor, tutoring, special conferences, test taking workshops. **ROTC:** Air Force, Army. **Placement/credit:** AP, CLEP General, institutional tests; 30 credit hours maximum for bachelor's degree.

ACADEMIC REQUIREMENTS. Freshmen must earn minimum GPA of 1.38 to continue in good standing. 73% of freshmen return for sophomore year. Students must declare major by end of second year. **Graduation requirements:** 128 hours for bachelor's (36 in major). Most students required to take courses in arts/fine arts, English, history, humanities, mathematics, philosophy/religion, biological/physical sciences, social sciences. **Additional information:** Certification on the secondary level in English, biology, mathematics, and social studies.

FRESHMAN ADMISSIONS. Selection criteria: High school record, class standing, recommendation, test scores, and college preparatory courses important. Students must submit record of 12th grade work in progress. **High school preparation:** 20 units required. Required and recommended units include biological science 1-2, English 4, mathematics 3, physical science 1-2, social science 2 and science 3. Foreign language 2 recommended. Social science must include 1 unit U.S. History. Sciences must include 1 unit laboratory science. **Test requirements:** SAT or ACT; score report by July 15.

1992 FRESHMAN CLASS PROFILE. 502 men applied, 411 accepted, 224 enrolled; 493 women applied, 402 accepted, 211 enrolled. 28% had high school GPA of 3.0 or higher, 58% between 2.0 and 2.99. 14% were in top tenth and 34% were in top quarter of graduating class. **Characteristics:** 93% from in state, 40% have minority backgrounds, 1% are foreign students. Average age is 19.

FALL-TERM APPLICATIONS. $25 fee, may be waived for applicants with need. Closing date July 15; priority given to applications received by June 30; applicants notified on a rolling basis. Audition required for music applicants. Interview recommended for borderline applicants. Deferred and early admission available.

STUDENT LIFE. Housing: Dormitories (men, women). **Activities:** Student government, student newspaper, television, yearbook, choral groups, concert band, drama, jazz band, musical theater, pep band, fraternities, sororities, Native American organization, black student organization, Baptist Student Union, International Student Club, Methodist campus ministry.

ATHLETICS. NCAA. **Intercollegiate:** Baseball M, basketball, cross-country, golf M, soccer M, softball W, track and field M, volleyball W, wrestling M. **Intramural:** Basketball, bowling, racquetball, soccer M, softball, table tennis, volleyball.

STUDENT SERVICES. Aptitude testing, career counseling, freshman orientation, health services, personal counseling, veterans counselor, services/facilities for handicapped.

ANNUAL EXPENSES. Tuition and fees (1992-93): $948, $5,018 additional for out-of-state students. **Room and board:** $2,530. **Books and supplies:** $450. **Other expenses:** $900.

FINANCIAL AID. 82% of grants, 88% of loans based on need. Academic, music/drama, art, athletic, alumni affiliation, minority scholarships available. **Aid applications:** No closing date; priority given to applications received by April 15; applicants notified on a rolling basis beginning on or about June 15; must reply within 2 weeks.

ADDRESS/TELEPHONE. Anthony Locklear, Director of Admissions, Pembroke State University, Pembroke, NC 28372. (919) 521-6000.

Pfeiffer College
Misenheimer, North Carolina — CB code: 5536

Admissions: 82% of applicants accepted
Based on:
- ••• School record, test scores
- •• Activities, interview, recommendations
- • Essay

Completion: 90% of freshmen end year in good standing
44% graduate, 28% of these enter graduate study

4-year private college of arts and sciences, coed, affiliated with United Methodist Church. Founded in 1885. **Accreditation:** Regional. **Undergraduate enrollment:** 326 men, 349 women full time; 56 men, 76 women part time. **Graduate enrollment:** 2 men, 4 women full time; 63 men, 40 women part time. **Faculty:** 91 total (47 full time), 40 with doctorates or other terminal degrees. **Location:** Rural campus in rural community; 40 miles from Charlotte, 60 miles from Winston-Salem. **Calendar:** Semester, limited summer session. **Microcomputers:** 49 located in libraries, classrooms, computer centers. **Special facilities:** Art gallery.

DEGREES OFFERED. BA, BS, MA, MBA. 124 bachelor's degrees awarded in 1992. 28% in business and management, 13% teacher education, 5% letters/literature, 21% parks/recreation, protective services, public affairs, 12% social sciences. Graduate degrees offered in 3 major fields of study.

UNDERGRADUATE MAJORS. Accounting, arts management, biology, business administration and management, business and management, chemistry, computer and information sciences, criminal justice studies, dramatic arts, economics, elementary education, English, health care administration, history, law enforcement and corrections, mathematics, music, music education, physical education, predentistry, preengineering, prelaw, premedicine, preveterinary, psychology, religion, religious education, religious music, secondary education, social studies education, sociology, special education, sports management, sports medicine.

ACADEMIC PROGRAMS. Accelerated program, cooperative education, double major, dual enrollment of high school students, honors program, independent study, internships, study abroad, teacher preparation, Washington semester; liberal arts/career combination in engineering. **Remedial services:** Learning center, reduced course load, remedial instruction, special counselor, tutoring. **ROTC:** Army. **Placement/credit:** AP, CLEP General and Subject, institutional tests; 40 credit hours maximum for bachelor's degree.

ACADEMIC REQUIREMENTS. Freshmen must earn minimum GPA of 1.3 to continue in good standing. 65% of freshmen return for sophomore year. Students must declare major by end of first year. **Graduation requirements:** 124 hours for bachelor's (50 in major). Most students required to take courses in arts/fine arts, English, history, mathematics, philosophy/religion, biological/physical sciences, social sciences. **Postgraduate studies:** 2% enter law school, 1% enter medical school, 5% enter MBA programs, 20% enter other graduate study.

FRESHMAN ADMISSIONS. Selection criteria: School achievement record, class rank, recommendations, and test scores reviewed. **High school preparation:** 16 units recommended. Required and recommended units include English 4. Biological science 1, foreign language 2, mathematics 3, physical science 2 and social science 4 recommended. Mathematics should include algebra I. **Test requirements:** SAT or ACT (SAT preferred); score report by August 15.

1992 FRESHMAN CLASS PROFILE. 390 men applied, 315 accepted, 81 enrolled; 290 women applied, 245 accepted, 67 enrolled. 18% had high school GPA of 3.0 or higher, 51% between 2.0 and 2.99. 7% were in top tenth and 26% were in top quarter of graduating class. **Academic background:** Mid 50% of enrolled freshmen had SAT-V between 340-440, SAT-M between 370-500. 92% submitted SAT scores. **Characteristics:** 61% from in state, 87% live in college housing, 8% have minority backgrounds, 1% are foreign students. Average age is 18.

FALL-TERM APPLICATIONS. $20 fee, may be waived for applicants with need. No closing date; priority given to applications received by March 15; applicants notified on a rolling basis. Audition required for music applicants. Interview recommended. CRDA. Deferred and early admission available.

STUDENT LIFE. Housing: Dormitories (men, women); apartment housing available. **Activities:** Student government, magazine, radio, student newspaper, yearbook, choral groups, concert band, dance, drama, jazz band, music ensembles, musical theater, hand bell choir, religious organizations, political groups, service clubs, professional clubs, Black Student Alliance.

ATHLETICS. NAIA, NCAA. **Intercollegiate:** Baseball M, basketball, cross-country, golf M, lacrosse M, soccer, softball W, swimming W, tennis, volleyball W. **Intramural:** Basketball, bowling, soccer, softball, table tennis, tennis, volleyball.

STUDENT SERVICES. Aptitude testing, career counseling, employment service for undergraduates, freshman orientation, health services, personal counseling, placement service for graduates, veterans counselor, services/facilities for handicapped.

ANNUAL EXPENSES. Tuition and fees (1992-93): $7,735. **Room and board:** $3,275. **Books and supplies:** $650. **Other expenses:** $650.

FINANCIAL AID. 96% of freshmen, 91% of continuing students receive some form of aid. 30% of grants, 92% of loans, 53% of jobs based on need. Academic, music/drama, athletic, state/district residency, religious affiliation scholarships available. **Aid applications:** No closing date; priority given to applications received by May 1; applicants notified on a rolling basis beginning on or about March 1; must reply within 2 weeks. **Additional information:** Incentive scholarship system allows students who perform well academically to obtain or increase scholarship.

ADDRESS/TELEPHONE. David Maltby, Dean of Admission and Financial Aid, Pfeiffer College, Misenheimer, NC 28109. (704) 463-1360. (800) 338-2060. Fax: (704) 463-1363.

Piedmont Bible College
Winston-Salem, North Carolina — CB code: 5555

Admissions: 96% of applicants accepted
Based on:
- ••• Essay, recommendations, religious affiliation/commitment
- •• Interview, school record

Completion: 80% of freshmen end year in good standing
50% graduate, 8% of these enter graduate study

5-year private Bible college, coed, affiliated with independent Baptist denomination. Founded in 1945. **Undergraduate enrollment:** 168 men, 77 women full time; 19 men, 22 women part time. **Faculty:** 39 total (29 full time), 9 with doctorates or other terminal degrees. **Location:** Urban campus in small city; 75 miles from Charlotte. **Calendar:** Semester, extensive summer session. **Microcomputers:** 17 located in libraries, computer centers. **Special facilities:** Old Salem Moravian Settlement.

DEGREES OFFERED. BA, BS. 46 bachelor's degrees awarded in 1992. 50% in teacher education, 50% philosophy, religion, theology.

UNDERGRADUATE MAJORS. Bible studies, education, education of the mentally handicapped, elementary education, music education, physical education, religious education, religious music, theological studies.

ACADEMIC PROGRAMS. Accelerated program, double major, internships, teacher preparation. **Remedial services:** Reduced course load, remedial instruction, special counselor. **Placement/credit:** AP, CLEP General and Subject.

ACADEMIC REQUIREMENTS. Freshmen must earn minimum GPA of 2.0 to continue in good standing. 48% of freshmen return for sophomore year. Students must declare major on application. **Graduation requirements:** 130 hours for bachelor's (47 in major). Most students required to take courses in computer science, English, history, mathematics, philosophy/religion, biological/physical sciences, social sciences.

FRESHMAN ADMISSIONS. Selection criteria: Student's life objectives and previous academic record important. Recommended units include biological science 1, English 4, foreign language 2, mathematics 1, physical science 1 and social science 2. **Test requirements:** SAT or ACT for placement and counseling only; score report by August 26.

1992 FRESHMAN CLASS PROFILE. 41 men applied, 39 accepted, 37 enrolled; 29 women applied, 28 accepted, 18 enrolled. **Academic background:** Mid 50% of enrolled freshmen had ACT composite between 16-21. 100% submitted ACT scores. **Characteristics:** 70% from in state, 57% commute, 9% have minority backgrounds, 1% are foreign students. Average age is 26.

FALL-TERM APPLICATIONS. $30 fee. No closing date; applicants notified on a rolling basis beginning on or about March 1; must reply by registration. Audition required for music program applicants. Essay required. Interview recommended. Deferred and early admission available.

STUDENT LIFE. Housing: Dormitories (men, women); apartment housing available. **Activities:** Student government, student newspaper, yearbook, choral groups, music ensembles, pep band, missions fellowship, Delta Epsilon Chi, preacher's fellowship, youth leader's fellowship, educator's fellowship. **Additional information:** Religious observance required.

ATHLETICS. Intercollegiate: Baseball M, basketball, volleyball W. **Intramural:** Basketball, soccer M, softball M, table tennis, volleyball.

STUDENT SERVICES. Freshman orientation, health services, personal counseling, placement service for graduates, veterans counselor.

ANNUAL EXPENSES. Tuition and fees: $4,090. **Room and board:** $2,600. **Books and supplies:** $450. **Other expenses:** $550.

FINANCIAL AID. 100% of freshmen, 86% of continuing students receive some form of aid. 99% of grants, 93% of loans, 22% of jobs based on need. 55 enrolled freshmen were judged to have need, all were offered aid. Academic, music/drama, leadership scholarships available. **Aid applications:** No closing date; applicants notified on a rolling basis beginning on or about March 1; must reply by May 1 or within 4 weeks if notified thereafter.

ADDRESS/TELEPHONE. Brian Cockram, Director of Admissions, Piedmont Bible College, 716 Franklin Street, Winston-Salem, NC 27101-5197. (919) 725-8344.

Piedmont Community College
Roxboro, North Carolina — CB code: 5518

2-year public community college, coed. Founded in 1970. **Accreditation:** Regional. **Undergraduate enrollment:** 250 men, 221 women full time; 265 men, 474 women part time. **Faculty:** 60 total (43 full time). **Location:** Rural campus in small town; 30 miles from Durham, 45 miles from Chapel Hill. **Calendar:** Quarter, limited summer session. Extensive evening/early morning classes. **Microcomputers:** 16 located in libraries, classrooms, computer centers. **Special facilities:** 4-mile nature trail. **Additional facts:** Branch campus in Caswell County. Correctional education offered at Hillsborough, Yanceyville, Blanch, and Roxboro.

DEGREES OFFERED. AAS. 52 associate degrees awarded in 1992. 29% in business and management, 18% computer sciences, 43% health sciences, 10% parks/recreation, protective services, public affairs.

UNDERGRADUATE MAJORS. Accounting, business administration and management, business and management, business and office, business computer/console/peripheral equipment operation, computer programming, cosmetology, criminal justice studies, gunsmithing, legal secretary, liberal/general studies, medical secretary, nursing, secretarial and related programs, social work, taxidermy.

ACADEMIC PROGRAMS. 2-year transfer program, cooperative education, double major, dual enrollment of high school students, independent study, internships, telecourses, cross-registration. **Remedial services:** Learning center, reduced course load, remedial instruction, special counselor, tutoring. **Placement/credit:** Institutional tests. Maximum of 50% of coursework may be completed through credit by examination.

ACADEMIC REQUIREMENTS. Freshmen must earn minimum GPA of 2.0 to continue in good standing. 80% of freshmen return for sophomore year. Students must declare major on application. **Graduation requirements:** 96 hours for associate (78 in major). Most students required to take courses in English, mathematics, social sciences.

FRESHMAN ADMISSIONS. Selection criteria: Open admissions. Selective admissions for nursing based on test scores, interview and recommendations. Nursing applicants must provide health data. **Test requirements:** Comparative Guidance and Placement Test (CGP).

1992 FRESHMAN CLASS PROFILE. 206 men, 166 women enrolled. **Characteristics:** 95% from in state, 100% commute, 45% have minority backgrounds. Average age is 24.

FALL-TERM APPLICATIONS. No fee. No closing date; applicants notified on a rolling basis. Interview required for nursing applicants. Deferred admission available. Certain certificate programs do not require high school diploma.

STUDENT LIFE. Activities: Student government, student newspaper, Phi Theta Kappa, Student Nursing Association, gunsmithing club, taxidermy club, cosmetology club.

ATHLETICS. Intramural: Basketball, softball, volleyball.

STUDENT SERVICES. Aptitude testing, career counseling, freshman orientation, on-campus day care, personal counseling, placement service for graduates, veterans counselor, services/facilities for handicapped.

ANNUAL EXPENSES. Tuition and fees (1992-93): $575, $3,959 additional for out-of-state students. **Books and supplies:** $500. **Other expenses:** $750.

FINANCIAL AID. 50% of freshmen, 50% of continuing students receive some form of aid. 95% of grants, all loans, all jobs based on need. 245 enrolled freshmen were judged to have need, 160 were offered aid. **Aid applications:** No closing date; priority given to applications received by April 15; applicants notified on a rolling basis; must reply within 2 weeks.

ADDRESS/TELEPHONE. Lizzie Hooker, Coordinator Admissions, Piedmont Community College, PO Box 1197, 1715 College Drive, Roxboro, NC 27573-1197. (919) 599-1181. Fax: (919) 597-3817.

Pitt Community College
Greenville, North Carolina — CB code: 5556

2-year public community college, coed. Founded in 1961. **Accreditation:** Regional. **Undergraduate enrollment:** 867 men, 1,257 women full time; 901 men, 1,440 women part time. **Faculty:** 233 total (113 full time), 1 with doctorate or other terminal degree. **Location:** Rural campus in large town; 85 miles from Raleigh. **Calendar:** Quarter, limited summer session. Extensive evening/early morning classes. **Microcomputers:** 45 located in computer centers.

DEGREES OFFERED. AA, AAS. 322 associate degrees awarded in 1992. 17% in business and management, 14% business/office and marketing/distribution, 20% health sciences, 23% allied health, 8% law.

UNDERGRADUATE MAJORS. Accounting, architectural technologies, architecture, business administration and management, business data programming, commercial art, construction, early childhood education, electronic technology, elementary education, finance, graphic arts technology, industrial technology, law enforcement and corrections technologies, legal assistant/paralegal, liberal/general studies, manufacturing technology, marketing and distribution, medical assistant, medical records technology, medical secretary, mental health/human services, nursing, occupational therapy assistant, personnel management, radiograph medical technology, respiratory therapy technology, secondary education, secretarial and related programs, trade and industrial supervision and management, ultrasound technology.

ACADEMIC PROGRAMS. 2-year transfer program, cooperative education, double major, dual enrollment of high school students, internships, telecourses. **Remedial services:** Learning center, preadmission summer program, reduced course load, remedial instruction, tutoring. **Placement/credit:** AP, CLEP General, institutional tests.

ACADEMIC REQUIREMENTS. Freshmen must earn minimum GPA of 2.0 to continue in good standing. 50% of freshmen return for sophomore year. Students must declare major on application. **Graduation requirements:** 97 hours for associate. Most students required to take courses in English, mathematics, social sciences.

FRESHMAN ADMISSIONS. Selection criteria: Open admissions. Special admissions requirements for allied health programs.

1992 FRESHMAN CLASS PROFILE. 162 men, 175 women enrolled. **Characteristics:** 99% from in state, 100% commute, 39% have minority backgrounds. Average age is 22.

FALL-TERM APPLICATIONS. No fee. No closing date; applicants notified on a rolling basis. Placement interview required for vocational and technical students.

STUDENT LIFE. Activities: Student government.

ATHLETICS. NJCAA. **Intercollegiate:** Basketball M, golf M, softball, tennis, volleyball.

STUDENT SERVICES. Aptitude testing, career counseling, employment service for undergraduates, personal counseling, placement service for graduates, veterans counselor, services/facilities for handicapped.

ANNUAL EXPENSES. Tuition and fees (projected): $575, $3,959 additional for out-of-state students. **Books and supplies:** $600. **Other expenses:** $400.

FINANCIAL AID. 22% of continuing students receive some form of aid. 94% of grants, 95% of loans, all jobs based on need. 1,200 enrolled freshmen were judged to have need, all were offered aid. Academic scholarships available. **Aid applications:** Closing date August 24; priority given to applications received by May 1; applicants notified on a rolling basis beginning on or about June 1; must reply by registration.

ADDRESS/TELEPHONE. Kathy O. Kinlaw, Registrar, Pitt Community College, PO Drawer 7007, Greenville, NC 27835-7007. (919) 355-4245. Fax: (919) 355-4401.

Queens College
Charlotte, North Carolina — CB code: 5560

Admissions: 80% of applicants accepted
Based on: ••• School record, test scores
•• Essay, interview, recommendations
• Activities, special talents
Completion: 94% of freshmen end year in good standing
53% graduate, 23% of these enter graduate study

4-year private liberal arts college, coed, affiliated with Presbyterian Church (USA). Founded in 1857. **Accreditation:** Regional. **Undergraduate enrollment:** 169 men, 447 women full time; 132 men, 538 women part time. **Graduate enrollment:** 39 men, 36 women full time; 95 men, 146 women part time. **Faculty:** 115 total (73 full time), 84 with doctorates or other terminal degrees. **Location:** Suburban campus in large city. **Calendar:** Semester, extensive summer session. Saturday and extensive evening/early morning classes. **Microcomputers:** 84 located in dormitories, libraries, classrooms, computer centers. **Special facilities:** 2 art galleries, rare books museum, recital hall. **Additional facts:** Internships and career opportunities available in Charlotte.

DEGREES OFFERED. BA, BS, MBA, MEd. 198 bachelor's degrees awarded in 1992. 23% in business and management, 17% communications, 8% education, 13% health sciences, 11% letters/literature, 9% life sciences, 6% social sciences. Graduate degrees offered in 3 major fields of study.

UNDERGRADUATE MAJORS. Accounting, advertising, art history, biochemistry, biology, business administration and management, business and management, communications, computer and information sciences, dramatic arts, early childhood education, education, elementary education, English, English literature, European studies, fine arts, French, history, international business management, journalism, mathematics, mathematics computer science, music, music education, music performance, music therapy, nursing, philosophy, political science and government, psychology, public relations, religion, secondary education, sociology, Spanish, studio art.

ACADEMIC PROGRAMS. Accelerated program, double major, dual enrollment of high school students, honors program, independent study, internships, study abroad, teacher preparation, visiting/exchange student program, Washington semester, cross-registration, Harvard Model U.N; combined bachelor's/graduate program in business administration. **Remedial services:** Reduced course load, remedial instruction, special counselor, tutoring, study skills/time management course. **Placement/credit:** AP, CLEP Subject, institutional tests; 43 credit hours maximum for bachelor's degree.

ACADEMIC REQUIREMENTS. Freshmen must earn minimum GPA of 1.8 to continue in good standing. 78% of freshmen return for sophomore year. Students must declare major by end of second year. **Graduation requirements:** 122 hours for bachelor's (30 in major). Most students required to take courses in arts/fine arts, English, foreign languages, history, humanities, mathematics, philosophy/religion, biological/physical sciences, social sciences. **Postgraduate studies:** 2% enter law school, 2% enter medical school, 7% enter MBA programs, 12% enter other graduate study. **Additional information:** Prelaw and premedical programs offered.

FRESHMAN ADMISSIONS. Selection criteria: High school courses taken, school achievement record, class rank and test scores are important. Extracurricular activities, recommendations, interview, highly considered. **High school preparation:** 16 units required. Required units include biological science 1, English 4, foreign language 2, mathematics 3 and social science 2. Chemistry recommended for nursing majors. **Test requirements:** SAT or ACT (SAT preferred).

1992 FRESHMAN CLASS PROFILE. 90 men applied, 72 accepted, 33 enrolled; 321 women applied, 256 accepted, 138 enrolled. 64% had high school GPA of 3.0 or higher, 36% between 2.0 and 2.99. 35% were in top tenth and 60% were in top quarter of graduating class. **Academic background:** Mid 50% of enrolled freshmen had SAT-V between 430-560, SAT-M between 470-570; ACT composite between 22-26. 91% submitted SAT scores, 9% submitted ACT scores. **Characteristics:** 31% from in state, 87% live in college housing, 15% have minority backgrounds, 7% are foreign students, 50% join fraternities/sororities. Average age is 19.

FALL-TERM APPLICATIONS. $25 fee, may be waived for applicants with need. No closing date; applicants notified on a rolling basis; must reply by May 1 or within 3 weeks if notified thereafter. Audition required for music, music therapist, drama applicants. Essay required. Interview recommended. Portfolio recommended for art applicants. CRDA. Deferred and early admission available. English composition and mathematics level 1 achievement tests recommended.

STUDENT LIFE. Housing: Dormitories (men, women, coed). **Activities:** Student government, film, magazine, student newspaper, yearbook, choral groups, dance, drama, jazz band, music ensembles, musical theater, symphony orchestra, fraternities, sororities, Students for Black Awareness, Fellowship of Christian Athletes, Organization Against Social Injustice and Suffering, Amnesty International, College Republicans, College Democrats, International Club, North Carolina student legislature, Justinian Society (pre-law).

ATHLETICS. NCAA. **Intercollegiate:** Basketball, golf M, soccer, softball W, tennis, volleyball W. **Intramural:** Badminton, basketball, bowling, cross-country, golf, gymnastics, horseback riding, sailing, skiing, soccer, softball, swimming, table tennis, tennis, volleyball.

STUDENT SERVICES. Aptitude testing, career counseling, employment service for undergraduates, freshman orientation, health services, personal counseling, placement service for graduates, special adviser for adult students, services/facilities for handicapped.

ANNUAL EXPENSES. Tuition and fees: $10,400. **Room and board:** $4,550. **Books and supplies:** $550. **Other expenses:** $900.

FINANCIAL AID. 90% of freshmen, 75% of continuing students receive some form of aid. 49% of grants, 80% of loans, 95% of jobs based on need. 102 enrolled freshmen were judged to have need, all were offered aid. Academic, music/drama, art, athletic, leadership, religious affiliation, minority scholarships available. **Aid applications:** No closing date; priority given to applications received by March 1; applicants notified on a rolling basis beginning on or about April 1; must reply by May 1 or within 3 weeks if notified thereafter.

ADDRESS/TELEPHONE. Dr. Steve Cloniger, Vice President for Enrollment Management, Queens College, 1900 Selwyn Avenue, Charlotte, NC 28274. (704) 337-2212. (800) 849-0202. Fax: (704) 337-2503.

Randolph Community College
Asheboro, North Carolina — CB code: 5585

2-year public technical college, coed. Founded in 1962. **Accreditation:** Regional. **Undergraduate enrollment:** 312 men, 377 women full time; 339 men, 520 women part time. **Faculty:** 70 total (45 full time), 1 with doctorate or other terminal degree. **Location:** Rural campus in large town; 65 miles from Charlotte. **Calendar:** Quarter. Extensive evening/early morning classes. **Microcomputers:** Located in libraries.

DEGREES OFFERED. AAS. 173 associate degrees awarded in 1992.

UNDERGRADUATE MAJORS. Accounting, business administration and management, commercial art, computer programming, electronic technology, horticulture, interior design, liberal/general studies, nursing, photographic technology, secretarial and related programs.

ACADEMIC PROGRAMS. 2-year transfer program, double major, internships. **Remedial services:** Learning center, remedial instruction, special counselor, tutoring.

ACADEMIC REQUIREMENTS. Students must declare major on application. **Graduation requirements:** 96 hours for associate. Most students required to take courses in English, mathematics, biological/physical sciences, social sciences.

FRESHMAN ADMISSIONS. Selection criteria: Open admissions. Selective admissions to nursing program based primarily on test scores. **Test requirements:** California Achievement Test required for placement.

1992 FRESHMAN CLASS PROFILE. 270 men and women enrolled. **Characteristics:** 98% from in state, 100% commute, 7% have minority backgrounds. Average age is 28.

FALL-TERM APPLICATIONS. No fee. No closing date; applicants notified on a rolling basis. Deferred admission available.

STUDENT LIFE. Activities: Student government, student newspaper.

STUDENT SERVICES. Aptitude testing, career counseling, employment service for undergraduates, personal counseling, placement service for graduates, special adviser for adult students, veterans counselor, services/facilities for handicapped.

ANNUAL EXPENSES. Tuition and fees (1992-93): $579, $3,959 additional for out-of-state students. **Books and supplies:** $800. **Other expenses:** $881.

FINANCIAL AID. 5% of freshmen, 20% of continuing students receive some form of aid. Grants, loans, jobs available. Academic scholarships available. **Aid applications:** Closing date May 1; applicants notified on or about June 15; must reply by July 15.

ADDRESS/TELEPHONE. O'Dene Suggs, Admissions Officer/Executive Secretary, Randolph Community College, PO Box 1009, Asheboro, NC 27204-1009. (919) 629-1471. Fax: (919) 629-4695.

Richmond Community College
Hamlet, North Carolina — CB code: 5588

2-year public community college, coed. Founded in 1964. **Accreditation:** Regional. **Undergraduate enrollment:** 197 men, 435 women full time; 159 men, 300 women part time. **Faculty:** 72 total (33 full time). **Location:** Rural campus in small town; 75 miles from Charlotte. **Calendar:** Quarter, limited summer session. Extensive evening/early morning classes. **Microcomputers:** 125 located in classrooms, computer centers.

DEGREES OFFERED. AA, AAS. 101 associate degrees awarded in 1992. 28% in business and management, 5% business/office and marketing/distribution, 7% computer sciences, 10% engineering technologies, 17% health sciences, 8% multi/interdisciplinary studies, 25% parks/recreation, protective services, public affairs.

UNDERGRADUATE MAJORS. Accounting, business and management, business and office, business data processing and related programs, business data programming, computer programming, criminal justice technology, education, electrical/electronics/communications engineering, law enforcement and corrections technologies, liberal/general studies, mechanical design technology, nursing, secretarial and related programs, social work.

ACADEMIC PROGRAMS. 2-year transfer program, cooperative education, double major, dual enrollment of high school students, independent study, student-designed major. **Remedial services:** Learning center, reduced course load, remedial instruction, tutoring. **Placement/credit:** Institutional tests; 15 credit hours maximum for associate degree.

ACADEMIC REQUIREMENTS. Freshmen must earn minimum GPA of 2.0 to continue in good standing. 50% of freshmen return for sophomore year. **Graduation requirements:** 115 hours for associate (100 in major). Most students required to take courses in computer science, English, mathematics, social sciences.

FRESHMAN ADMISSIONS. Selection criteria: Open admissions. Selective admissions to nursing program based on academic record and admission test scores. High school diploma not required for vocational programs.

1992 FRESHMAN CLASS PROFILE. 75 men, 87 women enrolled. **Characteristics:** 98% from in state, 100% commute, 30% have minority backgrounds. Average age is 20.

FALL-TERM APPLICATIONS. No fee. Closing date September 1; priority given to applications received by August 1; applicants notified on a rolling basis. Interview required for nursing applicants. Placement and counseling interview required for all other applicants.

STUDENT LIFE. Activities: Student government, student newspaper.

STUDENT SERVICES. Aptitude testing, career counseling, employment service for undergraduates, freshman orientation, health services, personal counseling, placement service for graduates, veterans counselor, services/facilities for handicapped.

ANNUAL EXPENSES. Tuition and fees (1992-93): $584, $3,959 additional for out-of-state students. **Books and supplies:** $450. **Other expenses:** $700.

FINANCIAL AID. 65% of freshmen, 60% of continuing students receive some form of aid. 87% of grants, 92% of loans, 81% of jobs based on need. Academic, leadership scholarships available. **Aid applications:** No closing date; priority given to applications received by August 1; applicants notified on a rolling basis beginning on or about August 1; must reply within 2 weeks.

ADDRESS/TELEPHONE. Teri P. Jacobs, Director of Admissions and Registrar, Richmond Community College, PO Box 1189, Hamlet, NC 28345. (919) 582-7120. Fax: (919) 582-7028.

Roanoke Bible College
Elizabeth City, North Carolina CB code: 5597

Admissions: 73% of applicants accepted
Based on:
••• Religious affiliation/commitment
•• Activities, essay, recommendations, school record, special talents, test scores
• Interview
Completion: 75% of freshmen end year in good standing
30% graduate, 10% of these enter graduate study

4-year private Bible college, coed, affiliated with Church of Christ. Founded in 1948. **Undergraduate enrollment:** 54 men, 42 women full time; 17 men, 13 women part time. **Faculty:** 14 total (7 full time), 1 with doctorate or other terminal degree. **Location:** Suburban campus in large town; 50 miles from Norfolk, Virginia. **Calendar:** Semester. **Microcomputers:** 5 located in dormitories, libraries.

DEGREES OFFERED. AAS, BA, BS. 9 associate degrees awarded in 1992. 100% in philosophy, religion, theology. 12 bachelor's degrees awarded. 100% in philosophy, religion, theology.

UNDERGRADUATE MAJORS. Associate: Bible studies. **Bachelor's:** Missionary studies, religious education, theological studies.

ACADEMIC PROGRAMS. Double major, internships, cross-registration. **Remedial services:** Learning center, reduced course load, remedial instruction. **Placement/credit:** AP, CLEP General and Subject; 8 credit hours maximum for associate degree; 16 credit hours maximum for bachelor's degree.

ACADEMIC REQUIREMENTS. Freshmen must earn minimum GPA of 1.8 to continue in good standing. 61% of freshmen return for sophomore year. Students must declare major by end of second year. **Graduation requirements:** 64 hours for associate (23 in major), 128 hours for bachelor's (42 in major). Most students required to take courses in English, history, humanities, philosophy/religion, social sciences. **Postgraduate studies:** 12% from 2-year programs enter 4-year programs. 10% enter other graduate study.

FRESHMAN ADMISSIONS. Selection criteria: Evidence of Christian character, school achievement record, test scores, school and community activities, recommendations important. **Test requirements:** SAT or ACT (SAT preferred); score report by August 5.

1992 FRESHMAN CLASS PROFILE. 36 men applied, 30 accepted, 23 enrolled; 57 women applied, 38 accepted, 18 enrolled. 24% had high school GPA of 3.0 or higher, 57% between 2.0 and 2.99. 30% were in top tenth and 39% were in top quarter of graduating class. **Academic background:** Mid 50% of enrolled freshmen had SAT-V between 370-410, SAT-M between 460-470. 55% submitted SAT scores. **Characteristics:** 85% live in college housing, 7% have minority backgrounds. Average age is 20.

FALL-TERM APPLICATIONS. $25 fee, may be waived for applicants with need. Closing date August 5; priority given to applications received by May 15; applicants notified on a rolling basis beginning on or about September 1. Interview recommended for borderline applicants. Deferred and early admission available.

STUDENT LIFE. Housing: Dormitories (men, women); apartment housing available. **Activities:** Student government, yearbook, choral groups, drama, music ensembles. **Additional information:** All students have opportunity to travel in choral group throughout country.

ATHLETICS. Intercollegiate: Basketball M. **Intramural:** Basketball, softball, tennis, track and field, volleyball.

STUDENT SERVICES. Career counseling, employment service for undergraduates, freshman orientation, personal counseling, placement service for graduates, services/facilities for handicapped.

ANNUAL EXPENSES. Tuition and fees (1992-93): $2,964. **Room and board:** $2,440. **Books and supplies:** $250. **Other expenses:** $250.

FINANCIAL AID. 68% of freshmen, 68% of continuing students receive some form of aid. All grants based on need. All jobs based on criteria other than need. 24 enrolled freshmen were judged to have need, all were offered aid. Academic, music/drama, leadership scholarships available. **Aid applications:** Closing date May 1; priority given to applications received by March 1; applicants notified on or about June 15; must reply by July 15.

ADDRESS/TELEPHONE. Chuck Holton, Director of Admissions, Roanoke Bible College, 714 First Street, Elizabeth City, NC 27909. (919) 338-5191. Fax: (919) 338-0801.

Roanoke-Chowan Community College
Ahoskie, North Carolina CB code: 5564

2-year public community college, coed. Founded in 1967. **Accreditation:** Regional. **Undergraduate enrollment:** 125 men, 369 women full time; 118 men, 262 women part time. **Faculty:** 66 total (27 full time). **Location:** Rural campus in small town; 60 miles from Greenville, 65 miles from Norfolk, Virginia. **Calendar:** Quarter, limited summer session. Extensive evening/early morning classes. **Microcomputers:** 100 located in libraries, classrooms, computer centers.

DEGREES OFFERED. AAS. 55 associate degrees awarded in 1992. 16% in business and management, 16% business/office and marketing/distribution, 7% computer sciences, 11% teacher education, 35% allied health, 9% parks/recreation, protective services, public affairs.

UNDERGRADUATE MAJORS. Architectural technologies, business administration and management, business and office, business data programming, computer programming, criminal justice technology, drafting, drug and alcohol technology, early childhood education, liberal/general studies, nursing, practical nursing, radiograph medical technology, rehabilitation counseling/services, secretarial and related programs, special education, teacher aide.

ACADEMIC PROGRAMS. 2-year transfer program, cooperative education, dual enrollment of high school students, independent study, internships, telecourses. **Remedial services:** Learning center, reduced course load, remedial instruction, special counselor, tutoring. **Placement/credit:** Institutional tests.

ACADEMIC REQUIREMENTS. Freshmen must earn minimum GPA of 1.7 to continue in good standing. 60% of freshmen return for sophomore year. Students must declare major by end of first year. **Graduation requirements:** 101 hours for associate (72 in major). Most students required to take courses in English, mathematics.

FRESHMAN ADMISSIONS. Selection criteria: Open admissions. Selective admissions to nursing program based on interview and test scores.

1992 FRESHMAN CLASS PROFILE. 47 men, 64 women enrolled. **Characteristics:** 100% from in state, 100% commute, 63% have minority backgrounds. Average age is 20.

FALL-TERM APPLICATIONS. No fee. No closing date; applicants notified on a rolling basis beginning on or about March 1. Interview required for nursing applicants.

STUDENT LIFE. Activities: Student government, choral groups.

ATHLETICS. Intramural: Basketball, softball, volleyball.

STUDENT SERVICES. Aptitude testing, career counseling, freshman orientation, on-campus day care, personal counseling, placement service for graduates, veterans counselor, services/facilities for handicapped.

ANNUAL EXPENSES. Tuition and fees (1992-93): $581, $3,959 additional for out-of-state students. **Books and supplies:** $360. **Other expenses:** $150.

FINANCIAL AID. 68% of freshmen, 38% of continuing students receive some form of aid. 97% of grants, 93% of loans, 94% of jobs based on need. 101 enrolled freshmen were judged to have need, all were offered aid. Academic, state/district residency, leadership scholarships available. **Aid applications:** No closing date; applicants notified on a rolling basis beginning on or about July 1.

ADDRESS/TELEPHONE. Sandra Copeland, Admissions Counselor, Roanoke-Chowan Community College, Route 2, Box 46-A, Ahoskie, NC 27910-9522. (919) 332-5921. Fax: (919) 332-2210.

Robeson Community College
Lumberton, North Carolina CB code: 5594

2-year public community, technical college, coed. Founded in 1965. **Accreditation:** Regional. **Undergraduate enrollment:** 261 men, 447 women full time; 182 men, 528 women part time. **Faculty:** 100 total (49 full time), 2 with doctorates or other terminal degrees. **Location:** Rural campus in large town; 30 miles from Fayetteville. **Calendar:** Quarter. Extensive evening/early morning classes. **Microcomputers:** 100 located in classrooms.

DEGREES OFFERED. AAS. 80 associate degrees awarded in 1992. 30% in business and management, 35% business/office and marketing/distribution, 15% computer sciences, 20% allied health.

UNDERGRADUATE MAJORS. Accounting, business administration and management, business and office, business computer/console/peripheral equipment operation, business data processing and related programs, computer programming, criminal justice technology, finance, industrial technology, liberal/general studies, marketing and distribution, nursing, respiratory therapy, respiratory therapy technology, secretarial and related programs.

ACADEMIC PROGRAMS. 2-year transfer program, double major, dual enrollment of high school students. **Remedial services:** Learning center, reduced course load, remedial instruction, special counselor, tutoring. **Placement/credit:** Institutional tests; 40 credit hours maximum for associate degree.

ACADEMIC REQUIREMENTS. Freshmen must earn minimum GPA of 2.0 to continue in good standing. 50% of freshmen return for sophomore year. Students must declare major on enrollment. **Graduation requirements:**

120 hours for associate. Most students required to take courses in computer science, English, humanities, mathematics, social sciences.

FRESHMAN ADMISSIONS. Selection criteria: Open admissions.

1992 FRESHMAN CLASS PROFILE. 214 men, 324 women enrolled. 1% had high school GPA of 3.0 or higher, 20% between 2.0 and 2.99. 25% were in top quarter of graduating class. **Characteristics:** 98% from in state, 100% commute, 61% have minority backgrounds. Average age is 21.

FALL-TERM APPLICATIONS. No fee. Closing date September 1; priority given to applications received by June 1; applicants notified on a rolling basis; must reply by registration. Interview recommended.

STUDENT LIFE. Activities: Student government, magazine, student newspaper, choral groups.

STUDENT SERVICES. Aptitude testing, career counseling, employment service for undergraduates, freshman orientation, health services, personal counseling, placement service for graduates, special adviser for adult students, veterans counselor, services/facilities for handicapped.

ANNUAL EXPENSES. Tuition and fees (1992-93): $575, $3,959 additional for out-of-state students. **Books and supplies:** $600. **Other expenses:** $75.

FINANCIAL AID. 62% of freshmen, 85% of continuing students receive some form of aid. All aid based on need. **Aid applications:** No closing date; priority given to applications received by May 15; applicants notified on a rolling basis beginning on or about July 31.

ADDRESS/TELEPHONE. Judith Revels, Director of Admissions, Robeson Community College, PO Box 1420, Lumberton, NC 28359. (919) 738-7101. Fax: (919) 671-4143.

Rockingham Community College
Wentworth, North Carolina CB code: 5582

2-year public community college, coed. Founded in 1963. **Accreditation:** Regional. **Undergraduate enrollment:** 1,001 men and women full time; 1,005 men and women part time. **Faculty:** 153 total (53 full time), 3 with doctorates or other terminal degrees. **Location:** Rural campus in rural community; 20 miles from Greensboro. **Calendar:** Quarter, extensive summer session. Saturday and extensive evening/early morning classes. **Microcomputers:** 50 located in libraries, classrooms, computer centers. **Special facilities:** Nature preserves and lakes; local historical collection.

DEGREES OFFERED. AA, AS, AAS. 171 associate degrees awarded in 1992.

UNDERGRADUATE MAJORS. Accounting, applied science, business administration and management, business and office, business computer/console/peripheral equipment operation, criminal justice technology, electromechanical technology, engineering, fine arts, law enforcement and corrections, legal assistant/paralegal, legal secretary, liberal/general studies, management information systems, medical records technology, medical secretary, microcomputer software, nursing, office supervision and management, personnel management, physical sciences, predentistry, preengineering, prelaw, premedicine, prepharmacy, preveterinary, secretarial and related programs, tourism, woodworking.

ACADEMIC PROGRAMS. 2-year transfer program, cooperative education, dual enrollment of high school students, independent study, student-designed major, preengineering program leading to transfer to North Carolina State University, North Carolina Agricultural and Technical State University, or University of North Carolina at Charlotte. **Remedial services:** Learning center, reduced course load, remedial instruction, special counselor, tutoring. **Placement/credit:** AP, CLEP Subject, institutional tests; 45 credit hours maximum for associate degree.

ACADEMIC REQUIREMENTS. Freshmen must earn minimum GPA of 1.75 to continue in good standing. Students must declare major on application. **Graduation requirements:** 96 hours for associate. Most students required to take courses in computer science, English, mathematics, biological/physical sciences, social sciences.

FRESHMAN ADMISSIONS. Selection criteria: Open admissions. Selective admissions to nursing and electromechanical technology programs. Nursing program requires 1 unit each of biology, algebra and chemistry. Electromechanical program requires preparation for college algebra. All business programs require algebra preparation at various levels. **Additional information:** Admissions interviewer arranges academic sequence and load to ensure success. Early identification of potential dropouts and intervention program available.

1992 FRESHMAN CLASS PROFILE. 568 men and women enrolled. **Characteristics:** 90% from in state, 100% commute, 22% have minority backgrounds, 1% are foreign students. Average age is 29.

FALL-TERM APPLICATIONS. No fee. No closing date; applicants notified on a rolling basis. Interview required for nursing applicants. Early admission available.

STUDENT LIFE. Activities: Student government, student newspaper, Phi Theta Kappa, nature study, astronomy, and science fiction clubs.

ATHLETICS. Intramural: Basketball, golf, softball, table tennis, tennis, volleyball.

STUDENT SERVICES. Aptitude testing, career counseling, employment service for undergraduates, on-campus day care, personal counseling, placement service for graduates, services/facilities for handicapped.

ANNUAL EXPENSES. Tuition and fees (1992-93): $584, $3,959 additional for out-of-state students. **Books and supplies:** $450. **Other expenses:** $1,000.

FINANCIAL AID. 25% of freshmen, 35% of continuing students receive some form of aid. 98% of grants, all loans, 67% of jobs based on need. 130 enrolled freshmen were judged to have need, all were offered aid. Academic, state/district residency scholarships available. **Aid applications:** No closing date; priority given to applications received by April 15; applicants notified on a rolling basis beginning on or about May 30; must reply within 10 days.

ADDRESS/TELEPHONE. Hal R. Griffin, Director of Admissions, Records, and Recruitment, Rockingham Community College, PO Box 38, Wentworth, NC 27375-0038. (919) 342-4261.

Rowan-Cabarrus Community College
Salisbury, North Carolina CB code: 5589

2-year public community, technical college, coed. Founded in 1961. **Accreditation:** Regional. **Undergraduate enrollment:** 276 men, 558 women full time; 398 men, 647 women part time. **Faculty:** 89 total, 1 with doctorate or other terminal degree. **Location:** Suburban campus in large town; 40 miles from Charlotte. **Calendar:** Quarter, extensive summer session. Extensive evening/early morning classes. **Microcomputers:** Located in libraries, classrooms, computer centers.

DEGREES OFFERED. AA, AAS. 140 associate degrees awarded in 1992. 5% in business and management, 50% business/office and marketing/distribution, 10% teacher education, 10% engineering technologies, 20% allied health, 5% parks/recreation, protective services, public affairs.

UNDERGRADUATE MAJORS. Accounting, business administration and management, business and office, business data processing and related programs, computer programming, criminal justice studies, drafting, drafting and design technology, early childhood education, electronic technology, engineering and engineering-related technologies, industrial technology, law enforcement and corrections technologies, liberal/general studies, manufacturing technology, marketing and distribution, medical secretary, nursing, radiograph medical technology, secretarial and related programs.

ACADEMIC PROGRAMS. 2-year transfer program, dual enrollment of high school students, telecourses. **Remedial services:** Learning center, reduced course load, remedial instruction, tutoring. **Placement/credit:** AP, CLEP General and Subject, institutional tests; 75 credit hours maximum for associate degree.

ACADEMIC REQUIREMENTS. Freshmen must earn minimum GPA of 2.0 to continue in good standing. 50% of freshmen return for sophomore year. Students must declare major on enrollment. **Graduation requirements:** 110 hours for associate. Most students required to take courses in English, mathematics, social sciences.

FRESHMAN ADMISSIONS. Selection criteria: Open admissions. Selective admissions to allied health programs.

1992 FRESHMAN CLASS PROFILE. 178 men, 244 women enrolled. **Characteristics:** 99% from in state, 100% commute, 17% have minority backgrounds. Average age is 29.

FALL-TERM APPLICATIONS. No fee. No closing date; applicants notified on a rolling basis. Interview required for allied health program applicants.

STUDENT LIFE. Activities: Student government, yearbook.

ATHLETICS. Intramural: Softball.

STUDENT SERVICES. Aptitude testing, career counseling, employment service for undergraduates, freshman orientation, on-campus day care, personal counseling, placement service for graduates, veterans counselor, services/facilities for handicapped.

ANNUAL EXPENSES. Tuition and fees (1992-93): $581, $3,959 additional for out-of-state students. **Books and supplies:** $430. **Other expenses:** $525.

FINANCIAL AID. 40% of freshmen, 60% of continuing students receive some form of aid. 96% of grants, all jobs based on need. 199 enrolled freshmen were judged to have need, 170 were offered aid. Academic, state/district residency scholarships available. **Aid applications:** No closing date; priority given to applications received by August 1; applicants notified on a rolling basis beginning on or about June 1; must reply within 2 weeks.

ADDRESS/TELEPHONE. Eddie Myers, Dir of Admissions, Rowan-Cabarrus Community College, PO Box 1595, Salisbury, NC 28145-1595. (704) 637-0760. Fax: (704) 633-6804.

St. Andrews Presbyterian College
Laurinburg, North Carolina CB code: 5214

Admissions: 95% of applicants accepted
Based on: ••• School record, test scores
•• Essay, interview, recommendations
• Activities, special talents
Completion: 90% of freshmen end year in good standing
55% graduate

4-year private liberal arts college, coed, affiliated with Presbyterian Church (USA). Founded in 1958. **Accreditation:** Regional. **Undergraduate enrollment:** 302 men, 315 women full time; 22 men, 23 women part time. **Faculty:** 66 total (42 full time), 38 with doctorates or other terminal degrees. **Location:** Suburban campus in large town; 40 miles from Fayetteville, 20 miles From Pinehurst. **Calendar:** 4-1-4, limited summer session. **Microcomputers:** 60 located in libraries, computer centers. **Special facilities:** Science laboratory with 3 electron microscopes, psychology laboratory complex, equestrian facilities, special support systems for physically disabled students, student art gallery, 640-acre nature preserve.

DEGREES OFFERED. BA, BS. 175 bachelor's degrees awarded in 1992. 30% in business and management, 5% education, 10% teacher education, 16% letters/literature, 17% life sciences, 14% psychology.

UNDERGRADUATE MAJORS. Allied health, art education, art history, arts management, Asian studies, biochemistry, biological and physical sciences, biology, business administration and management, business and management, business economics, chemistry, Chinese, communications, comparative literature, computer graphics, computer mathematics, creative writing, dramatic arts, education, elementary education, English, fine arts, foreign languages (multiple emphasis), foreign languages education, French, German, health education, health sciences, history, humanities, humanities and social sciences, international business management, international relations, international studies, Japanese, journalism, junior high education, mathematics, mathematics education, music, music business management, music history and appreciation, music performance, philosophy, physical education, political science and government, predentistry, preengineering, prelaw, premedicine, prepharmacy, preveterinary, psychology, religion, secondary education, Southeast Asian studies, theological studies.

ACADEMIC PROGRAMS. Double major, honors program, independent study, internships, student-designed major, study abroad, teacher preparation, visiting/exchange student program, Washington semester, cross-registration, courses offered abroad during winter or summer in Britain, Greece, India, Switzerland, Venezuela, China, Hawaii, Soviet Union; exchange programs with Stirling University, Scotland and Kansai Gaidai University, Japan; study at Brunnenburg Castle, Italy, and Beijing Normal College of Foreign Languages; liberal arts/career combination in engineering. **Remedial services:** Preadmission summer program, reduced course load, special counselor, tutoring, Supplemental Writing Program. **Placement/credit:** AP, CLEP General and Subject; 32 credit hours maximum for bachelor's degree.

ACADEMIC REQUIREMENTS. Freshmen must earn minimum GPA of 1.5 to continue in good standing. 75% of freshmen return for sophomore year. Students must declare major by end of second year. **Graduation requirements:** 127 hours for bachelor's (47 in major). Most students required to take courses in English, foreign languages, history, humanities, mathematics, philosophy/religion, biological/physical sciences, social sciences. **Additional information:** Academic programs include St. Andrew's General Education (SAGE).

FRESHMAN ADMISSIONS. Selection criteria: High school GPA, test scores, curriculum, type of high school, recommendations are very important. Interview is very important for applicants not meeting criteria. **High school preparation:** 16 units recommended. Recommended units include English 4, foreign language 2, mathematics 3, social science 2 and science 3. **Test requirements:** SAT or ACT (SAT preferred); score report by August 15.

1992 FRESHMAN CLASS PROFILE. 307 men applied, 286 accepted, 85 enrolled; 323 women applied, 314 accepted, 101 enrolled. 25% had high school GPA of 3.0 or higher, 65% between 2.0 and 2.99. **Academic background:** Mid 50% of enrolled freshmen had SAT-V between 450-550, SAT-M between 460-600. 92% submitted SAT scores. **Characteristics:** 35% from in state, 96% live in college housing, 19% have minority backgrounds, 4% are foreign students. Average age is 19.

FALL-TERM APPLICATIONS. $25 fee, may be waived for applicants with need. Closing date July 1; priority given to applications received by March 1; applicants notified on a rolling basis. Interview recommended for academically weak applicants. Essay recommended. CRDA. Deferred and early admission available.

STUDENT LIFE. Housing: Dormitories (men, women, coed); handicapped housing available. Special dormitory and independent living quarters for physically disabled. **Activities:** Student government, film, magazine, radio, student newspaper, yearbook, choral groups, drama, music ensembles, musical theater, improvisational theater, College Christian Union, Black Student Union, Young Democrats, Young Republicans, history club, World Culture Club, Eco-Action.

ATHLETICS. NAIA. **Intercollegiate:** Baseball M, basketball, cross-country, golf, horseback riding, rugby M, soccer, softball W, tennis, track and field M, volleyball W. **Intramural:** Badminton, baseball, basketball, bowling, handball, horseback riding, racquetball, soccer, softball W, swimming, table tennis, tennis, volleyball.

STUDENT SERVICES. Aptitude testing, career counseling, employment service for undergraduates, freshman orientation, health services, on-campus day care, personal counseling, placement service for graduates, special adviser for adult students, services/facilities for handicapped.

ANNUAL EXPENSES. Tuition and fees (1992-93): $9,410. **Room and board:** $4,155. **Books and supplies:** $300. **Other expenses:** $350.

FINANCIAL AID. 80% of freshmen, 80% of continuing students receive some form of aid. Grants, loans, jobs available. Academic, music/drama, art, athletic, state/district residency, leadership, alumni affiliation, religious affiliation, minority scholarships available. **Aid applications:** Closing date July 1; priority given to applications received by April 1; applicants notified on a rolling basis beginning on or about April 1; must reply by May 1 or within 4 weeks if notified thereafter.

ADDRESS/TELEPHONE. Peggy Floyd, Director of Admissions, St. Andrews Presbyterian College, 1700 Dogwood Mile, Laurinburg, NC 28352-9151. (919) 276-5555. (800) 763-0198. Fax: (919) 277-5020.

St. Augustine's College
Raleigh, North Carolina CB code: 5596

Admissions: 69% of applicants accepted
Based on: ••• School record
•• Special talents
• Activities, essay, recommendations, religious affiliation/commitment, test scores
Completion: 60% of freshmen end year in good standing
45% graduate, 38% of these enter graduate study

4-year private liberal arts college, coed, affiliated with Episcopal Church. Founded in 1867. **Accreditation:** Regional. **Undergraduate enrollment:** 748 men, 1,043 women full time; 61 men, 66 women part time. **Faculty:** 120 total (98 full time). **Location:** Urban campus in small city; 170 miles from Charlotte. **Calendar:** Semester. Extensive evening/early morning classes. **Microcomputers:** Located in libraries, classrooms, campus-wide network. **Special facilities:** Art gallery.

DEGREES OFFERED. BA, BS. 208 bachelor's degrees awarded in 1992. 58% in business and management, 6% communications, 12% computer sciences, 8% teacher education, 5% health sciences, 7% mathematics, 5% psychology.

UNDERGRADUATE MAJORS. Accounting, aerospace/aeronautical/astronautical engineering, Afro-American (black) studies, agricultural engineering, allied health, biology, business administration and management, business and management, business education, chemical engineering, chemistry, civil engineering, communications, computer and information sciences, criminal justice studies, criminology, early childhood education, economics, electrical/electronics/communications engineering, elementary education, English, English education, foreign languages education, French, German, health education, history, industrial engineering, journalism, materials engineering, mathematics, mathematics education, mechanical engineering, medical laboratory technologies, music, music education, physical education, physical sciences, physics, political science and government, prelaw, premedicine, psychology, radio/television broadcasting, science education, secondary education, social science education, social sciences, social studies education, social work, sociology, Spanish, special education, urban studies.

ACADEMIC PROGRAMS. Accelerated program, cooperative education, double major, honors program, independent study, internships, study abroad, teacher preparation, cross-registration; liberal arts/career combination in engineering. **Remedial services:** Reduced course load, remedial instruction, tutoring. **ROTC:** Air Force, Army. **Placement/credit:** Institutional tests.

ACADEMIC REQUIREMENTS. Freshmen must earn minimum GPA of 2.0 to continue in good standing. 70% of freshmen return for sophomore year. Students must declare major by end of second year. **Graduation requirements:** 126 hours for bachelor's (36 in major). Most students required to take courses in computer science, English, foreign languages, history, mathematics, philosophy/religion, biological/physical sciences, social sciences. **Postgraduate studies:** 30% from 2-year programs enter 4-year programs. 1% enter law school, 1% enter medical school, 3% enter MBA programs, 33% enter other graduate study.

FRESHMAN ADMISSIONS. Selection criteria: High school record, test scores, recommendations reviewed. **High school preparation:** 16 units required; 18 recommended. Required and recommended units include biological science 2, English 4-5, foreign language 2, mathematics 2, physical science 2-3 and social science 2-4. 6 electives recommended. **Test requirements:** SAT or ACT (SAT preferred); score report by August 1.

1992 FRESHMAN CLASS PROFILE. 1,005 men applied, 714 accepted, 307 enrolled; 1,619 women applied, 1,102 accepted, 395 enrolled. 35% had high school GPA of 3.0 or higher, 45% between 2.0 and 2.99. 40%

were in top tenth and 70% were in top quarter of graduating class. **Academic background:** Mid 50% of enrolled freshmen had SAT-V between 400-600, SAT-M between 350-650. 90% submitted SAT scores. **Characteristics:** 51% from in state, 85% live in college housing, 99% have minority backgrounds, 12% are foreign students, 30% join fraternities/sororities. Average age is 18.

FALL-TERM APPLICATIONS. $10 fee. Closing date August 1; applicants notified on a rolling basis. Essay recommended.

STUDENT LIFE. Housing: Dormitories (men, women). **Activities:** Student government, film, magazine, radio, student newspaper, television, yearbook, choral groups, concert band, drama, jazz band, musical theater, pep band, fraternities, sororities, religious organizations, Greek service organizations, fellowship organizations, academic clubs.

ATHLETICS. NCAA. **Intercollegiate:** Baseball M, basketball, bowling, cross-country, fencing, golf, softball W, tennis, track and field, volleyball W. **Intramural:** Baseball M, basketball, golf M, softball W, table tennis, tennis, track and field, volleyball W, wrestling M.

STUDENT SERVICES. Career counseling, employment service for undergraduates, freshman orientation, health services, personal counseling, placement service for graduates, veterans counselor, services/facilities for handicapped.

ANNUAL EXPENSES. Tuition and fees: $5,700. **Room and board:** $3,600. **Books and supplies:** $450. **Other expenses:** $1,300.

FINANCIAL AID. 94% of freshmen, 88% of continuing students receive some form of aid. 77% of grants, 99% of loans, 78% of jobs based on need. 570 enrolled freshmen were judged to have need, all were offered aid. Academic, music/drama, athletic, state/district residency scholarships available. **Aid applications:** No closing date; priority given to applications received by March 15; applicants notified on a rolling basis beginning on or about May 1; must reply within 2 weeks.

ADDRESS/TELEPHONE. Wanzo F. Hendrix, Director of Admissions and Retention, St. Augustine's College, 1315 Oak Avenue, Raleigh, NC 27610-2298. (919) 516-4000. Fax: (919) 828-0817.

St. Mary's College
Raleigh, North Carolina — CB code: 5600

Admissions: 82% of applicants accepted
Based on:
••• School record, test scores
•• Activities, essay, interview, recommendations
• Special talents
Completion: 91% of freshmen end year in good standing
98% enter 4-year programs

2-year private junior, liberal arts college, women only, affiliated with Episcopal Church. Founded in 1842. **Accreditation:** Regional. **Undergraduate enrollment:** 390 women full time. **Faculty:** 34 total (29 full time), 12 with doctorates or other terminal degrees. **Location:** Urban campus in small city; 143 miles from Charlotte. **Calendar:** Semester, limited summer session. **Microcomputers:** 45 located in dormitories, libraries, computer centers. **Additional facts:** Intermediate college providing last 2 years of high school and first 2 years of college.

DEGREES OFFERED. AA. 110 associate degrees awarded in 1992. 100% in multi/interdisciplinary studies.

UNDERGRADUATE MAJORS. Liberal/general studies.

ACADEMIC PROGRAMS. 2-year transfer program, accelerated program, internships, study abroad, cross-registration. **Placement/credit:** AP, institutional tests; 12 credit hours maximum for associate degree.

ACADEMIC REQUIREMENTS. Freshmen must earn minimum GPA of 1.5 to continue in good standing. 68% of freshmen return for sophomore year. **Graduation requirements:** 60 hours for associate. Most students required to take courses in arts/fine arts, English, foreign languages, history, mathematics, philosophy/religion, biological/physical sciences, social sciences.

FRESHMAN ADMISSIONS. Selection criteria: High school achievement and rank, test scores, character recommendations school and community activities, and interview important. **High school preparation:** 16 units required. Required and recommended units include biological science 1, English 4, foreign language 2-3, mathematics 3, physical science 1 and social science 1. Mathematics units should include 2 algebra, 1 geometry. 1 unit of US history also required. **Test requirements:** SAT or ACT; score report by June 1.

1992 FRESHMAN CLASS PROFILE. 341 women applied, 281 accepted, 207 enrolled. 25% had high school GPA of 3.0 or higher, 75% between 2.0 and 2.99. **Academic background:** Mid 50% of enrolled freshmen had SAT-V between 340-460, SAT-M between 390-490. 98% submitted SAT scores. **Characteristics:** 61% from in state, 90% live in college housing, 2% have minority backgrounds, 8% are foreign students. Average age is 18.

FALL-TERM APPLICATIONS. $25 fee, may be waived for applicants with need. No closing date; priority given to applications received by February 1; applicants notified on a rolling basis beginning on or about October 1; must reply within 2 weeks. Interview required. Essay required. Deferred and early admission available.

STUDENT LIFE. Housing: Dormitories (women). **Activities:** Student government, magazine, student newspaper, yearbook, student handbook, choral groups, dance, drama, music ensembles, musical theater, mime, synchronized swimming, YWCA, Altar Guild, Acolytes (church ushers), Vestry (church committee), Lay Readers, photography club, environmental club. **Additional information:** Religious observance required.

ATHLETICS. Intercollegiate: Tennis. **Intramural:** Archery, badminton, bowling, cross-country, golf, horseback riding, swimming, tennis, volleyball.

STUDENT SERVICES. Aptitude testing, career counseling, employment service for undergraduates, freshman orientation, health services, personal counseling, services/facilities for handicapped.

ANNUAL EXPENSES. Tuition and fees: $6,780. **Room and board:** $5,835. **Books and supplies:** $600. **Other expenses:** $1,400.

FINANCIAL AID. 33% of freshmen, 48% of continuing students receive some form of aid. 69% of grants, all loans, all jobs based on need. 30 enrolled freshmen were judged to have need, all were offered aid. Academic, music/drama, art, leadership, alumni affiliation, religious affiliation scholarships available. **Aid applications:** No closing date; priority given to applications received by April 1; applicants notified on a rolling basis beginning on or about April 15; must reply within 2 weeks.

ADDRESS/TELEPHONE. Jennette C. Herbert, Director of Admissions, St. Mary's College, 900 Hillsborough Street, Raleigh, NC 27603-1689. (919) 839-4100. Fax: (919) 832-4831.

Salem College
Winston-Salem, North Carolina — CB code: 5607

Admissions: 90% of applicants accepted
Based on:
••• Essay, school record
•• Activities, interview, recommendations, test scores
• Special talents
Completion: 98% of freshmen end year in good standing
64% graduate, 16% of these enter graduate study

4-year private liberal arts college, women only, affiliated with Moravian Church in America. Founded in 1772. **Accreditation:** Regional. **Undergraduate enrollment:** 3 men, 440 women full time; 50 men, 212 women part time. **Graduate enrollment:** 2 women full time; 3 men, 82 women part time. **Faculty:** 72 total (47 full time), 45 with doctorates or other terminal degrees. **Location:** Urban campus in small city. **Calendar:** 4-1-4, limited summer session. **Microcomputers:** 52 located in libraries, classrooms, computer centers. **Special facilities:** School of music. **Additional facts:** Male students may enroll in evening program only and may not reside at the college.

DEGREES OFFERED. BA, BS, MEd. 130 bachelor's degrees awarded in 1992. 7% in architecture and environmental design, 12% business and management, 25% communications, 7% teacher education, 9% languages, 10% letters/literature, 6% life sciences, 6% psychology, 10% social sciences. Graduate degrees offered in 3 major fields of study.

UNDERGRADUATE MAJORS. Accounting, American studies, art education, art history, arts management, biology, business administration and management, business and management, business economics, chemistry, clinical laboratory science, communications, economics, education, education of the emotionally handicapped, engineering, English, foreign languages education, French, German, health sciences, history, interior design, international business management, international relations, international studies, junior high education, management information systems, marketing management, mathematics, medical laboratory technologies, music, music business management, music education, music performance, philosophy, political science and government, predentistry, prelaw, premedicine, prepharmacy, preveterinary, psychology, reading education, religion, secondary education, sociology, Spanish, special education, studio art.

ACADEMIC PROGRAMS. Accelerated program, double major, dual enrollment of high school students, honors program, independent study, internships, student-designed major, study abroad, teacher preparation, visiting/exchange student program, United Nations semester, Washington semester, cross-registration; liberal arts/career combination in engineering, health sciences. **Remedial services:** Learning center, reduced course load, tutoring. **Placement/credit:** AP, CLEP Subject, institutional tests.

ACADEMIC REQUIREMENTS. Freshmen must earn minimum GPA of 1.2 to continue in good standing. 80% of freshmen return for sophomore year. Students must declare major by end of second year. **Graduation requirements:** 144 hours for bachelor's (40 in major). Most students required to take courses in arts/fine arts, English, foreign languages, history, mathematics, philosophy/religion, biological/physical sciences, social sciences. **Postgraduate studies:** 2% enter law school, 1% enter medical school, 1% enter MBA programs, 12% enter other graduate study. **Additional information:** Teacher Certification in English, mathematics, science, social science, social studies, foreign languages.

FRESHMAN ADMISSIONS. Selection criteria: School achievement record, essay or personal statement, test scores important. Recommendations, interview, extracurricular and community activities, talent, minority status considered. **High school preparation:** 16 units recommended. Recommended units include English 4, foreign language 2, mathematics 3, social science 2 and science 1. Mathematics recommendation includes 2 algebra and 1 geometry. **Test requirements:** SAT or ACT; score report by April 15.

1992 FRESHMAN CLASS PROFILE. 333 women applied, 299 accepted, 120 enrolled. 67% had high school GPA of 3.0 or higher, 27% between 2.0 and 2.99. **Academic background:** Mid 50% of enrolled freshmen had SAT-V between 430-550, SAT-M between 450-560. 74% submitted SAT scores. **Characteristics:** 43% from in state, 97% live in college housing, 10% have minority backgrounds, 1% are foreign students. Average age is 18.

FALL-TERM APPLICATIONS. $25 fee, may be waived for applicants with need. No closing date; priority given to applications received by March 1; applicants notified on a rolling basis; must reply by May 1 or within 2 weeks if notified thereafter. Audition required for music applicants. Essay required. Interview recommended. Portfolio recommended for art applicants. CRDA. Deferred and early admission available.

STUDENT LIFE. Housing: Dormitories (women). All full-time students under 23 years required to reside on-campus unless they reside with family within a 30 mile radius of the college. **Activities:** Student government, magazine, student newspaper, yearbook, choral groups, dance, drama, music ensembles, musical theater, symphony orchestra, College Christian Fellowship, Salem College Service Club, Model United Nations, ONUA (black students' organization), College Republicans, College Democrats, International Club, Catholic Student Association, Campus Activities Council, April Arts.

ATHLETICS. Intercollegiate: Basketball, cross-country, field hockey, horseback riding, soccer, swimming, tennis, volleyball. **Intramural:** Basketball, softball, swimming, volleyball.

STUDENT SERVICES. Aptitude testing, career counseling, freshman orientation, health services, personal counseling, placement service for graduates, special adviser for adult students, peer advising.

ANNUAL EXPENSES. Tuition and fees (1992-93): $9,450. Adult program fee $490 per course. **Room and board:** $5,790. **Books and supplies:** $600. **Other expenses:** $800.

FINANCIAL AID. 77% of freshmen, 54% of continuing students receive some form of aid. 58% of grants, 82% of loans, 84% of jobs based on need. Academic, music/drama, state/district residency, leadership, religious affiliation, minority scholarships available. **Aid applications:** Closing date August 1; priority given to applications received by March 1; applicants notified on a rolling basis beginning on or about February 12; must reply within 2 weeks.

ADDRESS/TELEPHONE. Katherine Knapp, Director of Admissions, Salem College, PO Box 10548, Winston-Salem, NC 27108. (919) 721-2621. (800) 327-2536. Fax: (919) 724-7102.

Sampson Community College
Clinton, North Carolina — CB code: 0505

2-year public community college, coed. Founded in 1965. **Accreditation:** Regional. **Undergraduate enrollment:** 181 men, 407 women full time; 142 men, 319 women part time. **Faculty:** 99 total (44 full time), 3 with doctorates or other terminal degrees. **Location:** Rural campus in small town; 30 miles from Fayetteville. **Calendar:** Quarter, limited summer session. Saturday and extensive evening/early morning classes. **Microcomputers:** 70 located in classrooms, computer centers.

DEGREES OFFERED. AAS. 105 associate degrees awarded in 1992. 31% in business and management, 12% business/office and marketing/distribution, 9% computer sciences, 18% education, 20% allied health.

UNDERGRADUATE MAJORS. Accounting, business administration and management, business and office, business data processing and related programs, computer programming, criminal justice technology, education, electronic technology, liberal/general studies, nursing, ornamental horticulture, secretarial and related programs.

ACADEMIC PROGRAMS. 2-year transfer program, cooperative education, dual enrollment of high school students, internships, telecourses, weekend college. **Remedial services:** Learning center, preadmission summer program, reduced course load, remedial instruction, special counselor, tutoring. **Placement/credit:** Institutional tests; 25 credit hours maximum for associate degree.

ACADEMIC REQUIREMENTS. Freshmen must earn minimum GPA of 1.6 to continue in good standing. 60% of freshmen return for sophomore year. Students must declare major on application. **Graduation requirements:** 120 hours for associate (80 in major). Most students required to take courses in English, mathematics, social sciences.

FRESHMAN ADMISSIONS. Selection criteria: Open admissions. Selective admissions to nursing and practical nursing. **High school preparation:** 16 units recommended. Recommended units include biological science 1, English 4, foreign language 3, mathematics 1, physical science 2 and social science 2. Algebra, chemistry and biology required for nursing programs.

1992 FRESHMAN CLASS PROFILE. 98 men, 218 women enrolled. **Characteristics:** 96% from in state, 100% commute, 34% have minority backgrounds. Average age is 24.

FALL-TERM APPLICATIONS. No fee. No closing date; applicants notified on a rolling basis. Interview required for Nursing applicants. Placement interview for all other applicants.

STUDENT LIFE. Activities: Student government, student newspaper, yearbook.

ATHLETICS. Intramural: Basketball M.

STUDENT SERVICES. Aptitude testing, career counseling, employment service for undergraduates, freshman orientation, personal counseling, placement service for graduates, special adviser for adult students, veterans counselor, services/facilities for handicapped.

ANNUAL EXPENSES. Tuition and fees (1992-93): $587, $3,969 additional for out-of-state students. **Books and supplies:** $600. **Other expenses:** $900.

FINANCIAL AID. 27% of freshmen, 50% of continuing students receive some form of aid. 97% of grants, 92% of loans, all jobs based on need. 255 enrolled freshmen were judged to have need, all were offered aid. Academic, state/district residency, minority scholarships available. **Aid applications:** No closing date; priority given to applications received by July 1; applicants notified on a rolling basis. **Additional information:** Short-term loans available to students waiting for federal aid to be approved. Covers tuition, fees and books only.

ADDRESS/TELEPHONE. William R. Jordan, Director of Admissions, Sampson Community College, PO Box 318, Clinton, NC 28328. (919) 592-8084 ext. 245. Fax: (919) 592-8048.

Sandhills Community College
Pinehurst, North Carolina — CB code: 5649

2-year public community college, coed. Founded in 1963. **Accreditation:** Regional. **Undergraduate enrollment:** 497 men, 923 women full time; 318 men, 563 women part time. **Faculty:** 130 total (100 full time), 6 with doctorates or other terminal degrees. **Location:** Rural campus in small town; 41 miles from Fayetteville, 71 miles from Raleigh. **Calendar:** Quarter, extensive summer session. Extensive evening/early morning classes. **Microcomputers:** 150 located in libraries, classrooms. **Special facilities:** Landscape garden, arboretum, hillside garden.

DEGREES OFFERED. AA, AS, AAS. 267 associate degrees awarded in 1992.

UNDERGRADUATE MAJORS. Accounting, architectural technologies, automotive mechanics, business administration and management, business data processing and related programs, business data programming, civil technology, computer and information sciences, computer engineering, computer programming, computer technology, criminal justice technology, data processing, electrical/electronics/communications engineering, electronic technology, engineering and engineering-related technologies, fine arts, golf course/turf management, horticulture, hotel/motel and restaurant management, human services technology, liberal/general studies, manufacturing technology, medical laboratory technologies, medical secretary, mental health/human services, music, nursing, radiograph medical technology, respiratory therapy technology, secretarial and related programs, studio art, substance abuse counseling, survey and mapping technology, teacher aide.

ACADEMIC PROGRAMS. 2-year transfer program, cooperative education, dual enrollment of high school students, honors program, independent study, internships, telecourses, 3rd and 4th year courses in business and economics, liberal studies, human services, and elementary education offered on campus evenings by St. Andrews Presbyterian College. **Remedial services:** Learning center, reduced course load, remedial instruction, special counselor, tutoring, mathematics laboratory, writing center. **Placement/credit:** AP, CLEP General and Subject, institutional tests.

ACADEMIC REQUIREMENTS. Freshmen must earn minimum GPA of 1.7 to continue in good standing. 57% of freshmen return for sophomore year. Students must declare major on enrollment. **Graduation requirements:** 96 hours for associate (60 in major). Most students required to take courses in arts/fine arts, English, humanities, mathematics, biological/physical sciences, social sciences.

FRESHMAN ADMISSIONS. Selection criteria: Open admissions. Specific scores on Comparative Guidance and Placement Test required for admission to landscape gardening, nursing and health sciences programs. Students not achieving these minimum scores may enroll in general college, take developmental courses and reapply for programs later. **Test requirements:** CGP program used for placement in English and mathematics. Stanford Diagnostic Test for reading placement.

1992 FRESHMAN CLASS PROFILE. 82 men, 133 women enrolled. **Characteristics:** 99% from in state, 100% commute, 38% have minority backgrounds. Average age is 25.

FALL-TERM APPLICATIONS. No fee. No closing date; applicants notified on a rolling basis.

STUDENT LIFE. Activities: Student government, student newspaper, choral groups, concert band, drama, jazz band, music ensembles, symphony orchestra, Minority Students for Academic and Cultural Enrichment, Circle-K, Young Democrats, Young Republicans.

ATHLETICS. Intercollegiate: Golf, softball, tennis, volleyball. **Intramural:** Basketball, racquetball, softball, table tennis, tennis, volleyball.

STUDENT SERVICES. Career counseling, employment service for

undergraduates, freshman orientation, personal counseling, placement service for graduates, veterans counselor, services/facilities for handicapped.

ANNUAL EXPENSES. Tuition and fees (1992-93): $578, $3,959 additional for out-of-state students. **Books and supplies:** $514. **Other expenses:** $578.

FINANCIAL AID. 40% of freshmen, 40% of continuing students receive some form of aid. 99% of grants, 88% of loans, 63% of jobs based on need. Academic, music/drama scholarships available. **Aid applications:** No closing date; priority given to applications received by June 1; applicants notified on a rolling basis beginning on or about July 15; must reply within 2 weeks.

ADDRESS/TELEPHONE. Carol Ewing, Director of Admissions, Sandhills Community College, 2200 Airport Road, Pinehurst, NC 28374. (919) 692-6185 ext. 204. Fax: (919) 692-2756.

Shaw University
Raleigh, North Carolina — CB code: 5612

4-year private liberal arts college, coed, affiliated with General Baptist State Convention of NC. Founded in 1865. **Accreditation:** Regional. **Undergraduate enrollment:** 1,017 men, 1,347 women full time; 37 men, 82 women part time. **Faculty:** 283 total (114 full time), 116 with doctorates or other terminal degrees. **Location:** Urban campus in small city. **Calendar:** Semester, limited summer session. Saturday and extensive evening/early morning classes. **Microcomputers:** 94 located in libraries, classrooms, computer centers. **Additional facts:** CAPE - Center for Alternative Programs of Education degree program with sites in 14 NC locations.

DEGREES OFFERED. AA, BA, BS. 15 associate degrees awarded in 1992. 100% in business and management. 288 bachelor's degrees awarded. 40% in business and management, 5% communications, 5% education, 20% parks/recreation, protective services, public affairs, 14% social sciences.

UNDERGRADUATE MAJORS. Associate: Accounting, business administration and management, criminal justice studies. **Bachelor's:** Accounting, behavioral sciences, biochemistry, business administration and management, chemistry, computer and information sciences, criminal justice studies, dramatic arts, education of the mentally handicapped, elementary education, English, history, international studies, liberal/general studies, mathematics, music, physical therapy, public administration, radio/television broadcasting, religion, secondary education, sociology, speech pathology/audiology.

ACADEMIC PROGRAMS. 2-year transfer program, double major, dual enrollment of high school students, external degree, independent study, internships, teacher preparation, cross-registration. **Remedial services:** Learning center, reduced course load, remedial instruction, special counselor, tutoring, developmental studies program. **ROTC:** Army. **Placement/credit:** 30 credit hours maximum for associate degree; 60 credit hours maximum for bachelor's degree.

ACADEMIC REQUIREMENTS. Freshmen must earn minimum GPA of 1.5 to continue in good standing. 68% of freshmen return for sophomore year. Students must declare major by end of second year. **Graduation requirements:** 60 hours for associate (15 in major), 120 hours for bachelor's (30 in major). Most students required to take courses in computer science, English, history, humanities, mathematics, biological/physical sciences, social sciences. **Additional information:** Alternative education program for working students offers Saturday and evening classes.

FRESHMAN ADMISSIONS. Selection criteria: 2.0 high school GPA. SAT scores and letters of recommendation considered. **High school preparation:** 13 units required. Required units include English 3, mathematics 2, social science 2 and science 2. 4 electives in English, foreign language, mathematics, science. **Test requirements:** ACH required of teacher education majors.

1992 FRESHMAN CLASS PROFILE. 1,136 men applied, 540 accepted, 317 enrolled; 1,795 women applied, 790 accepted, 436 enrolled. **Characteristics:** 58% from in state, 90% live in college housing, 97% have minority backgrounds. Average age is 19.

FALL-TERM APPLICATIONS. $25 fee, may be waived for applicants with need. Closing date August 10; applicants notified on a rolling basis; must reply within 2 weeks. Essay recommended.

STUDENT LIFE. Housing: Dormitories (men, women). **Activities:** Student government, radio, student newspaper, yearbook, choral groups, concert band, drama, jazz band, marching band, fraternities, sororities, NAACP, International Students' Organization. **Additional information:** Religious observance required.

ATHLETICS. NCAA. **Intercollegiate:** Baseball M, basketball, cross-country, softball W, tennis M, track and field, volleyball W. **Intramural:** Basketball, softball, table tennis.

STUDENT SERVICES. Career counseling, employment service for undergraduates, health services, personal counseling, placement service for graduates, special adviser for adult students, services/facilities for handicapped.

ANNUAL EXPENSES. Tuition and fees (1992-93): $4,894. **Room and board:** $3,325. **Books and supplies:** $850. **Other expenses:** $1,000.

FINANCIAL AID. 85% of freshmen, 90% of continuing students receive some form of aid. All grants, 85% of loans, all jobs based on need. **Aid applications:** Closing date February 1; applicants notified on or about July 30; must reply by August 10.

ADDRESS/TELEPHONE. Alfonza Carter, Director of Admissions, Shaw University, 118 East South Street, Raleigh, NC 27601. (919) 546-8220. Fax: (919) 546-8301.

Southeastern Baptist Theological Seminary
Wake Forest, North Carolina — CB code: 7050

2-year private seminary college, coed, affiliated with Southern Baptist Convention. Founded in 1950. **Accreditation:** Regional. **Undergraduate enrollment:** 48 men, 1 woman full time; 4 men, 3 women part time. **Graduate enrollment:** 516 men and women. **Faculty:** 48 total (26 full time), 32 with doctorates or other terminal degrees. **Location:** Rural campus in small town; 20 miles from Raleigh, 30 miles from Durham. **Calendar:** Semester, limited summer session. **Microcomputers:** 4 located in libraries.

DEGREES OFFERED. 31 associate degrees awarded in 1992. 100% in philosophy, religion, theology. Graduate degrees offered in 4 major fields of study.

UNDERGRADUATE MAJORS. Theological studies.

ACADEMIC PROGRAMS. Internships. **Remedial services:** Remedial instruction.

ACADEMIC REQUIREMENTS. Freshmen must earn minimum GPA of 2.0 to continue in good standing. 90% of freshmen return for sophomore year. Students must declare major on application. **Graduation requirements:** 56 hours for associate. Most students required to take courses in English, philosophy/religion.

FRESHMAN ADMISSIONS. Selection criteria: Open admissions. Applicants must be 30 years of age or older. Recommendations most important. **Test requirements:** Perdue high school English test required.

1992 FRESHMAN CLASS PROFILE. 25 men, 3 women enrolled. **Characteristics:** 60% from in state, 80% live in college housing, 11% have minority backgrounds. Average age is 35.

FALL-TERM APPLICATIONS. $10 fee. Closing date August 1; applicants notified on a rolling basis. Deferred admission available.

STUDENT LIFE. Housing: Dormitories (men, women); apartment housing available. **Activities:** Student government.

ATHLETICS. Intramural: Basketball, golf, racquetball, softball, tennis, volleyball.

STUDENT SERVICES. Career counseling, employment service for undergraduates, freshman orientation, health services, on-campus day care, personal counseling, placement service for graduates, special adviser for adult students, veterans counselor.

ANNUAL EXPENSES. Tuition and fees (1992-93): $1,050. **Room and board:** $1,575 room only. **Books and supplies:** $300.

FINANCIAL AID. 100% of freshmen receive some form of aid. Grants, loans, jobs available. **Aid applications:** Closing date August 1; applicants notified on a rolling basis. **Additional information:** Special endowment awards $300 to all freshmen.

ADDRESS/TELEPHONE. John Storcy, Director of Admissions, Southeastern Baptist Theological Seminary, P.O. Box 1889, Wake Forest, NC 27587-1889. (919) 556-3101. (800) 284-6317. Fax: (919) 556-3101.

Southeastern Community College
Whiteville, North Carolina — CB code: 5651

2-year public community college, coed. Founded in 1964. **Accreditation:** Regional. **Undergraduate enrollment:** 440 men, 710 women full time; 170 men, 410 women part time. **Faculty:** 75 total (54 full time), 3 with doctorates or other terminal degrees. **Location:** Rural campus in small town; 45 miles from Wilmington, 105 miles from Raleigh. **Calendar:** Quarter, limited summer session. Extensive evening/early morning classes. **Microcomputers:** 70 located in classrooms, computer centers.

DEGREES OFFERED. AA, AS, AAS. 113 associate degrees awarded in 1992. 9% in engineering technologies, 34% health sciences, 12% home economics, 21% multi/interdisciplinary studies, 11% parks/recreation, protective services, public affairs.

UNDERGRADUATE MAJORS. Biological and physical sciences, business administration and management, business data processing and related programs, child development/care/guidance, computer programming, criminal justice technology, early childhood education, electrical technology, elementary education, finance, fine arts, forest products processing technology, forestry production and processing, liberal/general studies, music, nursing, parks and recreation management, secretarial and related programs.

ACADEMIC PROGRAMS. 2-year transfer program, dual enrollment of high school students, independent study, internships, telecourses. **Remedial services:** Learning center, reduced course load, remedial instruction, special counselor, tutoring. **Placement/credit:** Institutional tests.

ACADEMIC REQUIREMENTS. Freshmen must earn minimum GPA of 2.0 to continue in good standing. 49% of freshmen return for sophomore year. Students must declare major on enrollment. **Graduation requirements:** 96 hours for associate (70 in major). Most students required to take courses in arts/fine arts, English, history, humanities, mathematics, biological/physical sciences, social sciences.

FRESHMAN ADMISSIONS. Selection criteria: Open admissions. Selective admissions to nursing programs. **Test requirements:** CGP required for nursing applicants for admissions. Institutional tests required for placement.

1992 FRESHMAN CLASS PROFILE. 120 men, 172 women enrolled. **Characteristics:** 100% from in state, 100% commute, 40% have minority backgrounds, 1% are foreign students. Average age is 27.

FALL-TERM APPLICATIONS. No fee. No closing date; applicants notified on a rolling basis. Interview required for nursing applicants. Deferred and early admission available.

STUDENT LIFE. Activities: Student government, art newspaper, literary magazine, choral groups, drama, piano, voice, Student Ambassadors.

ATHLETICS. NJCAA. **Intercollegiate:** Baseball M, softball W.

STUDENT SERVICES. Aptitude testing, career counseling, employment service for undergraduates, freshman orientation, on-campus day care, personal counseling, placement service for graduates, special adviser for adult students, veterans counselor, services/facilities for handicapped.

ANNUAL EXPENSES. Tuition and fees (1992-93): $586, $3,959 additional for out-of-state students. **Books and supplies:** $425. **Other expenses:** $900.

FINANCIAL AID. 32% of freshmen, 32% of continuing students receive some form of aid. 99% of grants, 94% of loans, all jobs based on need. Academic, athletic, leadership scholarships available. **Aid applications:** No closing date; priority given to applications received by April 1; applicants notified on a rolling basis beginning on or about July 30; must reply within 2 weeks.

ADDRESS/TELEPHONE. Julie Stocks, Dean for Student Development Services, Southeastern Community College, PO Box 151, Whiteville, NC 28472. (919) 642-7141 ext. 265. Fax: (919) 642-5658.

Southwestern Community College
Sylva, North Carolina — CB code: 5667

2-year public community college, coed. Founded in 1964. **Accreditation:** Regional. **Undergraduate enrollment:** 284 men, 481 women full time; 307 men, 522 women part time. **Faculty:** 103 total (47 full time), 2 with doctorates or other terminal degrees. **Location:** Rural campus in rural community; 48 miles from Asheville. **Calendar:** Quarter, limited summer session. Extensive evening/early morning classes. **Microcomputers:** Located in classrooms, computer centers. **Additional facts:** Three off-campus sites serving two adjoining counties.

DEGREES OFFERED. AA, AAS. 150 associate degrees awarded in 1992. 22% in business and management, 7% business/office and marketing/distribution, 9% teacher education, 11% engineering technologies, 22% allied health, 8% law, 10% visual and performing arts.

UNDERGRADUATE MAJORS. Accounting, automotive technology, business administration and management, business and management, business and office, business computer/console/peripheral equipment operation, business data programming, child development/care/guidance, clinical laboratory science, commercial art, computer programming, computer servicing technology, computer technology, criminal justice technology, drug and alcohol counseling, early childhood education, electrical/electronics/communications engineering, electronic technology, fashion design, fashion merchandising, finance, food management, food production/management/services, graphic arts technology, hotel/motel and restaurant management, legal assistant/paralegal, liberal/general studies, medical laboratory technologies, nursing, physical therapy assistant, radio/television broadcasting, radio/television technology, radiograph medical technology, real estate, respiratory therapy, respiratory therapy technology, science technologies, secretarial and related programs, trade and industrial education.

ACADEMIC PROGRAMS. 2-year transfer program, cooperative education, double major, dual enrollment of high school students, independent study, internships. **Remedial services:** Learning center, preadmission summer program, reduced course load, remedial instruction, special counselor, tutoring, services for learning disabled. **Placement/credit:** Institutional tests.

ACADEMIC REQUIREMENTS. Freshmen must earn minimum GPA of 2.0 to continue in good standing. 63% of freshmen return for sophomore year. Students must declare major by end of first year. **Graduation requirements:** 125 hours for associate. Most students required to take courses in English, mathematics.

FRESHMAN ADMISSIONS. Selection criteria: Open admissions. Selective admissions to allied health programs based on test scores, academic record, interview, and recommendations. Basic law and criminal justice programs require medical review. Algebra, biology, and chemistry required for allied health program applicants.

1992 FRESHMAN CLASS PROFILE. 212 men, 324 women enrolled. **Characteristics:** 91% from in state, 100% commute, 14% have minority backgrounds. Average age is 30.

FALL-TERM APPLICATIONS. No fee. No closing date; applicants notified on a rolling basis. Interview required for allied health applicants; recommended for all others. Deferred and early admission available.

STUDENT LIFE. Activities: Student government, film, radio, choral groups, Phi Theta Kappa, radiology club, drug and alcohol counseling organization, electronics club.

ATHLETICS. Intramural: Basketball, softball M, volleyball.

STUDENT SERVICES. Aptitude testing, career counseling, employment service for undergraduates, freshman orientation, health services, personal counseling, placement service for graduates, veterans counselor, computerized career planning, resume preparation, services/facilities for handicapped.

ANNUAL EXPENSES. Tuition and fees (1992-93): $581, $3,959 additional for out-of-state students. **Books and supplies:** $500. **Other expenses:** $630.

FINANCIAL AID. 36% of freshmen, 43% of continuing students receive some form of aid. All grants, 88% of loans, all jobs based on need. 370 enrolled freshmen were judged to have need, all were offered aid. **Aid applications:** No closing date; priority given to applications received by March 15; applicants notified on a rolling basis beginning on or about May 1; must reply within 2 weeks.

ADDRESS/TELEPHONE. Grady Corbin, Director of Admissions and Recruitment, Southwestern Community College, 275 Webster Road, Sylva, NC 28779. (704) 586-4091 ext. 217. Fax: (704) 586-4091.

Stanly Community College
Albemarle, North Carolina — CB code: 0496

2-year public community college, coed. Founded in 1971. **Accreditation:** Regional. **Undergraduate enrollment:** 242 men, 299 women full time; 387 men, 527 women part time. **Faculty:** 76 total (38 full time), 2 with doctorates or other terminal degrees. **Location:** Rural campus in large town; 30 miles from Charlotte. **Calendar:** Quarter, extensive summer session. Extensive evening/early morning classes. **Microcomputers:** Located in libraries, classrooms.

DEGREES OFFERED. AAS. 171 associate degrees awarded in 1992.

UNDERGRADUATE MAJORS. Accounting, biomedical equipment technology, business administration and management, business data programming, computer technology, criminal justice technology, drafting and design technology, electronic technology, legal secretary, liberal/general studies, marketing and distribution, medical secretary, nursing, occupational therapy assistant, physical therapy assistant, respiratory therapy technology, secretarial and related programs, teacher aide.

ACADEMIC PROGRAMS. 2-year transfer program, dual enrollment of high school students, telecourses. **Remedial services:** Preadmission summer program, remedial instruction, tutoring. **Placement/credit:** Institutional tests.

ACADEMIC REQUIREMENTS. Freshmen must earn minimum GPA of 1.5 to continue in good standing. 60% of freshmen return for sophomore year. **Graduation requirements:** 96 hours for associate.

FRESHMAN ADMISSIONS. Selection criteria: Open admissions.

1992 FRESHMAN CLASS PROFILE. 236 men, 345 women enrolled. **Characteristics:** 99% from in state, 100% commute, 14% have minority backgrounds. Average age is 19.

FALL-TERM APPLICATIONS. No fee. No closing date; applicants notified on a rolling basis beginning on or about January 15.

STUDENT LIFE. Activities: Student government, student newspaper.

STUDENT SERVICES. Aptitude testing, career counseling, employment service for undergraduates, personal counseling, placement service for graduates, veterans counselor, services/facilities for handicapped.

ANNUAL EXPENSES. Tuition and fees (1992-93): $578, $3,959 additional for out-of-state students. **Books and supplies:** $450. **Other expenses:** $1,200.

FINANCIAL AID. 90% of grants, 80% of loans, 89% of jobs based on need. Academic, state/district residency, leadership, minority scholarships available. **Aid applications:** No closing date; priority given to applications received by May 1; applicants notified on a rolling basis beginning on or about June 1; must reply within 1 week. **Additional information:** Approved school for veteran's education benefits.

ADDRESS/TELEPHONE. Ronnie Hinson, Director of Admissions and Placement, Stanly Community College, 141 College Drive, Albemarle, NC 28001. (704) 982-0121 ext. 234. Fax: (704) 982-0819.

Surry Community College
Dobson, North Carolina — CB code: 5656

2-year public community college, coed. Founded in 1964. **Accreditation:** Regional. **Undergraduate enrollment:** 572 men, 730 women full time; 646 men, 1,135 women part time. **Faculty:** 126 total (79 full time), 13 with doctorates or other terminal degrees. **Location:** Rural campus in rural community; 40 miles from Winston-Salem. **Calendar:** Quarter, extensive summer session. Extensive evening/early morning classes. **Microcomputers:** Located in classrooms.

DEGREES OFFERED. AA, AS, AAS. 290 associate degrees awarded in 1992. 15% in business and management, 6% business/office and market-

ing/distribution, 20% engineering technologies, 8% allied health, 40% multi/interdisciplinary studies, 7% trade and industry.

UNDERGRADUATE MAJORS. Accounting, agribusiness, agricultural sciences, automotive mechanics, automotive technology, business administration and management, business and office, business data processing and related programs, computer engineering, computer technology, criminal justice studies, criminal justice technology, drafting and design technology, electronic technology, horticultural science, law enforcement and corrections, law enforcement and corrections technologies, legal assistant/paralegal, legal secretary, liberal/general studies, machine tool operation/machine shop, marketing and distribution, mechanical engineering, medical secretary, nursing, practical nursing, secretarial and related programs.

ACADEMIC PROGRAMS. 2-year transfer program, accelerated program, double major, independent study. **Remedial services:** Learning center, reduced course load, remedial instruction, special counselor, tutoring. **Placement/credit:** AP, CLEP General and Subject, institutional tests.

ACADEMIC REQUIREMENTS. No policy requiring minimum GPA; records of students having academic difficulty are reviewed individually. 75% of freshmen return for sophomore year. **Graduation requirements:** 96 hours for associate. Most students required to take courses in English, mathematics, biological/physical sciences.

FRESHMAN ADMISSIONS. Selection criteria: Open admissions. Competitive admission to associate degree nursing program (RN) based primarily on academic standing; test scores considered. **Test requirements:** Nursing program applicants must take CGP Test given locally.

1992 FRESHMAN CLASS PROFILE. 120 men, 120 women enrolled. **Characteristics:** 80% from in state, 100% commute, 4% have minority backgrounds.

FALL-TERM APPLICATIONS. No fee. No closing date; applicants notified on a rolling basis. Interview required for nursing applicants.

STUDENT LIFE. Activities: Student government, student newspaper, yearbook, choral groups, drama.

ATHLETICS. Intramural: Basketball M, golf, softball, tennis, volleyball.

STUDENT SERVICES. Aptitude testing, career counseling, employment service for undergraduates, freshman orientation, personal counseling, placement service for graduates, veterans counselor, services/facilities for handicapped.

ANNUAL EXPENSES. Tuition and fees (1992-93): $575, $3,959 additional for out-of-state students. **Books and supplies:** $500. **Other expenses:** $495.

FINANCIAL AID. 50% of freshmen, 50% of continuing students receive some form of aid. 71% of grants, 95% of loans, 57% of jobs based on need. Academic scholarships available. **Aid applications:** No closing date; priority given to applications received by June 1; applicants notified on a rolling basis beginning on or about July 1; must reply within 2 weeks.

ADDRESS/TELEPHONE. Michael L. McHone, Dean of Admissions, Surry Community College, PO Box 304, Dobson, NC 27017. (919) 386-8121. Fax: (919) 386-8951.

Tri-County Community College

Murphy, North Carolina — CB code: 5785

2-year public community college, coed. Founded in 1964. **Accreditation:** Regional. **Undergraduate enrollment:** 117 men, 236 women full time; 168 men, 335 women part time. **Faculty:** 52 total (21 full time), 2 with doctorates or other terminal degrees. **Location:** Rural campus in rural community; 110 miles from Asheville, 96 miles from Chattanooga, Tennessee. **Calendar:** Quarter, extensive summer session. Extensive evening/early morning classes. **Microcomputers:** 42 located in libraries, computer centers.

DEGREES OFFERED. AA, AAS. 70 associate degrees awarded in 1992. 54% in business/office and marketing/distribution, 7% health sciences, 39% multi/interdisciplinary studies.

UNDERGRADUATE MAJORS. Accounting, automotive mechanics, business and office, business data programming, computer and information sciences, education, liberal/general studies, medical assistant, nursing, secretarial and related programs.

ACADEMIC PROGRAMS. 2-year transfer program, double major, dual enrollment of high school students, independent study, internships. **Remedial services:** Learning center, reduced course load, remedial instruction, special counselor, tutoring. **Placement/credit:** Institutional tests.

ACADEMIC REQUIREMENTS. Freshmen must earn minimum GPA of 1.5 to continue in good standing. 60% of freshmen return for sophomore year. Students must declare major on enrollment. **Graduation requirements:** 97 hours for associate. Most students required to take courses in English, mathematics.

FRESHMAN ADMISSIONS. Selection criteria: Open admissions.

1992 FRESHMAN CLASS PROFILE. 92 men, 189 women enrolled. **Characteristics:** 91% from in state, 100% commute, 7% have minority backgrounds. Average age is 29.

FALL-TERM APPLICATIONS. No fee. No closing date; applicants notified on a rolling basis. Interview required for placement and counseling. Deferred and early admission available.

STUDENT LIFE. Activities: Student government, student newspaper, drama, honor society.

STUDENT SERVICES. Aptitude testing, career counseling, employment service for undergraduates, personal counseling, placement service for graduates, veterans counselor, services/facilities for handicapped.

ANNUAL EXPENSES. Tuition and fees (1992-93): $570, $3,959 additional for out-of-state students. **Books and supplies:** $300. **Other expenses:** $450.

FINANCIAL AID. 44% of freshmen, 44% of continuing students receive some form of aid. Grants, loans, jobs available. **Aid applications:** No closing date; priority given to applications received by May 31; applicants notified on a rolling basis beginning on or about June 1; must reply within 4 weeks.

ADDRESS/TELEPHONE. Bob Jordan, Director of Admissions, Tri-County Community College, PO Box 40, Murphy, NC 28906. (704) 837-6810.

University of North Carolina at Asheville

Asheville, North Carolina — CB code: 5013

Admissions:	57% of applicants accepted
Based on:	••• School record
	•• Test scores
	• Activities, essay, interview, recommendations, special talents
Completion:	99% of freshmen end year in good standing
	34% graduate, 20% of these enter graduate study

4-year public university and liberal arts college, coed. Founded in 1927. **Accreditation:** Regional. **Undergraduate enrollment:** 971 men, 1,076 women full time; 437 men, 654 women part time. **Graduate enrollment:** 1 man full time; 18 men, 28 women part time. **Faculty:** 234 total (144 full time), 142 with doctorates or other terminal degrees. **Location:** Urban campus in small city; 129 miles from Charlotte, 150 from Atlanta, Georgia. **Calendar:** Semester, limited summer session. Extensive evening/early morning classes. **Microcomputers:** 177 located in libraries, classrooms, computer centers. **Special facilities:** Southern Highlands Research Center, botanical gardens, Jewish studies center, North Carolina Arboretum, Micro-Wave Teleconference Center, Environmental Quality Institute.

DEGREES OFFERED. BA, BS, BFA, M. 408 bachelor's degrees awarded in 1992. 27% in business and management, 6% communications, 5% computer sciences, 6% letters/literature, 5% life sciences, 11% psychology, 22% social sciences, 5% visual and performing arts. Graduate degrees offered in 1 major field of study.

UNDERGRADUATE MAJORS. Accounting, actuarial sciences, applied mathematics, atmospheric sciences and meteorology, biology, business administration and management, business and management, chemistry, classics, creative writing, dramatic arts, economics, engineering management, English literature, environmental science, financial management, fine arts, French, German, Greek (classical), health care administration, history, history/classics, information sciences and systems, journalism, Latin, marketing management, mathematics, music, personnel management, philosophy, physics, political science and government, political sociology, psychology, sociology, Spanish, statistics, systems analysis.

ACADEMIC PROGRAMS. Accelerated program, double major, dual enrollment of high school students, honors program, independent study, internships, student-designed major, study abroad, teacher preparation; liberal arts/career combination in engineering, forestry, health sciences. **Remedial services:** Learning center, preadmission summer program, reduced course load, remedial instruction, special counselor, tutoring. **Placement/credit:** AP, CLEP General and Subject, institutional tests; 30 credit hours maximum for bachelor's degree.

ACADEMIC REQUIREMENTS. Freshmen must earn minimum GPA of 2.0 to continue in good standing. 78% of freshmen return for sophomore year. Students must declare major by end of second year. **Graduation requirements:** 120 hours for bachelor's (36 in major). Most students required to take courses in arts/fine arts, English, foreign languages, humanities, mathematics, biological/physical sciences, social sciences. **Additional information:** Teacher certification programs at all levels in art, English, mathematics, reading, science, social studies, speech, and foreign languages.

FRESHMAN ADMISSIONS. Selection criteria: School achievement record, GPA, and class rank (top third) most important. Test scores, recommendations, interview, and extracurricular activities considered. **High school preparation:** 16 units required. Required units include biological science 1, English 4, foreign language 2, mathematics 3, physical science 1, social science 2 and science 3. Science units should include physical science, biology, and a third science (1 unit must be lab). One unit US history and 1 unit economics required. Mathematics must include algebra 1 & 2 and geometry. **Test requirements:** SAT or ACT (SAT preferred); score report by April 1.

1992 FRESHMAN CLASS PROFILE. 734 men applied, 392 accepted, 168 enrolled; 866 women applied, 520 accepted, 193 enrolled. 81% had high school GPA of 3.0 or higher, 19% between 2.0 and 2.99. 30% were in top tenth and 72% were in top quarter of graduating class. **Academic back-**

ground: Mid 50% of enrolled freshmen had SAT-V between 440-550, SAT-M between 500-600. 96% submitted SAT scores. **Characteristics:** 86% from in state, 70% live in college housing, 6% have minority backgrounds, 2% join fraternities/sororities. Average age is 18.

FALL-TERM APPLICATIONS. $25 fee, may be waived for applicants with need. Closing date April 1; priority given to applications received by October 1; applicants notified on a rolling basis; must reply by June 1. Interview recommended. Essay recommended. CRDA. Deferred and early admission available.

STUDENT LIFE. Housing: Dormitories (men, women, coed); apartment housing available. Suites available, many with direct main-frame computer access. **Activities:** Student government, magazine, student newspaper, television, choral groups, concert band, drama, jazz band, music ensembles, musical theater, pep band, symphony orchestra, fraternities, sororities, Young Democrats, Young Republicans, black association, women's association, veteran's association, service organizations, Baptist Student Union, International Student Association, Intervarsity Christian Fellowship, Habitat for Humanity.

ATHLETICS. NCAA. **Intercollegiate:** Baseball M, basketball, cross-country, golf M, soccer, tennis, track and field W, volleyball W. **Intramural:** Badminton, baseball M, basketball, cross-country, golf M, racquetball, soccer, softball, swimming, table tennis, tennis, volleyball, water polo.

STUDENT SERVICES. Aptitude testing, career counseling, employment service for undergraduates, freshman orientation, health services, personal counseling, placement service for graduates, special adviser for adult students, veterans counselor, Minority Student Affairs Office, services/facilities for handicapped.

ANNUAL EXPENSES. Tuition and fees (1992-93): $1,150, $5,108 additional for out-of-state students. **Room and board:** $3,000. **Books and supplies:** $600. **Other expenses:** $750.

FINANCIAL AID. 57% of freshmen, 26% of continuing students receive some form of aid. 55% of grants, 72% of loans, 22% of jobs based on need. 64 enrolled freshmen were judged to have need, all were offered aid. Academic, music/drama, art, athletic, leadership, alumni affiliation, minority scholarships available. **Aid applications:** No closing date; priority given to applications received by March 1; applicants notified on a rolling basis beginning on or about May 1; must reply within 2 weeks.

ADDRESS/TELEPHONE. John W. White, Director of Admissions, University of North Carolina at Asheville, One University Heights, Asheville, NC 28804-3299. (704) 251-6481.

University of North Carolina at Chapel Hill

Chapel Hill, North Carolina — CB code: 5816

Admissions: 36% of applicants accepted
Based on: ••• School record
•• Activities, test scores
• Essay, recommendations, special talents
Completion: 95% of freshmen end year in good standing
75% graduate

4-year public university, coed. Founded in 1789. **Accreditation:** Regional. **Undergraduate enrollment:** 5,620 men, 8,549 women full time; 474 men, 619 women part time. **Graduate enrollment:** 2,445 men, 2,553 women full time; 1,672 men, 2,012 women part time. **Faculty:** 2,452 total (2,223 full time), 2,298 with doctorates or other terminal degrees. **Location:** Suburban campus in large town; 30 miles from Raleigh, 45 miles from Greensboro. **Calendar:** Semester, extensive summer session. **Microcomputers:** Located in dormitories, libraries, classrooms, computer centers. **Special facilities:** Planetarium, observatory, art museum, arboretum, botanical gardens.

DEGREES OFFERED. BA, BS, BFA, MA, MS, MBA, MFA, MEd, MSW, PhD, EdD, DMD, MD, B. Pharm. 3,655 bachelor's degrees awarded in 1992. 16% in business and management, 11% communications, 6% teacher education, 11% health sciences, 7% letters/literature, 6% life sciences, 5% physical sciences, 6% psychology, 17% social sciences. Graduate degrees offered in 110 major fields of study.

UNDERGRADUATE MAJORS. African studies, Afro-American (black) studies, American studies, anthropology, applied mathematics, art history, Asian studies, astronomy, biological and physical sciences, biology, biometrics and biostatistics, business administration and management, chemistry, classics, clinical laboratory science, comparative literature, computer and information sciences, criminal justice studies, dental hygiene, dramatic arts, early childhood education, economics, elementary education, English, environmental health engineering, environmental science, foreign languages (multiple emphasis), French, geography, geology, German, Greek (classical), history, international relations, international studies, Italian, journalism, junior high education, Latin, Latin American studies, liberal/general studies, linguistics, mathematics, medical radiation dosimetry, music, music education, nursing, nutritional sciences, operations research, parks and recreation management, peace studies, pharmacy, philosophy, physical therapy, physics, political science and government, Portuguese, psychology, public health laboratory science, radio/television broadcasting, religion, Russian, Russian and Slavic studies, science education, secondary education, Slavic languages, social sciences, sociology, Spanish, speech, statistics, studio art.

ACADEMIC PROGRAMS. Accelerated program, double major, education specialist degree, honors program, independent study, internships, student-designed major, study abroad, teacher preparation, visiting/exchange student program, cross-registration; combined bachelor's/graduate program in medicine. **Remedial services:** Learning center, preadmission summer program, reduced course load, remedial instruction, tutoring. **ROTC:** Air Force, Army, Naval. **Placement/credit:** AP, CLEP Subject, institutional tests.

ACADEMIC REQUIREMENTS. Freshmen must earn minimum GPA of 1.5 to continue in good standing. Freshmen must also pass 24 semester hours. 94% of freshmen return for sophomore year. Students must declare major by end of second year. **Graduation requirements:** 120 hours for bachelor's. Most students required to take courses in arts/fine arts, English, foreign languages, history, humanities, mathematics, philosophy/religion, biological/physical sciences, social sciences.

FRESHMAN ADMISSIONS. Selection criteria: School achievement record and class rank (top 10% to 15% for in-state applicants, top 5% for out-of-state) most important. Test scores, activities, recommendations also considered. Special consideration to out-of-state children of alumni, minority applicants, and minority applicants whose parents attended any college in North Carolina. **High school preparation:** 16 units required. Required units include biological science 1, English 4, foreign language 2, mathematics 3, physical science 1 and social science 2. Students encouraged to exceed minimum requirements for better performance on required placement exams. **Test requirements:** SAT or ACT (SAT preferred); score report by January 15. 3 ACH may be required if applicant's school cannot provide class rank or GPA. Score report by January 15.

1992 FRESHMAN CLASS PROFILE. 7,144 men applied, 2,317 accepted, 1,266 enrolled; 8,992 women applied, 3,418 accepted, 1,983 enrolled. 97% had high school GPA of 3.0 or higher, 3% between 2.0 and 2.99. **Academic background:** Mid 50% of enrolled freshmen had SAT-V between 490-610, SAT-M between 550-680. 100% submitted SAT scores. **Characteristics:** 82% from in state, 99% live in college housing, 16% have minority backgrounds, 1% are foreign students, 25% join fraternities/sororities. Average age is 18.

FALL-TERM APPLICATIONS. $45 fee, may be waived for applicants with need. Closing date January 15; applicants notified on or about April 15; must reply by May 1. Audition required for music and drama applicants. Interview recommended for allied health applicants. Portfolio recommended for art applicants. Essay recommended. CRDA. Institutional early decision plan. Those applying by October 15 notified first week of December, those applying by November 15 notified by first week of February. All other applicants notified by April 15.

STUDENT LIFE. Housing: Dormitories (men, women, coed); apartment, fraternity, sorority, handicapped housing available. Students with interests in arts, international relations, or foreign languages may live in the culturally mixed Carmichale Dormitory (coed). **Activities:** Student government, film, magazine, radio, student newspaper, television, yearbook, choral groups, concert band, dance, drama, jazz band, marching band, music ensembles, musical theater, pep band, fraternities, sororities.

ATHLETICS. NCAA. **Intercollegiate:** Baseball M, basketball, cross-country, diving, fencing, field hockey W, football M, golf, gymnastics W, lacrosse M, soccer, softball W, swimming, tennis, track and field, volleyball W, wrestling M. **Intramural:** Badminton, basketball, bowling, cross-country, diving, fencing, field hockey W, golf, gymnastics W, handball, ice hockey M, lacrosse, racquetball, rugby M, sailing, skiing, soccer, softball, swimming, tennis, track and field, volleyball, water polo M, wrestling M.

STUDENT SERVICES. Aptitude testing, career counseling, employment service for undergraduates, freshman orientation, health services, personal counseling, placement service for graduates, veterans counselor, services/facilities for handicapped.

ANNUAL EXPENSES. Tuition and fees (1992-93): $1,261, $6,584 additional for out-of-state students. **Room and board:** $3,950. **Books and supplies:** $500. **Other expenses:** $1,050.

FINANCIAL AID. 40% of freshmen, 35% of continuing students receive some form of aid. 92% of grants, 82% of loans, all jobs based on need. 865 enrolled freshmen were judged to have need, 843 were offered aid. Academic, music/drama, athletic, leadership, minority scholarships available. **Aid applications:** No closing date; priority given to applications received by March 1; applicants notified on a rolling basis beginning on or about April 1; must reply within 3 weeks.

ADDRESS/TELEPHONE. Jim C. Walters, Asst Provost/Dir Undergrad Admis, University of North Carolina at Chapel Hill, Country Club Road, Monogram Building, CB #2200, Chapel Hill, NC 27599-2200. (919) 966-3621.

University of North Carolina at Charlotte

Charlotte, North Carolina CB code: 5105

Admissions: 75% of applicants accepted
Based on: ••• School record
•• Test scores
• Activities, interview, recommendations, special talents
Completion: 96% of freshmen end year in good standing
46% graduate

4-year public university, coed. Founded in 1946. **Accreditation:** Regional. **Undergraduate enrollment:** 5,014 men, 5,076 women full time; 1,505 men, 1,492 women part time. **Graduate enrollment:** 235 men, 253 women full time; 759 men, 1,029 women part time. **Faculty:** 872 total (640 full time), 552 with doctorates or other terminal degrees. **Location:** Urban campus in very large city; 10 miles from downtown. **Calendar:** Semester, limited summer session. Extensive evening/early morning classes. **Microcomputers:** 600 located in dormitories. **Special facilities:** Botanical and horticultural complex with controlled environment, 100-acre experimental ecological reserve, tropical rain forest conservatory.

DEGREES OFFERED. BA, BS, BArch, MA, MS, MBA, MEd. 2,222 bachelor's degrees awarded in 1992. 22% in business and management, 9% teacher education, 6% engineering, 5% engineering technologies, 6% health sciences, 6% letters/literature, 8% parks/recreation, protective services, public affairs, 8% psychology, 14% social sciences. Graduate degrees offered in 29 major fields of study.

UNDERGRADUATE MAJORS. Accounting, Afro-American (black) studies, anthropology, architecture, biology, business administration and management, chemistry, child development/care/guidance, civil engineering, civil technology, clinical laboratory science, computer and information sciences, dance, dramatic arts, earth sciences, economics, electrical technology, electrical/electronics/communications engineering, elementary education, English, fine arts, French, geography, German, history, human services, junior high education, law enforcement and corrections, manufacturing technology, mathematics, mechanical design technology, mechanical engineering, music performance, nursing, philosophy, physics, political science and government, psychology, religion, social work, sociology, Spanish, special education.

ACADEMIC PROGRAMS. Accelerated program, cooperative education, double major, dual enrollment of high school students, education specialist degree, external degree, honors program, independent study, internships, study abroad, teacher preparation, visiting/exchange student program, cross-registration, wilderness exploration program. **Remedial services:** Learning center, reduced course load, special counselor, tutoring, study skills improvement, computer assisted program instruction. **ROTC:** Air Force, Army. **Placement/credit:** AP, CLEP General and Subject, institutional tests; 32 credit hours maximum for bachelor's degree.

ACADEMIC REQUIREMENTS. Freshmen must earn minimum GPA of 2.0 to continue in good standing. 80% of freshmen return for sophomore year. Students must declare major by end of second year. **Graduation requirements:** 120 hours for bachelor's (30 in major). Most students required to take courses in arts/fine arts, English, foreign languages, history, humanities, mathematics, philosophy/religion, biological/physical sciences, social sciences.

FRESHMAN ADMISSIONS. Selection criteria: Course selection, predicted college GPA, high schhol rank and test score considered; rank weighted twice test score. **High school preparation:** 16 units required. Required units include biological science 1, English 4, foreign language 2, mathematics 3, physical science 1, social science 2 and science 1. Social sciences must include 1 US history; science unit must be laboratory course. **Test requirements:** SAT or ACT (SAT preferred); score report by July 1.

1992 FRESHMAN CLASS PROFILE. 2,791 men applied, 2,058 accepted, 799 enrolled; 2,958 women applied, 2,227 accepted, 842 enrolled. 21% were in top tenth and 61% were in top quarter of graduating class. **Academic background:** Mid 50% of enrolled freshmen had SAT-V between 400-480, SAT-M between 440-540. 99% submitted SAT scores. **Characteristics:** 83% from in state, 57% live in college housing, 22% have minority backgrounds, 3% are foreign students. Average age is 18.

FALL-TERM APPLICATIONS. $25 fee. Closing date July 1; applicants notified on a rolling basis beginning on or about December 15. Interview required for architecture, music applicants. Portfolio required for architecture applicants. Deferred and early admission available. Depending on date application is submitted, additional notification dates are February 1, and March 15.

STUDENT LIFE. Housing: Dormitories (women, coed); apartment, fraternity, handicapped housing available. Housing facilities designed specifically for disabled students in wheelchairs limited; apply early. Suite housing available. **Activities:** Student government, film, magazine, radio, student newspaper, television, yearbook, choral groups, concert band, dance, drama, jazz band, music ensembles, musical theater, pep band, symphony orchestra, fraternities, sororities, religious, political, ethnic, and social service organizations.

ATHLETICS. NCAA. **Intercollegiate:** Baseball M, basketball, cross-country, golf M, soccer M, softball W, swimming, tennis, volleyball W. **Intramural:** Badminton, basketball, bowling, golf, handball, racquetball, soccer, softball, swimming, table tennis, tennis, track and field, volleyball, water polo. **Clubs:** Rugby, lacrosse, crew, karate, waterskiing, badminton.

STUDENT SERVICES. Aptitude testing, career counseling, employment service for undergraduates, freshman orientation, health services, personal counseling, placement service for graduates, veterans counselor, services/facilities for handicapped.

ANNUAL EXPENSES. Tuition and fees (1992-93): $1,189, $5,672 additional for out-of-state students. **Room and board:** $2,842. **Books and supplies:** $550. **Other expenses:** $900.

FINANCIAL AID. 44% of freshmen, 44% of continuing students receive some form of aid. 78% of grants, 87% of loans, 24% of jobs based on need. 890 enrolled freshmen were judged to have need, all were offered aid. Academic, athletic, leadership scholarships available. **Aid applications:** No closing date; priority given to applications received by April 1; applicants notified on a rolling basis beginning on or about May 1; must reply within 2 weeks. **Additional information:** Installment plan offered for room and board costs.

ADDRESS/TELEPHONE. Kathi M. Baucom, Director of Admissions, University of North Carolina at Charlotte, University City Boulevard, Charlotte, NC 28223. (704) 547-2213.

University of North Carolina at Greensboro

Greensboro, North Carolina CB code: 5913

Admissions: 78% of applicants accepted
Based on: ••• School record, test scores
• Activities, recommendations, special talents
Completion: 97% of freshmen end year in good standing
48% graduate

4-year public university, coed. Founded in 1891. **Accreditation:** Regional. **Undergraduate enrollment:** 2,649 men, 4,937 women full time; 696 men, 1,055 women part time. **Graduate enrollment:** 340 men, 688 women full time; 548 men, 1,264 women part time. **Faculty:** 780 total (668 full time), 627 with doctorates or other terminal degrees. **Location:** Urban campus in small city; 300 miles from Washington, D.C. **Calendar:** Semester, extensive summer session. Extensive evening/early morning classes. **Microcomputers:** 800 located in libraries, classrooms, computer centers. **Special facilities:** Art gallery, observatory, Jackson Library special collections (Silva cello music collection, Randall Jarrell collection, women's studies collection).

DEGREES OFFERED. BA, BS, BFA, MA, MS, MBA, MFA, MEd, PhD, EdD. 1,698 bachelor's degrees awarded in 1992. 21% in business and management, 9% teacher education, 12% health sciences, 8% home economics, 10% letters/literature, 5% parks/recreation, protective services, public affairs, 11% social sciences, 5% visual and performing arts. Graduate degrees offered in 77 major fields of study.

UNDERGRADUATE MAJORS. Accounting, American studies, anthropology, archeology, art education, art history, biology, business administration and management, business and management, business data processing and related programs, business economics, business education, business home economics, chemistry, city/community/regional planning, classics, clinical laboratory science, communications, computer and information sciences, computer mathematics, dance, data processing, dramatic arts, early childhood education, economics, education of the deaf and hearing impaired, elementary education, English, European studies, family/consumer resource management, film arts, finance, fine arts, food management, food science and nutrition, French, geography, German, gerontology, Greek (classical), health education, history, home economics, home economics education, human environment and housing, human resources development, humanities and social sciences, individual and family development, information sciences and systems, insurance and risk management, interior design, international business management, international relations, international studies, interpreter for the deaf, junior high education, Latin, Latin American studies, liberal/general studies, linguistics, management information systems, marketing and distribution, marketing and distributive education, marketing management, mathematics, music, music education, music history and appreciation, music performance, music theory and composition, nursing, office supervision and management, painting, parks and recreation management, personnel management, philosophy, physical education, physics, political science and government, predentistry, prelaw, premedicine, prepharmacy, preveterinary, psychology, public administration, radio/television broadcasting, recreation and community services technologies, religion, rhetoric, Russian, Russian and Slavic studies, sculpture, secretarial and related programs, social work, sociology, Spanish, speech, speech correction, speech pathology/audiology, speech/communication/theater education, statistics, studio art, textiles and clothing, theater design, tourism, urban studies, Western European studies, women's studies.

ACADEMIC PROGRAMS. Accelerated program, double major, dual enrollment of high school students, education specialist degree, honors program, independent study, internships, student-designed major, study abroad, teacher preparation, telecourses, Washington semester, cross-registration, residential college classes taught in dormitories; combined bachelor's/graduate program in business administration. **Remedial services:** Learning center, reduced course load, remedial instruction, special counselor, tutoring, Handicapped Student Services, Services to International Students. **ROTC:** Air Force, Army. **Placement/credit:** AP, CLEP Subject, institutional tests; 12 credit hours maximum for bachelor's degree.

ACADEMIC REQUIREMENTS. Freshmen must earn minimum GPA of 1.3 to continue in good standing. 79% of freshmen return for sophomore year. Students must declare major by end of second year. **Graduation requirements:** 122 hours for bachelor's (60 in major). Most students required to take courses in English, history, humanities, mathematics, biological/physical sciences.

FRESHMAN ADMISSIONS. Selection criteria: Combined test scores and high school GPA based on academic courses most important. High school recommendations and activities considered. **High school preparation:** 16 units required. Required units include biological science 1, English 4, foreign language 2, mathematics 3, physical science 1 and social science 2. Social sciences must include 1 US history and 1 other history, economics, sociology or civics; science unit must be a laboratory course. **Test requirements:** SAT or ACT (SAT preferred); score report by August 20.

1992 FRESHMAN CLASS PROFILE. 1,801 men applied, 1,387 accepted, 515 enrolled; 3,645 women applied, 2,849 accepted, 1,007 enrolled. 50% had high school GPA of 3.0 or higher, 50% between 2.0 and 2.99. 18% were in top tenth and 51% were in top quarter of graduating class. **Academic background:** Mid 50% of enrolled freshmen had SAT-V between 410-510, SAT-M between 440-550. 98% submitted SAT scores. **Characteristics:** 81% from in state, 79% live in college housing, 12% have minority backgrounds, 1% are foreign students, 3% join fraternities/sororities. Average age is 19.

FALL-TERM APPLICATIONS. $25 fee, may be waived for applicants with need. Closing date August 1; applicants notified on a rolling basis; must reply by May 1 or within 4 weeks if notified thereafter. Audition required for music applicants. Portfolio required for art, interior design applicants. CRDA. Deferred and early admission available. EDP-S. Achievement test scores in specific subjects may qualify for credit.

STUDENT LIFE. Housing: Dormitories (men, women, coed); apartment, sorority housing available. Residential college (academic/residential program), International House available. Apartments for single and married students expected to open in fall 1993. **Activities:** Student government, film, magazine, radio, student newspaper, television, yearbook, choral groups, concert band, dance, drama, jazz band, music ensembles, musical theater, opera, pep band, symphony orchestra, fraternities, sororities, Alpha Phi Omega service fraternity, Association of Woman Students, Gamma Sigma Sigma service sorority, International Student Association, Neo-Black Society, North Carolina Student Legislature, Outing Club, club sports programs.

ATHLETICS. NCAA. **Intercollegiate:** Baseball M, basketball, cross-country M, golf, soccer, softball W, tennis, volleyball W. **Intramural:** Badminton, basketball, bowling, golf, racquetball, soccer, softball, swimming, table tennis, tennis, track and field, volleyball.

STUDENT SERVICES. Aptitude testing, career counseling, employment service for undergraduates, freshman orientation, health services, personal counseling, placement service for graduates, special adviser for adult students, veterans counselor, special counseling and tutoring services for disadvantaged or first generation college students, services/facilities for handicapped.

ANNUAL EXPENSES. Tuition and fees (1992-93): $1,540, $6,584 additional for out-of-state students. **Room and board:** $3,552. **Books and supplies:** $450. **Other expenses:** $840.

FINANCIAL AID. 42% of freshmen, 45% of continuing students receive some form of aid. 88% of grants, 80% of loans, 6% of jobs based on need. 491 enrolled freshmen were judged to have need, all were offered aid. Academic, music/drama, athletic, leadership, minority scholarships available. **Aid applications:** No closing date; priority given to applications received by March 1; applicants notified on a rolling basis beginning on or about April 1; must reply within 3 weeks.

ADDRESS/TELEPHONE. Charles E. Rickard, Director of Admissions, University of North Carolina at Greensboro, 1000 Spring Garden Street, Greensboro, NC 27412-5001. (919) 334-5901. Fax: (919) 334-5926.

University of North Carolina at Wilmington
Wilmington, North Carolina — CB code: 5907

Admissions: 54% of applicants accepted
Based on:
- ••• School record
- •• Test scores
- • Special talents

Completion: 94% of freshmen end year in good standing
38% graduate, 36% of these enter graduate study

4-year public university, coed. Founded in 1947. **Accreditation:** Regional. **Undergraduate enrollment:** 2,680 men, 3,675 women full time; 458 men, 673 women part time. **Graduate enrollment:** 38 men, 43 women full time; 130 men, 201 women part time. **Faculty:** 419 total (349 full time), 317 with doctorates or other terminal degrees. **Location:** Suburban campus in small city; 125 miles from Raleigh. **Calendar:** Semester, extensive summer session. Extensive evening/early morning classes. **Microcomputers:** 296 located in libraries. **Special facilities:** Art gallery, wildlife preserve, museum of world cultures, research vessel for marine biology laboratory.

DEGREES OFFERED. BA, BS, MA, MS, MBA. 1,297 bachelor's degrees awarded in 1992. 28% in business and management, 13% teacher education, 12% letters/literature, 9% physical sciences, 8% psychology, 12% social sciences. Graduate degrees offered in 13 major fields of study.

UNDERGRADUATE MAJORS. Accounting, anthropology, biology, business administration and management, business economics, chemistry, clinical laboratory science, computer and information sciences, criminal justice studies, elementary education, English, environmental science, finance, fine arts, French, geography, geology, history, junior high education, management information systems, marine biology, marketing management, mathematics, music, nursing, parks and recreation management, philosophy, physical education, physics, political science and government, psychology, religion, social sciences, social work, sociology, Spanish, special education, speech.

ACADEMIC PROGRAMS. Cooperative education, double major, honors program, independent study, internships, study abroad, teacher preparation, visiting/exchange student program. **Remedial services:** Learning center, reduced course load, remedial instruction, special counselor, tutoring. **Placement/credit:** AP, CLEP Subject, institutional tests.

ACADEMIC REQUIREMENTS. Freshmen must earn minimum GPA of 1.2 to continue in good standing. 77% of freshmen return for sophomore year. Students must declare major by end of first year. **Graduation requirements:** 124 hours for bachelor's. Most students required to take courses in English, foreign languages, history, mathematics, philosophy/religion, biological/physical sciences, social sciences. **Postgraduate studies:** 9% enter law school, 3% enter medical school, 8% enter MBA programs, 16% enter other graduate study.

FRESHMAN ADMISSIONS. Selection criteria: High school academic record and test scores important. **High school preparation:** 20 units required. Required and recommended units include biological science 1, English 4, mathematics 3, physical science 1, social science 2 and science 3. Foreign language 2 recommended. Additional unit of laboratory science required. One foreign language and 1 mathematics unit in 12th grade recommended. **Test requirements:** SAT or ACT; score report by February 15.

1992 FRESHMAN CLASS PROFILE. 2,704 men applied, 1,289 accepted, 461 enrolled; 3,701 women applied, 2,166 accepted, 776 enrolled. 65% had high school GPA of 3.0 or higher, 35% between 2.0 and 2.99. **Academic background:** Mid 50% of enrolled freshmen had SAT-V between 390-490, SAT-M between 430-550. 97% submitted SAT scores. **Characteristics:** 79% from in state, 74% live in college housing, 10% have minority backgrounds, 1% are foreign students. Average age is 19.

FALL-TERM APPLICATIONS. $25 fee. Closing date May 1; priority given to applications received by February 15; applicants notified on a rolling basis; must reply by May 15.

STUDENT LIFE. Housing: Dormitories (women, coed); apartment, handicapped housing available. **Activities:** Student government, magazine, radio, student newspaper, choral groups, concert band, dance, drama, jazz band, music ensembles, musical theater, pep band, symphony orchestra, readers theater, fraternities, sororities, Christian Fellowship, Black Student Union, academic clubs and organizations. **Additional information:** Area churches sponsor campus ministry for students, special programs, social, health and personal growth concerns.

ATHLETICS. NCAA. **Intercollegiate:** Baseball M, basketball, cross-country, diving, golf, soccer M, softball W, swimming, tennis, track and field, volleyball W. **Intramural:** Basketball, racquetball, soccer, softball, tennis, volleyball.

STUDENT SERVICES. Aptitude testing, career counseling, employment service for undergraduates, freshman orientation, health services, personal counseling, placement service for graduates, special adviser for adult students, veterans counselor, services/facilities for handicapped.

ANNUAL EXPENSES. Tuition and fees (1992-93): $1,344, $5,672 additional for out-of-state students. **Room and board:** $3,460. **Books and supplies:** $500. **Other expenses:** $1,087.

FINANCIAL AID. 38% of freshmen, 40% of continuing students receive some form of aid. 53% of grants, 97% of loans, 13% of jobs based on need. 520 enrolled freshmen were judged to have need, 450 were offered aid. Academic, music/drama, art, athletic, state/district residency, leadership, minority scholarships available. **Aid applications:** No closing date; priority given to applications received by March 15; applicants notified on a rolling basis beginning on or about April 1; must reply within 2 weeks.

ADDRESS/TELEPHONE. Diane M. Zeeman, Director of Undergraduate Admissions, University of North Carolina at Wilmington, 601 South College Road, Wilmington, NC 28403-3297. (919) 395-3243.

Vance-Granville Community College
Henderson, North Carolina — CB code: 0617

2-year public community college, coed. Founded in 1969. **Accreditation:** Regional. **Undergraduate enrollment:** 458 men, 728 women full time; 560

men, 933 women part time. **Faculty:** 150 total (70 full time), 9 with doctorates or other terminal degrees. **Location:** Rural campus in large town; 42 miles from Raleigh. **Calendar:** Quarter, extensive summer session. Extensive evening/early morning classes. **Microcomputers:** Located in libraries, classrooms, computer centers. **Additional facts:** 4 rural counties served with sites in Warrenton, Butner and Louisburg.

DEGREES OFFERED. AA, AS, AAS. 227 associate degrees awarded in 1992. 32% in business/office and marketing/distribution, 10% computer sciences, 6% allied health, 8% parks/recreation, protective services, public affairs, 22% trade and industry.

UNDERGRADUATE MAJORS. Accounting, anatomy, automotive technology, biology, business administration and management, business and office, business data entry equipment operation, business data processing and related programs, business data programming, cell biology, child development/care/guidance, computer programming, data processing, finance, industrial engineering, industrial technology, law enforcement and corrections technologies, liberal/general studies, marketing and distribution, mathematics, microcomputer software, nursing, pathology, human and animal, physiology, human and animal, precision metal work, radiograph medical technology, recreation and community services technologies, recreation therapy, secretarial and related programs, teacher aide, textile technology, zoology.

ACADEMIC PROGRAMS. 2-year transfer program, double major, dual enrollment of high school students, independent study, internships. **Remedial services:** Learning center, reduced course load, remedial instruction, special counselor, tutoring. **Placement/credit:** AP, CLEP General and Subject, institutional tests; 45 credit hours maximum for associate degree.

ACADEMIC REQUIREMENTS. Freshmen must earn minimum GPA of 2.0 to continue in good standing. 61% of freshmen return for sophomore year. Students must declare major on enrollment. **Graduation requirements:** 96 hours for associate (65 in major). Most students required to take courses in English, humanities, mathematics, social sciences.

FRESHMAN ADMISSIONS. Selection criteria: Open admissions. Selective admissions to nursing and radiologic technology programs, based on academic record, placement tests and residency.

1992 FRESHMAN CLASS PROFILE. 342 men, 738 women enrolled. 14% had high school GPA of 3.0 or higher, 64% between 2.0 and 2.99. **Characteristics:** 99% from in state, 100% commute, 40% have minority backgrounds. Average age is 26.

FALL-TERM APPLICATIONS. No fee. No closing date; applicants notified on a rolling basis. Interview required for nursing, radiologic technology applicants. Early admission available. College placement examinations required of all students.

STUDENT LIFE. Activities: Student government, student newspaper, drama, departmental clubs.

ATHLETICS. Intramural: Basketball, softball, table tennis, tennis, volleyball.

STUDENT SERVICES. Aptitude testing, career counseling, employment service for undergraduates, health services, on-campus day care, personal counseling, placement service for graduates, services/facilities for handicapped.

ANNUAL EXPENSES. Tuition and fees (1992-93): $584, $3,959 additional for out-of-state students. **Books and supplies:** $475. **Other expenses:** $400.

FINANCIAL AID. 45% of freshmen, 52% of continuing students receive some form of aid. Grants, loans, jobs available. Academic, state/district residency, minority scholarships available. **Aid applications:** Closing date July 1; applicants notified on or about August 15; must reply by August 20.

ADDRESS/TELEPHONE. Brenda W. Beck, Admissions Officer, Vance-Granville Community College, PO Box 917, Henderson, NC 27536. (919) 492-2061. Fax: (919) 430-0460.

Wake Forest University

Winston-Salem, North Carolina — CB code: 5885

Admissions: 43% of applicants accepted
Based on: ••• School record, test scores
•• Activities, essay, recommendations, special talents
• Religious affiliation/commitment
Completion: 97% of freshmen end year in good standing
85% graduate, 31% of these enter graduate study

4-year private university, coed. Founded in 1834. **Accreditation:** Regional. **Undergraduate enrollment:** 1,823 men, 1,773 women full time; 88 men, 57 women part time. **Graduate enrollment:** 923 men, 565 women full time; 316 men, 179 women part time. **Faculty:** 1,535 total (951 full time), 906 with doctorates or other terminal degrees. **Location:** Suburban campus in small city; 4 miles from downtown. **Calendar:** Semester, limited summer session. **Microcomputers:** 161 located in dormitories, libraries, classrooms, computer centers, campus-wide network. **Special facilities:** Anthropology museum, art gallery, archaeology laboratory, primate research station, laser physics laboratory.

DEGREES OFFERED. BA, BS, MA, MS, MBA, MEd, PhD, MD, JD. 819 bachelor's degrees awarded in 1992. 16% in business and management, 18% letters/literature, 9% life sciences, 7% psychology, 28% social sciences. Graduate degrees offered in 27 major fields of study.

UNDERGRADUATE MAJORS. Accounting, anthropology, art history, biology, business and management, chemistry, classics, communications, computer and information sciences, dramatic arts, economics, education, elementary education, English, French, German, Greek (classical), health and sports science, health sciences, history, junior high education, Latin, mathematics, medical laboratory technologies, microbiology, music, philosophy, physician's assistant, physics, political science and government, psychology, religion, rhetoric, Russian, secondary education, sociology, Spanish, studio art.

ACADEMIC PROGRAMS. Accelerated program, double major, honors program, independent study, internships, study abroad, teacher preparation, visiting/exchange student program, cross-registration, semester in London or Venice, and semester at Universities in Dijon, Salamanca, Berlin, Moscow, Beijing, and Japan; liberal arts/career combination in engineering, forestry, health sciences; combined bachelor's/graduate program in medicine, law. **Remedial services:** Learning center, reduced course load, special counselor, tutoring. **ROTC:** Army. **Placement/credit:** AP, CLEP Subject, IB, institutional tests; 64 credit hours maximum for bachelor's degree.

ACADEMIC REQUIREMENTS. Freshmen must earn minimum GPA of 1.45 to continue in good standing. 98% of freshmen return for sophomore year. Students must declare major by end of second year. **Graduation requirements:** 144 hours for bachelor's (40 in major). Most students required to take courses in arts/fine arts, English, foreign languages, history, humanities, mathematics, philosophy/religion, biological/physical sciences, social sciences. **Postgraduate studies:** 6% enter law school, 5% enter medical school, 1% enter MBA programs, 19% enter other graduate study. **Additional information:** Language courses available at all levels in Russian, Greek, Italian, and Hebrew. Elementary and intermediate courses available in Chinese and Japanese and elementary courses available in Hindi and Portuguese.

FRESHMAN ADMISSIONS. Selection criteria: High school curriculum and achievement, test scores, school and community activities, essay, personal recommendations, and special talents all important. **High school preparation:** 16 units required. Required and recommended units include English 4, foreign language 2-4, mathematics 3-4 and social science 2-4. Science 4 recommended. **Test requirements:** SAT; score report by January 15. For merit-based scholarships, English, Mathematics I or II, and 1 other ACH required. Score report by March 1.

1992 FRESHMAN CLASS PROFILE. 2,762 men applied, 1,184 accepted, 462 enrolled; 2,795 women applied, 1,200 accepted, 441 enrolled. 70% were in top tenth and 92% were in top quarter of graduating class. **Academic background:** Mid 50% of enrolled freshmen had SAT-V between 550-650, SAT-M between 600-700. 99% submitted SAT scores. **Characteristics:** 30% from in state, 98% live in college housing, 11% have minority backgrounds, 1% are foreign students, 35% join fraternities/sororities. Average age is 18.

FALL-TERM APPLICATIONS. $25 fee, may be waived for applicants with need. Closing date January 15; applicants notified on or about April 1; must reply by May 1. Essay required. Audition recommended for music, theater, art, dance, debate applicants. CRDA. Deferred and early admission available. EDP-S.

STUDENT LIFE. Housing: Dormitories (men, women, coed); apartment, fraternity, sorority, handicapped housing available. International house, theme housing and off-campus foreign language houses available. Housing guaranteed for 4 years. Substance-free housing available. **Activities:** Student government, magazine, radio, student newspaper, yearbook, choral groups, concert band, dance, drama, jazz band, marching band, music ensembles, musical theater, opera, pep band, symphony orchestra, fraternities, sororities, Black Students' Alliance, Young Democrats, Young Republicans, Alpha Phi Omega, International Club, InterVarsity Christian Fellowship, and other interdenominational and denominational groups, Amnesty International, Habitat for Humanity, Volunteer Service Corps.

ATHLETICS. NCAA. **Intercollegiate:** Baseball M, basketball, cross-country, field hockey W, football M, golf, soccer M, tennis, track and field. **Intramural:** Basketball, bowling, cross-country, diving, golf, horseback riding, ice hockey M, lacrosse, racquetball, rugby M, sailing, skin diving, soccer, softball, swimming, tennis, track and field, volleyball, water polo W.

STUDENT SERVICES. Aptitude testing, career counseling, employment service for undergraduates, freshman orientation, health services, personal counseling, placement service for graduates, services/facilities for handicapped.

ANNUAL EXPENSES. Tuition and fees: $13,000. **Room and board:** $4,280. **Books and supplies:** $500. **Other expenses:** $1,000.

FINANCIAL AID. 63% of freshmen, 60% of continuing students receive some form of aid. 34% of grants, 77% of loans, 14% of jobs based on need. 232 enrolled freshmen were judged to have need, all were offered aid. Academic, music/drama, art, athletic, state/district residency, leadership, religious affiliation, minority scholarships available. **Aid applications:** No closing date; priority given to applications received by March 1; applicants notified on a rolling basis beginning on or about April 15.

ADDRESS/TELEPHONE. W. G. Starling, Director of Admissions and Financial Aid, Wake Forest University, PO Box 7305, Winston-Salem, NC 27109. (919) 759-5201. Fax: (919) 759-6074.

Wake Technical Community College
Raleigh, North Carolina CB code: 5928

2-year public community college, coed. Founded in 1958. **Accreditation:** Regional. **Undergraduate enrollment:** 6,850 men and women. **Faculty:** 667 total (189 full time), 27 with doctorates or other terminal degrees. **Location:** Suburban campus in small city; 10 miles from downtown. **Calendar:** Quarter, extensive summer session. Saturday and extensive evening/early morning classes. **Microcomputers:** 62 located in classrooms, computer centers.

DEGREES OFFERED. AA, AS, AAS. 404 associate degrees awarded in 1992. 10% in business and management, 23% business/office and marketing/distribution, 8% computer sciences, 33% engineering technologies, 17% health sciences, 6% allied health.

UNDERGRADUATE MAJORS. Accounting, air pollution control technology, architectural technologies, automotive technology, business and management, business and office, business computer/console/peripheral equipment operation, business data processing and related programs, business data programming, chemical manufacturing technology, civil technology, computer and information sciences, computer programming, computer technology, early childhood education, electromechanical technology, electronic technology, emergency medical technologies, energy conservation and use technology, engineering and engineering-related technologies, food management, hospitality and recreation marketing, hotel/motel and restaurant management, industrial pharmaceutical technology, industrial technology, landscape architecture, law enforcement and corrections technologies, legal secretary, library assistant, manufacturing technology, marketing and distribution, medical laboratory technologies, medical secretary, nursing, radiograph medical technology, robotics, secretarial and related programs, survey and mapping technology.

ACADEMIC PROGRAMS. 2-year transfer program, cooperative education, double major, dual enrollment of high school students. **Remedial services:** Learning center, preadmission summer program, reduced course load, remedial instruction, special counselor, tutoring.

ACADEMIC REQUIREMENTS. Freshmen must earn minimum GPA of 1.6 to continue in good standing. 61% of freshmen return for sophomore year. Students must declare major on application. **Graduation requirements:** 106 hours for associate (80 in major). Most students required to take courses in arts/fine arts, computer science, English, history, humanities, mathematics, philosophy/religion, biological/physical sciences, social sciences.

FRESHMAN ADMISSIONS. Selection criteria: Open admissions. Selective admission to health programs based on test scores, school achievement record and interview. Recommended units include English 4 and mathematics 3. One chemistry required for nursing, medical laboratory, radiograph technology applicants.

1992 FRESHMAN CLASS PROFILE. 293 men, 303 women enrolled. 45% had high school GPA of 3.0 or higher, 49% between 2.0 and 2.99. **Characteristics:** 98% from in state, 100% commute, 32% have minority backgrounds, 2% are foreign students. Average age is 25.

FALL-TERM APPLICATIONS. No fee. No closing date; applicants notified on a rolling basis; must reply 2 weeks before beginning of fall quarter. Interview recommended. Deferred admission available.

STUDENT LIFE. Activities: Student government, radio, student newspaper.

ATHLETICS. Intramural: Basketball, golf M, softball.

STUDENT SERVICES. Aptitude testing, career counseling, employment service for undergraduates, freshman orientation, health services, on-campus day care, personal counseling, placement service for graduates, veterans counselor, services/facilities for handicapped.

ANNUAL EXPENSES. Tuition and fees (1992-93): $566, $3,959 additional for out-of-state students. **Books and supplies:** $400. **Other expenses:** $1,071.

FINANCIAL AID. 16% of freshmen, 12% of continuing students receive some form of aid. 78% of grants, 54% of loans, all jobs based on need. 543 enrolled freshmen were judged to have need, 429 were offered aid. Academic scholarships available. **Aid applications:** No closing date; priority given to applications received by August 31; applicants notified on a rolling basis beginning on or about July 1; must reply within 4 weeks.

ADDRESS/TELEPHONE. Robert L. Brown, Vice President of Student Services, Wake Technical Community College, 9101 Fayetteville Road, Raleigh, NC 27603. (919) 772-7500. Fax: (919) 779-3360.

Warren Wilson College
Swannanoa, North Carolina CB code: 5886

Admissions: 79% of applicants accepted
Based on: ••• School record
•• Essay, recommendations, test scores
• Activities, interview, special talents
Completion: 81% of freshmen end year in good standing

4-year private liberal arts college, coed, affiliated with Presbyterian Church (USA). Founded in 1894. **Accreditation:** Regional. **Undergraduate enrollment:** 207 men, 274 women full time; 2 men, 6 women part time. **Graduate enrollment:** 18 men, 54 women full time. **Faculty:** 70 total (44 full time), 30 with doctorates or other terminal degrees. **Location:** Rural campus in rural community; One mile from Asheville. **Calendar:** 4 consecutive 8-week terms. **Microcomputers:** 75 located in libraries, computer centers. **Special facilities:** 300-acre farm, 700-acre forest. **Additional facts:** Campus includes over 25 miles of hiking trails

DEGREES OFFERED. BA, MFA. 111 bachelor's degrees awarded in 1992. 15% in business and management, 8% education, 14% letters/literature, 20% life sciences, 6% mathematics, 22% social sciences. Graduate degrees offered in 1 major field of study.

UNDERGRADUATE MAJORS. Biology, business administration and management, chemistry, computer and information sciences, early childhood education, economics, education, elementary education, English, environmental science, history, humanities, humanities and social sciences, international studies, junior high education, liberal/general studies, mathematics, political science and government, premedicine, preveterinary, psychology, secondary education, social work.

ACADEMIC PROGRAMS. 2-year transfer program, double major, dual enrollment of high school students, honors program, independent study, internships, student-designed major, study abroad, teacher preparation, visiting/exchange student program, cross-registration; liberal arts/career combination in engineering, forestry, health sciences. **Remedial services:** Special counselor, tutoring. **Placement/credit:** AP, CLEP General and Subject, IB, institutional tests.

ACADEMIC REQUIREMENTS. Freshmen must earn minimum GPA of 1.75 to continue in good standing. 72% of freshmen return for sophomore year. Students must declare major by end of second year. **Graduation requirements:** 128 hours for bachelor's (36 in major). Most students required to take courses in arts/fine arts, English, history, mathematics, philosophy/religion, biological/physical sciences, social sciences.

FRESHMAN ADMISSIONS. Selection criteria: In order of importance, high school achievement, class rank, personal statement, recommendations, SAT or ACT scores, school and community activities. All records of examinations taken overseas required of foreign applicants. **High school preparation:** 12 units required. Required and recommended units include English 4, mathematics 3, social science 2 and science 2. Foreign language 2 recommended. Mathematics requirement includes algebra I and II, and geometry. Sciences must include 2 laboratories. **Test requirements:** SAT or ACT (SAT preferred); score report by May 1.

1992 FRESHMAN CLASS PROFILE. 299 men and women applied, 236 accepted; 46 men enrolled, 69 women enrolled. 42% had high school GPA of 3.0 or higher, 51% between 2.0 and 2.99. 25% were in top tenth and 38% were in top quarter of graduating class. **Academic background:** Mid 50% of enrolled freshmen had SAT-V between 440-600, SAT-M between 450-590; ACT composite between 16-30. 91% submitted SAT scores, 9% submitted ACT scores. **Characteristics:** 44% from in state, 99% live in college housing, 7% have minority backgrounds, 14% are foreign students. Average age is 18.

FALL-TERM APPLICATIONS. $25 fee, may be waived for applicants with need. Closing date July 1; priority given to applications received by March 15; applicants notified on a rolling basis beginning on or about September 1. Interview recommended. Essay recommended. CRDA. Deferred and early admission available.

STUDENT LIFE. Housing: Dormitories (men, women, coed). Limited number of apartments available for single parents and married students. **Activities:** Student government, film, student newspaper, yearbook, community government by full staff and 30-student caucus, choral groups, dance, drama, music ensembles, musical theater, mountain string band, youth fellowship, Students National Education Association, peace group, Amnesty International, Habitat for Humanity.

ATHLETICS. NAIA. **Intercollegiate:** Basketball, cross-country, soccer, swimming. **Intramural:** Basketball, cross-country, soccer, softball, swimming, table tennis, tennis, volleyball.

STUDENT SERVICES. Aptitude testing, career counseling, employment service for undergraduates, freshman orientation, health services, on-campus day care, personal counseling, special adviser for adult students.

ANNUAL EXPENSES. Tuition and fees: $10,015. **Room and board:** $2,852. **Books and supplies:** $500. **Other expenses:** $738.

FINANCIAL AID. 59% of freshmen, 79% of continuing students receive some form of aid. 70% of grants, 96% of loans, 24% of jobs based on need. 48 enrolled freshmen were judged to have need, all were offered aid. Academic, state/district residency, leadership scholarships available. **Aid**

applications: No closing date; priority given to applications received by April 15; applicants notified on a rolling basis beginning on or about May 1; must reply within 3 weeks. **Additional information:** All resident students required to work 15 hours per week in college's work program. Earnings credited toward college costs.

ADDRESS/TELEPHONE. Thomas Weede, Dean of Admission, Warren Wilson College, 701 Warren Wilson College Road, Swannanoa, NC 28778-2099. (704) 298-3325 ext. 245. (800) 934-3536. Fax: (704) 298-2161.

Wayne Community College
Goldsboro, North Carolina CB code: 5926

2-year public community college, coed. Founded in 1957. **Accreditation:** Regional. **Undergraduate enrollment:** 715 men, 995 women full time; 417 men, 617 women part time. **Faculty:** 137 total (87 full time), 4 with doctorates or other terminal degrees. **Location:** Suburban campus in large town; 55 miles from Raleigh. **Calendar:** Quarter, limited summer session. Extensive evening/early morning classes. **Microcomputers:** 64 located in libraries, classrooms.

DEGREES OFFERED. AA, AS, AAS. 268 associate degrees awarded in 1992. 8% in agriculture, 18% business and management, 10% business/office and marketing/distribution, 16% engineering technologies, 11% health sciences, 8% allied health, 18% multi/interdisciplinary studies, 5% parks/recreation, protective services, public affairs.

UNDERGRADUATE MAJORS. Accounting, aeronautical technology, agribusiness, animal sciences, automotive mechanics, automotive technology, biological and physical sciences, business and management, child development/care/guidance, computer programming, dental hygiene, developmental disabilities, drafting and design technology, engineering and engineering-related technologies, fashion merchandising, forestry and related sciences, gerontology, industrial technology, law enforcement and corrections technologies, legal secretary, liberal/general studies, marketing and distribution, medical secretary, mental health/human services, nursing, poultry, secretarial and related programs, soil sciences, wildlife management.

ACADEMIC PROGRAMS. 2-year transfer program, cooperative education, double major, dual enrollment of high school students, internships, telecourses. **Remedial services:** Learning center, reduced course load, remedial instruction, special counselor, tutoring. **Placement/credit:** AP, CLEP General and Subject, institutional tests.

ACADEMIC REQUIREMENTS. Freshmen must earn minimum GPA of 2.0 to continue in good standing. 75% of freshmen return for sophomore year. Students must declare major on enrollment. **Graduation requirements:** 110 hours for associate (60 in major). Most students required to take courses in computer science, English, mathematics, social sciences.

FRESHMAN ADMISSIONS. Selection criteria: Open admissions. Selective admissions to allied health programs based on placement test, academic record and interview.

1992 FRESHMAN CLASS PROFILE. 687 men and women enrolled. **Characteristics:** 86% from in state, 100% commute, 27% have minority backgrounds, 1% are foreign students. Average age is 27.

FALL-TERM APPLICATIONS. No fee. No closing date; applicants notified on a rolling basis. Interview required for allied health programs applicants. Placement interview required of all applicants. Deferred admission available.

STUDENT LIFE. Activities: Student government, student newspaper, yearbook, choral groups, concert band, fraternities. **Additional information:** Student government organizes sports program.

ATHLETICS. Intercollegiate: Basketball M, golf, softball, volleyball. **Intramural:** Table tennis.

STUDENT SERVICES. Aptitude testing, career counseling, employment service for undergraduates, freshman orientation, health services, personal counseling, placement service for graduates, veterans counselor, services/facilities for handicapped.

ANNUAL EXPENSES. Tuition and fees (1992-93): $584, $3,959 additional for out-of-state students. **Books and supplies:** $600. **Other expenses:** $400.

FINANCIAL AID. 16% of freshmen, 20% of continuing students receive some form of aid. All grants, 80% of loans, 85% of jobs based on need. 410 enrolled freshmen were judged to have need, 340 were offered aid. **Aid applications:** No closing date; priority given to applications received by April 15; applicants notified on a rolling basis beginning on or about July 30; must reply within 2 weeks.

ADDRESS/TELEPHONE. Susan M. Sasser, Director of Admissions and Records, Wayne Community College, Caller Box 8002, Goldsboro, NC 27533-8002. (919) 735-5151 ext. 238. Fax: (919) 736-3204.

Western Carolina University
Cullowhee, North Carolina CB code: 5897

Admissions: 77% of applicants accepted
Based on: ••• School record, test scores
• Activities, essay, interview, recommendations, special talents
Completion: 85% of freshmen end year in good standing
43% graduate, 12% of these enter graduate study

4-year public university, coed. Founded in 1889. **Accreditation:** Regional. **Undergraduate enrollment:** 2,602 men, 2,511 women full time; 230 men, 304 women part time. **Graduate enrollment:** 134 men, 167 women full time; 195 men, 433 women part time. **Faculty:** 430 total (324 full time), 235 with doctorates or other terminal degrees. **Location:** Rural campus in rural community; 55 miles from Asheville, 120 miles from Knoxville, Tennessee. **Calendar:** Semester, extensive summer session. Extensive evening/early morning classes. **Microcomputers:** 300 located in libraries, classrooms, computer centers. **Special facilities:** Mountain Heritage Center, Belk Art Gallery, Chelsea Gallery, Geology Museum.

DEGREES OFFERED. BA, BS, BFA, MA, MS, MBA, MEd. 896 bachelor's degrees awarded in 1992. 13% in business and management, 9% business/office and marketing/distribution, 11% education, 15% teacher education, 13% health sciences, 6% home economics, 7% parks/recreation, protective services, public affairs, 5% visual and performing arts. Graduate degrees offered in 42 major fields of study.

UNDERGRADUATE MAJORS. Accounting, anthropology, art education, biology, business administration and management, business administration law, business economics, business education, chemistry, child development/care/guidance, clinical laboratory science, communications, computer and information sciences, dramatic arts, education of exceptional children, education of the mentally handicapped, electronic technology, elementary education, emergency medical technologies, English, English education, environmental health, finance, fine arts, food science and nutrition, foreign languages education, French, geography, geology, German, health care administration, health education, history, home economics, home economics education, home furnishings and equipment management/production/services, human environment and housing, individual and family development, industrial arts education, international business management, junior high education, law enforcement and corrections, liberal/general studies, management science, manufacturing technology, marketing management, mathematics, mathematics education, medical records administration, music, music education, nursing, parks and recreation management, philosophy, physical education, physics, political science and government, psychology, radio/television broadcasting, renewable natural resources, science education, secondary education, secretarial and related programs, social science education, social sciences, social work, sociology, Spanish, special education, specific learning disabilities, speech correction, speech/communication/theater education, sports management, textiles and clothing, therapeutic recreation.

ACADEMIC PROGRAMS. Cooperative education, double major, dual enrollment of high school students, education specialist degree, honors program, independent study, internships, student-designed major, study abroad, teacher preparation, cross-registration. **Remedial services:** Learning center, preadmission summer program, reduced course load, remedial instruction, special counselor, tutoring. **ROTC:** Army. **Placement/credit:** AP, CLEP Subject, institutional tests; 48 credit hours maximum for bachelor's degree.

ACADEMIC REQUIREMENTS. Freshmen must earn minimum GPA of 2.0 to continue in good standing. 71% of freshmen return for sophomore year. Students must declare major by end of second year. **Graduation requirements:** 128 hours for bachelor's (45 in major). Most students required to take courses in computer science, English, history, humanities, mathematics, biological/physical sciences, social sciences. **Postgraduate studies:** 1% enter law school, 1% enter medical school, 3% enter MBA programs, 7% enter other graduate study.

FRESHMAN ADMISSIONS. Selection criteria: Careful consideration given to academic records, rank in class, and test scores. Recommendations optional, but will be considered if submitted. **High school preparation:** 13 units required. Required and recommended units include biological science 1, English 4, mathematics 3, physical science 1, social science 3 and science 1. Foreign language 2 recommended. **Test requirements:** SAT or ACT (SAT preferred); score report by July 15.

1992 FRESHMAN CLASS PROFILE. 1,734 men applied, 1,232 accepted, 524 enrolled; 1,508 women applied, 1,280 accepted, 545 enrolled. 32% had high school GPA of 3.0 or higher, 67% between 2.0 and 2.99. 11% were in top tenth and 31% were in top quarter of graduating class. **Academic background:** Mid 50% of enrolled freshmen had SAT-V between 360-450, SAT-M between 400-510. 99% submitted SAT scores. **Characteristics:** 90% from in state, 82% live in college housing, 6% have minority backgrounds, 1% are foreign students, 10% join fraternities/sororities. Average age is 18.

FALL-TERM APPLICATIONS. $20 fee, may be waived for applicants with need. Closing date May 1; priority given to applications received by December 1; applicants notified on a rolling basis; must reply within 4 weeks. Audition required for music applicants. Interview recommended.

Portfolio recommended for art applicants. Deferred and early admission available.

STUDENT LIFE. Housing: Dormitories (men, women); apartment, fraternity, sorority housing available. Sorority housing available within residence halls. **Activities:** Student government, film, radio, student newspaper, television, yearbook, choral groups, concert band, drama, jazz band, marching band, music ensembles, musical theater, opera, pep band, symphony orchestra, fraternities, sororities, black students association, forensics, Circle-K, College Democrats, College Republicans.

ATHLETICS. NCAA. **Intercollegiate:** Baseball M, basketball, cross-country, football M, golf M, tennis, track and field, volleyball W. **Intramural:** Archery, badminton, basketball, bowling, cross-country, fencing, golf, handball, racquetball, skiing, soccer, softball, swimming, table tennis, tennis, track and field, volleyball, water polo, wrestling M. **Clubs:** Wrestling, skiing.

STUDENT SERVICES. Aptitude testing, career counseling, employment service for undergraduates, freshman orientation, health services, personal counseling, placement service for graduates, veterans counselor, services/facilities for handicapped.

ANNUAL EXPENSES. Tuition and fees (1992-93): $1,375, $5,672 additional for out-of-state students. **Room and board:** $2,310. **Books and supplies:** $200. **Other expenses:** $756.

FINANCIAL AID. 40% of freshmen, 56% of continuing students receive some form of aid. 54% of grants, 88% of loans, 22% of jobs based on need. 432 enrolled freshmen were judged to have need, 422 were offered aid. Academic, music/drama, art, athletic, state/district residency, minority scholarships available. **Aid applications:** No closing date; priority given to applications received by April 1; applicants notified on a rolling basis beginning on or about April 15; must reply within 2 weeks.

ADDRESS/TELEPHONE. Drumont I. Bowman, Director of Admissions, Western Carolina University, Cullowhee, NC 28723. (704) 227-7317.

Western Piedmont Community College

Morganton, North Carolina CB code: 5922

2-year public community college, coed. Founded in 1964. **Accreditation:** Regional. **Undergraduate enrollment:** 376 men, 586 women full time; 706 men, 1,002 women part time. **Faculty:** 118 total (58 full time), 6 with doctorates or other terminal degrees. **Location:** Rural campus in large town; 60 miles from Asheville. **Calendar:** Quarter, extensive summer session. Extensive evening/early morning classes. **Microcomputers:** 150 located in libraries, classrooms, computer centers. **Special facilities:** Greenhouse, fitness and nature trails.

DEGREES OFFERED. AA, AS, AAS. 152 associate degrees awarded in 1992. 10% in business and management, 10% business/office and marketing/distribution, 10% computer sciences, 10% teacher education, 10% engineering technologies, 25% health sciences, 5% life sciences, 10% parks/recreation, protective services, public affairs, 5% social sciences, 5% visual and performing arts.

UNDERGRADUATE MAJORS. Accounting, agricultural sciences, biology, business administration and management, business and office, business data programming, civil engineering, computer technology, drafting, drafting and design technology, dramatic arts, drug and alcohol technology, education, elementary education, engineering and engineering-related technologies, finance, fine arts, forestry and related sciences, horticulture, industrial technology, information sciences and systems, interior design, journalism, law enforcement and corrections technologies, legal assistant/paralegal, legal secretary, liberal/general studies, marketing and distribution, marketing research, mathematics, medical assistant, medical laboratory technologies, medical secretary, nursing, predentistry, prelaw, premedicine, preveterinary, protective services, real estate, recreation therapy, science technologies, secondary education, secretarial and related programs, social sciences, systems analysis.

ACADEMIC PROGRAMS. 2-year transfer program, cooperative education, dual enrollment of high school students, internships. **Remedial services:** Learning center, reduced course load, remedial instruction, special counselor. **Placement/credit:** CLEP Subject, institutional tests; 15 credit hours maximum for associate degree.

ACADEMIC REQUIREMENTS. Freshmen must earn minimum GPA of 2.0 to continue in good standing. 50% of freshmen return for sophomore year. Students must declare major by end of first year. **Graduation requirements:** 96 hours for associate. Most students required to take courses in English, history, humanities, mathematics, biological/physical sciences, social sciences.

FRESHMAN ADMISSIONS. Selection criteria: Open admissions. Selective admissions for health programs.

1992 FRESHMAN CLASS PROFILE. 280 men, 328 women enrolled. **Characteristics:** 100% from in state, 100% commute, 7% have minority backgrounds.

FALL-TERM APPLICATIONS. No fee. No closing date; applicants notified on a rolling basis. Interview recommended for nursing, dental assistant, medical laboratory technician, medical office assistant applicants. Portfolio recommended for fine arts applicants. Early admission available. Application closing date for nursing, medical laboratory applicants April 15 for admission in fall.

STUDENT LIFE. Activities: Student government, student newspaper, drama, College Republicans, Young Democrats, Phi Beta Lambda, Phi Theta Kappa, Black Students Association.

ATHLETICS. Intramural: Basketball M, softball, volleyball W.

STUDENT SERVICES. Aptitude testing, career counseling, employment service for undergraduates, personal counseling, placement service for graduates, veterans counselor, services/facilities for handicapped.

ANNUAL EXPENSES. Tuition and fees (1992-93): $575, $3,959 additional for out-of-state students. **Books and supplies:** $500. **Other expenses:** $1,200.

FINANCIAL AID. 40% of freshmen, 45% of continuing students receive some form of aid. 93% of grants, all loans, all jobs based on need. 450 enrolled freshmen were judged to have need, 440 were offered aid. Academic, state/district residency scholarships available. **Aid applications:** No closing date; priority given to applications received by April 15; applicants notified on a rolling basis beginning on or about July 10; must reply within 2 weeks.

ADDRESS/TELEPHONE. Jim A. Reed, Director of Admissions, Western Piedmont Community College, 1001 Burkemont Avenue, Morganton, NC 28655. (704) 438-6051. Fax: (704) 438-6051.

Wilkes Community College

Wilkesboro, North Carolina CB code: 5921

2-year public community college, coed. Founded in 1965. **Accreditation:** Regional. **Undergraduate enrollment:** 425 men, 568 women full time; 310 men, 659 women part time. **Faculty:** 102 total (63 full time), 4 with doctorates or other terminal degrees. **Location:** Rural campus in small town; 50 miles from Winston-Salem. **Calendar:** Quarter, limited summer session. Saturday and extensive evening/early morning classes. **Microcomputers:** 75 located in libraries, classrooms, computer centers. **Special facilities:** John A. Walker Community Center. **Additional facts:** Campus on National Register of Public Gardens.

DEGREES OFFERED. AA, AS, AAS. 171 associate degrees awarded in 1992. 15% in business and management, 5% business/office and marketing/distribution, 5% computer sciences, 10% engineering technologies, 6% health sciences, 42% multi/interdisciplinary studies, 5% parks/recreation, protective services, public affairs.

UNDERGRADUATE MAJORS. Accounting, automotive mechanics, business administration and management, business and office, business data processing and related programs, computer and information sciences, construction, criminal justice technology, diesel engine mechanics, dramatic arts, education, electromechanical technology, electronic technology, fine arts, food management, hotel/motel and restaurant management, liberal/general studies, mathematics, music, nursing, radio/television broadcasting, radio/television technology, science technologies, secretarial and related programs, social work.

ACADEMIC PROGRAMS. 2-year transfer program, cooperative education, double major, dual enrollment of high school students, honors program, independent study. **Remedial services:** Learning center, preadmission summer program, reduced course load, remedial instruction, special counselor, tutoring. **Placement/credit:** AP, CLEP General, institutional tests; 25 credit hours maximum for associate degree.

ACADEMIC REQUIREMENTS. Freshmen must earn minimum GPA of 2.0 to continue in good standing. 60% of freshmen return for sophomore year. Students must declare major on enrollment. **Graduation requirements:** 96 hours for associate (50 in major). Most students required to take courses in computer science, English, humanities, mathematics, social sciences.

FRESHMAN ADMISSIONS. Selection criteria: Open admissions. Selective admissions for nursing and dental programs.

1992 FRESHMAN CLASS PROFILE. 210 men, 375 women enrolled. **Characteristics:** 99% from in state, 100% commute, 7% have minority backgrounds. Average age is 20.

FALL-TERM APPLICATIONS. No fee. No closing date; applicants notified on a rolling basis. Interview required for nursing, dental applicants. Deferred admission available.

STUDENT LIFE. Activities: Student government, film, magazine, radio, student newspaper, yearbook, choral groups, concert band, drama, jazz band, music ensembles, musical theater, symphony orchestra, Baptist Student Union, art club, Organization of Ebony Students, Phi Beta Lambda, Ye Hosts hotel and food service club, camera club, Phi Theta Kappa.

ATHLETICS. NJCAA. **Intercollegiate:** Basketball M, soccer, tennis M. **Intramural:** Basketball, softball, table tennis, tennis, volleyball. **Clubs:** Skiing.

STUDENT SERVICES. Aptitude testing, career counseling, employment service for undergraduates, freshman orientation, personal counseling, placement service for graduates, special adviser for adult students, veterans counselor, services/facilities for handicapped.

ANNUAL EXPENSES. Tuition and fees (1992-93): $577, $3,958 additional for out-of-state students. **Books and supplies:** $600. **Other expenses:** $1,125.

FINANCIAL AID. 26% of freshmen, 20% of continuing students re-

ceive some form of aid. All loans, 29% of jobs based on need. Academic, music/drama, art, state/district residency, leadership, minority scholarships available. **Aid applications:** Closing date April 1; applicants notified on a rolling basis beginning on or about April 1; must reply by August 21.

ADDRESS/TELEPHONE. Mac Warren, Director of Admissions, Wilkes Community College, PO Box 120, Wilkesboro, NC 28697-0120. (919) 651-8642 ext. 642. Fax: (919) 651-8749.

Wilson Technical Community College
Wilson, North Carolina CB code: 5930

2-year public technical college, coed. Founded in 1958. **Accreditation:** Regional. **Undergraduate enrollment:** 21 men, 392 women full time; 301 men, 387 women part time. **Faculty:** 74 total (42 full time), 1 with doctorate or other terminal degree. **Location:** Rural campus in large town; 50 miles from Raleigh. **Calendar:** Quarter, extensive summer session. Extensive evening/early morning classes. **Microcomputers:** Located in libraries.

DEGREES OFFERED. AAS. 76 associate degrees awarded in 1992. 37% in business and management, 17% business/office and marketing/distribution, 9% engineering technologies, 17% health sciences, 16% parks/recreation, protective services, public affairs.

UNDERGRADUATE MAJORS. Accounting, business administration and management, business data programming, child development/care/guidance, criminal justice technology, drafting, emergency medical technologies, energy conservation and use technology, engineering and engineering-related technologies, finance, fire protection, interpreter for the deaf, legal assistant/paralegal, liberal/general studies, manufacturing technology, mechanical design technology, nursing, secretarial and related programs, trade and industrial supervision and management.

ACADEMIC PROGRAMS. 2-year transfer program, cooperative education, double major, dual enrollment of high school students, internships, telecourses. **Remedial services:** Learning center, preadmission summer program, reduced course load, remedial instruction, special counselor, tutoring. **Placement/credit:** Institutional tests.

ACADEMIC REQUIREMENTS. Freshmen must earn minimum GPA of 2.0 to continue in good standing. 37% of freshmen return for sophomore year. Students must declare major on enrollment. **Graduation requirements:** 109 hours for associate. Most students required to take courses in English, mathematics, social sciences. **Additional information:** Special program assistance for hearing-impaired students.

FRESHMAN ADMISSIONS. Selection criteria: Open admissions. Selective admission for nursing based on test scores, high school record, skills, and experience. Health requirement for emergency medical technology. High school diploma not required for certificate programs.

1992 FRESHMAN CLASS PROFILE. 128 men, 131 women enrolled. **Characteristics:** 99% from in state, 100% commute, 34% have minority backgrounds. Average age is 22.

FALL-TERM APPLICATIONS. No fee. No closing date; applicants notified on a rolling basis beginning on or about January 1. Interview recommended. Deferred admission available. Accepted applicants to nursing program must reply by May 1.

STUDENT LIFE. Activities: Student government.

STUDENT SERVICES. Aptitude testing, career counseling, employment service for undergraduates, freshman orientation, personal counseling, placement service for graduates, veterans counselor, services/facilities for handicapped.

ANNUAL EXPENSES. Tuition and fees (1992-93): $572, $3,959 additional for out-of-state students. **Books and supplies:** $800. **Other expenses:** $2,500.

FINANCIAL AID. 30% of freshmen, 35% of continuing students receive some form of aid. All grants, 90% of loans, all jobs based on need. 250 enrolled freshmen were judged to have need, 200 were offered aid. **Aid applications:** No closing date; applicants notified on a rolling basis.

ADDRESS/TELEPHONE. Maurice Barnes, Counselor, Wilson Technical Community College, PO Box 4305, Wilson, NC 27893. (919) 291-1195. Fax: (919) 243-7148.

Wingate College
Wingate, North Carolina CB code: 5908

Admissions:	85% of applicants accepted
Based on:	••• School record
	•• Special talents, test scores
	• Activities, essay, interview, recommendations, religious affiliation/commitment
Completion:	90% of freshmen end year in good standing
	55% graduate, 22% of these enter graduate study

4-year private liberal arts college, coed, affiliated with Southern Baptist Convention. Founded in 1896. **Accreditation:** Regional. **Undergraduate enrollment:** 606 men, 606 women full time; 37 men, 124 women part time. **Graduate enrollment:** 1 man full time; 23 men, 21 women part time. **Faculty:** 107 total (85 full time), 62 with doctorates or other terminal degrees. **Location:** Suburban campus in small town; 20 miles from Charlotte. **Calendar:** Semester, limited summer session. **Microcomputers:** 80 located in dormitories, libraries, classrooms, computer centers. **Special facilities:** Outdoor recreation laboratory for parks and recreation administration majors, 11-acre lake.

DEGREES OFFERED. AA, AS, BA, BS, MBA, MEd. 12 associate degrees awarded in 1992. 40% in business and management, 20% allied health, 40% multi/interdisciplinary studies. 230 bachelor's degrees awarded. 24% in business and management, 14% communications, 10% teacher education, 12% health sciences, 14% parks/recreation, protective services, public affairs, 8% psychology, 5% social sciences. Graduate degrees offered in 3 major fields of study.

UNDERGRADUATE MAJORS. Associate: Accounting, business and management, business and office, liberal/general studies, management science, medical assistant, office supervision and management. **Bachelor's:** Accounting, allied health, American studies, art education, biology, business administration and management, business and management, business and office, business economics, chemistry, communications, computer and information sciences, drawing, early childhood education, economics, elementary education, English, English education, history, human services, humanities and social sciences, journalism, junior high education, liberal/general studies, management science, mathematics, mathematics education, music, music business management, music education, music performance, nursing, office supervision and management, painting, parks and recreation management, predentistry, preengineering, prelaw, premedicine, prepharmacy, preveterinary, psychology, public relations, radio/television broadcasting, reading education, religion, science education, secondary education, small business management and ownership, social science education, social sciences, social studies education, sociology, speech, sports medicine, studio art.

ACADEMIC PROGRAMS. 2-year transfer program, double major, dual enrollment of high school students, honors program, independent study, internships, study abroad, teacher preparation, cross-registration; liberal arts/career combination in engineering. **Remedial services:** Learning center, reduced course load, special counselor, tutoring, preadmission fall program. **ROTC:** Air Force, Army. **Placement/credit:** AP, CLEP General and Subject, institutional tests; 15 credit hours maximum for associate degree; 30 credit hours maximum for bachelor's degree.

ACADEMIC REQUIREMENTS. Freshmen must earn minimum GPA of 1.4 to continue in good standing. 80% of freshmen return for sophomore year. Students must declare major by end of second year. **Graduation requirements:** 64 hours for associate, 125 hours for bachelor's (30 in major). Most students required to take courses in arts/fine arts, computer science, English, foreign languages, history, humanities, mathematics, philosophy/religion, biological/physical sciences, social sciences. **Postgraduate studies:** 85% from 2-year programs enter 4-year programs. 1% enter law school, 1% enter medical school, 10% enter MBA programs, 10% enter other graduate study.

FRESHMAN ADMISSIONS. Selection criteria: School achievement record, class rank, test scores most important. **High school preparation:** 20 units recommended. Recommended units include biological science 1, English 4, mathematics 3, physical science 1, social science 2 and science 2. **Test requirements:** SAT or ACT; score report by August 15.

1992 FRESHMAN CLASS PROFILE. 631 men applied, 510 accepted, 195 enrolled; 527 women applied, 475 accepted, 183 enrolled. 20% had high school GPA of 3.0 or higher, 65% between 2.0 and 2.99. **Academic background:** Mid 50% of enrolled freshmen had SAT-V between 350-450, SAT-M between 370-460. 95% submitted SAT scores. **Characteristics:** 75% from in state, 85% live in college housing, 12% have minority backgrounds, 1% are foreign students. Average age is 18.

FALL-TERM APPLICATIONS. $20 fee, may be waived for applicants with need. Closing date August 15; applicants notified on a rolling basis; must reply by May 1 or within 2 weeks if notified thereafter. Audition required for music applicants. Interview recommended. Portfolio recommended for art applicants. Essay recommended. CRDA. Deferred and early admission available. Supporting test information and psychological evaluations for students with diagnosed learning disabilities required prior to admission.

STUDENT LIFE. Housing: Dormitories (men, women); apartment housing available. **Activities:** Student government, film, magazine, student newspaper, television, yearbook, choral groups, concert band, dance, drama, jazz band, marching band, music ensembles, pep band, fraternities, sororities, Christian Student Union, Young Democrats, Young Republicans, Black Student Coalition, Circle-K, Fellowship of Christian Athletics.

ATHLETICS. NAIA, NCAA. **Intercollegiate:** Baseball M, basketball, football M, golf M, soccer, softball W, tennis, volleyball W. **Intramural:** Basketball, bowling, diving, football, racquetball, softball, swimming, table tennis, tennis, volleyball, water polo.

STUDENT SERVICES. Aptitude testing, career counseling, employment service for undergraduates, freshman orientation, health services, personal counseling, placement service for graduates, services/facilities for handicapped.

ANNUAL EXPENSES. Tuition and fees (1992-93): $6,740. **Room and board:** $3,050. **Books and supplies:** $500. **Other expenses:** $800.

FINANCIAL AID. 75% of freshmen, 75% of continuing students receive some form of aid. 34% of grants, 67% of loans, 31% of jobs based on need. 250 enrolled freshmen were judged to have need, all were offered aid. Academic, music/drama, athletic, state/district residency, leadership scholarships available. **Aid applications:** No closing date; priority given to applications received by March 1; applicants notified on a rolling basis beginning on or about April 1; must reply within 2 weeks. **Additional information:** Tuition payment plans available with no interest charges for a $75 per year enrollment fee.

ADDRESS/TELEPHONE. Steve Poston, Vice President for Enrollment, Wingate College, Wingate, NC 28174-0157. (704) 233-8201. (800) 755-5550. Fax: (704) 233-8192.

Winston-Salem State University
Winston-Salem, North Carolina — CB code: 5909

Admissions: 75% of applicants accepted
Based on: ••• School record, test scores
•• Activities
• Essay, interview, recommendations
Completion: 75% of freshmen end year in good standing
15% enter graduate study

4-year public university, coed. Founded in 1892. **Accreditation:** Regional. **Undergraduate enrollment:** 700 men, 1,295 women full time; 253 men, 407 women part time. **Faculty:** 174 total (147 full time), 115 with doctorates or other terminal degrees. **Location:** Urban campus in small city; 28 miles from Greensboro. **Calendar:** Semester, limited summer session. Extensive evening/early morning classes. **Microcomputers:** 64 located in classrooms, computer centers. **Special facilities:** Art gallery.

DEGREES OFFERED. BA, BS. 280 bachelor's degrees awarded in 1992. 33% in business and management, 11% education, 14% allied health, 6% parks/recreation, protective services, public affairs, 14% social sciences.

UNDERGRADUATE MAJORS. Accounting, applied science, art education, biology, business administration and management, business economics, business education, chemistry, communications, computer and information sciences, elementary education, English, fine arts, history, junior high education, mathematics, medical laboratory technologies, music, music business management, music education, nursing, office supervision and management, physical education, political science and government, psychology, public administration, recreation therapy, sociology, Spanish, special education, sports management, urban studies.

ACADEMIC PROGRAMS. Cooperative education, double major, honors program, independent study, internships, teacher preparation, telecourses. **Remedial services:** Learning center, preadmission summer program, reduced course load, remedial instruction, special counselor, tutoring. **ROTC:** Army. **Placement/credit:** AP, CLEP Subject, institutional tests; 36 credit hours maximum for bachelor's degree.

ACADEMIC REQUIREMENTS. Freshmen must earn minimum GPA of 1.5 to continue in good standing. 70% of freshmen return for sophomore year. Students must declare major by end of second year. **Graduation requirements:** 127 hours for bachelor's. Most students required to take courses in English, history, humanities, mathematics, philosophy/religion, biological/physical sciences, social sciences.

FRESHMAN ADMISSIONS. Selection criteria: School achievement record, test scores, rank in top half of class, and character important. **High school preparation:** 16 units required. Required and recommended units include biological science 1, English 4, mathematics 3, physical science 1, social science 2 and science 1. Foreign language 2 recommended. Mathematics units must include or exceed algebra I, geometry and algebra II. **Test requirements:** SAT or ACT (SAT preferred); score report by August 1.

1992 FRESHMAN CLASS PROFILE. 419 men applied, 278 accepted, 129 enrolled; 694 women applied, 561 accepted, 279 enrolled. **Academic background:** Mid 50% of enrolled freshmen had SAT-V between 300-400, SAT-M between 300-400. 98% submitted SAT scores. **Characteristics:** 86% from in state, 60% live in college housing, 95% have minority backgrounds, 1% are foreign students, 10% join fraternities/sororities. Average age is 18.

FALL-TERM APPLICATIONS. $15 fee. No closing date; priority given to applications received by May 1; applicants notified on a rolling basis; must reply within 3 weeks. Audition required for music applicants. Interview recommended. Deferred admission available.

STUDENT LIFE. Housing: Dormitories (men, women, coed). **Activities:** Student government, radio, student newspaper, television, yearbook, choral groups, concert band, dance, drama, jazz band, marching band, music ensembles, pep band, symphony orchestra, fraternities, sororities, student religious council.

ATHLETICS. NCAA. **Intercollegiate:** Basketball, cross-country, football M, softball W, tennis, track and field, volleyball W.

STUDENT SERVICES. Career counseling, employment service for undergraduates, freshman orientation, health services, on-campus day care, personal counseling, placement service for graduates, special adviser for adult students, veterans counselor, services/facilities for handicapped.

ANNUAL EXPENSES. Tuition and fees (1992-93): $1,094, $5,018 additional for out-of-state students. **Room and board:** $2,762. **Books and supplies:** $600. **Other expenses:** $2,100.

FINANCIAL AID. 86% of freshmen, 90% of continuing students receive some form of aid. 85% of grants, 81% of loans, 96% of jobs based on need. Academic, music/drama, art, athletic, state/district residency, alumni affiliation, minority scholarships available. **Aid applications:** No closing date; priority given to applications received by June 1; applicants notified on a rolling basis beginning on or about May 25; must reply within 2 weeks.

ADDRESS/TELEPHONE. Van C. Wilson, Director of Admissions, Winston-Salem State University, 601 Martin Luther King Drive, Winston-Salem, NC 27110. (919) 750-2070. Fax: (919) 750-3210.

North Dakota

Bismarck State College
Bismarck, North Dakota CB code: 6041

2-year public community college, coed. Founded in 1939. **Accreditation:** Regional. **Undergraduate enrollment:** 910 men, 805 women full time; 263 men, 494 women part time. **Faculty:** 125 total (85 full time), 11 with doctorates or other terminal degrees. **Location:** Rural campus in small city; 200 miles from Fargo, 450 miles from Minneapolis-St. Paul, Minnesota. **Calendar:** Semester, limited summer session. Extensive evening/early morning classes. **Microcomputers:** 90 located in libraries, computer centers. **Special facilities:** 2 art galleries.

DEGREES OFFERED. AA, AS, AAS. 349 associate degrees awarded in 1992. 20% in business and management, 12% health sciences, 40% multi/interdisciplinary studies, 21% trade and industry.

UNDERGRADUATE MAJORS. Agribusiness, agricultural business and management, agricultural education, air conditioning/heating/refrigeration mechanics, art education, aviation computer technology, biology, business administration and management, business data processing and related programs, business education, carpentry, chemical manufacturing technology, chemistry, clinical laboratory science, commercial art, computer and information sciences, criminal justice studies, early childhood education, electrical and electronics equipment repair, electronic technology, engineering and engineering-related technologies, English, English education, German, hospitality and recreation marketing, hotel/motel and restaurant management, humanities and social sciences, industrial technology, law enforcement and corrections technologies, legal secretary, liberal/general studies, marketing and distribution, mathematics, mathematics education, medical laboratory technologies, medical secretary, music education, physical education, power plant operation and maintenance, precision metal work, predentistry, preengineering, prelaw, premedicine, prenursing, prepharmacy, psychology, public affairs, real estate, science education, secretarial and related programs, social science education, social sciences, Spanish, speech/communication/theater education, welding technology, word processing.

ACADEMIC PROGRAMS. 2-year transfer program, dual enrollment of high school students, internships. **Remedial services:** Learning center, remedial instruction, tutoring. **Placement/credit:** CLEP General and Subject, institutional tests; 30 credit hours maximum for associate degree.

ACADEMIC REQUIREMENTS. Freshmen must earn minimum GPA of 2.0 to continue in good standing. 25% of freshmen return for sophomore year. Students must declare major on application. **Graduation requirements:** 60 hours for associate. Most students required to take courses in English, humanities, mathematics, biological/physical sciences, social sciences.

FRESHMAN ADMISSIONS. Selection criteria: Open admissions. Selective admissions to some programs, based upon first-come, first-served. **Test requirements:** SAT or ACT for counseling; score report by August 15.

1992 FRESHMAN CLASS PROFILE. 511 men, 432 women enrolled. **Characteristics:** 92% commute. Average age is 19.

FALL-TERM APPLICATIONS. $20 fee. Closing date August 15; priority given to applications received by August 1; applicants notified on a rolling basis beginning on or about January 1. Interview required for specified program applicants. Portfolio recommended for graphic arts applicants. Deferred admission available.

STUDENT LIFE. Housing: Dormitories (men, women); apartment housing available. **Activities:** Student government, student newspaper, yearbook, choral groups, concert band, drama, jazz band, music ensembles, musical theater, pep band.

ATHLETICS. NAIA, NJCAA. **Intercollegiate:** Baseball M, basketball, cross-country, golf M, tennis, track and field, volleyball W, wrestling M. **Intramural:** Badminton, basketball, cross-country, golf, softball, volleyball.

STUDENT SERVICES. Career counseling, employment service for undergraduates, health services, on-campus day care, personal counseling, placement service for graduates, services/facilities for handicapped.

ANNUAL EXPENSES. Tuition and fees (projected): $1,665, $2,508 additional for out-of-state students. Additional tuition for Minnesota South Dakota, Montana, Manitoba, Saskatchewan residents $376. **Room and board:** $2,140. **Books and supplies:** $600. **Other expenses:** $1,600.

FINANCIAL AID. 80% of freshmen, 80% of continuing students receive some form of aid. 95% of grants, 72% of loans, 80% of jobs based on need. 665 enrolled freshmen were judged to have need, 618 were offered aid. Academic, music/drama, athletic scholarships available. **Aid applications:** No closing date; priority given to applications received by April 15; applicants notified on a rolling basis beginning on or about June 15; must reply within 15 days.

ADDRESS/TELEPHONE. Jason Karch, Registrar, Bismarck State College, 1500 Edwards Avenue, Bismarck, ND 58501. (701) 224-5426.

Dickinson State University
Dickinson, North Dakota CB code: 6477

4-year public university, coed. Founded in 1918. **Accreditation:** Regional. **Undergraduate enrollment:** 588 men, 801 women full time; 56 men, 160 women part time. **Faculty:** 90 total (72 full time), 27 with doctorates or other terminal degrees. **Location:** Rural campus in large town; 100 miles from Bismarck. **Calendar:** Semester, limited summer session. **Microcomputers:** 150 located in dormitories, libraries, classrooms, computer centers, campus-wide network. **Special facilities:** Art gallery, nature preserve.

DEGREES OFFERED. AA, AS, AAS, BA, BS. 58 associate degrees awarded in 1992. 51% in business/office and marketing/distribution, 42% health sciences. 198 bachelor's degrees awarded. 39% in business and management, 39% teacher education, 7% health sciences.

UNDERGRADUATE MAJORS. Associate: Agribusiness, agricultural business and management, business and office, legal secretary, liberal/general studies, medical secretary, nursing, office supervision and management, practical nursing, secretarial and related programs. **Bachelor's:** Accounting, agricultural business and management, art education, art history, behavioral sciences, biology, business administration and management, business and management, business education, chemistry, communications, computer and information sciences, dramatic arts, earth sciences, elementary education, English, English education, environmental science, foreign languages education, history, junior high education, liberal/general studies, mathematics, mathematics education, music, music education, music history and appreciation, nursing, physical education, physical sciences, political science and government, predentistry, prelaw, premedicine, science education, secondary education, social science education, social sciences, Spanish, speech, speech/communication/theater education, visual and performing arts.

ACADEMIC PROGRAMS. 2-year transfer program, double major, dual enrollment of high school students, independent study, internships, student-designed major, study abroad, teacher preparation, telecourses. **Remedial services:** Learning center, special counselor, tutoring. **Placement/credit:** AP, CLEP General and Subject, institutional tests; 8 credit hours maximum for associate degree; 15 credit hours maximum for bachelor's degree.

ACADEMIC REQUIREMENTS. Freshmen must earn minimum GPA of 1.6 to continue in good standing. 60% of freshmen return for sophomore year. Students must declare major by end of second year. **Graduation requirements:** 64 hours for associate, 128 hours for bachelor's (32 in major). Most students required to take courses in arts/fine arts, computer science, English, history, humanities, mathematics, biological/physical sciences, social sciences. **Postgraduate studies:** 40% from 2-year programs enter 4-year programs. 1% enter law school, 1% enter medical school, 7% enter other graduate study.

FRESHMAN ADMISSIONS. Selection criteria: Applicants must have high school diploma or GED, completion of college preparatory program. Nursing program has additional admission requirements. Required units include English 4, mathematics 3, social science 3 and science 3. **Test requirements:** SAT or ACT (ACT preferred); score report by August 15.

1992 FRESHMAN CLASS PROFILE. 150 men, 205 women enrolled. **Characteristics:** Average age is 19.

FALL-TERM APPLICATIONS. $20 fee. No closing date; priority given to applications received by June 1; applicants notified on a rolling basis. Deferred admission available. ACT recommended for counseling and research.

STUDENT LIFE. Housing: Dormitories (men, women, coed); apartment housing available. **Activities:** Student government, magazine, student newspaper, yearbook, choral groups, concert band, drama, jazz band, marching band, music ensembles, musical theater, pep band, fraternities, sororities, Catholic Student Association, United Ministries in Higher Education, business club, Student Education Association, student nurses' association.

ATHLETICS. NAIA. **Intercollegiate:** Baseball M, basketball, cross-country, football M, golf, tennis, track and field, volleyball W, wrestling M. **Intramural:** Basketball, softball, volleyball. **Clubs:** Varsity rodeo.

STUDENT SERVICES. Aptitude testing, career counseling, employment service for undergraduates, freshman orientation, health services, personal counseling, placement service for graduates, special adviser for adult students, services/facilities for handicapped.

ANNUAL EXPENSES. Tuition and fees (1992-93): $1,706, $2,550 additional for out-of-state students. Additional tuition for Minnesota, South Dakota, Montana, Manitoba, Saskatchewan residents, $378. **Room and board:** $1,950. **Books and supplies:** $400. **Other expenses:** $1,200.

FINANCIAL AID. 82% of freshmen, 90% of continuing students receive some form of aid. 86% of grants, 98% of loans, 90% of jobs based on need. 234 enrolled freshmen were judged to have need, all were offered aid. Academic, music/drama, art, athletic, state/district residency, leadership, minority scholarships available. **Aid applications:** No closing date; applicants notified on a rolling basis beginning on or about June 1; must reply within 2 weeks.

ADDRESS/TELEPHONE. Marshall Melbye, Director of Admissions/Registrar, Dickinson State University, Box 274, Dickinson, ND 58601-4896. (701) 227-2175. (800) 279-4295. Fax: (701) 227-2006.

Fort Bethold Community College
New Town, North Dakota CB code: 7304

2-year public community college, coed. Founded in 1973. **Accreditation:** Regional. **Undergraduate enrollment:** 32 men, 81 women full time; 50 men, 60 women part time. **Location:** Rural campus in small town; 70 miles between Minot and Williston. **Calendar:** Semester. **Additional facts:** Affiliated with American Indian Higher Education Consortium.

FRESHMAN ADMISSIONS. Selection criteria: Open admissions.

ANNUAL EXPENSES. Tuition and fees (projected): $1,600. **Books and supplies:** $400. **Other expenses:** $800.

ADDRESS/TELEPHONE. Rusty Mason, Admissions Director, Fort Bethold Community College, PO P.O. Box 490, New Town, ND 58763. (701) 627-3665. Fax: (701) 627-3609.

Jamestown College
Jamestown, North Dakota CB code: 6318

Admissions:	90% of applicants accepted
Based on:	••• School record
	•• Activities, interview, special talents, test scores
	• Recommendations
Completion:	80% of freshmen end year in good standing
	50% graduate, 10% of these enter graduate study

4-year private liberal arts college, coed, affiliated with Presbyterian Church (USA). Founded in 1883. **Accreditation:** Regional. **Undergraduate enrollment:** 477 men, 543 women full time; 21 men, 42 women part time. **Faculty:** 62 total (48 full time), 21 with doctorates or other terminal degrees. **Location:** Rural campus in large town; 100 miles from Fargo and Bismarck. **Calendar:** Semester, limited summer session. **Microcomputers:** 80 located in libraries, classrooms, computer centers.

DEGREES OFFERED. BA. 132 bachelor's degrees awarded in 1992. 19% in business and management, 20% teacher education, 19% health sciences, 6% life sciences, 10% psychology, 13% social sciences.

UNDERGRADUATE MAJORS. Accounting, actuarial sciences, arts management, biology, business administration and management, chemistry, computer and information sciences, elementary education, English, English education, fine arts, history, history/political science, information sciences and systems, mathematics, mathematics education, music, music education, nursing, philosophy, physical education, political science and government, predentistry, premedicine, prepharmacy, preveterinary, psychology, religion, religion/philosophy, science education, secondary education, social studies education.

ACADEMIC PROGRAMS. Cooperative education, double major, dual enrollment of high school students, honors program, independent study, internships, teacher preparation, cross-registration, medical technology and pharmacy programs with North Dakota State University; liberal arts/career combination in engineering, health sciences. **Remedial services:** Learning center, reduced course load, remedial instruction, special counselor, tutoring. **Placement/credit:** AP, CLEP General and Subject, institutional tests. Unlimited number of hours of credit by examination may be counted toward degree.

ACADEMIC REQUIREMENTS. Freshmen must earn minimum GPA of 1.7 to continue in good standing. 73% of freshmen return for sophomore year. Students must declare major by end of second year. **Graduation requirements:** 128 hours for bachelor's (36 in major). Most students required to take courses in arts/fine arts, computer science, English, history, mathematics, philosophy/religion, biological/physical sciences, social sciences.

FRESHMAN ADMISSIONS. Selection criteria: School achievement record most important. Test scores, special talents, interview, and school and community activities considered. **Test requirements:** SAT or ACT (ACT preferred); score report by August 20.

1992 FRESHMAN CLASS PROFILE. 450 men and women applied, 405 accepted; 152 men enrolled, 140 women enrolled. 63% had high school GPA of 3.0 or higher, 37% between 2.0 and 2.99. 15% were in top tenth and 37% were in top quarter of graduating class. **Academic background:** Mid 50% of enrolled freshmen had ACT composite between 19-25. 84% submitted ACT scores. **Characteristics:** 59% from in state, 90% live in college housing, 1% have minority backgrounds, 8% are foreign students. Average age is 19.

FALL-TERM APPLICATIONS. $20 fee, may be waived for applicants with need. No closing date; applicants notified on a rolling basis. Interview recommended. Audition recommended for music applicants. Portfolio recommended for art applicants. Deferred and early admission available.

STUDENT LIFE. Housing: Dormitories (coed); apartment housing available. **Activities:** Student government, magazine, student newspaper, yearbook, choral groups, concert band, drama, jazz band, music ensembles, pep band, Spurs, Jimmie Janes, honor societies. **Additional information:** Weekly chapel service available on campus. Non-alcoholic nightclub available.

ATHLETICS. NAIA. **Intercollegiate:** Baseball M, basketball, cross-country, football M, golf M, softball W, track and field, volleyball W, wrestling M. **Intramural:** Basketball, bowling, football, racquetball, soccer, softball, volleyball.

STUDENT SERVICES. Aptitude testing, career counseling, employment service for undergraduates, freshman orientation, personal counseling, placement service for graduates.

ANNUAL EXPENSES. Tuition and fees: $7,270. **Room and board:** $2,980. **Books and supplies:** $400. **Other expenses:** $400.

FINANCIAL AID. 97% of freshmen, 95% of continuing students receive some form of aid. 23% of grants, 87% of loans, 65% of jobs based on need. 221 enrolled freshmen were judged to have need, all were offered aid. Academic, music/drama, athletic, leadership scholarships available. **Aid applications:** No closing date; applicants notified on a rolling basis beginning on or about November 1; must reply within 3 weeks.

ADDRESS/TELEPHONE. Carol Schmeichel, Dean of Students, Jamestown College, PO 6081, Jamestown, ND 58401-9989. (701) 252-3467 ext. 2562. (800) 336-2554. Fax: (701) 253-2318.

Little Hoop Community College
Fort Totten, North Dakota CB code: 1306

2-year public community college, coed. Founded in 1974. **Accreditation:** Regional candidate. **Undergraduate enrollment:** 30 men, 37 women full time; 32 men, 74 women part time. **Faculty:** 18 total (11 full time). **Location:** Rural campus in rural community; 13 miles from Devils Lake. **Calendar:** Semester. **Microcomputers:** 30 located in computer centers.

DEGREES OFFERED. AA, AS, AAS. 10 associate degrees awarded in 1992. 40% in business and management, 40% teacher education, 20% trade and industry.

UNDERGRADUATE MAJORS. Accounting, bilingual/bicultural education, business and management, carpentry, education, secretarial and related programs, trade and industrial education, wildlife management.

ACADEMIC PROGRAMS. 2-year transfer program, cooperative education, independent study. **Remedial services:** Learning center, remedial instruction, tutoring.

ACADEMIC REQUIREMENTS. Freshmen must earn minimum GPA of 2.0 to continue in good standing. 61% of freshmen return for sophomore year. Students must declare major by end of first year. **Graduation requirements:** 60 hours for associate. Most students required to take courses in arts/fine arts, computer science, English, history, humanities, mathematics, biological/physical sciences, social sciences.

FRESHMAN ADMISSIONS. Selection criteria: Open admissions. **Test requirements:** TABE test required for placement and counseling. **Additional information:** School achievement record important for evaluation of applicants. Interview and minority status considered.

1992 FRESHMAN CLASS PROFILE. 47 men, 82 women enrolled. **Characteristics:** 100% commute. Average age is 28.

FALL-TERM APPLICATIONS. $10 fee. Closing date August 20; applicants notified on or about August 20. Early admission available.

STUDENT LIFE. Activities: Student government, drama, Indian club.

ATHLETICS. Intercollegiate: Basketball, bowling.

STUDENT SERVICES. Aptitude testing, career counseling, freshman orientation, on-campus day care, personal counseling, services/facilities for handicapped.

ANNUAL EXPENSES. Tuition and fees (1992-93): $1,130. **Books and supplies:** $175. **Other expenses:** $875.

FINANCIAL AID. Grants, loans, jobs available. **Aid applications:** Closing date August 20; applicants notified on a rolling basis.

ADDRESS/TELEPHONE. Dean Dauphinais, Director of Admissions/Registrar, Little Hoop Community College, PO Box 269, Fort Totten, ND 58335. (701) 766-4415. Fax: (701) 766-4077.

Mayville State University
Mayville, North Dakota CB code: 6478

4-year public liberal arts, teachers college, coed. Founded in 1889. **Accreditation:** Regional. **Undergraduate enrollment:** 346 men, 341 women full time; 24 men, 38 women part time. **Faculty:** 52 total (36 full time), 23 with doctorates or other terminal degrees. **Location:** Rural campus in small town; 60 miles from Fargo, 40 miles from Grand Forks. **Calendar:** Semester, limited summer session. **Microcomputers:** 65 located in libraries, classrooms, computer centers. **Special facilities:** Nature area.

DEGREES OFFERED. AA, BA, BS. 12 associate degrees awarded in 1992. 25% in business and management, 16% business/office and marketing/distribution, 59% education. 131 bachelor's degrees awarded. 26% in business and management, 62% teacher education.

UNDERGRADUATE MAJORS. Associate: Business administration and management, child development/care/guidance, early childhood education, secretarial and related programs. **Bachelor's:** Biology, business administration and management, business education, chemistry, computer and information sciences, elementary education, English, English education, health education, liberal/general studies, mathematics, mathematics education, physical education, physical sciences, science education, secondary education, secretarial and related programs, social science education, social sciences.

ACADEMIC PROGRAMS. Cooperative education, double major, internships, student-designed major, teacher preparation, telecourses. **Remedial services:** Learning center, preadmission summer program, remedial instruction, special counselor, tutoring, and reading laboratory. **Placement/credit:** AP, CLEP General and Subject, institutional tests; 15 credit hours maximum for associate degree; 30 credit hours maximum for bachelor's degree.

ACADEMIC REQUIREMENTS. Freshmen must earn minimum GPA of 2.0 to continue in good standing. 65% of freshmen return for sophomore year. Students must declare major by end of second year. **Graduation requirements:** 64 hours for associate (46 in major), 128 hours for bachelor's (72 in major). Most students required to take courses in computer science, English, history, humanities, mathematics, biological/physical sciences, social sciences. **Postgraduate studies:** 15% from 2-year programs enter 4-year programs.

FRESHMAN ADMISSIONS. Selection criteria: Open admissions. Applicants must have completed prerequisite college preparatory curriculum in high school to ensure acceptance. Minimum 2.0 GPA required for acceptance in good academic standing. **High school preparation:** 17 units required. Recommended units include biological science 1, English 4, foreign language 2, mathematics 3, physical science 2 and social science 3. One computer studies recommended. **Test requirements:** SAT or ACT (ACT preferred) for placement and counseling only; score report by September 2.

1992 FRESHMAN CLASS PROFILE. Academic background: Mid 50% of enrolled freshmen had ACT composite between 16-22. 89% submitted ACT scores. **Characteristics:** 67% from in state, 80% live in college housing, 8% have minority backgrounds, 1% are foreign students, 5% join fraternities/sororities. Average age is 18.

FALL-TERM APPLICATIONS. $20 fee. No closing date; applicants notified on a rolling basis. Interview recommended.

STUDENT LIFE. Housing: Dormitories (men, women); apartment housing available. **Activities:** Student government, film, student newspaper, yearbook, choral groups, concert band, debate and speech, fraternities, sororities, Newman Club, Inter-Varsity Christian Fellowship, Student Education Association, Young Democrats, Young Republicans, Lutheran Student Movement, Mature Educable Student Society, Outdoor Adventure Club.

ATHLETICS. NAIA. **Intercollegiate:** Baseball M, basketball, football M, softball W, volleyball W, wrestling M. **Intramural:** Badminton, basketball, racquetball, softball, tennis, volleyball.

STUDENT SERVICES. Aptitude testing, career counseling, employment service for undergraduates, freshman orientation, health services, on-campus day care, personal counseling, placement service for graduates, special adviser for adult students, veterans counselor, services/facilities for handicapped.

ANNUAL EXPENSES. Tuition and fees (1992-93): $1,755, $2,550 additional for out-of-state students. Additional tuition for Minnesota, South Dakota, Montana, Manitoba, Saskatchewan residents, $378. **Room and board:** $2,360. **Books and supplies:** $400. **Other expenses:** $1,140.

FINANCIAL AID. 81% of freshmen, 81% of continuing students receive some form of aid. 89% of grants, 83% of loans, all jobs based on need. 125 enrolled freshmen were judged to have need, all were offered aid. Athletic scholarships available. **Aid applications:** No closing date; priority given to applications received by April 15; applicants notified on a rolling basis beginning on or about April 1; must reply within 10 days.

ADDRESS/TELEPHONE. Ronald G. Brown, Director of Admissions, Mayville State University, 330 Third Street, Northeast, Mayville, ND 58257. (701) 786-4873. (800) 437-4104. Fax: (701) 786-4748.

Medcenter One College of Nursing
Bismarck, North Dakota — CB code: 7051

2-year upper-division private nursing college, coed. Founded in 1988. **Accreditation:** Regional. **Undergraduate enrollment:** 8 men, 88 women full time. **Faculty:** 18 total (16 full time), 3 with doctorates or other terminal degrees. **Location:** Urban campus in small city; 200 miles from Fargo. **Microcomputers:** Located in libraries, computer centers.

DEGREES OFFERED. BS. 43 bachelor's degrees awarded in 1992.

UNDERGRADUATE MAJORS. Nursing.

ACADEMIC REQUIREMENTS. Students must declare major on application. **Graduation requirements:** 128 hours for bachelor's (61 in major). Most students required to take courses in arts/fine arts, computer science, English, humanities, biological/physical sciences, social sciences.

STUDENT LIFE. Housing: Dormitories (men, women, coed). **Activities:** Student government.

STUDENT SERVICES. Health services, placement service for graduates.

ANNUAL EXPENSES. Tuition and fees: $5,510. **Room and board:** $2,640. **Books and supplies:** $1,040. **Other expenses:** $900.

FINANCIAL AID. 90% of continuing students receive some form of aid. 97% of grants, 63% of loans, all jobs based on need. scholarships available. **Aid applications:** No closing date; priority given to applications received by May 1; applicants notified on a rolling basis beginning on or about June 15; must reply within 2 weeks.

ADDRESS/TELEPHONE. Dr. Louis Rigley, Director of Student Services, Medcenter One College of Nursing, 512 North Seventh Street, Bismarck, ND 58501. (701) 224-6271.

Minot State University
Minot, North Dakota — CB code: 6479

4-year public university and liberal arts college, coed. Founded in 1913. **Accreditation:** Regional. **Undergraduate enrollment:** 1,233 men, 2,013 women full time; 161 men, 274 women part time. **Graduate enrollment:** 10 men, 37 women full time; 14 men, 35 women part time. **Faculty:** 204 total (166 full time), 74 with doctorates or other terminal degrees. **Location:** Suburban campus in large town; 194 miles from Bismarck. **Calendar:** Semester, limited summer session. **Microcomputers:** Located in dormitories, libraries, classrooms, computer centers.

DEGREES OFFERED. AA, AS, BA, BS, MA, MS, MEd. 80 associate degrees awarded in 1992. 31% in business and management, 52% business/office and marketing/distribution, 16% parks/recreation, protective services, public affairs. 520 bachelor's degrees awarded. 24% in business and management, 5% education, 19% teacher education, 8% health sciences, 14% parks/recreation, protective services, public affairs, 5% psychology, 6% social sciences, 5% visual and performing arts. Graduate degrees offered in 10 major fields of study.

UNDERGRADUATE MAJORS. Associate: Accounting, business data processing and related programs, criminal justice studies, development disabilities, legal secretary, medical secretary, office supervision and management, secretarial and related programs. **Bachelor's:** Accounting, art education, biology, business administration and management, business and management, business education, chemistry, clinical laboratory science, computer and information sciences, criminal justice studies, drug and alcohol addiction studies, earth sciences, economics, education of the deaf and hearing impaired, education of the mentally handicapped, elementary education, English, English education, finance, foreign languages education, French, German, history, liberal/general studies, management information systems, marketing management, mathematics, mathematics education, medical laboratory technologies, music, music education, nursing, physical education, physical sciences, physics, prelaw, premedicine, psychology, radio/television broadcasting, radiograph medical technology, science education, secondary education, social science education, social sciences, social studies education, social work, sociology, Spanish, speech correction, speech pathology/audiology, speech/communication/theater education, visual and performing arts.

ACADEMIC PROGRAMS. 2-year transfer program, double major, dual enrollment of high school students, honors program, independent study, internships, student-designed major, teacher preparation, telecourses, weekend college. **Remedial services:** Learning center, reduced course load, remedial instruction, special counselor, tutoring. **Placement/credit:** CLEP General, institutional tests.

ACADEMIC REQUIREMENTS. Freshmen must earn minimum GPA of 1.6 to continue in good standing. Students must declare major by end of second year. **Graduation requirements:** 128 hours for bachelor's (36 in major). Most students required to take courses in English, history, humanities, mathematics, biological/physical sciences, social sciences.

FRESHMAN ADMISSIONS. Selection criteria: College preparatory curriculum in high school required to ensure acceptance. **High school preparation:** 13 units required; 15 recommended. Required and recommended units include English 4, mathematics 3, social science 3 and science 3. Foreign language 2 recommended. Science should include at least 2 units of biology, chemistry, physics, or physical science. Social science should not include consumer education, cooperative marketing, orientation to social science, or marriage/family. **Test requirements:** ACT for placement and counseling only.

1992 FRESHMAN CLASS PROFILE. 760 men and women enrolled. **Characteristics:** 95% from in state, 60% live in college housing, 11% have minority backgrounds. Average age is 18.

FALL-TERM APPLICATIONS. $20 fee. No closing date; priority given to applications received by August 1; applicants notified on a rolling basis. CRDA. Deferred admission available.

STUDENT LIFE. Housing: Dormitories (men, women, coed); apartment housing available. Freshmen not required to live on campus. **Activities:** Student government, film, magazine, radio, student newspaper, television, yearbook, choral groups, concert band, dance, drama, jazz band, marching band, music ensembles, musical theater, opera, pep band, symphony orchestra, 4 major religious organizations on campus.

ATHLETICS. NAIA. **Intercollegiate:** Basketball, cross-country, football M, golf, tennis, track and field, volleyball W. **Intramural:** Basketball, volleyball.

STUDENT SERVICES. Aptitude testing, career counseling, employment service for undergraduates, freshman orientation, health services, personal counseling, placement service for graduates, special adviser for adult students, veterans counselor, minority counselor, services/facilities for handicapped.

ANNUAL EXPENSES. Tuition and fees (projected): $1,860, $2,860 additional for out-of-state students. Additional tuition for Minnesota, South Dakota, Montana, Manitoba, Saskatchewan residents, $420. **Room and board:** $2,571. **Books and supplies:** $600. **Other expenses:** $1,369.

FINANCIAL AID. 66% of freshmen, 66% of continuing students receive some form of aid. 99% of grants, 90% of loans, all jobs based on need. 371 enrolled freshmen were judged to have need, 364 were offered aid. Academic, music/drama, athletic scholarships available. **Aid applications:** No closing date; priority given to applications received by April 15; applicants notified on a rolling basis beginning on or about June 1; must reply within 2 weeks.

ADDRESS/TELEPHONE. Angela Kirhmeier, Senior Admissions Counselor, Minot State University, 500 University Avenue, West, Minot, ND 58702-5002. (701) 857-3350. Fax: (701) 839-6933.

North Dakota State College of Science
Wahpeton, North Dakota — CB code: 6476

2-year public junior, technical college, coed. Founded in 1903. **Accreditation:** Regional. **Undergraduate enrollment:** 1,250 men, 710 women full time; 78 men, 109 women part time. **Faculty:** 151 total (129 full time), 7 with doctorates or other terminal degrees. **Location:** Rural campus in small town; 50 miles from Fargo. **Calendar:** Semester, limited summer session. **Microcomputers:** 500 located in libraries, classrooms, computer centers.

DEGREES OFFERED. AA, AS, AAS. 542 associate degrees awarded in 1992. 8% in business and management, 10% business/office and marketing/distribution, 5% computer sciences, 29% engineering technologies, 18% allied health, 13% multi/interdisciplinary studies, 14% trade and industry.

UNDERGRADUATE MAJORS. Accounting, agribusiness, agricultural business and management, air conditioning/heating/refrigeration mechanics, air conditioning/heating/refrigeration technology, architectural technologies, automotive mechanics, business administration and management, business and office, business computer/console/peripheral equipment operation, business data processing and related programs, business data programming, civil technology, computer programming, computer servicing technology, dental hygiene, diesel engine mechanics, electrical technology, electromechanical technology, electronic technology, engineering and other disciplines, finance, food production/management/services, graphic and printing production, graphic arts technology, information sciences and systems, instrumentation technology, insurance and risk management, insurance marketing, legal secretary, liberal/general studies, machine tool operation/machine shop, marketing and distribution, mechanical design technology, medical records technology, medical secretary, microcomputer software, occupational therapy assistant, practical nursing, real estate, robotic and advanced welding technology, secretarial and related programs, welding technology, word processing.

ACADEMIC PROGRAMS. 2-year transfer program, computer delivered (on-line) credit-bearing course offerings, internships, telecourses. **Remedial services:** Learning center, preadmission summer program, reduced course load, remedial instruction, special counselor, tutoring. **Placement/credit:** AP, CLEP General and Subject, institutional tests.

ACADEMIC REQUIREMENTS. Freshmen must earn minimum GPA of 1.75 to continue in good standing. 83% of freshmen return for sophomore year. Students must declare major on application. **Graduation requirements:** 64 hours for associate. Most students required to take courses in computer science, English, mathematics, social sciences.

FRESHMAN ADMISSIONS. Selection criteria: Open admissions. Selective admission to allied health programs. Chemistry required for dental hygiene applicants. **Test requirements:** SAT or ACT (ACT preferred) for placement and counseling only; score report by September 1. California Psychological Inventory required for some health programs.

1992 FRESHMAN CLASS PROFILE. 584 men, 231 women enrolled. **Academic background:** Mid 50% of enrolled freshmen had ACT composite between 12-19. 80% submitted ACT scores. **Characteristics:** 68% from in state, 75% live in college housing, 4% have minority backgrounds, 1% are foreign students. Average age is 21.

FALL-TERM APPLICATIONS. $20 fee. No closing date; applicants notified on a rolling basis.

STUDENT LIFE. Housing: Dormitories (men, women, coed); apartment housing available. **Activities:** Student government, yearbook, choral groups, concert band, music ensembles, pep band.

ATHLETICS. NJCAA. **Intercollegiate:** Basketball, cross-country, football M, track and field, volleyball W, wrestling M. **Intramural:** Basketball, racquetball, softball, volleyball.

STUDENT SERVICES. Aptitude testing, career counseling, employment service for undergraduates, health services, on-campus day care, personal counseling, placement service for graduates, veterans counselor, services/facilities for handicapped.

ANNUAL EXPENSES. Tuition and fees (1992-93): $1,599, $2,424 additional for out-of-state students. Additional tuition for Minnesota, South Dakota, Montana, Saskatchewan, Manitoba residents $360. **Room and board:** $1,870. **Books and supplies:** $400. **Other expenses:** $1,255.

FINANCIAL AID. 81% of freshmen, 81% of continuing students receive some form of aid. 97% of grants, 82% of loans, 38% of jobs based on need. 564 enrolled freshmen were judged to have need, all were offered aid. Academic, music/drama, athletic, state/district residency, leadership scholarships available. **Aid applications:** No closing date; priority given to applications received by April 15; applicants notified on a rolling basis beginning on or about June 1; must reply within 2 weeks.

ADDRESS/TELEPHONE. Keath J. Borchert, Director of Enrollment, North Dakota State College of Science, 800 North 6 Street, Wahpeton, ND 58076. (701) 671-2201. Fax: (701) 671-2145.

North Dakota State University
Fargo, North Dakota — CB code: 6474

4-year public university, coed. Founded in 1890. **Accreditation:** Regional. **Undergraduate enrollment:** 4,215 men, 2,561 women full time; 720 men, 715 women part time. **Graduate enrollment:** 70 men, 36 women full time; 544 men, 368 women part time. **Faculty:** 569 total (538 full time), 414 with doctorates or other terminal degrees. **Location:** Urban campus in small city; 250 miles from Minneapolis-St. Paul, Minnesota, and Sioux Falls, South Dakota, and Winnepeg, Manitoba, Canada. **Calendar:** Semester, limited summer session. **Microcomputers:** 272 located in dormitories, libraries, classrooms, computer centers. **Special facilities:** Art gallery, Reineke Fine Arts Center (music), Institute for Regional Studies. **Additional facts:** Access to tri-college library system.

DEGREES OFFERED. BA, BS, BFA, BArch, MA, MS, MBA, MEd, PhD, B. Pharm. 1,470 bachelor's degrees awarded in 1992. 8% in agriculture, 8% architecture and environmental design, 12% business and management, 10% engineering, 11% engineering technologies, 9% health sciences, 7% home economics, 6% social sciences. Graduate degrees offered in 72 major fields of study.

UNDERGRADUATE MAJORS. Accounting, agricultural economics, agricultural education, agricultural engineering, agricultural mechanics, agricultural sciences, agronomy, animal sciences, architecture, athletic training, bacteriology, biological and physical sciences, biology, biotechnology, botany, business administration and management, chemistry, child development/care/guidance, civil engineering, clothing and textiles management/production/services, communications, computer and information sciences, computer engineering, construction engineering, construction management, corporate community fitness, dramatic arts, early childhood education, earth sciences, economics, electrical/electronics/communications engineering, elementary education, engineering, engineering physics, English, English education, entomology, environmental design, family/consumer resource management, fashion design, fine arts, fishing and fisheries, food science and nutrition, food sciences, foreign languages education, French, German, health sciences, history, home economics, home economics education, horticultural science, horticulture, hotel/motel and restaurant management, human environment and housing, humanities, humanities and social sciences, individual and family development, industrial engineering, institutional/home management/supporting programs, interior design, journalism, junior high education, landscape architecture, liberal/general studies, management information systems, marriage and family counseling, mathematics, mathematics education, mechanical engineering, medical laboratory technologies, microbiology, music, music education, nursing, ornamental horticulture, petroleum engineering, pharmacy, physical education, physical sciences, physics, plant pathology, plant sciences, political science and government, polymers and coatings, psychology, public relations, radio/television broadcasting, range management, recreation and community services technologies, respiratory therapy, science education, secondary education, social science education, social sciences, social studies education, sociology, soil sciences, Spanish, speech, speech/communication/theater education, sports medicine, statistics, textiles and clothing, transportation engineering, transportation management, wildlife management, zoology.

ACADEMIC PROGRAMS. Accelerated program, cooperative education, double major, dual enrollment of high school students, education specialist degree, honors program, independent study, internships, student-designed major, study abroad, teacher preparation, telecourses, cross-registration. **Remedial services:** Remedial instruction, special counselor, tutoring, student opportunity program. **ROTC:** Air Force, Army. **Placement/credit:** AP, CLEP General and Subject, IB, institutional tests.

ACADEMIC REQUIREMENTS. Freshmen must earn minimum GPA of 1.6 to continue in good standing. Sophomores must maintain 1.75 minimum GPA; juniors and seniors must maintain 2.0. Engineering, architecture, pharmacy and nursing programs require 2.0 GPA of all students. 70% of freshmen return for sophomore year. Students must declare major by end of second year. **Graduation requirements:** 122 hours for bachelor's (24 in major). Most students required to take courses in English, humanities, mathematics, biological/physical sciences, social sciences. **Postgraduate studies:** 1% enter law school, 1% enter medical school, 2% enter MBA programs, 11% enter other graduate study.

FRESHMAN ADMISSIONS. Selection criteria: All applicants must have completed college preparatory program in high school. Admissions to nursing, animal health, architecture, pharmacy, electrical and electronics engineering, mechanical engineering programs based on academic record and test scores. **High school preparation:** 17 units recommended. Required units include English 4, mathematics 3, social science 3 and science 3. **Test requirements:** SAT or ACT (ACT preferred) for placement and counseling only; score report by August 18. SAT or ACT required for admission to nursing, architecture, electrical and electronics engineering, mechanical engineering, pharmacy, and animal health technician training programs.

1992 FRESHMAN CLASS PROFILE. 964 men, 746 women enrolled. **Characteristics:** 61% from in state, 79% live in college housing, 1% have minority backgrounds, 2% are foreign students, 2% join fraternities/sororities. Average age is 18.

FALL-TERM APPLICATIONS. $20 fee. Closing date August 1; applicants notified on a rolling basis. Audition required for music applicants. Deferred admission available. Closing date for applications varies by program.

STUDENT LIFE. Housing: Dormitories (men, women, coed); apartment, fraternity, sorority, cooperative housing available. Freshmen under 19 not living with parents or guardians must live on campus. Limited mobile home facilities available. **Activities:** Student government, film, radio, student newspaper, television, choral groups, concert band, dance, drama, jazz band, marching band, music ensembles, musical theater, opera, pep band, symphony orchestra, fraternities, sororities, Newman Center, Lutheran Student Association, United Campus Ministry, Young Republicans, Young Democrats, Circle-K, Mortar Board, international student and campus service organizations, Students Older Than Average, sports clubs, Blue Key National Honor Fraternity, Phi Kappa Phi. **Additional information:** No alcoholic beverages allowed on campus.

ATHLETICS. NCAA. **Intercollegiate:** Baseball M, basketball, cross-country, football M, golf M, softball W, track and field, volleyball W, wrestling M. **Intramural:** Archery, badminton, basketball, cross-country, golf, ice hockey M, racquetball, skiing, soccer, softball, swimming, tennis, track and field, volleyball, water polo, wrestling M.

STUDENT SERVICES. Aptitude testing, career counseling, employment service for undergraduates, freshman orientation, health services, on-campus day care, personal counseling, placement service for graduates, special adviser for adult students, veterans counselor, minority students adviser, adviser for chemically dependent students, services/facilities for handicapped.

ANNUAL EXPENSES. Tuition and fees (1992-93): $2,033, $3,108 additional for out-of-state students. Tuition for Minnesota residents, $2,595; for Alaska, Colorado, Idaho, Montana, New Mexico, Utah and Wyoming, South Dakota, Manitoba, Saskatchewan, $3,120. **Room and board:** $2,482. **Books and supplies:** $475. **Other expenses:** $1,350.

FINANCIAL AID. 62% of freshmen, 55% of continuing students receive some form of aid. 86% of grants, 86% of loans based on need. 840 enrolled freshmen were judged to have need, all were offered aid. Academic scholarships available. **Aid applications:** Closing date April 15; priority given to applications received by March 15; applicants notified on or about June 30; must reply within 2 weeks.

ADDRESS/TELEPHONE. Robert Preloger, Assistant Dean Enrollment Management, North Dakota State University, PO Box 5596 University Station, Fargo, ND 58105. (701) 237-8643. (800) 488-NDSU. Fax: (701) 237-7050.

North Dakota State University: Bottineau
Bottineau, North Dakota — CB code: 1540

2-year public college of arts and sciences and agricultural and technical, branch campus, business, community, junior, liberal arts, technical college, coed. Founded in 1907. **Accreditation:** Regional. **Undergraduate enrollment:** 241 men, 133 women full time; 12 men, 25 women part time. **Faculty:** 28 total (21 full time), 3 with doctorates or other terminal degrees. **Location:** Rural campus in small town; 80 miles from Minot. **Calendar:** Semester. **Microcomputers:** 50 located in libraries, classrooms. **Special facilities:** Access to 4 million volumes through library computer network and statewide interactive video network where all 11 state campuses are networked. Headquarters for North Dakota Forest Service. Outdoor laboratories in state and federally owned refuges, forests, and parklands.

DEGREES OFFERED. AA, AS, AAS. 115 associate degrees awarded in 1992. 10% in agriculture, 10% business and management, 20% business/office and marketing/distribution, 30% life sciences, 30% multi/interdisciplinary studies.

UNDERGRADUATE MAJORS. Agribusiness, agricultural business and management, agricultural production, agricultural sciences, business administration and management, business and management, business and office, business computer/console/peripheral equipment operation, computer and information sciences, fishing and fisheries, forestry and related sciences, horticultural science, information sciences and systems, legal secretary, liberal/general studies, marketing and distribution, marketing management, mathematics, medical secretary, music, office supervision and management, ornamental horticulture, parks and recreation management, renewable natural resources, secretarial and related programs, wildlife management, zoology.

ACADEMIC PROGRAMS. 2-year transfer program, cooperative education, double major, dual enrollment of high school students, internships, telecourses. **Remedial services:** Learning center, reduced course load, remedial instruction, special counselor, tutoring, learning disabilities specialist. **Placement/credit:** Institutional tests; 12 credit hours maximum for associate degree.

ACADEMIC REQUIREMENTS. Freshmen must earn minimum GPA of 1.75 to continue in good standing. 65% of freshmen return for sophomore year. Students must declare major by end of first year. **Graduation requirements:** 61 hours for associate. Most students required to take courses in arts/fine arts, computer science, English, history, humanities, mathematics, biological/physical sciences, social sciences.

FRESHMAN ADMISSIONS. Selection criteria: Open admissions. **Test requirements:** SAT or ACT (ACT preferred) for placement and counseling only. **Additional information:** Application procedures include submission of ACT scores, high school or previous college, transcripts, medical history, and immunization records.

1992 FRESHMAN CLASS PROFILE. 145 men, 79 women enrolled. **Characteristics:** 60% from in state, 75% live in college housing, 6% have minority backgrounds, 7% are foreign students. Average age is 18.

FALL-TERM APPLICATIONS. $20 fee. No closing date; priority given to applications received by August 20; applicants notified on a rolling basis beginning on or about January 30. Deferred admission available.

STUDENT LIFE. Housing: Dormitories (men, women). **Activities:** Student government, choral groups, concert band, drama, pep band.

ATHLETICS. NJCAA. **Intercollegiate:** Baseball M, basketball, ice hockey M, volleyball W. **Intramural:** Badminton M, basketball, skiing M, softball, track and field, volleyball.

STUDENT SERVICES. Career counseling, employment service for undergraduates, freshman orientation, health services, personal counseling, placement service for graduates, veterans counselor.

ANNUAL EXPENSES. Tuition and fees (projected): $1,678, $2,550 additional for out-of-state students. Additional tuition for Minnesota, South Dakota, Montana, Saskatchewan, Manitoba residents, $360. **Room and board:** $2,100. **Books and supplies:** $600. **Other expenses:** $1,200.

FINANCIAL AID. 75% of freshmen, 75% of continuing students receive some form of aid. All grants, 85% of loans, all jobs based on need. 220 enrolled freshmen were judged to have need, all were offered aid. Academic, athletic, leadership, alumni affiliation scholarships available. **Aid applications:** No closing date; priority given to applications received by April 15; applicants notified on a rolling basis beginning on or about June 1; must reply within 2 weeks.

ADDRESS/TELEPHONE. Tom Berube, Admissions Counselor, North Dakota State University: Bottineau, First and Simrall Boulevard, Bottineau, ND 58318-1198. (701) 228-5469. Fax: (701)228-5468.

Standing Rock College
Fort Yates, North Dakota — CB code: 0310

2-year public community college, coed. Founded in 1971. **Accreditation:** Regional. **Undergraduate enrollment:** 203 men and women. **Faculty:** 29 total (23 full time), 3 with doctorates or other terminal degrees. **Location:** Rural campus in rural community; 75 miles from Bismark, 60 miles from Mobridge, South Dakota. **Calendar:** Semester, limited summer session. **Microcomputers:** 12 located in classrooms, computer centers.

DEGREES OFFERED. AA, AS, AAS. 35 associate degrees awarded in 1992. 10% in business and management, 24% business/office and marketing/distribution, 29% social sciences, 33% visual and performing arts.

UNDERGRADUATE MAJORS. Agricultural business and management, American Indian studies, business administration and management, business and office, computer and information sciences, criminal justice studies, marketing and distributive education, secretarial and related programs, small business management and ownership, social work, teacher aide.

ACADEMIC PROGRAMS. 2-year transfer program, cooperative education, independent study. **Remedial services:** Learning center, remedial instruction, special counselor.

ACADEMIC REQUIREMENTS. No policy requiring minimum GPA; records of students having academic difficulty are reviewed individually. 23% of freshmen return for sophomore year. **Graduation requirements:** Most students required to take courses in computer science, English, humanities, mathematics, biological/physical sciences, social sciences.

FRESHMAN ADMISSIONS. Selection criteria: Open admissions. **Additional information:** High school students may enroll with approval of Vice President of academic affairs and parents. Letters of recommendation from high school counselor or principal required.

1992 FRESHMAN CLASS PROFILE. 68 men and women enrolled. 20% had high school GPA of 3.0 or higher, 65% between 2.0 and 2.99. **Characteristics:** 40% from in state, 100% commute, 99% have minority backgrounds. Average age is 20.

FALL-TERM APPLICATIONS. $10 fee. No closing date; applicants notified on a rolling basis.

STUDENT LIFE. Activities: Student government, cultural club, Phi Beta Lambda, Rodeo Club.

ATHLETICS. Intercollegiate: Basketball, cross-country, volleyball.

STUDENT SERVICES. Aptitude testing, career counseling, em-

ployment service for undergraduates, freshman orientation, personal counseling, placement service for graduates, veterans counselor, services/facilities for handicapped.

ANNUAL EXPENSES. Tuition and fees: $1,870. **Books and supplies:** $500. **Other expenses:** $1,125.

FINANCIAL AID. 66% of freshmen, 90% of continuing students receive some form of aid. 94% of grants, all loans, all jobs based on need. 30 enrolled freshmen were judged to have need, all were offered aid. Academic, minority scholarships available. **Aid applications:** No closing date; priority given to applications received by April 15; applicants notified on a rolling basis beginning on or about July 15; must reply within 15 days.

ADDRESS/TELEPHONE. Linda Iron, Director of Admissions, Standing Rock College, HC1 Box 4, Fort Yates, ND 58538. (701) 854-3861. Fax: (701) 854-3403.

Trinity Bible College
Ellendale, North Dakota — CB code: 0356

4-year private Bible college, coed, affiliated with Assemblies of God. Founded in 1948. **Accreditation:** Regional. **Undergraduate enrollment:** 212 men, 170 women full time; 19 men, 18 women part time. **Faculty:** 30 total (17 full time), 3 with doctorates or other terminal degrees. **Location:** Rural campus in rural community; 60 miles from Jamestown, 38 miles from Aberdeen, South Dakota. **Calendar:** Semester, extensive summer session. **Microcomputers:** 20 located in classrooms, computer centers. **Special facilities:** Pentecostal Heritage Collection of rare and out-of-print works, teacher education laboratory, computer laboratory.

DEGREES OFFERED. AA, BA. 10 associate degrees awarded in 1992. 100% in business and management. 60 bachelor's degrees awarded. 5% in teacher education, 93% philosophy, religion, theology.

UNDERGRADUATE MAJORS. Associate: Bible studies, business administration and management, business and management, business and office, office supervision and management. **Bachelor's:** Bible studies, business and management, business and office, dramatic arts, elementary education, missionary studies, office supervision and management, psychology, religious education, religious music, theological studies.

ACADEMIC PROGRAMS. 2-year transfer program, double major, independent study, internships, teacher preparation. **Remedial services:** Learning center, reduced course load, remedial instruction, tutoring. **Placement/credit:** CLEP Subject, institutional tests; 30 credit hours maximum for bachelor's degree.

ACADEMIC REQUIREMENTS. Freshmen must earn minimum GPA of 1.5 to continue in good standing. Students must declare major on enrollment. **Graduation requirements:** 65 hours for associate (33 in major), 128 hours for bachelor's (38 in major). Most students required to take courses in English, history, mathematics, philosophy/religion, biological/physical sciences, social sciences. **Postgraduate studies:** 5% from 2-year programs enter 4-year programs. 4% enter other graduate study. **Additional information:** All students major in Biblical studies in conjunction with another major or minor of their choice.

FRESHMAN ADMISSIONS. Selection criteria: References, evidence of Christian testimony and lifestyle very important. **Test requirements:** SAT or ACT (ACT preferred) for placement and counseling only; score report by August 31. **Additional information:** High school record examined to determine if student should be placed under probation. Good references required as evidence of sound moral character and Christian conversion.

1992 FRESHMAN CLASS PROFILE. 85 men, 73 women enrolled. **Characteristics:** 15% from in state, 90% live in college housing, 7% have minority backgrounds. Average age is 20.

FALL-TERM APPLICATIONS. $15 fee. No closing date; priority given to applications received by August 24; applicants notified on a rolling basis. Essay required. Interview recommended. Deferred admission available.

STUDENT LIFE. Housing: Dormitories (men, women); apartment housing available. **Activities:** Student government, radio, yearbook, choral groups, drama, music ensembles, pep band, missions, photography, deaf clubs, ministry clubs. **Additional information:** Religious observance required.

ATHLETICS. Intercollegiate: Basketball, cross-country, football M, track and field, volleyball, wrestling M. **Intramural:** Basketball, football M, softball, volleyball, wrestling M.

STUDENT SERVICES. Aptitude testing, career counseling, employment service for undergraduates, freshman orientation, personal counseling, placement service for graduates, veterans counselor, services/facilities for handicapped.

ANNUAL EXPENSES. Tuition and fees: $4,734. **Room and board:** $2,994. **Books and supplies:** $450. **Other expenses:** $900.

FINANCIAL AID. 90% of freshmen, 95% of continuing students receive some form of aid. 75% of grants, 95% of loans, 99% of jobs based on need. 90 enrolled freshmen were judged to have need, all were offered aid. Academic, music/drama, state/district residency, leadership, religious affiliation, minority scholarships available. **Aid applications:** No closing date; priority given to applications received by March 1; applicants notified on a rolling basis beginning on or about April 1; must reply within 3 weeks.

ADDRESS/TELEPHONE. Vicki McRoberts, Director of Admissions, Trinity Bible College, 50 Sixth Avenue South, Ellendale, ND 58436-7150. (701) 349-3621. (800) 523-1603. Fax: (701) 349-5443.

Turtle Mountain Community College
Belcourt, North Dakota — CB code: 0352

2-year private community college, coed. Founded in 1972. **Accreditation:** Regional. **Undergraduate enrollment:** 550 men and women. **Faculty:** 44 total (17 full time), 1 with doctorate or other terminal degree. **Location:** Rural campus in small town; 90 miles from Devils Lake. **Calendar:** Quarter. **Microcomputers:** 53 located in computer centers. **Additional facts:** Chartered by the Turtle Mountain Chippewa Native Americans to serve their community.

DEGREES OFFERED. AA, AS, AAS. 75 associate degrees awarded in 1992.

UNDERGRADUATE MAJORS. American Indian studies, biology, business administration and management, community health work, computer and information sciences, education, elementary education, engineering, English education, history, home economics, journalism, liberal/general studies, mathematics, nursing, nursing education, predentistry, prelaw, premedicine, prepharmacy, preveterinary, public administration, science technologies, secondary education, social science education, social sciences, special education. gambling casino management.

ACADEMIC PROGRAMS. 2-year transfer program, dual enrollment of high school students, internships. **Remedial services:** Learning center, special counselor, tutoring. **Placement/credit:** CLEP General.

ACADEMIC REQUIREMENTS. Freshmen must earn minimum GPA of 1.5 to continue in good standing. Students must declare major on application. **Graduation requirements:** 92 hours for associate. Most students required to take courses in English, history, humanities, mathematics, biological/physical sciences, social sciences.

FRESHMAN ADMISSIONS. Selection criteria: Open admissions. **Test requirements:** ACT for placement and counseling only; score report by August 31.

1992 FRESHMAN CLASS PROFILE. 350 men and women enrolled. **Characteristics:** 100% from in state, 100% commute, 93% have minority backgrounds. Average age is 27.

FALL-TERM APPLICATIONS. No fee. No closing date; applicants notified on a rolling basis.

STUDENT LIFE. Activities: Student government, radio, student newspaper.

ATHLETICS. Intramural: Basketball, softball, volleyball.

STUDENT SERVICES. Career counseling, freshman orientation, personal counseling, veterans counselor, services/facilities for handicapped.

ANNUAL EXPENSES. Tuition and fees: $1,152. **Books and supplies:** $360. **Other expenses:** $1,320.

FINANCIAL AID. All grants, all jobs based on need. **Aid applications:** Closing date May 1; priority given to applications received by May 1; applicants notified on or about May 31; must reply within 2 weeks.

ADDRESS/TELEPHONE. Annette M. Charette, Admissions Officer, Turtle Mountain Community College, PO 340, Belcourt, ND 58316-0340. (701) 477-5605. Fax: (701) 477-5028.

United Tribes Technical College
Bismarck, North Dakota — CB code: 4915

2-year public technical college, coed. **Accreditation:** Regional. **Undergraduate enrollment:** 264 men and women. **Faculty:** 35 total. **Location:** Suburban campus in small city. **Calendar:** Semester.

DEGREES OFFERED. AAS. 45 associate degrees awarded in 1992.

UNDERGRADUATE MAJORS. Art marketing, elementary education.

FRESHMAN ADMISSIONS. Selection criteria: Open admissions. Must be 18 years of age and enrolled member of federally recognized tribe.

1992 FRESHMAN CLASS PROFILE. 150 men and women enrolled. **Characteristics:** 90% live in college housing.

FALL-TERM APPLICATIONS. No closing date.

ATHLETICS. Intercollegiate: Basketball.

ANNUAL EXPENSES. Tuition and fees: $2,740. **Room and board:** $2,400. **Books and supplies:** $400. **Other expenses:** $1,880.

FINANCIAL AID. 90% of freshmen, 100% of continuing students receive some form of aid. All grants, all jobs based on need. Academic, leadership, minority scholarships available. **Aid applications:** No closing date; priority given to applications received by May 29; applicants notified on a rolling basis beginning on or about May 29; must reply by July 31 or within 2 weeks if notified thereafter.

ADDRESS/TELEPHONE. Dr. David Gipp, President, United Tribes Technical College, 3315 University Drive, Bismarck, ND 58504. (701) 255-3285.

University of Mary
Bismarck, North Dakota CB code: 6428

Admissions: 91% of applicants accepted
Based on: ••• Recommendations, school record, test scores
• Activities, interview, special talents
Completion: 85% of freshmen end year in good standing
5% enter graduate study

4-year private university and liberal arts college, coed, affiliated with Roman Catholic Church. Founded in 1959. **Accreditation:** Regional. **Undergraduate enrollment:** 538 men, 863 women full time; 92 men, 207 women part time. **Graduate enrollment:** 1 man, 4 women full time; 46 men, 100 women part time. **Faculty:** 101 total (75 full time), 24 with doctorates or other terminal degrees. **Location:** Rural campus in small city; 6 miles from downtown. **Calendar:** Semester, limited summer session. **Microcomputers:** 40 located in libraries, classrooms, computer centers. **Special facilities:** Art gallery, fitness center. **Additional facts:** Butter Center offers evening classes.

DEGREES OFFERED. AA, BA, BS, M. 3 associate degrees awarded in 1992. 296 bachelor's degrees awarded. 34% in business and management, 12% teacher education, 24% health sciences, 8% allied health, 14% social sciences. Graduate degrees offered in 11 major fields of study.

UNDERGRADUATE MAJORS. Associate: Accounting, business and management, radiograph medical technology, respiratory therapy technology. **Bachelor's:** Accounting, athletic training, biological and physical sciences, biology, biology/chemistry/mathematics, business administration and management, business and management, Christian ministry, communications, computer and information sciences, early childhood education, education of the mentally handicapped, education of the physically handicapped, elementary education, English, English education, liberal/general studies, mathematics, mathematics education, medical laboratory technologies, music, music education, nursing, physical education, radiograph medical technology, respiratory therapy technology, science education, secondary education, social science education, social sciences, social work, special education.

ACADEMIC PROGRAMS. Cooperative education, double major, independent study, internships, study abroad, teacher preparation. **Remedial services:** Learning center, preadmission summer program, reduced course load, remedial instruction, special counselor, tutoring. **Placement/credit:** AP, CLEP General and Subject, institutional tests; 32 credit hours maximum for associate degree; 96 credit hours maximum for bachelor's degree.

ACADEMIC REQUIREMENTS. Freshmen must earn minimum GPA of 2.0 to continue in good standing. 84% of freshmen return for sophomore year. Students must declare major by end of second year. **Graduation requirements:** 64 hours for associate, 128 hours for bachelor's (44 in major). Most students required to take courses in arts/fine arts, English, mathematics, philosophy/religion, biological/physical sciences, social sciences. **Postgraduate studies:** 85% from 2-year programs enter 4-year programs. 1% enter law school, 1% enter medical school, 3% enter other graduate study.

FRESHMAN ADMISSIONS. Selection criteria: Applicants should be in top half of class and get counselor recommendation. Those not meeting requirements may be admitted after taking tests and acquiring study skills. Recommended units include English 4, mathematics 2, social science 3 and science 2. **Test requirements:** SAT or ACT (ACT preferred); score report by August 24.

1992 FRESHMAN CLASS PROFILE. 275 men applied, 244 accepted, 137 enrolled; 384 women applied, 357 accepted, 227 enrolled. 55% had high school GPA of 3.0 or higher, 42% between 2.0 and 2.99. 12% were in top tenth and 34% were in top quarter of graduating class. **Academic background:** Mid 50% of enrolled freshmen had ACT composite between 18-24. 93% submitted ACT scores. **Characteristics:** 82% from in state, 78% live in college housing, 6% have minority backgrounds, 1% are foreign students. Average age is 18.

FALL-TERM APPLICATIONS. $15 fee, may be waived for applicants with need. No closing date; priority given to applications received by June 1; applicants notified on a rolling basis; must reply by May 1 or within 4 weeks if notified thereafter. Audition required for music applicants. Interview recommended for academically weak applicants. CRDA. Deferred and early admission available.

STUDENT LIFE. Housing: Dormitories (men, women); apartment housing available. **Activities:** Student government, magazine, radio, student newspaper, television, yearbook, choral groups, concert band, drama, jazz band, music ensembles, musical theater, pep band, symphony orchestra, campus ministry, Sacred Hoop Indian Club, Spurs, Circle-K, Student Nurses Association, Young Democrats, College Republicans, Student Education Association, Social Work Club, Music Educators National Conference.

ATHLETICS. NAIA. **Intercollegiate:** Basketball, cross-country, football M, softball W, tennis, track and field, volleyball W, wrestling M. **Intramural:** Basketball, bowling, lacrosse, racquetball, softball, swimming, table tennis, tennis, volleyball, water polo.

STUDENT SERVICES. Aptitude testing, career counseling, employment service for undergraduates, freshman orientation, health services, personal counseling, placement service for graduates, special adviser for adult students, services/facilities for handicapped.

ANNUAL EXPENSES. Tuition and fees: $6,190. **Room and board:** $2,550. **Books and supplies:** $500. **Other expenses:** $700.

FINANCIAL AID. 94% of freshmen, 70% of continuing students receive some form of aid. 58% of grants, 82% of loans, 94% of jobs based on need. 286 enrolled freshmen were judged to have need, all were offered aid. Academic, music/drama, athletic, leadership scholarships available. **Aid applications:** No closing date; priority given to applications received by March 15; applicants notified on a rolling basis beginning on or about April 1; must reply by May 1 or within 2 weeks if notified thereafter.

ADDRESS/TELEPHONE. Steph Storey, Director of Admissions, University of Mary, 7500 University Drive, Bismarck, ND 58504-9652. (701) 255-7500 ext. 329. (800) 288-6279. Fax: (701) 255-7687.

University of North Dakota
Grand Forks, North Dakota CB code: 6878

Admissions: 85% of applicants accepted
Based on: ••• School record, test scores
•• Activities, essay, interview, recommendations
• Special talents
Completion: 74% of freshmen end year in good standing
43% graduate

4-year public university, coed. Founded in 1884. **Accreditation:** Regional. **Undergraduate enrollment:** 4,701 men, 4,000 women full time; 776 men, 914 women part time. **Graduate enrollment:** 468 men, 366 women full time; 461 men, 603 women part time. **Faculty:** 724 total (576 full time), 486 with doctorates or other terminal degrees. **Location:** Urban campus in small city; 320 miles from Minneapolis-St. Paul, 150 miles from Winnipeg, Canada. **Calendar:** Semester, extensive summer session. Saturday classes. **Microcomputers:** 3,700 located in dormitories, libraries, computer centers. **Special facilities:** US Weather Bureau observation station, atmospherium, Institute for Remote Sensing, energy research center, fine arts center, Chester Fritz Auditorium, Center for Aerospace Sciences.

DEGREES OFFERED. BA, BS, BFA, MA, MS, MBA, MFA, MEd, MSW, PhD, EdD, MD. 22 associate degrees awarded in 1992. 45% in business/office and marketing/distribution, 55% trade and industry. 1,729 bachelor's degrees awarded in 1992. 17% in business and management, 5% business/office and marketing/distribution, 6% communications, 8% education, 6% engineering, 5% health sciences, 7% allied health, 6% parks/recreation, protective services, public affairs, 5% psychology, 7% social sciences, 15% trade and industry. Graduate degrees offered in 57 major fields of study.

UNDERGRADUATE MAJORS. Accounting, advertising, air traffic control, air transportation, airline piloting and navigation, airport management, American Indian studies, American studies, anthropology, art education, atmospheric sciences and meteorology, aviation computer technology, aviation management, biological and physical sciences, biology, business and management, business economics, business education, chemical engineering, chemistry, civil engineering, computer and information sciences, criminal justice studies, cytotechnology, dramatic arts, early childhood education, earth sciences, economics, electrical/electronics/communications engineering, elementary education, engineering management, engineering physics, English, English education, environmental health engineering, finance, food science and nutrition, foreign languages (multiple emphasis), foreign languages education, French, geography, geological engineering, geology, German, history, home economics education, humanities, industrial arts education, industrial technology, international studies, journalism, junior high education, Latin, law enforcement and corrections, liberal/general studies, library science, marketing and distribution, marketing and distributive education, mathematics, mathematics education, mechanical engineering, medical laboratory technologies, music, music education, music performance, nursing, occupational therapy, office supervision and management, parks and recreation management, peace studies, philosophy, physical education, physical sciences, physical therapy, physics, political science and government, psychology, public administration, public relations, radio/television broadcasting, religion, retailing, Russian, Russian and Slavic studies, Scandinavian languages, science education, social science education, social sciences, social work, sociology, Spanish, special education, speech, speech pathology/audiology, speech/communication/theater education, sports medicine, textiles and clothing, transportation management, visual and performing arts, wildlife management.

ACADEMIC PROGRAMS. Accelerated program, cooperative education, double major, dual enrollment of high school students, education specialist degree, honors program, independent study, internships, student-designed major, study abroad, teacher preparation, visiting/exchange student program, weekend college. **Remedial services:** Learning center, reduced course load, special counselor, tutoring. **ROTC:** Army. **Placement/credit:** AP, CLEP Subject, IB, institutional tests; 30 credit hours maximum for bachelor's degree.

ACADEMIC REQUIREMENTS. Freshmen must earn minimum GPA of 2.0 to continue in good standing. 78% of freshmen return for sophomore year. Students must declare major by end of second year. **Graduation requirements:** 125 hours for bachelor's (30 in major). Most students required

to take courses in arts/fine arts, English, humanities, mathematics, biological/physical sciences, social sciences.

FRESHMAN ADMISSIONS. High school preparation: 18 units recommended. Required and recommended units include biological science 1, English 4, mathematics 3, physical science 1, social science 3 and science 1. Foreign language 2 recommended. 2 fine arts, and 1 computer science also recommended. Sciences require laboratory. Mathematics units should include algebra I, II and geometry. **Test requirements:** SAT or ACT (ACT preferred); score report by July 1.

1992 FRESHMAN CLASS PROFILE. 1,570 men applied, 1,325 accepted, 1,032 enrolled; 1,268 women applied, 1,084 accepted, 842 enrolled. 64% had high school GPA of 3.0 or higher, 34% between 2.0 and 2.99. 51% were in top quarter of graduating class. **Academic background:** Mid 50% of enrolled freshmen had SAT-V between 390-500, SAT-M between 440-590; ACT composite between 18-24. 9% submitted SAT scores, 77% submitted ACT scores. **Characteristics:** 58% from in state, 75% live in college housing, 4% have minority backgrounds, 4% are foreign students. Average age is 19.

FALL-TERM APPLICATIONS. $20 fee. Closing date July 1; priority given to applications received by March 1; applicants notified on a rolling basis. Interview recommended for out-of-state applicants. Essay recommended for out-of-state applicants. Deferred and early admission available.

STUDENT LIFE. Housing: Dormitories (men, women, coed); apartment, fraternity, sorority, cooperative housing available. Trailer space rental available. **Activities:** Student government, film, magazine, radio, student newspaper, television, choral groups, concert band, dance, drama, jazz band, marching band, music ensembles, musical theater, opera, pep band, fraternities, sororities, 120 student organizations.

ATHLETICS. NCAA. **Intercollegiate:** Baseball M, basketball, cross-country, diving, football M, golf M, ice hockey M, softball W, swimming, track and field, volleyball W, wrestling M. **Intramural:** Badminton, basketball, bowling, diving, football M, golf, ice hockey M, racquetball, softball, swimming, table tennis, tennis, track and field, volleyball, wrestling M.

STUDENT SERVICES. Aptitude testing, career counseling, employment service for undergraduates, freshman orientation, health services, on-campus day care, personal counseling, placement service for graduates, veterans counselor, Native American Programs Office, Office of Women's Programs, Office of Black Student Programs, student support services, services/facilities for handicapped.

ANNUAL EXPENSES. Tuition and fees (projected): $2,291, $3,231 additional for out-of-state students. Additional tuition for Minnesota residents, $590; for South Dakota, Montana, Saskatchewan, Manitoba residents, $1,055. **Room and board:** $2,720. **Books and supplies:** $450. **Other expenses:** $1,200.

FINANCIAL AID. 47% of freshmen, 83% of continuing students receive some form of aid. 90% of grants, 75% of loans, 34% of jobs based on need. 858 enrolled freshmen were judged to have need, all were offered aid. Academic, music/drama, art, athletic, leadership, minority scholarships available. **Aid applications:** No closing date; priority given to applications received by April 15; applicants notified on a rolling basis beginning on or about June 1; must reply within 15 days.

ADDRESS/TELEPHONE. Monty Nielsen, Director of Admissions and Records, University of North Dakota, PO Box 8070, Grand Forks, ND 58202-8357. (701) 777-3821. Fax: (701) 777-3650.

University of North Dakota: Lake Region
Devils Lake, North Dakota — CB code: 6163

2-year public community college, coed. Founded in 1941. **Accreditation:** Regional. **Undergraduate enrollment:** 175 men, 194 women full time; 121 men, 143 women part time. **Faculty:** 51 total (26 full time), 2 with doctorates or other terminal degrees. **Location:** Rural campus in small town; 90 miles from Grand Forks. **Calendar:** Semester, limited summer session. Extensive evening/early morning classes. **Microcomputers:** 70 located in dormitories, libraries, classrooms. **Additional facts:** Satellite center at Grand Forks Air Base.

DEGREES OFFERED. 120 associate degrees awarded in 1992. 18% in business/office and marketing/distribution, 8% home economics, 8% law, 49% multi/interdisciplinary studies, 10% trade and industry.

UNDERGRADUATE MAJORS. Accounting, aeronautical technology, agribusiness, agricultural business and management, agricultural sciences, automotive mechanics, automotive technology, business administration and management, business and management, business and office, business computer/console/peripheral equipment operation, business data processing and related programs, child development/care/guidance, electrical and electronics equipment repair, electronic technology, fashion merchandising, legal assistant/paralegal, legal secretary, liberal/general studies, marketing and distribution, medical secretary, office supervision and management, retailing, secretarial and related programs.

ACADEMIC PROGRAMS. 2-year transfer program, cooperative education, dual enrollment of high school students, internships, telecourses. **Remedial services:** Learning center, reduced course load, remedial instruction, special counselor, tutoring. **Placement/credit:** CLEP General and Subject, institutional tests.

ACADEMIC REQUIREMENTS. Freshmen must earn minimum GPA of 1.5 to continue in good standing. Students must declare major on application. **Graduation requirements:** 60 hours for associate (60 in major). Most students required to take courses in English, humanities, mathematics, social sciences.

FRESHMAN ADMISSIONS. Selection criteria: Open admissions. Selective admissions to peace officer training program, legal assistant program, and simulator maintenance technician program. **Test requirements:** SAT or ACT (ACT preferred) for counseling; score report by August 15.

1992 FRESHMAN CLASS PROFILE. 88 men, 108 women enrolled. **Academic background:** Mid 50% of enrolled freshmen had ACT composite between 15-21. 85% submitted ACT scores. **Characteristics:** 99% from in state, 60% commute, 5% have minority backgrounds. Average age is 26.

FALL-TERM APPLICATIONS. $20 fee. No closing date; applicants notified on a rolling basis. Interview required for peace officer training applicants. Essay required for legal assistants applicants. Deferred and early admission available.

STUDENT LIFE. Housing: Dormitories (men, women); apartment housing available. **Activities:** Student government, drama, Distributive Education Clubs of America, Vocational Industrial Clubs of America, Students Older than Average, Resident's Housing Association, Campus Crusade for Christ, Business Club, Legal Assistant Club, Simulator Maintenance Technician Club, Drama Club.

ATHLETICS. NJCAA. **Intercollegiate:** Basketball, volleyball W. **Intramural:** Basketball, softball, table tennis, volleyball.

STUDENT SERVICES. Aptitude testing, career counseling, employment service for undergraduates, freshman orientation, on-campus day care, personal counseling, placement service for graduates, veterans counselor, services/facilities for handicapped.

ANNUAL EXPENSES. Tuition and fees (projected): $1,723, $2,574 additional for out-of-state students. Additional tuition for Minnesota, South Dakota, Montana, Saskatchewan, Manitoba residents, $360. **Room and board:** $2,270. **Books and supplies:** $600. **Other expenses:** $1,300.

FINANCIAL AID. 87% of freshmen, 85% of continuing students receive some form of aid. All grants, 90% of loans, 96% of jobs based on need. Academic, athletic, leadership scholarships available. **Aid applications:** No closing date; priority given to applications received by March 15; applicants notified on a rolling basis beginning on or about June 1; must reply within 20 days.

ADDRESS/TELEPHONE. Daniel Johnson, Dean of Students, University of North Dakota: Lake Region, Highway 20 North, Devils Lake, ND 58301-1598. (701) 662-8683 ext. 315. (800) 443-1313. Fax: (701) 662-1570.

University of North Dakota: Williston
Williston, North Dakota — CB code: 6905

2-year public branch campus, junior college, coed. Founded in 1957. **Accreditation:** Regional. **Undergraduate enrollment:** 284 men, 358 women full time; 54 men, 129 women part time. **Faculty:** 45 total (30 full time), 1 with doctorate or other terminal degree. **Location:** Suburban campus in large town; 250 miles from Bismarck, 130 miles from Minot, 365 miles from Billings, Montana. **Calendar:** Semester. Extensive evening/early morning classes. **Microcomputers:** 100 located in dormitories, libraries, classrooms, computer centers. **Special facilities:** Interactive television. **Additional facts:** Students may enroll and complete lower, upper, and graduate level courses originating at other North Dakota campuses through Interactive Video Network.

DEGREES OFFERED. AA, AS, AAS. 151 associate degrees awarded in 1992. 12% in business/office and marketing/distribution, 11% allied health, 65% multi/interdisciplinary studies, 6% trade and industry.

UNDERGRADUATE MAJORS. Accounting, agribusiness, agricultural business and management, agricultural economics, agricultural sciences, automotive mechanics, automotive technology, business administration and management, business and management, business and office, business computer/console/peripheral equipment operation, business data programming, computer and information sciences, diesel engine mechanics, hazardous materials management, legal secretary, liberal/general studies, marketing and distribution, marketing management, medical secretary, physical therapy assistant, practical nursing, secretarial and related programs, word processing.

ACADEMIC PROGRAMS. 2-year transfer program, cooperative education, dual enrollment of high school students, honors program, internships, telecourses. **Remedial services:** Learning center, reduced course load, remedial instruction, tutoring. **Placement/credit:** AP, CLEP General and Subject, institutional tests; 15 credit hours maximum for associate degree.

ACADEMIC REQUIREMENTS. Freshmen must earn minimum GPA of 2.0 to continue in good standing. 80% of freshmen return for sophomore year. **Graduation requirements:** 62 hours for associate (45 in major). Most students required to take courses in computer science, English, humanities, mathematics, biological/physical sciences, social sciences.

FRESHMAN ADMISSIONS. Selection criteria: Open admissions. Selective admission process for practical nursing and physical therapist assistant programs. Recommended units include English 4, foreign language 1, mathematics 3, social science 3 and science 3. **Test requirements:** ACT for placement and counseling only; score report by August 20. **Additional information:** Medical form and immunization records required for applicants born after 1956.

1992 FRESHMAN CLASS PROFILE. 201 men, 263 women enrolled. **Characteristics:** 80% from in state, 70% commute, 10% have minority backgrounds, 2% are foreign students. Average age is 23.

FALL-TERM APPLICATIONS. $20 fee. No closing date; applicants notified on a rolling basis. Deferred and early admission available.

STUDENT LIFE. Housing: Dormitories (men, women, coed); apartment, handicapped housing available. Housing for men and women athletes only. **Activities:** Student government, choral groups, drama, music ensembles, Fellowship Among Christian Tetons (FACT).

ATHLETICS. NJCAA. **Intercollegiate:** Baseball M, basketball, volleyball W. **Intramural:** Basketball, bowling, golf, racquetball, softball, swimming, tennis, volleyball.

STUDENT SERVICES. Employment service for undergraduates, freshman orientation, personal counseling, placement service for graduates, services/facilities for handicapped.

ANNUAL EXPENSES. Tuition and fees (projected): $1,708, $2,424 additional for out-of-state students. Additional tuition for Minnesota, South Dakota, Montana, Manitoba, Saskatchewan residents, $360. **Room and board:** $1,000. **Books and supplies:** $600. **Other expenses:** $400.

FINANCIAL AID. 60% of continuing students receive some form of aid. 88% of grants, 87% of loans, 69% of jobs based on need. Academic, athletic, state/district residency, leadership scholarships available. **Aid applications:** No closing date; priority given to applications received by April 15; applicants notified on a rolling basis beginning on or about June 15.

ADDRESS/TELEPHONE. Jan Solem, Asst Registrar, University of North Dakota: Williston, PO Box 1326, 1426 University Avenue, Williston, ND 58802-1326. (701) 774-4210. Fax: (701) 774-4275.

Valley City State University
Valley City, North Dakota CB code: 6480

4-year public teachers college, coed. Founded in 1889. **Accreditation:** Regional. **Undergraduate enrollment:** 407 men, 424 women full time; 41 men, 131 women part time. **Faculty:** 68 total (54 full time), 21 with doctorates or other terminal degrees. **Location:** Rural campus in small town; 60 miles from Fargo. **Calendar:** Semester, limited summer session. **Microcomputers:** 230 located in libraries, classrooms, computer centers. **Special facilities:** Art gallery, planetarium.

DEGREES OFFERED. AA, BA, BS. 24 associate degrees awarded in 1992. 94% in business/office and marketing/distribution, 6% multi/interdisciplinary studies. 171 bachelor's degrees awarded. 18% in business and management, 61% teacher education, 15% multi/interdisciplinary studies.

UNDERGRADUATE MAJORS. Associate: Liberal/general studies, secretarial and related programs. **Bachelor's:** Art education, biology, business administration and management, business education, chemistry, elementary education, English, English education, fine arts, health education, history, industrial arts education, information sciences and systems, liberal/general studies, mathematics, mathematics education, music, music education, office supervision and management, physical education, science education, social science education, social sciences, Spanish, studio art, technical education.

ACADEMIC PROGRAMS. 2-year transfer program, double major, internships, teacher preparation. **Remedial services:** Learning center, remedial instruction, tutoring. **Placement/credit:** CLEP General.

ACADEMIC REQUIREMENTS. Freshmen must earn minimum GPA of 1.6 to continue in good standing. 60% of freshmen return for sophomore year. Students must declare major by end of first year. **Graduation requirements:** 64 hours for associate (40 in major), 128 hours for bachelor's (32 in major). Most students required to take courses in arts/fine arts, computer science, English, humanities, mathematics, biological/physical sciences, social sciences. **Postgraduate studies:** 20% from 2-year programs enter 4-year programs.

FRESHMAN ADMISSIONS. High school preparation: 13 units required. Required units include English 4, mathematics 3, social science 3 and science 3. **Test requirements:** SAT or ACT (ACT preferred); score report by August 20.

1992 FRESHMAN CLASS PROFILE. 193 men applied, 193 accepted, 122 enrolled; 126 women applied, 126 accepted, 104 enrolled. 55% had high school GPA of 3.0 or higher, 42% between 2.0 and 2.99. **Academic background:** Mid 50% of enrolled freshmen had ACT composite between 13-20. 95% submitted ACT scores. **Characteristics:** 92% from in state, 54% commute, 2% have minority backgrounds, 1% are foreign students. Average age is 18.

FALL-TERM APPLICATIONS. $20 fee. No closing date; applicants notified on a rolling basis beginning on or about November 1.

STUDENT LIFE. Housing: Dormitories (men, women, coed); apartment housing available. **Activities:** Student government, student newspaper, yearbook, choral groups, concert band, drama, jazz band, marching band, music ensembles, musical theater, pep band, fraternities, sororities.

ATHLETICS. NAIA. **Intercollegiate:** Baseball M, basketball, cross-country, football M, golf M, softball W, tennis, track and field, volleyball W, wrestling M. **Intramural:** Badminton, basketball, cross-country, racquetball, softball, volleyball, water polo, wrestling M.

STUDENT SERVICES. Aptitude testing, career counseling, employment service for undergraduates, freshman orientation, health services, on-campus day care, personal counseling, placement service for graduates, veterans counselor, services/facilities for handicapped.

ANNUAL EXPENSES. Tuition and fees (projected): $1,802, $2,550 additional for out-of-state students. Additional tuition for Minnesota, South Dakota, Montana, Manitoba, Saskatchewan residents, $378. **Room and board:** $2,510. **Books and supplies:** $600. **Other expenses:** $1,359.

FINANCIAL AID. 85% of freshmen, 74% of continuing students receive some form of aid. 84% of grants, 71% of loans, 28% of jobs based on need. 126 enrolled freshmen were judged to have need, all were offered aid. Academic, music/drama, art, athletic, state/district residency, leadership, alumni affiliation scholarships available. **Aid applications:** No closing date; priority given to applications received by April 15; applicants notified on a rolling basis beginning on or about June 15; must reply within 2 weeks.

ADDRESS/TELEPHONE. Monte Johnson, Director of Admissions, Valley City State University, Valley City, ND 58072. (701) 845-7412. (800) 532-8641. Fax: (701) 845-7245.

Ohio

Antioch College

Yellow Springs, Ohio CB code: 1017

Admissions: 78% of applicants accepted
Based on: ••• Interview, recommendations, school record
•• Activities, essay, test scores
• Special talents
Completion: 85% of freshmen end year in good standing
41% graduate

4-year private liberal arts college, coed. Founded in 1852. **Accreditation:** Regional. **Undergraduate enrollment:** 228 men, 339 women full time; 2 men part time. **Faculty:** 85 total (60 full time), 49 with doctorates or other terminal degrees. **Location:** Suburban campus in small town; 18 miles from Dayton. **Calendar:** Quarter. **Microcomputers:** 37 located in dormitories, libraries, computer centers. **Special facilities:** Glen Helen 1000-acre nature preserve.

DEGREES OFFERED. BA, BS. 126 bachelor's degrees awarded in 1992. 11% in communications, 6% teacher education, 12% letters/literature, 7% life sciences, 5% multi/interdisciplinary studies, 7% psychology, 6% social sciences, 29% visual and performing arts.

UNDERGRADUATE MAJORS. Afro-American (black) studies, anthropology, biology, business and management, chemistry, cinematography/film, communications, comparative literature, computer and information sciences, creative writing, cross-cultural studies, dance, dramatic arts, economics, education, elementary education, environmental science, European studies, geology, history, international studies, journalism, Latin American studies, liberal/general studies, literature and creative writing, mathematics, music, peace studies, philosophy, physics, political science and government, psychology, secondary education, social sciences, sociology, visual and performing arts, women's studies.

ACADEMIC PROGRAMS. Cooperative education, double major, independent study, internships, student-designed major, study abroad, teacher preparation, cross-registration, All students alternate on-campus study with minimum of 6 3-month cooperative job assignments across United States and abroad; liberal arts/career combination in engineering. **Remedial services:** Remedial instruction, tutoring. **Placement/credit:** AP, CLEP General and Subject, IB, institutional tests.

ACADEMIC REQUIREMENTS. No policy requiring minimum GPA; records of students having academic difficulty are reviewed individually. 72% of freshmen return for sophomore year. **Graduation requirements:** 160 hours for bachelor's (60 in major). Most students required to take courses in arts/fine arts, English, foreign languages, history, mathematics, biological/physical sciences, social sciences. **Additional information:** Students receive narrative evaluations instead of grades. Foreign language proficiency required.

FRESHMAN ADMISSIONS. Selection criteria: School achievement record and test scores considered equally with personal qualities (independence, creativity, initiative) as demonstrated by interview, essay, and references. College-preparatory program recommended.

1992 FRESHMAN CLASS PROFILE. 195 men applied, 141 accepted, 63 enrolled; 445 women applied, 355 accepted, 99 enrolled. 60% had high school GPA of 3.0 or higher, 37% between 2.0 and 2.99. 20% were in top tenth and 42% were in top quarter of graduating class. **Academic background:** Mid 50% of enrolled freshmen had SAT-V between 480-610, SAT-M between 470-600; ACT composite between 22-27. 70% submitted SAT scores, 28% submitted ACT scores. **Characteristics:** 12% from in state, 100% live in college housing, 14% have minority backgrounds, 1% are foreign students. Average age is 18.

FALL-TERM APPLICATIONS. $25 fee, may be waived for applicants with need. Closing date February 1; applicants notified on or about April 1; must reply by May 1 or within 2 weeks if notified thereafter. Essay required. Interview recommended. CRDA. Deferred and early admission available. Institutional early decision plan. SAT or ACT recommended.

STUDENT LIFE. Housing: Dormitories (coed). Living/learning dormitory units available for students studying foreign languages. Substance-free housing available. **Activities:** Student government, film, magazine, radio, student newspaper, television, Antioch Review, choral groups, dance, drama, women's center, men's group, Third World Alliance. **Additional information:** Students participate in government of college.

ATHLETICS. Intramural: Archery, badminton, fencing, handball, racquetball, soccer, softball, squash, swimming, tennis, track and field, volleyball.

STUDENT SERVICES. Career counseling, employment service for undergraduates, freshman orientation, health services, personal counseling.

ANNUAL EXPENSES. Tuition and fees: $16,356. **Room and board:** $3,176. **Books and supplies:** $400. **Other expenses:** $700.

FINANCIAL AID. 78% of freshmen, 77% of continuing students receive some form of aid. 92% of grants, 88% of loans, all jobs based on need. 130 enrolled freshmen were judged to have need, all were offered aid. Academic, state/district residency, leadership, minority scholarships available. **Aid applications:** No closing date; priority given to applications received by March 1; applicants notified on a rolling basis beginning on or about April 1; must reply by May 1 or within 2 weeks if notified thereafter. **Additional information:** Middle Income Assistance Program provides interest-free loans to students who qualify for little or no financial aid. Those loans are waived upon graduation from the college.

ADDRESS/TELEPHONE. James H. Williams, Jr, Dean of Admissions, Antioch College, 795 Livermore Street, Yellow Springs, OH 45387. (513) 767-6400. (800) 543-9436. Fax: (513) 767-1891.

Antioch School for Adult and Experiential Learning

Yellow Springs, Ohio CB code: 4527

3-year private liberal arts college, coed. Founded in 1988. **Accreditation:** Regional. **Undergraduate enrollment:** 240 men and women. **Graduate enrollment:** 347 men and women. **Faculty:** 38 total (11 full time), 21 with doctorates or other terminal degrees. **Location:** Suburban campus in small town; 18 miles from of Dayton. **Calendar:** Quarter, extensive summer session. **Microcomputers:** 13 located in libraries. **Special facilities:** Antioch College library facilities, Glen Helen Nature Reserve.

DEGREES OFFERED. BA, MA. 100 bachelor's degrees awarded in 1992. 68% in business and management, 32% social sciences. Graduate degrees offered in 2 major fields of study.

UNDERGRADUATE MAJORS. Behavioral sciences, business and management, humanities.

ACADEMIC PROGRAMS. Double major, external degree, independent study, student-designed major, weekend college, cross-registration. **Remedial services:** Reduced course load. **Placement/credit:** CLEP General and Subject; 45 credit hours maximum for bachelor's degree.

ACADEMIC REQUIREMENTS. Students must declare major by end of third year. **Graduation requirements:** 180 hours for bachelor's (38 in major). Most students required to take courses in English, humanities, biological/physical sciences, social sciences. **Additional information:** Residential Master of Arts degree in management offered exclusively on weekends.

FALL-TERM APPLICATIONS. $35 fee.

STUDENT SERVICES. Career counseling, personal counseling, special adviser for adult students.

ANNUAL EXPENSES. Tuition and fees (projected): $8,100. **Books and supplies:** $400.

FINANCIAL AID. 44% of continuing students receive some form of aid. All grants, 71% of loans, all jobs based on need. **Aid applications:** No closing date; applicants notified on a rolling basis; must reply by registration.

ADDRESS/TELEPHONE. Jane Bourden, Director of Recruitment and Public Relations, Antioch School for Adult and Experiential Learning, 800 Livermore Street, Yellow Springs, OH 45387. (513) 767-6321.

Antonelli Institute of Art and Photography

Cincinnati, Ohio CB code: 0611

2-year proprietary technical college, coed. Founded in 1947. **Undergraduate enrollment:** 170 men and women. **Faculty:** 18 total (5 full time), 1 with doctorate or other terminal degree. **Location:** Urban campus in large city; 55 miles from Dayton, 110 miles from Columbus. **Calendar:** Semester. **Microcomputers:** Located in computer centers. **Special facilities:** Computer graphics laboratory, complete darkroom and commercial studio facilities. **Additional facts:** Prepares students for careers in commercial art, photography, fashion merchandising, interior design, computerized office management.

DEGREES OFFERED. 130 associate degrees awarded in 1992. 10% in architecture and environmental design, 50% trade and industry, 40% visual and performing arts.

UNDERGRADUATE MAJORS. Commercial art, fashion merchandising, interior design, photographic technology, photography.

ACADEMIC PROGRAMS. Double major, internships. **Remedial services:** Tutoring. **Placement/credit:** Institutional tests.

ACADEMIC REQUIREMENTS. Freshmen must earn minimum GPA of 2.0 to continue in good standing. 75% of freshmen return for sophomore year. Students must declare major on application. **Graduation requirements:** 60 hours for associate. Most students required to take courses in English, social sciences.

FRESHMAN ADMISSIONS. Selection criteria: Interview and portfolio reviewed to determine interest, motivation, and ability.

1992 FRESHMAN CLASS PROFILE. 90 men and women enrolled. **Characteristics:** 70% from in state, 93% commute, 10% have minority backgrounds. Average age is 21.

FALL-TERM APPLICATIONS. $50 fee. No closing date; applicants notified on a rolling basis. Interview required. Portfolio recommended for commercial art, photography applicants.

STUDENT LIFE. Housing: Off-campus coeducational dormitory housing available at nearby College of Mount St. Joseph on the Ohio. **Activities:** Student newspaper, Alpha Beta Kappa honor society.

ATHLETICS. Intramural: Softball.

STUDENT SERVICES. Career counseling, employment service for undergraduates, freshman orientation, personal counseling, placement service for graduates, special adviser for adult students, veterans counselor, services/facilities for handicapped.

ANNUAL EXPENSES. Tuition and fees (1992-93): $6,990. Tuition for photography $7,990. **Room and board:** $3,480. **Books and supplies:** $1,500. **Other expenses:** $1,350.

FINANCIAL AID. 80% of freshmen, 75% of continuing students receive some form of aid. Grants, loans, jobs available. **Aid applications:** No closing date; applicants notified on a rolling basis.

ADDRESS/TELEPHONE. Brian K. Johnson, Director of Admissions and Placement, Antonelli Institute of Art and Photography, 124 East Seventh Street, Cincinnati, OH 45202. (513) 241-4338. Fax: (513) 241-9396.

Art Academy of Cincinnati
Cincinnati, Ohio CB code: 1002

Admissions:	63% of applicants accepted
Based on:	••• Interview, school record, special talents
	• Activities, recommendations, test scores
Completion:	90% of freshmen end year in good standing
	30% enter graduate study

4-year private art college, coed. Founded in 1869. **Accreditation:** Regional. **Undergraduate enrollment:** 109 men, 90 women full time; 15 men, 16 women part time. **Faculty:** 40 total (18 full time). **Location:** Urban campus in large city; one mile from downtown. **Calendar:** Semester, limited summer session. **Special facilities:** 2 art galleries, 1 in the school, 1 in Mt. Adams. **Additional facts:** Affiliated with (and attached to) Cincinnati Art Museum. Some shared facilities.

DEGREES OFFERED. AS, BFA, MA. 2 associate degrees awarded in 1992. 100% in visual and performing arts. 36 bachelor's degrees awarded. 100% in visual and performing arts. Graduate degrees offered in 1 major field of study.

UNDERGRADUATE MAJORS. Associate: Graphic arts technology, graphic design. **Bachelor's:** Art history, drawing, fine arts, graphic design, illustration design, painting, photography, printmaking, sculpture, studio art, visual and performing arts.

ACADEMIC PROGRAMS. Double major, independent study, internships, student-designed major, study abroad, visiting/exchange student program, cross-registration. **Remedial services:** Special counselor, tutoring. **Placement/credit:** AP, institutional tests.

ACADEMIC REQUIREMENTS. Freshmen must earn minimum GPA of 1.7 to continue in good standing. 75% of freshmen return for sophomore year. Students must declare major by end of first year. **Graduation requirements:** 62 hours for associate, 129 hours for bachelor's. Most students required to take courses in arts/fine arts, English, history, humanities, mathematics, philosophy/religion, biological/physical sciences, social sciences.

FRESHMAN ADMISSIONS. Selection criteria: Academic background, portfolio, and interview very important. **High school preparation:** 12 units recommended. Recommended units include English 4, mathematics 3, social science 1 and science 2. 3-4 units art recommended. **Test requirements:** SAT or ACT; score report by August 15.

1992 FRESHMAN CLASS PROFILE. 130 men and women applied, 82 accepted; 33 enrolled. 10% had high school GPA of 3.0 or higher, 70% between 2.0 and 2.99. **Academic background:** Mid 50% of enrolled freshmen had SAT-V between 400-550, SAT-M between 400-500; ACT composite between 12-23. 40% submitted SAT scores, 60% submitted ACT scores. **Characteristics:** 75% from in state, 100% commute, 15% have minority backgrounds, 1% are foreign students. Average age is 19.

FALL-TERM APPLICATIONS. $25 fee, may be waived for applicants with need. Closing date August 15; priority given to applications received by March 15; applicants notified on a rolling basis. Interview required for nearby (within 150 miles) applicants. Portfolio required.

STUDENT LIFE. Housing: Apartments and rooming houses near campus. **Activities:** Student government, film, student newspaper, group and individual art exhibitions.

ATHLETICS. Intramural: Basketball, soccer, volleyball.

STUDENT SERVICES. Career counseling, employment service for undergraduates, freshman orientation, health services, personal counseling, placement service for graduates, veterans counselor.

ANNUAL EXPENSES. Tuition and fees: $8,450. **Books and supplies:** $1,000. **Other expenses:** $590.

FINANCIAL AID. 84% of freshmen, 86% of continuing students receive some form of aid. 58% of grants, 83% of loans, 59% of jobs based on need. Academic, art scholarships available. **Aid applications:** No closing date; priority given to applications received by April 1; applicants notified on a rolling basis beginning on or about May 25; must reply by July 31 or within 4 weeks if notified thereafter. **Additional information:** 15 annual scholarships awarded to entering and transfer students and 50 to continuing students based on spring portfolio competition.

ADDRESS/TELEPHONE. Douglas Dobbins, Director of Admissions, Art Academy of Cincinnati, 1125 St. Gregory Street, Cincinnati, OH 45202-1597. (513) 721-5205. (800) 323-5692. Fax: (513) 562-8778.

Ashland University
Ashland, Ohio CB code: 1021

Admissions:	89% of applicants accepted
Based on:	••• School record
	•• Activities, essay, interview, recommendations, special talents, test scores
Completion:	95% of freshmen end year in good standing
	48% graduate, 8% of these enter graduate study

4-year private university, coed, affiliated with Brethren Church. Founded in 1878. **Accreditation:** Regional. **Undergraduate enrollment:** 884 men, 1,063 women full time; 234 men, 511 women part time. **Graduate enrollment:** 295 men, 250 women full time; 780 men, 1,166 women part time. **Faculty:** 202 total (195 full time), 80 with doctorates or other terminal degrees. **Location:** Rural campus in large town; 15 miles from Mansfield, 60 miles from Cleveland. **Calendar:** Semester, limited summer session. Saturday and extensive evening/early morning classes. **Microcomputers:** 100 located in classrooms, computer centers. **Special facilities:** Art gallery, Center for Public Affairs, Center for Business and Economic Research, convocation center, theater, fitness center, numismatic center.

DEGREES OFFERED. AA, BA, BS, MA, MBA, MEd, D, M.Div. 132 associate degrees awarded in 1992. 18% in business and management, 82% multi/interdisciplinary studies. 501 bachelor's degrees awarded. 21% in business and management, 8% business/office and marketing/distribution, 5% communications, 20% teacher education, 6% life sciences, 9% parks/recreation, protective services, public affairs, 14% social sciences. Graduate degrees offered in 9 major fields of study.

UNDERGRADUATE MAJORS. Associate: Business and office, criminal justice studies, liberal/general studies, radio/television broadcasting. **Bachelor's:** Accounting, American studies, art education, biochemistry, biological and physical sciences, biology, broadcast sales and station management, business administration and management, business and management, business economics, business education, chemistry, child development/care/guidance, communications, computer and information sciences, computer mathematics, creative writing, criminal justice studies, dramatic arts, early childhood education, earth sciences, economics, education, education of the mentally handicapped, education of the multiple handicapped, elementary education, English, English education, English literature, environmental science, fashion merchandising, finance, fine arts, food production/management/services, food science and nutrition, foreign languages education, French, geology, graphic design, health care administration, health education, history, home economics, home economics education, hotel/motel and restaurant management, illustration design, individual and family development, information sciences and systems, interior design, international studies, journalism, marketing and distribution, marketing management, mathematics, mathematics education, medical laboratory technologies, music, music education, music performance, music theory and composition, nursing, philosophy, physical education, physical sciences, physics, political science and government, predentistry, prelaw, premedicine, prepharmacy, preveterinary, psychology, public administration, public affairs, public relations, radio/television broadcasting, radio/television technology, recreation and community services technologies, religion, religious education, secondary education, social sciences, social work, sociology, Spanish, special education, specific learning disabilities, speech, speech/communication/theater education, sports communications, sports medicine, toxicology.

ACADEMIC PROGRAMS. Accelerated program, double major, dual enrollment of high school students, honors program, independent study, internships, study abroad, teacher preparation, New York semester, United Nations semester, Washington semester, cross-registration, pre-MBA courses for graduated nonbusiness majors, bachelor's degree completion program for RNs; liberal arts/career combination in engineering; combined bachelor's/graduate program in business administration. **Remedial services:** Reduced course load, remedial instruction, special counselor, tutoring, writing and reading labs, study strategy class. **ROTC:** Air Force. **Placement/credit:** AP, CLEP General and Subject, IB, institutional tests; 32 credit hours maximum for associate degree; 32 credit hours maximum for bachelor's degree.

ACADEMIC REQUIREMENTS. Freshmen must earn minimum GPA of 2.0 to continue in good standing. 70% of freshmen return for sophomore year. Students must declare major by end of second year. **Graduation requirements:** 64 hours for associate (21 in major), 128 hours for bachelor's (30 in major). Most students required to take courses in arts/fine arts, English, history, humanities, mathematics, philosophy/religion, biological/physical sciences, social sciences. **Postgraduate studies:** 1% from 2-year programs enter 4-year programs. 2% enter law school, 3% enter medical school, 1% enter MBA programs, 2% enter other graduate study.

FRESHMAN ADMISSIONS. Selection criteria: School achievement record most important. Counselor's recommendation and test scores also considered. **High school preparation:** 16 units recommended. Recommended units include biological science 2, English 4, foreign language 2, mathematics 3, physical science 2 and social science 3. **Test requirements:** SAT or ACT (ACT preferred); score report by August 25.

1992 FRESHMAN CLASS PROFILE. 1,557 men and women applied, 1,388 accepted; 297 men enrolled, 422 women enrolled. 37% had high school GPA of 3.0 or higher, 63% between 2.0 and 2.99. 9% were in top tenth and 33% were in top quarter of graduating class. **Academic background:** Mid 50% of enrolled freshmen had ACT composite between 19-23. 85% submitted ACT scores. **Characteristics:** 88% from in state, 95% live in college housing, 28% have minority backgrounds, 12% are foreign students, 25% join fraternities/sororities. Average age is 18.

FALL-TERM APPLICATIONS. $15 fee, may be waived for applicants with need. Closing date August 15; applicants notified on a rolling basis; must reply by May 1 or within 2 weeks if notified thereafter. Essay required. Interview recommended. Audition recommended for music, theater, ant applicants. Portfolio recommended for art applicants. Interview strongly recommended. CRDA. Deferred admission available.

STUDENT LIFE. Housing: Dormitories (men, women, coed); fraternity housing available. Honors and international floors available. **Activities:** Student government, radio, student newspaper, television, yearbook, annual literary publication, choral groups, concert band, dance, drama, jazz band, marching band, music ensembles, musical theater, pep band, symphony orchestra, madrigal singers, fraternities, sororities, Christian Fellowship, Newman Club, Bible studies group, Fellowship of Christian Athletes, international club, Black Student Union, political club, Martial Arts Club, Campus Activities Board, NAACP.

ATHLETICS. NCAA. **Intercollegiate:** Baseball M, basketball, cross-country, diving, football M, golf M, soccer, softball W, swimming, tennis, track and field, volleyball W, wrestling M. **Intramural:** Archery W, badminton, basketball, bowling M, cross-country, golf M, racquetball, skiing, softball, swimming, table tennis, volleyball, wrestling M.

STUDENT SERVICES. Aptitude testing, career counseling, employment service for undergraduates, freshman orientation, health services, on-campus day care, personal counseling, placement service for graduates, special adviser for adult students, veterans counselor.

ANNUAL EXPENSES. Tuition and fees: $10,933. **Room and board:** $4,520. **Books and supplies:** $500. **Other expenses:** $900.

FINANCIAL AID. 95% of freshmen, 95% of continuing students receive some form of aid. 77% of grants, 87% of loans, 47% of jobs based on need. 432 enrolled freshmen were judged to have need, all were offered aid. Academic, music/drama, art, athletic, state/district residency, leadership, alumni affiliation, religious affiliation, minority scholarships available. **Aid applications:** No closing date; priority given to applications received by March 15; applicants notified on a rolling basis beginning on or about April 1; must reply by May 1 or within 2 weeks if notified thereafter.

ADDRESS/TELEPHONE. Carl Gerbasi, Executive Director of Admissions and Financial Aid, Ashland University, 401 College Avenue, Ashland, OH 44805-9981. (419) 289-5052. Fax: (419) 289-5333.

Baldwin-Wallace College

Berea, Ohio — CB code: 1050

Admissions: 82% of applicants accepted
Based on:
- ••• School record
- •• Activities, recommendations, special talents, test scores
- • Essay, interview

Completion: 87% of freshmen end year in good standing
62% graduate, 10% of these enter graduate study

4-year private liberal arts college, coed, affiliated with United Methodist Church. Founded in 1845. **Accreditation:** Regional. **Undergraduate enrollment:** 1,037 men, 1,537 women full time; 494 men, 1,019 women part time. **Graduate enrollment:** 17 men, 19 women full time; 294 men, 295 women part time. **Faculty:** 288 total (154 full time), 153 with doctorates or other terminal degrees. **Location:** Suburban campus in large town; 15 miles from Cleveland. **Calendar:** Quarter, limited summer session. **Microcomputers:** 205 located in dormitories, libraries, classrooms, computer centers, campus-wide network. **Special facilities:** Observatory, 2 art galleries, 2 theaters, receation center, Student Activities Center, Conservatory of Music, computer center, 2 dance studios. **Additional facts:** Travel Abroad (seminars and student teaching)

DEGREES OFFERED. BA, BS, MBA, MEd. 818 bachelor's degrees awarded in 1992. 49% in business and management, 6% communications, 9% teacher education, 6% psychology, 6% social sciences, 5% visual and performing arts. Graduate degrees offered in 7 major fields of study.

UNDERGRADUATE MAJORS. Accounting, allied health, art education, art history, arts management, biology, business administration and management, business and management, business education, chemistry, clinical laboratory science, communications, computer and information sciences, computer programming, criminal justice studies, dance, dramatic arts, economics, education, elementary education, English, English education, English literature, finance, food science and nutrition, foreign languages education, French, geology, German, health education, health sciences, history, home economics, home economics education, individual and family development, information sciences and systems, international studies, junior high education, marketing and distributive education, marketing management, mathematics, mathematics education, medical laboratory technologies, music, music business management, music education, music history and appreciation, music performance, music theory and composition, music therapy, musical theater, philosophy, physical education, physics, political science and government, predentistry, preengineering, prelaw, premedicine, prepharmacy, preveterinary, psychology, radio/television broadcasting, religion, science education, secondary education, social sciences, social studies education, sociology, Spanish, specific learning disabilities, speech, speech correction, speech pathology/audiology, speech/communication/theater education, sports management, sports medicine, studio art, textiles and clothing.

ACADEMIC PROGRAMS. Double major, dual enrollment of high school students, honors program, independent study, internships, student-designed major, study abroad, teacher preparation, visiting/exchange student program, weekend college, United Nations semester, Washington semester, cross-registration, BS program in allied health fields with 3 local community colleges; liberal arts/career combination in engineering, forestry. **Remedial services:** Learning center, reduced course load, remedial instruction, special counselor, tutoring, writing laboratory, mathematics laboratory. **ROTC:** Air Force, Army. **Placement/credit:** AP, CLEP General and Subject, institutional tests.

ACADEMIC REQUIREMENTS. Freshmen must earn minimum GPA of 1.7 to continue in good standing. 85% of freshmen return for sophomore year. Students must declare major by end of second year. **Graduation requirements:** 186 hours for bachelor's (45 in major). Most students required to take courses in arts/fine arts, computer science, English, foreign languages, history, humanities, mathematics, philosophy/religion, biological/physical sciences, social sciences. **Postgraduate studies:** 1% enter law school, 1% enter medical school, 4% enter MBA programs, 4% enter other graduate study.

FRESHMAN ADMISSIONS. Selection criteria: School achievement record most important. Test scores, recommendations, class rank, extracurricular activities also considered. Special consideration to children of alumni and to rank in top half of class. **High school preparation:** 16 units recommended. Required units include English 4, foreign language 2, mathematics 3, social science 3 and science 3. Some flexibility in choice of subjects permitted. **Test requirements:** SAT or ACT; score report by July 1.

1992 FRESHMAN CLASS PROFILE. 674 men applied, 517 accepted, 250 enrolled; 776 women applied, 676 accepted, 339 enrolled. 67% had high school GPA of 3.0 or higher, 33% between 2.0 and 2.99. 28% were in top tenth and 60% were in top quarter of graduating class. **Academic background:** Mid 50% of enrolled freshmen had SAT-V between 380-520, SAT-M between 460-580; ACT composite between 20-25. 40% submitted SAT scores, 80% submitted ACT scores. **Characteristics:** 85% from in state, 76% live in college housing, 9% have minority backgrounds, 1% are foreign students, 19% join fraternities/sororities. Average age is 18.

FALL-TERM APPLICATIONS. $15 fee, may be waived for applicants with need. No closing date; priority given to applications received by April 1; applicants notified on a rolling basis. Audition required for music therapy, musical theater, music performance, music education applicants. Essay required. Interview recommended. Portfolio recommended for art applicants. CRDA. Deferred admission available.

STUDENT LIFE. Housing: Dormitories (men, women, coed); fraternity, sorority housing available. Students in Freshman Center required to stay entire freshman year. **Activities:** Student government, magazine, radio, student newspaper, yearbook, choral groups, concert band, dance, drama, jazz band, music ensembles, musical theater, opera, pep band, symphony orchestra, fraternities, sororities, Young Democrats, Young Republicans, Hillel, Newman Club, Religious Life Council, community service organizations, Fellowship of Christian Athletes, Black Student Alliance, World Student Alliance, Hispanic Student Association.

ATHLETICS. NCAA. **Intercollegiate:** Baseball M, basketball, cross-country, diving, football M, golf M, soccer, softball W, swimming, tennis, track and field, volleyball W, wrestling M. **Intramural:** Basketball, bowling, football M, golf, handball, ice hockey M, racquetball, rugby M, softball M, swimming, table tennis, tennis, track and field M, volleyball M, wrestling M.

STUDENT SERVICES. Aptitude testing, career counseling, employment service for undergraduates, freshman orientation, health services, on-campus day care, personal counseling, placement service for graduates, special adviser for adult students, veterans counselor, services/facilities for handicapped.

ANNUAL EXPENSES. Tuition and fees: $10,980. **Room and board:** $4,230. **Books and supplies:** $500. **Other expenses:** $250.

FINANCIAL AID. 95% of freshmen, 95% of continuing students receive some form of aid. 74% of grants, 77% of loans, 46% of jobs based on need. 330 enrolled freshmen were judged to have need, all were offered aid. Academic, music/drama, state/district residency, leadership, alumni affiliation, religious affiliation, minority scholarships available. **Aid applications:** No closing date; priority given to applications received by March 1; applicants notified on a rolling basis beginning on or about March 1; must reply by May 1 or within 3 weeks if notified thereafter.

ADDRESS/TELEPHONE. Juliann K. Baker, Director of Undergraduate Admissions, Baldwin-Wallace College, 275 Eastland Road, Berea, OH 44017-2088. (216) 826-2222. Fax: (216) 826-2329.

Belmont Technical College
St. Clairsville, Ohio CB code: 1072

2-year public technical college, coed. Founded in 1969. **Accreditation:** Regional. **Undergraduate enrollment:** 381 men, 745 women full time; 226 men, 398 women part time. **Faculty:** 130 total (34 full time). **Location:** Rural campus in small town; 15 miles from Wheeling, West Virginia. **Calendar:** Quarter, limited summer session. Saturday classes. **Microcomputers:** 85 located in classrooms, computer centers.

DEGREES OFFERED. AAS. 292 associate degrees awarded in 1992. 31% in business and management, 10% computer sciences, 21% engineering technologies, 9% health sciences, 24% allied health.

UNDERGRADUATE MAJORS. Accounting, air conditioning/heating/refrigeration mechanics, air conditioning/heating/refrigeration technology, business and management, business data programming, civil technology, computer programming, diesel engine mechanics, electromechanical technology, electronic technology, emergency medical technologies, historic preservation, mechanical design technology, medical assistant, medical social work, mental health/human services, microcomputer software, nursing, secretarial and related programs, welding technology.

ACADEMIC PROGRAMS. Double major, dual enrollment of high school students, internships, cross-registration, 2/2 program in industrial engineering with Wheeling College. **Remedial services:** Learning center, reduced course load, remedial instruction, special counselor, tutoring. **Placement/credit:** Institutional tests.

ACADEMIC REQUIREMENTS. Freshmen must earn minimum GPA of 1.5 to continue in good standing. Students must declare major on application. **Graduation requirements:** 100 hours for associate (80 in major). Most students required to take courses in computer science, English, mathematics, biological/physical sciences, social sciences.

FRESHMAN ADMISSIONS. Selection criteria: Open admissions. Selective admissions to nursing and paramedic programs based on test scores and interview. **Test requirements:** Applicants for associate in nursing, practical nursing, and paramedic applicants take admissions test on campus. All new full-time students must complete ASSET for purpose of course placement.

1992 FRESHMAN CLASS PROFILE. 372 men, 651 women enrolled. **Characteristics:** 85% from in state, 100% commute, 2% have minority backgrounds. Average age is 28.

FALL-TERM APPLICATIONS. $10 fee, may be waived for applicants with need. No closing date; applicants notified on a rolling basis beginning on or about January 1. Interview required for nursing and paramedic applicants; recommended for all others. Deferred and early admission available.

STUDENT LIFE. Activities: Choral groups.

STUDENT SERVICES. Aptitude testing, career counseling, employment service for undergraduates, freshman orientation, on-campus day care, personal counseling, placement service for graduates, special adviser for adult students, veterans counselor, services/facilities for handicapped.

ANNUAL EXPENSES. Tuition and fees (1992-93): $1,800, $630 additional for out-of-state students. **Books and supplies:** $450. **Other expenses:** $4,507.

FINANCIAL AID. 65% of continuing students receive some form of aid. Grants, loans, jobs available. Academic scholarships available. **Aid applications:** No closing date; applicants notified on a rolling basis beginning on or about June 1; must reply within 2 weeks.

ADDRESS/TELEPHONE. Thomas J. Tarowsky, Assistant Dean Student Services, Belmont Technical College, 120 Fox Shannon Place, St. Clairsville, OH 43950. (614) 695-9500. (800) 423-1188. Fax: (614) 695-2247.

Bliss College
Columbus, Ohio CB code: 1048

2-year proprietary branch campus, business college, coed. Founded in 1899. **Undergraduate enrollment:** 250 men and women. **Faculty:** 24 total (8 full time), 4 with doctorates or other terminal degrees. **Location:** Urban campus in very large city; 100 miles from of Cincinnati. **Calendar:** Quarter, extensive summer session. **Microcomputers:** 22 located in classrooms. **Additional facts:** Only National Shorthand Reporters Association approved training school in Columbus.

DEGREES OFFERED. 100 associate degrees awarded in 1992. 60% in business and management, 30% business/office and marketing/distribution, 10% computer sciences.

UNDERGRADUATE MAJORS. Accounting, business administration and management, computer programming, marketing and distribution.

ACADEMIC PROGRAMS. 2-year transfer program, accelerated program, double major, internships. **Remedial services:** Preparation for GED. **Placement/credit:** Institutional tests.

ACADEMIC REQUIREMENTS. Freshmen must earn minimum GPA of 1.75 to continue in good standing. 78% of freshmen return for sophomore year. Students must declare major on enrollment. **Graduation requirements:** 90 hours for associate. Most students required to take courses in computer science, English, mathematics.

FRESHMAN ADMISSIONS. Selection criteria: Interview and standardized entrance examination most important. **Test requirements:** Skadron Student Achievement Analysis required. **Additional information:** Applicants without high school diploma may be admitted under College Preparation Program.

1992 FRESHMAN CLASS PROFILE. 125 men and women enrolled. **Characteristics:** 95% from in state, 100% commute, 13% have minority backgrounds, 1% are foreign students. Average age is 24.

FALL-TERM APPLICATIONS. $100 fee. No closing date; priority given to applications received by September 5; applicants notified on a rolling basis; must reply by registration. Interview required. Deferred admission available.

STUDENT LIFE. Activities: Student government, student newspaper, Phi Beta Lambda.

ATHLETICS. Intramural: Basketball M, bowling, softball, table tennis, volleyball.

STUDENT SERVICES. Aptitude testing, career counseling, employment service for undergraduates, freshman orientation, on-campus day care, placement service for graduates, veterans counselor, services/facilities for handicapped.

ANNUAL EXPENSES. Tuition and fees (1992-93): $4,600. **Books and supplies:** $400.

FINANCIAL AID. 50% of freshmen, 50% of continuing students receive some form of aid. **Aid applications:** No closing date; applicants notified on a rolling basis.

ADDRESS/TELEPHONE. Walt Beckett, Admissions Coordinator, Bliss College, 3770 North High Street, Columbus, OH 43214. (614) 267-8355.

Bluffton College
Bluffton, Ohio CB code: 1067

Admissions: 84% of applicants accepted
Based on: ••• School record, test scores
•• Activities, interview, recommendations
• Essay, religious affiliation/commitment, special talents
Completion: 90% of freshmen end year in good standing
60% graduate, 6% of these enter graduate study

4-year private liberal arts college, coed, affiliated with General Conference, Mennonite Church. Founded in 1899. **Accreditation:** Regional. **Undergraduate enrollment:** 285 men, 354 women full time; 30 men, 54 women part time. **Faculty:** 79 total (54 full time), 34 with doctorates or other terminal degrees. **Location:** Rural campus in small town; 15 miles from Lima, 75 miles from Toledo. **Calendar:** Quarter, limited summer session. **Microcomputers:** 40 located in classrooms, computer centers. **Special facilities:** Mennonite historical library, 130-acre nature preserve, Peace Arts Center. **Additional facts:** Honor system used during exams. Christian faith, values and service to others emphasized.

DEGREES OFFERED. BA. 148 bachelor's degrees awarded in 1992. 38% in business and management, 20% teacher education, 5% parks/recreation, protective services, public affairs, 13% social sciences.

UNDERGRADUATE MAJORS. Accounting, art education, biological and physical sciences, biology, business administration and management, business and management, business economics, business education, chemistry, child development/care/guidance, clothing and textiles management/production/services, communications, computer and information sciences, criminal justice studies, early childhood education, economics, education, elementary education, English, English education, family/consumer resource management, fashion merchandising, food science and nutrition, health education, history, home economics, home economics education, humanities, humanities and social sciences, institutional management, junior high education, liberal/general studies, mathematics, mathematics education, music, music education, music performance, parks and recreation management, philosophy, physical education, physical sciences, physics, predentistry, prelaw, premedicine, preveterinary, psychology, religion, science education, secondary education, social sciences, social studies education, social work, sociology, Spanish, special education, speech, speech/communication/theater education, studio art, textiles and clothing, visual and performing arts.

ACADEMIC PROGRAMS. Double major, dual enrollment of high school students, honors program, independent study, internships, student-designed major, study abroad, teacher preparation, visiting/exchange student program, Washington semester, cross-registration, degree-completion program for working adults 25 years and older. **Remedial services:** Learning center, tutoring. **Placement/credit:** AP, CLEP General, institutional tests; 37 credit hours maximum for bachelor's degree.

ACADEMIC REQUIREMENTS. Freshmen must earn minimum GPA

of 1.6 to continue in good standing. 70% of freshmen return for sophomore year. Students must declare major by end of second year. **Graduation requirements:** 184 hours for bachelor's (55 in major). Most students required to take courses in arts/fine arts, English, history, mathematics, philosophy/religion, biological/physical sciences, social sciences.

FRESHMAN ADMISSIONS. Selection criteria: Class rank, school achievement record, and test scores very important. **High school preparation:** 16 units recommended. Recommended units include English 4, foreign language 3, mathematics 3, social science 3 and science 3. **Test requirements:** SAT or ACT; score report by August 15. **Additional information:** Campus visit and interview strongly recommended.

1992 FRESHMAN CLASS PROFILE. 231 men applied, 174 accepted, 77 enrolled; 226 women applied, 208 accepted, 102 enrolled. 64% had high school GPA of 3.0 or higher, 34% between 2.0 and 2.99. 21% were in top tenth and 52% were in top quarter of graduating class. **Academic background:** Mid 50% of enrolled freshmen had SAT-V between 380-510, SAT-M between 430-600; ACT composite between 20-25. 26% submitted SAT scores, 95% submitted ACT scores. **Characteristics:** 93% from in state, 95% live in college housing, 2% have minority backgrounds, 3% are foreign students. Average age is 19.

FALL-TERM APPLICATIONS. $20 fee, may be waived for applicants with need. Closing date August 15; priority given to applications received by June 1; applicants notified on a rolling basis. Essay required for academically weak applicants. Interview recommended. Audition recommended for music applicants. Portfolio recommended for art applicants. CRDA. Deferred and early admission available.

STUDENT LIFE. Housing: Dormitories (men, women). **Activities:** Student government, magazine, radio, student newspaper, yearbook, choral groups, concert band, drama, jazz band, music ensembles, musical theater, pep band, symphony orchestra, Black Student Union, departmental clubs, Brothers and Sisters in Christ, Peace Club, Habitat for Humanity, Fellowship of Christian Athletes, International Student Association. **Additional information:** No alcoholic beverages or tobacco allowed on campus. Honor system applies to all student activities. Students should feel comfortable with emphasis on faith and values. Voluntary chapel service once each week.

ATHLETICS. NCAA. **Intercollegiate:** Baseball M, basketball, cross-country, football M, golf M, soccer, softball W, tennis, track and field, volleyball W. **Intramural:** Archery, badminton, basketball, bowling, handball, racquetball, softball, table tennis, tennis, volleyball.

STUDENT SERVICES. Aptitude testing, career counseling, employment service for undergraduates, freshman orientation, health services, personal counseling, placement service for graduates, campus pastor, services/facilities for handicapped.

ANNUAL EXPENSES. Tuition and fees: $9,226. **Room and board:** $3,726. **Books and supplies:** $400. **Other expenses:** $800.

FINANCIAL AID. 90% of freshmen, 90% of continuing students receive some form of aid. 75% of grants, 88% of loans, 59% of jobs based on need. 160 enrolled freshmen were judged to have need, all were offered aid. Academic, music/drama, art, state/district residency, leadership, religious affiliation scholarships available. **Aid applications:** No closing date; priority given to applications received by May 15; applicants notified on a rolling basis beginning on or about February 15; must reply by May 1 or within 2 weeks if notified thereafter. **Additional information:** Tuition Equalization Program guarantees qualified students nonrepayable financial aid at least equal to the difference between Bluffton College tuition and the average Ohio public university tuition.

ADDRESS/TELEPHONE. Michael Hieronimus, Dean of Admissions, Bluffton College, 280 West College Avenue, Bluffton, OH 45817-1196. (419) 358-3257. (800) 488-3257. Fax: (419) 358-3323.

Bowling Green State University
Bowling Green, Ohio — CB code: 1069

Admissions: 75% of applicants accepted
Based on: ••• School record, test scores
• Activities, essay, interview, recommendations, special talents
Completion: 85% of freshmen end year in good standing
62% graduate, 15% of these enter graduate study

4-year public university, coed. Founded in 1910. **Accreditation:** Regional. **Undergraduate enrollment:** 5,792 men, 8,106 women full time; 537 men, 656 women part time. **Graduate enrollment:** 600 men, 656 women full time; 507 men, 648 women part time. **Faculty:** 852 total (680 full time), 547 with doctorates or other terminal degrees. **Location:** Rural campus in large town; 23 miles from Toledo. **Calendar:** Semester, limited summer session. Extensive evening/early morning classes. **Microcomputers:** 707 located in dormitories, libraries, computer centers. **Special facilities:** Planetarium, Lillian and Dorothy Gish Film Theater, sound recording archives, popular culture library, marine biology laboratory, educational memorabilia center. **Additional facts:** Evening degree programs and career counselling offered for adults in the greater community. Graduate level courses offered at Bryan, Bucyrus, Defiance, Findlay, Fremont, Elyria, Huron, Lima, Lorain, Mansfield, Marion, Tiffin, and Van Wert.

DEGREES OFFERED. BA, BS, BFA, MA, MS, MBA, MFA, MEd, PhD. 7 associate degrees awarded in 1992. 100% in business/office and marketing/distribution. 3,168 bachelor's degrees awarded. 23% in business and management, 12% communications, 19% teacher education, 6% health sciences, 6% parks/recreation, protective services, public affairs. Graduate degrees offered in 69 major fields of study.

UNDERGRADUATE MAJORS. Associate: Secretarial and related programs. **Bachelor's:** Accounting, actuarial sciences, advertising, aeronautical technology, American studies, apparel design and history, architectural technologies, art education, art history, art therapy, Asian studies, biochemistry, biology, business administration and management, business and management, business economics, business education, business statistics, ceramics, chemistry, child development/care/guidance, classics, clinical laboratory science, communications, computer and information sciences, crafts, creative writing, criminal justice studies, dance, dietetics, drafting and design technology, dramatic arts, drawing, early childhood education, earth sciences, economics, education, education of the deaf and hearing impaired, education of the emotionally handicapped, education of the mentally handicapped, education of the multiple handicapped, education of the physically handicapped, electronic technology, elementary education, energy conservation and use technology, English, English education, environmental design, environmental health engineering, environmental science, ethnic studies, family and community services, family/consumer resource management, fashion design, fashion merchandising, fiber/textiles/weaving, film arts, finance, fine arts, food production/management/services, food science and nutrition, foreign languages education, French, geochemistry, geography, geology, geophysics and seismology, German, gerontology, glass, graphic and printing production, graphic arts technology, graphic design, health care administration, health education, health sciences, history, home economics, home economics education, hotel/motel and restaurant management, human resources development, individual and family development, industrial technology, information sciences and systems, institutional management, institutional/home management/supporting programs, interior design, international business management, international studies, jazz, journalism, labor/industrial relations, Latin, Latin American studies, law enforcement and corrections, liberal/general studies, management information systems, manufacturing technology, marketing and distribution, marketing and distributive education, marketing management, mathematics, mathematics education, mechanical design technology, metal/jewelry, microbiology, music, music education, music history and appreciation, music performance, music theory and composition, musical theater, nursing, office supervision and management, operations research, painting, paleontology, parks and recreation management, personnel management, philosophy, photography, photojournalism, physical education, physical therapy, physics, political science and government, popular culture, pre-osteopathy, predentistry, prelaw, premedicine, printmaking, psychology, public administration, public relations, quality control technology, radio/television broadcasting, radio/television technology, recreation and community services technologies, religious music, Russian, Russian and Slavic studies, science education, sculpture, social studies education, social work, sociology, Spanish, special education, specific learning disabilities, speech correction, speech pathology/audiology, speech/communication/theater education, sports management, statistics, technical and business writing, technical education, trade and industrial education, visual and performing arts, women's studies.

ACADEMIC PROGRAMS. Accelerated program, cooperative education, double major, dual enrollment of high school students, education specialist degree, honors program, independent study, internships, student-designed major, study abroad, teacher preparation, telecourses, visiting/exchange student program, Washington semester, cross-registration; liberal arts/career combination in health sciences. **Remedial services:** Learning center, preadmission summer program, remedial instruction, tutoring, summer freshman program, basic skill learning laboratories. **ROTC:** Air Force, Army. **Placement/credit:** AP, CLEP Subject, institutional tests.

ACADEMIC REQUIREMENTS. Freshmen must earn minimum GPA of 2.0 to continue in good standing. 79% of freshmen return for sophomore year. Students must declare major by end of second year. **Graduation requirements:** 62 hours for associate (37 in major), 122 hours for bachelor's. Most students required to take courses in English, humanities, mathematics, biological/physical sciences, social sciences.

FRESHMAN ADMISSIONS. Selection criteria: Admissions decision based on high school sixth semester GPA, ACT or SAT test scores, and class rank. **High school preparation:** 16 units required. Required units include English 4, foreign language 2, mathematics 3, social science 3 and science 3. One unit visual/performing arts also required. 4 units mathematics recommended for business majors. **Test requirements:** SAT or ACT (ACT preferred); score report by February 1.

1992 FRESHMAN CLASS PROFILE. 3,245 men applied, 2,607 accepted, 1,155 enrolled; 5,822 women applied, 4,198 accepted, 1,822 enrolled. 56% had high school GPA of 3.0 or higher, 44% between 2.0 and 2.99. 13% were in top tenth and 45% were in top quarter of graduating class. **Academic background:** Mid 50% of enrolled freshmen had SAT-V between 400-510, SAT-M between 430-560; ACT composite between 20-24.

32% submitted SAT scores, 93% submitted ACT scores. **Characteristics:** 90% from in state, 91% live in college housing, 7% have minority backgrounds, 1% are foreign students, 20% join fraternities/sororities. Average age is 18.

FALL-TERM APPLICATIONS. $30 fee, may be waived for applicants with need. No closing date; priority given to applications received by February 1; applicants notified on a rolling basis beginning on or about November 15. Audition required for music applicants. Interview recommended. Portfolio recommended for art applicants. Deferred and early admission available.

STUDENT LIFE. Housing: Dormitories (men, women, coed); fraternity, sorority, handicapped housing available. Study areas, nonalcoholic wings, nonsmoking areas, international wing and honors housing offered. **Activities:** Student government, film, magazine, radio, student newspaper, television, yearbook, choral groups, concert band, dance, drama, jazz band, marching band, music ensembles, musical theater, opera, pep band, symphony orchestra, fraternities, sororities, Black Student Union, La Union de Estudiantes Latinos, social service organizations, World Student Association, African-American Graduate Student Association, African People's Association, Campus Crusade for Christ, College Democrats, College Republicans, Peace Coalition.

ATHLETICS. NCAA. **Intercollegiate:** Baseball M, basketball, cross-country, diving, football M, golf, gymnastics W, ice hockey M, soccer M, softball W, swimming, tennis, track and field, volleyball W. **Intramural:** Basketball, bowling, cross-country, football, golf, ice hockey M, racquetball, soccer, softball, tennis, track and field, volleyball, wrestling M.

STUDENT SERVICES. Career counseling, employment service for undergraduates, freshman orientation, health services, personal counseling, placement service for graduates, special adviser for adult students, veterans counselor, services/facilities for handicapped.

ANNUAL EXPENSES. Tuition and fees (1992-93): $3,334, $3,974 additional for out-of-state students. **Room and board:** $3,478. **Books and supplies:** $450. **Other expenses:** $1,206.

FINANCIAL AID. 55% of freshmen, 50% of continuing students receive some form of aid. 61% of grants, 79% of loans, 18% of jobs based on need. 1,632 enrolled freshmen were judged to have need, all were offered aid. Academic, music/drama, art, athletic, leadership, alumni affiliation, minority scholarships available. **Aid applications:** Closing date April 1; priority given to applications received by February 15; applicants notified on a rolling basis beginning on or about May 1; must reply within 3 weeks.

ADDRESS/TELEPHONE. John W. Martin, Director for Admissions, Bowling Green State University, McFall Center, Bowling Green, OH 43403-0080. (419) 372-2086. Fax: (419) 372-6955.

Bowling Green State University: Firelands College
Huron, Ohio — CB code: 0749

2-year public branch campus college, coed. Founded in 1967. **Accreditation:** Regional. **Undergraduate enrollment:** 1,406 men and women. **Faculty:** 75 total (36 full time), 22 with doctorates or other terminal degrees. **Location:** Rural campus in small town; 50 miles west of Cleveland, 60 miles east of Toledo. **Calendar:** Semester, limited summer session. **Microcomputers:** 230 located in classrooms, computer centers. **Special facilities:** Arboretum. **Additional facts:** Some graduate courses (primarily in education) and some upper-division courses offered. Upper-division program in nursing also available for registered nurses who hold associate's degree or have completed 3-year diploma program.

DEGREES OFFERED. AA, AS, AAS. 60 associate degrees awarded in 1992. 24% in business and management, 6% business/office and marketing/distribution, 6% computer sciences, 5% education, 7% engineering technologies, 24% allied health, 19% multi/interdisciplinary studies, 9% social sciences.

UNDERGRADUATE MAJORS. Accounting, allied health, biological and physical sciences, biology, business administration and management, business and management, business and office, business computer/console/peripheral equipment operation, business data processing and related programs, business data programming, chemistry, communications, computer and information sciences, computer programming, criminal justice studies, criminology, education, electrical technology, electronic technology, elementary education, engineering, engineering and engineering-related technologies, fine arts, geriatric services, health sciences, humanities, humanities and social sciences, industrial technology, liberal/general studies, management information systems, manufacturing technology, mathematics, medical records administration, medical records technology, nursing, physical sciences, physics, psychology, respiratory therapy, respiratory therapy technology, secondary education, secretarial and related programs, social sciences, social work, special education, trade and industrial supervision and management, visual and performing arts.

ACADEMIC PROGRAMS. 2-year transfer program, double major, dual enrollment of high school students, independent study, internships, student-designed major, teacher preparation, cross-registration. **Remedial services:** Learning center, preadmission summer program, reduced course load, remedial instruction, special counselor, tutoring. **Placement/credit:** AP, CLEP General and Subject, institutional tests; 15 credit hours maximum for associate degree.

ACADEMIC REQUIREMENTS. Freshmen must earn minimum GPA of 2.0 to continue in good standing. Students must declare major on application. **Graduation requirements:** 62 hours for associate (30 in major). Most students required to take courses in arts/fine arts, computer science, English, humanities, mathematics, biological/physical sciences, social sciences.

FRESHMAN ADMISSIONS. Selection criteria: Open admissions. Recommended units include English 4, foreign language 2, mathematics 3, social science 3 and science 3. College-preparatory program recommended, including 1 visual or performing arts. **Test requirements:** SAT or ACT (ACT preferred) for placement and counseling only; score report by August 1.

1992 FRESHMAN CLASS PROFILE. 306 men and women enrolled. 14% had high school GPA of 3.0 or higher, 66% between 2.0 and 2.99. **Academic background:** Mid 50% of enrolled freshmen had ACT composite between 19-23. 97% submitted ACT scores. **Characteristics:** 99% from in state, 100% commute, 4% have minority backgrounds.

FALL-TERM APPLICATIONS. $30 fee. Closing date July 23; applicants notified on a rolling basis. Deferred admission available.

STUDENT LIFE. Activities: Magazine, drama, musical theater, Social Science Club, Firelands College Bible Study, minority student union, student activities committee.

ATHLETICS. Intramural: Basketball, skiing, volleyball.

STUDENT SERVICES. Aptitude testing, career counseling, employment service for undergraduates, freshman orientation, personal counseling, placement service for graduates, special adviser for adult students, veterans counselor, services/facilities for handicapped.

ANNUAL EXPENSES. Tuition and fees (1992-93): $2,604, $3,974 additional for out-of-state students. **Books and supplies:** $400. **Other expenses:** $1,511.

FINANCIAL AID. 25% of continuing students receive some form of aid. 83% of grants, 93% of loans, 38% of jobs based on need. Academic, state/district residency, minority scholarships available. **Aid applications:** No closing date; priority given to applications received by April 1; applicants notified on a rolling basis beginning on or about April 15; must reply within 2 weeks.

ADDRESS/TELEPHONE. Jose L. Trevino, Director of Admissions and Marketing, Bowling Green State University: Firelands College, 901 Rye Beach Road, Huron, OH 44839. (419) 433-5560. Fax: (419) 433-9696.

Bradford School
Columbus, Ohio — CB code: 3952

2-year proprietary business college, coed. Founded in 1911. **Undergraduate enrollment:** 208 men and women. **Faculty:** 10 total (8 full time). **Location:** Suburban campus in very large city. **Calendar:** Semester, extensive summer session. **Microcomputers:** 86 located in classrooms. **Additional facts:** Prepares students to enter business world.

DEGREES OFFERED. 69 associate degrees awarded in 1992. 100% in business/office and marketing/distribution.

UNDERGRADUATE MAJORS. Accounting, graphic design, legal assistant/paralegal, retailing, secretarial and related programs, word processing.

ACADEMIC PROGRAMS. Internships.

ACADEMIC REQUIREMENTS. Freshmen must earn minimum GPA of 1.9 to continue in good standing. 80% of freshmen return for sophomore year. Students must declare major on application. **Graduation requirements:** 63 hours for associate (30 in major). Most students required to take courses in computer science, English, mathematics.

FRESHMAN ADMISSIONS. Selection criteria: Open admissions. Interview required to ensure interest in business education. **Additional information:** Student conditionally accepted based on high school transcript. Final transcript requested on graduation.

1992 FRESHMAN CLASS PROFILE. 477 men and women applied, 446 accepted; 157 enrolled. 12% had high school GPA of 3.0 or higher, 74% between 2.0 and 2.99. **Characteristics:** 100% from in state, 54% commute, 11% have minority backgrounds.

FALL-TERM APPLICATIONS. $45 fee. No closing date; applicants notified on a rolling basis; must reply by registration. Interview required. Deferred admission available.

STUDENT LIFE. Housing: Apartment housing available. **Activities:** Student government.

STUDENT SERVICES. Freshman orientation, personal counseling, placement service for graduates, services/facilities for handicapped.

ANNUAL EXPENSES. Tuition and fees (1992-93): $7,970. **Room and board:** $3,300 room only. **Books and supplies:** $800.

FINANCIAL AID. 85% of freshmen, 86% of continuing students receive some form of aid. 98% of grants, 58% of loans based on need. **Aid applications:** No closing date; applicants notified on a rolling basis.

ADDRESS/TELEPHONE. Pat Denton, Director of Admissions, Bradford School, 6170 Busch Boulevard, Columbus, OH 43229. (614) 846-9410. (800) 678-7981. Fax: (614) 846-9656.

Bryant & Stratton Business Institute: Cleveland West
Parma, Ohio CB code: 0577

2-year proprietary business, health science college, coed. Founded in 1854. **Undergraduate enrollment:** 59 men, 275 women full time; 31 men, 149 women part time. **Location:** Suburban campus in small city; 10 miles west of Cleveland. **Calendar:** Quarter. **Additional facts:** Provides business, computer and medical skills training leading to entry-level employment.

FRESHMAN ADMISSIONS. Selection criteria: High school transcript, Career Program Assessment Test, interview and essay most important.

ANNUAL EXPENSES. Tuition and fees (projected): $5,785. **Books and supplies:** $750.

ADDRESS/TELEPHONE. Daniel Reinbold, Director of Admissions, Bryant & Stratton Business Institute: Cleveland West, 12955 Snow Road, Parma, OH 44130. (216) 265-3151. Fax: (216) 265-0325.

Capital University
Columbus, Ohio CB code: 1099

Admissions: 76% of applicants accepted
Based on: ••• School record
•• Activities, recommendations, test scores
• Interview, special talents
Completion: 88% of freshmen end year in good standing
60% graduate, 19% of these enter graduate study

4-year private university and college of arts and sciences and music, nursing college, coed, affiliated with Evangelical Lutheran Church in America. Founded in 1830. **Accreditation:** Regional. **Undergraduate enrollment:** 549 men, 892 women full time; 381 men, 686 women part time. **Graduate enrollment:** 401 men, 237 women full time; 318 men, 216 women part time. **Faculty:** 161 total (105 full time), 106 with doctorates or other terminal degrees. **Location:** Suburban campus in very large city; 3 miles from downtown. **Calendar:** Semester, limited summer session. **Microcomputers:** 75 located in libraries, classrooms, computer centers, campus-wide network. **Special facilities:** Schumacher Art Gallery.

DEGREES OFFERED. BA, BFA, MBA, JD. 462 bachelor's degrees awarded in 1992. 19% in business and management, 5% communications, 12% teacher education, 14% health sciences, 5% multi/interdisciplinary studies, 20% social sciences, 13% visual and performing arts. Graduate degrees offered in 3 major fields of study.

UNDERGRADUATE MAJORS. Accounting, American literature, art education, art therapy, biological and physical sciences, biology, business administration and management, business and management, chemistry, communications, computer and information sciences, criminology, early childhood education, economics, elementary education, English, English education, English literature, finance, fine arts, foreign languages education, French, health education, history, human resources development, humanities and social sciences, international studies, jazz, junior high education, liberal/general studies, marketing management, mathematics, mathematics education, music, music education, music performance, music theory and composition, nursing, philosophy, physical education, political science and government, predentistry, prelaw, premedicine, prepharmacy, preveterinary, psychology, public administration, public relations, radio/television broadcasting, religion, religious education, science education, secondary education, social science education, social studies education, social work, sociology, Spanish, speech, sports medicine, technical and business writing, visual and performing arts.

ACADEMIC PROGRAMS. Accelerated program, double major, dual enrollment of high school students, independent study, internships, student-designed major, study abroad, teacher preparation, weekend college, Washington semester, cross-registration, 3-2 engineering program with Washington University, St. Louis, and Case Western Reserve, 3-2 occupational therapy program with Washington University, St. Louis, cooperative education for nursing students; liberal arts/career combination in engineering. **Remedial services:** Reduced course load, special counselor, tutoring. **ROTC:** Army. **Placement/credit:** AP, CLEP Subject, institutional tests; 27 credit hours maximum for bachelor's degree.

ACADEMIC REQUIREMENTS. Freshmen must earn minimum GPA of 2.0 to continue in good standing. 82% of freshmen return for sophomore year. Students must declare major by end of second year. **Graduation requirements:** 124 hours for bachelor's (30 in major). Most students required to take courses in arts/fine arts, English, history, humanities, mathematics, philosophy/religion, biological/physical sciences, social sciences. **Postgraduate studies:** 4% enter law school, 2% enter medical school, 3% enter MBA programs, 10% enter other graduate study. **Additional information:** Teacher certification available for learning disabilities and reading. Paralegal certification available from law school.

FRESHMAN ADMISSIONS. Selection criteria: Academic achievement in a college-preparatory curriculum most important. Recommendations, test scores, and extracurricular activities considered. **High school preparation:** 16 units required. Required units include English 4, foreign language 2, mathematics 3, social science 3 and science 3. Chemistry required for nursing applicants. One fine arts recommended. **Test requirements:** SAT or ACT; score report by May 1.

1992 FRESHMAN CLASS PROFILE. 556 men applied, 394 accepted, 116 enrolled; 760 women applied, 610 accepted, 218 enrolled. 73% had high school GPA of 3.0 or higher, 27% between 2.0 and 2.99. 36% were in top tenth and 72% were in top quarter of graduating class. **Academic background:** Mid 50% of enrolled freshmen had SAT-V between 400-520, SAT-M between 420-580; ACT composite between 20-25. 29% submitted SAT scores, 92% submitted ACT scores. **Characteristics:** 89% from in state, 77% live in college housing, 7% have minority backgrounds, 2% are foreign students, 25% join fraternities/sororities. Average age is 18.

FALL-TERM APPLICATIONS. $15 fee, may be waived for applicants with need. Closing date July 15; priority given to applications received by May 1; applicants notified on a rolling basis; must reply by May 1 or within 2 weeks if notified thereafter. Audition required for music applicants. Interview recommended. Portfolio recommended for art, art therapy applicants. CRDA. Deferred and early admission available.

STUDENT LIFE. Housing: Dormitories (men, women, coed). **Activities:** Student government, magazine, student newspaper, yearbook, choral groups, concert band, drama, jazz band, music ensembles, musical theater, opera, symphony orchestra, fraternities, sororities, University Congregation, Students for the Advancement of Afro-American Culture, Young Republicans, Campus Democrats, Circle-K, Ebony Brotherhood Association, International Student Association, Student Environmental Action Coalition, Capateers.

ATHLETICS. NCAA. **Intercollegiate:** Baseball M, basketball, football M, golf M, soccer, softball W, tennis, volleyball W, wrestling M. **Intramural:** Baseball M, basketball, bowling, football, soccer, softball, swimming, tennis, volleyball.

STUDENT SERVICES. Aptitude testing, career counseling, employment service for undergraduates, freshman orientation, health services, personal counseling, placement service for graduates, veterans counselor.

ANNUAL EXPENSES. Tuition and fees: $12,500. **Room and board:** $3,910. **Books and supplies:** $480. **Other expenses:** $670.

FINANCIAL AID. 90% of freshmen, 83% of continuing students receive some form of aid. 48% of grants, 85% of loans, 95% of jobs based on need. 258 enrolled freshmen were judged to have need, all were offered aid. Academic, music/drama, state/district residency, leadership, religious affiliation, minority scholarships available. **Aid applications:** Closing date July 15; priority given to applications received by March 1; applicants notified on a rolling basis beginning on or about April 1; must reply by May 1 or within 2 weeks if notified thereafter.

ADDRESS/TELEPHONE. Dr. Dolphus Henry, Associate Provost, Capital University, 2199 East Main Street, Columbus, OH 43209-2394. (614) 236-6101. (800) 289-6289. Fax: (614) 236-6820.

Case Western Reserve University
Cleveland, Ohio CB code: 1105

Admissions: 79% of applicants accepted
Based on: ••• School record, test scores
•• Activities, essay, interview, recommendations
• Special talents
Completion: 93% of freshmen end year in good standing
68% graduate, 33% of these enter graduate study

4-year private university, coed. Founded in 1826. **Accreditation:** Regional. **Undergraduate enrollment:** 1,739 men, 1,162 women full time; 267 men, 318 women part time. **Graduate enrollment:** 1,704 men, 1,587 women full time; 1,325 men, 1,054 women part time. **Faculty:** 1,742 total (1,695 full time), 1,644 with doctorates or other terminal degrees. **Location:** Urban campus in very large city; 4 miles from downtown. **Calendar:** Semester, limited summer session. **Microcomputers:** 200 located in dormitories, libraries, computer centers, campus-wide network. **Special facilities:** Biology field station; observatory; interdisciplinary research centers; art, natural history, and auto-aviation museums.

DEGREES OFFERED. BA, BS, MA, MS, MBA, MFA, MSW, PhD, DDS, MD, JD. 561 bachelor's degrees awarded in 1992. 11% in business and management, 33% engineering, 6% letters/literature, 7% life sciences, 7% physical sciences, 10% psychology, 13% social sciences. Graduate degrees offered in 88 major fields of study.

UNDERGRADUATE MAJORS. Accounting, aerospace/aeronautical/astronautical engineering, American literature, American studies, anthropology, applied mathematics, applied physics, art education, art history, Asian studies, astronomy, audio recording technology, biochemistry, bioengineering and biomedical engineering, biological and physical sciences, biology, business administration and management, business and management, chemical engineering, chemistry, civil engineering, classics, clinical laboratory science, communications, comparative literature, computer and information sciences, computer engineering, dance, dramatic arts, economics, electrical/electronics/communications engineering, engineering, engineering and other disciplines, English, English education, English literature, environmental geology, fluid and thermal engineering sciences, food science and nutrition, foreign languages education, French, geology, German, German studies, gerontology, history, history and philosophy of science and technology, industrial engineering, international relations, international studies, literature, macromolecular science, management science, materials engineering, mathematics, mathematics education, mechanical engineering, music, music education, music history and appreciation, music performance, nursing, nutritional sciences, philosophy, physics, political science and government, polymer science, prearchitecture, psychology, pure mathematics, religion, science education, secondary education, social studies education, sociology, Spanish, speech pathology/audiology, statistics, systems engineering, theater design.

ACADEMIC PROGRAMS. Accelerated program, cooperative education, double major, dual enrollment of high school students, honors program, independent study, internships, semester at sea, student-designed major, study abroad, teacher preparation, Washington semester, cross-registration; liberal arts/career combination in engineering, health sciences; combined bachelor's/graduate program in business administration. **Remedial services:** Learning center, preadmission summer program, reduced course load, remedial instruction, special counselor, tutoring. **ROTC:** Air Force, Army. **Placement/credit:** AP, IB, institutional tests.

ACADEMIC REQUIREMENTS. Freshmen must earn minimum GPA of 1.75 to continue in good standing. 92% of freshmen return for sophomore year. Students must declare major by end of second year. **Graduation requirements:** 120 hours for bachelor's (30 in major). Most students required to take courses in English, humanities, mathematics, biological/physical sciences, social sciences. **Postgraduate studies:** 4% enter law school, 8% enter medical school, 3% enter MBA programs, 18% enter other graduate study. **Additional information:** Pre-Professional Scholars Program gives talented undergraduates conditional acceptances to our graduate schools of medicine, dentistry, nursing, law, management, and social work.

FRESHMAN ADMISSIONS. Selection criteria: School achievement record and test scores. Special consideration to applicants from culturally, educationally, or economically disadvantaged backgrounds. School and community activities, essays, recommendations, and interview also considered. **High school preparation:** 16 units required. Required and recommended units include English 4, mathematics 3 and science 1. Foreign language 2 recommended. One chemistry and physics, 4 mathematics required for engineering, 2 laboratory science required for science, mathematics and premedical. **Test requirements:** SAT or ACT; score report by February 15. 3 ACH required of Preprofessional Scholars program applicants who take SAT. Score report by February 15.

1992 FRESHMAN CLASS PROFILE. 3,890 men and women applied, 3,083 accepted; 444 men enrolled, 323 women enrolled. 70% were in top tenth and 93% were in top quarter of graduating class. **Academic background:** Mid 50% of enrolled freshmen had SAT-V between 510-640, SAT-M between 610-730; ACT composite between 26-31. 85% submitted SAT scores, 58% submitted ACT scores. **Characteristics:** 57% from in state, 85% live in college housing, 23% have minority backgrounds, 6% are foreign students, 30% join fraternities/sororities. Average age is 18.

FALL-TERM APPLICATIONS. No fee. Closing date February 15; applicants notified on or about April 1; must reply by May 1. Audition required for music, music education applicants. Portfolio required for art education applicants. Essay required. Interview recommended. CRDA. Deferred and early admission available. EDP-F. 3 ACH recommended for applicants who take the SAT. Score report by February 1.

STUDENT LIFE. Housing: Dormitories (women, coed); fraternity, sorority housing available. Undergraduate students guaranteed housing; most are required to live on campus until age 21. Each dormitory room is hardwired to fiber-optic network. **Activities:** Student government, film, magazine, radio, student newspaper, yearbook, choral groups, concert band, dance, drama, jazz band, marching band, music ensembles, pep band, symphony orchestra, fraternities, sororities, University Christian Movement, Catholic Campus Ministry, Hillel Foundation, African-American Society, women's center, international club, College Democrats, College Republicans, Habitat for Humanity.

ATHLETICS. NCAA. **Intercollegiate:** Baseball M, basketball, cross-country, diving, fencing, football M, golf M, soccer, swimming, tennis, track and field, volleyball W, wrestling M. **Intramural:** Archery, badminton, basketball, bowling, cross-country, football M, golf, ice hockey, lacrosse, racquetball, rowing (crew), skiing, soccer, softball, squash, swimming, table tennis, tennis, track and field, volleyball, water polo M, wrestling M.

STUDENT SERVICES. Aptitude testing, career counseling, employment service for undergraduates, freshman orientation, health services, personal counseling, placement service for graduates, special adviser for adult students, veterans counselor, services/facilities for handicapped.

ANNUAL EXPENSES. Tuition and fees: $15,320. **Room and board:** $4,590. **Books and supplies:** $510. **Other expenses:** $1,140.

FINANCIAL AID. 77% of freshmen, 74% of continuing students receive some form of aid. Grants, loans, jobs available. Academic, music/drama, art, leadership scholarships available. **Aid applications:** No closing date; priority given to applications received by February 1; applicants notified on a rolling basis beginning on or about April 1; must reply by May 1 or within 2 weeks, whichever is later.

ADDRESS/TELEPHONE. William T. Conley, Dean of Undergraduate Admission, Case Western Reserve University, Tomlinson Hall, Cleveland, OH 44106-7055. (216) 368-4450. (800) 967-8898. Fax: (216) 368-5111.

Cedarville College
Cedarville, Ohio — CB code: 1151

Admissions: 86% of applicants accepted
Based on:
- ••• Essay, recommendations, religious affiliation/commitment, school record
- •• Test scores
- • Activities, special talents

Completion: 92% of freshmen end year in good standing
54% graduate, 7% of these enter graduate study

4-year private liberal arts college, coed, affiliated with General Association of Regular Baptist Churches. Founded in 1887. **Accreditation:** Regional. **Undergraduate enrollment:** 908 men, 1,192 women full time; 34 men, 38 women part time. **Faculty:** 163 total (122 full time), 71 with doctorates or other terminal degrees. **Location:** Rural campus in small town; 12 miles from Springfield, 20 miles from Dayton. **Calendar:** Quarter, limited summer session. **Microcomputers:** 400 located in dormitories, libraries, classrooms, computer centers. **Special facilities:** Observatory. **Additional facts:** Christian college with emphasis on academics and daily commitment to Christ.

DEGREES OFFERED. AA, BA, BS. 7 associate degrees awarded in 1992. 100% in business/office and marketing/distribution. 441 bachelor's degrees awarded. 19% in business and management, 10% communications, 26% teacher education, 7% health sciences, 5% philosophy, religion, theology, 5% psychology, 7% social sciences.

UNDERGRADUATE MAJORS. Associate: Secretarial and related programs. **Bachelor's:** Accounting, American studies, applied psychology, behavioral sciences, Bible studies, biological and physical sciences, biology, business administration and management, business and management, business communication technology, business economics, business education, chemistry, communications, computer and information sciences, criminal justice studies, electrical/electronics/communications engineering, elementary education, English, English education, finance, foreign languages education, health education, history, international business management, international studies, marketing and distribution, marketing management, mathematics, mathematics education, mechanical engineering, missionary studies, music, music education, nursing, physical education, political science and government, prelaw, psychology, public administration, radio/television broadcasting, radio/television technology, science education, secondary education, secretarial and related programs, social science education, social sciences, social studies education, social work, sociology, Spanish, speech, speech/communication/theater education, technical and business writing.

ACADEMIC PROGRAMS. 2-year transfer program, accelerated program, double major, dual enrollment of high school students, honors program, independent study, internships, study abroad, teacher preparation, telecourses; liberal arts/career combination in engineering, health sciences. **Remedial services:** Reduced course load, remedial instruction, special counselor, tutoring, Baldridge Reading Program. **ROTC:** Air Force, Army. **Placement/credit:** AP, CLEP General and Subject, institutional tests; 15 credit hours maximum for associate degree; 60 credit hours maximum for bachelor's degree.

ACADEMIC REQUIREMENTS. Freshmen must earn minimum GPA of 2.0 to continue in good standing. 75% of freshmen return for sophomore year. Students must declare major by end of second year. **Graduation requirements:** 96 hours for associate, 192 hours for bachelor's (48 in major). Most students required to take courses in arts/fine arts, English, foreign languages, history, humanities, mathematics, philosophy/religion, biological/physical sciences, social sciences. **Postgraduate studies:** 1% enter law school, 1% enter medical school, 1% enter MBA programs, 4% enter other graduate study.

FRESHMAN ADMISSIONS. Selection criteria: Clear testimony of personal faith in Jesus Christ, evidence of consistent Christian lifestyle, above-average academic performance (academic records, class rank, test scores), personal references considered. **High school preparation:** 15 units recommended. Recommended units include English 4, foreign language 2, mathematics 3, social science 3 and science 3. Additional mathematics and science recommended for nursing, science, engineering, and mathematics applicants. **Test requirements:** SAT or ACT (ACT preferred); score report by July 1.

1992 FRESHMAN CLASS PROFILE. 491 men applied, 415 accepted, 244 enrolled; 663 women applied, 583 accepted, 349 enrolled. 75% had high school GPA of 3.0 or higher, 24% between 2.0 and 2.99. 27% were in top tenth and 37% were in top quarter of graduating class. **Academic background:** Mid 50% of enrolled freshmen had SAT-V between 420-530, SAT-M between 440-590; ACT composite between 21-26. 52% submitted SAT scores, 71% submitted ACT scores. **Characteristics:** 32% from in state, 98% live in college housing, 3% have minority backgrounds, 1% are foreign students. Average age is 18.

FALL-TERM APPLICATIONS. $20 fee, may be waived for applicants

with need. No closing date; priority given to applications received by May 1; applicants notified on a rolling basis; must reply by May 1 or within 4 weeks if notified thereafter. Audition required for music majors applicants. Essay required. Interview recommended for marginal academic credentials applicants. CRDA. Deferred and early admission available. Students replying after May 1 admitted if openings exist.

STUDENT LIFE. Housing: Dormitories (men, women); apartment housing available. **Activities:** Student government, radio, student newspaper, television, yearbook, choral groups, concert band, drama, music ensembles, pep band, symphony orchestra, Christian ministries, College Republicans, Iota Chi, Emergency Medical Squad, Earth Stewardship Organization, Fellowship for World Missions. **Additional information:** Use of alcohol, tobacco, and drugs prohibited. Religious observance required.

ATHLETICS. NAIA. **Intercollegiate:** Baseball M, basketball, cross-country, golf M, soccer M, softball W, tennis, track and field, volleyball W. **Intramural:** Archery, badminton, basketball, bowling, golf, racquetball, skiing, soccer, softball, table tennis, tennis, volleyball.

STUDENT SERVICES. Aptitude testing, career counseling, employment service for undergraduates, freshman orientation, health services, personal counseling, placement service for graduates, veterans counselor, services/facilities for handicapped.

ANNUAL EXPENSES. Tuition and fees: $7,296. **Room and board:** $3,756. **Books and supplies:** $555. **Other expenses:** $1,015.

FINANCIAL AID. 81% of freshmen, 81% of continuing students receive some form of aid. 45% of grants, 89% of loans, 84% of jobs based on need. 359 enrolled freshmen were judged to have need, all were offered aid. Academic, music/drama, athletic, state/district residency, leadership scholarships available. **Aid applications:** No closing date; priority given to applications received by April 1; applicants notified on a rolling basis beginning on or about April 1; must reply within 2 weeks. **Additional information:** Ohio residents encouraged to submit Ohio choice resident form with admissions materials.

ADDRESS/TELEPHONE. David M. Ormsbee, Director of Admissions, Cedarville College, PO Box 601, Cedarville, OH 45314-0601. (513) 766-2211. (800) 777-2211. Fax: (513) 766-2760.

Central Ohio Technical College
Newark, Ohio CB code: 7331

2-year public technical college, coed. Founded in 1971. **Accreditation:** Regional. **Undergraduate enrollment:** 262 men, 652 women full time; 282 men, 664 women part time. **Faculty:** 109 total (51 full time), 6 with doctorates or other terminal degrees. **Location:** Suburban campus in large town; 45 miles from Columbus. **Calendar:** Quarter, limited summer session. **Microcomputers:** 40 located in computer centers. **Special facilities:** Campus shared with Ohio State University: Newark campus. **Additional facts:** Off-campus evening classes are taught in Mount Vernon and Coshocton.

DEGREES OFFERED. AS, AAS. 280 associate degrees awarded in 1992. 22% in business and management, 5% business/office and marketing/distribution, 6% computer sciences, 21% engineering technologies, 31% health sciences, 13% allied health.

UNDERGRADUATE MAJORS. Accounting, business administration and management, business and management, computer programming, criminal justice technology, drafting, drafting and design technology, electromechanical technology, electronic technology, finance, law enforcement and corrections technologies, legal secretary, manufacturing technology, mechanical design technology, medical secretary, nursing, physical therapy assistant, radiograph medical technology, secretarial and related programs, ultrasound technology.

ACADEMIC PROGRAMS. Cooperative education, double major, dual enrollment of high school students, honors program, internships, weekend college, cross-registration. **Remedial services:** Learning center, reduced course load, remedial instruction, special counselor, tutoring, developmental education. **Placement/credit:** Institutional tests.

ACADEMIC REQUIREMENTS. Freshmen must earn minimum GPA of 1.75 to continue in good standing. 65% of freshmen return for sophomore year. Students must declare major by end of first year. **Graduation requirements:** 100 hours for associate. Most students required to take courses in English, mathematics, social sciences.

FRESHMAN ADMISSIONS. Selection criteria: Open admissions. All health service applicants required to take placement test. Algebra and chemistry required for general nursing applicants. Algebra, chemistry, biology, and laboratory observation required for applicants to physical therapy assistant, radiology, and medical sonography programs. One chemistry, 1 algebra required for nursing; 1 chemistry, 1 algebra, 1 biology required for medical sonography, radiographic and physical therapist assistant; 1 alegebra required for computer programming and engineering programs.

1992 FRESHMAN CLASS PROFILE. 145 men, 338 women enrolled. **Characteristics:** 99% from in state, 94% commute, 3% have minority backgrounds. Average age is 29.

FALL-TERM APPLICATIONS. $15 fee, may be waived for applicants with need. Closing date September 15; priority given to applications received by June 15; applicants notified on a rolling basis. Deferred and early admission available.

STUDENT LIFE. Housing: Apartment housing available. **Activities:** Student government, choral groups, music ensembles.

ATHLETICS. Intercollegiate: Baseball M, basketball, softball W, volleyball W. **Intramural:** Badminton, basketball, table tennis, volleyball.

STUDENT SERVICES. Career counseling, employment service for undergraduates, on-campus day care, personal counseling, placement service for graduates, veterans counselor, services/facilities for handicapped.

ANNUAL EXPENSES. Tuition and fees (1992-93): $2,088, $864 additional for out-of-state students. **Books and supplies:** $600. **Other expenses:** $2,276.

FINANCIAL AID. 50% of freshmen, 50% of continuing students receive some form of aid. 97% of grants, 86% of loans, all jobs based on need. 258 enrolled freshmen were judged to have need, all were offered aid. Academic, minority scholarships available. **Aid applications:** No closing date; priority given to applications received by April 15; applicants notified on a rolling basis beginning on or about May 1; must reply within 3 weeks.

ADDRESS/TELEPHONE. John K. Merrin, Coordinator of Admissions, Central Ohio Technical College, 1179 University Drive, Newark, OH 43055. (614) 366-9222. Fax: (614) 366-5047.

Central State University
Wilberforce, Ohio CB code: 1107

4-year public university and college of arts and sciences and branch campus, business, teachers college, coed. Founded in 1887. **Accreditation:** Regional. **Undergraduate enrollment:** 3,261 men and women. **Faculty:** 156 total (129 full time), 74 with doctorates or other terminal degrees. **Location:** Rural campus in rural community; 18 miles from Dayton. **Calendar:** Quarter, limited summer session. Saturday and extensive evening/early morning classes. **Microcomputers:** Located in libraries, classrooms, computer centers. **Additional facts:** Historically black public university.

DEGREES OFFERED. AAS, BA, BS. 2 associate degrees awarded in 1992. 250 bachelor's degrees awarded.

UNDERGRADUATE MAJORS. Associate: Child development/care/guidance. **Bachelor's:** Accounting, anthropology, biology, business administration and management, business and management, business economics, chemistry, clinical laboratory science, communications, computer and information sciences, computer programming, dance, data processing, dramatic arts, early childhood education, earth sciences, economics, education, education of the culturally disadvantaged, education of the emotionally handicapped, education of the mentally handicapped, electrical/electronics/communications engineering, elementary education, English, English literature, finance, French, geography, geology, health sciences, history, information sciences and systems, international relations, journalism, junior high education, manufacturing technology, marketing management, mathematics, mechanical engineering, military science (Army), music, philosophy, physics, political science and government, prelaw, psychology, public administration, radio/television broadcasting, radio/television technology, remedial education, secondary education, secretarial and related programs, social sciences, social work, sociology, Spanish, special education, specific learning disabilities, speech, systems analysis, water and wastewater technology.

ACADEMIC PROGRAMS. Cooperative education, double major, honors program, independent study, internships, teacher preparation, weekend college, cross-registration; liberal arts/career combination in engineering. **Remedial services:** Learning center, reduced course load, remedial instruction, special counselor, tutoring. **ROTC:** Army. **Placement/credit:** CLEP General and Subject, institutional tests; 45 credit hours maximum for bachelor's degree.

ACADEMIC REQUIREMENTS. Freshmen must earn minimum GPA of 2.0 to continue in good standing. Students must declare major by end of second year. **Graduation requirements:** 111 hours for associate (39 in major), 189 hours for bachelor's (70 in major). Most students required to take courses in English, humanities, mathematics, biological/physical sciences, social sciences. **Postgraduate studies:** 90% from 2-year programs enter 4-year programs.

FRESHMAN ADMISSIONS. Selection criteria: Open admissions. Out-of-state residents must have 2.0 high school GPA. **High school preparation:** 16 units recommended. Recommended units include English 4, foreign language 2, mathematics 3, social science 3 and science 3. **Test requirements:** ACT for placement and counseling only.

1992 FRESHMAN CLASS PROFILE. 884 men and women enrolled. **Characteristics:** Average age is 18.

FALL-TERM APPLICATIONS. $15 fee, may be waived for applicants with need. Closing date August 1; applicants notified on a rolling basis. Interview recommended. Deferred and early admission available. ACT required for placement. Score report by September 1.

STUDENT LIFE. Housing: Dormitories (men, women). Honors dormitory available. **Activities:** Student government, radio, student newspaper, television, yearbook, choral groups, concert band, dance, drama, jazz band, marching band, music ensembles, musical theater, symphony orchestra, fraternities, sororities.

ATHLETICS. NAIA. **Intercollegiate:** Baseball M, basketball, cross-country M, football M, track and field, volleyball W. **Intramural:** Basketball M, racquetball, softball, swimming.

STUDENT SERVICES. Aptitude testing, career counseling, employment service for undergraduates, health services, personal counseling, placement service for graduates, veterans counselor.

ANNUAL EXPENSES. Tuition and fees (projected): $3,588, $3,588 additional for out-of-state students. **Room and board:** $1,489. **Books and supplies:** $604. **Other expenses:** $1,929.

FINANCIAL AID. 70% of freshmen, 85% of continuing students receive some form of aid. All grants, 61% of loans, 84% of jobs based on need. Academic, music/drama, art, state/district residency, leadership, alumni affiliation, religious affiliation, minority scholarships available. **Aid applications:** Closing date August 1; priority given to applications received by May 15; applicants notified on a rolling basis beginning on or about May 15; must reply within 2 weeks.

ADDRESS/TELEPHONE. Robert E. Johnson, Director of Admissions and Enrollment Mngmnt, Central State University, 1400 Brush Row Road, Wilberforce, OH 45384-3002. (513) 376-6348. Fax: (513) 376-6530.

Chatfield College
St. Martin, Ohio CB code: 1143

2-year private liberal arts college, coed, affiliated with Roman Catholic Church. Founded in 1970. **Accreditation:** Regional. **Undergraduate enrollment:** 14 men, 64 women full time; 19 men, 63 women part time. **Faculty:** 35 total, 3 with doctorates or other terminal degrees. **Location:** Rural campus in rural community; 40 miles from Cincinnati. **Calendar:** Semester, limited summer session. **Microcomputers:** Located in computer centers. **Additional facts:** Commitment to value-based education. Mainly serves adults, most of whom are working parents.

DEGREES OFFERED. AA. 19 associate degrees awarded in 1992. 100% in multi/interdisciplinary studies.

UNDERGRADUATE MAJORS. Business administration and management, business and management, fine arts, liberal/general studies, mental health/human services.

ACADEMIC PROGRAMS. 2-year transfer program, dual enrollment of high school students, independent study, internships, cross-registration, cooperative programs leading to bachelor of science in business and teaching certification with 2 local institutions. **Remedial services:** Learning center, preadmission summer program, remedial instruction, special counselor, tutoring, skills development program. **Placement/credit:** AP, CLEP General and Subject; 15 credit hours maximum for associate degree.

ACADEMIC REQUIREMENTS. Freshmen must earn minimum GPA of 2.0 to continue in good standing. Students must declare major by end of first year. **Graduation requirements:** 62 hours for associate (20 in major). Most students required to take courses in arts/fine arts, computer science, English, history, humanities, mathematics, philosophy/religion, biological/physical sciences, social sciences.

FRESHMAN ADMISSIONS. Selection criteria: Open admissions. **High school preparation:** 18 units recommended. Recommended units include English 4, foreign language 2, mathematics 2, social science 3 and science 2. Computer science recommended.

1992 FRESHMAN CLASS PROFILE. 10 men, 34 women enrolled. **Characteristics:** 100% from in state, 100% commute, 2% have minority backgrounds. Average age is 25.

FALL-TERM APPLICATIONS. $10 fee. No closing date; applicants notified on a rolling basis. Deferred and early admission available.

STUDENT SERVICES. Career counseling, personal counseling, special adviser for adult students, veterans counselor, services/facilities for handicapped.

ANNUAL EXPENSES. Tuition and fees: $4,590. **Books and supplies:** $444. **Other expenses:** $1,575.

FINANCIAL AID. 65% of freshmen, 60% of continuing students receive some form of aid. All aid based on need. 22 enrolled freshmen were judged to have need, all were offered aid. **Aid applications:** No closing date; priority given to applications received by July 15; applicants notified on a rolling basis beginning on or about May 1; must reply within 2 weeks. **Additional information:** Institutional grants/scholarships given primarily to first-year students to reduce debt load during initial year.

ADDRESS/TELEPHONE. Rebecca Cluxton, Director of Student Records and Financial Aid, Chatfield College, 20918 State Route 251, St. Martin, OH 45118-9705. (513) 875-3344.

Cincinnati Bible College and Seminary
Cincinnati, Ohio CB code: 1091

4-year private Bible college, coed, affiliated with Church of Christ/Christian Church. Founded in 1924. **Accreditation:** Regional. **Undergraduate enrollment:** 310 men, 209 women full time; 52 men, 39 women part time. **Graduate enrollment:** 57 men, 17 women full time; 166 men, 32 women part time. **Faculty:** 52 total (27 full time), 11 with doctorates or other terminal degrees. **Location:** Urban campus in large city. **Calendar:** Semester, limited summer session. **Microcomputers:** 12 located in computer centers. **Additional facts:** Member Greater Cincinnati Library Consortium and Greater Cincinnati Consortium of Colleges and Universities.

DEGREES OFFERED. AA, BA, BS, MA. 27 associate degrees awarded in 1992. 100% in philosophy, religion, theology. 56 bachelor's degrees awarded. 100% in philosophy, religion, theology. Graduate degrees offered in 2 major fields of study.

UNDERGRADUATE MAJORS. Associate: Bible studies. **Bachelor's:** Missionary studies, religious music, theological studies.

ACADEMIC PROGRAMS. Independent study, internships, cross-registration. **Remedial services:** Remedial instruction, tutoring. **Placement/credit:** AP, CLEP General and Subject, institutional tests.

ACADEMIC REQUIREMENTS. Freshmen must earn 2.0 GPA to be in good standing and minimum 1.5 by end of year to stay off probation/suspension. 75% of freshmen return for sophomore year. Students must declare major on enrollment. **Graduation requirements:** 66 hours for associate (26 in major), 132 hours for bachelor's (23 in major). Most students required to take courses in English, foreign languages, history, philosophy/religion, biological/physical sciences, social sciences. **Postgraduate studies:** 50% from 2-year programs enter 4-year programs. 25% enter other graduate study.

FRESHMAN ADMISSIONS. Selection criteria: Open admissions. College-preparatory program recommended. **Test requirements:** ACT for placement; score report by August 15.

1992 FRESHMAN CLASS PROFILE. 135 men, 75 women enrolled. 43% had high school GPA of 3.0 or higher, 47% between 2.0 and 2.99. **Academic background:** Mid 50% of enrolled freshmen had ACT composite between 14-19. 97% submitted ACT scores. **Characteristics:** 41% from in state, 95% live in college housing, 1% are foreign students. Average age is 19.

FALL-TERM APPLICATIONS. $35 fee. Closing date August 1; applicants notified on a rolling basis. Deferred admission available.

STUDENT LIFE. Housing: Dormitories (men, women); apartment housing available. **Activities:** Student government, student newspaper, yearbook, choral groups, concert band, drama, music ensembles.

ATHLETICS. Intercollegiate: Baseball M, basketball, golf M, soccer M, volleyball W. **Intramural:** Basketball, football M, track and field, volleyball.

STUDENT SERVICES. Career counseling, employment service for undergraduates, freshman orientation, health services, personal counseling, services/facilities for handicapped.

ANNUAL EXPENSES. Tuition and fees (1992-93): $3,872. **Room and board:** $3,124. **Books and supplies:** $500. **Other expenses:** $1,569.

FINANCIAL AID. 95% of freshmen, 63% of continuing students receive some form of aid. 86% of grants, 94% of loans, 18% of jobs based on need. 153 enrolled freshmen were judged to have need, all were offered aid. Academic, music/drama, leadership, alumni affiliation scholarships available. **Aid applications:** No closing date; priority given to applications received by May 1; applicants notified on a rolling basis beginning on or about June 1; must reply within 2 weeks.

ADDRESS/TELEPHONE. Phil Coleman, Director of Admissions, Cincinnati Bible College and Seminary, 2700 Glenway Avenue, PO Box 043200, Cincinnati, OH 45204-3200. (513) 244-8141. Fax: (513) 244-8140.

Cincinnati College of Mortuary Science
Cincinnati, Ohio CB code: 0945

4-year private college of mortuary science, coed. Founded in 1882. **Accreditation:** Regional. **Undergraduate enrollment:** 117 men, 28 women full time. **Faculty:** 18 total (6 full time), 6 with doctorates or other terminal degrees. **Location:** Urban campus in large city; 3 miles from downtown. **Calendar:** Quarter. **Additional facts:** Students with 2 years of college can obtain bachelor of mortuary science in 5 quarters. Program of study contingent on licensing requirements of state in which student will practice. Full access to Xavier University library and facilities.

DEGREES OFFERED. B. 58 associate degrees awarded in 1992. 26 bachelor's degrees awarded.

UNDERGRADUATE MAJORS. Funeral services/mortuary science. funeral services/mortuary science.

ACADEMIC PROGRAMS. 2-year transfer program, internships. **Remedial services:** Reduced course load, tutoring. **Placement/credit:** Institutional tests; 41 credit hours maximum for associate degree; 56 credit hours maximum for bachelor's degree.

ACADEMIC REQUIREMENTS. Freshmen must earn minimum GPA of 2.0 to continue in good standing. 85% of freshmen return for sophomore year. Students must declare major on application. **Graduation requirements:** 99 hours for associate (75 in major), 180 hours for bachelor's (90 in major). Most students required to take courses in arts/fine arts, computer science, English, history, humanities, biological/physical sciences, social sciences. **Postgraduate studies:** 60% from 2-year programs enter 4-year programs. 5% enter other graduate study.

FRESHMAN ADMISSIONS. Selection criteria: School achievement record most important. **High school preparation:** 15 units required. Required units include biological science 2, English 3, mathematics 1 and social science 2.

1992 FRESHMAN CLASS PROFILE. 13 men and women applied, 13 accepted; 10 enrolled. 17% had high school GPA of 3.0 or higher, 80% between 2.0 and 2.99. **Characteristics:** 45% from in state, 78% commute, 10% have minority backgrounds.

FALL-TERM APPLICATIONS. $25 fee. No closing date; applicants notified on a rolling basis; must reply within 3 weeks. Deferred admission available.

STUDENT LIFE. Housing: Cooperative housing available. **Activities:** Yearbook, professional fraternity. **Additional information:** Health services and athletic facilities available through Xavier University.

STUDENT SERVICES. Career counseling, employment service for undergraduates, health services, personal counseling, placement service for graduates, veterans counselor, services/facilities for handicapped.

ANNUAL EXPENSES. Tuition and fees: $7,210. **Books and supplies:** $750. **Other expenses:** $375.

FINANCIAL AID. 50% of freshmen, 50% of continuing students receive some form of aid. 74% of grants, all loans based on need. 8 enrolled freshmen were judged to have need, all were offered aid. **Aid applications:** No closing date; priority given to applications received by July 1; applicants notified on a rolling basis beginning on or about March 1; must reply within 2 weeks. **Additional information:** Several scholarships available plus Pell, Ohio grants for Ohio residents and student loans.

ADDRESS/TELEPHONE. Admissions Office, Cincinnati College of Mortuary Science, 3860 Pacific Avenue, Cincinnati, OH 45207-1033. (513) 745-3632.

Cincinnati Metropolitan College
St. Bernard, Ohio CB code: 3953

2-year proprietary business, health science, community, technical college, coed. Founded in 1964. **Undergraduate enrollment:** 150 men and women. **Location:** Urban campus in small town; within Cincinnati greater metropolitan area. **Calendar:** Quarter.

FRESHMAN ADMISSIONS. Selection criteria: Open admissions.

ANNUAL EXPENSES. Tuition and fees: $6,110. **Books and supplies:** $600. **Other expenses:** $2,000.

ADDRESS/TELEPHONE. Cynthia Wanner, Director of Admissions, Cincinnati Metropolitan College, 4320 Bertus Street, St. Bernard, OH 45217. (513) 242-0202.

Cincinnati Technical College
Cincinnati, Ohio CB code: 1984

2-year public technical college, coed. Founded in 1966. **Accreditation:** Regional. **Undergraduate enrollment:** 5,500 men and women. **Location:** Urban campus in large city; 5 miles from downtown. **Calendar:** Five 10-week terms. **Additional facts:** Two extention centers at local high schools for some credit courses.

FRESHMAN ADMISSIONS. Selection criteria: Open admissions. Selective admissions to some programs.

ANNUAL EXPENSES. Tuition and fees (1992-93): $2,226, $1,722 additional for out-of-state students. **Books and supplies:** $650. **Other expenses:** $900.

ADDRESS/TELEPHONE. John P. Wagner, Dean of Admissions, Cincinnati Technical College, 3520 Central Parkway, Cincinnati, OH 45223. (513) 861-7700.

Circleville Bible College
Circleville, Ohio CB code: 1088

4-year private Bible, teachers college, coed, affiliated with Churches of Christ in Christian Union. Founded in 1948. **Undergraduate enrollment:** 96 men, 55 women full time; 20 men, 17 women part time. **Faculty:** 20 total (13 full time), 3 with doctorates or other terminal degrees. **Location:** Rural campus in large town; 25 miles from Columbus. **Calendar:** Semester, limited summer session. **Special facilities:** Bible collection.

DEGREES OFFERED. AA, BA. 3 associate degrees awarded in 1992. 100% in philosophy, religion, theology. 20 bachelor's degrees awarded. 22% in teacher education, 78% philosophy, religion, theology.

UNDERGRADUATE MAJORS. Associate: Elementary education, junior high education, missionary studies, religious education, religious music, youth ministries. **Bachelor's:** Bible studies, Christian counseling, elementary education, evangelism and church growth, junior high education, missionary studies, religious education, religious music, theological studies, youth ministries.

ACADEMIC PROGRAMS. Double major, independent study, internships, teacher preparation, weekend college. **Remedial services:** Reduced course load, remedial instruction, special counselor, tutoring. **Placement/credit:** Institutional tests.

ACADEMIC REQUIREMENTS. Freshmen must earn minimum GPA of 2.0 to continue in good standing. Students must declare major by end of second year. **Graduation requirements:** 62 hours for associate (16 in major), 124 hours for bachelor's. Most students required to take courses in English, history, mathematics, philosophy/religion, biological/physical sciences, social sciences. **Postgraduate studies:** 8% from 2-year programs enter 4-year programs. 35% enter other graduate study.

FRESHMAN ADMISSIONS. Selection criteria: Positive Chistian testimony, potential for Christian service, sound academic performance, and personal character references important. **Test requirements:** SAT or ACT; score report by August 15. Students without SAT or ACT may be admitted conditionally but must meet test requirement at earliest opportunity.

1992 FRESHMAN CLASS PROFILE. 77 men and women enrolled. 25% had high school GPA of 3.0 or higher, 73% between 2.0 and 2.99. **Characteristics:** 80% from in state, 85% live in college housing, 1% have minority backgrounds. Average age is 19.

FALL-TERM APPLICATIONS. No fee. No closing date; applicants notified on a rolling basis. Essay required.

STUDENT LIFE. Housing: Dormitories (men, women); apartment housing available. **Activities:** Student government, yearbook, choral groups, drama, music ensembles, Rotoract, ministerial association, married couples association, student missionary association.

ATHLETICS. Intercollegiate: Basketball M, soccer M, volleyball W. **Intramural:** Basketball, bowling, golf, softball, table tennis, tennis, volleyball.

STUDENT SERVICES. Aptitude testing, career counseling, employment service for undergraduates, freshman orientation, personal counseling, veterans counselor.

ANNUAL EXPENSES. Tuition and fees (1992-93): $4,020. **Room and board:** $2,992. **Books and supplies:** $400. **Other expenses:** $910.

FINANCIAL AID. 95% of freshmen, 95% of continuing students receive some form of aid. Grants, loans, jobs available. **Aid applications:** No closing date; applicants notified on a rolling basis; must reply within 2 weeks. **Additional information:** Religious affiliation tuition discount.

ADDRESS/TELEPHONE. Mike Atkins, Director Enrollment Services, Circleville Bible College, Box 458, Circleville, OH 43113. (614) 477-7701.

Clark State Community College
Springfield, Ohio CB code: 0777

2-year public community college, coed. Founded in 1966. **Accreditation:** Regional. **Undergraduate enrollment:** 420 men, 823 women full time; 566 men, 1,304 women part time. **Faculty:** 370 total (73 full time), 31 with doctorates or other terminal degrees. **Location:** Suburban campus in small city; 30 miles from Dayton, 45 miles from Columbus. **Calendar:** Quarter, limited summer session. Saturday classes. **Microcomputers:** Located in libraries, classrooms. **Additional facts:** Branch campus at New Carlisle.

DEGREES OFFERED. AA, AS, AAS. 274 associate degrees awarded in 1992. 30% in business and management, 7% business/office and marketing/distribution, 5% computer sciences, 7% engineering technologies, 23% health sciences, 12% multi/interdisciplinary studies, 12% parks/recreation, protective services, public affairs.

UNDERGRADUATE MAJORS. Accounting, agribusiness, agricultural business and management, business administration and management, business and management, business and office, business data programming, child development/care/guidance, civil technology, commercial art, computer programming, court reporting, criminal justice technology, drafting and design technology, electrical technology, emergency medical technologies, finance, forensic studies, geriatric services, horticulture, information sciences and systems, law enforcement and corrections technologies, legal assistant/paralegal, legal secretary, manufacturing technology, mechanical design technology, medical laboratory technologies, medical secretary, nursing, ornamental horticulture, quality control technology, secretarial and related programs, social work, word processing.

ACADEMIC PROGRAMS. 2-year transfer program, cooperative education, double major, dual enrollment of high school students, internships, student-designed major, weekend college, cross-registration. **Remedial services:** Learning center, preadmission summer program, reduced course load, remedial instruction, tutoring. **Placement/credit:** AP, CLEP General and Subject, institutional tests; 24 credit hours maximum for associate degree.

ACADEMIC REQUIREMENTS. Freshmen must earn minimum GPA of 1.5 to continue in good standing. 70% of freshmen return for sophomore year. Students must declare major on application. **Graduation requirements:** 90 hours for associate (90 in major). Most students required to take courses in computer science, English, humanities, mathematics, philosophy/religion, social sciences.

FRESHMAN ADMISSIONS. Selection criteria: Open admissions. Nursing and allied health applicants must have high school chemistry and algebra or equivalent with a grade of 2.0 or better. Mathematics placement test with a score of 12 or better required for nursing. Recommended units include English 4, foreign language 2, mathematics 3, social science 3 and science 3. Algebra and chemistry required for nursing and medical technology. 2 units mathematics required for engineering programs.

1992 FRESHMAN CLASS PROFILE. 307 men, 526 women enrolled.

Characteristics: 99% from in state, 100% commute, 8% have minority backgrounds, 1% are foreign students. Average age is 25.

FALL-TERM APPLICATIONS. $15 fee. No closing date; applicants notified on a rolling basis beginning on or about February 1; must reply by May 1 or within 4 weeks if notified thereafter. CRDA. Early admission available. Early admission open to high school juniors and seniors. Placement test and high school approval required.

STUDENT LIFE. Activities: Student government, student newspaper, television, drama, professional and technological fraternities and sororities, interfaith campus ministry.

ATHLETICS. NJCAA. **Intercollegiate:** Basketball, golf M, volleyball W. **Intramural:** Basketball, bowling, golf, skiing, softball, swimming, table tennis, tennis, volleyball.

STUDENT SERVICES. Aptitude testing, career counseling, employment service for undergraduates, freshman orientation, health services, on-campus day care, personal counseling, placement service for graduates, veterans counselor, services/facilities for handicapped.

ANNUAL EXPENSES. Tuition and fees (1992-93): $2,183, $2,003 additional for out-of-state students. **Books and supplies:** $600. **Other expenses:** $750.

FINANCIAL AID. All grants, all jobs based on need. **Aid applications:** No closing date; applicants notified on a rolling basis.

ADDRESS/TELEPHONE. Todd Jones, Director of Admissions, Clark State Community College, PO Box 570, Springfield, OH 45501. (513) 325-0691. Fax: (513) 328-6142.

Cleveland College of Jewish Studies

Beachwood, Ohio CB code: 1190

4-year private liberal arts, teachers college, coed, affiliated with Jewish faith. Founded in 1963. **Accreditation:** Regional. **Undergraduate enrollment:** 2 men, 10 women full time; 150 men, 300 women part time. **Graduate enrollment:** 4 women full time; 10 men, 30 women part time. **Faculty:** 20 total (5 full time), 13 with doctorates or other terminal degrees. **Location:** Suburban campus in large town; 10 miles from Cleveland. **Calendar:** Semester, extensive summer session. **Special facilities:** College-sponsored museum exhibits. **Additional facts:** College specializes in Judaic and Hebrew Studies and teacher education.

DEGREES OFFERED. B, M. Graduate degrees offered in 5 major fields of study.

UNDERGRADUATE MAJORS. Bible studies, comparative literature, Hebrew, Jewish studies, Middle Eastern studies.

ACADEMIC PROGRAMS. Internships, study abroad, cross-registration.

ACADEMIC REQUIREMENTS. No policy requiring minimum GPA; records of students having academic difficulty are reviewed individually. Students must declare major on enrollment. **Graduation requirements:** 120 hours for bachelor's. **Additional information:** Continuing education program in Judaic and Hebrew studies.

FRESHMAN ADMISSIONS. Selection criteria: Open admissions. Graduation from Hebrew high school or good background in Hebrew language and Judaic subjects.

1992 FRESHMAN CLASS PROFILE. Characteristics: 95% from in state, 100% commute.

FALL-TERM APPLICATIONS. $25 fee. No closing date; applicants notified on a rolling basis. Deferred and early admission available.

STUDENT SERVICES. Career counseling.

ANNUAL EXPENSES. Tuition and fees (1992-93): $3,015. **Books and supplies:** $150.

FINANCIAL AID. Grants available. **Aid applications:** No closing date; applicants notified on a rolling basis.

ADDRESS/TELEPHONE. Director of Student Services, Cleveland College of Jewish Studies, 26500 Shaker Boulevard, Beachwood, OH 44122. (216) 464-4050. Fax: (216) 464-5827.

Cleveland Institute of Art

Cleveland, Ohio CB code: 1152

Admissions:	78% of applicants accepted
Based on:	••• School record, special talents
	•• Interview, test scores
	• Essay
Completion:	94% of freshmen end year in good standing
	47% graduate, 14% of these enter graduate study

5-year private art college, coed. Founded in 1882. **Accreditation:** Regional. **Undergraduate enrollment:** 246 men, 223 women full time; 11 men, 35 women part time. **Faculty:** 72 total (26 full time), 12 with doctorates or other terminal degrees. **Location:** Urban campus in very large city; 7 miles from downtown. **Calendar:** 4-1-4, limited summer session. **Microcomputers:** 20 located in libraries, computer centers. **Additional facts:** Within walking distance of Cleveland Art Museum, Museum of Natural History, Cleveland Health Museum, Western Reserve Historical Society, and Case Western Reserve University.

DEGREES OFFERED. BFA. 69 bachelor's degrees awarded in 1992. 100% in visual and performing arts.

UNDERGRADUATE MAJORS. Ceramics, drawing, enameling, fiber/textiles/weaving, glass, graphic design, illustration design, industrial design, interior design, medical illustrating, metal/jewelry, painting, photography, printmaking, sculpture.

ACADEMIC PROGRAMS. Accelerated program, double major, honors program, independent study, internships, student-designed major, study abroad, teacher preparation, New York semester, cross-registration. **Remedial services:** Reduced course load, remedial instruction, special counselor, tutoring. **Placement/credit:** AP, CLEP General and Subject, institutional tests.

ACADEMIC REQUIREMENTS. Freshmen must earn minimum GPA of 1.7 to continue in good standing. 90% of freshmen return for sophomore year. Students must declare major by end of second year. **Graduation requirements:** 179 hours for bachelor's (42 in major). Most students required to take courses in arts/fine arts, English. **Postgraduate studies:** 14% enter other graduate study.

FRESHMAN ADMISSIONS. Selection criteria: Portfolio, transcripts, statement of purpose, interview, and test scores are important. **High school preparation:** 15 units required. Required and recommended units include biological science 2, English 4, mathematics 3-4 and social science 4. Foreign language 1 and physical science 2 recommended. 2 years of art also required. **Test requirements:** SAT or ACT; score report by September 1.

1992 FRESHMAN CLASS PROFILE. 173 men applied, 138 accepted, 43 enrolled; 134 women applied, 101 accepted, 37 enrolled. 40% had high school GPA of 3.0 or higher, 52% between 2.0 and 2.99. **Academic background:** Mid 50% of enrolled freshmen had SAT-V between 420-510, SAT-M between 430-530; ACT composite between 19-24. 60% submitted SAT scores, 54% submitted ACT scores. **Characteristics:** 70% from in state, 50% commute, 11% have minority backgrounds, 3% are foreign students. Average age is 21.

FALL-TERM APPLICATIONS. $30 fee, may be waived for applicants with need. Closing date July 30; priority given to applications received by March 1; applicants notified on a rolling basis; must reply by May 1 or within 2 weeks if notified thereafter. Interview required. Portfolio required. Essay required. CRDA. Deferred admission available. EDP-F.

STUDENT LIFE. Housing: Dormitories (coed); fraternity, sorority, cooperative housing available. **Activities:** Student government, student newspaper, student art shows, fraternities, sororities. **Additional information:** Athletic facilities available through Case Western Reserve University.

ATHLETICS. Intramural: Volleyball.

STUDENT SERVICES. Career counseling, employment service for undergraduates, freshman orientation, health services, personal counseling, placement service for graduates, special adviser for adult students, veterans counselor, services/facilities for handicapped.

ANNUAL EXPENSES. Tuition and fees: $11,200. **Room and board:** $4,600. **Books and supplies:** $1,000. **Other expenses:** $800.

FINANCIAL AID. 60% of freshmen, 73% of continuing students receive some form of aid. 80% of grants, 76% of loans, all jobs based on need. Academic, art scholarships available. **Aid applications:** No closing date; priority given to applications received by April 20; applicants notified on a rolling basis beginning on or about January 15; must reply by May 1 or within 3 weeks if notified thereafter.

ADDRESS/TELEPHONE. Tom Steffen, Director of Admissions, Cleveland Institute of Art, 11141 East Boulevard, Cleveland, OH 44106. (216) 421-7418. (800) 223-4700. Fax: (216) 421-7438.

Cleveland Institute of Electronics

Cleveland, Ohio CB code: 0802

2-year proprietary technical college, coed. Founded in 1934. **Undergraduate enrollment:** 8,900 men and women. **Faculty:** 84 total (7 full time), 16 with doctorates or other terminal degrees. **Location:** Urban campus in very large city. **Calendar:** Continuous enrollment. **Additional facts:** Curriculum is entirely home study with no classroom attendance.

DEGREES OFFERED. AAS. 80 associate degrees awarded in 1992. 100% in engineering technologies.

UNDERGRADUATE MAJORS. Electronic technology.

ACADEMIC PROGRAMS. Independent study. **Placement/credit:** Institutional tests; 53 credit hours maximum for associate degree.

ACADEMIC REQUIREMENTS. Freshmen must earn minimum GPA of 2.0 to continue in good standing. Students must declare major on application. **Graduation requirements:** 106 hours for associate. Most students required to take courses in English.

FRESHMAN ADMISSIONS. Selection criteria: Open admissions.

1992 FRESHMAN CLASS PROFILE. 3,300 men and women enrolled.

FALL-TERM APPLICATIONS. No fee. No closing date; applicants notified on a rolling basis. Early admission available. High school students are permitted to enroll with signed approval of their parents and guidance counselors (if student is a minor).

STUDENT LIFE. Activities: Student newspaper.

STUDENT SERVICES. Employment service for undergraduates, veterans counselor.

ANNUAL EXPENSES. Tuition and fees (1992-93): Tuition and fees $1,000 per 6-month term.

FINANCIAL AID. 15% of freshmen, 15% of continuing students receive some form of aid. All grants, 80% of loans based on need. 300 enrolled freshmen were judged to have need, all were offered aid. Academic scholarships available. **Aid applications:** No closing date; applicants notified on a rolling basis; must reply within 30 days.

ADDRESS/TELEPHONE. Office of Mail Enrollments, Cleveland Institute of Electronics, 1776 East 17th Street, Cleveland, OH 44114-3679. (216) 781-9400. (800) 243-6446. Fax: (216) 781-0331.

Cleveland Institute of Music
Cleveland, Ohio CB code: 1124

4-year private music college, coed. Founded in 1920. **Accreditation:** Regional. **Undergraduate enrollment:** 181 men and women. **Graduate enrollment:** 169 men and women. **Faculty:** 107 total (36 full time). **Location:** Urban campus in very large city. **Calendar:** Semester, limited summer session. **Microcomputers:** 36 located in libraries, computer centers. **Special facilities:** Electronic music studios, audio recording facilities, 16,000 records/tapes/CDs.

DEGREES OFFERED. B, M, D. 46 bachelor's degrees awarded in 1992. 100% in visual and performing arts. Graduate degrees offered in 2 major fields of study.

UNDERGRADUATE MAJORS. Audio recording, eurhythmics, music performance, music theory and composition.

ACADEMIC PROGRAMS. Double major, independent study, cross-registration. **Remedial services:** Reduced course load, remedial instruction, tutoring. **Placement/credit:** AP, institutional tests.

ACADEMIC REQUIREMENTS. Freshmen must earn minimum GPA of 2.0 to continue in good standing. 87% of freshmen return for sophomore year. Students must declare major on application. **Graduation requirements:** 124 hours for bachelor's. Most students required to take courses in computer science, humanities.

FRESHMAN ADMISSIONS. Selection criteria: Audition most important. Interviews, test scores, high school record, and letters of recommendation also reviewed. **High school preparation:** 16 units recommended. Recommended units include English 4, foreign language 3, mathematics 3, social science 3 and science 3. **Test requirements:** SAT or ACT; score report by March 1. Institutional examinations including sight singing, keyboard harmony, general musicianship required. **Additional information:** Incoming students must have scholastic and musical skills prerequisite to entering highly intensive, professionally oriented program.

1992 FRESHMAN CLASS PROFILE. 47 men and women enrolled. 88% had high school GPA of 3.0 or higher, 12% between 2.0 and 2.99. **Characteristics:** 100% live in college housing, 14% have minority backgrounds, 17% are foreign students. Average age is 18.

FALL-TERM APPLICATIONS. $50 fee. Closing date January 15; applicants notified on or about April 1; must reply by May 1. Audition required. Essay required. Interview recommended. CRDA. Early admission available.

STUDENT LIFE. Housing: Dormitories (coed). **Activities:** Student government, choral groups, music ensembles, opera, symphony orchestra, Wind ensemble and jazz ensemble participation available through Case Western Reserve University. **Additional information:** Most student activities, athletics, and student services available through Case Western Reserve University.

STUDENT SERVICES. Career counseling, employment service for undergraduates, freshman orientation, health services, personal counseling, placement service for graduates, veterans counselor, services/facilities for handicapped.

ANNUAL EXPENSES. Tuition and fees (projected): $13,965. **Room and board:** $5,200. **Books and supplies:** $650. **Other expenses:** $650.

FINANCIAL AID. 90% of freshmen, 90% of continuing students receive some form of aid. 99% of grants, 95% of loans, 69% of jobs based on need. 31 enrolled freshmen were judged to have need, all were offered aid. Academic, music/drama scholarships available. **Aid applications:** No closing date; priority given to applications received by March 1; applicants notified on a rolling basis beginning on or about April 1; must reply by May 1 or within 2 weeks if notified thereafter.

ADDRESS/TELEPHONE. William Fay, Director of Admissions, Cleveland Institute of Music, 11021 East Boulevard, Cleveland, OH 44106. (216) 795-3107.

Cleveland State University
Cleveland, Ohio CB code: 1221

4-year public university, coed. Founded in 1964. **Accreditation:** Regional. **Undergraduate enrollment:** 4,134 men, 4,195 women full time; 2,232 men, 2,155 women part time. **Graduate enrollment:** 834 men, 619 women full time; 1,718 men, 2,312 women part time. **Faculty:** 688 total (570 full time), 534 with doctorates or other terminal degrees. **Location:** Urban campus in very large city. **Calendar:** Quarter, extensive summer session. Saturday and extensive evening/early morning classes. **Microcomputers:** Located in dormitories, computer centers.

DEGREES OFFERED. BA, BS, MA, MS, MBA, MEd, PhD, EdD, JD. 1,640 bachelor's degrees awarded in 1992. 25% in business and management, 10% communications, 6% teacher education, 8% engineering, 6% parks/recreation, protective services, public affairs, 7% psychology, 10% social sciences. Graduate degrees offered in 52 major fields of study.

UNDERGRADUATE MAJORS. Accounting, anthropology, art history, biology, biotechnology, business administration and management, business economics, business statistics, chemical engineering, chemistry, civil engineering, communications, computer and information sciences, dramatic arts, early childhood education, economics, education of the mentally handicapped, education of the multiple handicapped, electrical technology, electrical/electronics/communications engineering, electronic technology, elementary education, English, environmental science, finance, French, geology, German, history, industrial engineering, information sciences and systems, international relations, labor/industrial relations, liberal/general studies, linguistics, management information systems, manufacturing technology, marketing management, mathematics, mechanical engineering, medieval studies, music, music therapy, nursing, occupational therapy, philosophy, physical education, physical therapy, physics, political science and government, psychology, religion, secondary education, social sciences, social work, sociology, Spanish, speech pathology/audiology, sports management, studio art, urban studies.

ACADEMIC PROGRAMS. Accelerated program, cooperative education, double major, dual enrollment of high school students, education specialist degree, independent study, internships, student-designed major, study abroad, teacher preparation, visiting/exchange student program, cross-registration. **Remedial services:** Learning center, reduced course load, remedial instruction, special counselor, tutoring. **ROTC:** Army. **Placement/credit:** AP, CLEP General and Subject, institutional tests.

ACADEMIC REQUIREMENTS. Freshmen must earn minimum GPA of 1.7 to continue in good standing. 53% of freshmen return for sophomore year. Students must declare major by end of second year. **Graduation requirements:** 192 hours for bachelor's (48 in major). Most students required to take courses in English, humanities, mathematics, biological/physical sciences, social sciences. **Additional information:** Extensive evening and Saturday classes for working student population.

FRESHMAN ADMISSIONS. Selection criteria: Open admissions. Out-of-state applicants must meet selective admission requirements. **High school preparation:** 16 units recommended. Recommended units include English 4, foreign language 2, mathematics 3, social science 3 and science 3. **Test requirements:** SAT or ACT for placement and counseling only; score report by September 15.

1992 FRESHMAN CLASS PROFILE. 618 men, 590 women enrolled. **Academic background:** Mid 50% of enrolled freshmen had SAT-V between 350-470, SAT-M between 370-530; ACT composite between 13-23. 28% submitted SAT scores, 72% submitted ACT scores. **Characteristics:** 99% from in state, 99% commute, 23% have minority backgrounds, 1% join fraternities/sororities. Average age is 22.

FALL-TERM APPLICATIONS. $25 fee. No closing date; applicants notified on a rolling basis beginning on or about November 1. Audition required for music applicants. Deferred admission available. Applicants for fall admission urged to complete admission process by May 1.

STUDENT LIFE. Housing: Dormitories (coed); fraternity, handicapped housing available. Housing floors for law and graduate students, and quiet floors. Rooms for athletes. **Activities:** Student government, magazine, radio, student newspaper, choral groups, dance, drama, jazz band, music ensembles, opera, pep band, symphony orchestra, fraternities, sororities, Newman Center, Los Latinos Unidos, Hillel, University Christian Movement, Organization for Afro-American Unity, Lutheran Campus Ministry, International Students Organization, NAACP, Environmental Action Group, College Democrats and Republicans. **Additional information:** 150 student organizations.

ATHLETICS. NCAA. **Intercollegiate:** Baseball M, basketball, cross-country, diving, fencing, golf M, soccer M, softball W, swimming, tennis, track and field, volleyball W, wrestling M. **Intramural:** Badminton, basketball, bowling, cross-country, fencing, field hockey, golf, handball, racquetball, soccer, softball, swimming, table tennis, tennis, track and field, volleyball, water polo, wrestling M.

STUDENT SERVICES. Aptitude testing, career counseling, employment service for undergraduates, freshman orientation, health services, personal counseling, placement service for graduates, special adviser for adult students, veterans counselor, services/facilities for handicapped.

ANNUAL EXPENSES. Tuition and fees (projected): $3,090, $3,090 additional for out-of-state students. **Room and board:** $3,975. **Books and supplies:** $555. **Other expenses:** $865.

FINANCIAL AID. 33% of freshmen, 30% of continuing students receive some form of aid. 90% of grants, 92% of loans, 24% of jobs based on need. 525 enrolled freshmen were judged to have need, 470 were offered aid. Academic, music/drama, art, athletic, leadership, minority scholarships available. **Aid applications:** No closing date; priority given to applications received by April 15; applicants notified on a rolling basis beginning on or about May 15; must reply within 2 weeks.

ADDRESS/TELEPHONE. Ruth Ann Moyer, Director of Admissions, Cleveland State University, 1983 East 24 Street, 108 Fenn Tower, Cleveland, OH 44115-2403. (216) 687-3755. Fax: (216) 687-9366.

College of Mount St. Joseph
Cincinnati, Ohio — CB code: 1129

Admissions: 73% of applicants accepted
Based on:
••• School record, test scores
•• Activities, essay, interview, recommendations
• Special talents
Completion: 86% of freshmen end year in good standing
64% graduate, 10% of these enter graduate study

4-year private liberal arts college, coed, affiliated with Roman Catholic Church. Founded in 1920. **Accreditation:** Regional. **Undergraduate enrollment:** 352 men, 761 women full time; 256 men, 1,051 women part time. **Graduate enrollment:** 13 men, 23 women full time; 25 men, 113 women part time. **Faculty:** 218 total (98 full time), 59 with doctorates or other terminal degrees. **Location:** Suburban campus in large city; 7 miles from downtown. **Calendar:** Semester, limited summer session. **Microcomputers:** 60 located in libraries, computer centers. **Special facilities:** Music therapy clinic, art gallery. **Additional facts:** Project Excel program for learning disabled students.

DEGREES OFFERED. AA, AS, BA, BS, MA. 53 associate degrees awarded in 1992. 26% in business and management, 6% communications, 12% health sciences, 13% allied health, 6% law, 24% multi/interdisciplinary studies. 341 bachelor's degrees awarded. 22% in business and management, 6% communications, 18% teacher education, 19% health sciences, 5% life sciences, 11% multi/interdisciplinary studies, 5% parks/recreation, protective services, public affairs, 7% visual and performing arts. Graduate degrees offered in 2 major fields of study.

UNDERGRADUATE MAJORS. Associate: Accounting, business and management, communications, computer and information sciences, early childhood education, gerontology, graphic design, human services, interior design, legal assistant/paralegal, liberal/general studies, respiratory therapy. **Bachelor's:** Accounting, art education, biological and physical sciences, biology, business and management, chemistry, communications, computer and information sciences, elementary education, English, fine arts, food science and nutrition, gerontology, graphic design, health education, history, human services, humanities, interior design, legal assistant/paralegal, liberal/general studies, management communication, management of nursing, mathematics, mathematics computer science, mathematics/chemistry, medical laboratory technologies, music, nursing, physical education, religion, religious education, religious pastoral ministry, secondary education, social psychology, social work, special education, women's studies.

ACADEMIC PROGRAMS. 2-year transfer program, cooperative education, double major, dual enrollment of high school students, independent study, internships, student-designed major, study abroad, weekend college. **Remedial services:** Learning center, preadmission summer program, reduced course load, remedial instruction, special counselor, tutoring. **ROTC:** Air Force, Army. **Placement/credit:** AP, CLEP Subject, institutional tests; 32 credit hours maximum for associate degree; 64 credit hours maximum for bachelor's degree.

ACADEMIC REQUIREMENTS. Freshmen must earn minimum GPA of 2.0 to continue in good standing. 77% of freshmen return for sophomore year. Students must declare major by end of second year. **Graduation requirements:** 64 hours for associate, 128 hours for bachelor's. Most students required to take courses in arts/fine arts, computer science, English, history, mathematics, philosophy/religion, biological/physical sciences, social sciences. **Additional information:** Evening and weekend colleges offer 10 majors for adults. Project EXCEL provides assistance to students with lerning disabilities within the context of regular college curricula.

FRESHMAN ADMISSIONS. Selection criteria: School achievement record most important, followed by test scores. Recommendations also considered. **High school preparation:** 13 units required. Required and recommended units include English 4, mathematics 2, social science 2 and science 2. Foreign language 2 recommended. 1 unit fine arts also recommended. **Test requirements:** SAT or ACT; score report by August 28. **Additional information:** Applicants 23 years or older admitted to the college through the Office of Continuing Education.

1992 FRESHMAN CLASS PROFILE. 269 men applied, 169 accepted, 95 enrolled; 346 women applied, 283 accepted, 188 enrolled. 30% had high school GPA of 3.0 or higher, 70% between 2.0 and 2.99. 14% were in top tenth and 36% were in top quarter of graduating class. **Academic background:** Mid 50% of enrolled freshmen had SAT-V between 380-500, SAT-M between 400-550; ACT composite between 19-25. 55% submitted SAT scores, 85% submitted ACT scores. **Characteristics:** 92% from in state, 60% commute, 13% have minority backgrounds, 4% are foreign students. Average age is 18.

FALL-TERM APPLICATIONS. May be waived for applicants with need. Application fee $25, Project EXCEL, $60. Closing date August 15; applicants notified on a rolling basis; must reply by May 1 or within 4 weeks if notified thereafter. Audition required for music applicants. Interview recommended. Portfolio recommended for art applicants. Essay recommended. CRDA. Deferred and early admission available.

STUDENT LIFE. Housing: Dormitories (coed). All full-time matriculated, single students under 21 not residing with parent or legal guardian required to live on campus. **Activities:** Student government, radio, student newspaper, choral groups, concert band, jazz band, music ensembles, pep band, Student Council for Exceptional Children, Association of Black Students.

ATHLETICS. NAIA. **Intercollegiate:** Basketball W, football M, softball W, volleyball W. **Intramural:** Badminton, basketball, soccer, softball, swimming, table tennis, tennis, volleyball.

STUDENT SERVICES. Aptitude testing, career counseling, employment service for undergraduates, freshman orientation, health services, on-campus day care, personal counseling, placement service for graduates, special adviser for adult students, services/facilities for handicapped.

ANNUAL EXPENSES. Tuition and fees (1992-93): $8,740. **Room and board:** $4,080. **Books and supplies:** $400. **Other expenses:** $600.

FINANCIAL AID. 94% of freshmen, 85% of continuing students receive some form of aid. 60% of grants, 87% of loans, 86% of jobs based on need. 196 enrolled freshmen were judged to have need, all were offered aid. Academic, art, athletic, leadership scholarships available. **Aid applications:** No closing date; priority given to applications received by April 15; applicants notified on a rolling basis beginning on or about February 15.

ADDRESS/TELEPHONE. Edward Eckel, Director of Admission, College of Mount St. Joseph, 5701 Delhi Road, Cincinnati, OH 45233-1672. (513) 244-4531. (800) 654-9314. Fax: (513) 244-4222.

College of Wooster
Wooster, Ohio — CB code: 1134

Admissions: 89% of applicants accepted
Based on:
••• School record
•• Essay, recommendations, special talents, test scores
• Activities, interview
Completion: 90% of freshmen end year in good standing
93% graduate, 46% of these enter graduate study

4-year private liberal arts college, coed, affiliated with Presbyterian Church (USA). Founded in 1866. **Accreditation:** Regional. **Undergraduate enrollment:** 828 men, 866 women full time. **Faculty:** 178 total (154 full time), 152 with doctorates or other terminal degrees. **Location:** Rural campus in large town; 55 miles from Cleveland; 30 miles from Akron. **Calendar:** Semester, limited summer session. **Microcomputers:** 100 located in dormitories, libraries, classrooms, computer centers. **Special facilities:** Art gallery, museum. **Additional facts:** Independent institution founded by Presbyterians.

DEGREES OFFERED. BA. 424 bachelor's degrees awarded in 1992. 7% in business and management, 15% letters/literature, 8% physical sciences, 8% psychology, 34% social sciences, 10% visual and performing arts.

UNDERGRADUATE MAJORS. African studies, Afro-American (black) studies, American literature, archeology, art history, biology, business economics, chemistry, classics, communications, comparative literature, computer and information sciences, creative writing, dance, dramatic arts, East Asian studies, economics, elementary education, English, English literature, foreign languages (multiple emphasis), French, geology, German, Greek (classical), history, international relations, Italian, junior high education, Latin, Latin American studies, mathematics, Middle Eastern studies, music, music education, music history and appreciation, music performance, music therapy, philosophy, physics, political science and government, psychology, religion, Russian and Slavic studies, secondary education, social work, sociology, South Asian studies, Spanish, speech pathology/audiology, studio art, urban studies, Western European studies, women's studies.

ACADEMIC PROGRAMS. Double major, dual enrollment of high school students, independent study, internships, student-designed major, study abroad, teacher preparation, visiting/exchange student program, United Nations semester, Washington semester; liberal arts/career combination in engineering, forestry. **Remedial services:** Learning center, tutoring. **Placement/credit:** AP, institutional tests.

ACADEMIC REQUIREMENTS. Freshmen must earn minimum GPA of 2.0 to continue in good standing. 84% of freshmen return for sophomore year. Students must declare major by end of second year. **Graduation requirements:** Most students required to take courses in foreign languages, humanities, philosophy/religion, biological/physical sciences, social sciences. **Postgraduate studies:** 9% enter law school, 8% enter medical school, 3% enter MBA programs, 26% enter other graduate study. **Additional information:** Centers in 6 cities for urban internships in social sciences.

FRESHMAN ADMISSIONS. Selection criteria: Course pattern and academic performance most important. Recommendations, extracurricular activities, class rank, test scores, interview considered. **High school preparation:** 16 units recommended. Recommended units include English 4, foreign language 2, mathematics 3, social science 3 and science 3. Mathematics recommendation includes 2 algebra. **Test requirements:** SAT or ACT (SAT preferred); score report by March 1.

1992 FRESHMAN CLASS PROFILE. 1,023 men applied, 888 accepted, 219 enrolled; 989 women applied, 902 accepted, 240 enrolled. 56% had high school GPA of 3.0 or higher, 42% between 2.0 and 2.99. **Academic background:** Mid 50% of enrolled freshmen had SAT-V between 490-560, SAT-M between 520-600; ACT composite between 21-27. 91% submitted SAT scores, 51% submitted ACT scores. **Characteristics:** 33% from in state, 98% live in college housing, 10% have minority backgrounds, 6% are foreign students, 21% join fraternities/sororities. Average age is 18.

FALL-TERM APPLICATIONS. $25 fee, may be waived for applicants with need. Closing date February 15; applicants notified on or about April 1; must reply by May 1. Essay required. Interview recommended. Audition recommended for music applicants. Portfolio recommended for art applicants. CRDA. Deferred and early admission available. EDP-F.

STUDENT LIFE. Housing: Dormitories (men, women, coed). Program dormitories, special interest housing available. **Activities:** Student government, magazine, radio, student newspaper, television, yearbook, choral groups, concert band, dance, drama, jazz band, marching band, music ensembles, musical theater, opera, pep band, symphony orchestra, fraternities, sororities, variety of religious, ethnic, and social service organizations.

ATHLETICS. NCAA. **Intercollegiate:** Baseball M, basketball, cross-country, diving, field hockey W, football M, golf M, lacrosse, soccer, swimming, tennis, track and field, volleyball W. **Intramural:** Badminton, basketball, bowling, football M, golf, ice hockey M, racquetball, rugby, soccer, softball, swimming, tennis, volleyball, water polo M.

STUDENT SERVICES. Aptitude testing, career counseling, employment service for undergraduates, freshman orientation, health services, personal counseling, placement service for graduates, services/facilities for handicapped.

ANNUAL EXPENSES. Tuition and fees: Comprehensive fee: $19,865. **Books and supplies:** $450. **Other expenses:** $450.

FINANCIAL AID. 68% of freshmen, 70% of continuing students receive some form of aid. 89% of grants, all loans, all jobs based on need. 255 enrolled freshmen were judged to have need, all were offered aid. Academic, music/drama, minority scholarships available. **Aid applications:** No closing date; priority given to applications received by February 15; applicants notified on a rolling basis beginning on or about April 1; must reply by May 1 or within 2 weeks if notified thereafter.

ADDRESS/TELEPHONE. Hayden Schilling, Dean of Admissions, College of Wooster, Galpin Hall, Wooster, OH 44691-2363. (216) 263-2322. (800) 877-9905. Fax: (216) 263-2427.

Columbus College of Art and Design
Columbus, Ohio CB code: 1085

Admissions:	67% of applicants accepted
Based on:	••• Special talents
	•• Recommendations, school record
	• Activities, interview, test scores
Completion:	92% of freshmen end year in good standing
	45% graduate, 12% of these enter graduate study

4-year private art college, coed. Founded in 1879. **Accreditation:** Regional. **Undergraduate enrollment:** 1,208 men and women full time; 459 men and women part time. **Faculty:** 108 total (61 full time), 9 with doctorates or other terminal degrees. **Location:** Urban campus in very large city; in downtown area. **Calendar:** Semester, limited summer session. Extensive evening/early morning classes. **Special facilities:** Student exhibition hall, gallery, recreation center. **Additional facts:** Campus adjacent to Columbus Museum of Art.

DEGREES OFFERED. BFA. 144 bachelor's degrees awarded in 1992. 100% in visual and performing arts.

UNDERGRADUATE MAJORS. Advertising, fine arts, graphic design, illustration design, industrial design, interior design, photography.

ACADEMIC PROGRAMS. Double major, internships, weekend college, cross-registration. **Remedial services:** Reduced course load, remedial instruction, special counselor, tutoring.

ACADEMIC REQUIREMENTS. Freshmen must earn minimum GPA of 2.0 to continue in good standing. 88% of freshmen return for sophomore year. Students must declare major by end of first year. **Graduation requirements:** 145 hours for bachelor's (83 in major). Most students required to take courses in arts/fine arts, computer science, English, history, humanities, mathematics, philosophy/religion, biological/physical sciences, social sciences.

FRESHMAN ADMISSIONS. Selection criteria: Portfolio and minimum high school GPA of 2.0.

1992 FRESHMAN CLASS PROFILE. 653 men and women applied, 440 accepted; 334 enrolled. **Characteristics:** 75% from in state, 80% live in college housing, 10% have minority backgrounds, 2% are foreign students. Average age is 18.

FALL-TERM APPLICATIONS. $25 fee, may be waived for applicants with need. No closing date; priority given to applications received by June 15; applicants notified on a rolling basis; must reply within 6 weeks. Portfolio required. Interview recommended. Deferred admission available.

STUDENT LIFE. Housing: Dormitories (coed); apartment housing available. **Activities:** Student government, magazine, student newspaper, yearly art and literary publication, drama, Bible study, Black Student Alliance, nontraditional student resource group.

ATHLETICS. Intramural: Basketball M, soccer M, volleyball.

STUDENT SERVICES. Career counseling, employment service for undergraduates, freshman orientation, personal counseling, placement service for graduates, special adviser for adult students, veterans counselor, services/facilities for handicapped.

ANNUAL EXPENSES. Tuition and fees (1992-93): $8,600. **Room and board:** $4,800. **Books and supplies:** $1,100. **Other expenses:** $750.

FINANCIAL AID. 85% of freshmen, 85% of continuing students receive some form of aid. 56% of grants, 77% of loans, 54% of jobs based on need. 245 enrolled freshmen were judged to have need, all were offered aid. Art, state/district residency scholarships available. **Aid applications:** No closing date; priority given to applications received by May 3; applicants notified on a rolling basis beginning on or about June 15; must reply within 2 weeks. **Additional information:** Opportunities for selling art work, design contests offered, part- and full-time jobs available.

ADDRESS/TELEPHONE. Thomas E. Green, Director of Admissions, Columbus College of Art and Design, 107 North Ninth Street, Columbus, OH 43215-3875. (614) 224-9101. Fax: (614) 222-4040.

Columbus State Community College
Columbus, Ohio CB code: 1148

2-year public community college, coed. Founded in 1967. **Accreditation:** Regional. **Undergraduate enrollment:** 2,913 men, 3,227 women full time; 4,058 men, 6,312 women part time. **Faculty:** 842 total (184 full time), 112 with doctorates or other terminal degrees. **Location:** Urban campus in very large city. **Calendar:** Quarter, limited summer session. Saturday and extensive evening/early morning classes. **Microcomputers:** 380 located in libraries, classrooms, computer centers, campus-wide network. **Special facilities:** College-owned building for aviation maintenance program at Bolton Field Airport. **Additional facts:** Courses offered at 5 off-campus sites (Dublin, Gahanna, Westerville, London, Bolton Field).

DEGREES OFFERED. AA, AS, AAS. 1,085 associate degrees awarded in 1992. 30% in business and management, 14% engineering technologies, 19% health sciences, 6% allied health, 8% multi/interdisciplinary studies, 10% parks/recreation, protective services, public affairs.

UNDERGRADUATE MAJORS. Accounting, aeronautical technology, air conditioning/heating/refrigeration mechanics, air conditioning/heating/refrigeration technology, aircraft mechanics, allied health, animal sciences, architectural technologies, architecture, automotive mechanics, automotive technology, business administration and management, chef apprentice, child development/care/guidance, civil technology, clinical laboratory science, computer programming, computer servicing technology, computer technology, construction, construction management, contract management and procurement/purchasing, dental laboratory technology, dietetic aide/assistant, drafting, drafting and design technology, early childhood education, EDP auditing, electrical and electronics equipment repair, electromechanical technology, electronic technology, emergency medical technologies, engineering and engineering-related technologies, finance, financial management, food management, food production/management/services, food science and nutrition, gerontology, graphic and printing production, graphic arts technology, hotel/motel and restaurant management, interpreter for the deaf, landscape architecture, law enforcement and corrections technologies, legal assistant/paralegal, legal secretary, liberal/general studies, machine tool operation/machine shop, manufacturing technology, marketing and distribution, mechanical design technology, medical laboratory technologies, medical records administration, medical records technology, medical secretary, mental health/human services, microcomputer software, multicompetency health, nursing, occupational safety and health technology, personnel management, protective services, quality control technology, radiograph medical technology, real estate, rehabilitation counseling/services, respiratory therapy, respiratory therapy technology, retailing, secretarial and related programs, small business management and ownership, sports management, surgical technology, tourism, transportation and travel marketing, veterinarian's assistant.

ACADEMIC PROGRAMS. 2-year transfer program, cooperative education, double major, dual enrollment of high school students, independent study, internships, student-designed major, telecourses, cross-registration. **Remedial services:** Learning center, preadmission summer program, reduced course load, remedial instruction, special counselor, tutoring. **ROTC:** Army. **Placement/credit:** AP, institutional tests.

ACADEMIC REQUIREMENTS. Freshmen must earn minimum GPA of 2.0 to continue in good standing. 46% of freshmen return for sophomore year. **Graduation requirements:** 100 hours for associate (47 in major). Most students required to take courses in computer science, English, humanities, mathematics, biological/physical sciences, social sciences.

FRESHMAN ADMISSIONS. Selection criteria: Open admissions. Some technology programs have special admission requirements. Algebra required for some engineering, health, and computer science technology programs. Chemistry and biology required for some health programs.

1992 FRESHMAN CLASS PROFILE. 2,172 men, 2,791 women enrolled. 15% had high school GPA of 3.0 or higher, 56% between 2.0 and 2.99. 19% were in top quarter of graduating class. **Academic background:** Mid 50% of enrolled freshmen had ACT composite between 12-19. 24% submitted ACT scores. **Characteristics:** 97% from in state, 100% commute, 20% have minority backgrounds, 1% are foreign students. Average age is 26.

FALL-TERM APPLICATIONS. $10 fee. No closing date; applicants notified on a rolling basis. Interview required for most health and human service technologies, chef apprenticeship applicants. Deferred and early admission available. Most health programs admit students on a space-available basis; students are advised to apply early for these programs.

STUDENT LIFE. Housing: Students may live in dormitories of other local colleges if space available. **Activities:** Student government, student newspaper, fraternities, Black Student Association, Bible Fellowship, International Student Group.

ATHLETICS. NJCAA. **Intercollegiate:** Baseball M, basketball M, cross-country, golf, soccer M, softball W, volleyball W. **Intramural:** Badminton, basketball, bowling, golf, horseback riding W, soccer M, softball, table tennis, volleyball. **Clubs:** Equestrian W, cheerleading MW.

STUDENT SERVICES. Career counseling, employment service for undergraduates, freshman orientation, health services, personal counseling, placement service for graduates, special adviser for adult students, veterans counselor, services/facilities for handicapped.

ANNUAL EXPENSES. Tuition and fees (1992-93): $1,764, $2,052 additional for out-of-state students. **Books and supplies:** $600. **Other expenses:** $731.

FINANCIAL AID. 35% of freshmen, 38% of continuing students receive some form of aid. 99% of grants, 80% of loans, all jobs based on need. Academic, state/district residency, minority scholarships available. **Aid applications:** Closing date March 31; applicants notified on or about August 15; must reply within 3 weeks.

ADDRESS/TELEPHONE. Mary Jo Deerwester, Director of Admissions, Columbus State Community College, 550 East Spring Street, Columbus, OH 43216-1609. (614) 227-2453. (800) 621-6407. Fax: (614) 461-5117.

Cuyahoga Community College: Eastern Campus
Highland Hills, Ohio CB code: 1978

2-year public branch campus, community college, coed. Founded in 1971. **Accreditation:** Regional. **Undergraduate enrollment:** 5,858 men and women. **Faculty:** 234 total (59 full time), 105 with doctorates or other terminal degrees. **Location:** Suburban campus in small town; 3 miles from Cleveland. **Calendar:** Quarter, limited summer session. **Microcomputers:** 200 located in libraries, classrooms, computer centers. **Additional facts:** Comprehensive arts, music and theater programs. Off-campus offerings at local high schools and businesses. Two summer programs, 8 weeks and 5 1/2 weeks.

DEGREES OFFERED. AA, AS, AAS. 480 associate degrees awarded in 1992.

UNDERGRADUATE MAJORS. Accounting, business and management, business and office, business computer/console/peripheral equipment operation, business data processing and related programs, business data programming, child development/care/guidance, computer and information sciences, computer graphics, early childhood education, educational media technology, engineering and engineering-related technologies, finance, fine arts, graphic arts technology, graphic design, industrial technology, law enforcement and corrections technologies, liberal/general studies, marketing and distribution, nursing, office supervision and management, pharmacy technician, podiatric assistant, real estate, secretarial and related programs, transportation management, word processing.

ACADEMIC PROGRAMS. 2-year transfer program, accelerated program, cooperative education, dual enrollment of high school students, external degree, independent study, internships, teacher preparation, telecourses, weekend college, cross-registration. **Remedial services:** Learning center, remedial instruction, tutoring, comprehensive interdepartmental developmental education program. **Placement/credit:** AP, CLEP General, institutional tests; 45 credit hours maximum for associate degree.

ACADEMIC REQUIREMENTS. Freshmen must earn minimum GPA of 1.5 to continue in good standing. 60% of freshmen return for sophomore year. **Graduation requirements:** 93 hours for associate. Most students required to take courses in English, humanities, mathematics, biological/physical sciences.

FRESHMAN ADMISSIONS. Selection criteria: Open admissions. For health technologies, test scores, school GPA, subjects taken, and related work experience considered. **Test requirements:** SAT or ACT required for admission to some health technology programs.

1992 FRESHMAN CLASS PROFILE. 3,913 men and women enrolled. **Characteristics:** 100% commute. Average age is 28.

FALL-TERM APPLICATIONS. $10 fee. No closing date; applicants notified on a rolling basis beginning on or about January 1.

STUDENT LIFE. Activities: Student government, student newspaper, drama, music ensembles, musical theater, fraternities, sororities, political, journalism, Futurist, Bible, and ski clubs, art club, Phi Theta Kappa.

ATHLETICS. NJCAA. **Intercollegiate:** Basketball W, volleyball W. **Intramural:** Basketball, softball, volleyball.

STUDENT SERVICES. Aptitude testing, career counseling, employment service for undergraduates, freshman orientation, health services, on-campus day care, personal counseling, placement service for graduates, special adviser for adult students, veterans counselor, services/facilities for handicapped.

ANNUAL EXPENSES. Tuition and fees (1992-93): $1,440, $450 additional for out-of-district students, $2,340 additional for out-of-state students. **Books and supplies:** $675. **Other expenses:** $1,053.

FINANCIAL AID. 26% of freshmen, 40% of continuing students receive some form of aid. Grants, loans, jobs available. Academic, leadership scholarships available. **Aid applications:** No closing date; priority given to applications received by May 31; applicants notified on a rolling basis beginning on or about July 15.

ADDRESS/TELEPHONE. David Puffer, Director of Admissions, Cuyahoga Community College: Eastern Campus, 4250 Richmond Road, Highland Hills, OH 44122. (216) 464-3535.

Cuyahoga Community College: Metropolitan Campus ⇆
Cleveland, Ohio CB code: 1159

2-year public community college, coed. Founded in 1963. **Accreditation:** Regional. **Undergraduate enrollment:** 6,864 men and women. **Faculty:** 388 total (147 full time). **Location:** Urban campus in very large city; in downtown area. **Calendar:** Quarter, limited summer session. **Microcomputers:** Located in classrooms, computer centers. **Special facilities:** Unified technology center to provide business training.

DEGREES OFFERED. AA, AS, AAS. 400 associate degrees awarded in 1992.

UNDERGRADUATE MAJORS. Accounting, airline piloting and navigation, architecture, business administration and management, business and office, business computer/console/peripheral equipment operation, business data processing and related programs, civil engineering, clinical laboratory science, computer and information sciences, court reporting, data processing, dental assistant, dental hygiene, dental laboratory technology, dietetic aide/assistant, drafting, early childhood education, electrical technology, electrical/electronics/communications engineering, electronic technology, emergency medical technologies, engineering, engineering and engineering-related technologies, finance, fire control and safety technology, food management, food production/management/services, graphic arts technology, hospitality and recreation marketing, hotel/motel and restaurant management, industrial technology, instrumentation technology, interior design, journalism, law enforcement and corrections technologies, legal assistant/paralegal, liberal/general studies, library assistant, marketing and distribution, marketing management, mechanical design technology, mechanical engineering, medical assistant, medical laboratory technologies, medical records administration, medical records technology, mental health/human services, nursing, occupational therapy assistant, ophthalmic services, physical therapy assistant, physician's assistant, plant sciences, radio/television broadcasting, radio/television technology, radiograph medical technology, real estate, respiratory therapy, respiratory therapy technology, secretarial and related programs, small business management and ownership, trade and industrial supervision and management, transportation management.

ACADEMIC PROGRAMS. 2-year transfer program, accelerated program, computer delivered (on-line) credit-bearing course offerings, cooperative education, dual enrollment of high school students, honors program, independent study, internships, student-designed major, telecourses, visiting/exchange student program, cross-registration. **Remedial services:** Reduced course load, remedial instruction, special counselor, tutoring, comprehensive interdepartmental developmental education program. **ROTC:** Air Force. **Placement/credit:** AP, CLEP General, institutional tests; 45 credit hours maximum for associate degree.

ACADEMIC REQUIREMENTS. Freshmen must earn minimum GPA of 1.0 to continue in good standing. Students must declare major on application. **Graduation requirements:** 93 hours for associate (45 in major). Most students required to take courses in English, humanities, mathematics, social sciences.

FRESHMAN ADMISSIONS. Selection criteria: Open admissions. Selective admission for some health technology programs. **Test requirements:** SAT or ACT required for admission to some health technology programs. Nelson Denny Test.

1992 FRESHMAN CLASS PROFILE. 1,040 men and women enrolled. **Characteristics:** 99% from in state, 100% commute, 60% have minority backgrounds, 4% are foreign students.

FALL-TERM APPLICATIONS. $10 fee. No closing date.

STUDENT LIFE. Activities: Student government, magazine, student newspaper, television, choral groups, dance, drama, jazz band, musical theater, symphony orchestra, Hillel, Afro-American Society, Veterans Service Fraternity, Young Socialist Alliance, Student Coalition Against Racism, National Education Association, Hispanic Club.

ATHLETICS. Intercollegiate: Basketball M, soccer M, track and field, wrestling M. **Intramural:** Baseball, basketball, bowling, gymnastics, handball, racquetball, softball, tennis, volleyball.

STUDENT SERVICES. Aptitude testing, career counseling, employment service for undergraduates, freshman orientation, health services, on-campus day care, personal counseling, placement service for graduates, veterans counselor, services/facilities for handicapped.

ANNUAL EXPENSES. Tuition and fees (1992-93): $1,440, $450 additional for out-of-district students, $2,340 additional for out-of-state students. **Books and supplies:** $675. **Other expenses:** $1,053.

FINANCIAL AID. 70% of continuing students receive some form of aid. Grants, loans, jobs available. **Aid applications:** No closing date; applicants notified on a rolling basis beginning on or about August 1.

ADDRESS/TELEPHONE. Sammie Tyree Cox, Director of Admissions, Cuyahoga Community College: Metropolitan Campus, 2900 Community College Avenue, Cleveland, OH 44115-2878. (216) 241-5365.

Cuyahoga Community College: Western Campus
Parma, Ohio CB code: 1985

2-year public community college, coed. Founded in 1966. **Accreditation:** Regional. **Undergraduate enrollment:** 1,546 men, 2,134 women full time; 3,265 men, 6,016 women part time. **Faculty:** 626 total (159 full time), 63 with doctorates or other terminal degrees. **Location:** Suburban campus in small city; 15 miles from Cleveland. **Calendar:** Quarter, limited summer session. Saturday and extensive evening/early morning classes. **Microcomputers:** 195 located in libraries, computer centers.

DEGREES OFFERED. AA, AS, AAS. 660 associate degrees awarded in 1992.

UNDERGRADUATE MAJORS. Accounting, automotive technology, business and office, cardiovascular technology, computer and information sciences, court reporting, early childhood education, finance, graphic and printing production, labor/industrial relations, law enforcement and corrections technologies, legal assistant/paralegal, marketing and distribution, microcomputer software, nursing, office supervision and management, physician's assistant, radiograph medical technology, real estate, respiratory therapy technology, secretarial and related programs, small business management and ownership, surgical technology, technical studies, ultrasound technology, veterinarian's assistant, word processing.

ACADEMIC PROGRAMS. 2-year transfer program, cooperative education, dual enrollment of high school students, honors program, independent study, telecourses, weekend college, cross-registration, Automotive Technology with GM and Toyota; Dyke College, Kent State, Cleveland State Dual Admission Program. **Remedial services:** Learning center, remedial instruction, special counselor, tutoring, comprehensive interdepartmental developmental education program. **Placement/credit:** AP, CLEP General and Subject, institutional tests; 45 credit hours maximum for associate degree.

ACADEMIC REQUIREMENTS. Freshmen must earn minimum GPA of 1.5 to continue in good standing. Students must declare major on application. **Graduation requirements:** 93 hours for associate. Most students required to take courses in English, humanities, mathematics, social sciences.

FRESHMAN ADMISSIONS. Selection criteria: Selective admissions to health technologies based on test scores, high school GPA, subjects taken, and related work experience.

1992 FRESHMAN CLASS PROFILE. 1,091 men, 1,449 women enrolled. **Characteristics:** 99% from in state, 100% commute, 7% have minority backgrounds, 1% are foreign students.

FALL-TERM APPLICATIONS. $10 fee. No closing date; applicants notified on a rolling basis. Deferred and early admission available.

STUDENT LIFE. Activities: Student government, student newspaper, choral groups, concert band, dance, drama, jazz band, music ensembles, musical theater, fraternities, sororities, Christian Fellowship, International Students, Newman Campus Ministry, Circle-K, Los Latinos Unidos, Lebanese Students Organization.

ATHLETICS. NJCAA. **Intercollegiate:** Baseball M, cross-country, wrestling M.

STUDENT SERVICES. Aptitude testing, career counseling, employment service for undergraduates, freshman orientation, health services, on-campus day care, personal counseling, placement service for graduates, special adviser for adult students, veterans counselor, services/facilities for handicapped.

ANNUAL EXPENSES. Tuition and fees (1992-93): $1,440, $450 additional for out-of-district students, $2,340 additional for out-of-state students. **Books and supplies:** $675. **Other expenses:** $1,053.

FINANCIAL AID. 42% of continuing students receive some form of aid. 98% of grants, all loans, 53% of jobs based on need. Academic, music/drama, art, athletic, leadership, minority scholarships available. **Aid applications:** No closing date; applicants notified on a rolling basis beginning on or about April 1.

ADDRESS/TELEPHONE. Dr. Sharon A. Akridge, Director of Admissions and Records, Cuyahoga Community College: Western Campus, 11000 Pleasant Valley Road, Parma, OH 44130. (216) 987-5150. Fax: (216) 987-5050.

Davis Junior College of Business
Toledo, Ohio CB code: 2155

2-year proprietary junior college, coed. Founded in 1858. **Accreditation:** Regional candidate. **Undergraduate enrollment:** 106 men, 261 women full time; 56 men, 116 women part time. **Faculty:** 33 total (19 full time). **Location:** Urban campus in large city; 6 miles from downtown, 45 miles from Detroit. **Calendar:** Quarter. **Microcomputers:** 35 located in libraries, computer centers. **Special facilities:** Aviation center and large hanger at local airport. **Additional facts:** Professional pilot program available at aviation center 6 miles from campus.

DEGREES OFFERED. AS, AAS. 109 associate degrees awarded in 1992. 10% in architecture and environmental design, 26% business and management, 53% business/office and marketing/distribution, 11% allied health.

UNDERGRADUATE MAJORS. Accounting, aviation management, business and management, business and office, business data programming, commercial art, fashion merchandising, interior design, legal assistant/paralegal, medical assistant, secretarial and related programs, tourism.

ACADEMIC PROGRAMS. Internships. **Remedial services:** Reduced course load, remedial instruction, tutoring. **Placement/credit:** Institutional tests.

ACADEMIC REQUIREMENTS. Freshmen must earn minimum GPA of 2.0 to continue in good standing. 60% of freshmen return for sophomore year. Students must declare major on application. **Graduation requirements:** 92 hours for associate. Most students required to take courses in computer science, English, humanities, mathematics, social sciences.

FRESHMAN ADMISSIONS. Selection criteria: Standardized admissions test and interview required. **Test requirements:** School and College Ability Tests required (CPAT).

1992 FRESHMAN CLASS PROFILE. 132 men, 261 women enrolled. **Characteristics:** 82% from in state, 100% commute, 15% have minority backgrounds, 1% are foreign students.

FALL-TERM APPLICATIONS. $25 fee. No closing date; applicants notified on a rolling basis. Interview required. Deferred admission available.

STUDENT LIFE. Activities: Student government.

ATHLETICS. Intramural: Bowling, volleyball.

STUDENT SERVICES. Employment service for undergraduates, freshman orientation, personal counseling, placement service for graduates, services/facilities for handicapped.

ANNUAL EXPENSES. Tuition and fees (1992-93): $5,232. **Books and supplies:** $625. **Other expenses:** $1,800.

FINANCIAL AID. 80% of freshmen, 75% of continuing students receive some form of aid. All aid based on need. **Aid applications:** No closing date; applicants notified on a rolling basis.

ADDRESS/TELEPHONE. Diane Lambert, Director of Admissions, Davis Junior College of Business, 4747 Monroe, Toledo, OH 43623. (419) 473-2700.

Defiance College
Defiance, Ohio CB code: 1162

Admissions: 84% of applicants accepted
Based on: ••• School record
•• Interview, test scores
• Activities, essay, recommendations, special talents
Completion: 86% of freshmen end year in good standing
51% graduate, 4% of these enter graduate study

4-year private liberal arts college, coed, affiliated with United Church of Christ. Founded in 1850. **Accreditation:** Regional. **Undergraduate enrollment:** 348 men, 341 women full time; 106 men, 170 women part time. **Graduate enrollment:** 14 men, 56 women part time. **Faculty:** 77 total (57 full time), 23 with doctorates or other terminal degrees. **Location:** Rural campus in large town; 55 miles from Toledo, 45 miles from Fort Wayne, Indiana. **Calendar:** 4-4-1, extensive summer session. **Microcomputers:** 30 located in libraries, classrooms, computer centers. **Special facilities:** Women's Commission Art Gallery, Eisenhower Room, United Church of Christ Media Center, Indian Wars Collection, Kettering Genetics Center.

DEGREES OFFERED. AA, BA, BS, MA. 2 associate degrees awarded in 1992. 25% in business and management, 13% computer sciences, 37% parks/recreation, protective services, public affairs, 25% philosophy, religion, theology. 178 bachelor's degrees awarded. 32% in business and management, 29% teacher education, 5% law, 6% life sciences, 5% psychology, 7% social sciences.

UNDERGRADUATE MAJORS. Associate: Business administration and management, business and management, computer and information sciences, criminal justice studies, fine arts, liberal/general studies, religious education, therapeutic recreation. **Bachelor's:** Accounting, applied mathematics, art education, biology, business administration and management, business and management, business education, chemistry, Christian education, communications, comprehensive social science, computer and information sciences, criminal justice studies, early childhood education, education, education of the emotionally handicapped, education of the mentally handicapped, elementary education, English, English education, environmental science, finance, fine arts, health education, history, humanities and social sciences, industrial recreation, journalism, junior high education, liberal/general studies, marketing and distribution, marketing management, mathematics, mathematics education, medical laboratory technologies, municipal recreation, music, music education, philosophy, physical education, physical sciences, physics, predentistry, prelaw, premedicine, preveterinary, psychology, public relations, pure mathematics, radio/television broadcasting, reading education, recreation therapy, religion, religious education, restoration ecology, science education, secondary education, social science education, social studies education, social work, special education, specific learning disabilities, speech, speech/communication/theater education, sports management, sports medicine, therapeutic recreation, wellness.

ACADEMIC PROGRAMS. Accelerated program, cooperative education, double major, dual enrollment of high school students, independent study, internships, student-designed major, study abroad, teacher preparation, weekend college, cross-registration. **Remedial services:** Learning center, reduced course load, remedial instruction, special counselor, tutoring. **Placement/credit:** AP, CLEP General and Subject, institutional tests; 15 credit hours maximum for associate degree; 30 credit hours maximum for bachelor's degree.

ACADEMIC REQUIREMENTS. Freshmen must earn minimum GPA of 2.0 to continue in good standing. 56% of freshmen return for sophomore year. Students must declare major by end of second year. **Graduation requirements:** 60 hours for associate (30 in major), 120 hours for bachelor's (30 in major). Most students required to take courses in arts/fine arts, English, foreign languages, history, humanities, mathematics, philosophy/religion, biological/physical sciences, social sciences. **Postgraduate studies:** 13% from 2-year programs enter 4-year programs. 1% enter law school, 1% enter medical school, 1% enter MBA programs, 1% enter other graduate study. **Additional information:** Evening sessions available in many areas. Re-entry Student Seminar available for students over 23 to assist in transition.

FRESHMAN ADMISSIONS. Selection criteria: School achievement record, test scores, special talents important. Minimum 2.0 high school GPA, rank in top 60% percent of graduating class, 18 ACT composite or 700 SAT combined score. **High school preparation:** 15 units recommended. Recommended units include English 4, foreign language 2, mathematics 3, social science 3 and science 3. One unit of fine arts and 1 unit of word processing recommended. **Test requirements:** SAT or ACT (ACT preferred); score report by August 15.

1992 FRESHMAN CLASS PROFILE. 313 men applied, 257 accepted, 108 enrolled; 179 women applied, 154 accepted, 78 enrolled. **Characteristics:** 60% live in college housing. Average age is 18.

FALL-TERM APPLICATIONS. $25 fee, may be waived for applicants with need. No closing date; priority given to applications received by May 1; applicants notified on a rolling basis; must reply by May 1 or within 30 days. Interview recommended. Essay recommended. CRDA. Deferred and early admission available.

STUDENT LIFE. Housing: Dormitories (men, women); fraternity, sorority housing available. All freshmen, sophomore, and junior students, excluding married students, veterans, and commuting students living with parents or close relatives within the approved commuting distance, must reside in college housing and take their meals on campus. Quiet floors available. **Activities:** Student government, magazine, student newspaper, yearbook, choral groups, drama, musical theater, College Community Band, fraternities, sororities, Newman Club, Black Action Student Association, International Student Association, United Christian Student Fellowship, Fellowship of Christian Athletes, American Marketing Association, speech/debate team, Social Work Association, Circle K.

ATHLETICS. NCAA. **Intercollegiate:** Baseball M, basketball, cross-country, football M, golf M, soccer, softball W, tennis, track and field, volleyball W, wrestling M. **Intramural:** Badminton, basketball, bowling, cross-country, racquetball, soccer, softball, table tennis, tennis, volleyball.

STUDENT SERVICES. Career counseling, employment service for undergraduates, freshman orientation, health services, personal counseling, placement service for graduates, special adviser for adult students, career interest survey, services/facilities for handicapped.

ANNUAL EXPENSES. Tuition and fees: $9,950. **Room and board:** $3,530. **Books and supplies:** $500. **Other expenses:** $928.

FINANCIAL AID. 96% of freshmen, 80% of continuing students receive some form of aid. 79% of grants, 90% of loans, 66% of jobs based on need. 169 enrolled freshmen were judged to have need, all were offered aid. Academic, music/drama, state/district residency, leadership, alumni affiliation, religious affiliation scholarships available. **Aid applications:** No closing date; applicants notified on a rolling basis beginning on or about February 20; must reply by May 1 or within 3 weeks if notified thereafter.

ADDRESS/TELEPHONE. Penny D. Bell, Director of Admission, Defiance College, 701 North Clinton Street, Defiance, OH 43512-1695. (419) 783-2330. Fax: (419) 784-0426.

Denison University
Granville, Ohio — CB code: 1164

Admissions: 84% of applicants accepted
Based on: ••• School record, test scores
•• Activities, essay, recommendations, special talents
• Interview
Completion: 86% of freshmen end year in good standing
78% graduate, 21% of these enter graduate study

4-year private liberal arts college, coed. Founded in 1831. **Accreditation:** Regional. **Undergraduate enrollment:** 877 men, 985 women full time; 3 men, 18 women part time. **Faculty:** 247 total (232 full time), 154 with doctorates or other terminal degrees. **Location:** Rural campus in small town; 27 miles from Columbus. **Calendar:** 4-4-1. **Microcomputers:** 460 located in dormitories, libraries, classrooms, computer centers, campus-wide network. **Special facilities:** 275-acre biological reserve, Swasey Observatory, high resolution spectrometer lab, nuclear magnetic resonance spectrometer, planetarium.

DEGREES OFFERED. BA, BS, BFA. 500 bachelor's degrees awarded in 1992. 6% in communications, 7% languages, 15% letters/literature, 5% life sciences, 9% psychology, 38% social sciences, 8% visual and performing arts.

UNDERGRADUATE MAJORS. Afro-American (black) studies, anthropology, art history, biology, chemistry, cinematography/film, classics, communications, computer and information sciences, creative writing, dance, dramatic arts, East Asian studies, economics, education, English, English literature, French, geology, German, history, international studies, Latin American studies, mathematics, music, music education, philosophy, physical education, physics, political science and government, psychology, religion, sociology, Spanish, speech, studio art, Western European studies, women's studies.

ACADEMIC PROGRAMS. Double major, honors program, independent study, internships, semester at sea, student-designed major, study abroad, teacher preparation, visiting/exchange student program, New York semester, Washington semester, Greek studies program on-site in Greece taught by Denison faculty, Latin America Studies summer program in Cuernavaca; liberal arts/career combination in engineering, forestry, health sciences. **Remedial services:** Learning center, reduced course load, special counselor, tutoring. **Placement/credit:** AP, CLEP Subject, institutional tests.

ACADEMIC REQUIREMENTS. Freshmen must earn minimum GPA of 2.0 to continue in good standing. 86% of freshmen return for sophomore year. Students must declare major by end of second year. **Graduation requirements:** 127 hours for bachelor's (32 in major). Most students required to take courses in arts/fine arts, English, foreign languages, history, humanities, philosophy/religion, biological/physical sciences, social sciences. **Postgraduate studies:** 5% enter law school, 3% enter medical school, 3% enter MBA programs, 10% enter other graduate study. **Additional information:** Special curriculum for first-year students. All students must complete a course in minority or women's studies. Computer-based laboratories for teaching mathematics and economics. Generous resources to support student involvement in faculty research.

FRESHMAN ADMISSIONS. Selection criteria: Academic record, test scores, recommendations, school and community activities, essay and personal potential. Special consideration given to multicultural students, foreign applicants, fine arts applicants, and children of alumni. **High school preparation:** 16 units recommended. Recommended units include English 4, foreign language 3, mathematics 3, social science 3 and science 3. One unit fine arts also recommended. **Test requirements:** SAT or ACT; score report by March 1.

1992 FRESHMAN CLASS PROFILE. 1,366 men applied, 1,078 accepted, 269 enrolled; 1,432 women applied, 1,280 accepted, 301 enrolled. 31% were in top tenth and 53% were in top quarter of graduating class. **Academic background:** Mid 50% of enrolled freshmen had SAT-V between 450-560, SAT-M between 500-620; ACT composite between 25-29. 60% submitted SAT scores, 40% submitted ACT scores. **Characteristics:** 36% from in state, 99% live in college housing, 9% have minority backgrounds, 2% are foreign students, 55% join fraternities/sororities. Average age is 18.

FALL-TERM APPLICATIONS. $35 fee, may be waived for applicants with need. Closing date February 1; priority given to applications received by January 10; applicants notified on or about April 1; must reply by May 1. Essay required. Interview recommended. Audition recommended for music, theater, dance, art, and cinema applicants. Portfolio recommended for studio art applicants. CRDA. Deferred and early admission available. EDP-F. To be assured of academic scholarship consideration application must be received by January 10.

STUDENT LIFE. Housing: Dormitories (men, women, coed); fraternity, handicapped housing available. 3 student-constructed buildings using alternative energy resources accommodate 12 students. 3.2 GPA required for apartment-style living. Substance-free housing available. **Activities:** Student government, film, magazine, radio, student newspaper, yearbook, choral groups, concert band, dance, drama, jazz band, music ensembles, musical theater, symphony orchestra, fraternities, sororities, Black Student Union, International Students Association, community service, political union, Jewish and Christian organizations, College Life (spiritual fellowship), Amnesty International, Denison Recycling Project. **Additional information:** 600 leadership roles available on campus.

ATHLETICS. NCAA. **Intercollegiate:** Baseball M, basketball, cross-country, diving, field hockey W, football M, golf M, lacrosse, soccer, swimming, tennis, track and field, volleyball W. **Intramural:** Basketball, golf, horseback riding, ice hockey M, lacrosse M, racquetball, rifle, rugby, skiing, soccer, softball, squash, tennis, volleyball, wrestling M.

STUDENT SERVICES. Career counseling, employment service for undergraduates, freshman orientation, health services, personal counseling, placement service for graduates, services/facilities for handicapped.

ANNUAL EXPENSES. Tuition and fees: $16,730. **Room and board:** $4,450. **Books and supplies:** $500. **Other expenses:** $600.

FINANCIAL AID. 60% of freshmen, 57% of continuing students receive some form of aid. 70% of grants, 98% of loans, 58% of jobs based on need. 262 enrolled freshmen were judged to have need, all were offered aid. Academic, music/drama, art, state/district residency, leadership, minority scholarships available. **Aid applications:** No closing date; priority given to applications received by April 1; applicants notified on a rolling basis beginning on or about April 1; must reply by May 1 or within 2 weeks if notified thereafter.

ADDRESS/TELEPHONE. William W. Dennett, Dean of Admissions and Financial Aid, Denison University, PO Box H, Granville, OH 43023. (614) 587-6276. (800) 336-4766. Fax: (614) 587-6417.

DeVry Institute of Technology: Columbus

Columbus, Ohio CB code: 1605

Admissions: 92% of applicants accepted
Based on: ••• Test scores
Completion: 38% graduate

4-year proprietary business, technical college, coed. Founded in 1952. **Accreditation:** Regional. **Undergraduate enrollment:** 1,961 men, 377 women full time; 318 men, 96 women part time. **Faculty:** 97 total (62 full time). **Location:** Suburban campus in very large city; 5 miles from downtown. **Calendar:** Three continuous calendar terms. Extensive evening/early morning classes. **Microcomputers:** 190 located in computer centers.

DEGREES OFFERED. AAS, BS. 172 associate degrees awarded in 1992. 100% in engineering technologies. 428 bachelor's degrees awarded. 25% in business and management, 25% computer sciences, 50% engineering technologies.

UNDERGRADUATE MAJORS. Associate: Electronic technology. **Bachelor's:** Accounting, business administration and management, electronic technology, information sciences and systems.

ACADEMIC PROGRAMS. Accelerated program. **Remedial services:** Learning center, reduced course load, special counselor, tutoring, developmental coursework. **ROTC:** Air Force, Army. **Placement/credit:** Institutional tests; 31 credit hours maximum for associate degree; 47 credit hours maximum for bachelor's degree.

ACADEMIC REQUIREMENTS. Freshmen must earn minimum GPA of 2.0 to continue in good standing. 44% of freshmen return for sophomore year. Students must declare major on enrollment. **Graduation requirements:** 89 hours for associate, 134 hours for bachelor's. Most students required to take courses in computer science, English, history, humanities, mathematics, social sciences.

FRESHMAN ADMISSIONS. Selection criteria: Applicants must have high school diploma or equivalant, pass institutional entrance examination or submit acceptable ACT/SAT/WPCT scores, and be 17 years of age. **Test requirements:** SAT or ACT; score report by October 30. **Additional information:** New students may enter beginning of any semester.

1992 FRESHMAN CLASS PROFILE. 1,598 men and women applied, 1,473 accepted; 794 men enrolled, 140 women enrolled. **Characteristics:** 56% from in state, 100% commute, 21% have minority backgrounds, 1% are foreign students.

FALL-TERM APPLICATIONS. $25 fee. No closing date; applicants notified on a rolling basis; must reply within 4 weeks. Deferred admission available.

STUDENT LIFE. Housing: School-contracted furnished apartments available for single students. **Activities:** Student government, student newspaper, Data Processing Management Association (DPMA), Institute of Electrical and Electronic Engineers (IEEE).

ATHLETICS. Intramural: Basketball, football, soccer, softball, volleyball.

STUDENT SERVICES. Career counseling, employment service for undergraduates, freshman orientation, placement service for graduates, veterans counselor, services/facilities for handicapped.

ANNUAL EXPENSES. Tuition and fees (1992-93): $5,249. **Books and supplies:** $500. **Other expenses:** $1,911.

FINANCIAL AID. 80% of freshmen, 80% of continuing students receive some form of aid. All grants, 76% of loans, all jobs based on need. Academic scholarships available. **Aid applications:** No closing date; applicants notified on a rolling basis; must reply by registration. **Additional information:** Approximately 80% of students work part-time at jobs found through Institute.

ADDRESS/TELEPHONE. Richard Rodman, Director of Admissions, DeVry Institute of Technology: Columbus, 1350 Alum Creek Drive, Columbus, OH 43209-2764. (614) 253-1525. (800) 426-2206. Fax: (614) 252-4108.

Dyke College

Cleveland, Ohio CB code: 1178

4-year private business college, coed. Founded in 1848. **Accreditation:** Regional. **Undergraduate enrollment:** 1,426 men and women. **Faculty:** 92 total (32 full time). **Location:** Urban campus in very large city; in downtown area. **Calendar:** Semester, extensive summer session. **Microcomputers:** Located in libraries, computer centers.

DEGREES OFFERED. AS, BS. 22 associate degrees awarded in 1992. 168 bachelor's degrees awarded.

UNDERGRADUATE MAJORS. Associate: Accounting, business administration and management, business and management, business and office, legal assistant/paralegal, legal secretary, management science, marketing and distribution, marketing management, office supervision and management, public administration, real estate, secretarial and related programs, word processing. **Bachelor's:** Accounting, business administration and management, business and management, business and office, business economics, engineering management, finance, health care administration, humanities and social sciences, information processing administration, legal assistant/paralegal, management science, marketing and distribution, marketing management, office supervision and management, public administration, real estate, secretarial and related programs, social sciences, word processing.

ACADEMIC PROGRAMS. Accelerated program, cooperative education, double major, dual enrollment of high school students, external degree, independent study, internships, weekend college, cross-registration. **Remedial services:** Learning center, preadmission summer program, remedial instruction, special counselor, tutoring, Developmental Education Program. **Placement/credit:** AP, institutional tests.

ACADEMIC REQUIREMENTS. Freshmen must earn minimum GPA of 2.0 to continue in good standing. 65% of freshmen return for sophomore year. Students must declare major by end of second year. **Graduation requirements:** 63 hours for associate (21 in major), 126 hours for bachelor's (24 in major). Most students required to take courses in English, history, mathematics, biological/physical sciences, social sciences. **Postgraduate studies:** 50% from 2-year programs enter 4-year programs. 5% enter law school, 10% enter MBA programs, 5% enter other graduate study.

FRESHMAN ADMISSIONS. Selection criteria: High school GPA, test scores very important. **Test requirements:** SAT or ACT (ACT preferred); score report by August 15.

1992 FRESHMAN CLASS PROFILE. 194 men and women enrolled. 25% had high school GPA of 3.0 or higher, 70% between 2.0 and 2.99. **Characteristics:** 95% from in state, 100% commute, 40% have minority backgrounds. Average age is 21.

FALL-TERM APPLICATIONS. $25 fee. No closing date; applicants notified on a rolling basis; must reply by registration. Essay required for external degree applicants. Interview recommended. Deferred and early admission available.

STUDENT LIFE. Activities: Student government, student newspaper, yearbook, fraternities, sororities, Paralegal Association, Marketing Club, Administrative Management Society, Students in Free Enterprise.

ATHLETICS. NAIA, NSCAA. **Intercollegiate:** Basketball M.

STUDENT SERVICES. Aptitude testing, career counseling, employment service for undergraduates, freshman orientation, health services, personal counseling, placement service for graduates, veterans counselor, services/facilities for handicapped.

ANNUAL EXPENSES. Tuition and fees (1992-93): $5,300. **Books and supplies:** $544. **Other expenses:** $1,160.

FINANCIAL AID. 80% of freshmen, 80% of continuing students receive some form of aid. Academic, athletic, leadership scholarships available. **Aid applications:** No closing date; priority given to applications received by August 15; applicants notified on a rolling basis beginning on or about March 15; must reply within 2 weeks.

ADDRESS/TELEPHONE. Ron Wendeln, Director of Admissions, Dyke College, 112 Prospect Avenue, Cleveland, OH 44115. (216) 696-9000. Fax: (216) 696-6430.

Edison State Community College

Piqua, Ohio CB code: 1191

2-year public community college, coed. Founded in 1973. **Accreditation:**

Regional. **Undergraduate enrollment:** 379 men, 624 women full time; 757 men, 1,537 women part time. **Faculty:** 151 total (41 full time), 8 with doctorates or other terminal degrees. **Location:** Rural campus in large town; 25 miles from Dayton. **Calendar:** Semester, extensive summer session. Saturday and extensive evening/early morning classes. **Microcomputers:** 200 located in libraries, classrooms, computer centers.

DEGREES OFFERED. AA, AS, AAS. 269 associate degrees awarded in 1992. 21% in business and management, 10% business/office and marketing/distribution, 9% engineering technologies, 16% health sciences, 28% multi/interdisciplinary studies, 14% parks/recreation, protective services, public affairs.

UNDERGRADUATE MAJORS. Accounting, architectural technologies, biological and physical sciences, biology, business and management, business and office, business computer/console/peripheral equipment operation, business data processing and related programs, business data programming, civil technology, computer technology, criminal justice technology, data processing, drafting, education, electronic technology, engineering and engineering-related technologies, English, finance, fine arts, humanities and social sciences, industrial technology, law enforcement and corrections technologies, legal assistant/paralegal, legal secretary, liberal/general studies, manufacturing technology, marketing and distribution, mathematics, mechanical design technology, microcomputer software, nursing, physical sciences, preengineering, psychology, quality control technology, real estate, secretarial and related programs, social sciences, social work, word processing.

ACADEMIC PROGRAMS. 2-year transfer program, double major, dual enrollment of high school students, independent study, internships, student-designed major. **Remedial services:** Learning center, preadmission summer program, reduced course load, remedial instruction, special counselor, tutoring. **Placement/credit:** CLEP Subject, institutional tests; 45 credit hours maximum for associate degree.

ACADEMIC REQUIREMENTS. Freshmen must earn minimum GPA of 1.8 to continue in good standing. 44% of freshmen return for sophomore year. **Graduation requirements:** 90 hours for associate (45 in major). Most students required to take courses in arts/fine arts, computer science, English, humanities, mathematics, social sciences.

FRESHMAN ADMISSIONS. Selection criteria: Open admissions. Special admissions requirements for nursing program. **Test requirements:** SAT or ACT (ACT preferred) for placement and counseling only; score report by September 12.

1992 FRESHMAN CLASS PROFILE. 276 men, 452 women enrolled. **Academic background:** Mid 50% of enrolled freshmen had ACT composite between 15-19. 40% submitted ACT scores. **Characteristics:** 99% from in state, 100% commute, 3% have minority backgrounds. Average age is 30.

FALL-TERM APPLICATIONS. $15 fee. No closing date; applicants notified on a rolling basis. Deferred admission available.

STUDENT LIFE. Activities: Student government, student newspaper, drama, social sciences club, Business Professionals of America, National Student Nursing Association, Environmental Club.

ATHLETICS. NJCAA. **Intercollegiate:** Baseball M, basketball M, golf, softball W. **Intramural:** Softball, tennis.

STUDENT SERVICES. Aptitude testing, career counseling, employment service for undergraduates, freshman orientation, on-campus day care, personal counseling, placement service for graduates, veterans counselor, services/facilities for handicapped.

ANNUAL EXPENSES. Tuition and fees (1992-93): $1,845, $1,575 additional for out-of-state students. **Books and supplies:** $633. **Other expenses:** $400.

FINANCIAL AID. 26% of continuing students receive some form of aid. Grants, loans, jobs available. Academic, athletic scholarships available. **Aid applications:** Closing date April 1; applicants notified on a rolling basis beginning on or about May 15.

ADDRESS/TELEPHONE. Dr. Dotty Muir, Associate Dean Student Development, Edison State Community College, 1973 Edison Drive, Piqua, OH 45356. (513) 778-8600. Fax: (513) 778-1920.

ETI Technical College
Cleveland, Ohio — CB code: 0814

4-year proprietary technical college, coed. Founded in 1929. **Undergraduate enrollment:** 283 men and women. **Location:** Urban campus in very large city; 2 miles east of Cleveland Public Square. **Calendar:** 4 terms of 12 weeks each.

FRESHMAN ADMISSIONS. Selection criteria: Institutional test scores and interview most important.

ANNUAL EXPENSES. Tuition and fees: $5,955. **Room and board:** $2,100 room only. **Books and supplies:** $1,500. **Other expenses:** $500.

ADDRESS/TELEPHONE. Sonia Ross, Dean of Admissions, ETI Technical College, 4300 Euclid Avenue, Cleveland, OH 44103. (216) 431-4300.

Franciscan University of Steubenville
Steubenville, Ohio — CB code: 1133

Admissions: 85% of applicants accepted
Based on: ••• School record, test scores
• Activities, interview, recommendations, special talents
Completion: 90% of freshmen end year in good standing
61% graduate

4-year private university, coed, affiliated with Roman Catholic Church. Founded in 1946. **Accreditation:** Regional. **Undergraduate enrollment:** 537 men, 777 women full time; 62 men, 157 women part time. **Graduate enrollment:** 59 men, 53 women full time; 88 men, 76 women part time. **Faculty:** 128 total (87 full time), 64 with doctorates or other terminal degrees. **Location:** Urban campus in large town; 40 miles from Pittsburgh, Pennsylvania. **Calendar:** Semester, limited summer session. **Microcomputers:** 64 located in computer centers. **Special facilities:** Replica of Portiuncula (St. Mary of the Angels) Chapel as rebuilt by St. Francis of Assisi in 1207 and Tomb of the Unborn Child. **Additional facts:** Franciscan University committed to providing quality education consistent with the teaching authority of the Roman Catholic Church.

DEGREES OFFERED. AA, BS, MA, MS, MBA, MEd. 10 associate degrees awarded in 1992. 20% in business and management, 40% multi/interdisciplinary studies, 40% philosophy, religion, theology. 269 bachelor's degrees awarded. 20% in business and management, 16% teacher education, 6% health sciences, 16% philosophy, religion, theology, 20% psychology. Graduate degrees offered in 7 major fields of study.

UNDERGRADUATE MAJORS. Associate: Accounting, business and management, early childhood education, liberal/general studies, theological studies. **Bachelor's:** Accounting, biology, business administration and management, business and management, business economics, chemistry, clinical laboratory science, communications, computer and information sciences, criminal justice studies, dramatic arts, economics, education of the emotionally handicapped, education of the mentally handicapped, elementary education, engineering science, English, English literature, finance, French, history, humanities, humanities and Catholic culture, information sciences and systems, journalism, junior high education, marketing management, mathematics, medical laboratory technologies, nursing, philosophy, political science and government, predentistry, prelaw, premedicine, preveterinary, psychology, radio/television broadcasting, secondary education, sociology, Spanish, special education, theological studies.

ACADEMIC PROGRAMS. Accelerated program, double major, honors program, internships, study abroad, teacher preparation; combined bachelor's/graduate program in business administration. **Remedial services:** Reduced course load, special counselor, tutoring. **Placement/credit:** AP, CLEP General and Subject, institutional tests; 30 credit hours maximum for associate degree; 30 credit hours maximum for bachelor's degree.

ACADEMIC REQUIREMENTS. Freshmen must earn minimum GPA of 1.8 to continue in good standing. 80% of freshmen return for sophomore year. Students must declare major on enrollment. **Graduation requirements:** 60 hours for associate (12 in major), 124 hours for bachelor's (24 in major). Most students required to take courses in computer science, English, foreign languages, history, humanities, mathematics, philosophy/religion, biological/physical sciences, social sciences. **Additional information:** Students encouraged to spend 1 semester of sophomore year studying humanities core courses at branch campus in Gaming, Austria.

FRESHMAN ADMISSIONS. Selection criteria: Admission requirements include minimum 2.4 high school GPA, rank in top half of class, recommendations, interview when available, combined SAT verbal and mathematical score of 850 or Enhanced ACT composite of 19. **High school preparation:** 15 units required. Recommended units include biological science 3, English 3, foreign language 2, mathematics 3, physical science 1 and social science 3. 10 units in 4 of the following fields: English, foreign language, social science, mathematics, natural sciences. Remaining 5 units may be in other subjects counted toward graduation. Majors in chemistry, engineering science, or mathematics should have 2 units algebra and 2 units geometry/trigonometry. **Test requirements:** SAT or ACT; score report by July 31.

1992 FRESHMAN CLASS PROFILE. 216 men applied, 184 accepted, 106 enrolled; 338 women applied, 286 accepted, 138 enrolled. 60% had high school GPA of 3.0 or higher, 39% between 2.0 and 2.99. 21% were in top tenth and 48% were in top quarter of graduating class. **Academic background:** Mid 50% of enrolled freshmen had SAT-V between 420-550, SAT-M between 430-560; ACT composite between 19-26. 44% submitted SAT scores, 67% submitted ACT scores. **Characteristics:** 22% from in state, 87% live in college housing, 5% have minority backgrounds, 8% are foreign students, 1% join fraternities/sororities. Average age is 18.

FALL-TERM APPLICATIONS. $20 fee, may be waived for applicants with need. Closing date July 31; priority given to applications received by March 1; applicants notified on a rolling basis; must reply within 4 weeks. Interview recommended for academically weak applicants. Essay recommended for academically marginal applicants. Deferred and early admission available. Institutional early decision plan.

STUDENT LIFE. Housing: Dormitories (men, women). Household groups of 10-20 students in resident halls may develop distinctive environment for their group within the context of Christian and Franciscan perspective. **Activities:** Student government, radio, student newspaper, television, yearbook, choral groups, drama, fraternities, sororities, campus ministry, community service volunteer program, International Student Organization, Human Life Concerns (pro-life).

ATHLETICS. Intramural: Basketball, cross-country, racquetball, table tennis, tennis, volleyball.

STUDENT SERVICES. Aptitude testing, career counseling, employment service for undergraduates, freshman orientation, health services, personal counseling, placement service for graduates, veterans counselor.

ANNUAL EXPENSES. Tuition and fees: $9,180. **Room and board:** $4,200. **Books and supplies:** $600. **Other expenses:** $1,000.

FINANCIAL AID. 80% of freshmen, 82% of continuing students receive some form of aid. 74% of grants, 96% of loans, 86% of jobs based on need. 191 enrolled freshmen were judged to have need, all were offered aid. Academic scholarships available. **Aid applications:** Closing date May 1; priority given to applications received by March 1; applicants notified on a rolling basis beginning on or about April 1; must reply within 4 weeks.

ADDRESS/TELEPHONE. Margaret Weber, Director of Admissions, Franciscan University of Steubenville, 100 Franciscan Way, Steubenville, OH 43952-6701. (614) 283-6226. (800) 783-6220. Fax: (614) 283-6472.

Franklin University
Columbus, Ohio CB code: 1229

4-year private university, coed. Founded in 1902. **Accreditation:** Regional. **Undergraduate enrollment:** 551 men, 593 women full time; 1,185 men, 1,523 women part time. **Faculty:** 196 total (46 full time), 42 with doctorates or other terminal degrees. **Location:** Urban campus in very large city; in downtown area. **Calendar:** Trimester, limited summer session. Saturday and extensive evening/early morning classes. **Microcomputers:** 120 located in classrooms, computer centers. **Special facilities:** Art gallery. **Additional facts:** Credit courses offered at 7 off-campus suburban locations.

DEGREES OFFERED. AS, BS. 110 associate degrees awarded in 1992. 81% in business and management, 12% computer sciences, 7% engineering technologies. 651 bachelor's degrees awarded. 62% in business and management, 13% business/office and marketing/distribution, 8% computer sciences, 7% engineering technologies.

UNDERGRADUATE MAJORS. Associate: Accounting, business administration and management, computer and information sciences, electronic technology, mechanical design technology, public administration, real estate. **Bachelor's:** Accounting, business administration and management, communications, computer and information sciences, electronic technology, employee assistance counseling, finance, management information systems, management science, marketing and distribution, mechanical design technology, nursing, personnel management, public administration, real estate.

ACADEMIC PROGRAMS. Accelerated program, double major, dual enrollment of high school students, independent study, internships, study abroad, weekend college, cross-registration. **Remedial services:** Learning center, preadmission summer program, reduced course load, remedial instruction, special counselor, tutoring, Placement Profile Testing and free, noncredit workshops in study skills, mathematics anxiety, public speaking anxiety, career decisions, resume writing, and interviewing skills. **ROTC:** Air Force, Army. **Placement/credit:** AP, CLEP General and Subject, institutional tests; 30 credit hours maximum for associate degree; 70 credit hours maximum for bachelor's degree.

ACADEMIC REQUIREMENTS. Freshmen must earn minimum GPA of 1.1 to continue in good standing. 39% of freshmen return for sophomore year. Students must declare major on application. **Graduation requirements:** 64 hours for associate (16 in major), 124 hours for bachelor's (24 in major). Most students required to take courses in computer science, English, humanities, mathematics, biological/physical sciences, social sciences. **Additional information:** Bachelor of science degree programs in accounting, banking, business management, computer management, computer science, finance, human resources management, marketing, real estate for those who have bachelor of arts degree.

FRESHMAN ADMISSIONS. Selection criteria: Open admissions. Registered nursing license required for admission to BS in nursing program. Recommended units include mathematics 3. Strong mathematics background recommended for engineering technology applicants.

1992 FRESHMAN CLASS PROFILE. 54 men, 83 women enrolled. **Characteristics:** 99% from in state, 100% commute, 25% have minority backgrounds, 6% are foreign students. Average age is 24.

FALL-TERM APPLICATIONS. $25 fee, may be waived for applicants with need. No closing date; applicants notified on a rolling basis. Interview required. Deferred and early admission available. ACT used for placement purposes.

STUDENT LIFE. Activities: Student newspaper, International Students Association, Black Student Union.

ATHLETICS. Intercollegiate: Soccer M. **Intramural:** Basketball M, volleyball.

STUDENT SERVICES. Aptitude testing, career counseling, employment service for undergraduates, freshman orientation, personal counseling, placement service for graduates, veterans counselor, services/facilities for handicapped.

ANNUAL EXPENSES. Tuition and fees (1992-93): $4,110. **Books and supplies:** $450. **Other expenses:** $510.

FINANCIAL AID. 72% of grants, 80% of loans, all jobs based on need. 46 enrolled freshmen were judged to have need, all were offered aid. Academic, state/district residency, leadership, minority scholarships available. **Aid applications:** No closing date; priority given to applications received by May 30; applicants notified on a rolling basis beginning on or about July 1; must reply within 2 weeks.

ADDRESS/TELEPHONE. Kitty Miller, Director of Student Services, Franklin University, 201 South Grant Avenue, Columbus, OH 43215-5399. (614) 341-6231. Fax: (614) 221-7723.

God's Bible School and College
Cincinnati, Ohio CB code: 1238

4-year private Bible college, coed, interdenominational. Founded in 1900. **Undergraduate enrollment:** 62 men, 73 women full time; 18 men, 19 women part time. **Faculty:** 26 total (19 full time). **Location:** Urban campus in large city; one mile from downtown. **Calendar:** Semester, limited summer session.

DEGREES OFFERED. BA. 28 bachelor's degrees awarded in 1992.

UNDERGRADUATE MAJORS. Bible studies, education, English education, home economics, home economics education, mathematics, mathematics education, missionary studies, music education, psychology, religious education, religious music, secondary education, social science education, social sciences, theological studies.

ACADEMIC PROGRAMS. Double major. **Remedial services:** Learning center. **Placement/credit:** CLEP General and Subject, institutional tests.

ACADEMIC REQUIREMENTS. Freshmen must earn minimum GPA of 1.6 to continue in good standing. 50% of freshmen return for sophomore year. Students must declare major by end of first year. **Graduation requirements:** 128 hours for bachelor's (30 in major). Most students required to take courses in English, history, humanities, mathematics, philosophy/religion, biological/physical sciences, social sciences.

FRESHMAN ADMISSIONS. Selection criteria: Open admissions. 3 references recommended. Applicants of Wesleyan Armenian background encouraged. **High school preparation:** 17 units recommended. Recommended units include English 3, mathematics 2, social science 2 and science 2. **Test requirements:** SAT or ACT for placement and counseling only; score report by July 12.

1992 FRESHMAN CLASS PROFILE. 54 men and women enrolled. **Characteristics:** 31% from in state, 90% live in college housing, 7% have minority backgrounds, 3% are foreign students. Average age is 19.

FALL-TERM APPLICATIONS. $50 fee. Closing date July 12; applicants notified on a rolling basis. Deferred admission available.

STUDENT LIFE. Housing: Dormitories (men, women). **Activities:** Student government, yearbook, music ensembles, symphony orchestra.

ATHLETICS. Intramural: Basketball M, volleyball.

STUDENT SERVICES. Employment service for undergraduates, health services, placement service for graduates, veterans counselor.

ANNUAL EXPENSES. Tuition and fees: $3,160. **Room and board:** $2,450. **Books and supplies:** $300. **Other expenses:** $555.

FINANCIAL AID. 79% of freshmen, 86% of continuing students receive some form of aid. All grants, 96% of loans, 40% of jobs based on need. Academic, music/drama scholarships available. **Aid applications:** No closing date; priority given to applications received by June 1; applicants notified on a rolling basis. **Additional information:** Institutional work scholarships available.

ADDRESS/TELEPHONE. Carol Wiseman, Director of Admissions, God's Bible School and College, 1810 Young Street, Cincinnati, OH 45210. (513) 721-7944.

Heidelberg College
Tiffin, Ohio CB code: 1292

Admissions:	96% of applicants accepted
Based on:	••• School record
	•• Test scores
	• Activities, essay, interview, recommendations, special talents
Completion:	90% of freshmen end year in good standing
	62% graduate, 39% of these enter graduate study

4-year private liberal arts college, coed, affiliated with United Church of Christ. Founded in 1850. **Accreditation:** Regional. **Undergraduate enrollment:** 510 men, 424 women full time; 52 men, 48 women part time. **Graduate enrollment:** 43 men, 105 women part time. **Faculty:** 110 total (72 full time), 45 with doctorates or other terminal degrees. **Location:** Suburban campus in large town; 52 miles from Toledo, 100 miles from Detroit. **Calendar:** Semester, limited summer session. **Microcomputers:** 100 located in dormitories, libraries, classrooms, computer centers. **Special facilities:** Water quality laboratory, cadaver laboratory for anatomy students. **Additional facts:** Accelerated degree program offered in Maumee for students who have completed 39 hours of college-level work. Freshman-level credit courses offered at the American Universities League in Shin Yokohama, Japan.

DEGREES OFFERED. BA, BS, MA, MBA. 220 bachelor's degrees awarded in 1992. 23% in business and management, 5% communications, 8% education, 6% letters/literature, 12% life sciences, 7% psychology, 9% social sciences, 5% visual and performing arts. Graduate degrees offered in 5 major fields of study.

UNDERGRADUATE MAJORS. Accounting, allied health, anthropology, biological and physical sciences, biology, business administration and management, business and management, business economics, chemistry, communications, computer and information sciences, computer programming, criminal justice studies, dramatic arts, economics, education, education of the mentally handicapped, elementary education, English, English education, English literature, environmental science, foreign languages education, German, health care administration, health education, health sciences, history, humanities, humanities and social sciences, information sciences and systems, international business management, international relations, international studies, liberal/general studies, management science, mathematics, mathematics education, medical laboratory technologies, music, music business management, music education, music history and appreciation, music performance, music theory and composition, philosophy, physical education, physical sciences, physics, political science and government, predentistry, preengineering, prelaw, premedicine, preveterinary, psychology, public administration, public relations, radio/television broadcasting, religion, science education, secondary education, social science education, social sciences, social studies education, Spanish, specific learning disabilities, speech, speech/communication/theater education, sports medicine, technical education.

ACADEMIC PROGRAMS. Accelerated program, double major, dual enrollment of high school students, honors program, independent study, internships, semester at sea, student-designed major, study abroad, teacher preparation, weekend college, Washington semester, cross-registration; liberal arts/career combination in engineering, forestry. **Remedial services:** Learning center, reduced course load, tutoring. **Placement/credit:** AP, CLEP General and Subject, institutional tests; 30 credit hours maximum for bachelor's degree.

ACADEMIC REQUIREMENTS. Freshmen must earn minimum GPA of 1.7 to continue in good standing. 77% of freshmen return for sophomore year. Students must declare major by end of second year. **Graduation requirements:** 120 hours for bachelor's (42 in major). Most students required to take courses in arts/fine arts, computer science, English, foreign languages, history, humanities, mathematics, philosophy/religion, biological/physical sciences, social sciences.

FRESHMAN ADMISSIONS. Selection criteria: School achievement record most important, followed by test scores. Special talents, community activities, and leadership qualities also considered. **High school preparation:** 18 units required; 21 recommended. Required and recommended units include English 4, mathematics 3-4, social science 3-4 and science 3-4. Foreign language 2 recommended. **Test requirements:** SAT or ACT; score report by June 1.

1992 FRESHMAN CLASS PROFILE. 794 men and women applied, 763 accepted; 148 men enrolled, 93 women enrolled. 68% had high school GPA of 3.0 or higher, 32% between 2.0 and 2.99. 28% were in top tenth and 52% were in top quarter of graduating class. **Academic background:** Mid 50% of enrolled freshmen had SAT-V between 430-480, SAT-M between 430-480; ACT composite between 20-26. 32% submitted SAT scores, 81% submitted ACT scores. **Characteristics:** 70% from in state, 95% live in college housing, 4% have minority backgrounds, 7% are foreign students, 25% join fraternities/sororities. Average age is 18.

FALL-TERM APPLICATIONS. $20 fee. Closing date August 1; priority given to applications received by January 1; applicants notified on a rolling basis; must reply within 4 weeks. Interview required for academically weak applicants. Audition required for music applicants. Essay recommended. CRDA. Deferred and early admission available. EDP-S.

STUDENT LIFE. Housing: Dormitories (men, women, coed). Undergraduate specialty houses by major. **Activities:** Student government, magazine, radio, student newspaper, television, yearbook, choral groups, concert band, dance, drama, jazz band, marching band, music ensembles, musical theater, opera, pep band, symphony orchestra, fraternities, sororities, Black Student Union, Young Democrats, Young Republicans, Circle-K, religious organizations, World Student Union, Volunteers, Beta Beta Beta, political science organization.

ATHLETICS. NCAA. **Intercollegiate:** Baseball M, basketball, cross-country, football M, golf M, soccer, softball W, tennis, track and field, volleyball W, wrestling M. **Intramural:** Archery, baseball M, basketball, bowling, golf, lacrosse, soccer, softball, table tennis, volleyball.

STUDENT SERVICES. Career counseling, employment service for undergraduates, freshman orientation, health services, personal counseling, placement service for graduates, special adviser for adult students, services/facilities for handicapped.

ANNUAL EXPENSES. Tuition and fees (projected): $13,000. **Room and board:** $4,160. **Books and supplies:** $500. **Other expenses:** $500.

FINANCIAL AID. 93% of freshmen, 87% of continuing students receive some form of aid. 96% of grants, 99% of loans, 97% of jobs based on need. 210 enrolled freshmen were judged to have need, all were offered aid. Academic, music/drama, state/district residency, leadership, religious affiliation scholarships available. **Aid applications:** No closing date; priority given to applications received by April 1; applicants notified on a rolling basis beginning on or about March 1; must reply within 2 weeks.

ADDRESS/TELEPHONE. Stephen E. Eidson, Dean of Admission, Heidelberg College, 310 East Market Street, Tiffin, OH 44883-2462. (419) 448-2330. (800) 925-9250. Fax: (419) 448-2124.

Hiram College
Hiram, Ohio — CB code: 1297

Admissions:	81% of applicants accepted
Based on:	••• School record, test scores
	•• Interview, recommendations
	• Activities, essay, special talents
Completion:	95% of freshmen end year in good standing
	73% graduate, 31% of these enter graduate study

4-year private liberal arts college, coed, affiliated with Christian Church (Disciples of Christ). Founded in 1850. **Accreditation:** Regional. **Undergraduate enrollment:** 866 men and women full time. **Faculty:** 93 total (79 full time), 74 with doctorates or other terminal degrees. **Location:** Rural campus in rural community; 35 miles from Cleveland. **Calendar:** Quarter, limited summer session. **Microcomputers:** 150 located in dormitories, libraries, classrooms, computer centers, campus-wide network. **Special facilities:** 2 nature/science field research stations, observatory. **Additional facts:** Affiliated with John Cabot International University in Rome, Italy, Shoals Marine Laboratory in New Hampshire, the Institute of European Studies, and the Institute for Asian Studies. Exchange programs with Mithibai College of the University of Bombay, India, and Kansai University of Foreign Studies in Osaka, Japan.

DEGREES OFFERED. BA. 237 bachelor's degrees awarded in 1992.

UNDERGRADUATE MAJORS. Art history, biology, business and management, chemistry, classics, communications, computer and information sciences, dramatic arts, economics, elementary education, English, French, German, history, international business management, mathematics, music, philosophy, physics, political science and government, psychobiology, psychology, religion, social sciences, sociology, Spanish, studio art.

ACADEMIC PROGRAMS. Accelerated program, double major, dual enrollment of high school students, independent study, internships, student-designed major, study abroad, teacher preparation, weekend college, Washington semester; liberal arts/career combination in engineering, forestry, health sciences, business; combined bachelor's/graduate program in business administration. **Remedial services:** Reduced course load, tutoring, writing center. **Placement/credit:** AP, CLEP Subject, IB, institutional tests; 90 credit hours maximum for bachelor's degree.

ACADEMIC REQUIREMENTS. Freshmen must earn minimum GPA of 2.0 to continue in good standing. 84% of freshmen return for sophomore year. Students must declare major by end of second year. **Graduation requirements:** 180 hours for bachelor's (60 in major). Most students required to take courses in arts/fine arts, English, history, humanities, mathematics, philosophy/religion, biological/physical sciences, social sciences. **Postgraduate studies:** 3% enter law school, 3% enter medical school, 3% enter MBA programs, 22% enter other graduate study. **Additional information:** Secondary education certification in 23 different fields and three areas of special education. Pre-law and Pre-Veterinary programs offered.

FRESHMAN ADMISSIONS. Selection criteria: School record, test scores, character and teacher recommendations emphasized. Extracurricular participation important. Alumni relationship considered. **High school preparation:** 16 units required. Required and recommended units include English 4, mathematics 3-4, social science 3 and science 3. Biological science 1 and foreign language 2 recommended. **Test requirements:** SAT or ACT; score report by April 15. 3 ACH may be submitted in place of SAT or ACT.

1992 FRESHMAN CLASS PROFILE. 801 men and women applied, 647 accepted; 138 men enrolled, 131 women enrolled. 67% had high school GPA of 3.0 or higher, 31% between 2.0 and 2.99. 33% were in top tenth and 65% were in top quarter of graduating class. **Academic background:** Mid 50% of enrolled freshmen had SAT-V between 440-580, SAT-M between 420-590; ACT composite between 21-27. 52% submitted SAT scores, 87% submitted ACT scores. **Characteristics:** 78% from in state, 98% live in college housing, 10% have minority backgrounds. Average age is 18.

FALL-TERM APPLICATIONS. $20 fee, may be waived for applicants with need. Closing date April 15; applicants notified on a rolling basis; must reply by May 1 or within 2 weeks if notified thereafter. Interview recommended for academically marginal applicants. Essay recommended. CRDA. Deferred and early admission available.

STUDENT LIFE. Housing: Dormitories (women, coed). Residence halls have professionally trained residence directors and student resident advisers on each floor. Dormitories include 24-hour and 12-hour quiet floors. **Activities:** Student government, magazine, radio, student newspaper, yearbook, literary arts magazine, choral groups, concert band, drama, jazz band, music ensembles, musical theater, opera, chamber orchestra, African-American Students United, Environmental Awareness Club, Hiram Christian Fellowship, Network for Progressive Action, Hiram College Republicans, Model United Nations, National Organization of Women (NOW), Hiram Volunteer Association, International Students Organization.

ATHLETICS. NCAA. **Intercollegiate:** Baseball M, basketball, cross-country, diving, football M, golf, soccer, softball W, swimming, tennis, track and field, volleyball W. **Intramural:** Basketball, football, lacrosse, rugby, soccer, softball W, table tennis, volleyball, water polo M.

STUDENT SERVICES. Aptitude testing, career counseling, employment service for undergraduates, freshman orientation, health services, personal counseling, placement service for graduates, veterans counselor.

ANNUAL EXPENSES. Tuition and fees: $13,825. **Room and board:** $4,515. **Books and supplies:** $400. **Other expenses:** $900.

FINANCIAL AID. 85% of freshmen, 85% of continuing students receive some form of aid. 95% of grants, 94% of loans, 94% of jobs based on need. Academic, music/drama, state/district residency, leadership, religious affiliation, minority scholarships available. **Aid applications:** Closing date August 1; priority given to applications received by March 1; applicants notified on a rolling basis beginning on or about April 1; must reply by May 1 or within 2 weeks if notified thereafter.

ADDRESS/TELEPHONE. Gary Craig, Vice President for College Advancement and Dean of Admissions, Hiram College, PO Box 96, Rodefer House, Hiram, OH 44234. (216) 569-5169. (800) 362-5280. Fax: (216) 569-5944.

Hocking Technical College
Nelsonville, Ohio — CB code: 1822

2-year public technical college, coed. Founded in 1968. **Accreditation:** Regional. **Undergraduate enrollment:** 2,183 men, 1,664 women full time; 1,010 men, 1,091 women part time. **Faculty:** 210 total (186 full time), 11 with doctorates or other terminal degrees. **Location:** Rural campus in small town; 15 miles from Athens, 55 miles from Columbus. **Calendar:** Quarter, limited summer session. **Microcomputers:** Located in dormitories, classrooms, computer centers. **Special facilities:** Nature center, Robbins Crossing (living history village). **Additional facts:** Courses available at Perry, Fairfield, and Pickaway Centers and in 7 prisons.

DEGREES OFFERED. AAS. 632 associate degrees awarded in 1992. 21% in agriculture, 16% business and management, 8% business/office and marketing/distribution, 8% engineering technologies, 27% health sciences, 5% allied health, 12% parks/recreation, protective services, public affairs.

UNDERGRADUATE MAJORS. Accounting, automotive mechanics, automotive technology, business and management, business and office, business data processing and related programs, ceramic engineering, computer programming, criminal justice technology, dietetic aide/assistant, drafting, drafting and design technology, electrical/electronics/communications engineering, electronic technology, emergency medical technologies, fire control and safety technology, forestry and related sciences, hotel/motel and restaurant management, law enforcement and corrections technologies, marketing and distribution, materials engineering, medical assistant, medical records technology, nursing, parks and recreation management, secretarial and related programs, telecommunications, tourism, wildlife management.

ACADEMIC PROGRAMS. 2-year transfer program, accelerated program, cooperative education, double major, dual enrollment of high school students, independent study, internships, student-designed major, weekend college, cross-registration. **Remedial services:** Learning center, preadmission summer program, reduced course load, remedial instruction, special counselor, tutoring. **ROTC:** Army. **Placement/credit:** CLEP General, institutional tests.

ACADEMIC REQUIREMENTS. Freshmen must earn minimum GPA of 1.5 to continue in good standing. 70% of freshmen return for sophomore year. Students must declare major on application. **Graduation requirements:** 90 hours for associate (45 in major). Most students required to take courses in computer science, English, mathematics, social sciences. **Additional information:** Alternative education programs available.

FRESHMAN ADMISSIONS. Selection criteria: Open admissions. Selective admissions to nursing based on test scores. One algebra, 1 biology highly recommended for recreation/wildlife and forestry applicants. **Test requirements:** Entrance Examination for Schools of Nursing or Entrance Examination for Schools of Practical Nursing required of nursing applicants.

1992 FRESHMAN CLASS PROFILE. 1,470 men and women enrolled. **Characteristics:** 93% from in state, 70% commute, 1% have minority backgrounds, 1% are foreign students. Average age is 22.

FALL-TERM APPLICATIONS. $25 fee. No closing date; priority given to applications received by December 1; applicants notified on a rolling basis beginning on or about November 15; must reply within 4 weeks. Early admission available.

STUDENT LIFE. Housing: Dormitories (coed). Honors House. **Activities:** Student government, magazine, television, Phi Theta Kappa.

ATHLETICS. Intramural: Archery, basketball, bowling, golf, soccer, softball, table tennis, tennis, volleyball.

STUDENT SERVICES. Aptitude testing, career counseling, employment service for undergraduates, freshman orientation, health services, personal counseling, placement service for graduates, special adviser for adult students, veterans counselor, services/facilities for handicapped.

ANNUAL EXPENSES. Tuition and fees (1992-93): $1,773, $1,758 additional for out-of-state students. **Room and board:** $3,504. **Books and supplies:** $600. **Other expenses:** $1,189.

FINANCIAL AID. 98% of grants, 84% of loans, 93% of jobs based on need. Academic, state/district residency, leadership scholarships available. **Aid applications:** No closing date; priority given to applications received by April 30; applicants notified on a rolling basis beginning on or about June 1.

ADDRESS/TELEPHONE. Candace S. Vancko, Vice President Enrollment Management, Hocking Technical College, 3301 Hocking Parkway, Nelsonville, OH 45764-9704. (614) 753-3591 ext. 2160. Fax: (614) 753-4097.

ITT Technical Institute: Dayton
Dayton, Ohio — CB code: 7312

2-year proprietary technical college, coed. Founded in 1935. **Undergraduate enrollment:** 778 men, 132 women full time. **Faculty:** 31 total (29 full time). **Location:** Suburban campus in small city; 5 miles from downtown. **Calendar:** Quarter. **Microcomputers:** 89 located in libraries, classrooms.

DEGREES OFFERED. AAS. 150 associate degrees awarded in 1992. 75% in engineering technologies, 25% trade and industry.

UNDERGRADUATE MAJORS. Architectural technologies, architecture, carpentry, electronic technology, tool engineering.

ACADEMIC PROGRAMS. Remedial services: Learning center, remedial instruction, tutoring.

ACADEMIC REQUIREMENTS. Freshmen must earn minimum GPA of 1.9 to continue in good standing. Students must declare major on application. **Graduation requirements:** 110 hours for associate (87 in major). Most students required to take courses in humanities.

FRESHMAN ADMISSIONS. Selection criteria: Specialized on-site test results considered for certain courses. Recommended units include mathematics 2.

1992 FRESHMAN CLASS PROFILE. 215 men, 53 women enrolled. 10% had high school GPA of 3.0 or higher, 70% between 2.0 and 2.99. **Characteristics:** 98% from in state, 100% commute, 14% have minority backgrounds. Average age is 19.

FALL-TERM APPLICATIONS. $100 fee. Application fee refunded if student not accepted. No closing date; applicants notified on a rolling basis; must reply by registration. Interview required.

STUDENT LIFE. Activities: Student government.

STUDENT SERVICES. Career counseling, employment service for undergraduates, freshman orientation, placement service for graduates, services/facilities for handicapped.

ANNUAL EXPENSES. Tuition and fees (1992-93): $7,402. Tuition and fees are for 12-month period. **Books and supplies:** $1,400. **Other expenses:** $1,500.

FINANCIAL AID. 89% of freshmen, 88% of continuing students receive some form of aid. All grants, 79% of loans, all jobs based on need. **Aid applications:** No closing date; priority given to applications received by August 1; applicants notified on a rolling basis; must reply by registration.

ADDRESS/TELEPHONE. Claude Smith, Director of Education, ITT Technical Institute: Dayton, 3325 Stop Eight Road, Dayton, OH 45414. (513) 454-2267. Fax: (513) 454-2278.

ITT Technical Institute: Youngstown
Youngstown, Ohio — CB code: 0418

2-year proprietary technical college, coed. Founded in 1967. **Undergraduate enrollment:** 244 men, 128 women full time. **Faculty:** 19 total. **Location:** Urban campus in small city; 60 miles from Cleveland and 60 miles from Pittsburgh, Pennsylvania. **Calendar:** Quarter, extensive summer session. **Microcomputers:** Located in classrooms.

DEGREES OFFERED. AAS. 159 associate degrees awarded in 1992. 33% in business and management, 22% business/office and marketing/distribution, 44% engineering technologies.

UNDERGRADUATE MAJORS. Accounting, business and management, business computer/console/peripheral equipment operation, computer-aided drafting, drafting, drafting and design technology, electronic technology.

ACADEMIC PROGRAMS. Remedial services: Tutoring. **Placement/credit:** Institutional tests.

ACADEMIC REQUIREMENTS. Freshmen must earn minimum GPA of 1.9 to continue in good standing. 60% of freshmen return for sophomore year. Students must declare major on enrollment. **Graduation requirements:** 126 hours for associate (76 in major). Most students required to take courses in English, mathematics.

FRESHMAN ADMISSIONS. Selection criteria: Specialized on-site test scores considered for certain courses. **Test requirements:** Required tests are: (A)CPAT reading skills, (B)CPAT numerial skills, (C)CPAT language usage, (D)DAT mechanical reasoning, (E)DAT space relations. Secretarial, business management and accounting majors must take A,B and C. Electronics majors must take A and B. Drafting majors must take A,B,D and E.

1992 FRESHMAN CLASS PROFILE. 183 men, 43 women enrolled. **Characteristics:** 100% commute, 3% have minority backgrounds.

FALL-TERM APPLICATIONS. $100 fee. Application fee refunded if student not accepted. No closing date; applicants notified on a rolling basis; must reply by 5th day of class. Interview required.

STUDENT LIFE. Activities: American Institute of Design and Drafting club, Electronics Technicians Association (ETA), Collegiate Secretaries International (CSI).

STUDENT SERVICES. Employment service for undergraduates, personal counseling, placement service for graduates.

ANNUAL EXPENSES. Tuition and fees (1992-93): $7,402. Tuition and fees for 12-month period. Laboratory fees, $50 per quarter. **Books and supplies:** $1,000.

FINANCIAL AID. 91% of freshmen, 93% of continuing students receive some form of aid. All grants, 91% of loans, all jobs based on need. **Aid applications:** No closing date; priority given to applications received by September 29; applicants notified on a rolling basis; must reply by registration.

ADDRESS/TELEPHONE. Director of Recruitment, ITT Technical Institute: Youngstown, 655 Wick Avenue, Youngstown, OH 44501-0779. (216) 747-5555. (800) 832-5001. Fax: (216) 747-7718.

Jefferson Technical College
Steubenville, Ohio — CB code: 2264

2-year public technical college, coed. Founded in 1966. **Accreditation:** Regional. **Undergraduate enrollment:** 333 men, 545 women full time; 300 men, 513 women part time. **Faculty:** 97 total (53 full time), 3 with doctorates or other terminal degrees. **Location:** Suburban campus in large town; 30 miles from Pittsburgh, Pennsylvania. **Calendar:** Quarter, limited summer session. **Microcomputers:** 160 located in libraries, classrooms. **Special facilities:** Learning skills laboratory specializing in adult basic education.

DEGREES OFFERED. AAS. 235 associate degrees awarded in 1992. 31% in business and management, 9% business/office and marketing/distribution, 15% engineering technologies, 36% allied health, 9% parks/recreation, protective services, public affairs.

UNDERGRADUATE MAJORS. Accounting, business and management, business data processing and related programs, child development/care/guidance, dental assistant, drafting and design technology, electrical technology, electronic technology, finance, food management, geriatric technician, instrumentation and control, law enforcement and corrections technologies, legal secretary, mechanical design technology, medical assistant, medical laboratory technologies, medical secretary, protective services, radiograph medical technology, real estate, respiratory therapy technology, retailing, secretarial and related programs, welding technology.

ACADEMIC PROGRAMS. Double major, dual enrollment of high school students, honors program, independent study, internships. **Remedial services:** Learning center, preadmission summer program, remedial instruction, special counselor, tutoring. **Placement/credit:** CLEP General and Subject, institutional tests.

ACADEMIC REQUIREMENTS. Freshmen must earn minimum GPA of 2.0 to continue in good standing. 67% of freshmen return for sophomore year. Students must declare major on application. **Graduation requirements:** 95 hours for associate (63 in major). Most students required to take courses in English, mathematics.

FRESHMAN ADMISSIONS. Selection criteria: Open admissions. Selective admissions for all allied health technologies. **Test requirements:** ACT required for admission to radiology and medical laboratory, medical assisting, and dental assisting technologies. Psychological Corporation Entrance Examination for Schools of Practical Nursing required of nursing applicants.

1992 FRESHMAN CLASS PROFILE. 196 men, 300 women enrolled. **Characteristics:** 81% from in state, 100% commute, 5% have minority backgrounds. Average age is 19.

FALL-TERM APPLICATIONS. $15 fee. No closing date; applicants notified on a rolling basis. Interview required for health program applicants. Early admission available.

STUDENT LIFE. Housing: Students may live in dormitory of local university on space-available basis. **Activities:** Student government, student newspaper.

ATHLETICS. Intramural: Baseball, basketball, bowling, softball, table tennis, tennis, volleyball.

STUDENT SERVICES. Aptitude testing, career counseling, employment service for undergraduates, health services, on-campus day care, personal counseling, placement service for graduates, special adviser for adult students, veterans counselor, services/facilities for handicapped.

ANNUAL EXPENSES. Tuition and fees (1992-93): $1,575, $135 additional for out-of-district students, $675 additional for out-of-state students. Residents of 5 neighboring West Virginia counties eligible for in-state tuition rates. **Books and supplies:** $500. **Other expenses:** $400.

FINANCIAL AID. 55% of freshmen, 60% of continuing students receive some form of aid. 98% of grants, all loans, 22% of jobs based on need. Academic, leadership scholarships available. **Aid applications:** No closing date; priority given to applications received by June 1; applicants notified on a rolling basis beginning on or about June 15; must reply within 2 weeks.

ADDRESS/TELEPHONE. Chuck Mascellino, Director of Admissions, Jefferson Technical College, 4000 Sunset Boulevard, Steubenville, OH 43952. (614) 264-5591 ext. 230.

John Carroll University
University Heights, Ohio — CB code: 1342

Admissions:	85% of applicants accepted
Based on:	••• School record, test scores
	•• Activities, interview, recommendations
	• Essay, special talents
Completion:	95% of freshmen end year in good standing
	72% graduate, 30% of these enter graduate study

4-year private university, coed, affiliated with Roman Catholic Church. Founded in 1886. **Accreditation:** Regional. **Undergraduate enrollment:** 1,563 men, 1,554 women full time; 199 men, 216 women part time. **Graduate enrollment:** 42 men, 85 women full time; 293 men, 536 women part time. **Faculty:** 341 total (217 full time), 255 with doctorates or other terminal degrees. **Location:** Suburban campus in large town; 10 miles from Cleveland. **Calendar:** Semester, limited summer session. Extensive evening/early morning classes. **Microcomputers:** 320 located in dormitories, libraries, computer centers. **Special facilities:** G. K. Chesterton Library collection, U.S. Geological Service seismology station, Mitzie Verne Art Gallery, Ralph Vince Fitness Center. **Additional facts:** Jesuit institution.

DEGREES OFFERED. B, MA, MS, MBA, MEd. 815 bachelor's degrees awarded in 1992. 28% in business and management, 14% communications, 7% teacher education, 11% letters/literature, 5% life sciences, 6% psychology, 18% social sciences. Graduate degrees offered in 21 major fields of study.

UNDERGRADUATE MAJORS. Accounting, art history, biology, business administration and management, business and management, business economics, business logistics, chemistry, classics, communications, computer and information sciences, early childhood education, economics, education, elementary education, engineering physics, English, finance, French, German, Greek (classical), history, humanities, humanities and social sciences, junior high education, Latin, liberal/general studies, marketing management, mathematics, mathematics education, personnel management, philosophy, physical education, physics, political science and government, predentistry, premedicine, preveterinary, psychology, religion, secondary education, sociology, Spanish, transportation management.

ACADEMIC PROGRAMS. Accelerated program, cooperative education, double major, dual enrollment of high school students, honors program, independent study, internships, student-designed major, study abroad, teacher preparation, visiting/exchange student program, cross-registration; liberal arts/career combination in engineering. **Remedial services:** Reduced course load, special counselor, tutoring. **ROTC:** Army. **Placement/credit:** AP, CLEP General and Subject, institutional tests; 30 credit hours maximum for bachelor's degree.

ACADEMIC REQUIREMENTS. Freshmen must earn minimum GPA of 2.0 to continue in good standing. 88% of freshmen return for sophomore year. Students must declare major by end of second year. **Graduation requirements:** 128 hours for bachelor's (30 in major). Most students required to take courses in English, humanities, philosophy/religion, biological/physical sciences, social sciences. **Postgraduate studies:** 6% enter law school, 3% enter medical school, 1% enter MBA programs, 20% enter other graduate study.

FRESHMAN ADMISSIONS. Selection criteria: High school academic record, test scores, recommendations, class rank, extracurricular activities. Interview highly recommended. **High school preparation:** 16 units recommended. Recommended units include English 4, foreign language 3, mathematics 3, social science 2 and science 2. **Test requirements:** SAT or ACT; score report by July 1.

1992 FRESHMAN CLASS PROFILE. 1,054 men applied, 876 accepted, 354 enrolled; 1,099 women applied, 964 accepted, 386 enrolled. 64% had high school GPA of 3.0 or higher, 35% between 2.0 and 2.99. 24% were in top tenth and 56% were in top quarter of graduating class. **Academic background:** Mid 50% of enrolled freshmen had SAT-V between 450-600, SAT-M between 450-600; ACT composite between 21-26. 37% submitted SAT scores, 63% submitted ACT scores. **Characteristics:** 64% from in state, 83% live in college housing, 8% have minority backgrounds, 1% are foreign students. Average age is 18.

FALL-TERM APPLICATIONS. $25 fee, may be waived for applicants with need. No closing date; applicants notified on a rolling basis; must reply by May 1 or within 2 weeks if notified thereafter. Interview recommended. Essay recommended. CRDA. Deferred and early admission available.

STUDENT LIFE. Housing: Dormitories (men, women, coed). **Activities:** Student government, film, magazine, radio, student newspaper, television, yearbook, choral groups, concert band, dance, drama, jazz band, musical theater, pep band, fraternities, sororities, campus ministry, Black Students Association, Young Republicans, sports clubs, international students club, Christian Life Community, Young Democrats, Christmas in April, Project Gold. **Additional information:** 33-acre student villa located nearby.

ATHLETICS. NCAA. **Intercollegiate:** Baseball M, basketball, cross-country, diving, football M, golf M, ice hockey M, lacrosse, rugby M, sailing M, skiing, soccer, softball W, swimming, tennis, track and field, volleyball, wrestling M. **Intramural:** Baseball, basketball, field hockey W, ice hockey, racquetball, rowing (crew), softball, swimming, tennis, volleyball.

STUDENT SERVICES. Aptitude testing, career counseling, employment service for undergraduates, freshman orientation, health services, personal counseling, placement service for graduates, special adviser for adult students, services/facilities for handicapped.

ANNUAL EXPENSES. Tuition and fees: $11,060. **Room and board:** $5,450. **Books and supplies:** $600. **Other expenses:** $450.

FINANCIAL AID. 80% of freshmen, 70% of continuing students receive some form of aid. 68% of grants, 97% of loans, 88% of jobs based on need. 550 enrolled freshmen were judged to have need, all were offered aid. Academic, leadership, alumni affiliation, minority scholarships available. **Aid applications:** No closing date; priority given to applications received by March 1; applicants notified on a rolling basis; must reply by May 1 or within 4 weeks if notified thereafter. **Additional information:** Institutional form for need analysis required from upperclass and transfer students only.

ADDRESS/TELEPHONE. Laryn D. Runco, Director of Admissions, John Carroll University, 20700 North Park Boulevard, University Heights, OH 44118-4581. (216) 397-4294.

Kent State University
Kent, Ohio — CB code: 1367

Admissions: 88% of applicants accepted
Based on: ••• School record
•• Test scores
• Special talents
Completion: 66% of freshmen end year in good standing
35% graduate

4-year public university, coed. Founded in 1910. **Accreditation:** Regional. **Undergraduate enrollment:** 6,773 men, 8,766 women full time; 1,502 men, 1,804 women part time. **Graduate enrollment:** 943 men, 1,196 women full time; 1,027 men, 2,088 women part time. **Faculty:** 1,340 total (764 full time), 678 with doctorates or other terminal degrees. **Location:** Suburban campus in large town; 50 miles from Cleveland, 11 miles from Akron. **Calendar:** Semester, extensive summer session. **Microcomputers:** 800 located in dormitories, libraries, classrooms, computer centers. **Special facilities:** 287-acre airport, Liquid Crystal Institute, fashion museum, planetarium, ice arena. **Additional facts:** University consists of main campus and 7 regional campuses.

DEGREES OFFERED. BA, BS, BFA, BArch, MA, MS, MBA, MFA, MEd, PhD, EdD, MD. 2,810 bachelor's degrees awarded in 1992. 23% in business and management, 5% communications, 16% education, 8% health sciences, 5% home economics, 6% multi/interdisciplinary studies, 5% social sciences, 5% visual and performing arts. Graduate degrees offered in 104 major fields of study.

UNDERGRADUATE MAJORS. Accounting, advertising, aeronautical technology, aerospace technology and airway science, African studies, Afro-American (black) studies, air traffic control, airline piloting and navigation, American studies, anthropology, applied mathematics, architecture, art education, art history, Asian studies, aviation computer technology, aviation management, biological and physical sciences, biology, botany, business administration and management, business and management, business data programming, business economics, business education, chemistry, child development/care/guidance, cinematography/film, classics, clothing and textiles management/production/services, community health work, computer and information sciences, computer mathematics, computer programming, conservation and regulation, crafts, creative writing, criminal justice studies, criminology, cytotechnology, dance, dramatic arts, drawing, early childhood education, earth sciences, Eastern European studies, economics, education, education of exceptional children, education of the deaf and hearing impaired, education of the emotionally handicapped, education of the gifted and talented, education of the mentally handicapped, education of the multiple handicapped, education of the physically handicapped, electronic technology, elementary education, English, English education, ethnic heritage studies, family and community services, family/consumer resource management, fashion design, fashion merchandising, finance, fine arts, food management, food production/management/services, food science and nutrition, foreign languages education, forestry and related sciences, French, geography, geology, German, gerontology, graphic design, health education, history, home economics education, human environment and housing, human resources development, humanities, humanities and social sciences, individual and family development, industrial arts education, industrial design, industrial technology, information sciences and systems, interior design, international relations, international studies, Jewish studies, journalism, junior high education, labor/industrial relations, Latin, Latin American studies, law enforcement and corrections, liberal/general studies, management science, manufacturing technology, marketing and distribution, marketing and distributive education, marketing management, mathematics, mathematics education, medical laboratory technologies, music, music education, music performance, music theory and composition, musical theater, nursing, painting, parks and recreation management, peace studies, personnel management, philosophy, photography, physical education, physics, political science and government, predentistry, prelaw, premedicine, prepharmacy, preveterinary, psychology, public health laboratory science, public relations, pure mathematics, radio/television broadcasting, radio/television technology, real estate, recreation and community services technologies, recreation therapy, renewable natural resources, rhetoric, Russian, Russian and Slavic studies, science education, sculpture, secondary education, social sciences, social studies education, sociology, Spanish, speech pathology/audiology, speech/communication/theater education, studio art, telecommunications, tourism, trade and industrial education, visual and performing arts, women's studies, zoology.

ACADEMIC PROGRAMS. Accelerated program, cooperative education, double major, dual enrollment of high school students, education specialist degree, honors program, independent study, internships, student-designed major, study abroad, teacher preparation, visiting/exchange student program, weekend college, United Nations semester, Washington semester, cross-registration; liberal arts/career combination in forestry, health sciences, business; combined bachelor's/graduate program in medicine. **Remedial services:** Learning center, reduced course load, remedial instruction, special counselor, tutoring, writing clinic. **ROTC:** Air Force, Army. **Placement/credit:** AP, CLEP General and Subject, institutional tests; 30 credit hours maximum for bachelor's degree.

ACADEMIC REQUIREMENTS. Freshmen must earn minimum GPA of 2.0 to continue in good standing. 74% of freshmen return for sophomore year. Students must declare major by end of second year. **Graduation requirements:** 129 hours for bachelor's (32 in major). Most students required to take courses in arts/fine arts, English, humanities, mathematics, biological/physical sciences, social sciences.

FRESHMAN ADMISSIONS. Selection criteria: Selective admissions based on academic record, test scores, high school rank and course work. Selective admissions with varying criteria in nursing, education, business, fashion design and merchandising, architecture, interior design, journalism and mass communication, 6-year medical program, music, dance, honors college, and radio/TV. **High school preparation:** 16 units recommended. Recommended units include English 4, foreign language 3, mathematics 3, social science 3 and science 3. One unit of fine arts or third unit foreign language required for out-of-state students. **Test requirements:** SAT or ACT; score report by July 1.

1992 FRESHMAN CLASS PROFILE. 8,479 men and women applied, 7,422 accepted; 3,013 enrolled. 38% had high school GPA of 3.0 or higher, 60% between 2.0 and 2.99. **Academic background:** Mid 50% of enrolled freshmen had SAT-V between 360-480, SAT-M between 380-530; ACT composite between 17-23. 35% submitted SAT scores, 84% submitted ACT scores. **Characteristics:** 90% from in state, 69% live in college housing, 11% have minority backgrounds, 1% are foreign students, 7% join fraternities/sororities. Average age is 20.

FALL-TERM APPLICATIONS. $25 fee. Closing date March 15; applicants notified on a rolling basis beginning on or about October 1. Audition required for music, dance, musical theater applicants. Interview recommended for all students, required for medical students applicants. Early admission available. Application fee may be deferred for students with financial need.

STUDENT LIFE. Housing: Dormitories (men, women, coed); apartment, fraternity, sorority housing available. Single undergraduate students must live in college housing first 4 semesters, some exemptions granted. **Activities:** Student government, film, magazine, radio, student newspaper, television, choral groups, concert band, dance, drama, jazz band, marching band, music ensembles, musical theater, opera, pep band, symphony orchestra, fraternities, sororities, social service, political and religious organizations.

ATHLETICS. NCAA. **Intercollegiate:** Baseball M, basketball, cross-country, field hockey W, football M, golf M, gymnastics, ice hockey M, softball W, track and field, volleyball W, wrestling M. **Intramural:** Badminton, basketball, bowling, fencing, football, golf, gymnastics, horseback riding, ice hockey M, lacrosse M, racquetball, rowing (crew), rugby M, sailing, skiing, soccer, softball, swimming, tennis, track and field, volleyball, water polo, wrestling M.

STUDENT SERVICES. Aptitude testing, career counseling, employment service for undergraduates, freshman orientation, health services, on-campus day care, personal counseling, placement service for graduates, special adviser for adult students, veterans counselor, services/facilities for handicapped.

ANNUAL EXPENSES. Tuition and fees (1992-93): $3,596, $3,596 additional for out-of-state students. **Room and board:** $3,394. **Books and supplies:** $530. **Other expenses:** $1,310.

FINANCIAL AID. 70% of freshmen, 50% of continuing students re-

ceive some form of aid. 81% of grants, 96% of loans, 52% of jobs based on need. Academic, music/drama, art, athletic, alumni affiliation, minority scholarships available. **Aid applications:** Closing date April 1; priority given to applications received by February 14; applicants notified on a rolling basis beginning on or about March 1; must reply within 3 weeks.

ADDRESS/TELEPHONE. Bruce Riddle, Director of Admissions, Kent State University, PO Box 5190, Kent, OH 44242-0001. (216) 672-2444.

Kent State University: Ashtabula Regional Campus

Ashtabula, Ohio CB code: 1485

2-year public branch campus college, coed. Founded in 1958. **Accreditation:** Regional. **Undergraduate enrollment:** 130 men, 332 women full time; 170 men, 394 women part time. **Faculty:** 76 total (31 full time), 18 with doctorates or other terminal degrees. **Location:** Suburban campus in large town; 50 miles from Cleveland. **Calendar:** Semester, limited summer session. Saturday and extensive evening/early morning classes. **Microcomputers:** 45 located in libraries, computer centers.

DEGREES OFFERED. AA, AS, AAS. 86 associate degrees awarded in 1992. 19% in business and management, 6% computer sciences, 7% engineering technologies, 51% health sciences, 10% multi/interdisciplinary studies, 7% parks/recreation, protective services, public affairs.

UNDERGRADUATE MAJORS. Accounting, business and management, business and office, business data programming, chemical manufacturing technology, computer and information sciences, engineering and engineering-related technologies, industrial technology, law enforcement and corrections technologies, liberal/general studies, mechanical design technology, mental health/human services, nursing, plastic technology, real estate, secretarial and related programs.

ACADEMIC PROGRAMS. 2-year transfer program, dual enrollment of high school students, external degree, independent study, internships, student-designed major, telecourses, cross-registration. **Remedial services:** Learning center, remedial instruction, tutoring. **Placement/credit:** AP, CLEP General and Subject, institutional tests; 12 credit hours maximum for associate degree.

ACADEMIC REQUIREMENTS. Freshmen must earn minimum GPA of 2.0 to continue in good standing. 41% of freshmen return for sophomore year. **Graduation requirements:** 65 hours for associate (32 in major). Most students required to take courses in arts/fine arts, English, humanities, mathematics, biological/physical sciences, social sciences.

FRESHMAN ADMISSIONS. Selection criteria: Open admissions. Selective admissions to nursing and human services progams. College-preparatory program strongly recommended. **Test requirements:** SAT or ACT for placement; score report by August 1.

1992 FRESHMAN CLASS PROFILE. 143 men, 221 women enrolled. **Characteristics:** 99% from in state, 100% commute, 10% have minority backgrounds. Average age is 25.

FALL-TERM APPLICATIONS. $25 fee. No closing date; applicants notified on a rolling basis beginning on or about January 1. Early admission available.

STUDENT LIFE. Activities: Student government, radio, student newspaper, dance, drama, chamber orchestra, world affairs club, social issues club.

STUDENT SERVICES. Career counseling, employment service for undergraduates, freshman orientation, personal counseling, placement service for graduates, special adviser for adult students, veterans counselor, services/facilities for handicapped.

ANNUAL EXPENSES. Tuition and fees (1992-93): $2,885, $3,596 additional for out-of-state students. **Books and supplies:** $525. **Other expenses:** $1,380.

FINANCIAL AID. 51% of freshmen, 50% of continuing students receive some form of aid. All grants, 96% of loans, 86% of jobs based on need. **Aid applications:** Closing date August 1; priority given to applications received by February 15; applicants notified on a rolling basis beginning on or about June 15; must reply within 3 weeks.

ADDRESS/TELEPHONE. Robin McDermott, Admissions Officer, Kent State University: Ashtabula Regional Campus, 3325 West 13th Street, Ashtabula, OH 44004. (216) 964-3322 ext. 240. Fax: (216) 964-4269.

Kent State University: East Liverpool Regional Campus

East Liverpool, Ohio CB code: 0328

2-year public branch campus college, coed. Founded in 1965. **Accreditation:** Regional. **Undergraduate enrollment:** 155 men, 363 women full time; 99 men, 248 women part time. **Faculty:** 60 total (25 full time), 21 with doctorates or other terminal degrees. **Location:** Urban campus in large town; 40 miles from Pittsburgh, Pennsylvania. **Calendar:** Semester, extensive summer session. Saturday and extensive evening/early morning classes. **Microcomputers:** 45 located in computer centers.

DEGREES OFFERED. AA, AS. 113 associate degrees awarded in 1992. 17% in business and management, 75% health sciences, 8% multi/interdisciplinary studies.

UNDERGRADUATE MAJORS. Accounting, business administration and management, business data processing and related programs, business data programming, computer programming, finance, law enforcement and corrections technologies, legal assistant/paralegal, liberal/general studies, marketing and distribution, nursing, occupational therapy assistant, physical therapy assistant, real estate, small business management and ownership.

ACADEMIC PROGRAMS. 2-year transfer program, double major, dual enrollment of high school students, independent study, internships, student-designed major, cross-registration. **Remedial services:** Learning center, pre-admission summer program, reduced course load, remedial instruction, tutoring. **Placement/credit:** AP, CLEP General and Subject, institutional tests; 14 credit hours maximum for associate degree.

ACADEMIC REQUIREMENTS. Freshmen must earn minimum GPA of 2.0 to continue in good standing. 48% of freshmen return for sophomore year. Students must declare major by end of first year. **Graduation requirements:** 65 hours for associate (48 in major). Most students required to take courses in English, mathematics.

FRESHMAN ADMISSIONS. Selection criteria: Open admissions. Selective admissions for out-of-state, nursing, occupational therapy, and physical therapy applicants. **High school preparation:** 16 units recommended. Recommended units include English 4, foreign language 2, mathematics 3, social science 3 and science 3. One unit algebra, 1 unit chemistry, 1 unit biology required for nursing applicants. One unit algebra, 1 unit biology for physical therapy and occupational therapy. **Test requirements:** SAT or ACT (ACT preferred) for placement and counseling only; score report by August 1.

1992 FRESHMAN CLASS PROFILE. 88 men, 238 women enrolled. **Characteristics:** 95% from in state, 100% commute, 3% have minority backgrounds. Average age is 22.

FALL-TERM APPLICATIONS. $25 fee. No closing date; priority given to applications received by August 1; applicants notified on a rolling basis beginning on or about March 1. Interview recommended. Deferred and early admission available. All new applicants must complete Basic Skills Assessment Tests.

STUDENT LIFE. Activities: Student government, choral groups, drama, pep band.

ATHLETICS. Intramural: Basketball, bowling, golf, racquetball, softball, table tennis, volleyball.

STUDENT SERVICES. Career counseling, employment service for undergraduates, freshman orientation, personal counseling, placement service for graduates, veterans counselor, services/facilities for handicapped.

ANNUAL EXPENSES. Tuition and fees (1992-93): $2,885, $3,596 additional for out-of-state students. **Books and supplies:** $525. **Other expenses:** $1,315.

FINANCIAL AID. 65% of freshmen, 64% of continuing students receive some form of aid. All grants, 84% of loans, 31% of jobs based on need. Academic scholarships available. **Aid applications:** No closing date; priority given to applications received by April 1; applicants notified on a rolling basis beginning on or about May 1; must reply within 2 weeks.

ADDRESS/TELEPHONE. Darwin K. Smith, Director of Admissions, Kent State University: East Liverpool Regional Campus, 400 East Fourth Street, East Liverpool, OH 43920. (216) 385-3805. Fax: (216) 385-6348.

Kent State University: Salem Regional Campus

Salem, Ohio CB code: 0683

2-year public branch campus college, coed. Founded in 1962. **Accreditation:** Regional. **Undergraduate enrollment:** 157 men, 349 women full time; 169 men, 335 women part time. **Faculty:** 62 total (33 full time), 17 with doctorates or other terminal degrees. **Location:** Rural campus in large town. **Calendar:** Semester, limited summer session. **Microcomputers:** 75 located in computer centers. **Special facilities:** Learning (tutoring) laboratory, writer's workshop, career planning center, mathematics workshop. **Additional facts:** Graduate courses in education and business available. Graduate degrees granted through main campus.

DEGREES OFFERED. AA, AS, AAS. 74 associate degrees awarded in 1992. 16% in business and management, 5% business/office and marketing/distribution, 5% computer sciences, 6% engineering technologies, 62% allied health, 6% multi/interdisciplinary studies.

UNDERGRADUATE MAJORS. Accounting, business and management, business and office, business data programming, computer and information sciences, horticultural science, horticulture, liberal/general studies, mechanical design technology, mental health/human services, office supervision and management, radiograph medical technology, secretarial and related programs.

ACADEMIC PROGRAMS. Dual enrollment of high school students, internships, cross-registration. **Remedial services:** Learning center, remedial instruction, tutoring. **ROTC:** Air Force, Army. **Placement/credit:** AP, CLEP General and Subject, institutional tests; 24 credit hours maximum for associate degree.

ACADEMIC REQUIREMENTS. Freshmen must earn minimum GPA

of 2.0 to continue in good standing. **Graduation requirements:** 65 hours for associate. Most students required to take courses in English, humanities, mathematics, social sciences.

FRESHMAN ADMISSIONS. Selection criteria: Open admissions. **High school preparation:** 16 units recommended. Recommended units include English 4, foreign language 3, mathematics 3, social science 3 and science 3. One unit visual or performing arts may be substitiuted for 1 unit foreign language. **Test requirements:** SAT or ACT (ACT preferred) for placement and counseling only; score report by August 15. **Additional information:** Applicants who do not have a high school GPA of 2.5 with an ACT composite score of 21, or who have not completed a college preparatory curriculum with a GPA of 2.0, are required to take placement examinations and follow prescribed course work if deemed necessary through testing.

1992 FRESHMAN CLASS PROFILE. 231 men and women enrolled. **Characteristics:** 99% from in state, 100% commute, 1% have minority backgrounds. Average age is 25.

FALL-TERM APPLICATIONS. $25 fee. No closing date; applicants notified on a rolling basis beginning on or about October 1. Deferred and early admission available. Early admission available to high school juniors or seniors in top 15% of their class with ACT of 26 or above and GPA of 3.5 or higher.

STUDENT LIFE. Activities: Student government, student newspaper, choral groups, music ensembles, professional business and engineering clubs, art club, nontraditional student club.

ATHLETICS. NCAA. **Intramural:** Badminton, basketball, racquetball, skiing, table tennis, tennis, volleyball.

STUDENT SERVICES. Aptitude testing, career counseling, freshman orientation, personal counseling, placement service for graduates, special adviser for adult students, veterans counselor, services/facilities for handicapped.

ANNUAL EXPENSES. Tuition and fees (1992-93): $2,885, $3,596 additional for out-of-state students. **Books and supplies:** $525. **Other expenses:** $1,380.

FINANCIAL AID. 60% of continuing students receive some form of aid. Academic, leadership scholarships available. **Aid applications:** No closing date; priority given to applications received by February 15; applicants notified on a rolling basis beginning on or about July 1; must reply within 2 weeks.

ADDRESS/TELEPHONE. Marilyn Ward, Director of Admissions and Records, Kent State University: Salem Regional Campus, 2491 State Route 45 South, Salem, OH 44460. (216) 332-0361. Fax: (216) 332-9256.

Kent State University: Stark Campus
Canton, Ohio — CB code: 0585

2-year public branch campus college, coed. Founded in 1946. **Accreditation:** Regional. **Undergraduate enrollment:** 489 men, 637 women full time; 478 men, 764 women part time. **Faculty:** 131 total (63 full time), 42 with doctorates or other terminal degrees. **Location:** Suburban campus in small city; 14 miles from Akron, 60 miles from Cleveland. **Calendar:** Semester, limited summer session. **Microcomputers:** Located in libraries, classrooms, computer centers. **Additional facts:** Graduate courses in education available. Graduate degrees granted through main campus.

DEGREES OFFERED. AA, AS. 110 associate degrees awarded in 1992. 100% in multi/interdisciplinary studies.

UNDERGRADUATE MAJORS. Liberal/general studies.

ACADEMIC PROGRAMS. 2-year transfer program, double major, dual enrollment of high school students, honors program, independent study, student-designed major, cross-registration, access program for senior citizens. **Remedial services:** Learning center, reduced course load, remedial instruction, special counselor, tutoring, writing center. **Placement/credit:** AP, CLEP General and Subject, institutional tests; 24 credit hours maximum for associate degree.

ACADEMIC REQUIREMENTS. Freshmen must earn minimum GPA of 2.0 to continue in good standing. 60% of freshmen return for sophomore year. Students must declare major by end of first year. **Graduation requirements:** 65 hours for associate (16 in major). Most students required to take courses in arts/fine arts, English, foreign languages, history, mathematics, philosophy/religion, biological/physical sciences, social sciences. **Additional information:** Selected upper-division courses available.

FRESHMAN ADMISSIONS. Selection criteria: Open admissions. Applicants without 2.5 GPA and 21 ACT or 900 SAT score, or 2.0 GPA and 16 units specific college prepatory classes, admitted conditionally. **High school preparation:** 17 units recommended. Recommended units include biological science 1, English 4, foreign language 3, mathematics 3, physical science 3 and social science 3. One unit of fine arts may be substituted for 1 unit of foreign language. **Test requirements:** SAT or ACT (ACT preferred) for placement and counseling only; score report by May 1. Basic Skills Assessment Tests (institutional tests) required for placement.

1992 FRESHMAN CLASS PROFILE. 326 men, 443 women enrolled. 20% had high school GPA of 3.0 or higher, 58% between 2.0 and 2.99. **Academic background:** Mid 50% of enrolled freshmen had ACT composite between 13-20. 46% submitted ACT scores. **Characteristics:** 99% from in state, 100% commute, 7% have minority backgrounds. Average age is 19.

FALL-TERM APPLICATIONS. $25 fee. No closing date; priority given to applications received by August 1; applicants notified on a rolling basis. Audition required for music applicants. Portfolio required for art applicants. Essay required for honors college, early admission applicants. Interview recommended. Deferred and early admission available.

STUDENT LIFE. Activities: Student government, television, literary magazine, choral groups, concert band, drama, jazz band, music ensembles, musical theater, political science forum, Interfaith Campus Ministry, Academy of Life Sciences, student education association, ethnic awareness union.

ATHLETICS. Intercollegiate: Basketball, volleyball W. **Intramural:** Basketball, bowling, cross-country, golf, rugby, skiing, soccer, softball, tennis, volleyball.

STUDENT SERVICES. Aptitude testing, career counseling, employment service for undergraduates, freshman orientation, on-campus day care, personal counseling, veterans counselor, services/facilities for handicapped.

ANNUAL EXPENSES. Tuition and fees (1992-93): $2,885, $3,596 additional for out-of-state students. **Books and supplies:** $525. **Other expenses:** $1,315.

FINANCIAL AID. 30% of continuing students receive some form of aid. 99% of grants, all loans, all jobs based on need. Academic, minority scholarships available. **Aid applications:** No closing date; priority given to applications received by February 15; applicants notified on a rolling basis.

ADDRESS/TELEPHONE. Mary S. Southards, Registar and Director of Admissions, Kent State University: Stark Campus, 6000 Frank Avenue Northwest, Canton, OH 44720. (216) 499-9600. Fax: (216) 494-6121.

Kent State University: Trumbull Regional Campus
Warren, Ohio — CB code: 0593

2-year public branch campus college, coed. Founded in 1954. **Accreditation:** Regional. **Undergraduate enrollment:** 1,996 men and women. **Faculty:** 86 total (50 full time), 24 with doctorates or other terminal degrees. **Location:** Suburban campus in small city; 2 miles from downtown. **Calendar:** Semester, limited summer session. **Microcomputers:** 50 located in libraries, classrooms, computer centers. **Special facilities:** Art gallery.

DEGREES OFFERED. AA, AS, AAS. 107 associate degrees awarded in 1992. 16% in business and management, 10% business/office and marketing/distribution, 12% computer sciences, 15% engineering, 34% social sciences.

UNDERGRADUATE MAJORS. Accounting, automotive engineering, automotive technology, business administration and management, business and management, business and office, business computer/console/peripheral equipment operation, business data entry equipment operation, business data processing and related programs, business data programming, computer programming, computer technology, criminal justice studies, education, electrical technology, electrical/electronics/communications engineering, electronic technology, engineering and engineering-related technologies, engineering management, finance, food management, industrial engineering, industrial technology, law enforcement and corrections technologies, liberal/general studies, marketing and distribution, marketing management, mechanical design technology, mechanical engineering, nursing, office supervision and management, real estate, secretarial and related programs, small business management and ownership, tourism.

ACADEMIC PROGRAMS. 2-year transfer program, double major, dual enrollment of high school students, independent study, internships. **Remedial services:** Learning center, preadmission summer program, reduced course load, remedial instruction, special counselor, tutoring. **Placement/credit:** AP, CLEP General and Subject, institutional tests; 6 credit hours maximum for associate degree.

ACADEMIC REQUIREMENTS. Freshmen must earn minimum GPA of 2.0 to continue in good standing. 50% of freshmen return for sophomore year. Students must declare major by end of first year. **Graduation requirements:** 65 hours for associate (33 in major). Most students required to take courses in arts/fine arts, computer science, English, history, humanities, mathematics, philosophy/religion, biological/physical sciences.

FRESHMAN ADMISSIONS. Selection criteria: Open admissions. Current high school students are eligible for part-time admission with a 3.5 GPA, 26 ACT and letter of recommendation. **High school preparation:** 16 units recommended. Recommended units include English 4, foreign language 3, mathematics 3, social science 3 and science 3. **Test requirements:** SAT or ACT (ACT preferred) for placement; score report by August 18.

1992 FRESHMAN CLASS PROFILE. 615 men and women enrolled. 20% had high school GPA of 3.0 or higher, 50% between 2.0 and 2.99. **Characteristics:** 99% from in state, 100% commute, 7% have minority backgrounds. Average age is 26.

FALL-TERM APPLICATIONS. $25 fee. Closing date August 15; priority given to applications received by June 1; applicants notified on a rolling basis beginning on or about February 1. Deferred and early admission available. 3.5 GPA, college preparatory curriculum, and ACT minimum of

27 required for early admission. All incoming freshmen, regardless of age or GPA, required to take placement surveys prior to their first semester.

STUDENT LIFE. Activities: Student government, student newspaper, choral groups, drama, nontraditional student and minority student organizations, circle K, independent black/minority coalition, Kent Christian Fellowship, Trumbull Enviromental Council.

ATHLETICS. Intercollegiate: Baseball M, basketball, golf. **Intramural:** Basketball, skiing, tennis.

STUDENT SERVICES. Career counseling, employment service for undergraduates, freshman orientation, health services, personal counseling, placement service for graduates, special adviser for adult students, veterans counselor, services/facilities for handicapped.

ANNUAL EXPENSES. Tuition and fees (1992-93): $2,885, $3,596 additional for out-of-state students. **Books and supplies:** $525. **Other expenses:** $1,380.

FINANCIAL AID. 70% of freshmen, 70% of continuing students receive some form of aid. 97% of grants, 84% of loans, 20% of jobs based on need. Academic, state/district residency scholarships available. **Aid applications:** No closing date; priority given to applications received by April 1; applicants notified on a rolling basis beginning on or about June 1; must reply within 3 weeks.

ADDRESS/TELEPHONE. Barbara Brooks, Admissions Officer, Kent State University: Trumbull Regional Campus, 4314 Mahoning Avenue, Warren, OH 44483. (216) 847-0571 ext. 260. Fax: (216) 847-6172.

Kent State University: Tuscarawas Campus
New Philadelphia, Ohio CB code: 1434

2-year public branch campus college, coed. Founded in 1962. **Accreditation:** Regional. **Undergraduate enrollment:** 248 men, 372 women full time; 186 men, 392 women part time. **Faculty:** 85 total (33 full time), 19 with doctorates or other terminal degrees. **Location:** Rural campus in large town; 80 miles from Cleveland. **Calendar:** Semester, limited summer session. **Microcomputers:** 57 located in computer centers.

DEGREES OFFERED. AA, AS, AAS. 149 associate degrees awarded in 1992. 14% in business and management, 7% computer sciences, 11% engineering technologies, 45% health sciences, 19% multi/interdisciplinary studies.

UNDERGRADUATE MAJORS. Accounting, business and management, business and office, computer programming, criminal justice studies, electrical technology, electronic technology, engineering and engineering-related technologies, environmental science, industrial technology, liberal/general studies, nursing, secretarial and related programs.

ACADEMIC PROGRAMS. 2-year transfer program, double major, dual enrollment of high school students, honors program, independent study, internships, student-designed major. **Remedial services:** Learning center, reduced course load, remedial instruction, tutoring. **Placement/credit:** AP, CLEP General and Subject, institutional tests; 15 credit hours maximum for associate degree.

ACADEMIC REQUIREMENTS. Freshmen must earn minimum GPA of 2.0 to continue in good standing. 50% of freshmen return for sophomore year. Students must declare major on application. **Graduation requirements:** 65 hours for associate (30 in major). Most students required to take courses in English, humanities, mathematics, biological/physical sciences, social sciences.

FRESHMAN ADMISSIONS. Selection criteria: Open admissions. Selective admissions for out-of-state and nursing program applicants. **High school preparation:** 16 units recommended. Recommended units include English 4, foreign language 3, mathematics 3, social science 3 and science 3. College-preparatory program strongly recommended. **Test requirements:** SAT or ACT (ACT preferred) for placement and counseling only; score report by August 1. **Additional information:** Students under 21 or out of high school less than 3 years admitted unconditionally if 16 college preparatory units completed with 2.0 GPA or 2.5 GPA and ACT composite score of 19. Students admitted conditionally must complete recommended developmental course work.

1992 FRESHMAN CLASS PROFILE. 98 men, 172 women enrolled. **Characteristics:** 100% from in state, 100% commute, 2% have minority backgrounds. Average age is 25.

FALL-TERM APPLICATIONS. $25 fee. Closing date August 2; applicants notified on a rolling basis beginning on or about May 31. Deferred and early admission available. Institutional early decision plan.

STUDENT LIFE. Activities: Student government, music ensembles, Circle K.

ATHLETICS. Intramural: Basketball, volleyball.

STUDENT SERVICES. Career counseling, employment service for undergraduates, freshman orientation, on-campus day care, placement service for graduates, veterans counselor, services/facilities for handicapped.

ANNUAL EXPENSES. Tuition and fees (projected): $2,885, $3,596 additional for out-of-state students. **Books and supplies:** $530. **Other expenses:** $1,310.

FINANCIAL AID. 66% of freshmen, 68% of continuing students receive some form of aid. 97% of grants, 91% of loans, all jobs based on need. 102 enrolled freshmen were judged to have need, all were offered aid. Academic, state/district residency, leadership, minority scholarships available. **Aid applications:** Closing date April 1; priority given to applications received by February 15; applicants notified on a rolling basis beginning on or about April 15; must reply within 3 weeks. **Additional information:** OIG application form required for in-state students.

ADDRESS/TELEPHONE. Connie Espenschied, Admissions Officer, Kent State University: Tuscarawas Campus, University Drive Northeast, New Philadelphia, OH 44663-9447. (216) 339-3391 ext. 225. Fax: (216) 339-3321.

Kenyon College
Gambier, Ohio CB code: 1370

Admissions:	67% of applicants accepted
Based on:	••• School record
	•• Essay, test scores
	• Activities, interview, recommendations, special talents
Completion:	95% of freshmen end year in good standing
	85% graduate, 25% of these enter graduate study

4-year private liberal arts college, coed, affiliated with Episcopal Church. Founded in 1824. **Accreditation:** Regional. **Undergraduate enrollment:** 724 men, 764 women full time. **Faculty:** 172 total (140 full time), 133 with doctorates or other terminal degrees. **Location:** Rural campus in rural community; 50 miles from Columbus. **Calendar:** Semester. **Microcomputers:** 140 located in dormitories, libraries, classrooms, computer centers, campus-wide network. **Special facilities:** Art gallery, observatory.

DEGREES OFFERED. BA. 364 bachelor's degrees awarded in 1992. 24% in letters/literature, 6% life sciences, 5% multi/interdisciplinary studies, 6% philosophy, religion, theology, 10% psychology, 33% social sciences, 7% visual and performing arts.

UNDERGRADUATE MAJORS. Afro-American (black) studies, American literature, American studies, anthropology, applied mathematics, archeology, art history, Asian studies, biological and physical sciences, biology, chemistry, Chinese, classics, comparative literature, computer and information sciences, creative writing, dance, dramatic arts, East Asian studies, economics, English, English literature, European studies, foreign languages (multiple emphasis), French, German, Greek (classical), history, humanities and social sciences, international relations, international studies, Italian, Japanese, Latin, Latin American studies, mathematics, Middle Eastern studies, music, music history and appreciation, philosophy, physics, political science and government, predentistry, preengineering, prelaw, premedicine, preveterinary, psychology, pure mathematics, religion, Russian, Russian and Slavic studies, sociology, Spanish, studio art, women's studies.

ACADEMIC PROGRAMS. Accelerated program, double major, dual enrollment of high school students, honors program, independent study, internships, semester at sea, student-designed major, study abroad, visiting/exchange student program, New York semester, Integrated Program in Humane Studies; liberal arts/career combination in engineering; combined bachelor's/graduate program in business administration. **Remedial services:** Tutoring, writing center. **Placement/credit:** AP, IB, institutional tests.

ACADEMIC REQUIREMENTS. Freshmen must earn minimum GPA of 2.0 to continue in good standing. 92% of freshmen return for sophomore year. Students must declare major by end of second year. **Graduation requirements:** 128 hours for bachelor's (32 in major). Most students required to take courses in arts/fine arts, humanities, mathematics, biological/physical sciences, social sciences. **Postgraduate studies:** 5% enter law school, 3% enter medical school, 1% enter MBA programs, 16% enter other graduate study. **Additional information:** Freshmen and sophomores may enroll in Integrated Program in Humane Studies.

FRESHMAN ADMISSIONS. Selection criteria: Achievement record most important. Essays, school recommendations, test scores weighed equally. Children of alumni and minority applicants receive some consideration. **High school preparation:** 15 units required; 20 recommended. Required and recommended units include biological science 1, English 4, foreign language 2-3, mathematics 3-4, physical science 1 and social science 2. Science 3 recommended. Sciences include laboratory. **Test requirements:** SAT or ACT; score report by February 15.

1992 FRESHMAN CLASS PROFILE. 1,023 men applied, 646 accepted, 195 enrolled; 1,098 women applied, 781 accepted, 217 enrolled. 64% had high school GPA of 3.0 or higher, 36% between 2.0 and 2.99. 38% were in top tenth and 76% were in top quarter of graduating class. **Academic background:** Mid 50% of enrolled freshmen had SAT-V between 510-620, SAT-M between 550-650; ACT composite between 25-29. 96% submitted SAT scores, 42% submitted ACT scores. **Characteristics:** 20% from in state, 100% live in college housing, 11% have minority backgrounds, 4% are foreign students, 18% join fraternities/sororities. Average age is 18.

FALL-TERM APPLICATIONS. $35 fee, may be waived for applicants with need. Closing date February 15; applicants notified on or about April 1; must reply by May 1. Essay required. Interview recommended. CRDA. Deferred and early admission available. EDP-F. 2 early decision plans available. Option 1 has closing date of December 1 and December 15 notification; Option 2 has closing date of February 1 and February 15 notification.

STUDENT LIFE. Housing: Dormitories (men, women, coed); apartment, cooperative housing available. **Activities:** Student government, film, magazine, radio, student newspaper, television, yearbook, literary journal, opinion journal, nonfiction journal, choral groups, dance, drama, jazz band, music ensembles, musical theater, opera, pep band, symphony orchestra, brass, string, and woodwind chamber music groups, fraternities, sororities, Black Student Union, social service organizations, Christian fellowship, Hillel, Lesbian-Gay-Straight Alliance.

ATHLETICS. NCAA. **Intercollegiate:** Baseball M, basketball, cross-country, diving, field hockey W, football M, golf, lacrosse, soccer, swimming, tennis, track and field, volleyball W. **Intramural:** Basketball, bowling, cross-country, golf, horseback riding, ice hockey M, racquetball, rowing (crew), rugby, sailing, skiing, soccer, softball, squash, swimming, tennis, track and field, volleyball, water polo M.

STUDENT SERVICES. Career counseling, employment service for undergraduates, freshman orientation, health services, personal counseling, placement service for graduates, services/facilities for handicapped.

ANNUAL EXPENSES. Tuition and fees: $18,730. **Room and board:** $3,700. **Books and supplies:** $750. **Other expenses:** $320.

FINANCIAL AID. 40% of freshmen, 38% of continuing students receive some form of aid. 79% of grants, 99% of loans, 52% of jobs based on need. 201 enrolled freshmen were judged to have need, 159 were offered aid. Academic scholarships available. **Aid applications:** Closing date February 15; applicants notified on or about April 1; must reply by May 1.

ADDRESS/TELEPHONE. John W. Anderson, Dean of Admissions, Kenyon College, Ransom Hall, Gambier, OH 43022-9623. (614) 427-5000. (800) 848-2468. Fax: (614) 427-3077.

Kettering College of Medical Arts
Kettering, Ohio

CB code: 0602

2-year private health science, nursing college, coed, affiliated with Seventh-day Adventists. Founded in 1967. **Accreditation:** Regional. **Undergraduate enrollment:** 107 men, 236 women full time; 64 men, 317 women part time. **Faculty:** 58 total (49 full time), 5 with doctorates or other terminal degrees. **Location:** Suburban campus in small city; 5 miles from Dayton. **Calendar:** Semester, limited summer session. **Microcomputers:** 20 located in libraries, computer centers. **Additional facts:** Institution is educational division of the Kettering Medical Center.

DEGREES OFFERED. AS. 140 associate degrees awarded in 1992. 49% in health sciences, 51% allied health.

UNDERGRADUATE MAJORS. Allied health, biomedical equipment technology, medical radiation dosimetry, nuclear medical technology, nursing, physician's assistant, radiograph medical technology, respiratory therapy technology, ultrasound technology.

ACADEMIC PROGRAMS. Accelerated program, double major, cross-registration. **Remedial services:** Preadmission summer program, reduced course load, remedial instruction, tutoring. **Placement/credit:** AP, CLEP General and Subject, institutional tests.

ACADEMIC REQUIREMENTS. Freshmen must earn minimum GPA of 1.85 to continue in good standing. 85% of freshmen return for sophomore year. Students must declare major on application. **Graduation requirements:** 70 hours for associate (35 in major). Most students required to take courses in computer science, English, philosophy/religion, biological/physical sciences, social sciences.

FRESHMAN ADMISSIONS. Selection criteria: Test scores, references, high school GPA most important. **High school preparation:** 14 units recommended. Strong mathematics and science background recommended. **Test requirements:** ACT; score report by June 1.

1992 FRESHMAN CLASS PROFILE. 17 men, 65 women enrolled. 30% had high school GPA of 3.0 or higher, 65% between 2.0 and 2.99. **Academic background:** Mid 50% of enrolled freshmen had ACT composite between 20-30. 65% submitted ACT scores. **Characteristics:** 75% from in state, 75% commute, 20% have minority backgrounds, 3% are foreign students. Average age is 30.

FALL-TERM APPLICATIONS. $25 fee, may be waived for applicants with need. Closing date July 1; priority given to applications received by February 1; applicants notified on a rolling basis; must reply within 3 weeks. Interview recommended. Essay recommended. Interview required for physician assistant applicants; recommended for all applicants. Early admission available.

STUDENT LIFE. Housing: Dormitories (men, women). **Activities:** Yearbook, choral groups, music ensembles.

STUDENT SERVICES. Career counseling, employment service for undergraduates, freshman orientation, health services, personal counseling, placement service for graduates, veterans counselor, services/facilities for handicapped.

ANNUAL EXPENSES. Tuition and fees: $4,850. **Room and board:** $3,408. **Books and supplies:** $550. **Other expenses:** $130.

FINANCIAL AID. 57% of freshmen, 58% of continuing students receive some form of aid. All grants, 65% of loans, 50% of jobs based on need. **Aid applications:** No closing date; priority given to applications received by April 1; applicants notified on a rolling basis; must reply within 3 weeks.

ADDRESS/TELEPHONE. Sally Taylor, Director of Admissions, Kettering College of Medical Arts, 3737 Southern Boulevard, Kettering, OH 45429. (513) 296-7228. (800) 433-5262. Fax: (513) 296-4238.

Lake Erie College
Painesville, Ohio

CB code: 1391

Admissions:	83% of applicants accepted
Based on:	••• School record
	•• Activities, essay, interview, recommendations, test scores
	• Special talents
Completion:	60% of freshmen end year in good standing

4-year private liberal arts college, coed. Founded in 1856. **Accreditation:** Regional. **Undergraduate enrollment:** 71 men, 245 women full time; 94 men, 164 women part time. **Graduate enrollment:** 2 men, 2 women full time; 55 men, 60 women part time. **Faculty:** 68 total (32 full time), 32 with doctorates or other terminal degrees. **Location:** Urban campus in large town; 28 miles from Cleveland, 3 miles from Lake Erie. **Calendar:** Semester, limited summer session. Saturday and extensive evening/early morning classes. **Microcomputers:** 20 located in dormitories, libraries, computer centers. **Special facilities:** Art gallery, Indian museum, equestrian center.

DEGREES OFFERED. BA, BS, BFA, MBA. 154 bachelor's degrees awarded in 1992. 8% in agriculture, 55% business and management, 14% teacher education, 5% health sciences, 5% life sciences. Graduate degrees offered in 1 major field of study.

UNDERGRADUATE MAJORS. Accounting, biology, business administration and management, chemistry, communications, dance, elementary education, English, equestrian facility management, equestrian science, equine stud farm management, fine arts, foreign languages (multiple emphasis), French, German, health care administration, international business management, Italian, legal assistant/paralegal, liberal/general studies, mathematics, music, prelaw, premedicine, preveterinary, psychology, social sciences, Spanish.

ACADEMIC PROGRAMS. Double major, dual enrollment of high school students, independent study, internships, student-designed major, study abroad, teacher preparation. **Remedial services:** Learning center, reduced course load. **Placement/credit:** AP, CLEP General and Subject, institutional tests.

ACADEMIC REQUIREMENTS. Freshmen must earn minimum GPA of 2.0 to continue in good standing. 60% of freshmen return for sophomore year. Students must declare major by end of second year. **Graduation requirements:** 128 hours for bachelor's (40 in major). Most students required to take courses in arts/fine arts, computer science, English, foreign languages, history, humanities, mathematics, biological/physical sciences, social sciences.

FRESHMAN ADMISSIONS. Selection criteria: School achievement record, rank in top half of class, test scores, recommendations, and interview strongly considered. Special consideration of test scores for minority applicants. **High school preparation:** 17 units required. Required and recommended units include English 4, foreign language 2, mathematics 3, social science 3 and science 3. Biological science 2 and physical science 2 recommended. One fine arts and one physical education or health recommended. **Test requirements:** SAT or ACT (ACT preferred); score report by August 15.

1992 FRESHMAN CLASS PROFILE. 23 men applied, 13 accepted, 8 enrolled; 87 women applied, 78 accepted, 33 enrolled. 67% had high school GPA of 3.0 or higher, 30% between 2.0 and 2.99. **Academic background:** Mid 50% of enrolled freshmen had SAT-V between 370-490, SAT-M between 430-490; ACT composite between 20-24. 39% submitted SAT scores, 61% submitted ACT scores. **Characteristics:** 66% from in state, 61% live in college housing, 2% have minority backgrounds. Average age is 19.

FALL-TERM APPLICATIONS. $20 fee, may be waived for applicants with need. Closing date August 15; priority given to applications received by July 1; applicants notified on a rolling basis beginning on or about November 15; must reply within 8 weeks. Essay required. Interview recommended. Audition recommended for performing arts, equestrian studies applicants. Portfolio recommended for fine arts applicants. Deferred and early admission available.

STUDENT LIFE. Housing: Dormitories (men, women). **Activities:** Student government, yearbook, choral groups, dance, drama, honor, accounting, academic, and athletic associations, Black caucus, Women's Forum, foreign language clubs, professional organizations, riding club.

ATHLETICS. NAIA. **Intercollegiate:** Basketball, horseback riding, softball W, volleyball W. **Clubs:** Equestrian.

STUDENT SERVICES. Aptitude testing, career counseling, freshman orientation, personal counseling, placement service for graduates.

ANNUAL EXPENSES. Tuition and fees: $9,000. Equestrian fee $575 per course; student horse boarding fee $275 per month. **Room and board:** $4,400. **Books and supplies:** $500. **Other expenses:** $1,740.

FINANCIAL AID. Academic, music/drama, art, athletic, state/district residency, leadership scholarships available. **Aid applications:** No closing date; priority given to applications received by April 1; applicants notified on a rolling basis beginning on or about June 1; must reply within 4 weeks if notified before June 1, within 2 weeks if notified thereafter.

ADDRESS/TELEPHONE. Phyliss Hammerstrom, Director of Admissions, Lake Erie College, 391 West Washington Street, Painesville, OH 44077-3389. (216) 639-7879. (800) 533-4996. Fax: (216) 352-3533.

Lakeland Community College
Mentor, Ohio CB code: 1422

2-year public community college, coed. Founded in 1967. **Accreditation:** Regional. **Undergraduate enrollment:** 1,054 men, 1,345 women full time; 2,507 men, 4,268 women part time. **Faculty:** 420 total (109 full time), 44 with doctorates or other terminal degrees. **Location:** Suburban campus in large town; 15 miles from Cleveland. **Calendar:** Quarter, limited summer session. Saturday and extensive evening/early morning classes. **Microcomputers:** 325 located in libraries, classrooms, computer centers. **Special facilities:** Art gallery, planetarium, observatory, licensed preschool program laboratory.

DEGREES OFFERED. AA, AS, AAS. 575 associate degrees awarded in 1992. 19% in business and management, 6% business/office and marketing/distribution, 6% computer sciences, 12% engineering technologies, 10% health sciences, 24% allied health, 7% multi/interdisciplinary studies.

UNDERGRADUATE MAJORS. Accounting, biology, business administration and management, business and management, business data processing and related programs, cardiovascular perfusion, ceramics, chemistry, civil technology, clinical laboratory science, dental hygiene, early childhood education, economics, education, electronic technology, engineering, engineering science, fine arts, fire control and safety technology, fluid power, geography, geology, graphic arts technology, health sciences, history, hotel/motel and restaurant management, industrial technology, information sciences and systems, law enforcement and corrections technologies, legal assistant/paralegal, legal secretary, liberal/general studies, manufacturing technology, mathematics, mechanical design technology, medical laboratory technologies, medical secretary, microcomputer software, music, nuclear medical technology, nursing, office supervision and management, philosophy, photography, physical sciences, physics, political science and government, protective services, psychology, public administration, quality control technology, radiograph medical technology, radiology, respiratory therapy technology, science technologies, social sciences, sociology, transportation and travel marketing, welding technology, word processing.

ACADEMIC PROGRAMS. 2-year transfer program, cooperative education, dual enrollment of high school students, independent study, telecourses, weekend college. **Remedial services:** Learning center, reduced course load, remedial instruction, special counselor, tutoring. **Placement/credit:** AP, CLEP General, institutional tests.

ACADEMIC REQUIREMENTS. Freshmen must earn minimum GPA of 2.0 to continue in good standing. Students must declare major on application. **Graduation requirements:** 96 hours for associate. Most students required to take courses in computer science, English, mathematics.

FRESHMAN ADMISSIONS. Selection criteria: Open admissions. Selective admissions to health technology programs based on test scores and school achievement record. Health technology programs require algebra and laboratory chemistry. **Test requirements:** SAT or ACT required for health technology programs; score report by April 1.

1992 FRESHMAN CLASS PROFILE. 1,029 men applied, 1,029 accepted, 614 enrolled; 1,612 women applied, 1,612 accepted, 779 enrolled. **Characteristics:** 99% from in state, 100% commute. Average age is 28.

FALL-TERM APPLICATIONS. $15 fee, may be waived for applicants with need. No closing date; applicants notified on a rolling basis. Early admission available.

STUDENT LIFE. Activities: Student government, radio, student newspaper, television, choral groups, concert band, drama, jazz band.

ATHLETICS. NJCAA. **Intercollegiate:** Baseball M, basketball, soccer M, softball W, volleyball W, wrestling M. **Intramural:** Basketball, racquetball, skiing, tennis, volleyball.

STUDENT SERVICES. Aptitude testing, career counseling, employment service for undergraduates, freshman orientation, health services, on-campus day care, personal counseling, placement service for graduates, veterans counselor, services/facilities for handicapped.

ANNUAL EXPENSES. Tuition and fees (1992-93): $1,671, $291 additional for out-of-district students, $2,295 additional for out-of-state students. **Books and supplies:** $456. **Other expenses:** $1,053.

FINANCIAL AID. 89% of grants, 21% of loans, 33% of jobs based on need. Academic, music/drama, art, athletic, state/district residency, minority scholarships available. **Aid applications:** No closing date; priority given to applications received by March 1; applicants notified on a rolling basis; must reply within 10 days. **Additional information:** Quarterly loans available for tuition only.

ADDRESS/TELEPHONE. William Kraus, Director for Admissions/Registrar, Lakeland Community College, 7700 Clocktower Drive, Mentor, OH 44060-7594. (216) 953-7100. Fax: (216) 953-7269.

Lima Technical College
Lima, Ohio CB code: 0754

2-year public technical college, coed. Founded in 1971. **Accreditation:** Regional. **Undergraduate enrollment:** 431 men, 1,065 women full time; 486 men, 768 women part time. **Faculty:** 142 total (80 full time), 3 with doctorates or other terminal degrees. **Location:** Suburban campus in large town; 75 miles from Dayton. **Calendar:** Quarter, limited summer session. Saturday and extensive evening/early morning classes. **Microcomputers:** Located in libraries, classrooms, computer centers.

DEGREES OFFERED. AAS. 445 associate degrees awarded in 1992. 21% in business and management, 14% business/office and marketing/distribution, 13% engineering technologies, 40% allied health, 5% home economics, 5% law.

UNDERGRADUATE MAJORS. Accounting, business and management, business and office, business data programming, child development/care/guidance, computer programming, dental hygiene, dietetic aide/assistant, drafting, drafting and design technology, early childhood development, electronic technology, emergency medical technologies, engineering and engineering-related technologies, fashion merchandising, finance, flexible manufacturing systems, food production/management/services, food science and nutrition, industrial technology, law enforcement and corrections technologies, legal assistant/paralegal, legal secretary, marketing and distribution, marketing management, mechanical design technology, medical secretary, nursing, office supervision and management, physical therapy assistant, quality control technology, radiograph medical technology, respiratory therapy technology, retailing, robotics, secretarial and related programs, trade and industrial supervision and management, word processing.

ACADEMIC PROGRAMS. Double major, dual enrollment of high school students, independent study, internships, student-designed major, telecourses, cross-registration. **Remedial services:** Learning center, preadmission summer program, reduced course load, remedial instruction, special counselor, tutoring. **Placement/credit:** Institutional tests; 13 credit hours maximum for associate degree.

ACADEMIC REQUIREMENTS. Freshmen must earn minimum GPA of 2.0 to continue in good standing. Students must declare major on application. **Graduation requirements:** 100 hours for associate. Most students required to take courses in English. **Additional information:** Associate of technical studies degree program offered, integrating technology and business.

FRESHMAN ADMISSIONS. Selection criteria: Open admissions. Selective admissions to health programs. **Test requirements:** ACT for placement and counseling only.

1992 FRESHMAN CLASS PROFILE. 1,767 men and women enrolled. **Characteristics:** 100% from in state, 100% commute, 6% have minority backgrounds. Average age is 27.

FALL-TERM APPLICATIONS. $10 fee. No closing date; applicants notified on a rolling basis. Interview recommended for health programs applicants. Early admission available.

STUDENT LIFE. Activities: Student government, radio, student newspaper, choral groups, drama, music ensembles, sports clubs, academic area organizations, political party clubs, campus ministry, fellowship and Bible study.

ATHLETICS. Intercollegiate: Baseball M, basketball, golf, tennis, volleyball W. **Intramural:** Baseball M, basketball, bowling, golf, racquetball, skiing, softball, tennis, volleyball.

STUDENT SERVICES. Aptitude testing, career counseling, employment service for undergraduates, freshman orientation, on-campus day care, placement service for graduates, services/facilities for handicapped.

ANNUAL EXPENSES. Tuition and fees (projected): $1,950, $1,950 additional for out-of-state students. **Books and supplies:** $900. **Other expenses:** $450.

FINANCIAL AID. 50% of freshmen, 55% of continuing students receive some form of aid. 99% of grants, 86% of loans, all jobs based on need. Academic scholarships available. **Aid applications:** Closing date March 15; applicants notified on or about May 1; must reply within 2 weeks.

ADDRESS/TELEPHONE. William D. Hussey, VP Student Services, Lima Technical College, 4240 Campus Drive, Lima, OH 45804. (419) 221-1112 ext. 280. Fax: (419) 221-0450.

Lorain County Community College
Elyria, Ohio CB code: 1417

2-year public community college, coed. Founded in 1963. **Accreditation:** Regional. **Undergraduate enrollment:** 995 men, 1,638 women full time; 1,669 men, 3,389 women part time. **Faculty:** 343 total (118 full time), 24 with doctorates or other terminal degrees. **Location:** Suburban campus in small city; 26 miles from Cleveland. **Calendar:** Quarter, extensive summer session. **Microcomputers:** 150 located in libraries, classrooms, computer centers. **Special facilities:** 1000-seat performing arts center, advanced technologies center.

DEGREES OFFERED. AA, AS, AAS. 586 associate degrees awarded in 1992. 6% in business and management, 15% business/office and marketing/distribution, 6% teacher education, 23% engineering technologies, 5% health sciences, 16% allied health, 19% multi/interdisciplinary studies.

UNDERGRADUATE MAJORS. Accounting, biological and physical sciences, biology, business and management, business and office, business data processing and related programs, business data programming, chemical manufacturing technology, chemistry, computer and information sciences, early childhood education, electromechanical technology, elementary education, engineering, finance, fine arts, fire control and safety technology, human resources development, humanities and social sciences, industrial technology, instrumentation technology, journalism, law enforcement and corrections technologies, liberal/general studies, marketing and distribution, mathematics, mechanical design technology, mechanical engineering, medical laboratory technologies, music, music education, nuclear medical technology, nursing, physics, prelaw, premedicine, prepharmacy, preveterinary, psychology, quality control technology, radiograph medical technology, real estate, robotics, science technologies, secondary education, secretarial and related programs, social sciences, social studies education, sports medicine, tourism, visual and performing arts.

ACADEMIC PROGRAMS. 2-year transfer program, cooperative education, dual enrollment of high school students, independent study, study abroad, telecourses, weekend college. **Remedial services:** Learning center, preadmission summer program, reduced course load, remedial instruction, special counselor, tutoring. **Placement/credit:** AP, CLEP General and Subject, institutional tests; 30 credit hours maximum for associate degree.

ACADEMIC REQUIREMENTS. No policy requiring minimum GPA; records of students having academic difficulty are reviewed individually. 78% of freshmen return for sophomore year. **Graduation requirements:** 93 hours for associate (45 in major). Most students required to take courses in English, mathematics, biological/physical sciences, social sciences.

FRESHMAN ADMISSIONS. Selection criteria: Open admissions. **Test requirements:** SAT or ACT for placement and counseling only; score report by September 10.

1992 FRESHMAN CLASS PROFILE. 817 men, 1,322 women enrolled. **Characteristics:** 99% from in state, 100% commute, 6% have minority backgrounds, 1% are foreign students. Average age is 26.

FALL-TERM APPLICATIONS. $10 fee, may be waived for applicants with need. Closing date September 15; priority given to applications received by August 1; applicants notified on a rolling basis beginning on or about April 15. Deferred and early admission available.

STUDENT LIFE. Activities: Student government, film, student newspaper, television, literary magazine, choral groups, concert band, drama, jazz band, music ensembles, musical theater, symphony orchestra, forensics, Black Progressives, Los Unidos, Newman club, Christian Fellowship, Student Nurses Association, Phi Theta Kappa.

ATHLETICS. Intramural: Archery, badminton, basketball, bowling, cross-country, golf, racquetball, rifle, soccer, softball, tennis, volleyball.

STUDENT SERVICES. Aptitude testing, career counseling, employment service for undergraduates, freshman orientation, health services, on-campus day care, personal counseling, placement service for graduates, veterans counselor, services/facilities for handicapped.

ANNUAL EXPENSES. Tuition and fees (1992-93): $2,003, $450 additional for out-of-district students, $3,150 additional for out-of-state students. **Books and supplies:** $580. **Other expenses:** $950.

FINANCIAL AID. 34% of freshmen, 40% of continuing students receive some form of aid. 83% of grants, 94% of loans, 16% of jobs based on need. 834 enrolled freshmen were judged to have need, all were offered aid. Academic scholarships available. **Aid applications:** No closing date; applicants notified on a rolling basis beginning on or about September 17; must reply within 3 weeks.

ADDRESS/TELEPHONE. Dr. John Thrash, Jr, Director of Student Development, Transfer, and Placement, Lorain County Community College, 1005 North Abbe Road, Elyria, OH 44035-1697. (216) 365-4191. (800) 995-5222. Fax: (216) 365-4191.

Lourdes College
Sylvania, Ohio

CB code: 1427

4-year private liberal arts college, coed, affiliated with Roman Catholic Church. Founded in 1958. **Accreditation:** Regional. **Undergraduate enrollment:** 59 men, 304 women full time; 174 men, 932 women part time. **Faculty:** 138 total (63 full time), 28 with doctorates or other terminal degrees. **Location:** Suburban campus in large town; 10 miles from Toledo. **Calendar:** Semester, limited summer session. **Microcomputers:** 25 located in computer centers. **Special facilities:** Planetarium, nature preserve, art collections throughout campus halls.

DEGREES OFFERED. AA, AAS, BA, BS. 29 associate degrees awarded in 1992. 59% in allied health, 33% social sciences. 101 bachelor's degrees awarded. 45% in business and management, 24% health sciences, 8% psychology, 16% social sciences.

UNDERGRADUATE MAJORS. Associate: Art history, Bible studies, biological and physical sciences, biology, business and management, chemistry, child development/care/guidance, drawing, English, fiber/textiles/weaving, fine arts, French, gerontology, graphic arts technology, history, liberal/general studies, music, occupational therapy assistant, painting, printmaking, psychology, recreation and community services technologies, religion, sculpture, social sciences, social work, sociology, Spanish, studio art, teacher aide, theological studies. **Bachelor's:** Art history, Bible studies, biological and physical sciences, biology, business and management, chemistry, child development/care/guidance, English, fine arts, French, gerontology, history, human resources development, liberal/general studies, nursing, organizational behavior, personnel management, psychology, religion, small business management and ownership, social sciences, social work, sociology, theological studies.

ACADEMIC PROGRAMS. Double major, dual enrollment of high school students, independent study, internships, student-designed major, teacher preparation, weekend college; liberal arts/career combination in business. **Remedial services:** Learning center, reduced course load, remedial instruction, special counselor. **Placement/credit:** AP, CLEP General and Subject, institutional tests; 15 credit hours maximum for associate degree; 30 credit hours maximum for bachelor's degree.

ACADEMIC REQUIREMENTS. Freshmen must earn minimum GPA of 2.0 to continue in good standing. 85% of freshmen return for sophomore year. Students must declare major by end of second year. **Graduation requirements:** 64 hours for associate (24 in major), 128 hours for bachelor's (45 in major). Most students required to take courses in arts/fine arts, English, history, mathematics, philosophy/religion, biological/physical sciences, social sciences. **Postgraduate studies:** 90% from 2-year programs enter 4-year programs. 1% enter medical school, 1% enter MBA programs, 2% enter other graduate study.

FRESHMAN ADMISSIONS. Selection criteria: High school GPA, ACT or SAT scores, and interview most important. **High school preparation:** 14 units required; 19 recommended. Required and recommended units include English 4, mathematics 3, social science 3 and science 3. Foreign language 2 recommended. One unit fine or performing arts also recommended. **Test requirements:** SAT or ACT (ACT preferred); score report by August 15. **Additional information:** Special admission available for freshman with low GPA and high test scores (ACT/SAT) or low test scores and high GPA.

1992 FRESHMAN CLASS PROFILE. 93 men, 509 women enrolled. 33% had high school GPA of 3.0 or higher, 47% between 2.0 and 2.99. **Academic background:** Mid 50% of enrolled freshmen had ACT composite between 17-22. 88% submitted ACT scores. **Characteristics:** 93% from in state, 100% commute, 2% have minority backgrounds. Average age is 23.

FALL-TERM APPLICATIONS. $20 fee, may be waived for applicants with need. Closing date August 15; applicants notified on a rolling basis. Portfolio required for art applicants. Interview recommended. Essay recommended. CRDA. Deferred and early admission available.

STUDENT LIFE. Activities: Student government, student newspaper, choral groups, music ensembles, sororities, Theta Alpha Kappa (religious studies honor society), Phi Theta Kappa, Kappa Gamma Pi (Catholic College Graduate Honor Society), The Networker (social work). **Additional information:** Variety of art, music, and lecture series offered.

ATHLETICS. Intramural: Basketball, volleyball.

STUDENT SERVICES. Career counseling, freshman orientation, personal counseling, placement service for graduates, services/facilities for handicapped.

ANNUAL EXPENSES. Tuition and fees: $6,410. **Books and supplies:** $500. **Other expenses:** $682.

FINANCIAL AID. 29% of freshmen, 32% of continuing students receive some form of aid. All grants, 85% of loans, all jobs based on need. State/district residency scholarships available. **Aid applications:** No closing date; priority given to applications received by March 1; applicants notified on a rolling basis beginning on or about April 15; must reply within 30 days.

ADDRESS/TELEPHONE. Mary Ellen Briggs, Director of Admissions, Lourdes College, 6832 Convent Boulevard, Sylvania, OH 43560-2898. (419) 885-5291. (800) 878-3210. Fax: (419) 882-3987 ext. 299.

Malone College
Canton, Ohio

CB code: 1439

Admissions:		96% of applicants accepted
Based on:	•••	School record
	••	Activities, essay, recommendations, religious affiliation/commitment, test scores
	•	Interview, special talents
Completion:		85% of freshmen end year in good standing
		40% graduate, 8% of these enter graduate study

4-year private college of arts and sciences, coed, affiliated with Evangelical Friends Church. Founded in 1892. **Accreditation:** Regional. **Undergraduate enrollment:** 549 men, 889 women full time; 64 men, 201 women part time. **Graduate enrollment:** 19 men, 72 women part time. **Faculty:** 152 total (79 full time), 41 with doctorates or other terminal degrees. **Location:** Suburban campus in small city; 60 miles from Cleveland, 20 miles from Akron. **Calendar:** Semester, limited summer session. Saturday classes. **Microcomputers:** 59 located in libraries, classrooms, computer centers. **Special facilities:** National Football Hall of Fame, Canton Players Guild, Weaver Child Development Center. **Additional facts:** Interdenominational Christian environment. Reciprocal course agreement with Stark Technical College.

DEGREES OFFERED. AA, BA, BS, MA. 3 associate degrees awarded in 1992. 100% in teacher education. 338 bachelor's degrees awarded. 56% in business and management, 16% teacher education, 7% health sciences. Graduate degrees offered in 7 major fields of study.

UNDERGRADUATE MAJORS. Associate: Early childhood education. **Bachelor's:** Accounting, allied health, art education, Bible studies, biology, business administration and management, business and management, business education, chemistry, communications, computer and information sciences, elementary education, English, English education, fine arts, health education, history, journalism, liberal/general studies, mathematics, mathematics education, medical laboratory technologies, music, music education, music performance, nurse anesthetist, nursing, physical education, predentistry, prelaw, premedicine, prepharmacy, preveterinary, psychology, radio/television broadcasting, religion, religious education, religious music, science education, secondary education, social science education, social sciences, social studies education, social work, Spanish, specific learning disabilities, speech/communication/theater education, sports medicine, studio art, theological studies.

ACADEMIC PROGRAMS. Cooperative education, double major, dual enrollment of high school students, independent study, internships, student-designed major, study abroad, teacher preparation, visiting/exchange student program, Washington semester. **Remedial services:** Learning center, reduced course load, remedial instruction, special counselor, tutoring, freshman entry program for underprepared students. **Placement/credit:** AP, CLEP General and Subject, institutional tests; 20 credit hours maximum for bachelor's degree.

ACADEMIC REQUIREMENTS. Freshmen must earn minimum GPA of 2.0 to continue in good standing. 71% of freshmen return for sophomore year. Students must declare major by end of second year. **Graduation requirements:** 63 hours for associate, 124 hours for bachelor's (36 in major). Most students required to take courses in arts/fine arts, computer science, English, history, humanities, mathematics, philosophy/religion, biological/physical sciences, social sciences. **Postgraduate studies:** 2% enter law school, 1% enter medical school, 1% enter MBA programs, 4% enter other graduate study.

FRESHMAN ADMISSIONS. Selection criteria: High school record, test scores and recommendations most important. Interview also considered and encoruraged. **High school preparation:** 16 units recommended. Recommended units include English 4, foreign language 2, mathematics 3, social science 3 and science 3. One fine arts recommended. **Test requirements:** SAT or ACT (ACT preferred); score report by August 1.

1992 FRESHMAN CLASS PROFILE. 233 men applied, 227 accepted, 125 enrolled; 404 women applied, 385 accepted, 228 enrolled. 53% had high school GPA of 3.0 or higher, 46% between 2.0 and 2.99. 24% were in top tenth and 52% were in top quarter of graduating class. **Academic background:** Mid 50% of enrolled freshmen had SAT-V between 390-510, SAT-M between 420-570; ACT composite between 18-24. 11% submitted SAT scores, 92% submitted ACT scores. **Characteristics:** 94% from in state, 80% live in college housing, 2% have minority backgrounds. Average age is 18.

FALL-TERM APPLICATIONS. $20 fee, may be waived for applicants with need. No closing date; applicants notified on a rolling basis. Audition required for music applicants. Essay required. Interview recommended. CRDA. Deferred and early admission available.

STUDENT LIFE. Housing: Dormitories (men, women, coed); apartment housing available. Students required to live on campus unless 21 or older or commuting from home. Exceptions considered. **Activities:** Student government, film, magazine, radio, student newspaper, television, yearbook, choral groups, concert band, drama, jazz band, music ensembles, musical theater, pep band, interdenominational religious fellowship, Circle-K, Unity Under Christ, World Christian Coalition, Nurses Christian Fellowship, Habitat for Humanity, World Awareness & Social Issues Committee. **Additional information:** Christian institution with conservative campus lifestyle.

ATHLETICS. NAIA. **Intercollegiate:** Baseball M, basketball, cross-country, football M, golf M, soccer M, softball W, tennis, track and field, volleyball W. **Intramural:** Basketball, bowling, cross-country, racquetball, skiing, softball, table tennis, tennis, volleyball.

STUDENT SERVICES. Aptitude testing, career counseling, employment service for undergraduates, freshman orientation, health services, on-campus day care, personal counseling, placement service for graduates, special adviser for adult students, veterans counselor, services/facilities for handicapped.

ANNUAL EXPENSES. Tuition and fees: $9,172. **Room and board:** $3,400. **Books and supplies:** $450. **Other expenses:** $800.

FINANCIAL AID. 92% of freshmen, 68% of continuing students receive some form of aid. 64% of grants, 92% of loans, all jobs based on need. Academic, music/drama, athletic, state/district residency, leadership, religious affiliation scholarships available. **Aid applications:** Closing date July 31; priority given to applications received by March 31; applicants notified on a rolling basis beginning on or about March 3; must reply within 2 weeks.

ADDRESS/TELEPHONE. Lee J. Sommers, Dean of Admissions, Malone College, 515 25th Street Northwest, Canton, OH 44709-3897. (216) 471-8145. (800) 521-1146. Fax: (216) 454-6977.

Marietta College
Marietta, Ohio

CB code: 1444

Admissions:	60% of applicants accepted
Based on:	••• School record
	•• Recommendations, test scores
	• Activities, essay, interview, special talents
Completion:	88% of freshmen end year in good standing
	65% graduate, 13% of these enter graduate study

4-year private liberal arts college, coed. Founded in 1835. **Accreditation:** Regional. **Undergraduate enrollment:** 585 men, 508 women full time; 92 men, 132 women part time. **Graduate enrollment:** 13 men, 49 women part time. **Faculty:** 110 total (76 full time), 56 with doctorates or other terminal degrees. **Location:** Suburban campus in small city; 114 miles from Columbus. **Calendar:** Semester, limited summer session. Saturday and extensive evening/early morning classes. **Microcomputers:** 150 located in libraries, classrooms, computer centers. **Special facilities:** 14 operational oil wells, observatory, geology field station, natural gas laboratory, special collections library.

DEGREES OFFERED. AA, BA, BS, BFA, MA, MEd. 1 associate degree awarded in 1992. 100% in business and management. 265 bachelor's degrees awarded. 20% in business and management, 11% communications, 10% education, 6% engineering, 11% health sciences, 5% letters/literature, 7% life sciences, 7% psychology, 8% social sciences, 5% visual and performing arts. Graduate degrees offered in 3 major fields of study.

UNDERGRADUATE MAJORS. Associate: Business administration and management, liberal/general studies. **Bachelor's:** Accounting, advertising, allied health, applied mathematics, arts management, behavioral sciences, biochemistry, biological and physical sciences, biology, business administration and management, business and management, business communications, business economics, chemistry, computer and information sciences, computer mathematics, computer programming, dramatic arts, economics, education, elementary education, engineering, engineering and other disciplines, English, fine arts, forestry and related sciences, French, geology, history, human resources development, industrial engineering, information sciences and systems, international business management, journalism, liberal/general studies, marketing and distribution, marketing management, mathematics, music, petroleum engineering, philosophy, physics, political science and government, predentistry, prelaw, premedicine, prepharmacy, preveterinary, psychology, public relations, radio/television broadcasting, religion, renewable natural resources, secondary education, social sciences, Spanish, speech, sports medicine, studio art.

ACADEMIC PROGRAMS. Accelerated program, double major, dual enrollment of high school students, honors program, independent study, internships, semester at sea, student-designed major, study abroad, teacher preparation, visiting/exchange student program, Washington semester; liberal arts/career combination in engineering, forestry, health sciences. **Remedial services:** Preadmission summer program, reduced course load, remedial instruction, tutoring, writing laboratory, mathematics laboratory. **ROTC:** Army. **Placement/credit:** AP, CLEP General and Subject, institutional tests; 36 credit hours maximum for bachelor's degree.

ACADEMIC REQUIREMENTS. Freshmen must earn minimum GPA of 1.8 to continue in good standing. 78% of freshmen return for sophomore year. Students must declare major by end of second year. **Graduation requirements:** 60 hours for associate, 124 hours for bachelor's (30 in major). Most students required to take courses in arts/fine arts, English, humanities, mathematics, biological/physical sciences, social sciences. **Postgraduate studies:** 98% from 2-year programs enter 4-year programs. 1% enter law school, 3% enter medical school, 2% enter MBA programs, 7% enter other graduate study.

FRESHMAN ADMISSIONS. Selection criteria: High school curriculum, high school GPA, activities, recommendation, essay, test scores strongly considered. **High school preparation:** 13 units required; 15 recommended. Required and recommended units include English 4, mathematics 3, social science 3 and science 3. Foreign language 2 recommended. **Test requirements:** SAT or ACT; score report by August 1.

1992 FRESHMAN CLASS PROFILE. 1,078 men applied, 583 accepted, 220 enrolled; 565 women applied, 400 accepted, 150 enrolled. 65% had high school GPA of 3.0 or higher, 35% between 2.0 and 2.99. 27% were in top tenth and 51% were in top quarter of graduating class. **Academic background:** Mid 50% of enrolled freshmen had SAT-V between 430-540, SAT-M between 480-590; ACT composite between 21-26. 62% submitted SAT scores, 69% submitted ACT scores. **Characteristics:** 48% from in state, 94% live in college housing, 3% have minority backgrounds, 1% are foreign students, 36% join fraternities/sororities. Average age is 18.

FALL-TERM APPLICATIONS. $25 fee, may be waived for applicants with need. No closing date; applicants notified on a rolling basis; must reply by May 1 or within 4 weeks if notified thereafter. Essay required. Interview recommended. CRDA. Deferred and early admission available. EDP-F.

STUDENT LIFE. Housing: Dormitories (men, women, coed); fraternity, sorority housing available. Honors housing available. **Activities:** Student government, magazine, radio, student newspaper, television, yearbook, choral groups, concert band, drama, jazz band, music ensembles, musical theater, pep band, symphony orchestra, fraternities, sororities, Students for Environmental Action, Christian Fellowship, international student organization, public affairs forum, Bacchus-Alcohol Awareness, Democratic Club, Republican Club, Amnesty International.

ATHLETICS. NCAA. **Intercollegiate:** Baseball M, basketball, football M, golf M, lacrosse M, rowing (crew), soccer, softball W, tennis, volleyball W. **Intramural:** Baseball M, basketball, bowling, cross-country, football M, golf, handball, ice hockey M, lacrosse W, racquetball, rowing (crew), rugby M, soccer, softball, swimming, volleyball.

STUDENT SERVICES. Aptitude testing, career counseling, employment service for undergraduates, freshman orientation, health services, personal counseling, placement service for graduates, special adviser for adult students, veterans counselor, special freshmen advisers, services/facilities for handicapped.

ANNUAL EXPENSES. Tuition and fees: $13,170. **Room and board:** $3,770. **Books and supplies:** $430. **Other expenses:** $350.

FINANCIAL AID. 89% of freshmen, 83% of continuing students receive some form of aid. 96% of grants, 98% of loans, all jobs based on need. 163 enrolled freshmen were judged to have need, all were offered aid. Academic, music/drama, art scholarships available. **Aid applications:** No closing date; priority given to applications received by May 1; applicants notified on a rolling basis beginning on or about March 15; must reply by May 1 or within 2 weeks if notified thereafter.

ADDRESS/TELEPHONE. Dennis R. DePerro, Dean of Admission and Financial Aid, Marietta College, Fifth Street, Marietta, OH 45750-4005. (614) 374-4600. (800) 331-7896. Fax: (614) 374-4896.

Marion Technical College
Marion, Ohio — CB code: 0699

2-year public technical college, coed. Founded in 1971. **Accreditation:** Regional. **Undergraduate enrollment:** 234 men, 556 women full time; 304 men, 604 women part time. **Faculty:** 105 total (36 full time). **Location:** Suburban campus in large town; 45 miles from Columbus. **Calendar:** Quarter, limited summer session. Saturday and extensive evening/early morning classes. **Microcomputers:** 111 located in classrooms, computer centers. **Additional facts:** Common campus and some shared facilities with Ohio State University: Marion.

DEGREES OFFERED. AAS. 220 associate degrees awarded in 1992. 30% in business and management, 20% computer sciences, 10% engineering technologies, 37% health sciences.

UNDERGRADUATE MAJORS. Accounting, business and management, data processing, electrical technology, electronic technology, engineering and engineering-related technologies, finance, industrial technology, legal assistant/paralegal, marketing management, mechanical design technology, medical laboratory technologies, medical secretary, microcomputer software, multi-disciplinary studies, nursing.

ACADEMIC PROGRAMS. 2-year transfer program, double major, dual enrollment of high school students, independent study, student-designed major, weekend college. **Remedial services:** Learning center, reduced course load, remedial instruction, tutoring, developmental tutoring. **Placement/credit:** Institutional tests; 24 credit hours maximum for associate degree.

ACADEMIC REQUIREMENTS. Freshmen must earn minimum GPA of 2.0 to continue in good standing. Students must declare major on enrollment. **Graduation requirements:** 98 hours for associate. Most students required to take courses in computer science, English, social sciences.

FRESHMAN ADMISSIONS. Selection criteria: Open admissions. Selective admission to health technology programs. ACT scores required for health program applicants. Recommended units include English 4, foreign language 2, mathematics 2, social science 1 and science 2. Algebra, biology, and chemistry required for health technology applicants. Algebra required, physics recommended for engineering applicants. **Test requirements:** ACT required of health applicants for admissions, placement, and counseling; recommended for all other applicants for counseling.

1992 FRESHMAN CLASS PROFILE. 430 men, 795 women enrolled. **Characteristics:** 98% from in state, 100% commute, 4% have minority backgrounds. Average age is 30.

FALL-TERM APPLICATIONS. $10 fee, may be waived for applicants with need. No closing date; priority given to applications received by June 1; applicants notified on a rolling basis beginning on or about January 1. Interview required for health technologies, paralegal applicants. Early admission available. Placement testing in English and mathematics computation recommended for all applicants. ACT scores required for applicants to Health Programs. ASSET test required for applicants to paralegal program.

STUDENT LIFE. Activities: Student government, student newspaper, choral groups, Joint Activities Committee, Student Admission Committee, Campus Christian Fellowship, Program of Outdoor Pursuits Club, Cultural Arts Program. **Additional information:** Share campus and activities with the Ohio State University: Marion Branch.

ATHLETICS. Intercollegiate: Basketball, cross-country, golf, rugby M, soccer M, track and field, volleyball. **Intramural:** Archery, baseball M, basketball, cross-country, golf, handball, horseback riding, racquetball, rowing (crew), rugby, sailing, skiing, soccer, softball, swimming, table tennis, tennis, track and field, volleyball.

STUDENT SERVICES. Career counseling, employment service for undergraduates, freshman orientation, on-campus day care, placement service for graduates, special adviser for adult students, veterans counselor, services/facilities for handicapped.

ANNUAL EXPENSES. Tuition and fees: $2,160, $1,584 additional for out-of-state students. **Books and supplies:** $500.

FINANCIAL AID. 65% of freshmen, 65% of continuing students receive some form of aid. 95% of grants, 93% of loans, 41% of jobs based on need. 350 enrolled freshmen were judged to have need, 300 were offered aid. Academic, leadership, minority scholarships available. **Aid applications:** No closing date; priority given to applications received by July 1; applicants notified on a rolling basis beginning on or about July 15; must reply within 2 weeks.

ADDRESS/TELEPHONE. Joel Liles, Director of Admission/Career Services, Marion Technical College, 1467 Mount Vernon Avenue, Marion, OH 43302-5694. (614) 389-4636. Fax: (614) 389-6136.

Miami University: Hamilton Campus
Hamilton, Ohio — CB code: 1526

2-year public branch campus college, coed. Founded in 1968. **Accreditation:** Regional. **Undergraduate enrollment:** 307 men, 486 women full time. **Faculty:** 155 total (85 full time). **Location:** Urban campus in small city; 25 miles from Cincinnati. **Calendar:** Semester, limited summer session. Extensive evening/early morning classes. **Microcomputers:** 60 located in classrooms, computer centers.

DEGREES OFFERED. AA, AAS. 70 associate degrees awarded in 1992. 10% in business and management, 10% computer sciences, 10% engineering technologies, 70% health sciences.

UNDERGRADUATE MAJORS. Accounting, business and management, computer and information sciences, computer technology, drafting, electrical technology, electromechanical technology, engineering and engineering-related technologies, law enforcement and corrections technologies, liberal/general studies, management information systems, marketing management, nursing, office supervision and management, public affairs, secretarial and related programs.

ACADEMIC PROGRAMS. 2-year transfer program, cooperative education, double major, dual enrollment of high school students, honors program, independent study, study abroad, teacher preparation, cross-registration. **Remedial services:** Learning center, remedial instruction, special counselor, tutoring, learning assistance program. **ROTC:** Air Force, Naval. **Placement/credit:** AP, CLEP Subject, institutional tests; 32 credit hours maximum for associate degree.

ACADEMIC REQUIREMENTS. Freshmen must earn minimum GPA of 1.7 to continue in good standing. 60% of freshmen return for sophomore year. Students must declare major by end of first year. **Graduation requirements:** 64 hours for associate. Most students required to take courses in arts/fine arts, English, foreign languages, history, humanities, mathematics, philosophy/religion, biological/physical sciences, social sciences. **Additional information:** Some upper-division courses in education offered.

FRESHMAN ADMISSIONS. Selection criteria: Open admissions. Selective admissions to nursing program. **High school preparation:** 17 units recommended. Recommended units include biological science 3, English 4, foreign language 2, mathematics 3 and physical science 3. One fine arts also recommended. **Test requirements:** SAT or ACT for placement and counseling only; score report by August 1. SAT or ACT required for admission to nursing program. **Additional information:** Interviews recommended for all.

1992 FRESHMAN CLASS PROFILE. 337 men, 430 women enrolled. **Characteristics:** 99% from in state, 100% commute, 3% have minority backgrounds. Average age is 23.

FALL-TERM APPLICATIONS. $25 fee. No closing date; priority given to applications received by August 1; applicants notified on a rolling basis. Interview recommended for nursing applicants. CRDA. Priority date for nursing applicants February 1.

STUDENT LIFE. Activities: Student government, choral groups, drama, musical theater, service organizations, student nurse association, recycling group, adult association.

ATHLETICS. Intercollegiate: Basketball, golf M, tennis. **Intramural:** Baseball, basketball, golf, soccer, softball, table tennis, tennis, volleyball.

STUDENT SERVICES. Aptitude testing, career counseling, employment service for undergraduates, freshman orientation, on-campus day care, personal counseling, placement service for graduates, veterans counselor, services/facilities for handicapped.

ANNUAL EXPENSES. Tuition and fees (1992-93): $2,932, $4,590

additional for out-of-state students. **Books and supplies:** $480. **Other expenses:** $1,134.

FINANCIAL AID. 16% of freshmen, 40% of continuing students receive some form of aid. 94% of grants, 82% of loans, 14% of jobs based on need. 179 enrolled freshmen were judged to have need, 142 were offered aid. Academic, state/district residency, leadership, minority scholarships available. **Aid applications:** No closing date; priority given to applications received by February 15; applicants notified on a rolling basis beginning on or about April 1; must reply by May 1 or within 2 weeks if notified thereafter. **Additional information:** Special gift funds for needy, full-time black students who enter with appropriate academic record. No student need apply for admission prior to filing a financial aid application. Separate application required for scholarships, closing date January 31.

ADDRESS/TELEPHONE. T. Michael Smithson, Director of Admission and Financial Aid, Miami University: Hamilton Campus, 1601 Peck Boulevard, Hamilton, OH 45011. (513) 863-8833. Fax: (513) 863-1655.

Miami University: Middletown Campus
Middletown, Ohio — CB code: 1509

2-year public branch campus college, coed. Founded in 1963. **Accreditation:** Regional. **Undergraduate enrollment:** 2,333 men and women. **Graduate enrollment:** 40 men and women part time. **Faculty:** 61 total, 17 with doctorates or other terminal degrees. **Location:** Suburban campus in large town; 30 miles from Cincinnati, 20 miles from Dayton. **Calendar:** Semester, extensive summer session. **Microcomputers:** Located in classrooms, computer centers. **Special facilities:** Nature trail, government document collection (35,458 titles), 6800 audio-visual titles.

DEGREES OFFERED. AA, AS, AAS.

UNDERGRADUATE MAJORS. Accounting, business and management, business and office, business computer/console/peripheral equipment operation, business data programming, computer technology, electrical technology, English, finance, humanities and social sciences, liberal/general studies, marketing and distribution, mechanical design technology, nursing, secretarial and related programs.

ACADEMIC PROGRAMS. 2-year transfer program, double major, dual enrollment of high school students, independent study, internships, study abroad, teacher preparation, cross-registration. **Remedial services:** Learning center, preadmission summer program, reduced course load, remedial instruction, special counselor, tutoring. **ROTC:** Air Force, Army, Naval. **Placement/credit:** AP, CLEP Subject, institutional tests; 32 credit hours maximum for associate degree.

ACADEMIC REQUIREMENTS. Freshmen must earn minimum GPA of 1.7 to continue in good standing. 55% of freshmen return for sophomore year. Students must declare major on enrollment. **Graduation requirements:** 64 hours for associate (12 in major). Most students required to take courses in English, humanities, mathematics, biological/physical sciences, social sciences. **Additional information:** Upper-division courses offered in education.

FRESHMAN ADMISSIONS. Selection criteria: Open admissions. Special admission requirements for nursing program. Recommended units include English 4, foreign language 2, mathematics 3, social science 3 and science 3. One fine arts also recommended. **Test requirements:** SAT or ACT for placement and counseling only; score report by August 30.

1992 FRESHMAN CLASS PROFILE. 1,000 men and women enrolled. **Academic background:** Mid 50% of enrolled freshmen had ACT composite between 14-21. 60% submitted ACT scores. **Characteristics:** 99% from in state, 100% commute, 2% have minority backgrounds. Average age is 25.

FALL-TERM APPLICATIONS. $25 fee, may be waived for applicants with need. No closing date; applicants notified on a rolling basis beginning on or about January 1. Interview recommended for nursing applicants. Deferred and early admission available. Nursing applicants must apply by April 1.

STUDENT LIFE. Activities: Student government, radio, student newspaper, choral groups, drama, black student association, Model United Nations.

ATHLETICS. Intercollegiate: Basketball, golf M, tennis, volleyball W. **Intramural:** Badminton, basketball, bowling, golf, racquetball, softball, table tennis, tennis, volleyball.

STUDENT SERVICES. Aptitude testing, career counseling, employment service for undergraduates, freshman orientation, on-campus day care, personal counseling, placement service for graduates, special adviser for adult students, veterans counselor, services/facilities for handicapped.

ANNUAL EXPENSES. Tuition and fees (projected): $3,262, $5,222 additional for out-of-state students. **Books and supplies:** $500. **Other expenses:** $1,198.

FINANCIAL AID. 25% of freshmen, 35% of continuing students receive some form of aid. All grants, 84% of loans, all jobs based on need. 280 enrolled freshmen were judged to have need, 165 were offered aid. Academic, state/district residency, leadership, minority scholarships available. **Aid applications:** No closing date; priority given to applications received by March 1; applicants notified on a rolling basis beginning on or about April 10; must reply within 2 weeks.

ADDRESS/TELEPHONE. Mary Lu Flynn, Director of Admissions, Miami University: Middletown Campus, 4200 East University Blvd, Middletown, OH 45042. (513) 424-4444. Fax: (513) 424-4632.

Miami University: Oxford Campus
Oxford, Ohio — CB code: 1463

Admissions: 79% of applicants accepted
Based on: ••• School record, test scores
• Activities, essay, recommendations, special talents
Completion: 95% of freshmen end year in good standing
80% graduate

4-year public university, coed. Founded in 1809. **Accreditation:** Regional. **Undergraduate enrollment:** 6,868 men, 7,820 women full time; 624 men, 939 women part time. **Graduate enrollment:** 472 men, 480 women full time; 246 men, 532 women part time. **Faculty:** 1,027 total (858 full time), 823 with doctorates or other terminal degrees. **Location:** Rural campus in small town; 35 miles from Cincinnati, 46 miles from Dayton. **Calendar:** Semester, extensive summer session. **Microcomputers:** 512 located in dormitories, computer centers. **Special facilities:** Art museum, museum-home of William Holmes McGuffey.

DEGREES OFFERED. AA, BA, BS, BFA, MA, MS, MBA, MFA, MEd, PhD. 219 associate degrees awarded in 1992. 3,420 bachelor's degrees awarded. 25% in business and management, 14% business/office and marketing/distribution, 7% communications, 10% teacher education, 6% psychology, 13% social sciences. Graduate degrees offered in 64 major fields of study.

UNDERGRADUATE MAJORS. Associate: Liberal/general studies. **Bachelor's:** Accounting, Afro-American (black) studies, American studies, anthropology, art education, art history, botany, business administration and management, business and management, business economics, business statistics, chemistry, classics, communications, contract management and procurement/purchasing, creative writing, dramatic arts, economics, elementary education, engineering physics, English education, English literature, environmental design, family/consumer resource management, finance, fine arts, food management, food production/management/services, food science and nutrition, foreign languages education, French, geography, geology, German, Greek (classical), health education, history, home economics, home economics education, human environment and housing, institutional/home management/supporting programs, interior design, international relations, international studies, journalism, Latin, liberal/general studies, linguistics, Management engineering, management information systems, manufacturing technology, marketing and distribution, mathematics, mathematics education, medical laboratory technologies, microbiology, music, music education, nursing, office supervision and management, organizational behavior, paper engineering, personnel management, philosophy, physical education, physics, political science and government, psychology, public administration, public relations, radio/television broadcasting, radio/television technology, religion, retailing, Russian, science education, secondary education, social science education, social studies education, sociology, Spanish, special education, speech, speech correction, speech pathology/audiology, sports management, statistics, systems analysis, technical and business writing, urban studies, zoology.

ACADEMIC PROGRAMS. 2-year transfer program, cooperative education, double major, dual enrollment of high school students, education specialist degree, honors program, independent study, internships, student-designed major, study abroad, teacher preparation, visiting/exchange student program, cross-registration; liberal arts/career combination in engineering, forestry. **Remedial services:** Learning center, special counselor, tutoring, Academic Enhancement Program. **ROTC:** Air Force, Naval. **Placement/credit:** AP, CLEP Subject, IB, institutional tests; 32 credit hours maximum for bachelor's degree.

ACADEMIC REQUIREMENTS. Freshmen must earn minimum GPA of 1.7 to continue in good standing. 92% of freshmen return for sophomore year. Students must declare major by end of second year. **Graduation requirements:** 128 hours for bachelor's (64 in major). Most students required to take courses in arts/fine arts, English, humanities, mathematics, biological/physical sciences, social sciences.

FRESHMAN ADMISSIONS. Selection criteria: High school achievement record, test scores, extracurricular activities, and recommendations most important. Out-of-state students limited to 30% of freshmen class. **High school preparation:** 16 units required. Required units include biological science 1, English 4, foreign language 2, mathematics 3, physical science 2 and social science 3. One fine or performing arts also required. **Test requirements:** SAT or ACT; score report by February 28.

1992 FRESHMAN CLASS PROFILE. 9,102 men and women applied, 7,195 accepted; 1,347 men enrolled, 1,675 women enrolled. 41% were in top tenth and 78% were in top quarter of graduating class. **Academic background:** Mid 50% of enrolled freshmen had SAT-V between 480-570, SAT-M between 550-650; ACT composite between 24-28. 47% submitted SAT scores, 52% submitted ACT scores. **Characteristics:** 73% from in state, 97%

live in college housing, 6% have minority backgrounds, 1% are foreign students, 40% join fraternities/sororities. Average age is 18.

FALL-TERM APPLICATIONS. $30 fee, may be waived for applicants with need. Closing date January 31; applicants notified on or about March 15; must reply by May 1. Audition required for music, theater applicants. Portfolio required for art, architecture applicants. Essay recommended. CRDA. Deferred admission available. EDP-F. Dates for early decision plan: deadline for application November 1, notification by December 15, confirmation by January 15. Oates for early notification plan: application December 1, notification February 1, confirmation May 1.

STUDENT LIFE. Housing: Dormitories (men, women, coed); apartment, fraternity, handicapped housing available. All first year students live in first year student halls. Special arrangements include sorority suites in residence halls, honors hall, and international hall. **Activities:** Student government, magazine, radio, student newspaper, television, yearbook, student-run advertising agency, choral groups, concert band, dance, drama, jazz band, marching band, music ensembles, musical theater, opera, pep band, symphony orchestra, fraternities, sororities, Miami Service Network, Minority Affairs Council, United Campus Ministries, Black Student Association, Miami Student Foundation, Association of International Students.

ATHLETICS. NCAA. **Intercollegiate:** Archery, baseball M, basketball, cross-country, diving, fencing, field hockey W, football M, golf M, gymnastics, horseback riding, ice hockey M, lacrosse M, rifle, rowing (crew), rugby M, sailing, soccer, softball W, swimming, tennis, track and field, volleyball W, water polo M, wrestling M. **Intramural:** Badminton, basketball, boxing M, handball, horseback riding, ice hockey, racquetball, skiing, soccer, softball, squash, table tennis, tennis, volleyball, water polo.

STUDENT SERVICES. Aptitude testing, career counseling, employment service for undergraduates, freshman orientation, health services, personal counseling, placement service for graduates, veterans counselor, speech/hearing clinic, tutoring, services/facilities for handicapped.

ANNUAL EXPENSES. Tuition and fees (1992-93): $4,024, $4,590 additional for out-of-state students. **Room and board:** $3,360. **Books and supplies:** $500. **Other expenses:** $1,090.

FINANCIAL AID. 39% of freshmen, 49% of continuing students receive some form of aid. 34% of grants, 67% of loans, 15% of jobs based on need. 877 enrolled freshmen were judged to have need, 832 were offered aid. Academic, music/drama, art, athletic, state/district residency, leadership, minority scholarships available. **Aid applications:** No closing date; priority given to applications received by February 15; applicants notified on a rolling basis beginning on or about April 10; must reply by May 1 or within 2 weeks if notified thereafter.

ADDRESS/TELEPHONE. James S. McCoy, Assistant Vice President of Enrollment Services, Miami University: Oxford Campus, GLOS Admission Center, Grey Gables, Oxford, OH 45056. (513) 529-2531. Fax: (513) 529-1550.

Miami-Jacobs College

Dayton, Ohio — CB code: 1528

Admissions: 89% of applicants accepted
Based on: ••• Interview, test scores
Completion: 90% of freshmen end year in good standing
25% enter 4-year programs

2-year proprietary junior college, coed. Founded in 1860. **Undergraduate enrollment:** 30 men, 282 women full time; 5 men, 69 women part time. **Faculty:** 46 total (6 full time), 3 with doctorates or other terminal degrees. **Location:** Urban campus in small city; in downtown area. **Calendar:** Quarter, extensive summer session. Saturday classes. **Microcomputers:** 36 located in computer centers. **Special facilities:** Antique typewriter museum.

DEGREES OFFERED. AAS. 86 associate degrees awarded in 1992. 73% in business and management, 11% computer sciences, 16% allied health.

UNDERGRADUATE MAJORS. Accounting, business administration and management, business and management, business and office, business computer/console/peripheral equipment operation, business data entry equipment operation, business data processing and related programs, business data programming, computer programming, fashion merchandising, finance, legal secretary, marketing and distribution, marketing management, medical assistant, medical records technology, medical secretary, microcomputer software, office supervision and management, retailing, secretarial and related programs, tourism, word processing.

ACADEMIC PROGRAMS. Accelerated program, honors program, independent study, internships, cross-registration. **Remedial services:** Preadmission summer program, reduced course load, remedial instruction, special counselor, tutoring. **Placement/credit:** CLEP General and Subject, institutional tests; 45 credit hours maximum for associate degree.

ACADEMIC REQUIREMENTS. Freshmen must earn minimum GPA of 2.0 to continue in good standing. 70% of freshmen return for sophomore year. Students must declare major on application. **Graduation requirements:** 105 hours for associate (34 in major). Most students required to take courses in computer science, English, mathematics, social sciences. **Additional information:** College has dress code and attendance policy establishing patterns and habits to be carried over into employment setting.

FRESHMAN ADMISSIONS. Selection criteria: Institutional test scores and interview considered. **Test requirements:** SAT or ACT (ACT preferred); score report by August 1. Career Placement Assessment Test required for placement.

1992 FRESHMAN CLASS PROFILE. 14 men applied, 11 accepted, 11 enrolled; 97 women applied, 88 accepted, 88 enrolled. **Characteristics:** 100% from in state, 100% commute, 31% have minority backgrounds. Average age is 24.

FALL-TERM APPLICATIONS. $25 fee, may be waived for applicants with need. No closing date; applicants notified on a rolling basis; must reply within 4 weeks. Interview required. Deferred and early admission available.

STUDENT LIFE. Activities: Student newspaper.

STUDENT SERVICES. Aptitude testing, career counseling, employment service for undergraduates, freshman orientation, on-campus day care, personal counseling, placement service for graduates, special adviser for adult students, veterans counselor.

ANNUAL EXPENSES. Tuition and fees (1992-93): $3,750. **Books and supplies:** $850. **Other expenses:** $2,500.

FINANCIAL AID. 85% of freshmen, 80% of continuing students receive some form of aid. All grants, 96% of loans, all jobs based on need. **Aid applications:** No closing date; applicants notified on a rolling basis beginning on or about August 1.

ADDRESS/TELEPHONE. Darlene Waite, Director of Enrollment Management, Miami-Jacobs College, PO Box 1433, 400 East Second Street, Dayton, OH 45401. (513) 449-8277. Fax: (513) 461-5174.

Mount Union College

Alliance, Ohio — CB code: 1492

Admissions: 82% of applicants accepted
Based on: ••• School record, test scores
•• Interview, recommendations
• Activities, essay, special talents
Completion: 82% of freshmen end year in good standing
65% graduate, 24% of these enter graduate study

4-year private liberal arts college, coed, affiliated with United Methodist Church. Founded in 1846. **Accreditation:** Regional. **Undergraduate enrollment:** 714 men, 665 women full time; 29 men, 38 women part time. **Faculty:** 96 total (81 full time), 61 with doctorates or other terminal degrees. **Location:** Suburban campus in large town; 55 miles from Cleveland, 75 miles from Pittsburgh, Pennsylvania. **Calendar:** Semester, limited summer session. **Microcomputers:** 120 located in libraries, classrooms, computer centers. **Special facilities:** 2 observatories, 109 acre nature center for ecological studies, Crandall Art Gallery.

DEGREES OFFERED. BA, BS. 265 bachelor's degrees awarded in 1992. 35% in business and management, 7% communications, 5% computer sciences, 15% teacher education, 7% health sciences, 5% life sciences, 11% social sciences.

UNDERGRADUATE MAJORS. Accounting, American studies, art education, astronomy, biology, business administration and management, business economics, chemistry, communications, computer and information sciences, cytotechnology, dramatic arts, elementary education, English, English education, foreign languages education, French, geology, health education, history, information sciences and systems, international business management, junior high education, liberal/general studies, mathematics, mathematics education, medical laboratory technologies, music, music education, music performance, philosophy, physical education, physics, political science and government, preengineering, prelaw, psychology, religion, science education, secondary education, social science education, social studies education, social work, sociology, Spanish, specific learning disabilities, speech, speech/communication/theater education, sports management, sports medicine, studio art.

ACADEMIC PROGRAMS. Accelerated program, cooperative education, double major, dual enrollment of high school students, honors program, independent study, internships, semester at sea, student-designed major, study abroad, teacher preparation, Washington semester; liberal arts/career combination in engineering. **ROTC:** Air Force, Army. **Placement/credit:** AP, institutional tests; 15 credit hours maximum for bachelor's degree.

ACADEMIC REQUIREMENTS. Freshmen must earn minimum GPA of 1.6 to continue in good standing. 90% of freshmen return for sophomore year. Students must declare major by end of second year. **Graduation requirements:** 120 hours for bachelor's (30 in major). Most students required to take courses in arts/fine arts, English, history, humanities, mathematics, philosophy/religion, biological/physical sciences, social sciences. **Postgraduate studies:** 5% enter law school, 4% enter medical school, 4% enter MBA programs, 11% enter other graduate study. **Additional information:** All freshmen must take the Liberal Arts Experience Course.

FRESHMAN ADMISSIONS. Selection criteria: School achievement record, tests, and recommendations most important. Interview and extracurricular activities also considered. Special consideration to children of alumni.

High school preparation: 15 units recommended. Recommended units include biological science 1, English 4, foreign language 2, mathematics 3, physical science 2 and social science 3. **Test requirements:** SAT or ACT; score report by June 1.

1992 FRESHMAN CLASS PROFILE. 660 men applied, 507 accepted, 203 enrolled; 520 women applied, 457 accepted, 186 enrolled. 22% were in top tenth and 54% were in top quarter of graduating class. **Academic background:** Mid 50% of enrolled freshmen had SAT-V between 450-550, SAT-M between 480-550; ACT composite between 19-26. 38% submitted SAT scores, 83% submitted ACT scores. **Characteristics:** 82% from in state, 95% live in college housing, 9% have minority backgrounds, 6% are foreign students, 35% join fraternities/sororities. Average age is 18.

FALL-TERM APPLICATIONS. $20 fee, may be waived for applicants with need. No closing date; applicants notified on a rolling basis beginning on or about September 30; must reply and send deposit within 4 weeks, refundable until May 1. Audition required for music applicants. Portfolio required for art applicants. Essay required. Interview recommended. CRDA. Deferred admission available.

STUDENT LIFE. Housing: Dormitories (men, women, coed); fraternity, handicapped housing available. Small single sex college-owned residential homes converted to college housing available. **Activities:** Student government, magazine, radio, student newspaper, yearbook, choral groups, concert band, dance, drama, jazz band, marching band, music ensembles, musical theater, fraternities, sororities, Association of International Students, Black Student Union, religious organizations, Associated Women Students, Christian Science organization, Recycling Program.

ATHLETICS. NCAA. **Intercollegiate:** Baseball M, basketball, cross-country, diving, football M, golf M, soccer, softball W, swimming, tennis, track and field, volleyball W, wrestling M. **Intramural:** Badminton, basketball, fencing, racquetball, skiing, soccer, softball, volleyball.

STUDENT SERVICES. Aptitude testing, career counseling, freshman orientation, health services, personal counseling, placement service for graduates, services/facilities for handicapped.

ANNUAL EXPENSES. Tuition and fees: $12,320. **Room and board:** $3,530. **Books and supplies:** $450. **Other expenses:** $550.

FINANCIAL AID. 90% of freshmen, 97% of continuing students receive some form of aid. 79% of grants, 99% of loans, all jobs based on need. 357 enrolled freshmen were judged to have need, all were offered aid. Academic, music/drama, art, alumni affiliation, religious affiliation, minority scholarships available. **Aid applications:** No closing date; priority given to applications received by April 1; applicants notified on a rolling basis beginning on or about February 15; must reply within 4 weeks.

ADDRESS/TELEPHONE. Amy Tomko, Director of Admissions, Mount Union College, 1972 Clark Avenue, Alliance, OH 44601-3993. (216) 823-2590. (800) 334-6682. Fax: (216) 821-0425.

Mount Vernon Nazarene College
Mount Vernon, Ohio — CB code: 1531

4-year private college of arts and sciences and liberal arts college, coed, affiliated with Church of the Nazarene. Founded in 1964. **Accreditation:** Regional. **Undergraduate enrollment:** 1,112 men and women. **Graduate enrollment:** 14 men and women. **Location:** Suburban campus in large town; 37 miles from Columbus. **Calendar:** 4-1-4.

FRESHMAN ADMISSIONS. Selection criteria: School achievement record, ACT scores, references.

ANNUAL EXPENSES. Tuition and fees: $7,190. **Room and board:** $3,200. **Books and supplies:** $600. **Other expenses:** $1,100.

ADDRESS/TELEPHONE. Rev. Ron Hyson, Dean of Enrollment Services, Mount Vernon Nazarene College, 800 Martinsburg Road, Mount Vernon, OH 43050. (614) 397-6862 ext. 4500. (800) 782-2435. Fax: (614) 393-0511.

Muskingum Area Technical College
Zanesville, Ohio — CB code: 1535

2-year public technical college, coed. Founded in 1969. **Accreditation:** Regional. **Undergraduate enrollment:** 1,426 men and women full time; 1,275 men and women part time. **Graduate enrollment:** 1,326 men and women full time; 2,711 men and women part time. **Location:** Suburban campus in large town. **Calendar:** Quarter.

FRESHMAN ADMISSIONS. Selection criteria: Open admissions. Selective admissions to allied health programs.

ANNUAL EXPENSES. Tuition and fees (1992-93): $2,040, $1,350 additional for out-of-state students. **Books and supplies:** $675.

ADDRESS/TELEPHONE. Tim Shepfer, Director of Admissions, Muskingum Area Technical College, 1555 Newark Road, Zanesville, OH 43701. (614) 454-2501. (800) 686-8324. Fax: (614) 454-0035.

Muskingum College
New Concord, Ohio — CB code: 1496

Admissions:	82% of applicants accepted
Based on:	••• School record
	•• Recommendations, test scores
	• Activities, essay, interview, special talents
Completion:	85% of freshmen end year in good standing
	65% graduate, 15% of these enter graduate study

4-year private liberal arts college, coed, affiliated with Presbyterian Church (USA). Founded in 1837. **Accreditation:** Regional. **Undergraduate enrollment:** 529 men, 550 women full time. **Graduate enrollment:** 6 women full time; 9 men, 53 women part time. **Faculty:** 102 total (78 full time), 74 with doctorates or other terminal degrees. **Location:** Rural campus in small town; 70 miles from Columbus, 125 miles from Pittsburgh (PA). **Calendar:** Semester, limited summer session. **Microcomputers:** 40 located in dormitories, libraries, classrooms, computer centers, campus-wide network. **Special facilities:** McAllister Biology Station, Louis Palmer art gallery.

DEGREES OFFERED. BA, BS, MA. 230 bachelor's degrees awarded in 1992. 24% in business and management, 26% education, 8% letters/literature, 10% psychology, 8% social sciences, 6% visual and performing arts. Graduate degrees offered in 3 major fields of study.

UNDERGRADUATE MAJORS. Accounting, American studies, art education, biological and physical sciences, biology, business administration and management, business and management, business education, chemistry, communications, computer and information sciences, dramatic arts, earth sciences, economics, education, elementary education, English, fine arts, French, geology, German, history, humanities and social sciences, international business management, international relations, international studies, liberal/general studies, mathematics, medical laboratory technologies, music, music education, philosophy, physical education, physical sciences, physics, political science and government, predentistry, preengineering, prelaw, premedicine, preveterinary, psychology, public affairs, radio/television broadcasting, religion, religious education, secondary education, sociology, Spanish, special education, specific learning disabilities, speech.

ACADEMIC PROGRAMS. Accelerated program, double major, dual enrollment of high school students, independent study, internships, semester at sea, student-designed major, study abroad, teacher preparation, visiting/exchange student program, United Nations semester, Washington semester; liberal arts/career combination in engineering, health sciences. **Remedial services:** Learning center, reduced course load, special counselor, tutoring, PLUS (program for learning disabled students). **Placement/credit:** AP, CLEP General and Subject, institutional tests.

ACADEMIC REQUIREMENTS. Freshmen must earn minimum GPA of 2.0 to continue in good standing. 86% of freshmen return for sophomore year. Students must declare major by end of second year. **Graduation requirements:** 124 hours for bachelor's (30 in major). Most students required to take courses in English, history, humanities, mathematics, philosophy/religion, biological/physical sciences, social sciences. **Postgraduate studies:** 3% enter law school, 3% enter medical school, 2% enter MBA programs, 7% enter other graduate study.

FRESHMAN ADMISSIONS. Selection criteria: School achievement record most important. Test scores, recommendations, extracurricular activities, interview and children of alumni considered. **High school preparation:** 10 units required; 15 recommended. Required and recommended units include English 4, mathematics 2-3, social science 2-3 and science 2-3. Foreign language 2 recommended. **Test requirements:** SAT or ACT; score report by June 1.

1992 FRESHMAN CLASS PROFILE. 565 men applied, 434 accepted, 165 enrolled; 426 women applied, 382 accepted, 143 enrolled. 58% had high school GPA of 3.0 or higher, 39% between 2.0 and 2.99. 26% were in top tenth of graduating class. **Academic background:** Mid 50% of enrolled freshmen had SAT-V between 370-510, SAT-M between 430-540; ACT composite between 18-24. 42% submitted SAT scores, 87% submitted ACT scores. **Characteristics:** 83% from in state, 96% live in college housing, 3% have minority backgrounds, 1% are foreign students, 44% join fraternities/sororities. Average age is 18.

FALL-TERM APPLICATIONS. $15 fee, may be waived for applicants with need. Closing date August 1; priority given to applications received by May 1; applicants notified on a rolling basis; must reply by May 1 or within 2 weeks if notified thereafter. Interview recommended. Audition recommended for music applicants. Portfolio recommended for art applicants. Essay recommended. CRDA. Deferred admission available. Application deadline of March 1 for PLUS program.

STUDENT LIFE. Housing: Dormitories (men, women, coed); fraternity, sorority, cooperative housing available. Students selected for approved programs have option of living in special program cottages. **Activities:** Student government, magazine, radio, student newspaper, television, yearbook, choral groups, concert band, drama, jazz band, marching band, music ensembles, pep band, symphony orchestra, fraternities, sororities, Muskingum Christian Fellowship, Fellowship of Christian Athletes, international student organization, political awareness program, SADD, Habitat for Humanity.

ATHLETICS. NCAA. **Intercollegiate:** Baseball M, basketball, cross-country, football M, golf, soccer, softball W, tennis, track and field, volleyball W, wrestling M. **Intramural:** Baseball M, basketball, bowling, cross-country, golf, racquetball, rugby M, soccer M, softball, swimming, table tennis M, tennis, track and field, volleyball, wrestling M.

STUDENT SERVICES. Aptitude testing, career counseling, employment service for undergraduates, freshman orientation, health services, personal counseling, placement service for graduates, services/facilities for handicapped.

ANNUAL EXPENSES. Tuition and fees: $13,010. **Room and board:** $3,740. **Books and supplies:** $500. **Other expenses:** $700.

FINANCIAL AID. 88% of freshmen, 81% of continuing students receive some form of aid. 66% of grants, 96% of loans, 75% of jobs based on need. 257 enrolled freshmen were judged to have need, all were offered aid. Academic, music/drama, art, leadership, alumni affiliation, religious affiliation, minority scholarships available. **Aid applications:** Closing date August 1; priority given to applications received by March 1; applicants notified on a rolling basis beginning on or about March 1; must reply by May 1 or within 4 weeks if notified thereafter.

ADDRESS/TELEPHONE. Jeff Zellers, Dean of Enrollment, Muskingum College, New Concord, OH 43762. (614) 826-8137. (800) 752-6082. Fax: (614) 826-8404.

North Central Technical College
Mansfield, Ohio — CB code: 0721

2-year public technical college, coed. Founded in 1961. **Accreditation:** Regional. **Undergraduate enrollment:** 429 men, 877 women full time; 556 men, 1,041 women part time. **Faculty:** 180 total (75 full time), 6 with doctorates or other terminal degrees. **Location:** Suburban campus in small city; 70 miles from Cleveland and Columbus. **Calendar:** Quarter, limited summer session. Saturday and extensive evening/early morning classes. **Microcomputers:** 70 located in classrooms, computer centers. **Special facilities:** Art gallery, wooded hiking trails.

DEGREES OFFERED. AAS. 350 associate degrees awarded in 1992. 22% in business and management, 5% business/office and marketing/distribution, 8% computer sciences, 15% engineering technologies, 29% allied health, 19% parks/recreation, protective services, public affairs.

UNDERGRADUATE MAJORS. Accounting, biomedical equipment technology, business administration and management, business data programming, child day care management, computer programming, criminal justice technology, drafting and design technology, early childhood education, electronic technology, engineering and engineering-related technologies, financial management, hotel/motel and restaurant management, human services, information sciences and systems, law enforcement and corrections technologies, legal assistant/paralegal, manufacturing technology, mechanical design technology, mental health/human services, metal forming engineering technology, nursing, operations management, pharmacy technology, physical therapy assistant, radiograph medical technology, recreation therapy, respiratory therapy technology, secretarial and related programs, word processing.

ACADEMIC PROGRAMS. Double major, dual enrollment of high school students, weekend college. **Remedial services:** Learning center, remedial instruction, tutoring. **Placement/credit:** CLEP General and Subject, institutional tests.

ACADEMIC REQUIREMENTS. Freshmen must earn minimum GPA of 2.0 to continue in good standing. 40% of freshmen return for sophomore year. Students must declare major on application. **Graduation requirements:** 110 hours for associate. Most students required to take courses in English, humanities, mathematics, social sciences.

FRESHMAN ADMISSIONS. Selection criteria: Open admissions. Nursing, physical therapist assistant, radiology, respiratory therapy require ACT score, high school algebra and chemistry. Pharmacy technology requires high school algebra. One algebra and 1 chemistry required for nursing, physical therapist assistant, respiratory therapy, radiologic technology and pharmacy technology programs. **Test requirements:** ACT scores used for admission to registered nursing, physical therapist assistant, radiology, and respiratory therapy programs; score report by September 15.

1992 FRESHMAN CLASS PROFILE. 271 men, 491 women enrolled. **Characteristics:** 99% from in state, 100% commute, 7% have minority backgrounds. Average age is 24.

FALL-TERM APPLICATIONS. $35 fee. No closing date; applicants notified on a rolling basis. Interview recommended for all health and public service programs applicants. Deferred and early admission available. Applicants required to take college-administered ASSET test.

STUDENT LIFE. Activities: Student government, student newspaper, adult student organization, Substance Management Awareness Resource Team. **Additional information:** On-campus Arts and Lecture series.

ATHLETICS. Intramural: Basketball, golf, racquetball, softball, table tennis, tennis, volleyball.

STUDENT SERVICES. Career counseling, employment service for undergraduates, freshman orientation, personal counseling, placement service for graduates, veterans counselor, services/facilities for handicapped.

ANNUAL EXPENSES. Tuition and fees (projected): $2,115, $1,845 additional for out-of-state students. **Books and supplies:** $600.

FINANCIAL AID. 51% of freshmen, 47% of continuing students receive some form of aid. 87% of grants, 73% of loans, all jobs based on need. 438 enrolled freshmen were judged to have need, all were offered aid. Academic, state/district residency scholarships available. **Aid applications:** No closing date; priority given to applications received by April 1; applicants notified on a rolling basis beginning on or about June 30; must reply within 6 weeks.

ADDRESS/TELEPHONE. Mark Monnes, Director of Admissions, North Central Technical College, PO Box 698, Mansfield, OH 44901. (419) 755-4888. Fax: (419) 755-4750.

Northwest Technical College
Archbold, Ohio — CB code: 1235

2-year public technical college, coed. Founded in 1968. **Accreditation:** Regional. **Undergraduate enrollment:** 173 men, 405 women full time; 565 men, 911 women part time. **Faculty:** 114 total (38 full time), 7 with doctorates or other terminal degrees. **Location:** Rural campus in small town; 18 miles from Defiance, 45 miles from Toledo. **Calendar:** Quarter, limited summer session. Saturday and extensive evening/early morning classes. **Microcomputers:** 285 located in libraries, classrooms, computer centers.

DEGREES OFFERED. AAS. 178 associate degrees awarded in 1992. 26% in business and management, 14% business/office and marketing/distribution, 19% engineering technologies, 34% health sciences.

UNDERGRADUATE MAJORS. Accounting, agricultural business and management, agricultural mechanics, animal sciences, business and management, computer programming, construction, drafting and design technology, early childhood education, electromechanical technology, electronic technology, finance, food sciences, horticultural science, human resources development, industrial technology, legal secretary, marketing management, mechanical design technology, medical secretary, network programming, nursing, office supervision and management, plastic technology, quality control technology, real estate, retailing, secretarial and related programs, social sciences.

ACADEMIC PROGRAMS. Dual enrollment of high school students, independent study, internships, student-designed major, weekend college. **Remedial services:** Learning center, remedial instruction, special counselor, tutoring. **Placement/credit:** Institutional tests.

ACADEMIC REQUIREMENTS. Freshmen must earn minimum GPA of 2.0 to continue in good standing. 42% of freshmen return for sophomore year. Students must declare major on application. **Graduation requirements:** 105 hours for associate (55 in major). Most students required to take courses in computer science, English, mathematics, biological/physical sciences, social sciences.

FRESHMAN ADMISSIONS. Selection criteria: Open admissions. Recommended units include biological science 1, English 3, mathematics 3, physical science 1, social science 3 and science 1. College-preparatory program preferred. **Test requirements:** SAT or ACT (ACT preferred) for placement and counseling only; score report by September 7. CGP accepted in place of ACT or SAT.

1992 FRESHMAN CLASS PROFILE. 275 men, 328 women enrolled. 25% had high school GPA of 3.0 or higher, 53% between 2.0 and 2.99. 6% were in top tenth and 26% were in top quarter of graduating class. **Academic background:** Mid 50% of enrolled freshmen had ACT composite between 17-22. 33% submitted ACT scores. **Characteristics:** 96% from in state, 100% commute, 5% have minority backgrounds. Average age is 28.

FALL-TERM APPLICATIONS. $10 fee. No closing date; applicants notified on a rolling basis. Interview recommended for nursing applicants. Deferred and early admission available.

STUDENT LIFE. Activities: Student government, student activities bulletin, Phi Theta Kappa, Student Nurses Association (SNA).

ATHLETICS. Intramural: Basketball, bowling, table tennis, volleyball.

STUDENT SERVICES. Aptitude testing, career counseling, employment service for undergraduates, freshman orientation, on-campus day care, personal counseling, placement service for graduates, special adviser for adult students, veterans counselor, services/facilities for handicapped.

ANNUAL EXPENSES. Tuition and fees (projected): $2,358, $1,674 additional for out-of-state students. **Books and supplies:** $660. **Other expenses:** $450.

FINANCIAL AID. 98% of grants, 96% of loans, all jobs based on need. Academic scholarships available. **Aid applications:** No closing date; applicants notified on a rolling basis beginning on or about March 20.

ADDRESS/TELEPHONE. Dennis Gable, Admissions Coordinator, Northwest Technical College, PO 246A, Route 1, Archbold, OH 43502. (419) 267-5511 ext. 318.

Northwestern College
Lima, Ohio — CB code: 0816

2-year proprietary business, technical college, coed. Founded in 1920. **Accreditation:** Regional. **Undergraduate enrollment:** 813 men, 343 women full time; 39 men, 136 women part time. **Faculty:** 57 total (35 full time). **Loca-**

tion: Urban campus in large town; 75 miles from Toledo, 90 miles from Columbus. **Calendar:** Quarter and 6 week session. Saturday and extensive evening/early morning classes. **Microcomputers:** 20 located in computer centers.

DEGREES OFFERED. AAS. 247 associate degrees awarded in 1992. 32% in business and management, 19% business/office and marketing/distribution, 45% trade and industry.

UNDERGRADUATE MAJORS. Accounting, automotive mechanics, automotive technology, business administration and management, business computer/console/peripheral equipment operation, business data processing and related programs, diesel engine mechanics, legal assistant/paralegal, legal secretary, marketing and distribution, medical assistant, medical secretary, secretarial and related programs, tourism, word processing.

ACADEMIC PROGRAMS. 2-year transfer program, accelerated program, cooperative education, double major, external degree, weekend college. **Remedial services:** Reduced course load, remedial instruction, special counselor, tutoring. **Placement/credit:** CLEP General and Subject, institutional tests; 25 credit hours maximum for associate degree.

ACADEMIC REQUIREMENTS. Freshmen must earn minimum GPA of 2.0 to continue in good standing. 75% of freshmen return for sophomore year. Students must declare major on application. **Graduation requirements:** 108 hours for associate (75 in major). Most students required to take courses in computer science, English, mathematics. **Additional information:** Students wishing credit for life experience must register for 1-hour course in portfolio development offered by college.

FRESHMAN ADMISSIONS. Selection criteria: Open admissions.

1992 FRESHMAN CLASS PROFILE. 211 men, 204 women enrolled. **Characteristics:** 45% from in state, 6% have minority backgrounds. Average age is 18.

FALL-TERM APPLICATIONS. $50 fee. No closing date; applicants notified on a rolling basis. Deferred and early admission available.

STUDENT LIFE. Housing: Apartment housing available. All students not living with family must live in college housing.

ATHLETICS. Intramural: Basketball M, bowling, softball M, volleyball M.

STUDENT SERVICES. Career counseling, employment service for undergraduates, freshman orientation, personal counseling, placement service for graduates, veterans counselor, services/facilities for handicapped.

ANNUAL EXPENSES. Tuition and fees (projected): $6,993. **Room and board:** $1,950. **Books and supplies:** $600. **Other expenses:** $1,053.

FINANCIAL AID. 63% of freshmen, 56% of continuing students receive some form of aid. 94% of grants, 96% of loans, all jobs based on need. Academic, minority scholarships available. **Aid applications:** No closing date; applicants notified on a rolling basis; must reply within 2 weeks.

ADDRESS/TELEPHONE. Jeffrey A. Jarvis, Vice President of Admissions, Northwestern College, 1441 North Cable Road, Lima, OH 45805. (419) 227-3141. Fax: (419) 229-6926.

Notre Dame College of Ohio
South Euclid, Ohio — CB code: 1566

Admissions: 67% of applicants accepted
Based on:
- ••• School record
- •• Activities, recommendations, test scores
- • Essay, interview, religious affiliation/commitment, special talents

Completion: 80% of freshmen end year in good standing
60% graduate, 100% of these enter graduate study

4-year private liberal arts college, women only, affiliated with Roman Catholic Church. Founded in 1922. **Accreditation:** Regional. **Undergraduate enrollment:** 370 women full time; 10 men, 409 women part time. **Graduate enrollment:** 21 women part time. **Faculty:** 104 total (34 full time), 36 with doctorates or other terminal degrees. **Location:** Suburban campus in very large city; 12 miles from downtown Cleveland. **Calendar:** Semester, limited summer session. Saturday and extensive evening/early morning classes. **Microcomputers:** 33 located in libraries, classrooms, computer centers. **Additional facts:** Weekend College for women 25 and over.

DEGREES OFFERED. AA, BA, BS, MEd. 1 associate degree awarded in 1992. 100% in business and management. 118 bachelor's degrees awarded. 52% in business and management, 8% business/office and marketing/distribution, 8% teacher education, 5% life sciences, 5% psychology, 5% social sciences. Graduate degrees offered in 1 major field of study.

UNDERGRADUATE MAJORS. Associate: Business and management, legal assistant/paralegal, pastoral ministry. **Bachelor's:** Accounting, allied health, arts management, biochemistry, biology, business administration and management, business and management, business economics, chemistry, chemistry/biochemistry, clinical laboratory science, communications, cytotechnology, early childhood education, elementary education, English, finance, food science and nutrition, French, graphic communication, history, human resources development, international business management, junior high education, management information systems, marketing and distribution, marketing management, mathematics, nuclear medical technology, political science and government, predentistry, prelaw, premedicine, preveterinary, psychology, secondary education, social sciences, Spanish, studio art.

ACADEMIC PROGRAMS. Double major, independent study, internships, study abroad, teacher preparation, visiting/exchange student program, weekend college, cross-registration, program in engineering with Case Western Reserve University. **Remedial services:** Learning center, preadmission summer program, reduced course load, remedial instruction, special counselor, tutoring, writing laboratory. **Placement/credit:** AP, CLEP General and Subject, institutional tests.

ACADEMIC REQUIREMENTS. Freshmen must earn minimum GPA of 2.0 to continue in good standing. 70% of freshmen return for sophomore year. Students must declare major by end of second year. **Graduation requirements:** 64 hours for associate, 128 hours for bachelor's (36 in major). Most students required to take courses in arts/fine arts, English, foreign languages, history, mathematics, philosophy/religion, biological/physical sciences, social sciences. **Postgraduate studies:** 5% enter law school, 5% enter medical school, 32% enter MBA programs, 58% enter other graduate study.

FRESHMAN ADMISSIONS. Selection criteria: School achievement record most important, followed by recommendations and test scores. Applicants should be in top half of class and have 2.5 high school GPA. Extracurricular activities also considered. **High school preparation:** 15 units required. Required and recommended units include English 4, foreign language 2, mathematics 2, social science 2 and science 1-2. Science units must include 1 laboratory science. **Test requirements:** SAT or ACT.

1992 FRESHMAN CLASS PROFILE. 132 women applied, 88 accepted, 48 enrolled. 55% had high school GPA of 3.0 or higher, 39% between 2.0 and 2.99. 12% were in top tenth and 41% were in top quarter of graduating class. **Academic background:** Mid 50% of enrolled freshmen had SAT-V between 350-430, SAT-M between 320-430; ACT composite between 17-23. 34% submitted SAT scores, 70% submitted ACT scores. **Characteristics:** 86% from in state, 66% live in college housing, 27% have minority backgrounds. Average age is 18.

FALL-TERM APPLICATIONS. $20 fee, may be waived for applicants with need. No closing date; applicants notified on a rolling basis; must reply by May 1 or within 2 weeks if notified thereafter. Interview recommended. Essay recommended. Deferred admission available.

STUDENT LIFE. Housing: Dormitories (women). Weekend college students may use dormitories. **Activities:** Student government, magazine, student newspaper, drama, music ensembles, musical theater, Campus Ministry Board, Black Scholars, Current Affairs Forum.

ATHLETICS. NAIA. **Intercollegiate:** Basketball, softball, volleyball. **Intramural:** Basketball, skiing, softball, swimming, table tennis, tennis, volleyball.

STUDENT SERVICES. Aptitude testing, career counseling, employment service for undergraduates, freshman orientation, health services, on-campus day care, personal counseling, placement service for graduates, special adviser for adult students, adviser for minorities, services/facilities for handicapped.

ANNUAL EXPENSES. Tuition and fees: $7,200. **Room and board:** $3,690. **Books and supplies:** $500. **Other expenses:** $650.

FINANCIAL AID. 95% of freshmen, 84% of continuing students receive some form of aid. 69% of grants, 78% of loans, 89% of jobs based on need. Academic, leadership, alumni affiliation, religious affiliation scholarships available. **Aid applications:** Closing date July 15; priority given to applications received by March 1; applicants notified on a rolling basis beginning on or about March 1; must reply within 4 weeks.

ADDRESS/TELEPHONE. Mrs. Karen Poelking, Dean of Admissions and Records, Notre Dame College of Ohio, 4545 College Road, South Euclid, OH 44121. (216) 382-9806. Fax: (216) 381-1680 ext. 301.

Oberlin College
Oberlin, Ohio — CB code: 1587

Admissions: 65% of applicants accepted
Based on:
- ••• School record, test scores
- •• Activities, essay, recommendations, special talents
- • Interview

Completion: 97% of freshmen end year in good standing
85% graduate, 24% of these enter graduate study

4-year private college of arts and sciences and music college, coed. Founded in 1833. **Accreditation:** Regional. **Undergraduate enrollment:** 1,299 men, 1,528 women full time. **Graduate enrollment:** 23 men and women. **Faculty:** 277 total, 250 with doctorates or other terminal degrees. **Location:** Rural campus in small town; 34 miles west of Cleveland. **Calendar:** 4-1-4. **Microcomputers:** 250 located in dormitories, libraries, classrooms, computer centers. **Special facilities:** Art museum, observatory, bog. **Additional facts:** First coeducational college in the world. School consists of college of arts and sciences and conservatory of music.

DEGREES OFFERED. BA, MA. 760 bachelor's degrees awarded in 1992. 6% in area and ethnic studies, 17% letters/literature, 8% life sciences,

5% physical sciences, 22% social sciences, 20% visual and performing arts. Graduate degrees offered in 5 major fields of study.

UNDERGRADUATE MAJORS. Afro-American (black) studies, American studies, anthropology, archeology, art history, biochemistry, biology, chemistry, classics, comparative literature, computer and information sciences, creative writing, dance, dramatic arts, East Asian studies, economics, engineering, English, environmental science, French, geology, German, Greek (classical), history, Jewish studies, Latin, Latin American studies, mathematics, Middle Eastern studies, music, music education, music history and appreciation, music performance, music theory and composition, neurosciences, philosophy, physics, political science and government, prelaw, psychobiology, psychology, religion, Russian, Russian and Slavic studies, sociology, Spanish, studio art, urban studies, women's studies.

ACADEMIC PROGRAMS. Double major, honors program, independent study, internships, student-designed major, study abroad, visiting/exchange student program, New York semester, Washington semester, cross-registration, 3-2 engineering; liberal arts/career combination in engineering. **Remedial services:** Learning center, remedial instruction, special counselor, tutoring. **Placement/credit:** AP, IB, institutional tests.

ACADEMIC REQUIREMENTS. No policy requiring minimum GPA; records of students having academic difficulty are reviewed individually. 90% of freshmen return for sophomore year. Students must declare major by end of second year. **Graduation requirements:** 112 hours for bachelor's. Most students required to take courses in humanities, mathematics, biological/physical sciences, social sciences.

FRESHMAN ADMISSIONS. Selection criteria: For college of arts and sciences, school achievement record, school and community leadership activities, recommendations, interview, and test scores. Special consideration to applicants from minority and first generation college families and to foreign applicants. For conservatory, audition most important factor; admission extremely selective. Required and recommended units include English 4. Foreign language 3, mathematics 4, social science 3 and science 3 recommended. **Test requirements:** SAT or ACT; score report by March 1.

1992 FRESHMAN CLASS PROFILE. 1,557 men applied, 958 accepted, 255 enrolled; 2,128 women applied, 1,435 accepted, 363 enrolled. 56% were in top tenth and 77% were in top quarter of graduating class. **Academic background:** Mid 50% of enrolled freshmen had SAT-V between 550-660, SAT-M between 580-690. 97% submitted SAT scores. **Characteristics:** 11% from in state, 100% live in college housing, 28% have minority backgrounds, 3% are foreign students. Average age is 18.

FALL-TERM APPLICATIONS. $45 fee, may be waived for applicants with need. Closing date January 15; applicants notified on or about April 1; must reply by May 1. Audition required for conservatory applicants. Essay required for college of arts and sciences applicants. Interview recommended. Interview required for early admission candidates; recommended for all others. CRDA. Deferred and early admission available. EDP-F. 3 ACH, including English Composition, recommended for college of arts and science applicants. Closing date for applications to Conservatory of Music February 15.

STUDENT LIFE. Housing: Dormitories (men, women, coed); cooperative housing available. **Activities:** Student government, magazine, radio, student newspaper, yearbook, journals of philosophy and political science, literary magazines, choral groups, concert band, dance, drama, jazz band, music ensembles, musical theater, opera, symphony orchestra, early music, electronic music, religious, political, ethnic, and social service organizations.

ATHLETICS. NCAA. **Intercollegiate:** Baseball M, basketball, cross-country, diving, field hockey W, football M, lacrosse, soccer, swimming, tennis, track and field, volleyball W. **Intramural:** Baseball M, basketball, bowling, handball, horseback riding, racquetball, rugby M, soccer, softball, squash, table tennis, tennis, track and field, volleyball.

STUDENT SERVICES. Career counseling, employment service for undergraduates, freshman orientation, health services, personal counseling, placement service for graduates, services/facilities for handicapped.

ANNUAL EXPENSES. Tuition and fees: $18,950. **Room and board:** $5,620. **Books and supplies:** $575. **Other expenses:** $525.

FINANCIAL AID. 50% of freshmen, 70% of continuing students receive some form of aid. 94% of grants, all loans, all jobs based on need. 328 enrolled freshmen were judged to have need, all were offered aid. Academic, music/drama scholarships available. **Aid applications:** Closing date February 1; applicants notified on or about April 1; must reply by May 1 or within 2 weeks if notified thereafter.

ADDRESS/TELEPHONE. Debra Chermonte, Director of Admissions, Oberlin College, Carnegie Building, Oberlin, OH 44074. (216) 775-8411. (800) 622-OBIE. Fax: (216) 775-6905.

Ohio Dominican College
Columbus, Ohio — CB code: 1131

4-year private liberal arts college, coed, affiliated with Roman Catholic Church. Founded in 1911. **Accreditation:** Regional. **Undergraduate enrollment:** 431 men, 580 women full time; 123 men, 376 women part time. **Faculty:** 99 total (53 full time), 48 with doctorates or other terminal degrees. **Location:** Suburban campus in very large city; 4 miles from downtown. **Calendar:** Semester, limited summer session. **Microcomputers:** 33 located in computer centers. **Special facilities:** Wehrle Art Gallery.

DEGREES OFFERED. AA, AS, BA, BS. 10 associate degrees awarded in 1992. 100% in multi/interdisciplinary studies. 218 bachelor's degrees awarded. 22% in business and management, 7% communications, 23% teacher education, 10% multi/interdisciplinary studies, 6% psychology, 16% social sciences.

UNDERGRADUATE MAJORS. Associate: Chemistry, legal assistant/paralegal, liberal/general studies, library assistant, theological studies. **Bachelor's:** Accounting, art education, biology, business administration and management, business and management, chemistry, communications, computer programming, criminal justice studies, early childhood education, economics, education, education of the mentally handicapped, education of the multiple handicapped, elementary education, English, English education, fashion merchandising, foreign languages education, health care administration, history, international business management, liberal/general studies, library science, mathematics, mathematics education, philosophy, physical education, political science and government, prelaw, psychology, public relations, science education, secondary education, social science education, social sciences, social studies education, social work, sociology, special education, speech/communication/theater education, teaching English as a second language/foreign language, theological studies.

ACADEMIC PROGRAMS. Double major, dual enrollment of high school students, honors program, independent study, internships, student-designed major, study abroad, teacher preparation, weekend college, Washington semester, cross-registration. **Remedial services:** Learning center, reduced course load, remedial instruction, special counselor, tutoring. **Placement/credit:** AP, CLEP General and Subject, institutional tests. No limit on credit hours by examination, but residency requirement must be met.

ACADEMIC REQUIREMENTS. Freshmen must earn minimum GPA of 1.86 to continue in good standing. Students must declare major by end of first year. **Graduation requirements:** 62 hours for associate (20 in major), 124 hours for bachelor's (32 in major). Most students required to take courses in arts/fine arts, English, foreign languages, humanities, mathematics, philosophy/religion, biological/physical sciences, social sciences. **Postgraduate studies:** 70% from 2-year programs enter 4-year programs.

FRESHMAN ADMISSIONS. Selection criteria: High school GPA, curriculum most important, followed by class rank, test scores, interview, recommendations, and activities. **High school preparation:** 16 units recommended. Recommended units include English 4, foreign language 3, mathematics 3, social science 3 and science 3. **Test requirements:** SAT or ACT; score report by August 25. Prueba de Aptitud Academica for Spanish speaking applicants.

1992 FRESHMAN CLASS PROFILE. 94 men, 133 women enrolled. **Characteristics:** 81% from in state, 60% live in college housing, 9% have minority backgrounds, 14% are foreign students. Average age is 19.

FALL-TERM APPLICATIONS. No fee. $25 fee for international applicants. No closing date; priority given to applications received by April 1; applicants notified on a rolling basis; must reply within 4 weeks. Essay required. Interview required for in-state applicants; recommended for out-of-state. Deferred admission available.

STUDENT LIFE. Housing: Dormitories (women, coed). **Activities:** Student government, radio, student newspaper, literary magazine, choral groups, drama, campus ministry council, Black Student Union, international student club, Circle-K, Student Council for Exceptional Children, Association of Resident Students, Association of Commuter Students, social work club.

ATHLETICS. NAIA. **Intercollegiate:** Baseball M, basketball, soccer M, softball W, volleyball W. **Intramural:** Badminton, basketball, cross-country, golf, soccer, softball, table tennis, tennis, volleyball.

STUDENT SERVICES. Aptitude testing, career counseling, employment service for undergraduates, freshman orientation, health services, personal counseling, placement service for graduates, special adviser for adult students, veterans counselor, services/facilities for handicapped.

ANNUAL EXPENSES. Tuition and fees (1992-93): $7,370. **Room and board:** $3,930. **Books and supplies:** $350. **Other expenses:** $750.

FINANCIAL AID. 82% of freshmen, 87% of continuing students receive some form of aid. Academic, athletic scholarships available. **Aid applications:** No closing date; priority given to applications received by March 1; applicants notified on a rolling basis beginning on or about March 1; must reply within 2 weeks.

ADDRESS/TELEPHONE. James Sagona, Vice President for Admissions and Student Services, Ohio Dominican College, 1216 Sunbury Road, Columbus, OH 43219-2099. (614) 251-4500. Fax: (614) 252-0776.

Ohio Institute of Photography and Technology
Dayton, Ohio CB code: 3380

Admissions: 97% of applicants accepted
Based on: ••• Interview, special talents
•• Activities, recommendations, school record
• Test scores
Completion: 95% of freshmen end year in good standing
65% graduate, 1% of these enter 4-year programs

2-year proprietary technical college, coed. Founded in 1971. **Undergraduate enrollment:** 74 men, 40 women full time; 18 men, 22 women part time. **Faculty:** 23 total (7 full time), 2 with doctorates or other terminal degrees. **Location:** Suburban campus in small city; 55 miles from Cincinnati, 80 miles from Columbus. **Calendar:** Quarter. Saturday and extensive evening/early morning classes. **Special facilities:** Photographic laboratories including 30 black and white and 30 color enlargers, gallery, computer lab for electronic imaging.

DEGREES OFFERED. AAS. 27 associate degrees awarded in 1992. 48% in communications, 52% visual and performing arts.

UNDERGRADUATE MAJORS. Medical photography, photographic technology, photography, video.

ACADEMIC PROGRAMS. 2-year transfer program, double major, internships. **Remedial services:** Learning to Learn course. **Placement/credit:** Institutional tests.

ACADEMIC REQUIREMENTS. Freshmen must earn minimum GPA of 2.0 to continue in good standing. 84% of freshmen return for sophomore year. Students must declare major by end of first year. **Graduation requirements:** 102 hours for associate (66 in major). Most students required to take courses in English, humanities, social sciences. **Additional information:** Training directed toward technical and professional aspects of photography.

FRESHMAN ADMISSIONS. Selection criteria: High school achievement record, activities, previous photography experience important. Interview or 2 letters of recommendation required. **Test requirements:** Basic skills test in mathematics and English required of applicants with high school GPA below 2.0 and those out of high school over 10 years.

1992 FRESHMAN CLASS PROFILE. 59 men applied, 58 accepted, 31 enrolled; 36 women applied, 34 accepted, 19 enrolled. 20% had high school GPA of 3.0 or higher, 65% between 2.0 and 2.99. **Characteristics:** 73% from in state, 100% commute. Average age is 20.

FALL-TERM APPLICATIONS. $35 fee. No closing date; applicants notified on a rolling basis. Interview required. Portfolio recommended. Deferred and early admission available.

STUDENT LIFE. Housing: Sufficient housing available in area. **Activities:** Student government, student newspaper, photography competitions.

STUDENT SERVICES. Career counseling, employment service for undergraduates, freshman orientation, personal counseling, placement service for graduates, services/facilities for handicapped.

ANNUAL EXPENSES. Tuition and fees (1992-93): $8,580. **Books and supplies:** $1,400.

FINANCIAL AID. 58% of freshmen, 43% of continuing students receive some form of aid. All jobs based on need. 29 enrolled freshmen were judged to have need, all were offered aid. **Aid applications:** No closing date; applicants notified on a rolling basis beginning on or about March 1.

ADDRESS/TELEPHONE. Betty Landes, Admissions Representative, Ohio Institute of Photography and Technology, 2029 Edgefield Road, Dayton, OH 45439. (513) 294-6155. Fax: (513) 294-2259.

Ohio Northern University
Ada, Ohio CB code: 1591

Admissions: 89% of applicants accepted
Based on: ••• School record, test scores
• Activities, essay, interview, recommendations, special talents
Completion: 85% of freshmen end year in good standing
58% graduate, 14% of these enter graduate study

4-year private university, coed, affiliated with United Methodist Church. Founded in 1871. **Accreditation:** Regional. **Undergraduate enrollment:** 1,251 men, 1,105 women full time; 49 men, 29 women part time. **Graduate enrollment:** 304 men, 130 women full time; 1 man, 1 woman part time. **Faculty:** 254 total (179 full time), 173 with doctorates or other terminal degrees. **Location:** Rural campus in small town; 15 miles from Lima. **Calendar:** Quarter, limited summer session. **Microcomputers:** 140 located in dormitories, libraries, classrooms, computer centers, campus-wide network. **Special facilities:** Art gallery, nature center, performing arts center.

DEGREES OFFERED. BA, BS, BFA, B. Pharm, JD. 433 bachelor's degrees awarded in 1992. 8% in business and management, 11% business/office and marketing/distribution, 9% teacher education, 16% engineering, 24% health sciences, 6% life sciences. Graduate degrees offered in 2 major fields of study.

UNDERGRADUATE MAJORS. Accounting, biochemistry, biology, business administration and management, business economics, ceramics, chemistry, civil engineering, communications, computer and information sciences, criminal justice studies, dramatic arts, electrical/electronics/communications engineering, elementary education, engineering and other disciplines, English, environmental science, finance, fine arts, French, graphic design, health education, history, industrial technology, international relations, liberal/general studies, marketing management, mathematics, mechanical engineering, medical laboratory technologies, music, music education, music performance, musical theater, painting, pharmacy, philosophy, physical education, physics, political science and government, printmaking, psychology, public relations, radio/television broadcasting, religion, sculpture, sociology, Spanish, sports management, sports medicine.

ACADEMIC PROGRAMS. Cooperative education, double major, dual enrollment of high school students, independent study, internships, study abroad, teacher preparation, Washington semester; liberal arts/career combination in engineering; combined bachelor's/graduate program in law. **Remedial services:** Tutoring, communication skills center. **ROTC:** Air Force, Army. **Placement/credit:** AP, CLEP General and Subject, IB, institutional tests; 45 credit hours maximum for bachelor's degree.

ACADEMIC REQUIREMENTS. Freshmen must earn minimum GPA of 2.0 to continue in good standing. 78% of freshmen return for sophomore year. Students must declare major by end of second year. **Graduation requirements:** 182 hours for bachelor's (45 in major). Most students required to take courses in English, history, mathematics, philosophy/religion, biological/physical sciences, social sciences. **Postgraduate studies:** 2% enter law school, 2% enter medical school, 1% enter MBA programs, 9% enter other graduate study.

FRESHMAN ADMISSIONS. Selection criteria: Minimum ACT score of 20 for pharmacy and engineering applicants. **High school preparation:** 16 units required. Required and recommended units include English 4, mathematics 2-3, social science 2-3 and science 2-3. 4 units mathematics and science required for engineering applicants, 3 units mathematics and science required for pharmacy applicants. **Test requirements:** SAT or ACT; score report by August 15.

1992 FRESHMAN CLASS PROFILE. 1,152 men applied, 990 accepted, 369 enrolled; 1,014 women applied, 930 accepted, 328 enrolled. 65% had high school GPA of 3.0 or higher, 33% between 2.0 and 2.99. 36% were in top tenth and 65% were in top quarter of graduating class. **Academic background:** Mid 50% of enrolled freshmen had ACT composite between 20-26. 93% submitted ACT scores. **Characteristics:** 87% from in state, 97% live in college housing, 6% have minority backgrounds, 2% are foreign students, 24% join fraternities/sororities. Average age is 18.

FALL-TERM APPLICATIONS. $30 fee, may be waived for applicants with need. Closing date August 1; priority given to applications received by June 1; applicants notified on a rolling basis beginning on or about October 15; must reply by August 1. Interview recommended. Audition recommended for music applicants. Portfolio recommended for art applicants. Essay recommended. Deferred admission available.

STUDENT LIFE. Housing: Dormitories (men, women, coed); fraternity, sorority housing available. **Activities:** Student government, magazine, radio, student newspaper, television, yearbook, choral groups, concert band, drama, jazz band, marching band, music ensembles, musical theater, opera, pep band, symphony orchestra, chapel choir, mime troupe, fraternities, sororities, Christian Legal Society, Fellowship of Christian Athletes, University Religious Association Council, Black Student Union, Amnesty International, College Republicans, Black Law Student Association, International Club, Habitat for Humanity.

ATHLETICS. NCAA. **Intercollegiate:** Baseball M, basketball, cross-country, diving, football M, golf M, soccer, softball W, swimming, tennis, track and field, volleyball W, wrestling M. **Intramural:** Badminton, basketball, bowling, golf M, handball M, racquetball, softball, swimming, table tennis M, tennis, track and field, volleyball, wrestling M.

STUDENT SERVICES. Aptitude testing, career counseling, employment service for undergraduates, freshman orientation, health services, personal counseling, placement service for graduates, services/facilities for handicapped.

ANNUAL EXPENSES. Tuition and fees: $14,775. **Room and board:** $3,885. **Books and supplies:** $540. **Other expenses:** $525.

FINANCIAL AID. 90% of freshmen, 78% of continuing students receive some form of aid. 59% of grants, 85% of loans, 92% of jobs based on need. Academic, music/drama, art scholarships available. **Aid applications:** Closing date July 31; priority given to applications received by May 1; applicants notified on a rolling basis beginning on or about March 15; must reply within 2 weeks.

ADDRESS/TELEPHONE. Karen P. Condeni, Dean of Admissions and Financial Aid, Ohio Northern University, Ada, OH 45810-1599. (419) 772-2260. Fax: (419) 772-1932.

Ohio State University Agricultural Technical Institute
Wooster, Ohio CB code: 1009

2-year public agricultural and technical college, coed. Founded in 1971. **Accreditation:** Regional. **Undergraduate enrollment:** 432 men, 131 women full time; 106 men, 60 women part time. **Faculty:** 51 total (45 full time), 24 with doctorates or other terminal degrees. **Location:** Rural campus in large town; 30 miles from Akron. **Calendar:** Quarter, limited summer session. Saturday classes. **Microcomputers:** 50 located in dormitories, libraries, computer centers. **Special facilities:** 1800-acre farm operation/enterprise laboratory, horticulture complex including greenhouses and polyhouses, conservatory and display gardens.

DEGREES OFFERED. AAS.

UNDERGRADUATE MAJORS. Agribusiness, agricultural business and management, agricultural products and processing, agricultural/industrial power and equipment, agronomy, animal sciences, biological laboratory technology, business and management, conservation and regulation, construction, dairy, equestrian science, fluid power, food management, food production/management/services, forest products processing technology, industrial equipment maintenance and repair, marketing and distribution, office supervision and management, ornamental horticulture, range management, science technologies, small business management and ownership, soil sciences.

ACADEMIC PROGRAMS. Cooperative education, double major, dual enrollment of high school students, honors program, independent study, internships, student-designed major, weekend college. **Remedial services:** Learning center, reduced course load, remedial instruction, tutoring. **Placement/credit:** AP, CLEP Subject, institutional tests.

ACADEMIC REQUIREMENTS. Freshmen must earn minimum GPA of 2.0 to continue in good standing. 83% of freshmen return for sophomore year. Students must declare major on enrollment. **Graduation requirements:** 100 hours for associate. Most students required to take courses in computer science, English, mathematics, biological/physical sciences, social sciences. **Additional information:** One quarter of occupational internship required.

FRESHMAN ADMISSIONS. Selection criteria: Open admissions. Out-of-state applicants evaluated on basis of GPA, class rank, curriculum, principal/counselor recommendations, and SAT/ACT scores. Recommended units include English 4, mathematics 3, social science 2 and science 2. Recommended science units should include biology and chemistry. Physics recommended for engineering technology majors. **Test requirements:** SAT or ACT (ACT preferred) for placement and counseling only; score report by August 15.

1992 FRESHMAN CLASS PROFILE. 144 men, 53 women enrolled. 26% were in top tenth and 61% were in top quarter of graduating class. **Academic background:** Mid 50% of enrolled freshmen had SAT-V between 310-440, SAT-M between 370-530; ACT composite between 15-19. 6% submitted SAT scores, 81% submitted ACT scores. **Characteristics:** 98% from in state, 61% commute, 2% have minority backgrounds. Average age is 20.

FALL-TERM APPLICATIONS. $30 fee, may be waived for applicants with need. Closing date August 15; applicants notified on a rolling basis. Interview recommended. CRDA. Deferred and early admission available. Programs with limited enrollment may have earlier application closing dates.

STUDENT LIFE. Housing: Dormitories (coed). **Activities:** Student government, student newspaper, yearbook, Phi Theta Kappa.

ATHLETICS. Intramural: Basketball, racquetball, softball, volleyball.

STUDENT SERVICES. Career counseling, employment service for undergraduates, freshman orientation, health services, personal counseling, placement service for graduates, special adviser for adult students, veterans counselor, services/facilities for handicapped.

ANNUAL EXPENSES. Tuition and fees (1992-93): $2,700, $8,193 additional for out-of-state students. **Room and board:** $2,115 room only. **Books and supplies:** $483. **Other expenses:** $2,921.

FINANCIAL AID. Academic scholarships available. **Aid applications:** No closing date; applicants notified on a rolling basis; must reply within 2 weeks.

ADDRESS/TELEPHONE. Arnold L. Mokma, Coordinator, Admissions/Marketing, Ohio State University Agricultural Technical Institute, 1328 Dover Road, Wooster, OH 44691-4099. (216) 264-3911.

Ohio State University: Columbus Campus

Columbus, Ohio CB code: 1592

Admissions: 79% of applicants accepted
Based on: ••• School record
• Activities, essay, recommendations, special talents, test scores
Completion: 81% of freshmen end year in good standing
46% graduate

4-year public university, coed. Founded in 1870. **Accreditation:** Regional. **Undergraduate enrollment:** 17,531 men, 15,376 women full time; 3,268 men, 2,783 women part time. **Graduate enrollment:** 4,569 men, 3,704 women full time; 2,099 men, 2,943 women part time. **Faculty:** 3,823 total (2,944 full time), 3,635 with doctorates or other terminal degrees. **Location:** Urban campus in very large city; 3 miles from downtown. **Calendar:** Quarter, extensive summer session. Saturday and extensive evening/early morning classes. **Microcomputers:** 1,068 located in dormitories, libraries, classrooms, computer centers. **Special facilities:** Radio telescope, American Playwrights Theater, Dance Notation Bureau Extension Center for Educational Research, biological science laboratory on Lake Erie, campus airport, Barneby Center for Environmental Studies, research vessel Hydra on Lake Erie, nuclear research reactor, supercomputer facility, Wexner Center for the Arts, Hale Black Cultural Center.

DEGREES OFFERED. BA, BS, BFA, MA, MS, MBA, MFA, MEd, MSW, PhD, DDS, MD, OD, B. Pharm, Pharm D, DVM, JD. 414 associate degrees awarded in 1992. 36% in agriculture, 64% multi/interdisciplinary studies. 7,214 bachelor's degrees awarded in 1992. 18% in business and management, 5% business/office and marketing/distribution, 9% communications, 9% education, 8% engineering, 8% allied health, 6% home economics, 10% social sciences. Graduate degrees offered in 246 major fields of study.

UNDERGRADUATE MAJORS. Accounting, actuarial sciences, adult and continuing education research, advertising, aerospace science (Air Force), aerospace/aeronautical/astronautical engineering, African languages, African studies, Afro-American (black) studies, agribusiness, agricultural business and management, agricultural economics, agricultural education, agricultural engineering, agricultural production, agricultural products and processing, agricultural sciences, agronomy, American literature, American studies, analytical chemistry, animal sciences, anthropology, Arabic, architecture, art education, art history, Asian studies, astronomy, atomic/molecular physics, behavioral sciences, bilingual/bicultural education, biochemistry, biological and physical sciences, biology, botany, business administration and management, business and management, business economics, business education, business statistics, ceramic engineering, ceramics, chemical engineering, chemistry, child development/care/guidance, Chinese, cinematography/film, city/community/regional planning, civil engineering, classics, clothing and textiles management/production/services, communications, community health work, comparative literature, computer and information sciences, computer engineering, computer graphics, computer programming, conservation and regulation, crafts, criminal justice studies, criminology, dairy, dance, demography, dental hygiene, dramatic arts, drawing, early childhood education, earth sciences, economics, education, education administration, education of exceptional children, education of the deaf and hearing impaired, education of the emotionally handicapped, education of the gifted and talented, education of the mentally handicapped, education of the multiple handicapped, education of the physically handicapped, education of the visually handicapped, electrical/electronics/communications engineering, electron physics, elementary education, engineering, engineering mechanics, engineering physics, English, English education, English literature, entomology, environmental design, family and community services, family/consumer resource management, fashion design, fiber/textiles/weaving, film arts, finance, fine arts, fishing and fisheries, fluids and plasmas, food management, food production/management/services, food science and nutrition, food sciences, foreign languages (multiple emphasis), foreign languages education, forestry and related sciences, forestry production and processing, French, genetics, human and animal, geochemistry, geography, geology, geophysics and seismology, geriatric services, German, gerontology, glass, Greek (classical), Greek (modern), health education, health sciences, Hebrew, history, home economics, home economics education, home economics journalism, home furnishings and equipment management/production/services, horticultural science, horticulture, hospitality and recreation marketing, hotel/motel and restaurant management, human environment and housing, human resources development, humanities, humanities and social sciences, Indic languages, individual and family development, industrial design, industrial engineering, information sciences and systems, inorganic chemistry, institutional/home management/supporting programs, insurance and risk management, international business management, international relations, international studies, international/comparative home economics, Islamic studies, Italian, Japanese, jazz, Jewish studies, journalism, junior high education, labor/industrial relations, landscape architecture, Latin, liberal/general studies, linguistics, management information systems, management science, marketing and distribution, marketing and distributive education, marketing management, marketing research, marriage and family counseling, materials engineering, mathematics, mathematics education, mechanical engineering, medical illustrating, medical laboratory technologies, medical records administration, medieval studies, metallurgical engineering, microbiology, military science (Army), mining and mineral engineering, music, music education, music history and appreciation, music performance, music theory and composition, naval science (Navy, Marines), nuclear physics, nurse anesthetist, nursing, occupational therapy, operations research, optometry, organic chemistry, painting, paleontology, parks and recreation management, personal services, personnel management, petroleum engineering, pharmacy, philosophy, photography, physical chemistry, physical education, physical sciences, physical therapy, physics, plant pathology, plant protection, plant sciences, political science and government, poultry, printmaking, production and operations management, psychology, public affairs, public relations, quality control technology, radio/television broadcasting, radiograph medical technology, real estate, recreation and community services technologies, religion, renewable natural resources, respiratory therapy, respiratory therapy technology, rhetoric, rural sociology, Russian, Scandinavian languages, science education, sculpture, secondary education, Slavic languages, social science education, social sciences, social studies education, social work, sociology, soil sciences, solid state physics, Spanish, special education, specific learning disabilities, speech, speech correction, speech pathology/audiology, speech/communication/theater education, statistics, student counseling and personnel services, surveying and mapping sciences, systems analysis, systems engineering, textiles and clothing, trade and industrial education, transportation management, urban design, visual and performing arts, water resources, wildlife management, women's studies, zoology.

ACADEMIC PROGRAMS. Accelerated program, computer delivered (on-line) credit-bearing course offerings, cooperative education, double major, dual enrollment of high school students, honors program, independent study, internships, semester at sea, student-designed major, study abroad, visiting/exchange student program, weekend college, cross-registration; combined bachelor's/graduate program in business administration, medicine, law. **Remedial services:** Learning center, reduced course load, remedial instruction, special counselor, tutoring. **ROTC:** Air Force, Army, Naval. **Placement/credit:** AP, CLEP Subject, institutional tests; 45 credit hours maximum for bachelor's degree.

ACADEMIC REQUIREMENTS. Freshmen must earn minimum GPA of 2.0 to continue in good standing. 83% of freshmen return for sophomore year. Students must declare major by end of second year. **Graduation requirements:** 196 hours for bachelor's. Most students required to take courses in English, foreign languages, humanities, mathematics, biological/physical sciences, social sciences. **Additional information:** Freshman Foundation Program available for minority and Appalachian students from Ohio for special counseling, tutoring, and financial aid.

FRESHMAN ADMISSIONS. Selection criteria: Competitive admissions for freshman applicants to the Columbus campus. Open admissions for Ohio residents for all other campuses. **High school preparation:** 15 units required. Required and recommended units include English 4, foreign language 2-3, mathematics 3-4, social science 2 and science 2-3. One visual or performing arts also required, and 1 additional unit from any other academic unit. **Test requirements:** SAT or ACT (ACT preferred) for placement and counseling only; score report by March 1.

1992 FRESHMAN CLASS PROFILE. 8,527 men applied, 6,567 accepted, 2,773 enrolled; 7,631 women applied, 6,192 accepted, 2,638 enrolled. 26% were in top tenth and 55% were in top quarter of graduating class. **Academic background:** Mid 50% of enrolled freshmen had SAT-V between 400-540, SAT-M between 450-620; ACT composite between 20-26. 52% submitted SAT scores, 89% submitted ACT scores. **Characteristics:** 91% from in state, 75% live in college housing, 15% have minority backgrounds, 3% are foreign students, 16% join fraternities/sororities. Average age is 18.

FALL-TERM APPLICATIONS. $30 fee, may be waived for applicants with need. Closing date February 15; applicants notified on or about March 31; must reply by May 1. Audition required for dance, music applicants. Portfolio required. CRDA.

STUDENT LIFE. Housing: Dormitories (men, women, coed); apartment, fraternity, sorority, cooperative housing available. Honors living-learning center residence hall for agriculture and human ecology majors. **Activities:** Student government, film, magazine, radio, student newspaper, television, yearbook, choral groups, concert band, dance, drama, jazz band, marching band, music ensembles, musical theater, opera, pep band, symphony orchestra, folk dance, fraternities, sororities, campus ministry, nationality groups, International Student Association, Black student organizations, Ohio Staters.

ATHLETICS. NCAA. **Intercollegiate:** Baseball M, basketball, cross-country, diving, fencing, field hockey W, football M, golf, gymnastics, ice hockey M, lacrosse M, rifle, soccer M, softball W, swimming, tennis, track and field, volleyball, wrestling M. **Intramural:** Archery, badminton, basketball, bowling, cross-country, diving, fencing, golf, gymnastics, handball, ice hockey, lacrosse, racquetball, rifle, rowing (crew), rugby, sailing, skiing, soccer, softball, squash, swimming, table tennis, tennis, track and field, volleyball, water polo, wrestling.

STUDENT SERVICES. Aptitude testing, career counseling, employment service for undergraduates, freshman orientation, health services, on-campus day care, personal counseling, placement service for graduates, special adviser for adult students, veterans counselor, services/facilities for handicapped.

ANNUAL EXPENSES. Tuition and fees (1992-93): $2,799, $8,292 additional for out-of-state students. **Room and board:** $4,014. **Books and supplies:** $483. **Other expenses:** $647.

FINANCIAL AID. 65% of freshmen, 65% of continuing students receive some form of aid. Grants, loans, jobs available. Academic, music/drama, art, athletic, state/district residency, leadership, alumni affiliation, minority scholarships available. **Aid applications:** No closing date; priority given to applications received by February 15; applicants notified on a rolling basis beginning on or about April 15; must reply within 2 weeks.

ADDRESS/TELEPHONE. Dr. James J. Mager, Director of Admissions, Ohio State University: Columbus Campus, 1800 Cannon Drive, Columbus, OH 43210-1200. (614) 292-3980.

Ohio State University: Lima Campus

Lima, Ohio CB code: 1541

2-year public branch campus college, coed. Founded in 1960. **Accreditation:** Regional. **Undergraduate enrollment:** 411 men, 540 women full time; 134 men, 176 women part time. **Faculty:** 74 total (49 full time), 42 with doctorates or other terminal degrees. **Location:** Suburban campus in large town; 90 miles from Columbus. **Calendar:** Quarter, limited summer session. Saturday classes. **Microcomputers:** 66 located in libraries, computer centers. **Additional facts:** One 4-year program and some graduate courses in education offered.

DEGREES OFFERED. AA.

UNDERGRADUATE MAJORS. Liberal/general studies. elementary education.

ACADEMIC PROGRAMS. 2-year transfer program, dual enrollment of high school students, honors program, independent study, teacher preparation, cross-registration. **Remedial services:** Learning center, reduced course load, remedial instruction, special counselor. **Placement/credit:** AP, CLEP Subject, institutional tests; 45 credit hours maximum for associate degree.

ACADEMIC REQUIREMENTS. Freshmen must earn minimum GPA of 2.0 to continue in good standing. 61% of freshmen return for sophomore year. Students must declare major by end of first year. **Graduation requirements:** 90 hours for associate. Most students required to take courses in English, humanities, mathematics, biological/physical sciences, social sciences. **Additional information:** Students often leave campus after 1-3 years and complete bachelor's degree on Columbus campus.

FRESHMAN ADMISSIONS. Selection criteria: Open admissions. **High school preparation:** 15 units recommended. Recommended units include English 4, foreign language 2, mathematics 3, social science 2 and science 2. One visual or performing arts also recommended and 1 additional unit from any other recommended unit. **Test requirements:** SAT or ACT (ACT preferred) for placement and counseling only; score report by July 1.

1992 FRESHMAN CLASS PROFILE. 295 men applied, 283 accepted, 197 enrolled; 296 women applied, 279 accepted, 199 enrolled. 8% were in top tenth and 20% were in top quarter of graduating class. **Academic background:** Mid 50% of enrolled freshmen had SAT-V between 370-500, SAT-M between 380-560; ACT composite between 18-22. 9% submitted SAT scores, 83% submitted ACT scores. **Characteristics:** 99% from in state, 100% commute, 4% have minority backgrounds. Average age is 19.

FALL-TERM APPLICATIONS. $30 fee, may be waived for applicants with need. Closing date July 1; applicants notified on a rolling basis. CRDA. Early admission available.

STUDENT LIFE. Activities: Student government, radio, student newspaper, choral groups, drama, musical theater, social service organizations.

ATHLETICS. Intramural: Baseball M, basketball, bowling, golf M, soccer, softball, table tennis, tennis, volleyball.

STUDENT SERVICES. Aptitude testing, career counseling, employment service for undergraduates, freshman orientation, on-campus day care, personal counseling, placement service for graduates, special adviser for adult students, services/facilities for handicapped.

ANNUAL EXPENSES. Tuition and fees (1992-93): $2,700, $8,193 additional for out-of-state students. **Books and supplies:** $650. **Other expenses:** $400.

FINANCIAL AID. 45% of freshmen, 40% of continuing students receive some form of aid. 96% of grants, 90% of loans, all jobs based on need. 180 enrolled freshmen were judged to have need, all were offered aid. Academic, music/drama, art, state/district residency, leadership, alumni affiliation, minority scholarships available. **Aid applications:** No closing date; priority given to applications received by April 1; applicants notified on a rolling basis beginning on or about May 1; must reply within 2 weeks.

ADDRESS/TELEPHONE. Melissa Green, Assistant Director, Ohio State University: Lima Campus, 4240 Campus Drive, Lima, OH 45804-3596. (419) 221-1641.

Ohio State University: Mansfield Campus

Mansfield, Ohio CB code: 0744

2-year public branch campus college, coed. Founded in 1958. **Accreditation:** Regional. **Undergraduate enrollment:** 345 men, 517 women full time; 166 men, 299 women part time. **Faculty:** 75 total (43 full time), 49 with doctorates or other terminal degrees. **Location:** Suburban campus in small city; 67 miles from Columbus. **Calendar:** Quarter, limited summer session. Saturday classes. **Microcomputers:** 47 located in libraries, classrooms, computer centers. **Special facilities:** Louis Bromfield Archives and Reading room, educational enrichment laboratory, language laboratory, Conard Art Gallery, elementary education suite. **Additional facts:** One 4-year program and graduate courses in education offered.

DEGREES OFFERED. AA.

UNDERGRADUATE MAJORS. Liberal/general studies. elementary education.

ACADEMIC PROGRAMS. 2-year transfer program, cooperative education, dual enrollment of high school students, honors program, independent study, teacher preparation, weekend college. **Remedial services:** Learning center, reduced course load, remedial instruction, special counselor. **Placement/credit:** AP, CLEP Subject, institutional tests; 45 credit hours maximum for associate degree.

ACADEMIC REQUIREMENTS. Freshmen must earn minimum GPA of 2.0 to continue in good standing. 58% of freshmen return for sophomore year. Students must declare major on enrollment. **Graduation requirements:** 90 hours for associate. Most students required to take courses in English, humanities, mathematics, biological/physical sciences, social sciences. **Additional information:** Students offen leave campus after 1-3 years and complete bachelor's degree on Columbus campus.

FRESHMAN ADMISSIONS. Selection criteria: Open admissions. Competitive admissions for out-of-state applicants. **High school preparation:** 15 units recommended. Recommended units include English 4, foreign language 2, mathematics 3, social science 2 and science 2. One visual or performing arts also recommended and one additional unit from any one of the subject areas. **Test requirements:** SAT or ACT (ACT preferred) for placement and counseling only; score report by July 1.

1992 FRESHMAN CLASS PROFILE. 137 men, 179 women enrolled. 9% were in top tenth and 26% were in top quarter of graduating class. **Academic background:** Mid 50% of enrolled freshmen had SAT-V between 420-510, SAT-M between 470-560; ACT composite between 18-22. 3% submitted SAT scores, 79% submitted ACT scores. **Characteristics:** 99% from in state, 100% commute, 5% have minority backgrounds, 1% are foreign students. Average age is 19.

FALL-TERM APPLICATIONS. $30 fee, may be waived for applicants with need. Closing date July 1; applicants notified on a rolling basis. Essay required. CRDA. Deferred and early admission available.

STUDENT LIFE. Activities: Student government, student newspaper, choral groups, drama, musical theater, Black Culture Club.

ATHLETICS. Intramural: Basketball, bowling, golf, softball, table tennis, tennis, volleyball.

STUDENT SERVICES. Aptitude testing, career counseling, employment service for undergraduates, freshman orientation, personal counseling, placement service for graduates, special adviser for adult students, services/facilities for handicapped.

ANNUAL EXPENSES. Tuition and fees (1992-93): $2,700, $8,193 additional for out-of-state students. **Books and supplies:** $450. **Other expenses:** $2,335.

FINANCIAL AID. 40% of freshmen, 30% of continuing students receive some form of aid. Academic, music/drama, art, athletic, leadership, minority scholarships available. **Aid applications:** No closing date; priority given to applications received by April 1; applicants notified on a rolling basis beginning on or about May 27; must reply within 2 weeks.

ADDRESS/TELEPHONE. Henry Thomas, Assistant Director, Ohio State University: Mansfield Campus, 1680 University Drive, Mansfield, OH 44906. (419) 755-4226.

Ohio State University: Marion Campus

Marion, Ohio CB code: 0752

4-year public branch campus college, coed. Founded in 1957. **Accreditation:** Regional. **Undergraduate enrollment:** 381 men, 363 women full time; 111 men, 156 women part time. **Faculty:** 86 total (30 full time), 34 with doctorates or other terminal degrees. **Location:** Suburban campus in large town; 44 miles from Columbus. **Calendar:** Quarter, limited summer session. Saturday classes. **Microcomputers:** 130 located in computer centers.

DEGREES OFFERED. AA, BA, BS.

UNDERGRADUATE MAJORS. Associate: Liberal/general studies. **Bachelor's:** Accounting, education, elementary education, psychology.

ACADEMIC PROGRAMS. 2-year transfer program, cooperative education, double major, dual enrollment of high school students, honors program, independent study, student-designed major, teacher preparation, weekend college. **Remedial services:** Learning center, reduced course load, remedial instruction, special counselor, tutoring. **Placement/credit:** AP, CLEP Subject, institutional tests; 45 credit hours maximum for associate degree.

ACADEMIC REQUIREMENTS. Freshmen must earn minimum GPA of 2.0 to continue in good standing. 53% of freshmen return for sophomore year. Students must declare major by end of first year. **Graduation requirements:** 90 hours for associate, 196 hours for bachelor's. Most students required to take courses in English, humanities, mathematics, biological/physical sciences, social sciences.

FRESHMAN ADMISSIONS. Selection criteria: Open admissions. Selective admissions for out-of-state applicants. **High school preparation:** 15 units recommended. Recommended units include English 4, foreign language 2, mathematics 3, social science 2 and science 2. One performing or visual arts also recommended, plus 1 additional unit from other recommended units. **Test requirements:** SAT or ACT (ACT preferred) for placement and counseling only; score report by July 1.

1992 FRESHMAN CLASS PROFILE. 176 men, 124 women enrolled. 8% were in top tenth and 19% were in top quarter of graduating class. **Academic background:** Mid 50% of enrolled freshmen had SAT-V between 380-480, SAT-M between 430-550; ACT composite between 17-22. 8% submitted SAT scores, 70% submitted ACT scores. **Characteristics:** 100% from in state, 100% commute, 10% have minority backgrounds. Average age is 20.

FALL-TERM APPLICATIONS. $30 fee, may be waived for applicants with need. Closing date July 1; applicants notified on a rolling basis; must reply by July 1. CRDA. Early admission available.

STUDENT LIFE. Activities: Student government, choral groups, campus Christian group, nontraditional student group, foreign language club.

ATHLETICS. Intramural: Basketball, horseback riding, table tennis, volleyball. **Clubs:** Basketball W and volleyball W.

STUDENT SERVICES. Aptitude testing, career counseling, employment service for undergraduates, freshman orientation, on-campus day care, personal counseling, placement service for graduates, services/facilities for handicapped.

ANNUAL EXPENSES. Tuition and fees (1992-93): $2,700, $8,193 additional for out-of-state students. **Books and supplies:** $483. **Other expenses:** $2,500.

FINANCIAL AID. Academic scholarships available. **Aid applications:** No closing date; priority given to applications received by April 1; applicants notified on a rolling basis beginning on or about May 27; must reply within 2 weeks.

ADDRESS/TELEPHONE. Becky McConnell, Admissions, Ohio State University: Marion Campus, 1465 Mount Vernon Avenue, Marion, OH 43302. (614) 389-2361.

Ohio State University: Newark Campus

Newark, Ohio CB code: 0824

2-year public branch campus college, coed. Founded in 1957. **Accreditation:** Regional. **Undergraduate enrollment:** 523 men, 567 women full time; 161 men, 285 women part time. **Faculty:** 93 total (48 full time), 50 with doctorates or other terminal degrees. **Location:** Suburban campus in large town; 28 miles from Columbus. **Calendar:** Quarter, limited summer session. Saturday classes. **Microcomputers:** 36 located in libraries, computer centers. **Special facilities:** Art gallery, mathematics laboratory, writing laboratory. **Additional facts:** One 4-year program in elementary education and some graduate courses in education offered.

DEGREES OFFERED. AA.

UNDERGRADUATE MAJORS. Liberal/general studies. elementary education.

ACADEMIC PROGRAMS. 2-year transfer program, cooperative education, dual enrollment of high school students, honors program, independent study, student-designed major, teacher preparation, weekend college, cross-registration. **Remedial services:** Learning center, remedial instruction, tutoring, mathematics workshops. **Placement/credit:** AP, CLEP Subject, institutional tests; 45 credit hours maximum for associate degree.

ACADEMIC REQUIREMENTS. Freshmen must earn minimum GPA of 2.0 to continue in good standing. 55% of freshmen return for sophomore year. Students must declare major by end of first year. **Graduation requirements:** 90 hours for associate. Most students required to take courses in English, humanities, mathematics, biological/physical sciences, social sciences. **Additional information:** Students often leave campus after 1-3 years and complete bachelor's degree on Columbus campus.

FRESHMAN ADMISSIONS. Selection criteria: Open admissions. Selective admissions for out-of-state applicants based on college preparatory curriculum and rank in class. **High school preparation:** 15 units recommended. Recommended units include English 4, foreign language 2, mathematics 3, social science 2 and science 2. One visual or performing arts also recommended and 1 additional unit from any other subject area. **Test requirements:** SAT or ACT (ACT preferred) for placement and counseling only; score report by July 1.

1992 FRESHMAN CLASS PROFILE. 231 men, 231 women enrolled. 9% were in top tenth and 22% were in top quarter of graduating class. **Academic background:** Mid 50% of enrolled freshmen had SAT-V between 360-460, SAT-M between 390-500; ACT composite between 18-22. 20% submitted SAT scores, 75% submitted ACT scores. **Characteristics:** 93% from in state, 100% commute, 4% have minority backgrounds. Average age is 19.

FALL-TERM APPLICATIONS. $30 fee, may be waived for applicants with need. No closing date; priority given to applications received by February 15; applicants notified on a rolling basis. CRDA. Early admission available. ACT/SAT not required for those out of high school 3 years or more. College preparatory curriculum not required of those who graduated from high school before 1984.

STUDENT LIFE. Housing: Privately owned student apartments within 2 minute walk of campus. **Activities:** Student government, choral groups, drama, campus ministry, support groups minority organization.

ATHLETICS. Intramural: Baseball M, basketball, softball, table tennis, volleyball.

STUDENT SERVICES. Aptitude testing, career counseling, freshman orientation, on-campus day care, personal counseling, placement service for graduates, special adviser for adult students, returnee center, services/facilities for handicapped.

ANNUAL EXPENSES. Tuition and fees (1992-93): $2,700, $8,193

additional for out-of-state students. **Books and supplies:** $600. **Other expenses:** $2,276.

FINANCIAL AID. 30% of freshmen, 30% of continuing students receive some form of aid. Academic, minority scholarships available. **Aid applications:** No closing date; priority given to applications received by April 1; applicants notified on a rolling basis beginning on or about May 27.

ADDRESS/TELEPHONE. Ann Donahue, Coordinator of Admissions, Ohio State University: Newark Campus, University Drive, Newark, OH 43055. (614) 366-3321.

Ohio University
Athens, Ohio CB code: 1593

Admissions: 73% of applicants accepted
Based on: ••• School record
•• Test scores
• Activities, essay, interview, recommendations, special talents
Completion: 92% of freshmen end year in good standing
70% graduate, 26% of these enter graduate study

4-year public university, coed. Founded in 1804. **Accreditation:** Regional. **Undergraduate enrollment:** 6,731 men, 7,886 women full time; 273 men, 433 women part time. **Graduate enrollment:** 1,425 men, 1,042 women full time; 229 men, 229 women part time. **Faculty:** 1,029 total (769 full time), 830 with doctorates or other terminal degrees. **Location:** Rural campus in large town; 75 miles from Columbus. **Calendar:** Quarter, extensive summer session. **Microcomputers:** 804 located in dormitories, libraries, classrooms, computer centers, campus-wide network. **Special facilities:** University airport, nuclear accelerator, 2 art galleries, genetics research center, greenhouse, cartography center, meteorology center, contemporary history institute. **Additional facts:** First university established in state.

DEGREES OFFERED. AA, AS, AAS, BA, BS, BFA, MA, MS, MBA, MFA, MEd, PhD, DO. 377 associate degrees awarded in 1992. 19% in business/office and marketing/distribution, 19% health sciences, 53% multi/interdisciplinary studies, 7% social sciences. 3,447 bachelor's degrees awarded. 16% in business and management, 19% communications, 14% teacher education, 7% engineering, 5% health sciences, 5% multi/interdisciplinary studies, 8% social sciences, 5% visual and performing arts. Graduate degrees offered in 117 major fields of study.

UNDERGRADUATE MAJORS. Associate: Accounting, aeronautical technology, child development/care/guidance, fashion merchandising, food science and nutrition, interior design, law enforcement and corrections, manufacturing technology, nursing, office supervision and management, radio/television technology, secretarial and related programs. **Bachelor's:** Accounting, actuarial sciences, advertising, aeronautical technology, African studies, Afro-American (black) studies, agribusiness, airline piloting and navigation, anthropology, applied mathematics, art education, art history, Asian studies, aviation management, biochemistry, biomedical science, botany, business administration and management, business and management, business computer/console/peripheral equipment operation, business economics, business education, business home economics, business statistics, business systems analysis, cell biology, ceramics, chemical engineering, chemistry, child development/care/guidance, civil engineering, classics, clinical laboratory science, communications, community services, computer and information sciences, computer engineering, creative writing, criminal justice studies, criminology, dance, dramatic arts, drawing, early childhood education, Eastern European studies, economics, education of the emotionally handicapped, education of the mentally handicapped, education of the multiple handicapped, educational media technology, electrical/electronics/communications engineering, elementary education, engineering physics, English, English education, English literature, environmental science, experimental psychology, family and community services, family/consumer resource management, fashion merchandising, fiber/textiles/weaving, film arts, finance, food management, food production/management/services, food science and nutrition, foreign languages (multiple emphasis), foreign languages education, forensic studies, French, geography, geology, German, graphic design, Greek (classical), health care administration, health education, history, home economics, home economics education, human environment and housing, human resources development, individual and family development, industrial engineering, industrial technology, information sciences and systems, institutional/home management/supporting programs, interior design, international business management, international public service, international relations, international studies, journalism, junior high education, labor/industrial relations, Latin, Latin American studies, liberal/general studies, linguistics, management information systems, management science, marketing and distribution, marketing management, mathematics, mathematics education, mechanical engineering, medical social work, microbiology, mining and mineral engineering, music, music education, music history and appreciation, music performance, music theory and composition, music therapy, nursing, nutritional sciences, occupational safety and health technology, operations research, painting, parks and recreation management, personnel management, philosophy, photography, physical education, physical therapy, physics, political science and government, predentistry, prelaw, premedicine, prepharmacy, preveterinary, printmaking, psychology, public administration, public relations, pure mathematics, radio/television broadcasting, recreation and community services technologies, recreation therapy, science education, sculpture, small business management and ownership, social science education, social studies education, social work, sociology, Spanish, special education, specific learning disabilities, speech, speech correction, speech pathology/audiology, speech/communication/theater education, sports medicine, studio art, systems analysis, systems engineering, telecommunications, textiles and clothing, theater design, visual and performing arts, Western European studies, zoology.

ACADEMIC PROGRAMS. Accelerated program, cooperative education, double major, dual enrollment of high school students, external degree, honors program, independent study, internships, student-designed major, study abroad, teacher preparation, visiting/exchange student program. **Remedial services:** Learning center, remedial instruction, special counselor, tutoring. **ROTC:** Air Force, Army. **Placement/credit:** AP, CLEP Subject, institutional tests.

ACADEMIC REQUIREMENTS. Freshmen must earn minimum GPA of 2.0 to continue in good standing. 84% of freshmen return for sophomore year. Students must declare major by end of second year. **Graduation requirements:** 96 hours for associate (40 in major), 192 hours for bachelor's (50 in major). Most students required to take courses in arts/fine arts, English, humanities, mathematics, biological/physical sciences, social sciences. **Postgraduate studies:** 35% from 2-year programs enter 4-year programs. 2% enter law school, 1% enter medical school, 6% enter MBA programs, 17% enter other graduate study.

FRESHMAN ADMISSIONS. Selection criteria: High school record as represented by rank in class, GPA, and curriculum completed. Secondary criteria, test scores, and recommendation. Top third in class preferred. **High school preparation:** 17 units recommended. Recommended units include English 4, foreign language 2, mathematics 3, social science 3 and science 3. Science preparatory program required for physical therapy applicants. **Test requirements:** SAT or ACT (ACT preferred); score report by March 1.

1992 FRESHMAN CLASS PROFILE. 4,968 men applied, 3,398 accepted, 1,299 enrolled; 6,489 women applied, 4,976 accepted, 1,972 enrolled. 75% had high school GPA of 3.0 or higher, 25% between 2.0 and 2.99. 22% were in top tenth and 58% were in top quarter of graduating class. **Academic background:** Mid 50% of enrolled freshmen had SAT-V between 420-520, SAT-M between 460-580; ACT composite between 21-25. 58% submitted SAT scores, 87% submitted ACT scores. **Characteristics:** 86% from in state, 98% live in college housing, 6% have minority backgrounds, 1% are foreign students, 20% join fraternities/sororities. Average age is 18.

FALL-TERM APPLICATIONS. $25 fee, may be waived for applicants with need. Closing date March 1; priority given to applications received by January 1; applicants notified on a rolling basis; must reply by May 15. Portfolio required. Essay recommended. Audition recommended for theater applicants; required for music and dance applicants. CRDA. Deferred and early admission available.

STUDENT LIFE. Housing: Dormitories (men, women, coed); apartment, fraternity, sorority housing available. **Activities:** Student government, film, magazine, radio, student newspaper, television, yearbook, choral groups, concert band, dance, drama, jazz band, marching band, music ensembles, musical theater, opera, pep band, symphony orchestra, fraternities, sororities, over 300 professional, religious, ethnic, political, and social service organizations.

ATHLETICS. NCAA. **Intercollegiate:** Baseball M, basketball, cross-country, diving, field hockey W, football M, golf M, ice hockey M, lacrosse, rifle, rugby, sailing, skiing, soccer M, softball W, swimming, tennis, track and field, volleyball, wrestling M. **Intramural:** Archery, badminton, baseball M, basketball, bowling, boxing M, cross-country, diving, fencing, golf, gymnastics, handball, horseback riding, lacrosse, racquetball, soccer, softball, squash, swimming, table tennis, tennis, track and field, volleyball, water polo, wrestling M.

STUDENT SERVICES. Aptitude testing, career counseling, employment service for undergraduates, freshman orientation, health services, on-campus day care, personal counseling, placement service for graduates, veterans counselor, black resource center, student legal program, ombudsman, international student, affirmative action offices, women's center, services/facilities for handicapped.

ANNUAL EXPENSES. Tuition and fees: $3,234, $3,453 additional for out-of-state students. **Room and board:** $4,353. **Books and supplies:** $425. **Other expenses:** $1,200.

FINANCIAL AID. 52% of freshmen, 46% of continuing students receive some form of aid. 81% of grants based on need. Academic, music/drama, art, athletic, state/district residency, leadership, alumni affiliation, minority scholarships available. **Aid applications:** Closing date March 15; priority given to applications received by February 15; applicants notified on a rolling basis beginning on or about April 15; must reply within 3 weeks.

ADDRESS/TELEPHONE. N. Kip Howard, Director of Admissions, Ohio University, 120 Chubb Hall, Athens, OH 45701-2979. (614) 593-4100. Fax: (614) 593-0662.

Ohio University: Chillicothe Campus
Chillicothe, Ohio CB code: 0775

2-year public branch campus college, coed. Founded in 1946. **Accreditation:** Regional. **Undergraduate enrollment:** 1,748 men and women. **Faculty:** 75 total (27 full time), 11 with doctorates or other terminal degrees. **Location:** Rural campus in large town; 45 miles from Columbus. **Calendar:** Quarter, limited summer session. **Microcomputers:** Located in libraries, classrooms, computer centers. **Additional facts:** Bachelor's programs in management, elementary education, criminal justice, nursing, self-designed major. Degree granted by Ohio University main campus. Some graduate courses available.

DEGREES OFFERED. AA, AS, AAS. 110 associate degrees awarded in 1992.

UNDERGRADUATE MAJORS. Business administration and management, law enforcement and corrections, legal secretary, liberal/general studies, mathematics/science, medical secretary, mental health/human services, office supervision and management, protective services, secretarial and related programs, social work, word processing.

ACADEMIC PROGRAMS. 2-year transfer program, double major, dual enrollment of high school students, external degree, independent study, internships, student-designed major, study abroad, teacher preparation, telecourses, cross-registration. **Remedial services:** Reduced course load, remedial instruction, special counselor, tutoring. **ROTC:** Air Force, Army. **Placement/credit:** AP, CLEP Subject, institutional tests.

ACADEMIC REQUIREMENTS. Freshmen must earn minimum GPA of 2.0 to continue in good standing. 45% of freshmen return for sophomore year. Students must declare major by end of first year. **Graduation requirements:** 192 hours for associate. Most students required to take courses in arts/fine arts, English, humanities, mathematics, biological/physical sciences, social sciences.

FRESHMAN ADMISSIONS. Selection criteria: Open admissions. Business, communications, and engineering colleges require high school GPA and test scores. Recommended units include English 4, foreign language 2, mathematics 3, social science 3 and science 3. College-preparatory program strongly recommended including 1 visual or performing art. **Test requirements:** SAT or ACT (ACT preferred) for placement and counseling only; score report by September 1.

1992 FRESHMAN CLASS PROFILE. 450 men and women enrolled. **Characteristics:** 99% from in state, 100% commute, 3% have minority backgrounds. Average age is 27.

FALL-TERM APPLICATIONS. $15 fee, may be waived for applicants with need. No closing date; applicants notified on a rolling basis.

STUDENT LIFE. Activities: Student government, student newspaper, drama.

ATHLETICS. Intercollegiate: Baseball M, basketball, golf, tennis, volleyball W. **Intramural:** Basketball, skiing.

STUDENT SERVICES. Aptitude testing, career counseling, freshman orientation, personal counseling, placement service for graduates, veterans counselor, services/facilities for handicapped.

ANNUAL EXPENSES. Tuition and fees (1992-93): $2,613, $3,663 additional for out-of-state students. **Books and supplies:** $500.

FINANCIAL AID. 40% of freshmen, 40% of continuing students receive some form of aid. **Aid applications:** Closing date March 1; applicants notified on a rolling basis beginning on or about April 30.

ADDRESS/TELEPHONE. Richard R. Whitney, Director of Student Services, Ohio University: Chillicothe Campus, 571 West Fifth Street, PO Box 629, Chillicothe, OH 45601. (614) 774-7200 ext. 240.

Ohio University: Eastern Campus
St. Clairsville, Ohio CB code: 0828

2-year public branch campus college, coed. Founded in 1957. **Accreditation:** Regional. **Undergraduate enrollment:** 980 men and women. **Faculty:** 65 total (20 full time), 23 with doctorates or other terminal degrees. **Location:** Rural campus in small town; 15 miles from downtown. **Calendar:** Quarter, limited summer session. **Microcomputers:** Located in libraries, computer centers. **Special facilities:** Dysart Woods (laboratory) primeval oak forest, Great Western School (Little Red Schoolhouse), art gallery. **Additional facts:** Some bachelor's and masters degrees available.

DEGREES OFFERED. AA, AS, B, M. 30 associate degrees awarded in 1992. 12% in business and management, 62% teacher education, 20% health sciences, 6% multi/interdisciplinary studies. 71 bachelor's degrees awarded. Graduate degrees offered in 3 major fields of study.

UNDERGRADUATE MAJORS. Biological and physical sciences, fine arts, humanities, liberal/general studies. business and management, elementary education, liberal/general studies, nursing.

ACADEMIC PROGRAMS. 2-year transfer program, accelerated program, dual enrollment of high school students, external degree, independent study, student-designed major, teacher preparation, weekend college. **Remedial services:** Learning center, reduced course load, remedial instruction, special counselor, tutoring. **Placement/credit:** Institutional tests.

ACADEMIC REQUIREMENTS. Freshmen must earn minimum GPA of 2.0 to continue in good standing. 65% of freshmen return for sophomore year. Students must declare major by end of second year. **Graduation requirements:** 96 hours for associate (30 in major), 192 hours for bachelor's (45 in major). Most students required to take courses in arts/fine arts, English, humanities, mathematics, biological/physical sciences, social sciences. **Additional information:** Several degree programs offered through cross-registration with main campus.

FRESHMAN ADMISSIONS. Selection criteria: Open admissions. Selective admissions to some programs. Recommended units include English 4, foreign language 2, mathematics 4, social science 3 and science 3. **Test requirements:** SAT or ACT (ACT preferred) for placement and counseling only; score report by September 10.

1992 FRESHMAN CLASS PROFILE. 205 men and women enrolled. **Characteristics:** 98% from in state, 100% commute, 1% have minority backgrounds. Average age is 23.

FALL-TERM APPLICATIONS. $15 fee, may be waived for applicants with need. No closing date; priority given to applications received by September 10; applicants notified on a rolling basis. Deferred and early admission available.

STUDENT LIFE. Activities: Student government, literary journal, drama.

ATHLETICS. Intercollegiate: Basketball, golf M, volleyball W. **Intramural:** Basketball.

STUDENT SERVICES. Aptitude testing, career counseling, freshman orientation, on-campus day care, personal counseling, special adviser for adult students, services/facilities for handicapped.

ANNUAL EXPENSES. Tuition and fees (1992-93): $2,613, $3,663 additional for out-of-state students. **Books and supplies:** $390.

FINANCIAL AID. Aid applications: Closing date February 15; applicants notified on or about May 15. **Additional information:** All financial aid applications and awards administered by main campus at Athens.

ADDRESS/TELEPHONE. Barry K. Hess, Director of Student Services, Ohio University: Eastern Campus, 45425 National Road, St. Clairsville, OH 43950. (614) 695-1720.

Ohio University: Lancaster Campus
Lancaster, Ohio CB code: 0826

2-year public branch campus college, coed. Founded in 1968. **Accreditation:** Regional. **Undergraduate enrollment:** 2,068 men and women. **Faculty:** 109 total (39 full time), 17 with doctorates or other terminal degrees. **Location:** Suburban campus in large town; 30 miles of Columbus. **Calendar:** Quarter, limited summer session. **Microcomputers:** 98 located in libraries, computer centers. **Special facilities:** Art gallery, museum. **Additional facts:** Some bachelor's and master's degrees available.

DEGREES OFFERED. AAS. 60 associate degrees awarded in 1992. 20% in business and management, 30% business/office and marketing/distribution, 6% computer sciences, 40% engineering technologies.

UNDERGRADUATE MAJORS. Accounting, business and management, computer and information sciences, drafting and design technology, electronic technology, fine arts, industrial technology, liberal/general studies, manufacturing technology, secretarial and related programs.

ACADEMIC PROGRAMS. Double major, independent study, internships, student-designed major, cross-registration. **Remedial services:** Learning center, remedial instruction, tutoring. **ROTC:** Air Force, Army, Naval. **Placement/credit:** AP, institutional tests.

ACADEMIC REQUIREMENTS. Freshmen must earn minimum GPA of 2.0 to continue in good standing. 60% of freshmen return for sophomore year. **Graduation requirements:** 50 hours for associate. Most students required to take courses in English, humanities, mathematics, biological/physical sciences, social sciences.

FRESHMAN ADMISSIONS. Selection criteria: Open admissions. Selective admissions to business, engineering and communciation programs. **Test requirements:** SAT or ACT (ACT preferred) for counseling; score report by September 1.

1992 FRESHMAN CLASS PROFILE. 400 men and women enrolled. **Academic background:** Mid 50% of enrolled freshmen had ACT composite between 14-22. 63% submitted ACT scores. **Characteristics:** 99% from in state, 100% commute, 1% have minority backgrounds.

FALL-TERM APPLICATIONS. $15 fee, may be waived for applicants with need. No closing date; applicants notified on a rolling basis. Deferred admission available.

STUDENT LIFE. Activities: Student government, choral groups, drama, outdoor club, Young Democrats, Young Republicans, Christian fellowship, adult support group.

ATHLETICS. Intercollegiate: Baseball, basketball, golf, tennis. **Intramural:** Skiing, table tennis, volleyball.

STUDENT SERVICES. Career counseling, employment service for undergraduates, freshman orientation, on-campus day care, placement service for graduates, veterans counselor, services/facilities for handicapped.

ANNUAL EXPENSES. Tuition and fees (1992-93): $2,613, $3,663 additional for out-of-state students. **Books and supplies:** $500.

FINANCIAL AID. 17% of continuing students receive some form of aid. Grants, loans, jobs available. **Aid applications:** No closing date; priority given to applications received by February 15; applicants notified on a rolling basis; must reply within 2 weeks. **Additional information:** Scholarship application deadline April 1. FAF and student information sheets must be sent by February 15 for first priority consideration.

ADDRESS/TELEPHONE. Scott Shepherd, Director of Student Services, Ohio University: Lancaster Campus, 1570 Granville Pike, Lancaster, OH 43130. (614) 654-6711. Fax: (614) 687-9497.

Ohio University: Southern Campus at Ironton
Ironton, Ohio CB code: 4529

4-year public branch campus college, coed. Founded in 1956. **Accreditation:** Regional. **Undergraduate enrollment:** 326 men, 633 women full time; 336 men, 761 women part time. **Graduate enrollment:** 85 men, 217 women part time. **Faculty:** 122 total (12 full time), 2 with doctorates or other terminal degrees. **Location:** Rural campus in large town; 20 miles from Huntington, West Virginia. **Calendar:** Quarter. **Microcomputers:** Located in libraries, classrooms. **Special facilities:** Microwave link with main campus and other regional campuses.

DEGREES OFFERED. AA, AS, AAS, BA, BS, MBA, MEd. 51 associate degrees awarded in 1992. 134 bachelor's degrees awarded. Graduate degrees offered in 1 major field of study.

UNDERGRADUATE MAJORS. Associate: Business and management, communications, community services, computer and information sciences, elementary education, journalism, liberal/general studies, prelaw, sociology. **Bachelor's:** Business and management, elementary education, liberal/general studies, management science, nursing.

ACADEMIC PROGRAMS. 2-year transfer program, dual enrollment of high school students, teacher preparation. **Remedial services:** Tutoring. **Placement/credit:** Institutional tests.

ACADEMIC REQUIREMENTS. No policy requiring minimum GPA; records of students having academic difficulty are reviewed individually. Students must declare major by end of second year. **Graduation requirements:** 96 hours for associate, 192 hours for bachelor's. Most students required to take courses in arts/fine arts, English, mathematics, biological/physical sciences, social sciences.

FRESHMAN ADMISSIONS. Selection criteria: Open admissions. **Additional information:** Nursing applicants must have associate degree or diploma.

1992 FRESHMAN CLASS PROFILE. 245 men, 523 women enrolled.

FALL-TERM APPLICATIONS. $15 fee. No closing date; applicants notified on a rolling basis. Deferred admission available.

STUDENT LIFE. Activities: Student government, radio, student newspaper.

STUDENT SERVICES. Career counseling, freshman orientation, personal counseling, placement service for graduates, veterans counselor, services/facilities for handicapped.

ANNUAL EXPENSES. Tuition and fees (1992-93): $2,412, $105 additional for out-of-state students. **Books and supplies:** $450.

FINANCIAL AID. Aid applications: No closing date; applicants notified on a rolling basis; must reply within 10 days.

ADDRESS/TELEPHONE. Eric Cunningham, Assistant Director, Ohio University: Southern Campus at Ironton, 1804 Liberty Avenue, Ironton, OH 45638. (614) 533-4600. (800) 626-0513. Fax: (614) 533-4631.

Ohio University: Zanesville Campus
Zanesville, Ohio CB code: 0846

4-year public regional campus of university with selected upper-division and graduate courses, coed. Founded in 1946. **Accreditation:** Regional. **Undergraduate enrollment:** 243 men, 489 women full time; 131 men, 315 women part time. **Graduate enrollment:** 14 men, 40 women part time. **Faculty:** 52 total (30 full time), 9 with doctorates or other terminal degrees. **Location:** Rural campus in large town; 55 miles from Columbus. **Calendar:** Quarter, limited summer session. Extensive evening/early morning classes. **Microcomputers:** 42 located in libraries, computer centers. **Additional facts:** Various masters degrees in education sometimes given on Zanesville Campus through the auspices of the main university.

DEGREES OFFERED. AA, AS, AAS, BS. 93 associate degrees awarded in 1992. 13% in communications, 76% health sciences, 11% multi/interdisciplinary studies. 97 bachelor's degrees awarded. 9% in business and management, 48% teacher education, 14% health sciences, 10% multi/interdisciplinary studies, 6% parks/recreation, protective services, public affairs, 7% psychology, 6% social sciences.

UNDERGRADUATE MAJORS. Associate: Biological and physical sciences, humanities, humanities and social sciences, liberal/general studies, nursing, radio/television broadcasting, radio/television technology. **Bachelor's:** Criminal justice studies, elementary education, liberal/general studies, nursing, prelaw.

ACADEMIC PROGRAMS. 2-year transfer program, double major, dual enrollment of high school students, independent study, student-designed major, teacher preparation, cross-registration. **Remedial services:** Learning center, reduced course load, remedial instruction, special counselor, tutoring. **Placement/credit:** AP, institutional tests.

ACADEMIC REQUIREMENTS. Freshmen must earn minimum GPA of 2.0 to continue in good standing. Students must declare major by end of second year. **Graduation requirements:** 96 hours for associate (30 in major), 192 hours for bachelor's (45 in major). Most students required to take courses in English, humanities, mathematics, biological/physical sciences, social sciences.

FRESHMAN ADMISSIONS. Selection criteria: Open admissions. Nursing admissions based on National League for Nursing test scores, high school GPA, and class rank. Admission to Colleges of Business, Engineering, and Communication based on high school rank and ACT scores. Recommended units include English 4, foreign language 2, mathematics 3, social science 3 and science 3. One year of visual or performing arts recommended. **Test requirements:** SAT or ACT (ACT preferred) for counseling. National League for Nursing Pre-Nursing and Guidance Examination required for nursing applicants.

1992 FRESHMAN CLASS PROFILE. 204 men and women enrolled. **Characteristics:** 100% commute.

FALL-TERM APPLICATIONS. $15 fee, may be waived for applicants with need. Closing date August 28; priority given to applications received by July 4; applicants notified on a rolling basis. Interview recommended for nursing applicants. Deferred and early admission available.

STUDENT LIFE. Housing: Privately owned student apartments available adjacent to campus. **Activities:** Student government, drama, Cultural Events Committee, Student Nursing Association.

ATHLETICS. Intercollegiate: Baseball M, basketball, golf, tennis, volleyball W. **Intramural:** Badminton, basketball, bowling, golf, skiing, table tennis, tennis, volleyball.

STUDENT SERVICES. Career counseling, employment service for undergraduates, freshman orientation, personal counseling, placement service for graduates, veterans counselor, services/facilities for handicapped.

ANNUAL EXPENSES. Tuition and fees (1992-93): $3,663 additional for out-of-state students. **Books and supplies:** $500. **Other expenses:** $489.

FINANCIAL AID. 65% of continuing students receive some form of aid. 82% of grants, all loans, 19% of jobs based on need. Academic scholarships available. **Aid applications:** No closing date; priority given to applications received by February 15; applicants notified on a rolling basis beginning on or about May 1; must reply within 2 weeks.

ADDRESS/TELEPHONE. Kellie Doyle, Assistant Director of Student Services, Ohio University: Zanesville Campus, 1425 Newark Road, Zanesville, OH 43701. (614) 453-0762. Fax: (614) 453-6161.

Ohio Valley Business College
East Liverpool, Ohio CB code: 5852

2-year proprietary business college, coed. Founded in 1886. **Undergraduate enrollment:** 246 men and women. **Faculty:** 23 total (8 full time), 5 with doctorates or other terminal degrees. **Location:** Urban campus in large town; 30 miles from Youngstown, 35 miles from Pittsburgh, Pennsylvania. **Calendar:** Semester, limited summer session. **Microcomputers:** 18 located in computer centers.

DEGREES OFFERED. AAS. 35 associate degrees awarded in 1992. 45% in business and management, 23% computer sciences, 23% allied health, 10% law.

UNDERGRADUATE MAJORS. Accounting, business and management, business computer/console/peripheral equipment operation, computer and information sciences, dental assistant, legal assistant/paralegal, medical assistant, secretarial and related programs.

ACADEMIC PROGRAMS. Double major, internships. **Remedial services:** Reduced course load. **Placement/credit:** Institutional tests.

ACADEMIC REQUIREMENTS. Freshmen must earn minimum GPA of 1.5 to continue in good standing. 86% of freshmen return for sophomore year. Students must declare major on application. **Graduation requirements:** 69 hours for associate. Most students required to take courses in English, mathematics.

FRESHMAN ADMISSIONS. Selection criteria: CPAT scores most important.

1992 FRESHMAN CLASS PROFILE. 120 men and women enrolled. 10% had high school GPA of 3.0 or higher, 50% between 2.0 and 2.99. **Academic background:** Mid 50% of enrolled freshmen had ACT composite between 13-19. 10% submitted ACT scores. **Characteristics:** 85% from in state, 100% commute, 6% have minority backgrounds, 5% join fraternities/sororities. Average age is 28.

FALL-TERM APPLICATIONS. $50 fee. Closing date August 15; priority given to applications received by April 15; applicants notified on a rolling basis beginning on or about June 30; must reply by registration. Interview required.

STUDENT LIFE. Activities: Student government, film, magazine, fraternities.

STUDENT SERVICES. Employment service for undergraduates, personal counseling, placement service for graduates, services/facilities for handicapped.

ANNUAL EXPENSES. Tuition and fees: $3,315. Fees for medical and dental assistant programs total $350. **Books and supplies:** $425.

FINANCIAL AID. 80% of freshmen, 80% of continuing students receive some form of aid. 99% of grants, 88% of loans based on need. 83 enrolled freshmen were judged to have need, all were offered aid. **Aid applications:** Closing date August 30; priority given to applications received by April 15; applicants notified on a rolling basis; must reply within 6 weeks.

ADDRESS/TELEPHONE. Director, Ohio Valley Business College, 500 Maryland Street, P.O. Box 7000, East Liverpool, OH 43920. (216) 385-1070 ext. 12.

Ohio Wesleyan University

Delaware, Ohio — CB code: 1594

Admissions: 77% of applicants accepted
Based on:
- ••• School record
- •• Activities, essay, recommendations, special talents, test scores
- • Interview

Completion: 96% of freshmen end year in good standing
73% graduate, 30% of these enter graduate study

4-year private liberal arts college, coed, affiliated with United Methodist Church. Founded in 1842. **Accreditation:** Regional. **Undergraduate enrollment:** 979 men, 908 women full time; 12 men, 38 women part time. **Faculty:** 164 total (134 full time), 133 with doctorates or other terminal degrees. **Location:** Suburban campus in large town; 20 miles from Columbus. **Calendar:** Semester, limited summer session. **Microcomputers:** 130 located in dormitories, libraries, classrooms, computer centers. **Special facilities:** Art museum, observatory, US Department of Agriculture laboratories, two nature field study preserves, SETI Research Observatory in Flagstaff, AZ.

DEGREES OFFERED. BA, BFA. 440 bachelor's degrees awarded in 1992. 24% in business and management, 6% teacher education, 5% health sciences, 8% law, 6% letters/literature, 6% life sciences, 5% physical sciences, 7% psychology, 10% social sciences, 6% visual and performing arts.

UNDERGRADUATE MAJORS. Accounting, advertising, Afro-American (black) studies, anthropology, art history, astronomy, bacteriology, biology, botany, business administration and management, business and management, business economics, business statistics, chemistry, classics, computer and information sciences, creative writing, dance, dramatic arts, earth sciences, economics, education, elementary education, English, English education, English literature, environmental science, finance, fine arts, foreign languages (multiple emphasis), foreign languages education, French, genetics, human and animal, geography, geology, German, history, international business management, international relations, journalism, junior high education, marketing research, mathematics, mathematics education, microbiology, music, music education, music history and appreciation, music performance, philosophy, physical education, physics, plant genetics, political science and government, predentistry, prelaw, premedicine, preveterinary, psychology, public relations, radio/television broadcasting, reading education, religion, science education, secondary education, social science education, social sciences, social studies education, sociology, Spanish, speech/communication/theater education, urban studies, visual and performing arts, women's studies, zoology.

ACADEMIC PROGRAMS. Accelerated program, double major, honors program, independent study, internships, student-designed major, study abroad, teacher preparation, visiting/exchange student program, New York semester, Washington semester, cross-registration; liberal arts/career combination in engineering, health sciences. **Remedial services:** Writing center. **ROTC:** Air Force. **Placement/credit:** AP, institutional tests.

ACADEMIC REQUIREMENTS. Freshmen must earn minimum GPA of 1.75 to continue in good standing. 85% of freshmen return for sophomore year. Students must declare major by end of second year. **Graduation requirements:** 128 hours for bachelor's (43 in major). Most students required to take courses in arts/fine arts, English, foreign languages, history, humanities, mathematics, philosophy/religion, biological/physical sciences, social sciences. **Postgraduate studies:** 10% enter law school, 7% enter medical school, 5% enter MBA programs, 8% enter other graduate study.

FRESHMAN ADMISSIONS. Selection criteria: Secondary school record most important followed by curriculum, test scores, recommendations, essay, extracurricular activities, general aptitude, alumni affiliations. Special consideration given to minority applicants; art, music and theater talent, students involved in volunteerism and service, and children of alumni and siblings of current students or alumni. **High school preparation:** 16 units recommended. Recommended units include English 4, foreign language 3, mathematics 3, social science 3 and science 3. **Test requirements:** SAT or ACT; score report by March 1. If SAT/ACT scores differ significantly, highest score taken.

1992 FRESHMAN CLASS PROFILE. 1,276 men applied, 914 accepted, 250 enrolled; 989 women applied, 829 accepted, 241 enrolled. 34% were in top tenth and 58% were in top quarter of graduating class. **Academic background:** Mid 50% of enrolled freshmen had SAT-V between 470-570, SAT-M between 510-610; ACT composite between 22-28. 81% submitted SAT scores, 57% submitted ACT scores. **Characteristics:** 47% from in state, 97% live in college housing, 9% have minority backgrounds, 9% are foreign students, 45% join fraternities/sororities. Average age is 18.

FALL-TERM APPLICATIONS. $35 fee, may be waived for applicants with need. No closing date; priority given to applications received by March 1; applicants notified on a rolling basis beginning on or about April 1; must reply by May 1 or within 2 weeks if notified thereafter. Audition required for music degree applicants. Essay required. Interview recommended. Portfolio recommended for art applicants. CRDA. Deferred and early admission available. Institutional early decision plan. Early applicants notified on February 15 or March 10.

STUDENT LIFE. Housing: Dormitories (women, coed); fraternity, cooperative housing available. Special-interest housing available including international, language, fine arts, honors, performing arts, black culture, and peace and justice houses. **Activities:** Student government, magazine, radio, student newspaper, yearbook, Cable News Network, choral groups, concert band, dance, drama, jazz band, music ensembles, musical theater, opera, pep band, symphony orchestra, fraternities, sororities, Organization of Jewish Students, Christian Fellowship, Young Democrats, College Republicans, Democratic Socialists of America, Student Union on Black Awareness, Sisters United, Help Anonymous, Student Y, Women's Resource Center.

ATHLETICS. NCAA. **Intercollegiate:** Baseball M, basketball, cross-country, diving, field hockey W, football M, golf M, horseback riding, lacrosse, sailing, soccer, swimming, tennis, track and field, volleyball W. **Intramural:** Basketball, cross-country, football, golf, gymnastics, handball, ice hockey, racquetball, skin diving, soccer, softball, squash, swimming, tennis, volleyball, water polo M.

STUDENT SERVICES. Aptitude testing, career counseling, employment service for undergraduates, health services, personal counseling, placement service for graduates, services/facilities for handicapped.

ANNUAL EXPENSES. Tuition and fees: $15,726. **Room and board:** $5,382. **Books and supplies:** $450. **Other expenses:** $650.

FINANCIAL AID. 82% of freshmen, 74% of continuing students receive some form of aid. 71% of grants, 91% of loans, 77% of jobs based on need. 344 enrolled freshmen were judged to have need, all were offered aid. Academic, music/drama, art, state/district residency, leadership, religious affiliation, minority scholarships available. **Aid applications:** No closing date; priority given to applications received by March 1; applicants notified on a rolling basis beginning on or about April 1; must reply by May 1 or within 2 weeks if notified thereafter.

ADDRESS/TELEPHONE. Donald C. Bishop, Dean for Enrollment Management, Ohio Wesleyan University, Sandusky Street, Delaware, OH 43015. (614) 368-2000. (800) 922-8953. Fax: (614) 368-3314.

Otterbein College

Westerville, Ohio — CB code: 1597

Admissions: 80% of applicants accepted
Based on:
- ••• School record
- •• Test scores
- • Activities, interview, recommendations, special talents

Completion: 97% of freshmen end year in good standing
64% graduate, 13% of these enter graduate study

4-year private liberal arts college, coed, affiliated with United Methodist Church. Founded in 1847. **Accreditation:** Regional. **Undergraduate enrollment:** 641 men, 967 women full time; 323 men, 507 women part time. **Graduate enrollment:** 2 men full time; 17 men, 74 women part time. **Faculty:** 187 total (130 full time), 76 with doctorates or other terminal degrees. **Location:** Suburban campus in large town; 12 miles from Columbus. **Calendar:** Quarter, limited summer session. **Microcomputers:** 50 located in dormitories, libraries, classrooms, computer centers. **Special facilities:** Observatory, radio telescope, 3 performance stages, stables.

DEGREES OFFERED. BA, BS, BFA, MEd. 400 bachelor's degrees awarded in 1992. 26% in business and management, 14% communications, 13% teacher education, 7% health sciences, 5% letters/literature, 7% psychology, 9% visual and performing arts. Graduate degrees offered in 3 major fields of study.

UNDERGRADUATE MAJORS. Accounting, art education, biology, biomedical science, business administration and management, business and management, business economics, business/organizational communications, chemistry, communications, computer and information sciences, dance, dramatic arts, economics, education, elementary education, English, English education, environmental science, equestrian science, finance, foreign languages education, French, health education, history, interior design, international relations, international studies, journalism, junior high education, marketing management, mathematics, mathematics education, music, music business management, music education, music history and appreciation, music performance, music theory and composition, musical theater, nursing, nursing education, philosophy, physical education, physics, political science and government, predentistry, preengineering, prelaw, premedicine, prepharmacy, preveterinary, psychology, public relations, radio/television broadcasting, religion, science education, secondary education, social studies education, sociology, Spanish, speech/communication/theater education, sports medicine, technical theater, theater design, visual and performing arts.

ACADEMIC PROGRAMS. Accelerated program, double major, dual enrollment of high school students, honors program, independent study, internships, semester at sea, student-designed major, study abroad, teacher preparation, weekend college, Washington semester, cross-registration; liberal arts/career combination in forestry, health sciences. **Remedial services:** Learning center, reduced course load, remedial instruction, tutoring. **ROTC:** Air Force, Army, Naval. **Placement/credit:** AP, CLEP General and Subject, institutional tests; 60 credit hours maximum for bachelor's degree.

ACADEMIC REQUIREMENTS. Freshmen must earn minimum GPA of 2.0 to continue in good standing. 82% of freshmen return for sophomore year. Students must declare major by end of second year. **Graduation requirements:** 180 hours for bachelor's (50 in major). Most students required to take courses in arts/fine arts, English, foreign languages, humanities, mathematics, philosophy/religion, biological/physical sciences, social sciences. **Postgraduate studies:** 2% enter law school, 3% enter medical school, 2% enter MBA programs, 6% enter other graduate study.

FRESHMAN ADMISSIONS. Selection criteria: All credentials considered. School achievement record most important. **High school preparation:** 18 units recommended. Recommended units include biological science 1, English 4, foreign language 3, mathematics 3, physical science 1 and social science 3. 1 unit in fine arts recommended. **Test requirements:** SAT or ACT; score report by April 20. **Additional information:** Students applying between May 1 and June 1 accepted on space-available basis.

1992 FRESHMAN CLASS PROFILE. 584 men applied, 469 accepted, 164 enrolled; 913 women applied, 736 accepted, 263 enrolled. 68% had high school GPA of 3.0 or higher, 32% between 2.0 and 2.99. 13% were in top tenth and 23% were in top quarter of graduating class. **Academic background:** Mid 50% of enrolled freshmen had SAT-V between 410-540, SAT-M between 440-570; ACT composite between 20-26. 49% submitted SAT scores, 91% submitted ACT scores. **Characteristics:** 87% from in state, 87% live in college housing, 7% have minority backgrounds, 2% are foreign students, 45% join fraternities/sororities. Average age is 18.

FALL-TERM APPLICATIONS. $15 fee, may be waived for applicants with need. Closing date June 1; priority given to applications received by April 20; applicants notified on a rolling basis; must reply by May 1 or immediately if notified therafter. Audition required for theater, music applicants. Interview recommended. Portfolio recommended for visual art applicants. CRDA. Deferred admission available.

STUDENT LIFE. Housing: Dormitories (men, women); fraternity, sorority housing available. **Activities:** Student government, radio, student newspaper, television, yearbook, choral groups, concert band, dance, drama, jazz band, marching band, music ensembles, musical theater, opera, pep band, symphony orchestra, fraternities, sororities, Fellowship of Christian Athletes, Religious Activities Council, Christian Support Group, Afro-American Student Union.

ATHLETICS. NCAA. **Intercollegiate:** Baseball M, basketball, cross-country, football M, golf M, horseback riding, soccer, softball W, tennis, track and field, volleyball W. **Intramural:** Badminton W, basketball, bowling, football M, golf, racquetball, softball, table tennis, tennis, track and field M, volleyball.

STUDENT SERVICES. Career counseling, employment service for undergraduates, freshman orientation, health services, personal counseling, placement service for graduates, special adviser for adult students, services/facilities for handicapped.

ANNUAL EXPENSES. Tuition and fees: $12,192. **Room and board:** $4,314. **Books and supplies:** $400. **Other expenses:** $720.

FINANCIAL AID. 90% of freshmen, 90% of continuing students receive some form of aid. 69% of grants, 93% of loans, 83% of jobs based on need. Academic, music/drama, art, state/district residency, leadership, religious affiliation, minority scholarships available. **Aid applications:** Closing date April 15; priority given to applications received by March 1; applicants notified on a rolling basis beginning on or about February 15; must reply by May 1 or within 4 weeks if notified thereafter.

ADDRESS/TELEPHONE. Thomas H. Stein, Vice President of Admission and Financial Aid, Otterbein College, West College Avenue and Grove Street, Westerville, OH 43081. (614) 890-0004. Fax: (614) 898-1200.

Owens Technical College: Findlay Campus

Findlay, Ohio — CB code: 5487

2-year public technical college, coed. **Accreditation:** Regional. **Undergraduate enrollment:** 156 men, 225 women full time; 434 men, 484 women part time. **Faculty:** 60 total (10 full time). **Location:** Urban campus in large town; 45 minutes from Toledo. **Calendar:** Semester, limited summer session. **Microcomputers:** 50 located in classrooms, computer centers. **Special facilities:** University of Findlay facilities available.

DEGREES OFFERED. AS, AAS. 60 associate degrees awarded in 1992. 22% in business and management, 43% engineering technologies, 29% allied health, 6% parks/recreation, protective services, public affairs.

UNDERGRADUATE MAJORS. Business data programming, computer technology, drafting and design technology, early childhood education, electrical technology, electromechanical technology, electronic technology, engineering and engineering-related technologies, industrial technology, law enforcement and corrections technologies, marketing and distribution, marketing management, microcomputer software, nursing, secretarial and related programs, surgical technology, water and wastewater technology, word processing.

ACADEMIC PROGRAMS. Double major, dual enrollment of high school students, internships, student-designed major, telecourses. **Remedial services:** Preadmission summer program, reduced course load, remedial instruction, special counselor, tutoring. **Placement/credit:** Institutional tests.

ACADEMIC REQUIREMENTS. Freshmen must earn minimum GPA of 1.70 to continue in good standing. Students must declare major on enrollment. **Graduation requirements:** Most students required to take courses in computer science, English, humanities, social sciences.

FRESHMAN ADMISSIONS. Selection criteria: Open admissions. Health technologies required to submit high school and college transcript plus ACT scores. College Peace Officer Academy applicants must submit high school and college transcripts, ACT or ASSET scores, and LEADR scores.

1992 FRESHMAN CLASS PROFILE. 142 men, 174 women enrolled. **Academic background:** Mid 50% of enrolled freshmen had ACT composite between 12-19. 50% submitted ACT scores. **Characteristics:** 100% commute, 6% have minority backgrounds. Average age is 29.

FALL-TERM APPLICATIONS. No fee. Closing date August 28; applicants notified on a rolling basis. Deferred and early admission available. Acceptance reply required only of allied health applicants.

STUDENT LIFE. Housing: Housing available through special arrangement with the University of Findlay. **Activities:** Student government, student newspaper, pep band.

ATHLETICS. NJCAA. **Intercollegiate:** Basketball M. **Intramural:** Baseball M, basketball M, football M, softball.

STUDENT SERVICES. Aptitude testing, career counseling, employment service for undergraduates, freshman orientation, personal counseling, placement service for graduates, special adviser for adult students, veterans counselor, services/facilities for handicapped.

ANNUAL EXPENSES. Tuition and fees (1992-93): $1,724, $1,464 additional for out-of-state students. **Books and supplies:** $800. **Other expenses:** $800.

FINANCIAL AID. Grants, loans, jobs available. **Aid applications:** No closing date; applicants notified on a rolling basis.

ADDRESS/TELEPHONE. Mary Ann Frost, Enrollment Manager, Owens Technical College: Findlay Campus, 300 Davis Street, Findlay, OH 45840. (419) 423-6827. (800) FINDLAY.

Owens Technical College: Toledo

Toledo, Ohio — CB code: 1643

2-year public technical college, coed. Founded in 1966. **Accreditation:** Regional. **Undergraduate enrollment:** 1,255 men, 1,716 women full time; 3,152 men, 2,737 women part time. **Faculty:** 410 total (120 full time), 30 with doctorates or other terminal degrees. **Location:** Suburban campus in large city. **Calendar:** Semester, limited summer session. **Microcomputers:** 300 located in libraries, classrooms, computer centers. **Additional facts:** Branch campus in Findlay.

DEGREES OFFERED. AAS. 630 associate degrees awarded in 1992. 30% in business and management, 12% engineering technologies, 41% health sciences, 10% parks/recreation, protective services, public affairs, 7% trade and industry.

UNDERGRADUATE MAJORS. Accounting, agribusiness, air conditioning/heating/refrigeration mechanics, air conditioning/heating/refrigeration technology, architectural technologies, automotive mechanics, automotive technology, biomedical equipment technology, business and management, business data programming, child development/care/guidance, civil technology, computer graphics, computer programming, computer technology, dental hygiene, diesel engine mechanics, dietetic aide/assistant, drafting and design technology, early childhood education, electrical technology, electromechanical technology, electronic technology, engineering and engineering-related technologies, fashion merchandising, finance, food management, horticulture, hotel/motel and restaurant management, industrial technology, law enforcement and corrections technologies, manufacturing technology, marketing and distribution, marketing management, mechanical engineering, microcomputer software, nuclear medical technology, nursing, ophthalmic services, physical therapy assistant, quality control technology, radiograph medical technology, secretarial and related programs, surgical technology, ultrasound technology, word processing.

ACADEMIC PROGRAMS. Cooperative education, double major, dual enrollment of high school students, internships, student-designed major. **Remedial services:** Preadmission summer program, reduced course load, remedial instruction, special counselor, tutoring. **Placement/credit:** Institutional tests.

ACADEMIC REQUIREMENTS. Freshmen must earn minimum GPA of 1.7 to continue in good standing. Students must declare major on enrollment. **Graduation requirements:** 64 hours for associate (37 in major). Most students required to take courses in computer science, English, humanities, social sciences.

FRESHMAN ADMISSIONS. Selection criteria: Open admissions. Health technologies required to submit high school and college transcripts plus ACT test score. College Peace Officer Academy applicants must submit high school and college transcripts, ACT or ASSET score,and LEADR score. **Test requirements:** ACT required of allied health applicants.

1992 FRESHMAN CLASS PROFILE. 1,205 men, 1,204 women enrolled. **Academic background:** Mid 50% of enrolled freshmen had ACT composite between 12-19. 50% submitted ACT scores. **Characteristics:** 97% from in state, 100% commute, 11% have minority backgrounds, 2% are foreign students. Average age is 28.

FALL-TERM APPLICATIONS. No fee. Closing date August 28; applicants notified on a rolling basis; reply required only of allied health applicants. Deferred and early admission available. February 1 application deadline for dental hygiene and physical therapist assistant programs.

STUDENT LIFE. Activities: Student government, student newspaper, special interest clubs.

ATHLETICS. NJCAA. **Intercollegiate:** Basketball M. **Intramural:** Baseball M, basketball, golf, skiing, softball, table tennis, tennis, volleyball.

STUDENT SERVICES. Aptitude testing, career counseling, employment service for undergraduates, freshman orientation, health services, on-campus day care, personal counseling, placement service for graduates, special adviser for adult students, veterans counselor, services/facilities for handicapped.

ANNUAL EXPENSES. Tuition and fees (1992-93): $1,724, $1,464 additional for out-of-state students. **Books and supplies:** $800.

FINANCIAL AID. 40% of freshmen, 40% of continuing students receive some form of aid. Grants, loans, jobs available. Academic scholarships available. **Aid applications:** No closing date; priority given to applications received by March 15; applicants notified on a rolling basis beginning on or about May 1; must reply within 2 weeks.

ADDRESS/TELEPHONE. Mary Ann Frost, Enrollment Manager, Owens Technical College: Toledo, P.O. Box 10000, Toledo, OH 43699-1947. (419) 666-3282. Fax: (800) 466-9367 ext. 225.

Pontifical College Josephinum
Columbus, Ohio — CB code: 1348

Admissions:	93% of applicants accepted
Based on:	••• Recommendations, religious affiliation/commitment, school record, test scores
	• Activities, essay, interview
Completion:	99% of freshmen end year in good standing
	90% graduate, 77% of these enter graduate study

4-year private liberal arts, seminary college, men only, affiliated with Roman Catholic Church. Founded in 1892. **Accreditation:** Regional. **Undergraduate enrollment:** 52 men, 1 woman full time; 2 men, 3 women part time. **Graduate enrollment:** 67 men, 1 woman full time; 3 men, 8 women part time. **Faculty:** 60 total (26 full time), 24 with doctorates or other terminal degrees. **Location:** Suburban campus in very large city. **Calendar:** Semester. **Microcomputers:** 11 located in libraries, computer centers. **Additional facts:** Only seminary outside of Italy directly under Holy See. The Apostolic Pronuncio in the United States is chancellor. Applicants should have serious intentions of studying for Roman Catholic priesthood. Women who plan to enter graduate school to earn degree in theology may matriculate at undergraduate level.

DEGREES OFFERED. BA, MA, M.Div. 15 bachelor's degrees awarded in 1992. 19% in area and ethnic studies, 27% letters/literature, 27% philosophy, religion, theology, 27% psychology, 10% social sciences. Graduate degrees offered in 2 major fields of study.

UNDERGRADUATE MAJORS. English, English literature, history, Latin American studies, philosophy, psychology, religion.

ACADEMIC PROGRAMS. Accelerated program, double major, independent study. **Remedial services:** Learning center, reduced course load, remedial instruction, special counselor, tutoring. **Placement/credit:** AP, CLEP General and Subject, institutional tests; 30 credit hours maximum for bachelor's degree.

ACADEMIC REQUIREMENTS. Freshmen must earn minimum GPA of 1.75 to continue in good standing. 85% of freshmen return for sophomore year. Students must declare major by end of second year. **Graduation requirements:** 130 hours for bachelor's (30 in major). Most students required to take courses in English, foreign languages, history, mathematics, philosophy/religion, biological/physical sciences, social sciences. **Additional information:** Students participate in supervised field experience and clinical pastoral education.

FRESHMAN ADMISSIONS. Selection criteria: School achievement record, recommendations from pastor and director of vocations required. **High school preparation:** 10 units required; 18 recommended. Required and recommended units include English 4, foreign language 1-2, mathematics 2-4, physical science 1-2 and social science 2-4. Science 2 recommended. **Test requirements:** SAT or ACT; score report by August 24.

1992 FRESHMAN CLASS PROFILE. 15 men applied, 14 accepted, 14 enrolled. 5% had high school GPA of 3.0 or higher, 70% between 2.0 and 2.99. **Characteristics:** 21% from in state, 100% live in college housing, 14% have minority backgrounds. Average age is 21.

FALL-TERM APPLICATIONS. $15 fee, may be waived for applicants with need. No closing date; priority given to applications received by August 1; applicants notified on a rolling basis beginning on or about May 1; must reply within 3 weeks. Essay required. Interview recommended for undecided applicants. CRDA. EDP-S.

STUDENT LIFE. Housing: Dormitories (men). **Activities:** Student government, student newspaper, yearbook, choral groups, drama, jazz band, music ensembles, pep band, Latin American Studies Organization. **Additional information:** Religious observance required.

ATHLETICS. NSCAA. **Intercollegiate:** Basketball, soccer. **Intramural:** Basketball, bowling, gymnastics, handball, softball, swimming, table tennis, volleyball.

STUDENT SERVICES. Career counseling, health services, personal counseling, services/facilities for handicapped.

ANNUAL EXPENSES. Tuition and fees (projected): $5,227. **Room and board:** $3,532. **Books and supplies:** $350. **Other expenses:** $2,700.

FINANCIAL AID. 95% of freshmen, 75% of continuing students receive some form of aid. 88% of grants, 94% of loans, all jobs based on need. 3 enrolled freshmen were judged to have need, all were offered aid. Academic, state/district residency scholarships available. **Aid applications:** No closing date; priority given to applications received by June 30; applicants notified on a rolling basis beginning on or about August 15; must reply by August 30 or immediately if notified thereafter.

ADDRESS/TELEPHONE. Director of Admissions, Pontifical College Josephinum, 7625 North High Street, Columbus, OH 43085. (614) 885-5585 ext. 43. Fax: (614) 885-2307.

Rabbinical College of Telshe
Wickliffe, Ohio — CB code: 1660

4-year private rabbinical, teachers college, men only, affiliated with Jewish faith. Founded in 1941. **Undergraduate enrollment:** 700 men full time. **Graduate enrollment:** 100 men full time. **Location:** Suburban campus in small city. **Calendar:** Quarter.

FRESHMAN ADMISSIONS. Selection criteria: Personal interview and religious commitment most important.

ADDRESS/TELEPHONE. Office of Admissions, Rabbinical College of Telshe, 28400 Euclid Avenue, Wickliffe, OH 44092-2584. (216) 943-5300.

RETS Tech Center
Centerville, Ohio — CB code: 1610

2-year proprietary postsecondary technical school, coed. Founded in 1953. **Undergraduate enrollment:** 400 men and women. **Location:** Suburban campus in large town; 15 miles south of Dayton. **Calendar:** Quarter.

FRESHMAN ADMISSIONS. Selection criteria: Open admissions.

ANNUAL EXPENSES. Tuition and fees (1992-93): $6,700. **Books and supplies:** $700. **Other expenses:** $945.

ADDRESS/TELEPHONE. Kenneth Miller, Director of Admissions, RETS Technical Center, 116 Westpark Road, Centerville, OH 45459. (513) 433-3410. (800) 837-7387.

Shawnee State University
Portsmouth, Ohio — CB code: 1790

4-year public university, coed. Founded in 1975. **Accreditation:** Regional. **Undergraduate enrollment:** 3,636 men and women. **Location:** Suburban campus in large town; 90 miles south of Columbus. **Calendar:** Quarter.

FRESHMAN ADMISSIONS. Selection criteria: Open admissions. Selective admissions to allied health programs.

ANNUAL EXPENSES. Tuition and fees (1992-93): $2,409, $1,536 additional for out-of-state students. Some districts in Kentucky and West Virginia pay only $624 additional tuition. **Room and board:** $1,650 room only. **Books and supplies:** $420. **Other expenses:** $2,813.

ADDRESS/TELEPHONE. Rosemary Poston, Director of Admission/Counselor, Shawnee State University, 940 Second Street, Portsmouth, OH 45662. (614) 354-3205. Fax: (614) 355-2416.

Sinclair Community College
Dayton, Ohio — CB code: 1720

2-year public community college, coed. Founded in 1887. **Accreditation:** Regional. **Undergraduate enrollment:** 2,405 men, 3,819 women full time; 5,457 men, 9,119 women part time. **Faculty:** 933 total (373 full time), 43 with doctorates or other terminal degrees. **Location:** Urban campus in small city; 50 miles from Cincinnati. **Calendar:** Quarter, extensive summer session. Saturday and extensive evening/early morning classes. **Microcomputers:** Located in libraries, computer centers.

DEGREES OFFERED. AA, AS, AAS. 1,228 associate degrees awarded in 1992. 30% in business and management, 13% engineering technologies, 28% allied health, 12% multi/interdisciplinary studies, 7% visual and performing arts.

UNDERGRADUATE MAJORS. Accounting, air conditioning/heating/refrigeration mechanics, air conditioning/heating/refrigeration technology, architectural technologies, architecture, automotive mechanics, automotive technology, aviation management, business administration and management, business and office, child development/care/guidance, civil technology, commercial art, communications, computer and information sciences, contract management and procurement/purchasing, dance, dental hygiene, dietetic aide/assistant, drafting and design technology, dramatic arts, education of the multiple handicapped, electromechanical technology, electronic technology, emergency medical technologies, engineering and engineering-related technologies, finance, fine arts, fire control and safety technology, food production/management/services, food science and nutrition, graphic arts technology, hotel/motel and restaurant management, illustration design, industrial technology, interpreter for the deaf, labor/industrial relations, law enforcement and corrections technologies, legal assistant/paralegal, legal secretary, liberal/general studies, manufacturing technology, marketing and distribution, marketing management, mechanical design technology, medical records technology, mental health/human services, music, nursing, occupational safety and health technology, occupational therapy assistant, packaging engineering technology, physical education, physical therapy assistant, protective services, public affairs, quality control technology, radiograph medical technology, real estate, respiratory therapy, retailing, robotics, secretarial and related programs, social work, special education, surgical technology, theater design, tourism, trade and industrial supervision and management, transportation and travel marketing, transportation management, visual and performing arts.

ACADEMIC PROGRAMS. 2-year transfer program, cooperative education, double major, dual enrollment of high school students, honors program, independent study, internships, student-designed major, study abroad, telecourses, cross-registration. **Remedial services:** Learning center, preadmission summer program, reduced course load, remedial instruction, special counselor, tutoring. **ROTC:** Army. **Placement/credit:** AP, CLEP General and Subject, institutional tests; 45 credit hours maximum for associate degree.

ACADEMIC REQUIREMENTS. Freshmen must earn minimum GPA of 1.8 to continue in good standing. 70% of freshmen return for sophomore year. **Graduation requirements:** 90 hours for associate. Most students required to take courses in computer science, English, humanities, mathematics, biological/physical sciences.

FRESHMAN ADMISSIONS. Selection criteria: Open admissions. Selective admissions for allied health programs, based on test scores and school grades. Recommended high school units vary by program. **Test requirements:** Allied Health Aptitude Test required for medical records, physical therapy, radiology, dietetics, and respiratory therapy applicants. Psychological Corporation Nursing Entrance Examination for nursing, dental hygiene, and surgical applicants.

1992 FRESHMAN CLASS PROFILE. 1,828 men, 2,465 women enrolled. **Characteristics:** 99% from in state, 100% commute, 16% have minority backgrounds, 1% are foreign students. Average age is 29.

FALL-TERM APPLICATIONS. $10 fee. No closing date; applicants notified on a rolling basis. Interview required for allied health applicants. Early admission available. Institutional early decision plan. Closing dates for allied health program applications vary by program.

STUDENT LIFE. Activities: Student government, student newspaper, student handbook, choral groups, concert band, dance, drama, jazz band, music ensembles, musical theater, opera.

ATHLETICS. NJCAA. **Intercollegiate:** Baseball M, basketball, golf M, softball W, tennis, volleyball W. **Intramural:** Archery, badminton, basketball M, bowling, gymnastics, handball M, racquetball, softball M, swimming, table tennis, volleyball, wrestling M.

STUDENT SERVICES. Aptitude testing, career counseling, employment service for undergraduates, freshman orientation, on-campus day care, personal counseling, placement service for graduates, special adviser for adult students, veterans counselor, women's reentry program, services/facilities for handicapped.

ANNUAL EXPENSES. Tuition and fees (1992-93): $1,395, $630 additional for out-of-district students, $1,935 additional for out-of-state students. **Books and supplies:** $750. **Other expenses:** $1,700.

FINANCIAL AID. 6% of freshmen, 20% of continuing students receive some form of aid. All grants, 72% of loans, all jobs based on need. **Aid applications:** No closing date; priority given to applications received by April 15; applicants notified on a rolling basis beginning on or about June 15; must reply within 2 weeks.

ADDRESS/TELEPHONE. Sara Smith, Director of Admissions, Sinclair Community College, 444 West Third Street, Dayton, OH 45402. (513) 226-2963.

Southern Ohio College
Cincinnati, Ohio

CB code: 0297

2-year proprietary junior college, coed. Founded in 1927. **Accreditation:** Regional. **Undergraduate enrollment:** 292 men and women full time; 136 men and women part time. **Faculty:** 43 total (11 full time). **Location:** Urban campus in large city; 5 miles from downtown. **Calendar:** Quarter, extensive summer session. Extensive evening/early morning classes. **Microcomputers:** 50 located in classrooms, computer centers. **Additional facts:** 4 collegiate branch campuses located in Fairfield, Cincinnati, Akron, and Ft. Mitchell, Kentucky.

DEGREES OFFERED. AAS. 130 associate degrees awarded in 1992. 10% in business and management, 17% business/office and marketing/distribution, 24% communications, 25% computer sciences, 24% allied health.

UNDERGRADUATE MAJORS. Accounting, business administration and management, computer and information sciences, computer programming, medical assistant, ophthalmic services, radio/television technology, real estate, secretarial and related programs, tourism.

ACADEMIC PROGRAMS. Independent study, internships. **Remedial services:** Learning center, remedial instruction, special counselor, tutoring. **Placement/credit:** AP, CLEP General and Subject, institutional tests; 24 credit hours maximum for associate degree.

ACADEMIC REQUIREMENTS. Freshmen must earn minimum GPA of 1.3 to continue in good standing. Students must declare major on enrollment. **Graduation requirements:** 100 hours for associate (48 in major). Most students required to take courses in computer science, English, mathematics, social sciences.

FRESHMAN ADMISSIONS. Selection criteria: Must achieve minimum scores in reading, English, and mathematics on standardized tests. Interview required. **Test requirements:** Aptitude test required for computer programming applicants.

1992 FRESHMAN CLASS PROFILE. 150 men and women enrolled. **Characteristics:** 95% from in state, 100% commute, 40% have minority backgrounds. Average age is 27.

FALL-TERM APPLICATIONS. $100 fee. No closing date; applicants notified on a rolling basis; must reply within 1 week. Interview required. Deferred and early admission available.

STUDENT LIFE. Activities: Student government, film, professional organizations, Phi Beta Lambda, Alpha Sigma Lambda.

STUDENT SERVICES. Aptitude testing, career counseling, employment service for undergraduates, freshman orientation, on-campus day care, personal counseling, placement service for graduates, veterans counselor, services/facilities for handicapped.

ANNUAL EXPENSES. Tuition and fees (1992-93): $5,860. **Books and supplies:** $500.

FINANCIAL AID. 85% of freshmen, 80% of continuing students receive some form of aid. Academic scholarships available. **Aid applications:** No closing date; priority given to applications received by March 15; applicants notified on a rolling basis.

ADDRESS/TELEPHONE. Eunice Punghorst, Dean of Admission, Southern Ohio College, 1055 Laidlaw Avenue, Cincinnati, OH 45237. (513) 242-3791. Fax: (513) 242-2844.

Southern State Community College
Hillsboro, Ohio

CB code: 1752

2-year public community college, coed. Founded in 1975. **Accreditation:** Regional. **Undergraduate enrollment:** 261 men, 697 women full time; 227 men, 469 women part time. **Faculty:** 114 total (46 full time), 3 with doctorates or other terminal degrees. **Location:** Rural campus in small town; 60 miles from Cincinnati, 55 miles from Columbus. **Calendar:** Quarter, limited summer session. Saturday and extensive evening/early morning classes. **Microcomputers:** 111 located in libraries, classrooms, computer centers.

DEGREES OFFERED. AA, AS, AAS. 197 associate degrees awarded in 1992. 21% in business and management, 9% business/office and marketing/distribution, 5% engineering technologies, 18% health sciences, 8% allied health, 35% multi/interdisciplinary studies.

UNDERGRADUATE MAJORS. Accounting, agricultural production, business administration and management, computer graphics, computer programming, computer technology, drafting and design technology, education, electrical technology, electromechanical technology, electronic technology, liberal/general studies, medical assistant, nursing, real estate, robotics, secretarial and related programs.

ACADEMIC PROGRAMS. 2-year transfer program, dual enrollment of high school students, internships, cross-registration. **Remedial services:** Learning center, remedial instruction, tutoring. **Placement/credit:** CLEP General, institutional tests; 45 credit hours maximum for associate degree.

ACADEMIC REQUIREMENTS. Freshmen must earn minimum GPA of 1.5 to continue in good standing. Students must declare major on application. **Graduation requirements:** 90 hours for associate (54 in major). Most students required to take courses in English, mathematics.

FRESHMAN ADMISSIONS. Selection criteria: Open admissions.

1992 FRESHMAN CLASS PROFILE. 357 men, 847 women enrolled.

Characteristics: 99% from in state, 100% commute, 2% have minority backgrounds.

FALL-TERM APPLICATIONS. $15 fee. No closing date; applicants notified on a rolling basis beginning on or about January 1. Interview required for nursing applicants. Deferred and early admission available.

STUDENT LIFE. Activities: Student government, magazine, student newspaper, television, choral groups, drama, fraternities.

ATHLETICS. Intercollegiate: Basketball M, soccer M, volleyball W. **Intramural:** Archery, basketball, bowling, golf, soccer M, table tennis, tennis, volleyball.

STUDENT SERVICES. Aptitude testing, career counseling, freshman orientation, personal counseling, placement service for graduates, services/facilities for handicapped.

ANNUAL EXPENSES. Tuition and fees (1992-93): $2,552, $2,115 additional for out-of-state students. **Books and supplies:** $400.

FINANCIAL AID. 30% of freshmen, 37% of continuing students receive some form of aid. 88% of grants, 93% of loans, all jobs based on need. Academic, music/drama, art, leadership scholarships available. **Aid applications:** No closing date; priority given to applications received by July 1; applicants notified on a rolling basis beginning on or about July 1.

ADDRESS/TELEPHONE. Sherry Stout, Coordinator of Placement and Recruiting, Southern State Community College, 100 Hobart Drive, Hillsboro, OH 45133. (513) 393-3431. Fax: (513) 393-9370.

Stark Technical College
Canton, Ohio — CB code: 1688

2-year public technical college, coed. Founded in 1970. **Accreditation:** Regional. **Undergraduate enrollment:** 657 men, 1,155 women full time; 1,028 men, 1,697 women part time. **Faculty:** 196 total (99 full time), 7 with doctorates or other terminal degrees. **Location:** Suburban campus in small city; 50 miles from Cleveland. **Calendar:** Quarter, limited summer session. Saturday and extensive evening/early morning classes. **Microcomputers:** 100 located in classrooms, computer centers. **Additional facts:** All programs developed with input from local employers and professionals who serve on advisory committees with the purpose of designing and updating curricula to meet educational needs of the community.

DEGREES OFFERED. 430 associate degrees awarded in 1992. 41% in business/office and marketing/distribution, 34% engineering technologies, 25% allied health.

UNDERGRADUATE MAJORS. Accounting, automotive technology, business and office, civil technology, computer and information sciences, computer programming, court reporting, drafting and design technology, electrical and electronics equipment repair, electrical technology, electronic technology, engineering and engineering-related technologies, fashion merchandising, fire control and safety technology, hotel/motel and restaurant management, industrial equipment maintenance and repair, industrial technology, legal secretary, marketing and distribution, medical assistant, medical laboratory technologies, medical records technology, nursing, occupational therapy assistant, operation management, physical therapy assistant, respiratory therapy technology, secretarial and related programs, small business computer systems, word processing.

ACADEMIC PROGRAMS. Cooperative education, double major, dual enrollment of high school students, independent study, internships, student-designed major, cross-registration. **Remedial services:** Learning center, pre-admission summer program, reduced course load, remedial instruction, special counselor, tutoring. **Placement/credit:** Institutional tests; 12 credit hours maximum for associate degree.

ACADEMIC REQUIREMENTS. Freshmen must earn minimum GPA of 2.0 to continue in good standing. 60% of freshmen return for sophomore year. Students must declare major on application. **Graduation requirements:** 100 hours for associate (45 in major). Most students required to take courses in computer science, English, mathematics.

FRESHMAN ADMISSIONS. Selection criteria: Open admissions. Selective admissions to allied health programs. **Test requirements:** SAT or ACT (ACT preferred) for placement and counseling only.

1992 FRESHMAN CLASS PROFILE. 1,023 men, 1,983 women enrolled. 10% had high school GPA of 3.0 or higher, 60% between 2.0 and 2.99. **Characteristics:** 99% from in state, 100% commute, 7% have minority backgrounds. Average age is 28.

FALL-TERM APPLICATIONS. $35 fee. No closing date; priority given to applications received by June 1; applicants notified on a rolling basis. Interview recommended. Deferred and early admission available. ACT recommended for placement and counseling.

STUDENT LIFE. Activities: Student government, magazine, student newspaper, Bible study group, Circle-K.

ATHLETICS. Intramural: Basketball M, bowling, golf, skiing, softball, volleyball.

STUDENT SERVICES. Aptitude testing, career counseling, employment service for undergraduates, freshman orientation, on-campus day care, personal counseling, placement service for graduates, special adviser for adult students, veterans counselor, services/facilities for handicapped.

ANNUAL EXPENSES. Tuition and fees (1992-93): $2,700, $960 additional for out-of-state students. **Books and supplies:** $735. **Other expenses:** $1,475.

FINANCIAL AID. 40% of continuing students receive some form of aid. All grants, 89% of loans based on need. Academic, state/district residency scholarships available. **Aid applications:** No closing date; priority given to applications received by May 1; applicants notified on a rolling basis beginning on or about May 1; must reply within 2 weeks.

ADDRESS/TELEPHONE. Wallace Hoffer, Associate Dean Admissions, Stark Technical College, 6200 Frank Avenue, Northwest, Canton, OH 44720. (216) 494-6170 ext. 228. Fax: (216) 497-6313.

Terra Technical College
Fremont, Ohio — CB code: 0365

2-year public technical college, coed. Founded in 1968. **Accreditation:** Regional. **Undergraduate enrollment:** 493 men, 484 women full time; 1,065 men, 898 women part time. **Faculty:** 179 total (59 full time), 8 with doctorates or other terminal degrees. **Location:** Rural campus in large town; 27 miles from Toledo. **Calendar:** Quarter, limited summer session. Saturday and extensive evening/early morning classes. **Microcomputers:** 228 located in libraries, classrooms, computer centers. **Additional facts:** Evening teaching credit course available at Fostoria High School.

DEGREES OFFERED. AAS. 270 associate degrees awarded in 1992.

UNDERGRADUATE MAJORS. Accounting, air conditioning/heating/refrigeration technology, architectural technologies, automotive mechanics, automotive technology, business administration and management, business and management, business data entry equipment operation, business data programming, child development/care/guidance, computer programming, criminal justice technology, drafting, early childhood education, electrical technology, electromechanical technology, electronic technology, engineering and engineering-related technologies, finance, graphic and printing production, graphic arts technology, industrial technology, interpreter for the deaf, labor/industrial relations, law enforcement and corrections technologies, legal secretary, machine tool operation/machine shop, manufacturing technology, marketing and distribution, marketing management, mechanical design technology, medical secretary, nuclear engineering, nuclear technologies, plastic technology, precision metal work, quality control technology, real estate, robotics, secretarial and related programs, technical and business writing, welding technology.

ACADEMIC PROGRAMS. 2-year transfer program, accelerated program, double major, dual enrollment of high school students, independent study, internships, semester at sea, student-designed major, study abroad, weekend college. **Remedial services:** Learning center, reduced course load, remedial instruction, tutoring. **Placement/credit:** Institutional tests; 60 credit hours maximum for associate degree.

ACADEMIC REQUIREMENTS. Freshmen must earn minimum GPA of 2.0 to continue in good standing. 65% of freshmen return for sophomore year. Students must declare major on application. **Graduation requirements:** 102 hours for associate (50 in major). Most students required to take courses in computer science, English, mathematics, biological/physical sciences, social sciences.

FRESHMAN ADMISSIONS. Selection criteria: Open admissions. Law enforcement programs require director's approval. Algebra recommended for engineering and computer programming applicants.

1992 FRESHMAN CLASS PROFILE. 1,093 men, 1,074 women enrolled. **Characteristics:** 99% from in state, 100% commute, 5% have minority backgrounds.

FALL-TERM APPLICATIONS. $15 fee. No closing date; priority given to applications received by June 30; applicants notified on a rolling basis. Interview recommended. Portfolio recommended for graphics applicants. Deferred and early admission available. In-college mathematics and English testing recommended.

STUDENT LIFE. Activities: Student government, student newspaper, graphic arts communications annual, fraternities, sororities, Phi Theta Kappa, Early Childhood Education Association, Koinonia, Nuclear Power Association, Spanish club.

ATHLETICS. Intramural: Baseball M, basketball, bowling, football M, soccer, softball, table tennis, tennis, volleyball.

STUDENT SERVICES. Aptitude testing, career counseling, employment service for undergraduates, freshman orientation, on-campus day care, personal counseling, placement service for graduates, special adviser for adult students, veterans counselor, services/facilities for handicapped.

ANNUAL EXPENSES. Tuition and fees (1992-93): $1,905, $2,730 additional for out-of-state students. **Books and supplies:** $600. **Other expenses:** $400.

FINANCIAL AID. 60% of freshmen, 78% of continuing students receive some form of aid. 97% of grants, 90% of loans based on need. Academic, leadership scholarships available. **Aid applications:** No closing date; priority given to applications received by August 20; applicants notified on a rolling basis beginning on or about August 1; must reply within 1 week.

ADDRESS/TELEPHONE. Dennis W. Kayden, Director of Marketing and Enrollment Management, Terra Technical College, 2830 Napoleon Road, Fremont, OH 43420. (419) 334-3300 ext. 3491.

Tiffin University
Tiffin, Ohio CB code: 1817

Admissions: 92% of applicants accepted
Based on: ••• School record, test scores
• Essay, interview, recommendations
Completion: 70% of freshmen end year in good standing
34% graduate, 22% of these enter graduate study

4-year private business college, coed. Founded in 1888. **Accreditation:** Regional. **Undergraduate enrollment:** 375 men, 221 women full time; 134 men, 228 women part time. **Graduate enrollment:** 23 men, 11 women full time; 14 men, 8 women part time. **Faculty:** 65 total (25 full time), 20 with doctorates or other terminal degrees. **Location:** Rural campus in large town; 50 miles from Toledo, 90 miles from Columbus. **Calendar:** Semester, limited summer session. Saturday and extensive evening/early morning classes. **Microcomputers:** 30 located in libraries, computer centers. **Special facilities:** College-owned restaurant. **Additional facts:** Emphasis on business and criminal justice studies. Off-campus courses offered in Lima, Mansfield, Clyde, Fostoria, Willard and upper Sandusky.

DEGREES OFFERED. AAS, B, MBA. 32 associate degrees awarded in 1992. 27% in business and management. 131 bachelor's degrees awarded. 101% in business and management, 9% business/office and marketing/distribution, 10% computer sciences, 6% parks/recreation, protective services, public affairs. Graduate degrees offered in 1 major field of study.

UNDERGRADUATE MAJORS. Accounting, business administration and management, business and office, business computer/console/peripheral equipment operation, business data entry equipment operation, business data processing and related programs, computer programming, hotel/motel and restaurant management, law enforcement and corrections technologies. accounting, business administration and management, criminal justice studies, forensic studies, hotel/motel and restaurant management, information sciences and systems, international business management, law enforcement and corrections, office supervision and management.

ACADEMIC PROGRAMS. Double major, dual enrollment of high school students, independent study, internships, study abroad, weekend college. **Remedial services:** Learning center, preadmission summer program, reduced course load, remedial instruction, tutoring. **Placement/credit:** AP, CLEP General and Subject, institutional tests; 15 credit hours maximum for associate degree; 30 credit hours maximum for bachelor's degree.

ACADEMIC REQUIREMENTS. Freshmen must earn minimum GPA of 1.7 to continue in good standing. 55% of freshmen return for sophomore year. Students must declare major by end of first year. **Graduation requirements:** 60 hours for associate (36 in major), 120 hours for bachelor's (54 in major). Most students required to take courses in computer science, English, history, humanities, mathematics, philosophy/religion, social sciences. **Postgraduate studies:** 40% from 2-year programs enter 4-year programs. 3% enter law school, 17% enter MBA programs, 2% enter other graduate study.

FRESHMAN ADMISSIONS. Selection criteria: Minimum 2.0 high school GPA for nonconditional admissions. Recommended units include English 4, mathematics 3, social science 2 and science 2. Mathematics recommendation includes 1 algebra. **Test requirements:** SAT or ACT (ACT preferred); score report by August 15.

1992 FRESHMAN CLASS PROFILE. 383 men applied, 345 accepted, 135 enrolled; 194 women applied, 184 accepted, 71 enrolled. 18% had high school GPA of 3.0 or higher, 61% between 2.0 and 2.99. 9% were in top tenth and 21% were in top quarter of graduating class. **Academic background:** Mid 50% of enrolled freshmen had ACT composite between 17-20. 74% submitted ACT scores. **Characteristics:** 88% from in state, 67% live in college housing, 16% have minority backgrounds, 2% are foreign students, 10% join fraternities/sororities. Average age is 19.

FALL-TERM APPLICATIONS. $20 fee, may be waived for applicants with need. No closing date; applicants notified on a rolling basis; must reply within 8 weeks. Interview required for academically weak applicants. Deferred and early admission available.

STUDENT LIFE. Housing: Dormitories (coed); apartment, fraternity, sorority housing available. **Activities:** Student government, student newspaper, choral groups, fraternities, sororities, campus ministry club, Black united students, international students club, future activities board, DSK service fraternity, society for the advancement of management.

ATHLETICS. NAIA. **Intercollegiate:** Baseball M, basketball, cross-country, football M, golf M, soccer, softball W, tennis, volleyball W. **Intramural:** Basketball, skiing, soccer, softball M, table tennis, volleyball. **Clubs:** Skiing.

STUDENT SERVICES. Aptitude testing, career counseling, employment service for undergraduates, freshman orientation, personal counseling, placement service for graduates, special adviser for adult students, veterans counselor, services/facilities for handicapped.

ANNUAL EXPENSES. Tuition and fees: $7,100. **Room and board:** $3,700. **Books and supplies:** $500. **Other expenses:** $980.

FINANCIAL AID. 79% of freshmen, 63% of continuing students receive some form of aid. 57% of grants, 94% of loans, 77% of jobs based on need. Academic, athletic, state/district residency, leadership scholarships available. **Aid applications:** No closing date; priority given to applications received by March 31; applicants notified on a rolling basis beginning on or about March 31; must reply within 3 weeks.

ADDRESS/TELEPHONE. Kristine Boyle, Director of Admissions, Tiffin University, 155 Miami Street, Tiffin, OH 44883. (419) 447-6443. (800) 968-6446. Fax: (419) 447-9605.

Union Institute
Cincinnati, Ohio CB code: 0732

4-year private nontraditional university, coed. Founded in 1964. **Accreditation:** Regional. **Undergraduate enrollment:** 389 men and women. **Graduate enrollment:** 1,052 men and women. **Faculty:** 1,154 total (54 full time), 949 with doctorates or other terminal degrees. **Location:** Urban campus in large city. **Calendar:** Quarter. **Additional facts:** Non-campus-based institution with 5 undergraduate program sites: Cincinnati, Miami, San Diego, Los Angeles, Sacramento. Center for Public Policy in Washington, DC provides academic and technical support for policy development and research. Graduate school (doctoral only) operates external program from central office. Center for Women's Studies Office of Social Responsibility in Washington, DC.

DEGREES OFFERED. BA, BS, PhD. 100 bachelor's degrees awarded in 1992. 36% in business and management, 7% education, 8% health sciences, 9% multi/interdisciplinary studies, 25% psychology. Graduate degrees offered in 108 major fields of study.

UNDERGRADUATE MAJORS. Accounting, adult and continuing education research, African studies, Afro-American (black) studies, allied health, American literature, American studies, anthropology, applied mathematics, art history, Asian studies, biological and physical sciences, biology, business administration and management, business and management, chemistry, city/community/regional planning, clinical pastoral care, communications, comparative literature, computer and information sciences, creative writing, criminal justice studies, criminology, East Asian studies, economics, education, engineering and other disciplines, English, English literature, fine arts, foreign languages (multiple emphasis), geography, geology, health care administration, health sciences, history, human resources development, humanities, humanities and social sciences, information sciences and systems, international relations, international studies, journalism, labor/industrial relations, law , law enforcement and corrections, liberal/general studies, management information systems, marketing management, music, organizational behavior, personnel management, philosophy, physical sciences, physics, political science and government, prelaw, psychology, public administration, public affairs, public policy studies, religion, small business management and ownership, social psychology, social sciences, social work, sociology, special education, speech, taxation, theological studies, urban design, urban studies, visual and performing arts, women's studies.

ACADEMIC PROGRAMS. Double major, external degree, independent study, internships, student-designed major. **Remedial services:** Learning center, remedial instruction, special counselor.

ACADEMIC REQUIREMENTS. Students must declare major on application. **Graduation requirements:** 180 hours for bachelor's. Most students required to take courses in arts/fine arts, humanities, biological/physical sciences, social sciences. **Additional information:** Student-designed degree programs in any area where appropriate faculty available. Students may receive credit for traditional courses taken at other institutions.

FRESHMAN ADMISSIONS. Selection criteria: Interview important, school and community activities and recommendations considered. Evidence of ability to carry out self-directed learning.

1992 FRESHMAN CLASS PROFILE. Characteristics: 100% commute.

FALL-TERM APPLICATIONS. $50 fee. Closing date September 30; applicants notified on a rolling basis. Interview required. Essay required.

STUDENT SERVICES. Career counseling, personal counseling, special adviser for adult students, services/facilities for handicapped.

ANNUAL EXPENSES. Tuition and fees: $6,840. **Books and supplies:** $600.

FINANCIAL AID. 89% of continuing students receive some form of aid. Grants, loans, jobs available. **Aid applications:** No closing date; applicants notified on a rolling basis.

ADDRESS/TELEPHONE. Charles Cunning, PhD, Dean of the College of Undergraduate Studies, Union Institute, 440 East McMillan Street, Cincinnati, OH 45206-1947. (513) 861-6400. Fax: (513) 861-0779.

University of Akron
Akron, Ohio CB code: 1829

Admissions: 95% of applicants accepted
Based on: ••• School record, test scores
Completion: 80% of freshmen end year in good standing
39% enter graduate study

4-year public university, coed. Founded in 1870. **Accreditation:** Regional. **Undergraduate enrollment:** 8,790 men, 8,981 women full time; 2,304 men, 2,680 women part time. **Graduate enrollment:** 1,080 men, 890 women full time; 1,101 men, 1,253 women part time. **Faculty:** 2,137 total (1,115 full time), 616 with doctorates or other terminal degrees. **Location:** Urban campus in small city; 40 miles from Cleveland. **Calendar:** Semester, limited summer session. Saturday and extensive evening/early morning classes. **Microcomputers:** 1,000 located in libraries, classrooms, computer centers. **Special facilities:** 3 art galleries, performing arts hall, Bliss Political Science Institute.

DEGREES OFFERED. AA, AS, BA, BS, BFA, MA, MS, MBA, MFA, MEd, PhD, EdD. 720 associate degrees awarded in 1992. 23% in business and management, 14% business/office and marketing/distribution, 10% computer sciences, 15% engineering technologies, 8% allied health, 17% multi/interdisciplinary studies, 6% trade and industry, 5% visual and performing arts. 2,700 bachelor's degrees awarded. 22% in business and management, 9% business/office and marketing/distribution, 5% communications, 17% teacher education, 10% engineering, 5% engineering technologies, 9% health sciences, 5% visual and performing arts. Graduate degrees offered in 67 major fields of study.

UNDERGRADUATE MAJORS. Associate: Accounting, business and management, business and office, business data processing and related programs, business data programming, child development/care/guidance, commercial art, community services, computer and information sciences, criminal justice studies, criminal justice technology, data processing, drafting, drafting and design technology, electronic technology, engineering and engineering-related technologies, family and community services, fashion design, fashion merchandising, finance, fire control and safety technology, food management, graphic arts technology, hotel/motel and restaurant management, interpreter for the deaf, law enforcement and corrections, law enforcement and corrections technologies, legal secretary, liberal/general studies, library assistant, manufacturing technology, marketing and distribution, mechanical design technology, medical assistant, medical secretary, office supervision and management, radiograph medical technology, real estate, recreation and community services technologies, respiratory therapy technology, retailing, secretarial and related programs, small business management and ownership, surgical technology, survey and mapping technology, teacher aide, transportation and travel marketing, transportation management, word processing. **Bachelor's:** Accounting, advertising, anthropology, applied mathematics, art history, astronomy, astrophysics, bioengineering and biomedical engineering, biological and physical sciences, biology, botany, business administration and management, business economics, cell biology, ceramics, chemical engineering, chemistry, child development/care/guidance, civil engineering, classics, clothing and textiles management/production/services, communications, computer engineering, computer programming, crafts, cytotechnology, dance, dramatic arts, drawing, early childhood education, ecology, economics, education, education of the emotionally handicapped, education of the gifted and talented, education of the mentally handicapped, education of the physically handicapped, electrical/electronics/communications engineering, electronic technology, elementary education, enameling, engineering, engineering and other disciplines, English, fiber/textiles/weaving, finance, fine arts, food science and nutrition, French, geography, geology, geophysics and seismology, German, graphic and printing production, graphic design, Greek (classical), history, home economics, humanities, humanities and social sciences, individual and family development, international business management, journalism, Latin, law enforcement and corrections, marketing and distribution, mathematics, mechanical engineering, medical laboratory technologies, metal/jewelry, microbiology, music, music performance, music theory and composition, nursing, painting, philosophy, photography, physics, physiology, human and animal, political science and government, predentistry, prelaw, premedicine, prepharmacy, preveterinary, printmaking, psychology, public relations, radio/television broadcasting, radio/television technology, sculpture, secondary education, social work, sociology, Spanish, special education, specific learning disabilities, speech, speech correction, speech pathology/audiology, sports medicine, statistics, studio art, systems analysis, textiles and clothing, trade and industrial supervision and management, woodworking, zoology.

ACADEMIC PROGRAMS. Accelerated program, computer delivered (on-line) credit-bearing course offerings, cooperative education, dual enrollment of high school students, honors program, independent study, internships, student-designed major, study abroad, teacher preparation; combined bachelor's/graduate program in business administration, law. **Remedial services:** Learning center, reduced course load, remedial instruction, special counselor, tutoring. **ROTC:** Air Force, Army. **Placement/credit:** AP, CLEP General and Subject, institutional tests; 24 credit hours maximum for bachelor's degree.

ACADEMIC REQUIREMENTS. Freshmen must earn minimum GPA of 2.0 to continue in good standing. 80% of freshmen return for sophomore year. Students must declare major by end of second year. **Graduation requirements:** 64 hours for associate, 128 hours for bachelor's. Most students required to take courses in English, foreign languages, history, mathematics, biological/physical sciences, social sciences. **Postgraduate studies:** 14% from 2-year programs enter 4-year programs. 15% enter law school, 6% enter medical school, 18% enter MBA programs.

FRESHMAN ADMISSIONS. Selection criteria: Conditional/unconditional admissions policy for entering freshmen. Students with high school GPA less than 2.3 and lower than 16 ACT/650 SAT score with or without core curriculum, or high school GPA less than 2.8 and lower than 19 ACT/800 SAT score without the core curriculum admitted conditionally and required to complete one or more activities such as developmental courses, tutoring, learning laboratories and workshops, and/or summer school. Out-of-state applicants and applicants for campus housing must have minimum 2.8 high school GPA. **High school preparation:** 15 units recommended. Recommended units include English 4, foreign language 2, mathematics 3, social science 3 and science 3. Additional science and mathematics recommended for science, engineering, computer science, and nursing majors. **Test requirements:** SAT or ACT; score report by August 14.

1992 FRESHMAN CLASS PROFILE. 3,135 men applied, 2,966 accepted, 1,648 enrolled; 3,342 women applied, 3,166 accepted, 1,630 enrolled. 30% were in top quarter of graduating class. **Academic background:** Mid 50% of enrolled freshmen had SAT-V between 350-530, SAT-M between 400-580; ACT composite between 17-23. 15% submitted SAT scores, 76% submitted ACT scores. **Characteristics:** 97% from in state, 75% commute, 15% have minority backgrounds, 1% are foreign students, 3% join fraternities/sororities. Average age is 18.

FALL-TERM APPLICATIONS. $25 fee. Closing date August 14; applicants notified on a rolling basis. Audition required for music, dance applicants. Interview recommended for engineering, nursing applicants. Portfolio recommended for art, graphic design applicants. Early admission available. Closing date for applications is 2 weeks prior to start of each semester. Applicants who want to live in campus housing should complete application process by January 15.

STUDENT LIFE. Housing: Dormitories (men, women, coed); apartment, fraternity, sorority housing available. **Activities:** Student government, film, radio, student newspaper, television, yearbook, choral groups, concert band, dance, drama, jazz band, marching band, music ensembles, musical theater, opera, pep band, symphony orchestra, student faculty chamber orchestra, fraternities, sororities, religious organizations, Black United Students, International Students Association, Young Democrats, College Republicans.

ATHLETICS. NCAA. **Intercollegiate:** Baseball M, basketball, cross-country, football M, golf M, rifle, soccer M, softball W, tennis, track and field, volleyball W. **Intramural:** Badminton, basketball, bowling, cross-country, golf, racquetball, skiing, soccer, softball, swimming, table tennis, track and field, volleyball, wrestling M.

STUDENT SERVICES. Aptitude testing, career counseling, employment service for undergraduates, freshman orientation, health services, on-campus day care, personal counseling, placement service for graduates, special adviser for adult students, veterans counselor, advising services for disabled students, services/facilities for handicapped.

ANNUAL EXPENSES. Tuition and fees (projected): $2,953, $4,553 additional for out-of-state students. **Room and board:** $3,686. **Books and supplies:** $500. **Other expenses:** $1,000.

FINANCIAL AID. 50% of freshmen, 50% of continuing students receive some form of aid. 70% of grants, 88% of loans, 17% of jobs based on need. Academic, music/drama, art, athletic, minority scholarships available. **Aid applications:** Closing date May 1; priority given to applications received by April 1; applicants notified on a rolling basis beginning on or about April 15; must reply within 3 weeks. **Additional information:** Presidential and honor scholarships deadline February 1.

ADDRESS/TELEPHONE. Martha Booth, Associate Director of Admissions, University of Akron, 381 Buchtel Common, Akron, OH 44325-2001. (216) 972-7100.

University of Akron: Wayne College
Orrville, Ohio — CB code: 1892

2-year public branch campus, community, technical college, coed. Founded in 1972. **Accreditation:** Regional. **Undergraduate enrollment:** 1,438 men and women. **Faculty:** 165 total (24 full time). **Location:** Rural campus in small town; 30 miles from Akron. **Calendar:** Semester.

DEGREES OFFERED. AA, AS, AAS. 81 associate degrees awarded in 1992.

UNDERGRADUATE MAJORS. Business and management, international studies, mining and petroleum technologies, social services technology.

ACADEMIC PROGRAMS. Dual enrollment of high school students, honors program, independent study. **Remedial services:** Learning center, remedial instruction, tutoring.

ACADEMIC REQUIREMENTS. Freshmen must earn minimum GPA of 2.0 to continue in good standing. Students must declare major by end of first year. **Graduation requirements:** 64 hours for associate. Most students required to take courses in English, mathematics, biological/physical sciences, social sciences.

FRESHMAN ADMISSIONS. Selection criteria: Open admissions.

1992 FRESHMAN CLASS PROFILE. 266 men and women enrolled. **Characteristics:** 100% commute.

FALL-TERM APPLICATIONS. $20 fee. No closing date; applicants notified on a rolling basis.

ATHLETICS. Intercollegiate: Basketball, volleyball W.

ANNUAL EXPENSES. Tuition and fees (projected): $2,995, $4,540 additional for out-of-state students. **Books and supplies:** $550. **Other expenses:** $720.

ADDRESS/TELEPHONE. Admissions Office, University of Akron: Wayne College, 1901 Smucker Road, Orrville, OH 44667. (216) 683-2010. (800) 221-8308.

University of Cincinnati
Cincinnati, Ohio — CB code: 1833

Admissions: 84% of applicants accepted
Based on: ••• School record, test scores
• Activities, recommendations, special talents
Completion: 85% of freshmen end year in good standing

4-year public university, coed. Founded in 1819. **Accreditation:** Regional. **Undergraduate enrollment:** 5,550 men, 5,387 women full time; 1,119 men, 973 women part time. **Graduate enrollment:** 2,244 men, 1,895 women full time; 1,304 men, 1,717 women part time. **Faculty:** 968 total (943 full time), 730 with doctorates or other terminal degrees. **Location:** Urban campus in large city. **Calendar:** Quarter, extensive summer session. **Microcomputers:** 560 located in libraries, classrooms, computer centers. **Special facilities:** Observatory, river showboat.

DEGREES OFFERED. BA, BS, BFA, MA, MS, MBA, MFA, MEd, MSW, PhD, EdD, MD, B. Pharm. 2,759 bachelor's degrees awarded in 1992. 10% in architecture and environmental design, 22% business and management, 13% education, 14% engineering, 9% health sciences, 5% psychology, 9% social sciences. Graduate degrees offered in 96 major fields of study.

UNDERGRADUATE MAJORS. Accounting, aerospace/aeronautical/astronautical engineering, Afro-American (black) studies, anthropology, applied mathematics, architectural technologies, architecture, art education, art history, Asian studies, biochemistry, biology, business administration and management, business and management, chemical engineering, chemistry, city/community/regional planning, civil engineering, classics, clinical laboratory science, communications, community services, comparative literature, computer and information sciences, computer engineering, computer programming, construction, criminal justice studies, dance, data processing, dramatic arts, early childhood education, earth sciences, economics, education of the mentally handicapped, electrical technology, electrical/electronics/communications engineering, elementary education, engineering, engineering and other disciplines, engineering mechanics, engineering science, English, English literature, environmental health engineering, fashion design, finance, fine arts, fire control and safety technology, food science and nutrition, French, French studies, geography, geology, German, German studies, graphic design, health care administration, health education, history, humanities, industrial design, industrial engineering, information sciences and systems, interior design, international relations, international studies, investments and securities, jazz, Jewish studies, Latin American studies, liberal/general studies, linguistics, management information systems, management science, mathematics, mechanical engineering, metallurgical engineering, music, music education, music history and appreciation, music performance, music theory and composition, musical theater, nuclear engineering, nuclear medical technology, nursing, operations research, personnel management, pharmacy, philosophy, physics, political science and government, prelaw, psychology, public health laboratory science, radio/television broadcasting, real estate, secondary education, social work, sociology, Spanish, Spanish studies, special education, speech pathology/audiology, systems analysis, theater design, urban design, urban studies.

ACADEMIC PROGRAMS. Accelerated program, cooperative education, double major, honors program, independent study, internships, student-designed major, study abroad, teacher preparation, weekend college, Washington semester, cross-registration, Learning at Large (students earn college credit without attending regularly scheduled classes); combined bachelor's/graduate program in law. **Remedial services:** Preadmission summer program, remedial instruction, special counselor, tutoring. **ROTC:** Air Force, Army. **Placement/credit:** AP, CLEP General, institutional tests.

ACADEMIC REQUIREMENTS. Freshmen must earn minimum GPA of 2.0 to continue in good standing. 77% of freshmen return for sophomore year. Students must declare major by end of second year. **Graduation requirements:** 186 hours for bachelor's (54 in major). Most students required to take courses in English. **Additional information:** Some engineering programs require students to acquire personal computers.

FRESHMAN ADMISSIONS. Selection criteria: Class rank, test scores considered for baccalaureate programs. Special requirements vary for 4-year colleges. Same requirements for in-state and out-of-state students. **High school preparation:** 16 units required. Required units include English 4, foreign language 2, mathematics 3, social science 2 and science 2. One fine arts also required for 4-year colleges plus 2 additional units of any other required unit. Specific requirements may vary for each college. **Test requirements:** SAT or ACT; score report by July 1.

1992 FRESHMAN CLASS PROFILE. 3,332 men applied, 2,799 accepted, 1,103 enrolled; 3,095 women applied, 2,614 accepted, 1,002 enrolled. **Academic background:** Mid 50% of enrolled freshmen had SAT-V between 400-520, SAT-M between 450-600; ACT composite between 20-26. 63% submitted SAT scores, 86% submitted ACT scores. **Characteristics:** 85% commute. Average age is 19.

FALL-TERM APPLICATIONS. $30 fee, may be waived for applicants with need. No closing date; applicants notified on a rolling basis beginning on or about January 1; must reply by May 1 or within 2 weeks if notified thereafter. Interview required for music applicants. Audition required for dance, music applicants. CRDA.

STUDENT LIFE. Housing: Dormitories (men, women, coed); apartment, fraternity, sorority, cooperative housing available. **Activities:** Student government, film, magazine, radio, student newspaper, yearbook, choral groups, concert band, dance, drama, jazz band, marching band, music ensembles, musical theater, opera, pep band, symphony orchestra, fraternities, sororities.

ATHLETICS. NCAA. **Intercollegiate:** Baseball M, basketball, cross-country, diving, football M, golf, soccer, swimming, tennis, track and field M, volleyball W. **Intramural:** Archery W, badminton, baseball M, basketball, bowling, diving, golf, gymnastics W, handball, racquetball, soccer, softball, squash, swimming, table tennis, tennis, track and field, volleyball.

STUDENT SERVICES. Aptitude testing, career counseling, employment service for undergraduates, freshman orientation, health services, personal counseling, placement service for graduates, special adviser for adult students, veterans counselor, services/facilities for handicapped.

ANNUAL EXPENSES. Tuition and fees (1992-93): $3,372, $4,677 additional for out-of-state students. **Room and board:** $4,431. **Books and supplies:** $500. **Other expenses:** $1,195.

FINANCIAL AID. 65% of freshmen, 65% of continuing students receive some form of aid. 50% of grants, 90% of loans, all jobs based on need. 1,169 enrolled freshmen were judged to have need, 1,149 were offered aid. Academic, music/drama, art, athletic, leadership, minority scholarships available. **Aid applications:** No closing date; priority given to applications received by March 1; applicants notified on a rolling basis beginning on or about March 15; must reply by May 1 or within 2 weeks if notified thereafter.

ADDRESS/TELEPHONE. Rudolph F. Jones, Director of Admissions, University of Cincinnati, 100 Edward Center, Cincinnati, OH 45221-0091. (513) 556-1100. Fax: (513) 556-1105.

University of Cincinnati: Access Colleges
Cincinnati, Ohio — CB code: 7354

2-year public branch campus, community college, coed. **Accreditation:** Regional. **Undergraduate enrollment:** 3,184 men, 3,129 women full time; 3,607 men, 4,551 women part time. **Faculty:** 240 total (238 full time), 81 with doctorates or other terminal degrees. **Location:** Urban campus in large city. **Calendar:** Quarter. **Microcomputers:** 500 located in libraries, classrooms, computer centers. **Additional facts:** Baccalaureate and professional colleges on the same campus.

DEGREES OFFERED. AA, AS, AAS. 1,204 associate degrees awarded in 1992. 38% in business/office and marketing/distribution, 9% engineering technologies, 13% allied health, 19% multi/interdisciplinary studies, 9% social sciences.

UNDERGRADUATE MAJORS. Accounting, air conditioning/heating/refrigeration technology, architectural technologies, business and management, business and office, business computer/console/peripheral equipment operation, business data processing and related programs, business data programming, business systems analysis, chemical manufacturing technology, child development/care/guidance, commercial art, court reporting, dental hygiene, drafting and design technology, education, electrical technology, elementary education, energy conservation and use technology, engineering and engineering-related technologies, finance, fire control and safety technology, hospitality and recreation marketing, humanities, humanities and social sciences, industrial technology, information sciences and systems, legal assistant/paralegal, legal secretary, liberal/general studies, marketing and distribution, medical secretary, occupational safety and health technology, office supervision and management, physical therapy assistant, practical nursing, quality control technology, real estate, retailing, robotics, science technologies, secondary education, secretarial and related programs, social sciences, transportation and travel marketing, veterinarian's assistant, word processing.

ACADEMIC PROGRAMS. Cooperative education, double major, independent study, internships, student-designed major, cross-registration, Learning at Large (students earn college credit without attending regularly scheduled classes). **Remedial services:** Preadmission summer program, remedial instruction, special counselor, tutoring. **ROTC:** Air Force, Army. **Placement/credit:** AP, CLEP General, institutional tests.

ACADEMIC REQUIREMENTS. Freshmen must earn minimum GPA of 2.0 to continue in good standing. 63% of freshmen return for sophomore year. Students must declare major by end of first year. **Graduation requirements:** 100 hours for associate. Most students required to take courses in English.

FRESHMAN ADMISSIONS. Selection criteria: Open admissions.

High school preparation: 16 units recommended. Recommended units include English 4, foreign language 2, mathematics 3, social science 2 and science 2.

1992 FRESHMAN CLASS PROFILE. 2,010 men and women enrolled. **Academic background:** Mid 50% of enrolled freshmen had SAT-V between 310-430, SAT-M between 330-460; ACT composite between 16-20. 30% submitted SAT scores, 57% submitted ACT scores. **Characteristics:** 85% commute.

FALL-TERM APPLICATIONS. $30 fee, may be waived for applicants with need. No closing date; applicants notified on a rolling basis.

STUDENT LIFE. Housing: Dormitories (men, women, coed); apartment, fraternity, sorority, cooperative housing available. **Activities:** Student government, film, magazine, radio, student newspaper, yearbook, choral groups, concert band, dance, drama, jazz band, marching band, music ensembles, musical theater, opera, pep band, symphony orchestra, fraternities, sororities.

ATHLETICS. NCAA. **Intercollegiate:** Baseball M, basketball, cross-country, diving, football M, golf M, soccer, swimming, tennis, track and field, volleyball W.

STUDENT SERVICES. Aptitude testing, career counseling, employment service for undergraduates, freshman orientation, health services, personal counseling, placement service for graduates, special adviser for adult students, veterans counselor, services/facilities for handicapped.

ANNUAL EXPENSES. Tuition and fees (1992-93): $3,372, $4,677 additional for out-of-state students. **Room and board:** $4,431. **Books and supplies:** $500. **Other expenses:** $1,195.

FINANCIAL AID. 65% of freshmen, 65% of continuing students receive some form of aid. 76% of grants, 87% of loans, all jobs based on need. 1,262 enrolled freshmen were judged to have need, 1,242 were offered aid. Academic, music/drama, art, athletic, leadership, minority scholarships available. **Aid applications:** No closing date; priority given to applications received by March 1; applicants notified on a rolling basis beginning on or about March 15; must reply by May 1 or within 2 weeks if notified thereafter.

ADDRESS/TELEPHONE. Rudolph F. Jones, Director of Admissions, University of Cincinnati: Access Colleges, 100 Edwards Center, Cincinnati, OH 45221. (513) 556-1100. Fax: (513) 556-1105.

University of Cincinnati: Clermont College
Batavia, Ohio CB code: 3073

2-year public branch campus, community college, coed. Founded in 1972. **Accreditation:** Regional. **Undergraduate enrollment:** 302 men, 491 women full time; 286 men, 572 women part time. **Faculty:** 106 total (23 full time), 15 with doctorates or other terminal degrees. **Location:** Suburban campus in small town; 23 miles from Cincinnati. **Calendar:** Quarter, limited summer session. **Microcomputers:** Located in libraries, classrooms. **Additional facts:** College serves Clermont, Brown, and eastern Hamilton counties. One of 2 open-access branches of the university.

DEGREES OFFERED. AA, AS, AAS. 180 associate degrees awarded in 1992. 49% in business and management, 7% computer sciences, 10% teacher education, 6% engineering technologies, 21% multi/interdisciplinary studies, 7% social sciences.

UNDERGRADUATE MAJORS. Accounting, aviation management, business administration and management, business and management, business and office, computer programming, criminal justice studies, criminal justice technology, early childhood education, education, electrical technology, English, hotel/motel and restaurant management, human/social services technology, industrial technology, legal secretary, liberal/general studies, medical secretary, prelaw, prepharmacy, real estate, secondary education, secretarial and related programs, social work, urban studies, word processing.

ACADEMIC PROGRAMS. 2-year transfer program, double major, dual enrollment of high school students, independent study, internships, weekend college, cross-registration. **Remedial services:** Learning center, reduced course load, remedial instruction, special counselor, tutoring, developmental education program. **Placement/credit:** AP, CLEP Subject, institutional tests. 50% of hours needed for degree may be earned by examination.

ACADEMIC REQUIREMENTS. Freshmen must earn minimum GPA of 2.0 to continue in good standing. 60% of freshmen return for sophomore year. Students must declare major on application. **Graduation requirements:** 93 hours for associate. Most students required to take courses in English, mathematics, social sciences.

FRESHMAN ADMISSIONS. Selection criteria: Open admissions. **High school preparation:** 16 units recommended. Recommended units include English 4, foreign language 2, mathematics 3, social science 2 and science 2. One fine arts and 2 additional recommended units. **Test requirements:** ASSET test used for placement in English and mathematics.

1992 FRESHMAN CLASS PROFILE. 118 men, 195 women enrolled. **Academic background:** Mid 50% of enrolled freshmen had SAT-V between 320-390, SAT-M between 330-480; ACT composite between 17-21. 9% submitted SAT scores, 44% submitted ACT scores. **Characteristics:** 100% from in state, 100% commute, 2% have minority backgrounds. Average age is 23.

FALL-TERM APPLICATIONS. $30 fee, may be waived for applicants with need. Closing date September 1; applicants notified on a rolling basis beginning on or about March 1; must reply by May 1 or within 2 weeks if notified thereafter.

STUDENT LIFE. Activities: Student government, newsletter, drama, Christian Youth Fellowship.

ATHLETICS. Intramural: Baseball, basketball, bowling, softball, table tennis, tennis, volleyball.

STUDENT SERVICES. Aptitude testing, career counseling, employment service for undergraduates, freshman orientation, personal counseling, placement service for graduates, veterans counselor, services/facilities for handicapped.

ANNUAL EXPENSES. Tuition and fees (1992-93): $3,072, $4,461 additional for out-of-state students. **Books and supplies:** $520.

FINANCIAL AID. Academic, music/drama, art, leadership, minority scholarships available. **Aid applications:** No closing date; priority given to applications received by March 1; applicants notified on a rolling basis beginning on or about March 15; must reply by May 1 or within 2 weeks if notified thereafter. **Additional information:** All financial aid applications and awards administered through main campus.

ADDRESS/TELEPHONE. Robert W. Neel, Admissions Officer, University of Cincinnati: Clermont College, 725 College Drive, Batavia, OH 45103. (513) 732-5200.

University of Cincinnati: Raymond Walters College
Cincinnati, Ohio CB code: 0354

2-year public branch campus college, coed. Founded in 1967. **Accreditation:** Regional. **Undergraduate enrollment:** 598 men, 942 women full time; 862 men, 1,828 women part time. **Faculty:** 219 total (105 full time), 63 with doctorates or other terminal degrees. **Location:** Suburban campus in large city; 15 miles from downtown. **Calendar:** Quarter, limited summer session. Saturday classes. **Microcomputers:** 106 located in classrooms.

DEGREES OFFERED. AA, AAS. 387 associate degrees awarded in 1992. 9% in business and management, 26% business/office and marketing/distribution, 18% health sciences, 21% allied health, 9% multi/interdisciplinary studies, 5% trade and industry.

UNDERGRADUATE MAJORS. Accounting, automotive mechanics, biochemistry, biological laboratory technology, biology, business and management, business and office, business data programming, chemistry, commercial art, computer programming, dental hygiene, economics, education, elementary education, emergency medical technologies, industrial technology, legal secretary, liberal/general studies, library assistant, marketing and distribution, marketing management, medical laboratory technologies, medical radiation dosimetry, medical secretary, nuclear medical technology, nuclear technologies, nursing, office supervision and management, predentistry, prelaw, premedicine, prepharmacy, radiograph medical technology, real estate, secondary education, secretarial and related programs, social work, trade and industrial supervision and management, urban studies, veterinarian's assistant.

ACADEMIC PROGRAMS. 2-year transfer program, cooperative education, double major, dual enrollment of high school students, independent study, internships, student-designed major, study abroad, teacher preparation, in-house degree program with Ford/UAW. **Remedial services:** Learning center, preadmission summer program, reduced course load, remedial instruction, special counselor, tutoring. **Placement/credit:** AP, CLEP General and Subject, institutional tests; 22 credit hours maximum for associate degree.

ACADEMIC REQUIREMENTS. Freshmen must earn minimum GPA of 2.0 to continue in good standing. 50% of freshmen return for sophomore year. Students must declare major on enrollment. **Graduation requirements:** 90 hours for associate (36 in major). Most students required to take courses in English, mathematics.

FRESHMAN ADMISSIONS. Selection criteria: Open admissions. Allied Health programs have prerequisite requirements that must be met before entrance to clinical portion of programs. **Test requirements:** SAT or ACT. SAT or ACT required for allied health programs. ASSET test used for placement in mathematics, English, and general chemistry.

1992 FRESHMAN CLASS PROFILE. 160 men, 250 women enrolled. **Characteristics:** 98% from in state, 100% commute, 15% have minority backgrounds.

FALL-TERM APPLICATIONS. $30 fee, may be waived for applicants with need. No closing date; applicants notified on a rolling basis beginning on or about December 1. Portfolio recommended for commercial art applicants. Deferred and early admission available. Nursing, dental hygiene applicants begin acceptance process October 1.

STUDENT LIFE. Activities: Student government, student newspaper, fraternities, sororities, United Black Association, Baptist Student Union, Culture Club, Needy Family Project.

STUDENT SERVICES. Aptitude testing, career counseling, employment service for undergraduates, freshman orientation, health services,

on-campus day care, personal counseling, placement service for graduates, special adviser for adult students, veterans counselor, services/facilities for handicapped.

ANNUAL EXPENSES. Tuition and fees (1992-93): $3,072, $4,461 additional for out-of-state students. **Books and supplies:** $600. **Other expenses:** $900.

FINANCIAL AID. 25% of freshmen, 25% of continuing students receive some form of aid. 99% of grants, 86% of loans, all jobs based on need. Academic scholarships available. **Aid applications:** No closing date; priority given to applications received by March 1; applicants notified on a rolling basis beginning on or about March 15; must reply by May 1 or within 2 weeks if notified thereafter. **Additional information:** All financial aid applications and awards administered through main campus.

ADDRESS/TELEPHONE. Sharon R. Wilson, Assistant Dean for Student Services, University of Cincinnati: Raymond Walters College, 9555 Plainfield Road, Cincinnati, OH 45236. (513) 745-5700. Fax: (513) 745-5767.

University of Dayton
Dayton, Ohio — CB code: 1834

Admissions: 85% of applicants accepted
Based on:
••• School record
•• Activities, recommendations, special talents, test scores
• Essay, interview
Completion: 67% graduate, 32% of these enter graduate study

4-year private university, coed, affiliated with Roman Catholic Church. Founded in 1850. **Accreditation:** Regional. **Undergraduate enrollment:** 3,161 men, 2,938 women full time; 415 men, 284 women part time. **Graduate enrollment:** 773 men, 511 women full time; 765 men, 973 women part time. **Faculty:** 794 total (420 full time), 326 with doctorates or other terminal degrees. **Location:** Suburban campus in large city; 2 miles from downtown, 50 miles from Cincinnati. **Calendar:** Semester, extensive summer session. **Microcomputers:** 533 located in dormitories, classrooms, computer centers. **Special facilities:** Major research institute, student-operated store, Miriam Library.

DEGREES OFFERED. BA, BS, BFA, MA, MS, MBA, PhD, EdD. 1,683 bachelor's degrees awarded in 1992. 24% in business and management, 14% communications, 12% education, 12% engineering, 6% engineering technologies, 5% psychology, 8% social sciences. Graduate degrees offered in 52 major fields of study.

UNDERGRADUATE MAJORS. Accounting, American studies, anthropology, art education, biochemistry, biology, business administration and management, business and management, business economics, business education, chemical engineering, chemical process technology, chemistry, civil engineering, communications, computer and information sciences, computer science-physics, criminal justice studies, dramatic arts, early childhood education, economics, education of the mentally handicapped, education of the multiple handicapped, education of the physically handicapped, electrical/electronics/communications engineering, electronic technology, elementary education, engineering, engineering and engineering-related technologies, English, English education, environmental engineering technology, family/consumer resource management, fashion merchandising, finance, fine arts, food science and nutrition, foreign languages (multiple emphasis), French, geology, German, graphic design, health education, history, home economics, industrial technology, information sciences and systems, interior design, international relations, international studies, journalism, law enforcement and corrections, liberal/general studies, management information systems, manufacturing technology, marketing and distribution, marketing management, marketing research, mathematics, mathematics education, mechanical design technology, mechanical engineering, medical laboratory technologies, music, music education, music performance, music theory and composition, music therapy, nuclear medical technology, philosophy, photography, physical education, physical sciences, physics, political science and government, predentistry, prelaw, premedicine, psychology, public relations, radio/television broadcasting, religion, religious education, science education, secondary education, social sciences, social studies education, sociology, Spanish, special education, specific learning disabilities, speech, sports management, theological studies, visual and performing arts.

ACADEMIC PROGRAMS. Accelerated program, cooperative education, double major, education specialist degree, honors program, independent study, internships, student-designed major, study abroad, teacher preparation, cross-registration. **Remedial services:** Learning center, preadmission summer program, reduced course load, remedial instruction, special counselor, tutoring. **ROTC:** Air Force, Army. **Placement/credit:** AP, CLEP General and Subject, institutional tests; 46 credit hours maximum for bachelor's degree.

ACADEMIC REQUIREMENTS. Freshmen must earn minimum GPA of 1.7 to continue in good standing. 85% of freshmen return for sophomore year. Students must declare major by end of second year. **Graduation requirements:** 120 hours for bachelor's (60 in major). Most students required to take courses in arts/fine arts, English, history, humanities, mathematics, philosophy/religion, biological/physical sciences, social sciences. **Postgraduate studies:** 2% enter law school, 3% enter medical school, 2% enter MBA programs, 25% enter other graduate study.

FRESHMAN ADMISSIONS. Selection criteria: High school GPA in college preparatory courses most important. SAT or ACT results considered. Interview helpful. Recommendations and personal statement carefully considered. Leadership skills, extracurricular involvement, class rank also considered. **High school preparation:** 18 units recommended. Recommended units include English 4, foreign language 2, mathematics 3, social science 3 and science 2. 2 units of a single foreign language required for admission to College of Arts and Sciences. Requirement may be met during first year of study but credit not counted toward graduation. **Test requirements:** SAT or ACT; score report by August 1.

1992 FRESHMAN CLASS PROFILE. 2,906 men applied, 2,407 accepted, 873 enrolled; 2,584 women applied, 2,245 accepted, 793 enrolled. 24% were in top tenth and 49% were in top quarter of graduating class. **Academic background:** Mid 50% of enrolled freshmen had SAT-V between 440-550, SAT-M between 500-640; ACT composite between 22-27. 55% submitted SAT scores, 61% submitted ACT scores. **Characteristics:** 53% from in state, 95% live in college housing, 8% have minority backgrounds, 1% are foreign students. Average age is 18.

FALL-TERM APPLICATIONS. $25 fee, may be waived for applicants with need. No closing date; priority given to applications received by May 1; applicants notified on a rolling basis beginning on or about October 30; must reply within 8 weeks. Audition required for music, music therapy, music education applicants. Essay required. Interview recommended. CRDA. Deferred and early admission available.

STUDENT LIFE. Housing: Dormitories (men, women, coed); apartment, fraternity, sorority housing available. Out-of-town freshmen and sophomores required to live in residence halls. Upperclass students may choose to live in furnished, university-owned apartments or houses. Private houses and apartments available to juniors and seniors. **Activities:** Student government, radio, student newspaper, television, yearbook, choral groups, concert band, dance, drama, jazz band, marching band, music ensembles, musical theater, pep band, symphony orchestra, fraternities, sororities, over 20 service organizations, 60 professional clubs, honorary societies, Rudy's Fly-Buy (student-run convenience store).

ATHLETICS. NCAA. **Intercollegiate:** Baseball M, basketball, cross-country, football M, golf M, soccer, softball W, tennis, volleyball W, water polo M, wrestling M. **Intramural:** Badminton, baseball M, basketball, bowling, cross-country, diving, golf, handball, racquetball, rifle, soccer, softball, squash, swimming, table tennis, tennis, track and field, volleyball, water polo, wrestling.

STUDENT SERVICES. Aptitude testing, career counseling, employment service for undergraduates, freshman orientation, health services, on-campus day care, personal counseling, placement service for graduates, services/facilities for handicapped.

ANNUAL EXPENSES. Tuition and fees: $11,090. **Room and board:** $4,270. **Books and supplies:** $500. **Other expenses:** $900.

FINANCIAL AID. 89% of freshmen, 85% of continuing students receive some form of aid. 46% of grants, 97% of loans, 23% of jobs based on need. Academic, music/drama, art, athletic, state/district residency, leadership, minority scholarships available. **Aid applications:** No closing date; priority given to applications received by March 31; applicants notified on a rolling basis beginning on or about March 15; must reply within 4 weeks.

ADDRESS/TELEPHONE. Myron Achbach, Director of Admission, University of Dayton, 300 College Park Avenue, Dayton, OH 45469-1611. (513) 229-4411. (800) 837-7433. Fax: (513) 229-4545.

University of Findlay
Findlay, Ohio — CB code: 1223

Admissions: 85% of applicants accepted
Based on:
••• School record
•• Interview, test scores
• Activities, essay, recommendations, special talents
Completion: 70% of freshmen end year in good standing
40% graduate, 11% of these enter graduate study

4-year private university, coed, affiliated with Churches of God General Conference. Founded in 1882. **Accreditation:** Regional. **Undergraduate enrollment:** 982 men, 963 women full time; 1,164 men and women part time. **Graduate enrollment:** 162 men and women part time. **Faculty:** 255 total (155 full time). **Location:** Urban campus in large town; 45 miles from Toledo, 90 miles from Columbus. **Calendar:** Semester, limited summer session. Saturday classes. **Microcomputers:** 77 located in libraries, classrooms, computer centers. **Special facilities:** Planetarium, 2 equestrian farms, childrens-book-artists gallery.

DEGREES OFFERED. AA, BA, MA. 104 associate degrees awarded in 1992. 20% in agriculture, 30% business and management, 10% letters/literature, 15% multi/interdisciplinary studies, 20% social sciences. 234 bachelor's degrees awarded. 35% in business and management, 10% communications, 10% teacher education, 5% health sciences, 10% physical sciences, 12% social sciences. Graduate degrees offered in 1 major field of study.

UNDERGRADUATE MAJORS. Associate: Accounting, business administration and management, business and office, community services, computer and information sciences, environmental and hazardous materials management, equestrian science, equine management, liberal/general studies, nuclear medical technology, religion, secretarial and related programs, social sciences. **Bachelor's:** Accounting, advertising, art education, art history, art therapy, bilingual/bicultural education, biology, business administration and management, business economics, business education, business systems analysis, communications, computer and information sciences, creative writing, criminal justice studies, criminology, dramatic arts, ecology, economics, elementary education, English, English education, environmental and hazardous materials management, equestrian science, equine management, finance, foreign languages education, gerontology, health education, history, Japanese, journalism, junior high education, marketing management, mathematics, mathematics education, medical laboratory technologies, music education, nuclear medical technology, philosophy, physical education, political science and government, preengineering, prelaw, premedicine, preveterinary, psychology, public relations, radio/television broadcasting, religion, secondary education, social science education, social sciences, social studies education, social work, sociology, Spanish, special education, speech, speech/communication/theater education, systems analysis, technical and business writing, visual and performing arts.

ACADEMIC PROGRAMS. 2-year transfer program, accelerated program, double major, dual enrollment of high school students, honors program, independent study, internships, student-designed major, study abroad, teacher preparation, weekend college, Washington semester, 3-2 engineering; liberal arts/career combination in engineering, health sciences. **Remedial services:** Learning center, reduced course load, remedial instruction, special counselor, tutoring, foundations semester. **ROTC:** Air Force, Army. **Placement/credit:** AP, CLEP General and Subject; 30 credit hours maximum for bachelor's degree.

ACADEMIC REQUIREMENTS. Freshmen must earn minimum GPA of 2.0 to continue in good standing. 65% of freshmen return for sophomore year. Students must declare major by end of second year. **Graduation requirements:** 62 hours for associate (30 in major), 124 hours for bachelor's (36 in major). Most students required to take courses in arts/fine arts, computer science, English, history, mathematics, philosophy/religion, biological/physical sciences, social sciences. **Postgraduate studies:** 2% enter medical school, 9% enter other graduate study.

FRESHMAN ADMISSIONS. Selection criteria: School achievement record, curriculum, test scores, rank in top half of class, recommendations, interview. **High school preparation:** 16 units required. Required and recommended units include English 4. Biological science 1, foreign language 2, mathematics 2, physical science 1, social science 2 and science 2 recommended. **Test requirements:** SAT or ACT (ACT preferred); score report by August 1.

1992 FRESHMAN CLASS PROFILE. 1,054 men applied, 859 accepted, 226 enrolled; 777 women applied, 702 accepted, 206 enrolled. **Academic background:** Mid 50% of enrolled freshmen had ACT composite between 15-22. 80% submitted ACT scores. **Characteristics:** 84% from in state, 85% live in college housing, 12% have minority backgrounds, 6% are foreign students, 10% join fraternities/sororities. Average age is 18.

FALL-TERM APPLICATIONS. No fee. No closing date; priority given to applications received by April 1; applicants notified on a rolling basis; must reply by May 1 or within 4 weeks if notified thereafter. Interview recommended for foundations program applicants. CRDA. Deferred admission available. Early admission available to part-time applicants only.

STUDENT LIFE. Housing: Dormitories (men, women); fraternity, sorority housing available. **Activities:** Student government, magazine, radio, student newspaper, yearbook, choral groups, concert band, drama, jazz band, music ensembles, musical theater, pep band, fraternities, sororities, Circle-K, Black Student Union, Spanish, wilderness, and environmental clubs.

ATHLETICS. NAIA. **Intercollegiate:** Baseball M, basketball, cross-country, football M, golf M, soccer, softball W, swimming, tennis, track and field, volleyball W, wrestling M. **Intramural:** Softball.

STUDENT SERVICES. Career counseling, employment service for undergraduates, freshman orientation, health services, personal counseling, placement service for graduates, special adviser for adult students, veterans counselor, services/facilities for handicapped.

ANNUAL EXPENSES. Tuition and fees: $10,920. **Room and board:** $4,780. **Books and supplies:** $500. **Other expenses:** $600.

FINANCIAL AID. 85% of freshmen, 80% of continuing students receive some form of aid. 91% of grants, 89% of loans, 56% of jobs based on need. 350 enrolled freshmen were judged to have need, 330 were offered aid. Academic, music/drama, athletic, alumni affiliation, religious affiliation, minority scholarships available. **Aid applications:** Closing date August 1; priority given to applications received by April 1; applicants notified on a rolling basis beginning on or about March 15; must reply by May 1 or within 2 weeks if notified thereafter. **Additional information:** Grant for more than 1 child at school from same family.

ADDRESS/TELEPHONE. Dr. Mary Ellen Klein, Director of Admissions, University of Findlay, 1000 North Main Street, Findlay, OH 45840-3695. (419) 424-4540. (800) 548-0932. Fax: (419) 424-4822.

University of Rio Grande
Rio Grande, Ohio — CB code: 1663

4-year private university and college of arts and sciences and business, nursing, community, liberal arts, teachers, technical college, coed. Founded in 1876. **Accreditation:** Regional. **Undergraduate enrollment:** 763 men, 1,057 women full time; 96 men, 244 women part time. **Graduate enrollment:** 23 men, 90 women part time. **Faculty:** 112 total (87 full time), 30 with doctorates or other terminal degrees. **Location:** Rural campus in rural community; 12 miles from Gallipolis. **Calendar:** Quarter, limited summer session. Extensive evening/early morning classes. **Microcomputers:** 64 located in classrooms, computer centers. **Additional facts:** Contains public, state-supported 2-year community college component. Two branch campuses in Japan.

DEGREES OFFERED. AA, AS, AAS, BS, MEd. 172 associate degrees awarded in 1992. 20% in business and management, 25% health sciences, 8% social sciences, 35% trade and industry, 12% visual and performing arts. 182 bachelor's degrees awarded. 30% in business and management, 12% communications, 8% computer sciences, 23% teacher education, 6% physical sciences, 10% social sciences, 9% visual and performing arts. Graduate degrees offered in 2 major fields of study.

UNDERGRADUATE MAJORS. Associate: Accounting, biology, business administration and management, business and management, business and office, chemistry, child development/care/guidance, clinical laboratory science, communications, computer and information sciences, computer servicing technology, drafting, drafting and design technology, early childhood education, electrical and electronics equipment repair, electronic technology, fine arts, health sciences, history, legal secretary, manufacturing technology, mathematics, mechanical design technology, medical laboratory technologies, medical secretary, nursing, physical education, political science and government, psychology, secretarial and related programs, social work, sociology, technical studies, visual and performing arts, woodworking. **Bachelor's:** Accounting, American studies, art education, biology, business administration and management, business and management, business economics, business education, chemistry/physics, communications, computer and information sciences, early childhood education, elementary education, English, English education, fine arts, health education, history, humanities, humanities and social sciences, industrial technology, international business management, international studies, journalism, junior high education, marketing management, mathematics, mathematics education, music, music education, physical education, prelaw, psychology, public relations, reading education, science education, secondary education, social science education, social sciences, social studies education, social work, special education, speech, speech/communication/theater education, sport and exercise studies, sports management, visual and performing arts.

ACADEMIC PROGRAMS. 2-year transfer program, accelerated program, double major, dual enrollment of high school students, honors program, independent study, internships, student-designed major, teacher preparation, visiting/exchange student program. **Remedial services:** Learning center, preadmission summer program, reduced course load, remedial instruction, special counselor, tutoring. **ROTC:** Army. **Placement/credit:** AP, CLEP General and Subject, institutional tests.

ACADEMIC REQUIREMENTS. Freshmen must earn minimum GPA of 1.8 to continue in good standing. 60% of freshmen return for sophomore year. Students must declare major by end of second year. **Graduation requirements:** 95 hours for associate (30 in major), 190 hours for bachelor's (50 in major). Most students required to take courses in arts/fine arts, English, history, humanities, mathematics, philosophy/religion, biological/physical sciences, social sciences. **Postgraduate studies:** 30% from 2-year programs enter 4-year programs. 4% enter law school, 2% enter medical school, 5% enter MBA programs, 9% enter other graduate study.

FRESHMAN ADMISSIONS. Selection criteria: Open admissions. Selective admissions for nursing, medical laboratory technician, and education programs. Deferred admission for students demonstrating need for remedial work. **High school preparation:** 17 units recommended. Recommended units include English 4, foreign language 2, mathematics 3, social science 3 and science 3. Chemistry, algebra, biology required for nursing applicants. **Test requirements:** ACT for placement; score report by August 15. **Additional information:** Acceptance to education department occurs at end of sophomore year. Early application recommended for nursing program.

1992 FRESHMAN CLASS PROFILE. 247 men, 320 women enrolled. 30% had high school GPA of 3.0 or higher, 45% between 2.0 and 2.99. **Academic background:** Mid 50% of enrolled freshmen had ACT composite between 15-19. 95% submitted ACT scores. **Characteristics:** 93% from in state, 53% live in college housing, 3% have minority backgrounds, 7% are foreign students, 15% join fraternities/sororities. Average age is 20.

FALL-TERM APPLICATIONS. $15 fee, may be waived for applicants with need. Closing date August 1; priority given to applications received by

May 31; applicants notified on a rolling basis. Audition required for music applicants. Interview recommended for nursing, medical laboratory technologies, music, education applicants. Deferred admission available. ACT required for nursing, medical technology, education programs.

STUDENT LIFE. Housing: Dormitories (men, women). Private housing owned and operated by university available to responsible students. **Activities:** Student government, radio, student newspaper, television, yearbook, college information brochure, student handbook, choral groups, concert band, drama, jazz band, musical theater, pep band, symphony orchestra, fraternities, sororities, Student ambassadors for free enterprise, international student organization, Valley Artist Services, Handicapped Coalition, Young Republicans, Rio Christian Fellowship.

ATHLETICS. NAIA. **Intercollegiate:** Baseball M, basketball, cross-country, soccer M, softball W, track and field, volleyball W. **Intramural:** Archery, badminton, basketball, handball, horseback riding, racquetball, softball, swimming, tennis, water polo, wrestling M.

STUDENT SERVICES. Aptitude testing, career counseling, employment service for undergraduates, freshman orientation, health services, on-campus day care, personal counseling, placement service for graduates, veterans counselor, services/facilities for handicapped.

ANNUAL EXPENSES. Tuition and fees (1992-93): $2,277, $288 additional for out-of-district students, $3,306 additional for out-of-state students. **Room and board:** $3,150. **Books and supplies:** $600. **Other expenses:** $1,450.

FINANCIAL AID. 70% of freshmen, 82% of continuing students receive some form of aid. 78% of grants, 90% of loans, 35% of jobs based on need. 379 enrolled freshmen were judged to have need, all were offered aid. Academic, music/drama, athletic, leadership scholarships available. **Aid applications:** No closing date; priority given to applications received by April 15; applicants notified on a rolling basis beginning on or about April 30; must reply within 2 weeks.

ADDRESS/TELEPHONE. Mark Abell, Executive Director of Admissions and Enrollment Svcs, University of Rio Grande, Rio Grande, OH 45674. (614) 245-5353 ext. 208. Fax: (614) 245-9220.

University of Toledo
Toledo, Ohio — CB code: 1845

4-year public university, coed. Founded in 1872. **Accreditation:** Regional. **Undergraduate enrollment:** 7,691 men, 7,849 women full time; 2,608 men, 3,014 women part time. **Graduate enrollment:** 815 men, 523 women full time; 916 men, 1,125 women part time. **Faculty:** 1,532 total (680 full time), 710 with doctorates or other terminal degrees. **Location:** Suburban campus in large city; 6 miles from downtown Toledo. **Calendar:** Quarter, extensive summer session. Extensive evening/early morning classes. **Microcomputers:** 1,010 located in dormitories, libraries, classrooms, computer centers. **Special facilities:** 2 observatories, ion accelerator, arboretum, planetarium, linear laser and nuclear physics laboratory, art museum. **Additional facts:** Main campus offers baccalaureate and graduate programs. University Community and Technical College campus offers associate degree and certificate programs. Individual and interdepartmental bachelor's degrees also offered. Affiliated with Toledo Museum of Art and Medical College of Ohio at Toledo.

DEGREES OFFERED. AA, AAS, BA, BS, BFA, MA, MS, MBA, MEd, PhD, EdD, B. Pharm, Pharm D, JD. 655 associate degrees awarded in 1992. 17% in business and management, 12% business/office and marketing/distribution, 19% engineering technologies, 23% allied health, 9% law, 12% parks/recreation, protective services, public affairs. 2,285 bachelor's degrees awarded. 16% in business and management, 8% business/office and marketing/distribution, 5% communications, 14% education, 11% engineering, 13% multi/interdisciplinary studies. Graduate degrees offered in 72 major fields of study.

UNDERGRADUATE MAJORS. Associate: Accounting, air conditioning/heating/refrigeration technology, air pollution control technology, architectural technologies, architecture, business and management, business and office, business computer/console/peripheral equipment operation, business data entry equipment operation, business data processing and related programs, business data programming, cardiovascular technology, chemical manufacturing technology, civil technology, data processing, drafting, drafting and design technology, electrodiagnostic technologies, electronic technology, emergency medical technologies, engineering and engineering-related technologies, environmental control/protection, food management, food production/management/services, geriatric aide, gerontology, industrial technology, law enforcement and corrections technologies, legal assistant/paralegal, legal secretary, liberal/general studies, management information systems, manufacturing technology, marketing and distribution, marketing management, marketing research, mechanical design technology, medical assistant, medical records administration, medical records technology, medical secretary, mental health/human services, nursing, plastic technology, protective services, public affairs, quality control technology, real estate, recreation and community services technologies, respiratory therapy, respiratory therapy technology, retailing, science technologies, secretarial and related programs, transportation and travel marketing, transportation management, water and wastewater technology, word processing. **Bachelor's:** Accounting, adult and continuing education research, advertising, American studies, anthropology, applied mathematics, art education, art history, Asian studies, biology, business administration and management, business and management, business and office, business computer/console/peripheral equipment operation, business economics, business education, business statistics, chemical engineering, chemistry, cinematography/film, civil engineering, classics, clinical laboratory science, clinical psychology, communications, communications research, community health work, community services, comparative literature, computer and information sciences, computer engineering, computer mathematics, computer programming, construction, corrective therapy (kinesiotherapy), creative writing, criminal justice studies, dramatic arts, drawing, early childhood education, economics, education, education of the deaf and hearing impaired, education of the emotionally handicapped, education of the gifted and talented, education of the mentally handicapped, education of the multiple handicapped, education of the physically handicapped, education of the visually handicapped, educational media technology, electrical/electronics/communications engineering, electronic technology, elementary education, engineering, engineering physics, engineering science, English, English education, English literature, European studies, experimental psychology, finance, fine arts, foreign languages education, French, geography, geology, German, glass, Greek (classical), health care administration, health education, history, human resources development, humanities and social sciences, industrial engineering, information sciences and systems, institutional management, insurance and risk management, international business management, international relations, international studies, investments and securities, journalism, junior high education, labor/industrial relations, Latin, Latin American studies, liberal/general studies, linguistics, management information systems, manufacturing technology, marketing and distribution, marketing and distributive education, marketing management, marketing research, mathematics, mathematics education, mechanical engineering, medieval studies, Middle Eastern studies, motion picture technology, music, music education, nursing, operations research, painting, parks and recreation management, personnel management, pharmacy, philosophy, physical education, physical therapy, physics, political science and government, predentistry, prelaw, premedicine, printmaking, production management, psychology, public affairs, public health laboratory science, public relations, pure mathematics, radio/television broadcasting, radio/television technology, reading education, recreation therapy, science education, sculpture, secondary education, social science education, social studies education, social work, sociology, Spanish, special education, specific learning disabilities, speech, speech correction, speech pathology/audiology, speech/communication/theater education, sports medicine, statistics, systems analysis, technical education, telecommunications, trade and industrial education, transportation management, visual and performing arts, women's studies.

ACADEMIC PROGRAMS. 2-year transfer program, cooperative education, double major, dual enrollment of high school students, education specialist degree, honors program, independent study, internships, student-designed major, study abroad, teacher preparation, visiting/exchange student program, weekend college, cross-registration; combined bachelor's/graduate program in business administration, medicine, law. **Remedial services:** Learning center, preadmission summer program, reduced course load, remedial instruction, special counselor, tutoring, academic support services, student development programs. **ROTC:** Air Force, Army. **Placement/credit:** AP, CLEP General and Subject, institutional tests; 92 credit hours maximum for associate degree; 186 credit hours maximum for bachelor's degree.

ACADEMIC REQUIREMENTS. Freshmen must earn minimum GPA of 2.0 to continue in good standing. 72% of freshmen return for sophomore year. Students must declare major by end of first year. **Graduation requirements:** 92 hours for associate, 186 hours for bachelor's. Most students required to take courses in arts/fine arts, English, foreign languages, history, humanities, mathematics, biological/physical sciences, social sciences.

FRESHMAN ADMISSIONS. Selection criteria: Open admissions. Selective admissions for out-of-state students and for many programs. **High school preparation:** 16 units recommended. Recommended units include English 4, foreign language 3, mathematics 3, social science 3 and science 3. Science recommendation includes 2 laboratory science. 1 fine arts also recommended. 4 units of mathematics and science required of engineering applicants. 3 units of foreign language recommended for all arts and sciences and secondary education majors. **Test requirements:** SAT or ACT (ACT preferred) for placement and counseling only; score report by July 1. Deadline for SAT/ACT scores to be considered for fall term scholarships is January 28. **Additional information:** Students with 3.5 GPA and 25 ACT invited to apply for Honors Program.

1992 FRESHMAN CLASS PROFILE. 3,837 men applied, 3,701 accepted, 1,859 enrolled; 3,817 women applied, 3,707 accepted, 1,857 enrolled. 43% had high school GPA of 3.0 or higher, 46% between 2.0 and 2.99. **Academic background:** Mid 50% of enrolled freshmen had SAT-V between 380-520, SAT-M between 430-600; ACT composite between 18-24. 23% submitted SAT scores, 82% submitted ACT scores. **Characteristics:** 92% from in state, 65% live in college housing, 14% have minority backgrounds, 2% are foreign students, 6% join fraternities/sororities. Average age is 20.

FALL-TERM APPLICATIONS. $30 fee. Closing date September 13; priority given to applications received by September 1; applicants notified on a rolling basis. Audition required for music applicants. Interview recommended. Essay recommended. Deferred admission available. EDP-F. Freshman applicants desiring on-campus housing encouraged to apply in October.

STUDENT LIFE. Housing: Dormitories (men, women, coed); fraternity, sorority housing available. Free university bus service is available for students in off-campus housing and over 20 off-campus apartment complexes. **Activities:** Student government, film, radio, student newspaper, television, choral groups, concert band, dance, drama, jazz band, marching band, music ensembles, musical theater, pep band, fraternities, sororities, Black Student Union, Campus Crusade for Christ, Hillel, University Democrats, Newman Club, Volunteers In Action, MECHA-Latino Student Union, University YMCA, Student Environmental Coalition of Toledo.

ATHLETICS. NCAA. **Intercollegiate:** Baseball M, basketball, cross-country, diving, football M, golf M, softball W, swimming, tennis, track and field, volleyball W, wrestling M. **Intramural:** Badminton, basketball, bowling, cross-country, fencing, golf, ice hockey M, lacrosse, racquetball, rowing (crew), sailing, skiing, soccer, softball, swimming, table tennis, tennis, track and field, volleyball, wrestling M.

STUDENT SERVICES. Aptitude testing, career counseling, employment service for undergraduates, freshman orientation, health services, on-campus day care, personal counseling, placement service for graduates, special adviser for adult students, veterans counselor, services/facilities for handicapped.

ANNUAL EXPENSES. Tuition and fees (1992-93): $3,073, $4,305 additional for out-of-state students. **Room and board:** $3,053. **Books and supplies:** $550. **Other expenses:** $2,080.

FINANCIAL AID. 52% of freshmen, 51% of continuing students receive some form of aid. 78% of grants, 88% of loans, 51% of jobs based on need. 1,937 enrolled freshmen were judged to have need, 1,685 were offered aid. Academic, music/drama, art, athletic, minority scholarships available. **Aid applications:** No closing date; priority given to applications received by April 1; applicants notified on a rolling basis beginning on or about April 1; must reply within 4 weeks. **Additional information:** 4-year full scholarships for National Merit, National Achievement, andNational Hispanic finalists as well as 300 freshman merit scholarships offered annually; awards range from $500 to $4,500 and average $1,500.

ADDRESS/TELEPHONE. Richard J. Eastop, Dean of Admissions Services, University of Toledo, 2801 West Bancroft, Toledo, OH 43606-3398. (419) 537-2696. Fax: (419) 537-4504.

Urbana University
Urbana, Ohio — CB code: 1847

Admissions: 75% of applicants accepted
Based on: ••• School record, test scores
•• Essay, interview, recommendations
• Activities, special talents
Completion: 77% of freshmen end year in good standing
12% enter graduate study

4-year private liberal arts college, coed, affiliated with Swedenborgian Church. Founded in 1850. **Accreditation:** Regional. **Undergraduate enrollment:** 476 men, 284 women full time; 66 men, 126 women part time. **Faculty:** 78 total (34 full time), 25 with doctorates or other terminal degrees. **Location:** Rural campus in large town; 42 miles from Columbus, 49 miles from Dayton. **Calendar:** Semester, limited summer session. **Microcomputers:** 30 located in libraries, classrooms, computer centers. **Special facilities:** Rare book room in library, Swedenborgian Collection (books). **Additional facts:** 3 branch sites in Bellefontaine, Columbus, and Dayton.

DEGREES OFFERED. AA, BA, BS. 70 associate degrees awarded in 1992. 16% in business and management, 27% multi/interdisciplinary studies, 57% social sciences. 80 bachelor's degrees awarded. 53% in business and management, 18% teacher education, 5% physical sciences, 17% social sciences.

UNDERGRADUATE MAJORS. Associate: Business administration and management, liberal/general studies, social sciences. **Bachelor's:** Accounting, biological and physical sciences, biology, business administration and management, business and management, business economics, business education, chemistry, communications, community services, economics, education, elementary education, English, English education, finance, health education, history, humanities and social sciences, junior high education, law enforcement and corrections, marketing management, mathematics education, personnel management, philosophy, physical education, physical sciences, predentistry, prelaw, premedicine, psychology, recreation and community services technologies, religion, science education, secondary education, social psychology, social sciences, social studies education, social work, sociology, sports medicine.

ACADEMIC PROGRAMS. 2-year transfer program, accelerated program, double major, dual enrollment of high school students, independent study, internships, student-designed major, teacher preparation, cross-registration. **Remedial services:** Learning center, reduced course load, remedial instruction, special counselor, tutoring. **Placement/credit:** CLEP General and Subject, institutional tests; 12 credit hours maximum for associate degree; 12 credit hours maximum for bachelor's degree.

ACADEMIC REQUIREMENTS. Freshmen must earn minimum GPA of 1.7 to continue in good standing. 61% of freshmen return for sophomore year. Students must declare major by end of second year. **Graduation requirements:** 63 hours for associate (33 in major), 126 hours for bachelor's (87 in major). Most students required to take courses in arts/fine arts, English, history, humanities, mathematics, philosophy/religion, biological/physical sciences, social sciences. **Postgraduate studies:** 53% from 2-year programs enter 4-year programs. 8% enter MBA programs, 4% enter other graduate study.

FRESHMAN ADMISSIONS. Selection criteria: School achievement record, class rank or GPA, test scores, recommendations, interview. Special consideration given to children of alumni. **High school preparation:** 14 units recommended. Recommended units include English 4, mathematics 3, social science 4 and science 3. **Test requirements:** SAT or ACT; score report by August 15.

1992 FRESHMAN CLASS PROFILE. 235 men applied, 175 accepted, 98 enrolled; 98 women applied, 74 accepted, 57 enrolled. 20% had high school GPA of 3.0 or higher, 61% between 2.0 and 2.99. 7% were in top tenth and 22% were in top quarter of graduating class. **Academic background:** Mid 50% of enrolled freshmen had ACT composite between 17-20. 78% submitted ACT scores. **Characteristics:** 99% from in state, 70% commute, 35% have minority backgrounds, 1% are foreign students. Average age is 19.

FALL-TERM APPLICATIONS. $10 fee, may be waived for applicants with need. No closing date; priority given to applications received by May 1; applicants notified on a rolling basis beginning on or about January 1; must reply by May 1 or within 4 weeks if notified thereafter. Essay required. Interview recommended. CRDA. Deferred and early admission available. EDP-F.

STUDENT LIFE. Housing: Dormitories (men, women, coed). **Activities:** Student government, radio, student newspaper, yearbook, choral groups, drama, music ensembles, musical theater, pep band, International Friends Club, Black Awareness Organization.

ATHLETICS. NAIA. **Intercollegiate:** Baseball M, basketball, cross-country, football M, golf, softball W, track and field, volleyball W. **Intramural:** Basketball, bowling, handball, racquetball, softball, swimming, tennis, track and field, volleyball.

STUDENT SERVICES. Aptitude testing, career counseling, employment service for undergraduates, freshman orientation, health services, personal counseling, placement service for graduates, special adviser for adult students, veterans counselor, services/facilities for handicapped.

ANNUAL EXPENSES. Tuition and fees: $7,841. **Room and board:** $4,140. **Books and supplies:** $500. **Other expenses:** $600.

FINANCIAL AID. 100% of freshmen, 95% of continuing students receive some form of aid. 98% of grants, 95% of loans, all jobs based on need. Academic, music/drama, athletic, alumni affiliation, religious affiliation scholarships available. **Aid applications:** No closing date; priority given to applications received by May 1; applicants notified on a rolling basis beginning on or about February 1; must reply by May 1 or within 2 weeks if notified thereafter.

ADDRESS/TELEPHONE. Lori Botkin-Carpenter, Director of Admissions, Urbana University, 579 College Way, Urbana, OH 43078-2091. (513) 652-1301 ext. 356. Fax: (513) 652-3835.

Ursuline College
Pepper Pike, Ohio — CB code: 1848

4-year private liberal arts college, women only, affiliated with Roman Catholic Church. Founded in 1871. **Accreditation:** Regional. **Undergraduate enrollment:** 1,448 women. **Graduate enrollment:** 140 women. **Faculty:** 127 total (63 full time), 37 with doctorates or other terminal degrees. **Location:** Suburban campus in small town; 10 miles from Cleveland. **Calendar:** Semester, limited summer session. **Microcomputers:** 25 located in computer centers. **Special facilities:** Wassmer Gallery. **Additional facts:** Men admitted as degree-seeking students, but not housed in college dormitories.

DEGREES OFFERED. BA, BS, MA. 2 associate degrees awarded in 1992. 231 bachelor's degrees awarded in 1992. 10% in business and management, 8% business/office and marketing/distribution, 50% health sciences, 8% psychology. Graduate degrees offered in 3 major fields of study.

UNDERGRADUATE MAJORS. Accounting, American studies, arts management, behavioral sciences, biological and physical sciences, biology, business administration and management, education, elementary education, English, fashion merchandising, fine arts, health care administration, history, humanities, humanities and social sciences, individual and family development, interior design, liberal/general studies, mathematics, nursing, philosophy, prelaw, psychology, public relations, religion, social studies education, social work, sociology.

ACADEMIC PROGRAMS. Accelerated program, double major, dual enrollment of high school students, independent study, internships, student-designed major, teacher preparation, cross-registration, junior year program in fashion merchandising or design at Fashion Institute of Technology in

New York City, studies program is highly interactive liberal arts core curriculum designed to accommodate distinctive learning styles of women. **Remedial services:** Reduced course load, remedial instruction, special counselor, tutoring. **Placement/credit:** AP, CLEP Subject, institutional tests; 50 credit hours maximum for bachelor's degree.

ACADEMIC REQUIREMENTS. Freshmen must earn minimum GPA of 2.0 to continue in good standing. Students must declare major by end of first year. **Graduation requirements:** 128 hours for bachelor's (30 in major). Most students required to take courses in arts/fine arts, English, history, humanities, mathematics, philosophy/religion, biological/physical sciences, social sciences.

FRESHMAN ADMISSIONS. Selection criteria: School achievement record, recommendations, test scores, school and community activities. Applicants should be in top half of class. **High school preparation:** 17 units recommended. Recommended units include English 4, foreign language 2, mathematics 3, social science 3 and science 3. One fine or performing arts recommended. Nursing students should have chemistry. **Test requirements:** SAT or ACT; score report by August 20.

1992 FRESHMAN CLASS PROFILE. 31% had high school GPA of 3.0 or higher, 60% between 2.0 and 2.99. **Academic background:** Mid 50% of enrolled freshmen had SAT-V between 380-470, SAT-M between 390-490; ACT composite between 17-22. 41% submitted SAT scores, 81% submitted ACT scores. **Characteristics:** 92% from in state, 60% commute, 23% have minority backgrounds, 1% are foreign students. Average age is 18.

FALL-TERM APPLICATIONS. $25 fee, may be waived for applicants with need. No closing date; priority given to applications received by January 1; applicants notified on a rolling basis; must reply within 4 weeks. Essay required. Interview recommended. CRDA. Deferred and early admission available. Separate application required. Admission granted only to exceptional early admission candidates.

STUDENT LIFE. Housing: Dormitories (women). Single-person room available as space allows at additional charge. **Activities:** Student government, magazine, yearbook, choral groups, student nurses, education association, campus service and spiritual life committees, ethnic groups.

ATHLETICS. Intramural: Volleyball.

STUDENT SERVICES. Career counseling, employment service for undergraduates, freshman orientation, health services, personal counseling, placement service for graduates, special adviser for adult students, services/facilities for handicapped.

ANNUAL EXPENSES. Tuition and fees: $9,180. Additional $40 per credit hour for clinical nursing courses. **Room and board:** $4,000. **Books and supplies:** $450. **Other expenses:** $750.

FINANCIAL AID. 54% of continuing students receive some form of aid. 87% of loans, all jobs based on need. Academic scholarships available. **Aid applications:** No closing date; priority given to applications received by March 15; applicants notified on a rolling basis beginning on or about March 1; must reply within 2 weeks.

ADDRESS/TELEPHONE. Dennis Giacommino, Director of Admissions, Ursuline College, 2550 Lander Road, Pepper Pike, OH 44124-4398. (216) 449-4203. Fax: (216) 449-3180.

Virginia Marti College of Fashion and Art
Lakewood, Ohio — CB code: 0396

2-year proprietary art, business college, coed. Founded in 1966. **Undergraduate enrollment:** 150 men and women. **Faculty:** 31 total (4 full time), 3 with doctorates or other terminal degrees. **Location:** Urban campus in small city; 17 miles from Cleveland. **Calendar:** Quarter, extensive summer session. **Microcomputers:** 6 located in computer centers.

DEGREES OFFERED. 40 associate degrees awarded in 1992. 25% in architecture and environmental design, 70% home economics, 5% trade and industry.

UNDERGRADUATE MAJORS. Commercial art, fashion design, fashion merchandising, interior design.

ACADEMIC PROGRAMS. Dual enrollment of high school students, independent study, internships, study abroad. **Remedial services:** Remedial instruction, tutoring. **Placement/credit:** Institutional tests.

ACADEMIC REQUIREMENTS. Freshmen must earn minimum GPA of 2.0 to continue in good standing. 81% of freshmen return for sophomore year. Students must declare major on application. **Graduation requirements:** 105 hours for associate (105 in major). Most students required to take courses in arts/fine arts, English, history, humanities, mathematics.

FRESHMAN ADMISSIONS. Selection criteria: School achievement record, test scores and interview considered. Portfolio review required for commercial art and interior design majors. **Test requirements:** Career Ability Placement Survey (CAPS) required for admission.

1992 FRESHMAN CLASS PROFILE. 75 men and women enrolled. **Characteristics:** 100% commute.

FALL-TERM APPLICATIONS. $20 fee. No closing date; applicants notified on a rolling basis. Interview required. Portfolio required for commercial art, interior design, fashion design applicants. Essay required. Early admission available.

STUDENT LIFE. Activities: Student government, student newspaper, student art exhibitions and contests. **Additional information:** Students participate in yearly fashion shows, competitions, trips to New York, France, and Italy.

STUDENT SERVICES. Career counseling, employment service for undergraduates, freshman orientation, personal counseling, placement service for graduates, veterans counselor, services/facilities for handicapped.

ANNUAL EXPENSES. Tuition and fees (1992-93): $6,120. **Books and supplies:** $600. **Other expenses:** $1,512.

FINANCIAL AID. 34% of freshmen, 67% of continuing students receive some form of aid. Grants, loans available. Academic, art, state/district residency scholarships available. **Aid applications:** No closing date; priority given to applications received by May 30; applicants notified on a rolling basis; must reply by registration.

ADDRESS/TELEPHONE. June James, Director of Admissions, Virginia Marti College of Fashion and Art, 11724 Detroit Avenue, PO Box 580, Lakewood, OH 44107. (216) 221-8584. Fax: (216) 221-2311.

Walsh University
North Canton, Ohio — CB code: 1926

Admissions: 79% of applicants accepted
Based on:
- ••• School record, test scores
- •• Activities, essay, interview, recommendations
- • Religious affiliation/commitment, special talents

Completion: 82% of freshmen end year in good standing
21% enter graduate study

4-year private university, coed, affiliated with Roman Catholic Church. Founded in 1958. **Accreditation:** Regional. **Undergraduate enrollment:** 331 men, 480 women full time; 147 men, 373 women part time. **Graduate enrollment:** 3 men, 8 women full time; 63 men, 145 women part time. **Faculty:** 113 total (65 full time), 101 with doctorates or other terminal degrees. **Location:** Suburban campus in large town; 20 miles from Akron, 60 miles from Cleveland and Youngstown. **Calendar:** Semester, limited summer session. Saturday classes. **Microcomputers:** Located in libraries, classrooms, computer centers.

DEGREES OFFERED. AA, AS, BA, BS, MA. 55 associate degrees awarded in 1992. 160 bachelor's degrees awarded. Graduate degrees offered in 3 major fields of study.

UNDERGRADUATE MAJORS. Associate: Accounting, business administration and management, business and management, liberal/general studies, nursing. **Bachelor's:** Accounting, biological and physical sciences, biology, business administration and management, business and management, business education, chemistry, clinical laboratory science, communications, computer and information sciences, computer mathematics, computer programming, counseling psychology, early childhood education, education of the emotionally handicapped, education of the mentally handicapped, education of the multiple handicapped, elementary education, English, English education, finance, foreign languages (multiple emphasis), foreign languages education, French, history, humanities and social sciences, international studies, junior high education, liberal/general studies, mathematics, mathematics education, medical laboratory technologies, nursing, pastoral ministry, philosophy, physical education, political science and government, predentistry, prelaw, premedicine, prepharmacy, preveterinary, psychology, reading education, religion, religious education, science education, secondary education, social science education, social studies education, sociology, Spanish, special education, sports medicine, theological studies.

ACADEMIC PROGRAMS. Accelerated program, double major, dual enrollment of high school students, honors program, independent study, internships, student-designed major, teacher preparation, weekend college; liberal arts/career combination in forestry, health sciences. **Remedial services:** Learning center, preadmission summer program, reduced course load, remedial instruction, special counselor, tutoring, writing center. **Placement/credit:** AP, institutional tests; 30 credit hours maximum for bachelor's degree.

ACADEMIC REQUIREMENTS. Freshmen must earn minimum GPA of 1.75 to continue in good standing. 85% of freshmen return for sophomore year. Students must declare major by end of first year. **Graduation requirements:** 60 hours for associate, 130 hours for bachelor's (65 in major). Most students required to take courses in arts/fine arts, English, foreign languages, history, humanities, mathematics, philosophy/religion, biological/physical sciences, social sciences. **Postgraduate studies:** 65% from 2-year programs enter 4-year programs. 3% enter law school, 4% enter medical school, 3% enter MBA programs, 11% enter other graduate study.

FRESHMAN ADMISSIONS. Selection criteria: School achievement record, test scores, recommendations, interview considered. **High school preparation:** 16 units required. Required units include English 4, foreign language 2, mathematics 3, social science 3 and science 3. Algebra, biology, and chemistry required for nursing applicants. **Test requirements:** SAT or ACT (ACT preferred).

1992 FRESHMAN CLASS PROFILE. 420 men applied, 331 accepted, 195 enrolled; 512 women applied, 404 accepted, 238 enrolled. 65% had high school GPA of 3.0 or higher, 35% between 2.0 and 2.99. **Characteristics:**

96% from in state, 80% live in college housing, 8% have minority backgrounds, 2% are foreign students. Average age is 18.

FALL-TERM APPLICATIONS. $15 fee, may be waived for applicants with need. No closing date; applicants notified on a rolling basis; must reply by May 1 or immediately if notified thereafter. Interview recommended. Essay recommended. CRDA. Deferred and early admission available. EDP-F.

STUDENT LIFE. Housing: Dormitories (men, women, coed). **Activities:** Student government, radio, student newspaper, yearbook, dance, drama, musical theater, Social Action Committee, Bread for the World Committee, Circle-K, community building team, black student organization, international student club, Habitat for Humanity.

ATHLETICS. NAIA. **Intercollegiate:** Baseball M, basketball, cross-country, golf M, soccer, softball W, swimming W, tennis, track and field, volleyball W. **Intramural:** Baseball M, basketball, bowling, skiing, softball, table tennis, tennis, volleyball.

STUDENT SERVICES. Aptitude testing, career counseling, employment service for undergraduates, freshman orientation, health services, personal counseling, placement service for graduates, special adviser for adult students, veterans counselor, religious counseling, services/facilities for handicapped.

ANNUAL EXPENSES. Tuition and fees: $8,404. **Room and board:** $3,950. **Books and supplies:** $500. **Other expenses:** $500.

FINANCIAL AID. 94% of freshmen, 55% of continuing students receive some form of aid. 88% of grants, 82% of loans, 88% of jobs based on need. 247 enrolled freshmen were judged to have need, all were offered aid. Academic, athletic, state/district residency, leadership, alumni affiliation, minority scholarships available. **Aid applications:** Closing date August 1; priority given to applications received by March 1; applicants notified on or about August 15; must reply by May 1 or within 2 weeks if notified thereafter.

ADDRESS/TELEPHONE. Jim Abbuhl, Director of Enrollment Management, Walsh College, 2020 Easton Street, Northwest, North Canton, OH 44720-3396. (216) 499-7090 ext. 171. (800) 362-9846. Fax: (216) 499-8518.

Washington State Community College
Marietta, Ohio — CB code: 0381

2-year public community college, coed. Founded in 1971. **Accreditation:** Regional. **Undergraduate enrollment:** 1,794 men and women. **Location:** Suburban campus in large town; 112 miles from Columbus. **Calendar:** Quarter.

FRESHMAN ADMISSIONS. Selection criteria: Open admissions. Selective admissions for medical laboratory technology and nursing programs.

ANNUAL EXPENSES. Tuition and fees (projected): $2,089, $1,969 additional for out-of-state students. **Books and supplies:** $495. **Other expenses:** $995.

ADDRESS/TELEPHONE. Kevin L. Conley, Director of Admissions, Washington State Community College, 710 Colegate Drive, Marietta, OH 45750. (614) 374-8716. Fax: (614) 373-7496.

West Side Institute of Technology
Cleveland, Ohio — CB code: 0748

2-year proprietary technical college, coed. Founded in 1958. **Undergraduate enrollment:** 160 men and women full time; 148 men and women part time. **Location:** Urban campus in very large city; 5 miles from downtown. **Calendar:** Quarter.

FRESHMAN ADMISSIONS. Selection criteria: Score of 45 on Bennett Mechanical Comprehension Test.

ANNUAL EXPENSES. Tuition and fees (1992-93): $4,645. **Books and supplies:** $1,230. **Other expenses:** $1,353.

ADDRESS/TELEPHONE. Leonard Finkelhor, Director, West Side Institute of Technology, 9801 Walford Avenue, Cleveland, OH 44102. (216) 651-1656. Fax: (216) 651-4077.

Wilberforce University
Wilberforce, Ohio — CB code: 1906

Admissions: 55% of applicants accepted
Based on:
- ••• School record
- •• Activities, interview, recommendations, test scores
- • Essay, special talents

Completion: 75% of freshmen end year in good standing

4-year private liberal arts college, coed, affiliated with African Methodist Episcopal Church. Founded in 1856. **Accreditation:** Regional. **Undergraduate enrollment:** 350 men, 450 women full time. **Faculty:** 62 total (51 full time), 14 with doctorates or other terminal degrees. **Location:** Rural campus in rural community; 18 miles from Dayton. **Calendar:** Semester, extensive summer session. **Microcomputers:** 49 located in computer centers. **Special facilities:** African Methodist Episcopal Church archives. **Additional facts:** Cooperative education program required of all students.

DEGREES OFFERED. BA, BS. 100 bachelor's degrees awarded in 1992.

UNDERGRADUATE MAJORS. Accounting, biological and physical sciences, biology, business administration and management, business economics, chemical engineering, chemistry, civil engineering, comparative literature, computer and information sciences, economics, electrical/electronics/communications engineering, English, finance, fine arts, health care administration, information sciences and systems, journalism, liberal/general studies, marketing and distribution, mathematics, mechanical engineering, music, political science and government, psychology, sociology.

ACADEMIC PROGRAMS. Cooperative education, honors program, internships, study abroad, cross-registration; liberal arts/career combination in engineering, health sciences. **Remedial services:** Remedial instruction, special counselor, tutoring. **ROTC:** Air Force, Army. **Placement/credit:** AP, CLEP General and Subject, institutional tests; 30 credit hours maximum for bachelor's degree.

ACADEMIC REQUIREMENTS. Freshmen must earn minimum GPA of 1.5 to continue in good standing. 60% of freshmen return for sophomore year. Students must declare major by end of second year. **Graduation requirements:** 126 hours for bachelor's (45 in major). Most students required to take courses in arts/fine arts, computer science, English, history, humanities, mathematics, philosophy/religion, biological/physical sciences, social sciences. **Additional information:** Secondary education certification available for literature, art, and music majors.

FRESHMAN ADMISSIONS. Selection criteria: Class rank (top two-thirds), high school GPA, and test scores are most important. **High school preparation:** 15 units required. Required and recommended units include English 4, mathematics 2-3, social science 2 and science 2-3. Foreign language 2 recommended. **Test requirements:** SAT or ACT (ACT preferred); score report by July 1.

1992 FRESHMAN CLASS PROFILE. 1,198 men and women applied, 660 accepted; 195 enrolled. 10% had high school GPA of 3.0 or higher, 63% between 2.0 and 2.99. **Characteristics:** 57% from in state, 96% live in college housing, 99% have minority backgrounds, 20% join fraternities/sororities. Average age is 18.

FALL-TERM APPLICATIONS. $20 fee, may be waived for applicants with need. Closing date June 1; applicants notified on a rolling basis; must reply within 3 weeks. Interview recommended. Essay recommended. Deferred and early admission available.

STUDENT LIFE. Housing: Dormitories (men, women). **Activities:** Student government, radio, student newspaper, yearbook, choral groups, dance, drama, music ensembles, fraternities, sororities, Inter-Faith Fellowship, Interdenominational Ministerial Alliance, Alpha-Omega.

ATHLETICS. Intercollegiate: Basketball, track and field. **Intramural:** Baseball M, basketball M, softball, table tennis, tennis, volleyball.

STUDENT SERVICES. Career counseling, employment service for undergraduates, freshman orientation, health services, personal counseling, placement service for graduates, veterans counselor.

ANNUAL EXPENSES. Tuition and fees (projected): $6,984. **Room and board:** $3,562. **Books and supplies:** $550. **Other expenses:** $1,490.

FINANCIAL AID. 95% of freshmen, 96% of continuing students receive some form of aid. 96% of grants, 98% of loans, 99% of jobs based on need. 190 enrolled freshmen were judged to have need, all were offered aid. Academic, leadership, alumni affiliation, religious affiliation scholarships available. **Aid applications:** Closing date June 1; priority given to applications received by April 30; applicants notified on a rolling basis beginning on or about March 15; must reply within 2 weeks.

ADDRESS/TELEPHONE. Rick Mitchell, Director for Admissions, Wilberforce University, 1055 North Bickett Road, Wilberforce, OH 45384-1091. (513) 376-7321.

Wilmington College
Wilmington, Ohio — CB code: 1909

Admissions: 82% of applicants accepted
Based on:
- ••• Recommendations, school record, test scores
- •• Interview
- • Activities, essay, special talents

Completion: 88% of freshmen end year in good standing
55% graduate

4-year private liberal arts college, coed, affiliated with Wilmington Yearly Meeting of the Religious Society of Friends (Quaker). Founded in 1870. **Accreditation:** Regional. **Undergraduate enrollment:** 901 men and women. **Faculty:** 73 total (54 full time), 41 with doctorates or other terminal degrees. **Location:** Rural campus in large town; 50 miles from Cincinnati, 60 miles from Columbus. **Calendar:** Semester, limited summer session. **Microcomputers:** 27 located in classrooms, computer centers. **Special facilities:** 5 farms (1,500 acres) for agricultural program, greenhouse, herbarium, observatory, electron microscope, live animal area, sports medicine center, Peace Resource Center containing Hiroshima/Nagasaki Memorial collection. **Additional facts:** College dedicated to Quaker ideals of peace, service, and self-discipline. Branch campuses in Cincinnati and other locations. BA in business offered at Cincinnati branch and Wilmington evening program.

DEGREES OFFERED. BA, BS. 160 bachelor's degrees awarded in 1992. 7% in agriculture, 28% business and management, 5% business/office and marketing/distribution, 6% communications, 20% education, 10% psychology, 7% social sciences.

UNDERGRADUATE MAJORS. Accounting, agricultural sciences, art education, biology, business administration and management, business and management, chemistry, communications, computer and information sciences, criminal justice studies, dramatic arts, economics, education, elementary education, English, English education, foreign languages education, French, health education, history, industrial technology, liberal/general studies, marketing and distribution, marketing management, mathematics, mathematics education, music education, philosophy, physical education, predentistry, prelaw, premedicine, preveterinary, psychology, religion, science education, secondary education, social studies education, sociology, Spanish, sports medicine.

ACADEMIC PROGRAMS. Double major, dual enrollment of high school students, independent study, internships, student-designed major, study abroad, teacher preparation, Washington semester, cross-registration. **Remedial services:** Learning center, reduced course load, remedial instruction, special counselor, tutoring. **Placement/credit:** AP, CLEP General and Subject, institutional tests; 30 credit hours maximum for bachelor's degree.

ACADEMIC REQUIREMENTS. Freshmen must earn minimum GPA of 2.0 to continue in good standing. 77% of freshmen return for sophomore year. Students must declare major by end of second year. **Graduation requirements:** 124 hours for bachelor's (36 in major). Most students required to take courses in arts/fine arts, English, humanities, mathematics, biological/physical sciences, social sciences.

FRESHMAN ADMISSIONS. Selection criteria: Previous academic record, test scores, counselor recommendation, extracurricular activities, and interview considered. **High school preparation:** 16 units required. Required units include English 4, foreign language 2, mathematics 2, social science 2 and science 2. **Test requirements:** SAT or ACT (ACT preferred); score report by August 15.

1992 FRESHMAN CLASS PROFILE. 650 men and women applied, 530 accepted; 205 enrolled. **Characteristics:** 92% from in state, 80% live in college housing, 5% have minority backgrounds, 4% are foreign students. Average age is 18.

FALL-TERM APPLICATIONS. $15 fee. No closing date; priority given to applications received by August 15; applicants notified on a rolling basis beginning on or about December 1; must reply by May 1 or within 10 days if notified thereafter. Interview recommended. Essay recommended. CRDA. Deferred and early admission available.

STUDENT LIFE. Housing: Dormitories (men, women, coed); fraternity housing available. **Activities:** Student government, magazine, student newspaper, yearbook, choral groups, drama, jazz band, music ensembles, musical theater, fraternities, sororities, black, business, social service, international, education, and agriculture clubs, Christian Students, Young Friends (Quaker-Christian group), Catholic campus ministry, sports medicine association.

ATHLETICS. NCAA. **Intercollegiate:** Baseball M, basketball, cross-country, football M, golf M, soccer, softball W, tennis, track and field, volleyball W, wrestling M. **Intramural:** Basketball, racquetball, softball, squash, tennis, volleyball.

STUDENT SERVICES. Career counseling, employment service for undergraduates, freshman orientation, health services, personal counseling, placement service for graduates, special adviser for adult students, minority adviser, services/facilities for handicapped.

ANNUAL EXPENSES. Tuition and fees: $9,830. **Room and board:** $3,870. **Books and supplies:** $500. **Other expenses:** $1,186.

FINANCIAL AID. 90% of freshmen, 89% of continuing students receive some form of aid. 65% of grants, 95% of loans, 43% of jobs based on need. 194 enrolled freshmen were judged to have need, all were offered aid. Academic, music/drama, state/district residency, leadership, alumni affiliation, religious affiliation, minority scholarships available. **Aid applications:** No closing date; priority given to applications received by March 31; applicants notified on a rolling basis beginning on or about March 1; must reply within 2 weeks.

ADDRESS/TELEPHONE. Lawrence T. Lesick, Director of Admission, Wilmington College, Box 1325 Pyle Center, Wilmington, OH 45177. (800) 341-9318 ext. 260. (800) 341-9318. Fax: (513) 382-7077.

Wittenberg University
Springfield, Ohio — CB code: 1922

Admissions: 78% of applicants accepted
Based on:
••• Recommendations, school record
•• Activities, essay, interview, special talents
• Religious affiliation/commitment, test scores
Completion: 92% of freshmen end year in good standing
70% graduate, 24% of these enter graduate study

4-year private liberal arts college, coed, affiliated with Evangelical Lutheran Church in America. Founded in 1845. **Accreditation:** Regional. **Undergraduate enrollment:** 860 men, 1,182 women full time; 34 men, 77 women part time. **Faculty:** 186 total (156 full time), 172 with doctorates or other terminal degrees. **Location:** Suburban campus in small city; 25 miles from Dayton, 80 miles from Cincinnati. **Calendar:** Trimester, limited summer session. Extensive evening/early morning classes. **Microcomputers:** 150 located in dormitories, libraries, classrooms, computer centers.

DEGREES OFFERED. BA, BFA. 500 bachelor's degrees awarded in 1992. 6% in area and ethnic studies, 16% business and management, 10% education, 5% languages, 8% law, 12% life sciences, 7% psychology, 11% social sciences, 6% visual and performing arts.

UNDERGRADUATE MAJORS. Accounting, adult and continuing education research, American literature, American studies, art education, art history, behavioral sciences, biochemistry, biological and physical sciences, biology, biophysics, botany, business administration and management, business and management, business economics, business education, ceramics, chemistry, Chinese, city/community/regional planning, communications, comparative literature, computer and information sciences, computer mathematics, creative writing, dance, drawing, earth sciences, East Asian studies, economics, education, elementary education, engineering, English, English education, English literature, European studies, finance, fine arts, foreign languages (multiple emphasis), foreign languages education, forestry and related sciences, French, genetics, human and animal, geography, geology, German, graphic design, health education, health sciences, history, humanities, humanities and social sciences, international business management, international relations, international studies, Japanese, journalism, junior high education, liberal/general studies, marine biology, marketing management, mathematics, mathematics education, microbiology, music, music education, music performance, music theory and composition, musical theater, nursing, occupational therapy, operations research, optometry, painting, philosophy, physical education, physical sciences, physics, political science and government, predentistry, prelaw, premedicine, prepharmacy, preveterinary, printmaking, psychology, reading education, religion, religious music, Russian, Russian and Slavic studies, science education, science technologies, sculpture, secondary education, social science education, social sciences, social studies education, sociology, Spanish, special education, specific learning disabilities, speech, urban studies, visual and performing arts, women's studies, zoology.

ACADEMIC PROGRAMS. Accelerated program, double major, dual enrollment of high school students, honors program, independent study, internships, student-designed major, study abroad, teacher preparation, visiting/exchange student program, weekend college, Washington semester, cross-registration, semester programs with Duke University (marine biology), School of Visual Arts in New York, Camarillo Hospital in California, National Institutes of Health in Washington, D.C., Washington University (MO) (occupational therapy), 3-2 engineering program with Columbia University, Case Western, Georgia Tech, Washington University (MO); liberal arts/career combination in engineering, forestry, health sciences. **Remedial services:** Learning center, reduced course load, special counselor, tutoring, writers and mathematics workshops. **ROTC:** Air Force, Army. **Placement/credit:** AP, IB, institutional tests.

ACADEMIC REQUIREMENTS. Freshmen must earn minimum GPA of 2.0 to continue in good standing. 87% of freshmen return for sophomore year. Students must declare major by end of second year. **Graduation requirements:** 154 hours for bachelor's (52 in major). Most students required to take courses in arts/fine arts, English, foreign languages, humanities, mathematics, philosophy/religion, biological/physical sciences, social sciences. **Postgraduate studies:** 5% enter law school, 3% enter medical school, 4% enter MBA programs, 12% enter other graduate study.

FRESHMAN ADMISSIONS. Selection criteria: In order of importance: school achievement record, school attended, trend in work, test scores, counselor recommendation, extracurricular activities, and interview. Special consideration for children of alumni, minorities, Lutherans, residents of Clark County, and international students. **High school preparation:** 16 units required. Required units include English 4, foreign language 3, mathematics 3, social science 3 and science 3. **Test requirements:** SAT or ACT; score report by March 15. English ACH required of students who perform poorly on SAT or ACT, and learning disabled. Score report by March 15. **Additional information:** Each student's record evaluated individually. No cut off on rank, average, or test data.

1992 FRESHMAN CLASS PROFILE. 959 men applied, 703 accepted, 217 enrolled; 1,284 women applied, 1,050 accepted, 358 enrolled. 85% had high school GPA of 3.0 or higher, 15% between 2.0 and 2.99. 48% were in top tenth and 72% were in top quarter of graduating class. **Academic background:** Mid 50% of enrolled freshmen had SAT-V between 480-570, SAT-M between 510-620; ACT composite between 21-27. 45% submitted SAT scores, 55% submitted ACT scores. **Characteristics:** 52% from in state, 98% live in college housing, 15% have minority backgrounds, 6% are foreign students, 40% join fraternities/sororities. Average age is 18.

FALL-TERM APPLICATIONS. $40 fee, may be waived for applicants with need. Closing date March 15; applicants notified on or about March 15; must reply by May 1. Audition required for music applicants. Portfolio required for art applicants. Essay required. Interview recommended. Deferred and early admission available. Institutional early decision plan. Application closing date for early action is January 15; notification by February 15. Closing date for early decision is December 15; notification by February 15. Closing date for regular action is March 15 - notification by April 1.

STUDENT LIFE. Housing: Dormitories (men, women, coed); apartment, fraternity, sorority housing available. Substance free residence halls. **Activities:** Student government, magazine, radio, student newspaper, yearbook, literary magazines, departmental journals, choral groups, concert band, dance, drama, jazz band, music ensembles, musical theater, pep band, symphony orchestra, fraternities, sororities, Newman Club, Concerned Black Students, Community Volunteer Service, Weaver Chapel Association, Project Woman, International Student Organization. East Asian Studies Club, Hillel, Amnesty International.

ATHLETICS. NCAA. **Intercollegiate:** Baseball M, basketball, cross-country, diving, field hockey W, football M, golf M, lacrosse, soccer, softball W, swimming, tennis, track and field, volleyball W. **Intramural:** Badminton, basketball, bowling, diving, fencing, golf W, gymnastics, handball M, horseback riding, ice hockey M, racquetball, rugby, sailing, skiing, skin diving, soccer, softball, squash, swimming, table tennis, tennis, track and field, volleyball, water polo M.

STUDENT SERVICES. Aptitude testing, career counseling, employment service for undergraduates, freshman orientation, health services, on-campus day care, personal counseling, placement service for graduates, special adviser for adult students, veterans counselor, minority counselor, international counselor, women's programs, services/facilities for handicapped.

ANNUAL EXPENSES. Tuition and fees: $15,726. **Room and board:** $4,272. **Books and supplies:** $400. **Other expenses:** $800.

FINANCIAL AID. 50% of freshmen, 55% of continuing students receive some form of aid. 95% of grants, 92% of loans, 90% of jobs based on need. 321 enrolled freshmen were judged to have need, 320 were offered aid. Academic, music/drama, art, state/district residency, alumni affiliation, religious affiliation, minority scholarships available. **Aid applications:** No closing date; priority given to applications received by March 1; applicants notified on a rolling basis beginning on or about March 1; must reply by May 1 or within 2 weeks if notified thereafter.

ADDRESS/TELEPHONE. Kenneth G. Benne, Dean of Admissions, Wittenberg University, PO Box 720, Ward Street and North Wittenberg Avenue, Springfield, OH 45501. (513) 327-6314. (800) 677-7558. Fax: (513) 327-6340.

Wright State University
Dayton, Ohio — CB code: 1179

4-year public university, coed. Founded in 1964. **Accreditation:** Regional. **Undergraduate enrollment:** 4,665 men, 4,932 women full time; 1,582 men, 1,746 women part time. **Graduate enrollment:** 571 men, 625 women full time; 1,025 men, 1,693 women part time. **Faculty:** 1,013 total (710 full time), 568 with doctorates or other terminal degrees. **Location:** Suburban campus in small city; 10 miles from downtown Dayton. **Calendar:** Quarter, extensive summer session. **Microcomputers:** Located in dormitories, libraries, classrooms, computer centers. **Special facilities:** 2,200-acre biological preserve, garden of the senses accessible to handicapped, new athletic/entertainment complex, museum of contemporary art.

DEGREES OFFERED. BA, BS, BFA, MA, MS, MBA, MEd, PhD, MD. 1,720 bachelor's degrees awarded in 1992. 29% in business and management, 15% teacher education, 12% engineering, 11% health sciences, 6% multi/interdisciplinary studies, 27% physical sciences. Graduate degrees offered in 57 major fields of study.

UNDERGRADUATE MAJORS. Accounting, anthropology, applied mathematics, art education, art history, arts management, bioengineering and biomedical engineering, biology, business administration and management, business economics, business education, chemistry, cinematography/film, city/community/regional planning, classics, communications, computer and information sciences, computer engineering, criminal justice studies, dance, directing/stage management, dramatic arts, drawing, early childhood education, economics, education of the mentally handicapped, education of the multiple handicapped, education of the physically handicapped, electrical/electronics/communications engineering, elementary education, engineering physics, English, English education, environmental science, experimental psychology, film arts, finance, fine arts, fire protection, foreign languages (multiple emphasis), foreign languages education, French, geography, geology, geophysics and seismology, German, Greek (classical), history, human factors, human resources development, international studies, journalism, Latin, management information systems, marketing and distribution, materials engineering, mathematics, mathematics education, mechanical engineering, medical laboratory technologies, motion picture history, motion picture production, motion picture technology, music, music education, music history and appreciation, music performance, music theory and composition, nursing, operations research, painting, philosophy, photography, physical education, physics, political science and government, printmaking, psychology, public administration, public relations, pure mathematics, radio/television broadcasting, reading education, rehabilitation counseling/services, religion, science education, sculpture, secondary education, social science education, social studies education, social work, sociology, Spanish, special education, specific learning disabilities, speech/communication/theater education, statistics, theater design, theory and criticism, urban studies, visual and performing arts.

ACADEMIC PROGRAMS. Accelerated program, cooperative education, double major, dual enrollment of high school students, education specialist degree, honors program, independent study, internships, student-designed major, study abroad, teacher preparation, visiting/exchange student program, cross-registration. **Remedial services:** Learning center, preadmission summer program, reduced course load, remedial instruction, special counselor, tutoring. **ROTC:** Air Force, Army. **Placement/credit:** AP, CLEP Subject, institutional tests.

ACADEMIC REQUIREMENTS. Freshmen must earn minimum GPA of 2.0 to continue in good standing. 65% of freshmen return for sophomore year. Students must declare major by end of first year. **Graduation requirements:** 187 hours for bachelor's. Most students required to take courses in arts/fine arts, English, history, humanities, mathematics, biological/physical sciences, social sciences.

FRESHMAN ADMISSIONS. High school preparation: 16 units recommended. Recommended units include English 4, foreign language 2, mathematics 3, social science 3 and science 3. Mathematics recommendation includes 2 algebra. Social science recommendation includes 2 history. Art, music, or theater also recommended. Students not meeting course recommendations must make up deficiency prior to admission to program. **Test requirements:** SAT or ACT (ACT preferred); score report by May 1. SAT or ACT required for admission of out-of-state applicants.

1992 FRESHMAN CLASS PROFILE. 951 men, 1,068 women enrolled. 32% had high school GPA of 3.0 or higher, 55% between 2.0 and 2.99. 11% were in top tenth and 30% were in top quarter of graduating class. **Academic background:** Mid 50% of enrolled freshmen had SAT-V between 300-480, SAT-M between 330-530; ACT composite between 17-23. 37% submitted SAT scores, 96% submitted ACT scores. **Characteristics:** 94% from in state, 53% commute, 12% have minority backgrounds, 4% join fraternities/sororities. Average age is 19.

FALL-TERM APPLICATIONS. $25 fee. Closing date September 1; priority given to applications received by May 1; applicants notified on a rolling basis beginning on or about October 1. Audition required for music, acting, dance, directing/stage management applicants. Portfolio required for art, art education applicants. Deferred and early admission available. Application by January recommended for students desiring on-campus housing.

STUDENT LIFE. Housing: Dormitories (coed); apartment housing available. Handicapped accessible housing available. **Activities:** Student government, magazine, radio, student newspaper, television, yearbook, choral groups, concert band, dance, drama, jazz band, music ensembles, pep band, symphony orchestra, Drill Team, fraternities, sororities, Black Student Union, Baptist Student Union, Student Association for Escorts (SAFE) College Students for Special Wish, Fellowship of Christian Students, Circle-K, Model United Nations, Campus Crusade for Christ, Ohio College Democrats, Jewish Student Union. **Additional information:** Athletic facilities accessible to handicapped.

ATHLETICS. NCAA. **Intercollegiate:** Baseball M, basketball, cross-country, diving, golf M, soccer, softball W, swimming, tennis, volleyball W. **Intramural:** Archery, basketball, cross-country, golf, handball, lacrosse M, racquetball, soccer, softball, squash, table tennis, tennis, volleyball, wrestling M.

STUDENT SERVICES. Career counseling, employment service for undergraduates, freshman orientation, health services, on-campus day care, personal counseling, placement service for graduates, special adviser for adult students, veterans counselor, psychological services, services/facilities for handicapped.

ANNUAL EXPENSES. Tuition and fees (1992-93): $2,934, $2,934 additional for out-of-state students. **Room and board:** $3,579. **Books and supplies:** $650. **Other expenses:** $1,000.

FINANCIAL AID. 56% of freshmen, 49% of continuing students receive some form of aid. 79% of grants, 98% of loans, 41% of jobs based on need. 1,321 enrolled freshmen were judged to have need, all were offered aid. Academic, music/drama, art, athletic, state/district residency, leadership, minority scholarships available. **Aid applications:** No closing date; priority given to applications received by April 1; applicants notified on a rolling basis beginning on or about April 1; must reply within 2 weeks. **Additional information:** Academic scholarship applications must be submitted by February 1.

ADDRESS/TELEPHONE. Kenneth Davenport, Director of Admissions, Wright State University, 3640 Colonel Glenn Highway, Dayton, OH 45435. (513) 873-2211. Fax: (513) 873-3301.

Wright State University: Lake Campus
Celina, Ohio CB code: 1947

2-year public branch campus college, coed. Founded in 1969. **Accreditation:** Regional. **Undergraduate enrollment:** 158 men, 236 women full time; 203 men, 251 women part time. **Faculty:** 59 total (28 full time), 12 with doctorates or other terminal degrees. **Location:** Rural campus in small town; 70 miles from Dayton. **Calendar:** Quarter, limited summer session. Saturday and extensive evening/early morning classes. **Microcomputers:** 105 located in computer centers.

DEGREES OFFERED. AA, AS, AAS. 75 associate degrees awarded in 1992. 17% in business and management, 20% business/office and marketing/distribution, 33% engineering technologies, 15% trade and industry.

UNDERGRADUATE MAJORS. Accounting, biological and physical sciences, biology, business administration and management, business and management, business and office, business data processing and related programs, business economics, chemistry, communications, computer and information sciences, drafting, drafting and design technology, electronic technology, engineering and engineering-related technologies, English, geography, geology, history, industrial technology, legal secretary, manufacturing technology, marketing and distribution, mechanical design technology, medical secretary, psychology, secretarial and related programs, social sciences, social work, sociology, word processing.

ACADEMIC PROGRAMS. 2-year transfer program, double major, dual enrollment of high school students, honors program, independent study, internships, student-designed major, cross-registration. **Remedial services:** Learning center, preadmission summer program, reduced course load, remedial instruction, special counselor, tutoring. **Placement/credit:** AP, institutional tests.

ACADEMIC REQUIREMENTS. Freshmen must earn minimum GPA of 2.0 to continue in good standing. 70% of freshmen return for sophomore year. Students must declare major on application. **Graduation requirements:** 100 hours for associate. Most students required to take courses in arts/fine arts, computer science, English, foreign languages, history, humanities, mathematics, philosophy/religion, biological/physical sciences, social sciences.

FRESHMAN ADMISSIONS. Selection criteria: Open admissions. **High school preparation:** 16 units recommended. Recommended units include English 4, foreign language 2, mathematics 3, social science 3 and science 3. One unit of art recommended. **Test requirements:** SAT or ACT (ACT preferred) for placement and counseling only; score report by September 14.

1992 FRESHMAN CLASS PROFILE. 87 men, 89 women enrolled. **Academic background:** Mid 50% of enrolled freshmen had ACT composite between 18-23. 95% submitted ACT scores. **Characteristics:** 100% from in state, 100% commute, 1% have minority backgrounds. Average age is 23.

FALL-TERM APPLICATIONS. $25 fee. No closing date; applicants notified on a rolling basis beginning on or about September 1. Deferred and early admission available.

STUDENT LIFE. Activities: Student government, student newspaper, drama.

ATHLETICS. Intercollegiate: Basketball. **Intramural:** Table tennis.

STUDENT SERVICES. Aptitude testing, career counseling, freshman orientation, on-campus day care, personal counseling, placement service for graduates, veterans counselor, learning resource center for tutoring, services/facilities for handicapped.

ANNUAL EXPENSES. Tuition and fees (1992-93): $2,625, $2,625 additional for out-of-state students. **Books and supplies:** $650. **Other expenses:** $1,000.

FINANCIAL AID. 70% of freshmen, 50% of continuing students receive some form of aid. Academic, state/district residency, leadership scholarships available. **Aid applications:** No closing date; priority given to applications received by March 1; applicants notified on a rolling basis beginning on or about May 1; must reply within 3 weeks. **Additional information:** Academic scholarship application deadline February 1. All financial aid applications and awards administered by Dayton campus. Monies awarded for bothcampuses totaled $17,056,000.

ADDRESS/TELEPHONE. Carol Kill, Admissions Officer and Registrar, Wright State University: Lake Campus, 7600 State Route 703, Celina, OH 45822. (419) 586-2365 ext. 224. Fax: (419) 586-9048.

Xavier University
Cincinnati, Ohio CB code: 1965

Admissions: 91% of applicants accepted
Based on: ••• School record
•• Special talents, test scores
• Activities, essay, interview, recommendations
Completion: 90% of freshmen end year in good standing
62% graduate, 55% of these enter graduate study

4-year private university, coed, affiliated with Roman Catholic Church. Founded in 1831. **Accreditation:** Regional. **Undergraduate enrollment:** 1,382 men, 1,470 women full time; 388 men, 756 women part time. **Graduate enrollment:** 142 men, 113 women full time; 1,057 men, 1,065 women part time. **Faculty:** 411 total (231 full time), 209 with doctorates or other terminal degrees. **Location:** Suburban campus in large city; 5 miles from downtown. **Calendar:** Semester, limited summer session. Saturday classes. **Microcomputers:** 150 located in dormitories, libraries, classrooms, computer centers. **Special facilities:** Student-run professional art gallery, observatory.

DEGREES OFFERED. AA, AS, BA, BS, BFA, MA, MS, MBA, MEd. 51 associate degrees awarded in 1992. 10% in business and management, 6% communications, 57% health sciences, 25% allied health. 721 bachelor's degrees awarded. 33% in business and management, 11% communications, 6% teacher education, 13% letters/literature, 9% social sciences. Graduate degrees offered in 13 major fields of study.

UNDERGRADUATE MAJORS. Associate: Business and management, communications, criminal justice studies, early childhood education, French, history, liberal/general studies, nursing, political science and government, prepharmacy, psychology, public relations, radio/television broadcasting, radiograph medical technology, sociology, Spanish. **Bachelor's:** Accounting, advertising, applied science, art education, biological and physical sciences, biology, business administration and management, business and management, business economics, chemistry, classics, clinical laboratory science, communications, computer and information sciences, criminal justice studies, early childhood education, economics, education of exceptional children, education of the mentally handicapped, elementary education, English, finance, fine arts, French, German, Greek (classical), health education, history, human resources development, humanities, information sciences and systems, international relations, labor/industrial relations, Latin, liberal/general studies, management information systems, mathematics, Montessori education, music, music education, nursing, philosophy, physical education, physics, political science and government, predentistry, preengineering, prelaw, premedicine, preveterinary, psychology, public relations, radio/television broadcasting, secondary education, small business management and ownership, social work, sociology, Spanish, special education, specific learning disabilities, sports management, theological studies.

ACADEMIC PROGRAMS. Accelerated program, double major, dual enrollment of high school students, honors program, independent study, internships, study abroad, teacher preparation, visiting/exchange student program, weekend college, Washington semester, cross-registration; liberal arts/career combination in engineering, forestry. **Remedial services:** Preadmission summer program, reduced course load, remedial instruction, special counselor, tutoring, academic bridge program, writing and mathematics labs. **ROTC:** Army. **Placement/credit:** AP, CLEP General and Subject, IB, institutional tests.

ACADEMIC REQUIREMENTS. Freshmen must earn minimum GPA of 2.0 to continue in good standing. 88% of freshmen return for sophomore year. Students must declare major by end of second year. **Graduation requirements:** 60 hours for associate, 120 hours for bachelor's (30 in major). Most students required to take courses in arts/fine arts, English, foreign languages, history, humanities, mathematics, philosophy/religion, biological/physical sciences, social sciences. **Postgraduate studies:** 5% enter medical school, 50% enter other graduate study.

FRESHMAN ADMISSIONS. Selection criteria: Class rank, high school GPA, and test scores are criteria. Interview, activities, and recommendations considered in borderline cases. **High school preparation:** 15 units required. Required units include English 4, foreign language 2, mathematics 3, social science 2 and science 2. Additional social science or science may be substituted for language requirement. 2 elective courses are also recommended. **Test requirements:** SAT or ACT; score report by August 15.

1992 FRESHMAN CLASS PROFILE. 1,094 men applied, 1,002 accepted, 342 enrolled; 1,140 women applied, 1,030 accepted, 333 enrolled. 50% had high school GPA of 3.0 or higher, 49% between 2.0 and 2.99. 28% were in top tenth and 52% were in top quarter of graduating class. **Academic background:** Mid 50% of enrolled freshmen had SAT-V between 420-520, SAT-M between 460-590; ACT composite between 21-27. 75% submitted SAT scores, 76% submitted ACT scores. **Characteristics:** 64% from in state, 75% live in college housing, 13% have minority backgrounds. Average age is 19.

FALL-TERM APPLICATIONS. $25 fee, may be waived for applicants with need. Closing date August 15; priority given to applications received by April 1; applicants notified on a rolling basis beginning on or about November 1; must reply by May 1 or within 3 weeks if notified thereafter. Interview recommended for academically borderline applicants. Essay recommended for academically borderline applicants. CRDA. Deferred and early admission available. Recommend Prueba de Evaluacion test for applicants from Puerto Rico.

STUDENT LIFE. Housing: Dormitories (coed); apartment, handicapped housing available. Out-of-town freshmen and sophomores required to live in dormitories. Furnished apartments available for juniors and seniors. **Activities:** Student government, film, magazine, radio, student newspaper, television, yearbook, choral groups, concert band, drama, jazz band, music ensembles, musical theater, pep band, student volunteer services, Black Student Association, campus ministry, sports clubs, international student center, center for peace and justice.

ATHLETICS. NCAA. **Intercollegiate:** Baseball M, basketball, cross-country, diving, golf, rifle, soccer, swimming, tennis, volleyball W. **Intramural:** Basketball, boxing M, fencing, handball, racquetball, rowing (crew), rugby, sailing, soccer, softball, table tennis, tennis, volleyball.

STUDENT SERVICES. Aptitude testing, career counseling, employment service for undergraduates, freshman orientation, health services, personal counseling, placement service for graduates, special adviser for adult students, veterans counselor, services/facilities for handicapped.

ANNUAL EXPENSES. Tuition and fees: $10,970. **Room and board:** $4,740. **Books and supplies:** $500. **Other expenses:** $700.

FINANCIAL AID. 85% of freshmen, 82% of continuing students receive some form of aid. 46% of grants, 93% of loans, 70% of jobs based on need. Academic, music/drama, art, athletic, state/district residency, leadership, minority scholarships available. **Aid applications:** No closing date; priority given to applications received by April 15; applicants notified on a rolling basis beginning on or about March 1; must reply by May 1 or within 4 weeks if notified thereafter.

ADDRESS/TELEPHONE. Jay Leiendecker, Director of Admission, Xavier University, 3800 Victory Parkway, Cincinnati, OH 45207-5311. (513) 745-3301. (800) 344-4698. Fax: (513) 745-4319.

Youngstown State University

Youngstown, Ohio — CB code: 1975

4-year public university, coed. Founded in 1908. **Accreditation:** Regional. **Undergraduate enrollment:** 4,892 men, 4,815 women full time; 1,740 men, 2,122 women part time. **Graduate enrollment:** 84 men, 92 women full time; 412 men, 649 women part time. **Faculty:** 889 total (465 full time), 369 with doctorates or other terminal degrees. **Location:** Urban campus in small city; midway between Cleveland and Pittsburgh, Pennsylvania. **Calendar:** Quarter, limited summer session. Saturday and extensive evening/early morning classes. **Microcomputers:** 394 located in computer centers. **Special facilities:** John McDonough Museum of Art, Butler Institute of American Art (near campus), Ward Beecher Planetarium. **Additional facts:** University comprises colleges of arts and sciences, business administration, engineering, fine and performing arts, education, applied science and technology, graduate school.

DEGREES OFFERED. AA, AAS, BA, BS, BFA, MA, MS, MBA, MEd, EdD. 290 associate degrees awarded in 1992. 1,365 bachelor's degrees awarded. Graduate degrees offered in 33 major fields of study.

UNDERGRADUATE MAJORS. Associate: Accounting, advertising, business administration and management, business and office, business data processing and related programs, child development/care/guidance, civil technology, computer and information sciences, computer technology, court reporting, dental hygiene, dietetic aide/assistant, drafting, drafting and design technology, electrical technology, emergency medical technologies, food production/management/services, hotel/motel and restaurant management, labor/industrial relations, law enforcement and corrections technologies, marketing and distribution, mechanical design technology, medical assistant, medical laboratory technologies, respiratory therapy, respiratory therapy technology, secretarial and related programs, social work, transportation management. **Bachelor's:** Accounting, advertising, Afro-American (black) studies, allied health, American studies, anthropology, art education, art history, astronomy, biology, business administration and management, business and management, business education, chemical engineering, chemistry, civil engineering, civil technology, clinical laboratory science, communications, computer and information sciences, computer technology, criminology, dramatic arts, early childhood education, earth sciences, economics, education, education of the mentally handicapped, electrical technology, electrical/electronics/communications engineering, elementary education, English, English education, fashion merchandising, finance, food science and nutrition, foreign languages education, French, geography, geology, German, graphic design, health education, health sciences, history, home economics, home economics education, industrial engineering, Italian, labor/industrial relations, Latin, law enforcement and corrections, mall management, marketing and distribution, marketing management, mathematics, mathematics education, mechanical design technology, mechanical engineering, medical laboratory technologies, music education, music history and appreciation, music performance, music theory and composition, nursing, philosophy, physical education, physics, political science and government, predentistry, prelaw, premedicine, preveterinary, psychology, public administration, public relations, reading education, religion, retailing, Russian, science education, secondary education, social science education, social sciences, social studies education, social work, sociology, Spanish, special education, specific learning disabilities, speech, speech/communication/theater education, studio art, technical and business writing, telecommunications, transportation management, visual and performing arts.

ACADEMIC PROGRAMS. 2-year transfer program, accelerated program, double major, dual enrollment of high school students, honors program, internships, student-designed major, study abroad, teacher preparation, weekend college, 3-2 forestry program with Duke University; liberal arts/career combination in forestry; combined bachelor's/graduate program in medicine. **Remedial services:** Learning center, preadmission summer program, reduced course load, remedial instruction, special counselor, tutoring. **ROTC:** Army. **Placement/credit:** AP, CLEP Subject, institutional tests.

ACADEMIC REQUIREMENTS. Freshmen must earn minimum GPA of 1.7 to continue in good standing. 64% of freshmen return for sophomore year. Students must declare major on application. **Graduation requirements:** 96 hours for associate, 186 hours for bachelor's (45 in major). Most students required to take courses in English, history, humanities, mathematics, biological/physical sciences, social sciences. **Additional information:** High school course requirements must be met within first 90 hours of college work.

FRESHMAN ADMISSIONS. Selection criteria: Open admissions. Out-of-state applicants must be in top two-thirds of class; or have ACT composite score of 15 or higher; or a combined SAT score of 700 or higher. Selective admission for some programs. **High school preparation:** 16 units recommended. Recommended units include English 4, foreign language 2, mathematics 3, social science 2 and science 3. **Test requirements:** SAT or ACT for counseling; score report by July 15. **Additional information:** Those out of high school 2 years or more can waive general entrance examination unless required for specific program.

1992 FRESHMAN CLASS PROFILE. 1,034 men, 1,072 women enrolled. 9% were in top tenth and 27% were in top quarter of graduating class. **Characteristics:** 92% from in state, 95% commute, 11% have minority backgrounds, 1% are foreign students. Average age is 22.

FALL-TERM APPLICATIONS. $25 fee, may be waived for applicants with need. Closing date August 15; applicants notified on a rolling basis. Audition required for music applicants. Deferred and early admission available. Institutional early decision plan.

STUDENT LIFE. Housing: Dormitories (coed); apartment, fraternity, sorority housing available. **Activities:** Student government, magazine, radio, student newspaper, choral groups, concert band, dance, drama, jazz band, marching band, music ensembles, musical theater, opera, pep band, symphony orchestra, fraternities, sororities, coalition for animal rights, fellowship of christian athletes, College Republicans, Student Democrats, Pan African Student Union, National Panhelenic Council, voices in praise, students for a healthier planet, linematheque.

ATHLETICS. NCAA. **Intercollegiate:** Baseball M, basketball, cross-country, football M, golf M, softball W, tennis, track and field, volleyball W. **Intramural:** Badminton, basketball, bowling, football, golf, handball, racquetball, rifle, soccer, softball, squash, swimming, tennis, track and field, volleyball, water polo, wrestling M.

STUDENT SERVICES. Aptitude testing, career counseling, employment service for undergraduates, freshman orientation, health services, personal counseling, placement service for graduates, special adviser for adult students, veterans counselor, services/facilities for handicapped.

ANNUAL EXPENSES. Tuition and fees (1992-93): $2,589, $1,800 additional for out-of-state students. **Room and board:** $3,555. **Books and supplies:** $500. **Other expenses:** $950.

FINANCIAL AID. 60% of freshmen, 60% of continuing students receive some form of aid. Grants, loans, jobs available. Academic, music/drama, athletic, leadership, minority scholarships available. **Aid applications:** No closing date; priority given to applications received by April 1; applicants notified on a rolling basis beginning on or about May 30; must reply within 2 weeks.

ADDRESS/TELEPHONE. Dr. Harold Yiannaki, Director of Enrollment Services, Youngstown State University, 410 Wick Avenue, Youngstown, OH 44555-0001. (216) 742-3150. (800) 336-9978. Fax: (216) 742-1408.

Oklahoma

Bacone College
Muskogee, Oklahoma CB code: 6030

2-year private junior college, coed, affiliated with American Baptist Churches in the USA. Founded in 1880. **Accreditation:** Regional. **Undergraduate enrollment:** 686 men and women. **Faculty:** 35 total (23 full time), 4 with doctorates or other terminal degrees. **Location:** Suburban campus in large town; 60 miles from Tulsa. **Calendar:** Semester, limited summer session. **Microcomputers:** 32 located in libraries, classrooms. **Special facilities:** Ataloa Lodge Museum (Native American), Indian Collection Library. **Additional facts:** Unique American Indian heritage and commitment to serving American Indians. Guided by Christian principles.

DEGREES OFFERED. AA, AS, AAS. 97 associate degrees awarded in 1992.

UNDERGRADUATE MAJORS. Accounting, American Indian studies, biology, business administration and management, business and management, business data programming, chemistry, computer and information sciences, education, home economics, horticultural science, journalism, liberal/general studies, mathematics, medical assistant, medical records technology, nursing, physical sciences, psychology, radiograph medical technology, religion, secretarial and related programs, social sciences.

ACADEMIC PROGRAMS. 2-year transfer program, dual enrollment of high school students, weekend college, cross-registration. **Remedial services:** Learning center, remedial instruction, special counselor, tutoring, developmental courses. **Placement/credit:** CLEP Subject, institutional tests; 15 credit hours maximum for associate degree.

ACADEMIC REQUIREMENTS. Freshmen must earn minimum GPA of 1.6 to continue in good standing. 65% of freshmen return for sophomore year. Students must declare major by end of first year. **Graduation requirements:** 62 hours for associate. Most students required to take courses in arts/fine arts, English, history, humanities, mathematics, philosophy/religion, biological/physical sciences, social sciences.

FRESHMAN ADMISSIONS. Selection criteria: Open admissions. Required units include English 4, mathematics 3, social science 2 and science 2. **Test requirements:** SAT or ACT (ACT preferred) for placement and counseling only; score report by August 22.

1992 FRESHMAN CLASS PROFILE. 492 men and women enrolled. **Characteristics:** 76% from in state, 64% commute, 55% have minority backgrounds. Average age is 19.

FALL-TERM APPLICATIONS. $10 fee. No closing date; applicants notified on a rolling basis. Interview required for nursing, radiologic technology applicants. Deferred and early admission available.

STUDENT LIFE. Housing: Dormitories (men, women). **Activities:** Student government, radio, student newspaper, yearbook, choral groups, drama, Bacone Christian Fellowship, Bacone Indian Club, Black Student Union, Cultural Exchange Student Organization.

ATHLETICS. NJCAA. **Intercollegiate:** Baseball M, basketball, cross-country, softball W. **Intramural:** Badminton, basketball, cross-country, football, horseback riding, softball, table tennis, tennis, track and field, volleyball.

STUDENT SERVICES. Career counseling, employment service for undergraduates, health services, personal counseling.

ANNUAL EXPENSES. Tuition and fees: $3,450. **Room and board:** $2,900. **Books and supplies:** $600. **Other expenses:** $500.

FINANCIAL AID. 86% of freshmen, 88% of continuing students receive some form of aid. 94% of grants, 99% of loans, all jobs based on need. Athletic, leadership scholarships available. **Aid applications:** No closing date; priority given to applications received by May 1; applicants notified on a rolling basis beginning on or about May 1; must reply within 2 weeks.

ADDRESS/TELEPHONE. Dave Norfolk, Dean, Enrollment Management, Bacone College, 99 Bacone Road, Muskogee, OK 74403-1597. (918) 683-4581 ext. 340.

Bartlesville Wesleyan College
Bartlesville, Oklahoma CB code: 6135

4-year private liberal arts college, coed, affiliated with Wesleyan Church. Founded in 1910. **Accreditation:** Regional. **Undergraduate enrollment:** 135 men, 188 women full time; 70 men, 109 women part time. **Faculty:** 57 total (32 full time), 34 with doctorates or other terminal degrees. **Location:** Suburban campus in large town; 50 miles from Tulsa. **Calendar:** Semester, limited summer session. **Microcomputers:** 28 located in libraries, computer centers. **Special facilities:** Nature preserve. **Additional facts:** Dedicated to providing quality liberal arts education in a Christ-centered environment.

DEGREES OFFERED. AA, AAS, BA, BS. 20 associate degrees awarded in 1992. 25% in business and management, 25% business/office and marketing/distribution, 15% computer sciences, 5% letters/literature, 10% mathematics, 10% philosophy, religion, theology, 10% social sciences. 85 bachelor's degrees awarded. 20% in business and management, 5% business/office and marketing/distribution, 25% education, 5% letters/literature, 5% mathematics, 15% philosophy, religion, theology, 18% physical sciences, 5% social sciences.

UNDERGRADUATE MAJORS. Associate: Accounting, behavioral sciences, biology, business and management, chemistry, communications, computer and information sciences, finance, information sciences and systems, journalism, legal assistant/paralegal, legal secretary, liberal/general studies, linguistics, mathematics, philosophy, physical sciences, psychology, religion, secretarial and related programs, social sciences, sociology, teaching English as a second language/foreign language, theological studies. **Bachelor's:** Accounting, behavioral sciences, biology, business and management, business education, chemistry, communications, computer and information sciences, education, elementary education, English, English education, history, information sciences and systems, linguistics, mathematics, mathematics education, missionary studies, physical education, political science and government, predentistry, prelaw, premedicine, preveterinary, psychology, religion, science education, secondary education, social science education, social studies education, teaching English as a second language/foreign language.

ACADEMIC PROGRAMS. 2-year transfer program, double major, dual enrollment of high school students, independent study, internships, teacher preparation, cross-registration. **Remedial services:** Learning center, reduced course load, remedial instruction, special counselor, tutoring. **Placement/credit:** AP, CLEP General and Subject, institutional tests; 30 credit hours maximum for associate degree; 36 credit hours maximum for bachelor's degree.

ACADEMIC REQUIREMENTS. Freshmen must earn minimum GPA of 1.8 to continue in good standing. 88% of freshmen return for sophomore year. Students must declare major by end of second year. **Graduation requirements:** 64 hours for associate (15 in major), 126 hours for bachelor's (39 in major). Most students required to take courses in English, history, humanities, mathematics, philosophy/religion, biological/physical sciences, social sciences. **Postgraduate studies:** 50% from 2-year programs enter 4-year programs. 2% enter law school, 2% enter medical school, 4% enter MBA programs, 7% enter other graduate study.

FRESHMAN ADMISSIONS. Selection criteria: In addition to required high school study, students must rank in top two-thirds of class or have 2.0 GPA or have ACT score of 15. **High school preparation:** 15 units required. Required units include English 4, mathematics 2, social science 2 and science 1. One laboratory science unit also recommended. **Test requirements:** SAT or ACT (ACT preferred); score report by August 15.

1992 FRESHMAN CLASS PROFILE. 50 men, 61 women enrolled. **Academic background:** Mid 50% of enrolled freshmen had ACT composite between 16-26. 90% submitted ACT scores. **Characteristics:** 30% from in state, 91% live in college housing, 19% have minority backgrounds, 5% are foreign students. Average age is 19.

FALL-TERM APPLICATIONS. $25 fee, may be waived for applicants with need. No closing date; applicants notified on a rolling basis beginning on or about January 15. Interview recommended for academically weak, socially troubled applicants. Deferred and early admission available.

STUDENT LIFE. Housing: Dormitories (men, women). **Activities:** Student government, magazine, student newspaper, yearbook, choral groups, drama, music ensembles, pep band, Christian Services, Future Secretaries of America, Wesleyan Student Education Association, Campus Missionary Fellowship, Theology Fellowship, forensics. **Additional information:** Religious observance required.

ATHLETICS. NAIA. **Intercollegiate:** Basketball, cross-country, golf M, soccer, tennis, volleyball W. **Intramural:** Archery, badminton, basketball, golf, handball, racquetball, soccer, softball, swimming, table tennis, tennis, track and field, volleyball.

STUDENT SERVICES. Aptitude testing, career counseling, employment service for undergraduates, freshman orientation, health services, personal counseling, placement service for graduates, special adviser for adult students, veterans counselor, services/facilities for handicapped.

ANNUAL EXPENSES. Tuition and fees: $6,350. **Room and board:** $3,050. **Books and supplies:** $600. **Other expenses:** $1,000.

FINANCIAL AID. 85% of freshmen, 70% of continuing students receive some form of aid. 55% of grants, 76% of loans, all jobs based on need. Academic, music/drama, athletic, leadership, religious affiliation scholarships available. **Aid applications:** No closing date; priority given to applications received by March 1; applicants notified on a rolling basis beginning on or about April 1; must reply within 2 weeks.

ADDRESS/TELEPHONE. Bob Hubbard, Enrollment Services Administrator, Bartlesville Wesleyan College, 2201 Silver Lake Road, Bartlesville, OK 74006. (918) 335-6219. Fax: (918) 335-6210.

Cameron University
Lawton, Oklahoma CB code: 6080

Admissions: 95% of applicants accepted
Based on: ••• School record, test scores
• Special talents
Completion: 98% of freshmen end year in good standing
65% graduate, 10% of these enter graduate study

4-year public liberal arts college, coed. Founded in 1909. **Accreditation:** Regional. **Undergraduate enrollment:** 1,518 men, 1,986 women full time; 1,050 men, 1,182 women part time. **Graduate enrollment:** 28 men, 47 women full time; 80 men, 190 women part time. **Faculty:** 298 total (197 full time), 114 with doctorates or other terminal degrees. **Location:** Urban campus in small city; 100 miles from Oklahoma City. **Calendar:** Semester, limited summer session. Saturday classes. **Microcomputers:** 200 located in libraries, classrooms, computer centers. **Special facilities:** Art gallery.

DEGREES OFFERED. AS, AAS, BA, BS, BFA, MS, MBA, MEd. 254 associate degrees awarded in 1992. 10% in business/office and marketing/distribution, 10% engineering technologies, 25% health sciences, 27% multi/interdisciplinary studies, 28% parks/recreation, protective services, public affairs. 670 bachelor's degrees awarded. 6% in agriculture, 15% business and management, 5% communications, 7% computer sciences, 14% education, 6% health sciences, 6% life sciences, 10% parks/recreation, protective services, public affairs, 8% psychology, 8% social sciences. Graduate degrees offered in 4 major fields of study.

UNDERGRADUATE MAJORS. Associate: Business data processing and related programs, criminal justice studies, data processing, drafting, drafting and design technology, law enforcement and corrections technologies, liberal/general studies, nursing. **Bachelor's:** Accounting, agricultural education, agricultural sciences, biology, business administration and management, chemistry, clinical laboratory science, communications, computer and information sciences, criminal justice studies, drafting and design technology, education, electronic technology, elementary education, engineering and engineering-related technologies, English, foreign languages (multiple emphasis), history, home economics, human environment and housing, industrial technology, information sciences and systems, liberal/general studies, mathematics, music, physics, political science and government, psychology, sociology, speech, studio art, visual and performing arts.

ACADEMIC PROGRAMS. 2-year transfer program, double major, dual enrollment of high school students, honors program, independent study, teacher preparation, telecourses. **Remedial services:** Learning center, preadmission summer program, remedial instruction, tutoring. **ROTC:** Army. **Placement/credit:** AP, CLEP General and Subject, institutional tests; 45 credit hours maximum for associate degree; 64 credit hours maximum for bachelor's degree.

ACADEMIC REQUIREMENTS. Freshmen must earn minimum GPA of 1.7 to continue in good standing. 68% of freshmen return for sophomore year. Students must declare major by end of second year. **Graduation requirements:** 60 hours for associate (31 in major), 128 hours for bachelor's (40 in major). Most students required to take courses in English, history, humanities, mathematics, biological/physical sciences, social sciences. **Postgraduate studies:** 41% from 2-year programs enter 4-year programs. 1% enter MBA programs, 9% enter other graduate study.

FRESHMAN ADMISSIONS. Selection criteria: 2.7 GPA and rank in top one-half of class, or ACT composite score of 19 required for bachelor's degree programs. Open admissions for Associate degree candidates only. **High school preparation:** 11 units required. Required units include English 4, mathematics 3, social science 2 and science 2. **Test requirements:** SAT or ACT (ACT preferred); score report by August 23. Students limited to 9 credit hours if SAT/ACT scores not submitted before enrollment.

1992 FRESHMAN CLASS PROFILE. 7% were in top tenth and 21% were in top quarter of graduating class. **Academic background:** Mid 50% of enrolled freshmen had ACT composite between 16-21. 98% submitted ACT scores. **Characteristics:** 76% from in state, 90% commute, 20% have minority backgrounds, 6% join fraternities/sororities. Average age is 24.

FALL-TERM APPLICATIONS. $15 fee. No closing date; applicants notified on a rolling basis. Deferred admission available.

STUDENT LIFE. Housing: Dormitories (men, women). Quiet and wellness (no smoking) areas available. **Activities:** Student government, radio, student newspaper, yearbook, choral groups, concert band, dance, drama, jazz band, marching band, music ensembles, musical theater, opera, pep band, symphony orchestra, fraternities, sororities, Ebony Society, Intertribe Council, International Club, Cameron Campus Ministry, Baptist Student Union.

ATHLETICS. NCAA. **Intercollegiate:** Baseball M, basketball, football M, golf M, softball W, tennis W, volleyball W. **Intramural:** Badminton, basketball, softball, volleyball.

STUDENT SERVICES. Aptitude testing, career counseling, employment service for undergraduates, freshman orientation, personal counseling, placement service for graduates, veterans counselor, services/facilities for handicapped.

ANNUAL EXPENSES. Tuition and fees (1992-93): $1,413, $2,029 additional for out-of-state students. **Room and board:** $2,252. **Books and supplies:** $500. **Other expenses:** $900.

FINANCIAL AID. 62% of freshmen, 56% of continuing students receive some form of aid. 77% of grants, 90% of loans, 37% of jobs based on need. 532 enrolled freshmen were judged to have need, 510 were offered aid. Academic, music/drama, art, athletic, state/district residency, leadership, minority scholarships available. **Aid applications:** No closing date; priority given to applications received by May 15; applicants notified on a rolling basis beginning on or about April 10; must reply within 3 weeks.

ADDRESS/TELEPHONE. Zoe DuRant, Director of Admissions, Cameron University, 2800 West Gore Boulevard, Lawton, OK 73505-6377. (405) 581-2230. Fax: (405) 581-5514.

Carl Albert State College
Poteau, Oklahoma CB code: 1474

2-year public junior college, coed. Founded in 1932. **Accreditation:** Regional. **Undergraduate enrollment:** 1,979 men and women. **Location:** Rural campus in small town; 35 miles from Fort Smith, Arkansas. **Calendar:** Semester. **Microcomputers:** Located in libraries, classrooms, computer centers.

DEGREES OFFERED. AA, AS, AAS. 210 associate degrees awarded in 1992.

UNDERGRADUATE MAJORS. Accounting, agribusiness, architectural design and construction management, biology, business administration and management, business education, child development/care/guidance, computer and information sciences, early childhood education, electronic technology, English, fine arts, health, physical education and recreation, hotel/motel and restaurant management, industrial arts education, industrial management technology, liberal/general studies, materials engineering, mathematics, music, nursing, office supervision and management, physical sciences, pre-journalism, pre-nursing, prelaw, premedicine, prepharmacy, preveterinary, secretarial and related programs, social sciences, sociology/psychology, speech/theater, zoology.

ACADEMIC PROGRAMS. Cooperative education, dual enrollment of high school students, honors program, telecourses. **Remedial services:** Learning center, remedial instruction, tutoring.

ACADEMIC REQUIREMENTS. Students must declare major on enrollment. **Graduation requirements:** 60 hours for associate. Most students required to take courses in computer science, English, history, humanities, mathematics, biological/physical sciences, social sciences.

FRESHMAN ADMISSIONS. Selection criteria: Open admissions. **High school preparation:** 11 units required. Required units include English 4, mathematics 3, social science 2 and science 2. 2 sciences must be laboratory sciences. One social science unit must be in American history. **Test requirements:** SAT or ACT (ACT preferred) for counseling.

1992 FRESHMAN CLASS PROFILE. 1,061 men and women enrolled. **Characteristics:** 98% commute.

FALL-TERM APPLICATIONS. No fee. No closing date; applicants notified on a rolling basis.

STUDENT LIFE. Housing: Scholar's dorm on campus. **Activities:** Student government, student newspaper, choral groups, drama, music ensembles.

ATHLETICS. NJCAA. **Intercollegiate:** Baseball M, basketball M. **Clubs:** Rodeo.

STUDENT SERVICES. Career counseling, freshman orientation, on-campus day care, veterans counselor, services/facilities for handicapped.

ANNUAL EXPENSES. Tuition and fees (1992-93): $975, $1,590 additional for out-of-state students. **Books and supplies:** $500. **Other expenses:** $600.

FINANCIAL AID. 75% of continuing students receive some form of aid. 74% of grants, all loans, 72% of jobs based on need. **Aid applications:** No closing date; applicants notified on a rolling basis.

ADDRESS/TELEPHONE. Lynda Hicks, Director of Admissions, Carl Albert State College, PO 1507 South McKenna, Poteau, OK 74953-5208. (918) 647-8660 ext. 237. Fax: (918) 647-2980.

Connors State College
Warner, Oklahoma CB code: 6117

2-year public college of arts and sciences and agricultural and technical, junior college, coed. Founded in 1908. **Accreditation:** Regional. **Undergraduate enrollment:** 547 men, 1,053 women full time; 204 men, 575 women part time. **Faculty:** 111 total (47 full time), 10 with doctorates or other terminal degrees. **Location:** Rural campus in rural community; 20 miles from Muskagee, 50 miles from Fort Smith, Arkansas. **Calendar:** Semester, limited summer session. **Microcomputers:** 63 located in libraries, classrooms, computer centers.

DEGREES OFFERED. AA, AS, AAS. 290 associate degrees awarded in 1992. 28% in business and management, 6% business/office and marketing/distribution, 5% computer sciences, 12% education, 6% teacher education, 15% health sciences, 6% allied health.

UNDERGRADUATE MAJORS. Accounting, agribusiness, agricultural business and management, agricultural sciences, allied health, architecture, biology, botany, business administration and management, business and management, business and office, business data processing and related programs, chemistry, child development/care/guidance, communications, computer and information sciences, data processing, drafting, drawing, education, elementary education, engineering and engineering-related technologies, English, equestrian science, finance, gerontology, home economics, horticultural science, individual and family development, journalism, law enforcement and corrections technologies, legal secretary, liberal/general studies, marketing and distribution, mathematics, medical assistant, medical laboratory technologies, music, nursing, physical sciences, predentistry, prelaw, premedicine, prepharmacy, preveterinary, psychology, secondary education, secretarial and related programs, services to the aging, small business management and ownership, social sciences, sociology, soil sciences, zoology.

ACADEMIC PROGRAMS. 2-year transfer program, dual enrollment of high school students, internships, telecourses. **Remedial services:** Learning center, remedial instruction, tutoring. **Placement/credit:** AP, CLEP Subject, institutional tests; 18 credit hours maximum for associate degree.

ACADEMIC REQUIREMENTS. Freshmen must earn minimum GPA of 2.0 to continue in good standing. 66% of freshmen return for sophomore year. Students must declare major on enrollment. **Graduation requirements:** 60 hours for associate. Most students required to take courses in English, history, humanities, biological/physical sciences, social sciences.

FRESHMAN ADMISSIONS. Selection criteria: Open admissions. Selective admissions to nursing and equine programs. Recommended units include English 4, mathematics 3, social science 2 and science 2. **Test requirements:** SAT or ACT (ACT preferred) for placement and counseling only; score report by September 1.

1992 FRESHMAN CLASS PROFILE. 265 men, 408 women enrolled. **Characteristics:** 98% from in state, 90% commute, 29% have minority backgrounds, 1% are foreign students. Average age is 26.

FALL-TERM APPLICATIONS. No fee. No closing date; applicants notified on a rolling basis. Interview required for equine technology, nursing applicants. Early admission available. Admission available to all students 18 years or over or younger than 18 years with a high school diploma.

STUDENT LIFE. Housing: Dormitories (men, women); apartment housing available. **Activities:** Student government, magazine, student newspaper, jazz band, pep band, Phi Theta Kappa, Mu Alpha Theta, Aggie Club, Black Student Society, Indian Club, Business Club, English Club, Psychology Club.

ATHLETICS. NJCAA. **Intercollegiate:** Baseball M, basketball, softball W, tennis. **Intramural:** Basketball, softball, tennis, volleyball.

STUDENT SERVICES. Freshman orientation, health services, on-campus day care, personal counseling, veterans counselor, services/facilities for handicapped.

ANNUAL EXPENSES. Tuition and fees (1992-93): $960, $1,590 additional for out-of-state students. **Room and board:** $1,836. **Books and supplies:** $500. **Other expenses:** $1,000.

FINANCIAL AID. 68% of freshmen, 78% of continuing students receive some form of aid. 97% of grants, all loans, 31% of jobs based on need. 1,350 enrolled freshmen were judged to have need, all were offered aid. Academic, athletic scholarships available. **Aid applications:** No closing date; priority given to applications received by March 31; applicants notified on a rolling basis beginning on or about May 1; must reply within 3 weeks.

ADDRESS/TELEPHONE. Paul Wells, Registrar and Director of Admissions, Connors State College, Rt. 1 Box 1000, Warner, OK 74469-9700. (918) 463-6241. Fax: (918) 463-2233.

East Central University
Ada, Oklahoma CB code: 6186

Admissions: 94% of applicants accepted
Based on: ••• School record, test scores
• Recommendations, special talents
Completion: 90% of freshmen end year in good standing
24% graduate, 22% of these enter graduate study

4-year public university, coed. Founded in 1909. **Accreditation:** Regional. **Undergraduate enrollment:** 1,220 men, 1,556 women full time; 216 men, 572 women part time. **Graduate enrollment:** 23 men, 50 women full time; 146 men, 348 women part time. **Faculty:** 250 total (175 full time), 82 with doctorates or other terminal degrees. **Location:** Urban campus in large town; 86 miles from Oklahoma City. **Calendar:** Semester, extensive summer session. **Microcomputers:** Located in libraries, computer centers.

DEGREES OFFERED. BA, BS, MS, MEd. 608 bachelor's degrees awarded in 1992. 14% in business and management, 5% communications, 5% education, 20% teacher education, 6% health sciences, 5% life sciences, 8% parks/recreation, protective services, public affairs, 8% social sciences, 8% trade and industry. Graduate degrees offered in 8 major fields of study.

UNDERGRADUATE MAJORS. Accounting, art education, biology, business administration and management, business and management, business economics, business education, cartography, chemistry, communications, community services, comparative literature, computer and information sciences, criminal justice studies, criminology, dramatic arts, early childhood education, education of the mentally handicapped, education of the physically handicapped, elementary education, English, English education, environmental science, fashion merchandising, finance, fine arts, general industries, geography, history, home economics, home economics education, industrial arts education, industry and business, industry and science, interior design, journalism, law enforcement and corrections, legal assistant/paralegal, marketing management, mathematics, mathematics education, medical laboratory technologies, medical records technology, music, music education, nursing, office supervision and management, physical education, physics, political science and government, predentistry, prelaw, premedicine, prepharmacy, preveterinary, psychology, radio/television broadcasting, science education, secretarial and related programs, social studies education, social work, sociology, special education, speech, technical and business writing, trade and industrial education, trade and industrial supervision and management.

ACADEMIC PROGRAMS. Double major, dual enrollment of high school students, honors program, independent study, internships, teacher preparation, telecourses, visiting/exchange student program. **Remedial services:** Learning center, preadmission summer program, reduced course load, remedial instruction, special counselor, tutoring, writing skills center. **ROTC:** Army. **Placement/credit:** AP, CLEP Subject, institutional tests; 94 credit hours maximum for bachelor's degree.

ACADEMIC REQUIREMENTS. Freshmen must earn minimum GPA of 1.7 to continue in good standing. 61% of freshmen return for sophomore year. Students must declare major by end of second year. **Graduation requirements:** 124 hours for bachelor's (40 in major). Most students required to take courses in English, history, humanities, mathematics, biological/physical sciences, social sciences. **Postgraduate studies:** 1% enter law school, 1% enter medical school, 1% enter MBA programs, 19% enter other graduate study.

FRESHMAN ADMISSIONS. Selection criteria: Rank in top 55% of graduating class, 19 ACT score, 2.7 high school GPA and required course work. **High school preparation:** 11 units required. Required units include English 4, mathematics 3, social science 2 and science 2. **Test requirements:** ACT; score report by August 1.

1992 FRESHMAN CLASS PROFILE. 638 men and women applied, 600 accepted; 576 enrolled. 58% had high school GPA of 3.0 or higher, 38% between 2.0 and 2.99. **Characteristics:** 98% from in state, 50% commute, 13% have minority backgrounds, 1% are foreign students, 13% join fraternities/sororities. Average age is 20.

FALL-TERM APPLICATIONS. No fee. No closing date; applicants notified on a rolling basis. Deferred and early admission available.

STUDENT LIFE. Housing: Dormitories (men, women, coed); apartment, fraternity, sorority, handicapped housing available. **Activities:** Student government, student newspaper, yearbook, choral groups, dance, drama, jazz band, marching band, music ensembles, musical theater, pep band, fraternities, sororities, Black People's Union, Inter-Tribal Council, Baptist Students Union, United Campus Ministry, Young Democrats, Collegiate Republicans, Students with Disabilities, and Non-Traditional Students, Church of Christ Bible Chair.

ATHLETICS. NAIA. **Intercollegiate:** Baseball M, basketball, bowling W, football M, golf M, tennis M, track and field M. **Intramural:** Basketball, softball, volleyball.

STUDENT SERVICES. Aptitude testing, career counseling, employment service for undergraduates, freshman orientation, health services, on-campus day care, personal counseling, placement service for graduates, special adviser for adult students, veterans counselor, services/facilities for handicapped.

ANNUAL EXPENSES. Tuition and fees (1992-93): $1,438, $2,028 additional for out-of-state students. **Room and board:** $2,068. **Books and supplies:** $350. **Other expenses:** $1,200.

FINANCIAL AID. 59% of freshmen, 68% of continuing students receive some form of aid. Grants, loans, jobs available. Academic, music/drama, art, athletic, leadership, minority scholarships available. **Aid applications:** No closing date; priority given to applications received by April 1; applicants notified on a rolling basis beginning on or about June 1; must reply within 4 weeks.

ADDRESS/TELEPHONE. Pamla Armstrong, Registrar and Director of Admissions, East Central University, Ada, OK 74820-6899. (405) 332-8000 ext. 208. Fax: (405) 521-6516.

Eastern Oklahoma State College
Wilburton, Oklahoma CB code: 6189

2-year public community college, coed. Founded in 1908. **Accreditation:** Regional. **Undergraduate enrollment:** 557 men, 693 women full time; 253 men, 675 women part time. **Faculty:** 60 total (54 full time), 4 with doctorates or other terminal degrees. **Location:** Rural campus in small town; 32 miles from McAlester. **Calendar:** Semester, limited summer session. Extensive evening/early morning classes. **Microcomputers:** 100 located in libraries, classrooms, computer centers. **Special facilities:** Oklahoma Miner Training Institute, Department of Corrections-Center for Correction Officer Studies.

DEGREES OFFERED. AA, AS, AAS. 303 associate degrees awarded in 1992. 9% in agriculture, 12% business/office and marketing/distribution, 18% education, 13% engineering technologies, 20% allied health, 15% social sciences.

UNDERGRADUATE MAJORS. Accounting, agricultural economics, agricultural sciences, agronomy, animal sciences, biological and physical sciences, biology, business and management, business and office, business computer/console/peripheral equipment operation, business data entry equipment operation, business data processing and related programs, business data programming, chemistry, communications, computer and information sciences, drafting, drafting and design technology, dramatic arts, electronic technology, elementary education, engineering, engineering and other disciplines, English, fashion merchandising, fine arts, forestry and related sciences, health sciences, history, horticultural science, horticulture, humanities and social sciences, journalism, law enforcement and corrections, legal secretary, marketing and distribution, mathematics, medical laboratory technologies, music, nursing, occupational therapy, parks and recreation management, physical sciences, physical therapy, physics, political science and government, predentistry, premedicine, prepharmacy, preveterinary, psychology, public health laboratory science, public relations, range management, science technologies, secondary education, secretarial and related programs, social sciences, sociology, speech, wildlife management.

ACADEMIC PROGRAMS. 2-year transfer program, cooperative education, dual enrollment of high school students, honors program, internships, telecourses. **Remedial services:** Learning center, remedial instruction, special counselor, tutoring. **Placement/credit:** AP, CLEP Subject, institutional tests; 30 credit hours maximum for associate degree.

ACADEMIC REQUIREMENTS. Freshmen must earn minimum GPA of 1.7 to continue in good standing. 37% of freshmen return for sophomore year. Students must declare major by end of first year. **Graduation requirements:** 64 hours for associate (18 in major). Most students required to take courses in English, history, humanities, mathematics, biological/physical sciences, social sciences.

FRESHMAN ADMISSIONS. Selection criteria: Open admissions. Selective admission for out-of-state students, based on high school record. **High school preparation:** 11 units recommended. Recommended units include English 4, mathematics 3, social science 2 and science 2. **Test requirements:** ACT for placement and counseling only; score report by August 15.

1992 FRESHMAN CLASS PROFILE. 1,766 men and women enrolled. **Characteristics:** 98% from in state, 60% commute, 15% have minority backgrounds, 3% are foreign students.

FALL-TERM APPLICATIONS. $15 fee, may be waived for applicants with need. No closing date; priority given to applications received by August 31; applicants notified on a rolling basis. Interview required for nursing applicants. Deferred and early admission available.

STUDENT LIFE. Housing: Dormitories (men, women, coed); apartment housing available. **Activities:** Student government, student newspaper, yearbook, choral groups, drama, music ensembles, musical theater, pep band, Campus religious organizations, Afro-American and Native American clubs, professional clubs.

ATHLETICS. NJCAA. **Intercollegiate:** Baseball M, basketball, softball W. **Intramural:** Handball, racquetball, softball, swimming, table tennis, tennis, volleyball.

STUDENT SERVICES. Aptitude testing, career counseling, employment service for undergraduates, freshman orientation, personal counseling, placement service for graduates, special adviser for adult students, veterans counselor, services/facilities for handicapped.

ANNUAL EXPENSES. Tuition and fees (1992-93): $960, $1,590 additional for out-of-state students. **Room and board:** $2,124. **Books and supplies:** $500. **Other expenses:** $500.

FINANCIAL AID. 70% of freshmen, 82% of continuing students receive some form of aid. Grants, loans, jobs available. Academic, music/drama, athletic, leadership scholarships available. **Aid applications:** No closing date; priority given to applications received by March 1; applicants notified on a rolling basis beginning on or about June 1; must reply within 2 weeks.

ADDRESS/TELEPHONE. Jerry Smith, Registrar, Director of Admission and High School Relations, Eastern Oklahoma State College, 1301 West Main Street, Wilburton, OK 74578-4999. (918) 465-2361. Fax: (918) 465-2431.

Langston University
Langston, Oklahoma

CB code: 6361

4-year public liberal arts, teachers college, coed. Founded in 1897. **Accreditation:** Regional. **Undergraduate enrollment:** 1,340 men, 1,896 women full time; 178 men, 256 women part time. **Graduate enrollment:** 12 men, 28 women full time. **Faculty:** 116 total (66 full time), 21 with doctorates or other terminal degrees. **Location:** Rural campus in rural community; 40 miles from Oklahoma City, 90 miles from Tulsa. **Calendar:** Semester, limited summer session. **Microcomputers:** 100 located in libraries, classrooms, computer centers. **Special facilities:** M. B. Tolson Black Heritage Center housing 15,000 volumes, international dairy goat research facility.

DEGREES OFFERED. AA, AS, BA, BS, MEd. 403 bachelor's degrees awarded. Graduate degrees offered in 2 major fields of study.

UNDERGRADUATE MAJORS. Associate: Drafting, drafting and design technology, electrical technology. **Bachelor's:** Accounting, agricultural business and management, agricultural economics, agricultural sciences, animal sciences, biology, business administration and management, business and management, business education, chemistry, communications, computer and information sciences, economics, education, elementary education, English, environmental science, food science and nutrition, geography, gerontology, health care administration, history, home economics, home economics education, hotel/motel and restaurant management, individual and family development, law enforcement and corrections, mathematics, mathematics education, music education, music performance, nursing, personnel management, physical education, physical sciences, physical therapy, premedicine, preveterinary, psychology, radio/television broadcasting, radio/television technology, secondary education, secretarial and related programs, social sciences, social studies education, sociology, special education, textiles and clothing, urban studies, zoology.

ACADEMIC PROGRAMS. Cooperative education, double major, dual enrollment of high school students, honors program, internships, teacher preparation; liberal arts/career combination in health sciences. **Remedial services:** Learning center, reduced course load, remedial instruction, special counselor, tutoring, mathematics and writing laboratories. **Placement/credit:** Institutional tests; 16 credit hours maximum for associate degree; 30 credit hours maximum for bachelor's degree.

ACADEMIC REQUIREMENTS. Freshmen must earn minimum GPA of 2.0 to continue in good standing. Students must declare major by end of first year. **Graduation requirements:** 124 hours for bachelor's (64 in major). Most students required to take courses in English, history, mathematics, biological/physical sciences, social sciences.

FRESHMAN ADMISSIONS. Selection criteria: Minimum 2.7 GPA, test scores equally important. **High school preparation:** 11 units required; 15 recommended. Required and recommended units include English 4, mathematics 3, social science 2 and science 2. Biological science 4, foreign language 4 and physical science 4 recommended. Remaining units must be additional work in these areas or in computer science, speech, economics, geography, government, psychology, or sociology. Required mathematics units must begin with algebra I. Required social sciences units must include 1 US history. **Test requirements:** SAT or ACT (ACT preferred); score report by September 9. March 1 priority date for SAT or ACT scores.

1992 FRESHMAN CLASS PROFILE. 1,077 men and women enrolled. 25% had high school GPA of 3.0 or higher, 70% between 2.0 and 2.99. **Characteristics:** 80% from in state, 80% live in college housing, 50% have minority backgrounds, 9% are foreign students.

FALL-TERM APPLICATIONS. $15 fee. No closing date; priority given to applications received by March 1; applicants notified on a rolling basis. Audition recommended for music applicants. Early admission available.

STUDENT LIFE. Housing: Dormitories (men, women); apartment housing available. Nonlocal freshmen required to live on campus. **Activities:** Student government, radio, student newspaper, television, yearbook, choral groups, concert band, dance, drama, jazz band, marching band, music ensembles, fraternities, sororities.

ATHLETICS. NAIA. **Intercollegiate:** Baseball M, basketball, football M, track and field. **Intramural:** Basketball, soccer M, swimming, tennis M, volleyball.

STUDENT SERVICES. Aptitude testing, career counseling, employment service for undergraduates, health services, personal counseling, placement service for graduates.

ANNUAL EXPENSES. Tuition and fees (projected): $1,561, $2,232 additional for out-of-state students. **Room and board:** $2,499. **Books and supplies:** $446.

FINANCIAL AID. 38% of freshmen, 62% of continuing students receive some form of aid. 83% of grants, all loans, all jobs based on need. 433 enrolled freshmen were judged to have need, all were offered aid. Academic, music/drama, athletic, state/district residency, leadership, alumni affiliation, minority scholarships available. **Aid applications:** No closing date; priority given to applications received by March 1; applicants notified on a rolling basis beginning on or about April 15.

ADDRESS/TELEPHONE. Ronald K. Smith, Director of Admissions, Langston University, PO Box 728, Langston, OK 73050. (405) 466-2231.

Mid-America Bible College
Oklahoma City, Oklahoma

CB code: 0918

4-year private Bible college, coed, affiliated with Church of God. Founded in 1953. **Accreditation:** Regional. **Undergraduate enrollment:** 136 men, 80 women full time; 34 men, 40 women part time. **Faculty:** 30 total (16 full time), 10 with doctorates or other terminal degrees. **Location:** Suburban campus in very large city. **Calendar:** Semester, limited summer session. Saturday and extensive evening/early morning classes. **Microcomputers:** 8 located in classrooms, computer centers.

DEGREES OFFERED. AA, BA, BS. 10 associate degrees awarded in

1992. 100% in multi/interdisciplinary studies. 20 bachelor's degrees awarded.

UNDERGRADUATE MAJORS. Associate: Bible studies, liberal/general studies. **Bachelor's:** Behavioral sciences, business and management, elementary education, English, English education, music education, psychology, religion, religious education, religious music, secondary education, social science education, theological studies.

ACADEMIC PROGRAMS. Double major, dual enrollment of high school students, external degree, independent study, internships, teacher preparation. **Remedial services:** Reduced course load, remedial instruction. **Placement/credit:** AP, CLEP General and Subject, institutional tests; 15 credit hours maximum for bachelor's degree.

ACADEMIC REQUIREMENTS. Freshmen must earn minimum GPA of 1.75 to continue in good standing. Students must declare major by end of second year. **Graduation requirements:** 64 hours for associate (15 in major), 126 hours for bachelor's (30 in major). Most students required to take courses in arts/fine arts, English, history, mathematics, philosophy/religion, biological/physical sciences, social sciences. **Additional information:** Students must major in Bible/theology in addition to other majors offered.

FRESHMAN ADMISSIONS. Selection criteria: Open admissions. Open admissions policy, admitting applicants who feel calling to full-time Christian vocations or seek God's will for their lives in spiritual environment. Recommendations important. **High school preparation:** 16 units recommended. Recommended units include English 4, foreign language 2, mathematics 2, social science 2 and science 2. **Test requirements:** ACT for placement and counseling only; score report by August 26.

1992 FRESHMAN CLASS PROFILE. 26 men, 19 women enrolled. **Characteristics:** 30% from in state, 65% live in college housing, 10% have minority backgrounds, 3% are foreign students. Average age is 20.

FALL-TERM APPLICATIONS. $25 fee, may be waived for applicants with need. No closing date; priority given to applications received by August 20; applicants notified on a rolling basis; must reply by August 20 or immediately if notified thereafter. Recommendations required. Deferred and early admission available.

STUDENT LIFE. Housing: Dormitories (men, women). **Activities:** Student government, student newspaper, yearbook, choral groups, concert band, drama, music ensembles, musical theater. **Additional information:** No smoking or drinking allowed on campus. Religious observance required.

ATHLETICS. Intercollegiate: Baseball M, basketball, volleyball W. **Intramural:** Basketball, golf, softball, table tennis, volleyball.

STUDENT SERVICES. Career counseling, employment service for undergraduates, freshman orientation, health services, personal counseling, placement service for graduates, services/facilities for handicapped.

ANNUAL EXPENSES. Tuition and fees: $4,712. **Room and board:** $3,672. **Books and supplies:** $400. **Other expenses:** $1,530.

FINANCIAL AID. 75% of freshmen, 70% of continuing students receive some form of aid. Grants, loans, jobs available. Academic, alumni affiliation, religious affiliation, minority scholarships available. **Aid applications:** No closing date; priority given to applications received by June 1; applicants notified on a rolling basis.

ADDRESS/TELEPHONE. Tony O'Brien, Director of Admissions and Records/Registrar, Mid-America Bible College, 3500 Southwest 119th Street, Oklahoma City, OK 73170. (405) 691-3800. Fax: (405) 691-3961.

Murray State College
Tishomingo, Oklahoma — CB code: 6421

2-year public junior college, coed. Founded in 1908. **Accreditation:** Regional. **Undergraduate enrollment:** 1,667 men and women. **Location:** Rural campus in small town; 32 miles from Ardmore. **Calendar:** Semester.

FRESHMAN ADMISSIONS. Selection criteria: Open admissions.

ANNUAL EXPENSES. Tuition and fees (1992-93): $1,028, $1,911 additional for out-of-state students. **Room and board:** $2,430. **Books and supplies:** $500. **Other expenses:** $1,937.

ADDRESS/TELEPHONE. Director of Admissions, Murray State College, Tishomingo, OK 73460. (405) 371-2371.

National Education Center: Spartan School of Aeronautics Campus
Tulsa, Oklahoma — CB code: 0336

2-year proprietary technical college, coed. Founded in 1928. **Undergraduate enrollment:** 1,728 men and women. **Location:** Urban campus in large city; 10 miles from downtown, 100 miles from Oklahoma City. **Calendar:** Year-round, quarterly sessions, quarterly enrollment. **Additional facts:** Multi-campus institution. All campuses in Tulsa, 1 at Jones Airport.

FRESHMAN ADMISSIONS. Selection criteria: Open admissions.

ANNUAL EXPENSES. Tuition and fees: $6,910. Tuition and required fees vary by program, include books and tools. **Other expenses:** $1,260.

ADDRESS/TELEPHONE. Cheryl Kostoff, Director of Admissions, National Education Center: Spartan School of Aeronautics Campus, PO Box 582833, 8820 E. Pine, Tulsa, OK 74158-2833. (918) 836-6886 ext. 5108. (800) 331-2104. Fax: (918) 831-5287.

Northeastern Oklahoma Agricultural and Mechanical College
Miami, Oklahoma — CB code: 6484

2-year public junior college, coed. Founded in 1919. **Accreditation:** Regional. **Undergraduate enrollment:** 1,142 men, 1,159 women full time; 171 men, 253 women part time. **Faculty:** 112 total (95 full time), 8 with doctorates or other terminal degrees. **Location:** Urban campus in large town; 72 miles from Tulsa. **Calendar:** Semester, limited summer session. Extensive evening/early morning classes. **Microcomputers:** 85 located in libraries, classrooms, computer centers. **Special facilities:** College farm, equine center. **Additional facts:** Extension courses offered in neighboring towns.

DEGREES OFFERED. AA, AAS. 380 associate degrees awarded in 1992.

UNDERGRADUATE MAJORS. Accounting, agribusiness, agricultural economics, allied health, animal sciences, automotive technology, biological and physical sciences, biology, business administration and management, business and management, business and office, business computer/console/peripheral equipment operation, business data entry equipment operation, business data programming, carpentry, chemistry, child development/care/guidance, clinical laboratory science, commercial art, communications, computer programming, criminal justice studies, criminology, drafting, drafting and design technology, education, electromechanical technology, elementary education, engineering, engineering and engineering-related technologies, engineering mechanics, English, environmental design, equestrian science, fashion design, fashion merchandising, fine arts, food management, food science and nutrition, forest products processing technology, forestry and related sciences, geology, graphic arts technology, history, home economics, horticulture, hotel/motel and restaurant management, industrial technology, journalism, law enforcement and corrections technologies, legal secretary, marketing management, mathematics, mechanical design technology, mechanical engineering, medical laboratory technologies, medical secretary, music, nursing, physical sciences, physical therapy, physics, plant protection, political science and government, poultry, precision metal work, predentistry, preengineering, prelaw, premedicine, prepharmacy, psychology, radio/television broadcasting, range management, secondary education, secretarial and related programs, small business management and ownership, social sciences, social work, sociology, speech, tourism, welding technology, wildlife management, woodworking, word processing. automotive mechanics, construction.

ACADEMIC PROGRAMS. 2-year transfer program, accelerated program, dual enrollment of high school students, honors program, telecourses. **Remedial services:** Learning center, reduced course load, remedial instruction, special counselor, tutoring. **Placement/credit:** AP, CLEP Subject, institutional tests; 36 credit hours maximum for associate degree.

ACADEMIC REQUIREMENTS. Freshmen must earn minimum GPA of 1.5 to continue in good standing. Students must declare major on enrollment. **Graduation requirements:** 62 hours for associate (20 in major). Most students required to take courses in English, history, humanities, biological/physical sciences, social sciences.

FRESHMAN ADMISSIONS. Selection criteria: Open admissions. Selective admissions for out-of-state applicants: must have ACT composite score of 15 or be in top half of class. **High school preparation:** 11 units required. Required units include English 4, mathematics 3, social science 2 and science 2. **Test requirements:** ACT for placement and counseling only; score report by September 3.

1992 FRESHMAN CLASS PROFILE. 817 men, 739 women enrolled. **Characteristics:** 90% from in state, 50% commute, 12% have minority backgrounds, 3% are foreign students. Average age is 18.

FALL-TERM APPLICATIONS. No fee. No closing date; applicants notified on a rolling basis. Early admission available.

STUDENT LIFE. Housing: Dormitories (men, women); apartment housing available. **Activities:** Student government, student newspaper, yearbook, choral groups, concert band, drama, jazz band, marching band, music ensembles, musical theater, symphony orchestra, fraternities, ministerial alliance, Baptist Student Union, Afro-American, Aggiu Society, Phi Beta Lamda, OWLS, collegiates for Christ, home economics club, Young Democrats.

ATHLETICS. NJCAA. **Intercollegiate:** Baseball M, basketball, cross-country, football M, golf M, softball W, track and field, wrestling M. **Intramural:** Basketball, football M, softball, tennis, volleyball, wrestling M.

STUDENT SERVICES. Career counseling, employment service for undergraduates, freshman orientation, health services, personal counseling, special adviser for adult students, veterans counselor, services/facilities for handicapped.

ANNUAL EXPENSES. Tuition and fees (1992-93): $900, $1,590 additional for out-of-state students. **Room and board:** $2,124. **Books and supplies:** $400. **Other expenses:** $675.

FINANCIAL AID. Grants, loans, jobs available. Academic scholarships available. **Aid applications:** Closing date March 1; applicants notified on or about July 1; must reply within 2 weeks.

ADDRESS/TELEPHONE. K. Dale Patterson, Dean of Admissions, Northeastern Oklahoma Agricultural and Mechanical College, 200 I Street Northeast, Miami, OK 74354-6497. (918) 542-8441. (800) 678-3761. Fax: (918) 542-9759.

Northeastern State University
Tahlequah, Oklahoma CB code: 6485

Admissions: 75% of applicants accepted
Based on: ••• School record, test scores
• Special talents
Completion: 70% of freshmen end year in good standing
10% enter graduate study

4-year public university, coed. Founded in 1851. **Accreditation:** Regional. **Undergraduate enrollment:** 2,505 men, 2,809 women full time; 1,139 men, 1,139 women part time. **Graduate enrollment:** 194 men, 251 women full time; 832 men, 658 women part time. **Faculty:** 268 total (208 full time), 145 with doctorates or other terminal degrees. **Location:** Rural campus in large town; 60 miles from Tulsa, 30 miles from Muskogee. **Calendar:** Semester, extensive summer session. **Microcomputers:** 200 located in dormitories, libraries, classrooms, computer centers.

DEGREES OFFERED. BA, BS, BFA, MA, MS, MBA, MEd, OD. 1,190 bachelor's degrees awarded in 1992. Graduate degrees offered in 15 major fields of study.

UNDERGRADUATE MAJORS. Accounting, American Indian studies, biology, botany, business administration and management, business and management, business economics, cell biology, chemistry, clinical laboratory science, computer and information sciences, counseling psychology, criminal justice studies, criminology, dramatic arts, early childhood education, economics, education, education of the culturally disadvantaged, education of the emotionally handicapped, education of the mentally handicapped, education of the multiple handicapped, elementary education, engineering physics, English, English literature, finance, food science and nutrition, French, geography, geology, German, graphic arts technology, graphic design, health care administration, history, home economics, individual and family development, journalism, library science, marine biology, mathematics, medical radiation dosimetry, molecular biology, music, nursing, optometry, physical sciences, physics, political science and government, psychology, school psychology, secondary education, secretarial and related programs, social sciences, sociology, Spanish, special education, specific learning disabilities, speech correction, textiles and clothing, theater design, zoology.

ACADEMIC PROGRAMS. Cooperative education, double major, dual enrollment of high school students, internships, teacher preparation, cross-registration. **Remedial services:** Learning center, preadmission summer program, reduced course load, remedial instruction, special counselor, tutoring. **ROTC:** Army. **Placement/credit:** AP, CLEP Subject, institutional tests; 31 credit hours maximum for bachelor's degree.

ACADEMIC REQUIREMENTS. Freshmen must earn minimum GPA of 1.7 to continue in good standing. 65% of freshmen return for sophomore year. Students must declare major by end of second year. **Graduation requirements:** 124 hours for bachelor's (32 in major). Most students required to take courses in English, history, humanities, mathematics, biological/physical sciences, social sciences.

FRESHMAN ADMISSIONS. Selection criteria: 3.0 high school GPA and rank in top half of class very important. **High school preparation:** 11 units required; 15 recommended. Required and recommended units include biological science 1, English 4, mathematics 3, physical science 1 and social science 2. Foreign language 2 recommended. **Test requirements:** ACT; score report by August 10.

1992 FRESHMAN CLASS PROFILE. 773 men applied, 581 accepted, 413 enrolled; 944 women applied, 710 accepted, 505 enrolled. 80% had high school GPA of 3.0 or higher, 10% between 2.0 and 2.99. **Characteristics:** 90% from in state, 84% commute, 23% have minority backgrounds. Average age is 19.

FALL-TERM APPLICATIONS. No fee. Closing date August 1; applicants notified on a rolling basis; must reply by August 1 or within 2 weeks if notified thereafter. Audition required for music applicants. Interview recommended for music, drama applicants. Portfolio recommended for graphic art applicants. Deferred admission available. EDP-F.

STUDENT LIFE. Housing: Dormitories (men, women); apartment, fraternity, sorority housing available. **Activities:** Student government, student newspaper, television, yearbook, choral groups, concert band, dance, drama, jazz band, marching band, music ensembles, musical theater, pep band, fraternities, sororities, Native American Student Association.

ATHLETICS. NAIA. **Intercollegiate:** Baseball M, basketball, football M, golf M, soccer M, softball W, tennis, track and field M. **Intramural:** Basketball, softball, volleyball.

STUDENT SERVICES. Aptitude testing, career counseling, employment service for undergraduates, health services, personal counseling, placement service for graduates, special adviser for adult students, veterans counselor, services/facilities for handicapped.

ANNUAL EXPENSES. Tuition and fees (1992-93): $1,426, $2,028 additional for out-of-state students. **Room and board:** $2,400. **Books and supplies:** $350. **Other expenses:** $625.

FINANCIAL AID. 35% of freshmen, 65% of continuing students receive some form of aid. 95% of grants, 87% of loans, 41% of jobs based on need. Academic, music/drama, art, athletic, state/district residency, leadership scholarships available. **Aid applications:** No closing date; priority given to applications received by March 1; applicants notified on a rolling basis beginning on or about March 1; must reply by May 1 or within 4 weeks if notified thereafter.

ADDRESS/TELEPHONE. Noel T. Smith, Director of Admissions and Registrar, Northeastern State University, Tahlequah, OK 74464. (918) 456-5511 ext. 2130. Fax: (918) 458-2015.

Northern Oklahoma College
Tonkawa, Oklahoma CB code: 6486

2-year public community college, coed. Founded in 1901. **Accreditation:** Regional. **Undergraduate enrollment:** 2,250 men and women. **Location:** Rural campus in small town; 90 miles north of Oklahoma City, 70 miles south of Wichita, Kansas. **Calendar:** Semester.

FRESHMAN ADMISSIONS. Selection criteria: Open admissions. Out-of-state applicants must be in top half of high school class or have ACT composite score of 18.

ANNUAL EXPENSES. Tuition and fees: $870, $1,590 additional for out-of-state students. **Room and board:** $2,060. **Books and supplies:** $450. **Other expenses:** $500.

ADDRESS/TELEPHONE. Wanda Webb, Registrar, Northern Oklahoma College, 1220 East Grand Avenue, Tonkawa, OK 74653-0310. (405) 628-2581.

Northwestern Oklahoma State University
Alva, Oklahoma CB code: 6493

Admissions: 66% of applicants accepted
Based on: ••• School record, test scores
• Interview, special talents
Completion: 21% graduate

4-year public university, coed. Founded in 1897. **Accreditation:** Regional. **Undergraduate enrollment:** 644 men, 731 women full time; 213 men, 477 women part time. **Graduate enrollment:** 6 men, 8 women full time; 37 men, 99 women part time. **Faculty:** 121 total (85 full time), 37 with doctorates or other terminal degrees. **Location:** Rural campus in small town; 160 miles from Oklahoma City, 70 miles from Enid. **Calendar:** Semester, limited summer session. **Microcomputers:** 75 located in libraries, classrooms, computer centers.

DEGREES OFFERED. BA, BS, MS, MEd. 244 bachelor's degrees awarded in 1992. 6% in agriculture, 24% business and management, 25% teacher education, 9% health sciences, 6% allied health, 6% parks/recreation, protective services, public affairs, 8% social sciences. Graduate degrees offered in 7 major fields of study.

UNDERGRADUATE MAJORS. Accounting, agribusiness, agricultural ecology, biology, business administration and management, business education, chemistry, computer and information sciences, conservation and regulation, economics, education of the mentally handicapped, elementary education, English, English education, health education, history, home economics, home economics education, industrial arts education, industrial technology, information sciences and systems, journalism, law enforcement and corrections, library science, mathematics, mathematics education, medical laboratory technologies, music, music education, nursing, physical education, physics, political science and government, predentistry, preengineering, prelaw, premedicine, prepharmacy, preveterinary, psychology, public relations, radio/television broadcasting, science education, secondary education, social science education, social work, sociology, specific learning disabilities, speech and drama, speech/communication/theater education, trade and industrial education, vocational home economics, general, zoology.

ACADEMIC PROGRAMS. Double major, dual enrollment of high school students, independent study, teacher preparation, telecourses, 2+2 programs in many professional fields. **Remedial services:** Learning center, reduced course load, remedial instruction, special counselor, tutoring. **Placement/credit:** AP, CLEP Subject, institutional tests.

ACADEMIC REQUIREMENTS. Freshmen must earn minimum GPA of 1.7 to continue in good standing. 61% of freshmen return for sophomore year. Students must declare major by end of second year. **Graduation requirements:** 124 hours for bachelor's (40 in major). Most students required to take courses in arts/fine arts, computer science, English, history, humanities, mathematics, biological/physical sciences, social sciences.

FRESHMAN ADMISSIONS. Selection criteria: Applicants with 2.7 GPA and in top 50% of class or with ACT composite score of 19 admitted unconditionally. Others admitted provisionally. **High school preparation:** 20 units required. Required and recommended units include English 4, mathematics 3, social science 2 and science 2. Foreign language 2 recommended. Choice of 4 total units from following subject areas recommended: speech, computer science, economics, geography, government, psychology, sociology. 5 units of other electives also recommended. **Test requirements:** SAT or ACT (ACT preferred); score report by July 20.

1992 FRESHMAN CLASS PROFILE. 285 men applied, 189 accepted, 159 enrolled; 335 women applied, 221 accepted, 187 enrolled. **Academic background:** Mid 50% of enrolled freshmen had ACT composite between 18-24. 81% submitted ACT scores. **Characteristics:** 91% from in state, 53% live in college housing, 9% have minority backgrounds. Average age is 23.

FALL-TERM APPLICATIONS. No fee. No closing date; applicants notified on a rolling basis. Audition recommended for music applicants.

STUDENT LIFE. Housing: Dormitories (men, women); fraternity housing available. **Activities:** Student government, radio, student newspaper, television, yearbook, choral groups, concert band, drama, jazz band, marching band, music ensembles, musical theater, pep band, fraternities, sororities, Black Student Organization, International Student Organization, Non-traditional Students Club, Student Oklahoma Education Association, Fellowship of Christian Athletes.

ATHLETICS. NAIA. **Intercollegiate:** Baseball M, basketball, football M, tennis, track and field M. **Intramural:** Badminton, basketball, football M, racquetball, soccer, softball, table tennis, tennis, volleyball.

STUDENT SERVICES. Aptitude testing, career counseling, employment service for undergraduates, freshman orientation, health services, personal counseling, placement service for graduates, special adviser for adult students, veterans counselor, services/facilities for handicapped.

ANNUAL EXPENSES. Tuition and fees (1992-93): $1,330, $2,028 additional for out-of-state students. **Room and board:** $1,864. **Books and supplies:** $450. **Other expenses:** $1,000.

FINANCIAL AID. 65% of freshmen, 80% of continuing students receive some form of aid. 93% of grants, 96% of loans based on need. 260 enrolled freshmen were judged to have need, all were offered aid. Academic, music/drama, art, athletic, leadership scholarships available. **Aid applications:** No closing date; priority given to applications received by August 1; applicants notified on a rolling basis beginning on or about June 15; must reply within 2 weeks.

ADDRESS/TELEPHONE. S. L. White, Director of Pre-Admissions, Northwestern Oklahoma State University, 709 Oklahoma Boulevard, Alva, OK 73717. (405) 327-1700 ext. 213. (800) 299-6978. Fax: (405) 327-1881.

Oklahoma Baptist University

Shawnee, Oklahoma — CB code: 6541

Admissions: 90% of applicants accepted
Based on: ••• School record, test scores
• Activities, interview, recommendations
Completion: 91% of freshmen end year in good standing
68% graduate, 45% of these enter graduate study

4-year private university and liberal arts college, coed, affiliated with Southern Baptist Convention. Founded in 1910. **Accreditation:** Regional. **Undergraduate enrollment:** 681 men, 969 women full time; 332 men, 278 women part time. **Faculty:** 154 total (102 full time), 84 with doctorates or other terminal degrees. **Location:** Suburban campus in large town; 40 miles from Oklahoma City, 200 miles from Dallas. **Calendar:** Semester, limited summer session. **Microcomputers:** 220 located in classrooms, computer centers. **Special facilities:** Planetarium, natural science museum, greenhouses, telecommunications, fine arts centers, Baptist General Convention of Oklahoma Archives, Bailey Business Center.

DEGREES OFFERED. AA, BA, BS, BFA. 2 associate degrees awarded in 1992. 100% in philosophy, religion, theology. 300 bachelor's degrees awarded. 8% in business and management, 6% communications, 25% teacher education, 10% health sciences, 15% philosophy, religion, theology, 5% social sciences, 6% visual and performing arts.

UNDERGRADUATE MAJORS. Associate: Theological studies. **Bachelor's:** Accounting, American studies, art education, Bible studies, biology, business administration and management, business and management, business and office, business data processing and related programs, business education, chemistry, communications, computer and information sciences, dramatic arts, early childhood education, education, education administration, elementary education, engineering, English, English education, ethics, exercise science, family psychology, finance, fine arts, foreign languages (multiple emphasis), foreign languages education, French, German, history, humanities and social sciences, individual and family development, information sciences and systems, journalism, junior high education, management information systems, marketing and distribution, marketing management, mathematics, mathematics education, missionary studies, music, music education, music performance, music theory and composition, nursing, parks and recreation management, philosophy, physical education, physical sciences, physics, political science and government, predentistry, prelaw, premedicine, prepharmacy, preveterinary, psychology, public relations, radio/television broadcasting, religion, religious education, religious music, science education, secondary education, social science education, social sciences, social studies education, social work, sociology, Spanish, special education, speech, speech/communication/theater education, sports medicine, studio art, teaching English as a second language/foreign language, telecommunications, theological studies, visual and performing arts.

ACADEMIC PROGRAMS. Accelerated program, cooperative education, double major, dual enrollment of high school students, honors program, independent study, internships, student-designed major, study abroad, teacher preparation, visiting/exchange student program, cross-registration, exchange program with Seinan Gakuin University, Japan; liberal arts/career combination in engineering. **Remedial services:** Learning center, preadmission summer program, reduced course load, remedial instruction, special counselor, tutoring. **Placement/credit:** AP, CLEP Subject, institutional tests; 32 credit hours maximum for bachelor's degree.

ACADEMIC REQUIREMENTS. Freshmen must earn minimum GPA of 1.75 to continue in good standing. 67% of freshmen return for sophomore year. Students must declare major by end of first year. **Graduation requirements:** 128 hours for bachelor's (30 in major). Most students required to take courses in arts/fine arts, computer science, English, foreign languages, history, humanities, mathematics, philosophy/religion, biological/physical sciences, social sciences. **Postgraduate studies:** 6% enter law school, 2% enter medical school, 4% enter MBA programs, 33% enter other graduate study.

FRESHMAN ADMISSIONS. Selection criteria: School achievement record and test scores most important. Class rank in top half. **High school preparation:** 16 units recommended. Recommended units include English 4, foreign language 2, mathematics 2, social science 2 and science 2. Mathematics recommendation includes 1 algebra and 1 plane geometry. **Test requirements:** SAT or ACT (ACT preferred); score report by August 15.

1992 FRESHMAN CLASS PROFILE. 263 men applied, 237 accepted, 163 enrolled; 454 women applied, 408 accepted, 300 enrolled. 65% had high school GPA of 3.0 or higher, 26% between 2.0 and 2.99. **Academic background:** Mid 50% of enrolled freshmen had ACT composite between 20-27. 70% submitted ACT scores. **Characteristics:** 72% from in state, 86% live in college housing, 11% have minority backgrounds, 3% are foreign students. Average age is 18.

FALL-TERM APPLICATIONS. $25 fee, may be waived for applicants with need. Closing date August 15; priority given to applications received by April 1; applicants notified on a rolling basis. Interview recommended for borderline applicants. Audition recommended for drama, music applicants. Portfolio recommended for art applicants. Early admission available.

STUDENT LIFE. Housing: Dormitories (men, women); apartment housing available. **Activities:** Student government, magazine, radio, student newspaper, television, yearbook, choral groups, concert band, drama, jazz band, music ensembles, musical theater, opera, pep band, theater travel team, Baptist Student Union, Fellowship of Christian Athletes, social clubs, International Student Union, Black Student Fellowship.

ATHLETICS. NAIA. **Intercollegiate:** Baseball M, basketball, cross-country, golf M, softball W, tennis M, track and field. **Intramural:** Basketball, bowling, racquetball, soccer M, softball, swimming, table tennis, tennis, volleyball.

STUDENT SERVICES. Aptitude testing, career counseling, employment service for undergraduates, freshman orientation, health services, personal counseling, placement service for graduates, services/facilities for handicapped.

ANNUAL EXPENSES. Tuition and fees: $5,440. **Room and board:** $3,050. **Books and supplies:** $510. **Other expenses:** $1,250.

FINANCIAL AID. 79% of freshmen, 71% of continuing students receive some form of aid. 60% of grants, 93% of loans, 77% of jobs based on need. 397 enrolled freshmen were judged to have need, all were offered aid. Academic, music/drama, art, athletic, state/district residency, alumni affiliation, religious affiliation scholarships available. **Aid applications:** No closing date; priority given to applications received by March 1; applicants notified on a rolling basis beginning on or about April 15; must reply within 10 days. **Additional information:** Special scholarships for religious vocation students.

ADDRESS/TELEPHONE. Jody Johnson, Director of Admissions, Oklahoma Baptist University, 500 West University, Shawnee, OK 74801. (405) 275-2850. (800) 654-3285. Fax: (405) 878-2069.

Oklahoma Christian University of Science and Arts

Oklahoma City, Oklahoma — CB code: 6086

4-year private college of arts and sciences and engineering, liberal arts, teachers college, coed, affiliated with Church of Christ. Founded in 1950. **Accreditation:** Regional. **Undergraduate enrollment:** 733 men, 676 women full time; 96 men, 90 women part time. **Graduate enrollment:** 7 men full time; 34 men part time. **Faculty:** 132 total (81 full time), 57 with doctorates or other terminal degrees. **Location:** Suburban campus in large city. **Calendar:** Trimester, extensive summer session. **Microcomputers:** 107 located in libraries, computer centers. **Special facilities:** Enterprise Square U.S.A. (multimedia economics center).

DEGREES OFFERED. BA, BS, MA. 303 bachelor's degrees awarded in 1992. 16% in business and management, 7% business/office and marketing/distribution, 13% communications, 8% teacher education, 5% engineering, 5% life sciences, 11% philosophy, religion, theology, 7% psychology, 8% social sciences, 5% visual and performing arts. Graduate degrees offered in 2 major fields of study.

UNDERGRADUATE MAJORS. Accounting, advertising, art education, Bible studies, biochemistry, biology, business administration and management, business and management, chemistry, child development/care/guidance, clinical laboratory science, computer and information sciences, computer engineering, computer programming, creative writing, dramatic arts, early childhood education, electrical engineering/controls, electrical/electronics/communications engineering, elementary education, engineering physics, English, English education, family and community services, finance, graphic design, history, individual and family development, interior design, journalism, liberal/general studies, marketing and distribution, mathematics, mathematics education, mechanical engineering, missionary studies, music, music education, organizational communication, physical education, predentistry, prelaw, premedicine, psychology, public relations, radio/television broadcasting, religion, religious education, science education, social studies education, social work, sociology, Spanish, special education, speech, speech/communication/theater education, studio art, teaching English as a second language/foreign language, theological studies, youth ministry.

ACADEMIC PROGRAMS. Accelerated program, dual enrollment of high school students, independent study, internships, study abroad, teacher preparation, cross-registration; liberal arts/career combination in engineering. **Remedial services:** Learning center, preadmission summer program, remedial instruction, tutoring. **ROTC:** Air Force, Army. **Placement/credit:** AP, CLEP General and Subject, institutional tests; 60 credit hours maximum for bachelor's degree.

ACADEMIC REQUIREMENTS. Freshmen must earn minimum GPA of 1.6 to continue in good standing. Students must declare major by end of first year. **Graduation requirements:** 126 hours for bachelor's (55 in major). Most students required to take courses in arts/fine arts, English, history, humanities, mathematics, philosophy/religion, biological/physical sciences, social sciences.

FRESHMAN ADMISSIONS. High school preparation: 15 units recommended. Recommended units include biological science 2, English 4, mathematics 4, physical science 2 and social science 3. **Test requirements:** SAT or ACT (ACT preferred); score report by July 15.

1992 FRESHMAN CLASS PROFILE. 722 men and women applied, 708 accepted; 361 enrolled. **Characteristics:** 85% live in college housing, 12% have minority backgrounds. Average age is 18.

FALL-TERM APPLICATIONS. $10 fee. No closing date; applicants notified on a rolling basis. Deferred and early admission available.

STUDENT LIFE. Housing: Dormitories (men, women); apartment housing available. Single students must live on campus or with parents. Special arrangements considered. **Activities:** Student government, magazine, radio, student newspaper, television, yearbook, choral groups, concert band, drama, jazz band, music ensembles, musical theater, opera, pep band, Outreach, 14 social service clubs.

ATHLETICS. NAIA. **Intercollegiate:** Baseball M, basketball, cross-country, soccer, tennis M, track and field. **Intramural:** Basketball, cross-country, golf M, soccer, softball, swimming, table tennis, tennis, track and field, volleyball.

STUDENT SERVICES. Aptitude testing, career counseling, employment service for undergraduates, freshman orientation, health services, personal counseling, placement service for graduates, veterans counselor, services/facilities for handicapped.

ANNUAL EXPENSES. Tuition and fees (projected): $5,690. **Room and board:** $3,000. **Books and supplies:** $500. **Other expenses:** $850.

FINANCIAL AID. 82% of freshmen, 82% of continuing students receive some form of aid. 48% of grants, 79% of loans, 74% of jobs based on need. 208 enrolled freshmen were judged to have need, all were offered aid. Academic, music/drama, art, athletic, leadership scholarships available. **Aid applications:** Closing date July 31; priority given to applications received by April 15; applicants notified on a rolling basis beginning on or about April 15; must reply within 4 weeks.

ADDRESS/TELEPHONE. Bob Rowley, Director of Admissions, Oklahoma Christian University of Science and Arts, PO Box 11000, Oklahoma City, OK 73136-1100. (405) 425-5055. (800) 877-5010. Fax: (405) 425-5316.

Oklahoma City Community College
Oklahoma City, Oklahoma — CB code: 0270

2-year public community college, coed. Founded in 1969. **Accreditation:** Regional. **Undergraduate enrollment:** 1,299 men, 1,678 women full time; 2,963 men, 4,935 women part time. **Faculty:** 372 total (104 full time), 20 with doctorates or other terminal degrees. **Location:** Urban campus in large city. **Calendar:** Variable calendar, with 6 entry points per year. Saturday and extensive evening/early morning classes. **Microcomputers:** 65 located in libraries, computer centers.

DEGREES OFFERED. AA, AS, AAS. 474 associate degrees awarded in 1992. 14% in business and management, 5% communications, 5% computer sciences, 15% health sciences, 15% allied health, 8% life sciences, 5% mathematics, 5% psychology, 5% social sciences, 16% trade and industry.

UNDERGRADUATE MAJORS. Accounting, apparel and accessories marketing, automotive technology, biology, business and management, business data processing and related programs, chemistry, child development/care/guidance, commercial art, communications, comparative literature, computer-aided drafting and design, construction, credit union management, data processing, drafting, drafting and design technology, dramatic arts, electronic technology, emergency medical technologies, engineering and engineering-related technologies, finance, French, German, gerontology, graphic and printing production, graphic arts technology, history, humanities, insurance and risk management, insurance marketing, journalism, labor/industrial relations, law enforcement and corrections technologies, liberal/general studies, management science, manufacturing technology, mathematics, mechanical design technology, modern language, music, nursing, occupational therapy assistant, physical therapy assistant, physics, political science and government, preengineering, prelaw, protective services, psychology, radio/television broadcasting, real estate, recreation and community services technologies, secretarial and related programs, sociology, Spanish, tourism, visual and performing arts.

ACADEMIC PROGRAMS. 2-year transfer program, accelerated program, double major, dual enrollment of high school students, honors program, independent study, internships, student-designed major, telecourses, weekend college. **Remedial services:** Learning center, reduced course load, remedial instruction, special counselor, tutoring. **Placement/credit:** AP, CLEP Subject, institutional tests; 30 credit hours maximum for associate degree.

ACADEMIC REQUIREMENTS. Freshmen must complete 50% to 60% of courses attempted. 40% of freshmen return for sophomore year. Students must declare major by end of first year. **Graduation requirements:** 60 hours for associate (30 in major). Most students required to take courses in English, history, mathematics, social sciences.

FRESHMAN ADMISSIONS. Selection criteria: Open admissions. Reading testing required for entrance into nursing, physical therapy, and EMT programs. **High school preparation:** 9 units recommended. Recommended units include biological science 1, English 4, foreign language 3 and mathematics 1. **Test requirements:** SAT or ACT (ACT preferred) for placement and counseling only; score report by September 8. CPT or Nelson-Denny Reading Test required of nursing program applicants.

1992 FRESHMAN CLASS PROFILE. 3,467 men and women enrolled. 15% had high school GPA of 3.0 or higher, 30% between 2.0 and 2.99. **Academic background:** Mid 50% of enrolled freshmen had ACT composite between 15-21. 12% submitted ACT scores. **Characteristics:** 99% from in state, 100% commute. Average age is 30.

FALL-TERM APPLICATIONS. No fee. No closing date; applicants notified on a rolling basis. Deferred and early admission available.

STUDENT LIFE. Activities: Student government, magazine, student newspaper, choral groups, drama, Phi Theta Kappa.

ATHLETICS. Intercollegiate: Basketball, softball, volleyball. **Intramural:** Baseball, basketball, bowling, golf, soccer, softball, volleyball.

STUDENT SERVICES. Aptitude testing, career counseling, employment service for undergraduates, freshman orientation, on-campus day care, personal counseling, placement service for graduates, veterans counselor, services/facilities for handicapped.

ANNUAL EXPENSES. Tuition and fees (1992-93): $993, $1,590 additional for out-of-state students. **Books and supplies:** $675. **Other expenses:** $600.

FINANCIAL AID. 50% of freshmen, 60% of continuing students receive some form of aid. All grants, 80% of loans, all jobs based on need. Academic, state/district residency scholarships available. **Aid applications:** No closing date; priority given to applications received by July 1; applicants notified on a rolling basis; must reply by August 15 or within 2 weeks if notified thereafter.

ADDRESS/TELEPHONE. Gloria Barton, Registrar, Oklahoma City Community College, 7777 South May Avenue, Oklahoma City, OK 73159. (405) 682-7511. Fax: (405) 682-7585.

Oklahoma City University
Oklahoma City, Oklahoma — CB code: 6543

Admissions:	83% of applicants accepted
Based on:	••• School record, test scores
	•• Recommendations
	• Activities, interview
Completion:	81% of freshmen end year in good standing

4-year private university, coed, affiliated with United Methodist Church. Founded in 1904. **Accreditation:** Regional. **Undergraduate enrollment:** 796 men, 913 women full time; 185 men, 225 women part time. **Graduate enrollment:** 684 men, 1,032 women full time; 338 men, 277 women part time. **Faculty:** 263 total (152 full time), 90 with doctorates or other terminal degrees. **Location:** Urban campus in large city; Located 2 miles from downtown. **Calendar:** Semester, limited summer session. **Microcomputers:** 150 located in dormitories, libraries, classrooms, computer centers, campus-wide network. **Special facilities:** Hulsey Art Gallery, AT&T fiber optic information system network, Noble Center for Competitive Enterprise, Smith Chapel, Margaret E. Petree Recital Hall, Wooten Observatory.

DEGREES OFFERED. BA, BS, BFA, MA, MS, MBA, MFA, MEd. 326 bachelor's degrees awarded in 1992. 25% in business and management, 8% communications, 9% computer sciences, 6% health sciences, 10% visual and performing arts. Graduate degrees offered in 27 major fields of study.

UNDERGRADUATE MAJORS. Native American art. accounting, advertising, art education, Asian studies, biochemistry, biological and physical sciences, biology, business administration and management, business and management, business economics, chemistry, communications, computer and information sciences, criminal justice studies, criminology, dance, dance management, dramatic arts, economics, education, elementary education, English, English education, finance, fine arts, foreign languages education, French, German, health education, history, humanities, humanities and social sciences, international business management, journalism, law enforcement and corrections, liberal/general studies, management information systems, marketing management, mathematics, mathematics education, music, music business management, music education, music performance, music theory and composition, musical theater, nursing, philosophy, physical education, physical sciences, physics, political science and government, predentistry, prelaw, premedicine, prepharmacy, preveterinary, psychology, public relations, radio/television broadcasting, religion, religious arts, science education, secondary education, social studies education, social work, sociology, Spanish, speech, speech/communication/theater education.

ACADEMIC PROGRAMS. Accelerated program, double major, dual enrollment of high school students, education specialist degree, external degree, honors program, independent study, internships, study abroad, visiting/exchange student program, Washington semester; combined bachelor's/graduate program in business administration, law. **Remedial services:** Learning center, special counselor, tutoring. **ROTC:** Air Force, Army. **Placement/credit:** AP, CLEP Subject, institutional tests.

ACADEMIC REQUIREMENTS. Freshmen must earn minimum GPA of 2.0 to continue in good standing. 64% of freshmen return for sophomore year. Students must declare major on enrollment. **Graduation requirements:** 124 hours for bachelor's (66 in major). Most students required to take courses in arts/fine arts, computer science, English, foreign languages, history, humanities, mathematics, philosophy/religion, biological/physical sciences, social sciences.

FRESHMAN ADMISSIONS. Selection criteria: School achievement record and test scores most important. Class rank, admissions interview, and counselor recommendations also considered. Recommended units include English 4, foreign language 2, mathematics 3, social science 3 and science 3. Mathematics recommendation includes 1 algebra and 1 geometry. Science recommendation includes 1 laboratory science. **Test requirements:** SAT or ACT; score report by August 20.

1992 FRESHMAN CLASS PROFILE. 454 men applied, 365 accepted, 131 enrolled; 629 women applied, 537 accepted, 194 enrolled. 66% had high school GPA of 3.0 or higher, 32% between 2.0 and 2.99. 37% were in top quarter of graduating class. **Academic background:** Mid 50% of enrolled freshmen had SAT-V between 390-520, SAT-M between 430-560; ACT composite between 20-21. 17% submitted SAT scores, 74% submitted ACT scores. **Characteristics:** 81% from in state, 67% live in college housing, 17% have minority backgrounds, 35% join fraternities/sororities. Average age is 18.

FALL-TERM APPLICATIONS. $20 fee, may be waived for applicants with need. No closing date; applicants notified on a rolling basis. Audition required for dance, music applicants. Interview recommended. Portfolio recommended for art applicants. Deferred and early admission available.

STUDENT LIFE. Housing: Dormitories (men, women); apartment, fraternity housing available. Students under the age of 23 not living at home must live on campus. **Activities:** Student government, film, magazine, student newspaper, television, yearbook, choral groups, concert band, dance, drama, jazz band, music ensembles, musical theater, opera, pep band, symphony orchestra, fraternities, sororities, United Methodist Student Fellowship, Women's Christian Organization, Native American Student Organization, Jewish Student Organization, Black Student Union, Baptist Student Union, International Student Association, College Republicans.

ATHLETICS. NAIA. **Intercollegiate:** Baseball M, basketball, golf M, soccer M, softball W, tennis. **Intramural:** Basketball, golf M, softball, volleyball.

STUDENT SERVICES. Aptitude testing, career counseling, employment service for undergraduates, freshman orientation, health services, personal counseling, placement service for graduates, veterans counselor, office of handicap concerns, services/facilities for handicapped.

ANNUAL EXPENSES. Tuition and fees: $6,185. **Room and board:** $3,420. **Books and supplies:** $350. **Other expenses:** $947.

FINANCIAL AID. 49% of freshmen, 58% of continuing students receive some form of aid. 22% of grants, 76% of loans, 51% of jobs based on need. 158 enrolled freshmen were judged to have need, all were offered aid. Academic, music/drama, art, athletic, state/district residency, leadership, religious affiliation, minority scholarships available. **Aid applications:** No closing date; priority given to applications received by March 1; applicants notified on a rolling basis beginning on or about April 15; must reply within 2 weeks.

ADDRESS/TELEPHONE. Keith Hackett, Dean of Admissions, Oklahoma City University, 2501 North Blackwelder, Oklahoma City, OK 73106. (405) 521-5050. (800) 633-7242. Fax: (405) 521-5264.

Oklahoma Panhandle State University

Goodwell, Oklahoma — CB code: 6571

4-year public agricultural and technical, liberal arts, teachers college, coed. Founded in 1909. **Accreditation:** Regional. **Undergraduate enrollment:** 1,209 men and women. **Faculty:** 83 total (52 full time), 27 with doctorates or other terminal degrees. **Location:** Rural campus in rural community; 110 miles from Amarillo, Texas. **Calendar:** Semester, extensive summer session. **Microcomputers:** 50 located in classrooms, computer centers. **Special facilities:** Agronomy experiment station, livestock facilities, farming area.

DEGREES OFFERED. AA, AS, AAS, BA, BS. 8 associate degrees awarded in 1992. 149 bachelor's degrees awarded. 15% in agriculture, 7% business and management, 5% computer sciences, 12% teacher education, 6% life sciences, 10% physical sciences.

UNDERGRADUATE MAJORS. Associate: Drafting, fashion design, information sciences and systems, precision metal work, woodworking. **Bachelor's:** Accounting, agribusiness, agricultural education, agronomy, animal sciences, biology, business administration and management, business education, chemistry, clinical laboratory science, communications, computer and information sciences, elementary education, English, English education, history, home economics, home economics education, industrial arts, industrial arts education, mathematics, mathematics education, music, music education, physical education, physical sciences, plant sciences, psychology, recreation and community services technologies, science education, secondary education, secretarial and related programs, social science education, social sciences, soil sciences, speech, speech/communication/theater education.

ACADEMIC PROGRAMS. 2-year transfer program, double major, teacher preparation. **Remedial services:** Reduced course load, remedial instruction, tutoring. **Placement/credit:** AP, CLEP Subject; 34 credit hours maximum for associate degree; 60 credit hours maximum for bachelor's degree.

ACADEMIC REQUIREMENTS. Freshmen must earn minimum GPA of 1.7 to continue in good standing. 53% of freshmen return for sophomore year. Students must declare major by end of second year. **Graduation requirements:** 124 hours for bachelor's (36 in major). Most students required to take courses in English, history, humanities, mathematics, biological/physical sciences, social sciences.

FRESHMAN ADMISSIONS. Selection criteria: Applicants must meet 1 of 3 requirements: 2.8 minimum high school GPA, rank in top 60% of class, or ACT composite score of 15. **High school preparation:** 20 units required. Required units include English 4, mathematics 3, social science 2 and science 2. **Test requirements:** SAT or ACT (ACT preferred); score report by August 19. Minnesota Multiphasic Personality Inventory required for education applicants.

1992 FRESHMAN CLASS PROFILE. 251 men and women enrolled. **Academic background:** Mid 50% of enrolled freshmen had ACT composite between 14-20. 90% submitted ACT scores. **Characteristics:** 75% from in state, 80% live in college housing, 12% have minority backgrounds. Average age is 18.

FALL-TERM APPLICATIONS. No fee. No closing date; applicants notified on a rolling basis beginning on or about April 1. Deferred admission available.

STUDENT LIFE. Housing: Dormitories (men, women); apartment housing available. **Activities:** Student government, magazine, radio, student newspaper, television, yearbook, choral groups, concert band, drama, jazz band, marching band, music ensembles, pep band, Wesley Foundation, Baptist Student Union, Church of Christ Student Center, Apostolic Faith Center, Circle-K, Newman Club, Methodist Student Center.

ATHLETICS. NAIA. **Intercollegiate:** Basketball, football M. **Intramural:** Basketball, racquetball, softball, volleyball.

STUDENT SERVICES. Employment service for undergraduates, freshman orientation, health services, personal counseling, placement service for graduates.

ANNUAL EXPENSES. Tuition and fees (1992-93): $1,389, $2,029 additional for out-of-state students. Required fees include $90 book rental fee. **Room and board:** $1,800. **Other expenses:** $1,000.

FINANCIAL AID. 40% of freshmen, 50% of continuing students receive some form of aid. 64% of grants, 97% of loans, 18% of jobs based on need. 140 enrolled freshmen were judged to have need, all were offered aid. Academic, music/drama, athletic, leadership scholarships available. **Aid applications:** No closing date; priority given to applications received by August 25; applicants notified on a rolling basis beginning on or about June 15.

ADDRESS/TELEPHONE. Emma Schultz, Registrar/Director of Admissions, Oklahoma Panhandle State University, PO Box 430, Goodwell, OK 73939-0430. (405) 349-2611.

Oklahoma State University

Stillwater, Oklahoma CB code: 6546

Admissions: 80% of applicants accepted
Based on: ••• School record, test scores
• Special talents
Completion: 80% of freshmen end year in good standing
40% graduate

4-year public university, coed. Founded in 1890. **Accreditation:** Regional. **Undergraduate enrollment:** 7,037 men, 6,068 women full time; 901 men, 780 women part time. **Graduate enrollment:** 1,031 men, 544 women full time; 1,506 men, 1,341 women part time. **Faculty:** 1,130 total (1,043 full time), 1,006 with doctorates or other terminal degrees. **Location:** Rural campus in large town; 65 miles from Tulsa, 65 miles from Oklahoma City. **Calendar:** Semester, extensive summer session. **Microcomputers:** 800 located in dormitories, classrooms, computer centers. **Special facilities:** Branch campus in Kyoto, Japan.

DEGREES OFFERED. BA, BS, BFA, BArch, MA, MS, MBA, PhD, EdD, DO, DVM. 2,683 bachelor's degrees awarded in 1992. 9% in agriculture, 28% business and management, 6% education, 11% teacher education, 8% engineering, 6% engineering technologies, 9% home economics. Graduate degrees offered in 74 major fields of study.

UNDERGRADUATE MAJORS. Accounting, advertising, aerospace science (Air Force), aerospace/aeronautical/astronautical engineering, agribusiness, agricultural economics, agricultural education, agricultural engineering, agricultural sciences, agriculture communication, agronomy, animal sciences, architectural engineering, architecture, art history, aviation sciences, biochemistry, biological and physical sciences, biology, botany, business administration and management, business and management, business economics, chemical engineering, chemistry, child development/care/guidance, civil engineering, community health work, computer and information sciences, computer engineering, computer technology, construction management technology, ecology, economics, electrical/electronics/communications engineering, electronic technology, elementary education, engineering, engineering and engineering-related technologies, English, entomology, family and community services, family/consumer resource management, fashion design, finance, fine arts, fire control and safety technology, food science and nutrition, forestry and related sciences, French, geography, geology, German, health education, history, horticultural science, horticulture, hotel/motel and restaurant management, human resources development, individual and family development, industrial arts education, industrial engineering, information sciences and systems, interior design, journalism, landscape architecture, management information systems, management science, manufacturing technology, marketing and distribution, marketing management, mathematics, mechanical design technology, mechanical engineering, mechanical power technology, medical laboratory technologies, microbiology, military science (Army), music, music education, ornamental horticulture, philosophy, physical education, physical sciences, physics, physiology, human and animal, political science and government, preveterinary, psychology, public relations, radio/television broadcasting, range management, Russian, secondary education, sociology, Spanish, special education, speech, speech pathology/audiology, statistics, studio art, technical education, theater design, trade and industrial education, zoology.

ACADEMIC PROGRAMS. Cooperative education, double major, dual enrollment of high school students, education specialist degree, external degree, honors program, independent study, internships, semester at sea, student-designed major, study abroad, teacher preparation, telecourses, visiting/exchange student program. **Remedial services:** Learning center, reduced course load, remedial instruction, special counselor, tutoring. **ROTC:** Air Force, Army. **Placement/credit:** AP, CLEP Subject, institutional tests; 70 credit hours maximum for bachelor's degree.

ACADEMIC REQUIREMENTS. Freshmen must earn minimum GPA of 1.7 to continue in good standing. 75% of freshmen return for sophomore year. Students must declare major by end of second year. **Graduation requirements:** 120 hours for bachelor's (32 in major). Most students required to take courses in English, history, humanities, mathematics, philosophy/religion, biological/physical sciences, social sciences.

FRESHMAN ADMISSIONS. Selection criteria: To be in good academic standing, rank in top third of class and have GPA of 3.0 or above, or achieve a composite score at 21 or above on ACT or 990 or above on SAT. **High school preparation:** 11 units required. Required and recommended units include English 4, mathematics 3, social science 2 and science 2. Foreign language 2 recommended. **Test requirements:** SAT or ACT (ACT preferred); score report by August 15. **Additional information:** Early application encouraged.

1992 FRESHMAN CLASS PROFILE. 2,526 men applied, 1,918 accepted, 1,033 enrolled; 2,333 women applied, 1,962 accepted, 1,199 enrolled. 74% had high school GPA of 3.0 or higher, 25% between 2.0 and 2.99. 29% were in top tenth and 63% were in top quarter of graduating class. **Academic background:** Mid 50% of enrolled freshmen had SAT-V between 420-560, SAT-M between 470-620; ACT composite between 21-26. 26% submitted SAT scores, 90% submitted ACT scores. **Characteristics:** 84% from in state, 82% live in college housing, 12% have minority backgrounds, 2% are foreign students, 33% join fraternities/sororities. Average age is 19.

FALL-TERM APPLICATIONS. No fee. $10 fee for out-of-state applicants. No closing date; applicants notified on a rolling basis beginning on or about November 1; must reply by registration. Early admission available.

STUDENT LIFE. Housing: Dormitories (men, women, coed); apartment, fraternity, sorority housing available. **Activities:** Student government, film, magazine, radio, student newspaper, television, yearbook, choral groups, concert band, dance, drama, jazz band, marching band, music ensembles, musical theater, pep band, symphony orchestra, fraternities, sororities.

ATHLETICS. NCAA. **Intercollegiate:** Baseball M, basketball, cross-country, football M, golf, softball W, tennis, track and field, wrestling M. **Intramural:** Archery, badminton, basketball, bowling, cross-country, diving, fencing, golf, handball M, racquetball, soccer, softball, squash, swimming, table tennis, tennis, track and field, volleyball, water polo, wrestling M.

STUDENT SERVICES. Aptitude testing, career counseling, employment service for undergraduates, freshman orientation, health services, on-campus day care, personal counseling, placement service for graduates, special adviser for adult students, veterans counselor, services/facilities for handicapped.

ANNUAL EXPENSES. Tuition and fees (1992-93): $1,802, $3,191 additional for out-of-state students. **Room and board:** $3,070. **Books and supplies:** $720. **Other expenses:** $1,200.

FINANCIAL AID. 73% of freshmen, 65% of continuing students receive some form of aid. 59% of grants, 89% of loans, 17% of jobs based on need. 767 enrolled freshmen were judged to have need, 750 were offered aid. Academic, music/drama, art, athletic, state/district residency, leadership, alumni affiliation, minority scholarships available. **Aid applications:** No closing date; priority given to applications received by March 1; applicants notified on a rolling basis beginning on or about April 1; must reply within 2 weeks. **Additional information:** Priority date for scholarship applications March 1. Fall-term scholarship applicants notified on or about April 1.

ADDRESS/TELEPHONE. Norman N. Durham, Director of Admissions, Oklahoma State University, 104 Whitehurst Hall, Stillwater, OK 74078. (405) 744-6858. (800) 852-1255. Fax: (405) 744-8426.

Oklahoma State University: Oklahoma City

Oklahoma City, Oklahoma CB code: 1436

2-year public community, technical college, coed. Founded in 1961. **Accreditation:** Regional. **Undergraduate enrollment:** 656 men, 582 women full time; 1,459 men, 1,660 women part time. **Faculty:** 205 total (55 full time), 15 with doctorates or other terminal degrees. **Location:** Urban campus in very large city; 8 miles from downtown. **Calendar:** Semester, extensive summer session. Saturday and extensive evening/early morning classes. **Microcomputers:** 100 located in computer centers.

DEGREES OFFERED. AAS. 230 associate degrees awarded in 1992. 5% in architecture and environmental design, 7% business and management, 5% computer sciences, 35% engineering technologies, 45% health sciences.

UNDERGRADUATE MAJORS. Accounting, air conditioning/heating/refrigeration mechanics, air conditioning/heating/refrigeration technology, architectural technologies, architecture, business and management, business computer/console/peripheral equipment operation, business data processing and related programs, business data programming, business systems analysis, civil technology, computer programming, construction, drafting, drafting and design technology, electrical and electronics equipment repair, electronic technology, engineering, engineering and engineering-related technologies, equestrian science, equine racing, fire control and safety technology, fire protection, horticultural science, horticulture, industrial technology, instrumentation technology, international business management, interpreter for the deaf, law enforcement and corrections, law enforcement and corrections technologies, management science, nursing, petroleum engineering, residential design, survey and mapping technology, systems analysis, technical and business writing, toxicology, transportation management.

ACADEMIC PROGRAMS. Double major, dual enrollment of high school students, independent study. **Remedial services:** Learning center, remedial instruction, special counselor, tutoring. **Placement/credit:** AP, CLEP Subject, institutional tests; 33 credit hours maximum for associate degree.

ACADEMIC REQUIREMENTS. Freshmen must earn minimum GPA of 2.0 to continue in good standing. 40% of freshmen return for sophomore year. Students must declare major by end of first year. **Graduation requirements:** 70 hours for associate. Most students required to take courses in English, history.

FRESHMAN ADMISSIONS. Selection criteria: Open admissions. Applicants must complete 4 credits English, 3 mathematics (algebra 1 and 2, geometry), 2 history and 2 laboratory science before enrolling in freshman level courses in these subject areas. **Test requirements:** SAT or ACT (ACT preferred); score report by September 15.

1992 FRESHMAN CLASS PROFILE. 2,529 men and women enrolled. **Characteristics:** 100% commute.

FALL-TERM APPLICATIONS. No fee. $15 fee for out-of-state applicants. Closing date August 23; applicants notified on a rolling basis. Interview required for nursing applicants. Deferred and early admission available.

STUDENT LIFE. Activities: Student government, student newspaper, nursing, electronics, horticulture, data processing and law enforcement associations, special interest clubs.

ATHLETICS. Intramural: Soccer.

STUDENT SERVICES. Aptitude testing, career counseling, employment service for undergraduates, on-campus day care, personal counseling, placement service for graduates, special adviser for adult students, veterans counselor, learning programs for hearing and mobility impaired, services/facilities for handicapped.

ANNUAL EXPENSES. Tuition and fees: $1,298, $2,790 additional for out-of-state students. **Books and supplies:** $450. **Other expenses:** $1,800.

FINANCIAL AID. 30% of freshmen, 22% of continuing students receive some form of aid. 91% of grants, 77% of loans, 79% of jobs based on need. 750 enrolled freshmen were judged to have need, all were offered aid. Academic, state/district residency, leadership, alumni affiliation, minority scholarships available. **Aid applications:** No closing date; priority given to applications received by July 1; applicants notified on a rolling basis beginning on or about August 1; must reply within 2 weeks.

ADDRESS/TELEPHONE. Evelyn Wilson, Director of Admissions/Registrar, Oklahoma State University: Oklahoma City, 900 North Portland, Oklahoma City, OK 73107. (405) 947-4421. Fax: (405) 945-3289.

Oklahoma State University Technical Branch: Okmulgee

Okmulgee, Oklahoma — CB code: 3382

2-year public branch campus, technical college, coed. Founded in 1946. **Accreditation:** Regional. **Undergraduate enrollment:** 960 men, 575 women full time; 478 men, 287 women part time. **Faculty:** 144 total. **Location:** Rural campus in large town; 35 miles from Tulsa. **Calendar:** Trimester, limited summer session. **Microcomputers:** Located in dormitories, libraries, classrooms, computer centers. **Special facilities:** Noble Center for Advancing Technology.

DEGREES OFFERED. AAS. 420 associate degrees awarded in 1992. 16% in business and management, 81% trade and industry.

UNDERGRADUATE MAJORS. Accounting, air conditioning/heating/refrigeration mechanics, air conditioning/heating/refrigeration technology, automotive mechanics, automotive service management, business administration and management, business data processing and related programs, civil technology, commercial art, computer graphics, computer programming, construction, diesel engine mechanics, drafting, drafting and design technology, electrical and electronics equipment repair, electrical installation, electrical technology, electronic technology, engineering and engineering-related technologies, food management, graphic and printing production, graphic arts technology, graphic design, illustration design, legal secretary, machine tool operation/machine shop, manufacturing technology, marketing management, medical secretary, metal/jewelry, photography, plumbing/pipefitting/steamfitting, robotics, secretarial and related programs.

ACADEMIC PROGRAMS. Double major, dual enrollment of high school students, internships. **Remedial services:** Remedial instruction, tutoring. **Placement/credit:** CLEP Subject, institutional tests.

ACADEMIC REQUIREMENTS. Freshmen must earn minimum GPA of 2.0 to continue in good standing. 60% of freshmen return for sophomore year. Students must declare major on enrollment. **Graduation requirements:** 90 hours for associate. Most students required to take courses in English, history, mathematics, social sciences.

FRESHMAN ADMISSIONS. Selection criteria: Open admissions. Recommended units include English 4, mathematics 3, social science 2 and science 2. **Test requirements:** ACT for placement. Freshmen must report ACT score before end of first semester for counseling purposes.

1992 FRESHMAN CLASS PROFILE. 470 men, 280 women enrolled. 33% had high school GPA of 3.0 or higher, 30% between 2.0 and 2.99. **Characteristics:** Average age is 20.

FALL-TERM APPLICATIONS. No fee. Closing date August 25; applicants notified on a rolling basis; must reply by registration. Interview recommended. Deferred admission available.

STUDENT LIFE. Housing: Dormitories (men, coed); apartment housing available. **Activities:** Student government, radio.

ATHLETICS. Intramural: Basketball, softball, volleyball.

STUDENT SERVICES. Aptitude testing, career counseling, employment service for undergraduates, freshman orientation, health services, on-campus day care, personal counseling, placement service for graduates, veterans counselor, services/facilities for handicapped.

ANNUAL EXPENSES. Tuition and fees (1992-93): $1,214, $2,790 additional for out-of-state students. **Room and board:** $2,010. **Books and supplies:** $600. **Other expenses:** $900.

FINANCIAL AID. 60% of freshmen, 60% of continuing students receive some form of aid. Grants, loans, jobs available. **Aid applications:** No closing date; applicants notified on a rolling basis beginning on or about March 1.

ADDRESS/TELEPHONE. Susan Hill, Director of Admissions, Oklahoma State University Technical Branch: Okmulgee, 1801 East 4th Street, Okmulgee, OK 74447-3901. (918) 756-6211 ext. 252. (800) 722-4471. Fax: (918) 756-4157.

Oral Roberts University

Tulsa, Oklahoma — CB code: 6552

Admissions:	53% of applicants accepted
Based on:	••• Recommendations, school record, test scores
	•• Essay, religious affiliation/commitment
	• Activities, interview, special talents
Completion:	77% of freshmen end year in good standing
	44% graduate

4-year private university and liberal arts, teachers college, coed, interdenominational. Founded in 1965. **Accreditation:** Regional. **Undergraduate enrollment:** 1,146 men, 1,499 women full time; 61 men, 106 women part time. **Graduate enrollment:** 153 men, 160 women full time; 76 men, 90 women part time. **Faculty:** 180 total (145 full time), 94 with doctorates or other terminal degrees. **Location:** Suburban campus in large city; 7 miles from downtown. **Calendar:** Semester, limited summer session. **Microcomputers:** Located in libraries, computer centers. **Special facilities:** Closed circuit television in classrooms and dormitories.

DEGREES OFFERED. BA, BS, MA, MS, MBA, M.Div. 514 bachelor's degrees awarded in 1992. 15% in business and management, 10% business/office and marketing/distribution, 11% communications, 16% teacher education, 5% health sciences, 6% life sciences, 8% philosophy, religion, theology, 5% physical sciences, 6% visual and performing arts. Graduate degrees offered in 12 major fields of study.

UNDERGRADUATE MAJORS. Accounting, art education, biochemistry, biology, business administration and management, business and management, chemistry, church ministries/Christian education, church ministries/evangelistic, church ministries/pastoral, clinical laboratory science, commercial art, communications, computer and information sciences, drama/telefilm performance, dramatic arts, elementary education, engineering, engineering management, English Bible, English education, English literature, foreign languages education, French, German, health education, history, humanities, inter-cultural development, international business management, liberal/general studies, management information systems, marketing and distribution, mathematics, mathematics education, missionary studies, music, music education, music performance, music theory and composition, New Testament, nursing, Old Testament, physical education, physics, political science and government, predentistry, prelaw, premedicine, preoccupational therapy, preosteopathy, prepharmacy, preveterinary, psychology, radio/television broadcasting, religious education, religious music, science education, secondary education, social studies education, social work, Spanish, special education, studio art, telecommunications, theological and historical studies, theological studies, visual and performing arts.

ACADEMIC PROGRAMS. Accelerated program, cooperative education, double major, external degree, independent study, internships, student-designed major, study abroad, teacher preparation, Washington semester, cross-registration; combined bachelor's/graduate program in business administration. **Remedial services:** Learning center, reduced course load, remedial instruction, special counselor, tutoring, study skills course, 1 semester bridge classes. **ROTC:** Army. **Placement/credit:** AP, CLEP Subject, institutional tests; 18 credit hours maximum for bachelor's degree.

ACADEMIC REQUIREMENTS. Freshmen must earn minimum GPA of 1.5 to continue in good standing. 77% of freshmen return for sophomore year. Students must declare major by end of first year. **Graduation requirements:** 128 hours for bachelor's (30 in major). Most students required to take courses in arts/fine arts, English, foreign languages, history, humanities, mathematics, philosophy/religion, biological/physical sciences.

FRESHMAN ADMISSIONS. Selection criteria: School achievement record, test scores, personal essay, minister's recommendation, other recommendations, immunization records considered. **High school preparation:** 12 units required. Required and recommended units include English 4, foreign language 2-3, mathematics 2, social science 2 and science 2. Science requirement includes 1 laboratory science. Science majors may substitute additional mathematics for foreign language. **Test requirements:** SAT or ACT; score report by August 14.

1992 FRESHMAN CLASS PROFILE. 513 men applied, 281 accepted, 273 enrolled; 710 women applied, 369 accepted, 359 enrolled. 49% had high school GPA of 3.0 or higher, 41% between 2.0 and 2.99. 13% were in top tenth and 37% were in top quarter of graduating class. **Academic background:** Mid 50% of enrolled freshmen had SAT-V between 370-510, SAT-M between 380-550; ACT composite between 17-25. 44% submitted SAT scores, 48% submitted ACT scores. **Characteristics:** 25% from in state, 92% live in college housing, 36% have minority backgrounds, 6% are foreign students. Average age is 18.

FALL-TERM APPLICATIONS. $35 fee, may be waived for applicants with need. Closing date August 10; priority given to applications received by April 1; applicants notified on a rolling basis. Audition required for music applicants. Essay required. Interview recommended. Portfolio recommended for art applicants. Deferred and early admission available. EDP-F.

STUDENT LIFE. Housing: Dormitories (men, women); apartment housing available. Students under 25 years of age must live in university housing or with parents. **Activities:** Student government, film, radio, student newspaper, television, yearbook, creative writing publication, choral groups, concert band, drama, jazz band, music ensembles, musical theater, opera, pep band, symphony orchestra, live television band, Cutting Edge Outreach, International Students Association, Missions Club, Young Republicans, Young Democrats, Student Activist Society, Model United Nations. **Additional information:** Religious observance required.

ATHLETICS. NCAA. **Intercollegiate:** Baseball M, basketball, cross-country, diving M, golf M, soccer M, swimming M, tennis, track and field, volleyball W. **Intramural:** Badminton, basketball, bowling, cross-country, golf, racquetball, softball, swimming, table tennis, tennis, volleyball, wrestling M.

STUDENT SERVICES. Aptitude testing, career counseling, employment service for undergraduates, freshman orientation, health services, on-campus day care, personal counseling, placement service for graduates, veterans counselor, services/facilities for handicapped.

ANNUAL EXPENSES. Tuition and fees: $7,369. Graduate tuition varies according to program. **Room and board:** $4,044. **Books and supplies:** $600. **Other expenses:** $1,400.

FINANCIAL AID. 85% of freshmen, 80% of continuing students receive some form of aid. 39% of grants, 89% of loans, all jobs based on need. Academic, music/drama, art, athletic, leadership scholarships available. **Aid applications:** No closing date; priority given to applications received by April 1; applicants notified on a rolling basis beginning on or about April 15; must reply by May 1 or within 3 weeks if notified thereafter.

ADDRESS/TELEPHONE. Shawn Nichols, Director of Admissions, Oral Roberts University, 7777 South Lewis Avenue, Tulsa, OK 74171. (918) 495-6518. (800) 678-8876. Fax: (918) 495-6033.

Phillips University
Enid, Oklahoma — CB code: 6579

Admissions:	86% of applicants accepted
Based on:	••• School record, test scores
	•• Activities, essay, interview, recommendations
	• Religious affiliation/commitment, special talents
Completion:	90% of freshmen end year in good standing
	54% graduate, 18% of these enter graduate study

4-year private university and liberal arts college, coed, affiliated with Christian Church (Disciples of Christ). Founded in 1906. **Accreditation:** Regional. **Undergraduate enrollment:** 244 men, 351 women full time; 35 men, 64 women part time. **Graduate enrollment:** 42 men, 62 women full time. **Faculty:** 67 total (43 full time), 47 with doctorates or other terminal degrees. **Location:** Suburban campus in large town; 90 miles from Oklahoma City, 115 miles from Tulsa. **Calendar:** Semester, extensive summer session. Extensive evening/early morning classes. **Microcomputers:** 120 located in libraries, classrooms, computer centers. **Special facilities:** Music therapy clinic. **Additional facts:** Two branch campuses in Japan; Japanese language courses offered on Enid campus.

DEGREES OFFERED. AA, AS, BA, BS, BFA, MBA, MEd, M.Div. 4 associate degrees awarded in 1992. 100% in business and management. 102 bachelor's degrees awarded. 28% in business and management, 41% business/office and marketing/distribution, 22% education, 9% psychology. Graduate degrees offered in 6 major fields of study.

UNDERGRADUATE MAJORS. Associate: Business and management, ceramics, computer and information sciences, graphic design. **Bachelor's:** Accounting, American studies, art education, art history, Asian studies, aviation management, biology, business administration and management, business and management, chemistry, clinical laboratory science, communications, computer and information sciences, dramatic arts, education, elementary education, engineering and engineering-related technologies, English, English education, environmental science, European studies, fine arts, French, geology, history, international studies, library science, mathematics, mathematics education, medical laboratory technologies, music, music business management, music education, music therapy, painting, philosophy, physical education, physics, political science and government, predentistry, prelaw, premedicine, prepharmacy, preveterinary, psychology, religion, renewable natural resources, science education, secondary education, social studies education, sociology, Spanish, speech, sports management, sports medicine, studio art.

ACADEMIC PROGRAMS. Dual enrollment of high school students, independent study, internships, student-designed major, study abroad, visiting/exchange student program, weekend college, Washington semester; liberal arts/career combination in engineering. **Remedial services:** Learning center, remedial instruction, tutoring. **Placement/credit:** AP, CLEP Subject, institutional tests; 32 credit hours maximum for bachelor's degree.

ACADEMIC REQUIREMENTS. Freshmen must earn minimum GPA of 2.0 to continue in good standing. 58% of freshmen return for sophomore year. Students must declare major by end of first year. **Graduation requirements:** 64 hours for associate, 128 hours for bachelor's. Most students required to take courses in arts/fine arts, English, foreign languages, history, humanities, mathematics, philosophy/religion, biological/physical sciences, social sciences. **Postgraduate studies:** 4% enter law school, 4% enter medical school, 2% enter MBA programs, 8% enter other graduate study. **Additional information:** Students required to complete Phillips plus portfolio-personal vita of activity during academic program.

FRESHMAN ADMISSIONS. Selection criteria: 2.75 GPA, 18 ACT, ranking in top half of class required for regular admission. Campus visit and interview recommended. **High school preparation:** 16 units required. Required and recommended units include English 4, mathematics 3, physical science 2-3, social science 2-3 and science 2. Foreign language 2 recommended. **Test requirements:** SAT or ACT; score report by August 15. **Additional information:** Each application reviewed individually; conditional acceptance based on special circumstances.

1992 FRESHMAN CLASS PROFILE. 381 men and women applied, 327 accepted; 53 men enrolled, 123 women enrolled. 74% had high school GPA of 3.0 or higher, 25% between 2.0 and 2.99. 19% were in top tenth and 50% were in top quarter of graduating class. **Academic background:** Mid 50% of enrolled freshmen had ACT composite between 19-25. 89% submitted ACT scores. **Characteristics:** 85% from in state, 83% live in college housing, 17% have minority backgrounds, 6% are foreign students. Average age is 19.

FALL-TERM APPLICATIONS. $20 fee, may be waived for applicants with need. No closing date; applicants notified on a rolling basis; must reply by May 1 or within 2 weeks if notified thereafter. Audition required for music, drama applicants. Portfolio required for art applicants. Essay required. Interview recommended. Deferred admission available. Institutional early decision plan. Early Financial Awards are available to accepted students prior to February 1.

STUDENT LIFE. Housing: Dormitories (men, women); apartment housing available. **Activities:** Student government, student newspaper, television, yearbook, choral groups, concert band, drama, jazz band, music ensembles, musical theater, pep band, symphony orchestra, fraternities, sororities, men's service clubs, women's service clubs, Baptist Student Union, minority student organization, Fellowship of Christian Athletes, Disciples Student Fellowship, Amnesty International, Cosmopolitan Club.

ATHLETICS. NAIA. **Intercollegiate:** Basketball, golf M, tennis. **Intramural:** Badminton, basketball, golf M, racquetball, soccer, softball, table tennis, tennis, volleyball.

STUDENT SERVICES. Aptitude testing, career counseling, employment service for undergraduates, freshman orientation, health services, personal counseling, placement service for graduates, special adviser for adult students, veterans counselor, services/facilities for handicapped.

ANNUAL EXPENSES. Tuition and fees (1992-93): $8,524. **Room and board:** $2,820. **Books and supplies:** $700. **Other expenses:** $1,000.

FINANCIAL AID. 85% of freshmen, 88% of continuing students receive some form of aid. 47% of grants, 83% of loans, 51% of jobs based on need. 132 enrolled freshmen were judged to have need, all were offered aid. Academic, music/drama, art, athletic, leadership, religious affiliation scholarships available. **Aid applications:** Closing date August 15; priority given to applications received by May 1; must reply within 10 days.

ADDRESS/TELEPHONE. Alan Liebrecht, II, Director Admissions and Financial Aid, Phillips University, PO 100 S. University, 100 S. University Ave, Enid, OK 73701-6439. (405) 237-4433 ext. 203. Fax: (405) 237-1607.

Redlands Community College
El Reno, Oklahoma — CB code: 7324

2-year public community college, coed. Founded in 1938. **Accreditation:** Regional. **Undergraduate enrollment:** 1,908 men and women. **Faculty:** 110 total (31 full time), 19 with doctorates or other terminal degrees. **Location:** Rural campus in large town; 25 miles from Oklahoma City. **Calendar:** Semester, limited summer session. **Microcomputers:** 25 located in computer centers. **Special facilities:** 12.8 acre equine center for horse technology programs, 300-seat community cultural center with performance stage, Chianina cattle herd and bovine center for agriculture and ranch technology programs.

DEGREES OFFERED. AA, AS, AAS. 183 associate degrees awarded in 1992. 5% in agriculture, 10% business and management, 6% computer sciences, 15% education, 25% health sciences, 30% multi/interdisciplinary studies, 5% trade and industry.

UNDERGRADUATE MAJORS. Accounting, agribusiness, agricultural business and management, agricultural sciences, allied health, biological and physical sciences, biology, business administration and management, business and management, business and office, business computer/console/peripheral equipment operation, business data programming, chemistry, commercial art, communications, computer and information sciences, computer technology, criminal justice studies, earth sciences, electrical/electronics/communications engineering, electronic technology, engineering, engineering and engineering-related technologies, English, equestrian science, finance, fine arts, graphic and printing production, graphic arts technology, health sciences, history, horticulture, journalism, law enforcement and corrections technologies, liberal/general studies, marketing and distribution, mathematics, medical laboratory technologies, music, nursing, physical sciences, physics, political science and government, predentistry, premedicine, prepharmacy, psychology, real estate, science technologies, secretarial and related programs, social sciences, sociology, speech, visual and performing arts, word processing, zoology.

ACADEMIC PROGRAMS. 2-year transfer program, cooperative education, dual enrollment of high school students, honors program, independent study, internships, telecourses. **Remedial services:** Learning center, preadmission summer program, reduced course load, remedial instruction, special counselor, tutoring. **Placement/credit:** CLEP Subject, institutional tests; 30 credit hours maximum for associate degree.

ACADEMIC REQUIREMENTS. Freshmen must earn minimum GPA of 1.5 to continue in good standing. 50% of freshmen return for sophomore year. Students must declare major on enrollment. **Graduation requirements:** 64 hours for associate (32 in major). Most students required to take courses in English, history, humanities, mathematics, biological/physical sciences, social sciences.

FRESHMAN ADMISSIONS. Selection criteria: Open admissions. **Test requirements:** SAT or ACT (ACT preferred) for placement and counseling only; score report by August 25.

1992 FRESHMAN CLASS PROFILE. 693 men and women enrolled. 20% had high school GPA of 3.0 or higher, 50% between 2.0 and 2.99. **Characteristics:** 99% from in state, 100% commute, 19% have minority backgrounds, 1% are foreign students.

FALL-TERM APPLICATIONS. No fee. Closing date August 25; applicants notified on a rolling basis. Interview required for nursing applicants. Deferred and early admission available.

STUDENT LIFE. Activities: Student government, student newspaper, yearbook, drama.

ATHLETICS. NJCAA. **Intercollegiate:** Baseball M, basketball.

STUDENT SERVICES. Aptitude testing, career counseling, employment service for undergraduates, freshman orientation, personal counseling, veterans counselor, services/facilities for handicapped.

ANNUAL EXPENSES. Tuition and fees (1992-93): $960, $1,590 additional for out-of-state students. **Books and supplies:** $400. **Other expenses:** $1,200.

FINANCIAL AID. 22% of freshmen, 47% of continuing students receive some form of aid. 94% of grants, 89% of loans, all jobs based on need. 275 enrolled freshmen were judged to have need, all were offered aid. Academic, athletic, leadership scholarships available. **Aid applications:** Closing date April 15; priority given to applications received by March 30; applicants notified on or about May 1; must reply by May 15.

ADDRESS/TELEPHONE. George C. Roper, Director of Admissions, Redlands Community College, 1300 Country Club Road, El Reno, OK 73036. (405) 262-2552 ext. 221. Fax: (405) 262-7960.

Rogers State College
Claremore, Oklahoma — CB code: 6545

2-year public community college, coed. Founded in 1909. **Accreditation:** Regional. **Undergraduate enrollment:** 571 men, 1,114 women full time; 748 men, 1,489 women part time. **Faculty:** 190 total (80 full time), 9 with doctorates or other terminal degrees. **Location:** Suburban campus in large town; 25 miles from Tulsa. **Calendar:** Semester, extensive summer session. **Microcomputers:** Located in libraries. **Special facilities:** Rogers State Conservation Education Reserve.

DEGREES OFFERED. AA, AS, AAS. 245 associate degrees awarded in 1992. 32% in business and management, 10% computer sciences, 15% teacher education, 15% health sciences, 9% multi/interdisciplinary studies, 10% social sciences.

UNDERGRADUATE MAJORS. Accounting, agribusiness, art history, aviation management, biology, business administration and management, business and management, business and office, business computer/console/peripheral equipment operation, business data programming, business education, chemistry, computer programming, computer technology, court reporting, criminal justice studies, electrical and electronics equipment repair, electrical technology, electrical/electronics/communications engineering, elementary education, engineering, engineering and engineering-related technologies, English, equestrian science, gerontology, graphic arts technology, history, industrial arts education, interior design, journalism, law enforcement and corrections technologies, legal assistant/paralegal, liberal/general studies, mathematics, mathematics education, music, music (country/western), nursing, physical therapy assistant, physics, political science and government, prelaw, premedicine, prepharmacy, radio/television broadcasting, radio/television technology, range management, real estate, secondary education, secretarial and related programs.

ACADEMIC PROGRAMS. 2-year transfer program, cooperative education, dual enrollment of high school students, independent study, telecourses. **Remedial services:** Learning center, reduced course load, remedial instruction, special counselor, tutoring. **Placement/credit:** CLEP Subject, institutional tests; 30 credit hours maximum for associate degree.

ACADEMIC REQUIREMENTS. Freshmen must earn minimum GPA of 1.7 to continue in good standing. 55% of freshmen return for sophomore year. Students must declare major on enrollment. **Graduation requirements:** 60 hours for associate (18 in major). Most students required to take courses in English, history, humanities, mathematics, biological/physical sciences, social sciences.

FRESHMAN ADMISSIONS. Selection criteria: Open admissions. **High school preparation:** 11 units required. 11 units required for students pursuing AA degree: 4 english, 3 mathematics (including algebra I and II), 2 social sciences, 2 laboratory sciences. 4 additional units recommended: 1 speech, 1 computer science, 2 foreign language. **Test requirements:** SAT or ACT for placement and counseling only; score report by September 1.

1992 FRESHMAN CLASS PROFILE. 693 men, 1,297 women enrolled. **Characteristics:** 96% from in state, 97% commute, 13% have minority backgrounds, 3% are foreign students. Average age is 20.

FALL-TERM APPLICATIONS. No fee. No closing date; applicants notified on a rolling basis. Deferred admission available.

STUDENT LIFE. Housing: Dormitories (men, women). **Activities:** Student government, radio, television, yearbook, choral groups, music ensembles, musical theater, country-western band, Afro-American Society, Native American Association, Baptist Student Union, Young Republicans, Young Democrats, service organizations, SIFE Business Organization.

ATHLETICS. Intramural: Basketball, table tennis M, volleyball.

STUDENT SERVICES. Aptitude testing, career counseling, freshman orientation, on-campus day care, personal counseling, placement service for graduates, special adviser for adult students, veterans counselor, services/facilities for handicapped.

ANNUAL EXPENSES. Tuition and fees (1992-93): $1,134, $1,590 additional for out-of-state students. **Room and board:** $2,860. **Books and supplies:** $600. **Other expenses:** $1,000.

FINANCIAL AID. 46% of freshmen, 47% of continuing students receive some form of aid. 90% of grants, 95% of loans, all jobs based on need. Academic, music/drama, art, leadership, alumni affiliation scholarships available. **Aid applications:** No closing date; priority given to applications received by April 15; applicants notified on a rolling basis beginning on or about June 1; must reply within 3 weeks.

ADDRESS/TELEPHONE. Jane Summerlin, Director of Admissions/Registrar, Rogers State College, Will Rogers and College Hill, Claremore, OK 74017-2099. (918) 341-7510 ext. 319. (800) 333-7510 ext. 362. Fax: (918) 342-3811.

Rose State College
Midwest City, Oklahoma — CB code: 1462

2-year public community college, coed. Founded in 1968. **Accreditation:** Regional. **Undergraduate enrollment:** 3,177 men and women full time; 6,762 men and women part time. **Faculty:** 498 total (153 full time). **Location:** Urban campus in small city; 5 miles from Oklahoma City. **Calendar:** Semester, extensive summer session. **Microcomputers:** Located in libraries.

DEGREES OFFERED. AA, AS, AAS. 580 associate degrees awarded in 1992. 41% in business and management, 5% computer sciences, 9% engineering technologies, 18% multi/interdisciplinary studies, 9% social sciences.

UNDERGRADUATE MAJORS. Accounting, airline piloting and navigation, aviation management, biology, business administration and management, business and management, business and office, business computer/console/peripheral equipment operation, business data processing and related programs, business data programming, chemistry, child development/care/guidance, computer and information sciences, contract management and procurement/purchasing, court reporting, criminal justice studies, dental assistant, dental hygiene, drafting, drafting and design technology, electromechanical technology, electronic technology, elementary education, engineering, engineering and engineering-related technologies, engineering and other disciplines, English, fashion merchandising, finance, French, German, history, home economics, insurance and risk management, journalism, legal assistant/paralegal, legal secretary, liberal/general studies, library assistant, marketing and distribution, mathematics, mechanical design technology, medical laboratory technologies, medical records administration, medical records technology, medical secretary, music, nursing, office supervision and management, physics, political science and government, predentistry, preengineering, prelaw, premedicine, prepharmacy, preveterinary, psychology, public administration, quality control technology, radio/television broadcasting, radio/television technology, radiograph medical technology, real estate, respiratory therapy technology, secondary education, secretarial and related programs, small business management and ownership, sociology, Spanish, speech, water and wastewater technology, word processing.

ACADEMIC PROGRAMS. 2-year transfer program, double major, dual enrollment of high school students, honors program, internships, telecourses. **Remedial services:** Learning center, reduced course load, remedial instruction, special counselor, tutoring. **Placement/credit:** AP, CLEP Subject, institutional tests; 50 credit hours maximum for associate degree.

ACADEMIC REQUIREMENTS. Freshmen must earn minimum GPA

of 2.0 to continue in good standing. 75% of freshmen return for sophomore year. Students must declare major on enrollment. **Graduation requirements:** 62 hours for associate (25 in major). Most students required to take courses in English, history, humanities, mathematics, biological/physical sciences, social sciences.

FRESHMAN ADMISSIONS. Selection criteria: Open admissions. 4 English, 3 mathematics, 2 histories (1 American), 2 sciences required of applicants to associate of arts or sciences degree programs. **Test requirements:** SAT or ACT (ACT preferred) for placement and counseling only; score report by August 15.

1992 FRESHMAN CLASS PROFILE. 2,604 men and women enrolled. **Characteristics:** 99% from in state, 100% commute, 17% have minority backgrounds, 1% are foreign students.

FALL-TERM APPLICATIONS. $15 fee. No closing date; applicants notified on a rolling basis. Interview required for medical programs applicants.

STUDENT LIFE. Activities: Student government, student newspaper, choral groups, dance, drama, jazz band, music ensembles, Phi Theta Kappa.

ATHLETICS. NJCAA. **Intercollegiate:** Baseball M, basketball. **Intramural:** Basketball, bowling, diving, soccer, softball, swimming, table tennis, tennis, volleyball, water polo.

STUDENT SERVICES. Aptitude testing, career counseling, employment service for undergraduates, freshman orientation, health services, on-campus day care, personal counseling, placement service for graduates, special adviser for adult students, veterans counselor, services/facilities for handicapped.

ANNUAL EXPENSES. Tuition and fees (1992-93): $923, $1,590 additional for out-of-state students. **Books and supplies:** $625. **Other expenses:** $125.

FINANCIAL AID. 30% of freshmen, 35% of continuing students receive some form of aid. All aid based on need. Academic, music/drama, art, athletic, state/district residency, leadership, minority scholarships available. **Aid applications:** No closing date; priority given to applications received by May 1; applicants notified on a rolling basis; must reply within 2 weeks. **Additional information:** Rose State College requires 100% verification of all information for all recipients.

ADDRESS/TELEPHONE. Evelyn K. Hutchings, Registrar/Director of Admissions, Rose State College, 6420 Southeast 15th, Midwest City, OK 73110-2799. (405) 733-7673. Fax: (405) 736-0309.

St. Gregory's College
Shawnee, Oklahoma — CB code: 6621

2-year private liberal arts college, coed, affiliated with Roman Catholic Church. Founded in 1875. **Accreditation:** Regional. **Undergraduate enrollment:** 230 men and women full time; 98 men and women part time. **Faculty:** 37 total (16 full time), 12 with doctorates or other terminal degrees. **Location:** Rural campus in large town; 35 miles from Oklahoma City. **Calendar:** Semester. **Microcomputers:** 25 located in computer centers. **Special facilities:** Museum, art gallery.

DEGREES OFFERED. AA, AS. 57 associate degrees awarded in 1992.

UNDERGRADUATE MAJORS. Accounting, art history, biology, business and management, business data programming, computer programming, dramatic arts, education, education of the mentally handicapped, engineering, English, individual and family development, journalism, liberal/general studies, mathematics, music, physical sciences, psychology, religious education, visual and performing arts.

ACADEMIC PROGRAMS. 2-year transfer program, dual enrollment of high school students, honors program, cross-registration. **Remedial services:** Learning center, remedial instruction, special counselor, tutoring. **ROTC:** Air Force. **Placement/credit:** AP, CLEP Subject, institutional tests; 12 credit hours maximum for associate degree.

ACADEMIC REQUIREMENTS. Freshmen must earn minimum GPA of 2.0 to continue in good standing. 68% of freshmen return for sophomore year. Students must declare major on enrollment. **Graduation requirements:** 64 hours for associate. Most students required to take courses in arts/fine arts, English, history, humanities, mathematics, philosophy/religion, biological/physical sciences, social sciences.

FRESHMAN ADMISSIONS. Selection criteria: High school record, test scores, and interests. **High school preparation:** 15 units required. Required units include biological science 1, English 4, mathematics 3, physical science 1 and social science 6. **Test requirements:** SAT or ACT (ACT preferred); score report by August 20.

1992 FRESHMAN CLASS PROFILE. 162 men and women enrolled. 41% had high school GPA of 3.0 or higher, 52% between 2.0 and 2.99. **Characteristics:** 89% from in state, 85% live in college housing, 7% have minority backgrounds, 3% are foreign students.

FALL-TERM APPLICATIONS. $10 fee, may be waived for applicants with need. No closing date; priority given to applications received by August 1; applicants notified on a rolling basis. Essay recommended for academically weak applicants. CRDA. Deferred and early admission available. EDP-F.

STUDENT LIFE. Housing: Dormitories (men, women). **Activities:** Student government, film, student newspaper, yearbook, choral groups, drama, Knights of Columbus, Pax Corps, Intercollegiate Association of Women Students, academic honor society.

ATHLETICS. NJCAA. **Intercollegiate:** Basketball, fencing, golf, tennis. **Intramural:** Basketball, racquetball, soccer, softball, volleyball.

STUDENT SERVICES. Health services, personal counseling, services/facilities for handicapped.

ANNUAL EXPENSES. Tuition and fees: $4,520. **Room and board:** $3,100. **Books and supplies:** $590. **Other expenses:** $930.

FINANCIAL AID. 78% of freshmen, 74% of continuing students receive some form of aid. 52% of grants, 94% of loans, 29% of jobs based on need. 67 enrolled freshmen were judged to have need, all were offered aid. Academic, music/drama, art, athletic, leadership, alumni affiliation, religious affiliation, minority scholarships available. **Aid applications:** No closing date; priority given to applications received by June 1; applicants notified on a rolling basis beginning on or about March 15; must reply within 2 weeks.

ADDRESS/TELEPHONE. Director of Admissions, Director of Admissions, St. Gregory's College, 1900 West MacArthur Drive, Shawnee, OK 74801. (405) 273-9870.

Seminole Junior College
Seminole, Oklahoma — CB code: 0316

2-year public community college, coed. Founded in 1931. **Accreditation:** Regional. **Undergraduate enrollment:** 431 men, 648 women full time; 257 men, 554 women part time. **Faculty:** 62 total (41 full time), 8 with doctorates or other terminal degrees. **Location:** Rural campus in small town; 55 miles from Oklahoma City. **Calendar:** Semester, extensive summer session. Extensive evening/early morning classes. **Microcomputers:** Located in computer centers.

DEGREES OFFERED. AA, AS, AAS. 201 associate degrees awarded in 1992.

UNDERGRADUATE MAJORS. Accounting, art history, biological and physical sciences, biology, business administration and management, business and office, child development/care/guidance, computer and information sciences, education, engineering, English, health sciences, humanities and social sciences, journalism, law enforcement and corrections technologies, liberal/general studies, mathematics, medical laboratory technologies, music, nursing, physical sciences, psychology, secretarial and related programs, social sciences.

ACADEMIC PROGRAMS. 2-year transfer program, dual enrollment of high school students. **Remedial services:** Learning center, remedial instruction, special counselor, tutoring. **Placement/credit:** CLEP Subject, institutional tests; 30 credit hours maximum for associate degree.

ACADEMIC REQUIREMENTS. Freshmen must earn minimum GPA of 1.7 to continue in good standing. 70% of freshmen return for sophomore year. Students must declare major on application. **Graduation requirements:** 62 hours for associate. Most students required to take courses in arts/fine arts, English, foreign languages, history, humanities, mathematics, biological/physical sciences, social sciences.

FRESHMAN ADMISSIONS. Selection criteria: Open admissions. Additional requirements for admission to A.D. Nursing Program and MLT Program include minimum ACT composite score of 18 and minimum score of 15 on Nelson Denny Reading Test. **High school preparation:** 15 units required. Required units include English 4, mathematics 3, social science 2 and science 2. **Test requirements:** SAT or ACT (ACT preferred) for placement and counseling only; score report by September 1.

1992 FRESHMAN CLASS PROFILE. 410 men and women enrolled. **Characteristics:** 97% from in state, 97% commute, 20% have minority backgrounds, 1% are foreign students. Average age is 28.

FALL-TERM APPLICATIONS. $15 fee. No closing date; applicants notified on a rolling basis.

STUDENT LIFE. Housing: Dormitories (coed). **Activities:** Student government, student newspaper, pep band.

ATHLETICS. NJCAA. **Intramural:** Baseball M, basketball.

STUDENT SERVICES. Aptitude testing, career counseling, freshman orientation, personal counseling, veterans counselor, services/facilities for handicapped.

ANNUAL EXPENSES. Tuition and fees: $975, $1,590 additional for out-of-state students. **Room and board:** $1,880. **Books and supplies:** $315. **Other expenses:** $175.

FINANCIAL AID. 60% of freshmen, 45% of continuing students receive some form of aid. Grants, loans, jobs available. Academic, music/drama, athletic, state/district residency scholarships available. **Aid applications:** No closing date; priority given to applications received by May 1; applicants notified on a rolling basis beginning on or about March 1; must reply within 4 weeks.

ADDRESS/TELEPHONE. Wayne Day, Vice President for Student Affairs, Seminole Junior College, PO Box 351, 2701 State Street, Seminole, OK 74818-0351. (405) 382-9950. Fax: (405) 382-3122.

Southeastern Oklahoma State University
Durant, Oklahoma CB code: 6657

Admissions: 87% of applicants accepted
Based on: ••• School record
•• Test scores
• Special talents
Completion: 67% of freshmen end year in good standing
27% graduate, 40% of these enter graduate study

4-year public university, coed. Founded in 1909. **Accreditation:** Regional. **Undergraduate enrollment:** 1,369 men, 1,568 women full time; 251 men, 446 women part time. **Graduate enrollment:** 55 men, 81 women full time; 117 men, 222 women part time. **Faculty:** 221 total (174 full time), 99 with doctorates or other terminal degrees. **Location:** Rural campus in large town; 90 miles from Dallas, Texas. **Calendar:** Semester, extensive summer session. **Microcomputers:** 80 located in dormitories, libraries, classrooms, computer centers. **Special facilities:** Herbarium, equestrian facilities. **Additional facts:** Courses offered through Higher Education Centers at Ardmore and Idabel.

DEGREES OFFERED. BA, BS, MEd. 530 bachelor's degrees awarded in 1992. 24% in business and management, 41% teacher education, 5% engineering, 5% letters/literature, 8% social sciences. Graduate degrees offered in 20 major fields of study.

UNDERGRADUATE MAJORS. Accounting, aerospace/aeronautical/astronautical engineering, art education, automotive technology, biochemistry, biology, business administration and management, business and management, business and office, business economics, business education, chemistry, clinical laboratory science, communications, computer and information sciences, computer programming, criminal justice studies, criminology, drafting and design technology, dramatic arts, economics, education, electronic technology, elementary education, English, English education, fashion design, finance, fine arts, fishing and fisheries, foreign languages (multiple emphasis), foreign languages education, French, health education, history, home economics, home economics education, industrial arts education, industrial technology, information sciences and systems, institutional/home management/supporting programs, management information systems, management science, manufacturing technology, marketing management, mathematics, mathematics education, medical laboratory technologies, music, music education, music performance, music theory and composition, occupational safety and health technology, physical education, physics, political science and government, psychology, range management, recreation and community services technologies, renewable natural resources, science education, secondary education, secretarial and related programs, social science education, social sciences, sociology, soil sciences, Spanish, speech, technical education, visual and performing arts, wildlife management.

ACADEMIC PROGRAMS. Accelerated program, double major, dual enrollment of high school students, honors program, independent study, internships, teacher preparation. **Remedial services:** Learning center, reduced course load, remedial instruction, special counselor, tutoring. **Placement/credit:** AP, CLEP Subject, institutional tests; 60 credit hours maximum for bachelor's degree.

ACADEMIC REQUIREMENTS. Freshmen must earn minimum GPA of 1.7 to continue in good standing. 60% of freshmen return for sophomore year. Students must declare major by end of second year. **Graduation requirements:** 124 hours for bachelor's (30 in major). Most students required to take courses in arts/fine arts, English, history, mathematics, biological/physical sciences, social sciences. **Postgraduate studies:** 1% enter law school, 1% enter medical school, 3% enter MBA programs, 35% enter other graduate study. **Additional information:** Special programs in aviation, ecology, energy, health-related sciences, and criminology.

FRESHMAN ADMISSIONS. Selection criteria: High school transcript and test scores important. Applicants must have 2.8 high school GPA and rank in top of class to be considered. Applicants must score in top half on ACT scores. **High school preparation:** 20 units required. Required units include English 4, mathematics 3, social science 2 and science 2. **Test requirements:** ACT; score report by August 15.

1992 FRESHMAN CLASS PROFILE. 315 men applied, 269 accepted, 194 enrolled; 372 women applied, 328 accepted, 247 enrolled. **Academic background:** Mid 50% of enrolled freshmen had ACT composite between 17-22. 99% submitted ACT scores. **Characteristics:** 92% from in state, 65% commute, 45% have minority backgrounds, 1% are foreign students. Average age is 23.

FALL-TERM APPLICATIONS. No fee. No closing date; applicants notified on a rolling basis beginning on or about April 1. Audition required for music, drama applicants. CRDA. Deferred and early admission available. EDP-F.

STUDENT LIFE. Housing: Dormitories (men, women, coed); apartment, fraternity, sorority housing available. **Activities:** Student government, radio, student newspaper, yearbook, choral groups, concert band, drama, jazz band, marching band, music ensembles, musical theater, opera, pep band, fraternities, sororities, Native American Student Council, Fellowship of Christian Athletes, Circle-K.

ATHLETICS. NAIA. **Intercollegiate:** Baseball M, basketball, football M, golf M, tennis, track and field M. **Intramural:** Basketball, golf M, handball, racquetball, softball, table tennis, tennis, volleyball.

STUDENT SERVICES. Aptitude testing, career counseling, employment service for undergraduates, freshman orientation, health services, personal counseling, placement service for graduates, special adviser for adult students, veterans counselor, services/facilities for handicapped.

ANNUAL EXPENSES. Tuition and fees (1992-93): $1,334, $2,028 additional for out-of-state students. **Room and board:** $2,628. **Books and supplies:** $450. **Other expenses:** $992.

FINANCIAL AID. 60% of freshmen, 78% of continuing students receive some form of aid. 94% of grants, 93% of loans, 32% of jobs based on need. 323 enrolled freshmen were judged to have need, all were offered aid. Academic, music/drama, athletic, leadership, alumni affiliation, minority scholarships available. **Aid applications:** Closing date November 15; priority given to applications received by April 1; applicants notified on or about July 1; must reply within 1 week.

ADDRESS/TELEPHONE. Fred Stroup, Director of Admissions and Registrar, Southeastern Oklahoma State University, Station A, Durant, OK 74701. (405) 924-0121 ext. 240. Fax: (405) 924-8531.

Southern Nazarene University
Bethany, Oklahoma CB code: 6036

4-year private university and liberal arts college, coed, affiliated with Church of the Nazarene. Founded in 1899. **Accreditation:** Regional. **Undergraduate enrollment:** 574 men, 692 women full time; 141 men, 184 women part time. **Graduate enrollment:** 77 men, 92 women full time; 10 men, 10 women part time. **Faculty:** 108 total (68 full time), 44 with doctorates or other terminal degrees. **Location:** Suburban campus in large town; 10 miles from Oklahoma City. **Calendar:** Semester, limited summer session. **Microcomputers:** 75 located in libraries, classrooms, computer centers.

DEGREES OFFERED. AA, BA, BS, MA, MS. 2 associate degrees awarded in 1992. 373 bachelor's degrees awarded. Graduate degrees offered in 11 major fields of study.

UNDERGRADUATE MAJORS. Associate: Business administration and management, clothing and textiles management/production/services, communications, family/consumer resource management, fashion merchandising, individual and family development, interior design, office supervision and management. **Bachelor's:** Accounting, allied health, behavioral sciences, biology, business administration and management, business and management, chemistry, clinical laboratory science, communications, computer and information sciences, criminal justice studies, early childhood education, education, elementary education, English, family/consumer resource management, French, German, history, humanities and social sciences, international public service, international studies, journalism, marketing and distribution, mathematics, music, nursing, philosophy, physics, political science and government, psychology, radio/television technology, religion, religious education, religious music, secondary education, secretarial and related programs, social sciences, sociology, Spanish, speech, theological studies, visual and performing arts.

ACADEMIC PROGRAMS. Double major, dual enrollment of high school students, external degree, independent study, internships, student-designed major, study abroad, teacher preparation, Washington semester. **Remedial services:** Remedial instruction, special counselor, tutoring. **ROTC:** Army. **Placement/credit:** AP, CLEP General and Subject; 30 credit hours maximum for bachelor's degree.

ACADEMIC REQUIREMENTS. Freshmen must earn minimum GPA of 2.0 to continue in good standing. 72% of freshmen return for sophomore year. Students must declare major by end of second year. **Graduation requirements:** 62 hours for associate (18 in major), 124 hours for bachelor's (35 in major). Most students required to take courses in arts/fine arts, computer science, English, history, mathematics, philosophy/religion, biological/physical sciences, social sciences. **Postgraduate studies:** 2% enter law school, 5% enter medical school, 16% enter MBA programs, 20% enter other graduate study.

FRESHMAN ADMISSIONS. Selection criteria: School achievement record, character recommendations, test scores considered. Recommended units include biological science 1, English 4, foreign language 2, mathematics 3, physical science 1 and social science 2. One computer course recommended. **Test requirements:** SAT or ACT (ACT preferred) for placement and counseling only; score report by August 1.

1992 FRESHMAN CLASS PROFILE. 237 men and women enrolled. **Academic background:** Mid 50% of enrolled freshmen had ACT composite between 15-23. 80% submitted ACT scores. **Characteristics:** 50% from in state, 85% live in college housing, 10% have minority backgrounds, 4% are foreign students. Average age is 18.

FALL-TERM APPLICATIONS. $25 fee. Closing date August 1; priority given to applications received by May 1; applicants notified on a rolling basis. Interview recommended. Audition recommended for music applicants. Deferred admission available.

STUDENT LIFE. Housing: Dormitories (men, women); apartment housing available. Single students under 23 required to live on campus or with relatives. **Activities:** Student government, film, student newspaper, yearbook, choral groups, concert band, drama, jazz band, music ensembles, pep band, symphony orchestra, Gospel Team, Mission Crusaders, Circle-K.

ATHLETICS. NAIA. **Intercollegiate:** Basketball, soccer, softball M, tennis, volleyball W. **Intramural:** Basketball, football M, golf M, horseback riding M, softball, swimming, table tennis, tennis, track and field, volleyball.

STUDENT SERVICES. Aptitude testing, career counseling, employment service for undergraduates, freshman orientation, health services, personal counseling, placement service for graduates, services/facilities for handicapped.

ANNUAL EXPENSES. Tuition and fees: $6,176. **Room and board:** $3,642. **Books and supplies:** $400. **Other expenses:** $1,200.

FINANCIAL AID. 77% of freshmen, 75% of continuing students receive some form of aid. 44% of grants, 83% of loans, all jobs based on need. 172 enrolled freshmen were judged to have need, all were offered aid. Academic, music/drama, art, athletic, state/district residency, leadership, religious affiliation scholarships available. **Aid applications:** No closing date; priority given to applications received by March 1; applicants notified on a rolling basis beginning on or about June 15; must reply within 2 weeks.

ADDRESS/TELEPHONE. Jeffrey Williamson, Director of Admissions, Southern Nazarene University, 6729 Northwest 39th Expressway, Bethany, OK 73008-2694. (405) 789-6400 ext. 6324.

Southwestern College of Christian Ministries
Bethany, Oklahoma — CB code: 1433

4-year private Bible college, coed, affiliated with Pentecostal Holiness Church. Founded in 1946. **Accreditation:** Regional. **Undergraduate enrollment:** 155 men and women. **Faculty:** 25 total (7 full time), 5 with doctorates or other terminal degrees. **Location:** Suburban campus in large town; 10 miles from Oklahoma City. **Calendar:** Semester, limited summer session.

DEGREES OFFERED. AA, BA, BS. 10 associate degrees awarded in 1992. 100% in philosophy, religion, theology. 15 bachelor's degrees awarded. 100% in philosophy, religion, theology.

UNDERGRADUATE MAJORS. Associate: Religion. **Bachelor's:** Bible studies, Christian elementary education, missionary studies, religion, religious education, religious music, theological studies.

ACADEMIC PROGRAMS. Double major, dual enrollment of high school students, independent study, internships, cross-registration. **Remedial services:** Reduced course load, special counselor, tutoring, developmental English program. **Placement/credit:** CLEP General and Subject, institutional tests; 30 credit hours maximum for bachelor's degree.

ACADEMIC REQUIREMENTS. Freshmen must earn minimum GPA of 1.5 to continue in good standing. 72% of freshmen return for sophomore year. Students must declare major on enrollment. **Graduation requirements:** 65 hours for associate, 128 hours for bachelor's. Most students required to take courses in English, history, humanities, mathematics, philosophy/religion, biological/physical sciences, social sciences. **Postgraduate studies:** 60% from 2-year programs enter 4-year programs.

FRESHMAN ADMISSIONS. Selection criteria: Must have 1 of the following: GPA of 2.0, rank in top 67% of class; rank in top 50% of national 12th-grade ACT norms. Minister's recommendation important. **Test requirements:** SAT or ACT (ACT preferred); score report by August 25.

1992 FRESHMAN CLASS PROFILE. 39 men and women enrolled. 25% had high school GPA of 3.0 or higher, 71% between 2.0 and 2.99. **Characteristics:** 60% from in state, 67% live in college housing, 8% have minority backgrounds. Average age is 18.

FALL-TERM APPLICATIONS. $25 fee, may be waived for applicants with need. Closing date July 15; priority given to applications received by June 1; applicants notified on a rolling basis. Interview recommended. Essay recommended. Minister's recommendation required. Deferred and early admission available.

STUDENT LIFE. Housing: Dormitories (men, women); apartment housing available. **Activities:** Student government, student newspaper, yearbook, Heartline Newsletter, choral groups, drama, music ensembles, Southwestern Ministerial Association, Robert Hough Missionary Society, Christian Education Association. **Additional information:** Extracurricular Christian programs and activities emphasized. Mandatory dress code. Religious observance required.

ATHLETICS. Intercollegiate: Basketball M. **Intramural:** Baseball, basketball, football M, golf, softball, table tennis, volleyball.

STUDENT SERVICES. Aptitude testing, career counseling, employment service for undergraduates, freshman orientation, personal counseling, placement service for graduates, veterans counselor.

ANNUAL EXPENSES. Tuition and fees: $3,584. **Room and board:** $2,450. **Books and supplies:** $400. **Other expenses:** $1,000.

FINANCIAL AID. 80% of freshmen, 80% of continuing students receive some form of aid. All grants, 83% of loans, all jobs based on need. 60 enrolled freshmen were judged to have need, all were offered aid. Academic, music/drama, religious affiliation scholarships available. **Aid applications:** Closing date July 15; priority given to applications received by May 15; applicants notified on a rolling basis beginning on or about June 1; must reply by August 15.

ADDRESS/TELEPHONE. Dr. Douglas Jernigan, Dean of Academics, Southwestern College of Christian Ministries, PO Box 340, Bethany, OK 73008. (405) 789-7661. Fax: (405) 789-7661 ext.132.

Southwestern Oklahoma State University
Weatherford, Oklahoma — CB code: 6673

4-year public university, coed. Founded in 1901. **Accreditation:** Regional. **Undergraduate enrollment:** 3,500 men and women. **Graduate enrollment:** 2,000 men and women. **Faculty:** 240 total (229 full time), 135 with doctorates or other terminal degrees. **Location:** Rural campus in large town; 75 miles from Oklahoma City. **Calendar:** Semester, extensive summer session. **Microcomputers:** 80 located in libraries, classrooms, computer centers. **Additional facts:** Additional campus at Sayre offers lower division and remedial courses.

DEGREES OFFERED. AS, AAS, BA, BS, BFA, MS, MBA, MFA, MEd. 107 associate degrees awarded in 1992. 689 bachelor's degrees awarded. Graduate degrees offered in 24 major fields of study.

UNDERGRADUATE MAJORS. Associate: Liberal/general studies. **Bachelor's:** Accounting, allied health, art education, biology, biophysics, business administration and management, business and management, business computer/console/peripheral equipment operation, business data processing and related programs, business economics, business education, business statistics, chemistry, clinical laboratory science, communications, computer and information sciences, computer programming, criminal justice studies, dramatic arts, economics, education of the mentally handicapped, elementary education, engineering physics, English, English education, finance, geography, health care administration, history, home economics, home economics education, industrial arts education, industrial technology, journalism, library science, management information systems, management science, marketing and distribution, marketing management, mathematics, mathematics education, medical records administration, military science (Army), music education, music theory and composition, nursing, office supervision and management, personnel management, pharmacy, physical education, physical sciences, physics, political science and government, prelaw, psychology, recreation and community services technologies, religious music, retailing, science education, secondary education, secretarial and related programs, social science education, social sciences, social studies education, social work, sociology, specific learning disabilities, speech, speech/communication/theater education.

ACADEMIC PROGRAMS. Accelerated program, double major, dual enrollment of high school students, honors program, independent study, internships, teacher preparation, visiting/exchange student program; liberal arts/career combination in health sciences; combined bachelor's/graduate program in business administration. **Remedial services:** Preadmission summer program, reduced course load, remedial instruction, special counselor, tutoring. **Placement/credit:** AP, CLEP Subject, institutional tests; 62 credit hours maximum for bachelor's degree.

ACADEMIC REQUIREMENTS. Freshmen must earn minimum GPA of 2.0 to continue in good standing. 54% of freshmen return for sophomore year. Students must declare major by end of second year. **Graduation requirements:** 60 hours for associate (20 in major), 124 hours for bachelor's (40 in major). Most students required to take courses in English, history, humanities, mathematics, biological/physical sciences, social sciences. **Postgraduate studies:** 5% enter law school, 2% enter medical school, 5% enter MBA programs, 11% enter other graduate study. **Additional information:** Tutorial services available.

FRESHMAN ADMISSIONS. Selection criteria: 2.8 GPA, rank in top half of class, test scores considered. **High school preparation:** 11 units required. Required units include English 4, mathematics 3, social science 2 and science 2. **Test requirements:** SAT or ACT (ACT preferred); score report by August 15.

1992 FRESHMAN CLASS PROFILE. 950 men and women enrolled. 35% had high school GPA of 3.0 or higher, 60% between 2.0 and 2.99. **Academic background:** Mid 50% of enrolled freshmen had ACT composite between 19-27. 99% submitted ACT scores. **Characteristics:** 92% from in state, 70% live in college housing, 14% have minority backgrounds, 2% are foreign students, 5% join fraternities/sororities. Average age is 20.

FALL-TERM APPLICATIONS. $4 fee. Closing date August 18; applicants notified on a rolling basis; must reply by August 25 or within 2 weeks if notified thereafter. Interview required for pharmacy, nursing applicants. Deferred and early admission available.

STUDENT LIFE. Housing: Dormitories (men, women); apartment, fraternity, sorority housing available. Private rooms available on priority basis. Limited housing available for married students. **Activities:** Student government, student newspaper, yearbook, choral groups, concert band, dance, drama, jazz band, marching band, music ensembles, musical theater, pep band, symphony orchestra, fraternities, sororities, 5 religious organizations, 2 political organizations, and approximately 75 social and professional clubs.

ATHLETICS. NAIA. **Intercollegiate:** Baseball M, basketball, football M, golf M, tennis, track and field. **Intramural:** Archery, basketball, bowling, football M, gymnastics, handball, racquetball, rifle, sailing, skiing, skin diving, soccer, softball, swimming, table tennis, tennis, track and field, volleyball.

STUDENT SERVICES. Aptitude testing, career counseling, employment service for undergraduates, freshman orientation, health services, personal counseling, placement service for graduates, veterans counselor, services/facilities for handicapped.

ANNUAL EXPENSES. Tuition and fees (projected): $1,500, $2,250 additional for out-of-state students. **Room and board:** $2,330. **Books and supplies:** $500. **Other expenses:** $900.

FINANCIAL AID. 65% of freshmen, 65% of continuing students receive some form of aid. 75% of grants, 91% of loans, 24% of jobs based on need. 331 enrolled freshmen were judged to have need, all were offered aid. Academic, music/drama, art, athletic, leadership scholarships available. **Aid applications:** No closing date; applicants notified on a rolling basis beginning on or about April 1; must reply within 6 weeks.

ADDRESS/TELEPHONE. Bob Klaassen, Director of Admissions, Southwestern Oklahoma State University, 100 Campus Drive, Weatherford, OK 73096. (405) 774-3777. Fax: (405) 774-3795.

Tulsa Junior College

Tulsa, Oklahoma — CB code: 6839

2-year public junior college, coed. Founded in 1968. **Accreditation:** Regional. **Undergraduate enrollment:** 19,195 men and women. **Faculty:** 918 total (238 full time). **Location:** Urban campus in large city. **Calendar:** Semester, extensive summer session. **Microcomputers:** Located in computer centers. **Additional facts:** 3-campus institution.

DEGREES OFFERED. AA, AS, AAS. 1,270 associate degrees awarded in 1992.

UNDERGRADUATE MAJORS. Accounting, air conditioning/heating/refrigeration mechanics, air conditioning/heating/refrigeration technology, allied health, apparel and accessories marketing, astronomy, aviation sciences technology, biology, biomedical equipment technology, business and office, business computer/console/peripheral equipment operation, business data processing and related programs, business data programming, business economics, chemistry, clinical laboratory science, computer and information sciences, computer programming, criminal justice studies, dental hygiene, drafting, drafting and design technology, economics, education, electrical and electronics equipment repair, electrical technology, electromechanical technology, electronic technology, engineering, engineering and engineering-related technologies, English, finance, fire control and safety technology, food production/management/services, French, geography, geology, German, health sciences, history, horticultural science, hospitality and recreation marketing, humanities, industrial technology, insurance marketing, international business management, interpreter for the deaf, Italian, Japanese, law enforcement and corrections technologies, legal assistant/paralegal, legal secretary, liberal/general studies, library science, management information systems, marketing and distribution, marketing management, mathematics, mechanical design technology, medical assistant, medical laboratory technologies, medical secretary, music, nursing, occupational therapy assistant, personnel management, philosophy, physical education, physical sciences, physical therapy assistant, physics, plant pathology, political science and government, precision metal work, psychology, radiograph medical technology, real estate, respiratory therapy, respiratory therapy technology, robotics, Russian, science technologies, secretarial and related programs, small business management and ownership, social sciences, sociology, Spanish, speech, telecommunications, tourism.

ACADEMIC PROGRAMS. 2-year transfer program, dual enrollment of high school students, honors program, internships, cross-registration. **Remedial services:** Learning center, remedial instruction, special counselor, tutoring. **Placement/credit:** AP, CLEP Subject, institutional tests; 30 credit hours maximum for associate degree.

ACADEMIC REQUIREMENTS. Freshmen must earn minimum GPA of 2.0 to continue in good standing. Students must declare major on enrollment. **Graduation requirements:** 60 hours for associate. Most students required to take courses in English, history, social sciences. **Additional information:** Many short-period intensive courses within conventional semesters.

FRESHMAN ADMISSIONS. Selection criteria: Open admissions. Selective admissions to health-related, legal assistant, and administrative management programs. **Test requirements:** SAT or ACT (ACT preferred) for placement and counseling only; score report by August 15.

1992 FRESHMAN CLASS PROFILE. 3,872 men and women enrolled. **Characteristics:** 98% from in state, 100% commute, 14% have minority backgrounds, 1% are foreign students.

FALL-TERM APPLICATIONS. $15 fee. No closing date; applicants notified on a rolling basis. Interview required for nursing, health programs, legal assistant applicants.

STUDENT LIFE. Activities: Student government, student newspaper, choral groups, concert band, drama, jazz band, music ensembles.

ATHLETICS. Intramural: Basketball, soccer, softball, table tennis, tennis, volleyball.

STUDENT SERVICES. Aptitude testing, career counseling, employment service for undergraduates, freshman orientation, health services, personal counseling, placement service for graduates, veterans counselor, services/facilities for handicapped.

ANNUAL EXPENSES. Tuition and fees (1992-93): $945, $1,590 additional for out-of-state students. **Books and supplies:** $405. **Other expenses:** $678.

FINANCIAL AID. 30% of continuing students receive some form of aid. Grants, loans, jobs available. **Aid applications:** No closing date; priority given to applications received by April 1; applicants notified on a rolling basis beginning on or about May 1.

ADDRESS/TELEPHONE. Leanne C. Brewer, Director of Admissions and Records, Tulsa Junior College, 6111 East Skelly Drive, Tulsa, OK 74135-6198. (918) 631-7811. Fax: (918) 631-7910.

University of Central Oklahoma

Edmond, Oklahoma — CB code: 6091

Admissions:	94% of applicants accepted
Based on:	•• School record, test scores
	• Special talents
Completion:	72% of freshmen end year in good standing
	13% graduate

4-year public university, coed. Founded in 1890. **Accreditation:** Regional. **Undergraduate enrollment:** 3,338 men, 4,179 women full time; 1,910 men, 2,615 women part time. **Graduate enrollment:** 570 men, 597 women full time; 847 men, 1,783 women part time. **Faculty:** 640 total (386 full time), 310 with doctorates or other terminal degrees. **Location:** Suburban campus in small city; 12 miles from Oklahoma City. **Calendar:** Semester, extensive summer session. Extensive evening/early morning classes. **Microcomputers:** 139 located in dormitories, libraries, classrooms, computer centers. **Special facilities:** Museum. **Additional facts:** First institution in United States to offer B.S. degree in funeral service and one of only two programs. Nigh Institute, dedicated to study of state government, established by former Governor Nigh.

DEGREES OFFERED. BA, BS, MA, MS, MBA, MEd. 1,799 bachelor's degrees awarded in 1992. 28% in business and management, 6% communications, 5% computer sciences, 30% education, 5% health sciences, 8% social sciences. Graduate degrees offered in 51 major fields of study.

UNDERGRADUATE MAJORS. Accounting, actuarial sciences, advertising, allied health, applied mathematics, art education, biological and physical sciences, biology, business administration and management, business and management, business and office, business computer/console/peripheral equipment operation, business economics, business education, ceramics, chemistry, clinical laboratory science, commercial art, communications, computer and information sciences, computer mathematics, computer programming, criminal justice studies, data processing, dramatic arts, drawing, driver and safety education, early childhood education, economics, education, education of the emotionally handicapped, education of the mentally handicapped, education of the multiple handicapped, education of the physically handicapped, elementary education, English, English education, fashion design, fashion merchandising, finance, fine arts, food production/management/services, food science and nutrition, foreign languages (multiple emphasis), foreign languages education, French, funeral services/mortuary science, German, graphic design, health education, history, home economics, home economics education, hotel/motel and restaurant management, human resources development, individual and family development, industrial arts education, industrial technology, insurance and risk management, interior design, journalism, liberal/general studies, management science, marketing and distribution, marketing and distributive education, marketing management, mathematics, mathematics education, museum studies, music, music education, musical theater, nursing, office supervision and management, painting, personnel management, philosophy, photography, physical education, physics, political science and government, psychology, public administration, public relations, radio/television broadcasting, reading education, real estate, retailing, school psychology, science education, sculpture, secretarial and related programs, social sciences, social studies education, sociology, Spanish, special education, specific learning disabilities, speech, speech correction, speech pathology/audiology, textiles and clothing, trade and industrial education.

ACADEMIC PROGRAMS. Double major, dual enrollment of high school students, honors program, independent study, internships, telecourses. **Remedial services:** Reduced course load, remedial instruction. **ROTC:** Army. **Placement/credit:** AP, CLEP General and Subject, institutional tests; 94 credit hours maximum for bachelor's degree.

ACADEMIC REQUIREMENTS. Freshmen must earn minimum GPA of 1.7 to continue in good standing. 47% of freshmen return for sophomore year. Students must declare major by end of first year. **Graduation requirements:** 124 hours for bachelor's (36 in major). Most students required to take courses in English, history, humanities, philosophy/religion, biological/physical sciences, social sciences.

FRESHMAN ADMISSIONS. Selection criteria: High school graduates must have 2.7 GPA, rank in top 60% of class, or minimum enhanced ACT composite score of 19 or combined SAT score of 840. **High school**

preparation: 11 units required. Required units include English 4, mathematics 3, social science 2 and science 2. **Test requirements:** SAT or ACT (ACT preferred); score report by August 20.

1992 FRESHMAN CLASS PROFILE. 1,531 men applied, 1,427 accepted, 602 enrolled; 1,867 women applied, 1,764 accepted, 774 enrolled. 60% had high school GPA of 3.0 or higher, 39% between 2.0 and 2.99. 12% were in top tenth and 37% were in top quarter of graduating class. **Academic background:** Mid 50% of enrolled freshmen had ACT composite between 18-22. 95% submitted ACT scores. **Characteristics:** 92% from in state, 83% commute, 13% have minority backgrounds, 3% are foreign students, 1% join fraternities/sororities. Average age is 22.

FALL-TERM APPLICATIONS. $15 fee. No closing date; applicants notified on a rolling basis beginning on or about March 15. Early admission available.

STUDENT LIFE. Housing: Dormitories (men, women); apartment, fraternity, sorority housing available. **Activities:** Student government, radio, student newspaper, television, yearbook, choral groups, concert band, dance, drama, jazz band, marching band, music ensembles, musical theater, pep band, symphony orchestra, fraternities, sororities.

ATHLETICS. NCAA. **Intercollegiate:** Baseball M, basketball, cross-country, football M, golf M, softball W, tennis, track and field, volleyball W, wrestling M. **Intramural:** Baseball M, basketball, bowling, golf, soccer, softball, swimming, table tennis, tennis, track and field, volleyball, wrestling M.

STUDENT SERVICES. Aptitude testing, career counseling, employment service for undergraduates, health services, personal counseling, placement service for graduates, veterans counselor, services/facilities for handicapped.

ANNUAL EXPENSES. Tuition and fees (1992-93): $1,369, $2,028 additional for out-of-state students. **Room and board:** $2,150. **Books and supplies:** $500. **Other expenses:** $1,400.

FINANCIAL AID. 30% of freshmen, 41% of continuing students receive some form of aid. 67% of grants, 71% of loans, 23% of jobs based on need. Academic, music/drama, art, athletic, leadership, alumni affiliation, minority scholarships available. **Aid applications:** No closing date; priority given to applications received by June 1; applicants notified on a rolling basis beginning on or about July 1; must reply within 3 weeks.

ADDRESS/TELEPHONE. Suzzane Martin, Director of Admissions and Records/Registrar, University of Central Oklahoma, 100 North University Drive, Edmond, OK 73034-0151. (405) 341-2980 ext. 3366. Fax: (405) 341-4964.

University of Oklahoma
Norman, Oklahoma

CB code: 6879

Admissions: 86% of applicants accepted
Based on: ••• School record, test scores
• Recommendations, special talents
Completion: 88% of freshmen end year in good standing
37% graduate

4-year public university, coed. Founded in 1890. **Accreditation:** Regional. **Undergraduate enrollment:** 6,808 men, 5,614 women full time; 1,308 men, 1,223 women part time. **Graduate enrollment:** 1,346 men, 998 women full time; 1,359 men, 1,332 women part time. **Faculty:** 1,008 total (849 full time), 762 with doctorates or other terminal degrees. **Location:** Suburban campus in small city; 20 miles from Oklahoma City. **Calendar:** Semester, extensive summer session. **Microcomputers:** 500 located in dormitories, libraries, classrooms, computer centers. **Special facilities:** Museum of science and history, art museum, biological station, history of science collection, western history collection, national severe storms laboratory, energy center. **Additional facts:** Some programs offered through University Center at Tulsa, a consortium of 4 state universities.

DEGREES OFFERED. BA, BS, BFA, BArch, MA, MS, MBA, MFA, MEd, MSW, PhD, EdD, DMD, MD, B. Pharm. 2,511 bachelor's degrees awarded in 1992. 5% in architecture and environmental design, 24% business and management, 13% communications, 7% education, 12% engineering, 12% social sciences, 5% visual and performing arts. Graduate degrees offered in 88 major fields of study.

UNDERGRADUATE MAJORS. Accounting, advertising, aerospace/aeronautical/astronautical engineering, anthropology, architecture, art history, Asian studies, astronomy, astrophysics, atmospheric sciences and meteorology, botany, business administration and management, business and management, business economics, business statistics, ceramics, chemical engineering, chemistry, cinematography/film, civil engineering, clinical laboratory science, communications, computer and information sciences, computer engineering, construction, dance, dental hygiene, dramatic arts, early childhood education, earth sciences, economics, education of the mentally handicapped, electrical/electronics/communications engineering, elementary education, engineering, engineering physics, English, environmental design, environmental health engineering, environmental science, European studies, finance, fine arts, foreign languages education, French, geography, geological engineering, geology, geophysics and seismology, German, history, industrial engineering, interior design, international business management, journalism, Latin American studies, liberal/general studies, linguistics, logistics and materials management, management information systems, marketing management, mathematics, mathematics education, mechanical engineering, medical laboratory technologies, medical radiation dosimetry, metal/jewelry, microbiology, music, music education, music history and appreciation, music performance, music theory and composition, musical theater, nursing, occupational therapy, painting, petroleum engineering, petroleum land management, pharmacy, philosophy, photography, physical education, physical therapy, physician's assistant, physics, political science and government, printmaking, psychology, public administration, public relations, radio/television broadcasting, radiograph medical technology, real estate, religion, Russian, Russian and Slavic studies, science education, sculpture, social studies education, social work, sociology, Spanish, special education, specific learning disabilities, video, visual and performing arts, zoology.

ACADEMIC PROGRAMS. Accelerated program, cooperative education, dual enrollment of high school students, external degree, honors program, independent study, internships, semester at sea, student-designed major, study abroad, teacher preparation, telecourses, visiting/exchange student program, cross-registration; combined bachelor's/graduate program in business administration, law. **Remedial services:** Reduced course load, special counselor, tutoring. **ROTC:** Air Force, Army, Naval. **Placement/credit:** AP, CLEP Subject, IB, institutional tests; 31 credit hours maximum for bachelor's degree.

ACADEMIC REQUIREMENTS. Freshmen must earn minimum GPA of 1.7 to continue in good standing. 77% of freshmen return for sophomore year. Students must declare major by end of second year. **Graduation requirements:** 124 hours for bachelor's (30 in major). Most students required to take courses in English, foreign languages, history, humanities, mathematics, biological/physical sciences, social sciences.

FRESHMAN ADMISSIONS. Selection criteria: Rank in top third of class, and 3.0 GPA or test score plus 11 units in English (4), math (3), lab science (2), and history (2) required. Alternative admissions available to those who do not meet criteria. **High school preparation:** 11 units required. Required and recommended units include English 4, mathematics 3 and science 2. Foreign language 2 recommended. 2 units of history; 1 unit must be American history. **Test requirements:** SAT or ACT; score report by August 21. High school grade-point average and class rank may be used in place of test scores for admission purposes.

1992 FRESHMAN CLASS PROFILE. 2,531 men applied, 2,163 accepted, 1,244 enrolled; 2,328 women applied, 2,032 accepted, 1,178 enrolled. 79% had high school GPA of 3.0 or higher, 20% between 2.0 and 2.99. 32% were in top tenth and 60% were in top quarter of graduating class. **Academic background:** Mid 50% of enrolled freshmen had ACT composite between 21-27. 88% submitted ACT scores. **Characteristics:** 79% from in state, 80% live in college housing, 27% have minority backgrounds, 1% are foreign students, 30% join fraternities/sororities. Average age is 19.

FALL-TERM APPLICATIONS. $15 fee, may be waived for applicants with need. No closing date; applicants notified on a rolling basis. Audition required for drama, dance, music applicants. Early admission available. Institutional early decision plan. Freshman applicants should apply early in the fall term of senior year. ACT or SAT required. Admission on rolling basis after junior year and is based on GPA and class rank or test scores, plus 11 curricular units.

STUDENT LIFE. Housing: Dormitories (men, women, coed); apartment, fraternity, sorority housing available. **Activities:** Student government, film, magazine, radio, student newspaper, television, choral groups, concert band, dance, drama, jazz band, marching band, music ensembles, musical theater, opera, pep band, symphony orchestra, fraternities, sororities, American Indian Association, Black Student Association, Hispanic American Student Association, Asian-American Student Association.

ATHLETICS. NCAA. **Intercollegiate:** Baseball M, basketball, cross-country, football M, golf, gymnastics, softball W, tennis, track and field, volleyball W, wrestling M. **Intramural:** Badminton, basketball, bowling, cross-country, diving, fencing, golf, handball, lacrosse M, racquetball, rugby, sailing, soccer, softball, squash, swimming, table tennis, tennis, track and field, volleyball, water polo.

STUDENT SERVICES. Aptitude testing, career counseling, employment service for undergraduates, freshman orientation, health services, personal counseling, placement service for graduates, special adviser for adult students, veterans counselor, Minority Student Services, services/facilities for handicapped.

ANNUAL EXPENSES. Tuition and fees (1992-93): $1,783, $3,191 additional for out-of-state students. **Room and board:** $3,358. **Books and supplies:** $590. **Other expenses:** $1,752.

FINANCIAL AID. 55% of freshmen, 56% of continuing students receive some form of aid. 66% of grants, 86% of loans, 18% of jobs based on need. 1,074 enrolled freshmen were judged to have need, 1,011 were offered aid. Academic, music/drama, art, athletic, leadership, minority scholarships available. **Aid applications:** No closing date; priority given to applications received by March 1; applicants notified on a rolling basis; must reply within 4 weeks. **Additional information:** Institutional loans are available for early applicants who do not qualify for federal or state need-based aid (middle-income students).

ADDRESS/TELEPHONE. Marc Borish, Director of Admissions, University of Oklahoma, 407 West Boyd, Norman, OK 73069-0520. (405) 325-2151. (800) 234-6868.

University of Oklahoma Health Sciences Center
Oklahoma City, Oklahoma CB code: 0430

2-year upper-division public branch campus, health science, nursing, pharmacy college, coed. Founded in 1900. **Accreditation:** Regional. **Undergraduate enrollment:** 224 men, 689 women full time; 122 men, 149 women part time. **Graduate enrollment:** 660 men, 526 women full time; 230 men, 459 women part time. **Faculty:** 801 total (632 full time). **Location:** Urban campus in large city. **Calendar:** Semester, limited summer session. **Microcomputers:** Located in libraries, computer centers. **Additional facts:** Branch campus in Tulsa for completion of third and fourth year medical school.

DEGREES OFFERED. BS, MS, PhD, DDS, MD, Pharm D. 569 bachelor's degrees awarded in 1992. 74% in health sciences, 26% allied health. Graduate degrees offered in 29 major fields of study.

UNDERGRADUATE MAJORS. Clinical laboratory science, cytotechnology, dental hygiene, medical laboratory technologies, medical radiation dosimetry, nuclear medical technology, nursing, nutritional sciences, occupational therapy, pharmacy, physical therapy, physician's assistant, radiograph medical technology, ultrasound technology.

ACADEMIC PROGRAMS. Honors program, independent study, internships, telecourses, cross-registration; liberal arts/career combination in health sciences; combined bachelor's/graduate program in medicine. **Remedial services:** Preadmission summer program, reduced course load, tutoring, study skills, test-taking skills program. **Placement/credit:** AP, CLEP Subject, institutional tests; 32 credit hours maximum for bachelor's degree.

ACADEMIC REQUIREMENTS. Students must declare major on application. **Graduation requirements:** 124 hours for bachelor's. Most students required to take courses in biological/physical sciences, social sciences. **Postgraduate studies:** 2% enter medical school, 2% enter other graduate study.

STUDENT LIFE. Housing: Students may live in dorm located on main campus, 22 miles south of Health Sciences Center. **Activities:** Student government, student newspaper, yearbook, American Indian Student Organization, Black Medical Student Organization, Christian Medical Society, Black dental student association, Black pharmacy student association, Hispanic American student organization.

STUDENT SERVICES. Career counseling, health services, personal counseling, services/facilities for handicapped.

ANNUAL EXPENSES. Tuition and fees (1992-93): $1,545, $3,191 additional for out-of-state students. **Books and supplies:** $850. **Other expenses:** $1,521.

FINANCIAL AID. 49% of continuing students receive some form of aid. 99% of grants, 97% of loans based on need. **Aid applications:** No closing date; priority given to applications received by March 1; applicants notified on a rolling basis beginning on or about April 1; must reply within 6 weeks.

ADDRESS/TELEPHONE. Pam Hutcherson, Manager Student Admission, University of Oklahoma Health Sciences Center, 941 Stanton L. Young Boulevard, Oklahoma City, OK 73190. (405) 271-2359. Fax: (405) 271-2480.

University of Science and Arts of Oklahoma
Chickasha, Oklahoma CB code: 6544

4-year public liberal arts college, coed. Founded in 1908. **Accreditation:** Regional. **Undergraduate enrollment:** 1,653 men and women. **Faculty:** 60 total (54 full time), 38 with doctorates or other terminal degrees. **Location:** Rural campus in large town; 48 miles from Oklahoma City. **Calendar:** Trimester, limited summer session. **Microcomputers:** 50 located in libraries, classrooms, computer centers.

DEGREES OFFERED. BA, BS. 160 bachelor's degrees awarded in 1992. 30% in business and management, 8% computer sciences, 26% teacher education, 9% social sciences, 13% visual and performing arts.

UNDERGRADUATE MAJORS. Accounting, American Indian studies, art education, biology, business administration and management, business and management, business data processing and related programs, business economics, business education, chemistry, child development/care/guidance, communications, computer and information sciences, data processing, dramatic arts, economics, education of the deaf and hearing impaired, education of the mentally handicapped, elementary education, English, English education, fine arts, history, home economics, home economics education, liberal/general studies, mathematics, mathematics education, medical laboratory technologies, music, music education, physical education, physics, political science and government, psychology, reading education, retailing, science education, secondary education, social science education, social studies education, sociology, Spanish, specific learning disabilities, speech correction, speech/communication/theater education.

ACADEMIC PROGRAMS. Accelerated program, double major, dual enrollment of high school students, honors program, independent study. **Remedial services:** Learning center, reduced course load, remedial instruction, tutoring. **Placement/credit:** AP, CLEP Subject, institutional tests; 62 credit hours maximum for bachelor's degree.

ACADEMIC REQUIREMENTS. Freshmen must earn minimum GPA of 1.6 to continue in good standing. 54% of freshmen return for sophomore year. Students must declare major on application. **Graduation requirements:** 124 hours for bachelor's (40 in major). Most students required to take courses in arts/fine arts, computer science, English, history, humanities, mathematics, philosophy/religion, biological/physical sciences, social sciences. **Postgraduate studies:** 3% enter law school, 1% enter medical school, 11% enter MBA programs, 10% enter other graduate study. **Additional information:** 32 hours of the 52 hours general education core curriculum are team taught. These interdisciplinary courses are unique to this institution.

FRESHMAN ADMISSIONS. Selection criteria: Minimum 2.7 GPA and test scores important. **High school preparation:** 11 units required. Required and recommended units include English 4, mathematics 3, social science 2-3 and science 2. Biological science 1, foreign language 1 and physical science 1 recommended. **Test requirements:** SAT or ACT (ACT preferred); score report by August 1.

1992 FRESHMAN CLASS PROFILE. 227 men and women enrolled. 39% had high school GPA of 3.0 or higher, 61% between 2.0 and 2.99. **Academic background:** Mid 50% of enrolled freshmen had ACT composite between 18-23. 96% submitted ACT scores. **Characteristics:** 98% from in state, 50% commute, 21% have minority backgrounds. Average age is 19.

FALL-TERM APPLICATIONS. No fee. Closing date August 7; priority given to applications received by August 7; applicants notified on a rolling basis. Audition required.

STUDENT LIFE. Housing: Dormitories (men, women). **Activities:** Student government, student newspaper, yearbook, choral groups, concert band, dance, drama, jazz band, music ensembles, musical theater, pep band, Baptist Student Union, Church of Christ Bible Chair.

ATHLETICS. NAIA. **Intercollegiate:** Basketball, golf M, tennis. **Intramural:** Badminton, basketball, bowling, fencing, softball, swimming, tennis, volleyball.

STUDENT SERVICES. Aptitude testing, career counseling, employment service for undergraduates, freshman orientation, health services, personal counseling, placement service for graduates, veterans counselor, services/facilities for handicapped.

ANNUAL EXPENSES. Tuition and fees (projected): $1,380, $2,100 additional for out-of-state students. **Room and board:** $1,920. **Books and supplies:** $600. **Other expenses:** $1,200.

FINANCIAL AID. 79% of freshmen, 75% of continuing students receive some form of aid. 82% of grants, 85% of loans, all jobs based on need. Academic, music/drama, art, athletic, leadership scholarships available. **Aid applications:** No closing date; priority given to applications received by March 15; applicants notified on a rolling basis.

ADDRESS/TELEPHONE. Jack Hudson, Director of Admissions and Records, University of Science and Arts of Oklahoma, PO Box 82345, Chickasha, OK 73018. (405) 224-3140 ext. 204.

University of Tulsa
Tulsa, Oklahoma CB code: 6883

Admissions:	91% of applicants accepted
Based on:	••• School record
	•• Test scores
	• Activities, essay, interview, recommendations, special talents
Completion:	85% of freshmen end year in good standing
	50% graduate, 22% of these enter graduate study

4-year private university, coed, affiliated with Presbyterian Church (USA). Founded in 1894. **Accreditation:** Regional. **Undergraduate enrollment:** 1,446 men, 1,587 women full time; 181 men, 249 women part time. **Graduate enrollment:** 569 men, 371 women full time; 301 men, 218 women part time. **Faculty:** 439 total (335 full time), 384 with doctorates or other terminal degrees. **Location:** Urban campus in large city; 100 miles from Oklahoma City, 248 miles from Kansas City. **Calendar:** 4-4-1, limited summer session. **Microcomputers:** 250 located in dormitories, libraries, classrooms, computer centers, campus-wide network. **Special facilities:** Art gallery, biotechnology institute. **Additional facts:** Founded by United Presbyterian Church.

DEGREES OFFERED. BA, BS, BFA, MA, MS, MBA, MFA, MEd, PhD, JD. 600 bachelor's degrees awarded in 1992. 30% in business and management, 8% communications, 9% computer sciences, 13% engineering, 6% psychology, 6% social sciences, 6% visual and performing arts. Graduate degrees offered in 44 major fields of study.

UNDERGRADUATE MAJORS. Accounting, anthropology, applied mathematics, art education, art history, athletic training, biology, business administration and management, business economics, ceramics, chemical engineering, chemistry, communications, computer and information sciences, dramatic arts, drawing, earth sciences, economics, education, education of the deaf and hearing impaired, electrical/electronics/communications engineering, elementary education, engineering physics, English, English education, English literature, finance, fine arts, foreign languages education, French, geological engineering, geology, geophysical engineering, geophysics and seismology, graphic design, history, information sciences and systems, international studies, linguistics, management information systems, management science, marketing and distribution, marketing management, mathematics, mathematics education, mechanical engineering, music, music education, music performance, music theory and composition, musical theater, nursing, painting, petroleum engineering, philosophy, physics, political science and government, predentistry, prelaw, premedicine, prepharmacy, preveterinary, printmaking, psychology, real estate, science education, sculpture, secondary education, social science education, social studies education, sociology, Spanish, speech correction, speech pathology/audiology, visual and performing arts.

ACADEMIC PROGRAMS. Double major, dual enrollment of high school students, honors program, independent study, internships, semester at sea, student-designed major, study abroad, teacher preparation, Washington semester; combined bachelor's/graduate program in business administration. **Remedial services:** Reduced course load, tutoring, English Institute for International Students. **ROTC:** Army. **Placement/credit:** AP, CLEP Subject, IB, institutional tests; 36 credit hours maximum for bachelor's degree.

ACADEMIC REQUIREMENTS. Freshmen must earn minimum GPA of 2.0 to continue in good standing. 80% of freshmen return for sophomore year. Students must declare major by end of second year. **Graduation requirements:** 126 hours for bachelor's (30 in major). Most students required to take courses in arts/fine arts, computer science, English, foreign languages, history, humanities, mathematics, philosophy/religion, biological/physical sciences, social sciences. **Postgraduate studies:** 5% enter law school, 2% enter medical school, 3% enter MBA programs, 12% enter other graduate study.

FRESHMAN ADMISSIONS. Selection criteria: Primarily school achievement record and test scores. High school guidance counselor recommendations required. **High school preparation:** 15 units recommended. Recommended units include English 4, foreign language 2, mathematics 3, social science 3 and science 3. 4 mathematics and 4 physical science recommended for engineering and applied science students. **Test requirements:** SAT or ACT; score report by August 15.

1992 FRESHMAN CLASS PROFILE. 1,853 men and women applied, 1,680 accepted; 738 enrolled. 79% had high school GPA of 3.0 or higher, 20% between 2.0 and 2.99. 36% were in top tenth and 66% were in top quarter of graduating class. **Academic background:** Mid 50% of enrolled freshmen had SAT-V between 450-580, SAT-M between 500-650; ACT composite between 22-28. 31% submitted SAT scores, 69% submitted ACT scores. **Characteristics:** 58% from in state, 65% live in college housing, 18% have minority backgrounds, 6% are foreign students, 20% join fraternities/sororities. Average age is 18.

FALL-TERM APPLICATIONS. $25 fee, may be waived for applicants with need. No closing date; applicants notified on a rolling basis beginning on or about December 1. Audition required for music, theater applicants. Portfolio required for art applicants. Interview recommended. Essay recommended. CRDA. Deferred admission available.

STUDENT LIFE. Housing: Dormitories (men, women, coed); apartment, fraternity, sorority housing available. Honors house and honors condominium available. **Activities:** Student government, radio, student newspaper, television, yearbook, Coda Literary Journal, choral groups, concert band, drama, jazz band, marching band, music ensembles, musical theater, opera, pep band, symphony orchestra, fraternities, sororities, total of 120 clubs including Phi Beta Kappa, foreign student club, political affiliation clubs, preprofessional clubs, recreation, special interest, and student government organizations.

ATHLETICS. NCAA. **Intercollegiate:** Basketball M, cross-country, football M, golf, soccer, softball W, tennis, track and field, volleyball W. **Intramural:** Badminton, basketball, bowling, cross-country, diving, golf, racquetball, soccer, softball, squash, swimming, table tennis, tennis, track and field, volleyball, water polo, wrestling M.

STUDENT SERVICES. Aptitude testing, career counseling, employment service for undergraduates, freshman orientation, health services, personal counseling, placement service for graduates, special adviser for adult students, services/facilities for handicapped.

ANNUAL EXPENSES. Tuition and fees: $9,995. **Room and board:** $3,948. **Books and supplies:** $1,200. **Other expenses:** $1,350.

FINANCIAL AID. 75% of freshmen, 75% of continuing students receive some form of aid. 40% of grants, 86% of loans, 51% of jobs based on need. 326 enrolled freshmen were judged to have need, all were offered aid. Academic, music/drama, art, athletic, leadership scholarships available. **Aid applications:** No closing date; priority given to applications received by March 1; applicants notified on a rolling basis beginning on or about April 1; must reply by May 1 or within 2 weeks if notified thereafter.

ADDRESS/TELEPHONE. John Corso, Dean of Admission, University of Tulsa, 600 South College Avenue, Tulsa, OK 74104-3189. (918) 631-2307. (800) 331-3050. Fax: (918) 631-2033.

Western Oklahoma State College
Altus, Oklahoma CB code: 6020

2-year public community college, coed. Founded in 1926. **Accreditation:** Regional. **Undergraduate enrollment:** 1,803 men and women. **Faculty:** 81 total (41 full time), 3 with doctorates or other terminal degrees. **Location:** Rural campus in large town; 50 miles from Lawton. **Calendar:** Semester, limited summer session.

DEGREES OFFERED. AA, AS, AAS. 218 associate degrees awarded in 1992. 10% in business and management, 10% business/office and marketing/distribution, 5% teacher education, 63% multi/interdisciplinary studies.

UNDERGRADUATE MAJORS. Accounting, agribusiness, agricultural sciences, biology, business and office, business economics, communications, computer and information sciences, construction, drafting, education, elementary education, engineering, English education, fine arts, fire control and safety technology, graphic arts technology, home economics, industrial arts education, journalism, law enforcement and corrections technologies, liberal/general studies, marketing and distribution, mathematics, music, music education, nursing, photographic technology, psychology, real estate, secretarial and related programs, social sciences, Spanish, speech, visual and performing arts.

ACADEMIC PROGRAMS. 2-year transfer program, dual enrollment of high school students. **Remedial services:** Learning center, remedial instruction, tutoring. **Placement/credit:** AP, CLEP Subject; 30 credit hours maximum for associate degree.

ACADEMIC REQUIREMENTS. Upon completion of 24 credits students must earn minimum grade-point average of 1.6. 60% of freshmen return for sophomore year. Students must declare major by end of first year. **Graduation requirements:** 62 hours for associate (15 in major). Most students required to take courses in English, history, humanities, mathematics, biological/physical sciences, social sciences.

FRESHMAN ADMISSIONS. Selection criteria: Open admissions. **High school preparation:** 21 units recommended. Recommended units include English 4, mathematics 3, social science 2 and science 2. **Test requirements:** SAT or ACT (ACT preferred) for placement; score report by August 24.

1992 FRESHMAN CLASS PROFILE. 767 men and women enrolled. **Characteristics:** 99% from in state, 100% commute, 12% have minority backgrounds. Average age is 19.

FALL-TERM APPLICATIONS. $15 fee. No closing date; applicants notified on a rolling basis. Interview recommended for applicants who are not high school graduates. Deferred and early admission available. ACT required of all students. Must be taken before completion of degree requirements.

STUDENT LIFE. Activities: Student government, radio, student newspaper, choral groups, concert band, drama, jazz band, music ensembles, musical theater, pep band, Young Democrats, Young Republicans, Baptist Student Union, Christian Student Union.

ATHLETICS. NJCAA. **Intercollegiate:** Baseball M, basketball. **Intramural:** Basketball, volleyball. **Clubs:** Rodeo.

STUDENT SERVICES. Aptitude testing, career counseling, freshman orientation, health services, personal counseling, veterans counselor, services/facilities for handicapped.

ANNUAL EXPENSES. Tuition and fees (1992-93): $930, $1,590 additional for out-of-state students. **Books and supplies:** $450. **Other expenses:** $400.

FINANCIAL AID. 60% of freshmen, 60% of continuing students receive some form of aid. Grants, loans, jobs available. **Aid applications:** No closing date; priority given to applications received by March 30; applicants notified on a rolling basis beginning on or about April 30; must reply within 3 weeks.

ADDRESS/TELEPHONE. Larry Paxton, Director of Admissions and Registrar, Western Oklahoma State College, 2801 North Main Street, Altus, OK 73521. (405) 477-2000. Fax: (405) 521-6154.

Oregon

Bassist College

Portland, Oregon CB code: 4231

4-year proprietary college of design and merchandising, coed. Founded in 1963. **Accreditation:** Regional. **Undergraduate enrollment:** 250 men and women. **Faculty:** 16 total (10 full time), 3 with doctorates or other terminal degrees. **Location:** Urban campus in large city; 200 miles from Seattle, WA. **Calendar:** 4 terms of varying length; students attend all 4 terms. **Microcomputers:** 10 located in computer centers. **Special facilities:** Specialized library. **Additional facts:** Baccalaureate offered in combination with credits from accredited 4-year colleges. 12-week internship program mandatory, the first year a job in retail sales, the second year a job in student's specialty.

DEGREES OFFERED. B. 40 associate degrees awarded in 1992. 53% in architecture and environmental design, 15% business/office and marketing/distribution, 33% home economics. 4 bachelor's degrees awarded. 100% in architecture and environmental design.

UNDERGRADUATE MAJORS. Fashion design, industrial design, interior design, retailing. fashion design, industrial design, interior design, retailing.

ACADEMIC PROGRAMS. Accelerated program, independent study, internships. **Remedial services:** Tutoring. **Placement/credit:** AP, institutional tests.

ACADEMIC REQUIREMENTS. Freshmen must earn minimum GPA of 2.25 to continue in good standing. 73% of freshmen return for sophomore year. Students must declare major on application. **Graduation requirements:** 125 hours for associate (65 in major), 190 hours for bachelor's (70 in major). Most students required to take courses in arts/fine arts, computer science, English, history, humanities, mathematics, social sciences. **Postgraduate studies:** 20% from 2-year programs enter 4-year programs. 10% enter other graduate study. **Additional information:** Baccalaureate completion on part-time basis available. All students study history of western civilization, English composition, design, creative problem solving, business law. Senior paper or senior project required for baccalaureate.

FRESHMAN ADMISSIONS. Selection criteria: Interview and references very important. School GPA of 2.25 or score of at least 55 on GED required. Recommended units include English 3 and mathematics 1. For interior design, art and drafting recommended. For apparel design, sewing recommended. For industrial design, drafting, mathematics and physics recommended.

1992 FRESHMAN CLASS PROFILE. 3 men, 26 women enrolled. 32% had high school GPA of 3.0 or higher, 61% between 2.0 and 2.99. **Characteristics:** 59% from in state, 80% commute, 21% have minority backgrounds, 4% are foreign students. Average age is 22.

FALL-TERM APPLICATIONS. $200 fee. Closing date September 1; priority given to applications received by April 1; applicants notified on a rolling basis beginning on or about April 15; must reply by September 1. Interview required. Portfolio recommended. Essay recommended. Deferred and early admission available.

STUDENT LIFE. Housing: Dormitories (coed). Non-smoking environment available. **Activities:** Student government, student newspaper, Distributive Education Club, Interior Design Student Chapter.

STUDENT SERVICES. Career counseling, employment service for undergraduates, freshman orientation, personal counseling, placement service for graduates, special adviser for adult students, veterans counselor, services/facilities for handicapped.

ANNUAL EXPENSES. Tuition and fees: $9,000. **Room and board:** $2,850 room only. **Books and supplies:** $1,200. **Other expenses:** $1,200.

FINANCIAL AID. 91% of freshmen, 84% of continuing students receive some form of aid. 79% of grants, 55% of loans, all jobs based on need. 20 enrolled freshmen were judged to have need, all were offered aid. Academic, leadership, alumni affiliation scholarships available. **Aid applications:** No closing date; priority given to applications received by June 1; applicants notified on a rolling basis beginning on or about June 1; must reply within 3 weeks.

ADDRESS/TELEPHONE. Lynn Harrison, Officer, Bassist College, 2000 Southwest Fifth Avenue, Portland, OR 97201. (503) 228-6528. (800) 547-0937. Fax: (503) 228-4227.

Blue Mountain Community College

Pendleton, Oregon CB code: 4025

2-year public community college, coed. Founded in 1962. **Accreditation:** Regional. **Undergraduate enrollment:** 1,191 men and women full time; 4,397 men and women part time. **Faculty:** 188 total (68 full time). **Location:** Rural campus in large town; 200 miles from Portland. **Calendar:** Quarter, limited summer session. **Microcomputers:** 173 located in classrooms, computer centers. **Additional facts:** Located in an agricultural community.

DEGREES OFFERED. AA, AS, AAS. 207 associate degrees awarded in 1992.

UNDERGRADUATE MAJORS. Accounting, agribusiness, agricultural sciences, automotive technology, business and office, dental assistant, diesel engine mechanics, law enforcement and corrections technologies, liberal/general studies, marketing and distribution, mechanical design technology, medical records technology, nursing, practical nursing, precision metal work, protective services, radio/television broadcasting, secretarial and related programs, social work.

ACADEMIC PROGRAMS. 2-year transfer program. **Remedial services:** Learning center, remedial instruction, tutoring. **Placement/credit:** AP, CLEP General and Subject, institutional tests.

ACADEMIC REQUIREMENTS. Freshmen must earn minimum GPA of 2.0 to continue in good standing. **Graduation requirements:** 93 hours for associate. Most students required to take courses in English, humanities, mathematics, biological/physical sciences, social sciences.

FRESHMAN ADMISSIONS. Selection criteria: Open admissions. Selective admission to nursing program based on placement test and required course work. Dental assistant applicants must be high school graduates.

1992 FRESHMAN CLASS PROFILE. Characteristics: 95% from in state, 100% commute, 5% have minority backgrounds.

FALL-TERM APPLICATIONS. No fee. No closing date; applicants notified on a rolling basis. Early admission available.

STUDENT LIFE. Activities: Student government, radio, student newspaper, choral groups, concert band, drama, jazz band, music ensembles.

ATHLETICS. NJCAA. **Intercollegiate:** Baseball M, basketball, track and field, volleyball W. **Intramural:** Track and field.

STUDENT SERVICES. Aptitude testing, career counseling, employment service for undergraduates, personal counseling, placement service for graduates, services/facilities for handicapped.

ANNUAL EXPENSES. Tuition and fees (1992-93): $900, $1,440 additional for out-of-state students. Rates for foreign students vary. **Books and supplies:** $450. **Other expenses:** $900.

FINANCIAL AID. 80% of continuing students receive some form of aid. 98% of grants, all loans, all jobs based on need. Music/drama, athletic, leadership scholarships available. **Aid applications:** No closing date; priority given to applications received by March 30; applicants notified on a rolling basis beginning on or about May 15.

ADDRESS/TELEPHONE. Patrick Loughary, Dean of College and Student Services, Blue Mountain Community College, PO Box 100, Pendleton, OR 97801. (503) 276-1260. Fax: (503) 276-6119.

Central Oregon Community College

Bend, Oregon CB code: 4090

2-year public community college, coed. Founded in 1949. **Accreditation:** Regional. **Undergraduate enrollment:** 711 men, 722 women full time; 619 men, 1,086 women part time. **Faculty:** 184 total (84 full time), 28 with doctorates or other terminal degrees. **Location:** Rural campus in large town; 150 miles from Portland. **Calendar:** Quarter, limited summer session. **Microcomputers:** 110 located in dormitories, libraries, classrooms, computer centers. **Special facilities:** Art gallery, exercise physiology laboratory.

DEGREES OFFERED. AA, AS, AAS. 186 associate degrees awarded in 1992.

UNDERGRADUATE MAJORS. Accounting, agricultural sciences, allied health, anthropology, automotive mechanics, automotive technology, biological and physical sciences, biology, botany, business administration and management, business and management, business and office, business computer/console/peripheral equipment operation, business data entry equipment operation, business data processing and related programs, business data programming, ceramics, chemistry, communications, computer and information sciences, computer engineering, computer programming, computer servicing technology, computer technology, crafts, criminal justice studies, criminology, data processing, early childhood education, economics, education, education administration, electrical and electronics equipment repair, electrical technology, electrical/electronics/communications engineering, electronic technology, elementary education, engineering, engineering and engineering-related technologies, engineering and other disciplines, English, fine arts, fire control and safety technology, forestry and related sciences, forestry production and processing, French, geography, geology, German, health sciences, history, home economics, hotel/motel and restaurant management, humanities, humanities and social sciences, industrial engineering, industrial technology, information sciences and systems, journalism, junior high education, legal secretary, liberal/general studies, machine tool operation/machine shop, management information systems, management science, manufacturing technology, marketing and distribution, marketing management, mathematics, medical records administration, medical records technology, medical secretary, metal/jewelry, music, nursing, physical sciences, physics, political science and government, practical nursing, precision metal work, predentistry, preengineering, prelaw, premedicine, prepharmacy, preveterinary, protective services, psychology, public affairs, robotics, Russian, science technologies, secondary education, secretarial and related programs, social sciences, social work, sociology, Spanish, special education, teacher aide, visual and performing arts, welding technology, wildlife management, zoology.

ACADEMIC PROGRAMS. 2-year transfer program, cooperative education, double major, dual enrollment of high school students, internships, study abroad. **Remedial services:** Learning center, reduced course load, remedial instruction, special counselor, tutoring. **Placement/credit:** AP, CLEP General and Subject, institutional tests; 69 credit hours maximum for associate degree.

ACADEMIC REQUIREMENTS. To continue in good academic standing, freshmen must earn minimum 2.0 GPA and complete 65% of coursework attempted. 41% of freshmen return for sophomore year. Students must declare major on enrollment. **Graduation requirements:** 93 hours for associate. Most students required to take courses in English, humanities, mathematics, biological/physical sciences, social sciences.

FRESHMAN ADMISSIONS. Selection criteria: Open admissions. Selective admissions for nursing. One unit chemistry required for nursing program.

1992 FRESHMAN CLASS PROFILE. 442 men, 454 women enrolled. **Characteristics:** 80% from in state, 89% commute, 6% have minority backgrounds, 1% are foreign students. Average age is 22.

FALL-TERM APPLICATIONS. No fee. No closing date; priority given to applications received by May 30; applicants notified on a rolling basis beginning on or about January 15. CRDA. Deferred admission available. comparative guidance and placement program test.

STUDENT LIFE. Housing: Dormitories (coed). **Activities:** Student government, student newspaper, choral groups, concert band, dance, drama, jazz band, music ensembles, musical theater, symphony orchestra, wilderness training program.

ATHLETICS. NJCAA. **Intercollegiate:** Cross-country, skiing. **Intramural:** Archery, badminton, basketball, cross-country, football, golf, ice hockey, racquetball, skiing, soccer, softball, swimming, table tennis, tennis, track and field, volleyball.

STUDENT SERVICES. Aptitude testing, career counseling, employment service for undergraduates, freshman orientation, health services, personal counseling, placement service for graduates, special adviser for adult students, veterans counselor, off-campus child care, services/facilities for handicapped.

ANNUAL EXPENSES. Tuition and fees: $1,152, $558 additional for out-of-district students, $3,906 additional for out-of-state students. **Room and board:** $3,360. **Books and supplies:** $650. **Other expenses:** $700.

FINANCIAL AID. 33% of freshmen, 30% of continuing students receive some form of aid. 89% of grants, 85% of loans, all jobs based on need. Academic, music/drama, art, athletic, state/district residency scholarships available. **Aid applications:** No closing date; priority given to applications received by March 1; applicants notified on a rolling basis beginning on or about June 1; within 20 days. **Additional information:** Institution-sponsored short term loans. Extensive part-time student employment.

ADDRESS/TELEPHONE. Christine Kerlin, Director of Admissions, Central Oregon Community College, 2600 Northwest College Way, Bend, OR 97701-5998. (503) 383-7500. Fax: (503) 383-7503.

Chemeketa Community College
Salem, Oregon — CB code: 4745

2-year public community college, coed. Founded in 1962. **Accreditation:** Regional. **Undergraduate enrollment:** 1,347 men, 1,520 women full time; 6,741 men, 7,600 women part time. **Faculty:** 726 total (226 full time). **Location:** Suburban campus in small city; 45 miles from Portland. **Calendar:** Quarter, limited summer session. **Microcomputers:** 315 located in libraries, computer centers.

DEGREES OFFERED. AA, AS, AAS. 490 associate degrees awarded in 1992. 14% in business and management, 8% computer sciences, 8% engineering technologies, 19% allied health, 28% multi/interdisciplinary studies, 5% parks/recreation, protective services, public affairs, 15% trade and industry.

UNDERGRADUATE MAJORS. Accounting, architectural technologies, automotive mechanics, automotive technology, bilingual/bicultural education, business administration and management, business and office, business computer/console/peripheral equipment operation, business data processing and related programs, business data programming, child development/care/guidance, civil engineering, community health work, computer programming, computer servicing technology, computer technology, criminal justice technology, drafting, drafting and design technology, early childhood education, education of the deaf and hearing impaired, education of the emotionally handicapped, education of the mentally handicapped, education of the multiple handicapped, education of the physically handicapped, education of the visually handicapped, electrical and electronics equipment repair, electrical/electronics/communications engineering, electromechanical technology, electronic technology, emergency medical technologies, engineering and engineering-related technologies, finance, fire control and safety technology, fire protection, food management, food production/management/services, forestry and related sciences, gerontology, graphic and printing production, graphic arts technology, human resources development, law enforcement and corrections technologies, legal secretary, liberal/general studies, machine tool operation/machine shop, management science, manufacturing technology, mechanical design technology, medical secretary, mental health/human services, microcomputer software, nursing, office supervision and management, practical nursing, precision metal work, real estate, secretarial and related programs, social work, teacher aide, welding technology.

ACADEMIC PROGRAMS. 2-year transfer program, cooperative education, double major, dual enrollment of high school students, independent study, study abroad. **Remedial services:** Learning center, preadmission summer program, reduced course load, remedial instruction, tutoring. **Placement/credit:** AP, CLEP General and Subject, institutional tests.

ACADEMIC REQUIREMENTS. No policy requiring minimum GPA; records of students having academic difficulty are reviewed individually. 55% of freshmen return for sophomore year. Students must declare major on application. **Graduation requirements:** 93 hours for associate. Most students required to take courses in computer science, English, mathematics.

FRESHMAN ADMISSIONS. Selection criteria: Open admissions. Selective admissions to allied health and emergency services programs. High school diploma or GED tests required for health and fire control applicants.

1992 FRESHMAN CLASS PROFILE. 3,977 men, 4,408 women enrolled. **Characteristics:** 99% from in state, 100% commute, 12% have minority backgrounds, 1% are foreign students. Average age is 25.

FALL-TERM APPLICATIONS. No fee. No closing date; applicants notified on a rolling basis beginning on or about May 20. Interview required for health, fire control, graphic arts applicants. Early admission available.

STUDENT LIFE. Activities: Student government, student newspaper, drama.

ATHLETICS. NJCAA. **Intercollegiate:** Baseball M, basketball, soccer, track and field, volleyball W.

STUDENT SERVICES. Aptitude testing, career counseling, employment service for undergraduates, freshman orientation, on-campus day care, personal counseling, placement service for graduates, special adviser for adult students, veterans counselor, women's adviser (New Workforce), services/facilities for handicapped.

ANNUAL EXPENSES. Tuition and fees: $1,080, $3,024 additional for out-of-state students. **Books and supplies:** $600. **Other expenses:** $840.

FINANCIAL AID. 60% of freshmen, 60% of continuing students receive some form of aid. 97% of grants, 95% of loans, 80% of jobs based on need. Athletic, leadership scholarships available. **Aid applications:** Closing date September 4; priority given to applications received by April 1; applicants notified on a rolling basis beginning on or about June 30; must reply within 2 weeks.

ADDRESS/TELEPHONE. Alan C. Scott, Admissions Specialist, Chemeketa Community College, PO Box 14007, Salem, OR 97309-7070. (503) 399-5006. Fax: (503) 399-3918.

Clackamas Community College
Oregon City, Oregon — CB code: 4111

2-year public community college, coed. Founded in 1966. **Accreditation:** Regional. **Undergraduate enrollment:** 1,254 men, 1,159 women full time; 2,157 men, 2,051 women part time. **Faculty:** 512 total (148 full time), 18 with doctorates or other terminal degrees. **Location:** Suburban campus in small city; 15 miles from Portland. **Calendar:** Quarter, limited summer session. **Microcomputers:** 132 located in libraries, classrooms, computer centers. **Special facilities:** Environmental learning center, observatory.

DEGREES OFFERED. AA, AS, AAS. 346 associate degrees awarded in 1992. 5% in business and management, 12% engineering technologies, 10% health sciences, 58% multi/interdisciplinary studies, 6% parks/recreation, protective services, public affairs.

UNDERGRADUATE MAJORS. Accounting, automotive mechanics, automotive technology, biological and physical sciences, business administration and management, business and management, business and office, criminal justice technology, drafting, drafting and design technology, humanities and social sciences, industrial equipment maintenance and repair, industrial technology, law enforcement and corrections technologies, liberal/general studies, manufacturing technology, nursing, ornamental horticulture, social sciences, water and wastewater technology.

ACADEMIC PROGRAMS. 2-year transfer program, cooperative education, dual enrollment of high school students, honors program, internships, study abroad, visiting/exchange student program. **Remedial services:** Learning center, reduced course load, remedial instruction, special counselor, tutoring. **Placement/credit:** AP, CLEP General and Subject, institutional tests.

ACADEMIC REQUIREMENTS. Freshmen must earn minimum GPA of 2.0 to continue in good standing. 49% of freshmen return for sophomore year. Students must declare major on enrollment. **Graduation requirements:** 93 hours for associate (60 in major). Most students required to take courses in arts/fine arts, computer science, English, foreign languages, history, humanities, mathematics, philosophy/religion, biological/physical sciences, social sciences. **Additional information:** Some occupational technologies offered as self-paced programs.

FRESHMAN ADMISSIONS. Selection criteria: Open admissions. Special prerequisite requirements for nursing and medical assistant. Institutional examination and oral interview required for dispatcher training 911 program.

1992 FRESHMAN CLASS PROFILE. 724 men, 549 women enrolled. **Characteristics:** 99% from in state, 100% commute, 9% have minority backgrounds, 1% are foreign students. Average age is 24.

FALL-TERM APPLICATIONS. No fee. Closing date September 25; applicants notified on a rolling basis. Deferred and early admission available.

STUDENT LIFE. Activities: Student government, student newspaper, daily activities bulletin, choral groups, concert band, dance, drama, jazz band, music ensembles, symphony orchestra, Christian Support Group.

ATHLETICS. NJCAA. **Intercollegiate:** Baseball M, basketball, cross-country, softball W, track and field, volleyball W, wrestling M. **Intramural:** Baseball W, basketball, racquetball, softball W, tennis, volleyball.

STUDENT SERVICES. Aptitude testing, career counseling, employment service for undergraduates, freshman orientation, health services, on-campus day care, personal counseling, placement service for graduates, special adviser for adult students, veterans counselor, services/facilities for handicapped.

ANNUAL EXPENSES. Tuition and fees: $1,170, $2,925 additional for out-of-state students. **Books and supplies:** $600. **Other expenses:** $720.

FINANCIAL AID. 45% of freshmen, 43% of continuing students receive some form of aid. 85% of grants, 94% of loans, all jobs based on need. Academic, music/drama, art, athletic, state/district residency, leadership, minority scholarships available. **Aid applications:** No closing date; priority given to applications received by March 1; applicants notified on a rolling basis beginning on or about May 15; must reply within 3 weeks.

ADDRESS/TELEPHONE. Mary E. Dykes, Director of Admissions and Records, Clackamas Community College, 19600 South Molalla Avenue, Oregon City, OR 97045. (503) 657-6958 ext. 2254. Fax: (503) 655-5153.

Clatsop Community College
Astoria, Oregon CB code: 4089

2-year public community college, coed. Founded in 1958. **Accreditation:** Regional. **Undergraduate enrollment:** 166 men, 276 women full time; 587 men, 1,171 women part time. **Faculty:** 160 total (35 full time), 6 with doctorates or other terminal degrees. **Location:** Rural campus in large town; 100 miles from Portland. **Calendar:** Quarter, limited summer session. Saturday classes. **Microcomputers:** 30 located in classrooms, computer centers. **Special facilities:** 51-foot commercial fishing vessel.

DEGREES OFFERED. AA, AAS. 77 associate degrees awarded in 1992. 5% in agriculture, 11% business and management, 29% health sciences, 42% multi/interdisciplinary studies, 7% parks/recreation, protective services, public affairs, 5% trade and industry.

UNDERGRADUATE MAJORS. Accounting, business and management, business and office, business data processing and related programs, criminal justice technology, fire control and safety technology, industrial technology, liberal/general studies, nursing, secretarial and related programs.

ACADEMIC PROGRAMS. 2-year transfer program, cooperative education, double major, dual enrollment of high school students, student-designed major, telecourses. **Remedial services:** Learning center, reduced course load, remedial instruction, special counselor, tutoring. **Placement/credit:** CLEP General and Subject, institutional tests; 24 credit hours maximum for associate degree.

ACADEMIC REQUIREMENTS. Freshmen must earn minimum GPA of 2.0 to continue in good standing. Students must declare major on application. **Graduation requirements:** 90 hours for associate. Most students required to take courses in computer science, English, mathematics, social sciences.

FRESHMAN ADMISSIONS. Selection criteria: Open admissions. Special admissions requirements for nursing program applicants and international students.

1992 FRESHMAN CLASS PROFILE. 80 men, 113 women enrolled. **Characteristics:** 90% from in state, 100% commute, 3% have minority backgrounds, 1% are foreign students. Average age is 25.

FALL-TERM APPLICATIONS. No fee. No closing date; applicants notified on a rolling basis beginning on or about January 15. CRDA. Deferred and early admission available.

STUDENT LIFE. Activities: Student government, student newspaper, dance, drama, musical theater.

ATHLETICS. Intercollegiate: Fencing. **Intramural:** Basketball, fencing, golf, skiing, tennis, volleyball.

STUDENT SERVICES. Career counseling, employment service for undergraduates, freshman orientation, personal counseling, veterans counselor, services/facilities for handicapped.

ANNUAL EXPENSES. Tuition and fees (projected): $1,350, $4,185 additional for out-of-state students. **Books and supplies:** $660. **Other expenses:** $1,000.

FINANCIAL AID. 67% of freshmen, 55% of continuing students receive some form of aid. 98% of grants, all loans, all jobs based on need. Academic scholarships available. **Aid applications:** No closing date; priority given to applications received by March 1; applicants notified on a rolling basis beginning on or about June 1; must reply within 3 weeks.

ADDRESS/TELEPHONE. Linda Oldenkamp, Director of Admissions, Clatsop Community College, 16th and Jerome, Astoria, OR 97103. (503) 325-0910 ext. 2211. Fax: (503) 325-5738.

Concordia College
Portland, Oregon CB code: 4079

Admissions: 73% of applicants accepted
Based on:
••• School record, test scores
•• Interview, recommendations
• Activities, essay, religious affiliation/commitment, special talents
Completion: 70% of freshmen end year in good standing

4-year private liberal arts college, coed, affiliated with Lutheran Church—Missouri Synod. Founded in 1905. **Accreditation:** Regional. **Undergraduate enrollment:** 381 men, 410 women full time; 95 men, 180 women part time. **Faculty:** 83 total (41 full time), 33 with doctorates or other terminal degrees. **Location:** Suburban campus in large city; 5 miles from downtown. **Calendar:** Quarter, limited summer session. **Microcomputers:** 30 located in libraries, classrooms, computer centers. **Additional facts:** About 10% of students preparing for full-time service in Lutheran Church—Missouri Synod. 45% of freshmen are Lutheran.

DEGREES OFFERED. AA, BA, BS. 2 associate degrees awarded in 1992. 100% in business and management. 226 bachelor's degrees awarded. 50% in business and management, 30% teacher education, 10% health sciences, 8% multi/interdisciplinary studies.

UNDERGRADUATE MAJORS. Associate: Business administration and management, business and management, liberal/general studies, resident aid training for mentally handicapped. **Bachelor's:** Biology, business administration and management, business and management, chemistry, elementary education, fine arts, health care administration, health care/social work, human resources development, international business management, junior high education, liberal/general studies, marketing management, marketing research, psychology, religion, secondary education, small business management and ownership, social work.

ACADEMIC PROGRAMS. Accelerated program, double major, independent study, internships, study abroad, teacher preparation, cross-registration; liberal arts/career combination in health sciences. **Remedial services:** Learning center, reduced course load, remedial instruction, tutoring. **Placement/credit:** AP, CLEP General and Subject, institutional tests.

ACADEMIC REQUIREMENTS. Freshmen must earn minimum GPA of 1.65 to continue in good standing. 68% of freshmen return for sophomore year. Students must declare major by end of second year. **Graduation requirements:** 93 hours for associate (40 in major), 185 hours for bachelor's (65 in major). Most students required to take courses in arts/fine arts, computer science, English, humanities, mathematics, philosophy/religion, biological/physical sciences, social sciences. **Postgraduate studies:** 90% from 2-year programs enter 4-year programs.

FRESHMAN ADMISSIONS. Selection criteria: 2.5 high school GPA required or verbal SAT greater than 400. Recommended units include English 4, foreign language 2, mathematics 3, social science 3 and science 3. One music/art also recommended. **Test requirements:** SAT or ACT (SAT preferred); score report by September 1. Washington Pre-College Test scores accepted from Washington State residents.

1992 FRESHMAN CLASS PROFILE. 311 men and women applied, 226 accepted; 41 men enrolled, 59 women enrolled. 53% had high school GPA of 3.0 or higher, 45% between 2.0 and 2.99. 10% were in top tenth and 31% were in top quarter of graduating class. **Academic background:** Mid 50% of enrolled freshmen had SAT-V between 380-500, SAT-M between 410-560. 66% submitted SAT scores. **Characteristics:** 46% from in state, 70% live in college housing, 18% have minority backgrounds, 4% are foreign students. Average age is 18.

FALL-TERM APPLICATIONS. No fee. Closing date September 1; applicants notified on a rolling basis. Interview recommended. Deferred admission available.

STUDENT LIFE. Housing: Dormitories (men, women, coed). School rents nearby houses to married students and maintains a referral file. Homestay option for international students. **Activities:** Student government, film, yearbook, literary journal, choral groups, drama, music ensembles, social service organization, achievers club, Chi Beta Chi, Amnesty International, Students in Free Enterprise, Circle K. **Additional information:** Optional attendance for chapel services. Lutheran format and mixture of traditional and contemporary services offered.

ATHLETICS. NAIA. **Intercollegiate:** Baseball M, basketball, soccer M, softball W, volleyball W. **Intramural:** Badminton, basketball, golf, skiing, soccer M, softball, table tennis, tennis, volleyball. **Clubs:** Skiing.

STUDENT SERVICES. Career counseling, freshman orientation, health services, personal counseling.

ANNUAL EXPENSES. Tuition and fees: $9,300. **Room and board:** $3,000. **Books and supplies:** $500. **Other expenses:** $900.

FINANCIAL AID. 90% of freshmen, 75% of continuing students receive some form of aid. 79% of grants, 75% of loans, 73% of jobs based on need. 93 enrolled freshmen were judged to have need, all were offered aid. Academic, music/drama, athletic, religious affiliation scholarships available. **Aid applications:** No closing date; priority given to applications received by May 1; applicants notified on a rolling basis beginning on or about April 1; must reply by May 1 or within 3 weeks if notified thereafter.

ADDRESS/TELEPHONE. William H. Balke, Vice President, Admissions/Student Services, Concordia College, 2811 Northeast Holman, Portland, OR 97211-6099. (503) 288-9371. (800) 321-9371. Fax: (503) 280-8531.

Eastern Oregon State College
LaGrande, Oregon CB code: 4300

Admissions: 97% of applicants accepted
Based on: ••• School record
•• Essay, test scores
• Recommendations
Completion: 79% of freshmen end year in good standing
30% graduate, 10% of these enter graduate study

4-year public liberal arts college, coed. Founded in 1929. **Accreditation:** Regional. **Undergraduate enrollment:** 867 men, 951 women full time; 150 men, 150 women part time. **Graduate enrollment:** 12 men, 13 women full time; 1 woman part time. **Faculty:** 217 total (164 full time), 69 with doctorates or other terminal degrees. **Location:** Rural campus in large town; 260 miles from Portland, 180 miles from Boise, Idaho. **Calendar:** Quarter, limited summer session. **Microcomputers:** 78 located in dormitories, libraries, classrooms, computer centers. **Special facilities:** Anthropology museum, art gallery, wildlife habitat laboratory, education laboratory school.

DEGREES OFFERED. AS, BA, BS, M. 14 associate degrees awarded in 1992. 78% in business/office and marketing/distribution, 22% multi/interdisciplinary studies. 473 bachelor's degrees awarded. 16% in business and management, 5% teacher education, 5% life sciences, 48% multi/interdisciplinary studies, 5% psychology. Graduate degrees offered in 2 major fields of study.

UNDERGRADUATE MAJORS. Associate: Liberal/general studies, secretarial and related programs. **Bachelor's:** Agricultural business and management, agricultural economics, anthropology, biology, business economics, chemistry, dramatic arts, elementary education, English, fine arts, fire protection, geography and regional sciences, health sciences, history, liberal/general studies, mathematics, music, nursing, physical education, physics, predentistry, premedicine, prepharmacy, preveterinary, psychology, range management, secondary education, sociology, soil sciences.

ACADEMIC PROGRAMS. Accelerated program, cooperative education, double major, dual enrollment of high school students, external degree, independent study, internships, student-designed major, study abroad, teacher preparation, telecourses, visiting/exchange student program, weekend college, cross-registration; liberal arts/career combination in engineering, health sciences. **Remedial services:** Learning center, preadmission summer program, reduced course load, remedial instruction, special counselor, tutoring, special programs for Native American and Micronesian students. **Placement/credit:** AP, CLEP General and Subject, institutional tests; 45 credit hours maximum for bachelor's degree.

ACADEMIC REQUIREMENTS. Freshmen must earn minimum GPA of 2.5 to continue in good standing. 58% of freshmen return for sophomore year. Students must declare major by end of second year. **Graduation requirements:** 93 hours for associate, 186 hours for bachelor's. Most students required to take courses in arts/fine arts, English, humanities, mathematics, biological/physical sciences, social sciences. **Postgraduate studies:** 1% enter law school, 1% enter medical school, 1% enter MBA programs, 7% enter other graduate study.

FRESHMAN ADMISSIONS. Selection criteria: High school GPA of 2.0 required for regional residents (2.5 for out-of-district and out-of-state residents), or SAT combined score of 890, or ACT composite score of 21. Limited number of students not meeting requirements may be admitted. Students admitted on space available basis after August 1. **High school preparation:** 14 units required. Required units include English 4, mathematics 3, social science 3 and science 2. Science requirement includes 1 laboratory science. **Test requirements:** SAT or ACT (SAT preferred); score report by September 10. ACH required of students who do not meet high school subject requirements. Score report by September 10 Test of Standard Written English required for applicants taking ACT.

1992 FRESHMAN CLASS PROFILE. 595 men and women applied, 579 accepted; 191 men enrolled, 198 women enrolled. 56% had high school GPA of 3.0 or higher, 42% between 2.0 and 2.99. **Academic background:** Mid 50% of enrolled freshmen had SAT-V between 340-460, SAT-M between 370-510. 96% submitted SAT scores. **Characteristics:** 74% from in state, 25% live in college housing, 15% have minority backgrounds, 7% are foreign students. Average age is 18.

FALL-TERM APPLICATIONS. $40 fee. Closing date September 10; priority given to applications received by August 1; applicants notified on a rolling basis. Interview recommended for special admission applicants. Deferred and early admission available.

STUDENT LIFE. Housing: Dormitories (men, women, coed); apartment housing available. **Activities:** Student government, magazine, radio, student newspaper, choral groups, concert band, drama, jazz band, music ensembles, musical theater, pep band, symphony orchestra, over 60 campus organizations.

ATHLETICS. NAIA. **Intercollegiate:** Baseball M, basketball, cross-country, football M, skiing, track and field, volleyball W. **Intramural:** Badminton, basketball, racquetball, rifle, soccer, softball, swimming, tennis, volleyball.

STUDENT SERVICES. Aptitude testing, career counseling, employment service for undergraduates, freshman orientation, health services, personal counseling, placement service for graduates, veterans counselor, services/facilities for handicapped.

ANNUAL EXPENSES. Tuition and fees (1992-93): $2,445. **Room and board:** $3,200. **Books and supplies:** $450. **Other expenses:** $900.

FINANCIAL AID. 80% of freshmen, 75% of continuing students receive some form of aid. 86% of grants, 87% of loans, all jobs based on need. 285 enrolled freshmen were judged to have need, all were offered aid. Academic, music/drama, state/district residency, leadership, minority scholarships available. **Aid applications:** No closing date; applicants notified on a rolling basis; must reply within 3 weeks.

ADDRESS/TELEPHONE. Terral Schut, Director of Admissions/New Student Programs, Eastern Oregon State College, 1410 L Avenue, LaGrande, OR 97850-2899. (503) 962-3393. Fax: (503) 962-3849.

Eugene Bible College
Eugene, Oregon CB code: 4274

Admissions: 65% of applicants accepted
Based on: ••• Essay, recommendations, religious affiliation/commitment, school record
•• Activities, interview, test scores
• Special talents
Completion: 57% of freshmen end year in good standing
48% graduate, 25% of these enter graduate study

4-year private Bible college, coed, affiliated with Open Bible Standard Churches. Founded in 1925. **Undergraduate enrollment:** 94 men, 74 women full time; 15 men, 12 women part time. **Faculty:** 20 total (12 full time). **Location:** Urban campus in small city; 100 miles from Portland. **Calendar:** Quarter, limited summer session. **Microcomputers:** Located in computer centers.

DEGREES OFFERED. BA, BS. 20 bachelor's degrees awarded in 1992. 100% in philosophy, religion, theology.

UNDERGRADUATE MAJORS. Bible studies, missionary studies, religious education, religious music, theological studies.

ACADEMIC PROGRAMS. Independent study, internships. **Remedial services:** Tutoring. **Placement/credit:** Institutional tests.

ACADEMIC REQUIREMENTS. Freshmen must earn minimum GPA of 1.7 to continue in good standing. 60% of freshmen return for sophomore year. Students must declare major on enrollment. **Graduation requirements:** 187 hours for bachelor's (51 in major). Most students required to take courses in English, history, philosophy/religion, biological/physical sciences, social sciences.

FRESHMAN ADMISSIONS. Selection criteria: School achievement, test scores, and religious affiliation or commitment considered. **Test requirements:** SAT or ACT (SAT preferred); score report by September 1.

1992 FRESHMAN CLASS PROFILE. 88 men applied, 56 accepted, 37 enrolled; 74 women applied, 50 accepted, 37 enrolled. 43% had high school GPA of 3.0 or higher, 57% between 2.0 and 2.99. **Academic background:** Mid 50% of enrolled freshmen had SAT-V between 340-500, SAT-M between 320-510; ACT composite between 19-22. 90% submitted SAT scores, 10% submitted ACT scores. **Characteristics:** 55% from in state, 65% live in college housing, 7% have minority backgrounds. Average age is 21.

FALL-TERM APPLICATIONS. $25 fee. Closing date September 1; applicants notified on a rolling basis. Essay required. Interview recommended. Deferred admission available.

STUDENT LIFE. Housing: Dormitories (men, women); apartment housing available. **Activities:** Student government, yearbook, choral groups, drama, music ensembles, pep band, missions organizations. **Additional information:** Campus leadership roles provide opportunities for students to learn ministry skills. Religious observance required.

ATHLETICS. Intercollegiate: Basketball M. **Intramural:** Basketball M, football M, soccer M, volleyball.

STUDENT SERVICES. Aptitude testing, career counseling, employment service for undergraduates, freshman orientation, health services, personal counseling, placement service for graduates, veterans counselor, services/facilities for handicapped.

ANNUAL EXPENSES. Tuition and fees (projected): $4,020. **Room and board:** $2,610. **Books and supplies:** $600. **Other expenses:** $500.

FINANCIAL AID. 80% of freshmen, 75% of continuing students re-

ceive some form of aid. 99% of grants, 78% of loans, all jobs based on need. 28 enrolled freshmen were judged to have need, all were offered aid. Academic, music/drama, religious affiliation scholarships available. **Aid applications:** Closing date September 1; priority given to applications received by April 15; applicants notified on a rolling basis beginning on or about July 1; must reply within 4 weeks.

ADDRESS/TELEPHONE. Trent Combs, Director of Admissions, Eugene Bible College, 2155 Bailey Hill Road, Eugene, OR 97405. (503) 485-1780. (800) 322-2638. Fax: (503) 343-5801.

George Fox College
Newberg, Oregon — CB code: 4325

Admissions: 88% of applicants accepted
Based on:
- ••• School record, test scores
- •• Essay, recommendations
- • Activities, interview, religious affiliation/commitment, special talents

Completion: 93% of freshmen end year in good standing
48% graduate, 36% of these enter graduate study

4-year private liberal arts college, coed, affiliated with Northwest Yearly Meeting of Friends Church (Quaker). Founded in 1891. **Accreditation:** Regional. **Undergraduate enrollment:** 492 men, 721 women full time; 20 men, 17 women part time. **Graduate enrollment:** 56 men, 45 women full time; 56 men, 28 women part time. **Faculty:** 133 total (70 full time), 41 with doctorates or other terminal degrees. **Location:** Suburban campus in large town; 23 miles from Portland. **Calendar:** Semester. **Microcomputers:** 1,000 located in dormitories, libraries, classrooms, computer centers. Lease or purchase required**Special facilities:** Retreat center, Quaker museum, Quaker library.

DEGREES OFFERED. BA, BS, MA, MBA, D. 270 bachelor's degrees awarded in 1992. 19% in business and management, 8% communications, 21% teacher education, 5% letters/literature, 6% life sciences, 11% psychology, 8% social sciences, 9% visual and performing arts. Graduate degrees offered in 11 major fields of study.

UNDERGRADUATE MAJORS. American literature, Bible studies, biology, business and management, business economics, chemistry, civil engineering, communications, computer and information sciences, computer engineering, creative writing, electrical/electronics/communications engineering, elementary education, engineering, English education, English literature, history, home economics, home economics education, human resources development, international relations, international studies, liberal/general studies, mathematics, mathematics education, mechanical engineering, music, music education, music performance, physical education, predentistry, prelaw, premedicine, prepharmacy, preveterinary, psychology, radio/television technology, religion, science education, secondary education, social sciences, social studies education, social work, sociology, sports medicine, telecommunications, theological studies.

ACADEMIC PROGRAMS. Double major, dual enrollment of high school students, honors program, independent study, internships, student-designed major, study abroad, teacher preparation, visiting/exchange student program, Washington semester, cross-registration. **Remedial services:** Learning center, remedial instruction, special counselor, tutoring. **Placement/credit:** AP, CLEP General and Subject, IB, institutional tests; 32 credit hours maximum for bachelor's degree.

ACADEMIC REQUIREMENTS. Freshmen must earn minimum GPA of 2.1 to continue in good standing. 83% of freshmen return for sophomore year. Students must declare major by end of second year. **Graduation requirements:** 126 hours for bachelor's (40 in major). Most students required to take courses in English, history, humanities, mathematics, philosophy/religion, biological/physical sciences, social sciences. **Postgraduate studies:** 3% enter law school, 5% enter medical school, 7% enter MBA programs, 21% enter other graduate study.

FRESHMAN ADMISSIONS. Selection criteria: 75% of decision based on grade transcript, test scores, recommendations from teacher and counselor; 25% based on church, school, and community activities. **High school preparation:** 16 units recommended. Recommended units include English 4, foreign language 2, mathematics 2, social science 2 and science 3. **Test requirements:** SAT or ACT; score report by August 1.

1992 FRESHMAN CLASS PROFILE. 245 men applied, 211 accepted, 106 enrolled; 384 women applied, 340 accepted, 175 enrolled. 79% had high school GPA of 3.0 or higher, 21% between 2.0 and 2.99. **Academic background:** Mid 50% of enrolled freshmen had SAT-V between 410-570, SAT-M between 420-570. 85% submitted SAT scores. **Characteristics:** 59% from in state, 96% live in college housing, 4% have minority backgrounds, 17% are foreign students. Average age is 19.

FALL-TERM APPLICATIONS. $20 fee, may be waived for applicants with need. Closing date July 15; priority given to applications received by May 1; applicants notified on a rolling basis; must reply by May 1 or within 2 weeks if notified thereafter. Essay required. Interview recommended. Audition recommended for music, drama applicants. CRDA. Deferred and early admission available.

STUDENT LIFE. Housing: Dormitories (men, women); apartment housing available. **Activities:** Student government, radio, student newspaper, television, yearbook, student bulletin, choral groups, concert band, drama, jazz band, music ensembles, musical theater, pep band, chamber orchestra, stage band, Quaker Fellowship, Student Christian Union, Christian Service Committee. **Additional information:** Religious observance required.

ATHLETICS. NAIA. **Intercollegiate:** Baseball M, basketball, cross-country, soccer, softball W, track and field, volleyball W. **Intramural:** Badminton, basketball, handball, racquetball, table tennis, tennis, volleyball.

STUDENT SERVICES. Aptitude testing, career counseling, employment service for undergraduates, freshman orientation, health services, personal counseling, placement service for graduates, veterans counselor, services/facilities for handicapped.

ANNUAL EXPENSES. Tuition and fees: $11,740. **Room and board:** $3,890. **Books and supplies:** $400. **Other expenses:** $800.

FINANCIAL AID. 86% of freshmen, 83% of continuing students receive some form of aid. 29% of grants, 94% of loans, 82% of jobs based on need. 216 enrolled freshmen were judged to have need, 215 were offered aid. Academic, music/drama, athletic, state/district residency, leadership, religious affiliation, minority scholarships available. **Aid applications:** Closing date August 1; priority given to applications received by March 1; applicants notified on a rolling basis beginning on or about April 1; must reply by May 1 or within 3 weeks if notified thereafter. **Additional information:** Audition required for music and drama scholarships.

ADDRESS/TELEPHONE. Randall C. Comfort, Director of Admissions, George Fox College, 414 North Meridian, Newberg, OR 97132-9987. (503) 538-8383 ext. 234. Fax: (503) 538-7234.

ITT Technical Institute: Portland
Portland, Oregon — CB code: 0947

3-year proprietary technical college, coed. Founded in 1979. **Undergraduate enrollment:** 531 men, 64 women full time. **Faculty:** 31 total (27 full time), 1 with doctorate or other terminal degree. **Location:** Suburban campus in large city; 10 miles east of downtown. **Calendar:** Quarter, extensive summer session. **Microcomputers:** 80 located in libraries, classrooms, computer centers. Lease or purchase required**Additional facts:** Extension in Spokane.

DEGREES OFFERED. AAS, BA. 150 associate degrees awarded in 1992. 100% in engineering technologies. 60 bachelor's degrees awarded. 100% in engineering technologies.

UNDERGRADUATE MAJORS. Associate: Drafting and design technology, electronic technology, engineering and engineering-related technologies. **Bachelor's:** Manufacturing technology.

ACADEMIC PROGRAMS. Honors program. **Remedial services:** Learning center, tutoring, Preparatory courses in mathematics and algebra. **Placement/credit:** Institutional tests; 30 credit hours maximum for associate degree; 30 credit hours maximum for bachelor's degree.

ACADEMIC REQUIREMENTS. Freshmen must earn minimum GPA of 2.0 to continue in good standing. 70% of freshmen return for sophomore year. Students must declare major on application. **Graduation requirements:** Most students required to take courses in computer science, mathematics. **Postgraduate studies:** 18% from 2-year programs enter 4-year programs. 10% enter MBA programs.

FRESHMAN ADMISSIONS. Selection criteria: Institutional test scores very important. One unit algebra required. **Test requirements:** SRA Arithmetic Index, SRA Reading Index required of electronics applicants.

1992 FRESHMAN CLASS PROFILE. 282 men, 32 women enrolled. **Characteristics:** 4% have minority backgrounds. Average age is 22.

FALL-TERM APPLICATIONS. $100 fee. Application fee refunded if student not accepted. Closing date September 11; applicants notified on a rolling basis. Interview required. Deferred admission available.

STUDENT LIFE. Activities: Student government, student newspaper, computer club, student chapter of Society of Manufacturing Engineers.

ATHLETICS. Intramural: Baseball M, basketball M, bowling, golf, softball, volleyball.

STUDENT SERVICES. Career counseling, employment service for undergraduates, freshman orientation, personal counseling, placement service for graduates, veterans counselor, services/facilities for handicapped.

ANNUAL EXPENSES. Tuition and fees (1992-93): Tuition for 12-month period ranges from $7,202 to $8,545, depending on course of study. **Books and supplies:** $900.

FINANCIAL AID. 95% of freshmen, 95% of continuing students receive some form of aid. **Aid applications:** Closing date September 11; applicants notified on a rolling basis.

ADDRESS/TELEPHONE. Jack Kempt, Director of Recruitment, ITT Technical Institute: Portland, 6035 Northeast 78th Court, Portland, OR 97218-2854. (503) 255-6500. (800) 234-5488. Fax: (503) 255-6135.

Lane Community College
Eugene, Oregon — CB code: 4407

2-year public community college, coed. Founded in 1964. **Accreditation:**

Regional. **Undergraduate enrollment:** 2,069 men, 1,868 women full time; 3,018 men, 3,617 women part time. **Faculty:** 484 total (283 full time), 26 with doctorates or other terminal degrees. **Location:** Suburban campus in small city; 110 miles from Portland. **Calendar:** Quarter, extensive summer session. **Microcomputers:** 275 located in computer centers. **Additional facts:** Outreach centers in downtown Eugene, Cottage Grove, and Florence.

DEGREES OFFERED. AA, AS, AAS. 451 associate degrees awarded in 1992. 21% in business/office and marketing/distribution, 8% engineering technologies, 23% health sciences, 5% home economics, 10% multi/interdisciplinary studies, 8% parks/recreation, protective services, public affairs, 17% trade and industry.

UNDERGRADUATE MAJORS. Agricultural mechanics, air conditioning/heating/refrigeration mechanics, aircraft mechanics, airline piloting and navigation, automotive mechanics, business and management, business computer/console/peripheral equipment operation, business data programming, child development/care/guidance, computer and information sciences, construction, criminal justice studies, dental hygiene, diesel engine mechanics, drafting, electrical and electronics equipment repair, finance, fire control and safety technology, food production/management/services, graphic design, hotel/motel and restaurant management, industrial equipment maintenance and repair, industrial technology, laboratory technology, liberal/general studies, machine tool operation/machine shop, nursing, office supervision and management, radio/television broadcasting, radio/television technology, real estate, respiratory therapy technology, secretarial and related programs, social sciences, welding technology.

ACADEMIC PROGRAMS. 2-year transfer program, dual enrollment of high school students, independent study, internships, study abroad, telecourses, weekend college, cross-registration. **Remedial services:** Learning center, preadmission summer program, remedial instruction, special counselor, tutoring. **Placement/credit:** AP, CLEP General and Subject, institutional tests; 48 credit hours maximum for associate degree.

ACADEMIC REQUIREMENTS. Freshmen must earn minimum GPA of 2.0 to continue in good standing. 47% of freshmen return for sophomore year. Students must declare major on application. **Graduation requirements:** 93 hours for associate. Most students required to take courses in English, humanities, mathematics, biological/physical sciences, social sciences.

FRESHMAN ADMISSIONS. Selection criteria: Open admissions. Selective admissions to allied health and flight technology programs. **Test requirements:** Sequential Tests of Educational Progress for dental applicants, School and College Ability Tests for nursing applicants, and Nelson-Denny Reading Test for dental and medical assistant applicants.

1992 FRESHMAN CLASS PROFILE. 1,800 men, 1,821 women enrolled. **Characteristics:** 96% from in state, 100% commute, 8% have minority backgrounds, 3% are foreign students. Average age is 27.

FALL-TERM APPLICATIONS. No fee. No closing date; applicants notified on a rolling basis. CRDA. Early admission available.

STUDENT LIFE. Activities: Student government, magazine, radio, student newspaper, choral groups, concert band, dance, drama, jazz band, music ensembles, musical theater, Ospirg, Campus Ministry.

ATHLETICS. Intercollegiate: Basketball, track and field, volleyball W. **Intramural:** Baseball M, cross-country, volleyball.

STUDENT SERVICES. Aptitude testing, career counseling, employment service for undergraduates, freshman orientation, health services, on-campus day care, personal counseling, placement service for graduates, veterans counselor, services/facilities for handicapped.

ANNUAL EXPENSES. Tuition and fees (1992-93): $1,108, $2,925 additional for out-of-state students. **Books and supplies:** $795. **Other expenses:** $1,800.

FINANCIAL AID. 22% of freshmen, 22% of continuing students receive some form of aid. 96% of grants, 96% of loans, all jobs based on need. 1,672 enrolled freshmen were judged to have need, all were offered aid. Academic, music/drama, athletic, state/district residency, leadership scholarships available. **Aid applications:** No closing date; priority given to applications received by March 15; applicants notified on a rolling basis beginning on or about April 1; must reply within 2 weeks.

ADDRESS/TELEPHONE. Sharon Moore, Director of Admissions, Lane Community College, 4000 East 30th Avenue, Eugene, OR 97405. (503) 726-2207. Fax: (503) 747-1229.

Lewis and Clark College

Portland, Oregon — CB code: 4384

Admissions: 72% of applicants accepted
Based on:
- ••• School record
- •• Activities, essay, recommendations, special talents, test scores
- • Interview

Completion: 84% of freshmen end year in good standing
66% graduate

4-year private college of arts and sciences and liberal arts college, coed, affiliated with Presbyterian Church (USA). Founded in 1867. **Accreditation:** Regional. **Undergraduate enrollment:** 761 men, 944 women full time; 28 men, 34 women part time. **Faculty:** 155 total (122 full time), 127 with doctorates or other terminal degrees. **Location:** Suburban campus in large city; 5 miles from downtown. **Calendar:** Quarter, limited summer session. **Microcomputers:** 200 located in dormitories, libraries, computer centers. **Special facilities:** Theater with 2 stages, concert hall, observatory, 300-MHz Fourier-Transform Nuclear Magnetic Resonance variable temperature cryostat and super-conducting magnet, 5 super mac color graphics systems for digital video editing. **Additional facts:** More than 50% of students participate in one or more overseas programs before graduation.

DEGREES OFFERED. BA, BS, MA, MS, MEd, JD. 510 bachelor's degrees awarded in 1992. 9% in business and management, 8% communications, 5% languages, 10% letters/literature, 9% life sciences, 10% psychology, 29% social sciences, 7% visual and performing arts. Graduate degrees offered in 11 major fields of study.

UNDERGRADUATE MAJORS. Anthropology, art history, biochemistry, biological and physical sciences, biology, business administration and management, chemistry, communications, computer mathematics, dramatic arts, economics, English, fine arts, foreign languages (multiple emphasis), French, German, history, international relations, international studies, mathematics, music, music history and appreciation, philosophy, physics, political science and government, psychology, religion, sociology, Spanish.

ACADEMIC PROGRAMS. Accelerated program, double major, honors program, independent study, internships, student-designed major, study abroad, teacher preparation, New York semester, Washington semester, cross-registration; liberal arts/career combination in engineering. **Remedial services:** Reduced course load, special counselor, tutoring, writing and mathematics skills centers. **Placement/credit:** AP, IB, institutional tests; 50 credit hours maximum for bachelor's degree.

ACADEMIC REQUIREMENTS. Freshmen must earn minimum GPA of 2.0 to continue in good standing. 76% of freshmen return for sophomore year. Students must declare major by end of second year. **Graduation requirements:** 185 hours for bachelor's (60 in major). Most students required to take courses in arts/fine arts, English, foreign languages, humanities, mathematics, biological/physical sciences, social sciences. **Additional information:** Since 1962, more than 6000 students and 139 faculty members have participated in 309 study programs in 57 countries.

FRESHMAN ADMISSIONS. Selection criteria: School curriculum and achievement most important. Standardized tests recommendations, extracurricular involvement, essay and interview also considered. Recommended units include English 4, foreign language 2, mathematics 3 and social science 3. One unit fine arts recommended, 2-3 units laboratory science. **Test requirements:** SAT or ACT; score report by March 1. Scores optional for applicants using Portfolio Path, which requires 2 additional teacher recommendations and 3 to 5 samples of writing and graded work.

1992 FRESHMAN CLASS PROFILE. 1,112 men applied, 704 accepted, 164 enrolled; 1,405 women applied, 1,109 accepted, 245 enrolled. 84% had high school GPA of 3.0 or higher, 16% between 2.0 and 2.99. 37% were in top tenth and 66% were in top quarter of graduating class. **Academic background:** Mid 50% of enrolled freshmen had SAT-V between 480-580, SAT-M between 520-620; ACT composite between 24-29. 80% submitted SAT scores, 33% submitted ACT scores. **Characteristics:** 27% from in state, 92% live in college housing, 12% have minority backgrounds, 5% are foreign students, 1% join fraternities/sororities. Average age is 18.

FALL-TERM APPLICATIONS. $40 fee, may be waived for applicants with need. No closing date; priority given to applications received by February 1; applicants notified on or about April 1; must reply by May 1. Essay required. Interview recommended. CRDA. Deferred admission available. EDP-F; institutional early decision plan. Early Action Application Plan, due date December 15, nonbinding, students have until May 1 to make decision. Early Decision, due November 15, binding, deposit due January 1.

STUDENT LIFE. Housing: Dormitories (women, coed); handicapped housing available. Upperclass dormitory , foreign language floor available. **Activities:** Student government, film, magazine, radio, student newspaper, television, yearbook, student cross-cultural journal, literature review journal, choral groups, concert band, dance, drama, jazz band, music ensembles, musical theater, symphony orchestra, fraternities, volunteer service group, international affairs association, Halutzim (Jewish student union), Fellowship of Christian Athletes, Students United for American Cultural Awareness, Community Service Center, Hawaii Club, OSPIRG, Amnesty International, SISCAP (Students in Solidarity with Central American Peoples), Black Student Union. **Additional information:** Over 90% of students take advantage of college outdoors programs. All students eat in common dining room. Campus activities include films, lectures, concerts, plays, coffee houses.

ATHLETICS. NAIA. **Intercollegiate:** Baseball M, basketball, cross-country, football M, golf M, softball W, swimming, tennis, track and field, volleyball W. **Intramural:** Badminton, basketball, racquetball, soccer, softball, squash, tennis, volleyball, water polo. **Clubs:** Fencing, lacrosse, rowing, rugby, sailing, skiing, soccer.

STUDENT SERVICES. Career counseling, employment service for undergraduates, freshman orientation, health services, personal counseling, placement service for graduates, special adviser for adult students, veterans counselor, services/facilities for handicapped.

ANNUAL EXPENSES. Tuition and fees: $15,051. **Room and board:** $4,929. **Books and supplies:** $300. **Other expenses:** $750.

FINANCIAL AID. 76% of freshmen, 76% of continuing students receive some form of aid. Grants, loans, jobs available. Academic, music/drama, leadership scholarships available. **Aid applications:** No closing date; priority given to applications received by February 15; applicants notified on a rolling basis beginning on or about April 1; must reply by May 1 or within 2 weeks if notified thereafter.

ADDRESS/TELEPHONE. Michael B. Sexton, Dean of Admissions, Lewis and Clark College, LC Box 32, Portland, OR 97219-7899. (503) 768-7040. (800) 444-4111. Fax: (503) 768-7055.

Linfield College
McMinnville, Oregon — CB code: 4387

Admissions: 84% of applicants accepted
Based on:
- ••• School record
- •• Activities, essay, recommendations, special talents, test scores
- • Interview

Completion: 98% of freshmen end year in good standing
56% graduate, 16% of these enter graduate study

4-year private college of arts and sciences and liberal arts college, coed, affiliated with American Baptist Churches in the USA. Founded in 1849. **Accreditation:** Regional. **Undergraduate enrollment:** 635 men, 826 women full time; 20 men, 50 women part time. **Graduate enrollment:** 12 men, 17 women full time; 10 men, 36 women part time. **Faculty:** 113 total (99 full time), 105 with doctorates or other terminal degrees. **Location:** Suburban campus in large town; 38 miles from Portland. **Calendar:** 4-1-4, limited summer session. **Microcomputers:** 150 located in dormitories, computer centers. **Special facilities:** Art gallery, field station, wilderness cabin, observatory, research institute, aquatic center, microprobe scanner. **Additional facts:** Semester abroad for sophomores, juniors, seniors (with one year of language) at Linfield centers in England.

DEGREES OFFERED. BA, BS, MEd. 467 bachelor's degrees awarded in 1992. 39% in business and management, 8% education, 16% health sciences, 11% letters/literature, 8% social sciences. Graduate degrees offered in 3 major fields of study.

UNDERGRADUATE MAJORS. Accounting, anthropology, applied physics-electronics, art education, arts management, biology, business administration and management, business and management, business systems analysis, chemistry, clinical laboratory science, communications, computer and information sciences, creative writing, dramatic arts, early childhood education, economics, education, elementary education, engineering physics, English, finance, fine arts, French, German, health education, health sciences, history, international business management, journalism, junior high education, liberal/general studies, mathematics, mechanical engineering, music, music education, music performance, music theory and composition, nursing, philosophy, physical education, physical sciences, physics, political science and government, predentistry, prelaw, premedicine, preveterinary, psychology, radio/television broadcasting, religion, secondary education, sociology, Spanish, sports medicine, systems analysis.

ACADEMIC PROGRAMS. Accelerated program, cooperative education, double major, dual enrollment of high school students, external degree, honors program, independent study, internships, semester at sea, student-designed major, study abroad, teacher preparation, visiting/exchange student program, Washington semester, cross-registration, off-campus program for working adults; liberal arts/career combination in engineering, forestry, health sciences. **Remedial services:** Learning center, reduced course load, remedial instruction, special counselor, tutoring, writing center. **ROTC:** Air Force. **Placement/credit:** AP, CLEP General and Subject, institutional tests; 30 credit hours maximum for bachelor's degree.

ACADEMIC REQUIREMENTS. Freshmen must earn minimum GPA of 2.0 to continue in good standing. 76% of freshmen return for sophomore year. Students must declare major by end of second year. **Graduation requirements:** 125 hours for bachelor's (40 in major). Most students required to take courses in arts/fine arts, English, foreign languages, history, humanities, mathematics, philosophy/religion, biological/physical sciences, social sciences. **Postgraduate studies:** 2% enter law school, 3% enter medical school, 2% enter MBA programs, 9% enter other graduate study.

FRESHMAN ADMISSIONS. Selection criteria: High school grades, official transcripts, counselor's recommendation, 1 faculty recommendation, test scores, and written essays considered. **High school preparation:** 15 units recommended. Recommended units include biological science 2, English 4, foreign language 2, mathematics 2, physical science 2 and social science 3. **Test requirements:** SAT or ACT; score report by August 15. Applicants from Washington State may submit Washington Pre-College Test.

1992 FRESHMAN CLASS PROFILE. 630 men applied, 509 accepted, 217 enrolled; 739 women applied, 647 accepted, 284 enrolled. 82% had high school GPA of 3.0 or higher. 48% were in top tenth and 62% were in top quarter of graduating class. **Academic background:** Mid 50% of enrolled freshmen had SAT-V between 450-520, SAT-M between 490-640; ACT composite between 22-27. 90% submitted SAT scores, 32% submitted ACT scores. **Characteristics:** 62% from in state, 92% live in college housing, 10% have minority backgrounds, 10% are foreign students, 35% join fraternities/sororities. Average age is 18.

FALL-TERM APPLICATIONS. $30 fee, may be waived for applicants with need. No closing date; priority given to applications received by March 15; applicants notified on a rolling basis beginning on or about December 15; must reply by May 1 or within 2 weeks if notified thereafter. Essay required. Interview recommended. CRDA. Deferred and early admission available.

STUDENT LIFE. Housing: Dormitories (men, women, coed); apartment, fraternity housing available. College-owned houses and apartments near campus. **Activities:** Student government, magazine, radio, student newspaper, television, yearbook, choral groups, concert band, dance, drama, jazz band, music ensembles, musical theater, opera, pep band, symphony orchestra, fraternities, sororities, Fellowship of Christian Athletes, Minority Student Union, International Club, Hawaiian club, SPURS International, women's center, Campus Crusades, Volunteers in Mission, College Companions, Circle-K. **Additional information:** Out-of Door Program includes 6-day preorientation wilderness trip. January term offers environmental/survival courses in Cascade Mountains and New Zealand's South Island.

ATHLETICS. NAIA. **Intercollegiate:** Baseball M, basketball, cross-country, football M, golf M, soccer, softball W, swimming, tennis, track and field, volleyball W. **Intramural:** Basketball, bowling, fencing, handball, lacrosse, racquetball, sailing, skiing, softball, swimming, table tennis, tennis, volleyball, water polo.

STUDENT SERVICES. Aptitude testing, career counseling, employment service for undergraduates, freshman orientation, health services, on-campus day care, personal counseling, placement service for graduates, special adviser for adult students, veterans counselor, services/facilities for handicapped.

ANNUAL EXPENSES. Tuition and fees: $12,700. **Room and board:** $3,970. **Books and supplies:** $600. **Other expenses:** $900.

FINANCIAL AID. 91% of freshmen, 82% of continuing students receive some form of aid. 71% of grants, 92% of loans, 88% of jobs based on need. 286 enrolled freshmen were judged to have need, all were offered aid. Academic, music/drama scholarships available. **Aid applications:** No closing date; priority given to applications received by March 1; applicants notified on a rolling basis beginning on or about March 15; must reply by May 1 or within 2 weeks if notified thereafter.

ADDRESS/TELEPHONE. Thomas Meicho, Dean of Admissions, Linfield College, 900 S. Baker Street, McMinnville, OR 97128-6894. (503) 472-4121 ext. 213. Fax: (503) 472-9528.

Linn-Benton Community College
Albany, Oregon — CB code: 4413

2-year public community college, coed. Founded in 1966. **Accreditation:** Regional. **Undergraduate enrollment:** 1,293 men, 1,255 women full time; 1,679 men, 2,130 women part time. **Faculty:** 479 total (157 full time), 7 with doctorates or other terminal degrees. **Location:** Rural campus in large town; 70 miles from Portland. **Calendar:** Quarter, limited summer session. Extensive evening/early morning classes. **Microcomputers:** Located in classrooms, computer centers. **Additional facts:** Courses available at off-campus centers in Corvallis, Lebanon and Sweethome.

DEGREES OFFERED. AA, AS, AAS. 347 associate degrees awarded in 1992.

UNDERGRADUATE MAJORS. Accounting, agricultural business and management, agricultural production, agricultural sciences, air conditioning/heating/refrigeration mechanics, animal sciences, automotive mechanics, biology, business administration and management, business and management, business data processing and related programs, computer programming, criminal justice studies, diesel engine mechanics, drafting and design technology, dramatic arts, early childhood education, electronic technology, engineering, finance, fine arts, food production/management/services, graphic and printing production, graphic arts technology, graphic design, horticulture, humanities, journalism, law enforcement and corrections technologies, legal secretary, liberal/general studies, mathematics, medical secretary, metallurgy, nursing, precision metal work, secondary education, secretarial and related programs, social sciences, trade and industrial supervision and management, water and wastewater technology.

ACADEMIC PROGRAMS. 2-year transfer program, cooperative education, student-designed major, telecourses, evening degree program. **Remedial services:** Learning center, remedial instruction, tutoring. **ROTC:** Air Force, Army, Naval. **Placement/credit:** AP, CLEP General and Subject, institutional tests.

ACADEMIC REQUIREMENTS. Freshmen must earn minimum GPA of 2.0 to continue in good standing. Students must declare major on application. **Graduation requirements:** 90 hours for associate (70 in major). Most students required to take courses in computer science, English, history, humanities, mathematics, biological/physical sciences, social sciences.

FRESHMAN ADMISSIONS. Selection criteria: Open admissions. **Test requirements:** Comparative Guidance and Placement Examination required.

1992 FRESHMAN CLASS PROFILE. 375 men, 344 women enrolled.

Characteristics: 98% from in state, 100% commute, 7% have minority backgrounds, 1% are foreign students.

FALL-TERM APPLICATIONS. $20 fee. No closing date; priority given to applications received by July 15; applicants notified on a rolling basis.

STUDENT LIFE. Activities: Student government, student newspaper, choral groups, concert band, drama, jazz band, music ensembles, musical theater.

ATHLETICS. Intercollegiate: Baseball M, basketball, track and field, volleyball W.

STUDENT SERVICES. Aptitude testing, career counseling, employment service for undergraduates, freshman orientation, on-campus day care, personal counseling, placement service for graduates, special adviser for adult students, veterans counselor, tutorial services, services/facilities for handicapped.

ANNUAL EXPENSES. Tuition and fees: $1,260, $3,915 additional for out-of-state students. **Books and supplies:** $600. **Other expenses:** $810.

FINANCIAL AID. 50% of freshmen, 60% of continuing students receive some form of aid. 89% of grants, 94% of loans, 97% of jobs based on need. Academic, music/drama, art, athletic, leadership scholarships available. **Aid applications:** No closing date; priority given to applications received by April 1; applicants notified on a rolling basis beginning on or about June 15; must reply within 30 days.

ADDRESS/TELEPHONE. Diane Watson, Director of Admissions and Records, Linn-Benton Community College, 6500 Southwest Pacific Boulevard, Albany, OR 97321-3779. (503) 967-6105. Fax: (503) 967-6550.

Marylhurst College
Marylhurst, Oregon — CB code: 0440

4-year private liberal arts college, coed, affiliated with Roman Catholic Church. Founded in 1893. **Accreditation:** Regional. **Undergraduate enrollment:** 60 men, 171 women full time; 189 men, 628 women part time. **Graduate enrollment:** 20 men, 15 women full time; 65 men, 90 women part time. **Faculty:** 237 total (12 full time), 10 with doctorates or other terminal degrees. **Location:** Suburban campus in large town; 10 miles from Portland. **Calendar:** Quarter, limited summer session. Saturday and extensive evening/early morning classes. **Microcomputers:** 12 located in libraries. **Special facilities:** Art gallery. **Additional facts:** Most undergraduate students enter as third year students.

DEGREES OFFERED. BA, BS, BFA, MA, MS, MBA. 219 bachelor's degrees awarded in 1992. 23% in business and management, 16% communications, 22% multi/interdisciplinary studies, 27% social sciences, 10% visual and performing arts. Graduate degrees offered in 3 major fields of study.

UNDERGRADUATE MAJORS. Biological and physical sciences, business and management, clinical pastoral care, communications, earth sciences, fine arts, humanities, humanities and social sciences, interior design, liberal/general studies, music, music performance, music theory and composition, religion, religion and ethics, social sciences, visual and performing arts.

ACADEMIC PROGRAMS. Double major, independent study, internships, student-designed major, weekend college, cross-registration. **Remedial services:** Learning center, tutoring. **Placement/credit:** CLEP General and Subject, institutional tests; 45 credit hours maximum for bachelor's degree.

ACADEMIC REQUIREMENTS. Freshmen must earn minimum GPA of 2.0 to continue in good standing. Students must declare major on application. **Graduation requirements:** 180 hours for bachelor's (70 in major). Most students required to take courses in English, history, humanities, mathematics, philosophy/religion, biological/physical sciences, social sciences. **Postgraduate studies:** 5% enter law school, 10% enter MBA programs, 30% enter other graduate study.

FRESHMAN ADMISSIONS. Selection criteria: Open admissions.

1992 FRESHMAN CLASS PROFILE. Characteristics: 100% from in state, 100% commute, 3% have minority backgrounds. Average age is 35.

FALL-TERM APPLICATIONS. $73 fee. No closing date; applicants notified on a rolling basis. Interview required for prior learning experience program applicants. Audition required for music applicants.

STUDENT LIFE. Activities: Choral groups, music ensembles, symphony orchestra, Campus Ministry.

STUDENT SERVICES. Aptitude testing, career counseling, personal counseling, special adviser for adult students, veterans counselor, services/facilities for handicapped.

ANNUAL EXPENSES. Tuition and fees (1992-93): $7,644. **Books and supplies:** $500. **Other expenses:** $1,688.

FINANCIAL AID. 65% of freshmen, 65% of continuing students receive some form of aid. Grants, loans, jobs available. Music/drama, art, alumni affiliation scholarships available. **Aid applications:** No closing date; priority given to applications received by June 1; applicants notified on a rolling basis beginning on or about May 1; must reply within 4 weeks.

ADDRESS/TELEPHONE. Keith W. Protonentis, Registrar, Marylhurst College, Marylhurst, OR 97036. (503) 636-8141. (800) 634-9982. Fax: (503) 636-9526.

Mount Angel Seminary
St. Benedict, Oregon — CB code: 4491

4-year private seminary college, men only, affiliated with Roman Catholic Church. Founded in 1887. **Accreditation:** Regional. **Undergraduate enrollment:** 41 men full time. **Graduate enrollment:** 124 men. **Location:** Rural campus in small town; 40 miles from Portland. **Calendar:** Semester. **Additional facts:** All undergraduates are candidates for Roman Catholic priesthood.

FRESHMAN ADMISSIONS. Selection criteria: Primarily recommendations from sponsoring dioceses or clergymen, personal interview. Test scores considered. Adequate ESL scores for non-English speaking students.

ANNUAL EXPENSES. Tuition and fees: $4,000. **Room and board:** $3,500. **Books and supplies:** $400. **Other expenses:** $1,000.

ADDRESS/TELEPHONE. Sr. Georgetta Cunningham, Admissions Officer, Mount Angel Seminary, St. Benedict, OR 97373. (503) 845-3951.

Mount Hood Community College
Gresham, Oregon — CB code: 4508

2-year public community college, coed. Founded in 1965. **Accreditation:** Regional. **Undergraduate enrollment:** 1,695 men, 1,733 women full time; 1,940 men, 2,592 women part time. **Faculty:** 544 total (180 full time). **Location:** Suburban campus in small city; 12 miles from Portland. **Calendar:** Quarter, limited summer session. **Microcomputers:** Located in libraries, classrooms, computer centers. **Special facilities:** Planetarium, art gallery, solar observatory.

DEGREES OFFERED. AA, AS, AAS. 682 associate degrees awarded in 1992. 5% in architecture and environmental design, 10% business and management, 9% business/office and marketing/distribution, 5% communications, 13% teacher education, 6% engineering technologies, 6% health sciences, 18% allied health.

UNDERGRADUATE MAJORS. Accounting, airline piloting and navigation, architectural technologies, automotive technology, business and management, child development/care/guidance, civil technology, cosmetology, dental hygiene, drafting, electrical and electronics equipment repair, electronic technology, fire control and safety technology, fishing and fisheries, food sciences, forestry and related sciences, funeral services/mortuary science, graphic and printing production, graphic arts technology, graphic design, horticultural science, hospitality and recreation marketing, industrial technology, international business management, journalism, legal secretary, liberal/general studies, machine tool operation/machine shop, marketing and distribution, mechanical design technology, medical assistant, medical secretary, mental health/human services, nursing, occupational safety and health technology, occupational therapy assistant, ornamental horticulture, physical therapy assistant, radio/television broadcasting, respiratory therapy, respiratory therapy technology, retailing, robotics, small business management and ownership, surgical technology, tourism, word processing.

ACADEMIC PROGRAMS. 2-year transfer program, accelerated program, cooperative education, double major, dual enrollment of high school students, independent study, internships, study abroad, telecourses, visiting/exchange student program. **Remedial services:** Learning center, preadmission summer program, reduced course load, remedial instruction, tutoring. **Placement/credit:** AP, CLEP General and Subject, institutional tests; 45 credit hours maximum for associate degree.

ACADEMIC REQUIREMENTS. Freshmen must earn minimum GPA of 2.0 to continue in good standing. Students must declare major on application. **Graduation requirements:** 90 hours for associate. Most students required to take courses in computer science, English, humanities, mathematics, biological/physical sciences, social sciences.

FRESHMAN ADMISSIONS. Selection criteria: Open admissions. Selective admissions to some programs. Applicants to health services programs should have school minimum GPA of 2.0. Requirements for health programs include 1 algebra, 1 biology, and 1 chemistry. **Additional information:** Additional admission criteria required for professional and technical programs.

1992 FRESHMAN CLASS PROFILE. 1,112 men, 1,106 women enrolled. **Characteristics:** 95% from in state, 100% commute, 9% have minority backgrounds. Average age is 32.

FALL-TERM APPLICATIONS. No application fee, except for health programs. No closing date; priority given to applications received by September 1; applicants notified on a rolling basis. Interview required for most health services, cosmetology applicants. Deferred and early admission available. Most health services majors must apply between November 1 and March 30 for fall admission, College Placement Test required for chemistry, mathematics, writing or reading courses, application fee.

STUDENT LIFE. Activities: Student government, film, magazine, radio, student newspaper, television, choral groups, concert band, dance, drama, jazz band, music ensembles, musical theater, symphony orchestra.

ATHLETICS. Intercollegiate: Baseball M, basketball, cross-country, golf M, tennis, track and field, volleyball W. **Intramural:** Archery, badminton M, basketball, bowling, cross-country, golf, racquetball, skiing, soccer, softball, swimming, tennis, track and field, volleyball, wrestling M.

STUDENT SERVICES. Aptitude testing, career counseling, employment service for undergraduates, freshman orientation, health services, on-campus day care, personal counseling, placement service for graduates, veterans counselor, services/facilities for handicapped.

ANNUAL EXPENSES. Tuition and fees (projected): $1,302. Tuition for out-of-state students $100 per credit, foreign students $115 per credit. **Books and supplies:** $621. **Other expenses:** $540.

FINANCIAL AID. 45% of continuing students receive some form of aid. 67% of jobs based on need. Academic, music/drama, art, athletic, state/district residency, leadership scholarships available. **Aid applications:** No closing date; priority given to applications received by April 1; applicants notified on a rolling basis beginning on or about May 1; must reply within 2 weeks.

ADDRESS/TELEPHONE. Marilyn J. Kennedy, Registrar/Director of Admissions, Mount Hood Community College, 26000 Southeast Stark Street, Gresham, OR 97030. (503) 667-7391. Fax: (503) 667-7388.

Multnomah School of the Bible
Portland, Oregon — CB code: 4496

4-year private Bible, seminary college, coed, interdenominational. Founded in 1936. **Undergraduate enrollment:** 266 men, 188 women full time; 41 men, 26 women part time. **Graduate enrollment:** 70 men, 31 women full time; 36 men, 25 women part time. **Faculty:** 51 total (34 full time), 19 with doctorates or other terminal degrees. **Location:** Urban campus in large city. **Calendar:** Semester, limited summer session. **Microcomputers:** 12 located in libraries, computer centers. **Additional facts:** Emphasis on preparation for Christian ministries.

DEGREES OFFERED. BA, BS, MA, M.Div. 29 associate degrees awarded in 1992. 100% in philosophy, religion, theology. 53 bachelor's degrees awarded. 100% in philosophy, religion, theology. Graduate degrees offered in 3 major fields of study.

UNDERGRADUATE MAJORS. Associate: Bible studies. **Bachelor's:** Bible studies, biblical languages, religious education, theological studies.

ACADEMIC PROGRAMS. Double major. **Remedial services:** Reduced course load, remedial instruction. **Placement/credit:** AP, CLEP General and Subject; 12 credit hours maximum for associate degree; 12 credit hours maximum for bachelor's degree.

ACADEMIC REQUIREMENTS. Freshmen must earn minimum GPA of 2.0 to continue in good standing. 53% of freshmen return for sophomore year. **Graduation requirements:** 96 hours for associate (52 in major), 128 hours for bachelor's (52 in major). Most students required to take courses in English, history, philosophy/religion.

FRESHMAN ADMISSIONS. Selection criteria: School achievement record, test scores, and recommendations most important. **Test requirements:** SAT; score report by August 15.

1992 FRESHMAN CLASS PROFILE. 47 men, 72 women enrolled. **Characteristics:** 37% from in state, 65% live in college housing, 6% have minority backgrounds, 6% are foreign students. Average age is 22.

FALL-TERM APPLICATIONS. $25 fee. Closing date July 15; priority given to applications received by March 1; applicants notified on a rolling basis. Essay required. Deferred admission available.

STUDENT LIFE. Housing: Dormitories (men, women); apartment housing available. **Activities:** Student government, student newspaper, yearbook, choral groups, music ensembles, pep band. **Additional information:** Religious observance required.

ATHLETICS. Intercollegiate: Basketball M, soccer M, tennis, volleyball W. **Intramural:** Basketball, football M, volleyball.

STUDENT SERVICES. Employment service for undergraduates, freshman orientation, health services, personal counseling, placement service for graduates, veterans counselor, services/facilities for handicapped.

ANNUAL EXPENSES. Tuition and fees: $5,790. **Room and board:** $3,200. **Books and supplies:** $400. **Other expenses:** $900.

FINANCIAL AID. 80% of freshmen, 81% of continuing students receive some form of aid. 69% of grants, 77% of loans, 35% of jobs based on need. Academic, music/drama, leadership, religious affiliation scholarships available. **Aid applications:** No closing date; priority given to applications received by March 1; applicants notified on a rolling basis beginning on or about May 15; must reply within 2 weeks.

ADDRESS/TELEPHONE. Joyce L. Kehoe, Director of Admissions and Registrar, Multnomah School of the Bible, 8435 Northeast Glisan Street, Portland, OR 97220-5898. (503) 255-0332.

Northwest Christian College
Eugene, Oregon — CB code: 4543

4-year private Bible, liberal arts college, coed, affiliated with Christian Church (Disciples of Christ) and Christian Churches/Churches of Christ. Founded in 1895. **Accreditation:** Regional. **Undergraduate enrollment:** 115 men, 102 women full time; 31 men, 33 women part time. **Graduate enrollment:** 11 men, 15 women full time; 13 men, 5 women part time. **Faculty:** 23 total (11 full time), 8 with doctorates or other terminal degrees. **Location:** Urban campus in small city; 110 miles from Portland. **Calendar:** Quarter. **Microcomputers:** 7 located in libraries. **Special facilities:** Rare book and Bible collection.

DEGREES OFFERED. AA, BA, BS, MA. 5 associate degrees awarded in 1992. 51 bachelor's degrees awarded. Graduate degrees offered in 2 major fields of study.

UNDERGRADUATE MAJORS. Associate: Bible studies. **Bachelor's:** Anthropology, Asian studies, biblical languages, biology, church/society/family, communication ministry, communications, computer and information sciences, cross-cultural ministry, early childhood education, economics, English, French, geology, German, history, management communication, mathematics, organizational management, physics, political science and government, predentistry, prelaw, premedicine, psychology, religious education, religious music, Russian, sociology, Spanish.

ACADEMIC PROGRAMS. Double major, internships, combination degree program with University of Oregon. **Remedial services:** Preadmission summer program, reduced course load, special counselor, tutoring. **Placement/credit:** AP.

ACADEMIC REQUIREMENTS. Freshmen must earn minimum GPA of 2.0 to continue in good standing. 65% of freshmen return for sophomore year. Students must declare major by end of second year. **Graduation requirements:** 96 hours for associate, 186 hours for bachelor's (45 in major). Most students required to take courses in English, history, philosophy/religion, biological/physical sciences, social sciences. **Postgraduate studies:** 65% from 2-year programs enter 4-year programs.

FRESHMAN ADMISSIONS. Selection criteria: School achievement record, test scores, and two recommendations considered. **Test requirements:** SAT or ACT (SAT preferred) for placement and counseling only; score report by September 20.

1992 FRESHMAN CLASS PROFILE. 22 men, 32 women enrolled. **Characteristics:** 60% from in state, 79% live in college housing, 8% have minority backgrounds, 1% are foreign students. Average age is 19.

FALL-TERM APPLICATIONS. $25 fee. Closing date September 15; priority given to applications received by April 15; applicants notified on a rolling basis. Essay required. Deferred admission available.

STUDENT LIFE. Housing: Dormitories (men, women, coed); apartment housing available. **Activities:** Student government, student newspaper, yearbook, choral groups, music ensembles, pep band, ACTS, campus restoration ministry. **Additional information:** Campus observes Wellness Week, National Collegiate Alcohol Awareness Week, Martin Luther King day. Short-term service experiences through NW Medical teams. Religious observance required.

ATHLETICS. Intercollegiate: Basketball M, volleyball W. **Intramural:** Baseball M, basketball W, football M, soccer M, volleyball W.

STUDENT SERVICES. Aptitude testing, career counseling, employment service for undergraduates, freshman orientation, health services, personal counseling, placement service for graduates, veterans counselor.

ANNUAL EXPENSES. Tuition and fees (1992-93): $6,639. **Room and board:** $3,514. **Books and supplies:** $420. **Other expenses:** $1,536.

FINANCIAL AID. 93% of freshmen, 87% of continuing students receive some form of aid. 72% of grants, all loans, all jobs based on need. 23 enrolled freshmen were judged to have need, all were offered aid. Academic, religious affiliation scholarships available. **Aid applications:** No closing date; priority given to applications received by April 15; applicants notified on a rolling basis beginning on or about May 1; must reply within 2 weeks.

ADDRESS/TELEPHONE. Randolph Jones, Director of Admissions, Northwest Christian College, 828 East 11th Avenue, Eugene, OR 97401-9983. (503) 343-1641. (800) 888-1641. Fax: (503) 343-9159.

Oregon Health Sciences University
Portland, Oregon — CB code: 4900

4-year public university, coed. Founded in 1887. **Accreditation:** Regional. **Undergraduate enrollment:** 31 men, 289 women full time; 8 men, 64 women part time. **Graduate enrollment:** 510 men, 364 women full time; 14 men, 108 women part time. **Location:** Urban campus in large city. **Calendar:** Quarter. **Microcomputers:** Located in libraries, classrooms, computer centers.

DEGREES OFFERED. BS, MS, PhD, DDS, MD. 165 bachelor's degrees awarded in 1992. 76% in health sciences, 24% allied health. Graduate degrees offered in 11 major fields of study.

UNDERGRADUATE MAJORS. Dental hygiene, medical laboratory technologies, nursing.

ACADEMIC PROGRAMS. Visiting/exchange student program.

ACADEMIC REQUIREMENTS. Students must declare major on application. **Graduation requirements:** 186 hours for bachelor's (62 in major). Most students required to take courses in English, humanities, mathematics, biological/physical sciences, social sciences.

FRESHMAN ADMISSIONS. Selection criteria: Admissions requirements vary with program. Student not admitted directly from high school.

FALL-TERM APPLICATIONS. $40 fee.

STUDENT LIFE. Housing: Dormitories (coed); cooperative housing available. **Activities:** Student government, yearbook.

ATHLETICS. Intramural: Basketball, swimming, table tennis, tennis.

STUDENT SERVICES. Career counseling, health services, on-campus day care, personal counseling, services/facilities for handicapped.

ANNUAL EXPENSES. Tuition and fees (1992-93): $3,900, $4,215 additional for out-of-state students. Tuition/fees and estimated expenses for nursing program only. Costs for other programs vary. **Room and board:** $1,827 room only. **Books and supplies:** $500. **Other expenses:** $1,000.

FINANCIAL AID. Aid applications: No closing date; must reply within 15 days.

ADDRESS/TELEPHONE. Registrar's Office, Oregon Health Sciences University, 3181 SW Sam Jackson Road, Portland, OR 97201. (503) 494-7800.

Oregon Institute of Technology
Klamath Falls, Oregon CB code: 4587

Admissions:	98% of applicants accepted
Based on:	••• School record
	• Recommendations, test scores
Completion:	75% of freshmen end year in good standing
	5% enter graduate study

4-year public polytechnic institute, coed. Founded in 1946. **Accreditation:** Regional. **Undergraduate enrollment:** 1,207 men, 807 women full time; 400 men, 345 women part time. **Faculty:** 220 total (167 full time), 42 with doctorates or other terminal degrees. **Location:** Suburban campus in large town; 280 miles from Portland, 270 miles from Reno, Nevada. **Calendar:** Quarter, limited summer session. **Microcomputers:** 300 located in dormitories, libraries, classrooms, computer centers. **Special facilities:** Geo-heat center for research on direct uses of geothermal energy. **Additional facts:** Metro Campus in Portland offers upper-division courses in electronics engineering technology, manufacturing engineering technology, and industrial management.

DEGREES OFFERED. AA, AAS, BS. 299 associate degrees awarded in 1992. 16% in business and management, 58% engineering technologies, 13% allied health, 13% multi/interdisciplinary studies. 331 bachelor's degrees awarded. 12% in business and management, 64% engineering technologies, 24% health sciences.

UNDERGRADUATE MAJORS. Associate: Accounting, computer engineering, computer programming, computer software engineering technology, dental hygiene, electronic technology, engineering and engineering-related technologies, laser electro-optic technology, liberal/general studies, manufacturing technology, radiograph medical technology, secretarial and related programs. **Bachelor's:** Business administration and management, business data processing and related programs, civil technology, computer engineering, computer programming, computer software engineering technology, dental hygiene, electronic technology, laser electro-optic technology, manufacturing technology, mechanical design technology, medical radiation dosimetry, nursing, survey and mapping technology.

ACADEMIC PROGRAMS. 2-year transfer program, cooperative education, double major, honors program, internships. **Remedial services:** Learning center, reduced course load, remedial instruction, special counselor, tutoring. **Placement/credit:** AP, CLEP Subject, institutional tests; 25 credit hours maximum for associate degree; 50 credit hours maximum for bachelor's degree.

ACADEMIC REQUIREMENTS. Freshmen must earn minimum GPA of 2.0 to continue in good standing. 70% of freshmen return for sophomore year. Students must declare major on enrollment. **Graduation requirements:** 100 hours for associate (56 in major), 200 hours for bachelor's (112 in major). Most students required to take courses in computer science, English, humanities, mathematics, biological/physical sciences, social sciences. **Post-graduate studies:** 40% from 2-year programs enter 4-year programs.

FRESHMAN ADMISSIONS. Selection criteria: High school GPA of 2.50 or SAT combined score of 890 required. **High school preparation:** 14 units required. Required units include English 4, mathematics 3, social science 3 and science 2. 2 additional units from other college preparatory studies required. **Test requirements:** SAT or ACT (SAT preferred) for placement; score report by September 20.

1992 FRESHMAN CLASS PROFILE. 278 men applied, 272 accepted, 218 enrolled; 202 women applied, 197 accepted, 157 enrolled. 53% had high school GPA of 3.0 or higher, 43% between 2.0 and 2.99. **Characteristics:** 90% from in state, 70% commute, 14% have minority backgrounds, 1% are foreign students, 1% join fraternities/sororities. Average age is 21.

FALL-TERM APPLICATIONS. $35 fee. No closing date; applicants notified on a rolling basis. Deferred admission available.

STUDENT LIFE. Housing: Dormitories (coed); fraternity housing available. **Activities:** Student government, magazine, radio, student newspaper, pep band, fraternities, sororities, Newman Club, Latter Day Saints, Christan Fellowship, Afro American Club, Native American Club, International Student Club, Circle K. **Additional information:** Student clubs are very community oriented and compete for community service awards.

ATHLETICS. NAIA. **Intercollegiate:** Basketball M, softball W. **Intramural:** Basketball, sailing, skiing, softball, swimming.

STUDENT SERVICES. Aptitude testing, career counseling, employment service for undergraduates, freshman orientation, health services, personal counseling, placement service for graduates, special adviser for adult students, veterans counselor, services/facilities for handicapped.

ANNUAL EXPENSES. Tuition and fees (1992-93): $2,595, $4,083 additional for out-of-state students. **Room and board:** $3,315. **Books and supplies:** $500. **Other expenses:** $1,800.

FINANCIAL AID. 60% of freshmen, 60% of continuing students receive some form of aid. 92% of grants, 90% of loans, 25% of jobs based on need. Academic, state/district residency, minority scholarships available. **Aid applications:** No closing date; priority given to applications received by March 1; applicants notified on a rolling basis beginning on or about April 15; must reply within 3 weeks.

ADDRESS/TELEPHONE. Dr. Russ Lyon, Director of Enrollment Management, Oregon Institute of Technology, 3201 Campus Drive, Klamath Falls, OR 97601-8801. (503) 885-1150. (800) 343-6653. Fax: (503) 885-1115.

Oregon Polytechnic Institute
Portland, Oregon CB code: 1498

2-year proprietary technical college, coed. Founded in 1947. **Undergraduate enrollment:** 210 men, 50 women full time. **Faculty:** 17 total (8 full time), 1 with doctorate or other terminal degree. **Location:** Urban campus in large city. **Calendar:** Quarter, extensive summer session. **Microcomputers:** 10 located in computer centers.

DEGREES OFFERED. AAS. 53 associate degrees awarded in 1992. 100% in engineering technologies.

UNDERGRADUATE MAJORS. Computer programming, drafting and design technology, engineering and engineering-related technologies.

ACADEMIC PROGRAMS. Internships. **Remedial services:** Reduced course load, tutoring. **Placement/credit:** Institutional tests; 24 credit hours maximum for associate degree.

ACADEMIC REQUIREMENTS. Freshmen must earn minimum GPA of 2.0 to continue in good standing. 74% of freshmen return for sophomore year. Students must declare major on enrollment. **Graduation requirements:** 90 hours for associate. Most students required to take courses in computer science, English, mathematics.

FRESHMAN ADMISSIONS. Selection criteria: Test scores, interview, school achievement record considered. Recommended units include English 2, mathematics 3 and physical science 1. **Test requirements:** Institutional screening test required for admissions.

1992 FRESHMAN CLASS PROFILE. 120 men, 34 women enrolled. 30% had high school GPA of 3.0 or higher, 70% between 2.0 and 2.99. **Characteristics:** 83% from in state, 100% commute, 5% have minority backgrounds. Average age is 24.

FALL-TERM APPLICATIONS. $25 fee. No closing date; applicants notified on a rolling basis. Interview recommended. Deferred and early admission available.

STUDENT SERVICES. Career counseling, employment service for undergraduates, freshman orientation, placement service for graduates, services/facilities for handicapped.

ANNUAL EXPENSES. Tuition and fees (1992-93): $5,525. **Books and supplies:** $950. **Other expenses:** $700.

FINANCIAL AID. 90% of freshmen, 89% of continuing students receive some form of aid. All grants, 65% of loans, all jobs based on need. **Aid applications:** No closing date; priority given to applications received by May 30; applicants notified on a rolling basis beginning on or about July 1; must reply within 3 weeks.

ADDRESS/TELEPHONE. Admissions Office, Oregon Polytechnic Institute, 900 Southeast Sandy Boulevard, Portland, OR 97214. (503) 234-9333. Fax: (503) 233-0195.

Oregon State University
Corvallis, Oregon CB code: 4586

Admissions:	87% of applicants accepted
Based on:	••• School record, test scores
Completion:	92% of freshmen end year in good standing
	44% graduate

4-year public university, coed. Founded in 1868. **Accreditation:** Regional. **Undergraduate enrollment:** 11,430 men and women. **Graduate enrollment:** 2,906 men and women. **Faculty:** 2,240 total (1,663 full time), 1,188 with doctorates or other terminal degrees. **Location:** Suburban campus in large town; 80 miles from Portland, 45 miles from Eugene. **Calendar:** Quarter, extensive summer session. **Microcomputers:** 925 located in dormitories, libraries, computer centers. **Special facilities:** Peavy Arboretum, McDonald/Dunn Forest (13774 acres), Radiation Center (with TRIGA Mark II Nuclear Reactor), Hinsdale Wave Research Facility, Horner Museum, Mark O. Hatfield Marine Science Center Museum and Aquarium, Fairbanks Art Gallery, Giustina Gallery.

DEGREES OFFERED. BA, BS, BFA, MA, MS, MBA, MEd, PhD, EdD, DVM. 2,871 bachelor's degrees awarded in 1992. 8% in agriculture, 18% business and management, 5% communications, 7% education, 16% engineering, 6% home economics, 8% social sciences. Graduate degrees offered in 82 major fields of study.

UNDERGRADUATE MAJORS. Accounting, actuarial sciences, agricultural business and management, agricultural economics, agricultural sciences, agronomy, American studies, animal sciences, anthropology, applied mathematics, archeology, art history, atmospheric sciences and meteorology, biochemistry, biological and physical sciences, biology, biophysics, bioresources research, botany, business administration and management, business and management, chemical engineering, chemistry, child development/care/guidance, civil and forest engineering, civil engineering, clothing and textiles management/production/services, commercial and industrial fitness, communications, computer and information sciences, computer engineering, construction engineering management, dairy, dental assistant, dietetic aide/assistant, economics, electrical/electronics/communications engineering, engineering physics, English, entomology, environmental health and safety, environmental science, exercise and sport science, family and community services, family/consumer resource management, finance, financial management, fine arts, fishing and fisheries, food production/management/services, food science and nutrition, food sciences, forest engineering, forest products processing technology, forestry and related sciences, forestry production and processing, French, geography, geological engineering, geology, German, health care administration, health education, history, home economics, home economics communication, horticulture, human environment and housing, individual and family development, industrial engineering, institutional/home management/supporting programs, interior merchandising, international business management, international studies, liberal/general studies, management information systems, management science, manufacturing engineering, marketing management, mathematical science, mathematics, mechanical engineering, medical laboratory technologies, merchandising management, metallurgical engineering, microbiology, mining and mineral engineering, music, music history and appreciation, music performance, music theory and composition, nuclear engineering, parks and recreation management, pharmacy, philosophy, physical education, physics, plant protection, political science and government, poultry, predentistry, premedicine, prepharmacy, preveterinary, psychology, pure mathematics, radiation health physics, range management, sociology, Spanish, speech, studio art, textiles and clothing, trade and industrial education, visual and performing arts, wildlife management, zoology.

ACADEMIC PROGRAMS. Cooperative education, double major, dual enrollment of high school students, independent study, internships, student-designed major, study abroad, teacher preparation, telecourses, visiting/exchange student program, weekend college, cross-registration; combined bachelor's/graduate program in business administration. **Remedial services:** Learning center, remedial instruction, special counselor, tutoring, Communication Skills Center, English Language Institute, Mathematical Sciences Learning Center. **ROTC:** Air Force, Army, Naval. **Placement/credit:** AP, CLEP General and Subject, institutional tests.

ACADEMIC REQUIREMENTS. Freshmen must earn minimum GPA of 2.0 to continue in good standing. 78% of freshmen return for sophomore year. Students must declare major by end of second year. **Graduation requirements:** 192 hours for bachelor's (36 in major). Most students required to take courses in arts/fine arts, English, humanities, mathematics, biological/physical sciences, social sciences.

FRESHMAN ADMISSIONS. Selection criteria: 3.0 high school GPA most important. **High school preparation:** 14 units required. Required units include English 4, mathematics 3, social science 3 and science 2. 2 units from foreign language, computer science, fine and performing arts recommended. **Test requirements:** SAT or ACT; score report by August 15. 3 ACH required of applicants not meeting high school subject requirements. Score report by August 15. **Additional information:** Students not meeting admission requirements may petition for exception.

1992 FRESHMAN CLASS PROFILE. 4,544 men and women applied, 3,948 accepted; 1,722 enrolled. 81% had high school GPA of 3.0 or higher, 19% between 2.0 and 2.99. **Academic background:** Mid 50% of enrolled freshmen had SAT-V between 380-510, SAT-M between 440-590; ACT composite between 18-26. 92% submitted SAT scores, 5% submitted ACT scores. **Characteristics:** 80% from in state, 95% live in college housing, 16% have minority backgrounds, 3% are foreign students. Average age is 18.

FALL-TERM APPLICATIONS. $40 fee. Closing date March 1; applicants notified on a rolling basis; Must reply by May 25, or 3 weeks after notice of admission. CRDA. Deferred and early admission available. EDP-F.

STUDENT LIFE. Housing: Dormitories (men, women, coed); apartment, fraternity, sorority, cooperative housing available. Freshman enrolling within a year of high school graduation must live in a university residence hall, fraternity, sorority, or cooperative. **Activities:** Student government, film, magazine, radio, student newspaper, television, yearbook, choral groups, concert band, dance, drama, jazz band, music ensembles, musical theater, pep band, symphony orchestra, fraternities, sororities, Memorial Union Program Council, 253 student organizations, 47 student honor and recognition societies.

ATHLETICS. NCAA. **Intercollegiate:** Baseball M, basketball, football M, golf, gymnastics W, rowing (crew), soccer, softball W, swimming W, volleyball W, wrestling M. **Intramural:** Badminton, basketball, bowling, cross-country, football M, golf, racquetball, soccer, softball, swimming, tennis, track and field, volleyball, water polo, wrestling M.

STUDENT SERVICES. Aptitude testing, career counseling, employment service for undergraduates, freshman orientation, health services, on-campus day care, personal counseling, placement service for graduates, special adviser for adult students, veterans counselor, Educational Opportunities Program, Asian, black, Hispanic, and Native American cultural centers, Women's Center, Special Services Project, Experimental College, services/facilities for handicapped.

ANNUAL EXPENSES. Tuition and fees (1992-93): $2,691, $4,281 additional for out-of-state students. **Room and board:** $3,177. **Books and supplies:** $513. **Other expenses:** $1,717.

FINANCIAL AID. 60% of freshmen, 55% of continuing students receive some form of aid. 87% of grants, 88% of loans, all jobs based on need. Academic, music/drama, athletic, state/district residency, minority scholarships available. **Aid applications:** No closing date; priority given to applications received by March 1; applicants notified on a rolling basis beginning on or about April 15; must reply within 3 weeks.

ADDRESS/TELEPHONE. D. Kay Conrad, Director of Admissions, Oregon State University, Corvallis, OR 97331-2130. (503) 737-4411. Fax: (503) 737-2400.

Pacific Northwest College of Art
Portland, Oregon — CB code: 4504

4-year private art college, coed. Founded in 1909. **Accreditation:** Regional. **Undergraduate enrollment:** 77 men, 116 women full time; 1 man, 11 women part time. **Faculty:** 43 total (17 full time), 19 with doctorates or other terminal degrees. **Location:** Urban campus in large city. **Calendar:** Semester. **Microcomputers:** 24 located in computer centers. **Special facilities:** Art museum, film study center, student art gallery, computer graphics laboratory.

DEGREES OFFERED. BFA. 33 bachelor's degrees awarded in 1992. 100% in visual and performing arts.

UNDERGRADUATE MAJORS. Bookarts, ceramics, drawing, fiber/textiles/weaving, graphic design, illustration design, metal/jewelry, painting, photography, printmaking, sculpture, woodworking.

ACADEMIC PROGRAMS. Dual enrollment of high school students, independent study, internships, visiting/exchange student program, cross-registration, 5-year BA/BFA program with Reed College. **Placement/credit:** Institutional tests.

ACADEMIC REQUIREMENTS. Freshmen must earn minimum GPA of 2.0 to continue in good standing. 60% of freshmen return for sophomore year. Students must declare major by end of first year. **Graduation requirements:** 122 hours for bachelor's (39 in major). Most students required to take courses in arts/fine arts, English, humanities, biological/physical sciences, social sciences. **Additional information:** Individual studio space provided for fourth-year students. Thesis required as part of fourth-year curriculum.

FRESHMAN ADMISSIONS. Selection criteria: Drawing skills test and/or portfolio, 3 letters of recommendation, and essay most important. High school GPA average of at least 2.0 recommended. At least 1 year each of drawing and life drawing recommended.

1992 FRESHMAN CLASS PROFILE. 35% had high school GPA of 3.0 or higher, 47% between 2.0 and 2.99. **Characteristics:** 100% commute. Average age is 24.

FALL-TERM APPLICATIONS. $25 fee. Closing date August 15; priority given to applications received by April 15; applicants notified on a rolling basis beginning on or about October 1; must reply by August 20. Portfolio required. Essay required. Interview recommended. CRDA. Deferred admission available. SAT or ACT recommended.

STUDENT LIFE. Activities: Student government, student art exhibitions.

STUDENT SERVICES. Career counseling, employment service for undergraduates, freshman orientation, personal counseling, services/facilities for handicapped.

ANNUAL EXPENSES. Tuition and fees: $7,700. **Books and supplies:** $700. **Other expenses:** $3,500.

FINANCIAL AID. 50% of freshmen, 80% of continuing students receive some form of aid. 92% of grants, 90% of loans, all jobs based on need. 41 enrolled freshmen were judged to have need, all were offered aid. Academic, art scholarships available. **Aid applications:** No closing date; priority given to applications received by May 1; applicants notified on a rolling basis beginning on or about June 15; must reply by registration.

ADDRESS/TELEPHONE. Colin Page, Director of Admission, Pacific Northwest College of Art, 1219 Southwest Park Avenue, Portland, OR 97205-2486. (503) 226-0462. Fax: (503) 226-4842.

Pacific University
Forest Grove, Oregon CB code: 4601

Admissions: 89% of applicants accepted
Based on: ••• School record
•• Interview, recommendations, test scores
• Activities, essay, special talents
Completion: 87% of freshmen end year in good standing
52% graduate, 40% of these enter graduate study

4-year private university, coed, affiliated with United Church of Christ. Founded in 1849. **Accreditation:** Regional. **Undergraduate enrollment:** 368 men, 535 women full time; 16 men, 24 women part time. **Graduate enrollment:** 256 men, 318 women full time; 41 men, 64 women part time. **Faculty:** 199 total (112 full time). **Location:** Suburban campus in large town; 25 miles from Portland. **Calendar:** Semester, limited summer session. **Microcomputers:** 105 located in dormitories, libraries, computer centers. **Special facilities:** Wildlife refuge, museum, art gallery, arboretum.

DEGREES OFFERED. BA, BS, MA, MS, D, OD. 210 bachelor's degrees awarded in 1992. 15% in business and management, 11% education, 5% health sciences, 35% allied health, 7% letters/literature, 6% psychology, 9% social sciences. Graduate degrees offered in 8 major fields of study.

UNDERGRADUATE MAJORS. Biology, business administration and management, business and management, business and research, business economics, chemistry, Chinese, communications, computer and information sciences, creative writing, dramatic arts, economics, education, elementary education, English, fine arts, foreign languages (multiple emphasis), French, German, history, humanities, humanities and social sciences, international relations, international studies, Japanese, journalism, mathematics, music, music education, occupational therapy, philosophy, physical education, physical sciences, physics, political science and government, prelaw, premedicine, psychology, religion, social work, sociology, Spanish, telecommunications, visual and performing arts.

ACADEMIC PROGRAMS. Double major, honors program, independent study, internships, study abroad, teacher preparation, visiting/exchange student program, Washington semester, cross-registration, Peace and Conflict Studies Program; liberal arts/career combination in engineering, health sciences. **Remedial services:** Learning center, special counselor, tutoring. **ROTC:** Army. **Placement/credit:** AP, CLEP General and Subject, institutional tests.

ACADEMIC REQUIREMENTS. Freshmen must earn minimum of 2.0 in two-thirds of courses to continue in good academic standing. 73% of freshmen return for sophomore year. Students must declare major by end of second year. **Graduation requirements:** 124 hours for bachelor's (30 in major). Most students required to take courses in arts/fine arts, computer science, English, foreign languages, history, humanities, mathematics, philosophy/religion, biological/physical sciences, social sciences. **Postgraduate studies:** 6% enter law school, 8% enter medical school, 3% enter MBA programs, 23% enter other graduate study.

FRESHMAN ADMISSIONS. Selection criteria: Strength of high school program, academic GPA, test scores, course selection, and interview most important. Consideration also given to counselor recommendation, application essay, activity and leadership involvement. **High school preparation:** 16 units recommended. Recommended units include biological science 1, English 4, foreign language 2, mathematics 3, physical science 1 and social science 1. College-preparatory program strongly recommended. **Test requirements:** SAT or ACT; score report by August 15.

1992 FRESHMAN CLASS PROFILE. 387 men applied, 341 accepted, 91 enrolled; 616 women applied, 547 accepted, 152 enrolled. 85% had high school GPA of 3.0 or higher, 15% between 2.0 and 2.99. 42% were in top tenth and 33% were in top quarter of graduating class. **Academic background:** Mid 50% of enrolled freshmen had SAT-V between 410-510, SAT-M between 450-570; ACT composite between 21-26. 86% submitted SAT scores, 20% submitted ACT scores. **Characteristics:** 47% from in state, 96% live in college housing, 22% have minority backgrounds, 5% are foreign students, 32% join fraternities/sororities. Average age is 18.

FALL-TERM APPLICATIONS. $25 fee. Closing date May 1; priority given to applications received by March 15; applicants notified on a rolling basis beginning on or about February 1; must reply by June 1. Audition required for music applicants. Essay required. Interview recommended. Portfolio recommended for art applicants. CRDA. Deferred and early admission available. Institutional early decision plan. Accepted applicants urged to reply by May 1.

STUDENT LIFE. Housing: Dormitories (coed); apartment, handicapped housing available. **Activities:** Student government, magazine, radio, student newspaper, television, yearbook, Pacific Review (published poetry book), choral groups, concert band, dance, drama, jazz band, music ensembles, musical theater, opera, pep band, symphony orchestra, fraternities, sororities, Concerned Black Students, Hawaiian Club, Newman Club, Christian Fellowship, Politics and Law Forum, International Student Club, Spurs, Circle-K, Humanitarian Center. **Additional information:** Because of location, much interest and involvement in outdoor recreation, skiing, backpacking, rock climbing, river running.

ATHLETICS. NAIA. **Intercollegiate:** Baseball M, basketball, cross-country, golf, handball, soccer, softball W, swimming, tennis, track and field, volleyball W, wrestling M. **Intramural:** Basketball M, handball, racquetball, soccer, softball, volleyball.

STUDENT SERVICES. Aptitude testing, career counseling, employment service for undergraduates, freshman orientation, health services, on-campus day care, personal counseling, placement service for graduates, veterans counselor, handicapped utility clinic, services/facilities for handicapped.

ANNUAL EXPENSES. Tuition and fees: $13,490. **Room and board:** $3,815. **Books and supplies:** $400. **Other expenses:** $570.

FINANCIAL AID. 80% of freshmen, 87% of continuing students receive some form of aid. 74% of grants, 85% of loans, 85% of jobs based on need. Academic, music/drama, art, religious affiliation scholarships available. **Aid applications:** No closing date; priority given to applications received by March 15; applicants notified on a rolling basis; must reply within 3 weeks.

ADDRESS/TELEPHONE. Bart Howard, Dean of Admissions and Financial Aid, Pacific University, 2043 College Way, Forest Grove, OR 97116-1797. (503) 359-2218. (800) 677-6712. Fax: (503) 359-2242.

Portland Community College
Portland, Oregon CB code: 4617

2-year public community college, coed. Founded in 1961. **Accreditation:** Regional. **Undergraduate enrollment:** 42,868 men and women. **Faculty:** 1,086 total (376 full time), 85 with doctorates or other terminal degrees. **Location:** Urban campus in large city; main campus 5 miles from downtown. **Calendar:** Quarter, extensive summer session. **Microcomputers:** 200 located in computer centers. **Additional facts:** College has 3 comprehensive campuses and offers classes at several centers throughout the district.

DEGREES OFFERED. AA, AS, AAS. 983 associate degrees awarded in 1992. 9% in business and management, 7% business/office and marketing/distribution, 5% computer sciences, 17% allied health, 36% multi/interdisciplinary studies, 15% trade and industry.

UNDERGRADUATE MAJORS. Accounting, agricultural mechanics, aircraft mechanics, anthropology, architectural technologies, automotive mechanics, automotive technology, biology, biotechnology, business administration and management, business and office, business computer/console/peripheral equipment operation, business data entry equipment operation, business data programming, carpentry, chemistry, child development/care/guidance, civil technology, clinical laboratory science, commercial art, computer and information sciences, computer programming, computer servicing technology, computer software technician, computer technology, construction, criminal justice technology, dance, data processing, dental hygiene, dental laboratory technology, diesel engine mechanics, dietetic aide/assistant, drafting, drafting and design technology, dramatic arts, economics, education, electrical and electronics equipment repair, electronic technology, engineering, engineering and engineering-related technologies, English, finance, fine arts, fire control and safety technology, food production/management/services, French, geography, geology, German, graphic and printing production, graphic arts technology, history, home economics, hotel/motel and restaurant management, interior design, interpreter for the deaf, Japanese, journalism, landscape technology, law enforcement and corrections technologies, legal assistant/paralegal, legal secretary, liberal/general studies, library assistant, machine tool operation/machine shop, mathematics, mechanical design technology, medical laboratory technologies, medical records administration, medical records technology, metal/jewelry, microcomputer software, music, music performance, nursing, office supervision and management, ophthalmic services, optical technology, philosophy, physical sciences, physics, political science and government, practical nursing, precision metal work, predentistry, premedicine, prepharmacy, preveterinary, psychology, public administration, radiograph medical technology, real estate, Russian, secretarial and related programs, social sciences, sociology, Spanish, speech, tourism, trade and industrial education, ultrasound technology, veterinarian's assistant, welding technology, word processing.

ACADEMIC PROGRAMS. 2-year transfer program, dual enrollment of high school students, internships, study abroad, weekend college. **Remedial services:** Learning center, remedial instruction, tutoring. **Placement/credit:** AP, CLEP General and Subject, institutional tests; 45 credit hours maximum for associate degree.

ACADEMIC REQUIREMENTS. No policy requiring minimum GPA; records of students having academic difficulty are reviewed individually. Students must declare major on application. **Graduation requirements:** 90 hours for associate. Most students required to take courses in arts/fine arts, English, humanities, mathematics, biological/physical sciences, social sciences.

FRESHMAN ADMISSIONS. Selection criteria: Open admissions. Enrollment in certain programs or courses may require prequisite coursework or permission by a department representative. High school diploma required for some allied health programs.

1992 FRESHMAN CLASS PROFILE. 22,807 men and women enrolled. **Characteristics:** 99% from in state, 100% commute, 13% have minority backgrounds, 1% are foreign students.

FALL-TERM APPLICATIONS. No fee. No closing date; applicants notified on a rolling basis. Early admission available.

STUDENT LIFE. Activities: Student government, magazine, student newspaper, television, choral groups, dance, drama, jazz band.

ATHLETICS. NJCAA. **Intercollegiate:** Basketball, soccer M, volleyball W. **Intramural:** Archery, badminton, basketball, handball, racquetball, soccer, softball, swimming, table tennis, tennis, track and field, volleyball.

STUDENT SERVICES. Aptitude testing, career counseling, employment service for undergraduates, freshman orientation, health services, on-campus day care, personal counseling, placement service for graduates, veterans counselor, services/facilities for handicapped.

ANNUAL EXPENSES. Tuition and fees (projected): $1,305, $2,835 additional for out-of-state students. **Books and supplies:** $675. **Other expenses:** $720.

FINANCIAL AID. 15% of continuing students receive some form of aid. 98% of grants, 83% of loans, 50% of jobs based on need. Athletic scholarships available. **Aid applications:** No closing date; priority given to applications received by March 1; applicants notified on a rolling basis beginning on or about June 1; must reply within 3 weeks.

ADDRESS/TELEPHONE. Office of Admissions, Portland Community College, PO Box 19000, Portland, OR 97219-0990. (503) 244-6111 ext. 4519. (800) 634-7999. Fax: (503) 452-4988.

Portland State University
Portland, Oregon — CB code: 4610

Admissions: 90% of applicants accepted
Based on:
- ••• School record
- •• Test scores
- • Recommendations

Completion: 95% of freshmen end year in good standing

4-year public university, coed. Founded in 1946. **Accreditation:** Regional. **Undergraduate enrollment:** 3,060 men, 3,145 women full time; 2,184 men, 2,389 women part time. **Graduate enrollment:** 646 men, 722 women full time; 1,335 men, 1,531 women part time. **Faculty:** 954 total (760 full time), 449 with doctorates or other terminal degrees. **Location:** Urban campus in large city. **Calendar:** Quarter, extensive summer session. Extensive evening/early morning classes. **Microcomputers:** 350 located in computer centers, campus-wide network. **Special facilities:** Littman Gallery, White Gallery. **Additional facts:** Campus shared with Oregon Art Institute, Portland Center for the Performing Arts, and Oregon Historical Center. Courses offered at off-campus locations.

DEGREES OFFERED. BA, BS, MA, MS, MBA, MFA, MEd, MSW, PhD, EdD. 1,886 bachelor's degrees awarded in 1992. 18% in business and management, 8% business/office and marketing/distribution, 7% engineering, 9% letters/literature, 8% multi/interdisciplinary studies, 8% psychology, 20% social sciences, 5% visual and performing arts. Graduate degrees offered in 50 major fields of study.

UNDERGRADUATE MAJORS. Accounting, anthropology, biological and physical sciences, biology, business administration and management, business and management, business education, chemistry, civil engineering, computer and information sciences, computer engineering, dramatic arts, economics, electrical/electronics/communications engineering, English, finance, fine arts, foreign languages (multiple emphasis), French, geography, geology, German, health education, history, humanities and social sciences, international studies, Japanese, law enforcement and corrections, liberal/general studies, linguistics, marketing and distribution, mathematics, mechanical engineering, music, music performance, painting, philosophy, physics, political science and government, psychology, Russian, sculpture, secondary education, social sciences, sociology, Spanish, speech.

ACADEMIC PROGRAMS. Accelerated program, cooperative education, double major, dual enrollment of high school students, honors program, independent study, internships, student-designed major, study abroad, teacher preparation, telecourses, visiting/exchange student program, Washington semester, cross-registration. **Remedial services:** Preadmission summer program, reduced course load, special counselor, tutoring, remedial instruction offered through school of extended studies. **ROTC:** Air Force, Army. **Placement/credit:** AP, CLEP General and Subject, IB, institutional tests; 45 credit hours maximum for bachelor's degree.

ACADEMIC REQUIREMENTS. Freshmen must earn minimum GPA of 1.6 to continue in good standing. Students must declare major by end of second year. **Graduation requirements:** 186 hours for bachelor's. Most students required to take courses in English, biological/physical sciences, social sciences. **Additional information:** Community based service and research projects offer an opportunity to use the Portland area as a laboratory.

FRESHMAN ADMISSIONS. Selection criteria: High school GPA and completion of 14 specific approved courses most important. Test scores used to compensate for lower GPA. **High school preparation:** 14 units required. Required units include English 4, mathematics 3, social science 3 and science 2. 2 units in foreign language, computer science, or fine and performing arts required. **Test requirements:** SAT or ACT for placement; score report by June 1. 3 ACH may be submitted as alternative to high school subject requirement. ACH must include English, Mathematics Level I or II, and an additional test of students's choice. Score report by June 15 Test scores required for those with a high school grade-point average below 2.5.

1992 FRESHMAN CLASS PROFILE. 682 men applied, 597 accepted, 322 enrolled; 802 women applied, 739 accepted, 392 enrolled. 58% had high school GPA of 3.0 or higher, 40% between 2.0 and 2.99. **Academic background:** Mid 50% of enrolled freshmen had SAT-V between 360-500, SAT-M between 420-540; ACT composite between 18-24. 90% submitted SAT scores, 13% submitted ACT scores. **Characteristics:** 84% from in state, 86% commute, 24% have minority backgrounds, 2% are foreign students. Average age is 19.

FALL-TERM APPLICATIONS. $40 fee, may be waived for applicants with need. Closing date June 1; applicants notified on a rolling basis. Interviews recommended for those who do not meet regular admission requirements. CRDA. Deferred and early admission available.

STUDENT LIFE. Housing: Dormitories (coed); apartment, fraternity, sorority, handicapped housing available. Housing available through Portland Student Services, which operates non-profit coed dormitories and apartments on or near campus. **Activities:** Student government, magazine, student newspaper, yearbook, choral groups, concert band, dance, drama, jazz band, music ensembles, musical theater, opera, pep band, symphonic band, orchestra, fraternities, sororities, Campus Christian Ministry, student public interest research group, Black Cultural Affairs Board, United Indian Students in Higher Education, Women's Union, outdoor program, Disabled Student Union, Hispanic Student Union, Organization of International Students.

ATHLETICS. NCAA. **Intercollegiate:** Baseball M, basketball W, cross-country, football M, golf M, softball W, tennis W, track and field, volleyball W, wrestling M. **Intramural:** Archery, badminton, basketball, racquetball, soccer, softball, table tennis, tennis, volleyball.

STUDENT SERVICES. Aptitude testing, career counseling, employment service for undergraduates, freshman orientation, health services, on-campus day care, personal counseling, placement service for graduates, special adviser for adult students, veterans counselor, legal services, student resource center, services/facilities for handicapped.

ANNUAL EXPENSES. Tuition and fees (1992-93): $2,658, $4,281 additional for out-of-state students. **Books and supplies:** $750. **Other expenses:** $1,098.

FINANCIAL AID. 38% of freshmen, 46% of continuing students receive some form of aid. 78% of grants, 80% of loans, all jobs based on need. 243 enrolled freshmen were judged to have need, 231 were offered aid. Academic, music/drama, art, athletic, minority scholarships available. **Aid applications:** No closing date; priority given to applications received by March 1; applicants notified on a rolling basis beginning on or about April 1; must reply within 2 weeks.

ADDRESS/TELEPHONE. Jesse R. Welch, Director of Admissions, Portland State University, PO Box 751, Portland, OR 97207-0751. (503) 725-3511. (800) 547-8887. Fax: (503) 725-4882.

Reed College
Portland, Oregon — CB code: 4654

Admissions: 71% of applicants accepted
Based on:
- ••• Essay, school record
- •• Recommendations, test scores
- • Activities, interview, special talents

Completion: 94% of freshmen end year in good standing
67% graduate, 65% of these enter graduate study

4-year private liberal arts college, coed. Founded in 1910. **Accreditation:** Regional. **Undergraduate enrollment:** 596 men, 563 women full time; 20 men, 31 women part time. **Graduate enrollment:** 3 men, 3 women full time; 6 men, 8 women part time. **Faculty:** 133 total (105 full time), 106 with doctorates or other terminal degrees. **Location:** Suburban campus in large city; 5 miles from downtown. **Calendar:** Semester. **Microcomputers:** 150 located in libraries, classrooms, computer centers, campus-wide network. **Special facilities:** Nuclear research reactor, wildlife refuge, comprehensive science facilities, ski cabin on Mount Hood.

DEGREES OFFERED. BA, M. 296 bachelor's degrees awarded in 1992. 20% in letters/literature, 13% life sciences, 5% mathematics, 8% multi/interdisciplinary studies, 8% philosophy, religion, theology, 11% physical sciences, 7% psychology, 17% social sciences, 7% visual and performing arts. Graduate degrees offered in 1 major field of study.

UNDERGRADUATE MAJORS. American studies, anthropology, art history, biochemistry, biological and physical sciences, biology, chemistry, Chinese, classics, comparative literature, dance, dramatic arts, economics, English literature, fine arts, French, German, history, humanities and social sciences, international relations, liberal/general studies, linguistics, mathematics, medieval studies, music, philosophy, physics, political science and government, psychology, religion, Russian, sociology, Spanish.

ACADEMIC PROGRAMS. Accelerated program, double major, independent study, internships, student-designed major, study abroad, visiting/exchange student program, cross-registration; liberal arts/career combination in engineering, forestry, business. **Remedial services:** Tutoring. **ROTC:** Army. **Placement/credit:** AP, institutional tests; 32 credit hours maximum for bachelor's degree.

ACADEMIC REQUIREMENTS. No policy requiring minimum GPA; records of students having academic difficulty are reviewed individually. 90% of freshmen return for sophomore year. Students must declare major by end of second year. **Graduation requirements:** 120 hours for bachelor's. Most students required to take courses in arts/fine arts, humanities, biological/physical sciences, social sciences. **Postgraduate studies:** 7% enter law school, 5% enter medical school, 5% enter MBA programs, 48% enter other graduate study.

FRESHMAN ADMISSIONS. Selection criteria: Academic criteria most important, as demonstrated by grades, class rank, course selection, personal essays, recommendations, and test scores. No grade or test score cutoffs. Demonstrated ability, an inquisitive nature, academic motivation, and individual responsibility. Recommended units include English 4, foreign language 2, mathematics 4, social science 2 and science 2. **Test requirements:** SAT or ACT; score report by March 1. 3 ACH required for foreign students. Score report by March 1.

1992 FRESHMAN CLASS PROFILE. 865 men applied, 565 accepted, 137 enrolled; 990 women applied, 754 accepted, 173 enrolled. 97% had high school GPA of 3.0 or higher, 3% between 2.0 and 2.99. 57% were in top tenth and 83% were in top quarter of graduating class. **Academic background:** Mid 50% of enrolled freshmen had SAT-V between 570-670, SAT-M between 580-700. 98% submitted SAT scores. **Characteristics:** 7% from in state, 97% live in college housing, 14% have minority backgrounds, 16% are foreign students. Average age is 18.

FALL-TERM APPLICATIONS. $40 fee, may be waived for applicants with need. Closing date February 1; applicants notified on or about April 1; must reply by May 1. Essay required. Interview recommended. CRDA. Deferred and early admission available. EDP-F. 2 early decision plans: fall option (deadline December 1, notification December 15); winter option (deadline January 15, notification February 1).

STUDENT LIFE. Housing: Dormitories (men, women, coed); apartment, handicapped housing available. Most off-campus apartments and houses within 2 miles. 5 language houses available for upperclass students. **Activities:** Student government, film, magazine, radio, student newspaper, yearbook, poetry publications, research journal, choral groups, dance, drama, jazz band, music ensembles, musical theater, chamber orchestra, Christian Fellowship, Jewish Student Union, women's center, environmental coalition, politically active student groups, volunteer tutoring, language and outing clubs, student art gallery, public, cultural, and social affairs boards, poetry forum, sports clubs. **Additional information:** During January students may participate in noncredit, student-run, 2-week period of academic and nonacademic courses.

ATHLETICS. Intramural: Archery, badminton, basketball M, bowling, diving, fencing, golf, handball, horseback riding, racquetball, rowing (crew), rugby, sailing, skiing, soccer, softball, squash, swimming, tennis, volleyball, water polo M.

STUDENT SERVICES. Career counseling, employment service for undergraduates, freshman orientation, health services, personal counseling, placement service for graduates, special adviser for adult students, services/facilities for handicapped.

ANNUAL EXPENSES. Tuition and fees: $19,250. **Room and board:** $5,230. **Books and supplies:** $500. **Other expenses:** $450.

FINANCIAL AID. 45% of freshmen, 48% of continuing students receive some form of aid. All grants, 97% of loans, 18% of jobs based on need. 140 enrolled freshmen were judged to have need, 129 were offered aid. **Aid applications:** Closing date March 1; applicants notified on or about April 1; must reply by May 1.

ADDRESS/TELEPHONE. Robert J. Mansueto, Dean of Admission, Reed College, 3203 Southeast Woodstock Boulevard, Portland, OR 97202-8199. (503) 777-7511. (800) 547-4750. Fax: (503) 777-7775.

Rogue Community College
Grants Pass, Oregon — CB code: 4653

2-year public community college, coed. Founded in 1970. **Accreditation:** Regional. **Undergraduate enrollment:** 499 men, 703 women full time; 507 men, 939 women part time. **Faculty:** 345 total (65 full time), 4 with doctorates or other terminal degrees. **Location:** Rural campus in large town; 30 miles from Medford, 240 miles from Portland. **Calendar:** Quarter, limited summer session. **Microcomputers:** 96 located in classrooms, computer centers. **Special facilities:** Rogue Music Theater (outdoor bowl), Wiseman Art Gallery. **Additional facts:** Branch campus in Phoenix, learning centers in Medford, Ashland, Klamath Falls, and Cave Junction.

DEGREES OFFERED. AA, AAS. 126 associate degrees awarded in 1992. 10% in business and management, 10% business/office and marketing/distribution, 26% allied health, 14% letters/literature, 5% life sciences, 21% social sciences, 10% trade and industry.

UNDERGRADUATE MAJORS. Accounting, automotive mechanics, automotive technology, biological and physical sciences, business administration and management, business and office, computer and information sciences, criminal justice studies, diesel engine mechanics, electrical and electronics equipment repair, fine arts, fire control and safety technology, humanities, humanities and social sciences, liberal/general studies, mathematics, mechanical design technology, nursing, office supervision and management, physical sciences, practical nursing, respiratory therapy, respiratory therapy technology, secretarial and related programs, social sciences, visual and performing arts.

ACADEMIC PROGRAMS. 2-year transfer program, cooperative education, double major, dual enrollment of high school students, independent study, telecourses, cross-registration. **Remedial services:** Learning center, remedial instruction, special counselor, tutoring. **Placement/credit:** AP, CLEP General and Subject, institutional tests.

ACADEMIC REQUIREMENTS. Freshmen must earn minimum GPA of 2.0 to continue in good standing. 67% of freshmen return for sophomore year. Students must declare major on enrollment. **Graduation requirements:** 90 hours for associate (24 in major). Most students required to take courses in computer science, English, mathematics.

FRESHMAN ADMISSIONS. Selection criteria: Open admissions. Special admissions for nursing and respiratory therapy.

1992 FRESHMAN CLASS PROFILE. 100 men, 117 women enrolled. **Characteristics:** 99% from in state, 100% commute, 23% have minority backgrounds, 1% are foreign students. Average age is 19.

FALL-TERM APPLICATIONS. No fee. No closing date; applicants notified on a rolling basis. Interview required for allied health, nursing applicants. Early admission available.

STUDENT LIFE. Activities: Student government, student newspaper, choral groups, dance, drama, music ensembles, musical theater.

ATHLETICS. Intramural: Badminton, basketball, softball, tennis, volleyball.

STUDENT SERVICES. Aptitude testing, career counseling, employment service for undergraduates, freshman orientation, on-campus day care, personal counseling, placement service for graduates, veterans counselor, services/facilities for handicapped.

ANNUAL EXPENSES. Tuition and fees: $1,074, $612 additional for out-of-district students, $2,412 additional for out-of-state students. **Books and supplies:** $450. **Other expenses:** $825.

FINANCIAL AID. 70% of freshmen, 70% of continuing students receive some form of aid. 99% of grants, all loans, all jobs based on need. Academic, state/district residency, leadership scholarships available. **Aid applications:** No closing date; priority given to applications received by April 1; applicants notified on a rolling basis beginning on or about May 1; must reply within 2 weeks.

ADDRESS/TELEPHONE. Ted Risser, Director of Enrollment Services, Rogue Community College, 3345 Redwood Highway, Grants Pass, OR 97527. (503) 471-3500 ext. 254. Fax: (503) 471-3588.

Southern Oregon State College
Ashland, Oregon — CB code: 4702

Admissions:	83% of applicants accepted
Based on:	••• School record, test scores
	• Activities, interview, recommendations, special talents
Completion:	75% of freshmen end year in good standing
	40% enter graduate study

4-year public college of arts and sciences and teachers college, coed. Founded in 1926. **Accreditation:** Regional. **Undergraduate enrollment:** 1,584 men, 1,652 women full time; 362 men, 488 women part time. **Graduate enrollment:** 98 men, 115 women full time; 88 men, 142 women part time. **Faculty:** 348 total (278 full time), 193 with doctorates or other terminal degrees. **Location:** Suburban campus in large town; 10 miles from Medford. **Calendar:** Quarter, limited summer session. **Microcomputers:** Located in dormitories, libraries, classrooms, computer centers. **Special facilities:** Art galleries, art museum, history and natural history museums, herbarium, U.S. Fish and Wildfife Forensics Laboratory, greenhouses, invertebrate collection, theaters, concert auditorium, radio and television studios. **Additional facts:** College is one of 30 U.S. colleges designated by National Aeronautical and Space Administration (NASA) to do joint space research.

DEGREES OFFERED. AA, BA, BS, BFA, MA, MS, MBA. 21 associate degrees awarded in 1992. 55% in business/office and marketing/distribution, 45% multi/interdisciplinary studies. 713 bachelor's degrees awarded. 29% in business and management, 8% communications, 8% allied health, 11% multi/interdisciplinary studies, 8% psychology, 21% social sciences. Graduate degrees offered in 21 major fields of study.

UNDERGRADUATE MAJORS. Associate: Accounting, business administration and management, business and management, business and office, business/chemistry, business/mathematics, business/physics, dramatic arts, liberal/general studies, secretarial and related programs. **Bachelor's:** Accounting, applied mathematics, art history, biological and physical sciences, biology, business administration and management, business and management, chemistry, communications, computer and information sciences, computer mathematics, criminal justice studies, criminology, dramatic arts, economics, English, fine arts, foreign languages (multiple emphasis), geography, geology, history, humanities and social sciences, international relations, international studies, law enforcement and corrections, liberal/general studies, marketing management, mathematics, music, nursing, personnel management, physical sciences, physics, political science and government, predentistry, prelaw, premedicine, prepharmacy, preveterinary, psychology, social sciences, sociology, speech, statistics.

ACADEMIC PROGRAMS. Double major, dual enrollment of high school students, honors program, independent study, study abroad. **Remedial services:** Reduced course load, remedial instruction. **Placement/credit:** AP, CLEP General and Subject, institutional tests.

ACADEMIC REQUIREMENTS. Freshmen must earn minimum GPA of 2.0 to continue in good standing. 60% of freshmen return for sophomore year. Students must declare major by end of first year. **Graduation requirements:** 96 hours for associate (20 in major), 186 hours for bachelor's (50 in major). Most students required to take courses in arts/fine arts, English, humanities, biological/physical sciences, social sciences. **Postgraduate studies:** 80% from 2-year programs enter 4-year programs.

FRESHMAN ADMISSIONS. Selection criteria: High school GPA of 2.5 from state-accredited high school or ACT composite score of 20, or SAT combined score of 890. Special admission program for minorities, low-income, disadvantaged, and older students. **High school preparation:** 14 units required. Required units include science 2. **Test requirements:** SAT or ACT; score report by September 15. 3 ACH required of applicants not meeting high school subject requirements. Score report by September 15. **Additional information:** Requests for special admission for undergraduates reviewed individually.

1992 FRESHMAN CLASS PROFILE. 624 men applied, 521 accepted, 350 enrolled; 764 women applied, 636 accepted, 395 enrolled. **Academic background:** Mid 50% of enrolled freshmen had SAT-V between 400-520, SAT-M between 400-530. 93% submitted SAT scores. **Characteristics:** 90% from in state, 50% commute, 7% have minority backgrounds, 2% are foreign students. Average age is 19.

FALL-TERM APPLICATIONS. $40 fee. No closing date; priority given to applications received by June 1; applicants notified on a rolling basis beginning on or about November 1. Audition recommended for theater, music applicants. Portfolio recommended for art applicants. Deferred and early admission available.

STUDENT LIFE. Housing: Dormitories (men, women); apartment housing available. **Activities:** Student government, film, radio, student newspaper, television, yearbook, choral groups, concert band, dance, drama, marching band, musical theater, opera, symphony orchestra, club sports.

ATHLETICS. NAIA, NCAA. **Intercollegiate:** Basketball, cross-country, football M, skiing, swimming, track and field, volleyball W, wrestling M. **Intramural:** Badminton, basketball M, soccer M, softball, swimming, track and field, volleyball, wrestling M.

STUDENT SERVICES. Aptitude testing, career counseling, employment service for undergraduates, health services, on-campus day care, personal counseling, placement service for graduates, veterans counselor.

ANNUAL EXPENSES. Tuition and fees (projected): $2,635, $3,750 additional for out-of-state students. **Room and board:** $3,300. **Books and supplies:** $580. **Other expenses:** $1,545.

FINANCIAL AID. 60% of freshmen, 65% of continuing students receive some form of aid. 85% of grants, 87% of loans, 33% of jobs based on need. 649 enrolled freshmen were judged to have need, all were offered aid. Academic, music/drama, art, leadership, minority scholarships available. **Aid applications:** No closing date; priority given to applications received by March 1; applicants notified on a rolling basis beginning on or about May 20; must reply within 2 weeks.

ADDRESS/TELEPHONE. Allen H. Blaszak, Director of Admissions, Southern Oregon State College, Ashland, OR 97520-5032. (503) 552-6411. Fax: (503) 552-6429.

Southwestern Oregon Community College

Coos Bay, Oregon — CB code: 4729

2-year public community college, coed. Founded in 1961. **Accreditation:** Regional. **Undergraduate enrollment:** 5,377 men and women. **Location:** Rural campus in large town; 125 miles from Eugene. **Calendar:** Quarter.

FRESHMAN ADMISSIONS. Selection criteria: Open admissions. Selective admissions to some programs. Placement test, interview, high school chemistry and algebra required for nursing. Background check required for emergency response.

ANNUAL EXPENSES. Tuition and fees (projected): $1,082, $1,082 additional for out-of-state students. **Books and supplies:** $600. **Other expenses:** $510.

ADDRESS/TELEPHONE. Jean von Schweinitz, Director of Admissions and Records, Southwestern Oregon Community College, 1988 Newmark, Coos Bay, OR 97420. (503) 888-7420. Fax: (503) 888-7285.

Treasure Valley Community College

Ontario, Oregon — CB code: 4825

2-year public community college, coed. Founded in 1961. **Accreditation:** Regional. **Undergraduate enrollment:** 430 men, 374 women full time; 878 men, 1,321 women part time. **Faculty:** 69 total (44 full time), 2 with doctorates or other terminal degrees. **Location:** Rural campus in small town; 60 miles from Boise, Idaho. **Calendar:** Quarter, limited summer session. **Microcomputers:** 50 located in libraries, classrooms, computer centers.

DEGREES OFFERED. AA, AS, AAS. 190 associate degrees awarded in 1992.

UNDERGRADUATE MAJORS. Agribusiness, agricultural sciences, airline piloting and navigation, biology, business and management, business and office, business data entry equipment operation, business data programming, chemistry, communications, computer and information sciences, drafting, drafting and design technology, dramatic arts, education, elementary education, engineering, fine arts, forestry and related sciences, law enforcement and corrections technologies, legal secretary, liberal/general studies, marketing and distribution, mathematics, medical secretary, music, nursing, physical education, physical sciences, preengineering, prelaw, psychology, range management, secondary education, secretarial and related programs, social sciences, survey and mapping technology, surveying and mapping sciences, welding technology.

ACADEMIC PROGRAMS. 2-year transfer program, double major, dual enrollment of high school students, elementary education program with Eastern Oregon State College and satellite program with Boise State University. **Remedial services:** Learning center, reduced course load, remedial instruction, special counselor, tutoring. **Placement/credit:** AP, CLEP General and Subject, institutional tests.

ACADEMIC REQUIREMENTS. Freshmen must earn minimum GPA of 2.0 to continue in good standing. 45% of freshmen return for sophomore year. **Graduation requirements:** 96 hours for associate. Most students required to take courses in English, humanities, mathematics, biological/physical sciences, social sciences.

FRESHMAN ADMISSIONS. Selection criteria: Open admissions.

1992 FRESHMAN CLASS PROFILE. 1,121 men, 1,419 women enrolled. **Characteristics:** 90% from in state, 88% commute, 8% have minority backgrounds, 1% are foreign students. Average age is 19.

FALL-TERM APPLICATIONS. No fee. No closing date; applicants notified on a rolling basis. Early admission available.

STUDENT LIFE. Housing: Dormitories (men, women). **Activities:** Student government, choral groups, concert band, drama, jazz band, music ensembles, musical theater, pep band.

ATHLETICS. NJCAA. **Intercollegiate:** Baseball M, basketball, cross-country, golf M, track and field, volleyball W. **Intramural:** Basketball, softball, volleyball.

STUDENT SERVICES. Aptitude testing, career counseling, freshman orientation, health services, personal counseling, veterans counselor, services/facilities for handicapped.

ANNUAL EXPENSES. Tuition and fees (1992-93): $966, $864 additional for out-of-state students. **Room and board:** $3,111. **Books and supplies:** $350. **Other expenses:** $750.

FINANCIAL AID. 80% of freshmen, 80% of continuing students receive some form of aid. 84% of grants, 93% of loans, all jobs based on need. Academic, music/drama, art, athletic scholarships available. **Aid applications:** No closing date; priority given to applications received by April 1; applicants notified on a rolling basis beginning on or about May 1; must reply within 15 days.

ADDRESS/TELEPHONE. Ron Kulm, Director of Admissions, Treasure Valley Community College, 650 College Boulevard, Ontario, OR 97914. (503) 889-6493.

Umpqua Community College

Roseburg, Oregon — CB code: 4862

2-year public community college, coed. Founded in 1964. **Accreditation:** Regional. **Undergraduate enrollment:** 497 men, 550 women full time; 461 men, 604 women part time. **Faculty:** 185 total (65 full time), 9 with doctorates or other terminal degrees. **Location:** Rural campus in large town; 70 miles from Eugene. **Calendar:** Quarter, limited summer session. **Microcomputers:** 150 located in libraries, classrooms, computer centers. **Special facilities:** Art gallery.

DEGREES OFFERED. AA, AS, AAS. 206 associate degrees awarded in 1992. 28% in business/office and marketing/distribution, 28% health sciences, 27% multi/interdisciplinary studies, 14% trade and industry.

UNDERGRADUATE MAJORS. Accounting, automotive mechanics, automotive technology, business administration and management, business and management, business and office, business computer/console/peripheral equipment operation, business data entry equipment operation, business data processing and related programs, business data programming, child development/care/guidance, civil engineering, computer programming, electrical and electronics equipment repair, electronic technology, engineering and engineering-related technologies, fire control and safety technology, legal secretary, liberal/general studies, marketing and distribution, marketing management, medical secretary, microcomputer software, nursing, secretarial and related programs.

ACADEMIC PROGRAMS. 2-year transfer program, cooperative education, double major, dual enrollment of high school students, internships, telecourses. **Remedial services:** Learning center, preadmission summer program, reduced course load, remedial instruction, special counselor, tutoring. **Placement/credit:** AP, CLEP General and Subject, institutional tests; 45 credit hours maximum for associate degree.

ACADEMIC REQUIREMENTS. Freshmen must earn minimum GPA of 2.0 to continue in good standing. 38% of freshmen return for sophomore year. Students must declare major on enrollment. **Graduation requirements:** 93 hours for associate. Most students required to take courses in English, mathematics, social sciences.

FRESHMAN ADMISSIONS. Selection criteria: Open admissions. All students whose high school class has graduated admitted even if they did not graduate.

1992 FRESHMAN CLASS PROFILE. 529 men, 806 women enrolled. **Characteristics:** 97% from in state, 100% commute, 1% have minority backgrounds. Average age is 21.

FALL-TERM APPLICATIONS. No fee. Closing date August 15; applicants notified on a rolling basis. Deferred and early admission available.

STUDENT LIFE. Activities: Student government, student newspaper, choral groups, concert band, drama, jazz band, music ensembles, musical theater, pep band, Campus Challenge, professional organizations.

ATHLETICS. Intercollegiate: Basketball, cross-country, track and field, volleyball W. **Intramural:** Basketball, softball.

STUDENT SERVICES. Aptitude testing, career counseling, employment service for undergraduates, freshman orientation, on-campus day care, personal counseling, placement service for graduates, veterans counselor, services/facilities for handicapped.

ANNUAL EXPENSES. Tuition and fees (1992-93): $1,176, $3,268 additional for out-of-state students. **Books and supplies:** $540. **Other expenses:** $630.

FINANCIAL AID. 60% of freshmen, 60% of continuing students receive some form of aid. 99% of grants, all loans, 17% of jobs based on need. 525 enrolled freshmen were judged to have need, all were offered aid. Academic, state/district residency, leadership scholarships available. **Aid applications:** No closing date; priority given to applications received by March 1; applicants notified on a rolling basis beginning on or about June 1; must reply within 2 weeks.

ADDRESS/TELEPHONE. Dr. Larry H. Shipley, Director of Admissions and Records, Umpqua Community College, PO Box 967, Roseburg, OR 97470. (503) 440-4604. Fax: (503) 440-4637.

University of Oregon
Eugene, Oregon

CB code: 4846

Admissions: 77% of applicants accepted
Based on: ••• School record
•• Test scores
Completion: 84% of freshmen end year in good standing
48% graduate, 20% of these enter graduate study

4-year public university, coed. Founded in 1876. **Accreditation:** Regional. **Undergraduate enrollment:** 5,521 men, 5,620 women full time; 833 men, 793 women part time. **Graduate enrollment:** 1,507 men, 1,167 women full time; 318 men, 341 women part time. **Faculty:** 1,534 total (1,405 full time), 769 with doctorates or other terminal degrees. **Location:** Urban campus in small city; 110 miles from Portland. **Calendar:** Quarter, extensive summer session. **Microcomputers:** Located in dormitories, libraries, classrooms, computer centers, campus-wide network. **Special facilities:** Art and natural history museums, mountain observatory, herbarium, marine biology station at coast. **Additional facts:** Campus is registered arboretum with more than 300 species of trees, shrubs, and plants.

DEGREES OFFERED. BA, BS, BFA, MA, MS, MBA, MFA, PhD, EdD, JD. 2,931 bachelor's degrees awarded in 1992. 15% in business and management, 11% communications, 6% teacher education, 7% languages, 11% letters/literature, 5% parks/recreation, protective services, public affairs, 10% psychology, 15% social sciences, 5% visual and performing arts. Graduate degrees offered in 83 major fields of study.

UNDERGRADUATE MAJORS. Accounting, advertising, anthropology, architecture, art history, Asian studies, biological and physical sciences, biology, business administration and management, business and management, ceramics, chemistry, Chinese, classics, comparative literature, computer and information sciences, dance, dramatic arts, economics, English, English literature, fiber/textiles/weaving, finance, fine arts, foreign languages (multiple emphasis), French, geography, geology, German, Greek (classical), history, humanities and social sciences, interior design, Italian, Japanese, journalism, landscape architecture, Latin, liberal/general studies, linguistics, management information systems, marine biology, marketing management, mathematics, metal/jewelry, music, music education, music performance, music theory and composition, operations research, painting, philosophy, physics, political science and government, printmaking, psychology, public relations, radio/television broadcasting, religion, Russian, sculpture, sociology, Spanish, special education, speech pathology/audiology, telecommunications.

ACADEMIC PROGRAMS. Cooperative education, double major, honors program, independent study, internships, semester at sea, study abroad, teacher preparation, visiting/exchange student program, cross-registration; liberal arts/career combination in engineering; combined bachelor's/graduate program in business administration. **Remedial services:** Learning center, remedial instruction, tutoring. **ROTC:** Army. **Placement/credit:** AP, CLEP General and Subject, institutional tests.

ACADEMIC REQUIREMENTS. Freshmen must earn minimum GPA of 2.0 to continue in good standing. 82% of freshmen return for sophomore year. Students must declare major by end of second year. **Graduation requirements:** 186 hours for bachelor's (36 in major). Most students required to take courses in English, foreign languages, humanities, mathematics, biological/physical sciences, social sciences. **Postgraduate studies:** 2% enter law school, 2% enter medical school, 7% enter MBA programs, 9% enter other graduate study.

FRESHMAN ADMISSIONS. Selection criteria: 3.0 high school GPA. Test scores used to compensate for lower GPA. Minimum score of 30 on Test of Standard Written English. **High school preparation:** 14 units required. Required and recommended units include English 4, mathematics 3, social science 3 and science 2. Foreign language 2 recommended. **Test requirements:** SAT or ACT; score report by May 1. ACH required of students who do not meet course pattern requirement. Score report by May 1.

1992 FRESHMAN CLASS PROFILE. 3,407 men applied, 2,648 accepted, 1,566 enrolled; 3,752 women applied, 2,889 accepted, 1,607 enrolled. 85% had high school GPA of 3.0 or higher, 15% between 2.0 and 2.99. 20% were in top tenth and 48% were in top quarter of graduating class. **Academic background:** Mid 50% of enrolled freshmen had SAT-V between 440-570, SAT-M between 470-600. 97% submitted SAT scores. **Characteristics:** 65% from in state, 64% live in college housing, 12% have minority backgrounds, 2% are foreign students, 24% join fraternities/sororities. Average age is 19.

FALL-TERM APPLICATIONS. $50 fee. Closing date March 1; applicants notified on or about April 1; must reply by May 1. Audition required for music, dance applicants. Portfolio required for architecture, interior design, fine art, applied applied arts applicants. Early admission available. Application deadline for architecture, interior architecture is December 15, for landscape architecture, February 1.

STUDENT LIFE. Housing: Dormitories (men, women, coed); apartment, fraternity, sorority, cooperative housing available. **Activities:** Student government, film, magazine, radio, student newspaper, television, yearbook, choral groups, concert band, dance, drama, jazz band, marching band, music ensembles, musical theater, opera, pep band, symphony orchestra, fraternities, sororities, ethnic student unions, numerous religious organizations, political and environmental groups.

ATHLETICS. NCAA. **Intercollegiate:** Basketball, cross-country, football M, golf, softball W, tennis, track and field, volleyball W, wrestling M. **Intramural:** Archery, badminton, baseball M, basketball, bowling, cross-country, diving, fencing, field hockey, golf, handball, horseback riding, ice hockey M, lacrosse, racquetball, rowing (crew), rugby M, sailing, skiing, skin diving, soccer, softball, squash, swimming, table tennis, tennis, track and field, volleyball, water polo, wrestling M.

STUDENT SERVICES. Aptitude testing, career counseling, employment service for undergraduates, freshman orientation, health services, on-campus day care, personal counseling, placement service for graduates, special adviser for adult students, veterans counselor, athletes' counselor, minority counselor, services/facilities for handicapped.

ANNUAL EXPENSES. Tuition and fees (1992-93): $2,721, $5,130 additional for out-of-state students. **Room and board:** $3,212. **Books and supplies:** $425. **Other expenses:** $1,145.

FINANCIAL AID. 45% of freshmen, 45% of continuing students receive some form of aid. 90% of grants, 94% of loans, 56% of jobs based on need. Academic, music/drama, art, athletic, state/district residency, leadership scholarships available. **Aid applications:** No closing date; priority given to applications received by March 1; applicants notified on a rolling basis beginning on or about April 15; must reply within 4 weeks.

ADDRESS/TELEPHONE. James Buch, Director of Admissions, University of Oregon, 240 Oregon Hall, Eugene, OR 97403-1217. (503) 346-3201. Fax: (503) 346-5815.

University of Oregon: Robert Donald Clark Honors College
Eugene, Oregon CB code: 7353

Admissions: 59% of applicants accepted
Based on: ••• Essay, school record, test scores
•• Recommendations
• Activities, interview, special talents
Completion: 95% of freshmen end year in good standing
65% graduate, 40% of these enter graduate study

4-year public university, coed. **Accreditation:** Regional. **Undergraduate enrollment:** 150 men, 225 women full time. **Faculty:** 6 total, 6 with doctorates or other terminal degrees. **Location:** Urban campus in small city; 110 miles from Portland. **Calendar:** Quarter, extensive summer session. **Microcomputers:** Located in dormitories, classrooms, computer centers. **Special facilities:** Art and natural history museums, mountain observatory, herbarium, marine biology station at coast. **Additional facts:** Small liberal arts college within the University of Oregon. Honors college has resident faculty, its own seminar room, classroom, lounge, library and computer laboratory.

DEGREES OFFERED. BA. 59 bachelor's degrees awarded in 1992.

UNDERGRADUATE MAJORS. Accounting, advertising, anthropology, architecture, art history, Asian studies, biological and physical sciences, biology, business administration and management, business and management, ceramics, chemistry, Chinese, classics, comparative literature, computer and information sciences, dance, dramatic arts, economics, English, English literature, finance, fine arts, foreign languages (multiple emphasis), French, geography, geology, German, Greek (classical), history, humanities and social sciences, international public service, international relations, Italian, Japanese, journalism, Latin, liberal/general studies, linguistics, marine biology, marketing management, mathematics, metal/jewelry, music, music performance, music theory and composition, operations research, painting, philosophy, physics, political science and government, printmaking, psychology, public administration, public relations, radio/television broadcasting, religion, Russian, sculpture, social work, sociology, Spanish, special education, speech, speech correction, speech pathology/audiology, telecommunications.

ACADEMIC PROGRAMS. Cooperative education, double major, honors program, independent study, internships, semester at sea, study abroad, visiting/exchange student program; combined bachelor's/graduate program in business administration. **Remedial services:** Learning center, preadmission summer program, tutoring. **ROTC:** Army. **Placement/credit:** AP, CLEP General and Subject, institutional tests.

ACADEMIC REQUIREMENTS. No policy requiring minimum GPA; records of students having academic difficulty are reviewed individually. Students must complete 85% of all work attempted. 90% of freshmen return for sophomore year. Students must declare major by end of second year. **Graduation requirements:** 186 hours for bachelor's (36 in major). Most students required to take courses in English, foreign languages, history, humanities, mathematics, biological/physical sciences, social sciences. **Additional information:** All students graduating from Clark do research and write honors theses in their majors. All seniors are eligible for honors research fellowships.

FRESHMAN ADMISSIONS. Selection criteria: High school achievement, standardized test scores, recommendation, essay and activities are all important, interview, when possible. **High school preparation:** 14 units required. Required and recommended units include English 4, mathematics 3, social science 3 and science 2. Foreign language 2 recommended. **Test requirements:** SAT or ACT (SAT preferred). ACH required of some applicants.

1992 FRESHMAN CLASS PROFILE. 136 men applied, 80 accepted, 42 enrolled; 204 women applied, 121 accepted, 55 enrolled. 100% had high school GPA of 3.0 or higher. **Academic background:** Mid 50% of enrolled freshmen had SAT-V between 580-660, SAT-M between 580-680. 90% submitted SAT scores. **Characteristics:** 64% live in college housing. Average age is 19.

FALL-TERM APPLICATIONS. $40 fee. Closing date February 1; applicants notified on or about April 1; must reply by May 1. Audition required for music, dance applicants. Portfolio required for architecture, interior design applicants. Essay required. Early admission available. Application deadline for interior architecture, January 15; landscape architecture, February 1.

STUDENT LIFE. Housing: Dormitories (men, women, coed); apartment, fraternity, sorority, cooperative housing available. **Activities:** Student government, film, magazine, radio, student newspaper, television, yearbook, choral groups, concert band, dance, drama, jazz band, marching band, music ensembles, musical theater, opera, pep band, symphony orchestra, fraternities, sororities, more than 175 student organizations.

ATHLETICS. NCAA. **Intercollegiate:** Basketball, cross-country, football M, golf, softball W, tennis, track and field, volleyball W, wrestling M. **Intramural:** Archery, badminton, baseball, basketball, bowling, cross-country, fencing, field hockey, golf, handball, horseback riding, lacrosse, racquetball, rowing (crew), sailing, skiing, skin diving, soccer, softball, squash, swimming, table tennis, tennis, track and field, volleyball, water polo, wrestling M.

STUDENT SERVICES. Aptitude testing, career counseling, employment service for undergraduates, health services, on-campus day care, personal counseling, placement service for graduates, special adviser for adult students, veterans counselor, Y, services/facilities for handicapped.

ANNUAL EXPENSES. Tuition and fees (1992-93): $2,721, $5,130 additional for out-of-state students. **Room and board:** $3,212. **Books and supplies:** $450. **Other expenses:** $1,150.

FINANCIAL AID. Academic, music/drama, art, athletic, state/district residency, leadership scholarships available. **Aid applications:** No closing date; priority given to applications received by March 1; applicants notified on a rolling basis beginning on or about April 15; must reply within 4 weeks. **Additional information:** Fee remission scholarships now being offered to freshmen who have been admitted to the Clark Honors College.

ADDRESS/TELEPHONE. University of Oregon: Robert Donald Clark Honors College, Eugene, OR 97403-1293. (503) 346-5414.

University of Portland
Portland, Oregon CB code: 4847

4-year private university, coed, affiliated with Roman Catholic Church. Founded in 1901. **Accreditation:** Regional. **Undergraduate enrollment:** 2,599 men and women. **Graduate enrollment:** 467 men and women. **Faculty:** 200 total (129 full time), 186 with doctorates or other terminal degrees. **Location:** Urban campus in large city; 4 miles from city center. **Calendar:** Semester, extensive summer session. **Microcomputers:** 217 located in libraries, classrooms, computer centers. **Special facilities:** 5000-seat athletic convention facility, rare book collection, observatories.

DEGREES OFFERED. BA, BS, MA, MS, MBA, MFA, MEd. 410 bachelor's degrees awarded in 1992. 23% in business and management, 10% communications, 12% education, 19% engineering, 5% health sciences, 10% life sciences, 6% social sciences. Graduate degrees offered in 12 major fields of study.

UNDERGRADUATE MAJORS. Accounting, aerospace science (Air Force), allied health, biology, business administration and management, business and management, chemistry, civil engineering, communication management, communications, computer and information sciences, computer applications management, criminal justice studies, dramatic arts, electrical/electronics/communications engineering, elementary education, engineering management, engineering science, English, finance, foreign languages (multiple emphasis), health care administration, history, journalism, marketing management, mathematics, mechanical engineering, military science (Army), music, music education, nursing, philosophy, physical education, physics, political science and government, predentistry, prelaw, premedicine, prepharmacy, preveterinary, psychology, secondary education, social work, sociology, special education, theological studies.

ACADEMIC PROGRAMS. Accelerated program, double major, honors program, independent study, internships, student-designed major, study abroad, teacher preparation; combined bachelor's/graduate program in business administration. **Remedial services:** Learning center, special counselor, tutoring. **ROTC:** Air Force, Army. **Placement/credit:** AP, CLEP General and Subject, institutional tests.

ACADEMIC REQUIREMENTS. Freshmen must earn minimum GPA of 2.0 to continue in good standing. 78% of freshmen return for sophomore year. Students must declare major by end of second year. **Graduation requirements:** 120 hours for bachelor's. Most students required to take courses in arts/fine arts, English, history, mathematics, philosophy/religion, biological/physical sciences, social sciences. **Postgraduate studies:** 3% enter law school, 5% enter medical school, 5% enter MBA programs, 7% enter other graduate study. **Additional information:** Secondary education endorsements available in French, German, Spanish, Language Arts, Speech, Drama, Mathematics, Music, Biology, Physical Science, and Social Science.

FRESHMAN ADMISSIONS. Selection criteria: School achievement record, test scores, counselor recommendation considered. **High school preparation:** 16 units recommended. Recommended units include biological science 1, English 3, foreign language 2, mathematics 2, physical science 1 and social science 2. **Test requirements:** SAT or ACT; score report by August 15.

1992 FRESHMAN CLASS PROFILE. 70% had high school GPA of 3.0 or higher, 30% between 2.0 and 2.99. **Academic background:** Mid 50% of enrolled freshmen had SAT-V between 450-550, SAT-M between 470-570. 90% submitted SAT scores. **Characteristics:** 60% from in state, 84% live in college housing, 7% have minority backgrounds, 13% are foreign students, 5% join fraternities/sororities. Average age is 19.

FALL-TERM APPLICATIONS. $30 fee, may be waived for applicants with need. No closing date; priority given to applications received by August 15; applicants notified on a rolling basis. Deferred admission available.

STUDENT LIFE. Housing: Dormitories (men, women, coed). Housing guaranteed all 4 years. **Activities:** Student government, magazine, radio, student newspaper, television, yearbook, choral groups, concert band, dance, drama, jazz band, music ensembles, musical theater, pep band, symphony orchestra, fraternities, sororities, International Students Association, Association of African-American Students, Volunteer Services, clubs representing various student interests.

ATHLETICS. NCAA. **Intercollegiate:** Baseball M, basketball, cross-country, golf M, soccer, tennis, track and field, volleyball M. **Intramural:** Badminton, basketball M, rugby M, sailing, skiing, skin diving, softball, swimming, tennis, volleyball, water polo.

STUDENT SERVICES. Aptitude testing, career counseling, employment service for undergraduates, freshman orientation, health services, personal counseling, placement service for graduates, special adviser for adult students, veterans counselor, campus ministry services, services/facilities for handicapped.

ANNUAL EXPENSES. Tuition and fees: $11,040. **Room and board:** $3,940. **Books and supplies:** $600. **Other expenses:** $600.

FINANCIAL AID. 76% of freshmen, 80% of continuing students receive some form of aid. 60% of grants, 77% of loans, 17% of jobs based on need. 249 enrolled freshmen were judged to have need, all were offered aid. Academic, music/drama, athletic, leadership, alumni affiliation, religious affiliation scholarships available. **Aid applications:** No closing date; priority given to applications received by March 15; applicants notified on a rolling basis beginning on or about April 1; must reply within 3 weeks.

ADDRESS/TELEPHONE. Daniel B. Reilly, Director of Admissions, University of Portland, 5000 North Willamette Boulevard, Portland, OR 97203-5798. (503) 283-7147. (800) 227-4568. Fax: (503) 283-7399.

Warner Pacific College
Portland, Oregon — CB code: 4595

Admissions: 82% of applicants accepted
Based on:
••• Recommendations, school record
•• Essay, religious affiliation/commitment, test scores
• Activities, interview, special talents
Completion: 80% of freshmen end year in good standing
45% graduate, 15% of these enter graduate study

4-year private liberal arts college, coed, affiliated with Church of God. Founded in 1937. **Accreditation:** Regional. **Undergraduate enrollment:** 195 men, 282 women full time; 49 men, 65 women part time. **Graduate enrollment:** 12 men, 5 women full time; 1 man, 3 women part time. **Faculty:** 51 total (35 full time), 28 with doctorates or other terminal degrees. **Location:** Urban campus in large city; 44 miles from Salem, 10 miles from Vancouver, Washington. **Calendar:** Semester, extensive summer session. Extensive evening/early morning classes. **Microcomputers:** Located in libraries, computer centers. **Special facilities:** 2 electron microscopes, student-run shelter for the homeless, early childhood learning center, Mt. Tabor bicycling and hiking trails, 195-acre city park adjacent to campus. **Additional facts:** Co-operative programs with several area institutions, 3-2 nursing BS/RN program.

DEGREES OFFERED. AA, AS, BA, BS, M. 3 associate degrees awarded in 1992. 33% in philosophy, religion, theology, 67% social sciences. 66 bachelor's degrees awarded. 35% in business and management, 10% teacher education, 8% philosophy, religion, theology, 38% social sciences. Graduate degrees offered in 2 major fields of study.

UNDERGRADUATE MAJORS. Associate: Health sciences, mathematics, missionary studies, recreation and community services technologies, religious education, social sciences. **Bachelor's:** American studies, Bible studies, biological and physical sciences, biology, business administration and management, business economics, education, elementary education, English, English education, history, human development, humanities, humanities and social sciences, junior high education, liberal/general studies, marketing management, music, music education, music ministries, music performance, music theory and composition, nursing, physical education, physical sciences, predentistry, premedicine, prepharmacy, preveterinary, psychology, religion, religious education, religious music, science education, secondary education, social psychology, social science education, social sciences, social work, sociology, theological studies.

ACADEMIC PROGRAMS. Accelerated program, double major, external degree, independent study, internships, student-designed major, study abroad, teacher preparation, visiting/exchange student program, Washington semester, cross-registration; liberal arts/career combination in health sciences. **Remedial services:** Learning center, reduced course load, remedial instruction, special counselor, tutoring. **ROTC:** Air Force, Army. **Placement/credit:** AP, CLEP General and Subject, IB, institutional tests.

ACADEMIC REQUIREMENTS. Freshmen must earn minimum GPA of 2.0 to continue in good standing. 70% of freshmen return for sophomore year. Students must declare major by end of second year. **Graduation requirements:** 65 hours for associate, 124 hours for bachelor's (30 in major). Most students required to take courses in arts/fine arts, computer science, English, history, humanities, mathematics, philosophy/religion, biological/physical sciences, social sciences. **Postgraduate studies:** 30% from 2-year programs enter 4-year programs. 2% enter law school, 3% enter medical school, 7% enter MBA programs, 3% enter other graduate study. **Additional information:** Evening degree completions program for working adults offers bachelor of science degrees in business administration or human development.

FRESHMAN ADMISSIONS. Selection criteria: High school GPA important, recommendations, SAT or ACT scores, essay required. **High school preparation:** 12 units required. Required and recommended units include biological science 2, English 4, mathematics 2-3, physical science 1 and social science 3. Foreign language 2 recommended. **Test requirements:** SAT or ACT (SAT preferred); score report by August 1. ACH required of scholarship applicants. Scholarship applicants scores must be received by March 1, August 1 for credit.

1992 FRESHMAN CLASS PROFILE. 105 men and women applied, 86 accepted; 57 enrolled. 59% had high school GPA of 3.0 or higher, 40% between 2.0 and 2.99. **Characteristics:** 60% from in state, 70% live in college housing. Average age is 19.

FALL-TERM APPLICATIONS. $25 fee, may be waived for applicants with need. No closing date; priority given to applications received by June 1; applicants notified on a rolling basis. Audition required for music applicants. Essay required. Interview recommended for music, required for scholarship applica applicants. Deferred and early admission available.

STUDENT LIFE. Housing: Dormitories (men, women); apartment, handicapped housing available. **Activities:** Student government, student newspaper, yearbook, choral groups, concert band, drama, jazz band, music ensembles, pep band, women's organization, Christian Service Corps, missions outreach program, numerous student clubs. **Additional information:** Religious observance required.

ATHLETICS. NAIA. **Intramural:** Archery, badminton, baseball, basketball, bowling, boxing, cross-country, diving, field hockey, golf, gymnastics, handball, horseback riding, racquetball, rowing (crew) M, rugby M, sailing, skiing, skin diving, soccer M, softball, swimming, table tennis, tennis, track and field W, volleyball, wrestling M.

STUDENT SERVICES. Aptitude testing, career counseling, employment service for undergraduates, freshman orientation, health services, on-campus day care, personal counseling, placement service for graduates, special adviser for adult students, veterans counselor, services/facilities for handicapped.

ANNUAL EXPENSES. Tuition and fees (1992-93): $7,511. **Room and board:** $3,900. **Books and supplies:** $400. **Other expenses:** $850.

FINANCIAL AID. 58% of freshmen, 75% of continuing students receive some form of aid. 65% of grants, 87% of loans, 77% of jobs based on need. Academic, music/drama, alumni affiliation, religious affiliation, minority scholarships available. **Aid applications:** Closing date August 15; priority given to applications received by May 1; applicants notified on a rolling basis beginning on or about February 15; must reply within 4 weeks. **Additional information:** Church scholarship awards matched for returning students.

ADDRESS/TELEPHONE. Kenneth S.T. Thomas, Director of Admissions, Warner Pacific College, 2219 Southeast 68th Street, Portland, OR 97215. (503) 775-4366 ext. 512. (800) 582-7885. Fax: (503) 775-8853.

Western Baptist College
Salem, Oregon — CB code: 4956

4-year private Bible, liberal arts college, coed, affiliated with Baptist. Founded in 1936. **Accreditation:** Regional. **Undergraduate enrollment:** 213 men, 238 women full time; 11 men, 16 women part time. **Faculty:** 48 total (29 full time), 11 with doctorates or other terminal degrees. **Location:** Suburban campus in small city; 45 miles from Portland. **Calendar:** Semester, limited summer session. **Microcomputers:** 12 located in libraries, computer centers. **Special facilities:** Archaeological museum of Middle Eastern artifacts and replicas.

DEGREES OFFERED. AA, BA, BS. 10 associate degrees awarded in 1992. 30% in business and management, 30% allied health, 40% philosophy, religion, theology. 84 bachelor's degrees awarded. 19% in business and management, 27% education, 9% multi/interdisciplinary studies, 5% philosophy, religion, theology, 27% psychology, 13% social sciences.

UNDERGRADUATE MAJORS. Associate: Bible studies, business administration and management, business and management, liberal/general studies, prenursing, pretheology. **Bachelor's:** Accounting, Bible studies, business administration and management, business and management, elementary education, English, English education, finance, humanities, humanities and social sciences, junior high education, liberal/general studies, mathematics, mathematics education, missionary studies, music, music education, physical education, prelaw, psychology, religious education, religious music, secondary education, social sciences, social studies education, theological studies.

ACADEMIC PROGRAMS. Accelerated program, double major, independent study, internships, teacher preparation, cross-registration. **Remedial services:** Reduced course load, special counselor, tutoring. **ROTC:** Army. **Placement/credit:** AP, CLEP General and Subject, institutional tests; 15 credit hours maximum for associate degree; 30 credit hours maximum for bachelor's degree.

ACADEMIC REQUIREMENTS. Freshmen must earn minimum GPA of 2.0 to continue in good standing. 60% of freshmen return for sophomore year. Students must declare major by end of second year. **Graduation requirements:** 64 hours for associate (20 in major), 128 hours for bachelor's (30 in major). Most students required to take courses in arts/fine arts, computer science, English, history, humanities, mathematics, philosophy/religion, biological/physical sciences, social sciences.

FRESHMAN ADMISSIONS. Selection criteria: Commitment to Christianity, high school GPA, test scores, school and community activities. **Test requirements:** SAT or ACT; score report by September 1.

1992 FRESHMAN CLASS PROFILE. 57 men, 63 women enrolled. 56% had high school GPA of 3.0 or higher, 43% between 2.0 and 2.99. **Characteristics:** 42% from in state, 56% commute, 6% have minority backgrounds, 1% are foreign students. Average age is 18.

FALL-TERM APPLICATIONS. $25 fee. Closing date August 15; applicants notified on a rolling basis; must reply within 3 weeks. Audition required for music applicants. Essay required.

STUDENT LIFE. Housing: Dormitories (men, women). **Activities:** Student government, student newspaper, yearbook, choral groups, concert band, drama, music ensembles, Christian fellowships. **Additional information:** Many students from traditions other than Baptist.

ATHLETICS. NAIA. **Intercollegiate:** Baseball M, basketball, soccer M, volleyball W. **Intramural:** Basketball, soccer, softball, volleyball.

STUDENT SERVICES. Career counseling, employment service for undergraduates, freshman orientation, health services, personal counseling, placement service for graduates.

ANNUAL EXPENSES. Tuition and fees: $8,700. **Room and board:** $3,700. **Books and supplies:** $500. **Other expenses:** $990.

FINANCIAL AID. 92% of freshmen, 91% of continuing students receive some form of aid. 52% of grants, 90% of loans, 33% of jobs based on need. 67 enrolled freshmen were judged to have need, all were offered aid. Academic, music/drama, athletic, state/district residency, leadership, religious affiliation scholarships available. **Aid applications:** No closing date; priority given to applications received by February 15; applicants notified on a rolling basis beginning on or about April 1; must reply within 4 weeks.

ADDRESS/TELEPHONE. Palmer Muntz, Director of Admissions and Financial Aid, Western Baptist College, 5000 Deer Park Drive Southeast, Salem, OR 97301-9392. (503) 581-8600. (800) 845-3005. Fax: (503) 585-4316.

Western Oregon State College
Monmouth, Oregon — CB code: 4585

Admissions: 85% of applicants accepted
Based on: ••• School record
•• Test scores
Completion: 85% of freshmen end year in good standing

4-year public liberal arts college, coed. Founded in 1856. **Accreditation:** Regional. **Undergraduate enrollment:** 3,647 men and women. **Graduate enrollment:** 289 men and women. **Faculty:** 294 total (177 full time), 150 with doctorates or other terminal degrees. **Location:** Rural campus in small town; 15 miles from Salem. **Calendar:** Quarter, extensive summer session. **Microcomputers:** 120 located in dormitories, libraries, classrooms, computer centers. **Special facilities:** Jensen arctic museum.

DEGREES OFFERED. AA, BA, BS, MA, MS, MEd. 10 associate degrees awarded in 1992. 815 bachelor's degrees awarded. 14% in business and management, 43% teacher education, 9% parks/recreation, protective services, public affairs, 12% psychology, 8% social sciences. Graduate degrees offered in 24 major fields of study.

UNDERGRADUATE MAJORS. Associate: Liberal/general studies. **Bachelor's:** Bilingual/bicultural education, biological and physical sciences, biology, business and management, chemistry, communications, computer and information sciences, criminology, dramatic arts, economics, education, elementary education, English, English education, fine arts, fire protection, foreign languages (multiple emphasis), foreign languages education, geography, health education, history, humanities, humanities and social sciences, international studies, interpreter for the deaf, junior high education, law enforcement and corrections, liberal/general studies, mathematics, mathematics education, music, music education, physical education, physical sciences, political science and government, prelaw, psychology, public administration, science education, secondary education, social science education, social sciences, social studies education, sociology, Spanish, speech, speech/communication/theater education, teaching English as a second language/foreign language, visual and performing arts.

ACADEMIC PROGRAMS. Double major, dual enrollment of high school students, honors program, independent study, internships, student-designed major, study abroad, teacher preparation, telecourses. **Remedial services:** Learning center, special counselor, tutoring, remedial mathematics through local community college. **ROTC:** Air Force, Army. **Placement/credit:** AP, CLEP General and Subject, institutional tests; 48 credit hours maximum for bachelor's degree.

ACADEMIC REQUIREMENTS. Freshmen must earn minimum GPA of 2.0 to continue in good standing. 65% of freshmen return for sophomore year. Students must declare major by end of second year. **Graduation requirements:** 93 hours for associate (20 in major), 192 hours for bachelor's (72 in major). Most students required to take courses in arts/fine arts, computer science, English, foreign languages, history, humanities, mathematics, philosophy/religion, biological/physical sciences, social sciences.

FRESHMAN ADMISSIONS. Selection criteria: Completion of 14 college preparatory classes, 2.75 high school GPA or SAT combined score of 890, or ACT enhanced composite score of 21 important. **High school preparation:** 14 units required. Required and recommended units include English 4, mathematics 3, social science 3 and science 2. Foreign language 2 recommended. One laboratory science recommended. 2 additional units of college preparatory course work required. **Test requirements:** SAT or ACT (SAT preferred); score report by September 15. 3 ACH (including English Composition, Mathematics Level I or II, and a third subject of applicant's choice) required of applicants not meeting high school subject requirements. Score report by September 15. **Additional information:** Students who do not meet admissions requirements may petition admissions committee for admission as an exception. Limited number admitted under this category.

1992 FRESHMAN CLASS PROFILE. 65% had high school GPA of 3.0 or higher, 35% between 2.0 and 2.99. **Characteristics:** 94% from in state, 100% live in college housing, 5% have minority backgrounds, 3% are foreign students. Average age is 18.

FALL-TERM APPLICATIONS. $40 fee. Closing date April 15; applicants notified on a rolling basis.

STUDENT LIFE. Housing: Dormitories (coed); apartment housing available. Special interest option floors including health/wellness floor, outdoor recreation floor, and multicultural floor. Single parent/family housing. No alcohol permitted in residence halls even those over 21 years of age. **Activities:** Student government, magazine, student newspaper, television, yearbook, speech team, choral groups, concert band, dance, drama, jazz band, marching band, music ensembles, musical theater, symphony orchestra, Baptist Student Union, International Students Club, Big Brother/Big Sister, Western Oregon Peace Action Committee, Multicultural Student Union, Campus Crusade for Christ, Circle-K, Environmental Action Commitee, National Organization for Women (NOW).

ATHLETICS. NAIA. **Intercollegiate:** Baseball M, basketball, cross-country, football M, softball W, track and field, volleyball W. **Intramural:** Archery, badminton, basketball, bowling, cross-country, football M, handball, racquetball, rifle, soccer, softball, swimming, table tennis, tennis, track and field, volleyball, water polo, wrestling.

STUDENT SERVICES. Aptitude testing, career counseling, employment service for undergraduates, freshman orientation, health services, on-campus day care, personal counseling, placement service for graduates, special adviser for adult students, veterans counselor, Office of Minority Student Affairs, Office of International Education and Services, services/facilities for handicapped.

ANNUAL EXPENSES. Tuition and fees: $2,640, $4,170 additional for out-of-state students. **Room and board:** $3,540. **Books and supplies:** $630. **Other expenses:** $1,090.

FINANCIAL AID. 81% of freshmen, 61% of continuing students receive some form of aid. 79% of grants, 88% of loans, 22% of jobs based on need. 353 enrolled freshmen were judged to have need, all were offered aid. Academic, music/drama, art, state/district residency, leadership, minority scholarships available. **Aid applications:** No closing date; priority given to applications received by March 1; applicants notified on a rolling basis beginning on or about May 1; must reply within 3 weeks.

ADDRESS/TELEPHONE. Craig Kolins, Director of Admissions, Western Oregon State College, 345 North Monmouth Avenue, Monmouth, OR 97361-1394. (503) 838-8211. Fax: (503) 838-8289.

Willamette University
Salem, Oregon — CB code: 4954

Admissions: 80% of applicants accepted
Based on: ••• Recommendations, school record, test scores
•• Activities, essay, special talents
• Interview
Completion: 96% of freshmen end year in good standing
73% graduate, 35% of these enter graduate study

4-year private university and liberal arts college, coed, affiliated with United Methodist Church. Founded in 1842. **Accreditation:** Regional. **Undergraduate enrollment:** 733 men, 893 women full time; 25 men and women part time. **Graduate enrollment:** 447 men, 259 women full time; 42 men and women part time. **Faculty:** 247 total (159 full time), 148 with doctorates or other terminal degrees. **Location:** Suburban campus in small city; 45 miles from Portland. **Calendar:** Semester. **Microcomputers:** 110 located in dormitories, libraries, classrooms, computer centers. **Special facilities:** Art gallery, papers and memorabilia of Senator Mark O. Hatfield, botanical garden, Japanese garden, mountain retreat center, rural conference center. **Additional facts:** Campus located adjacent to Oregon state government legislative and judicial facilities which students utilize in internships.

DEGREES OFFERED. BA, BS, MA, JD. 363 bachelor's degrees awarded in 1992. 5% in area and ethnic studies, 11% business and management, 12% letters/literature, 11% life sciences, 5% mathematics, 12% psychology, 24% social sciences, 6% visual and performing arts. Graduate degrees offered in 23 major fields of study.

UNDERGRADUATE MAJORS. American studies, art history, Asian studies, biology, business economics, chemistry, computer and information sciences, dramatic arts, East Asian studies, Eastern European studies, economics, English, environmental science, French, German, history, humanities, international studies, Japanese, Latin American studies, mathematics, music, music education, music performance, music therapy, philosophy, physics, political science and government, psychology, religion, Russian and Slavic studies, sociology, Spanish, speech, studio art, Western European studies.

ACADEMIC PROGRAMS. Accelerated program, double major, dual enrollment of high school students, independent study, internships, study abroad, teacher preparation, visiting/exchange student program, United Nations semester, Washington semester, interdisciplinary freshman study program, field studies program in ecology (in Hawaii, Mexico and the Southwest, and Oregon); liberal arts/career combination in engineering. **Remedial services:** Reduced course load, tutoring. **Placement/credit:** AP, institutional tests; 28 credit hours maximum for bachelor's degree.

ACADEMIC REQUIREMENTS. Freshmen must earn minimum GPA of 2.0 to continue in good standing. 90% of freshmen return for sophomore year. Students must declare major by end of second year. **Graduation requirements:** 124 hours for bachelor's (32 in major). Most students required to take courses in arts/fine arts, English, foreign languages, history, humanities, mathematics, philosophy/religion, biological/physical sciences, social sciences. **Postgraduate studies:** 10% enter law school, 5% enter medical school, 5% enter MBA programs, 15% enter other graduate study.

FRESHMAN ADMISSIONS. Selection criteria: School record most important, followed by test scores, recommendations, school and community activities. Personal interview considered when available. **High school preparation:** 16 units recommended. Recommended units include English 4, foreign language 3, mathematics 3, social science 3 and science 3. **Test requirements:** SAT or ACT; score report by February 15.

1992 FRESHMAN CLASS PROFILE. 722 men applied, 536 accepted, 157 enrolled; 856 women applied, 721 accepted, 238 enrolled. 88% had high school GPA of 3.0 or higher, 12% between 2.0 and 2.99. 49% were in top tenth and 80% were in top quarter of graduating class. **Academic background:** Mid 50% of enrolled freshmen had SAT-V between 500-600, SAT-M between 540-650; ACT composite between 23-28. 96% submitted SAT scores, 35% submitted ACT scores. **Characteristics:** 49% from in state, 95% live in college housing, 14% have minority backgrounds, 5% are foreign students, 30% join fraternities/sororities. Average age is 18.

FALL-TERM APPLICATIONS. $35 fee, may be waived for applicants with need. Closing date June 1; priority given to applications received by February 1; applicants notified on or about April 1; must reply by May 1 or within 2 weeks if notified thereafter. Essay required. Interview recommended. Audition recommended for music applicants. Portfolio recommended for art applicants. CRDA. Deferred and early admission available. EDP-S.

STUDENT LIFE. Housing: Dormitories (coed); apartment, fraternity, sorority housing available. International studies house, nonsmoking residence hall, hall for people interested in social change, quiet study residence hall available. **Activities:** Student government, film, magazine, radio, student newspaper, yearbook, choral groups, concert band, dance, drama, jazz band, music ensembles, musical theater, opera, pep band, symphony orchestra, fraternities, sororities, minority student organizations, religious organizations, support groups, Circle-K. **Additional information:** Student involvement encouraged. Oldest and strongest university tradition is Freshman Glee, a marching and singing competition.

ATHLETICS. NAIA. **Intercollegiate:** Baseball M, basketball, cross-country, football M, golf M, lacrosse M, rugby M, soccer, softball W, swimming, tennis, track and field, volleyball W. **Intramural:** Badminton, basketball, cross-country, fencing, football M, golf M, handball, racquetball, skiing, soccer, softball, swimming, table tennis, tennis, track and field, volleyball, water polo M, wrestling M.

STUDENT SERVICES. Aptitude testing, career counseling, employment service for undergraduates, freshman orientation, health services, personal counseling, placement service for graduates, special adviser for adult students, veterans counselor, services/facilities for handicapped.

ANNUAL EXPENSES. Tuition and fees: $13,665. **Room and board:** $4,420. **Books and supplies:** $400. **Other expenses:** $720.

FINANCIAL AID. 70% of freshmen, 75% of continuing students receive some form of aid. 93% of grants, 92% of loans, 55% of jobs based on need. 300 enrolled freshmen were judged to have need, all were offered aid. Academic, music/drama, art scholarships available. **Aid applications:** Closing date June 1; priority given to applications received by February 15; applicants notified on or about April 1; must reply by May 1 or within 2 weeks if notified thereafter.

ADDRESS/TELEPHONE. James M. Sumner, Dean of University Admissions, Willamette University, 900 State Street, Salem, OR 97301-3922. (503) 370-6303. Fax: (503) 375-5363.

Pennsylvania

Academy of the New Church

Bryn Athyn, Pennsylvania CB code: 2002

4-year private liberal arts college, coed, affiliated with General Church of the New Jerusalem (Swedenborgian). Founded in 1876. **Accreditation:** Regional. **Undergraduate enrollment:** 49 men, 51 women full time; 6 men, 12 women part time. **Graduate enrollment:** 7 men full time; 3 men part time. **Faculty:** 39 total (23 full time), 10 with doctorates or other terminal degrees. **Location:** Suburban campus in rural community; 17 miles from Philadelphia. **Calendar:** Trimester. **Microcomputers:** 30 located in libraries, classrooms, computer centers. **Special facilities:** Glencairn Museum with medieval, Greek, and Egyptian artifacts. **Additional facts:** All resident students participate in campus work program to help defray expenses.

DEGREES OFFERED. AA, BA, BS, M.Div. 20 associate degrees awarded in 1992. 100% in multi/interdisciplinary studies. 12 bachelor's degrees awarded. 56% in education, 44% teacher education. Graduate degrees offered in 2 major fields of study.

UNDERGRADUATE MAJORS. Associate: Education, humanities and social sciences, liberal/general studies. **Bachelor's:** Education, elementary education, humanities and social sciences, liberal/general studies, religion.

ACADEMIC PROGRAMS. 2-year transfer program, cooperative education, independent study, internships, teacher preparation. **Remedial services:** Special counselor, tutoring. **Placement/credit:** AP.

ACADEMIC REQUIREMENTS. Freshmen must earn minimum GPA of 1.9 to continue in good standing. 80% of freshmen return for sophomore year. Students must declare major by end of second year. **Graduation requirements:** 68 hours for associate, 136 hours for bachelor's (36 in major). Most students required to take courses in computer science, English, history, humanities, philosophy/religion, biological/physical sciences, social sciences. **Postgraduate studies:** 60% from 2-year programs enter 4-year programs.

FRESHMAN ADMISSIONS. Selection criteria: Applicants expected to be baptized into, or have a mature interest in, the faith of the New Church. School achievement record and test scores considered. Interview mandatory for students from Academy of the New Church secondary schools; pastor's recommendation required of those from other schools. **High school preparation:** 16 units required. Students with less than 16 required high school course units accepted on probation. Must maintain 1.9 GPA during probationary period. **Test requirements:** SAT or ACT (SAT preferred) for placement and counseling only; score report by June 20.

1992 FRESHMAN CLASS PROFILE. 17 men applied, 17 accepted, 17 enrolled; 14 women applied, 14 accepted, 13 enrolled. **Academic background:** Mid 50% of enrolled freshmen had SAT-V between 400-570, SAT-M between 450-600. 90% submitted SAT scores. **Characteristics:** 49% from in state, 66% live in college housing, 24% are foreign students. Average age is 19.

FALL-TERM APPLICATIONS. No fee. No closing date; applicants notified on a rolling basis beginning on or about January 15. Interview required for nearby applicants. Essay required. Deferred and early admission available.

STUDENT LIFE. Housing: Dormitories (men, women). **Activities:** Student government, yearbook, choral groups, dance, drama, music ensembles, musical theater, symphony orchestra, missionary groups. **Additional information:** Religious observance required.

ATHLETICS. Intercollegiate: Badminton W, basketball W, ice hockey M, lacrosse, soccer M, volleyball W. **Intramural:** Archery, badminton, basketball M, ice hockey, racquetball, softball, volleyball.

STUDENT SERVICES. Career counseling, employment service for undergraduates, freshman orientation, health services, personal counseling.

ANNUAL EXPENSES. Tuition and fees (1992-93): $3,765. **Room and board:** $3,207. **Other expenses:** $1,200.

FINANCIAL AID. 62% of freshmen, 47% of continuing students receive some form of aid. 90% of grants, all loans, 79% of jobs based on need. 13 enrolled freshmen were judged to have need, all were offered aid. **Aid applications:** Closing date August 15; priority given to applications received by March 1; applicants notified on a rolling basis beginning on or about June 16; must reply by August 15.

ADDRESS/TELEPHONE. Brian L. Schnarr, Dean, Academy of the New Church, PO Box 717 ANCC, 2895 College Drive, Bryn Athyn, PA 19009. (215) 938-2543. Fax: (215) 938-2616.

Albright College

Reading, Pennsylvania CB code: 2004

Admissions:	85% of applicants accepted
Based on:	••• School record
	•• Activities, essay, interview, recommendations, test scores
	• Special talents
Completion:	90% of freshmen end year in good standing
	76% graduate, 51% of these enter graduate study

4-year private liberal arts college, coed, affiliated with United Methodist Church. Founded in 1856. **Accreditation:** Regional. **Undergraduate enrollment:** 574 men, 528 women full time; 205 men, 188 women part time. **Graduate enrollment:** 502 men, 452 women full time; 412 men, 401 women part time. **Faculty:** 120 total (89 full time), 71 with doctorates or other terminal degrees. **Location:** Suburban campus in small city; 50 miles from Philadelphia. **Calendar:** 4-1-4, extensive summer session. Extensive evening/early morning classes. **Microcomputers:** 104 located in dormitories, libraries, classrooms, computer centers. **Special facilities:** Art gallery, Center for the Arts, child development center, satellite dish for foreign language program, 2 electron microscopes.

DEGREES OFFERED. BA, BS. 338 bachelor's degrees awarded in 1992. 31% in business and management, 8% letters/literature, 12% life sciences, 14% psychology, 14% social sciences.

UNDERGRADUATE MAJORS. Accounting, American studies, biochemistry, biology, business administration and management, chemistry, child and family studies, clinical laboratory science, computer and information sciences, critical languages, economics, elementary education, engineering, English, English education, environmental science, fashion merchandising, finance, fine arts, food science and nutrition, foreign languages education, French, German, history, home economics, home economics education, international business management, marketing management, mathematics, mathematics education, philosophy, physics, political science and government, predentistry, prelaw, premedicine, prepharmacy, preveterinary, psychobiology, psychology, psychology/business, religion, science education, secondary education, social studies education, social work, sociology, Spanish, textiles and clothing.

ACADEMIC PROGRAMS. Accelerated program, double major, dual enrollment of high school students, honors program, independent study, internships, student-designed major, study abroad, teacher preparation, visiting/exchange student program, New York semester, Washington semester, 1-semester internships at Fashion Institute of Technology in New York City, and at Philadelphia College of Textiles and Sciences; liberal arts/career combination in engineering, forestry. **Remedial services:** Reduced course load, special counselor, tutoring, writing center. **Placement/credit:** AP, CLEP Subject; 28 credit hours maximum for bachelor's degree.

ACADEMIC REQUIREMENTS. Freshmen must earn minimum GPA of 1.7 to continue in good standing. 88% of freshmen return for sophomore year. Students must declare major by end of second year. **Graduation requirements:** 128 hours for bachelor's (64 in major). Most students required to take courses in arts/fine arts, English, foreign languages, history, humanities, philosophy/religion, biological/physical sciences, social sciences. **Postgraduate studies:** 8% enter law school, 10% enter medical school, 12% enter MBA programs, 21% enter other graduate study.

FRESHMAN ADMISSIONS. Selection criteria: High school performance (with emphasis on difficulty of curriculum pursued), personal statement, and test scores most important factors. Community service and extracurricular activity considered. **High school preparation:** 15 units required; 18 recommended. Required and recommended units include biological science 1, English 4, foreign language 2-3, mathematics 2-4, physical science 1-2 and social science 2-4. Bachelor of science applicants should have 1 additional unit in science and 1 in mathematics. **Test requirements:** SAT or ACT; score report by February 15.

1992 FRESHMAN CLASS PROFILE. 502 men applied, 412 accepted, 175 enrolled; 452 women applied, 401 accepted, 135 enrolled. 65% had high school GPA of 3.0 or higher, 35% between 2.0 and 2.99. 22% were in top tenth of graduating class. **Academic background:** Mid 50% of enrolled freshmen had SAT-V between 420-530, SAT-M between 460-590; ACT composite between 19-23. 94% submitted SAT scores, 5% submitted ACT scores. **Characteristics:** 52% from in state, 91% live in college housing, 8% have minority backgrounds, 6% are foreign students, 16% join fraternities/sororities. Average age is 18.

FALL-TERM APPLICATIONS. $25 fee, may be waived for applicants with need. Closing date February 15; applicants notified on a rolling basis beginning on or about December 15; must reply by May 1. Essay required. Interview recommended. Portfolio recommended for art applicants. Interview recommended for all students; required for adult and nontraditional students. CRDA. Deferred and early admission available. EDP-F.

STUDENT LIFE. Housing: Dormitories (men, women, coed); apartment housing available. Special interest residence hall for groups with common interest. **Activities:** Student government, film, magazine, radio, student newspaper, television, yearbook, choral groups, concert band, drama, jazz band, music ensembles, musical theater, pep band, fraternities, sororities, preprofessional and service organizations, Newman Association, Hillel, Christian Fellowship, African-American Society, Asian-American Society, International Students Organization, Amnesty International, Environmental Action Group, Albright Unity.

ATHLETICS. NCAA. **Intercollegiate:** Badminton W, baseball M, basketball, cross-country, field hockey W, football M, golf M, soccer M, softball W, swimming, tennis, track and field, volleyball W, wrestling M. **Intramural:** Badminton W, basketball, bowling, cross-country, field hockey W, lacrosse W, racquetball, soccer W, softball, swimming, table tennis, tennis, track and field, volleyball.

STUDENT SERVICES. Aptitude testing, career counseling, employment service for undergraduates, freshman orientation, health services, on-campus day care, personal counseling, placement service for graduates, special adviser for adult students, veterans counselor, services/facilities for handicapped.

ANNUAL EXPENSES. Tuition and fees: $15,010. **Room and board:** $4,250. **Books and supplies:** $500. **Other expenses:** $900.

FINANCIAL AID. 67% of freshmen, 88% of continuing students receive some form of aid. 88% of grants, 86% of loans, 51% of jobs based on need. 250 enrolled freshmen were judged to have need, all were offered aid. Academic, leadership scholarships available. **Aid applications:** Closing date April 1; priority given to applications received by March 1; applicants notified on a rolling basis beginning on or about March 1; must reply by May 1 or within 2 weeks if notified thereafter.

ADDRESS/TELEPHONE. William Stahler, Dean of Admissions and Financial Aid, Albright College, PO Box 15234, Reading, PA 19612-5234. (215) 921-7512. (800) 252-1856. Fax: (215) 921-7530.

Allegheny College
Meadville, Pennsylvania — CB code: 2006

Admissions: 73% of applicants accepted
Based on:
••• School record, test scores
•• Activities, essay, interview, recommendations
• Special talents
Completion: 95% of freshmen end year in good standing
71% graduate, 32% of these enter graduate study

4-year private liberal arts college, coed, affiliated with United Methodist Church. Founded in 1815. **Accreditation:** Regional. **Undergraduate enrollment:** 854 men, 878 women full time; 19 men, 32 women part time. **Graduate enrollment:** 1 woman part time. **Faculty:** 206 total (156 full time), 138 with doctorates or other terminal degrees. **Location:** Rural campus in large town; 90 miles from Pittsburgh, 90 miles from Cleveland. **Calendar:** Semester, limited summer session. **Microcomputers:** 330 located in libraries, classrooms, computer centers, campus-wide network. **Special facilities:** Ida Tarbell Papers, Colonial American Book Collection, observatory, planetarium, environmental studies field station, art galleries.

DEGREES OFFERED. BA, BS. 476 bachelor's degrees awarded in 1992. 7% in communications, 5% languages, 14% letters/literature, 10% life sciences, 6% multi/interdisciplinary studies, 6% physical sciences, 13% psychology, 29% social sciences, 5% visual and performing arts.

UNDERGRADUATE MAJORS. Anthropology, art history, biology, chemistry, classics, communications, computer and information sciences, dramatic arts, economics, elementary education, English, environmental geology, environmental science, environmental studies, French, geology, German, Greek (classical), history, international studies, journalism, Latin, mathematics, music, philosophy, physics, political science and government, predentistry, prelaw, premedicine, preveterinary, psychology, religion, rhetoric, Russian, secondary education, sociology, Spanish, studio art.

ACADEMIC PROGRAMS. Accelerated program, double major, dual enrollment of high school students, independent study, internships, semester at sea, student-designed major, study abroad, teacher preparation, visiting/exchange student program, New York semester, Washington semester, cross-registration, Appalachian semester, SEA maritime semester, Marine Sciences Semester with Duke University, 3-2 liberal arts career combination programs in engineering with Columbia University, Case Western Reserve University, University of Pittsburgh, Duke University, Washington University, 3-1 liberal arts career combinations in medical technology with Case Western Reserve University, University of Rochester, 3-2 liberal arts career combinations in medical technology with Thomas Jefferson University, 3-3 bachelor's/ master's program in physical therapy with Thomas Jefferson University, 3-2 bachelor's/master's programs in environmental management with Duke University, 3-2 bachelor's/master's programs in forestry with Duke University, University of Michigan; liberal arts/career combination in engineering, health sciences. **Remedial services:** Learning center, reduced course load, remedial instruction, special counselor, tutoring, writing center. **ROTC:** Army. **Placement/credit:** AP, CLEP General and Subject, IB, institutional tests; 20 credit hours maximum for bachelor's degree.

ACADEMIC REQUIREMENTS. Freshmen must earn minimum GPA of 2.0 to continue in good standing. 85% of freshmen return for sophomore year. Students must declare major by end of second year. **Graduation requirements:** 128 hours for bachelor's (32 in major). Most students required to take courses in arts/fine arts, English, humanities, mathematics, biological/physical sciences, social sciences. **Postgraduate studies:** 6% enter law school, 6% enter medical school, 2% enter MBA programs, 18% enter other graduate study. **Additional information:** Flexible and individual programs encouraged. Writing proficiency required; computer literacy promoted.

FRESHMAN ADMISSIONS. Selection criteria: High school achievement and rigor of program most important, test scores secondary. Personal qualities, interview, activities, recommendations and essay also important. Minority status, alumni ties, geography considered. **High school preparation:** 16 units recommended. Recommended units include English 4, foreign language 2, mathematics 3, social science 3 and science 3. **Test requirements:** SAT or ACT; score report by February 15.

1992 FRESHMAN CLASS PROFILE. 1,347 men applied, 911 accepted, 220 enrolled; 1,108 women applied, 885 accepted, 256 enrolled. 41% were in top tenth and 75% were in top quarter of graduating class. **Academic background:** Mid 50% of enrolled freshmen had SAT-V between 460-560, SAT-M between 510-620; ACT composite between 22-27. 92% submitted SAT scores, 34% submitted ACT scores. **Characteristics:** 53% from in state, 99% live in college housing, 7% have minority backgrounds, 2% are foreign students, 38% join fraternities/sororities. Average age is 18.

FALL-TERM APPLICATIONS. $30 fee, may be waived for applicants with need. Closing date February 15; applicants notified on or about April 1; must reply by May 1. Essay required. Interview recommended. CRDA. Deferred and early admission available. EDP-F. 2 recommendations required, 1 from guidance counselor and 1 from academic teacher. 2 early decision closings: Phase I-November 30, Phase II-January 15. Achievement tests recommended.

STUDENT LIFE. Housing: Dormitories (men, women, coed); apartment, fraternity housing available. German, French, Russian and Spanish language houses, music, theater, international studies, philosophy, and Black Culture houses available. Freshman only or freshman-upperclass combination in residence halls. Housing guaranteed for 4-years, if requested. **Activities:** Student government, magazine, radio, student newspaper, television, yearbook, national literary review, choral groups, concert band, dance, drama, jazz band, music ensembles, musical theater, opera, symphony orchestra, fraternities, sororities, Amnesty International, Advancement of Black Culture, Union Latina, Habitat for Humanity, Newman Association, Hillel, Christian Outreach, International Club, Circle-K, Society for Environmental Awareness.

ATHLETICS. NCAA. **Intercollegiate:** Baseball M, basketball, cross-country, diving, football M, golf M, soccer, softball W, swimming, tennis, track and field, volleyball W. **Intramural:** Badminton, basketball, bowling, cross-country, fencing, golf, ice hockey, lacrosse, racquetball, rugby M, skiing, soccer, softball, squash, swimming, table tennis, tennis, volleyball, wrestling M. **Clubs:** Ice hockey M, rugby M, volleyball M, cycling, fencing, lacrosse.

STUDENT SERVICES. Aptitude testing, career counseling, employment service for undergraduates, freshman orientation, health services, personal counseling, placement service for graduates, special adviser for adult students, minority student counseling, services/facilities for handicapped.

ANNUAL EXPENSES. Tuition and fees: $16,700. **Room and board:** $4,320. **Books and supplies:** $400. **Other expenses:** $400.

FINANCIAL AID. 86% of freshmen, 74% of continuing students receive some form of aid. 83% of grants, 87% of loans, 90% of jobs based on need. 364 enrolled freshmen were judged to have need, all were offered aid. Academic, music/drama, art, leadership, minority scholarships available. **Aid applications:** No closing date; priority given to applications received by February 15; applicants notified on a rolling basis beginning on or about April 1; must reply by May 1 or within 2 weeks if notified thereafter. **Additional information:** Complete financial aid for United States students with demonstrated need. Generous merit scholarship program.

ADDRESS/TELEPHONE. Gayle W. Pollock, Director of Admissions, Allegheny College, Meadville, PA 16335. (814) 332-4351. (800) 521-5293. Fax: (814) 337-0988.

Allentown College of St. Francis de Sales
Center Valley, Pennsylvania — CB code: 2021

Admissions: 77% of applicants accepted
Based on:
••• School record
•• Essay, interview, recommendations, test scores
• Activities, special talents
Completion: 85% of freshmen end year in good standing
57% graduate, 10% of these enter graduate study

4-year private liberal arts college, coed, affiliated with Roman Catholic Church. Founded in 1964. **Accreditation:** Regional. **Undergraduate enrollment:** 529 men, 601 women full time; 293 men, 345 women part time. **Graduate enrollment:** 166 men, 184 women part time. **Faculty:** 171 total (75 full time), 62 with doctorates or other terminal degrees. **Location:** Rural campus in rural community; 7 miles from Allentown and Bethlehem. **Calen-**

dar: Semester, limited summer session. **Microcomputers:** 60 located in libraries, computer centers. **Special facilities:** Performing arts center. **Additional facts:** Dedicated to the principles of Christian humanism.

DEGREES OFFERED. BA, BS, MS, MBA, MEd. 298 bachelor's degrees awarded in 1992. 31% in business and management, 13% business/office and marketing/distribution, 12% computer sciences, 7% health sciences, 16% social sciences. Graduate degrees offered in 7 major fields of study.

UNDERGRADUATE MAJORS. Accounting, biology, business administration and management, business and management, business communications, chemistry, communications, computer and information sciences, criminal justice studies, criminology, dance, dramatic arts, English, English education, finance, foreign languages (multiple emphasis), foreign languages education, French, liberal/general studies, marketing and distribution, marketing management, mathematics, mathematics education, medical laboratory technologies, nursing, political science and government, predentistry, prelaw, premedicine, preveterinary, psychology, science education, social studies education, Spanish, speech/communication/theater education, sports management, theater design, theological studies, visual and performing arts.

ACADEMIC PROGRAMS. Accelerated program, double major, dual enrollment of high school students, honors program, independent study, internships, study abroad, teacher preparation, Washington semester, cross-registration. **Remedial services:** Learning center, preadmission summer program, reduced course load, tutoring. **ROTC:** Army. **Placement/credit:** AP, CLEP General and Subject, institutional tests; 24 credit hours maximum for bachelor's degree.

ACADEMIC REQUIREMENTS. Freshmen must earn minimum GPA of 1.5 to continue in good standing. 85% of freshmen return for sophomore year. Students must declare major by end of second year. **Graduation requirements:** 120 hours for bachelor's (48 in major). Most students required to take courses in arts/fine arts, computer science, English, foreign languages, history, humanities, mathematics, philosophy/religion, biological/physical sciences, social sciences. **Postgraduate studies:** 1% enter law school, 2% enter medical school, 6% enter MBA programs, 1% enter other graduate study.

FRESHMAN ADMISSIONS. Selection criteria: High school achievement most important. SAT scores and recommendations also considered. **High school preparation:** 16 units required. Required units include English 4, foreign language 2, mathematics 2, social science 2 and science 2. Biology, chemistry, 3 math recommended for biology major. 3 math, including 2 algebra, recommended for business major. Chemistry, physics, 3 math recommended for chemistry major. Biology, chemistry, physics, 2 math recommended for nursing major. 2 biology, chemistry, or physics, and 3 math recommended for pre-med major. 4 math recommended for mathematics major. **Test requirements:** SAT or ACT (SAT preferred); score report by August 1. March 15 preferred date for test score reports.

1992 FRESHMAN CLASS PROFILE. 429 men applied, 312 accepted, 115 enrolled; 444 women applied, 362 accepted, 124 enrolled. **Academic background:** Mid 50% of enrolled freshmen had SAT-V between 400-510, SAT-M between 420-560. 99% submitted SAT scores. **Characteristics:** 70% from in state, 80% live in college housing, 7% have minority backgrounds, 1% are foreign students. Average age is 18.

FALL-TERM APPLICATIONS. $25 fee, may be waived for applicants with need. Closing date August 1; priority given to applications received by February 15; applicants notified on a rolling basis; must reply by May 1 or within 4 weeks if notified thereafter. Interview recommended. Audition recommended for theater, dance applicants. Essay recommended. CRDA. Deferred and early admission available. Readiness for college, academic achievement, educational plans, recommendations, and parental consent considered for admission.

STUDENT LIFE. Housing: Dormitories (men, women). Common-interest housing available. **Activities:** Student government, film, magazine, radio, student newspaper, yearbook, choral groups, dance, drama, music ensembles, musical theater, sororities, campus ministry, community service corps, Amnesty International, pre-law society, homeless outreach, debate club.

ATHLETICS. NCAA. **Intercollegiate:** Baseball M, basketball, cross-country, golf M, soccer M, softball W, tennis, track and field, volleyball W. **Intramural:** Basketball, soccer, softball, volleyball.

STUDENT SERVICES. Aptitude testing, career counseling, employment service for undergraduates, freshman orientation, health services, personal counseling, placement service for graduates, special adviser for adult students, veterans counselor, services/facilities for handicapped.

ANNUAL EXPENSES. Tuition and fees: $9,320. **Room and board:** $4,620. **Books and supplies:** $500. **Other expenses:** $800.

FINANCIAL AID. 90% of freshmen, 80% of continuing students receive some form of aid. 87% of grants, 51% of loans, 71% of jobs based on need. 175 enrolled freshmen were judged to have need, 153 were offered aid. Academic, music/drama, leadership scholarships available. **Aid applications:** Applicants notified on a rolling basis beginning on or about December 15; must reply by May 1 or within 2 weeks if notified thereafter.

ADDRESS/TELEPHONE. George C. Kelly, Jr, Vice President for Enrollment Management, Allentown College of St. Francis de Sales, 2755 Station Avenue, Center Valley, PA 18034-9568. (215) 282-1100 ext. 1277. (800) 228-5114. Fax: (215) 282-2342.

Alvernia College
Reading, Pennsylvania — CB code: 2431

Admissions: 76% of applicants accepted
Based on:
- ••• School record
- •• Test scores
- • Activities, essay, interview, recommendations, special talents

Completion: 80% of freshmen end year in good standing; 18% enter graduate study

4-year private liberal arts college, coed, affiliated with Roman Catholic Church. Founded in 1958. **Accreditation:** Regional. **Undergraduate enrollment:** 316 men, 507 women full time; 160 men, 343 women part time. **Faculty:** 115 total (58 full time), 36 with doctorates or other terminal degrees. **Location:** Suburban campus in small city; 60 miles from Philadelphia. **Calendar:** Semester, limited summer session. **Microcomputers:** 27 located in dormitories, classrooms, computer centers.

DEGREES OFFERED. AS, BA, BS. 53 associate degrees awarded in 1992. 28% in business and management, 72% health sciences. 169 bachelor's degrees awarded. 41% in business and management, 5% communications, 5% computer sciences, 14% education, 14% parks/recreation, protective services, public affairs, 9% social sciences.

UNDERGRADUATE MAJORS. Associate: Accounting, business administration and management, nursing, physical therapy assistant. **Bachelor's:** Accounting, addiction studies, biochemistry, biology, business administration and management, chemistry, clinical laboratory science, communications, computer and information sciences, criminal justice studies, early childhood education, education, elementary education, English, finance, history, liberal/general studies, marketing management, mathematics, music, nursing, philosophy, political science and government, psychology, secondary education, social sciences, social work, Spanish, theological studies.

ACADEMIC PROGRAMS. Double major, dual enrollment of high school students, independent study, internships, student-designed major, study abroad, teacher preparation, weekend college, Washington semester. **Remedial services:** Reduced course load, special counselor, tutoring, writing laboratory, study skills workshop. **Placement/credit:** AP, CLEP General and Subject, IB, institutional tests; 16 credit hours maximum for associate degree; 30 credit hours maximum for bachelor's degree.

ACADEMIC REQUIREMENTS. Freshmen must earn minimum GPA of 1.75 to continue in good standing. 75% of freshmen return for sophomore year. Students must declare major by end of first year. **Graduation requirements:** 66 hours for associate (33 in major), 123 hours for bachelor's (45 in major). Most students required to take courses in arts/fine arts, English, foreign languages, humanities, mathematics, philosophy/religion, biological/physical sciences, social sciences. **Postgraduate studies:** 50% from 2-year programs enter 4-year programs. 5% enter law school, 6% enter medical school, 7% enter MBA programs.

FRESHMAN ADMISSIONS. Selection criteria: School achievement record, test scores, activities, counselor's recommendation, and interview are considered. **High school preparation:** 16 units required. Required units include biological science 1, English 4, foreign language 2, mathematics 2, physical science 1 and social science 3. Chemistry and biology required for nursing majors. Physics or chemistry and biology required for physical therapy assistant majors. **Test requirements:** SAT or ACT; score report by August 30.

1992 FRESHMAN CLASS PROFILE. 196 men applied, 154 accepted, 79 enrolled; 283 women applied, 208 accepted, 101 enrolled. 21% had high school GPA of 3.0 or higher, 65% between 2.0 and 2.99. **Academic background:** Mid 50% of enrolled freshmen had SAT-V between 400-490, SAT-M between 400-480. 95% submitted SAT scores. **Characteristics:** 88% from in state, 80% live in college housing, 4% have minority backgrounds, 1% are foreign students. Average age is 18.

FALL-TERM APPLICATIONS. $25 fee, may be waived for applicants with need. No closing date; applicants notified on a rolling basis; must reply within 4 weeks. Interview recommended. Essay recommended. Interview required of nursing and physical therapist assistant applicants; recommended for all others. CRDA. Deferred and early admission available.

STUDENT LIFE. Housing: Dormitories (coed). Single sex townhouses available. **Activities:** Student government, magazine, student newspaper, yearbook, choral groups, drama, music ensembles, musical theater, veterans, religious, and science clubs.

ATHLETICS. NAIA. **Intercollegiate:** Baseball M, basketball, cross-country, field hockey W, golf, softball W, volleyball W. **Intramural:** Badminton, basketball W, bowling, field hockey W, soccer, softball, table tennis, tennis, volleyball.

STUDENT SERVICES. Career counseling, employment service for undergraduates, freshman orientation, health services, personal counseling, placement service for graduates, special adviser for adult students.

ANNUAL EXPENSES. Tuition and fees: $8,474. **Room and board:** $4,000. **Books and supplies:** $600. **Other expenses:** $600.

FINANCIAL AID. 85% of freshmen, 75% of continuing students receive some form of aid. 98% of grants, 71% of loans, 66% of jobs based on

need. Academic, athletic, leadership scholarships available. **Aid applications:** Closing date April 1; applicants notified on or about March 15; must reply within 4 weeks.

ADDRESS/TELEPHONE. Karin L. Allmendinger, Director of Admissions, Alvernia College, 400 St. Bernardine Street, Reading, PA 19607-1799. (215) 796-8220. Fax: (215) 796-8336.

American Institute of Design
Philadelphia, Pennsylvania CB code: 7326

2-year proprietary trade and technical School, coed. Founded in 1967. **Undergraduate enrollment:** 500 men and women. **Faculty:** 18 total (15 full time). **Location:** Urban campus in very large city. **Calendar:** Continuous enrollment. **Microcomputers:** 22 located in computer centers.

DEGREES OFFERED. 100 associate degrees awarded in 1992. 60% in architecture and environmental design, 40% engineering technologies.

UNDERGRADUATE MAJORS. Architectural technologies, architecture, civil technology, drafting, drafting and design technology, electromechanical technology, engineering and engineering-related technologies, interior design.

ACADEMIC REQUIREMENTS. No policy requiring minimum GPA; records of students having academic difficulty are reviewed individually. 80% of freshmen return for sophomore year. Students must declare major on enrollment. **Graduation requirements:** 84 hours for associate. Most students required to take courses in arts/fine arts, computer science, mathematics.

FRESHMAN ADMISSIONS. Selection criteria: Open admissions. Aptitude evaluation and interview required. School achievement record considered.

1992 FRESHMAN CLASS PROFILE. 300 men and women enrolled. **Characteristics:** 98% from in state, 100% commute, 30% have minority backgrounds. Average age is 18.

FALL-TERM APPLICATIONS. $90 fee. No closing date; applicants notified on a rolling basis. Interview required. Portfolio recommended.

STUDENT SERVICES. Career counseling, employment service for undergraduates, personal counseling, placement service for graduates, services/facilities for handicapped.

ANNUAL EXPENSES. Tuition and fees (1992-93): $15,315. **Books and supplies:** $928.

FINANCIAL AID. 90% of freshmen, 90% of continuing students receive some form of aid. **Aid applications:** No closing date; applicants notified on a rolling basis.

ADDRESS/TELEPHONE. Dorothy Miller, Director, American Institute of Design, 1616 Orthodox Street, Philadelphia, PA 19124. (215) 288-8200.

Antonelli Institute of Art and Photography
Plymouth Meeting, Pennsylvania CB code: 0971

2-year proprietary technical college, coed. Founded in 1938. **Undergraduate enrollment:** 165 men and women. **Faculty:** 29 total (17 full time). **Location:** Suburban campus in large town; 15 miles from Philadelphia. **Calendar:** Semester. **Microcomputers:** Located in computer centers.

DEGREES OFFERED. 45 associate degrees awarded in 1992. 100% in visual and performing arts.

UNDERGRADUATE MAJORS. Clothing and textiles management/production/services, fashion merchandising, graphic arts technology, industrial design, interior design, photographic technology, photography.

ACADEMIC PROGRAMS. Remedial services: Tutoring.

ACADEMIC REQUIREMENTS. Freshmen must earn minimum GPA of 2.0 to continue in good standing. 75% of freshmen return for sophomore year. Students must declare major on application. **Graduation requirements:** 60 hours for associate. Most students required to take courses in English, social sciences.

FRESHMAN ADMISSIONS. Selection criteria: Interview most important in determining interest, motivation, and ability.

1992 FRESHMAN CLASS PROFILE. 31 men, 31 women enrolled. **Characteristics:** 88% from in state, 90% commute, 5% have minority backgrounds, 6% are foreign students. Average age is 20.

FALL-TERM APPLICATIONS. $100 fee. No closing date; applicants notified on a rolling basis; must reply by registration. Interview recommended. Portfolio recommended for advanced placement applicants.

STUDENT LIFE. Housing: Dormitories (coed). **Activities:** Student newspaper, television.

ATHLETICS. Intramural: Baseball, basketball, softball, volleyball.

STUDENT SERVICES. Career counseling, employment service for undergraduates, personal counseling, placement service for graduates.

ANNUAL EXPENSES. Tuition and fees (1992-93): $8,470. **Room and board:** $3,850. **Books and supplies:** $1,320. **Other expenses:** $1,320.

FINANCIAL AID. 86% of freshmen, 90% of continuing students receive some form of aid. Grants, loans available. **Aid applications:** Closing date August 15; priority given to applications received by July 31; applicants notified on a rolling basis beginning on or about September 1; must reply within 2 weeks.

ADDRESS/TELEPHONE. Natalie Stevens, Director of Admissions, Antonelli Institute of Art and Photography, 2910 Jolly Road, Plymouth Meeting, PA 19462. (215) 275-3040. Fax: (215) 275-5630.

Art Institute of Philadelphia
Philadelphia, Pennsylvania CB code: 2033

2-year proprietary technical college, coed. Founded in 1966. **Undergraduate enrollment:** 1,200 men and women full time; 80 men and women part time. **Location:** Urban campus in very large city. **Calendar:** Quarter.

FRESHMAN ADMISSIONS. Selection criteria: Open admissions. High school diploma or GED required. Admissions interview highly recommended.

ANNUAL EXPENSES. Tuition and fees (projected): $8,411. **Books and supplies:** $897. **Other expenses:** $1,305.

ADDRESS/TELEPHONE. Barbara H. Browning, Director of Admissions, Art Institute of Philadelphia, 1622 Chestnut Street, Philadelphia, PA 19103-5198. (215) 567-7080. (800) 275-2474. Fax: (215) 567-7080.

Art Institute of Pittsburgh
Pittsburgh, Pennsylvania CB code: 2029

2-year proprietary art college, coed. Founded in 1921. **Undergraduate enrollment:** 2,297 men and women. **Faculty:** 121 total (104 full time). **Location:** Urban campus in large city; in downtown area. **Calendar:** Quarter, extensive summer session. **Microcomputers:** 110 located in classrooms. **Special facilities:** Photography laboratory, art gallery for students and faculty, traveling exhibits, 24-track recording studio.

DEGREES OFFERED. 615 associate degrees awarded in 1992. 25% in architecture and environmental design, 25% business/office and marketing/distribution, 25% trade and industry, 25% visual and performing arts.

UNDERGRADUATE MAJORS. Commercial art, fashion illustration, fashion merchandising, graphic arts technology, graphic design, illustration design, industrial design, interior design, music video business, photography, video, visual communication.

ACADEMIC PROGRAMS. Internships, cross-registration. **Remedial services:** Special counselor, tutoring.

ACADEMIC REQUIREMENTS. Freshmen must earn minimum GPA of 2.0 to continue in good standing. 89% of freshmen return for sophomore year. Students must declare major on enrollment. **Graduation requirements:** 120 hours for associate.

FRESHMAN ADMISSIONS. Selection criteria: Open admissions. Prefer students with demonstrated interest in chosen major.

1992 FRESHMAN CLASS PROFILE. 871 men and women enrolled. **Characteristics:** 50% from in state, 55% live in college housing, 7% have minority backgrounds. Average age is 19.

FALL-TERM APPLICATIONS. $50 fee. No closing date; applicants notified on a rolling basis; must reply within 2 weeks. Interview required. Deferred and early admission available. SAT recommended for placement. Portfolio considered if available.

STUDENT LIFE. Housing: Dormitories (coed); apartment housing available. **Activities:** Student government, radio, student newspaper, television, various community relations activities, international student organization, student success task force.

STUDENT SERVICES. Career counseling, employment service for undergraduates, freshman orientation, personal counseling, placement service for graduates, veterans counselor, services/facilities for handicapped.

ANNUAL EXPENSES. Tuition and fees (1992-93): $8,050. Tuition and fees vary according to program. **Room and board:** $5,340. **Books and supplies:** $1,073. **Other expenses:** $1,212.

FINANCIAL AID. 80% of freshmen, 80% of continuing students receive some form of aid. Grants, loans, jobs available. Academic, art, leadership scholarships available. **Aid applications:** No closing date; priority given to applications received by March 1; applicants notified on a rolling basis beginning on or about May 15; must reply within 1 week. **Additional information:** Internal scholarships available.

ADDRESS/TELEPHONE. Lee Colker, Director of Admissions, Art Institute of Pittsburgh, 526 Penn Avenue, Pittsburgh, PA 15222. (412) 263-6600. (800) 275-2470. Fax: (412) 263-6600.

Baptist Bible College of Pennsylvania
Clarks Summit, Pennsylvania CB code: 2036

4-year private Bible college, coed, affiliated with General Association of Regular Baptist Churches. Founded in 1932. **Accreditation:** Regional. **Undergraduate enrollment:** 592 men and women. **Graduate enrollment:** 30 men and women. **Faculty:** 42 total (35 full time), 17 with doctorates or other terminal degrees. **Location:** Suburban campus in small town; 5 miles from Scranton. **Calendar:** Semester, limited summer session. **Microcomputers:** Located in computer centers.

DEGREES OFFERED. AA, BS, BFA, MS, M.Div. 23 associate degrees awarded in 1992. 79 bachelor's degrees awarded. Graduate degrees offered in 3 major fields of study.

UNDERGRADUATE MAJORS. Associate: Liberal/general studies, secretarial and related programs. **Bachelor's:** Elementary education, religious education, religious music, secondary education, secretarial and related programs, theological studies.

ACADEMIC PROGRAMS. 2-year transfer program, double major, dual enrollment of high school students, independent study, internships, student-designed major, study abroad. **Remedial services:** Learning center, reduced course load, remedial instruction, tutoring. **ROTC:** Army. **Placement/credit:** AP, CLEP Subject; 6 credit hours maximum for associate degree; 6 credit hours maximum for bachelor's degree.

ACADEMIC REQUIREMENTS. Freshmen must earn minimum GPA of 2.0 to continue in good standing. 80% of freshmen return for sophomore year. Students must declare major by end of second year. **Graduation requirements:** 63 hours for associate, 124 hours for bachelor's (42 in major). Most students required to take courses in arts/fine arts, English, history, philosophy/religion, biological/physical sciences, social sciences. **Postgraduate studies:** 75% from 2-year programs enter 4-year programs.

FRESHMAN ADMISSIONS. Selection criteria: Special importance given to Christian character and purpose. **Test requirements:** SAT or ACT; score report by August 1.

1992 FRESHMAN CLASS PROFILE. 216 men and women enrolled. **Characteristics:** 20% from in state, 90% live in college housing, 2% have minority backgrounds, 1% are foreign students. Average age is 20.

FALL-TERM APPLICATIONS. $20 fee. Closing date August 15; priority given to applications received by May 15; applicants notified on a rolling basis; must reply within 2 weeks. Essay required. Interview recommended. Deferred and early admission available.

STUDENT LIFE. Housing: Dormitories (men, women); apartment housing available. **Activities:** Student government, student newspaper, yearbook, choral groups, drama, music ensembles, pep band, Pennsylvania State Forest Fire Crew, volunteer first aid squad and fire company, several religious and service groups.

ATHLETICS. NAIA. **Intercollegiate:** Basketball, cross-country, golf M, soccer M, track and field, volleyball, wrestling M. **Intramural:** Basketball, golf M, ice hockey M, skiing, soccer, softball M, volleyball.

STUDENT SERVICES. Career counseling, employment service for undergraduates, health services, personal counseling, placement service for graduates, special adviser for adult students, veterans counselor.

ANNUAL EXPENSES. Tuition and fees: $6,061. **Room and board:** $3,660. **Books and supplies:** $500. **Other expenses:** $600.

FINANCIAL AID. 85% of freshmen, 85% of continuing students receive some form of aid. All grants, 88% of loans based on need. All jobs based on criteria other than need. Academic, music/drama, leadership, religious affiliation scholarships available. **Aid applications:** Closing date April 1; applicants notified on a rolling basis beginning on or about May 15; must reply within 2 weeks.

ADDRESS/TELEPHONE. Timothy Mayo, Director of Admissions, Baptist Bible College of Pennsylvania, 538 Venard Road, Clarks Summit, PA 18411. (717) 587-1172.

Beaver College
Glenside, Pennsylvania — CB code: 2039

Admissions: 76% of applicants accepted
Based on:
- ••• School record
- •• Activities, essay, recommendations, test scores
- • Interview, special talents

Completion: 87% of freshmen end year in good standing
65% graduate, 17% of these enter graduate study

4-year private college of arts and sciences, coed, affiliated with Presbyterian Church (USA). Founded in 1853. **Accreditation:** Regional. **Undergraduate enrollment:** 190 men, 566 women full time; 181 men, 347 women part time. **Graduate enrollment:** 1,197 men and women. **Faculty:** 183 total (75 full time), 93 with doctorates or other terminal degrees. **Location:** Suburban campus in large town; 10 miles from center city Philadelphia. **Calendar:** Semester, limited summer session. **Microcomputers:** 37 located in libraries, classrooms, computer centers. **Special facilities:** Art gallery with focus on contemporary art and 8 exhibitions annually, observatory housing 14-inch Schmidt-Cassegraim telescope with extensive astrophotography capabilities. **Additional facts:** A division of the American Language Academy on campus.

DEGREES OFFERED. AA, AS, BA, BS, BFA, MA, MS, MEd. 15 associate degrees awarded in 1992. 56% in business and management, 44% computer sciences. 221 bachelor's degrees awarded. 18% in business and management, 12% computer sciences, 9% teacher education, 8% allied health, 5% letters/literature, 13% life sciences, 9% psychology, 6% social sciences, 13% visual and performing arts. Graduate degrees offered in 20 major fields of study.

UNDERGRADUATE MAJORS. Associate: Business and management, computer and information sciences, liberal/general studies. **Bachelor's:** Accounting, art education, art history, art therapy, artificial intelligence, biological and physical sciences, biology, business administration and management, business and chemistry, business and management, ceramics, chemistry, communications, computer and information sciences, computer programming, dramatic arts, early childhood education, elementary education, engineering, English, English education, finance, fine arts, graphic design, history, human resources development, illustration design, interior design, liberal/general studies, management information systems, marketing management, mathematics, mathematics education, medical illustrating, metal/jewelry, optometry, painting, personnel management, philosophy, photography, political science and government, printmaking, psychobiology, psychology, science education, secondary education, social studies education, sociology, special education, visual and performing arts.

ACADEMIC PROGRAMS. Accelerated program, cooperative education, double major, dual enrollment of high school students, honors program, independent study, internships, student-designed major, study abroad, teacher preparation, Washington semester, cross-registration; liberal arts/career combination in engineering. **Remedial services:** Reduced course load, special counselor, tutoring. **Placement/credit:** AP, CLEP General and Subject, institutional tests; 64 credit hours maximum for bachelor's degree.

ACADEMIC REQUIREMENTS. Freshmen must earn minimum GPA of 1.75 to continue in good standing. 84% of freshmen return for sophomore year. Students must declare major by end of second year. **Graduation requirements:** 60 hours for associate (21 in major), 128 hours for bachelor's (48 in major). Most students required to take courses in computer science, English, foreign languages, history, humanities, mathematics, biological/physical sciences, social sciences. **Postgraduate studies:** 75% from 2-year programs enter 4-year programs. 1% enter law school, 1% enter medical school, 1% enter MBA programs, 14% enter other graduate study. **Additional information:** Associate and bachelor's degree programs and postbaccalaureate certificate programs in business administration and computer science, associate program in art, and bachelor's program in communications offered in evening.

FRESHMAN ADMISSIONS. Selection criteria: Emphasis placed on academic record, including type of program followed, grades, and class rank. Test scores, counselor and teacher recommendations, character references, participation in school and community activities considered. Interview recommended. **High school preparation:** 16 units required. Required units include English 4, foreign language 2, mathematics 3, social science 3 and science 1. Additional units in foreign language, mathematics, or laboratory science recommended. Chemistry required for prenursing students. Strong background in science and mathematics recommended for applicants to prehealth professions and combined engineering programs. **Test requirements:** SAT or ACT; score report by August 15.

1992 FRESHMAN CLASS PROFILE. 721 men and women applied, 545 accepted; 173 enrolled. **Academic background:** Mid 50% of enrolled freshmen had SAT-V between 390-510, SAT-M between 430-550. 97% submitted SAT scores. **Characteristics:** 69% from in state, 60% live in college housing, 17% have minority backgrounds, 2% are foreign students. Average age is 18.

FALL-TERM APPLICATIONS. $25 fee, may be waived for applicants with need. No closing date; priority given to applications received by August 1; applicants notified on a rolling basis; must reply by May 1 or within 2 weeks if notified thereafter. Essay required. Interview recommended. Portfolio recommended for art applicants, required for science illustration applicants. CRDA. Deferred and early admission available. EDP-F. Supplementary materials demonstrating student's talents and potential recommended.

STUDENT LIFE. Housing: Dormitories (women, coed). Thomas Residence Hall designed as living/learning center offering variety of cultural and educational programs. **Activities:** Student government, magazine, radio, student newspaper, yearbook, choral groups, drama, musical theater, 35 clubs and organizations, including Christian Fellowship, Newman Club, Black Awareness Society, International Club, Hillel, Circle-K, Political Awareness Society, Inter-Varsity Christian Fellowship.

ATHLETICS. NAIA. **Intercollegiate:** Baseball M, basketball, cross-country, field hockey W, lacrosse W, soccer, softball W, tennis, track and field, volleyball W. **Intramural:** Basketball, skiing, soccer, softball, swimming, tennis, volleyball. **Clubs:** Horseback riding.

STUDENT SERVICES. Career counseling, employment service for undergraduates, freshman orientation, health services, on-campus day care, personal counseling, placement service for graduates, special adviser for adult students, writing center, learning resource center, services/facilities for handicapped.

ANNUAL EXPENSES. Tuition and fees (1992-93): $11,710. **Room and board:** $4,750. **Books and supplies:** $400. **Other expenses:** $550.

FINANCIAL AID. 76% of freshmen, 65% of continuing students receive some form of aid. 97% of grants, 70% of loans, 51% of jobs based on need. 92 enrolled freshmen were judged to have need, all were offered aid. Academic, music/drama, art, athletic, leadership scholarships available. **Aid applications:** Closing date April 15; priority given to applications received by March 15; applicants notified on a rolling basis beginning on or about March 15; must reply by May 1.

ADDRESS/TELEPHONE. Carolyn Pyatt, Vice President for Enrollment Management, Beaver College, Church and Easton Roads, Glenside, PA 19038-3295. (215) 572-2910. (800) 767-0031.

Berean Institute
Philadelphia, Pennsylvania CB code: 1045

2-year private vocational and technical college, coed. Founded in 1899. **Undergraduate enrollment:** 318 men and women. **Location:** Urban campus in very large city; in downtown area. **Calendar:** Semester.

FRESHMAN ADMISSIONS. Selection criteria: School achievement record, test scores, interview, and recommendations considered.

ANNUAL EXPENSES. Tuition and fees (projected): $2,663. Cosmetology students incur additional fees. Uniforms required. **Books and supplies:** $400. **Other expenses:** $500.

ADDRESS/TELEPHONE. Micki Blackman, Admissions Director, Berean Institute, 1901 West Girard Avenue, Philadelphia, PA 19130. (215) 763-4833.

Bloomsburg University of Pennsylvania
Bloomsburg, Pennsylvania CB code: 2646

Admissions: 40% of applicants accepted
Based on: ••• School record, test scores
•• Activities, recommendations
• Essay, special talents
Completion: 81% of freshmen end year in good standing
64% graduate, 10% of these enter graduate study

4-year public university, coed. Founded in 1839. **Accreditation:** Regional. **Undergraduate enrollment:** 2,268 men, 3,676 women full time; 336 men, 698 women part time. **Graduate enrollment:** 50 men, 123 women full time; 104 men, 296 women part time. **Faculty:** 398 total (369 full time), 231 with doctorates or other terminal degrees. **Location:** Rural campus in large town; 40 miles from Wilkes-Barre. **Calendar:** Semester, extensive summer session. **Microcomputers:** 250 located in classrooms, computer centers.

DEGREES OFFERED. AS, BA, BS, MA, MS, MBA, MEd. 1,256 bachelor's degrees awarded. 27% in business and management, 6% education, 20% teacher education, 5% health sciences, 11% social sciences. Graduate degrees offered in 19 major fields of study.

UNDERGRADUATE MAJORS. Associate: Allied health. **Bachelor's:** Accounting, anthropology, art history, biology, business administration and management, business economics, business education, chemistry, clinical chemistry, communications, computer and information sciences, dental hygiene, dramatic arts, early childhood education, earth sciences, economics, education of the mentally handicapped, education of the physically handicapped, elementary education, English, English education, foreign languages education, French, geography, geology, German, health enhancement practices, health physics, history, humanities, interpreter for the deaf, journalism, mathematics, mathematics education, medical laboratory technologies, music, natural science and mathematics, nursing, office supervision and management, philosophy, physics, political economics, political science and government, psychology, radiograph medical technology, science education, secondary education, social sciences, social studies education, social work, sociology, Spanish, speech, speech correction, studio art.

ACADEMIC PROGRAMS. Cooperative education, double major, dual enrollment of high school students, honors program, independent study, internships, study abroad, teacher preparation, telecourses, visiting/exchange student program; liberal arts/career combination in engineering. **Remedial services:** Learning center, preadmission summer program, reduced course load, remedial instruction, special counselor, tutoring. **ROTC:** Air Force, Army. **Placement/credit:** AP, CLEP General and Subject, institutional tests; 64 credit hours maximum for bachelor's degree.

ACADEMIC REQUIREMENTS. Freshmen must earn minimum GPA of 1.65 to continue in good standing. 85% of freshmen return for sophomore year. Students must declare major by end of second year. **Graduation requirements:** 64 hours for associate, 128 hours for bachelor's. Most students required to take courses in arts/fine arts, English, history, humanities, mathematics, philosophy/religion, biological/physical sciences, social sciences. **Postgraduate studies:** 1% enter law school, 1% enter medical school, 2% enter MBA programs, 6% enter other graduate study.

FRESHMAN ADMISSIONS. Selection criteria: School achievement record and test scores. School's recommendation considered in borderline cases. **High school preparation:** 16 units recommended. Recommended units include biological science 2, English 4, foreign language 2, mathematics 3, physical science 1 and social science 4. Additional mathematics or science units may be applied if foreign language units not met. **Test requirements:** SAT; score report by March 15. **Additional information:** Must submit nonrefundable advance deposit by March 1.

1992 FRESHMAN CLASS PROFILE. 2,528 men applied, 1,056 accepted, 351 enrolled; 4,524 women applied, 1,755 accepted, 704 enrolled. 22% had high school GPA of 3.0 or higher, 65% between 2.0 and 2.99. 15% were in top tenth and 55% were in top quarter of graduating class. **Academic background:** Mid 50% of enrolled freshmen had SAT-V between 430-500, SAT-M between 480-570. 90% submitted SAT scores. **Characteristics:** 86% from in state, 92% live in college housing, 8% have minority backgrounds, 1% are foreign students. Average age is 18.

FALL-TERM APPLICATIONS. $15 fee. No closing date; priority given to applications received by December 1; applicants notified on a rolling basis beginning on or about December 1. Early admission available. Nursing applicants encouraged to apply by December 1.

STUDENT LIFE. Housing: Dormitories (men, women, coed); apartment, fraternity, sorority housing available. **Activities:** Student government, magazine, radio, student newspaper, television, yearbook, choral groups, concert band, drama, jazz band, marching band, music ensembles, musical theater, pep band, symphony orchestra, fraternities, sororities, Newman Student Association, Christian Fellowship, Jewish Fellowship, Orthodox Christian Fellowship, Fellowship of Christian Athletes, Young Democrats, College Republicans, Commonwealth Association of Students, Black Cultural Society, Association of Hispanic Students. **Additional information:** Of students who commute, 48% live off-campus and 9% commute from home.

ATHLETICS. NCAA. **Intercollegiate:** Baseball M, basketball, cross-country, diving, field hockey W, football M, lacrosse W, soccer, softball W, swimming, tennis, track and field, wrestling M. **Intramural:** Badminton W, baseball M, basketball, bowling W, cross-country M, golf, gymnastics, handball M, racquetball, soccer M, softball, table tennis, tennis, track and field M, volleyball, water polo M, wrestling M.

STUDENT SERVICES. Aptitude testing, career counseling, employment service for undergraduates, freshman orientation, health services, on-campus day care, personal counseling, placement service for graduates, special adviser for adult students, veterans counselor, services/facilities for handicapped.

ANNUAL EXPENSES. Tuition and fees (1992-93): $3,068, $3,394 additional for out-of-state students. **Room and board:** $2,754. **Books and supplies:** $400. **Other expenses:** $1,400.

FINANCIAL AID. 80% of freshmen, 70% of continuing students receive some form of aid. Grants, loans, jobs available. Academic scholarships available. **Aid applications:** Closing date May 1; priority given to applications received by March 15; applicants notified on a rolling basis beginning on or about June 1; must reply within 20 days.

ADDRESS/TELEPHONE. Bernie Vinovrski, Director of Admissions, Bloomsburg University of Pennsylvania, Room 10, Ben Franklin Hall, Bloomsburg, PA 17815. (717) 389-4316.

Bradley Academy for the Visual Arts
York, Pennsylvania CB code: 1548

2-year proprietary art, technical college. **Undergraduate enrollment:** 220 men and women. **Location:** Suburban campus in large town.

FRESHMAN ADMISSIONS. Selection criteria: High school record and attendance, recommendations, and admissions interview most important. Portfolio review required for graphic design applicants.

ANNUAL EXPENSES. Tuition and fees: $3,895. **Books and supplies:** $500.

ADDRESS/TELEPHONE. Janet Stevens, Director of Admissions, Bradley Academy for the Visual Arts, 625 East Philadelphia Street, York, PA 17403. (717) 848-1447.

Bryn Mawr College
Bryn Mawr, Pennsylvania CB code: 2049

Admissions: 54% of applicants accepted
Based on: ••• School record
•• Activities, essay, recommendations, special talents, test scores
• Interview
Completion: 98% of freshmen end year in good standing
85% graduate, 52% of these enter graduate study

4-year private university and liberal arts college, women only. Founded in 1885. **Accreditation:** Regional. **Undergraduate enrollment:** 42 men, 1,205 women full time; 2 men, 91 women part time. **Graduate enrollment:** 392 men and women full time; 98 men, 148 women part time. **Faculty:** 225 total (158 full time), 215 with doctorates or other terminal degrees. **Location:** Suburban campus in small town; 11 miles from Philadelphia. **Calendar:** Semester, limited summer session. **Microcomputers:** 150 located in libraries, classrooms, computer centers. **Special facilities:** Museums. **Additional facts:** Academic exchange with Haverford College, Swarthmore College, and University of Pennsylvania. Extracurricular and social coordination with Haverford.

DEGREES OFFERED. BA, MA, MSW, PhD. 310 bachelor's degrees awarded in 1992. 16% in languages, 14% letters/literature, 7% life sciences,

6% multi/interdisciplinary studies, 7% physical sciences, 7% psychology, 33% social sciences. Graduate degrees offered in 28 major fields of study.

UNDERGRADUATE MAJORS. African studies, Afro-American (black) studies, anthropology, archeology, art history, astronomy, biochemistry, biology, chemistry, city/community/regional planning, classics, comparative literature, dance, dramatic arts, East Asian studies, economics, English, English literature, experimental psychology, fine arts, foreign languages (multiple emphasis), French, geology, German, Greek (classical), Hispanic American studies, history, international relations, Italian, Latin, law and social policy, mathematics, molecular biology, music, music history and appreciation, neurosciences, peace studies, philosophy, physics, political science and government, psychology, religion, Russian, Russian and Slavic studies, sociology, Spanish, urban studies, visual and performing arts, women's studies.

ACADEMIC PROGRAMS. Accelerated program, double major, honors program, independent study, internships, student-designed major, study abroad, teacher preparation, visiting/exchange student program, cross-registration, archaeological excavations in Turkey, Greece and Siberia; anthropological excavations in Alaska and Kenya; summer language institutes and program in international economic relations in France, Germany, Italy, Spain, and Russia; exchange with Spelman College, Georgia; liberal arts/career combination in engineering; combined bachelor's/graduate program in business administration. **Remedial services:** Preadmission summer program, reduced course load, special counselor, tutoring. **ROTC:** Air Force, Army, Naval. **Placement/credit:** AP, IB, institutional tests; 60 credit hours maximum for bachelor's degree.

ACADEMIC REQUIREMENTS. Freshmen must earn minimum GPA of 2.0 in at least half of their courses. 94% of freshmen return for sophomore year. Students must declare major by end of second year. **Graduation requirements:** 128 hours for bachelor's (32 in major). Most students required to take courses in English, foreign languages, humanities, mathematics, biological/physical sciences, social sciences. **Postgraduate studies:** 10% enter law school, 8% enter medical school, 5% enter MBA programs, 29% enter other graduate study.

FRESHMAN ADMISSIONS. Selection criteria: School achievement record most important. Test scores, recommendations, interview, school and community activities, extracurricular achievements important. **High school preparation:** 16 units required; 18 recommended. Required and recommended units include English 4, foreign language 3-4, mathematics 3-4, social science 1-2 and science 1-3. **Test requirements:** SAT or ACT (SAT preferred); score report by February 15. 3 ACH (including English Composition) required. Score report by February 15.

1992 FRESHMAN CLASS PROFILE. 1,400 women applied, 755 accepted, 275 enrolled. 62% were in top tenth and 90% were in top quarter of graduating class. **Academic background:** Mid 50% of enrolled freshmen had SAT-V between 570-670, SAT-M between 570-680. 99% submitted SAT scores. **Characteristics:** 7% from in state, 99% live in college housing, 28% have minority backgrounds, 10% are foreign students. Average age is 18.

FALL-TERM APPLICATIONS. $40 fee, may be waived for applicants with need. Closing date January 15; applicants notified on or about April 10; must reply by May 1. Interview required. Essay required. CRDA. Deferred and early admission available. EDP-F. Winter early decision plan also available. Application deadline January 1; notification by February 1.

STUDENT LIFE. Housing: Dormitories (women, coed); apartment, cooperative housing available. Students may live at Haverford College. Foreign language houses available to students studying French, German, Italian, Russian, Spanish. **Activities:** Student government, magazine, radio, student newspaper, yearbook, choral groups, dance, drama, jazz band, music ensembles, musical theater, symphony orchestra, international student, ethnic, political, and religious organizations, social action and service groups. **Additional information:** Strong student self government, student participation on trustees and most important faculty committees and councils.

ATHLETICS. NCAA. **Intercollegiate:** Badminton, basketball, cross-country, field hockey, lacrosse, soccer, swimming, tennis, volleyball. **Intramural:** Archery, badminton, basketball, cross-country, fencing, golf, gymnastics, horseback riding, ice hockey, rugby, sailing, softball, squash, track and field, volleyball.

STUDENT SERVICES. Career counseling, employment service for undergraduates, freshman orientation, health services, personal counseling, placement service for graduates, special adviser for adult students, services/facilities for handicapped.

ANNUAL EXPENSES. Tuition and fees: $17,660. **Room and board:** $6,450. **Books and supplies:** $530. **Other expenses:** $750.

FINANCIAL AID. 48% of freshmen, 48% of continuing students receive some form of aid. All grants, all loans, 62% of jobs based on need. 143 enrolled freshmen were judged to have need, 139 were offered aid. **Aid applications:** Closing date January 15; applicants notified on or about April 15; must reply by May 1.

ADDRESS/TELEPHONE. Elizabeth G. Vermey, Director of Admissions, Bryn Mawr College, Bryn Mawr, PA 19010. (215) 526-5152. Fax: (215) 526-7471.

Bucknell University
Lewisburg, Pennsylvania

CB code: 2050

Admissions:	58% of applicants accepted
Based on:	••• School record, test scores
	•• Activities, recommendations
	• Essay, interview, special talents
Completion:	95% of freshmen end year in good standing
	88% graduate, 27% of these enter graduate study

4-year private university, coed. Founded in 1846. **Accreditation:** Regional. **Undergraduate enrollment:** 1,820 men, 1,490 women full time; 19 men, 32 women part time. **Graduate enrollment:** 56 men, 75 women full time; 60 men, 51 women part time. **Faculty:** 268 total (238 full time), 238 with doctorates or other terminal degrees. **Location:** Rural campus in small town; 150 miles from Philadelphia, 130 miles from Baltimore, Maryland. **Calendar:** Semester, extensive summer session. **Microcomputers:** 650 located in dormitories, libraries, classrooms, computer centers. **Special facilities:** Art gallery, observatory, race and gender center, environmental science preserve, center for performing arts, poetry center, women's resource center, multicultural center, science center.

DEGREES OFFERED. BA, BS, MA, MS. 813 bachelor's degrees awarded in 1992. 13% in business and management, 16% engineering, 7% letters/literature, 13% physical sciences, 7% psychology, 25% social sciences. Graduate degrees offered in 29 major fields of study.

UNDERGRADUATE MAJORS. Accounting, American literature, analytical chemistry, anthropology, applied mathematics, art history, Asian studies, biochemistry, biological and physical sciences, biology, biophysics, business administration and management, business and management, cell biology, chemical engineering, chemistry, civil engineering, classics, clinical psychology, comparative literature, computer and information sciences, computer engineering, computer mathematics, computer programming, counseling psychology, creative writing, developmental psychology, dramatic arts, drawing, early childhood education, East Asian studies, economics, education administration, educational testing, evaluation, and measurement, electrical/electronics/communications engineering, elementary education, engineering and other disciplines, English, English literature, environmental science, experimental psychology, finance, foreign languages education, French, geography, geology, German, Greek (classical), hemispheric studies, higher education research, history, humanities and social sciences, inorganic chemistry, international relations, international studies, investments and securities, Japanese, junior high education, Latin, Latin American studies, linguistics, marketing management, mathematics, mathematics education, mechanical engineering, military science (Army), music, music education, music history and appreciation, music performance, music theory and composition, nuclear physics, organic chemistry, organizational behavior, painting, personnel management, philosophy, physical chemistry, physics, physiological psychology, political science and government, predentistry, prelaw, premedicine, preveterinary, psychology, pure mathematics, religion, Russian, science education, sculpture, secondary education, social psychology, social studies education, sociology, Spanish, statistics, studio art, women's studies.

ACADEMIC PROGRAMS. Double major, honors program, independent study, internships, semester at sea, student-designed major, study abroad, teacher preparation, visiting/exchange student program, United Nations semester, Washington semester; liberal arts/career combination in engineering; combined bachelor's/graduate program in business administration. **Remedial services:** Special counselor, tutoring. **ROTC:** Army. **Placement/credit:** AP, CLEP Subject, IB; 56 credit hours maximum for bachelor's degree.

ACADEMIC REQUIREMENTS. Freshmen must earn minimum GPA of 1.8 to continue in good standing. 96% of freshmen return for sophomore year. Students must declare major by end of second year. **Graduation requirements:** 128 hours for bachelor's (32 in major). Most students required to take courses in English, history, philosophy/religion, biological/physical sciences, social sciences. **Postgraduate studies:** 7% enter law school, 3% enter medical school, 3% enter MBA programs, 14% enter other graduate study.

FRESHMAN ADMISSIONS. Selection criteria: Emphasis on school achievement. Test scores, activities, alumni relationship important. Essay considered. **High school preparation:** 16 units required; 20 recommended. Required and recommended units include biological science 1, English 4, foreign language 2-4, mathematics 3-4, physical science 1 and social science 4. **Test requirements:** SAT or ACT (SAT preferred); score report by March 1. Foreign language ACH required of applicants planning to continue that language in college. Score report by July 31.

1992 FRESHMAN CLASS PROFILE. 3,397 men applied, 1,922 accepted, 464 enrolled; 2,798 women applied, 1,653 accepted, 425 enrolled. 92% had high school GPA of 3.0 or higher, 8% between 2.0 and 2.99. 52% were in top tenth and 80% were in top quarter of graduating class. **Academic background:** Mid 50% of enrolled freshmen had SAT-V between 510-590, SAT-M between 590-670. 99% submitted SAT scores. **Characteristics:** 28% from in state, 99% live in college housing, 6% have minority backgrounds, 4% are foreign students. Average age is 18.

FALL-TERM APPLICATIONS. $35 fee, may be waived for applicants

with need. Closing date January 1; applicants notified on or about April 1; must reply by May 1. Audition required for music applicants. Essay required. Interview recommended. Portfolio recommended for art applicants. CRDA. Deferred and early admission available. EDP-F.

STUDENT LIFE. Housing: Dormitories (men, women, coed); apartment, fraternity housing available. **Activities:** Student government, magazine, radio, student newspaper, television, yearbook, choral groups, concert band, dance, drama, jazz band, marching band, music ensembles, musical theater, opera, pep band, symphony orchestra, fraternities, sororities, Hillel, Newman Club, Black Student Alliance, Fellowship of Christian Athletes, CUMBRE, Race and Gender Resource Center, Office of International Education, multicultural affairs.

ATHLETICS. NCAA. **Intercollegiate:** Baseball M, basketball, cross-country, diving, field hockey W, football M, golf M, horseback riding W, ice hockey M, lacrosse, rifle, rowing (crew), rugby, sailing, skiing M, soccer, softball W, swimming, tennis, track and field, volleyball, water polo, wrestling M. **Intramural:** Badminton W, basketball, bowling, cross-country, fencing, golf, gymnastics, handball, racquetball, soccer, softball, squash, swimming, tennis, track and field M, volleyball, water polo W, wrestling M.

STUDENT SERVICES. Aptitude testing, career counseling, freshman orientation, health services, on-campus day care, personal counseling, placement service for graduates, multicultural adviser, services/facilities for handicapped.

ANNUAL EXPENSES. Tuition and fees: $17,730. **Room and board:** $4,590. **Books and supplies:** $600. **Other expenses:** $1,200.

FINANCIAL AID. 60% of freshmen, 60% of continuing students receive some form of aid. All grants, 72% of loans, 31% of jobs based on need. 327 enrolled freshmen were judged to have need, all were offered aid. **Aid applications:** Closing date February 15; applicants notified on or about April 5; must reply by May 1.

ADDRESS/TELEPHONE. Mark D. Davies, Director of Admission, Bucknell University, Lewisburg, PA 17837-9988. (717) 524-1101. Fax: (717) 524-3760.

Bucks County Community College
Newtown, Pennsylvania — CB code: 2066

2-year public community college, coed. Founded in 1964. **Accreditation:** Regional. **Undergraduate enrollment:** 1,562 men, 1,779 women full time; 3,442 men, 4,565 women part time. **Faculty:** 384 total (201 full time), 23 with doctorates or other terminal degrees. **Location:** Suburban campus in small town; 35 miles from Philadelphia. **Calendar:** Semester, limited summer session. Saturday and extensive evening/early morning classes. **Microcomputers:** Located in libraries, classrooms, computer centers. **Special facilities:** Wellness center, Hicks Art Center. **Additional facts:** Credit courses available at 8 off-campus locations.

DEGREES OFFERED. AA. 430 associate degrees awarded in 1992. 34% in business and management, 6% education, 23% health sciences, 14% multi/interdisciplinary studies, 5% visual and performing arts.

UNDERGRADUATE MAJORS. Accounting, allied health, American studies, biology, business administration and management, business and management, business and office, business data processing and related programs, business data programming, chemistry, cinematography/film, communications, computer and information sciences, computer programming, criminal justice studies, dietetic aide/assistant, drafting, early childhood education, education, electrical and electronics equipment repair, engineering, engineering and engineering-related technologies, finance, fine arts, food management, food production/management/services, graphic arts technology, graphic design, health education, health sciences, hotel/motel and restaurant management, human resources development, humanities and social sciences, institutional management, journalism, labor/industrial relations, law enforcement and corrections technologies, legal secretary, liberal/general studies, marketing management, mathematics, medical secretary, mental health/human services, music, nursing, office supervision and management, physical education, psychology, radio/television broadcasting, real estate, retailing, secretarial and related programs, small business management and ownership, social sciences, telecommunications, visual and performing arts.

ACADEMIC PROGRAMS. 2-year transfer program, cooperative education, dual enrollment of high school students, honors program, independent study, internships, student-designed major, study abroad. **Remedial services:** Learning center, preadmission summer program, reduced course load, remedial instruction, special counselor, tutoring. **Placement/credit:** AP, CLEP General and Subject, institutional tests; 30 credit hours maximum for associate degree.

ACADEMIC REQUIREMENTS. Freshmen must earn minimum GPA of 1.7 to continue in good standing. 48% of freshmen return for sophomore year. Students must declare major on application. **Graduation requirements:** 62 hours for associate. Most students required to take courses in English, history, mathematics, philosophy/religion, biological/physical sciences.

FRESHMAN ADMISSIONS. Selection criteria: Open admissions. Selective admissions to nursing, fine arts, chef apprenticeship, music, and fine woodworking programs. **Test requirements:** Nelson-Denny and institutional tests required for placement.

1992 FRESHMAN CLASS PROFILE. 2,771 men and women enrolled. **Characteristics:** 99% from in state, 100% commute. Average age is 21.

FALL-TERM APPLICATIONS. $30 fee, may be waived for applicants with need. Closing date May 1; applicants notified on a rolling basis; must reply within 4 weeks. Interview required for chef apprentice, nursing, fine arts, fine woodworking applicants. Audition required for music applicants. Portfolio required for art, fine woodworking applicants. Essay required for chef apprentice applicants. Deferred and early admission available.

STUDENT LIFE. Activities: Student government, magazine, radio, student newspaper, choral groups, dance, drama, jazz band, music ensembles, sororities, Society for the Advancement of Management, Hillel, Human Rights, Inter-Varsity Christian Fellowship, Open Door, Third World Cultural Society, Hotel/Motel Club, Glass Art Society, Armenian Club, Woodcrafter's Guild.

ATHLETICS. NJCAA. **Intercollegiate:** Baseball M, basketball, cross-country, field hockey W, golf, horseback riding, soccer M, softball W, tennis. **Intramural:** Baseball M, basketball, horseback riding, skiing, soccer M, softball, swimming, volleyball, water polo.

STUDENT SERVICES. Aptitude testing, career counseling, employment service for undergraduates, freshman orientation, health services, on-campus day care, personal counseling, placement service for graduates, special adviser for adult students, veterans counselor, Continuing Education for Mature Students, community services, services/facilities for handicapped.

ANNUAL EXPENSES. Tuition and fees (projected): $1,855, $1,820 additional for out-of-district students, $3,640 additional for out-of-state students. **Books and supplies:** $500. **Other expenses:** $1,350.

FINANCIAL AID. 99% of grants, all loans, all jobs based on need. Academic, music/drama, art, state/district residency, leadership, minority scholarships available. **Aid applications:** No closing date; priority given to applications received by May 1; applicants notified on a rolling basis beginning on or about June 1; must reply within 2 weeks.

ADDRESS/TELEPHONE. Elizabeth M. Kulick, Director of Admissions, Records, and Registration, Bucks County Community College, Swamp Road, Newtown, PA 18940. (215) 968-8100 ext. 8119.

Butler County Community College
Butler, Pennsylvania — CB code: 2069

2-year public community college, coed. Founded in 1965. **Accreditation:** Regional. **Undergraduate enrollment:** 3,290 men and women. **Faculty:** 191 total (79 full time), 17 with doctorates or other terminal degrees. **Location:** Suburban campus in large town; 35 miles from Pittsburgh. **Calendar:** Semester, limited summer session. **Microcomputers:** Located in libraries, classrooms, computer centers. **Special facilities:** Nature trail, observatory, open-air theater.

DEGREES OFFERED. AA, AS, AAS. 380 associate degrees awarded in 1992. 30% in business and management, 5% computer sciences, 8% teacher education, 10% health sciences, 15% multi/interdisciplinary studies, 20% trade and industry.

UNDERGRADUATE MAJORS. Accounting, architectural technologies, architecture, atmospheric sciences and meteorology, biological and physical sciences, biology, business administration and management, business and management, business and office, business data processing and related programs, business data programming, civil technology, computer programming, data processing, drafting, drafting and design technology, early childhood education, education, electromechanical technology, electronic technology, elementary education, engineering, engineering and engineering-related technologies, English, food management, food production/management/services, hospitality and recreation marketing, humanities, humanities and social sciences, industrial technology, instrumentation technology, legal secretary, liberal/general studies, marketing and distribution, mathematics, mechanical design technology, medical assistant, medical secretary, nursing, parks and recreation management, physical sciences, retailing, science technologies, secondary education, secretarial and related programs, word processing.

ACADEMIC PROGRAMS. 2-year transfer program, double major, independent study, internships. **Remedial services:** Learning center, preadmission summer program, reduced course load, remedial instruction, tutoring. **Placement/credit:** AP, institutional tests; 45 credit hours maximum for associate degree.

ACADEMIC REQUIREMENTS. Freshmen must earn minimum GPA of 1.8 to continue in good standing. Students must declare major on enrollment. **Graduation requirements:** 63 hours for associate. Most students required to take courses in English, humanities, mathematics, social sciences.

FRESHMAN ADMISSIONS. Selection criteria: Open admissions. Selective admissions to nursing and metrology programs based on test scores, high school record, interview. **Test requirements:** Asset Placement Test required of incoming students.

1992 FRESHMAN CLASS PROFILE. 1,009 men and women enrolled. **Characteristics:** 99% from in state, 100% commute. Average age is 23.

FALL-TERM APPLICATIONS. $10 fee, may be waived for applicants with need. Closing date August 15; priority given to applications received by May 1; applicants notified on a rolling basis beginning on or about January

15. Interview recommended for nursing, metrology applicants. CRDA. Deferred and early admission available.

STUDENT LIFE. Activities: Student government, radio, student newspaper, yearbook, choral groups, drama, jazz band, pep band, Christian outreach organization.

ATHLETICS. Intercollegiate: Baseball M, basketball M, golf, softball W, tennis, volleyball W. **Intramural:** Badminton, basketball, handball M, racquetball, soccer, softball, table tennis, tennis, volleyball.

STUDENT SERVICES. Career counseling, employment service for undergraduates, freshman orientation, on-campus day care, personal counseling, placement service for graduates, special adviser for adult students, veterans counselor, services/facilities for handicapped.

ANNUAL EXPENSES. Tuition and fees (projected): $1,182, $1,140 additional for out-of-district students, $2,280 additional for out-of-state students. **Books and supplies:** $558. **Other expenses:** $900.

FINANCIAL AID. 55% of freshmen, 70% of continuing students receive some form of aid. 97% of grants, 56% of loans, 79% of jobs based on need. Academic scholarships available. **Aid applications:** Closing date May 1; priority given to applications received by April 16; applicants notified on or about May 15; must reply within 2 weeks.

ADDRESS/TELEPHONE. William L. Miller, Director of Admissions, Butler County Community College, PO Box 1203, Butler, PA 16003-1203. (412) 287-8711 ext. 344.

Cabrini College
Radnor, Pennsylvania — CB code: 2071

Admissions:	79% of applicants accepted
Based on:	••• School record
	•• Essay, interview, recommendations, test scores
	• Activities, special talents
Completion:	85% of freshmen end year in good standing
	55% graduate, 23% of these enter graduate study

4-year private college of arts and sciences, coed, affiliated with Roman Catholic Church. Founded in 1957. **Accreditation:** Regional. **Undergraduate enrollment:** 326 men, 700 women full time; 106 men, 311 women part time. **Graduate enrollment:** 4 men, 4 women full time; 48 men, 327 women part time. **Faculty:** 117 total (43 full time), 44 with doctorates or other terminal degrees. **Location:** Suburban campus in large town; 18 miles from Philadelphia. **Calendar:** Semester, extensive summer session. **Microcomputers:** 30 located in computer centers. **Special facilities:** Preschool, 30-acre preserve for environmental studies. **Additional facts:** College sponsored by Missionary Sisters of the Sacred Heart, international religious order serving 6 continents.

DEGREES OFFERED. BA, BS, MEd. 242 bachelor's degrees awarded in 1992. 30% in business and management, 19% communications, 6% education, 19% teacher education, 9% social sciences. Graduate degrees offered in 1 major field of study.

UNDERGRADUATE MAJORS. Accounting, American studies, arts management, biology, business administration and management, chemistry, communications, computer and information sciences, early childhood education, education of the emotionally handicapped, education of the mentally handicapped, education of the multiple handicapped, education of the physically handicapped, elementary education, English, English education, fine arts, foreign languages education, French, history, human resources development, junior high education, liberal/general studies, marketing management, mathematics, mathematics education, organizational management, philosophy, political science and government, psychology, religion, science education, secondary education, social studies education, social work, sociology, Spanish, special education, specific learning disabilities.

ACADEMIC PROGRAMS. Accelerated program, cooperative education, double major, dual enrollment of high school students, honors program, independent study, internships, student-designed major, study abroad, teacher preparation, exchange programs with Eastern College, Villanova University, and Rosemont College. **Remedial services:** Learning center, reduced course load, remedial instruction, special counselor, tutoring. **ROTC:** Army. **Placement/credit:** AP, CLEP Subject, IB, institutional tests.

ACADEMIC REQUIREMENTS. Freshmen must earn minimum GPA of 2.0 to continue in good standing. 71% of freshmen return for sophomore year. Students must declare major by end of second year. **Graduation requirements:** 123 hours for bachelor's. Most students required to take courses in arts/fine arts, computer science, English, foreign languages, history, humanities, mathematics, philosophy/religion, biological/physical sciences, social sciences. **Postgraduate studies:** 9% enter law school, 1% enter medical school, 3% enter MBA programs, 10% enter other graduate study. **Additional information:** Education fieldwork opportunities provided through children's school. Students required to complete 10 hours community service for junior seminar. 4 year cooperative program offered.

FRESHMAN ADMISSIONS. Selection criteria: School achievement record, recommendations, test scores, academic potential, and personal qualities. Special consideration for children of alumni and minorities. **High school preparation:** 17 units required. Required units include English 4, foreign language 2, mathematics 3, social science 3 and science 3. 2 arts and humanities also required. Additional mathematics and science units recommended for science students. **Test requirements:** SAT or ACT (SAT preferred); score report by December 30.

1992 FRESHMAN CLASS PROFILE. 160 men applied, 101 accepted, 46 enrolled; 387 women applied, 333 accepted, 115 enrolled. 29% had high school GPA of 3.0 or higher, 70% between 2.0 and 2.99. 11% were in top tenth and 23% were in top quarter of graduating class. **Academic background:** Mid 50% of enrolled freshmen had SAT-V between 350-480, SAT-M between 360-530. 99% submitted SAT scores. **Characteristics:** 65% from in state, 75% live in college housing, 10% have minority backgrounds, 1% are foreign students. Average age is 18.

FALL-TERM APPLICATIONS. $25 fee, may be waived for applicants with need. Applicants notified on a rolling basis; must reply by May 1. Essay required. Interview recommended. Portfolio recommended for art applicants. CRDA. Deferred and early admission available.

STUDENT LIFE. Housing: Dormitories (men, women, coed); handicapped housing available. 7 family-style houses available. **Activities:** Student government, film, magazine, radio, student newspaper, television, yearbook, choral groups, dance, drama, jazz band, music ensembles, Black Student Alliance, Project Outreach, campus ministry, student service and social action organizations, Prison Literacy, Outreach to the Homeless, Respect Life.

ATHLETICS. NCAA. **Intercollegiate:** Basketball, cross-country, field hockey W, soccer M, softball W, tennis, track and field, volleyball W. **Intramural:** Basketball, bowling, football M, soccer M, softball M, tennis, volleyball M, wrestling M.

STUDENT SERVICES. Aptitude testing, career counseling, employment service for undergraduates, freshman orientation, health services, personal counseling, placement service for graduates, special adviser for adult students, graduate opportunities office, services/facilities for handicapped.

ANNUAL EXPENSES. Tuition and fees (projected): $10,200. **Room and board:** $5,790. **Books and supplies:** $665. **Other expenses:** $1,075.

FINANCIAL AID. 75% of freshmen, 77% of continuing students receive some form of aid. 90% of grants, 80% of loans, all jobs based on need. 120 enrolled freshmen were judged to have need, 114 were offered aid. Academic, state/district residency, leadership, alumni affiliation scholarships available. **Aid applications:** No closing date; priority given to applications received by April 1; applicants notified on a rolling basis beginning on or about February 15; must reply within 2 weeks.

ADDRESS/TELEPHONE. Nancy Gardner, Admissions Director, Cabrini College, 610 King of Prussia Road, Radnor, PA 19087-3699. (215) 971-8552. (800) 848-1003. Fax: (215) 971-8539.

California University of Pennsylvania
California, Pennsylvania — CB code: 2647

Admissions:	55% of applicants accepted
Based on:	••• School record
	•• Recommendations, test scores
	• Activities, essay, interview, special talents
Completion:	75% of freshmen end year in good standing
	50% graduate, 20% of these enter graduate study

4-year public university, coed. Founded in 1852. **Accreditation:** Regional. **Undergraduate enrollment:** 2,464 men, 2,323 women full time; 269 men, 520 women part time. **Graduate enrollment:** 160 men, 206 women full time; 196 men, 346 women part time. **Faculty:** 321 total, 159 with doctorates or other terminal degrees. **Location:** Rural campus in small town; 45 miles from Pittsburgh. **Calendar:** Semester, limited summer session. **Microcomputers:** 708 located in libraries, classrooms, computer centers. **Special facilities:** Fine arts museum and gallery.

DEGREES OFFERED. AS, AAS, BA, BS, MA, MS, MEd. 40 associate degrees awarded in 1992. 40% in business and management, 8% computer sciences, 44% engineering technologies, 6% trade and industry. 972 bachelor's degrees awarded. 18% in business and management, 9% education, 18% teacher education, 13% engineering technologies, 6% letters/literature, 5% life sciences, 11% social sciences. Graduate degrees offered in 59 major fields of study.

UNDERGRADUATE MAJORS. Associate: Accounting, business administration and management, business and management, business data programming, community services, computer graphics, computer programming, drafting, drafting and design technology, early childhood education, education, emergency medical technologies, emergency/disaster science, fashion illustration, gerontology, graphic and printing production, graphic arts technology, information sciences and systems, management information systems, marketing and distribution, music video business, public affairs, robotics, teacher aide, visual communication. **Bachelor's:** Accounting, advertising, allied health, American literature, American studies, anthropology, applied mathematics, art history, atmospheric sciences and meteorology, biological and physical sciences, biology, botany, business administration and management, business and management, business economics, chemical engineering, chemistry, city/community/regional planning, clinical laboratory science, commercial art, communications, computer and information sciences, computer graphics, computer mathematics, computer programming, computer technology, conservation and regulation, creative writing, dental hygiene, drafting and design technology, dramatic arts, driver and safety education, early childhood education, earth sciences, Eastern European studies, ecology, economics, education, education of the culturally disadvantaged, education of the deaf and hearing impaired, education of the emotionally handicapped, education of the gifted and talented, education of the mentally handicapped, education of the multiple handicapped, education of the physically handicapped, educational media technology, electrical technology, elementary education, energy conservation and use technology, engineering, engineering and engineering-related technologies, engineering and other disciplines, English, English education, English literature, environmental science, European studies, finance, fine arts, foreign languages (multiple emphasis), foreign languages education, French, geography, geology, German, gerontology, graphic and printing production, graphic arts technology, graphic design, health sciences, history, human resources development, humanities and social sciences, industrial and organizational psychology, industrial arts education, industrial design, industrial engineering, industrial technology, information sciences and systems, international business management, international relations, international studies, journalism, junior high education, liberal/general studies, management information systems, manufacturing technology, marketing and distribution, marketing management, mathematics, mathematics education, mechanical design technology, mechanical engineering, medical laboratory technologies, military science (Army), nurse anesthetist, nursing, oceanography, parks and recreation management, personnel management, philosophy, physical sciences, physics, political science and government, predentistry, prelaw, premedicine, prepharmacy, preveterinary, psychology, public administration, public relations, radio/television broadcasting, radio/television technology, radiograph medical technology, reading education, recreation and community services technologies, Russian, Russian and Slavic studies, science education, science technologies, secondary education, Slavic languages, social science education, social sciences, social studies education, social work, sociology, soil sciences, Spanish, special education, specific learning disabilities, speech, speech correction, speech pathology/audiology, sports medicine, technical and business writing, technical education, theater design, tourism, trade and industrial education, trade and industrial supervision and management, transportation and travel marketing, urban design, urban planning technology, urban studies, visual and performing arts, water and wastewater technology, water resources, wildlife management.

ACADEMIC PROGRAMS. Accelerated program, cooperative education, double major, dual enrollment of high school students, education specialist degree, honors program, independent study, internships, student-designed major, study abroad, teacher preparation, visiting/exchange student program; liberal arts/career combination in engineering, health sciences. **Remedial services:** Learning center, reduced course load, remedial instruction, special counselor, tutoring. **ROTC:** Army. **Placement/credit:** AP, CLEP General and Subject, institutional tests; 15 credit hours maximum for associate degree; 60 credit hours maximum for bachelor's degree.

ACADEMIC REQUIREMENTS. Freshmen must earn minimum GPA of 2.0 to continue in good standing. 80% of freshmen return for sophomore year. Students must declare major by end of first year. **Graduation requirements:** 64 hours for associate, 128 hours for bachelor's. Most students required to take courses in English, humanities, biological/physical sciences, social sciences. **Postgraduate studies:** 37% from 2-year programs enter 4-year programs. 1% enter law school, 2% enter medical school, 5% enter MBA programs, 12% enter other graduate study. **Additional information:** Bachelor's of science in nursing and certified registered nurse anesthesia open only to registered nurses.

FRESHMAN ADMISSIONS. Selection criteria: School achievement record, test scores, activities, recommendations, interview. **High school preparation:** 14 units required; 17 recommended. Required and recommended units include biological science 1, English 4, foreign language 1-2, mathematics 3-4, physical science 1-2 and social science 4. **Test requirements:** SAT or ACT (SAT preferred); score report by August 1. English placement examination required.

1992 FRESHMAN CLASS PROFILE. 1,402 men applied, 792 accepted, 554 enrolled; 1,344 women applied, 713 accepted, 474 enrolled. 23% had high school GPA of 3.0 or higher, 74% between 2.0 and 2.99. 5% were in top tenth and 19% were in top quarter of graduating class. **Academic background:** Mid 50% of enrolled freshmen had SAT-V between 330-420, SAT-M between 350-470. 90% submitted SAT scores. **Characteristics:** 93% from in state, 60% commute, 7% have minority backgrounds, 1% are foreign students, 13% join fraternities/sororities. Average age is 18.

FALL-TERM APPLICATIONS. $25 fee, may be waived for applicants with need. Closing date August 1; priority given to applications received by May 1; applicants notified on a rolling basis; must reply by registration. Interview recommended. Essay recommended. Deferred and early admission available. EDP-F.

STUDENT LIFE. Housing: Dormitories (men, women, coed); fraternity, sorority, handicapped housing available. **Activities:** Student government, film, magazine, radio, student newspaper, television, yearbook, choral groups, concert band, drama, jazz band, marching band, music ensembles, musical theater, pep band, symphony orchestra, fraternities, sororities.

ATHLETICS. NCAA. **Intercollegiate:** Baseball M, basketball, cross-country, fencing, football M, rugby, soccer, softball W, tennis W, track and field, volleyball W, wrestling M. **Intramural:** Badminton W, basketball, handball, racquetball, skiing, soccer, softball, swimming, table tennis, tennis, track and field, volleyball, wrestling M.

STUDENT SERVICES. Aptitude testing, career counseling, employment service for undergraduates, freshman orientation, health services, on-campus day care, personal counseling, placement service for graduates, veterans counselor, women's center, services/facilities for handicapped.

ANNUAL EXPENSES. Tuition and fees (1992-93): $3,384, $3,394 additional for out-of-state students. **Room and board:** $3,460. **Books and supplies:** $400. **Other expenses:** $1,275.

FINANCIAL AID. 74% of freshmen, 69% of continuing students receive some form of aid. 84% of grants, 68% of loans, 26% of jobs based on need. 670 enrolled freshmen were judged to have need, 630 were offered aid. Academic, music/drama, athletic, state/district residency, minority scholarships available. **Aid applications:** No closing date; priority given to applications received by April 1; applicants notified on a rolling basis beginning on or about April 1; must reply within 25 days.

ADDRESS/TELEPHONE. Norman G. Hasbrouck, Dean for Enrollment Management and Academic Services, California University of Pennsylvania, 250 University Avenue, California, PA 15419-1394. (412) 938-4404. Fax: (412) 938-5832.

Carlow College
Pittsburgh, Pennsylvania

CB code: 2421

Admissions: 81% of applicants accepted
Based on:
- ••• School record
- •• Test scores
- • Activities, essay, interview, recommendations, special talents

Completion: 53% graduate, 24% of these enter graduate study

4-year private liberal arts college, women only, affiliated with Roman Catholic Church. Founded in 1929. **Accreditation:** Regional. **Undergraduate enrollment:** 61 men, 692 women full time; 81 men, 776 women part time. **Graduate enrollment:** 3 women full time; 2 men, 53 women part time. **Faculty:** 200 total (55 full time), 74 with doctorates or other terminal degrees. **Location:** Urban campus in large city; 3 miles from downtown. **Calendar:** Semester, limited summer session. **Microcomputers:** 50 located in libraries, computer centers. **Special facilities:** On-campus preschool and elementary school for education students, media center. **Additional facts:** Sponsored by Sisters of Mercy. 9% of enrolled students are men.

DEGREES OFFERED. BA, BS, MEd. 184 bachelor's degrees awarded in 1992. 16% in business and management, 17% communications, 10% teacher education, 31% health sciences, 5% life sciences, 7% multi/interdisciplinary studies. Graduate degrees offered in 2 major fields of study.

UNDERGRADUATE MAJORS. Accounting, art education, art history, art therapy, biology, business and management, communication business management, communications, comprehensive social studies, early childhood education, elementary education, English, English and business management, fine arts, health sciences, history, information management, liberal/general studies, mathematics, mathematics/computer science, nursing, philosophy, physical therapy, predentistry, prelaw, premedicine, preosteopathy, prepharmacy, prepodiatry, preveterinary, psychology, social science education, sociology and anthropology, special education, theological studies, writing.

ACADEMIC PROGRAMS. Accelerated program, double major, education specialist degree, honors program, independent study, internships, student-designed major, study abroad, teacher preparation, weekend college, cross-registration. **Remedial services:** Learning center, reduced course load, remedial instruction, special counselor, tutoring. **ROTC:** Air Force, Army, Naval. **Placement/credit:** CLEP General and Subject, institutional tests.

ACADEMIC REQUIREMENTS. Freshmen must earn minimum GPA of 2.0 to continue in good standing. 70% of freshmen return for sophomore year. Students must declare major by end of second year. **Graduation requirements:** 120 hours for bachelor's (44 in major). Most students required to take courses in arts/fine arts, English, history, humanities, mathematics, philosophy/religion, biological/physical sciences, social sciences. **Postgraduate studies:** 2% enter MBA programs, 22% enter other graduate study.

FRESHMAN ADMISSIONS. Selection criteria: School achievement record, class rank, test scores, recommendations important. 3.0 GPA, rank in upper two-fifths in class preferred. **High school preparation:** 18 units required. Required units include English 4, mathematics 3 and science 3. 4 arts and humanities and 4 electives also required. **Test requirements:** SAT or ACT (SAT preferred). **Additional information:** Nontraditional freshmen admitted for 1-semester assessment period and provided with special academic adviser and support program.

1992 FRESHMAN CLASS PROFILE. 14 men applied, 11 accepted, 7 enrolled; 314 women applied, 255 accepted, 142 enrolled. **Characteristics:**

93% from in state, 63% live in college housing, 11% have minority backgrounds, 1% are foreign students. Average age is 18.

FALL-TERM APPLICATIONS. $20 fee, may be waived for applicants with need. No closing date; applicants notified on a rolling basis; must reply within 4 weeks or upon receipt of financial aid offer, whichever comes first. Portfolio required for art applicants. Interview recommended. Deferred and early admission available. EDP-F.

STUDENT LIFE. Housing: Dormitories (women). **Activities:** Student government, student newspaper, choral groups, drama, music ensembles, YMCA volunteers, campus ministry, commuter students association, resident students association, international students association, Celtic Boosters club, honor societies, biology club, philosophy club, United Black Students.

ATHLETICS. NAIA. **Intercollegiate:** Basketball, cross-country, volleyball. **Intramural:** Basketball, volleyball.

STUDENT SERVICES. Aptitude testing, career counseling, employment service for undergraduates, freshman orientation, health services, on-campus day care, personal counseling, placement service for graduates, special adviser for adult students, services/facilities for handicapped.

ANNUAL EXPENSES. Tuition and fees (1992-93): $9,190. **Room and board:** $4,100. **Books and supplies:** $500. **Other expenses:** $1,200.

FINANCIAL AID. 94% of freshmen, 88% of continuing students receive some form of aid. 79% of grants, all loans, all jobs based on need. 135 enrolled freshmen were judged to have need, all were offered aid. Academic, art, athletic, leadership, alumni affiliation, religious affiliation, minority scholarships available. **Aid applications:** No closing date; priority given to applications received by March 15; applicants notified on a rolling basis; must reply within 4 weeks.

ADDRESS/TELEPHONE. James Enrietti, Vice President for Enrollment Management, Carlow College, 3333 Fifth Avenue, Pittsburgh, PA 15213-3165. (412) 578-6059. (800) 333-CARLOW.

Carnegie Mellon University
Pittsburgh, Pennsylvania

CB code: 2074

Admissions: 60% of applicants accepted
Based on: ••• School record, test scores
•• Activities, interview, recommendations
• Essay, special talents
Completion: 95% of freshmen end year in good standing
69% graduate, 30% of these enter graduate study

4-year private university, coed. Founded in 1900. **Accreditation:** Regional. **Undergraduate enrollment:** 2,903 men, 1,243 women full time; 99 men, 58 women part time. **Graduate enrollment:** 1,374 men, 422 women full time; 525 men, 343 women part time. **Faculty:** 996 total (821 full time), 660 with doctorates or other terminal degrees. **Location:** Urban campus in large city; 5 miles from downtown. **Calendar:** Semester, limited summer session. **Microcomputers:** 390 located in dormitories, libraries, classrooms, computer centers. **Special facilities:** 4 art galleries, concert hall, 3 theaters.

DEGREES OFFERED. BA, BS, BFA, BArch, MA, MS, MBA, MFA, PhD. 897 bachelor's degrees awarded in 1992. 5% in architecture and environmental design, 11% business and management, 26% engineering, 6% letters/literature, 14% mathematics, 7% physical sciences, 7% social sciences, 18% visual and performing arts. Graduate degrees offered in 118 major fields of study.

UNDERGRADUATE MAJORS. Actuarial sciences, American literature, analytical chemistry, applied mathematics, architecture, atomic/molecular physics, biochemistry, bioengineering and biomedical engineering, biological and physical sciences, biology, biomedical science, biophysics, business administration and management, business and management, business economics, business statistics, cell biology, ceramics, chemical engineering, chemistry, civil engineering, cognitive psychology, communications, comparative literature, computer and information sciences, computer engineering, computer mathematics, computer programming, crafts, creative writing, developmental psychology, dramatic arts, drawing, economics, electrical/electronics/communications engineering, elementary particle physics, enameling, engineering, engineering and other disciplines, engineering science, English, English literature, environmental health engineering, European studies, experimental psychology, fiber/textiles/weaving, fluids and plasmas, French, genetics, human and animal, German, glass, graphic arts technology, graphic design, history, humanities, humanities and social sciences, illustration design, industrial and organizational psychology, industrial design, information sciences and systems, inorganic chemistry, international business management, international relations, jazz, journalism, linguistics, management information systems, management science, marketing management, marketing research, materials engineering, mathematics, mechanical engineering, metal/jewelry, metallurgical engineering, metallurgy, molecular biology, music, music education, music performance, music theory and composition, musical theater, operations research, organic chemistry, organizational behavior, painting, philosophy, physical chemistry, physical sciences, physics, political science and government, printmaking, psychology, public administration, public affairs, public policy studies, pure mathematics, quantitative psychology, robotics, sculpture, social psychology, social sciences, sociology, Spanish, statistics, studio art, systems analysis, systems engineering, technical and business writing, theater design, toxicology, urban studies, visual and performing arts.

ACADEMIC PROGRAMS. Accelerated program, cooperative education, double major, dual enrollment of high school students, honors program, independent study, internships, student-designed major, study abroad, teacher preparation, visiting/exchange student program, Washington semester, cross-registration, Semester abroad programs in Keio University Program (Tokyo, Japan), Institute National Polytechnique du Lorraine (Nancy, France), Ecole Polytechnique Federale de Lausanne (Switzerland) Carnegie Mellon Study Center (Tours, France). **Remedial services:** Learning center, preadmission summer program, special counselor, tutoring, communications skills center. **ROTC:** Air Force, Army, Naval. **Placement/credit:** AP, institutional tests.

ACADEMIC REQUIREMENTS. Minimum GPA (typically 2.0) required to continue in good academic standing varies among colleges. 86% of freshmen return for sophomore year. Students must declare major by end of first year. **Graduation requirements:** 96 hours for bachelor's (30 in major). Most students required to take courses in computer science, English, history, humanities, mathematics, philosophy/religion, biological/physical sciences, social sciences. **Postgraduate studies:** 5% enter law school, 5% enter medical school, 7% enter MBA programs, 13% enter other graduate study. **Additional information:** Fine arts students must declare a major upon application, engineering and science students by end of first year, liberal arts and business students by end of second year.

FRESHMAN ADMISSIONS. Selection criteria: School academic record, class rank, test scores, recommendations, school and community activities, interview. Special consideration given to children of alumni, minority applicants. **High school preparation:** 16 units required. High school academic unit requirements vary by college. **Test requirements:** SAT or ACT; score report by February 15. 3 ACH required of engineering, science, humanities, social science, industrial management, and architecture applicants. Score report by February 15.

1992 FRESHMAN CLASS PROFILE. 5,438 men applied, 3,345 accepted, 789 enrolled; 2,769 women applied, 1,619 accepted, 355 enrolled. 91% had high school GPA of 3.0 or higher, 9% between 2.0 and 2.99. **Academic background:** Mid 50% of enrolled freshmen had SAT-V between 500-600, SAT-M between 590-730. 90% submitted SAT scores. **Characteristics:** 27% from in state, 98% live in college housing, 28% have minority backgrounds, 10% are foreign students, 25% join fraternities/sororities. Average age is 18.

FALL-TERM APPLICATIONS. $50 fee, may be waived for applicants with need. Closing date February 1; applicants notified on or about April 15; must reply by May 1. Audition required for drama, music applicants. Portfolio required for art, graphic and industrial design, drama design applicants. Essay required. Interview recommended. CRDA. Deferred and early admission available. EDP-F.

STUDENT LIFE. Housing: Dormitories (men, women, coed); apartment, fraternity, sorority, cooperative housing available. **Activities:** Student government, magazine, radio, student newspaper, yearbook, choral groups, concert band, drama, jazz band, marching band, music ensembles, musical theater, opera, pep band, symphony orchestra, student art gallery, Beaux Arts Ball, fraternities, sororities, Alpha Phi Omega, Hillel, Christian student organizations, minority women's club, service club, professional clubs, International Student Organization, National Society of Black Engineers, Society of Women Engineers.

ATHLETICS. NCAA. **Intercollegiate:** Basketball, cross-country, football M, golf M, rifle M, soccer, swimming, tennis, track and field, volleyball W. **Intramural:** Badminton, basketball, bowling, cross-country, fencing, golf, ice hockey M, racquetball, soccer, softball, swimming, table tennis, tennis, track and field, volleyball, water polo, wrestling M. **Clubs:** Baseball, floor hockey, lacrosse, rowing, rugby, intramural billiards.

STUDENT SERVICES. Aptitude testing, career counseling, employment service for undergraduates, freshman orientation, health services, on-campus day care, personal counseling, placement service for graduates, international student counselor, services/facilities for handicapped.

ANNUAL EXPENSES. Tuition and fees: $17,060. Freshmen pay additional $160 orientation fee.Graduate per credit hour charge ranges from $471 to $810 depending on program of study. **Room and board:** $5,540. **Books and supplies:** $450. **Other expenses:** $1,050.

FINANCIAL AID. 70% of freshmen, 67% of continuing students receive some form of aid. 96% of grants, 81% of loans, 71% of jobs based on need. 686 enrolled freshmen were judged to have need, 683 were offered aid. Academic, music/drama, art, leadership, alumni affiliation, minority scholarships available. **Aid applications:** No closing date; priority given to applications received by February 15; applicants notified on a rolling basis beginning on or about April 15; must reply by May 1 or within 3 weeks if notified thereafter.

ADDRESS/TELEPHONE. Michael Steidel, Director of Admissions, Carnegie Mellon University, 5000 Forbes Avenue, Pittsburgh, PA 15213-3890. (412) 268-2082. Fax: (412) 268-7838.

Cedar Crest College
Allentown, Pennsylvania CB code: 2079

Admissions: 82% of applicants accepted
Based on: ••• School record
•• Activities, essay, interview, recommendations, test scores
• Special talents
Completion: 75% of freshmen end year in good standing
58% graduate, 30% of these enter graduate study

4-year private liberal arts college, women only, affiliated with United Church of Christ. Founded in 1867. **Accreditation:** Regional. **Undergraduate enrollment:** 16 men, 645 women full time; 64 men, 617 women part time. **Faculty:** 141 total (64 full time), 82 with doctorates or other terminal degrees. **Location:** Suburban campus in small city; 55 miles from Philadelphia, 100 miles from New York City. **Calendar:** Semester, extensive summer session. **Microcomputers:** 60 located in dormitories, computer centers. **Special facilities:** Art gallery, Hawk Wildlife sanctuary, outdoor Greek theater, archaeological dig, registered arboretum. **Additional facts:** Men admitted to evening and weekend division and daytime programs in nursing, medical technology and nuclear medicine programs. Returning women students admitted to PORTAL Program.

DEGREES OFFERED. BA, BS. 175 bachelor's degrees awarded in 1992. 29% in business and management, 26% health sciences, 14% psychology, 7% social sciences.

UNDERGRADUATE MAJORS. Accounting, biochemistry, bioengineering and biomedical engineering, biology, business administration and management, business and management, chemistry, communications, comparative literature, computer and information sciences, dramatic arts, elementary education, English, fine arts, foreign languages (multiple emphasis), French, genetic engineering technology, German, history, liberal/general studies, mathematics, medical laboratory technologies, music, nuclear medical technology, nursing, philosophy, political science and government, psychology, public administration, science education, secondary education, social work, sociology, Spanish.

ACADEMIC PROGRAMS. Double major, dual enrollment of high school students, honors program, independent study, internships, student-designed major, study abroad, teacher preparation, visiting/exchange student program, weekend college, Washington semester, cross-registration; liberal arts/career combination in engineering, health sciences. **Remedial services:** Learning center, reduced course load, remedial instruction, special counselor, tutoring, 1 credit freshman course emphasizing study skills, communications. **ROTC:** Army. **Placement/credit:** AP, CLEP General and Subject, institutional tests; 12 credit hours maximum for bachelor's degree.

ACADEMIC REQUIREMENTS. Freshmen must earn minimum GPA of 1.8 to continue in good standing. 83% of freshmen return for sophomore year. Students must declare major by end of second year. **Graduation requirements:** 120 hours for bachelor's. Most students required to take courses in arts/fine arts, English, foreign languages, history, humanities, mathematics, biological/physical sciences, social sciences. **Additional information:** School nurse and addictions counselor certification available.

FRESHMAN ADMISSIONS. Selection criteria: Secondary school curriculum and grades most important. Test scores, special talents, potential for academic and personal growth considered. Foreign applicants welcome. **High school preparation:** 16 units required. Required units include biological science 1, English 4, foreign language 2, mathematics 3, physical science 1, social science 3 and science 1. Special natural science requirements for nuclear medicine and nursing. **Test requirements:** SAT or ACT (SAT preferred); score report by August 15.

1992 FRESHMAN CLASS PROFILE. 689 women applied, 567 accepted, 183 enrolled. 51% had high school GPA of 3.0 or higher, 44% between 2.0 and 2.99. 20% were in top tenth and 45% were in top quarter of graduating class. **Academic background:** Mid 50% of enrolled freshmen had SAT-V between 440-460, SAT-M between 480-490. 99% submitted SAT scores. **Characteristics:** 61% from in state, 91% live in college housing, 16% have minority backgrounds, 5% are foreign students. Average age is 18.

FALL-TERM APPLICATIONS. $30 fee, may be waived for applicants with need. No closing date; applicants notified on a rolling basis beginning on or about September 15; must reply by May 1 or within 3 weeks if notified thereafter. Essay required. Interview recommended. Audition recommended for music, theater applicants. Portfolio recommended for art applicants. CRDA. Deferred and early admission available.

STUDENT LIFE. Housing: Dormitories (women). **Activities:** Student government, student newspaper, yearbook, choral groups, dance, drama, musical theater, Newman Club, Minority Awareness Association, Hillel, Crest Christian Fellowship, Amnesty International, Alpha Omega Chi service organization, international student organization, student environmental association, peer network group. **Additional information:** Students vote on Board of Trustees and participate in most important committees. Cocurricular activities strongly encouraged for community participation and individual leadership development.

ATHLETICS. NCAA. **Intercollegiate:** Badminton, basketball, cross-country, field hockey, lacrosse, tennis, track and field, volleyball. **Intramural:** Basketball, tennis, track and field, volleyball.

STUDENT SERVICES. Career counseling, employment service for undergraduates, freshman orientation, health services, on-campus day care, personal counseling, placement service for graduates, special adviser for adult students.

ANNUAL EXPENSES. Tuition and fees: $13,720. **Room and board:** $5,210. **Books and supplies:** $500. **Other expenses:** $500.

FINANCIAL AID. 90% of freshmen, 85% of continuing students receive some form of aid. 91% of grants, 74% of loans, all jobs based on need. 168 enrolled freshmen were judged to have need, all were offered aid. Academic scholarships available. **Aid applications:** No closing date; priority given to applications received by May 1; applicants notified on a rolling basis beginning on or about October 1; must reply within 3 weeks. **Additional information:** College-developed aid program, SAVE (Supplemental Aid for Value in Education). Parents apply for up to $3,000 per year. College contributes 25% as grant, remainder is loan with interest-only payments during in-college years.

ADDRESS/TELEPHONE. Barbara Strickler, MBA, Vice President for Enrollment, Cedar Crest College, 100 College Drive, Allentown, PA 18104-6196. (215) 740-3780. (800) 360-1222. Fax: (215) 437-5955.

Central Pennsylvania Business School
Summerdale, Pennsylvania CB code: 1061

2-year proprietary business college, coed. Founded in 1922. **Accreditation:** Regional. **Undergraduate enrollment:** 90 men, 440 women full time; 14 men, 57 women part time. **Faculty:** 54 total (23 full time), 3 with doctorates or other terminal degrees. **Location:** Suburban campus in small town; 5 miles from Harrisburg. **Calendar:** Trimester, extensive summer session. **Microcomputers:** 75 located in libraries, classrooms, computer centers. **Special facilities:** Museum of central Pennsylvania artifacts.

DEGREES OFFERED. 248 associate degrees awarded in 1992. 19% in business and management, 50% business/office and marketing/distribution, 5% communications, 25% allied health.

UNDERGRADUATE MAJORS. Accounting, aviation management, business administration and management, child development/care/guidance, communications, court reporting, finance, hotel/motel and restaurant management, human resources development, information sciences and systems, legal assistant/paralegal, legal secretary, marketing management, medical assistant, medical secretary, office supervision and management, personnel management, physical therapy assistant, retailing, secretarial and related programs, small business management and ownership, tourism.

ACADEMIC PROGRAMS. Double major, internships. **Remedial services:** Reduced course load, remedial instruction, special counselor, tutoring. **Placement/credit:** AP, CLEP General and Subject.

ACADEMIC REQUIREMENTS. Freshmen must earn minimum GPA of 1.5 to continue in good standing. 60% of freshmen return for sophomore year. Students must declare major on application. **Graduation requirements:** 75 hours for associate. Most students required to take courses in computer science, English, humanities.

FRESHMAN ADMISSIONS. Selection criteria: Open admissions. Selective admission to some programs. High School achievement and admissions interview very important.

1992 FRESHMAN CLASS PROFILE. 85 men applied, 72 accepted, 59 enrolled; 503 women applied, 484 accepted, 280 enrolled. 25% had high school GPA of 3.0 or higher, 69% between 2.0 and 2.99. **Characteristics:** 90% from in state, 65% live in college housing, 4% have minority backgrounds. Average age is 18.

FALL-TERM APPLICATIONS. No fee. Closing date August 30; applicants notified on a rolling basis; must reply within 2 weeks. Interview recommended. Interview required of academically weak applicants, physical therapist assistant and legal assistant applicants; recommended for all others. Deferred and early admission available.

STUDENT LIFE. Housing: Dormitories (coed). **Activities:** Student government, radio, student newspaper, yearbook, Campus Christian Fellowship, Allied Medical Health Club, Travel Club, Collegiate Secreturies International.

ATHLETICS. Intercollegiate: Basketball, cross-country, golf, softball W, volleyball W. **Intramural:** Bowling, cross-country, skiing, softball, tennis, volleyball.

STUDENT SERVICES. Career counseling, employment service for undergraduates, freshman orientation, personal counseling, placement service for graduates, special adviser for adult students, services/facilities for handicapped.

ANNUAL EXPENSES. Tuition and fees: $5,250. **Room and board:** $2,590 room only. **Books and supplies:** $696. **Other expenses:** $748.

FINANCIAL AID. 47% of freshmen, 53% of continuing students receive some form of aid. All grants, 72% of loans, all jobs based on need. Academic scholarships available. **Aid applications:** No closing date; priority given to applications received by May 1; applicants notified on a rolling basis beginning on or about July 1; must reply within 2 weeks.

ADDRESS/TELEPHONE. David T. Bradley, Director for Admission Services, Central Pennsylvania Business School, College Hill Road, Summerdale, PA 17093-0309. (717) 732-0702 ext. 201. (800) 759-2727 ext. 201. Fax: (717) 732-5254.

Chatham College

Pittsburgh, Pennsylvania — CB code: 2081

Admissions: 86% of applicants accepted
Based on: ••• Interview, school record, test scores
•• Activities, essay, recommendations
• Special talents
Completion: 90% of freshmen end year in good standing
56% graduate, 33% of these enter graduate study

4-year private liberal arts college, women only. Founded in 1869. **Accreditation:** Regional. **Undergraduate enrollment:** 468 women full time; 151 women part time. **Faculty:** 56 total (47 full time), 49 with doctorates or other terminal degrees. **Location:** Urban campus in large city; 8 miles from downtown. **Calendar:** 4-1-4, limited summer session. **Microcomputers:** 50 located in libraries, classrooms, computer centers. **Special facilities:** Media center, greenhouse, art gallery.

DEGREES OFFERED. BA, BS. 102 bachelor's degrees awarded in 1992. 12% in business and management, 17% communications, 12% letters/literature, 6% life sciences, 15% psychology, 20% social sciences.

UNDERGRADUATE MAJORS. American literature, art history, biological and physical sciences, biology, business and management, business economics, chemistry, communications, computer and information sciences, dramatic arts, early childhood education, economics, elementary education, English, English education, English literature, fine arts, foreign languages (multiple emphasis), foreign languages education, French, history, humanities, humanities and social sciences, information sciences and systems, international business management, international relations, junior high education, liberal/general studies, management science, mathematics, mathematics education, music, music performance, philosophy, political science and government, psychology, religion, science education, secondary education, social studies education, Spanish.

ACADEMIC PROGRAMS. Accelerated program, dual enrollment of high school students, independent study, internships, student-designed major, study abroad, teacher preparation, visiting/exchange student program, Washington semester, cross-registration, cooperative degree program with Pittsburgh Ballet Theatre School. **Remedial services:** Learning center, preadmission summer program, special counselor, tutoring. **ROTC:** Air Force, Army, Naval. **Placement/credit:** AP, CLEP General, institutional tests.

ACADEMIC REQUIREMENTS. Freshmen must earn minimum GPA of 2.0 to continue in good standing. 75% of freshmen return for sophomore year. Students must declare major by end of second year. **Graduation requirements:** 126 hours for bachelor's (42 in major). Most students required to take courses in computer science, English, history, mathematics, biological/physical sciences. **Postgraduate studies:** 9% enter law school, 6% enter medical school, 3% enter MBA programs, 15% enter other graduate study. **Additional information:** Student designed interdepartmental majors available.

FRESHMAN ADMISSIONS. Selection criteria: School achievement record, test scores, essay, activities, and recommendations most important. **High school preparation:** 15 units required. Required and recommended units include English 4, foreign language 2-3, mathematics 3, social science 3 and science 3. Science units must include 2 laboratory sciences. **Test requirements:** SAT or ACT; score report by March 31.

1992 FRESHMAN CLASS PROFILE. 211 women applied, 182 accepted, 100 enrolled. 70% had high school GPA of 3.0 or higher, 26% between 2.0 and 2.99. 35% were in top tenth and 62% were in top quarter of graduating class. **Academic background:** Mid 50% of enrolled freshmen had SAT-V between 430-560, SAT-M between 420-550; ACT composite between 18-26. 83% submitted SAT scores, 17% submitted ACT scores. **Characteristics:** 78% from in state, 75% live in college housing, 19% have minority backgrounds, 3% are foreign students. Average age is 18.

FALL-TERM APPLICATIONS. $25 fee, may be waived for applicants with need. Closing date March 31; priority given to applications received by December 1; applicants notified on or about April 15; must reply by May 1. Interview required. Audition required. Essay required. Portfolio recommended for art applicants. CRDA. Deferred and early admission available. EDP-F.

STUDENT LIFE. Housing: Dormitories (women); apartment housing available. Residence hall specifically designed for adult students (Berry Hall) featuring efficiency apartments created to meet needs of single women, single mothers with one child (under age 10), or handicapped female students available. **Activities:** Student government, magazine, radio, student newspaper, yearbook, choral groups, dance, drama, music ensembles, musical theater, theater touring company, Mortar Board, Phi Beta Kappa, Black Student Union, Christian Fellowship, Hillel, Women's Issues and Actions Forum, environmental group, international student association, house board, judicial board.

ATHLETICS. Intercollegiate: Tennis, volleyball. **Intramural:** Badminton, bowling, golf, rowing (crew), swimming, tennis, volleyball.

STUDENT SERVICES. Aptitude testing, career counseling, employment service for undergraduates, freshman orientation, health services, personal counseling, placement service for graduates, special adviser for adult students, services/facilities for handicapped.

ANNUAL EXPENSES. Tuition and fees: $12,780. **Room and board:** $5,230. **Books and supplies:** $400. **Other expenses:** $850.

FINANCIAL AID. 94% of freshmen, 85% of continuing students receive some form of aid. Grants, loans, jobs available. 72 enrolled freshmen were judged to have need, all were offered aid. Academic, music/drama, leadership, alumni affiliation scholarships available. **Aid applications:** No closing date; priority given to applications received by March 15; applicants notified on a rolling basis beginning on or about March 15; must reply within 2 weeks.

ADDRESS/TELEPHONE. Denise Marie Michalka, Associate Director of Admissions, Chatham College, Woodland Road, Pittsburgh, PA 15232-9987. (412) 365-1290. (800) 837-1290. Fax: (412) 365-1609.

Chestnut Hill College

Philadelphia, Pennsylvania — CB code: 2082

Admissions: 74% of applicants accepted
Based on: ••• School record, test scores
•• Activities, interview, recommendations
• Essay, special talents
Completion: 95% of freshmen end year in good standing
70% graduate, 16% of these enter graduate study

4-year private liberal arts college, women only, affiliated with Roman Catholic Church. Founded in 1924. **Accreditation:** Regional. **Undergraduate enrollment:** 556 women full time; 62 men, 293 women part time. **Graduate enrollment:** 83 men, 357 women part time. **Faculty:** 120 total (61 full time), 51 with doctorates or other terminal degrees. **Location:** Suburban campus in very large city; 17 miles from center city Philadelphia. **Calendar:** Semester, extensive summer session. Extensive evening/early morning classes. **Microcomputers:** 100 located in dormitories, libraries, computer centers. **Special facilities:** Observatory and planetarium, nationally recognized Irish literature collection, technology center, neighboring art galleries, art museum, arboretum, concert park, stables, 2 nature centers. **Additional facts:** Men over 23 may matriculate part-time through continuing education and graduate school.

DEGREES OFFERED. AA, BA, BS, MA, MS, MEd. 1 associate degree awarded in 1992. 100% in business and management. 130 bachelor's degrees awarded. 14% in business and management, 35% teacher education, 12% letters/literature, 5% life sciences, 7% psychology, 14% social sciences, 7% visual and performing arts. Graduate degrees offered in 3 major fields of study.

UNDERGRADUATE MAJORS. Associate: Accounting, art history, business and management, chemistry, French, history, music, psychology, sociology, Spanish, studio art. **Bachelor's:** Accounting, art history, biochemistry, biology, business and management, chemistry, classics, computer and mathematical sciences, early childhood education, early childhood/elementary education, economics, elementary education, English literature, fine arts, French, German, history, marketing management, mathematics, molecular biology, music, music education, political science and government, psychology, sociology, Spanish, studio art.

ACADEMIC PROGRAMS. Accelerated program, cooperative education, double major, dual enrollment of high school students, education specialist degree, honors program, independent study, internships, student-designed major, study abroad, teacher preparation, visiting/exchange student program, cross-registration, 2-2 double bachelor's program in biology (or chemistry) and medical technology with Thomas Jefferson University School of Allied Health Sciences, bachelor's/doctoral program with Pennsylvania College of Podiatric Medicine; liberal arts/career combination in health sciences. **Remedial services:** Preadmission summer program, tutoring, writing enrichment center, mathematics center. **ROTC:** Army. **Placement/credit:** AP, CLEP Subject, institutional tests; 12 credit hours maximum for bachelor's degree.

ACADEMIC REQUIREMENTS. Freshmen must earn minimum GPA of 1.75 to continue in good standing. 83% of freshmen return for sophomore year. Students must declare major by end of second year. **Graduation requirements:** 60 hours for associate, 120 hours for bachelor's (36 in major). Most students required to take courses in arts/fine arts, computer science, English, foreign languages, history, humanities, mathematics, philosophy/religion, biological/physical sciences, social sciences. **Postgraduate studies:** 1% enter law school, 15% enter other graduate study. **Additional information:** Montessori certification available with elementary and pre-elementary education. Secondary education certification available in major field of study. American Chemical Society certification also available.

FRESHMAN ADMISSIONS. Selection criteria: Rank in class, type and quality of secondary education, test scores, recommendations, extracurricular and community activities, ability to demonstrate short-term goals.

High school preparation: 16 units required; 19 recommended. Required and recommended units include English 4, foreign language 2-3, mathematics 3-4, social science 4 and science 3-4. **Test requirements:** SAT or ACT (SAT preferred); score report by April 1. Prueba de Aptitud Academica for Spanish speaking applicants.

1992 FRESHMAN CLASS PROFILE. 337 women applied, 250 accepted, 134 enrolled. 25% were in top tenth and 63% were in top quarter of graduating class. **Characteristics:** 75% from in state, 78% live in college housing, 19% have minority backgrounds, 1% are foreign students. Average age is 18.

FALL-TERM APPLICATIONS. $25 fee, may be waived for applicants with need. No closing date; applicants notified on a rolling basis beginning on or about October 1. Audition required for music, music education applicants. Interview recommended. Portfolio recommended for studio art applicants. Essay recommended. CRDA. Deferred and early admission available.

STUDENT LIFE. Housing: Dormitories (women). Facilities for handicapped available in dormitories. **Activities:** Student government, magazine, student newspaper, yearbook, foreign language newspaper, choral groups, drama, jazz band, music ensembles, opera, symphony orchestra, madrigal singers, campus ministry group, more than 12 academic interest clubs, political and social service groups, business club, College Republicans, cultural awareness society, PeaceNet, Phi Beta Lambda.

ATHLETICS. Intercollegiate: Basketball, field hockey, lacrosse, softball, tennis, volleyball. **Intramural:** Archery, badminton, basketball, swimming, volleyball.

STUDENT SERVICES. Aptitude testing, career counseling, employment service for undergraduates, freshman orientation, health services, on-campus day care, personal counseling, placement service for graduates, special adviser for adult students, services/facilities for handicapped.

ANNUAL EXPENSES. Tuition and fees (1992-93): $8,950. **Room and board:** $4,450. **Books and supplies:** $680. **Other expenses:** $350.

FINANCIAL AID. 65% of freshmen, 66% of continuing students receive some form of aid. 71% of grants, 60% of loans, 73% of jobs based on need. 76 enrolled freshmen were judged to have need, all were offered aid. Academic, leadership scholarships available. **Aid applications:** No closing date; priority given to applications received by March 15; applicants notified on a rolling basis beginning on or about March 1; must reply by May 1 or within 3 weeks if notified thereafter. **Additional information:** 4-year, full-tuition and partial-tuition awards based on academic merit offered. Application priority date is January 15 for merit-based scholarships.

ADDRESS/TELEPHONE. Margaret Anne Birtwistle, SSJ, Director of Admissions, Chestnut Hill College, 9601 Germantown Avenue, Philadelphia, PA 19118-2695. (215) 248-7001. (800) 248-0052. Fax: (215) 248-7155.

Cheyney University of Pennsylvania
Cheyney, Pennsylvania CB code: 2648

4-year public university and liberal arts, teachers college, coed. Founded in 1837. **Accreditation:** Regional. **Undergraduate enrollment:** 570 men, 627 women full time; 32 men, 31 women part time. **Graduate enrollment:** 13 men, 32 women full time; 83 men, 160 women part time. **Faculty:** 91 total, 42 with doctorates or other terminal degrees. **Location:** Rural campus in rural community; 25 miles from Philadelphia. **Calendar:** Semester, limited summer session. **Microcomputers:** 50 located in libraries, classrooms, computer centers. **Special facilities:** Planetarium, ethnic studies collection, weather station, theater arts center, radio station. **Additional facts:** Courses offered at Philadelphia Urban Center.

DEGREES OFFERED. BA, BS, MS, MEd. 148 bachelor's degrees awarded in 1992. 30% in business and management, 5% communications, 25% teacher education, 6% engineering technologies, 17% parks/recreation, protective services, public affairs. Graduate degrees offered in 7 major fields of study.

UNDERGRADUATE MAJORS. Biological and physical sciences, biology, business and management, business education, chemistry, communications, computer and information sciences, dramatic arts, early childhood education, economics, elementary education, English, English education, fine arts, food science and nutrition, foreign languages education, geography, history, home economics education, hotel/motel and restaurant management, industrial arts education, industrial technology, mathematics, mathematics education, medical laboratory technologies, music, music business management, parks and recreation management, political science and government, psychology, radio/television technology, science education, secondary education, social science education, social sciences, social work, special education, technical education, textiles and clothing, trade and industrial supervision and management.

ACADEMIC PROGRAMS. Cooperative education, double major, dual enrollment of high school students, education specialist degree, independent study, internships, study abroad, teacher preparation, cross-registration. **Remedial services:** Learning center, preadmission summer program, reduced course load, remedial instruction, special counselor, tutoring. **ROTC:** Army. **Placement/credit:** CLEP General and Subject, institutional tests; 23 credit hours maximum for bachelor's degree.

ACADEMIC REQUIREMENTS. Freshmen must earn minimum GPA of 1.6 to continue in good standing. Students must declare major by end of first year. **Graduation requirements:** 128 hours for bachelor's (55 in major). Most students required to take courses in English, humanities, mathematics, biological/physical sciences, social sciences. **Additional information:** African-American heritage and health and physical education courses required for most students.

FRESHMAN ADMISSIONS. Selection criteria: Test scores, class rank, high school GPA, counselor recommendation, extracurricular activities. Recommended units include English 4, mathematics 3, social science 3 and science 2. **Test requirements:** SAT or ACT (SAT preferred); score report by June 30.

1992 FRESHMAN CLASS PROFILE. 518 men applied, 416 accepted, 192 enrolled; 564 women applied, 428 accepted, 185 enrolled. **Characteristics:** 73% from in state, 86% live in college housing, 99% have minority backgrounds, 1% are foreign students, 4% join fraternities/sororities. Average age is 18.

FALL-TERM APPLICATIONS. $20 fee, may be waived for applicants with need. No closing date; priority given to applications received by June 30; applicants notified on a rolling basis beginning on or about January 1; must reply within 30 days. Interview recommended. Essay recommended. EDP-S.

STUDENT LIFE. Housing: Dormitories (men, women, coed). Freshmen only dormitory available. **Activities:** Student government, film, radio, student newspaper, television, yearbook, choral groups, concert band, dance, drama, jazz band, marching band, music ensembles, fraternities, sororities, Students In Praise Society, Muslim Students Organization, DEX/NSBL Business Club, Toastmasters International, Association of Resident Students, International Students Association, Commuting Students Association, education club, chess club, Math and Computer Science Club, National Council of Negro Women. **Additional information:** Ecumenical services held on campus.

ATHLETICS. NCAA. **Intercollegiate:** Basketball, cross-country, football M, soccer M, tennis, track and field, volleyball W, wrestling M. **Intramural:** Archery, badminton, basketball, diving, football M, softball, swimming, tennis, volleyball, water polo.

STUDENT SERVICES. Aptitude testing, career counseling, employment service for undergraduates, freshman orientation, health services, personal counseling, placement service for graduates, veterans counselor, services/facilities for handicapped.

ANNUAL EXPENSES. Tuition and fees (1992-93): $2,938, $3,394 additional for out-of-state students. **Room and board:** $3,540. **Books and supplies:** $400. **Other expenses:** $1,000.

FINANCIAL AID. 78% of freshmen, 84% of continuing students receive some form of aid. Grants, loans, jobs available. Academic, music/drama, athletic, minority scholarships available. **Aid applications:** Closing date May 1; priority given to applications received by April 1; applicants notified on a rolling basis; must reply within 2 weeks.

ADDRESS/TELEPHONE. William Byrd, Director of Admissions, Cheyney University of Pennsylvania, Cheyney and Creek Roads, Cheyney, PA 19319-0019. (215) 399-2275. (800) 223-3608. Fax: (215) 399-2415.

CHI Institute
Southampton, Pennsylvania CB code: 3386

Admissions: 46% of applicants accepted
Based on: ••• Test scores
•• Interview
• School record
Completion: 70% of freshmen end year in good standing

2-year proprietary technical institute, coed. Founded in 1981. **Undergraduate enrollment:** 500 men and women. **Faculty:** 30 total (20 full time). **Location:** Suburban campus in large town; One mile from Philadelphia. **Calendar:** Semester. **Microcomputers:** 36 located in classrooms.

DEGREES OFFERED. AAS. 170 associate degrees awarded in 1992. 100% in engineering technologies.

UNDERGRADUATE MAJORS. Computer technology, engineering and engineering-related technologies.

ACADEMIC REQUIREMENTS. 70% of freshmen return for sophomore year.

FRESHMAN ADMISSIONS. Selection criteria: Institutional aptitude evaluation test most important. Interview also important. **Test requirements:** Institutional aptitude evaluation test required.

1992 FRESHMAN CLASS PROFILE. Characteristics: 100% commute, 4% have minority backgrounds. Average age is 24.

FALL-TERM APPLICATIONS. No fee. No closing date; applicants notified on a rolling basis. Interview required.

ANNUAL EXPENSES. Tuition and fees: $6,700. Tuition and fees include books and supplies.

FINANCIAL AID. 88% of freshmen, 88% of continuing students receive some form of aid. **Aid applications:** Closing date September 20; applicants notified on a rolling basis.

ADDRESS/TELEPHONE. Kevin Quinn, Admissions Director, CHI Institute, 520 Street Road, Southampton, PA 18966. (215) 357-5100.

Churchman Business School
Easton, Pennsylvania CB code: 3954

Admissions: 82% of applicants accepted
Based on: ••• School record
•• Interview, test scores
Completion: 86% of freshmen end year in good standing
84% graduate, 30% of these enter 4-year programs

2-year proprietary business college, coed. Founded in 1911. **Undergraduate enrollment:** 80 men, 94 women full time; 18 men, 60 women part time. **Faculty:** 10 total (8 full time). **Location:** Urban campus in large town; 60 miles from New York City. **Calendar:** Trimester. **Microcomputers:** 25 located in computer centers.

DEGREES OFFERED. 68 associate degrees awarded in 1992. 63% in business and management, 37% business/office and marketing/distribution.

UNDERGRADUATE MAJORS. Accounting, business administration and management, business and management, business and office, legal secretary, medical secretary, secretarial and related programs.

ACADEMIC PROGRAMS. 2-year transfer program, accelerated program, dual enrollment of high school students, independent study. **Remedial services:** Reduced course load, remedial instruction, special counselor, tutoring. **Placement/credit:** Institutional tests; 30 credit hours maximum for associate degree.

ACADEMIC REQUIREMENTS. Freshmen must earn minimum GPA of 2.5 to continue in good standing. 85% of freshmen return for sophomore year. Students must declare major on enrollment. **Graduation requirements:** 84 hours for associate (75 in major). Most students required to take courses in computer science, English, mathematics. **Additional information:** Students can transfer to Fort Lauderdale College and completer bachelor's degree in 9 more months.

FRESHMAN ADMISSIONS. Selection criteria: Applicants should have minimum 2.0 GPA. Personal interview and test scores important. **Test requirements:** Institutional test required.

1992 FRESHMAN CLASS PROFILE. 74 men applied, 60 accepted, 31 enrolled; 103 women applied, 86 accepted, 79 enrolled. 31% had high school GPA of 3.0 or higher, 56% between 2.0 and 2.99. 8% were in top tenth and 21% were in top quarter of graduating class. **Characteristics:** 58% from in state, 100% commute, 8% have minority backgrounds. Average age is 19.

FALL-TERM APPLICATIONS. $25 fee, may be waived for applicants with need. Closing date August 20; applicants notified on a rolling basis; must reply within 5 days. Interview recommended. Deferred and early admission available.

STUDENT LIFE. Activities: Student government, yearbook.

ATHLETICS. Intramural: Baseball, bowling, golf, skiing, softball, table tennis, volleyball.

STUDENT SERVICES. Career counseling, employment service for undergraduates, freshman orientation, personal counseling, placement service for graduates.

ANNUAL EXPENSES. Tuition and fees (1992-93): $4,285. **Books and supplies:** $675.

FINANCIAL AID. 65% of freshmen, 63% of continuing students receive some form of aid. Grants, loans available. 66 enrolled freshmen were judged to have need, all were offered aid. **Aid applications:** Closing date August 1; applicants notified on or about August 20.

ADDRESS/TELEPHONE. Paula Leffel, Admissions Officer, Churchman Business School, 355 Spring Garden Street, Easton, PA 18042. (215) 258-5345.

Clarion University of Pennsylvania
Clarion, Pennsylvania CB code: 2649

Admissions: 82% of applicants accepted
Based on: ••• School record
•• Test scores
• Activities, essay, interview, recommendations, special talents
Completion: 55% graduate

4-year public university, coed. Founded in 1867. **Accreditation:** Regional. **Undergraduate enrollment:** 2,083 men, 2,870 women full time; 169 men, 499 women part time. **Graduate enrollment:** 84 men, 171 women full time; 64 men, 149 women part time. **Faculty:** 374 total (341 full time), 194 with doctorates or other terminal degrees. **Location:** Rural campus in small town; 85 miles from Pittsburgh, 90 miles from Erie. **Calendar:** Semester, limited summer session. **Microcomputers:** 200 located in dormitories, libraries, classrooms, computer centers, campus-wide network. **Special facilities:** Art gallery, planetarium, greenhouse, archaeology dig and display. **Additional facts:** Venango campus at Oil City. West Penn hospital School of Nursing comprises third campus.

DEGREES OFFERED. AA, AS, BA, BS, BFA, MA, MS, MBA, MEd. 72 associate degrees awarded in 1992. 25% in business/office and marketing/distribution, 60% health sciences, 27% allied health, 14% law. 1,037 bachelor's degrees awarded. 26% in business and management, 15% communications, 35% teacher education, 5% allied health, 5% psychology. Graduate degrees offered in 14 major fields of study.

UNDERGRADUATE MAJORS. Associate: Accounting, business and management, business data processing and related programs, business data programming, business systems analysis, data processing, legal assistant/paralegal, legal secretary, liberal/general studies, nursing, office supervision and management, rehabilitation counseling/services, secretarial and related programs. **Bachelor's:** Accounting, actuarial sciences, advertising, anthropology, applied mathematics, biological and physical sciences, biological laboratory technology, biology, business administration and management, business and management, business economics, chemistry, clinical laboratory science, communications, computer and information sciences, computer programming, dramatic arts, early childhood education, earth sciences, economics, education, education of the deaf and hearing impaired, education of the mentally handicapped, education of the multiple handicapped, elementary education, English, English education, finance, fine arts, foreign languages education, French, geography, geology, German, habilitative sciences, history, humanities, humanities and social sciences, information sciences and systems, junior high education, labor/industrial relations, liberal/general studies, library science, marketing and distribution, marketing management, mathematics, mathematics education, molecular biology, music, music business management, music education, music performance, musical theater, nursing, philosophy, physical sciences, physics, political science and government, psychology, real estate, rehabilitation counseling/services, science education, secondary education, social sciences, social studies education, sociology, Spanish, special education, speech, speech pathology/audiology, speech/communication/theater education, studio art, systems analysis.

ACADEMIC PROGRAMS. Accelerated program, double major, honors program, independent study, internships, study abroad, teacher preparation, visiting/exchange student program, New York semester, Washington semester, co-op engineering program with 2 affiliate schools; combined bachelor's/graduate program in business administration. **Remedial services:** Learning center, preadmission summer program, reduced course load, remedial instruction, special counselor, tutoring, writing center. **Placement/credit:** AP, CLEP General and Subject, institutional tests; 38 credit hours maximum for bachelor's degree.

ACADEMIC REQUIREMENTS. Freshmen must earn minimum GPA of 2.0 to continue in good standing. 80% of freshmen return for sophomore year. Students must declare major by end of second year. **Graduation requirements:** 62 hours for associate (48 in major), 128 hours for bachelor's (80 in major). Most students required to take courses in arts/fine arts, computer science, English, history, humanities, mathematics, biological/physical sciences, social sciences.

FRESHMAN ADMISSIONS. Selection criteria: School achievement record and test scores. Record must reflect college preparatory course of study. **High school preparation:** 16 units required. Required and recommended units include English 4, mathematics 3-4, social science 4 and science 3-4. Foreign language 2 recommended. **Test requirements:** SAT or ACT (SAT preferred); score report by May 1.

1992 FRESHMAN CLASS PROFILE. 1,399 men applied, 1,105 accepted, 441 enrolled; 1,922 women applied, 1,615 accepted, 749 enrolled. **Characteristics:** 92% from in state, 4% have minority backgrounds, 2% are foreign students, 10% join fraternities/sororities.

FALL-TERM APPLICATIONS. $15 fee. Closing date May 1; priority given to applications received by December 1; applicants notified on a rolling basis beginning on or about October 1; must reply by May 1 or within 4 weeks if notified thereafter. Audition required for music, theater applicants. Portfolio required for art applicants. Interview recommended. Essay recommended. Interview required of nursing applicants; recommended for all others. CRDA. Deferred and early admission available.

STUDENT LIFE. Housing: Dormitories (men, women, coed); fraternity, sorority, handicapped housing available. **Activities:** Student government, film, magazine, radio, student newspaper, television, yearbook, choral groups, concert band, dance, drama, jazz band, marching band, music ensembles, musical theater, opera, pep band, symphony orchestra, fraternities, sororities, Christian and black student organizations, Young Democrats, Young Republicans, Circle-K, service fraternities and sororities.

ATHLETICS. NAIA, NCAA. **Intercollegiate:** Baseball M, basketball, cross-country, diving, football M, golf M, softball W, swimming, tennis W, track and field, volleyball W, wrestling M. **Intramural:** Badminton, baseball W, basketball, bowling, boxing M, golf, handball, racquetball, soccer, softball, swimming, table tennis, tennis, volleyball, wrestling M.

STUDENT SERVICES. Aptitude testing, career counseling, employment service for undergraduates, freshman orientation, health services, on-campus day care, personal counseling, placement service for graduates, special adviser for adult students, veterans counselor, services/facilities for handicapped.

ANNUAL EXPENSES. Tuition and fees (1992-93): $3,328, $3,394

additional for out-of-state students. **Room and board:** $2,786. **Books and supplies:** $450. **Other expenses:** $600.

FINANCIAL AID. 76% of freshmen, 70% of continuing students receive some form of aid. 69% of grants, 62% of loans, 13% of jobs based on need. Academic, music/drama, art, athletic, leadership, alumni affiliation scholarships available. **Aid applications:** Closing date May 1; priority given to applications received by March 15; applicants notified on a rolling basis beginning on or about April 15; must reply within 2 weeks. **Additional information:** Application closing date for academic scholarships, March 15; for APSGFSA, May 1.

ADDRESS/TELEPHONE. John S. Shropshire, Dean of Enrollment Management and Academic Records, Clarion University of Pennsylvania, Admissions Office - Carlson Library Bldg, Clarion, PA 16214. (814) 226-2306. Fax: (814) 226-2030.

College Misericordia
Dallas, Pennsylvania CB code: 2087

Admissions: 64% of applicants accepted
Based on: ••• Activities, interview, school record
•• Test scores
• Essay, recommendations, special talents
Completion: 90% of freshmen end year in good standing
80% graduate, 12% of these enter graduate study

4-year private liberal arts college, coed, affiliated with Roman Catholic Church. Founded in 1924. **Accreditation:** Regional. **Undergraduate enrollment:** 242 men, 769 women full time; 134 men, 403 women part time. **Graduate enrollment:** 3 men, 17 women full time; 24 men, 98 women part time. **Faculty:** 131 total (74 full time), 30 with doctorates or other terminal degrees. **Location:** Suburban campus in large town; 9 miles from Wilkes-Barre, 20 miles from Scranton. **Calendar:** Semester, limited summer session. **Microcomputers:** 24 located in libraries, computer centers. **Special facilities:** Art gallery, computer science center, health and recreation center.

DEGREES OFFERED. AS, BA, BS, MS. 250 bachelor's degrees awarded. 19% in business and management, 13% education, 43% allied health, 7% multi/interdisciplinary studies, 10% social sciences. Graduate degrees offered in 5 major fields of study.

UNDERGRADUATE MAJORS. Associate: Radiograph medical technology. **Bachelor's:** Accounting, biology, business administration and management, chemistry, computer and information sciences, early childhood education, education, elementary education, English, history, information sciences and systems, liberal/general studies, management information systems, marketing and distribution, marketing management, mathematics, medical laboratory technologies, nursing, occupational therapy, physical therapy, predentistry, prelaw, premedicine, preveterinary, psychology, radiograph medical technology, secondary education, social work, special education.

ACADEMIC PROGRAMS. Accelerated program, cooperative education, double major, dual enrollment of high school students, honors program, independent study, internships, student-designed major, study abroad, teacher preparation, visiting/exchange student program, weekend college, cross-registration, 5-year bachelor's/master's in social work with Marywood College. **Remedial services:** Learning center, preadmission summer program, reduced course load, remedial instruction, special counselor, tutoring, Act 101 program for state residents. **ROTC:** Air Force, Army. **Placement/credit:** AP, CLEP General and Subject, institutional tests; 30 credit hours maximum for bachelor's degree.

ACADEMIC REQUIREMENTS. Freshmen must earn minimum GPA of 2.0 to continue in good standing. 90% of freshmen return for sophomore year. Students must declare major by end of first year. **Graduation requirements:** 120 hours for bachelor's (66 in major). Most students required to take courses in arts/fine arts, English, history, humanities, mathematics, philosophy/religion, biological/physical sciences, social sciences. **Postgraduate studies:** 5% enter law school, 1% enter medical school, 1% enter MBA programs, 5% enter other graduate study.

FRESHMAN ADMISSIONS. Selection criteria: In order of importance: high school achievement, test scores, character, recommendations from school teachers or counselors. Special consideration given to children of alumni and disadvantaged students. Foreign applicants encouraged. **High school preparation:** 16 units required. 2 units science and algebra required for allied health applicants. Strong mathematics background required for computer science, physical therapy, chemistry and biology applicants. **Test requirements:** SAT or ACT (SAT preferred); score report by August 28. **Additional information:** Entrance to all health science programs highly competitive, with greater emphasis on SAT scores.

1992 FRESHMAN CLASS PROFILE. 390 men applied, 240 accepted, 112 enrolled; 905 women applied, 587 accepted, 287 enrolled. 65% had high school GPA of 3.0 or higher, 35% between 2.0 and 2.99. **Academic background:** Mid 50% of enrolled freshmen had SAT-V between 410-550, SAT-M between 420-590. 90% submitted SAT scores. **Characteristics:** 76% from in state, 74% live in college housing, 6% have minority backgrounds, 1% are foreign students. Average age is 18.

FALL-TERM APPLICATIONS. $15 fee, may be waived for applicants with need. No closing date; applicants notified on a rolling basis; must reply within 4 weeks. Interview required for occupational therapy applicants. Deferred and early admission available. Institutional early decision plan.

STUDENT LIFE. Housing: Dormitories (men, women, coed). **Activities:** Student government, magazine, student newspaper, yearbook, choral groups, concert band, dance, drama, jazz band, music ensembles, symphony orchestra, resident professional chamber orchestra, fraternities, sororities, Young Democrats, Young Republicans, Student Nurses Association, Student Council for Exceptional Children, Circle-K, Campus Ministry, Ambassadors Club.

ATHLETICS. NCAA. **Intercollegiate:** Baseball M, basketball, field hockey W, golf M, soccer, softball W, volleyball W. **Intramural:** Baseball M, basketball, cross-country, football, golf, lacrosse M, racquetball, skiing, soccer, softball, tennis, track and field, volleyball.

STUDENT SERVICES. Aptitude testing, career counseling, employment service for undergraduates, freshman orientation, health services, on-campus day care, personal counseling, placement service for graduates, special adviser for adult students, Learning disabled program, services/facilities for handicapped.

ANNUAL EXPENSES. Tuition and fees (1992-93): $9,500. **Room and board:** $4,868. **Books and supplies:** $500. **Other expenses:** $400.

FINANCIAL AID. 95% of freshmen, 95% of continuing students receive some form of aid. 78% of grants, 97% of loans, 49% of jobs based on need. 231 enrolled freshmen were judged to have need, all were offered aid. Academic scholarships available. **Aid applications:** Closing date April 1; priority given to applications received by March 1; applicants notified on or about April 1; must reply within 2 weeks.

ADDRESS/TELEPHONE. Michael Joseph, Dean of Enrollment Management, College Misericordia, 301 Lake Street, Dallas, PA 18612-9984. (717) 674-4449. (800) 852-7675. Fax: (717) 675-2441.

Community College of Allegheny County: Allegheny Campus
Pittsburgh, Pennsylvania CB code: 2156

2-year public community college, coed. Founded in 1966. **Accreditation:** Regional. **Undergraduate enrollment:** 7,583 men and women. **Faculty:** 1,305 total (144 full time), 66 with doctorates or other terminal degrees. **Location:** Urban campus in large city; 150 miles from Clevelend, Ohio, 200 miles from Harrisburg. **Calendar:** Semester, extensive summer session. **Microcomputers:** 404 located in classrooms, computer centers. **Additional facts:** 3 additional campuses in suburbs and over 200 off-campus sites for credit and noncredit offerings.

DEGREES OFFERED. 1,080 associate degrees awarded in 1992. 15% in business and management, 10% business/office and marketing/distribution, 10% computer sciences, 10% teacher education, 5% engineering, 10% engineering technologies, 20% health sciences, 20% allied health.

UNDERGRADUATE MAJORS. Accounting, aeronautical technology, air conditioning/heating/refrigeration mechanics, air conditioning/heating/refrigeration technology, allied health, apparel and accessories marketing, automotive mechanics, automotive technology, aviation computer technology, aviation management, behavioral sciences, biology, business administration and management, business and management, business and office, business data entry equipment operation, business data processing and related programs, business data programming, business economics, carpentry, chemical manufacturing technology, chemistry, child development/care/guidance, commercial art, communications, court reporting, criminal justice studies, data processing, dietetic aide/assistant, drafting, drafting and design technology, education, electromechanical technology, elementary education, engineering and engineering-related technologies, finance, fine arts, fire control and safety technology, food management, food production/management/services, food science and nutrition, French, German, graphic and printing production, graphic arts technology, histological technician, hospitality and recreation marketing, hotel/motel and restaurant management, humanities and social sciences, industrial technology, information sciences and systems, insurance and risk management, Italian, journalism, labor/industrial relations, law enforcement and corrections technologies, legal assistant/paralegal, legal secretary, liberal/general studies, marketing and distribution, marketing management, mathematics, mechanical design technology, medical assistant, medical laboratory technologies, medical records technology, medical secretary, mental health/human services, music, nuclear medical technology, nuclear technologies, nurse anesthetist, nursing, occupational therapy assistant, physics, practical nursing, precision metal work, psychology, public administration, radiograph medical technology, real estate, recreation and community services technologies, respiratory therapy, respiratory therapy technology, retailing, Russian, science technologies, secondary education, secretarial and related programs, social sciences, Spanish, surgical technology, ultrasound technology, word processing.

ACADEMIC PROGRAMS. 2-year transfer program, cooperative education, dual enrollment of high school students, honors program, independent study, internships, cross-registration. **Remedial services:** Learning center, preadmission summer program, reduced course load, remedial instruction, special counselor, tutoring. **ROTC:** Air Force, Army. **Placement/credit:** AP, CLEP General and Subject, institutional tests; 30 credit hours maximum for associate degree.

ACADEMIC REQUIREMENTS. Freshmen must earn minimum GPA of 2.0 to continue in good standing. 58% of freshmen return for sophomore year. Students must declare major on application. **Graduation requirements:** 62 hours for associate (24 in major). Most students required to take courses in computer science, English, history, mathematics, biological/physical sciences, social sciences.

FRESHMAN ADMISSIONS. Selection criteria: Open admissions. Allied health fields have some science and mathematics requirements.

1992 FRESHMAN CLASS PROFILE. 3,364 men and women enrolled. **Characteristics:** 99% from in state, 100% commute, 27% have minority backgrounds, 1% are foreign students. Average age is 26.

FALL-TERM APPLICATIONS. No fee. No closing date; priority given to applications received by August 21; applicants notified on a rolling basis beginning on or about January 25; must reply within 2 weeks. Interview recommended for allied health, nursing applicants. Audition recommended for music applicants. Deferred admission available.

STUDENT LIFE. Activities: Student government, film, magazine, student newspaper, television, yearbook, choral groups, concert band, dance, drama, music ensembles, musical theater.

ATHLETICS. NJCAA. **Intercollegiate:** Baseball M, basketball, cross-country W, golf M, soccer M, softball W, tennis. **Intramural:** Archery, baseball, cross-country, field hockey, golf, handball, racquetball, softball, swimming, tennis, volleyball.

STUDENT SERVICES. Career counseling, employment service for undergraduates, health services, on-campus day care, personal counseling, placement service for graduates, veterans counselor, women's center, services/facilities for handicapped.

ANNUAL EXPENSES. Tuition and fees: $1,528, $1,416 additional for out-of-district students, $2,832 additional for out-of-state students. **Books and supplies:** $500. **Other expenses:** $950.

FINANCIAL AID. 45% of freshmen, 38% of continuing students receive some form of aid. 99% of grants, 34% of loans, all jobs based on need. Academic, athletic, leadership scholarships available. **Aid applications:** No closing date; priority given to applications received by May 1; applicants notified on a rolling basis beginning on or about July 1; must reply within 10 days.

ADDRESS/TELEPHONE. Charlene M. Dukes, Director of Admissions, Community College of Allegheny County: Allegheny Campus, 808 Ridge Avenue, Pittsburgh, PA 15212. (412) 237-2511.

Community College of Allegheny County: Boyce Campus

Monroeville, Pennsylvania — CB code: 2122

2-year public community college, coed. Founded in 1966. **Accreditation:** Regional. **Undergraduate enrollment:** 4,639 men and women. **Faculty:** 811 total (80 full time), 39 with doctorates or other terminal degrees. **Location:** Suburban campus in large town; 18 miles from Pittsburgh. **Calendar:** Semester, extensive summer session. **Microcomputers:** 321 located in classrooms, computer centers.

DEGREES OFFERED. AA, AS, AAS. 880 associate degrees awarded in 1992. 15% in business and management, 10% business/office and marketing/distribution, 10% computer sciences, 10% teacher education, 5% engineering, 10% engineering technologies, 20% health sciences, 20% allied health.

UNDERGRADUATE MAJORS. Accounting, air conditioning/heating/refrigeration mechanics, air conditioning/heating/refrigeration technology, anthropology, behavioral sciences, biology, business administration and management, business and management, business and office, business computer/console/peripheral equipment operation, business data processing and related programs, business data programming, business systems analysis, chemistry, civil engineering, civil technology, commercial art, computer and information sciences, computer engineering, computer programming, computer servicing technology, computer technology, criminal justice studies, criminal justice technology, data processing, drafting, drafting and design technology, education, electrical and electronics equipment repair, electrical technology, electrical/electronics/communications engineering, electronic technology, elementary education, engineering, engineering and engineering-related technologies, engineering science, fashion merchandising, finance, fine arts, fire control and safety technology, graphic arts technology, hotel/motel and restaurant management, humanities, industrial engineering, industrial technology, information sciences and systems, journalism, legal secretary, marketing management, mathematics, mechanical design technology, medical secretary, microcomputer software, nursing, occupational therapy assistant, office supervision and management, personnel management, physical therapy assistant, physics, preengineering, premedicine, psychology, radiograph medical technology, real estate, robotics, secondary education, secretarial and related programs, small business management and ownership, social sciences, sociology, surgical technology, trade and industrial supervision and management, ultrasound technology, welding technology, word processing.

ACADEMIC PROGRAMS. 2-year transfer program, cooperative education, dual enrollment of high school students, honors program, independent study, teacher preparation, weekend college, cross-registration. **Remedial services:** Learning center, preadmission summer program, reduced course load, remedial instruction, special counselor, tutoring. **Placement/credit:** AP, CLEP General and Subject, institutional tests; 12 credit hours maximum for associate degree.

ACADEMIC REQUIREMENTS. Freshmen must earn minimum GPA of 2.0 to continue in good standing. 60% of freshmen return for sophomore year. Students must declare major on enrollment. **Graduation requirements:** 60 hours for associate (40 in major). Most students required to take courses in computer science, English, history, humanities, mathematics, biological/physical sciences, social sciences.

FRESHMAN ADMISSIONS. Selection criteria: Open admissions. **Test requirements:** TSWE, Iowa Silent Reading test, and local math required for placement.

1992 FRESHMAN CLASS PROFILE. 1,697 men and women enrolled. **Characteristics:** 100% commute.

FALL-TERM APPLICATIONS. No fee. No closing date; applicants notified on a rolling basis; must reply within 15 days. Interview recommended.

STUDENT LIFE. Activities: Student government, film, magazine, student newspaper, television, choral groups, concert band, dance, drama, jazz band, music ensembles, symphony orchestra.

ATHLETICS. NJCAA. **Intercollegiate:** Basketball, golf, softball W.

STUDENT SERVICES. Aptitude testing, career counseling, employment service for undergraduates, freshman orientation, health services, on-campus day care, personal counseling, placement service for graduates, special adviser for adult students, veterans counselor, services/facilities for handicapped.

ANNUAL EXPENSES. Tuition and fees (1992-93): $1,806, $1,680 additional for out-of-district students, $3,360 additional for out-of-state students. **Books and supplies:** $475. **Other expenses:** $1,000.

FINANCIAL AID. 24% of freshmen, 24% of continuing students receive some form of aid. Grants, loans, jobs available. 1,232 enrolled freshmen were judged to have need, all were offered aid. Academic, music/drama, art, athletic scholarships available. **Aid applications:** No closing date; priority given to applications received by May 1; applicants notified on a rolling basis; must reply by registration.

ADDRESS/TELEPHONE. Mary Ellen Gray, Director of Admissions, Community College of Allegheny County: Boyce Campus, 595 Beatty Road, Monroeville, PA 15146. (412) 371-8651. Fax: (412) 733-4397.

Community College of Allegheny County: North Campus

Pittsburgh, Pennsylvania — CB code: 2025

2-year public community college, coed. Founded in 1972. **Accreditation:** Regional. **Undergraduate enrollment:** 4,587 men and women. **Faculty:** 1,575 total (45 full time), 21 with doctorates or other terminal degrees. **Location:** Suburban campus in large city; 9 miles from Pittsburgh. **Calendar:** Semester, extensive summer session. **Microcomputers:** 210 located in classrooms, computer centers.

DEGREES OFFERED. AA, AS, AAS. 470 associate degrees awarded in 1992. 15% in business and management, 10% business/office and marketing/distribution, 10% computer sciences, 10% teacher education, 5% engineering, 10% engineering technologies, 20% health sciences, 20% allied health.

UNDERGRADUATE MAJORS. Accounting, air conditioning/heating/refrigeration mechanics, air conditioning/heating/refrigeration technology, anthropology, behavioral sciences, biology, business administration and management, business and management, business and office, business computer/console/peripheral equipment operation, business data processing and related programs, business data programming, business systems analysis, chemistry, civil engineering, civil technology, commercial art, computer and information sciences, computer engineering, computer programming, computer servicing technology, computer technology, data processing, drafting, drafting and design technology, education, electrical and electronics equipment repair, electrical technology, electrical/electronics/communications engineering, electronic technology, elementary education, engineering, engineering and engineering-related technologies, engineering science, fashion merchandising, finance, hotel/motel and restaurant management, humanities, industrial engineering, industrial technology, information sciences and systems, journalism, legal secretary, marketing management, mathematics, mechanical design technology, medical secretary, microcomputer software, nursing, occupational therapy assistant, office supervision and management, personnel management, physical therapy assistant, physics, preengineering, premedicine, psychology, radiograph medical technology, real estate, robotics, secondary education, secretarial and related programs, small business management and ownership, social sciences, sociology, surgical technology, trade and industrial supervision and management, ultrasound technology, welding technology, word processing.

ACADEMIC PROGRAMS. 2-year transfer program, cooperative education, dual enrollment of high school students, honors program, independent study, teacher preparation, weekend college, cross-registration. **Remedial services:** Learning center, preadmission summer program, reduced course load, remedial instruction, special counselor, tutoring. **Placement/credit:** AP, CLEP General and Subject, institutional tests; 12 credit hours maximum for associate degree.

ACADEMIC REQUIREMENTS. Freshmen must earn minimum GPA of 2.0 to continue in good standing. 60% of freshmen return for sophomore year. **Graduation requirements:** 60 hours for associate (40 in major). Most students required to take courses in computer science, English, history, humanities, mathematics, biological/physical sciences, social sciences.

FRESHMAN ADMISSIONS. Selection criteria: Open admissions.

1992 FRESHMAN CLASS PROFILE. 1,230 men and women enrolled. **Characteristics:** 100% commute.

FALL-TERM APPLICATIONS. No fee. No closing date; applicants notified on a rolling basis; must reply within 15 days. Interview recommended.

STUDENT LIFE. Activities: Student government, student newspaper.

STUDENT SERVICES. Aptitude testing, career counseling, employment service for undergraduates, freshman orientation, health services, on-campus day care, personal counseling, placement service for graduates, special adviser for adult students, veterans counselor, services/facilities for handicapped.

ANNUAL EXPENSES. Tuition and fees: $1,528, $1,416 additional for out-of-district students, $2,832 additional for out-of-state students. **Books and supplies:** $500. **Other expenses:** $950.

FINANCIAL AID. 24% of freshmen, 24% of continuing students receive some form of aid. 98% of grants, 33% of loans, 38% of jobs based on need. Academic, athletic scholarships available. **Aid applications:** No closing date; priority given to applications received by May 1; applicants notified on a rolling basis beginning on or about June 1; must reply within 2 weeks.

ADDRESS/TELEPHONE. Ray Oyler, Director of Admissions, Community College of Allegheny County: North Campus, 8701 Perry Highway, Pittsburgh, PA 15237. (412) 931-8500. Fax: (412) 369-3626.

Community College of Allegheny County: South Campus
West Mifflin, Pennsylvania — CB code: 2123

2-year public community college, coed. Founded in 1967. **Accreditation:** Regional. **Undergraduate enrollment:** 5,686 men and women. **Faculty:** 822 total (88 full time), 44 with doctorates or other terminal degrees. **Location:** Suburban campus in large town; 15 miles from Pittsburgh. **Calendar:** Semester, extensive summer session. **Microcomputers:** 252 located in classrooms, computer centers.

DEGREES OFFERED. AA, AS, AAS. 990 associate degrees awarded in 1992. 15% in business and management, 10% business/office and marketing/distribution, 10% computer sciences, 10% teacher education, 5% engineering, 10% engineering technologies, 20% health sciences, 20% allied health.

UNDERGRADUATE MAJORS. Accounting, air conditioning/heating/refrigeration mechanics, air conditioning/heating/refrigeration technology, anthropology, architectural engineering, architectural technologies, aviation management, behavioral sciences, biology, business and management, business and office, business computer/console/peripheral equipment operation, business data processing and related programs, business data programming, business systems analysis, chemistry, civil engineering, civil technology, commercial art, computer and information sciences, computer engineering, computer programming, computer servicing technology, computer technology, data processing, drafting, drafting and design technology, education, electrical and electronics equipment repair, electrical technology, electrical/electronics/communications engineering, electronic technology, elementary education, engineering, engineering and engineering-related technologies, engineering physics, engineering science, fashion merchandising, finance, fine arts, graphic arts technology, humanities, industrial engineering, industrial technology, information sciences and systems, journalism, legal secretary, marketing management, mathematics, mechanical design technology, medical laboratory technologies, medical secretary, microcomputer software, nursing, occupational therapy assistant, office supervision and management, ophthalmic services, personnel management, physical therapy assistant, physics, preengineering, premedicine, psychology, radiograph medical technology, real estate, robotics, secondary education, secretarial and related programs, small business management and ownership, social sciences, surgical technology, trade and industrial supervision and management, ultrasound technology, welding technology, word processing.

ACADEMIC PROGRAMS. 2-year transfer program, cooperative education, dual enrollment of high school students, honors program, independent study, teacher preparation, weekend college, cross-registration. **Remedial services:** Learning center, preadmission summer program, reduced course load, remedial instruction, special counselor, tutoring. **Placement/credit:** AP, CLEP General and Subject, institutional tests; 12 credit hours maximum for associate degree.

ACADEMIC REQUIREMENTS. 60% of freshmen return for sophomore year. **Graduation requirements:** 60 hours for associate (40 in major). Most students required to take courses in computer science, English, history, humanities, mathematics, biological/physical sciences, social sciences.

FRESHMAN ADMISSIONS. Selection criteria: Open admissions.

1992 FRESHMAN CLASS PROFILE. 2,149 men and women enrolled. **Characteristics:** 100% commute.

FALL-TERM APPLICATIONS. No fee. No closing date; applicants notified on a rolling basis; must reply within 15 days. Interview recommended.

STUDENT LIFE. Activities: Student government, film, magazine, student newspaper, television, choral groups, concert band, dance, drama, jazz band, music ensembles.

ATHLETICS. NJCAA. **Intercollegiate:** Basketball, golf, softball W.

STUDENT SERVICES. Aptitude testing, career counseling, employment service for undergraduates, freshman orientation, health services, on-campus day care, personal counseling, placement service for graduates, special adviser for adult students, veterans counselor, services/facilities for handicapped.

ANNUAL EXPENSES. Tuition and fees: $1,528, $1,416 additional for out-of-district students, $2,832 additional for out-of-state students. **Books and supplies:** $500. **Other expenses:** $950.

FINANCIAL AID. 24% of freshmen, 24% of continuing students receive some form of aid. 96% of grants, 46% of loans, all jobs based on need. 1,200 enrolled freshmen were judged to have need, all were offered aid. Academic, music/drama, art, athletic scholarships available. **Aid applications:** Closing date May 1; applicants notified on a rolling basis; must reply by registration.

ADDRESS/TELEPHONE. William Plumb, Director of Admissions, Community College of Allegheny County: South Campus, 1750 Clairton Road, West Mifflin, PA 15122. (412) 469-1100. Fax: (412) 469-1506.

Community College of Beaver County
Monaca, Pennsylvania — CB code: 2126

2-year public community college, coed. Founded in 1966. **Accreditation:** Regional. **Undergraduate enrollment:** 785 men, 644 women full time; 501 men, 897 women part time. **Faculty:** 149 total (57 full time), 11 with doctorates or other terminal degrees. **Location:** Suburban campus in small town; 30 miles from Pittsburgh. **Calendar:** Semester, limited summer session. Saturday and extensive evening/early morning classes. **Microcomputers:** 220 located in libraries, classrooms, computer centers. **Special facilities:** Student-monitored control tower for air traffic control program. **Additional facts:** Aviation sciences facility approximately 15 miles from campus at Beaver County Airport.

DEGREES OFFERED. AA, AS. 392 associate degrees awarded in 1992. 25% in business and management, 10% business/office and marketing/distribution, 8% communications, 8% computer sciences, 10% education, 21% allied health, 16% trade and industry.

UNDERGRADUATE MAJORS. Accounting, air traffic control, airline piloting and navigation, architectural technologies, architecture, automotive mechanics, automotive technology, aviation computer technology, aviation management, biological and physical sciences, biology, business administration and management, business and management, business and office, business data entry equipment operation, business data processing and related programs, business data programming, computer and information sciences, diesel engine mechanics, drafting, drafting and design technology, education, electrical and electronics equipment repair, electronic technology, engineering and engineering-related technologies, finance, human resources development, humanities and social sciences, information sciences and systems, law enforcement and corrections technologies, liberal/general studies, medical laboratory technologies, medical secretary, nuclear technologies, nursing, office supervision and management, photographic technology, practical nursing, public affairs, public relations, radio/television technology, robotics, secretarial and related programs, social sciences, telecommunications, welding technology, word processing.

ACADEMIC PROGRAMS. 2-year transfer program, double major, dual enrollment of high school students, internships, weekend college, cross-registration. **Remedial services:** Learning center, preadmission summer program, reduced course load, remedial instruction, special counselor, tutoring. **Placement/credit:** CLEP General and Subject, institutional tests; 45 credit hours maximum for associate degree.

ACADEMIC REQUIREMENTS. Freshmen must earn minimum GPA of 1.5 to continue in good standing. 71% of freshmen return for sophomore year. Students must declare major on application. **Graduation requirements:** 60 hours for associate (37 in major). Most students required to take courses in English, social sciences.

FRESHMAN ADMISSIONS. Selection criteria: Open admissions. Applicants to nursing program must rank in top 50% of high school class, medical laboratory technician applicants in top 25%. Medical laboratory technician applicants must have ACT composite score of at least 19. **Test**

requirements: Nursing applicants must have National League of Nursing test.

1992 FRESHMAN CLASS PROFILE. 379 men, 366 women enrolled. 20% had high school GPA of 3.0 or higher, 30% between 2.0 and 2.99. **Academic background:** Mid 50% of enrolled freshmen had ACT composite between 14-18. 25% submitted ACT scores. **Characteristics:** 99% from in state, 100% commute, 5% have minority backgrounds. Average age is 22.

FALL-TERM APPLICATIONS. $20 fee, may be waived for applicants with need. No closing date; priority given to applications received by June 1; applicants notified on a rolling basis; must reply by registration. Interview recommended. Interview required for nursing, medical laboratory technician applicants; recommended for all others. Deferred and early admission available. Application deadline January 20 for nursing, April 1 for medical laboratory technician; must reply within 3 weeks of notification.

STUDENT LIFE. Activities: Student government, student newspaper, fraternities, sororities.

ATHLETICS. NJCAA. **Intercollegiate:** Baseball M, basketball, golf, softball W, tennis, volleyball W. **Intramural:** Basketball, bowling, golf, softball, table tennis, tennis, volleyball.

STUDENT SERVICES. Career counseling, employment service for undergraduates, freshman orientation, on-campus day care, personal counseling, placement service for graduates, services/facilities for handicapped.

ANNUAL EXPENSES. Tuition and fees: $1,760, $2,010 additional for out-of-district students, $4,020 additional for out-of-state students. **Books and supplies:** $500. **Other expenses:** $900.

FINANCIAL AID. 61% of freshmen, 63% of continuing students receive some form of aid. 99% of grants, 87% of loans, all jobs based on need. 625 enrolled freshmen were judged to have need, 550 were offered aid. Academic scholarships available. **Aid applications:** No closing date; priority given to applications received by May 1; applicants notified on a rolling basis beginning on or about August 1.

ADDRESS/TELEPHONE. Scott Ensworth, Director of Admissions, Community College of Beaver County, One Campus Drive, Monaca, PA 15061. (412) 775-8561 ext. 101. Fax: (412) 775-4055.

Community College of Philadelphia
Philadelphia, Pennsylvania CB code: 2682

2-year public community college, coed. Founded in 1965. **Accreditation:** Regional. **Undergraduate enrollment:** 2,138 men, 3,609 women full time; 4,449 men, 9,280 women part time. **Faculty:** 1,170 total (350 full time), 85 with doctorates or other terminal degrees. **Location:** Urban campus in very large city. **Calendar:** Semester, extensive summer session. Saturday and extensive evening/early morning classes. **Microcomputers:** 350 located in libraries, classrooms. **Additional facts:** Regional centers located in northeast, northwest, and west Philadelphia. Many additional temporary facilities located throughout the city.

DEGREES OFFERED. AA, AS, AAS. 949 associate degrees awarded in 1992. 7% in business and management, 15% business/office and marketing/distribution, 15% health sciences, 11% allied health, 36% multi/interdisciplinary studies.

UNDERGRADUATE MAJORS. Accounting, architectural technologies, automotive mechanics, biomedical equipment technology, business and management, business and office, business data entry equipment operation, business data processing and related programs, business data programming, business education, chemical manufacturing technology, child development/care/guidance, computer and information sciences, computer technology, construction, criminal justice studies, dental hygiene, dietetic aide/assistant, early childhood education, education, electronic technology, engineering, engineering and engineering-related technologies, fashion merchandising, finance, fire control and safety technology, hotel/motel and restaurant management, instrumentation technology, international business management, interpreter for the deaf, law enforcement and corrections technologies, legal assistant/paralegal, liberal/general studies, library assistant, marketing and distribution, medical assistant, medical laboratory technologies, medical records administration, medical records technology, mental health/human services, music, nursing, photographic technology, photography, radiograph medical technology, real estate, respiratory therapy technology, retailing, science technologies, secretarial and related programs, studio art, word processing.

ACADEMIC PROGRAMS. 2-year transfer program, dual enrollment of high school students, honors program, internships, telecourses, weekend college. **Remedial services:** Learning center, preadmission summer program, reduced course load, remedial instruction, special counselor, tutoring, English as a Second Language, bilingual services. **Placement/credit:** AP, institutional tests; 30 credit hours maximum for associate degree.

ACADEMIC REQUIREMENTS. Freshmen must earn minimum GPA of 2.0 to continue in good standing. 50% of freshmen return for sophomore year. Students must declare major on enrollment. **Graduation requirements:** 60 hours for associate (30 in major). Most students required to take courses in English, mathematics, biological/physical sciences, social sciences.

FRESHMAN ADMISSIONS. Selection criteria: Open admissions. Selective admission to allied health and some other technical programs. One chemistry, 2 mathematics, required of allied health applicants.

1992 FRESHMAN CLASS PROFILE. 1,939 men, 3,336 women enrolled. **Characteristics:** 99% from in state, 100% commute, 53% have minority backgrounds. Average age is 24.

FALL-TERM APPLICATIONS. $20 fee. No closing date; applicants notified on a rolling basis. Interview required for early childhood education applicants. Audition required for music applicants. Portfolio required for art applicants. Early admission available.

STUDENT LIFE. Activities: Student government, radio, student newspaper, television, yearbook, literary journal, choral groups, dance, drama, jazz band, music ensembles, Christian Coalition, Newman Club, Hillel, Black Student Congress, Latin American Student Organization, Phi Theta Kappa, Muslim Student Association, Vietnamese Student Organization, Asian-American Association.

ATHLETICS. Intercollegiate: Baseball M, basketball, cross-country, soccer M, softball W, volleyball W. **Intramural:** Basketball, soccer, softball, tennis, track and field, volleyball.

STUDENT SERVICES. Aptitude testing, career counseling, employment service for undergraduates, health services, personal counseling, placement service for graduates, services/facilities for handicapped.

ANNUAL EXPENSES. Tuition and fees (1992-93): $1,810, $1,770 additional for out-of-district students, $3,540 additional for out-of-state students. **Books and supplies:** $455. **Other expenses:** $575.

FINANCIAL AID. 40% of freshmen, 40% of continuing students receive some form of aid. All grants, all loans, 77% of jobs based on need. Academic scholarships available. **Aid applications:** Closing date May 1; applicants notified on or about July 15.

ADDRESS/TELEPHONE. Kathleen Hetherington, Division Dean for Student Systems, Community College of Philadelphia, 1700 Spring Garden Street, Philadelphia, PA 19130-3991. (215) 751-8010.

Curtis Institute of Music
Philadelphia, Pennsylvania CB code: 2100

4-year private music conservatory, coed. Founded in 1924. **Accreditation:** Regional candidate. **Undergraduate enrollment:** 61 men, 84 women full time. **Graduate enrollment:** 12 men, 13 women full time. **Faculty:** 72 total (2 full time), 9 with doctorates or other terminal degrees. **Location:** Urban campus in very large city. **Calendar:** Semester. **Microcomputers:** 5 located in computer centers. **Special facilities:** 61,486 titles in audio-visual materials and sheet music for performance purposes. **Additional facts:** Accredited by National Association of Schools of Music.

DEGREES OFFERED. B, M. 25 bachelor's degrees awarded in 1992. 100% in visual and performing arts.

UNDERGRADUATE MAJORS. Music performance, music theory and composition.

ACADEMIC PROGRAMS. Dual enrollment of high school students. **Remedial services:** Tutoring. **Placement/credit:** AP, institutional tests.

ACADEMIC REQUIREMENTS. No policy requiring minimum GPA; records of students having academic difficulty are reviewed individually. Students must maintain a GPA of 2.0 in academic (non-music) courses. 95% of freshmen return for sophomore year. Students must declare major on application. **Graduation requirements:** 128 hours for bachelor's (98 in major). Most students required to take courses in English, history.

FRESHMAN ADMISSIONS. Selection criteria: Admission based on talent shown in audition rather than advancement already obtained, and limited to those whose inherent musical gift shows promise. Test scores considered for applicants to bachelor's degree program. Major emphasis on applied music activities. **Test requirements:** SAT; score report by January 15. English Composition ACH required. Score report by January 15.

1992 FRESHMAN CLASS PROFILE. 10 men, 10 women enrolled. **Characteristics:** 10% from in state, 100% commute, 30% have minority backgrounds, 31% are foreign students. Average age is 18.

FALL-TERM APPLICATIONS. $60 fee, may be waived for applicants with need. Additional $85 audition fee. Closing date January 15; applicants notified on a rolling basis beginning on or about March 15; must reply immediately. Audition required.

STUDENT LIFE. Activities: Student government, music ensembles, opera, symphony orchestra.

STUDENT SERVICES. Career counseling, freshman orientation, personal counseling, services/facilities for handicapped.

ANNUAL EXPENSES. Tuition and fees (1992-93): $500. Students pay required fees only; there is no tuition. **Books and supplies:** $250. **Other expenses:** $1,795.

FINANCIAL AID. 100% of freshmen, 100% of continuing students receive some form of aid. All grants, 62% of loans, all jobs based on need. 3 enrolled freshmen were judged to have need, all were offered aid. Music/drama scholarships available. **Aid applications:** Closing date June 1; priority given to applications received by May 1; applicants notified on or about July 31; must reply within 3 weeks. **Additional information:** All students accepted on full-tuition scholarship basis.

ADDRESS/TELEPHONE. Judi Gattone, Admissions and Financial Aid Officer, Curtis Institute of Music, 1726 Locust Street, Philadelphia, PA 19103. (215) 893-5252. Fax: (215) 893-9065.

Dean Institute of Technology
Pittsburgh, Pennsylvania CB code: 2199

2-year proprietary technical college, coed. Founded in 1948. **Undergraduate enrollment:** 112 men, 2 women full time; 44 men, 1 woman part time. **Faculty:** 16 total (9 full time). **Location:** Urban campus in large city; 3 miles from downtown. **Calendar:** Quarter, extensive summer session. **Microcomputers:** 6 located in classrooms.

DEGREES OFFERED. AAS. 40 associate degrees awarded in 1992. 100% in engineering technologies.

UNDERGRADUATE MAJORS. Drafting and design technology, electrical technology.

ACADEMIC PROGRAMS. Placement/credit: Institutional tests; 12 credit hours maximum for associate degree.

ACADEMIC REQUIREMENTS. Freshmen must earn minimum GPA of 2.5 to continue in good standing. 90% of freshmen return for sophomore year. Students must declare major on application. **Graduation requirements:** 60 hours for associate. Most students required to take courses in mathematics.

FRESHMAN ADMISSIONS. Selection criteria: Open admissions.

1992 FRESHMAN CLASS PROFILE. 79 men enrolled. 5% had high school GPA of 3.0 or higher, 10% between 2.0 and 2.99. **Characteristics:** 95% from in state, 100% commute, 12% have minority backgrounds, 10% are foreign students. Average age is 23.

FALL-TERM APPLICATIONS. $50 fee. No closing date; applicants notified on a rolling basis. Interview required. Deferred admission available.

STUDENT SERVICES. Career counseling, personal counseling, placement service for graduates, veterans counselor, services/facilities for handicapped.

ANNUAL EXPENSES. Tuition and fees (1992-93): $4,900. **Books and supplies:** $500.

FINANCIAL AID. 85% of freshmen, 85% of continuing students receive some form of aid. All grants, all loans based on need. 30 enrolled freshmen were judged to have need, all were offered aid. **Aid applications:** Closing date August 1; applicants notified on a rolling basis.

ADDRESS/TELEPHONE. William Nichie, Admissions Director, Dean Institute of Technology, 1501 West Liberty Avenue, Pittsburgh, PA 15226. (412) 531-4433. Fax: (412) 531-4435.

Delaware County Community College
Media, Pennsylvania CB code: 2125

2-year public community college, coed. Founded in 1967. **Accreditation:** Regional. **Undergraduate enrollment:** 1,884 men, 1,786 women full time; 2,526 men, 4,073 women part time. **Faculty:** 486 total (132 full time), 18 with doctorates or other terminal degrees. **Location:** Suburban campus in large town; 20 miles from Philadelphia. **Calendar:** Semester, limited summer session. Saturday and extensive evening/early morning classes. **Microcomputers:** 250 located in classrooms, computer centers. **Special facilities:** CAD laboratory, solar laboratory, art gallery. **Additional facts:** Off-campus sites in 5 centers.

DEGREES OFFERED. AA, AS, AAS. 824 associate degrees awarded in 1992. 25% in business and management, 5% computer sciences, 8% teacher education, 5% engineering technologies, 14% health sciences, 29% multi/interdisciplinary studies, 5% parks/recreation, protective services, public affairs.

UNDERGRADUATE MAJORS. Accounting, air conditioning/heating/refrigeration technology, allied health, architectural technologies, biological and physical sciences, biomedical equipment technology, business administration and management, business and management, computer and information sciences, computer programming, computer servicing technology, construction, criminal justice technology, data processing, drafting and design technology, early childhood education, electronic technology, energy conservation and use technology, engineering, finance, fire control and safety technology, graphic design, hotel/motel and restaurant management, liberal/general studies, manufacturing technology, marketing management, mechanical design technology, medical assistant, microcomputer software, nursing, office supervision and management, plastic technology, respiratory therapy technology, retailing, small business management and ownership, surgical technology, telecommunications.

ACADEMIC PROGRAMS. 2-year transfer program, accelerated program, cooperative education, double major, independent study, internships, student-designed major, study abroad. **Remedial services:** Learning center, preadmission summer program, reduced course load, remedial instruction, tutoring. **Placement/credit:** AP, CLEP General and Subject, institutional tests; 45 credit hours maximum for associate degree.

ACADEMIC REQUIREMENTS. Freshmen must earn minimum GPA of 1.75 to continue in good standing. 58% of freshmen return for sophomore year. Students must declare major on application. **Graduation requirements:** 60 hours for associate. Most students required to take courses in English, humanities, mathematics, biological/physical sciences, social sciences.

FRESHMAN ADMISSIONS. Selection criteria: Open admissions. Selective admission to nursing, respiratory therapy, and surgical technology programs. **Test requirements:** If submitted, ACT, SAT or ACH scores used for advising.

1992 FRESHMAN CLASS PROFILE. 1,230 men, 1,397 women enrolled. **Characteristics:** 97% from in state, 100% commute, 10% have minority backgrounds, 1% are foreign students. Average age is 25.

FALL-TERM APPLICATIONS. $10 fee, may be waived for applicants with need. No closing date; applicants notified on a rolling basis; must reply within 2 weeks. Interview recommended. Deferred and early admission available. Limited-admission programs have differing closing dates for applications.

STUDENT LIFE. Activities: Student government, magazine, radio, student newspaper, choral groups, concert band, drama, music ensembles, symphony orchestra, Asian American Association, Black Student Union, Christian Fellowship, International club, Multicultural Affairs Council, Newman Club, Phi Beta Kappa.

ATHLETICS. Intercollegiate: Baseball M, basketball, golf, soccer M, softball W, tennis, volleyball. **Intramural:** Basketball, bowling, volleyball. **Clubs:** Cross-country.

STUDENT SERVICES. Aptitude testing, career counseling, employment service for undergraduates, freshman orientation, health services, on-campus day care, personal counseling, placement service for graduates, veterans counselor, services/facilities for handicapped.

ANNUAL EXPENSES. Tuition and fees (1992-93): $1,240, $1,200 additional for out-of-district students, $2,400 additional for out-of-state students. Additional fees for out-of-district and out-of-state students are $260. **Books and supplies:** $400. **Other expenses:** $1,580.

FINANCIAL AID. 30% of freshmen, 30% of continuing students receive some form of aid. 96% of grants, all loans, 52% of jobs based on need. **Aid applications:** No closing date; priority given to applications received by May 1; applicants notified on a rolling basis beginning on or about June 14. **Additional information:** COPE grants offered to educationally and economically disadvantaged students.

ADDRESS/TELEPHONE. Joseph D. Piorkowski, Director of Admissions, Delaware County Community College, 901 South Media Line Road, Media, PA 19063-1094. (215) 359-5050.

Delaware Valley College
Doylestown, Pennsylvania CB code: 2510

Admissions: 88% of applicants accepted
Based on: ••• School record, test scores
•• Recommendations
• Activities, essay, interview, special talents
Completion: 86% of freshmen end year in good standing
57% graduate, 17% of these enter graduate study

4-year private agricultural and technical, business college, coed. Founded in 1896. **Accreditation:** Regional. **Undergraduate enrollment:** 698 men, 508 women full time; 34 men, 46 women part time. **Faculty:** 106 total (72 full time), 38 with doctorates or other terminal degrees. **Location:** Suburban campus in large town; 30 miles from Philadelphia, 70 miles from New York City. **Calendar:** Semester, extensive summer session. **Microcomputers:** 50 located in libraries, classrooms, computer centers. **Special facilities:** Equine facility with horse ring, indoor and outdoor animal farms, arboretum greenhouses, tissue culture laboratories.

DEGREES OFFERED. AS, BA, BS. 13 associate degrees awarded in 1992. 93% in agriculture, 7% business and management. 254 bachelor's degrees awarded. 51% in agriculture, 35% business and management, 9% life sciences.

UNDERGRADUATE MAJORS. Associate: Business and management, equestrian science. **Bachelor's:** Accounting, agribusiness, agricultural education, agronomy, animal sciences, applied mathematics, biology, business administration and management, business education, chemistry, criminal justice studies, dairy, English, English education, environmental design, equestrian science, food management, food sciences, horticultural science, horticulture, information sciences and systems, marketing management, mathematics education, ornamental horticulture, plant sciences, science education.

ACADEMIC PROGRAMS. Cooperative education, dual enrollment of high school students, honors program, internships, teacher preparation, cross-registration. **Remedial services:** Learning center, reduced course load, remedial instruction, special counselor, tutoring. **ROTC:** Army. **Placement/credit:** AP, CLEP General and Subject, institutional tests.

ACADEMIC REQUIREMENTS. Freshmen must earn minimum GPA of 2.0 to continue in good standing. 75% of freshmen return for sophomore year. Students must declare major by end of first year. **Graduation requirements:** 128 hours for bachelor's. Most students required to take courses in computer science, English, history, mathematics, philosophy/religion, biological/physical sciences, social sciences. **Postgraduate studies:** 45% from 2-

year programs enter 4-year programs. 4% enter medical school, 2% enter MBA programs, 11% enter other graduate study.

FRESHMAN ADMISSIONS. Selection criteria: Academic achievement, class rank, test scores, letters of recommendation from mathematics or science teacher and guidance counselor, grades in mathematics and science considered. Interview recommended. **High school preparation:** 15 units required. Required units include biological science 1, English 3, mathematics 2, physical science 1 and social science 2. For business administration 1 unit science only. Agriculture, biology, and chemistry majors need 6 additional units, business majors 7. **Test requirements:** SAT or ACT; score report by May 1.

1992 FRESHMAN CLASS PROFILE. 801 men applied, 683 accepted, 267 enrolled; 657 women applied, 606 accepted, 228 enrolled. 52% had high school GPA of 3.0 or higher, 46% between 2.0 and 2.99. 14% were in top tenth and 36% were in top quarter of graduating class. **Academic background:** Mid 50% of enrolled freshmen had SAT-V between 380-490, SAT-M between 410-530. 98% submitted SAT scores. **Characteristics:** 68% from in state, 74% live in college housing, 5% have minority backgrounds, 1% are foreign students. Average age is 20.

FALL-TERM APPLICATIONS. $35 fee, may be waived for applicants with need. No closing date; applicants notified on a rolling basis beginning on or about October 15; must reply within 4 weeks. Interview recommended for - applicants. Deferred admission available.

STUDENT LIFE. Housing: Dormitories (men, women, coed). **Activities:** Student government, magazine, radio, student newspaper, yearbook, choral groups, concert band, drama, pep band, Christian Fellowship, Hillel, Future Farmers of America, minority leadership coalition, environmental awareness club, Alpha Phi Omega, DVC volunteer corps, Newman club, equine club, business club.

ATHLETICS. NCAA. **Intercollegiate:** Baseball M, basketball, cross-country, field hockey W, football M, golf M, softball W, track and field, volleyball W, wrestling M. **Intramural:** Basketball, bowling, cross-country, football M, golf, horseback riding, lacrosse M, racquetball, soccer M, softball, tennis, volleyball. **Clubs:** Horseback riding.

STUDENT SERVICES. Career counseling, employment service for undergraduates, freshman orientation, health services, personal counseling, placement service for graduates.

ANNUAL EXPENSES. Tuition and fees: $11,645. **Room and board:** $4,785. **Books and supplies:** $500. **Other expenses:** $1,000.

FINANCIAL AID. 82% of freshmen, 72% of continuing students receive some form of aid. 75% of grants, 85% of loans, 69% of jobs based on need. 348 enrolled freshmen were judged to have need, all were offered aid. Academic, leadership, alumni affiliation scholarships available. **Aid applications:** Closing date April 1; priority given to applications received by March 1; applicants notified on a rolling basis beginning on or about March 1; must reply within 4 weeks.

ADDRESS/TELEPHONE. Stephen W. Zenko, Director of Admissions, Delaware Valley College, 700 East Butler Avenue, Doylestown, PA 18901-2697. (215) 345-1500 ext. 2211. (800) 2-DELVAL. Fax: (215) 345-5277.

Dickinson College

Carlisle, Pennsylvania CB code: 2186

Admissions: 76% of applicants accepted
Based on: ••• Recommendations, school record, test scores
•• Activities, essay, special talents
• Interview
Completion: 96% of freshmen end year in good standing
85% graduate, 12% of these enter graduate study

4-year private liberal arts college, coed. Founded in 1773. **Accreditation:** Regional. **Undergraduate enrollment:** 869 men, 1,118 women full time; 24 men, 36 women part time. **Faculty:** 179 total (146 full time), 161 with doctorates or other terminal degrees. **Location:** Suburban campus in large town; 18 miles from Harrisburg, 100 miles from Philadelphia. **Calendar:** Semester, limited summer session. **Microcomputers:** 450 located in dormitories, libraries, classrooms, computer centers, campus-wide network. **Special facilities:** Center for the arts (including art gallery), planetarium and multiple telescope observatory, intercontinental satellite communications with study abroad programs. **Additional facts:** Located in historic district of old central Pennsylvania county seat.

DEGREES OFFERED. BA, BS. 582 bachelor's degrees awarded in 1992. 5% in area and ethnic studies, 14% languages, 11% letters/literature, 5% life sciences, 12% multi/interdisciplinary studies, 5% physical sciences, 5% psychology, 34% social sciences.

UNDERGRADUATE MAJORS. American studies, anthropology, biology, chemistry, computer and information sciences, dramatic arts, East Asian studies, economics, English, fine arts, French, geology, German, Greek (classical), history, international studies, Italian studies, Jewish studies, Latin, mathematics, music, philosophy, physics, policy and management studies, policy management studies, policy management studies, political science and government, psychology, religion, Russian, Russian and Slavic studies, sociology, Spanish.

ACADEMIC PROGRAMS. Accelerated program, double major, honors program, independent study, internships, student-designed major, study abroad, teacher preparation, visiting/exchange student program, Washington semester, cross-registration, summer language-immersion programs in 6 European cities: Moscow, Bologna, Rome, Bremen, Toulouse and Malaga; liberal arts/career combination in engineering. **Remedial services:** Special counselor, tutoring, writing center. **ROTC:** Army. **Placement/credit:** AP, IB, institutional tests.

ACADEMIC REQUIREMENTS. Freshmen must earn minimum GPA of 1.75 to continue in good standing. 94% of freshmen return for sophomore year. Students must declare major by end of second year. **Graduation requirements:** 136 hours for bachelor's (40 in major). Most students required to take courses in arts/fine arts, foreign languages, humanities, biological/physical sciences, social sciences. **Postgraduate studies:** 2% enter law school, 1% enter medical school, 1% enter MBA programs, 8% enter other graduate study. **Additional information:** Certificates in interdepartmental programs offered in Latin American studies, environmental studies, and women's studies in conjunction with bachelor's degree. Prebusiness, law and premedical preparation available in conjunction with major offerings listed.

FRESHMAN ADMISSIONS. Selection criteria: Academic potential as shown by school achievement record, standardized test results important. Extracurricular activities, motivation, personal character considered, counselor recommendation required. Special consideration given to nonwhite applicants. Preference given to academically qualified children of alumni if they satisfy above mentioned criteria on base equal to other applicants. **High school preparation:** 16 units required. Required and recommended units include English 4, foreign language 2-3, mathematics 3, social science 2 and science 3. **Test requirements:** SAT or ACT; score report by March 1.

1992 FRESHMAN CLASS PROFILE. 1,500 men applied, 1,045 accepted, 231 enrolled; 1,953 women applied, 1,591 accepted, 344 enrolled. 35% were in top tenth and 72% were in top quarter of graduating class. **Academic background:** Mid 50% of enrolled freshmen had SAT-V between 490-580, SAT-M between 520-620. 99% submitted SAT scores. **Characteristics:** 38% from in state, 100% live in college housing, 6% have minority backgrounds, 3% are foreign students. Average age is 18.

FALL-TERM APPLICATIONS. $35 fee, may be waived for applicants with need. Closing date February 20; applicants notified on or about March 30; must reply by May 1. Essay required. Interview recommended. CRDA. Deferred and early admission available. EDP-F.

STUDENT LIFE. Housing: Dormitories (men, women, coed); fraternity, sorority, handicapped housing available. Language houses, arts house, environmental house, multi-cultural house, Hillel house, Congress of African Students house, Asian house. All groups including fraternity and sorority chapters apply each year to college's housing board for group living space in college facilities. **Activities:** Student government, film, magazine, radio, student newspaper, yearbook, choral groups, concert band, dance, drama, jazz band, music ensembles, musical theater, opera, pep band, symphony orchestra, debate, fraternities, sororities, public affairs, social service, religious, black, Hispanic, Korean, East Asian, and other foreign student organizations, College Democrats, Young Republicans. **Additional information:** Student-run public affairs symposium on major topics presented annually. Multi-cultural week and series of cultural events planned by student committee. Social hall separate from college-operated student union functions under student supervision.

ATHLETICS. NCAA. **Intercollegiate:** Baseball M, basketball, cross-country, field hockey W, football M, golf M, lacrosse, soccer, softball W, swimming, tennis, track and field, volleyball W. **Intramural:** Badminton, basketball, bowling, fencing, field hockey W, football, golf, horseback riding, ice hockey M, racquetball, rugby M, skiing, soccer, softball, squash, swimming, table tennis, tennis, volleyball, water polo M.

STUDENT SERVICES. Aptitude testing, career counseling, employment service for undergraduates, freshman orientation, health services, on-campus day care, personal counseling, placement service for graduates, special adviser for adult students, Needs of handicapped students met individually on case by case basis, 70% of facilities accessible to handicapped, services/facilities for handicapped.

ANNUAL EXPENSES. Tuition and fees: $17,775. **Room and board:** $4,930. **Books and supplies:** $445. **Other expenses:** $900.

FINANCIAL AID. 62% of freshmen, 65% of continuing students receive some form of aid. All grants, 91% of loans, 43% of jobs based on need. 302 enrolled freshmen were judged to have need, all were offered aid. Academic, leadership scholarships available. **Aid applications:** Closing date February 15; applicants notified on or about April 10; must reply by May 1. **Additional information:** Flexible financing system available.

ADDRESS/TELEPHONE. J. Larry Mench, Dean of Admissions and Enrollment, Dickinson College, P O Box 1773, Carlisle, PA 17013-2896. (717) 245-1231. Fax: (717) 245-1899.

Drexel University

Philadelphia, Pennsylvania CB code: 2194

Admissions: 82% of applicants accepted
Based on: ••• School record
•• Activities, essay, recommendations, special talents, test scores
• Interview
Completion: 77% of freshmen end year in good standing
52% graduate, 19% of these enter graduate study

5-year private university, coed. Founded in 1891. **Accreditation:** Regional. **Undergraduate enrollment:** 3,838 men, 1,809 women full time; 1,552 men, 612 women part time. **Graduate enrollment:** 625 men, 373 women full time; 1,470 men, 759 women part time. **Faculty:** 841 total (430 full time), 413 with doctorates or other terminal degrees. **Location:** Urban campus in very large city. **Calendar:** Quarter, extensive summer session. **Microcomputers:** 6,500 located in dormitories, libraries, classrooms, computer centers. Lease or purchase required**Special facilities:** Museum, observatory, rifle range. **Additional facts:** Cooperative Education program incorporates related work experiences into academic curriculum. Most undergraduate programs require up to 18 months work experience within 5-year program of study.

DEGREES OFFERED. BS, BArch, MS, MBA, PhD. 1,616 bachelor's degrees awarded in 1992. 37% in business and management, 6% computer sciences, 32% engineering, 5% visual and performing arts. Graduate degrees offered in 57 major fields of study.

UNDERGRADUATE MAJORS. Accounting, anthropology, architectural engineering, architecture, atmospheric sciences and meteorology, biochemistry, biological and physical sciences, biology, biophysics, business administration and management, business and management, business economics, business statistics, chemical engineering, chemistry, civil engineering, communications, comparative literature, computer and information sciences, computer engineering, electrical/electronics/communications engineering, engineering, engineering and engineering-related technologies, engineering science, environmental science, fashion design, fashion merchandising, film arts, finance, food science and nutrition, food sciences, graphic and printing production, graphic design, history, hotel/motel and restaurant management, human resources development, humanities and social sciences, industrial engineering, information sciences and systems, inorganic chemistry, interior design, International area studies, investments and securities, labor/industrial relations, management information systems, marketing management, materials engineering, mathematics, mathematics education, mechanical engineering, music, nutritional sciences, operations research, organic chemistry, personnel management, photography, physics, political science and government, psychology, retailing, science education, sociology, systems analysis, visual and performing arts.

ACADEMIC PROGRAMS. Accelerated program, cooperative education, honors program, independent study, study abroad, teacher preparation, 3+3 programs with Lincoln University, Indiana University of Pennsylvania and Eastern Mennonite College. **Remedial services:** Preadmission summer program, reduced course load, remedial instruction, special counselor, tutoring, reading clinic. **ROTC:** Air Force, Army, Naval. **Placement/credit:** AP, institutional tests.

ACADEMIC REQUIREMENTS. Freshmen must earn minimum GPA of 1.6 to continue in good standing. Students must declare major by end of second year. **Graduation requirements:** 180 hours for bachelor's. Most students required to take courses in computer science, English, history, mathematics, biological/physical sciences, social sciences. **Postgraduate studies:** 1% enter law school, 1% enter medical school, 5% enter MBA programs, 12% enter other graduate study.

FRESHMAN ADMISSIONS. Selection criteria: Emphasis on class rank, academic average, counselor's recommendation, test scores. School, community, church activities, and employment also considered. Required units include 2 algebra, 1 laboratory science. Trigonometry and 1 additional laboratory science required of engineering, science, and commerce and engineering applicants. **Test requirements:** SAT or ACT (SAT preferred); score report by March 1. 3 ACH (including English Composition, Mathematics Level I or II, and Chemistry or Physics or Biology) required of engineering, commerce and engineering, and science applicants. Score report by March 1.

1992 FRESHMAN CLASS PROFILE. 2,190 men applied, 1,818 accepted, 878 enrolled; 1,209 women applied, 970 accepted, 414 enrolled. 61% had high school GPA of 3.0 or higher, 38% between 2.0 and 2.99. 25% were in top tenth and 57% were in top quarter of graduating class. **Academic background:** Mid 50% of enrolled freshmen had SAT-V between 400-510, SAT-M between 490-620. 82% submitted SAT scores. **Characteristics:** 64% from in state, 58% live in college housing, 23% have minority backgrounds, 5% are foreign students, 10% join fraternities/sororities. Average age is 18.

FALL-TERM APPLICATIONS. $25 fee, may be waived for applicants with need. Closing date March 1; applicants notified on a rolling basis beginning on or about January 1; must reply by registration. Audition required for music applicants. Essay required. Interview recommended. Deferred and early admission available. EDP-F.

STUDENT LIFE. Housing: Dormitories (coed); fraternity, sorority, handicapped housing available. **Activities:** Student government, film, magazine, radio, student newspaper, television, yearbook, choral groups, concert band, dance, drama, jazz band, music ensembles, musical theater, pep band, symphony orchestra, fraternities, sororities, Protestant ministries, Newman Club, Hillel Club, Alpha Phi Omega, African-American Organization, Amnesty International, sports clubs, professional societies, environmental groups.

ATHLETICS. NAIA, NCAA. **Intercollegiate:** Baseball M, basketball, cross-country M, diving, field hockey W, golf M, lacrosse, rowing (crew), soccer M, softball W, swimming, tennis, track and field M, volleyball W, wrestling M. **Intramural:** Badminton, baseball, basketball, fencing, football M, ice hockey M, rifle, rugby, sailing, softball, squash, table tennis, tennis, volleyball, water polo.

STUDENT SERVICES. Aptitude testing, career counseling, employment service for undergraduates, freshman orientation, health services, personal counseling, placement service for graduates, special adviser for adult students, services/facilities for handicapped.

ANNUAL EXPENSES. Tuition and fees (1992-93): $11,635. **Room and board:** $5,437. **Books and supplies:** $500. **Other expenses:** $1,500.

FINANCIAL AID. 76% of freshmen, 85% of continuing students receive some form of aid. 75% of grants, 78% of loans, all jobs based on need. 760 enrolled freshmen were judged to have need, 745 were offered aid. Academic, music/drama, art, athletic, alumni affiliation scholarships available. **Aid applications:** No closing date; priority given to applications received by May 1; applicants notified on a rolling basis beginning on or about April 1; must reply by May 1 or within 2 weeks if notified thereafter. **Additional information:** Cooperative program provides earnings for 95% of students.

ADDRESS/TELEPHONE. Donald G. Dickason, Vice President for Enrollment Management, Drexel University, 32nd and Chestnut Streets, Philadelphia, PA 19104. (215) 895-2400. (800) 2-DREXEL. Fax: (215) 895-5939.

DuBois Business College

DuBois, Pennsylvania CB code: 3886

2-year proprietary business college, coed. Founded in 1885. **Undergraduate enrollment:** 40 men, 265 women full time. **Faculty:** 14 total (12 full time). **Location:** Suburban campus in large town; 100 miles from Pittsburgh. **Calendar:** Quarter. **Microcomputers:** 100 located in classrooms, computer centers.

DEGREES OFFERED. 110 associate degrees awarded in 1992. 50% in business and management, 50% business/office and marketing/distribution.

UNDERGRADUATE MAJORS. Accounting, business administration and management, business and management, legal secretary, medical secretary, secretarial and related programs.

ACADEMIC PROGRAMS. Cooperative education, internships. **Remedial services:** Reduced course load, remedial instruction, tutoring. **Placement/credit:** Institutional tests.

ACADEMIC REQUIREMENTS. Freshmen must earn minimum GPA of 2.0 to continue in good standing. Students must declare major on application. **Graduation requirements:** 78 hours for associate (78 in major).

FRESHMAN ADMISSIONS. Selection criteria: Open admissions. Courses in shorthand, accounting, computer, typing, law, psychology, and speech recommended.

1992 FRESHMAN CLASS PROFILE. 47 men applied, 40 accepted, 25 enrolled; 278 women applied, 265 accepted, 145 enrolled. 57% had high school GPA of 3.0 or higher, 40% between 2.0 and 2.99. **Characteristics:** 99% from in state, 70% commute, 2% have minority backgrounds, 10% join fraternities/sororities. Average age is 22.

FALL-TERM APPLICATIONS. $25 fee, may be waived for applicants with need. No closing date; applicants notified on a rolling basis. Interview recommended.

STUDENT LIFE. Housing: Dormitories (women); cooperative housing available. **Activities:** Student government, student newspaper, fraternities, sororities, accounting club, secretaries club.

ATHLETICS. Intramural: Volleyball.

STUDENT SERVICES. Career counseling, employment service for undergraduates, personal counseling, placement service for graduates, special adviser for adult students, veterans counselor, services/facilities for handicapped.

ANNUAL EXPENSES. Tuition and fees: $4,825. **Room and board:** $4,300. **Books and supplies:** $450.

FINANCIAL AID. 90% of freshmen, 90% of continuing students receive some form of aid. All grants, 79% of loans based on need. **Aid applications:** Closing date August 1; applicants notified on a rolling basis; must reply by registration.

ADDRESS/TELEPHONE. Scott Dixon, Admissions Representative, DuBois Business College, PO Box O, DuBois, PA 15801. (814) 371-6920. (800) 692-6213.

Duquesne University
Pittsburgh, Pennsylvania CB code: 2196

4-year private university, coed, affiliated with Roman Catholic Church. Founded in 1878. **Accreditation:** Regional. **Undergraduate enrollment:** 2,551 men, 2,719 women full time; 709 men and women part time. **Graduate enrollment:** 730 men, 720 women full time; 710 men, 1,000 women part time. **Faculty:** 593 total (309 full time), 256 with doctorates or other terminal degrees. **Location:** Urban campus in large city. **Calendar:** Semester, extensive summer session. **Microcomputers:** 215 located in dormitories, libraries, classrooms, computer centers. **Special facilities:** Manufacturing pharmacy, Kurzweil 250 digital keyboard, Tamburitzan Cultural Center, computerized language laboratory, Simon Silverman Phenomenology Center.

DEGREES OFFERED. BA, BS, MA, MS, MBA, MEd, PhD, B. Pharm, Pharm D, JD. 915 bachelor's degrees awarded in 1992. 26% in business and management, 10% communications, 11% teacher education, 20% health sciences, 9% social sciences. Graduate degrees offered in 64 major fields of study.

UNDERGRADUATE MAJORS. Accounting, advertising, athletic training, biochemistry, biology, business administration and management, business and management, business economics, chemistry, classics, communications, computer and information sciences, computer mathematics, computer programming, corporate communication, criminal justice studies, criminology, early childhood education, economics, education of exceptional children, education of the deaf and hearing impaired, education of the emotionally handicapped, education of the mentally handicapped, education of the multiple handicapped, education of the physically handicapped, education of the visually handicapped, elementary education, engineering and other disciplines, English, English education, English literature, finance, foreign languages (multiple emphasis), foreign languages education, French, German, Greek (classical), history, human resources development, information sciences and systems, international business management, investments and securities, jazz, journalism, Latin, linguistics, logistics, management information systems, management science, marketing management, marketing research, mathematics, mathematics education, media arts, medical records administration, microbiology, music education, music performance, music technology, nursing, perfusion technology, personnel management, pharmacology, human and animal, pharmacy, philosophy, physics, political science and government, predentistry, prelaw, premedicine, preveterinary, psychology, public relations, radio/television broadcasting, radio/television technology, real estate, religion, religious music, secondary education, social work, sociology, sound recording technology, Spanish, special education, speech, systems analysis, theological studies.

ACADEMIC PROGRAMS. Accelerated program, cooperative education, double major, dual enrollment of high school students, honors program, independent study, internships, student-designed major, study abroad, teacher preparation, Washington semester, cross-registration, 3-2 binary program in engineering with Case Western Reserve and Florida Institute of Technology, 3-3 early admission law and early admission medical program with The Medical College of Pennsylvania; liberal arts/career combination in engineering; combined bachelor's/graduate program in business administration, medicine, law. **Remedial services:** Learning center, preadmission summer program, reduced course load, remedial instruction, special counselor, tutoring. **ROTC:** Air Force, Army. **Placement/credit:** AP, CLEP General and Subject, institutional tests; 60 credit hours maximum for bachelor's degree.

ACADEMIC REQUIREMENTS. Freshmen must earn minimum GPA of 2.0 to continue in good standing. 90% of freshmen return for sophomore year. Students must declare major by end of second year. **Graduation requirements:** 120 hours for bachelor's (24 in major). Most students required to take courses in arts/fine arts, English, foreign languages, history, humanities, mathematics, philosophy/religion, biological/physical sciences, social sciences. **Postgraduate studies:** 8% enter law school, 2% enter medical school, 12% enter MBA programs, 22% enter other graduate study. **Additional information:** 27-credit core curriculum integrated throughout 7 schools on campus. Majors declared upon application for some programs.

FRESHMAN ADMISSIONS. Selection criteria: School achievement record, class rank, test scores, counselor recommendation, interview, and activities considered. Special talent or alumni affiliation. **High school preparation:** 16 units required. Required units include English 4. Total of 8 units in mathematics, social studies, foreign language, and science required in any combination. For applicants in mathematics or science, 7 units in mathematics and science required. **Test requirements:** SAT or ACT (SAT preferred); score report by July 1.

1992 FRESHMAN CLASS PROFILE. 1,029 men and women enrolled. **Academic background:** Mid 50% of enrolled freshmen had SAT-V between 410-570, SAT-M between 460-570. 96% submitted SAT scores. **Characteristics:** 82% from in state, 72% live in college housing, 8% have minority backgrounds, 3% are foreign students. Average age is 18.

FALL-TERM APPLICATIONS. $40 fee, may be waived for applicants with need. Closing date July 1; priority given to applications received by January 1; applicants notified on a rolling basis; must reply by May 1 or within 2 weeks if notified thereafter. Audition required for music applicants. Essay required. Interview recommended. CRDA. Deferred and early admission available. EDP-F. Early decision plan application by November 15.

STUDENT LIFE. Housing: Dormitories (coed); fraternity, sorority, handicapped housing available. **Activities:** Student government, magazine, radio, student newspaper, television, yearbook, student activities board, choral groups, concert band, dance, drama, jazz band, music ensembles, pep band, symphony orchestra, fraternities, sororities, United Nations organization, YMCA, ethnic, religious, and social service organizations, Black Student Union.

ATHLETICS. NCAA. **Intercollegiate:** Baseball M, basketball, cross-country, diving, football M, golf, ice hockey M, lacrosse M, rifle, rowing (crew), soccer, swimming, tennis, track and field, volleyball W, wrestling M. **Intramural:** Basketball, bowling, gymnastics M, ice hockey M, racquetball, soccer, softball, table tennis, tennis, volleyball, water polo M. **Clubs:** Bowling.

STUDENT SERVICES. Aptitude testing, career counseling, employment service for undergraduates, freshman orientation, health services, on-campus day care, personal counseling, placement service for graduates, special adviser for adult students, services/facilities for handicapped.

ANNUAL EXPENSES. Tuition and fees (1992-93): $10,470. **Room and board:** $4,875. **Books and supplies:** $400. **Other expenses:** $450.

FINANCIAL AID. 75% of freshmen, 78% of continuing students receive some form of aid. 64% of grants, 69% of loans, 63% of jobs based on need. 665 enrolled freshmen were judged to have need, all were offered aid. Academic, music/drama, athletic, religious affiliation, minority scholarships available. **Aid applications:** Closing date May 1; applicants notified on a rolling basis beginning on or about February 15; must reply by May 1 or within 3 weeks if notified thereafter.

ADDRESS/TELEPHONE. Rev. Thomas Schaefer, Director of Admissions, Duquesne University, 600 Forbes Avenue, Pittsburgh, PA 15282-0201. (412) 434-6220. (800) 456-0590. Fax: (412) 434-5644.

East Stroudsburg University of Pennsylvania
East Stroudsburg, Pennsylvania CB code: 2650

Admissions:		46% of applicants accepted
Based on:	•••	School record
	••	Test scores
	•	Activities, essay, recommendations, special talents
Completion:		85% of freshmen end year in good standing
		45% graduate, 16% of these enter graduate study

4-year public university, coed. Founded in 1893. **Accreditation:** Regional. **Undergraduate enrollment:** 1,728 men, 2,144 women full time; 306 men, 386 women part time. **Graduate enrollment:** 94 men, 112 women full time; 186 men, 396 women part time. **Faculty:** 273 total (260 full time), 169 with doctorates or other terminal degrees. **Location:** Rural campus in small town; 40 miles from Allentown and Scranton. **Calendar:** Semester, extensive summer session. **Microcomputers:** 150 located in libraries, classrooms, computer centers. **Special facilities:** 30-acre ecological studies area.

DEGREES OFFERED. AS, BA, BS, MA, MS, MEd. 803 bachelor's degrees awarded. 15% in business and management, 8% communications, 7% education, 28% teacher education, 5% letters/literature, 7% life sciences, 13% social sciences. Graduate degrees offered in 12 major fields of study.

UNDERGRADUATE MAJORS. Associate: Educational media technology. **Bachelor's:** Biochemistry, biological and physical sciences, biology, biophysics, business administration and management, chemistry, clinical laboratory science, communications, computer and information sciences, dramatic arts, early childhood education, earth sciences, economics, elementary education, English, English education, environmental science, fine arts, foreign languages education, French, geography, German, health education, history, marine biology, mathematics, mathematics education, music, nursing, parks and recreation management, philosophy, physical education, physical sciences, physics, political science and government, premedicine, prepharmacy, psychology, rehabilitation counseling/services, science education, secondary education, social studies education, sociology, Spanish, special education, speech, speech correction, speech pathology/audiology, speech/communication/theater education, visual and performing arts.

ACADEMIC PROGRAMS. Double major, honors program, independent study, internships, student-designed major, study abroad, teacher preparation, visiting/exchange student program; liberal arts/career combination in engineering, health sciences. **Remedial services:** Learning center, preadmission summer program, reduced course load, remedial instruction, special counselor, tutoring. **ROTC:** Air Force, Army. **Placement/credit:** AP, CLEP General and Subject, institutional tests; 24 credit hours maximum for bachelor's degree.

ACADEMIC REQUIREMENTS. Freshmen must earn minimum GPA of 1.76 to continue in good standing. 75% of freshmen return for sophomore year. Students must declare major by end of second year. **Graduation requirements:** 60 hours for associate (27 in major), 128 hours for bachelor's (30 in major). Most students required to take courses in arts/fine arts, English, humanities, biological/physical sciences, social sciences.

FRESHMAN ADMISSIONS. Selection criteria: High school achievement, test scores, intended curriculum. Top third of class and SAT combined score of 850 preferred. 16 academic units required of nursing applicants, including 4 English, 3 social studies, 2 mathematics (including 1 algebra), 2 laboratory sciences. **Test requirements:** SAT or ACT (SAT preferred); score report by February 15. Foreign language ACH required of foreign language majors. Score report by March 1.

1992 FRESHMAN CLASS PROFILE. 4,472 men and women applied, 2,055 accepted; 266 men enrolled, 375 women enrolled. **Academic background:** Mid 50% of enrolled freshmen had SAT-V between 380-470, SAT-M between 430-540. 83% submitted SAT scores. **Characteristics:** 75% from in state, 80% live in college housing, 7% have minority backgrounds, 1% are foreign students, 10% join fraternities/sororities. Average age is 19.

FALL-TERM APPLICATIONS. $25 fee, may be waived for applicants with need. Closing date March 1; priority given to applications received by January 1; applicants notified on or about March 1; must reply by April 1 or within 3 weeks if notified thereafter. Essay recommended. Deferred and early admission available.

STUDENT LIFE. Housing: Dormitories (men, women, coed); apartment, fraternity housing available. **Activities:** Student government, radio, student newspaper, yearbook, choral groups, concert band, dance, drama, jazz band, marching band, music ensembles, musical theater, pep band, fraternities, sororities, Latin American Students Association, Campus Democrats, Young Republicans, Black Student Association, Fellowship of Christian Athletes, Newman Club.

ATHLETICS. NCAA. **Intercollegiate:** Baseball M, basketball, cross-country, field hockey W, football M, lacrosse W, soccer, softball W, tennis, track and field, volleyball, wrestling M. **Intramural:** Badminton, basketball, racquetball, softball, tennis, volleyball.

STUDENT SERVICES. Aptitude testing, career counseling, employment service for undergraduates, freshman orientation, health services, on-campus day care, personal counseling, placement service for graduates, special adviser for adult students, veterans counselor, services/facilities for handicapped.

ANNUAL EXPENSES. Tuition and fees (1992-93): $3,352, $3,394 additional for out-of-state students. **Room and board:** $3,040. **Books and supplies:** $450. **Other expenses:** $750.

FINANCIAL AID. 77% of freshmen, 72% of continuing students receive some form of aid. 84% of grants, 50% of loans, 17% of jobs based on need. 468 enrolled freshmen were judged to have need, all were offered aid. Academic, athletic, minority scholarships available. **Aid applications:** Closing date March 15; applicants notified on or about June 1; must reply within 2 weeks.

ADDRESS/TELEPHONE. Alan T. Chesterton, Director of Admissions, East Stroudsburg University of Pennsylvania, East Stroudsburg, PA 18301. (717) 424-3542.

Eastern College
St. Davids, Pennsylvania CB code: 2220

Admissions: 88% of applicants accepted
Based on:
- ••• School record
- •• Essay, recommendations, religious affiliation/commitment, test scores
- • Activities, interview, special talents

Completion: 92% of freshmen end year in good standing
50% graduate, 15% of these enter graduate study

4-year private liberal arts college, coed, affiliated with American Baptist Churches in the USA. Founded in 1952. **Accreditation:** Regional. **Undergraduate enrollment:** 433 men, 600 women full time; 73 men, 270 women part time. **Graduate enrollment:** 67 men, 37 women full time; 110 men, 155 women part time. **Faculty:** 141 total (47 full time), 57 with doctorates or other terminal degrees. **Location:** Suburban campus in small town; 10 miles from Philadelphia, near Valley Forge. **Calendar:** Semester, limited summer session. **Microcomputers:** 35 located in computer centers. **Special facilities:** Planetarium.

DEGREES OFFERED. AS, BA, BS, MS, MBA, MEd. 23 associate degrees awarded in 1992. 100% in multi/interdisciplinary studies. 269 bachelor's degrees awarded. 43% in business and management, 13% teacher education, 11% health sciences, 6% philosophy, religion, theology, 6% psychology, 7% social sciences. Graduate degrees offered in 3 major fields of study.

UNDERGRADUATE MAJORS. Associate: Liberal/general studies. **Bachelor's:** Accounting, art history, astronomy, Bible studies, biology, business administration and management, chemistry, clinical laboratory science, communications, communications education, creative writing, economics, elementary education, English education, English literature, French, health and physical education, health care administration, history, mathematics, music, nursing, organizational management, philosophy, philosophy/religion, political science and government, psychology, secondary education, social work, sociology, Spanish, studio art, youth ministries.

ACADEMIC PROGRAMS. Accelerated program, double major, dual enrollment of high school students, honors program, independent study, internships, student-designed major, study abroad, teacher preparation, visiting/exchange student program, Washington semester, cross-registration, BS in nursing for registered nurses, BA in organizational management for adult students. **Remedial services:** Learning center, preadmission summer program, reduced course load, remedial instruction, special counselor, tutoring. **ROTC:** Air Force, Army. **Placement/credit:** AP, CLEP Subject, institutional tests; 60 credit hours maximum for bachelor's degree.

ACADEMIC REQUIREMENTS. Freshmen must earn minimum GPA of 1.67 to continue in good standing. 76% of freshmen return for sophomore year. Students must declare major by end of second year. **Graduation requirements:** 127 hours for bachelor's. Most students required to take courses in computer science, English, foreign languages, history, mathematics, philosophy/religion, biological/physical sciences, social sciences. **Postgraduate studies:** 1% enter law school, 2% enter medical school, 1% enter MBA programs, 11% enter other graduate study. **Additional information:** Bilingual (Spanish) program in business and economics.

FRESHMAN ADMISSIONS. Selection criteria: Recommendations, class rank, and SAT or ACT scores considered. Answer to question regarding faith also considered. **High school preparation:** 9 units recommended. **Test requirements:** SAT or ACT; score report by August 1. **Additional information:** Waiver of requirements for students age 22 or older.

1992 FRESHMAN CLASS PROFILE. 125 men applied, 110 accepted, 54 enrolled; 303 women applied, 267 accepted, 130 enrolled. 14% were in top tenth and 28% were in top quarter of graduating class. **Academic background:** Mid 50% of enrolled freshmen had SAT-V between 400-530, SAT-M between 380-570; ACT composite between 20-26. 91% submitted SAT scores, 2% submitted ACT scores. **Characteristics:** 51% from in state, 76% live in college housing, 12% have minority backgrounds, 3% are foreign students. Average age is 21.

FALL-TERM APPLICATIONS. $25 fee. No closing date; priority given to applications received by May 1; applicants notified on a rolling basis beginning on or about September 15. Essay required. Interview recommended. Deferred and early admission available.

STUDENT LIFE. Housing: Dormitories (coed); apartment housing available. Students required to live on campus unless they receive permission from Dean of Student Office. **Activities:** Student government, magazine, radio, student newspaper, yearbook, choral groups, dance, drama, jazz band, marching band, clowning, Christian Coalition, Black Student League, gospel teams, Missions Program, Evangelical Association for the Promotion of Education.

ATHLETICS. NCAA. **Intercollegiate:** Baseball M, basketball, cross-country, field hockey W, lacrosse W, soccer, softball W, tennis, volleyball W. **Intramural:** Badminton, basketball, bowling, cross-country, golf, racquetball, soccer, softball, table tennis, tennis, volleyball. **Clubs:** Volleyball M, intramural touch football.

STUDENT SERVICES. Aptitude testing, career counseling, employment service for undergraduates, freshman orientation, health services, personal counseling, placement service for graduates, special adviser for adult students, spiritual life coordinator, international student advisor, services/facilities for handicapped.

ANNUAL EXPENSES. Tuition and fees (1992-93): $9,875. **Room and board:** $4,130. **Books and supplies:** $400. **Other expenses:** $970.

FINANCIAL AID. 80% of freshmen, 81% of continuing students receive some form of aid. 69% of grants, 79% of loans, 73% of jobs based on need. 137 enrolled freshmen were judged to have need, all were offered aid. Academic, leadership, minority scholarships available. **Aid applications:** No closing date; priority given to applications received by April 15; applicants notified on a rolling basis beginning on or about March 1; must reply by May 1 or within 2 weeks if notified thereafter.

ADDRESS/TELEPHONE. Dr. Ronald Keller, Vice President for Enrollment Management, Eastern College, 10 Fairview Drive, St. Davids, PA 19087-3696. (215) 341-5967.

Edinboro University of Pennsylvania
Edinboro, Pennsylvania CB code: 2651

Admissions: 70% of applicants accepted
Based on:
- ••• School record
- •• Activities, test scores
- • Essay, interview, recommendations, special talents

Completion: 48% graduate

4-year public university, coed. Founded in 1857. **Accreditation:** Regional. **Undergraduate enrollment:** 2,922 men, 3,752 women full time; 330 men, 533 women part time. **Graduate enrollment:** 88 men, 181 women full time; 90 men, 306 women part time. **Faculty:** 417 total (399 full time), 221 with doctorates or other terminal degrees. **Location:** Rural campus in small town; 18 miles from Erie. **Calendar:** Semester, extensive summer session. Extensive evening/early morning classes. **Microcomputers:** 204 located in classrooms, computer centers. **Special facilities:** 2 art galleries, observatory, planetarium, natural wildlife museum, on-campus preschool to grade 4, robotics laboratory. **Additional facts:** Offers extensive programs and services for physically and learning disabled students. Operates the Porreco Center in Erie.

DEGREES OFFERED. AA, AS, AAS, BA, BS, BFA, MA, MS, MFA, MEd. 73 associate degrees awarded in 1992. 30% in business and management, 11% computer sciences, 11% teacher education, 11% engineering technologies, 16% health sciences, 14% multi/interdisciplinary studies, 7% parks/recreation, protective services, public affairs. 1,074 bachelor's degrees awarded. 13% in business and management, 10% communications, 28% teacher education, 5% health sciences, 10% parks/recreation, protective services, public affairs, 7% psychology, 5% social sciences, 7% visual and performing arts. Graduate degrees offered in 29 major fields of study.

UNDERGRADUATE MAJORS. Associate: Biomedical equipment technology, business and management, clinical laboratory science, computer and information sciences, criminal justice technology, digital electronics technology, early childhood education, engineering and engineering-related technologies, human services, liberal/general studies, manufacturing technology, teacher aide. **Bachelor's:** Accounting, Afro-American (black) studies, anthropology, art education, art history, biochemistry, biological and physical sciences, biology, business and management, business economics, ceramics, chemistry, cinematography/film, clinical laboratory science, communications, computer and information sciences, criminal justice studies, dramatic arts, drawing, early childhood education, earth sciences, economics, education, education of the mentally handicapped, elementary education, engineering and other disciplines, English, English education, environmental science, fiber/textiles/weaving, fine arts, food science and nutrition, foreign languages (multiple emphasis), foreign languages education, French, geography, geology, German, graphic arts technology, health education, history, humanities, humanities and social sciences, liberal/general studies, mathematics, mathematics education, metal/jewelry, music, music education, nuclear medical technology, nursing, painting, philosophy, photography, physical education, physical sciences, physics, political science and government, predentistry, prelaw, premedicine, prepharmacy, preveterinary, printmaking, psychology, Russian, science education, sculpture, secondary education, social sciences, social studies education, social work, sociology, Spanish, special education, speech correction, trade and industrial supervision and management.

ACADEMIC PROGRAMS. Accelerated program, cooperative education, dual enrollment of high school students, education specialist degree, honors program, independent study, internships, student-designed major, study abroad, teacher preparation, visiting/exchange student program, Washington semester, technical trade experience credited toward BS degree. **Remedial services:** Learning center, preadmission summer program, reduced course load, remedial instruction, special counselor, tutoring. **ROTC:** Army. **Placement/credit:** AP, CLEP General and Subject, institutional tests; 30 credit hours maximum for bachelor's degree.

ACADEMIC REQUIREMENTS. Freshmen must earn minimum GPA of 1.6 to continue in good standing. 72% of freshmen return for sophomore year. Students must declare major by end of second year. **Graduation requirements:** 62 hours for associate (30 in major), 128 hours for bachelor's (68 in major). Most students required to take courses in English.

FRESHMAN ADMISSIONS. Selection criteria: Primary importance given high school GPA and class rank. Recommendations and test scores also reviewed. **High school preparation:** 17 units recommended. Recommended units include foreign language 2, mathematics 3, social science 4 and science 4. **Test requirements:** SAT or ACT (SAT preferred); score report by August 29.

1992 FRESHMAN CLASS PROFILE. 2,021 men applied, 1,302 accepted, 658 enrolled; 2,407 women applied, 1,813 accepted, 888 enrolled. **Academic background:** Mid 50% of enrolled freshmen had SAT-V between 390-480, SAT-M between 400-510. 90% submitted SAT scores. **Characteristics:** 82% from in state, 81% live in college housing, 6% have minority backgrounds, 2% are foreign students. Average age is 19.

FALL-TERM APPLICATIONS. $20 fee. No closing date; applicants notified on a rolling basis; Students accepted by February 1 must reply by March 1. Students accepted after February 1 must reply within 30 days. Audition required for music applicants. Interview recommended. Deferred and early admission available.

STUDENT LIFE. Housing: Dormitories (men, women, coed); handicapped housing available. Honors dormitory available. **Activities:** Student government, film, radio, student newspaper, yearbook, choral groups, concert band, dance, drama, jazz band, marching band, music ensembles, symphony orchestra, fraternities, sororities, service organizations, campus ministries, minority student union.

ATHLETICS. NCAA. **Intercollegiate:** Baseball M, basketball, cross-country, diving, football M, golf M, softball W, swimming, tennis, track and field, volleyball W, wrestling M. **Intramural:** Basketball, bowling, cross-country, golf, racquetball, soccer, softball, table tennis, volleyball, water polo, wrestling M.

STUDENT SERVICES. Career counseling, employment service for undergraduates, freshman orientation, health services, on-campus day care, personal counseling, placement service for graduates, special adviser for adult students, veterans counselor, services/facilities for handicapped.

ANNUAL EXPENSES. Tuition and fees (projected): $3,352, $3,294 additional for out-of-state students. **Room and board:** $3,260. **Books and supplies:** $500. **Other expenses:** $1,088.

FINANCIAL AID. 80% of freshmen, 80% of continuing students receive some form of aid. 96% of grants, 75% of loans, 67% of jobs based on need. 1,200 enrolled freshmen were judged to have need, all were offered aid. Academic, athletic, minority scholarships available. **Aid applications:** Closing date May 1; applicants notified on a rolling basis beginning on or about June 20; must reply within 2 weeks.

ADDRESS/TELEPHONE. Terrence Carlin, Assistant Vice President for Admissions, Edinboro University of Pennsylvania, Edinboro, PA 16444. (814) 732-2761. Fax: (814) 732-2420.

Electronic Institutes: Middletown
Middletown, Pennsylvania CB code: 1313

2-year private technical college, coed. Founded in 1959. **Undergraduate enrollment:** 172 men, 4 women full time. **Faculty:** 13 total. **Location:** Suburban campus in large town; 6 miles from Harrisburg. **Calendar:** Trimester, extensive summer session. **Microcomputers:** 32 located in libraries, classrooms.

DEGREES OFFERED. 65 associate degrees awarded in 1992. 100% in engineering technologies.

UNDERGRADUATE MAJORS. Computer technology, electronic technology.

ACADEMIC PROGRAMS. Placement/credit: Institutional tests.

ACADEMIC REQUIREMENTS. Freshmen must earn minimum GPA of 2.0 to continue in good standing. 81% of freshmen return for sophomore year. Students must declare major on application.

FRESHMAN ADMISSIONS. Selection criteria: Test scores and school achievement record important, recommendations considered. 1 algebra required. **Test requirements:** Otis Series aptitude test required.

1992 FRESHMAN CLASS PROFILE. 53 men, 2 women enrolled. **Characteristics:** 100% from in state, 100% commute, 5% have minority backgrounds.

FALL-TERM APPLICATIONS. $10 fee. No closing date; applicants notified on a rolling basis. Interview required.

STUDENT SERVICES. Aptitude testing, career counseling, employment service for undergraduates, personal counseling, placement service for graduates, veterans counselor, test site for NABERS certification, services/facilities for handicapped.

ANNUAL EXPENSES. Tuition and fees (1992-93): $4,950. **Books and supplies:** $155. **Other expenses:** $1,350.

FINANCIAL AID. Aid applications: No closing date; priority given to applications received by August 1; applicants notified on a rolling basis.

ADDRESS/TELEPHONE. James S. Owens, Admissions Director, Electronic Institutes: Middletown, 19 Jamesway Plaza, Middletown, PA 17057-4851. (717) 944-2731.

Electronic Institutes: Pittsburgh
Pittsburgh, Pennsylvania CB code: 2229

2-year private technical college, coed. Founded in 1955. **Undergraduate enrollment:** 136 men and women. **Faculty:** 8 total. **Location:** Urban campus in large city; 6 miles from downtown Pittsburgh. **Calendar:** Trimester. **Microcomputers:** 16 located in libraries, computer centers.

DEGREES OFFERED. 29 associate degrees awarded in 1992. 100% in trade and industry.

UNDERGRADUATE MAJORS. Computer technology, electrical and electronics equipment repair.

ACADEMIC PROGRAMS. Remedial services: Tutoring. **Placement/credit:** Institutional tests.

ACADEMIC REQUIREMENTS. Freshmen must earn minimum GPA of 1.5 to continue in good standing. 79% of freshmen return for sophomore year. Students must declare major on application. **Graduation requirements:** Most students required to take courses in computer science, English, mathematics, biological/physical sciences.

FRESHMAN ADMISSIONS. Selection criteria: Open admissions. 1 year high school algebra and interview required for admission.

1992 FRESHMAN CLASS PROFILE. 56 men and women enrolled. 22% had high school GPA of 3.0 or higher, 44% between 2.0 and 2.99. **Characteristics:** 100% commute. Average age is 19.

FALL-TERM APPLICATIONS. $10 fee. No closing date; priority given to applications received by August 1; applicants notified on a rolling basis beginning on or about August 15; must reply within 4 weeks. Interview required. Deferred admission available.

STUDENT LIFE. Activities: Student newspaper.

STUDENT SERVICES. Employment service for undergraduates, personal counseling, placement service for graduates, services/facilities for handicapped.

ANNUAL EXPENSES. Tuition and fees: $7,350. Tuition and required fees $14,550 for 24-month electronic and computer technology program;

$9,750 for 16-month electrical technology program. **Books and supplies:** $500.

FINANCIAL AID. 90% of freshmen, 86% of continuing students receive some form of aid. All grants, 96% of loans based on need. **Aid applications:** No closing date; priority given to applications received by August 1; applicants notified on a rolling basis beginning on or about August 1; must reply within 30 days. **Additional information:** Scholarship available for dependents of professional educadors.

ADDRESS/TELEPHONE. Ron Kubitz, Chief Admission Officer, Electronic Institutes: Pittsburgh, 4634 Browns Hill Road, Pittsburgh, PA 15217. (412) 521-8686.

Elizabethtown College
Elizabethtown, Pennsylvania CB code: 2225

Admissions: 76% of applicants accepted
Based on: ••• School record
•• Recommendations, special talents, test scores
• Activities, essay, interview, religious affiliation/commitment
Completion: 84% of freshmen end year in good standing
62% graduate, 16% of these enter graduate study

4-year private liberal arts college, coed, affiliated with Church of the Brethren. Founded in 1899. **Accreditation:** Regional. **Undergraduate enrollment:** 513 men, 1,035 women full time; 125 men, 191 women part time. **Faculty:** 157 total (105 full time), 76 with doctorates or other terminal degrees. **Location:** Suburban campus in small town; 10 miles from Hershey, 20 miles from Harrisburg and Lancaster. **Calendar:** Semester, limited summer session. **Microcomputers:** 150 located in libraries, classrooms, computer centers. **Special facilities:** John W. Hess Art Gallery, Young Center for study of Anabaptist and Pietist groups.

DEGREES OFFERED. BA, BS. 325 bachelor's degrees awarded in 1992. 34% in business and management, 11% communications, 12% teacher education, 11% allied health, 6% letters/literature, 5% psychology, 11% social sciences.

UNDERGRADUATE MAJORS. Accounting, actuarial sciences, applied mathematics, biochemistry, biology, business administration and management, business and management, business economics, chemical physics, chemistry, chemistry management, child psychology, communications, comparative literature, computer and information sciences, computer engineering, cytotechnology, dental hygiene, early childhood education, economics, elementary education, engineering, engineering physics, English, English education, environmental science, finance, fine arts, foreign languages (multiple emphasis), forestry and related sciences, French, German, history, industrial engineering, information sciences and systems, international business management, international studies, journalism, junior high education, management information systems, marketing management, mathematics, mathematics education, medical laboratory technologies, music, music education, music therapy, nursing, occupational therapy, peace studies, philosophy, physical therapy, physics, political science and government, predentistry, preengineering, prelaw, premedicine, prepharmacy, preveterinary, psychology, public administration, public relations, pure mathematics, radio/television broadcasting, radiograph medical technology, religion, science education, secondary education, social studies education, social work, sociology, sociology/anthropology, Spanish, statistics, technical and business writing, ultrasound technology, visual and performing arts.

ACADEMIC PROGRAMS. Double major, dual enrollment of high school students, external degree, independent study, internships, semester at sea, study abroad, teacher preparation, 2-2 programs and 2-3 (p/t) programs with Thomas Jefferson University in nursing, physical therapy, cytotechnology, radiology, dental hygiene, 3-2 with Penn State in engineering, 3-2 with Duke in forestry and environmental management, capital semester internship in Harrisburg; liberal arts/career combination in engineering. **Remedial services:** Learning center, reduced course load, special counselor, tutoring, Special Advising Program for students with less than adequate academic credentials. **Placement/credit:** AP, CLEP General and Subject, IB, institutional tests; 64 credit hours maximum for bachelor's degree.

ACADEMIC REQUIREMENTS. Freshmen must earn minimum GPA of 1.7 to continue in good standing. 81% of freshmen return for sophomore year. Students must declare major by end of second year. **Graduation requirements:** 125 hours for bachelor's (39 in major). Most students required to take courses in arts/fine arts, English, foreign languages, history, mathematics, philosophy/religion, biological/physical sciences, social sciences. **Postgraduate studies:** 2% enter law school, 1% enter medical school, 2% enter MBA programs, 11% enter other graduate study.

FRESHMAN ADMISSIONS. Selection criteria: School achievement record most important. Extracurricular activities also considered. Applicants should be in top quarter of class with combined SAT score of 950. **High school preparation:** 16 units required. Required units include English 4, foreign language 2, mathematics 3, social science 2 and science 2. Sciences should be laboratory sciences. 3 academic electives required. **Test requirements:** SAT or ACT.

1992 FRESHMAN CLASS PROFILE. 713 men applied, 533 accepted, 192 enrolled; 1,531 women applied, 1,174 accepted, 422 enrolled. 32% were in top tenth and 67% were in top quarter of graduating class. **Academic background:** Mid 50% of enrolled freshmen had SAT-V between 440-540, SAT-M between 490-540. 98% submitted SAT scores. **Characteristics:** 62% from in state, 90% live in college housing, 2% have minority backgrounds, 2% are foreign students. Average age is 18.

FALL-TERM APPLICATIONS. $20 fee, may be waived for applicants with need. No closing date; priority given to applications received by March 15; applicants notified on a rolling basis beginning on or about November 1; must reply by May 1 or within 2 weeks if notified thereafter. Audition required for music, music education, music therapy applicants. Essay required. Interview recommended. Interview required for occupational therapy. CRDA. Deferred and early admission available. December 15 closing date for occupational therapy program.

STUDENT LIFE. Housing: Dormitories (men, women, coed); apartment, cooperative housing available. Guaranteed housing for all 4 years of study. **Activities:** Student government, radio, student newspaper, television, yearbook, forensics, literary magazine, choral groups, concert band, drama, jazz band, music ensembles, musical theater, symphony orchestra, brass ensemble, string ensemble, woodwind ensembles, Sock and Buskin, Alpha Psi Omega, Newman Club, intervarsity fellowship, international club, Concepts of Hillel, Circle-K, Habitat for Humanity, Amnesty International, student senate, African-American Cultural Society, Color United.

ATHLETICS. NCAA. **Intercollegiate:** Baseball M, basketball, cross-country, field hockey W, golf, soccer, softball W, swimming, tennis, volleyball W, wrestling M. **Intramural:** Basketball, racquetball, skiing, soccer, softball, tennis, track and field, volleyball. **Clubs:** Track, volleyball M touch football.

STUDENT SERVICES. Aptitude testing, career counseling, employment service for undergraduates, freshman orientation, health services, personal counseling, placement service for graduates, special adviser for adult students, services/facilities for handicapped.

ANNUAL EXPENSES. Tuition and fees: $13,600. **Room and board:** $4,250. **Books and supplies:** $500. **Other expenses:** $600.

FINANCIAL AID. 81% of freshmen, 68% of continuing students receive some form of aid. 69% of grants, 67% of loans, 11% of jobs based on need. 337 enrolled freshmen were judged to have need, all were offered aid. Academic, music/drama scholarships available. **Aid applications:** Closing date April 1; priority given to applications received by March 1; applicants notified on a rolling basis; must reply by May 1. **Additional information:** Application deadline for academic scholarships March 1.

ADDRESS/TELEPHONE. Ronald D. Potier, Director of Admissions, Elizabethtown College, Leffler House, 1 Alpha Drive, Elizabethtown, PA 17022-2298. (717) 361-1400. Fax: (717) 361-1167.

Franklin and Marshall College
Lancaster, Pennsylvania CB code: 2261

Admissions: 58% of applicants accepted
Based on: ••• School record
•• Activities, essay, interview, recommendations, special talents, test scores
Completion: 97% of freshmen end year in good standing
83% graduate, 33% of these enter graduate study

4-year private liberal arts college, coed, historical relationship with United Church of Christ. Founded in 1787. **Accreditation:** Regional. **Undergraduate enrollment:** 984 men, 810 women full time; 17 men, 26 women part time. **Faculty:** 194 total (168 full time), 172 with doctorates or other terminal degrees. **Location:** Suburban campus in small city; 60 miles from Philadelphia. **Calendar:** Semester, limited summer session. **Microcomputers:** 100 located in libraries, classrooms, computer centers, campus-wide network. **Special facilities:** Observatory, planetarium, natural history/science museum, science library, art gallery, retail sales complex, bronze casting foundry.

DEGREES OFFERED. BA. 449 bachelor's degrees awarded in 1992. 5% in area and ethnic studies, 14% business and management, 12% letters/literature, 7% life sciences, 9% physical sciences, 33% social sciences, 5% visual and performing arts.

UNDERGRADUATE MAJORS. Accounting, American studies, anthropology, art history, biology, business administration and management, chemistry, classics, dramatic arts, economics, English, French, geology, German, Greek (classical), history, Latin, mathematics, music, neurosciences, philosophy, physics, political science and government, psychology, religion, sociology, Spanish, studio art.

ACADEMIC PROGRAMS. Accelerated program, double major, honors program, independent study, internships, semester at sea, student-designed major, study abroad, visiting/exchange student program, New York semester, Washington semester, semesters in Paris and at School of Visual Arts in New York City; liberal arts/career combination in engineering, forestry. **Remedial services:** Reduced course load, special counselor, tutoring, writing center, pre enrollment summer program. **Placement/credit:** AP, CLEP Subject, IB, institutional tests; 44 credit hours maximum for bachelor's degree.

ACADEMIC REQUIREMENTS. Freshmen must earn minimum GPA of 1.60 to continue in good standing. 95% of freshmen return for sophomore year. Students must declare major by end of second year. **Graduation requirements:** 128 hours for bachelor's (32 in major). Most students required to take courses in arts/fine arts, English, history, humanities, philosophy/religion, biological/physical sciences, social sciences. **Postgraduate studies:** 10% enter law school, 9% enter medical school, 2% enter MBA programs, 12% enter other graduate study. **Additional information:** 3 interdisciplinary minors offered: Asian studies, women's studies, and environmental studies.

FRESHMAN ADMISSIONS. Selection criteria: School achievement record, test scores, extracurricular activities, counselor's and teacher's recommendation, essay considered. Recommended units include English 4, foreign language 3, mathematics 4, social science 3 and science 3. **Test requirements:** SAT or ACT; score report by February 1. English Composition ACH required. Students in top 10 percent of graduating class not required to submit test scores. Score report by March 1. **Additional information:** Students in top 10% of class may submit 2 graded writing samples in lieu of standardized tests.

1992 FRESHMAN CLASS PROFILE. 1,911 men applied, 1,021 accepted, 262 enrolled; 1,609 women applied, 1,021 accepted, 224 enrolled. 43% were in top tenth of graduating class. **Academic background:** Mid 50% of enrolled freshmen had SAT-V between 500-600, SAT-M between 560-660. 94% submitted SAT scores. **Characteristics:** 34% from in state, 99% live in college housing, 19% have minority backgrounds, 7% are foreign students. Average age is 18.

FALL-TERM APPLICATIONS. $35 fee, may be waived for applicants with need. Closing date February 1; applicants notified on or about April 1; must reply by May 1. Essay required. Interview recommended. Interview required for early decision applicants, strongly recommended for other applicants. Auditions and portfolios are recommended for all students who wish to demonstrate a particular talent. CRDA. Deferred and early admission available. EDP-F. First choice early decision applications accepted between November 15 and January 15. Applicant notified 1 month after receipt of completed application.

STUDENT LIFE. Housing: Dormitories (coed); apartment housing available. Freshmen and sophomores required to live in college housing. French house, co-op house, arts house, International House are available to upperclass students. **Activities:** Student government, magazine, radio, student newspaper, television, yearbook, choral groups, concert band, dance, drama, jazz band, music ensembles, musical theater, pep band, symphony orchestra, Association of Spanish Cultures, Black Student Union, East Asian Society, Catholic Campus Community, Hillel, Intervarsity Christian Fellowship, Habitat for Humanity, Voices for Women, Peace Forum, Coalition for Choice. **Additional information:** Although the College no longer recognizes or supports Greek organizations, 9 fraternities and 3 sororities remain as independent social organizations.

ATHLETICS. NCAA. **Intercollegiate:** Baseball M, basketball, cross-country, field hockey W, football M, golf, lacrosse, soccer, softball W, squash, swimming, tennis, track and field, volleyball W, wrestling M. **Intramural:** Archery, badminton, basketball, bowling, cross-country, football M, racquetball, soccer, softball, squash, swimming, table tennis, tennis, track and field, volleyball, wrestling M. **Clubs:** Badminton, fencing, ice hockey, rowing, rugby, sailing, volleyball, cricket, skiing, water polo.

STUDENT SERVICES. Aptitude testing, career counseling, employment service for undergraduates, freshman orientation, health services, on-campus day care, personal counseling, placement service for graduates, services/facilities for handicapped.

ANNUAL EXPENSES. Tuition and fees: Comprehensive fee: $23,655. **Books and supplies:** $590. **Other expenses:** $880.

FINANCIAL AID. 60% of freshmen, 61% of continuing students receive some form of aid. 97% of grants, 89% of loans, 55% of jobs based on need. 239 enrolled freshmen were judged to have need, all were offered aid. Academic scholarships available. **Aid applications:** Closing date March 1; applicants notified on or about April 5; must reply by May 1.

ADDRESS/TELEPHONE. Peter W. Van Buskirk, Director of Admissions, Franklin and Marshall College, PO Box 3003, Lancaster, PA 17604-3003. (717) 291-3951. Fax: (717) 291-4389.

Gannon University

Erie, Pennsylvania CB code: 2270

Admissions: 77% of applicants accepted
Based on: ••• School record
•• Essay, recommendations, test scores
• Activities, interview
Completion: 50% graduate, 22% of these enter graduate study

4-year private university and liberal arts college, coed, affiliated with Roman Catholic Church. Founded in 1925. **Accreditation:** Regional. **Undergraduate enrollment:** 1,253 men, 1,366 women full time; 380 men, 636 women part time. **Graduate enrollment:** 67 men, 70 women full time; 210 men, 315 women part time. **Faculty:** 345 total (217 full time), 125 with doctorates or other terminal degrees. **Location:** Urban campus in small city; 125 miles from Pittsburgh, 100 miles from Cleveland, Ohio. **Calendar:** Semester, limited summer session. Graduate summer courses available. Saturday classes. **Microcomputers:** 250 located in libraries, classrooms, computer centers. **Special facilities:** Erie Historical Museum and Planetarium.

DEGREES OFFERED. AA, AS, BA, BS, MA, MS, MBA, MEd. 200 associate degrees awarded in 1992. 8% in business and management, 12% engineering technologies, 72% health sciences, 5% law. 577 bachelor's degrees awarded. 10% in business and management, 9% business/office and marketing/distribution, 8% teacher education, 10% engineering, 15% engineering technologies, 15% health sciences, 12% physical sciences, 6% social sciences. Graduate degrees offered in 21 major fields of study.

UNDERGRADUATE MAJORS. Associate: Accounting, business administration and management, business and management, business and office, early childhood education, electrical technology, engineering and engineering-related technologies, funeral services/mortuary science, humanities, industrial technology, legal assistant/paralegal, legal secretary, marketing management, medical records technology, medical secretary, nursing, office supervision and management, radiograph medical technology, recreation therapy, respiratory therapy, robotics, secretarial and related programs. **Bachelor's:** Accounting, anthropology, art education, bilingual/bicultural education, biology, business administration and management, business and management, business economics, business education, chemical engineering, chemistry, clinical laboratory science, communications, computer and information sciences, criminal justice studies, dramatic arts, early childhood education, earth sciences, economics, education, electrical technology, electrical/electronics/communications engineering, elementary education, engineering and engineering-related technologies, English, English education, finance, fine arts, foreign languages (multiple emphasis), foreign languages education, French, funeral services/mortuary science, German, history, humanities and social sciences, industrial distribution, industrial engineering, industrial technology, information sciences and systems, international business management, international studies, journalism, legal assistant/paralegal, liberal/general studies, management information systems, management science, marketing and distribution, marketing management, mathematics, mathematics education, mechanical engineering, medical laboratory technologies, military science (Army), nursing, occupational therapy, philosophy, physician's assistant, physics, political science and government, predentistry, prelaw, premedicine, prepharmacy, preveterinary, psychology, radio/television broadcasting, recreation therapy, respiratory therapy, science education, secondary education, social science education, social sciences, social work, sociology, Spanish, special education, teaching English as a second language/foreign language, theological studies.

ACADEMIC PROGRAMS. 2-year transfer program, accelerated program, cooperative education, double major, dual enrollment of high school students, honors program, independent study, internships, study abroad, teacher preparation, weekend college, Washington semester, cross-registration; combined bachelor's/graduate program in business administration. **Remedial services:** Learning center, reduced course load, remedial instruction, special counselor, tutoring, Commonwealth Academic Achievement Program, a general studies program to bring academically capable students to college-level work. **ROTC:** Army. **Placement/credit:** AP, CLEP General and Subject, institutional tests; 40 credit hours maximum for bachelor's degree.

ACADEMIC REQUIREMENTS. Freshmen must earn minimum GPA of 2.0 to continue in good standing. 73% of freshmen return for sophomore year. Students must declare major on application. **Graduation requirements:** 64 hours for associate, 128 hours for bachelor's. Most students required to take courses in arts/fine arts, English, foreign languages, history, humanities, mathematics, philosophy/religion, biological/physical sciences, social sciences. **Postgraduate studies:** 4% enter law school, 3% enter medical school, 5% enter MBA programs, 10% enter other graduate study.

FRESHMAN ADMISSIONS. Selection criteria: High school record including course selection, GPA, class rank, standardized test scores, recommendations, personal statement and interview considered in this order of importance. **High school preparation:** 16 units required; 18 recommended. Required and recommended units include English 4-4, mathematics 3-4, social science 4 and science 3-4. Foreign language 2 recommended. The College of Health Sciences and College of Science and Engineering require at least 3 units mathematics and science, 4 preferred. School of Business Administration requires at least 3 units mathematics, 4 preferred. Some programs require 2 units foreign language. **Test requirements:** SAT or ACT; score report by July 1.

1992 FRESHMAN CLASS PROFILE. 1,017 men applied, 761 accepted, 280 enrolled; 1,041 women applied, 830 accepted, 350 enrolled. 15% were in top tenth and 38% were in top quarter of graduating class. **Academic background:** Mid 50% of enrolled freshmen had SAT-V between 410-510, SAT-M between 470-580; ACT composite between 21-24. 91% submitted SAT scores, 22% submitted ACT scores. **Characteristics:** 81% from in state, 63% live in college housing, 8% have minority backgrounds, 1% are foreign students, 10% join fraternities/sororities. Average age is 21.

FALL-TERM APPLICATIONS. $25 fee, may be waived for applicants with need. No closing date; applicants notified on a rolling basis; must reply by May 1 or within 3 weeks if notified thereafter. Interview recommended. Essay recommended. CRDA. Deferred and early admission available.

STUDENT LIFE. Housing: Dormitories (men, women); apartment, fraternity, sorority housing available. **Activities:** Student government, magazine, radio, student newspaper, television, yearbook, choral groups, drama, musical theater, pep band, symphony orchestra, fraternities, sororities, Catholic Services Organization.

ATHLETICS. NCAA. **Intercollegiate:** Baseball M, basketball, cross-country M, diving, football M, golf M, ice hockey M, soccer, softball W, swimming, tennis, volleyball W, wrestling M. **Intramural:** Badminton, basketball, bowling, cross-country M, diving, football M, golf M, handball M, racquetball, sailing, skiing, soccer, softball W, swimming, table tennis, tennis, volleyball, wrestling M. **Clubs:** Hockey M volleyballM.

STUDENT SERVICES. Aptitude testing, career counseling, employment service for undergraduates, freshman orientation, health services, personal counseling, placement service for graduates, special adviser for adult students, veterans counselor, services/facilities for handicapped.

ANNUAL EXPENSES. Tuition and fees: $9,838. **Room and board:** $4,040. **Books and supplies:** $508. **Other expenses:** $911.

FINANCIAL AID. 86% of freshmen, 86% of continuing students receive some form of aid. 95% of grants, 88% of loans, 96% of jobs based on need. 544 enrolled freshmen were judged to have need, all were offered aid. Academic, athletic scholarships available. **Aid applications:** No closing date; priority given to applications received by March 1; applicants notified on a rolling basis beginning on or about February 1; must reply within 30 days.

ADDRESS/TELEPHONE. Joyce Scheid-Gilman, Director of Freshmen/Transfer Admissions, Gannon University, University Square, Erie, PA 16541-0001. (814) 871-7240. (800) GANNON U. Fax: (814) 452-6277.

Geneva College
Beaver Falls, Pennsylvania — CB code: 2273

Admissions: 81% of applicants accepted
Based on:
••• School record, test scores
•• Essay, interview, recommendations
• Activities, special talents
Completion: 86% of freshmen end year in good standing
55% graduate, 14% of these enter graduate study

4-year private liberal arts college, coed, affiliated with Reformed Presbyterian Church of North America. Founded in 1848. **Accreditation:** Regional. **Undergraduate enrollment:** 637 men, 637 women full time; 146 men, 121 women part time. **Graduate enrollment:** 4 men, 10 women full time; 12 men, 27 women part time. **Faculty:** 102 total (51 full time), 34 with doctorates or other terminal degrees. **Location:** Suburban campus in large town; 35 miles from Pittsburgh. **Calendar:** Semester, extensive summer session. **Microcomputers:** 100 located in libraries, computer centers. **Special facilities:** Collection of artifacts and records of Pittsburgh steel industry. **Additional facts:** Education through Biblically based programs and services.

DEGREES OFFERED. AS, BA, BS, MA. 2 associate degrees awarded in 1992. 50% in business and management, 50% business/office and marketing/distribution. 319 bachelor's degrees awarded. 46% in business and management, 17% teacher education, 6% engineering, 7% physical sciences, 5% psychology. Graduate degrees offered in 1 major field of study.

UNDERGRADUATE MAJORS. Associate: Business administration and management, engineering. **Bachelor's:** Accounting, applied mathematics, aviation management, Bible studies, biology, business and management, business economics, business education, chemical engineering, chemistry, civil engineering, communications, computer and information sciences, counseling psychology, creative writing, economics, education, electrical/electronics/communications engineering, elementary education, engineering, English, English education, English literature, foreign languages education, history, human resources development, industrial engineering, management information systems, mathematics, mathematics education, mechanical engineering, medical laboratory technologies, missionary studies, music, music business management, music education, music performance, philosophy, physical sciences, physics, political science and government, practical nursing, psychology, radio/television broadcasting, science education, secondary education, social studies education, sociology, Spanish, speech, speech correction, speech pathology/audiology, speech/communication/theater education, youth ministries.

ACADEMIC PROGRAMS. Accelerated program, double major, dual enrollment of high school students, honors program, independent study, internships, student-designed major, study abroad, Washington semester, cross-registration, cooperative program in aviation/business administration with Community College of Beaver County; liberal arts/career combination in health sciences. **Remedial services:** Reduced course load, remedial instruction, special counselor, tutoring. **Placement/credit:** AP, CLEP General and Subject, institutional tests; 30 credit hours maximum for bachelor's degree.

ACADEMIC REQUIREMENTS. Freshmen must earn minimum GPA of 2.0 to continue in good standing. 75% of freshmen return for sophomore year. Students must declare major by end of second year. **Graduation requirements:** 63 hours for associate (30 in major), 126 hours for bachelor's (42 in major). Most students required to take courses in English, humanities, philosophy/religion, biological/physical sciences, social sciences.

FRESHMAN ADMISSIONS. Selection criteria: Academic performance and test scores most important. Interview, recommendations, and activities also considered. **High school preparation:** 16 units required. Required units include English 4, foreign language 2, mathematics 2, physical science 1 and social science 3. **Test requirements:** SAT or ACT; score report by August 1.

1992 FRESHMAN CLASS PROFILE. 602 men and women applied, 486 accepted; 131 men enrolled, 116 women enrolled. **Academic background:** Mid 50% of enrolled freshmen had SAT-V between 390-500, SAT-M between 430-550. 86% submitted SAT scores. **Characteristics:** 70% from in state, 62% live in college housing, 6% have minority backgrounds, 1% are foreign students. Average age is 18.

FALL-TERM APPLICATIONS. $15 fee, may be waived for applicants with need. No closing date; priority given to applications received by July 31; applicants notified on a rolling basis; must reply within 3 weeks. Essay required. Interview recommended. Audition recommended for music applicants. Deferred and early admission available.

STUDENT LIFE. Housing: Dormitories (men, women). Students must live on campus unless married, commuting, or over the age of 24. Apartments for married graduate students available to rent. **Activities:** Student government, magazine, radio, student newspaper, television, yearbook, video yearbook, choral groups, concert band, drama, jazz band, marching band, music ensembles, musical theater, pep band, forensics, African-American student union, international student club, Christian ministry organizations, community service club. **Additional information:** Smoking, drinking, social or ballroom dancing not permitted on campus.

ATHLETICS. NAIA. **Intercollegiate:** Baseball M, basketball, cross-country, football M, soccer, softball W, tennis, track and field, volleyball W. **Intramural:** Basketball, bowling, ice hockey M, racquetball, soccer, softball, table tennis, tennis, volleyball. **Clubs:** Skiing.

STUDENT SERVICES. Aptitude testing, career counseling, employment service for undergraduates, freshman orientation, health services, personal counseling, placement service for graduates, special adviser for adult students, services/facilities for handicapped.

ANNUAL EXPENSES. Tuition and fees (1992-93): $8,164. **Room and board:** $3,980. **Books and supplies:** $500. **Other expenses:** $1,100.

FINANCIAL AID. 91% of freshmen, 90% of continuing students receive some form of aid. 81% of grants, 86% of loans, 31% of jobs based on need. 230 enrolled freshmen were judged to have need, 215 were offered aid. Academic, music/drama, religious affiliation scholarships available. **Aid applications:** No closing date; priority given to applications received by April 15; applicants notified on a rolling basis beginning on or about March 1; must reply within 3 weeks. **Additional information:** Academic scholarships to all applicants who rank in top 10% with SAT of 1000 or ACT of 24 with a 3.0 GPA (SAT of 1100 or ACT of 26, with a 3.0 GPA).Scholarships for National Merit finalists and semifinalists. Grants for members of controlling church.

ADDRESS/TELEPHONE. Dr. William J. Katip, Vice President for Enrollment Management, Geneva College, 3200 College Avenue, Beaver Falls, PA 15010-3599. (412) 847-6500. (800) 847-8255. Fax: (412) 847-5017.

Gettysburg College
Gettysburg, Pennsylvania — CB code: 2275

Admissions: 69% of applicants accepted
Based on:
••• Recommendations, school record, test scores
•• Activities, essay, special talents
• Interview, religious affiliation/commitment
Completion: 90% of freshmen end year in good standing
80% graduate, 40% of these enter graduate study

4-year private liberal arts college, coed, affiliated with Lutheran Church. Founded in 1832. **Accreditation:** Regional. **Undergraduate enrollment:** 1,065 men, 1,043 women full time; 8 men, 20 women part time. **Faculty:** 193 total (154 full time), 156 with doctorates or other terminal degrees. **Location:** Suburban campus in small town; 36 miles from Harrisburg, 80 miles from Washington, D.C. **Calendar:** Semester, limited summer session. **Microcomputers:** 500 located in dormitories, libraries, classrooms, computer centers, campus-wide network. **Special facilities:** Observatory, planetarium, facilities for fine and performing arts (including art gallery), intercultural resources center, women's resource center.

DEGREES OFFERED. BA, BS. 490 bachelor's degrees awarded in 1992. 18% in business and management, 5% languages, 10% letters/literature, 6% life sciences, 6% psychology, 31% social sciences.

UNDERGRADUATE MAJORS. Accounting, Afro-American (black) studies, American literature, American studies, anthropology, applied mathematics, art history, Asian studies, biochemistry, biological and physical sciences, biology, business administration and management, business economics, chemistry, classics, communications, comparative literature, computer and information sciences, dramatic arts, economics, elementary education, engineering, English, English education, English literature, environmental science, European studies, foreign languages education, French, German,

Greek (classical), health education, history, human resources development, humanities, humanities and social sciences, international business management, international relations, international studies, Latin, liberal/general studies, mathematics, mathematics education, music, music education, peace studies, philosophy, physical education, physics, political science and government, predentistry, prelaw, premedicine, prepharmacy, preveterinary, psychology, religion, science education, secondary education, small business management and ownership, social science education, social studies education, sociology, Spanish, sports medicine, statistics, studio art, women's studies.

ACADEMIC PROGRAMS. Accelerated program, double major, honors program, independent study, internships, semester at sea, student-designed major, study abroad, teacher preparation, United Nations semester, Washington semester, cross-registration; liberal arts/career combination in engineering, forestry. **Remedial services:** Tutoring, writing center. **Placement/credit:** AP, IB, institutional tests.

ACADEMIC REQUIREMENTS. Freshmen must earn minimum GPA of 2.0 to continue in good standing. 89% of freshmen return for sophomore year. Students must declare major by end of second year. **Graduation requirements:** 123 hours for bachelor's (35 in major). Most students required to take courses in arts/fine arts, English, foreign languages, history, humanities, philosophy/religion, biological/physical sciences, social sciences. **Postgraduate studies:** 6% enter law school, 4% enter medical school, 10% enter MBA programs, 20% enter other graduate study.

FRESHMAN ADMISSIONS. Selection criteria: Academic record, test scores, recommendations, activities. Special consideration given to children of alumni, minority applicants, and to students who represent geographic and cultural diversity. **High school preparation:** 16 units recommended. Recommended units include English 4, foreign language 3, mathematics 3, social science 3 and science 3. Well-rounded academic preparation required. Participation in accelerated, enriched, and advanced placement courses desirable. **Test requirements:** SAT or ACT; score report by February 15.

1992 FRESHMAN CLASS PROFILE. 1,938 men applied, 1,269 accepted, 282 enrolled; 1,658 women applied, 1,197 accepted, 290 enrolled. 93% had high school GPA of 3.0 or higher, 7% between 2.0 and 2.99. 43% were in top tenth and 75% were in top quarter of graduating class. **Academic background:** Mid 50% of enrolled freshmen had SAT-V between 500-580, SAT-M between 550-640; ACT composite between 24-28. 95% submitted SAT scores, 5% submitted ACT scores. **Characteristics:** 25% from in state, 99% live in college housing, 8% have minority backgrounds, 4% are foreign students, 50% join fraternities/sororities. Average age is 18.

FALL-TERM APPLICATIONS. $35 fee, may be waived for applicants with need. Closing date February 15; applicants notified on or about April 1; must reply by May 1. Audition required for music applicants. Essay required. Interview recommended. Portfolio recommended for art applicants. CRDA. Deferred and early admission available. EDP-F.

STUDENT LIFE. Housing: Dormitories (men, women, coed); apartment, fraternity housing available. Special interest houses available. **Activities:** Student government, film, magazine, radio, student newspaper, television, yearbook, scholarly review, choral groups, concert band, dance, drama, jazz band, marching band, music ensembles, musical theater, symphony orchestra, fraternities, sororities, model United Nations, Intercollegiate Conference on Government, Young Republicans, Young Democrats, Black Student Union, Chapel Council program, Migrant Worker program, Fellowship of Christian Athletes, Hillel, Alpha Phi Omega service organization, International Student Group, Women's Action Group. **Additional information:** Of students who commute, 1% commute from home and 14% live in off-campus housing.

ATHLETICS. NCAA. **Intercollegiate:** Baseball M, basketball, cross-country, field hockey W, football M, golf, lacrosse, soccer, softball W, swimming, tennis, track and field, volleyball W, wrestling M. **Intramural:** Badminton, basketball, boxing M, gymnastics, horseback riding, ice hockey M, rugby M, skiing, soccer, softball, swimming, table tennis, tennis, volleyball, water polo M.

STUDENT SERVICES. Career counseling, employment service for undergraduates, freshman orientation, health services, personal counseling, placement service for graduates, services/facilities for handicapped.

ANNUAL EXPENSES. Tuition and fees: $18,870. **Room and board:** $4,090. **Books and supplies:** $300. **Other expenses:** $500.

FINANCIAL AID. 42% of freshmen, 38% of continuing students receive some form of aid. 99% of grants, 52% of loans, 50% of jobs based on need. 290 enrolled freshmen were judged to have need, all were offered aid. **Aid applications:** Closing date February 15; applicants notified on or about April 10; must reply by May 1.

ADDRESS/TELEPHONE. Delwin K. Gustafson, Dean of Admissions, Gettysburg College, Eisenhower House, Gettysburg, PA 17325-1484. (717) 337-6100. (800) 431-0803. Fax: (717) 337-6145.

Gratz College
Melrose Park, Pennsylvania — CB code: 2280

4-year private liberal arts college, coed, affiliated with Jewish faith. Founded in 1895. **Accreditation:** Regional. **Undergraduate enrollment:** 2 men, 6 women full time; 15 men, 55 women part time. **Graduate enrollment:** 8 men, 20 women full time; 19 men, 95 women part time. **Faculty:** 19 total (8 full time), 19 with doctorates or other terminal degrees. **Location:** Suburban campus in very large city; 12 miles from downtown Philadelphia. **Calendar:** Semester, limited summer session. **Special facilities:** Jewish music library and rare book collection, oral history Holocaust archives, Holocaust Awareness Museum. **Additional facts:** Continuing education courses in locations throughout Delaware Valley.

DEGREES OFFERED. BA, MA. 5 bachelor's degrees awarded in 1992. 100% in area and ethnic studies. Graduate degrees offered in 4 major fields of study.

UNDERGRADUATE MAJORS. Jewish studies, Middle Eastern studies.

ACADEMIC PROGRAMS. Independent study, internships, study abroad, cross-registration, double master's programs in Jewish education/Jewish music/Jewish studies. **Remedial services:** Reduced course load, remedial instruction, tutoring. **Placement/credit:** Institutional tests; 16 credit hours maximum for bachelor's degree.

ACADEMIC REQUIREMENTS. No policy requiring minimum GPA; records of students having academic difficulty are reviewed individually. 50% of freshmen return for sophomore year. **Graduation requirements:** 78 hours for bachelor's. Most students required to take courses in arts/fine arts, foreign languages, history, humanities, philosophy/religion, social sciences. **Additional information:** All education programs relate specifically to the Jewish school. For bachelor's in Jewish studies 40 liberal arts credits from another accredited college or university required.

FRESHMAN ADMISSIONS. Selection criteria: Open admissions.

1992 FRESHMAN CLASS PROFILE. 2 men, 4 women enrolled. **Characteristics:** 50% from in state, 100% commute, 50% are foreign students. Average age is 26.

FALL-TERM APPLICATIONS. $25 fee. No closing date; applicants notified on a rolling basis. Essay required. Interview recommended. Deferred and early admission available.

STUDENT LIFE. Activities: Choral groups, dance.

STUDENT SERVICES. Career counseling, on-campus day care, personal counseling, placement service for graduates, special adviser for adult students, services/facilities for handicapped.

ANNUAL EXPENSES. Tuition and fees (1992-93): $4,200. **Books and supplies:** $600.

FINANCIAL AID. 38% of freshmen, 30% of continuing students receive some form of aid. All grants based on need. **Aid applications:** No closing date; priority given to applications received by September 15; applicants notified on a rolling basis beginning on or about November 1. **Additional information:** Institutional work-study program available.

ADDRESS/TELEPHONE. Naomi Zvirman, Director Enrollment Management, Gratz College, Old York Road and Melrose Avenue, Melrose Park, PA 19126. (215) 635-7300. Fax: (215) 635-7320.

Grove City College
Grove City, Pennsylvania — CB code: 2277

Admissions: 43% of applicants accepted
Based on:
••• School record
•• Activities, essay, recommendations, special talents, test scores
• Interview, religious affiliation/commitment
Completion: 85% of freshmen end year in good standing
78% graduate, 15% of these enter graduate study

4-year private liberal arts college, coed, affiliated with Presbyterian Church (USA). Founded in 1876. **Accreditation:** Regional. **Undergraduate enrollment:** 1,095 men, 1,084 women full time; 20 men, 18 women part time. **Faculty:** 140 total (116 full time), 69 with doctorates or other terminal degrees. **Location:** Rural campus in small town; 60 miles from Pittsburgh. **Calendar:** Semester. **Microcomputers:** 155 located in libraries, classrooms, computer centers. **Special facilities:** J. Howard Pew Fine Arts Center.

DEGREES OFFERED. BA, BS. 484 bachelor's degrees awarded in 1992. 35% in business and management, 6% communications, 13% teacher education, 7% engineering, 6% life sciences, 6% psychology, 9% social sciences.

UNDERGRADUATE MAJORS. Accounting, American literature, biochemistry, biology, business administration and management, business and office, chemistry, Christian ministries, communications, computer and information sciences, economics, electrical/electronics/communications engineering, elementary education, English education, English literature, foreign languages education, French, history, international business management, management information systems, marketing and distribution, marketing management, mathematics, mathematics education, mechanical engineering, molecular biology, music, music business management, music education, philosophy, physics, political science and government, predentistry, prelaw, premedicine, preveterinary, psychology, religion, science education, secondary education, social science education, social studies education, Spanish.

ACADEMIC PROGRAMS. Accelerated program, double major, dual enrollment of high school students, honors program, independent study, internships, student-designed major, study abroad, teacher preparation. **Remedial services:** Reduced course load, tutoring. **Placement/credit:** AP, CLEP Subject.

ACADEMIC REQUIREMENTS. Freshmen must earn minimum GPA of 2.0 to continue in good standing. 83% of freshmen return for sophomore year. Students must declare major by end of second year. **Graduation requirements:** 128 hours for bachelor's (30 in major). Most students required to take courses in English, foreign languages, humanities, mathematics, philosophy/religion, biological/physical sciences, social sciences. **Postgraduate studies:** 2% enter law school, 2% enter medical school, 2% enter MBA programs, 9% enter other graduate study. **Additional information:** All students required to complete 3-year interdisciplinary humanities sequence which includes religion, philosophy, history, philosophy of science, literature, art, and music.

FRESHMAN ADMISSIONS. Selection criteria: High school record, GPA or class rank, test scores, recommendations, interview, character, and extracurricular activities. **High school preparation:** 15 units recommended. Recommended units include biological science 1, English 4, foreign language 3, mathematics 3, physical science 1 and social science 2. Engineering, science, and mathematics applicants must have 4 units in mathematics and 4 in science. **Test requirements:** SAT or ACT; score report by March 1.

1992 FRESHMAN CLASS PROFILE. 1,283 men applied, 588 accepted, 310 enrolled; 1,321 women applied, 539 accepted, 308 enrolled. 51% were in top tenth and 82% were in top quarter of graduating class. **Academic background:** Mid 50% of enrolled freshmen had SAT-V between 470-570, SAT-M between 550-650; ACT composite between 23-28. 88% submitted SAT scores, 26% submitted ACT scores. **Characteristics:** 63% from in state, 87% live in college housing, 1% have minority backgrounds, 1% are foreign students, 44% join fraternities/sororities. Average age is 18.

FALL-TERM APPLICATIONS. $20 fee. Closing date February 15; priority given to applications received by November 15; applicants notified on or about March 15; must reply by May 1. Audition required for music applicants. Essay required. Interview recommended. Deferred and early admission available. EDP-F. Early decision applications close November 15; applicants notified on December 1.

STUDENT LIFE. Housing: Dormitories (men, women). Dormitory housing required all 4 years, except for those commuting from home. **Activities:** Student government, radio, student newspaper, yearbook, literary journal, choral groups, concert band, dance, drama, jazz band, marching band, music ensembles, musical theater, pep band, symphony orchestra, fraternities, sororities, many Christian, political, and social service organizations. **Additional information:** Alcohol and resident freshmen's cars not permitted on campus. Chapel program consists of lectures, vespers, and seminars; students must attend 16 events per semester.

ATHLETICS. NCAA. **Intercollegiate:** Baseball M, basketball, cross-country, diving, football M, golf, soccer, softball W, swimming, tennis, track and field, volleyball W. **Intramural:** Basketball, bowling, golf M, handball M, racquetball, soccer M, softball, swimming W, tennis, volleyball.

STUDENT SERVICES. Career counseling, freshman orientation, health services, personal counseling, placement service for graduates, services/facilities for handicapped.

ANNUAL EXPENSES. Tuition and fees: $4,976. **Room and board:** $2,894. **Books and supplies:** $525. **Other expenses:** $350.

FINANCIAL AID. 53% of freshmen, 50% of continuing students receive some form of aid. 64% of grants, 71% of loans, 63% of jobs based on need. 252 enrolled freshmen were judged to have need, 237 were offered aid. Academic, leadership scholarships available. **Aid applications:** Closing date May 1; applicants notified on or about June 1. **Additional information:** Institutional aid applications required for institutional scholarships, loans, and student employment.

ADDRESS/TELEPHONE. Jeffrey C. Mincey, Director of Admissions, Grove City College, 100 Campus Drive, Grove City, PA 16127-2104. (412) 458-2100.

Gwynedd-Mercy College
Gwynedd Valley, Pennsylvania CB code: 2278

Admissions: 60% of applicants accepted
Based on: ••• School record, test scores
• Activities, interview, recommendations
Completion: 92% of freshmen end year in good standing
81% graduate

4-year private college of arts and sciences, coed, affiliated with Roman Catholic Church. Founded in 1948. **Accreditation:** Regional. **Undergraduate enrollment:** 134 men, 560 women full time; 216 men, 927 women part time. **Graduate enrollment:** 1 man, 17 women full time; 15 men, 146 women part time. **Faculty:** 173 total (94 full time), 38 with doctorates or other terminal degrees. **Location:** Suburban campus in large town; 20 miles from downtown Philadelphia. **Calendar:** Semester, limited summer session. **Microcomputers:** 61 located in computer centers. **Special facilities:** Extensive Abraham Lincoln-era collection and center for creative studies in library, nursery laboratory school for early childhood education majors. **Additional facts:** Affiliated with the Religious Sisters of Mercy.

DEGREES OFFERED. AA, AS, BA, BS, MS, MEd. 153 associate degrees awarded in 1992. 6% in business and management, 58% health sciences, 29% allied health, 5% multi/interdisciplinary studies. 218 bachelor's degrees awarded. 24% in business and management, 7% computer sciences, 24% teacher education, 12% health sciences, 8% allied health, 7% letters/literature, 6% psychology. Graduate degrees offered in 3 major fields of study.

UNDERGRADUATE MAJORS. Associate: Accounting, biological and physical sciences, business administration and management, cardiovascular technology, computer programming, liberal/general studies, medical records administration, medical records technology, natural science, nursing, radiation technology, respiratory therapy, respiratory therapy technology. **Bachelor's:** Accounting, basic clinical health sciences, behavioral and social gerontology, biology, business administration and management, business education, clinical laboratory science, computer and information sciences, early childhood education, education of the mentally handicapped, education of the physically handicapped, elementary education, English, english drama, English education, English literature, english media, english/communications, gerontology, health care administration, health sciences, history, junior high education, mathematics, mathematics education, mathematics/computers, medical laboratory technologies, medical records administration, medical records technology, nursing, predentistry, prelaw, premedicine, preveterinary, psychology, science education, secondary education, social studies education, sociology, special education.

ACADEMIC PROGRAMS. Double major, dual enrollment of high school students, internships, teacher preparation. **Remedial services:** Reduced course load, tutoring, basic skills tutoring. **ROTC:** Army. **Placement/credit:** AP, CLEP General and Subject, institutional tests; 30 credit hours maximum for associate degree; 60 credit hours maximum for bachelor's degree.

ACADEMIC REQUIREMENTS. Freshmen must earn minimum GPA of 1.8 to continue in good standing. 78% of freshmen return for sophomore year. Students must declare major on application. **Graduation requirements:** 64 hours for associate (34 in major), 125 hours for bachelor's (60 in major). Most students required to take courses in English, history, humanities, mathematics, philosophy/religion, biological/physical sciences, social sciences. **Additional information:** Many academic programs structured to allow students to obtain associate degree before bachelor's degree. Teacher certification programs available in biology, business, English, mathematics, social studies, elementary, early childhood and special education.

FRESHMAN ADMISSIONS. Selection criteria: School achievement record most important, followed by test scores, recommendations, and extracurricular activities. Nursing program very competitive. **High school preparation:** 16 units required. Required and recommended units include English 4, mathematics 3, social science 1 and science 3. Foreign language 2 recommended. Chemistry required for applicants to nursing, cardiovascular, biology, medical technology programs. Biology required for cardiovascular, health records programs. Physics required for radiation therapy, medical technology, biology programs. Chemistry or physics required for respiratory therapy. **Test requirements:** SAT or ACT (SAT preferred); score report by July 15. **Additional information:** Study of English as a second language available prior to admission.

1992 FRESHMAN CLASS PROFILE. 73 men applied, 38 accepted, 23 enrolled; 409 women applied, 252 accepted, 79 enrolled. 17% were in top tenth and 58% were in top quarter of graduating class. **Academic background:** Mid 50% of enrolled freshmen had SAT-V between 410-500, SAT-M between 410-480. 96% submitted SAT scores. **Characteristics:** 94% from in state, 65% commute, 20% have minority backgrounds, 2% are foreign students. Average age is 25.

FALL-TERM APPLICATIONS. $25 fee, may be waived for applicants with need. No closing date; priority given to applications received by January 1; applicants notified on a rolling basis; must reply within 8 weeks. Interview recommended. Interview required for allied health applicants. Deferred and early admission available. Nursing program usually filled by February 1.

STUDENT LIFE. Housing: Dormitories (coed). **Activities:** Student government, magazine, student newspaper, yearbook, choral groups, drama, business society, honor societies, Mercy Corps, resident council, commuter club, education club, peer counseling, foreign student organization, psychology/sociology club, campus ministry.

ATHLETICS. NAIA. **Intercollegiate:** Basketball, cross-country, field hockey W, golf M, lacrosse W, tennis, volleyball W. **Intramural:** Volleyball.

STUDENT SERVICES. Aptitude testing, career counseling, employment service for undergraduates, freshman orientation, health services, on-campus day care, personal counseling, placement service for graduates, special adviser for adult students, peer counseling, services/facilities for handicapped.

ANNUAL EXPENSES. Tuition and fees: $10,200. Tuition and fees for nursing and allied health programs is $10,960. **Room and board:** $5,250. **Books and supplies:** $500. **Other expenses:** $600.

FINANCIAL AID. 82% of freshmen, 91% of continuing students receive some form of aid. 92% of grants, 71% of loans, 74% of jobs based on need. Academic, leadership, alumni affiliation scholarships available. **Aid**

applications: No closing date; priority given to applications received by March 15; applicants notified on a rolling basis beginning on or about March 20; must reply within 4 weeks. Applicants notified after May 1 must reply within 2 weeks.

ADDRESS/TELEPHONE. Marjorie S. DeSimone, M.A, Dean of Admissions, Gwynedd-Mercy College, Sumneytown Pike, Gwynedd Valley, PA 19437. (215) 646-7300 ext. 510. (800) DIAL-GMC. Fax: (215) 641-5596.

Hahnemann University School of Health Sciences and Humanities

Philadelphia, Pennsylvania — CB code: 2306

Admissions:	39% of applicants accepted
Based on:	••• Interview, school record
	•• Essay, recommendations, test scores
	• Activities
Completion:	90% of freshmen end year in good standing
	25% enter graduate study

4-year private health science, nursing college, coed. Founded in 1848. **Accreditation:** Regional. **Undergraduate enrollment:** 208 men, 461 women full time; 54 men, 195 women part time. **Faculty:** 595 total (165 full time). **Location:** Urban campus in very large city; 60 miles from Atlantic City, New Jersey, 110 miles from New York City. **Calendar:** Semester, limited summer session. **Microcomputers:** 74 located in libraries, computer centers. **Special facilities:** Art gallery, Truex Anatomy Museum. **Additional facts:** Undergraduate college part of large teaching hospital. Nontraditional campus environment in Center City, Philadelphia, with cultural, historical, art, and entertainment facilities.

DEGREES OFFERED. AA, AS, BS, MA, MS, PhD. 120 associate degrees awarded in 1992. 100% in allied health. 90 bachelor's degrees awarded. 100% in allied health. Graduate degrees offered in 21 major fields of study.

UNDERGRADUATE MAJORS. Associate: Cardiovascular perfusion, emergency medical technologies, humanities and social sciences, medical laboratory technologies, mental health/human services, nursing, physical therapy assistant, physician's assistant, radiograph medical technology. **Bachelor's:** Cardiovascular perfusion, emergency medical technologies, health sciences and society, medical laboratory technologies, mental health/human services, nursing, occupational and environmental health, physician's assistant, premedicine.

ACADEMIC PROGRAMS. Cooperative education, independent study. **Remedial services:** Reduced course load, remedial instruction, special counselor, tutoring, Pre-entrance diagnostic examinations, HEART. **Placement/credit:** AP, CLEP Subject, institutional tests; 20 credit hours maximum for bachelor's degree.

ACADEMIC REQUIREMENTS. Freshmen must earn minimum GPA of 2.0 to continue in good standing. 88% of freshmen return for sophomore year. Students must declare major on application. **Graduation requirements:** 60 hours for associate, 120 hours for bachelor's. Most students required to take courses in computer science, English, humanities, mathematics, biological/physical sciences, social sciences. **Postgraduate studies:** 30% from 2-year programs enter 4-year programs.

FRESHMAN ADMISSIONS. Selection criteria: Admissions criteria vary by program and include SAT or ACT test scores, references, class rank, course of study, high school GPA, and personal interviews. **High school preparation:** 16 units required. Required and recommended units include biological science 2, English 4, mathematics 2, physical science 1 and social science 3. Foreign language 2 recommended. Most programs require biology, chemistry, mathematics, sometimes physics, and 6 electives. Applicants to bachelor's nursing program must be RNs or have pending licenses. Physician assistant program applicants must be out of high school at least 2 years at time of matriculation. Applicants to cardiovascular perfusion technology program must have completed 45 hours for associate of science degree and 60 hours for bachelor of science. **Test requirements:** SAT or ACT; score report by June 1. SAT or ACT scores required for associate degree nursing and physician assistant programs unless 30 semester hours or 40 quarter hours completed at time of application. Scores not required for other associate of science programs if applicant out of high school for at least 5 years.

1992 FRESHMAN CLASS PROFILE. 80 men applied, 37 accepted, 42 enrolled; 285 women applied, 107 accepted, 90 enrolled. **Characteristics:** 90% commute. Average age is 27.

FALL-TERM APPLICATIONS. $25 fee, may be waived for applicants with need. No closing date; priority given to applications received by March 1; applicants notified on a rolling basis; must reply within 20 days. Essay required. Interview requirements vary by program. Deferred admission available. Applications for all programs accepted until classes are filled. Applicants encouraged to apply early for nursing and radiologic technology programs.

STUDENT LIFE. Housing: Dormitories (coed); apartment housing available. One building exclusively for student housing. **Activities:** Student government, magazine, student newspaper, yearbook, Newman Club, Hillel, Minority Student Association.

ATHLETICS. Intramural: Basketball, football, racquetball, softball, volleyball.

STUDENT SERVICES. Aptitude testing, career counseling, employment service for undergraduates, freshman orientation, health services, personal counseling, placement service for graduates, services/facilities for handicapped.

ANNUAL EXPENSES. Tuition and fees (1992-93): $8,260. **Room and board:** $4,800 room only. **Books and supplies:** $650. **Other expenses:** $2,500.

FINANCIAL AID. All grants, 83% of loans, all jobs based on need. Academic scholarships available. **Aid applications:** Closing date May 31; priority given to applications received by May 1; applicants notified on or about July 5; must reply by August 5.

ADDRESS/TELEPHONE. Londa Tuzi, Director of Admissions, Hahnemann University School of Health Sciences and Humanities, 201 North 15th Street, Mail Stop 506, Philadelphia, PA 19102-1192. (215) 762-8288. Fax: (215) 246-5347.

Harcum Junior College

Bryn Mawr, Pennsylvania — CB code: 2287

2-year private junior college, women only. Founded in 1915. **Accreditation:** Regional. **Undergraduate enrollment:** 44 men, 539 women full time; 47 men, 168 women part time. **Faculty:** 91 total (37 full time), 8 with doctorates or other terminal degrees. **Location:** Suburban campus in large town; 10 miles from Philadelphia. **Calendar:** Semester, limited summer session. Extensive evening/early morning classes. **Microcomputers:** Located in classrooms, computer centers. **Additional facts:** Men in limited number of programs, primarily animal sciences, allied health, and continuing education.

DEGREES OFFERED. AA, AS. 193 associate degrees awarded in 1992. 24% in business/office and marketing/distribution, 57% allied health, 8% multi/interdisciplinary studies, 10% visual and performing arts.

UNDERGRADUATE MAJORS. Advertising, allied health, animal sciences, business and management, business and office, business computer/console/peripheral equipment operation, business data processing and related programs, communications, computer and information sciences, dental assistant, dental hygiene, early childhood education, education of exceptional children, equestrian science, fashion design, fashion merchandising, fine arts, graphic design, hotel/motel and restaurant management, illustration design, interior design, legal assistant/paralegal, legal secretary, liberal/general studies, medical assistant, medical laboratory technologies, occupational therapy assistant, office supervision and management, physical therapy assistant, recreation therapy, retailing, secretarial and related programs, social sciences, teacher aide, tourism, veterinarian's assistant.

ACADEMIC PROGRAMS. 2-year transfer program, double major, internships, study abroad. **Remedial services:** Learning center, preadmission summer program, reduced course load, remedial instruction, special counselor, tutoring, study skills course. **Placement/credit:** AP, CLEP General and Subject, institutional tests.

ACADEMIC REQUIREMENTS. Freshmen must earn minimum GPA of 2.0 to continue in good standing. 75% of freshmen return for sophomore year. Students must declare major on enrollment. **Graduation requirements:** 64 hours for associate (60 in major). Most students required to take courses in computer science, English, humanities, mathematics, social sciences.

FRESHMAN ADMISSIONS. Selection criteria: School record and recommendation of primary importance. Required units for veterinarian's assistant, laboratory animal science, dental hygiene, and physical therapy assistant programs include 2 algebra, geometry, biology, chemistry. Chemistry required for medical technician program. **Test requirements:** SAT; score report by June 1. SAT required for admission to veterinarian's assistant, animal health technician, physical therapy assistant, laboratory animal science, and dental hygiene programs.

1992 FRESHMAN CLASS PROFILE. 20 men, 201 women enrolled. **Characteristics:** 77% from in state, 60% commute, 21% have minority backgrounds, 9% are foreign students. Average age is 20.

FALL-TERM APPLICATIONS. $15 fee, may be waived for applicants with need. No closing date; applicants notified on a rolling basis; must reply within 8 weeks. Interview recommended. Interview required of borderline applicants; recommended for all others. Deferred and early admission available.

STUDENT LIFE. Housing: Dormitories (men, women). **Activities:** Student government, magazine, student newspaper, yearbook, choral groups, dance, drama, musical theater, interfaith council, organization of black students, campus guides, peer resource counseling program, Hillel, volunteer corps.

ATHLETICS. NAIA. **Intercollegiate:** Badminton, field hockey, softball, tennis, volleyball. **Intramural:** Badminton, field hockey, horseback riding, softball, tennis, volleyball.

STUDENT SERVICES. Aptitude testing, career counseling, employment service for undergraduates, freshman orientation, health services,

personal counseling, placement service for graduates, special adviser for adult students, veterans counselor, services/facilities for handicapped.

ANNUAL EXPENSES. Tuition and fees (1992-93): $7,070. **Room and board:** $4,300. **Books and supplies:** $400. **Other expenses:** $1,500.

FINANCIAL AID. 77% of freshmen, 67% of continuing students receive some form of aid. 99% of grants, 86% of loans, all jobs based on need. Academic, art, state/district residency, leadership, alumni affiliation scholarships available. **Aid applications:** No closing date; priority given to applications received by May 1; applicants notified on a rolling basis; must reply within 3 weeks.

ADDRESS/TELEPHONE. Mary M. Pontius, Dean of Admissions, Harcum Junior College, Morris and Montgomery Avenues, Bryn Mawr, PA 19010-3476. (215) 526-6050. (800) 345-2600. Fax: (215) 526-6086.

Harrisburg Area Community College
Harrisburg, Pennsylvania CB code: 2309

2-year public community college, coed. **Accreditation:** Regional. **Undergraduate enrollment:** 1,895 men, 2,298 women full time; 2,656 men, 4,712 women part time. **Faculty:** 440 total (140 full time), 23 with doctorates or other terminal degrees. **Location:** Urban campus in small city. **Calendar:** Semester, limited summer session. Saturday and extensive evening/early morning classes. **Microcomputers:** 300 located in libraries, classrooms, computer centers. **Additional facts:** 2 branch campuses in addition to main campus.

DEGREES OFFERED. AA. 815 associate degrees awarded in 1992. 30% in business and management, 5% education, 13% engineering technologies, 14% allied health, 5% parks/recreation, protective services, public affairs, 12% social sciences.

UNDERGRADUATE MAJORS. Accounting, architectural technologies, art education, automotive technology, biology, business administration and management, business and management, business and office, business data processing and related programs, business data programming, business education, chemistry, child development/care/guidance, communications, computer mathematics, construction, criminal justice studies, dental hygiene, education, electronic technology, elementary education, emergency medical technologies, engineering and engineering-related technologies, English education, finance, fire control and safety technology, food management, food production/management/services, graphic arts technology, graphic design, hospitality and recreation marketing, hotel/motel and restaurant management, industrial technology, information sciences and systems, law enforcement and corrections technologies, legal assistant/paralegal, legal secretary, liberal/general studies, management information systems, manufacturing technology, marketing management, mathematics, mathematics education, mechanical design technology, medical assistant, medical laboratory technologies, microcomputer software, nuclear medical technology, nursing, photographic technology, photography, physical education, physical sciences, prechiropractic, psychology, public affairs, radiograph medical technology, real estate, respiratory therapy, respiratory therapy technology, retailing, science education, secondary education, secretarial and related programs, social science education, social sciences, teacher aide, tourism, transportation management.

ACADEMIC PROGRAMS. 2-year transfer program, double major, dual enrollment of high school students, honors program, independent study, internships, student-designed major, study abroad, dual admissions with 6 United Negro College Fund institutions, with Penn State Harrisburg Capital College, and with Cheney University of Pennsylvania. **Remedial services:** Learning center, preadmission summer program, reduced course load, remedial instruction, special counselor, tutoring. **ROTC:** Army. **Placement/credit:** AP, CLEP General and Subject, institutional tests; 30 credit hours maximum for associate degree.

ACADEMIC REQUIREMENTS. Freshmen must earn minimum GPA of 1.2 to continue in good standing. 50% of freshmen return for sophomore year. **Graduation requirements:** 61 hours for associate. Most students required to take courses in arts/fine arts, English, humanities, mathematics, biological/physical sciences, social sciences.

FRESHMAN ADMISSIONS. Selection criteria: Open admissions. Selective admissions for allied health programs and chef's apprenticeship. **Test requirements:** ACT required for allied health programs; score report by February 1. Institutional mathematics, English, and reading tests required for counseling.

1992 FRESHMAN CLASS PROFILE. 1,401 men, 1,807 women enrolled. **Characteristics:** 99% from in state, 100% commute, 8% have minority backgrounds, 1% are foreign students.

FALL-TERM APPLICATIONS. $25 fee. No closing date; applicants notified on a rolling basis. Interview required for allied health, chef's apprenticeship applicants. Essay required for chef's apprenticeship applicants. Early admission available.

STUDENT LIFE. Activities: Student government, film, radio, student newspaper, choral groups, drama, jazz band, music ensembles, musical theater, fraternities, sororities, Black Student Union, Volunteers Interested in People, Asian-American Club, Latino Club, International Student Club.

ATHLETICS. Intramural: Badminton, basketball, racquetball, soccer, softball, swimming, table tennis, tennis, volleyball.

STUDENT SERVICES. Career counseling, employment service for undergraduates, on-campus day care, personal counseling, placement service for graduates, veterans counselor, services/facilities for handicapped.

ANNUAL EXPENSES. Tuition and fees (1992-93): $1,500, $1,440 additional for out-of-district students, $2,880 additional for out-of-state students. Out-of-district students pay an additional capital fee of $2 per credit and out-of-state and foreign students pay an additional capital fee of $4 per credit. **Books and supplies:** $500. **Other expenses:** $600.

FINANCIAL AID. 35% of continuing students receive some form of aid. 46% of loans, 28% of jobs based on need. 896 enrolled freshmen were judged to have need, all were offered aid. Academic, art, state/district residency, leadership scholarships available. **Aid applications:** Closing date June 1; applicants notified on or about July 1; must reply within 4 weeks.

ADDRESS/TELEPHONE. Alterman Jackson, Director of Admissions and Marketing, Harrisburg Area Community College, 1 HACC Drive, Harrisburg, PA 17110-2999. (717) 780-2400.

Haverford College
Haverford, Pennsylvania CB code: 2289

Admissions:	44% of applicants accepted
Based on:	••• Activities, recommendations, school record, test scores
	•• Essay, interview, special talents
Completion:	99% of freshmen end year in good standing
	92% graduate, 28% of these enter graduate study

4-year private college of arts and sciences and liberal arts college, coed. Founded in 1833. **Accreditation:** Regional. **Undergraduate enrollment:** 619 men, 519 women full time. **Faculty:** 107 total (95 full time), 100 with doctorates or other terminal degrees. **Location:** Suburban campus in large town; 10 miles from Philadelphia. **Calendar:** Semester. **Microcomputers:** 120 located in dormitories, libraries, classrooms, computer centers, campus-wide network. **Special facilities:** Strawbridge Observatory, Comfort Art Gallery, campus designated as arboretum. **Additional facts:** Close academic and social exchange with Bryn Mawr College. Students take courses and major at either college. Students may also enroll in courses at Swarthmore College and University of Pennsylvania. Integrated library computer system links Haverford libraries with those of Bryn Mawr and Swarthmore.

DEGREES OFFERED. BA, BS. 271 bachelor's degrees awarded in 1992. 5% in languages, 11% letters/literature, 11% life sciences, 9% philosophy, religion, theology, 9% physical sciences, 8% psychology, 42% social sciences.

UNDERGRADUATE MAJORS. Anthropology, archeology, art history, Asian studies, astronomy, biology, chemistry, classics, comparative literature, economics, English, fine arts, French, geology, German, Greek (classical), history, Italian, Latin, mathematics, music, philosophy, physics, political science and government, psychology, religion, Russian, sociology, Spanish, urban studies.

ACADEMIC PROGRAMS. Accelerated program, double major, independent study, internships, student-designed major, study abroad, teacher preparation, visiting/exchange student program, cross-registration, exchange programs with Spelman College (Georgia), Claremont McKenna College and Pitzer College (California); liberal arts/career combination in engineering. **Remedial services:** Special counselor, tutoring. **Placement/credit:** AP, IB, institutional tests; 16 credit hours maximum for bachelor's degree.

ACADEMIC REQUIREMENTS. No policy requiring minimum GPA; records of students having academic difficulty are reviewed individually. 99% of freshmen return for sophomore year. Students must declare major by end of second year. **Graduation requirements:** 128 hours for bachelor's (40 in major). Most students required to take courses in English, foreign languages, humanities, mathematics, biological/physical sciences, social sciences. **Postgraduate studies:** 5% enter law school, 10% enter medical school, 1% enter MBA programs, 12% enter other graduate study. **Additional information:** Academic Flexibility Program allows for advanced independent work and interdepartmental majors. Ample opportunity for student-faculty research. Senior seminars, a comprehensive examination and/or senior thesis required for completion of all major programs. Student-run honor code allows unsupervised examinations.

FRESHMAN ADMISSIONS. Selection criteria: School record, test scores, extracurricular achievements, and recommendations considered. College seeks diversity of social, economic, and geographic backgrounds. Minority applicants encouraged. Some preference to children of alumni. **High school preparation:** 12 units required. Required and recommended units include English 4, foreign language 3, mathematics 3-4, social science 1 and science 1-2. **Test requirements:** SAT; score report by February 1. 3 ACH required (including English Composition with essay). Score report by February 1.

1992 FRESHMAN CLASS PROFILE. 1,119 men applied, 442 accepted, 156 enrolled; 964 women applied, 476 accepted, 145 enrolled. 74% were in top tenth and 96% were in top quarter of graduating class. **Academic**

background: Mid 50% of enrolled freshmen had SAT-V between 580-670, SAT-M between 620-710. 100% submitted SAT scores. **Characteristics:** 14% from in state, 100% live in college housing, 19% have minority backgrounds, 2% are foreign students. Average age is 18.

FALL-TERM APPLICATIONS. $45 fee, may be waived for applicants with need. Closing date January 15; applicants notified on or about April 15; must reply by May 1. Essay required. Interview required of applicants within 150 miles of college, recommended for others. CRDA. Deferred and early admission available. EDP-F. Deferred admission not available to Early Decision applicants.

STUDENT LIFE. Housing: Dormitories (men, women, coed); apartment housing available. Students may live at Bryn Mawr College through dormitory exchange program. Students at both colleges may eat meals on either campus. **Activities:** Student government, magazine, radio, student newspaper, yearbook, choral groups, dance, drama, jazz band, music ensembles, musical theater, symphony orchestra, Quaker Activities Committee, Islamic Union, Hillel, Christian Fellowship, Environmental Action Committee, Black Students League, Puerto Rican Students at Haverford, Asian Students Association, Bisexual/Gay/Lesbian Alliance. **Additional information:** Student conduct regulated by academic and social honor code. Students serve on campus governance and policy-making committees.

ATHLETICS. NCAA. **Intercollegiate:** Baseball M, basketball, cross-country, fencing, field hockey W, lacrosse, soccer, tennis, track and field, volleyball W. **Intramural:** Basketball, ice hockey, rugby, sailing, soccer, softball, squash, swimming, volleyball.

STUDENT SERVICES. Aptitude testing, career counseling, employment service for undergraduates, freshman orientation, health services, personal counseling, placement service for graduates, services/facilities for handicapped.

ANNUAL EXPENSES. Tuition and fees: $18,000. Additional $135 for freshman orientation. **Room and board:** $5,950. **Books and supplies:** $650. **Other expenses:** $925.

FINANCIAL AID. 45% of freshmen, 45% of continuing students receive some form of aid. All grants, all loans based on need. 111 enrolled freshmen were judged to have need, all were offered aid. **Aid applications:** Closing date January 31; applicants notified on or about April 15; must reply by May 1.

ADDRESS/TELEPHONE. Delsie Z. Phillips, Director of Admissions, Haverford College, 370 Lancaster Avenue, Haverford, PA 19041-1392. (215) 896-1350. Fax: (215) 896-1338.

Holy Family College
Philadelphia, Pennsylvania — CB code: 2297

4-year private liberal arts college, coed, affiliated with Roman Catholic Church. Founded in 1954. **Accreditation:** Regional. **Undergraduate enrollment:** 262 men, 804 women full time; 279 men, 825 women part time. **Graduate enrollment:** 40 men, 170 women part time. **Faculty:** 224 total (79 full time), 60 with doctorates or other terminal degrees. **Location:** Suburban campus in very large city; 15 miles from downtown. **Calendar:** Semester, extensive summer session. Saturday and extensive evening/early morning classes. **Microcomputers:** 67 located in libraries, computer centers. **Special facilities:** Early childhood center with nursery school and kindergarten.

DEGREES OFFERED. AA, BA, BS, MEd. 8 associate degrees awarded in 1992. 100% in allied health. 281 bachelor's degrees awarded. 23% in business and management, 26% teacher education, 28% health sciences, 5% letters/literature, 6% psychology. Graduate degrees offered in 3 major fields of study.

UNDERGRADUATE MAJORS. Associate: Radiograph medical technology. **Bachelor's:** Accounting, biochemistry, biological and physical sciences, biology, business administration and management, business and management, chemistry, clinical laboratory science, communications, computer and information sciences, criminal justice studies, early childhood education, economics, education of the emotionally handicapped, education of the mentally handicapped, elementary education, English, English education, fine arts, fire control and safety technology, foreign languages education, French, history, humanities, humanities and social sciences, industrial and organizational psychology, information sciences and systems, international business management, management information systems, marketing and distribution, marketing management, mathematics, mathematics education, medical laboratory technologies, nursing, philosophy, predentistry, premedicine, prepharmacy, preveterinary, psychobiology, psychology, religion, religious education, science education, secondary education, social sciences, social studies education, social work, sociology, Spanish, special education.

ACADEMIC PROGRAMS. Accelerated program, cooperative education, double major, dual enrollment of high school students, independent study, internships, study abroad, teacher preparation; liberal arts/career combination in health sciences. **Remedial services:** Learning center, preadmission summer program, reduced course load, special counselor, tutoring. **Placement/credit:** AP, CLEP Subject, institutional tests; 30 credit hours maximum for bachelor's degree.

ACADEMIC REQUIREMENTS. Freshmen must earn minimum GPA of 2.0 to continue in good standing. Nursing and education students must maintain 2.5 GPA; medical technology students, 3.0. 80% of freshmen return for sophomore year. Students must declare major by end of second year. **Graduation requirements:** 60 hours for associate (24 in major), 126 hours for bachelor's (30 in major). Most students required to take courses in English, foreign languages, history, humanities, mathematics, philosophy/religion, biological/physical sciences, social sciences. **Postgraduate studies:** 2% enter law school, 2% enter medical school, 19% enter MBA programs, 9% enter other graduate study. **Additional information:** Most curricula offer students internships or co-op experiences.

FRESHMAN ADMISSIONS. Selection criteria: High school record most important, followed by recommendations and test scores. Motivation, school and community activities considered. **High school preparation:** 16 units required. Required and recommended units include English 4, foreign language 2-4, mathematics 2-4, physical science 2-4, social science 2-3 and science 1. **Test requirements:** SAT or ACT; score report by July 1.

1992 FRESHMAN CLASS PROFILE. 141 men, 451 women enrolled. 79% had high school GPA of 3.0 or higher, 21% between 2.0 and 2.99. 19% were in top tenth and 40% were in top quarter of graduating class. **Academic background:** Mid 50% of enrolled freshmen had SAT-V between 410-480, SAT-M between 420-510. 97% submitted SAT scores. **Characteristics:** 93% from in state, 100% commute, 4% have minority backgrounds, 4% are foreign students. Average age is 18.

FALL-TERM APPLICATIONS. $25 fee, may be waived for applicants with need. Closing date July 1; applicants notified on a rolling basis; must reply within 6 weeks. Interview recommended. Essay recommended. Deferred and early admission available.

STUDENT LIFE. Activities: Student government, magazine, radio, student newspaper, yearbook, intercollegiate publication, choral groups, drama, community health and welfare organizations, social and departmental clubs, honor societies, campus ministry team. **Additional information:** Mature and intelligent student conduct expected in accordance with college's interests, standards, and ideals.

ATHLETICS. NAIA. **Intercollegiate:** Basketball, soccer M, softball W. **Intramural:** Basketball M, volleyball.

STUDENT SERVICES. Aptitude testing, career counseling, employment service for undergraduates, freshman orientation, health services, personal counseling, placement service for graduates, special adviser for adult students, services/facilities for handicapped.

ANNUAL EXPENSES. Tuition and fees (1992-93): $7,600. **Books and supplies:** $500. **Other expenses:** $850.

FINANCIAL AID. 88% of freshmen, 89% of continuing students receive some form of aid. 96% of grants, 97% of loans, all jobs based on need. 159 enrolled freshmen were judged to have need, all were offered aid. Academic, athletic scholarships available. **Aid applications:** Closing date June 1; priority given to applications received by February 15; applicants notified on a rolling basis beginning on or about March 15; must reply within 2 weeks.

ADDRESS/TELEPHONE. Dr. Mott R. Linn, Director of Admissions, Holy Family College, Grant and Frankford Avenues, Philadelphia, PA 19114-2094. (215) 637-3050. Fax: (215) 632-8067.

Hussian School of Art
Philadelphia, Pennsylvania — CB code: 7309

4-year proprietary school of art and commercial art, coed. Founded in 1946. **Undergraduate enrollment:** 148 men and women. **Location:** Urban campus in very large city. **Calendar:** Semester.

FRESHMAN ADMISSIONS. Selection criteria: Interview, art portfolio important.

ANNUAL EXPENSES. Tuition and fees: $6,240. **Books and supplies:** $800. **Other expenses:** $1,600.

ADDRESS/TELEPHONE. Andrea Kane, Admissions Director, Hussian School of Art, 1010 Arch Street, Philadelphia, PA 19107. (215) 238-9000. Fax: (215) 238-0848.

ICS Center for Degree Studies
Scranton, Pennsylvania — CB code: 7313

2-year proprietary business, technical college, coed. Founded in 1975. **Undergraduate enrollment:** 4,286 men and women. **Faculty:** 38 total (20 full time). **Location:** Suburban campus in small city; 175 miles from Philadelphia. **Calendar:** Continuous enrollment and study sequence. **Additional facts:** No formal classes. Students establish own study pace with specially prepared instructional materials and have free telephone access to instructors.

DEGREES OFFERED. 347 associate degrees awarded in 1992. 77% in business and management, 23% engineering technologies.

UNDERGRADUATE MAJORS. Accounting, business and office, civil technology, computer and information sciences, electrical technology, electronic technology, finance, marketing and distribution.

ACADEMIC PROGRAMS. External degree, independent study. **Placement/credit:** AP, CLEP General.

ACADEMIC REQUIREMENTS. Freshmen must earn minimum GPA of 1.6 to continue in good standing. Students allowed 18 months to complete semester (15-18 credit hours). 25% of freshmen return for sophomore year. Students must declare major on application. **Graduation requirements:** 60 hours for associate.

FRESHMAN ADMISSIONS. Selection criteria: Open admissions.

1992 FRESHMAN CLASS PROFILE. Characteristics: 18% from in state.

FALL-TERM APPLICATIONS. No fee. No closing date; applicants notified on a rolling basis.

ANNUAL EXPENSES. Tuition and fees (1992-93): $689 tuition and required fees for first semester varies according to related equipment charges

ADDRESS/TELEPHONE. Director, ICS Center for Degree Studies, Oak Street and Pawnee Avenue, Scranton, PA 18515. (717) 342-7701. Fax: (717) 342-7707.

Immaculata College
Immaculata, Pennsylvania — CB code: 2320

4-year private liberal arts college, women only, affiliated with Roman Catholic Church. Founded in 1920. **Accreditation:** Regional. **Undergraduate enrollment:** 17 men, 532 women full time; 241 men, 1,278 women part time. **Graduate enrollment:** 4 men, 31 women full time; 68 men, 351 women part time. **Faculty:** 176 total (64 full time), 95 with doctorates or other terminal degrees. **Location:** Suburban campus in small town; 20 miles from Philadelphia. **Calendar:** Semester, limited summer session. **Microcomputers:** 75 located in libraries, classrooms, computer centers. **Additional facts:** Men attend only in evening division and graduate programs.

DEGREES OFFERED. AA, AS, BA, BS, MA, EdD. 21 associate degrees awarded in 1992. 198 bachelor's degrees awarded. 15% in business and management, 7% home economics, 25% letters/literature, 12% life sciences, 19% psychology, 11% social sciences. Graduate degrees offered in 10 major fields of study.

UNDERGRADUATE MAJORS. Associate: Accounting, art history, business and office, ceramics, creative writing, drawing, fashion merchandising, food management, French, German, Italian, Latin, liberal/general studies, marketing management, museum studies, painting, physics, printmaking, real estate, religious music, Russian, sculpture, Spanish, studio art, theological studies. **Bachelor's:** Accounting, American literature, biochemistry, biology, business administration and management, chemistry, comparative literature, computer and information sciences, counseling psychology, early childhood education, economics, elementary education, English, English education, English literature, family/consumer resource management, fashion merchandising, food management, food production/management/services, food science and nutrition, foreign languages (multiple emphasis), foreign languages education, French, German, history, home economics, home economics education, humanities and social sciences, international relations, junior high education, Latin, mathematics, mathematics education, music, music education, music therapy, nursing, nutritional education, political science and government, predentistry, prelaw, premedicine, prepharmacy, preveterinary, psychology, science education, secondary education, social science education, social studies education, social work, sociology, Spanish, technical and business writing, textiles and clothing.

ACADEMIC PROGRAMS. Accelerated program, double major, dual enrollment of high school students, honors program, independent study, internships, student-designed major, study abroad, teacher preparation. **Remedial services:** Learning center, preadmission summer program, reduced course load, remedial instruction, special counselor, tutoring, Pennsylvania Act 101 academic development program. **Placement/credit:** AP, CLEP General and Subject, institutional tests; 30 credit hours maximum for associate degree; 63 credit hours maximum for bachelor's degree.

ACADEMIC REQUIREMENTS. Freshmen must earn minimum GPA of 2.0 to continue in good standing. 87% of freshmen return for sophomore year. Students must declare major by end of second year. **Graduation requirements:** 64 hours for associate (30 in major), 126 hours for bachelor's (36 in major). Most students required to take courses in computer science, English, foreign languages, history, humanities, mathematics, philosophy/religion, biological/physical sciences, social sciences. **Postgraduate studies:** 2% enter law school, 5% enter medical school, 1% enter MBA programs, 21% enter other graduate study. **Additional information:** Theology study required of Roman Catholic students only.

FRESHMAN ADMISSIONS. Selection criteria: Class rank, academic program, test scores, counselor recommendation, minimum 2.3 GPA considered. **High school preparation:** 16 units required; 20 recommended. Required and recommended units include biological science 1-2, English 4, foreign language 2-3, mathematics 2-3, physical science 1-2 and social science 2-3. Music required for music majors. **Test requirements:** SAT or ACT (SAT preferred); score report by February 15.

1992 FRESHMAN CLASS PROFILE. 78 men, 509 women enrolled. 57% had high school GPA of 3.0 or higher, 41% between 2.0 and 2.99. **Academic background:** Mid 50% of enrolled freshmen had SAT-V between 450-520, SAT-M between 450-510. 98% submitted SAT scores. **Characteristics:** 58% from in state, 89% live in college housing, 16% have minority backgrounds, 5% are foreign students. Average age is 21.

FALL-TERM APPLICATIONS. $25 fee, may be waived for applicants with need. Closing date June 1; priority given to applications received by March 1; applicants notified on a rolling basis beginning on or about November 1; must reply by May 1 or within 3 weeks if notified thereafter. Audition required for music applicants. Interview recommended. CRDA. Deferred and early admission available.

STUDENT LIFE. Housing: Dormitories (women). **Activities:** Student government, magazine, student newspaper, yearbook, choral groups, drama, jazz band, music ensembles, musical theater, symphony orchestra, campus ministry, gospel choir, International Relations Society.

ATHLETICS. NCAA. **Intercollegiate:** Basketball, field hockey, softball, tennis, volleyball. **Intramural:** Archery, badminton, fencing, swimming.

STUDENT SERVICES. Aptitude testing, career counseling, employment service for undergraduates, freshman orientation, health services, personal counseling, placement service for graduates, special adviser for adult students, veterans counselor, services/facilities for handicapped.

ANNUAL EXPENSES. Tuition and fees: $9,600. Graduate students charged $350 per credit hour. Graduate students charged $436 per hour at 700 level. **Room and board:** $5,110. **Books and supplies:** $500. **Other expenses:** $1,000.

FINANCIAL AID. 70% of freshmen, 68% of continuing students receive some form of aid. 24% of grants, 70% of loans, 73% of jobs based on need. Academic, music/drama, athletic, state/district residency, religious affiliation scholarships available. **Aid applications:** Closing date May 1; priority given to applications received by March 1; applicants notified on a rolling basis beginning on or about April 1; must reply by May 1 or within 4 weeks if notified thereafter.

ADDRESS/TELEPHONE. Sr. Claudine M. Hagerty, Director of Admission, Immaculata College, Route 352 and King Road, Immaculata, PA 19345. (215) 647-4400. Fax: (215) 640-5828.

Indiana University of Pennsylvania
Indiana, Pennsylvania — CB code: 2652

Admissions:	46% of applicants accepted
Based on:	••• School record, test scores
	• Activities, recommendations, special talents
Completion:	82% of freshmen end year in good standing
	80% graduate

4-year public university, coed. Founded in 1875. **Accreditation:** Regional. **Undergraduate enrollment:** 12,825 men and women. **Graduate enrollment:** 1,532 men and women. **Faculty:** 805 total (720 full time), 468 with doctorates or other terminal degrees. **Location:** Rural campus in large town; 50 miles from Pittsburgh. **Calendar:** Semester, extensive summer session. **Microcomputers:** 290 located in dormitories, computer centers. **Special facilities:** Art galleries, museums, Breezedale (a restored Victorian mansion). **Additional facts:** Branch campuses located in Punxsutawney and Kittanning.

DEGREES OFFERED. AA, BA, BS, BFA, MA, MS, MBA, MFA, MEd, PhD, EdD. 30 associate degrees awarded in 1992. 2,000 bachelor's degrees awarded. Graduate degrees offered in 45 major fields of study.

UNDERGRADUATE MAJORS. Associate: Business administration and management, liberal/general studies. **Bachelor's:** Accounting, anthropology, applied mathematics, art education, art history, biochemistry, biology, business administration and management, business and management, business and office, business economics, business education, chemistry, child development/care/guidance, city/community/regional planning, clinical laboratory science, community services, computer and information sciences, criminology, dramatic arts, early childhood education, earth sciences, economics, education, education of exceptional children, education of the deaf and hearing impaired, education of the mentally handicapped, educational supervision, elementary education, engineering management, English, English education, family and community services, family/consumer resource management, fashion merchandising, finance, fine arts, food management, food production/management/services, food science and nutrition, food sciences, foreign languages education, French, geography, geology, geoscience, German, health education, history, home economics, home economics education, hotel/motel and restaurant management, human environment and housing, individual and family development, information sciences and systems, institutional management, interior design, international relations, jazz, journalism, junior high education, management information systems, marketing and distributive education, mathematics, mathematics education, medical laboratory technologies, music, music education, music history and appreciation, music performance, music theory and composition, nursing, nutritional education, office supervision and management, personnel management, philosophy, physical education, physics, political science and government, predentistry, preengineering, prelaw, premedicine, prepharmacy, preveterinary, psychology, public affairs, public policy studies, respiratory therapy, safety sciences, science education, secondary education, social science education, social sciences, social studies education, sociology, Spanish, special education, speech correction, speech pathology/audiology, studio art, systems analysis, textiles and clothing, visual and performing arts, vocational education.

ACADEMIC PROGRAMS. Accelerated program, cooperative education, double major, dual enrollment of high school students, education specialist degree, honors program, independent study, internships, student-designed major, study abroad, teacher preparation, visiting/exchange student program, Washington semester, cooperative and accelerated programs available in family medicine, podiatric medicine, and optometry; liberal arts/career combination in engineering, forestry, health sciences; combined bachelor's/graduate program in business administration. **Remedial services:** Learning center, preadmission summer program, remedial instruction, special counselor, tutoring, writing center. **ROTC:** Army. **Placement/credit:** AP, CLEP General and Subject, institutional tests. Unlimited number of hours of credit by examination may be counted toward degree.

ACADEMIC REQUIREMENTS. Freshmen must earn minimum GPA of 2.0 to continue in good standing. Freshmen must earn minimum 2.0 GPA. Business majors must earn 2.4, criminology 2.5 and education 2.5. 82% of freshmen return for sophomore year. Students must declare major on application. **Graduation requirements:** 60 hours for associate, 124 hours for bachelor's (36 in major). Most students required to take courses in arts/fine arts, English, humanities, mathematics, biological/physical sciences, social sciences.

FRESHMAN ADMISSIONS. Selection criteria: School achievement record, recommendations, test scores, extracurricular activities, and high school rank important. College-preparatory program recommended. **Test requirements:** SAT or ACT (SAT preferred); score report by January 1.

1992 FRESHMAN CLASS PROFILE. 7,805 men and women applied, 3,589 accepted; 1,425 enrolled. **Academic background:** Mid 50% of enrolled freshmen had SAT-V between 420-510, SAT-M between 470-560. 98% submitted SAT scores. **Characteristics:** 93% from in state, 72% live in college housing, 14% have minority backgrounds, 3% are foreign students. Average age is 18.

FALL-TERM APPLICATIONS. $20 fee, may be waived for applicants with need. No closing date; applicants notified on a rolling basis beginning on or about January 1; must reply by April 15 or within 2 weeks if notified thereafter. Audition required for music applicants. Portfolio required for art applicants. Deferred and early admission available. EDP-F.

STUDENT LIFE. Housing: Dormitories (men, women, coed); apartment, fraternity housing available. **Activities:** Student government, film, radio, student newspaper, television, yearbook, choral groups, concert band, dance, drama, jazz band, marching band, musical theater, symphony orchestra, fraternities, sororities, Alpha Phi Omega National Service Fraternity (coeducational), Gamma Sigma Sigma Service Sorority, Black Cultural Center, Campus Crusade for Christ, Coalition for Christian Outreach, Newman Center.

ATHLETICS. NAIA, NCAA. **Intercollegiate:** Baseball M, basketball, cross-country, diving, field hockey W, football M, golf M, gymnastics W, rifle, softball W, swimming, tennis W, track and field, volleyball W. **Intramural:** Archery, badminton, baseball M, basketball, bowling, cross-country, fencing M, football M, golf, handball M, horseback riding, ice hockey M, racquetball, rifle, rugby, sailing, skiing, soccer W, softball, swimming, table tennis, tennis, track and field, volleyball, water polo, wrestling M.

STUDENT SERVICES. Aptitude testing, career counseling, employment service for undergraduates, freshman orientation, health services, on-campus day care, personal counseling, placement service for graduates, special adviser for adult students, veterans counselor, speech and hearing clinics, services/facilities for handicapped.

ANNUAL EXPENSES. Tuition and fees (1992-93): $3,157, $3,394 additional for out-of-state students. **Room and board:** $2,834. **Books and supplies:** $500. **Other expenses:** $1,400.

FINANCIAL AID. 83% of freshmen, 83% of continuing students receive some form of aid. All grants, 96% of loans, 35% of jobs based on need. Academic, music/drama, art, athletic, state/district residency, leadership, minority scholarships available. **Aid applications:** No closing date; priority given to applications received by May 1; applicants notified on a rolling basis beginning on or about June 1; must reply immediately.

ADDRESS/TELEPHONE. Nancy Newkerk, Dean of Admissions, Indiana University of Pennsylvania, 216 Pratt Hall, Indiana, PA 15705-1088. (412) 357-2230. Fax: (412) 357-6213.

Johnson Technical Institute
Scranton, Pennsylvania — CB code: 1542

Admissions: 90% of applicants accepted
Based on:
- ••• School record, test scores
- •• Activities, interview, recommendations
- • Essay

Completion: 80% of freshmen end year in good standing
77% graduate, 10% of these enter 4-year programs

2-year private technical college, coed. Founded in 1916. **Undergraduate enrollment:** 327 men, 19 women full time; 11 men part time. **Faculty:** 21 total. **Location:** Suburban campus in small city; 117 miles from Philadelphia, 125 miles from New York City. **Calendar:** Semester, limited summer session. **Microcomputers:** 16 located in libraries, classrooms. **Special facilities:** Materials test laboratory.

DEGREES OFFERED. 142 associate degrees awarded in 1992. 100% in trade and industry.

UNDERGRADUATE MAJORS. Automotive mechanics, automotive technology, biomedical equipment technology, carpentry, construction, diesel engine mechanics, drafting, drafting and design technology, electrical and electronics equipment repair, electronic technology, machine tool operation/machine shop, mechanical design technology, precision metal work, welding technology, woodworking.

ACADEMIC PROGRAMS. Internships. **Remedial services:** Learning center, preadmission summer program, reduced course load, remedial instruction, special counselor, tutoring. **Placement/credit:** Institutional tests.

ACADEMIC REQUIREMENTS. Freshmen must earn minimum GPA of 2.0 to continue in good standing. 78% of freshmen return for sophomore year. Students must declare major on enrollment. **Graduation requirements:** 76 hours for associate (40 in major). Most students required to take courses in English, mathematics. **Additional information:** Extensive shop and laboratory components.

FRESHMAN ADMISSIONS. Selection criteria: High school record, test scores, recommendations, interview. **High school preparation:** 5 units required. Required units include English 4 and mathematics 1. **Test requirements:** SAT or ACT; score report by August 15. Institutional entrance examination required for applicants who have not taken SAT or ACT.

1992 FRESHMAN CLASS PROFILE. 339 men applied, 305 accepted, 201 enrolled; 8 women applied, 8 accepted, 8 enrolled. 10% had high school GPA of 3.0 or higher, 60% between 2.0 and 2.99. 6% were in top tenth and 12% were in top quarter of graduating class. **Characteristics:** 93% from in state, 87% commute, 2% have minority backgrounds, 3% join fraternities/sororities. Average age is 19.

FALL-TERM APPLICATIONS. $10 fee, may be waived for applicants with need. No closing date; applicants notified on a rolling basis; must reply within 2 weeks. Interview recommended. Interview required of local applicants; recommended for all others. Deferred admission available.

STUDENT LIFE. Housing: Apartment housing available. **Activities:** Student government, yearbook, fraternities.

ATHLETICS. Intramural: Badminton, basketball, skiing, softball, swimming, table tennis, volleyball.

STUDENT SERVICES. Aptitude testing, career counseling, employment service for undergraduates, freshman orientation, personal counseling, placement service for graduates, veterans counselor.

ANNUAL EXPENSES. Tuition and fees (projected): $5,296. **Room and board:** $2,041 room only. **Books and supplies:** $400. **Other expenses:** $1,305.

FINANCIAL AID. 80% of freshmen, 85% of continuing students receive some form of aid. All grants, 77% of loans based on need. Academic scholarships available. **Aid applications:** No closing date; priority given to applications received by August 1; applicants notified on a rolling basis beginning on or about May 15; must reply within 2 weeks.

ADDRESS/TELEPHONE. Harry Dickinson, Vice President for Institutional Advancement, Johnson Technical Institute, 3427 North Main Avenue, Scranton, PA 18508. (717) 342-6404 ext. 15. Fax: (717) 348-2181.

Juniata College
Huntingdon, Pennsylvania — CB code: 2341

Admissions: 82% of applicants accepted
Based on:
- ••• School record, test scores
- •• Essay, interview, special talents
- • Activities, recommendations, religious affiliation/commitment

Completion: 92% of freshmen end year in good standing
75% graduate, 33% of these enter graduate study

4-year private liberal arts college, coed, affiliated with Church of the Brethren. Founded in 1876. **Accreditation:** Regional. **Undergraduate enrollment:** 475 men, 555 women full time; 15 men, 20 women part time. **Faculty:** 113 total (75 full time), 65 with doctorates or other terminal degrees. **Location:** Rural campus in small town; 30 miles from Altoona and from State College. **Calendar:** Semester, limited summer session. **Microcomputers:** 90 located in libraries, classrooms, computer centers. **Special facilities:** Nature preserve, Raystown Lake Environmental Studies Field Station, Shoemaker Art Gallery, Paul E. Hickes Observatory. **Additional facts:** Students develop own majors, Programs of Emphasis, with help of advisers.

DEGREES OFFERED. BA, BS. 250 bachelor's degrees awarded in 1992. 15% in business and management, 7% communications, 9% teacher education, 10% health sciences, 12% life sciences, 5% multi/interdisciplinary studies, 7% physical sciences, 8% psychology, 7% social sciences.

UNDERGRADUATE MAJORS. Accounting, allied health, anthropology, art history, biochemistry, biological and physical sciences, biology, biophysics, botany, business administration and management, business and management, business economics, chemistry, communications, computer and information sciences, computer programming, counseling psychology, criminology, cytotechnology, dental hygiene, early childhood education, ecology, economics, education, elementary education, English, English education, environmental science, experimental psychology, finance, fine arts, foreign languages (multiple emphasis), foreign languages education, forestry and related sciences, French, geology, German, health sciences, history, human resources development, humanities, humanities and social sciences, industrial and organizational psychology, international business management, international relations, international studies, labor/industrial relations, liberal/general studies, management information systems, marine biology, marketing and distribution, marketing management, mathematics, mathematics education, medical laboratory technologies, microbiology, nursing, occupational therapy, peace studies, personnel management, philosophy, physical sciences, physical therapy, physics, political science and government, predentistry, preengineering, prelaw, premedicine, prepharmacy, prepodiatry, preveterinary, psychobiology, psychology, public administration, public relations, radiograph medical technology, religion, religious education, Russian, school psychology, science education, secondary education, social sciences, social studies education, social work, sociology, Spanish, ultrasound technology, urban studies, visual and performing arts, zoology.

ACADEMIC PROGRAMS. Accelerated program, double major, dual enrollment of high school students, independent study, internships, student-designed major, study abroad, teacher preparation, visiting/exchange student program, Washington semester, biological research opportunities with cooperating colleges and research institutions; liberal arts/career combination in engineering, forestry, health sciences. **Placement/credit:** AP, IB, institutional tests. Unlimited number of hours of credit by examination may be counted toward degree.

ACADEMIC REQUIREMENTS. Freshmen must earn minimum GPA of 1.66 to continue in good standing. 94% of freshmen return for sophomore year. Students must declare major by end of first year. **Graduation requirements:** 120 hours for bachelor's (45 in major). Most students required to take courses in arts/fine arts, computer science, English, humanities, biological/physical sciences, social sciences. **Postgraduate studies:** 3% enter law school, 6% enter medical school, 1% enter MBA programs, 23% enter other graduate study. **Additional information:** General education interdisciplinary courses study a people during an epoch in time and analyze contemporary ethical issues.

FRESHMAN ADMISSIONS. Selection criteria: School achievement record most important. Test scores, school and community activities, recommendations also important. Geographical distribution considered. **High school preparation:** 16 units required. Required units include English 4 and foreign language 2. 10 units must be distributed among mathematics, social studies, and laboratory science. **Test requirements:** SAT or ACT; score report by March 1.

1992 FRESHMAN CLASS PROFILE. 459 men applied, 377 accepted, 125 enrolled; 479 women applied, 393 accepted, 134 enrolled. 85% had high school GPA of 3.0 or higher, 15% between 2.0 and 2.99. 33% were in top tenth and 70% were in top quarter of graduating class. **Academic background:** Mid 50% of enrolled freshmen had SAT-V between 460-530, SAT-M between 500-580. 90% submitted SAT scores. **Characteristics:** 76% from in state, 96% live in college housing, 3% have minority backgrounds, 2% are foreign students. Average age is 18.

FALL-TERM APPLICATIONS. $30 fee, may be waived for applicants with need. Closing date March 1; applicants notified on a rolling basis; must reply by May 1 or within 4 weeks if notified thereafter. Essay required. Interview recommended. CRDA. Deferred and early admission available. EDP-F. November 15 early decision deadline, notification by December 15.

STUDENT LIFE. Housing: Dormitories (men, women, coed); apartment housing available. On-campus housing available to all students for 4 years. **Activities:** Student government, magazine, radio, student newspaper, yearbook, choral groups, concert band, drama, jazz band, marching band, music ensembles, musical theater, opera, pep band, chamber orchestra, Deputation Club, Catholic Council, Jewish Student Association, Social Service Club, Women's Action Committee, Campus Ministry Board, Committee on Multiculturalism, International Club, Amnesty International, African American Student Association.

ATHLETICS. NCAA. **Intercollegiate:** Baseball M, basketball, cross-country, field hockey W, football M, golf, soccer M, softball W, swimming, tennis, track and field, volleyball, wrestling M. **Intramural:** Badminton, basketball, field hockey W, gymnastics, handball, ice hockey M, lacrosse, racquetball, rugby, skiing, soccer M, softball, swimming, table tennis, tennis, track and field, volleyball, water polo, wrestling M. **Clubs:** Water polo W.

STUDENT SERVICES. Aptitude testing, career counseling, employment service for undergraduates, freshman orientation, health services, personal counseling, placement service for graduates, special adviser for adult students, services/facilities for handicapped.

ANNUAL EXPENSES. Tuition and fees: $14,150. **Room and board:** $4,240. **Books and supplies:** $450. **Other expenses:** $420.

FINANCIAL AID. 80% of freshmen, 77% of continuing students receive some form of aid. 91% of grants, 84% of loans, 34% of jobs based on need. 201 enrolled freshmen were judged to have need, 200 were offered aid. Academic, music/drama, art, leadership, religious affiliation scholarships available. **Aid applications:** No closing date; priority given to applications received by March 1; applicants notified on a rolling basis beginning on or about March 1; must reply by May 1 or within 2 weeks if notified thereafter.

ADDRESS/TELEPHONE. Carlton E. Surbeck, III, Director of Admissions, Juniata College, 1800 Moore Street, Huntingdon, PA 16652-2119. (814) 643-4310 ext. 420. (800) 526-1970 ext. 420. Fax: (814) 643-3620.

Keystone Junior College
La Plume, Pennsylvania — CB code: 2351

Admissions:	77% of applicants accepted
Based on:	••• Interview
	•• Recommendations
	• Activities, essay, school record, special talents, test scores
Completion:	65% of freshmen end year in good standing
	33% graduate, 65% of these enter 4-year programs

2-year private junior college, coed. Founded in 1868. **Accreditation:** Regional. **Undergraduate enrollment:** 279 men, 296 women full time; 147 men, 326 women part time. **Faculty:** 102 total (43 full time), 15 with doctorates or other terminal degrees. **Location:** Rural campus in small town; 15 miles from Scranton. **Calendar:** Semester, limited summer session. **Microcomputers:** 71 located in libraries, classrooms, computer centers. **Special facilities:** Observatory, Platt Learning Center, Zukowski Language Laboratory, Children's Center, Linder Art Gallery.

DEGREES OFFERED. AA, AS. 196 associate degrees awarded in 1992. 27% in business and management, 8% communications, 13% teacher education, 25% multi/interdisciplinary studies, 6% social sciences, 8% visual and performing arts.

UNDERGRADUATE MAJORS. Allied health, biochemistry, biology, business administration and management, business and management, business and office, child development/care/guidance, communications, computer and information sciences, cytotechnology, dental hygiene, early childhood education, education, environmental science, fashion merchandising, fine arts, food management, food production/management/services, forest products processing technology, forestry and related sciences, forestry production and processing, hotel/motel and restaurant management, human services, journalism, landscape architecture, liberal/general studies, marketing and distribution, medical laboratory technologies, nursing, occupational therapy, physical sciences, physical therapy, radiograph medical technology, studio art, tourism, transportation and travel marketing, ultrasound technology.

ACADEMIC PROGRAMS. 2-year transfer program, cooperative education, double major, dual enrollment of high school students, independent study, internships, student-designed major, weekend college, cross-registration, 2-2 programs with various 4-year institutions in art, education, human services, computer management, communications, business, engineering, general studies, allied health, environmental science, forestry. **Remedial services:** Learning center, reduced course load, remedial instruction, special counselor, tutoring, developmental education. **ROTC:** Air Force, Army. **Placement/credit:** AP, CLEP General and Subject, institutional tests; 12 credit hours maximum for associate degree.

ACADEMIC REQUIREMENTS. Freshmen must earn minimum GPA of 2.0 to continue in good standing. 53% of freshmen return for sophomore year. Students must declare major on enrollment. **Graduation requirements:** 70 hours for associate (34 in major). Most students required to take courses in arts/fine arts, English, humanities, mathematics, biological/physical sciences, social sciences.

FRESHMAN ADMISSIONS. Selection criteria: Interview, school achievement record, extracurricular activities, test scores, class rank, recommendations, preparation in proposed major area of study considered. **High school preparation:** 16 units recommended. Recommended units include English 4, foreign language 2, mathematics 2, social science 2 and science 2. Science recommendation includes 1 laboratory science. Foreign language recommended for art communications and liberal arts curricula. Foreign language and 3 math recommended for allied health, environmental science and forestry, and science curricula.

1992 FRESHMAN CLASS PROFILE. 675 men applied, 490 accepted, 215 enrolled; 593 women applied, 483 accepted, 286 enrolled. 3% were in top tenth and 12% were in top quarter of graduating class. **Academic background:** Mid 50% of enrolled freshmen had SAT-V between 290-400, SAT-M between 310-410. 62% submitted SAT scores. **Characteristics:** 82% from in state, 54% commute, 7% have minority backgrounds, 4% are foreign students. Average age is 18.

FALL-TERM APPLICATIONS. $20 fee, may be waived for applicants with need. No closing date; applicants notified on a rolling basis; must reply within 4 weeks of acceptance or as noted in acceptance letter. Interview recommended. Essay recommended. Art portfolio or recommendation from art teacher required of art applicants. Deferred and early admission available.

STUDENT LIFE. Housing: Dormitories (men, women, coed). Special interest dorms available. **Activities:** Student government, magazine, radio, student newspaper, yearbook, choral groups, drama, musical theater, concert/lecture series, art society, Varsity K, multi-ethnic cultural association, computer club, science club, business club, Phi Theta Kappa (honorary fraternity), engineering club, campus ministry, theater club.

ATHLETICS. NJCAA. **Intercollegiate:** Baseball M, basketball, soccer, softball W, volleyball W. **Intramural:** Archery, badminton, basketball, bowling, cross-country, football, racquetball, soccer, softball, table tennis, tennis, volleyball.

STUDENT SERVICES. Career counseling, employment service for undergraduates, freshman orientation, health services, personal counseling, placement service for graduates, special adviser for adult students, veterans counselor, services/facilities for handicapped.

ANNUAL EXPENSES. Tuition and fees: $8,260. **Room and board:** $4,900. **Books and supplies:** $600. **Other expenses:** $1,226.

FINANCIAL AID. 76% of freshmen, 73% of continuing students receive some form of aid. 95% of grants, 83% of loans, 62% of jobs based on need. 252 enrolled freshmen were judged to have need, 251 were offered aid. Academic scholarships available. **Aid applications:** No closing date; priority given to applications received by May 1; applicants notified on a rolling basis beginning on or about March 1; must reply by May 1 or within 3 weeks if notified thereafter.

ADDRESS/TELEPHONE. Kevin McIntyre, Director of Admissions, Keystone Junior College, PO Box 50, La Plume, PA 18440-0200. (717) 945-5141. (800) 824-2764. Fax: (717) 945-7977.

King's College

Wilkes-Barre, Pennsylvania — CB code: 2353

Admissions: 74% of applicants accepted
Based on:
••• School record
•• Test scores
• Activities, essay, interview, recommendations, special talents
Completion: 85% of freshmen end year in good standing
69% graduate, 16% of these enter graduate study

4-year private liberal arts college, coed, affiliated with Roman Catholic Church. Founded in 1946. **Accreditation:** Regional. **Undergraduate enrollment:** 898 men, 873 women full time; 175 men, 366 women part time. **Graduate enrollment:** 28 men, 16 women part time. **Faculty:** 171 total (106 full time), 71 with doctorates or other terminal degrees. **Location:** Urban campus in small city; 110 miles from Philadelphia, 140 miles from New York City. **Calendar:** Semester, extensive summer session. Saturday and extensive evening/early morning classes. **Microcomputers:** 225 located in libraries, classrooms, computer centers. **Special facilities:** Electron microscope, robotics laboratory, molecular biology laboratory.

DEGREES OFFERED. AA, AS, BA, BS, MS. 17 associate degrees awarded in 1992. 29% in business and management, 24% computer sciences, 41% law, 6% parks/recreation, protective services, public affairs. 515 bachelor's degrees awarded. 39% in business and management, 7% communications, 6% computer sciences, 6% education, 6% letters/literature, 5% psychology, 24% social sciences. Graduate degrees offered in 3 major fields of study.

UNDERGRADUATE MAJORS. Associate: Accounting, business administration and management, computer and information sciences, criminal justice studies, gerontology, information sciences and systems, law enforcement and corrections, legal assistant/paralegal, management information systems, marketing management, systems analysis. **Bachelor's:** Accounting, biological and physical sciences, biology, business administration and management, chemistry, clinical laboratory science, communications, computer and information sciences, criminal justice studies, dramatic arts, early childhood education, economics, elementary education, English, finance, French, gerontology, health care administration, history, human resources development, industrial and organizational psychology, information sciences and systems, international business management, law enforcement and corrections, management information systems, marketing management, mathematics, medical laboratory technologies, philosophy, physician's assistant, physics, political science and government, prelaw, psychology, radio/television technology, religion, secondary education, sociology, Spanish, special education, systems analysis, theological studies.

ACADEMIC PROGRAMS. Double major, dual enrollment of high school students, honors program, independent study, internships, study abroad, teacher preparation, visiting/exchange student program, Washington semester, cross-registration, preprofessional programs in dentistry, medicine, pharmacy, veterinary science; 2-3 and 3-2 program in preengineering. **Remedial services:** Learning center, preadmission summer program, reduced course load, special counselor, tutoring. **ROTC:** Air Force, Army. **Placement/credit:** AP, CLEP Subject, IB, institutional tests; 30 credit hours maximum for bachelor's degree.

ACADEMIC REQUIREMENTS. Freshmen must earn minimum GPA of 2.0 to continue in good standing. 84% of freshmen return for sophomore year. Students must declare major by end of second year. **Graduation requirements:** 60 hours for associate (30 in major), 123 hours for bachelor's (60 in major). Most students required to take courses in English, foreign languages, history, humanities, mathematics, philosophy/religion, biological/physical sciences, social sciences. **Postgraduate studies:** 2% enter law school, 2% enter medical school, 4% enter MBA programs, 8% enter other graduate study.

FRESHMAN ADMISSIONS. Selection criteria: School record and achievement, intended major, counselor's recommendation, test scores, class rank. **High school preparation:** 15 units required. Required units include English 4, foreign language 2, mathematics 3, social science 3 and science 3. Applicants for science, mathematics, computer science, and preengineering programs should have 4 mathematics, 1 physics. **Test requirements:** SAT or ACT (SAT preferred); score report by August 1.

1992 FRESHMAN CLASS PROFILE. 985 men applied, 676 accepted, 258 enrolled; 584 women applied, 490 accepted, 214 enrolled. 20% were in top tenth and 51% were in top quarter of graduating class. **Academic background:** Mid 50% of enrolled freshmen had SAT-V between 410-500, SAT-M between 440-560. 99% submitted SAT scores. **Characteristics:** 61% from in state, 79% live in college housing, 1% have minority backgrounds, 1% are foreign students, 1% join fraternities/sororities. Average age is 18.

FALL-TERM APPLICATIONS. $30 fee, may be waived for applicants with need. Closing date August 15; applicants notified on a rolling basis; must reply by May 1 or within 3 weeks if notified thereafter. Interview recommended. Essay recommended. CRDA. Deferred and early admission available. EDP-F.

STUDENT LIFE. Housing: Dormitories (men, women); apartment housing available. **Activities:** Student government, radio, student newspaper, television, yearbook, choral groups, drama, jazz band, debate team, campus ministry, and more than 45 social, political, and religious organizations.

ATHLETICS. NCAA. **Intercollegiate:** Baseball M, basketball, cross-country, diving, field hockey W, football M, golf M, rifle, soccer, softball W, swimming, tennis, volleyball W, wrestling M. **Intramural:** Basketball, bowling, racquetball, rifle, rowing (crew), softball, table tennis, volleyball.

STUDENT SERVICES. Aptitude testing, career counseling, employment service for undergraduates, freshman orientation, health services, personal counseling, placement service for graduates, special adviser for adult students, services/facilities for handicapped.

ANNUAL EXPENSES. Tuition and fees: $10,600. **Room and board:** $4,820. **Books and supplies:** $525. **Other expenses:** $1,765.

FINANCIAL AID. 81% of freshmen, 74% of continuing students receive some form of aid. 92% of grants, 77% of loans, 93% of jobs based on need. 313 enrolled freshmen were judged to have need, all were offered aid. Academic, leadership scholarships available. **Aid applications:** No closing date; priority given to applications received by March 1; applicants notified on a rolling basis beginning on or about March 1; must reply within 3 weeks.

ADDRESS/TELEPHONE. Daniel Conry, Dean of Admissions, King's College, 133 North River Street, Wilkes-Barre, PA 18711-0801. (717) 826-5858. (800) 955-5777. Fax: (717) 825-9049.

Kutztown University of Pennsylvania

Kutztown, Pennsylvania — CB code: 2653

Admissions: 48% of applicants accepted
Based on:
••• Recommendations, school record, test scores
•• Special talents
• Activities, essay
Completion: 47% graduate, 15% of these enter graduate study

4-year public university, coed. Founded in 1866. **Accreditation:** Regional. **Undergraduate enrollment:** 2,522 men, 3,344 women full time; 285 men, 633 women part time. **Graduate enrollment:** 71 men, 91 women full time; 213 men, 631 women part time. **Faculty:** 400 total (346 full time), 208 with doctorates or other terminal degrees. **Location:** Rural campus in small town; 15 miles from Allentown and Reading, 90 miles from Philadelphia. **Calendar:** 4-1-4, extensive summer session. **Microcomputers:** 500 located in libraries, classrooms, computer centers. **Special facilities:** Observatory, seismograph, on-campus preschool, art gallery, cartography lab.

DEGREES OFFERED. BA, BS, BFA, MA, MS, MBA, MEd. 1,162 bachelor's degrees awarded in 1992. 8% in communications, 34% teacher education, 13% social sciences, 14% visual and performing arts. Graduate degrees offered in 19 major fields of study.

UNDERGRADUATE MAJORS. Accounting, American studies, anthropology, art education, biological and physical sciences, biology, business administration and management, business economics, chemistry, communication design, computer and information sciences, crafts, criminal justice studies, dramatic arts, earth sciences, economics, education of the mentally handicapped, education of the physically handicapped, education of the visually handicapped, elementary education, English, environmental science, fine arts, French, geography, geology, German, history, international business management, liberal/general studies, library science, management science, marine biology, marketing management, mathematics, medical laboratory technologies, music, nursing, philosophy, physics, physics/engineering, political science and government, psychology, public administration, radio/television broadcasting, Russian, Russian and Slavic studies, secondary education, social work, sociology, Spanish, special education, speech, speech correction, studio art, visual and performing arts.

ACADEMIC PROGRAMS. Accelerated program, double major, dual enrollment of high school students, honors program, independent study, internships, student-designed major, study abroad, teacher preparation, visiting/exchange student program; liberal arts/career combination in engineering; combined bachelor's/graduate program in business administration. **Remedial services:** Learning center, preadmission summer program, remedial instruction, special counselor, tutoring. **ROTC:** Air Force, Army. **Placement/credit:** AP, CLEP General and Subject, institutional tests; 24 credit hours maximum for bachelor's degree.

ACADEMIC REQUIREMENTS. Freshmen must earn minimum GPA of 1.65 to continue in good standing. 79% of freshmen return for sophomore year. Students must declare major by end of second year. **Graduation requirements:** 128 hours for bachelor's (32 in major). Most students required to take courses in arts/fine arts, computer science, English, foreign languages, history, humanities, mathematics, philosophy/religion, biological/physical sciences, social sciences.

FRESHMAN ADMISSIONS. Selection criteria: Test scores and class rank most important. In borderline cases, school and community activities and recommendations considered. Special consideration for minorities. **High school preparation:** 16 units required. Required units include English 4, foreign language 2, mathematics 3, social science 4 and science 2. Course recommendations vary for specific programs. **Test requirements:** SAT or ACT (SAT preferred); score report by April 15. 2 ACH (including Biology and Chemistry) required of medical technology applicants. Score report by March 1 National League for Nursing Pre-admissions and Classification Test required of registered nursing applicants, art test for communication design applicants.

1992 FRESHMAN CLASS PROFILE. 2,546 men applied, 1,272 accepted, 530 enrolled; 3,334 women applied, 1,568 accepted, 720 enrolled. 57% had high school GPA of 3.0 or higher, 37% between 2.0 and 2.99. 10% were in top tenth and 34% were in top quarter of graduating class. **Academic background:** Mid 50% of enrolled freshmen had SAT-V between 400-480, SAT-M between 420-530. 99% submitted SAT scores. **Characteristics:** 17% from in state, 84% live in college housing, 2% have minority backgrounds, 1% are foreign students, 4% join fraternities/sororities. Average age is 18.

FALL-TERM APPLICATIONS. $20 fee, may be waived for applicants with need. Closing date March 1; priority given to applications received by January 1; applicants notified on a rolling basis beginning on or about November 15; must reply by May 1 or within 3 weeks if notified thereafter. Interview recommended for marginal applicants. Essay recommended. CRDA. Deferred and early admission available.

STUDENT LIFE. Housing: Dormitories (men, women, coed); handicapped housing available. Special interest housing available. **Activities:** Student government, film, magazine, radio, student newspaper, television, yearbook, choral groups, concert band, dance, drama, jazz band, marching band, music ensembles, musical theater, opera, pep band, symphony orchestra, fraternities, sororities, Black Student Union, Newman Association, Fellowship of Christian Athletes, Lutheran Campus Ministry, Inter-Varsity Christian Fellowship, Associated Campus Ministries, Latino Student Association, Minority Achievement Coalition, Women's Action Group.

ATHLETICS. NCAA. **Intercollegiate:** Baseball M, basketball, cross-country, diving, field hockey W, football M, soccer, softball W, swimming, tennis, track and field, volleyball W, wrestling M. **Intramural:** Archery, badminton, baseball M, basketball, cross-country, handball, horseback riding, ice hockey M, lacrosse M, racquetball, rifle, rugby M, skiing, skin diving, soccer, softball, swimming, table tennis, tennis, track and field, volleyball, water polo, wrestling M.

STUDENT SERVICES. Aptitude testing, career counseling, employment service for undergraduates, freshman orientation, health services, on-campus day care, personal counseling, placement service for graduates, special adviser for adult students, veterans counselor, services/facilities for handicapped.

ANNUAL EXPENSES. Tuition and fees (projected): $3,690, $3,810 additional for out-of-state students. **Room and board:** $2,970. **Books and supplies:** $550. **Other expenses:** $1,750.

FINANCIAL AID. 85% of freshmen, 75% of continuing students receive some form of aid. 94% of grants, 50% of loans, 17% of jobs based on need. 1,063 enrolled freshmen were judged to have need, all were offered aid. Academic, art, athletic, leadership, minority scholarships available. **Aid applications:** Closing date March 15; applicants notified on or about May 1; must reply within 4 weeks.

ADDRESS/TELEPHONE. George McKinley, Director of Admissions, Kutztown University of Pennsylvania, College Hill, Kutztown, PA 19530. (215) 683-4060. Fax: (215) 683-4010.

La Roche College
Pittsburgh, Pennsylvania

CB code: 2379

4-year private liberal arts college, coed, affiliated with Roman Catholic Church. Founded in 1963. **Accreditation:** Regional. **Undergraduate enrollment:** 226 men, 379 women full time; 173 men, 657 women part time. **Graduate enrollment:** 20 men, 29 women full time; 70 men, 209 women part time. **Faculty:** 123 total (44 full time), 38 with doctorates or other terminal degrees. **Location:** Suburban campus in large city; 10 miles from downtown. **Calendar:** Semester, limited summer session. **Microcomputers:** 40 located in libraries, computer centers. **Special facilities:** Art gallery. **Additional facts:** Founded by Sisters of Divine Providence.

DEGREES OFFERED. BA, BS, MS. 279 bachelor's degrees awarded in 1992. 7% in architecture and environmental design, 34% business and management, 25% health sciences, 6% letters/literature, 8% psychology, 10% visual and performing arts. Graduate degrees offered in 5 major fields of study.

UNDERGRADUATE MAJORS. Accounting, behavioral sciences, biology, business administration and management, chemistry, chemistry management, clinical laboratory science, communications, computer and information sciences, English, English literature, finance, graphic arts technology, graphic design, history, human services, information sciences and systems, interior design, international business management, medical laboratory technologies, nursing, predentistry, prelaw, premedicine, preveterinary, psychobiology, psychology, radiograph medical technology, religion, religious education, respiratory therapy technology, social sciences, sociology, technical and business writing.

ACADEMIC PROGRAMS. Accelerated program, dual enrollment of high school students, honors program, independent study, internships, cross-registration. **Remedial services:** Learning center, preadmission summer program, reduced course load, remedial instruction, special counselor, tutoring. **ROTC:** Air Force, Army. **Placement/credit:** AP, CLEP General and Subject, institutional tests; 60 credit hours maximum for bachelor's degree.

ACADEMIC REQUIREMENTS. Freshmen must earn minimum GPA of 1.8 to continue in good standing. 60% of freshmen return for sophomore year. Students must declare major by end of second year. **Graduation requirements:** 120 hours for bachelor's (30 in major). Most students required to take courses in computer science, English, history, humanities, mathematics, biological/physical sciences, social sciences.

FRESHMAN ADMISSIONS. Selection criteria: College preparatory curriculum required. Depth and rigor of curriculum considered, rank in upper 50% preferred. Standardized test scores required and considered in relation to other factors. Recommendation from guidance counselor required. Extra-curricular involvements considered. Interviews recommended. **High school preparation:** 16 units recommended. Recommended units include English 4, foreign language 2, mathematics 3, social science 4 and science 3. **Test requirements:** SAT or ACT (SAT preferred); score report by May 30.

1992 FRESHMAN CLASS PROFILE. 40 men, 88 women enrolled. 21% had high school GPA of 3.0 or higher, 61% between 2.0 and 2.99. **Academic background:** Mid 50% of enrolled freshmen had SAT-V between 320-450, SAT-M between 370-480. 93% submitted SAT scores. **Characteristics:** 88% from in state, 73% live in college housing, 4% have minority backgrounds, 2% are foreign students, 5% join fraternities/sororities. Average age is 19.

FALL-TERM APPLICATIONS. $25 fee, may be waived for applicants with need. No closing date; applicants notified on a rolling basis. Interview recommended. Deferred and early admission available. Institutional early decision plan.

STUDENT LIFE. Housing: Dormitories (coed). Student housing limited. Spaces filled on first come first served basis. **Activities:** Student government, film, magazine, student newspaper, yearbook, handbook, drama, fraternities, sororities, campus ministry, professional organizations, Project Forward, multicultural Organization, student senate.

ATHLETICS. NAIA. **Intercollegiate:** Baseball M, soccer M, softball W, volleyball W. **Intramural:** Basketball, football M, golf, skiing, soccer, softball, table tennis, tennis, volleyball.

STUDENT SERVICES. Aptitude testing, career counseling, employment service for undergraduates, freshman orientation, health services, personal counseling, placement service for graduates, special adviser for adult students, veterans counselor, services/facilities for handicapped.

ANNUAL EXPENSES. Tuition and fees: $8,682. **Room and board:** $4,555. **Books and supplies:** $600. **Other expenses:** $1,000.

FINANCIAL AID. 82% of freshmen, 75% of continuing students receive some form of aid. 94% of grants, 72% of loans, 99% of jobs based on need. 96 enrolled freshmen were judged to have need, all were offered aid. Academic, leadership, alumni affiliation, religious affiliation, minority scholarships available. **Aid applications:** No closing date; priority given to applications received by May 1; applicants notified on a rolling basis beginning on or about February 15; must reply within 4 weeks.

ADDRESS/TELEPHONE. Barry Duerr, Director of Admissions, La Roche College, 9000 Babcock Boulevard, Pittsburgh, PA 15237. (412) 367-9241.

La Salle University
Philadelphia, Pennsylvania CB code: 2363

Admissions: 65% of applicants accepted
Based on: ••• School record, test scores
•• Essay, interview, recommendations
• Activities, special talents
Completion: 87% of freshmen end year in good standing
80% graduate, 17% of these enter graduate study

4-year private university and liberal arts college, coed, affiliated with Roman Catholic Church. Founded in 1863. **Accreditation:** Regional. **Undergraduate enrollment:** 1,630 men, 1,526 women full time; 477 men, 1,119 women part time. **Graduate enrollment:** 40 men, 43 women full time; 536 men, 590 women part time. **Faculty:** 324 total (228 full time), 214 with doctorates or other terminal degrees. **Location:** Urban campus in very large city; 6 miles from downtown. **Calendar:** Semester, extensive summer session. Saturday and extensive evening/early morning classes. **Microcomputers:** 181 located in libraries, classrooms, computer centers. **Special facilities:** Language laboratory, art museum, urban studies center, Penlym Biology Station. **Additional facts:** School of continuing studies and graduate programs offered at 4 off-campus sites.

DEGREES OFFERED. AA, AS, BA, BS, BFA, MA, MBA, MEd. 43 associate degrees awarded in 1992. 65% in business and management, 6% business/office and marketing/distribution, 10% communications, 10% education, 6% health sciences. 948 bachelor's degrees awarded. 32% in business and management, 10% communications, 10% education, 5% letters/literature, 8% life sciences, 7% physical sciences, 6% psychology, 16% social sciences. Graduate degrees offered in 25 major fields of study.

UNDERGRADUATE MAJORS. Associate: Accounting, Bible studies, business administration and management, business and office, business data processing and related programs, business data programming, computer programming, finance, health care administration, health sciences, humanities, information sciences and systems, insurance marketing, law enforcement and corrections technologies, liberal/general studies, marketing and distribution, public affairs. **Bachelor's:** Accounting, advertising, American literature, art history, Bible studies, biochemistry, biological and physical sciences, biology, business administration and management, business and management, business computer/console/peripheral equipment operation, business economics, business statistics, chemistry, classics, clinical psychology, communications, comparative literature, computer and information sciences, computer mathematics, computer programming, counseling psychology, creative writing, criminal justice studies, criminology, data processing, earth sciences, economics, education, education of the emotionally handicapped, education of the mentally handicapped, education of the multiple handicapped, education of the physically handicapped, elementary education, English, English education, English literature, experimental psychology, finance, foreign languages education, French, geology, German, Greek (classical), health care administration, health sciences, history, human resources development, humanities, humanities and social sciences, industrial and organizational psychology, information sciences and systems, insurance marketing, Italian, journalism, junior high education, labor/industrial relations, Latin, law enforcement and corrections, liberal/general studies, management information systems, management science, marketing and distribution, marketing management, mathematics, mathematics education, music, music history and appreciation, nursing, operations research, optometry, organizational behavior, personnel management, philosophy, physical sciences, physics, political science and government, predentistry, prelaw, premedicine, prepharmacy, preveterinary, psychology, public administration, public relations, radio/television broadcasting, religion, religious education, Russian, school psychology, science education, secondary education, small business management and ownership, social psychology, social science education, social sciences, social studies education, social work, sociology, Spanish, special education, statistics, theological studies, urban studies.

ACADEMIC PROGRAMS. Accelerated program, cooperative education, double major, dual enrollment of high school students, honors program, independent study, internships, student-designed major, study abroad, teacher preparation, visiting/exchange student program, cross-registration, 2+2 with Thomas Jefferson University; combined bachelor's/graduate program in business administration. **Remedial services:** Learning center, preadmission summer program, reduced course load, remedial instruction, special counselor, tutoring. **ROTC:** Air Force, Army, Naval. **Placement/credit:** AP, CLEP General and Subject, institutional tests; 70 credit hours maximum for bachelor's degree.

ACADEMIC REQUIREMENTS. Freshmen must earn minimum GPA of 1.5 to continue in good standing. 90% of freshmen return for sophomore year. Students must declare major by end of second year. **Graduation requirements:** 120 hours for bachelor's (45 in major). Most students required to take courses in computer science, English, history, mathematics, philosophy/religion, biological/physical sciences, social sciences. **Postgraduate studies:** 4% enter law school, 3% enter medical school, 2% enter MBA programs, 8% enter other graduate study. **Additional information:** Associate degree offered only through evening division.

FRESHMAN ADMISSIONS. Selection criteria: High school GPA, class rank, test scores most important. Activities, recommendations, and interview considered. Special consideration given to relatives of alumni. **High school preparation:** 16 units required. Required units include biological science 1, English 4, foreign language 2, mathematics 3 and social science 2. 1 natural science also required. Social science must include 1 history. **Test requirements:** SAT or ACT (SAT preferred); score report by July 1. **Additional information:** Admission through Academic Discovery Program (ADP) provides counseling and tutorial support for students who need academic assistance and meet certain criteria of financial need.

1992 FRESHMAN CLASS PROFILE. 1,416 men applied, 919 accepted, 302 enrolled; 1,534 women applied, 996 accepted, 328 enrolled. 62% had high school GPA of 3.0 or higher, 38% between 2.0 and 2.99. 25% were in top tenth and 76% were in top quarter of graduating class. **Academic background:** Mid 50% of enrolled freshmen had SAT-V between 470-550, SAT-M between 490-590. 100% submitted SAT scores. **Characteristics:** 68% from in state, 67% live in college housing, 16% have minority backgrounds, 2% are foreign students, 2% join fraternities/sororities. Average age is 18.

FALL-TERM APPLICATIONS. $20 fee, may be waived for applicants with need. Closing date August 15; priority given to applications received by May 1; applicants notified on a rolling basis; must reply by May 1 or within 2 weeks if notified thereafter. Essay required. Interview recommended. CRDA. Deferred and early admission available.

STUDENT LIFE. Housing: Dormitories (coed); apartment, fraternity, sorority housing available. **Activities:** Student government, film, magazine, radio, student newspaper, television, yearbook, choral groups, concert band, drama, jazz band, music ensembles, musical theater, pep band, fraternities, sororities, Black Student Union, campus ministry, Hillel, women's center, international club, social work association, veterans club, Young Socialist Alliance, student council for exceptional children, urban center. **Additional information:** Non-alcoholic night club and eatery available to all students 7 days a week.

ATHLETICS. NCAA. **Intercollegiate:** Baseball M, basketball, cross-country, diving, field hockey W, golf, ice hockey M, rifle, rowing (crew), soccer, softball W, swimming, tennis, track and field, volleyball W, wrestling M. **Intramural:** Basketball, diving, golf, handball, ice hockey M, racquetball, rugby M, skiing, soccer, softball, squash, swimming, table tennis, tennis, volleyball, water polo.

STUDENT SERVICES. Career counseling, employment service for undergraduates, freshman orientation, health services, on-campus day care, personal counseling, placement service for graduates, special adviser for adult students, veterans counselor, services/facilities for handicapped.

ANNUAL EXPENSES. Tuition and fees (1992-93): $10,970. **Room and board:** $5,140. **Books and supplies:** $500.

FINANCIAL AID. 70% of freshmen, 70% of continuing students receive some form of aid. 54% of grants, 85% of loans, 30% of jobs based on need. 437 enrolled freshmen were judged to have need, 413 were offered aid. Academic, athletic, religious affiliation scholarships available. **Aid applications:** Closing date February 15; applicants notified on a rolling basis beginning on or about April 1; must reply by May 1 or within 2 weeks if notified thereafter.

ADDRESS/TELEPHONE. Br. Gerald Fitzgerald, FSC, Director of Admissions, La Salle University, 20th Street and Olney Avenue, Philadelphia, PA 19141. (215) 951-1500. (800) 328-1910.

Lackawanna Junior College
Scranton, Pennsylvania CB code: 2373

2-year private junior college, coed. Founded in 1894. **Accreditation:** Regional. **Undergraduate enrollment:** 173 men, 256 women full time; 97 men, 265 women part time. **Faculty:** 68 total (25 full time). **Location:** Urban campus in small city. **Calendar:** Semester, limited summer session. Saturday and extensive evening/early morning classes. **Microcomputers:** 100 located in libraries, computer centers. **Additional facts:** Additional centers at Hazelton and Honesdale. Affiliations with American Institute of Banking and ACT 120 mandatory police training.

DEGREES OFFERED. AA, AS. 111 associate degrees awarded in 1992. 30% in business and management, 35% business/office and marketing/distribution, 10% computer sciences, 10% multi/interdisciplinary studies, 15% social sciences.

UNDERGRADUATE MAJORS. Accounting, business administration and management, business and management, business and office, computer and information sciences, criminology, finance, law enforcement and corrections technologies, legal assistant/paralegal, liberal/general studies, management information systems, marketing and distribution, medical secretary, office supervision and management, retailing, secretarial and related programs.

ACADEMIC PROGRAMS. 2-year transfer program, cooperative education, double major, independent study, weekend college. **Remedial services:** Learning center, preadmission summer program, reduced course load, remedial instruction, special counselor, tutoring, Act 101 support service program. **Placement/credit:** AP, CLEP General and Subject, institutional tests; 32 credit hours maximum for associate degree.

ACADEMIC REQUIREMENTS. Freshmen must earn minimum GPA of 2.0 to continue in good standing. 80% of freshmen return for sophomore

year. Students must declare major on enrollment. **Graduation requirements:** 64 hours for associate (32 in major). Most students required to take courses in computer science, English, humanities, mathematics, social sciences. **Additional information:** Career PREP Center offers career development planning and career placement to residents of Northeastern Pennsylvania free of charge.

FRESHMAN ADMISSIONS. Selection criteria: Open admissions. **High school preparation:** 21 units recommended. Recommended units include English 4, mathematics 3, social science 1 and science 3. **Test requirements:** SAT or ACT (SAT preferred) for placement and counseling only; score report by September 6.

1992 FRESHMAN CLASS PROFILE. 223 men and women enrolled. 20% had high school GPA of 3.0 or higher, 60% between 2.0 and 2.99. **Academic background:** Mid 50% of enrolled freshmen had SAT-V between 300-400, SAT-M between 300-400. 65% submitted SAT scores. **Characteristics:** 99% from in state, 100% commute, 1% have minority backgrounds. Average age is 19.

FALL-TERM APPLICATIONS. $35 fee, may be waived for applicants with need. No closing date; applicants notified on a rolling basis; must reply within 4 weeks. Interview recommended. Deferred and early admission available.

STUDENT LIFE. Activities: Student government, student newspaper, yearbook.

ATHLETICS. NJCAA. **Intercollegiate:** Baseball M, basketball, football M, softball W.

STUDENT SERVICES. Aptitude testing, career counseling, employment service for undergraduates, freshman orientation, personal counseling, placement service for graduates, special adviser for adult students, veterans counselor, services/facilities for handicapped.

ANNUAL EXPENSES. Tuition and fees: $5,920. **Books and supplies:** $516. **Other expenses:** $2,400.

FINANCIAL AID. 80% of freshmen, 80% of continuing students receive some form of aid. 97% of grants, 89% of loans, 95% of jobs based on need. 194 enrolled freshmen were judged to have need, 150 were offered aid. Academic, athletic, leadership scholarships available. **Aid applications:** No closing date; priority given to applications received by May 1; applicants notified on a rolling basis beginning on or about May 1; must reply within 2 weeks.

ADDRESS/TELEPHONE. Nadine Oliver, Director of Admissions and Career Prep Center, Lackawanna Junior College, 901 Prospect Avenue, Scranton, PA 18505. (717) 961-7841. Fax: (717) 961-7858.

Lafayette College

Easton, Pennsylvania CB code: 2361

Admissions: 58% of applicants accepted
Based on: ••• School record
•• Activities, essay, recommendations, special talents, test scores
• Interview
Completion: 94% of freshmen end year in good standing
92% graduate, 25% of these enter graduate study

4-year private college of arts and sciences and engineering college, coed, affiliated with Presbyterian Church (USA). Founded in 1826. **Accreditation:** Regional. **Undergraduate enrollment:** 1,099 men, 871 women full time; 181 men, 59 women part time. **Faculty:** 227 total (174 full time), 176 with doctorates or other terminal degrees. **Location:** Suburban campus in large town; 80 miles from New York City, 60 miles from Philadelphia. **Calendar:** Semester, limited summer session. Extensive evening/early morning classes. **Microcomputers:** 150 located in libraries, classrooms, computer centers, campus-wide network. **Special facilities:** Advanced computer aided design laboratory in engineering lab, satellite downlink capability in language lab, transmission electron microscope, scanning electron microscope.

DEGREES OFFERED. BA, BS. 533 bachelor's degrees awarded in 1992. 21% in engineering, 10% letters/literature, 11% life sciences, 6% psychology, 38% social sciences.

UNDERGRADUATE MAJORS. American studies, anthropology, biochemistry, biological and physical sciences, biology, chemical engineering, chemistry, civil engineering, computer and information sciences, economics, electrical/electronics/communications engineering, engineering, engineering and other disciplines, English, fine arts, French, geology, German, history, humanities and social sciences, international relations, international studies, mathematics, mechanical engineering, music history and appreciation, philosophy, physics, political science and government, psychobiology, psychology, religion, Russian, sociology, Spanish.

ACADEMIC PROGRAMS. Double major, dual enrollment of high school students, honors program, independent study, internships, semester at sea, student-designed major, study abroad, visiting/exchange student program, Washington semester, cross-registration; liberal arts/career combination in engineering. **Remedial services:** Reduced course load, special counselor, tutoring. **ROTC:** Army. **Placement/credit:** AP, IB, institutional tests.

ACADEMIC REQUIREMENTS. No policy requiring minimum GPA; records of students having academic difficulty are reviewed individually. 94% of freshmen return for sophomore year. Students must declare major by end of second year. **Graduation requirements:** 120 hours for bachelor's (36 in major). Most students required to take courses in English, humanities, mathematics, biological/physical sciences, social sciences. **Postgraduate studies:** 7% enter law school, 6% enter medical school, 12% enter other graduate study. **Additional information:** Self-designed majors include psychobiology, pre-architecture, area studies. Interdisiplinary minors also offered.

FRESHMAN ADMISSIONS. Selection criteria: Academic performance, class rank, quality of courses taken, personal qualities, extracurricular record, recommendations, and standardized test results are important factors. Special consideration to applicants who will contribute diversity to student body. **High school preparation:** 16 units required. Required units include English 4, foreign language 2, mathematics 3 and science 2. 4 mathematics, chemistry, physics required of bachelor's of science degree candidates. **Test requirements:** SAT or ACT (SAT preferred); score report by March 1.

1992 FRESHMAN CLASS PROFILE. 2,458 men applied, 1,335 accepted, 312 enrolled; 1,581 women applied, 1,026 accepted, 265 enrolled. **Academic background:** Mid 50% of enrolled freshmen had SAT-V between 500-590, SAT-M between 570-680. 99% submitted SAT scores. **Characteristics:** 24% from in state, 99% live in college housing, 6% have minority backgrounds, 5% are foreign students, 60% join fraternities/sororities. Average age is 18.

FALL-TERM APPLICATIONS. $40 fee, may be waived for applicants with need. Closing date January 15; applicants notified on or about April 1; must reply by May 1. Portfolio required for art applicants. Essay required. Interview recommended. CRDA. Deferred and early admission available. EDP-F. Two early decision deadlines: November 1 and January 1. Candidates applying for early decision will be continuously reviewed until final admissions decisions are reached. Regular decision candidates filing by December 1 receive notification of their status by February 1.

STUDENT LIFE. Housing: Dormitories (men, women, coed); apartment, fraternity, sorority, cooperative housing available. Scholars house, Black Cultural Center, Hillel House, arts house, special interest group floors in residence halls available. **Activities:** Student government, magazine, radio, student newspaper, yearbook, choral groups, concert band, drama, jazz band, music ensembles, pep band, symphony orchestra, free performing arts series, fraternities, sororities, Hillel, Association for Black Collegians, International Student Association, Association for Lafayette Women, Muslim Student Association, Apartheid Awareness Association, Lafayette Activities Forum, Lafayette Environmental Awareness and Protection Group, Community Outreach Center, Association of Students Interested in Asia. **Additional information:** Over 100 student-run college funded groups and organizations focusing on environmental, political, service, and social issues. Services/facilities for visual or hearing impaired students and for speech or communication disorders available on individual need basis.

ATHLETICS. NCAA. **Intercollegiate:** Baseball M, basketball, cross-country, diving, fencing, field hockey W, football M, golf, lacrosse, rowing (crew), rugby M, skiing, soccer, softball W, swimming, tennis, track and field, volleyball W, wrestling M. **Intramural:** Badminton, basketball, bowling, cross-country, football M, horseback riding, racquetball, skiing, soccer, softball, squash, swimming, table tennis, tennis, track and field, volleyball, water polo, wrestling M. **Clubs:** Cricket, martial arts, ultimate frisbee, weightlifting, horseback riding, crew, rugby, squash.

STUDENT SERVICES. Career counseling, employment service for undergraduates, freshman orientation, health services, on-campus day care, personal counseling, placement service for graduates, special adviser for adult students, services/facilities for handicapped.

ANNUAL EXPENSES. Tuition and fees: $17,950. **Room and board:** $5,500. **Books and supplies:** $550. **Other expenses:** $900.

FINANCIAL AID. 60% of freshmen, 58% of continuing students receive some form of aid. All grants, 84% of loans, 39% of jobs based on need. 260 enrolled freshmen were judged to have need, all were offered aid. **Aid applications:** No closing date; priority given to applications received by February 15; applicants notified on a rolling basis beginning on or about March 19; must reply by May 1 or within 1 week if notified thereafter. **Additional information:** Parent loans through bank with college absorbing interest while student enrolled. Family has 8 years after graduation to repay. Not limited to those demonstrating need.

ADDRESS/TELEPHONE. G. Gary Ripple, Director of Admissions, Lafayette College, 118 Markle Hall, Easton, PA 18042-1770. (215) 250-5100. Fax: (215) 250-9850.

Lancaster Bible College
Lancaster, Pennsylvania CB code: 2388

Admissions: 87% of applicants accepted
Based on: ••• Religious affiliation/commitment
•• Essay, interview, recommendations, school record
• Activities, special talents, test scores
Completion: 93% of freshmen end year in good standing
49% graduate, 10% of these enter graduate study

4-year private Bible college, coed, nondenominational. Founded in 1933. **Accreditation:** Regional. **Undergraduate enrollment:** 151 men, 141 women full time; 79 men, 69 women part time. **Faculty:** 40 total (25 full time), 12 with doctorates or other terminal degrees. **Location:** Suburban campus in small city; 64 miles from Philadelphia. **Calendar:** Semester, limited summer session. **Microcomputers:** 15 located in computer centers.

DEGREES OFFERED. AS, BS. 16 associate degrees awarded in 1992. 50 bachelor's degrees awarded. 100% in philosophy, religion, theology.

UNDERGRADUATE MAJORS. Associate: Bible studies, secretarial and related programs. **Bachelor's:** Bible studies, missionary studies, religion, religious education, religious music, theological studies.

ACADEMIC PROGRAMS. Independent study, internships, study abroad, teacher preparation. **Remedial services:** Preadmission summer program, reduced course load, remedial instruction, special counselor, tutoring. **Placement/credit:** AP, CLEP Subject; 15 credit hours maximum for associate degree; 30 credit hours maximum for bachelor's degree.

ACADEMIC REQUIREMENTS. Freshmen must earn minimum GPA of 1.5 to continue in good standing. 69% of freshmen return for sophomore year. Students must declare major by end of first year. **Graduation requirements:** 62 hours for associate (24 in major), 122 hours for bachelor's (48 in major). Most students required to take courses in English, history, mathematics, philosophy/religion, biological/physical sciences, social sciences. **Postgraduate studies:** 25% from 2-year programs enter 4-year programs.

FRESHMAN ADMISSIONS. Selection criteria: Academic ability and interest in religious professions. Recommendation from friend, pastor, teacher, or school official important. **Test requirements:** ACT for placement and counseling only.

1992 FRESHMAN CLASS PROFILE. 82 men applied, 68 accepted, 50 enrolled; 58 women applied, 54 accepted, 33 enrolled. 50% had high school GPA of 3.0 or higher, 39% between 2.0 and 2.99. 3% were in top tenth and 30% were in top quarter of graduating class. **Academic background:** Mid 50% of enrolled freshmen had ACT composite between 16-22. 73% submitted ACT scores. **Characteristics:** 71% from in state, 59% live in college housing, 7% have minority backgrounds. Average age is 21.

FALL-TERM APPLICATIONS. $15 fee, may be waived for applicants with need. No closing date; priority given to applications received by August 1; applicants notified on a rolling basis; must reply as soon as possible. Audition required for religious music applicants. Essay required. Interview recommended. Deferred and early admission available.

STUDENT LIFE. Housing: Dormitories (men, women); apartment housing available. **Activities:** Student government, student newspaper, yearbook, choral groups, drama, music ensembles. **Additional information:** Religious observance required.

ATHLETICS. Intercollegiate: Baseball M, basketball, soccer M, softball W, tennis, volleyball W. **Intramural:** Basketball, volleyball.

STUDENT SERVICES. Employment service for undergraduates, freshman orientation, health services, personal counseling, placement service for graduates, services/facilities for handicapped.

ANNUAL EXPENSES. Tuition and fees: $7,410. **Room and board:** $3,300. **Books and supplies:** $450. **Other expenses:** $1,400.

FINANCIAL AID. 94% of freshmen, 86% of continuing students receive some form of aid. 54% of grants, all loans, all jobs based on need. 56 enrolled freshmen were judged to have need, all were offered aid. Academic, music/drama, leadership, alumni affiliation, minority scholarships available. **Aid applications:** No closing date; priority given to applications received by June 1; applicants notified on a rolling basis beginning on or about April 15; must reply by August 1 or within 2 weeks of contract date.

ADDRESS/TELEPHONE. Joanne Roper, Director of Admissions, Lancaster Bible College, 901 Eden Road, Lancaster, PA 17601. (717) 560-8271. (800) 544-7335. Fax: (717) 560-8213.

Lansdale School of Business
North Wales, Pennsylvania CB code: 5853

2-year proprietary business college, coed. **Undergraduate enrollment:** 270 men and women. **Location:** Suburban campus in small town; 25 miles north of Philadelphia. **Calendar:** Semester.

FRESHMAN ADMISSIONS. Selection criteria: Open admissions.

ANNUAL EXPENSES. Tuition and fees (1992-93): $4,960. **Books and supplies:** $425.

ADDRESS/TELEPHONE. Marianne Hylinski, Director of Admissions, Lansdale School of Business, 201 Church Road, North Wales, PA 19454. (215) 699-5700.

Lebanon Valley College of Pennsylvania
Annville, Pennsylvania CB code: 2364

Admissions: 75% of applicants accepted
Based on: ••• School record
•• Interview, recommendations
• Activities, essay, special talents, test scores
Completion: 81% of freshmen end year in good standing
70% graduate, 16% of these enter graduate study

4-year private liberal arts college, coed, affiliated with United Methodist Church. Founded in 1866. **Accreditation:** Regional. **Undergraduate enrollment:** 489 men, 382 women full time; 152 men, 332 women part time. **Graduate enrollment:** 126 men, 40 women part time. **Faculty:** 89 total (66 full time), 56 with doctorates or other terminal degrees. **Location:** Rural campus in small town; 7 miles from Hershey. **Calendar:** Semester, limited summer session. **Microcomputers:** 180 located in dormitories, libraries, classrooms, computer centers, campus-wide network. **Additional facts:** Candidate for accreditation for master's in business program.

DEGREES OFFERED. BA, BS, MBA. 11 associate degrees awarded in 1992. 238 bachelor's degrees awarded. 24% in business and management, 15% teacher education, 6% letters/literature, 12% life sciences, 9% mathematics, 5% physical sciences, 5% psychology, 12% social sciences. Graduate degrees offered in 1 major field of study.

UNDERGRADUATE MAJORS. Associate: Business and management, liberal/general studies. **Bachelor's:** Accounting, actuarial sciences, allied health, American studies, biochemistry, biology, business and management, chemistry, clinical laboratory science, computer and information sciences, cytotechnology, dental hygiene, economics, elementary education, engineering, English, foreign languages (multiple emphasis), forestry and related sciences, French, German, health care administration, history, hotel/motel and restaurant management, information sciences and systems, international business management, liberal/general studies, mathematics, medical laboratory technologies, music, music education, music performance, occupational therapy, philosophy, physical therapy, physics, political science and government, practical nursing, psychobiology, psychology, radiograph medical technology, religion, religious music, secondary education, social work, sociology, sound recording technologies, Spanish, ultrasound technology.

ACADEMIC PROGRAMS. 2-year transfer program, double major, dual enrollment of high school students, honors program, independent study, internships, student-designed major, study abroad, teacher preparation, visiting/exchange student program, weekend college, Washington semester; liberal arts/career combination in engineering, forestry, health sciences; combined bachelor's/graduate program in business administration. **Remedial services:** Learning center, reduced course load, special counselor, tutoring. **ROTC:** Army. **Placement/credit:** AP, CLEP General and Subject, institutional tests; 30 credit hours maximum for bachelor's degree.

ACADEMIC REQUIREMENTS. Freshmen must earn minimum GPA of 1.6 to continue in good standing. 85% of freshmen return for sophomore year. Students must declare major by end of second year. **Graduation requirements:** 60 hours for associate, 122 hours for bachelor's (27 in major). Most students required to take courses in arts/fine arts, computer science, English, foreign languages, history, humanities, mathematics, philosophy/religion, biological/physical sciences, social sciences. **Additional information:** A master's in business administration program available on a part-time basis, evenings and weekends. Individualized major in conjunction with Pennsylvania School of Art and Design (PSAD); student attends PSAD for 3 years then completes 40 credit hours at LVC.

FRESHMAN ADMISSIONS. Selection criteria: High school achievement record most important. Recommendations, test scores, school or community activities evaluated. **High school preparation:** 16 units required. Required units include biological science 2, English 4, foreign language 2, mathematics 2, physical science 1 and social science 2. **Test requirements:** SAT or ACT (SAT preferred).

1992 FRESHMAN CLASS PROFILE. 708 men applied, 493 accepted, 162 enrolled; 492 women applied, 406 accepted, 126 enrolled. 27% were in top tenth and 55% were in top quarter of graduating class. **Academic background:** Mid 50% of enrolled freshmen had SAT-V between 400-510, SAT-M between 440-580. 99% submitted SAT scores. **Characteristics:** 83% from in state, 89% live in college housing, 5% have minority backgrounds, 4% are foreign students, 12% join fraternities/sororities. Average age is 18.

FALL-TERM APPLICATIONS. $25 fee, may be waived for applicants with need. No closing date; priority given to applications received by April 1; applicants notified on a rolling basis. Audition required for music applicants. Interview recommended. CRDA. Deferred and early admission available. Candidates must reply by May 1 or within 2-4 weeks if notified thereafter.

STUDENT LIFE. Housing: Dormitories (men, women, coed). **Activities:** Student government, radio, student newspaper, yearbook, choral groups, concert band, dance, drama, jazz band, marching band, music ensembles, musical theater, symphony orchestra, fraternities, sororities, Fellowship of Christian Athletes, service fraternities, College Republicans, Young Democrats, Black Culture Club, SAFE (Student Action for the Earth), Hispanic Culture Club.

ATHLETICS. NCAA. **Intercollegiate:** Baseball M, basketball, cross-country, field hockey W, football M, golf M, soccer M, softball W, swimming, tennis, track and field, volleyball W, wrestling M. **Intramural:** Archery, badminton, baseball M, basketball, bowling, cross-country, football M, golf M, handball, lacrosse M, racquetball, softball, squash, swimming, table tennis, tennis, track and field M, volleyball, wrestling M.

STUDENT SERVICES. Aptitude testing, career counseling, employment service for undergraduates, freshman orientation, health services, on-campus day care, personal counseling, placement service for graduates, special adviser for adult students, veterans counselor, services/facilities for handicapped.

ANNUAL EXPENSES. Tuition and fees: $13,700. **Room and board:** $4,600. **Books and supplies:** $425. **Other expenses:** $600.

FINANCIAL AID. 78% of freshmen, 80% of continuing students receive some form of aid. 87% of grants, 91% of loans, 53% of jobs based on need. Academic, leadership scholarships available. **Aid applications:** No closing date; priority given to applications received by March 1; applicants notified on a rolling basis beginning on or about March 1.

ADDRESS/TELEPHONE. William J. Brown, Jr, Director of Admission, Lebanon Valley College of Pennsylvania, 101 North College Avenue, Annville, PA 17003-0501. (717) 867-6181. (800) 445-6181. Fax: (717) 867-6026.

Lehigh County Community College
Schnecksville, Pennsylvania — CB code: 2381

2-year public community college, coed. Founded in 1966. **Accreditation:** Regional. **Undergraduate enrollment:** 732 men, 886 women full time; 1,197 men, 2,267 women part time. **Faculty:** 209 total (80 full time), 10 with doctorates or other terminal degrees. **Location:** Rural campus in rural community; 8 miles from Allentown. **Calendar:** Semester, limited summer session. **Microcomputers:** 125 located in libraries, classrooms, computer centers.

DEGREES OFFERED. AA, AS, AAS. 527 associate degrees awarded in 1992. 15% in business and management, 7% business/office and marketing/distribution, 9% education, 23% allied health, 13% multi/interdisciplinary studies, 12% parks/recreation, protective services, public affairs, 12% trade and industry.

UNDERGRADUATE MAJORS. Accounting, air conditioning/heating/refrigeration mechanics, air conditioning/heating/refrigeration technology, airline piloting and navigation, apparel and accessories marketing, automotive mechanics, automotive technology, aviation management, biomedical equipment technology, business administration and management, business and office, business data processing and related programs, business data programming, computer and information sciences, computer programming, criminal justice studies, data processing, drafting, drafting and design technology, early childhood education, education, electrical technology, electrical/electronics/communications engineering, electronic technology, engineering, fashion merchandising, hotel/motel and restaurant management, humanities, humanities and social sciences, industrial technology, information sciences and systems, law enforcement and corrections, legal secretary, marketing and distribution, mathematics, mechanical design technology, medical assistant, medical records administration, medical records technology, medical secretary, nursing, occupational therapy assistant, physical therapy assistant, purchasing and materials management, radio/television technology, real estate, respiratory therapy, respiratory therapy technology, secretarial and related programs, social sciences, tourism, transportation and travel marketing, word processing.

ACADEMIC PROGRAMS. 2-year transfer program, telecourses, cross-registration. **Remedial services:** Learning center, preadmission summer program, reduced course load, remedial instruction, special counselor, tutoring, basic skills development. **ROTC:** Army. **Placement/credit:** AP, CLEP General and Subject, institutional tests; 18 credit hours maximum for associate degree.

ACADEMIC REQUIREMENTS. Freshmen must earn minimum GPA of 2.0 to continue in good standing. 40% of freshmen return for sophomore year. Students must declare major on enrollment. **Graduation requirements:** 60 hours for associate (36 in major). Most students required to take courses in English, mathematics, biological/physical sciences, social sciences.

FRESHMAN ADMISSIONS. Selection criteria: Open admissions. Selective admission to aviation and some allied health programs. Special requirements for allied health program and nursing. **Test requirements:** Course placement test required. **Additional information:** High school diploma or GED required of allied health applicants, professional pilot applicants, or applicants under the age of 18.

1992 FRESHMAN CLASS PROFILE. 453 men, 771 women enrolled. **Characteristics:** 99% from in state, 100% commute, 6% have minority backgrounds, 1% are foreign students. Average age is 25.

FALL-TERM APPLICATIONS. $20 fee. No closing date; applicants notified on a rolling basis. Interview required for allied health, aviation, early childhood, automotive applicants.

STUDENT LIFE. Activities: Student government, radio, student newspaper, yearbook.

ATHLETICS. NJCAA. **Intercollegiate:** Basketball M, golf, tennis, volleyball W. **Intramural:** Baseball M, basketball, field hockey W, racquetball, soccer M, softball, table tennis, tennis, volleyball.

STUDENT SERVICES. Aptitude testing, career counseling, employment service for undergraduates, freshman orientation, health services, on-campus day care, personal counseling, placement service for graduates, special adviser for adult students, veterans counselor, services/facilities for handicapped.

ANNUAL EXPENSES. Tuition and fees (1992-93): $1,455, $1,530 additional for out-of-district students, $3,060 additional for out-of-state students. **Books and supplies:** $500. **Other expenses:** $400.

FINANCIAL AID. 30% of freshmen, 30% of continuing students receive some form of aid. 85% of grants, 99% of loans, 66% of jobs based on need. Academic scholarships available. **Aid applications:** No closing date; priority given to applications received by March 31; applicants notified on a rolling basis beginning on or about July 1; must reply within 10 days.

ADDRESS/TELEPHONE. David F. Moyer, Director of Admissions, Lehigh County Community College, 4525 Education Park Drive, Schnecksville, PA 18078-2598. (215) 799-1117. Fax: (215) 799-1159.

Lehigh University
Bethlehem, Pennsylvania — CB code: 2365

Admissions:	64% of applicants accepted
Based on:	••• School record
	•• Activities, test scores
	• Essay, interview, recommendations, special talents
Completion:	95% of freshmen end year in good standing
	86% graduate, 15% of these enter graduate study

4-year private university, coed. Founded in 1865. **Accreditation:** Regional. **Undergraduate enrollment:** 2,817 men, 1,561 women full time; 54 men, 41 women part time. **Graduate enrollment:** 607 men, 328 women full time; 641 men, 501 women part time. **Faculty:** 503 total (418 full time), 414 with doctorates or other terminal degrees. **Location:** Suburban campus in small city; 90 miles from New York City, 60 miles from Philadelphia. **Calendar:** Semester, limited summer session. **Microcomputers:** 435 located in dormitories, libraries, classrooms, computer centers, campus-wide network. **Special facilities:** 3 art galleries, Van de Graaf accelerator, CAD-CAM laboratories, robotics laboratories, microprobe, electron microscope, ATLAS (world view room).

DEGREES OFFERED. BA, BS, MA, MS, MBA, MEd, PhD, EdD. 1,070 bachelor's degrees awarded in 1992. 24% in business and management, 34% engineering, 5% life sciences, 5% psychology, 16% social sciences. Graduate degrees offered in 51 major fields of study.

UNDERGRADUATE MAJORS. Accounting, American studies, anthropology, architecture, biochemistry, biological and physical sciences, biology, business administration and management, business economics, chemical engineering, chemistry, civil engineering, classics, cognitive psychology, computer and information sciences, computer engineering, dramatic arts, East Asian studies, economics, electrical/electronics/communications engineering, engineering and other disciplines, engineering mechanics, engineering physics, English, environmental science, finance, fine arts, French, geology, geophysics and seismology, German, history, humanities, humanities and social sciences, industrial engineering, international careers, international relations, international studies, journalism, journalism/science writing, Latin American studies, liberal/general studies, marketing and distribution, materials engineering, mathematics, mechanical engineering, metallurgical engineering, molecular biology, music, neurosciences, philosophy, physics, political science and government, predentistry, premedicine, psychology, religion, Russian, social psychology, social sciences, sociology, Spanish, statistics, urban studies.

ACADEMIC PROGRAMS. Accelerated program, double major, dual enrollment of high school students, honors program, independent study, internships, semester at sea, student-designed major, study abroad, telecourses, New York semester, Washington semester, cross-registration; liberal arts/career combination in engineering; combined bachelor's/graduate program in business administration, medicine. **Remedial services:** Learning center, preadmission summer program, reduced course load, tutoring. **ROTC:** Air Force, Army. **Placement/credit:** AP, IB, institutional tests.

ACADEMIC REQUIREMENTS. Freshmen must earn minimum GPA of 1.6 to continue in good standing. 93% of freshmen return for sophomore year. Students must declare major by end of second year. **Graduation requirements:** 121 hours for bachelor's. Most students required to take courses in English, humanities, mathematics, biological/physical sciences, social sciences. **Postgraduate studies:** 4% enter law school, 2% enter medical school, 9% enter other graduate study.

FRESHMAN ADMISSIONS. Selection criteria: School achievement record, test scores, involvement in extracurricular activities are important. Consideration given to diverse backgrounds and interests. **High school preparation:** 16 units required. Required and recommended units include English 4, foreign language 2, mathematics 4 and science 2. Social science 4 recommended. Chemistry required and physics recommended for engineering and science candidates. Waivers in mathematics granted by some departments to well qualified candidates. **Test requirements:** SAT or ACT; score report by March 1. 3 ACH (including English Composition) required. Mathematics Level I or II and chemistry or physics required of engineering applicants. Score report by July 1.

1992 FRESHMAN CLASS PROFILE. 3,995 men applied, 2,524 accepted, 738 enrolled; 2,317 women applied, 1,539 accepted, 394 enrolled. 40% were in top tenth and 72% were in top quarter of graduating class. **Academic background:** Mid 50% of enrolled freshmen had SAT-V between 470-570, SAT-M between 570-670. 100% submitted SAT scores. **Characteristics:** 26% from in state, 98% live in college housing, 5% have minority backgrounds, 2% are foreign students, 50% join fraternities/sororities. Average age is 18.

FALL-TERM APPLICATIONS. $40 fee, may be waived for applicants with need. Closing date February 15; priority given to applications received by January 1; applicants notified on or about April 1; must reply by May 1. Essay required. Interview recommended. CRDA. Deferred and early admission available. EDP-F; institutional early decision plan. Students may send applications directly or submit them to a high school official.

STUDENT LIFE. Housing: Dormitories (coed); apartment, fraternity, sorority housing available. Special interest housing on campus and one residential college. **Activities:** Student government, magazine, radio, student newspaper, yearbook, choral groups, concert band, dance, drama, jazz band, marching band, music ensembles, musical theater, fraternities, sororities, over 125 clubs and honor societies, cultural groups. **Additional information:** Few students leave campus on weekends.

ATHLETICS. NCAA. **Intercollegiate:** Baseball M, basketball, cross-country, diving, field hockey W, football M, golf M, ice hockey M, lacrosse, rifle, skiing, soccer, softball W, swimming, tennis, track and field, volleyball W, wrestling M. **Intramural:** Badminton, baseball M, basketball, bowling, boxing M, cross-country, fencing, golf, gymnastics, horseback riding, rugby M, sailing, skiing, soccer, softball, squash, swimming, table tennis, tennis, track and field, volleyball, water polo M, wrestling M. **Clubs:** Rugby M, rowing.

STUDENT SERVICES. Aptitude testing, career counseling, employment service for undergraduates, freshman orientation, health services, on-campus day care, personal counseling, placement service for graduates, veterans counselor, services/facilities for handicapped.

ANNUAL EXPENSES. Tuition and fees: $17,750. $250 fee for engineering students. $390 per-credit-hour for college of education summer graduate students. **Room and board:** $5,500. **Books and supplies:** $650. **Other expenses:** $1,100.

FINANCIAL AID. 52% of freshmen, 50% of continuing students receive some form of aid. 94% of grants, 91% of loans, all jobs based on need. 508 enrolled freshmen were judged to have need, all were offered aid. Academic scholarships available. **Aid applications:** Closing date February 5; applicants notified on or about April 10; must reply by May 1.

ADDRESS/TELEPHONE. Patricia G. Boig, Director of Admissions, Lehigh University, Alumni Memorial Building, 27 Memorial Drive West, Bethlehem, PA 18015-3094. (215) 758-3100. Fax: (215) 758-4361.

Lincoln Technical Institute
Allentown, Pennsylvania — CB code: 2741

2-year proprietary technical college, coed. Founded in 1949. **Undergraduate enrollment:** 650 men and women. **Location:** Suburban campus in small city. **Calendar:** Semester.

DEGREES OFFERED. AS.

UNDERGRADUATE MAJORS. Electrical/electronics/communications engineering.

FRESHMAN ADMISSIONS. Selection criteria: Open admissions.

1992 FRESHMAN CLASS PROFILE. 200 men and women enrolled. **Characteristics:** 80% commute.

FALL-TERM APPLICATIONS. $100 fee. No closing date; applicants notified on a rolling basis.

STUDENT LIFE. Housing: Apartment housing available.

ANNUAL EXPENSES. Tuition and fees (1992-93): $5,472. Tuition and fees vary for part-time programs and degree programs other than electronics technology. **Books and supplies:** $750.

ADDRESS/TELEPHONE. Brian Santangelo, Director of Admissions, Lincoln Technical Institute, 5151 Tilghman Street, Allentown, PA 18104. (215) 398-5301.

Lincoln University
Lincoln University, Pennsylvania — CB code: 2367

Admissions: 67% of applicants accepted
Based on:
••• Essay
•• Activities, recommendations, school record, special talents, test scores
• Interview
Completion: 86% of freshmen end year in good standing
23% graduate, 51% of these enter graduate study

4-year private university and liberal arts college, coed. Founded in 1854. **Accreditation:** Regional. **Undergraduate enrollment:** 508 men, 741 women full time; 13 men, 17 women part time. **Graduate enrollment:** 78 men, 117 women full time; 3 women part time. **Faculty:** 144 total (90 full time), 72 with doctorates or other terminal degrees. **Location:** Rural campus in rural community; 45 miles from Philadelphia. **Calendar:** Trimester, limited summer session. **Microcomputers:** 125 located in dormitories, libraries, classrooms, computer centers, campus-wide network. **Special facilities:** Special collections library.

DEGREES OFFERED. BA, BS, M. 207 bachelor's degrees awarded in 1992. 29% in business and management, 5% computer sciences, 9% education, 9% psychology, 24% social sciences.

UNDERGRADUATE MAJORS. Accounting, art education, biology, business administration and management, business economics, chemistry, Chinese, communications, computer and information sciences, criminal justice studies, early childhood education, economics, education, elementary education, engineering and engineering-related technologies, English, English education, finance, foreign languages education, French, health education, history, human services, industrial and organizational psychology, international public service, journalism, mathematics, mathematics education, music, music education, philosophy, physical education, physical sciences, physics, political science and government, preengineering, psychology, public affairs, recreation and community services technologies, recreation therapy, religious education, Russian, science education, secondary education, social studies education, social work, sociology, Spanish.

ACADEMIC PROGRAMS. Accelerated program, cooperative education, double major, dual enrollment of high school students, honors program, independent study, internships, study abroad, teacher preparation, visiting/exchange student program, joint programs in communications and journalism with Temple University; 2-2 in advanced science/engineering with Drexel University, Pennsylvania State University, University of Pittsburgh, Lafayette University, and New Jersey Institute of Technology; liberal arts/career combination in engineering. **Remedial services:** Learning center, preadmission summer program, reduced course load, remedial instruction, special counselor, tutoring. **ROTC:** Air Force. **Placement/credit:** AP, CLEP General and Subject, institutional tests.

ACADEMIC REQUIREMENTS. Freshmen must earn minimum GPA of 2.0 to continue in good standing. 74% of freshmen return for sophomore year. Students must declare major by end of second year. **Graduation requirements:** 120 hours for bachelor's (24 in major). Most students required to take courses in arts/fine arts, computer science, English, foreign languages, history, humanities, mathematics, philosophy/religion, biological/physical sciences, social sciences. **Postgraduate studies:** 1% enter medical school, 10% enter MBA programs, 40% enter other graduate study.

FRESHMAN ADMISSIONS. Selection criteria: 2.0 high school GPA, test scores, school and community activities, counselor's recommendation, writing sample. **High school preparation:** 21 units required. Required and recommended units include English 4, mathematics 3, social science 3 and science 3. Foreign language 2 recommended. 2 arts or humanities, 1 health and physical education, and 5 electives required. **Test requirements:** SAT or ACT (SAT preferred); score report by August 22.

1992 FRESHMAN CLASS PROFILE. 626 men applied, 380 accepted, 138 enrolled; 1,136 women applied, 797 accepted, 228 enrolled. 25% had high school GPA of 3.0 or higher, 75% between 2.0 and 2.99. **Academic background:** Mid 50% of enrolled freshmen had SAT-V between 310-420, SAT-M between 330-430. 97% submitted SAT scores. **Characteristics:** 36% from in state, 99% live in college housing, 98% have minority backgrounds, 1% are foreign students. Average age is 18.

FALL-TERM APPLICATIONS. $10 fee, may be waived for applicants with need. No closing date; applicants notified on a rolling basis; must reply within 2 weeks. Essay required. Interview recommended for borderline applicants. Deferred and early admission available. EDP-F.

STUDENT LIFE. Housing: Dormitories (men, women, coed). **Activities:** Student government, film, radio, student newspaper, yearbook, choral groups, concert band, dance, drama, jazz band, music ensembles, fraternities, sororities, gospel ensemble, Music Educator National Conference, Mu Phi Alpha, Tolson Society, Thurgood Marshall Law Society, Phi Kappa Epsilon Honor Society, many social and religious organizations.

ATHLETICS. NCAA. **Intercollegiate:** Baseball M, basketball, cross-country, soccer M, swimming, tennis, track and field, volleyball, wrestling M. **Intramural:** Archery, badminton, baseball M, basketball, bowling, cross-country, football M, softball, swimming, table tennis, tennis, track and field, volleyball, wrestling M.

STUDENT SERVICES. Career counseling, employment service for undergraduates, freshman orientation, health services, personal counseling, placement service for graduates, services/facilities for handicapped.

ANNUAL EXPENSES. Tuition and fees (1992-93): $2,960, $1,420 additional for out-of-state students. Fees for out-of-state undergraduate students are $380, graduate students $425. **Room and board:** $2,800. **Books and supplies:** $485. **Other expenses:** $1,016.

FINANCIAL AID. 91% of freshmen, 90% of continuing students receive some form of aid. 87% of grants, 73% of loans, 69% of jobs based on need. 301 enrolled freshmen were judged to have need, all were offered aid. Academic, music/drama, alumni affiliation scholarships available. **Aid applications:** No closing date; priority given to applications received by March 1; applicants notified on a rolling basis beginning on or about May 1; must reply by June 15.

ADDRESS/TELEPHONE. Jimmy Arrington, Director of Admissions, Lincoln University, Lincoln Hall, Lincoln University, PA 19352-0999. (215) 932-8300 ext. 206.

Lock Haven University of Pennsylvania
Lock Haven, Pennsylvania CB code: 2654

Admissions: 76% of applicants accepted
Based on: ••• School record
•• Test scores
• Activities, interview, recommendations, special talents
Completion: 85% of freshmen end year in good standing
50% graduate, 12% of these enter graduate study

4-year public university, coed. Founded in 1870. **Accreditation:** Regional. **Undergraduate enrollment:** 1,605 men, 1,999 women full time; 123 men, 152 women part time. **Graduate enrollment:** 1 man full time; 6 men, 10 women part time. **Faculty:** 226 total (214 full time), 112 with doctorates or other terminal degrees. **Location:** Rural campus in small town; 26 miles from Williamsport, 35 miles from State College. **Calendar:** Semester, limited summer session. **Microcomputers:** 100 located in dormitories, libraries, classrooms, computer centers, campus-wide network. **Special facilities:** Model United Nations with translation capabilities, theater, rural retreat conference center, human performance lab with cadaver dissection, electron microscope, primate laboratory. **Additional facts:** Branch campus in Clearfield.

DEGREES OFFERED. AS, BA, BS, BFA, MA. 578 bachelor's degrees awarded. Graduate degrees offered in 1 major field of study.

UNDERGRADUATE MAJORS. Associate: Nursing. **Bachelor's:** Aerospace/aeronautical/astronautical engineering, agricultural engineering, anthropology, biochemistry, biology, business and management, ceramic engineering, chemical engineering, chemistry, clinical laboratory science, communications, computer and information sciences, computer mathematics, computer programming, dramatic arts, early childhood education, earth sciences, economics, education of the emotionally handicapped, education of the mentally handicapped, education of the physically handicapped, electrical/electronics/communications engineering, elementary education, engineering, engineering mechanics, engineering science, English, English education, environmental health engineering, environmental science, fine arts, foreign languages education, French, geography, German, health education, health sciences, history, industrial engineering, information sciences and systems, international and comparative education, international relations, international studies, journalism, junior high education, Latin American studies, liberal/general studies, library science, management information systems, management science, mathematics, mathematics education, mechanical engineering, medical laboratory technologies, metallurgical engineering, mining and mineral engineering, music, music performance, nuclear engineering, parks and recreation management, petroleum engineering, philosophy, physical education, physical sciences, physics, political science and government, predentistry, prelaw, premedicine, prepharmacy, preveterinary, psychology, public relations, radio/television broadcasting, science education, secondary education, social science education, social sciences, social studies education, social work, sociology, Spanish, special education, specific learning disabilities, speech, speech/communication/theater education, sports medicine.

ACADEMIC PROGRAMS. Accelerated program, double major, dual enrollment of high school students, education specialist degree, honors program, independent study, internships, student-designed major, study abroad, teacher preparation, visiting/exchange student program, exchange with institutions in Taiwan, Russia, Australia, France, England, Poland, Germany, Scotland, Costa Rica, China, Japan, Yugoslavia, Mexico, 2-2 program in music education with Clarion University of Pennsylvania and Millersville University of Pennsylvania; liberal arts/career combination in engineering, health sciences. **Remedial services:** Reduced course load, special counselor, tutoring, ACT 101 Educational Opportunity Program for state residents. **ROTC:** Army. **Placement/credit:** AP, CLEP General and Subject, institutional tests; 30 credit hours maximum for bachelor's degree.

ACADEMIC REQUIREMENTS. 79% of freshmen return for sophomore year. Students must declare major by end of second year. **Graduation requirements:** 60 hours for associate, 128 hours for bachelor's. Most students required to take courses in English, foreign languages, history, humanities, mathematics, philosophy/religion, biological/physical sciences, social sciences. **Postgraduate studies:** 1% enter law school, 1% enter medical school, 1% enter MBA programs, 9% enter other graduate study. **Additional information:** Freshman with fewer than 18.5 credits must have 1.5 minimum GPA. Second semester freshman must have 1.7 minimum GPA.

FRESHMAN ADMISSIONS. Selection criteria: School achievement record, class rank, test scores. **High school preparation:** 16 units required; 17 recommended. Required and recommended units include biological science 1, English 4, foreign language 2, mathematics 3-4, physical science 2 and social science 4. 4 units mathematics required for mathematics, computer science, biology, physics, and chemistry majors. Biology, chemistry, physics required for health science majors. Biology, anatomy/physiology, chemistry recommended for health and physical education majors. **Test requirements:** SAT or ACT; score report by March 1. Preferred score report date December 15.

1992 FRESHMAN CLASS PROFILE. 1,736 men applied, 1,294 accepted, 399 enrolled; 2,239 women applied, 1,740 accepted, 524 enrolled. **Academic background:** Mid 50% of enrolled freshmen had SAT-V between 420-500, SAT-M between 470-570. 95% submitted SAT scores. **Characteristics:** 81% from in state, 95% live in college housing, 4% have minority backgrounds, 2% are foreign students. Average age is 18.

FALL-TERM APPLICATIONS. $20 fee, may be waived for applicants with need. No closing date; priority given to applications received by December 15; applicants notified on a rolling basis; must reply by March 1 or within 30 days if notified after February 15. Interview required for social work applicants. Audition required for music applicants. Deferred and early admission available. Institutional early decision plan.

STUDENT LIFE. Housing: Dormitories (men, women, coed); apartment, fraternity, sorority, handicapped housing available. **Activities:** Student government, film, radio, student newspaper, television, literary publication, choral groups, concert band, dance, drama, jazz band, marching band, music ensembles, musical theater, pep band, symphony orchestra, fraternities, sororities, Newman Club, Black Cultural Society, Campus Crusade, Commonwealth Association of Students, Fellowship of Christian Athletes, Social Service Society, Full Gospel Fellowship, model United Nations, New Life Student Fellowship.

ATHLETICS. NCAA. **Intercollegiate:** Baseball M, basketball, cross-country, diving W, field hockey W, football M, golf M, lacrosse W, soccer M, softball W, swimming W, track and field, volleyball W, wrestling M. **Intramural:** Badminton, basketball, boxing M, cross-country, field hockey W, golf, ice hockey M, racquetball, rugby M, skiing, soccer, softball, volleyball, water polo M, wrestling M. **Clubs:** Intramural women's water polo.

STUDENT SERVICES. Aptitude testing, career counseling, employment service for undergraduates, freshman orientation, health services, personal counseling, placement service for graduates, special adviser for adult students, veterans counselor, services/facilities for handicapped.

ANNUAL EXPENSES. Tuition and fees (1992-93): $3,260, $3,394 additional for out-of-state students. **Room and board:** $3,524. **Books and supplies:** $450. **Other expenses:** $1,000.

FINANCIAL AID. 80% of freshmen, 85% of continuing students receive some form of aid. 89% of grants, 54% of loans, 38% of jobs based on need. 470 enrolled freshmen were judged to have need, all were offered aid. Academic, music/drama, athletic, leadership, minority scholarships available. **Aid applications:** No closing date; priority given to applications received by April 15; applicants notified on a rolling basis beginning on or about May 15; must reply within 4 weeks.

ADDRESS/TELEPHONE. Joseph Coldren, Director of Admissions, Lock Haven University of Pennsylvania, Akeley Building, Lock Haven, PA 17745. (717) 893-2027. (800) 233-8978. Fax: (717) 893-2201.

Luzerne County Community College
Nanticoke, Pennsylvania CB code: 2382

2-year public community college, coed. Founded in 1966. **Accreditation:** Regional. **Undergraduate enrollment:** 1,264 men, 1,450 women full time; 1,656 men, 2,766 women part time. **Faculty:** 468 total (177 full time), 14 with doctorates or other terminal degrees. **Location:** Suburban campus in large town; 8 miles from Wilkes-Barre. **Calendar:** Semester, extensive summer session. Saturday classes. **Microcomputers:** 20 located in libraries, classrooms, computer centers. **Special facilities:** Advanced technology center, printing laboratory, radio station, television production studio.

DEGREES OFFERED. AA, AS, AAS. 1,000 associate degrees awarded in 1992. 23% in business and management, 8% business/office and marketing/distribution, 5% computer sciences, 5% education, 5% engineering technologies, 23% allied health, 24% social sciences.

UNDERGRADUATE MAJORS. Accounting, aeronautical technology, airline piloting and navigation, architectural technologies, architecture, automotive mechanics, aviation management, biological and physical sciences, business administration and management, business and management, business and office, business data processing and related programs, business economics, child development/care/guidance, commercial art, computer and information sciences, computer graphics, criminal justice technology, dental assistant, dental hygiene, drafting, drafting and design technology, education, electrical installation, electrical technology, electromechanical technology, electronic technology, elementary education, emergency medical technologies, engineering and engineering-related technologies, finance, fire control and safety technology, food management, food production/management/services, graphic and printing production, graphic arts technology, health care administration, hospitality and recreation marketing, hotel/motel and restaurant management, humanities and social sciences, information sciences and systems, international business management, journalism, laser electro-optic technology, legal secretary, liberal/general studies, mathematics, mechanical design technology, nursing, office supervision and management, photographic technology, physical education, physical sciences, prepharmacy, radio/television broadcasting, real estate, respiratory therapy technology, robotics, secondary education, secretarial and related programs, social sciences, surgical technology, telecommunications, tourism.

ACADEMIC PROGRAMS. 2-year transfer program, double major, dual enrollment of high school students, external degree, honors program, independent study, internships, telecourses, weekend college. **Remedial services:** Learning center, preadmission summer program, reduced course load, remedial instruction, special counselor, tutoring, special programs for disadvantaged students. **ROTC:** Air Force. **Placement/credit:** AP, CLEP General and Subject, institutional tests; 30 credit hours maximum for associate degree.

ACADEMIC REQUIREMENTS. Freshmen must earn minimum GPA of 1.7 to continue in good standing. 60% of freshmen return for sophomore year. Students must declare major on application. **Graduation requirements:** 60 hours for associate (30 in major). Most students required to take courses in English, history, humanities, mathematics, biological/physical sciences, social sciences. **Additional information:** Students interested in prelaw enroll in social science program.

FRESHMAN ADMISSIONS. Selection criteria: Open admissions. High school record and test scores considered for admission to allied health programs. One algebra, 1 chemistry, 1 biology required of nursing, respiratory therapy, and dental hygiene applicants. **Test requirements:** National League for Nursing, Pre-nursing and Guidance Examination required for nursing applicants. Placement test required upon admission.

1992 FRESHMAN CLASS PROFILE. 1,054 men, 1,300 women enrolled. **Characteristics:** 100% from in state, 100% commute, 2% have minority backgrounds. Average age is 20.

FALL-TERM APPLICATIONS. $20 fee, may be waived for applicants with need. Closing date August 15; applicants notified on a rolling basis; must reply within 3 weeks. Interview recommended for allied health applicants. Deferred and early admission available.

STUDENT LIFE. Activities: Student government, magazine, radio, student newspaper, choral groups, concert band, drama, Circle-K, Christocentric, various special interest clubs.

ATHLETICS. Intercollegiate: Baseball M, basketball, cross-country, golf, softball W, volleyball W. **Intramural:** Basketball, bowling, fencing, gymnastics, volleyball.

STUDENT SERVICES. Aptitude testing, career counseling, employment service for undergraduates, freshman orientation, health services, personal counseling, placement service for graduates, special adviser for adult students, veterans counselor, services/facilities for handicapped.

ANNUAL EXPENSES. Tuition and fees (1992-93): $1,470, $1,320 additional for out-of-district students, $2,640 additional for out-of-state students. **Books and supplies:** $375. **Other expenses:** $625.

FINANCIAL AID. 80% of freshmen, 75% of continuing students receive some form of aid. All aid based on need. 860 enrolled freshmen were judged to have need, 790 were offered aid. Academic, leadership scholarships available. **Aid applications:** No closing date; priority given to applications received by April 15; applicants notified on a rolling basis beginning on or about July 1; must reply immediately.

ADDRESS/TELEPHONE. Thomas P. Leary, Dean, Admissions and Student Affairs, Luzerne County Community College, 1333 Prospect Street, Nanticoke, PA 18634-9804. (717) 735-8300. (800) 377-LCCC. Fax: (717) 821-1525.

Lycoming College
Williamsport, Pennsylvania

CB code: 2372

Admissions: 83% of applicants accepted
Based on:
••• School record
•• Interview, test scores
• Activities, essay, recommendations, special talents
Completion: 93% of freshmen end year in good standing
11% enter graduate study

4-year private liberal arts college, coed, affiliated with United Methodist Church. Founded in 1812. **Accreditation:** Regional. **Undergraduate enrollment:** 654 men, 692 women full time; 35 men, 97 women part time. **Faculty:** 108 total (79 full time), 69 with doctorates or other terminal degrees. **Location:** Suburban campus in small city; 90 miles from Harrisburg, 185 miles from Philadelphia. **Calendar:** 4-4-1. **Microcomputers:** 120 located in libraries, classrooms, computer centers. **Special facilities:** Planetarium, art gallery, electronic music studio, nursing skills laboratory.

DEGREES OFFERED. BA, BS, BFA. 263 bachelor's degrees awarded in 1992. 20% in business and management, 9% communications, 7% health sciences, 10% life sciences, 8% multi/interdisciplinary studies, 13% psychology, 15% social sciences, 5% visual and performing arts.

UNDERGRADUATE MAJORS. Accounting, advertising, American studies, anthropology, art education, art history, astronomy, biological and physical sciences, biology, business administration and management, business and management, chemistry, clinical laboratory science, communications, comparative literature, computer and information sciences, creative writing, criminal justice studies, criminology, dramatic arts, economics, elementary education, English, English education, environmental science, fine arts, foreign languages education, forestry and related sciences, French, German, history, humanities and social sciences, international relations, international studies, journalism, law enforcement and corrections, liberal/general studies, mathematics, mathematics education, Middle Eastern studies, music, music education, nursing, philosophy, photography, physics, political science and government, predentistry, prelaw, premedicine, prepharmacy, preveterinary, psychology, public relations, radio/television broadcasting, religion, science education, sculpture, secondary education, social studies education, sociology, Spanish, visual and performing arts.

ACADEMIC PROGRAMS. Accelerated program, double major, honors program, independent study, internships, student-designed major, study abroad, teacher preparation, Washington semester, cross-registration, cooperative BFA in sculpture with Johnson Atelier, Princeton, New Jersey; liberal arts/career combination in engineering, forestry, health sciences. **Remedial services:** Learning center, reduced course load, remedial instruction, special counselor, tutoring, writing center. **ROTC:** Army. **Placement/credit:** AP, CLEP General and Subject, institutional tests; 64 credit hours maximum for bachelor's degree.

ACADEMIC REQUIREMENTS. Freshmen must earn minimum GPA of 1.85 to continue in good standing. 82% of freshmen return for sophomore year. Students must declare major by end of second year. **Graduation requirements:** 128 hours for bachelor's. Most students required to take courses in arts/fine arts, English, foreign languages, history, mathematics, philosophy/religion, biological/physical sciences, social sciences. **Postgraduate studies:** 3% enter law school, 3% enter medical school, 1% enter MBA programs, 4% enter other graduate study. **Additional information:** Students may design their own majors in interdisciplinary studies.

FRESHMAN ADMISSIONS. Selection criteria: Academic achievement as reflected in school record, class rank, and test scores most important. Curriculum, counselor and teacher recommendations also considered. **High school preparation:** 16 units required. Required units include English 4, foreign language 2, mathematics 3, social science 2 and science 2. **Test requirements:** SAT or ACT; score report by August 1.

1992 FRESHMAN CLASS PROFILE. 713 men applied, 562 accepted, 212 enrolled; 599 women applied, 530 accepted, 212 enrolled. 18% were in top tenth and 38% were in top quarter of graduating class. **Academic background:** Mid 50% of enrolled freshmen had SAT-V between 410-590, SAT-M between 420-610. 92% submitted SAT scores. **Characteristics:** 69% from in state, 85% live in college housing, 5% have minority backgrounds, 2% are foreign students, 20% join fraternities/sororities. Average age is 18.

FALL-TERM APPLICATIONS. $25 fee. No closing date; priority given to applications received by April 1; applicants notified on a rolling basis beginning on or about September 15; must reply by May 1 or within 4 weeks if notified thereafter. Portfolio required for sculpture; recommended for other art applicants applicants. Interview recommended. Audition recommended. Essay recommended. CRDA. Deferred and early admission available.

STUDENT LIFE. Housing: Dormitories (men, women, coed); fraternity, sorority housing available. **Activities:** Student government, magazine, radio, student newspaper, television, yearbook, choral groups, concert band, dance, drama, jazz band, music ensembles, musical theater, fraternities, sororities, religious, ethnic, political, and social service organizations.

ATHLETICS. NCAA. **Intercollegiate:** Basketball, cross-country, field hockey W, football M, golf, soccer M, softball W, swimming, tennis, track and field, volleyball W, wrestling M. **Intramural:** Basketball, bowling, lacrosse M, skiing, softball, volleyball, water polo, wrestling M.

STUDENT SERVICES. Career counseling, employment service for undergraduates, freshman orientation, health services, personal counseling, placement service for graduates, services/facilities for handicapped.

ANNUAL EXPENSES. Tuition and fees (1992-93): $12,000. **Room and board:** $4,100. **Books and supplies:** $500. **Other expenses:** $600.

FINANCIAL AID. 70% of freshmen, 78% of continuing students receive some form of aid. 88% of grants, 83% of loans, 46% of jobs based on need. 281 enrolled freshmen were judged to have need, all were offered aid. Academic, music/drama, art scholarships available. **Aid applications:** No closing date; priority given to applications received by May 1; applicants notified on a rolling basis beginning on or about March 1; must reply by May 1 or within 3 weeks if notified thereafter.

ADDRESS/TELEPHONE. James Spencer, Dean of Admissions and Financial Aid, Lycoming College, Washington Boulevard, Williamsport, PA 17701. (717) 321-4026. (800) 345-3920. Fax: (717) 321-4337.

Manor Junior College
Jenkintown, Pennsylvania — CB code: 2260

Admissions: 72% of applicants accepted
Based on: ••• Interview, school record, test scores
•• Activities
• Essay, recommendations, special talents
Completion: 85% of freshmen end year in good standing
40% enter 4-year programs

2-year private junior college, coed, affiliated with Ukrainian Catholic Church. Founded in 1947. **Accreditation:** Regional. **Undergraduate enrollment:** 75 men, 322 women full time; 39 men, 101 women part time. **Faculty:** 84 total (17 full time), 19 with doctorates or other terminal degrees. **Location:** Suburban campus in small town; 15 miles from downtown Philadelphia. **Calendar:** Semester, limited summer session. **Microcomputers:** 50 located in libraries, classrooms, computer centers. **Special facilities:** Law library, Ukrainian Heritage Studies Center, dental health center.

DEGREES OFFERED. AA, AS. 81 associate degrees awarded in 1992. 12% in business and management, 10% business/office and marketing/distribution, 32% allied health, 27% law, 19% multi/interdisciplinary studies.

UNDERGRADUATE MAJORS. Accounting, allied health, business administration and management, business and management, business and office, business data entry equipment operation, business data processing and related programs, clinical laboratory science, court reporting, dental assistant, early childhood education, education, humanities and social sciences, information sciences and systems, legal assistant/paralegal, legal secretary, liberal/general studies, medical laboratory technologies, medical secretary, mental health/human services, office supervision and management, preveterinary, psychology, secretarial and related programs, veterinarian's assistant, word processing.

ACADEMIC PROGRAMS. 2-year transfer program, double major, dual enrollment of high school students, honors program, independent study, internships, cross-registration. **Remedial services:** Learning center, preadmission summer program, reduced course load, remedial instruction, special counselor, tutoring. **Placement/credit:** AP, CLEP General and Subject, institutional tests; 30 credit hours maximum for associate degree.

ACADEMIC REQUIREMENTS. Freshmen must earn minimum GPA of 2.0 to continue in good standing. 65% of freshmen return for sophomore year. Students must declare major on enrollment. **Graduation requirements:** 60 hours for associate (24 in major). Most students required to take courses in computer science, English, history, mathematics, philosophy/religion, biological/physical sciences, social sciences.

FRESHMAN ADMISSIONS. Selection criteria: Class rank, high school GPA, high school course selection, recommendation of counselor or teacher, and SAT or ACT scores in addition to interview with admissions counselor and program coordinator. Recommended SAT mathematical 350; recommended SAT verbal 400. Manor Junior College Entrance Test required of all applicants, except those holding Bachelor's degree. **High school preparation:** 16 units required. Required units include biological science 2, English 4, foreign language 2, mathematics 2 and social science 1. Language units may be waived for secretarial and allied health programs. One biology, 1 chemistry required for medical laboratory technician applicants. **Test requirements:** SAT or ACT (ACT preferred).

1992 FRESHMAN CLASS PROFILE. 98 men applied, 68 accepted, 51 enrolled; 341 women applied, 246 accepted, 167 enrolled. 33% had high school GPA of 3.0 or higher, 45% between 2.0 and 2.99. **Academic background:** Mid 50% of enrolled freshmen had SAT-V between 320-450, SAT-M between 300-500. 75% submitted SAT scores. **Characteristics:** 85% from in state, 80% commute, 12% have minority backgrounds, 9% are foreign students. Average age is 20.

FALL-TERM APPLICATIONS. $20 fee, may be waived for applicants with need. Closing date September 1; applicants notified on a rolling basis; must reply within 2 weeks. Interview required. Deferred and early admission available.

STUDENT LIFE. Housing: Dormitories (coed). Housing arranged within local community for foreign students. **Activities:** Student government, yearbook, International Club, Students United for Nature.

ATHLETICS. NJCAA. **Intercollegiate:** Basketball, soccer M, volleyball W. **Intramural:** Volleyball W.

STUDENT SERVICES. Career counseling, employment service for undergraduates, freshman orientation, personal counseling, placement service for graduates, special adviser for adult students.

ANNUAL EXPENSES. Tuition and fees (1992-93): $6,496. **Room and board:** $3,120. **Books and supplies:** $450. **Other expenses:** $1,400.

FINANCIAL AID. 90% of freshmen, 86% of continuing students receive some form of aid. 89% of grants, 78% of loans, 93% of jobs based on need. Academic, athletic, leadership, minority scholarships available. **Aid applications:** Closing date August 15; priority given to applications received by March 15; applicants notified on a rolling basis beginning on or about May 1; must reply within 2 weeks.

ADDRESS/TELEPHONE. I. Jerry Czenstuch, Dean of Admissions, Manor Junior College, 700 Fox Chase Road, Jenkintown, PA 19046-3399. (215) 885-2360.

Mansfield University of Pennsylvania
Mansfield, Pennsylvania — CB code: 2655

Admissions: 57% of applicants accepted
Based on: ••• School record, test scores
• Activities, essay, interview, recommendations, special talents
Completion: 85% of freshmen end year in good standing
45% graduate, 16% of these enter graduate study

4-year public university, coed. Founded in 1857. **Accreditation:** Regional. **Undergraduate enrollment:** 1,153 men, 1,554 women full time; 71 men, 137 women part time. **Graduate enrollment:** 81 men, 227 women full time. **Faculty:** 189 total (178 full time), 88 with doctorates or other terminal degrees. **Location:** Rural campus in small town; 50 miles from Williamsport, 26 miles from Corning, New York. **Calendar:** Semester, limited summer session. **Microcomputers:** 100 located in dormitories, libraries, classrooms, computer centers. **Special facilities:** Planetarium, solar collector, science museum, animal collection, 2 art galleries.

DEGREES OFFERED. AA, AS, BA, BS, MA, MS, MEd. 29 associate degrees awarded in 1992. 100% in allied health. 551 bachelor's degrees awarded. 14% in business and management, 6% communications, 22% teacher education, 10% health sciences, 6% home economics, 10% parks/recreation, protective services, public affairs, 6% psychology, 6% social sciences. Graduate degrees offered in 9 major fields of study.

UNDERGRADUATE MAJORS. Associate: Radiograph medical technology, respiratory therapy, respiratory therapy technology. **Bachelor's:** Actuarial sciences, anthropology, apparel and accessories marketing, art education, art history, biology, business administration and management, chemistry, city/community/regional planning, clinical laboratory science, communications, computer and information sciences, counseling psychology, criminal justice studies, earth sciences, economics, elementary education, English, English education, English literature, fashion design, fashion merchandising, fishing and fisheries, food sciences, foreign languages education, French, geography, German, history, information sciences and systems, journalism, liberal/general studies, mathematics, mathematics education, music business management, music education, music history and appreciation, music performance, music theory and composition, music therapy, nursing, personnel management, philosophy, physics, political science and government, preengineering, prelaw, psychology, public relations, radio/television broadcasting, science education, secondary education, social science education, social studies education, social work, sociology, Spanish, special education, speech, statistics, studio art, systems analysis, tourism, transportation and travel marketing.

ACADEMIC PROGRAMS. Accelerated program, double major, dual enrollment of high school students, honors program, independent study, internships, student-designed major, study abroad, teacher preparation, cross-registration, semester exchange program with 6 Pennsylvania colleges; liberal arts/career combination in engineering, health sciences. **Remedial services:** Learning center, preadmission summer program, reduced course load, remedial instruction, special counselor, tutoring. **ROTC:** Army. **Placement/credit:** AP, CLEP Subject, institutional tests; 12 credit hours maximum for bachelor's degree.

ACADEMIC REQUIREMENTS. Freshmen must earn minimum GPA of 2.0 to continue in good standing. 78% of freshmen return for sophomore year. Students must declare major by end of second year. **Graduation requirements:** 67 hours for associate (45 in major), 128 hours for bachelor's (60 in major). Most students required to take courses in arts/fine arts, English, humanities, mathematics, biological/physical sciences, social sciences. **Postgraduate studies:** 3% enter law school, 1% enter medical school, 2% enter MBA programs, 10% enter other graduate study.

FRESHMAN ADMISSIONS. Selection criteria: Class rank, high school curriculum, test scores, counselor's recommendation, extracurricular activities. Special consideration given to applicants eligible for Equal Education Opportunity Program. Entry competitive in X-ray technology, respiratory therapy, fisheries, music, and art programs. **High school preparation:** 16 units required. Required and recommended units include biological science 2, English 4, mathematics 3, physical science 1 and social science 3. Foreign language 2 recommended. **Test requirements:** SAT or ACT; score report by July 15.

1992 FRESHMAN CLASS PROFILE. 2,766 men and women applied, 1,566 accepted; 607 enrolled. 52% had high school GPA of 3.0 or higher, 44% between 2.0 and 2.99. **Characteristics:** 67% from in state, 87% live in college housing, 9% have minority backgrounds, 2% are foreign students, 15% join fraternities/sororities. Average age is 19.

FALL-TERM APPLICATIONS. $15 fee, may be waived for applicants with need. Closing date July 15; priority given to applications received by

December 1; applicants notified on a rolling basis; must reply by May 1 or within 4 weeks if notified thereafter. Interview required for music, art, health professions applicants. Audition required for music applicants. Portfolio required for art applicants. Essay recommended for X-ray technology, respiratory therapy, academically weak applicants. Deferred and early admission available. Applicants to competitive programs should apply by January 15.

STUDENT LIFE. Housing: Dormitories (men, women, coed); fraternity, sorority housing available. **Activities:** Student government, magazine, radio, student newspaper, television, yearbook, choral groups, concert band, drama, jazz band, marching band, music ensembles, musical theater, pep band, symphony orchestra, fraternities, sororities, Black Awarenesss Association, Inter-Varsity Christian Fellowship, Commonwealth Association of Students.

ATHLETICS. NCAA. **Intercollegiate:** Baseball M, basketball, cross-country, diving W, field hockey W, football M, softball W, swimming W, track and field, wrestling M. **Intramural:** Badminton, basketball, golf, racquetball, skiing, soccer M, softball, volleyball, water polo. **Clubs:** Waterpolo W.

STUDENT SERVICES. Aptitude testing, career counseling, employment service for undergraduates, freshman orientation, health services, personal counseling, placement service for graduates, special adviser for adult students, veterans counselor, services/facilities for handicapped.

ANNUAL EXPENSES. Tuition and fees (projected): $3,304, $4,824 additional for out-of-state students. **Room and board:** $2,988. **Books and supplies:** $650. **Other expenses:** $800.

FINANCIAL AID. 78% of freshmen, 75% of continuing students receive some form of aid. 91% of grants, 67% of loans, 38% of jobs based on need. 398 enrolled freshmen were judged to have need, 380 were offered aid. Academic, music/drama, art, athletic, state/district residency, leadership, minority scholarships available. **Aid applications:** Closing date April 15; applicants notified on or about June 1; must reply within 4 weeks.

ADDRESS/TELEPHONE. John J. Abplanalp, Director of Admissions and Enrollment Services, Mansfield University of Pennsylvania, Beecher House, Mansfield, PA 16933. (717) 662-4243. Fax: (717) 662-4996.

Marywood College
Scranton, Pennsylvania — CB code: 2407

Admissions: 74% of applicants accepted
Based on: ••• School record, test scores
•• Recommendations
• Activities, interview, special talents
Completion: 95% of freshmen end year in good standing
58% graduate, 12% of these enter graduate study

4-year private liberal arts college, coed, affiliated with Roman Catholic Church. Founded in 1915. **Accreditation:** Regional. **Undergraduate enrollment:** 269 men, 1,149 women full time; 124 men, 316 women part time. **Graduate enrollment:** 66 men, 218 women full time; 199 men, 561 women part time. **Faculty:** 216 total (146 full time), 137 with doctorates or other terminal degrees. **Location:** Suburban campus in small city; 110 miles from Philadelphia, 120 miles from New York City. **Calendar:** Semester, extensive summer session. **Microcomputers:** 225 located in dormitories, libraries, computer centers. **Special facilities:** Museum, Suraci Art Gallery, early childhood center, radio and television station with computerized editing facility, contemporary gallery, electronic learning labs. **Additional facts:** Graduate schools offer courses at Cedarhust College, Divine Providence Hospital. Off-campus degree program available.

DEGREES OFFERED. AA, BA, BS, BFA, MA, MS, MBA, MFA, MSW. 100% in law. 310 bachelor's degrees awarded. 20% in business and management, 6% business/office and marketing/distribution, 7% communications, 11% teacher education, 10% health sciences, 6% parks/recreation, protective services, public affairs, 6% psychology, 14% visual and performing arts. Graduate degrees offered in 40 major fields of study.

UNDERGRADUATE MAJORS. Associate: Legal assistant/paralegal. **Bachelor's:** Accounting, advertising, art education, arts management, biology, business administration and management, business and management, ceramics, clinical psychology, communications, computer and information sciences, criminal justice studies, dramatic arts, drawing, early childhood education, education, education of the deaf and hearing impaired, elementary education, English, English education, environmental science, environmental studies, fashion merchandising, finance, fine arts, food science and nutrition, foreign languages education, French, graphic design, health care administration, health education, home economics, home economics education, hotel/motel and restaurant management, illustration design, information sciences and systems, interior design, international business management, junior high education, legal assistant/paralegal, management information systems, marketing management, mathematics, mathematics education, medical laboratory technologies, metal/jewelry, music, music education, music performance, music therapy, musical theater, nursing, nutritional education, painting, photography, physical education, prelaw, printmaking, psychology, public relations, radio/television broadcasting, radio/television technology, religion, religious music, science education, sculpture, secondary education, social science education, social sciences, social studies education, social work, sociology, Spanish, special education, speech, speech correction, speech pathology/audiology, speech/communication/theater education, sports medicine, visual and performing arts.

ACADEMIC PROGRAMS. Accelerated program, double major, dual enrollment of high school students, external degree, honors program, independent study, internships, student-designed major, study abroad, teacher preparation, telecourses, weekend college, New York semester. **Remedial services:** Learning center, preadmission summer program, reduced course load, remedial instruction, special counselor, tutoring. **ROTC:** Air Force, Army. **Placement/credit:** AP, CLEP General and Subject, institutional tests; 18 credit hours maximum for bachelor's degree.

ACADEMIC REQUIREMENTS. Freshmen must earn minimum GPA of 2.0 overall and 2.5 in major. 77% of freshmen return for sophomore year. Students must declare major by end of first year. **Graduation requirements:** 63 hours for associate (30 in major), 126 hours for bachelor's (36 in major). Most students required to take courses in arts/fine arts, computer science, English, foreign languages, history, humanities, mathematics, philosophy/religion, biological/physical sciences, social sciences. **Postgraduate studies:** 1% enter law school, 1% enter medical school, 1% enter MBA programs, 9% enter other graduate study.

FRESHMAN ADMISSIONS. Selection criteria: School achievement record most important, followed by test scores and recommendations. **High school preparation:** 16 units required. Required units include biological science 1, English 4, mathematics 2 and social science 3. Biological science must be laboratory science. **Test requirements:** SAT or ACT (SAT preferred); score report by September 1.

1992 FRESHMAN CLASS PROFILE. 256 men applied, 181 accepted, 53 enrolled; 919 women applied, 693 accepted, 207 enrolled. 2% were in top tenth and 6% were in top quarter of graduating class. **Academic background:** Mid 50% of enrolled freshmen had SAT-V between 380-490, SAT-M between 400-520. 90% submitted SAT scores. **Characteristics:** 72% from in state, 60% commute, 3% have minority backgrounds. Average age is 20.

FALL-TERM APPLICATIONS. $20 fee, may be waived for applicants with need. No closing date; applicants notified on a rolling basis. Audition required for music applicants. Interview recommended. Portfolio recommended for art applicants. CRDA. Deferred and early admission available.

STUDENT LIFE. Housing: Dormitories (men, women); apartment housing available. **Activities:** Student government, film, magazine, radio, student newspaper, television, yearbook, choral groups, concert band, drama, jazz band, music ensembles, musical theater, opera, symphony orchestra, Pennsylvania Association of Retarded Children, Council of Exceptional Children, Volunteers in Action, Campus Ministry, Drug and Alcohol Referral Service, Multicultural Awareness Club, Teresa Maxis Center for Peace and Justice, National Association for Music Therapy.

ATHLETICS. NCAA. **Intercollegiate:** Basketball, field hockey W, softball W, tennis, volleyball W. **Intramural:** Badminton, basketball, bowling, field hockey W, golf, racquetball, soccer M, softball, swimming, table tennis, tennis, volleyball. **Clubs:** Skiing, karate.

STUDENT SERVICES. Aptitude testing, career counseling, employment service for undergraduates, freshman orientation, health services, on-campus day care, personal counseling, special adviser for adult students, services/facilities for handicapped.

ANNUAL EXPENSES. Tuition and fees: $10,590. **Room and board:** $4,300. **Books and supplies:** $500. **Other expenses:** $700.

FINANCIAL AID. 90% of freshmen, 80% of continuing students receive some form of aid. All jobs based on need. Academic, music/drama, art, leadership, minority scholarships available. **Aid applications:** No closing date; priority given to applications received by February 15; applicants notified on a rolling basis beginning on or about March 1; must reply by May 1 or within 2 weeks if notified thereafter.

ADDRESS/TELEPHONE. Gary Sherman, Director of Admissions, Marywood College, 2300 Adams Avenue, Scranton, PA 18509-9989. (717) 348-6234. (800) 346-5014. Fax: (717) 348-1899.

McCarrie Schools of Health Sciences and Technology
Philadelphia, Pennsylvania — CB code: 1053

2-year proprietary health science, technical college, coed. Founded in 1917. **Undergraduate enrollment:** 560 men and women. **Faculty:** 23 total (21 full time). **Location:** Urban campus in very large city. **Calendar:** Continuous enrollment. Extensive evening/early morning classes. **Additional facts:** Programs are job oriented.

DEGREES OFFERED. 89 associate degrees awarded in 1992. 100% in allied health.

UNDERGRADUATE MAJORS. Clinical laboratory science, dental laboratory technology, legal assistant/paralegal, medical laboratory technologies, medical secretary, ophthalmic services, secretarial and related programs.

ACADEMIC PROGRAMS. 2-year transfer program, internships. **Remedial services:** Remedial instruction, tutoring.

ACADEMIC REQUIREMENTS. Freshmen must earn minimum GPA of 2.0 to continue in good standing.

FRESHMAN ADMISSIONS. Selection criteria: Open admissions. **Test requirements:** Institutional test required for admission.

1992 FRESHMAN CLASS PROFILE. 40% had high school GPA of 3.0 or higher, 40% between 2.0 and 2.99. 15% were in top quarter of graduating class. **Characteristics:** 95% from in state, 100% commute, 56% have minority backgrounds. Average age is 19.

FALL-TERM APPLICATIONS. No fee. No closing date; applicants notified on a rolling basis. Interview required. Deferred admission available.

STUDENT LIFE. Activities: Student government, student newspaper.

STUDENT SERVICES. Career counseling, employment service for undergraduates, placement service for graduates, services/facilities for handicapped.

ANNUAL EXPENSES. Tuition and fees (1992-93): Tuition varies from program to program. Ranging from $3500 to $8900. **Books and supplies:** $325.

FINANCIAL AID. 95% of freshmen, 85% of continuing students receive some form of aid. Grants, loans available. **Aid applications:** No closing date; applicants notified on a rolling basis; must reply within 2 weeks.

ADDRESS/TELEPHONE. Wally McKenzie, Director of Admissions, McCarrie Schools of Health Sciences and Technology, 512 South Broad Street, Philadelphia, PA 19146-1613. (215) 545-7772. Fax: (215) 545-8305.

Mercyhurst College
Erie, Pennsylvania — CB code: 2410

Admissions: 77% of applicants accepted
Based on:
••• School record, special talents
•• Interview, test scores
• Activities, recommendations
Completion: 93% of freshmen end year in good standing
60% graduate, 16% of these enter graduate study

4-year private liberal arts college, coed, affiliated with Roman Catholic Church. Founded in 1926. **Accreditation:** Regional. **Undergraduate enrollment:** 826 men, 1,005 women full time; 193 men, 235 women part time. **Graduate enrollment:** 9 men, 13 women full time; 11 men, 18 women part time. **Faculty:** 145 total (96 full time), 70 with doctorates or other terminal degrees. **Location:** Suburban campus in small city; 100 miles from Pittsburgh; 90 miles from Buffalo, New York. **Calendar:** 3-3-3. Saturday and extensive evening/early morning classes. **Microcomputers:** 120 located in libraries, classrooms, computer centers. **Special facilities:** Observatory, Cummings Art Gallery, Archeological Institute. **Additional facts:** Certificate programs and credit courses offered at centers in Corry and North East.

DEGREES OFFERED. AA, AS, BA, BS, MS. 30 associate degrees awarded in 1992. 72% in business and management, 7% business/office and marketing/distribution, 21% social sciences. 280 bachelor's degrees awarded. 21% in business and management, 18% business/office and marketing/distribution, 5% communications, 9% education, 5% home economics, 19% social sciences, 9% visual and performing arts. Graduate degrees offered in 2 major fields of study.

UNDERGRADUATE MAJORS. Associate: Business and management, business and office, criminal justice studies, hospitality and recreation marketing, hotel/motel and restaurant management, insurance and risk management, law enforcement and corrections, law enforcement and corrections technologies, legal secretary, marketing and distribution, medical secretary, office supervision and management, religious education, secretarial and related programs. **Bachelor's:** Accounting, anthropology, archeology, art education, art therapy, biology, business administration and management, business and management, business education, ceramics, chemistry, clinical laboratory science, communications, computer and information sciences, criminal justice studies, dance, drawing, early childhood education, earth sciences, earth-space science education, education of the emotionally handicapped, education of the mentally handicapped, elementary education, engineering, English, English education, environmental science, fashion merchandising, fiber/textiles/weaving, finance, fine arts, food science and nutrition, geology, graphic design, history, home economics, home economics education, hotel/motel and restaurant management, human environment and housing, humanities and social sciences, institutional/home management/supporting programs, insurance and risk management, interior design, journalism, law enforcement and corrections, management information systems, mathematics, mathematics education, medical laboratory technologies, medical records technology, music, music education, music performance, music therapy, nursing, painting, philosophy, physics, political science and government, predentistry, premedicine, prepharmacy, preveterinary, psychology, public administration, public relations, radio/television broadcasting, religion, religious education, science education, sculpture, secondary education, social science education, social sciences, social work, sociology, special education, specific learning disabilities, sports medicine, studio art, textiles and clothing.

ACADEMIC PROGRAMS. Accelerated program, cooperative education, double major, dual enrollment of high school students, honors program, independent study, internships, student-designed major, study abroad, teacher preparation, weekend college, New York semester, Washington semester, cross-registration; liberal arts/career combination in engineering, business. **Remedial services:** Learning center, preadmission summer program, reduced course load, remedial instruction, special counselor, tutoring. **ROTC:** Army. **Placement/credit:** AP, CLEP Subject, IB, institutional tests; 30 credit hours maximum for bachelor's degree.

ACADEMIC REQUIREMENTS. Freshmen must earn minimum GPA of 1.75 to continue in good standing. 75% of freshmen return for sophomore year. Students must declare major by end of second year. **Graduation requirements:** 60 hours for associate (36 in major), 120 hours for bachelor's (45 in major). Most students required to take courses in arts/fine arts, computer science, English, foreign languages, history, humanities, mathematics, philosophy/religion, biological/physical sciences, social sciences. **Postgraduate studies:** 2% enter law school, 2% enter medical school, 3% enter MBA programs, 9% enter other graduate study. **Additional information:** Education department offers graduate student-taught special education programs for learning disabled students.

FRESHMAN ADMISSIONS. Selection criteria: School activities, high school GPA, class rank, recommendations, and test scores. Interview also considered. **High school preparation:** 14 units recommended. Recommended units include English 4, foreign language 2, mathematics 2, social science 4 and science 2. **Test requirements:** SAT or ACT; score report by August 30.

1992 FRESHMAN CLASS PROFILE. 847 men applied, 615 accepted, 189 enrolled; 768 women applied, 622 accepted, 236 enrolled. 45% had high school GPA of 3.0 or higher, 55% between 2.0 and 2.99. 9% were in top tenth and 34% were in top quarter of graduating class. **Academic background:** Mid 50% of enrolled freshmen had SAT-V between 420-530, SAT-M between 450-550; ACT composite between 20-25. 73% submitted SAT scores, 36% submitted ACT scores. **Characteristics:** 62% from in state, 82% live in college housing, 12% have minority backgrounds, 5% are foreign students. Average age is 18.

FALL-TERM APPLICATIONS. $25 fee, may be waived for applicants with need. No closing date; priority given to applications received by May 1; applicants notified on a rolling basis beginning on or about January 15. Audition required for music, dance applicants. Portfolio required. Interview recommended. CRDA. Deferred and early admission available.

STUDENT LIFE. Housing: Dormitories (men, women); apartment housing available. **Activities:** Student government, film, magazine, radio, student newspaper, television, yearbook, choral groups, dance, drama, jazz band, music ensembles, musical theater, opera, pep band, symphony orchestra, campus ministry.

ATHLETICS. NCAA. **Intercollegiate:** Baseball M, basketball, cross-country, football M, golf, ice hockey M, rowing (crew), soccer, softball W, tennis, volleyball W. **Intramural:** Badminton W, basketball, bowling, ice hockey M, skiing, soccer, table tennis.

STUDENT SERVICES. Aptitude testing, career counseling, employment service for undergraduates, freshman orientation, health services, on-campus day care, personal counseling, placement service for graduates, special adviser for adult students, veterans counselor, services/facilities for handicapped.

ANNUAL EXPENSES. Tuition and fees: $9,838. **Room and board:** $3,650. **Books and supplies:** $465. **Other expenses:** $800.

FINANCIAL AID. 95% of freshmen, 80% of continuing students receive some form of aid. 65% of grants, 98% of loans, all jobs based on need. 118 enrolled freshmen were judged to have need, all were offered aid. Academic, music/drama, art, athletic, leadership, alumni affiliation, religious affiliation, minority scholarships available. **Aid applications:** No closing date; priority given to applications received by March 15; applicants notified on a rolling basis beginning on or about March 16; must reply within 3 weeks.

ADDRESS/TELEPHONE. Andrew Roth, Dean of Enrollment, Mercyhurst College, Glenwood Hills, Erie, PA 16546. (814) 824-2202. (800) 825-1926. Fax: (814) 824-2071.

Messiah College
Grantham, Pennsylvania — CB code: 2411

Admissions: 82% of applicants accepted
Based on:
••• Religious affiliation/commitment, school record
•• Essay, recommendations, test scores
• Activities, interview, special talents
Completion: 91% of freshmen end year in good standing
70% graduate, 22% of these enter graduate study

4-year private liberal arts college, coed, affiliated with Brethren in Christ Church. Founded in 1909. **Accreditation:** Regional. **Undergraduate enrollment:** 886 men, 1,308 women full time; 21 men, 47 women part time. **Faculty:** 219 total (159 full time), 110 with doctorates or other terminal degrees. **Location:** Suburban campus in small town; 10 miles from Harrisburg, 20 miles from Gettysburg. **Calendar:** 4-1-4, extensive summer session. **Microcomputers:** Located in libraries, classrooms, computer centers. **Special facilities:** College-operated archives of the Brethren in Christ Church. **Addi-**

tional facts: Curriculum designed to help students integrate Christian faith with learning and develop Christian world view.

DEGREES OFFERED. BA, BS. 523 bachelor's degrees awarded in 1992. 18% in business and management, 6% communications, 6% computer sciences, 15% teacher education, 9% allied health, 9% letters/literature, 6% life sciences, 6% multi/interdisciplinary studies, 6% social sciences.

UNDERGRADUATE MAJORS. Accounting, art history, behavioral sciences, biochemistry, biological and physical sciences, biology, business administration and management, business and management, business data processing and related programs, business data programming, business economics, chemistry, civil engineering, clinical laboratory science, clinical psychology, communications, computer and information sciences, computer programming, dramatic arts, early childhood education, education, electrical/electronics/communications engineering, elementary education, engineering, engineering mechanics, English, English education, English literature, experimental psychology, food science and nutrition, French, German, health education, history, home economics, home economics education, human environment and housing, human resources development, humanities, humanities and social sciences, information sciences and systems, journalism, junior high education, liberal/general studies, marketing and distribution, marketing management, mathematics, mathematics education, mechanical engineering, music, music education, nursing, occupational therapy, physical education, physical therapy, physics, political science and government, predentistry, prelaw, premedicine, preveterinary, psychology, radio/television broadcasting, religion, religious education, religious music, science education, secondary education, social science education, social studies education, social work, sociology, Spanish, speech, sports medicine, textiles and clothing, theological studies, visual and performing arts.

ACADEMIC PROGRAMS. Accelerated program, double major, dual enrollment of high school students, independent study, internships, student-designed major, study abroad, teacher preparation, visiting/exchange student program, Washington semester, cross-registration. **Remedial services:** Preadmission summer program, reduced course load, remedial instruction, special counselor. **Placement/credit:** AP, CLEP General and Subject, institutional tests; 24 credit hours maximum for bachelor's degree.

ACADEMIC REQUIREMENTS. Freshmen must earn minimum GPA of 1.8 to continue in good standing. 85% of freshmen return for sophomore year. Students must declare major by end of first year. **Graduation requirements:** 126 hours for bachelor's. Most students required to take courses in arts/fine arts, English, foreign languages, history, humanities, mathematics, philosophy/religion, biological/physical sciences, social sciences. **Postgraduate studies:** 3% enter law school, 3% enter medical school, 4% enter MBA programs, 12% enter other graduate study.

FRESHMAN ADMISSIONS. Selection criteria: Minimum requirements include rank in top half of class, acceptable test scores, and recommendations. High school GPA and personal statement also considered. Special consideration given to minority applicants. **High school preparation:** 16 units required. Required units include biological science 1, English 4, foreign language 2, mathematics 2, physical science 1 and social science 2. **Test requirements:** SAT or ACT; score report by May 1. **Additional information:** Statement of Christian commitment and agreement to live by campus ethos also required.

1992 FRESHMAN CLASS PROFILE. 602 men applied, 468 accepted, 217 enrolled; 902 women applied, 763 accepted, 354 enrolled. 85% had high school GPA of 3.0 or higher, 15% between 2.0 and 2.99. 27% were in top tenth and 62% were in top quarter of graduating class. **Academic background:** Mid 50% of enrolled freshmen had SAT-V between 430-560, SAT-M between 480-590; ACT composite between 21-27. 95% submitted SAT scores, 3% submitted ACT scores. **Characteristics:** 48% from in state, 97% live in college housing, 8% have minority backgrounds, 2% are foreign students. Average age is 18.

FALL-TERM APPLICATIONS. $20 fee, may be waived for applicants with need. Closing date May 1; priority given to applications received by March 1; applicants notified on a rolling basis; must reply by May 1. Audition required for music applicants. Essay required. Interview recommended. Portfolio recommended for art applicants. CRDA. Deferred and early admission available.

STUDENT LIFE. Housing: Dormitories (men, women); apartment housing available. **Activities:** Student government, magazine, radio, student newspaper, yearbook, choral groups, concert band, drama, jazz band, music ensembles, musical theater, opera, pep band, symphony orchestra, religious organizations, peace society, international student club, Young Republicans, Young Democrats, multi-cultural student organization.

ATHLETICS. NCAA. **Intercollegiate:** Baseball M, basketball, cross-country, field hockey W, golf M, soccer, softball W, tennis, track and field, volleyball W, wrestling M. **Intramural:** Badminton, basketball, bowling, handball, ice hockey M, soccer, softball, table tennis, tennis, volleyball.

STUDENT SERVICES. Aptitude testing, career counseling, employment service for undergraduates, health services, personal counseling, placement service for graduates, services/facilities for handicapped.

ANNUAL EXPENSES. Tuition and fees: $9,804. **Room and board:** $4,890. **Books and supplies:** $450. **Other expenses:** $800.

FINANCIAL AID. 86% of freshmen, 85% of continuing students receive some form of aid. 71% of grants, 79% of loans, 67% of jobs based on need. 386 enrolled freshmen were judged to have need, all were offered aid. Academic, leadership scholarships available. **Aid applications:** No closing date; priority given to applications received by April 1; applicants notified on a rolling basis beginning on or about May 1; must reply within 4 weeks. **Additional information:** Merit-base scholarships offered to students with outstanding academic ability and leadership traits.

ADDRESS/TELEPHONE. Ron E. Long, Vice President for Admissions, Financial Aid, and Communications, Messiah College, Grantham, PA 17027-0800. (717) 691-6000 ext. 6000. (800) 233-4220. Fax: (717) 691-6025.

Millersville University of Pennsylvania

Millersville, Pennsylvania CB code: 2656

Admissions: 49% of applicants accepted
Based on: ••• School record, test scores
•• Recommendations
• Activities, interview, special talents
Completion: 76% of freshmen end year in good standing
64% graduate

4-year public university, coed. Founded in 1855. **Accreditation:** Regional. **Undergraduate enrollment:** 2,205 men, 3,148 women full time; 563 men, 1,111 women part time. **Graduate enrollment:** 44 men, 78 women full time; 154 men, 488 women part time. **Faculty:** 401 total (325 full time), 235 with doctorates or other terminal degrees. **Location:** Suburban campus in small town; 3 miles from Lancaster, 35 miles from Harrisburg. **Calendar:** 4-1-4, limited summer session. Extensive evening/early morning classes. **Microcomputers:** 287 located in dormitories, libraries, classrooms, computer centers. **Special facilities:** Elizabeth Jenkins Early Childhood Center, foreign language laboratory, 2 art galleries. **Additional facts:** Located in heart of Pennsylvania Dutch country.

DEGREES OFFERED. AA, AS, BA, BS, BFA, MA, MS, MEd. 1 associate degree awarded in 1992. 1,166 bachelor's degrees awarded. 14% in business and management, 30% teacher education, 5% engineering technologies, 5% letters/literature, 6% life sciences, 7% psychology, 8% social sciences. Graduate degrees offered in 17 major fields of study.

UNDERGRADUATE MAJORS. Associate: Chemistry, computer and information sciences, gerontology, liberal/general studies. **Bachelor's:** Anthropology, art education, atmospheric sciences and meteorology, biology, business administration and management, chemistry, communications, computer and information sciences, earth sciences, economics, elementary education, English, fine arts, French, geography, geology, German, Greek (classical), history, industrial arts education, industrial technology, international studies, Latin, mathematics, music, music education, nursing, occupational safety and health technology, oceanography, philosophy, physics, political science and government, psychology, Russian, social studies education, social work, sociology, Spanish, special education.

ACADEMIC PROGRAMS. Accelerated program, cooperative education, double major, dual enrollment of high school students, honors program, independent study, internships, study abroad, teacher preparation, visiting/exchange student program, cross-registration; liberal arts/career combination in engineering. **Remedial services:** Learning center, preadmission summer program, reduced course load, remedial instruction, special counselor, tutoring. **ROTC:** Army. **Placement/credit:** AP, CLEP General and Subject, IB, institutional tests; 60 credit hours maximum for bachelor's degree.

ACADEMIC REQUIREMENTS. Freshmen must earn minimum GPA of 1.75 to continue in good standing. 87% of freshmen return for sophomore year. Students must declare major by end of second year. **Graduation requirements:** 60 hours for associate (30 in major), 120 hours for bachelor's (30 in major). Most students required to take courses in English, humanities, mathematics, biological/physical sciences, social sciences. **Additional information:** All students must complete at least 4 courses with a significant writing component(beyond freshman composition) and 2 interdisciplinary perspectives courses designed to integrate different areas of knowledge.

FRESHMAN ADMISSIONS. Selection criteria: Class rank (top 40%) most important, followed by test scores, recommendations. Special consideration to students with special talents and minority students. **High school preparation:** 13 units required; 17 recommended. Required and recommended units include English 4, mathematics 3-4, social science 4 and science 2-3. Foreign language 2 recommended. one science laboratory course required. **Test requirements:** SAT or ACT (SAT preferred); score report by March 1. Applicants without SAT scores may enroll as non-degree students and be admitted to degree-seeking status after completing 15 credits with 2.0 GPA. **Additional information:** Educationally and economically disadvantaged students may be admitted to PACE enrichment program if they demonstrate potential for college success.

1992 FRESHMAN CLASS PROFILE. 2,446 men applied, 1,112 accepted, 374 enrolled; 3,691 women applied, 1,884 accepted, 643 enrolled. 25% were in top tenth and 62% were in top quarter of graduating class. **Academic background:** Mid 50% of enrolled freshmen had SAT-V between 440-530, SAT-M between 490-580. 87% submitted SAT scores. **Characteristics:** 88% from in state, 90% live in college housing, 14% have minority backgrounds, 2% are foreign students, 3% join fraternities/sororities. Average age is 18.

FALL-TERM APPLICATIONS. $20 fee, may be waived for applicants with need. No closing date; priority given to applications received by April 1; applicants notified on a rolling basis beginning on or about October 1; must reply by April 1 or within 15 days if notified after March 15. Audition required for music applicants. Portfolio recommended for art applicants. Interview required for applicants to disadvantaged program; recommended for all others. Deferred and early admission available. Extensions for accepted applicants until May 1, granted upon request.

STUDENT LIFE. Housing: Dormitories (men, women, coed). Academic interest housing available for several subject areas. University-affiliated apartments for single students adjacent to campus. **Activities:** Student government, magazine, radio, student newspaper, yearbook, choral groups, concert band, drama, jazz band, marching band, music ensembles, musical theater, pep band, symphony orchestra, fraternities, sororities, Hillel, Black Campus Ministry, Campus Crusade for Christ, Newman Association, Black Student Union, College Republicans, Circle-K, Inter-Varsity Christian Fellowship, Alpha Phi Omega.

ATHLETICS. NCAA. **Intercollegiate:** Baseball M, basketball, cross-country, field hockey W, football M, golf M, lacrosse W, soccer M, softball W, swimming W, tennis, track and field, volleyball W, wrestling M. **Intramural:** Archery, badminton, basketball, bowling, cross-country, fencing, ice hockey, lacrosse, rugby, soccer, softball, swimming, tennis, track and field, volleyball, water polo.

STUDENT SERVICES. Aptitude testing, career counseling, employment service for undergraduates, freshman orientation, health services, on-campus day care, personal counseling, placement service for graduates, special adviser for adult students, veterans counselor, services/facilities for handicapped.

ANNUAL EXPENSES. Tuition and fees (1992-93): $3,488, $3,394 additional for out-of-state students. **Room and board:** $3,620. **Books and supplies:** $450. **Other expenses:** $958.

FINANCIAL AID. 70% of freshmen, 70% of continuing students receive some form of aid. 58% of grants, 49% of loans, 10% of jobs based on need. 515 enrolled freshmen were judged to have need, 493 were offered aid. Academic, music/drama, art, athletic, minority scholarships available. **Aid applications:** Closing date May 1; applicants notified on or about July 15; must reply within 20 days.

ADDRESS/TELEPHONE. Darrell C. Davis, Director of Admissions, Millersville University of Pennsylvania, PO Box 1002, Millersville, PA 17551-0302. (717) 872-3030. Fax: (717) 872-2022.

Montgomery County Community College
Blue Bell, Pennsylvania — CB code: 2445

2-year public community college, coed. Founded in 1964. **Accreditation:** Regional. **Undergraduate enrollment:** 9,400 men and women. **Faculty:** 412 total (152 full time), 47 with doctorates or other terminal degrees. **Location:** Suburban campus in rural community; 5 miles from Norristown. **Calendar:** Semester, extensive summer session. **Microcomputers:** 300 located in libraries, classrooms, computer centers. **Special facilities:** Art gallery, learning assistance laboratory, computer center, dental hygiene clinic, job placement center. **Additional facts:** 8 county high schools utilized for credit-course offerings. Availability varies by semester.

DEGREES OFFERED. AA, AS, AAS. 650 associate degrees awarded in 1992. 18% in business and management, 13% business/office and marketing/distribution, 6% computer sciences, 10% teacher education, 23% allied health, 10% multi/interdisciplinary studies, 8% social sciences.

UNDERGRADUATE MAJORS. Accounting, automotive mechanics, automotive technology, biology, business administration and management, business and management, business and office, business data processing and related programs, communications, computer and information sciences, criminal justice studies, data processing, dental hygiene, drafting, drafting and design technology, early childhood education, electronic technology, elementary education, engineering and engineering-related technologies, fine arts, fire control and safety technology, food production/management/services, graphic arts technology, hospitality and recreation marketing, hotel/motel and restaurant management, humanities and social sciences, information sciences and systems, law enforcement and corrections technologies, legal secretary, liberal/general studies, marketing and distribution, marketing management, mathematics, medical laboratory technologies, medical secretary, mental health/human services, mid-range computing, nursing, physical education, physical sciences, real estate, secondary education, secretarial and related programs, social sciences, teacher aide, word processing.

ACADEMIC PROGRAMS. 2-year transfer program, dual enrollment of high school students, honors program, independent study, internships, teacher preparation, telecourses. **Remedial services:** Learning center, reduced course load, remedial instruction, special counselor, tutoring, mandatory placement tests, placement into developmental courses. **Placement/credit:** AP, CLEP Subject, institutional tests; 30 credit hours maximum for associate degree.

ACADEMIC REQUIREMENTS. Freshmen must earn minimum GPA of 2.0 to continue in good standing. 65% of freshmen return for sophomore year. Students must declare major by end of first year. **Graduation requirements:** 60 hours for associate. Most students required to take courses in English, history, mathematics, social sciences.

FRESHMAN ADMISSIONS. Selection criteria: Open admissions. Selective admissions to allied health, art, and human services programs. County residents given priority. Biology, chemistry, and algebra required of nursing and medical laboratory technician applicants, chemistry of dental hygiene applicants. **Test requirements:** ACT or SAT required for allied health applicants; score report by August 1.

1992 FRESHMAN CLASS PROFILE. 2,400 men and women enrolled. **Characteristics:** 99% from in state, 100% commute, 12% have minority backgrounds, 1% are foreign students. Average age is 20.

FALL-TERM APPLICATIONS. $20 fee. No closing date; applicants notified on a rolling basis. Deferred and early admission available. EDP-F.

STUDENT LIFE. Activities: Student government, magazine, radio, student newspaper, television, choral groups, drama, African American Club, Asian Club, Service Club, International Club, Newman Club, Environmental Club, Creative Art Club, Writers Club, Meridian Club, Community Service Club.

ATHLETICS. Intercollegiate: Baseball M, soccer M, tennis M. **Intramural:** Basketball M, bowling, racquetball, table tennis, tennis, volleyball.

STUDENT SERVICES. Career counseling, employment service for undergraduates, freshman orientation, health services, on-campus day care, personal counseling, placement service for graduates, veterans counselor, services/facilities for handicapped.

ANNUAL EXPENSES. Tuition and fees (1992-93): $1,890, $3,000 additional for out-of-district students, $4,500 additional for out-of-state students. **Books and supplies:** $550. **Other expenses:** $975.

FINANCIAL AID. 16% of freshmen, 16% of continuing students receive some form of aid. 99% of grants, 58% of loans, all jobs based on need. 1,300 enrolled freshmen were judged to have need, 796 were offered aid. Academic, state/district residency, leadership scholarships available. **Aid applications:** No closing date; priority given to applications received by May 1; applicants notified on a rolling basis.

ADDRESS/TELEPHONE. Dennis J. Murphy, Director of Admissions and Records, Montgomery County Community College, 340 De Kalb Pike, Blue Bell, PA 19422-0758. (215) 641-6550. Fax: (215) 653-0585.

Moore College of Art and Design ⇚⇛
Philadelphia, Pennsylvania — CB code: 2417

Admissions:	81% of applicants accepted
Based on:	••• School record, special talents
	•• Essay, interview, recommendations, test scores
	• Activities
Completion:	95% of freshmen end year in good standing
	5% enter graduate study

4-year private art college, women only. Founded in 1844. **Accreditation:** Regional. **Undergraduate enrollment:** 400 women full time; 50 women part time. **Faculty:** 70 total (51 full time), 8 with doctorates or other terminal degrees. **Location:** Urban campus in very large city; 90 miles from New York City. **Calendar:** Semester. **Microcomputers:** 35 located in libraries, classrooms, computer centers. **Special facilities:** 2 nationally recognized art galleries. **Additional facts:** Nation's only women's art college that prepares women for careers in fine and design arts.

DEGREES OFFERED. BFA. 100% in visual and performing arts. 103 bachelor's degrees awarded in 1992. 100% in visual and performing arts.

UNDERGRADUATE MAJORS. Art education, ceramics, drawing, fiber/textiles/weaving, fine arts, graphic design, illustration design, interior design, metal/jewelry, painting, photographic technology, photography, printmaking, sculpture, studio art, textiles and clothing, visual and performing arts.

ACADEMIC PROGRAMS. Accelerated program, cooperative education, double major, dual enrollment of high school students, independent study, internships, student-designed major, study abroad, teacher preparation, cross-registration. **Remedial services:** Learning center, preadmission summer program, reduced course load, special counselor, tutoring. **Placement/credit:** AP, CLEP General and Subject, institutional tests.

ACADEMIC REQUIREMENTS. Freshmen must earn minimum GPA of 2.0 to continue in good standing. 85% of freshmen return for sophomore year. Students must declare major by end of first year. **Graduation requirements:** 124 hours for bachelor's (60 in major). Most students required to take courses in arts/fine arts, English, history, humanities, social sciences. **Additional information:** Computer graphics software that can be applied to all major areas of study available.

FRESHMAN ADMISSIONS. Selection criteria: High school record, reference (preferably from student's art teacher), interview, portfolio, and test scores important. **High school preparation:** 14 units recommended. Recommended units include English 4, foreign language 2, mathematics 2, physical science 2 and social science 4. 3 art recommended. **Test requirements:** SAT or ACT; score report by August 15.

1992 FRESHMAN CLASS PROFILE. 242 women applied, 195 accepted, 101 enrolled. 43% had high school GPA of 3.0 or higher, 55% between 2.0 and 2.99. **Academic background:** Mid 50% of enrolled freshmen had SAT-V between 390-510, SAT-M between 370-500. 100% submitted SAT scores. **Characteristics:** 70% from in state, 50% commute, 15% have minority backgrounds, 5% are foreign students. Average age is 18.

FALL-TERM APPLICATIONS. $35 fee, may be waived for applicants with need. No closing date; priority given to applications received by April 1; applicants notified on a rolling basis; must reply by May 1 or within 2 weeks if notified thereafter. Portfolio required. Interview recommended. Essay recommended. CRDA. Deferred and early admission available. EDP-F.

STUDENT LIFE. Housing: Dormitories (women); apartment housing available. **Activities:** Student government, student newspaper, yearbook, Black Student Union, Moore Environmental Action Now (MEAN). **Additional information:** Access to city's major museums, other colleges and universities, and entertainment.

STUDENT SERVICES. Career counseling, employment service for undergraduates, freshman orientation, health services, personal counseling, placement service for graduates, special adviser for adult students, services/facilities for handicapped.

ANNUAL EXPENSES. Tuition and fees (projected): $13,725. **Room and board:** $5,250. **Books and supplies:** $800. **Other expenses:** $1,000.

FINANCIAL AID. 90% of freshmen, 70% of continuing students receive some form of aid. 94% of grants, 91% of loans, all jobs based on need. 79 enrolled freshmen were judged to have need, all were offered aid. Art scholarships available. **Aid applications:** No closing date; priority given to applications received by April 1; applicants notified on a rolling basis; must reply within 2 weeks.

ADDRESS/TELEPHONE. Claire E. Gallicano, Director of Admissions, Moore College of Art and Design, The Parkway at Twentieth Street, Philadelphia, PA 19103-1179. (215) 568-4515 ext. 1105. (800) 523-2025. Fax: (215) 568-8017.

Moravian College

Bethlehem, Pennsylvania CB code: 2418

Admissions: 76% of applicants accepted
Based on: ••• School record, test scores
•• Activities, essay, interview, recommendations, special talents
• Religious affiliation/commitment
Completion: 90% of freshmen end year in good standing
75% graduate, 17% of these enter graduate study

4-year private liberal arts college, coed, affiliated with Moravian Church in America. Founded in 1742. **Accreditation:** Regional. **Undergraduate enrollment:** 581 men, 567 women full time; 8 men, 10 women part time. **Graduate enrollment:** 3 men full time; 109 men, 46 women part time. **Faculty:** 129 total (84 full time), 81 with doctorates or other terminal degrees. **Location:** Suburban campus in small city; 60 miles from Philadelphia, 90 miles from New York City. **Calendar:** Semester, extensive summer session. **Microcomputers:** 100 located in computer centers. **Special facilities:** Payne Art Gallery, Foy Concert Hall.

DEGREES OFFERED. BA, BS, MBA, M.Div. 257 bachelor's degrees awarded in 1992. 27% in business and management, 6% computer sciences, 9% teacher education, 6% letters/literature, 5% life sciences, 12% psychology, 19% social sciences, 8% visual and performing arts. Graduate degrees offered in 3 major fields of study.

UNDERGRADUATE MAJORS. Accounting, art history, biology, business administration and management, business economics, chemistry, classics, clinical psychology, computer and information sciences, counseling psychology, criminology, earth sciences, economics, elementary education, engineering, English, English education, experimental psychology, foreign languages education, forestry and related sciences, French, geology, German, graphic design, history, industrial and organizational psychology, information sciences and systems, international business management, jazz, journalism, mathematics, mathematics education, medical laboratory technologies, music, music education, music history and appreciation, music performance, music theory and composition, occupational therapy, philosophy, physics, political science and government, predentistry, prelaw, premedicine, preveterinary, psychology, religion, science education, secondary education, social sciences, social studies education, sociology, Spanish, studio art.

ACADEMIC PROGRAMS. Double major, dual enrollment of high school students, honors program, independent study, internships, student-designed major, study abroad, teacher preparation, Washington semester, cross-registration, allied health program with Thomas Jefferson University; forestry program cooperative with Duke University, North Carolina; engineering programs cooperative with Lafayette College, University of Pennsylvania, Lehigh University, and Washington University (MO); liberal arts/career combination in engineering, forestry, health sciences. **Remedial services:** Tutoring, Developmental Writing Center, study skills workshops. **ROTC:** Army. **Placement/credit:** CLEP General and Subject, institutional tests.

ACADEMIC REQUIREMENTS. Freshmen must earn minimum GPA of 1.35 to continue in good standing. 86% of freshmen return for sophomore year. Students must declare major by end of second year. **Graduation requirements:** 128 hours for bachelor's (36 in major). Most students required to take courses in arts/fine arts, English, foreign languages, history, humanities, mathematics, philosophy/religion, biological/physical sciences, social sciences. **Postgraduate studies:** 2% enter law school, 3% enter medical school, 2% enter MBA programs, 10% enter other graduate study. **Additional information:** 4-year program of academic and career counseling, and career placement/graduate study program in final two years, has produced a first-year graduate placement of more than 95% in past five years.

FRESHMAN ADMISSIONS. Selection criteria: Class rank, SAT scores (middle 50% score between 930-1130), high school record (3.0 high school GPA in college preparatory program preferred) very important. Essay and recommendations from teachers and counselors important. High school activities, community involvement, volunteer activities, and work experience also considered. **High school preparation:** 16 units required. Required and recommended units include English 4, foreign language 2, mathematics 3-4, social science 2 and science 2. 4 mathematics for business or science students recommended. **Test requirements:** SAT or ACT (SAT preferred); score report by March 1. No ACH requirement, but if submitted used for placement. **Additional information:** Early applications encouraged.

1992 FRESHMAN CLASS PROFILE. 467 men applied, 356 accepted, 152 enrolled; 484 women applied, 371 accepted, 142 enrolled. 90% had high school GPA of 3.0 or higher, 10% between 2.0 and 2.99. 23% were in top tenth and 52% were in top quarter of graduating class. **Academic background:** Mid 50% of enrolled freshmen had SAT-V between 440-540, SAT-M between 480-580. 98% submitted SAT scores. **Characteristics:** 49% from in state, 89% live in college housing, 4% have minority backgrounds, 2% are foreign students. Average age is 18.

FALL-TERM APPLICATIONS. $25 fee, may be waived for applicants with need. Closing date March 1; priority given to applications received by January 31; applicants notified on or about March 15; must reply by May 1. Audition required for music applicants. Essay required. Interview recommended. Portfolio recommended for studio art applicants. CRDA. Deferred and early admission available. EDP-F. Early decision application deadline December 15; notification date January 15.

STUDENT LIFE. Housing: Dormitories (men, women, coed); fraternity, sorority housing available. College housing guaranteed all 4 years. Townhouse and apartment arrangements available for upperclassmen. **Activities:** Student government, magazine, radio, student newspaper, yearbook, choral groups, concert band, dance, drama, jazz band, music ensembles, musical theater, pep band, symphony orchestra, fraternities, sororities, Hillel, Newman, Intervarsity Christian Fellowship, Alpha Phi Omega,Sigma Tau Sigma, sports clubs, Society for Political and Economic Consciousness, Black Student Union.

ATHLETICS. NCAA. **Intercollegiate:** Baseball M, basketball, cross-country, field hockey W, football M, golf M, horseback riding W, soccer M, softball W, tennis, track and field, volleyball W, wrestling M. **Intramural:** Basketball, football M, handball, ice hockey M, lacrosse M, racquetball, soccer, softball, table tennis, tennis, volleyball.

STUDENT SERVICES. Aptitude testing, career counseling, employment service for undergraduates, freshman orientation, health services, personal counseling, placement service for graduates, special adviser for adult students, veterans counselor.

ANNUAL EXPENSES. Tuition and fees (1992-93): $13,696. **Room and board:** $4,264. **Books and supplies:** $500. **Other expenses:** $962.

FINANCIAL AID. 73% of freshmen, 73% of continuing students receive some form of aid. 99% of grants, 74% of loans, 33% of jobs based on need. 211 enrolled freshmen were judged to have need, all were offered aid. Academic scholarships available. **Aid applications:** Closing date March 15; priority given to applications received by February 15; applicants notified on or about April 15; must reply by May 1 or within 2 weeks if notified thereafter.

ADDRESS/TELEPHONE. Bernard J. Story, Director of Admissions, Moravian College, 1200 Main Street, Bethlehem, PA 18018. (215) 861-1320. Fax: (215) 861-3919.

Mount Aloysius College

Cresson, Pennsylvania CB code: 2420

Admissions: 60% of applicants accepted
Based on: ••• Interview, school record
•• Recommendations, test scores
• Activities, essay
Completion: 80% of freshmen end year in good standing

4-year private institution, coed, Religious Sisters of Mercy. Founded in 1939. **Accreditation:** Regional. **Undergraduate enrollment:** 263 men, 738 women full time; 16 men, 52 women part time. **Faculty:** 88 total (40 full time), 12 with doctorates or other terminal degrees. **Location:** Rural campus in small town; 7 miles from Altoona, 28 miles from Johnstown. **Calendar:** Semester, limited summer session. Saturday classes. **Microcomputers:** 45 located in computer centers.

DEGREES OFFERED. AA, AS, BA, BS. 326 associate degrees awarded in 1992. 15% in business and management, 57% allied health, 12% multi/interdisciplinary studies, 8% social sciences.

UNDERGRADUATE MAJORS. Associate: Accounting, business administration and management, computer and information sciences, criminology, hotel/motel and restaurant management, interpreter for the deaf, legal assistant/paralegal, liberal/general studies, medical assistant, medical laboratory technologies, nursing, occupational therapy assistant, public administration, teacher aide, theological studies, tourism. **Bachelor's:** Nursing, professional studies, public administration.

ACADEMIC PROGRAMS. 2-year transfer program, independent study, internships, weekend college. **Remedial services:** Learning center, preadmission summer program, reduced course load, remedial instruction, special counselor, tutoring. **Placement/credit:** CLEP Subject, institutional tests; 15 credit hours maximum for associate degree; 30 credit hours maximum for bachelor's degree.

ACADEMIC REQUIREMENTS. Freshmen must earn minimum GPA of 2.0 to continue in good standing. 65% of freshmen return for sophomore year. Students must declare major on enrollment. **Graduation requirements:** 60 hours for associate (24 in major), 120 hours for bachelor's (30 in major). Most students required to take courses in computer science, English, humanities, mathematics, philosophy/religion, biological/physical sciences. **Postgraduate studies:** 25% from 2-year programs enter 4-year programs. **Additional information:** Applicants to baccalaureate program must have earned associate degree prior to being accepted.

FRESHMAN ADMISSIONS. Selection criteria: Official high school transcript, SAT or ACT scores, and personal interview are required. Nursing students required to have combined SAT score of 800, combined ACT score of 20, and minimum high school GPA of 2.5. Recommended units include biological science 2, English 4, mathematics 2, social science 4 and science 2. Algebra, chemistry, and biology required for nursing applicants. Biology required for medical assistant and occupational therapy assistant applicants. Typing required for legal assistant applicants. **Test requirements:** SAT or ACT.

1992 FRESHMAN CLASS PROFILE. 311 men applied, 187 accepted, 186 enrolled; 837 women applied, 504 accepted, 504 enrolled. **Characteristics:** 94% from in state, 91% commute, 2% have minority backgrounds, 3% are foreign students. Average age is 28.

FALL-TERM APPLICATIONS. $15 fee, may be waived for applicants with need. No closing date; applicants notified on a rolling basis; must reply within 2 weeks. Interview required for occupational therapy assistant, cardiovascular technology, surgical technology, nursing applicants; recommended for medical assistant applicants. Deferred and early admission available. Test scores must be received by end of first week of term.

STUDENT LIFE. Housing: Dormitories (men, women). Dormitory rooms for the hearing impaired available. **Activities:** Student government, student newspaper, yearbook, choral groups, music ensembles, campus ministry, nursing, occupational therapy assistant, business, hospitality, medical assistant, and art clubs.

ATHLETICS. NJCAA. **Intercollegiate:** Basketball, soccer M, softball W, volleyball W. **Intramural:** Baseball, basketball, soccer, softball, tennis, volleyball.

STUDENT SERVICES. Aptitude testing, career counseling, employment service for undergraduates, freshman orientation, health services, on-campus day care, personal counseling, placement service for graduates, veterans counselor, services/facilities for handicapped.

ANNUAL EXPENSES. Tuition and fees (1992-93): $7,190. **Room and board:** $3,320. **Books and supplies:** $550. **Other expenses:** $1,100.

FINANCIAL AID. 89% of freshmen, 87% of continuing students receive some form of aid. 76% of grants, 91% of loans, all jobs based on need. 649 enrolled freshmen were judged to have need, all were offered aid. Academic, athletic scholarships available. **Aid applications:** Closing date August 1; priority given to applications received by May 1; applicants notified on or about August 1; must reply within 3 weeks.

ADDRESS/TELEPHONE. Sylvia Ghezzi Hirsch, Director of Admissions, Mount Aloysius College, 1 College Drive, Cresson, PA 16630. (814) 886-4131 ext. 227. Fax: (814) 886-5061.

Muhlenberg College

Allentown, Pennsylvania — CB code: 2424

Admissions: 78% of applicants accepted
Based on:
- ••• School record
- •• Activities, essay, recommendations, special talents, test scores
- • Interview

Completion: 95% of freshmen end year in good standing
80% graduate, 31% of these enter graduate study

4-year private liberal arts college, coed, affiliated with Lutheran Church. Founded in 1848. **Accreditation:** Regional. **Undergraduate enrollment:** 762 men, 879 women full time; 36 men, 32 women part time. **Faculty:** 162 total (110 full time), 96 with doctorates or other terminal degrees. **Location:** Suburban campus in small city; 55 miles from Philadelphia, 90 miles from New York City. **Calendar:** Semester, limited summer session. **Microcomputers:** 151 located in libraries, classrooms, computer centers. **Special facilities:** Theater complex, electronic music studio, natural history museum, 38-acre environmental field station, greenhouse, art gallery, electron microscopes, isolation laboratories, 20-foot boat for marine studies. **Additional facts:** Joint library system with Cedar Crest College. Interlibrary loan with 5 cooperating institutions.

DEGREES OFFERED. BA, BS. 413 bachelor's degrees awarded in 1992. 22% in business and management, 5% communications, 10% letters/literature, 16% life sciences, 6% multi/interdisciplinary studies, 11% psychology, 16% social sciences.

UNDERGRADUATE MAJORS. Accounting, American studies, biological and physical sciences, biology, business administration and management, chemistry, classics, communications, computer and information sciences, dramatic arts, economics, English, fine arts, French, German, Greek (classical), history, human resources development, humanities, humanities and social sciences, international relations, international studies, Latin, mathematics, music, philosophy, philosophy/political thought, physics, political economy, political science and government, psychology, religion, Russian and Slavic studies, social work, sociology, Spanish.

ACADEMIC PROGRAMS. Accelerated program, double major, honors program, independent study, internships, student-designed major, study abroad, teacher preparation, visiting/exchange student program, Washington semester, cross-registration, 3+2 engineering and nursing programs with Columbia University, 3+2 engineering program with Washington University, 3+2 forestry program with Duke University, 3+4 accelerated dental program with University of Pennsylvania, 4+4 dual admission medical program with Hahnemann University School of Medicine, study abroad with Lehigh Valley Association of Independent Colleges; liberal arts/career combination in engineering, forestry, health sciences. **Remedial services:** Learning center, reduced course load, tutoring, writing center. **ROTC:** Army. **Placement/credit:** AP, CLEP Subject, institutional tests; 51 credit hours maximum for bachelor's degree.

ACADEMIC REQUIREMENTS. Freshmen must earn minimum GPA of 1.5 to continue in good standing. 93% of freshmen return for sophomore year. Students must declare major by end of second year. **Graduation requirements:** 136 hours for bachelor's (40 in major). Most students required to take courses in arts/fine arts, English, foreign languages, history, humanities, mathematics, philosophy/religion, biological/physical sciences, social sciences. **Postgraduate studies:** 6% enter law school, 9% enter medical school, 1% enter MBA programs, 15% enter other graduate study. **Additional information:** Many interdisciplinary majors with concentrations in women's studies, environmental studies, Asian studies, Latin American studies, and African-American studies.

FRESHMAN ADMISSIONS. Selection criteria: High school courses, grades, class rank; test scores; personal qualities; essay; activities considered. **High school preparation:** 16 units required. Required and recommended units include biological science 1, English 4, foreign language 2-3, mathematics 3-4, physical science 1 and social science 3. Advanced Placement and accelerated courses encouraged. **Test requirements:** SAT or ACT; score report by March 1.

1992 FRESHMAN CLASS PROFILE. 1,218 men applied, 881 accepted, 218 enrolled; 1,237 women applied, 1,022 accepted, 249 enrolled. 91% had high school GPA of 3.0 or higher, 9% between 2.0 and 2.99. 30% were in top tenth and 65% were in top quarter of graduating class. **Academic background:** Mid 50% of enrolled freshmen had SAT-V between 440-580, SAT-M between 490-640; ACT composite between 20-28. 93% submitted SAT scores, 5% submitted ACT scores. **Characteristics:** 33% from in state, 99% live in college housing, 9% have minority backgrounds, 1% are foreign students, 40% join fraternities/sororities. Average age is 18.

FALL-TERM APPLICATIONS. $30 fee, may be waived for applicants with need. Closing date February 15; applicants notified on or about April 1; must reply by May 1. Essay required. Interview recommended. Audition recommended for music, drama applicants. Portfolio recommended for art applicants. CRDA. Deferred and early admission available. EDP-F.

STUDENT LIFE. Housing: Dormitories (women, coed); apartment, fraternity, sorority housing available. Theme-oriented houses available. **Activities:** Student government, magazine, radio, student newspaper, yearbook, choral groups, concert band, dance, drama, jazz band, music ensembles, musical theater, opera, pep band, Muhlenberg Theater Association, fraternities, sororities, Amnesty International, Christian Association, Lutheran Student Movement, Newman Club, Hillel, Habitat for Humanity, International Affairs Club, International Student Association, Black Student Association, Alpha Phi Omega.

ATHLETICS. NCAA. **Intercollegiate:** Baseball M, basketball, cross-country, field hockey W, football M, golf M, lacrosse W, soccer, softball W, tennis, track and field, volleyball W, wrestling M. **Intramural:** Badminton, basketball, ice hockey M, lacrosse M, racquetball, rugby M, soccer, softball, squash, swimming, table tennis, tennis, volleyball.

STUDENT SERVICES. Aptitude testing, career counseling, employment service for undergraduates, freshman orientation, health services, personal counseling, placement service for graduates, special adviser for adult students, services/facilities for handicapped.

ANNUAL EXPENSES. Tuition and fees (1992-93): $15,740. **Room and board:** $4,260. **Books and supplies:** $550. **Other expenses:** $800.

FINANCIAL AID. 63% of freshmen, 60% of continuing students receive some form of aid. 85% of grants, 70% of loans, 55% of jobs based on need. 223 enrolled freshmen were judged to have need, 222 were offered aid. Academic, state/district residency, leadership, religious affiliation scholarships available. **Aid applications:** Closing date March 15; applicants notified on or about April 1; must reply by May 1. **Additional information:** Merit scholarships for academic and extracurricular achievement.

ADDRESS/TELEPHONE. Christopher Hooker-Haring, Director of Admissions, Muhlenberg College, 2400 Chew Street, Allentown, PA 18104. (215) 821-3200. Fax: (215) 821-3234.

National Education Center: Vale Tech Campus
Blairsville, Pennsylvania — CB code: 1578

2-year proprietary technical college, coed. Founded in 1946. **Undergraduate enrollment:** 374 men and women. **Faculty:** 22 total (20 full time). **Location:** Rural campus in small town; 45 miles from Pittsburgh. **Calendar:** Ten 5-week modules per year.

DEGREES OFFERED. 169 associate degrees awarded in 1992. 100% in trade and industry.

UNDERGRADUATE MAJORS. Automotive mechanics.

ACADEMIC REQUIREMENTS. Freshmen must earn minimum GPA of 2.0 to continue in good standing.

FRESHMAN ADMISSIONS. Selection criteria: Open admissions.

1992 FRESHMAN CLASS PROFILE. 307 men and women enrolled. **Characteristics:** 90% from in state, 63% live in college housing, 2% have minority backgrounds.

FALL-TERM APPLICATIONS. $50 fee. No closing date; applicants notified on a rolling basis; must reply within 2 weeks. Interview required. Deferred admission available.

STUDENT LIFE. Housing: Dormitories (men).

ATHLETICS. Intramural: Basketball, softball.

STUDENT SERVICES. Employment service for undergraduates, placement service for graduates.

ANNUAL EXPENSES. Tuition and fees (projected): $5,706. **Room and board:** $960 room only. **Books and supplies:** $761. **Other expenses:** $938.

FINANCIAL AID. 88% of freshmen, 90% of continuing students receive some form of aid. **Aid applications:** No closing date; applicants notified on a rolling basis.

ADDRESS/TELEPHONE. Alan Spencer, Director of Admissions, National Education Center: Vale Tech Campus, 135 West Market Street, Blairsville, PA 15717. (412) 459-9500. Fax: (412) 459-6499.

Neumann College
Aston, Pennsylvania — CB code: 2628

4-year private liberal arts college, coed, affiliated with Roman Catholic Church. Founded in 1965. **Accreditation:** Regional. **Undergraduate enrollment:** 114 men, 348 women full time; 143 men, 521 women part time. **Graduate enrollment:** 9 women full time; 14 men, 40 women part time. **Faculty:** 112 total (49 full time), 30 with doctorates or other terminal degrees. **Location:** Suburban campus in large town; 15 miles from Philadelphia, 9 miles from Wilmington, Delaware. **Calendar:** Semester, limited summer session. Saturday and extensive evening/early morning classes. **Microcomputers:** 47 located in libraries, computer centers.

DEGREES OFFERED. AA, BA, BS, MS. 9 associate degrees awarded in 1992. 100% in multi/interdisciplinary studies. 191 bachelor's degrees awarded. 14% in business and management, 12% teacher education, 22% health sciences, 42% multi/interdisciplinary studies.

UNDERGRADUATE MAJORS. Associate: Liberal/general studies. **Bachelor's:** Accounting, biology, business administration and management, clinical laboratory science, communications, computer and information sciences, elementary education, English, liberal/general studies, marketing and distribution, nursing, political science and government, prelaw, psychology, religion, secondary education.

ACADEMIC PROGRAMS. Cooperative education, double major, honors program, independent study, student-designed major, teacher preparation. **Remedial services:** Learning center, preadmission summer program, reduced course load, remedial instruction, tutoring. **Placement/credit:** AP, CLEP General and Subject, institutional tests; 24 credit hours maximum for bachelor's degree.

ACADEMIC REQUIREMENTS. Freshmen must earn minimum GPA of 2.0 to continue in good standing. 86% of freshmen return for sophomore year. Students must declare major by end of second year. **Graduation requirements:** 60 hours for associate, 121 hours for bachelor's (45 in major). Most students required to take courses in arts/fine arts, computer science, English, foreign languages, history, humanities, mathematics, philosophy/religion, biological/physical sciences, social sciences. **Postgraduate studies:** 8% enter other graduate study.

FRESHMAN ADMISSIONS. Selection criteria: School achievement record most important. Applicants must rank in top two-fifths of class. Test scores, interview, school and community activities and recommendations also considered. **High school preparation:** 16 units required. Required units include English 4, foreign language 2, mathematics 2, social science 2 and science 2. Biology and chemistry required of nursing, biology, and medical technology applicants. Physics recommended for biology and medical technology applicants. **Test requirements:** SAT or ACT; score report by August 15.

1992 FRESHMAN CLASS PROFILE. 21 men, 74 women enrolled. 41% had high school GPA of 3.0 or higher, 59% between 2.0 and 2.99. **Academic background:** Mid 50% of enrolled freshmen had SAT-V between 360-460, SAT-M between 370-490. 99% submitted SAT scores. **Characteristics:** 75% from in state, 100% commute, 19% have minority backgrounds. Average age is 18.

FALL-TERM APPLICATIONS. $25 fee, may be waived for applicants with need. Closing date August 1; priority given to applications received by May 1; applicants notified on a rolling basis; must reply by May 1 or within 4 weeks if notified thereafter. Interview recommended. CRDA. Deferred and early admission available.

STUDENT LIFE. Activities: Student government, student newspaper, yearbook, choral groups, music ensembles, musical theater, fraternities, campus ministry, nursing club, science club, social/behavioral science club.

ATHLETICS. NAIA. **Intercollegiate:** Baseball M, basketball, cross-country, softball W, tennis, volleyball W. **Intramural:** Badminton, basketball, softball, table tennis, tennis, volleyball.

STUDENT SERVICES. Aptitude testing, career counseling, employment service for undergraduates, freshman orientation, health services, on-campus day care, personal counseling, placement service for graduates, special adviser for adult students, services/facilities for handicapped.

ANNUAL EXPENSES. Tuition and fees (1992-93): $9,406. **Books and supplies:** $650. **Other expenses:** $500.

FINANCIAL AID. 79% of freshmen, 64% of continuing students receive some form of aid. 75% of grants, 66% of loans, 71% of jobs based on need. Academic, athletic, leadership scholarships available. **Aid applications:** Closing date April 30; priority given to applications received by March 15; applicants notified on a rolling basis beginning on or about June 30; must reply within 2 weeks.

ADDRESS/TELEPHONE. Mark Osborn, Director of Admissions, Neumann College, Concord Road, Aston, PA 19014-1297. (215) 558-5616. Fax: (215) 459-1370.

Northampton County Area Community College
Bethlehem, Pennsylvania — CB code: 2573

2-year public community college, coed. Founded in 1966. **Accreditation:** Regional. **Undergraduate enrollment:** 1,052 men, 1,223 women full time; 1,378 men, 3,072 women part time. **Faculty:** 372 total (94 full time), 38 with doctorates or other terminal degrees. **Location:** Suburban campus in small city; 60 miles from Philadelphia. **Calendar:** Semester, limited summer session. **Microcomputers:** 310 located in libraries, classrooms. **Additional facts:** College-At-Home Program for students who cannot attend classes regularly. 3 off-campus sites: Monroe County Center, Slate Belt Center, Center City Bethlehem.

DEGREES OFFERED. AA, AS, AAS. 558 associate degrees awarded in 1992. 15% in business/office and marketing/distribution, 6% teacher education, 10% engineering technologies, 19% health sciences, 16% allied health, 8% home economics.

UNDERGRADUATE MAJORS. Accounting, architectural technologies, automotive technology, biology, business administration and management, business and office, chemistry, child development/care/guidance, commercial art, computer and information sciences, computer graphics, criminal justice studies, data processing, dental hygiene, drafting and design technology, electromechanical technology, electronic technology, elementary education, engineering, fashion merchandising, finance, fire control and safety technology, funeral services/mortuary science, graphic arts technology, hotel/motel and restaurant management, industrial equipment maintenance and repair, information sciences and systems, interior design, legal secretary, liberal/general studies, library assistant, mathematics, medical laboratory technologies, medical secretary, nursing, office supervision and management, radio/television broadcasting, radiograph medical technology, secretarial and related programs, tourism, welding technology.

ACADEMIC PROGRAMS. 2-year transfer program, accelerated program, cooperative education, dual enrollment of high school students, honors program, independent study, internships, dual admission program with Moravian College, Allentown College, Cedar Crest College, Centenary College, Muhlenberg College; advanced admission with Cheyney and Lincoln University. **Remedial services:** Learning center, reduced course load, remedial instruction, special counselor, tutoring. **ROTC:** Air Force, Army. **Placement/credit:** AP, CLEP General and Subject, institutional tests; 30 credit hours maximum for associate degree.

ACADEMIC REQUIREMENTS. Freshmen must earn minimum GPA of 2.0 to continue in good standing. 59% of freshmen return for sophomore year. Students must declare major on enrollment. **Graduation requirements:** 60 hours for associate. Most students required to take courses in computer science, English, mathematics, biological/physical sciences, social sciences.

FRESHMAN ADMISSIONS. Selection criteria: Open admissions. Selective admissions to allied health programs and advertising design. Special subject requirements for allied health programs.

1992 FRESHMAN CLASS PROFILE. 956 men applied, 918 accepted, 622 enrolled; 1,565 women applied, 1,439 accepted, 1,037 enrolled.

FALL-TERM APPLICATIONS. $20 fee, may be waived for applicants with need. No closing date; priority given to applications received by March 1; applicants notified on a rolling basis beginning on or about November 15; must reply by June 15 or within 2 weeks if notified thereafter. Interview required for allied health applicants. Portfolio required for advertising design applicants. Deferred and early admission available.

STUDENT LIFE. Housing: Dormitories (coed); apartment housing available. Apartments available for 48 students on first-come, first-served basis. One dormitory accommodates 101 students. **Activities:** Student government, film, radio, student newspaper, television, choral groups, drama, music ensembles, United Students, disabled student organization, adult student organization.

ATHLETICS. Intercollegiate: Baseball M, basketball, bowling, golf M, softball W, tennis, volleyball. **Intramural:** Basketball M, bowling, golf, handball, racquetball, softball, volleyball.

STUDENT SERVICES. Aptitude testing, career counseling, employment service for undergraduates, freshman orientation, health services, on-campus day care, personal counseling, placement service for graduates, special adviser for adult students, support services for nontraditional students, disabled student services, services/facilities for handicapped.

ANNUAL EXPENSES. Tuition and fees: $1,770, $1,890 additional for out-of-district students, $3,780 additional for out-of-state students. **Room and board:** $3,700. **Books and supplies:** $600. **Other expenses:** $1,000.

FINANCIAL AID. 36% of freshmen, 15% of continuing students receive some form of aid. 91% of grants, 61% of loans, 83% of jobs based on need. Academic, athletic, state/district residency, leadership, minority scholarships available. **Aid applications:** No closing date; priority given to applications received by March 31; applicants notified on a rolling basis beginning on or about July 1; must reply within 2 weeks.

ADDRESS/TELEPHONE. Maria Teresa Donate, Director of Admissions, Northampton County Area Community College, 3835 Green Pond Road, Bethlehem, PA 18017. (215) 861-5500.

Peirce Junior College
Philadelphia, Pennsylvania CB code: 2674

2-year private business, junior college, coed. Founded in 1865. **Accreditation:** Regional. **Undergraduate enrollment:** 143 men, 531 women full time; 91 men, 239 women part time. **Location:** Urban campus in very large city. **Calendar:** Semester.

FRESHMAN ADMISSIONS. Selection criteria: School achievement record very important. Placement test scores, interview, SAT scores important.

ANNUAL EXPENSES. Tuition and fees (1992-93): $5,900. **Room and board:** $2,800 room only. **Books and supplies:** $500. **Other expenses:** $2,090.

ADDRESS/TELEPHONE. H. David Schleicher, Director of Admissions and Financial Aid, Peirce Junior College, 1420 Pine Street, Philadelphia, PA 19102. (215) 545-6400 ext. 214.

Penn State Allentown Campus
Fogelsville, Pennsylvania

2-year public branch campus college, coed. **Accreditation:** Regional. **Undergraduate enrollment:** 296 men, 129 women full time; 60 men, 102 women part time. **Location:** Suburban campus in rural community. **Calendar:** Semester. **Additional facts:** Students may take first 2 years of most Penn State baccalaureate programs and then transfer to University Park, Erie Behrend College, or Harrisburg Capital College campuses to complete degree.

FRESHMAN ADMISSIONS. Selection criteria: Requirements vary by program. Evaluation index based on SAT scores and high school record. Special consideration to children of alumni and minority applicants.

ANNUAL EXPENSES. Tuition and fees (1992-93): $4,474, $5,170 additional for out-of-state students. **Books and supplies:** $406. **Other expenses:** $1,794.

ADDRESS/TELEPHONE. Admissions Officer, Penn State Allentown Campus, Academic Building, Fogelsville, PA 18051-9733. (215) 821-6577.

Penn State Altoona Campus
Altoona, Pennsylvania

2-year public branch campus college, coed. Founded in 1929. **Accreditation:** Regional. **Undergraduate enrollment:** 1,145 men, 987 women full time; 147 men, 219 women part time. **Location:** Suburban campus in small city. **Calendar:** Semester. **Additional facts:** Selected complete associate degree programs offered. Students may also take first 2 years of most Penn State baccalaureate programs and then transfer to University Park, Erie Behrend College, or Harrisburg Capital College campuses to complete degree.

FRESHMAN ADMISSIONS. Selection criteria: Requirements vary by program. Evaluation index based on SAT scores and high school record. Special consideration to children of alumni and minority applicants.

ANNUAL EXPENSES. Tuition and fees (1992-93): $4,474, $5,170 additional for out-of-state students. **Room and board:** $3,790. **Books and supplies:** $440. **Other expenses:** $2,124.

ADDRESS/TELEPHONE. Admissions Officer, Penn State Altoona Campus, Ivyside Park, Altoona, PA 16601-3760. (814) 949-5466.

Penn State Beaver Campus
Monaca, Pennsylvania

2-year public branch campus college, coed. Founded in 1964. **Accreditation:** Regional. **Undergraduate enrollment:** 485 men, 271 women full time; 51 men, 57 women part time. **Location:** Suburban campus in small town. **Calendar:** Semester. **Additional facts:** Selected complete associate degree programs offered. Students may also take first 2 years of most Penn State baccalaureate programs and then transfer to University Park, Erie Behrend College, or Harrisburg Capital College campuses to complete degree.

FRESHMAN ADMISSIONS. Selection criteria: Requirements vary by program. Evaluation index based on SAT scores and high school record. Special consideration to children of alumni and minority applicants.

ANNUAL EXPENSES. Tuition and fees (1992-93): $4,474, $5,170 additional for out-of-state students. **Room and board:** $3,790. **Books and supplies:** $440. **Other expenses:** $2,124.

ADDRESS/TELEPHONE. Admissions Officer, Penn State Beaver Campus, Brodhead Road, Monaca, PA 15061. (412) 773-3800.

Penn State Berks Campus
Reading, Pennsylvania

2-year public branch campus college, coed. Founded in 1924. **Accreditation:** Regional. **Undergraduate enrollment:** 719 men, 451 women full time; 302 men, 184 women part time. **Location:** Suburban campus in small city. **Calendar:** Semester. **Additional facts:** Selected complete associate degree programs offered. Students may also take first 2 years of most Penn State baccalaureate programs and then transfer to University Park, Erie Behrend College, or Harrisburg Capital College campuses to complete degree.

FRESHMAN ADMISSIONS. Selection criteria: Requirements vary by program. Evaluation index based on SAT scores and high school record. Special consideration to children of alumni and minority applicants.

ANNUAL EXPENSES. Tuition and fees (1992-93): $4,474, $5,170 additional for out-of-state students. **Room and board:** $3,790. **Books and supplies:** $440. **Other expenses:** $2,124.

ADDRESS/TELEPHONE. Admissions Officer, Penn State Berks Campus, PO Box 7009, Tulpehocken Road, Reading, PA 19610-6009. (215) 320-4864.

Penn State Delaware County Campus
Media, Pennsylvania

2-year public branch campus college, coed. Founded in 1966. **Accreditation:** Regional. **Undergraduate enrollment:** 638 men, 366 women full time; 201 men, 348 women part time. **Location:** Suburban campus in small town. **Calendar:** Semester. **Additional facts:** Selected complete associate degree programs offered. Students may also take first 2 years of most Penn State baccalaureate programs and then transfer to University Park, Erie Behrend College, or Harrisburg Capital College campuses to complete degree.

FRESHMAN ADMISSIONS. Selection criteria: Requirements vary by

additional for out-of-state students. **Books and supplies:** $440. **Other expenses:** $1,794.

ADDRESS/TELEPHONE. Admissions Officer, Penn State Shenango Campus, 147 Shenango Avenue, Sharon, PA 16146. (412) 983-5830.

Penn State University Park Campus

University Park, Pennsylvania CB code: 2660

Admissions: 51% of applicants accepted
Based on: ••• School record, test scores
• Activities, recommendations
Completion: 56% graduate

4-year public university, coed. Founded in 1855. **Accreditation:** Regional. **Undergraduate enrollment:** 16,636 men, 12,966 women full time; 1,200 men, 1,003 women part time. **Graduate enrollment:** 2,622 men, 1,627 women full time; 1,269 men, 1,123 women part time. **Faculty:** 2,672 total (2,348 full time), 1,681 with doctorates or other terminal degrees. **Location:** Suburban campus in large town; 90 miles from Harrisburg. **Calendar:** Semester, extensive summer session. **Microcomputers:** 1,737 located in libraries, classrooms, computer centers. **Special facilities:** Museums of art, entomology, anthropology, earth and mineral sciences, weather station, Stone Valley Recreational Center. **Additional facts:** Main campus and administrative center of university. Some associate degree programs offered at University Park, but primarily offered only at 2-year campuses and Erie Behrend College. First 2 years of most University Park programs also offered at 2-year campuses and Erie Behrend College.

DEGREES OFFERED. AA, AS, BA, BS, BFA, BArch, MA, MS, MBA, MFA, MEd, PhD, EdD. 90 associate degrees awarded in 1992. 9% in agriculture, 20% business and management, 66% multi/interdisciplinary studies. 8,361 bachelor's degrees awarded. 23% in business and management, 5% communications, 8% teacher education, 14% engineering, 5% health sciences, 6% multi/interdisciplinary studies, 6% parks/recreation, protective services, public affairs, 6% social sciences. Graduate degrees offered in 112 major fields of study.

UNDERGRADUATE MAJORS. Associate: Agricultural business and management, architectural technologies, biomedical equipment technology, biotechnology, business and management, computer and information sciences, computer technology, dietetic aide/assistant, electronic technology, individual and family development, institutional management, liberal/general studies, materials engineering, mechanical design technology, medical laboratory technologies, nuclear technologies, physical therapy assistant, radiograph medical technology, science technologies, social sciences, sociology, solar heating and cooling technology, survey and mapping technology, telecommunications, wildlife management. **Bachelor's:** Accounting, actuarial sciences, advertising, aerospace/aeronautical/astronautical engineering, Afro-American (black) studies, agricultural business and management, agricultural economics, agricultural education, agricultural engineering, agricultural mechanics, agricultural sciences, agronomy, American studies, animal sciences, anthropology, architectural engineering, architecture, art education, art history, astronomy, astrophysics, atmospheric sciences and meteorology, biochemistry, biological and physical sciences, biology, business administration and management, business economics, cell biology, ceramic engineering, chemical engineering, chemistry, civil engineering, classics, communications, comparative literature, computer and information sciences, computer engineering, criminal justice studies, dramatic arts, earth sciences, East Asian studies, economics, education of the physically handicapped, electrical/electronics/communications engineering, elementary education, engineering science, English, entomology, exercise and sport science, film arts, finance, fine arts, fishing and fisheries, food science and nutrition, food sciences, forest products processing technology, forestry and related sciences, French, geography, geosciences, German, health care administration, health education, history, home economics education, horticultural science, individual and family development, industrial engineering, institutional management, insurance and risk management, international business management, international public service, Italian, journalism, labor/industrial relations, landscape architecture, Latin American studies, leisure studies, liberal/general studies, linguistics, management information systems, management science, marketing management, materials engineering, mathematics, mechanical engineering, medieval studies, metallurgical engineering, microbiology, mineral economics, mining and mineral engineering, mining and petroleum technologies, molecular biology, music, music education, nuclear engineering, nursing, petroleum engineering, philosophy, physics, plant sciences, political science and government, poultry, prelaw, premedicine, psychology, public affairs, radio/television broadcasting, real estate, religion, renewable natural resources, Russian, secondary education, social work, sociology, soil sciences, Spanish, special education, speech, speech pathology/audiology, trade and industrial education, transportation management.

ACADEMIC PROGRAMS. Cooperative education, double major, honors program, independent study, internships, student-designed major, study abroad, teacher preparation; liberal arts/career combination in engineering, health sciences; combined bachelor's/graduate program in medicine. **Remedial services:** Learning center, remedial instruction, special counselor, tutoring, Educational Opportunity Program, developmental year program. **ROTC:** Air Force, Army, Naval. **Placement/credit:** AP, CLEP General and Subject, institutional tests; 60 credit hours maximum for bachelor's degree.

ACADEMIC REQUIREMENTS. Freshmen must earn minimum GPA of 2.0 to continue in good standing. Higher GPA requirements in some departments. 84% of freshmen return for sophomore year. Students must declare major by end of second year. **Graduation requirements:** 60 hours for associate, 120 hours for bachelor's. Most students required to take courses in arts/fine arts, English, humanities, mathematics, biological/physical sciences, social sciences.

FRESHMAN ADMISSIONS. Selection criteria: Requirements vary by college. Evaluation index based on SAT scores and high school record. Special consideration to children of alumni and minority applicants. **High school preparation:** 15 units required. Required units include English 4, mathematics 3, social science 2 and science 3. Additional requirements for some programs. 3 additional units required in arts and humanities. **Test requirements:** SAT or ACT (SAT preferred); score report by November 30.

1992 FRESHMAN CLASS PROFILE. 12,588 men applied, 6,151 accepted, 2,318 enrolled; 10,342 women applied, 5,627 accepted, 2,067 enrolled. 85% had high school GPA of 3.0 or higher, 14% between 2.0 and 2.99. 42% were in top tenth and 90% were in top quarter of graduating class. **Academic background:** Mid 50% of enrolled freshmen had SAT-V between 450-550, SAT-M between 520-650. 94% submitted SAT scores. **Characteristics:** 71% from in state, 86% live in college housing, 11% have minority backgrounds, 1% are foreign students. Average age is 18.

FALL-TERM APPLICATIONS. $35 fee, may be waived for applicants with need. No closing date; priority given to applications received by November 30; applicants notified on a rolling basis beginning on or about November 1; must reply by March 1 or within 2 weeks if notified thereafter. All freshman applications processed at main campus.

STUDENT LIFE. Housing: Dormitories (men, women); apartment, fraternity, sorority housing available. **Activities:** Student government, film, magazine, radio, student newspaper, television, yearbook, choral groups, concert band, dance, drama, jazz band, marching band, music ensembles, musical theater, pep band, symphony orchestra, fraternities, sororities, approximately 415 student organizations.

ATHLETICS. NCAA. **Intercollegiate:** Baseball M, basketball, cross-country, diving, fencing, field hockey W, football M, golf, gymnastics, lacrosse, soccer M, softball W, swimming, tennis, track and field, volleyball, wrestling M. **Intramural:** Badminton, basketball, bowling M, cross-country, field hockey W, football M, golf, handball M, racquetball, soccer, softball, squash, swimming, tennis, track and field, volleyball, wrestling M.

STUDENT SERVICES. Aptitude testing, career counseling, employment service for undergraduates, freshman orientation, health services, personal counseling, placement service for graduates, special adviser for adult students, veterans counselor, services/facilities for handicapped.

ANNUAL EXPENSES. Tuition and fees (1992-93): $4,618, $5,026 additional for out-of-state students. **Room and board:** $3,790. **Books and supplies:** $440. **Other expenses:** $2,124.

FINANCIAL AID. 60% of freshmen, 73% of continuing students receive some form of aid. 63% of grants, 74% of loans, 24% of jobs based on need. Academic, music/drama, art, athletic scholarships available. **Aid applications:** No closing date; priority given to applications received by March 15; applicants notified on a rolling basis beginning on or about April 1; must reply within 4 weeks.

ADDRESS/TELEPHONE. Anna M. Griswold, Director of Admissions and Assistant Vice President for Academic Services, Penn State University Park Campus, 201 Shields Building, Box 3000, University Park, PA 16802. (814) 865-5471.

Penn State Wilkes-Barre Campus

Lehman, Pennsylvania

2-year public branch campus college, coed. Founded in 1916. **Accreditation:** Regional. **Undergraduate enrollment:** 417 men, 172 women full time; 173 men, 72 women part time. **Location:** Suburban campus in small city. **Calendar:** Semester. **Additional facts:** Selected complete associate degree progams offered. Students may also take first 2 years of most Penn State baccalaureate programs and then transfer to University Park, Erie Behrend College, or Harrisburg Capital College campuses to complete degree.

FRESHMAN ADMISSIONS. Selection criteria: Requirements vary by program. Evaluation index based on SAT scores and high school record. Special consideration to children of alumni and minority applicants.

ANNUAL EXPENSES. Tuition and fees (1992-93): $4,474, $5,170 additional for out-of-state students. **Books and supplies:** $440. **Other expenses:** $1,794.

ADDRESS/TELEPHONE. Admissions Officer, Penn State Wilkes-Barre Campus, PO Box PSU, Lehman, PA 18627. (717) 675-2171. (800) 426-2358.

Penn State Worthington-Scranton Campus
Dunmore, Pennsylvania

2-year public branch campus college, coed. Founded in 1923. **Accreditation:** Regional. **Undergraduate enrollment:** 493 men, 393 women full time; 122 men, 140 women part time. **Location:** Suburban campus in large town. **Calendar:** Semester. **Additional facts:** Selected complete associate degree programs offered. Students may also take first 2 years of most Penn State baccalaureate programs and then transfer to University Park, Erie Behrend College, or Harrisburg Capital College campuses to complete degree.

FRESHMAN ADMISSIONS. Selection criteria: Requirements vary by program. Evaluation index based on SAT scores and high school record. Special consideration to children of alumni and minority applicants.

ANNUAL EXPENSES. Tuition and fees (1992-93): $4,474, $5,170 additional for out-of-state students. **Books and supplies:** $440. **Other expenses:** $1,794.

ADDRESS/TELEPHONE. Admissions Officer, Penn State Worthington-Scranton Campus, 120 Ridge View Drive, Dunmore, PA 18512. (717) 963-4757.

Penn State York Campus
York, Pennsylvania

2-year public branch campus college, coed. Founded in 1926. **Accreditation:** Regional. **Undergraduate enrollment:** 575 men, 338 women full time; 545 men, 351 women part time. **Location:** Suburban campus in large town. **Calendar:** Semester. **Additional facts:** Selected complete associate degree programs offered. Students may also take first 2 years of most Penn State baccalaureate programs and then transfer to University Park, Erie Behrend College, or Harrisburg Capital College campuses to complete degree.

FRESHMAN ADMISSIONS. Selection criteria: Requirements vary by program. Evaluation index based on SAT scores and high school record. Special consideration to children of alumni and minority applicants.

ANNUAL EXPENSES. Tuition and fees (1992-93): $4,474, $5,170 additional for out-of-state students. **Books and supplies:** $440. **Other expenses:** $1,794.

ADDRESS/TELEPHONE. Admissions Office, Penn State York Campus, 1031 Edgecomb Avenue, York, PA 17403. (717) 771-4040.

Penn Technical Institute
Pittsburgh, Pennsylvania — CB code: 0646

2-year proprietary technical institute, coed. Founded in 1947. **Undergraduate enrollment:** 176 men, 8 women full time; 25 men, 3 women part time. **Faculty:** 9 total. **Location:** Urban campus in large city. **Calendar:** Quarter. **Microcomputers:** 90 located in classrooms. **Additional facts:** One-program institution offering general electronics technology with applications to areas such as computers, industrial electronics, robotics, medical electronics, consumer electronics, telecommunications.

DEGREES OFFERED. 110 associate degrees awarded in 1992. 100% in engineering technologies.

UNDERGRADUATE MAJORS. Electronic technology.

ACADEMIC PROGRAMS. Placement/credit: Institutional tests.

ACADEMIC REQUIREMENTS. Freshmen must earn minimum GPA of 2.0 to continue in good standing. 75% of freshmen return for sophomore year. Students must declare major on application. **Graduation requirements:** 70 hours for associate (53 in major). Most students required to take courses in mathematics.

FRESHMAN ADMISSIONS. Selection criteria: Open admissions. One unit algebra required.

1992 FRESHMAN CLASS PROFILE. 49 men, 6 women enrolled. **Characteristics:** 99% from in state, 100% commute, 9% have minority backgrounds. Average age is 23.

FALL-TERM APPLICATIONS. No fee. No closing date; applicants notified on a rolling basis. Interview required. Deferred admission available.

STUDENT LIFE. Activities: Student government.

STUDENT SERVICES. Career counseling, employment service for undergraduates, placement service for graduates.

ANNUAL EXPENSES. Tuition and fees (1992-93): $6,420. **Books and supplies:** $600. **Other expenses:** $1,000.

FINANCIAL AID. Grants, loans available. **Aid applications:** No closing date; applicants notified on a rolling basis.

ADDRESS/TELEPHONE. Louis A. Dimasi, Director of Admissions, Penn Technical Institute, 110 Ninth Street, Pittsburgh, PA 15222. (412) 355-0455.

Pennco Tech
Bristol, Pennsylvania — CB code: 0380

2-year proprietary technical training institute, coed. Founded in 1973. **Undergraduate enrollment:** 403 men and women. **Location:** Suburban campus in large town; 18 miles from Philadelphia. **Calendar:** Modular, year-round calendar. **Additional facts:** Branch campus in Blackwood, New Jersey.

FRESHMAN ADMISSIONS. Selection criteria: Institution's entrance examination and campus interview most important.

ANNUAL EXPENSES. Tuition and fees: $6,715. Tuition ranges from $3800 to $15000, depending on program. **Room and board:** $2,100 room only. **Books and supplies:** $800.

ADDRESS/TELEPHONE. Michael Hobyak, Director of Admissions, Pennco Tech, 3815 Otter Street, Bristol, PA 19007. (215) 824-3200.

Pennsylvania College of Technology
Williamsport, Pennsylvania — CB code: 2989

4-year public technical college, coed. Founded in 1965. **Accreditation:** Regional. **Undergraduate enrollment:** 2,329 men, 1,445 women full time; 446 men, 684 women part time. **Faculty:** 327 total (204 full time), 26 with doctorates or other terminal degrees. **Location:** Urban campus in large town; 85 miles from Harrisburg, 70 miles from Wilkes-Barre. **Calendar:** Semester, limited summer session. Saturday and extensive evening/early morning classes. **Microcomputers:** 575 located in libraries, classrooms, computer centers. **Additional facts:** Professional and transfer programs offered.

DEGREES OFFERED. AA, AAS, BS. 901 associate degrees awarded in 1992. 5% in agriculture, 17% business and management, 10% business/office and marketing/distribution, 17% engineering technologies, 6% health sciences, 8% allied health, 6% home economics, 21% trade and industry.

UNDERGRADUATE MAJORS. Associate: Accounting, air conditioning/heating/refrigeration mechanics, aircraft mechanics, architectural technologies, automotive specialist, automotive technology, biomedical equipment technology, business administration and management, business data processing and related programs, child development/care/guidance, civil technology, commercial art, computer servicing technology, construction, dental hygiene, diesel engine mechanics, drafting, early childhood education, electrical technology, electronic technology, engineering and engineering-related technologies, food production/management/services, forest products processing technology, forestry production and processing, graphic and printing production, graphic arts technology, horticulture, illustration design, industrial equipment maintenance and repair, industrial technology, journalism, laser electro-optic technology, legal assistant/paralegal, legal secretary, liberal/general studies, manufacturing technology, mechanical design technology, medical secretary, mental health/human services, nursing, occupational therapy assistant, ornamental horticulture, plastic technology, precision metal work, public relations, quality control technology, radio/television technology, radiograph medical technology, retailing, secretarial and related programs, telecommunications technology, welding technology, word processing. **Bachelor's:** Construction, dental hygiene, manufacturing technology, plastic technology, precision metal work.

ACADEMIC PROGRAMS. 2-year transfer program, accelerated program, cooperative education, double major, internships, student-designed major, weekend college, cross-registration. **Remedial services:** Learning center, preadmission summer program, remedial instruction, special counselor, tutoring. **Placement/credit:** AP, CLEP General and Subject, institutional tests; 30 credit hours maximum for associate degree.

ACADEMIC REQUIREMENTS. Freshmen must earn minimum GPA of 2.0 to continue in good standing. 68% of freshmen return for sophomore year. Students must declare major on application. **Graduation requirements:** 62 hours for associate, 120 hours for bachelor's. Most students required to take courses in computer science, English, humanities, mathematics, biological/physical sciences, social sciences. **Postgraduate studies:** 13% from 2-year programs enter 4-year programs.

FRESHMAN ADMISSIONS. Selection criteria: Open admissions. College's placement test determines admission to some programs. **Test requirements:** SAT required of dental hygiene, radiography, occupational therapy assistant, nursing applicants.

1992 FRESHMAN CLASS PROFILE. 931 men, 565 women enrolled. 6% were in top tenth and 15% were in top quarter of graduating class. **Characteristics:** 99% from in state, 100% commute, 4% have minority backgrounds. Average age is 22.

FALL-TERM APPLICATIONS. $20 fee, may be waived for applicants with need. No closing date; applicants notified on a rolling basis; must reply within 4 weeks. Interview recommended for dental hygiene, occupational therapy assistant, radiologic technology, surgical technology, nursing, practical nursing applicants. Portfolio recommended. Deferred and early admission available. Institutional early decision plan. Freshmen required to take placemnt test prior to scheduling.

STUDENT LIFE. Activities: Student government, radio, Alpha Omega (Christian) Fellowship, Phi Beta Lambda, Human Services Club, Multi-Cultural Society, Student Government Association, Women's Forum.

ATHLETICS. Intercollegiate: Baseball M, cross-country, golf, softball W, tennis. **Intramural:** Badminton, basketball, bowling, cross-country, golf, racquetball, skiing, soccer, softball, table tennis, tennis, volleyball, wrestling M.

STUDENT SERVICES. Aptitude testing, career counseling, employment service for undergraduates, freshman orientation, health services,

personal counseling, placement service for graduates, special adviser for adult students, veterans counselor, services/facilities for handicapped.

ANNUAL EXPENSES. Tuition and fees: $5,500, $2,500 additional for out-of-state students. **Books and supplies:** $800. **Other expenses:** $1,800.

FINANCIAL AID. 70% of freshmen, 70% of continuing students receive some form of aid. 99% of grants, 95% of loans, all jobs based on need. Academic, leadership scholarships available. **Aid applications:** No closing date; priority given to applications received by March 1; applicants notified on a rolling basis beginning on or about May 15; must reply within 10 days.

ADDRESS/TELEPHONE. Chester D. Schuman, Director of Admissions, Pennsylvania College of Technology, One College Avenue, Williamsport, PA 17701-5799. (717) 327-4761.

Pennsylvania Institute of Technology
Media, Pennsylvania CB code: 2675

2-year private technical college, coed. Founded in 1953. **Accreditation:** Regional. **Undergraduate enrollment:** 551 men and women. **Faculty:** 32 total (18 full time), 3 with doctorates or other terminal degrees. **Location:** Suburban campus in small town; 13 miles from Philadelphia, 15 miles from Wilmington, Delaware. **Calendar:** Quarter, extensive summer session. **Microcomputers:** Located in classrooms, computer centers.

DEGREES OFFERED. 70 associate degrees awarded in 1992. 8% in business and management, 17% business/office and marketing/distribution, 8% computer sciences, 67% engineering technologies.

UNDERGRADUATE MAJORS. Aeronautical technology, aerospace/aeronautical/astronautical engineering, allied health, architectural engineering, architectural technologies, architecture, business and office, civil engineering, civil technology, computer engineering, computer servicing technology, computer technology, drafting and design technology, electrical/electronics/communications engineering, electromechanical technology, electronic technology, engineering and engineering-related technologies, health care administration, health sciences, manufacturing technology, mechanical design technology, mechanical engineering, medical records administration, medical records technology, microcomputer software, radio/television technology, robotics, secretarial and related programs, telecommunications, word processing.

ACADEMIC PROGRAMS. 2-year transfer program, cooperative education, double major, independent study, internships. **Remedial services:** Learning center, reduced course load, remedial instruction, special counselor, tutoring, pretechnology curriculum. **Placement/credit:** AP, CLEP General and Subject, institutional tests; 60 credit hours maximum for associate degree.

ACADEMIC REQUIREMENTS. Freshmen must earn minimum GPA of 1.70 to continue in good standing. 63% of freshmen return for sophomore year. Students must declare major on application. **Graduation requirements:** 66 hours for associate (45 in major). Most students required to take courses in computer science, English, humanities, mathematics, biological/physical sciences. **Additional information:** Curricula designed to prepare students for positions in industry through combination of general education and job specific courses.

FRESHMAN ADMISSIONS. Selection criteria: Open admissions. **Test requirements:** Differential Aptitude Tests used for placement.

1992 FRESHMAN CLASS PROFILE. 151 men, 110 women enrolled. **Characteristics:** 100% commute. Average age is 24.

FALL-TERM APPLICATIONS. $50 fee, may be waived for applicants with need. No closing date; applicants notified on a rolling basis. Interview required. Essay required. Deferred and early admission available. Placement test required in English, mathematics.

STUDENT LIFE. Activities: Student government, radio, amateur radio club.

ATHLETICS. Intramural: Basketball M, football M, softball M.

STUDENT SERVICES. Aptitude testing, career counseling, employment service for undergraduates, freshman orientation, personal counseling, placement service for graduates, special adviser for adult students, veterans counselor, student services program, tutoring program, services/facilities for handicapped.

ANNUAL EXPENSES. Tuition and fees (projected): $6,903. **Books and supplies:** $700.

FINANCIAL AID. 71% of continuing students receive some form of aid. All grants, 72% of loans, all jobs based on need. Academic scholarships available. **Aid applications:** Closing date August 1; applicants notified on a rolling basis beginning on or about July 1; must reply immediately.

ADDRESS/TELEPHONE. John S. Founds, Director of Institutional Advancement, Pennsylvania Institute of Technology, 800 Manchester Avenue, Media, PA 19063-4098. (215) 565-7900. (800) 422-0025. Fax: (215) 565-7909.

Philadelphia College of Bible
Langhorne, Pennsylvania CB code: 2661

Admissions: 47% of applicants accepted
Based on: ••• Essay, recommendations, religious affiliation/commitment, school record, test scores
•• Interview, special talents
• Activities
Completion: 80% of freshmen end year in good standing
50% graduate, 25% of these enter graduate study

4-year private Bible college, coed, nondenominational. Founded in 1913. **Accreditation:** Regional. **Undergraduate enrollment:** 315 men, 317 women full time; 72 men, 56 women part time. **Graduate enrollment:** 1 man full time; 57 men, 50 women part time. **Faculty:** 91 total (49 full time), 24 with doctorates or other terminal degrees. **Location:** Suburban campus in small town; 17 miles from Philadelphia, 5 miles from Trenton. **Calendar:** Semester, limited summer session. Saturday and extensive evening/early morning classes. **Microcomputers:** 45 located in libraries, computer centers. **Additional facts:** Educates for professional church-related vocations in evangelical Protestant tradition.

DEGREES OFFERED. AA, BS, MS. 131 bachelor's degrees awarded. 15% in teacher education, 7% parks/recreation, protective services, public affairs, 70% philosophy, religion, theology, 8% visual and performing arts. Graduate degrees offered in 3 major fields of study.

UNDERGRADUATE MAJORS. Associate: Bible studies. **Bachelor's:** Bible studies, biblical languages, counseling psychology, early childhood education, elementary education, English education, mathematics education, missionary studies, music, music education, music performance, music theory and composition, physical education, religious education, religious music, secondary education, social studies education, social work.

ACADEMIC PROGRAMS. Double major, independent study, internships, study abroad, teacher preparation, cooperative agreement with Bucks County Community College. **Remedial services:** Learning center, reduced course load, remedial instruction, special counselor, tutoring, AIMS Program. **Placement/credit:** AP, CLEP General and Subject, institutional tests; 60 credit hours maximum for bachelor's degree.

ACADEMIC REQUIREMENTS. Freshmen must earn minimum GPA of 1.5 to continue in good standing. 75% of freshmen return for sophomore year. Students must declare major by end of first year. **Graduation requirements:** 64 hours for associate (64 in major), 128 hours for bachelor's (72 in major). Most students required to take courses in arts/fine arts, English, foreign languages, history, humanities, mathematics, philosophy/religion, biological/physical sciences, social sciences. **Postgraduate studies:** 25% enter other graduate study. **Additional information:** Limited summer graduate courses available.

FRESHMAN ADMISSIONS. Selection criteria: High school GPA, pastor's references, autobiography, SAT or ACT scores, and application required. **High school preparation:** 15 units recommended. Recommended units include English 4, foreign language 2, mathematics 1, social science 3 and science 2. **Test requirements:** SAT or ACT (SAT preferred); score report by August 30. **Additional information:** Applicants not meeting academic admissions requirements may be admitted and placed in remedial program.

1992 FRESHMAN CLASS PROFILE. 320 men applied, 161 accepted, 130 enrolled; 317 women applied, 137 accepted, 130 enrolled. 59% had high school GPA of 3.0 or higher, 36% between 2.0 and 2.99. 14% were in top tenth and 15% were in top quarter of graduating class. **Characteristics:** 51% from in state, 75% live in college housing, 18% have minority backgrounds, 8% are foreign students. Average age is 21.

FALL-TERM APPLICATIONS. $15 fee, may be waived for applicants with need. No closing date; applicants notified on a rolling basis. Audition required for music applicants. Essay required. Interview recommended. Deferred and early admission available.

STUDENT LIFE. Housing: Dormitories (men, women); apartment housing available. **Activities:** Student government, student newspaper, yearbook, choral groups, concert band, drama, music ensembles, symphony orchestra, student missionary fellowship, All-College Social Committee, class organizations, Commuter Council, Married Couples' Fellowship, Resident Council, student senate, student theological society, African-American Association, BASIC. **Additional information:** Religious observance required.

ATHLETICS. Intercollegiate: Baseball M, basketball, cross-country, field hockey W, soccer M, softball W, tennis, track and field. **Intramural:** Basketball, golf, softball, swimming, table tennis, tennis, volleyball.

STUDENT SERVICES. Career counseling, employment service for undergraduates, freshman orientation, health services, personal counseling, placement service for graduates, veterans counselor, services/facilities for handicapped.

ANNUAL EXPENSES. Tuition and fees: $7,140. **Room and board:** $4,060. **Books and supplies:** $550. **Other expenses:** $870.

FINANCIAL AID. 71% of freshmen, 82% of continuing students receive some form of aid. 74% of grants, 87% of loans, 35% of jobs based on need. 86 enrolled freshmen were judged to have need, all were offered aid. Academic, music/drama, leadership, alumni affiliation scholarships available.

Aid applications: No closing date; priority given to applications received by May 1; applicants notified on a rolling basis beginning on or about March 1; must reply within 2 weeks.

ADDRESS/TELEPHONE. Fran Emmons, Director of Admissions, Philadelphia College of Bible, 200 Manor Avenue, Langhorne, PA 19047-2992. (215) 752-5915. Fax: (215) 752-5812.

Philadelphia College of Pharmacy and Science
Philadelphia, Pennsylvania CB code: 2663

Admissions: 71% of applicants accepted
Based on:
- ••• School record, test scores
- •• Interview
- • Activities, essay, recommendations, special talents

Completion: 83% of freshmen end year in good standing
80% graduate, 12% of these enter graduate study

4-year private health science, pharmacy college, coed. Founded in 1821. **Accreditation:** Regional. **Undergraduate enrollment:** 605 men, 1,040 women full time; 5 men, 4 women part time. **Graduate enrollment:** 26 men, 25 women full time; 11 men, 10 women part time. **Faculty:** 198 total (158 full time), 139 with doctorates or other terminal degrees. **Location:** Urban campus in very large city. **Calendar:** Semester, limited summer session. **Microcomputers:** 34 located in libraries, classrooms, computer centers. **Special facilities:** History of pharmacy collection.

DEGREES OFFERED. BS, MS, PhD, B. Pharm, Pharm D. 253 bachelor's degrees awarded in 1992. 75% in health sciences, 24% life sciences. Graduate degrees offered in 6 major fields of study.

UNDERGRADUATE MAJORS. Biochemistry, biology, chemistry, clinical laboratory science, medical laboratory technologies, microbiology, pharmacology, human and animal, pharmacy, toxicology.

ACADEMIC PROGRAMS. Dual enrollment of high school students, internships; combined bachelor's/graduate program in business administration. **Remedial services:** Learning center, preadmission summer program, remedial instruction, tutoring. **ROTC:** Army. **Placement/credit:** CLEP General and Subject, institutional tests.

ACADEMIC REQUIREMENTS. Freshmen must earn minimum GPA of 2.0 to continue in good standing. 82% of freshmen return for sophomore year. Students must declare major on application. **Graduation requirements:** 174 hours for bachelor's (42 in major). Most students required to take courses in computer science, English, humanities, mathematics, biological/physical sciences. **Postgraduate studies:** 6% enter medical school, 2% enter MBA programs, 4% enter other graduate study.

FRESHMAN ADMISSIONS. Selection criteria: High school curriculum, GPA, class rank, test scores, essay, and motivation. **High school preparation:** 16 units required. Required units include biological science 1, English 4, mathematics 3 and physical science 2. Strong background in science and mathematics recommended. **Test requirements:** SAT; score report by June 1. ACH required of applicants with low SAT scores. Score report by May 1. **Additional information:** Physical therapy majors must show evidence of 20 hours of volunteer experience prior to application.

1992 FRESHMAN CLASS PROFILE. 464 men applied, 328 accepted, 138 enrolled; 696 women applied, 493 accepted, 236 enrolled. 95% had high school GPA of 3.0 or higher, 5% between 2.0 and 2.99. 50% were in top tenth and 89% were in top quarter of graduating class. **Academic background:** Mid 50% of enrolled freshmen had SAT-V between 450-560, SAT-M between 490-610. 97% submitted SAT scores. **Characteristics:** 67% from in state, 80% live in college housing, 24% have minority backgrounds, 1% are foreign students, 18% join fraternities/sororities. Average age is 19.

FALL-TERM APPLICATIONS. $25 fee, may be waived for applicants with need. No closing date; applicants notified on a rolling basis; must reply by April 15 or within 2 weeks if notified thereafter. Interview required for physical therapy applicants. Essay required. Deferred and early admission available.

STUDENT LIFE. Housing: Dormitories (coed); apartment, fraternity housing available. **Activities:** Student government, magazine, radio, student newspaper, yearbook, choral groups, drama, musical theater, fraternities, sororities, professional organizations, religious groups, Black Academic Achievement Society.

ATHLETICS. NAIA. **Intercollegiate:** Baseball M, basketball, cross-country, golf, rifle, softball W, tennis, volleyball W. **Intramural:** Archery, badminton, basketball, bowling, rifle, softball W, table tennis, volleyball.

STUDENT SERVICES. Career counseling, employment service for undergraduates, freshman orientation, health services, personal counseling, placement service for graduates, services/facilities for handicapped.

ANNUAL EXPENSES. Tuition and fees (1992-93): $10,770. **Room and board:** $4,700. **Books and supplies:** $500. **Other expenses:** $800.

FINANCIAL AID. 75% of freshmen, 75% of continuing students receive some form of aid. 60% of grants, 93% of loans, 28% of jobs based on need. 280 enrolled freshmen were judged to have need, all were offered aid. Academic, athletic, minority scholarships available. **Aid applications:** Closing date April 15; priority given to applications received by March 15; applicants notified on or about April 15; must reply within 3 weeks.

ADDRESS/TELEPHONE. Louis L. Hegyes, Director of Admissions, Philadelphia College of Pharmacy and Science, 600 South 43rd Street, Philadelphia, PA 19104-4495. (215) 596-8810. Fax: (215) 895-1100.

Philadelphia College of Textiles and Science
Philadelphia, Pennsylvania CB code: 2666

Admissions: 70% of applicants accepted
Based on:
- ••• School record
- •• Activities, essay, interview, test scores
- • Recommendations, special talents

Completion: 75% of freshmen end year in good standing
60% graduate, 8% of these enter graduate study

4-year private college of business, design, textiles, and science (pre-med), fashion, and architecture, coed. Founded in 1884. **Accreditation:** Regional. **Undergraduate enrollment:** 576 men, 1,128 women full time; 337 men, 739 women part time. **Graduate enrollment:** 62 men, 42 women full time; 289 men, 184 women part time. **Faculty:** 296 total (89 full time), 180 with doctorates or other terminal degrees. **Location:** Suburban campus in very large city; 9 miles from downtown Philadelphia. **Calendar:** Semester, extensive summer session. **Microcomputers:** 120 located in libraries, computer centers. **Special facilities:** Paley Design Center, computer-aided design laboratories. **Additional facts:** Advantage, a selective co-op program, available for most majors.

DEGREES OFFERED. BS, BArch, MS, MBA. 6 associate degrees awarded in 1992. 33% in business and management, 17% business/office and marketing/distribution, 50% home economics. 483 bachelor's degrees awarded. 11% in architecture and environmental design, 42% business and management, 16% business/office and marketing/distribution, 7% health sciences, 17% visual and performing arts. Graduate degrees offered in 11 major fields of study.

UNDERGRADUATE MAJORS. Associate: Accounting, business and management, business data processing and related programs, clothing and textiles management/production/services. **Bachelor's:** Accounting, apparel and accessories marketing, applied mathematics, applied textile chemistry, architecture, biochemistry, biological and physical sciences, biology, business administration and management, business and management, chemistry, clothing and textiles management/production/services, color science, computer and information sciences, computer programming, fashion design, fashion merchandising, fiber/textiles/weaving, finance, information sciences and systems, interior design, international business management, life science, management information systems, marketing and distribution, marketing management, predentistry, premedicine, preveterinary, product brand management, psychology, retailing, small business management and ownership, textile chemistry, textile design, textile engineering, textile management and marketing, textile technology, textiles and clothing.

ACADEMIC PROGRAMS. Cooperative education, double major, dual enrollment of high school students, honors program, independent study, internships, study abroad, visiting/exchange student program; combined bachelor's/graduate program in business administration. **Remedial services:** Learning center, preadmission summer program, reduced course load, remedial instruction, special counselor, tutoring, writing center. **Placement/credit:** AP, CLEP Subject, institutional tests; 60 credit hours maximum for bachelor's degree.

ACADEMIC REQUIREMENTS. Freshmen must earn minimum GPA of 2.0 to continue in good standing. 77% of freshmen return for sophomore year. Students must declare major by end of second year. **Graduation requirements:** 121 hours for bachelor's (63 in major). Most students required to take courses in English, foreign languages, history, mathematics, biological/physical sciences, social sciences.

FRESHMAN ADMISSIONS. Selection criteria: Academic record and class rank most important. Test scores, extracurricular activities, counselor's recommendation and interview considered. **High school preparation:** 16 units recommended. Recommended units include English 4, mathematics 3 and science 2. **Test requirements:** SAT or ACT; score report by July 1.

1992 FRESHMAN CLASS PROFILE. 822 men applied, 514 accepted, 182 enrolled; 1,340 women applied, 998 accepted, 342 enrolled. 67% had high school GPA of 3.0 or higher, 31% between 2.0 and 2.99. **Academic background:** Mid 50% of enrolled freshmen had SAT-V between 360-450, SAT-M between 400-500. 95% submitted SAT scores. **Characteristics:** 58% from in state, 62% live in college housing, 20% have minority backgrounds, 8% are foreign students. Average age is 18.

FALL-TERM APPLICATIONS. $20 fee, may be waived for applicants with need. No closing date; applicants notified on a rolling basis; must reply within 4 weeks. Interview recommended. Deferred and early admission available.

STUDENT LIFE. Housing: Dormitories (coed); apartment housing available. **Activities:** Student government, radio, student newspaper, yearbook, photography, choral groups, drama, cheerleading, fraternities, sororities, 10 professional (major-related) organizations, International Society,

Black Awareness Society, Hillel, Textile Christian Fellowship, Special Olympics.

ATHLETICS. NCAA. **Intercollegiate:** Baseball M, basketball, cross-country, field hockey W, golf M, lacrosse W, soccer, softball W, tennis, track and field. **Intramural:** Basketball, softball, table tennis, tennis.

STUDENT SERVICES. Aptitude testing, career counseling, employment service for undergraduates, freshman orientation, health services, personal counseling, placement service for graduates, special adviser for adult students.

ANNUAL EXPENSES. Tuition and fees (1992-93): $10,344. **Room and board:** $4,798. **Books and supplies:** $500. **Other expenses:** $1,038.

FINANCIAL AID. 73% of freshmen, 69% of continuing students receive some form of aid. 42% of jobs based on need. 201 enrolled freshmen were judged to have need, all were offered aid. Academic, athletic, leadership, minority scholarships available. **Aid applications:** No closing date; applicants notified on a rolling basis beginning on or about May 15; must reply within 3 weeks.

ADDRESS/TELEPHONE. David B. Conway, Dean of Admissions, Philadelphia College of Textiles and Science, School House Lane and Henry Avenue, Philadelphia, PA 19144-5497. (215) 951-2800. Fax: (215) 951-2615.

Pittsburgh Institute of Aeronautics
Pittsburgh, Pennsylvania CB code: 0652

2-year private aviation maintenance technician institution, coed. Founded in 1929. **Undergraduate enrollment:** 900 men, 15 women full time. **Location:** Suburban campus in large city; 8 miles south of Pittsburgh. **Calendar:** Quarter or semester, depending on program. **Additional facts:** Located on an active county airport.

FRESHMAN ADMISSIONS. Selection criteria: Open admissions. Institutional examination for avionics program. Interview strongly recommended for all applicants.

ANNUAL EXPENSES. Tuition and fees (projected): $11,964 for 6-semester avionics program; $10,458 for 7-quarter aeronautical maintenance technician program. **Books and supplies:** $1,645. **Other expenses:** $800.

ADDRESS/TELEPHONE. Sundae Kerr, Director of Admissions and Registrar, Pittsburgh Institute of Aeronautics, PO Box 10897, Pittsburgh, PA 15236. (412) 462-9011. (800) 444-1440. Fax: (412) 466-0513.

Pittsburgh Institute of Mortuary Science
Pittsburgh, Pennsylvania CB code: 7030

2-year private technical college, coed. Founded in 1939. **Undergraduate enrollment:** 84 men, 29 women full time; 5 men part time. **Graduate enrollment:** 14 men and women. **Faculty:** 16 total (4 full time), 3 with doctorates or other terminal degrees. **Location:** Urban campus in large city. **Calendar:** Trimester, extensive summer session. **Microcomputers:** Located in classrooms. **Additional facts:** Accredited by American Board of Funeral Services Education, Inc.

DEGREES OFFERED. 17 associate degrees awarded in 1992. 100% in business and management.

UNDERGRADUATE MAJORS. Funeral services management, funeral services/mortuary science.

ACADEMIC PROGRAMS. 2-year transfer program. **Remedial services:** Reduced course load, tutoring. **Placement/credit:** Institutional tests.

ACADEMIC REQUIREMENTS. Freshmen must earn minimum GPA of 2.0 to continue in good standing. Students must declare major on application. **Graduation requirements:** 96 hours for associate (60 in major). Most students required to take courses in arts/fine arts, computer science, history, philosophy/religion, biological/physical sciences, social sciences. **Additional information:** Four-pronged approach to funeral service management via natural sciences, social sciences, mortuary sciences, and the humanities. Students with associate degrees will also earn a diploma in embalming and funeral directing.

FRESHMAN ADMISSIONS. Selection criteria: Open admissions. Student must meet individual state requirements for preprofessional education.

1992 FRESHMAN CLASS PROFILE. 52 men, 21 women enrolled. **Characteristics:** 100% commute, 8% have minority backgrounds. Average age is 26.

FALL-TERM APPLICATIONS. $30 fee. Closing date September 24; priority given to applications received by September 1; applicants notified on a rolling basis; must reply by registration. Interview required. Deferred admission available.

STUDENT LIFE. Housing: Housing available at local funeral homes. **Activities:** Student government.

STUDENT SERVICES. Career counseling, employment service for undergraduates, freshman orientation, personal counseling, placement service for graduates, veterans counselor, services/facilities for handicapped.

ANNUAL EXPENSES. Tuition and fees (1992-93): $7,660.

FINANCIAL AID. All grants, 92% of loans based on need. Academic scholarships available. **Aid applications:** No closing date; applicants notified on a rolling basis.

ADDRESS/TELEPHONE. Jeanette G. Matthews, Registrar, Pittsburgh Institute of Mortuary Science, 5808 Baum Boulevard, Pittsburgh, PA 15206-3706. (412) 362-8500. (800) 933-5808. Fax: (412) 362-1684.

Pittsburgh Technical Institute
Pittsburgh, Pennsylvania CB code: 0382

2-year proprietary technical college, coed. Founded in 1946. **Undergraduate enrollment:** 418 men and women. **Faculty:** 31 total (28 full time). **Location:** Urban campus in large city; located in downtown. **Calendar:** Semester. **Microcomputers:** 26 located in computer centers.

DEGREES OFFERED. 150 associate degrees awarded in 1992. 100% in engineering technologies.

UNDERGRADUATE MAJORS. Computer graphics, drafting and design technology, graphic design, interior design.

ACADEMIC PROGRAMS. Independent study. **Remedial services:** Remedial instruction, tutoring. **Placement/credit:** AP, institutional tests.

ACADEMIC REQUIREMENTS. Freshmen must earn minimum GPA of 1.0 to continue in good standing. 90% of freshmen return for sophomore year. **Graduation requirements:** 90 hours for associate. Most students required to take courses in English, mathematics.

FRESHMAN ADMISSIONS. Selection criteria: Open admissions.

1992 FRESHMAN CLASS PROFILE. 257 men and women enrolled. **Characteristics:** 83% from in state, 72% commute, 6% have minority backgrounds. Average age is 18.

FALL-TERM APPLICATIONS. $40 fee, may be waived for applicants with need. No closing date; applicants notified on a rolling basis. Interview required. Deferred admission available.

STUDENT LIFE. Housing: Apartment housing available. **Activities:** Student newspaper, student activities committee.

ATHLETICS. Intramural: Basketball, volleyball.

STUDENT SERVICES. Career counseling, employment service for undergraduates, freshman orientation, personal counseling, placement service for graduates, services/facilities for handicapped.

ANNUAL EXPENSES. Tuition and fees (1992-93): $15,900. **Room and board:** $5,400 room only. **Books and supplies:** $800. **Other expenses:** $1,416.

FINANCIAL AID. 92% of grants, 96% of loans, all jobs based on need. Academic scholarships available. **Aid applications:** No closing date; applicants notified on a rolling basis.

ADDRESS/TELEPHONE. Gary Johnson, Vice President for Admissions, Pittsburgh Technical Institute, 635 Smithfield Street, Pittsburgh, PA 15222. (412) 471-1011. Fax: (412) 471-7501.

Point Park College
Pittsburgh, Pennsylvania CB code: 2676

Admissions: 80% of applicants accepted
Based on:
- ••• School record
- •• Interview, test scores
- • Activities, essay, recommendations, special talents

Completion: 63% of freshmen end year in good standing
15% enter graduate study

4-year private professionally oriented in arts, business, communications, and technology, coed. Founded in 1960. **Accreditation:** Regional. **Undergraduate enrollment:** 514 men, 660 women full time; 879 men, 689 women part time. **Graduate enrollment:** 15 men, 7 women full time; 39 men, 31 women part time. **Faculty:** 197 total (70 full time), 40 with doctorates or other terminal degrees. **Location:** Urban campus in large city; Located in downtown. **Calendar:** Semester, limited summer session. Saturday and extensive evening/early morning classes. **Microcomputers:** 81 located in computer centers. **Special facilities:** Pittsburgh Playhouse Theater Complex, children's school.

DEGREES OFFERED. AA, AS, BA, BS, BFA, MA, MBA. 25 associate degrees awarded in 1992. 80% in business and management, 13% communications, 7% computer sciences. 424 bachelor's degrees awarded. 36% in business and management, 5% communications, 31% engineering technologies, 19% visual and performing arts. Graduate degrees offered in 3 major fields of study.

UNDERGRADUATE MAJORS. Associate: Accounting, allied health, business and management, civil technology, communications, computer and information sciences, early childhood education, electrical technology, finance, funeral services/mortuary science, journalism, legal assistant/paralegal, liberal/general studies, mechanical design technology, public administration, respiratory therapy technology. **Bachelor's:** Accounting, arts management, behavioral sciences, biology, business and management, cinematography/film, civil technology, communications, computer and information sciences, dance, dramatic arts, education, electrical technology, elementary education, English, English education, environmental science, funeral services/mortuary science, graphic design, health sciences, history, hotel/motel and restaurant management, human resources development, illustration design, international studies, journalism, legal assistant/paralegal, mathematics education, mechanical design technology, photography, political science and government, psychology, public administration, science education, secondary education, social science education, social sciences, speech/communication/theater education.

ACADEMIC PROGRAMS. Accelerated program, double major, independent study, internships, student-designed major, teacher preparation, weekend college, Washington semester, cross-registration, cooperative programs in film and video production with Pittsburgh filmmakers, and photography and visual arts and design with the Art Institute of Pittsburgh; liberal arts/career combination in health sciences. **Remedial services:** Learning center, preadmission summer program, reduced course load, remedial instruction, special counselor, tutoring, alternative testing formats. **ROTC:** Air Force, Army. **Placement/credit:** AP, CLEP General and Subject, institutional tests; 30 credit hours maximum for associate degree; 60 credit hours maximum for bachelor's degree.

ACADEMIC REQUIREMENTS. Freshmen must earn minimum GPA of 1.5 to continue in good standing. 72% of freshmen return for sophomore year. Students must declare major by end of second year. **Graduation requirements:** 60 hours for associate (35 in major), 120 hours for bachelor's (55 in major). Most students required to take courses in English, humanities, biological/physical sciences, social sciences. **Postgraduate studies:** 2% enter law school, 5% enter MBA programs, 8% enter other graduate study.

FRESHMAN ADMISSIONS. Selection criteria: High school record, class rank, test scores, school and community activities considered. Recommendations and interview used for some applicants. **High school preparation:** 16 units recommended. Recommended units include English 4, mathematics 2, social science 2 and science 1. 4 electives recommended. **Test requirements:** SAT or ACT; score report by August 1.

1992 FRESHMAN CLASS PROFILE. 701 men and women applied, 564 accepted; 76 men enrolled, 118 women enrolled. 35% had high school GPA of 3.0 or higher, 60% between 2.0 and 2.99. 11% were in top tenth and 39% were in top quarter of graduating class. **Academic background:** Mid 50% of enrolled freshmen had SAT-V between 360-470, SAT-M between 360-480; ACT composite between 16-23. 95% submitted SAT scores, 5% submitted ACT scores. **Characteristics:** 75% from in state, 52% commute, 18% have minority backgrounds, 7% are foreign students, 3% join fraternities/sororities. Average age is 18.

FALL-TERM APPLICATIONS. May be waived for applicants with need. $30 for full-time students, $20 for part-time students. No closing date; applicants notified on a rolling basis; must reply by May 1 or within 2 weeks if notified thereafter. Audition required for dance, theater arts, performing arts management applicants. Interview recommended. Portfolio recommended for photography, multimedia applicants. Essay recommended. CRDA. Deferred and early admission available.

STUDENT LIFE. Housing: Dormitories (coed); apartment housing available. Quiet floors available. Single gender floors available. **Activities:** Student government, magazine, radio, student newspaper, television, yearbook, choral groups, dance, drama, musical theater, fraternities, sororities, campus ministry, International Club, Black Active Students Intercollegiate Struggle, BiGALA (bisexual, gay, and lesbian alliance).

ATHLETICS. NAIA. **Intercollegiate:** Baseball M, basketball, soccer M, softball W, volleyball W. **Intramural:** Basketball M, field hockey M, football M, tennis, volleyball.

STUDENT SERVICES. Career counseling, employment service for undergraduates, freshman orientation, health services, on-campus day care, personal counseling, placement service for graduates, veterans counselor, services/facilities for handicapped.

ANNUAL EXPENSES. Tuition and fees: $9,312. **Room and board:** $4,610. **Books and supplies:** $400. **Other expenses:** $450.

FINANCIAL AID. 79% of freshmen, 79% of continuing students receive some form of aid. 74% of grants, 99% of loans, 87% of jobs based on need. 146 enrolled freshmen were judged to have need, all were offered aid. Academic, music/drama, art, athletic, alumni affiliation scholarships available. **Aid applications:** No closing date; priority given to applications received by May 1; applicants notified on a rolling basis beginning on or about January 15; must reply by May 1 or within 2 weeks if notified thereafter.

ADDRESS/TELEPHONE. John Kudlac, PhD, Executive Officer of Enrollment Management, Point Park College, 201 Wood Street, Pittsburgh, PA 15222. (412) 392-3430. (800) 321-0129. Fax: (412) 391-1980.

Reading Area Community College
Reading, Pennsylvania — CB code: 2743

2-year public community college, coed. Founded in 1971. **Accreditation:** Regional. **Undergraduate enrollment:** 320 men, 681 women full time; 773 men, 1,642 women part time. **Faculty:** 193 total (57 full time), 4 with doctorates or other terminal degrees. **Location:** Urban campus in small city; 55 miles from Philadelphia. **Calendar:** Three 10-week terms per year. Saturday and extensive evening/early morning classes. **Microcomputers:** 90 located in libraries, computer centers. **Additional facts:** Certificate and associate degree credit courses offered to members of the American Institute of Banking.

DEGREES OFFERED. AA, AAS. 231 associate degrees awarded in 1992. 17% in business and management, 7% business/office and marketing/distribution, 7% education, 42% allied health, 5% letters/literature, 6% multi/interdisciplinary studies, 6% trade and industry.

UNDERGRADUATE MAJORS. Accounting, automotive mechanics, automotive technology, biological and physical sciences, biology, business administration and management, business and management, business and office, business data processing and related programs, business education, chemistry, child development/care/guidance, clinical laboratory science, computer programming, criminology, data processing, early childhood education, education, electrical technology, electrical/electronics/communications engineering, electronic technology, elementary education, engineering, engineering and engineering-related technologies, finance, gerontology, human resources development, humanities, industrial engineering, industrial laboratory technology, industrial technology, junior high education, law enforcement and corrections technologies, legal secretary, liberal/general studies, lightwave engineering technology, machine tool operation/machine shop, mechanical engineering, medical laboratory technologies, medical secretary, medical word processing, mental health/human services, nursing, office supervision and management, personnel management, practical nursing, predentistry, preengineering, prelaw, premedicine, prepharmacy, psychology, public administration, radiograph medical technology, respiratory therapy technology, science technologies, secondary education, secretarial and related programs, small business management and ownership, social sciences, social work, telecommunications, tourism, trade and industrial supervision and management, word processing.

ACADEMIC PROGRAMS. 2-year transfer program, cooperative education, dual enrollment of high school students, independent study, internships, student-designed major, telecourses, weekend college. **Remedial services:** Learning center, preadmission summer program, reduced course load, remedial instruction, special counselor, tutoring, study skills and personal development. **Placement/credit:** AP, CLEP General and Subject, institutional tests; 45 credit hours maximum for associate degree.

ACADEMIC REQUIREMENTS. Freshmen must earn minimum GPA of 2.0 to continue in good standing. 50% of freshmen return for sophomore year. Students must declare major on application. **Graduation requirements:** 60 hours for associate (40 in major). Most students required to take courses in English, humanities, mathematics, biological/physical sciences, social sciences.

FRESHMAN ADMISSIONS. Selection criteria: Open admissions. Selective admission to nursing programs and clinical portion of medical laboratory technician program. 16 units required for nursing program, including 4 English, 3 social studies, 2 mathematics (1 must be algebra), and 2 science with related laboratory or equivalent. **Test requirements:** Institutionally-designed placement test required of all applicants.

1992 FRESHMAN CLASS PROFILE. 275 men, 448 women enrolled. **Characteristics:** 98% from in state, 100% commute, 15% have minority backgrounds, 1% are foreign students.

FALL-TERM APPLICATIONS. $10 fee. No closing date; applicants notified on a rolling basis. Interview recommended. Deferred and early admission available.

STUDENT LIFE. Activities: Student government, radio, student newspaper, television, yearbook.

ATHLETICS. Intercollegiate: Basketball M, cross-country, volleyball W. **Intramural:** Basketball M, cross-country, volleyball W.

STUDENT SERVICES. Aptitude testing, career counseling, employment service for undergraduates, freshman orientation, on-campus day care, personal counseling, placement service for graduates, veterans counselor, services/facilities for handicapped.

ANNUAL EXPENSES. Tuition and fees (projected): $1,680, $1,620 additional for out-of-district students, $3,240 additional for out-of-state students. Additional fees for out-of-district and out-of-state students are $90. **Books and supplies:** $450. **Other expenses:** $1,200.

FINANCIAL AID. 66% of freshmen, 27% of continuing students receive some form of aid. 97% of grants, 97% of loans, 53% of jobs based on need. Academic, leadership scholarships available. **Aid applications:** No closing date; priority given to applications received by September 1; applicants notified on a rolling basis beginning on or about July 1; must reply within 2 weeks.

ADDRESS/TELEPHONE. Bridget Danielle Bauer, Admissions Coordinator, Reading Area Community College, PO Box 1706, 10 South Second Street, Reading, PA 19603-1706. (800) 626-1665. Fax: (215) 375-8255.

RETS Education Center
Broomall, Pennsylvania — CB code: 3398

2-year proprietary technical college, coed. **Undergraduate enrollment:** 440 men and women. **Location:** Suburban campus in large town; 7 miles from Philadelphia. **Calendar:** Quarter. **Additional facts:** Education geared to job market.

FRESHMAN ADMISSIONS. Selection criteria: Institutional examination most important. Interview and recommendations also important.

ANNUAL EXPENSES. Tuition and fees (1992-93): $10,900 for 2-year electronic engineering technology program, $7,300 for 1-year basic electronics and computer technology program. **Books and supplies:** $350.

ADDRESS/TELEPHONE. Director of Admissions, RETS Education Center, Westchester Pike and Main Road, Broomall, PA 19008. (215) 353-7630. (800) 336-7696. Fax: (215) 359-1370.

Robert Morris College
Coraopolis, Pennsylvania CB code: 2769

Admissions: 92% of applicants accepted
Based on:
••• School record
•• Test scores
• Activities, essay, interview, recommendations
Completion: 81% of freshmen end year in good standing
45% graduate

4-year private business college, coed. Founded in 1921. **Accreditation:** Regional. **Undergraduate enrollment:** 1,421 men, 1,330 women full time; 756 men, 1,242 women part time. **Graduate enrollment:** 432 men, 274 women part time. **Faculty:** 238 total (132 full time), 91 with doctorates or other terminal degrees. **Location:** Suburban campus in large town; 15 miles from Pittsburgh. **Calendar:** Semester, limited summer session. Saturday and extensive evening/early morning classes. **Microcomputers:** 300 located in classrooms, computer centers. **Special facilities:** Executive education center, convention and exhibit hall. **Additional facts:** Main campus at Coraopolis is both residential and commuter. Pittsburgh center serves commuting students only.

DEGREES OFFERED. AA, AS, BA, BS, MS, MBA. 140 associate degrees awarded in 1992. 71% in business and management, 22% business/office and marketing/distribution, 7% multi/interdisciplinary studies. 711 bachelor's degrees awarded. 81% in business and management, 5% business/office and marketing/distribution, 9% computer sciences. Graduate degrees offered in 16 major fields of study.

UNDERGRADUATE MAJORS. Associate: Biological and physical sciences, business and management, business and office, humanities and social sciences, legal secretary, liberal/general studies, medical secretary, radiograph medical technology, science technologies, secretarial and related programs, word processing. **Bachelor's:** Accounting, aviation management, business administration and management, business and management, business and office, business economics, business education, communications, communications management, computer and information sciences, English, English education, finance, health care administration, human resources development, marketing and distribution, marketing management, office supervision and management, personnel management, secondary education, secretarial and related programs, sports management, systems analysis, transportation management.

ACADEMIC PROGRAMS. Cooperative education, double major, internships, study abroad, teacher preparation, telecourses, weekend college, cross-registration. **Remedial services:** Learning center, preadmission summer program, reduced course load, remedial instruction, special counselor, tutoring. **ROTC:** Air Force, Army. **Placement/credit:** AP, CLEP General and Subject, institutional tests; 30 credit hours maximum for associate degree; 60 credit hours maximum for bachelor's degree.

ACADEMIC REQUIREMENTS. Freshmen must earn minimum GPA of 2.0 to continue in good standing. 82% of freshmen return for sophomore year. Students must declare major on application. **Graduation requirements:** 60 hours for associate (21 in major), 120 hours for bachelor's (24 in major). Most students required to take courses in computer science, English, history, humanities, mathematics, biological/physical sciences, social sciences. **Postgraduate studies:** 60% from 2-year programs enter 4-year programs.

FRESHMAN ADMISSIONS. Selection criteria: Academic potential, high school GPA, class rank, test scores, and evidence of motivation important. **High school preparation:** 16 units recommended. Recommended units include English 4, mathematics 3, social science 3 and science 2. **Test requirements:** SAT or ACT (SAT preferred); score report by August 15.

1992 FRESHMAN CLASS PROFILE. 387 men applied, 338 accepted, 211 enrolled; 449 women applied, 430 accepted, 250 enrolled. 37% had high school GPA of 3.0 or higher, 54% between 2.0 and 2.99. **Academic background:** Mid 50% of enrolled freshmen had SAT-V between 380-480, SAT-M between 400-510; ACT composite between 11-18. 86% submitted SAT scores, 12% submitted ACT scores. **Characteristics:** 93% from in state, 60% commute, 7% have minority backgrounds, 1% are foreign students, 5% join fraternities/sororities. Average age is 18.

FALL-TERM APPLICATIONS. $20 fee, may be waived for applicants with need. No closing date; applicants notified on a rolling basis; must reply by May 1 or within 4 weeks if notified thereafter. Interview recommended. Interview required of restricted-status applicants; recommended for all others. CRDA. Deferred and early admission available.

STUDENT LIFE. Housing: Dormitories (men, women). **Activities:** Student government, film, magazine, student newspaper, television, yearbook, choral groups, dance, drama, music ensembles, musical theater, pep band, drill team, fraternities, sororities, Minority Student Organization, R-Move, Alpha Phi Omega, International Student Organization, Alpha Chi, College Republicans.

ATHLETICS. NCAA. **Intercollegiate:** Basketball, cross-country, golf, soccer, softball W, tennis, track and field, volleyball W. **Intramural:** Basketball, bowling, boxing, handball, softball, table tennis, volleyball.

STUDENT SERVICES. Aptitude testing, career counseling, employment service for undergraduates, freshman orientation, health services, personal counseling, placement service for graduates, special adviser for adult students, veterans counselor, services/facilities for handicapped.

ANNUAL EXPENSES. Tuition and fees: $6,300. Students attending main campus pay an additional $370 campus fee. **Room and board:** $4,106. **Books and supplies:** $500. **Other expenses:** $600.

FINANCIAL AID. 70% of freshmen, 73% of continuing students receive some form of aid. 89% of grants, 59% of loans, 18% of jobs based on need. Academic, athletic, leadership, minority scholarships available. **Aid applications:** Closing date May 1; applicants notified on or about April 15; must reply within 3 weeks.

ADDRESS/TELEPHONE. Dr. Helen Mullen, Dean of Enrollment, Robert Morris College, Narrows Run Road, Coraopolis, PA 15108-1189. (412) 262-8206. (800) 762-0097. Fax: (412) 262-5958.

Rosemont College
Rosemont, Pennsylvania CB code: 2763

Admissions: 71% of applicants accepted
Based on:
••• School record
•• Activities, essay, interview, recommendations, test scores
• Special talents
Completion: 95% of freshmen end year in good standing
75% graduate, 16% of these enter graduate study

4-year private liberal arts college, women only, affiliated with Roman Catholic Church. Founded in 1921. **Accreditation:** Regional. **Undergraduate enrollment:** 450 women full time; 150 women part time. **Graduate enrollment:** 3 women full time; 42 men, 20 women part time. **Faculty:** 94 total (47 full time), 78 with doctorates or other terminal degrees. **Location:** Suburban campus in small town; 11 miles from Philadelphia. **Calendar:** Semester, extensive summer session. **Microcomputers:** Located in libraries, computer centers.

DEGREES OFFERED. BA, BS, BFA, MEd. 125 bachelor's degrees awarded in 1992. 10% in business and management, 14% letters/literature, 24% psychology, 31% social sciences, 11% visual and performing arts.

UNDERGRADUATE MAJORS. Accounting, American studies, art history, biology, business administration and management, business economics, chemistry, dramatic arts, economics, English literature, fine arts, foreign languages (multiple emphasis), French, German, history, humanities and social sciences, Italian, mathematics, philosophy, political science and government, psychology, religion, social sciences, sociology, Spanish.

ACADEMIC PROGRAMS. Accelerated program, double major, honors program, independent study, internships, student-designed major, study abroad, teacher preparation, Washington semester, cross-registration, summer program in Italy. **Remedial services:** Learning center, reduced course load, special counselor, tutoring, study skills program, writing center. **Placement/credit:** AP, CLEP General, institutional tests. Maximum of 9 semester hours of credit through CLEP may be counted toward degree.

ACADEMIC REQUIREMENTS. Freshmen must earn minimum GPA of 2.0 to continue in good standing. 90% of freshmen return for sophomore year. Students must declare major by end of second year. **Graduation requirements:** 120 hours for bachelor's (36 in major). Most students required to take courses in arts/fine arts, English, foreign languages, history, mathematics, philosophy/religion, biological/physical sciences, social sciences.

FRESHMAN ADMISSIONS. Selection criteria: School achievement record and curriculum, recommendations, test scores, extracurricular activities strongly considered. **High school preparation:** 16 units required. Required units include English 4, foreign language 2, mathematics 2, social science 2 and science 1. **Test requirements:** SAT; score report by August 15.

1992 FRESHMAN CLASS PROFILE. 370 women applied, 262 accepted, 154 enrolled. **Academic background:** Mid 50% of enrolled freshmen had SAT-V between 460-550, SAT-M between 460-550. 99% submitted SAT scores. **Characteristics:** 42% from in state, 85% live in college housing, 8% have minority backgrounds, 1% are foreign students. Average age is 18.

FALL-TERM APPLICATIONS. $35 fee, may be waived for applicants with need. No closing date; applicants notified on a rolling basis; must reply by May 1 or within 4 weeks if notified thereafter. Essay required. Interview recommended. CRDA. Deferred admission available. Early admission granted to students who complete high school in 3 years and receive diploma.

STUDENT LIFE. Housing: Dormitories (women). **Activities:** Student government, magazine, student newspaper, yearbook, choral groups, drama, campus ministry, peace colloquium, holistic health, psychology club, prelaw club.

ATHLETICS. Intercollegiate: Basketball, field hockey, softball, tennis, volleyball. **Intramural:** Cross-country. **Clubs:** Varsity badminton.

STUDENT SERVICES. Career counseling, health services, on-campus day care, personal counseling, special adviser for adult students.

ANNUAL EXPENSES. Tuition and fees: $11,075. Graduate tuition and fees are $825 per course. **Room and board:** $5,700. **Books and supplies:** $700. **Other expenses:** $700.

FINANCIAL AID. 50% of freshmen, 50% of continuing students receive some form of aid. 74% of grants, 82% of loans, 61% of jobs based on need. 56 enrolled freshmen were judged to have need, all were offered aid. Academic, art, leadership, alumni affiliation, religious affiliation, minority scholarships available. **Aid applications:** No closing date; priority given to applications received by February 15; applicants notified on a rolling basis beginning on or about April 1; must reply by May 1 or within 2 weeks if notified thereafter.

ADDRESS/TELEPHONE. Linda de Simone, Director of Enrollment Management, Rosemont College, Rosemont, PA 19010. (215) 525-6420. (800) 331-0708.

St. Charles Borromeo Seminary
Overbrook, Pennsylvania CB code: 2794

Admissions: 79% of applicants accepted
Based on:
••• Activities, essay, interview, recommendations, religious affiliation/commitment, school record
•• Test scores
• Special talents
Completion: 98% of freshmen end year in good standing
90% graduate, 90% of these enter graduate study

4-year private seminary college and graduate school of theology, men only, affiliated with Roman Catholic Church. Founded in 1832. **Accreditation:** Regional. **Undergraduate enrollment:** 86 men full time; 27 men, 90 women part time. **Graduate enrollment:** 162 men full time; 50 men, 76 women part time. **Faculty:** 56 total (37 full time), 24 with doctorates or other terminal degrees. **Location:** Suburban campus in large town; 4 miles from Philadelphia. **Calendar:** Semester, limited summer session. Summer courses available for graduate students. **Microcomputers:** 16 located on campus. **Special facilities:** Ryan Memorial Library, rare book and special collections, fine arts collection. **Additional facts:** College and Theology Divisions enroll full-time students preparing for Roman Catholic priesthood. Religious Studies Division enrolls part-time undergraduate and graduate students who wish to pursue theological studies. Part-time programs open to men and women.

DEGREES OFFERED. BA, MA, M.Div. 13 bachelor's degrees awarded in 1992. 25% in multi/interdisciplinary studies, 75% philosophy, religion, theology. Graduate degrees offered in 2 major fields of study.

UNDERGRADUATE MAJORS. Philosophy.

ACADEMIC PROGRAMS. Accelerated program, dual enrollment of high school students, independent study, cross-registration. **Remedial services:** Reduced course load, special counselor, tutoring. **Placement/credit:** AP, institutional tests.

ACADEMIC REQUIREMENTS. Freshmen must earn minimum GPA of 1.8 to continue in good standing. 90% of freshmen return for sophomore year. Students must declare major by end of second year. **Graduation requirements:** 125 hours for bachelor's (33 in major). Most students required to take courses in arts/fine arts, English, foreign languages, history, humanities, mathematics, philosophy/religion, biological/physical sciences, social sciences. **Additional information:** Strong emphasis on philosophy, theology, classical languages and the liberal arts.

FRESHMAN ADMISSIONS. Selection criteria: Letters of recommendation, interviews, SAT/ACT scores considered. Psychological evaluation and sponsorship by a diocese or religious community required for applicants to college and theology divisions. **High school preparation:** 20 units recommended. Required and recommended units include English 4, mathematics 3 and social science 3. Foreign language 2 and science 3 recommended. 3-4 units of religious education recommended. GED accepted on individual basis. **Test requirements:** SAT or ACT; score report by June 1. **Additional information:** Seminary applicants holding bachelor's degree from accredited institution may enter special pretheology program in college division.

1992 FRESHMAN CLASS PROFILE. 14 men applied, 11 accepted, 11 enrolled. **Academic background:** Mid 50% of enrolled freshmen had SAT-V between 390-550, SAT-M between 390-470. 75% submitted SAT scores. **Characteristics:** 73% from in state, 100% live in college housing, 27% have minority backgrounds. Average age is 21.

FALL-TERM APPLICATIONS. No fee. No closing date; priority given to applications received by March 1; applicants notified on a rolling basis beginning on or about March 1; must reply within 4 weeks. Interview required. Essay required. Deferred admission available. Pre-entrance program available for students with deferred admission. Level of admission dependent on student's academic background, in particular, background in philosophy, theology, and classical languages.

STUDENT LIFE. Housing: Dormitories (men). On-campus housing available for seminarians in college and theology divisions. Summer housing available to students in religious studies division. **Activities:** Student government, yearbook, drama, Seminarians for Human Life. **Additional information:** Athletic facilities, including pool, available on campus. Religious observance required.

ATHLETICS. Intramural: Basketball, volleyball.

STUDENT SERVICES. Aptitude testing, freshman orientation, health services, personal counseling, services/facilities for handicapped.

ANNUAL EXPENSES. Tuition and fees: $5,500. **Room and board:** $3,500. **Books and supplies:** $800. **Other expenses:** $2,200.

FINANCIAL AID. 80% of freshmen, 80% of continuing students receive some form of aid. 5% of grants, 98% of loans, all jobs based on need. 8 enrolled freshmen were judged to have need, all were offered aid. Religious affiliation scholarships available. **Aid applications:** Closing date August 1; priority given to applications received by April 1; applicants notified on or about September 1; must reply within 4 weeks. **Additional information:** Scholarships offered to full-time students studying for the priesthood.

ADDRESS/TELEPHONE. Rev. Michael J. Kelly, Dean of Formation/College Division, St. Charles Borromeo Seminary, 1000 East Wynnewood Road, Overbrook, PA 19096-3099. (215) 667-3394. Fax: (215) 664-7913.

St. Francis College
Loretto, Pennsylvania CB code: 2797

Admissions: 79% of applicants accepted
Based on:
••• School record
•• Test scores
• Activities, essay, interview, recommendations, special talents
Completion: 92% of freshmen end year in good standing
60% graduate, 15% of these enter graduate study

4-year private liberal arts college, coed, affiliated with Roman Catholic Church. Founded in 1847. **Accreditation:** Regional. **Undergraduate enrollment:** 541 men, 595 women full time; 9 men, 15 women part time. **Graduate enrollment:** 159 men, 213 women part time. **Faculty:** 93 total (67 full time), 50 with doctorates or other terminal degrees. **Location:** Rural campus in rural community; 80 miles from Pittsburgh, 20 miles from Altoona. **Calendar:** Semester, extensive summer session. **Microcomputers:** 40 located in dormitories, libraries, computer centers. **Special facilities:** Southern Alleghenies Museum of Art.

DEGREES OFFERED. AA, AS, BA, BS, MA, MBA, MEd. 17 associate degrees awarded in 1992. 82% in business and management, 18% computer sciences. 194 bachelor's degrees awarded. 41% in business and management, 14% teacher education, 5% health sciences, 9% allied health, 7% life sciences, 6% multi/interdisciplinary studies, 10% social sciences. Graduate degrees offered in 5 major fields of study.

UNDERGRADUATE MAJORS. Associate: Business data processing and related programs, data processing, electromechanical technology, real estate. **Bachelor's:** Accounting, American studies, anthropology, biology, business economics, chemistry, communications, computer and information sciences, criminology, economics, elementary education, engineering, English, English literature, environmental science, French, history, international business management, management science, marine biology, mathematics, medical laboratory technologies, nursing, philosophy, physician's assistant, political science and government, predentistry, prelaw, premedicine, preveterinary, psychology, public administration, religion, social work, sociology, Spanish.

ACADEMIC PROGRAMS. Accelerated program, double major, honors program, independent study, internships, semester at sea, student-designed major, study abroad, teacher preparation, Washington semester, 5-year master of forestry and master of environmental management program with Duke University; liberal arts/career combination in engineering, forestry, health sciences. **Remedial services:** Learning center, preadmission summer program, reduced course load, special counselor, tutoring. **ROTC:** Army. **Placement/credit:** AP, CLEP Subject, institutional tests; 30 credit hours maximum for bachelor's degree.

ACADEMIC REQUIREMENTS. Freshmen must earn minimum GPA of 1.75 to continue in good standing. 76% of freshmen return for sophomore year. Students must declare major by end of second year. **Graduation requirements:** 63 hours for associate, 128 hours for bachelor's. Most students required to take courses in arts/fine arts, English, history, mathematics, philosophy/religion, biological/physical sciences, social sciences. **Postgraduate studies:** 1% enter law school, 2% enter medical school, 3% enter MBA programs, 9% enter other graduate study.

FRESHMAN ADMISSIONS. Selection criteria: High school record most important. Counselors' recommendations, test scores, major area of interest, activities, honors, relationship to alumni also considered. Interview and campus visit highly recommended. **High school preparation:** 16 units required. Required and recommended units include English 4, mathematics 2, social science 2 and science 1. Foreign language 2 recommended. One natural science for nonscience majors, 2 for science majors also required. One science unit must include laboratory. Remaining units in academic electives. **Test requirements:** SAT or ACT; score report by August 23.

1992 FRESHMAN CLASS PROFILE. 981 men and women applied, 775 accepted; 147 men enrolled, 143 women enrolled. 67% had high school GPA of 3.0 or higher, 32% between 2.0 and 2.99. **Academic background:** Mid 50% of enrolled freshmen had SAT-V between 410-530, SAT-M between 420-580. 92% submitted SAT scores. **Characteristics:** 75% from in state, 75% live in college housing, 5% have minority backgrounds, 1% are foreign students. Average age is 18.

FALL-TERM APPLICATIONS. $20 fee, may be waived for applicants with need. Closing date August 1; applicants notified on a rolling basis; must reply by May 1 or within 5 weeks if notified thereafter. Interview recommended. Essay recommended. CRDA. Deferred and early admission available. Institutional early decision plan. Earliest decisions sent to applicants beginning of November. Deposit due in March, refundable until May 1.

STUDENT LIFE. Housing: Dormitories (men, women); apartment, fraternity, sorority housing available. Housing guaranteed on campus for 4 years. All students required to live on campus until 21st birthday unless commuter status. **Activities:** Student government, magazine, radio, student newspaper, television, yearbook, choral groups, drama, music ensembles, pep band, fraternities, sororities, Secular Franciscan Order, student activities organization, multi-cultural awareness club, Historian's Round Table, Knights of Columbus, Dorothy Day Peace and Justice Center, current affairs club, pro-life club, pre-law club.

ATHLETICS. NCAA. **Intercollegiate:** Basketball, cross-country, football M, golf, soccer, softball W, tennis, track and field, volleyball. **Intramural:** Basketball, cross-country, golf, skiing, soccer, softball, swimming, table tennis, tennis, track and field, volleyball.

STUDENT SERVICES. Aptitude testing, career counseling, employment service for undergraduates, freshman orientation, health services, personal counseling, placement service for graduates, special adviser for adult students, veterans counselor.

ANNUAL EXPENSES. Tuition and fees: $11,124. **Room and board:** $4,720. **Books and supplies:** $475. **Other expenses:** $800.

FINANCIAL AID. 92% of freshmen, 86% of continuing students receive some form of aid. 87% of grants, 90% of loans, 66% of jobs based on need. 261 enrolled freshmen were judged to have need, all were offered aid. Academic, athletic, leadership, alumni affiliation, minority scholarships available. **Aid applications:** Closing date May 1; applicants notified on a rolling basis beginning on or about February 15; must reply within 5 weeks.

ADDRESS/TELEPHONE. Gerard J. Rooney, Dean of Admissions, St. Francis College, PO Box 600, Loretto, PA 15940-0600. (814) 472-3100. (800) 342-5732. Fax: (814) 472-3044.

St. Joseph's University
Philadelphia, Pennsylvania — CB code: 2801

Admissions: 79% of applicants accepted
Based on: ••• School record
•• Essay, recommendations, test scores
• Activities, interview, special talents
Completion: 94% of freshmen end year in good standing
78% graduate, 22% of these enter graduate study

4-year private university, coed, affiliated with Roman Catholic Church. Founded in 1851. **Accreditation:** Regional. **Undergraduate enrollment:** 1,200 men, 1,328 women full time; 536 men, 745 women part time. **Graduate enrollment:** 137 men, 144 women full time; 1,315 men, 1,507 women part time. **Faculty:** 350 total (159 full time), 141 with doctorates or other terminal degrees. **Location:** Suburban campus in very large city; 8 miles from center city Philadelphia. **Calendar:** Semester, extensive summer session. Extensive evening/early morning classes. **Microcomputers:** Located in dormitories, libraries, classrooms, computer centers. **Additional facts:** Affiliated with the Jesuit Order.

DEGREES OFFERED. AA, AS, BA, BS, MA, MS, MBA. 8 associate degrees awarded in 1992. 25% in business and management, 25% business/office and marketing/distribution, 50% social sciences. 658 bachelor's degrees awarded. 28% in business and management, 23% business/office and marketing/distribution, 6% computer sciences, 5% education, 6% letters/literature, 6% life sciences, 5% psychology, 17% social sciences. Graduate degrees offered in 32 major fields of study.

UNDERGRADUATE MAJORS. Associate: Accounting, biology, business administration and management, business and management, chemistry, computer and information sciences, contract management and procurement/purchasing, criminal justice studies, finance, labor/industrial relations, marketing and distribution, marketing management. **Bachelor's:** Accounting, biology, business administration and management, business and management, business education, chemistry, computer and information sciences, contract management and procurement/purchasing, criminal justice studies, economics, elementary education, English, English education, finance, fine arts, food marketing, foreign languages education, French, German, health care administration, history, humanities, humanities and social sciences, information sciences and systems, international relations, labor/industrial relations, management information systems, management science, marketing and distribution, marketing management, mathematics, mathematics education, organizational behavior, pharmacy, philosophy, physics, political science and government, psychology, public administration, science education, secondary education, social sciences, social studies education, sociology, Spanish, theological studies.

ACADEMIC PROGRAMS. 2-year transfer program, accelerated program, cooperative education, double major, honors program, independent study, internships, student-designed major, study abroad, teacher preparation, visiting/exchange student program, Washington semester. **Remedial services:** Learning center, preadmission summer program, reduced course load, special counselor, tutoring, ACT 101 for state residents. **ROTC:** Air Force. **Placement/credit:** AP, institutional tests.

ACADEMIC REQUIREMENTS. Freshmen must earn minimum GPA of 1.6 to continue in good standing. 89% of freshmen return for sophomore year. Students must declare major by end of first year. **Graduation requirements:** 60 hours for associate (30 in major), 120 hours for bachelor's (60 in major). Most students required to take courses in English, foreign languages, history, humanities, mathematics, philosophy/religion, biological/physical sciences, social sciences. **Postgraduate studies:** 5% enter law school, 5% enter medical school, 6% enter MBA programs, 6% enter other graduate study. **Additional information:** Associate degrees offered in part-time university college only.

FRESHMAN ADMISSIONS. Selection criteria: School curriculum and achievement record most important. Rank in top two-fifths of class, test scores, school recommendations, and activities also considered. **High school preparation:** 12 units required. Required and recommended units include biological science 1, English 4, foreign language 2-3, mathematics 3-4, physical science 1 and social science 1-3. **Test requirements:** SAT or ACT (SAT preferred); score report by March 1.

1992 FRESHMAN CLASS PROFILE. 1,113 men applied, 868 accepted, 267 enrolled; 1,152 women applied, 921 accepted, 291 enrolled. **Academic background:** Mid 50% of enrolled freshmen had SAT-V between 420-550, SAT-M between 450-600. 98% submitted SAT scores. **Characteristics:** 61% from in state, 79% live in college housing, 11% have minority backgrounds, 2% are foreign students. Average age is 18.

FALL-TERM APPLICATIONS. $30 fee, may be waived for applicants with need. No closing date; applicants notified on a rolling basis. Essay required. Interview recommended. CRDA. Deferred and early admission available.

STUDENT LIFE. Housing: Dormitories (men, women, coed); apartment, handicapped housing available. State-of-the-art student residence with computer network capabilities. **Activities:** Student government, magazine, radio, student newspaper, yearbook, choral groups, dance, drama, jazz band, music ensembles, musical theater, pep band, fraternities, sororities, Black Awareness Society, community action program, international students association, political science association, Bread for the World, language clubs, campus ministry, Hand-in-Hand, Model United Nations Association, Amnesty International.

ATHLETICS. NCAA. **Intercollegiate:** Baseball M, basketball, cross-country, golf M, lacrosse, soccer M, softball W, tennis, track and field. **Intramural:** Basketball, football M, golf M, ice hockey M, racquetball, rowing (crew), rugby M, soccer W, softball, tennis, volleyball.

STUDENT SERVICES. Aptitude testing, career counseling, employment service for undergraduates, freshman orientation, health services, personal counseling, placement service for graduates, special adviser for adult students, women's center, services/facilities for handicapped.

ANNUAL EXPENSES. Tuition and fees: $12,000. Science, computer science and business majors, tuition $11,950. **Room and board:** $5,700. **Books and supplies:** $500. **Other expenses:** $1,155.

FINANCIAL AID. 85% of freshmen, 78% of continuing students receive some form of aid. All grants, all jobs based on need. 401 enrolled freshmen were judged to have need, all were offered aid. Academic, athletic scholarships available. **Aid applications:** Closing date March 1; applicants notified on a rolling basis beginning on or about March 15; must reply by May 1 or within 2 weeks if notified thereafter.

ADDRESS/TELEPHONE. Dr. Thomas Huddleston, Associate Vice President for Enrollment, St. Joseph's University, 5600 City Avenue, Philadelphia, PA 19131. (215) 660-1300. Fax: (215) 473-0001.

St. Vincent College
Latrobe, Pennsylvania CB code: 2808

Admissions: 84% of applicants accepted
Based on: ••• School record
•• Test scores
• Activities, essay, interview, recommendations, special talents
Completion: 90% of freshmen end year in good standing
63% graduate, 26% of these enter graduate study

4-year private liberal arts college, coed, affiliated with Roman Catholic Church. Founded in 1846. **Accreditation:** Regional. **Undergraduate enrollment:** 526 men, 501 women full time; 114 men, 107 women part time. **Graduate enrollment:** 24 men and women full time; 23 men and women part time. **Faculty:** 103 total (67 full time), 53 with doctorates or other terminal degrees. **Location:** Rural campus in large town; 35 miles from Pittsburgh. **Calendar:** Semester, extensive summer session. **Microcomputers:** 90 located in classrooms, computer centers. **Special facilities:** Planetarium, art gallery, observatory, radio telescope. **Additional facts:** Affiliated with Order of Saint Benedict.

DEGREES OFFERED. BA, BS, M, M.Div. 232 bachelor's degrees awarded in 1992. 22% in business and management, 5% communications, 7% letters/literature, 10% life sciences, 7% mathematics, 9% multi/interdisciplinary studies, 6% physical sciences, 12% psychology, 16% social sciences. Graduate degrees offered in 2 major fields of study.

UNDERGRADUATE MAJORS. Accounting, art education, art therapy, arts management, biochemistry, biology, business administration and management, business and management, chemistry, child development/care/guidance, clothing and textiles management/production/services, communications, computer and information sciences, dramatic arts, economics, engineering and other disciplines, English, environmental management, environmental science, family/consumer resource management, fashion merchandising, finance, fine arts, food production/management/services, food science and nutrition, French, graphic design, history, home economics, home economics education, home furnishings and equipment management/production/services, institutional/home management/supporting programs, interior design, liberal/general studies, mathematics, medical laboratory technologies, music, music education, music performance, philosophy, photography, physics, political science and government, preengineering, prelaw, psychology, religious education, religious music, retailing, social work, sociology, Spanish, studio art, visual and performing arts.

ACADEMIC PROGRAMS. Cooperative education, double major, dual enrollment of high school students, honors program, independent study, internships, student-designed major, study abroad, teacher preparation, visiting/exchange student program, Washington semester, cross-registration; liberal arts/career combination in engineering, health sciences. **Remedial services:** Learning center, preadmission summer program, reduced course load, special counselor, tutoring. **ROTC:** Air Force. **Placement/credit:** AP, CLEP General and Subject, IB; 62 credit hours maximum for bachelor's degree.

ACADEMIC REQUIREMENTS. Freshmen must earn minimum GPA of 2.0 to continue in good standing. 85% of freshmen return for sophomore year. Students must declare major by end of second year. **Graduation requirements:** 124 hours for bachelor's (30 in major). Most students required to take courses in English, foreign languages, history, mathematics, philosophy/religion, biological/physical sciences, social sciences. **Postgraduate studies:** 5% enter law school, 5% enter medical school, 5% enter MBA programs, 11% enter other graduate study. **Additional information:** College attempts to place career orientation in context of broader human and religious values.

FRESHMAN ADMISSIONS. Selection criteria: Class rank, test scores, school achievement record. Interview and recommendations from school counselor also considered. **High school preparation:** 15 units required. Required and recommended units include English 4, mathematics 2, social science 3 and science 1. Foreign language 2 recommended. For 3-2 engineering program applicants, 1 geometry, 1 intermediate algebra, .5 trigonometry, and 1 physics required. **Test requirements:** SAT or ACT (SAT preferred); score report by May 1. Prueba de Aptitud Academica for Spanish speaking applicants.

1992 FRESHMAN CLASS PROFILE. 343 men applied, 268 accepted, 116 enrolled; 359 women applied, 321 accepted, 152 enrolled. 25% were in top tenth and 40% were in top quarter of graduating class. **Academic background:** Mid 50% of enrolled freshmen had SAT-V between 400-510, SAT-M between 430-560. 98% submitted SAT scores. **Characteristics:** 81% from in state, 89% live in college housing, 5% have minority backgrounds, 1% are foreign students. Average age is 18.

FALL-TERM APPLICATIONS. $20 fee, may be waived for applicants with need. Closing date May 1; priority given to applications received by February 1; applicants notified on a rolling basis; must reply by May 1 or within 3 weeks if notified thereafter. Audition required for music, theater applicants. Portfolio required for art applicants. Interview recommended. Essay recommended. CRDA. Deferred and early admission available.

STUDENT LIFE. Housing: Dormitories (coed). Single occupancy quiet study dormitory available. **Activities:** Student government, film, magazine, radio, student newspaper, yearbook, choral groups, concert band, drama, music ensembles, musical theater, campus ministry, cultural awareness club, Pro-life Club.

ATHLETICS. NAIA. **Intercollegiate:** Baseball M, basketball, cross-country, lacrosse M, soccer M, softball W, tennis M, volleyball W. **Intramural:** Basketball, bowling, skiing, softball, swimming M, table tennis, tennis, volleyball.

STUDENT SERVICES. Aptitude testing, career counseling, employment service for undergraduates, freshman orientation, health services, personal counseling, placement service for graduates, special adviser for adult students, veterans counselor, services/facilities for handicapped.

ANNUAL EXPENSES. Tuition and fees (projected): $10,318. **Room and board:** $3,766. **Books and supplies:** $500. **Other expenses:** $1,700.

FINANCIAL AID. 80% of freshmen, 80% of continuing students receive some form of aid. 71% of grants, 77% of loans, 63% of jobs based on need. Academic, music/drama, athletic, leadership scholarships available. **Aid applications:** Closing date May 1; priority given to applications received by March 1; applicants notified on a rolling basis beginning on or about February 15; must reply by May 1 or within 3 weeks if notified thereafter.

ADDRESS/TELEPHONE. Rev. Earl J. Henry, OSB, Dean of Admission and Financial Aid, St. Vincent College, Latrobe, PA 15650-2690. (412) 537-4540. Fax: (412) 537-5445.

Seton Hill College
Greensburg, Pennsylvania CB code: 2812

Admissions: 83% of applicants accepted
Based on: ••• Interview, school record, test scores
•• Activities, recommendations
• Essay, special talents
Completion: 97% of freshmen end year in good standing
55% graduate, 23% of these enter graduate study

4-year private liberal arts college, women only, affiliated with Roman Catholic Church. Founded in 1883. **Accreditation:** Regional. **Undergraduate enrollment:** 47 men, 700 women full time; 29 men, 212 women part time. **Faculty:** 105 total (56 full time), 64 with doctorates or other terminal degrees. **Location:** Suburban campus in large town; 30 miles from Pittsburgh. **Calendar:** Semester, extensive summer session. Extensive evening/early morning classes. **Microcomputers:** 75 located in dormitories, libraries, classrooms, computer centers. **Special facilities:** Art gallery, theater, performance hall, child development center, kindergarten, fitness center, writing laboratory, tutoring laboratory, national center for women in business, folklife documentation center. **Additional facts:** Bachelor of fine arts offered to men and women.

DEGREES OFFERED. BA, BS, BFA. 167 bachelor's degrees awarded in 1992. 17% in business and management, 5% communications, 7% home economics, 9% letters/literature, 5% mathematics, 6% multi/interdisciplinary studies, 14% psychology, 10% social sciences, 21% visual and performing arts.

UNDERGRADUATE MAJORS. Accounting, actuarial sciences, applied mathematics, art education, art history, art therapy, arts management, biochemistry, biology, business administration and management, business and management, business economics, ceramics, chemistry, child development/care/guidance, clinical laboratory science, communications, computer and information sciences, computer programming, dramatic arts, drawing, early childhood education, economics, elementary education, English, English education, family and community services, family studies research and evaluation, family/consumer resource management, fashion merchandising, fiber/textiles/weaving, finance, fine arts, food management, food production/management/services, food science and nutrition, foreign languages education, French, geriatric services, graphic arts technology, graphic design, history, home economics, home economics education, human environment and housing, human resources development, humanities and social sciences, illustration design, individual and family development, institutional/home management/supporting programs, interior design, international business management, journalism, management information systems, marketing management, mathematics, mathematics education, medical laboratory technologies, metal/jewelry, music, music education, music performance, nursing, painting, personnel management, philosophy, photography, physics, political science and government, predentistry, preengineering, prelaw, premedicine, preveterinary, printmaking, psychology, public relations, radio/television broadcasting, religion, religious education, religious music, retailing, sacred music, science education, sculpture, secondary education, small business management and ownership, social sciences, social studies education, social work, sociology, Spanish, studio art, textiles and clothing, theological studies.

ACADEMIC PROGRAMS. Accelerated program, double major, honors program, independent study, internships, student-designed major, study abroad, teacher preparation, visiting/exchange student program, New York semester, United Nations semester, Washington semester, cross-registration; liberal arts/career combination in engineering, health sciences. **Remedial services:** Learning center, preadmission summer program, reduced course load, remedial instruction, special counselor, tutoring. **Placement/credit:** AP, CLEP General and Subject, institutional tests; 32 credit hours maximum for bachelor's degree.

ACADEMIC REQUIREMENTS. Freshmen must earn minimum GPA of 2.0 to continue in good standing. 78% of freshmen return for sophomore year. Students must declare major by end of second year. **Graduation requirements:** 128 hours for bachelor's. Most students required to take courses in arts/fine arts, English, foreign languages, history, humanities, mathematics, philosophy/religion, biological/physical sciences, social sciences. **Postgraduate studies:** 6% enter law school, 5% enter medical school, 3% enter MBA programs, 9% enter other graduate study. **Additional information:** Accredited dietetics program; Pennsylvania certification in early childhood, elementary, and secondary education; American Chemical Society accreditation.

FRESHMAN ADMISSIONS. Selection criteria: School achievement record most important, followed by test scores and recommendations. Applicants from minorities or low-income families encouraged; accepted on basis of motivation and potential. **High school preparation:** 15 units required. Required and recommended units include English 4, mathematics 2, physical science 1 and social science 2. Foreign language 2 recommended. **Test requirements:** SAT or ACT; score report by August 15. Prueba de Aptitud Academica for Spanish speaking applicants.

1992 FRESHMAN CLASS PROFILE. 34 men applied, 24 accepted, 10 enrolled; 641 women applied, 536 accepted, 150 enrolled. 18% were in top tenth and 47% were in top quarter of graduating class. **Academic background:** Mid 50% of enrolled freshmen had SAT-V between 420-520, SAT-M between 410-540. 88% submitted SAT scores. **Characteristics:** 78% from in state, 85% live in college housing, 18% have minority backgrounds, 2% are foreign students. Average age is 18.

FALL-TERM APPLICATIONS. $20 fee, may be waived for applicants with need. No closing date; priority given to applications received by July 1; applicants notified on a rolling basis; must reply within 3 weeks. Audition required for music, theater applicants. Portfolio required for art applicants. Interview recommended. Essay recommended. CRDA. Deferred and early admission available.

STUDENT LIFE. Housing: Dormitories (men, women). Housing guaranteed all 4 years for full time students. **Activities:** Student government, film, magazine, student newspaper, television, yearbook, choral groups, concert band, dance, drama, jazz band, music ensembles, musical theater, symphony orchestra, political awareness society, volunteer service through campus ministry, liturgical groups, Respect for Life, voluntary income tax assistance chapter, World Hunger Organization, skiing club, Operation Christmas Basket, Students United for Continued Cultural Experience and Setonian Support. **Additional information:** Freshman seminar choices coordinated with residence hall assignments.

ATHLETICS. NAIA. **Intercollegiate:** Basketball, cross-country, soccer, softball, tennis, volleyball. **Intramural:** Badminton, basketball, horseback riding, soccer, softball, table tennis, volleyball. **Clubs:** Intercollegiate horseback riding.

STUDENT SERVICES. Aptitude testing, career counseling, employment service for undergraduates, freshman orientation, health services, on-campus day care, personal counseling, placement service for graduates, special adviser for adult students, services/facilities for handicapped.

ANNUAL EXPENSES. Tuition and fees: $10,530. **Room and board:** $3,980. **Books and supplies:** $500. **Other expenses:** $1,500.

FINANCIAL AID. 83% of freshmen, 69% of continuing students receive some form of aid. 84% of grants, 90% of loans, all jobs based on need. 148 enrolled freshmen were judged to have need, all were offered aid. Academic, music/drama, art, athletic, state/district residency, leadership, alumni affiliation, religious affiliation, minority scholarships available. **Aid applications:** Closing date August 1; priority given to applications received by May 1; applicants notified on a rolling basis beginning on or about December 1; must reply by May 1 or within 2 weeks if notified thereafter. **Additional information:** Presidential scholarships available. Awards range up to $4,500 per year. Scholarships for Girl Scout Gold awardees, Hugh O'Brien Youth, and Governor's School of Excellence participants.

ADDRESS/TELEPHONE. Cynthia Wolley, Director of Admissions, Seton Hill College, Greensburg, PA 15601-1599. (412) 838-4255. (800) 826-6234. Fax: (412) 838-4203.

Shippensburg University of Pensylvania

Shippensburg, Pennsylvania — CB code: 2657

Admissions: 57% of applicants accepted
Based on: ••• School record, test scores
• Recommendations
Completion: 93% of freshmen end year in good standing
64% graduate

4-year public university and college of arts and sciences and business, teachers college, coed. Founded in 1871. **Accreditation:** Regional. **Undergraduate enrollment:** 2,459 men, 2,857 women full time; 121 men, 182 women part time. **Graduate enrollment:** 110 men, 104 women full time; 352 men, 503 women part time. **Faculty:** 371 total (323 full time), 253 with doctorates or other terminal degrees. **Location:** Rural campus in small town; 40 miles from Harrisburg. **Calendar:** Semester, extensive summer session. **Microcomputers:** 174 located in dormitories, libraries, classrooms, computer centers, campus-wide network. **Special facilities:** On-campus elementary school for student teachers, electron microscope, NMR spectrometer, planetarium, art gallery, fashion archives, women's center, vertebrate museum.

DEGREES OFFERED. BA, BS, MA, MS, MEd. 1,154 bachelor's degrees awarded in 1992. 26% in business and management, 6% communications, 14% teacher education, 9% letters/literature, 15% parks/recreation, protective services, public affairs, 7% psychology, 10% social sciences. Graduate degrees offered in 18 major fields of study.

UNDERGRADUATE MAJORS. Accounting, applied physics, biology, business administration and management, business data processing and related programs, business economics, business education, chemistry, computer and information sciences, criminal justice studies, earth sciences, economics, elementary education, engineering physics, English, finance, fine arts, French, geoenvironmental studies, geography, German, history, interdisciplinary arts, journalism, labor/industrial relations, management information systems, management science, marketing management, mathematics, medical laboratory technologies, office supervision and management, physics, political science and government, psychology, public administration, real estate, social work, sociology, Spanish, speech, urban studies.

ACADEMIC PROGRAMS. Double major, dual enrollment of high school students, education specialist degree, honors program, independent study, internships, study abroad, teacher preparation, Washington semester, cross-registration, 3+2 engineering program with University of Maryland and Pennsylvania State University, 4+1 dual degree program in biology or chemistry and medical technology; liberal arts/career combination in engineering, health sciences. **Remedial services:** Learning center, preadmission summer program, reduced course load, remedial instruction, special counselor, tutoring. **ROTC:** Army. **Placement/credit:** AP, CLEP General and Subject, institutional tests; 30 credit hours maximum for bachelor's degree.

ACADEMIC REQUIREMENTS. Freshmen must earn minimum GPA of 2.0 to continue in good standing. 82% of freshmen return for sophomore year. Students must declare major by end of second year. **Graduation requirements:** 120 hours for bachelor's (66 in major). Most students required to take courses in English, history, humanities, mathematics, biological/physical sciences, social sciences.

FRESHMAN ADMISSIONS. Selection criteria: Secondary school record and test scores important. Special consideration given to applicants from academically and economically disadvantaged backgrounds. **High school preparation:** 14 units recommended. Recommended units include English 4, foreign language 2, mathematics 3, social science 3 and science 3. **Test requirements:** SAT or ACT (SAT preferred); score report by March 1. **Additional information:** Equal opportunity program (ACT 101) available for educationally and economically disadvantaged students.

1992 FRESHMAN CLASS PROFILE. 2,588 men applied, 1,416 accepted, 566 enrolled; 3,082 women applied, 1,798 accepted, 676 enrolled. 10% were in top tenth and 39% were in top quarter of graduating class. **Academic background:** Mid 50% of enrolled freshmen had SAT-V between 420-490, SAT-M between 470-560. 99% submitted SAT scores. **Characteristics:** 87% from in state, 86% live in college housing, 5% have minority backgrounds, 1% are foreign students, 15% join fraternities/sororities. Average age is 18.

FALL-TERM APPLICATIONS. $20 fee, may be waived for applicants with need. No closing date; priority given to applications received by February 1; applicants notified on a rolling basis beginning on or about October 1; must reply by March 1 or within 30 days if notified thereafter. Deferred and early admission available.

STUDENT LIFE. Housing: Dormitories (men, women, coed); apartment, handicapped housing available. **Activities:** Student government, magazine, radio, student newspaper, television, yearbook, choral groups, concert band, dance, drama, jazz band, marching band, music ensembles, musical theater, symphony orchestra, college-community orchestra, fraternities, sororities, Afro-American student organization, Fellowship of Christian Athletes, Christian Fellowship, Jewish Student Organization, The Big Brother-Big Sister Program, United Ministry of Higher Education, international student organization, nontraditional student organization, T.O.U.C.H. **Additional information:** Handicapped students accomodated on as needed basis.

ATHLETICS. NCAA. **Intercollegiate:** Baseball M, basketball, field hockey W, football M, lacrosse W, soccer M, softball W, swimming, tennis W, track and field, volleyball W, wrestling M. **Intramural:** Basketball, bowling M, cross-country M, golf M, racquetball, softball, swimming M, table tennis M, tennis, track and field M, volleyball, wrestling M.

STUDENT SERVICES. Aptitude testing, career counseling, employment service for undergraduates, freshman orientation, health services, on-campus day care, personal counseling, placement service for graduates, special adviser for adult students, veterans counselor, services/facilities for handicapped.

ANNUAL EXPENSES. Tuition and fees (1992-93): $3,388, $3,394 additional for out-of-state students. **Room and board:** $3,132. **Books and supplies:** $400. **Other expenses:** $1,100.

FINANCIAL AID. 57% of freshmen, 60% of continuing students re-

ceive some form of aid. 93% of grants, 44% of loans, 22% of jobs based on need. 930 enrolled freshmen were judged to have need, all were offered aid. Academic, athletic, state/district residency, leadership, minority scholarships available. **Aid applications:** No closing date; priority given to applications received by May 1; applicants notified on a rolling basis beginning on or about May 1; must reply within 2 weeks.

ADDRESS/TELEPHONE. Doyle Bickers, Dean of Admissions, Shippensburg University of Pennsylvania, Shippensburg, PA 17257. (717) 532-1231. Fax: (717) 532-1273.

Slippery Rock University of Pennsylvania
Slippery Rock, Pennsylvania CB code: 2658

Admissions: 60% of applicants accepted
Based on: ••• School record
•• Essay, test scores
• Activities, interview, recommendations, special talents
Completion: 73% of freshmen end year in good standing
44% graduate, 22% of these enter graduate study

4-year public university, coed. Founded in 1889. **Accreditation:** Regional. **Undergraduate enrollment:** 2,752 men, 3,266 women full time; 316 men, 690 women part time. **Graduate enrollment:** 115 men, 192 women full time; 132 men, 314 women part time. **Faculty:** 408 total (374 full time), 255 with doctorates or other terminal degrees. **Location:** Rural campus in small town; 50 miles from Pittsburgh. **Calendar:** Semester, extensive summer session. **Microcomputers:** 200 located in dormitories, libraries, classrooms, computer centers. **Special facilities:** Jennings Environmental Education Center, McKeever Environmental Learning Center.

DEGREES OFFERED. BA, BS, BFA, MA, MS, MEd. 1,168 bachelor's degrees awarded in 1992. 21% in business and management, 5% communications, 38% teacher education, 5% health sciences, 8% social sciences. Graduate degrees offered in 15 major fields of study.

UNDERGRADUATE MAJORS. Accounting, administration of special education, allied health, anthropology, applied science, biological laboratory technology, biology, business administration and management, business economics, chemistry, communications, computer and information sciences, cytotechnology, dance, dramatic arts, earth sciences, economics, education of the emotionally handicapped, education of the mentally handicapped, education of the physically handicapped, elementary education, English, English education, environmental education, environmental science, finance, fine arts, foreign languages education, French, geography, geology, German, health education, history, liberal/general studies, marketing management, mathematics, mathematics education, medical laboratory technologies, music, music education, music performance, music theory and composition, nursing, occupational health and safety management, parks and recreation management, philosophy, physical education, physical sciences, physics, political science and government, psychology, public administration, rural/urban studies, science education, secondary education, social science education, social sciences, social studies education, social work, sociology, Spanish, special education, specific learning disabilities, speech/communication/theater education, technical and business writing, visual and performing arts.

ACADEMIC PROGRAMS. Accelerated program, double major, dual enrollment of high school students, honors program, independent study, internships, study abroad, teacher preparation, visiting/exchange student program; liberal arts/career combination in engineering. **Remedial services:** Learning center, preadmission summer program, reduced course load, remedial instruction, special counselor, tutoring, special 5-week summer program. **ROTC:** Army. **Placement/credit:** AP, CLEP General and Subject, institutional tests; 45 credit hours maximum for bachelor's degree.

ACADEMIC REQUIREMENTS. Freshmen must earn minimum GPA of 2.0 to continue in good standing. Students must declare major by end of second year. **Graduation requirements:** 128 hours for bachelor's (30 in major). Most students required to take courses in arts/fine arts, English, foreign languages, humanities, mathematics, biological/physical sciences, social sciences. **Postgraduate studies:** 2% enter law school, 2% enter medical school, 15% enter MBA programs, 3% enter other graduate study.

FRESHMAN ADMISSIONS. Selection criteria: Above average grades in college-preparatory curriculum, rank in top three-fifths of class, average SAT or ACT scores. Special consideration given to minority applicants. **High school preparation:** 16 units recommended. Recommended units include biological science 1, English 4, foreign language 2, mathematics 3, physical science 2 and social science 4. **Test requirements:** SAT or ACT (ACT preferred); score report by April 15.

1992 FRESHMAN CLASS PROFILE. 2,219 men applied, 1,142 accepted, 521 enrolled; 2,446 women applied, 1,634 accepted, 662 enrolled. 48% had high school GPA of 3.0 or higher, 52% between 2.0 and 2.99. 10% were in top tenth and 42% were in top quarter of graduating class. **Academic background:** Mid 50% of enrolled freshmen had SAT-V between 380-470, SAT-M between 420-530. 90% submitted SAT scores. **Characteristics:** 80% from in state, 82% live in college housing, 7% have minority backgrounds, 2% are foreign students, 7% join fraternities/sororities. Average age is 18.

FALL-TERM APPLICATIONS. $25 fee, may be waived for applicants with need. Closing date May 1; priority given to applications received by April 1; applicants notified on a rolling basis; must reply by May 1 or within 4 weeks if notified thereafter. Audition required for music, music therapy, music education applicants. Interview recommended. Essay recommended. CRDA. Deferred and early admission available. Institutional early decision plan. Early admissions candidates must rank in top-quarter of class, have a combined SAT score of 950 or ACT composite score over 20, have above average grades in a college-preparatory curriculum, and have permission of their school.

STUDENT LIFE. Housing: Dormitories (men, women, coed). **Activities:** Student government, film, radio, student newspaper, television, yearbook, college union programming boards, choral groups, concert band, dance, drama, jazz band, marching band, music ensembles, musical theater, opera, symphony orchestra, gospel choir, fraternities, sororities, Black service groups, other social service organizations, international club. **Additional information:** 3% of freshmen live in town and 15% commute.

ATHLETICS. NCAA. **Intercollegiate:** Baseball M, basketball, cross-country, diving, field hockey W, football M, golf, soccer M, softball W, swimming, tennis, track and field, volleyball W, wrestling M. **Intramural:** Basketball, racquetball, soccer, softball, track and field, volleyball, wrestling M.

STUDENT SERVICES. Aptitude testing, career counseling, employment service for undergraduates, freshman orientation, health services, on-campus day care, personal counseling, placement service for graduates, veterans counselor, services/facilities for handicapped.

ANNUAL EXPENSES. Tuition and fees (projected): $3,510, $4,730 additional for out-of-state students. **Room and board:** $3,364. **Books and supplies:** $500. **Other expenses:** $1,276.

FINANCIAL AID. 80% of freshmen, 80% of continuing students receive some form of aid. 75% of grants, 68% of loans, 22% of jobs based on need. 760 enrolled freshmen were judged to have need, 684 were offered aid. Academic, music/drama, art, athletic, leadership, minority scholarships available. **Aid applications:** No closing date; priority given to applications received by May 1; applicants notified on a rolling basis beginning on or about May 15; must reply within 2 weeks. **Additional information:** May 1 closing date for Pennsylvania state grants.

ADDRESS/TELEPHONE. David Collins, Director of Admissions, Slippery Rock University of Pennsylvania, Slippery Rock, PA 16057. (412) 738-2015. (800) 558-9740.

Susquehanna University
Selinsgrove, Pennsylvania CB code: 2820

Admissions: 72% of applicants accepted
Based on: ••• School record
•• Essay, interview, recommendations, special talents, test scores
• Activities, religious affiliation/commitment
Completion: 88% of freshmen end year in good standing
78% graduate, 16% of these enter graduate study

4-year private university with liberal arts, business, music, and fine arts, coed, affiliated with Lutheran Church. Founded in 1858. **Accreditation:** Regional. **Undergraduate enrollment:** 696 men, 689 women full time; 19 men, 43 women part time. **Faculty:** 136 total (102 full time), 90 with doctorates or other terminal degrees. **Location:** Rural campus in small town; 50 miles from Harrisburg, 150 miles from Philadelphia and Washington, D.C. **Calendar:** Semester, limited summer session. **Microcomputers:** 85 located in libraries, classrooms, computer centers. **Special facilities:** Hepner Ecology Field Station, film library, music library, rare book room, 24-hour study center, arboretum, observatory, art gallery, 450-seat teaching theater.

DEGREES OFFERED. BA, BS. 268 bachelor's degrees awarded in 1992. 32% in business and management, 14% communications, 9% teacher education, 6% letters/literature, 6% psychology, 16% social sciences.

UNDERGRADUATE MAJORS. Accounting, art history, biochemistry, biology, business administration and management, business economics, chemistry, communications, computer and information sciences, dramatic arts, economics, elementary education, English, fine arts, foreign languages (multiple emphasis), French, geoscience/environmental science, German, Greek (classical), history, information sciences and systems, international studies, Latin, mathematics, music, music education, music performance, philosophy, physics, political science and government, predentistry, prelaw, premedicine, preveterinary, psychology, religion, religious music, sociology, Spanish.

ACADEMIC PROGRAMS. Accelerated program, double major, honors program, independent study, internships, student-designed major, study abroad, teacher preparation, visiting/exchange student program, United Nations semester, Washington semester, summer study in Oxford (England), Philadelphia or Harrisburg urban semester, Appalachian semester, semester at Drew University, Denmark International program, internships abroad; liberal arts/career combination in engineering, forestry, health sciences. **Remedial services:** Preadmission summer program, reduced course load, tutoring, writing clinic, study skills sessions. **ROTC:** Army. **Placement/credit:** AP, CLEP General and Subject, IB, institutional tests; 64 credit hours maximum for bachelor's degree.

ACADEMIC REQUIREMENTS. Freshmen must earn minimum GPA of 2.0 to continue in good standing. 90% of freshmen return for sophomore year. Students must declare major by end of second year. **Graduation requirements:** 128 hours for bachelor's (42 in major). Most students required to take courses in arts/fine arts, computer science, English, foreign languages, history, humanities, mathematics, philosophy/religion, biological/physical sciences, social sciences. **Postgraduate studies:** 3% enter law school, 1% enter medical school, 2% enter MBA programs, 10% enter other graduate study. **Additional information:** Cross-registration available with Shenshu University in Japan, Konstantz University in Germany and Yaroslavl University in Russia.

FRESHMAN ADMISSIONS. Selection criteria: School record and class rank most important, test scores secondary. Application essay, interview, teacher and counselor evaluations, activities, and interest in the university also considered. Special consideration given to minority applicants. **High school preparation:** 18 units required. Required and recommended units include English 4, foreign language 2-3, mathematics 3-4, social science 3 and science 3-4. **Test requirements:** SAT or ACT (SAT preferred); score report by March 15. ACH recommended but not required.

1992 FRESHMAN CLASS PROFILE. 981 men applied, 646 accepted, 181 enrolled; 914 women applied, 712 accepted, 226 enrolled. 22% were in top tenth and 51% were in top quarter of graduating class. **Academic background:** Mid 50% of enrolled freshmen had SAT-V between 450-570, SAT-M between 510-610. 98% submitted SAT scores. **Characteristics:** 50% from in state, 98% live in college housing, 7% have minority backgrounds, 1% are foreign students, 30% join fraternities/sororities. Average age is 18.

FALL-TERM APPLICATIONS. $25 fee, may be waived for applicants with need. No closing date; priority given to applications received by March 15; applicants notified on a rolling basis beginning on or about January 15; must reply by May 1. Audition required for music applicants. Portfolio required for art applicants. Essay required. Interview recommended. CRDA. Deferred and early admission available. EDP-F. English Composition ACH and 1 or 2 other ACH tests recommended for admission and placement.

STUDENT LIFE. Housing: Dormitories (women, coed); fraternity, sorority, cooperative housing available. Volunteer services living group, International Student House available. **Activities:** Student government, film, magazine, radio, student newspaper, yearbook, choral groups, concert band, dance, drama, jazz band, music ensembles, musical theater, opera, pep band, fraternities, sororities, voluntary services program to campus and community, Catholic campus ministry, chapel council, International Club, Student Association for Cultural Awareness, Habitat for Humanity, Student Environmental Action Coalition, N.O.W., Black Student Union, Amnesty International.

ATHLETICS. NCAA. **Intercollegiate:** Baseball M, basketball, cross-country, diving, field hockey W, football M, golf M, lacrosse W, rowing (crew), soccer M, softball W, swimming, tennis, track and field, volleyball W, wrestling M. **Intramural:** Baseball M, basketball, field hockey W, football M, ice hockey M, rugby M, skiing, soccer, softball, volleyball, water polo.

STUDENT SERVICES. Aptitude testing, career counseling, employment service for undergraduates, freshman orientation, health services, personal counseling, placement service for graduates, special adviser for adult students, veterans counselor, services/facilities for handicapped.

ANNUAL EXPENSES. Tuition and fees (1992-93): $14,780. **Room and board:** $4,200. **Books and supplies:** $400. **Other expenses:** $600.

FINANCIAL AID. 64% of freshmen, 67% of continuing students receive some form of aid. 93% of grants, 74% of loans, 87% of jobs based on need. 232 enrolled freshmen were judged to have need, all were offered aid. Academic, music/drama, leadership, religious affiliation, minority scholarships available. **Aid applications:** Closing date May 1; priority given to applications received by March 1; applicants notified on a rolling basis beginning on or about February 1; must reply by May 1 or within 2 weeks if notified thereafter. **Additional information:** Graduated pay scale for college work-study program.

ADDRESS/TELEPHONE. J. Richard Ziegler, Director of Admissions, Susquehanna University, 514 University Avenue, Selinsgrove, PA 17870-1001. (717) 372-4260. (800) 326-9672.

Swarthmore College

Swarthmore, Pennsylvania — CB code: 2821

Admissions: 31% of applicants accepted
Based on:
••• Activities, recommendations, school record
•• Special talents, test scores
• Essay, interview
Completion: 95% of freshmen end year in good standing
90% graduate, 50% of these enter graduate study

4-year private liberal arts college, coed. Founded in 1864. **Accreditation:** Regional. **Undergraduate enrollment:** 670 men, 599 women full time. **Faculty:** 171 total (146 full time), 152 with doctorates or other terminal degrees. **Location:** Suburban campus in small town; 11 miles from Philadelphia. **Calendar:** Semester. **Microcomputers:** 150 located in dormitories, libraries, classrooms, computer centers, campus-wide network. **Special facilities:** Arboretum, peace collection in library, Sproul Observatory, Friends Historical Library, Lang Performing Arts Center. **Additional facts:** Quaker tradition.

DEGREES OFFERED. BA, BS. 400 bachelor's degrees awarded in 1992. 5% in engineering, 8% languages, 19% letters/literature, 10% life sciences, 8% mathematics, 5% multi/interdisciplinary studies, 7% philosophy, religion, theology, 7% physical sciences, 12% psychology, 15% social sciences.

UNDERGRADUATE MAJORS. Afro-American (black) studies, anthropology, art history, Asian studies, astronomy, astrophysics, biochemistry, biological and physical sciences, biology, chemistry, Chinese, civil engineering, classics, comparative literature, computer and information sciences, computer engineering, economics, electrical/electronics/communications engineering, engineering, engineering and other disciplines, engineering science, English literature, environmental health engineering, French, German, Greek (classical), history, humanities and social sciences, international relations, international studies, Latin, liberal/general studies, linguistics, mathematics, mechanical engineering, music, peace studies, philosophy, physics, political science and government, psychobiology, psycholinguistics, psychology, religion, Russian, sociology, Spanish, visual and performing arts, women's studies.

ACADEMIC PROGRAMS. Accelerated program, double major, honors program, independent study, internships, student-designed major, study abroad, teacher preparation, visiting/exchange student program, cross-registration, cooperative exchange programs with Tufts, Howard, and Rice Universities and Pomona, Mills, and Middlebury Colleges; liberal arts/career combination in engineering. **Remedial services:** Preadmission summer program, reduced course load, special counselor, tutoring, special program for economically and educationally disadvantaged students. **Placement/credit:** AP, institutional tests.

ACADEMIC REQUIREMENTS. No policy requiring minimum GPA; records of students having academic difficulty are reviewed individually. 98% of freshmen return for sophomore year. Students must declare major by end of second year. **Graduation requirements:** 128 hours for bachelor's (32 in major). Most students required to take courses in humanities, biological/physical sciences, social sciences. **Postgraduate studies:** 7% enter law school, 6% enter medical school, 2% enter MBA programs, 35% enter other graduate study.

FRESHMAN ADMISSIONS. Selection criteria: High school GPA, recommendations, test scores, essay, reading and experience in school and out, character, social responsibility, intellectual capacity considered. **High school preparation:** 16 units recommended. Recommended units include English 4, foreign language 3, mathematics 3, social science 3 and science 3. Literature, art, music, and laboratory science recommended. Engineering majors should have 4 mathematics (including algebra, geometry, trigonometry) plus chemistry and physics. **Test requirements:** SAT or ACT (SAT preferred); score report by February 1. 3 ACH (including English Composition) required of all applicants. Mathematics ACH required of engineering applicants. Score report by February 1.

1992 FRESHMAN CLASS PROFILE. 1,705 men applied, 520 accepted, 181 enrolled; 1,666 women applied, 535 accepted, 173 enrolled. 75% were in top tenth and 96% were in top quarter of graduating class. **Academic background:** Mid 50% of enrolled freshmen had SAT-V between 580-690, SAT-M between 630-720. 99% submitted SAT scores. **Characteristics:** 10% from in state, 100% live in college housing, 23% have minority backgrounds, 5% are foreign students, 3% join fraternities/sororities. Average age is 18.

FALL-TERM APPLICATIONS. $45 fee, may be waived for applicants with need. Closing date February 1; applicants notified on or about April 8; must reply by May 1. Essay required. Interview recommended. CRDA. Deferred admission available. EDP-F.

STUDENT LIFE. Housing: Dormitories (men, women, coed). Dormitory blocks and language halls available. **Activities:** Student government, magazine, radio, student newspaper, yearbook, choral groups, dance, drama, jazz band, music ensembles, musical theater, symphony orchestra, early music ensemble, fraternities, Catholic, Protestant, and Jewish student organizations, Women's Center, Black Cultural Center, Swarthmore Afro-American Student Society, Chester Tutorial Program, Hispanic Organization for Latino Awareness, Swarthmore Asian Organization, Community Service Program (CIVIC).

ATHLETICS. NCAA. **Intercollegiate:** Baseball M, basketball, cross-country, diving, field hockey W, football M, golf M, lacrosse, soccer, softball W, swimming, tennis, track and field, volleyball W, wrestling M. **Intramural:** Badminton, basketball, handball, horseback riding, ice hockey, rugby, sailing, soccer, softball, squash, tennis, volleyball, water polo. **Clubs:** Badminton.

STUDENT SERVICES. Aptitude testing, career counseling, employment service for undergraduates, freshman orientation, health services, personal counseling, placement service for graduates, services/facilities for handicapped.

ANNUAL EXPENSES. Tuition and fees: $18,482. **Room and board:** $6,300. **Books and supplies:** $700. **Other expenses:** $738.

FINANCIAL AID. 44% of freshmen, 47% of continuing students receive some form of aid. All grants, all loans, 67% of jobs based on need. 155 enrolled freshmen were judged to have need, all were offered aid. **Aid applications:** Closing date April 1; priority given to applications received by February 1; applicants notified on or about April 1; must reply by May 1.

ADDRESS/TELEPHONE. Robert A. Barr, Jr, Dean of Admissions, Swarthmore College, 500 College Avenue, Swarthmore, PA 19081-1397. (215) 328-8300.

Talmudical Yeshiva of Philadelphia
Philadelphia, Pennsylvania CB code: 1037

4-year private rabbinical college, men only, affiliated with Jewish faith. Founded in 1953. **Undergraduate enrollment:** 116 men full time. **Graduate enrollment:** 1 man full time. **Location:** Suburban campus in very large city. **Calendar:** Trimester. **Additional facts:** First Talmudic degree and ordination available.

FRESHMAN ADMISSIONS. Selection criteria: Institutional examinations.

ADDRESS/TELEPHONE. Rabbi Elya Svei, Dean, Talmudical Yeshiva of Philadelphia, 6063 Drexel Road, Philadelphia, PA 19131. (215) 473-1212. Fax: (215) 477-5065.

Temple University
Philadelphia, Pennsylvania CB code: 2906

Admissions:	64% of applicants accepted
Based on:	••• School record, test scores
	• Activities, essay, interview, recommendations, special talents
Completion:	40% graduate

4-year public university, coed. Founded in 1884. **Accreditation:** Regional. **Undergraduate enrollment:** 7,498 men, 7,785 women full time; 1,696 men, 1,906 women part time. **Graduate enrollment:** 4,837 men and women full time; 4,014 men and women part time. **Faculty:** 2,650 total (1,698 full time), 1,460 with doctorates or other terminal degrees. **Location:** Urban campus in very large city. **Calendar:** Semester, extensive summer session. Extensive evening/early morning classes. **Microcomputers:** 1,200 located in libraries, computer centers, campus-wide network. **Special facilities:** Art gallery at Center City Campus. **Additional facts:** Other campuses include suburban Ambler and Tyler School of Art, Health Sciences Center in North Philadelphia, Center City Campus in Philadelphia's central business district, New School of Music, and Temple Abroad in Rome, Tokyo, London, and Dublin.

DEGREES OFFERED. AA, AS, BA, BS, BFA, BArch, MA, MS, MBA, MFA, MEd, MSW, PhD, EdD, DDS, MD, B. Pharm, Pharm D, JD. 142 associate degrees awarded in 1992. 3,672 bachelor's degrees awarded. 27% in business and management, 13% communications, 9% education, 5% engineering, 7% health sciences, 5% psychology, 5% social sciences. Graduate degrees offered in 115 major fields of study.

UNDERGRADUATE MAJORS. Associate: Horticulture, humanities, humanities and social sciences, landscape architecture. **Bachelor's:** Accounting, actuarial sciences, Afro-American (black) studies, American studies, anthropology, architecture, art education, art history, Asian studies, biochemistry, biology, business administration and management, business economics, business statistics, ceramics, chemistry, civil engineering, classics, computer programming, crafts, criminal justice studies, dance, dramatic arts, early childhood education, economics, electrical/electronics/communications engineering, elementary education, English, English education, environmental health engineering, fiber/textiles/weaving, finance, foreign languages education, French, geography, geology, German, graphic design, health education, Hebrew, history, horticultural science, human resources development, industrial arts education, information sciences and systems, insurance and risk management, international business management, Italian, journalism, labor/industrial relations, landscape architecture, linguistics, marketing and distributive education, marketing management, mathematical economics, mathematics, mathematics education, mechanical engineering, medical records administration, metal/jewelry, music, music education, music history and appreciation, music performance, music theory and composition, music therapy, nursing, occupational therapy, painting, parks and recreation management, pharmacy, philosophy, photography, physical education, physics, political science and government, printmaking, psychology, Puerto Rican studies, radio/television broadcasting, real estate, religion, Russian, science education, sculpture, secondary education, social studies education, social work, sociology, Spanish, special education, speech, speech pathology/audiology, trade and industrial education, urban studies, visual and performing arts, women's studies.

ACADEMIC PROGRAMS. 2-year transfer program, accelerated program, cooperative education, double major, education specialist degree, honors program, independent study, internships, student-designed major, study abroad, teacher preparation, visiting/exchange student program, cross-registration; combined bachelor's/graduate program in business administration. **Remedial services:** Learning center, preadmission summer program, reduced course load, remedial instruction, special counselor, tutoring. **ROTC:** Army. **Placement/credit:** AP, CLEP General and Subject, institutional tests; 8 credit hours maximum for bachelor's degree.

ACADEMIC REQUIREMENTS. Freshmen must earn minimum GPA of 2.0 to continue in good standing. 71% of freshmen return for sophomore year. Students must declare major by end of second year. **Graduation requirements:** 68 hours for associate, 120 hours for bachelor's. Most students required to take courses in arts/fine arts, English, humanities, mathematics, biological/physical sciences, social sciences.

FRESHMAN ADMISSIONS. Selection criteria: School achievement record, test scores, class rank most important. Recommendations and interview considered. **High school preparation:** 16 units required. Required and recommended units include English 4-4, foreign language 2-3 and mathematics 2-3. Social science 2 and science 2 recommended. One history, 1 laboratory science required. 3 of the additional 6 required units should be in foreign language, mathematics, or social sciences. **Test requirements:** SAT or ACT; score report by June 15.

1992 FRESHMAN CLASS PROFILE. 7,987 men and women applied, 5,145 accepted; 2,399 enrolled. **Academic background:** Mid 50% of enrolled freshmen had SAT-V between 410-510, SAT-M between 450-560. 84% submitted SAT scores. **Characteristics:** 73% from in state, 65% commute, 40% have minority backgrounds. Average age is 18.

FALL-TERM APPLICATIONS. $30 fee, may be waived for applicants with need. Closing date June 15; applicants notified on a rolling basis; must reply by May 1 or within 3 weeks if notified thereafter. Audition required for music, dance applicants. Interview recommended. Essay recommended. Interview required for allied health, recommended for horticulture, landscape design. Portfolio required for art, recommended for architecture. Early admission available. Fine arts applicants must apply by March 29, physical therapy applicants by January 31, College of Music applicants by May 31.

STUDENT LIFE. Housing: Dormitories (coed); apartment, fraternity, handicapped housing available. **Activities:** Student government, film, magazine, radio, student newspaper, television, yearbook, choral groups, concert band, dance, drama, jazz band, marching band, music ensembles, musical theater, opera, symphony orchestra, fraternities, sororities, Newman Club, Hillel, Young Democrats, Young Republicans, international student association, professional organizations, public service, cultural, departmental, educational, honorary, sport, and special interest organizations.

ATHLETICS. NCAA. **Intercollegiate:** Baseball M, basketball, fencing W, field hockey W, football M, golf M, gymnastics, lacrosse W, rowing (crew), soccer, softball W, tennis, track and field, volleyball W. **Intramural:** Badminton, basketball, bowling, boxing M, field hockey, golf, handball, racquetball, soccer M, softball, tennis, track and field, volleyball, water polo.

STUDENT SERVICES. Aptitude testing, career counseling, employment service for undergraduates, health services, on-campus day care, personal counseling, placement service for graduates, special adviser for adult students, veterans counselor, services/facilities for handicapped.

ANNUAL EXPENSES. Tuition and fees (1992-93): $5,013, $4,212 additional for out-of-state students. **Room and board:** $4,950. **Books and supplies:** $550. **Other expenses:** $7,506.

FINANCIAL AID. 61% of freshmen, 60% of continuing students receive some form of aid. All grants, 94% of loans, all jobs based on need. 1,898 enrolled freshmen were judged to have need, all were offered aid. Academic, music/drama, athletic scholarships available. **Aid applications:** Closing date May 1; applicants notified on a rolling basis beginning on or about March 1; must reply by May 1 or within 3 weeks if notified thereafter.

ADDRESS/TELEPHONE. Randy Miller, Director of Admissions, Temple University, Conwell Hall, Philadelphia, PA 19122-1803. (215) 787-7200.

Thaddeus Stevens State School of Technology
Lancaster, Pennsylvania CB code: 0560

Admissions:	58% of applicants accepted
Based on:	••• School record, test scores
	•• Activities, recommendations
	• Essay, interview, special talents
Completion:	50% of freshmen end year in good standing
	48% graduate, 12% of these enter 4-year programs

2-year public vocational/technical college, coed. Founded in 1905. **Accreditation:** Regional. **Undergraduate enrollment:** 436 men, 33 women full time. **Faculty:** 48 total (38 full time). **Location:** Urban campus in small city; 60 miles from Philadelphia, 30 miles from Harrisburg. **Calendar:** Semester. **Microcomputers:** 32 located in libraries, classrooms, computer centers.

DEGREES OFFERED. AA, AAS. 117 associate degrees awarded in 1992. 100% in trade and industry.

UNDERGRADUATE MAJORS. Air conditioning/heating/refrigeration mechanics, architecture, automotive mechanics, business and office, drafting (mechanical), drafting and design technology, electrical and electronics equipment repair, electrical installation, graphic and printing production, legal secretary, machine tool operation/machine shop, specialized technology.

ACADEMIC PROGRAMS. Remedial services: Learning center, preadmission summer program, reduced course load, remedial instruction, special counselor, tutoring, Spring semester preadmission program. **Placement/credit:** Institutional tests.

ACADEMIC REQUIREMENTS. Freshmen must earn minimum GPA of 1.75 to continue in good standing. 50% of freshmen return for sophomore year. Students must declare major on application. **Graduation requirements:** 64 hours for associate (28 in major). Most students required to take courses in English, mathematics, biological/physical sciences, social sciences. **Additional information:** Modern technological equipment kept current with industry standards.

FRESHMAN ADMISSIONS. Selection criteria: Priority given to orphans and financially needy students. Admission based on school achievement record and institutional placement examination (ACT ASSET). **High school preparation:** 14 units required. Required and recommended units include English 4, mathematics 3-4 and science 2-4. Physical science 2 recommended. Algebra required for entry to some associate degree programs. **Test requirements:** ACT/ASSET required of all applicants (except college graduates).

1992 FRESHMAN CLASS PROFILE. 20% had high school GPA of 3.0 or higher, 65% between 2.0 and 2.99. **Characteristics:** 100% from in state, 75% live in college housing, 21% have minority backgrounds. Average age is 21.

FALL-TERM APPLICATIONS. No fee. Closing date July 30; priority given to applications received by March 1; applicants notified on a rolling basis beginning on or about March 1; must reply within 4 weeks. Interview recommended for associate of specialized technology applicants. Deferred admission available.

STUDENT LIFE. Housing: Dormitories (men, women). **Activities:** Student government, student newspaper, yearbook, fraternities, Bible study group, dormitory council.

ATHLETICS. NJCAA. **Intercollegiate:** Basketball M, cross-country, football M, track and field M, wrestling M. **Intramural:** Archery, badminton, basketball, bowling, fencing, golf, soccer, softball, table tennis, tennis, track and field, volleyball, wrestling M.

STUDENT SERVICES. Career counseling, employment service for undergraduates, freshman orientation, health services, personal counseling, placement service for graduates, special adviser for adult students, services/facilities for handicapped.

ANNUAL EXPENSES. Tuition and fees (1992-93): Cost of books room and board, and fees included in tuition. **Comprehensive fee:** $7,000.

FINANCIAL AID. 90% of freshmen, 85% of continuing students receive some form of aid. Grants, loans available. 119 enrolled freshmen were judged to have need, all were offered aid. **Aid applications:** No closing date; applicants notified on a rolling basis; must reply within 15 days. **Additional information:** Tuition, room and board free for students with adjusted family income of $15,000 or less.

ADDRESS/TELEPHONE. George Burke, Director of Enrollment Services, Thaddeus Stevens State School of Technology, 750 East King Street, Lancaster, PA 17602. Fax: (717) 396-7186. (800) THAD-TEC (instate only).

Thiel College
Greenville, Pennsylvania — CB code: 2910

Admissions:	87% of applicants accepted
Based on:	••• School record
	•• Interview, test scores
	• Activities, essay, recommendations, special talents
Completion:	75% of freshmen end year in good standing
	54% graduate, 28% of these enter graduate study

4-year private liberal arts college, coed, affiliated with Evangelical Lutheran Church in America. Founded in 1866. **Accreditation:** Regional. **Undergraduate enrollment:** 377 men, 372 women full time; 39 men, 104 women part time. **Faculty:** 100 total (61 full time). **Location:** Rural campus in large town; 75 miles from Pittsburgh, 75 miles from Cleveland. **Calendar:** Semester, limited summer session. **Microcomputers:** Located in libraries, computer centers. **Special facilities:** Sawhill-Georgian Room, CAD-CAM computer system, Sampson Art Gallery, Brucker Wildlife Sanctuary.

DEGREES OFFERED. AA, BA, BS. 4 associate degrees awarded in 1992. 50% in business and management, 50% computer sciences. 164 bachelor's degrees awarded. 34% in business and management, 6% communications, 7% health sciences, 8% languages, 7% physical sciences, 6% psychology, 17% social sciences, 5% visual and performing arts.

UNDERGRADUATE MAJORS. Associate: Accounting, computer and information sciences, liberal/general studies. **Bachelor's:** Accounting, actuarial sciences, biology, business administration and management, chemical engineering, chemistry, clinical laboratory science, communications, computer and information sciences, computer engineering, cytotechnology, engineering physics, English, environmental science, foreign languages (multiple emphasis), forestry and related sciences, French, geology, history, international business management, materials engineering, mathematics, medical laboratory technologies, nursing, philosophy, physics, political science and government, psychology, religion, religious education, respiratory therapy technology, sociology, Spanish, speech and hearing science, speech pathology/audiology, studio art.

ACADEMIC PROGRAMS. Cooperative education, double major, dual enrollment of high school students, honors program, independent study, internships, study abroad, teacher preparation, visiting/exchange student program, United Nations semester, Washington semester; liberal arts/career combination in engineering, forestry, health sciences. **Remedial services:** Learning center, reduced course load, remedial instruction, special counselor, tutoring. **Placement/credit:** AP, CLEP General and Subject, institutional tests; 30 credit hours maximum for associate degree; 60 credit hours maximum for bachelor's degree.

ACADEMIC REQUIREMENTS. Freshmen must earn minimum GPA of 2.0 to continue in good standing. 82% of freshmen return for sophomore year. Students must declare major by end of second year. **Graduation requirements:** 64 hours for associate (25 in major), 124 hours for bachelor's (40 in major). Most students required to take courses in arts/fine arts, computer science, English, foreign languages, history, humanities, mathematics, philosophy/religion, biological/physical sciences, social sciences. **Postgraduate studies:** 90% from 2-year programs enter 4-year programs. 1% enter law school, 12% enter medical school, 5% enter MBA programs, 10% enter other graduate study.

FRESHMAN ADMISSIONS. Selection criteria: High school GPA, class rank, curriculum, and recommendations important. **High school preparation:** 16 units recommended. Recommended units include English 4, foreign language 2, mathematics 2, social science 3 and science 2. **Test requirements:** SAT or ACT.

1992 FRESHMAN CLASS PROFILE. 445 men applied, 366 accepted, 98 enrolled; 321 women applied, 300 accepted, 103 enrolled. **Characteristics:** 80% live in college housing. Average age is 18.

FALL-TERM APPLICATIONS. $25 fee, may be waived for applicants with need. No closing date; applicants notified on a rolling basis; must reply within 4 weeks. Interview recommended. Essay recommended. Deferred and early admission available. ACT or SAT recommended for admissions and placement.

STUDENT LIFE. Housing: Dormitories (men, women, coed); fraternity housing available. **Activities:** Student government, radio, student newspaper, yearbook, choral groups, concert band, dance, drama, music ensembles, musical theater, pep band, symphony orchestra, fraternities, sororities, Model United Nations, Organization of Black Collegiates, Lutheran Youth Encounter, international students organization, debate group, drama group.

ATHLETICS. NCAA. **Intercollegiate:** Baseball M, basketball, cross-country, football M, golf, softball W, tennis, track and field, volleyball W, wrestling M. **Intramural:** Basketball, soccer, softball, tennis, volleyball.

STUDENT SERVICES. Aptitude testing, career counseling, employment service for undergraduates, freshman orientation, health services, personal counseling, placement service for graduates, special adviser for adult students, services/facilities for handicapped.

ANNUAL EXPENSES. Tuition and fees (1992-93): $9,953. **Room and board:** $4,505. **Books and supplies:** $600. **Other expenses:** $1,280.

FINANCIAL AID. 94% of freshmen, 96% of continuing students receive some form of aid. 99% of grants, 78% of loans, all jobs based on need. Academic, leadership, religious affiliation scholarships available. **Aid applications:** No closing date; priority given to applications received by April 1; applicants notified on a rolling basis beginning on or about February 15; must reply within 2 weeks.

ADDRESS/TELEPHONE. David J. Rhodes, Director of Admissions, Thiel College, College Avenue, Greenville, PA 16125. (412) 589-2345.

Thomas Jefferson University: College of Allied Health Sciences
Philadelphia, Pennsylvania — CB code: 2903

2-year upper-division private university, college of allied health sciences, coed. Founded in 1824. **Accreditation:** Regional. **Undergraduate enrollment:** 1,515 men and women full time. **Graduate enrollment:** 135 men and women. **Faculty:** 83 total (68 full time), 15 with doctorates or other terminal degrees. **Location:** Urban campus in very large city. **Calendar:** Semester, limited summer session. **Microcomputers:** 300 located in libraries, computer centers. **Special facilities:** Rare book collection. **Additional facts:** Associate degree programs available in evening division.

DEGREES OFFERED. BS, MS, D. 354 bachelor's degrees awarded in 1992. 40% in health sciences, 60% allied health. Graduate degrees offered in 3 major fields of study.

UNDERGRADUATE MAJORS. Liberal/general studies. cytotechnology, dental hygiene, diagnostic imaging radiography, medical laboratory technologies, nursing, occupational therapy, radiograph medical technology, ultrasound technology.

ACADEMIC PROGRAMS. Honors program, independent study, internships; liberal arts/career combination in health sciences. **Remedial services:** Tutoring, reading and study skills program. **ROTC:** Air Force. **Placement/credit:** CLEP Subject.

ACADEMIC REQUIREMENTS. Students must declare major on application. **Graduation requirements:** 120 hours for bachelor's. Most students required to take courses in computer science, English, humanities, mathematics, biological/physical sciences, social sciences. **Postgraduate studies:** 1% enter law school, 2% enter medical school, 3% enter MBA programs, 30% enter other graduate study. **Additional information:** PACE (Plan Ahead College Education Program) allows qualified high school seniors to reserve a place for future enrollment.

STUDENT LIFE. Housing: Dormitories (coed); apartment housing available. **Activities:** Student government, student newspaper, yearbook, choral groups, concert band, drama, minority outreach program.

ATHLETICS. Intramural: Basketball, golf, racquetball, rugby, softball, squash, swimming, table tennis, tennis, volleyball.

STUDENT SERVICES. Aptitude testing, career counseling, employment service for undergraduates, health services, on-campus day care, personal counseling, placement service for graduates, special adviser for adult students, services/facilities for handicapped.

ANNUAL EXPENSES. Tuition and fees (projected): $13,750. **Room and board:** $5,070. **Books and supplies:** $1,050. **Other expenses:** $600.

FINANCIAL AID. 75% of continuing students receive some form of aid. All grants, 86% of loans, all jobs based on need. Academic scholarships available. **Aid applications:** Closing date May 1; applicants notified on a rolling basis beginning on or about May 31; must reply within 1 week.

ADDRESS/TELEPHONE. Thomas J. Coyne, Director of Admissions and Enrollment Management, Thomas Jefferson University: College of Allied Health Sciences, 130 Ninth Street, Edison Building, Suite 1600, Philadelphia, PA 19107. (215) 955-8890. (800) 247-6933. Fax: (215) 955-8890.

Triangle Tech: Erie School
Erie, Pennsylvania CB code: 1572

2-year proprietary technical college, coed. Founded in 1976. **Undergraduate enrollment:** 154 men, 10 women full time; 8 men, 2 women part time. **Faculty:** 16 total (14 full time). **Location:** Urban campus in small city; 100 miles from Cleveland, Ohio, Buffalo, New York, and Pittsburgh. **Calendar:** Trimester. **Microcomputers:** Located in computer centers.

DEGREES OFFERED. 101 associate degrees awarded in 1992. 100% in trade and industry.

UNDERGRADUATE MAJORS. Drafting, electrical and electronics equipment repair, electrical installation.

ACADEMIC PROGRAMS. Remedial services: Remedial instruction, tutoring. **Placement/credit:** Institutional tests; 18 credit hours maximum for associate degree.

ACADEMIC REQUIREMENTS. Freshmen must earn minimum GPA of 1.5 to continue in good standing. 85% of freshmen return for sophomore year.

FRESHMAN ADMISSIONS. Selection criteria: Open admissions.

1992 FRESHMAN CLASS PROFILE. 80 men, 6 women enrolled. **Characteristics:** 90% from in state, 100% commute, 4% have minority backgrounds. Average age is 20.

FALL-TERM APPLICATIONS. $75 fee. No closing date; applicants notified on a rolling basis. Interview required. Deferred and early admission available.

STUDENT LIFE. Activities: Student government.

STUDENT SERVICES. Personal counseling, placement service for graduates.

ANNUAL EXPENSES. Tuition and fees (1992-93): $11,700 tuition and required fees for 2-year degree programs. **Books and supplies:** $1,159.

ADDRESS/TELEPHONE. John Mazzarese, Director of Admissions, Triangle Tech: Erie School, 2000 Liberty Street, Erie, PA 16502-2594. (814) 453-6016. Fax: (814) 454-2818.

Triangle Tech: Greensburg School
Greensburg, Pennsylvania CB code: 0658

2-year proprietary technical college, coed. Founded in 1944. **Undergraduate enrollment:** 225 men and women. **Faculty:** 18 total (15 full time). **Location:** Rural campus in large town; 30 miles from Pittsburgh. **Calendar:** Semester, extensive summer session. **Microcomputers:** Located in computer centers. Lease or purchase required**Additional facts:** Concentrated technical training, computer aided drafting, transport refrigeration programs offered.

DEGREES OFFERED. 110 associate degrees awarded in 1992.

UNDERGRADUATE MAJORS. Air conditioning/heating/refrigeration mechanics, air conditioning/heating/refrigeration technology, drafting, drafting and design technology.

ACADEMIC PROGRAMS. Remedial services: Remedial instruction, tutoring. **Placement/credit:** Institutional tests.

ACADEMIC REQUIREMENTS. Freshmen must earn minimum GPA of 2.0 to continue in good standing. 79% of freshmen return for sophomore year. Students must declare major on application. **Graduation requirements:** 72 hours for associate. Most students required to take courses in mathematics.

FRESHMAN ADMISSIONS. Selection criteria: Open admissions.

1992 FRESHMAN CLASS PROFILE. 40 men and women enrolled. **Characteristics:** 98% from in state, 100% commute, 6% have minority backgrounds. Average age is 23.

FALL-TERM APPLICATIONS. No fee. No closing date; applicants notified on a rolling basis; must reply within 2 weeks. Interview required. Deferred and early admission available.

STUDENT LIFE. Activities: Student government, student newspaper.

STUDENT SERVICES. Career counseling, employment service for undergraduates, freshman orientation, personal counseling, placement service for graduates, veterans counselor, services/facilities for handicapped.

ANNUAL EXPENSES. Tuition and fees (1992-93): $5,628. Tuition for refrigeration, heating, and air conditioning program is $5,073 with fees of $148. **Books and supplies:** $750. **Other expenses:** $825.

FINANCIAL AID. 80% of freshmen, 80% of continuing students receive some form of aid. 99% of grants, 76% of loans, all jobs based on need. **Aid applications:** No closing date; applicants notified on a rolling basis.

ADDRESS/TELEPHONE. John Mazzarese, Corporate Director of Admissions, Triangle Tech: Greensburg School, 900 Greengate North Plaza, Greensburg, PA 15601. (412) 832-1050. (800) 472-4351. Fax: (412) 834-0325.

Triangle Tech: Pittsburgh Campus
Pittsburgh, Pennsylvania CB code: 0734

2-year proprietary technical college, coed. Founded in 1944. **Undergraduate enrollment:** 282 men and women full time; 85 men and women part time. **Faculty:** 30 total (20 full time). **Location:** Urban campus in large city. **Calendar:** Semester.

DEGREES OFFERED. 105 associate degrees awarded in 1992. 50% in engineering technologies, 50% trade and industry.

UNDERGRADUATE MAJORS. Air conditioning/heating/refrigeration technology, computer aided drafting and design, drafting and design technology, maintainence electronics, mechanical design technology.

ACADEMIC REQUIREMENTS. Students must declare major on enrollment. **Graduation requirements:** 72 hours for associate (72 in major). Most students required to take courses in mathematics.

FRESHMAN ADMISSIONS. Selection criteria: School achievement record, interview, test scores most important. Recommendations, school and community activities considered.

1992 FRESHMAN CLASS PROFILE. 130 men and women applied, 124 accepted; 101 enrolled. **Characteristics:** 100% commute.

FALL-TERM APPLICATIONS. No fee. No closing date; applicants notified on a rolling basis. Interview required.

STUDENT SERVICES. Placement service for graduates.

ANNUAL EXPENSES. Tuition and fees (projected): $5,850. **Books and supplies:** $1,450. **Other expenses:** $1,305.

FINANCIAL AID. 90% of freshmen, 95% of continuing students receive some form of aid. 99% of grants, 74% of loans, all jobs based on need. Academic scholarships available. **Aid applications:** No closing date; applicants notified on a rolling basis.

ADDRESS/TELEPHONE. Paula J. Korbe, Director of Admissions, Triangle Tech: Pittsburgh Campus, 1940 Perrysville Avenue, Pittsburgh, PA 15214-3897. (412) 359-1000. Fax: (412) 359-1012.

University of the Arts
Philadelphia, Pennsylvania CB code: 2664

Admissions: 63% of applicants accepted
Based on:
- ••• School record, special talents
- •• Essay, interview, recommendations
- • Activities, test scores

Completion: 90% of freshmen end year in good standing
48% graduate

4-year private university of visual and performing arts, coed. Founded in 1870. **Accreditation:** Regional. **Undergraduate enrollment:** 592 men, 614 women full time; 26 men, 74 women part time. **Graduate enrollment:** 21 men, 66 women full time; 6 men, 21 women part time. **Faculty:** 294 total (85 full time), 101 with doctorates or other terminal degrees. **Location:** Urban campus in very large city; 90 miles from New York City and located in Philadelphia's Center City. **Calendar:** Semester, limited summer session. Saturday classes. **Microcomputers:** 85 located in dormitories, libraries, classrooms, computer centers. **Special facilities:** Extensive galleries, electronic media laboratories, video editing studio, Oxberry animation stand, MIDI and recording studios, analog and digital electronic music studios, music calligraphy laboratory, Borowsky Center for Publication Arts, laser scanner laboratory, industrial design computer-aided product design center, several performance facilities.

DEGREES OFFERED. AA, BS, BFA, MA, MFA. 2 associate degrees awarded in 1992. 100% in visual and performing arts. 305 bachelor's degrees awarded. 95% in visual and performing arts. Graduate degrees offered in 6 major fields of study.

UNDERGRADUATE MAJORS. Associate: Graphic arts technology, illustration design, interior design. **Bachelor's:** Architecture, ceramics, cinematography/film, dance, dance education, dramatic arts, fiber/textiles/weaving, film animation, film arts, graphic arts technology, graphic design, illustration design, industrial design, jazz, metal/jewelry, music performance, music theory and composition, musical theater, painting, photography, printmaking, sculpture, wood.

ACADEMIC PROGRAMS. Accelerated program, double major, dual enrollment of high school students, independent study, internships, study abroad, teacher preparation, visiting/exchange student program, cross-registration, exchange with Brighton Polytechnic, England; Ravensbourne College of Design, England; Tokyo School of Art, Japan. **Remedial services:** Learning center, preadmission summer program, reduced course load, remedial instruction, special counselor, tutoring. **Placement/credit:** AP, CLEP General and Subject, institutional tests; 6 credit hours maximum for associate degree. Limit on hours of credit by examination counted toward bachelor's degree varies.

ACADEMIC REQUIREMENTS. Freshmen must earn minimum GPA of 2.0 to continue in good standing. 80% of freshmen return for sophomore year. Students must declare major on application. **Graduation requirements:** 66 hours for associate (17 in major), 123 hours for bachelor's (45 in major). Most students required to take courses in arts/fine arts, English, history, humanities, philosophy/religion, biological/physical sciences, social sciences. **Postgraduate studies:** 1% from 2-year programs enter 4-year programs. **Additional information:** Credit for course work may be given to entering freshmen by portfolio review (awarded after first year) or audition and placement testing. Art and design students declare major at end of first year, dance students at end of second year.

FRESHMAN ADMISSIONS. Selection criteria: Academic records, art work portfolio, audition, SAT or ACT scores, statement of purpose, and letters of recommendation. Special consideration given to minorities. **High school preparation:** 14 units required. Required and recommended units include English 4, mathematics 2, social science 1 and science 2. Biological science 1, foreign language 2 and physical science 1 recommended. Coursework in art, dance, music, or theater as appropriate for specific programs recommended. **Test requirements:** SAT or ACT (SAT preferred); score report by August 15. Class placement in English composition though SAT/ACT scores. ACH not required, but August 15 store deadline for placing, counseling and/or credit. **Additional information:** Applicants for whom English is not first language must submit TOEFL score before application considered.

1992 FRESHMAN CLASS PROFILE. 1,276 men and women applied, 805 accepted; 122 men enrolled, 130 women enrolled. 27% had high school GPA of 3.0 or higher, 63% between 2.0 and 2.99. 5% were in top tenth and 21% were in top quarter of graduating class. **Academic background:** Mid 50% of enrolled freshmen had SAT-V between 400-500, SAT-M between 400-500. 97% submitted SAT scores. **Characteristics:** 44% from in state, 56% live in college housing, 21% have minority backgrounds, 2% are foreign students. Average age is 18.

FALL-TERM APPLICATIONS. $30 fee, may be waived for applicants with need. No closing date; priority given to applications received by April 1; applicants notified on a rolling basis. Audition required for performing arts applicants. Portfolio required for visual arts applicants. Essay required for performing arts, visual arts applicants. Interview recommended. CRDA. Deferred and early admission available. Portfolio or audition, permission of secondary school required.

STUDENT LIFE. Housing: Dormitories (coed); apartment housing available. All housing in apartment-style units. **Activities:** Student government, choral groups, dance, drama, jazz band, music ensembles, musical theater, opera, symphony orchestra, new music ensemble, arts council, orientation committee, Afro-American student union, Artists' Christian Fellowship, student congress, Society for Ecological Education. **Additional information:** Full range of social, recreational, issue-oriented, multicultural, and wellness programming.

ATHLETICS. Intramural: Volleyball.

STUDENT SERVICES. Career counseling, employment service for undergraduates, freshman orientation, health services, personal counseling, placement service for graduates, special adviser for adult students, veterans counselor, ESL support, services/facilities for handicapped.

ANNUAL EXPENSES. Tuition and fees: $12,170. **Room and board:** $5,250. **Books and supplies:** $1,500. **Other expenses:** $580.

FINANCIAL AID. 91% of freshmen, 43% of continuing students receive some form of aid. 89% of grants, 99% of loans, 86% of jobs based on need. Academic, music/drama, art scholarships available. **Aid applications:** No closing date; priority given to applications received by February 15; applicants notified on a rolling basis beginning on or about February 15; must reply by May 1 or within 2 weeks if notified thereafter.

ADDRESS/TELEPHONE. Barbara Elliott, Director of Admissions, University of the Arts, Broad and Pine Streets, Philadelphia, PA 19102. (215) 875-4808. (800) 272-3790. Fax: (215) 875-5467.

University of Pennsylvania
Philadelphia, Pennsylvania

CB code: 2926

Admissions:	40% of applicants accepted
Based on:	••• Activities, school record, test scores
	•• Essay, recommendations, special talents
Completion:	97% of freshmen end year in good standing
	88% graduate, 28% of these enter graduate study

4-year private university, coed. Founded in 1740. **Accreditation:** Regional. **Undergraduate enrollment:** 5,173 men, 3,872 women full time; 320 men, 228 women part time. **Graduate enrollment:** 4,950 men, 3,834 women full time; 914 men, 1,387 women part time. **Faculty:** 3,916 total (1,959 full time), 1,939 with doctorates or other terminal degrees. **Location:** Urban campus in very large city; located in Philadelphia, less than 1 mile from center city. **Calendar:** Semester, limited summer session. Extensive evening/early morning classes. **Microcomputers:** 450 located in dormitories, libraries, classrooms, computer centers. **Special facilities:** Archaeology museum, Institute of Contemporary Art, arboretum, astronomical observatory, Large Animal Research Center, state-of-art computer workstations in engineering school.

DEGREES OFFERED. AA, BA, BS, BFA, MA, MS, MBA, MFA, MEd, MSW, PhD, EdD, DDS, DMD, MD, DVM, JD. 32 associate degrees awarded in 1992. 95% in business and management, 5% social sciences. 2,673 bachelor's degrees awarded. 26% in business and management, 8% engineering, 8% letters/literature, 8% psychology, 27% social sciences. Graduate degrees offered in 138 major fields of study.

UNDERGRADUATE MAJORS. Associate: Accounting, anthropology, art conservation, art history, astronomy, biochemistry, biology, business administration and management, business and management, chemistry, comparative literature, economics, elementary education, English, English literature, environmental design, French, geology, German, history, insurance and risk management, Italian, management science, marketing management, mathematics, music, philosophy, physics, political science and government, Portuguese, religion, Russian, social sciences, sociology, Spanish, urban studies, women's studies. **Bachelor's:** Accounting, actuarial sciences, American studies, anthropology, art conservation, art history, astronomy, biochemistry, bioengineering and biomedical engineering, biological and physical sciences, biology, biophysics, business administration and management, business and management, chemical engineering, chemistry, civil engineering, classics, communications, comparative literature, computer and information sciences, computer engineering, dramatic arts, East Asian studies, economics, education, electrical/electronics/communications engineering, elementary education, engineering and other disciplines, English, English education, English literature, entrepreneurship, environmental design, environmental science, finance, fine arts, folklore and mythology, French, geology, German, Greek (classical), health care administration, Hebrew, history, human resources development, humanities and social sciences, industrial and organizational psychology, information sciences and systems, insurance and risk management, international business management, international relations, international studies, Italian, Japanese, labor/industrial relations, liberal/general studies, linguistics, management science, marketing management, materials engineering, mathematics, mechanical engineering, molecular biology, music, nursing, organizational behavior, philosophy, physics, physiological psychology, political science and government, Portuguese, prearchitecture, psychology, public policy studies, real estate, religion, robotics, Russian, Scandinavian languages, social sciences, sociology, South Asian studies, Spanish, statistics, systems engineering, transportation and travel marketing, transportation management, urban design, urban studies, women's studies.

ACADEMIC PROGRAMS. Accelerated program, double major, honors program, independent study, internships, semester at sea, student-designed major, study abroad, teacher preparation, visiting/exchange student program, cross-registration, combined degree programs offered by Wharton School of Business, College of Engineering and Applied Science, and College of Arts and Sciences; liberal arts/career combination in engineering, business; combined bachelor's/graduate program in business administration. **Remedial services:** Learning center, preadmission summer program, remedial instruction, tutoring, submatriculation into many masters programs. **ROTC:** Air Force, Army, Naval. **Placement/credit:** AP, IB, institutional tests. No maximum number of semester hours of credit by examination counted toward degree.

ACADEMIC REQUIREMENTS. Freshmen must earn minimum GPA of 2.0 to continue in good standing. 97% of freshmen return for sophomore year. Students must declare major by end of second year. **Graduation requirements:** 54 hours for associate, 96 hours for bachelor's (36 in major). Most students required to take courses in foreign languages, humanities, biological/physical sciences. **Postgraduate studies:** 10% enter law school, 7%

enter medical school, 1% enter MBA programs, 10% enter other graduate study.

FRESHMAN ADMISSIONS. Selection criteria: School achievement record, test scores most important. Counselor/teacher recommendations, essays, and extracurricular activities given considerable weight. Special consideration to alumni children. **High school preparation:** 17 units recommended. Recommended units include English 4, foreign language 3, mathematics 4, social science 3 and science 3. **Test requirements:** SAT or ACT; score report by February 1. 3 ACH (including English Composition) required of all applicants. Mathematics Level I or II required of business (Wharton School) and engineering applicants. Score report by February 1. **Additional information:** Interested in diverse geographic, economic, racial, ethnic student body.

1992 FRESHMAN CLASS PROFILE. 7,284 men applied, 2,789 accepted, 1,303 enrolled; 5,190 women applied, 2,159 accepted, 992 enrolled. 83% were in top tenth and 94% were in top quarter of graduating class. **Academic background:** Mid 50% of enrolled freshmen had SAT-V between 550-650, SAT-M between 650-740; ACT composite between 27-30. 99% submitted SAT scores, 15% submitted ACT scores. **Characteristics:** 19% from in state, 97% live in college housing, 33% have minority backgrounds, 9% are foreign students. Average age is 18.

FALL-TERM APPLICATIONS. $55 fee, may be waived for applicants with need. Closing date January 1; applicants notified on or about April 8; must reply by May 1. Essay required. Portfolio recommended for fine arts, design of the environment applicants. CRDA. Deferred and early admission available. EDP-F. Rolling admissions for nursing applicants; notification begins on or about February 2.

STUDENT LIFE. Housing: Dormitories (coed); apartment, fraternity, sorority housing available. **Activities:** Student government, film, magazine, radio, student newspaper, television, yearbook, choral groups, concert band, dance, drama, jazz band, marching band, music ensembles, musical theater, pep band, symphony orchestra, fraternities, sororities, various religious, political, ethnic, social service organizations, and sports clubs.

ATHLETICS. NAIA, NCAA. **Intercollegiate:** Baseball, basketball, cross-country, diving, fencing, field hockey W, football M, golf M, gymnastics, lacrosse, rowing (crew), soccer, softball W, squash, swimming, tennis, track and field, volleyball W, wrestling M. **Intramural:** Badminton, basketball, bowling, cross-country, football, horseback riding, ice hockey, rugby, sailing, skiing, soccer, softball, squash, swimming, tennis, track and field, volleyball, water polo, wrestling M.

STUDENT SERVICES. Career counseling, employment service for undergraduates, freshman orientation, health services, on-campus day care, personal counseling, placement service for graduates, special adviser for adult students, veterans counselor, services/facilities for handicapped.

ANNUAL EXPENSES. Tuition and fees: $17,838. **Room and board:** $6,800. **Books and supplies:** $500. **Other expenses:** $1,242.

FINANCIAL AID. 45% of freshmen, 45% of continuing students receive some form of aid. **Aid applications:** No closing date; priority given to applications received by February 15; applicants notified on a rolling basis beginning on or about April 1; must reply by May 1.

ADDRESS/TELEPHONE. Willis J. Stetson, Jr, Dean of Admissions, University of Pennsylvania, One College Hall, Philadelphia, PA 19104-6376. (215) 898-7507. Fax: (215) 898-9670.

University of Pittsburgh
Pittsburgh, Pennsylvania

CB code: 2927

Admissions: 75% of applicants accepted
Based on:
- ••• School record, test scores
- • Activities, essay, interview, recommendations, special talents

Completion: 60% graduate, 35% of these enter graduate study

4-year public university, coed. Founded in 1787. **Accreditation:** Regional. **Undergraduate enrollment:** 6,835 men, 6,520 women full time; 2,178 men, 2,379 women part time. **Graduate enrollment:** 3,292 men, 2,642 women full time; 1,772 men, 2,234 women part time. **Faculty:** 3,312 total (2,756 full time), 2,475 with doctorates or other terminal degrees. **Location:** Urban campus in large city; 3 miles from downtown Pittsburgh. **Calendar:** Fall, spring, summer terms. 2 summer sessions run concurrently with summer term. Saturday and extensive evening/early morning classes. **Microcomputers:** 600 located in dormitories, libraries, classrooms, computer centers, campus-wide network. **Special facilities:** Allegheny Observatory, art galleries, Nationality Rooms, Stephen Foster Memorial, Heinz Memorial Chapel, Pymatuning Laboratory of Ecology. **Additional facts:** Regional campuses in Johnstown, Bradford, Titusville, and Greensburg.

DEGREES OFFERED. BA, BS, MA, MS, MBA, MFA, MEd, MSW, PhD, EdD, DMD, MD, Pharm D, JD. 3,126 bachelor's degrees awarded in 1992. 9% in business and management, 10% engineering, 10% health sciences, 14% law, 14% letters/literature, 7% psychology, 19% social sciences. Graduate degrees offered in 86 major fields of study.

UNDERGRADUATE MAJORS. Accounting, Afro-American (black) studies, anthropology, applied mathematics, architectural studies, biochemistry, biological and physical sciences, biology, biophysics, business and management, business education, chemical engineering, chemistry, child development/care/guidance, Chinese, cinematography/film, civil engineering, classics, clinical laboratory science, communications, computer and information sciences, creative writing, criminal justice studies, dramatic arts, economics, electrical/electronics/communications engineering, engineering, engineering physics, English, English literature, fine arts, food science and nutrition, French, geology, German, health, physical education, and recreation, history, history and philosophy of science, humanities, humanities and social sciences, industrial engineering, information sciences and systems, Italian, Japanese, law , liberal/general studies, linguistics, marketing and distributive education, materials engineering, mathematics, mathematics/computer science, mathematics/economics, mathematics/philosophy, mathematics/psychology, mathematics/sociology, mechanical engineering, medical laboratory technologies, medical records administration, metallurgical engineering, microbiology, music, neurosciences, nursing, nutritional sciences, occupational therapy, pharmacy, philosophy, physical sciences, physics, polish, political science and government, psychology, public administration, religion, Russian, Slavic languages, social sciences, social work, sociology, Spanish, speech, statistics, studio art, trade and industrial education, urban studies.

ACADEMIC PROGRAMS. Accelerated program, cooperative education, double major, dual enrollment of high school students, external degree, honors program, independent study, internships, semester at sea, student-designed major, study abroad, teacher preparation, weekend college, Washington semester, cross-registration, freshman seminars, early admission to master's programs in many areas for exceptional students, 5-year joint degree liberal arts-engineering program; liberal arts/career combination in engineering; combined bachelor's/graduate program in medicine. **Remedial services:** Learning center, preadmission summer program, reduced course load, remedial instruction, special counselor, tutoring, writing workshop, provisional admission. **ROTC:** Air Force, Army, Naval. **Placement/credit:** AP, CLEP General, IB, institutional tests.

ACADEMIC REQUIREMENTS. Freshmen must earn minimum GPA of 2.0 to continue in good standing. 88% of freshmen return for sophomore year. Students must declare major by end of second year. **Graduation requirements:** 120 hours for bachelor's (24 in major). Most students required to take courses in arts/fine arts, English, foreign languages, history, mathematics, philosophy/religion, biological/physical sciences, social sciences. **Postgraduate studies:** 3% enter law school, 2% enter medical school, 5% enter MBA programs, 25% enter other graduate study.

FRESHMAN ADMISSIONS. Selection criteria: High school record, class rank, test scores, and activities. Consideration given to minorites and relatives of alumni. **High school preparation:** 15 units required. Required and recommended units include English 4, mathematics 3, social science 1 and science 3. Foreign language 3 recommended. 4 electives required with 3 in single foreign language recommended. School of Engineering requires 4 English, 2 algebra, 1 geometry, 1 trigonometry/solid geometry, 1 history, 1 chemistry, 1 physics and 4 1/2 academic electives. School of Nursing requires 4 English, 3 social studies, 5 academic electives with 2 foreign language recommended, 1 algebra I, 1 plane geometry or algebra II, 2 laboratory science (one must be in chemistry). **Test requirements:** SAT or ACT; score report by September 1. Michigan Test of English Language Proficiency required for some applicants. **Additional information:** College of General Studies applicants apply directly to that college, not to the office of admissions and financial aid.

1992 FRESHMAN CLASS PROFILE. 4,372 men applied, 3,194 accepted, 1,097 enrolled; 4,250 women applied, 3,298 accepted, 1,189 enrolled. 23% were in top tenth and 56% were in top quarter of graduating class. **Academic background:** Mid 50% of enrolled freshmen had SAT-V between 420-520, SAT-M between 480-590. 98% submitted SAT scores. **Characteristics:** 88% from in state, 88% live in college housing, 14% have minority backgrounds, 1% are foreign students. Average age is 18.

FALL-TERM APPLICATIONS. $30 fee, may be waived for applicants with need. No closing date; applicants notified on a rolling basis; must reply by May 1 or within 2 weeks if notified thereafter. Audition required for music applicants. Interview recommended. Essay recommended. CRDA. Deferred and early admission available.

STUDENT LIFE. Housing: Dormitories (women, coed); fraternity, sorority housing available. **Activities:** Student government, magazine, radio, student newspaper, yearbook, Pitt Program Council, central programming organization for social, cultural, and entertainment activities, choral groups, concert band, dance, drama, jazz band, marching band, music ensembles, pep band, fraternities, sororities.

ATHLETICS. NCAA. **Intercollegiate:** Baseball M, basketball, cross-country, diving, football M, gymnastics, soccer M, swimming, tennis, track and field, volleyball W, wrestling M. **Intramural:** Basketball, football, handball, racquetball, soccer, softball, squash, swimming, volleyball, wrestling M.

STUDENT SERVICES. Aptitude testing, career counseling, employment service for undergraduates, freshman orientation, health services, on-campus day care, personal counseling, placement service for graduates, special adviser for adult students, veterans counselor, commuter student service, services/facilities for handicapped.

ANNUAL EXPENSES. Tuition and fees (1992-93): $4,922, $5,144

additional for out-of-state students. **Room and board:** $4,130. **Books and supplies:** $400. **Other expenses:** $900.

FINANCIAL AID. 74% of freshmen, 74% of continuing students receive some form of aid. 85% of grants, 83% of loans, all jobs based on need. Academic, athletic, leadership, minority scholarships available. **Aid applications:** No closing date; priority given to applications received by March 1; applicants notified on a rolling basis beginning on or about April 1; must reply by May 1 or within 2 weeks if notified thereafter.

ADDRESS/TELEPHONE. Betsy A. Porter, Director of Admissions and Financial Aid, University of Pittsburgh, Bruce Hall, Second Floor, Pittsburgh, PA 15260. (412) 624-PITT. Fax: (412) 648-8815.

University of Pittsburgh at Bradford
Bradford, Pennsylvania CB code: 2935

Admissions: 91% of applicants accepted
Based on: ••• School record, test scores
•• Interview
• Activities, essay, recommendations
Completion: 98% of freshmen end year in good standing
25% enter graduate study

4-year public liberal arts college, coed. Founded in 1963. **Accreditation:** Regional. **Undergraduate enrollment:** 465 men, 464 women full time. **Faculty:** 95 total (60 full time), 48 with doctorates or other terminal degrees. **Location:** Rural campus in large town; 79 miles from Buffalo, New York. **Calendar:** Semester, extensive summer session. **Microcomputers:** 55 located in libraries, computer centers. **Special facilities:** Access to University of Pittsburgh holdings via computer catalog system.

DEGREES OFFERED. AS, BA, BS. 22 associate degrees awarded in 1992. 9% in computer sciences, 91% health sciences. 75 bachelor's degrees awarded. 32% in business and management, 7% communications, 9% computer sciences, 5% letters/literature, 7% life sciences, 20% multi/interdisciplinary studies, 12% psychology.

UNDERGRADUATE MAJORS. Associate: Computer programming, nursing. **Bachelor's:** American studies, applied mathematics, biological and physical sciences, biology, business and management, chemistry, communications, computer and information sciences, economics, education, English education, geology, history, human relations, humanities, liberal/general studies, mathematics education, physical sciences, political science and government, predentistry, prelaw, premedicine, prepharmacy, preveterinary, psychology, public relations, science education, social science education, social sciences, social studies education.

ACADEMIC PROGRAMS. Accelerated program, double major, independent study, internships, semester at sea, student-designed major, study abroad, teacher preparation, cross-registration. **Remedial services:** Learning center, preadmission summer program, reduced course load, remedial instruction, special counselor, tutoring. **ROTC:** Army. **Placement/credit:** AP, CLEP General, institutional tests; 30 credit hours maximum for bachelor's degree.

ACADEMIC REQUIREMENTS. Freshmen must earn minimum GPA of 2.0 to continue in good standing. 90% of freshmen return for sophomore year. Students must declare major by end of second year. **Graduation requirements:** 60 hours for associate (30 in major), 120 hours for bachelor's (60 in major). Most students required to take courses in English, humanities, mathematics, biological/physical sciences, social sciences. **Postgraduate studies:** 12% from 2-year programs enter 4-year programs. 1% enter law school, 1% enter medical school, 13% enter MBA programs, 10% enter other graduate study.

FRESHMAN ADMISSIONS. Selection criteria: School achievement record, test scores, self-evaluation, interview, and recommendations. **High school preparation:** 15 units required; 20 recommended. Required and recommended units include biological science 1, English 4, foreign language 2-3, mathematics 1-4 and social science 4. 2 laboratory science also required. Engineering majors required to take chemistry, physics, and trigonometry. **Test requirements:** SAT or ACT; score report by July 1.

1992 FRESHMAN CLASS PROFILE. 548 men and women applied, 499 accepted; 230 enrolled. 60% had high school GPA of 3.0 or higher, 30% between 2.0 and 2.99. **Academic background:** Mid 50% of enrolled freshmen had SAT-V between 410-490, SAT-M between 450-520. 99% submitted SAT scores. **Characteristics:** 90% from in state, 63% live in college housing, 3% have minority backgrounds, 1% are foreign students, 7% join fraternities/sororities. Average age is 19.

FALL-TERM APPLICATIONS. $30 fee, may be waived for applicants with need. Closing date July 1; priority given to applications received by May 1; applicants notified on a rolling basis; must reply by May 1 or within 2 weeks if notified thereafter. Interview recommended. Essay recommended for nursing applicants. CRDA. Deferred and early admission available. EDP-F.

STUDENT LIFE. Housing: Dormitories (coed); handicapped housing available. Apartment-style housing available. **Activities:** Student government, magazine, radio, student newspaper, television, yearbook, literary magazine, choral groups, drama, jazz band, pep band, fraternities, sororities, Campus Ministry, community service club, Black Action Committee, Harvest Christian Fellowship, Alpha Lambda Delta (freshman honorary), Alpha Phi Omega (social services fraternity).

ATHLETICS. NAIA. **Intercollegiate:** Basketball, cross-country, golf M, soccer M, volleyball W. **Intramural:** Badminton, basketball, bowling, football M, racquetball, skiing, soccer, softball W, table tennis, tennis, volleyball.

STUDENT SERVICES. Aptitude testing, career counseling, employment service for undergraduates, freshman orientation, health services, personal counseling, placement service for graduates, special adviser for adult students, services/facilities for handicapped.

ANNUAL EXPENSES. Tuition and fees (projected): $5,300, $5,400 additional for out-of-state students. **Room and board:** $4,100. **Books and supplies:** $500. **Other expenses:** $500.

FINANCIAL AID. 58% of freshmen, 77% of continuing students receive some form of aid. 71% of grants, 77% of loans, 44% of jobs based on need. 155 enrolled freshmen were judged to have need, all were offered aid. Academic, athletic, state/district residency scholarships available. **Aid applications:** Closing date March 1; applicants notified on or about April 1; must reply by May 1 or within 2 weeks if notified thereafter.

ADDRESS/TELEPHONE. Philip Alletto, Director of Admissions, University of Pittsburgh at Bradford, 300 Campus Drive, Bradford, PA 16701-2898. (814) 362-7555. (800) UPB-1787. Fax: (814) 362-7684.

University of Pittsburgh at Greensburg
Greensburg, Pennsylvania CB code: 2936

Admissions: 77% of applicants accepted
Based on: ••• School record, test scores
• Activities, essay, interview, recommendations, special talents
Completion: 60% of freshmen end year in good standing
50% graduate

4-year public regional campus of university, coed. Founded in 1963. **Accreditation:** Regional. **Undergraduate enrollment:** 524 men, 511 women full time; 193 men, 209 women part time. **Faculty:** 89 total (59 full time), 63 with doctorates or other terminal degrees. **Location:** Suburban campus in large town; 30 miles from Pittsburgh. **Calendar:** Trimester, limited summer session. Saturday and extensive evening/early morning classes. **Microcomputers:** 30 located in computer centers. **Special facilities:** Inter-library loan system links all university system libraries. **Additional facts:** Situated on 165 acres of former private estate including wildlife sanctuary and nature trail.

DEGREES OFFERED. BA, BS. 216 bachelor's degrees awarded in 1992. 35% in business and management, 9% communications, 5% letters/literature, 5% life sciences, 20% psychology, 19% social sciences, 20% trade and industry, 19% visual and performing arts.

UNDERGRADUATE MAJORS. Accounting, applied mathematics, biology, business administration and management, creative writing, criminal justice studies, criminology, English, English literature, humanities, information sciences and systems, journalism, law enforcement and corrections, political science and government, predentistry, prelaw, premedicine, psychology, social sciences.

ACADEMIC PROGRAMS. Accelerated program, double major, dual enrollment of high school students, independent study, internships, semester at sea, student-designed major, weekend college, Washington semester, cross-registration. **Remedial services:** Reduced course load, remedial instruction, tutoring, Study Skills Series. **Placement/credit:** AP, CLEP General, institutional tests; 30 credit hours maximum for bachelor's degree.

ACADEMIC REQUIREMENTS. Freshmen must earn minimum GPA of 2.0 to continue in good standing. 65% of freshmen return for sophomore year. Students must declare major by end of second year. **Graduation requirements:** 120 hours for bachelor's (30 in major). Most students required to take courses in English, humanities, mathematics, social sciences.

FRESHMAN ADMISSIONS. Selection criteria: School achievement record most important, followed by SAT/ACT scores. **High school preparation:** 15 units required. Required and recommended units include English 4, mathematics 2-3, social science 1-3 and science 1-2. Foreign language 3 recommended. For engineering applicants 2 algebra, 1 geometry, 1 trigonometry, 1 physics required; calculus and computer science recommended. **Test requirements:** SAT or ACT; score report by July 30.

1992 FRESHMAN CLASS PROFILE. 342 men applied, 255 accepted, 176 enrolled; 371 women applied, 295 accepted, 215 enrolled. 12% were in top tenth and 35% were in top quarter of graduating class. **Academic background:** Mid 50% of enrolled freshmen had SAT-V between 370-470, SAT-M between 410-550. 95% submitted SAT scores. **Characteristics:** 99% from in state, 73% commute, 2% have minority backgrounds. Average age is 18.

FALL-TERM APPLICATIONS. $30 fee, may be waived for applicants with need. Closing date August 1; applicants notified on a rolling basis; must reply by May 1 or within 3 weeks if notified thereafter. Interview recommended. Essay recommended. CRDA. Deferred and early admission available.

STUDENT LIFE. Housing: Dormitories (coed); apartment housing available. **Activities:** Student government, film, magazine, student newspaper, drama, clubs associated with academic subjects, Ambassadors, Interfaith Fellowship, Black Awareness, Circle-K.

ATHLETICS. Intramural: Baseball M, basketball M, racquetball, skiing, soccer M, table tennis, tennis, volleyball.

STUDENT SERVICES. Aptitude testing, career counseling, freshman orientation, health services, personal counseling, placement service for graduates, special adviser for adult students, services/facilities for handicapped.

ANNUAL EXPENSES. Tuition and fees (projected): $5,168, $5,420 additional for out-of-state students. **Room and board:** $3,620. **Books and supplies:** $550. **Other expenses:** $900.

FINANCIAL AID. 87% of freshmen, 70% of continuing students receive some form of aid. All grants, 71% of loans, all jobs based on need. 265 enrolled freshmen were judged to have need, all were offered aid. **Aid applications:** Closing date May 1; applicants notified on a rolling basis beginning on or about April 1; must reply by May 1 or within 2 weeks if notified thereafter.

ADDRESS/TELEPHONE. Larry J. Whatule, Director of Admissions and Financial Aid, University of Pittsburgh at Greensburg, 1150 Mount Pleasant Road, Greensburg, PA 15601-5898. (412) 836-9880. Fax: (414) 836-9901.

University of Pittsburgh at Johnstown
Johnstown, Pennsylvania CB code: 2934

Admissions: 68% of applicants accepted
Based on:
••• School record
•• Test scores
• Activities, essay, interview, recommendations, special talents
Completion: 94% of freshmen end year in good standing
20% enter graduate study

4-year public college of arts and sciences and engineering college, coed. Founded in 1927. **Accreditation:** Regional. **Undergraduate enrollment:** 1,342 men, 1,351 women full time; 226 men, 322 women part time. **Faculty:** 192 total (143 full time), 94 with doctorates or other terminal degrees. **Location:** Suburban campus in small city; 70 miles from Pittsburgh. **Calendar:** Modified trimester. Saturday and extensive evening/early morning classes. **Microcomputers:** 170 located in computer centers, campus-wide network. **Special facilities:** 40-acre nature preserve maintained by biology department, performing arts center, chapel.

DEGREES OFFERED. AS, BA, BS. 19 associate degrees awarded in 1992. 100% in allied health. 499 bachelor's degrees awarded. 25% in business and management, 5% computer sciences, 25% teacher education, 11% engineering technologies, 10% life sciences, 5% social sciences.

UNDERGRADUATE MAJORS. Associate: Respiratory therapy. **Bachelor's:** Accounting, American studies, biological and physical sciences, biology, business administration and management, business and management, business economics, chemistry, civil engineering technologies, civil technology, communications, computer and information sciences, creative writing, dramatic arts, ecology, economics, electrical/electronics/communications engineering, elementary education, English education, English literature, finance, geography, geology, history, humanities, humanities and social sciences, journalism, liberal/general studies, mathematics, mathematics education, mechanical engineering technologies, physical sciences, political science and government, predentistry, prelaw, premedicine, preveterinary, psychology, science education, secondary education, social sciences, sociology, speech/communication/theater education.

ACADEMIC PROGRAMS. Accelerated program, double major, dual enrollment of high school students, independent study, internships, semester at sea, student-designed major, study abroad, teacher preparation, Washington semester, cross-registration, medical technologies program in cooperation with local hospital. **Remedial services:** Learning center, special counselor, tutoring. **Placement/credit:** AP, CLEP General, institutional tests.

ACADEMIC REQUIREMENTS. Freshmen must earn minimum GPA of 2.0 to continue in good standing. 89% of freshmen return for sophomore year. Students must declare major by end of second year. **Graduation requirements:** 86 hours for associate, 120 hours for bachelor's. Most students required to take courses in English, history, humanities, mathematics, biological/physical sciences, social sciences. **Postgraduate studies:** 2% enter law school, 3% enter medical school, 3% enter MBA programs, 12% enter other graduate study.

FRESHMAN ADMISSIONS. Selection criteria: High school achievement, test scores, curriculum, class rank, recommendations, and self-evaluation. **High school preparation:** 15 units required. Required units include English 4, foreign language 2, mathematics 3, social science 4 and science 1. Laboratory science also required. Trigonometry, physics, and chemistry instead of foreign language, required for engineering technology program. **Test requirements:** SAT or ACT; score report by April 1.

1992 FRESHMAN CLASS PROFILE. 1,019 men applied, 672 accepted, 346 enrolled; 1,038 women applied, 730 accepted, 364 enrolled. 63% had high school GPA of 3.0 or higher, 36% between 2.0 and 2.99. **Academic background:** Mid 50% of enrolled freshmen had SAT-V between 420-520, SAT-M between 460-560. 99% submitted SAT scores. **Characteristics:** 99% from in state, 62% live in college housing, 2% have minority backgrounds, 1% are foreign students, 10% join fraternities/sororities. Average age is 18.

FALL-TERM APPLICATIONS. $30 fee, may be waived for applicants with need. No closing date; priority given to applications received by March 15; applicants notified on a rolling basis beginning on or about October 1; must reply by May 1 or within 2 weeks if notified thereafter. Essay required. Interview recommended. CRDA. Deferred and early admission available.

STUDENT LIFE. Housing: Dormitories (men, women); apartment, fraternity, sorority housing available. Guaranteed 4-year housing. **Activities:** Student government, magazine, radio, student newspaper, yearbook, choral groups, concert band, dance, drama, music ensembles, musical theater, pep band, symphony orchestra, fraternities, sororities, Newman Students Association, Circle K, Black Action Society, Time Out Christian Fellowship, Student Council on World Affairs, Amnesty International, Veterans in Pitt, Mu Upsilon Mu, Students for Ethical Treatment of Animals.

ATHLETICS. NCAA. **Intercollegiate:** Baseball M, basketball, cross-country W, soccer M, track and field W, volleyball W, wrestling M. **Intramural:** Archery, baseball M, basketball, bowling, cross-country, golf M, ice hockey M, rifle, rugby M, skiing, soccer, softball, swimming, table tennis, tennis, track and field, volleyball, wrestling M.

STUDENT SERVICES. Aptitude testing, career counseling, employment service for undergraduates, freshman orientation, health services, personal counseling, placement service for graduates, special adviser for adult students, veterans counselor, services/facilities for handicapped.

ANNUAL EXPENSES. Tuition and fees (1992-93): $4,966, $5,144 additional for out-of-state students. Engineering students tuition, in-state $5,900, additional out-of-state $6,810. **Room and board:** $3,544. **Books and supplies:** $600. **Other expenses:** $1,500.

FINANCIAL AID. 83% of freshmen, 84% of continuing students receive some form of aid. 87% of grants, 73% of loans, 67% of jobs based on need. Academic, athletic, state/district residency, minority scholarships available. **Aid applications:** No closing date; priority given to applications received by April 1; applicants notified on a rolling basis beginning on or about April 1.

ADDRESS/TELEPHONE. Thomas J. Wonders, Director of Admissions and Student Aid, University of Pittsburgh at Johnstown, 133 Biddle Hall, Johnstown, PA 15904. (814) 269-7050. Fax: (814) 269-7044.

University of Pittsburgh at Titusville
Titusville, Pennsylvania CB code: 2937

2-year public college of arts and sciences and branch campus college, coed. Founded in 1963. **Accreditation:** Regional. **Undergraduate enrollment:** 424 men and women. **Faculty:** 37 total (22 full time). **Location:** Suburban campus in small town; 95 miles from Pittsburgh, 45 miles from Erie. **Calendar:** Trimester, limited summer session. **Microcomputers:** 40 located in computer centers. **Additional facts:** Students may relocate into programs at any University of Pittsburgh campus.

DEGREES OFFERED. AA, AS. 10 associate degrees awarded in 1992. 100% in business and management.

UNDERGRADUATE MAJORS. Accounting, business and management, liberal/general studies, management information systems, natural science, supervision (engineering).

ACADEMIC PROGRAMS. 2-year transfer program, dual enrollment of high school students, cross-registration. **Remedial services:** Learning center, reduced course load, remedial instruction, special counselor, tutoring. **Placement/credit:** AP, institutional tests; 15 credit hours maximum for associate degree.

ACADEMIC REQUIREMENTS. Freshmen must earn minimum GPA of 2.0 to continue in good standing. 70% of freshmen return for sophomore year. Students must declare major by end of first year. **Graduation requirements:** 60 hours for associate. Most students required to take courses in arts/fine arts, English, foreign languages, humanities, mathematics, philosophy/religion, biological/physical sciences, social sciences.

FRESHMAN ADMISSIONS. Selection criteria: Class rank, test scores, recommendations from high school, personal qualifications considered. **High school preparation:** 15 units required; 19 recommended. Required and recommended units include English 4, foreign language 2, mathematics 3, social science 1-3 and science 1-3. 2 laboratory science also required. Precalculus and physics instead of foreign language required of engineering applicants. **Test requirements:** SAT or ACT (SAT preferred); score report by June 1.

1992 FRESHMAN CLASS PROFILE. 186 men and women enrolled. 26% had high school GPA of 3.0 or higher, 71% between 2.0 and 2.99. **Academic background:** Mid 50% of enrolled freshmen had SAT-V between 390-490, SAT-M between 410-500. 98% submitted SAT scores. **Characteristics:** 94% from in state, 90% live in college housing, 1% have minority backgrounds, 1% are foreign students. Average age is 18.

FALL-TERM APPLICATIONS. $30 fee, may be waived for applicants with need. No closing date; priority given to applications received by May 1; applicants notified on a rolling basis; must reply by May 1 or within 3 weeks if notified thereafter. Interview recommended. CRDA. Deferred and early admission available.

STUDENT LIFE. Housing: Dormitories (coed). Townhouse style housing facilities available. **Activities:** Student government, yearbook, choral groups, drama, academic honor fraternity, Campus Christian Fellowship. **Additional information:** Students strongly urged to participate in activities program.

ATHLETICS. Intramural: Basketball, bowling, field hockey M, handball, racquetball, skiing, soccer M, softball, squash, swimming, table tennis, tennis, volleyball.

STUDENT SERVICES. Aptitude testing, career counseling, employment service for undergraduates, freshman orientation, health services, personal counseling, placement service for graduates, special adviser for adult students.

ANNUAL EXPENSES. Tuition and fees (projected): $5,010, $5,200 additional for out-of-state students. **Room and board:** $3,970. **Books and supplies:** $500. **Other expenses:** $500.

FINANCIAL AID. 87% of freshmen, 80% of continuing students receive some form of aid. 97% of grants, 79% of loans, 83% of jobs based on need. Academic scholarships available. **Aid applications:** Closing date May 1; applicants notified on a rolling basis beginning on or about April 1; must reply by May 1 or within 3 weeks if notified thereafter.

ADDRESS/TELEPHONE. Jamie Mowat, Director of Admissions and Financial Aid, University of Pittsburgh at Titusville, McKinney Hall, 504 East Main Street, Titusville, PA 16354. (814) 827-4427. Fax: (814) 827-4448.

University of Scranton

Scranton, Pennsylvania — CB code: 2929

Admissions: 62% of applicants accepted
Based on:
••• School record, test scores
•• Activities, recommendations
• Essay, interview, special talents
Completion: 94% of freshmen end year in good standing
84% graduate, 35% of these enter graduate study

4-year private university, coed, affiliated with Roman Catholic Church. Founded in 1888. **Accreditation:** Regional. **Undergraduate enrollment:** 1,791 men, 1,948 women full time; 233 men, 332 women part time. **Graduate enrollment:** 79 men, 99 women full time; 258 men, 321 women part time. **Faculty:** 409 total (256 full time), 185 with doctorates or other terminal degrees. **Location:** Urban campus in small city; 125 miles from New York City, 125 miles from Philadelphia. **Calendar:** 4-1-4, extensive summer session. Extensive evening/early morning classes. **Microcomputers:** 308 located in dormitories, libraries, classrooms, computer centers, campus-wide network. **Special facilities:** Art gallery, fine arts center, Center for University Music Program, Conservatory for Horticulture. **Additional facts:** Affiliated with Society of Jesus.

DEGREES OFFERED. AA, AS, BA, BS, MA, MS, MBA. 18 associate degrees awarded in 1992. 944 bachelor's degrees awarded. 28% in business and management, 7% communications, 5% teacher education, 7% health sciences, 5% letters/literature, 9% life sciences, 5% parks/recreation, protective services, public affairs, 5% psychology, 10% social sciences. Graduate degrees offered in 16 major fields of study.

UNDERGRADUATE MAJORS. Associate: Business administration and management, computer and information sciences, criminal justice studies, electrical/electronics/communications engineering, fine arts, gerontology, health and human services, health care administration, law enforcement and corrections, political science and government, preengineering, public administration, social relations/gerontology. **Bachelor's:** Accounting, advertising, biochemistry, biology, biophysics, business administration and management, business and management, business economics, chemistry, chemistry/business, chemistry/computers, classics, clinical laboratory science, communications, computer and information sciences, computer engineering, criminal justice studies, economics, electrical/electronics/communications engineering, electronics/business, elementary education, English, English education, finance, foreign languages (multiple emphasis), foreign languages education, French, German, gerontology, Greek (classical), health and human services, health care administration, history, information sciences and systems, international language/business, international relations, international studies, journalism, Latin, law enforcement and corrections, marketing management, mathematics, mathematics education, neurosciences, nursing, occupational therapy, philosophy, physical therapy, physics, political science and government, predentistry, prelaw, premedicine, prepharmacy, preveterinary, production and operations management, psychology, public administration, public relations, radio/television broadcasting, science education, secondary education, social science education, social studies education, sociology, Spanish, theological studies.

ACADEMIC PROGRAMS. Accelerated program, double major, honors program, independent study, internships, semester at sea, student-designed major, study abroad, teacher preparation, United Nations semester, Washington semester, cross-registration, 4- and 5-year master's degree programs; liberal arts/career combination in engineering; combined bachelor's/graduate program in business administration. **Remedial services:** Learning center, tutoring, special academic development program for risk and educationally disadvantaged students. **ROTC:** Air Force, Army. **Placement/credit:** AP, CLEP General and Subject, institutional tests; 30 credit hours maximum for bachelor's degree.

ACADEMIC REQUIREMENTS. Freshmen must earn minimum GPA of 2.0 to continue in good standing. 94% of freshmen return for sophomore year. Students must declare major by end of first year. **Graduation requirements:** 60 hours for associate (18 in major), 127 hours for bachelor's (36 in major). Most students required to take courses in English, humanities, mathematics, philosophy/religion, biological/physical sciences, social sciences. **Postgraduate studies:** 7% enter law school, 10% enter medical school, 3% enter MBA programs, 15% enter other graduate study.

FRESHMAN ADMISSIONS. Selection criteria: School achievement record most important, followed by test scores and recommendations. **High school preparation:** 18 units required; 20 recommended. Required and recommended units include biological science 1-2, English 4, foreign language 2, mathematics 3-4, physical science 2 and social science 3-4. Science and business students should have 4 units of mathematics; science students, 4 science. **Test requirements:** SAT or ACT (SAT preferred); score report by May 1. **Additional information:** Physical therapy applicants are encouraged to do clinical observation and submit documentation as part of their application.

1992 FRESHMAN CLASS PROFILE. 1,776 men applied, 1,178 accepted, 404 enrolled; 2,582 women applied, 1,503 accepted, 503 enrolled. 85% had high school GPA of 3.0 or higher, 15% between 2.0 and 2.99. 29% were in top tenth and 60% were in top quarter of graduating class. **Academic background:** Mid 50% of enrolled freshmen had SAT-V between 460-540, SAT-M between 510-600. 99% submitted SAT scores. **Characteristics:** 51% from in state, 76% live in college housing, 3% have minority backgrounds. Average age is 18.

FALL-TERM APPLICATIONS. $30 fee, may be waived for applicants with need. Closing date March 1; priority given to applications received by February 1; applicants notified on a rolling basis; must reply by May 1. Interview recommended. Essay recommended. CRDA. Deferred and early admission available.

STUDENT LIFE. Housing: Dormitories (men, women, coed). Housing available for handicapped students. Theme houses (French, Spanish, international, service, education, arts) offered. Housing guaranteed for 4 years. **Activities:** Student government, film, magazine, radio, student newspaper, yearbook, debating, camera club, choral groups, concert band, drama, jazz band, music ensembles, musical theater, pep band, religious and social service organizations, veterans club, Young Democrats, Young Republicans, professional clubs, international students club, campus ministry, sports clubs, collegiate volunteers, multi-cultural club.

ATHLETICS. NCAA. **Intercollegiate:** Baseball M, basketball, cross-country, field hockey W, golf M, ice hockey M, lacrosse M, soccer, softball W, swimming, tennis, volleyball W, wrestling M. **Intramural:** Baseball M, basketball, bowling, cross-country, golf, handball, horseback riding, lacrosse, racquetball, rowing (crew), rugby, skiing, soccer, softball, swimming, table tennis, tennis, track and field, volleyball, water polo M, wrestling M. **Clubs:** Water polo W.

STUDENT SERVICES. Aptitude testing, career counseling, employment service for undergraduates, freshman orientation, health services, personal counseling, placement service for graduates, special adviser for adult students, veterans counselor, services/facilities for handicapped.

ANNUAL EXPENSES. Tuition and fees (1992-93): $10,095. **Room and board:** $5,112. **Books and supplies:** $500. **Other expenses:** $500.

FINANCIAL AID. 76% of freshmen, 80% of continuing students receive some form of aid. 88% of grants, 73% of loans, 72% of jobs based on need. 602 enrolled freshmen were judged to have need, 553 were offered aid. Academic, minority scholarships available. **Aid applications:** No closing date; priority given to applications received by February 15; applicants notified on a rolling basis beginning on or about March 15. **Additional information:** All applicants including scholarship candidates, must complete needs analysis document.

ADDRESS/TELEPHONE. Rev. Bernard R. McIlhenny, SJ, Dean of Admissions, University of Scranton, 800 Linden Street, Scranton, PA 18510-4699. (717) 941-7540. Fax: (717) 941-6369.

Ursinus College
Collegeville, Pennsylvania CB code: 2931

Admissions:	81% of applicants accepted
Based on:	••• School record
	•• Activities, recommendations, special talents, test scores
	• Essay, interview
Completion:	72% of freshmen end year in good standing
	75% graduate, 21% of these enter graduate study

4-year private liberal arts college, coed, affiliated with United Church of Christ. Founded in 1869. **Accreditation:** Regional. **Undergraduate enrollment:** 539 men, 558 women full time; 10 men, 6 women part time. **Faculty:** 120 total (93 full time), 91 with doctorates or other terminal degrees. **Location:** Suburban campus in small town; 25 miles from Philadelphia. **Calendar:** Semester, limited summer session. **Microcomputers:** 100 located in dormitories, libraries, classrooms, computer centers. **Special facilities:** Philip I. Berman Art Museum, observatory, Pennsylvania German studies archive.

DEGREES OFFERED. BA, BS. 323 bachelor's degrees awarded in 1992. 15% in business and management, 7% communications, 8% teacher education, 12% health sciences, 5% languages, 11% letters/literature, 8% physical sciences, 10% psychology, 17% social sciences.

UNDERGRADUATE MAJORS. Allied health, American public policy, anthropology, applied mathematics, applied mathematics/economics, biochemistry, biology, biophysics, business administration and management, business economics, chemistry, communications, computer and information sciences, East Asian studies, economics, English, foreign languages education, French, German, Greek (classical), health education, history, international relations, Japanese, Latin, mathematics, mathematics/computer science, philosophy, philosophy and religion, physical education, physics, political science and government, predentistry, prelaw, premedicine, preveterinary, psychology, religion, secondary education, sociology, Spanish.

ACADEMIC PROGRAMS. Accelerated program, double major, dual enrollment of high school students, honors program, independent study, internships, semester at sea, student-designed major, study abroad, teacher preparation, United Nations semester, Washington semester; liberal arts/career combination in engineering. **Placement/credit:** AP, CLEP Subject, institutional tests; 30 credit hours maximum for bachelor's degree.

ACADEMIC REQUIREMENTS. Freshmen must earn minimum GPA of 2.0 to continue in good standing. 91% of freshmen return for sophomore year. Students must declare major by end of first year. **Graduation requirements:** 128 hours for bachelor's (32 in major). Most students required to take courses in arts/fine arts, English, foreign languages, humanities, mathematics, biological/physical sciences, social sciences. **Postgraduate studies:** 2% enter law school, 5% enter medical school, 1% enter MBA programs, 13% enter other graduate study.

FRESHMAN ADMISSIONS. Selection criteria: Academic achievement of primary importance, including courses taken, grades received. Test scores also important. Personality, motivation, and activities considered. Rank in top fifth of class preferred. Alumni children and minorities receive special consideration. **High school preparation:** 16 units required; 20 recommended. Required and recommended units include English 4, foreign language 2-4, mathematics 3-4, social science 1-3 and science 1-3. Laboratory science 1 also required. Science majors should have a minumum of 4 units each in mathematics and science. **Test requirements:** SAT or ACT (SAT preferred); score report by February 15. ACH tests in English, mathematics, and 1 test of applicant's choice strongly recommended. Score report by February 15.

1992 FRESHMAN CLASS PROFILE. 731 men applied, 569 accepted, 208 enrolled; 669 women applied, 562 accepted, 202 enrolled. 95% had high school GPA of 3.0 or higher, 5% between 2.0 and 2.99. 45% were in top tenth and 70% were in top quarter of graduating class. **Academic background:** Mid 50% of enrolled freshmen had SAT-V between 460-560, SAT-M between 520-630. 94% submitted SAT scores. **Characteristics:** 61% from in state, 93% live in college housing, 13% have minority backgrounds, 1% are foreign students, 30% join fraternities/sororities. Average age is 18.

FALL-TERM APPLICATIONS. $30 fee, may be waived for applicants with need. Closing date February 15; applicants notified on or about April 1; must reply by May 1. Essay required. Interview recommended. CRDA. Deferred and early admission available. EDP-F. Students encouraged to apply in fall of their senior year. ACH strongly recommended. All students should take English Composition ACH. Science majors should take Mathematics-Level I or II and 1 science ACH.

STUDENT LIFE. Housing: Dormitories (men, women, coed). Approximately half student body housed in 24 homes that make up the college's Victorian residential village. **Activities:** Student government, magazine, radio, student newspaper, television, yearbook, choral groups, concert band, dance, drama, jazz band, music ensembles, musical theater, pep band, fraternities, sororities, Young Republicans, Young Democrats, religious and Bible study groups, minority student union, organization of Jewish students.

ATHLETICS. NCAA. **Intercollegiate:** Baseball M, basketball, cross-country, field hockey W, football M, golf, gymnastics W, lacrosse W, soccer M, softball W, swimming, tennis, track and field, volleyball W, wrestling M. **Intramural:** Basketball, fencing, handball, horseback riding, lacrosse M, racquetball, sailing, skiing, softball, squash, swimming, table tennis, tennis, volleyball, water polo M.

STUDENT SERVICES. Aptitude testing, career counseling, employment service for undergraduates, freshman orientation, health services, personal counseling, placement service for graduates, special adviser for adult students, services/facilities for handicapped.

ANNUAL EXPENSES. Tuition and fees: $14,265. **Room and board:** $4,900. **Books and supplies:** $500. **Other expenses:** $800.

FINANCIAL AID. 77% of freshmen, 74% of continuing students receive some form of aid. 74% of grants, 93% of loans, 33% of jobs based on need. 370 enrolled freshmen were judged to have need, all were offered aid. Academic, music/drama, art, leadership scholarships available. **Aid applications:** Closing date February 15; applicants notified on or about April 1; must reply by May 1 or within 2 weeks if notified thereafter.

ADDRESS/TELEPHONE. Richard G. DiFeliciantonio, Director of Admissions, Ursinus College, Box 1000 Main Street, Collegeville, PA 19426. (215) 489-4111. Fax: (215) 489-0627.

Valley Forge Christian College
Phoenixville, Pennsylvania CB code: 2579

4-year private Bible college, coed, affiliated with Assemblies of God. Founded in 1938. **Undergraduate enrollment:** 519 men and women. **Faculty:** 36 total (18 full time), 4 with doctorates or other terminal degrees. **Location:** Rural campus in large town; 25 miles from Philadelphia. **Calendar:** Semester, limited summer session. **Microcomputers:** Located in libraries.

DEGREES OFFERED. B. 62 bachelor's degrees awarded in 1992. 100% in philosophy, religion, theology.

UNDERGRADUATE MAJORS. Bible studies, missionary studies, religious education, religious music, theological studies.

ACADEMIC PROGRAMS. Accelerated program, double major, dual enrollment of high school students, honors program, independent study, internships, study abroad. **Remedial services:** Preadmission summer program, reduced course load, remedial instruction, special counselor. **Placement/credit:** AP, CLEP General and Subject, institutional tests; 30 credit hours maximum for bachelor's degree.

ACADEMIC REQUIREMENTS. Freshmen must earn minimum GPA of 1.6 to continue in good standing. 68% of freshmen return for sophomore year. Students must declare major by end of first year. **Graduation requirements:** 126 hours for bachelor's (40 in major). Most students required to take courses in English, history, humanities, mathematics, philosophy/religion, biological/physical sciences, social sciences.

FRESHMAN ADMISSIONS. Selection criteria: School achievement record, church leader and pastor recommendations, SAT or ACT scores. Recommended units include biological science 2, English 4, foreign language 2, mathematics 2, physical science 2 and social science 4. **Test requirements:** SAT or ACT (SAT preferred); score report by August 1.

1992 FRESHMAN CLASS PROFILE. 213 men and women enrolled. 32% had high school GPA of 3.0 or higher, 60% between 2.0 and 2.99. **Characteristics:** 30% from in state, 90% live in college housing, 8% have minority backgrounds, 2% are foreign students. Average age is 19.

FALL-TERM APPLICATIONS. $25 fee. Closing date August 1; applicants notified on a rolling basis. Essay required. Interview recommended. CRDA. Deferred and early admission available. EDP-F.

STUDENT LIFE. Housing: Dormitories (men, women); apartment housing available. **Activities:** Student government, student newspaper, yearbook, choral groups, concert band, drama, music ensembles. **Additional information:** Religious observance required.

ATHLETICS. Intercollegiate: Baseball M, basketball, cross-country M, soccer M, softball W, volleyball W. **Intramural:** Basketball, handball W, softball M, volleyball.

STUDENT SERVICES. Aptitude testing, career counseling, employment service for undergraduates, freshman orientation, health services, personal counseling, placement service for graduates, veterans counselor, services/facilities for handicapped.

ANNUAL EXPENSES. Tuition and fees: $4,196. **Room and board:** $3,022. **Books and supplies:** $450. **Other expenses:** $1,200.

FINANCIAL AID. 75% of freshmen, 84% of continuing students receive some form of aid. 89% of grants, 78% of loans, 82% of jobs based on need. 104 enrolled freshmen were judged to have need, 102 were offered aid. Academic, music/drama, state/district residency, leadership, alumni affiliation, religious affiliation, minority scholarships available. **Aid applications:** No closing date; priority given to applications received by May 1; applicants notified on a rolling basis; must reply within 2 weeks.

ADDRESS/TELEPHONE. Jim Barco, Director of Admissions, Valley Forge Christian College, 1401 Charlestown Road, Phoenixville, PA 19460. (215) 935-0450. (800) 432-VFCC. Fax: (215) 935-9353.

Valley Forge Military College
Wayne, Pennsylvania CB code: 2955

Admissions: 88% of applicants accepted
Based on: ••• Interview, test scores
•• Activities, recommendations, school record
• Essay, special talents
Completion: 90% of freshmen end year in good standing
88% enter 4-year programs

2-year private junior, military college, men only, nondenominational. Founded in 1928. **Accreditation:** Regional. **Undergraduate enrollment:** 148 men full time. **Faculty:** 23 total (11 full time), 2 with doctorates or other terminal degrees. **Location:** Suburban campus in small town; 15 miles from Philadelphia. **Calendar:** Semester. **Microcomputers:** 12 located in libraries, classrooms, computer centers.

DEGREES OFFERED. AA, AS. 42 associate degrees awarded in 1992. 31% in business and management, 45% multi/interdisciplinary studies, 17% parks/recreation, protective services, public affairs.

UNDERGRADUATE MAJORS. Business administration and management, business and management, criminal justice studies, liberal/general studies, military science (Army), music, physical sciences.

ACADEMIC PROGRAMS. 2-year transfer program, double major, dual enrollment of high school students, honors program. **Remedial services:** Reduced course load, remedial instruction, tutoring. **ROTC:** Air Force, Army. **Placement/credit:** AP, institutional tests; 30 credit hours maximum for associate degree.

ACADEMIC REQUIREMENTS. Freshmen must earn minimum GPA of 1.75 to continue in good standing. 78% of freshmen return for sophomore year. Students must declare major by end of first year. **Graduation requirements:** 60 hours for associate. Most students required to take courses in English, foreign languages, history, mathematics, biological/physical sciences.

FRESHMAN ADMISSIONS. Selection criteria: School achievement record, test scores, and personal character most important. Recommended units include biological science 1, English 4, mathematics 2 and physical science 2. **Test requirements:** SAT or ACT (SAT preferred); score report by August 17.

1992 FRESHMAN CLASS PROFILE. 165 men applied, 145 accepted, 101 enrolled. **Academic background:** Mid 50% of enrolled freshmen had SAT-V between 370-430, SAT-M between 420-480. 90% submitted SAT scores. **Characteristics:** 33% from in state, 100% live in college housing, 10% have minority backgrounds, 14% are foreign students. Average age is 18.

FALL-TERM APPLICATIONS. $25 fee. No closing date; applicants notified on a rolling basis. Interview recommended. CRDA. Deferred and early admission available.

STUDENT LIFE. Housing: Dormitories (men). **Activities:** Student government, radio, student newspaper, yearbook, choral groups, concert band, jazz band, marching band, service organization, sports clubs. **Additional information:** Religious observance required.

ATHLETICS. Intercollegiate: Basketball, cross-country, football, rifle, soccer, tennis. **Intramural:** Baseball, basketball, bowling, football, golf, lacrosse, rugby, softball, volleyball. **Clubs:** Intercollegiate horseback riding.

STUDENT SERVICES. Aptitude testing, career counseling, freshman orientation, health services, personal counseling, placement service for graduates.

ANNUAL EXPENSES. Tuition and fees: $10,470. **Room and board:** $6,350. **Comprehensive fee:** $16,820. **Books and supplies:** $450. **Other expenses:** $250.

FINANCIAL AID. 80% of freshmen, 65% of continuing students receive some form of aid. 77% of grants, 95% of loans, all jobs based on need. Music/drama, athletic scholarships available. **Aid applications:** No closing date; priority given to applications received by May 1; applicants notified on a rolling basis beginning on or about July 15; must reply by May 1 or within 2 weeks if notified thereafter. **Additional information:** Students enrolled in advanced military science program can receive up to $4,000 from federal government. In addition, competitively awarded ROTC scholarships pay average of another $6,600 per year for direct educational expenses.

ADDRESS/TELEPHONE. Col. Richard M. Artz, Director of Admissions and Registrar, Valley Forge Military College, 1001 Eagle Road, Wayne, PA 19087-3695. (215) 688-3151 ext. 261. (800) 234-8362. Fax: (215) 668-1545.

Villanova University
Villanova, Pennsylvania CB code: 2959

Admissions: 76% of applicants accepted
Based on: ••• School record, test scores
•• Essay
• Activities, recommendations, special talents
Completion: 93% of freshmen end year in good standing
85% graduate, 32% of these enter graduate study

4-year private university, coed, affiliated with Roman Catholic Church. Founded in 1842. **Accreditation:** Regional. **Undergraduate enrollment:** 3,130 men, 3,069 women full time; 853 men, 750 women part time. **Graduate enrollment:** 581 men, 510 women full time; 1,274 men, 1,123 women part time. **Faculty:** 898 total (552 full time), 743 with doctorates or other terminal degrees. **Location:** Suburban campus in small town; 12 miles from Philadelphia. **Calendar:** Semester, extensive summer session. Extensive evening/early morning classes. **Microcomputers:** 200 located in libraries, classrooms, computer centers. **Special facilities:** Astronomy and astrophysics observatories, art gallery, electron microscope, research with NASA, arboretum.

DEGREES OFFERED. AA, AS, BA, BS, MA, MS, MBA, PhD, JD. 9 associate degrees awarded in 1992. 100% in letters/literature. 1,843 bachelor's degrees awarded. 33% in business and management, 6% communications, 13% engineering, 7% health sciences, 7% letters/literature, 6% life sciences, 5% psychology, 12% social sciences. Graduate degrees offered in 25 major fields of study.

UNDERGRADUATE MAJORS. Associate: Biological and physical sciences, liberal/general studies. **Bachelor's:** Accounting, astronomy, atmospheric sciences and meteorology, biological and physical sciences, biology, business administration and management, business and management, business economics, chemical engineering, chemistry, civil engineering, classics, communications, computer and information sciences, computer engineering, cytotechnology, dental hygiene, diagnostic imaging, economics, electrical/electronics/communications engineering, English, finance, French, geography, German, history, human services, international business management, liberal/general studies, marketing management, mathematics, mechanical engineering, medical laboratory technologies, naval science (Navy, Marines), nursing, optometry, philosophy, physical therapy, physics, planetarium education and management, political science and government, predentistry, premedicine, psychology, religion, secondary education, sociology, Spanish.

ACADEMIC PROGRAMS. 2-year transfer program, accelerated program, double major, dual enrollment of high school students, honors program, independent study, internships, study abroad, teacher preparation, Washington semester, cross-registration, cooperative certification programs in elementary education with Rosemont College and in special education with Cabrini College; liberal arts/career combination in health sciences; combined bachelor's/graduate program in medicine. **Remedial services:** Preadmission summer program, reduced course load, remedial instruction, special counselor, tutoring, Academic Advancement Program. **ROTC:** Air Force, Army, Naval. **Placement/credit:** AP, institutional tests; 30 credit hours maximum for bachelor's degree.

ACADEMIC REQUIREMENTS. 92% of freshmen return for sophomore year. Students must declare major by end of second year. **Graduation requirements:** 60 hours for associate, 122 hours for bachelor's (30 in major). Most students required to take courses in arts/fine arts, English, history, humanities, mathematics, philosophy/religion, biological/physical sciences, social sciences. **Postgraduate studies:** 7% enter law school, 2% enter medical school, 1% enter MBA programs, 22% enter other graduate study. **Additional information:** Freshmen minimum GPA varies by college.

FRESHMAN ADMISSIONS. Selection criteria: High school record, class rank, standardized test scores, counselor recommendation, essay, extra curricular activities considered. **High school preparation:** 16 units required. Required units include biological science 1, English 4, foreign language 2, mathematics 4, physical science 2 and social science 3. **Test requirements:** SAT or ACT (SAT preferred); score report by January 31. Foreign language ACH required of liberal arts and science applicants. German preferred language test for science majors. Score report by June 15.

1992 FRESHMAN CLASS PROFILE. 3,363 men applied, 2,556 accepted, 842 enrolled; 3,248 women applied, 2,498 accepted, 851 enrolled. 32% were in top tenth of graduating class. **Academic background:** Mid 50% of enrolled freshmen had SAT-V between 480-580, SAT-M between 550-650. 95% submitted SAT scores. **Characteristics:** 30% from in state, 89% live in college housing, 8% have minority backgrounds, 1% are foreign students, 30% join fraternities/sororities. Average age is 18.

FALL-TERM APPLICATIONS. $40 fee, may be waived for applicants with need. Closing date January 15; applicants notified on or about April 1; must reply by May 1. Essay required. CRDA. Deferred and early admission available. Institutional early decision plan. Application date for early action December 15; accepted applicants notified January 15. Commuting students notified of decisions on a rolling basis beginning January 15.

STUDENT LIFE. Housing: Dormitories (men, women, coed). On-campus housing available for transfer students on space available basis. **Activities:** Student government, magazine, radio, student newspaper, yearbook, choral groups, concert band, dance, drama, jazz band, marching band, music ensembles, musical theater, pep band, fraternities, sororities, Special Olympics, Amnesty International, Villanovans for Life, Black Cultural Society, Big Brother/Sister, Committee for the Homeless, Villanova Environmental Group, Project Sunshine, University Christian Outreach, International Club, various club sports.

ATHLETICS. NCAA. **Intercollegiate:** Baseball M, basketball, cross-country, diving, field hockey W, football M, golf M, ice hockey M, lacrosse, soccer, softball W, swimming, tennis, track and field, volleyball W, water polo M. **Intramural:** Basketball, field hockey W, football M, skiing, soccer, softball, volleyball. **Clubs:** Intramural touch football W.

STUDENT SERVICES. Aptitude testing, career counseling, employment service for undergraduates, freshman orientation, health services, personal counseling, placement service for graduates, special adviser for adult students, services/facilities for handicapped.

ANNUAL EXPENSES. Tuition and fees: $14,460. Tuition and fees vary by program. **Room and board:** $6,060. **Books and supplies:** $800. **Other expenses:** $1,200.

FINANCIAL AID. 63% of freshmen, 60% of continuing students receive some form of aid. 48% of grants, 71% of loans, 40% of jobs based on need. 755 enrolled freshmen were judged to have need, all were offered aid. Academic, athletic, religious affiliation, minority scholarships available. **Aid applications:** Closing date March 15; priority given to applications received by February 15; applicants notified on or about April 1; must reply by May 1.

ADDRESS/TELEPHONE. Stephen R. Merritt, Director of Admissions, Villanova University, Villanova, PA 19085-1672. (215) 645-4000. (800) 338-7927. Fax: (215) 645-6450.

Washington and Jefferson College
Washington, Pennsylvania — CB code: 2967

Admissions: 80% of applicants accepted
Based on: ••• School record
•• Activities, interview, recommendations, test scores
• Essay, special talents
Completion: 93% of freshmen end year in good standing
84% graduate, 60% of these enter graduate study

4-year private liberal arts college, coed. Founded in 1781. **Accreditation:** Regional. **Undergraduate enrollment:** 624 men, 520 women full time; 7 men, 9 women part time. **Faculty:** 98 total (86 full time), 71 with doctorates or other terminal degrees. **Location:** Suburban campus in large town; 25 miles from Pittsburgh. **Calendar:** 4-1-4, limited summer session. **Microcomputers:** 203 located in libraries, classrooms, computer centers. **Special facilities:** Abernathy Biological Field Station, extensive library containing microfilm, recordings, slides and musical scores.

DEGREES OFFERED. BA. 262 bachelor's degrees awarded in 1992. 30% in business and management, 6% languages, 9% letters/literature, 14% life sciences, 8% physical sciences, 7% psychology, 22% social sciences.

UNDERGRADUATE MAJORS. Accounting, art education, biology, business administration and management, business and management, chemistry, computer and information sciences, economics, English, English education, entrepreneurial studies, foreign languages education, French, German, history, liberal/general studies, mathematics, mathematics education, medical laboratory technologies, philosophy, physics, political science and government, predentistry, prelaw, premedicine, preveterinary, psychology, science education, secondary education, social studies education, sociology, Spanish.

ACADEMIC PROGRAMS. Accelerated program, double major, dual enrollment of high school students, honors program, independent study, internships, student-designed major, study abroad, teacher preparation, Washington semester; liberal arts/career combination in engineering, health sciences. **Remedial services:** Preadmission summer program, reduced course load, remedial instruction, tutoring. **Placement/credit:** AP, CLEP General and Subject, institutional tests; 72 credit hours maximum for bachelor's degree.

ACADEMIC REQUIREMENTS. No policy requiring minimum GPA; records of students having academic difficulty are reviewed individually. 92% of freshmen return for sophomore year. Students must declare major by end of second year. **Graduation requirements:** 144 hours for bachelor's. Most students required to take courses in arts/fine arts, English, history, humanities, mathematics, philosophy/religion, biological/physical sciences, social sciences. **Postgraduate studies:** 18% enter law school, 21% enter medical school, 5% enter MBA programs, 16% enter other graduate study.

FRESHMAN ADMISSIONS. Selection criteria: Academic and extracurricular interests and achievements, character, recommendation from guidance counselor or principal, class rank, test scores, interview. **High school preparation:** 15 units required. Required units include English 3, foreign language 2, mathematics 3, social science 2 and science 1. **Test requirements:** SAT or ACT; score report by March 1. 3 ACH (including English Composition) required of applicants submitting SAT scores. Score report by September 1.

1992 FRESHMAN CLASS PROFILE. 95% had high school GPA of 3.0 or higher, 5% between 2.0 and 2.99. **Academic background:** Mid 50% of enrolled freshmen had SAT-V between 460-590, SAT-M between 490-630; ACT composite between 19-25. 93% submitted SAT scores, 7% submitted ACT scores. **Characteristics:** 70% from in state, 95% live in college housing, 10% have minority backgrounds, 1% are foreign students, 53% join fraternities/sororities. Average age is 18.

FALL-TERM APPLICATIONS. $25 fee, may be waived for applicants with need. Closing date March 1; applicants notified on a rolling basis beginning on or about January 15; must reply by May 1. Interview recommended. Essay recommended. CRDA. Deferred and early admission available. EDP-F.

STUDENT LIFE. Housing: Dormitories (men, women, coed); fraternity, cooperative housing available. **Activities:** Student government, magazine, radio, student newspaper, yearbook, choral groups, concert band, drama, jazz band, music ensembles, pep band, fraternities, sororities, Newman Club, Student Christian Association, Hillel, premedical and other special interest clubs, Young Republicans, Women's Council.

ATHLETICS. NCAA. **Intercollegiate:** Baseball M, basketball, cross-country, diving, football M, golf M, lacrosse M, soccer, softball W, swimming, tennis, track and field, volleyball W, wrestling M. **Intramural:** Basketball, bowling, diving, handball, racquetball, softball, squash, swimming, table tennis, tennis, track and field, volleyball, wrestling M.

STUDENT SERVICES. Career counseling, employment service for undergraduates, freshman orientation, health services, personal counseling, placement service for graduates, special adviser for adult students, veterans counselor, peer counseling.

ANNUAL EXPENSES. Tuition and fees: $15,620. **Room and board:** $3,740. **Books and supplies:** $200. **Other expenses:** $500.

FINANCIAL AID. 84% of freshmen, 78% of continuing students receive some form of aid. 90% of grants, 84% of loans, all jobs based on need. 262 enrolled freshmen were judged to have need, 261 were offered aid. Academic scholarships available. **Aid applications:** No closing date; priority given to applications received by March 15; applicants notified on a rolling basis beginning on or about February 15; must reply by May 1 or within 15 days if notified thereafter.

ADDRESS/TELEPHONE. Thomas P. O'Connor, Director of Admissions, Washington and Jefferson College, South Lincoln Street, Washington, PA 15301. (412) 223-6025. Fax: (412) 223-5271.

Waynesburg College
Waynesburg, Pennsylvania — CB code: 2969

Admissions: 75% of applicants accepted
Based on: ••• Interview, school record
•• Activities, essay, recommendations
• Test scores
Completion: 50% graduate, 18% of these enter graduate study

4-year private liberal arts college, coed, affiliated with Presbyterian Church (USA). Founded in 1849. **Accreditation:** Regional. **Undergraduate enrollment:** 520 men, 719 women full time; 24 men, 45 women part time. **Graduate enrollment:** 3 women full time; 24 men, 13 women part time. **Faculty:** 100 total (66 full time), 41 with doctorates or other terminal degrees. **Location:** Rural campus in small town; 50 miles from Pittsburgh. **Calendar:** Semester, extensive summer session. **Microcomputers:** 250 located in libraries, classrooms, computer centers. **Special facilities:** Geological museum, historical museum, art gallery.

DEGREES OFFERED. AA, AS, BA, BS, MBA. 17 associate degrees awarded in 1992. 35% in business and management, 29% business/office and marketing/distribution, 24% multi/interdisciplinary studies, 12% visual and performing arts. 225 bachelor's degrees awarded. 28% in business and management, 8% communications, 12% teacher education, 26% health sciences, 8% parks/recreation, protective services, public affairs. Graduate degrees offered in 1 major field of study.

UNDERGRADUATE MAJORS. Associate: Business administration and management, business and office, finance, legal secretary, liberal/general studies, medical secretary, secretarial and related programs, visual and performing arts. **Bachelor's:** Accounting, biology, business administration and management, business and management, business education, chemistry, clinical laboratory science, communications, computer and information sciences, criminal justice studies, economics, elementary education, English, English education, finance, hazardous materials management, history, journalism, management science, marketing management, mathematics, mathematics education, nursing, political science and government, predentistry, prelaw, premedicine, psychology, public administration, radio/television broadcasting, science education, secondary education, small business management and ownership, social sciences, social studies education, sociology, sports information broadcasting, sports medicine, visual and performing arts.

ACADEMIC PROGRAMS. Accelerated program, double major, dual enrollment of high school students, honors program, independent study, internships, study abroad, teacher preparation; liberal arts/career combination in engineering. **Remedial services:** Learning center, preadmission summer program, reduced course load, special counselor, tutoring. **Placement/credit:** AP, CLEP General and Subject, institutional tests; 15 credit hours maximum for bachelor's degree.

ACADEMIC REQUIREMENTS. Freshmen must earn minimum GPA of 2.0 to continue in good standing. 75% of freshmen return for sophomore year. Students must declare major by end of second year. **Graduation requirements:** 60 hours for associate (30 in major), 124 hours for bachelor's (45 in major). Most students required to take courses in arts/fine arts, computer science, English, history, humanities, mathematics, philosophy/religion, biological/physical sciences, social sciences. **Postgraduate studies:** 80% from 2-year programs enter 4-year programs. 18% enter other graduate study. **Additional information:** Nursing majors must complete 126 credit hours for bachelor of science degree.

FRESHMAN ADMISSIONS. Selection criteria: High school achievement and activities, community activities, interview, and recommendations considered. **High school preparation:** 16 units required. Required and recommended units include English 4, mathematics 3, social science 2 and science 2. Biological science 2, foreign language 2 and physical science 1 recommended.

1992 FRESHMAN CLASS PROFILE. 745 men applied, 511 accepted, 194 enrolled; 588 women applied, 495 accepted, 248 enrolled. 35% had high school GPA of 3.0 or higher, 60% between 2.0 and 2.99. **Characteristics:** 86% from in state, 78% live in college housing, 6% have minority backgrounds, 1% are foreign students, 10% join fraternities/sororities. Average age is 18.

FALL-TERM APPLICATIONS. $15 fee. No closing date; priority given to applications received by September 1; applicants notified on a rolling basis; must reply within 8 weeks. Interview recommended. Essay recommended. Early admission available.

STUDENT LIFE. Housing: Dormitories (men, women, coed). **Activities:** Student government, magazine, radio, student newspaper, television, yearbook, choral groups, concert band, drama, jazz band, marching band, music ensembles, musical theater, pep band, fraternities, sororities, Fellowship of Christian Athletes, Newman Club, International Student Organization, Black Student Union, Waynesburg Christian Fellowship, Bonner Scholars (service group).

ATHLETICS. NCAA. **Intercollegiate:** Baseball M, basketball, football M, golf M, soccer, softball W, tennis, volleyball W, wrestling M. **Intramural:** Archery, baseball, basketball M, bowling, cross-country, golf, racquetball, soccer, softball, table tennis, tennis, volleyball W.

STUDENT SERVICES. Aptitude testing, career counseling, employment service for undergraduates, freshman orientation, health services, personal counseling, placement service for graduates, special adviser for adult students, services/facilities for handicapped.

ANNUAL EXPENSES. Tuition and fees: $8,580. **Room and board:** $3,380. **Books and supplies:** $500. **Other expenses:** $751.

FINANCIAL AID. 93% of freshmen, 83% of continuing students receive some form of aid. 88% of grants, 88% of loans, 30% of jobs based on need. 404 enrolled freshmen were judged to have need, all were offered aid. Academic, leadership scholarships available. **Aid applications:** No closing date; priority given to applications received by March 15; applicants notified on a rolling basis beginning on or about January 1; must reply within 2 weeks.

ADDRESS/TELEPHONE. Robin L. Moore, Director of Admissions, Waynesburg College, 51 West College Street, Waynesburg, PA 15370. (412) 852-3248. (800) 225-7393. Fax: (412) 627-6416.

West Chester University of Pennsylvania

West Chester, Pennsylvania — CB code: 2659

Admissions:	51% of applicants accepted
Based on:	••• School record
	•• Essay, test scores
	• Activities, interview, recommendations, special talents
Completion:	90% of freshmen end year in good standing
	45% graduate, 14% of these enter graduate study

4-year public university, coed. Founded in 1871. **Accreditation:** Regional. **Undergraduate enrollment:** 2,920 men, 4,763 women full time; 906 men, 1,193 women part time. **Graduate enrollment:** 139 men, 268 women full time; 532 men, 1,085 women part time. **Faculty:** 659 total (612 full time), 402 with doctorates or other terminal degrees. **Location:** Suburban campus in large town; 23 miles from Philadelphia. **Calendar:** Semester, extensive summer session. Saturday classes. **Microcomputers:** 238 located in dormitories, libraries, classrooms, computer centers. **Special facilities:** Darlington Herbarium, Robert B. Gordon Natural Area for Environmental Studies, music library, IGA Art Gallery, planetarium.

DEGREES OFFERED. AA, AS, BA, BS, BFA, MA, MS, MBA, MEd. 10 associate degrees awarded in 1992. 10% in communications, 70% allied health, 20% multi/interdisciplinary studies. 1,598 bachelor's degrees awarded. 17% in business and management, 35% education, 5% health sciences, 7% letters/literature, 7% multi/interdisciplinary studies, 9% parks/recreation, protective services, public affairs, 6% social sciences. Graduate degrees offered in 57 major fields of study.

UNDERGRADUATE MAJORS. Associate: Applied media technology, graphic arts technology, industrial arts, liberal/general studies, respiratory therapy, respiratory therapy technology. **Bachelor's:** Accounting, allied health, American literature, American studies, anthropology, astronomy, athletic training, biochemistry, biology, business administration and management, business economics, cell biology, chemistry, clinical chemistry, cognitive psychology, communications, community health work, comparative literature, computer and information sciences, criminal justice studies, dental assistant, dental hygiene, dramatic arts, early childhood education, earth sciences, ecology, elementary education, English education, English literature, environmental health, fine arts, foreign languages education, forensic chemistry, French, geochemistry, geography, geology, German, gerontology, health care administration, health education, history, international relations, jazz, Latin, liberal/general studies, marketing management, mathematics, mathematics education, microbiology, molecular biology, music, music education, music history and appreciation, music performance, music theory and composition, neonatal/pediatric care, nursing, philosophy, physical education, physics, planetary science, political science and government, preengineering, prelaw, premedicine, psychology, public health laboratory science, religion, Russian, science education, social science education, social studies education, social work, sociology, Spanish, special education, speech, speech correction, speech pathology/audiology, studio art.

ACADEMIC PROGRAMS. 2-year transfer program, accelerated program, double major, honors program, independent study, internships, student-designed major, study abroad, teacher preparation, visiting/exchange student program, cross-registration; liberal arts/career combination in engineering. **Remedial services:** Learning center, preadmission summer program, reduced course load, remedial instruction, special counselor, tutoring. **Placement/credit:** AP, CLEP Subject, institutional tests; 30 credit hours maximum for bachelor's degree.

ACADEMIC REQUIREMENTS. Freshmen must earn minimum GPA of 2.0 to continue in good standing. 80% of freshmen return for sophomore year. Students must declare major on application. **Graduation requirements:** 64 hours for associate (30 in major), 128 hours for bachelor's (30 in major). Most students required to take courses in arts/fine arts, English, foreign languages, history, humanities, mathematics, philosophy/religion, biological/physical sciences, social sciences. **Postgraduate studies:** 30% from 2-year programs enter 4-year programs.

FRESHMAN ADMISSIONS. Selection criteria: School achievement record, class rank, and test scores. **High school preparation:** 16 units recommended. Recommended units include biological science 2, English 4, foreign language 2, mathematics 3, physical science 1 and social science 4. **Test requirements:** SAT or ACT (SAT preferred); score report by July 1.

1992 FRESHMAN CLASS PROFILE. 2,579 men applied, 1,223 accepted, 498 enrolled; 3,963 women applied, 2,118 accepted, 887 enrolled. 50% had high school GPA of 3.0 or higher, 50% between 2.0 and 2.99. 11% were in top tenth and 41% were in top quarter of graduating class. **Academic background:** Mid 50% of enrolled freshmen had SAT-V between 410-490, SAT-M between 450-550. 99% submitted SAT scores. **Characteristics:** 79% from in state, 87% live in college housing, 12% have minority backgrounds, 1% are foreign students, 10% join fraternities/sororities. Average age is 18.

FALL-TERM APPLICATIONS. $25 fee, may be waived for applicants with need. Closing date April 1; priority given to applications received by February 1; applicants notified on a rolling basis; must reply by March 15 or within 4 weeks if notified thereafter. Extension may be requested and granted until May 1. Audition required for music applicants. Essay required. Interview recommended for athletic training, respiratory care, music, preprofessional program applicants. Deferred and early admission available. All early admission candidates must interview with admissions officer.

STUDENT LIFE. Housing: Dormitories (women, coed); fraternity housing available. **Activities:** Student government, film, magazine, radio, student newspaper, television, yearbook, choral groups, concert band, dance, drama, jazz band, marching band, music ensembles, musical theater, opera, symphony orchestra, fraternities, sororities, Hillel, Newman Club, Crusade for Christ, International Student Association, Black Student Union, Spanish Student Union, variety of social service organizations.

ATHLETICS. NCAA. **Intercollegiate:** Baseball M, basketball, cross-country, diving, field hockey W, football M, golf M, gymnastics W, lacrosse, soccer, softball W, swimming, tennis, track and field, volleyball W. **Intramural:** Badminton, baseball M, basketball, boxing M, cross-country, fencing, football M, ice hockey M, racquetball, rugby, skiing, soccer W, tennis, volleyball, water polo.

STUDENT SERVICES. Aptitude testing, career counseling, employment service for undergraduates, freshman orientation, health services, on-campus day care, personal counseling, placement service for graduates, special adviser for adult students, veterans counselor, services/facilities for handicapped.

ANNUAL EXPENSES. Tuition and fees (1992-93): $3,158, $3,394 additional for out-of-state students. **Room and board:** $3,630. **Books and supplies:** $450. **Other expenses:** $1,000.

FINANCIAL AID. 65% of freshmen, 50% of continuing students receive some form of aid. 71% of grants, 49% of loans, 17% of jobs based on need. 1,000 enrolled freshmen were judged to have need, 950 were offered aid. Academic, music/drama, athletic, alumni affiliation, minority scholarships available. **Aid applications:** No closing date; priority given to applications received by March 15; applicants notified on a rolling basis beginning on or about April 15; must reply within 3 weeks.

ADDRESS/TELEPHONE. Marsha Haug, Director of Admissions, West Chester University of Pennsylvania, Messikomer Hall, West Chester, PA 19383. (215) 436-3411.

Westminster College
New Wilmington, Pennsylvania CB code: 2975

Admissions: 85% of applicants accepted
Based on: ••• School record, test scores
•• Activities, essay, interview, recommendations
• Special talents
Completion: 90% of freshmen end year in good standing
19% enter graduate study

4-year private liberal arts college, coed, affiliated with Presbyterian Church (USA). Founded in 1852. **Accreditation:** Regional. **Undergraduate enrollment:** 593 men, 754 women full time; 30 men, 56 women part time. **Graduate enrollment:** 45 men, 63 women part time. **Faculty:** 140 total (98 full time), 86 with doctorates or other terminal degrees. **Location:** Rural campus in small town; 60 miles from Pittsburgh, 17 miles from Youngstown, Ohio. **Calendar:** 4-1-4, limited summer session. Extensive evening/early morning classes. **Microcomputers:** 160 located in libraries, classrooms, computer centers. **Special facilities:** Art gallery, observatory, environmental outdoor laboratory, planetarium, electron microscopes, radar defractor.

DEGREES OFFERED. BA, BS, MEd. 324 bachelor's degrees awarded in 1992. 27% in business and management, 9% communications, 16% teacher education, 10% life sciences, 5% mathematics, 17% social sciences. Graduate degrees offered in 5 major fields of study.

UNDERGRADUATE MAJORS. Accounting, art education, biology, business administration and management, business economics, chemistry, cognitive science, communications, computer and information sciences, dramatic arts, economics, elementary education, English, environmental science, French, German, history, industrial and organizational psychology, information sciences and systems, intercultural studies, international business management, international relations, labor/industrial relations, Latin, management science, mathematics, molecular biology, music, music education, music performance, organizational behavior, philosophy, physics, political science and government, preengineering, prelaw, psychobiology, psychology, public relations, radio/television broadcasting, religion, religious education, religious music, secondary education, sociology, Spanish, studio art, telecommunications.

ACADEMIC PROGRAMS. Accelerated program, double major, honors program, independent study, internships, semester at sea, student-designed major, study abroad, teacher preparation, visiting/exchange student program, Washington semester, 3-2 engineering programs with Case Western Reserve University (OH), Penn State, Washington University(MO); liberal arts/career combination in engineering. **Remedial services:** Learning center, reduced course load, tutoring, college reading and study skills program. **Placement/credit:** AP, CLEP General, institutional tests.

ACADEMIC REQUIREMENTS. Freshmen must earn minimum GPA of 1.8 to continue in good standing. 94% of freshmen return for sophomore year. Students must declare major by end of second year. **Graduation requirements:** 126 hours for bachelor's (35 in major). Most students required to take courses in arts/fine arts, computer science, English, foreign languages, history, humanities, mathematics, philosophy/religion, biological/physical sciences, social sciences. **Postgraduate studies:** 3% enter law school, 3% enter medical school, 2% enter MBA programs, 11% enter other graduate study.

FRESHMAN ADMISSIONS. Selection criteria: Test scores, class rank, minimum 2.5 GPA, recommendations, activities. **High school preparation:** 16 units required; 20 recommended. Required and recommended units include English 4, foreign language 2, mathematics 3-4, social science 2-4 and science 2-3. **Test requirements:** SAT or ACT; score report by July 1.

1992 FRESHMAN CLASS PROFILE. 502 men applied, 399 accepted, 150 enrolled; 546 women applied, 496 accepted, 216 enrolled. 55% had high school GPA of 3.0 or higher, 45% between 2.0 and 2.99. **Academic background:** Mid 50% of enrolled freshmen had SAT-V between 420-520, SAT-M between 460-570; ACT composite between 21-27. 91% submitted SAT scores, 45% submitted ACT scores. **Characteristics:** 80% from in state, 97% live in college housing, 1% have minority backgrounds, 45% join fraternities/sororities. Average age is 18.

FALL-TERM APPLICATIONS. $20 fee, may be waived for applicants with need. No closing date; priority given to applications received by March 1; applicants notified on a rolling basis beginning on or about October 1; must reply by May 1 or within 4 weeks if notified thereafter. Essay required. Interview recommended. Audition recommended for music applicants. Portfolio recommended for art applicants. CRDA. Deferred and early admission available.

STUDENT LIFE. Housing: Dormitories (men, women); fraternity housing available. **Activities:** Student government, magazine, radio, student newspaper, television, yearbook, choral groups, concert band, dance, drama, jazz band, marching band, music ensembles, symphony orchestra, fraternities, sororities, Fellowship of Christian Athletes, mock convention, clown ministry, service organizations, social awareness and action groups, Students in Action who Value the Environment (SAVE), Habitat for Humanity.

ATHLETICS. NAIA. **Intercollegiate:** Baseball M, basketball, cross-country, diving, football M, golf M, soccer M, softball W, swimming, tennis, track and field M, volleyball W. **Intramural:** Basketball, racquetball, rugby M, skiing, soccer W, softball, volleyball.

STUDENT SERVICES. Aptitude testing, career counseling, employment service for undergraduates, freshman orientation, health services, personal counseling, placement service for graduates, special adviser for adult students, services/facilities for handicapped.

ANNUAL EXPENSES. Tuition and fees: $11,770. **Room and board:** $3,270. **Books and supplies:** $425. **Other expenses:** $675.

FINANCIAL AID. 70% of freshmen, 70% of continuing students receive some form of aid. 78% of grants, all loans, 54% of jobs based on need. 269 enrolled freshmen were judged to have need, all were offered aid. Academic, music/drama, athletic, leadership, alumni affiliation scholarships available. **Aid applications:** Closing date June 30; priority given to applications received by May 1; applicants notified on a rolling basis beginning on or about March 1; must reply by May 1 or within 4 weeks if notified thereafter.

ADDRESS/TELEPHONE. R. Dana Paul, Director of Admissions, Westminster College, South Market Street, New Wilmington, PA 16172-0001. (412) 946-7100. Fax: (412) 946-7171.

Westmoreland County Community College
Youngwood, Pennsylvania CB code: 2968

2-year public community college, coed. Founded in 1970. **Accreditation:** Regional. **Undergraduate enrollment:** 1,158 men, 1,387 women full time; 1,505 men, 2,797 women part time. **Faculty:** 442 total (87 full time), 15 with doctorates or other terminal degrees. **Location:** Rural campus in small town; 30 miles from Pittsburgh. **Calendar:** Semester, limited summer session. Saturday and extensive evening/early morning classes. **Microcomputers:** 240 located in classrooms, computer centers.

DEGREES OFFERED. AA, AAS. 537 associate degrees awarded in 1992. 19% in business and management, 14% business/office and marketing/distribution, 6% computer sciences, 5% engineering technologies, 20% health sciences, 9% home economics, 5% law, 8% multi/interdisciplinary studies, 9% trade and industry.

UNDERGRADUATE MAJORS. Accounting, air conditioning/heating/refrigeration mechanics, air conditioning/heating/refrigeration technology, air traffic control, business administration and management, business and office, business data programming, child development/care/guidance, clinical laboratory science, commercial art, computer and information sciences, criminal justice studies, data processing, dental hygiene, dietetic aide/assistant, drafting, drafting and design technology, education, educational media technology, electrical and electronics equipment repair, electrical/electronics/communications engineering, electronic technology, engineering, engineering and engineering-related technologies, fashion merchandising, finance, fire control and safety technology, food management, food production/management/services, food science and nutrition, graphic and printing production, graphic arts technology, graphic design, hospitality and recreation marketing, hotel/motel and restaurant management, information sciences and systems, law , law enforcement and corrections technologies, legal assistant/paralegal, legal secretary, liberal/general studies, medical laboratory technologies, medical secretary, nuclear technologies, nursing, office supervision and management, ophthalmic services, ornamental horticulture, photographic technology, photography, practical nursing, precision metal work, prelaw, public affairs, retailing, robotics, secretarial and related programs, welding technology, word processing.

ACADEMIC PROGRAMS. 2-year transfer program, cooperative education, double major, honors program, internships, student-designed major, telecourses, cross-registration. **Remedial services:** Learning center, remedial instruction, tutoring, ACT 101 program. **Placement/credit:** Institutional tests; 30 credit hours maximum for associate degree.

ACADEMIC REQUIREMENTS. Freshmen must earn minimum GPA of 2.0 to continue in good standing. 63% of freshmen return for sophomore year. Students must declare major on application. **Graduation requirements:** 60 hours for associate (30 in major). Most students required to take courses in computer science, English, mathematics, social sciences.

FRESHMAN ADMISSIONS. Selection criteria: Open admissions. Nursing applicants required to take Comparative Guidance and Placement test, submit application prior to November 30 of year prior to enrollment in fall semester, and submit satisfactory results from preentrance physicals.

1992 FRESHMAN CLASS PROFILE. 717 men, 857 women enrolled.

Characteristics: 99% from in state, 100% commute, 2% have minority backgrounds. Average age is 26.

FALL-TERM APPLICATIONS. $10 fee, may be waived for applicants with need. No closing date; priority given to applications received by July 1; applicants notified on a rolling basis. Interview recommended. Early admission available.

STUDENT LIFE. Activities: Student government, student newspaper, student life handbook, choral groups, drama, fraternities, religious club.

ATHLETICS. NJCAA. **Intercollegiate:** Baseball M, golf, softball W, tennis, volleyball W. **Intramural:** Basketball M, ice hockey M, racquetball, softball.

STUDENT SERVICES. Aptitude testing, career counseling, employment service for undergraduates, freshman orientation, health services, on-campus day care, personal counseling, placement service for graduates, veterans counselor, services/facilities for handicapped.

ANNUAL EXPENSES. Tuition and fees (1992-93): $1,193, $1,320 additional for out-of-district students, $2,490 additional for out-of-state students. **Books and supplies:** $400. **Other expenses:** $100.

FINANCIAL AID. 63% of freshmen, 63% of continuing students receive some form of aid. All grants, 99% of loans, 75% of jobs based on need. 580 enrolled freshmen were judged to have need, all were offered aid. scholarships available. **Aid applications:** No closing date; priority given to applications received by May 1; applicants notified on a rolling basis; must reply within 2 weeks.

ADDRESS/TELEPHONE. John R. Sparks, Director of Enrollment Management, Westmoreland County Community College, Armburst Road, College Station, Youngwood, PA 15697. (412) 925-4062. Fax: (412) 925-1150.

Widener University
Chester, Pennsylvania — CB code: 2642

Admissions: 78% of applicants accepted
Based on:
••• School record, test scores
•• Interview, special talents
• Activities, essay, recommendations
Completion: 84% of freshmen end year in good standing
83% graduate, 52% of these enter graduate study

4-year private university, coed. Founded in 1821. **Accreditation:** Regional. **Undergraduate enrollment:** 1,307 men, 1,070 women full time; 153 men and women part time. **Graduate enrollment:** 2,525 men and women full time; 1,739 men and women part time. **Faculty:** 394 total (196 full time), 351 with doctorates or other terminal degrees. **Location:** Suburban campus in small city; 15 miles from Philadelphia. **Calendar:** Semester, limited summer session. Extensive evening/early morning classes. **Microcomputers:** Located in libraries, classrooms, computer centers. **Special facilities:** Art museum.

DEGREES OFFERED. BA, BS, MA, MS, MBA, MEd, MSW, EdD, JD. 450 bachelor's degrees awarded in 1992. Graduate degrees offered in 31 major fields of study.

UNDERGRADUATE MAJORS. Accounting, allied health, applied mathematics, behavioral sciences, biology, business administration and management, business and management, business economics, chemical engineering, chemistry, civil engineering, communications, community psychology, computer and information sciences, early childhood education, economics, educational media technology, electrical/electronics/communications engineering, elementary education, engineering, engineering management, English, environmental science, finance, French, German, health sciences, history, hotel/motel and restaurant management, human resources development, humanities and social sciences, information sciences and systems, international business management, journalism, management information systems, mathematics, mechanical engineering, media studies, military science (Army), nursing, physical sciences, physics, political science and government, predentistry, prelaw, premedicine, preveterinary, psychology, public relations, radiograph medical technology, secondary education, social sciences, social work, sociology, Spanish.

ACADEMIC PROGRAMS. Accelerated program, cooperative education, double major, dual enrollment of high school students, honors program, independent study, internships, student-designed major, study abroad, teacher preparation, visiting/exchange student program, weekend college, Washington semester, cross-registration; combined bachelor's/graduate program in business administration. **Remedial services:** Learning center, reduced course load, remedial instruction, special counselor, tutoring, special programs for minority students. **ROTC:** Air Force, Army. **Placement/credit:** AP, CLEP General and Subject, institutional tests. Maximum of 90 semester hours of credit by examination may be counted toward engineering degree, 75 semester hours in all other majors.

ACADEMIC REQUIREMENTS. No policy requiring minimum GPA; records of students having academic difficulty are reviewed individually. 93% of freshmen return for sophomore year. Students must declare major on enrollment. **Graduation requirements:** 128 hours for bachelor's (30 in major). Most students required to take courses in English, humanities, mathematics, biological/physical sciences. **Postgraduate studies:** 14% enter law school, 6% enter medical school, 17% enter MBA programs, 15% enter other graduate study.

FRESHMAN ADMISSIONS. Selection criteria: School achievement record most important, followed by test scores. Activities and recommendations considered. Importance of class rank depends on quality of secondary school and quality of program taken. **High school preparation:** 16 units required; 17 recommended. Required and recommended units include biological science 1, English 4, foreign language 2-3, mathematics 3-4, physical science 2 and social science 2-3. **Test requirements:** SAT or ACT (SAT preferred); score report by May 1.

1992 FRESHMAN CLASS PROFILE. 1,860 men and women applied, 1,445 accepted; 574 enrolled. 54% had high school GPA of 3.0 or higher, 45% between 2.0 and 2.99. **Academic background:** Mid 50% of enrolled freshmen had SAT-V between 440-550, SAT-M between 450-560. 99% submitted SAT scores. **Characteristics:** 45% from in state, 59% live in college housing, 14% have minority backgrounds, 3% are foreign students, 7% join fraternities/sororities. Average age is 18.

FALL-TERM APPLICATIONS. $25 fee, may be waived for applicants with need. Closing date April 1; priority given to applications received by February 1; applicants notified on a rolling basis; must reply by May 1 or within 2 weeks if notified thereafter. Interview recommended. CRDA. Deferred and early admission available.

STUDENT LIFE. Housing: Dormitories (men, women, coed); apartment, fraternity, sorority housing available. Undergraduates must live at home or in college approved housing. **Activities:** Student government, magazine, radio, student newspaper, yearbook, choral groups, concert band, drama, jazz band, music ensembles, musical theater, pep band, fraternities, sororities, Hillel, Newman Apostolate, Christian fellowship, Hispanic-American society, international club, black student union, political affairs club, Greek Orthodox club.

ATHLETICS. NCAA. **Intercollegiate:** Baseball M, basketball, cross-country, diving, field hockey W, football M, golf M, lacrosse, rifle M, soccer, softball W, squash M, swimming, tennis, track and field, volleyball W. **Intramural:** Basketball, bowling, soccer M, softball M.

STUDENT SERVICES. Aptitude testing, career counseling, employment service for undergraduates, freshman orientation, health services, on-campus day care, personal counseling, placement service for graduates, special adviser for adult students, veterans counselor, services/facilities for handicapped.

ANNUAL EXPENSES. Tuition and fees (1992-93): $11,120. **Room and board:** $4,830. **Books and supplies:** $500. **Other expenses:** $900.

FINANCIAL AID. 87% of freshmen, 65% of continuing students receive some form of aid. 77% of grants, 81% of loans, 52% of jobs based on need. 307 enrolled freshmen were judged to have need, 301 were offered aid. Academic, music/drama scholarships available. **Aid applications:** Closing date April 1; priority given to applications received by March 1; applicants notified on or about April 15; must reply by May 1.

ADDRESS/TELEPHONE. Dr. Michael Mahoney, Director of University Admissions, Widener University, 1 University Way, Chester, PA 19013. (215) 499-4124. Fax: (215) 876-9751.

Wilkes University
Wilkes-Barre, Pennsylvania — CB code: 2977

Admissions: 85% of applicants accepted
Based on:
••• School record, test scores
•• Activities, interview, recommendations
• Essay, special talents
Completion: 86% of freshmen end year in good standing
55% graduate, 23% of these enter graduate study

4-year private university, coed. Founded in 1933. **Accreditation:** Regional. **Undergraduate enrollment:** 2,425 men and women. **Graduate enrollment:** 740 men and women. **Faculty:** 243 total (148 full time), 133 with doctorates or other terminal degrees. **Location:** Urban campus in small city; 100 miles from Philadelphia, 140 miles from New York City. **Calendar:** Semester, extensive summer session. **Microcomputers:** 210 located in libraries, classrooms, computer centers. **Special facilities:** Performing arts center, Sordoni Art Gallery.

DEGREES OFFERED. BA, BS, BFA, MS, MBA, MEd. 500 bachelor's degrees awarded in 1992. 32% in business and management, 7% communications, 9% engineering, 19% health sciences, 6% life sciences, 9% psychology, 8% social sciences. Graduate degrees offered in 14 major fields of study.

UNDERGRADUATE MAJORS. Accounting, art education, biochemistry, biology, business administration and management, business and management, chemistry, communications, computer and information sciences, dramatic arts, early childhood education, earth sciences, economics, electrical/electronics/communications engineering, elementary education, engineering management, engineering science, English, English education, environmental health engineering, environmental science, fine arts, foreign languages education, French, German, history, home economics education, information sciences and systems, international studies, liberal/general studies, materials engineering, mathematics, mathematics education, mechanical engineering, medical laboratory technologies, music education, music performance, nursing, occupational therapy, philosophy, physical therapy, physics, political science and government, predentistry, premedicine, prepharmacy, preveterinary, psychology, science education, secondary education, social science education, social studies education, sociology, Spanish.

ACADEMIC PROGRAMS. Accelerated program, cooperative education, double major, dual enrollment of high school students, honors program, independent study, internships, student-designed major, study abroad, teacher preparation, weekend college, cross-registration; liberal arts/career combination in health sciences; combined bachelor's/graduate program in business administration. **Remedial services:** Learning center, preadmission summer program, reduced course load, special counselor, tutoring. **ROTC:** Air Force, Army. **Placement/credit:** AP, CLEP Subject, institutional tests. credit by examination may be given to within 30 credits of graduation.

ACADEMIC REQUIREMENTS. Freshmen must earn minimum GPA of 1.7 to continue in good standing. 80% of freshmen return for sophomore year. Students must declare major by end of second year. **Graduation requirements:** 126 hours for bachelor's (30 in major). Most students required to take courses in arts/fine arts, computer science, English, foreign languages, history, humanities, mathematics, philosophy/religion, biological/physical sciences, social sciences. **Postgraduate studies:** 5% enter law school, 7% enter medical school, 2% enter MBA programs, 9% enter other graduate study.

FRESHMAN ADMISSIONS. Selection criteria: Test scores, class rank, GPA, curriculum considered. **High school preparation:** 18 units required. Required units include English 4, foreign language 2, mathematics 3 and science 3. One laboratory science also required. **Test requirements:** SAT or ACT; score report by August 15.

1992 FRESHMAN CLASS PROFILE. 1,698 men and women applied, 1,450 accepted; 410 enrolled. 42% had high school GPA of 3.0 or higher, 46% between 2.0 and 2.99. **Academic background:** Mid 50% of enrolled freshmen had SAT-V between 370-490, SAT-M between 410-550. 97% submitted SAT scores. **Characteristics:** 75% from in state, 65% live in college housing, 2% have minority backgrounds, 1% are foreign students. Average age is 18.

FALL-TERM APPLICATIONS. $25 fee, may be waived for applicants with need. No closing date; applicants notified on a rolling basis; must reply by May 1 or within 3 weeks if notified thereafter. Audition required for music applicants. Portfolio required. Interview recommended. CRDA. Deferred and early admission available.

STUDENT LIFE. Housing: Dormitories (men, women, coed). **Activities:** Student government, magazine, radio, student newspaper, television, yearbook, choral groups, concert band, drama, jazz band, music ensembles, musical theater, pep band, symphony orchestra, service sorority, Circle-K.

ATHLETICS. NCAA. **Intercollegiate:** Baseball M, basketball, cross-country, field hockey W, football M, golf M, soccer, softball W, tennis, volleyball W, wrestling M. **Intramural:** Basketball M, bowling, football M, ice hockey M, racquetball, rowing (crew), rugby M, skiing, softball, volleyball.

STUDENT SERVICES. Aptitude testing, career counseling, employment service for undergraduates, freshman orientation, health services, personal counseling, placement service for graduates, special adviser for adult students, veterans counselor, services/facilities for handicapped.

ANNUAL EXPENSES. Tuition and fees: $10,898. **Room and board:** $4,830. **Books and supplies:** $550. **Other expenses:** $750.

FINANCIAL AID. 90% of freshmen, 88% of continuing students receive some form of aid. 98% of grants, 79% of loans, 78% of jobs based on need. 319 enrolled freshmen were judged to have need, 317 were offered aid. Academic, music/drama, art, athletic, state/district residency, leadership, alumni affiliation, minority scholarships available. **Aid applications:** No closing date; priority given to applications received by June 1; applicants notified on a rolling basis beginning on or about March 1; must reply by May 1 or within 3 weeks if notified thereafter.

ADDRESS/TELEPHONE. Emory Guffrovich, Dean of Admissions, Wilkes University, 170 South Franklin Street, Wilkes-Barre, PA 18766-0001. (717) 831-4400. (800) 537-4444. Fax: (717) 824-0733.

Williamson Free School of Mechanical Trades
Media, Pennsylvania CB code: 0765

Admissions: 27% of applicants accepted
Based on: ••• School record
•• Interview, recommendations, test scores
• Activities, essay, special talents
Completion: 90% of freshmen end year in good standing

3-year private technical college, men only, nondenominational. Founded in 1888. **Undergraduate enrollment:** 250 men full time. **Faculty:** 25 total (14 full time). **Location:** Suburban campus in small town; 14 miles from Philadelphia, 14 miles from Wilmington, Delaware. **Calendar:** Semester. **Microcomputers:** 17 located in classrooms, computer centers. **Special facilities:** Natural arboretum.

DEGREES OFFERED. 38 associate degrees awarded in 1992. 73% in engineering technologies, 27% trade and industry.

UNDERGRADUATE MAJORS. Construction, horticulture, machine tool operation/machine shop, mechanical design technology, power plant operation and maintenance, structural coating technology, structural coatings technology.

ACADEMIC PROGRAMS. Internships. **Remedial services:** Preadmission summer program, tutoring. **Placement/credit:** Institutional tests.

ACADEMIC REQUIREMENTS. Freshmen must earn minimum GPA of 1.7 to continue in good standing. 90% of freshmen return for sophomore year. Students must declare major by end of first year. **Graduation requirements:** 140 hours for associate (70 in major). Most students required to take courses in computer science, English, mathematics, philosophy/religion, biological/physical sciences. **Postgraduate studies:** 5% from 2-year programs enter 4-year programs.

FRESHMAN ADMISSIONS. Selection criteria: Family economic need, high school performance, letters of character reference, interview. First consideration given to applicants with 2.0 or better average in mathematics, science, and English. **High school preparation:** 7 units required. Required units include English 3, mathematics 2 and physical science 2. Mathematics units must include algebra I and geometry. Science units should include chemistry and physics. Biology recommended for horticulture students only. **Test requirements:** Armed Services Vocational Aptitude Battery (ASVAB) required. **Additional information:** Applicant must have reached 16th birthday, but not have passed 20th birthday prior to June of year of admission.

1992 FRESHMAN CLASS PROFILE. 352 men applied, 94 accepted, 94 enrolled. 25% had high school GPA of 3.0 or higher, 75% between 2.0 and 2.99. 5% were in top tenth and 20% were in top quarter of graduating class. **Characteristics:** 85% from in state, 100% live in college housing, 3% have minority backgrounds. Average age is 18.

FALL-TERM APPLICATIONS. No fee. Closing date May 1; priority given to applications received by April 15; applicants notified on or about May 31; must reply by June 15. Interview required. Audition recommended. Essay recommended. Students who apply before November 30 will be brought in for January testing and interview session.

STUDENT LIFE. Housing: Dormitories (men). **Activities:** Student government, magazine, yearbook, choral groups, pep band, Campus Crusade for Christ, Bible study groups, VICA. **Additional information:** Student life carefully structured, including prescribed daily schedule, dress code, required chapel, and clearly defined privileges and responsibilities. Religious observance required.

ATHLETICS. NJCAA. **Intercollegiate:** Baseball, basketball, cross-country, football, soccer, wrestling. **Intramural:** Archery, basketball, handball, racquetball, table tennis, volleyball.

STUDENT SERVICES. Career counseling, employment service for undergraduates, freshman orientation, health services, personal counseling, placement service for graduates.

ANNUAL EXPENSES. Tuition and fees (1992-93): $175. Tuition, room and board are free. **Books and supplies:** $60. **Other expenses:** $400.

FINANCIAL AID. 100% of freshmen, 100% of continuing students receive some form of aid. 93 enrolled freshmen were judged to have need, all were offered aid. **Aid applications:** Closing date May 1; priority given to applications received by April 15. **Additional information:** Williamson is an endowed, private, vocational-technical school which awards scholarships covering tuition, room and board, and text books to all students accepted for admission.

ADDRESS/TELEPHONE. Ken Horton, Director of Admissions, Williamson Free School of Mechanical Trades, 106 South New Middletown Road, Media, PA 19063-5299. (215) 566-1776. Fax: (215) 566-6502.

Wilson College
Chambersburg, Pennsylvania CB code: 2979

4-year private liberal arts college, women only, affiliated with Presbyterian Church (USA). Founded in 1869. **Accreditation:** Regional. **Undergraduate enrollment:** 174 women full time; 2 women part time. **Faculty:** 42 total (36 full time), 28 with doctorates or other terminal degrees. **Location:** Rural campus in large town; 90 miles from Washington, D.C., 145 miles from Philadelphia. **Calendar:** 4-1-4. **Microcomputers:** 60 located in dormitories, libraries, classrooms, computer centers. **Special facilities:** Art gallery, stables, classics collection, electron microscope, natural history museum. **Additional facts:** Men admitted to continuing studies division, adult learning program, associate degree programs, teacher intern program.

DEGREES OFFERED. AA, BA, BS. 31 bachelor's degrees awarded. 13% in agriculture, 18% business and management, 20% allied health, 23% life sciences, 10% social sciences.

UNDERGRADUATE MAJORS. Associate: Information sciences and systems, liberal/general studies. **Bachelor's:** Behavioral sciences, biology, business economics, chemistry, communications, elementary education, English, equestrian science, fine arts, foreign languages (multiple emphasis), history, international studies, mathematics, philosophy, political science and government, religion, veterinarian's assistant.

ACADEMIC PROGRAMS. Independent study, internships, student-designed major, study abroad, teacher preparation, visiting/exchange student program, United Nations semester, Washington semester, cross-registration, 3-2 program in nursing and 2-4 program in biodental with University of Pennsylvania, exchange program with Aichi Shututoku University, Japan. **Remedial services:** Learning center, reduced course load, remedial instruction, special counselor, tutoring. **Placement/credit:** AP, CLEP General and Subject, institutional tests; 13 credit hours maximum for associate degree; 13 credit hours maximum for bachelor's degree.

ACADEMIC REQUIREMENTS. Freshmen must earn minimum GPA of 1.7 to continue in good standing. 75% of freshmen return for sophomore year. Students must declare major by end of second year. **Graduation requirements:** 60 hours for associate, 120 hours for bachelor's (46 in major). Most students required to take courses in computer science, English, foreign languages, humanities, mathematics, biological/physical sciences, social sciences. **Postgraduate studies:** 5% enter law school, 2% enter medical school, 5% enter MBA programs, 4% enter other graduate study.

FRESHMAN ADMISSIONS. Selection criteria: School achievement record, class rank, test scores, interview, noncurricular activities considered. **High school preparation:** 15 units required. Required units include English 4, foreign language 2, mathematics 3, social science 4 and science 2. **Test requirements:** SAT or ACT; score report by June 15.

1992 FRESHMAN CLASS PROFILE. 48 women enrolled. 30% had high school GPA of 3.0 or higher, 70% between 2.0 and 2.99. **Academic background:** Mid 50% of enrolled freshmen had SAT-V between 450-580, SAT-M between 450-550. 100% submitted SAT scores. **Characteristics:** 54% from in state, 89% live in college housing, 2% have minority backgrounds, 6% are foreign students. Average age is 18.

FALL-TERM APPLICATIONS. $20 fee, may be waived for applicants with need. No closing date; priority given to applications received by March 1; applicants notified on a rolling basis; must reply by May 1 or as soon as possible if notified thereafter. Essay required. Interview recommended. CRDA. Deferred and early admission available.

STUDENT LIFE. Housing: Dormitories (women). Students of sophomore standing or above guaranteed single residence hall room. **Activities:** Student government, magazine, student newspaper, yearbook, choral groups, dance, drama, music ensembles, religious activities committee, language clubs, riding club, interfaith support group, Muhibbah Club (International), Catholic student group.

ATHLETICS. Intercollegiate: Field hockey, horseback riding, softball, tennis, volleyball. **Intramural:** Archery, badminton, basketball, bowling, field hockey, gymnastics, horseback riding, soccer, softball, swimming, tennis, volleyball.

STUDENT SERVICES. Aptitude testing, career counseling, employment service for undergraduates, freshman orientation, health services, on-campus day care, personal counseling, placement service for graduates, special adviser for adult students, spiritual life coordinator, services/facilities for handicapped.

ANNUAL EXPENSES. Tuition and fees: $11,546. **Room and board:** $5,084. **Books and supplies:** $450. **Other expenses:** $350.

FINANCIAL AID. 77% of freshmen, 82% of continuing students receive some form of aid. 79% of grants, 79% of loans, 76% of jobs based on need. 34 enrolled freshmen were judged to have need, all were offered aid. Academic, state/district residency, leadership, alumni affiliation, religious affiliation scholarships available. **Aid applications:** Closing date April 30; applicants notified on a rolling basis; must reply by May 1 or within 3 weeks if notified thereafter. **Additional information:** Out-of-state students must apply for home-state grants.

ADDRESS/TELEPHONE. Karen Jewell, Director of Admissions, Wilson College, 1015 Philadelphia Avenue, Chambersburg, PA 17201-1285. (717) 264-4141 ext. 223. (800) 421-8402. Fax: (717) 264-1578.

Yeshivath Beth Moshe
Scranton, Pennsylvania — CB code: 1657

4-year private rabbinical college, men only, affiliated with Jewish faith. Founded in 1965. **Undergraduate enrollment:** 42 men full time. **Graduate enrollment:** 27 men full time. **Location:** Suburban campus in small city. **Additional facts:** First and second Talmudic degrees offered. Ordination available.

FRESHMAN ADMISSIONS. Selection criteria: Extensive oral examination given. Religious commitment important.

ADDRESS/TELEPHONE. Office of Dean, Yeshivath Beth Moshe, 930 Hickory Street, Scranton, PA 18505. (717) 346-1747.

York College of Pennsylvania
York, Pennsylvania — CB code: 2991

Admissions: 56% of applicants accepted
Based on:
- ••• School record
- •• Test scores
- • Activities, interview, recommendations, special talents

Completion: 87% of freshmen end year in good standing
65% graduate, 25% of these enter graduate study

4-year private liberal arts college, coed. Founded in 1787. **Accreditation:** Regional. **Undergraduate enrollment:** 1,227 men, 1,748 women full time; 698 men, 1,157 women part time. **Graduate enrollment:** 79 men, 33 women part time. **Faculty:** 286 total (120 full time), 90 with doctorates or other terminal degrees. **Location:** Suburban campus in small city; 46 miles from Baltimore, Maryland, 95 miles from Philadelphia. **Calendar:** Semester, extensive summer session. **Microcomputers:** 200 located in classrooms, computer centers. **Special facilities:** Abraham Lincoln artifacts collection, rare books collection, oral history room.

DEGREES OFFERED. AA, AS, BA, BS, BFA, MBA. 65 associate degrees awarded in 1992. 43% in business and management, 25% business/office and marketing/distribution, 14% multi/interdisciplinary studies, 5% parks/recreation, protective services, public affairs. 656 bachelor's degrees awarded. 17% in business and management, 10% business/office and marketing/distribution, 5% communications, 18% teacher education, 11% health sciences, 11% parks/recreation, protective services, public affairs, 5% psychology, 7% social sciences. Graduate degrees offered in 1 major field of study.

UNDERGRADUATE MAJORS. Associate: Business administration and management, chemistry, computer and information sciences, engineering, fine arts, foreign languages (multiple emphasis), forensic studies, law enforcement and corrections, law enforcement and corrections technologies, legal secretary, liberal/general studies, mathematics, medical secretary, music, office supervision and management, philosophy, physics, radio/television broadcasting, respiratory therapy, retailing, secretarial and related programs. **Bachelor's:** Accounting, behavioral sciences, biology, business administration and management, business education, clinical laboratory science, communications, computer and information sciences, elementary education, engineering management, English, English education, fine arts, history, humanities, international relations, international studies, Latin American studies, law enforcement and corrections, marketing and distribution, mathematics education, medical records administration, music, nuclear medical technology, nursing, office supervision and management, physical sciences, political science and government, predentistry, prelaw, premedicine, prepharmacy, preveterinary, psychology, public administration, radio/television broadcasting, recreation and community services technologies, recreation therapy, respiratory therapy, science education, secondary education, social studies education, sociology, speech.

ACADEMIC PROGRAMS. 2-year transfer program, double major, dual enrollment of high school students, honors program, independent study, internships, study abroad, teacher preparation, Washington semester; liberal arts/career combination in engineering. **Remedial services:** Learning center, reduced course load, remedial instruction, tutoring, writing center. **Placement/credit:** AP, CLEP General and Subject, institutional tests; 60 credit hours maximum for bachelor's degree.

ACADEMIC REQUIREMENTS. Freshmen must earn minimum GPA of 1.7 to continue in good standing. 83% of freshmen return for sophomore year. Students must declare major by end of second year. **Graduation requirements:** 62 hours for associate, 124 hours for bachelor's. Most students required to take courses in arts/fine arts, English, foreign languages, history, humanities, mathematics, philosophy/religion, biological/physical sciences, social sciences.

FRESHMAN ADMISSIONS. Selection criteria: High school record, standardized test results, and personal qualities most important. **High school preparation:** 15 units required. Required units include biological science 1, English 4, foreign language 2, mathematics 3, physical science 2 and social science 3. 1 biology, 2 chemistry, and 2 algebra required of nursing applicants. **Test requirements:** SAT or ACT; score report by August 1.

1992 FRESHMAN CLASS PROFILE. 1,359 men applied, 773 accepted, 292 enrolled; 1,893 women applied, 1,041 accepted, 454 enrolled. 78% had high school GPA of 3.0 or higher, 22% between 2.0 and 2.99. **Academic background:** Mid 50% of enrolled freshmen had SAT-V between 440-530, SAT-M between 480-570. 99% submitted SAT scores. **Characteristics:** 52% from in state, 64% live in college housing, 5% have minority backgrounds, 1% are foreign students, 17% join fraternities/sororities. Average age is 18.

FALL-TERM APPLICATIONS. $20 fee, may be waived for applicants with need. No closing date; applicants notified on a rolling basis; must reply by March 1 or within 30 days if notified thereafter. Audition required for music applicants. Interview recommended for academically borderline applicants. Portfolio recommended for art applicants. Deferred and early admission available.

STUDENT LIFE. Housing: Dormitories (men, women, coed); apart-

ment, fraternity, sorority housing available. Residence halls, minidorms featuring units of 10 students, suites, sponsored houses and apartments, and off-campus living arrangements available. **Activities:** Student government, magazine, radio, student newspaper, television, yearbook, forensic club, choral groups, concert band, drama, jazz band, music ensembles, musical theater, pep band, symphony orchestra, fraternities, sororities, Circle-K, Black Student Union, International Student Club, Hillel, Catholic Campus Ministry, Intervarsity Christian Fellowship, History Intercultural and Political Science Club, Alcohol and Drug Education Committee, Committee for Social Awareness, Christian Life Fellowship. **Additional information:** Student government participates in college decisions and sponsors wide spectrum of student activities. Campus chapel offers full range of religious services. Over 70 student organizations on campus. Computer facilities and software programs available 120 hours per week for students. Career services result in 90% employment of graduates.

ATHLETICS. NCAA. **Intercollegiate:** Baseball M, basketball, cross-country M, field hockey W, golf M, soccer M, softball W, swimming, tennis, track and field M, volleyball W, wrestling M. **Intramural:** Badminton, basketball, rugby M, soccer M, softball, swimming, tennis, track and field, volleyball, water polo M, wrestling M.

STUDENT SERVICES. Career counseling, employment service for undergraduates, freshman orientation, health services, personal counseling, placement service for graduates, special adviser for adult students, veterans counselor, services/facilities for handicapped.

ANNUAL EXPENSES. Tuition and fees: $4,995. **Room and board:** $3,350. **Books and supplies:** $500. **Other expenses:** $850.

FINANCIAL AID. 65% of freshmen, 58% of continuing students receive some form of aid. 83% of grants, 58% of loans, 72% of jobs based on need. 283 enrolled freshmen were judged to have need, all were offered aid. Academic, music/drama, art, state/district residency, leadership, alumni affiliation, minority scholarships available. **Aid applications:** No closing date; priority given to applications received by April 15; applicants notified on a rolling basis beginning on or about February 15; must reply within 2 weeks. **Additional information:** Trustee honors scholarships for full tuition offered to students with top 20% class rank and combined SAT score over 1100. Presidential, valedictionaian and salutatonain scholarships of one-half tuition or Dean's scholarships of one third tuition for students with top 40% class rank and combined SAT score o.

ADDRESS/TELEPHONE. Nancy L. Spataro, Director of Admissions, York College of Pennsylvania, Country Club Road, York, PA 17403-3426. (717) 846-7788.

Puerto Rico

American University of Puerto Rico

Bayamon, Puerto Rico CB code: 0961

4-year private business, teachers college, coed. Founded in 1963. **Accreditation:** Regional. **Undergraduate enrollment:** 1,490 men, 2,198 women full time; 251 men, 420 women part time. **Faculty:** 235 total (102 full time), 13 with doctorates or other terminal degrees. **Location:** Urban campus in small city; 12 miles from San Juan. **Calendar:** Semester, limited summer session. Saturday classes. **Microcomputers:** 75 located in computer centers. **Additional facts:** Branch campuses at Manati and Dorado. Classes conducted in Spanish.

DEGREES OFFERED. AA, AS, BA. 225 associate degrees awarded in 1992. 212 bachelor's degrees awarded.

UNDERGRADUATE MAJORS. Associate: Accounting, business and office, communications, computer programming, liberal/general studies, secretarial and related programs. **Bachelor's:** Accounting, business and management, business education, communications, educational media technology, elementary education, mathematics education, physical education, purchasing management, recreation and community services technologies, secondary education, secretarial and related programs, special education, teaching English as a second language/foreign language, word processing.

ACADEMIC PROGRAMS. 2-year transfer program, cooperative education, honors program, internships. **Remedial services:** Learning center, reduced course load, special counselor, tutoring. **ROTC:** Army. **Placement/credit:** Institutional tests.

ACADEMIC REQUIREMENTS. Freshmen must earn minimum GPA of 2.0 to continue in good standing. 63% of freshmen return for sophomore year. Students must declare major by end of first year. **Graduation requirements:** 68 hours for associate (16 in major), 129 hours for bachelor's (27 in major). Most students required to take courses in computer science, English, history, humanities, mathematics, philosophy/religion, biological/physical sciences, social sciences. **Postgraduate studies:** 45% from 2-year programs enter 4-year programs.

FRESHMAN ADMISSIONS. Selection criteria: Open admissions. **High school preparation:** 15 units required. Required units include biological science 2, English 3, foreign language 3, mathematics 2, social science 1.5 and science 3.5. **Test requirements:** Prueba de Aptitud Academica for Spanish speaking applicants.

1992 FRESHMAN CLASS PROFILE. 388 men, 506 women enrolled. **Characteristics:** 100% from in state, 100% commute. Average age is 19.

FALL-TERM APPLICATIONS. $15 fee, may be waived for applicants with need. Closing date July 1; applicants notified on or about July 31; must reply within 2 weeks.

STUDENT LIFE. Activities: Student government.

ATHLETICS. NCAA. **Intercollegiate:** Basketball, table tennis, tennis, track and field, volleyball. **Intramural:** Basketball, boxing M, softball M, volleyball.

STUDENT SERVICES. Career counseling, employment service for undergraduates, freshman orientation, health services, personal counseling, veterans counselor, services/facilities for handicapped.

ANNUAL EXPENSES. Tuition and fees (1992-93): $2,400. **Books and supplies:** $400.

FINANCIAL AID. 72% of freshmen, 77% of continuing students receive some form of aid. All aid based on need. **Aid applications:** Closing date June 30; priority given to applications received by May 31; applicants notified on or about August 31; must reply within 2 weeks.

ADDRESS/TELEPHONE. Margarita Cruz, Director of Admissions, American University of Puerto Rico, PO Box 2037, Bayamon, PR 00960-2037. (809) 798-2040 ext. 229. Fax: (809) 785-7377.

Bayamon Central University

Bayamon, Puerto Rico CB code: 0840

Admissions:	70% of applicants accepted
Based on:	••• School record, test scores
	•• Essay
	• Activities, interview, recommendations, special talents
Completion:	46% graduate

4-year private university, coed, affiliated with Roman Catholic Church. Founded in 1970. **Accreditation:** Regional. **Undergraduate enrollment:** 929 men, 1,441 women full time; 150 men, 216 women part time. **Graduate enrollment:** 45 men, 22 women full time; 32 men, 860 women part time. **Faculty:** 112 total (63 full time), 22 with doctorates or other terminal degrees. **Location:** Suburban campus in small city; 9 miles from San Juan. **Calendar:** Semester, limited summer session. Saturday and extensive evening/early morning classes. **Microcomputers:** Located in computer centers. **Special facilities:** Library of Dominican Order.

DEGREES OFFERED. AA, BA, BS, MA. 10 associate degrees awarded in 1992. 30% in business and management, 20% business/office and marketing/distribution, 30% communications, 20% computer sciences. 271 bachelor's degrees awarded. 10% in business and management, 10% business/office and marketing/distribution, 8% communications, 5% education, 18% teacher education, 24% health sciences, 8% parks/recreation, protective services, public affairs. Graduate degrees offered in 1 major field of study.

UNDERGRADUATE MAJORS. Associate: Business and management, computer and information sciences, educational media technology, management information systems, secretarial and related programs. **Bachelor's:** Accounting, biological and physical sciences, biology, business and management, chemistry, computer and information sciences, educational media technology, elementary education, English, English education, journalism, management information systems, management science, marketing and distribution, mathematics education, nursing, philosophy, physical education, psychology, religion, science education, secondary education, secretarial and related programs, social work, Spanish, special education.

ACADEMIC PROGRAMS. Double major, independent study. **Remedial services:** Learning center, reduced course load, special counselor, tutoring. **ROTC:** Air Force, Army. **Placement/credit:** AP.

ACADEMIC REQUIREMENTS. Freshmen must earn minimum GPA of 2.0 to continue in good standing. 64% of freshmen return for sophomore year. Students must declare major on application. **Graduation requirements:** 71 hours for associate (36 in major), 131 hours for bachelor's (36 in major). Most students required to take courses in computer science, English, history, humanities, mathematics, philosophy/religion, biological/physical sciences, social sciences. **Additional information:** All classroom instruction conducted in Spanish. Core curriculum includes courses in Spanish. Course in methodology of learning must be satisfactorily completed.

FRESHMAN ADMISSIONS. Selection criteria: Minimum 2.0 high school GPA. Fluency in Spanish, basic knowledge of English necessary. **High school preparation:** 15 units required. Required units include English 3, mathematics 3, social science 3 and science 1. 3 Spanish also required. **Test requirements:** Prueba de Aptitud Academica for Spanish speaking applicants. SAT or ACT accepted from English-speaking students. **Additional information:** Conditional admission to those identified as having underdeveloped academic potential.

1992 FRESHMAN CLASS PROFILE. 301 men applied, 253 accepted, 224 enrolled; 685 women applied, 440 accepted, 373 enrolled. 18% had high school GPA of 3.0 or higher, 60% between 2.0 and 2.99. **Characteristics:** 99% from in state, 100% commute, 100% have minority backgrounds, 1% are foreign students. Average age is 18.

FALL-TERM APPLICATIONS. $15 fee. Closing date August 15; priority given to applications received by April 15; applicants notified on a rolling basis; must reply by August 15 or within 2 weeks if notified thereafter. Interview recommended for academically weak applicants. Essay recommended. Deferred admission available.

STUDENT LIFE. Activities: Student government, student newspaper, various cultural, religious, and social activities. **Additional information:** Virtually all students come from Spanish-speaking background.

ATHLETICS. Intercollegiate: Basketball, cross-country, softball, table tennis, tennis, track and field, volleyball. **Intramural:** Basketball, volleyball.

STUDENT SERVICES. Career counseling, employment service for undergraduates, health services, personal counseling, placement service for graduates, services/facilities for handicapped.

ANNUAL EXPENSES. Tuition and fees (1992-93): $2,350. **Books and supplies:** $400. **Other expenses:** $800.

FINANCIAL AID. 94% of freshmen, 91% of continuing students receive some form of aid. 95% of grants, all loans, all jobs based on need. Academic, athletic scholarships available. **Aid applications:** Closing date August 1; applicants notified on a rolling basis beginning on or about August 2; must reply by August 20.

ADDRESS/TELEPHONE. Cristina Hernandez, Director of Admissions, Bayamon Central University, PO Box 1725, Bayamon, PR 00960-1725. (809) 786-3030 ext. 202. Fax: (809) 740-2200.

Caribbean University

Bayamon, Puerto Rico CB code: 0779

4-year private college of arts and sciences and business, liberal arts college, coed. Founded in 1969. **Accreditation:** Regional. **Undergraduate enrollment:** 871 men, 1,234 women full time; 394 men, 702 women part time. **Graduate enrollment:** 1 man, 3 women full time; 3 men, 10 women part time. **Faculty:** 133 total (57 full time), 5 with doctorates or other terminal degrees. **Location:** Suburban campus in small city; 12 miles from San Juan. **Calendar:** Semester. Saturday and extensive evening/early morning classes. **Microcomputers:** 80 located in classrooms, computer centers. **Additional facts:** Extension centers in Carolina, Vega Baja, and Ponce.

DEGREES OFFERED. AA, AS, BA, BS, MEd. 89 associate degrees awarded in 1992. 17 bachelor's degrees awarded. Graduate degrees offered in 2 major fields of study.

UNDERGRADUATE MAJORS. Associate: Accounting, business and management, business and office, computer and information sciences, engineering and engineering-related technologies, finance, insurance marketing, law enforcement and corrections, legal secretary, marketing and distribution, medical secretary, real estate, secretarial and related programs. **Bachelor's:** Accounting, biology, business administration and management, business and management, business education, civil engineering, computer and information sciences, computer programming, criminology, education, elementary education, English education, industrial engineering, marketing and distribution, marketing management, mathematics education, nursing, premedicine, science education, secondary education, secretarial and related programs, social sciences, Spanish, special education, systems analysis.

ACADEMIC PROGRAMS. Honors program, teacher preparation; liberal arts/career combination in engineering. **Remedial services:** Learning center, remedial instruction, special counselor, tutoring. **ROTC:** Army. **Placement/credit:** CLEP Subject.

ACADEMIC REQUIREMENTS. Freshmen must earn minimum GPA of 1.6 to continue in good standing. Students must declare major on application. **Graduation requirements:** 77 hours for associate, 133 hours for bachelor's. Most students required to take courses in computer science, English, history, humanities, mathematics, biological/physical sciences, social sciences. **Postgraduate studies:** 83% from 2-year programs enter 4-year programs.

FRESHMAN ADMISSIONS. Selection criteria: School achievement record, test scores, and interview considered. **Test requirements:** Prueba de Aptitud Academica for Spanish speaking applicants. SAT required of English-speaking applicants, score report by August 1. PAA and ACH score reports by August 15.

1992 FRESHMAN CLASS PROFILE. 371 men, 423 women enrolled. 40% had high school GPA of 3.0 or higher, 55% between 2.0 and 2.99. **Characteristics:** 95% from in state, 100% commute, 100% have minority backgrounds. Average age is 19.

FALL-TERM APPLICATIONS. $15 fee. No closing date; applicants notified on a rolling basis beginning on or about August 15; must reply within 2 weeks. Interview recommended for academically weak applicants. Deferred and early admission available.

STUDENT LIFE. Activities: Student government, choral groups, drama.

ATHLETICS. Intramural: Basketball, cross-country, gymnastics, table tennis, tennis, track and field, volleyball.

STUDENT SERVICES. Aptitude testing, career counseling, employment service for undergraduates, freshman orientation, health services, personal counseling, placement service for graduates, veterans counselor, services/facilities for handicapped.

ANNUAL EXPENSES. Tuition and fees (1992-93): $2,550. **Books and supplies:** $640. **Other expenses:** $1,950.

FINANCIAL AID. 87% of freshmen, 85% of continuing students receive some form of aid. All aid based on need. State/district residency scholarships available. **Aid applications:** No closing date; priority given to applications received by July 30; applicants notified on a rolling basis.

ADDRESS/TELEPHONE. Angel Diaz, Admissions Director, Caribbean University, PO Box 493, Bayamon, PR 00960-0493. (809) 780-0070. Fax: (809) 785-0101.

Colegio Universitario del Este
Carolina, Puerto Rico — CB code: 0883

4-year private college of arts and sciences and business college, coed. Founded in 1949. **Accreditation:** Regional. **Undergraduate enrollment:** 1,316 men, 2,583 women full time; 186 men, 338 women part time. **Faculty:** 277 total (63 full time), 21 with doctorates or other terminal degrees. **Location:** Urban campus in large city; within greater San Juan. **Calendar:** Semester, limited summer session. **Microcomputers:** Located in classrooms, computer centers.

DEGREES OFFERED. AA, AS, BA, BS. 399 associate degrees awarded in 1992. 31% in business and management, 22% business/office and marketing/distribution, 13% health sciences, 6% law, 26% parks/recreation, protective services, public affairs.

UNDERGRADUATE MAJORS. Associate: Accounting, allied health, automotive technology, business and management, business and office, business computer/console/peripheral equipment operation, business data entry equipment operation, business data processing and related programs, business systems analysis, community psychology, community services, computer programming, criminology, data processing, gerontology, health sciences, law enforcement and corrections technologies, legal assistant/paralegal, liberal/general studies, marketing and distribution, medical records administration, pharmacy, public affairs, radiograph medical technology, recreation and community services technologies, secretarial and related programs, social sciences, social work, ultrasound technology, word processing. **Bachelor's:** Office supervision and management, secretarial and related programs, social work.

ACADEMIC PROGRAMS. 2-year transfer program, independent study, internships, weekend college. **Remedial services:** Reduced course load, remedial instruction, special counselor, tutoring. **Placement/credit:** AP.

ACADEMIC REQUIREMENTS. Freshmen must earn minimum GPA of 1.5 to continue in good standing. 57% of freshmen return for sophomore year. Students must declare major on enrollment. **Graduation requirements:** 78 hours for associate. Most students required to take courses in English, history, humanities, social sciences.

FRESHMAN ADMISSIONS. Selection criteria: Open admissions. **Test requirements:** Prueba de Aptitud Academica for Spanish speaking applicants. SAT required of English-speaking freshman applicants. No test requirements for applicants aged 25 or older.

1992 FRESHMAN CLASS PROFILE. 1,679 men and women applied, 1,281 accepted; 433 men enrolled, 703 women enrolled. 10% had high school GPA of 3.0 or higher, 56% between 2.0 and 2.99. **Characteristics:** 100% commute. Average age is 18.

FALL-TERM APPLICATIONS. $15 fee. No closing date; priority given to applications received by March 30; applicants notified on a rolling basis beginning on or about April 15; must reply within 2 weeks. Interview recommended for health, law enforcement applicants. Deferred admission available.

STUDENT LIFE. Activities: Student government, student newspaper, choral groups, dance, Phi Theta Kappa, Future Secretaries of America, nursing club.

ATHLETICS. Intercollegiate: Basketball, table tennis, track and field, volleyball. **Intramural:** Basketball, table tennis, volleyball.

STUDENT SERVICES. Aptitude testing, career counseling, health services, personal counseling, placement service for graduates, veterans counselor.

ANNUAL EXPENSES. Tuition and fees (1992-93): $2,750. **Books and supplies:** $300. **Other expenses:** $1,045.

FINANCIAL AID. 90% of freshmen, 85% of continuing students receive some form of aid. **Aid applications:** Closing date May 30; priority given to applications received by March 30; applicants notified on or about July 30.

ADDRESS/TELEPHONE. Maria Caraballo, Director of Admissions, Colegio Universitario del Este, PO Box 2010, Carolina, PR 00983-2010. (809) 257-7373. Fax: (809) 257-7373 ext. 4000.

Columbia College
Caguas, Puerto Rico — CB code: 2315

4-year proprietary business, technical college, coed. Founded in 1966. **Undergraduate enrollment:** 979 men and women. **Location:** Urban campus in small city; 15 miles from San Juan. **Calendar:** Quarter.

FRESHMAN ADMISSIONS. Selection criteria: Open admissions.

ANNUAL EXPENSES. Tuition and fees (projected): $3,423. **Books and supplies:** $468. **Other expenses:** $331.

ADDRESS/TELEPHONE. Julio Perez, Admissions Officer, Columbia College, PO Box 8517, Caguas, PR 00626. (809) 743-4041.

Conservatory of Music of Puerto Rico
Santurce, Puerto Rico — CB code: 1115

4-year public music college, coed. Founded in 1959. **Accreditation:** Regional. **Undergraduate enrollment:** 288 men and women. **Location:** Urban campus in large city; within greater San Juan. **Calendar:** Semester.

FRESHMAN ADMISSIONS. Selection criteria: Musical ability very important. School achievement record, test scores, recommendations also considered.

ANNUAL EXPENSES. Tuition and fees (1992-93): $660. **Books and supplies:** $400. **Other expenses:** $450.

ADDRESS/TELEPHONE. Zulma Palos de Santini, Director of Admissions, Conservatory of Music of Puerto Rico, PO Box 41227 Minillas, Santurce, PR 00940. (809) 751-0160. Fax: (809) 758-8268.

Electronic Data Processing College of Puerto Rico
Hato Rey, Puerto Rico — CB code: 2243

4-year proprietary university and technical college, coed. Founded in 1968. **Undergraduate enrollment:** 497 men, 305 women full time; 85 men, 52 women part time. **Graduate enrollment:** 24 men, 13 women full time; 9 men, 2 women part time. **Location:** Urban campus in very large city. **Calendar:** Semester. **Additional facts:** Branch campus in San Sebastian offers 2-year programs and certificates.

FRESHMAN ADMISSIONS. Selection criteria: Minimum high school GPA of 2.0 required.

ANNUAL EXPENSES. Tuition and fees (1992-93): $2,749. **Books and supplies:** $465. **Other expenses:** $1,455.

ADDRESS/TELEPHONE. Elsie Zayas, Admissions Director, Electronic Data Processing College of Puerto Rico, 555 Munoz Rivera Avenue, Hato Rey, PR 00918. (809) 765-3560 ext. 4702. Fax: (809) 765-2650.

Escuela de Artes Plasticas de Puerto Rico
San Juan, Puerto Rico CB code: 7036

4-year public art college, coed. Founded in 1965. **Accreditation:** Regional candidate. **Undergraduate enrollment:** 209 men and women. **Faculty:** 40 total (9 full time). **Location:** Urban campus in large city; Located in natural park at historic El Morro Fortress in Old San Juan. **Calendar:** Semester, limited summer session.

DEGREES OFFERED. BFA. 26 bachelor's degrees awarded in 1992. 100% in visual and performing arts.

UNDERGRADUATE MAJORS. Art education, graphic arts technology, painting, sculpture.

ACADEMIC PROGRAMS. Teacher preparation. **Remedial services:** Preadmission summer program, reduced course load, special counselor. **Placement/credit:** Institutional tests.

ACADEMIC REQUIREMENTS. Freshmen must earn minimum GPA of 1.65 to continue in good standing. 70% of freshmen return for sophomore year. Students must declare major by end of first year. **Graduation requirements:** 144 hours for bachelor's (39 in major). Most students required to take courses in arts/fine arts, English, history, mathematics, philosophy/religion, social sciences.

FRESHMAN ADMISSIONS. Selection criteria: Applicants must complete preadmissions studio course during 3 weeks in summer. Admissions committee interviews each candidate and reviews portfolio. **Additional information:** Intensive workshop in image conceptualization offered. Students learn the relationships between different techniques of expression in drawing and painting.

1992 FRESHMAN CLASS PROFILE. 20 men, 14 women enrolled. **Characteristics:** 96% from in state, 100% commute, 96% have minority backgrounds, 4% are foreign students.

FALL-TERM APPLICATIONS. $20 fee. Closing date May 16; applicants notified on a rolling basis beginning on or about July 5; must reply by registration. Interview required. Portfolio required.

STUDENT LIFE. Activities: Student government, film, magazine, radio, student newspaper, dance, music ensembles.

STUDENT SERVICES. Freshman orientation, personal counseling.

ANNUAL EXPENSES. Tuition and fees (projected): $906. **Books and supplies:** $2,000. **Other expenses:** $1,260.

FINANCIAL AID. 54% of freshmen, 61% of continuing students receive some form of aid. All grants, all jobs based on need. 19 enrolled freshmen were judged to have need, all were offered aid. **Aid applications:** No closing date; must reply by registration.

ADDRESS/TELEPHONE. Alma Santiago, Dean of Student Affairs, Escuela de Artes Plasticas de Puerto Rico, Apartado 1112, San Juan, PR 00902-1112. (809) 725-8120 ext. 230/239. Fax: (809) 725-8111.

Huertas Junior College
Caguas, Puerto Rico CB code: 3406

2-year proprietary junior college, coed. **Undergraduate enrollment:** 2,248 men and women. **Faculty:** 82 total (23 full time), 6 with doctorates or other terminal degrees. **Location:** Urban campus in small city; 24 miles from metropolitan area. **Calendar:** Trimester. Extensive evening/early morning classes. **Microcomputers:** 50 located in classrooms, computer centers.

DEGREES OFFERED. AS. 192 associate degrees awarded in 1992.

UNDERGRADUATE MAJORS. Dental assistant, pharmacy.

ACADEMIC PROGRAMS. Internships. **Remedial services:** Remedial instruction, special counselor, tutoring.

ACADEMIC REQUIREMENTS. Freshmen must earn minimum GPA of 1.5 to continue in good standing. Students must declare major on application. **Graduation requirements:** 78 hours for associate (56 in major). Most students required to take courses in English, mathematics, biological/physical sciences.

FRESHMAN ADMISSIONS. Selection criteria: Open admissions.

1992 FRESHMAN CLASS PROFILE. 1,141 men and women enrolled. **Characteristics:** 100% from in state, 100% commute, 100% have minority backgrounds. Average age is 21.

FALL-TERM APPLICATIONS. $30 fee. No closing date. Interview recommended.

STUDENT LIFE. Activities: Student government, film, magazine, radio, student newspaper, television, yearbook, choral groups.

ATHLETICS. Intercollegiate: Basketball M, volleyball M. **Intramural:** Basketball, volleyball.

STUDENT SERVICES. Aptitude testing, career counseling, employment service for undergraduates, freshman orientation, personal counseling, placement service for graduates, veterans counselor, services/facilities for handicapped.

ANNUAL EXPENSES. Tuition and fees: $2,985. **Books and supplies:** $600. **Other expenses:** $600.

FINANCIAL AID. 95% of freshmen, 95% of continuing students receive some form of aid. All aid based on need. **Aid applications:** No closing date; applicants notified on a rolling basis; must reply within 10 days.

ADDRESS/TELEPHONE. Barbara Hassim, Director of Admissions, Huertas Junior College, PO Box 8429, Caguas, PR 00726. (809) 743-1242.

ICPR Junior College
Hato Rey, Puerto Rico CB code: 7315

2-year proprietary business, junior college, coed. Founded in 1946. **Accreditation:** Regional. **Undergraduate enrollment:** 109 men, 213 women full time; 4 men, 17 women part time. **Location:** Urban campus in large city; within greater San Juan. **Calendar:** Trimester. **Additional facts:** Multicampus institution with main campus in Hato Rey and branch campuses in Arecibo and Mayaguez.

FRESHMAN ADMISSIONS. Selection criteria: Open admissions.

ANNUAL EXPENSES. Tuition and fees (1992-93): $2,476. **Books and supplies:** $465. **Other expenses:** $875.

ADDRESS/TELEPHONE. Ines M. Caban, Admissions Director, ICPR Junior College, PO Box 304, Hato Rey, PR 00919. (809) 763-1010. Fax: (809) 763-7249.

Inter American University of Puerto Rico: Aguadilla Campus
Aguadilla, Puerto Rico CB code: 2042

4-year private college of arts and sciences. **Accreditation:** Regional. **Undergraduate enrollment:** 3,288 men and women full time; 746 men and women part time. **Graduate enrollment:** 3,288 men and women full time; 746 men and women part time. **Location:** Rural campus in large town; 10 miles from Aguadilla, 66 miles from Areciba. Saturday and extensive evening/early morning classes.

FRESHMAN ADMISSIONS. Selection criteria: Regular program requires minimum 2.0 GPA from accredited secondary school and combined score of 800 on SAT or PAA.

ADDRESS/TELEPHONE. Doris Perez, Admissions Director, Inter American University of Puerto Rico: Aguadilla Campus, Box 20000, Aguadilla, PR 00605. Fax: (809) 882-3020.

Inter American University of Puerto Rico: Arecibo Campus
Arecibo, Puerto Rico CB code: 1411

Admissions:	74% of applicants accepted
Based on:	••• School record, test scores
	• Essay, interview, recommendations, special talents
Completion:	67% of freshmen end year in good standing
	63% graduate

4-year private college of arts and sciences, coed. Founded in 1957. **Accreditation:** Regional. **Undergraduate enrollment:** 1,044 men, 2,357 women full time; 431 men, 677 women part time. **Faculty:** 231 total (93 full time), 29 with doctorates or other terminal degrees. **Location:** Urban campus in small city; 45 miles from San Juan metropolitan area. **Calendar:** Semester, limited summer session. **Microcomputers:** 156 located in libraries, computer centers.

DEGREES OFFERED. AA, AAS, BA, BS. 74 associate degrees awarded in 1992. 62% in business and management, 15% business/office and marketing/distribution, 22% health sciences. 445 bachelor's degrees awarded. 33% in business and management, 8% business/office and marketing/distribution, 21% education, 9% health sciences, 9% life sciences, 18% social sciences.

UNDERGRADUATE MAJORS. Associate: Accounting, business and management, business and office, chemical manufacturing technology, computer and information sciences, elementary education, medical laboratory technologies, nursing, secretarial and related programs. **Bachelor's:** Accounting, biology, business and management, chemical manufacturing technology, chemistry, computer and information sciences, criminal justice studies, criminology, early childhood education, elementary education, English, English education, health sciences, marketing and distribution, marketing management, mathematics, microbiology, nursing, premedicine, psychology, secondary education, secretarial and related programs, social work, Spanish, special education, specific learning disabilities, teaching English as a second language/foreign language.

ACADEMIC PROGRAMS. Cooperative education, honors program, independent study, internships, teacher preparation. **Remedial services:** Preadmission summer program, remedial instruction, tutoring. **Placement/credit:** AP, institutional tests; 15 credit hours maximum for associate degree; 15 credit hours maximum for bachelor's degree.

ACADEMIC REQUIREMENTS. Freshmen must earn minimum GPA of 1.5 to continue in good standing. 78% of freshmen return for sophomore year. Students must declare major by end of first year. **Graduation requirements:** 65 hours for associate (26 in major), 124 hours for bachelor's (39 in major). Most students required to take courses in arts/fine arts, computer science, English, history, humanities, mathematics, philosophy/religion, biological/physical sciences, social sciences. **Postgraduate studies:** 87% from 2-year programs enter 4-year programs.

FRESHMAN ADMISSIONS. Selection criteria: Minimum 2.0 high school GPA. Test scores considered, minimum admission index of 800 required. **High school preparation:** 15 units required. Required units include biological science 1, English 3, foreign language 3, mathematics 3, physical science 1, social science 3 and science 1. **Test requirements:** Prueba de Aptitud Academica for Spanish speaking applicants. SAT required of English-speaking applicants. Score reports by August 3. **Additional information:** Special admissions policies apply to adults aged 21 years or older.

1992 FRESHMAN CLASS PROFILE. 1,755 men and women applied, 1,301 accepted; 341 men enrolled, 724 women enrolled. 25% had high school GPA of 3.0 or higher, 75% between 2.0 and 2.99. **Characteristics:** 100% from in state, 100% commute, 100% have minority backgrounds. Average age is 18.

FALL-TERM APPLICATIONS. $15 fee. Closing date May 15; priority given to applications received by May 1; applicants notified on a rolling basis; must reply within 2 weeks. Interview recommended for academically weak applicants. Deferred and early admission available.

STUDENT LIFE. Activities: Student government, yearbook, choral groups, drama, fraternities, sororities, Baptist Unity, Young Catholics Association, Criminal Justice Association, Haziel Evangelical Association, Future Social Workers Association, Bahai Association, Student Counseling Association, Society for Human Resources.

ATHLETICS. Intercollegiate: Basketball, soccer, softball, table tennis, tennis, track and field, volleyball. **Intramural:** Basketball, soccer, softball, table tennis, tennis, track and field, volleyball.

STUDENT SERVICES. Career counseling, employment service for undergraduates, freshman orientation, health services, personal counseling, special adviser for adult students, veterans counselor, services/facilities for handicapped.

ANNUAL EXPENSES. Tuition and fees: $3,154. **Books and supplies:** $640. **Other expenses:** $880.

FINANCIAL AID. 85% of freshmen, 95% of continuing students receive some form of aid. All aid based on need. **Aid applications:** No closing date; priority given to applications received by April 29; applicants notified on a rolling basis; must reply by registration.

ADDRESS/TELEPHONE. Provi Montalvo, Admissions Director, Inter American University of Puerto Rico: Arecibo Campus, Box UI, Arecibo, PR 00613. (809) 878-5195. Fax: (809) 880-1624.

Inter American University of Puerto Rico: Barranquitas Campus

Barranquitas, Puerto Rico — CB code: 2067

4-year private institution. **Accreditation:** Regional. **Undergraduate enrollment:** 1,478 men and women.

ADDRESS/TELEPHONE. Inter American University of Puerto Rico: Barranquitas Campus, P.O. Box 517, Barranquitas, PR 00794.

Inter American University of Puerto Rico: Bayamon Campus

Bayamon, Puerto Rico — CB code: 2043

4-year private institution. **Accreditation:** Regional. **Undergraduate enrollment:** 4,890 men and women.

ADDRESS/TELEPHONE. Inter American University of Puerto Rico: Bayamon Campus, RD 174 Minillas Industrial Park, Bayamon, PR 00619.

Inter American University of Puerto Rico: Fajardo Campus

Fajardo, Puerto Rico — CB code: 2065

4-year private institution. **Accreditation:** Regional. **Undergraduate enrollment:** 1,942 men and women.

ADDRESS/TELEPHONE. Inter American University of Puerto Rico: Fajardo Campus, P.O. Box 1029, Fajardo, PR 00738.

Inter American University of Puerto Rico: Guayama Campus

Guayama, Puerto Rico — CB code: 2077

4-year private institution. **Accreditation:** Regional. **Undergraduate enrollment:** 1,748 men and women. **Faculty:** 114 total (38 full time), 5 with doctorates or other terminal degrees. **Location:** Urban campus in large town. Saturday and extensive evening/early morning classes. **Microcomputers:** Located in classrooms, computer centers. Lease or purchase required

DEGREES OFFERED. AA, AS, AAS, BA, BS.

UNDERGRADUATE MAJORS. Associate: Accounting, business administration and management, education, elementary education, nursing, secretarial and related programs. **Bachelor's:** Business administration and management, education, elementary education, nursing, secretarial and related programs.

ACADEMIC PROGRAMS. Accelerated program, cooperative education, double major, dual enrollment of high school students, external degree, independent study, study abroad, visiting/exchange student program. **Remedial services:** Learning center, remedial instruction, tutoring. **ROTC:** Army.

ACADEMIC REQUIREMENTS. Students must declare major by end of first year. **Graduation requirements:** 128 hours for bachelor's (61 in major). Most students required to take courses in arts/fine arts, computer science, English, foreign languages, history, mathematics, philosophy/religion, biological/physical sciences, social sciences.

FRESHMAN ADMISSIONS. Selection criteria: High school graduates must have 2.0 GPA and 800 admission index. **Test requirements:** Prueba de Aptitud Academica for Spanish speaking applicants. SAT accepted. Score reports must be received by May 15.

1992 FRESHMAN CLASS PROFILE. 458 men and women enrolled. **Characteristics:** 100% commute. Average age is 18.

FALL-TERM APPLICATIONS. $15 fee. No closing date; priority given to applications received by May 15; applicants notified on a rolling basis beginning on or about April 1; must reply within 3 weeks. Interview required. Early admission available.

STUDENT LIFE. Activities: Student government, magazine, radio, choral groups, dance, drama, religious circle.

ATHLETICS. NSCAA. **Intercollegiate:** Baseball, basketball, cross-country. **Intramural:** Baseball, basketball, cross-country, swimming, table tennis, tennis.

STUDENT SERVICES. Aptitude testing, career counseling, employment service for undergraduates, freshman orientation, health services, on-campus day care, personal counseling, placement service for graduates, special adviser for adult students, veterans counselor, services/facilities for handicapped.

ANNUAL EXPENSES. Tuition and fees (1992-93): $2,734. **Books and supplies:** $640.

FINANCIAL AID. 98% of freshmen, 92% of continuing students receive some form of aid. 18% of grants, all loans, all jobs based on need. **Aid applications:** Closing date April 29; applicants notified on or about June 15; must reply by July 30.

ADDRESS/TELEPHONE. Laura E. Ferrer Sanchez, Admission Director, Inter American University of Puerto Rico: Guayama Campus, P.O. Box 1559, Guayama, PR 00784. Fax: (809) 864-8232.

Inter American University of Puerto Rico: Metropolitan Campus

San Juan, Puerto Rico — CB code: 0873

4-year private university, coed. Founded in 1962. **Accreditation:** Regional. **Undergraduate enrollment:** 3,899 men, 5,139 women full time; 1,182 men, 1,728 women part time. **Graduate enrollment:** 138 men, 386 women full time; 483 men, 945 women part time. **Faculty:** 662 total (256 full time), 209 with doctorates or other terminal degrees. **Location:** Urban campus in large city; 9 miles from San Juan. **Calendar:** Semester, limited summer session. Saturday and extensive evening/early morning classes.

DEGREES OFFERED. AA, AS, AAS, BA, BS, MA, MS, MBA, EdD, OD. 23 associate degrees awarded in 1992. 992 bachelor's degrees awarded. Graduate degrees offered in 23 major fields of study.

UNDERGRADUATE MAJORS. Associate: Accounting, business and management, secretarial and related programs. **Bachelor's:** Accounting, biology, business and management, business economics, chemistry, computer and information sciences, criminal justice studies, electronic technology, elementary education, English, English education, English literature, finance, history, management information systems, marketing management, mathematics, mathematics education, medical laboratory technologies, nursing, physical education, physical sciences, political science and government, psychology, public administration, science education, secretarial and related programs, social sciences, social studies education, social work, sociology, Spanish, special education, teaching English as a second language/foreign language.

ACADEMIC PROGRAMS. Accelerated program, double major, honors program, independent study, internships, study abroad. **Remedial services:** Preadmission summer program, remedial instruction. **Placement/credit:** CLEP General, institutional tests; 15 credit hours maximum for associate degree; 15 credit hours maximum for bachelor's degree.

ACADEMIC REQUIREMENTS. Freshmen must earn minimum GPA of 1.5 to continue in good standing. Students must declare major by end of first year. **Graduation requirements:** 65 hours for associate (26 in major), 124 hours for bachelor's (39 in major). Most students required to take courses in history, humanities, mathematics, philosophy/religion, biological/physical sciences, social sciences. **Additional information:** Adult education programs available.

FRESHMAN ADMISSIONS. Selection criteria: School grade average and test scores important. **High school preparation:** 15 units required. **Test**

requirements: Prueba de Aptitud Academica for Spanish speaking applicants. SAT required of English-speaking applicants. Score report by May 1. **Additional information:** Special admissions policies apply to adults aged 21 years or older.

1992 FRESHMAN CLASS PROFILE. 1,014 men, 1,156 women enrolled. 23% had high school GPA of 3.0 or higher, 73% between 2.0 and 2.99. **Characteristics:** 100% commute.

FALL-TERM APPLICATIONS. $15 fee. Closing date May 15; applicants notified on a rolling basis; must reply by registration. Early admission available.

STUDENT LIFE. Activities: Student government, choral groups, drama.

ATHLETICS. Intercollegiate: Basketball, softball, swimming, tennis, track and field, volleyball, wrestling M. **Intramural:** Basketball, softball, table tennis, tennis, volleyball. **Clubs:** Intercollegiate table tennis.

STUDENT SERVICES. Career counseling, employment service for undergraduates, freshman orientation, health services, personal counseling, placement service for graduates, veterans counselor, services/facilities for handicapped.

ANNUAL EXPENSES. Tuition and fees (1992-93): $2,608. **Room and board:** $2,916. **Books and supplies:** $590. **Other expenses:** $880.

FINANCIAL AID. 85% of freshmen, 95% of continuing students receive some form of aid. All aid based on need. **Aid applications:** Closing date April 30.

ADDRESS/TELEPHONE. Magal Gonzalez-Figueroa, Director of Admissions, Inter American University of Puerto Rico: Metropolitan Campus, PO Box 1293, Hato Rey, Rio Piedras, PR 00919. (809) 758-8000.

Inter American University of Puerto Rico: Ponce Campus

Mercedita, Puerto Rico CB code: 3531

4-year private institution. **Accreditation:** Regional. **Undergraduate enrollment:** 3,555 men and women.

ADDRESS/TELEPHONE. Inter American University of Puerto Rico: Ponce Campus, Barrio Sabanetas Carretera 1, Mercedita, PR 00715.

Inter American University of Puerto Rico: San German Campus

San German, Puerto Rico CB code: 0946

4-year private university, coed. Founded in 1912. **Accreditation:** Regional. **Undergraduate enrollment:** 1,756 men, 2,567 women full time; 385 men, 474 women part time. **Graduate enrollment:** 38 men, 60 women full time; 222 men, 439 women part time. **Faculty:** 318 total (158 full time), 68 with doctorates or other terminal degrees. **Location:** Suburban campus in large town; 14 miles from Mayaguez, 104 miles from San Juan. **Calendar:** Semester. **Microcomputers:** 208 located in libraries, classrooms, computer centers. **Special facilities:** Nature preserve, botanical garden, museum.

DEGREES OFFERED. AS, BA, BS, MA, MBA, MEd. 33 associate degrees awarded in 1992. 15% in business/office and marketing/distribution, 49% health sciences, 36% allied health. 757 bachelor's degrees awarded. 38% in business and management, 5% computer sciences, 16% teacher education, 8% health sciences, 9% life sciences, 5% social sciences. Graduate degrees offered in 16 major fields of study.

UNDERGRADUATE MAJORS. Associate: Accounting, business administration and management, business and management, business and office, business data programming, education, medical records administration, radiograph medical technology, secretarial and related programs, word processing. **Bachelor's:** Accounting, art education, biological and physical sciences, biology, biomedical science, business administration and management, business and management, business and office, business data programming, business economics, ceramics, chemistry, computer and information sciences, drawing, economics, education, electronic technology, elementary education, English, English education, fine arts, history, junior high education, linguistics, management information systems, marketing management, mathematics, mathematics education, medical laboratory technologies, microbiology, music education, music performance, nursing, painting, photography, physical education, political science and government, premedicine, psychology, public administration, pure mathematics, science education, secondary education, secretarial and related programs, social sciences, social studies education, sociology, Spanish, special education, teaching English as a second language/foreign language, word processing.

ACADEMIC PROGRAMS. Accelerated program, cooperative education, double major, dual enrollment of high school students, honors program, independent study, internships, study abroad, teacher preparation, cross-registration; combined bachelor's/graduate program in business administration. **Remedial services:** Learning center, reduced course load, remedial instruction, special counselor, tutoring. **ROTC:** Air Force, Army, Naval. **Placement/credit:** CLEP General, institutional tests.

ACADEMIC REQUIREMENTS. Freshmen must earn minimum GPA of 2.0 to continue in good standing. 87% of freshmen return for sophomore year. Students must declare major on application. **Graduation requirements:** 60 hours for associate (30 in major), 129 hours for bachelor's (60 in major). Most students required to take courses in arts/fine arts, English, foreign languages, history, mathematics, philosophy/religion, biological/physical sciences, social sciences. **Additional information:** BEST program (Bilingual English-Spanish Track) enables students to learn English or Spanish while taking courses in their native language.

FRESHMAN ADMISSIONS. Selection criteria: High school GPA, test scores considered. **High school preparation:** 15 units recommended. Recommended units include biological science 1, English 3, mathematics 3, physical science 1, social science 2 and science 1. 3 units of Spanish required of Spanish-speaking students. **Test requirements:** Prueba de Aptitud Academica for Spanish speaking applicants. SAT required of English-speaking applicants, score report by May 15.

1992 FRESHMAN CLASS PROFILE. 993 men and women enrolled. 34% had high school GPA of 3.0 or higher, 62% between 2.0 and 2.99. **Characteristics:** 98% from in state, 15% live in college housing, 99% have minority backgrounds, 1% are foreign students, 20% join fraternities/sororities. Average age is 18.

FALL-TERM APPLICATIONS. $15 fee. Closing date May 15; applicants notified on a rolling basis beginning on or about February 15; must reply within 2 weeks. Interview recommended. Audition recommended for music applicants. Portfolio recommended for art applicants. Essay recommended. Deferred and early admission available.

STUDENT LIFE. Housing: Dormitories (men, women); apartment housing available. **Activities:** Student government, student newspaper, choral groups, concert band, dance, drama, jazz band, marching band, music ensembles, pep band, fraternities, sororities, Bajai Association, Student Bible Union, International Students Organization, Counselors Students Association, Catholic Student Organization, Bilingual English-Spanish Organization (BESO).

ATHLETICS. Intercollegiate: Basketball, cross-country, soccer M, softball, swimming, table tennis, tennis, track and field, volleyball, wrestling M. **Intramural:** Basketball, cross-country, handball W, softball, table tennis, tennis, track and field, volleyball, water polo W.

STUDENT SERVICES. Career counseling, employment service for undergraduates, freshman orientation, health services, on-campus day care, personal counseling, placement service for graduates, special adviser for adult students, veterans counselor, services/facilities for handicapped.

ANNUAL EXPENSES. Tuition and fees (1992-93): $2,500. **Room and board:** $2,050. **Books and supplies:** $700. **Other expenses:** $800.

FINANCIAL AID. 80% of freshmen, 90% of continuing students receive some form of aid. All aid based on need. **Aid applications:** Closing date April 30; applicants notified on or about June 15; must reply by August 1.

ADDRESS/TELEPHONE. Mildred Camacho, Director of Admissions, Inter American Univ Puerto Rico: San German Campus, Call Box 5100, San German, PR 00683. (809) 892-3090. Fax: (809) 892-6350.

Pontifical Catholic University of Puerto Rico

Ponce, Puerto Rico CB code: 0910

Admissions:	81% of applicants accepted
Based on:	••• School record
	•• Test scores
	• Essay, special talents
Completion:	75% of freshmen end year in good standing

4-year private university, coed, affiliated with Roman Catholic Church. Founded in 1948. **Accreditation:** Regional. **Undergraduate enrollment:** 3,322 men, 6,040 women full time; 682 men, 1,160 women part time. **Graduate enrollment:** 299 men, 314 women full time; 182 men, 367 women part time. **Faculty:** 676 total (456 full time), 60 with doctorates or other terminal degrees. **Location:** Urban campus in small city; 60 miles south of San Juan. **Calendar:** Semester, limited summer session. **Microcomputers:** 360 located in libraries, computer centers. **Special facilities:** Multipurpose building including theater, courts, pool, and gym.

DEGREES OFFERED. AA, AS, AAS, BA, BS, MA, MS, MBA, JD. 54 associate degrees awarded in 1992. 35% in business and management, 22% business/office and marketing/distribution, 26% computer sciences, 17% allied health. 1,148 bachelor's degrees awarded. 30% in business and management, 14% business/office and marketing/distribution, 16% teacher education, 11% health sciences, 9% life sciences. Graduate degrees offered in 14 major fields of study.

UNDERGRADUATE MAJORS. Associate: Business and office, computer programming, education, fashion design, gerontology, liberal/general studies, secretarial and related programs, teacher aide. **Bachelor's:** Accounting, art education, biology, business administration and management, business and management, business data processing and related programs, business economics, business education, chemistry, communications, criminology, education, elementary education, English, English education, finance, fine arts, French, gerontology, hispanic studies, history, home economics, home economics education, marketing and distribution, mathematics, mathematics education, medical laboratory technologies, music, music education, nursing, philosophy, physical education, physics, political science and government, psychology, public administration, science education, secondary education, secretarial and related programs, social sciences, social studies education, social work, sociology, Spanish, special education, teaching English as a second language/foreign language, theological studies.

ACADEMIC PROGRAMS. Accelerated program, double major, dual enrollment of high school students, honors program, independent study, internships, study abroad, visiting/exchange student program; liberal arts/career combination in health sciences; combined bachelor's/graduate program in business administration, law. **Remedial services:** Learning center, preadmission summer program, reduced course load, remedial instruction, tutoring. **ROTC:** Army. **Placement/credit:** AP, institutional tests; 30 credit hours maximum for bachelor's degree.

ACADEMIC REQUIREMENTS. Freshmen must earn minimum GPA of 2.0 to continue in good standing. 96% of freshmen return for sophomore year. Students must declare major by end of first year. **Graduation requirements:** 72 hours for associate (15 in major), 139 hours for bachelor's (30 in major). Most students required to take courses in computer science, English, foreign languages, history, humanities, mathematics, philosophy/religion, biological/physical sciences, social sciences.

FRESHMAN ADMISSIONS. Selection criteria: School achievement record, test scores considered. **High school preparation:** 10 units required. Required units include biological science 1, English 3, foreign language 3, mathematics 2 and science 1. One history recommended. 10 units required for 3-year high schools, 15 units for 4-year high schools. **Test requirements:** Prueba de Aptitud Academica for Spanish speaking applicants. SAT required of English-speaking applicants. Score reports by July 15.

1992 FRESHMAN CLASS PROFILE. 1,459 men applied, 1,144 accepted, 853 enrolled; 2,291 women applied, 1,889 accepted, 1,384 enrolled. 23% had high school GPA of 3.0 or higher, 77% between 2.0 and 2.99. **Characteristics:** 99% from in state, 95% commute, 100% have minority backgrounds, 1% are foreign students. Average age is 19.

FALL-TERM APPLICATIONS. $15 fee, may be waived for applicants with need. Closing date July 15; applicants notified on a rolling basis beginning on or about February 15; must reply by April 30 or within 2 weeks if notified thereafter. Interview required for special program applicants. Early admission available.

STUDENT LIFE. Housing: Dormitories (men, women). **Activities:** Student government, film, radio, student newspaper, television, yearbook, choral groups, dance, drama, marching band, musical theater, pep band, fraternities, sororities, Pi Gamma Mu, Phi Alpha Theta, Beta Beta Beta, Phi Delta Kappa, honor society for business students, pioneer students in Christ and Mary, Miles Jesu, Knights of Columbus.

ATHLETICS. NCAA. **Intercollegiate:** Baseball, basketball, cross-country, diving, soccer, softball, swimming, table tennis, tennis, track and field, volleyball, water polo M, wrestling M. **Intramural:** Archery, baseball, basketball, cross-country, diving, softball, swimming, table tennis, tennis, track and field, volleyball, wrestling M.

STUDENT SERVICES. Aptitude testing, career counseling, employment service for undergraduates, freshman orientation, health services, personal counseling, placement service for graduates, veterans counselor, services/facilities for handicapped.

ANNUAL EXPENSES. Tuition and fees (1992-93): $2,413. **Room and board:** $2,452. **Books and supplies:** $350. **Other expenses:** $1,050.

FINANCIAL AID. 88% of freshmen, 82% of continuing students receive some form of aid. 99% of grants, all loans, 86% of jobs based on need. Music/drama, art, athletic, religious affiliation scholarships available. **Aid applications:** No closing date; priority given to applications received by June 24; applicants notified on a rolling basis beginning on or about August 1; must reply within 2 weeks.

ADDRESS/TELEPHONE. Carilin Catasus de Frau, Director of Admissions, Pontifical Catholic University of Puerto Rico, Las Americas Ave, Station 6, Ponce, PR 00732. (809) 841-2000 ext. 426. Fax: (809) 840-4295.

Technological College of the Municipality of San Juan
Hato Rey, Puerto Rico CB code: 0391

2-year public nursing, technical college, coed. Founded in 1972. **Accreditation:** Regional. **Undergraduate enrollment:** 457 men, 448 women full time; 83 men, 74 women part time. **Faculty:** 80 total (44 full time). **Location:** Urban campus in large city; in downtown area. **Calendar:** Semester. **Microcomputers:** Located in computer centers. **Special facilities:** Language laboratory, learning resource center, amphitheater. **Additional facts:** All programs and services of institution oriented to meet needs of San Juan community, particularly those from socio-economically disadvantaged areas.

DEGREES OFFERED. AAS. 194 associate degrees awarded in 1992. 13% in business/office and marketing/distribution, 17% computer sciences, 14% engineering technologies, 52% health sciences.

UNDERGRADUATE MAJORS. Accounting, bilingual secretary, computer programming, electronic technology, nursing, secretarial and related programs.

ACADEMIC PROGRAMS. Internships. **Remedial services:** Learning center, remedial instruction, special counselor, tutoring, speed reading project, language laboratory.

ACADEMIC REQUIREMENTS. Freshmen must earn minimum GPA of 1.6 to continue in good standing. 63% of freshmen return for sophomore year. Students must declare major on application. **Graduation requirements:** 73 hours for associate (41 in major). Most students required to take courses in computer science, English, humanities, mathematics, social sciences. **Additional information:** Basic Development Year: special program through which students can improve basic skills in English, Spanish, and mathematics, and receive introduction to content areas related to program of study. At end of year, students admitted to program as regular students if they meet requirements for associate's degree.

FRESHMAN ADMISSIONS. Selection criteria: Combined College Board test scores of 2,000 or more and 2.0 high school GPA required for regular students. Special consideration and priority to applicants from low-income families. **High school preparation:** 10 units required. Required units include biological science 1, English 3, mathematics 2, social science 2 and science 2. 3 Spanish and 2 elective courses required. Biological science and algebra recommended for nursing program applicants, physical science for electronic program applicants. **Test requirements:** Prueba de Aptitud Academica for Spanish speaking applicants. SAT accepted from U.S. applicants. Score reports by July 15. **Additional information:** Through Basic Development Year program, special consideration given to those whose high school GPA is less than 2.00 and combined College Board test scores below 2000.

1992 FRESHMAN CLASS PROFILE. 160 men, 153 women enrolled. 32% had high school GPA of 3.0 or higher, 44% between 2.0 and 2.99. **Characteristics:** 87% from in state, 100% commute, 100% have minority backgrounds, 3% are foreign students. Average age is 21.

FALL-TERM APPLICATIONS. No fee. Closing date July 31; priority given to applications received by April 30; applicants notified on or about June 1; must reply by July 15. Interview required for nursing applicants.

STUDENT LIFE. Activities: Student government.

ATHLETICS. Intercollegiate: Volleyball. **Intramural:** Basketball M, cross-country, racquetball, softball M, table tennis, volleyball.

STUDENT SERVICES. Career counseling, employment service for undergraduates, freshman orientation, health services, personal counseling, placement service for graduates, veterans counselor, services/facilities for handicapped.

ANNUAL EXPENSES. Tuition and fees: $655. **Room and board:** $1,800. **Books and supplies:** $540. **Other expenses:** $800.

FINANCIAL AID. 98% of freshmen receive some form of aid. All grants, all jobs based on need. 945 enrolled freshmen were judged to have need, 199 were offered aid. **Aid applications:** Closing date September 30; applicants notified on or about October 30.

ADDRESS/TELEPHONE. Ruth E. Vicens, Admissions Officer, Technological College of San Juan, Jose R. Oliver Street, Tres Monjitas Industrial Park, Hato Rey, PR 00936. (809) 250-7111 ext. 249/250. Fax: (809) 250-7395.

Turabo University
Gurabo, Puerto Rico CB code: 0780

Admissions: 82% of applicants accepted
Based on: ••• School record
•• Interview, test scores
• Special talents
Completion: 80% of freshmen end year in good standing

4-year private university, coed. Founded in 1972. **Accreditation:** Regional. **Undergraduate enrollment:** 2,460 men, 3,709 women full time; 355 men, 424 women part time. **Graduate enrollment:** 39 men, 39 women full time; 330 men, 417 women part time. **Faculty:** 366 total (108 full time), 53 with doctorates or other terminal degrees. **Location:** Urban campus in small city; 17 miles from San Juan. **Calendar:** Semester, limited summer session. **Microcomputers:** Located in computer centers. **Special facilities:** Museum. **Additional facts:** 4 off-campus sites.

DEGREES OFFERED. AS, BA, BS, MBA, MEd. 67 associate degrees awarded in 1992. 67% in business and management, 33% business/office and marketing/distribution. 706 bachelor's degrees awarded. 32% in business and management, 10% business/office and marketing/distribution, 29% education, 7% psychology, 19% social sciences. Graduate degrees offered in 5 major fields of study.

UNDERGRADUATE MAJORS. Associate: Accounting, biology, business administration and management, business and office, education, liberal/general studies, science technologies, secretarial and related programs, teacher aide. **Bachelor's:** Accounting, biology, business administration and management, business and management, chemistry, computer and information sciences, criminology, economics, education, education of the deaf and hearing impaired, education of the emotionally handicapped, education of the mentally handicapped, elementary education, engineering, manufacturing technology, marketing management, mechanical engineering, political science and government, psychology, secondary education, secretarial and related programs, social sciences, sociology, special education, specific learning disabilities.

ACADEMIC PROGRAMS. 2-year transfer program, honors program. **Remedial services:** Remedial instruction, special counselor, tutoring, Basic Skills Institute. **Placement/credit:** AP, CLEP General and Subject, institutional tests.

ACADEMIC REQUIREMENTS. Freshmen must earn minimum GPA of 1.6 to continue in good standing. 66% of freshmen return for sophomore year. **Graduation requirements:** 75 hours for associate, 129 hours for bachelor's (24 in major).

FRESHMAN ADMISSIONS. Selection criteria: Minimum 2.0 high school GPA for secretarial applicants, 2.5 for science applicants. **High school preparation:** 15 units required. Required units include English 3, foreign language 3, mathematics 2, social science 2 and science 2. **Test requirements:** Prueba de Aptitud Academica for Spanish speaking applicants. SAT required for admission to honors and science programs.

1992 FRESHMAN CLASS PROFILE. 2,100 men and women applied, 1,717 accepted; 645 men enrolled, 829 women enrolled. 16% had high school GPA of 3.0 or higher, 58% between 2.0 and 2.99. **Characteristics:** 100% from in state, 100% commute. Average age is 19.

FALL-TERM APPLICATIONS. $15 fee. $15 application fee for undergraduate, $25 for graduate. No closing date; applicants notified on a rolling basis beginning on or about March 1. Interview required for applicants with less than 2.0 high school GPA.

STUDENT LIFE. Activities: Student government, choral groups, dance, drama, music ensembles.

ATHLETICS. Intercollegiate: Basketball, cross-country, softball, track and field, volleyball. **Intramural:** Basketball, softball, table tennis, volleyball.

STUDENT SERVICES. Aptitude testing, career counseling, employment service for undergraduates, freshman orientation, health services, personal counseling, placement service for graduates, services/facilities for handicapped.

ANNUAL EXPENSES. Tuition and fees (1992-93): $2,750. **Books and supplies:** $300. **Other expenses:** $1,045.

FINANCIAL AID. 80% of freshmen, 90% of continuing students receive some form of aid. **Aid applications:** No closing date; applicants notified on a rolling basis beginning on or about July 15.

ADDRESS/TELEPHONE. Jesus Torres, Admissions Director, Turabo University, PO Box 3030, Gurabo, PR 00778. (809) 746-3009.

Universidad Adventista de las Antillas
Mayaguez, Puerto Rico — CB code: 1020

4-year private liberal arts college, coed, affiliated with Seventh-day Adventists. Founded in 1957. **Accreditation:** Regional. **Undergraduate enrollment:** 294 men, 468 women full time; 33 men, 59 women part time. **Faculty:** 66 total (45 full time), 10 with doctorates or other terminal degrees. **Location:** Suburban campus in small city; 100 miles from San Juan. **Calendar:** Semester, limited summer session. **Microcomputers:** 75 located in computer centers.

DEGREES OFFERED. AA, AS, BA, BS. 34 associate degrees awarded in 1992. 12% in business and management, 12% business/office and marketing/distribution, 76% health sciences. 88 bachelor's degrees awarded. 6% in business and management, 18% business/office and marketing/distribution, 5% computer sciences, 18% teacher education, 37% health sciences, 6% life sciences, 8% philosophy, religion, theology.

UNDERGRADUATE MAJORS. Associate: Business administration and management, computer and information sciences, medical records technology, medical secretary, nursing, practical nursing, religion, respiratory therapy technology, secretarial and related programs, word processing. **Bachelor's:** Biology, business administration and management, chemistry, computer and information sciences, computer programming, elementary education, history, music, music education, music performance, nursing, practical nursing, religion, secondary education, secretarial and related programs, Spanish, systems analysis, theological studies.

ACADEMIC PROGRAMS. Double major, honors program, internships. **Remedial services:** Learning center, reduced course load, remedial instruction, special counselor, tutoring. **Placement/credit:** AP, CLEP Subject, institutional tests; 12 credit hours maximum for associate degree; 12 credit hours maximum for bachelor's degree.

ACADEMIC REQUIREMENTS. Freshmen must earn minimum GPA of 2.0 to continue in good standing. 54% of freshmen return for sophomore year. Students must declare major on enrollment. **Graduation requirements:** 64 hours for associate (44 in major), 128 hours for bachelor's (54 in major). Most students required to take courses in arts/fine arts, computer science, English, foreign languages, history, mathematics, philosophy/religion, biological/physical sciences. **Postgraduate studies:** 67% from 2-year programs enter 4-year programs.

FRESHMAN ADMISSIONS. Selection criteria: Recommendations, test scores important. Minimum 2.0 GPA required. **High school preparation:** 15 units required. Required units include biological science 1, English 3, mathematics 2, physical science 1, social science 2 and science 1. 3 Spanish, 2 electives required. **Test requirements:** Prueba de Aptitud Academica for Spanish speaking applicants. SAT or ACT required for English-speaking applicants. Score reports by August 10.

1992 FRESHMAN CLASS PROFILE. 89 men, 141 women enrolled. 30% had high school GPA of 3.0 or higher, 55% between 2.0 and 2.99. **Characteristics:** 92% from in state, 63% commute, 8% are foreign students. Average age is 19.

FALL-TERM APPLICATIONS. $15 fee. Closing date July 31; applicants notified on a rolling basis. Interview required for nursing applicants. Deferred admission available.

STUDENT LIFE. Housing: Dormitories (men, women); apartment housing available. **Activities:** Student government, student newspaper, yearbook, choral groups, drama, music ensembles, fraternities, sororities, Medical Cadets Corps. **Additional information:** Religious environment designed for Seventh-day Adventist student.

ATHLETICS. Intramural: Basketball M, gymnastics, soccer M, softball M, swimming, table tennis, track and field, volleyball.

STUDENT SERVICES. Aptitude testing, career counseling, health services, personal counseling, placement service for graduates.

ANNUAL EXPENSES. Tuition and fees (1992-93): $2,728. **Room and board:** $1,960. **Books and supplies:** $300. **Other expenses:** $500.

FINANCIAL AID. 89% of freshmen, 73% of continuing students receive some form of aid. All aid based on need. **Aid applications:** No closing date; applicants notified on a rolling basis beginning on or about August 15; must reply within 3 weeks.

ADDRESS/TELEPHONE. Wilma Gonzalez, Director of Admissions, Universidad Adventista de las Antillas, PO Box 118, Mayaguez, PR 00681. (809) 834-9595. Fax: (809) 834-9597.

Universidad Metropolitana
Rio Piedras, Puerto Rico — CB code: 1519

Admissions: 66% of applicants accepted
Based on: ••• School record, test scores
Completion: 69% of freshmen end year in good standing

4-year private university and college of arts and sciences, coed. Founded in 1985. **Accreditation:** Regional. **Undergraduate enrollment:** 1,492 men, 2,884 women full time; 304 men, 537 women part time. **Graduate enrollment:** 4 men, 23 women full time; 88 men, 104 women part time. **Faculty:** 278 total (99 full time), 40 with doctorates or other terminal degrees. **Location:** Urban campus in large city; 3 miles from San Juan. **Calendar:** Semester, limited summer session. **Microcomputers:** Located in computer centers.

DEGREES OFFERED. AS, AAS, BA, BS, MBA, MEd. 76 associate degrees awarded in 1992. 96% in allied health. 418 bachelor's degrees awarded. 49% in business and management, 28% education, 14% health sciences, 5% life sciences.

UNDERGRADUATE MAJORS. Associate: Biological and physical sciences, computer programming, liberal/general studies, medical records technology, nursing, respiratory therapy technology. **Bachelor's:** Accounting, bilingual/bicultural education, biological and physical sciences, biology, business administration and management, business and management, business and office, computer and information sciences, computer programming, education, education of the physically handicapped, elementary education, English education, finance, gerontology, human resources development, information sciences and systems, management information systems, marketing management, mathematics, mathematics education, nursing, premedicine, psychology, respiratory therapy technology, science education, secondary education, social sciences, special education.

ACADEMIC PROGRAMS. Honors program, telecourses. **Remedial services:** Remedial instruction, special counselor, tutoring. **ROTC:** Army.

ACADEMIC REQUIREMENTS. Freshmen must earn minimum GPA of 1.6 to continue in good standing. 54% of freshmen return for sophomore year. Students must declare major on application. **Graduation requirements:** 75 hours for associate (34 in major), 136 hours for bachelor's (33 in major). Most students required to take courses in English, mathematics, biological/physical sciences, social sciences.

FRESHMAN ADMISSIONS. Selection criteria: School achievement record and test scores considered. **Test requirements:** Prueba de Aptitud Academica for Spanish speaking applicants. SAT required of English-speaking applicants. **Additional information:** Foreign applicants must have college credits.

1992 FRESHMAN CLASS PROFILE. 2,222 men and women applied, 1,458 accepted; 400 men enrolled, 714 women enrolled. 14% had high school GPA of 3.0 or higher, 61% between 2.0 and 2.99. **Characteristics:** 100% commute, 100% have minority backgrounds.

FALL-TERM APPLICATIONS. $15 application fee for undergraduate, $25 for graduate. Closing date July 30; applicants notified on a rolling basis. Interview required for academically weak applicants. Deferred and early admission available.

STUDENT LIFE. Activities: Student government, student newspaper, choral groups, drama, fraternities, business students association.

ATHLETICS. Intramural: Basketball, softball, volleyball.

STUDENT SERVICES. Career counseling, employment service for

undergraduates, health services, personal counseling, placement service for graduates, services/facilities for handicapped.

ANNUAL EXPENSES. Tuition and fees: $2,940. **Books and supplies:** $300. **Other expenses:** $1,045.

FINANCIAL AID. 95% of continuing students receive some form of aid. All aid based on need. **Aid applications:** Closing date June 30; applicants notified on or about July 30; must reply by August 15.

ADDRESS/TELEPHONE. Carmen Rosado, Director of Admissions, Universidad Metropolitana, Apartado 21150, Rio Piedras, PR 00928. (809) 765-6262.

Universidad Politecnica de Puerto Rico
Hato Rey, Puerto Rico — CB code: 0614

Admissions: 89% of applicants accepted
Based on: ••• School record
•• Test scores
• Essay, interview, recommendations
Completion: 60% of freshmen end year in good standing
2% enter graduate study

5-year private engineering college, coed. Founded in 1966. **Accreditation:** Regional. **Undergraduate enrollment:** 2,974 men, 593 women full time; 997 men, 156 women part time. **Graduate enrollment:** 37 men, 3 women full time; 11 men, 1 woman part time. **Faculty:** 189 total (63 full time), 8 with doctorates or other terminal degrees. **Location:** Urban campus in large city; 3 miles from San Juan. **Calendar:** Quarter, extensive summer session. **Microcomputers:** Located in libraries, computer centers.

DEGREES OFFERED. BS, MBA. 133 bachelor's degrees awarded in 1992. 100% in engineering. Graduate degrees offered in 1 major field of study.

UNDERGRADUATE MAJORS. Business and management, civil engineering, electrical/electronics/communications engineering, industrial engineering, mechanical engineering, surveying and mapping sciences.

ACADEMIC PROGRAMS. Cooperative education. **Remedial services:** Preadmission summer program, reduced course load, remedial instruction, special counselor, tutoring. **ROTC:** Air Force, Army. **Placement/credit:** AP.

ACADEMIC REQUIREMENTS. Freshmen must earn minimum GPA of 2.0 to continue in good standing. 50% of freshmen return for sophomore year. Students must declare major on application. **Graduation requirements:** 176 hours for bachelor's (39 in major). Most students required to take courses in computer science, English, history, humanities, mathematics, biological/physical sciences, social sciences.

FRESHMAN ADMISSIONS. Selection criteria: Minimum 2.5 high school GPA and PAA combined score of 1300 required. **High school preparation:** 15 units required. **Test requirements:** SAT required of English-speaking applicants, score report by July 31. PAA and 3 ACH required of applicants under age 25, score reports by July 17.

1992 FRESHMAN CLASS PROFILE. 45% had high school GPA of 3.0 or higher, 53% between 2.0 and 2.99. **Characteristics:** 100% from in state, 100% commute, 90% have minority backgrounds. Average age is 18.

FALL-TERM APPLICATIONS. $30 fee. Closing date July 15; applicants notified on or about July 30. Deferred admission available.

STUDENT LIFE. Activities: Student government, student newspaper, fraternities, University Bible Association, Drugs and Alcohol Committee.

ATHLETICS. Intercollegiate: Basketball, cross-country, softball, table tennis, tennis, volleyball. **Intramural:** Basketball, softball, table tennis, volleyball.

STUDENT SERVICES. Aptitude testing, career counseling, employment service for undergraduates, health services, personal counseling, placement service for graduates, veterans counselor.

ANNUAL EXPENSES. Tuition and fees (projected): $3,300. **Books and supplies:** $1,016. **Other expenses:** $952.

FINANCIAL AID. 76% of freshmen, 72% of continuing students receive some form of aid. All grants, all loans, 83% of jobs based on need. **Aid applications:** Closing date June 30; priority given to applications received by May 31; applicants notified on or about August 15; must reply by September 15.

ADDRESS/TELEPHONE. Teresa Cardona, Admission Director, Universidad Politecnica de Puerto Rico, 377 Ponce de Leon Avenue, Hato Rey, PR 00918. (809) 754-8000. Fax: (809) 763-8919.

University of Puerto Rico: Aguadilla
Aguadilla, Puerto Rico — CB code: 0983

2-year public college of arts and sciences and technical college, coed. Founded in 1972. **Accreditation:** Regional. **Undergraduate enrollment:** 557 men, 748 women full time; 69 men, 61 women part time. **Faculty:** 82 total (81 full time), 12 with doctorates or other terminal degrees. **Location:** Suburban campus in small city; 81 miles from San Juan. **Calendar:** Semester, limited summer session. **Microcomputers:** 57 located in libraries, computer centers.

DEGREES OFFERED. AA, AS. 147 associate degrees awarded in 1992. 35% in business and management, 26% business/office and marketing/distribution, 9% computer sciences, 19% engineering technologies, 5% life sciences, 6% multi/interdisciplinary studies.

UNDERGRADUATE MAJORS. Biology, business administration and management, computer programming, electronic technology, liberal/general studies, quality control technology, secretarial and related programs, toxicology.

ACADEMIC PROGRAMS. 2-year transfer program, dual enrollment of high school students, honors program. **Remedial services:** Learning center, remedial instruction, tutoring. **Placement/credit:** AP, CLEP General and Subject, institutional tests; 12 credit hours maximum for associate degree.

ACADEMIC REQUIREMENTS. Students must earn minimum GPA of 2.0 upon completion of 24 semester hours to remain in good academic standing. 69% of freshmen return for sophomore year. Students must declare major on application. **Graduation requirements:** 69 hours for associate. Most students required to take courses in English, social sciences.

FRESHMAN ADMISSIONS. Selection criteria: School GPA, test scores important. Recommended units include English 3, mathematics 2 and social science 2. Spanish 3 also recommended. **Test requirements:** Prueba de Aptitud Academica for Spanish speaking applicants. SAT required of English-speaking applicants. Score reports by February 28.

1992 FRESHMAN CLASS PROFILE. 561 men, 321 women enrolled. **Characteristics:** 100% from in state, 100% commute, 100% have minority backgrounds.

FALL-TERM APPLICATIONS. $15 fee. Closing date January 30; priority given to applications received by November 30; applicants notified on or about May 15; must reply by May 30. Early admission available.

STUDENT LIFE. Activities: Student government, student newspaper, choral groups, drama, fraternities, sororities, Organizacion Juventud en Cristo, Estudiantes Orientadores, Juventud Accion Catolica, Teatro Experimental 80, Asociacion de Ciencias Secretariales, Bio-Study, Asociacion Quality Control (ASQS), Federacion Adventistas Universitarios (FADU).

ATHLETICS. Intercollegiate: Basketball, cross-country, softball W, tennis, track and field, volleyball. **Intramural:** Basketball M, cross-country, softball M, table tennis, volleyball. **Clubs:** Softball M, table tennis.

STUDENT SERVICES. Aptitude testing, career counseling, employment service for undergraduates, health services, personal counseling, placement service for graduates, services/facilities for handicapped.

ANNUAL EXPENSES. Tuition and fees: $970. Students from the US, but outside PR, pay their home state's non-resident tuition amount. **Books and supplies:** $800. **Other expenses:** $600.

FINANCIAL AID. 60% of freshmen, 70% of continuing students receive some form of aid. All aid based on need. 354 enrolled freshmen were judged to have need, 238 were offered aid. **Aid applications:** Closing date June 30; applicants notified on a rolling basis; must reply within 1 week.

ADDRESS/TELEPHONE. Melba Serrano, Admissions Officer, University of Puerto Rico: Aguadilla, PO Box 160, Ramey Station, Aguadilla, PR 00604. (809) 890-2681.

University of Puerto Rico: Arecibo Campus
Arecibo, Puerto Rico — CB code: 0911

4-year public university, coed. Founded in 1967. **Accreditation:** Regional. **Undergraduate enrollment:** 3,407 men and women. **Location:** Urban campus in small city; 48 miles from San Juan. **Calendar:** Semester.

FRESHMAN ADMISSIONS. Selection criteria: School achievement record, test scores.

ANNUAL EXPENSES. Tuition and fees (1992-93): $970. Students from the U.S., but outside Puerto Rico, pay their home state's non-resident tuition amount. **Books and supplies:** $800. **Other expenses:** $3,410.

ADDRESS/TELEPHONE. Margarita Saenz, Admissions Officer, University of Puerto Rico: Arecibo Campus, PO Box 4010, Arecibo, PR 00613. (809) 878-2830. Fax: (809) 880-4972.

University of Puerto Rico: Bayamon Technological University College
Bayamon, Puerto Rico — CB code: 0852

4-year public technical college, coed. Founded in 1971. **Accreditation:** Regional. **Undergraduate enrollment:** 1,363 men, 1,807 women full time; 363 men, 490 women part time. **Faculty:** 227 total (194 full time), 38 with doctorates or other terminal degrees. **Location:** Suburban campus in small city; 9 miles from San Juan. **Calendar:** Semester, limited summer session. Saturday and extensive evening/early morning classes. **Microcomputers:** 270 located in computer centers.

DEGREES OFFERED. AA, AS, BA. 286 associate degrees awarded in 1992. 23% in business and management, 30% business/office and marketing/distribution, 12% computer sciences, 29% engineering technologies, 5% multi/interdisciplinary studies. 465 bachelor's degrees awarded. 41% in business and management, 23% business/office and marketing/distribution, 9% computer sciences, 11% teacher education, 17% engineering technologies.

UNDERGRADUATE MAJORS. Associate: Accounting, business administration and management, business and management, civil technology, computer and information sciences, drafting and design technology, electronic technology, finance, industrial technology, instrumentation technology, liberal/general studies, marketing and distribution, mechanical design technology, secretarial and related programs, survey and mapping technology. **Bachelor's:** Accounting, business administration and management, business and management, computer and information sciences, early childhood education, education of the physically handicapped, electronic technology, elementary education, finance, marketing and distribution, materials management technologies, secretarial and related programs.

ACADEMIC PROGRAMS. 2-year transfer program, cooperative education, double major, honors program, cross-registration. **Remedial services:** Preadmission summer program, reduced course load, special counselor, tutoring. **ROTC:** Army. **Placement/credit:** AP.

ACADEMIC REQUIREMENTS. Freshmen must earn minimum GPA of 1.8 to continue in good standing. 75% of freshmen return for sophomore year. Students must declare major on application. **Graduation requirements:** 69 hours for associate (35 in major), 133 hours for bachelor's (48 in major). Most students required to take courses in English, mathematics, biological/physical sciences, social sciences. **Postgraduate studies:** 29% from 2-year programs enter 4-year programs.

FRESHMAN ADMISSIONS. Selection criteria: High school GPA and test scores most important. Higher scores required of applicants to bachelor's programs. Special consideration given to applicants with special talents or handicaps. **High school preparation:** 12 units required. Required units include biological science 1, English 3, mathematics 3, physical science 1 and social science 1. 3 units Spanish also required. **Test requirements:** Prueba de Aptitud Academica for Spanish speaking applicants. SAT and 3 ACH (English, Spanish, Math) accepted for English speaking applicants from U.S. mainland. Score reports by February 15.

1992 FRESHMAN CLASS PROFILE. 360 men, 477 women enrolled. **Academic background:** Mid 50% of enrolled freshmen had SAT-V between 500-600, SAT-M between 520-630. 100% submitted SAT scores. **Characteristics:** 100% from in state, 100% commute, 100% have minority backgrounds. Average age is 18.

FALL-TERM APPLICATIONS. $15 fee. Closing date January 31; priority given to applications received by December 10; applicants notified on or about February 25; must reply by March 30.

STUDENT LIFE. Activities: Student government, student newspaper, choral groups, concert band, drama, jazz band.

ATHLETICS. Intercollegiate: Basketball, table tennis, tennis, track and field, volleyball, wrestling M. **Intramural:** Table tennis, tennis, volleyball.

STUDENT SERVICES. Aptitude testing, career counseling, employment service for undergraduates, freshman orientation, health services, personal counseling, placement service for graduates, special adviser for adult students, services/facilities for handicapped.

ANNUAL EXPENSES. Tuition and fees (1992-93): $970. Tuition for associate degree program is $20 per credit hour. Students from the U.S., but outside Puerto Rico, pay their home state's non-resident tuition amount. **Books and supplies:** $800. **Other expenses:** $600.

FINANCIAL AID. 55% of freshmen, 66% of continuing students receive some form of aid. All aid based on need. Academic, athletic scholarships available. **Aid applications:** Closing date June 28; applicants notified on or about July 12.

ADDRESS/TELEPHONE. Pedro Martinez, Director of Admissions, University of Puerto Rico: Bayamon Technological University College, State Road 174 Km. 2.8, Bayamon, PR 00619-1919. (809) 786-6615. Fax: (809) 798-1595 ext. 236.

University of Puerto Rico: Carolina Regional College

Carolina, Puerto Rico — CB code: 3891

Admissions:	25% of applicants accepted
Based on:	••• School record, test scores
	• Activities, special talents
Completion:	76% of freshmen end year in good standing
	11% go on to graduate

2-year public community college, coed. Founded in 1974. **Accreditation:** Regional. **Undergraduate enrollment:** 478 men, 877 women full time; 206 men, 286 women part time. **Faculty:** 93 total (82 full time), 12 with doctorates or other terminal degrees. **Location:** Urban campus in small city; 10 miles from San Juan. **Calendar:** 3 terms of 12 weeks each. **Microcomputers:** 76 located in libraries, classrooms, computer centers.

DEGREES OFFERED. AA, AS. 189 associate degrees awarded in 1992. 12% in architecture and environmental design, 32% business and management, 14% business/office and marketing/distribution, 13% communications, 5% education, 5% engineering, 5% engineering technologies, 6% visual and performing arts.

UNDERGRADUATE MAJORS. Advertising, automotive mechanics, biological and physical sciences, education, education of the physically handicapped, finance, graphic and printing production, graphic arts technology, hotel/motel and restaurant management, humanities, insurance and risk management, interior design, law enforcement and corrections, mechanical engineering, predentistry, premedicine, prepharmacy, preveterinary, secretarial and related programs, social sciences. insurance and risk management.

ACADEMIC PROGRAMS. 2-year transfer program. **Remedial services:** Learning center, remedial instruction, tutoring. **ROTC:** Air Force, Army. **Placement/credit:** AP.

ACADEMIC REQUIREMENTS. Freshmen must earn minimum GPA of 1.5 to continue in good standing. 75% of freshmen return for sophomore year. Students must declare major by end of first year. **Graduation requirements:** 68 hours for associate (18 in major). Most students required to take courses in English, humanities, mathematics, biological/physical sciences, social sciences.

FRESHMAN ADMISSIONS. Selection criteria: High school GPA and test scores important. **High school preparation:** 15 units required. Required units include biological science 1, English 3, foreign language 3, mathematics 2, physical science 1 and social science 3. **Test requirements:** Prueba de Aptitud Academica for Spanish speaking applicants. SAT required of English-speaking applicants. Score reports by March 15.

1992 FRESHMAN CLASS PROFILE. 774 men applied, 191 accepted, 191 enrolled; 1,644 women applied, 409 accepted, 409 enrolled. **Characteristics:** 100% commute, 100% have minority backgrounds. Average age is 18.

FALL-TERM APPLICATIONS. $15 fee. Closing date December 10; applicants notified on or about April 15; must reply by May 25. Interview recommended for exceptional ability applicants. Portfolio recommended for art applicants.

STUDENT LIFE. Activities: Student government, choral groups, dance, drama, music ensembles, religious, departmental, and athletic organizations.

ATHLETICS. Intercollegiate: Basketball, cross-country, softball, table tennis, tennis, track and field, volleyball. **Intramural:** Basketball, cross-country, softball, table tennis, tennis, track and field, volleyball.

STUDENT SERVICES. Aptitude testing, career counseling, employment service for undergraduates, freshman orientation, health services, personal counseling, placement service for graduates, veterans counselor, services/facilities for handicapped.

ANNUAL EXPENSES. Tuition and fees: $970. Students from the U.S., but outside Puerto Rico, pay their home state's non-resident tuition amount **Books and supplies:** $800. **Other expenses:** $600.

FINANCIAL AID. 60% of freshmen, 54% of continuing students receive some form of aid. All grants, all jobs based on need. 420 enrolled freshmen were judged to have need, all were offered aid. Academic, music/drama, athletic scholarships available. **Aid applications:** Closing date May 28; priority given to applications received by May 14.

ADDRESS/TELEPHONE. Ivonne Calderon, Admissions Officer, University of Puerto Rico: Carolina Regional College, PO Box 4800, Carolina, PR 00984-4800. (809) 257-0000 ext. 3224. Fax: (809) 750-7940.

University of Puerto Rico: Cayey University College

Cayey, Puerto Rico — CB code: 0981

4-year public college of arts and sciences, coed. Founded in 1967. **Accreditation:** Regional. **Undergraduate enrollment:** 996 men, 1,919 women full time; 105 men, 216 women part time. **Faculty:** 184 total (174 full time), 63 with doctorates or other terminal degrees. **Location:** Urban campus in large town; 30 from San Juan. **Calendar:** Semester, limited summer session. Saturday classes. **Microcomputers:** 90 located in computer centers. **Special facilities:** Art museum.

DEGREES OFFERED. AA, AS, BA, BS. 30 associate degrees awarded in 1992. 100% in business/office and marketing/distribution. 372 bachelor's degrees awarded. 30% in business and management, 18% teacher education, 16% life sciences, 7% physical sciences, 9% psychology, 14% social sciences.

UNDERGRADUATE MAJORS. Associate: Secretarial and related programs. **Bachelor's:** Accounting, biology, business administration and management, business and management, chemistry, economics, elementary education, English, English education, humanities, mathematics, mathematics education, mental health/human services, physical education, psychology, science education, secondary education, social science education, social sciences, sociology, Spanish.

ACADEMIC PROGRAMS. 2-year transfer program, accelerated program, double major, teacher preparation, visiting/exchange student program, Washington semester, Ortega y Gasset Foundation study abroad program in Spain. **Remedial services:** Preadmission summer program, remedial instruction, tutoring. **ROTC:** Army. **Placement/credit:** AP.

ACADEMIC REQUIREMENTS. Freshmen must earn minimum GPA of 2.0 to continue in good standing. 74% of freshmen return for sophomore year. Students must declare major on application. **Graduation requirements:** 72 hours for associate (45 in major), 129 hours for bachelor's (40 in major). Most students required to take courses in English, humanities, mathematics, biological/physical sciences, social sciences.

FRESHMAN ADMISSIONS. Selection criteria: School achievement record, test scores important. **High school preparation:** 15 units required. Required units include English 3, mathematics 3, social science 3 and science 3. 3 units Spanish required. **Test requirements:** Prueba de Aptitud Academica for Spanish speaking applicants. SAT required of English-speaking applicants, score report by February 15.

1992 FRESHMAN CLASS PROFILE. 254 men, 483 women enrolled. 77% had high school GPA of 3.0 or higher, 23% between 2.0 and 2.99. **Characteristics:** 100% from in state, 100% commute. Average age is 18.

FALL-TERM APPLICATIONS. $15 fee. Closing date February 15; applicants notified on or about May 1; must reply by May 20. Interview recommended for music, theater applicants.

STUDENT LIFE. Activities: Student government, choral groups, concert band, drama, marching band, music ensembles, pep band, fraternities, sororities, many religious, political, and social service organizations including theater group, statehood movement group, Rene Marques literary society, natural sciences honorary association, Association of Future Economists of Puerto Rico.

ATHLETICS. Intercollegiate: Baseball M, basketball M, softball M, swimming, tennis M, track and field, volleyball M, wrestling M. **Intramural:** Baseball, basketball, football M, softball M, swimming, track and field, volleyball M, wrestling M.

STUDENT SERVICES. Career counseling, employment service for undergraduates, freshman orientation, health services, personal counseling, placement service for graduates, veterans counselor, services/facilities for handicapped.

ANNUAL EXPENSES. Tuition and fees: $970. Students from the U.S., but outside Puerto Rico, pay their home state's non-resident tuition amount. **Books and supplies:** $800. **Other expenses:** $600.

FINANCIAL AID. 79% of freshmen, 75% of continuing students receive some form of aid. All aid based on need. Alumni affiliation, religious affiliation scholarships available. **Aid applications:** Closing date June 30; priority given to applications received by May 31; applicants notified on or about July 30; must reply immediately.

ADDRESS/TELEPHONE. Josefina Hernandez, Director of Admissions, University of Puerto Rico: Cayey University College, Antonio R. Barcelo Avenue, Cayey, PR 00633. (809) 738-2161 ext. 2057. Fax: (809) 738-8039.

University of Puerto Rico: Humacao University College

Humacao, Puerto Rico — CB code: 0874

Admissions:	64% of applicants accepted
Based on:	••• School record, test scores
	• Special talents
Completion:	85% of freshmen end year in good standing
	36% graduate

4-year public liberal arts and sciences university college, coed. Founded in 1962. **Accreditation:** Regional. **Undergraduate enrollment:** 1,098 men, 2,198 women full time; 211 men, 377 women part time. **Faculty:** 243 total (216 full time), 64 with doctorates or other terminal degrees. **Location:** Suburban campus in small city; 5 miles from downtown, 30 miles from San Juan. **Calendar:** Semester, limited summer session. Extensive evening/early morning classes. **Microcomputers:** 159 located in libraries, computer centers. **Special facilities:** Observatory, census data center, Casa Roig Museum, plain pigeon endangered species project.

DEGREES OFFERED. AA, AS, BA, BS. 181 associate degrees awarded in 1992. 20% in business and management, 19% business/office and marketing/distribution, 14% communications, 15% engineering technologies, 27% allied health. 429 bachelor's degrees awarded. 42% in business and management, 11% business/office and marketing/distribution, 8% teacher education, 5% health sciences, 11% life sciences, 9% parks/recreation, protective services, public affairs, 10% physical sciences.

UNDERGRADUATE MAJORS. Associate: Accounting, business administration and management, chemical manufacturing technology, educational media technology, electronic technology, liberal/general studies, nursing, occupational therapy assistant, physical therapy assistant, secretarial and related programs. **Bachelor's:** Accounting, biology, business administration and management, business and management, computer mathematics, electron physics, elementary education, human resources development, industrial chemistry, marine biology, microbiology, nursing, secretarial and related programs, social work, teaching English as a second language/foreign language, wildlife management.

ACADEMIC PROGRAMS. 2-year transfer program, honors program, internships, teacher preparation, visiting/exchange student program. **Remedial services:** Remedial instruction, special counselor, tutoring. **ROTC:** Army. **Placement/credit:** AP, institutional tests; 40 credit hours maximum for associate degree; 40 credit hours maximum for bachelor's degree.

ACADEMIC REQUIREMENTS. Freshmen must earn minimum GPA of 1.6 to continue in good standing. 85% of freshmen return for sophomore year. Students must declare major on application. **Graduation requirements:** 71 hours for associate, 132 hours for bachelor's. Most students required to take courses in English, foreign languages, humanities, mathematics, biological/physical sciences, social sciences. **Postgraduate studies:** 16% from 2-year programs enter 4-year programs. **Additional information:** Course work conducted in Spanish.

FRESHMAN ADMISSIONS. Selection criteria: High school achievement record and test scores important. Recommended units include English 3, foreign language 3, mathematics 2, social science 3 and science 2. **Test requirements:** Prueba de Aptitud Academica for Spanish speaking applicants. SAT required of English-speaking applicants. Score reports by February 15. **Additional information:** Non-native speakers of Spanish required to prove fluency through institutional examinations, interviews.

1992 FRESHMAN CLASS PROFILE. 622 men applied, 391 accepted, 310 enrolled; 1,020 women applied, 661 accepted, 557 enrolled. 78% had high school GPA of 3.0 or higher, 22% between 2.0 and 2.99. **Characteristics:** 100% commute, 100% have minority backgrounds. Average age is 18.

FALL-TERM APPLICATIONS. $15 fee. Closing date December 10; applicants notified on or about April 15; must reply by May 30.

STUDENT LIFE. Activities: Student government, film, student newspaper, choral groups, concert band, drama, fraternities, various religious and social service organizations.

ATHLETICS. Intercollegiate: Basketball, cross-country, soccer M, softball, swimming, table tennis, tennis, track and field, volleyball, wrestling M. **Intramural:** Basketball M, cross-country, soccer M, softball, swimming, table tennis, tennis, track and field, volleyball M, water polo M, wrestling M.

STUDENT SERVICES. Aptitude testing, career counseling, employment service for undergraduates, freshman orientation, health services, personal counseling, placement service for graduates, services/facilities for handicapped.

ANNUAL EXPENSES. Tuition and fees (1992-93): $970. Students from the U.S., but outside Puerto Rico, pay their home state non-resident tuition. **Books and supplies:** $800. **Other expenses:** $600.

FINANCIAL AID. 84% of freshmen, 80% of continuing students receive some form of aid. All aid based on need. 710 enrolled freshmen were judged to have need, all were offered aid. **Aid applications:** Closing date June 30; applicants notified on a rolling basis beginning on or about July 30; must reply by August 15.

ADDRESS/TELEPHONE. Inara Ferrer, Admissions Officer, University of Puerto Rico: Humacao University College, CUH Station, Humacao, PR 00791. (809) 850-0000 ext. 9301.

University of Puerto Rico: La Montana Regional College

Utuado, Puerto Rico — CB code: 3893

2-year public agricultural and technical college, coed. Founded in 1979. **Accreditation:** Regional. **Undergraduate enrollment:** 268 men, 371 women full time; 26 men, 32 women part time. **Faculty:** 49 total, 4 with doctorates or other terminal degrees. **Location:** Rural campus in large town; 20 miles from Arecibo. **Calendar:** Semester, limited summer session. **Microcomputers:** 90 located in computer centers. **Special facilities:** 180-acre farm.

DEGREES OFFERED. AS, AAS. 100 associate degrees awarded in 1992. 64% in agriculture, 24% business and management, 7% business/office and marketing/distribution, 5% life sciences.

UNDERGRADUATE MAJORS. Accounting, agricultural business and management, animal sciences, biology, business and management, food sciences, horticulture, plant protection, secretarial and related programs.

ACADEMIC PROGRAMS. 2-year transfer program, dual enrollment of high school students, internships, teacher preparation. **Remedial services:** Reduced course load, remedial instruction, tutoring.

ACADEMIC REQUIREMENTS. Freshmen must earn minimum GPA of 1.81 to continue in good standing. 70% of freshmen return for sophomore year. Students must declare major on application. **Graduation requirements:** 70 hours for associate. Most students required to take courses in English, foreign languages, mathematics, biological/physical sciences, social sciences.

FRESHMAN ADMISSIONS. Selection criteria: School GPA and test scores important. **High school preparation:** 15 units required. Required units include biological science 1, English 3, foreign language 3, mathematics 2, physical science 1 and social science 2. **Test requirements:** Prueba de Aptitud Academica for Spanish speaking applicants. SAT required of English-speaking students; score report by June 10.

1992 FRESHMAN CLASS PROFILE. 307 men and women enrolled. **Characteristics:** 100% from in state, 100% commute, 100% have minority backgrounds. Average age is 18.

FALL-TERM APPLICATIONS. $15 fee, may be waived for applicants with need. Closing date November 30; applicants notified on or about May 31; must reply by June 30. Interview recommended.

STUDENT LIFE. Activities: Student government, choral groups, dance, drama, fraternities, sororities.

ATHLETICS. Intercollegiate: Basketball, cross-country, swimming, track and field, volleyball. **Intramural:** Basketball, cross-country, fencing, gymnastics, softball, swimming, table tennis, track and field, volleyball.

STUDENT SERVICES. Aptitude testing, career counseling, freshman orientation, health services, personal counseling, placement service for graduates, services/facilities for handicapped.

ANNUAL EXPENSES. Tuition and fees: $970. Students from the U.S., but outside P.R., pay their home state's non-resident tuition amount. **Books and supplies:** $900. **Other expenses:** $600.

FINANCIAL AID. 92% of freshmen, 90% of continuing students receive some form of aid. All grants, all jobs based on need. All loans based on criteria other than need. 213 enrolled freshmen were judged to have need, all were offered aid. Music/drama, athletic scholarships available. **Aid applications:** No closing date; priority given to applications received by May 31; applicants notified on a rolling basis beginning on or about September 30; must reply within 4 weeks.

ADDRESS/TELEPHONE. Naidez Casalduc, Admissions Officer, University of Puerto Rico: La Montana Regional College, PO Call Box 2500, Utuado, PR 00641-2500. (809) 894-2828 ext. 264. Fax: (809) 894-2891.

University of Puerto Rico: Mayaguez Campus

Mayaguez, Puerto Rico CB code: 0912

Admissions: 79% of applicants accepted
Based on: ••• School record, test scores
• Special talents
Completion: 96% of freshmen end year in good standing
36% graduate, 5% of these enter graduate study

4-year public university, coed. Founded in 1911. **Accreditation:** Regional. **Undergraduate enrollment:** 4,997 men, 4,600 women full time; 290 men, 342 women part time. **Graduate enrollment:** 383 men, 196 women full time; 5 men, 6 women part time. **Faculty:** 703 total (662 full time), 347 with doctorates or other terminal degrees. **Location:** Urban campus in small city; 100 miles from San Juan. **Calendar:** Semester, limited summer session. **Microcomputers:** 600 located in libraries, classrooms, computer centers, campus-wide network. **Special facilities:** Planetarium, botanical garden, fine arts museum, agricultural extension service, agricultural experimental station, natural history collection, resource center for science and engineering. **Additional facts:** Most courses conducted in Spanish. Students must have working knowledge of Spanish and English.

DEGREES OFFERED. AA, AAS, BA, BS, MA, MS, MBA, PhD. 20 associate degrees awarded in 1992. 20% in business/office and marketing/distribution, 80% health sciences. 1,281 bachelor's degrees awarded. 5% in agriculture, 13% business and management, 5% business/office and marketing/distribution, 44% engineering, 5% health sciences, 9% life sciences, 5% social sciences. Graduate degrees offered in 25 major fields of study.

UNDERGRADUATE MAJORS. Associate: Nursing, secretarial and related programs. **Bachelor's:** Accounting, agribusiness, agricultural economics, agricultural education, agricultural mechanics, agricultural sciences, agronomy, animal sciences, art history, biology, business administration and management, business economics, chemical engineering, chemistry, civil engineering, comparative literature, computer engineering, computer mathematics, economics, electrical/electronics/communications engineering, English, English education, finance, fine arts, French, geology, history, horticultural science, horticulture, industrial engineering, information sciences and systems, marketing and distribution, mathematics, mathematics education, mechanical engineering, microbiology, nursing, organizational behavior, philosophy, physical education, physical sciences, physics, plant protection, political science and government, premedicine, psychology, pure mathematics, secretarial and related programs, social sciences, sociology, Spanish, surveying and mapping sciences.

ACADEMIC PROGRAMS. 2-year transfer program, cooperative education, double major, internships, study abroad, teacher preparation, visiting/exchange student program, international agricultural programs, sea grant program, resource center for science and engineering publications. **Remedial services:** Reduced course load, remedial instruction, special counselor, tutoring. **ROTC:** Air Force, Army. **Placement/credit:** Institutional tests; 30 credit hours maximum for bachelor's degree.

ACADEMIC REQUIREMENTS. Freshmen must earn minimum GPA of 1.7 to continue in good standing. 90% of freshmen return for sophomore year. Students must declare major on application. **Graduation requirements:** 76 hours for associate, 139 hours for bachelor's. Most students required to take courses in English, foreign languages, history, humanities, mathematics, biological/physical sciences, social sciences.

FRESHMAN ADMISSIONS. Selection criteria: High school GPA and test scores important. **High school preparation:** 15 units required. **Test requirements:** Prueba de Aptitud Academica for Spanish speaking applicants. SAT required of English-speaking applicants.

1992 FRESHMAN CLASS PROFILE. 1,728 men applied, 1,339 accepted, 1,104 enrolled; 1,610 women applied, 1,297 accepted, 1,059 enrolled. 56% had high school GPA of 3.0 or higher, 44% between 2.0 and 2.99. **Characteristics:** 99% from in state, 100% commute, 99% have minority backgrounds. Average age is 18.

FALL-TERM APPLICATIONS. $15 fee. Closing date February 28; applicants notified on or about May 15; must reply by June 1.

STUDENT LIFE. Housing: Housing available near campus. **Activities:** Student government, magazine, student newspaper, yearbook, choral groups, concert band, dance, drama, jazz band, marching band, pep band, fraternities, sororities, international associations, model of United Nations council.

ATHLETICS. NCAA. **Intercollegiate:** Baseball M, basketball, cross-country, gymnastics, soccer M, softball, swimming, table tennis, tennis, track and field, volleyball, water polo M, wrestling M. **Intramural:** Archery, baseball M, basketball, cross-country, racquetball, soccer M, softball, swimming, table tennis, tennis, volleyball, water polo M, wrestling M.

STUDENT SERVICES. Aptitude testing, career counseling, employment service for undergraduates, freshman orientation, health services, personal counseling, placement service for graduates, veterans counselor, services/facilities for handicapped.

ANNUAL EXPENSES. Tuition and fees (1992-93): $970. Tuition for out-of-state students varies by state of residence. **Books and supplies:** $900. **Other expenses:** $600.

FINANCIAL AID. 73% of freshmen, 73% of continuing students receive some form of aid. 95% of grants, all loans, all jobs based on need. 1,414 enrolled freshmen were judged to have need, all were offered aid. Academic, music/drama, athletic, state/district residency scholarships available. **Aid applications:** Closing date June 29; applicants notified on or about September 30; must reply by October 15.

ADDRESS/TELEPHONE. Ivonne Ramirez, Director of Admissions, University of Puerto Rico: Mayaguez Campus, PO Box 5000, College Station, Mayaguez, PR 00681-5000. (809) 832-4040 ext. 2400. Fax: (809) 834-3031.

University of Puerto Rico: Medical Sciences Campus

Rio Piedras, Puerto Rico CB code: 0631

4-year public university, coed. Founded in 1950. **Accreditation:** Regional. **Undergraduate enrollment:** 116 men, 737 women full time; 32 men, 164 women part time. **Graduate enrollment:** 474 men, 821 women full time; 90 men, 130 women part time. **Faculty:** 719 total (642 full time), 649 with doctorates or other terminal degrees. **Location:** Urban campus in large city. **Calendar:** Most bachelor's programs are by trimester. For graduate programs, some are by trimester, some by semester. Saturday and extensive evening/early morning classes. **Microcomputers:** Located in computer centers.

DEGREES OFFERED. AS, BS, MS, D, DMD, MD, B. Pharm. 47 associate degrees awarded in 1992. 100% in allied health. 303 bachelor's degrees awarded. 20% in health sciences, 80% allied health. Graduate degrees offered in 23 major fields of study.

UNDERGRADUATE MAJORS. Associate: Dental assistant, dental hygiene, emergency medical technologies, ophthalmic services, radiograph medical technology. **Bachelor's:** Animal sciences, cytotechnology, health education, health sciences, medical laboratory technologies, nuclear medical technology, nursing, occupational therapy, pharmacy, physical therapy, speech pathology/audiology, veterinarian's assistant.

ACADEMIC PROGRAMS. Internships, visiting/exchange student program. **Remedial services:** Tutoring.

ACADEMIC REQUIREMENTS. No policy requiring minimum GPA; records of students having academic difficulty are reviewed individually. Students must declare major on application. **Graduation requirements:** 91 hours for associate (61 in major), 132 hours for bachelor's (65 in major). Most students required to take courses in English, humanities, mathematics, biological/physical sciences, social sciences.

FRESHMAN ADMISSIONS. Selection criteria: Must have 1 or more years of college (30-99 credits) for admission. Test scores required for some programs. GPA requirement varies for each program. Personal interview, evaluations from faculty considered.

1992 FRESHMAN CLASS PROFILE. Characteristics: 100% from in state, 100% commute, 100% have minority backgrounds. Average age is 19.

FALL-TERM APPLICATIONS. $25 fee. Closing date December 15; applicants notified on or about May 30; must reply within 2 weeks. Interview recommended.

STUDENT LIFE. Activities: Student government, choral groups, fraternities, sororities.

ATHLETICS. Intramural: Basketball M, softball M.

STUDENT SERVICES. Career counseling, health services, personal counseling, services/facilities for handicapped.

ANNUAL EXPENSES. Tuition and fees (1992-93): $970. Students from the U.S., but outside Puerto Rico, pay their home state's non-resident tuitiion amount. **Books and supplies:** $350. **Other expenses:** $600.

FINANCIAL AID. 88% of freshmen, 79% of continuing students receive some form of aid. All grants based on need. **Aid applications:** No closing date; priority given to applications received by April 30; applicants notified on a rolling basis beginning on or about June 30; must reply within 2 weeks.

ADDRESS/TELEPHONE. Rita Aponte, Central Admissions Office Director, University of Puerto Rico: Med Sci Campus, GPO Box 365067, Rio Piedras, San Juan, PR 00936-5067. (809) 758-2525 ext. 1791.

University of Puerto Rico: Ponce Technological University College
Ponce, Puerto Rico CB code: 0836

4-year public branch campus, technical college, coed. Founded in 1970. **Accreditation:** Regional. **Undergraduate enrollment:** 734 men, 1,261 women full time; 118 men, 150 women part time. **Faculty:** 122 total (116 full time), 20 with doctorates or other terminal degrees. **Location:** Urban campus in small city; 68 miles from San Juan. **Calendar:** Semester, limited summer session. **Microcomputers:** 73 located in classrooms, computer centers. **Special facilities:** Ponce Center for Historical Studies and Museum of History, Archeology, and Popular Arts.

DEGREES OFFERED. AA, AS, BA, BS. 205 associate degrees awarded in 1992. 195 bachelor's degrees awarded.

UNDERGRADUATE MAJORS. Associate: Accounting, biology, business administration and management, chemistry, civil technology, computer and information sciences, drafting, drafting and design technology, elementary education, industrial technology, liberal/general studies, marketing management, mathematics, occupational therapy assistant, physical therapy assistant, physics, precision metal work, secretarial and related programs, social sciences. **Bachelor's:** Accounting, business administration and management, computer and information sciences, elementary education, marketing management, secretarial and related programs.

ACADEMIC PROGRAMS. 2-year transfer program, dual enrollment of high school students, honors program, internships. **Remedial services:** Remedial instruction, tutoring. **ROTC:** Army.

ACADEMIC REQUIREMENTS. Students must earn minimum GPA of 1.75 for first 24 credit hours to continue in good academic standing. 84% of freshmen return for sophomore year. Students must declare major on application. **Graduation requirements:** 73 hours for associate, 128 hours for bachelor's. Most students required to take courses in English, mathematics.

FRESHMAN ADMISSIONS. Selection criteria: Admission based on general application index which is a combination of high school GPA and College Board test scores. **High school preparation:** 15 units required. Required units include biological science 2, English 3, mathematics 2, physical science 1 and social science 3. 3 units Spanish also required. **Test requirements:** Prueba de Aptitud Academica for Spanish speaking applicants. SAT accepted in place of ACH. Score reports by June 1.

1992 FRESHMAN CLASS PROFILE. 244 men, 401 women enrolled. **Characteristics:** 100% from in state, 100% commute, 100% have minority backgrounds. Average age is 18.

FALL-TERM APPLICATIONS. $15 fee. Closing date December 13; applicants notified on or about April 25; must reply by May 22. Interview required for academically weak, special ability applicants.

STUDENT LIFE. Activities: Student government, student newspaper, television, choral groups, concert band, dance, drama, fraternities, Catholic, Christian, and Baptist youth organizations.

ATHLETICS. NCAA. **Intercollegiate:** Basketball, cross-country, softball, table tennis, tennis, track and field, volleyball. **Intramural:** Basketball, cross-country, gymnastics, softball, table tennis, tennis, track and field, volleyball.

STUDENT SERVICES. Aptitude testing, career counseling, employment service for undergraduates, freshman orientation, health services, personal counseling, placement service for graduates, veterans counselor, services/facilities for handicapped.

ANNUAL EXPENSES. Tuition and fees: $970. Students from the U.S., but outside Puerto Rico, pay the home state's non-resident tuition amount. **Books and supplies:** $800. **Other expenses:** $600.

FINANCIAL AID. 80% of freshmen, 90% of continuing students receive some form of aid. 96% of grants, all loans, all jobs based on need. 619 enrolled freshmen were judged to have need, all were offered aid. Academic, music/drama, athletic scholarships available. **Aid applications:** Closing date June 10; applicants notified on or about October 15; must reply within 10 days.

ADDRESS/TELEPHONE. William Rodriguez Mercado, Admissions Officer, University of Puerto Rico: Ponce Technological University College, PO Box 7186, Ponce, PR 00732. (809) 844-8181. Fax: (809) 840-8108.

University of Puerto Rico: Rio Piedras Campus
Rio Piedras, Puerto Rico CB code: 0979

4-year public university, coed. Founded in 1903. **Accreditation:** Regional. **Undergraduate enrollment:** 3,279 men, 8,442 women full time; 1,150 men, 2,797 women part time. **Graduate enrollment:** 343 men, 861 women full time; 687 men, 1,723 women part time. **Faculty:** 1,476 total (1,290 full time), 564 with doctorates or other terminal degrees. **Location:** Urban campus in large city; 10 miles from downtown. **Calendar:** Semester, limited summer session. Saturday and extensive evening/early morning classes. **Microcomputers:** 154 located in dormitories, libraries, classrooms, computer centers. **Special facilities:** Museums, art galleries, theater. **Additional facts:** Most courses conducted in Spanish. Students must have working knowledge of Spanish and English.

DEGREES OFFERED. AS, BA, BS, BArch, MA, MS, MBA, MEd, MSW, PhD, EdD, JD. 9 associate degrees awarded in 1992. 100% in business/office and marketing/distribution. 2,549 bachelor's degrees awarded. 28% in business and management, 14% teacher education, 6% life sciences, 11% multi/interdisciplinary studies, 8% psychology, 10% social sciences. Graduate degrees offered in 45 major fields of study.

UNDERGRADUATE MAJORS. Associate: Secretarial and related programs. **Bachelor's:** Accounting, agricultural extension, anthropology, art education, art history, biological and physical sciences, biology, business and management, business economics, business education, business statistics, chemistry, child development/care/guidance, communications, comparative literature, computer and information sciences, cooperativism, dramatic arts, economics, elementary education, English, English education, environmental design, environmental science, finance, fine arts, food science and nutrition, foreign languages education, French, geography, history, home economics, home economics education, human resources development, humanities and social sciences, industrial arts education, labor/industrial relations, liberal/general studies, management information systems, marketing management, mathematics, mathematics education, music, music education, operations research, philosophy, physical education, physics, political science and government, psychology, recreation and community services technologies, science education, secondary education, secretarial and related programs, social science education, social sciences, social studies education, social work, sociology, Spanish, special education, speech, speech/communication/theater education, teaching English as a second language/foreign language.

ACADEMIC PROGRAMS. Double major, honors program, internships, study abroad, visiting/exchange student program, exchange programs with many colleges and universities in United States, Spain, France, Mexico, Brazil, Costa Rica. **Remedial services:** Learning center, preadmission summer program, remedial instruction, tutoring. **ROTC:** Air Force, Army. **Placement/credit:** AP, institutional tests; 30 credit hours maximum for bachelor's degree.

ACADEMIC REQUIREMENTS. Freshmen must earn minimum GPA of 1.8 to continue in good standing. 83% of freshmen return for sophomore year. Students must declare major on application. **Graduation requirements:** 77 hours for associate, 135 hours for bachelor's (30 in major). Most students required to take courses in English, foreign languages, humanities, mathematics, biological/physical sciences, social sciences. **Additional information:** Bachelor's degree must be completed within 10 years with general GPA of 2.0. Last 28 credits must be taken at Rio Piedras campus.

FRESHMAN ADMISSIONS. Selection criteria: High school GPA and test scores important. Minimum admission index required varies for each program. **Test requirements:** Prueba de Aptitud Academica for Spanish speaking applicants. SAT accepted from English-speaking applicants.

1992 FRESHMAN CLASS PROFILE. 469 men, 1,670 women enrolled. **Characteristics:** 100% from in state, 90% commute, 100% have minority backgrounds. Average age is 18.

FALL-TERM APPLICATIONS. $15 fee. Closing date December 10; applicants notified on or about May 10; must reply by June 15 or immediately if notified thereafter.

STUDENT LIFE. Housing: Dormitories (coed). **Activities:** Student government, film, magazine, radio, student newspaper, television, yearbook, choral groups, dance, drama, jazz band, musical theater, fraternities, sororities, Various religious, political, social service organizations. **Additional information:** Students represented in university administration.

ATHLETICS. Intercollegiate: Basketball, cross-country, gymnastics, soccer M, softball, swimming, table tennis, tennis, track and field, volleyball, water polo M, wrestling M. **Intramural:** Basketball, cross-country, gymnastics, soccer M, softball, swimming, table tennis, tennis, track and field, volleyball, water polo, wrestling M.

STUDENT SERVICES. Aptitude testing, career counseling, employment service for undergraduates, freshman orientation, health services, personal counseling, placement service for graduates, special adviser for adult students, veterans counselor, services/facilities for handicapped.

ANNUAL EXPENSES. Tuition and fees (1992-93): $970. Students from the U.S., but outside Puerto Rico, pay their home state's non-resident tuition amount. **Room and board:** $2,890. **Books and supplies:** $800. **Other expenses:** $600.

FINANCIAL AID. All grants, all jobs based on need. Academic, music/drama, art, athletic scholarships available. **Aid applications:** Closing date May 31; applicants notified on or about September 7. **Additional information:** Tuition fees waived for honor students, athletes, members of music chorus, and others with special talents.

ADDRESS/TELEPHONE. Maria M. Rosado, Director of Admissions, University of Puerto Rico: Rio Piedras Campus, PO Box 21907, UPR Station, Rio Piedras, PR 00931-1907. (809) 764-7290. Fax: (809) 763-4265.

University of the Sacred Heart
Santurce, Puerto Rico CB code: 0913

4-year private university, coed, affiliated with Roman Catholic Church. Founded in 1935. **Accreditation:** Regional. **Undergraduate enrollment:** 1,218 men, 2,468 women full time; 405 men, 662 women part time. **Graduate enrollment:** 21 men, 54 women full time; 79 men, 123 women part time. **Fac-**

ulty: 366 total (180 full time), 57 with doctorates or other terminal degrees. **Location:** Urban campus in large city; within greater San Juan. **Calendar:** Semester, extensive summer session. **Microcomputers:** 198 located in libraries, classrooms, computer centers. **Special facilities:** Museo de Arte Contemporaneo. **Additional facts:** Campus is historical and educational landmark.

DEGREES OFFERED. AA, AS, BA, BS, MA, MBA. 65 associate degrees awarded in 1992. 667 bachelor's degrees awarded. Graduate degrees offered in 3 major fields of study.

UNDERGRADUATE MAJORS. Associate: Accounting, computer and information sciences, marketing management, nursing, physical education, secretarial and related programs, tourism. **Bachelor's:** Accounting, advertising, bilingual/bicultural education, biology, business administration and management, business and management, chemistry, computer and information sciences, dramatic arts, elementary education, engineering, English, French, history, international and comparative education, journalism, law , management science, marketing and distribution, marketing management, mathematics, nursing, physical fitness, psychology, radio/television broadcasting, secretarial and related programs, social work, Spanish, telecommunications, tourism, urban studies, visual and performing arts.

ACADEMIC PROGRAMS. Cooperative education, double major, dual enrollment of high school students, honors program, independent study, internships, teacher preparation, cross-registration, cooperative programs with Seton Hall University (New Jersey) and Marquette University (Wisconsin). **Remedial services:** Preadmission summer program, reduced course load, remedial instruction, tutoring. **Placement/credit:** AP, institutional tests.

ACADEMIC REQUIREMENTS. Freshmen must earn minimum GPA of 1.5 to continue in good standing. Students must declare major on application. **Graduation requirements:** 71 hours for associate (29 in major), 137 hours for bachelor's (36 in major). Most students required to take courses in arts/fine arts, computer science, English, humanities, philosophy/religion, biological/physical sciences, social sciences.

FRESHMAN ADMISSIONS. Selection criteria: High school GPA and test scores most important. **High school preparation:** 15 units recommended. Recommended units include English 3, foreign language 3, mathematics 3, social science 2 and science 2. **Test requirements:** Prueba de Aptitud Academica for Spanish speaking applicants. SAT accepted.

1992 FRESHMAN CLASS PROFILE. 561 men applied, 370 accepted, 255 enrolled; 1,051 women applied, 720 accepted, 494 enrolled. 40% had high school GPA of 3.0 or higher, 53% between 2.0 and 2.99. **Characteristics:** 99% from in state, 99% commute, 100% have minority backgrounds, 1% are foreign students.

FALL-TERM APPLICATIONS. $15 fee. Closing date June 30; priority given to applications received by December 15; applicants notified on a rolling basis. Interview required for nursing applicants. Early admission available. SAT scores considered if student has taken it.

STUDENT LIFE. Housing: Dormitories (women). **Activities:** Student government, film, magazine, radio, student newspaper, television, choral groups, drama, student singing groups, pastoral services.

ATHLETICS. Intercollegiate: Basketball M, cross-country, swimming, tennis, track and field, volleyball. **Intramural:** Basketball M, table tennis, tennis, volleyball. **Clubs:** Judo, weightlifting, billiards.

STUDENT SERVICES. Aptitude testing, career counseling, employment service for undergraduates, freshman orientation, health services, personal counseling, placement service for graduates, veterans counselor, services/facilities for handicapped.

ANNUAL EXPENSES. Tuition and fees (1992-93): $2,690. **Room and board:** $1,200 room only. **Books and supplies:** $500. **Other expenses:** $640.

FINANCIAL AID. All aid based on need. 381 enrolled freshmen were judged to have need, 369 were offered aid. **Aid applications:** Closing date June 30; applicants notified on or about July 31; must reply within 2 weeks.

ADDRESS/TELEPHONE. Melvin Rosario, Director of Admissions, University of the Sacred Heart, PO Box 12383, Loiza Station, Santurce, PR 00914. (809) 728-1602. Fax: (809) 728-1515 ext. 506.

Rhode Island

Brown University
Providence, Rhode Island — CB code: 3094

Admissions: 24% of applicants accepted
Based on:
- ••• School record
- •• Activities, essay, recommendations, special talents
- • Interview, test scores

Completion: 98% of freshmen end year in good standing
91% graduate, 30% of these enter graduate study

4-year private university, coed. Founded in 1764. **Accreditation:** Regional. **Undergraduate enrollment:** 2,810 men, 2,747 women full time; 146 men, 203 women part time. **Graduate enrollment:** 914 men, 661 women full time; 65 men, 47 women part time. **Faculty:** 663 total (548 full time), 649 with doctorates of other terminal degrees. **Location:** Urban campus in small city; 50 miles from Boston. **Calendar:** semester. **Microcomputers:** 300 located in dormitories, libraries, computer centers, campus-wide network. **Special facilities:** Haffenreffer Museum of Anthropology, Bell Art Gallery, Ladd Observatory.

DEGREES OFFERED. BA, BS, MA, MS, MFA, PhD, MD. 1,488 bachelor's degrees awarded in 1992. 24% in letters/literature, 16% life sciences, 13% physical sciences, 47% social sciences. Graduate degrees offered in 81 major fields of study.

UNDERGRADUATE MAJORS. Afro-American (black) studies, American literature, American studies, analytical chemistry, anthropology, applied mathematics, archeology, art history, Asian studies, astronomy, astrophysics, biochemistry, bioengineering and biomedical engineering, biological and physical sciences, biology, biophysics, business economics, cell biology, chemical engineering, chemistry, Chinese, civil engineering, classics, comparative literature, computer and information sciences, creative writing, developmental psychology, dramatic arts, East Asian studies, economics, education, electrical/electronics/communications engineering, engineering, engineering and other disciplines, English, English literature, environmental health engineering, environmental science, European studies, experimental psychology, French, geochemistry, geology, geophysics and seismology, German, Greek (classical), Hebrew, Hispanic American studies, history, humanities and social sciences, information sciences and systems, inorganic chemistry, international relations, international studies, Italian, Jewish studies, Latin, Latin American studies, liberal/general studies, linguistics, Literature and society, marine biology, materials engineering, mathematics, mechanical engineering, molecular biology, music, music history and appreciation, neurosciences, nuclear engineering, nuclear physics, organic chemistry, philosophy, physical chemistry, physics, physiological psychology, political science and government, Portuguese, psychology, psychometrics, quantitative psychology, religion, Russian, Russian and Slavic studies, Slavic languages, sociology, South Asian studies, Spanish, statistics, studio art, systems analysis, urban studies, women's studies.

ACADEMIC PROGRAMS. Accelerated program, double major, honors program, independent study, internships, student-designed major, study abroad, teacher preparation, visiting/exchange student program, cross-registration; combined bachelor's/graduate program in medicine. **Remedial services:** Reduced course load, tutoring, writing center. **Placement/credit:** AP, institutional tests.

ACADEMIC REQUIREMENTS. No policy requiring minimum GPA; records of students having academic difficulty are reviewed individually. Freshmen must pass at least 7 courses in 2 consecutive semesters to continue in good academic standing. 96% of freshmen return for sophomore year. Students must declare major by end of second year. **Graduation requirements:** 120 hours for bachelor's (40 in major). **Postgraduate studies:** 10% enter law school, 10% enter medical school, 1% enter MBA programs, 9% enter other graduate study. **Additional information:** Nonrestrictive curriculum requires motivation, independence, and creativity.

FRESHMAN ADMISSIONS. Selection criteria: School achievement record, extracurricular activities, recommendations, personal essay and test scores strongly considered. There is no cut-off for GPA or test scores, interviews are not required, and decisions are made on an individual basis. **High school preparation:** 16 units required. Required units include biological science 1, English 4, foreign language 3, mathematics 3, physical science 2 and social science 2. One unit arts recommended. Familiarity with computer programming language encouraged. Chemistry and 1 physics required of bachelor of science candidates. **Test requirements:** SAT or ACT; score report by March 1. 3 ACH required. Score report by March 1.

1992 FRESHMAN CLASS PROFILE. 6,141 men applied, 1,412 accepted, 723 enrolled; 6,053 women applied, 1,541 accepted, 741 enrolled. 98% had high school GPA of 3.0 or higher, 2% between 2.0 and 2.99. 80% were in top tenth and 93% were in top quarter of graduating class. **Academic background:** Mid 50% of enrolled freshmen had SAT-V between 560-680, SAT-M between 630-730. 89% submitted SAT scores. **Characteristics:** 100% live in college housing, 29% have minority backgrounds, 9% are foreign students. Average age is 18.

FALL-TERM APPLICATIONS. $55 fee, may be waived for applicants with need. Closing date January 1; applicants notified on or about April 1; must reply by May 1. Essay required. Portfolio recommended for art and music applicants. CRDA. Deferred and early admission available. Institutional early decision plan. Closing date for early action applications November 1; notification December 15.

STUDENT LIFE. Housing: Dormitories (women, coed); apartment, fraternity, sorority, cooperative housing available. Language houses available. **Activities:** Student government, film, magazine, radio, student newspaper, television, yearbook, choral groups, concert band, dance, drama, jazz band, marching band, music ensembles, musical theater, pep band, symphony orchestra, fraternities, sororities, religious, political, ethnic, and social service organizations.

ATHLETICS. NCAA. **Intercollegiate:** Baseball M, basketball, cross-country, diving, fencing, field hockey W, football M, golf M, gymnastics W, ice hockey, lacrosse, rowing (crew), rugby M, sailing, skiing, soccer, softball W, squash, swimming, tennis, track and field, volleyball, water polo, wrestling M. **Intramural:** Archery, badminton, basketball, field hockey, ice hockey, soccer, softball, squash, swimming, tennis, volleyball, water polo.

STUDENT SERVICES. Career counseling, employment service for undergraduates, freshman orientation, health services, personal counseling, placement service for graduates, special adviser for adult students, services/facilities for handicapped.

ANNUAL EXPENSES. Tuition and fees: $19,006. **Room and board:** $5,612. **Books and supplies:** $680. **Other expenses:** $1,200.

FINANCIAL AID. 40% of freshmen, 39% of continuing students receive some form of aid. All aid based on need. 556 enrolled freshmen were judged to have need, all were offered aid. **Aid applications:** Closing date January 1; applicants notified on or about April 1; must reply by May 1.

ADDRESS/TELEPHONE. Eric Widmer, Dean of Admissions and Financial Aid, Brown University, PO Box 1876, Providence, RI 02912. (401) 863-2378. Fax: (401) 863-9300.

Bryant College
Smithfield, Rhode Island — CB code: 3095

Admissions: 72% of applicants accepted
Based on:
- ••• School record
- •• Test scores
- • Activities, essay, interview, recommendations, special talents

Completion: 88% of freshmen end year in good standing
76% graduate, 6% of these enter graduate study

4-year private business college, coed. Founded in 1863. **Accreditation:** Regional. **Undergraduate enrollment:** 1,588 men, 1,156 women full time; 405 men, 720 women part time. **Graduate enrollment:** 33 men, 40 women full time; 436 men, 249 women part time. **Faculty:** 218 total (141 full time), 123 with doctorates or other terminal degrees. **Location:** Suburban campus in large town; 40 miles from Boston, 12 miles from Providence. **Calendar:** Semester, extensive summer session. Saturday and extensive evening/early morning classes. **Microcomputers:** 300 located in classrooms, computer centers. **Special facilities:** Koffler Technology Center.

DEGREES OFFERED. AS, BA, BS, MS, MBA. 14 associate degrees awarded in 1992. 100% in business and management. 867 bachelor's degrees awarded. 92% in business and management, 5% computer sciences. Graduate degrees offered in 12 major fields of study.

UNDERGRADUATE MAJORS. Associate: Liberal/general studies. **Bachelor's:** Accounting, actuarial sciences, business administration and management, business and management, business economics, communications, computer and information sciences, economics, English, finance, history, international studies, marketing management, technical and business writing.

ACADEMIC PROGRAMS. Accelerated program, double major, honors program, internships, semester at sea, study abroad; combined bachelor's/graduate program in business administration. **Remedial services:** Reduced course load, special counselor, tutoring. **ROTC:** Army. **Placement/credit:** AP, CLEP Subject, institutional tests; 30 credit hours maximum for bachelor's degree.

ACADEMIC REQUIREMENTS. Freshmen must earn minimum GPA of 2.0 to continue in good standing. 88% of freshmen return for sophomore year. Students must declare major by end of second year. **Graduation requirements:** 120 hours for bachelor's (18 in major). Most students required to take courses in computer science, English, humanities, mathematics, biological/physical sciences, social sciences. **Postgraduate studies:** 2% enter law school, 3% enter MBA programs, 1% enter other graduate study.

FRESHMAN ADMISSIONS. Selection criteria: Secondary school curriculum, GPA, test scores, and guidance counselor's recommendation considered. **High school preparation:** 16 units required. Required units include English 4, mathematics 3, social science 2 and science 1. Mathematics must include algebra 1 and 2. **Test requirements:** SAT or ACT; score report by March 31.

1992 FRESHMAN CLASS PROFILE. 1,432 men applied, 1,011 accepted, 496 enrolled; 988 women applied, 734 accepted, 355 enrolled. 18% were in top tenth and 51% were in top quarter of graduating class. **Academic background:** Mid 50% of enrolled freshmen had SAT-V between 410-490, SAT-M between 500-600; ACT composite between 22-25. 95% submitted SAT scores, 5% submitted ACT scores. **Characteristics:** 16% from in state, 88% live in college housing, 8% have minority backgrounds, 2% are foreign students, 13% join fraternities/sororities. Average age is 18.

FALL-TERM APPLICATIONS. $20 fee, may be waived for applicants with need. No closing date; applicants notified on a rolling basis beginning on or about March 1; must reply by May 1 or within 2 weeks if notified thereafter. Essay required. Interview recommended. CRDA. Deferred and early admission available. EDP-F.

STUDENT LIFE. Housing: Dormitories (men, women, coed); apartment, fraternity, sorority housing available. Senior Townhouse Village. **Activities:** Student government, radio, student newspaper, yearbook, dance, drama, musical theater, fraternities, sororities, Multi-cultural student union, International Students Organization, Newman Club, Hillel, Big Sisters, Student Alumni Assembly, Special Olympics, Environmental Action Club, Hunger Coalition, Greek president's council.

ATHLETICS. NCAA. **Intercollegiate:** Baseball M, basketball, bowling M, cross-country, golf, soccer, softball W, tennis, track and field, volleyball W. **Intramural:** Basketball, soccer, softball, tennis, volleyball.

STUDENT SERVICES. Aptitude testing, career counseling, employment service for undergraduates, freshman orientation, health services, personal counseling, placement service for graduates, services/facilities for handicapped.

ANNUAL EXPENSES. Tuition and fees: $12,120. **Room and board:** $6,225. **Books and supplies:** $500. **Other expenses:** $700.

FINANCIAL AID. 62% of freshmen, 58% of continuing students receive some form of aid. 91% of grants, 94% of loans, 34% of jobs based on need. Academic, athletic scholarships available. **Aid applications:** Closing date February 15; applicants notified on or about April 1; must reply by May 1.

ADDRESS/TELEPHONE. Roy A. Nelson, Director of Admission, Bryant College, 1150 Douglas Pike, Smithfield, RI 02917-1285. (401) 232-6100. (800) 622-7001. Fax: (401) 232-6319.

Community College of Rhode Island
Warwick, Rhode Island — CB code: 3733

2-year public community college, coed. Founded in 1964. **Accreditation:** Regional. **Undergraduate enrollment:** 2,362 men, 3,140 women full time; 4,336 men, 8,148 women part time. **Faculty:** 719 total (304 full time), 54 with doctorates or other terminal degrees. **Location:** Suburban campus in small city. **Calendar:** Semester, extensive summer session. **Microcomputers:** Located in computer centers. **Special facilities:** Observatory, art gallery. **Additional facts:** Additional campuses in Lincoln and Providence.

DEGREES OFFERED. AA, AS, AAS. 1,393 associate degrees awarded in 1992.

UNDERGRADUATE MAJORS. Accounting, biological and physical sciences, business administration and management, business and management, business and office, chemical manufacturing technology, child development/care/guidance, clinical laboratory science, computer engineering, computer programming, computer technology, dental hygiene, dramatic arts, early childhood, education, education of the mentally handicapped, electrical/electronics/communications engineering, electronic technology, elementary education, engineering, engineering and engineering-related technologies, fashion merchandising, fire control and safety technology, gerontology, industrial equipment maintenance and repair, instrumentation technology, jazz, labor/industrial relations, law enforcement and corrections, legal secretary, liberal/general studies, machine tool operation/machine shop, mechanical design technology, mechanical engineering, medical assistant, medical laboratory technologies, medical secretary, mental health/human services, music, nursing, physical therapy assistant, radiograph medical technology, real estate, respiratory therapy, retailing, social work, special education, specific learning disabilities, substance abuse counseling, technical education, technical studies, urban studies, visual and performing arts.

ACADEMIC PROGRAMS. 2-year transfer program, cooperative education, double major, dual enrollment of high school students, honors program, internships, study abroad, telecourses, weekend college, cross-registration. **Remedial services:** Learning center, remedial instruction, special counselor, tutoring. **ROTC:** Army. **Placement/credit:** CLEP General and Subject; 30 credit hours maximum for associate degree.

ACADEMIC REQUIREMENTS. Freshmen must earn minimum GPA of 1.0 to continue in good standing. Students must declare major on application. **Graduation requirements:** 60 hours for associate. Most students required to take courses in arts/fine arts, English, mathematics, social sciences.

FRESHMAN ADMISSIONS. Selection criteria: Open admissions. Open admissions for New England residents for most programs. For programs with limited enrollment, high school record and in house testing in mathematics, English, and/or chemistry may be required. Some programs may require mathematics and science background. Special considerations for nursing and allied health applicants.

1992 FRESHMAN CLASS PROFILE. 6,549 men and women applied, 5,207 accepted; 1,100 men enrolled, 1,709 women enrolled. **Characteristics:** 91% from in state, 18% have minority backgrounds, 1% are foreign students.

FALL-TERM APPLICATIONS. $20 fee, may be waived for applicants with need. Closing date September 5; applicants notified on a rolling basis beginning on or about January 1; must reply by September 5. Deferred and early admission available.

STUDENT LIFE. Activities: Student government, radio, student newspaper, yearbook, choral groups, concert band, dance, drama, jazz band, music ensembles, Black Americans Student Association, Latin American Student Organization, Shielders, Spanish Club, German Club, Portuguese Club, French Club, South East Asian Club, ABLE, Minority Mentor Program, Distributive Education Club of America, New Americans.

ATHLETICS. NJCAA. **Intercollegiate:** Baseball M, basketball, cross-country, golf, ice hockey M, soccer M, softball W, tennis, track and field, volleyball W. **Intramural:** Badminton, basketball, golf, soccer, swimming, tennis, track and field, volleyball.

STUDENT SERVICES. Aptitude testing, career counseling, employment service for undergraduates, freshman orientation, health services, on-campus day care, personal counseling, placement service for graduates, veterans counselor, minority mentor program, services/facilities for handicapped.

ANNUAL EXPENSES. Tuition and fees (1992-93): $1,496, $2,188 additional for out-of-state students. **Books and supplies:** $450. **Other expenses:** $700.

FINANCIAL AID. 40% of freshmen, 35% of continuing students receive some form of aid. All grants, all loans based on need. **Aid applications:** No closing date; applicants notified on a rolling basis beginning on or about May 1; must reply within 2 weeks.

ADDRESS/TELEPHONE. Joseph P. DiMaria, Dean of Admissions and Records, Community College of Rhode Island, 400 East Avenue, Warwick, RI 02886-1807. (401) 825-2285. Fax: (401) 825-2418.

Johnson & Wales University
Providence, Rhode Island — CB code: 3465

Admissions:	79% of applicants accepted
Based on:	••• Interview, school record
	• Activities, essay, recommendations, special talents, test scores
Completion:	80% of freshmen end year in good standing
	13% enter graduate study

4-year private university, coed. Founded in 1914. **Undergraduate enrollment:** 3,359 men, 2,872 women full time; 491 men, 643 women part time. **Graduate enrollment:** 204 men, 188 women full time; 94 men, 69 women part time. **Faculty:** 277 total (169 full time), 37 with doctorates or other terminal degrees. **Location:** Urban campus in small city; 200 miles from New York City, 50 miles from Boston. **Calendar:** Trimester, limited summer session. **Microcomputers:** 120 located in dormitories, libraries, classrooms, computer centers. **Special facilities:** 3 college-operated hotels and restaurants, banquet facilities, a lobster kiosk, a retail store, and travel agency for internship training. **Additional facts:** Culinary arts program offered at branch campuses in Charleston, South Carolina, Norfolk, Virginia, North Miami, Flordia.

DEGREES OFFERED. AS, AAS, BS, MS, MBA. 1,799 associate degrees awarded in 1992. 13% in business and management, 72% home economics, 6% parks/recreation, protective services, public affairs. 966 bachelor's degrees awarded. 10% in business and management, 12% business/office and marketing/distribution, 71% home economics. Graduate degrees offered in 3 major fields of study.

UNDERGRADUATE MAJORS. Associate: Accounting, advertising, business administration and management, business and management, business and office, business computer/console/peripheral equipment operation, business data processing and related programs, business data programming, computer and information sciences, computer systems management, drafting and design technology, electrical/electronics/communications engineering, electronic technology, engineering and engineering-related technologies, entrepreneurship, equestrian science, fashion design, fashion merchandising, finance, food management, food production/management/services, food retailing, health care/hospitality management, hospitality and recreation marketing, hotel/motel and restaurant management, institutional management, investments and securities, legal assistant/paralegal, legal secretary, management science, marketing and distribution, marketing management, pastry arts, public relations, recreation and community services technologies, retailing, secretarial and related programs, small business management and ownership, tourism, word processing. **Bachelor's:** Accounting, advertising, business administration and management, business and management, business and office, business data processing and related programs, business education, computer and information sciences, computer systems management, court reporting, data processing, electrical/electronics/communications engineering, engineering and engineering-related technologies, equestrian science, food management, food production/management/services, health care administration, hospitality and recreation marketing, hotel/motel and restaurant management, information sciences and systems, institutional management, international business management, legal assistant/paralegal, management science, marketing and distribution, marketing management, office supervision and management, retailing, tourism.

ACADEMIC PROGRAMS. 2-year transfer program, accelerated program, cooperative education, double major, dual enrollment of high school students, honors program, independent study, internships, study abroad, teacher preparation, visiting/exchange student program, weekend college; liberal arts/career combination in engineering. **Remedial services:** Learning center, preadmission summer program, reduced course load, remedial instruction, special counselor, tutoring. **ROTC:** Army. **Placement/credit:** AP, CLEP General and Subject, institutional tests.

ACADEMIC REQUIREMENTS. Freshmen must earn minimum GPA of 2.0 to continue in good standing. 90% of freshmen return for sophomore year. Students must declare major by end of first year. **Graduation requirements:** 66 hours for associate (30 in major), 126 hours for bachelor's (65 in major). Most students required to take courses in computer science, English, foreign languages, history, humanities, mathematics, social sciences. **Post-graduate studies:** 64% from 2-year programs enter 4-year programs. 3% enter MBA programs, 10% enter other graduate study. **Additional information:** Students enrolled in 4-year programs earn both associate and bachelor's degrees, which may be in complementary or separate disciplines. Most associate programs include 1-term internship on campus.

FRESHMAN ADMISSIONS. Selection criteria: Admissions decisions are based on class rank, grades, and other documentation specifically requested. **High school preparation:** 13 units recommended. Recommended units include English 4, mathematics 2, social science 2 and science 1.

1992 FRESHMAN CLASS PROFILE. 4,153 men applied, 3,343 accepted, 864 enrolled; 5,322 women applied, 4,115 accepted, 751 enrolled. **Characteristics:** 29% from in state, 68% live in college housing, 21% have minority backgrounds, 5% are foreign students, 5% join fraternities/sororities. Average age is 18.

FALL-TERM APPLICATIONS. $25 fee, may be waived for applicants with need. No closing date; applicants notified on a rolling basis; must reply within 2 weeks. Interview recommended. Essay recommended. Interview recommended for all. Interview and letter of recommendation generally required of students in bottom quarter of class. Deferred and early admission available.

STUDENT LIFE. Housing: Dormitories (women, coed). **Activities:** Student government, student newspaper, yearbook, choral groups, dance, drama, fraternities, sororities, preprofessional clubs.

ATHLETICS. Intercollegiate: Horseback riding, ice hockey M, soccer M. **Intramural:** Basketball, bowling, golf, ice hockey, racquetball, skiing, soccer, softball, swimming, table tennis, tennis, volleyball.

STUDENT SERVICES. Aptitude testing, career counseling, employment service for undergraduates, freshman orientation, health services, personal counseling, placement service for graduates, veterans counselor, services/facilities for handicapped.

ANNUAL EXPENSES. Tuition and fees: $9,510. **Room and board:** $4,485. **Books and supplies:** $500. **Other expenses:** $500.

FINANCIAL AID. 82% of freshmen, 84% of continuing students receive some form of aid. 62% of grants, 87% of loans, 35% of jobs based on need. Academic, leadership scholarships available. **Aid applications:** No closing date; priority given to applications received by March 1; applicants notified on a rolling basis beginning on or about March 1; must reply within 2 weeks. **Additional information:** 10% tuition reduction offered to children of educators.

ADDRESS/TELEPHONE. Mark S. Burke, Director of Enrollment Management, Johnson & Wales University, 8 Abbott Park Place, Providence, RI 02903-3703. (401) 456-1000. (800) 343-2565. Fax: (401) 456-1835.

New England Institute of Technology
Warwick, Rhode Island — CB code: 0339

2-year private technical college, coed. Founded in 1940. **Accreditation:** Regional. **Undergraduate enrollment:** 2,300 men and women. **Faculty:** 128 total (67 full time), 11 with doctorates or other terminal degrees. **Location:** Suburban campus in small city; 50 miles from Boston. **Calendar:** Quarter, extensive summer session. **Microcomputers:** Located in libraries, classrooms, computer centers. **Special facilities:** Special technical research library as designated by the state.

DEGREES OFFERED. AS. 850 associate degrees awarded in 1992. 90 bachelor's degrees awarded.

UNDERGRADUATE MAJORS. Air conditioning/heating/refrigeration mechanics, air conditioning/heating/refrigeration technology, automotive mechanics, automotive technology, carpentry, computer programming, drafting, drafting and design technology, electrical technology, electronic technology, manufacturing technology, marine maintenance, mechanical design technology, medical assistant, medical secretary, plumbing/pipefitting/steamfitting, secretarial and related programs, telecommunications, video.

ACADEMIC PROGRAMS. Cooperative education, double major, internships. **Remedial services:** Learning center, preadmission summer program, reduced course load, remedial instruction, tutoring. **Placement/credit:** CLEP General and Subject, institutional tests; 51 credit hours maximum for associate degree.

ACADEMIC REQUIREMENTS. Freshmen must earn minimum GPA of 1.9 to continue in good standing. 85% of freshmen return for sophomore year. Students must declare major on enrollment. **Graduation requirements:** 196 hours for bachelor's. Most students required to take courses in English, history, humanities, mathematics, social sciences.

FRESHMAN ADMISSIONS. Selection criteria: Open admissions.

1992 FRESHMAN CLASS PROFILE. 900 men and women enrolled. **Characteristics:** 70% from in state, 100% commute, 28% have minority backgrounds, 1% are foreign students. Average age is 22.

FALL-TERM APPLICATIONS. No fee. No closing date; applicants notified on a rolling basis; must reply within 4 weeks. Interview required. Portfolio recommended for drafting applicants. Deferred and early admission available.

STUDENT LIFE. Activities: Magazine.

STUDENT SERVICES. Career counseling, employment service for undergraduates, personal counseling, placement service for graduates, veterans counselor, services/facilities for handicapped.

ANNUAL EXPENSES. Tuition and fees: $8,955. **Books and supplies:** $600. **Other expenses:** $1,872.

FINANCIAL AID. 80% of freshmen, 80% of continuing students receive some form of aid. All grants, 63% of loans, all jobs based on need. **Aid applications:** No closing date; priority given to applications received by June 1; applicants notified on a rolling basis beginning on or about June 15; must reply within 2 weeks. **Additional information:** Tuition at time of first enrollment guaranteed all students for 2 years.

ADDRESS/TELEPHONE. Nick Azzarone, Director of Admissions, New England Institute of Technology, 2500 Post Road, Warwick, RI 02886. (401) 467-7744. (800) 736-7744. Fax: (401) 738-5122.

New England Technical College
Warwick, Rhode Island — CB code: 1864

2-year upper-division private technical college, coed. Founded in 1991. **Undergraduate enrollment:** 164 men and women. **Location:** Suburban campus in small city; 50 miles south of Boston. **Calendar:** Quarter.

ANNUAL EXPENSES. Tuition and fees: $8,955. **Books and supplies:** $600. **Other expenses:** $1,000.

ADDRESS/TELEPHONE. Nick Azzarone, Director of Admissions, New England Institute of Technology, 2500 Post Road, Warwick, RI 02886. (401) 467-7744. (800) 736-7744. Fax: (401) 738-5122.

Providence College
Providence, Rhode Island — CB code: 3693

Admissions: 62% of applicants accepted
Based on:
••• School record
•• Activities, essay, special talents, test scores
• Interview, recommendations
Completion: 98% of freshmen end year in good standing
88% graduate, 30% of these enter graduate study

4-year private college of arts and sciences, coed, affiliated with Roman Catholic Church. Founded in 1917. **Accreditation:** Regional. **Undergraduate enrollment:** 1,732 men, 2,015 women full time; 616 men, 882 women part time. **Graduate enrollment:** 25 men, 4 women full time; 321 men, 519 women part time. **Faculty:** 303 total (256 full time), 196 with doctorates or other terminal degrees. **Location:** Suburban campus in small city; 50 miles from Boston. **Calendar:** Semester, limited summer session. Saturday and extensive evening/early morning classes. **Microcomputers:** 144 located in classrooms, computer centers. **Special facilities:** Blackfriars Theatre, Hunt-Cavanaugh Art Building, Science Center Complex, Peterson Recreation Center. **Additional facts:** Associate degrees offered only in evening division.

DEGREES OFFERED. AA, AS, BA, BS, MA, MS, MBA, MEd, PhD. 9 associate degrees awarded in 1992. 35% in business and management, 30% health sciences, 35% parks/recreation, protective services, public affairs. 1,027 bachelor's degrees awarded. 35% in business and management, 8% education, 9% letters/literature, 9% multi/interdisciplinary studies, 21% social sciences. Graduate degrees offered in 8 major fields of study.

UNDERGRADUATE MAJORS. Associate: Business and management, fire control and safety technology, health care administration, labor/industrial relations, legal assistant/paralegal, liberal/general studies, office supervision and management, youth ministry. **Bachelor's:** Accounting, American studies, art history, biology, business administration and management, business and management, business economics, chemistry, computer and information sciences, computer mathematics, dramatic arts, economics, elementary education, English, English education, finance, fire control and safety technology, foreign languages education, French, health care administration, history, humanities, humanities and social sciences, Italian, Latin American studies, liberal/general studies, marketing management, mathematics, mathematics education, music, philosophy, political science and government, preengineering, premedicine, psychology, religion, science education, secondary education, social sciences, social studies education, social work, sociology, Spanish, special education, studio art, systems engineering, youth ministry.

ACADEMIC PROGRAMS. 2-year transfer program, double major, honors program, independent study, internships, student-designed major, study abroad, teacher preparation, visiting/exchange student program, cross-registration; liberal arts/career combination in engineering; combined bachelor's/graduate program in business administration. **Remedial services:** Learning center, reduced course load, special counselor, tutoring. **ROTC:** Army. **Placement/credit:** AP, CLEP Subject, IB, institutional tests.

ACADEMIC REQUIREMENTS. Freshmen must earn minimum GPA of 1.6 to continue in good standing. 95% of freshmen return for sophomore year. Students must declare major by end of second year. **Graduation requirements:** 57 hours for associate, 116 hours for bachelor's (30 in major). Most students required to take courses in arts/fine arts, English, history, mathematics, philosophy/religion, biological/physical sciences, social sciences. **Postgraduate studies:** 8% enter law school, 4% enter medical school, 5% enter MBA programs, 13% enter other graduate study.

FRESHMAN ADMISSIONS. Selection criteria: Emphasis placed on scholastic ability, motivation, character, and seriousness of purpose. School record, recommendations, and results of standardized ability and achievement tests considered. **High school preparation:** 18 units required. Required and recommended units include English 4, foreign language 3-4, mathematics 3-4, social science 2-3 and science 2-3. **Test requirements:** SAT or ACT; score report by February 1. Prueba de Aptitud Academica for Spanish speaking applicants.

1992 FRESHMAN CLASS PROFILE. 2,208 men applied, 1,407 accepted, 413 enrolled; 2,898 women applied, 1,744 accepted, 528 enrolled. 21% were in top tenth and 58% were in top quarter of graduating class. **Academic background:** Mid 50% of enrolled freshmen had SAT-V between 440-530, SAT-M between 490-590. 94% submitted SAT scores. **Characteristics:** 14% from in state, 95% live in college housing, 8% have minority backgrounds, 1% are foreign students. Average age is 18.

FALL-TERM APPLICATIONS. $30 fee, may be waived for applicants with need. Closing date February 1; applicants notified on or about April 1; must reply by May 1. Essay required. Interview recommended. Audition recommended for music applicants. Portfolio recommended for art applicants. CRDA. Deferred and early admission available. Institutional early decision plan. 3 ACH (including English Composition with essay) recommended. January test scores latest accepted.

STUDENT LIFE. Housing: Dormitories (men, women); apartment, handicapped housing available. **Activities:** Student government, magazine, radio, student newspaper, yearbook, choral groups, concert band, dance, drama, jazz band, music ensembles, musical theater, pep band, Afro-American Society, Big Brothers and Sisters, Council for Exceptional Children, International Society, social organization, service organization.

ATHLETICS. NCAA. **Intercollegiate:** Baseball M, basketball, cross-country, diving, field hockey W, golf M, ice hockey, lacrosse M, racquetball, rugby, soccer, softball W, swimming, tennis, track and field, volleyball W. **Intramural:** Basketball, bowling, football M, handball, ice hockey, racquetball, rifle, rowing (crew), skiing, softball, squash, swimming, tennis, volleyball, water polo, wrestling M.

STUDENT SERVICES. Aptitude testing, career counseling, employment service for undergraduates, freshman orientation, health services, personal counseling, placement service for graduates, services/facilities for handicapped.

ANNUAL EXPENSES. Tuition and fees (projected): $13,350. **Room and board:** $5,900. **Books and supplies:** $450. **Other expenses:** $1,100.

FINANCIAL AID. 58% of freshmen, 58% of continuing students receive some form of aid. 91% of grants, 99% of loans, 54% of jobs based on need. 428 enrolled freshmen were judged to have need, all were offered aid. Academic, athletic, minority scholarships available. **Aid applications:** Closing date February 15; applicants notified on or about April 1; must reply by May 1. **Additional information:** Tuition Payment Agreement Plan (TPA) provides families with a monthly payment plan that divides charges into 10 monthly installments.

ADDRESS/TELEPHONE. Michael G. Backes, Dean of Admissions, Providence College, River Avenue and Eaton Street, Providence, RI 02918-0001. (401) 865-2535. Fax: (401) 865-2628.

Rhode Island College
Providence, Rhode Island — CB code: 3724

Admissions: 71% of applicants accepted
Based on:
- ••• School record
- •• Essay
- • Activities, interview, recommendations, special talents, test scores

Completion: 80% of freshmen end year in good standing
45% graduate

4-year public comprehensive college, coed. Founded in 1854. **Accreditation:** Regional. **Undergraduate enrollment:** 7,580 men and women. **Graduate enrollment:** 2,213 men and women. **Faculty:** 501 total (375 full time), 268 with doctorates or other terminal degrees. **Location:** Suburban campus in small city; 4 miles from downtown. **Calendar:** Semester, extensive summer session. Saturday classes. **Microcomputers:** 200 located in libraries, classrooms, computer centers. **Special facilities:** Bannister Art Gallery specializing in faculty and student exhibitions.

DEGREES OFFERED. BA, BS, BFA, MA, MS, MEd, MSW. 990 bachelor's degrees awarded in 1992. Graduate degrees offered in 43 major fields of study.

UNDERGRADUATE MAJORS. Accounting, African studies, Afro-American (black) studies, anthropology, art education, art history, bilingual/bicultural education, biology, business administration and management, business and management, business economics, chemistry, clinical laboratory science, communications, computer and information sciences, computer programming, criminal justice studies, dramatic arts, drawing, early childhood education, economics, education of exceptional children, education of the emotionally handicapped, education of the mentally handicapped, education of the multiple handicapped, education of the physically handicapped, elementary education, engineering and engineering-related technologies, English, English education, English literature, film arts, fine arts, foreign languages education, French, geography, gerontology, health education, history, human resources development, industrial arts education, industrial technology, information sciences and systems, junior high education, labor/industrial relations, Latin American studies, liberal/general studies, management information systems, marketing management, mathematics, mathematics education, medical laboratory technologies, medieval studies, music, music education, music performance, nursing, painting, personnel management, philosophy, physical education, physical sciences, physics, political science and government, predentistry, premedicine, preveterinary, psychology, public administration, public relations, radio/television broadcasting, radiograph medical technology, science education, sculpture, secondary education, social sciences, social studies education, social work, sociology, Spanish, speech/communication/theater education, studio art, technical education, trade and industrial education, urban studies, women's studies.

ACADEMIC PROGRAMS. Cooperative education, double major, dual enrollment of high school students, honors program, independent study, internships, student-designed major, study abroad, teacher preparation, visiting/exchange student program, cross-registration. **Remedial services:** Learning center, preadmission summer program, reduced course load, special counselor, tutoring. **ROTC:** Army. **Placement/credit:** AP, CLEP General and Subject, institutional tests.

ACADEMIC REQUIREMENTS. Freshmen must earn minimum GPA of 1.55 to continue in good standing. 70% of freshmen return for sophomore year. Students must declare major by end of second year. **Graduation requirements:** 120 hours for bachelor's. Most students required to take courses in arts/fine arts, English, history, mathematics, philosophy/religion, biological/physical sciences, social sciences.

FRESHMAN ADMISSIONS. Selection criteria: Performance in high school most important, followed by test scores, interviews, references. Minority, bilingual, disadvantaged status considered. **High school preparation:** 18 units required. Required units include biological science 1, English 4, foreign language 2, mathematics 3, physical science 1, social science 1 and science 2. One history, .5 units in arts, and .5 units in computer literacy also required. **Test requirements:** SAT or ACT (SAT preferred); score report by June 1.

1992 FRESHMAN CLASS PROFILE. 789 men applied, 531 accepted, 331 enrolled; 1,671 women applied, 1,204 accepted, 703 enrolled. **Academic background:** Mid 50% of enrolled freshmen had SAT-V between 370-470, SAT-M between 380-510. 100% submitted SAT scores. **Characteristics:** 87% from in state, 80% commute, 15% have minority backgrounds, 1% are foreign students, 2% join fraternities/sororities. Average age is 18.

FALL-TERM APPLICATIONS. $25 fee, may be waived for applicants with need. Closing date May 1; priority given to applications received by March 1; applicants notified on a rolling basis beginning on or about January 15; must reply by May 1 or within 2 weeks if notified thereafter. Audition required for music performance applicants. Portfolio required for bachelor of fine arts applicants. Essay required. Interview recommended. CRDA. Deferred and early admission available.

STUDENT LIFE. Housing: Dormitories (women, coed). **Activities:** Student government, radio, student newspaper, television, yearbook, choral groups, concert band, dance, drama, jazz band, music ensembles, musical theater, symphony orchestra, children's theater, fraternities, sororities, Catholic, Protestant, and Jewish religious organizations, black student organization, international students society, Lusophile Society, Latin American Student Organization, disabled student organization.

ATHLETICS. NCAA. **Intercollegiate:** Baseball M, basketball, cross-country, gymnastics W, soccer M, softball W, tennis, track and field, volleyball W, wrestling M. **Intramural:** Basketball, bowling, field hockey M, softball, tennis, volleyball.

STUDENT SERVICES. Aptitude testing, career counseling, employment service for undergraduates, freshman orientation, health services, on-campus day care, personal counseling, placement service for graduates, special adviser for adult students, veterans counselor, services/facilities for handicapped.

ANNUAL EXPENSES. Tuition and fees (1992-93): $2,498, $3,959 additional for out-of-state students. **Room and board:** $4,979. **Books and supplies:** $500. **Other expenses:** $1,000.

FINANCIAL AID. 40% of freshmen, 45% of continuing students receive some form of aid. 97% of grants, 85% of loans, all jobs based on need. 400 enrolled freshmen were judged to have need, all were offered aid. Academic, music/drama, art scholarships available. **Aid applications:** Closing date March 1; applicants notified on a rolling basis beginning on or about April 15; must reply by July 1.

ADDRESS/TELEPHONE. William H. Hurry Jr, Dean of Admissions and Financial Aid, Rhode Island College, Craig-Lee Hall, 154, Providence, RI 02908. (401) 456-8234. Fax: (401) 456-8379.

Rhode Island School of Design

Providence, Rhode Island — CB code: 3726

Admissions: 47% of applicants accepted
Based on: ••• School record, special talents
•• Essay, test scores
• Activities, recommendations
Completion: 98% of freshmen end year in good standing
85% graduate, 5% of these enter graduate study

4-year private art college, coed. Founded in 1877. **Accreditation:** Regional. **Undergraduate enrollment:** 819 men, 1,025 women full time. **Graduate enrollment:** 62 men, 80 women full time. **Faculty:** 286 total (103 full time). **Location:** Urban campus in small city; 52 miles from Boston, 200 miles from New York City. **Calendar:** 4-1-4, limited summer session. **Microcomputers:** 163 located in dormitories, libraries, classrooms, computer centers. **Special facilities:** Fine art and design museum, extensive photograph and clipping collections, slide collection, recreational farm on Narragansett Bay, nature laboratory.

DEGREES OFFERED. BFA, BArch, MFA. 496 bachelor's degrees awarded in 1992. 30% in architecture and environmental design, 70% visual and performing arts. Graduate degrees offered in 11 major fields of study.

UNDERGRADUATE MAJORS. Architecture, ceramics, cinematography/film, fashion design, fiber/textiles/weaving, film animation, glass, graphic design, illustration design, industrial design, interior design, landscape architecture, metal/jewelry, painting, photography, printmaking, sculpture, video.

ACADEMIC PROGRAMS. Independent study, internships, study abroad, teacher preparation, visiting/exchange student program, cross-registration. **Remedial services:** Remedial instruction. **Placement/credit:** AP.

ACADEMIC REQUIREMENTS. Freshmen must earn minimum GPA of 1.8 to continue in good standing. 93% of freshmen return for sophomore year. Students must declare major by end of first year. **Graduation requirements:** 126 hours for bachelor's (54 in major). Most students required to take courses in arts/fine arts, English, history, humanities, philosophy/religion, social sciences. **Additional information:** Fifth year for professional degrees in architectural studies.

FRESHMAN ADMISSIONS. Selection criteria: For architectural studies applicants: high school GPA, test scores, class rank most important; visual material may also be considered. For fine arts applicants: portfolio, drawing assignment, and academic record equally important. Architecture applicants must have 2 algebra, .5 trigonometry, 1 science. **Test requirements:** SAT or ACT (SAT preferred); score report by February 15. SAT or ACT required for admission of architecture applicants, for placement of art and design applicants.

1992 FRESHMAN CLASS PROFILE. 824 men applied, 391 accepted, 167 enrolled; 930 women applied, 442 accepted, 207 enrolled. 48% had high school GPA of 3.0 or higher, 50% between 2.0 and 2.99. 23% were in top tenth and 51% were in top quarter of graduating class. **Academic background:** Mid 50% of enrolled freshmen had SAT-V between 450-600, SAT-M between 500-600. 98% submitted SAT scores. **Characteristics:** 5% from in state, 92% live in college housing, 18% have minority backgrounds, 12% are foreign students. Average age is 18.

FALL-TERM APPLICATIONS. $35 fee, may be waived for applicants with need. Closing date January 21; applicants notified on or about April 1; must reply by May 1. Essay required. Portfolio required for fine arts and design applicants; recommended for architectural studies applicants. CRDA. Deferred and early admission available.

STUDENT LIFE. Housing: Dormitories (coed); apartment housing available. Freshman housing available in a chemical-free environment. **Activities:** Student government, film, student newspaper, yearbook, photography portfolio, silkscreen portfolio, dance, drama, all major religions represented on campus, professional societies, clubs.

ATHLETICS. Intramural: Baseball, basketball, ice hockey, sailing, skiing, soccer, softball, swimming, tennis, volleyball.

STUDENT SERVICES. Career counseling, employment service for undergraduates, freshman orientation, health services, personal counseling, placement service for graduates, adviser for international and minority students, services/facilities for handicapped.

ANNUAL EXPENSES. Tuition and fees: $15,900. **Room and board:** $6,415. **Books and supplies:** $1,300. **Other expenses:** $1,100.

FINANCIAL AID. 57% of freshmen, 64% of continuing students receive some form of aid. Grants, loans, jobs available. Academic, art scholarships available. **Aid applications:** Closing date February 15; applicants notified on or about April 1; must reply by May 1.

ADDRESS/TELEPHONE. Edward Newhall, Director of Admissions, Rhode Island School of Design, 2 College Street, Providence, RI 02903. (401) 454-6300. Fax: (401) 454-6309.

Roger Williams University

Bristol, Rhode Island — CB code: 3729

Admissions: 85% of applicants accepted
Based on: ••• School record
•• Essay, special talents
• Activities, interview, recommendations, test scores
Completion: 84% of freshmen end year in good standing
55% graduate, 10% of these enter graduate study

4-year private university, coed. Founded in 1956. **Accreditation:** Regional. **Undergraduate enrollment:** 1,108 men, 899 women full time; 932 men, 672 women part time. **Faculty:** 239 total (114 full time), 68 with doctorates or other terminal degrees. **Location:** Suburban campus in large town; 18 miles from Providence, 10 miles from Newport. **Calendar:** 4-1-4, limited summer session. **Microcomputers:** 175 located in libraries, classrooms, computer centers. **Special facilities:** Library has study carrels with computer access to mainframe. **Additional facts:** Continuing education evening division in Providence and Bristol. Associate degree offered only in continuing education evening division. 5-year bachelor of architecture program offered.

DEGREES OFFERED. AA, AS, BA, BS, BFA, BArch. 83 associate degrees awarded in 1992. 471 bachelor's degrees awarded. 17% in architecture and environmental design, 32% business and management, 5% communications, 8% engineering, 5% law, 9% psychology, 8% visual and performing arts.

UNDERGRADUATE MAJORS. Associate: Engineering and engineering-related technologies, liberal/general studies. **Bachelor's:** Accounting, architecture, biology, business administration and management, business and management, chemistry, communications, computer and information sciences, construction, creative writing, dance, dramatic arts, engineering, English, historic preservation, history, humanities and social sciences, law enforcement and corrections, legal assistant/paralegal, management information systems, marine biology, marketing management, mathematics, philosophy, political science and government, predentistry, premedicine, preveterinary, psychology, public administration, studio art.

ACADEMIC PROGRAMS. Accelerated program, cooperative education, double major, external degree, independent study, internships, student-designed major, study abroad, teacher preparation; liberal arts/career combination in forestry. **Remedial services:** Learning center, reduced course load, remedial instruction, tutoring. **ROTC:** Army. **Placement/credit:** AP, CLEP General and Subject, IB, institutional tests; 30 credit hours maximum for bachelor's degree.

ACADEMIC REQUIREMENTS. Freshmen must earn minimum GPA of 1.4 to continue in good standing. Full-time freshmen must pass 18 semester hours during their first year to continue in good academic standing. 80% of freshmen return for sophomore year. Students must declare major by end of second year. **Graduation requirements:** 120 hours for bachelor's (30 in major). Most students required to take courses in arts/fine arts, English, history, humanities, mathematics, biological/physical sciences, social sciences. **Postgraduate studies:** 1% enter law school, 2% enter medical school, 4% enter MBA programs, 3% enter other graduate study. **Additional information:** Teacher certification in elementary and early childhood education available.

FRESHMAN ADMISSIONS. Selection criteria: High school record, rank in class, recommendations of counselor and teachers, interview, standardized test scores considered. **High school preparation:** 16 units recommended. Recommended units include biological science 1, English 4, mathematics 3, physical science 1 and social science 2. Specific subject requirements vary with intended major. **Test requirements:** SAT or ACT (SAT preferred); score report by March 1.

1992 FRESHMAN CLASS PROFILE. 1,638 men applied, 1,384 accepted, 320 enrolled; 1,341 women applied, 1,134 accepted, 270 enrolled. 35% had high school GPA of 3.0 or higher, 65% between 2.0 and 2.99. **Academic background:** Mid 50% of enrolled freshmen had SAT-V between 380-460, SAT-M between 430-510. 87% submitted SAT scores. **Characteristics:** 12% from in state, 85% live in college housing, 4% have minority backgrounds, 4% are foreign students. Average age is 18.

FALL-TERM APPLICATIONS. $35 fee, may be waived for applicants with need. No closing date; applicants notified on a rolling basis; must reply by May 1 or within 4 weeks if notified thereafter. Portfolio required for art, architecture applicants. Interview recommended. Essay recommended. CRDA. Deferred and early admission available. Fall-term application deadline for architecture applicants February 1.

STUDENT LIFE. Housing: Dormitories (men, women, coed); apartment housing available. **Activities:** Student government, magazine, radio, student newspaper, yearbook, choral groups, dance, drama, jazz band, musical theater, Hillel, Christian Fellowship, Minority Affairs Committee, Environmental Action, International Students Association, Model United Nations, Volunteer Center.

ATHLETICS. NCAA. **Intercollegiate:** Baseball M, basketball, cross-country, golf, horseback riding, ice hockey M, lacrosse M, sailing, soccer, softball W, tennis, volleyball, wrestling M. **Intramural:** Basketball, rugby M, soccer W, softball, tennis, volleyball.

STUDENT SERVICES. Aptitude testing, career counseling, employment service for undergraduates, freshman orientation, health services, personal counseling, placement service for graduates, special adviser for adult students, veterans counselor, special services for veterans, services/facilities for handicapped.

ANNUAL EXPENSES. Tuition and fees (1992-93): $11,370. **Room and board:** $5,330. **Books and supplies:** $500. **Other expenses:** $300.

FINANCIAL AID. 44% of freshmen, 44% of continuing students receive some form of aid. 96% of grants, all loans, all jobs based on need. Academic, state/district residency, leadership, minority scholarships available. **Aid applications:** No closing date; priority given to applications received by March 1; applicants notified on a rolling basis beginning on or about March 1; must reply by May 1 or within 2 weeks if notified thereafter.

ADDRESS/TELEPHONE. William B. Galloway, Dean of Admission, Roger Williams University, Ferry Road, Bristol, RI 02809-2923. (401) 254-3500. (800) 458-7144.

Salve Regina University
Newport, Rhode Island

CB code: 3759

Admissions: 93% of applicants accepted
Based on:
••• School record
•• Activities, essay, interview, recommendations
• Special talents, test scores
Completion: 92% of freshmen end year in good standing
90% graduate, 74% of these enter graduate study

4-year private university and college of arts and sciences, coed, affiliated with Roman Catholic Church. Founded in 1934. **Accreditation:** Regional. **Undergraduate enrollment:** 449 men, 1,026 women full time; 67 men, 188 women part time. **Graduate enrollment:** 28 men, 31 women full time; 235 men, 290 women part time. **Faculty:** 212 total (114 full time), 104 with doctorates or other terminal degrees. **Location:** Suburban campus in large town; 40 miles from Providence. **Calendar:** Semester, limited summer session. **Microcomputers:** 90 located in libraries, computer centers. **Special facilities:** Art gallery, theater.

DEGREES OFFERED. AA, AS, BA, BS, MA, MS, MBA, MEd, PhD. 7 associate degrees awarded in 1992. 17% in business and management, 17% multi/interdisciplinary studies, 66% parks/recreation, protective services, public affairs. 361 bachelor's degrees awarded. 22% in business and management, 15% teacher education, 12% health sciences, 7% letters/literature, 12% parks/recreation, protective services, public affairs, 5% psychology, 8% social sciences, 6% visual and performing arts. Graduate degrees offered in 15 major fields of study.

UNDERGRADUATE MAJORS. Associate: Business and management, criminal justice studies, humanities. **Bachelor's:** Accounting, American studies, anthropology, applied mathematics, biology, business and management, chemistry, clinical laboratory science, computer programming, criminal justice studies, dramatic arts, economics, education, elementary education, English, English literature, French, history, information sciences and systems, management information systems, mathematics, medical laboratory technologies, music, music education, music performance, nursing, philosophy, political science and government, predentistry, prelaw, premedicine, prepharmacy, preveterinary, psychology, religion, secondary education, social work, sociology, Spanish, special education, speech/communication/theater education, studio art.

ACADEMIC PROGRAMS. 2-year transfer program, accelerated program, double major, dual enrollment of high school students, education specialist degree, independent study, internships, study abroad, teacher preparation, visiting/exchange student program; combined bachelor's/graduate program in business administration. **Remedial services:** Reduced course load, special counselor, tutoring. **ROTC:** Army. **Placement/credit:** AP, CLEP General and Subject, IB, institutional tests.

ACADEMIC REQUIREMENTS. Freshmen must earn minimum GPA of 2.0 to continue in good standing. 95% of freshmen return for sophomore year. Students must declare major by end of first year. **Graduation requirements:** 64 hours for associate (21 in major), 128 hours for bachelor's (36 in major). Most students required to take courses in arts/fine arts, computer science, English, foreign languages, history, humanities, mathematics, philosophy/religion, biological/physical sciences, social sciences. **Postgraduate studies:** 99% from 2-year programs enter 4-year programs.

FRESHMAN ADMISSIONS. Selection criteria: High school achievement most important, followed by rank in top half of high school class, test scores, recommendations, autobiography, activities, interview. Special consideration given to applicants from minorities and low income families. **High school preparation:** 16 units recommended. Recommended units include English 4, foreign language 2, mathematics 3, social science 1 and science 2. No more than 2 of 4 electives accepted in vocational subjects. **Test requirements:** SAT or ACT (SAT preferred).

1992 FRESHMAN CLASS PROFILE. 339 men applied, 315 accepted, 122 enrolled; 1,014 women applied, 943 accepted, 281 enrolled. **Characteristics:** 20% from in state, 90% live in college housing, 5% have minority backgrounds, 1% are foreign students. Average age is 18.

FALL-TERM APPLICATIONS. $25 fee, may be waived for applicants with need. No closing date; applicants notified on a rolling basis; must reply by May 1 or date specified if notified thereafter. Essay required. Interview recommended. CRDA. Deferred and early admission available. EDP-S.

STUDENT LIFE. Housing: Dormitories (men, women); apartment housing available. Apartment program in local community operated by college for upper-division students. **Activities:** Student government, student newspaper, yearbook, student senate newsletters, choral groups, concert band, dance, drama, jazz band, music ensembles, pep band, campus ministry, Council for Exceptional Children, student life, housing and academic senates, Mercy Honor Society, Learning Unlimited, Emerald Society, Administration of Justice Club, student nurse organization, Sigma Phi Sigma.

ATHLETICS. NCAA. **Intercollegiate:** Baseball M, basketball, cross-country, field hockey W, football M, golf, horseback riding, ice hockey M, rugby M, sailing, soccer, softball W, tennis, track and field. **Intramural:** Basketball, bowling, boxing M, field hockey W, golf, handball, lacrosse M, racquetball, sailing, soccer, softball, swimming, tennis, track and field, volleyball, water polo.

STUDENT SERVICES. Aptitude testing, career counseling, employment service for undergraduates, freshman orientation, health services, personal counseling, placement service for graduates, veterans counselor, services/facilities for handicapped.

ANNUAL EXPENSES. Tuition and fees: $13,800. **Room and board:** $6,300. **Books and supplies:** $500. **Other expenses:** $900.

FINANCIAL AID. 63% of freshmen, 52% of continuing students receive some form of aid. 96% of grants, 92% of loans, 41% of jobs based on need. 235 enrolled freshmen were judged to have need, all were offered aid. Alumni affiliation, religious affiliation, minority scholarships available. **Aid applications:** No closing date; priority given to applications received by March 1; applicants notified on a rolling basis beginning on or about April 1; must reply by May 1 or within 2 weeks if notified thereafter.

ADDRESS/TELEPHONE. Sr. Roselina McKillop, RSM, Dean of Admissions, Salve Regina University, 100 Ochre Point Avenue, Newport, RI 02840-4192. (401) 847-6650 ext. 2908. Fax: (401) 847-6650 ext. 2990.

University of Rhode Island
Kingston, Rhode Island

CB code: 3919

Admissions: 70% of applicants accepted
Based on:
••• School record
•• Test scores
• Activities, interview, recommendations, special talents
Completion: 80% of freshmen end year in good standing
57% graduate

4-year public university, coed. Founded in 1892. **Accreditation:** Regional. **Undergraduate enrollment:** 4,207 men, 4,807 women full time; 1,176 men, 1,580 women part time. **Graduate enrollment:** 538 men, 585 women full time; 1,195 men, 1,363 women part time. **Faculty:** 750 total (723 full time), 598 with doctorates or other terminal degrees. **Location:** Rural campus in small town; 30 miles from Providence. **Calendar:** Semester, extensive summer session. **Microcomputers:** 580 located in libraries, classrooms, computer centers. **Special facilities:** Center for robotics research, animal science farm, planetarium, Watson House Museum, Narragansett Bay Campus for Marine Sciences, American historic textiles museum, aquaculture center, fisheries and marine technology laboratory, biotechnology center, human performance laboratory. **Additional facts:** College of Continuing Education in Providence offers credit-bearing courses for degree and nondegree part-time students.

DEGREES OFFERED. AS, BA, BS, BFA, MA, MS, MBA, PhD, Pharm D. 9 associate degrees awarded in 1992. 100% in allied health. 2,308 bachelor's degrees awarded. 10% in business and management, 7% communications, 6% teacher education, 7% engineering, 6% health sciences, 8% letters/literature, 19% multi/interdisciplinary studies, 7% parks/recreation, protective services, public affairs, 8% psychology, 8% social sciences. Graduate degrees offered in 71 major fields of study.

UNDERGRADUATE MAJORS. Associate: Dental hygiene. **Bachelor's:** Accounting, animal sciences, anthropology, art history, biological laboratory technology, biology, botany, business administration and management, business and management, chemical engineering, chemistry, civil engineering, classics, communicative disorders, comparative literature, computer and information sciences, computer engineering, dental hygiene, dietetic aide/assistant, dramatic arts, economics, electrical/electronics/communications engineering, elementary education, English, family/consumer resource management, fashion design, fashion merchandising, finance, fine arts, fishing and fisheries, food production/management/services, food science and nutrition, food sciences, French, geology, German, history, home economics, individual and family development, industrial engineering, Italian, journalism, landscape architecture, Latin American studies, liberal/general studies, linguistics, management information systems, management science, marine affairs, marine affairs, marketing management, materials engineering, mathematics, mechanical engineering, medical laboratory technologies, microbiology, music, music education, music history and appreciation, music performance, music theory and composition, nursing, ocean engineering, operations research, personnel management, pharmacy, philosophy, physical education, physics, plant sciences, political science and government, psychology, public affairs, renewable natural resources, Russian, secondary education, sociology, soil sciences, Spanish, speech, statistics, studio art, textiles and clothing, urban horticulture and turf management, urban studies, wildlife management, women's studies, zoology.

ACADEMIC PROGRAMS. Double major, dual enrollment of high school students, honors program, independent study, internships, student-designed major, study abroad, teacher preparation, visiting/exchange student program, 5 year pharmacy program, 5 year physical therapy program. **Remedial services:** Learning center, preadmission summer program, special counselor, tutoring. **ROTC:** Army. **Placement/credit:** AP, CLEP General and Subject, institutional tests; 90 credit hours maximum for bachelor's degree.

ACADEMIC REQUIREMENTS. Freshmen must earn minimum GPA of 2.0 to continue in good standing. 74% of freshmen return for sophomore year. Students must declare major by end of second year. **Graduation requirements:** 71 hours for associate, 130 hours for bachelor's. Most students required to take courses in arts/fine arts, English, foreign languages, history, humanities, mathematics, biological/physical sciences, social sciences.

FRESHMAN ADMISSIONS. Selection criteria: School record primary, test scores secondary. Interview recommended. Extracurricular activities considered. Economically and socially disadvantaged students from Rhode Island admitted through special program for talent development. **High school preparation:** 18 units required. Required units include English 4, foreign language 2, mathematics 3, physical science 2, social science 2 and science 2. Specific unit requirements vary by college. **Test requirements:** SAT or ACT; score report by March 15. **Additional information:** SAT not required for those out of high school 3 years or more.

1992 FRESHMAN CLASS PROFILE. 11% were in top tenth and 28% were in top quarter of graduating class. **Academic background:** Mid 50% of enrolled freshmen had SAT-V between 400-490, SAT-M between 450-560. 95% submitted SAT scores. **Characteristics:** 46% from in state, 90% live in college housing, 8% have minority backgrounds, 1% are foreign students. Average age is 19.

FALL-TERM APPLICATIONS. $30 fee, may be waived for applicants with need. Closing date March 1; applicants notified on a rolling basis; must reply by May 1. Audition required for music applicants. Interview recommended. CRDA. Early admission available. Institutional early decision plan.

STUDENT LIFE. Housing: Dormitories (women, coed); apartment, fraternity, sorority housing available. Wellness dormitory for students who agree to refrain from using cigarettes, drugs and alcohol. **Activities:** Student government, magazine, radio, student newspaper, television, yearbook, choral groups, concert band, dance, drama, jazz band, marching band, music ensembles, musical theater, pep band, symphony orchestra, woodwind quartet and quintet, string and brass quartets, opera workshop, fraternities, sororities, Catholic Student Association, Hillel, Native American Association, ethnic clubs, Little Brother/Little Sister, World Hunger Committee, Women's Resource Center, Older Students Association, International Student Association, Model United Nations.

ATHLETICS. NCAA. **Intercollegiate:** Baseball M, basketball, cross-country, diving, field hockey W, football M, golf M, gymnastics W, soccer, softball, swimming, tennis, track and field, volleyball W. **Intramural:** Badminton, basketball, cross-country, fencing, football M, golf, gymnastics, rugby, soccer, swimming W, tennis, volleyball, water polo, wrestling M. **Clubs:** Horseback riding, ice hockey, lacrosse, rowing, rugby, sailing, skiing, volleyball, walter polo.

STUDENT SERVICES. Aptitude testing, career counseling, employment service for undergraduates, freshman orientation, health services, personal counseling, placement service for graduates, special adviser for adult students, veterans counselor, services/facilities for handicapped.

ANNUAL EXPENSES. Tuition and fees (1992-93): $3,540, $6,434 additional for out-of-state students. **Room and board:** $5,024. **Books and supplies:** $600. **Other expenses:** $1,332.

FINANCIAL AID. 60% of freshmen, 63% of continuing students receive some form of aid. 84% of grants, 82% of loans, all jobs based on need. 1,182 enrolled freshmen were judged to have need, all were offered aid. Academic, music/drama, athletic, alumni affiliation scholarships available. **Aid applications:** No closing date; priority given to applications received by March 1; applicants notified on a rolling basis beginning on or about March 1; must reply by May 1 or within 15 days if notified thereafter.

ADDRESS/TELEPHONE. David G. Taggart, Dean of Admissions and Financial Aid, University of Rhode Island, Green Hall, Kingston, RI 02881-0806. (401) 792-9800.

South Carolina

Aiken Technical College
Aiken, South Carolina CB code: 5037

2-year public community, technical college, coed. Founded in 1972. **Accreditation:** Regional. **Undergraduate enrollment:** 357 men, 468 women full time; 667 men, 884 women part time. **Faculty:** 124 total (56 full time). **Location:** Rural campus in large town; 8 miles from Aiken, 10 miles from Augusta, Georgia. **Calendar:** Semester, extensive summer session. Saturday classes. **Microcomputers:** 300 located in libraries, classrooms, computer centers.

DEGREES OFFERED. AA, AS, AAS. 141 associate degrees awarded in 1992. 38% in business and management, 38% engineering technologies, 6% home economics, 8% multi/interdisciplinary studies, 8% trade and industry.

UNDERGRADUATE MAJORS. Accounting, air conditioning/heating/refrigeration technology, automotive mechanics, automotive technology, business administration and management, business and management, business computer/console/peripheral equipment operation, computer technology, drafting and design technology, electromechanical technology, electronic technology, engineering and engineering-related technologies, human services, industrial equipment maintenance and repair, industrial technology, liberal/general studies, machine tool operation/machine shop, marketing management, mechanical design technology, nuclear technologies, trade and industrial education, welding technology.

ACADEMIC PROGRAMS. 2-year transfer program, cooperative education, double major, internships. **Remedial services:** Learning center, reduced course load, remedial instruction, special counselor, tutoring. **Placement/credit:** CLEP General and Subject, institutional tests; 49 credit hours maximum for associate degree.

ACADEMIC REQUIREMENTS. Freshmen must earn minimum GPA of 1.75 to continue in good standing. Students must declare major by end of first year. **Graduation requirements:** 66 hours for associate (24 in major). Most students required to take courses in computer science, English, humanities, mathematics, social sciences.

FRESHMAN ADMISSIONS. Selection criteria: Open admissions. **High school preparation:** 18 units recommended. Recommended units include biological science 1, English 4, foreign language 2, mathematics 4, physical science 1 and social science 6. High school diploma or GED required for all associate degree programs, engineering technologies and practical nursing programs. **Test requirements:** SAT or ACT (SAT preferred) for placement and counseling only; score report by August 15. ASSET test used for counseling and placement.

1992 FRESHMAN CLASS PROFILE. 250 men, 281 women enrolled. 3% were in top tenth and 12% were in top quarter of graduating class. **Characteristics:** 92% from in state, 100% commute, 33% have minority backgrounds. Average age is 24.

FALL-TERM APPLICATIONS. $15 fee. Closing date August 30; priority given to applications received by August 25; applicants notified on a rolling basis; must reply by August 30. Interview recommended. CRDA. Deferred admission available. SAT recommended.

STUDENT LIFE. Activities: Student government, student newspaper, Phi Theta Kappa Honor Society.

ATHLETICS. Intramural: Basketball, softball, volleyball.

STUDENT SERVICES. Aptitude testing, career counseling, employment service for undergraduates, freshman orientation, on-campus day care, personal counseling, placement service for graduates, special adviser for adult students, veterans counselor, services/facilities for handicapped.

ANNUAL EXPENSES. Tuition and fees (1992-93): $720, $30 additional for out-of-state students. **Books and supplies:** $450. **Other expenses:** $750.

FINANCIAL AID. 39% of freshmen, 37% of continuing students receive some form of aid. 98% of grants, all loans, all jobs based on need. 193 enrolled freshmen were judged to have need, 144 were offered aid. Academic scholarships available. **Aid applications:** No closing date; priority given to applications received by May 1; applicants notified on a rolling basis beginning on or about June 1; must reply within 10 days.

ADDRESS/TELEPHONE. Dean of Student Services, Aiken Technical College, PO Drawer 696, Aiken, SC 29802-0696. (803) 593-9231 ext. 249. Fax: (803)593-6526.

Allen University
Columbia, South Carolina CB code: 5006

4-year private liberal arts college, coed, affiliated with African Methodist Episcopal Church. Founded in 1870. **Accreditation:** Regional. **Undergraduate enrollment:** 195 men and women. **Faculty:** 39 total (25 full time). **Location:** Urban campus in small city. **Calendar:** Semester, limited summer session. **Microcomputers:** Located in libraries, classrooms, computer centers.

DEGREES OFFERED. AA, BA, BS. 17 bachelor's degrees awarded.

UNDERGRADUATE MAJORS. Associate: Science technologies, secretarial and related programs. **Bachelor's:** American studies, biology, business administration and management, education, elementary education, English, history, mathematics, music, political science and government, secretarial and related programs, social sciences, sociology.

ACADEMIC PROGRAMS. Honors program, independent study, internships. **Remedial services:** Learning center, tutoring. **ROTC:** Army. **Placement/credit:** Institutional tests.

ACADEMIC REQUIREMENTS. Freshmen must earn minimum GPA of 2.0 to continue in good standing. 85% of freshmen return for sophomore year. Students must declare major by end of second year. **Graduation requirements:** Most students required to take courses in arts/fine arts, computer science, English, foreign languages, history, humanities, mathematics, philosophy/religion, biological/physical sciences, social sciences.

FRESHMAN ADMISSIONS. Selection criteria: Open admissions.

1992 FRESHMAN CLASS PROFILE. 91 women enrolled. **Characteristics:** 70% from in state, 98% live in college housing, 99% have minority backgrounds, 2% are foreign students. Average age is 18.

FALL-TERM APPLICATIONS. $10 fee, may be waived for applicants with need. No closing date; applicants notified on a rolling basis; must reply by January 14. Interview recommended. Deferred and early admission available.

STUDENT LIFE. Housing: Dormitories (men, women). **Activities:** Student government, film, magazine, radio, student newspaper, television, yearbook, choral groups, dance, drama, fraternities, sororities. **Additional information:** Religious observance required.

ATHLETICS. NAIA. **Intercollegiate:** Baseball M, basketball M, track and field M.

STUDENT SERVICES. Career counseling, personal counseling, placement service for graduates, services/facilities for handicapped.

ANNUAL EXPENSES. Tuition and fees (1992-93): $4,750. **Room and board:** $2,900. **Books and supplies:** $300.

FINANCIAL AID. 100% of freshmen, 98% of continuing students receive some form of aid. **Aid applications:** No closing date; priority given to applications received by May 15; applicants notified on a rolling basis; must reply within 30 days.

ADDRESS/TELEPHONE. Kimberly Oggs, Coordinator of Enrollment Management, Allen University, 1530 Harden Street, Columbia, SC 29204. (803) 254-4165. Fax: (803) 376-5709.

Anderson College
Anderson, South Carolina CB code: 5008

4-year private liberal arts college, coed, affiliated with Southern Baptist Convention. Founded in 1911. **Accreditation:** Regional. **Undergraduate enrollment:** 408 men, 498 women full time; 99 men, 167 women part time. **Faculty:** 78 total (58 full time), 28 with doctorates or other terminal degrees. **Location:** Suburban campus in large town; 32 miles from Greenville. **Calendar:** Semester, limited summer session. **Microcomputers:** 31 located in computer centers. **Special facilities:** Gallant Art Gallery, Center Stage Anderson (fine arts center cultural program), on-campus audio recording studio.

DEGREES OFFERED. AA, BA, BS. 81 associate degrees awarded in 1992.

UNDERGRADUATE MAJORS. Associate: Business administration and management, business and management, fashion merchandising, liberal/general studies, marketing and distribution, music. **Bachelor's:** Business administration and management, business and management, communications, comparative literature, dramatic arts, drawing, elementary education, English, fashion merchandising, graphic design, journalism, junior high education, liberal/general studies, marketing and distribution, marketing management, music, music education, music performance, painting, psychology, radio/television broadcasting, religion, speech, sports management, studio art.

ACADEMIC PROGRAMS. 2-year transfer program, honors program, independent study, internships, study abroad, teacher preparation. **Remedial services:** Preadmission summer program, reduced course load, remedial instruction, special counselor, writing laboratory, mathematics laboratory. **ROTC:** Air Force, Army. **Placement/credit:** AP, CLEP Subject, institutional tests; 24 credit hours maximum for associate degree; 24 credit hours maximum for bachelor's degree.

ACADEMIC REQUIREMENTS. Freshmen must earn minimum GPA of 1.45 to continue in good standing. 64% of freshmen return for sophomore year. Students must declare major by end of second year. **Graduation requirements:** 64 hours for associate, 128 hours for bachelor's (36 in major). Most students required to take courses in arts/fine arts, English, humanities, mathematics, philosophy/religion, biological/physical sciences, social sciences. **Postgraduate studies:** 80% from 2-year programs enter 4-year programs. **Additional information:** Fashion merchandising internships available for freshmen and sophomores.

FRESHMAN ADMISSIONS. Selection criteria: High school achievement record and recommendations considered. Minimum high school GPA of 2.0 and SAT combined score of 700 preferred. Each applicant considered individually. Applicants not meeting these guidelines may be admitted into developmental studies program. **High school preparation:** 20 units recommended. Recommended units include English 4, foreign language 2, mathematics 3, social science 2 and science 4. **Test requirements:** SAT or ACT (SAT preferred); score report by August 15.

1992 FRESHMAN CLASS PROFILE. 148 men, 170 women enrolled. **Academic background:** Mid 50% of enrolled freshmen had SAT-V between 350-450, SAT-M between 350-500. 95% submitted SAT scores. **Characteristics:** 80% from in state, 55% live in college housing, 15% have minority backgrounds, 3% are foreign students. Average age is 18.

FALL-TERM APPLICATIONS. $20 fee, may be waived for applicants with need. Closing date August 15; priority given to applications received by March 15; applicants notified on a rolling basis beginning on or about October 1; must reply by June 1. Interview recommended. CRDA. Deferred and early admission available. Recommendations, further grades, or interview may be required for academically weak. Applicants with diagnosed learning disabilities must meet regular requirements and supply summary of recent (within 1 year of enrollment) diagnostic testing.

STUDENT LIFE. Housing: Dormitories (men, women); apartment housing available. Apartment styled housing for both men and women available. **Activities:** Student government, magazine, student newspaper, television, yearbook, literary magazine, choral groups, concert band, dance, drama, jazz band, music ensembles, musical theater, pep band, symphony orchestra, campus ministries, Phi Theta Kappa.

ATHLETICS. NJCAA. **Intercollegiate:** Baseball M, basketball, cross-country, golf M, soccer, softball W, table tennis, tennis, track and field, volleyball W, wrestling M. **Intramural:** Basketball, bowling, horseback riding, racquetball, soccer, softball, swimming, table tennis, tennis, volleyball W.

STUDENT SERVICES. Career counseling, employment service for undergraduates, freshman orientation, health services, personal counseling, placement service for graduates, special adviser for adult students, veterans counselor, services/facilities for handicapped.

ANNUAL EXPENSES. Tuition and fees: $8,320. **Room and board:** $3,900. **Books and supplies:** $600. **Other expenses:** $1,450.

FINANCIAL AID. 82% of freshmen, 88% of continuing students receive some form of aid. Grants, loans, jobs available. Academic, music/drama, art, athletic, state/district residency, leadership, alumni affiliation, religious affiliation scholarships available. **Aid applications:** No closing date; priority given to applications received by April 1; applicants notified on a rolling basis beginning on or about March 13; must reply within 3 weeks.

ADDRESS/TELEPHONE. Carl D. Lockman, Director of Admissions, Anderson College, 316 Boulevard, Anderson, SC 29621. (803) 231-2030. (800) 542-3594. Fax: (803) 231-2004.

Benedict College
Columbia, South Carolina — CB code: 5056

4-year private liberal arts college, coed, affiliated with American Baptist Churches in the USA. Founded in 1870. **Accreditation:** Regional. **Undergraduate enrollment:** 385 men, 711 women full time; 48 men, 63 women part time. **Faculty:** 115 total (86 full time), 40 with doctorates or other terminal degrees. **Location:** Urban campus in small city; 110 miles from Greenville, 120 miles from Charleston. **Calendar:** Semester, limited summer session. **Microcomputers:** Located in libraries, classrooms, computer centers. **Special facilities:** Computer-assisted instruction facilities.

DEGREES OFFERED. BA, BS. 180 bachelor's degrees awarded in 1992. 35% in business and management, 12% education, 5% letters/literature, 5% life sciences, 28% social sciences.

UNDERGRADUATE MAJORS. Accounting, art education, biology, business administration and management, chemistry, computer and information sciences, criminal justice studies, criminology, early childhood education, economics, elementary education, engineering physics, English, English education, environmental science, finance, journalism, law enforcement and corrections, mathematics, mathematics education, music education, parks and recreation management, physics, political science and government, public administration, radio/television broadcasting, religion, science education, secretarial and related programs, social sciences, social studies education, social work, special education.

ACADEMIC PROGRAMS. Accelerated program, double major, dual enrollment of high school students, external degree, honors program, internships, teacher preparation, weekend college; liberal arts/career combination in engineering. **Remedial services:** Learning center, preadmission summer program, reduced course load, remedial instruction, special counselor, tutoring, language and mathematics laboratory. **ROTC:** Air Force, Army. **Placement/credit:** AP, CLEP General and Subject, institutional tests; 24 credit hours maximum for bachelor's degree.

ACADEMIC REQUIREMENTS. Freshmen must earn minimum GPA of 2.0 to continue in good standing. 60% of freshmen return for sophomore year. Students must declare major by end of second year. **Graduation requirements:** 125 hours for bachelor's (24 in major). Most students required to take courses in arts/fine arts, computer science, English, foreign languages, history, humanities, mathematics, philosophy/religion, biological/physical sciences, social sciences.

FRESHMAN ADMISSIONS. Selection criteria: Open admissions. **High school preparation:** 20 units recommended. Recommended units include English 4, mathematics 3, social science 3 and science 2. One unit physical education or ROTC also recommended. **Test requirements:** SAT or ACT for counseling; score report by August 1.

1992 FRESHMAN CLASS PROFILE. 425 men applied, 280 accepted, 97 enrolled; 733 women applied, 518 accepted, 154 enrolled. **Characteristics:** 86% from in state, 100% have minority backgrounds, 1% are foreign students. Average age is 18.

FALL-TERM APPLICATIONS. $25 fee, may be waived for applicants with need. No closing date; applicants notified on a rolling basis; must reply within 4 weeks. Deferred and early admission available.

STUDENT LIFE. Housing: Dormitories (men, women). **Activities:** Student government, radio, student newspaper, yearbook, choral groups, concert band, dance, drama, jazz band, fraternities, sororities, Gordon-Jenkins Theological Association.

ATHLETICS. NAIA. **Intercollegiate:** Baseball M, basketball, cross-country M, softball M, track and field. **Intramural:** Baseball M, basketball, softball W, volleyball W.

STUDENT SERVICES. Aptitude testing, career counseling, employment service for undergraduates, freshman orientation, health services, personal counseling, placement service for graduates, special adviser for adult students, veterans counselor.

ANNUAL EXPENSES. Tuition and fees: $5,534. **Room and board:** $2,892. **Books and supplies:** $700. **Other expenses:** $1,070.

FINANCIAL AID. 80% of freshmen, 87% of continuing students receive some form of aid. All grants, 96% of loans, 92% of jobs based on need. Academic, athletic scholarships available. **Aid applications:** No closing date; priority given to applications received by April 15; applicants notified on a rolling basis beginning on or about January 1; must reply within 10 days.

ADDRESS/TELEPHONE. LeRoy R. Brown, Director of Admissions and Records, Benedict College, Harden and Blanding Streets, Columbia, SC 29204. (803) 253-5143. (800) 868-6598. Fax: (803) 253-5085.

Central Carolina Technical College
Sumter, South Carolina — CB code: 5665

2-year public technical college, coed. Founded in 1963. **Accreditation:** Regional. **Undergraduate enrollment:** 358 men, 557 women full time; 570 men, 922 women part time. **Faculty:** 66 total, 1 with doctorate or other terminal degree. **Location:** Suburban campus in large town; 45 miles from Columbia. **Calendar:** Semester, limited summer session. Saturday and extensive evening/early morning classes. **Microcomputers:** 75 located in classrooms, computer centers.

DEGREES OFFERED. AA, AS. 144 associate degrees awarded in 1992.

UNDERGRADUATE MAJORS. Accounting, agricultural sciences, automotive technology, business and management, business and office, civil technology, criminal justice technology, data processing, drafting and design technology, electronic technology, fashion merchandising, industrial equipment maintenance and repair, legal assistant/paralegal, marketing and distribution, nursing, precision metal work, secretarial and related programs.

ACADEMIC PROGRAMS. 2-year transfer program, cooperative education, independent study, internships. **Remedial services:** Learning center, reduced course load, remedial instruction, special counselor, tutoring. **Placement/credit:** AP, CLEP General and Subject, institutional tests; 15 credit hours maximum for associate degree.

ACADEMIC REQUIREMENTS. Freshmen must earn minimum GPA of 2.0 to continue in good standing. 60% of freshmen return for sophomore year. Students must declare major on enrollment. **Graduation requirements:** 69 hours for associate (27 in major). Most students required to take courses in English, mathematics, social sciences.

FRESHMAN ADMISSIONS. Selection criteria: Open admissions. Selective admissions to nursing program. Minimum SAT-verbal score of 400 and SAT-mathematical score of 400 required of nursing applicants. High school diploma and transcript required for nursing, associate in arts, and associate in science. **Test requirements:** SAT or ACT for placement and counseling only; score report by August 31.

1992 FRESHMAN CLASS PROFILE. 535 men and women enrolled. **Characteristics:** 99% from in state, 100% commute, 38% have minority backgrounds. Average age is 23.

FALL-TERM APPLICATIONS. $20 fee, may be waived for applicants with need. No closing date; applicants notified on a rolling basis. Interview required for nursing applicants. Deferred and early admission available.

STUDENT LIFE. Activities: Student government.

ATHLETICS. Intramural: Basketball, softball.

STUDENT SERVICES. Aptitude testing, career counseling, employment service for undergraduates, freshman orientation, personal counseling, placement service for graduates, veterans counselor, services/facilities for handicapped.

ANNUAL EXPENSES. Tuition and fees: $726, $194 additional for out-of-district students, $554 additional for out-of-state students. **Books and supplies:** $750. **Other expenses:** $1,000.

FINANCIAL AID. 50% of freshmen, 50% of continuing students receive some form of aid. 98% of grants, 91% of loans, 89% of jobs based on need. **Aid applications:** No closing date; priority given to applications received by August 1; applicants notified on a rolling basis; must reply within 2 weeks.

ADDRESS/TELEPHONE. Jack H. Wise, Director of Admissions/Registrar, Central Carolina Technical College, 506 Guignard Drive, Sumter, SC 29150. (803) 778-6605. (800) 221-8711 ext. 205. Fax: (803) 773-4859.

Central Wesleyan College
Central, South Carolina CB code: 5896

Admissions: 86% of applicants accepted
Based on:
- ••• School record
- •• Religious affiliation/commitment, test scores
- • Activities, interview, recommendations, special talents

Completion: 90% of freshmen end year in good standing
44% graduate, 34% of these enter graduate study

4-year private liberal arts college, coed, affiliated with Wesleyan Church. Founded in 1906. **Accreditation:** Regional. **Undergraduate enrollment:** 445 men, 598 women full time; 8 men, 23 women part time. **Graduate enrollment:** 44 men, 36 women full time. **Faculty:** 148 total (43 full time), 52 with doctorates or other terminal degrees. **Location:** Rural campus in rural community; 25 miles from Greenville. **Calendar:** Semester, limited summer session. Saturday and extensive evening/early morning classes. **Microcomputers:** 35 located in libraries, computer centers. **Additional facts:** Christian world view emphasized.

DEGREES OFFERED. AS, BA, BS, MA. 17 associate degrees awarded in 1992. 100% in business and management. 187 bachelor's degrees awarded. 64% in business and management, 13% teacher education, 5% philosophy, religion, theology, 9% psychology. Graduate degrees offered in 1 major field of study.

UNDERGRADUATE MAJORS. Associate: Business and management. **Bachelor's:** Accounting, biology, business administration and management, chemistry, elementary education, English, history, mathematics, medical laboratory technologies, music, personnel management, physical education, psychology, religion, social sciences, special education.

ACADEMIC PROGRAMS. 2-year transfer program, double major, dual enrollment of high school students, external degree, honors program, independent study, internships, teacher preparation, Washington semester, cross-registration, criminal justice program with 2-year schools in area; medical technology with city hospital. **Remedial services:** Learning center, reduced course load, remedial instruction, special counselor, tutoring. **ROTC:** Army. **Placement/credit:** AP, CLEP Subject, institutional tests; 21 credit hours maximum for bachelor's degree.

ACADEMIC REQUIREMENTS. Freshmen must earn minimum GPA of 1.6 to continue in good standing. 64% of freshmen return for sophomore year. Students must declare major by end of second year. **Graduation requirements:** 64 hours for associate (25 in major), 128 hours for bachelor's (32 in major). Most students required to take courses in arts/fine arts, computer science, English, history, humanities, mathematics, philosophy/religion, biological/physical sciences, social sciences. **Postgraduate studies:** 60% from 2-year programs enter 4-year programs. 2% enter law school, 2% enter medical school, 10% enter MBA programs, 20% enter other graduate study. **Additional information:** Master of arts in management of organizations and Christian ministries, bachelor of business administration, bachelor of accounting (5 year program) offered.

FRESHMAN ADMISSIONS. Selection criteria: GPA, class rank, and test scores. Recommendations also considered. Students admitted on conditional basis if combined SAT score is less than 740, or high school GPA is less than 2.0, and rank in bottom half of class. Students admitted conditionally take a limited number of course hours and are on academic warning. **High school preparation:** 20 units required. Required units include English 4, mathematics 2, social science 2 and science 2. **Test requirements:** SAT or ACT (SAT preferred); score report by December 14. Freshmen may be admitted provisionally and submit SAT scores by end of first semester.

1992 FRESHMAN CLASS PROFILE. 56 men applied, 47 accepted, 31 enrolled; 84 women applied, 74 accepted, 48 enrolled. 23% had high school GPA of 3.0 or higher, 57% between 2.0 and 2.99. 10% were in top tenth and 28% were in top quarter of graduating class. **Academic background:** Mid 50% of enrolled freshmen had SAT-V between 320-470, SAT-M between 370-490; ACT composite between 18-23. 92% submitted SAT scores, 8% submitted ACT scores. **Characteristics:** 58% from in state, 89% live in college housing, 13% have minority backgrounds. Average age is 19.

FALL-TERM APPLICATIONS. $15 fee, may be waived for applicants with need. Closing date July 31; applicants notified on a rolling basis beginning on or about October 1. Audition required for music applicants. Interview recommended for applicants with special physical, emotional problems. Deferred admission available.

STUDENT LIFE. Housing: Dormitories (men, women). **Activities:** Student government, magazine, student newspaper, yearbook, choral groups, drama, music ensembles, pep band, Christian service organization. **Additional information:** Students must agree to abide by social rules of college. Religious observance required.

ATHLETICS. NAIA. **Intercollegiate:** Baseball M, basketball, golf M, soccer M, softball W, volleyball W. **Intramural:** Basketball, skiing, soccer, softball, table tennis, tennis, volleyball.

STUDENT SERVICES. Career counseling, employment service for undergraduates, freshman orientation, health services, personal counseling, placement service for graduates, veterans counselor, services/facilities for handicapped.

ANNUAL EXPENSES. Tuition and fees: $8,100. **Room and board:** $3,080. **Books and supplies:** $800. **Other expenses:** $500.

FINANCIAL AID. 97% of freshmen, 92% of continuing students receive some form of aid. 51% of grants, 73% of loans, 77% of jobs based on need. 75 enrolled freshmen were judged to have need, all were offered aid. Academic, music/drama, athletic, leadership, alumni affiliation, religious affiliation scholarships available. **Aid applications:** No closing date; priority given to applications received by April 15; applicants notified on a rolling basis beginning on or about March 15; must reply within 10 days.

ADDRESS/TELEPHONE. Tim Wilkerson, Dean of Enrollment Management, Central Wesleyan College, PO Box 1020, Central, SC 29630-1020. (803) 639-2453. (800) 289-1292. Fax: (803) 639-0826.

Charleston Southern University
Charleston, South Carolina CB code: 5079

4-year private liberal arts college, coed, affiliated with Southern Baptist Convention. Founded in 1964. **Accreditation:** Regional. **Undergraduate enrollment:** 678 men, 792 women full time; 335 men, 419 women part time. **Graduate enrollment:** 15 men, 5 women full time; 73 men, 174 women part time. **Faculty:** 124 total (74 full time), 54 with doctorates or other terminal degrees. **Location:** Suburban campus in small city; 15 miles from downtown. **Calendar:** 4-1-4, extensive summer session. Extensive evening/early morning classes. **Microcomputers:** 150 located in libraries, classrooms, computer centers. **Special facilities:** South Carolina Earthquake Education Research Center.

DEGREES OFFERED. AA, AS, BA, BS, MBA, MEd. 5 associate degrees awarded in 1992. 269 bachelor's degrees awarded. 35% in business and management, 10% business/office and marketing/distribution, 12% education, 6% parks/recreation, protective services, public affairs, 6% philosophy, religion, theology, 6% psychology, 14% social sciences. Graduate degrees offered in 7 major fields of study.

UNDERGRADUATE MAJORS. Associate: Business and office, computer programming, liberal/general studies. **Bachelor's:** Accounting, applied mathematics, biological and physical sciences, biology, business administration and management, business and management, business and office, business economics, chemistry, computer and information sciences, criminal justice studies, dramatic arts, early childhood education, education, elementary education, English, history, humanities, humanities and social sciences, information sciences and systems, management information systems, marketing and distribution, marketing management, mathematics, mathematics education, music education, music performance, music therapy, physical education, physics, political science and government, predentistry, preengineering, prelaw, premedicine, prepharmacy, psychology, religion, religious music, science education, secondary education, sociology, Spanish, speech.

ACADEMIC PROGRAMS. 2-year transfer program, accelerated program, double major, honors program, internships, teacher preparation, cross-registration; liberal arts/career combination in engineering, health sciences. **Remedial services:** Remedial instruction, tutoring. **ROTC:** Air Force. **Placement/credit:** AP, CLEP General and Subject, institutional tests; 30 credit hours maximum for bachelor's degree.

ACADEMIC REQUIREMENTS. Freshmen must earn minimum GPA of 1.4 to continue in good standing. 70% of freshmen return for sophomore year. Students must declare major by end of second year. **Graduation requirements:** 64 hours for associate (36 in major), 125 hours for bachelor's (36 in major). Most students required to take courses in arts/fine arts, computer science, English, foreign languages, history, mathematics, philosophy/religion, biological/physical sciences, social sciences.

FRESHMAN ADMISSIONS. Selection criteria: School achievement record, test scores, GPA, class rank most important. Interview, recommendations, and minority status considered. **High school preparation:** 16 units required. **Test requirements:** SAT or ACT (SAT preferred). **Additional information:** Applicants without required number of high school credits or with low test scores will be referred to College Foundation Studies Program.

1992 FRESHMAN CLASS PROFILE. 318 men, 283 women enrolled. **Characteristics:** 90% from in state, 60% live in college housing, 27% have minority backgrounds, 1% are foreign students. Average age is 19.

FALL-TERM APPLICATIONS. $25 fee, may be waived for applicants with need. No closing date; applicants notified on a rolling basis; must reply within 2 weeks. Interview recommended. Audition recommended for music applicants. Essay recommended. Deferred and early admission available.

STUDENT LIFE. Housing: Dormitories (men, women); apartment housing available. **Activities:** Student government, magazine, student newspaper, yearbook, choral groups, concert band, drama, jazz band, marching band, music ensembles, pep band, College Republicans, Young Democrats, Afro-American Society, International Club, Baptist Student Union, Fellowship of Christian Athletes, Campus Crusade, numerous service clubs.

ATHLETICS. NCAA. **Intercollegiate:** Baseball M, basketball, cross-country, football M, golf, soccer, softball W, tennis, track and field, volleyball W. **Intramural:** Basketball, softball, volleyball.

STUDENT SERVICES. Aptitude testing, career counseling, employment service for undergraduates, freshman orientation, health services, personal counseling, placement service for graduates, special adviser for adult students, veterans counselor, services/facilities for handicapped.

ANNUAL EXPENSES. Tuition and fees: $7,292. **Room and board:** $2,990. **Books and supplies:** $750. **Other expenses:** $1,125.

FINANCIAL AID. 90% of freshmen, 98% of continuing students receive some form of aid. 64% of grants, 77% of loans, 79% of jobs based on need. Academic, art, athletic, leadership, religious affiliation scholarships available. **Aid applications:** No closing date; priority given to applications received by March 1; applicants notified on a rolling basis beginning on or about April 1; must reply within 2 weeks.

ADDRESS/TELEPHONE. Melinda Mitchum, Director of Recruitment, Charleston Southern University, PO Box 10087, 9200 University Boulevard, Charleston, SC 29411. (803) 863-7050. (800) 947-7474. Fax: (803) 863-7070.

Chesterfield-Marlboro Technical College
Cheraw, South Carolina — CB code: 5095

2-year public technical college, coed. Founded in 1969. **Accreditation:** Regional. **Undergraduate enrollment:** 128 men, 150 women full time; 236 men, 446 women part time. **Faculty:** 68 total (28 full time), 2 with doctorates or other terminal degrees. **Location:** Rural campus in small town; 89 miles from Columbia. **Calendar:** Semester, extensive summer session. **Microcomputers:** 125 located in libraries, classrooms, computer centers. **Additional facts:** Commuter college with high percentage of nontraditional students.

DEGREES OFFERED. AA, AS. 86 associate degrees awarded in 1992. 44% in business and management, 10% business/office and marketing/distribution, 11% computer sciences, 16% engineering technologies, 29% multi/interdisciplinary studies.

UNDERGRADUATE MAJORS. Accounting, air conditioning/heating/refrigeration mechanics, air conditioning/heating/refrigeration technology, automotive technology, business and management, business and office, business data processing and related programs, business data programming, data processing, drafting, electronic technology, industrial equipment maintenance and repair, liberal/general studies, mechanical design technology, medical laboratory technologies, nursing, precision metal work, secretarial and related programs.

ACADEMIC PROGRAMS. 2-year transfer program, independent study, cross-registration. **Remedial services:** Remedial instruction, tutoring. **Placement/credit:** AP, CLEP Subject, institutional tests. Credit by examination limited to 50% of quarter hours required for degree.

ACADEMIC REQUIREMENTS. Freshmen must earn minimum GPA of 2.0 to continue in good standing. 65% of freshmen return for sophomore year. Students must declare major on application. **Graduation requirements:** 99 hours for associate (52 in major). Most students required to take courses in English, mathematics.

FRESHMAN ADMISSIONS. Selection criteria: Open admissions. Selective admissions to some programs. SAT combined score of 800 required for nursing applicants. Algebra I and II, chemistry with laboratory required for nursing applicants. **Additional information:** ACT/ASSET and English language proficiency required for placement.

1992 FRESHMAN CLASS PROFILE. 96 men, 127 women enrolled. **Characteristics:** 99% from in state, 100% commute, 31% have minority backgrounds. Average age is 18.

FALL-TERM APPLICATIONS. $15 fee. No closing date; applicants notified on a rolling basis. Interview recommended. Deferred and early admission available.

STUDENT LIFE. Activities: Student government, service-leadership organization.

STUDENT SERVICES. Career counseling, employment service for undergraduates, personal counseling, placement service for graduates, veterans counselor.

ANNUAL EXPENSES. Tuition and fees (1992-93): $675, $50 additional for out-of-district students, $330 additional for out-of-state students. **Books and supplies:** $600. **Other expenses:** $1,884.

FINANCIAL AID. 53% of freshmen, 40% of continuing students receive some form of aid. 99% of grants, 98% of jobs based on need. **Aid applications:** No closing date; applicants notified on a rolling basis; must reply within 8 weeks.

ADDRESS/TELEPHONE. Mary K. Newton, Assistant Dean of Students, Chesterfield-Marlboro Technical College, PO Drawer 1007, Cheraw, SC 29520. (803) 537-5286.

The Citadel
Charleston, South Carolina — CB code: 5108

Admissions:	85% of applicants accepted
Based on:	••• School record, test scores
	•• Activities, recommendations
	• Interview, special talents
Completion:	91% of freshmen end year in good standing
	69% graduate, 11% of these enter graduate study

4-year public liberal arts, military college, men only. Founded in 1842. **Accreditation:** Regional. **Undergraduate enrollment:** 2,035 men, 3 women full time; 110 men, 37 women part time. **Graduate enrollment:** 51 men, 89 women full time; 307 men, 2,039 women part time. **Faculty:** 195 total (164 full time), 178 with doctorates or other terminal degrees. **Location:** Urban campus in small city. **Calendar:** Semester, extensive summer session. **Microcomputers:** 175 located in libraries, classrooms, computer centers. **Special facilities:** Museum of The Citadel. **Additional facts:** Graduate program and evening college open to women.

DEGREES OFFERED. BA, BS, MA, MBA, MEd. 447 bachelor's degrees awarded in 1992. 43% in business and management, 6% education, 10% engineering, 6% letters/literature, 5% life sciences, 23% social sciences. Graduate degrees offered in 20 major fields of study.

UNDERGRADUATE MAJORS. Biology, business and management, chemistry, civil engineering, computer and information sciences, education, electrical/electronics/communications engineering, English, foreign languages (multiple emphasis), French, German, history, mathematics, physical education, physics, political science and government, psychology, Spanish.

ACADEMIC PROGRAMS. Double major, education specialist degree, honors program, teacher preparation, cross-registration. **Remedial services:** Special counselor, tutoring, writing laboratory, mathematics laboratory. **ROTC:** Air Force, Army, Naval. **Placement/credit:** AP, CLEP Subject, institutional tests.

ACADEMIC REQUIREMENTS. Freshmen must earn minimum GPA of 1.1 to continue in good standing. Graduated GPA. Students must also successfully complete 24 semester hours per year. 84% of freshmen return for sophomore year. Students must declare major on enrollment. **Graduation requirements:** 124 hours for bachelor's (45 in major). Most students required to take courses in English, foreign languages, history, mathematics, biological/physical sciences, social sciences. **Postgraduate studies:** 2% enter law school, 3% enter medical school, 3% enter MBA programs, 3% enter other graduate study. **Additional information:** 4 years of ROTC required.

FRESHMAN ADMISSIONS. Selection criteria: Admissions based on class rank, SAT scores, GPA, alumni recommendations, extracurricular activities. **High school preparation:** 15 units required. Required units include English 4, foreign language 2, mathematics 3, social science 2 and science 2. One unit of physical education or ROTC also required; 1 unit advanced mathematics or computer science or 1 unit world history, world geography, or western civilization. **Test requirements:** SAT or ACT (SAT preferred); score report by June 1.

1992 FRESHMAN CLASS PROFILE. 1,493 men applied, 1,276 accepted, 629 enrolled. **Academic background:** Mid 50% of enrolled freshmen had SAT-V between 490-560, SAT-M between 530-600. 90% submitted SAT scores. **Characteristics:** 50% from in state, 100% live in college housing, 7% have minority backgrounds, 1% are foreign students. Average age is 18.

FALL-TERM APPLICATIONS. $25 fee. Closing date June 1; priority given to applications received by March 1; applicants notified on a rolling basis; must reply within 4 weeks. Interview recommended. Deferred admission available. Mathematics ACH (level II) recommended for engineering and science majors; used for placement when available.

STUDENT LIFE. Housing: Dormitories (men). **Activities:** Student government, magazine, student newspaper, yearbook, choral groups, drama, jazz band, marching band, music ensembles, pep band, drill teams.

ATHLETICS. NCAA. **Intercollegiate:** Baseball, basketball, cross-country, fencing, football, golf, lacrosse, rifle, rowing (crew), rugby, sailing, soccer, tennis, track and field, wrestling. **Intramural:** Badminton, basketball, bowling, boxing, field hockey, football, gymnastics, handball, racquetball, skin diving, soccer, softball, swimming, table tennis, tennis, volleyball, water polo, wrestling.

STUDENT SERVICES. Aptitude testing, career counseling, employment service for undergraduates, freshman orientation, health services, personal counseling, placement service for graduates, veterans counselor, limited testing and counseling for learning disabled students, services/facilities for handicapped.

ANNUAL EXPENSES. Tuition and fees (1992-93): $2,949, $3,710 additional for out-of-state students. Fees for uniforms and other special costs additional. **Room and board:** $2,369. **Books and supplies:** $630. **Other expenses:** $850.

FINANCIAL AID. 60% of freshmen, 50% of continuing students receive some form of aid. Grants, loans, jobs available. Academic, athletic, state/district residency, leadership, religious affiliation scholarships available. **Aid applications:** No closing date; priority given to applications received by March 15; applicants notified on a rolling basis beginning on or about May

1; must reply within 2 weeks. **Additional information:** Scholarship application closing date January 15.

ADDRESS/TELEPHONE. Maj. Wallace West, Director of Admissions, The Citadel, Citadel Station, Charleston, SC 29409. (803) 792-5230. Fax: (803) 792-5230.

Claflin College
Orangeburg, South Carolina — CB code: 5109

Admissions: 73% of applicants accepted
Based on:
- ••• School record, test scores
- •• Recommendations
- • Activities, essay, interview, special talents

Completion: 90% of freshmen end year in good standing

4-year private liberal arts college, coed, affiliated with United Methodist Church. Founded in 1869. **Accreditation:** Regional. **Undergraduate enrollment:** 360 men, 547 women full time; 9 men, 24 women part time. **Faculty:** 59 total (54 full time), 36 with doctorates or other terminal degrees. **Location:** Urban campus in large town; 40 miles from Columbia. **Calendar:** Semester, limited summer session. **Microcomputers:** Located in libraries, computer centers.

DEGREES OFFERED. BA, BS. 120 bachelor's degrees awarded in 1992. 14% in business and management, 18% education, 16% life sciences, 52% social sciences.

UNDERGRADUATE MAJORS. Art education, biology, business administration and management, business and computer science, chemistry, computer and information sciences, education, elementary education, engineering and engineering-related technologies, English, English education, fine arts, history, mathematics, mathematics and computer science, mathematics education, music, office supervision and management, physical education, secondary education, social sciences, sociology, theological studies.

ACADEMIC PROGRAMS. Double major, honors program, internships, cross-registration. **Remedial services:** Learning center, reduced course load, remedial instruction, special counselor, tutoring. **ROTC:** Air Force, Army. **Placement/credit:** AP; 18 credit hours maximum for bachelor's degree.

ACADEMIC REQUIREMENTS. Freshmen must earn minimum GPA of 1.65 to continue in good standing. 70% of freshmen return for sophomore year. Students must declare major on application. **Graduation requirements:** 124 hours for bachelor's (38 in major). Most students required to take courses in computer science, English, foreign languages, humanities, mathematics, biological/physical sciences.

FRESHMAN ADMISSIONS. Selection criteria: School achievement record, SAT, recommendation of high school officials, personal background, experience, apparent character traits, educational objectives, and health record considered. **High school preparation:** 16 units required; 18 recommended. Recommended units include biological science 1, English 4, foreign language 2, mathematics 2, physical science 1 and social science 1. **Test requirements:** SAT or ACT (SAT preferred); score report by September 1.

1992 FRESHMAN CLASS PROFILE. 308 men applied, 226 accepted, 173 enrolled; 462 women applied, 338 accepted, 236 enrolled. **Academic background:** Mid 50% of enrolled freshmen had SAT-V between 300-400, SAT-M between 300-400. 100% submitted SAT scores. **Characteristics:** 90% from in state, 75% live in college housing, 99% have minority backgrounds. Average age is 18.

FALL-TERM APPLICATIONS. $10 fee, may be waived for applicants with need. No closing date; priority given to applications received by July 30; applicants notified on a rolling basis; must reply within 6 weeks.

STUDENT LIFE. Housing: Dormitories (men, women). **Activities:** Student government, student newspaper, yearbook, choral groups, concert band, drama, marching band, music ensembles, pep band, fraternities, sororities.

ATHLETICS. NAIA. **Intercollegiate:** Basketball, softball W, track and field M, volleyball W. **Intramural:** Badminton, baseball M, basketball, softball, volleyball.

STUDENT SERVICES. Career counseling, employment service for undergraduates, health services, personal counseling, placement service for graduates, veterans counselor, services/facilities for handicapped.

ANNUAL EXPENSES. Tuition and fees (projected): $4,412. **Room and board:** $2,400. **Books and supplies:** $550. **Other expenses:** $1,125.

FINANCIAL AID. 93% of freshmen, 94% of continuing students receive some form of aid. All aid based on need. 385 enrolled freshmen were judged to have need, all were offered aid. **Aid applications:** Closing date June 1; applicants notified on a rolling basis beginning on or about June 1; must reply within 2 weeks.

ADDRESS/TELEPHONE. George F. Lee, Director of Admissions and Records, Claflin College, 700 College Avenue, NE, Orangeburg, SC 29115. (803) 534-2710. Fax: (803) 531-2860.

Clemson University
Clemson, South Carolina — CB code: 5111

Admissions: 67% of applicants accepted
Based on:
- ••• School record, test scores
- •• Special talents
- • Essay, recommendations

Completion: 93% of freshmen end year in good standing
65% graduate, 22% of these enter graduate study

4-year public university, coed. Founded in 1889. **Accreditation:** Regional. **Undergraduate enrollment:** 7,021 men, 5,467 women full time; 488 men, 329 women part time. **Graduate enrollment:** 1,485 men, 643 women full time; 829 men, 1,404 women part time. **Faculty:** 1,266 total (1,131 full time), 929 with doctorates or other terminal degrees. **Location:** Suburban campus in small town; 32 miles from Greenville, 125 miles from Atlanta, Georgia. **Calendar:** Semester, extensive summer session. **Microcomputers:** 1,000 located in libraries, classrooms, computer centers. **Special facilities:** Planetarium, agricultural and forestry experimental facilities.

DEGREES OFFERED. BA, BS, BFA, MA, MS, MBA, MFA, MEd, PhD, EdD. 2,602 bachelor's degrees awarded in 1992. 5% in architecture and environmental design, 31% business and management, 11% teacher education, 20% engineering, 5% life sciences, 7% social sciences. Graduate degrees offered in 63 major fields of study.

UNDERGRADUATE MAJORS. Accounting, agribusiness, agricultural economics, agricultural education, agricultural engineering, agricultural mechanics, agronomy, animal sciences, architecture, biochemistry, biology, business administration and management, ceramic engineering, chemical engineering, chemistry, civil engineering, clothing and textiles management/production/services, computer and information sciences, computer engineering, construction science and management, dairy, early childhood education, economics, electrical/electronics/communications engineering, elementary education, engineering analysis, English, entomology, finance, fine arts, fishing and fisheries, food sciences, forest products processing technology, forestry and related sciences, French, geology, German, graphic arts technology, health sciences, history, horticultural science, horticulture, industrial engineering, information sciences and systems, landscape architecture, language and international trade, marketing management, mathematics, mechanical engineering, medical laboratory technologies, microbiology, nursing, packaging science, parks and recreation management, philosophy, physics, plant pathology, plant sciences, political science and government, poultry, predentistry, prelaw, premedicine, prepharmacy, preveterinary, psychology, secondary education, sociology, Spanish, special education, textile technology, trade and industrial education, trade and industrial supervision and management.

ACADEMIC PROGRAMS. Cooperative education, double major, dual enrollment of high school students, education specialist degree, honors program, study abroad, teacher preparation, visiting/exchange student program. **Remedial services:** Learning center, preadmission summer program, tutoring. **ROTC:** Air Force, Army. **Placement/credit:** AP, CLEP Subject, institutional tests.

ACADEMIC REQUIREMENTS. Freshmen must earn minimum GPA of 1.60 to continue in good standing. 87% of freshmen return for sophomore year. Students must declare major on application. **Graduation requirements:** 130 hours for bachelor's (25 in major). Most students required to take courses in English, humanities, mathematics, biological/physical sciences, social sciences.

FRESHMAN ADMISSIONS. Selection criteria: Primarily class rank, test scores and choice of major. Counselor's recommendation important in marginal cases. Some preference given to children of alumni and state residents. **High school preparation:** 14 units required. Required units include biological science 1, English 4, foreign language 2, mathematics 3, physical science 1 and social science 3. **Test requirements:** SAT or ACT (SAT preferred); score report by March 1. Mathematics Level II ACH required of applicants whose major includes mathematical analysis, finite probability, or calculus in first semester of freshman year. Applicants from schools which do not compute class rank encouraged to submit 3 ACH scores. Score report by June 1.

1992 FRESHMAN CLASS PROFILE. 4,260 men applied, 2,807 accepted, 1,297 enrolled; 3,783 women applied, 2,591 accepted, 1,172 enrolled. 36% were in top tenth and 68% were in top quarter of graduating class. **Academic background:** Mid 50% of enrolled freshmen had SAT-V between 430-520, SAT-M between 500-620. 99% submitted SAT scores. **Characteristics:** 68% from in state, 90% live in college housing, 10% have minority backgrounds, 1% are foreign students, 25% join fraternities/sororities. Average age is 18.

FALL-TERM APPLICATIONS. $35 fee, may be waived for applicants with need. No closing date; applicants notified on a rolling basis beginning on or about October 15; depending on date of application, notification dates are March 1, Aprill, and May 1. Candidates with March or April Dates may request an extension to May 1. Interview recommended for architecture applicants. Portfolio recommended for architecture applicants. Essay recommended. CRDA. Early admission available.

STUDENT LIFE. Housing: Dormitories (men, women, coed); apart-

ment, fraternity, sorority, handicapped housing available. Housing guaranteed to entering freshmen and students consistently continuing in on-campus housing. **Activities:** Student government, magazine, radio, student newspaper, yearbook, choral groups, concert band, dance, drama, jazz band, marching band, music ensembles, pep band, fraternities, sororities, religious organizations, Young Democrats, Young Republicans, minority awareness organizations, Blue Key, Alpha Phi Omega, Mortarboard, Omicron Delta Kappa.

ATHLETICS. NCAA. **Intercollegiate:** Baseball M, basketball, cross-country, diving, football M, golf M, soccer M, swimming, tennis, track and field, volleyball W, wrestling M. **Intramural:** Badminton, basketball, bowling, cross-country, diving, fencing, field hockey W, gymnastics, handball, lacrosse, racquetball, rowing (crew), rugby M, sailing, skiing, soccer, softball, swimming, table tennis, tennis, track and field, volleyball, water polo, wrestling M.

STUDENT SERVICES. Aptitude testing, career counseling, employment service for undergraduates, freshman orientation, health services, personal counseling, placement service for graduates, veterans counselor, services/facilities for handicapped.

ANNUAL EXPENSES. Tuition and fees (projected): $2,930, $4,918 additional for out-of-state students. **Room and board:** $3,610. **Books and supplies:** $766. **Other expenses:** $1,521.

FINANCIAL AID. 59% of freshmen, 55% of continuing students receive some form of aid. 45% of grants, 93% of loans, 13% of jobs based on need. 684 enrolled freshmen were judged to have need, 657 were offered aid. Academic, music/drama, athletic, state/district residency, leadership, minority scholarships available. **Aid applications:** No closing date; priority given to applications received by April 1; applicants notified on or about May 15; must reply within 3 weeks. **Additional information:** Credit on portion of room and board extended by deferred note. Application closing date for scholarships March 1, notification on or about May 20.

ADDRESS/TELEPHONE. Michael R. Heintze, Director of Admissions, Clemson University, 105 Sikes Hall, Box 345124, Clemson, SC 29634-5124. (803) 656-2287. Fax: (803) 656-0622.

Coker College
Hartsville, South Carolina — CB code: 5112

4-year private liberal arts college, coed. Founded in 1908. **Accreditation:** Regional. **Undergraduate enrollment:** 252 men, 397 women full time; 103 men, 93 women part time. **Faculty:** 109 total (58 full time). **Location:** Suburban campus in large town; 70 miles from Columbia, 80 miles from Charlotte, North Carolina. **Calendar:** Semester, limited summer session. Saturday and extensive evening/early morning classes. **Microcomputers:** 40 located in libraries, classrooms, computer centers. **Special facilities:** Botanical gardens, art gallery, state-of-the-art science facility.

DEGREES OFFERED. BA, BS. 136 bachelor's degrees awarded in 1992. 22% in business and management, 7% business/office and marketing/distribution, 24% education, 27% social sciences, 12% visual and performing arts.

UNDERGRADUATE MAJORS. Accounting, art education, biology, business administration and management, business and management, chemistry, clinical laboratory science, communications, counseling psychology, criminal justice studies, criminology, dance, dramatic arts, early childhood education, education, elementary education, English, English education, finance, fine arts, French, graphic design, history, humanities and social sciences, journalism, marketing and distribution, marketing management, mathematics, mathematics education, music, music education, music performance, photography, physical education, political science and government, prelaw, premedicine, prepharmacy, preveterinary, psychology, religion, science education, social sciences, social work, sociology, Spanish, special education, sports medicine.

ACADEMIC PROGRAMS. Cooperative education, double major, dual enrollment of high school students, independent study, internships, student-designed major, study abroad, teacher preparation, visiting/exchange student program. **Remedial services:** Reduced course load, special counselor, tutoring. **Placement/credit:** AP, CLEP General and Subject, institutional tests.

ACADEMIC REQUIREMENTS. Freshmen must earn minimum GPA of 1.5 to continue in good standing. 75% of freshmen return for sophomore year. Students must declare major by end of second year. **Graduation requirements:** 120 hours for bachelor's (30 in major). Most students required to take courses in arts/fine arts, English, history, humanities, mathematics, philosophy/religion, biological/physical sciences, social sciences. **Postgraduate studies:** 1% enter law school, 1% enter medical school, 2% enter MBA programs, 39% enter other graduate study. **Additional information:** Classes limited to 20 students. Most classes taught by round table discussion.

FRESHMAN ADMISSIONS. Selection criteria: Primary emphasis on school academic record and test scores. Recommendations and class rank also used to determine status. Applicants must rank in top half of class and have GPA of 2.0 or better. **High school preparation:** 7 units required. Required units include English 4 and mathematics 3. **Test requirements:** SAT or ACT (SAT preferred); score report by August 15.

1992 FRESHMAN CLASS PROFILE. 131 men, 155 women enrolled. 41% had high school GPA of 3.0 or higher, 53% between 2.0 and 2.99. 24% were in top tenth and 56% were in top quarter of graduating class. **Academic background:** Mid 50% of enrolled freshmen had SAT-V between 380-470, SAT-M between 400-530. 89% submitted SAT scores. **Characteristics:** 90% from in state, 86% live in college housing, 14% have minority backgrounds, 1% are foreign students. Average age is 18.

FALL-TERM APPLICATIONS. $15 fee, may be waived for applicants with need. Closing date August 15; priority given to applications received by March 1; applicants notified on a rolling basis; must reply within 4 weeks unless extension is requested. Audition required for music, dance, drama, art applicants. Essay required. Interview recommended. Portfolio recommended for art applicants. Deferred and early admission available.

STUDENT LIFE. Housing: Dormitories (men, women, coed). **Activities:** Student government, student newspaper, yearbook, choral groups, dance, drama, jazz band, music ensembles, musical theater, Fellowship of Christian Students, Student National Education Association, religious clubs, service club, Amnesty International.

ATHLETICS. NAIA. **Intercollegiate:** Baseball M, basketball, golf M, soccer, softball W, tennis, volleyball W. **Intramural:** Badminton, basketball, football M, golf, handball, racquetball, rowing (crew) W, sailing, swimming, table tennis, tennis, volleyball, water polo.

STUDENT SERVICES. Aptitude testing, career counseling, employment service for undergraduates, freshman orientation, health services, personal counseling, placement service for graduates, special adviser for adult students, services/facilities for handicapped.

ANNUAL EXPENSES. Tuition and fees (projected): $9,510. **Room and board:** $4,280. **Books and supplies:** $750. **Other expenses:** $900.

FINANCIAL AID. 75% of freshmen, 86% of continuing students receive some form of aid. All grants, 86% of loans, all jobs based on need. Academic, music/drama, art, athletic, leadership scholarships available. **Aid applications:** No closing date; applicants notified on a rolling basis beginning on or about May 1; must reply within 2 weeks.

ADDRESS/TELEPHONE. Stephen B. Terry, Vice President of Enrollment Management, Coker College, 300 E. College Ave, Hartsville, SC 29550. (803) 383-8050. (800) 950-1908. Fax: (803) 383-8095.

College of Charleston
Charleston, South Carolina — CB code: 5113

Admissions:	62% of applicants accepted
Based on:	••• School record, test scores
	•• Recommendations
	• Activities, essay, interview, special talents
Completion:	95% of freshmen end year in good standing
	48% graduate, 33% of these enter graduate study

4-year public liberal arts college, coed. Founded in 1770. **Accreditation:** Regional. **Undergraduate enrollment:** 2,466 men, 4,030 women full time; 523 men, 802 women part time. **Faculty:** 538 total (313 full time), 268 with doctorates or other terminal degrees. **Location:** Urban campus in small city; downtown location. **Calendar:** Semester, limited summer session. 3-week May interim session. Saturday and extensive evening/early morning classes. **Microcomputers:** 400 located in dormitories, libraries, classrooms, computer centers, campus-wide network. **Special facilities:** Early childhood development center, broadcast museum, Halsey Art Gallery, observatory, sailing marina, Afro-American Research Center, Bronze Casting Foundary, marine sciences station, honors center.

DEGREES OFFERED. BA, BS. 1,131 bachelor's degrees awarded in 1992. 20% in business and management, 15% teacher education, 6% letters/literature, 10% life sciences, 10% psychology, 22% social sciences, 6% visual and performing arts. Graduate degrees offered in 1 major field of study.

UNDERGRADUATE MAJORS. Accounting, anthropology, art history, biochemistry, biology, business administration and management, chemistry, classics, communications, computer and information sciences, dramatic arts, economics, elementary education, English, French, geology, German, history, information sciences and systems, marine biology, mathematics, music, philosophy, physical education, physics, political science and government, predentistry, premedicine, psychology, sociology, Spanish, special education, studio art, urban studies.

ACADEMIC PROGRAMS. Accelerated program, cooperative education, double major, dual enrollment of high school students, honors program, independent study, internships, semester at sea, study abroad, teacher preparation, visiting/exchange student program, Washington semester, cross-registration; liberal arts/career combination in engineering, health sciences. **Remedial services:** Learning center, preadmission summer program, reduced course load, remedial instruction, special counselor, tutoring, learning strategies course. **ROTC:** Air Force. **Placement/credit:** AP, CLEP Subject, institutional tests; 30 credit hours maximum for bachelor's degree.

ACADEMIC REQUIREMENTS. Freshmen must earn minimum GPA of 1.5 to continue in good standing. 82% of freshmen return for sophomore year. Students must declare major by end of second year. **Graduation requirements:** 122 hours for bachelor's (36 in major). Most students required to take courses in English, foreign languages, history, humanities, mathematics, biological/physical sciences, social sciences. **Postgraduate studies:** 3% enter law school, 3% enter medical school, 3% enter MBA programs, 24% enter other graduate study. **Additional information:** Minimum credit hours required in major varies from 24 to 43, depending on field.

FRESHMAN ADMISSIONS. Selection criteria: School grades, class rank, and curriculum most important, then SAT scores. Recommendations and activities helpful in borderline cases. **High school preparation:** 16 units required. Required units include English 4, foreign language 2, mathematics 3, social science 3 and science 2. Mathematics requirement includes 2 algebra. Science requirement must be laboratory. Social science recommendation .5 economics and .5 government. Two units of same foreign language. One additional unit of advanced mathematics, computer science, world history, world geography, or western civilization required. **Test requirements:** SAT or ACT; score report by June 15.

1992 FRESHMAN CLASS PROFILE. 1,606 men applied, 970 accepted, 396 enrolled; 2,909 women applied, 1,823 accepted, 733 enrolled. 47% had high school GPA of 3.0 or higher, 51% between 2.0 and 2.99. 25% were in top tenth and 60% were in top quarter of graduating class. **Academic background:** Mid 50% of enrolled freshmen had SAT-V between 430-520, SAT-M between 480-570; ACT composite between 20-24. 92% submitted SAT scores, 8% submitted ACT scores. **Characteristics:** 68% from in state, 63% live in college housing, 8% have minority backgrounds, 2% are foreign students, 30% join fraternities/sororities. Average age is 19.

FALL-TERM APPLICATIONS. $25 fee, may be waived for applicants with need. Closing date June 1; priority given to applications received by January 1; applicants notified on a rolling basis; must reply within 4 weeks. Interview recommended. Essay recommended for academically weak; special circumstances applicants. CRDA. Deferred and early admission available. March 1 application date recommended for residence hall students. Admissions deposit refundable until May 1 for fall semester, December 1 for spring semester.

STUDENT LIFE. Housing: Dormitories (men, women, coed); fraternity, sorority housing available. Restored old Charleston houses used as dormitories. Some dormitories with kitchen facilities in suite. International Students House. 45% of undergraduates live on-campus or within walking or biking distance. **Activities:** Student government, magazine, student newspaper, yearbook, literary magazine, choral groups, concert band, dance, drama, jazz band, music ensembles, musical theater, pep band, symphony orchestra, fraternities, sororities, Alpha Phi Omega, International Club, Student Union for Minority Affairs, equestrian club, political organizations, religious organizations council, Peer Mentor Association, college activities board, Environmental Club, Student Sailing Association.

ATHLETICS. NCAA. **Intercollegiate:** Baseball M, basketball, cross-country, diving, golf, horseback riding, sailing, soccer, softball W, swimming, tennis, volleyball W. **Intramural:** Badminton, basketball, diving, golf, racquetball, rowing (crew), rugby M, soccer, softball, squash, swimming, table tennis, tennis, volleyball, water polo.

STUDENT SERVICES. Aptitude testing, career counseling, employment service for undergraduates, freshman orientation, health services, on-campus day care, personal counseling, placement service for graduates, special adviser for adult students, veterans counselor, college skills laboratory, services/facilities for handicapped.

ANNUAL EXPENSES. Tuition and fees: $2,950, $2,950 additional for out-of-state students. **Room and board:** $3,300. **Books and supplies:** $648. **Other expenses:** $2,255.

FINANCIAL AID. 63% of freshmen, 57% of continuing students receive some form of aid. 75% of grants, 96% of loans, 13% of jobs based on need. Academic, music/drama, art, athletic, state/district residency, leadership, alumni affiliation, minority scholarships available. **Aid applications:** No closing date; priority given to applications received by April 15; applicants notified on a rolling basis beginning on or about May 15; must reply within 3 weeks. **Additional information:** Foreign students not eligible for financial aid.

ADDRESS/TELEPHONE. Donald Burkard, Dean of Admissions, College of Charleston, 66 George Street, Charleston, SC 29424. (803) 792-5670. Fax: (803) 792-5505.

Columbia Bible College and Seminary
Columbia, South Carolina — CB code: 5116

Admissions: 87% of applicants accepted
Based on:
- ••• Recommendations, school record
- •• Activities, essay, religious affiliation/commitment, test scores
- • Interview, special talents

Completion: 75% of freshmen end year in good standing; 37% graduate

4-year private Bible college, coed, affiliated with interdenominational/evangelical. Founded in 1923. **Accreditation:** Regional. **Undergraduate enrollment:** 207 men, 162 women full time; 24 men, 32 women part time. **Graduate enrollment:** 9 men, 14 women full time; 3 men, 15 women part time. **Faculty:** 44 total (25 full time), 21 with doctorates or other terminal degrees. **Location:** Suburban campus in small city; 6 miles from city center. **Calendar:** Semester, limited summer session. **Microcomputers:** 36 located in libraries, computer centers.

DEGREES OFFERED. AA, BA, BS, MEd, M.Div. 5 associate degrees awarded in 1992. 100% in philosophy, religion, theology. 123 bachelor's degrees awarded. 100% in philosophy, religion, theology. Graduate degrees offered in 5 major fields of study.

UNDERGRADUATE MAJORS. Associate: Bible studies. **Bachelor's:** Bible studies, biblical languages, elementary education, humanities, missionary studies, religious education, religious music, theological studies.

ACADEMIC PROGRAMS. Double major, independent study, internships, study abroad. **Remedial services:** Reduced course load, tutoring. **Placement/credit:** AP, CLEP General and Subject.

ACADEMIC REQUIREMENTS. Freshmen must earn minimum GPA of 2.0 to continue in good standing. 66% of freshmen return for sophomore year. Students must declare major by end of second year. **Graduation requirements:** 65 hours for associate (23 in major), 128 hours for bachelor's (32 in major). Most students required to take courses in arts/fine arts, English, history, humanities, mathematics, philosophy/religion, biological/physical sciences, social sciences. **Additional information:** All students major in bible; double majors include bible teaching, biblical languages, church ministries, elementary education, humanities, intercultural studies, music, pastoral ministries, and youth ministries. Minors offered in bible teaching and intercultural studies. Two graduate level degrees are offered in education: Master of Arts in teaching and Master of Education.

FRESHMAN ADMISSIONS. Selection criteria: Potential suitability for church-related vocation. School achievement, test scores, class rank and grades, recommendations from pastor, teachers, friends, employers, as well as personal testimony considered. Recommended units include English 4, foreign language 2, mathematics 2, social science 2 and science 1. **Test requirements:** SAT or ACT; score report by August 1.

1992 FRESHMAN CLASS PROFILE. 67 men applied, 54 accepted, 27 enrolled; 61 women applied, 57 accepted, 31 enrolled. 51% had high school GPA of 3.0 or higher, 36% between 2.0 and 2.99. **Academic background:** Mid 50% of enrolled freshmen had SAT-V between 370-500, SAT-M between 400-550; ACT composite between 16-20. 84% submitted SAT scores, 16% submitted ACT scores. **Characteristics:** 45% from in state, 73% live in college housing, 3% have minority backgrounds, 2% are foreign students. Average age is 22.

FALL-TERM APPLICATIONS. $20 fee. No closing date; priority given to applications received by May 1; applicants notified on a rolling basis beginning on or about September 1; must reply within 3 weeks. Audition required for church music applicants. Essay required. Deferred admission available.

STUDENT LIFE. Housing: Dormitories (men, women). **Activities:** Student government, radio, yearbook, choral groups, drama, music ensembles, Student Foreign Missions Fellowship. **Additional information:** Religious observance required.

ATHLETICS. Intramural: Basketball M, soccer M, softball, tennis, volleyball.

STUDENT SERVICES. Career counseling, freshman orientation, health services, on-campus day care, personal counseling, placement service for graduates, special adviser for adult students, veterans counselor.

ANNUAL EXPENSES. Tuition and fees: $6,270. **Room and board:** $3,262. **Books and supplies:** $350. **Other expenses:** $410.

FINANCIAL AID. 65% of continuing students receive some form of aid. 93% of grants, 96% of loans, 32% of jobs based on need. Academic, music/drama, leadership scholarships available. **Aid applications:** No closing date; priority given to applications received by March 10; applicants notified on a rolling basis beginning on or about May 15; must reply within 2 weeks. **Additional information:** Spouse scholarship program and special short quarter scholarships for missionaries on furlough.

ADDRESS/TELEPHONE. Frank J. Bedell, Director of Admissions, Columbia Bible College and Seminary, PO Box 3122, Columbia, SC 29230-3122. (803) 754-4100 ext. 3024. (800) 777-2227. Fax: (803) 786-4209.

Columbia College
Columbia, South Carolina — CB code: 5117

Admissions: 80% of applicants accepted
Based on:
- ••• School record, test scores
- •• Special talents
- • Activities, essay, interview, recommendations

Completion: 90% of freshmen end year in good standing; 54% graduate

4-year private liberal arts college, women only, affiliated with United Methodist Church. Founded in 1854. **Accreditation:** Regional. **Undergraduate enrollment:** 944 women full time; 249 women part time. **Graduate enrollment:** 3 women full time; 32 women part time. **Faculty:** 77 total (68 full time), 49 with doctorates or other terminal degrees. **Location:** Urban campus in large city. **Calendar:** Semester, extensive summer session. Extensive evening/early morning classes. **Microcomputers:** 80 located in libraries, classrooms, computer centers. **Special facilities:** Art galleries, leadership center for women.

DEGREES OFFERED. BA, BFA, MEd. 249 bachelor's degrees awarded in 1992. 18% in business and management, 28% education, 5% letters/literature, 13% parks/recreation, protective services, public affairs, 5% psychology, 5% social sciences, 13% visual and performing arts. Graduate degrees offered in 1 major field of study.

UNDERGRADUATE MAJORS. Accounting, art education, biology, business administration and management, chemistry, communications, creative writing, dance, dramatic arts, early childhood education, education, education of the mentally handicapped, elementary education, English, English education, English literature, fine arts, French, German, health education, history, humanities and social sciences, mathematics, mathematics education, medical laboratory technologies, music, music education, music history and appreciation, music performance, music theory and composition, physical education, physical sciences, prelaw, premedicine, psychology, public affairs, religion, religious education, religious music, science education, secondary education, social science education, social studies education, social work, sociology, Spanish, special education, speech correction, studio art.

ACADEMIC PROGRAMS. Double major, dual enrollment of high school students, honors program, independent study, internships, student-designed major, teacher preparation, visiting/exchange student program. **Remedial services:** Learning center, reduced course load, remedial instruction. **Placement/credit:** AP, CLEP General and Subject, institutional tests.

ACADEMIC REQUIREMENTS. Freshmen must earn minimum GPA of 2.0 to continue in good standing. Freshmen must earn minimum GPA of 2.0 based on a 6.0 scale. 75% of freshmen return for sophomore year. Students must declare major by end of second year. **Graduation requirements:** 127 hours for bachelor's. Most students required to take courses in arts/fine arts, English, foreign languages, history, mathematics, philosophy/religion, biological/physical sciences, social sciences.

FRESHMAN ADMISSIONS. Selection criteria: School record counts 60%, test scores 40%. Recommendations, interview, any other academic indicators considered in borderline cases. **High school preparation:** 16 units recommended. Recommended units include English 4, foreign language 2, mathematics 3, social science 3 and science 2. 2.5 units in aesthetics (music, dance, art) also recommended. **Test requirements:** SAT or ACT; score report by August 1.

1992 FRESHMAN CLASS PROFILE. 711 women applied, 567 accepted, 261 enrolled. 19% were in top tenth and 52% were in top quarter of graduating class. **Academic background:** Mid 50% of enrolled freshmen had SAT-V between 390-480, SAT-M between 400-500. 96% submitted SAT scores. **Characteristics:** 90% from in state, 81% live in college housing, 24% have minority backgrounds. Average age is 18.

FALL-TERM APPLICATIONS. $20 fee, may be waived for applicants with need. Closing date August 10; priority given to applications received by March 15; applicants notified on a rolling basis; must reply by May 1 or within 4 weeks if notified thereafter. Interview recommended. Audition recommended for music, dance applicants. Portfolio recommended for art applicants. Essay recommended for borderline applicants. CRDA. Deferred and early admission available.

STUDENT LIFE. Housing: Dormitories (women). **Activities:** Student government, magazine, student newspaper, yearbook, choral groups, concert band, dance, drama, music ensembles, musical theater, opera, Young Republicans, Young Democrats, Council on Community Action, speakers bureau, religious organizations, student alumnae ambassadors, presidential aides.

ATHLETICS. NAIA. **Intercollegiate:** Tennis, volleyball. **Intramural:** Softball, swimming, tennis, volleyball.

STUDENT SERVICES. Aptitude testing, career counseling, employment service for undergraduates, freshman orientation, health services, personal counseling, placement service for graduates, special adviser for adult students, services/facilities for handicapped.

ANNUAL EXPENSES. Tuition and fees: $9,750. **Room and board:** $3,770. **Books and supplies:** $650. **Other expenses:** $1,500.

FINANCIAL AID. 91% of freshmen, 75% of continuing students receive some form of aid. 67% of grants, 71% of loans, 57% of jobs based on need. 225 enrolled freshmen were judged to have need, all were offered aid. Academic, music/drama, art, athletic, leadership scholarships available. **Aid applications:** No closing date; priority given to applications received by April 1; applicants notified on a rolling basis beginning on or about March 1; must reply by May 1 or within 2 weeks if notified thereafter.

ADDRESS/TELEPHONE. Dr. J Joseph Mitchell, Vice President of Enrollment Management, Columbia College, Columbia College Drive, Columbia, SC 29203-5998. (803) 786-3871. Fax: (803) 786-3674.

Columbia Junior College of Business
Columbia, South Carolina — CB code: 5097

2-year proprietary business, junior college, coed. Founded in 1935. **Undergraduate enrollment:** 400 men and women. **Faculty:** 45 total (10 full time), 17 with doctorates or other terminal degrees. **Location:** Suburban campus in small city. **Calendar:** Quarter, limited summer session. **Microcomputers:** 25 located in classrooms, computer centers.

DEGREES OFFERED. 100 associate degrees awarded in 1992. 42% in business and management, 10% business/office and marketing/distribution, 28% computer sciences, 20% law.

UNDERGRADUATE MAJORS. Accounting, business administration and management, business data processing and related programs, computer and information sciences, data processing, fashion merchandising, legal assistant/paralegal, medical assistant, secretarial and related programs, word processing.

ACADEMIC PROGRAMS. Double major, internships. **Remedial services:** Reduced course load, remedial instruction, special counselor, tutoring.

ACADEMIC REQUIREMENTS. Freshmen must earn minimum GPA of 2.0 to continue in good standing. 65% of freshmen return for sophomore year. Students must declare major on enrollment. **Graduation requirements:** 99 hours for associate. Most students required to take courses in English, history, humanities, mathematics, social sciences.

FRESHMAN ADMISSIONS. Selection criteria: Open admissions. **Test requirements:** SAT or ACT may be submitted in place of required institutional tests for placement. Score report by September 15.

1992 FRESHMAN CLASS PROFILE. 140 men and women enrolled. **Characteristics:** 50% from in state, 65% live in college housing, 98% have minority backgrounds. Average age is 18.

FALL-TERM APPLICATIONS. $10 fee, may be waived for applicants with need. No closing date; priority given to applications received by May 1; applicants notified on a rolling basis. Interview required. CRDA. Deferred and early admission available. EDP-F.

STUDENT LIFE. Housing: Dormitories (men, women); apartment housing available. **Activities:** Student government, student newspaper, choral groups, drama, fraternities, sororities.

STUDENT SERVICES. Career counseling, employment service for undergraduates, freshman orientation, personal counseling, placement service for graduates, veterans counselor, services/facilities for handicapped.

ANNUAL EXPENSES. Tuition and fees (1992-93): $3,045. **Room and board:** $1,350 room only. **Books and supplies:** $375. **Other expenses:** $300.

FINANCIAL AID. 76% of freshmen, 67% of continuing students receive some form of aid. Grants, loans, jobs available. Academic, state/district residency, leadership scholarships available. **Aid applications:** No closing date; priority given to applications received by May 30; applicants notified on a rolling basis beginning on or about May 30; must reply by July 1 or within 2 weeks if notified thereafter.

ADDRESS/TELEPHONE. Virginia Dordal, Corporate Administrative Specialist, Columbia Junior College of Business, 3810 Main Street, Columbia, SC 29203. (803) 799-9082.

Converse College
Spartanburg, South Carolina — CB code: 5121

Admissions: 92% of applicants accepted
Based on: ••• School record, test scores
• Activities, essay, interview, recommendations, special talents
Completion: 95% of freshmen end year in good standing
60% graduate, 10% of these enter graduate study

4-year private college of arts and sciences and music college, women only. Founded in 1889. **Accreditation:** Regional. **Undergraduate enrollment:** 704 women full time; 1 man, 77 women part time. **Graduate enrollment:** 11 men, 74 women full time; 41 men, 212 women part time. **Faculty:** 94 total (86 full time), 67 with doctorates or other terminal degrees. **Location:** Urban campus in small city; 70 miles from Charlotte, North Carolina, 180 miles from Atlanta, Georgia. **Calendar:** 4-2-4. **Microcomputers:** 40 located in dormitories, libraries, classrooms, computer centers. **Special facilities:** Music library containing 15,500 scores and 16,600 recordings. **Additional facts:** Men admitted to graduate programs in education and music.

DEGREES OFFERED. BA, BS, BFA, MEd. 190 bachelor's degrees awarded in 1992. 13% in business and management, 20% teacher education, 6% languages, 9% letters/literature, 8% psychology, 10% social sciences, 17% visual and performing arts. Graduate degrees offered in 13 major fields of study.

UNDERGRADUATE MAJORS. Accounting, art history, biology, business administration and management, chemistry, clinical laboratory science, computer and information sciences, dramatic arts, early childhood education, economics, education of the deaf and hearing impaired, education of the emotionally handicapped, education of the mentally handicapped, elementary education, English, foreign languages (multiple emphasis), French, history, interior design, international business management, marketing and distribution, mathematics, music, music history and appreciation, music performance, music theory and composition, political science and government, predentistry, prelaw, premedicine, prepharmacy, preveterinary, psychology, religion, sociology, Spanish, special education, specific learning disabilities, studio art.

ACADEMIC PROGRAMS. Accelerated program, double major, education specialist degree, honors program, independent study, internships, study abroad, teacher preparation, cross-registration. **Remedial services:** Reduced course load, tutoring, writing center, study center. **ROTC:** Army. **Placement/credit:** AP, CLEP General and Subject, institutional tests; 30 credit hours maximum for bachelor's degree.

ACADEMIC REQUIREMENTS. Freshmen must earn minimum GPA of 1.4 to continue in good standing. 77% of freshmen return for sophomore year. Students must declare major by end of second year. **Graduation requirements:** 120 hours for bachelor's (36 in major). Most students required to take courses in arts/fine arts, computer science, English, foreign languages, history, humanities, mathematics, philosophy/religion, biological/physical sciences, social sciences. **Postgraduate studies:** 2% enter law school, 1% enter medical school, 2% enter MBA programs, 5% enter other graduate study.

FRESHMAN ADMISSIONS. Selection criteria: School record, class rank, test scores, extracurricular activities, and school recommendation considered. **High school preparation:** 16 units required. Required units include English 4, foreign language 2, mathematics 3, social science 1 and science 2. **Test requirements:** SAT or ACT (SAT preferred); score report by August 1.

1992 FRESHMAN CLASS PROFILE. 503 women applied, 465 accepted, 199 enrolled. 65% had high school GPA of 3.0 or higher, 35% between 2.0 and 2.99. **Academic background:** Mid 50% of enrolled freshmen had SAT-V between 450-550, SAT-M between 450-550. 90% submitted SAT scores. **Characteristics:** 60% from in state, 91% live in college housing, 5% have minority backgrounds, 1% are foreign students. Average age is 18.

FALL-TERM APPLICATIONS. $25 fee, may be waived for applicants with need. Closing date April 1; priority given to applications received by February 15; applicants notified on a rolling basis; must reply by May 1. Audition required for music applicants. Interview recommended. CRDA. Deferred and early admission available.

STUDENT LIFE. Housing: Dormitories (women). **Activities:** Student government, magazine, student newspaper, yearbook, choral groups, dance, drama, music ensembles, musical theater, opera, symphony orchestra, show choir, Student Christian Association, student activities committee, Young Democrats, Young Republicans, community service organizations, honor organizations. **Additional information:** Honor tradition built on mutual trust and responsibility is basis of campus life.

ATHLETICS. NAIA. **Intercollegiate:** Basketball, cross-country, horseback riding, soccer, tennis, volleyball. **Intramural:** Basketball, swimming, volleyball.

STUDENT SERVICES. Aptitude testing, career counseling, employment service for undergraduates, freshman orientation, health services, personal counseling, placement service for graduates, special adviser for adult students, services/facilities for handicapped.

ANNUAL EXPENSES. Tuition and fees: $12,050. **Room and board:** $3,700. **Books and supplies:** $500. **Other expenses:** $700.

FINANCIAL AID. 86% of freshmen, 74% of continuing students receive some form of aid. 28% of grants, 88% of loans, all jobs based on need. 116 enrolled freshmen were judged to have need, 109 were offered aid. Academic, music/drama, athletic, leadership scholarships available. **Aid applications:** No closing date; priority given to applications received by March 15; applicants notified on a rolling basis beginning on or about February 1; must reply by May 1 or within 2 weeks if notified thereafter.

ADDRESS/TELEPHONE. Dr. Martha E. Rogers, Dean of Admissions, Converse College, 580 East Main Street, Spartanburg, SC 29302-0006. (803) 596-9040. (800) 766-1125. Fax: (803) 583-2563.

Denmark Technical College
Denmark, South Carolina — CB code: 5744

2-year public technical college, coed. Founded in 1948. **Accreditation:** Regional. **Undergraduate enrollment:** 217 men, 245 women full time; 76 men, 59 women part time. **Faculty:** 49 total (42 full time), 4 with doctorates or other terminal degrees. **Location:** Rural campus in small town; 55 miles from Columbia. **Calendar:** Semester, extensive summer session. **Microcomputers:** 75 located in libraries, classrooms.

DEGREES OFFERED. AA, AS. 75 associate degrees awarded in 1992. 45% in business/office and marketing/distribution, 35% computer sciences, 5% engineering technologies, 15% parks/recreation, protective services, public affairs.

UNDERGRADUATE MAJORS. Automotive technology, business and office, computer programming, criminal justice technology, electronic technology, secretarial and related programs.

ACADEMIC PROGRAMS. 2-year transfer program, cooperative education, independent study, internships, cross-registration. **Remedial services:** Learning center, reduced course load, remedial instruction, special counselor, tutoring. **ROTC:** Army. **Placement/credit:** AP, institutional tests.

ACADEMIC REQUIREMENTS. Freshmen must earn minimum GPA of 1.5 to continue in good standing. 40% of freshmen return for sophomore year. Students must declare major on application. **Graduation requirements:** Most students required to take courses in English, mathematics.

FRESHMAN ADMISSIONS. Selection criteria: Open admissions. Selective admission to some programs. Recommended units include English 4, foreign language 2, mathematics 4, social science 2 and science 2. College preparatory program required for A.A and A.S. transfer college programs.

1992 FRESHMAN CLASS PROFILE. 240 men, 220 women enrolled. **Characteristics:** 98% from in state, 60% live in college housing, 99% have minority backgrounds. Average age is 18.

FALL-TERM APPLICATIONS. $5 fee, may be waived for applicants with need. No closing date; applicants notified on a rolling basis beginning on or about April 1. Interview recommended. Deferred admission available.

STUDENT LIFE. Housing: Dormitories (men, women). **Activities:** Student government, student newspaper, yearbook, choral groups, fraternities, sororities, Student Christian Association.

ATHLETICS. Intercollegiate: Baseball M, basketball, softball W. **Intramural:** Basketball.

STUDENT SERVICES. Career counseling, employment service for undergraduates, freshman orientation, health services, personal counseling, placement service for graduates, veterans counselor, free bus service for students in Allendale, Barnwell, and Bamberg counties, services/facilities for handicapped.

ANNUAL EXPENSES. Tuition and fees: $1,030, $430 additional for out-of-state students. **Room and board:** $3,927. **Books and supplies:** $500. **Other expenses:** $1,600.

FINANCIAL AID. 95% of freshmen, 96% of continuing students receive some form of aid. 99% of grants, 99% of loans, all jobs based on need. Academic scholarships available. **Aid applications:** Closing date August 15; priority given to applications received by May 1; applicants notified on a rolling basis beginning on or about May 15; must reply within 2 weeks.

ADDRESS/TELEPHONE. Enrollment Services, Denmark Technical College, PO Box 327, Denmark, SC 29042-0327. (803) 793-3301. Fax: (803) 793-5942.

Erskine College
Due West, South Carolina — CB code: 5188

Admissions: 89% of applicants accepted
Based on:
••• School record
•• Recommendations, test scores
• Activities, essay, interview, religious affiliation/commitment
Completion: 80% of freshmen end year in good standing
63% graduate, 40% of these enter graduate study

4-year private liberal arts college, coed, affiliated with Associate Reformed Presbyterian Church. Founded in 1839. **Accreditation:** Regional. **Undergraduate enrollment:** 251 men, 285 women full time; 19 men, 21 women part time. **Faculty:** 46 total (39 full time), 40 with doctorates or other terminal degrees. **Location:** Rural campus in rural community; 18 miles from Anderson. **Calendar:** 4-1-4, limited summer session. **Microcomputers:** 100 located in libraries, classrooms, computer centers. **Additional facts:** Affiliated with Erskine Theological Seminary.

DEGREES OFFERED. BA, BS. 122 bachelor's degrees awarded in 1992. 18% in business and management, 16% education, 10% letters/literature, 11% life sciences, 5% mathematics, 7% philosophy, religion, theology, 10% physical sciences, 19% social sciences.

UNDERGRADUATE MAJORS. Accounting, allied health, behavioral sciences, biological and physical sciences, biology, business and management, business economics, chemistry, early childhood education, education, elementary education, English, English education, foreign languages education, French, history, junior high education, mathematics, mathematics education, medical laboratory technologies, military science (Army), music, music education, music performance, physical education, physics, predentistry, prelaw, premedicine, prepharmacy, preveterinary, psychology, religion, religious education, science education, secondary education, social studies education, Spanish, special education.

ACADEMIC PROGRAMS. Double major, dual enrollment of high school students, independent study, internships, study abroad, teacher preparation, cross-registration; liberal arts/career combination in engineering, health sciences. **Placement/credit:** AP, CLEP Subject, institutional tests.

ACADEMIC REQUIREMENTS. Freshmen must earn minimum GPA of 1.6 to continue in good standing. 88% of freshmen return for sophomore year. Students must declare major by end of second year. **Graduation requirements:** 124 hours for bachelor's (33 in major). Most students required to take courses in arts/fine arts, computer science, English, foreign languages, history, humanities, mathematics, philosophy/religion, biological/physical sciences, social sciences.

FRESHMAN ADMISSIONS. Selection criteria: School achievement record, with special emphasis on advanced placement and honor courses, most important. Test scores, counselor recommendations, class rank, activities also considered. Special consideration given to members of supporting church and alumni children. **High school preparation:** 14 units required. Required and recommended units include English 4 and mathematics 2-4. Biological science 1, foreign language 2 and physical science 2 recommended. Biology, chemistry, physics, and history highly recommended. **Test requirements:** SAT or ACT (SAT preferred); score report by August 15.

1992 FRESHMAN CLASS PROFILE. 297 men applied, 237 accepted, 87 enrolled; 358 women applied, 345 accepted, 94 enrolled. 45% were in top tenth and 69% were in top quarter of graduating class. **Academic background:** Mid 50% of enrolled freshmen had SAT-V between 430-530, SAT-M between 430-600; ACT composite between 21-24. 90% submitted SAT scores, 10% submitted ACT scores. **Characteristics:** 79% from in state, 93% live in college housing, 4% have minority backgrounds, 35% join fraternities/sororities. Average age is 18.

FALL-TERM APPLICATIONS. $15 fee, may be waived for applicants with need. Closing date August 15; applicants notified on a rolling basis; must reply by May 1. Interview required for academically weak applicants. CRDA. Deferred admission available.

STUDENT LIFE. Housing: Dormitories (men, women). **Activities:** Student government, magazine, student newspaper, television, yearbook, choral groups, concert band, drama, jazz band, music ensembles, musical theater, pep band, fraternities, sororities, National honor societies for academics, drama, and leadership, Organized Black Student Christian Association, denominational organizations, Judicial Council, Fellowship of Christian Athletes.

ATHLETICS. NCAA. **Intercollegiate:** Baseball M, basketball, cross-country, golf M, soccer, softball W, tennis, volleyball W. **Intramural:** Basketball, horseback riding, racquetball, soccer, softball, table tennis, volleyball.

STUDENT SERVICES. Career counseling, freshman orientation, health services, personal counseling, placement service for graduates, special adviser for adult students, word processing center, services/facilities for handicapped.

ANNUAL EXPENSES. Tuition and fees: $10,630. **Room and board:** $3,728. **Books and supplies:** $475. **Other expenses:** $726.

FINANCIAL AID. 81% of freshmen, 75% of continuing students receive some form of aid. 56% of grants, 80% of loans, 85% of jobs based on need. 154 enrolled freshmen were judged to have need, all were offered aid. Academic, music/drama, athletic, state/district residency, leadership, religious affiliation scholarships available. **Aid applications:** No closing date; priority given to applications received by March 15; applicants notified on a rolling basis beginning on or about March 15; must reply by May 1 or within 3 weeks if notified thereafter.

ADDRESS/TELEPHONE. Dorothy J. Carter, Director of Admissions and Financial Aid, Erskine College, Washington Street, Due West, SC 29639-0176. (803) 379-8838. (800) 241-8721. Fax: (803) 379-8759.

Florence-Darlington Technical College

Florence, South Carolina — CB code: 5207

2-year public technical college, coed. Founded in 1964. **Accreditation:** Regional. **Undergraduate enrollment:** 489 men, 704 women full time; 426 men, 1,020 women part time. **Faculty:** 221 total (89 full time), 8 with doctorates or other terminal degrees. **Location:** Suburban campus in large town; 80 miles from Columbia. **Calendar:** Semester, limited summer session. **Microcomputers:** Located in classrooms, computer centers.

DEGREES OFFERED. AA, AS. 338 associate degrees awarded in 1992. 7% in business and management, 5% business/office and marketing/distribution, 12% engineering technologies, 29% health sciences, 15% allied health, 5% law, 12% parks/recreation, protective services, public affairs, 10% trade and industry.

UNDERGRADUATE MAJORS. Accounting, air conditioning/heating/refrigeration mechanics, aircraft mechanics, automotive mechanics, automotive technology, business data processing and related programs, civil technology, computer and information sciences, criminal justice technology, dental hygiene, electronic technology, engineering and engineering-related technologies, fashion merchandising, funeral services/mortuary science, legal assistant/paralegal, machine tool operation/machine shop, marketing and distribution, medical laboratory technologies, medical records technology, nursing, physical therapy assistant, radiograph medical technology, respiratory therapy technology, secretarial and related programs, small business management and ownership.

ACADEMIC PROGRAMS. 2-year transfer program, dual enrollment of high school students, independent study, internships, cross-registration, cooperative program with Greenville Technical College for Physical Therapy, Fayetteville Technical College for Funeral Services. **Remedial services:** Learning center, reduced course load, remedial instruction, tutoring. **ROTC:** Army. **Placement/credit:** AP, CLEP General and Subject, institutional tests; 60 credit hours maximum for associate degree.

ACADEMIC REQUIREMENTS. Freshmen must earn minimum GPA of 2.0 to continue in good standing. 75% of freshmen return for sophomore year. Students must declare major on application. **Graduation requirements:** 96 hours for associate (80 in major). Most students required to take courses in English, mathematics.

FRESHMAN ADMISSIONS. Selection criteria: Open admissions. Selective admissions to some programs. SAT or ACT required of nursing, and radiologic technology applicants. Institutional placement test required of applicants to all other programs who do not submit satisfactory SAT scores. **High school preparation:** 20 units recommended. Recommended units include English 4, mathematics 3, social science 3 and science 2. Algebra I, biology, and chemistry required for health programs. **Test requirements:** SAT or ACT (SAT preferred) for placement; score report by August 15.

1992 FRESHMAN CLASS PROFILE. 253 men, 389 women enrolled. **Characteristics:** 99% from in state, 100% commute, 28% have minority backgrounds. Average age is 22.

FALL-TERM APPLICATIONS. $15 fee, may be waived for applicants with need. Closing date August 10; applicants notified on a rolling basis beginning on or about January 1. Interview required for nursing, allied health applicants. Deferred and early admission available. SAT required for some programs. Computerized Placement Test (CPT) administered at college as alternative to SAT for most programs.

STUDENT LIFE. Activities: Student government, student newspaper, yearbook, fraternities, sororities.

STUDENT SERVICES. Aptitude testing, career counseling, employment service for undergraduates, freshman orientation, personal counseling, placement service for graduates, veterans counselor, services/facilities for handicapped.

ANNUAL EXPENSES. Tuition and fees (1992-93): $910, $150 additional for out-of-district students, $376 additional for out-of-state students. **Books and supplies:** $700. **Other expenses:** $700.

FINANCIAL AID. 52% of freshmen, 18% of continuing students receive some form of aid. All grants, 86% of loans, all jobs based on need. **Aid applications:** No closing date; priority given to applications received by May 1; applicants notified on a rolling basis beginning on or about July 1; must reply within 2 weeks.

ADDRESS/TELEPHONE. Perry T. Kirven, Director of Admissions, Florence-Darlington Technical College, P.O. Box 100548, Florence, SC 29501-0548. (803) 661-8151. Fax: (803) 661-8041.

Francis Marion University

Florence, South Carolina — CB code: 5442

Admissions: 93% of applicants accepted
Based on: ••• School record, test scores
• Essay, recommendations
Completion: 75% of freshmen end year in good standing

4-year public liberal arts college, coed. Founded in 1970. **Accreditation:** Regional. **Undergraduate enrollment:** 1,468 men, 1,790 women full time; 205 men, 279 women part time. **Graduate enrollment:** 7 men, 8 women full time; 46 men, 172 women part time. **Faculty:** 209 total (160 full time), 139 with doctorates or other terminal degrees. **Location:** Rural campus in large town; 7 miles from downtown, 80 miles from Columbia. **Calendar:** Semester, limited summer session. **Microcomputers:** 159 located in computer centers. **Special facilities:** Planetarium, observatory.

DEGREES OFFERED. BA, BS, MS, MBA, MEd. 2 associate degrees awarded in 1992. 100% in multi/interdisciplinary studies. 542 bachelor's degrees awarded in 1992. 26% in business and management, 17% teacher education, 8% letters/literature, 8% life sciences, 6% psychology, 22% social sciences. Graduate degrees offered in 11 major fields of study.

UNDERGRADUATE MAJORS. Accounting, art education, biology, business administration and management, business economics, chemistry, civil technology, communications, computer and information sciences, dramatic arts, early childhood education, economics, electronic technology, elementary education, English, finance, forestry and related sciences, French, geography, health physics, history, information sciences and systems, liberal/general studies, management science, marketing management, mathematics, medical laboratory technologies, nuclear physics, nursing, philosophy, physics, political science and government, predentistry, prelaw, premedicine, prepharmacy, preveterinary, psychology, religion, sociology, Spanish, studio art.

ACADEMIC PROGRAMS. Accelerated program, cooperative education, double major, dual enrollment of high school students, honors program, independent study, internships, teacher preparation, cross-registration; liberal arts/career combination in engineering. **Remedial services:** Preadmission summer program, reduced course load, remedial instruction. **ROTC:** Army. **Placement/credit:** AP, CLEP Subject, institutional tests.

ACADEMIC REQUIREMENTS. Freshmen must earn minimum GPA of 1.9 to continue in good standing. 69% of freshmen return for sophomore year. Students must declare major by end of second year. **Graduation requirements:** 120 hours for bachelor's (30 in major). Most students required to take courses in English, history, humanities, mathematics, biological/physical sciences, social sciences.

FRESHMAN ADMISSIONS. Selection criteria: College-preparatory curriculum very important, also test scores, class rank. **High school preparation:** 16 units required. Required and recommended units include biological science 1, English 4, foreign language 2, mathematics 3-4, physical science 1 and social science 3. Science 3 recommended. One unit advanced mathematics, computer science, world history, world geography, or western civilization also required. Science must be laboratory sciences. One unit of physical education or ROTC required. **Test requirements:** SAT or ACT (SAT preferred); score report by August 15. **Additional information:** Students with the required college-preparatory curriculum and minimum SAT score of 900 automatically accepted. Students with high school course prerequistes but less than 900 on SAT accepted on basis of predicted GPA using SAT scores and class rank.

1992 FRESHMAN CLASS PROFILE. 693 men applied, 651 accepted, 392 enrolled; 944 women applied, 868 accepted, 495 enrolled. **Characteristics:** 95% from in state, 73% live in college housing, 18% have minority backgrounds, 1% are foreign students. Average age is 18.

FALL-TERM APPLICATIONS. $25 fee, may be waived for applicants with need. No closing date; applicants notified on a rolling basis. Deferred admission available. May 1 reply date for dormitory students.

STUDENT LIFE. Housing: Dormitories (coed); apartment, fraternity, handicapped housing available. On-campus housing limited. Students advised to apply for admission and housing by Fall of their senior year in high school. **Activities:** Student government, magazine, student newspaper, yearbook, choral groups, drama, fraternities, sororities, Baptist Student Union, College Democrats, College Republicans, NAACP, Collegiate Civitans, Rotoract, Christian Fellowship, Episcopal College Churchmen, Minority Student Association, Circle-K.

ATHLETICS. NCAA. **Intercollegiate:** Baseball M, basketball, cross-country, golf M, soccer M, softball W, tennis, track and field M, volleyball W. **Intramural:** Basketball, bowling, diving, golf M, racquetball, soccer M, softball, swimming, table tennis, tennis, track and field, volleyball.

STUDENT SERVICES. Aptitude testing, career counseling, employment service for undergraduates, freshman orientation, health services, personal counseling, placement service for graduates, special adviser for adult students, veterans counselor, services/facilities for handicapped.

ANNUAL EXPENSES. Tuition and fees (1992-93): $2,460, $2,460 additional for out-of-state students. **Room and board:** $3,078. **Books and supplies:** $400. **Other expenses:** $860.

FINANCIAL AID. 53% of continuing students receive some form of aid. 56% of grants, 82% of loans, 25% of jobs based on need. Academic, music/drama, art, athletic, minority scholarships available. **Aid applications:** No closing date; priority given to applications received by March 1; applicants notified on a rolling basis beginning on or about July 1; must reply within 2 weeks.

ADDRESS/TELEPHONE. Marvin W. Lynch, Director of Admissions, Francis Marion University, PO Box 100547, Florence, SC 29501-0547. (803) 661-1231. Fax: (803) 661-1219.

Furman University
Greenville, South Carolina — CB code: 5222

Admissions: 72% of applicants accepted
Based on:
••• School record
•• Essay, special talents, test scores
• Activities, recommendations
Completion: 95% of freshmen end year in good standing
80% graduate, 49% of these enter graduate study

4-year private liberal arts college, coed, with an historic relationship to South Carolina Baptist Convention. Founded in 1826. **Accreditation:** Regional. **Undergraduate enrollment:** 1,150 men, 1,324 women full time; 128 men, 437 women part time. **Graduate enrollment:** 61 men, 401 women full time. **Faculty:** 237 total (227 full time), 191 with doctorates or other terminal degrees. **Location:** Suburban campus in small city; 100 miles from Columbia, 100 miles from Charlotte, North Carolina. **Calendar:** 3-2-3. **Microcomputers:** 160 located in classrooms, computer centers. **Special facilities:** Observatory.

DEGREES OFFERED. BA, BS, MA, MS. 603 bachelor's degrees awarded in 1992. 19% in business and management, 6% letters/literature, 12% life sciences, 5% philosophy, religion, theology, 7% physical sciences, 25% social sciences, 7% visual and performing arts. Graduate degrees offered in 9 major fields of study.

UNDERGRADUATE MAJORS. Accounting, Asian studies, biology, business administration and management, chemistry, classics, computer and information sciences, computer mathematics, dramatic arts, early childhood education, economics, education of the mentally handicapped, elementary education, English, fine arts, French, geology, German, Greek (classical), history, Latin, mathematics, music, music history and appreciation, music performance, music theory and composition, philosophy, physics, political science and government, preengineering, psychology, religion, sociology, Spanish, special education, specific learning disabilities, urban studies.

ACADEMIC PROGRAMS. Cooperative education, double major, dual enrollment of high school students, independent study, internships, student-designed major, study abroad, teacher preparation, Washington semester; liberal arts/career combination in engineering, forestry, health sciences. **Remedial services:** Tutoring. **ROTC:** Army. **Placement/credit:** AP, institutional tests.

ACADEMIC REQUIREMENTS. Freshmen must earn minimum GPA of 1.62 to continue in good standing. 90% of freshmen return for sophomore year. Students must declare major by end of second year. **Graduation requirements:** 128 hours for bachelor's (32 in major). Most students required to take courses in arts/fine arts, English, foreign languages, history, humanities, mathematics, philosophy/religion, biological/physical sciences, social sciences. **Postgraduate studies:** 15% enter law school, 12% enter medical school, 5% enter MBA programs, 17% enter other graduate study.

FRESHMAN ADMISSIONS. Selection criteria: High school record, including courses taken, grades, class rank, most important, then SAT scores, particularly verbal. Special talents such as fine arts, athletic ability, writing ability considered. Special consideration given to children of alumni and to minorities. **High school preparation:** 18 units required; 20 recommended. Required and recommended units include English 4, foreign language 2-3, mathematics 3-4, social science 3-3 and science 2-3. Mathematics must include 2 algebra, 1 geometry. Two years of the same foreign language. **Test requirements:** SAT or ACT; score report by February 1.

1992 FRESHMAN CLASS PROFILE. 1,175 men applied, 875 accepted, 335 enrolled; 1,478 women applied, 1,027 accepted, 408 enrolled. 90% had high school GPA of 3.0 or higher, 10% between 2.0 and 2.99. **Academic background:** Mid 50% of enrolled freshmen had SAT-V between 480-580, SAT-M between 540-650; ACT composite between 24-28. 97% submitted SAT scores, 29% submitted ACT scores. **Characteristics:** 35% from in state, 98% live in college housing, 5% have minority backgrounds, 1% are foreign students, 30% join fraternities/sororities. Average age is 18.

FALL-TERM APPLICATIONS. $25 fee, may be waived for applicants with need. Closing date February 1; applicants notified on or about March 15; must reply by May 1. Audition required for music applicants. Essay required. Portfolio recommended for art applicants. CRDA. Early admission available. Institutional early decision plan. Early decision applications due December 1. Applicants notified by December 27. Accepted applicants must respond by February 1.

STUDENT LIFE. Housing: Dormitories (men, women, coed); apartment housing available. **Activities:** Student government, magazine, radio, student newspaper, yearbook, choral groups, concert band, dance, drama, jazz band, marching band, music ensembles, musical theater, opera, pep band, symphony orchestra, fraternities, sororities, Black Student League, Association of Jewish Students, Newman Club, Collegiate Educational Service Corporation.

ATHLETICS. NCAA. **Intercollegiate:** Baseball M, basketball, cross-country, football M, golf, soccer M, softball W, tennis, track and field, volleyball W. **Intramural:** Badminton, baseball, basketball, bowling, cross-country, field hockey W, golf, handball, racquetball, rowing (crew), rugby W, soccer, softball, swimming, table tennis, tennis, volleyball, water polo. **Clubs:** Sailing, skiing.

STUDENT SERVICES. Aptitude testing, career counseling, employment service for undergraduates, freshman orientation, health services, personal counseling, placement service for graduates, services/facilities for handicapped.

ANNUAL EXPENSES. Tuition and fees: $12,605. **Room and board:** $3,952. **Books and supplies:** $600. **Other expenses:** $750.

FINANCIAL AID. 42% of freshmen, 72% of continuing students receive some form of aid. 69% of grants, 94% of loans, 55% of jobs based on need. 472 enrolled freshmen were judged to have need, all were offered aid. Academic, music/drama, art, athletic, leadership, alumni affiliation, religious affiliation scholarships available. **Aid applications:** Closing date February 1; applicants notified on or about March 15; must reply by May 1. **Additional information:** 5-point comprehensive education financing plan includes financial aid packaging, money management counseling, debt management counseling.

ADDRESS/TELEPHONE. J. Carey Thompson, Director of Admissions, Furman University, Poinsett Highway, Greenville, SC 29613-0645. (803) 294-2034. Fax: (803) 294-3127.

Greenville Technical College
Greenville, South Carolina — CB code: 5278

2-year public community, technical college, coed. Founded in 1962. **Accreditation:** Regional. **Undergraduate enrollment:** 8,814 men and women. **Faculty:** 429 total (117 full time), 45 with doctorates or other terminal degrees. **Location:** Suburban campus in small city; 100 miles from Columbia, 100 miles from Charlotte, North Carolina. **Calendar:** Semester, extensive summer session. **Special facilities:** Technical Resource Center, Child Development Center. **Additional facts:** A limited number of classes offered at greater Greer and Golden Strip sites.

DEGREES OFFERED. AA, AS, AAS. 709 associate degrees awarded in 1992. 9% in business and management, 13% business/office and marketing/distribution, 10% engineering technologies, 14% health sciences, 11% allied health, 5% multi/interdisciplinary studies, 36% trade and industry.

UNDERGRADUATE MAJORS. Accounting, aircraft mechanics, architectural technologies, automotive mechanics, automotive technology, biological and physical sciences, computer programming, computer servicing technology, construction, contract management and procurement/purchasing, criminal justice technology, dental hygiene, drafting, drafting and design technology, electrical and electronics equipment repair, electronic technology, emergency medical technologies, engineering and engineering-related technologies, food management, food production/management/services, industrial technology, legal assistant/paralegal, liberal/general studies, machine tool operation/machine shop, management science, manufacturing technology, marketing and distribution, marketing management, mechanical design technology, medical laboratory technologies, nursing, physical therapy assistant, radiograph medical technology, respiratory therapy, respiratory therapy technology, secretarial and related programs, telecommunications.

ACADEMIC PROGRAMS. 2-year transfer program, cooperative education, weekend college. **Remedial services:** Reduced course load, remedial instruction, special counselor, tutoring. **Placement/credit:** AP, CLEP Subject, institutional tests.

ACADEMIC REQUIREMENTS. No policy requiring minimum GPA; records of students having academic difficulty are reviewed individually. Students must declare major on application. **Graduation requirements:** 96 hours for associate. Most students required to take courses in English, mathematics, social sciences.

FRESHMAN ADMISSIONS. Selection criteria: Selective admissions to programs. Minimum SAT, ACT, or ASSET scores required and high school courses required for some programs in allied health and nursing. For health programs, algebra, biology, and chemistry required for most and recommended for all applicants. Algebra required for engineering. **Test requirements:** SAT or ACT (SAT preferred); score report by August 1. **Additional information:** ACT/ASSET scores may be submitted in place of SAT or ACT scores.

1992 FRESHMAN CLASS PROFILE. Characteristics: 99% from in state, 100% commute.

FALL-TERM APPLICATIONS. $15 fee, may be waived for applicants with need. No closing date; priority given to applications received by March 1; applicants notified on a rolling basis; must reply within 4 weeks for specified programs. Portfolio required for visual arts applicants. Interview required for allied health sciences, nursing, child care, communication arts, and aircraft mechanic applicants; recommended for all others. Deferred admission available. Most allied health courses start only in September. Application by January 30 strongly advised. Some programs filled by early spring.

STUDENT LIFE. Activities: Student government, national academic/service honor society.

STUDENT SERVICES. Aptitude testing, career counseling, employment service for undergraduates, freshman orientation, health services, on-campus day care, personal counseling, placement service for graduates, veterans counselor, services/facilities for handicapped.

ANNUAL EXPENSES. Tuition and fees (1992-93): $906, $72 additional for out-of-district students, $540 additional for out-of-state students. **Books and supplies:** $500. **Other expenses:** $1,250.

FINANCIAL AID. 34% of freshmen, 21% of continuing students receive some form of aid. 90% of grants, 96% of loans, all jobs based on need. Academic, art, state/district residency, leadership scholarships available. **Aid applications:** No closing date; priority given to applications received by May 1; applicants notified on a rolling basis beginning on or about June 20; must reply within 2 weeks.

ADDRESS/TELEPHONE. Nancy Hagan, Director of Admissions and Assessment, Greenville Technical College, PO Box 5616, Station B, Greenville, SC 29606-5616. (803) 250-8109.

Horry-Georgetown Technical College
Conway, South Carolina — CB code: 5305

2-year public technical college, coed. Founded in 1965. **Accreditation:** Regional. **Undergraduate enrollment:** 2,456 men and women. **Faculty:** 137 total (51 full time), 3 with doctorates or other terminal degrees. **Location:** Rural campus in large town; 4 miles from Conway, 8 miles from Myrtle Beach. **Calendar:** Semester. **Microcomputers:** Located in classrooms, computer centers.

DEGREES OFFERED. 269 associate degrees awarded in 1992.

UNDERGRADUATE MAJORS. Air conditioning/heating/refrigeration mechanics, automotive mechanics, business and management, civil technology, computer technology, criminal justice technology, data processing, electrical and electronics equipment repair, electronic technology, food production/management/services, forestry and related sciences, hotel/motel and restaurant management, occupational safety and health technology, ornamental horticulture, parks and recreation management, precision metal work, recreation and community services technologies, secretarial and related programs.

ACADEMIC PROGRAMS. Independent study, internships, visiting/exchange student program. **Remedial services:** Learning center, reduced course load, remedial instruction, tutoring. **Placement/credit:** AP, institutional tests.

ACADEMIC REQUIREMENTS. Freshmen must earn minimum GPA of 1.6 to continue in good standing. 50% of freshmen return for sophomore year. Students must declare major on application. **Graduation requirements:** 116 hours for associate (74 in major). Most students required to take courses in English, mathematics, social sciences.

FRESHMAN ADMISSIONS. Selection criteria: Open admissions. Selective admission to certain programs. Algebra I, II required for electronics engineering and data processing. **Test requirements:** SAT for placement.

1992 FRESHMAN CLASS PROFILE. 800 men and women enrolled. 3% had high school GPA of 3.0 or higher, 35% between 2.0 and 2.99. 5% were in top tenth and 25% were in top quarter of graduating class. **Characteristics:** 95% from in state, 100% commute, 17% have minority backgrounds, 1% are foreign students. Average age is 25.

FALL-TERM APPLICATIONS. $10 fee. No closing date; applicants notified on a rolling basis.

STUDENT LIFE. Activities: Student government.

STUDENT SERVICES. Aptitude testing, career counseling, personal counseling, placement service for graduates, veterans counselor, financial aid counselor, services/facilities for handicapped.

ANNUAL EXPENSES. Tuition and fees (1992-93): $900, $900 additional for out-of-state students. **Books and supplies:** $300.

FINANCIAL AID. Grants, loans, jobs available. 300 enrolled freshmen were judged to have need, all were offered aid. Academic scholarships available. **Aid applications:** Closing date May 1; priority given to applications received by April 1; applicants notified on or about July 1; must reply by July 15.

ADDRESS/TELEPHONE. L. Carlyle Dixon, Director of Admissions, Horry-Georgetown Technical College, Highway 501 East, PO Box 1966, Conway, SC 29526-1966. (803) 347-3186.

Lander University
Greenwood, South Carolina — CB code: 5363

Admissions: 88% of applicants accepted
Based on: ••• Recommendations, school record, test scores
• Activities, essay, interview, special talents
Completion: 95% of freshmen end year in good standing
6% enter graduate study

4-year public liberal arts college, coed. Founded in 1872. **Accreditation:** Regional. **Undergraduate enrollment:** 688 men, 1,223 women full time; 129 men, 155 women part time. **Graduate enrollment:** 1 man, 5 women full time; 41 men, 279 women part time. **Faculty:** 152 total (126 full time), 97 with doctorates or other terminal degrees. **Location:** Urban campus in large town; 75 miles from Columbia. **Calendar:** Semester, limited summer session. **Microcomputers:** 100 located in libraries. **Special facilities:** Cultural center with art gallery.

DEGREES OFFERED. BA, BS, BFA, MEd. 314 bachelor's degrees awarded in 1992. 23% in business and management, 30% teacher education, 6% health sciences, 6% psychology, 9% social sciences. Graduate degrees offered in 1 major field of study.

UNDERGRADUATE MAJORS. Accounting, art education, biology, business administration and management, business and management, business economics, chemistry, clinical laboratory science, computer and information sciences, dramatic arts, early childhood education, elementary education, English, English education, excercise studies, fine arts, French, history, liberal/general studies, marketing management, mathematics, mathematics education, medical laboratory technologies, music, music education, nursing, physical education, political science and government, predentistry, prelaw, premedicine, prepharmacy, preveterinary, psychology, science education, social studies education, sociology, special education, speech/communication/theater education.

ACADEMIC PROGRAMS. Accelerated program, cooperative education, double major, dual enrollment of high school students, honors program, independent study, internships, student-designed major, study abroad, teacher preparation, visiting/exchange student program, dual degree in engineering with Clemson University; liberal arts/career combination in engineering, health sciences; combined bachelor's/graduate program in business administration. **Remedial services:** Learning center, preadmission summer program, reduced course load, remedial instruction, special counselor, tutoring. **ROTC:** Army. **Placement/credit:** AP, CLEP Subject, institutional tests; 30 credit hours maximum for bachelor's degree.

ACADEMIC REQUIREMENTS. Freshmen must earn minimum GPA of 2.0 to continue in good standing. 71% of freshmen return for sophomore year. Students must declare major by end of second year. **Graduation requirements:** 124 hours for bachelor's (30 in major). Most students required to take courses in arts/fine arts, computer science, English, foreign languages, history, humanities, mathematics, biological/physical sciences, social sciences. **Postgraduate studies:** 1% enter law school, 1% enter medical school, 3% enter MBA programs, 1% enter other graduate study.

FRESHMAN ADMISSIONS. Selection criteria: Test scores, class rank, curriculum, and recommendations weighed equally. Out-of-state students must rank in top half of graduating class. **High school preparation:** 18 units required; 20 recommended. Required units include English 4, foreign language 2, mathematics 3, social science 3 and science 2. One unit physical education or ROTC also required. **Test requirements:** SAT or ACT; score report by August 1.

1992 FRESHMAN CLASS PROFILE. 304 men applied, 258 accepted, 132 enrolled; 643 women applied, 575 accepted, 284 enrolled. **Characteristics:** 91% from in state, 55% live in college housing, 17% have minority backgrounds, 1% are foreign students, 2% join fraternities/sororities. Average age is 20.

FALL-TERM APPLICATIONS. $15 fee, may be waived for applicants with need. No closing date; priority given to applications received by August 7; applicants notified on a rolling basis. Audition required for music applicants. Interview recommended for art, music applicants. Portfolio recommended for art applicants. Deferred and early admission available.

STUDENT LIFE. Housing: Dormitories (men, women). **Activities:** Student government, magazine, student newspaper, yearbook, choral groups, concert band, dance, drama, jazz band, music ensembles, musical theater, pep band, fraternities, sororities, Baptist Student Union, Lander Bible Study, Chi Sigma, Young Democrats, College Republicans, Minorities on the Move, Blue Key, Alpha Kappa Gamma.

ATHLETICS. NCAA. **Intercollegiate:** Basketball, cross-country, soccer M, softball W, tennis. **Intramural:** Basketball, bowling, golf, soccer, softball, swimming, tennis, track and field, volleyball.

STUDENT SERVICES. Aptitude testing, career counseling, employment service for undergraduates, freshman orientation, health services, personal counseling, placement service for graduates, special adviser for adult students, veterans counselor, services/facilities for handicapped.

ANNUAL EXPENSES. Tuition and fees (1992-93): $2,920, $1,248 additional for out-of-state students. **Room and board:** $2,930. **Books and supplies:** $485. **Other expenses:** $1,150.

FINANCIAL AID. 45% of freshmen, 48% of continuing students receive some form of aid. 75% of grants, 83% of loans, 33% of jobs based on need. 220 enrolled freshmen were judged to have need, 173 were offered aid. Academic, music/drama, art, athletic, leadership, minority scholarships available. **Aid applications:** No closing date; priority given to applications received by April 15; applicants notified on a rolling basis beginning on or about June 1; must reply within 2 weeks.

ADDRESS/TELEPHONE. Jacquelyn DeVore Roark, Director of Admissions, Lander University, Stanley Avenue, Greenwood, SC 29649. (803) 229-8307. (800) 768-3600. Fax: (803) 229-8890.

Limestone College
Gaffney, South Carolina — CB code: 5366

4-year private liberal arts college, coed. Founded in 1845. **Accreditation:** Regional. **Faculty:** 40 total (29 full time), 14 with doctorates or other terminal degrees. **Location:** Suburban campus in large town; 50 miles from Greenville, 50 miles from Charlotte, North Carolina. **Calendar:** Semester, limited summer session. Saturday and extensive evening/early morning classes. **Microcomputers:** Located in classrooms, computer centers. **Special facilities:** Observatory. **Additional facts:** 26 branch campuses statewide. Adult evening program constitutes three-fourths of total student enrollment.

DEGREES OFFERED. AA, BA, BS, BFA. 20 associate degrees awarded in 1992. 90% in business and management, 10% multi/interdisciplinary studies. 200 bachelor's degrees awarded. 50% in business and management, 25% education, 10% physical sciences, 10% visual and performing arts.

UNDERGRADUATE MAJORS. Associate: Business and management, computer and information sciences, education, liberal/general studies. **Bachelor's:** Accounting, art education, biological and physical sciences, biology, business administration and management, business and management, business economics, chemistry, computer and information sciences, counseling psychology, education, elementary education, English, English education, history, humanities and social sciences, liberal/general studies, marketing management, mathematics, mathematics education, music, music education, music performance, physical education, physical sciences, prelaw, psychology, secondary education, social sciences, social studies education, social work, student counseling and personnel services, studio art.

ACADEMIC PROGRAMS. 2-year transfer program, accelerated program, double major, dual enrollment of high school students, honors program, independent study, internships, student-designed major, teacher preparation, weekend college, alternative learning program for learning disabled. **Remedial services:** Learning center, reduced course load, remedial instruction, tutoring. **Placement/credit:** AP, CLEP General and Subject; 60 credit hours maximum for bachelor's degree.

ACADEMIC REQUIREMENTS. Freshmen must earn minimum GPA of 1.5 to continue in good standing. 65% of freshmen return for sophomore year. Students must declare major by end of second year. **Graduation requirements:** 63 hours for associate (9 in major), 120 hours for bachelor's (15 in major). Most students required to take courses in arts/fine arts, computer science, English, history, mathematics, philosophy/religion, biological/physical sciences, social sciences. **Postgraduate studies:** 95% from 2-year programs enter 4-year programs.

FRESHMAN ADMISSIONS. Selection criteria: SAT combined score of 700 and GPA of 2.0. Admissions committee must approve all applicants who do not meet these standards. **High school preparation:** 18 units recommended. Recommended units include biological science 2, English 4, foreign language 2, mathematics 3, physical science 2 and social science 2. Mathematics recommendation includes 2 algebra, 1 geometry. **Test requirements:** SAT or ACT; score report by August 1.

1992 FRESHMAN CLASS PROFILE. 20% had high school GPA of 3.0 or higher, 70% between 2.0 and 2.99. 9% were in top tenth and 35% were in top quarter of graduating class. **Characteristics:** 75% live in college housing, 1% are foreign students, 40% join fraternities/sororities. Average age is 18.

FALL-TERM APPLICATIONS. $15 fee, may be waived for applicants with need. No closing date; priority given to applications received by March 31; applicants notified on a rolling basis; must reply within 4 weeks. Audition required for music, music education applicants. Portfolio required for art education, studio art applicants. Interview recommended. Interview required for lower-ranking applicants; recommended for all others. Deferred admission available.

STUDENT LIFE. Housing: Dormitories (men, women); apartment housing available. **Activities:** Student government, magazine, student newspaper, yearbook, choral groups, concert band, dance, drama, jazz band, music ensembles, musical theater, pep band, symphony orchestra, fraternities, sororities.

ATHLETICS. NAIA, NCAA. **Intercollegiate:** Baseball M, basketball, golf M, lacrosse M, soccer, softball W, tennis M, volleyball W. **Intramural:** Basketball, golf, lacrosse M, racquetball, skiing, soccer, softball, swimming, table tennis, tennis, volleyball.

STUDENT SERVICES. Aptitude testing, career counseling, employment service for undergraduates, freshman orientation, health services, personal counseling, placement service for graduates, special adviser for adult students, veterans counselor.

ANNUAL EXPENSES. Tuition and fees: $7,200. **Room and board:** $3,500. **Books and supplies:** $690. **Other expenses:** $837.

FINANCIAL AID. 98% of freshmen, 98% of continuing students receive some form of aid. 97% of grants, 81% of loans, all jobs based on need. Academic, music/drama, art, athletic, state/district residency, leadership, religious affiliation scholarships available. **Aid applications:** No closing date; priority given to applications received by March 30; applicants notified on a rolling basis beginning on or about February 1; must reply within 10 days.

ADDRESS/TELEPHONE. Sherri R. Hortin, Director of Admissions, Limestone College, 1115 College Drive, Gaffney, SC 29340. (803) 489-7151 ext. 300. (800) 345-3792. Fax: (803) 487-8706.

Medical University of South Carolina
Charleston, South Carolina — CB code: 5407

2-year upper-division public university and health science college, coed. Founded in 1824. **Accreditation:** Regional. **Undergraduate enrollment:** 139 men, 544 women full time; 44 men, 268 women part time. **Graduate enrollment:** 650 men, 459 women full time; 38 men, 149 women part time. **Faculty:** 2,435 total (845 full time), 577 with doctorates or other terminal degrees. **Location:** Urban campus in small city; 350 miles from Atlanta, Georgia. **Calendar:** Semester. Extensive evening/early morning classes. **Microcomputers:** 70 located in libraries, classrooms. **Special facilities:** Waring Historical Library, MacCauley Dental Museum.

DEGREES OFFERED. BS, MS, PhD, DMD, MD, B. Pharm, Pharm D. 308 bachelor's degrees awarded in 1992. 54% in health sciences, 46% allied health. Graduate degrees offered in 22 major fields of study.

UNDERGRADUATE MAJORS. Cytotechnology, health sciences, medical laboratory technologies, medical records administration, medical records technology, nuclear medical technology, nursing, occupational therapy, pharmacy, physical therapy, respiratory therapy.

ACADEMIC PROGRAMS. Internships, cross-registration. **Placement/credit:** CLEP General and Subject; 30 credit hours maximum for bachelor's degree.

ACADEMIC REQUIREMENTS. Students must declare major on application. **Graduation requirements:** 128 hours for bachelor's (128 in major). Most students required to take courses in biological/physical sciences. **Postgraduate studies:** 2% enter other graduate study.

ADMISSIONS. Admissions based on transcripts, test scores, interview, and references.

FALL-TERM APPLICATIONS. $35 fee.

STUDENT LIFE. Activities: Student government, film, choral groups, Christian Medical Society, Campus Crusade, Student Union, Community Help Initiative, South Carolina Health Initiative, Minority Student Union, Student National Medical Association.

STUDENT SERVICES. Career counseling, health services, personal counseling, veterans counselor, services/facilities for handicapped.

ANNUAL EXPENSES. Tuition and fees (1992-93): $2,330, $4,030 additional for out-of-state students. Tuition reported only for nursing and pharmacy. Tuition, fees, room and board varies from college to college.

FINANCIAL AID. Aid applications: No closing date; applicants notified on a rolling basis.

ADDRESS/TELEPHONE. Wanda L. Taylor, Director of Admissions, Medical University of South Carolina, 171 Ashley Avenue, Charleston, SC 29425-2970. (803) 792-3281.

Midlands Technical College
Columbia, South Carolina CB code: 5584

2-year public community, technical college, coed. Founded in 1974. **Accreditation:** Regional. **Undergraduate enrollment:** 1,547 men, 2,131 women full time; 2,006 men, 2,979 women part time. **Faculty:** 375 total (205 full time), 20 with doctorates or other terminal degrees. **Location:** Urban campus in small city. **Calendar:** Semester, extensive summer session. **Microcomputers:** Located in libraries, computer centers. **Additional facts:** College operates Airport Campus, Beltline Campus and Harbison Center within metropolitan area.

DEGREES OFFERED. AA, AS. 815 associate degrees awarded in 1992. 22% in business and management, 6% computer sciences, 28% health sciences, 8% law, 13% multi/interdisciplinary studies, 10% parks/recreation, protective services, public affairs, 6% trade and industry.

UNDERGRADUATE MAJORS. Accounting, air conditioning/heating/refrigeration mechanics, architectural technologies, automotive technology, business administration and management, business data programming, civil technology, court reporting, criminal justice technology, dental hygiene, diesel engine mechanics, drafting and design technology, electrical technology, electronic technology, engineering and engineering-related technologies, finance, graphic and printing production, graphic arts technology, human services, legal assistant/paralegal, legal secretary, liberal/general studies, marketing and distribution, marketing management, mechanical design technology, medical laboratory technologies, medical records technology, medical secretary, mental health/human services, nursing, office supervision and management, precision metal work, radiograph medical technology, respiratory therapy technology, secretarial and related programs, telecommunications, word processing.

ACADEMIC PROGRAMS. 2-year transfer program, cooperative education, weekend college. **Remedial services:** Learning center, preadmission summer program, reduced course load, remedial instruction, special counselor, tutoring. **Placement/credit:** AP, CLEP Subject, institutional tests.

ACADEMIC REQUIREMENTS. Freshmen must earn minimum GPA of 1.5 to continue in good standing. Students must declare major by end of first year. **Graduation requirements:** Most students required to take courses in English, mathematics, social sciences.

FRESHMAN ADMISSIONS. Selection criteria: Open admissions. High school record, SAT, ACT, or college placement test scores, interviews and recommendations considered for nursing applicants. **Test requirements:** National League for Nursing Test required of nursing applicants in place of SAT or ACT. **Additional information:** Admissions cut-off scores (SAT, ACT, College Placement) established for full admission into each program. Students falling below cut-off scores may enter in development studies.

1992 FRESHMAN CLASS PROFILE. 699 men, 824 women enrolled. **Characteristics:** 99% from in state, 100% commute, 32% have minority backgrounds. Average age is 25.

FALL-TERM APPLICATIONS. $20 fee. No closing date; priority given to applications received by July 30; applicants notified on a rolling basis. Interview required for allied health, nursing applicants. Deferred and early admission available.

STUDENT LIFE. Activities: Student government, student newspaper.

ATHLETICS. Intramural: Basketball M, football M, softball, volleyball.

STUDENT SERVICES. Aptitude testing, career counseling, employment service for undergraduates, personal counseling, placement service for graduates, special adviser for adult students, veterans counselor, women's center, services/facilities for handicapped.

ANNUAL EXPENSES. Tuition and fees: $990, $248 additional for out-of-district students, $990 additional for out-of-state students. **Books and supplies:** $300. **Other expenses:** $600.

FINANCIAL AID. 45% of freshmen, 50% of continuing students receive some form of aid. Grants, jobs available. Academic scholarships available. **Aid applications:** No closing date; priority given to applications received by June 1; applicants notified on a rolling basis; must reply within 2 weeks.

ADDRESS/TELEPHONE. Richard Tinney, Director of Admissions, Midlands Technical College, PO Box 2408, Columbia, SC 29202. (803) 738-7764. Fax: (803) 738-7821.

Morris College ⇹
Sumter, South Carolina CB code: 5418

4-year private liberal arts college, coed, affiliated with Southern Baptist Convention. Founded in 1908. **Accreditation:** Regional. **Undergraduate enrollment:** 272 men, 503 women full time; 8 men, 9 women part time. **Faculty:** 65 total (44 full time), 23 with doctorates or other terminal degrees. **Location:** Urban campus in large town; 45 miles from Columbia. **Calendar:** Semester, limited summer session. **Microcomputers:** 121 located in libraries, computer centers.

DEGREES OFFERED. BA, BS, BFA. 135 bachelor's degrees awarded in 1992. 30% in business and management, 10% multi/interdisciplinary studies, 5% parks/recreation, protective services, public affairs, 37% social sciences.

UNDERGRADUATE MAJORS. Biology, biology education, business administration and management, community health work, criminal justice studies, early childhood education, elementary education, English, English education, fine arts, health sciences, history, history education, international relations, liberal/general studies, mathematics, mathematics education, political science and government, predentistry, prelaw, premedicine, prepharmacy, preveterinary, recreation and community services technologies, religious education, secondary education, social sciences, social studies education, sociology.

ACADEMIC PROGRAMS. Cooperative education, honors program, internships, teacher preparation. **Remedial services:** Learning center, reduced course load, remedial instruction, special counselor, tutoring. **ROTC:** Army. **Placement/credit:** CLEP General and Subject, institutional tests.

ACADEMIC REQUIREMENTS. Freshmen must earn minimum GPA of 2.0 to continue in good standing. 55% of freshmen return for sophomore year. Students must declare major by end of second year. **Graduation requirements:** 124 hours for bachelor's (30 in major). Most students required to take courses in arts/fine arts, English, history, humanities, mathematics, philosophy/religion, biological/physical sciences, social sciences. **Postgraduate studies:** 1% enter law school, 1% enter MBA programs, 10% enter other graduate study.

FRESHMAN ADMISSIONS. Selection criteria: Open admissions. **High school preparation:** 20 units recommended. Recommended units include English 4, mathematics 3, physical science 1, social science 3 and science 2. 7 units of electives recommended; 1 may be in physical education.

1992 FRESHMAN CLASS PROFILE. 116 men, 179 women enrolled. 30% had high school GPA of 3.0 or higher, 56% between 2.0 and 2.99. 4% were in top tenth and 12% were in top quarter of graduating class. **Characteristics:** 80% from in state, 88% live in college housing, 100% have minority backgrounds. Average age is 19.

FALL-TERM APPLICATIONS. $10 fee, may be waived for applicants with need. No closing date; applicants notified on a rolling basis. Interview recommended.

STUDENT LIFE. Housing: Dormitories (men, women). **Activities:** Student government, film, magazine, radio, student newspaper, television, yearbook, choral groups, dance, drama, music ensembles, fraternities, sororities, Baptist Student Union, NAACP, Alpha Phi Omega.

ATHLETICS. NAIA. **Intercollegiate:** Baseball M, basketball, softball W, track and field. **Intramural:** Baseball, basketball, volleyball.

STUDENT SERVICES. Aptitude testing, career counseling, employment service for undergraduates, freshman orientation, health services, personal counseling, placement service for graduates, special adviser for adult students, veterans counselor.

ANNUAL EXPENSES. Tuition and fees: $4,405. **Room and board:** $2,475. **Books and supplies:** $725. **Other expenses:** $1,000.

FINANCIAL AID. 95% of freshmen, 92% of continuing students receive some form of aid. Grants, loans, jobs available. Academic scholarships available. **Aid applications:** No closing date; priority given to applications received by April 30; applicants notified on a rolling basis beginning on or about June 1; must reply within 10 days.

ADDRESS/TELEPHONE. Queen W. Spann, Director of Admission and Records, Morris College, 100 West College Street, Sumter, SC 29150-3599. (803) 775-9371 ext. 225. Fax: (803) 773-3687.

Newberry College ⇹
Newberry, South Carolina CB code: 5493

4-year private liberal arts college, coed, affiliated with Evangelical Lutheran Church in America. Founded in 1856. **Accreditation:** Regional. **Undergraduate enrollment:** 401 men, 302 women full time; 20 men, 21 women part time. **Faculty:** 65 total (43 full time), 38 with doctorates or other terminal degrees. **Location:** Suburban campus in large town; 40 miles from Columbia. **Calendar:** Semester, limited summer session. **Microcomputers:** 30 located in libraries, classrooms, computer centers.

DEGREES OFFERED. BA, BS. 101 bachelor's degrees awarded in 1992. 42% in business and management, 19% teacher education, 5% letters/literature, 7% mathematics, 16% social sciences, 5% visual and performing arts.

UNDERGRADUATE MAJORS. Accounting, allied health, arts management, biology, business administration and management, business and management, business economics, chemistry, communications, computer and information sciences, dramatic arts, early childhood education, economics, education, elementary education, English, foreign languages (multiple emphasis), French, history, international business management, international relations, mathematics, music, music education, music performance, music theory and composition, philosophy, physical education, physical sciences, political science and government, religious music, sociology, Spanish, speech, studio art.

ACADEMIC PROGRAMS. Cooperative education, double major, dual enrollment of high school students, independent study, internships, study abroad, teacher preparation, dual degree programs in engineering with Clemson University, Georgia Institute of Technology; liberal arts/career combination in engineering, health sciences. **Remedial services:** Learning center, reduced course load, remedial instruction. **ROTC:** Army. **Placement/credit:** AP, CLEP General and Subject, institutional tests; 30 credit hours maximum for bachelor's degree.

ACADEMIC REQUIREMENTS. Freshmen must earn minimum GPA of 1.5 to continue in good standing. 77% of freshmen return for sophomore year. Students must declare major by end of second year. **Graduation requirements:** 126 hours for bachelor's. Most students required to take courses in arts/fine arts, English, foreign languages, history, humanities, mathematics, philosophy/religion, biological/physical sciences, social sciences.

FRESHMAN ADMISSIONS. Selection criteria: High school record, class rank, extracurricular activities, test scores. Recommendations and interview strongly encouraged. **High school preparation:** 18 units recommended. Recommended units include English 4, foreign language 2, mathematics 2, social science 2 and science 2. **Test requirements:** SAT or ACT (SAT preferred); score report by July 1.

1992 FRESHMAN CLASS PROFILE. 94 men, 84 women enrolled. 20% had high school GPA of 3.0 or higher, 68% between 2.0 and 2.99. **Academic background:** Mid 50% of enrolled freshmen had SAT-V between 370-480, SAT-M between 390-520. 98% submitted SAT scores. **Characteristics:** 84% from in state, 80% live in college housing, 20% have minority backgrounds, 1% are foreign students, 32% join fraternities/sororities. Average age is 18.

FALL-TERM APPLICATIONS. $15 fee, may be waived for applicants with need. Closing date August 1; applicants notified on a rolling basis; must reply by May 1 or within 4 weeks if notified thereafter. Audition required for music, drama applicants. Portfolio required for art applicants. Interview recommended. CRDA. Deferred and early admission available.

STUDENT LIFE. Housing: Dormitories (men, women, coed). **Activities:** Student government, magazine, radio, student newspaper, yearbook, choral groups, concert band, dance, drama, jazz band, marching band, music ensembles, musical theater, pep band, symphony orchestra, community orchestra, fraternities, sororities, Lutheran Student Movement, Baptist Student Union, Young Republicans, Intervarsity, Fellowship of Christian Athletes, Students Organized for Community Service, South Carolina State Student Legislature.

ATHLETICS. NCAA. **Intercollegiate:** Baseball M, basketball, football M, golf M, softball W, tennis, volleyball W. **Intramural:** Basketball, football M, softball, volleyball W.

STUDENT SERVICES. Aptitude testing, career counseling, employment service for undergraduates, freshman orientation, health services, personal counseling, placement service for graduates, services/facilities for handicapped.

ANNUAL EXPENSES. Tuition and fees (1992-93): $7,900. **Room and board:** $3,100. **Books and supplies:** $450. **Other expenses:** $100.

FINANCIAL AID. 90% of freshmen, 90% of continuing students receive some form of aid. 91% of grants, 95% of loans, 79% of jobs based on need. Academic, music/drama, athletic, leadership, religious affiliation scholarships available. **Aid applications:** Closing date August 1; priority given to applications received by May 1; applicants notified on a rolling basis beginning on or about March 1; must reply by May 1 or within 2 weeks if notified thereafter.

ADDRESS/TELEPHONE. Director of Admissions, Newberry College, 2100 College Street, Newberry, SC 29108. (803) 321-5127. (800) 845-4955. Fax: (803) 321-5232.

Nielsen Electronics Institute
Charleston, South Carolina — CB code: 0340

2-year proprietary technical college, coed. Founded in 1965. **Undergraduate enrollment:** 216 men and women. **Location:** Urban campus in small city; in downtown Charleston. **Calendar:** Quarter.

FRESHMAN ADMISSIONS. Selection criteria: Open admissions.

ADDRESS/TELEPHONE. Gustave Roberts, Nielsen Electronics Institute, 1600 Meeting Street, Charleston, SC 29405. (803) 722-2344.

North Greenville College
Tigerville, South Carolina — CB code: 5498

Admissions: 80% of applicants accepted
Based on:
- ••• School record, test scores
- •• Religious affiliation/commitment, special talents
- • Essay

Completion: 92% of freshmen end year in good standing
35% graduate, 80% of these enter 4-year programs

2-year private junior, liberal arts college, coed, affiliated with Southern Baptist Convention. Founded in 1892. **Accreditation:** Regional. **Undergraduate enrollment:** 305 men, 148 women full time; 18 men, 5 women part time. **Faculty:** 47 total (29 full time), 13 with doctorates or other terminal degrees. **Location:** Rural campus in rural community; 18 miles from Greenville, 54 miles from Ashville. **Calendar:** Semester, limited summer session. **Microcomputers:** 34 located in libraries, computer centers. **Special facilities:** Antique Bible collection. **Additional facts:** Cooperative program where students enroll in work relating to their majors, especially in business and religion.

DEGREES OFFERED. AA, AS, B. 44 associate degrees awarded in 1992. 20% in business and management, 6% teacher education, 5% life sciences, 25% multi/interdisciplinary studies, 5% parks/recreation, protective services, public affairs, 6% physical sciences, 5% social sciences.

UNDERGRADUATE MAJORS. Accounting, allied health, biology, business administration and management, business and office, chemistry, communications, computer and information sciences, education, elementary education, English, fine arts, liberal/general studies, mathematics, music, physical sciences, physics, preengineering, prelaw, premedicine, prenursing, psychology, secondary education, social sciences, speech/communication/theater education, visual and performing arts. religion, religious music.

ACADEMIC PROGRAMS. 2-year transfer program, cooperative education, double major, honors program, independent study. **Remedial services:** Learning center, reduced course load, remedial instruction, special counselor, tutoring, developmental courses. **Placement/credit:** AP, CLEP General and Subject, institutional tests; 12 credit hours maximum for associate degree.

ACADEMIC REQUIREMENTS. Freshmen must earn minimum GPA of 1.25 to continue in good standing. 53% of freshmen return for sophomore year. **Graduation requirements:** 68 hours for associate (18 in major). Most students required to take courses in arts/fine arts, computer science, English, foreign languages, history, humanities, mathematics, philosophy/religion, biological/physical sciences, social sciences. **Additional information:** Limited 4 year bachelor degree programs in church music and religion.

FRESHMAN ADMISSIONS. Selection criteria: SAT/ACT minimum considered in admissions decisions and for PGPA (predicted Grade Point Average) after 1 year. Placement testing available in place of ACT/SAT scores. Automatic admission if SAT-verbal score over 400. Must have state high school diploma or GED. Certificates not allowed. **Test requirements:** Placement examinations waived for those submitting SAT score of 400 or greater on either section. **Additional information:** College Board Computerized Placement Test required for those with less than 400 SAT verbal or predicted 1.7 GPA in freshman year.

1992 FRESHMAN CLASS PROFILE. 632 men and women applied, 508 accepted; 156 men enrolled, 76 women enrolled. 18% had high school GPA of 3.0 or higher, 35% between 2.0 and 2.99. **Academic background:** Mid 50% of enrolled freshmen had SAT-V between 260-410, SAT-M between 300-450. 65% submitted SAT scores. **Characteristics:** 79% from in state, 98% live in college housing, 24% have minority backgrounds, 1% are foreign students. Average age is 19.

FALL-TERM APPLICATIONS. $15 fee, may be waived for applicants with need. Closing date August 20; priority given to applications received by August 1; applicants notified on a rolling basis; must reply within 4 weeks. Audition required for music applicants. Essay required for marginal applicants in English applicants. CRDA. Deferred and early admission available. EDP-F.

STUDENT LIFE. Housing: Dormitories (men, women); apartment housing available. Several modular units available for male students. **Activities:** Student government, student newspaper, yearbook, literary magazine, choral groups, concert band, drama, jazz band, marching band, music ensembles, pep band, Baptist Student Union, Fellowship of Christian Athletes. **Additional information:** Religious observance required.

ATHLETICS. NJCAA. **Intercollegiate:** Baseball M, basketball, football M, golf M, soccer, softball W, tennis M, volleyball W. **Intramural:** Badminton, basketball, bowling, cross-country M, golf, soccer, softball, swimming, table tennis, tennis, track and field, volleyball, water polo M.

STUDENT SERVICES. Aptitude testing, career counseling, freshman orientation, health services, personal counseling, services/facilities for handicapped.

ANNUAL EXPENSES. Tuition and fees (1992-93): $5,900. **Room and board:** $3,400. **Books and supplies:** $500. **Other expenses:** $500.

FINANCIAL AID. 94% of freshmen, 98% of continuing students receive some form of aid. All aid based on need. Academic, music/drama, art, athletic, state/district residency, leadership, alumni affiliation, religious affiliation, minority scholarships available. **Aid applications:** No closing date; priority given to applications received by June 1; applicants notified on a rolling basis beginning on or about June 1; must reply within 2 weeks.

ADDRESS/TELEPHONE. Gary Wells, Executive Director of Admissions, North Greenville College, PO Box 1892, Tigerville, SC 29688-1892. (803) 895-1410 ext. 350. Fax: (803) 895-1410.

Orangeburg-Calhoun Technical College
Orangeburg, South Carolina — CB code: 5527

2-year public technical college, coed. Founded in 1966. **Accreditation:** Regional. **Undergraduate enrollment:** 320 men, 613 women full time; 239 men, 671 women part time. **Location:** Rural campus in large town; 75 miles from Charleston, 45 miles from Columbia. **Calendar:** Semester.

FRESHMAN ADMISSIONS. Selection criteria: Open admissions.

Selective admissions to nursing and allied health programs based on school achievement record, test scores. The college uses ASSET by American College Testing as its course placement instrument. SAT or ACT test may be submitted in place of ASSET tests.

ANNUAL EXPENSES. Tuition and fees: $800, $200 additional for out-of-district students, $400 additional for out-of-state students. **Books and supplies:** $400. **Other expenses:** $500.

ADDRESS/TELEPHONE. Dana Rickards, Field Representative, Orangeburg-Calhoun Technical College, 3250 St. Matthews Road, Orangeburg, SC 29115. (803) 536-0311. Fax: (803) 531-4364.

Piedmont Technical College
Greenwood, South Carolina — CB code: 5550

2-year public community, technical college, coed. Founded in 1966. **Accreditation:** Regional. **Undergraduate enrollment:** 488 men, 836 women full time; 619 men, 804 women part time. **Location:** Suburban campus in large town; 75 miles northwest of Columbia, 50 miles south of Greenville. **Calendar:** Semester.

FRESHMAN ADMISSIONS. Selection criteria: Open admissions. Selective admissions to health science programs.

ANNUAL EXPENSES. Tuition and fees (projected): $975, $225 additional for out-of-district students, $525 additional for out-of-state students. **Books and supplies:** $600. **Other expenses:** $800.

ADDRESS/TELEPHONE. Martha J. Barnette, Director of Admissions, Piedmont Technical College, PO Drawer 1467, Greenwood, SC 29648. (803) 941-8324. (800) 868-5528. Fax: (803) 941-8555.

Presbyterian College
Clinton, South Carolina — CB code: 5540

Admissions: 78% of applicants accepted
Based on:
••• School record, test scores
•• Essay, recommendations
• Activities, interview, special talents
Completion: 90% of freshmen end year in good standing
80% graduate, 35% of these enter graduate study

4-year private liberal arts college, coed, affiliated with Presbyterian Church (USA). Founded in 1880. **Accreditation:** Regional. **Undergraduate enrollment:** 617 men, 550 women full time; 8 men, 9 women part time. **Faculty:** 109 total (74 full time), 72 with doctorates or other terminal degrees. **Location:** Suburban campus in large town; 40 miles from Greenville, 35 miles from Spartanburg. **Calendar:** Semester, limited summer session. **Microcomputers:** 100 located in libraries, classrooms, computer centers. **Special facilities:** 6 buildings on 212-acre campus listed on National Register of Historic Places. Art gallery, scanning electron and transmission microscopes, Brookgreen Gardens ecological research center. **Additional facts:** Academic student exchange with Turku University in Finland; Oxford University summer study program; biology department sponsored ecological research in Australia, Africa, Galapagos Islands, Alaska.

DEGREES OFFERED. BA, BS. 266 bachelor's degrees awarded in 1992. 30% in business and management, 8% teacher education, 7% letters/literature, 11% life sciences, 6% mathematics, 9% psychology, 17% social sciences.

UNDERGRADUATE MAJORS. Accounting, art education, biology, business administration and management, business economics, chemistry, dramatic arts, economics, education, elementary education, English, English education, fine arts, foreign languages (multiple emphasis), foreign languages education, French, German, history, mathematics, mathematics education, music, music education, philosophy and religion, physics, political science and government, psychology, religion, science education, social sciences, social studies education, sociology, Spanish, special education, speech/communication/theater education.

ACADEMIC PROGRAMS. Accelerated program, double major, dual enrollment of high school students, honors program, independent study, internships, study abroad, teacher preparation, Washington semester; liberal arts/career combination in engineering, forestry, health sciences. **ROTC:** Army. **Placement/credit:** AP, CLEP Subject, IB, institutional tests.

ACADEMIC REQUIREMENTS. Freshmen must earn minimum GPA of 1.52 to continue in good standing. 86% of freshmen return for sophomore year. Students must declare major by end of second year. **Graduation requirements:** 122 hours for bachelor's (30 in major). Most students required to take courses in arts/fine arts, English, foreign languages, history, humanities, mathematics, philosophy/religion, biological/physical sciences, social sciences. **Postgraduate studies:** 4% enter law school, 9% enter medical school, 5% enter MBA programs, 17% enter other graduate study. **Additional information:** Honors program Dean's Freshman Honors Seminar, The Great Books Seminar for sophmores, and independent research within a major field of interest for juniors or seniors. Off-campus internships provide students with experience in their area of study.

FRESHMAN ADMISSIONS. Selection criteria: Rigor of high school curriculum most important, followed by test scores and high school recommendation. Extracurricular involvement and interview considered in some cases. **High school preparation:** 16 units required. Required and recommended units include English 4, foreign language 2-3, mathematics 3, social science 2-2 and science 3. Science recommendation includes 2 or more units of laboratory science for science majors. **Test requirements:** SAT or ACT; score report by June 1.

1992 FRESHMAN CLASS PROFILE. 611 men applied, 452 accepted, 187 enrolled; 621 women applied, 506 accepted, 161 enrolled. 85% had high school GPA of 3.0 or higher, 15% between 2.0 and 2.99. 47% were in top tenth and 80% were in top quarter of graduating class. **Academic background:** Mid 50% of enrolled freshmen had SAT-V between 480-560, SAT-M between 530-610; ACT composite between 23-30. 80% submitted SAT scores, 20% submitted ACT scores. **Characteristics:** 41% from in state, 99% live in college housing, 6% have minority backgrounds, 44% join fraternities/sororities. Average age is 17.

FALL-TERM APPLICATIONS. $30 fee, may be waived for applicants with need. Closing date April 1; priority given to applications received by March 15; applicants notified on a rolling basis; must reply by May 1. Essay required. Interview recommended. CRDA. Deferred and early admission available.

STUDENT LIFE. Housing: Dormitories (men, women); apartment, fraternity housing available. Freshmen, sophomores, and juniors required to live on campus. **Activities:** Student government, magazine, radio, student newspaper, yearbook, literary publication, choral groups, concert band, drama, music ensembles, pep band, fraternities, sororities, volunteer organizations in variety of service areas, minority student union, young Democrats and Republicans, interdenominational. **Additional information:** Approximately 75% of all students participate in intramural sports. Students live by an honor code which governs conduct inside and outside the classroom. The Cultural Enrichment Program requires students to attend (40) on-campus cultural events as part of their graduation requirement.

ATHLETICS. NAIA, NCAA. **Intercollegiate:** Baseball M, basketball, cross-country M, football M, golf, rifle, soccer, tennis, track and field, volleyball W. **Intramural:** Basketball, bowling, football M, golf, racquetball, soccer, softball, swimming, table tennis, tennis, volleyball.

STUDENT SERVICES. Aptitude testing, career counseling, employment service for undergraduates, freshman orientation, health services, personal counseling, placement service for graduates, services/facilities for handicapped.

ANNUAL EXPENSES. Tuition and fees: $11,984. **Room and board:** $3,416. **Books and supplies:** $554. **Other expenses:** $916.

FINANCIAL AID. 80% of freshmen, 75% of continuing students receive some form of aid. 57% of grants, 77% of loans, 21% of jobs based on need. 173 enrolled freshmen were judged to have need, all were offered aid. Academic, music/drama, athletic, state/district residency, leadership, religious affiliation, minority scholarships available. **Aid applications:** Closing date June 1; priority given to applications received by March 1; applicants notified on a rolling basis beginning on or about January 1; must reply by May 1 or within 20 days if notified thereafter. **Additional information:** Tuition gift certificates available.

ADDRESS/TELEPHONE. Margaret Williamson, VP Enrollment/Dean of Admis, Presbyterian College, South Broad Street, Clinton, SC 29325-9989. (803) 833-8230. (800) 476-7272. Fax: (803) 833-8481.

South Carolina State University
Orangeburg, South Carolina — CB code: 5618

4-year public university and liberal arts college, coed. Founded in 1896. **Accreditation:** Regional. **Undergraduate enrollment:** 1,810 men, 2,343 women full time; 134 men, 339 women part time. **Graduate enrollment:** 8 men, 30 women full time; 115 men, 292 women part time. **Faculty:** 277 total, 161 with doctorates or other terminal degrees. **Location:** Urban campus in large town; 40 miles from Columbia, 70 miles from Charleston. **Calendar:** Semester, limited summer session. **Microcomputers:** Located in classrooms, computer centers. **Special facilities:** Planetarium.

DEGREES OFFERED. BA, BS, MA, MS, MEd, EdD. 555 bachelor's degrees awarded in 1992. 14% in business and management, 19% business/office and marketing/distribution, 12% teacher education, 11% engineering technologies, 16% parks/recreation, protective services, public affairs, 7% psychology. Graduate degrees offered in 11 major fields of study.

UNDERGRADUATE MAJORS. Accounting, agribusiness, art education, biology, business administration and management, business economics, business education, chemistry, child development/care/guidance, civil technology, computer and information sciences, criminal justice studies, dramatic arts, electrical technology, elementary education, English, English education, fine arts, food production/management/services, food science and nutrition, foreign languages education, French, health education, history, home economics, home economics education, industrial arts education, industrial technology, marketing and distribution, mathematics, mathematics education, mechanical design technology, music, music education, nursing, office supervision and management, physical education, physics, political science and government, prelaw, printmaking, psychology, secondary education, social sciences, social studies education, social work, sociology, Spanish, special education, speech pathology/audiology, speech/communication/theater education.

ACADEMIC PROGRAMS. Cooperative education, dual enrollment of high school students, education specialist degree, honors program, internships, study abroad, visiting/exchange student program, cross-registration; liberal arts/career combination in health sciences. **Remedial services:** Learning center, remedial instruction, tutoring. **ROTC:** Air Force, Army. **Placement/credit:** AP, institutional tests; 30 credit hours maximum for bachelor's degree.

ACADEMIC REQUIREMENTS. Freshmen must earn minimum GPA of 1.4 to continue in good standing. 80% of freshmen return for sophomore year. Students must declare major by end of first year. **Graduation requirements:** 120 hours for bachelor's (72 in major). Most students required to take courses in computer science, English, humanities, mathematics, biological/physical sciences, social sciences. **Postgraduate studies:** 2% enter law school, 2% enter medical school, 2% enter MBA programs, 11% enter other graduate study.

FRESHMAN ADMISSIONS. Selection criteria: Class rank, GPA, SAT scores. **High school preparation:** 16 units required. Required units include English 4, foreign language 2, mathematics 3, social science 3 and science 2. One unit of advanced mathematics, computer science, world history, world geography, or western civilization required. **Test requirements:** SAT or ACT (SAT preferred); score report by July 31.

1992 FRESHMAN CLASS PROFILE. 336 men, 367 women enrolled. 30% had high school GPA of 3.0 or higher, 60% between 2.0 and 2.99. **Characteristics:** 87% from in state, 96% live in college housing, 99% have minority backgrounds. Average age is 18.

FALL-TERM APPLICATIONS. $10 fee. $15 fee for out-of-state applicants. Closing date July 31; applicants notified on a rolling basis; must reply within 2 weeks. Audition required for music education applicants. Portfolio required for art education applicants. Deferred admission available.

STUDENT LIFE. Housing: Dormitories (men, women); apartment housing available. **Activities:** Student government, radio, student newspaper, yearbook, choral groups, concert band, dance, drama, jazz band, marching band, pep band, fraternities, sororities.

ATHLETICS. NCAA. **Intercollegiate:** Basketball, cross-country, football M, golf M, tennis, track and field, volleyball W, wrestling M. **Intramural:** Basketball, softball M.

STUDENT SERVICES. Career counseling, freshman orientation, health services, personal counseling, placement service for graduates, special adviser for adult students, veterans counselor, services/facilities for handicapped.

ANNUAL EXPENSES. Tuition and fees (1992-93): $2,200, $2,180 additional for out-of-state students. **Room and board:** $2,736. **Books and supplies:** $400. **Other expenses:** $700.

FINANCIAL AID. 72% of grants, 82% of jobs based on need. Academic, music/drama, athletic, alumni affiliation, religious affiliation, minority scholarships available. **Aid applications:** No closing date; priority given to applications received by June 1; applicants notified on a rolling basis beginning on or about June 15.

ADDRESS/TELEPHONE. Benny R. Mayfield, Dean of Enrollment Management, South Carolina State University, Orangeburg, SC 29117-0001. (803) 536-7185.

Spartanburg Methodist College

Spartanburg, South Carolina CB code: 5627

Admissions:	75% of applicants accepted
Based on:	••• School record, test scores
	•• Interview, religious affiliation/commitment, special talents
	• Activities, recommendations
Completion:	70% of freshmen end year in good standing
	48% graduate, 87% of these enter 4-year programs

2-year private junior college, coed, affiliated with United Methodist Church. Founded in 1911. **Accreditation:** Regional. **Undergraduate enrollment:** 364 men, 344 women full time; 17 men, 21 women part time. **Faculty:** 54 total (49 full time). **Location:** Suburban campus in small city; 67 miles from Charlotte, North Carolina, 200 miles from Atlanta, Georgia. **Calendar:** Semester, limited summer session. Saturday and extensive evening/early morning classes. **Microcomputers:** 40 located in libraries, computer centers.

DEGREES OFFERED. AA, AS. 171 associate degrees awarded in 1992.

UNDERGRADUATE MAJORS. Chiropractic, criminal justice studies, criminal justice technology, early childhood education, teacher aide.

ACADEMIC PROGRAMS. 2-year transfer program, independent study. **Remedial services:** Learning center, preadmission summer program, remedial instruction, tutoring. **ROTC:** Army. **Placement/credit:** AP, CLEP Subject, institutional tests; 15 credit hours maximum for associate degree.

ACADEMIC REQUIREMENTS. Freshmen must earn minimum GPA of 1.5 to continue in good standing. 65% of freshmen return for sophomore year. Students must declare major on enrollment. **Graduation requirements:** 64 hours for associate (30 in major). Most students required to take courses in English, history, humanities, mathematics, philosophy/religion, biological/physical sciences, social sciences.

FRESHMAN ADMISSIONS. Selection criteria: School record, class rank in top half, combined SAT score of 620. Consideration given to children of alumni and needy applicants. Recommended units include English 4, foreign language 2, mathematics 4, social science 2 and science 2. **Test requirements:** SAT or ACT; score report by August 27.

1992 FRESHMAN CLASS PROFILE. 721 men applied, 531 accepted, 220 enrolled; 560 women applied, 433 accepted, 210 enrolled. 4% were in top tenth and 17% were in top quarter of graduating class. **Characteristics:** 99% from in state, 58% live in college housing, 20% have minority backgrounds, 2% are foreign students. Average age is 18.

FALL-TERM APPLICATIONS. $20 fee, may be waived for applicants with need. No closing date; applicants notified on a rolling basis beginning on or about September 2; must reply by last day to drop/add courses. Interview recommended. Audition recommended. Portfolio recommended. Deferred admission available. Submit application, high school transcript and SAT/ACT scores. Applicant notified of decision within a week.

STUDENT LIFE. Housing: Dormitories (men, women). **Activities:** Student government, student newspaper, yearbook, choral groups, drama, music ensembles, pep band, fraternities, College Christian Movement.

ATHLETICS. NJCAA. **Intercollegiate:** Baseball M, basketball, golf M, soccer, softball W, tennis W, volleyball W. **Intramural:** Basketball, bowling, softball, table tennis, tennis, volleyball.

STUDENT SERVICES. Aptitude testing, career counseling, employment service for undergraduates, freshman orientation, health services, personal counseling, placement service for graduates, veterans counselor.

ANNUAL EXPENSES. Tuition and fees: $5,850. **Room and board:** $3,660. **Books and supplies:** $500. **Other expenses:** $500.

FINANCIAL AID. 83% of freshmen, 76% of continuing students receive some form of aid. 97% of grants, 98% of loans, 42% of jobs based on need. 315 enrolled freshmen were judged to have need, all were offered aid. Academic, music/drama, athletic, state/district residency, leadership, alumni affiliation, religious affiliation scholarships available. **Aid applications:** No closing date; priority given to applications received by June 1; applicants notified on a rolling basis beginning on or about June 1; must reply within 2 weeks.

ADDRESS/TELEPHONE. Kevin Comer, Director of Admissions, Spartanburg Methodist College, 1200 Textile Road, Spartanburg, SC 29301. (803) 587-4212. Fax: (803) 574-6919.

Spartanburg Technical College

Spartanburg, South Carolina CB code: 5668

2-year public technical college, coed. Founded in 1961. **Accreditation:** Regional. **Undergraduate enrollment:** 2,575 men and women. **Faculty:** 201 total (100 full time), 3 with doctorates or other terminal degrees. **Location:** Suburban campus in large town; 4 miles from downtown. **Calendar:** Semester, limited summer session. **Microcomputers:** Located in computer centers.

DEGREES OFFERED. AA, AS, AAS. 236 associate degrees awarded in 1992. 31% in business/office and marketing/distribution, 19% engineering technologies, 27% allied health, 12% trade and industry.

UNDERGRADUATE MAJORS. Accounting, air conditioning/heating/refrigeration mechanics, air conditioning/heating/refrigeration technology, automotive mechanics, automotive technology, business and management, civil technology, computer and information sciences, computer programming, drafting, drafting and design technology, electrical and electronics equipment repair, electronic technology, engineering and engineering-related technologies, horticulture, industrial technology, machine tool operation/machine shop, manufacturing technology, marketing and distribution, mechanical design technology, medical laboratory technologies, medical secretary, nuclear technologies, radiograph medical technology, respiratory therapy technology, secretarial and related programs, technical education.

ACADEMIC PROGRAMS. Cooperative education, double major, independent study, weekend college. **Remedial services:** Learning center, remedial instruction, special counselor, tutoring. **Placement/credit:** Institutional tests.

ACADEMIC REQUIREMENTS. Freshmen must earn minimum GPA of 2.0 to continue in good standing. Students must declare major on enrollment. **Graduation requirements:** 98 hours for associate (45 in major). Most students required to take courses in English, mathematics.

FRESHMAN ADMISSIONS. Selection criteria: Open admissions. Selective admissions to some programs. One biology and/or chemistry and 1 algebra required for most health programs. Algebra required for all engineering and computer programs. **Test requirements:** Test of Adult Basic Education required for admissions. Programmer's Aptitude Test required for computer programming and data processing.

1992 FRESHMAN CLASS PROFILE. 738 men and women enrolled.

FALL-TERM APPLICATIONS. $10 fee. No closing date; applicants notified on a rolling basis; must reply within 2 weeks. Interview required for health program, computer programming, data processing operations, academically weak applicants. Essay recommended. Deferred and early admission available.

STUDENT LIFE. Activities: Student government, radio, student newspaper, television.

ATHLETICS. Intercollegiate: Volleyball M. **Intramural:** Softball, tennis, volleyball.

STUDENT SERVICES. Aptitude testing, career counseling, health services, personal counseling, placement service for graduates, veterans counselor, services/facilities for handicapped.

ANNUAL EXPENSES. Tuition and fees (1992-93): $750, $190 additional for out-of-district students, $750 additional for out-of-state students. **Books and supplies:** $500. **Other expenses:** $600.

FINANCIAL AID. 38% of freshmen, 18% of continuing students receive some form of aid. Grants, loans, jobs available. 202 enrolled freshmen were judged to have need, all were offered aid. **Aid applications:** Closing date May 1; priority given to applications received by February 28; applicants notified on a rolling basis beginning on or about May 1; must reply as soon as possible.

ADDRESS/TELEPHONE. Art Decker, Coordinator of Admissions, Spartanburg Technical College, PO Box 4386, Spartanburg, SC 29305. (803) 591-3800.

Technical College of the Lowcountry
Beaufort, South Carolina — CB code: 5047

2-year public community, technical college, coed. Founded in 1972. **Accreditation:** Regional. **Undergraduate enrollment:** 92 men, 327 women full time; 337 men, 662 women part time. **Faculty:** 67 total (41 full time), 1 with doctorate or other terminal degree. **Location:** Rural campus in large town; 45 miles from Savannah, Georgia, 70 miles from Charleston. **Calendar:** Semester, limited summer session. **Microcomputers:** Located in computer centers. **Additional facts:** Several off-campus extension locations, including Hampton, Hilton Head, Parris Island, and Marine Corps Air Station.

DEGREES OFFERED. AA, AS, AAS. 71 associate degrees awarded in 1992. 8% in business and management, 13% business/office and marketing/distribution, 33% health sciences, 6% law, 11% parks/recreation, protective services, public affairs, 26% trade and industry.

UNDERGRADUATE MAJORS. Air conditioning/heating/refrigeration mechanics, automotive mechanics, business and management, business and office, business computer/console/peripheral equipment operation, business data entry equipment operation, business data processing and related programs, business data programming, computer and information sciences, construction, criminal justice technology, data processing, electrical and electronics equipment repair, electrical/electronics/communications engineering, horticulture, hospitality and recreation marketing, hotel/motel and restaurant management, legal assistant/paralegal, legal secretary, nursing, office supervision and management, secretarial and related programs.

ACADEMIC PROGRAMS. 2-year transfer program, double major, dual enrollment of high school students, independent study, internships, cross-registration. **Remedial services:** Learning center, preadmission summer program, reduced course load, remedial instruction, special counselor, tutoring. **Placement/credit:** AP, CLEP General and Subject, institutional tests. All but 30 hours of credit by examination may be counted toward associate degree.

ACADEMIC REQUIREMENTS. Freshmen must earn minimum GPA of 1.5 to continue in good standing. 30 quarter hours residency required. 50% of freshmen return for sophomore year. Students must declare major on application. **Graduation requirements:** 105 hours for associate. Most students required to take courses in English, mathematics.

FRESHMAN ADMISSIONS. Selection criteria: Open admissions. **Test requirements:** SAT or ACT for placement and counseling only; score report by August 15.

1992 FRESHMAN CLASS PROFILE. 137 men, 125 women enrolled. **Characteristics:** 95% from in state, 100% commute, 34% have minority backgrounds. Average age is 31.

FALL-TERM APPLICATIONS. $15 fee, may be waived for applicants with need. No closing date; applicants notified on a rolling basis beginning on or about May 1. Interview recommended for nursing applicants. Deferred admission available.

STUDENT LIFE. Activities: Student government, student newspaper, Phi Theta Kappa, Rotaract Club, professional societies.

ATHLETICS. Intramural: Tennis.

STUDENT SERVICES. Aptitude testing, career counseling, employment service for undergraduates, personal counseling, placement service for graduates, veterans counselor.

ANNUAL EXPENSES. Tuition and fees (1992-93): $916, $110 additional for out-of-district students, $314 additional for out-of-state students. **Books and supplies:** $410. **Other expenses:** $1,600.

FINANCIAL AID. 55% of freshmen, 45% of continuing students receive some form of aid. All aid based on need. 98 enrolled freshmen were judged to have need, all were offered aid. **Aid applications:** Closing date May 1; applicants notified on a rolling basis beginning on or about July 1.

ADDRESS/TELEPHONE. James Millen, Coordinator of Admissions, Technical College of the Lowcountry, PO Box 1288, 100 Ribaut Road, Beaufort, SC 29902-1288. (803) 525-8324. Fax: (803) 525-8330.

Tri-County Technical College
Pendleton, South Carolina — CB code: 5789

2-year public community, technical college, coed. Founded in 1962. **Accreditation:** Regional. **Undergraduate enrollment:** 873 men, 934 women full time; 551 men, 797 women part time. **Faculty:** 259 total (110 full time), 12 with doctorates or other terminal degrees. **Location:** Rural campus in small town; 5 miles from Clemson. **Calendar:** Semester, limited summer session. **Microcomputers:** 237 located in classrooms, computer centers. **Special facilities:** Ampitheater.

DEGREES OFFERED. AA, AS, AAS. 418 associate degrees awarded in 1992. 17% in business and management, 9% computer sciences, 19% engineering technologies, 19% health sciences, 12% multi/interdisciplinary studies, 19% trade and industry.

UNDERGRADUATE MAJORS. Accounting, air conditioning/heating/refrigeration technology, business and management, business and office, computer programming, data processing, electrical technology, electromechanical technology, electronic technology, industrial equipment maintenance and repair, law enforcement and corrections technologies, liberal/general studies, machine tool operation/machine shop, marketing management, mechanical design technology, medical laboratory technologies, microcomputer software, nursing, quality control technology, radio/television technology, secretarial and related programs, textile technology, veterinarian's assistant.

ACADEMIC PROGRAMS. 2-year transfer program, cooperative education, double major, dual enrollment of high school students, student-designed major, study abroad, visiting/exchange student program. **Remedial services:** Learning center, preadmission summer program, reduced course load, remedial instruction, special counselor, tutoring. **ROTC:** Air Force, Army. **Placement/credit:** AP, CLEP General and Subject, institutional tests.

ACADEMIC REQUIREMENTS. No policy requiring minimum GPA; records of students having academic difficulty are reviewed individually. 65% of freshmen return for sophomore year. Students must declare major on enrollment. **Graduation requirements:** Most students required to take courses in English, humanities, mathematics, social sciences.

FRESHMAN ADMISSIONS. Selection criteria: Open admissions. Selective admissions to nursing (RN), medical laboratory, sugical technology, dental assisting, practical nursing(LPN) and veterinary technology programs. Chemistry, biology, and algebra required for nursing, medical laboratory, practical nursing, surgical technology, dental assisting, and veterinary technology.

1992 FRESHMAN CLASS PROFILE. 316 men, 419 women enrolled. **Characteristics:** 98% from in state, 100% commute, 11% have minority backgrounds. Average age is 26.

FALL-TERM APPLICATIONS. No fee. No closing date; applicants notified on a rolling basis. Interview required. CRDA. Early admission available.

STUDENT LIFE. Activities: Student government, student newspaper, choral groups, Minority Student Association.

STUDENT SERVICES. Aptitude testing, career counseling, employment service for undergraduates, freshman orientation, on-campus day care, personal counseling, placement service for graduates, veterans counselor, services/facilities for handicapped.

ANNUAL EXPENSES. Tuition and fees (1992-93): $762, $690 additional for out-of-state students. **Books and supplies:** $480. **Other expenses:** $1,295.

FINANCIAL AID. 35% of continuing students receive some form of aid. 74% of grants, all loans, all jobs based on need. Academic, leadership scholarships available. **Aid applications:** No closing date; priority given to applications received by June 1; applicants notified on a rolling basis beginning on or about June 15; must reply within 2 weeks.

ADDRESS/TELEPHONE. David Shirley, Assistant Dean of Students, Tri-County Technical College, PO Drawer 587, Pendleton, SC 29670. (803) 646-8361 ext. 2200. Fax: (803) 646-8256.

Trident Technical College
Charleston, South Carolina — CB code: 5049

2-year public community, technical college, coed. Founded in 1964. **Accreditation:** Regional. **Undergraduate enrollment:** 1,405 men, 1,789 women full time; 2,435 men, 3,531 women part time. **Faculty:** 442 total (185 full time), 25 with doctorates or other terminal degrees. **Location:** Urban campus in small city; 10 miles from downtown. **Calendar:** Semester. Saturday and extensive evening/early morning classes. **Microcomputers:** 1,000 located in libraries, classrooms, computer centers. **Special facilities:** Computer Integrated Manufacturing Center.

DEGREES OFFERED. AA, AS. 662 associate degrees awarded in 1992. 14% in business and management, 5% business/office and marketing/

distribution, 8% engineering technologies, 13% health sciences, 15% allied health, 5% law, 27% multi/interdisciplinary studies.

UNDERGRADUATE MAJORS. Accounting, aircraft mechanics, business administration and management, business and management, business and office, business data programming, chemical manufacturing technology, civil technology, computer programming, criminal justice technology, dental hygiene, electronic technology, engineering and engineering-related technologies, graphic arts technology, horticulture, hotel/motel and restaurant management, legal assistant/paralegal, liberal/general studies, manufacturing technology, marketing and distribution, mechanical design technology, medical laboratory technologies, nursing, occupational therapy assistant, physical therapy assistant, precision metal work, radio/television broadcasting, radiograph medical technology, respiratory therapy technology, secretarial and related programs.

ACADEMIC PROGRAMS. 2-year transfer program, accelerated program, cooperative education, double major, dual enrollment of high school students, independent study, internships, cross-registration, 2+2 program with the University of South Carolina's College of Engineering. **Remedial services:** Learning center, reduced course load, remedial instruction, special counselor, tutoring. **Placement/credit:** AP, CLEP General and Subject, institutional tests.

ACADEMIC REQUIREMENTS. Freshmen must earn minimum GPA of 2.0 to continue in good standing. Students must declare major on application. **Graduation requirements:** 90 hours for associate (24 in major). Most students required to take courses in computer science, English, mathematics, social sciences.

FRESHMAN ADMISSIONS. Selection criteria: Open admissions. **Test requirements:** SAT or ACT for placement.

1992 FRESHMAN CLASS PROFILE. 460 men, 652 women enrolled. **Characteristics:** 98% from in state, 100% commute, 24% have minority backgrounds, 1% are foreign students.

FALL-TERM APPLICATIONS. $20 fee. No closing date; applicants notified on a rolling basis. Early admission available. Applicants to early admissions program must rank in upper half of high school class and must have combined SAT score of 800 or ACT composite score of 17.

STUDENT LIFE. Activities: Student government, student newspaper, choral groups, International Club, Disabled Students Association, Phi Theta Kappa, French Club, S.C. Black Student Association.

STUDENT SERVICES. Aptitude testing, career counseling, employment service for undergraduates, freshman orientation, personal counseling, placement service for graduates, veterans counselor, services/facilities for handicapped.

ANNUAL EXPENSES. Tuition and fees (1992-93): $830, $160 additional for out-of-district students, $708 additional for out-of-state students. **Books and supplies:** $650. **Other expenses:** $1,000.

FINANCIAL AID. 63% of continuing students receive some form of aid. 91% of grants, 87% of loans, 52% of jobs based on need. Academic, leadership scholarships available. **Aid applications:** No closing date; priority given to applications received by May 1; applicants notified on a rolling basis beginning on or about August 1; must reply within 6 weeks.

ADDRESS/TELEPHONE. Lynne Ankersen, Director of Admissions, Trident Technical College, PO Box 10367, Charleston, SC 29411. (803) 572-6123. Fax: (803) 572-6109.

University of South Carolina
Columbia, South Carolina — CB code: 5818

Admissions: 82% of applicants accepted
Based on: ••• School record, test scores
• Essay, recommendations, special talents
Completion: 97% of freshmen end year in good standing
56% graduate, 16% of these enter graduate study

4-year public university, coed. Founded in 1801. **Accreditation:** Regional. **Undergraduate enrollment:** 6,435 men, 7,112 women full time; 1,113 men, 1,482 women part time. **Graduate enrollment:** 2,311 men, 2,192 women full time; 1,870 men, 3,956 women part time. **Faculty:** 1,589 total (1,220 full time), 855 with doctorates or other terminal degrees. **Location:** Urban campus in small city; 221 miles from Atlanta, Georgia, 94 miles from Charlotte, North Carolina. **Calendar:** Semester, extensive summer session. Saturday and extensive evening/early morning classes. **Microcomputers:** 1,400 located in libraries, classrooms, computer centers, campus-wide network. **Special facilities:** McKissick Museums (art galleries, archives, geological exhibits, exhibitions of Twentieth Century-Fox Movietone newsreels), Baruch Institute for Marine Biology and Coastal Research, Koger Center for the Arts.

DEGREES OFFERED. BA, BS, BFA, MA, MS, MBA, MFA, MEd, MSW, PhD, EdD, MD, B. Pharm, Pharm D, JD. 3,062 bachelor's degrees awarded in 1992. 23% in business and management, 10% business/office and marketing/distribution, 7% communications, 6% engineering, 6% health sciences, 5% letters/literature, 8% multi/interdisciplinary studies, 6% psychology, 11% social sciences. Graduate degrees offered in 93 major fields of study.

UNDERGRADUATE MAJORS. Accounting, advertising, Afro-American (black) studies, anthropology, art education, art history, biological and physical sciences, biology, business administration and management, business economics, chemical engineering, chemistry, civil engineering, classics, communications, computer and information sciences, computer engineering, criminal justice studies, criminology, dramatic arts, economics, electrical/electronics/communications engineering, English, European studies, exercise science, experimental psychology, film arts, finance, French, geography, geology, geophysics and seismology, German, graphic design, Greek (classical), history, hotel/motel and restaurant management, humanities and social sciences, insurance and risk management, international relations, Italian, journalism, Latin, Latin American studies, liberal/general studies, management science, marine biology, marketing and distribution, mathematics, mechanical engineering, medical laboratory technologies, music, music education, nursing, office supervision and management, pharmacy, philosophy, photography, physical education, physics, political science and government, public relations, radio/television broadcasting, radio/television technology, real estate, religion, retailing, sociology, Spanish, speech, sports management, statistics, studio art, tourism.

ACADEMIC PROGRAMS. Accelerated program, cooperative education, double major, dual enrollment of high school students, education specialist degree, honors program, independent study, internships, student-designed major, study abroad, teacher preparation, telecourses, visiting/exchange student program. **Remedial services:** Learning center, reduced course load, remedial instruction, special counselor, tutoring. **ROTC:** Air Force, Army, Naval. **Placement/credit:** AP, CLEP Subject, institutional tests. Maximum number of semester hours of credit by examination allowed varies according to degree and program of study.

ACADEMIC REQUIREMENTS. Freshmen must earn minimum GPA of 2.0 to continue in good standing. Students suspended when grade points fall 24 points below that required for 2.0. 80% of freshmen return for sophomore year. Students must declare major by end of first year. **Graduation requirements:** 120 hours for bachelor's (24 in major). Most students required to take courses in arts/fine arts, English, foreign languages, history, humanities, mathematics, biological/physical sciences, social sciences.

FRESHMAN ADMISSIONS. Selection criteria: High school courses, grades, rank, and SAT/ACT scores used to determine admission. Student must have minimum 2.0 GPA in 16 core courses for admission. **High school preparation:** 16 units required. Required units include English 4, foreign language 2, mathematics 3, social science 3 and science 2. 2 science laboratory units from biology, chemistry, or physics required. 1 college preparatory elective unit from English, mathematics, social studies, laboratory science, or foreign language required. **Test requirements:** SAT or ACT (SAT preferred); score report by August 1.

1992 FRESHMAN CLASS PROFILE. 3,458 men applied, 2,734 accepted, 1,121 enrolled; 3,873 women applied, 3,259 accepted, 1,305 enrolled. 34% had high school GPA of 3.0 or higher, 64% between 2.0 and 2.99. 24% were in top tenth and 56% were in top quarter of graduating class. **Academic background:** Mid 50% of enrolled freshmen had SAT-V between 390-500, SAT-M between 430-560; ACT composite between 19-25. 98% submitted SAT scores, 1% submitted ACT scores. **Characteristics:** 76% from in state, 76% live in college housing, 26% have minority backgrounds, 1% are foreign students, 25% join fraternities/sororities. Average age is 18.

FALL-TERM APPLICATIONS. $25 fee. Fee may be waived for South Carolina residents with financial need. No closing date; priority given to applications received by February 1; applicants notified on a rolling basis. CRDA.

STUDENT LIFE. Housing: Dormitories (men, women, coed); apartment, fraternity, sorority, handicapped housing available. Some courses taught in residence halls each semester. Special housing available for honors students. **Activities:** Student government, magazine, radio, student newspaper, yearbook, choral groups, concert band, dance, drama, jazz band, marching band, music ensembles, musical theater, opera, pep band, symphony orchestra, fraternities, sororities, Association of Afro-American Students, over 20 religios organizations, 4 political organizations, over 10 service organizations.

ATHLETICS. NCAA. **Intercollegiate:** Baseball M, basketball, cross-country, diving, football M, golf, soccer M, softball W, swimming, tennis, track and field M, volleyball W. **Intramural:** Badminton, basketball, bowling, golf, racquetball, soccer, softball, swimming, table tennis, tennis, track and field, volleyball.

STUDENT SERVICES. Aptitude testing, career counseling, employment service for undergraduates, freshman orientation, health services, on-campus day care, personal counseling, placement service for graduates, special adviser for adult students, veterans counselor, services/facilities for handicapped.

ANNUAL EXPENSES. Tuition and fees: $2,843, $4,228 additional for out-of-state students. **Room and board:** $3,086. **Books and supplies:** $440. **Other expenses:** $910.

FINANCIAL AID. 25% of freshmen, 45% of continuing students receive some form of aid. 35% of grants, 86% of loans, 25% of jobs based on need. 831 enrolled freshmen were judged to have need, 632 were offered aid. Academic, music/drama, art, athletic, state/district residency, leadership, alumni affiliation, minority scholarships available. **Aid applications:** No closing date; priority given to applications received by April 15; applicants notified on a rolling basis beginning on or about May 1; must reply within 2 weeks.

ADDRESS/TELEPHONE. Terry L. Davis, Director of Admissions, University of South Carolina, Lieber College, Columbia, SC 29208. (803) 777-7700. (800) 868-5872. Fax: (803) 777-0101.

University of South Carolina at Aiken
Aiken, South Carolina CB code: 5840

4-year public liberal arts college, coed. Founded in 1961. **Accreditation:** Regional. **Undergraduate enrollment:** 746 men, 1,146 women full time; 415 men, 900 women part time. **Graduate enrollment:** 550 men and women. **Faculty:** 232 total (110 full time), 113 with doctorates or other terminal degrees. **Location:** Suburban campus in large town; 15 miles from Augusta, Georgia, 55 miles from Columbia. **Calendar:** Semester, limited summer session. **Microcomputers:** 100 located in computer centers. **Special facilities:** Etherredge Fine Arts Center, Ruth Patrick Science Center.

DEGREES OFFERED. AA, AS, BA, BS, M. 70 associate degrees awarded in 1992. 90% in health sciences, 10% parks/recreation, protective services, public affairs. 310 bachelor's degrees awarded. 31% in business and management, 23% teacher education, 22% health sciences. Graduate degrees offered in 1 major field of study.

UNDERGRADUATE MAJORS. Associate: Criminal justice studies, law enforcement and corrections technologies, nursing. **Bachelor's:** Accounting, biology, business administration and management, business and management, business economics, chemistry, community services, computer mathematics, early childhood education, economics, education, elementary education, English, English education, finance, history, humanities and social sciences, junior high education, liberal/general studies, marketing and distribution, mathematics education, nursing, physical education, political science and government, prelaw, psychology, science education, secondary education, social science education, social studies education, social work, sociology, sports management.

ACADEMIC PROGRAMS. 2-year transfer program, accelerated program, cooperative education, double major, dual enrollment of high school students, education specialist degree, honors program, independent study, internships, student-designed major, teacher preparation, cross-registration; combined bachelor's/graduate program in business administration. **Remedial services:** Reduced course load, tutoring, mathematics and writing laboratories. **ROTC:** Army. **Placement/credit:** AP, CLEP Subject, institutional tests; 30 credit hours maximum for bachelor's degree.

ACADEMIC REQUIREMENTS. Freshmen must earn minimum GPA of 1.2 to continue in good standing. 40% of freshmen return for sophomore year. Students must declare major by end of second year. **Graduation requirements:** 60 hours for associate, 120 hours for bachelor's. Most students required to take courses in English, foreign languages, history, mathematics, biological/physical sciences, social sciences. **Postgraduate studies:** 27% from 2-year programs enter 4-year programs.

FRESHMAN ADMISSIONS. Selection criteria: Class rank, test scores, GPA important. Interview, school recommendation also considered. **High school preparation:** 16 units required. Required units include biological science 1, English 4, foreign language 2, mathematics 3, physical science 1 and social science 3. Physical education or ROTC, 2 units laboratory science, 1 unit computer science or advanced mathematics also required. **Test requirements:** SAT or ACT (SAT preferred); score report by August 1.

1992 FRESHMAN CLASS PROFILE. 281 men, 456 women enrolled. **Academic background:** Mid 50% of enrolled freshmen had SAT-V between 350-450, SAT-M between 350-450. 95% submitted SAT scores. **Characteristics:** 80% from in state, 90% commute, 19% have minority backgrounds, 1% join fraternities/sororities. Average age is 19.

FALL-TERM APPLICATIONS. $25 fee, may be waived for applicants with need. Closing date August 20; priority given to applications received by August 1; applicants notified on a rolling basis. Interview recommended. Audition recommended. Portfolio recommended. Essay recommended. Deferred and early admission available.

STUDENT LIFE. Housing: Apartment housing available. Privately owned and operated fully furnished apartments available on-campus. **Activities:** Student government, magazine, radio, student newspaper, choral groups, concert band, dance, drama, musical theater, pep band, fraternities, sororities, Campus Crusade for Christ, honor societies, Student Alummi Association, Pacer Union Board, High Adventure Club.

ATHLETICS. NCAA. **Intercollegiate:** Baseball M, basketball, cross-country, golf M, soccer M, softball W, tennis, volleyball W. **Intramural:** Basketball, softball, table tennis, tennis, volleyball, wrestling M.

STUDENT SERVICES. Aptitude testing, career counseling, employment service for undergraduates, freshman orientation, on-campus day care, personal counseling, placement service for graduates, special adviser for adult students, veterans counselor, services/facilities for handicapped.

ANNUAL EXPENSES. Tuition and fees (1992-93): $2,145, $3,180 additional for out-of-state students. **Books and supplies:** $440. **Other expenses:** $910.

FINANCIAL AID. 40% of freshmen, 39% of continuing students receive some form of aid. 46% of grants, 94% of loans, 39% of jobs based on need. 175 enrolled freshmen were judged to have need, 150 were offered aid. Academic, music/drama, athletic, state/district residency, leadership scholarships available. **Aid applications:** No closing date; priority given to applications received by March 15; applicants notified on a rolling basis beginning on or about May 30; must reply within 2 weeks.

ADDRESS/TELEPHONE. Randy R. Duckett, Associate Dean of Students, University of South Carolina at Aiken, 171 University Parkway, Aiken, SC 29801. (803) 641-3366. Fax: (803) 641-3516.

University of South Carolina at Beaufort
Beaufort, South Carolina CB code: 5845

2-year public branch campus college, coed. Founded in 1959. **Accreditation:** Regional. **Undergraduate enrollment:** 1,040 men and women. **Faculty:** 63 total (23 full time), 11 with doctorates or other terminal degrees. **Location:** Urban campus in large town; 72 miles from Charleston, 42 miles from Savannah, Georgia. **Calendar:** Semester, limited summer session. **Microcomputers:** Located in computer centers. **Special facilities:** Pritchard's Island, a 1600-acre undeveloped island used for research, instruction, and as a center for the Loggerhead Sea Turtle Conservation Project.

DEGREES OFFERED. AA, AS. 80 associate degrees awarded in 1992. 100% in multi/interdisciplinary studies.

UNDERGRADUATE MAJORS. Liberal/general studies.

ACADEMIC PROGRAMS. 2-year transfer program, dual enrollment of high school students, honors program, independent study, student-designed major, telecourses, cross-registration. **Remedial services:** Learning center, remedial instruction, tutoring. **Placement/credit:** CLEP Subject, institutional tests; 30 credit hours maximum for associate degree.

ACADEMIC REQUIREMENTS. Freshmen must earn minimum GPA of 2.0 to continue in good standing. Freshmen must pass 50% of course credits to continue in good standing. 75% of freshmen return for sophomore year. **Graduation requirements:** 60 hours for associate. Most students required to take courses in English, history, mathematics, biological/physical sciences, social sciences. **Additional information:** Bachelor's degrees in early childhood education and business management offered in association with University of South Carolina at Aiken.

FRESHMAN ADMISSIONS. Selection criteria: SAT or ACT, rank in class important. Minimum 2.0 GPA. **High school preparation:** 14 units recommended. Recommended units include English 4, foreign language 2, mathematics 3, social science 3 and science 2. 2 additional units from any recommended subject area. Computer course recommended. **Test requirements:** SAT or ACT (SAT preferred); score report by August 25.

1992 FRESHMAN CLASS PROFILE. 132 men and women enrolled. **Characteristics:** 99% from in state, 100% commute, 30% have minority backgrounds. Average age is 18.

FALL-TERM APPLICATIONS. $25 fee. No closing date; applicants notified on a rolling basis beginning on or about July 1. Deferred and early admission available.

STUDENT LIFE. Activities: Student government, student newspaper, yearbook, Gamma Beta Phi Honors Society, Black Student Organization.

ATHLETICS. Intramural: Basketball, bowling, golf, softball, tennis.

STUDENT SERVICES. Aptitude testing, career counseling, employment service for undergraduates, freshman orientation, personal counseling, veterans counselor, services/facilities for handicapped.

ANNUAL EXPENSES. Tuition and fees (1992-93): $1,425, $2,200 additional for out-of-state students. **Books and supplies:** $440. **Other expenses:** $910.

FINANCIAL AID. 80% of freshmen, 51% of continuing students receive some form of aid. Grants, loans, jobs available. Academic scholarships available. **Aid applications:** No closing date; priority given to applications received by April 15; applicants notified on a rolling basis beginning on or about June 1; must reply within 2 weeks.

ADDRESS/TELEPHONE. Anita M. Folsom, Director of Admissions, University of South Carolina at Beaufort, 800 Carteret Street, Beaufort, SC 29902. (803) 521-4100. Fax: (803) 521-4198.

University of South Carolina: Coastal Carolina College
Conway, South Carolina CB code: 5837

Admissions:	67% of applicants accepted
Based on:	••• School record
	•• Recommendations, test scores
	• Activities, interview, special talents
Completion:	85% of freshmen end year in good standing
	40% enter graduate study

4-year public liberal arts college, coed. Founded in 1954. **Accreditation:** Regional. **Undergraduate enrollment:** 1,459 men, 1,654 women full time; 316 men, 594 women part time. **Faculty:** 253 total (176 full time), 119 with doctorates or other terminal degrees. **Location:** Suburban campus in small city; 9 miles from Myrtle Beach. **Calendar:** Semester, extensive summer session. Extensive evening/early morning classes. **Microcomputers:** 110 located in classrooms, computer centers. **Additional facts:** Unique marine science program with local waterfront laboratory for conducting extensive research projects.

DEGREES OFFERED. BA, BS. 55 associate degrees awarded in 1992. 58% in health sciences, 42% multi/interdisciplinary studies. 508 bachelor's degrees awarded in 1992. 31% in business and management, 29% teacher education, 6% letters/literature, 6% life sciences, 8% psychology, 10% social sciences.

UNDERGRADUATE MAJORS. Accounting, applied mathematics, art education, biology, business administration and management, business and management, computer and information sciences, dramatic arts, early childhood education, education, elementary education, English, English education, finance, history, liberal/general studies, marine biology, marketing management, mathematics education, music education, physical education, political science and government, predentistry, prelaw, premedicine, prepharmacy, preveterinary, psychology, real estate, secondary education, social studies education, sociology, studio art.

ACADEMIC PROGRAMS. Accelerated program, double major, dual enrollment of high school students, honors program, independent study, internships, student-designed major, study abroad, teacher preparation, cross-registration. **Remedial services:** Learning center, preadmission summer program, reduced course load, remedial instruction, special counselor, tutoring. **Placement/credit:** AP, CLEP Subject, institutional tests; 30 credit hours maximum for bachelor's degree.

ACADEMIC REQUIREMENTS. Freshmen must earn minimum GPA of 2.0 to continue in good standing. 70% of freshmen return for sophomore year. Students must declare major by end of second year. **Graduation requirements:** 120 hours for bachelor's. Most students required to take courses in arts/fine arts, computer science, English, foreign languages, history, humanities, mathematics, philosophy/religion, biological/physical sciences, social sciences.

FRESHMAN ADMISSIONS. Selection criteria: High school record, class rank most important (predictive GPA ratio used). Test scores considered (mathematics second, verbal first in priority). **High school preparation:** 21 units required. Required units include English 4, foreign language 2, mathematics 3, social science 3 and science 2. **Test requirements:** SAT or ACT; score report by August 15.

1992 FRESHMAN CLASS PROFILE. 1,628 men and women applied, 1,090 accepted; 307 men enrolled, 328 women enrolled. 9% were in top tenth and 30% were in top quarter of graduating class. **Characteristics:** 84% from in state, 80% commute, 12% have minority backgrounds, 1% are foreign students, 8% join fraternities/sororities. Average age is 19.

FALL-TERM APPLICATIONS. $25 fee, may be waived for applicants with need. Closing date August 15; applicants notified on a rolling basis. Audition required for music education applicants. Interview recommended. Deferred and early admission available.

STUDENT LIFE. Housing: Dormitories (coed); apartment housing available. **Activities:** Student government, magazine, student newspaper, yearbook, choral groups, dance, drama, jazz band, music ensembles, musical theater, pep band, fraternities, sororities, Afro-American organization, Alpha Phi Omega, Omicrom Delta Kappa, Sigma Phi Epsilon, Fellowship of Christian Athletes.

ATHLETICS. NCAA. **Intercollegiate:** Baseball M, basketball, cross-country, golf, soccer M, softball W, tennis, track and field, volleyball W. **Intramural:** Badminton, basketball, cross-country, golf, handball, racquetball, soccer, softball, tennis, volleyball.

STUDENT SERVICES. Aptitude testing, career counseling, employment service for undergraduates, freshman orientation, health services, personal counseling, placement service for graduates, special adviser for adult students, veterans counselor, services/facilities for handicapped.

ANNUAL EXPENSES. Tuition and fees: $2,195, $3,254 additional for out-of-state students. **Room and board:** $2,390 room only. **Books and supplies:** $440. **Other expenses:** $910.

FINANCIAL AID. 45% of freshmen, 47% of continuing students receive some form of aid. 44% of jobs based on need. Academic, athletic, leadership, minority scholarships available. **Aid applications:** Closing date April 1; applicants notified on a rolling basis; must reply by May 1.

ADDRESS/TELEPHONE. Ed Cerny, Director of Admissions, University of South Carolina: Coastal Carolina College, PO Box 1954, Conway, SC 29526. (803) 349-2026. (800) 277-7000. Fax: (803) 349-2127.

University of South Carolina at Lancaster

Lancaster, South Carolina — CB code: 5849

2-year public branch campus college, coed. Founded in 1959. **Accreditation:** Regional. **Undergraduate enrollment:** 1,031 men and women. **Location:** Urban campus in large town; 50 miles north of Columbia, South Carolina; 40 miles south of Charlotte, North Carolina. **Calendar:** Semester.

FRESHMAN ADMISSIONS. Selection criteria: Open admissions. School achievement record, test scores, and recommendations considered for 2-year transfer program applicants. Special consideration given minority applicants.

ANNUAL EXPENSES. Tuition and fees: $1,425, $2,200 additional for out-of-state students. **Books and supplies:** $440. **Other expenses:** $910.

ADDRESS/TELEPHONE. Barbara M. Watkins, Associate Dean Administration, University of South Carolina at Lancaster, PO Box 889, Lancaster, SC 29721. (803) 285-7471. Fax: (803) 285-4348.

University of South Carolina: Salkehatchie Regional Campus

Allendale, South Carolina — CB code: 5847

2-year public branch campus college, coed. Founded in 1965. **Accreditation:** Regional. **Undergraduate enrollment:** 137 men, 275 women full time; 207 men, 414 women part time. **Faculty:** 35 total (21 full time), 14 with doctorates or other terminal degrees. **Location:** Rural campus in small town; 82 miles from Columbia, 80 miles from Charleston. **Calendar:** Semester, limited summer session. **Microcomputers:** 50 located in computer centers. **Special facilities:** College-operated civic arts center.

DEGREES OFFERED. AA, AS. 84 associate degrees awarded in 1992. 100% in multi/interdisciplinary studies.

UNDERGRADUATE MAJORS. Liberal/general studies.

ACADEMIC PROGRAMS. 2-year transfer program, dual enrollment of high school students, independent study, student-designed major, study abroad, cross-registration. **Remedial services:** Learning center, preadmission summer program, reduced course load, remedial instruction, tutoring. **Placement/credit:** AP, CLEP Subject, institutional tests; 15 credit hours maximum for associate degree.

ACADEMIC REQUIREMENTS. Freshmen must earn minimum GPA of 2.0 to continue in good standing. 60% of freshmen return for sophomore year. Students must declare major by end of first year. **Graduation requirements:** 60 hours for associate. Most students required to take courses in English, mathematics, biological/physical sciences, social sciences.

FRESHMAN ADMISSIONS. Selection criteria: Open admissions. **High school preparation:** 20 units recommended. Recommended units include English 4, foreign language 2, mathematics 3, social science 3 and science 2. **Test requirements:** SAT or ACT (SAT preferred) for placement and counseling only; score report by August 20.

1992 FRESHMAN CLASS PROFILE. 86 men, 164 women enrolled. 15% had high school GPA of 3.0 or higher, 65% between 2.0 and 2.99. 15% were in top tenth and 65% were in top quarter of graduating class. **Academic background:** Mid 50% of enrolled freshmen had SAT-V between 300-350, SAT-M between 340-380. 75% submitted SAT scores. **Characteristics:** 99% from in state, 100% commute, 32% have minority backgrounds. Average age is 22.

FALL-TERM APPLICATIONS. $25 fee, may be waived for applicants with need. No closing date; priority given to applications received by August 24; applicants notified on a rolling basis.

STUDENT LIFE. Activities: Student government, student newspaper, choral groups, drama, Black Student Union.

ATHLETICS. NJCAA. **Intercollegiate:** Baseball M, basketball M. **Intramural:** Basketball, soccer, softball W, table tennis, tennis, volleyball.

STUDENT SERVICES. Career counseling, freshman orientation, personal counseling, veterans counselor, services/facilities for handicapped.

ANNUAL EXPENSES. Tuition and fees: $1,425, $2,200 additional for out-of-state students. **Books and supplies:** $440. **Other expenses:** $910.

FINANCIAL AID. 52% of freshmen, 62% of continuing students receive some form of aid. 83% of grants, 86% of loans, 68% of jobs based on need. 194 enrolled freshmen were judged to have need, all were offered aid. Academic, athletic, state/district residency scholarships available. **Aid applications:** No closing date; priority given to applications received by April 15; applicants notified on a rolling basis beginning on or about June 1; must reply within 2 weeks.

ADDRESS/TELEPHONE. Jane Brewer, Associate Dean for Student Services, University of South Carolina: Salkehatchie Regional Campus, PO Box 617, Allendale, SC 29810. (803) 584-3446. Fax: (803) 584-5038.

University of South Carolina at Spartanburg

Spartanburg, South Carolina — CB code: 5850

Admissions: 58% of applicants accepted
Based on: ••• School record, test scores
• Recommendations
Completion: 75% of freshmen end year in good standing

4-year public university, coed. Founded in 1967. **Accreditation:** Regional. **Undergraduate enrollment:** 944 men, 1,455 women full time; 419 men, 721 women part time. **Faculty:** 239 total (164 full time), 114 with doctorates or other terminal degrees. **Location:** Suburban campus in small city; 65 miles from Charlotte, North Carolina, 30 miles from Greenville. **Calendar:** Semester, extensive summer session. **Microcomputers:** 160 located in libraries, computer centers. **Special facilities:** Performing arts building, including 450-seat theater, arts studies film theater, recital hall, language laboratory, Quality Institute. **Additional facts:** Located near foothills of Blue Ridge Mountains on 298-acre campus.

DEGREES OFFERED. AS, BA, BS. 73 associate degrees awarded in 1992. 100% in health sciences. 435 bachelor's degrees awarded. 29% in business and management, 15% teacher education, 9% health sciences, 7% letters/literature, 14% multi/interdisciplinary studies, 8% psychology, 13% social sciences.

UNDERGRADUATE MAJORS. Associate: Nursing. **Bachelor's:** Biology, business administration and management, chemistry, communications, computer and information sciences, criminal justice studies, early childhood education, elementary education, English, history, international studies, liberal/general studies, mathematics, nursing, physical education, political science and government, psychology, secondary education, sociology.

ACADEMIC PROGRAMS. Dual enrollment of high school students, independent study, student-designed major, study abroad, teacher preparation, visiting/exchange student program, cross-registration. **Remedial services:** Learning center, reduced course load, special counselor, tutoring. **ROTC:** Army. **Placement/credit:** AP, CLEP Subject, institutional tests; 30 credit hours maximum for bachelor's degree.

ACADEMIC REQUIREMENTS. Freshmen must earn minimum GPA of 1.5 to continue in good standing. 72% of freshmen return for sophomore year. Students must declare major by end of second year. **Graduation requirements:** 65 hours for associate (38 in major), 120 hours for bachelor's (80 in major). Most students required to take courses in arts/fine arts, computer science, English, history, humanities, mathematics, biological/physical sciences, social sciences.

FRESHMAN ADMISSIONS. Selection criteria: 2.0 high school GPA, combined 700 SAT or 18 ACT scores very important. **High school preparation:** 20 units required. Required units include biological science 1, English 4, foreign language 2, mathematics 3, physical science 1 and social science 3. Students must also offer 1 unit of physical education or ROTC, and 1 unit selected from advanced mathematics, computer science, world history, world geography, or western civilization. **Test requirements:** SAT or ACT (SAT preferred); score report by August 15.

1992 FRESHMAN CLASS PROFILE. 375 men applied, 226 accepted, 170 enrolled; 638 women applied, 363 accepted, 259 enrolled. 41% had high school GPA of 3.0 or higher, 56% between 2.0 and 2.99. **Academic background:** Mid 50% of enrolled freshmen had SAT-V between 350-460, SAT-M between 380-490. 87% submitted SAT scores. **Characteristics:** 95% from in state, 85% commute, 16% have minority backgrounds, 1% are foreign students, 2% join fraternities/sororities. Average age is 20.

FALL-TERM APPLICATIONS. $25 fee. No closing date; priority given to applications received by August 15; applicants notified on a rolling basis beginning on or about October 1. CRDA. Deferred and early admission available.

STUDENT LIFE. Housing: Apartment housing available. Privately-owned and managed on-campus apartment housing available for 400 undergraduates. **Activities:** Student government, film, magazine, student newspaper, television, yearbook, video, choral groups, dance, drama, jazz band, pep band, fraternities, sororities, Afro-American Association, Student Nurses Association, Baptist Student Union, Political Awareness Club, paraprofessional advisement and leadership staff, Honors Society, professional fraternities, Literary Society.

ATHLETICS. NCAA. **Intercollegiate:** Baseball M, basketball, cross-country M, soccer M, softball W, tennis, volleyball W. **Intramural:** Archery, baseball M, basketball, bowling, cross-country, handball, racquetball, skiing, soccer, softball, table tennis, tennis, track and field, volleyball.

STUDENT SERVICES. Aptitude testing, career counseling, employment service for undergraduates, freshman orientation, health services, on-campus day care, personal counseling, placement service for graduates, special adviser for adult students, veterans counselor, services/facilities for handicapped.

ANNUAL EXPENSES. Tuition and fees (1992-93): $2,145, $3,180 additional for out-of-state students. Privately owned apartments available on campus at $795 per semester. Meal plan available. **Books and supplies:** $440. **Other expenses:** $910.

FINANCIAL AID. 43% of freshmen, 43% of continuing students receive some form of aid. 73% of grants, all loans, 47% of jobs based on need. Academic, music/drama, athletic, state/district residency, leadership, minority scholarships available. **Aid applications:** Closing date July 1; priority given to applications received by April 15; applicants notified on a rolling basis beginning on or about June 1; must reply within 2 weeks. **Additional information:** Tuition waivers for children of disabled or deceased South Carolina resident service personnel. Out-of-state students receiving minimum $250 per semester scholarship pay in-state fees.

ADDRESS/TELEPHONE. Donette Stewart, Director of Admissions, University of South Carolina at Spartanburg, 800 University Way, Spartanburg, SC 29303. (803) 599-2246. Fax: (803) 599-2375.

University of South Carolina at Sumter
Sumter, South Carolina CB code: 5821

2-year public branch campus college, coed. Founded in 1966. **Accreditation:** Regional. **Undergraduate enrollment:** 307 men, 520 women full time; 273 men, 400 women part time. **Faculty:** 93 total (53 full time), 34 with doctorates or other terminal degrees. **Location:** Urban campus in large town; 47 miles from Columbia. **Calendar:** Semester, limited summer session. **Microcomputers:** 38 located in libraries, computer centers. **Additional facts:** Upper-division courses leading to degree in business administration, education, or interdisciplinary studies available; degree conferred under auspices of other University of South Carolina system campuses.

DEGREES OFFERED. AA, AS. 237 associate degrees awarded in 1992. 100% in multi/interdisciplinary studies.

UNDERGRADUATE MAJORS. Liberal/general studies.

ACADEMIC PROGRAMS. 2-year transfer program, dual enrollment of high school students, cross-registration. **Remedial services:** Remedial instruction, special counselor, tutoring. **Placement/credit:** AP, institutional tests; 30 credit hours maximum for associate degree.

ACADEMIC REQUIREMENTS. Freshmen must earn minimum GPA of 2.0 to continue in good standing. **Graduation requirements:** 60 hours for associate. Most students required to take courses in English, foreign languages, humanities, mathematics, biological/physical sciences, social sciences.

FRESHMAN ADMISSIONS. Selection criteria: Test scores and class rank. Entering freshman must have 2.15 GPA. **High school preparation:** 20 units required. Required units include English 4, foreign language 2, mathematics 3, social science 3 and science 2. **Test requirements:** SAT or ACT; score report by August 20. **Additional information:** All freshmen required to take writing proficieny test, the Nelson Denny Reading Test, and foreign language test. Placement in mathematics may require additional testing.

1992 FRESHMAN CLASS PROFILE. Characteristics: 99% from in state, 100% commute, 17% have minority backgrounds, 2% are foreign students. Average age is 21.

FALL-TERM APPLICATIONS. $25 fee, may be waived for applicants with need. No closing date; priority given to applications received by August 20; applicants notified on a rolling basis. Interview required for academically marginal applicants. Limited concurrent enrollment for high school seniors available.

STUDENT LIFE. Activities: Student government, student newspaper, choral groups, drama, Gospel Choir, Afro-American, Apeiron, Baptist student clubs, campus activities board, Circle K, Student Art Guild, Student Education Association, Student Government Association, Wargamers, Student Nursing Organization.

ATHLETICS. Intramural: Badminton, basketball, bowling, golf, racquetball, soccer M, softball, table tennis, tennis, volleyball.

STUDENT SERVICES. Aptitude testing, career counseling, employment service for undergraduates, freshman orientation, personal counseling, veterans counselor, services/facilities for handicapped.

ANNUAL EXPENSES. Tuition and fees: $1,425, $2,200 additional for out-of-state students. **Books and supplies:** $440. **Other expenses:** $910.

FINANCIAL AID. 33% of freshmen, 38% of continuing students receive some form of aid. 80% of grants, 97% of loans, 84% of jobs based on need. Academic, minority scholarships available. **Aid applications:** No closing date; priority given to applications received by April 15; applicants notified on a rolling basis beginning on or about June 15; must reply within 2 weeks.

ADDRESS/TELEPHONE. William R. Ferrell III, PhD, Director of Enrollment Management, University of South Carolina at Sumter, Miller Road, Sumter, SC 29150. (803) 775-6341 ext. 3288. Fax: (803) 775-2170.

University of South Carolina at Union
Union, South Carolina CB code: 5846

2-year public branch campus college, coed. Founded in 1965. **Accreditation:** Regional. **Undergraduate enrollment:** 432 men and women. **Faculty:** 40 total (15 full time), 12 with doctorates or other terminal degrees. **Location:** Rural campus in large town; 30 miles from Spartanburg, 60 miles from Columbia. **Calendar:** Semester, limited summer session. Saturday and extensive evening/early morning classes. **Microcomputers:** Located in computer centers. **Additional facts:** Off-campus site at Laurens offers full range of courses.

DEGREES OFFERED. AA, AS. 25 associate degrees awarded in 1992. 100% in multi/interdisciplinary studies.

UNDERGRADUATE MAJORS. Liberal/general studies.

ACADEMIC PROGRAMS. 2-year transfer program, dual enrollment of high school students, independent study, internships, student-designed major, telecourses, cross-registration. **Remedial services:** Preadmission summer program, reduced course load, remedial instruction, special counselor, tutoring. **Placement/credit:** AP, CLEP Subject, institutional tests.

ACADEMIC REQUIREMENTS. No policy requiring minimum GPA; records of students having academic difficulty are reviewed individually. 60% of freshmen return for sophomore year. **Graduation requirements:** 60 hours for associate. Most students required to take courses in English, humanities, mathematics, social sciences. **Additional information:** Upper division courses leading to bachelor's degree in interdisciplinary studies available. Degree awarded by Columbia campus.

FRESHMAN ADMISSIONS. Selection criteria: Successful completion of high school course requirements. **High school preparation:** 20 units required. Required units include English 4, foreign language 2, mathematics 3, social science 3 and science 2. **Test requirements:** SAT or ACT for placement. **Additional information:** Students with high school diploma or GED but without required high school curriculum units may be admitted into Opportunity Program based on school achievement record and SAT or ACT scores.

1992 FRESHMAN CLASS PROFILE. 300 men and women enrolled. **Characteristics:** 99% from in state, 100% commute, 17% have minority backgrounds. Average age is 22.

FALL-TERM APPLICATIONS. $25 fee, may be waived for applicants with need. No closing date; applicants notified on a rolling basis beginning on or about June 1.

STUDENT LIFE. Activities: Student government, magazine, student newspaper, drama, pep band, music club, Afro-American and political groups, student media association, computer club, history club, art club, travel club, music club, biology club.

ATHLETICS. Intercollegiate: Basketball M, softball W. **Intramural:** Baseball, basketball, bowling, gymnastics, racquetball, skiing, softball, table tennis, tennis, volleyball. **Clubs:** Skiing, hiking, sailing.

STUDENT SERVICES. Aptitude testing, career counseling, employment service for undergraduates, freshman orientation, on-campus day care, personal counseling, special adviser for adult students, services/facilities for handicapped.

ANNUAL EXPENSES. Tuition and fees: $1,425, $2,200 additional for out-of-state students. **Books and supplies:** $440. **Other expenses:** $910.

FINANCIAL AID. 70% of freshmen, 90% of continuing students receive some form of aid. Grants, loans, jobs available. 110 enrolled freshmen were judged to have need, all were offered aid. Academic scholarships available. **Aid applications:** Closing date August 15; priority given to applications received by May 15; applicants notified on a rolling basis beginning on or about July 15.

ADDRESS/TELEPHONE. Terry Young, Director of Enrollment Services, University of South Carolina at Union, PO Drawer 729, 401 East Main Street, Union, SC 29379. (803) 429-8728. (800) 768-5566. Fax: (803) 427-3682.

Voorhees College
Denmark, South Carolina — CB code: 5863

4-year private liberal arts college, coed, affiliated with Episcopal Church. Founded in 1897. **Accreditation:** Regional. **Undergraduate enrollment:** 278 men, 354 women full time; 8 men, 25 women part time. **Faculty:** 33 total (29 full time), 14 with doctorates or other terminal degrees. **Location:** Rural campus in small town; 50 miles from Columbia. **Calendar:** Semester, extensive summer session. **Microcomputers:** 70 located in libraries, classrooms, computer centers.

DEGREES OFFERED. BS. 72 bachelor's degrees awarded in 1992.

UNDERGRADUATE MAJORS. Biology, business administration and management, computer and information sciences, criminal justice studies, mathematics, political science and government, sociology.

ACADEMIC PROGRAMS. Cooperative education, honors program, independent study, internships. **Remedial services:** Learning center, reduced course load, remedial instruction, special counselor, tutoring. **ROTC:** Army. **Placement/credit:** Institutional tests.

ACADEMIC REQUIREMENTS. Freshmen must earn minimum GPA of 2.0 to continue in good standing. 40% of freshmen return for sophomore year. Students must declare major by end of second year. **Graduation requirements:** 78 hours for associate, 122 hours for bachelor's. Most students required to take courses in computer science, English, history, mathematics, philosophy/religion, biological/physical sciences, social sciences. **Postgraduate studies:** 50% from 2-year programs enter 4-year programs.

FRESHMAN ADMISSIONS. Selection criteria: Open admissions. **High school preparation:** 20 units recommended. Recommended units include English 4, foreign language 2, mathematics 3, physical science 2 and social science 2. 7 additional electives also recommended. **Test requirements:** SAT or ACT for placement and counseling only; score report by August 22.

1992 FRESHMAN CLASS PROFILE. 117 men, 147 women enrolled. **Characteristics:** 90% from in state, 95% live in college housing, 99% have minority backgrounds, 1% are foreign students. Average age is 18.

FALL-TERM APPLICATIONS. $10 fee. No closing date; applicants notified on a rolling basis; must reply within 2 weeks. Deferred admission available.

STUDENT LIFE. Housing: Dormitories (men, women). **Activities:** Student government, student newspaper, yearbook, choral groups, dance, drama, pep band, fraternities, sororities.

ATHLETICS. NAIA. **Intercollegiate:** Baseball M, basketball, cross-country, softball W, track and field, volleyball W. **Intramural:** Basketball, softball W, tennis.

STUDENT SERVICES. Aptitude testing, career counseling, employment service for undergraduates, health services, personal counseling, placement service for graduates, special adviser for adult students, services/facilities for handicapped.

ANNUAL EXPENSES. Tuition and fees: $4,250. **Room and board:** $2,522. **Books and supplies:** $500. **Other expenses:** $1,500.

FINANCIAL AID. 96% of freshmen, 94% of continuing students receive some form of aid. 93% of grants, all loans, all jobs based on need. 204 enrolled freshmen were judged to have need, all were offered aid. Academic scholarships available. **Aid applications:** No closing date; applicants notified on a rolling basis beginning on or about June 15; must reply within 2 weeks.

ADDRESS/TELEPHONE. Samuel Blackwell, Director of Admissions and Recruitment, Voorhees College, Voorhees Road, Denmark, SC 29042. (803) 793-3351. Fax: (803) 793-4584.

Williamsburg Technical College
Kingstree, South Carolina — CB code: 5892

2-year public community, technical college, coed. Founded in 1969. **Accreditation:** Regional. **Undergraduate enrollment:** 27 men, 96 women full time; 130 men, 309 women part time. **Faculty:** 38 total (12 full time), 1 with doctorate or other terminal degree. **Location:** Rural campus in small town; 75 miles from Charleston, 40 miles from Florence. **Calendar:** Semester, limited summer session. Extensive evening/early morning classes. **Microcomputers:** 50 located in libraries, classrooms, computer centers.

DEGREES OFFERED. AA, AS. 34 associate degrees awarded in 1992. 37% in business and management, 10% business/office and marketing/distribution, 7% engineering technologies, 33% letters/literature, 33% multi/interdisciplinary studies, 13% trade and industry.

UNDERGRADUATE MAJORS. Biological and physical sciences, business and management, drafting, liberal/general studies, machine tool operation/machine shop, occupational safety and health technology, secretarial and related programs.

ACADEMIC PROGRAMS. 2-year transfer program, dual enrollment of high school students, honors program, telecourses. **Remedial services:** Learning center, remedial instruction, tutoring. **Placement/credit:** AP, CLEP Subject; 18 credit hours maximum for associate degree.

ACADEMIC REQUIREMENTS. Freshmen must earn minimum GPA of 2.0 to continue in good standing. 30% of freshmen return for sophomore year. Students must declare major on enrollment. **Graduation requirements:** 65 hours for associate. Most students required to take courses in computer science, English, mathematics.

FRESHMAN ADMISSIONS. Selection criteria: Open admissions. **Additional information:** Academically weak students must enroll in Applied Studies Program.

1992 FRESHMAN CLASS PROFILE. 44 men, 81 women enrolled. **Characteristics:** 100% from in state, 100% commute, 43% have minority backgrounds.

FALL-TERM APPLICATIONS. $10 fee. No closing date; applicants notified on a rolling basis.

STUDENT LIFE. Activities: Student government.

STUDENT SERVICES. Career counseling, placement service for graduates, veterans counselor, services/facilities for handicapped.

ANNUAL EXPENSES. Tuition and fees: $600. **Books and supplies:** $400.

FINANCIAL AID. 43% of freshmen, 48% of continuing students receive some form of aid. All grants, all jobs based on need. Academic, state/district residency, leadership scholarships available. **Aid applications:** Closing date May 1; applicants notified on a rolling basis; must reply within 1 week in most cases. **Additional information:** Certain requests for deferment of tuition payment may be honored.

ADDRESS/TELEPHONE. Donald W. Melton, Admissions Coordinator, Williamsburg Technical College, 601 Lane Road, Kingstree, SC 29556-4197. (803) 354-2021 ext. 27. (803) 354-7269.

Winthrop University
Rock Hill, South Carolina — CB code: 5910

Admissions: 73% of applicants accepted
Based on:
••• School record, test scores
•• Essay, recommendations
• Activities, interview, special talents
Completion: 88% of freshmen end year in good standing
44% graduate

4-year public university, coed. Founded in 1886. **Accreditation:** Regional. **Undergraduate enrollment:** 1,101 men, 2,406 women full time; 187 men, 413 women part time. **Graduate enrollment:** 116 men, 191 women full time; 194 men, 417 women part time. **Faculty:** 420 total (297 full time), 264 with doctorates or other terminal degrees. **Location:** Urban campus in large town; 23 miles from Charlotte, North Carolina. **Calendar:** Semester, extensive summer session. **Microcomputers:** 250 located in classrooms, computer centers. **Special facilities:** Rutledge Art Galleries, Winthrop Woods, MacFeat Nursery Laboratory.

DEGREES OFFERED. BA, BS, BFA, MA, MS, MBA, MFA, MEd. 676 bachelor's degrees awarded in 1992. 31% in business and management, 6% communications, 20% teacher education, 7% psychology, 10% social sciences, 11% visual and performing arts. Graduate degrees offered in 22 major fields of study.

UNDERGRADUATE MAJORS. Art history, biology, business administration and management, business education, chemistry, communications, computer and information sciences, dance, dramatic arts, early childhood education, elementary education, English, fine arts, food science and nutrition, foreign languages (multiple emphasis), history, home economics, home economics education, marketing and distributive education, mathematics, medical laboratory technologies, music, music education, music performance, philosophy, physical education, political science and government, psychology, religion, social work, sociology, special education, speech.

ACADEMIC PROGRAMS. Cooperative education, double major, dual enrollment of high school students, education specialist degree, honors program, independent study, internships, study abroad, teacher preparation, telecourses, visiting/exchange student program, United Nations semester, cross-registration. **Remedial services:** Preadmission summer program, special counselor, tutoring. **Placement/credit:** AP, CLEP Subject, institutional tests; 30 credit hours maximum for bachelor's degree.

ACADEMIC REQUIREMENTS. Freshmen must earn minimum GPA of 1.4 to continue in good standing. 75% of freshmen return for sophomore year. Students must declare major by end of first year. **Graduation requirements:** 124 hours for bachelor's (30 in major). Most students required to take courses in English, foreign languages, history, humanities, mathematics, philosophy/religion, biological/physical sciences, social sciences.

FRESHMAN ADMISSIONS. Selection criteria: School achievement record, test scores, counselor recommendations, school and community activities. **High school preparation:** 16 units required. Required units include English 4, foreign language 2, mathematics 3, social science 3 and science 2. Mathematics must include algebra I and II. Science must include 2 laboratory science. Social sciences must include 1 unit of US history, 2 units social studies. One unit of physical education or ROTC, 1 unit from advanced mathematics, computer science, world history, world geography, or western civilizations required. **Test requirements:** SAT or ACT (SAT preferred); score report by May 1.

1992 FRESHMAN CLASS PROFILE. 2,172 men and women applied, 1,576 accepted; 189 men enrolled, 616 women enrolled. 22% were in top tenth and 62% were in top quarter of graduating class. **Academic background:** Mid 50% of enrolled freshmen had SAT-V between 410-520, SAT-M between 450-550; ACT composite between 16-20. 89% submitted SAT scores, 11% submitted ACT scores. **Characteristics:** 85% from in state, 88% live in college housing, 24% have minority backgrounds, 1% are foreign students. Average age is 18.

FALL-TERM APPLICATIONS. $35 fee, may be waived for applicants with need. Closing date May 1; must reply by May 1. Audition required for music applicants. Interview recommended. Portfolio recommended for art applicants. Essay recommended. CRDA. 7 monthly notification dates for fall between November and May on the 21st of the month.

STUDENT LIFE. Housing: Dormitories (men, women, coed); apartment, fraternity, sorority housing available. **Activities:** Student government, magazine, student newspaper, yearbook, choral groups, concert band, dance, drama, jazz band, music ensembles, musical theater, pep band, symphony orchestra, chamber ensemble, opera workshop, fraternities, sororities, campus ministries, state student legislature, Christian fellowship, Ebonites, Democratic and Republican clubs, Council for Exceptional Children, SADD. **Additional information:** 102 clubs and organizations.

ATHLETICS. NCAA. **Intercollegiate:** Baseball M, basketball, cross-country, golf, soccer M, softball W, tennis, track and field, volleyball W. **Intramural:** Badminton, basketball, cross-country, football M, golf, handball, racquetball, soccer, softball, swimming, tennis, volleyball.

STUDENT SERVICES. Career counseling, employment service for undergraduates, freshman orientation, health services, personal counseling, placement service for graduates, special adviser for adult students, veterans counselor, language center, math center, writing center, services/facilities for handicapped.

ANNUAL EXPENSES. Tuition and fees (1992-93): $3,116, $2,400 additional for out-of-state students. **Room and board:** $3,132. **Books and supplies:** $440. **Other expenses:** $775.

FINANCIAL AID. 68% of freshmen, 47% of continuing students receive some form of aid. 63% of grants, 86% of loans, 22% of jobs based on need. 326 enrolled freshmen were judged to have need, 313 were offered aid. Academic, music/drama, art, athletic scholarships available. **Aid applications:** No closing date; priority given to applications received by May 1; applicants notified on a rolling basis beginning on or about March 30; must reply within 3 weeks. **Additional information:** Academic scholarships ranging from half tuition to full tuition are awarded to approximately one third of the entering freshman class each year.

ADDRESS/TELEPHONE. James Black, Dean of Enrollment Management, Winthrop University, 701 Oakland Avenue, Rock Hill, SC 29733. (803) 323-2191. Fax: (803) 323-2137.

Wofford College

Spartanburg, South Carolina — CB code: 5912

Admissions: 77% of applicants accepted
Based on: ••• School record
•• Essay, test scores
• Activities, interview, recommendations, special talents
Completion: 92% of freshmen end year in good standing
70% graduate, 31% of these enter graduate study

4-year private liberal arts college, coed, affiliated with United Methodist Church. Founded in 1854. **Accreditation:** Regional. **Undergraduate enrollment:** 661 men, 425 women full time; 23 men, 18 women part time. **Faculty:** 80 total (64 full time), 58 with doctorates or other terminal degrees. **Location:** Urban campus in small city; 70 miles from Charlotte, North Carolina, 180 miles from Atlanta, Georgia. **Calendar:** 4-1-4, limited summer session. **Microcomputers:** 130 located in libraries, classrooms, computer centers. **Special facilities:** Franklin W. Olin building, housing departments of foreign languages, mathematics, computer science, and education, incorporates advanced video and computer technology.

DEGREES OFFERED. BA, BS. 287 bachelor's degrees awarded in 1992. 23% in business and management, 6% languages, 14% letters/literature, 11% life sciences, 5% multi/interdisciplinary studies, 8% psychology, 22% social sciences.

UNDERGRADUATE MAJORS. Accounting, art history, biology, business economics, chemistry, computer mathematics, economics, English, finance, French, German, history, humanities, intercultural studies, mathematics, philosophy, physics, political philosophy and economy, political science and government, predentistry, prelaw, premedicine, prepharmacy, preveterinary, psychology, religion, sociology, Spanish.

ACADEMIC PROGRAMS. Accelerated program, cooperative education, double major, dual enrollment of high school students, honors program, independent study, internships, student-designed major, study abroad, teacher preparation, cross-registration, Presidential International Scholar program; liberal arts/career combination in engineering, health sciences. **Remedial services:** Tutoring, reading and writing laboratory. **ROTC:** Army. **Placement/credit:** AP, CLEP Subject, institutional tests; 30 credit hours maximum for bachelor's degree.

ACADEMIC REQUIREMENTS. Freshmen must earn minimum GPA of 1.8 to continue in good standing. 89% of freshmen return for sophomore year. Students must declare major by end of second year. **Graduation requirements:** 124 hours for bachelor's (31 in major). Most students required to take courses in arts/fine arts, English, foreign languages, history, humanities, mathematics, philosophy/religion, biological/physical sciences, social sciences. **Postgraduate studies:** 5% enter law school, 8% enter medical school, 4% enter MBA programs, 14% enter other graduate study. **Additional information:** January Interim Program devoted to internships, foreign travel, independent study, and other nontraditional academic pursuits.

FRESHMAN ADMISSIONS. Selection criteria: Most applicants rank in top fifth of class. Test scores important. School recommendation, leadership, extracurricular activities considered. Minority applications encouraged. **High school preparation:** 16 units required. Required units include English 4, foreign language 2, mathematics 4, social science 2 and science 3. **Test requirements:** SAT or ACT; score report by February 1.

1992 FRESHMAN CLASS PROFILE. 766 men applied, 545 accepted, 156 enrolled; 543 women applied, 457 accepted, 133 enrolled. 90% had high school GPA of 3.0 or higher, 10% between 2.0 and 2.99. 41% were in top tenth and 78% were in top quarter of graduating class. **Academic background:** Mid 50% of enrolled freshmen had SAT-V between 450-570, SAT-M between 500-600; ACT composite between 22-26. 90% submitted SAT scores, 10% submitted ACT scores. **Characteristics:** 67% from in state, 93% live in college housing, 11% have minority backgrounds, 52% join fraternities/sororities. Average age is 18.

FALL-TERM APPLICATIONS. May be waived for applicants with need. Closing date February 1; priority given to applications received by December 1; applicants notified on or about March 15; must reply by May 1. Essay required. Interview recommended. CRDA. Deferred and early admission available. Institutional early decision plan. Regular application deadline February 1; notification, March 1.

STUDENT LIFE. Housing: Dormitories (men, women); fraternity housing available. **Activities:** Student government, magazine, student newspaper, yearbook, choral groups, drama, music ensembles, musical theater, pep band, fraternities, sororities, Wesley Fellowship, Baptist Student Union, Association of African-American Students, Student Volunteer Services, Young Democrats and Republicans, Phi Beta Kappa. **Additional information:** Many student-initiated activities, such as fencing club, Wofford Theater Workshop.

ATHLETICS. NCAA. **Intercollegiate:** Baseball M, basketball, cross-country, football M, golf M, soccer M, tennis, volleyball W. **Intramural:** Basketball, bowling, racquetball, softball, table tennis, tennis, volleyball. **Clubs:** Fencing, rifle.

STUDENT SERVICES. Aptitude testing, career counseling, employment service for undergraduates, freshman orientation, health services,

personal counseling, placement service for graduates, veterans counselor, services/facilities for handicapped.

ANNUAL EXPENSES. Tuition and fees: $11,480. **Room and board:** $4,150. **Books and supplies:** $585. **Other expenses:** $915.

FINANCIAL AID. 70% of freshmen, 75% of continuing students receive some form of aid. 51% of grants, 94% of loans, 49% of jobs based on need. 180 enrolled freshmen were judged to have need, all were offered aid. Academic, music/drama, athletic, leadership, religious affiliation, minority scholarships available. **Aid applications:** No closing date; priority given to applications received by March 15; applicants notified on a rolling basis beginning on or about March 15; must reply by May 1 or within 2 weeks if notified thereafter.

ADDRESS/TELEPHONE. Charles H. Gray, Director of Admissions, Wofford College, 429 North Church Street, Spartanburg, SC 29303-3663. (803) 597-4130. Fax: (803) 597-4149.

York Technical College
Rock Hill, South Carolina — CB code: 5989

2-year public technical college, coed. Founded in 1962. **Accreditation:** Regional. **Undergraduate enrollment:** 1,441 men and women full time; 1,901 men and women part time. **Faculty:** 250 total (150 full time). **Location:** Suburban campus in large town; 18 miles from Charlotte, North Carolina. **Calendar:** Semester, extensive summer session. Saturday and extensive evening/early morning classes. **Microcomputers:** 125 located in computer centers. **Additional facts:** Member of Charlotte Area Consortium of Colleges and Universities.

DEGREES OFFERED. AA, AS, AAS. 359 associate degrees awarded in 1992.

UNDERGRADUATE MAJORS. Accounting, air conditioning/heating/refrigeration mechanics, air conditioning/heating/refrigeration technology, automotive mechanics, automotive technology, business and management, business and office, civil technology, clinical laboratory science, computer programming, computer servicing technology, computer technology, dental hygiene, diesel engine mechanics, drafting and design technology, electrical and electronics equipment repair, electromechanical technology, electronic technology, industrial equipment maintenance and repair, industrial technology, machine tool operation/machine shop, mechanical design technology, medical laboratory technologies, nursing, office supervision and management, radiograph medical technology, secretarial and related programs.

ACADEMIC PROGRAMS. 2-year transfer program, dual enrollment of high school students, honors program, weekend college. **Remedial services:** Learning center, reduced course load, remedial instruction, special counselor, tutoring. **Placement/credit:** AP, CLEP Subject, institutional tests.

ACADEMIC REQUIREMENTS. Freshmen must earn minimum GPA of 2.0 to continue in good standing. Students must declare major on application. **Graduation requirements:** 60 hours for associate. Most students required to take courses in English, mathematics, social sciences.

FRESHMAN ADMISSIONS. Selection criteria: Open admissions. Selective admission to nursing and human services program. One chemistry course required for admission into dental hygiene and nursing programs. **Additional information:** Institutional exams used for placement.

1992 FRESHMAN CLASS PROFILE. 334 men, 367 women enrolled. **Characteristics:** 100% commute, 17% have minority backgrounds. Average age is 26.

FALL-TERM APPLICATIONS. No fee. No closing date; applicants notified on a rolling basis.

STUDENT LIFE. Activities: Student government, student newspaper, Phi Theta Kappa.

STUDENT SERVICES. Aptitude testing, career counseling, employment service for undergraduates, freshman orientation, on-campus day care, personal counseling, placement service for graduates, veterans counselor, women's center, services/facilities for handicapped.

ANNUAL EXPENSES. Tuition and fees: $615, $123 additional for out-of-district students, $615 additional for out-of-state students. **Books and supplies:** $450.

FINANCIAL AID. 38% of freshmen, 38% of continuing students receive some form of aid. 98% of grants, 95% of loans, all jobs based on need. Academic scholarships available. **Aid applications:** No closing date; priority given to applications received by March 31; applicants notified on a rolling basis.

ADDRESS/TELEPHONE. Kenny Aldridge, Admissions Officer, York Technical College, 452 South Anderson Road, Rock Hill, SC 29730. (803) 327-8008. Fax: (803) 327-8059.

South Dakota

Augustana College
Sioux Falls, South Dakota — CB code: 6015

Admissions: 95% of applicants accepted
Based on: ••• School record, test scores
•• Activities, interview, recommendations
• Essay, religious affiliation/commitment, special talents
Completion: 90% of freshmen end year in good standing
60% graduate, 30% of these enter graduate study

4-year private liberal arts college, coed, affiliated with Evangelical Lutheran Church in America. Founded in 1860. **Accreditation:** Regional. **Undergraduate enrollment:** 558 men, 934 women full time; 97 men, 187 women part time. **Graduate enrollment:** 1 man, 2 women full time; 9 men, 27 women part time. **Faculty:** 142 total (109 full time), 82 with doctorates or other terminal degrees. **Location:** Suburban campus in small city; 160 miles from Omaha, Nebraska, 230 miles from Minneapolis-St. Paul. **Calendar:** 4-1-4, extensive summer session. **Microcomputers:** 146 located in libraries, classrooms, computer centers. **Special facilities:** Center for Western Studies (museum, archives, special art and literary collections), Eide-Darlymple Gallery, Bicentennial Prairie Garden and Heritage Park, Berdahl-Rolvaag House. **Additional facts:** New College, a center for adult learners.

DEGREES OFFERED. AA, BA, MA. 3 associate degrees awarded in 1992. 100% in multi/interdisciplinary studies. 364 bachelor's degrees awarded. 19% in business and management, 7% communications, 17% education, 13% health sciences, 8% letters/literature, 9% life sciences, 5% psychology, 8% social sciences. Graduate degrees offered in 13 major fields of study.

UNDERGRADUATE MAJORS. Associate: Aviation management, business data programming, library assistant. **Bachelor's:** Accounting, applied mathematics, art education, biochemistry, biological and physical sciences, biology, biophysics, business administration and management, business and management, business economics, chemistry, city/community/regional planning, classics, communications, comparative literature, computer and information sciences, dramatic arts, early childhood education, earth sciences, economics, education, education of the culturally disadvantaged, education of the deaf and hearing impaired, education of the emotionally handicapped, education of the mentally handicapped, education of the multiple handicapped, education of the physically handicapped, elementary education, engineering and other disciplines, engineering physics, English, English education, environmental science, fine arts, foreign languages education, French, geography, German, Greek (classical), health care administration, health education, history, humanities and social sciences, information sciences and systems, international relations, journalism, junior high education, liberal/general studies, mathematics, mathematics education, medical laboratory technologies, music, music education, nursing, philosophy, physical education, physics, political science and government, predentistry, preengineering, prelaw, premedicine, prepharmacy, preveterinary, psychology, religion, science education, secondary education, social studies education, social work, sociology, Spanish, special education, specific learning disabilities, speech, speech correction, speech pathology/audiology, speech/communication/theater education.

ACADEMIC PROGRAMS. Accelerated program, double major, dual enrollment of high school students, honors program, independent study, internships, student-designed major, study abroad, teacher preparation, cross-registration; liberal arts/career combination in engineering, health sciences. **Remedial services:** Learning center, preadmission summer program, reduced course load, remedial instruction, special counselor, tutoring, fall foundation program for freshmen on probation. **Placement/credit:** AP, CLEP Subject, IB, institutional tests; 32 credit hours maximum for bachelor's degree.

ACADEMIC REQUIREMENTS. Freshmen must earn minimum GPA of 1.6 to continue in good standing. 80% of freshmen return for sophomore year. Students must declare major by end of second year. **Graduation requirements:** 65 hours for associate (30 in major), 130 hours for bachelor's (36 in major). Most students required to take courses in arts/fine arts, computer science, English, foreign languages, history, humanities, mathematics, philosophy/religion, biological/physical sciences, social sciences. **Postgraduate studies:** 10% enter law school, 10% enter medical school, 5% enter MBA programs, 5% enter other graduate study.

FRESHMAN ADMISSIONS. Selection criteria: School record, class rank, test scores, college entrance examinations, and 2 recommendations required. **High school preparation:** 14 units recommended. Recommended units include biological science 2, English 4, foreign language 2, mathematics 3, physical science 1 and social science 2. **Test requirements:** SAT or ACT (ACT preferred); score report by September 1.

1992 FRESHMAN CLASS PROFILE. 731 men and women applied, 694 accepted; 132 men enrolled, 262 women enrolled. 68% had high school GPA of 3.0 or higher, 30% between 2.0 and 2.99. 17% were in top tenth and 52% were in top quarter of graduating class. **Academic background:** Mid 50% of enrolled freshmen had SAT-V between 420-550, SAT-M between 390-640; ACT composite between 21-26. 7% submitted SAT scores, 87% submitted ACT scores. **Characteristics:** 55% from in state, 75% live in college housing, 3% have minority backgrounds, 3% are foreign students. Average age is 18.

FALL-TERM APPLICATIONS. $25 fee. Closing date August 15; priority given to applications received by February 15; applicants notified on a rolling basis; must reply by May 1 or within 10 days if notified thereafter. Audition required for music applicants. Interview recommended. Portfolio recommended for art applicants. Deferred and early admission available.

STUDENT LIFE. Housing: Dormitories (coed); apartment housing available. **Activities:** Student government, magazine, radio, student newspaper, yearbook, choral groups, concert band, drama, jazz band, music ensembles, musical theater, pep band, symphony orchestra, Lutheran-ELCA congregation, Christian Athletes, Circle-K, Young Democrats, College Republicans, community service board, Environmental Club, International Students Club.

ATHLETICS. NCAA. **Intercollegiate:** Baseball M, basketball, cross-country, football M, softball W, tennis, track and field, volleyball W, wrestling M. **Intramural:** Basketball, bowling, handball, racquetball, skiing, softball, swimming, tennis, volleyball.

STUDENT SERVICES. Aptitude testing, career counseling, employment service for undergraduates, freshman orientation, health services, on-campus day care, personal counseling, placement service for graduates, special adviser for adult students, veterans counselor, services/facilities for handicapped.

ANNUAL EXPENSES. Tuition and fees: $10,300. **Room and board:** $3,120. **Books and supplies:** $600. **Other expenses:** $800.

FINANCIAL AID. 85% of freshmen, 85% of continuing students receive some form of aid. 87% of loans, 86% of jobs based on need. 308 enrolled freshmen were judged to have need, all were offered aid. Academic, music/drama, art, athletic, state/district residency, leadership, alumni affiliation, religious affiliation scholarships available. **Aid applications:** No closing date; priority given to applications received by April 15; applicants notified on a rolling basis beginning on or about April 1; must reply within 2 weeks.

ADDRESS/TELEPHONE. Susan Bies, Director of Admissions, Augustana College, 29th and Summit Avenue, Sioux Falls, SD 57197-9990. (605) 336-5516. (800) 727-2844. Fax: (605) 336-4903.

Black Hills State University
Spearfish, South Dakota — CB code: 6042

4-year public liberal arts, teachers college, coed. Founded in 1883. **Accreditation:** Regional. **Undergraduate enrollment:** 951 men, 1,334 women full time; 192 men, 288 women part time. **Graduate enrollment:** 2 men, 2 women full time; 10 men, 35 women part time. **Faculty:** 103 total (94 full time), 49 with doctorates or other terminal degrees. **Location:** Rural campus in small town; 45 miles from Rapid City, in Black Hills. **Calendar:** Semester, extensive summer session. **Microcomputers:** 200 located in dormitories, libraries, classrooms. **Special facilities:** E. Y. Berry Congressional Library, Leland D. Case Library for Western Historical Studies, Donald E. Young Sport and Fitness Center. **Additional facts:** Evening degree program available at Ellsworth Air Force Base campus in Rapid City.

DEGREES OFFERED. AA, AS, BA, BS, MS. 39 associate degrees awarded in 1992. 209 bachelor's degrees awarded. 20% in business and management, 8% communications, 31% education, 9% psychology, 11% social sciences, 5% trade and industry. Graduate degrees offered in 2 major fields of study.

UNDERGRADUATE MAJORS. Associate: Business and office, drafting, graphic arts technology, hospitality and recreation marketing, hotel/motel and restaurant management, liberal/general studies, public relations, radio/television broadcasting, radio/television technology, secretarial and related programs. **Bachelor's:** Accounting, art education, biological and physical sciences, biology, business administration and management, business and management, business education, chemistry, commercial art, communications, community services, dramatic arts, education, elementary education, English, English education, fine arts, foreign languages education, geriatric services, gerontology, graphic arts technology, health education, health sciences, history, hospitality and recreation marketing, hotel/motel and restaurant management, humanities and social sciences, industrial arts education, journalism, law enforcement and corrections, library assistant, library science, marketing and distribution, marketing management, mathematics, mathematics education, mental health/human services, music, music education, music performance, music theory and composition, physical education, physical sciences, political science and government, prelaw, psychology, public relations, radio/television broadcasting, science education, secondary education, secretarial and related programs, social science education, social sciences, social studies education, sociology, Spanish, special education, speech, speech/communication/theater education, tourism, trade and industrial education, visual and performing arts.

ACADEMIC PROGRAMS. 2-year transfer program, cooperative education, double major, dual enrollment of high school students, independent study, internships, cross-registration; liberal arts/career combination in health sciences. **Remedial services:** Learning center, preadmission summer program, reduced course load, remedial instruction, special counselor, tutoring. **ROTC:** Army. **Placement/credit:** AP, CLEP Subject, institutional tests; 32 credit hours maximum for bachelor's degree.

ACADEMIC REQUIREMENTS. Freshmen must earn minimum GPA of 2.0 to continue in good standing. 45% of freshmen return for sophomore year. Students must declare major by end of second year. **Graduation requirements:** 64 hours for associate (42 in major), 128 hours for bachelor's (48 in major). Most students required to take courses in arts/fine arts, English, history, humanities, mathematics, biological/physical sciences, social sciences. **Postgraduate studies:** 41% from 2-year programs enter 4-year programs. 1% enter law school, 1% enter medical school, 1% enter MBA programs, 1% enter other graduate study.

FRESHMAN ADMISSIONS. Selection criteria: Open admissions. Open admissions to associate degree programs. For bachelor's degree programs, minimum ACT composite score of 20 or class rank in top two-thirds (in-state applicants), top half (out-of-state applicants), or minimum GPA 2.0 in requi. **High school preparation:** 13 units required. Required units include English 4, mathematics 3, social science 3 and science 3. .5 fine arts, .5 computer science. **Test requirements:** SAT or ACT (ACT preferred); score report by October 1.

1992 FRESHMAN CLASS PROFILE. 375 men applied, 375 accepted, 248 enrolled; 516 women applied, 516 accepted, 318 enrolled. 5% were in top tenth and 18% were in top quarter of graduating class. **Academic background:** Mid 50% of enrolled freshmen had ACT composite between 18-23. 98% submitted ACT scores. **Characteristics:** 74% from in state, 57% live in college housing, 10% have minority backgrounds, 1% are foreign students, 5% join fraternities/sororities. Average age is 19.

FALL-TERM APPLICATIONS. $15 fee. No closing date; priority given to applications received by August 1; applicants notified on a rolling basis. Audition required for music applicants. Interview recommended. Portfolio recommended for art applicants. CRDA. Deferred and early admission available.

STUDENT LIFE. Housing: Dormitories (men, women, coed). Off-campus housing list provided by Residence Life Office. **Activities:** Student government, radio, student newspaper, yearbook, choral groups, concert band, dance, drama, jazz band, music ensembles, musical theater, pep band, fraternities, sororities, Native American Special Services, Inter-Greek Council, United Ministry, Veterans Club, Young Democrats, Young Republicans.

ATHLETICS. NAIA. **Intercollegiate:** Basketball, cross-country, football M, track and field, volleyball W. **Intramural:** Archery, badminton, basketball, bowling, golf, gymnastics, racquetball, rugby, skiing, soccer, softball, swimming, table tennis, tennis, volleyball.

STUDENT SERVICES. Aptitude testing, career counseling, employment service for undergraduates, freshman orientation, health services, on-campus day care, personal counseling, placement service for graduates, veterans counselor, services/facilities for handicapped.

ANNUAL EXPENSES. Tuition and fees (projected): $2,012, $1,560 additional for out-of-state students. Minnesota and Wyoming residents pay in-state tuition. Reduced out-of-state tuition for Western Undergraduate Exchange students. **Room and board:** $2,504. **Books and supplies:** $500. **Other expenses:** $1,250.

FINANCIAL AID. 76% of freshmen, 70% of continuing students receive some form of aid. 94% of grants, 91% of loans, 55% of jobs based on need. 314 enrolled freshmen were judged to have need, 304 were offered aid. Academic, music/drama, art, athletic, state/district residency, leadership, minority scholarships available. **Aid applications:** No closing date; priority given to applications received by April 1; applicants notified on a rolling basis beginning on or about May 15; must reply by June 1 or within 2 weeks if notified thereafter. **Additional information:** Out-of-state students may qualify for resident tuition. Wyoming and Minnesota students pay the same as South Dakota. College participates in Western Undergraduate Exchange Program.

ADDRESS/TELEPHONE. April Meeker, Director of Admissions and Records, Black Hills State University, 1200 University Avenue, Spearfish, SD 57799-9502. (605) 642-6343. (800) 255-2478. Fax: (605) 642-6214.

Dakota State University
Madison, South Dakota — CB code: 6247

Admissions: 88% of applicants accepted
Based on: ••• School record, test scores
• Activities, recommendations
Completion: 93% of freshmen end year in good standing
3% enter graduate study

4-year public university, coed. Founded in 1881. **Accreditation:** Regional. **Undergraduate enrollment:** 470 men, 642 women full time; 61 men, 331 women part time. **Faculty:** 68 total (55 full time), 23 with doctorates or other terminal degrees. **Location:** Rural campus in small town; 50 miles from Sioux Falls. **Calendar:** Semester, limited summer session. **Microcomputers:** 184 located in dormitories, libraries, classrooms, computer centers, campus-wide network. **Special facilities:** Smith-Zimmerman Museum.

DEGREES OFFERED. AA, AS, AAS, BS. 56 associate degrees awarded in 1992. 37% in business and management, 31% business/office and marketing/distribution, 6% computer sciences, 26% allied health. 125 bachelor's degrees awarded. 46% in business and management, 11% computer sciences, 22% education, 10% allied health, 5% letters/literature, 5% life sciences.

UNDERGRADUATE MAJORS. Associate: Business administration and management, business and management, business and office, clinical laboratory science, computer programming, liberal/general studies, medical laboratory technologies, medical records administration, medical records technology, respiratory therapy, respiratory therapy technology, secretarial and related programs. **Bachelor's:** Art education, arts management, biological and physical sciences, biology, business administration and management, business and management, business education, chemistry, chemistry for information systems, computer and information sciences, computer education, computer mathematics, computer programming, early childhood education, education, elementary education, English, English education, English for information systems, fine arts, health education, information sciences and systems, junior high education, marketing and distributive education, mathematics, mathematics education, medical records administration, medical records technology, music, music business management, music education, physical education, physics, physics for information systems, prelaw, premedicine, respiratory therapy, respiratory therapy technology, science education, secondary education, speech/communication/theater education, technical and business writing, technical education, technology management, trade and industrial education.

ACADEMIC PROGRAMS. 2-year transfer program, cooperative education, double major, dual enrollment of high school students, honors program, independent study, internships, study abroad, teacher preparation. **Remedial services:** Learning center, reduced course load, remedial instruction, special counselor, tutoring, reading development and study skills. **Placement/credit:** CLEP Subject, institutional tests; 32 credit hours maximum for bachelor's degree.

ACADEMIC REQUIREMENTS. Freshmen must earn minimum GPA of 2.0 to continue in good standing. 74% of freshmen return for sophomore year. Students must declare major on application. **Graduation requirements:** 64 hours for associate (35 in major), 128 hours for bachelor's (85 in major). Most students required to take courses in arts/fine arts, computer science, English, mathematics, biological/physical sciences, social sciences. **Postgraduate studies:** 22% from 2-year programs enter 4-year programs. 1% enter law school, 2% enter MBA programs.

FRESHMAN ADMISSIONS. Selection criteria: All students must be in top two-thirds of class or have minimum ACT composite scores of 20. Underqualified applicants considered. High school minimum GPA of 2.0 in core courses also required. Recommended units include English 4, foreign language 2, mathematics 2, social science 3 and science 3. 1 fine arts, .5 computer science also recommended. **Test requirements:** SAT or ACT (ACT preferred); score report by September 1.

1992 FRESHMAN CLASS PROFILE. 1,080 men and women applied, 950 accepted; 248 men enrolled, 311 women enrolled. **Academic background:** Mid 50% of enrolled freshmen had ACT composite between 15-22. 66% submitted ACT scores. **Characteristics:** 93% from in state, 70% live in college housing, 3% have minority backgrounds, 4% are foreign students.

FALL-TERM APPLICATIONS. $15 fee, may be waived for applicants with need. No closing date; applicants notified on a rolling basis. Deferred admission available.

STUDENT LIFE. Housing: Dormitories (men, women, coed). **Activities:** Student government, radio, student newspaper, yearbook, choral groups, concert band, drama, marching band, music ensembles, musical theater, pep band, stage band.

ATHLETICS. NAIA. **Intercollegiate:** Basketball, cross-country, football M, track and field, volleyball W. **Intramural:** Archery, badminton, baseball M, basketball, bowling, boxing M, golf, softball, track and field, volleyball. **Clubs:** Baseball, softball, tennis, golf, weight-lifting, soccer, karate.

STUDENT SERVICES. Aptitude testing, career counseling, employment service for undergraduates, freshman orientation, health services, personal counseling, placement service for graduates, veterans counselor, services/facilities for handicapped.

ANNUAL EXPENSES. Tuition and fees (projected): $2,111. **Room and board:** $2,480. **Books and supplies:** $600. **Other expenses:** $750.

FINANCIAL AID. 70% of freshmen, 59% of continuing students receive some form of aid. All grants, 80% of loans, 26% of jobs based on need. Academic, music/drama, athletic scholarships available. **Aid applications:** No closing date; priority given to applications received by March 1; applicants notified on a rolling basis beginning on or about May 1; must reply within 2 weeks. **Additional information:** Application deadline for grants and scholarships is April 1. No deadline for loan and job applications.

ADDRESS/TELEPHONE. Mark Weiss, Director of Admissions, Dakota State University, Heston Hall, Madison, SD 57042. (605) 256-5139. Fax: (605) 256-5316.

Dakota Wesleyan University
Mitchell, South Dakota CB code: 6155

Admissions: 64% of applicants accepted
Based on: ••• School record, test scores
•• Activities, recommendations
• Essay, special talents
Completion: 93% of freshmen end year in good standing
62% graduate, 15% of these enter graduate study

4-year private liberal arts college, coed, affiliated with United Methodist Church. Founded in 1885. **Accreditation:** Regional. **Undergraduate enrollment:** 222 men, 316 women full time; 58 men, 169 women part time. **Graduate enrollment:** 1 woman part time. **Faculty:** 82 total (45 full time), 15 with doctorates or other terminal degrees. **Location:** Rural campus in large town; 70 miles from Sioux Falls. **Calendar:** Semester, limited summer session. **Microcomputers:** 60 located in libraries, computer centers. **Additional facts:** Campuses in Wagner and Chamberlain offer AA degree in general studies.

DEGREES OFFERED. AA, BA, MA. 37 associate degrees awarded in 1992. 10% in business/office and marketing/distribution, 82% health sciences, 8% multi/interdisciplinary studies. 85 bachelor's degrees awarded. 36% in business and management, 12% education, 10% life sciences, 12% psychology, 22% social sciences. Graduate degrees offered in 2 major fields of study.

UNDERGRADUATE MAJORS. Associate: Business administration and management, business and management, business and office, criminal justice studies, criminology, liberal/general studies, nursing. **Bachelor's:** Accounting, agribusiness, American Indian studies, art education, biology, business administration and management, business and management, business and office, business education, chemistry, communications, creative writing, education, elementary education, English, English education, finance, fine arts, history, journalism, marketing and distribution, mathematics, mathematics education, mental health/human services, philosophy, physical education, political science and government, predentistry, preengineering, prelaw, premedicine, prepharmacy, preveterinary, psychology, religion, science education, secondary education, social science education, social sciences, social studies education, sociology, speech, sports medicine.

ACADEMIC PROGRAMS. 2-year transfer program, double major, dual enrollment of high school students, honors program, independent study, internships, student-designed major. **Remedial services:** Preadmission summer program, reduced course load, remedial instruction, special counselor, tutoring. **Placement/credit:** CLEP General and Subject, institutional tests; 12 credit hours maximum for associate degree; 63 credit hours maximum for bachelor's degree.

ACADEMIC REQUIREMENTS. Freshmen must earn minimum GPA of 1.5 to continue in good standing. 68% of freshmen return for sophomore year. Students must declare major by end of first year. **Graduation requirements:** 62 hours for associate (32 in major), 125 hours for bachelor's (38 in major). Most students required to take courses in arts/fine arts, English, history, mathematics, philosophy/religion, biological/physical sciences, social sciences. **Postgraduate studies:** 10% from 2-year programs enter 4-year programs.

FRESHMAN ADMISSIONS. Selection criteria: High school record, test scores, school activities, personal interview considered. Recommendations and personal interview used for marginal students. **Test requirements:** SAT or ACT (ACT preferred); score report by September 1. Institutional examinations in reading, writing, mathematics.

1992 FRESHMAN CLASS PROFILE. 518 men and women applied, 330 accepted; 57 men enrolled, 78 women enrolled. **Characteristics:** 76% from in state, 58% commute, 9% have minority backgrounds. Average age is 23.

FALL-TERM APPLICATIONS. $15 fee, may be waived for applicants with need. Closing date September 10; priority given to applications received by April 1; applicants notified on a rolling basis; must reply within 4 weeks.

STUDENT LIFE. Housing: Dormitories (men, women). **Activities:** Student government, student newspaper, yearbook, choral groups, dance, drama, music ensembles, musical theater, pep band, Fellowship of Christian Athletes, variety of religious, ethnic, minority, political, and service groups.

ATHLETICS. NAIA. **Intercollegiate:** Baseball M, basketball, cross-country, football M, track and field, volleyball W. **Intramural:** Basketball, football M, handball, racquetball, softball, volleyball.

STUDENT SERVICES. Aptitude testing, career counseling, employment service for undergraduates, freshman orientation, health services, personal counseling, placement service for graduates, special adviser for adult students, services/facilities for handicapped.

ANNUAL EXPENSES. Tuition and fees: $7,110. **Room and board:** $2,600. **Books and supplies:** $550. **Other expenses:** $920.

FINANCIAL AID. 95% of freshmen, 92% of continuing students receive some form of aid. 47% of grants, 76% of loans, 42% of jobs based on need. 95 enrolled freshmen were judged to have need, all were offered aid. Academic, music/drama, art, athletic, state/district residency, leadership, alumni affiliation, religious affiliation, minority scholarships available. **Aid applications:** No closing date; priority given to applications received by March 15; applicants notified on a rolling basis beginning on or about April 1; must reply within 2 weeks.

ADDRESS/TELEPHONE. Melinda Larson, Director of Admissions, Dakota Wesleyan University, 1200 West University Boulevard, Mitchell, SD 57301-4398. (605) 995-2650. (800) 333-8506. Fax: (605) 995-2699.

Huron University
Huron, South Dakota CB code: 6279

4-year proprietary university and business, nursing, liberal arts, teachers college, coed. Founded in 1883. **Accreditation:** Regional. **Undergraduate enrollment:** 148 men, 203 women full time; 14 men, 38 women part time. **Graduate enrollment:** 15 men, 4 women full time; 6 men, 6 women part time. **Faculty:** 36 total (19 full time), 10 with doctorates or other terminal degrees. **Location:** Rural campus in large town; 125 miles from Sioux Falls. **Calendar:** Semester, limited summer session. **Microcomputers:** 21 located in libraries, computer centers. **Special facilities:** College archives. **Additional facts:** Branch campuses in Sioux Falls, London (England), Tokyo (Japan).

DEGREES OFFERED. AA, AS, AAS, BA, BS, MBA. 46 associate degrees awarded in 1992. 39% in business and management, 54% health sciences, 7% multi/interdisciplinary studies. 57 bachelor's degrees awarded. 33% in business and management, 32% teacher education, 7% multi/interdisciplinary studies, 19% parks/recreation, protective services, public affairs, 9% social sciences. Graduate degrees offered in 1 major field of study.

UNDERGRADUATE MAJORS. Associate: Business administration and management, business data processing and related programs, communications, criminal justice studies, education, liberal/general studies, nursing, public relations, social work, tourism, transportation and travel marketing. **Bachelor's:** Accounting, business administration and management, business education, communications, criminal justice studies, education, elementary education, health education, liberal/general studies, physical education, prelaw, public relations, science education, secondary education, social science education, social work.

ACADEMIC PROGRAMS. 2-year transfer program, double major, internships, student-designed major, study abroad, teacher preparation, visiting/exchange student program; combined bachelor's/graduate program in business administration. **Remedial services:** Learning center, reduced course load, remedial instruction, tutoring, study and communication skills clinic and pretesting. **Placement/credit:** CLEP Subject, institutional tests; 21 credit hours maximum for bachelor's degree.

ACADEMIC REQUIREMENTS. Freshmen must earn minimum GPA of 1.6 to continue in good standing. 61% of freshmen return for sophomore year. Students must declare major by end of first year. **Graduation requirements:** 60 hours for associate, 120 hours for bachelor's. Most students required to take courses in computer science, English, history, humanities, mathematics, biological/physical sciences, social sciences. **Postgraduate studies:** 8% from 2-year programs enter 4-year programs.

FRESHMAN ADMISSIONS. Selection criteria: Test scores, GPA of 2.0, and top quarter of graduating class required. Exceptions made with personal interview. **Test requirements:** SAT or ACT (ACT preferred); score report by September 15.

1992 FRESHMAN CLASS PROFILE. Academic background: Mid 50% of enrolled freshmen had ACT composite between 16-22. 63% submitted ACT scores. **Characteristics:** 46% from in state, 62% live in college housing, 13% have minority backgrounds, 20% are foreign students. Average age is 21.

FALL-TERM APPLICATIONS. No fee. Closing date September 5; applicants notified on a rolling basis; must reply by September 5. Deferred and early admission available.

STUDENT LIFE. Housing: Dormitories (men, women, coed). Students under 21 required to live in college housing unless veteran or living with family. **Activities:** Student government, student newspaper, drama, Lakota Oyate (Native American club), Phi Beta Lambda, Sigma Alpha Pi, international club, Student Nurses Association, Student National Education Association.

ATHLETICS. NAIA. **Intercollegiate:** Baseball M, basketball, football M, track and field, volleyball W. **Intramural:** Baseball M, basketball, softball, swimming, table tennis.

STUDENT SERVICES. Career counseling, employment service for undergraduates, freshman orientation, personal counseling, placement service for graduates, veterans counselor, services/facilities for handicapped.

ANNUAL EXPENSES. Tuition and fees: $6,850. **Room and board:** $2,940. **Books and supplies:** $600. **Other expenses:** $960.

FINANCIAL AID. 97% of freshmen, 97% of continuing students receive some form of aid. Grants, loans, jobs available. 99 enrolled freshmen were judged to have need, all were offered aid. Academic, athletic scholarships available. **Aid applications:** No closing date; applicants notified on a rolling basis beginning on or about May 15; must reply within 15 days.

ADDRESS/TELEPHONE. Robert West, Director of Admissions, Huron University, 333 Ninth Southwest, Huron, SD 57350. (605) 352-8721. (800) 843-0026. Fax: (605) 352-7421.

Kilian Community College
Sioux Falls, South Dakota CB code: 6149

2-year private community college, coed. Founded in 1976. **Accreditation:** Regional. **Undergraduate enrollment:** 11 men, 60 women full time; 28 men, 86 women part time. **Faculty:** 52 total, 12 with doctorates or other terminal degrees. **Location:** Urban campus in small city; 180 miles from Omaha, Nebraska, 240 miles from Minneapolis-St. Paul. **Calendar:** Quarter. **Microcomputers:** 26 located in classrooms. **Additional facts:** College Without Walls primarily serving adults. Classes held citywide, with majority scheduled in evening. Cooperative library services with Sioux Falls College.

DEGREES OFFERED. AA, AS, AAS. 27 associate degrees awarded in 1992. 19% in business and management, 55% business/office and marketing/distribution, 25% law.

UNDERGRADUATE MAJORS. Accounting, business and management, business and office, computer programming, criminal justice studies, education, fire control and safety technology, health sciences, legal assistant/paralegal, legal secretary, medical records technology, medical secretary, office supervision and management, secretarial and related programs.

ACADEMIC PROGRAMS. 2-year transfer program, cooperative education, dual enrollment of high school students, independent study, internships, cross-registration. **Remedial services:** Reduced course load, special counselor, tutoring. **Placement/credit:** CLEP General and Subject, institutional tests; 18 credit hours maximum for associate degree.

ACADEMIC REQUIREMENTS. Freshmen must earn minimum GPA of 2.0 to continue in good standing. 80% of freshmen return for sophomore year. Students must declare major on enrollment. **Graduation requirements:** 96 hours for associate (54 in major). Most students required to take courses in arts/fine arts, computer science, English, history, humanities, mathematics, biological/physical sciences, social sciences. **Additional information:** Emphasis on job skills for adult learners.

FRESHMAN ADMISSIONS. Selection criteria: Open admissions. Students admitted without high school diploma must complete GED tests before completion of college program.

1992 FRESHMAN CLASS PROFILE. 16 men, 46 women enrolled. **Characteristics:** 97% from in state, 100% commute, 1% have minority backgrounds, 1% are foreign students. Average age is 29.

FALL-TERM APPLICATIONS. $10 fee. No closing date; applicants notified on a rolling basis. Interview recommended. Deferred admission available.

STUDENT LIFE. Housing: Housing available at Augustana College and Sioux Falls College. **Activities:** Student government, student newspaper.

STUDENT SERVICES. Aptitude testing, career counseling, employment service for undergraduates, freshman orientation, personal counseling, placement service for graduates, special adviser for adult students, veterans counselor, services/facilities for handicapped.

ANNUAL EXPENSES. Tuition and fees (1992-93): $3,185. **Books and supplies:** $400. **Other expenses:** $400.

FINANCIAL AID. 80% of freshmen, 80% of continuing students receive some form of aid. Grants, loans, jobs available. **Aid applications:** No closing date; applicants notified on a rolling basis beginning on or about July 15; must reply within 3 weeks.

ADDRESS/TELEPHONE. Kevin Kennedy, Director of Admissions, Kilian Community College, 1600 South Menlo Avenue, Sioux Falls, SD 57105-1698. (605) 336-1711. (800) 888-1147. Fax: (605) 336-2606.

Lake Area Vocational Technical Institute
Watertown, South Dakota CB code: 0717

2-year public technical college, coed. Founded in 1965. **Accreditation:** Regional. **Undergraduate enrollment:** 625 men, 351 women full time; 10 men, 59 women part time. **Faculty:** 71 total (65 full time), 1 with doctorate or other terminal degree. **Location:** Rural campus in large town; 90 miles from Sioux Falls, 120 miles from Fargo, North Dakota. **Calendar:** Semester, limited summer session. **Microcomputers:** 70 located in classrooms, computer centers, campus-wide network.

DEGREES OFFERED. AAS. 56 associate degrees awarded in 1992. 27% in agriculture, 43% business and management, 25% computer sciences, 5% health sciences.

UNDERGRADUATE MAJORS. Accounting, agribusiness, agricultural mechanics, aircraft mechanics, automotive mechanics, business and management, business and office, carpentry, civil technology, clinical laboratory science, computer and information sciences, computer programming, diesel engine mechanics, drafting and design technology, electrical and electronics equipment repair, finance, marketing management, nursing, survey and mapping technology.

ACADEMIC PROGRAMS. 2-year transfer program, internships. **Remedial services:** Learning center, preadmission summer program, reduced course load, tutoring.

ACADEMIC REQUIREMENTS. Freshmen must earn minimum GPA of 2.0 to continue in good standing. Students must declare major on application. **Graduation requirements:** 78 hours for associate. Most students required to take courses in computer science.

FRESHMAN ADMISSIONS. Selection criteria: Open admissions. Specific programs may specify certain criteria and require preadmission testing.

1992 FRESHMAN CLASS PROFILE. 257 men, 262 women enrolled. **Characteristics:** 100% commute. Average age is 19.

FALL-TERM APPLICATIONS. $15 fee. No closing date; applicants notified on a rolling basis. Interview required for medical laboratory technician applicants. Deferred admission available.

STUDENT LIFE. Activities: Yearbook.

ATHLETICS. Intramural: Basketball, bowling, softball, volleyball.

STUDENT SERVICES. Aptitude testing, career counseling, employment service for undergraduates, freshman orientation, health services, on-campus day care, personal counseling, placement service for graduates, veterans counselor, services/facilities for handicapped.

ANNUAL EXPENSES. Tuition and fees (1992-93):

ADDRESS/TELEPHONE. Dale Dobberpuhg, Curriculum Coordinator, Lake Area Vocational Technical Institute, P.O. Box 730, Watertown, SD 57201-0730. (605) 886-5872. (800) 657-4344. Fax: (605) 886-2824.

Mitchell Vocational Technical Institute
Mitchell, South Dakota CB code: 7038

2-year public agricultural and technical, technical college, coed. Founded in 1968. **Accreditation:** Regional. **Undergraduate enrollment:** 463 men, 82 women full time; 3 men, 12 women part time. **Faculty:** 54 total (50 full time). **Location:** Rural campus in large town; 70 miles from Sioux Falls. **Calendar:** Quarter, limited summer session. **Microcomputers:** 40 located in libraries, classrooms, computer centers. **Special facilities:** Satellite communications earth station, teleconference studio.

DEGREES OFFERED. AAS. 92 associate degrees awarded in 1992. 10% in computer sciences, 90% trade and industry.

UNDERGRADUATE MAJORS. Accounting, agribusiness, agricultural business and management, agricultural mechanics, agricultural production, air conditioning/heating/refrigeration mechanics, air conditioning/heating/refrigeration technology, automotive mechanics, automotive technology, business and office, business computer/console/peripheral equipment operation, carpentry, computer servicing technology, computer technology, construction, drafting and design technology, electrical and electronics equipment repair, electrical installation, electrical technology, electronic technology, food production/management/services, laser electro-optic technology, legal secretary, medical secretary, radio/television technology, robotics, secretarial and related programs, systems analysis, telecommunications, word processing.

ACADEMIC PROGRAMS. Independent study, internships. **Remedial services:** Learning center, preadmission summer program, remedial instruction, tutoring. **Placement/credit:** Institutional tests.

ACADEMIC REQUIREMENTS. Freshmen must earn minimum GPA of 2.0 to continue in good standing. Students must declare major on enrollment. **Graduation requirements:** Most students required to take courses in computer science, English, mathematics, social sciences.

FRESHMAN ADMISSIONS. Selection criteria: Open admissions. **High school preparation:** 16 units recommended. Recommended units include biological science 1, English 4, mathematics 2, physical science 1 and social science 2. **Test requirements:** ACT.

1992 FRESHMAN CLASS PROFILE. 210 men and women enrolled. **Characteristics:** 95% from in state, 100% commute, 7% have minority backgrounds. Average age is 22.

FALL-TERM APPLICATIONS. $25 fee. No closing date; applicants notified on a rolling basis; August 15. Interview recommended. Deferred admission available. The Test for Adult Basic Education required for placement.

STUDENT LIFE. Activities: Student government, yearbook.

ATHLETICS. Intercollegiate: Basketball M. **Intramural:** Basketball, bowling, softball, volleyball.

STUDENT SERVICES. Aptitude testing, career counseling, employment service for undergraduates, on-campus day care, personal counseling, placement service for graduates, special adviser for adult students, services/facilities for handicapped.

ANNUAL EXPENSES. Tuition and fees: $2,100. **Books and supplies:** $750. **Other expenses:** $750.

FINANCIAL AID. 100% of freshmen, 94% of continuing students receive some form of aid. All grants, 82% of loans, all jobs based on need. **Aid applications:** No closing date; applicants notified on a rolling basis; must reply within 3 weeks.

ADDRESS/TELEPHONE. Lance B. Carter, Director of Student Services, Mitchell Vocational Technical Institute, 821 North Capital, Mitchell, SD 57301. (605) 995-3024. (800) 952-0042. Fax: (605) 996-3299.

Mount Marty College
Yankton, South Dakota — CB code: 6416

Admissions:	99% of applicants accepted
Based on:	••• School record, test scores
	•• Interview
	• Recommendations
Completion:	85% of freshmen end year in good standing
	60% graduate, 6% of these enter graduate study

4-year private liberal arts college, coed, affiliated with Roman Catholic Church. Founded in 1936. **Accreditation:** Regional. **Undergraduate enrollment:** 184 men, 399 women full time; 195 men, 272 women part time. **Graduate enrollment:** 9 men, 8 women full time; 17 men, 20 women part time. **Faculty:** 71 total (36 full time), 24 with doctorates or other terminal degrees. **Location:** Rural campus in large town; 75 miles from Sioux Falls, 60 miles from Sioux City, Iowa. **Calendar:** 4-1-4, limited summer session. Extensive evening/early morning classes. **Microcomputers:** 72 located in libraries, classrooms, computer centers. **Special facilities:** Hospital.

DEGREES OFFERED. AA, AS, BA, BS, MS. 14 associate degrees awarded in 1992. 93 bachelor's degrees awarded. Graduate degrees offered in 1 major field of study.

UNDERGRADUATE MAJORS. Associate: Accounting, business administration and management, secretarial and related programs. **Bachelor's:** Accounting, biological and physical sciences, biology, business administration and management, business and management, chemistry, clinical laboratory science, communications, education, elementary education, English, English education, food science and nutrition, health care administration, hotel/motel and restaurant management, humanities and social sciences, junior high education, liberal/general studies, mathematics, mathematics education, music, music education, nursing, physical education, religion, religious education, science education, secondary education, social science education, social sciences.

ACADEMIC PROGRAMS. Accelerated program, double major, honors program, independent study, internships, student-designed major; liberal arts/career combination in engineering. **Remedial services:** Learning center, preadmission summer program, reduced course load, remedial instruction, special counselor, tutoring. **ROTC:** Army. **Placement/credit:** CLEP Subject, institutional tests; 30 credit hours maximum for associate degree; 30 credit hours maximum for bachelor's degree.

ACADEMIC REQUIREMENTS. Freshmen must earn minimum GPA of 2.0 to continue in good standing. 80% of freshmen return for sophomore year. Students must declare major by end of second year. **Graduation requirements:** 60 hours for associate, 128 hours for bachelor's. Most students required to take courses in arts/fine arts, English, history, humanities, mathematics, philosophy/religion, biological/physical sciences, social sciences. **Postgraduate studies:** 10% from 2-year programs enter 4-year programs. 1% enter law school, 1% enter medical school, 2% enter MBA programs, 2% enter other graduate study.

FRESHMAN ADMISSIONS. Selection criteria: School achievement record, test scores, interview considered. Out-of-state applicants welcome. Special consideration for minority and low-income applicants. **Test requirements:** SAT or ACT; score report by August 30.

1992 FRESHMAN CLASS PROFILE. 229 men and women applied, 226 accepted; 40 men enrolled, 89 women enrolled. 60% had high school GPA of 3.0 or higher, 37% between 2.0 and 2.99. **Academic background:** Mid 50% of enrolled freshmen had ACT composite between 18-23. 90% submitted ACT scores. **Characteristics:** 50% from in state, 75% live in college housing, 5% have minority backgrounds, 1% are foreign students. Average age is 20.

FALL-TERM APPLICATIONS. $10 fee, may be waived for applicants with need. Closing date August 30; priority given to applications received by March 1; applicants notified on a rolling basis. Interview required for nursing anesthesia applicants. Audition recommended for music, theater applicants. Interview recommended of all applicants. Deferred admission available. EDP-F.

STUDENT LIFE. Housing: Dormitories (men, women). All unmarried undergraduates under 21 required to live in college housing unless living with family. **Activities:** Student government, magazine, radio, student newspaper, choral groups, concert band, drama, jazz band, music ensembles, musical theater, pep band, nonpartisan political club, social service club, Christian Life Committee, Fellowship of Christian Athletes, Pastoral Council.

ATHLETICS. NAIA. **Intercollegiate:** Baseball M, basketball, volleyball W. **Intramural:** Basketball, softball.

STUDENT SERVICES. Aptitude testing, career counseling, employment service for undergraduates, freshman orientation, health services, on-campus day care, personal counseling, placement service for graduates, special adviser for adult students, veterans counselor, services/facilities for handicapped.

ANNUAL EXPENSES. Tuition and fees: $7,470. **Room and board:** $2,980. **Books and supplies:** $500. **Other expenses:** $900.

FINANCIAL AID. 97% of freshmen, 98% of continuing students receive some form of aid. 74% of grants, 92% of loans, 83% of jobs based on need. 124 enrolled freshmen were judged to have need, all were offered aid. Academic, music/drama, athletic, leadership, religious affiliation, minority scholarships available. **Aid applications:** No closing date; priority given to applications received by March 1; applicants notified on a rolling basis beginning on or about April 1; must reply within 2 weeks. **Additional information:** March 1 deadline for institutional scholarships.

ADDRESS/TELEPHONE. Paula Tacke, Director of Admissions, Mount Marty College, 1105 West Eighth Street, Yankton, SD 57078-3724. (800) 658-4552. (800) 658-4552. Fax: (605) 668-1357.

National College
Rapid City, South Dakota — CB code: 6464

4-year proprietary business, technical college, coed. Founded in 1941. **Accreditation:** Regional. **Undergraduate enrollment:** 149 men, 250 women full time; 55 men, 55 women part time. **Faculty:** 46 total (28 full time), 2 with doctorates or other terminal degrees. **Location:** Suburban campus in small city; 400 miles from Denver, Colorado. **Calendar:** Quarter, extensive summer session. Extensive evening/early morning classes. **Microcomputers:** 35 located in libraries, classrooms, computer centers. **Special facilities:** Medical, animal health laboratories. **Additional facts:** Branch campuses in 5 states offer degrees mainly in business administration, computer information services, travel/airline careers.

DEGREES OFFERED. AS, BS. 121 associate degrees awarded in 1992. 55 bachelor's degrees awarded.

UNDERGRADUATE MAJORS. Associate: Accounting, business administration and management, business and management, business and office, business computer/console/peripheral equipment operation, business data processing and related programs, business data programming, computer and information sciences, computer programming, computer technology, data processing, electronic technology, flight attendants, legal assistant/paralegal, legal secretary, liberal/general studies, marketing management, medical assistant, medical records administration, medical secretary, office supervision and management, secretarial and related programs, survey and mapping technology, transportation and travel marketing, veterinarian's assistant, word processing. **Bachelor's:** Accounting, business administration and management, business and management, business data processing and related programs, business data programming, computer and information sciences, computer programming, data processing, information sciences and systems, legal assistant/paralegal, marketing management, tourism.

ACADEMIC PROGRAMS. Accelerated program, cooperative education, double major, independent study, internships. **Remedial services:** Learning center, reduced course load, remedial instruction, special counselor, tutoring. **ROTC:** Army. **Placement/credit:** AP, CLEP General and Subject, institutional tests; 90 credit hours maximum for bachelor's degree.

ACADEMIC REQUIREMENTS. Freshmen must earn minimum GPA of 2.0 to continue in good standing. 52% of freshmen return for sophomore year. Students must declare major on enrollment. **Graduation requirements:** 96 hours for associate, 192 hours for bachelor's. Most students required to take courses in computer science, English, humanities, mathematics, biological/physical sciences, social sciences. **Postgraduate studies:** 3% enter MBA programs, 2% enter other graduate study. **Additional information:** Applied management program for students with associate degree in business, health, or technical fields, who desire to continue their education in management.

FRESHMAN ADMISSIONS. Selection criteria: Open admissions. Algebra helpful for computer technology. Science recommended for health program students. **Test requirements:** SAT or ACT (ACT preferred) for placement and counseling only; score report by September 1.

1992 FRESHMAN CLASS PROFILE. 290 men and women enrolled. **Academic background:** Mid 50% of enrolled freshmen had ACT composite between 13-20. 100% submitted ACT scores. **Characteristics:** 50% commute, 21% have minority backgrounds.

FALL-TERM APPLICATIONS. $25 fee. Closing date September 14; priority given to applications received by June 1; applicants notified on a rolling basis. Interview recommended. Deferred admission available.

STUDENT LIFE. Housing: Dormitories (men, women); fraternity, sorority housing available. Placement in private home where student works in exchange for room and board possible. **Activities:** Student government, student newspaper, choral groups, fraternities, sororities, Baptist Student Union.

ATHLETICS. NSCAA. **Intramural:** Basketball, bowling, football, skiing, softball, volleyball. **Clubs:** Rodeo.

STUDENT SERVICES. Career counseling, employment service for undergraduates, freshman orientation, health services, personal counseling, placement service for graduates, veterans counselor, day care subsidy, services/facilities for handicapped.

ANNUAL EXPENSES. Tuition and fees (1992-93): $6,260. **Room and board:** $3,129. **Books and supplies:** $600. **Other expenses:** $900.

FINANCIAL AID. 94% of freshmen, 89% of continuing students receive some form of aid. All grants, 91% of loans, 55% of jobs based on need. Academic, leadership, alumni affiliation scholarships available. **Aid applications:** No closing date; priority given to applications received by March 15; applicants notified on a rolling basis beginning on or about April 1; must reply within 4 weeks.

ADDRESS/TELEPHONE. Keith Carlyle, Director of High School Admissions, National College, PO Box 1780, Rapid City, SD 57709-1780. (605) 394-4820. (800) 843-8892. Fax: (605) 394-4871.

Northern State University
Aberdeen, South Dakota CB code: 6487

4-year public college of arts and sciences and business, teachers college, coed. Founded in 1901. **Accreditation:** Regional. **Undergraduate enrollment:** 2,135 men and women full time; 494 men and women part time. **Graduate enrollment:** 50 men and women full time; 166 men and women part time. **Faculty:** 149 total (120 full time), 72 with doctorates or other terminal degrees. **Location:** Urban campus in large town; 285 miles from Minneapolis-St. Paul. **Calendar:** Semester, extensive summer session. Extensive evening/early morning classes. **Microcomputers:** 500 located in dormitories, classrooms, computer centers. **Special facilities:** Physical education and convocation center, art galleries.

DEGREES OFFERED. AA, AS, BA, BS, MEd. 70 associate degrees awarded in 1992. 25% in business and management, 25% business/office and marketing/distribution, 20% computer sciences, 5% multi/interdisciplinary studies, 15% social sciences, 10% trade and industry. 370 bachelor's degrees awarded. 40% in business and management, 20% business/office and marketing/distribution, 30% teacher education. Graduate degrees offered in 13 major fields of study.

UNDERGRADUATE MAJORS. Associate: Accounting, business and office, business data processing and related programs, drafting, industrial technology, liberal/general studies, marketing and distribution, preengineering, public affairs, secretarial and related programs. **Bachelor's:** Accounting, art education, biological and physical sciences, biology, business administration and management, business and management, business education, chemistry, clinical laboratory science, community services, criminal justice studies, dramatic arts, economics, education of the emotionally handicapped, education of the mentally handicapped, education of the physically handicapped, education of the visually handicapped, elementary education, English, English education, environmental science, finance, fine arts, foreign languages education, French, German, history, humanities and social sciences, industrial arts education, industrial technology, international business management, mathematics, mathematics education, music, music education, physical education, political science and government, psychology, recreation and community services technologies, science education, secretarial and related programs, social science education, sociology, Spanish, special education, specific learning disabilities, speech, speech correction, speech pathology/audiology, speech/communication/theater education.

ACADEMIC PROGRAMS. 2-year transfer program, double major, dual enrollment of high school students, honors program, independent study, internships, study abroad, teacher preparation, telecourses, visiting/exchange student program, Washington semester, cross-registration; liberal arts/career combination in health sciences. **Remedial services:** Learning center, preadmission summer program, reduced course load, remedial instruction, special counselor, tutoring. **Placement/credit:** AP, CLEP General and Subject, institutional tests; 16 credit hours maximum for bachelor's degree.

ACADEMIC REQUIREMENTS. Freshmen must earn minimum GPA of 1.6 to continue in good standing. 83% of freshmen return for sophomore year. Students must declare major by end of second year. **Graduation requirements:** 64 hours for associate, 128 hours for bachelor's. Most students required to take courses in English, history, mathematics, biological/physical sciences, social sciences. **Postgraduate studies:** 60% from 2-year programs enter 4-year programs.

FRESHMAN ADMISSIONS. Selection criteria: Applicants to 4-year programs must meet the following: GPA in required courses, or rank in top two-thirds of class for South Dakota and Minnesota residents, top half all other states, or minimum enhanced ACT composite score of 20. Open admissions to 2-year programs. **High school preparation:** 13 units required. Required units include English 4, foreign language 3, mathematics 3, social science 3 and science 3. Mathematics units must be geometry and algebra. Social science units must be American government, American history, geography. Science units must be laboratory science in biology, chemistry, or physics. .5 fine arts, and .5 computer science also required. **Test requirements:** SAT or ACT (ACT preferred); score report by August 15. **Additional information:** Applicants lacking required high school units admitted provisionally. Equivalent work must be completed within 2 years.

1992 FRESHMAN CLASS PROFILE. 282 men, 341 women enrolled. 47% had high school GPA of 3.0 or higher, 47% between 2.0 and 2.99. **Academic background:** Mid 50% of enrolled freshmen had ACT composite between 16-24. 100% submitted ACT scores. **Characteristics:** 95% from in state, 70% live in college housing, 2% have minority backgrounds. Average age is 19.

FALL-TERM APPLICATIONS. $15 fee. No closing date; priority given to applications received by July 12; applicants notified on a rolling basis. Audition required for band, vocal music applicants. Interview recommended for borderline applicants. Portfolio recommended for art applicants. CRDA. Deferred and early admission available. EDP-F.

STUDENT LIFE. Housing: Dormitories (men, women, coed). Married graduate student housing available for summer session only. **Activities:** Student government, student newspaper, yearbook, choral groups, concert band, drama, jazz band, marching band, music ensembles, musical theater, pep band, symphony orchestra, Circle-K, Native American Student Association, College Democrats, College Republicans, Fellowship of Christian Athletes, SPURS, veterans club, Newman Club, United Ministries in Higher Education.

ATHLETICS. NAIA. **Intercollegiate:** Baseball M, basketball, cross-country, football M, golf, softball W, tennis, track and field, volleyball W, wrestling M. **Intramural:** Badminton, baseball M, basketball, bowling, field hockey, racquetball, softball W, tennis, volleyball.

STUDENT SERVICES. Aptitude testing, career counseling, employment service for undergraduates, freshman orientation, health services, on-campus day care, personal counseling, placement service for graduates, special adviser for adult students, veterans counselor, services/facilities for handicapped.

ANNUAL EXPENSES. Tuition and fees (projected): $2,006, $1,568 additional for out-of-state students. Minnesota, North Dakota, and Wyoming residents pay in-state tuition. **Room and board:** $2,399. **Books and supplies:** $550. **Other expenses:** $1,100.

FINANCIAL AID. 75% of freshmen, 75% of continuing students receive some form of aid. 86% of grants, 84% of loans, 62% of jobs based on need. 399 enrolled freshmen were judged to have need, 374 were offered aid. Academic, music/drama, art, athletic, leadership, minority scholarships available. **Aid applications:** No closing date; priority given to applications received by March 1; applicants notified on a rolling basis beginning on or about May 15; must reply within 2 weeks.

ADDRESS/TELEPHONE. Steve Ochsner, Director of Admissions, Northern State University, 1200 South Jay Street, Aberdeen, SD 57401. (605) 622-2544.

Oglala Lakota College
Kyle, South Dakota CB code: 1430

4-year public college of arts and sciences, coed. Founded in 1971. **Accreditation:** Regional. **Undergraduate enrollment:** 1,038 men and women. **Faculty:** 120 total (90 full time). **Location:** Rural campus in rural community; 90 miles from Rapid City. **Calendar:** Semester, extensive summer session. Extensive evening/early morning classes. **Additional facts:** Serves Oglala Lakota reservation.

DEGREES OFFERED. AA, AAS, BS, M. 85 associate degrees awarded in 1992. 27 bachelor's degrees awarded. Graduate degrees offered in 1 major field of study.

UNDERGRADUATE MAJORS. Associate: Law enforcement and corrections technologies, liberal/general studies, nursing, practical nursing, recreation and community services technologies, teacher aide. **Bachelor's:** American Indian studies, business administration and management, elementary education, history, human services.

ACADEMIC PROGRAMS. Remedial services: Learning center, reduced course load, remedial instruction, special counselor, tutoring. **Placement/credit:** Institutional tests; 13 credit hours maximum for bachelor's degree.

ACADEMIC REQUIREMENTS. Freshmen must earn minimum GPA of 1.50 to continue in good standing. 64% of freshmen return for sophomore year. **Additional information:** College is one of 2 tribally chartered, fully accredited institutions in the United States.

FRESHMAN ADMISSIONS. Selection criteria: Open admissions.

1992 FRESHMAN CLASS PROFILE. 200 men and women enrolled. **Characteristics:** 100% commute, 95% have minority backgrounds.

FALL-TERM APPLICATIONS. No fee. No closing date; applicants notified on a rolling basis.

STUDENT LIFE. Activities: Student government, student newspaper.

ATHLETICS. NJCAA. **Intercollegiate:** Basketball, cross-country, volleyball.

STUDENT SERVICES. Aptitude testing, career counseling, personal counseling.

ANNUAL EXPENSES. Tuition and fees (1992-93): $1,590. **Books and supplies:** $200. **Other expenses:** $450.

FINANCIAL AID. 95% of continuing students receive some form of aid. Grants available. **Aid applications:** No closing date; applicants notified on a rolling basis. **Additional information:** Deadline for applications for Bureau of Indian Affairs Higher Education Grants, is March 15; applicants notified early summer.

ADDRESS/TELEPHONE. Office of Admissions, Oglala Lakota College, Box 490, Kyle, SD 57752. (605) 455-2321.

Presentation College
Aberdeen, South Dakota CB code: 6582

4-year private health science, nursing college, coed, affiliated with Roman Catholic Church. Founded in 1951. **Accreditation:** Regional. **Undergraduate enrollment:** 40 men, 245 women full time; 20 men, 128 women part time.

Faculty: 48 total (24 full time), 2 with doctorates or other terminal degrees. **Location:** Rural campus in large town; 200 from Sioux Falls, 280 miles from Minneapolis-St. Paul. **Calendar:** Semester, limited summer session. **Microcomputers:** Located in computer centers. **Special facilities:** Member of the South Dakota library network M.

DEGREES OFFERED. AA, AS, BA, BS. 126 associate degrees awarded in 1992. 18% in business and management, 63% health sciences, 12% allied health. 43 bachelor's degrees awarded. 33% in business and management, 43% health sciences, 23% allied health.

UNDERGRADUATE MAJORS. Associate: Accounting, business and management, business and office, business computer/console/peripheral equipment operation, business data processing and related programs, business data programming, computer programming, education, histology, hotel/motel and restaurant management, medical laboratory technologies, medical records technology, medical secretary, nursing, office supervision and management, radiograph medical technology, religious education, social work. **Bachelor's:** Allied health management, nursing, social work.

ACADEMIC PROGRAMS. 2-year transfer program, external degree, internships. **Remedial services:** Learning center, reduced course load, remedial instruction, tutoring. **Placement/credit:** CLEP Subject; 12 credit hours maximum for associate degree.

ACADEMIC REQUIREMENTS. Freshmen must earn minimum GPA of 2.0 to continue in good standing. 68% of freshmen return for sophomore year. Students must declare major by end of first year. **Graduation requirements:** 64 hours for associate (32 in major), 128 hours for bachelor's (36 in major). Most students required to take courses in English, philosophy/religion, social sciences. **Postgraduate studies:** 12% from 2-year programs enter 4-year programs.

FRESHMAN ADMISSIONS. Selection criteria: Open admissions. Selective admissions to allied health programs: high school transcript, class rank, 2 references required. ACT test scores required for radiologic technician. ASSET required for all programs. **High school preparation:** 16 units recommended. Recommended units include English 4, mathematics 1, social science 2 and science 1. CPR certificate required of nursing applicants. **Test requirements:** ACT for placement and counseling only. ACT used for admissions to allied health programs.

1992 FRESHMAN CLASS PROFILE. 17 men, 70 women enrolled. 31% had high school GPA of 3.0 or higher, 42% between 2.0 and 2.99. 3% were in top tenth and 16% were in top quarter of graduating class. **Characteristics:** 87% from in state, 70% commute, 26% have minority backgrounds, 1% are foreign students. Average age is 24.

FALL-TERM APPLICATIONS. $10 fee, may be waived for applicants with need. Closing date September 1; priority given to applications received by May 1; applicants notified on a rolling basis; must reply by April 2 or within 4 weeks if notified thereafter. Deferred and early admission available. EDP-F.

STUDENT LIFE. Housing: Dormitories (men, women). **Activities:** Student government, student newspaper, yearbook, choral groups, Native American Club, Teachers of Tomorrow, Shalom, Friends in Christ.

ATHLETICS. Intramural: Basketball, table tennis, volleyball.

STUDENT SERVICES. Aptitude testing, career counseling, employment service for undergraduates, freshman orientation, health services, on-campus day care, personal counseling, placement service for graduates, special adviser for adult students, veterans counselor, services/facilities for handicapped.

ANNUAL EXPENSES. Tuition and fees (1992-93): $6,320. **Room and board:** $3,046. **Books and supplies:** $600. **Other expenses:** $850.

FINANCIAL AID. 89% of freshmen, 91% of continuing students receive some form of aid. 80% of grants, all loans, all jobs based on need. Academic, religious affiliation scholarships available. **Aid applications:** No closing date; priority given to applications received by March 1; applicants notified on a rolling basis beginning on or about March 1; must reply within 2 weeks.

ADDRESS/TELEPHONE. Ms. Kathy Gerdes, Director of Admissions, Presentation College, 1500 North Main Street, Aberdeen, SD 57401. (605) 225-0420. (800) 437-6060. Fax: (605) 229-8489.

Sinte Gleska University
Rosebud, South Dakota — CB code: 7328

4-year public liberal arts college, coed. Founded in 1970. **Accreditation:** Regional. **Undergraduate enrollment:** 108 men, 219 women full time; 58 men, 179 women part time. **Graduate enrollment:** 22 men, 75 women part time. **Faculty:** 50 total (30 full time), 7 with doctorates or other terminal degrees. **Location:** Rural campus in rural community; 90 miles from Pierre, 240 miles from Sioux Falls. **Calendar:** Semester, limited summer session. **Microcomputers:** 30 located in libraries, computer centers. **Additional facts:** College tribally controlled and charted by Rosebud Sicangu Lakota Tribe (Sioux).

DEGREES OFFERED. AA, AAS, BA, BS, MEd. 15 associate degrees awarded in 1992. 7 bachelor's degrees awarded. Graduate degrees offered in 1 major field of study.

UNDERGRADUATE MAJORS. Associate: Accounting, business administration and management, business and management, business and office, data processing, education, liberal/general studies, renewable natural resources, social sciences, teacher aide. **Bachelor's:** Business and management, education, elementary education, social sciences.

ACADEMIC PROGRAMS. Double major, dual enrollment of high school students, independent study, internships. **Remedial services:** Learning center, reduced course load, remedial instruction, special counselor, tutoring.

ACADEMIC REQUIREMENTS. Freshmen must earn minimum GPA of 1.5 to continue in good standing. Students must declare major on enrollment. **Graduation requirements:** 70 hours for associate (70 in major), 128 hours for bachelor's (128 in major). Most students required to take courses in English, foreign languages, history, humanities, mathematics, social sciences. **Postgraduate studies:** 70% from 2-year programs enter 4-year programs. 45% enter other graduate study. **Additional information:** One of 18 colleges with membership in American Indian Higher Education Consortium.

FRESHMAN ADMISSIONS. Selection criteria: Open admissions. First-time freshmen administered TASK test for placement in remedial or freshman-level classes.

1992 FRESHMAN CLASS PROFILE. 123 men, 257 women enrolled. **Characteristics:** 92% from in state.

FALL-TERM APPLICATIONS. No fee. No closing date. Early admission available.

STUDENT LIFE. Activities: Student government.

ATHLETICS. Intramural: Basketball, football M, softball, volleyball.

STUDENT SERVICES. Aptitude testing, career counseling, personal counseling, special adviser for adult students, veterans counselor, services/facilities for handicapped.

ANNUAL EXPENSES. Tuition and fees (1992-93): $1,580. **Books and supplies:** $400. **Other expenses:** $400.

ADDRESS/TELEPHONE. Michelle Zephier, Admissions Director, Sinte Gleska University, PO Box 490, Spotted Tail Drive, Rosebud, SD 57570. (605) 747-2263. Fax: (605) 747-2098.

Sioux Falls College
Sioux Falls, South Dakota — CB code: 6651

4-year private liberal arts college, coed, affiliated with American Baptist Churches in the USA. Founded in 1883. **Accreditation:** Regional. **Undergraduate enrollment:** 255 men, 327 women full time; 98 men, 181 women part time. **Graduate enrollment:** 45 women part time. **Faculty:** 72 total (35 full time), 26 with doctorates or other terminal degrees. **Location:** Suburban campus in small city; 250 miles from Minneapolis-St. Paul, 180 miles from Omaha. **Calendar:** 4-1-4, limited summer session. Saturday and extensive evening/early morning classes. **Microcomputers:** 58 located in libraries, classrooms, computer centers. **Special facilities:** Fine arts gallery, wellness/fitness facility, computerized library system linked with 5 city libraries and statewide library system. **Additional facts:** Only college in the Dakotas to offer majors in Wellness Management and Wellness/Fitness Instruction.

DEGREES OFFERED. AA, BA, BS, MEd. 1 associate degree awarded in 1992. 100% in education. 152 bachelor's degrees awarded. 43% in business and management, 11% communications, 13% teacher education, 8% letters/literature, 8% psychology, 8% social sciences. Graduate degrees offered in 1 major field of study.

UNDERGRADUATE MAJORS. Associate: Bible studies, business and management, early childhood education, liberal/general studies, preengineering, secretarial and related programs, social sciences. **Bachelor's:** Accounting, applied mathematics, art education, biology, business administration and management, business and management, chemistry, clinical laboratory science, communications, computer and information sciences, computer programming, dramatic arts, education, elementary education, English, English education, fine arts, health education, health sciences, history, humanities and social sciences, information sciences and systems, junior high education, liberal/general studies, management information systems, marketing management, mathematics, mathematics education, music, music education, music performance, music theory and composition, office supervision and management, organizational behavior, philosophy, physical education, political science and government, predentistry, prelaw, premedicine, prepharmacy, preveterinary, psychology, public relations, radio/television broadcasting, radio/television technology, radiograph medical technology, religion, science education, secondary education, social science education, social sciences, social work, sociology, speech, speech/communication/theater education, wellness and fitness leadership, wellness program management.

ACADEMIC PROGRAMS. 2-year transfer program, double major, dual enrollment of high school students, external degree, honors program, independent study, internships, student-designed major, study abroad, teacher preparation, visiting/exchange student program, Washington semester, cross-registration, 3-2 engineering program with South Dakota State University. 3-3 ministerial program with North American Baptist Seminary leading to master's of divinity. 2-2 program with North American Baptist College; liberal arts/career combination in engineering. **Remedial services:** Preadmission summer program, reduced course load, remedial instruction, special counselor, tutoring. **Placement/credit:** AP, CLEP Subject; 32 credit hours maximum for bachelor's degree.

ACADEMIC REQUIREMENTS. Freshmen must earn minimum GPA of 1.5 to continue in good standing. 53% of freshmen return for sophomore year. Students must declare major by end of second year. **Graduation requirements:** 64 hours for associate (20 in major), 128 hours for bachelor's (30 in major). Most students required to take courses in arts/fine arts, computer science, English, history, humanities, mathematics, philosophy/religion, biological/physical sciences, social sciences. **Postgraduate studies:** 50% from 2-year programs enter 4-year programs. 1% enter law school, 3% enter medical school, 6% enter MBA programs, 10% enter other graduate study. **Additional information:** Degree completion program offered for adults 25 and older with 64 hours previous education.

FRESHMAN ADMISSIONS. Selection criteria: Test scores, high school record, and rank in top half of graduating class important. Recommended units include English 4, mathematics 3, social science 3 and science 2. 1 unit computer recommended. **Test requirements:** SAT or ACT; score report by September 1.

1992 FRESHMAN CLASS PROFILE. 67 men, 96 women enrolled. 43% had high school GPA of 3.0 or higher, 43% between 2.0 and 2.99. **Academic background:** Mid 50% of enrolled freshmen had ACT composite between 19-24. 85% submitted ACT scores. **Characteristics:** 61% from in state, 89% live in college housing, 2% have minority backgrounds, 1% are foreign students. Average age is 18.

FALL-TERM APPLICATIONS. $20 fee. No closing date; applicants notified on a rolling basis; must reply by registration. Audition required for music, theater applicants. Portfolio recommended for art applicants. Deferred and early admission available.

STUDENT LIFE. Housing: Dormitories (men, women, coed); apartment housing available. Freshmen, sophomores required to live in college housing, unless over 20 years of age, or given permission by Vice President for Enrollment Management. **Activities:** Student government, radio, student newspaper, television, yearbook, choral groups, concert band, drama, jazz band, music ensembles, musical theater, pep band, nontraditional student association, student volunteer groups, religious organizations, Fellowship of Christian Athletes.

ATHLETICS. NAIA. **Intercollegiate:** Basketball, cross-country, football M, tennis, track and field, volleyball W. **Intramural:** Basketball, golf, racquetball, softball, tennis, volleyball.

STUDENT SERVICES. Aptitude testing, career counseling, employment service for undergraduates, freshman orientation, health services, personal counseling, placement service for graduates, special adviser for adult students, veterans counselor, center for women, services/facilities for handicapped.

ANNUAL EXPENSES. Tuition and fees (1992-93): $7,996. **Room and board:** $3,084. **Books and supplies:** $600. **Other expenses:** $900.

FINANCIAL AID. 94% of freshmen, 94% of continuing students receive some form of aid. 43% of grants, 92% of loans, 77% of jobs based on need. 148 enrolled freshmen were judged to have need, all were offered aid. Academic, music/drama, athletic, leadership, religious affiliation, minority scholarships available. **Aid applications:** No closing date; priority given to applications received by April 1; applicants notified on a rolling basis beginning on or about April 1; must reply within 2 weeks.

ADDRESS/TELEPHONE. Susan Reese, Director of Admissions, Sioux Falls College, 1501 South Prairie Avenue, Sioux Falls, SD 57105. (605) 331-6600. (800) 888-1047. Fax: (605) 331-6615.

Sisseton-Wahpeton Community College
Sisseton, South Dakota CB code: 3403

2-year public community college, coed. Founded in 1979. **Accreditation:** Regional. **Undergraduate enrollment:** 79 men, 106 women full time; 3 men, 11 women part time. **Faculty:** 20 total (11 full time). **Location:** Rural campus in rural community; 48 miles from Watertown. **Calendar:** Semester. **Microcomputers:** 26 located in classrooms, computer centers. **Special facilities:** Indians in North America book collection. **Additional facts:** Member of the American Indian Higher Education Consortium.

DEGREES OFFERED. AA, AAS. 19 associate degrees awarded in 1992. 16% in business and management, 8% business/office and marketing/distribution, 34% education, 10% allied health, 20% trade and industry.

UNDERGRADUATE MAJORS. Accounting, agricultural production, American Indian studies, business and office, business data entry equipment operation, business data processing and related programs, carpentry, early childhood education, education, electrical installation, masonry/tile setting, Native American languages, nursing, plumbing/pipefitting/steamfitting, rehabilitation counseling/services, retailing, social work.

ACADEMIC PROGRAMS. 2-year transfer program, independent study, internships. **Remedial services:** Tutoring, GED program and Adult Education. **Placement/credit:** Institutional tests.

ACADEMIC REQUIREMENTS. 95% of freshmen return for sophomore year. Students must declare major on application. **Graduation requirements:** 96 hours for associate. Most students required to take courses in computer science, English, foreign languages, history, humanities, mathematics, biological/physical sciences, social sciences.

FRESHMAN ADMISSIONS. Selection criteria: Open admissions. **High school preparation:** 16 units recommended. Recommended units include English 4, mathematics 4, physical science 4 and science 4. **Additional information:** Students entering vocational program may complete GED certificate while enrolled in classes.

1992 FRESHMAN CLASS PROFILE. 71 men, 84 women enrolled. **Characteristics:** 98% from in state, 100% commute, 94% have minority backgrounds. Average age is 26.

FALL-TERM APPLICATIONS. No fee. Closing date September 2; priority given to applications received by August 24; applicants notified on a rolling basis beginning on or about August 24.

STUDENT LIFE. Activities: Student government, student senate.

STUDENT SERVICES. Career counseling, freshman orientation, personal counseling, career interest testing, services/facilities for handicapped.

ANNUAL EXPENSES. Tuition and fees (1992-93): $2,475. **Books and supplies:** $375.

FINANCIAL AID. 98% of freshmen, 99% of continuing students receive some form of aid. Grants, loans, jobs available. 49 enrolled freshmen were judged to have need, all were offered aid. **Aid applications:** No closing date; applicants notified on a rolling basis.

ADDRESS/TELEPHONE. Darlene Redday, Admissions Clerk, Sisseton-Wahpeton Community College, PO Box 689, Sisseton, SD 57262-0689. (605) 698-3966. Fax: (605) 698-3132.

South Dakota School of Mines and Technology
Rapid City, South Dakota CB code: 6652

4-year public university and engineering college, coed. Founded in 1885. **Accreditation:** Regional. **Undergraduate enrollment:** 1,217 men, 432 women full time; 229 men, 299 women part time. **Graduate enrollment:** 121 men, 21 women full time; 124 men, 16 women part time. **Faculty:** 139 total (122 full time), 108 with doctorates or other terminal degrees. **Location:** Urban campus in small city; 350 miles northeast of Denver, Colorado. **Calendar:** Semester, limited summer session. **Microcomputers:** 310 located in libraries, classrooms, computer centers. **Special facilities:** Geology museum, art gallery.

DEGREES OFFERED. BS, MS, PhD. 227 bachelor's degrees awarded in 1992. 8% in computer sciences, 81% engineering, 5% physical sciences. Graduate degrees offered in 15 major fields of study.

UNDERGRADUATE MAJORS. Chemical engineering, chemistry, civil engineering, computer and information sciences, electrical/electronics/communications engineering, geological engineering, geology, industrial engineering, mathematics, mechanical engineering, metallurgical engineering, mining and mineral engineering, physics.

ACADEMIC PROGRAMS. Cooperative education, double major, dual enrollment of high school students, independent study. **Remedial services:** Learning center, reduced course load, remedial instruction, special counselor, tutoring, slide/tape modules for individualized instruction. **ROTC:** Army. **Placement/credit:** AP, CLEP Subject, institutional tests; 27 credit hours maximum for bachelor's degree.

ACADEMIC REQUIREMENTS. Freshmen must earn minimum GPA of 1.8 to continue in good standing. 71% of freshmen return for sophomore year. Students must declare major by end of first year. **Graduation requirements:** 136 hours for bachelor's (48 in major). Most students required to take courses in computer science, English, humanities, mathematics, biological/physical sciences, social sciences. **Postgraduate studies:** 1% enter law school, 1% enter medical school, 2% enter MBA programs, 6% enter other graduate study.

FRESHMAN ADMISSIONS. Selection criteria: Specified core curriculum with cumulative GPA of 2.0 and rank in top half of class. **High school preparation:** 13 units required; 15 recommended. Required and recommended units include English 4, mathematics 3, social science 3 and science 3. Foreign language 2 recommended. .5 unit computer science, .5 unit fine arts required. Science units must be laboratory. Mathematics must be algebra and higher level. **Test requirements:** SAT or ACT (ACT preferred); score report by August 15.

1992 FRESHMAN CLASS PROFILE. 293 men, 115 women enrolled. 67% had high school GPA of 3.0 or higher, 26% between 2.0 and 2.99. 26% were in top tenth and 54% were in top quarter of graduating class. **Academic background:** Mid 50% of enrolled freshmen had ACT composite between 21-26. 74% submitted ACT scores. **Characteristics:** 76% from in state, 65% live in college housing, 5% have minority backgrounds, 1% are foreign students, 5% join fraternities/sororities.

FALL-TERM APPLICATIONS. $15 fee. Closing date August 15; applicants notified on a rolling basis.

STUDENT LIFE. Housing: Dormitories (men, women); fraternity, sorority housing available. **Activities:** Student government, radio, student newspaper, yearbook, choral groups, concert band, drama, jazz band, marching band, music ensembles, pep band, fraternities, sororities, Circle-K, United Ministries of Higher Education, Young Republicans, Inter-Varsity Christian Fellowship.

ATHLETICS. NAIA. **Intercollegiate:** Basketball, cross-country, football M, track and field, volleyball W. **Intramural:** Basketball, golf, racquetball, skiing, softball, swimming, track and field, volleyball.

STUDENT SERVICES. Career counseling, employment service for undergraduates, freshman orientation, health services, personal counseling, placement service for graduates, services/facilities for handicapped.

ANNUAL EXPENSES. Tuition and fees (projected): $2,594, $2,092 additional for out-of-state students. **Room and board:** $2,620. **Books and supplies:** $500. **Other expenses:** $1,152.

FINANCIAL AID. 48% of freshmen, 46% of continuing students receive some form of aid. 85% of grants, 77% of loans, 35% of jobs based on need. 178 enrolled freshmen were judged to have need, all were offered aid. Academic, athletic scholarships available. **Aid applications:** No closing date; priority given to applications received by April 1; applicants notified on a rolling basis beginning on or about April 15; must reply within 2 weeks. **Additional information:** Closing date for scholarship applications February 15.

ADDRESS/TELEPHONE. Gary A. Bjordal, Director of Admissions, South Dakota School of Mines and Technology, 501 East St. Joseph Street, Rapid City, SD 57701-3995. (605) 394-2400. (800) 544-8162. Fax: (605) 394-6131.

South Dakota State University
Brookings, South Dakota CB code: 6653

Admissions: 94% of applicants accepted
Based on: ••• School record, test scores
•• Special talents
• Interview, recommendations
Completion: 85% of freshmen end year in good standing
60% graduate, 15% of these enter graduate study

4-year public university, coed. Founded in 1881. **Accreditation:** Regional. **Undergraduate enrollment:** 3,573 men, 3,061 women full time; 311 men, 575 women part time. **Graduate enrollment:** 296 men and women full time; 606 men and women part time. **Faculty:** 500 total (451 full time), 286 with doctorates or other terminal degrees. **Location:** Rural campus in large town; 50 miles from Sioux Falls. **Calendar:** Semester, limited summer session. Saturday and extensive evening/early morning classes. **Microcomputers:** 160 located in dormitories, libraries, classrooms, computer centers. **Special facilities:** McCrory Gardens, art center, Agricultural Heritage Museum, Northern Plains Biostress Laboratory.

DEGREES OFFERED. AS, BA, BS, MA, MS, MEd, PhD, Pharm D. 17 associate degrees awarded in 1992. 100% in agriculture. 1,163 bachelor's degrees awarded. 14% in agriculture, 13% engineering, 18% health sciences, 6% home economics, 21% social sciences. Graduate degrees offered in 29 major fields of study.

UNDERGRADUATE MAJORS. Associate: Agricultural sciences. **Bachelor's:** Advertising, aerospace science (Air Force), agribusiness, agricultural economics, agricultural education, agricultural engineering, agricultural sciences, agronomy, animal sciences, art education, biochemistry, biology, business economics, chemistry, child development/care/guidance, civil engineering, clinical laboratory science, clothing and textiles management/production/services, communications, computer and information sciences, dairy, early childhood education, economics, electrical/electronics/communications engineering, electronic technology, elementary education, engineering physics, English, English education, environmental science, family/consumer resource management, fashion merchandising, fine arts, fishing and fisheries, food science and nutrition, food sciences, foreign languages education, geography, German, graphic design, health education, history, home economics education, home economics journalism, horticultural science, horticulture, hotel/motel and restaurant management, individual and family development, institutional management, institutional/home management/supporting programs, interior design, journalism, junior high education, landscape architecture, liberal/general studies, materials engineering, mathematics, mathematics education, mechanical engineering, microbiology, military science (Army), music, music business management, music education, music performance, nursing, parks and recreation management, pharmacy, physical education, physics, plant sciences, political science and government, predentistry, prelaw, premedicine, preveterinary, psychology, radio/television broadcasting, range management, renewable natural resources, rural sociology, science education, secondary education, social science education, social studies education, sociology, soil sciences, Spanish, speech, speech correction, speech/communication/theater education, sports medicine, technical education, textiles and clothing, wildlife management.

ACADEMIC PROGRAMS. Accelerated program, cooperative education, double major, dual enrollment of high school students, honors program, independent study, internships, teacher preparation, visiting/exchange student program, New York semester. **Remedial services:** Reduced course load, tutoring. **ROTC:** Air Force, Army. **Placement/credit:** AP, CLEP General and Subject, institutional tests; 34 credit hours maximum for bachelor's degree.

ACADEMIC REQUIREMENTS. Freshmen must earn minimum GPA of 1.5 to continue in good standing. 76% of freshmen return for sophomore year. Students must declare major by end of second year. **Graduation requirements:** 64 hours for associate (16 in major), 128 hours for bachelor's (30 in major). Most students required to take courses in English, humanities, mathematics, biological/physical sciences, social sciences. **Postgraduate studies:** 40% from 2-year programs enter 4-year programs. 1% enter law school, 1% enter medical school, 1% enter MBA programs, 12% enter other graduate study. **Additional information:** Extensive evening and weekend degree-awarding classes available at Sioux Falls Center for Public Higher Education.

FRESHMAN ADMISSIONS. Selection criteria: School achievement record and test scores most important. **High school preparation:** 12 units required. Required units include English 4, mathematics 2, social science 3 and science 2. .5 computer science, .5 fine arts also required. Minimum of 3 units required for either mathematics or science. 2 advanced mathematics and 3 laboratory science or vice versa required. **Test requirements:** ACT; score report by August 1.

1992 FRESHMAN CLASS PROFILE. 2,437 men and women applied, 2,279 accepted; 1,534 enrolled. 15% were in top tenth and 38% were in top quarter of graduating class. **Academic background:** Mid 50% of enrolled freshmen had ACT composite between 18-25. 90% submitted ACT scores. **Characteristics:** 75% from in state, 95% live in college housing, 1% have minority backgrounds, 2% are foreign students. Average age is 18.

FALL-TERM APPLICATIONS. $15 fee. Closing date August 15; priority given to applications received by January 15; applicants notified on a rolling basis. Interview recommended. Deferred admission available.

STUDENT LIFE. Housing: Dormitories (coed); apartment, fraternity, sorority housing available. Limited single rooms with optional meal plan for upperclassmen. Students out of high school for less than 2 years required to live in campus housing unless living with family. **Activities:** Student government, radio, student newspaper, television, yearbook, choral groups, concert band, dance, drama, jazz band, marching band, music ensembles, musical theater, pep band, symphony orchestra, fraternities, sororities, 160 student organizations.

ATHLETICS. NCAA. **Intercollegiate:** Baseball M, basketball, cross-country, diving, football M, golf, softball W, swimming, tennis, track and field, volleyball W, wrestling M. **Intramural:** Badminton, basketball, cross-country, diving, fencing, golf, racquetball, soccer, softball, swimming, table tennis, tennis, track and field, volleyball, water polo, wrestling M.

STUDENT SERVICES. Aptitude testing, career counseling, employment service for undergraduates, freshman orientation, health services, personal counseling, placement service for graduates, special adviser for adult students, veterans counselor, adviser and services for nontraditional students, services/facilities for handicapped.

ANNUAL EXPENSES. Tuition and fees (1992-93): $2,030, $1,722 additional for out-of-state students. **Room and board:** $2,448. **Books and supplies:** $560. **Other expenses:** $1,170.

FINANCIAL AID. 82% of freshmen, 82% of continuing students receive some form of aid. Grants, loans, jobs available. 950 enrolled freshmen were judged to have need, all were offered aid. Academic, music/drama, art, athletic, state/district residency, leadership, minority scholarships available. **Aid applications:** No closing date; priority given to applications received by March 15; applicants notified on a rolling basis beginning on or about April 1; must reply within 3 weeks.

ADDRESS/TELEPHONE. Tracy Welsh, Director of Admissions, South Dakota State University, PO Box 2201, Brookings, SD 57007-0649. (605) 688-4121.

Southeast Vo-Tech Institute
Sioux Falls, South Dakota CB code: 7054

2-year public technical college. **Accreditation:** Regional. **Undergraduate enrollment:** 828 men and women. **Location:** Urban campus in small city. **Calendar:** Quarter.

FRESHMAN ADMISSIONS. Selection criteria: Must take in-house tests for admission.

ANNUAL EXPENSES. Tuition and fees: $1,910. **Books and supplies:** $500. **Other expenses:** $1,350.

ADDRESS/TELEPHONE. Leni Warwick, Director of Admissions/Public Relations, Southeast Vo-Tech Institute, 2301 Career Place, Sioux Falls, SD 57107. (605) 331-7624. Fax: (605) 331-7906.

University of South Dakota
Vermillion, South Dakota CB code: 6881

4-year public university, coed. Founded in 1862. **Accreditation:** Regional. **Undergraduate enrollment:** 2,470 men, 2,875 women full time; 409 men, 802 women part time. **Graduate enrollment:** 516 men, 468 women full time; 470 men, 683 women part time. **Faculty:** 521 total (493 full time), 377 with doctorates or other terminal degrees. **Location:** Rural campus in large town; 65 miles from Sioux Falls, 35 miles from Sioux City, Iowa. **Calendar:** Semester, extensive summer session. **Microcomputers:** 253 located in dormitories, libraries, classrooms, computer centers. **Special facilities:** Art gallery, music center, South Dakota history museums.

DEGREES OFFERED. AA, BA, BS, BFA, MA, MS, MBA, MFA, PhD, EdD, MD. 181 associate degrees awarded in 1992. 83% in health sciences, 14% allied health. 732 bachelor's degrees awarded. 27% in business and management, 5% communications, 17% teacher education, 9% health sciences, 5% letters/literature, 8% parks/recreation, protective services, public affairs, 7% psychology, 6% social sciences. Graduate degrees offered in 45 major fields of study.

UNDERGRADUATE MAJORS. Associate: Criminal justice studies, dental hygiene, nursing. **Bachelor's:** Accounting, advertising, alcohol and drug abuse studies, anthropology, art education, biological and physical sciences, biology, business administration and management, business economics, chemistry, classics, clinical laboratory science, communications, computer and information sciences, criminal justice studies, dental hygiene, dramatic arts, earth sciences, economics, elementary education, English, English education, foreign languages education, French, German, Greek (classical), health care administration, health education, history, humanities, journalism, Latin, liberal/general studies, mathematics, mathematics education, music education, music performance, nurse anesthetist, parks and recreation management, philosophy, physical education, physics, political science and government, psychology, public relations, radio/television broadcasting, science education, secondary education, social science education, social studies education, social work, sociology, Spanish, special education, speech, speech correction, speech pathology/audiology, speech/communication/theater education, statistics, studio art.

ACADEMIC PROGRAMS. Accelerated program, double major, dual enrollment of high school students, education specialist degree, external degree, honors program, independent study, internships, student-designed major, study abroad, teacher preparation, telecourses, visiting/exchange student program. **Remedial services:** Preadmission summer program, reduced course load, remedial instruction, tutoring. **ROTC:** Army. **Placement/credit:** AP, CLEP Subject, institutional tests; 30 credit hours maximum for bachelor's degree.

ACADEMIC REQUIREMENTS. Freshmen must earn minimum GPA of 1.65 to continue in good standing. Students must declare major by end of second year. **Graduation requirements:** 71 hours for associate (36 in major), 128 hours for bachelor's (36 in major). Most students required to take courses in arts/fine arts, English, humanities, mathematics, biological/physical sciences, social sciences.

FRESHMAN ADMISSIONS. Selection criteria: Acceptance in good standing granted if applicant has GPA of 2.0 or above in required courses. ACT scores and class rank also considered. **High school preparation:** 13 units required. Required and recommended units include English 4, mathematics 2-3, social science 3 and science 2-3. Foreign language 2 recommended. .5 computer science and .5 fine arts also required. **Test requirements:** SAT or ACT (ACT preferred); score report by September 4. **Additional information:** Applicants lacking required high school units admitted provisionally.

1992 FRESHMAN CLASS PROFILE. Characteristics: 67% from in state, 53% live in college housing, 6% have minority backgrounds, 2% are foreign students, 6% join fraternities/sororities.

FALL-TERM APPLICATIONS. $15 fee. No closing date; applicants notified on a rolling basis. Interview recommended for dental hygiene, nursing, physician assistant applicants. Deferred admission available. February 15 closing date for application to dental hygiene program. February 15 closing date for application to nursing program.

STUDENT LIFE. Housing: Dormitories (women, coed); apartment, fraternity, sorority, handicapped housing available. Students required to live in residence halls for first 2 years unless living in fraternity or sorority housing. **Activities:** Student government, radio, student newspaper, television, yearbook, choral groups, concert band, dance, drama, jazz band, marching band, music ensembles, musical theater, opera, pep band, symphony orchestra, madrigal, stage band, fraternities, sororities, Young Democrats, Young Republicans, several campus religious centers, academic fraternities, honor groups.

ATHLETICS. NCAA. **Intercollegiate:** Baseball M, basketball, cross-country, diving, football M, softball W, swimming, tennis, track and field, volleyball W. **Intramural:** Badminton, baseball M, basketball, bowling, cross-country, diving, golf, racquetball, rugby M, soccer, softball, swimming, tennis, track and field, volleyball, water polo, wrestling M.

STUDENT SERVICES. Aptitude testing, career counseling, employment service for undergraduates, freshman orientation, health services, on-campus day care, personal counseling, placement service for graduates, special adviser for adult students, veterans counselor, services/facilities for handicapped.

ANNUAL EXPENSES. Tuition and fees (1992-93): $2,073, $1,722 additional for out-of-state students. **Room and board:** $2,420. **Books and supplies:** $650. **Other expenses:** $1,050.

FINANCIAL AID. 81% of freshmen, 81% of continuing students receive some form of aid. 70% of grants, 85% of loans, 28% of jobs based on need. 880 enrolled freshmen were judged to have need, all were offered aid. Academic, music/drama, art, athletic, minority scholarships available. **Aid applications:** No closing date; priority given to applications received by February 15; applicants notified on a rolling basis beginning on or about May 1; must reply within 2 weeks.

ADDRESS/TELEPHONE. David Lorenz, Director of Admissions, University of South Dakota, 414 East Clark, Vermillion, SD 57069-2390. (605) 677-5434. Fax: (605) 677-5073.

Western Dakota Vocational Technical Institute
Rapid City, South Dakota — CB code: 6393

2-year public technical college, coed. **Accreditation:** Regional. **Undergraduate enrollment:** 334 men, 269 women full time; 6 men, 54 women part time. **Faculty:** 53 total (45 full time), 2 with doctorates or other terminal degrees. **Location:** Rural campus in small city; about 3 miles from downtown. **Calendar:** Semester. Extensive evening/early morning classes. **Microcomputers:** 75 located in libraries, classrooms, computer centers. **Special facilities:** 500-acre operating ranch for agricultural production students.

DEGREES OFFERED. AAS. 118 associate degrees awarded in 1992. 13% in architecture and environmental design, 20% business and management, 16% business/office and marketing/distribution, 28% computer sciences, 19% trade and industry.

UNDERGRADUATE MAJORS. Accounting, agribusiness, agricultural production, automotive mechanics, automotive technology, business and management, business and office, computer servicing technology, diesel engine mechanics, drafting and design technology, electrical and electronics equipment repair, electrical technology, electromechanical technology, electronic technology, equestrian science, industrial equipment maintenance and repair, law enforcement and corrections, legal assistant/paralegal, secretarial and related programs.

ACADEMIC PROGRAMS. Internships. **Remedial services:** Preadmission summer program, reduced course load, remedial instruction, special counselor, tutoring. **Placement/credit:** Institutional tests; 35 credit hours maximum for associate degree.

ACADEMIC REQUIREMENTS. Freshmen must earn minimum GPA of 2.0 to continue in good standing. 85% of freshmen return for sophomore year. Students must declare major on application. **Graduation requirements:** 71 hours for associate (71 in major). Most students required to take courses in computer science, English, humanities, mathematics, social sciences.

FRESHMAN ADMISSIONS. Selection criteria: Open admissions. Selected criteria for nursing, law enforcement, child development and paralegal programs. Recommended units include English 4 and mathematics 2. **Additional information:** Any person 16 years of age or older and able to profit from instruction may be eligible for admission.

1992 FRESHMAN CLASS PROFILE. 152 men, 153 women enrolled. 16% had high school GPA of 3.0 or higher, 48% between 2.0 and 2.99. **Characteristics:** 95% from in state, 100% commute, 13% have minority backgrounds. Average age is 25.

FALL-TERM APPLICATIONS. $10 fee. No closing date; priority given to applications received by July 1; applicants notified on a rolling basis; must reply within 10 days. Interview required for law enforcement, practical nursing, paralegal applicants. Require Test of Adult Basic Education unless other recent test results indicate ability to benefit from instruction.

STUDENT LIFE. Housing: Limited services/facilities available for learning disabled. **Activities:** Student government, Native American Club.

STUDENT SERVICES. Aptitude testing, career counseling, employment service for undergraduates, freshman orientation, on-campus day care, personal counseling, placement service for graduates, special adviser for adult students, single parent/displaced homemaker counselor, prevocational brush-up courses, services/facilities for handicapped.

ANNUAL EXPENSES. Tuition and fees: $2,082. Tool fees required for some programs, ranging from $400 to $1600. **Books and supplies:** $600.

FINANCIAL AID. 80% of freshmen, 80% of continuing students receive some form of aid. 97% of grants, 84% of loans, all jobs based on need. 295 enrolled freshmen were judged to have need, all were offered aid. Leadership scholarships available. **Aid applications:** No closing date; priority given to applications received by July 1; applicants notified on a rolling basis beginning on or about June 26; must reply within 10 days.

ADDRESS/TELEPHONE. Nancy Richter, Assistant Director/Student Services, Western Dakota Vocational Technical Institute, 1600 Sedivy Lane, Rapid City, SD 57701. (605) 394-4034.

Tennessee

American Baptist College of ABT Seminary
Nashville, Tennessee CB code: 0511

4-year private Bible college, coed, affiliated with Southern Baptist Convention. Founded in 1924. **Undergraduate enrollment:** 199 men and women full time; 32 men and women part time. **Faculty:** 15 total (8 full time). **Location:** Urban campus in large city. **Calendar:** Semester.

DEGREES OFFERED. BA. 32 bachelor's degrees awarded in 1992.

UNDERGRADUATE MAJORS. Bible studies, business administration and management, theological studies.

ACADEMIC PROGRAMS. Double major.

ACADEMIC REQUIREMENTS. All students major in Bible studies or theology. Additional major in business administration optional.

FRESHMAN ADMISSIONS. Selection criteria: Admissions committee selects applicants best qualified to benefit from opportunities offered by college.

1992 FRESHMAN CLASS PROFILE. 41 men and women enrolled. **Characteristics:** 74% commute.

FALL-TERM APPLICATIONS. $15 fee. Closing date July 1; applicants notified on a rolling basis; must reply within 2 weeks. Essay required.

STUDENT LIFE. Housing: Dormitories (men, women); apartment housing available.

ANNUAL EXPENSES. Tuition and fees (1992-93): $2,000. **Room and board:** $1,984. **Books and supplies:** $400.

FINANCIAL AID. Grants, loans, jobs available. **Aid applications:** No closing date; applicants notified on a rolling basis; must reply within 2 weeks.

ADDRESS/TELEPHONE. Georgia Larnes, Director of Admissions, American Baptist College of ABT Seminary, 1800 Whites Creek Pike, Nashville, TN 37207. (615) 262-1369.

American Technical Institute
Brunswick, Tennessee CB code: 7040

4-year private college of nuclear engineering technology, coed. **Accreditation:** Regional. **Undergraduate enrollment:** 850 men and women. **Location:** Suburban campus in very large city; within greater-Memphis metropolitan area. **Calendar:** Semester. **Additional facts:** Students must be employed at one of the following nuclear facilities: Entergy Corporation (Port Gibson, MS), Gulf States Utilities (St. Francisville, LA), the Georgia Power Company (Plant Hatch at Baxley, GA or Plant Vogtle at Waynesboro, GA). All teaching takes place at these locations.

FRESHMAN ADMISSIONS. Selection criteria: Students must be employed by Entergy Corporation, Gulf States Utilities, or the Georgia Power Company.

ADDRESS/TELEPHONE. Dr. Donald R. Brady, Dean of Admissions and Special Programs, American Technical Institute, 8760 Baylor Road, Box 8, Brunswick, TN 38014. (901) 382-5857.

Aquinas Junior College
Nashville, Tennessee CB code: 7318

2-year private junior college, coed, affiliated with Roman Catholic Church. Founded in 1961. **Accreditation:** Regional. **Undergraduate enrollment:** 100 men, 120 women full time; 22 men, 148 women part time. **Faculty:** 46 total (35 full time). **Location:** Urban campus in large city. **Calendar:** Semester. **Microcomputers:** 22 located in libraries, classrooms.

DEGREES OFFERED. AA, AS. 92 associate degrees awarded in 1992.

UNDERGRADUATE MAJORS. Criminal justice studies, liberal/general studies, nursing.

ACADEMIC PROGRAMS. 2-year transfer program. **Placement/credit:** Institutional tests.

ACADEMIC REQUIREMENTS. Freshmen must earn minimum GPA of 2.0 to continue in good standing. Students must declare major on application. **Graduation requirements:** 62 hours for associate. Most students required to take courses in English, history, mathematics, philosophy/religion, biological/physical sciences.

FRESHMAN ADMISSIONS. Selection criteria: School achievement record, test scores, recommendations, interview important. School and community activities considered. **High school preparation:** 16 units required. Required and recommended units include English 4, mathematics 2, social science 2 and science 2. Foreign language 2 recommended. **Test requirements:** SAT or ACT (ACT preferred); score report by July 31.

1992 FRESHMAN CLASS PROFILE. 280 men and women enrolled.

FALL-TERM APPLICATIONS. $15 fee. Closing date July 31; applicants notified on a rolling basis. Interview required. Essay required.

STUDENT LIFE. Activities: Student government, student newspaper.

ATHLETICS. NJCAA. **Intercollegiate:** Baseball M, basketball M.

STUDENT SERVICES. Freshman orientation.

ANNUAL EXPENSES. Tuition and fees (projected): $4,310. **Books and supplies:** $500. **Other expenses:** $650.

FINANCIAL AID. 5% of freshmen, 38% of continuing students receive some form of aid. All grants, 60% of loans, all jobs based on need. 16 enrolled freshmen were judged to have need, all were offered aid. Academic scholarships available. **Aid applications:** No closing date; applicants notified on a rolling basis; must reply within 3 weeks.

ADDRESS/TELEPHONE. Sr. Mary Julius, OP, Director of Admissions, Aquinas Junior College, 4210 Harding Road, Nashville, TN 37205. (615) 297-7545. Fax: (615) 297-7557 ext. 253.

Austin Peay State University
Clarksville, Tennessee CB code: 1028

4-year public university, coed. Founded in 1927. **Accreditation:** Regional. **Undergraduate enrollment:** 1,769 men, 2,739 women full time; 1,808 men, 1,087 women part time. **Graduate enrollment:** 32 men, 53 women full time; 78 men, 250 women part time. **Faculty:** 364 total (239 full time), 155 with doctorates or other terminal degrees. **Location:** Urban campus in small city; 45 miles from Nashville. **Calendar:** Semester, limited summer session. Saturday classes. **Microcomputers:** 70 located in classrooms. **Special facilities:** Art gallery, biological museum.

DEGREES OFFERED. AS, BA, BS, BFA, MA, MS, MEd. 111 associate degrees awarded in 1992. 22% in business/office and marketing/distribution, 78% multi/interdisciplinary studies. 607 bachelor's degrees awarded. 6% in architecture and environmental design, 21% business and management, 22% education, 12% health sciences, 6% psychology, 6% social sciences, 8% visual and performing arts. Graduate degrees offered in 19 major fields of study.

UNDERGRADUATE MAJORS. Associate: Advertising, automotive mechanics, automotive technology, business and office, business data processing and related programs, computer and information sciences, construction, electrical and electronics equipment repair, electronic technology, food science and nutrition, law enforcement and corrections, liberal/general studies, radio/television broadcasting, secretarial and related programs, welding technology. **Bachelor's:** Accounting, agricultural sciences, biology, business administration and management, business and management, business economics, chemistry, city/community/regional planning, clinical laboratory science, communications, computer and information sciences, counseling psychology, dental hygiene, dramatic arts, early childhood education, economics, education administration, electronic technology, elementary education, engineering and engineering-related technologies, English, English literature, finance, fine arts, foreign languages (multiple emphasis), geology, health education, health sciences, history, information sciences and systems, journalism, manufacturing technology, mathematics, medical laboratory technologies, medical radiation dosimetry, music, nuclear medical technology, nursing, office supervision and management, philosophy, physical education, physical therapy, physics, political science and government, psychology, public administration, radio/television technology, radiograph medical technology, secondary education, secretarial and related programs, social work, sociology, special education, speech, urban studies, visual and performing arts.

ACADEMIC PROGRAMS. 2-year transfer program, accelerated program, double major, dual enrollment of high school students, education specialist degree, honors program, independent study, internships, study abroad, teacher preparation; liberal arts/career combination in health sciences. **Remedial services:** Learning center, remedial instruction, special counselor, tutoring, special assessment testing. **ROTC:** Army. **Placement/credit:** AP, CLEP General and Subject, institutional tests; 32 credit hours maximum for associate degree; 64 credit hours maximum for bachelor's degree.

ACADEMIC REQUIREMENTS. Freshmen must earn minimum GPA of 1.5 to continue in good standing. 55% of freshmen return for sophomore year. Students must declare major on application. **Graduation requirements:** 64 hours for associate, 128 hours for bachelor's. Most students required to take courses in arts/fine arts, computer science, English, history, humanities, mathematics, biological/physical sciences, social sciences.

FRESHMAN ADMISSIONS. Selection criteria: SAT combined score of 720 to 740, ACT composite score of 19, or minimum high school GPA of 2.75. Additional testing required if criteria not met. **High school preparation:** 14 units required. Required units include English 4, foreign language 2, mathematics 3, social science 2 and science 2. Mathematics units should be algebra I and II, 1 geometry or advanced mathematics. Science units should include 1 laboratory science. Social science units should be 1 social studies, 1 US history. Foreign language units must be in 1 language. 1 visual and/or performing arts also required. **Test requirements:** SAT or ACT (ACT preferred); score report by June 30.

1992 FRESHMAN CLASS PROFILE. 298 men, 487 women enrolled. **Academic background:** Mid 50% of enrolled freshmen had ACT composite between 13-19. 99% submitted ACT scores. **Characteristics:** 85% from in state, 60% commute, 24% have minority backgrounds, 1% are foreign students, 20% join fraternities/sororities. Average age is 20.

FALL-TERM APPLICATIONS. $5 fee. Closing date August 15; applicants notified on a rolling basis. Essay recommended. Deferred and early admission available.

STUDENT LIFE. Housing: Dormitories (men, women, coed); apartment, fraternity housing available. **Activities:** Student government, radio, student newspaper, television, yearbook, literary journal, choral groups, concert band, dance, drama, jazz band, marching band, music ensembles, musical theater, pep band, symphony orchestra, fraternities, sororities, S.T.O.M.P., Baptist Student Union, Wesley Foundation, Church of Christ Student Center, Catholic Community Organization.

ATHLETICS. NCAA. **Intercollegiate:** Baseball M, basketball, cross-country, football M, golf, softball W, tennis, track and field, volleyball W. **Intramural:** Badminton, basketball, bowling, gymnastics, handball, racquetball, rifle, soccer, softball, swimming, table tennis, tennis, volleyball, wrestling M.

STUDENT SERVICES. Aptitude testing, career counseling, employment service for undergraduates, freshman orientation, health services, on-campus day care, personal counseling, placement service for graduates, special adviser for adult students, veterans counselor, services/facilities for handicapped.

ANNUAL EXPENSES. Tuition and fees (1992-93): $1,726, $3,602 additional for out-of-state students. **Room and board:** $2,750. **Books and supplies:** $465. **Other expenses:** $1,500.

FINANCIAL AID. 70% of freshmen, 70% of continuing students receive some form of aid. 67% of grants, 94% of loans, 30% of jobs based on need. Academic, music/drama, art, athletic, leadership, alumni affiliation, religious affiliation, minority scholarships available. **Aid applications:** No closing date; priority given to applications received by April 1; applicants notified on a rolling basis beginning on or about June 1; must reply within 2 weeks.

ADDRESS/TELEPHONE. Mr. Charles McCorkle, Director of Admissions, Austin Peay State University, P.O. Box 4548, Clarksville, TN 37044. (615) 648-7661. (800) 844-APSU. Fax: (615) 648-7475.

Belmont University
Nashville, Tennessee CB code: 1058

4-year private university, coed, affiliated with Southern Baptist Convention. Founded in 1951. **Accreditation:** Regional. **Undergraduate enrollment:** 851 men, 1,107 women full time; 250 men, 395 women part time. **Graduate enrollment:** 80 men, 86 women full time; 41 men, 55 women part time. **Faculty:** 298 total (143 full time), 141 with doctorates or other terminal degrees. **Location:** Urban campus in large city; 250 miles from Atlanta, Georgia, and St. Louis, Missouri. **Calendar:** Semester. **Microcomputers:** 99 located in computer centers. **Special facilities:** 22-track recording studio, 140-year-old antebellum mansion.

DEGREES OFFERED. BA, BS, MBA, MEd. 6 associate degrees awarded in 1992. 100% in business/office and marketing/distribution. 470 bachelor's degrees awarded in 1992. 28% in business and management, 10% business/office and marketing/distribution, 5% communications, 9% teacher education, 7% allied health, 5% letters/literature, 7% psychology, 5% social sciences, 8% visual and performing arts. Graduate degrees offered in 4 major fields of study.

UNDERGRADUATE MAJORS. Accounting, art history, behavioral sciences, biology, business administration and management, business and management, business economics, chemistry, communications, computer and information sciences, computer programming, criminal justice studies, dramatic arts, economics, education, elementary education, engineering physics, English, finance, fine arts, French, history, hotel/motel and restaurant management, imaging technology, information sciences and systems, international relations, journalism, library science, mathematics, medical laboratory technologies, music, music education, nursing, philosophy, physical sciences, physics, political science and government, prelaw, psychology, radio/television broadcasting, radio/television technology, religion, religious education, religious music, science and engineering, science education, secondary education, secretarial and related programs, social work, sociology, Spanish, speech, systems analysis, visual and performing arts.

ACADEMIC PROGRAMS. Accelerated program, cooperative education, double major, honors program, independent study, internships, study abroad, teacher preparation; liberal arts/career combination in engineering, health sciences. **Remedial services:** Preadmission summer program, reduced course load, remedial instruction, tutoring. **ROTC:** Air Force, Army, Naval. **Placement/credit:** AP, CLEP General and Subject, institutional tests; 12 credit hours maximum for associate degree; 24 credit hours maximum for bachelor's degree.

ACADEMIC REQUIREMENTS. Freshmen must earn minimum GPA of 2.0 to continue in good standing. 63% of freshmen return for sophomore year. Students must declare major on application. **Graduation requirements:** 64 hours for associate (25 in major), 128 hours for bachelor's (30 in major). Most students required to take courses in English, history, humanities, mathematics, philosophy/religion, biological/physical sciences, social sciences. **Postgraduate studies:** 1% enter law school, 1% enter medical school, 6% enter MBA programs, 4% enter other graduate study.

FRESHMAN ADMISSIONS. Selection criteria: Admissions based on test scores, GPA, class rank, recommendations of guidance counselor. **High school preparation:** 10 units required. Required units include English 4 and mathematics 2. 4 units from foreign language, social studies, or science required. **Test requirements:** SAT or ACT (ACT preferred); score report by August 1.

1992 FRESHMAN CLASS PROFILE. 377 men, 518 women enrolled. 73% had high school GPA of 3.0 or higher, 26% between 2.0 and 2.99. **Characteristics:** 72% from in state, 60% commute, 5% have minority backgrounds, 5% are foreign students. Average age is 21.

FALL-TERM APPLICATIONS. $25 fee, may be waived for applicants with need. Closing date August 3; priority given to applications received by May 1; applicants notified on a rolling basis; must reply as soon as possible. Audition required for music applicants. Interview recommended for probationary or academically weak applicants. Deferred and early admission available.

STUDENT LIFE. Housing: Dormitories (men, women); apartment, handicapped housing available. **Activities:** Student government, student newspaper, yearbook, choral groups, concert band, drama, jazz band, marching band, music ensembles, musical theater, opera, pep band, symphony orchestra, fraternities, sororities, Baptist Student Union, International Student Association, Christian Music Society, Democrats, Students for America, Campus Crusade for Christ, Fellowship of Christian Athletes.

ATHLETICS. NAIA. **Intercollegiate:** Baseball M, basketball, cross-country, golf, soccer M, softball W, tennis, track and field, volleyball W. **Intramural:** Basketball, golf M, racquetball, softball, table tennis, tennis, volleyball.

STUDENT SERVICES. Career counseling, employment service for undergraduates, freshman orientation, health services, personal counseling, placement service for graduates, special adviser for adult students, veterans counselor, special adviser for minority students, services/facilities for handicapped.

ANNUAL EXPENSES. Tuition and fees: $7,300. Graduate program in business on a trimester academic year, students pay $400 or $448 per credit hour. Graduate program in education on a semester academic year, students pay $318 per credit. **Room and board:** $3,490. **Books and supplies:** $580. **Other expenses:** $900.

FINANCIAL AID. 70% of freshmen, 75% of continuing students receive some form of aid. 72% of grants, 81% of loans, 25% of jobs based on need. Academic, music/drama, athletic, alumni affiliation, religious affiliation scholarships available. **Aid applications:** No closing date; priority given to applications received by March 15; applicants notified on a rolling basis beginning on or about May 15; must reply within 2 weeks.

ADDRESS/TELEPHONE. Claude Pressnell, Director of Admissions, Belmont University, 1900 Belmont Boulevard, Nashville, TN 37212-3757. (615) 385-6785.

Bethel College
McKenzie, Tennessee CB code: 1063

4-year private liberal arts college, coed, affiliated with Cumberland Presbyterian Church. Founded in 1842. **Accreditation:** Regional. **Undergraduate enrollment:** 421 men and women. **Graduate enrollment:** 10 men and women full time; 40 men and women part time. **Faculty:** 48 total (30 full time), 18 with doctorates or other terminal degrees. **Location:** Rural campus in small town; 115 miles from Nashville, 120 miles from Memphis. **Calendar:** Semester, limited summer session. **Microcomputers:** Located in libraries, classrooms, computer centers. **Special facilities:** Tennessee Wildlife Agency Research Laboratory.

DEGREES OFFERED. BA, BS, MA, MEd. 60 bachelor's degrees awarded in 1992. Graduate degrees offered in 1 major field of study.

UNDERGRADUATE MAJORS. Accounting, actuarial sciences, applied mathematics, art education, biological and physical sciences, biology, business administration and management, business and management, communications, elementary education, English, fine arts, health education, humanities and social sciences, mathematics education, music, physical education, psychology, religion, religious education, science education, secondary education, social sciences, special education, written communication.

ACADEMIC PROGRAMS. Accelerated program, double major, dual enrollment of high school students, honors program, independent study, internships, student-designed major, teacher preparation, cross-registration; liberal arts/career combination in engineering. **Remedial services:** Learning center, preadmission summer program, reduced course load, remedial instruction, special counselor, tutoring. **Placement/credit:** AP, CLEP General and Subject, institutional tests; 45 credit hours maximum for bachelor's degree.

ACADEMIC REQUIREMENTS. Freshmen must earn minimum GPA of 1.5 to continue in good standing. Academically restricted freshmen limited to 14 quarter hours during first 2 quarters and must earn 2.0 GPA by end of second quarter. 72% of freshmen return for sophomore year. Students must declare major by end of second year. **Graduation requirements:** 128 hours for bachelor's (50 in major). Most students required to take courses in computer science, English, history, humanities, mathematics, philosophy/religion, biological/physical sciences, social sciences. **Additional information:** Beyond Campus internship program, including at least 1 quarter of field experience and offering up to 16 hours of credit, required.

FRESHMAN ADMISSIONS. Selection criteria: Minimum SAT or ACT score and rank in top half of high school class preferred. Counselor recommendation, interview considered for academically marginal applicants. **High school preparation:** 14 units required. Required units include English 4, mathematics 3, social science 2 and science 2. One fine arts also required. **Test requirements:** SAT or ACT (ACT preferred); score report by August 1.

1992 FRESHMAN CLASS PROFILE. 128 men and women enrolled. **Academic background:** Mid 50% of enrolled freshmen had ACT composite between 14-21. 75% submitted ACT scores. **Characteristics:** 81% from in state, 78% live in college housing, 10% have minority backgrounds, 4% are foreign students. Average age is 19.

FALL-TERM APPLICATIONS. $10 fee, may be waived for applicants with need. Closing date August 1; priority given to applications received by April 1; applicants notified on a rolling basis. Interview recommended. Deferred and early admission available.

STUDENT LIFE. Housing: Dormitories (men, women); apartment housing available. **Activities:** Student government, student newspaper, yearbook, choral groups, drama, music ensembles, musical theater, fraternities, sororities, Fellowship of Christian Athletes, Young Democrats, Christian fellowship, Black Students United, International Club, honor societies, Young Republicans.

ATHLETICS. NAIA. **Intercollegiate:** Baseball M, basketball, football M, golf M, softball W, tennis W. **Intramural:** Basketball, softball, swimming, table tennis, volleyball.

STUDENT SERVICES. Aptitude testing, career counseling, employment service for undergraduates, freshman orientation, personal counseling, placement service for graduates, veterans counselor, adult learner support group, services/facilities for handicapped.

ANNUAL EXPENSES. Tuition and fees (1992-93): $5,250. **Room and board:** $2,650. **Books and supplies:** $500. **Other expenses:** $1,000.

FINANCIAL AID. 90% of freshmen, 84% of continuing students receive some form of aid. Grants, loans, jobs available. Academic, music/drama, athletic, leadership, religious affiliation scholarships available. **Aid applications:** No closing date; priority given to applications received by May 1; applicants notified on a rolling basis; must reply within 3 weeks.

ADDRESS/TELEPHONE. Joseph Rigell, Assistant to President, Bethel College, Cherry Street, McKenzie, TN 38201. (901) 352-1000. (800) 441-4940. Fax: (901) 352-1008.

Bristol University
Bristol, Tennessee — CB code: 0972

4-year proprietary business college, coed. Founded in 1895. **Undergraduate enrollment:** 72 men, 84 women full time; 31 men, 27 women part time. **Graduate enrollment:** 37 men, 43 women full time; 24 men, 22 women part time. **Faculty:** 74 total (38 full time). **Location:** Urban campus in large town; 110 miles from Knoxville, 140 miles from Roanoke, Virginia. **Calendar:** Twelve-month module system divided into two five-month semesters and one two-month summer mini-session. Each class lasts one month and is worth three semester credit hours. Saturday and extensive evening/early morning classes.

DEGREES OFFERED. AA, BS, MBA. 36 associate degrees awarded in 1992. 42 bachelor's degrees awarded. Graduate degrees offered in 14 major fields of study.

UNDERGRADUATE MAJORS. Associate: Accounting, business and office, business computer/console/peripheral equipment operation, business data programming, business economics, business statistics, computer and information sciences, court reporting, finance, hospitality and recreation marketing, human resources development, institutional management, international business management, labor/industrial relations, legal assistant/paralegal, management information systems, marketing and distribution, marketing management, medical records technology, music business management, office supervision and management, operations research, organizational behavior, parks and recreation management, personnel management, public relations, real estate, secretarial and related programs, small business management and ownership. **Bachelor's:** Business administration and management, business and management, business economics, business statistics, computer and information sciences, human resources development, institutional management, international business management, labor/industrial relations, legal assistant/paralegal, management information systems, marketing management, music business management, operations research, organizational behavior, parks and recreation management, personnel management, real estate, small business management and ownership.

ACADEMIC PROGRAMS. Accelerated program, honors program, independent study, internships; combined bachelor's/graduate program in business administration. **Placement/credit:** Institutional tests.

ACADEMIC REQUIREMENTS. Freshmen must earn minimum GPA of 2.0 to continue in good standing. Students must declare major by end of first year. **Graduation requirements:** 60 hours for associate (15 in major), 120 hours for bachelor's (24 in major). Most students required to take courses in computer science, English, history, humanities, mathematics, philosophy/religion. **Postgraduate studies:** 35% from 2-year programs enter 4-year programs.

FRESHMAN ADMISSIONS. Selection criteria: GPA and interview most important. Minimum GPA 2.0.

1992 FRESHMAN CLASS PROFILE. 113 men and women enrolled. **Characteristics:** 60% from in state, 100% commute, 5% have minority backgrounds, 1% are foreign students.

FALL-TERM APPLICATIONS. $10 fee. No closing date; applicants notified on a rolling basis. Interview required.

STUDENT LIFE. Activities: Student newspaper, sororities.

ATHLETICS. Intercollegiate: Baseball M, tennis M.

STUDENT SERVICES. Employment service for undergraduates, personal counseling.

ANNUAL EXPENSES. Tuition and fees (1992-93): $6,000. Tuition and fees includes books and supplies.

FINANCIAL AID. 60% of freshmen, 55% of continuing students receive some form of aid. All grants, 89% of loans, all jobs based on need. **Aid applications:** No closing date; applicants notified on a rolling basis.

ADDRESS/TELEPHONE. Gill Payne, Director of Admissions, Bristol University, PO Box 4366, Suite 300, 1241 Volunteer Parkway, Executive Park, Bristol, TN 37625. (615) 968-1442. (800) 366-1442. Fax: (615) 968-9087.

Carson-Newman College
Jefferson City, Tennessee — CB code: 1102

Admissions:	86% of applicants accepted
Based on:	••• School record
	•• Activities, recommendations, test scores
	• Essay, interview, religious affiliation/ commitment, special talents
Completion:	80% of freshmen end year in good standing
	57% graduate, 35% of these enter graduate study

4-year private liberal arts college, coed, affiliated with Southern Baptist Convention. Founded in 1851. **Accreditation:** Regional. **Undergraduate enrollment:** 756 men, 929 women full time; 53 men, 138 women part time. **Graduate enrollment:** 16 men, 18 women full time; 14 men, 61 women part time. **Faculty:** 182 total (115 full time), 71 with doctorates or other terminal degrees. **Location:** Rural campus in small town; 30 miles from Knoxville. **Calendar:** 4-4-1, extensive summer session. Saturday classes. **Microcomputers:** 80 located in dormitories, libraries, classrooms, computer centers, campus-wide network. **Special facilities:** Appalachia Museum, art gallery.

DEGREES OFFERED. AA, BA, BS, MA, MEd. 2 associate degrees awarded in 1992. 100% in philosophy, religion, theology. 430 bachelor's degrees awarded. 17% in business and management, 10% communications, 18% education, 7% life sciences, 7% psychology, 18% social sciences. Graduate degrees offered in 3 major fields of study.

UNDERGRADUATE MAJORS. Associate: Theological studies. **Bachelor's:** Accounting, art education, biology, business administration and management, business and management, business economics, chemistry, child development/care/guidance, clothing and textiles management/production/services, communications, dietetics, early childhood education, education, elementary education, English, family/consumer resource management, fashion design, fashion merchandising, fine arts, food science and nutrition, French, geography, geology, German, health education, history, home economics, home economics education, home furnishings and equipment management/production/services, information sciences and systems, interior design, journalism, junior high education, liberal/general studies, mathematics, mathematics education, mental health/human services, military science (Army), music, music education, music performance, nursing, philosophy, photography, physical education, physics, political science and government, predentistry, prelaw, premedicine, prepharmacy, preveterinary, psychology, radio/television broadcasting, religion, religious music, science education, secondary education, social science education, social studies education, sociology, Spanish, special education, speech, speech/communication/theater education, textiles and clothing, visual and performing arts.

ACADEMIC PROGRAMS. Accelerated program, double major, dual enrollment of high school students, honors program, independent study, internships, student-designed major, study abroad, teacher preparation, weekend college, Washington semester; liberal arts/career combination in engineering, health sciences. **Remedial services:** Learning center, preadmission summer program, reduced course load, remedial instruction, special counselor, tutoring. **ROTC:** Army. **Placement/credit:** AP, CLEP General and Subject, institutional tests; 32 credit hours maximum for associate degree; 32 credit hours maximum for bachelor's degree.

ACADEMIC REQUIREMENTS. Freshmen must earn minimum GPA of 2.0 to continue in good standing. 71% of freshmen return for sophomore year. Students must declare major by end of second year. **Graduation requirements:** 64 hours for associate, 128 hours for bachelor's (40 in major). Most students required to take courses in arts/fine arts, English, foreign languages, history, humanities, mathematics, philosophy/religion, biological/

physical sciences, social sciences. **Postgraduate studies:** 2% enter law school, 1% enter medical school, 2% enter MBA programs, 30% enter other graduate study.

FRESHMAN ADMISSIONS. Selection criteria: Minimum 2.0 high school GPA, rank in top half of class, test scores important. Minimum requirement 19 ACT, 800 SAT. **High school preparation:** 20 units required. Required and recommended units include English 4, mathematics 2-3, social science 2 and science 2. Biological science 2, foreign language 2 and physical science 1 recommended. **Test requirements:** SAT or ACT (ACT preferred); score report by August 1. **Additional information:** Extremely high acceptance rate to medical school and professional programs.

1992 FRESHMAN CLASS PROFILE. 980 men and women applied, 841 accepted; 401 enrolled. 60% had high school GPA of 3.0 or higher, 39% between 2.0 and 2.99. 15% were in top tenth and 30% were in top quarter of graduating class. **Academic background:** Mid 50% of enrolled freshmen had ACT composite between 19-25. 90% submitted ACT scores. **Characteristics:** 69% from in state, 80% live in college housing, 6% have minority backgrounds, 1% are foreign students. Average age is 19.

FALL-TERM APPLICATIONS. $25 fee, may be waived for applicants with need. Closing date April 1; priority given to applications received by December 1; applicants notified on a rolling basis; must reply by May 1 or within 4 weeks if notified thereafter. Audition required for music applicants. Portfolio required for art applicants. Interview recommended for academically weak applicants. Deferred and early admission available. Institutional early decision plan. Biology and chemistry ACH recommended for premedicine applicants.

STUDENT LIFE. Housing: Dormitories (men, women); apartment housing available. Honors house available. **Activities:** Student government, film, magazine, radio, student newspaper, television, yearbook, choral groups, concert band, drama, jazz band, marching band, music ensembles, musical theater, pep band, forensics, Baptist Student Union, Fellowship of Christian Athletes, honor societies, Appalachian Outreach, Bonners Scholars Community Service. **Additional information:** Religious observance required.

ATHLETICS. NCAA. **Intercollegiate:** Baseball M, basketball, cross-country, football M, golf M, soccer, softball W, tennis, track and field, volleyball W, wrestling M. **Intramural:** Badminton, basketball, bowling, golf, soccer, softball, table tennis, tennis, volleyball.

STUDENT SERVICES. Aptitude testing, career counseling, employment service for undergraduates, freshman orientation, health services, personal counseling, placement service for graduates, special adviser for adult students, veterans counselor, services/facilities for handicapped.

ANNUAL EXPENSES. Tuition and fees (1992-93): $7,140. **Room and board:** $2,850. **Books and supplies:** $400. **Other expenses:** $700.

FINANCIAL AID. 91% of freshmen, 89% of continuing students receive some form of aid. 80% of grants, 87% of loans, 85% of jobs based on need. 384 enrolled freshmen were judged to have need, all were offered aid. Academic, music/drama, art, athletic, state/district residency, leadership, alumni affiliation, religious affiliation scholarships available. **Aid applications:** No closing date; priority given to applications received by April 1; applicants notified on a rolling basis beginning on or about March 1; must reply within 2 weeks.

ADDRESS/TELEPHONE. Sheryl Gray, Director of Undergraduate Admissions, Carson-Newman College, Russell Avenue, Jefferson City, TN 37760. (615) 471-3223. (800) 678-9061. Fax: (615) 471-3502.

Chattanooga State Technical Community College
Chattanooga, Tennessee — CB code: 1084

2-year public community, technical college, coed. Founded in 1963. **Accreditation:** Regional. **Undergraduate enrollment:** 1,456 men, 2,047 women full time; 1,924 men, 3,516 women part time. **Faculty:** 185 total. **Location:** Suburban campus in small city; 129 miles from Nashville. **Calendar:** Semester, limited summer session. Saturday and extensive evening/early morning classes. **Microcomputers:** Located in libraries, classrooms, computer centers. **Special facilities:** Computer-integrated manufacturing center. **Additional facts:** Credit-bearing courses offered at various off-campus locations. ITFS courses and video courses for home study also available.

DEGREES OFFERED. AA, AS, AAS. 435 associate degrees awarded in 1992. 9% in business/office and marketing/distribution, 6% computer sciences, 7% engineering technologies, 6% health sciences, 31% allied health, 14% multi/interdisciplinary studies, 25% trade and industry.

UNDERGRADUATE MAJORS. Accounting, air conditioning/heating/refrigeration mechanics, allied health, automotive mechanics, aviation management, business administration and management, business and management, business and office, business data processing and related programs, business data programming, chemical manufacturing technology, child development/care/guidance, commercial art, computer and information sciences, computer servicing technology, construction, court reporting, data processing, dental assistant, dental hygiene, dental laboratory technology, diesel engine mechanics, drafting, drafting and design technology, early childhood education, electrical and electronics equipment repair, electrical installation, electrical technology, electronic technology, finance, fire control and safety technology, food production/management/services, graphic and printing production, graphic arts technology, graphic design, health care administration, industrial equipment maintenance and repair, information sciences and systems, instrumentation technology, interpreter for the deaf, legal assistant/paralegal, legal secretary, liberal/general studies, machine tool operation/machine shop, marketing and distribution, mechanical design technology, medical records technology, medical secretary, microcomputer software, nuclear medical technology, nuclear technologies, nursing, physical distribution, physical therapy assistant, power plant operation and maintenance, precision metal work, radio/television broadcasting, radiograph medical technology, respiratory therapy technology, retailing, robotics, secretarial and related programs, small business management and ownership, special education, survey and mapping technology.

ACADEMIC PROGRAMS. 2-year transfer program, cooperative education, double major, dual enrollment of high school students, honors program, independent study, internships, student-designed major, telecourses, weekend college, cross-registration. **Remedial services:** Learning center, preadmission summer program, reduced course load, remedial instruction, special counselor, tutoring. **ROTC:** Army. **Placement/credit:** AP, CLEP General and Subject, institutional tests.

ACADEMIC REQUIREMENTS. Freshmen must earn minimum GPA of 1.4 to continue in good standing. 38% of freshmen return for sophomore year. Students must declare major by end of first year. **Graduation requirements:** 64 hours for associate (39 in major). Most students required to take courses in arts/fine arts, computer science, English, history, humanities, mathematics, biological/physical sciences, social sciences.

FRESHMAN ADMISSIONS. Selection criteria: Open admissions. **High school preparation:** 15 units recommended. Recommended units include English 4, foreign language 1, mathematics 4, social science 4 and science 2. Specific requirements for allied health applicants. **Test requirements:** SAT or ACT (ACT preferred) for placement; score report by August 21. National standardized dental assisting and dental hygiene tests required of applicants to these programs. AAPP for first-time freshmen over 21 and those with ACT below 18.

1992 FRESHMAN CLASS PROFILE. 562 men, 783 women enrolled. 20% had high school GPA of 3.0 or higher, 59% between 2.0 and 2.99. **Academic background:** Mid 50% of enrolled freshmen had SAT-V between 330-460, SAT-M between 340-600; ACT composite between 13-27. 8% submitted SAT scores, 93% submitted ACT scores. **Characteristics:** 100% commute, 12% have minority backgrounds. Average age is 21.

FALL-TERM APPLICATIONS. $5 fee. Closing date August 15; applicants notified on a rolling basis beginning on or about June 1; must reply by registration. Interview required for allied health, nursing applicants. Early admission available.

STUDENT LIFE. Activities: Student government, magazine, radio, student newspaper, television, choral groups, jazz band, music ensembles, dance band, Baptist Student Union.

ATHLETICS. NJCAA. **Intercollegiate:** Baseball M, basketball. **Intramural:** Archery, racquetball, soccer, softball, tennis.

STUDENT SERVICES. Aptitude testing, career counseling, employment service for undergraduates, freshman orientation, on-campus day care, personal counseling, placement service for graduates, special adviser for adult students, services/facilities for handicapped.

ANNUAL EXPENSES. Tuition and fees (1992-93): $920, $2,600 additional for out-of-state students. **Books and supplies:** $440. **Other expenses:** $1,700.

FINANCIAL AID. 39% of freshmen, 46% of continuing students receive some form of aid. 82% of grants, 76% of loans, 37% of jobs based on need. Academic, music/drama, art, athletic, leadership, alumni affiliation, minority scholarships available. **Aid applications:** No closing date; priority given to applications received by April 1; applicants notified on a rolling basis beginning on or about May 1; must reply within 2 weeks.

ADDRESS/TELEPHONE. Ellis Forrester, Dir Admissions/Records, Chattanooga State Technical Community College, 4501 Amnicola Highway, Chattanooga, TN 37406. (615) 697-4401.

Christian Brothers University
Memphis, Tennessee — CB code: 1121

4-year private university and college of arts and sciences and business, engineering college, coed, affiliated with Roman Catholic Church. Founded in 1871. **Accreditation:** Regional. **Undergraduate enrollment:** 602 men, 431 women full time; 30 men, 17 women part time. **Graduate enrollment:** 208 men and women. **Faculty:** 149 total (106 full time), 83 with doctorates or other terminal degrees. **Location:** Urban campus in very large city; 150 miles from Little Rock, Arkansas; 200 miles from Nashville. **Calendar:** Semester, limited summer session. **Microcomputers:** 133 located in libraries, classrooms, computer centers. **Special facilities:** Center for telecommunications/information systems, college archives.

DEGREES OFFERED. BA, BS, MS, MBA, MEd. 313 bachelor's degrees awarded in 1992. 47% in business and management, 22% engineering, 7% physical sciences, 7% psychology. Graduate degrees offered in 7 major fields of study.

UNDERGRADUATE MAJORS. Accounting, biological and physical

sciences, biology, business administration and management, business and management, business economics, chemical engineering, chemistry, civil engineering, clinical laboratory science, computer and information sciences, computer engineering, dramatic arts, electrical/electronics/communications engineering, elementary education, engineering physics, English, English for corporate communications and management, finance, history, humanities and social sciences, information sciences and systems, journalism, management information systems, marketing and distribution, marketing management, mathematics, mechanical engineering, medical laboratory technologies, music performance, physics, prelaw, psychology, secondary education, telecommunications, telecommunications/information systems management, visual and performing arts.

ACADEMIC PROGRAMS. Accelerated program, double major, dual enrollment of high school students, honors program, independent study, internships, teacher preparation, cross-registration. **Remedial services:** Learning center, preadmission summer program, reduced course load, tutoring. **ROTC:** Air Force, Army, Naval. **Placement/credit:** AP, CLEP Subject, institutional tests; 30 credit hours maximum for bachelor's degree.

ACADEMIC REQUIREMENTS. Freshmen must earn minimum GPA of 1.5 to continue in good standing. 75% of freshmen return for sophomore year. Students must declare major by end of second year. **Graduation requirements:** 128 hours for bachelor's (50 in major). Most students required to take courses in computer science, English, mathematics, philosophy/religion, biological/physical sciences, social sciences. **Postgraduate studies:** 12% enter law school, 6% enter medical school, 24% enter MBA programs, 58% enter other graduate study.

FRESHMAN ADMISSIONS. Selection criteria: Test scores, 2.0 GPA, and rank in top two-thirds of class. Recommended units include English 4, mathematics 4 and science 4. College-preparatory program required of engineering applicants. **Test requirements:** SAT or ACT (ACT preferred); score report by May 1.

1992 FRESHMAN CLASS PROFILE. 228 men and women enrolled. 46% had high school GPA of 3.0 or higher, 48% between 2.0 and 2.99. **Academic background:** Mid 50% of enrolled freshmen had SAT-V between 410-540, SAT-M between 450-630; ACT composite between 20-26. 26% submitted SAT scores, 85% submitted ACT scores. **Characteristics:** 68% from in state, 64% commute, 19% have minority backgrounds, 4% are foreign students. Average age is 19.

FALL-TERM APPLICATIONS. $25 fee, may be waived for applicants with need. Closing date July 15; priority given to applications received by April 15; applicants notified on a rolling basis; must reply by July 15. Interview recommended. Essay recommended. CRDA. Deferred and early admission available.

STUDENT LIFE. Housing: Dormitories (men, women); apartment housing available. Juniors and seniors may live in on-campus apartments. Freshmen from outside Shelby County required to live on campus. **Activities:** Student government, magazine, student newspaper, yearbook, choral groups, drama, musical theater, fraternities, sororities, Black Student Association, Knights of Columbus, Women's Association to Motivate Spirit, professional, honor, and social organizations.

ATHLETICS. NAIA. **Intercollegiate:** Baseball M, basketball, soccer, softball W, tennis, volleyball W. **Intramural:** Basketball, bowling, golf, handball, racquetball, soccer M, softball, swimming, table tennis, tennis, track and field, volleyball.

STUDENT SERVICES. Aptitude testing, career counseling, employment service for undergraduates, freshman orientation, health services, personal counseling, placement service for graduates, veterans counselor, services/facilities for handicapped.

ANNUAL EXPENSES. Tuition and fees (1992-93): $8,090. Engineering student tuition is $8,340. **Room and board:** $3,080. **Books and supplies:** $600.

FINANCIAL AID. 97% of freshmen, 73% of continuing students receive some form of aid. 37% of grants, 80% of loans, 40% of jobs based on need. Academic, music/drama, athletic, alumni affiliation, minority scholarships available. **Aid applications:** No closing date; priority given to applications received by April 1; applicants notified on a rolling basis beginning on or about March 1; must reply within 3 weeks. **Additional information:** ROTC scholarships available to qualified applicants.

ADDRESS/TELEPHONE. Steve Pochard, Dean of Admissions, Christian Brothers University, 650 East Parkway South, Memphis, TN 38104-5581. (901) 722-0205. (800) 278-7576. Fax: (901) 722-0494.

Cleveland State Community College
Cleveland, Tennessee — CB code: 2848

2-year public community college, coed. Founded in 1967. **Accreditation:** Regional. **Undergraduate enrollment:** 651 men, 945 women full time; 751 men, 1,249 women part time. **Faculty:** 184 total (72 full time), 23 with doctorates or other terminal degrees. **Location:** Suburban campus in large town; 30 miles from Chattanooga. **Calendar:** Semester, extensive summer session. Saturday and extensive evening/early morning classes. **Microcomputers:** 160 located in libraries, classrooms, computer centers. **Special facilities:** Observatory, nature trail, fitness center.

DEGREES OFFERED. AA, AS, AAS. 284 associate degrees awarded in 1992. 22% in business/office and marketing/distribution, 8% engineering technologies, 22% health sciences, 41% multi/interdisciplinary studies.

UNDERGRADUATE MAJORS. Architectural technologies, business and management, business and office, elementary education, fine arts, industrial technology, legal assistant/paralegal, liberal/general studies, medical laboratory technologies, mental health/human services, music, nursing, secondary education, secretarial and related programs, trade and industrial supervision and management.

ACADEMIC PROGRAMS. 2-year transfer program, cooperative education, internships, cross-registration. **Remedial services:** Learning center, reduced course load, remedial instruction, special counselor, tutoring, assessment. **Placement/credit:** AP, CLEP Subject, institutional tests; 18 credit hours maximum for associate degree.

ACADEMIC REQUIREMENTS. Freshmen must earn minimum GPA of 1.4 to continue in good standing. 60% of freshmen return for sophomore year. Students must declare major on application. **Graduation requirements:** 64 hours for associate (24 in major). Most students required to take courses in computer science, English, humanities, mathematics, biological/physical sciences, social sciences.

FRESHMAN ADMISSIONS. Selection criteria: Open admissions. Program admission required for nursing and medical laboratory technician. College-preparatory program required for transfer programs: 14 total academic units, 4 English, 2 foreign language, 3 mathematics, 1 social science, 2 science, 1 US history, 1 visual or performing arts. Same units recommended for career/technical programs. **Test requirements:** SAT or ACT (ACT preferred) for placement; score report by August 15. Test score reports must be received by registration day for fall-term admissions. **Additional information:** All admitted students with ACT below 19 subject to basic skills assessment prior to enrollment.

1992 FRESHMAN CLASS PROFILE. 244 men, 371 women enrolled. 40% had high school GPA of 3.0 or higher, 50% between 2.0 and 2.99. **Academic background:** Mid 50% of enrolled freshmen had ACT composite between 11-20. 82% submitted ACT scores. **Characteristics:** 99% from in state, 100% commute, 4% have minority backgrounds. Average age is 24.

FALL-TERM APPLICATIONS. $5 fee. No closing date; applicants notified on a rolling basis; must reply by registration. Deferred and early admission available.

STUDENT LIFE. Activities: Student government, student newspaper, choral groups, drama, music ensembles, Baptist Student Union, Student Government Association, Methodist Campus Ministry, Black Student Association, Circle-K.

ATHLETICS. NJCAA. **Intercollegiate:** Baseball M, basketball, golf M, tennis. **Intramural:** Badminton, basketball, softball, table tennis, tennis, volleyball.

STUDENT SERVICES. Aptitude testing, career counseling, employment service for undergraduates, freshman orientation, personal counseling, placement service for graduates, special adviser for adult students, veterans counselor, services/facilities for handicapped.

ANNUAL EXPENSES. Tuition and fees (1992-93): $916, $2,600 additional for out-of-state students. **Books and supplies:** $475. **Other expenses:** $800.

FINANCIAL AID. 30% of freshmen, 12% of continuing students receive some form of aid. All grants, 80% of loans, 57% of jobs based on need. Academic, leadership, alumni affiliation, minority scholarships available. **Aid applications:** No closing date; priority given to applications received by May 15; applicants notified on a rolling basis beginning on or about July 15; must reply within 2 weeks.

ADDRESS/TELEPHONE. Francis Williams, Director of Student Information Systems and Services, Cleveland State Community College, PO Box 3570, Norman Chapel Road, Cleveland, TN 37320-3570. (615) 472-7141 ext. 212. Fax: (615) 478-6225.

Columbia State Community College
Columbia, Tennessee — CB code: 1081

2-year public community college, coed. Founded in 1966. **Accreditation:** Regional. **Undergraduate enrollment:** 544 men, 1,010 women full time; 661 men, 1,506 women part time. **Faculty:** 193 total (87 full time), 13 with doctorates or other terminal degrees. **Location:** Rural campus in large town; 40 miles from Nashville. **Calendar:** Semester, limited summer session.

DEGREES OFFERED. AA, AS, AAS. 311 associate degrees awarded in 1992. 5% in business/office and marketing/distribution, 50% allied health, 38% multi/interdisciplinary studies.

UNDERGRADUATE MAJORS. Accounting, agricultural sciences, biology, business and management, business data programming, chemistry, computer and information sciences, computer programming, education, electronic technology, elementary education, engineering, engineering and engineering-related technologies, English, industrial technology, liberal/general studies, marketing and distribution, mathematics, medical laboratory technologies, music, nursing, psychology, radiograph medical technology, respiratory therapy technology, secondary education, secretarial and related programs, social sciences, veterinarian's assistant.

ACADEMIC PROGRAMS. 2-year transfer program, dual enrollment of high school students. **Remedial services:** Remedial instruction. **Placement/credit:** AP, CLEP Subject, institutional tests.

ACADEMIC REQUIREMENTS. Freshmen must earn minimum GPA of 1.6 to continue in good standing. 42% of freshmen return for sophomore year. **Graduation requirements:** 66 hours for associate. Most students required to take courses in computer science, English, history, mathematics, biological/physical sciences, social sciences.

FRESHMAN ADMISSIONS. Selection criteria: Open admissions. **Test requirements:** ACT for placement and counseling only; score report by August 15.

1992 FRESHMAN CLASS PROFILE. 272 men, 449 women enrolled. **Academic background:** Mid 50% of enrolled freshmen had ACT composite between 13-20. 80% submitted ACT scores. **Characteristics:** 98% from in state, 100% commute, 7% have minority backgrounds.

FALL-TERM APPLICATIONS. $5 fee. Closing date August 15; applicants notified on a rolling basis; must reply by registration. Early admission available.

STUDENT LIFE. Activities: Student government, choral groups, drama.

ATHLETICS. NJCAA. **Intercollegiate:** Baseball M, basketball, golf M. **Intramural:** Basketball, softball M, table tennis, volleyball.

STUDENT SERVICES. Employment service for undergraduates, health services, personal counseling, placement service for graduates, services/facilities for handicapped.

ANNUAL EXPENSES. Tuition and fees (1992-93): $910, $2,600 additional for out-of-state students. **Books and supplies:** $420. **Other expenses:** $610.

FINANCIAL AID. 65% of freshmen, 55% of continuing students receive some form of aid. 72% of grants, 86% of loans, 59% of jobs based on need. 305 enrolled freshmen were judged to have need, 279 were offered aid. Academic, athletic, leadership, minority scholarships available. **Aid applications:** No closing date; priority given to applications received by April 1; applicants notified on a rolling basis beginning on or about May 15; must reply within 2 weeks.

ADDRESS/TELEPHONE. Sharon Bowen, Dir of Admissions/Registrar, Columbia State Community College, Columbia, TN 38401. (615) 388-0120. Fax: (615) 388-8714.

Crichton College
Memphis, Tennessee — CB code: 0704

4-year private liberal arts college, coed, interdenominational. Founded in 1944. **Accreditation:** Regional. **Undergraduate enrollment:** 96 men, 138 women full time; 45 men, 62 women part time. **Faculty:** 36 total (14 full time), 16 with doctorates or other terminal degrees. **Location:** Suburban campus in very large city. **Calendar:** 4-1-4, limited summer session. Saturday and extensive evening/early morning classes. **Microcomputers:** 15 located in libraries, computer centers.

DEGREES OFFERED. BA, BS. 44 bachelor's degrees awarded in 1992. 16% in business and management, 43% teacher education, 23% philosophy, religion, theology, 18% psychology.

UNDERGRADUATE MAJORS. Bible studies, biology, business administration and management, elementary education, English, English education, junior high education, liberal/general studies, music education, psychology, religious music, secondary education.

ACADEMIC PROGRAMS. Double major, independent study, internships, teacher preparation; liberal arts/career combination in business. **Remedial services:** Reduced course load, remedial instruction, special counselor. **Placement/credit:** AP, CLEP Subject, institutional tests; 30 credit hours maximum for bachelor's degree.

ACADEMIC REQUIREMENTS. Freshmen must earn minimum GPA of 1.5 to continue in good standing. 50% of freshmen return for sophomore year. Students must declare major on enrollment. **Graduation requirements:** 128 hours for bachelor's (30 in major). Most students required to take courses in arts/fine arts, computer science, English, history, humanities, mathematics, philosophy/religion, biological/physical sciences, social sciences.

FRESHMAN ADMISSIONS. Selection criteria: School achievement record, test scores, interview, references, Christian testimony considered. **High school preparation:** 14 units required. Required units include English 3, foreign language 3, mathematics 3, social science 3 and science 2. **Test requirements:** SAT or ACT (ACT preferred); score report by August 1.

1992 FRESHMAN CLASS PROFILE. 18 men, 34 women enrolled. **Academic background:** Mid 50% of enrolled freshmen had ACT composite between 14-20. 100% submitted ACT scores. **Characteristics:** 73% from in state, 97% commute, 27% have minority backgrounds, 1% are foreign students. Average age is 23.

FALL-TERM APPLICATIONS. $25 fee, may be waived for applicants with need. No closing date; priority given to applications received by July 1; applicants notified on a rolling basis beginning on or about August 1. Interview recommended. Essay recommended. Deferred and early admission available. Placement tests required for applicants without ACT scores.

STUDENT LIFE. Housing: Dormitories (men, women). **Activities:** Student government, student newspaper, yearbook, newsletter, choral groups, music ensembles, social clubs. **Additional information:** Religious observance required.

ATHLETICS. Intercollegiate: Basketball, volleyball. **Intramural:** Basketball, bowling, golf, soccer M, softball, table tennis, tennis, volleyball.

STUDENT SERVICES. Career counseling, freshman orientation, personal counseling, veterans counselor, services/facilities for handicapped.

ANNUAL EXPENSES. Tuition and fees: $4,750. **Room and board:** $750 room only. **Books and supplies:** $500. **Other expenses:** $2,000.

FINANCIAL AID. 89% of freshmen, 78% of continuing students receive some form of aid. 58% of grants, 87% of loans, 89% of jobs based on need. Academic, music/drama, leadership, alumni affiliation scholarships available. **Aid applications:** No closing date; priority given to applications received by July 15; applicants notified on a rolling basis; must reply within 2 weeks.

ADDRESS/TELEPHONE. Lee S. Ferguson, Director of Admissions, Crichton College, 6655 Winchester Road, PO Box 757830, Memphis, TN 38175-7830. (901) 367-9800. (800) 524-5554.

Cumberland University
Lebanon, Tennessee — CB code: 1146

4-year private university and liberal arts college, coed. Founded in 1842. **Accreditation:** Regional. **Undergraduate enrollment:** 283 men, 338 women full time; 76 men, 178 women part time. **Graduate enrollment:** 6 men, 25 women part time. **Faculty:** 75 total (50 full time), 33 with doctorates or other terminal degrees. **Location:** Urban campus in large town; 30 miles from Nashville. **Calendar:** Semester, limited summer session. **Microcomputers:** 28 located in libraries, computer centers.

DEGREES OFFERED. AA, AS, BA, BS, MA, MS. 6 associate degrees awarded in 1992. 125 bachelor's degrees awarded. Graduate degrees offered in 1 major field of study.

UNDERGRADUATE MAJORS. Associate: Biology, business and management, chemistry, health sciences, history, mathematics, physics, science technologies, social sciences. **Bachelor's:** Accounting, biology, business and management, chemistry, computer and information sciences, education, elementary education, health sciences, history, junior high education, marketing management, mathematics, physical sciences, predentistry, prelaw, premedicine, prepharmacy, preveterinary, psychology, secondary education, social sciences.

ACADEMIC PROGRAMS. Cooperative education, honors program, teacher preparation. **Remedial services:** Reduced course load, remedial instruction, tutoring. **Placement/credit:** 16 credit hours maximum for bachelor's degree.

ACADEMIC REQUIREMENTS. Freshmen must earn minimum GPA of 1.5 to continue in good standing. 55% of freshmen return for sophomore year. Students must declare major by end of second year. **Graduation requirements:** 64 hours for associate, 128 hours for bachelor's. Most students required to take courses in arts/fine arts, computer science, English, history, humanities, mathematics, philosophy/religion, biological/physical sciences, social sciences. **Postgraduate studies:** 75% from 2-year programs enter 4-year programs. 2% enter law school, 1% enter medical school, 5% enter MBA programs, 5% enter other graduate study. **Additional information:** Selection of major or minor not required.

FRESHMAN ADMISSIONS. Selection criteria: High school academic record and standardized test scores most important. **Test requirements:** SAT or ACT; score report by September 10.

1992 FRESHMAN CLASS PROFILE. 226 men and women enrolled. **Characteristics:** 80% from in state, 50% commute, 20% have minority backgrounds, 1% are foreign students, 10% join fraternities/sororities. Average age is 19.

FALL-TERM APPLICATIONS. $25 fee, may be waived for applicants with need. No closing date; applicants notified on a rolling basis. Interview recommended for academically weak applicants. Early admission available. Permission of high school principal or guidance counselor required for early admission.

STUDENT LIFE. Housing: Dormitories (men, women). **Activities:** Student government, radio, student newspaper, yearbook, choral groups, fraternities, sororities, Baptist student union, black student association. **Additional information:** Participation in extracurricular programs encouraged.

ATHLETICS. NAIA. **Intercollegiate:** Baseball M, basketball, cross-country, football M, golf, soccer M, softball W, tennis, volleyball W. **Intramural:** Volleyball.

STUDENT SERVICES. Career counseling, employment service for undergraduates, freshman orientation, personal counseling, placement service for graduates, special adviser for adult students, mentor groups for counseling, services/facilities for handicapped.

ANNUAL EXPENSES. Tuition and fees (1992-93): $5,200. **Room and board:** $2,900. **Books and supplies:** $450.

FINANCIAL AID. 70% of freshmen, 70% of continuing students receive some form of aid. Grants, loans, jobs available. Academic, athletic, leadership scholarships available. **Aid applications:** No closing date; priority given to applications received by March 1; applicants notified on a rolling basis.

ADDRESS/TELEPHONE. Lex C. Suite, Associate Director of Admissions, Cumberland University, South Greenwood Street, Lebanon, TN 37087. (615) 444-2562. (800) 467-0562. Fax: (615) 444-2569.

David Lipscomb University

Nashville, Tennessee CB code: 1161

Admissions: 85% of applicants accepted
Based on: ••• School record, test scores
•• Recommendations
• Activities, essay, interview
Completion: 85% of freshmen end year in good standing
49% graduate, 13% of these enter graduate study

4-year private liberal arts college, coed, affiliated with Church of Christ. Founded in 1891. **Accreditation:** Regional. **Undergraduate enrollment:** 901 men, 958 women full time; 118 men, 165 women part time. **Graduate enrollment:** 15 men, 1 woman full time; 65 men, 4 women part time. **Faculty:** 175 total (110 full time), 94 with doctorates or other terminal degrees. **Location:** Suburban campus in very large city; 4 miles from downtown. **Calendar:** Semester, extensive summer session. **Microcomputers:** 180 located in dormitories, libraries, classrooms, computer centers, campus-wide network.

DEGREES OFFERED. BA, BS, MA. 389 bachelor's degrees awarded in 1992. 22% in business and management, 11% business/office and marketing/distribution, 9% communications, 15% teacher education, 6% life sciences, 6% psychology, 6% social sciences. Graduate degrees offered in 3 major fields of study.

UNDERGRADUATE MAJORS. Accounting, American studies, applied mathematics, Bible studies, biblical languages, biochemistry, biology, business administration and management, business and management, business economics, chemistry, communications, computer and information sciences, elementary education, engineering science, English, English education, family/consumer resource management, fashion merchandising, finance, food management, food production/management/services, food science and nutrition, foreign languages education, French, German, history, home economics, information sciences and systems, journalism, marketing and distribution, mathematics, mathematics education, medical laboratory technologies, music, music education, music performance, office supervision and management, philosophy, physical education, physics, political science and government, predentistry, preengineering, premedicine, prepharmacy, preveterinary, psychology, public administration, public relations, science education, social sciences, social studies education, social work, Spanish, speech, speech/communication/theater education, studio art, urban studies.

ACADEMIC PROGRAMS. Accelerated program, double major, dual enrollment of high school students, honors program, internships, study abroad, teacher preparation, cross-registration, 3-1 bachelor's programs in health professions at clinical facilities; liberal arts/career combination in engineering, health sciences. **Remedial services:** Learning center, reduced course load, remedial instruction, special counselor, tutoring. **ROTC:** Air Force. **Placement/credit:** AP, CLEP General and Subject, IB, institutional tests; 30 credit hours maximum for bachelor's degree.

ACADEMIC REQUIREMENTS. Freshmen must earn minimum GPA of 1.7 to continue in good standing. 75% of freshmen return for sophomore year. Students must declare major by end of second year. **Graduation requirements:** 132 hours for bachelor's. Most students required to take courses in arts/fine arts, English, history, humanities, mathematics, philosophy/religion, biological/physical sciences, social sciences. **Postgraduate studies:** 5% enter law school, 4% enter medical school, 4% enter MBA programs.

FRESHMAN ADMISSIONS. Selection criteria: School achievement record, test scores and references weighed equally. **High school preparation:** 14 units required. Required units include English 4, foreign language 2, mathematics 2, social science 2 and science 2. 2 elective units from languages, social sciences, mathematics, and natural sciences required. Credits in computer sciences highly recommeded. **Test requirements:** SAT or ACT; score report by May 15.

1992 FRESHMAN CLASS PROFILE. 375 men applied, 309 accepted, 219 enrolled; 444 women applied, 387 accepted, 271 enrolled. 66% had high school GPA of 3.0 or higher, 33% between 2.0 and 2.99. **Academic background:** Mid 50% of enrolled freshmen had ACT composite between 20-26. 86% submitted ACT scores. **Characteristics:** 57% from in state, 78% live in college housing, 4% have minority backgrounds. Average age is 18.

FALL-TERM APPLICATIONS. $25 fee, may be waived for applicants with need. Closing date May 15; applicants notified on or about December 1; must reply within 4 weeks. Audition required for music applicants. Portfolio required for art applicants. Interview recommended for music, art, honors program applicants. Essay recommended. Early admission available.

STUDENT LIFE. Housing: Dormitories (men, women). Out-of-town undergraduates required to live on campus, except for seniors and students 22 or older. **Activities:** Student government, radio, student newspaper, television, yearbook, choral groups, concert band, drama, jazz band, music ensembles, musical theater, pep band, social service organizations, College Republicans, Young Democrats, honorary societies, social clubs. **Additional information:** Daily chapel service and Bible studies required. Religious observance required.

ATHLETICS. NAIA. **Intercollegiate:** Baseball M, basketball, cross-country M, golf M, soccer M, tennis, track and field M, volleyball W. **Intramural:** Badminton, basketball, racquetball M, softball, volleyball.

STUDENT SERVICES. Aptitude testing, career counseling, employment service for undergraduates, freshman orientation, health services, personal counseling, placement service for graduates, special adviser for adult students, veterans counselor.

ANNUAL EXPENSES. Tuition and fees (1992-93): $5,940. **Room and board:** $3,798. **Books and supplies:** $475. **Other expenses:** $650.

FINANCIAL AID. 71% of continuing students receive some form of aid. 42% of grants, 93% of loans, all jobs based on need. Academic, music/drama, art, athletic, leadership, religious affiliation scholarships available. **Aid applications:** No closing date; priority given to applications received by April 15; applicants notified on a rolling basis beginning on or about May 15; must reply within 2 weeks.

ADDRESS/TELEPHONE. Jerry Masterson, Dean of Enrollment, David Lipscomb University, Granny White Pike, Nashville, TN 37204-3951. (615) 269-1776. (800) 333-4358. Fax: (615) 269-1796.

Draughons Junior College of Business: Nashville

Nashville, Tennessee CB code: 0821

2-year proprietary business, junior college, coed. Founded in 1884. **Undergraduate enrollment:** 42 men, 116 women full time; 39 men, 173 women part time. **Faculty:** 28 total (11 full time), 3 with doctorates or other terminal degrees. **Location:** Urban campus in very large city. **Calendar:** Semester, limited summer session. Saturday classes. **Microcomputers:** 45 located in classrooms, computer centers. **Additional facts:** Daytime and evening programs of study. Branch campuses in Clarksville and Bowling Green (KY).

DEGREES OFFERED. AS. 90 associate degrees awarded in 1992. 35% in business and management, 50% business/office and marketing/distribution, 15% computer sciences.

UNDERGRADUATE MAJORS. Accounting, business and management, business data processing and related programs, business data programming, computer programming, data processing, fashion merchandising, legal assistant/paralegal, medical assistant, secretarial and related programs, word processing.

ACADEMIC PROGRAMS. Double major, internships. **Remedial services:** Reduced course load, remedial instruction, developmental education courses in English grammar, mathematics, comprehension, and study skills. **Placement/credit:** Institutional tests; 15 credit hours maximum for associate degree.

ACADEMIC REQUIREMENTS. Freshmen must earn minimum GPA of 2.0 to continue in good standing. 50% of freshmen return for sophomore year. Students must declare major on application. **Graduation requirements:** 60 hours for associate (42 in major). Most students required to take courses in computer science, English, history, humanities, mathematics, social sciences.

FRESHMAN ADMISSIONS. Selection criteria: Open admissions. **Test requirements:** ACT for placement and counseling only; score report by August 1. College Board AP examinations required for placement.

1992 FRESHMAN CLASS PROFILE. 35 men applied, 26 accepted, 26 enrolled; 117 women applied, 91 accepted, 91 enrolled. **Characteristics:** 95% from in state, 100% commute, 41% have minority backgrounds, 1% are foreign students.

FALL-TERM APPLICATIONS. $10 fee. No closing date; applicants notified on a rolling basis. Interview required. Deferred admission available.

STUDENT LIFE. Activities: Student government, student newspaper.

ATHLETICS. Intramural: Softball, volleyball.

STUDENT SERVICES. Career counseling, employment service for undergraduates, freshman orientation, personal counseling, placement service for graduates, special adviser for adult students, services/facilities for handicapped.

ANNUAL EXPENSES. Tuition and fees (projected): $4,010. **Books and supplies:** $500.

FINANCIAL AID. 82% of freshmen, 82% of continuing students receive some form of aid. All grants, 76% of loans, all jobs based on need. State/district residency scholarships available. **Aid applications:** No closing date; applicants notified on a rolling basis. **Additional information:** Financial Aid Form for in-state applicants must be filed before June 1.

ADDRESS/TELEPHONE. William R. Greene, Director of Admissions, Draughons Junior College of Business: Nashville, Plus Park at Pavilion Boulevard, Nashville, TN 37217. (615) 361-7555. Fax: (615) 367-2736.

Dyersburg State Community College

Dyersburg, Tennessee CB code: 7323

2-year public community college, coed. Founded in 1967. **Accreditation:** Regional. **Undergraduate enrollment:** 384 men, 655 women full time; 335

men, 545 women part time. **Faculty:** 135 total (47 full time), 21 with doctorates or other terminal degrees. **Location:** Rural campus in large town; 78 miles from Memphis. **Calendar:** Semester, limited summer session. **Microcomputers:** 87 located in libraries, classrooms. **Special facilities:** Computer-managed interactive video equipment used for instruction.

DEGREES OFFERED. AA, AS, AAS. 144 associate degrees awarded in 1992. 12% in business and management, 17% business/office and marketing/distribution, 17% education, 7% engineering technologies, 23% allied health, 13% multi/interdisciplinary studies, 5% psychology.

UNDERGRADUATE MAJORS. Allied health, biology, business administration and management, business and office, business data processing and related programs, business data programming, chemistry, computer and information sciences, computer programming, criminal justice studies, education, emergency medical technologies, engineering, engineering and engineering-related technologies, English, finance, health sciences, history, humanities and social sciences, industrial technology, information sciences and systems, law enforcement and corrections technologies, liberal/general studies, management information systems, manufacturing technology, marketing and distribution, marketing management, mathematics, music, nursing, office supervision and management, premedicine, preveterinary, psychology, respiratory therapy technology, secretarial and related programs, social sciences, sociology.

ACADEMIC PROGRAMS. 2-year transfer program, cooperative education, dual enrollment of high school students, independent study, internships, telecourses. **Remedial services:** Learning center, reduced course load, remedial instruction, special counselor, tutoring. **Placement/credit:** AP, CLEP Subject, institutional tests; 24 credit hours maximum for associate degree.

ACADEMIC REQUIREMENTS. Freshmen must earn minimum GPA of 1.4 to continue in good standing. 24% of freshmen return for sophomore year. Students must declare major on application. **Graduation requirements:** 64 hours for associate (27 in major). Most students required to take courses in computer science, English, humanities, mathematics, social sciences.

FRESHMAN ADMISSIONS. Selection criteria: Open admissions. **High school preparation:** 14 units recommended. Recommended units include biological science 1, English 4, foreign language 2, mathematics 3, social science 2 and science 1. **Test requirements:** SAT or ACT (ACT preferred) for placement and counseling only; score report by August 15.

1992 FRESHMAN CLASS PROFILE. 164 men, 229 women enrolled. 21% had high school GPA of 3.0 or higher, 65% between 2.0 and 2.99. **Academic background:** Mid 50% of enrolled freshmen had ACT composite between 15-20. 78% submitted ACT scores. **Characteristics:** 99% from in state, 100% commute, 15% have minority backgrounds. Average age is 21.

FALL-TERM APPLICATIONS. $5 fee. Fee may be waived for applicants over 60 years of age. No closing date; applicants notified on a rolling basis. Deferred admission available.

STUDENT LIFE. Activities: Student government, student newspaper, television, choral groups, concert band, drama, music ensembles, symphony orchestra, Baptist Student Union, American Chemical Society Affiliates, Black Organization for Successful Students, Data Processing Management Association, Dyersburg State Business and Office Systems Association, Student Nurses Association.

ATHLETICS. NJCAA. **Intercollegiate:** Baseball M, basketball. **Intramural:** Badminton, basketball, softball, table tennis, volleyball.

STUDENT SERVICES. Aptitude testing, career counseling, employment service for undergraduates, freshman orientation, health services, personal counseling, placement service for graduates, veterans counselor, services/facilities for handicapped.

ANNUAL EXPENSES. Tuition and fees (1992-93): $916, $2,600 additional for out-of-state students. **Books and supplies:** $400. **Other expenses:** $480.

FINANCIAL AID. 53% of freshmen, 50% of continuing students receive some form of aid. 97% of grants, 89% of loans, 61% of jobs based on need. Academic, music/drama, athletic, state/district residency, leadership, minority scholarships available. **Aid applications:** No closing date; priority given to applications received by March 15; applicants notified on a rolling basis beginning on or about April 15; must reply within 2 weeks.

ADDRESS/TELEPHONE. J. Dan Gullett, Coordinator of Records and Admissions, Dyersburg State Community College, PO Box 648, Dyersburg, TN 38025-0648. (901) 286-3200. Fax: (901) 286-3333.

East Tennessee State University
Johnson City, Tennessee — CB code: 1198

Admissions:	83% of applicants accepted
Based on:	••• School record
	•• Test scores
	• Activities, interview
Completion:	80% of freshmen end year in good standing
	45% graduate, 14% of these enter graduate study

4-year public university, coed. Founded in 1911. **Accreditation:** Regional. **Undergraduate enrollment:** 3,276 men, 4,434 women full time; 790 men, 1,423 women part time. **Graduate enrollment:** 75 men, 91 women full time; 632 men, 890 women part time. **Faculty:** 629 total (464 full time), 440 with doctorates or other terminal degrees. **Location:** Suburban campus in small city; 100 miles from Knoxville. 200 miles from Roanoke, Virginia. **Calendar:** Semester, extensive summer session. Extensive evening/early morning classes. **Microcomputers:** 80 located in computer centers. **Special facilities:** Museum, archives of Appalachia, art gallery, planetarium. **Additional facts:** Additional campus in Kingsport.

DEGREES OFFERED. AS, BA, BS, BFA, MA, MS, MBA, MFA, MEd, PhD, EdD, MD. 150 associate degrees awarded in 1992. 50% in engineering technologies, 50% allied health. 1,200 bachelor's degrees awarded. 10% in business and management, 5% business/office and marketing/distribution, 5% communications, 5% computer sciences, 10% education, 10% teacher education, 10% engineering technologies, 12% health sciences, 5% psychology, 5% social sciences, 5% visual and performing arts. Graduate degrees offered in 49 major fields of study.

UNDERGRADUATE MAJORS. Associate: Dental assistant, dental hygiene, dental laboratory technology, drafting, drafting and design technology, medical assistant, medical laboratory technologies, nursing, radiograph medical technology, respiratory therapy technology, surgical technology, survey and mapping technology. **Bachelor's:** Accounting, advertising, anthropology, art education, art history, biology, business administration and management, business and office, business economics, business education, ceramics, chemistry, child development/care/guidance, clinical laboratory science, clothing and textiles management/production/services, commercial art, communications, computer and information sciences, computer programming, crafts, criminal justice studies, curriculum and instruction, drafting, drafting and design technology, dramatic arts, drawing, early childhood education, economics, electronic technology, elementary education, engineering and engineering-related technologies, English, English education, environmental science, fiber/textiles/weaving, finance, fine arts, food science and nutrition, foreign languages education, French, geography, geology, German, graphic design, health care administration, health education, health sciences, history, home economics, home economics education, home furnishings and equipment management/production/services, humanities and social sciences, industrial arts education, information sciences and systems, journalism, junior high education, law enforcement and corrections, manufacturing technology, marketing and distribution, marketing management, mathematics, mathematics education, metal/jewelry, microbiology, music, music education, nursing, nutritional education, office supervision and management, painting, philosophy, physical education, physics, political science and government, predentistry, prelaw, premedicine, prepharmacy, preveterinary, psychology, public relations, radio/television broadcasting, reading education, science education, sculpture, secondary education, social science education, social sciences, social studies education, social work, sociology, Spanish, special education, speech, speech correction, speech pathology/audiology, studio art, survey and mapping technology, trade and industrial education.

ACADEMIC PROGRAMS. Accelerated program, cooperative education, double major, dual enrollment of high school students, education specialist degree, honors program, independent study, internships, study abroad, teacher preparation, telecourses, cross-registration; liberal arts/career combination in health sciences; combined bachelor's/graduate program in medicine. **Remedial services:** Reduced course load, remedial instruction, special counselor, tutoring. **ROTC:** Army. **Placement/credit:** AP, CLEP General and Subject, institutional tests; 25 credit hours maximum for associate degree; 25 credit hours maximum for bachelor's degree.

ACADEMIC REQUIREMENTS. Freshmen must earn minimum GPA of 1.7 to continue in good standing. 73% of freshmen return for sophomore year. Students must declare major by end of first year. **Graduation requirements:** 64 hours for associate (24 in major), 128 hours for bachelor's (34 in major). Most students required to take courses in arts/fine arts, computer science, English, history, humanities, mathematics, philosophy/religion, biological/physical sciences, social sciences. **Postgraduate studies:** 2% enter law school, 2% enter medical school, 4% enter MBA programs, 6% enter other graduate study.

FRESHMAN ADMISSIONS. Selection criteria: Completion of 14 specific high school units required by state. Minimum 2.3 GPA and ACT composite score of 19 or combined SAT scores of 800 required. **High school preparation:** 14 units required. Required and recommended units include biological science 1, English 4, foreign language 2, mathematics 3-4, physical science 1 and social science 2. One unit visual/performing arts also required. **Test requirements:** SAT or ACT (ACT preferred); score report by August 1.

1992 FRESHMAN CLASS PROFILE. 1,780 men applied, 1,486 accepted, 639 enrolled; 1,853 women applied, 1,547 accepted, 984 enrolled. 40% had high school GPA of 3.0 or higher, 58% between 2.0 and 2.99. **Academic background:** Mid 50% of enrolled freshmen had ACT composite between 16-23. 75% submitted ACT scores. **Characteristics:** 84% from in state, 65% commute, 6% have minority backgrounds, 1% are foreign students. Average age is 19.

FALL-TERM APPLICATIONS. $5 fee. Closing date August 15; priority given to applications received by August 1; applicants notified on a rolling basis. Interview required for nursing, dental hygiene, paramedical applicants. Audition required for music applicants. Portfolio recommended for art applicants. Deferred and early admission available.

STUDENT LIFE. Housing: Dormitories (men, women); apartment, fraternity, sorority housing available. **Activities:** Student government, film, magazine, radio, student newspaper, television, yearbook, choral groups, concert band, dance, drama, jazz band, marching band, music ensembles, musical theater, pep band, symphony orchestra, fraternities, sororities, Baptist Student Union, Campus Crusade, Catholic Center, Christian Student Fellowship, Fellowship of Christian Athletes, Presbyterian Ministry, Episcopal Ministry, Real Life Fellowship, Wesley Foundation (Methodist), Black Affairs Association.

ATHLETICS. NCAA. **Intercollegiate:** Baseball M, basketball, cross-country, football M, golf M, tennis, track and field, volleyball W. **Intramural:** Archery, badminton, basketball, bowling, cross-country, handball, racquetball, skiing, softball, swimming, table tennis, tennis, track and field, volleyball.

STUDENT SERVICES. Aptitude testing, career counseling, freshman orientation, health services, on-campus day care, personal counseling, placement service for graduates, special adviser for adult students, veterans counselor, services/facilities for handicapped.

ANNUAL EXPENSES. Tuition and fees (1992-93): $1,560, $3,602 additional for out-of-state students. **Room and board:** $1,300 room only. **Books and supplies:** $600. **Other expenses:** $1,200.

FINANCIAL AID. 40% of freshmen, 52% of continuing students receive some form of aid. 48% of grants, 77% of loans, 63% of jobs based on need. Academic, music/drama, art, athletic, state/district residency, leadership, minority scholarships available. **Aid applications:** No closing date; priority given to applications received by April 15; applicants notified on a rolling basis beginning on or about May 15; must reply within 2 weeks. **Additional information:** Housing costs payable by installment.

ADDRESS/TELEPHONE. Dr. Nancy Garland, Dean of Admissions, East Tennessee State University, PO Box 70731, Johnson City, TN 37614-0002. (615) 929-4213. (800) 462-3878. Fax: (615) 461-7156.

Fisk University
Nashville, Tennessee

CB code: 1224

4-year private liberal arts college, coed, affiliated with United Church of Christ. Founded in 1866. **Accreditation:** Regional. **Undergraduate enrollment:** 228 men, 603 women full time; 10 men, 4 women part time. **Graduate enrollment:** 7 men, 9 women full time; 9 men, 2 women part time. **Faculty:** 80 total (62 full time), 49 with doctorates or other terminal degrees. **Location:** Urban campus in very large city; 216 miles from Memphis, 225 miles from Atlanta, Georgia. **Calendar:** Semester. **Microcomputers:** Located in libraries, classrooms, computer centers. **Special facilities:** Van Vechten Art Gallery.

DEGREES OFFERED. BA, BS, BFA, MA. 153 bachelor's degrees awarded in 1992. 25% in business and management, 5% computer sciences, 10% health sciences, 5% languages, 15% mathematics, 5% philosophy, religion, theology, 10% physical sciences, 10% psychology, 10% social sciences, 5% visual and performing arts. Graduate degrees offered in 6 major fields of study.

UNDERGRADUATE MAJORS. Accounting, art history, biology, business administration and management, business and management, business economics, chemistry, computer and information sciences, dramatic arts, economics, elementary education, English, finance, French, geology, history, mathematics, music, music history and appreciation, physics, political science and government, premedicine, psychology, public administration, religion and philosophical studies, sociology, Spanish, speech.

ACADEMIC PROGRAMS. Cooperative education, double major, honors program, independent study, internships, student-designed major, study abroad, teacher preparation, cross-registration, 2-2 program with Rush-Presbyterian St. Luke's Medical Center in nursing; liberal arts/career combination in engineering. **Remedial services:** Learning center, special counselor, tutoring. **ROTC:** Air Force, Army, Naval. **Placement/credit:** AP, institutional tests; 30 credit hours maximum for bachelor's degree.

ACADEMIC REQUIREMENTS. Freshmen must earn minimum GPA of 2.0 to continue in good standing. 65% of freshmen return for sophomore year. Students must declare major by end of second year. **Graduation requirements:** 120 hours for bachelor's (30 in major). Most students required to take courses in computer science, English, foreign languages, history, mathematics, philosophy/religion, biological/physical sciences, social sciences. **Postgraduate studies:** 10% enter law school, 20% enter medical school, 30% enter other graduate study.

FRESHMAN ADMISSIONS. Selection criteria: School achievement record, class rank, test scores, recommendations, activities. **High school preparation:** 15 units recommended. Recommended units include English 4, foreign language 1, mathematics 2, social science 1 and science 1. One algebra and 1 geometry recommended. **Test requirements:** SAT or ACT. Submission of SAT or ACT scores by June 15 strongly recommended. SAT preferred.

1992 FRESHMAN CLASS PROFILE. 238 men and women enrolled. 45% had high school GPA of 3.0 or higher, 53% between 2.0 and 2.99. 18% were in top tenth and 35% were in top quarter of graduating class. **Characteristics:** 23% from in state, 95% live in college housing, 99% have minority backgrounds, 1% are foreign students. Average age is 18.

FALL-TERM APPLICATIONS. $25 fee, may be waived for applicants with need. No closing date; priority given to applications received by March 15; applicants notified on a rolling basis; must reply within 30 days. Audition recommended for music applicants. Essay recommended. Deferred and early admission available. December 1 closing date for early admission applications.

STUDENT LIFE. Housing: Dormitories (men, women); apartment housing available. **Activities:** Student government, film, magazine, radio, student newspaper, yearbook, choral groups, dance, drama, jazz band, music ensembles, fraternities, sororities, Baptist Student Union, Canterbury Club, Fisk-Meharry Catholic Association, Methodist group.

ATHLETICS. NCAA. **Intercollegiate:** Baseball M, basketball, cross-country, golf, tennis, track and field, volleyball W. **Intramural:** Baseball M, basketball, softball, volleyball W.

STUDENT SERVICES. Career counseling, employment service for undergraduates, freshman orientation, health services, personal counseling, placement service for graduates, veterans counselor, services/facilities for handicapped.

ANNUAL EXPENSES. Tuition and fees: $6,305. **Room and board:** $3,690. **Books and supplies:** $600. **Other expenses:** $1,750.

FINANCIAL AID. 80% of freshmen, 87% of continuing students receive some form of aid. 66% of grants, 85% of loans, all jobs based on need. Academic scholarships available. **Aid applications:** No closing date; priority given to applications received by April 20; applicants notified on a rolling basis beginning on or about April 30; must reply within 2 weeks.

ADDRESS/TELEPHONE. Harrison F. DeShields, Jr, Director of Admissions and Records, Fisk University, 17th Avenue North, Nashville, TN 37208. (615) 329-8665. (800) 443-FISK. Fax: (615) 329-8715.

Free Will Baptist Bible College
Nashville, Tennessee

CB code: 1232

4-year private Bible college, coed, affiliated with Free Will Baptists. Founded in 1942. **Undergraduate enrollment:** 146 men, 120 women full time; 25 men, 9 women part time. **Faculty:** 25 total (21 full time), 9 with doctorates or other terminal degrees. **Location:** Suburban campus in large city. **Calendar:** Semester, limited summer session. **Microcomputers:** Located in libraries, classrooms, computer centers.

DEGREES OFFERED. AA, AS, BA, BS. 4 associate degrees awarded in 1992. 50% in business/office and marketing/distribution, 50% philosophy, religion, theology. 37 bachelor's degrees awarded. 5% in business and management, 43% teacher education, 5% letters/literature, 47% philosophy, religion, theology.

UNDERGRADUATE MAJORS. Associate: Accounting, Bible studies, liberal/general studies, religious education, secretarial and related programs. **Bachelor's:** Accounting, bible education, Bible studies, business and management, early childhood education, elementary education, English, English education, missionary studies, physical education, religious education, religious music, secondary education, theological studies.

ACADEMIC PROGRAMS. 2-year transfer program, double major, independent study, internships, student-designed major, teacher preparation. **Remedial services:** Reduced course load, remedial instruction. **ROTC:** Air Force, Army. **Placement/credit:** AP, CLEP General and Subject; 16 credit hours maximum for bachelor's degree.

ACADEMIC REQUIREMENTS. Freshmen must earn minimum GPA of 1.5 to continue in good standing. Students must declare major by end of second year. **Graduation requirements:** 64 hours for associate (20 in major), 124 hours for bachelor's (30 in major). Most students required to take courses in English, history, humanities, mathematics, philosophy/religion, biological/physical sciences, social sciences.

FRESHMAN ADMISSIONS. Selection criteria: Open admissions. References certifying evangelical Christian faith and character required. **Test requirements:** ACT for placement and counseling only; score report by August 15. **Additional information:** Applicants without high school diploma or GED must pass GED prior to receiving degree.

1992 FRESHMAN CLASS PROFILE. 41 men, 37 women enrolled. 41% had high school GPA of 3.0 or higher, 43% between 2.0 and 2.99. 13% were in top tenth and 38% were in top quarter of graduating class. **Academic background:** Mid 50% of enrolled freshmen had ACT composite between 16-21. 97% submitted ACT scores. **Characteristics:** 27% from in state, 89% live in college housing, 1% are foreign students. Average age is 18.

FALL-TERM APPLICATIONS. $25 fee. No closing date; priority given to applications received by April 15; applicants notified on a rolling basis. Deferred and early admission available.

STUDENT LIFE. Housing: Dormitories (men, women). Single students required to live on campus, unless living with parents. **Activities:** Student government, yearbook, choral groups, drama, music ensembles, ministerial and missionary organizations, Christian service assignments for all students, Organization for Business Students. **Additional information:** Religious observance required.

ATHLETICS. Intercollegiate: Basketball M. **Intramural:** Badminton W, basketball, soccer M, softball, swimming, table tennis M, tennis, volleyball.

STUDENT SERVICES. Career counseling, freshman orientation, personal counseling.

ANNUAL EXPENSES. Tuition and fees: $3,777. **Room and board:** $2,980. **Books and supplies:** $390. **Other expenses:** $1,478.

FINANCIAL AID. 75% of freshmen, 66% of continuing students receive some form of aid. 91% of grants, 99% of loans, all jobs based on need. 78 enrolled freshmen were judged to have need, all were offered aid. Music/drama, art, religious affiliation scholarships available. **Aid applications:** No closing date; priority given to applications received by April 15; applicants notified on a rolling basis beginning on or about July 1; must reply by registration.

ADDRESS/TELEPHONE. Dr. Charles E. Hampton, Registrar, Free Will Baptist Bible College, 3606 West End Avenue, Nashville, TN 37205-0117. (615) 383-1340. (800) SOFWBBC.

Freed-Hardeman University
Henderson, Tennessee CB code: 1230

Admissions: 61% of applicants accepted
Based on: ••• Recommendations, school record, test scores
•• Activities, interview
Completion: 95% of freshmen end year in good standing
36% graduate, 17% of these enter graduate study

4-year private liberal arts college, coed, affiliated with Church of Christ. Founded in 1869. **Accreditation:** Regional. **Undergraduate enrollment:** 507 men, 580 women full time; 16 men, 26 women part time. **Graduate enrollment:** 8 men, 20 women full time; 33 men, 42 women part time. **Faculty:** 87 total (76 full time), 51 with doctorates or other terminal degrees. **Location:** Rural campus in small town; 17 miles from Jackson. **Calendar:** Semester, limited summer session. **Microcomputers:** 87 located in libraries. **Special facilities:** Art gallery.

DEGREES OFFERED. BA, BS, MEd. 127 bachelor's degrees awarded in 1992. 24% in business and management, 5% business/office and marketing/distribution, 7% communications, 6% computer sciences, 20% teacher education, 5% home economics, 5% multi/interdisciplinary studies, 6% parks/recreation, protective services, public affairs, 10% philosophy, religion, theology. Graduate degrees offered in 1 major field of study.

UNDERGRADUATE MAJORS. Accounting, agribusiness, American studies, art education, behavioral and social studies, Bible studies, biology, business administration and management, chemistry, clinical laboratory science, communications, computer and information sciences, dramatic arts, early childhood education, elementary education, English, English education, fashion design, finance, fine arts, foreign languages education, health education, history, home economics, human environment and housing, individual and family development, information sciences and systems, liberal/general studies, marketing and distribution, mathematics, mathematics education, missionary studies, music, music education, natural sciences and mathematics, organizational communications, physical education, physical sciences, preengineering, psychology, public relations, radio/television broadcasting, science education, secondary education, social studies education, social work, world culture.

ACADEMIC PROGRAMS. 2-year transfer program, accelerated program, cooperative education, double major, honors program, independent study, internships, student-designed major, study abroad, teacher preparation, cross-registration; liberal arts/career combination in engineering, health sciences. **Remedial services:** Learning center, preadmission summer program, reduced course load, remedial instruction, special counselor, tutoring. **Placement/credit:** AP, CLEP General and Subject, institutional tests; 33 credit hours maximum for bachelor's degree.

ACADEMIC REQUIREMENTS. Freshmen must earn minimum GPA of 1.6 to continue in good standing. 68% of freshmen return for sophomore year. Students must declare major by end of first year. **Graduation requirements:** 132 hours for bachelor's (30 in major). Most students required to take courses in computer science, English, history, humanities, mathematics, philosophy/religion, biological/physical sciences, social sciences. **Additional information:** Students enrolled for 12 or more undergraduate hours must register for Bible class.

FRESHMAN ADMISSIONS. Selection criteria: Admissions based on school achievement record, test scores, references. Recommended units include English 4, mathematics 2, social science 2 and science 2. Additional science and mathematics courses recommended. **Test requirements:** ACT; score report by August 26. **Additional information:** Applicants without minimum test score or high school GPA may be admitted on probation after further evaluation.

1992 FRESHMAN CLASS PROFILE. 353 men applied, 218 accepted, 130 enrolled; 531 women applied, 318 accepted, 156 enrolled. 58% had high school GPA of 3.0 or higher, 37% between 2.0 and 2.99. **Academic background:** Mid 50% of enrolled freshmen had ACT composite between 18-24. 93% submitted ACT scores. **Characteristics:** 50% from in state, 87% live in college housing, 6% have minority backgrounds, 3% are foreign students. Average age is 19.

FALL-TERM APPLICATIONS. No fee. Closing date September 1; applicants notified on a rolling basis; must reply by registration. Interview recommended. Deferred and early admission available.

STUDENT LIFE. Housing: Dormitories (men, women). Residence rooms equipped for optional access to cable TV and college computer network. **Activities:** Student government, radio, student newspaper, television, yearbook, choral groups, concert band, drama, musical theater, pep band, Collegiate Civitans, Totalife, Evangelism Forum, Preachers Club, DAC Club, Student-Alumni Association, Young Democrats, College Republicans. **Additional information:** Henderson Church of Christ facilities adjacent to campus.

ATHLETICS. NAIA. **Intercollegiate:** Baseball M, basketball, golf M, softball W, tennis, volleyball W. **Intramural:** Badminton, basketball, bowling, cross-country, golf, softball, swimming, table tennis, tennis, volleyball.

STUDENT SERVICES. Aptitude testing, career counseling, employment service for undergraduates, freshman orientation, health services, personal counseling, placement service for graduates, services/facilities for handicapped.

ANNUAL EXPENSES. Tuition and fees: $5,940. **Room and board:** $3,020. **Books and supplies:** $575. **Other expenses:** $850.

FINANCIAL AID. 84% of freshmen, 84% of continuing students receive some form of aid. 44% of grants, 85% of loans, 76% of jobs based on need. 236 enrolled freshmen were judged to have need, all were offered aid. Academic, music/drama, art, athletic, leadership scholarships available. **Aid applications:** No closing date; priority given to applications received by April 1; applicants notified on a rolling basis beginning on or about March 1; must reply within 2 weeks.

ADDRESS/TELEPHONE. Paul Pinckley, Director of Admissions, Freed-Hardeman University, 158 East Main Street, Henderson, TN 38340. (901) 989-6651. (800) 342-7837. Fax: (901) 989-6065.

Hiwassee College
Madisonville, Tennessee CB code: 1298

2-year private junior college, coed, affiliated with United Methodist Church. Founded in 1849. **Accreditation:** Regional. **Undergraduate enrollment:** 204 men, 208 women full time; 19 men, 50 women part time. **Faculty:** 36 total (25 full time), 7 with doctorates or other terminal degrees. **Location:** Rural campus in small town; 40 miles from Knoxville. **Calendar:** Semester, limited summer session. **Microcomputers:** 44 located in classrooms, computer centers. **Special facilities:** Equestrian center, nature preserve. **Additional facts:** Christian principles emphasized; involvement in total campus life encouraged.

DEGREES OFFERED. AA, AAS. 115 associate degrees awarded in 1992.

UNDERGRADUATE MAJORS. Accounting, aeronautical technology, agribusiness, agricultural economics, agricultural engineering, animal sciences, Bible studies, biology, business administration and management, business and management, business and office, business computer/console/peripheral equipment operation, business data programming, chemistry, communications, computer and information sciences, computer graphics, computer programming, dental hygiene, education, elementary education, engineering, engineering and engineering-related technologies, equestrian science, fashion design, food science and nutrition, food sciences, forestry and related sciences, home economics, industrial technology, liberal/general studies, library assistant, marketing management, mathematics, medical laboratory technologies, music, music performance, ornamental horticulture, physical therapy, physics, plant sciences, preengineering, prelaw, psychology, recreation and community services technologies, science technologies, secondary education, secretarial and related programs, sociology, soil sciences, special education, teacher aide, textile technology, textiles and clothing.

ACADEMIC PROGRAMS. 2-year transfer program, dual enrollment of high school students, honors program, independent study, internships, visiting/exchange student program. **Remedial services:** Learning center, remedial instruction, special counselor, tutoring. **Placement/credit:** AP, CLEP General and Subject, institutional tests; 33 credit hours maximum for associate degree.

ACADEMIC REQUIREMENTS. Freshmen must earn minimum GPA of 1.5 to continue in good standing. 58% of freshmen return for sophomore year. **Graduation requirements:** 66 hours for associate. Most students required to take courses in arts/fine arts, English, history, humanities, mathematics, philosophy/religion, biological/physical sciences, social sciences.

FRESHMAN ADMISSIONS. Selection criteria: Minimum high school GPA of 2.0, class rank in top two-thirds, and test scores. **Test requirements:** SAT or ACT; score report by August 1.

1992 FRESHMAN CLASS PROFILE. 122 men, 133 women enrolled. **Characteristics:** 74% from in state, 69% live in college housing, 23% have minority backgrounds, 1% are foreign students. Average age is 19.

FALL-TERM APPLICATIONS. $10 fee, may be waived for applicants with need. Closing date August 1; applicants notified on a rolling basis. Interview recommended for academically weak applicants.

STUDENT LIFE. Housing: Dormitories (men, women). **Activities:** Student government, student newspaper, yearbook, choral groups, dance, drama, musical theater.

ATHLETICS. NJCAA. **Intercollegiate:** Baseball M, basketball, horseback riding, softball W. **Intramural:** Basketball, football, softball, volleyball.

STUDENT SERVICES. Aptitude testing, career counseling, freshman orientation, personal counseling, special adviser for adult students, services/facilities for handicapped.

ANNUAL EXPENSES. Tuition and fees (1992-93): $4,200. **Room and board:** $2,700. **Books and supplies:** $350. **Other expenses:** $800.

FINANCIAL AID. 75% of freshmen, 75% of continuing students receive some form of aid. All grants, 97% of loans, all jobs based on need. Academic, music/drama, athletic, state/district residency, leadership, alumni affiliation, religious affiliation, minority scholarships available. **Aid applications:** No closing date; priority given to applications received by May 1; applicants notified on a rolling basis beginning on or about May 20; must reply within 2 weeks.

ADDRESS/TELEPHONE. Carl Pagles, Director of Admissions, Hiwassee College, Madisonville, TN 37354. (615) 442-3283.

ITT Technical Institute: Nashville

Nashville, Tennessee — CB code: 7025

2-year proprietary technical college, coed. **Undergraduate enrollment:** 635 men and women. **Faculty:** 20 total (19 full time). **Location:** Urban campus in very large city. **Calendar:** Quarter. Extensive evening/early morning classes. **Microcomputers:** 55 located in libraries, classrooms, computer centers.

DEGREES OFFERED. AAS. 269 associate degrees awarded in 1992. 100% in engineering technologies.

UNDERGRADUATE MAJORS. Computer-aided drafting, electronic technology.

ACADEMIC PROGRAMS. Remedial services: Learning center, tutoring. **Placement/credit:** Institutional tests.

ACADEMIC REQUIREMENTS. Freshmen must earn minimum GPA of 1.7 to continue in good standing. 75% of freshmen return for sophomore year. Students must declare major on application. **Graduation requirements:** 91 hours for associate. Most students required to take courses in computer science, mathematics.

FRESHMAN ADMISSIONS. Selection criteria: Institution's entrance examination in reading and mathematics most important. Recommended units include mathematics 3.

1992 FRESHMAN CLASS PROFILE. 301 men and women enrolled.

FALL-TERM APPLICATIONS. $100 fee. Application fee returned if student not accepted. No closing date; applicants notified on a rolling basis. Interview required.

STUDENT LIFE. Housing: Assistance provided in locating roommates, housing and car pooling. **Activities:** Student government, student newspaper.

STUDENT SERVICES. Career counseling, employment service for undergraduates, placement service for graduates, services/facilities for handicapped.

ANNUAL EXPENSES. Tuition and fees (1992-93): Tuition for 18-month computer-aided drafting program $12,817; books, supplies, and tools, $1,000. Tuition for 2-year electronics program $14,405; books and supplies, $1,500. Laboratory fees, $50 per quarter.

FINANCIAL AID. Aid applications: No closing date; applicants notified on a rolling basis.

ADDRESS/TELEPHONE. James Eller, Director of Recruitment, ITT Technical Institute: Nashville, PO PO Box 148029, 441 Donelson Pike, Nashville, TN 37214-8029. (615) 889-8700.

Jackson State Community College

Jackson, Tennessee — CB code: 2266

2-year public community college, coed. Founded in 1965. **Accreditation:** Regional. **Undergraduate enrollment:** 3,461 men and women. **Location:** Suburban campus in small city; 80 miles northeast of Memphis. **Calendar:** Semester.

FRESHMAN ADMISSIONS. Selection criteria: Open admissions.

ANNUAL EXPENSES. Tuition and fees (1992-93): $916, $2,600 additional for out-of-state students. **Books and supplies:** $400. **Other expenses:** $614.

ADDRESS/TELEPHONE. John L. Johnson, Director of Admissions/Records, Jackson State Community College, 2046 North Parkway, Jackson, TN 38301-3797. (901) 424-3520. Fax: (901) 425-2647.

John A. Gupton College

Nashville, Tennessee — CB code: 0539

2-year private college of funeral service, coed. Founded in 1946. **Accreditation:** Regional. **Undergraduate enrollment:** 50 men and women. **Location:** Urban campus in large city. **Calendar:** Semester.

FRESHMAN ADMISSIONS. Selection criteria: 2 letters of recommendation, test scores most important criteria for admissions.

ANNUAL EXPENSES. Tuition and fees (1992-93): $6,856. **Books and supplies:** $650.

ADDRESS/TELEPHONE. Bernadean Gupton, Dean, John A. Gupton College, 2507 West End Avenue, Nashville, TN 37203. (615) 327-3927.

Johnson Bible College

Knoxville, Tennessee — CB code: 1345

Admissions: 74% of applicants accepted
Based on: ••• Recommendations, religious affiliation/commitment, school record, test scores
• Essay, interview
Completion: 75% of freshmen end year in good standing
35% graduate, 2% of these enter graduate study

4-year private Bible college, coed, affiliated with Christian Church. Founded in 1893. **Accreditation:** Regional. **Undergraduate enrollment:** 228 men, 187 women full time; 11 men, 10 women part time. **Graduate enrollment:** 5 men full time; 46 men, 1 woman part time. **Faculty:** 28 total (20 full time), 10 with doctorates or other terminal degrees. **Location:** Rural campus in small city; 12 miles from town. **Calendar:** Semester, limited summer session. **Microcomputers:** 45 located in libraries, computer centers.

DEGREES OFFERED. AS, BA, BS, MA. 3 associate degrees awarded in 1992. 100% in philosophy, religion, theology. 43 bachelor's degrees awarded. 12% in teacher education, 87% philosophy, religion, theology. Graduate degrees offered in 1 major field of study.

UNDERGRADUATE MAJORS. Associate: Bible studies. **Bachelor's:** Bible studies, early childhood education, elementary education, junior high education, music, religious music, theological studies.

ACADEMIC PROGRAMS. Double major, internships, teacher preparation. **Remedial services:** Learning center, remedial instruction, special counselor. **Placement/credit:** AP, CLEP General and Subject, institutional tests; 18 credit hours maximum for associate degree; 18 credit hours maximum for bachelor's degree.

ACADEMIC REQUIREMENTS. Freshmen must earn minimum GPA of 1.5 to continue in good standing. 63% of freshmen return for sophomore year. Students must declare major on application. **Graduation requirements:** 66 hours for associate (19 in major), 132 hours for bachelor's (30 in major). Most students required to take courses in arts/fine arts, English, history, humanities, mathematics, philosophy/religion, biological/physical sciences, social sciences. **Postgraduate studies:** 2% enter other graduate study. **Additional information:** All degree programs have major in Bible, 2 programs have double majors: church music and Bible, teacher education and Bible.

FRESHMAN ADMISSIONS. Selection criteria: High school transcript and 3 references, 1 from minister required. High school percentile rank of 8 or above and ACT score of 10 or above (enhanced 14 or above) important. **High school preparation:** 16 units required. Required units include English 4, foreign language 2, mathematics 2, social science 2 and science 2. 2 history courses required. **Test requirements:** ACT; score report by August 1. **Additional information:** Enrolled on probation if ranked in bottom third of high school graduating class.

1992 FRESHMAN CLASS PROFILE. 67 men applied, 53 accepted, 40 enrolled; 97 women applied, 68 accepted, 59 enrolled. 51% had high school GPA of 3.0 or higher, 41% between 2.0 and 2.99. 20% were in top tenth and 43% were in top quarter of graduating class. **Academic background:** Mid 50% of enrolled freshmen had ACT composite between 18-24. 92% submitted ACT scores. **Characteristics:** 15% from in state, 95% live in college housing, 2% have minority backgrounds, 1% are foreign students. Average age is 20.

FALL-TERM APPLICATIONS. $35 fee. Closing date August 26; priority given to applications received by August 1; applicants notified on a rolling basis; must reply by registration. Audition required for music applicants. Interview recommended. Deferred and early admission available.

STUDENT LIFE. Housing: Dormitories (men, women); apartment housing available. Mobile homes and duplex houses available for family units. **Activities:** Student government, radio, television, yearbook, choral groups, drama, music ensembles. **Additional information:** Religious observance required.

ATHLETICS. Intercollegiate: Baseball M, basketball, soccer, volleyball W. **Intramural:** Archery, badminton, basketball, softball, swimming, tennis, volleyball.

STUDENT SERVICES. Career counseling, employment service for undergraduates, freshman orientation, health services, personal counseling, placement service for graduates, veterans counselor, services/facilities for handicapped.

ANNUAL EXPENSES. Tuition and fees (1992-93): $3,650. **Room and board:** $2,800. **Books and supplies:** $600. **Other expenses:** $700.

FINANCIAL AID. 80% of freshmen, 85% of continuing students receive some form of aid. 68% of grants, 99% of loans, 95% of jobs based on

need. Academic, music/drama, leadership, minority scholarships available. **Aid applications:** No closing date; priority given to applications received by July 1; applicants notified on a rolling basis beginning on or about March 1; must reply by registration.

ADDRESS/TELEPHONE. Larry Green, Director of Admissions, Johnson Bible College, 7900 Johnson Drive, Knoxville, TN 37998. (615) 573-4517 ext. 2233. Fax: (615) 579-2336.

King College
Bristol, Tennessee — CB code: 1371

Admissions: 73% of applicants accepted
Based on:
- ••• Interview, school record
- •• Religious affiliation/commitment, test scores
- • Activities, essay, recommendations, special talents

Completion: 85% of freshmen end year in good standing
80% graduate, 10% of these enter graduate study

4-year private liberal arts college, coed, affiliated with Presbyterian Church (USA). Founded in 1867. **Accreditation:** Regional. **Undergraduate enrollment:** 237 men, 269 women full time; 21 men, 31 women part time. **Faculty:** 64 total (40 full time), 27 with doctorates or other terminal degrees. **Location:** Suburban campus in large town; 110 miles from Knoxville, 95 miles from Asheville, North Carolina. **Calendar:** 4-4-1, limited summer session. Extensive evening/early morning classes. **Microcomputers:** 60 located in dormitories, libraries, classrooms, computer centers, campus-wide network. Lease or purchase required**Special facilities:** Observatory, nuclear physics laboratory. **Additional facts:** Christian values emphasized.

DEGREES OFFERED. BA, BS. 96 bachelor's degrees awarded in 1992. 21% in business and management, 23% letters/literature, 5% life sciences, 8% philosophy, religion, theology, 11% psychology, 27% social sciences.

UNDERGRADUATE MAJORS. Behavioral sciences, biology, business administration and management, business economics, chemistry, clinical laboratory science, English, fine arts, foreign languages (multiple emphasis), French, history, mathematics, physics, political science and government, psychology, religion.

ACADEMIC PROGRAMS. Double major, independent study, internships, study abroad, teacher preparation, visiting/exchange student program, Washington semester, cross-registration; liberal arts/career combination in engineering. **Remedial services:** Reduced course load, tutoring. **ROTC:** Army. **Placement/credit:** AP, CLEP General and Subject, IB; 30 credit hours maximum for bachelor's degree.

ACADEMIC REQUIREMENTS. Freshmen must earn minimum GPA of 1.6 to continue in good standing. 85% of freshmen return for sophomore year. Students must declare major by end of second year. **Graduation requirements:** 124 hours for bachelor's (36 in major). Most students required to take courses in arts/fine arts, English, foreign languages, history, mathematics, philosophy/religion, biological/physical sciences, social sciences. **Postgraduate studies:** 1% enter law school, 2% enter medical school, 5% enter MBA programs, 2% enter other graduate study.

FRESHMAN ADMISSIONS. Selection criteria: Minimum SAT combined score of 900 or ACT composite score of 23 and rank in top half of class preferred. High school GPA, recommendations, autobiographical statement considered. **High school preparation:** 16 units required. Recommended units include English 4, foreign language 2, mathematics 3, social science 2 and science 1. Mathematics units should include 2 algebra, 1 geometry. 5 units from foreign language, history, or social studies, 4 units from natural science, or advanced mathematics also recommended. **Test requirements:** SAT or ACT; score report by June 1.

1992 FRESHMAN CLASS PROFILE. 209 men applied, 150 accepted, 59 enrolled; 240 women applied, 178 accepted, 64 enrolled. 51% had high school GPA of 3.0 or higher, 46% between 2.0 and 2.99. **Academic background:** Mid 50% of enrolled freshmen had SAT-V between 410-510, SAT-M between 440-570; ACT composite between 21-26. 68% submitted SAT scores, 39% submitted ACT scores. **Characteristics:** 56% from in state, 84% live in college housing, 11% have minority backgrounds, 9% are foreign students. Average age is 18.

FALL-TERM APPLICATIONS. $50 fee, may be waived for applicants with need. Closing date August 25; priority given to applications received by March 1; applicants notified on a rolling basis; must reply immediately. Essay required. Interview recommended. Deferred and early admission available.

STUDENT LIFE. Housing: Dormitories (men, women, coed). **Activities:** Student government, student newspaper, yearbook, choral groups, drama, student Christian association, literary societies.

ATHLETICS. NAIA. **Intercollegiate:** Baseball M, basketball, cross-country, golf M, soccer M, softball W, tennis, volleyball W. **Intramural:** Badminton, basketball, soccer, softball, table tennis, volleyball.

STUDENT SERVICES. Career counseling, employment service for undergraduates, freshman orientation, health services, personal counseling, placement service for graduates, services/facilities for handicapped.

ANNUAL EXPENSES. Tuition and fees: $8,250. **Room and board:** $3,250. **Books and supplies:** $500. **Other expenses:** $1,200.

FINANCIAL AID. 90% of freshmen, 90% of continuing students receive some form of aid. 91% of grants, 93% of loans, 73% of jobs based on need. 99 enrolled freshmen were judged to have need, all were offered aid. Academic, music/drama, athletic, religious affiliation scholarships available. **Aid applications:** No closing date; priority given to applications received by March 1; applicants notified on a rolling basis; must reply within 2 weeks.

ADDRESS/TELEPHONE. Roger Kieffer, Dean of Admissions, King College, 1350 King College Road, Bristol, TN 37620-2699. (615) 968-1187. Fax: (615) 968-4456.

Knoxville Business College
Knoxville, Tennessee — CB code: 0711

2-year proprietary junior college, coed. Founded in 1882. **Undergraduate enrollment:** 70 men, 209 women full time; 6 men, 86 women part time. **Faculty:** 25 total (11 full time), 7 with doctorates or other terminal degrees. **Location:** Urban campus in small city; 1 mile from downtown. **Calendar:** Quarter, extensive summer session. Extensive evening/early morning classes. **Microcomputers:** 50 located in classrooms, computer centers.

DEGREES OFFERED. AS. 48 associate degrees awarded in 1992. 38% in business and management, 30% business/office and marketing/distribution, 30% law.

UNDERGRADUATE MAJORS. Accounting, business and management, computer and information sciences, hotel/motel and restaurant management, legal assistant/paralegal, office supervision and management, secretarial and related programs.

ACADEMIC PROGRAMS. Accelerated program, double major, dual enrollment of high school students, internships. **Remedial services:** Reduced course load, remedial instruction, tutoring. **Placement/credit:** AP, institutional tests; 24 credit hours maximum for associate degree.

ACADEMIC REQUIREMENTS. Freshmen must earn minimum GPA of 2.0 to continue in good standing. 55% of freshmen return for sophomore year. Students must declare major on application. **Graduation requirements:** 104 hours for associate (40 in major). Most students required to take courses in computer science, English, history, mathematics, social sciences.

FRESHMAN ADMISSIONS. Selection criteria: CPAT examination required. **Test requirements:** SAT or ACT.

1992 FRESHMAN CLASS PROFILE. 22 men, 67 women enrolled. **Characteristics:** 99% from in state, 100% commute, 16% have minority backgrounds, 1% are foreign students. Average age is 22.

FALL-TERM APPLICATIONS. $25 fee. No closing date; applicants notified on a rolling basis. Interview required. Early admission available.

STUDENT LIFE. Activities: Student government, student newspaper, Collegiate Secretaries International, Accounting Society, Paralegal Association, Student Affairs Advisory Council, Hotel Association.

STUDENT SERVICES. Aptitude testing, career counseling, employment service for undergraduates, freshman orientation, placement service for graduates, veterans counselor, services/facilities for handicapped.

ANNUAL EXPENSES. Tuition and fees (1992-93): $4,800. Required computer fees vary by program. **Books and supplies:** $550. **Other expenses:** $1,000.

FINANCIAL AID. 95% of freshmen, 95% of continuing students receive some form of aid. 99% of grants, all loans, all jobs based on need. **Aid applications:** No closing date; applicants notified on a rolling basis.

ADDRESS/TELEPHONE. Nelson Bridge, Admissions Director, Knoxville Business College, 720 N. Fifth Ave, Knoxville, TN 37917. (615) 524-3043.

Knoxville College
Knoxville, Tennessee — CB code: 1373

4-year private liberal arts college, coed, affiliated with Presbyterian Church (USA). Founded in 1875. **Accreditation:** Regional. **Undergraduate enrollment:** 914 men and women. **Faculty:** 79 total (66 full time), 37 with doctorates or other terminal degrees. **Location:** Urban campus in small city; 177 miles from Nashville. **Calendar:** Semester, extensive summer session. **Microcomputers:** 50 located in classrooms, computer centers.

DEGREES OFFERED. AA, BA, BS. 35 associate degrees awarded in 1992. 100% in allied health. 59 bachelor's degrees awarded. 34% in business and management, 15% business/office and marketing/distribution, 20% communications, 6% teacher education, 9% mathematics.

UNDERGRADUATE MAJORS. Associate: Medical assistant, science technologies, secretarial and related programs. **Bachelor's:** Accounting, allied health, biological and physical sciences, biology, business and management, business economics, chemistry, communications, economics, education, elementary education, English, English literature, health education, history, hotel/motel and restaurant management, humanities and social sciences, junior high education, liberal/general studies, mathematics, music, physical education, physical sciences, physics, political science and government, prelaw, psychology, recreation and community services technologies, secondary education, secretarial and related programs, sociology, zoology.

ACADEMIC PROGRAMS. Cooperative education, double major, independent study, internships, cross-registration; liberal arts/career combination in engineering. **Remedial services:** Remedial instruction, special counselor, tutoring. **ROTC:** Air Force, Army. **Placement/credit:** AP.

ACADEMIC REQUIREMENTS. Freshmen must earn minimum GPA of 1.5 to continue in good standing. 75% of freshmen return for sophomore year. Students must declare major by end of second year. **Graduation requirements:** 65 hours for associate, 124 hours for bachelor's (45 in major). Most students required to take courses in arts/fine arts, computer science, English, history, humanities, mathematics, philosophy/religion, biological/physical sciences, social sciences.

FRESHMAN ADMISSIONS. Selection criteria: Minimum 2.0 high school GPA, recommendations. Students with GPA between 1.7 and 1.99 may be admitted with provisional status. **High school preparation:** 11 units required. Required units include biological science 1, English 3, foreign language 2, mathematics 2, physical science 2 and social science 1. **Test requirements:** SAT or ACT; score report by September 1.

1992 FRESHMAN CLASS PROFILE. 258 men and women enrolled. **Characteristics:** 65% from in state, 95% live in college housing, 99% have minority backgrounds, 2% are foreign students. Average age is 19.

FALL-TERM APPLICATIONS. $15 fee, may be waived for applicants with need. No closing date; applicants notified on a rolling basis beginning on or about January 2. Audition required for music applicants. Essay recommended. Deferred admission available.

STUDENT LIFE. Housing: Dormitories (men, women). **Activities:** Student government, student newspaper, yearbook, choral groups, concert band, dance, drama, jazz band, marching band, music ensembles, musical theater, opera, pep band, fraternities, sororities, Christian Fellowship Society, Black Awareness Organization.

ATHLETICS. Intercollegiate: Baseball M, basketball, football M, tennis, track and field, volleyball W. **Intramural:** Badminton M, basketball M, softball, table tennis, volleyball.

STUDENT SERVICES. Career counseling, employment service for undergraduates, freshman orientation, health services, personal counseling, placement service for graduates.

ANNUAL EXPENSES. Tuition and fees: $5,470. **Room and board:** $2,850. **Books and supplies:** $600. **Other expenses:** $1,730.

FINANCIAL AID. 99% of freshmen, 99% of continuing students receive some form of aid. 64% of grants, 88% of loans, 39% of jobs based on need. 220 enrolled freshmen were judged to have need, all were offered aid. Academic, music/drama, leadership, religious affiliation scholarships available. **Aid applications:** No closing date; priority given to applications received by May 31; applicants notified on a rolling basis beginning on or about March 1; must reply within 30 days.

ADDRESS/TELEPHONE. Robert Thomas, Director of Admissions, Knoxville College, 901 College Street, Knoxville, TN 37921. (615) 524-6568. (800) 743-5669. Fax: (615) 524-6686.

Lambuth University
Jackson, Tennessee — CB code: 1394

Admissions: 53% of applicants accepted
Based on: ••• Recommendations, school record, test scores
•• Activities, essay, interview, special talents
Completion: 50% graduate

4-year private liberal arts college, coed, affiliated with United Methodist Church. Founded in 1843. **Accreditation:** Regional. **Undergraduate enrollment:** 426 men, 416 women full time; 151 men, 160 women part time. **Faculty:** 84 total (41 full time), 26 with doctorates or other terminal degrees. **Location:** Urban campus in small city; 80 miles from Memphis. **Calendar:** Semester, limited summer session. Extensive evening/early morning classes. **Microcomputers:** 37 located in libraries, classrooms, computer centers. **Special facilities:** Planetarium, art and interior design complex, Oxley Biological Field Station.

DEGREES OFFERED. BA, BS. 179 bachelor's degrees awarded in 1992.

UNDERGRADUATE MAJORS. Accounting, advertising, art education, biological and physical sciences, biology, business administration and management, business and management, business and office, business data processing and related programs, business economics, chemistry, communications, computer and information sciences, computer programming, data processing, dramatic arts, early childhood education, education, education of exceptional children, education of the deaf and hearing impaired, elementary education, English, English education, fashion merchandising, fine arts, foreign languages (multiple emphasis), foreign languages education, French, German, health education, history, history/political science, home economics, home economics education, humanities, humanities and social sciences, interior design, international relations, journalism, junior high education, liberal/general studies, library science, management information systems, marketing and distribution, marketing management, marketing research, mathematics, mathematics education, music, music education, music performance, philosophy, physical education, physical sciences, physics, predentistry, preengineering, prelaw, premedicine, prepharmacy, psychology, public relations, radio/television broadcasting, reading education, religion, science education, secondary education, social sciences, social studies education, social work, sociology, Spanish, special education, speech, speech correction, speech pathology/audiology, speech/communication/theater education, studio art, visual and performing arts.

ACADEMIC PROGRAMS. Double major, dual enrollment of high school students, honors program, independent study, internships, student-designed major, study abroad, teacher preparation, Washington semester, cross-registration. **Remedial services:** Learning center, preadmission summer program, reduced course load, special counselor, tutoring. **Placement/credit:** AP, CLEP General and Subject, institutional tests; 32 credit hours maximum for bachelor's degree.

ACADEMIC REQUIREMENTS. Freshmen must earn minimum GPA of 1.75 to continue in good standing. 66% of freshmen return for sophomore year. Students must declare major by end of second year. **Graduation requirements:** 128 hours for bachelor's (40 in major). Most students required to take courses in arts/fine arts, computer science, English, humanities, mathematics, philosophy/religion, biological/physical sciences, social sciences.

FRESHMAN ADMISSIONS. Selection criteria: High school record, test scores, recommendation of counselor considered. **Test requirements:** SAT or ACT; score report by August 1.

1992 FRESHMAN CLASS PROFILE. 20% were in top tenth and 40% were in top quarter of graduating class. **Characteristics:** 70% live in college housing. Average age is 18.

FALL-TERM APPLICATIONS. $10 fee, may be waived for applicants with need. No closing date; applicants notified on a rolling basis; must reply by May 1 or within 2 weeks if notified thereafter. Interview recommended. Audition recommended for music, drama applicants. Portfolio recommended for art applicants. Essay recommended. CRDA. Deferred and early admission available.

STUDENT LIFE. Housing: Dormitories (men, women); apartment, fraternity, sorority housing available. **Activities:** Student government, radio, student newspaper, television, yearbook, literary publication, small television laboratory, choral groups, concert band, drama, jazz band, music ensembles, musical theater, pep band, fraternities, sororities, Black Student Union, Campus Congregation, International Students Club.

ATHLETICS. NAIA. **Intercollegiate:** Baseball M, basketball, football M, golf M, soccer, softball W, tennis, volleyball W. **Intramural:** Badminton, basketball, cross-country, golf, racquetball, soccer M, softball, swimming, table tennis, tennis, volleyball.

STUDENT SERVICES. Aptitude testing, career counseling, employment service for undergraduates, freshman orientation, health services, personal counseling, placement service for graduates, special adviser for adult students, services/facilities for handicapped.

ANNUAL EXPENSES. Tuition and fees (1992-93): $4,834. **Room and board:** $3,160. **Books and supplies:** $400. **Other expenses:** $1,200.

FINANCIAL AID. 75% of freshmen, 75% of continuing students receive some form of aid. Grants, loans, jobs available. Academic, music/drama, art, athletic, leadership, religious affiliation scholarships available. **Aid applications:** No closing date; priority given to applications received by March 15; applicants notified on a rolling basis beginning on or about April 15; must reply within 4 weeks.

ADDRESS/TELEPHONE. Nancy Tipton, Director of Student Recruitment, Lambuth University, Lambuth Boulevard, Jackson, TN 38301-5296. (901) 425-3223. (800) LAMBUTH ext. 223. Fax: (901) 423-1990.

Lane College
Jackson, Tennessee — CB code: 1395

Admissions: 66% of applicants accepted
Based on: ••• Recommendations, school record
•• Activities, special talents, test scores
• Essay, interview
Completion: 87% of freshmen end year in good standing
25% graduate, 33% of these enter graduate study

4-year private liberal arts college, coed, affiliated with Christian Methodist Episcopal Church. Founded in 1882. **Accreditation:** Regional. **Undergraduate enrollment:** 251 men, 265 women full time; 11 men, 7 women part time. **Faculty:** 41 total (39 full time), 14 with doctorates or other terminal degrees. **Location:** Suburban campus in small city; 80 miles from Memphis, 126 miles from Nashville. **Calendar:** Semester, limited summer session. **Microcomputers:** 60 located in libraries, classrooms, computer centers.

DEGREES OFFERED. BA, BS. 60 bachelor's degrees awarded in 1992. 30% in business and management, 15% communications, 16% teacher education, 7% health sciences, 7% life sciences, 15% social sciences.

UNDERGRADUATE MAJORS. Biology, business and management, chemistry, communications, computer and information sciences, computer science/mathematics, elementary education, engineering, English, history, mathematics, music, physical education, predentistry, prelaw, premedicine, prenursing, religion, sociology.

ACADEMIC PROGRAMS. Accelerated program, cooperative education, honors program, independent study, internships, Minority Biomedical Research Support Program, Health Careers Opportunity Program, Minority Science Improvement Program, MARC Honors Undergraduate Research Training Program. **Remedial services:** Learning center, remedial instruction, tutoring. **Placement/credit:** AP, CLEP Subject; 32 credit hours maximum for bachelor's degree.

ACADEMIC REQUIREMENTS. Freshmen must earn minimum GPA of 1.25 to continue in good standing. 65% of freshmen return for sophomore year. Students must declare major by end of second year. **Graduation requirements:** 124 hours for bachelor's (35 in major). Most students required to take courses in arts/fine arts, computer science, English, foreign languages, history, humanities, mathematics, philosophy/religion, biological/physical sciences, social sciences.

FRESHMAN ADMISSIONS. Selection criteria: 2.0 GPA or ACT composite score of 13 or other supporting evidence of ability to do college-level work. **High school preparation:** 10 units required. Required and recommended units include English 4, mathematics 2, social science 2 and science 2. Biological science 2 and foreign language 2 recommended. **Test requirements:** SAT or ACT (ACT preferred); score report by July 15.

1992 FRESHMAN CLASS PROFILE. 171 men applied, 111 accepted, 69 enrolled; 183 women applied, 123 accepted, 65 enrolled. 12% had high school GPA of 3.0 or higher, 70% between 2.0 and 2.99. **Characteristics:** 46% from in state, 93% live in college housing, 100% have minority backgrounds. Average age is 19.

FALL-TERM APPLICATIONS. $10 fee, may be waived for applicants with need. Closing date August 1; priority given to applications received by May 15; applicants notified on a rolling basis; must reply by June 15. Interview recommended. Audition recommended. Early admission available. ACT or SAT examinations should be taken by December prior to planned entrance.

STUDENT LIFE. Housing: Dormitories (men, women). College housing available. **Activities:** Student government, student newspaper, yearbook, choral groups, drama, marching band, music ensembles, fraternities, sororities, Student Ministerial Alliance, Student Christian Association, Pre-Alumni Council.

ATHLETICS. NCAA. **Intercollegiate:** Baseball M, basketball, cross-country W, football M, track and field, volleyball W. **Intramural:** Basketball, softball, swimming, table tennis, tennis, volleyball M.

STUDENT SERVICES. Career counseling, employment service for undergraduates, freshman orientation, health services, personal counseling, placement service for graduates, veterans counselor, services/facilities for handicapped.

ANNUAL EXPENSES. Tuition and fees (1992-93): $4,557. **Room and board:** $2,544. **Books and supplies:** $400. **Other expenses:** $900.

FINANCIAL AID. 97% of freshmen, 94% of continuing students receive some form of aid. **Aid applications:** Closing date August 1; priority given to applications received by May 15; applicants notified on a rolling basis.

ADDRESS/TELEPHONE. Ella Ruth Maddox, Director of Admissions, Lane College, 545 Lane Avenue, Jackson, TN 38301. (901) 426-7500. Fax: (901)423-4931.

Lee College
Cleveland, Tennessee — CB code: 1401

4-year private liberal arts college, coed, affiliated with Church of God. Founded in 1918. **Accreditation:** Regional. **Undergraduate enrollment:** 1,922 men and women. **Faculty:** 163 total (76 full time), 46 with doctorates or other terminal degrees. **Location:** Urban campus in large town; 30 miles from Chattanooga. **Calendar:** Semester, limited summer session. **Microcomputers:** Located in computer centers.

DEGREES OFFERED. BA, BS. 310 bachelor's degrees awarded in 1992. 7% in business and management, 17% business/office and marketing/distribution, 6% communications, 17% teacher education, 5% life sciences, 17% philosophy, religion, theology, 11% psychology, 9% social sciences.

UNDERGRADUATE MAJORS. Accounting, Bible studies, biological and physical sciences, biology, business administration and management, business and management, chemistry, communications, early childhood education, elementary education, English, foreign languages (multiple emphasis), history, human development, information sciences and systems, mathematics, medical laboratory technologies, missionary studies, music performance, office supervision and management, physical education, psychology, religious education, religious music, secondary education, social sciences, sociology.

ACADEMIC PROGRAMS. Double major, honors program, independent study, internships, study abroad, teacher preparation, Washington semester; liberal arts/career combination in health sciences. **Remedial services:** Learning center, preadmission summer program, reduced course load, remedial instruction, special counselor, tutoring. **Placement/credit:** AP, CLEP Subject; 30 credit hours maximum for bachelor's degree.

ACADEMIC REQUIREMENTS. Freshmen must earn minimum GPA of 1.5 to continue in good standing. 60% of freshmen return for sophomore year. Students must declare major by end of second year. **Graduation requirements:** 130 hours for bachelor's (30 in major). Most students required to take courses in arts/fine arts, English, history, humanities, mathematics, philosophy/religion, biological/physical sciences, social sciences.

FRESHMAN ADMISSIONS. Selection criteria: School achievement record and test scores considered. **Test requirements:** SAT or ACT; score report by August 25.

1992 FRESHMAN CLASS PROFILE. 384 men and women enrolled. **Characteristics:** 13% from in state, 85% live in college housing, 9% have minority backgrounds, 2% are foreign students. Average age is 20.

FALL-TERM APPLICATIONS. $25 fee. No closing date; applicants notified on a rolling basis. Audition required for music applicants. Deferred and early admission available.

STUDENT LIFE. Housing: Dormitories (men, women); apartment housing available. **Activities:** Student government, magazine, student newspaper, yearbook, choral groups, concert band, drama, music ensembles, musical theater, opera, pep band, symphony orchestra, fraternities, sororities.

ATHLETICS. NAIA. **Intercollegiate:** Basketball, golf M, soccer, softball W, tennis, volleyball W. **Intramural:** Baseball, basketball, racquetball, softball, tennis, volleyball.

STUDENT SERVICES. Aptitude testing, career counseling, freshman orientation, health services, personal counseling, placement service for graduates, veterans counselor, services/facilities for handicapped.

ANNUAL EXPENSES. Tuition and fees: $4,692. **Room and board:** $3,160. **Books and supplies:** $500. **Other expenses:** $840.

FINANCIAL AID. 90% of freshmen, 93% of continuing students receive some form of aid. 79% of grants, 84% of loans, all jobs based on need. 227 enrolled freshmen were judged to have need, 225 were offered aid. Academic, music/drama, athletic, state/district residency, leadership, alumni affiliation, religious affiliation, minority scholarships available. **Aid applications:** No closing date; priority given to applications received by April 15; applicants notified on a rolling basis beginning on or about April 1; must reply within 2 weeks.

ADDRESS/TELEPHONE. Gary Ray, Director of Admissions, Lee College, Cleveland, TN 37311. (615) 472-2111. (800) LEE-9930. Fax: (615) 478-7075.

LeMoyne-Owen College
Memphis, Tennessee — CB code: 1403

Admissions:	84% of applicants accepted
Based on:	••• School record, test scores
	•• Activities, essay, interview, recommendations, special talents
Completion:	85% of freshmen end year in good standing
	42% enter graduate study

4-year private liberal arts college, coed, affiliated with United Church of Christ and Tennessee Baptist Convention. Founded in 1862. **Accreditation:** Regional. **Undergraduate enrollment:** 1,200 men and women. **Graduate enrollment:** 40 men, 110 women full time. **Faculty:** 100 total (75 full time), 65 with doctorates or other terminal degrees. **Location:** Urban campus in very large city; 200 miles from Nashville. **Calendar:** Semester, extensive summer session. Saturday and extensive evening/early morning classes. **Microcomputers:** 60 located in dormitories, libraries, classrooms, computer centers, campus-wide network. **Special facilities:** Art gallery. **Additional facts:** Four off-campus sites.

DEGREES OFFERED. BA, BS, MS, MEd. 142 bachelor's degrees awarded in 1992. 40% in business and management, 20% computer sciences, 5% teacher education, 5% engineering, 20% mathematics, 10% social sciences. Graduate degrees offered in 2 major fields of study.

UNDERGRADUATE MAJORS. Accounting, biochemistry, biological and physical sciences, biology, business administration and management, chemistry, computer and information sciences, computer programming, economics, education, elementary education, engineering, English, health and fitness/wellness, history, humanities and social sciences, junior high education, mathematics, political science and government, secondary education, social sciences, social work, sociology, visual and performing arts.

ACADEMIC PROGRAMS. Cooperative education, double major, dual enrollment of high school students, honors program, internships, student-designed major, study abroad, teacher preparation, telecourses, visiting/exchange student program, weekend college, cross-registration; liberal arts/career combination in engineering, health sciences. **Remedial services:** Learning center, preadmission summer program, reduced course load, remedial instruction, special counselor, tutoring. **ROTC:** Air Force, Army, Naval. **Placement/credit:** AP, institutional tests; 30 credit hours maximum for bachelor's degree.

ACADEMIC REQUIREMENTS. Freshmen must earn minimum GPA of 2.0 to continue in good standing. 65% of freshmen return for sophomore year. Students must declare major by end of second year. **Graduation requirements:** 130 hours for bachelor's. Most students required to take courses in arts/fine arts, computer science, English, history, humanities, mathematics, philosophy/religion, biological/physical sciences, social sciences. **Postgraduate studies:** 8% enter law school, 8% enter medical school, 10% enter MBA programs, 16% enter other graduate study.

FRESHMAN ADMISSIONS. Selection criteria: High school transcript, test scores, letter of recommendation, and interview considered. Special consideration given to children of alumni. **High school preparation:** 20 units required. **Test requirements:** SAT or ACT (ACT preferred); score report by July 30.

1992 FRESHMAN CLASS PROFILE. 576 men applied, 500 accepted, 180 enrolled; 594 women applied, 480 accepted, 221 enrolled. 27% had high school GPA of 3.0 or higher, 73% between 2.0 and 2.99. 30% were in top tenth and 30% were in top quarter of graduating class. **Characteristics:** 95% from in state, 90% commute, 100% have minority backgrounds, 1% are foreign students. Average age is 18.

FALL-TERM APPLICATIONS. $25 fee, may be waived for applicants with need. Closing date June 15; priority given to applications received by May 15; applicants notified on a rolling basis; must reply within 2 weeks. Interview required. Essay required. Deferred and early admission available.

STUDENT LIFE. Housing: Dormitories (men, women). **Activities:** Student government, student newspaper, yearbook, choral groups, dance, drama, jazz band, music ensembles, fraternities, sororities, NAACP, Social Work Club, Students for Free Enterprise, Operation Push.

ATHLETICS. NCAA. **Intercollegiate:** Baseball M, basketball, cross-country M. **Intramural:** Badminton, baseball M, basketball, cross-country M, golf, gymnastics, softball, swimming, tennis, track and field, volleyball.

STUDENT SERVICES. Aptitude testing, career counseling, employment service for undergraduates, freshman orientation, health services, on-campus day care, personal counseling, placement service for graduates, special adviser for adult students, veterans counselor.

ANNUAL EXPENSES. Tuition and fees (1992-93): $3,750. **Books and supplies:** $400. **Other expenses:** $900.

FINANCIAL AID. 88% of freshmen, 95% of continuing students receive some form of aid. **Aid applications:** No closing date; priority given to applications received by April 15; applicants notified on a rolling basis beginning on or about April 1; must reply within 10 days.

ADDRESS/TELEPHONE. Marie Milam, Director of Admissions, LeMoyne-Owen College, 807 Walker Avenue, Memphis, TN 38126. (901) 942-7302. (800) 737-7778. Fax: (901) 942-7810.

Lincoln Memorial University
Harrogate, Tennessee — CB code: 1408

Admissions: 76% of applicants accepted
Based on:
- ••• School record
- •• Recommendations
- • Essay, interview, test scores

Completion: 76% of freshmen end year in good standing
46% graduate, 20% of these enter graduate study

4-year private liberal arts college, coed. Founded in 1897. **Accreditation:** Regional. **Undergraduate enrollment:** 377 men, 591 women full time; 81 men, 560 women part time. **Graduate enrollment:** 1 man, 2 women full time; 84 men, 164 women part time. **Faculty:** 139 total (66 full time), 71 with doctorates or other terminal degrees. **Location:** Rural campus in rural community; 50 miles from Knoxville. **Calendar:** Semester, limited summer session. **Microcomputers:** 40 located in computer centers. **Special facilities:** Abraham Lincoln Library and Museum.

DEGREES OFFERED. AA, AS, BA, BS, MEd. 108 associate degrees awarded in 1992. 5% in business/office and marketing/distribution, 90% allied health. 177 bachelor's degrees awarded. 15% in business and management, 8% communications, 30% education, 10% health sciences, 5% allied health, 7% letters/literature, 5% parks/recreation, protective services, public affairs, 5% social sciences. Graduate degrees offered in 4 major fields of study.

UNDERGRADUATE MAJORS. Associate: Business and management, computer and information sciences, liberal/general studies, nursing, secretarial and related programs, veterinarian's assistant. **Bachelor's:** Accounting, art education, biology, business administration and management, business and management, business and office, business economics, business education, chemistry, clinical laboratory science, communications, early childhood education, economics, education, elementary education, English, English education, finance, fine arts, health education, history, humanities and social sciences, junior high education, liberal/general studies, marketing management, mathematics, mathematics education, medical laboratory technologies, nursing, physical education, predentistry, prelaw, premedicine, prepharmacy, preveterinary, psychology, radio/television broadcasting, science education, secondary education, secretarial and related programs, social science education, social sciences, social studies education, social work, sports medicine, visual and performing arts, wildlife management.

ACADEMIC PROGRAMS. Accelerated program, double major, dual enrollment of high school students, honors program, independent study, internships, teacher preparation. **Remedial services:** Learning center, preadmission summer program, reduced course load, remedial instruction, special counselor, tutoring. **Placement/credit:** AP, CLEP General and Subject, institutional tests; 30 credit hours maximum for associate degree; 30 credit hours maximum for bachelor's degree.

ACADEMIC REQUIREMENTS. Freshmen must earn minimum GPA of 2.0 to continue in good standing. 70% of freshmen return for sophomore year. Students must declare major by end of second year. **Graduation requirements:** 64 hours for associate (34 in major), 128 hours for bachelor's (50 in major). Most students required to take courses in arts/fine arts, computer science, English, history, humanities, mathematics, biological/physical sciences, social sciences. **Postgraduate studies:** 25% from 2-year programs enter 4-year programs. 2% enter law school, 3% enter medical school, 5% enter MBA programs, 10% enter other graduate study.

FRESHMAN ADMISSIONS. Selection criteria: School achievement record and recommendations most important criteria. **High school preparation:** 18 units required. Required and recommended units include English 4, mathematics 2, social science 2 and science 2. Biological science 1 and physical science 2 recommended. **Test requirements:** SAT or ACT (ACT preferred); score report by August 2.

1992 FRESHMAN CLASS PROFILE. 330 men applied, 270 accepted, 220 enrolled; 480 women applied, 346 accepted, 295 enrolled. 68% had high school GPA of 3.0 or higher, 32% between 2.0 and 2.99. 23% were in top tenth and 47% were in top quarter of graduating class. **Academic background:** Mid 50% of enrolled freshmen had ACT composite between 19-26. 80% submitted ACT scores. **Characteristics:** 55% from in state, 60% commute, 3% have minority backgrounds, 7% are foreign students. Average age is 20.

FALL-TERM APPLICATIONS. $25 fee, may be waived for applicants with need. No closing date; applicants notified on a rolling basis. Audition required for music applicants. Interview recommended. Portfolio recommended for art applicants. Essay recommended. Deferred and early admission available.

STUDENT LIFE. Housing: Dormitories (men, women, coed); apartment housing available. **Activities:** Student government, radio, student newspaper, television, yearbook, choral groups, concert band, dance, drama, musical theater, pep band, dinner theater, fraternities, sororities, Baptist Student Union, Wesley Foundation.

ATHLETICS. NCAA. **Intercollegiate:** Baseball M, basketball, cross-country, golf M, soccer M, softball W, tennis, volleyball W. **Intramural:** Badminton, basketball, soccer M, softball, swimming, table tennis, volleyball.

STUDENT SERVICES. Career counseling, freshman orientation, on-campus day care, personal counseling, placement service for graduates, veterans counselor.

ANNUAL EXPENSES. Tuition and fees: $5,530. **Room and board:** $2,688. **Books and supplies:** $550. **Other expenses:** $1,200.

FINANCIAL AID. 70% of freshmen, 72% of continuing students receive some form of aid. 70% of grants, 96% of loans, all jobs based on need. 135 enrolled freshmen were judged to have need, all were offered aid. Academic, music/drama, athletic scholarships available. **Aid applications:** No closing date; priority given to applications received by April 1; applicants notified on a rolling basis beginning on or about April 15; must reply within 2 weeks.

ADDRESS/TELEPHONE. Conrad Daniels, Dean of Admissions, Lincoln Memorial University, Cumberland Gap Parkway, Harrogate, TN 37752. (615) 869-3611. Fax: (615) 869-4825.

Martin Methodist College
Pulaski, Tennessee — CB code: 1449

2-year private liberal arts college, coed, affiliated with United Methodist Church. Founded in 1870. **Accreditation:** Regional. **Undergraduate enrollment:** 155 men, 124 women full time; 43 men, 99 women part time. **Location:** Rural campus in small town; 70 miles south of Nashville and 40 miles north of Huntsville, Alabama. **Calendar:** Semester. **Additional facts:** Candidate for accreditation as BS degree granting 4 year institution.

FRESHMAN ADMISSIONS. Selection criteria: Minimum 2.0 high school GPA and ACT composite score of 16 preferred.

ANNUAL EXPENSES. Tuition and fees: $5,000. **Room and board:** $2,900. **Books and supplies:** $260.

ADDRESS/TELEPHONE. William E. Rutherford, Dean of Admissions, Martin Methodist College, 433 West Madison, Pulaski, TN 38478-2799. (615) 363-9804. (800) 467-1273. Fax: (615) 363-9818.

Maryville College

Maryville, Tennessee CB code: 1454

Admissions: 64% of applicants accepted
Based on: ••• School record, test scores
• Activities, essay, interview, recommendations, special talents
Completion: 82% of freshmen end year in good standing
38% graduate, 23% of these enter graduate study

4-year private liberal arts college, coed, affiliated with Presbyterian Church (USA). Founded in 1819. **Accreditation:** Regional. **Undergraduate enrollment:** 311 men, 347 women full time; 61 men, 123 women part time. **Faculty:** 74 total (49 full time), 40 with doctorates or other terminal degrees. **Location:** Suburban campus in large town; 15 miles from Knoxville. **Calendar:** 4-1-4, limited summer session. **Microcomputers:** 60 located in libraries, computer centers. **Special facilities:** Sutton Science Center, fine arts center, ropes course.

DEGREES OFFERED. BA, BS. 115 bachelor's degrees awarded in 1992. 23% in business and management, 7% teacher education, 20% allied health, 12% letters/literature, 7% multi/interdisciplinary studies, 6% psychology, 11% social sciences.

UNDERGRADUATE MAJORS. Biological and physical sciences, biology, business administration and management, business and management, business economics, chemistry, chemistry for the health professions, computer and information sciences, computer mathematics, computer programming, computer sciences/business, economics, elementary education, engineering and engineering-related technologies, engineering and other disciplines, English, environmental science, fine arts, health sciences, history, international studies, interpreter for the deaf, liberal/general studies, mathematics, microcomputer software, music, music education, music performance, nursing, physical education, political science and government, predentistry, prelaw, premedicine, prepharmacy, preveterinary, psychology, public administration, religion, secondary education, sociology, Spanish, speech-theatre, statistics, visual and performing arts, writing/communication.

ACADEMIC PROGRAMS. Double major, dual enrollment of high school students, honors program, independent study, internships, student-designed major, study abroad, teacher preparation, visiting/exchange student program, weekend college, Washington semester; liberal arts/career combination in engineering, health sciences; combined bachelor's/graduate program in business administration. **Remedial services:** Learning center, reduced course load, tutoring. **Placement/credit:** AP, CLEP General and Subject, institutional tests; 32 credit hours maximum for bachelor's degree.

ACADEMIC REQUIREMENTS. Freshmen must earn minimum GPA of 2.0 to continue in good standing. 62% of freshmen return for sophomore year. Students must declare major by end of second year. **Graduation requirements:** 128 hours for bachelor's (30 in major). Most students required to take courses in arts/fine arts, English, foreign languages, history, humanities, mathematics, philosophy/religion, biological/physical sciences, social sciences. **Postgraduate studies:** 1% enter law school, 2% enter medical school, 2% enter MBA programs, 18% enter other graduate study.

FRESHMAN ADMISSIONS. Selection criteria: School achievement record, test scores considered. 3.0 school GPA, rank in top half of class preferred. SAT 800 or above, ACT 20 or above. **High school preparation:** 15 units required. Required and recommended units include biological science 1, English 4, mathematics 2 and social science 1. Foreign language 2 recommended. **Test requirements:** SAT or ACT; score report by September 1.

1992 FRESHMAN CLASS PROFILE. 448 men applied, 220 accepted, 98 enrolled; 419 women applied, 337 accepted, 97 enrolled. 43% had high school GPA of 3.0 or higher, 55% between 2.0 and 2.99. 23% were in top tenth and 62% were in top quarter of graduating class. **Academic background:** Mid 50% of enrolled freshmen had SAT-V between 390-490, SAT-M between 430-580; ACT composite between 19-25. 46% submitted SAT scores, 77% submitted ACT scores. **Characteristics:** 59% from in state, 65% live in college housing, 7% have minority backgrounds, 1% are foreign students. Average age is 18.

FALL-TERM APPLICATIONS. $25 fee, may be waived for applicants with need. Closing date August 1; priority given to applications received by February 1; applicants notified on a rolling basis; must reply by May 1. Audition required for music applicants. Interview recommended. Portfolio recommended for art applicants. Essay recommended. CRDA. Deferred and early admission available.

STUDENT LIFE. Housing: Dormitories (men, women, coed). **Activities:** Student government, student newspaper, yearbook, choral groups, concert band, dance, drama, jazz band, music ensembles, musical theater, opera, symphony orchestra, outdoor club, Black Students Association, Circle-K, Religious Life Council, Playhouse Association, Inter-Varsity Christian Fellowship, Fellowship of Christian Athletes, Baptist Student Union, worship and religious programs committee, peace education task force, world concerns committee.

ATHLETICS. NCAA. **Intercollegiate:** Baseball M, basketball, football M, soccer, softball W, volleyball W. **Intramural:** Basketball, bowling, golf, racquetball, soccer W, softball, table tennis, tennis, volleyball.

STUDENT SERVICES. Career counseling, employment service for undergraduates, freshman orientation, health services, personal counseling, placement service for graduates, services/facilities for handicapped.

ANNUAL EXPENSES. Tuition and fees (1992-93): $9,580. **Room and board:** $3,865. **Books and supplies:** $475. **Other expenses:** $500.

FINANCIAL AID. 87% of freshmen, 85% of continuing students receive some form of aid. 55% of grants, 89% of loans, 73% of jobs based on need. 109 enrolled freshmen were judged to have need, all were offered aid. Academic, music/drama, art, state/district residency, leadership, religious affiliation, minority scholarships available. **Aid applications:** No closing date; priority given to applications received by March 1; applicants notified on a rolling basis beginning on or about March 15; must reply by May 1 or within 2 weeks if notified thereafter.

ADDRESS/TELEPHONE. Donna F. Davis, VP Admissions/Enrollment, Maryville College, 502 East Lamar Alexander Parkway, Maryville, TN 37801. (615) 981-8092. (800) 597-2687. Fax: (615) 983-0581.

Memphis College of Art

Memphis, Tennessee CB code: 1511

Admissions: 86% of applicants accepted
Based on: ••• School record, special talents
•• Essay, recommendations, test scores
• Activities, interview
Completion: 85% of freshmen end year in good standing
60% graduate, 20% of these enter graduate study

4-year private art college, coed. Founded in 1936. **Accreditation:** Regional. **Undergraduate enrollment:** 131 men, 78 women full time; 9 men, 18 women part time. **Graduate enrollment:** 9 men, 21 women full time; 1 woman part time. **Faculty:** 46 total (16 full time). **Location:** Urban campus in very large city; 500 miles from New Orleans, Louisiana, 700 miles from Dallas, Texas. **Calendar:** Semester, limited summer session. **Microcomputers:** Located in libraries, classrooms, computer centers. **Special facilities:** Three on-campus galleries for faculty, student and visiting artist exhibitions. **Additional facts:** Situated in 324-acre city park with bicycle trails and golf course. Students have access to Memphis Brooks Museum of Art and Overton Park Zoo. A consortium with four other colleges provides greater selection of liberal studies classes.

DEGREES OFFERED. BFA, MFA. 40 bachelor's degrees awarded in 1992. 100% in visual and performing arts. Graduate degrees offered in 7 major fields of study.

UNDERGRADUATE MAJORS. Advertising, ceramics, commercial art, crafts, drawing, fiber/textiles/weaving, fine arts, graphic arts technology, graphic design, illustration design, metal/jewelry, painting, papermaking, printmaking, sculpture, studio art, visual and performing arts.

ACADEMIC PROGRAMS. Double major, dual enrollment of high school students, independent study, internships, study abroad, visiting/exchange student program, New York semester, cross-registration. **Remedial services:** Reduced course load, remedial instruction, tutoring. **Placement/credit:** AP, CLEP General and Subject, IB, institutional tests.

ACADEMIC REQUIREMENTS. Freshmen must earn minimum GPA of 1.5 to continue in good standing. 80% of freshmen return for sophomore year. Students must declare major by end of second year. **Graduation requirements:** 129 hours for bachelor's (33 in major). Most students required to take courses in arts/fine arts, English, history, humanities, social sciences. **Additional information:** Foundation courses incorporate computer use in design and color theory.

FRESHMAN ADMISSIONS. Selection criteria: Art portfolio, high school transcript, ACT composite score or SAT scores, and letter of recommendation from art teacher, essay considered for admission. Portfolio should include 10 to 20 pieces of work, originals or slides, with focus on direct observational drawing. **Test requirements:** SAT or ACT; score report by August 1. **Additional information:** Applicants scoring 23 or above on ACT or 980 or above on SAT have 1 point added to portfolio score; students scoring 15 or below on ACT or 620 or below on SAT have 1 point subtracted.

1992 FRESHMAN CLASS PROFILE. 85 men applied, 74 accepted, 35 enrolled; 60 women applied, 50 accepted, 20 enrolled. **Characteristics:** 45% from in state, 97% commute, 22% have minority backgrounds, 5% are foreign students. Average age is 18.

FALL-TERM APPLICATIONS. $25 fee, may be waived for applicants with need. No closing date; priority given to applications received by June 15; applicants notified on a rolling basis beginning on or about December 1; must reply within 3 weeks. Portfolio required. Essay required. Interview recommended. CRDA. Deferred and early admission available.

STUDENT LIFE. Housing: Apartment housing available. Considerable assistance in matching roommates and helping students find affordable housing within walking distance. **Activities:** Student government, student newspaper, International Student Club.

STUDENT SERVICES. Career counseling, employment service for undergraduates, freshman orientation, personal counseling, placement service for graduates, special adviser for adult students, veterans counselor, services/facilities for handicapped.

ANNUAL EXPENSES. Tuition and fees (1992-93): $8,590. **Room and board:** $4,600. **Books and supplies:** $1,000. **Other expenses:** $225.

FINANCIAL AID. 84% of freshmen, 86% of continuing students receive some form of aid. Grants, loans, jobs available. Academic, art, leadership scholarships available. **Aid applications:** No closing date; priority given to applications received by April 1; applicants notified on a rolling basis; must reply within 3 weeks.

ADDRESS/TELEPHONE. Susan Miller, Director of Admissions, Memphis College of Art, Overton Park, Memphis, TN 38112. (901) 726-4085 ext. 30. (800) 727-1088. Fax: (901) 726-9371.

Memphis State University
Memphis, Tennessee CB code: 1459

Admissions: 67% of applicants accepted
Based on: ••• School record, test scores
• Recommendations, special talents
Completion: 58% of freshmen end year in good standing
30% graduate

4-year public university, coed. Founded in 1912. **Accreditation:** Regional. **Undergraduate enrollment:** 4,965 men, 5,614 women full time; 2,201 men, 2,987 women part time. **Graduate enrollment:** 982 men, 917 women full time; 1,173 men, 1,739 women part time. **Faculty:** 1,057 total (755 full time), 560 with doctorates or other terminal degrees. **Location:** Urban campus in very large city; 10 miles from downtown. **Calendar:** Semester, extensive summer session. **Microcomputers:** Located in dormitories, libraries, classrooms, computer centers, campus-wide network. **Special facilities:** Chucalissa Indian Village, speech and hearing center, art gallery (featuring Egyptian collection), earthquake information center.

DEGREES OFFERED. BA, BS, BFA, MA, MS, MBA, MFA, MEd, PhD, EdD. 2,047 bachelor's degrees awarded in 1992. 28% in business and management, 10% business/office and marketing/distribution, 10% education, 9% engineering, 6% social sciences, 5% visual and performing arts. Graduate degrees offered in 55 major fields of study.

UNDERGRADUATE MAJORS. Accounting, American studies, anthropology, architectural technologies, art history, biology, business administration and management, business economics, chemistry, civil engineering, clinical laboratory science, commercial music, computer and information sciences, computer servicing technology, criminal justice studies, dramatic arts, early childhood education, economics, electrical/electronics/communications engineering, electronic technology, elementary education, English, finance, fine arts, foreign languages (multiple emphasis), geography, geology, health education, history, home economics, humanities, humanities and social sciences, information sciences and systems, insurance and risk management, international business management, international relations, journalism, Latin American studies, liberal/general studies, management information systems, manufacturing technology, marketing and distribution, marketing management, mathematics, mechanical engineering, music, music business management, nursing, office supervision and management, parks and recreation management, philosophy, physical education, physical sciences, physics, political science and government, psychology, real estate, rehabilitation counseling/services, social work, sociology, special education, transportation and travel marketing, urban studies, visual and performing arts.

ACADEMIC PROGRAMS. Double major, dual enrollment of high school students, education specialist degree, honors program, independent study, internships, student-designed major, study abroad, teacher preparation, telecourses, visiting/exchange student program. **Remedial services:** Learning center, preadmission summer program, remedial instruction, special counselor, tutoring, remedial/developmental program. **ROTC:** Air Force, Army, Naval. **Placement/credit:** AP, CLEP Subject, institutional tests; 24 credit hours maximum for bachelor's degree.

ACADEMIC REQUIREMENTS. Freshmen must earn minimum GPA of 2.0 to continue in good standing. 80% of freshmen return for sophomore year. Students must declare major by end of second year. **Graduation requirements:** 132 hours for bachelor's. Most students required to take courses in arts/fine arts, computer science, English, history, humanities, mathematics, biological/physical sciences, social sciences.

FRESHMAN ADMISSIONS. Selection criteria: Test scores most important. High school GPA considered if SAT combined score is below 800 or ACT composite score is below 20. Out-of-state applicants must also rank in top half of graduating class. **High school preparation:** 18 units required. Required units include English 4, foreign language 2, mathematics 3, social science 2 and science 2. One unit visual and/or performing arts also required. **Test requirements:** SAT or ACT (ACT preferred); score report by August 15.

1992 FRESHMAN CLASS PROFILE. 3,785 men and women applied, 2,538 accepted; 737 men enrolled, 884 women enrolled. 50% had high school GPA of 3.0 or higher, 46% between 2.0 and 2.99. **Academic background:** Mid 50% of enrolled freshmen had ACT composite between 19-21. 91% submitted ACT scores. **Characteristics:** 87% from in state, 70% commute, 23% have minority backgrounds, 1% are foreign students, 87% join fraternities/sororities. Average age is 18.

FALL-TERM APPLICATIONS. $5 fee. Closing date August 1; applicants notified on a rolling basis; must reply by registration. Interview required for university college applicants. Audition required for music applicants. Portfolio required for fine arts applicants. Early admission available.

STUDENT LIFE. Housing: Dormitories (men, women); apartment, fraternity, handicapped housing available. **Activities:** Student government, film, magazine, radio, student newspaper, television, yearbook, choral groups, concert band, dance, drama, jazz band, marching band, music ensembles, musical theater, opera, pep band, symphony orchestra, fraternities, sororities, all major organizations.

ATHLETICS. NCAA. **Intercollegiate:** Baseball M, basketball, cross-country M, football M, golf, soccer M, tennis, track and field M, volleyball W. **Intramural:** Archery, badminton, basketball, bowling, boxing M, fencing M, golf, rugby, soccer M, softball, swimming, table tennis, tennis, track and field, volleyball.

STUDENT SERVICES. Aptitude testing, career counseling, employment service for undergraduates, freshman orientation, health services, personal counseling, placement service for graduates, special adviser for adult students, veterans counselor, psychological services center, services/facilities for handicapped.

ANNUAL EXPENSES. Tuition and fees (1992-93): $1,748, $3,602 additional for out-of-state students. **Room and board:** $3,040. **Books and supplies:** $850. **Other expenses:** $715.

FINANCIAL AID. 50% of freshmen, 40% of continuing students receive some form of aid. 61% of grants, 81% of loans, 17% of jobs based on need. Academic, music/drama, art, athletic, state/district residency, leadership scholarships available. **Aid applications:** No closing date; priority given to applications received by April 1; applicants notified on a rolling basis beginning on or about June 1; must reply within 2 weeks.

ADDRESS/TELEPHONE. Dr. John Y. Eubank, Jr, Dean of Admissions and Records, Memphis State University, Memphis, TN 38152. (901) 678-2101. (800) 669-9678. Fax: (901) 678-2983.

Middle Tennessee State University
Murfreesboro, Tennessee CB code: 1466

Admissions: 77% of applicants accepted
Based on: ••• School record, test scores
Completion: 85% of freshmen end year in good standing
42% graduate

4-year public university, coed. Founded in 1911. **Accreditation:** Regional. **Undergraduate enrollment:** 5,969 men, 6,376 women full time; 1,186 men, 1,480 women part time. **Graduate enrollment:** 705 men and women full time; 1,071 men and women part time. **Faculty:** 877 total (677 full time), 425 with doctorates or other terminal degrees. **Location:** Suburban campus in large town; 32 miles from Nashville. **Calendar:** Semester, extensive summer session. Extensive evening/early morning classes. **Microcomputers:** 200 located in dormitories, libraries, classrooms, computer centers, campus-wide network. **Special facilities:** 3 recording studios, observatory, flight simulators, weather center, electronic music laboratory, digital audio edit laboratory, sateleite mapping equipment, seismograph, 3 television studios, electronic newsroom, radio television mobile production laboratory, CNN affiliation.

DEGREES OFFERED. AA, BA, BS, MA, MS, MBA, MEd, D. 18 associate degrees awarded in 1992. 2,121 bachelor's degrees awarded. Graduate degrees offered in 34 major fields of study.

UNDERGRADUATE MAJORS. Associate: Court reporting, law enforcement and corrections technologies, secretarial and related programs. **Bachelor's:** Accounting, actuarial sciences, advertising, aerospace/aeronautical/astronautical engineering, agribusiness, animal sciences, anthropology, biology, business administration and management, business and office, business economics, chemistry, city/community/regional planning, clinical laboratory science, communications, computer and information sciences, computer technology, criminal justice studies, dramatic arts, early childhood education, earth sciences, economics, education, electrical technology, elementary education, engineering and engineering-related technologies, English, English education, environmental science, fashion merchandising, finance, food science and nutrition, foreign languages (multiple emphasis), French, geography, German, historic preservation, history, home economics, home economics education, humanities and social sciences, industrial arts education, industrial technology, information sciences and systems, interior design, international relations, journalism, law enforcement and corrections, manufacturing technology, marketing research, mathematics, mathematics education, military science (Army), music, music business management, music education, nursing, office supervision and management, philosophy, photography, physical education, physical sciences, physics, plant sciences, political science and government, predentistry, prelaw, premedicine, prepharmacy, preveterinary, psychology, public relations, radio/television broadcasting, social sciences, social work, sociology, soil sciences, Spanish, special education, speech correction, studio art, urban studies.

ACADEMIC PROGRAMS. Cooperative education, double major, dual enrollment of high school students, education specialist degree, honors program, independent study, internships, student-designed major, study abroad, teacher preparation, cross-registration; liberal arts/career combination in engineering, forestry, health sciences. **Remedial services:** Learning center, preadmission summer program, reduced course load, remedial instruction, special counselor, tutoring. **ROTC:** Army. **Placement/credit:** AP, CLEP General and Subject, institutional tests; 66 credit hours maximum for bachelor's degree.

ACADEMIC REQUIREMENTS. Freshmen must earn minimum GPA of 2.0 to continue in good standing. 73% of freshmen return for sophomore year. Students must declare major by end of second year. **Graduation requirements:** 67 hours for associate (33 in major), 132 hours for bachelor's. Most students required to take courses in arts/fine arts, computer science, English, history, humanities, mathematics, biological/physical sciences, social sciences.

FRESHMAN ADMISSIONS. Selection criteria: Must meet high school curriculum requirements and have 2.0 high school GPA or ACT composite score of 19. **High school preparation:** 14 units required. Required units include English 4, foreign language 2, mathematics 3, social science 2 and science 2. Required foreign language units must be in single language. Mathematics units must include algebra I and II and geometry or other advanced mathematics. One unit visual or performing arts, 1 unit US history and 1 unit global studies also required. **Test requirements:** SAT or ACT (ACT preferred); score report by July 1. SAT accepted from out-of-state applicants. Tennessee residents must have ACT. Institution's academic assessment test required for applicants scoring 19 or below on ACT or scoring less than 19 in mathematics or English.

1992 FRESHMAN CLASS PROFILE. 4,406 men and women applied, 3,401 accepted; 2,154 enrolled. **Characteristics:** 95% from in state, 55% commute, 14% have minority backgrounds, 1% are foreign students, 1% join fraternities/sororities. Average age is 22.

FALL-TERM APPLICATIONS. $5 fee. Closing date July 1; applicants notified on a rolling basis. Deferred and early admission available.

STUDENT LIFE. Housing: Dormitories (men, women); apartment, fraternity, handicapped housing available. **Activities:** Student government, film, magazine, radio, student newspaper, television, yearbook, choral groups, concert band, dance, drama, jazz band, marching band, music ensembles, musical theater, opera, symphony orchestra, fraternities, sororities, honor, professional, and departmental societies, special interest groups, religious organizations.

ATHLETICS. NCAA. **Intercollegiate:** Baseball M, basketball, cross-country, football M, golf M, horseback riding, rifle, softball W, tennis, track and field, volleyball W. **Intramural:** Basketball M, boxing M, rugby M, soccer, softball, swimming, tennis, volleyball.

STUDENT SERVICES. Aptitude testing, career counseling, employment service for undergraduates, freshman orientation, health services, on-campus day care, personal counseling, placement service for graduates, special adviser for adult students, veterans counselor, services/facilities for handicapped.

ANNUAL EXPENSES. Tuition and fees (1992-93): $1,594, $3,602 additional for out-of-state students. **Room and board:** $2,102. **Books and supplies:** $175.

FINANCIAL AID. 60% of freshmen, 65% of continuing students receive some form of aid. Academic, athletic, leadership scholarships available. **Aid applications:** Closing date May 15; priority given to applications received by March 15; applicants notified on a rolling basis beginning on or about April 1; must reply within 2 weeks.

ADDRESS/TELEPHONE. Lynn Palmer, Director of Admissions, Middle Tennessee State University, Murfreesboro, TN 37132. (615) 898-2300. (800) 433-MTSU. Fax: (615) 898-5538.

Milligan College

Milligan College, Tennessee — CB code: 1469

Admissions: 77% of applicants accepted
Based on: •• Activities, recommendations, religious affiliation/commitment, school record, test scores
• Essay, interview, special talents
Completion: 78% of freshmen end year in good standing
45% graduate, 20% of these enter graduate study

4-year private liberal arts college, coed, affiliated with independent Christian churches. Founded in 1866. **Accreditation:** Regional. **Undergraduate enrollment:** 269 men, 376 women full time; 13 men, 38 women part time. **Graduate enrollment:** 7 men, 10 women full time; 1 man, 23 women part time. **Faculty:** 78 total (53 full time), 39 with doctorates or other terminal degrees. **Location:** Suburban campus in large town; 3 miles from Johnson City. **Calendar:** Semester, limited summer session. **Microcomputers:** 48 located in libraries, computer centers. **Additional facts:** 9 hours of Bible study and twice-weekly convocation required.

DEGREES OFFERED. AS, BA, BS, MEd. 1 associate degree awarded in 1992. 100% in business/office and marketing/distribution. 163 bachelor's degrees awarded. 34% in business and management, 14% communications, 7% teacher education, 6% philosophy, religion, theology, 12% psychology, 9% social sciences. Graduate degrees offered in 2 major fields of study.

UNDERGRADUATE MAJORS. Associate: Teacher aide. **Bachelor's:** Accounting, Bible studies, biology, business and management, business economics, chemistry, clinical laboratory science, communications, computer and information sciences, elementary education, English, English education, health care administration, history, humanities and social sciences, legal assistant/paralegal, mathematics, mathematics education, missionary studies, music, music education, nursing, physical education, psychology, religious education, religious music, science education, secondary education, secretarial and related programs, social studies education, social work, sociology, special education.

ACADEMIC PROGRAMS. Accelerated program, double major, independent study, internships, study abroad, teacher preparation, Washington semester, cross-registration. **Remedial services:** Preadmission summer program, reduced course load, remedial instruction, tutoring. **ROTC:** Army. **Placement/credit:** AP, CLEP General and Subject, institutional tests; 32 credit hours maximum for bachelor's degree.

ACADEMIC REQUIREMENTS. Freshmen must earn minimum GPA of 2.0 to continue in good standing. 68% of freshmen return for sophomore year. Students must declare major by end of second year. **Graduation requirements:** 64 hours for associate (33 in major), 128 hours for bachelor's (36 in major). Most students required to take courses in arts/fine arts, English, history, humanities, mathematics, philosophy/religion, biological/physical sciences, social sciences.

FRESHMAN ADMISSIONS. Selection criteria: Academic work, test scores, and references from minister or church leader and high school principal or counselor required for admission. **High school preparation:** 16 units recommended. Recommended units include biological science 1, English 4, foreign language 2, mathematics 3, physical science 1 and social science 2. **Test requirements:** SAT or ACT (ACT preferred); score report by August 1.

1992 FRESHMAN CLASS PROFILE. 442 men and women applied, 339 accepted; 64 men enrolled, 132 women enrolled. 57% had high school GPA of 3.0 or higher, 40% between 2.0 and 2.99. **Academic background:** Mid 50% of enrolled freshmen had SAT-V between 390-530, SAT-M between 410-580; ACT composite between 19-26. 40% submitted SAT scores, 75% submitted ACT scores. **Characteristics:** 31% from in state, 90% live in college housing, 5% have minority backgrounds, 1% are foreign students. Average age is 18.

FALL-TERM APPLICATIONS. $25 fee, may be waived for applicants with need. Closing date August 1; priority given to applications received by April 1; applicants notified on a rolling basis; must reply by August 15. Interview recommended for early admission applicants. Audition recommended for music applicants. Essay recommended. Deferred and early admission available.

STUDENT LIFE. Housing: Dormitories (men, women); apartment housing available. Students must live in college housing unless married or living with members of immediate family. **Activities:** Student government, film, magazine, radio, student newspaper, television, yearbook, choral groups, concert band, drama, music ensembles, musical theater, opera, pep band, symphony orchestra, service groups, professional organizations for most majors. **Additional information:** Alcoholic beverages and dancing not permitted.

ATHLETICS. NAIA. **Intercollegiate:** Baseball M, basketball, golf M, soccer M, softball W, tennis, volleyball W. **Intramural:** Archery, badminton, baseball M, basketball, field hockey W, racquetball M, softball, table tennis, volleyball, wrestling M.

STUDENT SERVICES. Aptitude testing, career counseling, employment service for undergraduates, freshman orientation, health services, personal counseling, placement service for graduates, special adviser for adult students, services/facilities for handicapped.

ANNUAL EXPENSES. Tuition and fees (projected): $7,590. **Room and board:** $3,100. **Books and supplies:** $550. **Other expenses:** $940.

FINANCIAL AID. 93% of freshmen, 90% of continuing students receive some form of aid. 93% of grants, 84% of loans, 95% of jobs based on need. Academic, music/drama, art, athletic, leadership scholarships available. **Aid applications:** No closing date; priority given to applications received by March 15; applicants notified on a rolling basis beginning on or about April 15; must reply within 2 weeks.

ADDRESS/TELEPHONE. Michael A. Johnson, Director of Admissions, Milligan College, Milligan College, TN 37682. (615) 461-8730. (800) 262-8337.

Motlow State Community College

Tullahoma, Tennessee — CB code: 1543

2-year public community college, coed. Founded in 1969. **Accreditation:** Regional. **Undergraduate enrollment:** 569 men, 1,122 women full time; 477 men, 1,043 women part time. **Faculty:** 238 total (68 full time), 31 with doctorates or other terminal degrees. **Location:** Rural campus in large town; 65 miles from Nashville. **Calendar:** Semester, limited summer session. **Microcomputers:** 245 located in libraries, classrooms, computer centers. **Additional facts:** Off-campus sites in Minnville and Fayetteville.

DEGREES OFFERED. AA, AS, AAS. 263 associate degrees awarded in 1992.

UNDERGRADUATE MAJORS. Accounting, aeronautical technology, aerospace/aeronautical/astronautical engineering, agribusiness, architectural engineering, biological and physical sciences, biology, business administration and management, business and management, business and office, business data entry equipment operation, business data processing and related programs, business data programming, business economics, business statistics, chemistry, communications, computer and information sciences, computer graphics, computer programming, criminology, data processing, economics, education, electronic technology, elementary education, engineering, engineering and engineering-related technologies, engineering and other disciplines, English, finance, fine arts, geography, health sciences, history, humanities and social sciences, industrial engineering, information sciences and systems, insurance and risk management, insurance marketing, liberal/general studies, marketing and distribution, marketing research, mathematics, medical assistant, medical laboratory technologies, medical records technology, music, nursing, occupational therapy assistant, office supervision and management, philosophy, physical chemistry, physical sciences, physical therapy assistant, physics, physiology, human and animal, political science and government, psychology, radiograph medical technology, real estate, respiratory therapy technology, school psychology, science technologies, secondary education, secretarial and related programs, social sciences, sociology, systems analysis, visual and performing arts.

ACADEMIC PROGRAMS. 2-year transfer program, cooperative education, double major, honors program. **Remedial services:** Learning center, preadmission summer program, reduced course load, remedial instruction, special counselor, tutoring. **Placement/credit:** AP, CLEP Subject, institutional tests; 24 credit hours maximum for associate degree.

ACADEMIC REQUIREMENTS. Freshmen must earn minimum GPA of 1.8 to continue in good standing. Students must declare major on application. **Graduation requirements:** 66 hours for associate. Most students required to take courses in computer science, English, history, humanities, mathematics, social sciences.

FRESHMAN ADMISSIONS. Selection criteria: Open admissions. **High school preparation:** 16 units required. Required units include biological science 2, English 4, foreign language 2, mathematics 3, physical science 1, social science 2 and science 2. **Test requirements:** ACT for placement and counseling only; score report by August 3. ACT score reports must be received before registration.

1992 FRESHMAN CLASS PROFILE. 240 men, 432 women enrolled. **Characteristics:** 98% from in state, 100% commute, 5% have minority backgrounds, 1% are foreign students. Average age is 19.

FALL-TERM APPLICATIONS. $5 fee. Closing date August 25; priority given to applications received by July 19; applicants notified on a rolling basis. Interview required for nursing applicants. Deferred and early admission available.

STUDENT LIFE. Activities: Student government, magazine, radio, student newspaper, television, choral groups, drama, pep band, Baptist Student Union.

ATHLETICS. Intercollegiate: Basketball, golf M. **Intramural:** Baseball M, basketball, football M, softball, table tennis, tennis, volleyball.

STUDENT SERVICES. Aptitude testing, career counseling, employment service for undergraduates, freshman orientation, health services, personal counseling, placement service for graduates, special adviser for adult students, veterans counselor, services/facilities for handicapped.

ANNUAL EXPENSES. Tuition and fees (1992-93): $922, $2,600 additional for out-of-state students. **Books and supplies:** $400. **Other expenses:** $3,200.

FINANCIAL AID. 62% of freshmen, 55% of continuing students receive some form of aid. 93% of grants, 90% of loans, 66% of jobs based on need. Academic, music/drama, athletic, leadership, minority scholarships available. **Aid applications:** No closing date; priority given to applications received by May 1; applicants notified on a rolling basis beginning on or about July 1; must reply within 2 weeks.

ADDRESS/TELEPHONE. Ed Kilgour, Director of Admissions and Records, Motlow State Community College, PO Box 88100, Tullahoma, TN 37388-8100. (615) 455-8511. Fax: (615) 454-0059.

Nashville State Technical Institute
Nashville, Tennessee CB code: 0850

2-year public technical college, coed. Founded in 1969. **Accreditation:** Regional. **Undergraduate enrollment:** 727 men, 680 women full time; 2,358 men, 2,317 women part time. **Faculty:** 294 total (94 full time), 23 with doctorates or other terminal degrees. **Location:** Suburban campus in large city; 5 miles from downtown. **Calendar:** Semester, limited summer session. Saturday and extensive evening/early morning classes. **Microcomputers:** 518 located in libraries, classrooms, computer centers.

DEGREES OFFERED. AAS. 278 associate degrees awarded in 1992. 14% in business and management, 6% business/office and marketing/distribution, 37% computer sciences, 37% engineering technologies, 6% allied health.

UNDERGRADUATE MAJORS. Accounting, architectural technologies, automotive technology, business and management, business and office, civil technology, computer servicing technology, computer technology, data processing, electrical technology, electronic technology, engineering and engineering-related technologies, finance, graphic design, industrial technology, information sciences and systems, legal secretary, mechanical design technology, occupational therapy assistant, office supervision and management, photography, small business management and ownership.

ACADEMIC PROGRAMS. Cooperative education, telecourses. **Remedial services:** Learning center, preadmission summer program, reduced course load, remedial instruction, special counselor, tutoring. **Placement/credit:** AP, CLEP General and Subject, institutional tests; 20 credit hours maximum for associate degree.

ACADEMIC REQUIREMENTS. Freshmen must earn minimum GPA of 1.75 to continue in good standing. 64% of freshmen return for sophomore year. Students must declare major on application. **Graduation requirements:** 64 hours for associate. Most students required to take courses in computer science, English, humanities, mathematics, social sciences.

FRESHMAN ADMISSIONS. Selection criteria: Open admissions. Recommended units include English 4, foreign language 2, mathematics 3, social science 2 and science 2. 1 visual/performing arts recommended. **Test requirements:** SAT or ACT (ACT preferred) for placement and counseling only; score report by August 20. Test waived for applicants 21 years of age or older.

1992 FRESHMAN CLASS PROFILE. 937 men, 1,119 women enrolled. **Characteristics:** 94% from in state, 100% commute, 18% have minority backgrounds, 1% are foreign students.

FALL-TERM APPLICATIONS. $5 fee. No closing date; applicants notified on a rolling basis. Interview required for occupational therapy assistant, automotive services technology, surgical technology applicants. Deferred admission available. Automotive services technology applicants must have automobile dealer sponsorship prior to acceptance.

STUDENT LIFE. Activities: Student government, magazine, Black Student Organization, International Student Organization.

ATHLETICS. Intramural: Softball, table tennis, volleyball.

STUDENT SERVICES. Aptitude testing, career counseling, employment service for undergraduates, freshman orientation, personal counseling, placement service for graduates, special adviser for adult students, veterans counselor, services/facilities for handicapped.

ANNUAL EXPENSES. Tuition and fees (1992-93): $908, $2,600 additional for out-of-state students. **Books and supplies:** $400.

FINANCIAL AID. 10% of freshmen, 20% of continuing students receive some form of aid. 90% of grants, 84% of loans, all jobs based on need. Academic scholarships available. **Aid applications:** No closing date; priority given to applications received by May 1; applicants notified on a rolling basis beginning on or about June 1; must reply within 2 weeks.

ADDRESS/TELEPHONE. Eddie Pawlawski, Director of Admissions, Nashville State Technical Institute, 120 White Bridge Road, Nashville, TN 37209. (615) 353-3333. Fax: (615) 353-3243.

Northeast State Technical Community College
Blountville, Tennessee CB code: 0453

2-year public community, technical college, coed. Founded in 1965. **Accreditation:** Regional. **Undergraduate enrollment:** 914 men, 714 women full time; 1,015 men, 821 women part time. **Faculty:** 230 total (70 full time). **Location:** Suburban campus in small city; 12 miles from Johnson City, 10 miles from Kingsport and Bristol. **Calendar:** Semester. **Microcomputers:** 100 located in libraries, classrooms, computer centers.

DEGREES OFFERED. AA, AS, AAS. 188 associate degrees awarded in 1992. 25% in business/office and marketing/distribution, 25% engineering technologies, 25% multi/interdisciplinary studies, 25% trade and industry.

UNDERGRADUATE MAJORS. Accounting, automotive mechanics, automotive technology, business administration and management, business data processing and related programs, business data programming, chemical manufacturing technology, computer technology, diesel engine mechanics, drafting and design technology, electrical installation, electrical technology, electronic technology, emergency medical technologies, finance, industrial equipment maintenance and repair, information sciences and systems, instrumentation technology, liberal/general studies, machine tool operation/machine shop, manufacturing technology, mechanical design technology, secretarial and related programs, welding technology.

ACADEMIC PROGRAMS. 2-year transfer program, cooperative education, double major, dual enrollment of high school students, honors program. **Remedial services:** Learning center, preadmission summer program, reduced course load, remedial instruction, special counselor, tutoring. **Placement/credit:** AP, CLEP General and Subject, institutional tests; 18 credit hours maximum for associate degree.

ACADEMIC REQUIREMENTS. Freshmen must earn minimum GPA of 1.75 to continue in good standing. Students with 36 or more semester hours must earn 2.0 to continue in good standing. 50% of freshmen return for sophomore year. Students must declare major on application. **Graduation requirements:** 64 hours for associate. Most students required to take courses in computer science, English, humanities, mathematics, biological/physical sciences, social sciences.

FRESHMAN ADMISSIONS. Selection criteria: Open admissions. **High school preparation:** 20 units recommended. Recommended units include English 4, mathematics 3, physical science 1 and social science 1. **Test requirements:** ACT for placement and counseling only; score report by August 29. Academic Assessment Placement Program test required for applicants 21 and older, and freshman applicants under 21 with ACT composite score below 16.

1992 FRESHMAN CLASS PROFILE. 387 men, 315 women enrolled. **Characteristics:** 98% from in state, 100% commute, 3% have minority backgrounds. Average age is 21.

FALL-TERM APPLICATIONS. $5 fee. Closing date August 29; applicants notified on a rolling basis beginning on or about August 1. Early admission available.

STUDENT LIFE. Activities: Student government, student newspaper.

STUDENT SERVICES. Aptitude testing, career counseling, freshman orientation, personal counseling, placement service for graduates, veterans counselor, services/facilities for handicapped.

ANNUAL EXPENSES. Tuition and fees (1992-93): $910, $2,600 additional for out-of-state students. **Books and supplies:** $500. **Other expenses:** $890.

FINANCIAL AID. 36% of freshmen, 58% of continuing students receive some form of aid. 87% of grants, 79% of loans, all jobs based on need. Academic, leadership, minority scholarships available. **Aid applications:** No closing date; priority given to applications received by August 1; applicants notified on a rolling basis beginning on or about June 1.

ADDRESS/TELEPHONE. Rebecca Sensabaugh, Coordinator of Enrollment and Student Records, Northeast State Technical Community College, PO Box 246, Blountville, TN 37617. (615) 323-3191. Fax: (615) 323-3083.

O'More College of Design
Franklin, Tennessee — CB code: 1545

4-year private professional school of interior design, fashion merchandising, design, and graphic art design, coed. Founded in 1970. **Undergraduate enrollment:** 6 men, 100 women full time; 25 women part time. **Location:** Suburban campus in large town; 15 miles from Nashville. **Calendar:** Semester. **Additional facts:** Housed in 2 historic mansions. Accredited by Foundation for Interior Design Education Research.

FRESHMAN ADMISSIONS. Selection criteria: High school record and interview most important. Minimum 2.0 GPA. Exceptions to 2.0 GPA considered.

ANNUAL EXPENSES. Tuition and fees (1992-93): $6,600. **Room and board:** $3,000 room only. **Books and supplies:** $750.

ADDRESS/TELEPHONE. Thomas L. Campbell, Registrar/Dean of Admissions, O'More College of Design, PO Box 908, Franklin, TN 37065-0908. (615) 794-4254. Fax: (615) 790-1662.

Pellissippi State Technical Community College
Knoxville, Tennessee — CB code: 0319

2-year public community, technical college, coed. Founded in 1974. **Accreditation:** Regional. **Undergraduate enrollment:** 1,956 men, 2,001 women full time; 1,504 men, 2,377 women part time. **Faculty:** 451 total (151 full time). **Location:** Suburban campus in small city; 17 miles from downtown. **Calendar:** Semester, extensive summer session. **Microcomputers:** 600 located in libraries, classrooms, computer centers, campus-wide network. **Special facilities:** State-of-the-art technology laboratories.

DEGREES OFFERED. AA, AS, AAS. 305 associate degrees awarded in 1992.

UNDERGRADUATE MAJORS. Accounting, automotive mechanics, business administration and management, business data processing and related programs, business data programming, chemical manufacturing technology, civil technology, computer and information sciences, computer graphics, computer mathematics, computer programming, computer servicing technology, computer technology, data processing, drafting, drafting and design technology, educational media technology, electrical and electronics equipment repair, electrical technology, electronic technology, engineering and engineering-related technologies, finance, industrial technology, information sciences and systems, laser electro-optic technology, legal assistant/paralegal, legal secretary, management science, manufacturing technology, marketing and distribution, marketing management, mechanical design technology, medical secretary, office supervision and management, prelaw, quality control technology, radio/television technology, secretarial and related programs, word processing.

ACADEMIC PROGRAMS. 2-year transfer program, cooperative education, double major, dual enrollment of high school students, internships, telecourses, weekend college. **Remedial services:** Learning center, preadmission summer program, reduced course load, remedial instruction, special counselor, tutoring, peer counseling. **Placement/credit:** AP, CLEP General and Subject, institutional tests; 36 credit hours maximum for associate degree.

ACADEMIC REQUIREMENTS. Freshmen must earn minimum GPA of 2.0 to continue in good standing. 60% of freshmen return for sophomore year. Students must declare major on application. **Graduation requirements:** 66 hours for associate (36 in major). Most students required to take courses in arts/fine arts, computer science, English, foreign languages, history, humanities, mathematics, biological/physical sciences, social sciences.

FRESHMAN ADMISSIONS. Selection criteria: Open admissions. **Test requirements:** SAT or ACT (ACT preferred) for placement and counseling only; score report by August 28. Institutional placement test may be substituted for SAT or ACT. **Additional information:** All applicants to computer accounting and computer science technology conditionally accepted pending completion of 4 courses with grade of 2.0 or better, and with minimum 2.5 GPA.

1992 FRESHMAN CLASS PROFILE. 1,306 men, 1,278 women enrolled. **Characteristics:** 99% from in state, 100% commute, 8% have minority backgrounds. Average age is 22.

FALL-TERM APPLICATIONS. $5 fee. No closing date; applicants notified on a rolling basis. Deferred and early admission available.

STUDENT LIFE. Activities: Student government, magazine, student newspaper, television, choral groups, drama, jazz band, music ensembles, American Society of Certified Engineering Technicians, Data Processing Management Association, Student Management Association, American Institute of Design Drafting, American Society of Electrical Engineers.

ATHLETICS. Intercollegiate: Soccer W. **Intramural:** Basketball, bowling, soccer M, table tennis, tennis, volleyball.

STUDENT SERVICES. Aptitude testing, career counseling, employment service for undergraduates, freshman orientation, health services, personal counseling, placement service for graduates, special adviser for adult students, veterans counselor, services/facilities for handicapped.

ANNUAL EXPENSES. Tuition and fees (1992-93): $944, $2,600 additional for out-of-state students. **Books and supplies:** $400. **Other expenses:** $1,300.

FINANCIAL AID. 29% of freshmen, 32% of continuing students receive some form of aid. 98% of grants, 86% of loans, all jobs based on need. 600 enrolled freshmen were judged to have need, all were offered aid. Academic, music/drama, art, state/district residency, leadership, minority scholarships available. **Aid applications:** Closing date July 1; applicants notified on or about August 15.

ADDRESS/TELEPHONE. Harris Moeller, Dean of Student Affairs, Pellissippi State Technical Community College, PO Box 22990, Knoxville, TN 37933-0990. (615) 694-6570. Fax: (615) 539-7016.

Rhodes College
Memphis, Tennessee — CB code: 1730

Admissions:	77% of applicants accepted
Based on:	••• School record
	•• Activities, essay, interview, recommendations, test scores
	• Special talents
Completion:	96% of freshmen end year in good standing
	76% graduate, 37% of these enter graduate study

4-year private liberal arts college, coed, affiliated with Presbyterian Church (USA). Founded in 1848. **Accreditation:** Regional. **Undergraduate enrollment:** 599 men, 744 women full time; 22 men, 49 women part time. **Faculty:** 154 total (121 full time), 141 with doctorates or other terminal degrees. **Location:** Suburban campus in very large city; 4 miles from downtown. **Calendar:** Semester. **Microcomputers:** 120 located in libraries, classrooms, computer centers, campus-wide network. **Special facilities:** Physics tower, theater, arboretum, scanning electron microscope, cell culture facility, nuclear magnetic resonance instrument. **Additional facts:** 13 buildings listed on National Register of Historic Places.

DEGREES OFFERED. BA, BS, MS. 278 bachelor's degrees awarded in 1992. 13% in business and management, 6% letters/literature, 13% life sciences, 6% philosophy, religion, theology, 5% physical sciences, 9% psychology, 37% social sciences. Graduate degrees offered in 1 major field of study.

UNDERGRADUATE MAJORS. American studies, anthropology, art history, biochemistry, biology, business and management, chemistry, classics, computer and information sciences, dramatic arts, economics, English, French, German, history, international business management, international studies, Latin American studies, mathematics, music, philosophy, physics, political science and government, psychology, religion, Russian and Slavic studies, sociology, Spanish, studio art, urban studies.

ACADEMIC PROGRAMS. Accelerated program, double major, honors program, independent study, internships, student-designed major, study abroad, teacher preparation, visiting/exchange student program, Washington semester, cross-registration, science semester at Oak Ridge National Laboratory; exchange programs with University of Tubingen, Germany, Kansai Gaidai University in Osaka, Japan and Russian universities through the American Collegiate Consortium; summer study at Oxford University, England; 17-week European Studies Program includes 4 weeks summer study at Rhodes College or University of the South and 13 weeks abroad during fall semester. **Remedial services:** Tutoring, composition laboratory. **ROTC:** Air Force, Army. **Placement/credit:** AP, IB, institutional tests; 28 credit hours maximum for bachelor's degree.

ACADEMIC REQUIREMENTS. Freshmen must earn minimum GPA of 1.6 to continue in good standing. 91% of freshmen return for sophomore year. Students must declare major by end of second year. **Graduation requirements:** 112 hours for bachelor's. Most students required to take courses in arts/fine arts, English, foreign languages, humanities, philosophy/religion, biological/physical sciences, social sciences. **Postgraduate studies:** 8% enter law school, 8% enter medical school, 3% enter MBA programs, 18% enter other graduate study. **Additional information:** Model United Nations program, opportunities for participation in computer-simulated international negotiating, strong mock trial program; teacher certification for secondary school.

FRESHMAN ADMISSIONS. Selection criteria: Academic record, standardized test scores, and class rank most important. Recommendations, essay, school and community activities important. Applications sought from and special consideration given to international students, minorities, and children of alumni. **High school preparation:** 16 units required. Required and recommended units include English 4, foreign language 2 and mathematics 3. Social science 2 and science 2 recommended. 4 mathematics recommended for applicants in mathematics, natural science, computer science, and economics. **Test requirements:** SAT or ACT; score report by February 1.

1992 FRESHMAN CLASS PROFILE. 900 men applied, 658 accepted, 160 enrolled; 1,084 women applied, 870 accepted, 206 enrolled. 88% had high school GPA of 3.0 or higher, 12% between 2.0 and 2.99. 59% were in top tenth and 88% were in top quarter of graduating class. **Academic background:** Mid 50% of enrolled freshmen had SAT-V between 520-640, SAT-M between 570-670; ACT composite between 25-30. 74% submitted SAT scores, 70% submitted ACT scores. **Characteristics:** 32% from in state, 98% live in college housing, 11% have minority backgrounds, 2% are foreign students, 58% join fraternities/sororities. Average age is 18.

FALL-TERM APPLICATIONS. $30 fee, may be waived for applicants with need. No closing date; priority given to applications received by February 1; applicants notified on a rolling basis beginning on or about April 1; must reply by May 1 or within 2 weeks if notified thereafter. Essay required. Interview recommended. CRDA. Deferred and early admission available. EDP-F.

STUDENT LIFE. Housing: Dormitories (men, women). Academic interest housing, some with foreign language emphasis, available. **Activities:** Student government, magazine, student newspaper, yearbook, science journal, choral groups, dance, drama, music ensembles, musical theater, pep band, fraternities, sororities, Black Student Association, Kinney (social service), Inter-Varsity Christian Fellowship, Young Democrats, Young Republicans, Religious Life Commission, Baptist Student Union, International House, Habitat for Humanity, historically black sororities.

ATHLETICS. NCAA. **Intercollegiate:** Baseball M, basketball, cross-country, football M, golf M, soccer, tennis, track and field, volleyball W. **Intramural:** Basketball, racquetball, soccer, softball, swimming, tennis, volleyball, water polo.

STUDENT SERVICES. Aptitude testing, career counseling, employment service for undergraduates, freshman orientation, health services, personal counseling, placement service for graduates, special adviser for adult students, services/facilities for handicapped.

ANNUAL EXPENSES. Tuition and fees: $14,916. **Room and board:** $4,709. **Books and supplies:** $500. **Other expenses:** $800.

FINANCIAL AID. 76% of freshmen, 69% of continuing students receive some form of aid. 58% of grants, 95% of loans, 89% of jobs based on need. 196 enrolled freshmen were judged to have need, all were offered aid. Academic, music/drama, art, religious affiliation, minority scholarships available. **Aid applications:** No closing date; priority given to applications received by March 1; applicants notified on a rolling basis beginning on or about April 1; must reply by May 1 or within 2 weeks if notified thereafter. **Additional information:** College attempts to provide adequate financial resources to every student admitted during the regular admission process. Auditions required for theater and music achievement awards and art achievement awards. Interviews recommended for merit scholarships.

ADDRESS/TELEPHONE. David J. Wottle, Dean of Admissions and Financial Aid, Rhodes College, 2000 North Parkway, Memphis, TN 38112-1690. (901) 726-3700. (800) 844-5969. Fax: (901) 726-3719.

Roane State Community College
Harriman, Tennessee — CB code: 1656

2-year public community college, coed. Founded in 1971. **Accreditation:** Regional. **Undergraduate enrollment:** 1,045 men, 1,809 women full time; 1,033 men, 1,955 women part time. **Faculty:** 257 total (132 full time), 23 with doctorates or other terminal degrees. **Location:** Rural campus in small town; 40 miles from Knoxville. **Calendar:** Semester, limited summer session. **Microcomputers:** 159 located in libraries, computer centers. **Special facilities:** Writing center.

DEGREES OFFERED. AA, AS, AAS. 333 associate degrees awarded in 1992. 15% in business and management, 8% computer sciences, 8% education, 9% engineering technologies, 45% allied health, 10% multi/interdisciplinary studies.

UNDERGRADUATE MAJORS. Accounting, art education, biological and physical sciences, biology, business administration and management, business and management, business and office, business data processing and related programs, business education, computer and information sciences, dental hygiene, early childhood education, elementary education, engineering, engineering and engineering-related technologies, finance, fine arts, health physics technology, insurance and risk management, law enforcement and corrections technologies, liberal/general studies, mathematics, medical laboratory technologies, medical records technology, medical secretary, music, music education, nuclear medical technology, nursing, optical technology, pharmacy, physical education, physical sciences, physical therapy assistant, predentistry, premedicine, prepharmacy, radiograph medical technology, respiratory therapy, respiratory therapy technology, secondary education, secretarial and related programs, small business management and ownership, social sciences, special education, word processing.

ACADEMIC PROGRAMS. 2-year transfer program, cooperative education, dual enrollment of high school students, honors program, independent study, internships, teacher preparation. **Remedial services:** Learning center, remedial instruction, special counselor, tutoring, writing center. **Placement/credit:** AP, CLEP General and Subject, institutional tests; 30 credit hours maximum for associate degree.

ACADEMIC REQUIREMENTS. Freshmen must earn minimum GPA of 1.4 to continue in good standing. 45% of freshmen return for sophomore year. Students must declare major by end of first year. **Graduation requirements:** 68 hours for associate. Most students required to take courses in computer science, English, mathematics, biological/physical sciences, social sciences.

FRESHMAN ADMISSIONS. Selection criteria: Open admissions. Minimum ACT score of 20 required for nursing program. **High school preparation:** 20 units required. Required units include English 4, foreign language 2, mathematics 3, social science 2 and science 2. **Test requirements:** SAT or ACT (ACT preferred) for placement and counseling only; score report by August 15. SAT or ACT not required of applicants 21 years of age or older.

1992 FRESHMAN CLASS PROFILE. 354 men, 586 women enrolled. 34% had high school GPA of 3.0 or higher, 56% between 2.0 and 2.99. **Characteristics:** 99% from in state, 100% commute, 4% have minority backgrounds, 1% are foreign students. Average age is 18.

FALL-TERM APPLICATIONS. $5 fee. Closing date August 14; applicants notified on a rolling basis; must reply by registration. Interview required for allied health program applicants. Audition required for music applicants. Deferred and early admission available.

STUDENT LIFE. Activities: Student government, radio, student newspaper, yearbook, choral groups, concert band, drama, jazz band, music ensembles, Baptist Student Union.

ATHLETICS. NJCAA. **Intercollegiate:** Baseball M, basketball. **Intramural:** Basketball, soccer M, softball, volleyball.

STUDENT SERVICES. Aptitude testing, career counseling, employment service for undergraduates, freshman orientation, health services, personal counseling, placement service for graduates, veterans counselor, services/facilities for handicapped.

ANNUAL EXPENSES. Tuition and fees (1992-93): $914, $2,600 additional for out-of-state students. **Books and supplies:** $400. **Other expenses:** $750.

FINANCIAL AID. 35% of freshmen, 31% of continuing students receive some form of aid. 88% of grants, 92% of loans, 56% of jobs based on need. Academic, music/drama, art, athletic, minority scholarships available. **Aid applications:** No closing date; priority given to applications received by May 1; applicants notified on a rolling basis beginning on or about July 1; must reply within 2 weeks.

ADDRESS/TELEPHONE. John Neill, Director Admissions and Records, Roane State Community College, Route 8, Box 69, Patton Lane, Harriman, TN 37748. (615) 354-3000 ext. 4523. Fax: (615) 354-3000 ext. 4462.

Shelby State Community College
Memphis, Tennessee — CB code: 0274

2-year public community college, coed. Founded in 1970. **Accreditation:** Regional. **Undergraduate enrollment:** 1,048 men, 2,226 women full time; 1,087 men, 2,627 women part time. **Faculty:** 354 total (121 full time), 15 with doctorates or other terminal degrees. **Location:** Urban campus in very large city. **Calendar:** Semester, extensive summer session. Saturday and extensive evening/early morning classes. **Microcomputers:** 200 located in libraries, classrooms, computer centers.

DEGREES OFFERED. AA, AS, AAS. 254 associate degrees awarded in 1992. 5% in business and management, 38% health sciences, 20% allied health, 5% home economics, 23% multi/interdisciplinary studies, 7% parks/recreation, protective services, public affairs.

UNDERGRADUATE MAJORS. Accounting, Afro-American (black) studies, biological and physical sciences, business administration and management, clothing and textiles management/production/services, criminal justice studies, early childhood education, education, emergency medical technologies, English, family and community services, fashion merchandising, fine arts, food production/management/services, French, legal secretary, liberal/general studies, mathematics, medical assistant, medical laboratory technologies, medical secretary, nursing, occupational therapy assistant, physical therapy assistant, radiograph medical technology, secretarial and related programs, Spanish.

ACADEMIC PROGRAMS. 2-year transfer program, cooperative education, dual enrollment of high school students, independent study, internships, telecourses, weekend college. **Remedial services:** Learning center, preadmission summer program, remedial instruction, special counselor, tutoring, special orientation course. **ROTC:** Air Force, Army. **Placement/credit:** CLEP General and Subject, institutional tests; 42 credit hours maximum for associate degree.

ACADEMIC REQUIREMENTS. Freshmen must earn minimum GPA of 1.4 to continue in good standing. Students must declare major on application. **Graduation requirements:** 64 hours for associate (12 in major). Most students required to take courses in arts/fine arts, computer science, English, history, mathematics, philosophy/religion, biological/physical sciences, social sciences.

FRESHMAN ADMISSIONS. Selection criteria: Open admissions. Special requirements for admission to nursing, allied health, nutrition, and dietetics programs. **High school preparation:** 14 units recommended. Recommended units include English 4, foreign language 2, mathematics 3, social science 2 and science 2. One visual/performing arts also recommended. **Test requirements:** ACT for placement; score report by September 1. ACT not required of applicants 21 years of age or older.

1992 FRESHMAN CLASS PROFILE. 361 men, 606 women enrolled. 14% had high school GPA of 3.0 or higher, 33% between 2.0 and 2.99. **Academic background:** Mid 50% of enrolled freshmen had ACT composite between 14-18. 63% submitted ACT scores. **Characteristics:** 97% from in state, 100% commute, 68% have minority backgrounds. Average age is 21.

FALL-TERM APPLICATIONS. $5 fee. No closing date; applicants notified on a rolling basis; must reply by registration. Deferred and early admission available. Applicants aged 21 or over should take the AAPP, statewide placement test, if college-level English and mathematics course have not been successfully completed.

STUDENT LIFE. Activities: Student government, student newspaper, academic subject area clubs, choral groups, concert band, drama, jazz band, music ensembles, NAACP, Christian Fellowship, PUSH.

ATHLETICS. NJCAA. **Intercollegiate:** Baseball M, basketball, golf M. **Intramural:** Basketball, racquetball, softball, tennis, volleyball.

STUDENT SERVICES. Aptitude testing, career counseling, employment service for undergraduates, freshman orientation, on-campus day care, personal counseling, placement service for graduates, veterans counselor, services/facilities for handicapped.

ANNUAL EXPENSES. Tuition and fees (1992-93): $906, $2,600 additional for out-of-state students. **Books and supplies:** $400. **Other expenses:** $675.

FINANCIAL AID. 42% of freshmen, 42% of continuing students receive some form of aid. All grants based on need. Academic, music/drama, art, athletic, leadership, minority scholarships available. **Aid applications:** No closing date; priority given to applications received by May 1; applicants notified on a rolling basis beginning on or about July 1; must reply within 2 weeks.

ADDRESS/TELEPHONE. Verna Crockett, Director of Admissions and Records, Shelby State Community College, PO Box 40568, Memphis, TN 38174-0568. (901) 544-5900. Fax: (901) 544-5920.

Southern College of Seventh-day Adventists

Collegedale, Tennessee CB code: 1727

4-year private liberal arts college, coed, affiliated with Seventh-day Adventists. Founded in 1892. **Accreditation:** Regional. **Undergraduate enrollment:** 563 men, 635 women full time; 99 men, 197 women part time. **Faculty:** 158 total (153 full time), 44 with doctorates or other terminal degrees. **Location:** Rural campus in small town; 18 miles from Chattanooga. **Calendar:** Semester, limited summer session. **Microcomputers:** Located in libraries, classrooms, computer centers. **Special facilities:** Lincoln collection, Anton Memorial Organ.

DEGREES OFFERED. AA, AS, BA, BS. 133 associate degrees awarded in 1992. 13% in business and management, 67% health sciences, 13% allied health. 229 bachelor's degrees awarded. 9% in business and management, 18% business/office and marketing/distribution, 18% health sciences, 5% languages, 9% life sciences, 9% philosophy, religion, theology, 6% psychology, 8% social sciences.

UNDERGRADUATE MAJORS. Associate: Accounting, business and office, business data processing and related programs, computer and information sciences, computer graphics, engineering, food production/management/services, industrial technology, legal secretary, medical secretary, nursing, occupational therapy, occupational therapy assistant, physical therapy, secretarial and related programs. **Bachelor's:** Accounting, behavioral sciences, biology, business administration and management, business and management, chemistry, clinical laboratory science, computer and information sciences, elementary education, English, French, German, health care administration, history, journalism, marketing and distribution, mathematics, music, nursing, occupational therapy, occupational therapy assistant, office supervision and management, physical therapy, physics, psychology, public relations, radio/television broadcasting, radio/television technology, religion, religious education, secretarial and related programs, social sciences, Spanish, speech, theological studies.

ACADEMIC PROGRAMS. 2-year transfer program, accelerated program, cooperative education, double major, dual enrollment of high school students, honors program, internships, study abroad, teacher preparation. **Remedial services:** Learning center, reduced course load, remedial instruction, special counselor, tutoring. **Placement/credit:** AP, CLEP Subject; 31 credit hours maximum for bachelor's degree.

ACADEMIC REQUIREMENTS. Freshmen must earn minimum GPA of 2.0 to continue in good standing. 64% of freshmen return for sophomore year. Students must declare major on application. **Graduation requirements:** 68 hours for associate (18 in major), 124 hours for bachelor's (30 in major). Most students required to take courses in arts/fine arts, English, foreign languages, history, humanities, mathematics, philosophy/religion, biological/physical sciences, social sciences. **Postgraduate studies:** 19% from 2-year programs enter 4-year programs.

FRESHMAN ADMISSIONS. Selection criteria: School achievement record, test scores, and recommendations. **High school preparation:** 18 units required. Required units include biological science 2, English 4, foreign language 2, mathematics 2, social science 2 and science 2. **Test requirements:** ACT; score report by August 30.

1992 FRESHMAN CLASS PROFILE. 166 men, 203 women enrolled. **Academic background:** Mid 50% of enrolled freshmen had ACT composite between 18-23. 97% submitted ACT scores. **Characteristics:** 90% live in college housing. Average age is 18.

FALL-TERM APPLICATIONS. $20 fee, may be waived for applicants with need. Closing date August 15; applicants notified on a rolling basis; must reply within 3 weeks. Audition required for music, gymnastics applicants. Essay required. Interview recommended. Deferred and early admission available.

STUDENT LIFE. Housing: Dormitories (men, women); apartment housing available. **Activities:** Student government, film, radio, student newspaper, television, yearbook, choral groups, concert band, drama, music ensembles, symphony orchestra. **Additional information:** Religious observance required.

ATHLETICS. Intramural: Badminton, basketball, golf, gymnastics, racquetball, sailing, soccer, softball, swimming, tennis, track and field, volleyball.

STUDENT SERVICES. Aptitude testing, career counseling, employment service for undergraduates, freshman orientation, health services, on-campus day care, personal counseling, placement service for graduates, veterans counselor, services/facilities for handicapped.

ANNUAL EXPENSES. Tuition and fees: $7,988. **Room and board:** $3,360. **Books and supplies:** $480. **Other expenses:** $525.

FINANCIAL AID. 85% of freshmen, 64% of continuing students receive some form of aid. 38% of grants, 86% of loans, 20% of jobs based on need. 190 enrolled freshmen were judged to have need, 182 were offered aid. Academic, music/drama, leadership scholarships available. **Aid applications:** No closing date; priority given to applications received by May 1; applicants notified on a rolling basis beginning on or about May 1; must reply within 2 weeks.

ADDRESS/TELEPHONE. Dr. Ronald M. Barrow, Vice President for Admissions and College Relations, Southern College of Seventh-day Adventists, PO Box 370, Collegedale, TN 37315. (615) 238-2844. (800) 768-8437. Fax: (615) 238-3005.

State Technical Institute at Memphis

Memphis, Tennessee CB code: 0281

2-year public technical college, coed. Founded in 1967. **Accreditation:** Regional. **Undergraduate enrollment:** 1,549 men, 1,597 women full time; 3,318 men, 4,055 women part time. **Faculty:** 527 total (154 full time), 23 with doctorates or other terminal degrees. **Location:** Suburban campus in very large city; within city limits. **Calendar:** Semester, extensive summer session. Saturday and extensive evening/early morning classes. **Microcomputers:** 567 located in classrooms, computer centers. **Additional facts:** Classes offered at 43 off-campus sites.

DEGREES OFFERED. AAS. 624 associate degrees awarded in 1992. 33% in business and management, 28% computer sciences, 39% engineering technologies.

UNDERGRADUATE MAJORS. Accounting, architectural technologies, automotive technology, biomedical equipment technology, business and management, business computer/console/peripheral equipment operation, business data processing and related programs, chemical manufacturing technology, civil technology, computer and information sciences, computer technology, court reporting, electrical technology, electronic technology, finance, graphic and printing production, hotel/motel and restaurant management, industrial equipment maintenance and repair, industrial technology, information sciences and systems, legal assistant/paralegal, legal secretary, mechanical design technology, microcomputer software, telecommunications, telecommunications engineering technology, trade and industrial supervision and management.

ACADEMIC PROGRAMS. Cooperative education, double major, dual enrollment of high school students, independent study, student-designed major, weekend college, on-site extension courses at business, industry and government installations. **Remedial services:** Learning center, reduced course load, remedial instruction, special counselor, tutoring. **ROTC:** Air Force, Army. **Placement/credit:** CLEP General and Subject, institutional tests; 24 credit hours maximum for associate degree.

ACADEMIC REQUIREMENTS. Freshmen must earn minimum GPA of 2.0 to continue in good standing. Students must declare major on application. **Graduation requirements:** 73 hours for associate. Most students required to take courses in English, humanities, mathematics, social sciences.

FRESHMAN ADMISSIONS. Selection criteria: Open admissions. Recommended units include English 4, mathematics 2, social science 1 and science 1. **Test requirements:** ACT for placement and counseling only; score report by September 1. Applicants 21 and older and those having ACT composite score of 19 required to take assessment tests for placement and counseling.

1992 FRESHMAN CLASS PROFILE. 563 men, 490 women enrolled. **Academic background:** Mid 50% of enrolled freshmen had ACT composite between 13-18. 77% submitted ACT scores. **Characteristics:** 98% from in state, 100% commute, 46% have minority backgrounds. Average age is 22.

FALL-TERM APPLICATIONS. $5 fee. No closing date; applicants notified on a rolling basis beginning on or about July 1; must reply by registration. Deferred and early admission available.

STUDENT LIFE. Activities: Student government, student newspaper, religious and social service organizations.

STUDENT SERVICES. Aptitude testing, career counseling, employment service for undergraduates, freshman orientation, on-campus day care, personal counseling, placement service for graduates, veterans counselor, services/facilities for handicapped.

ANNUAL EXPENSES. Tuition and fees (1992-93): $902, $2,600 additional for out-of-state students. **Books and supplies:** $600. **Other expenses:** $675.

FINANCIAL AID. 25% of freshmen, 30% of continuing students receive some form of aid. 82% of grants, 1% of loans, all jobs based on need. Academic scholarships available. **Aid applications:** No closing date; priority given to applications received by March 15; applicants notified on a rolling basis beginning on or about May 1; must reply within 10 days.

ADDRESS/TELEPHONE. Jana Turner, Director of Admissions, State Technical Institute at Memphis, 5983 Macon Cove, Memphis, TN 38134. (901) 377-4111. Fax: (901) 373-2503.

Tennessee Institute of Electronics
Knoxville, Tennessee — CB code: 0446

2-year proprietary technical college, coed. Founded in 1947. **Undergraduate enrollment:** 110 men and women. **Location:** Suburban campus in small city. **Calendar:** Quarter.

FRESHMAN ADMISSIONS. Selection criteria: Test scores and interview considered.

ANNUAL EXPENSES. Tuition and fees (1992-93): $3,314. $6,627 in tuition and fees for 18-month program. **Books and supplies:** $325. **Other expenses:** $1,143.

ADDRESS/TELEPHONE. Nancy Rackley, Vice President, Tennessee Institute of Electronics, 3203 Tazewell Pike, Knoxville, TN 37918. (615) 688-9422.

Tennessee State University
Nashville, Tennessee — CB code: 1803

Admissions: 57% of applicants accepted
Based on: ••• School record, test scores
• Special talents
Completion: 75% of freshmen end year in good standing
29% graduate, 12% of these enter graduate study

4-year public university, coed. Founded in 1912. **Accreditation:** Regional. **Undergraduate enrollment:** 1,889 men, 2,793 women full time; 723 men, 1,200 women part time. **Graduate enrollment:** 89 men, 143 women full time; 278 men, 475 women part time. **Faculty:** 425 total (320 full time), 210 with doctorates or other terminal degrees. **Location:** Urban campus in large city. **Calendar:** Semester, limited summer session. Extensive evening/early morning classes. **Microcomputers:** Located in computer centers.

DEGREES OFFERED. AAS, BA, BS, MA, MS, MBA, MEd, PhD, EdD. 120 associate degrees awarded in 1992. 80% in health sciences, 15% allied health. 510 bachelor's degrees awarded. Graduate degrees offered in 20 major fields of study.

UNDERGRADUATE MAJORS. Associate: Accounting, dental hygiene, fire control and safety technology, liberal/general studies, medical records technology, nursing, practical nursing, public affairs, secretarial and related programs. **Bachelor's:** Accounting, aerospace science (Air Force), aerospace/aeronautical/astronautical engineering, agricultural sciences, animal sciences, architectural engineering, architecture, art history, biochemistry, biological and physical sciences, biology, business administration and management, business and management, business economics, chemistry, civil engineering, clinical laboratory science, communications, computer and information sciences, computer programming, criminal justice studies, dental hygiene, dramatic arts, early childhood education, education, electrical/electronics/communications engineering, elementary education, engineering, engineering and other disciplines, English, food science and nutrition, French, health care administration, history, home economics, humanities and social sciences, individual and family development, journalism, law enforcement and corrections, liberal/general studies, mathematics, mechanical engineering, medical records administration, music, nursing, physical education, physical sciences, physics, political science and government, psychology, secondary education, secretarial and related programs, social sciences, social work, sociology, soil sciences, Spanish, special education, speech pathology/audiology, textiles and clothing.

ACADEMIC PROGRAMS. 2-year transfer program, cooperative education, honors program, independent study, teacher preparation, visiting/exchange student program, weekend college, cross-registration; combined bachelor's/graduate program in business administration. **Remedial services:** Learning center, remedial instruction, special counselor, tutoring. **ROTC:** Air Force. **Placement/credit:** AP, CLEP Subject, institutional tests; 33 credit hours maximum for bachelor's degree.

ACADEMIC REQUIREMENTS. Freshmen must earn minimum GPA of 1.6 to continue in good standing. 50% of freshmen return for sophomore year. Students must declare major by end of first year. **Graduation requirements:** 76 hours for associate, 132 hours for bachelor's. Most students required to take courses in computer science, English, history, humanities, mathematics, biological/physical sciences, social sciences. **Postgraduate studies:** 25% from 2-year programs enter 4-year programs.

FRESHMAN ADMISSIONS. Selection criteria: School achievement record, test scores considered. **High school preparation:** 16 units required. Required units include English 4, foreign language 2, mathematics 3, social science 2 and science 2. Units required of engineering majors: plane and solid geometry, trigonometry, 1 physics, 1 chemistry. One science unit must be with laboratory. One visual and/or performing arts recommended. **Test requirements:** SAT or ACT; score report by August 1.

1992 FRESHMAN CLASS PROFILE. 1,285 men applied, 669 accepted, 327 enrolled; 1,946 women applied, 1,164 accepted, 464 enrolled. 15% had high school GPA of 3.0 or higher, 84% between 2.0 and 2.99. **Academic background:** Mid 50% of enrolled freshmen had ACT composite between 18-22. 70% submitted ACT scores. **Characteristics:** 71% from in state, 75% commute, 87% have minority backgrounds, 4% are foreign students. Average age is 18.

FALL-TERM APPLICATIONS. $5 fee, may be waived for applicants with need. Closing date August 1; applicants notified on a rolling basis. Interview required for allied health, nursing, physical therapy applicants. CRDA. Deferred and early admission available.

STUDENT LIFE. Housing: Dormitories (men, women). **Activities:** Student government, film, radio, student newspaper, yearbook, choral groups, concert band, dance, drama, jazz band, marching band, music ensembles, musical theater, pep band, fraternities, sororities, religious organizations, foreign student organization.

ATHLETICS. NCAA. **Intercollegiate:** Baseball M, basketball, football M, golf M, tennis, track and field, volleyball M. **Intramural:** Basketball, racquetball, tennis, track and field, volleyball.

STUDENT SERVICES. Aptitude testing, career counseling, employment service for undergraduates, freshman orientation, health services, on-campus day care, personal counseling, placement service for graduates, veterans counselor, services/facilities for handicapped.

ANNUAL EXPENSES. Tuition and fees (1992-93): $1,632, $3,602 additional for out-of-state students. **Room and board:** $2,640. **Books and supplies:** $400. **Other expenses:** $700.

FINANCIAL AID. 80% of freshmen, 68% of continuing students receive some form of aid. 76% of grants, 97% of loans, 67% of jobs based on need. 525 enrolled freshmen were judged to have need, 500 were offered aid. Academic, music/drama, athletic, state/district residency, leadership, alumni affiliation, minority scholarships available. **Aid applications:** No closing date; priority given to applications received by April 1; applicants notified on a rolling basis beginning on or about July 10; must reply within 2 weeks.

ADDRESS/TELEPHONE. Erskine Vanderbilt, Dean of Admissions, Tennessee State University, 3500 John Merritt Boulevard, Nashville, TN 37203. (615) 320-3729. Fax: (615) 320-3747.

Tennessee Technological University
Cookeville, Tennessee CB code: 1804

4-year public university and engineering college, coed. Founded in 1915. **Accreditation:** Regional. **Undergraduate enrollment:** 3,569 men, 2,898 women full time; 886 men and women part time. **Graduate enrollment:** 104 men, 49 women full time; 347 men, 391 women part time. **Faculty:** 393 total (373 full time), 295 with doctorates or other terminal degrees. **Location:** Rural campus in large town; 80 miles from Nashville. **Calendar:** Semester, limited summer session. **Microcomputers:** 225 located in libraries, classrooms, computer centers. **Special facilities:** Joe L. Evins Appalachian Center for Crafts, Tech Aqua Center, cooperative fishery research unit.

DEGREES OFFERED. AA, BA, BS, BFA, MA, MS, MBA, PhD. 34 associate degrees awarded in 1992. 100% in parks/recreation, protective services, public affairs. 984 bachelor's degrees awarded. 16% in business and management, 18% teacher education, 22% engineering, 7% home economics, 7% physical sciences. Graduate degrees offered in 25 major fields of study.

UNDERGRADUATE MAJORS. Associate: Criminal justice studies. **Bachelor's:** Accounting, agribusiness, agricultural business and management, agricultural economics, agricultural education, agricultural engineering, agricultural sciences, agronomy, animal sciences, applied physics, art education, biochemistry, biology, business administration and management, business and management, chemical engineering, chemistry, child development/care/guidance, civil engineering, computer and information sciences, crafts, early childhood education, economics, education, electrical/electronics/communications engineering, elementary education, engineering, English, English education, family/consumer resource management, fashion design, fashion merchandising, finance, fine arts, food science and nutrition, foreign languages education, French, geology, German, health education, history, home economics, home economics education, horticulture, individual and family development, industrial arts education, industrial engineering, industrial technology, information sciences and systems, interior design, journalism, labor/industrial relations, management information systems, marine biology, marketing and distribution, mathematics, mathematics education, mechanical engineering, music, music education, music therapy, nursing, personnel management, physical education, physics, plant sciences, political science and government, prelaw, psychology, renewable natural resources, science education, secondary education, social science education, sociology, soil sciences, Spanish, special education, speech/communication/theater education, systems analysis, technical and business writing, textiles and clothing, trade and industrial education, wildlife management.

ACADEMIC PROGRAMS. Accelerated program, cooperative education, double major, dual enrollment of high school students, education specialist degree, honors program, independent study, internships, teacher preparation. **Remedial services:** Learning center, preadmission summer program, reduced course load, remedial instruction, tutoring. **ROTC:** Army. **Placement/credit:** AP, CLEP Subject, institutional tests; 33 credit hours maximum for bachelor's degree.

ACADEMIC REQUIREMENTS. Freshmen must earn minimum GPA of 1.4 to continue in good standing. 65% of freshmen return for sophomore year. Students must declare major on application. **Graduation requirements:** 66 hours for associate, 132 hours for bachelor's. Most students required to take courses in computer science, English, history, humanities, mathematics, biological/physical sciences, social sciences. **Postgraduate studies:** 3% enter MBA programs, 15% enter other graduate study.

FRESHMAN ADMISSIONS. Selection criteria: 2.35 high school GPA required. Engineering applicants need ACT mathematics score of 20 and composite score of 20. Computer science and mathematics applicants need ACT mathematics score of 20 and composite score of 20. 250 students may be admitted under open admission. **High school preparation:** 13 units required. Required units include English 4, foreign language 2, mathematics 3, social science 2 and science 2. Mathematics units must include algebra I and II and geometry or advanced mathematics course. Science units must be biology, chemistry, or physics with laboratories. Foreign language units must be in single language. Social science units must include 1 US history. 1 unit visual and/or performing arts also required. **Test requirements:** ACT; score report by August 1.

1992 FRESHMAN CLASS PROFILE. 1,622 men and women enrolled. 44% had high school GPA of 3.0 or higher, 48% between 2.0 and 2.99. **Characteristics:** 96% from in state, 80% live in college housing, 6% have minority backgrounds, 2% are foreign students, 12% join fraternities/sororities. Average age is 19.

FALL-TERM APPLICATIONS. $5 fee. No closing date; applicants notified on a rolling basis; must reply 2 weeks prior to registration. Interview recommended. Audition recommended for music applicants. Portfolio recommended for arts, crafts applicants. Early admission available.

STUDENT LIFE. Housing: Dormitories (men, women); apartment, fraternity housing available. Students required to live in college housing for first 2 years. **Activities:** Student government, magazine, radio, student newspaper, television, yearbook, choral groups, concert band, dance, drama, jazz band, marching band, music ensembles, musical theater, pep band, symphony orchestra, fraternities, sororities, several honors, foreign student, and religious organizations.

ATHLETICS. NCAA. **Intercollegiate:** Baseball M, basketball, cross-country M, football M, golf, rifle, softball W, tennis, volleyball W. **Intramural:** Basketball, handball, racquetball, rugby M, soccer, softball, track and field M, volleyball, wrestling M.

STUDENT SERVICES. Aptitude testing, career counseling, employment service for undergraduates, freshman orientation, health services, on-campus day care, personal counseling, placement service for graduates, veterans counselor, services/facilities for handicapped.

ANNUAL EXPENSES. Tuition and fees (1992-93): $1,634, $3,602 additional for out-of-state students. **Room and board:** $3,000. **Books and supplies:** $670. **Other expenses:** $670.

FINANCIAL AID. 65% of freshmen, 60% of continuing students receive some form of aid. 57% of grants, 89% of loans, 13% of jobs based on need. Academic, music/drama, athletic, state/district residency, leadership, alumni affiliation, minority scholarships available. **Aid applications:** No closing date; priority given to applications received by March 15; applicants notified on a rolling basis; must reply within 2 weeks.

ADDRESS/TELEPHONE. Dr. James C. Perry, Director of Admissions, Tennessee Technological University, PO Box 5006, Cookeville, TN 38505. (615) 372-3888. Fax: (615) 372-3898.

Tennessee Temple University
Chattanooga, Tennessee CB code: 1818

4-year private university and college of arts and sciences and Bible college, coed, affiliated with Independent Baptist Church. Founded in 1946. **Undergraduate enrollment:** 373 men, 361 women full time; 82 men, 49 women part time. **Graduate enrollment:** 17 men, 1 woman full time; 29 men, 2 women part time. **Faculty:** 81 total (66 full time). **Location:** Urban campus in small city; 120 miles from Atlanta, Georgia. **Calendar:** Semester, limited summer session. Extensive evening/early morning classes. **Microcomputers:** 50 located in libraries, computer centers.

DEGREES OFFERED. AA, AS, BA, BS, MA, MS, PhD, EdD, M.Div. 2 associate degrees awarded in 1992. 166 bachelor's degrees awarded. 17% in business and management, 5% communications, 17% education, 31% philosophy, religion, theology, 16% psychology, 5% visual and performing arts. Graduate degrees offered in 5 major fields of study.

UNDERGRADUATE MAJORS. Associate: Bible studies, education, home economics, secretarial and related programs. **Bachelor's:** Accounting, biblical languages, biology, business administration and management, business and management, communications, computer and information sciences, early childhood education, education of the deaf and hearing impaired, elementary education, English, history, liberal/general studies, missionary studies, music, music performance, music theory and composition, office supervision and management, physical sciences, psychology, religious education, secondary education, secretarial and related programs, theological studies.

ACADEMIC PROGRAMS. Double major, dual enrollment of high school students, external degree, honors program, independent study, internships, teacher preparation. **Remedial services:** Reduced course load, remedial instruction, special counselor, tutoring. **ROTC:** Army. **Placement/credit:** AP, CLEP General and Subject, institutional tests; 32 credit hours maximum for bachelor's degree.

ACADEMIC REQUIREMENTS. Freshmen must earn minimum GPA of 1.5 to continue in good standing. 70% of freshmen return for sophomore year. Students must declare major by end of first year. **Graduation requirements:** 64 hours for associate (26 in major), 128 hours for bachelor's (30 in major). Most students required to take courses in arts/fine arts, computer science, English, history, mathematics, philosophy/religion, biological/physical sciences, social sciences. **Postgraduate studies:** 10% from 2-year programs enter 4-year programs.

FRESHMAN ADMISSIONS. Selection criteria: Personal references and salvation experience considered. **High school preparation:** 18 units required. Required and recommended units include English 4, mathematics 2, physical science 2 and social science 2-3. Foreign language 2 recommended. **Test requirements:** SAT or ACT (ACT preferred); score report by September 28.

1992 FRESHMAN CLASS PROFILE. 90 men, 83 women enrolled. **Characteristics:** 13% from in state, 65% live in college housing, 8% have minority backgrounds, 100% join fraternities/sororities. Average age is 18.

FALL-TERM APPLICATIONS. $15 fee, may be waived for applicants with need. Closing date September 10; priority given to applications received by March 1; applicants notified on a rolling basis; must reply within 3 weeks. Essay recommended. Deferred admission available. Transcripts from all institutions attended, ACT or SAT scores, pastor's reference, two personal references, and $100 confirmation fee required.

STUDENT LIFE. Housing: Dormitories (men, women); apartment housing available. **Activities:** Student government, magazine, radio, yearbook, choral groups, concert band, drama, music ensembles, opera, pep band, symphony orchestra, debate, fraternities, sororities, Student Mission

Fellowship, Word of Life Clubs. **Additional information:** Religious observance required.

ATHLETICS. Intercollegiate: Basketball, soccer M, volleyball W. **Intramural:** Baseball, basketball, football M, golf M, table tennis, tennis.

STUDENT SERVICES. Career counseling, employment service for undergraduates, freshman orientation, health services, on-campus day care, personal counseling, placement service for graduates, veterans counselor, services/facilities for handicapped.

ANNUAL EXPENSES. Tuition and fees (1992-93): $4,130. **Room and board:** $3,370. **Books and supplies:** $450. **Other expenses:** $900.

FINANCIAL AID. 60% of freshmen, 77% of continuing students receive some form of aid. All grants, 99% of loans, all jobs based on need. 7 enrolled freshmen were judged to have need, all were offered aid. Academic, music/drama, athletic, leadership, alumni affiliation scholarships available. **Aid applications:** No closing date; priority given to applications received by March 31; applicants notified on a rolling basis beginning on or about May 1; must reply by August 1 or within 2 weeks if notified thereafter.

ADDRESS/TELEPHONE. Dr. Paul Martin, Director of Admissions, Tennessee Temple University, 1815 Union Avenue, Chattanooga, TN 37404. (615) 493-4100 ext. 4213. (800) 553-4050. Fax: (615) 493-4497.

Tennessee Wesleyan College
Athens, Tennessee CB code: 1805

4-year private liberal arts college, coed, affiliated with United Methodist Church. Founded in 1857. **Accreditation:** Regional. **Undergraduate enrollment:** 228 men, 209 women full time; 56 men, 139 women part time. **Faculty:** 66 total (32 full time), 26 with doctorates or other terminal degrees. **Location:** Urban campus in large town; 57 miles from Chattanooga and Knoxville. **Calendar:** Semester, extensive summer session. **Microcomputers:** 79 located in libraries, classrooms, computer centers.

DEGREES OFFERED. BA, BS. 142 bachelor's degrees awarded in 1992. 32% in business and management, 5% communications, 16% teacher education, 5% letters/literature, 13% life sciences, 13% psychology, 7% social sciences.

UNDERGRADUATE MAJORS. Accounting, aviation management, biological and physical sciences, biology, business administration and management, business and management, business education, chemistry, communications, comparative literature, computer and information sciences, early childhood education, education, elementary education, English, English education, English literature, health education, history, humanities and social sciences, junior high education, liberal/general studies, mathematics, mathematics education, music, music education, music performance, optometry, physical education, psychology, religion, science education, secondary education, social science education, social sciences, social studies education, social work.

ACADEMIC PROGRAMS. Double major, dual enrollment of high school students, independent study, internships, student-designed major, study abroad, teacher preparation. **Remedial services:** Learning center, reduced course load, remedial instruction, tutoring. **Placement/credit:** AP, CLEP General and Subject, institutional tests; 12 credit hours maximum for bachelor's degree.

ACADEMIC REQUIREMENTS. Freshmen must earn minimum GPA of 2.0 to continue in good standing. 69% of freshmen return for sophomore year. Students must declare major by end of first year. **Graduation requirements:** 128 hours for bachelor's. Most students required to take courses in arts/fine arts, English, history, humanities, mathematics, philosophy/religion, biological/physical sciences, social sciences.

FRESHMAN ADMISSIONS. Selection criteria: SAT or ACT scores, class rank, high school achievement. **High school preparation:** 17 units recommended. Recommended units include biological science 2, English 4, foreign language 2, mathematics 2, physical science 1 and social science 2. **Test requirements:** SAT or ACT (ACT preferred); score report by August 15.

1992 FRESHMAN CLASS PROFILE. 55 men, 25 women enrolled. 43% had high school GPA of 3.0 or higher, 57% between 2.0 and 2.99. 34% were in top quarter of graduating class. **Characteristics:** Average age is 18.

FALL-TERM APPLICATIONS. $25 fee, may be waived for applicants with need. No closing date; applicants notified on a rolling basis; must reply within 4 weeks. Interview required for academically weak applicants. Audition required for music applicants. Essay recommended. Deferred and early admission available.

STUDENT LIFE. Housing: Dormitories (men, women). **Activities:** Student government, magazine, radio, student newspaper, yearbook, choral groups, drama, music ensembles, musical theater, sororities, Circle-K, Independent Women and Men (social organization), international students club, Wesleyan Christian Fellowship, Baptist Student Union, masqued players, political science club, biology club, Society for the Advancement of Management, Fellowship of Christian Athletes.

ATHLETICS. NAIA. **Intercollegiate:** Baseball M, basketball, football M, golf M, soccer, softball W, tennis. **Intramural:** Archery, badminton, basketball, bowling, sailing, softball, swimming, table tennis, tennis M, volleyball.

STUDENT SERVICES. Aptitude testing, career counseling, employment service for undergraduates, freshman orientation, health services, personal counseling, placement service for graduates, services/facilities for handicapped.

ANNUAL EXPENSES. Tuition and fees: $6,520. **Room and board:** $3,340. **Books and supplies:** $400. **Other expenses:** $1,200.

FINANCIAL AID. 95% of freshmen, 77% of continuing students receive some form of aid. 35% of grants, 94% of loans, 54% of jobs based on need. Academic, music/drama, athletic, leadership, religious affiliation, minority scholarships available. **Aid applications:** Closing date July 31; priority given to applications received by April 1; applicants notified on a rolling basis beginning on or about April 1; must reply within 2 weeks.

ADDRESS/TELEPHONE. Jim Harrison, Dean of Enrollment, Tennessee Wesleyan College, PO Box 40, Athens, TN 37371-0040. (615) 745-7504. Fax: (615) 744-9968.

Trevecca Nazarene College
Nashville, Tennessee CB code: 1809

4-year private liberal arts college, coed, affiliated with Church of the Nazarene. Founded in 1901. **Accreditation:** Regional. **Undergraduate enrollment:** 383 men, 472 women full time; 71 men, 141 women part time. **Graduate enrollment:** 96 men, 186 women full time; 14 men, 23 women part time. **Faculty:** 130 total (85 full time), 67 with doctorates or other terminal degrees. **Location:** Suburban campus in large city. **Calendar:** Semester, limited summer session. **Microcomputers:** Located in libraries, computer centers.

DEGREES OFFERED. AA, AS, BA, BS, MA, MEd. 8 associate degrees awarded in 1992. 254 bachelor's degrees awarded. 48% in business and management, 16% business/office and marketing/distribution, 5% communications, 8% education, 5% allied health, 7% philosophy, religion, theology, 5% social sciences. Graduate degrees offered in 5 major fields of study.

UNDERGRADUATE MAJORS. Associate: Bible studies, computer and information sciences, liberal/general studies, marketing and distribution, medical assistant, medical records administration, medical records technology, secretarial and related programs. **Bachelor's:** Accounting, behavioral sciences, biological and physical sciences, biology, business administration and management, business and management, business data processing and related programs, business education, chemistry, clinical laboratory science, communications, computer and information sciences, dramatic arts, early childhood education, education, education of the deaf and hearing impaired, education of the multiple handicapped, education of the visually handicapped, elementary education, English, history, human resources development, humanities and social sciences, junior high education, management information systems, mathematics, music, music business management, music education, music history and appreciation, office supervision and management, physical therapy, physician's assistant, psychology, radio/television broadcasting, religion, religious education, religious music, science education, secondary education, secretarial and related programs, social science education, social sciences, sociology, special education, speech, speech correction, theological studies.

ACADEMIC PROGRAMS. Double major, dual enrollment of high school students, independent study, internships, teacher preparation. **Remedial services:** Learning center, remedial instruction, special counselor, tutoring. **ROTC:** Air Force, Army, Naval. **Placement/credit:** AP, CLEP General, institutional tests; 15 credit hours maximum for associate degree; 30 credit hours maximum for bachelor's degree.

ACADEMIC REQUIREMENTS. Freshmen must earn minimum GPA of 1.6 to continue in good standing. 68% of freshmen return for sophomore year. **Graduation requirements:** 64 hours for associate (20 in major), 128 hours for bachelor's (30 in major). Most students required to take courses in English, history, mathematics, philosophy/religion, biological/physical sciences, social sciences. **Postgraduate studies:** 50% from 2-year programs enter 4-year programs.

FRESHMAN ADMISSIONS. Selection criteria: Open admissions. **Test requirements:** SAT or ACT (ACT preferred) for placement and counseling only; score report by September 1.

1992 FRESHMAN CLASS PROFILE. 83 men, 100 women enrolled. **Characteristics:** 46% from in state, 71% live in college housing, 6% have minority backgrounds, 2% are foreign students. Average age is 20.

FALL-TERM APPLICATIONS. $25 fee. No closing date; applicants notified on a rolling basis beginning on or about January 1. Deferred and early admission available.

STUDENT LIFE. Housing: Dormitories (men, women); apartment housing available. **Activities:** Student government, magazine, radio, student newspaper, yearbook, choral groups, concert band, drama, jazz band, marching band, music ensembles, musical theater, opera, pep band, Christian Workers Association, Circle-K, Civitans, Young Democrats, Young Republicans, Junior Chamber of Commerce, Sigma Society, Civinettes, campus ministries, Rotoract, Theta Chi.

ATHLETICS. NAIA. **Intercollegiate:** Baseball M, basketball M, softball W, volleyball W. **Intramural:** Archery, badminton, bowling, golf M, handball M, racquetball, softball, swimming, table tennis, tennis, wrestling M.

STUDENT SERVICES. Aptitude testing, career counseling, employment service for undergraduates, freshman orientation, health services,

on-campus day care, personal counseling, placement service for graduates, special adviser for adult students, veterans counselor.

ANNUAL EXPENSES. Tuition and fees (1992-93): $5,850. **Room and board:** $3,054. **Books and supplies:** $450. **Other expenses:** $650.

FINANCIAL AID. 95% of freshmen, 91% of continuing students receive some form of aid. Grants, loans, jobs available. **Aid applications:** No closing date; priority given to applications received by April 15; applicants notified on a rolling basis beginning on or about May 15; must reply within 4 weeks.

ADDRESS/TELEPHONE. Jan Forman, Dean of Enrollment Services, Trevecca Nazarene College, 333 Murfreesboro Road, Nashville, TN 37210. (615) 248-1320. Fax: (615) 248-7728.

Tusculum College

Greeneville, Tennessee — CB code: 1812

Admissions: 70% of applicants accepted
Based on: ••• School record, test scores
•• Essay, recommendations
• Activities, interview, special talents
Completion: 89% of freshmen end year in good standing
44% graduate, 20% of these enter graduate study

4-year private liberal arts college, coed, affiliated with Presbyterian Church (USA). Founded in 1794. **Accreditation:** Regional. **Undergraduate enrollment:** 438 men, 441 women full time; 19 men, 32 women part time. **Graduate enrollment:** 39 men, 71 women full time. **Faculty:** 88 total (25 full time), 55 with doctorates or other terminal degrees. **Location:** Rural campus in large town; 70 miles from Knoxville, 30 miles from Johnson City. **Calendar:** Semester, limited summer session. **Microcomputers:** 25 located in libraries, classrooms, computer centers. **Special facilities:** 3 special library collections, including Charles Coffin Collection (original college library), college archives, and Andrew Johnson Library and Museum.

DEGREES OFFERED. BA, BS, MEd. 360 bachelor's degrees awarded in 1992. 78% in business and management, 10% teacher education. Graduate degrees offered in 1 major field of study.

UNDERGRADUATE MAJORS. Biology, business and management, clinical laboratory science, communications, computer and information sciences, early childhood education, elementary education, English, English literature, environmental science, junior high education, mathematics/computer science, organizational behavior, physical education, predentistry, premedicine, prepharmacy, preveterinary, psychology, secondary education, social sciences, special education, telecommunications, visual and performing arts.

ACADEMIC PROGRAMS. Accelerated program, independent study, internships, student-designed major, teacher preparation. **Remedial services:** Learning center, reduced course load, remedial instruction, special counselor, tutoring. **Placement/credit:** AP, CLEP General and Subject; 30 credit hours maximum for bachelor's degree.

ACADEMIC REQUIREMENTS. Freshmen must earn minimum GPA of 1.75 to continue in good standing. 84% of freshmen return for sophomore year. Students must declare major by end of second year. **Graduation requirements:** 128 hours for bachelor's (38 in major). Most students required to take courses in arts/fine arts, computer science, English, foreign languages, history, mathematics, philosophy/religion, biological/physical sciences, social sciences. **Postgraduate studies:** 1% enter law school, 2% enter medical school, 5% enter MBA programs, 12% enter other graduate study.

FRESHMAN ADMISSIONS. Selection criteria: Applicant should rank in top half of class and have minimum 2.0 high school GPA. Conditional acceptances granted at discretion of Admissions and Academic Standards Committee. Recommended units include English 4, foreign language 2, mathematics 3, social science 2 and science 2. **Test requirements:** SAT or ACT; score report by August 15.

1992 FRESHMAN CLASS PROFILE. 359 men applied, 241 accepted, 81 enrolled; 203 women applied, 151 accepted, 57 enrolled. 28% had high school GPA of 3.0 or higher, 67% between 2.0 and 2.99. **Academic background:** Mid 50% of enrolled freshmen had SAT-V between 320-450, SAT-M between 370-510; ACT composite between 16-22. 44% submitted SAT scores, 73% submitted ACT scores. **Characteristics:** 50% from in state, 66% live in college housing, 29% have minority backgrounds, 1% are foreign students. Average age is 18.

FALL-TERM APPLICATIONS. No fee. No closing date; applicants notified on a rolling basis; must reply within 4 weeks. Essay required. Interview recommended. Deferred and early admission available.

STUDENT LIFE. Housing: Dormitories (men, women). **Activities:** Student government, radio, student newspaper, television, yearbook, choral groups, drama, Social Service Club, Student Christian Association, Bonwandi, Alpha Chi, Circle-K, biology club, Council for Exceptional Children, Students in Free Enterprise (SIFE).

ATHLETICS. NAIA. **Intercollegiate:** Baseball M, basketball, cross-country, football M, golf M, soccer, softball W, tennis, volleyball W. **Intramural:** Basketball, football M, golf, soccer, softball, swimming, tennis, volleyball.

STUDENT SERVICES. Career counseling, employment service for undergraduates, freshman orientation, health services, personal counseling, placement service for graduates, veterans counselor, peer counseling, services/facilities for handicapped.

ANNUAL EXPENSES. Tuition and fees (1992-93): $6,600. **Room and board:** $3,200. **Books and supplies:** $550. **Other expenses:** $800.

FINANCIAL AID. 95% of freshmen, 90% of continuing students receive some form of aid. 84% of grants, 59% of loans, all jobs based on need. 107 enrolled freshmen were judged to have need, all were offered aid. Academic, athletic scholarships available. **Aid applications:** No closing date; priority given to applications received by April 1; applicants notified on a rolling basis beginning on or about February 1; must reply within 2 weeks.

ADDRESS/TELEPHONE. Mark Stokes, Vice President Student/Auxillary Services, Tusculum College, Tusculum Station, Greeneville, TN 37743. (615) 636-7300 ext. 310. (800) 251-0256. Fax: (615) 638-7166.

Union University

Jackson, Tennessee — CB code: 1826

4-year private liberal arts college, coed, affiliated with Southern Baptist Convention. Founded in 1823. **Accreditation:** Regional. **Undergraduate enrollment:** 549 men, 988 women full time; 344 men and women part time. **Graduate enrollment:** 74 men and women full time; 7 men and women part time. **Faculty:** 147 total (119 full time), 46 with doctorates or other terminal degrees. **Location:** Suburban campus in small city; 80 miles from Memphis, 120 miles from Nashville. **Calendar:** 4-1-4, extensive summer session. Extensive evening/early morning classes. **Microcomputers:** 100 located in libraries, classrooms, computer centers. **Special facilities:** Aquatic center, fine and performing arts center, creative communications center and art gallery. **Additional facts:** Nursing program at satellite campus in Memphis.

DEGREES OFFERED. AS, BA, BS, MEd. 41 associate degrees awarded in 1992. 100% in health sciences. 330 bachelor's degrees awarded. 25% in business and management, 7% communications, 16% education, 8% health sciences, 9% life sciences, 6% physical sciences, 6% social sciences, 5% visual and performing arts. Graduate degrees offered in 18 major fields of study.

UNDERGRADUATE MAJORS. Associate: Nursing. **Bachelor's:** Accounting, advertising, American literature, art education, biology, business administration and management, business and management, business economics, business education, chemistry, clinical laboratory science, communications, computer and information sciences, computer programming, cytotechnology, dramatic arts, early childhood education, economics, education, elementary education, English, English education, English literature, finance, fine arts, foreign languages education, French, graphic design, Greek (classical), health care administration, health education, health sciences, history, journalism, junior high education, marketing and distributive education, marketing management, mathematics, mathematics education, medical laboratory technologies, medical records administration, music, music education, music performance, music/instrumental, music/piano, music/voice, nursing, optometry, pharmacy, philosophy, physical education, physical sciences, physical therapy, physics, podiatry or podiatric medicine, predentistry, preengineering, prelaw, premedicine, prepharmacy, preveterinary, psychology, public relations, radio/television broadcasting, religion, religious education, religious music, science education, secondary education, social science education, social sciences, social studies education, social work, sociology, Spanish, special education, speech, sports medicine, theological studies.

ACADEMIC PROGRAMS. Accelerated program, double major, honors program, independent study, internships, study abroad, teacher preparation, visiting/exchange student program, cross-registration; liberal arts/career combination in engineering, health sciences. **Remedial services:** Learning center, preadmission summer program, reduced course load, tutoring. **Placement/credit:** AP, CLEP Subject, institutional tests; 32 credit hours maximum for bachelor's degree.

ACADEMIC REQUIREMENTS. Freshmen must earn minimum GPA of 2.0 to continue in good standing. 89% of freshmen return for sophomore year. Students must declare major by end of first year. **Graduation requirements:** 128 hours for bachelor's (39 in major). Most students required to take courses in arts/fine arts, computer science, English, history, humanities, mathematics, philosophy/religion, biological/physical sciences, social sciences. **Postgraduate studies:** 5% enter law school, 5% enter medical school, 10% enter MBA programs, 20% enter other graduate study. **Additional information:** Special studies available for qualified students.

FRESHMAN ADMISSIONS. Selection criteria: Minimum ACT-20, combined SAT-820 and 2.5 GPA required for freshmen. **High school preparation:** 15 units required; 21 recommended. Required and recommended units include biological science 2-4, English 4, foreign language 2, mathematics 2-4, physical science 3 and social science 2-3. Science 3 recommended. Required units must be from among the following: natural science, social science, social science, English, mathematics. **Test requirements:** SAT or ACT (ACT preferred); score report by August 28.

1992 FRESHMAN CLASS PROFILE. 193 men, 445 women enrolled. **Characteristics:** 81% from in state, 51% commute, 8% have minority backgrounds, 1% are foreign students, 24% join fraternities/sororities. Average age is 18.

FALL-TERM APPLICATIONS. $10 fee. Closing date August 1; priority given to applications received by December 1; applicants notified on a rolling basis; must reply by May 1 or within 3 weeks if notified thereafter. Audition required for music applicants. Interview recommended. Portfolio recommended for art, communications applicants. Deferred and early admission available.

STUDENT LIFE. Housing: Dormitories (men, women); apartment housing available. All college housing is in private bedroom apartment units with shared living rooms. 82% have kitchens. **Activities:** Student government, magazine, radio, student newspaper, television, yearbook, choral groups, concert band, drama, jazz band, music ensembles, musical theater, opera, pep band, symphony orchestra, fraternities, sororities, Baptist Student Union, Baptist Young Women, Fellowship of Christian Athletes, Ministerial Association, Black Christian Fellowship, International Club, Student Activity Council. **Additional information:** Teams of students serve in area churches for weekend revivals.

ATHLETICS. NAIA. **Intercollegiate:** Baseball M, basketball, golf M, tennis. **Intramural:** Archery, badminton, basketball, bowling, cross-country, diving, golf, racquetball, skiing, soccer, softball, swimming, table tennis, tennis, volleyball.

STUDENT SERVICES. Aptitude testing, career counseling, employment service for undergraduates, freshman orientation, health services, personal counseling, placement service for graduates, veterans counselor, services/facilities for handicapped.

ANNUAL EXPENSES. Tuition and fees (1992-93): $4,900. **Room and board:** $2,630. **Books and supplies:** $500. **Other expenses:** $400.

FINANCIAL AID. 79% of freshmen, 77% of continuing students receive some form of aid. 71% of grants, 93% of loans, all jobs based on need. 294 enrolled freshmen were judged to have need, 275 were offered aid. Academic, music/drama, art, athletic, leadership, alumni affiliation scholarships available. **Aid applications:** Closing date August 1; priority given to applications received by May 15; applicants notified on a rolling basis beginning on or about June 15; must reply by May 1 or within 20 days if notified thereafter.

ADDRESS/TELEPHONE. Carroll Griffin, Director of Admissions, Union University, 2447 Highway 45 Bypass, North, Jackson, TN 38305. (901) 668-1818 ext. 206. Fax: (901) 668-3886.

University of the South
Sewanee, Tennessee — CB code: 1842

Admissions: 66% of applicants accepted
Based on:
••• School record
•• Activities, essay, recommendations, test scores
• Interview, special talents
Completion: 98% of freshmen end year in good standing
79% graduate, 30% of these enter graduate study

4-year private university and seminary college, coed, affiliated with Episcopal Church. Founded in 1857. **Accreditation:** Regional. **Undergraduate enrollment:** 586 men, 537 women full time; 5 men, 14 women part time. **Graduate enrollment:** 43 men, 25 women full time; 3 men, 1 woman part time. **Faculty:** 141 total (113 full time), 117 with doctorates or other terminal degrees. **Location:** Rural campus in small town; 45 miles from Chattanooga, 90 miles from Nashville. **Calendar:** Semester, limited summer session. **Microcomputers:** 45 located in dormitories, libraries, classrooms, computer centers. **Special facilities:** Art gallery, observatory, 10,000-acre wooded campus, 131,500 government documents in library.

DEGREES OFFERED. BA, BS, MA, D, M.Div. 236 bachelor's degrees awarded in 1992. 15% in letters/literature, 8% multi/interdisciplinary studies, 12% philosophy, religion, theology, 8% physical sciences, 8% psychology, 25% social sciences, 10% visual and performing arts. Graduate degrees offered in 3 major fields of study.

UNDERGRADUATE MAJORS. American studies, anthropology, art history, biological and physical sciences, biology, chemistry, classics, comparative literature, computer science and mathematics, dramatic arts, economics, English, English literature, fine arts, forestry and related sciences, French, geology, German, German studies, Greek (classical), history, humanities and social sciences, Latin, mathematics, medieval studies, music, philosophy, physics, political science and government, predentistry, preengineering, prelaw, premedicine, preveterinary, psychology, religion, renewable natural resources, Russian, Russian and Slavic studies, social science/foreign language, Spanish, studio art, Third World studies.

ACADEMIC PROGRAMS. Accelerated program, double major, honors program, independent study, internships, semester at sea, student-designed major, study abroad, teacher preparation, Washington semester, Oak Ridge semester in experimental science, summer science program on St. Catherines Island, Georgia; liberal arts/career combination in engineering, forestry. **Remedial services:** Special counselor, tutoring. **Placement/credit:** AP, institutional tests; 60 credit hours maximum for bachelor's degree.

ACADEMIC REQUIREMENTS. Freshmen must earn minimum GPA of 1.2 to continue in good standing. Freshmen must complete 18 semester hours and earn minimum 15 credits to remain in good standing. 98% of freshmen return for sophomore year. Students must declare major by end of second year. **Graduation requirements:** 123 hours for bachelor's (40 in major). Most students required to take courses in arts/fine arts, English, foreign languages, history, mathematics, philosophy/religion, biological/physical sciences, social sciences. **Postgraduate studies:** 8% enter law school, 4% enter medical school, 3% enter MBA programs, 15% enter other graduate study.

FRESHMAN ADMISSIONS. Selection criteria: School achievement record, recommendations, extracurricular activities, test scores, and essay. Some special consideration given to children of alumni and minority applicants. **High school preparation:** 15 units required. Required and recommended units include English 4, foreign language 2, mathematics 3-4, social science 2 and science 2. **Test requirements:** SAT or ACT; score report by February 1.

1992 FRESHMAN CLASS PROFILE. 765 men applied, 472 accepted, 165 enrolled; 654 women applied, 468 accepted, 169 enrolled. 66% had high school GPA of 3.0 or higher, 34% between 2.0 and 2.99. 45% were in top tenth and 77% were in top quarter of graduating class. **Academic background:** Mid 50% of enrolled freshmen had SAT-V between 500-610, SAT-M between 540-640; ACT composite between 24-28. 83% submitted SAT scores, 53% submitted ACT scores. **Characteristics:** 20% from in state, 100% live in college housing, 6% have minority backgrounds, 1% are foreign students, 60% join fraternities/sororities. Average age is 18.

FALL-TERM APPLICATIONS. $35 fee, may be waived for applicants with need. Closing date February 1; applicants notified on or about April 1; must reply by May 1. Essay required. Interview recommended. CRDA. Deferred and early admission available. EDP-F. Closing date for early decision applications November 15; notification date December 15.

STUDENT LIFE. Housing: Dormitories (men, women, coed); apartment housing available. German, French, Spanish, Russian language houses available. **Activities:** Student government, film, magazine, radio, student newspaper, yearbook, choral groups, dance, drama, jazz band, music ensembles, musical theater, pep band, symphony orchestra, fraternities, sororities, student-operated activities, tutoring center for disadvantaged youths, various religious organizations, Big Brother-Big Sister program. **Additional information:** Student-administered honor code strictly observed.

ATHLETICS. NCAA. **Intercollegiate:** Baseball M, basketball, cross-country, diving, fencing, field hockey W, football M, golf M, horseback riding, lacrosse M, rowing (crew), rugby M, skiing, soccer, softball W, swimming, tennis, track and field, volleyball W. **Intramural:** Basketball, cross-country, diving, golf, handball, racquetball, skin diving, soccer, softball, swimming, table tennis, tennis, track and field, volleyball, wrestling M.

STUDENT SERVICES. Aptitude testing, career counseling, employment service for undergraduates, freshman orientation, health services, on-campus day care, personal counseling, placement service for graduates, services/facilities for handicapped.

ANNUAL EXPENSES. Tuition and fees: $14,910. **Room and board:** $3,920. **Books and supplies:** $450. **Other expenses:** $810.

FINANCIAL AID. 62% of freshmen, 55% of continuing students receive some form of aid. 85% of grants, 98% of loans, 69% of jobs based on need. 158 enrolled freshmen were judged to have need, all were offered aid. Academic, leadership, religious affiliation, minority scholarships available. **Aid applications:** No closing date; priority given to applications received by March 1; applicants notified on a rolling basis beginning on or about April 1; must reply within 30 days.

ADDRESS/TELEPHONE. Robert M. Hedrick, Director of Admission, University of the South, 735 University Avenue, Sewanee, TN 37375-1000. (615) 598-1238. (800) 522-2234. Fax: (615) 598-1667.

University of Tennessee: Chattanooga
Chattanooga, Tennessee — CB code: 1831

Admissions: 66% of applicants accepted
Based on:
••• School record, test scores
• Essay, recommendations
Completion: 75% of freshmen end year in good standing
25% enter graduate study

4-year public university, coed. Founded in 1886. **Accreditation:** Regional. **Undergraduate enrollment:** 2,491 men, 2,758 women full time; 764 men, 1,011 women part time. **Graduate enrollment:** 122 men, 133 women full time; 380 men, 488 women part time. **Faculty:** 495 total (292 full time), 225 with doctorates or other terminal degrees. **Location:** Urban campus in large city; 130 miles from Nashville, 118 miles from Atlanta, Georgia. **Calendar:** Semester, extensive summer session. Extensive evening/early morning classes. **Microcomputers:** Located in dormitories, libraries, classrooms, computer centers. **Special facilities:** 2 art galleries, theater, observatory.

DEGREES OFFERED. BA, BS, BFA, MA, MS, MBA, MEd. 999 bachelor's degrees awarded in 1992. 29% in business and management, 15% teacher education, 5% engineering, 10% psychology, 12% social sciences. Graduate degrees offered in 43 major fields of study.

UNDERGRADUATE MAJORS. Accounting, actuarial sciences, advertising, American studies, anthropology, applied mathematics, art education, biological and physical sciences, biology, business administration and management, business and management, business economics, business home economics, chemical engineering, chemistry, civil engineering, classics, clinical laboratory science, communications, community services, computer and information sciences, criminal justice studies, dramatic arts, drawing, early childhood education, earth sciences, education, electrical/electronics/communications engineering, elementary education, engineering, engineering management, English, English education, English literature, environmental science, family/consumer resource management, finance, food production/management/services, food science and nutrition, foreign languages education, French, geology, Greek (classical), health education, history, home economics, humanities, humanities and social sciences, individual and family development, industrial engineering, information sciences and systems, journalism, Latin, law enforcement and corrections, liberal/general studies, management science, marketing management, mathematics, mathematics education, mechanical engineering, music, music education, music performance, music theory and composition, nursing, painting, personnel management, philosophy, physical education, physical sciences, physical therapy, physics, political science and government, predentistry, prelaw, premedicine, prepharmacy, preveterinary, psychology, public relations, radio/television broadcasting, religion, science education, sculpture, secondary education, social science education, social sciences, social work, sociology, Spanish, special education, speech, systems analysis, urban studies.

ACADEMIC PROGRAMS. Cooperative education, double major, dual enrollment of high school students, honors program, independent study, internships, study abroad, teacher preparation, cooperative program in criminal justice with Cleveland State Community College. **Remedial services:** Learning center, reduced course load, remedial instruction, special counselor, tutoring, college access program for learning disabled students. **ROTC:** Army. **Placement/credit:** AP, CLEP Subject, institutional tests; 30 credit hours maximum for bachelor's degree.

ACADEMIC REQUIREMENTS. Freshmen must earn minimum GPA of 1.0 to continue in good standing. 70% of freshmen return for sophomore year. Students must declare major by end of second year. **Graduation requirements:** 128 hours for bachelor's (35 in major). Most students required to take courses in arts/fine arts, English, mathematics, biological/physical sciences, social sciences.

FRESHMAN ADMISSIONS. Selection criteria: High school curriculum and GPA (minimum 2.75), test scores, special talents, recommendations, essay or personal statement considered. Conditional admission for those with GPA between 2.0 and 2.74 and SAT combined score between 640 and 899 or ACT composite score between 12 and 19. **High school preparation:** 13 units required; 15 recommended. Required and recommended units include English 4, foreign language 2, mathematics 3, social science 2 and science 2. Biological science 2 and physical science 2 recommended. Foreign language units must be in same language. Social science units should be US history and World/European history or World geography. 2 required science units must be laboratory sciences. **Test requirements:** SAT or ACT (ACT preferred); score report by August 27.

1992 FRESHMAN CLASS PROFILE. 1,887 men and women applied, 1,251 accepted; 370 men enrolled, 455 women enrolled. **Characteristics:** 85% from in state, 83% commute, 18% have minority backgrounds, 1% are foreign students, 6% join fraternities/sororities. Average age is 20.

FALL-TERM APPLICATIONS. $15 fee. Closing date August 1; applicants notified on a rolling basis; must reply by registration. Essay recommended. Early admission available.

STUDENT LIFE. Housing: Dormitories (women, coed); apartment, fraternity housing available. Housing with different types of programming and supervision provided. **Activities:** Student government, magazine, radio, student newspaper, yearbook, choral groups, concert band, dance, drama, jazz band, marching band, music ensembles, musical theater, opera, pep band, symphony orchestra, fraternities, sororities, several religious, political, ethnic, and social service organizations.

ATHLETICS. NCAA. **Intercollegiate:** Basketball, cross-country, football M, golf, rifle, rowing (crew), tennis, track and field, volleyball W, wrestling M. **Intramural:** Badminton, baseball M, basketball, fencing, golf, racquetball, soccer, softball W, swimming, tennis, track and field, volleyball, water polo, wrestling M.

STUDENT SERVICES. Aptitude testing, career counseling, employment service for undergraduates, freshman orientation, health services, on-campus day care, personal counseling, placement service for graduates, special adviser for adult students, veterans counselor, adult services center, services/facilities for handicapped.

ANNUAL EXPENSES. Tuition and fees (1992-93): $1,670, $3,600 additional for out-of-state students. **Room and board:** $1,390 room only. **Books and supplies:** $525. **Other expenses:** $850.

FINANCIAL AID. 70% of freshmen, 50% of continuing students receive some form of aid. Academic, music/drama, art, athletic, leadership, alumni affiliation, minority scholarships available. **Aid applications:** No closing date; priority given to applications received by March 1; applicants notified on a rolling basis beginning on or about July 1; must reply within 3 weeks.

ADDRESS/TELEPHONE. Patsy Reynolds, Director of Admissions, University of Tennessee: Chattanooga, 615 McCallie Avenue, Chattanooga, TN 37403. (615) 755-4662. (800) 882-6627. Fax: (615) 755-4025.

University of Tennessee: Knoxville
Knoxville, Tennessee

CB code: 1843

4-year public university, coed. Founded in 1794. **Accreditation:** Regional. **Undergraduate enrollment:** 8,662 men, 7,687 women full time; 1,433 men, 1,560 women part time. **Graduate enrollment:** 1,751 men, 1,785 women full time; 1,531 men, 1,589 women part time. **Faculty:** 1,155 total (1,110 full time). **Location:** Urban campus in large city; 224 miles from Atlanta, Georgia, 178 miles from Nashville. **Calendar:** Semester, extensive summer session. Extensive evening/early morning classes. **Microcomputers:** 1,500 located in dormitories, libraries, classrooms, computer centers. **Special facilities:** Museum, 2 theaters.

DEGREES OFFERED. BA, BS, BFA, BArch, MA, MS, MBA, MFA, MSW, PhD, EdD, DVM, JD. 3,308 bachelor's degrees awarded in 1992. 22% in business and management, 5% communications, 8% teacher education, 10% engineering, 5% letters/literature, 6% psychology, 14% social sciences. Graduate degrees offered in 96 major fields of study.

UNDERGRADUATE MAJORS. Accounting, advertising, aerospace/aeronautical/astronautical engineering, Afro-American (black) studies, agribusiness, agricultural economics, agricultural engineering, American studies, ancient Mediterranean civilizations, animal sciences, anthropology, architecture, art education, art history, Asian studies, biochemistry, biology, botany, business administration and management, business and management, business economics, business education, business statistics, chemical engineering, chemistry, child development/care/guidance, cinematography/film, civil engineering, classics, clinical laboratory science, clothing and textiles management/production/services, community services, comparative literature, computer and information sciences, creative writing, cultural studies, dance, dramatic arts, Eastern European studies, economics, electrical/electronics/communications engineering, elementary education, engineering physics, engineering science, English, English education, English literature, finance, fishing and fisheries, food science and nutrition, food sciences, foreign languages education, forestry and related sciences, French, geography, geology, German, graphic design, health education, history, home economics, home economics education, hotel/motel and restaurant management, human services, illustration design, industrial arts education, industrial engineering, interior design, international business management, Italian, journalism, Latin American studies, linguistics, marketing and distribution, marketing and distributive education, marketing research, materials science, mathematics, mathematics education, mechanical engineering, medical records administration, medieval studies, microbiology, music, music education, nuclear engineering, nursing, nutritional sciences, ornamental horticulture, personnel management, philosophy, physical education, physics, plant sciences, political science and government, practical nursing, precytotechnology, predentistry, premedicine, prepharmacy, preveterinary, psychology, public administration, radio/television broadcasting, recreation and community services technologies, religion, Russian, Russian and Slavic studies, science education, secondary education, Slavic languages, social science education, social studies education, social work, sociology, soil sciences, Spanish, special education, speech, speech pathology/audiology, statistics, studio art, technical education, textiles and clothing, trade and industrial education, transportation management, urban studies, vocational-technical education, wildlife management, women's studies, zoology.

ACADEMIC PROGRAMS. Cooperative education, double major, dual enrollment of high school students, education specialist degree, honors program, independent study, internships, student-designed major, study abroad, teacher preparation, visiting/exchange student program, cross-registration; liberal arts/career combination in health sciences; combined bachelor's/graduate program in business administration, medicine, law. **Remedial services:** Tutoring. **ROTC:** Air Force, Army. **Placement/credit:** AP, CLEP General and Subject, institutional tests; 25 credit hours maximum for bachelor's degree.

ACADEMIC REQUIREMENTS. Freshmen must earn minimum GPA of 2.0 to continue in good standing. 81% of freshmen return for sophomore year. Students must declare major by end of second year. **Graduation requirements:** 124 hours for bachelor's (50 in major). Most students required to take courses in arts/fine arts, English, foreign languages, history, humanities, mathematics, philosophy/religion, biological/physical sciences, social sciences.

FRESHMAN ADMISSIONS. Selection criteria: Automatic admission for in-state applicants with 2.75 high school GPA and SAT combined score of 720 or ACT composite score of 18. Others admitted according to scale of high school GPA and test scores. Out-of-state applicants must have minimum 2.25 high school GPA. Required test score determined by GPA. **High school preparation:** 13 units required. Required units include English 4, foreign language 2, mathematics 3, social science 2 and science 2. Social science units must be 1 US history and either world history, European history, or world geography. Mathematics units must include algebra I, algebra II, and 1 unit of either geometry, trigonometry, advanced mathematics, or calculus. One unit of fine or performing arts required. Sciences include 2 units of a natural science of which one must be a laboratory science. **Test requirements:** SAT or ACT; score report by July 1. **Additional information:** Students must be admitted by February 1 prior to fall entry term to be considered for academic scholarships. Students may apply for housing at the same time they apply for admissions.

1992 FRESHMAN CLASS PROFILE. 1,618 men, 1,601 women enrolled. 59% had high school GPA of 3.0 or higher, 39% between 2.0 and 2.99. 27% were in top tenth and 53% were in top quarter of graduating class. **Academic background:** Mid 50% of enrolled freshmen had SAT-V between 410-530, SAT-M between 460-590; ACT composite between 20-26. 45% submitted SAT scores, 85% submitted ACT scores. **Characteristics:** 82% from in state, 76% live in college housing, 10% have minority backgrounds, 1% are foreign students. Average age is 19.

FALL-TERM APPLICATIONS. $15 fee, may be waived for applicants with need. Closing date July 1; priority given to applications received by February 1; applicants notified on a rolling basis. Audition required for music applicants. Essay required for architecture review applicants. Interview recommended for marginally prepared, reentry applicants. Portfolio recommended for architecture review applicants. Questionnaire required for applicants not meeting automatic admissions requirements. Early admission available.

STUDENT LIFE. Housing: Dormitories (men, women, coed); apartment, fraternity housing available. Foreign language housing available. Freshmen must live on campus unless residing with parent or legal guardian. **Activities:** Student government, film, magazine, radio, student newspaper, television, yearbook, choral groups, concert band, dance, drama, jazz band, marching band, music ensembles, musical theater, opera, pep band, symphony orchestra, fraternities, sororities, Black Cultural Center, variety of student political, ethnic, social, and service organizations, women's center.

ATHLETICS. NCAA. **Intercollegiate:** Baseball M, basketball, cross-country, diving, football M, golf, swimming, tennis, track and field, volleyball W. **Intramural:** Badminton, basketball, bowling, cross-country, golf, skin diving, soccer, softball, swimming, table tennis, tennis, track and field, volleyball. **Clubs:** Gymnastics, handball, equestrian, ice hockey, lacrosse, racquetball, rowing, rugby, sailing.

STUDENT SERVICES. Aptitude testing, career counseling, employment service for undergraduates, freshman orientation, health services, on-campus day care, personal counseling, placement service for graduates, special adviser for adult students, veterans counselor, services/facilities for handicapped.

ANNUAL EXPENSES. Tuition and fees (1992-93): $1,898, $3,600 additional for out-of-state students. **Room and board:** $3,166. **Books and supplies:** $760. **Other expenses:** $1,432.

FINANCIAL AID. 50% of freshmen, 50% of continuing students receive some form of aid. 68% of grants, 92% of loans, 44% of jobs based on need. 1,536 enrolled freshmen were judged to have need, 1,284 were offered aid. Academic, music/drama, art, athletic, state/district residency, leadership, alumni affiliation, minority scholarships available. **Aid applications:** No closing date; priority given to applications received by April 1; applicants notified on a rolling basis beginning on or about April 1; must reply within 3 weeks. **Additional information:** Application priority date for scholarships February 1.

ADDRESS/TELEPHONE. Gordon Stanley, Director of Admissions, University of Tennessee: Knoxville, 320 Student Services Building, Knoxville, TN 37996-0230. (615) 974-2184.

University of Tennessee: Martin

Martin, Tennessee — CB code: 1844

Admissions:	92% of applicants accepted
Based on:	••• School record, test scores
	• Activities, essay, interview, recommendations
Completion:	70% of freshmen end year in good standing
	25% graduate, 25% of these enter graduate study

4-year public university, coed. Founded in 1927. **Accreditation:** Regional. **Undergraduate enrollment:** 2,149 men, 2,542 women full time; 256 men, 449 women part time. **Graduate enrollment:** 14 men, 14 women full time; 54 men, 149 women part time. **Faculty:** 270 total (220 full time), 140 with doctorates or other terminal degrees. **Location:** Rural campus in small town; 130 miles from Memphis, 56 miles from Paducah, Kentucky. **Calendar:** Semester, extensive summer session. **Microcomputers:** Located in dormitories, classrooms, computer centers. **Special facilities:** Museum archives, nature preserve at Realfoot Lake State Resort. **Additional facts:** Campus listed in National Botanical Register. Courses maybe taken at 20 off-campus sites.

DEGREES OFFERED. BA, BS, BFA, MS, MBA, MEd. 620 bachelor's degrees awarded in 1992. 8% in agriculture, 25% business and management, 5% communications, 21% teacher education, 6% life sciences, 9% parks/recreation, protective services, public affairs. Graduate degrees offered in 5 major fields of study.

UNDERGRADUATE MAJORS. Accounting, agribusiness, agricultural education, agricultural sciences, animal sciences, art education, biology, business administration and management, business economics, business education, chemistry, civil technology, computer and information sciences, conservation and regulation, criminal justice studies, dance, dramatic arts, early childhood education, economics, electrical technology, elementary education, English, English education, finance, foreign languages education, French, geography, geology, German, history, home economics, home economics education, international business management, international studies, journalism, management information systems, marketing management, mathematics, mathematics education, mechanical design technology, music, music education, music performance, nursing, office supervision and management, parks and recreation management, physical education, plant sciences, political science and government, predentistry, premedicine, prepharmacy, preveterinary, psychology, public administration, public relations, radio/television broadcasting, renewable natural resources, science education, social studies education, social work, sociology, soil sciences, Spanish, studio art, wildlife management.

ACADEMIC PROGRAMS. 2-year transfer program, cooperative education, double major, dual enrollment of high school students, honors program, independent study, internships, student-designed major, study abroad, teacher preparation, visiting/exchange student program. **Remedial services:** Learning center, reduced course load, remedial instruction, special counselor, tutoring, qualified admissions program. **ROTC:** Army. **Placement/credit:** AP, CLEP General and Subject, institutional tests; 30 credit hours maximum for bachelor's degree.

ACADEMIC REQUIREMENTS. Freshmen must earn minimum GPA of 2.0 to continue in good standing. 70% of freshmen return for sophomore year. Students must declare major by end of second year. **Graduation requirements:** 130 hours for bachelor's. Most students required to take courses in computer science, English, humanities, mathematics, biological/physical sciences, social sciences.

FRESHMAN ADMISSIONS. Selection criteria: School achievement record and test scores. 2.6 GPA or minimum ACT composite score of 19 or equivalent SAT score. **High school preparation:** 14 units required. Required units include English 4, foreign language 2, mathematics 3 and social science 2. Requirements include algebra I and II plus additional unit in geometry or advanced mathematics; 1 laboratory course in biology, chemistry, or physics; 1 U.S. history and additional unit in European history, world history, or geography, 2 units in natural sciences, and 1 unit in fine or performing arts. **Test requirements:** SAT or ACT (ACT preferred); score report by August 1.

1992 FRESHMAN CLASS PROFILE. 800 men applied, 740 accepted, 474 enrolled; 900 women applied, 820 accepted, 654 enrolled. 59% had high school GPA of 3.0 or higher, 40% between 2.0 and 2.99. **Academic background:** Mid 50% of enrolled freshmen had ACT composite between 12-26. 95% submitted ACT scores. **Characteristics:** 96% from in state, 85% live in college housing, 37% have minority backgrounds, 2% are foreign students, 12% join fraternities/sororities. Average age is 18.

FALL-TERM APPLICATIONS. $10 fee. Closing date August 8; priority given to applications received by August 1; applicants notified on a rolling basis; must reply within 2 weeks. Early admission available. Institutional early decision plan.

STUDENT LIFE. Housing: Dormitories (men, women, coed); apartment, fraternity housing available. Freshmen must live on campus. Honors floors available. Both limited and no open house hours housing available. **Activities:** Student government, radio, student newspaper, television, yearbook, choral groups, concert band, dance, drama, jazz band, marching band, music ensembles, musical theater, opera, pep band, symphony orchestra, fraternities, sororities, 90 social and service organizations.

ATHLETICS. NCAA. **Intercollegiate:** Baseball M, basketball, cross-country, football M, golf M, rifle, softball W, tennis, volleyball W. **Intramural:** Badminton, basketball, bowling, diving, fencing, field hockey, golf M, gymnastics, handball, racquetball, skin diving, soccer, softball, swimming, table tennis, tennis, track and field, volleyball, wrestling.

STUDENT SERVICES. Career counseling, employment service for undergraduates, freshman orientation, health services, on-campus day care, personal counseling, placement service for graduates, special adviser for adult students, veterans counselor, services/facilities for handicapped.

ANNUAL EXPENSES. Tuition and fees (1992-93): $1,728, $3,600 additional for out-of-state students. **Room and board:** $2,830. **Books and supplies:** $640. **Other expenses:** $1,591.

FINANCIAL AID. 65% of freshmen, 55% of continuing students receive some form of aid. 68% of grants, 78% of loans, 33% of jobs based on need. Academic, music/drama, athletic, leadership, minority scholarships available. **Aid applications:** No closing date; priority given to applications received by March 1; applicants notified on a rolling basis beginning on or about May 1; must reply within 2 weeks.

ADDRESS/TELEPHONE. Paul Kelley, Executive Director of Admissions and Records, University of Tennessee: Martin, Admin Bldng Room 201, Martin, TN 38238. (901) 587-7020. (800) 829-8861.

University of Tennessee: Memphis

Memphis, Tennessee CB code: 1850

2-year upper-division public health science college, coed. Founded in 1911. **Accreditation:** Regional. **Undergraduate enrollment:** 60 men, 337 women full time; 3 men, 21 women part time. **Graduate enrollment:** 862 men, 580 women full time; 5 men, 84 women part time. **Faculty:** 992 total (798 full time), 991 with doctorates or other terminal degrees. **Location:** Urban campus in very large city; 220 miles from Nashville, 299 miles from St. Louis, Missouri. **Calendar:** Semester, limited summer session. **Microcomputers:** 100 located in libraries, classrooms, computer centers.

DEGREES OFFERED. BS, MS, PhD, DDS, MD, Pharm D. 228 bachelor's degrees awarded in 1992. 45% in health sciences, 55% allied health. Graduate degrees offered in 16 major fields of study.

UNDERGRADUATE MAJORS. Cytotechnology, dental hygiene, medical laboratory technologies, medical records administration, medical records technology, nursing, occupational therapy, physical therapy.

ACADEMIC PROGRAMS. Accelerated program, internships, telecourses, visiting/exchange student program, cross-registration. **Remedial services:** Learning center, preadmission summer program, reduced course load, special counselor, tutoring.

ACADEMIC REQUIREMENTS. Students must declare major on application. **Graduation requirements:** 198 hours for bachelor's. Most students required to take courses in English, history, biological/physical sciences, social sciences.

STUDENT LIFE. Housing: Dormitories (coed); fraternity housing available. **Activities:** Student government, student newspaper, yearbook, fraternities, sororities, Baptist Student Union, United Methodist Fellowship, Catholic Student Association, Black Student Association, International Student Association.

ATHLETICS. Intramural: Badminton, basketball, bowling, golf, handball, racquetball, soccer, softball, squash, swimming, table tennis, tennis, volleyball, water polo.

STUDENT SERVICES. Career counseling, employment service for undergraduates, health services, personal counseling, placement service for graduates, services/facilities for handicapped.

ANNUAL EXPENSES. Tuition and fees (1992-93): $1,686, $3,600 additional for out-of-state students. **Room and board:** $3,970. **Books and supplies:** $1,097. **Other expenses:** $1,527.

FINANCIAL AID. 68% of continuing students receive some form of aid. 97% of grants, 83% of loans, all jobs based on need. Academic, minority scholarships available. **Aid applications:** No closing date; priority given to applications received by February 15; applicants notified on a rolling basis beginning on or about April 15; must reply within 2 weeks. **Additional information:** Scholarships available to defray out-of-state portion of fees charged to out-of-state minority students.

ADDRESS/TELEPHONE. Nelson Strother, Assistant Vice Chancellor Enrollment Management, University of Tennessee: Memphis, 800 Madison Avenue, Memphis, TN 38163. (901) 528-5560. Fax: (901) 528-7585.

Vanderbilt University

Nashville, Tennessee CB code: 1871

Admissions:	58% of applicants accepted
Based on:	••• School record
	•• Essay, recommendations, test scores
	• Activities, special talents
Completion:	94% of freshmen end year in good standing
	80% graduate, 70% of these enter graduate study

4-year private university, coed. Founded in 1873. **Accreditation:** Regional. **Undergraduate enrollment:** 2,867 men, 2,636 women full time; 44 men, 32 women part time. **Graduate enrollment:** 1,975 men, 1,578 women full time; 205 men, 387 women part time. **Faculty:** 1,861 total (1,590 full time), 1,542 with doctorates or other terminal degrees. **Location:** Urban campus in large city; 240 miles from Atlanta, Georgia, 300 miles from St. Louis, Missouri. **Calendar:** Semester, limited summer session. Saturday and extensive evening/early morning classes. **Microcomputers:** 400 located in dormitories, libraries, classrooms, computer centers. **Special facilities:** 2 observatories, free electron laser, electron microscopes, television news archive, national arboretum, 3 art galleries.

DEGREES OFFERED. BA, BS, MA, MS, MBA, MEd, PhD, EdD, MD, M.Div. 1,236 bachelor's degrees awarded in 1992. 17% in engineering, 8% letters/literature, 5% life sciences, 5% mathematics, 16% psychology, 26% social sciences. Graduate degrees offered in 69 major fields of study.

UNDERGRADUATE MAJORS. Afro-American (black) studies, anthropology, bioengineering and biomedical engineering, biology, chemical engineering, chemistry, civil engineering, classics, communications, computer and information sciences, dramatic arts, early childhood education, East Asian studies, economics, education, education of the mentally handicapped, education of the multiple handicapped, electrical/electronics/communications engineering, elementary education, engineering, engineering science, English, European studies, fine arts, French, geology, German, history, human resources development, Latin American studies, liberal/general studies, linguistics, mathematics, mechanical engineering, molecular biology, music history and appreciation, music performance, music theory and composition, philosophy, physics, physics/astronomy, political science and government, Portuguese, psychology, public policy studies, religion, Russian, secondary education, sociology, Spanish, special education, urban studies, visual and performing arts.

ACADEMIC PROGRAMS. Accelerated program, double major, dual enrollment of high school students, education specialist degree, external degree, honors program, independent study, internships, student-designed major, study abroad, teacher preparation, visiting/exchange student program, weekend college, Washington semester, cross-registration; liberal arts/career combination in engineering; combined bachelor's/graduate program in business administration, medicine, law. **Remedial services:** Learning center, special counselor, tutoring. **ROTC:** Air Force, Army, Naval. **Placement/credit:** AP, institutional tests; 30 credit hours maximum for bachelor's degree.

ACADEMIC REQUIREMENTS. Freshmen must earn minimum GPA of 1.8 to continue in good standing. 90% of freshmen return for sophomore year. Students must declare major by end of second year. **Graduation requirements:** 120 hours for bachelor's (27 in major). Most students required to take courses in English, foreign languages, history, humanities, mathematics, biological/physical sciences, social sciences. **Postgraduate studies:** 16% enter law school, 8% enter medical school, 14% enter MBA programs, 32% enter other graduate study. **Additional information:** All undergraduates take portion of course work in College of Arts and Science.

FRESHMAN ADMISSIONS. Selection criteria: Academic achievement, class rank, recommendation, test scores, activities. **High school preparation:** 15 units required. Required and recommended units include English 4, foreign language 2 and mathematics 3. Social science 1 and science 1 recommended. Additional unit in mathematics and 2 in science recommended for engineering applicants. **Test requirements:** SAT or ACT (SAT preferred); score report by February 15. 3 ACH (including English Composition and Mathematics Level I, II, or IIC) required of all applicants. Foreign language ACH recommended for liberal arts applicants, science ACH recommended for engineering applicants. Score report by February 15.

1992 FRESHMAN CLASS PROFILE. 3,926 men applied, 2,321 accepted, 767 enrolled; 3,627 women applied, 2,054 accepted, 641 enrolled. 84% had high school GPA of 3.0 or higher, 15% between 2.0 and 2.99. 64% were in top tenth and 90% were in top quarter of graduating class. **Academic background:** Mid 50% of enrolled freshmen had SAT-V between 510-610, SAT-M between 580-690; ACT composite between 25-30. 95% submitted SAT scores, 53% submitted ACT scores. **Characteristics:** 13% from in state, 99% live in college housing, 13% have minority backgrounds, 1% are foreign students, 50% join fraternities/sororities. Average age is 18.

FALL-TERM APPLICATIONS. $50 fee, may be waived for applicants with need. No closing date; priority given to applications received by January 15; applicants notified on a rolling basis beginning on or about April 1. Audition required for music applicants. Essay required. CRDA. Deferred and early admission available. EDP-F. Applications for education, engineering, and music accepted after February 1 if space available. January 15 priority date for engineering, music and Peabody College.

STUDENT LIFE. Housing: Dormitories (men, women, coed); apartment, handicapped housing available. McTyeire International House designed for students with strong interest in foreign languages, McGill dormitory for students with interest in philosophy, Mayfield living/learning centers for students with any common interests. **Activities:** Student government, film, magazine, radio, student newspaper, television, yearbook, choral groups, concert band, dance, drama, jazz band, marching band, music ensembles, musical theater, opera, pep band, symphony orchestra, fraternities, sororities, 247 campus organizations including Campus Crusade for Christ, Jewish Student Union, College Republicans, Young Democrats, Hispanic Student Association, Habitat for Humanity, NAACP, Asian-American Students Association, Vanderbilt Women's Political Caucus, Alternative Spring Break Volunteer Program.

ATHLETICS. NCAA. **Intercollegiate:** Baseball M, basketball, cross-country, football M, golf, soccer, tennis. **Intramural:** Badminton, basketball, bowling, diving, field hockey W, golf, racquetball, soccer, softball, squash, swimming, table tennis, tennis, track and field, volleyball, water polo, wrestling.

STUDENT SERVICES. Aptitude testing, career counseling, employment service for undergraduates, freshman orientation, health services, on-campus day care, personal counseling, placement service for graduates, women's center, black cultural center, services/facilities for handicapped.

ANNUAL EXPENSES. Tuition and fees: $17,202. **Room and board:** $6,220. **Books and supplies:** $550. **Other expenses:** $550.

FINANCIAL AID. 49% of freshmen, 46% of continuing students receive some form of aid. 75% of grants, 97% of loans, 26% of jobs based on need. 516 enrolled freshmen were judged to have need, all were offered aid. Academic, music/drama, athletic, state/district residency, minority scholarships available. **Aid applications:** No closing date; priority given to applications received by February 15; applicants notified on a rolling basis beginning on or about April 1; must reply by May 1 or within 2 weeks if notified thereafter. **Additional information:** Various payment plans available.

ADDRESS/TELEPHONE. Neill F. Sanders, Dean of Undergraduate Admissions, Vanderbilt University, 2305 West End Avenue, Nashville, TN 37203-1700. (615) 322-2561. Fax: (615) 343-7765.

Volunteer State Community College
Gallatin, Tennessee CB code: 1881

2-year public community college, coed. Founded in 1970. **Accreditation:** Regional. **Undergraduate enrollment:** 1,046 men, 1,486 women full time; 828 men, 1,858 women part time. **Faculty:** 276 total (102 full time), 22 with doctorates or other terminal degrees. **Location:** Suburban campus in large town; 25 miles from downtown Nashville. **Calendar:** Semester, limited summer session. Saturday and extensive evening/early morning classes. **Microcomputers:** 170 located in classrooms.

DEGREES OFFERED. AA, AS, AAS. 225 associate degrees awarded in 1992. 18% in business and management, 7% teacher education, 33% allied health, 34% multi/interdisciplinary studies.

UNDERGRADUATE MAJORS. Business and management, business data processing and related programs, communications, dental assistant, elementary education, emergency medical technologies, engineering, fine arts, humanities, legal assistant/paralegal, liberal/general studies, marketing and distribution, medical records technology, physical therapy assistant, predentistry, premedicine, prepharmacy, preveterinary, radiograph medical technology, respiratory therapy, secondary education.

ACADEMIC PROGRAMS. 2-year transfer program, double major, dual enrollment of high school students, honors program, independent study, telecourses. **Remedial services:** Learning center, reduced course load, remedial instruction, special counselor, tutoring. **Placement/credit:** AP, CLEP General and Subject, institutional tests; 12 credit hours maximum for associate degree.

ACADEMIC REQUIREMENTS. Freshmen must earn minimum GPA of 2.0 to continue in good standing. 59% of freshmen return for sophomore year. Students must declare major on enrollment. **Graduation requirements:** 67 hours for associate (43 in major). Most students required to take courses in arts/fine arts, computer science, English, history, humanities, mathematics, biological/physical sciences, social sciences.

FRESHMAN ADMISSIONS. Selection criteria: Open admissions. Allied health students screened into programs after completing designated amount of college course work. Screening based on GPA and interview. **High school preparation:** 14 units required. Required units include English 4, foreign language 2, mathematics 3, physical science 2 and social science 1. One unit in US history and 1 unit in visual and/or performing arts also required. **Test requirements:** ACT for placement and counseling only; score report by August 30.

1992 FRESHMAN CLASS PROFILE. 373 men, 594 women enrolled. **Characteristics:** 94% from in state, 100% commute, 9% have minority backgrounds. Average age is 21.

FALL-TERM APPLICATIONS. $5 fee. Closing date August 20; applicants notified on a rolling basis. Interview required for allied health applicants. Deferred and early admission available.

STUDENT LIFE. Activities: Student government, radio, student newspaper, choral groups, drama, Baptist Student Union, African-American Student Union, Gamma Beta Phi, Student Government Association, Returning Women's Organization.

ATHLETICS. NJCAA. **Intercollegiate:** Baseball M, basketball. **Intramural:** Basketball, volleyball.

STUDENT SERVICES. Aptitude testing, career counseling, employment service for undergraduates, freshman orientation, health services, personal counseling, placement service for graduates, veterans counselor, services/facilities for handicapped.

ANNUAL EXPENSES. Tuition and fees (1992-93): $910, $2,600 additional for out-of-state students. **Books and supplies:** $500. **Other expenses:** $400.

FINANCIAL AID. 40% of continuing students receive some form of aid. 85% of grants, 79% of loans, 63% of jobs based on need. Academic, athletic, minority scholarships available. **Aid applications:** No closing date; priority given to applications received by April 15; applicants notified on a rolling basis beginning on or about July 1; must reply within 2 weeks.

ADDRESS/TELEPHONE. Janice R. Roark, Dir, Admissions and Records, Volunteer State Community College, 1360 Nashville Pike, Gallatin, TN 37066. (615) 452-8600. Fax: (615) 452-8600 ext. 502.

Walters State Community College
Morristown, Tennessee CB code: 1893

2-year public community college, coed. Founded in 1970. **Accreditation:** Regional. **Undergraduate enrollment:** 973 men, 1,522 women full time; 1,181 men, 1,751 women part time. **Faculty:** 253 total (111 full time), 27 with doctorates or other terminal degrees. **Location:** Suburban campus in large town; 45 miles from Knoxville. **Calendar:** Semester, extensive summer session. **Microcomputers:** 100 located in libraries, classrooms.

DEGREES OFFERED. AA, AS, AAS. 384 associate degrees awarded in 1992. 11% in business and management, 6% computer sciences, 38% health sciences, 28% multi/interdisciplinary studies, 6% parks/recreation, protective services, public affairs.

UNDERGRADUATE MAJORS. Agricultural sciences, business and management, business and office, business data processing and related programs, child development/care/guidance, computer and information sciences, education, elementary education, engineering, environmental science, fine arts, horticultural science, industrial technology, law enforcement and corrections technologies, liberal/general studies, medical laboratory technologies, music, nursing, ornamental horticulture, physical therapy assistant, prechiropractic, predentistry, premedical technology, premedicine, preoptometric, prepharmacy, radiograph medical technology, secondary education, secretarial and related programs.

ACADEMIC PROGRAMS. 2-year transfer program, honors program, telecourses. **Remedial services:** Remedial instruction, special counselor, tutoring. **ROTC:** Army. **Placement/credit:** AP, CLEP Subject, institutional tests.

ACADEMIC REQUIREMENTS. Graduated GPA requirements used to determine good academic standing. 56% of freshmen return for sophomore year. Students must declare major on application. **Graduation requirements:** 64 hours for associate. Most students required to take courses in computer science, English, humanities, mathematics, biological/physical sciences, social sciences.

FRESHMAN ADMISSIONS. Selection criteria: Open admissions. Selective admissions to nursing, criminal justice, and education programs. College-preparatory program required for 2-year transfer program: 1 unit biological science, 4 English, 2 foreign language, 3 mathematics, 1 physical science, 2 social science, 1 visual or performing arts. Same preparation recommended for all students. **Test requirements:** SAT or ACT for placement; score report by August 1. ACT not required of applicants 21 years of age or older, but must take Academic Assessment Placement Program Test. Placement test required for applicants with ACT scores below 18.

1992 FRESHMAN CLASS PROFILE. 358 men, 551 women enrolled. **Characteristics:** 99% from in state, 100% commute, 4% have minority backgrounds.

FALL-TERM APPLICATIONS. $5 fee. No closing date; applicants notified on a rolling basis. Early admission available.

STUDENT LIFE. Activities: Student government, student newspaper, choral groups, drama.

ATHLETICS. NJCAA. **Intercollegiate:** Baseball M, basketball. **Intramural:** Basketball, softball, tennis, volleyball.

STUDENT SERVICES. Career counseling, employment service for undergraduates, health services, personal counseling, placement service for graduates, veterans counselor, services/facilities for handicapped.

ANNUAL EXPENSES. Tuition and fees (1992-93): $910, $2,600 additional for out-of-state students. **Books and supplies:** $500. **Other expenses:** $900.

FINANCIAL AID. 15% of freshmen, 23% of continuing students receive some form of aid. 87% of grants, 84% of loans, 69% of jobs based on need. 325 enrolled freshmen were judged to have need, 320 were offered aid. Academic, music/drama, athletic, leadership, alumni affiliation, religious affiliation, minority scholarships available. **Aid applications:** No closing date; priority given to applications received by March 31; applicants notified on a rolling basis beginning on or about May 15; must reply within 3 weeks.

ADDRESS/TELEPHONE. Dr. R. Lynn Gilmore, Dean of Admissions, Walters State Community College, 500 South Davy Crockett Parkway, Morristown, TN 37813-6899. (615) 587-WSCC. Fax: (615) 587-9222.

William Jennings Bryan College
Dayton, Tennessee CB code: 1908

Admissions: 74% of applicants accepted
Based on: ••• Recommendations, religious affiliation/commitment, school record
•• Activities, test scores
• Essay, interview, special talents
Completion: 85% of freshmen end year in good standing
48% graduate, 20% of these enter graduate study

4-year private liberal arts college, coed, interdenominational. Founded in 1930. **Accreditation:** Regional. **Undergraduate enrollment:** 180 men, 223 women full time; 3 men, 4 women part time. **Faculty:** 55 total (27 full time), 20 with doctorates or other terminal degrees. **Location:** Rural campus in small town; 40 miles from Chattanooga. **Calendar:** Semester, limited summer session. **Microcomputers:** 125 located in dormitories, computer centers. **Special facilities:** Natural history museum. **Additional facts:** All courses taught from Christian perspective. All faculty sign statement of faith annually.

DEGREES OFFERED. AA, AS, BA, BS. 4 associate degrees awarded in 1992. 100% in business and management. 71 bachelor's degrees awarded. 22% in business and management, 16% teacher education, 5% letters/literature, 6% mathematics, 6% multi/interdisciplinary studies, 14% philosophy, religion, theology, 10% psychology, 8% social sciences, 9% visual and performing arts.

UNDERGRADUATE MAJORS. Associate: Business administration and management, liberal/general studies. **Bachelor's:** Accounting, Bible studies, biology, business administration and management, communications, elementary education, English, English education, history, liberal/general studies, mathematics, mathematics education, music, music and religious education, music education, prelaw, psychology, religious education, science education, social studies education.

ACADEMIC PROGRAMS. Double major, dual enrollment of high school students, independent study, internships, student-designed major, study abroad, teacher preparation, Washington semester. **Remedial services:** Reduced course load, remedial instruction, special counselor, tutoring. **Placement/credit:** AP, CLEP Subject, IB, institutional tests; 30 credit hours maximum for associate degree; 31 credit hours maximum for bachelor's degree.

ACADEMIC REQUIREMENTS. Freshmen must earn minimum GPA of 1.75 to continue in good standing. 68% of freshmen return for sophomore year. Students must declare major by end of second year. **Graduation requirements:** 60 hours for associate (36 in major), 124 hours for bachelor's (30 in major). Most students required to take courses in arts/fine arts, English, foreign languages, history, humanities, mathematics, philosophy/religion, biological/physical sciences, social sciences.

FRESHMAN ADMISSIONS. Selection criteria: High school record, Christian character supported by references, and SAT or ACT scores. **High school preparation:** 20 units recommended. Recommended units include English 4, foreign language 2, mathematics 3, social science 3 and science 3. **Test requirements:** ACT; score report by August 1. ACT composite score of 23 or SAT combined score of 1000 or Pre-Professional Skills Test required of all teacher education applicants.

1992 FRESHMAN CLASS PROFILE. 329 men and women applied, 244 accepted; 50 men enrolled, 58 women enrolled. 66% had high school GPA of 3.0 or higher, 34% between 2.0 and 2.99. **Characteristics:** 40% from in state, 99% live in college housing, 1% have minority backgrounds, 4% are foreign students. Average age is 18.

FALL-TERM APPLICATIONS. $20 fee, may be waived for applicants with need. Closing date July 31; priority given to applications received by May 1; applicants notified on a rolling basis; must reply by August 15. Interview required for marginal applicants. Essay recommended. CRDA. Deferred and early admission available.

STUDENT LIFE. Housing: Dormitories (men, women); apartment housing available. **Activities:** Student government, student newspaper, yearbook, choral groups, concert band, drama, music ensembles, Christian service organization, community tutoring program, Practical Christian Involvement, Students for Life, international students organization. **Additional information:** Religious observance required.

ATHLETICS. NAIA. **Intercollegiate:** Basketball, cross-country, soccer M, volleyball W. **Intramural:** Basketball, football M, soccer, softball, table tennis, tennis, volleyball.

STUDENT SERVICES. Aptitude testing, career counseling, employment service for undergraduates, freshman orientation, personal counseling, placement service for graduates, services/facilities for handicapped.

ANNUAL EXPENSES. Tuition and fees: $7,690. **Room and board:** $3,950. **Books and supplies:** $450. **Other expenses:** $800.

FINANCIAL AID. 88% of freshmen, 88% of continuing students receive some form of aid. 63% of grants, 88% of loans, 83% of jobs based on need. 95 enrolled freshmen were judged to have need, all were offered aid. Academic, music/drama, athletic, leadership scholarships available. **Aid applications:** No closing date; priority given to applications received by May 1; applicants notified on a rolling basis beginning on or about May 15; must reply within 4 weeks.

ADDRESS/TELEPHONE. Thomas A. Shaw, Director of Admissions, William Jennings Bryan College, PO Box 7000, Bryan Drive, Dayton, TN 37321-7000. (615) 775-2041 ext. 204. (800) 277-9522. Fax: (615) 775-7330.

Texas

Abilene Christian University
Abilene, Texas CB code: 6001

Admissions: 50% of applicants accepted
Based on: ••• School record
•• Activities, interview, recommendations, test scores
• Special talents
Completion: 90% of freshmen end year in good standing
49% graduate, 38% of these enter graduate study

4-year private university and liberal arts college, coed, affiliated with Church of Christ. Founded in 1906. **Accreditation:** Regional. **Undergraduate enrollment:** 1,509 men, 1,441 women full time; 209 men, 287 women part time. **Graduate enrollment:** 151 men, 83 women full time; 214 men, 150 women part time. **Faculty:** 227 total (165 full time), 171 with doctorates or other terminal degrees. **Location:** Suburban campus in small city; 180 miles from Dallas. **Calendar:** Semester, limited summer session. Saturday and extensive evening/early morning classes. **Microcomputers:** 475 located in libraries, classrooms, computer centers. **Special facilities:** Shore Art Gallery, observatory, college farm (for agriculture majors), center for Biblical studies, West Texas Voice Institute. **Additional facts:** Campus Abroad programs in Germany, Belgium, France, Greece, Australia, Spain, Japan, and England.

DEGREES OFFERED. AA, AS, BA, BS, BFA, MA, MS, MBA, MEd, D, M.Div. 7 associate degrees awarded in 1992. 10% in agriculture, 30% health sciences, 20% home economics, 20% philosophy, religion, theology, 20% trade and industry. 669 bachelor's degrees awarded. 10% in business and management, 6% business/office and marketing/distribution, 12% communications, 23% education, 7% health sciences, 7% philosophy, religion, theology, 7% physical sciences, 6% psychology, 6% social sciences. Graduate degrees offered in 26 major fields of study.

UNDERGRADUATE MAJORS. Associate: Agricultural sciences, Bible studies, business computer/console/peripheral equipment operation, child development/care/guidance, construction, drafting, industrial technology, nursing, word processing. **Bachelor's:** Accounting, advertising, agribusiness, agricultural sciences, agronomy, animal sciences, applied mathematics, art education, art history, arts management, Bible studies, biblical languages, bilingual/bicultural education, biochemistry, biology, business administration and management, business and management, business education, chemistry, clinical laboratory science, communication disorders, communication theory, communications, computer and information sciences, corporate communication, corporate fitness, corporate video, criminal justice studies, dramatic arts, early childhood education, education of exceptional children, education of the gifted and talented, education of the mentally handicapped, electrical/electronics/communications engineering, engineering physics, English, English education, exercise and sport science, fashion merchandising, finance, fine arts, food science and nutrition, foreign languages education, French, geology, German, graphic design, Greek (classical), history, home economics, home economics education, human resources development, individual and family development, industrial arts education, interior design, international business management, international studies, journalism, management science, marketing and distribution, marketing management, mathematics, mathematics education, missionary studies, music, music education, music performance, nursing, parks and recreation management, photo journalism, photographic technology, physical education, physical sciences, physics, political science and government, predentistry, premedicine, preveterinary, psychology, public policy studies, public relations, radio/television broadcasting, radio/television technology, range management, recreation therapy, religious communication, religious education, religious journalism, school psychology, science education, social studies education, social work, sociology, Spanish, speech, speech correction, speech pathology/audiology, speech/communication/theater education, telecommunications, theological studies, visual and performing arts.

ACADEMIC PROGRAMS. Accelerated program, cooperative education, double major, dual enrollment of high school students, education specialist degree, honors program, independent study, student-designed major, study abroad, teacher preparation, cross-registration; combined bachelor's/graduate program in medicine. **Remedial services:** Learning center, preadmission summer program, reduced course load, remedial instruction, special counselor, tutoring. **ROTC:** Army. **Placement/credit:** AP, CLEP Subject, institutional tests; 15 credit hours maximum for associate degree; 30 credit hours maximum for bachelor's degree.

ACADEMIC REQUIREMENTS. Freshmen must earn minimum GPA of 2.0 to continue in good standing. 77% of freshmen return for sophomore year. Students must declare major by end of second year. **Graduation requirements:** 66 hours for associate (31 in major), 128 hours for bachelor's (36 in major). Most students required to take courses in arts/fine arts, English, history, humanities, mathematics, philosophy/religion, biological/physical sciences, social sciences. **Postgraduate studies:** 40% from 2-year programs enter 4-year programs. 3% enter law school, 6% enter medical school, 10% enter MBA programs, 19% enter other graduate study.

FRESHMAN ADMISSIONS. Selection criteria: Rank in top 75% of class and score 19 on ACT composite or 850 on combined SAT. **High school preparation:** 15 units required. Required and recommended units include English 4, mathematics 2, social science 2 and science 2. Foreign language 2 recommended. Science requirement must be laboratory science in either biology, chemistry or physics. **Test requirements:** SAT or ACT (ACT preferred); score report by August 15. **Additional information:** ACT administered on campus if not taken previously.

1992 FRESHMAN CLASS PROFILE. 725 men applied, 372 accepted, 503 enrolled; 774 women applied, 377 accepted, 521 enrolled. 74% had high school GPA of 3.0 or higher, 25% between 2.0 and 2.99. 20% were in top tenth and 44% were in top quarter of graduating class. **Academic background:** Mid 50% of enrolled freshmen had SAT-V between 370-520, SAT-M between 410-580; ACT composite between 17-23. 52% submitted SAT scores, 94% submitted ACT scores. **Characteristics:** 70% from in state, 90% live in college housing, 9% have minority backgrounds, 1% are foreign students. Average age is 19.

FALL-TERM APPLICATIONS. $25 fee. No closing date; applicants notified on a rolling basis beginning on or about January 1. Audition required for music, debate, forensics applicants. Interview recommended. Deferred and early admission available. ACH tests in English, mathematics, and science recommended.

STUDENT LIFE. Housing: Dormitories (men, women); apartment housing available. **Activities:** Student government, magazine, radio, student newspaper, television, yearbook, choral groups, concert band, drama, jazz band, marching band, music ensembles, musical theater, symphony orchestra, honorary society, Campus Service Organization, Blue Key, Student Foundation, Young Republicans, Mission Outreach, Missionary Apprentice Resource Corps, Global Campaigns.

ATHLETICS. NCAA. **Intercollegiate:** Basketball, cross-country, football M, golf M, tennis, track and field, volleyball W. **Intramural:** Badminton, baseball, basketball, bowling, gymnastics, handball, racquetball, soccer M, softball, swimming M, tennis, track and field, volleyball, water polo M.

STUDENT SERVICES. Aptitude testing, career counseling, employment service for undergraduates, freshman orientation, health services, personal counseling, placement service for graduates, special adviser for adult students, veterans counselor, services/facilities for handicapped.

ANNUAL EXPENSES. Tuition and fees: $7,370. **Room and board:** $3,400. **Books and supplies:** $450. **Other expenses:** $1,250.

FINANCIAL AID. 75% of freshmen, 65% of continuing students receive some form of aid. 57% of grants, 70% of loans, 27% of jobs based on need. 446 enrolled freshmen were judged to have need, 437 were offered aid. Academic, music/drama, art, athletic, leadership, alumni affiliation, religious affiliation, minority scholarships available. **Aid applications:** No closing date; priority given to applications received by March 1; applicants notified on a rolling basis beginning on or about April 1; must reply by registration.

ADDRESS/TELEPHONE. Don King, Director of Admissions, Abilene Christian University, ACU Station Box 6000, Abilene, TX 79699. (915) 674-2653. (800) 888-0228. Fax: (915) 674-2130.

Alvin Community College
Alvin, Texas CB code: 6005

2-year public community college, coed. Founded in 1948. **Accreditation:** Regional. **Undergraduate enrollment:** 685 men, 899 women full time; 1,069 men, 1,253 women part time. **Faculty:** 141 total (102 full time), 25 with doctorates or other terminal degrees. **Location:** Suburban campus in large town; 25 miles from Houston. **Calendar:** Semester, extensive summer session. **Microcomputers:** 75 located in classrooms, computer centers. **Special facilities:** Art gallery, firing range, recording studio, fitness center. **Additional facts:** Campus operated radio station and child care center. Court reporting program, law enforcement program with indoor firing range.

DEGREES OFFERED. AA, AS, AAS. 411 associate degrees awarded in 1992.

UNDERGRADUATE MAJORS. Accounting, air conditioning/heating/refrigeration mechanics, air conditioning/heating/refrigeration technology, biology, business administration and management, child development/care/guidance, computer programming, court reporting, criminal justice studies, drafting, drafting and design technology, dramatic arts, electrical and electronics equipment repair, electronic technology, fashion merchandising, fine arts, law enforcement and corrections, law enforcement and corrections technologies, legal assistant/paralegal, legal secretary, liberal/general studies, marketing and distribution, mathematics, medical laboratory technologies, medical secretary, mental health/human services, music, music performance, musical theater, nursing, physical education, physical sciences, radio/television broadcasting, respiratory therapy technology, secretarial and related programs, welding technology.

ACADEMIC PROGRAMS. 2-year transfer program, dual enrollment of high school students, internships, weekend college, cross-registration. **Remedial services:** Learning center, reduced course load, remedial instruction, special counselor, tutoring. **Placement/credit:** CLEP General and Subject, institutional tests.

ACADEMIC REQUIREMENTS. Freshmen must earn minimum GPA of 2.0 to continue in good standing. Students must declare major on application. **Graduation requirements:** 64 hours for associate. Most students required to take courses in computer science, English, history, mathematics, biological/physical sciences, social sciences.

FRESHMAN ADMISSIONS. Selection criteria: Open admissions. Selective admissions to nursing, respiratory therapy, medical laboratory technology, criminal justice, court reporting, and musical theater programs. TASP (Texas Academic Skills Program) policies must be adhered to. **High school preparation:** 22 units recommended. Recommended units include biological science 1, English 4, foreign language 2, mathematics 3, physical science 2 and social science 3. Units recommended: 1.5 physical education, .5 health.

1992 FRESHMAN CLASS PROFILE. 389 men, 300 women enrolled. **Characteristics:** 98% from in state, 100% commute, 17% have minority backgrounds. Average age is 25.

FALL-TERM APPLICATIONS. No fee. Closing date August 17; priority given to applications received by July 20; applicants notified on a rolling basis. Interview required for nursing, respiratory therapy, medical laboratory technology, court reporting applicants. Audition required for music, musical theater applicants.

STUDENT LIFE. Activities: Student government, magazine, radio, student newspaper, television, choral groups, concert band, drama, jazz band, music ensembles, musical theater, Catholic association, Baptist association, Phi Theta Kappa, honorary drama fraternity, Pan American College Forum, Latter-Day Saints Student Organization, various associations related to specific fields of study.

ATHLETICS. NJCAA. **Intercollegiate:** Baseball M, golf, tennis, volleyball W. **Intramural:** Bowling, racquetball, table tennis.

STUDENT SERVICES. Aptitude testing, career counseling, employment service for undergraduates, freshman orientation, on-campus day care, personal counseling, placement service for graduates, veterans counselor, services/facilities for handicapped.

ANNUAL EXPENSES. Tuition and fees (1992-93): $420, $300 additional for out-of-district students, $300 additional for out-of-state students. **Books and supplies:** $385. **Other expenses:** $1,017.

FINANCIAL AID. 23% of freshmen, 26% of continuing students receive some form of aid. Grants, loans, jobs available. 322 enrolled freshmen were judged to have need, all were offered aid. Academic, music/drama, art, athletic, state/district residency scholarships available. **Aid applications:** No closing date; priority given to applications received by June 15; applicants notified on a rolling basis beginning on or about July 10; must reply within 2 weeks. **Additional information:** Short-term loans available.

ADDRESS/TELEPHONE. David N. Mclane, Registrar, Alvin Community College, 3110 Mustang Road, Alvin, TX 77511-4898. (713) 388-4636. Fax: (713) 388-4895.

Amarillo College
Amarillo, Texas CB code: 6006

2-year public community college, coed. Founded in 1929. **Accreditation:** Regional. **Undergraduate enrollment:** 703 men, 1,241 women full time; 1,681 men, 2,925 women part time. **Faculty:** 365 total (196 full time), 16 with doctorates or other terminal degrees. **Location:** Urban campus in small city; 300 miles from Dallas, Denver, Colorado, and Oklahoma City, Oklahoma. **Calendar:** Semester, extensive summer session. Saturday and extensive evening/early morning classes. **Microcomputers:** Located in libraries, classrooms, computer centers. **Special facilities:** Amarillo art center.

DEGREES OFFERED. AA, AS, AAS. 469 associate degrees awarded in 1992.

UNDERGRADUATE MAJORS. Accounting, air conditioning/heating/refrigeration mechanics, architectural engineering, architecture, automotive mechanics, biology, business and management, business and office, business computer/console/peripheral equipment operation, business data entry equipment operation, business data processing and related programs, business data programming, chemical engineering, chemistry, child development/care/guidance, civil engineering, computer and information sciences, computer engineering, computer programming, court reporting, criminal justice technology, dental hygiene, diesel engine mechanics, drafting, drafting and design technology, dramatic arts, electrical and electronics equipment repair, electrical/electronics/communications engineering, electronic technology, elementary education, emergency medical technologies, engineering, engineering and engineering-related technologies, English, fashion merchandising, finance, fine arts, fire control and safety technology, geology, graphic arts technology, home economics, industrial equipment maintenance and repair, instrumentation technology, journalism, legal secretary, liberal/general studies, management science, marketing and distribution, mathematics, mechanical engineering, medical laboratory technologies, medical radiation dosimetry, medical secretary, microcomputer software, music, nuclear medical technology, nursing, office supervision and management, petroleum engineering, photographic technology, physical sciences, physical therapy assistant, physics, predentistry, preengineering, premedicine, prepharmacy, preveterinary, psychology, radio/television broadcasting, radio/television technology, radiograph medical technology, real estate, religion, respiratory therapy, respiratory therapy technology, retailing, secondary education, secretarial and related programs, social sciences, tourism, veterinarian's assistant, word processing.

ACADEMIC PROGRAMS. 2-year transfer program, dual enrollment of high school students, honors program, telecourses. **Remedial services:** Learning center, remedial instruction, special counselor, tutoring. **Placement/credit:** AP, CLEP Subject, institutional tests; 9 credit hours maximum for associate degree.

ACADEMIC REQUIREMENTS. Freshmen must earn minimum GPA of 2.0 to continue in good standing. 46% of freshmen return for sophomore year. Students must declare major by end of first year. **Graduation requirements:** 62 hours for associate (24 in major). Most students required to take courses in English, history, mathematics, biological/physical sciences, social sciences.

FRESHMAN ADMISSIONS. Selection criteria: Open admissions.

1992 FRESHMAN CLASS PROFILE. 1,196 men and women enrolled. **Characteristics:** 95% from in state, 100% commute, 18% have minority backgrounds. Average age is 28.

FALL-TERM APPLICATIONS. No fee. No closing date; priority given to applications received by July 1; applicants notified on a rolling basis beginning on or about April 1.

STUDENT LIFE. Activities: Student government, magazine, radio, student newspaper, television, choral groups, concert band, dance, drama, jazz band, music ensembles, musical theater, opera.

ATHLETICS. Intramural: Basketball, tennis, volleyball.

STUDENT SERVICES. Aptitude testing, career counseling, employment service for undergraduates, freshman orientation, on-campus day care, personal counseling, placement service for graduates, special adviser for adult students, services/facilities for handicapped.

ANNUAL EXPENSES. Tuition and fees (1992-93): $470, $222 additional for out-of-district students, $1,081 additional for out-of-state students. **Books and supplies:** $525. **Other expenses:** $851.

FINANCIAL AID. 38% of freshmen, 62% of continuing students receive some form of aid. 87% of grants, 94% of loans, all jobs based on need. Academic scholarships available. **Aid applications:** No closing date; priority given to applications received by June 1; applicants notified on a rolling basis beginning on or about August 1; must reply within 2 weeks.

ADDRESS/TELEPHONE. Registrar's Office, Amarillo College, PO Box 447, Amarillo, TX 79178. (806) 371-5030. Fax: (806) 371-5370.

Amber University
Garland, Texas CB code: 6140

2-year upper-division private university, coed, nondenominational. Founded in 1971. **Accreditation:** Regional. **Undergraduate enrollment:** 40 men, 55 women full time; 224 men, 354 women part time. **Graduate enrollment:** 130 men, 140 women full time; 237 men, 353 women part time. **Faculty:** 41 total (16 full time), 31 with doctorates or other terminal degrees. **Location:** Suburban campus in small city; 12 miles from downtown Dallas. **Calendar:** Four 10-week sessions. Saturday and extensive evening/early morning classes. **Microcomputers:** Located in libraries, computer centers.

DEGREES OFFERED. BA, BS, MA, MS, MBA. 220 bachelor's degrees awarded in 1992. 90% in business and management, 10% multi/interdisciplinary studies. Graduate degrees offered in 3 major fields of study.

UNDERGRADUATE MAJORS. Accounting, business administration and management, business and management, liberal/general studies, management technology.

ACADEMIC PROGRAMS. Independent study. **Placement/credit:** AP, CLEP General and Subject; 30 credit hours maximum for bachelor's degree.

ACADEMIC REQUIREMENTS. Graduation requirements: 126 hours for bachelor's (39 in major). Most students required to take courses in English, history, humanities, mathematics, philosophy/religion, biological/physical sciences, social sciences. **Postgraduate studies:** 20% enter MBA programs, 20% enter other graduate study.

STUDENT SERVICES. Career counseling, personal counseling, placement service for graduates, special adviser for adult students, veterans counselor, services/facilities for handicapped.

ANNUAL EXPENSES. Tuition and fees (1992-93): $3,750. **Books and supplies:** $350.

FINANCIAL AID. 5% of continuing students receive some form of aid. Grants available. **Aid applications:** Closing date July 1; applicants notified on or about September 1.

ADDRESS/TELEPHONE. Judy George, Manager for Admissions, Amber University, 1700 Eastgate Drive, Garland, TX 75041-5595. (214) 279-6511 ext. 80. Fax: (214) 279-9773.

Angelina College
Lufkin, Texas CB code: 6025

2-year public community college, coed. Founded in 1966. **Accreditation:** Regional. **Undergraduate enrollment:** 3,395 men and women. **Faculty:** 191 total (102 full time), 14 with doctorates or other terminal degrees. **Location:** Suburban campus in large town; 125 miles from Houston. **Calendar:** Semester, extensive summer session. **Microcomputers:** 100 located in libraries, classrooms, computer centers. **Special facilities:** Computer-aided design laboratory, environmental trail in 20 acres of hardwood forest. **Additional facts:** Teaching centers located in five contiguous counties.

DEGREES OFFERED. AA, AS, AAS. 197 associate degrees awarded in 1992. 12% in business/office and marketing/distribution, 9% education, 39% allied health, 8% letters/literature, 20% trade and industry.

UNDERGRADUATE MAJORS. Accounting, agricultural sciences, automotive mechanics, automotive technology, biology, business administration and management, business and management, business and office, business computer/console/peripheral equipment operation, business data processing and related programs, business data programming, chemistry, child development/care/guidance, computer and information sciences, criminal justice studies, data processing, diesel engine mechanics, drafting, drafting and design technology, dramatic arts, education, education of the mentally handicapped, electrical and electronics equipment repair, electrical technology, electromechanical technology, electronic technology, elementary education, emergency medical technologies, engineering, engineering and engineering-related technologies, English, fine arts, industrial equipment maintenance and repair, industrial technology, journalism, law enforcement and corrections, law enforcement and corrections technologies, liberal/general studies, marketing management, mathematics, mechanical design technology, mental health/human services, music, nursing, physical sciences, physical therapy assistant, physics, postal service management, power plant operation and maintenance, practical nursing, predentistry, prelaw, premedicine, prepharmacy, preveterinary, psychology, radiograph medical technology, real estate, respiratory therapy, respiratory therapy technology, science technologies, secondary education, secretarial and related programs, social sciences, social work, speech, teacher aide, welding technology.

ACADEMIC PROGRAMS. 2-year transfer program, accelerated program, dual enrollment of high school students, internships, telecourses. **Remedial services:** Learning center, reduced course load, remedial instruction, special counselor, tutoring. **Placement/credit:** AP, CLEP Subject, institutional tests; 15 credit hours maximum for associate degree.

ACADEMIC REQUIREMENTS. Freshmen must earn minimum GPA of 1.75 to continue in good standing. 60% of freshmen return for sophomore year. Students must declare major on application. **Graduation requirements:** 63 hours for associate (24 in major). Most students required to take courses in arts/fine arts, English, history, mathematics, biological/physical sciences, social sciences. **Additional information:** All students must take Texas Academic Skills Programs test before completion of 9 semester hours. Physical education requirements waived for veterans, adults 25 and over, and some part-time students.

FRESHMAN ADMISSIONS. Selection criteria: Open admissions. Selective admissions to nursing and radiologic technology programs. **Test requirements:** General Aptitute Test Battery required of nursing applicants. ASSET Student Success Package used for placement. State-mandated TASP test required.

1992 FRESHMAN CLASS PROFILE. 913 men and women enrolled. **Characteristics:** 95% from in state, 98% commute, 16% have minority backgrounds. Average age is 24.

FALL-TERM APPLICATIONS. No fee. No closing date; priority given to applications received by July 1; applicants notified on a rolling basis. Interview required for radiologic technology, nursing, respiratory therapy applicants. Deferred admission available.

STUDENT LIFE. Housing: Dormitories (coed). 5 modern apartment buildings nearby, some offering student discounts. **Activities:** Student government, student newspaper, yearbook, choral groups, dance, drama, music ensembles, musical theater, community band, fraternities, sororities, Baptist Student Union.

ATHLETICS. NJCAA. **Intercollegiate:** Baseball M, basketball. **Intramural:** Badminton, bowling, golf, gymnastics, handball, racquetball, soccer, softball, swimming, table tennis, tennis, track and field, volleyball.

STUDENT SERVICES. Aptitude testing, career counseling, employment service for undergraduates, freshman orientation, health services, personal counseling, placement service for graduates, special adviser for adult students, veterans counselor, services/facilities for handicapped.

ANNUAL EXPENSES. Tuition and fees: $588, $158 additional for out-of-district students, $300 additional for out-of-state students. **Room and board:** $2,440. **Books and supplies:** $590. **Other expenses:** $550.

FINANCIAL AID. 27% of freshmen, 20% of continuing students receive some form of aid. 86% of grants, all jobs based on need. All loans based on criteria other than need. 568 enrolled freshmen were judged to have need, all were offered aid. Academic, music/drama, art, athletic, leadership, minority scholarships available. **Aid applications:** No closing date; priority given to applications received by June 15; applicants notified on a rolling basis beginning on or about July 15; must reply by June 1 or within 3 weeks if notified thereafter.

ADDRESS/TELEPHONE. Jill Hill, Registrar, Angelina College, PO Box 1768, Lufkin, TX 75902-1768. (409) 639-1301. Fax: (409) 639-4299.

Angelo State University
San Angelo, Texas CB code: 6644

Admissions:	52% of applicants accepted
Based on:	••• School record, test scores
Completion:	70% of freshmen end year in good standing
	25% enter graduate study

4-year public university, coed. Founded in 1928. **Accreditation:** Regional. **Undergraduate enrollment:** 1,937 men, 2,257 women full time; 578 men, 820 women part time. **Graduate enrollment:** 40 men, 39 women full time; 176 men, 255 women part time. **Faculty:** 240 total (211 full time), 133 with doctorates or other terminal degrees. **Location:** Suburban campus in small city; 215 miles from San Antonio, 259 miles from Dallas. **Calendar:** Semester, extensive summer session. **Microcomputers:** 250 located in dormitories, libraries, classrooms, computer centers. **Special facilities:** Spitz Planetarium.

DEGREES OFFERED. AS, BA, BS, MA, MS, MBA, MEd. 146 associate degrees awarded in 1992. 100% in health sciences. 798 bachelor's degrees awarded. 23% in business and management, 7% business/office and marketing/distribution, 5% computer sciences, 12% teacher education, 5% letters/literature, 5% life sciences, 7% mathematics, 6% physical sciences, 8% psychology, 9% social sciences. Graduate degrees offered in 22 major fields of study.

UNDERGRADUATE MAJORS. Associate: Nursing. **Bachelor's:** Accounting, agribusiness, animal sciences, art education, biology, business administration and management, business and management, business economics, business education, chemistry, clinical laboratory science, computer and information sciences, criminal justice studies, dramatic arts, early childhood education, economics, elementary education, English, English education, finance, fine arts, foreign languages education, French, history, journalism, marketing management, mathematics, mathematics education, music, music education, nursing, physical education, physics, political science and government, predentistry, premedicine, psychology, range management, real estate, science education, social studies education, sociology, Spanish, special education, speech, speech/communication/theater education, wildlife management.

ACADEMIC PROGRAMS. Double major, internships, study abroad; liberal arts/career combination in engineering. **Remedial services:** Learning center, preadmission summer program, reduced course load, remedial instruction. **ROTC:** Air Force. **Placement/credit:** AP, CLEP General and Subject, institutional tests.

ACADEMIC REQUIREMENTS. Freshmen must earn minimum GPA of 2.0 to continue in good standing. 63% of freshmen return for sophomore year. Students must declare major by end of second year. **Graduation requirements:** 60 hours for associate (30 in major), 130 hours for bachelor's (30 in major). Most students required to take courses in arts/fine arts, English, history, mathematics, biological/physical sciences. **Postgraduate studies:** 2% enter law school, 2% enter medical school, 9% enter MBA programs, 12% enter other graduate study.

FRESHMAN ADMISSIONS. Selection criteria: Rank in top quarter of class. If rank in 2nd quarter, minimum ACT score must be 17 or SAT 700; third quarter, ACT 23 or SAT 920; fourth quarter, ACT 30 or SAT 1200. **High school preparation:** 22 units recommended. Recommended units include foreign language 2, mathematics 3, social science 3 and science 3. College-preparatory program recommended. **Test requirements:** SAT or ACT; score report by August 19.

1992 FRESHMAN CLASS PROFILE. 1,539 men applied, 777 accepted, 768 enrolled; 1,996 women applied, 1,048 accepted, 1,011 enrolled. 3% were in top tenth and 58% were in top quarter of graduating class. **Academic background:** Mid 50% of enrolled freshmen had SAT-V between 380-510, SAT-M between 420-580; ACT composite between 20-27. 51% submitted SAT scores, 49% submitted ACT scores. **Characteristics:** 97% from in state, 60% live in college housing, 21% have minority backgrounds, 1% are foreign students, 3% join fraternities/sororities. Average age is 19.

FALL-TERM APPLICATIONS. No fee. No closing date; priority given to applications received by August 19; applicants notified on a rolling basis. Interview required of applicants not meeting normal admission requirements. Deferred and early admission available.

STUDENT LIFE. Housing: Dormitories (men, women); apartment housing available. **Activities:** Student government, magazine, student newspaper, yearbook, choral groups, concert band, dance, drama, jazz band, marching band, music ensembles, musical theater, fraternities, sororities, black students association, Mexican American group, Alpha Phi Omega, Baptist Student Union, Church of Christ Bible study center, Newman Club, campus ministries, International Student Association.

ATHLETICS. NCAA. **Intercollegiate:** Basketball, cross-country, football M, track and field, volleyball W. **Intramural:** Archery, badminton, basketball, bowling, golf, racquetball, soccer, softball, swimming, table tennis, tennis, volleyball.

STUDENT SERVICES. Aptitude testing, career counseling, employment service for undergraduates, freshman orientation, health services, personal counseling, placement service for graduates, veterans counselor, services/facilities for handicapped.

ANNUAL EXPENSES. Tuition and fees: $1,489, $4,080 additional for out-of-state students. **Room and board:** $3,592. **Books and supplies:** $450. **Other expenses:** $1,320.

FINANCIAL AID. 50% of continuing students receive some form of aid. 63% of grants, 81% of loans, all jobs based on need. Academic scholarships available. **Aid applications:** No closing date; priority given to applications received by July 15; applicants notified on a rolling basis beginning on or about March 1; must reply within 2 weeks.

ADDRESS/TELEPHONE. Lorri Morris, Assistant Director of Admissions, Angelo State University, 2601 West Avenue N, San Angelo, TX 76909. (915) 942-2041. Fax: (915) 942-2038.

Arlington Baptist College
Arlington, Texas — CB code: 6039

4-year private Bible college, coed, affiliated with World Baptist Fellowship. Founded in 1939. **Undergraduate enrollment:** 67 men, 37 women full time; 28 men, 17 women part time. **Faculty:** 17 total (7 full time), 2 with doctorates or other terminal degrees. **Location:** Urban campus in large city; 25 miles from Fort Worth and Dallas. **Calendar:** Semester, limited summer session. Extensive evening/early morning classes.

DEGREES OFFERED. BA, BS. 22 bachelor's degrees awarded in 1992.

UNDERGRADUATE MAJORS. Bible studies, biblical languages, elementary education, missionary studies, music, religious education, religious music, theological studies.

ACADEMIC PROGRAMS. Double major, independent study. **Remedial services:** Remedial instruction, audit program. **Placement/credit:** CLEP Subject, institutional tests.

ACADEMIC REQUIREMENTS. Freshmen must earn minimum GPA of 2.0 to continue in good standing. 50% of freshmen return for sophomore year. Students must declare major by end of second year. **Graduation requirements:** 128 hours for bachelor's (30 in major). Most students required to take courses in English, history, mathematics, philosophy/religion, biological/physical sciences, social sciences.

FRESHMAN ADMISSIONS. Selection criteria: Open admissions. **High school preparation:** 16 units recommended. Recommended units include English 3, mathematics 2, social science 3 and science 1. **Test requirements:** SAT or ACT for counseling; score report by August 16. **Additional information:** Specific standards of Christian conduct and recommendation by clergy most important.

1992 FRESHMAN CLASS PROFILE. 24 men applied, 23 accepted, 24 enrolled; 12 women applied, 12 accepted, 13 enrolled. **Characteristics:** 78% from in state, 54% live in college housing, 4% have minority backgrounds, 3% are foreign students. Average age is 19.

FALL-TERM APPLICATIONS. $15 fee. No closing date; applicants notified on a rolling basis; must reply by August 16. Audition required for music applicants. Essay required. Interview recommended. Deferred admission available.

STUDENT LIFE. Housing: Dormitories (men, women). **Activities:** Student government, student newspaper, yearbook, choral groups, drama, music ensembles, Student Missionary Association, Student Preachers' Fellowship, International Students Fellowship. **Additional information:** On-campus chapel services available. Religious observance required.

ATHLETICS. Intramural: Basketball, soccer M, softball, table tennis, tennis, volleyball.

STUDENT SERVICES. Career counseling, employment service for undergraduates, freshman orientation, personal counseling, placement service for graduates, veterans counselor.

ANNUAL EXPENSES. Tuition and fees (1992-93): $2,050. **Room and board:** $1,320 room only. **Books and supplies:** $700. **Other expenses:** $720.

FINANCIAL AID. 95% of freshmen, 95% of continuing students receive some form of aid. All grants, 71% of loans, all jobs based on need. 24 enrolled freshmen were judged to have need, all were offered aid. Religious affiliation scholarships available. **Aid applications:** No closing date; priority given to applications received by August 15; applicants notified on a rolling basis.

ADDRESS/TELEPHONE. Helen Sullivan, Director of Admissions/Registrar, Arlington Baptist College, 3001 West Division, Arlington, TX 76012-3425. (817) 461-8741.

Austin College
Sherman, Texas — CB code: 6016

Admissions: 84% of applicants accepted
Based on: ••• School record, test scores
•• Interview, recommendations
• Activities, essay, special talents
Completion: 86% of freshmen end year in good standing
65% graduate, 36% of these enter graduate study

4-year private liberal arts college, coed, affiliated with Presbyterian Church (USA). Founded in 1849. **Accreditation:** Regional. **Undergraduate enrollment:** 542 men, 559 women full time; 3 men, 15 women part time. **Graduate enrollment:** 5 men, 19 women full time; 1 man, 2 women part time. **Faculty:** 113 total (96 full time), 73 with doctorates or other terminal degrees. **Location:** Suburban campus in large town; 60 miles from Dallas. **Calendar:** 4-1-4, limited summer session. **Microcomputers:** 70 located in dormitories, libraries, computer centers. **Special facilities:** 100-acre Sneed Environmental Research Area near Lake Texoma, Abell Library Center, 26-acre lake recreation area, AC Tissue Culture Facility for the study of cellular molecular interactions of eukaryotic cells.

DEGREES OFFERED. BA, MA. 288 bachelor's degrees awarded in 1992. 18% in business and management, 6% communications, 10% letters/literature, 13% life sciences, 14% psychology, 22% social sciences. Graduate degrees offered in 2 major fields of study.

UNDERGRADUATE MAJORS. American studies, biology, business and management, chemistry, classics, communications, computer and information sciences, economics, English, fine arts, French, German, history, international relations, Latin American studies, mathematics, music, philosophy, physical education, physics, political science and government, psychology, religion, sociology, Spanish.

ACADEMIC PROGRAMS. Accelerated program, double major, honors program, independent study, internships, student-designed major, study abroad, teacher preparation, telecourses, Washington semester; liberal arts/career combination in engineering. **Remedial services:** Learning center, reduced course load, special counselor, tutoring. **Placement/credit:** AP, CLEP Subject, institutional tests.

ACADEMIC REQUIREMENTS. Freshmen must earn minimum GPA of 2.0 to continue in good standing. 81% of freshmen return for sophomore year. Students must declare major by end of second year. **Graduation requirements:** 136 hours for bachelor's (28 in major). Most students required to take courses in arts/fine arts, computer science, English, foreign languages, history, humanities, mathematics, philosophy/religion, biological/physical sciences, social sciences. **Postgraduate studies:** 4% enter law school, 7% enter medical school, 2% enter MBA programs, 23% enter other graduate study.

FRESHMAN ADMISSIONS. Selection criteria: School achievement record, test scores, recommendations, out of class accomplishment, and essay considered. **High school preparation:** 14 units recommended. Recommended units include English 4, foreign language 2, mathematics 3, social science 2 and science 2. Science units should include 1 laboratory science. Math should include algebra and geometry. One unit in fine arts also recommended. 2 units in foreign language should be of the same language. **Test requirements:** SAT or ACT; score report by June 15.

1992 FRESHMAN CLASS PROFILE. 386 men applied, 303 accepted, 144 enrolled; 420 women applied, 373 accepted, 146 enrolled. 41% were in top tenth and 62% were in top quarter of graduating class. **Academic background:** Mid 50% of enrolled freshmen had SAT-V between 440-560, SAT-M between 490-610; ACT composite between 21-27. 92% submitted SAT scores, 48% submitted ACT scores. **Characteristics:** 91% from in state, 98% live in college housing, 18% have minority backgrounds, 1% are foreign students. Average age is 18.

FALL-TERM APPLICATIONS. $25 fee, may be waived for applicants with need. No closing date; priority given to applications received by March 15; applicants notified on a rolling basis beginning on or about April 1; must reply by May 1 or within 2 weeks if notified thereafter. Essay required. Interview recommended. Audition recommended for music applicants. Portfolio recommended for art applicants. CRDA. Deferred and early admission available.

STUDENT LIFE. Housing: Dormitories (men, women, coed); apartment housing available. **Activities:** Student government, film, magazine, student newspaper, yearbook, choral groups, drama, jazz band, music ensembles, musical theater, pep band, symphony orchestra, fraternities, sororities, Alpha Phi Omega, Intervarsity Christian Fellowship, Fellowship of Christian Athletes, Haverim, Student International Organization, Black Expressions, Student Development Board, Young Democrats, Young Republicans. **Additional information:** Recreational facilities available through Austin College Lake Campus, 20 miles away on Lake Texoma.

ATHLETICS. NAIA. **Intercollegiate:** Baseball M, basketball, diving, football M, golf M, soccer M, swimming, tennis, track and field, volleyball W. **Intramural:** Baseball, basketball, diving, gymnastics, handball, racquetball, softball, swimming, table tennis, tennis, volleyball.

STUDENT SERVICES. Aptitude testing, career counseling, employment service for undergraduates, freshman orientation, health services,

on-campus day care, personal counseling, placement service for graduates, services/facilities for handicapped.

ANNUAL EXPENSES. Tuition and fees: $10,865. Undergraduates and graduates pay $865 per course during summer term. **Room and board:** $4,134. **Books and supplies:** $400. **Other expenses:** $950.

FINANCIAL AID. 80% of freshmen, 75% of continuing students receive some form of aid. 91% of grants, 98% of loans, 89% of jobs based on need. 167 enrolled freshmen were judged to have need, all were offered aid. Academic, music/drama, art, leadership, alumni affiliation, religious affiliation scholarships available. **Aid applications:** No closing date; priority given to applications received by May 1; applicants notified on a rolling basis beginning on or about February 1; must reply by May 1 or within 4 weeks if notified thereafter.

ADDRESS/TELEPHONE. Rodney Oto, Dean of Admission and Financial Aid, Austin College, PO Box 1177, 900 North Grand, Suite 6N, Sherman, TX 75091-1177. (903) 813-2387. (800) 442-5363. Fax: (903) 813-3199.

Austin Community College
Austin, Texas — CB code: 6759

2-year public community college, coed. Founded in 1972. **Accreditation:** Regional. **Undergraduate enrollment:** 3,271 men, 3,065 women full time; 8,247 men, 10,603 women part time. **Faculty:** 1,334 total (265 full time), 54 with doctorates or other terminal degrees. **Location:** Urban campus in large city; main campuses in downtown area. **Calendar:** Semester, extensive summer session. **Microcomputers:** Located in libraries, classrooms, computer centers.

DEGREES OFFERED. AA, AS, AAS. 61 associate degrees awarded in 1992. 22% in business and management, 8% engineering, 12% health sciences, 6% allied health, 31% trade and industry.

UNDERGRADUATE MAJORS. Accounting, air conditioning/heating/refrigeration mechanics, air conditioning/heating/refrigeration technology, applications support, architecture, astronomy, automotive mechanics, automotive technology, biology, building trades, business administration and management, business and management, business and office, business data processing and related programs, business data programming, business systems analysis, chemistry, clinical laboratory science, commercial art, communications, computer and information sciences, computer technology, dance, data processing, drafting and design technology, dramatic arts, economics, electronic technology, emergency medical technologies, engineering, fashion merchandising, finance, fine arts, fire control and safety technology, food management, food production/management/services, French, geology, German, graphic and printing production, graphic arts technology, history, hotel/motel and restaurant management, human resources development, individual and family development, information sciences and systems, institutional/home management/supporting programs, insurance marketing, interpreter for the deaf, landscape architecture, law enforcement and corrections technologies, legal assistant/paralegal, legal secretary, liberal/general studies, manufacturing technology, marketing and distribution, mathematics, medical laboratory technologies, medical secretary, mental health/human services, music, nursing, occupational therapy assistant, photographic technology, photography, physical sciences, physical therapy assistant, physician's assistant, physics, political science and government, practical nursing, precision metal work, predentistry, premedicine, prepharmacy, preveterinary, psychology, quality control technology, radio/television broadcasting, radiograph medical technology, real estate, retailing, science technologies, secretarial and related programs, social work, sociology, Spanish, surgical technology, survey and mapping technology, technical and business writing, welding technology, word processing.

ACADEMIC PROGRAMS. 2-year transfer program, dual enrollment of high school students, independent study, internships, study abroad. **Remedial services:** Learning center, reduced course load, remedial instruction, tutoring. **ROTC:** Air Force, Army. **Placement/credit:** CLEP General and Subject, institutional tests; 30 credit hours maximum for associate degree.

ACADEMIC REQUIREMENTS. Freshmen must earn minimum GPA of 2.0 to continue in good standing. Students must declare major on application. **Graduation requirements:** 60 hours for associate. Most students required to take courses in English, history, social sciences.

FRESHMAN ADMISSIONS. Selection criteria: Open admissions.

1992 FRESHMAN CLASS PROFILE. 6,102 men and women enrolled. **Characteristics:** 98% from in state, 100% commute, 26% have minority backgrounds, 3% are foreign students. Average age is 20.

FALL-TERM APPLICATIONS. No fee. No closing date; priority given to applications received by August 15; applicants notified on or about August 15. Deferred and early admission available.

STUDENT LIFE. Activities: Student newspaper, choral groups, dance, drama, jazz band, Phi Theta Kappa honor society.

ATHLETICS. Intramural: Baseball M, basketball M, gymnastics M, soccer M, softball M.

STUDENT SERVICES. Aptitude testing, career counseling, employment service for undergraduates, personal counseling, placement service for graduates, veterans counselor, services/facilities for handicapped.

ANNUAL EXPENSES. Tuition and fees: $794, $392 additional for out-of-district students, $2,688 additional for out-of-state students. **Books and supplies:** $440. **Other expenses:** $1,236.

FINANCIAL AID. 20% of continuing students receive some form of aid. All grants, 78% of loans, all jobs based on need. Academic scholarships available. **Aid applications:** Closing date April 1; priority given to applications received by February 15; applicants notified on a rolling basis beginning on or about June 30; must reply within 2 weeks.

ADDRESS/TELEPHONE. Clifton Van Dyke, Director of Admissions and Records, Austin Community College, 5930 Middle Fiskville Road, Austin, TX 78752-4390. (512) 483-7000. Fax: (512) 483-7789.

Baptist Missionary Association Theological Seminary
Jacksonville, Texas — CB code: 7042

4-year private Bible, seminary college, coed, affiliated with Baptist Missionary Association. Founded in 1955. **Accreditation:** Regional. **Undergraduate enrollment:** 10 men full time; 21 men, 1 woman part time. **Graduate enrollment:** 11 men, 2 women full time; 20 men, 1 woman part time. **Faculty:** 13 total (9 full time), 11 with doctorates or other terminal degrees. **Location:** Rural campus in large town; 120 miles from Dallas. **Calendar:** Semester, limited summer session. **Microcomputers:** 2 located in libraries.

DEGREES OFFERED. BA, MA, M.Div. 2 associate degrees awarded in 1992. 100% in philosophy, religion, theology. 6 bachelor's degrees awarded. 100% in philosophy, religion, theology. Graduate degrees offered in 3 major fields of study.

UNDERGRADUATE MAJORS. Associate: Theological studies. **Bachelor's:** Religion.

ACADEMIC PROGRAMS. Internships.

ACADEMIC REQUIREMENTS. Freshmen must earn minimum GPA of 2.0 to continue in good standing. 80% of freshmen return for sophomore year. Students must declare major on enrollment. **Graduation requirements:** 66 hours for associate, 66 hours for bachelor's (30 in major). Most students required to take courses in English, history, mathematics, philosophy/religion, biological/physical sciences. **Postgraduate studies:** 50% from 2-year programs enter 4-year programs. 80% enter other graduate study.

1992 FRESHMAN CLASS PROFILE. 12 men applied, 12 accepted, 12 enrolled.

FALL-TERM APPLICATIONS. $20 fee. Closing date August 15; priority given to applications received by July 15; applicants notified on a rolling basis; must reply by registration. Interview required.

STUDENT LIFE. Housing: Apartment housing available. **Activities:** Student government.

STUDENT SERVICES. Career counseling, personal counseling.

ANNUAL EXPENSES. Tuition and fees: $1,260. **Room and board:** $1,500 room only. **Books and supplies:** $450. **Other expenses:** $1,200.

FINANCIAL AID. 26% of continuing students receive some form of aid. All aid based on need. **Aid applications:** Closing date September 4; priority given to applications received by August 1; applicants notified on a rolling basis; must reply by registration.

ADDRESS/TELEPHONE. Wilbur K. Benningfield, Dean/Registrar, Baptist Missionary Association Theological Seminary, 1530 East Pine Street, Jacksonville, TX 75766-5414. (903) 586-2501. Fax: (903) 586-0378.

Bauder Fashion College
Arlington, Texas — CB code: 6068

2-year proprietary college of merchandising and design, coed. Founded in 1967. **Accreditation:** Regional. **Undergraduate enrollment:** 17 men, 221 women full time. **Faculty:** 39 total (32 full time), 4 with doctorates or other terminal degrees. **Location:** Suburban campus in large city; 18 miles from Dallas, 12 miles from Fort Worth. **Calendar:** Quarter, extensive summer session. **Microcomputers:** 34 located in libraries, classrooms. **Special facilities:** Interior and fashion design resource libraries.

DEGREES OFFERED. AA. 107 associate degrees awarded in 1992.

UNDERGRADUATE MAJORS. Fashion design, fashion merchandising, interior design.

ACADEMIC PROGRAMS. Internships. **Remedial services:** Remedial instruction, tutoring. **Placement/credit:** Institutional tests.

ACADEMIC REQUIREMENTS. Freshmen must earn minimum GPA of 2.0 to continue in good standing. Students must declare major on enrollment. **Graduation requirements:** 105 hours for associate (76 in major). Most students required to take courses in arts/fine arts, computer science, English, mathematics, social sciences.

FRESHMAN ADMISSIONS. Selection criteria: School achievement record, recommendations considered. Admissions standards moderately difficult. 2.0 GPA and interview recommended.

1992 FRESHMAN CLASS PROFILE. 147 men and women enrolled. 15% had high school GPA of 3.0 or higher, 83% between 2.0 and 2.99. **Characteristics:** 49% from in state, 73% live in college housing, 8% have minority backgrounds, 1% are foreign students. Average age is 18.

FALL-TERM APPLICATIONS. $50 fee. No closing date; applicants notified on a rolling basis. Interview recommended. Deferred admission available.

STUDENT LIFE. Housing: Dormitories (women); apartment housing available. **Activities:** Student government, student newspaper, yearbook, organizations related to fashion design industry.

ATHLETICS. Intramural: Basketball, softball, volleyball.

STUDENT SERVICES. Career counseling, employment service for undergraduates, personal counseling, placement service for graduates.

ANNUAL EXPENSES. Tuition and fees (1992-93): $5,990. **Room and board:** $2,980. **Books and supplies:** $800.

FINANCIAL AID. 40% of freshmen, 40% of continuing students receive some form of aid. Grants, loans available. 125 enrolled freshmen were judged to have need, all were offered aid. Academic scholarships available. **Aid applications:** Closing date July 1; applicants notified on or about September 1; must reply within 15 days.

ADDRESS/TELEPHONE. Beverly Gooch, Director of Admissions, Bauder Fashion College, 508 South Center Street, Arlington, TX 76010. (817) 261-7586. (800) 255-9216. Fax: (817) 274-9701.

Baylor College of Dentistry
Dallas, Texas CB code: 6059

2-year upper-division private college of dentistry, coed. Founded in 1905. **Accreditation:** Regional. **Undergraduate enrollment:** 38 women full time; 3 women part time. **Graduate enrollment:** 242 men, 164 women full time; 15 men, 9 women part time. **Faculty:** 198 total (103 full time), 184 with doctorates or other terminal degrees. **Location:** Urban campus in very large city. **Calendar:** Quarter. **Microcomputers:** 25 located in libraries.

DEGREES OFFERED. BS, MS, D, DDS, DMD. 14 bachelor's degrees awarded in 1992. 100% in allied health. Graduate degrees offered in 8 major fields of study.

UNDERGRADUATE MAJORS. Dental hygiene.

ACADEMIC PROGRAMS. Internships. **Remedial services:** Remedial instruction.

ACADEMIC REQUIREMENTS. Students must declare major on application. **Graduation requirements:** 130 hours for bachelor's (55 in major). Most students required to take courses in English, history, humanities, mathematics, biological/physical sciences, social sciences. **Additional information:** Participation in research activities under faculty sponsorship and annual research fellowships awarded by college offered.

STUDENT LIFE. Housing: Baylor Medical Center nursing dormitory housing available for students. **Activities:** Student government, yearbook, fraternities.

STUDENT SERVICES. Employment service for undergraduates, health services, personal counseling, services/facilities for handicapped.

ANNUAL EXPENSES. Tuition and fees: $1,750. Additional fees: $2,480 for instruments, books, supplies and uniforms. **Books and supplies:** $2,480. **Other expenses:** $6,800.

FINANCIAL AID. 54% of continuing students receive some form of aid. All grants, 77% of loans based on need. **Aid applications:** Closing date June 1; applicants notified on or about July 1.

ADDRESS/TELEPHONE. Jack Long, Director, Baylor College of Dentistry, 3302 Gaston Avenue, Dallas, TX 75246-2098. (214) 828-8230. Fax: (214) 828-8346.

Baylor University
Waco, Texas CB code: 6032

4-year private university, coed, affiliated with Baptist General Conference. Founded in 1845. **Accreditation:** Regional. **Undergraduate enrollment:** 4,393 men, 5,492 women full time; 195 men, 341 women part time. **Graduate enrollment:** 666 men, 489 women full time; 304 men, 305 women part time. **Faculty:** 636 total (589 full time). **Location:** Urban campus in small city; 100 miles from Dallas-Fort Worth, 100 miles from Austin. **Calendar:** Semester, extensive summer session. **Microcomputers:** 250 located in dormitories, libraries, classrooms, computer centers. **Special facilities:** Strecker Museum of Natural Science, extensive collection of Elizabeth and Robert Browning's works.

DEGREES OFFERED. BA, BS, BFA, MA, MS, MBA, MFA, PhD, EdD, JD. 1,964 bachelor's degrees awarded in 1992. 27% in business and management, 8% business/office and marketing/distribution, 7% communications, 9% teacher education, 5% health sciences, 5% letters/literature, 7% life sciences, 6% psychology, 8% social sciences. Graduate degrees offered in 59 major fields of study.

UNDERGRADUATE MAJORS. Accounting, airline piloting and navigation, American studies, anthropology, archeology, art education, art history, Asian studies, biblical languages, biology, business administration and management, business and management, business economics, business education, business-broadcasting, business-journalism, chemistry, classics, communications, computer and information sciences, dramatic arts, earth sciences, economics, education, elementary education, engineering, English, English education, environmental science, fashion design, fashion merchandising, finance, food science and nutrition, foreign languages education, forestry and related sciences, French, geology, geophysics and seismology, German, Greek (classical), health education, history, home economics, human resources development, individual and family development, information sciences and systems, insurance and risk management, interior design, international business management, international public service, journalism, Latin, Latin American studies, law , liberal/general studies, management information systems, marketing and distribution, marketing management, mathematics, mathematics education, medical laboratory technologies, museum studies, music, music education, music history and appreciation, music performance, music theory and composition, nursing, operations research, philosophy, physical education, physics, political science and government, predentistry, premedicine, prepharmacy, psychology, public administration, real estate, recreation and community services technologies, religion, religious music, Russian, Russian and Slavic studies, science education, secondary education, small business management and ownership, social science education, social studies education, social work, sociology, Spanish, speech, speech correction, speech pathology/audiology, speech/communication/theater education, studio art, telecommunications, urban studies, visual and performing arts.

ACADEMIC PROGRAMS. Accelerated program, double major, education specialist degree, honors program, independent study, internships, student-designed major, study abroad, teacher preparation, visiting/exchange student program; combined bachelor's/graduate program in medicine, law. **Remedial services:** Learning center, reduced course load, special counselor, tutoring. **ROTC:** Air Force. **Placement/credit:** AP, CLEP Subject, institutional tests; 60 credit hours maximum for bachelor's degree.

ACADEMIC REQUIREMENTS. Freshmen must earn minimum GPA of 2.0 to continue in good standing. 85% of freshmen return for sophomore year. Students must declare major by end of second year. **Graduation requirements:** 124 hours for bachelor's (27 in major). Most students required to take courses in arts/fine arts, English, foreign languages, history, mathematics, philosophy/religion, biological/physical sciences, social sciences.

FRESHMAN ADMISSIONS. Selection criteria: Class rank in top half, preferably top quarter. Test scores, recommendations considered. Special consideration for children of alumni. **High school preparation:** 16 units required. Required and recommended units include English 4, mathematics 2-3, social science 2 and science 2-3. Foreign language 2 recommended. **Test requirements:** SAT or ACT; score report by April 1.

1992 FRESHMAN CLASS PROFILE. 965 men, 1,402 women enrolled. 70% were in top quarter of graduating class. **Academic background:** Mid 50% of enrolled freshmen had SAT-V between 430-540, SAT-M between 500-620; ACT composite between 21-25. 63% submitted SAT scores, 37% submitted ACT scores. **Characteristics:** 74% from in state, 98% live in college housing, 19% have minority backgrounds, 1% are foreign students. Average age is 19.

FALL-TERM APPLICATIONS. $25 fee. No closing date; applicants notified on a rolling basis. Interview recommended for marginal applicants. Audition recommended for music applicants. Portfolio recommended for art applicants. CRDA. Deferred and early admission available.

STUDENT LIFE. Housing: Dormitories (men, women); apartment housing available. **Activities:** Student government, film, magazine, radio, student newspaper, television, yearbook, choral groups, concert band, drama, jazz band, marching band, music ensembles, musical theater, opera, pep band, symphony orchestra, fraternities, sororities, Baptist, Methodist, and Catholic student organizations, College Republicans, Young Democrats, Black Students at Baylor, Hispanic Culture Association, Oriental Student Association, Chamber of Commerce, and Service League.

ATHLETICS. NCAA. **Intercollegiate:** Baseball M, basketball, cross-country, football M, golf, lacrosse M, soccer, tennis, track and field, volleyball W. **Intramural:** Badminton, basketball, bowling, cross-country, fencing, golf, horseback riding, lacrosse, racquetball, rifle, sailing, soccer, softball, swimming, tennis, track and field, volleyball.

STUDENT SERVICES. Aptitude testing, career counseling, employment service for undergraduates, freshman orientation, health services, personal counseling, placement service for graduates, services/facilities for handicapped.

ANNUAL EXPENSES. Tuition and fees: $7,070. **Room and board:** $3,920. **Books and supplies:** $600. **Other expenses:** $1,346.

FINANCIAL AID. 67% of freshmen, 64% of continuing students receive some form of aid. Grants, loans, jobs available. 1,082 enrolled freshmen were judged to have need, all were offered aid. Academic, music/drama, art, athletic, state/district residency, leadership, religious affiliation, minority scholarships available. **Aid applications:** No closing date; priority given to applications received by May 1; applicants notified on a rolling basis; must reply within 2 weeks.

ADDRESS/TELEPHONE. Herman D. Thomas, Director of Admissions, Baylor University, PO Box 97056, Waco, TX 76798-7056. (817) 755-3435. Fax: (817) 755-3843.

Bee County College
Beeville, Texas CB code: 6055

2-year public community college, coed. Founded in 1965. **Accreditation:** Regional. **Undergraduate enrollment:** 2,289 men and women. **Faculty:** 117 total (74 full time), 12 with doctorates or other terminal degrees. **Location:** Rural campus in large town; 60 miles from Corpus Christi. **Calendar:** Semester, limited summer session. **Microcomputers:** Located in computer centers. **Special facilities:** Art gallery.

DEGREES OFFERED. AA, AS, AAS. 342 associate degrees awarded in 1992.

UNDERGRADUATE MAJORS. Accounting, agricultural sciences, air conditioning/heating/refrigeration mechanics, automotive mechanics, biology, business administration and management, business and office, business computer/console/peripheral equipment operation, business data processing and related programs, chemistry, child development/care/guidance, computer and information sciences, criminal justice studies, dental hygiene, diesel engine mechanics, drafting and design technology, education, elementary education, engineering, English, fashion merchandising, finance, fire control and safety technology, French, geology, German, graphic arts technology, history, home economics, law enforcement and corrections technologies, liberal/general studies, marketing and distribution, mathematics, music, nursing, physical sciences, physics, political science and government, predentistry, prelaw, premedicine, prepharmacy, preveterinary, psychology, radio/television technology, real estate, secondary education, secretarial and related programs, sociology, Spanish, speech, studio art, visual and performing arts, welding technology, word processing.

ACADEMIC PROGRAMS. 2-year transfer program, dual enrollment of high school students, internships. **Remedial services:** Learning center, remedial instruction, special counselor, tutoring. **Placement/credit:** CLEP Subject, institutional tests; 30 credit hours maximum for associate degree.

ACADEMIC REQUIREMENTS. Freshmen must earn minimum GPA of 1.5 to continue in good standing. Students must declare major by end of first year. **Graduation requirements:** 60 hours for associate. Most students required to take courses in English, mathematics.

FRESHMAN ADMISSIONS. Selection criteria: Open admissions.

1992 FRESHMAN CLASS PROFILE. 652 men and women enrolled. **Characteristics:** 99% from in state, 93% commute, 66% have minority backgrounds. Average age is 26.

FALL-TERM APPLICATIONS. No fee. No closing date; applicants notified on a rolling basis. Deferred admission available.

STUDENT LIFE. Housing: Dormitories (men, women); apartment housing available. **Activities:** Student government, choral groups, concert band, drama, music ensembles, musical theater, Baptist Student Union, Newman Club.

ATHLETICS. Intramural: Archery, badminton, basketball, bowling, softball, swimming, table tennis, track and field.

STUDENT SERVICES. Aptitude testing, career counseling, employment service for undergraduates, on-campus day care, personal counseling, placement service for graduates, veterans counselor, services/facilities for handicapped.

ANNUAL EXPENSES. Tuition and fees (1992-93): $400, $300 additional for out-of-district students, $840 additional for out-of-state students. **Room and board:** $2,110. **Books and supplies:** $500. **Other expenses:** $605.

FINANCIAL AID. 50% of freshmen, 50% of continuing students receive some form of aid. 93% of grants, all jobs based on need. Academic, music/drama, art scholarships available. **Aid applications:** No closing date; priority given to applications received by April 1; applicants notified on a rolling basis beginning on or about June 15; must reply within 2 weeks.

ADDRESS/TELEPHONE. Anne Nicholson, Registrar and Director Admissions, Bee County College, 3800 Charco Road, Beeville, TX 78102. (512) 358-3130 ext. 245. Fax: (512) 358-3973.

Blinn College
Brenham, Texas CB code: 6043

2-year public junior college, coed. Founded in 1883. **Accreditation:** Regional. **Undergraduate enrollment:** 2,566 men, 2,074 women full time; 1,422 men, 2,043 women part time. **Faculty:** 326 total (162 full time), 51 with doctorates or other terminal degrees. **Location:** Rural campus in large town; 79 miles from Houston. **Calendar:** Semester, limited summer session. **Microcomputers:** 420 located in libraries, classrooms, computer centers. **Special facilities:** Star of the Republic Museum, Texas Baseball Hall of Fame.

DEGREES OFFERED. AA, AAS. 386 associate degrees awarded in 1992.

UNDERGRADUATE MAJORS. Agricultural sciences, biology, business and management, business and office, chemistry, computer and information sciences, English, home economics, liberal/general studies, mathematics, nursing, physics, Spanish.

ACADEMIC PROGRAMS. 2-year transfer program, dual enrollment of high school students, cross-registration. **Remedial services:** Learning center, reduced course load, remedial instruction, special counselor, tutoring. **Placement/credit:** AP, CLEP Subject, institutional tests; 10 credit hours maximum for associate degree.

ACADEMIC REQUIREMENTS. Freshmen must earn minimum GPA of 2.0 to continue in good standing. 32% of freshmen return for sophomore year. Students must declare major by end of first year. **Graduation requirements:** 62 hours for associate (12 in major). Most students required to take courses in English, history, humanities, mathematics, biological/physical sciences, social sciences.

FRESHMAN ADMISSIONS. Selection criteria: Open admissions. **Test requirements:** SAT or ACT for placement.

1992 FRESHMAN CLASS PROFILE. 2,832 men, 3,002 women enrolled. **Characteristics:** 97% from in state, 90% commute, 16% have minority backgrounds, 2% are foreign students. Average age is 20.

FALL-TERM APPLICATIONS. No fee. No closing date; applicants notified on a rolling basis beginning on or about May 30. Deferred and early admission available.

STUDENT LIFE. Housing: Dormitories (men, women). **Activities:** Student government, student newspaper, choral groups, concert band, dance, drama, jazz band, marching band, music ensembles, musical theater, pep band, Baptist Student Union, Circle K International, Phi Theta Kappa, Fellowship of Christian Athletes.

ATHLETICS. NJCAA. **Intercollegiate:** Baseball M, basketball, cross-country M, football M, track and field M. **Intramural:** Baseball M, basketball, bowling, cross-country, softball, table tennis, track and field, volleyball.

STUDENT SERVICES. Career counseling, freshman orientation, personal counseling, veterans counselor, services/facilities for handicapped.

ANNUAL EXPENSES. Tuition and fees: $804, $240 additional for out-of-district students, $1,650 additional for out-of-state students. **Room and board:** $7,412. **Books and supplies:** $526. **Other expenses:** $1,036.

FINANCIAL AID. 30% of freshmen, 30% of continuing students receive some form of aid. 88% of grants, 70% of loans based on need. Academic, music/drama, athletic, minority scholarships available. **Aid applications:** No closing date; priority given to applications received by July 1; applicants notified on a rolling basis beginning on or about August 1.

ADDRESS/TELEPHONE. Dr. Don R. Stafford, Vice President for Student Services, Blinn College, 902 College Avenue, Brenham, TX 77833. (409) 830-4140. Fax: (409) 830-1416.

Brazosport College
Lake Jackson, Texas CB code: 6054

2-year public community college, coed. Founded in 1948. **Accreditation:** Regional. **Undergraduate enrollment:** 421 men, 496 women full time; 1,194 men, 1,235 women part time. **Faculty:** 162 total (68 full time), 12 with doctorates or other terminal degrees. **Location:** Suburban campus in large town; 50 miles from Houston. **Calendar:** Semester, extensive summer session. **Microcomputers:** Located in libraries, classrooms, computer centers. **Special facilities:** Chemical unit operations laboratory.

DEGREES OFFERED. AA, AS, AAS. 163 associate degrees awarded in 1992.

UNDERGRADUATE MAJORS. Air conditioning/heating/refrigeration mechanics, air conditioning/heating/refrigeration technology, automotive mechanics, automotive technology, biology, business and management, business and office, carpentry, chemical manufacturing technology, chemistry, child development/care/guidance, communications, computer and information sciences, computer programming, computer technology, construction, criminal justice technology, data processing, diesel engine mechanics, drafting, drafting and design technology, education, electrical and electronics equipment repair, electrical technology, electronic technology, elementary education, engineering, engineering and engineering-related technologies, English, finance, fine arts, food management, food production/management/services, history, industrial equipment maintenance and repair, industrial technology, information sciences and systems, instrumentation technology, legal secretary, liberal/general studies, marketing management, mathematics, medical secretary, music, nursing, physics, plumbing/pipefitting/steamfitting, political science and government, practical nursing, prelaw, psychology, quality control technology, real estate, secondary education, secretarial and related programs, social sciences, sociology, Spanish, vehicle and equipment operation, welding technology, word processing.

ACADEMIC PROGRAMS. 2-year transfer program, cooperative education, dual enrollment of high school students, internships, cross-registration. **Remedial services:** Learning center, reduced course load, remedial instruction, tutoring. **Placement/credit:** CLEP Subject, institutional tests; 15 credit hours maximum for associate degree.

ACADEMIC REQUIREMENTS. No policy requiring minimum GPA; records of students having academic difficulty are reviewed individually. 75% of freshmen return for sophomore year. **Graduation requirements:** 62 hours for associate. Most students required to take courses in English, history, mathematics, biological/physical sciences, social sciences.

FRESHMAN ADMISSIONS. Selection criteria: Open admissions. Selective admissions to nursing programs.

1992 FRESHMAN CLASS PROFILE. 1,081 men, 1,009 women enrolled. **Characteristics:** 99% from in state, 100% commute.

FALL-TERM APPLICATIONS. No fee. Closing date August 15; applicants notified on a rolling basis beginning on or about January 15. Early admission available.

STUDENT LIFE. Activities: Student government, magazine, student newspaper, choral groups, concert band, drama, jazz band, musical theater, Newman Club, Baptist Student Union, Phi Theta Kappa, Afro-American Club, Chicano Club, Wesley organization, student senate.

ATHLETICS. Intramural: Baseball, basketball, bowling, racquetball, soccer, softball, table tennis, tennis, volleyball.

STUDENT SERVICES. Aptitude testing, career counseling, employment service for undergraduates, freshman orientation, personal counseling, placement service for graduates, veterans counselor, services/facilities for handicapped.

ANNUAL EXPENSES. Tuition and fees: $460, $150 additional for out-of-district students, $1,650 additional for out-of-state students. **Books and supplies:** $540. **Other expenses:** $880.

FINANCIAL AID. 21% of freshmen, 24% of continuing students receive some form of aid. 77% of grants based on need. All loans, jobs based on criteria other than need. Academic, leadership scholarships available. **Aid applications:** No closing date; priority given to applications received by August 1; applicants notified on a rolling basis beginning on or about May 1.

ADDRESS/TELEPHONE. James Barta, Director Admissions and Registrar, Brazosport College, 500 College Drive, Lake Jackson, TX 77566. (409) 265-6131 ext. 216.

Brookhaven College
Farmers Branch, Texas — CB code: 6070

2-year public community college, coed. Founded in 1965. **Accreditation:** Regional. **Undergraduate enrollment:** 8,752 men and women. **Location:** Suburban campus in large town; right outside Dallas. **Calendar:** Semester. **Microcomputers:** Located in classrooms, computer centers.

DEGREES OFFERED. AA, AS, AAS. 143 associate degrees awarded in 1992.

UNDERGRADUATE MAJORS. Accounting, advertising art, automotive mechanics, automotive technology, business administration and management, business data programming, business systems analysis, child development/care/guidance, commercial art, computer programming, electrical technology, electromechanical technology, fashion merchandising, industrial technology, information sciences and systems, legal secretary, manufacturing technology, marketing management, nursing, office supervision and management, quality control technology, robotics, small business management and ownership, transportation management, word processing.

ACADEMIC PROGRAMS. 2-year transfer program, cooperative education, dual enrollment of high school students, honors program, study abroad, weekend college. **Remedial services:** Remedial instruction, special counselor, tutoring.

ACADEMIC REQUIREMENTS. Freshmen must earn minimum GPA of 2.0 to continue in good standing. Students must declare major by end of first year. **Graduation requirements:** Most students required to take courses in English, history, mathematics, social sciences.

FRESHMAN ADMISSIONS. Selection criteria: Open admissions.

1992 FRESHMAN CLASS PROFILE. 2,917 men and women enrolled. **Characteristics:** 100% commute.

FALL-TERM APPLICATIONS. $5 fee. No closing date; applicants notified on a rolling basis.

STUDENT LIFE. Activities: Film, student newspaper, choral groups, drama, music ensembles, musical theater.

ATHLETICS. NJCAA. **Intercollegiate:** Baseball M, golf M, soccer M, tennis. **Intramural:** Soccer.

STUDENT SERVICES. Aptitude testing, career counseling, employment service for undergraduates, freshman orientation, health services, personal counseling, placement service for graduates, special adviser for adult students, veterans counselor, services/facilities for handicapped.

ANNUAL EXPENSES. Tuition and fees (1992-93): $450, $570 additional for out-of-district students, $1,470 additional for out-of-state students. **Books and supplies:** $390. **Other expenses:** $1,245.

FINANCIAL AID. 68% of freshmen, 32% of continuing students receive some form of aid. Grants, loans, jobs available. Academic scholarships available. **Aid applications:** No closing date; priority given to applications received by July 1; applicants notified on a rolling basis. **Additional information:** Some tuition waivers available based upon state residency.

ADDRESS/TELEPHONE. Barbara Burke, Director of Admissions and Registrar, Brookhaven College, 3939 Valley View Lane, Farmers Branch, TX 75244. (214) 620-4700.

Cedar Valley College
Lancaster, Texas — CB code: 6148

2-year public community college, coed. Founded in 1974. **Accreditation:** Regional. **Undergraduate enrollment:** 459 men, 454 women full time; 900 men, 1,462 women part time. **Location:** Suburban campus in large town; 10 miles from Dallas. **Calendar:** Semester, limited summer session. **Microcomputers:** Located in libraries.

DEGREES OFFERED. 250 associate degrees awarded in 1992.

UNDERGRADUATE MAJORS. Accounting, agricultural sciences, air conditioning/heating/refrigeration mechanics, automotive mechanics, automotive technology, biology, business and management, business and office, business data processing and related programs, computer and information sciences, education, fashion merchandising, legal secretary, liberal/general studies, marketing and distribution, mathematics, office supervision and management, psychology, secretarial and related programs, small business management and ownership, social sciences.

ACADEMIC PROGRAMS. Cooperative education, dual enrollment of high school students, telecourses, visiting/exchange student program. **Remedial services:** Remedial instruction, special counselor, tutoring. **Placement/credit:** CLEP Subject, institutional tests; 45 credit hours maximum for associate degree.

ACADEMIC REQUIREMENTS. Freshmen must earn minimum GPA of 2.0 to continue in good standing. **Graduation requirements:** 61 hours for associate. Most students required to take courses in arts/fine arts, English, history, humanities, mathematics, biological/physical sciences, social sciences.

FRESHMAN ADMISSIONS. Selection criteria: Open admissions.

1992 FRESHMAN CLASS PROFILE. Characteristics: 99% from in state, 100% commute.

FALL-TERM APPLICATIONS. No fee. No closing date; applicants notified on a rolling basis.

STUDENT LIFE. Activities: Student newspaper, choral groups, jazz band, music ensembles.

ATHLETICS. Intercollegiate: Baseball M, basketball M. **Intramural:** Track and field W.

STUDENT SERVICES. Aptitude testing, career counseling, employment service for undergraduates, health services, personal counseling, placement service for graduates, services/facilities for handicapped.

ANNUAL EXPENSES. Tuition and fees (1992-93): $450, $570 additional for out-of-district students, $1,470 additional for out-of-state students. **Books and supplies:** $600. **Other expenses:** $1,045.

FINANCIAL AID. 35% of freshmen, 35% of continuing students receive some form of aid. All grants, 98% of loans, all jobs based on need. Academic, music/drama, art, state/district residency, leadership, minority scholarships available. **Aid applications:** No closing date; applicants notified on a rolling basis.

ADDRESS/TELEPHONE. John W. Williamson, Director of Admissions and Registrar, Cedar Valley College, 3030 North Dallas Avenue, Lancaster, TX 75134. (214) 372-8200.

Central Texas College
Killeen, Texas — CB code: 6130

2-year public community, technical college, coed. Founded in 1965. **Accreditation:** Regional. **Undergraduate enrollment:** 880 men, 1,174 women full time; 2,345 men, 2,426 women part time. **Faculty:** 300 total (108 full time), 34 with doctorates or other terminal degrees. **Location:** Suburban campus in small city; 5 miles from downtown. **Calendar:** Semester, extensive summer session. Extensive evening/early morning classes. **Microcomputers:** 60 located in libraries, computer centers. **Additional facts:** Continental, international campuses.

DEGREES OFFERED. AA, AS, AAS. 560 associate degrees awarded in 1992. 20% in business and management, 8% allied health, 36% multi/interdisciplinary studies, 5% social sciences, 12% trade and industry.

UNDERGRADUATE MAJORS. Accounting, agricultural business and management, agricultural sciences, air conditioning/heating/refrigeration mechanics, air conditioning/heating/refrigeration technology, airline piloting and navigation, animal sciences, architecture, automotive mechanics, automotive technology, biological and physical sciences, biology, business and management, business and office, business computer/console/peripheral equipment operation, business data entry equipment operation, business data processing and related programs, business data programming, chemistry, child development/care/guidance, clinical laboratory science, commercial art, communications, computer and information sciences, computer programming, computer servicing technology, criminal justice technology, diesel engine mechanics, drafting, drafting and design technology, education, electrical and electronics equipment repair, engineering, engineering and engineering-related technologies, engineering and other disciplines, English, equestrian science, finance, fine arts, food management, French, geology, German, graphic and printing production, graphic arts technology, hospitality and recreation marketing, hotel/motel and restaurant management, humanities, humanities and social sciences, industrial technology, journalism, law enforcement and corrections technologies, legal assistant/paralegal, liberal/general studies, maintenance technology, marketing and distribution, marketing management, masonry/tile setting, mathematics, medical laboratory technologies, music history and appreciation, nursing, office supervision and management, physical sciences, physics, practical nursing, prelaw, premedicine, protective services, psychology, radio/television broadcasting, radio/television technology, real estate, robotics, secretarial and related programs, social sciences, social work, soil sciences, Spanish, speech, systems analysis, telecommunications, visual and performing arts, welding technology, word processing. agricultural production.

ACADEMIC PROGRAMS. 2-year transfer program, dual enrollment of high school students, independent study, internships, telecourses, cross-registration. **Remedial services:** Learning center, reduced course load, remedial instruction, special counselor, tutoring. **Placement/credit:** AP, CLEP General and Subject, institutional tests; 49 credit hours maximum for associate degree.

ACADEMIC REQUIREMENTS. Freshmen must earn minimum GPA of 2.0 to continue in good standing. Students must declare major on enrollment. **Graduation requirements:** 64 hours for associate (36 in major). Most students required to take courses in arts/fine arts, computer science, English, history, humanities, mathematics, social sciences.

FRESHMAN ADMISSIONS. Selection criteria: Open admissions. Pre-TASP exam for placement required in the fall. Selective admissions to registered nursing program based upon successful completion of 10 selected credit hours. **High school preparation:** 21 units recommended. Recommended units include English 4, mathematics 3, social science 3 and science 2. **Test requirements:** SAT or ACT for placement and counseling only; score report by August 23.

1992 FRESHMAN CLASS PROFILE. 544 men, 499 women enrolled. **Characteristics:** 98% from in state, 97% commute, 40% have minority backgrounds, 2% are foreign students. Average age is 25.

FALL-TERM APPLICATIONS. No fee. No closing date; applicants notified on a rolling basis. Interview required for nursing, medical laboratory technician applicants. Audition recommended for music applicants. Portfolio recommended for art applicants. CRDA. Deferred and early admission available. EDP-F.

STUDENT LIFE. Housing: Dormitories (coed); apartment housing available. **Activities:** Student government, radio, student newspaper, television, choral groups, Baptist Student Union, sports clubs, ethnic clubs.

ATHLETICS. Intramural: Badminton, basketball, bowling, golf, soccer, softball, table tennis, tennis, volleyball.

STUDENT SERVICES. Aptitude testing, career counseling, employment service for undergraduates, freshman orientation, on-campus day care, personal counseling, placement service for graduates, veterans counselor, services/facilities for handicapped.

ANNUAL EXPENSES. Tuition and fees: $696, $1,400 additional for out-of-state students. **Room and board:** $2,995. **Books and supplies:** $800. **Other expenses:** $1,531.

FINANCIAL AID. 21% of freshmen, 12% of continuing students receive some form of aid. 94% of grants, all loans, all jobs based on need. Academic, leadership, minority scholarships available. **Aid applications:** Closing date August 1; priority given to applications received by July 1; applicants notified on or about August 10.

ADDRESS/TELEPHONE. Bill Alexander, Dean of Admissions and Counseling, Central Texas College, PO Box 1800, Killeen, TX 76540-9990. (817) 526-1104. (800) 792-3348 ext. 1104. Fax: (817) 526-0817.

Cisco Junior College
Cisco, Texas CB code: 6096

2-year public junior college, coed. Founded in 1940. **Accreditation:** Regional. **Undergraduate enrollment:** 576 men, 516 women full time; 600 men, 864 women part time. **Faculty:** 123 total (68 full time), 3 with doctorates or other terminal degrees. **Location:** Rural campus in small town; 100 miles from Fort Worth. **Calendar:** Semester, limited summer session. **Microcomputers:** Located in classrooms. **Special facilities:** Museum.

DEGREES OFFERED. AA, AS, AAS. 136 associate degrees awarded in 1992.

UNDERGRADUATE MAJORS. Accounting, agribusiness, agricultural sciences, automotive technology, business and office, business data entry equipment operation, business data processing and related programs, business data programming, computer and information sciences, drafting, engineering and engineering-related technologies, finance, fire control and safety technology, law enforcement and corrections technologies, liberal/general studies, marketing and distribution, personal services, photographic technology, plant sciences, practical nursing, range management, real estate, recreation and community services technologies, secretarial and related programs, teacher aide.

ACADEMIC PROGRAMS. 2-year transfer program, dual enrollment of high school students. **Remedial services:** Remedial instruction, tutoring. **Placement/credit:** CLEP Subject; 22 credit hours maximum for associate degree.

ACADEMIC REQUIREMENTS. Freshmen must earn minimum GPA of 1.75 to continue in good standing. Full-time students must pass 9 hours per semester, part-time students must pass 66% of hours for which they enroll. 65% of freshmen return for sophomore year. Students must declare major on enrollment. **Graduation requirements:** 63 hours for associate. Most students required to take courses in English, history, mathematics, biological/physical sciences.

FRESHMAN ADMISSIONS. Selection criteria: Open admissions. **Test requirements:** SAT or ACT for placement and counseling only.

1992 FRESHMAN CLASS PROFILE. 729 men and women enrolled. **Characteristics:** 90% from in state, 70% commute, 30% have minority backgrounds. Average age is 28.

FALL-TERM APPLICATIONS. No fee. No closing date; applicants notified on a rolling basis. Deferred and early admission available.

STUDENT LIFE. Housing: Dormitories (men, women). **Activities:** Student government, student newspaper, yearbook, choral groups, concert band, drama, marching band, music ensembles.

ATHLETICS. Intercollegiate: Basketball, football M. **Intramural:** Basketball, track and field.

STUDENT SERVICES. Health services, personal counseling, services/facilities for handicapped.

ANNUAL EXPENSES. Tuition and fees: $630, $120 additional for out-of-district students, $426 additional for out-of-state students. **Room and board:** $1,950. **Books and supplies:** $500. **Other expenses:** $600.

FINANCIAL AID. 50% of freshmen, 50% of continuing students receive some form of aid. 76% of grants, all loans, all jobs based on need. Academic, music/drama, athletic scholarships available. **Aid applications:** No closing date; priority given to applications received by August 15; applicants notified on a rolling basis beginning on or about August 15; must reply within 15 days.

ADDRESS/TELEPHONE. Olin Odom, Dean Admissions and Registrar, Cisco Junior College, Route 3, Box 3, Cisco, TX 76437. (817) 442-2567.

Clarendon College
Clarendon, Texas CB code: 6097

2-year public junior college, coed. Founded in 1898. **Accreditation:** Regional. **Undergraduate enrollment:** 785 men and women. **Faculty:** 31 total. **Location:** Rural campus in rural community; 60 miles from Amarillo. **Calendar:** Semester, limited summer session. **Microcomputers:** Located in computer centers.

DEGREES OFFERED. AA, AS, AAS. 120 associate degrees awarded in 1992.

UNDERGRADUATE MAJORS. Automotive technology, business and office, law enforcement and corrections technologies, liberal/general studies, personal services, photographic technology, practical nursing, real estate, secretarial and related programs.

ACADEMIC PROGRAMS. Dual enrollment of high school students. **Remedial services:** Learning center, remedial instruction. **Placement/credit:** CLEP General and Subject; 30 credit hours maximum for associate degree.

ACADEMIC REQUIREMENTS. Freshmen must earn minimum GPA of 1.5 to continue in good standing. 60% of freshmen return for sophomore year. **Graduation requirements:** 62 hours for associate (50 in major).

FRESHMAN ADMISSIONS. Selection criteria: Open admissions. All nursing applicants must pass pre-entrance examination, provide 3 personal references, and interview with vocational nursing instructor. **High school preparation:** 15 units recommended. Recommended units include biological science 1, English 3, mathematics 2 and social science 2. Students must complete requirements with 7 electives. **Test requirements:** SAT or ACT (ACT preferred) for counseling; score report by July 15.

1992 FRESHMAN CLASS PROFILE. 192 men and women enrolled. **Characteristics:** 75% from in state, 60% live in college housing, 4% have minority backgrounds. Average age is 18.

FALL-TERM APPLICATIONS. No fee. No closing date; priority given to applications received by August 15; applicants notified on a rolling basis. Early admission available.

STUDENT LIFE. Housing: Dormitories (men, women). **Activities:** Student government, yearbook, choral groups, drama, college dance band, Intercollegiate and intramural rodeo.

ATHLETICS. NSCAA. **Intercollegiate:** Basketball. **Intramural:** Basketball, golf, softball, tennis, volleyball.

STUDENT SERVICES. Career counseling, personal counseling, services/facilities for handicapped.

ANNUAL EXPENSES. Tuition and fees (1992-93): $620, $60 additional for out-of-district students, $4,482 additional for out-of-state students. **Room and board:** $1,550. **Books and supplies:** $350. **Other expenses:** $1,000.

FINANCIAL AID. 80% of freshmen, 75% of continuing students receive some form of aid. **Aid applications:** No closing date; priority given to applications received by August 1; applicants notified on a rolling basis beginning on or about June 1; must reply within 4 weeks.

ADDRESS/TELEPHONE. Lissa Parish, Director of Admissions/Development, Clarendon College, PO Box 968, Clarendon, TX 79226. (806) 874-3571.

College of the Mainland
Texas City, Texas — CB code: 6133

2-year public community college, coed. Founded in 1966. **Accreditation:** Regional. **Undergraduate enrollment:** 467 men, 596 women full time; 1,013 men, 1,807 women part time. **Faculty:** 84 total (83 full time), 16 with doctorates or other terminal degrees. **Location:** Suburban campus in large town; 25 miles from Houston. **Calendar:** Semester, extensive summer session. **Microcomputers:** Located in libraries, classrooms, computer centers. **Special facilities:** Art gallery.

DEGREES OFFERED. AA, AS, AAS. 158 associate degrees awarded in 1992. 15% in business and management, 7% business/office and marketing/distribution, 9% education, 5% engineering technologies, 27% health sciences, 6% multi/interdisciplinary studies, 8% parks/recreation, protective services, public affairs.

UNDERGRADUATE MAJORS. Accounting, air conditioning/heating/refrigeration mechanics, allied health, behavioral sciences, biological and physical sciences, business administration and management, business and management, business and office, business data entry equipment operation, business data processing and related programs, business data programming, child development/care/guidance, data processing, drafting, economics, electrical installation, elementary education, engineering and other disciplines, finance, fine arts, fire control and safety technology, history, humanities and social sciences, labor/industrial relations, law enforcement and corrections technologies, liberal/general studies, marketing and distribution, mathematics, music, nursing, office supervision and management, political science and government, practical nursing, psychology, public affairs, real estate, science technologies, secondary education, secretarial and related programs, social work, sociology.

ACADEMIC PROGRAMS. 2-year transfer program, cooperative education, cross-registration. **Remedial services:** Learning center, remedial instruction, tutoring. **Placement/credit:** AP, CLEP Subject, institutional tests; 24 credit hours maximum for associate degree.

ACADEMIC REQUIREMENTS. No policy requiring minimum GPA; records of students having academic difficulty are reviewed individually. **Graduation requirements:** 62 hours for associate. Most students required to take courses in English, history, mathematics, social sciences.

FRESHMAN ADMISSIONS. Selection criteria: Open admissions. Selective admissions to nursing program and for all foreign applicants. **Test requirements:** SAT or ACT for placement and counseling only; score report by August 1.

1992 FRESHMAN CLASS PROFILE. 338 men, 441 women enrolled. **Characteristics:** 100% commute. Average age is 29.

FALL-TERM APPLICATIONS. No fee. No closing date; priority given to applications received by August 20; applicants notified on a rolling basis. Early admission available.

STUDENT LIFE. Activities: Student government, student newspaper, choral groups, concert band, drama, musical theater.

ATHLETICS. Intramural: Baseball, basketball, bowling, racquetball, tennis, volleyball.

STUDENT SERVICES. Aptitude testing, career counseling, employment service for undergraduates, on-campus day care, personal counseling, placement service for graduates, veterans counselor, services/facilities for handicapped.

ANNUAL EXPENSES. Tuition and fees: $341, $290 additional for out-of-district students, $960 additional for out-of-state students. **Room and board:** $1,880. **Books and supplies:** $427. **Other expenses:** $1,005.

FINANCIAL AID. 92% of freshmen, 8% of continuing students receive some form of aid. 92% of grants, all loans, 57% of jobs based on need. 105 enrolled freshmen were judged to have need, 93 were offered aid. Academic, music/drama, art, leadership scholarships available. **Aid applications:** No closing date; applicants notified on a rolling basis. **Additional information:** Large student employment program, short-term loans available for tuition payment plan.

ADDRESS/TELEPHONE. Dr. Robert A. Johnston, Director of Admissions and Records/Registrar, College of the Mainland, 1200 Amburn Rd, Texas City, TX 77591. (409) 938-1211 ext. 243. Fax: (409) 938-1306.

Collin County Community College District
McKinney, Texas — CB code: 1951

2-year public community college, coed. Founded in 1985. **Accreditation:** Regional. **Undergraduate enrollment:** 1,415 men, 1,336 women full time; 2,720 men, 4,119 women part time. **Faculty:** 528 total (116 full time), 122 with doctorates or other terminal degrees. **Location:** Suburban campus in large town; 25 miles from Dallas. **Calendar:** Semester. **Microcomputers:** 500 located in libraries, classrooms, computer centers, campus-wide network. **Additional facts:** Two campuses: McKinney and Plano.

DEGREES OFFERED. AA, AS, AAS. 209 associate degrees awarded in 1992. 17% in business and management, 19% business/office and marketing/distribution, 11% health sciences, 9% letters/literature, 5% parks/recreation, protective services, public affairs.

UNDERGRADUATE MAJORS. Accounting, biological and physical sciences, biology, business and management, business and office, chemistry, child development/care/guidance, commercial art, computer and information sciences, criminal justice studies, drafting and design technology, economics, education, electrical technology, electronic technology, emergency medical technologies, engineering, English, fashion merchandising, fine arts, fire control and safety technology, French, geography, geology, health education, health sciences, history, horticulture, Latin, legal assistant/paralegal, marketing and distribution, mathematics, medical secretary, microcomputer software, music, nursing, office supervision and management, philosophy, photography, physics, political science and government, predentistry, prelaw, premedicine, preveterinary, psychology, real estate, respiratory therapy technology, secretarial and related programs, small business management and ownership, sociology, Spanish, speech, theater design.

ACADEMIC PROGRAMS. 2-year transfer program, accelerated program, cooperative education, dual enrollment of high school students, honors program, internships, study abroad, telecourses. **Remedial services:** Learning center, remedial instruction, special counselor, tutoring. **Placement/credit:** AP, CLEP Subject, institutional tests; 18 credit hours maximum for associate degree.

ACADEMIC REQUIREMENTS. Students must declare major on application. **Graduation requirements:** 60 hours for associate (16 in major). Most students required to take courses in computer science, English, history, humanities, mathematics, biological/physical sciences, social sciences.

FRESHMAN ADMISSIONS. Selection criteria: Open admissions. Concurrent high school enrollment requires high school transcript, letter of permission, assessment testing and interview. Special requirements for nursing and emergency medical technician. Students on suspension require transcripts and interview.

1992 FRESHMAN CLASS PROFILE. 1,798 men and women enrolled. **Characteristics:** 97% from in state, 100% commute, 12% have minority backgrounds, 1% are foreign students. Average age is 28.

FALL-TERM APPLICATIONS. No fee. No closing date; applicants notified on a rolling basis.

STUDENT LIFE. Activities: Magazine, student newspaper, choral groups, concert band, dance, drama, jazz band, music ensembles, Baptist Student Union, Black Student Union, College Republicans, Advocates for Child Development, Collin Nursing Student Association, Students for Political Awareness.

ATHLETICS. NJCAA. **Intercollegiate:** Baseball M, basketball M, tennis, volleyball W. **Intramural:** Softball.

STUDENT SERVICES. Aptitude testing, career counseling, employment service for undergraduates, freshman orientation, personal counseling, placement service for graduates, veterans counselor, services/facilities for handicapped.

ANNUAL EXPENSES. Tuition and fees: $588, $280 additional for out-of-district students, $1,260 additional for out-of-state students. **Books and supplies:** $433. **Other expenses:** $1,086.

FINANCIAL AID. 10% of freshmen, 10% of continuing students receive some form of aid. 99% of grants, 81% of loans, 27% of jobs based on need. 790 enrolled freshmen were judged to have need, all were offered aid. Academic, music/drama, art, athletic, state/district residency, leadership scholarships available. **Aid applications:** No closing date; priority given to applications received by June 1; applicants notified on a rolling basis beginning on or about July 15; must reply within 2 weeks.

ADDRESS/TELEPHONE. Toni P. Allen, Dean of Enrollment Management, Collin County Community College District, 2200 West University, McKinney, TX 75070-2906. (214) 548-6742. Fax: (214) 548-5636.

Commonwealth Institute of Funeral Service
Houston, Texas — CB code: 7031

2-year private mortuary college, coed. Founded in 1988. **Undergraduate enrollment:** 94 men, 30 women full time. **Faculty:** 6 total (4 full time). **Location:** Urban campus in very large city. **Calendar:** Quarter. **Microcomputers:** 6 located in computer centers. **Special facilities:** Museum, television studio, theater. **Additional facts:** Accredited by American Board of Funeral Service Education, Inc.

DEGREES OFFERED. AAS. 38 associate degrees awarded in 1992. 100% in parks/recreation, protective services, public affairs.

UNDERGRADUATE MAJORS. Funeral services/mortuary science.

ACADEMIC REQUIREMENTS. Freshmen must earn minimum GPA of 2.0 to continue in good standing. Students must declare major on application. **Graduation requirements:** 75 hours for associate (75 in major). Most students required to take courses in computer science, biological/physical sciences, social sciences.

FRESHMAN ADMISSIONS. Selection criteria: Open admissions.

1992 FRESHMAN CLASS PROFILE. 94 men, 30 women enrolled. **Characteristics:** 80% from in state, 100% commute, 50% have minority backgrounds, 30% join fraternities/sororities. Average age is 24.

FALL-TERM APPLICATIONS. $25 fee. No closing date; applicants notified on a rolling basis; must reply immediately.

STUDENT LIFE. Housing: Local funeral homes provide student employees accommodations while attending college. **Activities:** Fraternities.

STUDENT SERVICES. Freshman orientation, services/facilities for handicapped.

ANNUAL EXPENSES. Tuition and fees: $6,075. Tuition for 12-month certificate program is $6,000 including fees and books. Associate degree program is an additional $1,500. **Other expenses:** $100.

FINANCIAL AID. 60% of freshmen, 50% of continuing students receive some form of aid. All grants, 45% of loans based on need. 60 enrolled freshmen were judged to have need, all were offered aid. Leadership scholarships available. **Aid applications:** No closing date; priority given to applications received by July 16; applicants notified on a rolling basis; must reply by registration.

ADDRESS/TELEPHONE. Commonwealth Institute of Funeral Service, 415 Barren Springs Drive, Houston, TX 77090-5913. (713) 873-0262. (800) 628-1580. Fax: (713) 873-0264.

Concordia Lutheran College
Austin, Texas

CB code: 6127

Admissions: 82% of applicants accepted
Based on: ••• School record, test scores
• Activities, essay, interview, recommendations, religious affiliation/commitment, special talents
Completion: 90% of freshmen end year in good standing
22% enter graduate study

4-year private liberal arts college, coed, affiliated with Lutheran Church—Missouri Synod. Founded in 1926. **Accreditation:** Regional. **Undergraduate enrollment:** 220 men, 303 women full time; 76 men, 95 women part time. **Faculty:** 57 total (37 full time), 34 with doctorates or other terminal degrees. **Location:** Urban campus in large city; centrally located. **Calendar:** Semester, limited summer session. Extensive evening/early morning classes. **Microcomputers:** 30 located in libraries, classrooms, computer centers.

DEGREES OFFERED. AA, BA. 2 associate degrees awarded in 1992. 90 bachelor's degrees awarded. 41% in business and management, 19% communications, 25% teacher education, 9% social sciences.

UNDERGRADUATE MAJORS. Associate: Liberal/general studies. **Bachelor's:** Accounting, art education, behavioral sciences, business and management, communications, earth sciences, elementary education, English, English education, environmental science, liberal/general studies, mathematics education, Mexican American studies, music, music education, physical education, predentistry, prelaw, premedicine, reading education, religious music, science education, secondary education, social science education, social sciences, social studies education, Spanish.

ACADEMIC PROGRAMS. Double major, dual enrollment of high school students, independent study, internships, telecourses, cross-registration. **Remedial services:** Learning center, reduced course load, remedial instruction, special counselor, tutoring. **ROTC:** Air Force, Army, Naval. **Placement/credit:** AP, CLEP Subject, institutional tests; 15 credit hours maximum for associate degree; 30 credit hours maximum for bachelor's degree.

ACADEMIC REQUIREMENTS. Freshmen must earn minimum GPA of 2.0 to continue in good standing. 77% of freshmen return for sophomore year. Students must declare major by end of second year. **Graduation requirements:** 64 hours for associate, 128 hours for bachelor's (36 in major). Most students required to take courses in arts/fine arts, computer science, English, history, humanities, mathematics, philosophy/religion, biological/physical sciences, social sciences. **Postgraduate studies:** 85% from 2-year programs enter 4-year programs. 1% enter law school, 1% enter medical school, 5% enter MBA programs, 15% enter other graduate study.

FRESHMAN ADMISSIONS. Selection criteria: School achievement record, test scores, and 2.5 GPA. **Test requirements:** SAT or ACT; score report by August 15.

1992 FRESHMAN CLASS PROFILE. 169 men applied, 139 accepted, 70 enrolled; 169 women applied, 139 accepted, 85 enrolled. 60% had high school GPA of 3.0 or higher, 40% between 2.0 and 2.99. **Academic background:** Mid 50% of enrolled freshmen had SAT-V between 380-470, SAT-M between 390-520; ACT composite between 15-22. 78% submitted SAT scores, 76% submitted ACT scores. **Characteristics:** 88% from in state, 55% live in college housing, 12% have minority backgrounds, 2% are foreign students. Average age is 19.

FALL-TERM APPLICATIONS. $25 fee, may be waived for applicants with need. Closing date March 15; priority given to applications received by March 15; applicants notified on a rolling basis. Interview required for academically weak applicants. Deferred and early admission available. Accepted dormitory applicants must reply by August 15. Financial assistance recipients must reply within 30 days.

STUDENT LIFE. Housing: Dormitories (men, women, coed). **Activities:** Student government, student newspaper, television, yearbook, choral groups, drama, jazz band, music ensembles, musical theater, pep band, community social service organization, religious organization, Spanish club, honors societies.

ATHLETICS. NAIA. **Intercollegiate:** Baseball M, basketball, golf M, tennis, volleyball W. **Intramural:** Badminton, basketball, bowling, field hockey M, football M, golf, handball, racquetball, soccer M, softball, table tennis, tennis, volleyball.

STUDENT SERVICES. Aptitude testing, career counseling, employment service for undergraduates, freshman orientation, personal counseling, placement service for graduates, special adviser for adult students, veterans counselor, tutoring, substance abuse counseling, services/facilities for handicapped.

ANNUAL EXPENSES. Tuition and fees: $6,760. **Room and board:** $3,500. **Books and supplies:** $450. **Other expenses:** $1,050.

FINANCIAL AID. 80% of freshmen, 75% of continuing students receive some form of aid. 80% of grants, 83% of loans, 81% of jobs based on need. 79 enrolled freshmen were judged to have need, all were offered aid. Academic, music/drama, athletic, leadership scholarships available. **Aid applications:** Closing date July 1; priority given to applications received by April 15; applicants notified on a rolling basis beginning on or about February 1; must reply within 2 weeks.

ADDRESS/TELEPHONE. Kurt Senske, Dir Recruitment/Registration, Concordia Lutheran College, 3400 Interstate 35 North, Austin, TX 78705-2799. (512) 452-7661. (800) 285-4CLC. Fax: (512) 459-8517.

Cooke County College
Gainesville, Texas

CB code: 6245

2-year public community college, coed. Founded in 1924. **Accreditation:** Regional. **Undergraduate enrollment:** 475 men, 641 women full time; 1,151 men, 1,801 women part time. **Faculty:** 185 total (74 full time), 15 with doctorates or other terminal degrees. **Location:** Rural campus in large town; 70 miles from Dallas. **Calendar:** Semester, extensive summer session. Extensive evening/early morning classes. **Microcomputers:** 60 located in classrooms. **Special facilities:** Planetarium, experimental farm, cattle center, horse arena.

DEGREES OFFERED. AA, AS, AAS. 189 associate degrees awarded in 1992. 5% in business and management, 12% business/office and marketing/distribution, 26% allied health, 37% multi/interdisciplinary studies, 12% social sciences, 5% trade and industry.

UNDERGRADUATE MAJORS. Agricultural sciences, automotive mechanics, automotive technology, biological and physical sciences, business and management, business and office, business data entry equipment operation, business data processing and related programs, business data programming, criminal justice studies, criminology, data processing, diesel engine mechanics, drafting, drafting and design technology, electronic technology, emergency medical technologies, engineering and engineering-related technologies, equestrian science, humanities and social sciences, law enforcement and corrections technologies, legal assistant/paralegal, legal secretary, liberal/general studies, machine tool operation/machine shop, marketing and distribution, microcomputer software, nursing, occupational therapy assistant, photographic technology, precision metal work, real estate, science technologies, secretarial and related programs, welding technology.

ACADEMIC PROGRAMS. 2-year transfer program, dual enrollment of high school students, telecourses, cross-registration. **Remedial services:** Learning center, remedial instruction, tutoring. **Placement/credit:** CLEP Subject, institutional tests; 18 credit hours maximum for associate degree.

ACADEMIC REQUIREMENTS. Freshmen must earn minimum GPA of 2.0 to continue in good standing. 56% of freshmen return for sophomore year. Students must declare major on application. **Graduation requirements:** 62 hours for associate. Most students required to take courses in English, history, mathematics, biological/physical sciences, social sciences.

FRESHMAN ADMISSIONS. Selection criteria: Open admissions. **High school preparation:** 16 units recommended. Recommended units include English 4, mathematics 2, social science 2 and science 2.

1992 FRESHMAN CLASS PROFILE. 1,229 men and women enrolled. **Characteristics:** 94% from in state, 98% commute, 7% have minority backgrounds, 1% are foreign students.

FALL-TERM APPLICATIONS. No fee. No closing date; applicants notified on a rolling basis. CRDA. Deferred and early admission available. EDP-F. High school transcript, proof of state residency, pre-TASP placement.

STUDENT LIFE. Housing: Dormitories (coed). **Activities:** Student government, magazine, choral groups, drama, music ensembles, Baptist Student Union, Collegiate Vocational Future Farmers of America, honor society, Catholic Campus Community, Nursing Student Association, Criminal Justice Club, Methodist Student Organization, computer club. **Additional information:** Intercollegiate rodeo and scholarships available to students.

ATHLETICS. NJCAA. **Intercollegiate:** Baseball M, tennis W, volleyball W. **Intramural:** Badminton, basketball, bowling, golf, racquetball, softball, table tennis, tennis, track and field, volleyball.

STUDENT SERVICES. Aptitude testing, career counseling, employment service for undergraduates, freshman orientation, personal counseling, special adviser for adult students, veterans counselor, women's services, services/facilities for handicapped.

ANNUAL EXPENSES. Tuition and fees (1992-93): $600, $300 additional for out-of-state students. **Room and board:** $2,300. **Books and supplies:** $450. **Other expenses:** $1,075.

FINANCIAL AID. 30% of freshmen, 35% of continuing students receive some form of aid. 80% of grants, 87% of loans, 65% of jobs based on need. Academic, music/drama, athletic scholarships available. **Aid applications:** Closing date June 1; applicants notified on a rolling basis beginning on or about August 1; must reply within 4 weeks. **Additional information:** Intercollegiate rodeo and scholarships available to students.

ADDRESS/TELEPHONE. Janie Neighbors, Director of Admissions, Cooke County College, 1525 West California, Gainesville, TX 76240. (817) 668-7731. Fax: (817) 668-6049.

Corpus Christi State University
Corpus Christi, Texas — CB code: 0366

2-year upper-division public university, coed. Founded in 1971. **Accreditation:** Regional. **Undergraduate enrollment:** 445 men, 749 women full time; 733 men, 1,293 women part time. **Graduate enrollment:** 107 men, 130 women full time; 304 men, 664 women part time. **Faculty:** 279 total (122 full time). **Location:** Suburban campus in large city; 150 miles from San Antonio. **Calendar:** Semester, extensive summer session. Extensive evening/early morning classes. **Microcomputers:** 145 located in libraries, classrooms, computer centers. **Special facilities:** Weil Art Gallery, National Spill Control School, Conrad Blucher Institute for Surveying and Science, Center for Coastal Studies. **Additional facts:** Campus located on island.

DEGREES OFFERED. BA, BS, BFA, MA, MS, MBA, EdD. 626 bachelor's degrees awarded in 1992. 26% in business and management, 28% teacher education, 6% health sciences, 6% parks/recreation, protective services, public affairs, 8% psychology, 5% social sciences, 6% visual and performing arts. Graduate degrees offered in 15 major fields of study.

UNDERGRADUATE MAJORS. Accounting, biology, business administration and management, business and management, chemistry, clinical laboratory science, communications, computer and information sciences, criminal justice studies, criminology, elementary education, English, finance, fine arts, geology, history, humanities and social sciences, information sciences and systems, marketing management, mathematics, music, nursing, occupational management, physical education, political science and government, psychology, secondary education, sociology, Spanish, special education, trade and industrial education.

ACADEMIC PROGRAMS. Internships, teacher preparation. **ROTC:** Army. **Placement/credit:** Institutional tests.

ACADEMIC REQUIREMENTS. Students must declare major on enrollment. **Graduation requirements:** 124 hours for bachelor's (30 in major). Most students required to take courses in English, history, mathematics, biological/physical sciences, social sciences.

STUDENT LIFE. Housing: Dormitories (coed); apartment housing available. **Activities:** Student government, film, student newspaper, choral groups, concert band, drama, jazz band, music ensembles, musical theater, Baptist Student Union, Campus Catholic Community, Friends Meeting, LDS Students Association, Amigos.

ATHLETICS. Intramural: Badminton, baseball, basketball, cross-country, golf, gymnastics, handball, racquetball, sailing, softball, swimming, table tennis, tennis, volleyball.

STUDENT SERVICES. Career counseling, employment service for undergraduates, health services, personal counseling, placement service for graduates, veterans counselor, services/facilities for handicapped.

ANNUAL EXPENSES. Tuition and fees: $1,427, $4,080 additional for out-of-state students. **Room and board:** $1,100 room only. **Books and supplies:** $425. **Other expenses:** $1,100.

FINANCIAL AID. 34% of continuing students receive some form of aid. Grants, loans, jobs available. Academic, music/drama, art scholarships available. **Aid applications:** Closing date April 1; applicants notified on a rolling basis beginning on or about May 1; must reply within 2 weeks.

ADDRESS/TELEPHONE. Mary Margaret Dechant, Director of Admissions, Corpus Christi State University, 6300 Ocean Drive, Corpus Christi, TX 78412. (512) 994-2624. Fax: (512) 993-4204.

Criswell College
Dallas, Texas — CB code: 0794

4-year private Bible, seminary college, coed, affiliated with Southern Baptist Convention. Founded in 1970. **Accreditation:** Regional. **Undergraduate enrollment:** 127 men, 26 women full time; 101 men, 18 women part time. **Graduate enrollment:** 41 men, 2 women full time; 20 men part time. **Faculty:** 25 total (15 full time), 17 with doctorates or other terminal degrees. **Location:** Urban campus in very large city; located downtown. **Calendar:** Semester. **Microcomputers:** Located in classrooms.

DEGREES OFFERED. AA, BA, MA, M.Div. 1 associate degree awarded in 1992. 90% in philosophy, religion, theology, 10% social sciences. 24 bachelor's degrees awarded. 80% in philosophy, religion, theology, 20% social sciences. Graduate degrees offered in 4 major fields of study.

UNDERGRADUATE MAJORS. Associate: Bible studies, missionary studies. **Bachelor's:** Bible studies, Biblical counseling, missionary studies.

ACADEMIC PROGRAMS. Accelerated program, double major, dual enrollment of high school students. **Remedial services:** Reduced course load.

ACADEMIC REQUIREMENTS. Freshmen must earn minimum GPA of 2.0 to continue in good standing. Students must declare major on application. **Graduation requirements:** 63 hours for associate (36 in major), 129 hours for bachelor's (60 in major). Most students required to take courses in computer science, English, foreign languages, history, philosophy/religion, biological/physical sciences. **Additional information:** Students must pass oral examination during final semester.

FRESHMAN ADMISSIONS. Selection criteria: SAT or ACT scores and 3 letters of recommendation required. **Test requirements:** SAT or ACT (SAT preferred); score report by July 30.

1992 FRESHMAN CLASS PROFILE. 95 men applied, 85 accepted, 45 enrolled; 30 women applied, 25 accepted, 5 enrolled. **Characteristics:** 61% from in state, 100% commute, 3% are foreign students.

FALL-TERM APPLICATIONS. $30 fee. Closing date July 30; priority given to applications received by July 20; applicants notified on or about July 30. Essay required. Interview recommended. Deferred admission available.

STUDENT LIFE. Activities: Student government, missionary fellowship. **Additional information:** Religious observance required.

STUDENT SERVICES. Aptitude testing, employment service for undergraduates, freshman orientation, personal counseling, veterans counselor, services/facilities for handicapped.

ANNUAL EXPENSES. Tuition and fees (1992-93): $2,650. **Books and supplies:** $200.

FINANCIAL AID. 20% of freshmen, 25% of continuing students receive some form of aid. All grants, all jobs based on need. 25 enrolled freshmen were judged to have need, all were offered aid. Religious affiliation scholarships available. **Aid applications:** Closing date July 15; applicants notified on or about August 1.

ADDRESS/TELEPHONE. Dr. Luis L. Pantoja, Jr, Dean Admissions and Records, Criswell College, 4010 Gaston Avenue, Dallas, TX 75246. (214) 821-5433. (800) 899-0012. Fax: (214) 818-1310.

Dallas Baptist University
Dallas, Texas — CB code: 6159

4-year private university, coed, affiliated with Southern Baptist Convention. Founded in 1965. **Accreditation:** Regional. **Undergraduate enrollment:** 382 men, 448 women full time; 695 men, 812 women part time. **Graduate enrollment:** 47 men, 37 women full time; 191 men, 100 women part time. **Faculty:** 175 total (61 full time), 31 with doctorates or other terminal degrees. **Location:** Suburban campus in very large city; 13 miles from downtown. **Calendar:** 4-1-4, extensive summer session. Saturday and extensive evening/early morning classes. **Microcomputers:** 56 located in libraries, computer centers.

DEGREES OFFERED. AA, BA, BS, MA, MBA, MEd. 484 bachelor's degrees awarded. 50% in business and management, 7% computer sciences, 8% multi/interdisciplinary studies, 8% parks/recreation, protective services, public affairs, 7% philosophy, religion, theology. Graduate degrees offered in 13 major fields of study.

UNDERGRADUATE MAJORS. Associate: Business administration and management, liberal/general studies. **Bachelor's:** Accounting, aviation management, biology, business administration and management, business and management, business economics, computer and information sciences, counseling psychology, criminal justice studies, criminology, early childhood education, economics, education, elementary education, engineering and engineering-related technologies, engineering management, English, English education, finance, history, information sciences and systems, law enforcement and corrections, liberal/general studies, management information systems, management science, marketing management, mathematics, mathematics education, music, music education, music performance, physical education, political science and government, prelaw, premedicine, prepharmacy, preveterinary, psychology, reading education, real estate, religion, religious education, religious music, science education, secondary education, social science education, social studies education, social work, sociology, visual and performing arts.

ACADEMIC PROGRAMS. Double major, dual enrollment of high school students, education specialist degree, honors program, independent study, internships, teacher preparation, weekend college, Washington semester. **ROTC:** Air Force, Army. **Placement/credit:** AP, CLEP Subject, institutional tests.

ACADEMIC REQUIREMENTS. Freshmen must earn minimum GPA of 2.0 to continue in good standing. 59% of freshmen return for sophomore year. Students must declare major by end of second year. **Graduation requirements:** 60 hours for associate, 126 hours for bachelor's (24 in major). Most students required to take courses in arts/fine arts, computer science, English, history, humanities, mathematics, philosophy/religion, biological/physical sciences, social sciences.

FRESHMAN ADMISSIONS. Selection criteria: All factors considered for admission, including test scores, classrank, and GPA. **Test requirements:** SAT or ACT.

1992 FRESHMAN CLASS PROFILE. 124 men and women enrolled. 23% were in top tenth and 45% were in top quarter of graduating class. **Academic background:** Mid 50% of enrolled freshmen had SAT-V between 370-490, SAT-M between 380-520; ACT composite between 17-23. 80% submitted SAT scores, 49% submitted ACT scores. **Characteristics:** 83% from in state, 58% live in college housing, 23% have minority backgrounds, 6% are foreign students. Average age is 19.

FALL-TERM APPLICATIONS. $25 fee. No closing date; applicants notified on a rolling basis. Interview recommended. Essay recommended for academically weak applicants. Deferred and early admission available.

STUDENT LIFE. Housing: Dormitories (men, women). **Activities:** Student government, yearbook, choral groups, concert band, drama, music ensembles, musical theater, handbell choir, symphonic winds ensemble, Baptist Student Union, Ministerial Alliance, Fellowship of Christian Athletes, Students for America, Student Government Association, Gateway players, Habitat for Humanity, Ephphatha, Chi Gamma Kappa, Kappa Alpha Chi. **Additional information:** Religious observance required.

ATHLETICS. NAIA. **Intercollegiate:** Baseball M, soccer M, volleyball W. **Intramural:** Baseball, basketball, cross-country, golf, soccer M, softball, table tennis, tennis, volleyball.

STUDENT SERVICES. Aptitude testing, employment service for undergraduates, freshman orientation, health services, personal counseling, placement service for graduates, special adviser for adult students, veterans counselor, services/facilities for handicapped.

ANNUAL EXPENSES. Tuition and fees (1992-93): $6,000. **Room and board:** $3,130. **Books and supplies:** $572. **Other expenses:** $1,036.

FINANCIAL AID. 87% of freshmen, 62% of continuing students receive some form of aid. Grants, loans, jobs available. Academic, music/drama, art, athletic, alumni affiliation, religious affiliation scholarships available. **Aid applications:** No closing date; priority given to applications received by May 1; applicants notified on a rolling basis beginning on or about May 1; must reply within 2 weeks.

ADDRESS/TELEPHONE. John Plotts, Director of Admissions, Dallas Baptist University, 3000 Mountain Creek Parkway, Dallas, TX 75211-9800. (214) 333-5360. Fax: (214) 333-5115.

Dallas Christian College
Dallas, Texas CB code: 0792

4-year private Bible college, coed, affiliated with Christian interdenominational. Founded in 1950. **Undergraduate enrollment:** 40 men, 25 women full time; 13 men, 9 women part time. **Faculty:** 30 total (5 full time), 4 with doctorates or other terminal degrees. **Location:** Suburban campus in very large city; 10 miles from downtown. **Calendar:** 4-1-4. Extensive evening/early morning classes. **Microcomputers:** 6 located in libraries, computer centers.

DEGREES OFFERED. AA, BA, BS. 100% in business and management. 9 bachelor's degrees awarded. 25% in education, 75% philosophy, religion, theology.

UNDERGRADUATE MAJORS. Associate: Business and management, liberal/general studies, secretarial and related programs. **Bachelor's:** Bible studies, biblical languages, education, missionary studies, religious education, religious music.

ACADEMIC PROGRAMS. Internships. **Remedial services:** Reduced course load, remedial instruction. **Placement/credit:** AP, CLEP Subject, institutional tests.

ACADEMIC REQUIREMENTS. Freshmen must earn minimum GPA of 1.8 to continue in good standing. Sophomores must maintain 1.9 GPA, juniors and seniors 2.0. 80% of freshmen return for sophomore year. Students must declare major by end of first year. **Graduation requirements:** 68 hours for associate, 132 hours for bachelor's (44 in major). Most students required to take courses in arts/fine arts, English, foreign languages, history, mathematics, philosophy/religion, biological/physical sciences. **Postgraduate studies:** 20% from 2-year programs enter 4-year programs.

FRESHMAN ADMISSIONS. Selection criteria: School record and recommendation, followed by test scores. Must be in top three-fourths of class and have ACT composite score above 20th percentile. **Test requirements:** SAT or ACT (ACT preferred); score report by August 10.

1992 FRESHMAN CLASS PROFILE. 6 men applied, 6 accepted, 6 enrolled; 8 women applied, 8 accepted, 8 enrolled. 44% had high school GPA of 3.0 or higher, 29% between 2.0 and 2.99. 29% were in top tenth and 57% were in top quarter of graduating class. **Academic background:** Mid 50% of enrolled freshmen had ACT composite between 19-25. 100% submitted ACT scores. **Characteristics:** 71% from in state, 79% live in college housing, 7% have minority backgrounds. Average age is 19.

FALL-TERM APPLICATIONS. $20 fee, may be waived for applicants with need. Closing date August 15; applicants notified on a rolling basis. Interview recommended. Essay recommended. Deferred admission available.

STUDENT LIFE. Housing: Dormitories (men, women). **Activities:** Student government, yearbook, choral groups, drama, music ensembles. **Additional information:** All resident students as well as those taking 12 hours or more required to attend campus chapel services 3 times a week. Devotional services available in dormitories. Students encouraged to participate in local churches.

ATHLETICS. Intercollegiate: Basketball M, soccer M. **Intramural:** Volleyball.

STUDENT SERVICES. Employment service for undergraduates, freshman orientation, health services, personal counseling, placement service for graduates.

ANNUAL EXPENSES. Tuition and fees: $2,790. **Room and board:** $2,790. **Books and supplies:** $650. **Other expenses:** $625.

FINANCIAL AID. 71% of freshmen, 86% of continuing students receive some form of aid. All aid based on need. Academic, music/drama, leadership, religious affiliation scholarships available. **Aid applications:** Closing date August 1; priority given to applications received by July 1; applicants notified on a rolling basis beginning on or about July 15; must reply by August 1.

ADDRESS/TELEPHONE. Mark Worley, Director of Admissions and Church Relations, Dallas Christian College, 2700 Christian Parkway, Dallas, TX 75234-7299. (214) 241-3371. (800) 688-1029. Fax: (214) 241-8021.

Dallas Institute of Funeral Service
Dallas, Texas CB code: 7032

1-year private mortuary college, coed. **Accreditation:** Regional. **Undergraduate enrollment:** 144 men and women. **Faculty:** 8 total (5 full time), 1 with doctorate or other terminal degree. **Location:** Urban campus in very large city. **Calendar:** Quarter. **Additional facts:** Accredited by American Board of Funeral Service Education, Inc.

DEGREES OFFERED. AAS. 50 associate degrees awarded in 1992.

UNDERGRADUATE MAJORS. Funeral services/mortuary science.

FRESHMAN ADMISSIONS. Selection criteria: Open admissions.

1992 FRESHMAN CLASS PROFILE. 144 men and women enrolled. **Characteristics:** 100% commute.

FALL-TERM APPLICATIONS. No closing date.

ANNUAL EXPENSES. Tuition and fees: $5,225. Tuition for 12-month certificate program is $5225 including fees and books payable in quarterly installments. Associate degree program is an additional $1,250. **Other expenses:** $1,190.

FINANCIAL AID. 55% of freshmen, 43% of continuing students receive some form of aid. 99% of grants, 81% of loans based on need. Academic scholarships available. **Aid applications:** No closing date; applicants notified on a rolling basis; must reply by registration.

ADDRESS/TELEPHONE. Dallas Institute of Funeral Service, 3909 South Buckner Boulevard, Dallas, TX 75227. (214) 388-5466.

Del Mar College
Corpus Christi, Texas CB code: 6160

2-year public community college, coed. Founded in 1935. **Accreditation:** Regional. **Undergraduate enrollment:** 1,633 men, 2,232 women full time; 2,966 men, 4,828 women part time. **Faculty:** 557 total (296 full time), 60 with doctorates or other terminal degrees. **Location:** Urban campus in large city; 155 miles from San Antonio. **Calendar:** Semester, extensive summer session. **Microcomputers:** Located in libraries, classrooms, computer centers. **Special facilities:** Joseph Cain Art Gallery, Virginia Stone English Learning Laboratory. **Additional facts:** Courses taught at 16 off-campus sites in the Coastal Bend Region.

DEGREES OFFERED. AA, AS, AAS. 623 associate degrees awarded in 1992. 13% in business and management, 5% computer sciences, 12% engineering technologies, 18% health sciences, 12% allied health, 5% law, 8% multi/interdisciplinary studies.

UNDERGRADUATE MAJORS. Accounting, air conditioning/heating/refrigeration mechanics, architectural technologies, art education, automotive mechanics, automotive technology, biology, business administration and management, business and office, business computer/console/peripheral equipment operation, business data processing and related programs, business data programming, chemistry, child development/care/guidance, computer and information sciences, court reporting, criminal justice studies, dental assistant, dental hygiene, diesel engine mechanics, drafting and design technology, dramatic arts, education, electrical and electronics equipment repair, electrical technology, electrical/electronics/communications engineering, electronic technology, engineering and engineering-related technologies, English, English education, finance, fire control and safety technology, food production/management/services, geography, geology, health education, history, hotel/motel and restaurant management, journalism, legal assistant/paralegal, legal secretary, liberal/general studies, machine tool operation/machine shop, marketing and distribution, marketing management, mathematics, medical laboratory technologies, mental health/human services, microcomputer software, music education, music performance, music theory and composition, nursing, physical education, physics, political science and government, practical nursing, predentistry, preengineering, prelaw, premedicine, prepharmacy, preveterinary, psychology, public administration, public affairs, radio/television broadcasting, radiograph medical technology, real estate, respiratory therapy technology, secretarial and related programs, social work, sociology, speech, studio art, surgical technology, trade and industrial supervision and management, ultrasound technology, welding technology.

ACADEMIC PROGRAMS. 2-year transfer program, dual enrollment of high school students, honors program, independent study, internships, telecourses. **Remedial services:** Learning center, remedial instruction, tutoring. **ROTC:** Army. **Placement/credit:** CLEP Subject, institutional tests; 30 credit hours maximum for associate degree.

ACADEMIC REQUIREMENTS. Freshmen must earn minimum GPA of 2.0 to continue in good standing. 60% of freshmen return for sophomore year. Students must declare major on application. **Graduation requirements:** 62 hours for associate. Most students required to take courses in English, history, mathematics, social sciences.

FRESHMAN ADMISSIONS. Selection criteria: Open admissions. Selective admissions to health science programs. **Test requirements:** SAT or ACT for placement and counseling only; score report by August 31. Dental Hygiene Aptitude Test used for placement for dental hygiene applicants.

1992 FRESHMAN CLASS PROFILE. 1,028 men, 1,329 women enrolled. **Academic background:** Mid 50% of enrolled freshmen had SAT-V between 330-450, SAT-M between 340-470; ACT composite between 13-19. 20% submitted SAT scores, 60% submitted ACT scores. **Characteristics:** 98% from in state, 100% commute, 58% have minority backgrounds. Average age is 23.

FALL-TERM APPLICATIONS. No fee. No closing date; applicants notified on a rolling basis. Interview required for health sciences applicants. Early admission available. College placement test will be arranged if ACT/SAT not taken.

STUDENT LIFE. Activities: Student government, radio, student newspaper, television, choral groups, concert band, dance, drama, jazz band, music ensembles, opera.

ATHLETICS. Intramural: Badminton, basketball, bowling, cross-country, golf, racquetball, sailing, softball, swimming, table tennis, tennis, track and field, volleyball.

STUDENT SERVICES. Career counseling, employment service for undergraduates, freshman orientation, personal counseling, placement service for graduates, veterans counselor, services/facilities for handicapped.

ANNUAL EXPENSES. Tuition and fees: $480, $150 additional for out-of-district students, $900 additional for out-of-state students. **Books and supplies:** $400. **Other expenses:** $810.

FINANCIAL AID. 40% of freshmen, 34% of continuing students receive some form of aid. 93% of grants, 82% of loans, 52% of jobs based on need. Academic, music/drama, art, state/district residency, leadership, alumni affiliation, minority scholarships available. **Aid applications:** No closing date; priority given to applications received by May 1; applicants notified on a rolling basis beginning on or about July 1; must reply within 2 weeks.

ADDRESS/TELEPHONE. Joseph Estrada, Registrar and Director of Admissions, Del Mar College, 101 Baldwin Street, Corpus Christi, TX 78404-3897. (512) 886-1398. Fax: (512) 886-1595.

DeVry Institute of Technology: Irving

Irving, Texas — CB code: 6180

Admissions: 92% of applicants accepted
Based on: ••• Test scores
• Interview
Completion: 28% graduate

4-year proprietary business, technical college, coed. Founded in 1969. **Accreditation:** Regional. **Undergraduate enrollment:** 1,289 men, 281 women full time; 422 men, 149 women part time. **Faculty:** 53 total (52 full time), 2 with doctorates or other terminal degrees. **Location:** Suburban campus in small city; 12 miles from Dallas. **Calendar:** Three continuous calendar terms. Extensive evening/early morning classes. **Microcomputers:** 160 located in computer centers.

DEGREES OFFERED. AAS, BS. 190 associate degrees awarded in 1992. 100% in engineering technologies. 242 bachelor's degrees awarded. 22% in business and management, 38% computer sciences, 40% engineering technologies.

UNDERGRADUATE MAJORS. Associate: Electronic technology. **Bachelor's:** Accounting, business administration and management, electronic technology, information sciences and systems.

ACADEMIC PROGRAMS. Accelerated program, cooperative education. **Remedial services:** Learning center, reduced course load, remedial instruction, special counselor, tutoring, developmental coursework. **Placement/credit:** Institutional tests; 30 credit hours maximum for associate degree; 55 credit hours maximum for bachelor's degree.

ACADEMIC REQUIREMENTS. Freshmen must earn minimum GPA of 2.0 to continue in good standing. 48% of freshmen return for sophomore year. Students must declare major on enrollment. **Graduation requirements:** 87 hours for associate, 134 hours for bachelor's. Most students required to take courses in computer science, English, history, humanities, mathematics, social sciences.

FRESHMAN ADMISSIONS. Selection criteria: Applicants must have high school diploma or equivalant, pass institutional entrance examination or submit acceptable ACT/SAT/WPCT scores, and be 17 years of age. **Test requirements:** SAT or ACT. **Additional information:** New students may enter at beginning of any semester.

1992 FRESHMAN CLASS PROFILE. 1,083 men and women applied, 997 accepted; 384 men enrolled, 101 women enrolled. **Characteristics:** 87% from in state, 100% commute, 74% have minority backgrounds, 2% are foreign students.

FALL-TERM APPLICATIONS. $25 fee. Closing date November 4; applicants notified on a rolling basis; must reply within 4 weeks. Interview required. Deferred admission available.

STUDENT LIFE. Housing: School-contracted furnished apartments available for single students. **Activities:** Student government, student newspaper, Data Processing Management Association (DPMA) Institute of Electrical and Electronic Engineers (IEEE).

ATHLETICS. Intramural: Basketball, football, softball, volleyball.

STUDENT SERVICES. Career counseling, employment service for undergraduates, freshman orientation, placement service for graduates, veterans counselor, services/facilities for handicapped.

ANNUAL EXPENSES. Tuition and fees: $5,609. **Books and supplies:** $525. **Other expenses:** $1,928.

FINANCIAL AID. 82% of freshmen, 85% of continuing students receive some form of aid. All grants, 61% of loans, all jobs based on need. Academic scholarships available. **Aid applications:** No closing date; applicants notified on a rolling basis; must reply immediately. **Additional information:** Approximately 80% of students work part-time at jobs found through Institute.

ADDRESS/TELEPHONE. Danny Millan, Director of Admissions, DeVry Institute of Technology: Irving, 4250 North Beltline Road, Irving, TX 75038-4299. (214) 258-6330. (800) 243-3879. Fax: (214) 659-1748.

East Texas Baptist University

Marshall, Texas — CB code: 6187

4-year private liberal arts college, coed, affiliated with Southern Baptist Convention. Founded in 1912. **Accreditation:** Regional. **Undergraduate enrollment:** 439 men, 573 women full time; 63 men, 115 women part time. **Graduate enrollment:** 2 men, 1 woman full time; 4 men, 7 women part time. **Faculty:** 79 total (56 full time), 46 with doctorates or other terminal degrees. **Location:** Suburban campus in large town; 35 miles from Shreveport, Louisiana, 20 miles from Longview. **Calendar:** 4-1-4, extensive summer session. **Microcomputers:** 50 located in computer centers. **Additional facts:** University assumes that the liberal arts form the surest foundation for education and that the Christian faith provides the surest foundation for life.

DEGREES OFFERED. AA, AAS, BA, BS, MBA. 1 associate degree awarded in 1992. 100% in business/office and marketing/distribution. 144 bachelor's degrees awarded. 22% in business and management, 5% communications, 26% teacher education, 17% philosophy, religion, theology, 10% social sciences.

UNDERGRADUATE MAJORS. Associate: Allied health, business administration and management, business and office, legal assistant/paralegal, liberal/general studies, medical laboratory technologies. **Bachelor's:** Accounting, behavioral sciences, biology, business administration and management, business and management, business and office, business data processing and related programs, business education, chemistry, clinical laboratory science, communications, computer and information sciences, dramatic arts, elementary education, English, English education, foreign languages education, history, junior high education, mathematics, mathematics education, medical laboratory technologies, music, music education, nursing, physical education, psychology, reading education, religion, religious education, religious music, science education, secondary education, social science education, social studies education, sociology, Spanish, speech, speech/communication/theater education, theological studies.

ACADEMIC PROGRAMS. Accelerated program, double major, dual enrollment of high school students, honors program, independent study, internships, teacher preparation. **Remedial services:** Preadmission summer program, reduced course load, remedial instruction, special counselor, tutoring. **Placement/credit:** AP, CLEP Subject, institutional tests; 30 credit hours maximum for bachelor's degree.

ACADEMIC REQUIREMENTS. Freshmen must earn minimum GPA of 1.75 to continue in good standing. 65% of freshmen return for sophomore year. Students must declare major by end of second year. **Graduation requirements:** 66 hours for associate, 128 hours for bachelor's (30 in major). Most students required to take courses in arts/fine arts, computer science, English, history, humanities, mathematics, philosophy/religion, biological/physical sciences, social sciences. **Postgraduate studies:** 1% enter law school, 1% enter medical school, 50% enter MBA programs, 15% enter other graduate study.

FRESHMAN ADMISSIONS. Selection criteria: School achievement record and test scores most important. Applicants should be in top half of class. **High school preparation:** 16 units required. Required units include English 4, mathematics 2, social science 2 and science 2. **Test requirements:**

SAT or ACT (ACT preferred); score report by August 1. **Additional information:** Applicants must also take Texas Academic Skills Program (TASP) test prior to completing admissions process.

1992 FRESHMAN CLASS PROFILE. 117 men, 172 women enrolled. 68% had high school GPA of 3.0 or higher, 31% between 2.0 and 2.99. **Academic background:** Mid 50% of enrolled freshmen had ACT composite between 17-23. 91% submitted ACT scores. **Characteristics:** 91% from in state, 78% live in college housing, 18% have minority backgrounds, 11% are foreign students. Average age is 21.

FALL-TERM APPLICATIONS. $25 fee, may be waived for applicants with need. No closing date; priority given to applications received by August 1; applicants notified on a rolling basis. Interview recommended for academically deficient applicants. Audition recommended for music, speech, theater arts applicants. Deferred and early admission available.

STUDENT LIFE. Housing: Dormitories (men, women); apartment, handicapped housing available. **Activities:** Student government, student newspaper, yearbook, choral groups, concert band, drama, music ensembles, musical theater, pep band, Baptist Student Union.

ATHLETICS. NAIA. **Intercollegiate:** Baseball M, basketball. **Intramural:** Archery, badminton, basketball, bowling, cross-country, golf, handball, racquetball, soccer, softball, table tennis, tennis, volleyball.

STUDENT SERVICES. Aptitude testing, career counseling, employment service for undergraduates, freshman orientation, health services, personal counseling, placement service for graduates, special adviser for adult students.

ANNUAL EXPENSES. Tuition and fees: $5,100. **Room and board:** $2,780. **Books and supplies:** $515. **Other expenses:** $960.

FINANCIAL AID. 77% of freshmen, 87% of continuing students receive some form of aid. 59% of grants, 69% of loans, 53% of jobs based on need. Academic, music/drama, athletic, state/district residency, leadership, religious affiliation scholarships available. **Aid applications:** No closing date; priority given to applications received by June 1; applicants notified on a rolling basis beginning on or about May 15; must reply within 3 weeks.

ADDRESS/TELEPHONE. Mike Davis, Director of Admissions, East Texas Baptist University, 1209 North Grove, Marshall, TX 75670-1498. (903) 935-7963 ext. 225. Fax: (903) 935-3447.

East Texas State University

Commerce, Texas — CB code: 6188

Admissions:	66% of applicants accepted
Based on:	••• School record, test scores
Completion:	80% of freshmen end year in good standing
	55% graduate

4-year public university, coed. Founded in 1889. **Accreditation:** Regional. **Undergraduate enrollment:** 1,808 men, 2,337 women full time; 608 men, 732 women part time. **Graduate enrollment:** 300 men, 346 women full time; 830 men, 1,383 women part time. **Faculty:** 383 total (235 full time), 211 with doctorates or other terminal degrees. **Location:** Rural campus in small town; 60 miles northeast of Dallas. **Calendar:** Semester, extensive summer session. **Microcomputers:** 130 located in dormitories, libraries, classrooms, computer centers. **Special facilities:** University farm (instructional), radio and television station, art gallery, Zeppa Recreational and Workout Center. **Additional facts:** Metroplex commuter facility in Garland, offers graduate courses for credit.

DEGREES OFFERED. BA, BS, BFA, MA, MS, MBA, MFA, MEd, PhD, EdD. 826 bachelor's degrees awarded in 1992. 20% in business and management, 5% communications, 13% education, 10% multi/interdisciplinary studies, 5% psychology, 12% social sciences, 6% visual and performing arts. Graduate degrees offered in 57 major fields of study.

UNDERGRADUATE MAJORS. Accounting, advertising, advertising art, agricultural economics, agricultural sciences, animal sciences, anthropology, biological and physical sciences, biology, business administration and management, business and management, business and office, business economics, business education, business systems analysis, ceramics, chemistry, commercial art, communications, computer and information sciences, construction, criminal justice studies, criminology, dramatic arts, earth sciences, economics, English, environmental science, finance, fine arts, French, geography, geology, German, graphic and printing production, graphic design, health care administration, health sciences, history, human resources development, humanities and social sciences, illustration design, industrial technology, information sciences and systems, journalism, legal assistant/paralegal, liberal/general studies, management information systems, manufacturing technology, marketing management, mathematics, music, music education, music performance, music theory and composition, office supervision and management, operations research, painting, personnel management, photography, physics, plant sciences, political science and government, predentistry, prelaw, premedicine, preveterinary, printmaking, psychology, radio/television broadcasting, sculpture, social sciences, social work, sociology, soil sciences, Spanish, speech/communication/theater education, student counseling and personnel services, visual and performing arts, vocational education.

ACADEMIC PROGRAMS. Accelerated program, cooperative education, double major, dual enrollment of high school students, external degree, honors program, independent study, internships, study abroad, teacher preparation, cross-registration. **Remedial services:** Learning center, preadmission summer program, remedial instruction, tutoring. **Placement/credit:** AP, CLEP General and Subject, institutional tests.

ACADEMIC REQUIREMENTS. Freshmen must earn minimum GPA of 2.0 to continue in good standing. 60% of freshmen return for sophomore year. Students must declare major by end of second year. **Graduation requirements:** 126 hours for bachelor's (30 in major). Most students required to take courses in arts/fine arts, English, history, humanities, mathematics, biological/physical sciences, social sciences.

FRESHMAN ADMISSIONS. Selection criteria: ACT or SAT scores most important, followed by high school grades and class rank. Students admitted with ACT scores 17-19 or SAT scores 700-790 based on 50% chance of success. **High school preparation:** 14 units recommended. Recommended units include English 4, foreign language 2, mathematics 3, social science 3 and science 2. **Test requirements:** SAT or ACT; score report by August 15.

1992 FRESHMAN CLASS PROFILE. 2,088 men and women applied, 1,387 accepted; 313 men enrolled, 354 women enrolled. **Characteristics:** 95% from in state, 36% live in college housing, 25% have minority backgrounds.

FALL-TERM APPLICATIONS. No fee. $25 fee for international applicants. Closing date August 20; priority given to applications received by August 10; applicants notified on a rolling basis. Portfolio required for advertising art applicants. Audition recommended for music applicants. Deferred admission available. High school seniors may enroll part-time before graduation with consent of high school principal if they meet requirements.

STUDENT LIFE. Housing: Dormitories (men, women, coed); apartment, sorority housing available. Special art, honors, and athletics houses available. **Activities:** Student government, film, magazine, radio, student newspaper, television, choral groups, concert band, dance, drama, jazz band, music ensembles, musical theater, opera, pep band, symphony orchestra, fraternities, sororities, Baptist Student Union, Church of Christ Bible Chair Catholic Newman Club, University Christian Center, Young Democrats, Association Cultural de Hispanos-Americans (ACHA), Chinese Student Association, Muslim Society, NAACP, Thai Students Association, Alpha Phi Omega. **Additional information:** Holistic needs of students met in atmosphere of cultural diversity.

ATHLETICS. NCAA. **Intercollegiate:** Basketball, cross-country, football M, golf M, track and field, volleyball W. **Intramural:** Archery, badminton, baseball M, basketball, bowling, cross-country, golf, racquetball, softball, swimming, table tennis, tennis, track and field, volleyball.

STUDENT SERVICES. Aptitude testing, career counseling, employment service for undergraduates, freshman orientation, health services, on-campus day care, personal counseling, placement service for graduates, veterans counselor, services/facilities for handicapped.

ANNUAL EXPENSES. Tuition and fees: $1,381, $4,080 additional for out-of-state students. **Room and board:** $3,500. **Books and supplies:** $600. **Other expenses:** $950.

FINANCIAL AID. All grants, 90% of loans, all jobs based on need. Minority scholarships available. **Aid applications:** Closing date October 1; priority given to applications received by March 1; applicants notified on a rolling basis beginning on or about June 1; must reply within 10 days.

ADDRESS/TELEPHONE. Suzzanne Woodley, Director of Admissions, East Texas State University, East Texas Station, Commerce, TX 75429-3011. (903) 886-5081. Fax: (903) 886-5888.

East Texas State University at Texarkana

Texarkana, Texas — CB code: 6206

2-year upper-division public university, coed. Founded in 1971. **Accreditation:** Regional. **Undergraduate enrollment:** 845 men and women. **Graduate enrollment:** 539 men and women. **Faculty:** 57 total (34 full time), 34 with doctorates or other terminal degrees. **Location:** Suburban campus in small city; 180 miles from Dallas; 145 miles from Little Rock, Arkansas. **Calendar:** Semester, limited summer session. Saturday and extensive evening/early morning classes. **Microcomputers:** Located in libraries. **Additional facts:** Courses scheduled so students can work and go to school.

DEGREES OFFERED. BA, BS, MA, MS, MBA, MEd. 241 bachelor's degrees awarded in 1992. 26% in business and management, 36% teacher education, 26% multi/interdisciplinary studies, 7% psychology. Graduate degrees offered in 8 major fields of study.

UNDERGRADUATE MAJORS. Accounting, business administration and management, business and management, English, history, liberal/general studies, management information systems, marketing management, mathematics, psychology.

ACADEMIC PROGRAMS. Double major, independent study, student-designed major, teacher preparation, cross-registration. **Placement/credit:** CLEP General and Subject, institutional tests.

ACADEMIC REQUIREMENTS. To continue in good academic standing, students must earn minimum 2.0 grade-point average. Students must declare major on application. **Graduation requirements:** 126 hours for bachelor's (24 in major). Most students required to take courses in computer science, English, history, mathematics, biological/physical sciences, social sciences.

STUDENT LIFE. 1992 freshman class profile: 100% commute. **Activities:** Student government, student newspaper, television, concert band, drama, jazz band, music ensembles, musical theater, opera, symphony orchestra, Psi Chi, Phi Beta Lambda, Phi Alpha Theta, Sigma Tau Delta, University Historians, English Club, Psych Club, Kappa Delta Pi, Accounting Club, Multicultural Association.

STUDENT SERVICES. Career counseling, employment service for undergraduates, personal counseling, placement service for graduates, veterans counselor, services/facilities for handicapped.

ANNUAL EXPENSES. Tuition and fees: $1,350, $4,080 additional for out-of-state students. **Books and supplies:** $650. **Other expenses:** $970.

FINANCIAL AID. 17% of continuing students receive some form of aid. 96% of grants, 94% of loans, all jobs based on need. Academic, state/district residency, leadership, minority scholarships available. **Aid applications:** Closing date November 1; priority given to applications received by May 1; applicants notified on a rolling basis beginning on or about February 15; must reply within 10 days.

ADDRESS/TELEPHONE. Sandra Rogers, Director of Academic and Student Services, East Texas State University at Texarkana, PO Box 5518, 2600 North Robison Road, Texarkana, TX 75505-0518. (903) 838-6514. Fax: (903) 832-8890.

Eastfield College
Mesquite, Texas — CB code: 6201

2-year public community college, coed. Founded in 1970. **Accreditation:** Regional. **Undergraduate enrollment:** 1,232 men, 1,281 women full time; 3,048 men, 4,527 women part time. **Faculty:** 345 total (125 full time). **Location:** Suburban campus in small city; 1 mile from Dallas. **Calendar:** Semester, limited summer session. Saturday and extensive evening/early morning classes. **Microcomputers:** Located in libraries, computer centers. **Special facilities:** Art gallery.

DEGREES OFFERED. AA, AAS. 800 associate degrees awarded in 1992.

UNDERGRADUATE MAJORS. Accounting, air conditioning/heating/refrigeration mechanics, air conditioning/heating/refrigeration technology, automotive mechanics, automotive technology, business and management, business and office, business computer/console/peripheral equipment operation, business data processing and related programs, business data programming, computer and information sciences, computer programming, drafting, drafting and design technology, education of the deaf and hearing impaired, electronic technology, graphic and printing production, graphic arts technology, instrumentation technology, interpreter for the deaf, legal secretary, liberal/general studies, mechanical design technology, microcomputer software, precision metal work, recreation and community services technologies, secretarial and related programs, social work, telecommunications, transportation management.

ACADEMIC PROGRAMS. 2-year transfer program, cooperative education, honors program, independent study, telecourses. **Remedial services:** Learning center, preadmission summer program, remedial instruction, special counselor, tutoring. **Placement/credit:** AP, CLEP Subject, institutional tests; 15 credit hours maximum for associate degree.

ACADEMIC REQUIREMENTS. Freshmen must earn minimum GPA of 2.0 to continue in good standing. 60% of freshmen return for sophomore year. Students must declare major by end of first year. **Graduation requirements:** 60 hours for associate. Most students required to take courses in English, history, humanities, mathematics, biological/physical sciences.

FRESHMAN ADMISSIONS. Selection criteria: Open admissions.

1992 FRESHMAN CLASS PROFILE. 3,023 men, 4,165 women enrolled. **Characteristics:** 100% commute.

FALL-TERM APPLICATIONS. No fee. No closing date; applicants notified on a rolling basis. Interview recommended for foreign applicants. CRDA. Early admission available.

STUDENT LIFE. Activities: Student government, student newspaper, social science journal, choral groups, concert band, dance, drama, jazz band, music ensembles, musical theater.

ATHLETICS. NJCAA. **Intercollegiate:** Baseball M, basketball M. **Intramural:** Archery, baseball M, basketball M, bowling, golf M, gymnastics, tennis, volleyball, wrestling M.

STUDENT SERVICES. Career counseling, employment service for undergraduates, health services, personal counseling, placement service for graduates, veterans counselor, services/facilities for handicapped.

ANNUAL EXPENSES. Tuition and fees (1992-93): $450, $570 additional for out-of-district students, $1,470 additional for out-of-state students. **Books and supplies:** $400. **Other expenses:** $935.

FINANCIAL AID. 25% of continuing students receive some form of aid. Grants, loans, jobs available. **Aid applications:** Closing date June 1; applicants notified on a rolling basis beginning on or about April 15.

ADDRESS/TELEPHONE. Bobbie Trout, Director of Admissions and Registrar, Eastfield College, 3737 Motley Drive, Mesquite, TX 75150-1212. (214) 324-7100. Fax: (214) 324-7183.

El Centro College
Dallas, Texas — CB code: 6199

2-year public community college, coed. Founded in 1966. **Accreditation:** Regional. **Undergraduate enrollment:** 425 men, 797 women full time; 1,656 men, 3,503 women part time. **Faculty:** 431 total (130 full time), 69 with doctorates or other terminal degrees. **Location:** Urban campus in very large city. **Calendar:** Semester, limited summer session. Saturday and extensive evening/early morning classes. **Microcomputers:** 120 located in classrooms, computer centers. **Special facilities:** Art gallery.

DEGREES OFFERED. AA, AAS. 54 associate degrees awarded in 1992. 15% in business and management, 48% health sciences, 12% home economics, 18% multi/interdisciplinary studies, 6% visual and performing arts.

UNDERGRADUATE MAJORS. Accounting, architectural technologies, architecture, business administration and management, business and management, business and office, business computer/console/peripheral equipment operation, business data entry equipment operation, business data processing and related programs, business data programming, business systems analysis, clinical laboratory science, computer and information sciences, computer programming, criminal justice studies, data processing, fashion design, fine arts, fire control and safety technology, fire protection, food production/management/services, hotel/motel and restaurant management, information sciences and systems, interior design, Invasive cardiovascular technology, law enforcement and corrections technologies, legal assistant/paralegal, legal secretary, liberal/general studies, medical assistant, medical laboratory technologies, medical records administration, medical records technology, nursing, office supervision and management, pattern drafting, radiograph medical technology, respiratory therapy, respiratory therapy technology, secretarial and related programs, sonargraphy, ultrasound technology.

ACADEMIC PROGRAMS. 2-year transfer program, cooperative education, double major, dual enrollment of high school students, honors program, internships, study abroad, teacher preparation, telecourses, weekend college, cross-registration. **Remedial services:** Learning center, preadmission summer program, reduced course load, remedial instruction, special counselor, tutoring. **Placement/credit:** AP, CLEP Subject, institutional tests; 45 credit hours maximum for associate degree.

ACADEMIC REQUIREMENTS. Freshmen must earn minimum GPA of 2.0 to continue in good standing. 42% of freshmen return for sophomore year. Students must declare major by end of first year. **Graduation requirements:** 62 hours for associate. Most students required to take courses in arts/fine arts, English, history, humanities, mathematics, biological/physical sciences, social sciences.

FRESHMAN ADMISSIONS. Selection criteria: Open admissions. **Test requirements:** Institutional test may be substituted for SAT or ACT.

1992 FRESHMAN CLASS PROFILE. 1,406 men, 2,880 women enrolled. **Characteristics:** 99% from in state, 56% have minority backgrounds, 1% are foreign students. Average age is 29.

FALL-TERM APPLICATIONS. No fee. No closing date; applicants notified on a rolling basis beginning on or about June 1. Interview recommended for foreign applicants. Deferred and early admission available. SAT or ACT recommended for placement and counseling.

STUDENT LIFE. Activities: Student government, magazine, student newspaper, choral groups, dance, drama, jazz band, music ensembles, musical theater, Phi Theta Kappa.

ATHLETICS. Intramural: Basketball M, softball.

STUDENT SERVICES. Aptitude testing, career counseling, employment service for undergraduates, health services, personal counseling, placement service for graduates, veterans counselor, services/facilities for handicapped.

ANNUAL EXPENSES. Tuition and fees (1992-93): $450, $570 additional for out-of-district students, $1,470 additional for out-of-state students. **Books and supplies:** $600. **Other expenses:** $600.

FINANCIAL AID. 24% of freshmen, 20% of continuing students receive some form of aid. Grants, loans, jobs available. Academic, music/drama, art, state/district residency, minority scholarships available. **Aid applications:** No closing date; priority given to applications received by July 1; applicants notified on a rolling basis; must reply within 2 weeks. **Additional information:** Interview required for financial aid applicants.

ADDRESS/TELEPHONE. Robert Bennett, Registrar and Director of Admissions, El Centro College, Main and Lamar, Dallas, TX 75202. (214) 746-2311. Fax: (214) 746-2335.

El Paso Community College
El Paso, Texas — CB code: 6203

2-year public community college, coed. Founded in 1969. **Accreditation:**

Regional. **Undergraduate enrollment:** 3,097 men, 5,653 women full time; 3,981 men, 5,748 women part time. **Faculty:** 1,154 total (326 full time), 73 with doctorates or other terminal degrees. **Location:** Urban campus in very large city; 3 miles from Juarez, Mexico. **Calendar:** Semester, extensive summer session. **Microcomputers:** Located in libraries, computer centers. **Additional facts:** Multicampus institution. Teaching locations at Fort Bliss, local schools, community centers, women's satellite centers, and on-site at local businesses, as requested.

DEGREES OFFERED. AA, AS, AAS. 801 associate degrees awarded in 1992. 17% in business and management, 17% communications, 7% computer sciences, 6% education, 19% health sciences, 8% multi/interdisciplinary studies, 18% social sciences.

UNDERGRADUATE MAJORS. vocational nursing, accounting, air conditioning/heating/refrigeration technology, allied health, architecture, automotive technology, biology, business administration and management, business and management, business data processing and related programs, chemistry, child development/care/guidance, clothing and textiles management/production/services, commercial art, communications disorder science, computer and information sciences, computer programming, computer servicing technology, construction, court reporting, dental assistant, dental hygiene, dietetic aide/assistant, drafting, drafting and design technology, dramatic arts, electronic technology, elementary education, engineering and engineering-related technologies, English, fashion design, fashion illustration, fashion merchandising, finance, fine arts, fire control and safety technology, food management, foreign languages (multiple emphasis), geology, history, hotel/motel and restaurant management, humanities, interior design, international business management, international relations, interpreter for the deaf, journalism, law enforcement and corrections technologies, legal assistant/paralegal, liberal/general studies, management science, mathematics, media production, medical assistant, medical laboratory technologies, medical radiation dosimetry, medical records technology, mental health/human services, microcomputer software, mid-management, music, nursing, office supervision and management, ophthalmic services, photographic technology, physical education, physical therapy assistant, physics, political science and government, practical nursing, pre-nursing, predentistry, preengineering, premedicine, prepharmacy, preveterinary, psychology, public relations, radio/television broadcasting, radiograph medical technology, real estate, respiratory therapy technology, secondary education, social sciences, sociology, speech, surgical technology, technical and business writing, technical communications, tourism, women's studies.

ACADEMIC PROGRAMS. 2-year transfer program, cooperative education, double major, dual enrollment of high school students, honors program, independent study, internships, telecourses, weekend college, cross-registration. **Remedial services:** Learning center, remedial instruction, special counselor, tutoring, computer-assisted instruction (CAI). **Placement/credit:** AP, CLEP General and Subject, institutional tests; 45 credit hours maximum for associate degree.

ACADEMIC REQUIREMENTS. Freshmen must earn minimum GPA of 2.0 to continue in good standing. Students must declare major on enrollment. **Graduation requirements:** 60 hours for associate. Most students required to take courses in English, foreign languages, history, mathematics, biological/physical sciences, social sciences.

FRESHMAN ADMISSIONS. Selection criteria: Open admissions. Selective admissions to some health occupations programs. **Test requirements:** Nelson-Denny Reading Test and institutional mathematics test required for admission to health programs. Assessment test required of all first-time degree-seeking freshmen.

1992 FRESHMAN CLASS PROFILE. 3,679 men and women enrolled. **Characteristics:** 93% from in state, 100% commute, 77% have minority backgrounds, 1% are foreign students.

FALL-TERM APPLICATIONS. $10 fee, may be waived for applicants with need. Closing date July 31. Deferred admission available.

STUDENT LIFE. Activities: Student government, film, radio, student newspaper, television, choral groups, dance, drama, music ensembles, Phi Theta Kappa.

ATHLETICS. Intramural: Basketball, bowling, racquetball, soccer, softball, table tennis, tennis, track and field, volleyball.

STUDENT SERVICES. Aptitude testing, career counseling, employment service for undergraduates, health services, personal counseling, placement service for graduates, veterans counselor, women's resource center, services/facilities for handicapped.

ANNUAL EXPENSES. Tuition and fees (1992-93): $721, $2,063 additional for out-of-state students. **Books and supplies:** $435. **Other expenses:** $915.

FINANCIAL AID. 65% of freshmen, 65% of continuing students receive some form of aid. 99% of grants, 92% of loans, 96% of jobs based on need. Academic, leadership, minority scholarships available. **Aid applications:** Closing date June 1; applicants notified on or about July 15; must reply within 2 weeks.

ADDRESS/TELEPHONE. Tim Nugent, Director of Admissions, El Paso Community College, PO Box 20500, El Paso, TX 79998. (915) 594-2579. Fax: (915) 594-2161.

Frank Phillips College
Borger, Texas — CB code: 6222

2-year public junior college, coed. Founded in 1948. **Accreditation:** Regional. **Undergraduate enrollment:** 976 men and women. **Faculty:** 96 total (39 full time), 3 with doctorates or other terminal degrees. **Location:** Rural campus in large town; 60 miles from Amarillo. **Calendar:** Semester, limited summer session. **Microcomputers:** Located in computer centers. **Special facilities:** Instructional television to three off-campus sites in towns approximately 1.5 hours from Borger. **Additional facts:** Guaranteed transfer program.

DEGREES OFFERED. AA, AS, AAS. 64 associate degrees awarded in 1992.

UNDERGRADUATE MAJORS. Accounting, agribusiness, agricultural business and management, agricultural sciences, American studies, anatomy, applied mathematics, art history, bacteriology, biological and physical sciences, biology, botany, business and management, business and office, business data entry equipment operation, business data processing and related programs, business data programming, chemical manufacturing technology, chemistry, criminology, dramatic arts, economics, education, elementary education, engineering, engineering and other disciplines, English, English literature, finance, fine arts, French, geography, graphic arts technology, history, home economics, humanities and social sciences, journalism, law enforcement and corrections technologies, liberal/general studies, linguistics, marketing and distribution, mathematics, mechanical engineering, music, music history and appreciation, personal services, physical sciences, physics, political science and government, practical nursing, psychology, radio/television broadcasting, range management, real estate, secondary education, secretarial and related programs, social sciences, social work, sociology, Spanish, visual and performing arts, zoology.

ACADEMIC PROGRAMS. 2-year transfer program, cooperative education. **Remedial services:** Learning center, remedial instruction, special counselor, tutoring. **Placement/credit:** CLEP Subject, institutional tests; 24 credit hours maximum for associate degree.

ACADEMIC REQUIREMENTS. Freshmen must earn minimum GPA of 1.5 to continue in good standing. 70% of freshmen return for sophomore year.

FRESHMAN ADMISSIONS. Selection criteria: Open admissions. **Additional information:** Guidelines set by Texas Academic Skills Program are followed.

1992 FRESHMAN CLASS PROFILE. 255 men and women enrolled. **Characteristics:** 98% from in state, 65% commute, 7% have minority backgrounds. Average age is 18.

FALL-TERM APPLICATIONS. No fee. No closing date; applicants notified on a rolling basis. Audition required for music applicants. Portfolio recommended for art applicants. CRDA. Early admission available. EDP-F.

STUDENT LIFE. Housing: Dormitories (men, women). **Activities:** Student government, student newspaper, choral groups, drama, music ensembles, musical theater, Circle-K, Baptist Student Union, 11 clubs and organizations.

ATHLETICS. NJCAA. **Intercollegiate:** Baseball M, basketball. **Intramural:** Racquetball, softball, table tennis, tennis, volleyball.

STUDENT SERVICES. Aptitude testing, career counseling, employment service for undergraduates, freshman orientation, personal counseling, placement service for graduates, special adviser for adult students, veterans counselor, services/facilities for handicapped.

ANNUAL EXPENSES. Tuition and fees (1992-93): $630, $60 additional for out-of-district students, $120 additional for out-of-state students. **Room and board:** $1,800. **Books and supplies:** $475. **Other expenses:** $900.

FINANCIAL AID. 42% of freshmen, 23% of continuing students receive some form of aid. 59% of grants, 96% of loans, 3% of jobs based on need. 31 enrolled freshmen were judged to have need, all were offered aid. Academic, music/drama, athletic scholarships available. **Aid applications:** No closing date; priority given to applications received by July 1; applicants notified on a rolling basis beginning on or about July 13; must reply within 2 weeks.

ADDRESS/TELEPHONE. Christi Rummez, Admission Assistant, Frank Phillips College, PO Box 5118, Borger, TX 79008-5118. (806) 274-5311 ext. 20.

Galveston College
Galveston, Texas — CB code: 6255

2-year public community college, coed. Founded in 1967. **Accreditation:** Regional. **Undergraduate enrollment:** 271 men, 371 women full time; 526 men, 1,161 women part time. **Faculty:** 120 total (51 full time), 19 with doctorates or other terminal degrees. **Location:** Urban campus in small city; 50 miles from Houston. **Calendar:** Semester, limited summer session. **Microcomputers:** Located in libraries.

DEGREES OFFERED. AAS. 160 associate degrees awarded in 1992.

UNDERGRADUATE MAJORS. Accounting, allied health, biology, business administration and management, business and office, business computer/console/peripheral equipment operation, chemical manufacturing technology, chemistry, criminal justice technology, finance, fine arts, fire control and safety technology, graphic arts technology, hospitality and recreation marketing, hotel/motel and restaurant management, law enforcement and corrections technologies, liberal/general studies, marketing and distribution, mathematics, medical records technology, microcomputer software, nuclear medical technology, nursing, ornamental horticulture, physics, psychology, public affairs, radiograph medical technology, real estate, science technologies, secretarial and related programs, social work, sociology, teacher aide, visual and performing arts.

ACADEMIC PROGRAMS. 2-year transfer program, dual enrollment of high school students, honors program, internships, telecourses. **Remedial services:** Learning center, remedial instruction, special counselor, tutoring. **Placement/credit:** AP, CLEP Subject; 24 credit hours maximum for associate degree.

ACADEMIC REQUIREMENTS. Freshmen must earn minimum GPA of 2.0 to continue in good standing. Students must declare major by end of first year. **Graduation requirements:** 60 hours for associate. Most students required to take courses in English, history, mathematics.

FRESHMAN ADMISSIONS. Selection criteria: Open admissions. **Test requirements:** ACT/ASSET may be substituted for ACT.

1992 FRESHMAN CLASS PROFILE. 179 men, 245 women enrolled. **Characteristics:** 99% from in state, 100% commute.

FALL-TERM APPLICATIONS. No fee. No closing date; applicants notified on a rolling basis. Early admission available.

STUDENT LIFE. Activities: Student government, magazine, student newspaper, choral groups, drama, music ensembles.

ATHLETICS. Intercollegiate: Baseball M, bowling, golf, tennis, volleyball W.

STUDENT SERVICES. Career counseling, employment service for undergraduates, on-campus day care, personal counseling, placement service for graduates, veterans counselor, services/facilities for handicapped.

ANNUAL EXPENSES. Tuition and fees: $538, $336 additional for out-of-state students. **Books and supplies:** $566. **Other expenses:** $1,390.

FINANCIAL AID. 18% of freshmen, 29% of continuing students receive some form of aid. 88% of grants, 82% of loans, all jobs based on need. 203 enrolled freshmen were judged to have need, 150 were offered aid. Academic, music/drama, athletic scholarships available. **Aid applications:** No closing date; priority given to applications received by June 1; applicants notified on a rolling basis beginning on or about August 1.

ADDRESS/TELEPHONE. Gene Moore, Dean of Admissions and Student Records, Galveston College, 4015 Avenue Q, Galveston, TX 77550. (409) 763-6551 ext. 232.

Grayson County College
Denison, Texas CB code: 6254

2-year public community college, coed. Founded in 1963. **Accreditation:** Regional. **Undergraduate enrollment:** 555 men, 718 women full time; 799 men, 1,282 women part time. **Faculty:** 132 total (63 full time), 10 with doctorates or other terminal degrees. **Location:** Rural campus in large town; 7 miles from Sherman, 75 miles from Dallas. **Calendar:** Semester, limited summer session. Saturday and extensive evening/early morning classes. **Microcomputers:** Located in libraries, classrooms. **Special facilities:** College vineyard.

DEGREES OFFERED. AA, AS, AAS. 415 associate degrees awarded in 1992. 20% in business and management, 8% business/office and marketing/distribution, 6% computer sciences, 8% teacher education, 21% health sciences, 5% life sciences, 6% multi/interdisciplinary studies, 16% trade and industry.

UNDERGRADUATE MAJORS. Accounting, air conditioning/heating/refrigeration mechanics, air conditioning/heating/refrigeration technology, biology, business and management, business and office, business data processing and related programs, chemistry, computer programming, cosmetology, cosmetology instructor, criminal justice technology, drafting, drafting and design technology, dramatic arts, education, electrical and electronics equipment repair, electrical technology, elementary education, emergency medical technologies, engineering, engineering and engineering-related technologies, finance, fine arts, geology, golf course and turf grass management, industrial equipment maintenance and repair, landscape design maintenance, law enforcement and corrections technologies, legal assistant/paralegal, liberal/general studies, mathematics, mechanical design technology, medical laboratory technologies, microcomputer software, music, nursing, office supervision and management, physical education, physics, precision metal work, predentistry, prelaw, premedicine, prepharmacy, psychology, real estate, secondary education, secretarial and related programs, sociology, speech, viticulture and enology, welding technology.

ACADEMIC PROGRAMS. 2-year transfer program, dual enrollment of high school students, honors program, internships, telecourses. **Remedial services:** Learning center, reduced course load, remedial instruction, special counselor, tutoring, developmental mathematics, reading and writing programs. **Placement/credit:** AP, CLEP Subject, institutional tests; 32 credit hours maximum for associate degree.

ACADEMIC REQUIREMENTS. Freshmen must earn minimum GPA of 2.0 to continue in good standing. 56% of freshmen return for sophomore year. **Graduation requirements:** 65 hours for associate. Most students required to take courses in arts/fine arts, computer science, English, history, humanities, mathematics, biological/physical sciences, social sciences.

FRESHMAN ADMISSIONS. Selection criteria: Open admissions.

1992 FRESHMAN CLASS PROFILE. 291 men, 348 women enrolled. **Characteristics:** 98% from in state, 97% commute, 8% have minority backgrounds.

FALL-TERM APPLICATIONS. No fee. Closing date August 25; applicants notified on a rolling basis. Early admission available.

STUDENT LIFE. Housing: Dormitories (men, women). **Activities:** Student government, choral groups, drama, jazz band, music ensembles.

ATHLETICS. NJCAA. **Intercollegiate:** Basketball, golf M. **Intramural:** Basketball, softball, tennis, volleyball.

STUDENT SERVICES. Aptitude testing, personal counseling, veterans counselor, services/facilities for handicapped.

ANNUAL EXPENSES. Tuition and fees (1992-93): $613, $114 additional for out-of-district students, $1,144 additional for out-of-state students. **Room and board:** $3,102. **Books and supplies:** $434. **Other expenses:** $918.

FINANCIAL AID. 28% of freshmen, 25% of continuing students receive some form of aid. 74% of grants, 79% of loans, 90% of jobs based on need. Academic, music/drama, art, athletic, leadership scholarships available. **Aid applications:** No closing date; applicants notified on a rolling basis; must reply within 5 weeks. **Additional information:** Short term loans available.

ADDRESS/TELEPHONE. Dr. David L. Petrash, Associate Vice President for Admissions and Records, Grayson County College, 6101 Grayson Drive, Denison, TX 75020. (903) 465-6030. Fax: (903) 463-5284.

Hardin-Simmons University
Abilene, Texas CB code: 6268

Admissions:	95% of applicants accepted
Based on:	••• School record, test scores
	• Interview, recommendations, special talents
Completion:	80% of freshmen end year in good standing
	35% graduate, 20% of these enter graduate study

4-year private university, coed, Affiliated with Baptist General Convention of Texas. Founded in 1891. **Accreditation:** Regional. **Undergraduate enrollment:** 658 men, 714 women full time; 175 men, 255 women part time. **Graduate enrollment:** 22 men, 29 women full time; 50 men, 47 women part time. **Faculty:** 140 total (101 full time), 87 with doctorates or other terminal degrees. **Location:** Urban campus in small city; 150 miles from Fort Worth. **Calendar:** Semester, extensive summer session. **Microcomputers:** 125 located in libraries, classrooms, computer centers. **Special facilities:** Rare and fine book room, science research center, observatory, chapel. **Additional facts:** University consists of college of arts and sciences; schools of business, education, music, nursing, and theology; and graduate school.

DEGREES OFFERED. AS, BA, BS, MA, MBA, MEd. 8 associate degrees awarded in 1992. 100% in allied health. 221 bachelor's degrees awarded. 13% in business and management, 22% teacher education, 5% health sciences, 6% letters/literature, 14% parks/recreation, protective services, public affairs, 9% philosophy, religion, theology, 7% psychology, 6% social sciences, 8% visual and performing arts. Graduate degrees offered in 13 major fields of study.

UNDERGRADUATE MAJORS. Associate: Nursing. **Bachelor's:** Accounting, agricultural sciences, art education, Bible studies, bilingual/bicultural education, biology, business administration and management, business education, chemistry, clinical laboratory science, communications, computer and information sciences, computer education, criminal justice studies, dramatic arts, earth sciences, elementary education, English, English education, exercise physiology, finance, foreign languages education, French, geology, German, health education, history, history education, law enforcement and corrections, management information systems, management science, marketing management, mathematics, mathematics education, medical laboratory technologies, music, music education, music performance, music theory and composition, nursing, philosophy, physical education, physics, political science and government, predentistry, prelaw, premedicine, psychology, psychology education, public relations, reading education, religious education, religious music, science education, social science education, social studies education, social work, sociology, Spanish, speech, speech correction, speech pathology/audiology, speech/communication/theater education, theological studies.

ACADEMIC PROGRAMS. 2-year transfer program, double major, dual enrollment of high school students, education specialist degree, independent study, internships, study abroad, teacher preparation, Washington semester, cross-registration. **Remedial services:** Reduced course load, remedial instruction, special counselor, tutoring, computerized review and drill in mathematics. **ROTC:** Army. **Placement/credit:** AP, CLEP Subject, IB, institutional tests; 32 credit hours maximum for bachelor's degree.

ACADEMIC REQUIREMENTS. Freshmen must earn minimum GPA of 1.6 to continue in good standing. Students must have GPA of 1.8 for 33-

48 hours; 2.0 for 49 or more hours; 2.0 required for graduation in both major and minor fields. Programs leading to teacher certification require 2.50. 59% of freshmen return for sophomore year. Students must declare major by end of second year. **Graduation requirements:** 72 hours for associate (36 in major), 124 hours for bachelor's (30 in major). Most students required to take courses in computer science, English, history, humanities, mathematics, philosophy/religion, biological/physical sciences, social sciences.

FRESHMAN ADMISSIONS. High school preparation: 16 units required. Required units include English 3, mathematics 2, social science 2 and science 2. Mathematics must include algebra I and above. **Test requirements:** SAT or ACT; score report by July 31.

1992 FRESHMAN CLASS PROFILE. 514 men and women applied, 490 accepted; 241 men enrolled, 205 women enrolled. 16% were in top tenth and 40% were in top quarter of graduating class. **Academic background:** Mid 50% of enrolled freshmen had SAT-V between 380-500, SAT-M between 400-550; ACT composite between 18-24. 67% submitted SAT scores, 67% submitted ACT scores. **Characteristics:** 68% from in state, 60% commute, 18% have minority backgrounds, 1% are foreign students. Average age is 21.

FALL-TERM APPLICATIONS. $25 fee. No closing date; priority given to applications received by August 1; applicants notified on a rolling basis. Audition required for music applicants. Interview recommended. Deferred and early admission available.

STUDENT LIFE. Housing: Dormitories (men, women); apartment housing available. All freshmen must live on campus unless living with parents. **Activities:** Student government, magazine, student newspaper, yearbook, choral groups, concert band, drama, jazz band, marching band, music ensembles, musical theater, opera, symphony orchestra, fraternities, sororities, Baptist Student Union, social clubs, service organizations.

ATHLETICS. NAIA. **Intercollegiate:** Baseball M, basketball, football M, golf, soccer, tennis, volleyball W. **Intramural:** Badminton, baseball M, basketball, bowling, golf, racquetball, soccer, softball, tennis, volleyball.

STUDENT SERVICES. Career counseling, employment service for undergraduates, freshman orientation, health services, personal counseling, placement service for graduates, services/facilities for handicapped.

ANNUAL EXPENSES. Tuition and fees: $6,480. **Room and board:** $2,980. **Books and supplies:** $700. **Other expenses:** $1,284.

FINANCIAL AID. 72% of freshmen, 75% of continuing students receive some form of aid. 45% of grants, 68% of loans, 31% of jobs based on need. 220 enrolled freshmen were judged to have need, 219 were offered aid. Academic, music/drama, art, athletic, leadership, alumni affiliation, religious affiliation, minority scholarships available. **Aid applications:** No closing date; priority given to applications received by March 15; applicants notified on a rolling basis beginning on or about June 1; must reply within 10 days. **Additional information:** Academic scholarships for tuition only range from $1,000 to $3,000 per semester and are available for students with composite scores of 24 and above on ACT or 1010 and above on SAT.

ADDRESS/TELEPHONE. Laura Moore, Dir University Relations/Admissions, Hardin-Simmons University, 2200 Hickory, Drawer M, Abilene, TX 79698. (915) 670-1206. (800) 568-2692.

Hill College
Hillsboro, Texas — CB code: 6285

2-year public junior college, coed. Founded in 1962. **Accreditation:** Regional. **Undergraduate enrollment:** 422 men, 413 women full time; 389 men, 567 women part time. **Faculty:** 90 total (48 full time). **Location:** Rural campus in small town; 64 miles from Dallas. **Calendar:** Semester, limited summer session. **Microcomputers:** Located in classrooms, computer centers. **Special facilities:** History complex including gun museum and Civil War research center.

DEGREES OFFERED. AA, AS, AAS. 84 associate degrees awarded in 1992.

UNDERGRADUATE MAJORS. Agribusiness, agricultural sciences, air conditioning/heating/refrigeration mechanics, automotive mechanics, automotive technology, biology, botany, business and management, business and office, business data entry equipment operation, business data processing and related programs, business data programming, chemistry, commercial art, communications, computer and information sciences, computer programming, criminal justice studies, data processing, drafting, drafting and design technology, education, electronic technology, engineering, engineering and engineering-related technologies, English, fine arts, food production/management/services, geology, industrial technology, journalism, law enforcement and corrections technologies, liberal/general studies, marketing and distribution, mathematics, music, nursing, office supervision and management, physical sciences, physics, practical nursing, precision metal work, prelaw, psychology, real estate, robotics, science technologies, secretarial and related programs, social sciences, word processing, zoology.

ACADEMIC PROGRAMS. 2-year transfer program, cooperative education, dual enrollment of high school students, internships. **Remedial services:** Learning center, reduced course load, remedial instruction, special counselor, tutoring. **Placement/credit:** CLEP General and Subject, institutional tests; 24 credit hours maximum for associate degree.

ACADEMIC REQUIREMENTS. Freshmen must earn minimum GPA of 2.0 to continue in good standing. Students must declare major by end of first year. **Graduation requirements:** 62 hours for associate. Most students required to take courses in computer science, English, history, humanities, mathematics, social sciences.

FRESHMAN ADMISSIONS. Selection criteria: Open admissions. **Test requirements:** ACT for placement and counseling only; score report by September 1.

1992 FRESHMAN CLASS PROFILE. 374 men, 368 women enrolled. **Characteristics:** 95% from in state, 85% commute, 12% have minority backgrounds.

FALL-TERM APPLICATIONS. No fee. No closing date; applicants notified on a rolling basis.

STUDENT LIFE. Housing: Dormitories (men, women, coed). **Activities:** Student government, film, magazine, student newspaper, yearbook, choral groups, concert band, dance, drama, jazz band, music ensembles, pep band, Circle-K, Young Democrats, Young Republicans, Black Student Union, Baptist Student Union.

ATHLETICS. NJCAA. **Intercollegiate:** Baseball M, basketball, soccer M, softball W, tennis, track and field, volleyball W.

STUDENT SERVICES. Aptitude testing, career counseling, freshman orientation, personal counseling.

ANNUAL EXPENSES. Tuition and fees: $705, $180 additional for out-of-district students, $580 additional for out-of-state students. **Room and board:** $2,500. **Books and supplies:** $526. **Other expenses:** $937.

FINANCIAL AID. 60% of freshmen, 60% of continuing students receive some form of aid. 72% of grants, all loans, all jobs based on need. 590 enrolled freshmen were judged to have need, all were offered aid. Academic, music/drama, athletic, state/district residency, leadership scholarships available. **Aid applications:** No closing date; priority given to applications received by August 1; applicants notified on a rolling basis.

ADDRESS/TELEPHONE. Registrar's Office, Hill College, PO Box 619, Hillsboro, TX 76645. (817) 582-2555.

Houston Baptist University ⇎
Houston, Texas — CB code: 6282

Admissions:	68% of applicants accepted
Based on:	••• Recommendations, test scores
	•• School record, special talents
	• Activities, essay, interview
Completion:	83% of freshmen end year in good standing
	40% enter graduate study

4-year private university and liberal arts college, coed, affiliated with Baptist General Convention of Texas. Founded in 1960. **Accreditation:** Regional. **Undergraduate enrollment:** 467 men, 811 women full time; 121 men, 301 women part time. **Graduate enrollment:** 108 men, 116 women full time; 81 men, 195 women part time. **Faculty:** 145 total (107 full time), 94 with doctorates or other terminal degrees. **Location:** Suburban campus in very large city; in southwest part of city. **Calendar:** Quarter, extensive summer session. **Microcomputers:** 83 located in libraries, computer centers. **Special facilities:** Museum.

DEGREES OFFERED. BA, BS, MA, MS, MBA, MEd. 21 associate degrees awarded in 1992. 100% in health sciences. 217 bachelor's degrees awarded. Graduate degrees offered in 10 major fields of study.

UNDERGRADUATE MAJORS. Associate: Nursing. **Bachelor's:** Accounting, art education, biology, business administration and management, business economics, chemical engineering, chemistry, civil engineering, clinical laboratory science, communications, developmental psychology, early childhood education, economics, education, electrical/electronics/communications engineering, elementary education, engineering, English, finance, fine arts, French, history, industrial engineering, information sciences and systems, marketing management, mathematics, mechanical engineering, music, music education, nuclear medical technology, nursing, political science and government, psychology, religion, religious music, secondary education, social work, sociology, Spanish, special education, specific learning disabilities, speech, student counseling and personnel services.

ACADEMIC PROGRAMS. Double major, dual enrollment of high school students, independent study, internships, study abroad, telecourses. **Remedial services:** Reduced course load. **Placement/credit:** AP, CLEP General and Subject, institutional tests.

ACADEMIC REQUIREMENTS. Freshmen must earn minimum GPA of 1.8 to continue in good standing. 58% of freshmen return for sophomore year. Students must declare major by end of second year. **Graduation requirements:** 72 hours for associate, 130 hours for bachelor's. Most students required to take courses in computer science, English, foreign languages, history, mathematics, philosophy/religion, biological/physical sciences, social sciences.

FRESHMAN ADMISSIONS. Selection criteria: School achievement record, test scores, class rank, special talents, and skills most important. **Test requirements:** SAT or ACT (SAT preferred); score report by August 15.

1992 FRESHMAN CLASS PROFILE. 165 men applied, 104 accepted,

65 enrolled; 292 women applied, 206 accepted, 123 enrolled. **Academic background:** Mid 50% of enrolled freshmen had SAT-V between 430-450, SAT-M between 480-500. 98% submitted SAT scores. **Characteristics:** 92% from in state, 88% commute, 47% have minority backgrounds, 5% are foreign students, 18% join fraternities/sororities. Average age is 18.

FALL-TERM APPLICATIONS. $25 fee. Closing date June 1; priority given to applications received by May 1; applicants notified on a rolling basis; must reply by May 15. Audition required for music applicants. Portfolio required for art applicants. Essay required. Interview recommended for academically weak applicants. Deferred and early admission available.

STUDENT LIFE. Housing: Dormitories (men, women); apartment housing available. **Activities:** Student government, student newspaper, television, yearbook, choral groups, concert band, drama, jazz band, music ensembles, musical theater, opera, pep band, symphony orchestra, fraternities, sororities, Christian Life on Campus, Psi Chi, social work organization, nursing association, international club, FCA, Omicron Delta Kappa.

ATHLETICS. NAIA. **Intercollegiate:** Baseball M, basketball M, softball W, volleyball W. **Intramural:** Badminton, basketball, bowling, football M, softball, table tennis, tennis, track and field, volleyball.

STUDENT SERVICES. Employment service for undergraduates, freshman orientation, health services, personal counseling, placement service for graduates, services/facilities for handicapped.

ANNUAL EXPENSES. Tuition and fees (1992-93): $6,230. **Room and board:** $2,340. **Books and supplies:** $525. **Other expenses:** $1,370.

FINANCIAL AID. 70% of freshmen, 70% of continuing students receive some form of aid. 62% of grants, 76% of loans, all jobs based on need. Academic, music/drama, art, athletic, religious affiliation scholarships available. **Aid applications:** No closing date; priority given to applications received by May 1; applicants notified on a rolling basis beginning on or about July 1; must reply within 2 weeks.

ADDRESS/TELEPHONE. Phil Kimrey, Director of Admissions, Houston Baptist University, 7502 Fondren Road, Houston, TX 77074. (713) 995-3210. (800) 969-3210. Fax: (713)995-3209.

Houston Community College
Houston, Texas — CB code: 0929

2-year public community college, coed. Founded in 1971. **Accreditation:** Regional. **Undergraduate enrollment:** 4,202 men, 4,309 women full time; 16,684 men, 20,726 women part time. **Faculty:** 2,587 total (487 full time), 284 with doctorates or other terminal degrees. **Location:** Urban campus in very large city. **Calendar:** Semester, extensive summer session. Saturday and extensive evening/early morning classes. **Microcomputers:** 375 located in libraries, classrooms, computer centers. **Additional facts:** Multicampus system. Student may attend campus of choice.

DEGREES OFFERED. AA, AS, AAS. 959 associate degrees awarded in 1992. 13% in business and management, 5% engineering technologies, 23% health sciences, 12% allied health, 31% multi/interdisciplinary studies.

UNDERGRADUATE MAJORS. Accounting, agricultural sciences, bilingual/bicultural education, biological and physical sciences, biology, building science technology, business administration and management, business and management, business and office, chemical manufacturing technology, chemistry, child development/care/guidance, civil technology, commercial art, commercial music, comparative literature, computer servicing technology, court reporting, criminal justice studies, data processing, drafting and design technology, dramatic arts, earth sciences, economics, electronic technology, elementary education, engineering and engineering-related technologies, English, fashion design, fashion merchandising, fine arts, fire control and safety technology, fire protection, foreign languages (multiple emphasis), graphic arts technology, history, home economics, home furnishings and equipment management/production/services, horticulture, hotel/motel and restaurant management, illustration design, interior design, interpreter for the deaf, journalism, law enforcement and corrections technologies, legal assistant/paralegal, liberal/general studies, manufacturing technology, mathematics, mechanical design technology, medical laboratory technologies, medical records technology, mental health/human services, mining and petroleum technologies, music, music performance, music theory and composition, nuclear medical technology, nursing, occupational therapy assistant, philosophy, photographic technology, physical therapy assistant, physics, piano pedogogy, political science and government, predentistry, preengineering, premedicine, prepharmacy, preveterinary, psychology, radiograph medical technology, real estate, secondary education, secretarial and related programs, sociology, speech, technical and business writing, technical communications, tourism, video, word processing.

ACADEMIC PROGRAMS. 2-year transfer program, computer delivered (on-line) credit-bearing course offerings, cooperative education, dual enrollment of high school students, internships, telecourses, visiting/exchange student program, weekend college. **Remedial services:** Learning center, remedial instruction, tutoring. **ROTC:** Army. **Placement/credit:** AP, CLEP General and Subject, institutional tests; 15 credit hours maximum for associate degree.

ACADEMIC REQUIREMENTS. Freshmen must earn minimum GPA of 2.0 to continue in good standing. 55% of freshmen return for sophomore year. **Graduation requirements:** 60 hours for associate. Most students required to take courses in English, mathematics, social sciences.

FRESHMAN ADMISSIONS. Selection criteria: Open admissions. High school transcript, assessment, and personal interview required for admission to health programs.

1992 FRESHMAN CLASS PROFILE. 2,210 men applied, 2,210 accepted, 2,210 enrolled; 2,474 women applied, 2,474 accepted, 2,474 enrolled. **Characteristics:** 96% from in state, 100% commute, 49% have minority backgrounds, 2% are foreign students. Average age is 23.

FALL-TERM APPLICATIONS. No fee. No closing date; applicants notified on a rolling basis. Interview required for health careers applicants. High school diploma required for students under age 18.

STUDENT LIFE. Activities: Student government, magazine, student newspaper, choral groups, concert band, dance, drama, jazz band, music ensembles, musical theater, opera, International student association, Vietnamese student association, United Student Council, Black Student Union, Association of Latin American Students, Phi Theta Kappa.

ATHLETICS. Intramural: Basketball M, bowling, golf, soccer, softball, table tennis, tennis, volleyball.

STUDENT SERVICES. Aptitude testing, career counseling, employment service for undergraduates, freshman orientation, on-campus day care, personal counseling, placement service for graduates, veterans counselor, women's support services, services/facilities for handicapped.

ANNUAL EXPENSES. Tuition and fees (projected): $738, $360 additional for out-of-district students, $1,380 additional for out-of-state students. **Books and supplies:** $1,000. **Other expenses:** $1,328.

FINANCIAL AID. 14% of freshmen, 15% of continuing students receive some form of aid. 99% of grants, 97% of loans, all jobs based on need. 4,330 enrolled freshmen were judged to have need, all were offered aid. **Aid applications:** No closing date; priority given to applications received by April 15; applicants notified on a rolling basis; must reply within 2 weeks.

ADDRESS/TELEPHONE. Dona G. Harris, Assoc VC Enrollment Services, Houston Community College, PO Box 7849, Houston, TX 77270. (713) 868-0763. Fax: (713) 869-5743.

Howard College
Big Spring, Texas — CB code: 6277

2-year public community college, coed. Founded in 1945. **Accreditation:** Regional. **Undergraduate enrollment:** 423 men, 613 women full time; 509 men, 849 women part time. **Faculty:** 190 total (95 full time), 9 with doctorates or other terminal degrees. **Location:** Rural campus in large town; 95 miles from Lubbock, 40 miles from Midland. **Calendar:** Semester, limited summer session. **Microcomputers:** Located in libraries, computer centers. **Special facilities:** Rodeo arena.

DEGREES OFFERED. AA, AS, AAS. 127 associate degrees awarded in 1992.

UNDERGRADUATE MAJORS. Accounting, agribusiness, agricultural economics, agricultural sciences, agronomy, anatomy, art history, automotive mechanics, automotive technology, biology, botany, business and management, business and office, business data entry equipment operation, business data processing and related programs, business data programming, chemistry, communications, computer and information sciences, dental hygiene, drafting, dramatic arts, education, emergency medical technologies, engineering, English, finance, fine arts, fire control and safety technology, fire protection, geology, law enforcement and corrections technologies, liberal/general studies, management information systems, marketing and distribution, mathematics, medical laboratory technologies, microbiology, music, nursing, physical sciences, physical therapy assistant, physics, practical nursing, predentistry, premedicine, prepharmacy, psychology, radiograph medical technology, real estate, rehabilitation counseling/services, secretarial and related programs, social sciences, soil sciences, speech, visual and performing arts, zoology.

ACADEMIC PROGRAMS. 2-year transfer program, dual enrollment of high school students, cross-registration. **Remedial services:** Learning center, preadmission summer program, reduced course load, remedial instruction, special counselor, tutoring. **Placement/credit:** AP, CLEP General and Subject, institutional tests; 18 credit hours maximum for associate degree.

ACADEMIC REQUIREMENTS. Freshmen must earn minimum GPA of 2.0 to continue in good standing. 40% of freshmen return for sophomore year. Students must declare major on enrollment. **Graduation requirements:** 62 hours for associate. Most students required to take courses in computer science, English, history, humanities, mathematics, biological/physical sciences, social sciences.

FRESHMAN ADMISSIONS. Selection criteria: Open admissions. **Test requirements:** SAT or ACT for placement and counseling only; score report by August 24.

1992 FRESHMAN CLASS PROFILE. 664 men, 988 women enrolled. **Characteristics:** 81% from in state, 79% commute, 27% have minority backgrounds, 1% are foreign students. Average age is 20.

FALL-TERM APPLICATIONS. No fee. Closing date August 24; applicants notified on a rolling basis beginning on or about June 10. Interview required for dental hygiene, degree and licensed vocational nursing, cosmetology applicants. Early admission available.

STUDENT LIFE. Housing: Dormitories (men, women). **Activities:** Student government, magazine, yearbook, choral groups, concert band, dance, drama, jazz band, music ensembles, musical theater, Phi Theta Kappa honor fraternity.

ATHLETICS. NJCAA. **Intercollegiate:** Baseball M, basketball. **Intramural:** Basketball, bowling, golf, handball, racquetball, softball, tennis, volleyball.

STUDENT SERVICES. Aptitude testing, career counseling, employment service for undergraduates, freshman orientation, personal counseling, placement service for graduates, veterans counselor, services/facilities for handicapped.

ANNUAL EXPENSES. Tuition and fees: $780, $50 additional for out-of-district students, $400 additional for out-of-state students. Nonresident students required to pay $200 fee per semester, plus $16 per additional semester hour taken. **Room and board:** $2,100. **Books and supplies:** $350. **Other expenses:** $1,175.

FINANCIAL AID. 60% of freshmen, 60% of continuing students receive some form of aid. 87% of grants, 90% of loans, all jobs based on need. Academic, music/drama, art, athletic, leadership scholarships available. **Aid applications:** No closing date; priority given to applications received by April 1; applicants notified on a rolling basis beginning on or about July 15; must reply within 2 weeks.

ADDRESS/TELEPHONE. Dusty Johnston, Vice President Student/Instructional Services, Howard College, 1001 Birdwell Lane, Big Spring, TX 79720. (915) 264-5000. Fax: (915) 264-5082.

Howard Payne University
Brownwood, Texas CB code: 6278

Admissions: 79% of applicants accepted
Based on: ••• School record, test scores
• Essay, interview, recommendations
Completion: 85% of freshmen end year in good standing
30% enter graduate study

4-year private liberal arts college, coed, affiliated with Southern Baptist Convention. Founded in 1889. **Accreditation:** Regional. **Undergraduate enrollment:** 539 men, 515 women full time; 125 men, 114 women part time. **Faculty:** 108 total (84 full time), 58 with doctorates or other terminal degrees. **Location:** Rural campus in large town; 150 miles from Dallas, 77 miles from Abilene. **Calendar:** Semester, limited summer session. **Special facilities:** Douglas MacArthur Academy of Freedom.

DEGREES OFFERED. BA, BS. 185 bachelor's degrees awarded in 1992. 19% in business and management, 12% teacher education, 13% letters/literature, 16% philosophy, religion, theology, 16% social sciences.

UNDERGRADUATE MAJORS. Accounting, art education, Bible studies, biblical languages, biology, business and management, business education, chemistry, clinical laboratory science, communications, computer and information sciences, dramatic arts, economics, elementary education, English, English education, environmental science, foreign languages education, Greek (classical), history, liberal/general studies, marketing and distribution, mathematics, mathematics education, music, music education, philosophy, physical education, political science and government, psychology, religious education, religious music, secondary education, secretarial and related programs, social science education, social sciences, social studies education, sociology, Spanish, speech, speech/communication/theater education, studio art, theological studies.

ACADEMIC PROGRAMS. Double major, dual enrollment of high school students, honors program, internships, teacher preparation, telecourses. **Remedial services:** Reduced course load, remedial instruction, special counselor, tutoring. **Placement/credit:** AP, CLEP Subject, institutional tests; 30 credit hours maximum for bachelor's degree.

ACADEMIC REQUIREMENTS. Freshmen must earn minimum GPA of 1.5 to continue in good standing. 58% of freshmen return for sophomore year. Students must declare major by end of second year. **Graduation requirements:** 128 hours for bachelor's (30 in major). Most students required to take courses in arts/fine arts, computer science, English, foreign languages, history, mathematics, philosophy/religion, biological/physical sciences, social sciences. **Postgraduate studies:** 3% enter law school, 2% enter medical school, 5% enter MBA programs, 20% enter other graduate study.

FRESHMAN ADMISSIONS. Selection criteria: ACT score of 19 or above or SAT at least 830, or B average throughout high school, or rank in top half of class. Those not meeting these requirements eligible for provisional or conditional admission. **High school preparation:** 15 units required. Recommended units include English 3, mathematics 2, social science 1 and science 2. The remaining credits must be among those listed in the approved courses provided by the Texas Education Agency. **Test requirements:** SAT or ACT; score report by August 15.

1992 FRESHMAN CLASS PROFILE. 401 men applied, 316 accepted, 173 enrolled; 385 women applied, 303 accepted, 157 enrolled. 72% had high school GPA of 3.0 or higher, 26% between 2.0 and 2.99. 37% were in top quarter of graduating class. **Characteristics:** 90% from in state, 70% live in college housing, 17% have minority backgrounds. Average age is 18.

FALL-TERM APPLICATIONS. $25 fee. No closing date; priority given to applications received by August 15; applicants notified on a rolling basis. Audition recommended for music applicants. Interview required for academy program applicants; recommended for all others. Interview may be required by Admissions Committee. Deferred and early admission available. Placement tests in Math/English may be required before advisement and registration based on subject scores on ACT/SAT tests.

STUDENT LIFE. Housing: Dormitories (men, women); apartment housing available. **Activities:** Student government, magazine, student newspaper, television, yearbook, choral groups, concert band, drama, jazz band, marching band, music ensembles, musical theater, opera, Baptist Student Union, Ministerial Association, Delta Pi, Delta Omicron,Kappa Kappa Psi, Sigma Alph, Tau Beta Sigma, Soul Alpha Delta Kappa, Delta Chi Rho, Delta Pi, Phi Beta Lambada. **Additional information:** Religious observance required.

ATHLETICS. NAIA, NCAA. **Intercollegiate:** Baseball M, basketball, cross-country, football M, golf M, tennis, track and field M, volleyball W. **Intramural:** Basketball, volleyball.

STUDENT SERVICES. Aptitude testing, career counseling, employment service for undergraduates, freshman orientation, health services, personal counseling, placement service for graduates, veterans counselor, services/facilities for handicapped.

ANNUAL EXPENSES. Tuition and fees: $5,070. **Room and board:** $2,820. **Books and supplies:** $450. **Other expenses:** $1,250.

FINANCIAL AID. 75% of freshmen, 80% of continuing students receive some form of aid. 57% of grants, 74% of loans, 72% of jobs based on need. Academic, music/drama, art, leadership, alumni affiliation scholarships available. **Aid applications:** No closing date; priority given to applications received by May 1; applicants notified on a rolling basis; must reply within 2 weeks.

ADDRESS/TELEPHONE. Veta Young, Director of Admissions, Howard Payne University, Howard Payne Station, Box 174, Brownwood, TX 76801-2794. (915) 646-2502 ext. 2803. (800) 950-8468. Fax: (915) 643-7835.

Huston-Tillotson College
Austin, Texas CB code: 6280

4-year private liberal arts college, coed, affiliated with United Church of Christ and United Methodist Church. Founded in 1876. **Accreditation:** Regional. **Undergraduate enrollment:** 215 men, 249 women full time; 30 men, 72 women part time. **Faculty:** 48 total (40 full time), 21 with doctorates or other terminal degrees. **Location:** Urban campus in large city; 78 miles from San Antonio. **Calendar:** Semester, limited summer session. Saturday and extensive evening/early morning classes. **Microcomputers:** 60 located in libraries, classrooms, computer centers.

DEGREES OFFERED. BA, BS. 70 bachelor's degrees awarded in 1992. 10% in business and management, 33% business/office and marketing/distribution, 10% communications, 10% computer sciences, 7% teacher education, 8% physical sciences, 11% social sciences.

UNDERGRADUATE MAJORS. Accounting, biology, business administration and management, business and office, chemistry, communications, computer and information sciences, economics, education, elementary education, engineering, English, finance, history, hotel/motel and restaurant management, human resources development, marketing and distribution, marketing management, mathematics, music, personnel management, physical education, political science and government, predentistry, prelaw, premedicine, prepharmacy, radio/television broadcasting, secondary education, sociology.

ACADEMIC PROGRAMS. Cooperative education, double major, honors program, internships, teacher preparation, weekend college; liberal arts/career combination in engineering, health sciences. **Remedial services:** Learning center, remedial instruction, special counselor, tutoring. **Placement/credit:** Institutional tests; 15 credit hours maximum for bachelor's degree.

ACADEMIC REQUIREMENTS. Freshmen must earn minimum GPA of 1.5 to continue in good standing. 57% of freshmen return for sophomore year. Students must declare major by end of second year. **Graduation requirements:** 120 hours for bachelor's (30 in major). Most students required to take courses in computer science, English, foreign languages, history, humanities, mathematics, philosophy/religion, biological/physical sciences, social sciences. **Postgraduate studies:** 4% enter law school, 10% enter medical school, 21% enter other graduate study.

FRESHMAN ADMISSIONS. Selection criteria: School achievement record important. Test scores and interview considered. **High school preparation:** 18 units required. Required units include English 4, mathematics 3, social science 2 and science 2. **Test requirements:** SAT or ACT.

1992 FRESHMAN CLASS PROFILE. 33 men, 44 women enrolled. **Characteristics:** 64% live in college housing, 98% have minority backgrounds, 7% join fraternities/sororities. Average age is 18.

FALL-TERM APPLICATIONS. $15 fee. No closing date; priority given to applications received by March 1; applicants notified on a rolling basis beginning on or about May 1. Interview recommended. Audition recommended. Deferred and early admission available.

STUDENT LIFE. Housing: Dormitories (coed). **Activities:** Student government, student newspaper, television, yearbook, choral groups, drama, music ensembles, fraternities, sororities, Brothers and Sisters in Christ.

ATHLETICS. NAIA. **Intercollegiate:** Baseball M, basketball, volleyball W. **Intramural:** Badminton, basketball, soccer M, table tennis, volleyball.

STUDENT SERVICES. Aptitude testing, career counseling, employment service for undergraduates, freshman orientation, health services, personal counseling, placement service for graduates, special adviser for adult students, veterans counselor, services/facilities for handicapped.

ANNUAL EXPENSES. Tuition and fees (1992-93): $4,650. **Room and board:** $3,450. **Books and supplies:** $500. **Other expenses:** $1,088.

FINANCIAL AID. 95% of freshmen, 89% of continuing students receive some form of aid. All grants, 69% of loans, 91% of jobs based on need. **Aid applications:** Closing date May 1; applicants notified on or about May 15; must reply by June 1.

ADDRESS/TELEPHONE. Donnie J. Scott, Director of Admissions, Huston-Tillotson College, 900 Chicon Street, Austin, TX 78702. (512) 476-7421. (800) 321-7421. Fax: (512) 474-0762.

Incarnate Word College
San Antonio, Texas — CB code: 6303

Admissions: 19% of applicants accepted
Based on:
- ••• School record
- •• Test scores
- • Activities, interview, recommendations, special talents

Completion: 78% of freshmen end year in good standing
20% enter graduate study

4-year private liberal arts college, coed, affiliated with Roman Catholic Church. Founded in 1881. **Accreditation:** Regional. **Undergraduate enrollment:** 476 men, 1,212 women full time; 155 men, 439 women part time. **Graduate enrollment:** 19 men, 47 women full time; 152 men, 301 women part time. **Faculty:** 196 total (119 full time), 78 with doctorates or other terminal degrees. **Location:** Urban campus in very large city; 5 miles from downtown. **Calendar:** 4-4-1, limited summer session. **Microcomputers:** Located in computer centers. **Special facilities:** Elizabeth Huth Maddux teaching theater. **Additional facts:** Off-campus full credit courses available at USAA, Kelly Airforce Base, Randolph Airforce Base, City Public Service Board, Santa Rosa Hospital, Saint Rose Hospital.

DEGREES OFFERED. BA, BS, MA, MS, MBA, MEd. 276 bachelor's degrees awarded in 1992. 31% in business and management, 9% communications, 18% health sciences, 6% psychology, 10% social sciences, 8% visual and performing arts. Graduate degrees offered in 21 major fields of study.

UNDERGRADUATE MAJORS. Accounting, allied health, art education, art history, biology, business administration and management, business and management, business education, chemistry, clinical laboratory science, communications, dramatic arts, early childhood education, education of the emotionally handicapped, education of the mentally handicapped, elementary education, English, English education, fashion design, fashion merchandising, finance, food science and nutrition, history, hotel/motel and restaurant management, interior design, international business management, management information systems, marketing and distribution, mathematics, mathematics education, medical laboratory technologies, music, music education, music performance, nuclear medical technology, nursing, philosophy, physical education, political science and government, psychology, reading education, religion, science education, secondary education, social studies education, sociology, Spanish, special education, speech, speech/communication/theater education.

ACADEMIC PROGRAMS. Accelerated program, double major, dual enrollment of high school students, education specialist degree, independent study, internships, study abroad, teacher preparation, visiting/exchange student program, cross-registration; combined bachelor's/graduate program in business administration. **Remedial services:** Learning center, preadmission summer program, reduced course load, remedial instruction, special counselor, tutoring. **ROTC:** Army. **Placement/credit:** AP, CLEP General and Subject, institutional tests.

ACADEMIC REQUIREMENTS. Freshmen must earn minimum GPA of 2.0 to continue in good standing. 70% of freshmen return for sophomore year. Students must declare major by end of second year. **Graduation requirements:** 128 hours for bachelor's (30 in major). Most students required to take courses in arts/fine arts, computer science, English, foreign languages, history, humanities, mathematics, philosophy/religion, biological/physical sciences, social sciences. **Postgraduate studies:** 1% enter law school, 1% enter medical school, 6% enter MBA programs, 12% enter other graduate study.

FRESHMAN ADMISSIONS. Selection criteria: Test scores and school achievement record most important. Interview helpful. **High school preparation:** 16 units required. Required units include English 4, foreign language 2, mathematics 2, social science 3 and science 2. One hour fine arts required. **Test requirements:** SAT or ACT; score report by August 15.

1992 FRESHMAN CLASS PROFILE. 649 men applied, 114 accepted, 114 enrolled; 1,571 women applied, 298 accepted, 298 enrolled. **Academic background:** Mid 50% of enrolled freshmen had SAT-V between 320-430, SAT-M between 370-470; ACT composite between 16-22. 58% submitted SAT scores, 40% submitted ACT scores. **Characteristics:** 82% from in state, 78% commute, 68% have minority backgrounds, 3% are foreign students. Average age is 21.

FALL-TERM APPLICATIONS. $15 fee, may be waived for applicants with need. Closing date August 31; priority given to applications received by April 1; applicants notified on a rolling basis beginning on or about November 1; must reply within 30 days. Interview recommended for academically weak applicants. Deferred and early admission available. Academic Skills Placement Tests.

STUDENT LIFE. Housing: Dormitories (men, women, coed); apartment housing available. **Activities:** Student government, student newspaper, yearbook, choral groups, dance, drama, jazz band, music ensembles, musical theater, fraternities, sororities, Black Student Union, Student Ambassadors, service fraternity, International Student Association. **Additional information:** Incarnate Word College offers training for leaders at an annual retreat.

ATHLETICS. NAIA. **Intercollegiate:** Baseball M, basketball, cross-country, soccer, softball W, tennis, volleyball W. **Intramural:** Archery, badminton, basketball, bowling, cross-country, golf, handball, racquetball, soccer, softball, swimming, table tennis, tennis, track and field, volleyball.

STUDENT SERVICES. Aptitude testing, career counseling, employment service for undergraduates, freshman orientation, health services, personal counseling, placement service for graduates, services/facilities for handicapped.

ANNUAL EXPENSES. Tuition and fees: $8,325. **Room and board:** $4,060. **Books and supplies:** $750. **Other expenses:** $1,875.

FINANCIAL AID. 62% of freshmen, 60% of continuing students receive some form of aid. 64% of grants, 70% of loans, 90% of jobs based on need. 203 enrolled freshmen were judged to have need, all were offered aid. Academic, music/drama, art, athletic, leadership, religious affiliation, minority scholarships available. **Aid applications:** No closing date; priority given to applications received by April 1; applicants notified on a rolling basis beginning on or about April 15; must reply within 4 weeks. **Additional information:** Students encouraged to pursue outside scholarship programs.

ADDRESS/TELEPHONE. Sr. Sally Mitchell, Dean of Enrollment Services, Incarnate Word College, 4301 Broadway, San Antonio, TX 78209-6397. (210) 829-6000. Fax: (210) 829-1220.

Institute for Christian Studies
Austin, Texas — CB code: 4969

2-year upper-division private Bible college, coed, affiliated with Church of Christ. **Accreditation:** Regional. **Undergraduate enrollment:** 29 men, 2 women full time; 16 men, 9 women part time. **Faculty:** 10 total (5 full time), 6 with doctorates or other terminal degrees. **Location:** Urban campus in large city; in downtown Austin. **Calendar:** Semester, limited summer session. Extensive evening/early morning classes. **Microcomputers:** 2 located in libraries.

DEGREES OFFERED. BA, BS. 13 bachelor's degrees awarded in 1992. 100% in philosophy, religion, theology.

UNDERGRADUATE MAJORS. Bible studies, religion.

ACADEMIC PROGRAMS. Internships. **Remedial services:** Special counselor, tutoring. **Placement/credit:** CLEP General and Subject; 18 credit hours maximum for bachelor's degree.

ACADEMIC REQUIREMENTS. Students must declare major on application. **Graduation requirements:** 122 hours for associate, 122 hours for bachelor's (68 in major). Most students required to take courses in arts/fine arts, English, history, mathematics, philosophy/religion, biological/physical sciences, social sciences.

STUDENT LIFE. Housing: Dormitories (coed). **Activities:** Student government, student newspaper.

STUDENT SERVICES. Personal counseling, services/facilities for handicapped.

ANNUAL EXPENSES. Tuition and fees (1992-93): $910. **Room and board:** $1,500. **Books and supplies:** $120.

FINANCIAL AID. 95% of continuing students receive some form of aid. 93% of grants, all loans based on need. Academic, religious affiliation scholarships available. **Aid applications:** Closing date June 15; applicants notified on or about September 1. **Additional information:** Government loans, generous scholarships for students taking at least 12 hours.

ADDRESS/TELEPHONE. Cindy Lippe, Director of Admissions, Institute for Christian Studies, 1909 University Avenue, Austin, TX 78705. (512) 476-2772.

ITT Technical Institute: Arlington
Arlington, Texas CB code: 3572

2-year proprietary technical/career training institute, coed. **Undergraduate enrollment:** 513 men and women. **Location:** Suburban campus in large city; 15 miles from Fort Worth, 15 miles from Dallas. **Calendar:** Quarter.

FRESHMAN ADMISSIONS. Selection criteria: High school transcript (2.0 or better in algebra), mathematics and reading tests. CPAT test used for admissions.

ANNUAL EXPENSES. Tuition and fees (1992-93): $7,402. Tuition for 18-month computer-aided drafting program $12,817; books, supplies, and tools $1,300. Tuition for 2-year electronics program $14,405; books andsupplies $1,500. Laboratory fees $30 per quarter. **Books and supplies:** $750. **Other expenses:** $1,496.

ADDRESS/TELEPHONE. Frank Cave, Director of Education, ITT Technical Institute: Arlington, 2201 Arlington Downs Road, Arlington, TX 76011. (817) 640-7100.

ITT Technical Institute: Houston
Houston, Texas CB code: 3573

2-year proprietary technical/career training center, coed. **Undergraduate enrollment:** 587 men, 77 women full time. **Faculty:** 22 total, 1 with doctorate or other terminal degree. **Location:** Suburban campus in very large city. **Calendar:** Quarter. Extensive evening/early morning classes. **Microcomputers:** 90 located in libraries, classrooms, computer centers.

DEGREES OFFERED. AAS. 280 associate degrees awarded in 1992. 100% in engineering technologies.

UNDERGRADUATE MAJORS. Architectural technologies, drafting and design technology, electrical/electronics/communications engineering.

ACADEMIC PROGRAMS. Remedial services: Tutoring.

ACADEMIC REQUIREMENTS. Freshmen must earn minimum GPA of 1.5 to continue in good standing. 70% of freshmen return for sophomore year. Students must declare major on enrollment. **Graduation requirements:** 123 hours for associate (123 in major). Most students required to take courses in computer science, humanities, mathematics, biological/physical sciences, social sciences.

FRESHMAN ADMISSIONS. Selection criteria: Institutional entrance examination. One algebra required.

1992 FRESHMAN CLASS PROFILE. 306 men and women enrolled. **Characteristics:** 100% commute. Average age is 19.

FALL-TERM APPLICATIONS. $100 fee. Closing date September 18; applicants notified on a rolling basis. Interview required.

STUDENT LIFE. Activities: Student government.

STUDENT SERVICES. Employment service for undergraduates, freshman orientation, placement service for graduates, services/facilities for handicapped.

ANNUAL EXPENSES. Tuition and fees (1992-93): Tuition for 18-month computer-aided drafting program $12,817; books, supplies, and tools, $1,200. Tuition for 2-year electronics program $14,405; books and supplies $1,700. Laboratory fees, $50 per quarter. **Books and supplies:** $500.

FINANCIAL AID. 85% of freshmen, 85% of continuing students receive some form of aid. **Aid applications:** No closing date; applicants notified on a rolling basis.

ADDRESS/TELEPHONE. Gary Updike, Sales Manager, ITT Technical Institute: Houston, 9421 West Sam Houston Parkway, Houston, TX 77099. (713) 270-1634. Fax: (713) 270-8251.

Jacksonville College
Jacksonville, Texas CB code: 6317

2-year private Christian liberal arts college, coed, affiliated with Baptist Missionary Association of Texas. Founded in 1899. **Accreditation:** Regional. **Undergraduate enrollment:** 118 men, 154 women full time; 18 men, 42 women part time. **Faculty:** 32 total (14 full time), 1 with doctorate or other terminal degree. **Location:** Suburban campus in large town; 120 miles from Dallas, 25 miles from Tyler. **Calendar:** Semester, limited summer session. **Microcomputers:** 30 located in libraries, classrooms, computer centers.

DEGREES OFFERED. AA, AS. 40 associate degrees awarded in 1992. 100% in teacher education.

UNDERGRADUATE MAJORS. Art education, science education, secretarial and related programs.

ACADEMIC PROGRAMS. 2-year transfer program, dual enrollment of high school students. **Remedial services:** Reduced course load, remedial instruction, tutoring. **Placement/credit:** Institutional tests.

ACADEMIC REQUIREMENTS. Freshmen must earn minimum GPA of 1.5 to continue in good standing. 55% of freshmen return for sophomore year. Students must declare major by end of first year. **Graduation requirements:** 64 hours for associate. Most students required to take courses in computer science, English, foreign languages, history, mathematics, philosophy/religion, biological/physical sciences, social sciences.

FRESHMAN ADMISSIONS. Selection criteria: Open admissions. **Test requirements:** SAT or ACT for placement and counseling only.

1992 FRESHMAN CLASS PROFILE. 50 men, 61 women enrolled. **Characteristics:** 90% from in state, 75% live in college housing, 31% have minority backgrounds, 2% are foreign students. Average age is 18.

FALL-TERM APPLICATIONS. $10 fee, may be waived for applicants with need. No closing date; priority given to applications received by August 15; applicants notified on a rolling basis. Interview recommended. Deferred admission available.

STUDENT LIFE. Housing: Dormitories (men, women); apartment housing available. **Activities:** Student government, student newspaper, yearbook, choral groups, concert band, drama, music ensembles, International Student Organization, Ministerial Alliance.

ATHLETICS. NJCAA. **Intercollegiate:** Basketball M. **Intramural:** Basketball, softball, table tennis, tennis, volleyball.

STUDENT SERVICES. Career counseling, freshman orientation, health services, personal counseling, services/facilities for handicapped.

ANNUAL EXPENSES. Tuition and fees: $2,520. **Room and board:** $2,496. **Books and supplies:** $400.

FINANCIAL AID. 94% of freshmen, 89% of continuing students receive some form of aid. 64% of grants, 79% of loans, all jobs based on need. Academic, music/drama, athletic scholarships available. **Aid applications:** No closing date; priority given to applications received by June 10; applicants notified on a rolling basis beginning on or about June 15; Notified applicants must reply by August 1 or within 2 weeks if notified thereafter.

ADDRESS/TELEPHONE. Jeffrey Davis, Director of Admissions, Jacksonville College, 500 West Pine Street, Jacksonville, TX 75766. (903) 586-2518. (800) 256-8JBC. Fax: (903) 586-0743.

Jarvis Christian College
Hawkins, Texas CB code: 6319

4-year private liberal arts college, coed, affiliated with Christian Church (Disciples of Christ). Founded in 1912. **Accreditation:** Regional. **Undergraduate enrollment:** 256 men, 318 women full time; 10 men, 13 women part time. **Faculty:** 46 total (40 full time), 24 with doctorates or other terminal degrees. **Location:** Rural campus in rural community; 100 miles from Dallas, 100 miles from Shreveport, Louisiana. **Calendar:** Semester, limited summer session. **Microcomputers:** 40 located in libraries, computer centers. **Special facilities:** Observatory, natatorium.

DEGREES OFFERED. BA, BS. 61 bachelor's degrees awarded in 1992. 31% in business and management, 7% computer sciences, 10% education, 10% letters/literature, 5% life sciences, 8% mathematics, 5% physical sciences, 23% social sciences.

UNDERGRADUATE MAJORS. Accounting, biology, business administration and management, chemistry, computer and information sciences, elementary education, English, English education, health education, history, management science, marketing management, mathematics, mathematics education, music, music education, physical education, political science and government, prelaw, religion, science education, secondary education, social sciences, social studies education, sociology, special education.

ACADEMIC PROGRAMS. Cooperative education, double major, honors program, internships, teacher preparation; liberal arts/career combination in engineering; combined bachelor's/graduate program in law. **Remedial services:** Learning center, reduced course load, remedial instruction, special counselor, tutoring. **Placement/credit:** CLEP General and Subject, institutional tests; 18 credit hours maximum for bachelor's degree.

ACADEMIC REQUIREMENTS. Freshmen must earn minimum GPA of 1.5 to continue in good standing. 55% of freshmen return for sophomore year. Students must declare major by end of second year. **Graduation requirements:** 124 hours for bachelor's (30 in major). Most students required to take courses in English, history, humanities, mathematics, philosophy/religion, biological/physical sciences. **Postgraduate studies:** 10% enter other graduate study.

FRESHMAN ADMISSIONS. Selection criteria: Open admissions. **Test requirements:** SAT or ACT (ACT preferred).

1992 FRESHMAN CLASS PROFILE. 56 men, 72 women enrolled. 54% had high school GPA of 3.0 or higher, 32% between 2.0 and 2.99. **Characteristics:** 100% live in college housing. Average age is 18.

FALL-TERM APPLICATIONS. $15 fee, may be waived for applicants with need. No closing date; applicants notified on a rolling basis beginning on or about January 25; August 15. Essay required. Interview recommended. Deferred and early admission available.

STUDENT LIFE. Housing: Dormitories (men, women); apartment housing available. Single parents housing available on limited basis. **Activities:** Student government, student newspaper, yearbook, choral groups, concert band, drama, jazz band, music ensembles, fraternities, sororities, Student Minister's Association, The United Campus Christian Fellowship, pre-Law club, National Society of Black Accountants, Student National Educational Association, Students in Free Enterprise, Phi Beta Lambda English Club, College Church.

ATHLETICS. NAIA. **Intercollegiate:** Baseball M, basketball, cross-country M, softball W, track and field, volleyball. **Intramural:** Baseball, basketball, football M, swimming, tennis, track and field, volleyball.

STUDENT SERVICES. Aptitude testing, career counseling, employment service for undergraduates, freshman orientation, health services, on-campus day care, personal counseling, placement service for graduates, services/facilities for handicapped.

ANNUAL EXPENSES. Tuition and fees (1992-93): $4,015. **Room and board:** $2,999. **Books and supplies:** $300. **Other expenses:** $900.

FINANCIAL AID. 95% of freshmen, 95% of continuing students receive some form of aid. All grants, 99% of loans, all jobs based on need. Academic, music/drama, state/district residency, leadership, religious affiliation scholarships available. **Aid applications:** No closing date; priority given to applications received by July 30; applicants notified on a rolling basis; must reply within 2 weeks.

ADDRESS/TELEPHONE. Linda Rutherford, Director of Recruitment and Admissions, Jarvis Christian College, PO Drawer G, Hawkins, TX 75765. (903) 769-2174 ext. 233. Fax: (903) 769-4842.

Kilgore College
Kilgore, Texas CB code: 6341

2-year public community college, coed. Founded in 1935. **Accreditation:** Regional. **Undergraduate enrollment:** 4,423 men and women. **Faculty:** 188 total (138 full time), 12 with doctorates or other terminal degrees. **Location:** Rural campus in large town; 120 miles from Dallas. **Calendar:** Semester, limited summer session. **Microcomputers:** Located in libraries, computer centers. **Special facilities:** Experimental farm.

DEGREES OFFERED. AA, AS, AAS. 450 associate degrees awarded in 1992.

UNDERGRADUATE MAJORS. Accounting, agricultural sciences, automotive technology, Bible studies, biology, business and management, business and office, business data entry equipment operation, business data processing and related programs, chemical engineering, chemical manufacturing technology, chemistry, civil engineering, data processing, diesel engine mechanics, drafting, dramatic arts, economics, electrical/electronics/communications engineering, elementary education, engineering and engineering-related technologies, English, fashion merchandising, finance, fire control and safety technology, French, German, graphic and printing production, graphic arts technology, history, instrumentation technology, journalism, law enforcement and corrections technologies, liberal/general studies, marketing and distribution, mathematics, mechanical engineering, medical laboratory technologies, medical records technology, music, nursing, organic chemistry, petroleum engineering, photographic technology, photography, physical sciences, practical nursing, precision metal work, psychology, radio/television broadcasting, real estate, secondary education, secretarial and related programs, social sciences, sociology, Spanish, surgical technology, trade and industrial supervision and management, visual and performing arts.

ACADEMIC PROGRAMS. 2-year transfer program, dual enrollment of high school students, internships. **Remedial services:** Learning center, reduced course load, remedial instruction. **Placement/credit:** AP, CLEP Subject, institutional tests; 14 credit hours maximum for associate degree.

ACADEMIC REQUIREMENTS. Freshmen must earn minimum GPA of 2.0 to continue in good standing. 60% of freshmen return for sophomore year. Students must declare major on application. **Graduation requirements:** 64 hours for associate. Most students required to take courses in computer science, English, history, mathematics, biological/physical sciences, social sciences.

FRESHMAN ADMISSIONS. Selection criteria: Open admissions. **Test requirements:** SAT or ACT (ACT preferred) for placement and counseling only; score report by August 15.

1992 FRESHMAN CLASS PROFILE. 2,372 men and women enrolled. **Characteristics:** 97% from in state, 90% commute, 12% have minority backgrounds. Average age is 19.

FALL-TERM APPLICATIONS. No fee. No closing date; priority given to applications received by August 15; applicants notified on a rolling basis.

STUDENT LIFE. Housing: Dormitories (men, women). **Activities:** Student government, radio, student newspaper, television, yearbook, choral groups, concert band, dance, drama, marching band, Rangerettes, fraternities, sororities, church organizations, rodeo club.

ATHLETICS. NJCAA. **Intercollegiate:** Basketball, football M, tennis. **Intramural:** Badminton, bowling, handball, racquetball, softball, swimming, tennis, volleyball.

STUDENT SERVICES. Career counseling, employment service for undergraduates, freshman orientation, personal counseling, placement service for graduates, veterans counselor, services/facilities for handicapped.

ANNUAL EXPENSES. Tuition and fees (1992-93): $330, $480 additional for out-of-state students. **Room and board:** $2,200. **Books and supplies:** $450. **Other expenses:** $1,000.

FINANCIAL AID. 13% of freshmen, 13% of continuing students receive some form of aid. Grants, loans, jobs available. Academic scholarships available. **Aid applications:** No closing date; priority given to applications received by August 1; applicants notified on a rolling basis beginning on or about August 1; must reply within 2 weeks.

ADDRESS/TELEPHONE. Dana M. Ransom, Director of Admissions, Kilgore College, 1100 Broadway, Kilgore, TX 75662-3299. (903) 983-8209. Fax: (903) 983-8607.

Lamar University—Beaumont
Beaumont, Texas CB code: 6360

Admissions: 80% of applicants accepted
Based on: ••• School record, test scores
• Activities, essay, recommendations, special talents
Completion: 46% of freshmen end year in good standing
22% graduate

4-year public university, coed. Founded in 1923. **Accreditation:** Regional. **Undergraduate enrollment:** 3,001 men, 3,177 women full time; 1,972 men, 2,521 women part time. **Graduate enrollment:** 330 men, 110 women full time; 171 men, 151 women part time. **Faculty:** 466 total (371 full time), 282 with doctorates or other terminal degrees. **Location:** Urban campus in small city; 75 miles from Houston. **Calendar:** Semester, limited summer session. **Microcomputers:** Located in dormitories, libraries, classrooms, computer centers. **Special facilities:** Dishman Art Gallery, Texas Energy Museum, Center for Coastal and Marine Studies, Space Exploration Center, environmental chemistry laboratory.

DEGREES OFFERED. AAS, BA, BS, BFA, MA, MS, MBA, MEd, D. 162 associate degrees awarded in 1992. 10% in engineering technologies, 70% health sciences, 16% allied health, 12% parks/recreation, protective services, public affairs. 858 bachelor's degrees awarded. 20% in business and management, 13% education, 7% engineering, 6% health sciences, 10% multi/interdisciplinary studies, 10% parks/recreation, protective services, public affairs, 7% social sciences. Graduate degrees offered in 47 major fields of study.

UNDERGRADUATE MAJORS. Associate: Air conditioning/heating/refrigeration mechanics, business data processing and related programs, child development/care/guidance, dental hygiene, drafting, drafting and design technology, electronic technology, fire control and safety technology, food management, instrumentation technology, law enforcement and corrections technologies, marketing and distribution, nursing, occupational safety and health technology, petroleum technology, radiograph medical technology, real estate, respiratory therapy, respiratory therapy technology, robotics, secretarial and related programs. **Bachelor's:** Accounting, advertising, applied mathematics, biology, business administration and management, business and management, business economics, chemical engineering, chemistry, civil engineering, clothing and textiles management/production/services, communications, computer and information sciences, criminal justice studies, criminology, dance, dramatic arts, earth sciences, economics, education of the deaf and hearing impaired, electrical/electronics/communications engineering, engineering and engineering-related technologies, engineering management, English, environmental health engineering, environmental science, family and community services, fashion design, fashion merchandising, finance, fine arts, food science and nutrition, French, geology, German, graphic design, history, home economics, humanities and social sciences, industrial engineering, industrial technology, information sciences and systems, interdisciplinary studies, interior design, interpreter for the deaf, law enforcement and corrections, liberal/general studies, management information systems, marine biology, marketing management, mathematics, mechanical engineering, medical laboratory technologies, music, music performance, music theory and composition, nursing, oceanography, office supervision and management, personnel management, physics, political science and government, predentistry, prelaw, premedicine, prepharmacy, psychology, retailing, social work, sociology, Spanish, specific learning disabilities, speech, speech pathology/audiology, studio art.

ACADEMIC PROGRAMS. Accelerated program, cooperative education, double major, dual enrollment of high school students, honors program, independent study, internships, study abroad, teacher preparation, weekend college. **Remedial services:** Learning center, reduced course load, remedial instruction, special counselor, tutoring. **ROTC:** Army. **Placement/credit:** AP, CLEP Subject, institutional tests; 15 credit hours maximum for associate degree; 30 credit hours maximum for bachelor's degree.

ACADEMIC REQUIREMENTS. Freshmen must earn minimum GPA of 2.0 to continue in good standing. 66% of freshmen return for sophomore year. Students must declare major by end of second year. **Graduation requirements:** 60 hours for associate (24 in major), 127 hours for bachelor's (24 in major). Most students required to take courses in arts/fine arts, computer science, English, foreign languages, history, humanities, mathematics, philosophy/religion, biological/physical sciences, social sciences.

FRESHMAN ADMISSIONS. Selection criteria: Admission decision based on high school class rank, SAT scores, and completion of 14 high school units of college preparatory courses. **High school preparation:** 14 units required. Required and recommended units include English 4, mathematics 3, social science 2.5 and science 2. Foreign language 2 recommended. 2.5 college preparatory electives. **Test requirements:** SAT or ACT (SAT preferred); score report by August 1.

1992 FRESHMAN CLASS PROFILE. 1,167 men applied, 965 accepted, 608 enrolled; 1,487 women applied, 1,163 accepted, 668 enrolled. 10% were in top tenth and 17% were in top quarter of graduating class. **Academic background:** Mid 50% of enrolled freshmen had SAT-V between 300-450, SAT-M between 320-460. 75% submitted SAT scores. **Characteristics:** 98% from in state, 85% commute, 29% have minority backgrounds, 5% are foreign students, 2% join fraternities/sororities. Average age is 19.

FALL-TERM APPLICATIONS. No fee. Closing date August 1; priority given to applications received by March 1; applicants notified on a rolling basis. Essay recommended. Interview required of students accepted with GED tests. Early admission available.

STUDENT LIFE. Housing: Dormitories (men, women); apartment, fraternity, sorority housing available. 24-hour quiet floors and wings; honor floors and wings. **Activities:** Student government, student newspaper, choral groups, concert band, dance, drama, jazz band, music ensembles, musical theater, opera, pep band, symphony orchestra, fraternities, sororities, religious, professional, honor, service,sports, special interest organizations.

ATHLETICS. NCAA. **Intercollegiate:** Baseball M, basketball, cross-country, golf, soccer M, tennis, track and field, volleyball W. **Intramural:** Badminton, basketball, bowling, cross-country, golf, handball M, racquetball, sailing, softball, swimming, table tennis, tennis, track and field, volleyball.

STUDENT SERVICES. Aptitude testing, career counseling, employment service for undergraduates, freshman orientation, health services, on-campus day care, personal counseling, placement service for graduates, special adviser for adult students, veterans counselor, learning assistance, services/facilities for handicapped.

ANNUAL EXPENSES. Tuition and fees: $1,404, $4,080 additional for out-of-state students. **Room and board:** $2,878. **Books and supplies:** $698. **Other expenses:** $1,794.

FINANCIAL AID. 31% of freshmen, 38% of continuing students receive some form of aid. 83% of grants, all loans, 41% of jobs based on need. 743 enrolled freshmen were judged to have need, all were offered aid. Academic, music/drama, art, athletic, state/district residency, leadership, alumni affiliation, minority scholarships available. **Aid applications:** No closing date; priority given to applications received by April 1; applicants notified on a rolling basis beginning on or about April 15; must reply within 2 weeks.

ADDRESS/TELEPHONE. James C. Rush, Director Academic Services, Lamar University—Beaumont, PO Box 10009, Beaumont, TX 77710. (409) 880-8888. (800) 458-7558. Fax: (409) 880-8463.

Laredo Junior College
Laredo, Texas — CB code: 6362

2-year public community college, coed. Founded in 1946. **Accreditation:** Regional. **Undergraduate enrollment:** 1,118 men, 1,320 women full time; 1,421 men, 2,084 women part time. **Faculty:** 340 total (168 full time), 23 with doctorates or other terminal degrees. **Location:** Urban campus in small city; 150 miles from San Antonio, and 140 miles from Corpus Christi. **Calendar:** Semester. **Microcomputers:** 250 located in libraries, classrooms, computer centers. **Special facilities:** Special collections relating to regional history, museums, Abraham Kazen Papers.

DEGREES OFFERED. AA, AAS. 264 associate degrees awarded in 1992. 8% in business and management, 6% business/office and marketing/distribution, 8% computer sciences, 5% education, 8% health sciences, 8% allied health, 39% multi/interdisciplinary studies, 14% parks/recreation, protective services, public affairs.

UNDERGRADUATE MAJORS. Accounting, business and office, business data entry equipment operation, business data programming, child development/care/guidance, clinical laboratory science, computer programming, construction, early childhood education, electrical installation, electrical technology, electronic technology, emergency medical technologies, finance, fire protection, hotel/motel and restaurant management, Import-export, international business management, law enforcement and corrections, legal secretary, liberal/general studies, marketing and distribution, marketing management, medical records technology, nursing, physical therapy assistant, radiograph medical technology, real estate, retailing, secretarial and related programs, word processing.

ACADEMIC PROGRAMS. 2-year transfer program, dual enrollment of high school students, honors program, visiting/exchange student program, cross-registration. **Remedial services:** Learning center, remedial instruction, tutoring. **Placement/credit:** CLEP General and Subject, institutional tests; 30 credit hours maximum for associate degree.

ACADEMIC REQUIREMENTS. Freshmen must earn minimum GPA of 1.5 to continue in good standing. 65% of freshmen return for sophomore year. Students must declare major on enrollment. **Graduation requirements:** 60 hours for associate (24 in major). Most students required to take courses in arts/fine arts, computer science, English, history, mathematics, biological/physical sciences, social sciences. **Additional information:** Mandatory assessment program provides effective educational services for students.

FRESHMAN ADMISSIONS. Selection criteria: Open admissions. Special admissions requirements for some programs.

1992 FRESHMAN CLASS PROFILE. 589 men applied, 589 accepted, 589 enrolled; 655 women applied, 655 accepted, 655 enrolled. **Characteristics:** 96% from in state, 98% commute, 3% are foreign students. Average age is 19.

FALL-TERM APPLICATIONS. No fee. No closing date; applicants notified on a rolling basis. Early admission available.

STUDENT LIFE. Housing: Dormitories (coed). **Activities:** Student government, student newspaper, choral groups, concert band, dance, drama, jazz band, music ensembles, musical theater, opera, symphony orchestra.

ATHLETICS. NJCAA. **Intercollegiate:** Baseball M, tennis, volleyball W. **Intramural:** Baseball, basketball, bowling, football M, golf, handball, racquetball, softball, tennis, volleyball.

STUDENT SERVICES. Career counseling, employment service for undergraduates, freshman orientation, health services, personal counseling, placement service for graduates, veterans counselor, services/facilities for handicapped.

ANNUAL EXPENSES. Tuition and fees: $576, $1,170 additional for out-of-district students, $1,950 additional for out-of-state students. **Room and board:** $3,320. **Books and supplies:** $485. **Other expenses:** $1,818.

FINANCIAL AID. 61% of freshmen, 56% of continuing students receive some form of aid. 95% of grants, 99% of loans, all jobs based on need. Academic, music/drama, athletic scholarships available. **Aid applications:** No closing date; priority given to applications received by May 1; applicants notified on a rolling basis.

ADDRESS/TELEPHONE. Warren Haslam, Associate Dean for Enrollment Management, Laredo Junior College, West End Washington Street, Laredo, TX 78040-4395. (210) 721-5109.

Laredo State University
Laredo, Texas — CB code: 0359

2-year upper-division public university, coed. Founded in 1969. **Accreditation:** Regional. **Undergraduate enrollment:** 89 men, 228 women full time; 169 men, 308 women part time. **Graduate enrollment:** 57 men, 52 women full time; 196 men, 348 women part time. **Faculty:** 63 total (32 full time), 34 with doctorates or other terminal degrees. **Location:** Urban campus in small city; 150 miles from San Antonio. **Calendar:** Semester, extensive summer session. Saturday and extensive evening/early morning classes. **Microcomputers:** 60 located in libraries, classrooms. **Special facilities:** Nuevo Santander Museum.

DEGREES OFFERED. BA, BS, MA, MS, MBA. 165 bachelor's degrees awarded in 1992. 26% in business and management, 5% computer sciences, 26% teacher education, 38% social sciences. Graduate degrees offered in 15 major fields of study.

UNDERGRADUATE MAJORS. Accounting, bilingual/bicultural education, business and management, business economics, computer and information sciences, early childhood education, economics, elementary education, English, finance, history, law enforcement and corrections, liberal/general studies, management information systems, marketing management, mathematics, political science and government, psychology, reading education, secondary education, sociology, Spanish, transportation management.

ACADEMIC PROGRAMS. Double major, independent study, internships. **Remedial services:** Learning center, remedial instruction.

ACADEMIC REQUIREMENTS. Students must declare major on enrollment. **Graduation requirements:** 128 hours for associate (24 in major), 24 hours for bachelor's (60 in major). Most students required to take courses in computer science, English, history, mathematics, biological/physical sciences. **Postgraduate studies:** 15% enter MBA programs, 5% enter other graduate study.

STUDENT LIFE. Housing: Housing may be arranged through Laredo Junior College. **Activities:** Student government.

STUDENT SERVICES. Career counseling, employment service for undergraduates, personal counseling, placement service for graduates, veterans counselor, services/facilities for handicapped.

ANNUAL EXPENSES. Tuition and fees: $1,110, $4,080 additional for out-of-state students. **Room and board:** $3,302. **Books and supplies:** $549. **Other expenses:** $1,569.

FINANCIAL AID. 35% of continuing students receive some form of aid. 98% of grants, 91% of loans, all jobs based on need. Academic, leadership scholarships available. **Aid applications:** No closing date; priority given to applications received by June 30; applicants notified on a rolling basis beginning on or about October 1; must reply within 2 weeks.

ADDRESS/TELEPHONE. Maria R. Rosillo, Dir Admissions/Advisement, Laredo State University, 1 West End Washington Street, Laredo, TX 78040-9960. (210) 722-8001. Fax: (210) 726-4603.

Lee College
Baytown, Texas — CB code: 6363

2-year public community college, coed. Founded in 1934. **Accreditation:** Regional. **Undergraduate enrollment:** 619 men, 872 women full time; 2,638 men, 1,407 women part time. **Faculty:** 223 total (110 full time), 13 with doctorates or other terminal degrees. **Location:** Urban campus in small city; 25 miles from Houston. **Calendar:** Semester, limited summer session. Saturday classes. **Microcomputers:** Located in classrooms, computer centers.

DEGREES OFFERED. AA, AS, AAS. 306 associate degrees awarded in 1992. 9% in business and management, 21% business/office and marketing/distribution, 5% computer sciences, 17% engineering technologies, 15% health sciences, 20% multi/interdisciplinary studies, 8% trade and industry.

UNDERGRADUATE MAJORS. Accounting, air conditioning/heating/refrigeration mechanics, automotive mechanics, automotive technology, business administration and management, business and management, business and office, business computer/console/peripheral equipment operation, business data entry equipment operation, business data processing and related programs, business data programming, communications, computer programming, diesel engine mechanics, drafting, electromechanical technology, elementary education, engineering, engineering and engineering-related technologies, French, German, graphic and printing production, graphic arts technology, horticultural science, industrial technology, instrumentation technology, law enforcement and corrections technologies, legal assistant/paralegal, legal secretary, liberal/general studies, marketing and distribution, mathematics, mechanical design technology, medical records administration, medical secretary, music, nursing, photographic technology, precision metal work, real estate, rehabilitation counseling/services, science technologies, secretarial and related programs, Spanish, visual and performing arts, word processing.

ACADEMIC PROGRAMS. 2-year transfer program, cooperative education, dual enrollment of high school students, honors program, independent study, internships, telecourses, weekend college. **Remedial services:** Remedial instruction, special counselor, tutoring. **Placement/credit:** Institutional tests; 15 credit hours maximum for associate degree.

ACADEMIC REQUIREMENTS. Freshmen must earn minimum GPA of 2.0 to continue in good standing. 45% of freshmen return for sophomore year. Students must declare major on enrollment. **Graduation requirements:** 64 hours for associate. Most students required to take courses in arts/fine arts, English, history, humanities, mathematics, biological/physical sciences, social sciences.

FRESHMAN ADMISSIONS. Selection criteria: Open admissions. All students must take institutional placement examination or TASP.

1992 FRESHMAN CLASS PROFILE. 2,208 men, 1,498 women enrolled. **Characteristics:** 95% from in state, 100% commute, 24% have minority backgrounds. Average age is 22.

FALL-TERM APPLICATIONS. No fee. $25 fee for foreign applicants. No closing date; applicants notified on a rolling basis. Deferred and early admission available.

STUDENT LIFE. Activities: Student government, film, magazine, student newspaper, choral groups, concert band, dance, drama, jazz band, music ensembles, Baptist Student Union.

ATHLETICS. NJCAA. **Intercollegiate:** Baseball M, basketball M, volleyball W.

STUDENT SERVICES. Aptitude testing, career counseling, employment service for undergraduates, freshman orientation, personal counseling, veterans counselor, job placement, services/facilities for handicapped.

ANNUAL EXPENSES. Tuition and fees (projected): $455, $360 additional for out-of-district students, $840 additional for out-of-state students. **Books and supplies:** $500. **Other expenses:** $1,037.

FINANCIAL AID. 19% of freshmen, 17% of continuing students receive some form of aid. 79% of grants, 85% of loans, 15% of jobs based on need. 110 enrolled freshmen were judged to have need, 108 were offered aid. Academic, music/drama, art, athletic scholarships available. **Aid applications:** No closing date; priority given to applications received by July 1; applicants notified on a rolling basis.

ADDRESS/TELEPHONE. Tom Sanders, Dean, Student Devlpmt/Planning, Lee College, P.O. Box 818, Baytown, TX 77522-0818. (713) 427-5611.

LeTourneau University
Longview, Texas — CB code: 6365

4-year private university, coed, nondenominational. Founded in 1946. **Accreditation:** Regional. **Undergraduate enrollment:** 1,075 men, 423 women full time; 48 men, 32 women part time. **Faculty:** 119 total (49 full time), 33 with doctorates or other terminal degrees. **Location:** Suburban campus in small city; 130 miles from Dallas. **Calendar:** Semester, limited summer session. Saturday and extensive evening/early morning classes. **Microcomputers:** 300 located in libraries, classrooms, computer centers. **Special facilities:** Microprocessor and robotics laboratory, CAD/CAM facilities. **Additional facts:** Branch campuses in Tyler, Dallas, Houston, Hurst, Euliss and Bedford.

DEGREES OFFERED. AS, BA, BS, MBA. 14 associate degrees awarded in 1992. 100% in trade and industry. 345 bachelor's degrees awarded. 36% in business and management, 7% computer sciences, 14% engineering, 37% engineering technologies.

UNDERGRADUATE MAJORS. Associate: Aeronautical technology, aircraft mechanics, automotive technology, drafting, drafting and design technology, mechanical design technology. **Bachelor's:** Accounting, aeronautical technology, airline piloting and navigation, Bible studies, biology, business administration and management, business and management, chemistry, clinical laboratory science, computer and information sciences, computer mathematics, computer programming, computer science and engineering, computer science and engineering technology, education, electrical technology, electrical/electronics/communications engineering, engineering, engineering and engineering-related technologies, English, health sciences, history, marketing and distribution, mathematics, mechanical engineering, political science and government, prelaw, premedicine, preveterinary, public administration, secondary education, trade and industrial supervision and management, welding technology.

ACADEMIC PROGRAMS. Accelerated program, cooperative education, double major, education specialist degree, honors program, independent study, internships, teacher preparation, Washington semester. **Remedial services:** Preadmission summer program, remedial instruction, special counselor, tutoring. **Placement/credit:** AP, CLEP Subject, IB, institutional tests; 30 credit hours maximum for bachelor's degree.

ACADEMIC REQUIREMENTS. Freshmen must earn minimum GPA of 2.0 to continue in good standing. 73% of freshmen return for sophomore year. Students must declare major on enrollment. **Graduation requirements:** 72 hours for associate (24 in major), 126 hours for bachelor's (30 in major). Most students required to take courses in computer science, English, history, humanities, mathematics, philosophy/religion, biological/physical sciences, social sciences.

FRESHMAN ADMISSIONS. Selection criteria: Applicants should meet at least 2 of the following criteria: top half of graduating class, minimum ACT composite score of 20; or minimum combined SAT score of 800, GPA of 2.0. Personal statement on Christian belief required. **High school preparation:** 16 units required. Required units include English 4, mathematics 2, social science 2 and science 1. Foreign language recommended. 4 mathematics (including trigonometry), recommended for engineering applicants. **Test requirements:** SAT or ACT.

1992 FRESHMAN CLASS PROFILE. 158 men, 26 women enrolled. 72% had high school GPA of 3.0 or higher, 28% between 2.0 and 2.99. **Academic background:** Mid 50% of enrolled freshmen had SAT-V between 410-560, SAT-M between 460-630; ACT composite between 20-27. 73% submitted SAT scores, 54% submitted ACT scores. **Characteristics:** 20% from in state, 87% live in college housing, 13% have minority backgrounds, 6% are foreign students. Average age is 18.

FALL-TERM APPLICATIONS. $20 fee, may be waived for applicants with need. Closing date August 15; priority given to applications received by July 1; applicants notified on a rolling basis. Essay required. CRDA. Deferred and early admission available.

STUDENT LIFE. Housing: Dormitories (men, women); apartment housing available. Residential societies available. **Activities:** Student government, student newspaper, yearbook, choral groups, concert band, drama, music ensembles, pep band, international student organization. **Additional information:** Religious observance required.

ATHLETICS. NAIA. **Intercollegiate:** Baseball M, basketball M, cross-country, soccer M, volleyball W. **Intramural:** Badminton, basketball, bowling, cross-country, golf M, racquetball, soccer, softball, swimming, table tennis, tennis, track and field, volleyball, wrestling M.

STUDENT SERVICES. Career counseling, employment service for undergraduates, freshman orientation, health services, personal counseling, placement service for graduates, services/facilities for handicapped.

ANNUAL EXPENSES. Tuition and fees: $7,940. **Room and board:** $3,860. **Books and supplies:** $600. **Other expenses:** $900.

FINANCIAL AID. 78% of freshmen, 76% of continuing students receive some form of aid. 77% of grants, 92% of loans, 39% of jobs based on need. Academic, athletic, leadership scholarships available. **Aid applications:** No closing date; priority given to applications received by February 15; applicants notified on a rolling basis beginning on or about February 5; must reply by May 1 or within 3 weeks if notified thereafter.

ADDRESS/TELEPHONE. Howard Wilson, Director of Enrollment Management, LeTourneau University, PO Box 7001, 2100 South Mobberly Avenue, Longview, TX 75607-7001. (903) 753-0231 ext. 240. (800) 759-8811. Fax: (903) 237-2730.

Lon Morris College
Jacksonville, Texas — CB code: 6369

2-year private junior, liberal arts college, coed, affiliated with United Methodist Church. Founded in 1873. **Accreditation:** Regional. **Undergraduate enrollment:** 317 men and women. **Faculty:** 33 total (18 full time), 6 with doctorates or other terminal degrees. **Location:** Suburban campus in large town; 100 miles from Dallas; 25 miles from Tyler. **Calendar:** Semester. **Microcomputers:** Located in libraries, classrooms, computer centers. **Special facilities:** Art gallery.

DEGREES OFFERED. AA, AS. 68 associate degrees awarded in 1992.

UNDERGRADUATE MAJORS. American literature, anatomy, art history, astronomy, Bible studies, biology, botany, business and management, business and office, business computer/console/peripheral equipment operation, chemistry, computer and information sciences, computer graphics, computer programming, crafts, creative writing, dance, dramatic arts, drawing, economics, education, elementary education, engineering, English, English literature, French, health sciences, history, home economics, humanities and social sciences, inorganic chemistry, liberal/general studies, mathematics, microbiology, music, music history and appreciation, music performance, music theory and composition, organic chemistry, painting, philosophy, physical sciences, physics, political science and government, predentistry, prelaw, premedicine, prepharmacy, preveterinary, printmaking, psychology, religion, secondary education, social sciences, sociology, Spanish, speech, studio art, theater design, theological studies, visual and performing arts, word processing, zoology.

ACADEMIC PROGRAMS. 2-year transfer program, dual enrollment of high school students, independent study. **Remedial services:** Reduced course load, remedial instruction, tutoring, reading efficiency classes. **Placement/credit:** AP, CLEP General and Subject, institutional tests; 15 credit hours maximum for associate degree.

ACADEMIC REQUIREMENTS. Freshmen must earn minimum GPA of 1.2 to continue in good standing. 69% of freshmen return for sophomore year. **Graduation requirements:** 62 hours for associate. Most students required to take courses in arts/fine arts, English, history, mathematics, philosophy/religion, biological/physical sciences, social sciences. **Additional information:** Quality education through personalized attention from qualified faculty in stimulating campus atmosphere.

FRESHMAN ADMISSIONS. **Selection criteria:** School achievement record, minimum GPA of 2.0, recommendation, test scores, interview most important. **High school preparation:** 10 units required. Required and recommended units include English 4, mathematics 2, social science 2 and science 2. Foreign language 1 recommended. **Test requirements:** SAT or ACT; score report by September 1.

1992 FRESHMAN CLASS PROFILE. 265 men and women enrolled. **Characteristics:** Average age is 19.

FALL-TERM APPLICATIONS. $20 fee, may be waived for applicants with need. No closing date; applicants notified on a rolling basis. Audition required for choral, drama applicants. Interview recommended for academically weak applicants. Portfolio recommended for art applicants. Deferred and early admission available.

STUDENT LIFE. **Housing:** Dormitories (men, women). **Activities:** Student government, student newspaper, yearbook, choral groups, concert band, dance, drama, jazz band, music ensembles, musical theater, fraternities, sororities, Student Christian Movement, ecology club, APO.

ATHLETICS. NJCAA. **Intercollegiate:** Baseball M, basketball M, golf M. **Intramural:** Baseball, basketball, soccer M, softball, table tennis, tennis, volleyball.

STUDENT SERVICES. Career counseling, employment service for undergraduates, health services, personal counseling.

ANNUAL EXPENSES. **Tuition and fees (1992-93):** $4,354. **Room and board:** $3,266. **Books and supplies:** $450. **Other expenses:** $1,510.

FINANCIAL AID. 90% of freshmen, 90% of continuing students receive some form of aid. 43% of grants, 96% of loans, 47% of jobs based on need. 200 enrolled freshmen were judged to have need, all were offered aid. Academic, music/drama, art, athletic, state/district residency, leadership, religious affiliation scholarships available. **Aid applications:** No closing date; priority given to applications received by June 1; applicants notified on a rolling basis beginning on or about April 1; must reply within 3 weeks.

ADDRESS/TELEPHONE. Craig Gould, Director of Admissions, Lon Morris College, LMC Station, Jacksonville, TX 75766. (903) 586-2471. (800) 594-2201. Fax: (903) 586-1194.

Lubbock Christian University
Lubbock, Texas — CB code: 6378

4-year private university and liberal arts college, coed, affiliated with Church of Christ. Founded in 1957. **Accreditation:** Regional. **Undergraduate enrollment:** 401 men, 485 women full time; 106 men, 123 women part time. **Graduate enrollment:** 9 men full time; 9 men, 1 woman part time. **Faculty:** 97 total (54 full time), 36 with doctorates or other terminal degrees. **Location:** Suburban campus in small city; 300 miles from Dallas. **Calendar:** Semester, limited summer session. **Microcomputers:** 30 located in computer centers.

DEGREES OFFERED. AS, BA, BS, MA, MS. 6 associate degrees awarded in 1992. 100% in computer sciences. 198 bachelor's degrees awarded. 20% in business and management, 32% teacher education, 16% multi/interdisciplinary studies, 7% psychology, 9% social sciences. Graduate degrees offered in 1 major field of study.

UNDERGRADUATE MAJORS. **Associate:** Liberal/general studies, secretarial and related programs. **Bachelor's:** Accounting, agribusiness, agricultural sciences, art education, Bible studies, biblical languages, biology, business administration and management, business and management, chemistry, communications, computer and information sciences, education, elementary education, English, English education, finance, fine arts, graphic design, history, home economics, home economics education, interior design, journalism, liberal/general studies, mathematics, mathematics education, missionary studies, music, music education, nursing, physical education, predentistry, prelaw, premedicine, prepharmacy, preveterinary, psychology, public relations, religion, religious education, science education, secondary education, secretarial and related programs, social science education, social work, sociology, Spanish, speech, speech/communication/theater education, sports medicine, theological studies.

ACADEMIC PROGRAMS. 2-year transfer program, double major, dual enrollment of high school students, internships, student-designed major, study abroad, teacher preparation, cross-registration; liberal arts/career combination in engineering, health sciences. **Remedial services:** Learning center, preadmission summer program, reduced course load, remedial instruction, special counselor, tutoring. **ROTC:** Air Force, Army, Naval. **Placement/credit:** AP, CLEP General and Subject; 45 credit hours maximum for bachelor's degree.

ACADEMIC REQUIREMENTS. Freshmen must earn minimum GPA of 1.7 to continue in good standing. 60% of freshmen return for sophomore year. Students must declare major by end of second year. **Graduation requirements:** 132 hours for bachelor's (30 in major). Most students required to take courses in arts/fine arts, computer science, English, history, humanities, mathematics, philosophy/religion, biological/physical sciences, social sciences. **Postgraduate studies:** 1% from 2-year programs enter 4-year programs. 2% enter law school, 2% enter medical school, 5% enter MBA programs, 12% enter other graduate study. **Additional information:** Engineering degrees offered in conjunction with Texas Tech University.

FRESHMAN ADMISSIONS. **Selection criteria:** ACT scores, school grade average, and/or limited interviews. Recommendations frequently used. Special consideration given to those who demonstrate financial need either through recommendation or interview. Required units include English 4, mathematics 3, social science 2 and science 3. **Test requirements:** SAT or ACT (ACT preferred); score report by August 1.

1992 FRESHMAN CLASS PROFILE. 214 men applied, 214 accepted, 214 enrolled; 251 women applied, 251 accepted, 251 enrolled. 13% were in top tenth and 30% were in top quarter of graduating class. **Characteristics:** 31% from in state, 56% live in college housing, 7% have minority backgrounds, 1% are foreign students. Average age is 18.

FALL-TERM APPLICATIONS. $10 fee. Closing date August 1; applicants notified on a rolling basis. Interview recommended. Audition recommended for music applicants. Deferred and early admission available.

STUDENT LIFE. **Housing:** Dormitories (men, women); apartment housing available. **Activities:** Student government, student newspaper, yearbook, choral groups, concert band, drama, jazz band, music ensembles, musical theater, 5 social clubs for women, 5 for men.

ATHLETICS. NAIA. **Intercollegiate:** Baseball M, basketball, cross-country, golf, track and field, volleyball W. **Intramural:** Badminton, basketball, bowling, cross-country, soccer, softball, table tennis, tennis, volleyball.

STUDENT SERVICES. Aptitude testing, career counseling, employment service for undergraduates, freshman orientation, health services, personal counseling, placement service for graduates, special adviser for adult students, veterans counselor, services/facilities for handicapped.

ANNUAL EXPENSES. **Tuition and fees (1992-93):** $6,450. **Room and board:** $2,600. **Books and supplies:** $317. **Other expenses:** $1,055.

FINANCIAL AID. 90% of freshmen, 96% of continuing students receive some form of aid. Grants, loans, jobs available. **Aid applications:** Closing date August 1; priority given to applications received by July 1; applicants notified on a rolling basis beginning on or about March 1; must reply within 2 weeks.

ADDRESS/TELEPHONE. Steve German, Dean of Admissions, Lubbock Christian University, 5601 19th Street, Lubbock, TX 79407. (806) 792-3221 ext. 260. Fax: (806) 796-8917.

McLennan Community College
Waco, Texas — CB code: 6429

2-year public community college, coed. Founded in 1965. **Accreditation:** Regional. **Undergraduate enrollment:** 845 men, 1,489 women full time; 1,225 men, 2,175 women part time. **Location:** Urban campus in small city; 100 miles from Dallas and Austin. **Calendar:** Semester.

FRESHMAN ADMISSIONS. **Selection criteria:** Open admissions.

ANNUAL EXPENSES. **Tuition and fees:** $660, $150 additional for out-of-district students, $1,980 additional for out-of-state students. **Books and supplies:** $484. **Other expenses:** $1,398.

ADDRESS/TELEPHONE. Willie R. Hobbs, Director of Admissions and Registrar, McLennan Community College, 1400 College Drive, Waco, TX 76708. (817) 750-3622. Fax: (817) 756-0934.

McMurry University

Abilene, Texas CB code: 6402

Admissions: 79% of applicants accepted
Based on: ••• School record, test scores
•• Activities, essay, interview, recommendations
• Special talents
Completion: 76% of freshmen end year in good standing
24% graduate, 24% of these enter graduate study

4-year private liberal arts college, coed, affiliated with United Methodist Church. Founded in 1923. **Accreditation:** Regional. **Undergraduate enrollment:** 427 men, 508 women full time; 296 men, 287 women part time. **Faculty:** 121 total (68 full time), 56 with doctorates or other terminal degrees. **Location:** Suburban campus in small city; 155 miles from Fort Worth, 180 miles from Dallas. **Calendar:** 4-4-1, extensive summer session. Saturday and extensive evening/early morning classes. **Microcomputers:** 79 located in libraries, classrooms, computer centers. **Additional facts:** Off-campus extension at Dyes Air Force Base.

DEGREES OFFERED. AA, AS, BA, BS, BFA. 20 associate degrees awarded in 1992. 20% in business and management, 5% business/office and marketing/distribution, 75% health sciences. 195 bachelor's degrees awarded. 24% in business and management, 38% teacher education, 8% social sciences.

UNDERGRADUATE MAJORS. Associate: Business and management, business and office, liberal/general studies, nursing, secretarial and related programs. **Bachelor's:** Accounting, applied mathematics, applied sociology, art education, bilingual/bicultural education, biology, business administration and management, business and management, business economics, business education, ceramics, chemistry, communications, computer and information sciences, criminal justice studies, dramatic arts, education, elementary education, English, English education, finance, foreign languages education, history, legal assistant/paralegal, marketing and distribution, mathematics, mathematics education, music, music education, music performance, nursing, painting, philosophy, physical education, physical sciences, political science and government, predentistry, prelaw, premedicine, prepharmacy, preveterinary, psychology, reading education, religion, religious education, religious music, science education, secondary education, secretarial and related programs, social science education, social studies education, sociology, Spanish, speech/communication/theater education, visual and performing arts.

ACADEMIC PROGRAMS. Accelerated program, double major, dual enrollment of high school students, honors program, independent study, internships, study abroad, teacher preparation, cross-registration. **Remedial services:** Learning center, preadmission summer program, remedial instruction, tutoring. **ROTC:** Army. **Placement/credit:** AP, CLEP Subject, institutional tests; 45 credit hours maximum for associate degree; 45 credit hours maximum for bachelor's degree.

ACADEMIC REQUIREMENTS. Freshmen must earn minimum GPA of 1.7 to continue in good standing. 61% of freshmen return for sophomore year. Students must declare major by end of second year. **Graduation requirements:** 66 hours for associate, 126 hours for bachelor's (27 in major). Most students required to take courses in arts/fine arts, English, foreign languages, history, humanities, mathematics, philosophy/religion, biological/physical sciences, social sciences. **Postgraduate studies:** 1% enter law school, 1% enter medical school, 4% enter MBA programs, 18% enter other graduate study. **Additional information:** Students receive credit for nontraditional courses on and off campus during 3-week May term.

FRESHMAN ADMISSIONS. Selection criteria: School achievement record and test scores most important. Applicants must be in top 50% of high school class. **High school preparation:** 14 units required. Required units include English 4, foreign language 2, mathematics 3, social science 3 and science 2. 2 foreign language or 2 additional units in mathematics and/or science recommended. **Test requirements:** SAT or ACT; score report by August 15.

1992 FRESHMAN CLASS PROFILE. 363 men applied, 278 accepted, 136 enrolled; 219 women applied, 180 accepted, 114 enrolled. 52% had high school GPA of 3.0 or higher, 47% between 2.0 and 2.99. 24% were in top tenth and 52% were in top quarter of graduating class. **Academic background:** Mid 50% of enrolled freshmen had SAT-V between 360-480, SAT-M between 390-550; ACT composite between 19-23. 55% submitted SAT scores, 71% submitted ACT scores. **Characteristics:** 91% from in state, 88% live in college housing, 26% have minority backgrounds, 1% are foreign students, 35% join fraternities/sororities. Average age is 18.

FALL-TERM APPLICATIONS. $20 fee. Closing date August 15; priority given to applications received by March 15; applicants notified on a rolling basis; must reply by May 1 or within 2 weeks if notified thereafter. Audition required for music, theater applicants. Essay required for borderline applicants. Interview recommended. Portfolio recommended for art applicants. Deferred and early admission available.

STUDENT LIFE. Housing: Dormitories (men, women). **Activities:** Student government, magazine, student newspaper, yearbook, choral groups, concert band, drama, jazz band, marching band, music ensembles, musical theater, fraternities, sororities, Alpha Phi Omega, service organization, Fellowship of Christian Athletes, campus ministries, Christian Outreach.

ATHLETICS. NAIA. **Intercollegiate:** Basketball, football M, golf M, tennis, volleyball W. **Intramural:** Badminton, basketball, racquetball, soccer, softball, swimming, tennis, volleyball.

STUDENT SERVICES. Aptitude testing, career counseling, employment service for undergraduates, freshman orientation, health services, personal counseling, placement service for graduates, veterans counselor.

ANNUAL EXPENSES. Tuition and fees: $7,040. **Room and board:** $3,100. **Books and supplies:** $400. **Other expenses:** $1,480.

FINANCIAL AID. 79% of freshmen, 83% of continuing students receive some form of aid. 51% of grants, 84% of loans, 61% of jobs based on need. Academic, music/drama, art, leadership, religious affiliation, minority scholarships available. **Aid applications:** No closing date; priority given to applications received by March 15; applicants notified on a rolling basis beginning on or about February 15; must reply within 2 weeks.

ADDRESS/TELEPHONE. Becki Bryant, Director of Admissions, McMurry University, South 14th and Sayles Boulevard, Abilene, TX 79697-0001. (915) 691-6226. Fax: (915) 691-6599.

Midland College

Midland, Texas CB code: 6459

2-year public community college, coed. Founded in 1969. **Accreditation:** Regional. **Undergraduate enrollment:** 542 men, 781 women full time; 1,021 men, 1,531 women part time. **Faculty:** 231 total (88 full time), 37 with doctorates or other terminal degrees. **Location:** Suburban campus in small city; 300 miles from El Paso, 300 miles from Dallas. **Calendar:** Semester, extensive summer session. Extensive evening/early morning classes. **Special facilities:** Multipurpose 5,000-seat Chaparral Center, McCormick Art Gallery.

DEGREES OFFERED. AA, AS, AAS. 255 associate degrees awarded in 1992. 35% in business and management, 5% business/office and marketing/distribution, 6% communications, 15% computer sciences, 9% allied health, 12% social sciences, 8% trade and industry.

UNDERGRADUATE MAJORS. Accounting, air conditioning/heating/refrigeration mechanics, air conditioning/heating/refrigeration technology, alcohol and drug counseling, architectural technologies, architecture, automotive mechanics, automotive technology, biology, business administration and management, business and management, business and office, business computer/console/peripheral equipment operation, business data entry equipment operation, business data processing and related programs, business data programming, business economics, chemistry, child development/care/guidance, communications, computer and information sciences, computer programming, criminal justice technology, dance, data processing, diesel engine mechanics, drafting, drafting and design technology, economics, electrical and electronics equipment repair, electronic technology, English, fashion merchandising, fine arts, fire control and safety technology, fire protection, French, graphic and printing production, graphic arts technology, history, journalism, law enforcement and corrections technologies, legal assistant/paralegal, legal secretary, liberal/general studies, management science, marketing and distribution, marketing management, mathematics, music, music performance, nursing, photographic technology, physical sciences, physics, political science and government, predentistry, prelaw, premedicine, prepharmacy, psychology, radio/television broadcasting, radiograph medical technology, real estate, respiratory therapy, respiratory therapy technology, secretarial and related programs, small business management and ownership, social sciences, sociology, Spanish, speech, teacher aide, veterinarian's assistant, welding technology.

ACADEMIC PROGRAMS. 2-year transfer program, cooperative education, dual enrollment of high school students, internships, student-designed major, cross-registration. **Remedial services:** Learning center, reduced course load, remedial instruction, special counselor, tutoring. **Placement/credit:** CLEP Subject, IB, institutional tests; 15 credit hours maximum for associate degree.

ACADEMIC REQUIREMENTS. Freshmen must earn minimum GPA of 2.0 to continue in good standing. 50% of freshmen return for sophomore year. Students must declare major by end of first year. **Graduation requirements:** 63 hours for associate (15 in major). Most students required to take courses in English, history, humanities, mathematics, biological/physical sciences, social sciences.

FRESHMAN ADMISSIONS. Selection criteria: Open admissions. Admissions decision to nursing made by faculty committee. **Test requirements:** SAT or ACT for counseling; score report by August 27.

1992 FRESHMAN CLASS PROFILE. 1,100 men applied, 1,100 accepted, 1,100 enrolled; 1,650 women applied, 1,650 accepted, 1,650 enrolled. **Characteristics:** 95% from in state, 100% commute, 17% have minority backgrounds, 1% are foreign students. Average age is 26.

FALL-TERM APPLICATIONS. No fee. No closing date; priority given to applications received by August 26; applicants notified on a rolling basis.

STUDENT LIFE. Activities: Student government, film, magazine, radio, student newspaper, television, choral groups, dance, drama, jazz band, music ensembles, musical theater, opera, symphony orchestra, Baptist Student

Union, religious groups, international, ethnic, service clubs, management fraternity, law enforcement club.

ATHLETICS. NJCAA. **Intercollegiate:** Basketball M, golf M, tennis.

STUDENT SERVICES. Aptitude testing, career counseling, employment service for undergraduates, health services, on-campus day care, personal counseling, placement service for graduates, special adviser for adult students, veterans counselor, services/facilities for handicapped.

ANNUAL EXPENSES. Tuition and fees (1992-93): $642, $48 additional for out-of-district students, $366 additional for out-of-state students. **Books and supplies:** $400. **Other expenses:** $1,210.

FINANCIAL AID. 24% of freshmen, 14% of continuing students receive some form of aid. 56% of grants, all loans, all jobs based on need. Academic, music/drama, art, athletic scholarships available. **Aid applications:** No closing date; priority given to applications received by June 1; applicants notified on a rolling basis beginning on or about August 1; must reply within 2 weeks.

ADDRESS/TELEPHONE. Dr. Donald Cates, Director of Admissions, Midland College, 3600 North Garfield, Midland, TX 79705. (915) 685-4502.

Midwestern State University
Wichita Falls, Texas — CB code: 6408

4-year public university and liberal arts college, coed. Founded in 1922. **Accreditation:** Regional. **Undergraduate enrollment:** 1,648 men, 1,684 women full time; 715 men, 1,002 women part time. **Graduate enrollment:** 68 men, 89 women full time; 262 men, 289 women part time. **Faculty:** 225 total (155 full time), 104 with doctorates or other terminal degrees. **Location:** Suburban campus in small city; 130 miles from Dallas-Fort Worth. **Calendar:** 4-1-4, extensive summer session. Saturday and extensive evening/early morning classes. **Microcomputers:** 220 located in dormitories, libraries, classrooms, computer centers. **Special facilities:** Kurzweil reading machine for the blind, art gallery , planetarium, greenhouse.

DEGREES OFFERED. AAS, BA, BS, BFA, MA, MS, MBA, MEd. 61 associate degrees awarded in 1992. 97% in health sciences. 535 bachelor's degrees awarded. 21% in business and management, 12% education, 12% health sciences, 5% life sciences, 10% multi/interdisciplinary studies, 5% psychology, 16% social sciences. Graduate degrees offered in 16 major fields of study.

UNDERGRADUATE MAJORS. Associate: Radiograph medical technology. **Bachelor's:** Accounting, art education, biology, business administration and management, business and management, business economics, business education, chemical manufacturing technology, chemistry, clinical laboratory science, communications, computer and information sciences, criminal justice studies, dental hygiene, dramatic arts, early childhood education, economics, education, electronic technology, elementary education, engineering and engineering-related technologies, English, English education, finance, fine arts, foreign languages education, geology, geophysics and seismology, history, humanities, journalism, management science, manufacturing technology, marketing and distribution, mathematics, mathematics education, medical laboratory technologies, music, music education, nursing, physical education, political science and government, psychology, radiograph medical technology, science education, secondary education, social studies education, social work, sociology, Spanish, special education, speech, speech/communication/theater education.

ACADEMIC PROGRAMS. Accelerated program, cooperative education, double major, dual enrollment of high school students, honors program, independent study, internships, study abroad; liberal arts/career combination in health sciences. **Remedial services:** Learning center, reduced course load, remedial instruction, special counselor, tutoring, writing laboratory, mathematics laboratories, study and test-taking skills workshops. **Placement/credit:** AP, CLEP Subject, institutional tests; 30 credit hours maximum for bachelor's degree.

ACADEMIC REQUIREMENTS. Freshmen must earn minimum GPA of 1.7 to continue in good standing. 63% of freshmen return for sophomore year. Students must declare major by end of second year. **Graduation requirements:** 64 hours for associate (15 in major), 120 hours for bachelor's (30 in major). Most students required to take courses in arts/fine arts, computer science, English, foreign languages, history, humanities, mathematics, biological/physical sciences, social sciences.

FRESHMAN ADMISSIONS. Selection criteria: SAT combined score of 800 or ACT composite score of 20, or rank above 60th percentile in graduating class for unconditional admission. Admissions committee may grant exceptions. **High school preparation:** 6 units required; 8 recommended. Required and recommended units include English 4 and mathematics 2. Foreign language 4, social science 2 and science 2 recommended. **Test requirements:** SAT or ACT; score report by August 7.

1992 FRESHMAN CLASS PROFILE. 1,371 men applied, 1,371 accepted, 832 enrolled; 1,370 women applied, 1,368 accepted, 861 enrolled. **Characteristics:** 90% from in state, 67% commute, 9% have minority backgrounds, 1% are foreign students, 15% join fraternities/sororities. Average age is 22.

FALL-TERM APPLICATIONS. No fee. $50 fee for foreign applicants. Closing date August 7; applicants notified on a rolling basis. Audition required for applied music applicants. Deferred admission available.

STUDENT LIFE. Housing: Dormitories (men, women, coed); apartment, fraternity housing available. Off-campus apartments available through the University meet overflow dormitory space demands. **Activities:** Student government, magazine, student newspaper, television, yearbook, choral groups, concert band, drama, jazz band, marching band, music ensembles, musical theater, pep band, fraternities, sororities, Methodist Student Foundation, Baptist Student Center, Catholic campus ministries, Student Ambassadors, Black Student Union, Organization of Hispanic Students, International Students Association, University Democrats, College Republicans, Amnesty International. **Additional information:** Active general academic and special interest honor societies available.

ATHLETICS. NAIA, NCAA. **Intercollegiate:** Basketball, cross-country, football M, golf M, rifle, soccer M, swimming, tennis, track and field, volleyball W. **Intramural:** Archery, badminton, basketball, bowling, golf, sailing, soccer M, softball, swimming, table tennis, tennis, track and field, volleyball.

STUDENT SERVICES. Aptitude testing, career counseling, employment service for undergraduates, freshman orientation, health services, personal counseling, placement service for graduates, veterans counselor, mathematics and writing laboratories, international English language institute, services/facilities for handicapped.

ANNUAL EXPENSES. Tuition and fees: $1,636, $4,080 additional for out-of-state students. **Room and board:** $3,144. **Books and supplies:** $630. **Other expenses:** $938.

FINANCIAL AID. 44% of freshmen, 37% of continuing students receive some form of aid. 70% of grants, 89% of loans, 9% of jobs based on need. Academic, music/drama, art, athletic, leadership, minority scholarships available. **Aid applications:** No closing date; priority given to applications received by April 1; applicants notified on a rolling basis beginning on or about April 1; must reply within 4 weeks.

ADDRESS/TELEPHONE. Billye Tims, Registrar, Midwestern State University, 3410 Taft Boulevard, Wichita Falls, TX 76308. (817) 689-4321. (817) 842-1922. Fax: (817) 689-4302.

Miss Wade's Fashion Merchandising College
Dallas, Texas — CB code: 1537

Admissions:	93% of applicants accepted
Based on:	••• Interview
	• Activities, recommendations, school record
Completion:	80% of freshmen end year in good standing
	65% graduate, 25% of these enter 4-year programs

2-year proprietary art, business, junior college, coed. Founded in 1965. **Accreditation:** Regional. **Undergraduate enrollment:** 27 men, 300 women full time. **Faculty:** 13 total (11 full time), 5 with doctorates or other terminal degrees. **Location:** Urban campus in very large city; 2 miles from downtown. **Calendar:** Trimester, extensive summer session. **Microcomputers:** 50 located in libraries, classrooms, computer centers. **Additional facts:** Located inside Dallas Market Center complex-the world's largest wholesale merchandising complex and home of the International Apparel Mart.

DEGREES OFFERED. AA. 170 associate degrees awarded in 1992. 25% in architecture and environmental design, 50% business/office and marketing/distribution, 25% home economics.

UNDERGRADUATE MAJORS. Fashion design, fashion merchandising, interior design.

ACADEMIC PROGRAMS. Double major, internships, study abroad. **Remedial services:** Learning center, remedial instruction, special counselor, tutoring.

ACADEMIC REQUIREMENTS. Freshmen must earn minimum GPA of 2.0 to continue in good standing. 70% of freshmen return for sophomore year. Students must declare major by end of first year. **Graduation requirements:** 76 hours for associate (45 in major). Most students required to take courses in arts/fine arts, computer science, English, humanities, mathematics, biological/physical sciences, social sciences. **Additional information:** All students attend 4 consecutive trimesters to complete associate degree in 16 months. New students may enter at beginning of any trimester. Associate degree graduates may complete additional term of advanced study in professional certificate programs in computer-aided design and marketing.

FRESHMAN ADMISSIONS. Selection criteria: Interview very important. School achievement record, recommendations, school and community activities considered.

1992 FRESHMAN CLASS PROFILE. 81 men applied, 75 accepted, 9 enrolled; 708 women applied, 660 accepted, 154 enrolled. 40% had high school GPA of 3.0 or higher, 50% between 2.0 and 2.99. **Characteristics:** 65% from in state, 55% commute, 39% have minority backgrounds, 1% are foreign students. Average age is 20.

FALL-TERM APPLICATIONS. No fee. No closing date; applicants notified on a rolling basis; must reply within 6 weeks. Interview required. Deferred admission available.

STUDENT LIFE. Housing: Apartment housing available. **Activities:**

Student government, student newspaper, television, yearbook, fashion shows, fraternities, sororities.

STUDENT SERVICES. Aptitude testing, career counseling, employment service for undergraduates, freshman orientation, health services, personal counseling, placement service for graduates, special adviser for adult students, veterans counselor, services/facilities for handicapped.

ANNUAL EXPENSES. Tuition and fees: $4,985. **Room and board:** $1,870 room only. **Books and supplies:** $575. **Other expenses:** $936.

FINANCIAL AID. 85% of freshmen, 85% of continuing students receive some form of aid. All grants, 46% of loans, all jobs based on need. 124 enrolled freshmen were judged to have need, all were offered aid. **Aid applications:** No closing date; applicants notified on a rolling basis; must reply immediately. **Additional information:** Individual financial plans developed for each student depending on need, grant and loan eligibility, monthly payments (self-help) and down payment.

ADDRESS/TELEPHONE. Charles L. Restivo, Director of Admissions, Miss Wade's Fashion Merchandising College, PO Box 586343, International Apparel Mart, Suite M5120, Apparel Mart, Dallas, TX 75258. (214) 637-3530. (800) 624-4850. Fax: (214) 637-0827.

Mountain View College
Dallas, Texas — CB code: 6438

2-year public community college, coed. Founded in 1970. **Accreditation:** Regional. **Undergraduate enrollment:** 1,741 men, 1,689 women full time; 1,414 men, 1,714 women part time. **Faculty:** 207 total (86 full time), 45 with doctorates or other terminal degrees. **Location:** Suburban campus in very large city; 8 miles from downtown. **Calendar:** Semester, extensive summer session. Saturday classes. **Microcomputers:** Located in libraries, computer centers.

DEGREES OFFERED. 200 associate degrees awarded in 1992.

UNDERGRADUATE MAJORS. Accounting, aeronautical technology, air traffic control, airline piloting and navigation, architecture, aviation management, business administration and management, business and management, business and office, business computer/console/peripheral equipment operation, business data entry equipment operation, business data processing and related programs, business data programming, computer and information sciences, data processing, drafting, electrical and electronics equipment repair, electrical technology, electrical/electronics/communications engineering, electromechanical technology, electronic technology, legal secretary, liberal/general studies, marketing and distribution, office supervision and management, precision metal work, quality control technology, secretarial and related programs, welding technology.

ACADEMIC PROGRAMS. 2-year transfer program, accelerated program, cooperative education, dual enrollment of high school students, honors program, independent study, telecourses. **Remedial services:** Learning center, reduced course load, remedial instruction, tutoring. **Placement/credit:** AP, CLEP Subject, institutional tests; 45 credit hours maximum for associate degree.

ACADEMIC REQUIREMENTS. Freshmen must earn minimum GPA of 2.0 to continue in good standing. 52% of freshmen return for sophomore year. Students must declare major on application. **Graduation requirements:** 61 hours for associate. Most students required to take courses in English, history, mathematics, biological/physical sciences, social sciences.

FRESHMAN ADMISSIONS. Selection criteria: Open admissions. **Test requirements:** SAT or ACT for placement.

1992 FRESHMAN CLASS PROFILE. 2,425 men, 2,464 women enrolled. **Characteristics:** 98% from in state, 100% commute, 35% have minority backgrounds. Average age is 24.

FALL-TERM APPLICATIONS. No fee. No closing date; applicants notified on a rolling basis. Interview recommended. Early admission available.

STUDENT LIFE. Activities: Student government, radio, student newspaper, choral groups, concert band, dance, drama, music ensembles, musical theater, symphony orchestra.

ATHLETICS. Intramural: Basketball M, tennis, volleyball.

STUDENT SERVICES. Aptitude testing, career counseling, employment service for undergraduates, health services, on-campus day care, personal counseling, placement service for graduates, veterans counselor, services/facilities for handicapped.

ANNUAL EXPENSES. Tuition and fees (1992-93): $450, $570 additional for out-of-district students, $1,470 additional for out-of-state students. **Books and supplies:** $600. **Other expenses:** $1,045.

FINANCIAL AID. 12% of freshmen, 12% of continuing students receive some form of aid. 96% of grants, 71% of loans, 48% of jobs based on need. **Aid applications:** No closing date; priority given to applications received by June 1; applicants notified on a rolling basis; must reply immediately.

ADDRESS/TELEPHONE. Juan C. Torres, Director Admissions and Registrar, Mountain View College, 4849 West Illinois Avenue, Dallas, TX 75211-6599. (214) 333-8603. Fax: (214) 333-8708.

Navarro College
Corsicana, Texas — CB code: 6465

2-year public community college, coed. Founded in 1946. **Accreditation:** Regional. **Undergraduate enrollment:** 863 men, 905 women full time; 417 men, 1,025 women part time. **Faculty:** 160 total (69 full time), 5 with doctorates or other terminal degrees. **Location:** Rural campus in large town; 50 miles from Dallas. **Calendar:** Semester, limited summer session. **Microcomputers:** Located in classrooms.

DEGREES OFFERED. AA, AS, AAS. 256 associate degrees awarded in 1992.

UNDERGRADUATE MAJORS. Accounting, agribusiness, agricultural sciences, behavioral sciences, biological and physical sciences, biology, business and office, business data entry equipment operation, business data processing and related programs, business data programming, child development/care/guidance, choral music, clinical laboratory science, commercial art, communications, computer and information sciences, criminal justice studies, drafting, elementary education, emergency medical technologies, engineering, finance, fire control and safety technology, graphic arts technology, humanities and social sciences, industrial technology, instrumental music, law enforcement and corrections technologies, liberal/general studies, marketing and distribution, mathematics, medical laboratory technologies, mining and petroleum technologies, music, nursing, practical nursing, precision metal work, predentistry, premedicine, prepharmacy, preveterinary, psychology, radio/television broadcasting, radiograph medical technology, range management, real estate, science technologies, secondary education, secretarial and related programs, social sciences, taxation.

ACADEMIC PROGRAMS. 2-year transfer program, honors program, independent study, internships, telecourses. **Remedial services:** Learning center, reduced course load, remedial instruction, special counselor, tutoring. **Placement/credit:** CLEP General and Subject, institutional tests; 30 credit hours maximum for associate degree.

ACADEMIC REQUIREMENTS. Freshmen must earn minimum GPA of 2.0 to continue in good standing. **Graduation requirements:** 63 hours for associate (22 in major). Most students required to take courses in arts/fine arts, computer science, English, history, mathematics, biological/physical sciences.

FRESHMAN ADMISSIONS. Selection criteria: Open admissions. **Test requirements:** SAT or ACT (ACT preferred) for placement and counseling only; score report by September 1.

1992 FRESHMAN CLASS PROFILE. 922 men, 1,341 women enrolled. **Characteristics:** 98% from in state, 84% live in college housing, 28% have minority backgrounds.

FALL-TERM APPLICATIONS. No fee. No closing date; applicants notified on a rolling basis.

STUDENT LIFE. Housing: Dormitories (men, women, coed); apartment housing available. **Activities:** Student government, student newspaper, television, choral groups, concert band, drama, jazz band, marching band, music ensembles, pep band, fraternities, sororities, religious organizations, honorary and special interest clubs.

ATHLETICS. NJCAA. **Intercollegiate:** Baseball M, basketball, football M, golf, tennis. **Intramural:** Softball, swimming.

STUDENT SERVICES. Aptitude testing, career counseling, employment service for undergraduates, freshman orientation, personal counseling, placement service for graduates, veterans counselor.

ANNUAL EXPENSES. Tuition and fees (1992-93): $740, $120 additional for out-of-district students, $264 additional for out-of-state students. **Room and board:** $2,740. **Books and supplies:** $416. **Other expenses:** $811.

FINANCIAL AID. 30% of freshmen, 25% of continuing students receive some form of aid. 99% of grants, 84% of loans, all jobs based on need. Academic, music/drama, art, athletic scholarships available. **Aid applications:** No closing date; priority given to applications received by June 1; applicants notified on a rolling basis beginning on or about May 1; must reply within 2 weeks.

ADDRESS/TELEPHONE. Helen Thornton, Registrar, Navarro College, 3200 West Seventh Avenue, Corsicana, TX 75110. (903) 874-6501. Fax: (903) 876-4636.

North Harris Montgomery Community College District
Houston, Texas — CB code: 6508

2-year public community college, coed. Founded in 1972. **Accreditation:** Regional. **Undergraduate enrollment:** 2,724 men, 3,127 women full time; 4,954 men, 8,053 women part time. **Faculty:** 921 total (303 full time), 116 with doctorates or other terminal degrees. **Location:** Suburban campus in very large city; 20 miles from downtown. **Calendar:** Semester, extensive summer session. Saturday and extensive evening/early morning classes. **Microcomputers:** 150 located in libraries, classrooms, computer centers. **Special facilities:** Art gallery. **Additional facts:** Campuses in Kingwood, Tomball, and Aldine-Westfield.

DEGREES OFFERED. AA, AAS. 654 associate degrees awarded in 1992. 23% in business and management, 5% teacher education, 5% engineering technologies, 25% health sciences, 24% multi/interdisciplinary studies, 6% trade and industry.

UNDERGRADUATE MAJORS. Accounting, aeronautical technology, air conditioning/heating/refrigeration mechanics, art education, automotive mechanics, biology, biotechnology, business administration and management, business and office, business computer/console/peripheral equipment operation, business data programming, chemistry, child development/care/guidance, computer and information sciences, criminal justice studies, data processing, drafting and design technology, dramatic arts, education, electronic technology, elementary education, emergency medical technologies, engineering, finance, fine arts, geology, health education, information sciences and systems, interior design, journalism, law enforcement and corrections technologies, legal assistant/paralegal, liberal/general studies, marketing and distribution, mathematics, mental health/human services, music, nursing, office supervision and management, personal services, photographic technology, physical education, physics, predentistry, premedicine, prepharmacy, preveterinary, psychology, real estate, respiratory therapy, respiratory therapy technology, secondary education, speech, tourism, veterinarian's assistant, welding technology.

ACADEMIC PROGRAMS. 2-year transfer program, computer delivered (on-line) credit-bearing course offerings, dual enrollment of high school students, independent study, telecourses. **Remedial services:** Learning center, reduced course load, remedial instruction, tutoring. **Placement/credit:** CLEP Subject, institutional tests; 18 credit hours maximum for associate degree.

ACADEMIC REQUIREMENTS. Freshmen must earn minimum GPA of 2.0 to continue in good standing. 50% of freshmen return for sophomore year. Students must declare major by end of first year. **Graduation requirements:** 62 hours for associate. Most students required to take courses in English, history, mathematics, social sciences.

FRESHMAN ADMISSIONS. Selection criteria: Open admissions. Admission screening for nursing and respiratory therapy. **Test requirements:** SAT or ACT (ACT preferred) for placement and counseling only; score report by August 20.

1992 FRESHMAN CLASS PROFILE. 1,643 men, 2,021 women enrolled. **Characteristics:** 96% from in state, 100% commute, 19% have minority backgrounds, 1% are foreign students. Average age is 20.

FALL-TERM APPLICATIONS. No fee. No closing date; applicants notified on a rolling basis. Early admission available.

STUDENT LIFE. Activities: Magazine, student newspaper, choral groups, drama, jazz band, music ensembles, musical theater, pep band, Phi Theta Kappa, Baptist Student Union, student nurses association, art forum, international student association, Piney Woods Wildlife Society.

ATHLETICS. Intramural: Badminton, basketball, bowling, golf, racquetball, soccer, softball, table tennis, tennis, volleyball.

STUDENT SERVICES. Aptitude testing, career counseling, employment service for undergraduates, freshman orientation, personal counseling, placement service for graduates, veterans counselor, services/facilities for handicapped.

ANNUAL EXPENSES. Tuition and fees (1992-93): $474, $600 additional for out-of-district students, $900 additional for out-of-state students. **Books and supplies:** $530. **Other expenses:** $964.

FINANCIAL AID. 15% of freshmen, 24% of continuing students receive some form of aid. 83% of grants, 85% of loans, 24% of jobs based on need. **Aid applications:** No closing date; priority given to applications received by April 15; applicants notified on a rolling basis beginning on or about July 1.

ADDRESS/TELEPHONE. Teresa Phillips, Director of Academic Services, North Harris Montgomery Community College District, 250 North Sam Houston Parkway East, Houston, TX 77060-2000. (713) 591-3500 ext. 583. Fax: (713) 591-3513.

North Lake College
Irving, Texas — CB code: 6519

2-year public community college, coed. Founded in 1977. **Accreditation:** Regional. **Undergraduate enrollment:** 896 men, 762 women full time; 2,196 men, 2,845 women part time. **Faculty:** 292 total (92 full time), 42 with doctorates or other terminal degrees. **Location:** Suburban campus in small city; 15 miles from Dallas. **Calendar:** Semester, limited summer session.

DEGREES OFFERED. AA, AAS. 315 associate degrees awarded in 1992.

UNDERGRADUATE MAJORS. Accounting, business and office, business data processing and related programs, carpentry, computer and information sciences, data processing, electrical installation, electronic technology, liberal/general studies, management science, real estate, secretarial and related programs, video.

ACADEMIC PROGRAMS. 2-year transfer program, accelerated program, dual enrollment of high school students, honors program, internships, study abroad, cross-registration. **Remedial services:** Learning center, remedial instruction. **Placement/credit:** CLEP Subject; 15 credit hours maximum for associate degree.

ACADEMIC REQUIREMENTS. Freshmen must earn minimum GPA of 2.0 to continue in good standing. **Graduation requirements:** 61 hours for associate. Most students required to take courses in English, mathematics.

FRESHMAN ADMISSIONS. Selection criteria: Open admissions.

1992 FRESHMAN CLASS PROFILE. 1,163 men and women enrolled. **Characteristics:** 97% from in state, 100% commute, 1% are foreign students.

FALL-TERM APPLICATIONS. No fee. No closing date; applicants notified on a rolling basis. Deferred admission available.

STUDENT LIFE. Activities: Student government, student newspaper, drama, jazz band, music ensembles.

ATHLETICS. NJCAA.

STUDENT SERVICES. Career counseling, employment service for undergraduates, health services, personal counseling, placement service for graduates, veterans counselor, services/facilities for handicapped.

ANNUAL EXPENSES. Tuition and fees (1992-93): $450, $570 additional for out-of-district students, $1,470 additional for out-of-state students. **Books and supplies:** $400.

FINANCIAL AID. 10% of continuing students receive some form of aid. Grants, loans, jobs available. Academic scholarships available. **Aid applications:** No closing date; priority given to applications received by July 1; applicants notified on a rolling basis.

ADDRESS/TELEPHONE. Stephen P. Twenge, Director of Admissions and Registration, North Lake College, 5001 North MacArthur Boulevard, Irving, TX 75038-3899. (214) 659-5225.

Northeast Texas Community College
Mount Pleasant, Texas — CB code: 6531

2-year public community college, coed. Founded in 1984. **Accreditation:** Regional. **Undergraduate enrollment:** 402 men, 561 women full time; 296 men, 765 women part time. **Faculty:** 94 total (39 full time), 17 with doctorates or other terminal degrees. **Location:** Rural campus in large town; 60 miles from Texarkana, 118 miles from Dallas. **Calendar:** Semester, extensive summer session. Extensive evening/early morning classes. **Microcomputers:** 150 located in libraries, classrooms.

DEGREES OFFERED. AA, AS, AAS. 119 associate degrees awarded in 1992.

UNDERGRADUATE MAJORS. Accounting, agricultural sciences, air conditioning/heating/refrigeration technology, automotive technology, business and management, computer and information sciences, criminal justice studies, diesel engine mechanics, finance, legal secretary, marketing management, medical secretary, practical nursing, ranch management, real estate, secretarial and related programs, small engine technology, welding technology.

ACADEMIC PROGRAMS. 2-year transfer program, dual enrollment of high school students. **Remedial services:** Learning center, remedial instruction, tutoring. **Placement/credit:** CLEP Subject; 15 credit hours maximum for associate degree.

ACADEMIC REQUIREMENTS. Freshmen must earn minimum GPA of 2.0 to continue in good standing. 58% of freshmen return for sophomore year. Students must declare major by end of first year. **Graduation requirements:** 62 hours for associate. Most students required to take courses in computer science, English, history, humanities, mathematics, biological/physical sciences, social sciences.

FRESHMAN ADMISSIONS. Selection criteria: Open admissions.

1992 FRESHMAN CLASS PROFILE. 218 men, 324 women enrolled. **Characteristics:** 99% from in state, 89% commute, 3% have minority backgrounds. Average age is 20.

FALL-TERM APPLICATIONS. No fee. No closing date; applicants notified on a rolling basis.

STUDENT LIFE. Housing: Dormitories (men, women). **Activities:** Student government, magazine, student newspaper, choral groups, drama, music ensembles, Student Coordinating Board, Baptist Student Union.

ATHLETICS. NJCAA. **Intercollegiate:** Baseball M. **Intramural:** Basketball M, softball, tennis, volleyball.

STUDENT SERVICES. Aptitude testing, career counseling, employment service for undergraduates, freshman orientation, personal counseling, veterans counselor, services/facilities for handicapped.

ANNUAL EXPENSES. Tuition and fees: $570, $240 additional for out-of-district students, $760 additional for out-of-state students. **Room and board:** $2,700. **Books and supplies:** $530. **Other expenses:** $1,350.

FINANCIAL AID. 92% of grants, all loans, 86% of jobs based on need. Academic, music/drama, art scholarships available. **Aid applications:** No closing date; priority given to applications received by May 1; applicants notified on a rolling basis beginning on or about June 15; must reply within 2 weeks.

ADDRESS/TELEPHONE. Phil Ebensberger, Director Admissions, Northeast Texas Community College, PO Box 1307, Mount Pleasant, TX 75455-1307. (903) 572-1911 ext. 213. Fax: (903) 572-6712.

Northwood University: Texas Campus
Cedar Hill, Texas CB code: 6499

4-year private university and business college, coed. Founded in 1959. **Accreditation:** Regional. **Undergraduate enrollment:** 328 men, 215 women full time; 5 men, 3 women part time. **Faculty:** 26 total (16 full time), 3 with doctorates or other terminal degrees. **Location:** Rural campus in large town; 15 miles from downtown Dallas, 25 miles from Fort Worth. **Calendar:** Quarter. **Microcomputers:** 20 located in computer centers. **Special facilities:** 350 acres wooded campus, nature exercise trail. **Additional facts:** 3 residential campuses in Texas, Florida, and Michigan, 24 outreach centers, and the Margaret Chase Smith Library Center in Maine.

DEGREES OFFERED. AA, B. 47 associate degrees awarded in 1992. 90% in business and management, 5% business/office and marketing/distribution, 5% communications. 69 bachelor's degrees awarded. 100% in business and management.

UNDERGRADUATE MAJORS. Advertising, automotive aftermarket management, automotive marketing, business and management, fashion merchandising, hotel/motel and restaurant management. automotive marketing management, business administration and management, business and management, international business management, marketing management.

ACADEMIC PROGRAMS. Accelerated program, double major, external degree, honors program, independent study, internships, study abroad, weekend college, cross-registration, 3-1 articulation program with Dallas County Community Colleges and Tarrant County Community College, 2-2 adult degree completion program with Bauder Fashion College. **Remedial services:** Tutoring. **Placement/credit:** CLEP Subject, institutional tests; 4 credit hours maximum for associate degree; 4 credit hours maximum for bachelor's degree.

ACADEMIC REQUIREMENTS. Freshmen must earn minimum GPA of 2.0 to continue in good standing. 94% of freshmen return for sophomore year. Students must declare major on application. **Graduation requirements:** 90 hours for associate (36 in major), 180 hours for bachelor's (36 in major). Most students required to take courses in computer science, English, humanities, mathematics, philosophy/religion, biological/physical sciences, social sciences. **Postgraduate studies:** 95% from 2-year programs enter 4-year programs. 1% enter law school, 5% enter MBA programs.

FRESHMAN ADMISSIONS. Selection criteria: School achievement record school and community activities considered, as well as test scores, personal interview, major academic interest. Recommended units include English 4, mathematics 3 and social science 2. **Test requirements:** SAT or ACT (SAT preferred); score report by June 1.

1992 FRESHMAN CLASS PROFILE. 197 men applied, 197 accepted, 39 enrolled; 149 women applied, 149 accepted, 32 enrolled. **Characteristics:** 100% live in college housing. Average age is 18.

FALL-TERM APPLICATIONS. $15 fee, may be waived for applicants with need. No closing date; applicants notified on a rolling basis. Interview recommended.

STUDENT LIFE. Housing: Dormitories (men, women); apartment housing available. **Activities:** Student government, student newspaper, yearbook, fraternities, sororities.

ATHLETICS. NAIA. **Intercollegiate:** Baseball M, cross-country. **Intramural:** Basketball, bowling, softball, tennis, volleyball.

STUDENT SERVICES. Career counseling, employment service for undergraduates, freshman orientation, health services, personal counseling, placement service for graduates.

ANNUAL EXPENSES. Tuition and fees: $9,126. **Room and board:** $4,334. **Books and supplies:** $525. **Other expenses:** $4,335.

FINANCIAL AID. 80% of freshmen, 80% of continuing students receive some form of aid. Grants, loans, jobs available. Academic, athletic, leadership, minority scholarships available. **Aid applications:** No closing date; priority given to applications received by March 31; applicants notified on a rolling basis beginning on or about March 31; must reply within 10 days.

ADDRESS/TELEPHONE. James Hickerson, Director of Admissions, Northwood University: Texas Campus, PO Box 58, Cedar Hill, TX 75104-0058. (214) 291-1541. (800) 927-9663. Fax: (214) 291-3824.

Odessa College
Odessa, Texas CB code: 6540

2-year public community college, coed. Founded in 1946. **Accreditation:** Regional. **Undergraduate enrollment:** 830 men, 859 women full time; 1,315 men, 1,881 women part time. **Faculty:** 252 total (138 full time), 26 with doctorates or other terminal degrees. **Location:** Urban campus in small city; 140 miles from Lubbock, 290 miles from El Paso, 350 miles from Dallas. **Calendar:** Semester, limited summer session. Saturday and extensive evening/early morning classes. **Microcomputers:** 230 located in libraries, classrooms, computer centers. **Special facilities:** Globe Theater of the Southwest, sports center, tennis center, business incubator. **Additional facts:** Extension centers in Pecos, Monahans, Andrews, Crane, Kermit, McCamey, and Pyote.

DEGREES OFFERED. AA, AS, AAS. 289 associate degrees awarded in 1992. 9% in engineering technologies, 21% health sciences, 14% allied health, 34% multi/interdisciplinary studies, 8% parks/recreation, protective services, public affairs.

UNDERGRADUATE MAJORS. Air conditioning/heating/refrigeration mechanics, automotive mechanics, automotive technology, business and management, business and office, carpentry, child development/care/guidance, computer and information sciences, construction, diesel engine mechanics, drafting, economics, electrical technology, electronic technology, emergency medical technologies, fashion merchandising, fire protection, food production/management/services, law enforcement and corrections technologies, liberal/general studies, machine tool operation/machine shop, marketing management, medical laboratory technologies, mental health/human services, mining and petroleum technologies, nursing, photographic technology, physical therapy assistant, power plant operation and maintenance, precision metal work, radio/television broadcasting, radiograph medical technology, respiratory therapy, respiratory therapy technology, secretarial and related programs, surgical technology, teacher aide, trade and industrial supervision and management.

ACADEMIC PROGRAMS. 2-year transfer program, dual enrollment of high school students, honors program, telecourses, cross-registration. **Remedial services:** Learning center, reduced course load, remedial instruction, special counselor, tutoring, placement testing, diagnostic testing. **Placement/credit:** AP, CLEP Subject, institutional tests; 15 credit hours maximum for associate degree.

ACADEMIC REQUIREMENTS. Freshmen must earn minimum GPA of 2.0 to continue in good standing. Students must declare major on enrollment. **Graduation requirements:** 63 hours for associate. Most students required to take courses in English, history, mathematics, biological/physical sciences, social sciences.

FRESHMAN ADMISSIONS. Selection criteria: Open admissions. Special admissions for several programs like nursing, allied health, music, and law enforcement.

1992 FRESHMAN CLASS PROFILE. 549 men, 552 women enrolled. **Characteristics:** 98% from in state, 96% commute, 32% have minority backgrounds, 1% are foreign students. Average age is 27.

FALL-TERM APPLICATIONS. No fee. No closing date; applicants notified on a rolling basis. Deferred and early admission available.

STUDENT LIFE. Housing: Dormitories (men, women). Men's and women's dormitories reserved for athletes. **Activities:** Student government, radio, television, choral groups, concert band, dance, jazz band, symphony orchestra, Baptist Student Union, Women's Student Union, Black Organization of Successful Students (BOSS), Student Alliance of Latinos Succeeding Academically (SALSA), Changing Attitudes Helping Ourselves Overcome the Situation (CAHOOTS).

ATHLETICS. NJCAA. **Intercollegiate:** Baseball M, basketball, golf M, tennis, track and field. **Intramural:** Basketball, bowling, racquetball, softball, table tennis, tennis. **Clubs:** Rodeo.

STUDENT SERVICES. Aptitude testing, career counseling, employment service for undergraduates, freshman orientation, health services, personal counseling, placement service for graduates, veterans counselor, services/facilities for handicapped.

ANNUAL EXPENSES. Tuition and fees: $500, $80 additional for out-of-district students, $240 additional for out-of-state students. **Room and board:** $2,875. **Books and supplies:** $400. **Other expenses:** $3,705.

FINANCIAL AID. 31% of freshmen, 26% of continuing students receive some form of aid. 70% of grants, 92% of loans, 22% of jobs based on need. 372 enrolled freshmen were judged to have need, all were offered aid. Academic, music/drama, art, athletic, state/district residency, minority scholarships available. **Aid applications:** No closing date; priority given to applications received by June 1; applicants notified on a rolling basis beginning on or about June 15; must reply within 15 days.

ADDRESS/TELEPHONE. Dr. Mary Koeninger, Director of Admissions and Registrar, Odessa College, 201 West University, Odessa, TX 79764-7127. (915) 335-6575. Fax: (915) 335-6860.

Our Lady of the Lake University of San Antonio
San Antonio, Texas CB code: 6550

Admissions:	65% of applicants accepted
Based on:	••• School record, test scores
Completion:	61% of freshmen end year in good standing
	24% graduate, 55% of these enter graduate study

4-year private university, coed, affiliated with Roman Catholic Church. Founded in 1911. **Accreditation:** Regional. **Undergraduate enrollment:** 285 men, 928 women full time; 238 men, 661 women part time. **Graduate enrollment:** 62 men, 210 women full time; 178 men, 385 women part time. **Faculty:** 171 total (95 full time), 62 with doctorates or other terminal degrees. **Location:** Urban campus in very large city. **Calendar:** 4-1-4, limited summer session. **Microcomputers:** 125 located in libraries, computer centers.

DEGREES OFFERED. BA, BS, MA, MS, MBA, MEd, MSW, D. 265 bachelor's degrees awarded in 1992. 5% in area and ethnic studies, 41% business and management, 8% computer sciences, 5% teacher education, 5%

multi/interdisciplinary studies, 13% philosophy, religion, theology, 7% psychology, 5% social sciences. Graduate degrees offered in 14 major fields of study.

UNDERGRADUATE MAJORS. Accounting, American studies, biology, business administration and management, business and management, chemistry, clinical laboratory science, communications, computer and information sciences, dramatic arts, elementary education, English, liberal/general studies, mathematics, music, philosophy, psychology, public administration, radio/television technology, religion, secondary education, social sciences, social work, sociology, Spanish, special education, speech, speech pathology/audiology.

ACADEMIC PROGRAMS. Accelerated program, double major, dual enrollment of high school students, independent study, internships, study abroad, teacher preparation, weekend college, cross-registration; liberal arts/career combination in engineering. **Remedial services:** Learning center, reduced course load, remedial instruction, special counselor, tutoring. **ROTC:** Army. **Placement/credit:** AP, CLEP General and Subject, institutional tests.

ACADEMIC REQUIREMENTS. Freshmen must earn minimum GPA of 1.75 to continue in good standing. 61% of freshmen return for sophomore year. Students must declare major by end of second year. **Graduation requirements:** 128 hours for bachelor's (30 in major). Most students required to take courses in English, history, mathematics, philosophy/religion, biological/physical sciences, social sciences.

FRESHMAN ADMISSIONS. Selection criteria: High school academic record important. **High school preparation:** 16 units required. Required units include English 4, foreign language 2, mathematics 2, social science 3 and science 2. **Test requirements:** SAT or ACT; score report by August 15.

1992 FRESHMAN CLASS PROFILE. 1,975 men and women applied, 1,290 accepted; 74 men enrolled, 245 women enrolled. 61% had high school GPA of 3.0 or higher, 39% between 2.0 and 2.99. 18% were in top tenth and 45% were in top quarter of graduating class. **Characteristics:** 99% from in state, 63% commute, 87% have minority backgrounds, 1% are foreign students. Average age is 19.

FALL-TERM APPLICATIONS. $15 fee, may be waived for applicants with need. No closing date; applicants notified on a rolling basis. CRDA. Deferred and early admission available. EDP-F.

STUDENT LIFE. Housing: Dormitories (men, women, coed). **Activities:** Student government, student newspaper, yearbook, choral groups, drama, religious organizations, black and Hispanic clubs.

ATHLETICS. Intramural: Basketball, soccer M, softball, volleyball.

STUDENT SERVICES. Career counseling, employment service for undergraduates, freshman orientation, health services, personal counseling, placement service for graduates, special adviser for adult students, veterans counselor, services/facilities for handicapped.

ANNUAL EXPENSES. Tuition and fees: $8,180. **Room and board:** $3,756. **Books and supplies:** $750. **Other expenses:** $1,532.

FINANCIAL AID. 71% of freshmen, 85% of continuing students receive some form of aid. 76% of grants, 84% of loans, all jobs based on need. Academic, music/drama, state/district residency, alumni affiliation, minority scholarships available. **Aid applications:** Closing date July 15; priority given to applications received by April 15; applicants notified on a rolling basis beginning on or about March 1; must reply by May 1 or within 2 weeks if notified thereafter.

ADDRESS/TELEPHONE. Loretta Schlegel, Director of Enrollment Management, Our Lady of the Lake University of San Antonio, 411 Southwest 24th Street, San Antonio, TX 78207-4689. (210) 434-6711. Fax: (210) 436-0824.

Palo Alto College
San Antonio, Texas CB code: 3730

2-year public community college, coed. Founded in 1987. **Accreditation:** Regional. **Undergraduate enrollment:** 744 men, 1,116 women full time; 1,736 men, 2,604 women part time. **Faculty:** 311 total (101 full time), 20 with doctorates or other terminal degrees. **Location:** Urban campus in very large city. **Calendar:** Semester, limited summer session. Saturday and extensive evening/early morning classes. **Microcomputers:** 50 located in libraries, classrooms, computer centers. **Special facilities:** FAA Aviation Education Resource Center.

DEGREES OFFERED. AA, AS, AAS. 56 associate degrees awarded in 1992.

UNDERGRADUATE MAJORS. Airline piloting and navigation, architecture, aviation management, biology, business administration and management, business and management, business and office, chemistry, computer and information sciences, economics, education, engineering and engineering-related technologies, finance, fine arts, history, horticulture, mathematics, microcomputer software, nursing, philosophy, physics, pneudraulics, political science and government, predentistry, prelaw, premedicine, preveterinary, psychology, sociology.

ACADEMIC PROGRAMS. 2-year transfer program, cooperative education, dual enrollment of high school students, honors program, telecourses. **Remedial services:** Learning center, remedial instruction, special counselor, tutoring. **Placement/credit:** Institutional tests; 32 credit hours maximum for associate degree.

ACADEMIC REQUIREMENTS. Freshmen must earn minimum GPA of 2.0 to continue in good standing. **Graduation requirements:** 60 hours for associate (18 in major). Most students required to take courses in computer science, English, history, mathematics, biological/physical sciences, social sciences.

FRESHMAN ADMISSIONS. Selection criteria: Open admissions.

1992 FRESHMAN CLASS PROFILE. 1,765 men, 2,695 women enrolled. **Characteristics:** 87% from in state, 100% commute.

FALL-TERM APPLICATIONS. No fee. Closing date September 6. Early admission available.

STUDENT LIFE. Activities: Student newspaper, drama.

STUDENT SERVICES. Aptitude testing, career counseling, freshman orientation, health services, personal counseling, veterans counselor, services/facilities for handicapped.

ANNUAL EXPENSES. Tuition and fees (1992-93): $510, $750 additional for out-of-state students. Out-of-district and out-of-state students pay general fee of $250.

FINANCIAL AID. 20% of continuing students receive some form of aid. Grants, loans available. **Aid applications:** Closing date June 1; applicants notified on or about October 31.

ADDRESS/TELEPHONE. F. P. Terrell, Director of Admissions and Records, Palo Alto College, 1400 West Villaret, San Antonio, TX 78224. (210) 921-5000.

Panola College
Carthage, Texas CB code: 6572

2-year public community, junior college, coed. Founded in 1947. **Accreditation:** Regional. **Undergraduate enrollment:** 862 men and women full time; 735 men and women part time. **Faculty:** 61 total (43 full time), 2 with doctorates or other terminal degrees. **Location:** Rural campus in small town; 40 miles from Shreveport, Louisiana, 35 miles from Longview. **Calendar:** Semester, limited summer session. **Microcomputers:** Located in libraries, classrooms, computer centers. **Additional facts:** Campuses in Marshall and Center.

DEGREES OFFERED. AA, AS, AAS. 99 associate degrees awarded in 1992.

UNDERGRADUATE MAJORS. Accounting, advertising, agribusiness, agricultural sciences, anatomy, automotive technology, biology, business and management, business and office, business computer/console/peripheral equipment operation, business data entry equipment operation, business data processing and related programs, business data programming, chemistry, communications, computer programming, data processing, early childhood education, economics, education, elementary education, engineering, English, finance, fine arts, history, journalism, junior high education, liberal/general studies, management information systems, mathematics, music, personal services, personnel management, physical sciences, physics, political science and government, practical nursing, precision metal work, predentistry, prelaw, premedicine, prepharmacy, preveterinary, psychology, real estate, secondary education, secretarial and related programs, social sciences, teacher aide.

ACADEMIC PROGRAMS. 2-year transfer program, dual enrollment of high school students. **Remedial services:** Learning center, reduced course load, remedial instruction, special counselor, tutoring. **Placement/credit:** AP, CLEP Subject, institutional tests; 12 credit hours maximum for associate degree.

ACADEMIC REQUIREMENTS. Freshmen must earn minimum GPA of 2.0 to continue in good standing. Students must declare major on enrollment. **Graduation requirements:** 62 hours for associate. Most students required to take courses in arts/fine arts, English, foreign languages, history, mathematics, biological/physical sciences, social sciences.

FRESHMAN ADMISSIONS. Selection criteria: Open admissions. Selective admissions to some programs. **Test requirements:** SAT or ACT for placement and counseling only.

1992 FRESHMAN CLASS PROFILE. 385 men, 696 women enrolled. **Characteristics:** 90% from in state, 88% commute, 15% have minority backgrounds. Average age is 18.

FALL-TERM APPLICATIONS. No fee. No closing date; applicants notified on a rolling basis. Interview required for licensed vocational nursing applicants. Early admission available.

STUDENT LIFE. Housing: Dormitories (men, women). **Activities:** Student government, magazine, student newspaper, choral groups, concert band, drama, music ensembles, musical theater, service and school spirit clubs.

ATHLETICS. NJCAA. **Intercollegiate:** Baseball M, basketball. **Intramural:** Badminton, baseball, basketball, racquetball, table tennis, tennis, volleyball.

STUDENT SERVICES. Aptitude testing, career counseling, personal counseling, veterans counselor, services/facilities for handicapped.

ANNUAL EXPENSES. Tuition and fees (1992-93): $440, $150 additional for out-of-district students, $400 additional for out-of-state students. **Room and board:** $1,990. **Books and supplies:** $400. **Other expenses:** $300.

FINANCIAL AID. 40% of freshmen, 40% of continuing students receive some form of aid. Grants, loans, jobs available. 174 enrolled freshmen were judged to have need, 170 were offered aid. Academic, music/drama, athletic scholarships available. **Aid applications:** No closing date; priority given to applications received by June 1; applicants notified on a rolling basis beginning on or about July 1; must reply within 1 week.

ADDRESS/TELEPHONE. Betsy Wheat, Dean of Admissions/Student Svcs, Panola College, 1109 West Panola Street, Carthage, TX 75633. (214) 693-2037. (800) 776-8153. Fax: (214) 693-2018.

Paris Junior College

Paris, Texas — CB code: 6573

2-year public community, junior college, coed. Founded in 1924. **Accreditation:** Regional. **Undergraduate enrollment:** 514 men, 655 women full time; 468 men, 752 women part time. **Faculty:** 118 total (90 full time), 2 with doctorates or other terminal degrees. **Location:** Rural campus in large town; 110 miles from Dallas. **Calendar:** Semester, limited summer session. **Microcomputers:** Located in libraries. **Special facilities:** Regional archives, collection of historical documents and artifacts of region, biological field laboratory with nature trails.

DEGREES OFFERED. AA, AS, AAS. 171 associate degrees awarded in 1992. 5% in computer sciences, 5% education, 10% health sciences, 10% allied health, 6% letters/literature, 5% life sciences, 5% physical sciences, 40% trade and industry.

UNDERGRADUATE MAJORS. Accounting, agricultural sciences, air conditioning/heating/refrigeration mechanics, air conditioning/heating/refrigeration technology, biology, business administration and management, business and management, business and office, business data processing and related programs, carpentry, chemistry, data processing, drafting and design technology, dramatic arts, education, electronic technology, English, fine arts, foreign languages (multiple emphasis), French, German, health sciences, history, journalism, liberal/general studies, machine tool operation/machine shop, mathematics, medical records technology, metal/jewelry, music, nursing, physical sciences, physics, political science and government, practical nursing, precision metal work, predentistry, prelaw, premedicine, prepharmacy, preveterinary, psychology, real estate, secretarial and related programs, sociology, Spanish, speech, watch repair, welding technology.

ACADEMIC PROGRAMS. 2-year transfer program, accelerated program, dual enrollment of high school students, cross-registration. **Remedial services:** Learning center, reduced course load, remedial instruction, special counselor, tutoring. **Placement/credit:** CLEP General and Subject, institutional tests.

ACADEMIC REQUIREMENTS. Freshmen must earn minimum GPA of 1.5 to continue in good standing. Students must declare major on enrollment. **Graduation requirements:** 64 hours for associate. Most students required to take courses in English, history, mathematics, biological/physical sciences, social sciences.

FRESHMAN ADMISSIONS. Selection criteria: Open admissions. Selective admissions to nursing program.

1992 FRESHMAN CLASS PROFILE. 715 men, 925 women enrolled. **Characteristics:** 87% from in state, 88% commute, 15% have minority backgrounds, 4% are foreign students. Average age is 24.

FALL-TERM APPLICATIONS. No fee. No closing date; applicants notified on a rolling basis. Interview required for nursing applicants.

STUDENT LIFE. Housing: Dormitories (men, women); apartment housing available. **Activities:** Student government, magazine, student newspaper, choral groups, drama, music ensembles, musical theater, Baptist Student Union, Afro-American Club, honorary business fraternity, honorary scholastic fraternity, United Campus Ministry.

ATHLETICS. NJCAA. **Intercollegiate:** Baseball M, basketball, golf M, tennis, track and field. **Intramural:** Baseball, basketball M, bowling, football M, soccer, softball, table tennis, tennis, track and field, volleyball.

STUDENT SERVICES. Career counseling, employment service for undergraduates, freshman orientation, health services, personal counseling, placement service for graduates, veterans counselor, services/facilities for handicapped.

ANNUAL EXPENSES. Tuition and fees (1992-93): $2,130, $1,440 additional for out-of-district students, $5,400 additional for out-of-state students. **Room and board:** $2,584. **Books and supplies:** $400.

FINANCIAL AID. 44% of freshmen, 56% of continuing students receive some form of aid. Grants, loans, jobs available. **Aid applications:** No closing date; priority given to applications received by April 1; applicants notified on a rolling basis beginning on or about April 15; must reply within 10 days.

ADDRESS/TELEPHONE. Brad Bankhead, Director of Admissions, Paris Junior College, 2400 Clarksville Street, Paris, TX 75460. (903) 785-7661. (800) 232-5804.

Paul Quinn College

Dallas, Texas — CB code: 6577

4-year private liberal arts college, coed, affiliated with African Methodist Episcopal Church. Founded in 1872. **Accreditation:** Regional. **Undergraduate enrollment:** 789 men and women. **Faculty:** 58 total (35 full time), 19 with doctorates or other terminal degrees. **Location:** Urban campus in very large city; 95 miles from Dallas, 105 miles from Austin. **Calendar:** Semester, limited summer session. **Microcomputers:** 30 located in classrooms, computer centers.

DEGREES OFFERED. BA, BS. 98 bachelor's degrees awarded in 1992. 42% in business and management, 24% teacher education, 6% health sciences, 10% parks/recreation, protective services, public affairs, 8% social sciences.

UNDERGRADUATE MAJORS. Accounting, biology, business and management, business and office, business economics, clinical laboratory science, computer and information sciences, computer technology, criminal justice studies, drafting and design technology, elementary education, English, history, laser electro-optic technology, mathematics, music, occupational safety and health technology, religion, secondary education, social work, sociology.

ACADEMIC PROGRAMS. Cooperative education, double major, honors program, internships, program with Texas State Technical Institute leading to Bachelor of Applied Science in 24 fields. **Remedial services:** Reduced course load, remedial instruction, special counselor, tutoring. **ROTC:** Air Force. **Placement/credit:** CLEP General; 12 credit hours maximum for bachelor's degree.

ACADEMIC REQUIREMENTS. Freshmen must earn minimum GPA of 2.0 to continue in good standing. Students must declare major by end of second year. **Graduation requirements:** 128 hours for bachelor's (36 in major). Most students required to take courses in arts/fine arts, computer science, English, history, mathematics, philosophy/religion, biological/physical sciences, social sciences.

FRESHMAN ADMISSIONS. Selection criteria: Open admissions. **Test requirements:** SAT or ACT (ACT preferred) for counseling; score report by August 1.

1992 FRESHMAN CLASS PROFILE. 245 men and women enrolled. **Characteristics:** 70% from in state, 75% live in college housing, 99% have minority backgrounds, 1% are foreign students, 5% join fraternities/sororities. Average age is 18.

FALL-TERM APPLICATIONS. No fee. No closing date; applicants notified on a rolling basis. Deferred admission available. EDP-F.

STUDENT LIFE. Housing: Dormitories (men, women). **Activities:** Student government, student newspaper, yearbook, choral groups, dance, drama, fraternities, sororities, Student Ministerial Council, Christian Student Organization.

ATHLETICS. NAIA. **Intercollegiate:** Baseball M, basketball, softball W, track and field, volleyball. **Intramural:** Basketball, softball, table tennis, volleyball.

STUDENT SERVICES. Aptitude testing, career counseling, employment service for undergraduates, freshman orientation, health services, personal counseling.

ANNUAL EXPENSES. Tuition and fees (1992-93): $3,635. **Room and board:** $2,975. **Books and supplies:** $400. **Other expenses:** $700.

FINANCIAL AID. 75% of freshmen, 85% of continuing students receive some form of aid. Grants, loans, jobs available. Academic scholarships available. **Aid applications:** No closing date; applicants notified on a rolling basis beginning on or about July 15; must reply by August 15 or within 2 weeks if notified thereafter.

ADDRESS/TELEPHONE. Marilyn Marshall, Director of Admissions and Support Services, Paul Quinn College, 3837 Simpson Stuart Road, Dallas, TX 75241. (214) 302-3547. Fax: (214) 371-1016.

Prairie View A&M University

Prairie View, Texas — CB code: 6580

Admissions: 77% of applicants accepted
Based on: ••• School record, test scores
• Essay, recommendations, special talents
Completion: 70% of freshmen end year in good standing

4-year public university, coed. Founded in 1876. **Accreditation:** Regional. **Undergraduate enrollment:** 2,272 men, 2,208 women full time; 216 men, 242 women part time. **Graduate enrollment:** 74 men, 97 women full time; 182 men, 369 women part time. **Faculty:** 303 total (284 full time), 161 with doctorates or other terminal degrees. **Location:** Rural campus in small town; 45 miles from Houston. **Calendar:** Semester, extensive summer session. **Microcomputers:** 75 located in libraries, classrooms, computer centers. **Special facilities:** Nuclear magnetic resonance spectrometric differentiator, scanning calorimeter, high pressure liquid chromatograph, solid state engineering laboratory, computer-aided design and drafting laboratory, Center for Learning and Teaching Effectiveness, International Dairy Goat Research Center, Accelerate Learning Resource Center, Cooperative Agricultural Research

Center. **Additional facts:** Historically black college, second oldest educational institution in state, land-grant institution.

DEGREES OFFERED. BA, BS, BArch, MA, MS, MBA, MEd. 547 bachelor's degrees awarded in 1992. 6% in agriculture, 15% business and management, 12% education, 17% engineering, 7% engineering technologies, 5% health sciences, 8% life sciences, 10% social sciences. Graduate degrees offered in 32 major fields of study.

UNDERGRADUATE MAJORS. Accounting, agricultural economics, agricultural engineering, agricultural sciences, agronomy, animal sciences, architecture, biology, business economics, business education, chemical engineering, chemistry, civil engineering, communications, computer and information sciences, computer technology, computer-aided drafting and design, drafting and design technology, dramatic arts, electrical technology, electrical/electronics/communications engineering, elementary education, English, family and community services, fashion design, finance, food science and nutrition, geography, health education, history, individual and family development, industrial arts education, industrial technology, journalism, law enforcement and corrections, management science, marketing management, mathematics, mechanical design technology, mechanical engineering, music, music performance, nursing, office supervision and management, physical education, physics, political science and government, psychology, radio/television broadcasting, secondary education, social work, sociology, Spanish, speech, speech correction, trade and industrial education.

ACADEMIC PROGRAMS. Cooperative education, double major, dual enrollment of high school students, education specialist degree, honors program, independent study, internships, teacher preparation, telecourses; combined bachelor's/graduate program in business administration. **Remedial services:** Learning center, reduced course load, remedial instruction, special counselor, tutoring. **ROTC:** Army, Naval. **Placement/credit:** AP, CLEP General and Subject, institutional tests; 30 credit hours maximum for bachelor's degree.

ACADEMIC REQUIREMENTS. Freshmen must earn minimum GPA of 2.0 to continue in good standing. 60% of freshmen return for sophomore year. Students must declare major by end of second year. **Graduation requirements:** 120 hours for bachelor's. Most students required to take courses in English, history, humanities, mathematics, biological/physical sciences, social sciences. **Additional information:** Honors college provides for informal participation in symposia and seminars.

FRESHMAN ADMISSIONS. Selection criteria: Applicants must be in top half of graduating class, have 2.0 GPA, and SAT combined score of 700 or ACT composite score of 17. **High school preparation:** 16 units recommended. Recommended units include English 4, mathematics 3, social science 3 and science 2. 4 electives also recommended. **Test requirements:** SAT or ACT. **Additional information:** SAT/ACT scores must be submitted before second semester.

1992 FRESHMAN CLASS PROFILE. 1,426 men applied, 1,052 accepted, 633 enrolled; 1,353 women applied, 1,088 accepted, 596 enrolled. 25% had high school GPA of 3.0 or higher, 65% between 2.0 and 2.99. **Characteristics:** 70% from in state, 90% live in college housing, 91% have minority backgrounds, 5% are foreign students, 38% join fraternities/sororities. Average age is 18.

FALL-TERM APPLICATIONS. No fee. No closing date; applicants notified on a rolling basis. Essay required for honors college applicants. Deferred and early admission available.

STUDENT LIFE. Housing: Dormitories (men, women). **Activities:** Student government, radio, student newspaper, yearbook, choral groups, concert band, dance, drama, jazz band, marching band, music ensembles, musical theater, symphony orchestra, fraternities, sororities, Baptist Student Movement, Wesley Foundation.

ATHLETICS. NAIA, NCAA. **Intercollegiate:** Baseball M, basketball, cross-country, football M, golf M, tennis, track and field, volleyball W. **Intramural:** Basketball, golf, gymnastics, horseback riding, softball, swimming, table tennis, tennis, track and field, volleyball.

STUDENT SERVICES. Aptitude testing, career counseling, employment service for undergraduates, freshman orientation, health services, personal counseling, placement service for graduates, veterans counselor, services/facilities for handicapped.

ANNUAL EXPENSES. Tuition and fees: $1,568, $4,080 additional for out-of-state students. **Room and board:** $3,500. **Books and supplies:** $581. **Other expenses:** $1,473.

FINANCIAL AID. 85% of freshmen, 85% of continuing students receive some form of aid. 70% of grants, 97% of loans, 78% of jobs based on need. Academic, music/drama, art, athletic, minority scholarships available. **Aid applications:** No closing date; priority given to applications received by April 16; applicants notified on a rolling basis beginning on or about June 1; must reply within 2 weeks.

ADDRESS/TELEPHONE. Robert Ford, Director Admissions/Records, Prairie View A&M University, PO PO Box 2777, Prairie View, TX 77446. (409) 857-2626. (800) 334-1807. Fax: (409) 857-2699.

Ranger Junior College
Ranger, Texas — CB code: 6608

2-year public junior college, coed. Founded in 1926. **Accreditation:** Regional. **Undergraduate enrollment:** 373 men, 136 women full time; 58 men, 159 women part time. **Faculty:** 51 total (28 full time), 6 with doctorates or other terminal degrees. **Location:** Rural campus in small town; 85 miles from Fort Worth. **Calendar:** Semester, limited summer session. **Microcomputers:** 30 located in computer centers.

DEGREES OFFERED. AA, AS, AAS. 29 associate degrees awarded in 1992.

UNDERGRADUATE MAJORS. Automotive mechanics, automotive technology, business computer/console/peripheral equipment operation, computer and information sciences, education, elementary education, English education, liberal/general studies, mathematics, mathematics education, music education, physical education, secondary education, secretarial and related programs, social sciences, welding technology.

ACADEMIC PROGRAMS. 2-year transfer program, dual enrollment of high school students, honors program. **Remedial services:** Learning center, reduced course load, remedial instruction. **Placement/credit:** CLEP General and Subject, institutional tests; 12 credit hours maximum for associate degree.

ACADEMIC REQUIREMENTS. Freshmen must earn minimum GPA of 1.7 to continue in good standing. 65% of freshmen return for sophomore year. Students must declare major on enrollment. **Graduation requirements:** 62 hours for associate. Most students required to take courses in English, history, mathematics, biological/physical sciences, social sciences.

FRESHMAN ADMISSIONS. Selection criteria: Open admissions.

1992 FRESHMAN CLASS PROFILE. 223 men, 109 women enrolled. **Characteristics:** 97% from in state, 80% live in college housing, 43% have minority backgrounds, 1% are foreign students. Average age is 19.

FALL-TERM APPLICATIONS. No fee. No closing date; applicants notified on a rolling basis beginning on or about August 1. Early admission available.

STUDENT LIFE. Housing: Dormitories (men, women). **Activities:** Student government, student newspaper, choral groups, concert band, dance, jazz band, marching band, music ensembles, pep band.

ATHLETICS. NJCAA. **Intercollegiate:** Baseball M, basketball, football M, softball W, track and field. **Intramural:** Basketball, softball.

STUDENT SERVICES. Aptitude testing, career counseling, employment service for undergraduates, freshman orientation, health services, personal counseling, placement service for graduates, veterans counselor, services/facilities for handicapped.

ANNUAL EXPENSES. Tuition and fees: $750, $20 additional for out-of-district students, $120 additional for out-of-state students. **Room and board:** $2,401. **Books and supplies:** $440. **Other expenses:** $809.

FINANCIAL AID. 75% of freshmen, 75% of continuing students receive some form of aid. 57% of grants, all jobs based on need. 168 enrolled freshmen were judged to have need, all were offered aid. Academic, music/drama, athletic, leadership scholarships available. **Aid applications:** Closing date July 31; priority given to applications received by August 1; applicants notified on a rolling basis beginning on or about May 1; must reply within 2 weeks.

ADDRESS/TELEPHONE. Jim W. Cockburn, Associate Dean of Admissions, Ranger Junior College, College Circle, Ranger, TX 76470. (817) 647-3234. Fax: (817) 647-1656.

Rice University
Houston, Texas — CB code: 6609

4-year private university, coed. Founded in 1891. **Accreditation:** Regional. **Undergraduate enrollment:** 2,695 men and women. **Graduate enrollment:** 1,322 men and women. **Faculty:** 584 total (434 full time), 412 with doctorates or other terminal degrees. **Location:** Urban campus in very large city; 3 miles from downtown. **Calendar:** Semester, limited summer session. **Microcomputers:** 200 located in dormitories, computer centers. **Special facilities:** Museum, art gallery, outdoor biology laboratory.

DEGREES OFFERED. BA, BS, MA, MS, MBA, PhD. 679 bachelor's degrees awarded in 1992. Graduate degrees offered in 45 major fields of study.

UNDERGRADUATE MAJORS. Ancient Mediterranean civilization, anthropology, applied mathematics, archeology, architecture, art history, Asian studies, behavioral sciences, biochemistry, biological and physical sciences, biology, biophysics, business administration and management, business and management, chemical engineering, chemistry, civil engineering, classics, cognitive sciences, computer and information sciences, computer engineering, economics, electrical/electronics/communications engineering, English, environmental health engineering, fine arts, French, geology, geophysics and seismology, German, Greek (classical), history, humanities and social sciences, Latin, Latin American studies, legal studies, liberal/general studies, linguistics, materials engineering, mathematical sciences, mathematics, mechanical engineering, metallurgical engineering, music, music history and appreciation, music performance, music theory and composition, philosophy, physical chemistry, physical education, physics, policy studies, political science and government, psychology, religion, Russian, Russian and Slavic studies, sociology, Spanish, statistics, studio art, visual and performing arts, women's studies.

ACADEMIC PROGRAMS. Double major, dual enrollment of high school students, honors program, independent study, internships, student-designed major, study abroad, teacher preparation, visiting/exchange student program, semester exchange programs with Swarthmore College, Texas Southern University, Williams College, Trinity College of Cambridge University; liberal arts/career combination in engineering; combined bachelor's/graduate program in business administration. **Remedial services:** Tutoring. **ROTC:** Army, Naval. **Placement/credit:** AP, CLEP General and Subject, institutional tests.

ACADEMIC REQUIREMENTS. Freshmen must earn minimum GPA of 1.67 to continue in good standing. 95% of freshmen return for sophomore year. Students must declare major by end of second year. **Graduation requirements:** 120 hours for bachelor's (30 in major). Most students required to take courses in humanities, biological/physical sciences, social sciences. **Postgraduate studies:** 10% enter law school, 8% enter medical school, 3% enter MBA programs, 26% enter other graduate study.

FRESHMAN ADMISSIONS. Selection criteria: School achievement record, test scores, interview, teacher and counselor recommendations, and application essay most important. **High school preparation:** 16 units required. Required and recommended units include English 4, foreign language 2, mathematics 3-4, social science 2 and science 2. Biological science 1 recommended. Trigonometry, physics, and chemistry required of engineering and natural science majors. **Test requirements:** SAT; score report by March 1. 3 ACH (including English Composition) required of all applicants. Mathematics Level I or II, and physics or chemistry required of engineering and natural science applicants. Score report by March 1 Music theory test required for music applicants.

1992 FRESHMAN CLASS PROFILE. 650 men and women enrolled. **Academic background:** Mid 50% of enrolled freshmen had SAT-V between 570-690, SAT-M between 640-750. 100% submitted SAT scores. **Characteristics:** 47% from in state, 96% live in college housing, 29% have minority backgrounds, 2% are foreign students. Average age is 18.

FALL-TERM APPLICATIONS. No fee. Closing date January 2; applicants notified on or about April 1; must reply by May 1. Interview required. Audition required for music applicants. Essay required. Portfolio recommended for architecture applicants. CRDA. Deferred and early admission available. EDP-S. Early decision application deadline November 1, notification December 1. Interim decision plan available, application deadline December 1, notification February 1, reply date March 1.

STUDENT LIFE. Housing: Dormitories (coed). Residential college system is center of campus social life. **Activities:** Student government, film, magazine, radio, student newspaper, yearbook, choral groups, concert band, dance, drama, jazz band, marching band, music ensembles, musical theater, pep band, symphony orchestra, Mexican American Organization, Hillel, Black Student Union, Young Democrats, Young Republicans, Chinese Students Association, Campus Crusade, Baptist Student Union, Catholic Student Center, International Students Association, Society of Women Engineers, RSVP (Rice Student Volunteer Program).

ATHLETICS. NCAA. **Intercollegiate:** Baseball M, basketball, bowling, cross-country, diving, football M, golf M, lacrosse M, sailing, swimming, tennis, track and field, volleyball W. **Intramural:** Badminton, basketball, fencing, racquetball, rowing (crew), soccer, softball, squash M, swimming, table tennis, tennis, track and field, volleyball.

STUDENT SERVICES. Career counseling, employment service for undergraduates, freshman orientation, health services, personal counseling, placement service for graduates, services/facilities for handicapped.

ANNUAL EXPENSES. Tuition and fees: $9,650. **Room and board:** $5,460. **Books and supplies:** $425. **Other expenses:** $1,300.

FINANCIAL AID. 91% of freshmen, 76% of continuing students receive some form of aid. 54% of grants, 97% of loans, 14% of jobs based on need. Academic, music/drama, athletic, minority scholarships available. **Aid applications:** Closing date June 1; priority given to applications received by March 1; applicants notified on a rolling basis beginning on or about April 1; must reply by May 1 or within 2 weeks if notified thereafter.

ADDRESS/TELEPHONE. Ron Moss, Director of Admissions, Rice University, PO Box 1892, Houston, TX 77251. (800) 527-6957.

Richland College

Dallas, Texas CB code: 6607

2-year public community college, coed. Founded in 1972. **Accreditation:** Regional. **Undergraduate enrollment:** 2,043 men, 1,953 women full time; 4,035 men, 5,196 women part time. **Faculty:** 500 total (150 full time), 101 with doctorates or other terminal degrees. **Location:** Suburban campus in very large city; 15 miles from downtown. **Calendar:** Semester, extensive summer session. **Microcomputers:** 200 located in classrooms, computer centers. **Special facilities:** Planetarium, Laser Light Theater, Brazos Art Gallery, Lakeside Art Gallery, Horticulture's Demonstration Garden.

DEGREES OFFERED. AA, AS. 331 associate degrees awarded in 1992.

UNDERGRADUATE MAJORS. Accounting, bilingual/bicultural education, business administration and management, business computer/console/peripheral equipment operation, business data processing and related programs, business data programming, computer and information sciences, data processing, electromechanical technology, electronic technology, engineering and engineering-related technologies, horticultural science, horticulture, information sciences and systems, interior design, international business management, legal secretary, liberal/general studies, manufacturing technology, mechanical design technology, ornamental horticulture, quality control technology, real estate, robotics, secretarial and related programs, small business management and ownership, teacher aide.

ACADEMIC PROGRAMS. 2-year transfer program, cooperative education, dual enrollment of high school students, honors program, internships, study abroad, telecourses, weekend college, cross-registration. **Remedial services:** Learning center, remedial instruction, special counselor, tutoring. **Placement/credit:** AP, CLEP Subject, institutional tests; 45 credit hours maximum for associate degree.

ACADEMIC REQUIREMENTS. Freshmen must earn minimum GPA of 2.0 to continue in good standing. 20% of freshmen return for sophomore year. Students must declare major on enrollment. **Graduation requirements:** 61 hours for associate. Most students required to take courses in arts/fine arts, computer science, English, history, humanities, mathematics, biological/physical sciences, social sciences.

FRESHMAN ADMISSIONS. Selection criteria: Open admissions.

1992 FRESHMAN CLASS PROFILE. 4,393 men, 5,201 women enrolled. **Characteristics:** 96% from in state, 100% commute.

FALL-TERM APPLICATIONS. No fee. No closing date; applicants notified on a rolling basis. Early admission available.

STUDENT LIFE. Activities: Student government, student newspaper, choral groups, concert band, dance, drama, jazz band, music ensembles, musical theater.

ATHLETICS. NJCAA. **Intercollegiate:** Baseball M, basketball M, soccer, volleyball W. **Intramural:** Basketball M, soccer, softball, tennis, volleyball.

STUDENT SERVICES. Aptitude testing, career counseling, employment service for undergraduates, freshman orientation, health services, personal counseling, placement service for graduates, special adviser for adult students, services/facilities for handicapped.

ANNUAL EXPENSES. Tuition and fees (1992-93): $450, $570 additional for out-of-district students, $1,470 additional for out-of-state students. **Books and supplies:** $350. **Other expenses:** $935.

FINANCIAL AID. 10% of freshmen, 10% of continuing students receive some form of aid. 99% of grants, 86% of loans, 45% of jobs based on need. 500 enrolled freshmen were judged to have need, 300 were offered aid. Academic scholarships available. **Aid applications:** No closing date; priority given to applications received by June 1; applicants notified on a rolling basis; must reply within 2 weeks.

ADDRESS/TELEPHONE. Gary Matney, Registrar and Director of Admissions, Richland College, 12800 Abrams Road, Dallas, TX 75243-2199. (214) 238-6100. Fax: (214) 238-6149.

St. Edward's University

Austin, Texas CB code: 6619

Admissions: 73% of applicants accepted
Based on: ••• School record, test scores
• Activities, essay, interview, recommendations, special talents
Completion: 80% of freshmen end year in good standing
35% graduate

4-year private university and liberal arts college, coed, affiliated with Roman Catholic Church. Founded in 1885. **Accreditation:** Regional. **Undergraduate enrollment:** 738 men, 941 women full time; 412 men, 540 women part time. **Graduate enrollment:** 28 men, 30 women full time; 183 men, 175 women part time. **Faculty:** 211 total (95 full time), 97 with doctorates or other terminal degrees. **Location:** Urban campus in large city; 80 miles from San Antonio, 180 miles from Dallas. **Calendar:** Semester, limited summer session. **Microcomputers:** 135 located in dormitories, libraries, classrooms, computer centers, campus-wide network. **Special facilities:** Fine arts facility which includes photography laboratory, historic main building.

DEGREES OFFERED. BA, BS, MA, MBA. 432 bachelor's degrees awarded in 1992. 31% in business and management, 5% communications, 6% computer sciences, 5% teacher education, 8% letters/literature, 5% life sciences, 6% multi/interdisciplinary studies, 20% social sciences, 7% visual and performing arts. Graduate degrees offered in 3 major fields of study.

UNDERGRADUATE MAJORS. Accounting, art education, bilingual/bicultural education, biology, business administration and management, business education, chemistry, communications, computer and information sciences, computer programming, computer science education, creative writing, criminal justice studies, dramatic arts, economics, elementary education,

English, English education, English literature, finance, fine arts, foreign languages education, history, international studies, liberal/general studies, marketing management, mathematics, mathematics education, philosophy, photo communications, physical education, political science and government, predentistry, prelaw, premedicine, prepharmacy, preveterinary, psychology, reading education, religion, science education, secondary education, social studies education, social work, sociology, Spanish and international business, Spanish/liberal arts, speech/communication/theater education.

ACADEMIC PROGRAMS. Cooperative education, double major, external degree, honors program, independent study, internships, study abroad, teacher preparation; combined bachelor's/graduate program in business administration. **Remedial services:** Learning center, reduced course load, remedial instruction, special counselor, tutoring. **ROTC:** Air Force, Army, Naval. **Placement/credit:** AP, CLEP General and Subject, institutional tests; 30 credit hours maximum for bachelor's degree.

ACADEMIC REQUIREMENTS. Freshmen must earn minimum GPA of 2.0 to continue in good standing. 70% of freshmen return for sophomore year. Students must declare major by end of second year. **Graduation requirements:** 120 hours for bachelor's (45 in major). Most students required to take courses in arts/fine arts, computer science, English, foreign languages, history, humanities, mathematics, philosophy/religion, biological/physical sciences, social sciences.

FRESHMAN ADMISSIONS. Selection criteria: High school record, rank in top half of class, composite test scores in top 50th percentile nationally. **High school preparation:** 15 units recommended. Recommended units include biological science 1, English 4, foreign language 2, mathematics 3, physical science 2 and social science 3. **Test requirements:** SAT or ACT (SAT preferred); score report by August 1.

1992 FRESHMAN CLASS PROFILE. 1,376 men and women applied, 1,009 accepted; 139 men enrolled, 192 women enrolled. **Academic background:** Mid 50% of enrolled freshmen had SAT-V between 400-480, SAT-M between 420-540; ACT composite between 19-23. 88% submitted SAT scores, 60% submitted ACT scores. **Characteristics:** 90% from in state, 78% live in college housing, 44% have minority backgrounds, 3% are foreign students. Average age is 18.

FALL-TERM APPLICATIONS. $25 fee, may be waived for applicants with need. Closing date August 1; applicants notified on a rolling basis. Interview recommended. CRDA. Deferred admission available. Students without high school diploma must take GED for auditing purposes.

STUDENT LIFE. Housing: Dormitories (men, women). Suites available for both women and men. **Activities:** Student government, film, magazine, student newspaper, Arete-academic journal, choral groups, dance, drama, jazz band, music ensembles, musical theater, campus ministry, Delta Sigma Pi business fraternity, Phi Alpha Delta (pre-law fraternity), environmental group, criminal justice fraternity, drama fraternity, College Republicans, Young Democrats, Hunger Awareness Organization, Pax Christi.

ATHLETICS. NAIA. **Intercollegiate:** Baseball M, basketball, golf M, soccer, softball W, tennis, volleyball W. **Intramural:** Basketball, racquetball, soccer, softball, swimming, volleyball.

STUDENT SERVICES. Aptitude testing, career counseling, employment service for undergraduates, freshman orientation, health services, personal counseling, placement service for graduates, special adviser for adult students, veterans counselor, services/facilities for handicapped.

ANNUAL EXPENSES. Tuition and fees (1992-93): $8,376. **Room and board:** $3,625. **Books and supplies:** $550. **Other expenses:** $1,520.

FINANCIAL AID. 73% of freshmen, 55% of continuing students receive some form of aid. 77% of grants, 83% of loans, 53% of jobs based on need. 217 enrolled freshmen were judged to have need, all were offered aid. Academic, athletic scholarships available. **Aid applications:** Closing date August 15; priority given to applications received by March 1; applicants notified on a rolling basis beginning on or about March 1; must reply by May 1 or within 2 weeks if notified thereafter.

ADDRESS/TELEPHONE. Megan Murphy, Director of Admissions, St. Edward's University, 3001 South Congress Avenue, Austin, TX 78704-6489. (512) 448-8500. Fax: (512) 448-8492.

St. Mary's University

San Antonio, Texas — CB code: 6637

Admissions: 82% of applicants accepted
Based on: ••• School record, test scores
•• Activities, essay, special talents
• Interview, recommendations
Completion: 90% of freshmen end year in good standing
65% graduate, 50% of these enter graduate study

4-year private university, coed, affiliated with Roman Catholic Church. Founded in 1852. **Accreditation:** Regional. **Undergraduate enrollment:** 938 men, 1,269 women full time; 155 men, 233 women part time. **Graduate enrollment:** 501 men, 440 women full time; 245 men, 226 women part time. **Faculty:** 302 total (170 full time), 253 with doctorates or other terminal degrees. **Location:** Suburban campus in very large city; 5 miles from downtown. **Calendar:** Semester, limited summer session. **Microcomputers:** 100 located in dormitories, libraries, classrooms, computer centers.

DEGREES OFFERED. BA, BS, MA, MS, MBA, PhD. 494 bachelor's degrees awarded in 1992. 32% in business and management, 9% letters/literature, 17% life sciences, 7% multi/interdisciplinary studies, 14% social sciences. Graduate degrees offered in 31 major fields of study.

UNDERGRADUATE MAJORS. Accounting, applied physics, applied theology, biochemistry, biology, biotechnology, business administration and management, business education, chemistry, communications, computer and information sciences, computer engineering, criminal justice studies, earth sciences, economics, electrical/electronics/communications engineering, elementary education, engineering, engineering science, English, English education, finance, foreign languages education, French, German, history, human resources development, industrial engineering, information sciences and systems, international business management, international relations, junior high education, Latin American studies, liberal/general studies, management information systems, marketing management, mathematics, mathematics education, medical laboratory technologies, multinational organizational studies, music, music education, organizational administration, philosophy, physical education, physics, political science and government, predentistry, premedicine, prepharmacy, psychology, reading education, science education, secondary education, small business management and ownership, social science education, social studies education, sociology, Spanish, speech, speech/communication/theater education, theological studies.

ACADEMIC PROGRAMS. Accelerated program, cooperative education, double major, honors program, independent study, internships, study abroad, teacher preparation, Washington semester, cross-registration; liberal arts/career combination in engineering. **Remedial services:** Learning center, preadmission summer program, reduced course load, remedial instruction, special counselor, tutoring. **ROTC:** Army. **Placement/credit:** AP, CLEP General and Subject, institutional tests; 30 credit hours maximum for bachelor's degree.

ACADEMIC REQUIREMENTS. Freshmen must earn minimum GPA of 1.7 to continue in good standing. 88% of freshmen return for sophomore year. Students must declare major by end of second year. **Graduation requirements:** 128 hours for bachelor's (30 in major). Most students required to take courses in arts/fine arts, computer science, English, foreign languages, humanities, mathematics, philosophy/religion, biological/physical sciences, social sciences. **Postgraduate studies:** 12% enter law school, 10% enter medical school, 15% enter MBA programs, 13% enter other graduate study.

FRESHMAN ADMISSIONS. Selection criteria: SAT and ACT scores at the 50th percentile required for students in top half of class, 2.5 GPA or better required in college preparatory program. **High school preparation:** 16 units required. Required units include English 4, foreign language 2, mathematics 3, social science 2 and science 2. 4 mathematics and 4 science preferred for science programs and engineering. 3 academic electives recommended. **Test requirements:** SAT or ACT; score report by August 15.

1992 FRESHMAN CLASS PROFILE. 532 men applied, 424 accepted, 233 enrolled; 784 women applied, 654 accepted, 316 enrolled. 76% had high school GPA of 3.0 or higher, 21% between 2.0 and 2.99. 30% were in top tenth and 61% were in top quarter of graduating class. **Academic background:** Mid 50% of enrolled freshmen had SAT-V between 390-480, SAT-M between 430-530; ACT composite between 20-23. 77% submitted SAT scores, 57% submitted ACT scores. **Characteristics:** 86% from in state, 65% live in college housing, 73% have minority backgrounds, 3% are foreign students, 20% join fraternities/sororities. Average age is 18.

FALL-TERM APPLICATIONS. $15 fee, may be waived for applicants with need. Closing date August 15; priority given to applications received by March 1; applicants notified on a rolling basis; must reply by May 1 or within 2 weeks if notified thereafter. Audition required. Essay required. Interview recommended. Portfolio recommended. CRDA. Deferred admission available.

STUDENT LIFE. Housing: Dormitories (men, women, coed); handicapped housing available. **Activities:** Student government, student newspaper, choral groups, concert band, drama, jazz band, music ensembles, musical theater, pep band, fraternities, sororities, campus ministry, political science association, black and Mexican American student organizations, service organizations, departmental clubs and organizations, honor and service fraternities.

ATHLETICS. NAIA. **Intercollegiate:** Baseball M, basketball, golf M, soccer, softball W, tennis, volleyball W. **Intramural:** Basketball, bowling, golf, rifle, soccer, softball, swimming, table tennis, tennis, volleyball.

STUDENT SERVICES. Aptitude testing, career counseling, employment service for undergraduates, freshman orientation, health services, personal counseling, placement service for graduates, veterans counselor, services/facilities for handicapped.

ANNUAL EXPENSES. Tuition and fees: $8,536. **Room and board:** $3,440. **Books and supplies:** $500. **Other expenses:** $1,000.

FINANCIAL AID. 73% of freshmen, 62% of continuing students receive some form of aid. 84% of grants, 65% of loans, all jobs based on need. Academic, music/drama, athletic, state/district residency, minority scholarships available. **Aid applications:** No closing date; priority given to applications received by April 1; applicants notified on a rolling basis beginning on or about February 1; must reply by May 1 or within 2 weeks if notified thereafter.

ADDRESS/TELEPHONE. Dr. Barry Abrams, Vice President of Enrollment Management, St. Mary's University, One Camino Santa Maria, San Antonio, TX 78228-8503. (512) 436-3126. Fax: (512) 436-3500.

St. Philip's College

San Antonio, Texas — CB code: 6642

2-year public community college, coed. Founded in 1898. **Accreditation:** Regional. **Undergraduate enrollment:** 1,074 men, 1,195 women full time; 1,932 men, 1,962 women part time. **Faculty:** 351 total (172 full time), 21 with doctorates or other terminal degrees. **Location:** Urban campus in very large city; One mile from downtown San Antonio. **Calendar:** Semester, extensive summer session. Saturday and extensive evening/early morning classes. **Microcomputers:** 255 located in libraries, classrooms, computer centers. **Additional facts:** Ten percent of courses held at off-campus sites.

DEGREES OFFERED. AA, AS, AAS. 357 associate degrees awarded in 1992. 5% in business and management, 16% business/office and marketing/distribution, 5% computer sciences, 8% engineering technologies, 26% allied health, 5% home economics, 25% trade and industry.

UNDERGRADUATE MAJORS. Accounting, air conditioning/heating/refrigeration mechanics, air conditioning/heating/refrigeration technology, aircraft mechanics, auto body repair, automotive mechanics, automotive technology, biology, biomedical equipment technology, business administration and management, business and management, business and office, business data processing and related programs, business data programming, chemistry, computer and information sciences, computer programming, computer servicing technology, construction, diesel engine mechanics, dietetic aide/assistant, drafting, drafting and design technology, dramatic arts, economics, electrical installation, electrical technology, electronic technology, English, fine arts, food management, food production/management/services, health sciences, history, hotel/motel and restaurant management, interior design, legal secretary, liberal/general studies, machine tool operation/machine shop, mathematics, medical laboratory technologies, medical records technology, medical secretary, music, occupational therapy assistant, physical therapy assistant, plumbing/pipefitting/steamfitting, political science and government, power plant operation and maintenance, practical nursing, predentistry, preengineering, prelaw, premedicine, psychology, radiograph medical technology, secretarial and related programs, sociology, Spanish, speech, teacher aide, teacher education, textiles and clothing, tourism, urban studies, welding technology, word processing.

ACADEMIC PROGRAMS. 2-year transfer program, dual enrollment of high school students, internships, teacher preparation, telecourses, weekend college, cross-registration. **Remedial services:** Learning center, preadmission summer program, reduced course load, remedial instruction, special counselor, tutoring. **ROTC:** Army. **Placement/credit:** CLEP General and Subject, institutional tests; 32 credit hours maximum for associate degree.

ACADEMIC REQUIREMENTS. Freshmen must earn minimum GPA of 2.0 to continue in good standing. 44% of freshmen return for sophomore year. Students must declare major by end of first year. **Graduation requirements:** 64 hours for associate (30 in major). Most students required to take courses in English, history, mathematics, social sciences.

FRESHMAN ADMISSIONS. Selection criteria: Open admissions. **High school preparation:** 15 units recommended. Recommended units include English 3, foreign language 2, mathematics 2, social science 2 and science 2.

1992 FRESHMAN CLASS PROFILE. 407 men, 448 women enrolled. **Characteristics:** 99% from in state, 100% commute, 68% have minority backgrounds, 1% are foreign students.

FALL-TERM APPLICATIONS. No fee. Closing date August 20. Early admission available. Students who have not taken SAT or ACT tests must take Pre-TASP examination upon admission.

STUDENT LIFE. Activities: Student government, student newspaper, choral groups, drama, jazz band, music ensembles, musical theater, Phi Theta Kappa, Black Educational Network, Phi Beta, Inroads In Unity, Alamo Golden Tigers.

ATHLETICS. Intramural: Basketball, swimming, table tennis, tennis, volleyball.

STUDENT SERVICES. Aptitude testing, career counseling, employment service for undergraduates, freshman orientation, health services, personal counseling, placement service for graduates, veterans counselor, services/facilities for handicapped.

ANNUAL EXPENSES. Tuition and fees (1992-93): $570, $390 additional for out-of-district students, $1,290 additional for out-of-state students. Out-of-district/state students pay additional $190 required fees. **Books and supplies:** $275. **Other expenses:** $700.

FINANCIAL AID. 34% of freshmen, 34% of continuing students receive some form of aid. 98% of grants, all loans, all jobs based on need. Academic, music/drama scholarships available. **Aid applications:** Closing date June 1; applicants notified on or about August 1; must reply by August 10.

ADDRESS/TELEPHONE. Harry Stine, Director Admissions and Records, St. Philip's College, 1801 Martin Luther King Boulevard, San Antonio, TX 78203-2098. (512) 531-3200.

Sam Houston State University

Huntsville, Texas — CB code: 6643

Admissions:	71% of applicants accepted
Based on:	••• School record, test scores
	• Recommendations, special talents
Completion:	50% of freshmen end year in good standing
	32% graduate

4-year public university, coed. Founded in 1879. **Accreditation:** Regional. **Undergraduate enrollment:** 4,077 men, 4,657 women full time; 1,008 men, 1,094 women part time. **Graduate enrollment:** 233 men, 272 women full time; 372 men, 699 women part time. **Faculty:** 483 total (348 full time). **Location:** Suburban campus in large town; 69 miles from Houston. **Calendar:** Semester, extensive summer session. **Microcomputers:** 249 located in libraries, classrooms, computer centers. **Special facilities:** Sam Houston Museum near campus, agricultural center.

DEGREES OFFERED. BA, BS, MA, MS, MBA, PhD. 1,457 bachelor's degrees awarded in 1992. 5% in agriculture, 23% business and management, 5% communications, 14% teacher education, 20% social sciences, 6% visual and performing arts. Graduate degrees offered in 49 major fields of study.

UNDERGRADUATE MAJORS. Accounting, agribusiness, agricultural education, agricultural mechanics, agricultural sciences, animal sciences, art education, biology, business administration and management, business and management, business economics, business education, chemistry, clinical laboratory science, communications, computer and information sciences, criminology, dance, dramatic arts, economics, elementary education, English, environmental science, fashion design, finance, fine arts, food production/management/services, food science and nutrition, French, geography, geology, German, graphic design, health education, history, home economics, home economics education, home furnishings and equipment management/production/services, horticulture, humanities, industrial arts education, industrial technology, international business management, journalism, law enforcement and corrections, marketing and distribution, marketing management, mathematics, medical laboratory technologies, music, music education, music performance, music theory and composition, music therapy, office supervision and management, photographic technology, photography, physical education, physics, political science and government, psychology, radio/television broadcasting, secondary education, social work, sociology, Spanish, speech, studio art, trade and industrial education.

ACADEMIC PROGRAMS. Double major, dual enrollment of high school students, honors program, internships. **Remedial services:** Learning center, preadmission summer program, reduced course load, remedial instruction, tutoring. **ROTC:** Army. **Placement/credit:** AP, CLEP Subject, institutional tests.

ACADEMIC REQUIREMENTS. Freshmen must earn minimum GPA of 2.0 to continue in good standing. 67% of freshmen return for sophomore year. Students must declare major by end of second year. **Graduation requirements:** 128 hours for bachelor's (30 in major). Most students required to take courses in arts/fine arts, English, history, mathematics, biological/physical sciences, social sciences.

FRESHMAN ADMISSIONS. Selection criteria: Test scores and school achievement record considered. Recommended units include English 4, mathematics 2, social science 2 and science 2. **Test requirements:** SAT or ACT; score report by August 22.

1992 FRESHMAN CLASS PROFILE. 4,582 men and women applied, 3,249 accepted; 711 men enrolled, 892 women enrolled. **Academic background:** Mid 50% of enrolled freshmen had ACT composite between 17-21. 42% submitted ACT scores. **Characteristics:** 97% from in state, 90% live in college housing, 25% have minority backgrounds, 1% are foreign students. Average age is 19.

FALL-TERM APPLICATIONS. No fee. No closing date; applicants notified on a rolling basis. Deferred and early admission available.

STUDENT LIFE. Housing: Dormitories (men, women, coed); apartment, fraternity, sorority housing available. **Activities:** Student government, film, radio, student newspaper, television, yearbook, choral groups, concert band, dance, drama, jazz band, marching band, music ensembles, musical theater, opera, pep band, symphony orchestra, fraternities, sororities.

ATHLETICS. NCAA. **Intercollegiate:** Baseball M, basketball, cross-country M, football M, golf, rifle, soccer M, softball W, tennis, volleyball W. **Intramural:** Badminton, basketball, bowling, diving, golf, handball, lacrosse M, racquetball, softball, swimming, table tennis, tennis, volleyball, water polo.

STUDENT SERVICES. Aptitude testing, career counseling, employment service for undergraduates, freshman orientation, health services, personal counseling, placement service for graduates, services/facilities for handicapped.

ANNUAL EXPENSES. Tuition and fees: $1,536, $4,080 additional for

out-of-state students. **Room and board:** $3,380. **Books and supplies:** $498. **Other expenses:** $1,282.

FINANCIAL AID. 31% of freshmen, 30% of continuing students receive some form of aid. 77% of grants, 91% of loans, all jobs based on need. 963 enrolled freshmen were judged to have need, all were offered aid. Academic, music/drama, art, athletic, leadership, alumni affiliation, minority scholarships available. **Aid applications:** Closing date May 31; priority given to applications received by March 31; applicants notified on or about June 15; must reply within 2 weeks.

ADDRESS/TELEPHONE. Joey Chandler, Director of Admissions, Sam Houston State University, Box 2418, Huntsville, TX 77341-2418. (409) 294-1056. Fax: (409) 294-1465.

San Antonio College
San Antonio, Texas CB code: 6645

2-year public community college, coed. Founded in 1925. **Accreditation:** Regional. **Undergraduate enrollment:** 21,103 men and women. **Faculty:** 917 total (480 full time), 73 with doctorates or other terminal degrees. **Location:** Urban campus in very large city; in downtown area. **Calendar:** Semester, extensive summer session. **Microcomputers:** Located in computer centers. **Special facilities:** Planetarium.

DEGREES OFFERED. AA, AS, AAS. 763 associate degrees awarded in 1992.

UNDERGRADUATE MAJORS. Accounting, allied health, architecture, biological and physical sciences, business administration and management, business and management, business and office, business computer/console/peripheral equipment operation, business data processing and related programs, business data programming, business systems analysis, computer and information sciences, computer programming, criminal justice technology, data processing, dental assistant, drafting, drafting and design technology, education, electronic technology, engineering and engineering-related technologies, fire control and safety technology, funeral services/mortuary science, graphic design, journalism, law enforcement and corrections technologies, legal assistant/paralegal, legal secretary, liberal/general studies, medical assistant, mental health/human services, metal/jewelry, nursing, physical therapy, physician's assistant, predentistry, prelaw, premedicine, prepharmacy, preveterinary, protective services, public administration, public affairs, radio/television technology, real estate, secretarial and related programs, word processing.

ACADEMIC PROGRAMS. 2-year transfer program, cooperative education, double major, dual enrollment of high school students, honors program, internships, study abroad, telecourses, weekend college, cross-registration. **Remedial services:** Learning center, reduced course load, remedial instruction, special counselor, tutoring, guided studies and team teaching. **Placement/credit:** AP, CLEP Subject, institutional tests; 32 credit hours maximum for associate degree.

ACADEMIC REQUIREMENTS. Freshmen must earn minimum GPA of 2.0 to continue in good standing. **Graduation requirements:** 66 hours for associate. Most students required to take courses in English, history, mathematics, biological/physical sciences, social sciences. **Additional information:** Students in Texas public colleges must pass the Texas Academic Skills Program test before they are awarded a degree. Test must be taken before end of semester in which 15th college level credit is earned.

FRESHMAN ADMISSIONS. Selection criteria: Open admissions. Nursing requires 2.02 GPA, satisfactory completion of human anatomy and physiology, and Nelson-Denny Reading score. **Test requirements:** SAT or ACT for placement and counseling only; score report by August 20. **Additional information:** Students with no ACT of SAT scores must take ASSET.

1992 FRESHMAN CLASS PROFILE. 3,156 men and women enrolled. **Academic background:** Mid 50% of enrolled freshmen had ACT composite between 13-17. 10% submitted ACT scores. **Characteristics:** 100% commute.

FALL-TERM APPLICATIONS. No fee. No closing date; applicants notified on a rolling basis. Early admission available. Nursing applicants must apply by January 15.

STUDENT LIFE. Housing: Special program places students in homes of elderly residents who have spare rooms and need assistance. **Activities:** Student government, film, magazine, radio, student newspaper, television, choral groups, concert band, dance, drama, music ensembles, musical theater, symphony orchestra, Baptist Student Center, Catholic Student Center, Methodist Student Center, Church of Christ Student Center, Black Student Alliance, United Mexican-American Students, College Republicans, Young Democrats, Young Socialist Alliance.

ATHLETICS. Intramural: Basketball, cross-country, fencing, golf, racquetball, soccer, softball, swimming, tennis, volleyball, water polo.

STUDENT SERVICES. Aptitude testing, career counseling, employment service for undergraduates, freshman orientation, health services, on-campus day care, personal counseling, placement service for graduates, special adviser for adult students, veterans counselor, services/facilities for handicapped.

ANNUAL EXPENSES. Tuition and fees (1992-93): $624, $390 additional for out-of-district students, $1,290 additional for out-of-state students. **Books and supplies:** $720. **Other expenses:** $1,627.

FINANCIAL AID. 40% of freshmen, 40% of continuing students receive some form of aid. 98% of grants, 77% of loans, all jobs based on need. Academic, music/drama, art, state/district residency, leadership, minority scholarships available. **Aid applications:** No closing date; priority given to applications received by May 1; applicants notified on a rolling basis; must reply within 10 days.

ADDRESS/TELEPHONE. Phyllis McCarley, Director Admissions and Registrar, San Antonio College, 1300 San Pedro Avenue, San Antonio, TX 78212-4299. (512) 733-2300.

San Jacinto College: Central Campus
Pasadena, Texas CB code: 6694

2-year public community college, coed. Founded in 1960. **Accreditation:** Regional. **Undergraduate enrollment:** 10,263 men and women. **Location:** Suburban campus in small city; 20 miles from Houston. **Calendar:** Semester.

FRESHMAN ADMISSIONS. Selection criteria: Open admissions. Selective admissions to health science program.

ANNUAL EXPENSES. Tuition and fees (1992-93): $430, $300 additional for out-of-district students, $990 additional for out-of-state students. **Books and supplies:** $400. **Other expenses:** $1,209.

ADDRESS/TELEPHONE. Dr. Del Long, Director of Admissions, San Jacinto College: Central Campus, 8060 Spencer Highway, PO Box 2007, Pasadena, TX 77501-2007. (713) 476-1816. Fax: (713) 476-1892.

San Jacinto College: North
Houston, Texas CB code: 6729

2-year public community college, coed. Founded in 1974. **Accreditation:** Regional. **Undergraduate enrollment:** 4,291 men and women. **Faculty:** 212 total (77 full time). **Location:** Suburban campus in very large city; 15 miles from downtown. **Calendar:** Semester, limited summer session. **Microcomputers:** Located in classrooms, computer centers. **Special facilities:** Art gallery, nature preserve.

DEGREES OFFERED. AA, AS, AAS. 97 associate degrees awarded in 1992. 27% in business and management, 16% business/office and marketing/distribution, 7% letters/literature, 7% social sciences, 30% trade and industry.

UNDERGRADUATE MAJORS. Accounting, advertising, air conditioning/heating/refrigeration mechanics, air conditioning/heating/refrigeration technology, biology, business administration and management, business and management, business and office, business data entry equipment operation, business data processing and related programs, business data programming, carpentry, chemistry, child development/care/guidance, construction, criminal justice studies, data processing, diesel engine mechanics, drafting, drafting and design technology, education, electrical installation, electrical technology, electronic technology, elementary education, English, finance, food management, food production/management/services, food science and nutrition, history, interior design, law enforcement and corrections technologies, legal assistant/paralegal, legal secretary, liberal/general studies, mathematics, medical secretary, music, office supervision and management, practical nursing, protective services, psychology, real estate, secretarial and related programs, Spanish, speech, studio art, welding technology.

ACADEMIC PROGRAMS. 2-year transfer program, accelerated program, dual enrollment of high school students, honors program, internships, telecourses, weekend college, cross-registration. **Remedial services:** Learning center, remedial instruction. **Placement/credit:** CLEP General and Subject, institutional tests; 12 credit hours maximum for associate degree.

ACADEMIC REQUIREMENTS. Freshmen must earn minimum GPA of 1.5 to continue in good standing. 25% of freshmen return for sophomore year. Students must declare major on enrollment. **Graduation requirements:** 62 hours for associate (12 in major). Most students required to take courses in English, history, mathematics, social sciences.

FRESHMAN ADMISSIONS. Selection criteria: Open admissions. Recommended units include English 4, mathematics 3 and science 2. **Test requirements:** Psychological Services Bureau test required of nursing applicants.

1992 FRESHMAN CLASS PROFILE. 2,459 men and women enrolled. **Characteristics:** 99% from in state, 100% commute, 30% have minority backgrounds. Average age is 26.

FALL-TERM APPLICATIONS. No fee. No closing date; applicants notified on a rolling basis. Interview required for nursing applicants. Early admission available.

STUDENT LIFE. Activities: Student government, choral groups, dance, drama, jazz band, musical theater, pep band, Baptist organization, Circle-K, Young Democrats, Distributive Education Clubs of America, business club, historical society, Spanish society, Rotaract.

ATHLETICS. NJCAA. **Intercollegiate:** Baseball M, basketball W, golf. **Intramural:** Badminton, basketball, racquetball, softball, swimming, tennis, volleyball.

STUDENT SERVICES. Aptitude testing, career counseling, em-

ployment service for undergraduates, freshman orientation, on-campus day care, veterans counselor, services/facilities for handicapped.

ANNUAL EXPENSES. Tuition and fees (projected): $430, $300 additional for out-of-district students, $990 additional for out-of-state students. **Books and supplies:** $500. **Other expenses:** $1,583.

FINANCIAL AID. 15% of freshmen, 8% of continuing students receive some form of aid. 88% of grants, 95% of loans based on need. All jobs based on criteria other than need. 327 enrolled freshmen were judged to have need, all were offered aid. Academic, music/drama, art, athletic, leadership scholarships available. **Aid applications:** No closing date; priority given to applications received by June 1; applicants notified on a rolling basis beginning on or about August 1; must reply within 10 days.

ADDRESS/TELEPHONE. Wanda W. Simpson, Registrar, San Jacinto College: North, 5800 Uvalde, Houston, TX 77049. (713) 458-4050.

Schreiner College
Kerrville, Texas — CB code: 6647

Admissions: 75% of applicants accepted
Based on: ••• School record
•• Activities, interview, test scores
• Essay, recommendations, special talents
Completion: 80% of freshmen end year in good standing
16% enter graduate study

4-year private liberal arts college, coed, affiliated with Presbyterian Church (USA). Founded in 1923. **Accreditation:** Regional. **Undergraduate enrollment:** 261 men, 263 women full time; 25 men, 63 women part time. **Faculty:** 64 total (44 full time), 32 with doctorates or other terminal degrees. **Location:** Rural campus in large town; 55 miles from San Antonio. **Calendar:** 4-1-4, limited summer session. **Microcomputers:** 36 located in libraries, classrooms, computer centers.

DEGREES OFFERED. AA, AAS, BA. 12 associate degrees awarded in 1992. 42% in business and management, 58% letters/literature. 64 bachelor's degrees awarded. 42% in business and management, 11% teacher education, 7% law, 16% letters/literature, 15% psychology.

UNDERGRADUATE MAJORS. Associate: Biology, business and office, computer and information sciences, engineering, engineering and engineering-related technologies, English literature, liberal/general studies, secretarial and related programs. **Bachelor's:** Accounting, art education, biochemistry, biology, business administration and management, business and management, education, elementary education, English, English education, English literature, exercise science, history, humanities, liberal/general studies, marketing management, mathematics, mathematics education, philosophy, physical education, predentistry, prelaw, premedicine, prepharmacy, preveterinary, psychology, real estate, religion, secondary education, social science education.

ACADEMIC PROGRAMS. Double major, dual enrollment of high school students, honors program, internships, student-designed major, study abroad, teacher preparation, visiting/exchange student program, United Nations semester; liberal arts/career combination in engineering. **Remedial services:** Learning center, reduced course load, remedial instruction, special counselor, tutoring. **Placement/credit:** AP, institutional tests.

ACADEMIC REQUIREMENTS. Freshmen must earn minimum GPA of 1.8 to continue in good standing. 50% of freshmen return for sophomore year. Students must declare major by end of second year. **Graduation requirements:** 64 hours for associate, 128 hours for bachelor's (24 in major). Most students required to take courses in computer science, English, foreign languages, history, humanities, mathematics, philosophy/religion, biological/physical sciences. **Postgraduate studies:** 65% from 2-year programs enter 4-year programs. 2% enter law school, 1% enter medical school, 2% enter MBA programs, 11% enter other graduate study.

FRESHMAN ADMISSIONS. Selection criteria: High school courses taken, grades, class rank, extracurricular activities, test scores, recommendations, interviews considered. **High school preparation:** 21 units required. Required and recommended units include English 4, mathematics 3, social science 2 and science 2. Foreign language 2 recommended. **Test requirements:** SAT or ACT; score report by August 15. ACH required of students seeking advanced placement. Score report by August 1.

1992 FRESHMAN CLASS PROFILE. 443 men applied, 324 accepted, 107 enrolled; 379 women applied, 296 accepted, 90 enrolled. 28% were in top tenth and 54% were in top quarter of graduating class. **Academic background:** Mid 50% of enrolled freshmen had SAT-V between 360-460, SAT-M between 380-540; ACT composite between 17-22. 61% submitted SAT scores, 49% submitted ACT scores. **Characteristics:** 91% from in state, 69% live in college housing, 16% have minority backgrounds, 2% are foreign students. Average age is 18.

FALL-TERM APPLICATIONS. $20 fee, may be waived for applicants with need. Closing date August 1; priority given to applications received by July 1; applicants notified on a rolling basis; must reply by May 1. Interview recommended. Portfolio recommended for fine arts applicants. Essay required of applicants not meeting certain admissions standards. CRDA. Deferred and early admission available.

STUDENT LIFE. Housing: Dormitories (men, women, coed); apartment housing available. Freshmen may pick roommates in advance. Smoking and nonsmoking rooms available. **Activities:** Student government, magazine, student newspaper, choral groups, drama, Student Senate, international students organization, men's and women's social clubs, Young Republicans, Young Democrats, runners club, biking club, campus ministry group, Babtist Student Union.

ATHLETICS. NAIA. **Intercollegiate:** Baseball M, basketball, cross-country, soccer, tennis, volleyball W. **Intramural:** Basketball, racquetball, soccer, softball, swimming, table tennis, tennis, track and field, volleyball. **Clubs:** Running, biking.

STUDENT SERVICES. Aptitude testing, career counseling, employment service for undergraduates, freshman orientation, health services, personal counseling, placement service for graduates, special adviser for adult students, services/facilities for handicapped.

ANNUAL EXPENSES. Tuition and fees: $8,650. **Room and board:** $5,900. **Books and supplies:** $500. **Other expenses:** $1,116.

FINANCIAL AID. 83% of freshmen, 85% of continuing students receive some form of aid. 62% of grants, 79% of loans, 70% of jobs based on need. 103 enrolled freshmen were judged to have need, all were offered aid. Academic, music/drama, athletic, state/district residency, leadership, religious affiliation scholarships available. **Aid applications:** No closing date; priority given to applications received by April 15; applicants notified on a rolling basis beginning on or about February 15; must reply by May 1 or within 3 weeks if notified thereafter.

ADDRESS/TELEPHONE. Dewayne Bannister, VP of Admissions, Schreiner College, 2100 Memorial Boulevard, Kerrville, TX 78028. (210) 896-5411. (800) 343-4919. Fax: (210) 896-3232.

South Plains College
Levelland, Texas — CB code: 6695

2-year public community, junior college, coed. Founded in 1957. **Accreditation:** Regional. **Undergraduate enrollment:** 1,343 men, 1,522 women full time; 1,316 men, 1,779 women part time. **Faculty:** 358 total (268 full time), 22 with doctorates or other terminal degrees. **Location:** Suburban campus in large town; 30 miles from Lubbock. **Calendar:** Semester, extensive summer session. Saturday and extensive evening/early morning classes. **Microcomputers:** Located in classrooms, computer centers.

DEGREES OFFERED. AA, AS, AAS. 498 associate degrees awarded in 1992.

UNDERGRADUATE MAJORS. Accounting, agribusiness, agricultural sciences, air conditioning/heating/refrigeration mechanics, air conditioning/heating/refrigeration technology, automotive mechanics, automotive technology, biology, botany, business and office, business data processing and related programs, chemistry, commercial art, computer mathematics, computer servicing technology, country/bluegrass music, criminology, data processing, diesel engine mechanics, drafting, drafting and design technology, electrical and electronics equipment repair, electronic technology, engineering, English, fashion merchandising, food management, food production/management/services, food science and nutrition, history, home economics, information sciences and systems, journalism, law enforcement and corrections, law enforcement and corrections technologies, legal secretary, liberal/general studies, machine tool operation/machine shop, marketing and distribution, mathematics, medical records technology, medical secretary, mental health/human services, microcomputer software, mining and petroleum technologies, music, nursing, physics, political science and government, practical nursing, precision metal work, predentistry, prelaw, premedicine, prepharmacy, preveterinary, psychology, radiograph medical technology, real estate, respiratory therapy technology, secretarial and related programs, sound technology, sports medicine, telecommunications, video, welding technology, zoology.

ACADEMIC PROGRAMS. 2-year transfer program, dual enrollment of high school students. **Remedial services:** Learning center, remedial instruction, tutoring. **Placement/credit:** CLEP Subject, institutional tests; 15 credit hours maximum for associate degree.

ACADEMIC REQUIREMENTS. Freshmen must earn minimum GPA of 2.0 to continue in good standing. 77% of freshmen return for sophomore year. **Graduation requirements:** 62 hours for associate. Most students required to take courses in English, history, mathematics, biological/physical sciences, social sciences.

FRESHMAN ADMISSIONS. Selection criteria: Open admissions. Selective admissions to allied health programs. **Test requirements:** SAT or ACT (ACT preferred) for counseling; score report by August 30.

1992 FRESHMAN CLASS PROFILE. Characteristics: 95% from in state, 80% commute, 20% have minority backgrounds, 1% are foreign students. Average age is 20.

FALL-TERM APPLICATIONS. No fee. No closing date; applicants notified on a rolling basis. Interview required for health care applicants. Early admission available.

STUDENT LIFE. Housing: Dormitories (men, women); apartment housing available. **Activities:** Student government, magazine, radio, student newspaper, television, yearbook, choral groups, concert band, dance, drama, jazz band, music ensembles, pep band.

ATHLETICS. NJCAA. **Intercollegiate:** Basketball, cross-country M, track and field M. **Intramural:** Basketball, racquetball, softball, table tennis, volleyball.

STUDENT SERVICES. Aptitude testing, career counseling, employment service for undergraduates, freshman orientation, health services, personal counseling, placement service for graduates, veterans counselor, services/facilities for handicapped.

ANNUAL EXPENSES. Tuition and fees: $936, $480 additional for out-of-state students. **Room and board:** $2,300. **Books and supplies:** $400. **Other expenses:** $1,100.

FINANCIAL AID. 30% of freshmen, 25% of continuing students receive some form of aid. 85% of grants, all loans, 48% of jobs based on need. Academic, music/drama, art, athletic, leadership scholarships available. **Aid applications:** No closing date; priority given to applications received by June 10; applicants notified on a rolling basis beginning on or about June 30; must reply within 2 weeks.

ADDRESS/TELEPHONE. Bobby James, Dean of Admissions and Records, South Plains College, 1400 College Avenue, Levelland, TX 79336. (806) 894-9611 ext. 210. Fax: (806) 894-5274.

Southern Methodist University ⇎
Dallas, Texas — CB code: 6660

Admissions: 68% of applicants accepted
Based on:
- ••• School record
- •• Activities, test scores
- • Essay, interview, recommendations, special talents

Completion: 93% of freshmen end year in good standing
71% graduate, 26% of these enter graduate study

4-year private university, coed, affiliated with United Methodist Church. Founded in 1911. **Accreditation:** Regional. **Undergraduate enrollment:** 2,473 men, 2,573 women full time; 103 men, 139 women part time. **Graduate enrollment:** 978 men, 646 women full time; 1,068 men, 558 women part time. **Faculty:** 643 total (484 full time), 421 with doctorates or other terminal degrees. **Location:** Suburban campus in very large city; 5 miles from downtown. **Calendar:** Semester, limited summer session. **Microcomputers:** 250 located in dormitories, libraries, classrooms, computer centers, campus-wide network. **Special facilities:** Meadows Museum, Elizabeth Meadows Sculpture Garden, art gallery, radio station, Southwest Film/Video Archives, laboratories, research facilities. **Additional facts:** Campus in New Mexico, study abroad programs in France, England, Austria, Denmark, Japan, Spain, Russia, Italy.

DEGREES OFFERED. BA, BS, BFA, MA, MS, MBA, MFA, PhD, JD, M.Div. 1,324 bachelor's degrees awarded in 1992. 7% in area and ethnic studies, 24% business and management, 17% communications, 5% letters/literature, 7% psychology, 20% social sciences, 5% visual and performing arts. Graduate degrees offered in 46 major fields of study.

UNDERGRADUATE MAJORS. Accounting, advertising, Afro-American (black) studies, anthropology, art history, biochemistry, biology, business administration and management, business and management, chemistry, cinematography/film, computer and information sciences, computer engineering, creative writing, dance, dramatic arts, economics, electrical/electronics/communications engineering, English literature, environmental geology, finance, fine arts, foreign languages (multiple emphasis), French, geology, geophysics and seismology, German, history, humanities, international studies, journalism, Latin American studies, management information systems, marketing management, mathematics, mechanical engineering, Mexican American studies, music, music education, music history and appreciation, music performance, music theory and composition, music therapy, organizational behavior, philosophy, physics, piano pedagogy, political science and government, psychology, public relations, radio/television broadcasting, radio/television technology, real estate, religion, Russian, Russian and Slavic studies, social sciences, sociology, Spanish, statistics, systems analysis, Western European studies.

ACADEMIC PROGRAMS. Cooperative education, double major, honors program, independent study, internships, student-designed major, study abroad, teacher preparation, visiting/exchange student program; combined bachelor's/graduate program in business administration. **Remedial services:** Learning center, special counselor, tutoring, Learning Enhancement Center provides support and individualized tutoring to students. No specific remedial programs. **ROTC:** Air Force, Army. **Placement/credit:** AP, CLEP Subject, IB, institutional tests.

ACADEMIC REQUIREMENTS. Freshmen must earn minimum GPA of 2.0 to continue in good standing. Majors in engineering, business, journalism, broadcast, and film require minimum GPA of 2.5. 84% of freshmen return for sophomore year. Students must declare major by end of second year. **Graduation requirements:** 120 hours for bachelor's (30 in major). Most students required to take courses in English, foreign languages, history, humanities, mathematics, biological/physical sciences, social sciences. **Post-graduate studies:** 7% enter law school, 3% enter medical school, 5% enter MBA programs, 11% enter other graduate study.

FRESHMAN ADMISSIONS. Selection criteria: High school curriculum, GPA, class rank, test scores, recommendations, student essay, school accreditation, character and personality, extracurricular participation all considered. **High school preparation:** 15 units required. Required units include English 4, foreign language 2, mathematics 3, social science 3 and science 3. **Test requirements:** SAT or ACT; score report by January 15. ACH scores not required but recommended. Score report by January 15.

1992 FRESHMAN CLASS PROFILE. 4,748 men and women applied, 3,207 accepted; 586 men enrolled, 635 women enrolled. **Academic background:** Mid 50% of enrolled freshmen had ACT composite between 21-26. 53% submitted ACT scores. **Characteristics:** 49% from in state, 96% live in college housing, 19% have minority backgrounds, 3% are foreign students, 34% join fraternities/sororities. Average age is 18.

FALL-TERM APPLICATIONS. $40 fee, may be waived for applicants with need. Closing date April 1; priority given to applications received by January 15; applicants notified on or about March 15; must reply by May 1. Audition required for performing arts applicants. Essay required. Interview recommended. Portfolio recommended for studio art applicants. CRDA. Deferred admission available. Institutional early decision plan.

STUDENT LIFE. Housing: Dormitories (men, women, coed); apartment, fraternity, sorority housing available. Honors houses, special interest houses, substance free floors, international floor available. **Activities:** Student government, film, radio, student newspaper, yearbook, choral groups, concert band, drama, jazz band, marching band, music ensembles, musical theater, opera, pep band, symphony orchestra, 155 special interest organizations, fraternities, sororities, Association of Black Students, Catholic Campus Ministry, Campus Y, College Hispanic American Students, College Republicans, Jewish Student Association/Hillel, Mobilization of Volunteer Efforts, Organization of International Students, United Methodist Campus Ministry, Young Democrats.

ATHLETICS. NCAA. **Intercollegiate:** Baseball M, basketball, cross-country, diving, football M, golf, soccer, swimming, tennis, track and field. **Intramural:** Badminton, basketball, bowling, diving, football, racquetball, skiing, soccer, softball, swimming, table tennis, tennis, volleyball, wrestling M.

STUDENT SERVICES. Aptitude testing, career counseling, employment service for undergraduates, freshman orientation, health services, on-campus day care, personal counseling, placement service for graduates, special adviser for adult students, legal clinic, services/facilities for handicapped.

ANNUAL EXPENSES. Tuition and fees: $13,580. **Room and board:** $4,940. **Books and supplies:** $576. **Other expenses:** $1,100.

FINANCIAL AID. 80% of freshmen, 68% of continuing students receive some form of aid. 47% of grants, 93% of loans, all jobs based on need. 495 enrolled freshmen were judged to have need, all were offered aid. Academic, music/drama, art, athletic, leadership, alumni affiliation, religious affiliation, minority scholarships available. **Aid applications:** No closing date; priority given to applications received by February 1; applicants notified on a rolling basis beginning on or about March 15; must reply by May 1 or within 2 weeks if notified thereafter.

ADDRESS/TELEPHONE. Ron W Moss, Director of Admissions, Southern Methodist University, PO Box 296, 6425 Boaz Street, Dallas, TX 75275-0296. (214) 768-2058. (800) 323-0672. Fax: (214) 768-4138.

Southwest Texas Junior College
Uvalde, Texas — CB code: 6666

2-year public junior college, coed. Founded in 1946. **Accreditation:** Regional. **Undergraduate enrollment:** 2,859 men and women. **Faculty:** 117 total (58 full time), 23 with doctorates or other terminal degrees. **Location:** Rural campus in large town; 80 miles from San Antonio, 70 miles from Del Rio. **Calendar:** Semester, limited summer session. **Microcomputers:** Located in classrooms, computer centers.

DEGREES OFFERED. AA, AS, AAS. 250 associate degrees awarded in 1992.

UNDERGRADUATE MAJORS. Business computer/console/peripheral equipment operation, business data entry equipment operation, business data processing and related programs, business data programming, computer and information sciences, data processing, liberal/general studies, mechanical design technology, practical nursing, science technologies, secretarial and related programs.

ACADEMIC PROGRAMS. 2-year transfer program, dual enrollment of high school students. **Remedial services:** Special counselor, tutoring. **Placement/credit:** CLEP Subject.

ACADEMIC REQUIREMENTS. Freshmen must earn minimum GPA of 2.0 to continue in good standing. 60% of freshmen return for sophomore year. Students must declare major by end of second year. **Graduation requirements:** 60 hours for associate. Most students required to take courses in English, history, mathematics, biological/physical sciences, social sciences.

FRESHMAN ADMISSIONS. Selection criteria: Open admissions. **Test requirements:** ACT for counseling.

1992 FRESHMAN CLASS PROFILE. 715 men and women enrolled. **Characteristics:** 90% from in state, 93% commute. Average age is 24.

FALL-TERM APPLICATIONS. No fee. No closing date; applicants notified on a rolling basis.

STUDENT LIFE. Housing: Dormitories (men, women, coed). **Activities:** Magazine, radio, student newspaper, yearbook, drama.

ATHLETICS. Intramural: Baseball, basketball, golf, racquetball, softball, swimming, tennis, volleyball. **Clubs:** Rodeo.

STUDENT SERVICES. Aptitude testing, career counseling, employment service for undergraduates, health services, personal counseling, placement service for graduates, veterans counselor, services/facilities for handicapped.

ANNUAL EXPENSES. Tuition and fees (1992-93): $806, $240 additional for out-of-district students, $1,380 additional for out-of-state students. **Room and board:** $1,980. **Books and supplies:** $350. **Other expenses:** $411.

FINANCIAL AID. 37% of freshmen, 30% of continuing students receive some form of aid. Grants, loans, jobs available. Academic scholarships available. **Aid applications:** No closing date; priority given to applications received by June 15; applicants notified on a rolling basis beginning on or about June 1; must reply within 2 weeks.

ADDRESS/TELEPHONE. John Allen Davis, Director of Admissions and Registrar, Southwest Texas Junior College, Garner Field Road, Uvalde, TX 78801. (512) 278-4401.

Southwest Texas State University
San Marcos, Texas — CB code: 6667

4-year public university, coed. Founded in 1899. **Accreditation:** Regional. **Undergraduate enrollment:** 6,857 men, 7,693 women full time; 1,949 men, 1,998 women part time. **Graduate enrollment:** 80 men, 80 women full time; 833 men, 991 women part time. **Faculty:** 902 total (661 full time), 777 with doctorates or other terminal degrees. **Location:** Suburban campus in large town; 30 miles from Austin and 49 miles from San Antonio. **Calendar:** Semester, extensive summer session. Saturday and extensive evening/early morning classes. **Microcomputers:** Located in dormitories, libraries, classrooms, computer centers, campus-wide network.

DEGREES OFFERED. AAS, BA, BS, BFA, MA, MS, MBA, MEd, MD, B. Pharm, DVM. 24 associate degrees awarded in 1992. 100% in allied health. 2,694 bachelor's degrees awarded. 13% in business and management, 6% business/office and marketing/distribution, 6% communications, 13% education, 6% home economics, 7% parks/recreation, protective services, public affairs, 5% psychology, 10% social sciences, 7% trade and industry. Graduate degrees offered in 55 major fields of study.

UNDERGRADUATE MAJORS. Associate: Respiratory therapy technology. **Bachelor's:** Accounting, African studies, agribusiness, agricultural business and management, agricultural education, agricultural mechanics, agricultural production, agricultural sciences, allied health, American studies, animal sciences, anthropology, architectural technologies, art education, Asian studies, bilingual/bicultural education, biological and physical sciences, biology, botany, business administration and management, business and management, business economics, business education, chemistry, city/community/regional planning, commercial art, computer and information sciences, criminal justice studies, curriculum and instruction, dramatic arts, driver and safety education, early childhood education, economics, education, elementary education, engineering and engineering-related technologies, English, English education, environmental science, European studies, exercise sciences/physiology and movement studies, family/consumer resource management, fashion merchandising, finance, fine arts, food science and nutrition, foreign languages education, French, geography, German, graphic and printing production, health care administration, health education, health sciences, history, home economics, home economics education, horticultural science, horticulture, individual and family development, industrial arts education, industrial technology, information sciences and systems, interior design, international relations, international studies, journalism, law enforcement and corrections, management information systems, management science, manufacturing technology, marine biology, marketing management, mathematics, mathematics education, medical laboratory technologies, medical records administration, microbiology, Middle Eastern studies, music, music education, music performance, musical theater, occupational therapy, office supervision and management, parks and recreation management, philosophy, physical education, physical therapy, physics, physiology, human and animal, plant sciences, political science and government, psychology, public administration, range management, reading education, respiratory therapy, science education, secondary education, social sciences, social work, sociology, soil sciences, Spanish, speech, speech correction, speech pathology/audiology, speech/communication/theater education, sports medicine, studio art, textiles and clothing, trade and industrial education, wildlife sciences, zoology.

ACADEMIC PROGRAMS. Double major, dual enrollment of high school students, honors program, independent study, internships, study abroad, teacher preparation, cross-registration. **Remedial services:** Learning center, preadmission summer program, remedial instruction, special counselor, tutoring. **ROTC:** Air Force, Army. **Placement/credit:** AP, CLEP General and Subject, institutional tests; 30 credit hours maximum for bachelor's degree.

ACADEMIC REQUIREMENTS. Freshmen must earn minimum GPA of 2.0 to continue in good standing. Business school and education students must maintain 2.5 GPA. 60% of freshmen return for sophomore year. Students must declare major by end of second year. **Graduation requirements:** 72 hours for associate (40 in major), 128 hours for bachelor's (30 in major). Most students required to take courses in arts/fine arts, English, foreign languages, history, humanities, mathematics, philosophy/religion, biological/physical sciences, social sciences. **Postgraduate studies:** 1% enter law school, 9% enter MBA programs, 33% enter other graduate study.

FRESHMAN ADMISSIONS. Selection criteria: No minimum for top 10%. Next 15%, minimum of 800 SAT or 20 ACT; 2nd quarter, 900 SAT or 22 ACT; 3rd quarter, 1000 SAT or 24 ACT; 4th quarter, 1100 SAT or 26 ACT. **High school preparation:** 14 units required; 16 recommended. Required and recommended units include English 4, foreign language 2, mathematics 3-4, social science 3 and science 2-3. **Test requirements:** SAT or ACT; score report by July 1.

1992 FRESHMAN CLASS PROFILE. 909 men, 1,346 women enrolled. 12% were in top tenth and 45% were in top quarter of graduating class. **Academic background:** Mid 50% of enrolled freshmen had SAT-V between 360-470, SAT-M between 410-520; ACT composite between 18-22. 78% submitted SAT scores, 54% submitted ACT scores. **Characteristics:** 98% from in state, 79% live in college housing, 27% have minority backgrounds, 1% are foreign students, 15% join fraternities/sororities. Average age is 21.

FALL-TERM APPLICATIONS. No fee. Closing date July 1; applicants notified on a rolling basis. Portfolio required for art applicants. Audition recommended for music applicants. CRDA. Deferred and early admission available.

STUDENT LIFE. Housing: Dormitories (men, women, coed); apartment, fraternity, sorority, cooperative housing available. **Activities:** Student government, film, magazine, radio, student newspaper, television, yearbook, choral groups, concert band, dance, drama, jazz band, marching band, music ensembles, musical theater, opera, symphony orchestra, fraternities, sororities, over 150 social, service, religious, political, and professional organizations.

ATHLETICS. NCAA. **Intercollegiate:** Baseball M, basketball, cross-country, football M, golf M, softball W, tennis, track and field, volleyball W. **Intramural:** Basketball, bowling, cross-country, diving, gymnastics, racquetball, softball, swimming, table tennis, tennis, track and field, volleyball, wrestling.

STUDENT SERVICES. Aptitude testing, career counseling, employment service for undergraduates, freshman orientation, health services, personal counseling, placement service for graduates, veterans counselor, veterans affairs, services/facilities for handicapped.

ANNUAL EXPENSES. Tuition and fees: $1,240, $4,080 additional for out-of-state students. **Room and board:** $3,854. **Books and supplies:** $500. **Other expenses:** $1,970.

FINANCIAL AID. 50% of freshmen, 32% of continuing students receive some form of aid. 74% of grants, 89% of loans, 17% of jobs based on need. 844 enrolled freshmen were judged to have need, 759 were offered aid. Academic, music/drama, athletic, leadership, minority scholarships available. **Aid applications:** No closing date; priority given to applications received by April 1; applicants notified on a rolling basis beginning on or about June 1; must reply within 2 weeks.

ADDRESS/TELEPHONE. Fernando A. Yarrito, Director of Admissions, Southwest Texas State University, 601 University Drive, San Marcos, TX 78666. (512) 245-2364.

Southwestern Adventist College
Keene, Texas — CB code: 6671

4-year private liberal arts college, coed, affiliated with Seventh-day Adventists. Founded in 1893. **Accreditation:** Regional. **Undergraduate enrollment:** 284 men, 318 women full time; 91 men, 158 women part time. **Graduate enrollment:** 3 men, 8 women part time. **Faculty:** 69 total (53 full time), 22 with doctorates or other terminal degrees. **Location:** Rural campus in small town; 55 miles from Dallas and 25 miles from Fort Worth. **Calendar:** Semester, limited summer session. **Microcomputers:** 28 located in libraries, classrooms, computer centers. **Special facilities:** Thomsen observatory, Museum of Student Life.

DEGREES OFFERED. AS, BA, BS, MEd. 33 associate degrees awarded in 1992. 95% in allied health. 93 bachelor's degrees awarded. 25% in business and management, 5% business/office and marketing/distribution, 7% communications, 7% computer sciences, 21% teacher education, 8% allied health, 5% languages, 7% life sciences, 7% philosophy, religion, theology. Graduate degrees offered in 1 major field of study.

UNDERGRADUATE MAJORS. Associate: Health sciences, information sciences and systems, legal secretary, medical secretary, nursing, office information systems, office supervision and management, secretarial and related programs, social work. **Bachelor's:** Accounting, biology, biometrics and biostatistics, business administration and management, business and management, chemistry, computer and information sciences, corporate communications, elementary education, English, history, information sciences and systems, international relations, journalism, long-term health care administration, mathematics, medical laboratory technologies, nursing, office information systems, office supervision and management, physics, psychology, radio/television broadcasting, religion, secretarial and related programs, social sciences, social work, theological studies.

ACADEMIC PROGRAMS. Accelerated program, cooperative education, double major, external degree, honors program, independent study, internships, student-designed major, study abroad, teacher preparation, cross-registration. **Remedial services:** Reduced course load, special counselor, tutoring. **Placement/credit:** CLEP General, institutional tests.

ACADEMIC REQUIREMENTS. Freshmen must earn minimum GPA of 1.5 to continue in good standing. 66% of freshmen return for sophomore year. Students must declare major by end of second year. **Graduation requirements:** 64 hours for associate, 128 hours for bachelor's (27 in major). Most students required to take courses in arts/fine arts, English, history, mathematics, philosophy/religion, biological/physical sciences, social sciences. **Postgraduate studies:** 4% enter medical school, 4% enter MBA programs, 9% enter other graduate study.

FRESHMAN ADMISSIONS. Selection criteria: Open admissions. High school record and test scores very important. Recommended units include biological science 1, English 4, mathematics 2, physical science 1 and social science 2.5. **Test requirements:** SAT or ACT (SAT preferred) for placement and counseling only; score report by September 15.

1992 FRESHMAN CLASS PROFILE. 96 men, 93 women enrolled. **Characteristics:** 53% from in state, 65% commute, 25% have minority backgrounds, 6% are foreign students. Average age is 20.

FALL-TERM APPLICATIONS. No fee. No closing date; applicants notified on a rolling basis. Interview recommended for those with unsatisfactory character references. Deferred admission available.

STUDENT LIFE. Housing: Dormitories (men, women); apartment housing available. **Activities:** Student government, radio, student newspaper, television, yearbook, choral groups, concert band, drama, music ensembles, musical theater, pep band, symphony orchestra, campus ministries, multicultural student organization.

ATHLETICS. Intercollegiate: Baseball M, basketball M, volleyball W. **Intramural:** Basketball, football, gymnastics, racquetball, skiing, soccer, softball, swimming, table tennis, tennis, volleyball.

STUDENT SERVICES. Aptitude testing, career counseling, employment service for undergraduates, freshman orientation, health services, personal counseling, placement service for graduates, special adviser for adult students, veterans counselor, visitation days, services/facilities for handicapped.

ANNUAL EXPENSES. Tuition and fees: $7,064. **Room and board:** $3,466. **Books and supplies:** $430. **Other expenses:** $1,088.

FINANCIAL AID. 75% of freshmen, 70% of continuing students receive some form of aid. 54% of grants, 91% of loans, 22% of jobs based on need. 135 enrolled freshmen were judged to have need, all were offered aid. Academic, music/drama, leadership scholarships available. **Aid applications:** No closing date; priority given to applications received by March 15; applicants notified on a rolling basis beginning on or about May 1; must reply within 2 weeks.

ADDRESS/TELEPHONE. Flavia Illingworth, Admissions of Counselor, Southwestern Adventist College, PO Box 567, Keene, TX 76059. (817) 645-3921 ext. 294. (800) 433-2240. Fax: (817) 556-4744.

Southwestern Assemblies of God College
Waxahachie, Texas — CB code: 6669

4-year private Bible college, coed, affiliated with Assemblies of God. Founded in 1927. **Accreditation:** Regional. **Undergraduate enrollment:** 287 men, 288 women full time; 113 men, 73 women part time. **Faculty:** 29 total (18 full time), 12 with doctorates or other terminal degrees. **Location:** Suburban campus in large town; 20 miles from Dallas. **Calendar:** Semester, limited summer session. **Microcomputers:** 27 located in libraries, computer centers.

DEGREES OFFERED. AA, BA, BS. 24 associate degrees awarded in 1992. 30% in business and management, 8% communications, 23% philosophy, religion, theology, 30% psychology. 87 bachelor's degrees awarded. 14% in business and management, 10% teacher education, 74% philosophy, religion, theology.

UNDERGRADUATE MAJORS. Associate: Bible studies, business administration and management, business and management, communications, education, English, journalism, psychology, social sciences, Spanish. **Bachelor's:** Bible studies, business administration and management, business and management, elementary education, missionary studies, music, religious education, religious music.

ACADEMIC PROGRAMS. Double major, dual enrollment of high school students, external degree, independent study, internships, teacher preparation. **Remedial services:** Learning center, reduced course load, remedial instruction, special counselor, tutoring. **Placement/credit:** CLEP General and Subject, institutional tests; 15 credit hours maximum for associate degree; 30 credit hours maximum for bachelor's degree.

ACADEMIC REQUIREMENTS. Freshmen must earn minimum GPA of 1.75 to continue in good standing. 55% of freshmen return for sophomore year. Students must declare major on enrollment. **Graduation requirements:** 66 hours for associate (9 in major), 126 hours for bachelor's (51 in major). Most students required to take courses in computer science, English, history, mathematics, philosophy/religion, biological/physical sciences, social sciences. **Postgraduate studies:** 75% from 2-year programs enter 4-year programs.

FRESHMAN ADMISSIONS. Selection criteria: Open admissions. **Test requirements:** ACT for placement and counseling only; score report by August 30. **Additional information:** One personal reference and one reference from a minister required.

1992 FRESHMAN CLASS PROFILE. 56 men, 91 women enrolled. 50% had high school GPA of 3.0 or higher, 45% between 2.0 and 2.99. **Academic background:** Mid 50% of enrolled freshmen had ACT composite between 13-23. 100% submitted ACT scores. **Characteristics:** 74% from in state, 77% live in college housing, 15% have minority backgrounds. Average age is 19.

FALL-TERM APPLICATIONS. $30 fee. No closing date; priority given to applications received by August 1; applicants notified on a rolling basis. Interview recommended. Essay recommended. Deferred and early admission available.

STUDENT LIFE. Housing: Dormitories (men, women, coed); apartment housing available. Unmarried students 23 and under required to live in college housing unless alternative arrangements agreed to upon enrollment. **Activities:** Student government, student newspaper, yearbook, choral groups, drama, music ensembles, musical theater. **Additional information:** Dress code observed. Religious observance required.

ATHLETICS. Intercollegiate: Basketball M, volleyball W. **Intramural:** Basketball, softball, table tennis, tennis, volleyball.

STUDENT SERVICES. Career counseling, employment service for undergraduates, freshman orientation, health services, personal counseling, placement service for graduates, special adviser for adult students, veterans counselor, services/facilities for handicapped.

ANNUAL EXPENSES. Tuition and fees: $2,900. **Room and board:** $2,762. **Books and supplies:** $481. **Other expenses:** $1,272.

FINANCIAL AID. 75% of freshmen, 75% of continuing students receive some form of aid. 76% of grants, 88% of loans, 71% of jobs based on need. 67 enrolled freshmen were judged to have need, all were offered aid. Academic, music/drama, leadership, religious affiliation scholarships available. **Aid applications:** No closing date; priority given to applications received by March 1; applicants notified on a rolling basis beginning on or about May 15; must reply within 2 weeks.

ADDRESS/TELEPHONE. Greg Dufrene, Director of Admissions, Southwestern Assemblies of God College, 1200 Sycamore Street, Waxahachie, TX 75165. (214) 937-4010. (800) 262-SAGC. Fax: (214) 923-0488.

Southwestern Christian College
Terrell, Texas — CB code: 6705

4-year private Bible, liberal arts college, coed, affiliated with Church of Christ. Founded in 1949. **Accreditation:** Regional. **Undergraduate enrollment:** 116 men, 96 women full time; 16 men, 16 women part time. **Faculty:** 20 total (17 full time). **Location:** Rural campus in large town; 30 miles from Dallas. **Calendar:** Semester. **Microcomputers:** Located in computer centers.

DEGREES OFFERED. AA, AS, BA, BS. 60 associate degrees awarded in 1992. 30% in business and management, 15% computer sciences, 5% health sciences, 40% philosophy, religion, theology, 5% psychology. 19 bachelor's degrees awarded. 100% in philosophy, religion, theology.

UNDERGRADUATE MAJORS. Associate: Accounting, Bible studies, business data entry equipment operation, business data processing and related programs, business data programming, computer and information sciences, education, elementary education, engineering, liberal/general studies, mathematics, science technologies, secondary education, secretarial and related programs. **Bachelor's:** Religious education, theological studies.

ACADEMIC PROGRAMS. 2-year transfer program, independent study, internships. **Remedial services:** Learning center, reduced course load, remedial instruction, special counselor. **Placement/credit:** Institutional tests; 8 credit hours maximum for associate degree; 16 credit hours maximum for bachelor's degree.

ACADEMIC REQUIREMENTS. Freshmen must earn minimum GPA of 2.0 to continue in good standing. 65% of freshmen return for sophomore year. Students must declare major by end of second year. **Graduation requirements:** 62 hours for associate, 124 hours for bachelor's. Most students required to take courses in computer science, English, history, humanities, mathematics, philosophy/religion, biological/physical sciences. **Postgraduate studies:** 90% from 2-year programs enter 4-year programs.

FRESHMAN ADMISSIONS. Selection criteria: Open admissions.

1992 FRESHMAN CLASS PROFILE. 47 men applied, 47 accepted, 47 enrolled; 57 women applied, 57 accepted, 57 enrolled. **Characteristics:**

15% from in state, 94% live in college housing, 87% have minority backgrounds, 20% are foreign students. Average age is 18.

FALL-TERM APPLICATIONS. $10 fee. Closing date July 31; applicants notified on a rolling basis. Interview recommended. CRDA. Deferred and early admission available. EDP-F.

STUDENT LIFE. Housing: Dormitories (men, women). **Activities:** Student government, student newspaper, yearbook, choral groups, drama, jazz band, music ensembles, pep band. **Additional information:** High moral standards required. Profanity, vulgarity, gambling, drinking alcoholic beverages, attending dances or places of questionable amusement against college's ideals and rules.

ATHLETICS. NJCAA. **Intercollegiate:** Basketball, track and field.

STUDENT SERVICES. Career counseling, freshman orientation, personal counseling.

ANNUAL EXPENSES. Tuition and fees: $4,386. **Room and board:** $2,793. **Books and supplies:** $460. **Other expenses:** $400.

FINANCIAL AID. 90% of freshmen, 92% of continuing students receive some form of aid. All grants, 98% of loans, all jobs based on need. 8 enrolled freshmen were judged to have need, all were offered aid. Academic, music/drama, athletic scholarships available. **Aid applications:** Closing date July 15; applicants notified on a rolling basis beginning on or about July 15; must reply by August 23.

ADDRESS/TELEPHONE. Gerald Lee, Director of Admissions, Southwestern Christian College, PO Box 10, Terrell, TX 75160. (214) 524-3341. (800) 733-7922. Fax: (214) 563-7133.

Southwestern University

Georgetown, Texas — CB code: 6674

Admissions: 69% of applicants accepted
Based on: ••• School record
•• Essay, interview, recommendations, test scores
• Activities, special talents
Completion: 95% of freshmen end year in good standing
70% graduate, 31% of these enter graduate study

4-year private liberal arts college, coed, affiliated with United Methodist Church. Founded in 1840. **Accreditation:** Regional. **Undergraduate enrollment:** 535 men, 626 women full time; 17 men, 24 women part time. **Faculty:** 128 total (84 full time), 87 with doctorates or other terminal degrees. **Location:** Suburban campus in large town; 28 miles from Austin. **Calendar:** Semester, limited summer session. **Microcomputers:** 172 located in dormitories, libraries, classrooms, computer centers.

DEGREES OFFERED. BA, BS, BFA. 279 bachelor's degrees awarded in 1992. 17% in business and management, 6% life sciences, 5% physical sciences, 9% psychology, 30% social sciences, 15% visual and performing arts.

UNDERGRADUATE MAJORS. Accounting, American studies, animal behavior, animal sciences, art history, biological and physical sciences, biology, business administration and management, business and management, chemistry, classics, communications, computer and information sciences, dramatic arts, economics, English, experimental psychology, foreign languages (multiple emphasis), French, German, history, international studies, Latin, mathematics, medical laboratory technologies, music, music history and appreciation, philosophy, physics, political science and government, psychology, religion, religious education, religious music, social sciences, sociology, Spanish, theological studies, visual and performing arts, women's studies.

ACADEMIC PROGRAMS. Accelerated program, double major, dual enrollment of high school students, education specialist degree, honors program, independent study, internships, student-designed major, study abroad, teacher preparation, visiting/exchange student program, Washington semester; liberal arts/career combination in engineering. **Remedial services:** Tutoring. **Placement/credit:** AP, CLEP Subject, institutional tests.

ACADEMIC REQUIREMENTS. Freshmen must earn minimum GPA of 2.0 to continue in good standing. 86% of freshmen return for sophomore year. Students must declare major by end of second year. **Graduation requirements:** 122 hours for bachelor's (30 in major). Most students required to take courses in arts/fine arts, computer science, English, foreign languages, humanities, mathematics, philosophy/religion, biological/physical sciences, social sciences. **Postgraduate studies:** 8% enter law school, 6% enter medical school, 7% enter MBA programs, 10% enter other graduate study. **Additional information:** Students must demonstrate computer skills and grasp of major through special project, course, or examination prior to graduation.

FRESHMAN ADMISSIONS. Selection criteria: In order of importance: high school academic record, recommendations, test scores, interview, essay. Strong college preparatory program with 3.0 GPA preferred. **High school preparation:** 16 units recommended. Recommended units include English 4, foreign language 2, mathematics 3, social science 3 and science 2. **Test requirements:** SAT or ACT; score report by April 1.

1992 FRESHMAN CLASS PROFILE. 519 men applied, 379 accepted, 141 enrolled; 695 women applied, 456 accepted, 177 enrolled. 88% had high school GPA of 3.0 or higher, 12% between 2.0 and 2.99. 50% were in top tenth and 82% were in top quarter of graduating class. **Academic background:** Mid 50% of enrolled freshmen had SAT-V between 480-580, SAT-M between 520-630; ACT composite between 23-28. 95% submitted SAT scores, 51% submitted ACT scores. **Characteristics:** 90% from in state, 98% live in college housing, 21% have minority backgrounds, 2% are foreign students, 33% join fraternities/sororities. Average age is 19.

FALL-TERM APPLICATIONS. $25 fee, may be waived for applicants with need. Closing date February 15; priority given to applications received by January 1; applicants notified on a rolling basis; must reply by May 1. Audition required for music, theater applicants. Portfolio required for art applicants. Essay required. Interview recommended. CRDA. Deferred and early admission available. EDP-F. Applicants accepted after February 15 if space allows.

STUDENT LIFE. Housing: Dormitories (men, women, coed); fraternity housing available. **Activities:** Student government, magazine, student newspaper, yearbook, choral groups, concert band, dance, drama, jazz band, music ensembles, musical theater, opera, symphony orchestra, fraternities, sororities.

ATHLETICS. NCAA. **Intercollegiate:** Baseball M, basketball, cross-country, golf, soccer, tennis, volleyball W. **Intramural:** Archery, basketball, bowling, diving M, golf, racquetball M, soccer M, softball, swimming, table tennis, tennis, track and field. **Clubs:** Lacrosse, soccer, cross-country, fencing, softball W, volleyball M.

STUDENT SERVICES. Aptitude testing, career counseling, employment service for undergraduates, freshman orientation, health services, personal counseling, placement service for graduates, services/facilities for handicapped.

ANNUAL EXPENSES. Tuition and fees (1992-93): $10,300. **Room and board:** $4,257. **Books and supplies:** $500. **Other expenses:** $770.

FINANCIAL AID. 68% of freshmen, 68% of continuing students receive some form of aid. 70% of grants, 98% of loans, 79% of jobs based on need. 187 enrolled freshmen were judged to have need, all were offered aid. Academic, music/drama, art, minority scholarships available. **Aid applications:** Closing date March 15; applicants notified on a rolling basis; must reply by May 1 or within 10 days if notified thereafter.

ADDRESS/TELEPHONE. John W. Lind, VP Enrollment Management, Southwestern University, University at Maple, Georgetown, TX 78626. (512) 863-1200. (800) 252-3166. Fax: (512) 863-5788.

Stephen F. Austin State University

Nacogdoches, Texas — CB code: 6682

4-year public university, coed. Founded in 1923. **Accreditation:** Regional. **Undergraduate enrollment:** 4,543 men, 5,528 women full time; 569 men, 655 women part time. **Graduate enrollment:** 403 men, 495 women full time; 268 men, 260 women part time. **Faculty:** 710 total (450 full time), 450 with doctorates or other terminal degrees. **Location:** Rural campus in large town; 140 miles from Houston, and 60 miles from Longview. **Calendar:** Semester, extensive summer session. **Microcomputers:** 515 located in dormitories, libraries, classrooms, computer centers. **Special facilities:** Computerized observatory, experimental forest, art gallery.

DEGREES OFFERED. BA, BS, BFA, MA, MS, MBA, MFA, MEd, D. 2,032 bachelor's degrees awarded in 1992. 13% in business and management, 8% business/office and marketing/distribution, 9% communications, 6% education, 20% teacher education, 5% life sciences, 13% social sciences. Graduate degrees offered in 33 major fields of study.

UNDERGRADUATE MAJORS. Accounting, agribusiness, agricultural economics, agricultural sciences, agronomy, animal sciences, biology, business administration and management, business and management, business and office, business computer/console/peripheral equipment operation, business data programming, business economics, chemistry, clinical laboratory science, communications, computer and information sciences, criminal justice studies, dramatic arts, education of the deaf and hearing impaired, education of the mentally handicapped, education of the visually handicapped, English, environmental science, family/consumer resource management, fashion merchandising, finance, fine arts, food science and nutrition, food sciences, forest products processing technology, forestry and related sciences, forestry production and processing, French, geography, geology, gerontology, history, home economics, horticultural science, horticulture, human environment and housing, humanities, individual and family development, interior design, journalism, marketing and distribution, marketing management, mathematics, music, nursing, office supervision and management, parks and recreation management, physics, political science and government, predentistry, premedicine, prepharmacy, preveterinary, psychology, public administration, radio/television broadcasting, radio/television technology, range management, rehabilitation counseling/services, secretarial and related programs, social foundations, social work, sociology, Spanish, special education, specific learning disabilities, speech correction, speech pathology/audiology, wildlife management.

ACADEMIC PROGRAMS. Accelerated program, double major, dual enrollment of high school students, internships, teacher preparation; liberal arts/career combination in forestry. **Remedial services:** Learning center, preadmission summer program, reduced course load, remedial instruction, special counselor, tutoring, writing skills laboratory. **ROTC:** Army. **Placement/credit:** AP, IB, institutional tests; 32 credit hours maximum for bachelor's degree.

ACADEMIC REQUIREMENTS. Freshmen must earn minimum GPA of 1.5 to continue in good standing. 70% of freshmen return for sophomore year. Students must declare major by end of second year. **Graduation requirements:** 130 hours for bachelor's (36 in major). Most students required to take courses in arts/fine arts, English, history, mathematics, biological/physical sciences, social sciences.

FRESHMAN ADMISSIONS. Selection criteria: Student must be in top half of high school graduating class or have combined SAT score of 900 or composite ACT score of 21. Recommended units include biological science 1, English 4, foreign language 2, mathematics 4, social science 2 and science 3. **Test requirements:** SAT or ACT; score report by August 30.

1992 FRESHMAN CLASS PROFILE. 912 men, 1,257 women enrolled. 90% had high school GPA of 3.0 or higher, 10% between 2.0 and 2.99. 5% were in top tenth and 20% were in top quarter of graduating class. **Academic background:** Mid 50% of enrolled freshmen had SAT-V between 380-490, SAT-M between 390-510; ACT composite between 16-23. 72% submitted SAT scores, 27% submitted ACT scores. **Characteristics:** 99% from in state, 85% live in college housing, 12% have minority backgrounds, 11% join fraternities/sororities. Average age is 18.

FALL-TERM APPLICATIONS. No fee. No closing date; priority given to applications received by April 1; applicants notified on a rolling basis. CRDA. Deferred and early admission available.

STUDENT LIFE. Housing: Dormitories (men, women, coed); apartment, fraternity, sorority housing available. Students must live in college housing until they complete 60 semester hours. **Activities:** Student government, radio, student newspaper, television, yearbook, choral groups, concert band, dance, drama, jazz band, marching band, music ensembles, musical theater, opera, pep band, symphony orchestra, fraternities, sororities.

ATHLETICS. NCAA. **Intercollegiate:** Baseball M, basketball, cross-country, football M, golf M, softball W, track and field, volleyball W. **Intramural:** Basketball, handball, lacrosse M, racquetball, rugby M, soccer, softball, swimming, tennis, track and field, volleyball.

STUDENT SERVICES. Aptitude testing, career counseling, employment service for undergraduates, freshman orientation, health services, on-campus day care, personal counseling, placement service for graduates, special adviser for adult students, veterans counselor, services/facilities for handicapped.

ANNUAL EXPENSES. Tuition and fees: $1,450, $4,080 additional for out-of-state students. **Room and board:** $3,768. **Books and supplies:** $500. **Other expenses:** $900.

FINANCIAL AID. 45% of freshmen, 60% of continuing students receive some form of aid. 73% of grants, 77% of loans, all jobs based on need. Academic, music/drama, athletic scholarships available. **Aid applications:** Closing date June 1; priority given to applications received by April 1; applicants notified on a rolling basis beginning on or about August 1; must reply within 10 days.

ADDRESS/TELEPHONE. Judd Staples, Director of Admissions, Stephen F. Austin State University, PO Box 13051, SFA Station, Nacogdoches, TX. (409) 568-2504. Fax: (409) 568-3849.

Sul Ross State University
Alpine, Texas — CB code: 6685

4-year public university, coed. Founded in 1917. **Accreditation:** Regional. **Undergraduate enrollment:** 740 men, 702 women full time; 138 men, 283 women part time. **Graduate enrollment:** 93 men, 75 women full time; 291 men, 384 women part time. **Faculty:** 165 total (101 full time), 96 with doctorates or other terminal degrees. **Location:** Rural campus in small town; 140 miles from Odessa. **Calendar:** Semester, limited summer session. **Microcomputers:** 150 located in libraries, classrooms, computer centers. **Special facilities:** Museum of the Big Bend, Range Animal Science Ranch, observatory, Chihuahuauan Desert Research Center. **Additional facts:** Off-campus upper-level and graduate programs available in Del Rio, Eagle Pass, and Uvalde.

DEGREES OFFERED. AAS, BA, BS, BFA, MA, MS, MBA, MEd. 5 associate degrees awarded in 1992. 100% in agriculture. 195 bachelor's degrees awarded. 15% in agriculture, 11% business and management, 33% teacher education, 5% life sciences, 10% parks/recreation, protective services, public affairs, 8% psychology. Graduate degrees offered in 25 major fields of study.

UNDERGRADUATE MAJORS. Associate: Agricultural products and processing, animal health technology, practical nursing. **Bachelor's:** Accounting, agribusiness, agricultural business and management, animal health management, animal sciences, art education, biology, business administration and management, business and management, business education, chemistry, communications, criminal justice studies, dramatic arts, elementary education, English, equestrian science, finance, fine arts, geology, history, industrial arts education, marketing and distribution, mathematics, music, music education, physical education, political science and government, psychology, range management, science education, secretarial and related programs, social sciences, Spanish, studio art, wildlife management.

ACADEMIC PROGRAMS. Dual enrollment of high school students, independent study, internships, teacher preparation. **Remedial services:** Reduced course load, remedial instruction, special counselor, tutoring. **Placement/credit:** AP, CLEP General and Subject, institutional tests; 30 credit hours maximum for bachelor's degree.

ACADEMIC REQUIREMENTS. Freshmen must earn minimum GPA of 2.0 to continue in good standing. 41% of freshmen return for sophomore year. Students must declare major by end of second year. **Graduation requirements:** 70 hours for associate (49 in major), 130 hours for bachelor's (44 in major). Most students required to take courses in arts/fine arts, computer science, English, history, humanities, mathematics, biological/physical sciences, social sciences.

FRESHMAN ADMISSIONS. Selection criteria: Open admissions. Students must meet one of following criteria: ACT score of 20 or SAT score of 800, rank in top half of graduating class; 50% probability of earning 2.0 GPA. Probational admission for all other applicants. **High school preparation:** 21 units required. Required units include English 4, mathematics 3, social science 3 and science 2. One algebra required. **Test requirements:** SAT or ACT; score report by August 24.

1992 FRESHMAN CLASS PROFILE. 159 men, 134 women enrolled. 3% were in top tenth and 18% were in top quarter of graduating class. **Academic background:** Mid 50% of enrolled freshmen had SAT-V between 280-380, SAT-M between 330-440; ACT composite between 14-19. 41% submitted SAT scores, 59% submitted ACT scores. **Characteristics:** 97% from in state, 86% live in college housing, 52% have minority backgrounds. Average age is 20.

FALL-TERM APPLICATIONS. No fee. No closing date; applicants notified on a rolling basis. Deferred and early admission available.

STUDENT LIFE. Housing: Dormitories (men, women, coed); apartment housing available. **Activities:** Student government, magazine, radio, student newspaper, yearbook, choral groups, concert band, drama, jazz band, music ensembles, musical theater, pep band, symphony orchestra, Wesley Foundation, Newman Club, Baptist Student Union, Fellowship of Christian Athletes, Spanish club, black and international student associations.

ATHLETICS. NAIA. **Intercollegiate:** Baseball M, basketball, football M, tennis, track and field, volleyball W. **Intramural:** Basketball, softball, volleyball.

STUDENT SERVICES. Aptitude testing, career counseling, employment service for undergraduates, freshman orientation, health services, personal counseling, placement service for graduates, veterans counselor, services/facilities for handicapped.

ANNUAL EXPENSES. Tuition and fees: $1,461, $4,080 additional for out-of-state students. **Room and board:** $2,990. **Books and supplies:** $650. **Other expenses:** $1,150.

FINANCIAL AID. 60% of continuing students receive some form of aid. All loans, 50% of jobs based on need. Academic, music/drama, leadership, alumni affiliation scholarships available. **Aid applications:** No closing date; priority given to applications received by April 1; applicants notified on a rolling basis beginning on or about May 1; must reply within 2 weeks.

ADDRESS/TELEPHONE. Dorothy M. Leavitt, Director of Admissions and Records, Sul Ross State University, PO Box C-2, Alpine, TX 79832. (915) 837-8052. Fax: (915) 837-8046.

Tarleton State University
Stephenville, Texas — CB code: 6817

Admissions: 78% of applicants accepted
Based on: ••• School record
•• Test scores
Completion: 28% graduate

4-year public university, coed. Founded in 1899. **Accreditation:** Regional. **Undergraduate enrollment:** 2,521 men, 2,339 women full time; 305 men, 435 women part time. **Graduate enrollment:** 112 men, 101 women full time; 224 men, 388 women part time. **Faculty:** 223 total (221 full time), 136 with doctorates or other terminal degrees. **Location:** Rural campus in large town; 65 miles from Fort Worth. **Calendar:** Semester, extensive summer session. Extensive evening/early morning classes. **Microcomputers:** 400 located in libraries, computer centers. **Special facilities:** University farm and equine center.

DEGREES OFFERED. BA, BS, BFA, MA, MS, MBA, MEd. 65 associate degrees awarded in 1992. 100% in health sciences. 875 bachelor's degrees awarded. Graduate degrees offered in 14 major fields of study.

UNDERGRADUATE MAJORS. Associate: Nursing, practical nursing. **Bachelor's:** Accounting, agribusiness, agricultural economics, agricultural education, agricultural mechanics, agricultural sciences, animal sciences, biology, business administration and management, business and management, business and office, business education, chemistry, communications, computer and information sciences, criminal justice studies, economics, education, elementary education, English, equestrian science, fashion merchandising, finance, geology, history, home economics, home economics education, horticultural science, human resources development, hydrology, industrial technology, law enforcement and corrections, marketing and distribution, marketing management, mathematics, medical laboratory technologies, music, office supervision and management, personnel management, physical education, physics, plant sciences, political science and government, predentistry, preengineering, prelaw, premedicine, prepharmacy, preveterinary, range management, social work, sociology, soil sciences, Spanish, speech, water and wastewater technology.

ACADEMIC PROGRAMS. Accelerated program, double major, dual enrollment of high school students, honors program, telecourses, specialized bachelor of applied arts and science degree for students with practical work experience in field of study. **Remedial services:** Learning center, preadmission summer program, reduced course load, remedial instruction, special counselor, tutoring. **ROTC:** Army. **Placement/credit:** AP, CLEP Subject, institutional tests.

ACADEMIC REQUIREMENTS. Freshmen must earn minimum GPA of 1.75 to continue in good standing. 56% of freshmen return for sophomore year. Students must declare major by end of second year. **Graduation requirements:** 82 hours for associate, 128 hours for bachelor's. Most students required to take courses in arts/fine arts, computer science, English, history, humanities, mathematics, biological/physical sciences, social sciences. **Postgraduate studies:** 35% from 2-year programs enter 4-year programs.

FRESHMAN ADMISSIONS. Recommended units include English 4 and mathematics 3. **Test requirements:** SAT or ACT; score report by August 1.

1992 FRESHMAN CLASS PROFILE. 832 men applied, 654 accepted, 535 enrolled; 702 women applied, 538 accepted, 462 enrolled. 28% were in top quarter of graduating class. **Academic background:** Mid 50% of enrolled freshmen had SAT-V between 340-430, SAT-M between 380-500; ACT composite between 18-21. 61% submitted SAT scores, 52% submitted ACT scores. **Characteristics:** 99% from in state, 62% live in college housing, 3% have minority backgrounds, 1% are foreign students, 7% join fraternities/sororities. Average age is 19.

FALL-TERM APPLICATIONS. $20 fee, may be waived for applicants with need. Closing date August 3; applicants notified on a rolling basis beginning on or about March 1. Deferred and early admission available.

STUDENT LIFE. Housing: Dormitories (men, women, coed); fraternity housing available. **Activities:** Student government, student newspaper, yearbook, choral groups, concert band, drama, jazz band, marching band, music ensembles, musical theater, fraternities, sororities, Los Tejanos, Chinese Student Association, Progressive United Black Student Organization, Student Social Work Association, Alpha Phi Omega, Gamma Sigma Sigma, Circle K, Fellowship of Christian Athletes, Fellowship of Christian Cowboys, College Republicans, Young Democrats.

ATHLETICS. NAIA. **Intercollegiate:** Baseball M, basketball, football M, golf, tennis, track and field, volleyball W. **Intramural:** Basketball, cross-country, football, golf, racquetball, rifle, softball, tennis, volleyball.

STUDENT SERVICES. Aptitude testing, career counseling, employment service for undergraduates, freshman orientation, health services, on-campus day care, personal counseling, placement service for graduates, veterans counselor, services/facilities for handicapped.

ANNUAL EXPENSES. Tuition and fees: $1,478, $4,080 additional for out-of-state students. **Room and board:** $3,100. **Books and supplies:** $425. **Other expenses:** $1,266.

FINANCIAL AID. 20% of freshmen, 45% of continuing students receive some form of aid. Grants, loans, jobs available. Academic, music/drama, leadership, minority scholarships available. **Aid applications:** No closing date; priority given to applications received by June 1; applicants notified on a rolling basis.

ADDRESS/TELEPHONE. Gail Mayfield, Director of Admissions, Tarleton State University, PO Box T-2003 Tarleton Station, Stephenville, TX 76402. (817) 968-9125. Fax: (817) 968-9389.

Tarrant County Junior College
Fort Worth, Texas CB code: 6834

2-year public community college, coed. Founded in 1965. **Accreditation:** Regional. **Undergraduate enrollment:** 3,748 men, 4,241 women full time; 9,183 men, 12,031 women part time. **Faculty:** 1,019 total (429 full time), 146 with doctorates or other terminal degrees. **Location:** Urban campus in large city. **Calendar:** Semester, extensive summer session. **Microcomputers:** 700 located in libraries, classrooms, computer centers. **Additional facts:** Multicampus institution.

DEGREES OFFERED. AA, AAS. 1,397 associate degrees awarded in 1992.

UNDERGRADUATE MAJORS. Accounting, aeronautical technology, air conditioning/heating/refrigeration mechanics, aircraft mechanics, architectural technologies, automotive mechanics, automotive technology, business and management, business and office, child development/care/guidance, civil technology, construction, data processing, dental hygiene, drafting and design technology, educational media technology, electromechanical technology, electronic technology, emergency medical technologies, engineering and engineering-related technologies, fashion merchandising, fire control and safety technology, food production/management/services, graphic and printing production, horticultural science, interpreter for the deaf, law enforcement and corrections technologies, legal assistant/paralegal, liberal/general studies, marketing and distribution, medical laboratory technologies, medical records technology, mental health/human services, nursing, physical therapy assistant, precision metal work, quality control technology, radiograph medical technology, real estate, respiratory therapy technology, small business management and ownership, trade and industrial supervision and management, welding technology.

ACADEMIC PROGRAMS. 2-year transfer program, dual enrollment of high school students, honors program, telecourses. **Remedial services:** Learning center, preadmission summer program, reduced course load, remedial instruction, special counselor, tutoring. **ROTC:** Army. **Placement/credit:** AP, CLEP General and Subject, institutional tests; 18 credit hours maximum for associate degree.

ACADEMIC REQUIREMENTS. Freshmen must earn minimum GPA of 2.0 to continue in good standing. Students must declare major on enrollment. **Graduation requirements:** 64 hours for associate. Most students required to take courses in English, mathematics, biological/physical sciences. **Additional information:** Major can be changed at any time.

FRESHMAN ADMISSIONS. Selection criteria: Open admissions. Applicants to nursing and allied health programs must submit separate application.

1992 FRESHMAN CLASS PROFILE. 2,222 men, 2,754 women enrolled. **Characteristics:** 99% from in state, 100% commute, 22% have minority backgrounds.

FALL-TERM APPLICATIONS. $10 fee. No closing date; applicants notified on a rolling basis. Early admission available. Applicants 18 years of age or older not having high school diploma may be admitted on individual basis.

STUDENT LIFE. Activities: Student government, student newspaper, choral groups, dance, drama, music ensembles.

ATHLETICS. Intramural: Basketball M, table tennis.

STUDENT SERVICES. Aptitude testing, career counseling, employment service for undergraduates, health services, personal counseling, placement service for graduates, veterans counselor, services/facilities for handicapped.

ANNUAL EXPENSES. Tuition and fees (1992-93): $450, $240 additional for out-of-district students, $3,180 additional for out-of-state students. **Books and supplies:** $540. **Other expenses:** $1,218.

FINANCIAL AID. 10% of freshmen, 10% of continuing students receive some form of aid. 98% of grants, 87% of loans, 44% of jobs based on need. Academic, music/drama scholarships available. **Aid applications:** No closing date; priority given to applications received by April 15; applicants notified on a rolling basis beginning on or about June 1; must reply within 2 weeks.

ADDRESS/TELEPHONE. Cathie Jackson, Director Admissions and Records, Tarrant County Junior College, 1500 Houston Street, Fort Worth, TX 76102-6599. (817) 336-7851.

Temple Junior College
Temple, Texas CB code: 6818

2-year public community college, coed. Founded in 1926. **Accreditation:** Regional. **Undergraduate enrollment:** 431 men, 595 women full time; 290 men, 532 women part time. **Faculty:** 123 total (77 full time), 16 with doctorates or other terminal degrees. **Location:** Urban campus in large town; 65 miles from Austin. **Calendar:** Semester, limited summer session. **Microcomputers:** 14 located on campus.

DEGREES OFFERED. AA, AAS. 132 associate degrees awarded in 1992.

UNDERGRADUATE MAJORS. Automotive mechanics, automotive technology, business and management, business and office, business data processing and related programs, business data programming, computer programming, data processing, drafting, drafting and design technology, electronic technology, fashion merchandising, fire control and safety technology, law enforcement and corrections technologies, liberal/general studies, marketing and distribution, medical laboratory technologies, medical secretary, real estate, respiratory therapy technology, secretarial and related programs.

ACADEMIC PROGRAMS. 2-year transfer program, dual enrollment of high school students. **Remedial services:** Learning center, tutoring, developmental studies. **Placement/credit:** AP, CLEP Subject, institutional tests; 24 credit hours maximum for associate degree.

ACADEMIC REQUIREMENTS. Freshmen must earn minimum GPA of 2.0 to continue in good standing. 75% of freshmen return for sophomore year. Students must declare major on application. **Graduation requirements:** 64 hours for associate. Most students required to take courses in English, history, humanities, mathematics, biological/physical sciences, social sciences. **Additional information:** Students must pass TASP (Texas Academic Skills Program) test before earning more than 15 semester hours. Students demonstrating successful completion of at least 3 semester hours of credit prior to start of fall semester may be excluded from TASP requirements.

FRESHMAN ADMISSIONS. Selection criteria: Open admissions.

Limited enrollment in allied health programs; interview required. **Additional information:** All students must take Texas Academic Skills Test.

1992 FRESHMAN CLASS PROFILE. 1,114 men and women enrolled. **Characteristics:** 98% from in state, 97% commute, 21% have minority backgrounds. Average age is 26.

FALL-TERM APPLICATIONS. No fee. Closing date September 1; applicants notified on a rolling basis beginning on or about June 1. Interview required for allied health applicants. Early admission available.

STUDENT LIFE. Housing: Dormitories (coed). **Activities:** Student government, student newspaper, choral groups, concert band, drama, jazz band, music ensembles, musical theater, Baptist Student Union, United Methodist Student Fellowship, Pentecostal Student Fellowship, Church of Christ Student Fellowship, Newman Club, Circle-K, Black American Cultural Club.

ATHLETICS. NJCAA. **Intercollegiate:** Basketball, golf M, tennis. **Intramural:** Baseball, basketball M, golf, racquetball, softball W, swimming, tennis.

STUDENT SERVICES. Aptitude testing, career counseling, employment service for undergraduates, freshman orientation, personal counseling, placement service for graduates, veterans counselor, services/facilities for handicapped.

ANNUAL EXPENSES. Tuition and fees: $720, $390 additional for out-of-district students, $1,410 additional for out-of-state students. **Room and board:** $3,500. **Books and supplies:** $520. **Other expenses:** $1,061.

FINANCIAL AID. 52% of freshmen, 52% of continuing students receive some form of aid. 71% of grants, 95% of loans, 46% of jobs based on need. Academic, music/drama, athletic, leadership scholarships available. **Aid applications:** No closing date; priority given to applications received by August 1; applicants notified on a rolling basis beginning on or about May 1; must reply by May 1 or within 2 weeks if notified thereafter.

ADDRESS/TELEPHONE. A. C. Hervey, Director of Admission and Records, Temple Junior College, 2600 South First Street, Temple, TX 76504-7435. (817) 773-9961. Fax: (817) 773-7841.

Texarkana College
Texarkana, Texas CB code: 6819

2-year public community college, coed. Founded in 1927. **Accreditation:** Regional. **Undergraduate enrollment:** 666 men, 982 women full time; 888 men, 1,591 women part time. **Faculty:** 212 total (128 full time), 6 with doctorates or other terminal degrees. **Location:** Urban campus in small city; 80 miles from Shreveport, Louisiana, 180 miles from Dallas, 130 miles from Little Rock, Arkansas on Texas/Arkansas border. **Calendar:** Semester, limited summer session. **Microcomputers:** Located in computer centers. **Special facilities:** 365-acre farm.

DEGREES OFFERED. AA, AS, AAS. 240 associate degrees awarded in 1992. 10% in business and management, 10% business/office and marketing/distribution, 5% communications, 5% computer sciences, 25% allied health, 20% letters/literature, 5% mathematics, 20% social sciences.

UNDERGRADUATE MAJORS. Agricultural business and management, biological and physical sciences, business administration and management, business and office, business data processing and related programs, emergency medical technologies, fashion merchandising, finance, humanities, humanities and social sciences, law enforcement and corrections technologies, liberal/general studies, nursing, radio/television broadcasting, real estate, science technologies, secretarial and related programs.

ACADEMIC PROGRAMS. 2-year transfer program, cooperative education, dual enrollment of high school students, internships, study abroad, cross-registration. **Remedial services:** Remedial instruction. **Placement/credit:** AP, CLEP General and Subject; 14 credit hours maximum for associate degree.

ACADEMIC REQUIREMENTS. Freshmen must earn minimum GPA of 1.5 to continue in good standing. 37% of freshmen return for sophomore year. Students must declare major by end of first year. **Graduation requirements:** 62 hours for associate (18 in major). Most students required to take courses in English, mathematics.

FRESHMAN ADMISSIONS. Selection criteria: Open admissions. **Test requirements:** SAT or ACT (ACT preferred) for placement and counseling only; score report by September 1.

1992 FRESHMAN CLASS PROFILE. 939 men, 1,444 women enrolled. 18% had high school GPA of 3.0 or higher, 68% between 2.0 and 2.99. **Characteristics:** 70% from in state, 100% commute, 13% have minority backgrounds. Average age is 18.

FALL-TERM APPLICATIONS. No fee. No closing date; applicants notified on a rolling basis. Interview recommended for nursing applicants. Deferred and early admission available.

STUDENT LIFE. Activities: Student government, magazine, radio, student newspaper, choral groups, concert band, drama, musical theater, pep band.

ATHLETICS. NJCAA. **Intercollegiate:** Baseball M, golf M. **Intramural:** Archery, badminton, basketball, bowling, handball, racquetball, sailing, skin diving, swimming, tennis, volleyball.

STUDENT SERVICES. Aptitude testing, career counseling, employment service for undergraduates, freshman orientation, personal counseling, veterans counselor, services/facilities for handicapped.

ANNUAL EXPENSES. Tuition and fees (1992-93): $690, $150 additional for out-of-district students, $440 additional for out-of-state students. Arkansas residents pay tuition and fees of out-of-district student (additional $150). **Books and supplies:** $650. **Other expenses:** $1,200.

FINANCIAL AID. 10% of continuing students receive some form of aid. Grants, jobs available. **Aid applications:** Closing date July 15; priority given to applications received by June 1; applicants notified on or about August 1; must reply by August 15.

ADDRESS/TELEPHONE. Steve Middlebrooks, Director of Admissions and Registrar, Texarkana College, 2500 North Robison Road, Texarkana, TX 75599. (903) 838-4541 ext. 358. Fax: (903) 832-5030.

Texas A&I University
Kingsville, Texas CB code: 6822

4-year public university, coed. Founded in 1925. **Accreditation:** Regional. **Undergraduate enrollment:** 2,258 men, 2,114 women full time; 385 men, 545 women part time. **Graduate enrollment:** 189 men, 162 women full time; 343 men, 418 women part time. **Faculty:** 258 total (206 full time). **Location:** Rural campus in large town; 40 miles from Corpus Christi, 250 miles from Houston, 150 miles from San Antonio. **Calendar:** Semester, extensive summer session. Saturday classes. **Microcomputers:** 85 located in libraries, classrooms, computer centers. **Special facilities:** Connor Museum of South Texas (history, anthropology, archaeology), Kleberg Research Institute (South Texas biology, botany, and wildlife research), equine facilities, observatory, college-operated farms, research center for citrus in Weslaco, art gallery.

DEGREES OFFERED. BA, BS, BFA, MA, MS, MBA, MFA, MEd, EdD. 693 bachelor's degrees awarded in 1992. 10% in agriculture, 25% business and management, 15% teacher education, 25% engineering, 5% mathematics, 5% physical sciences, 15% social sciences. Graduate degrees offered in 48 major fields of study.

UNDERGRADUATE MAJORS. Accounting, agribusiness, agricultural education, animal sciences, art education, bilingual/bicultural education, biology, business and management, chemical engineering, chemistry, civil engineering, communications, computer and information sciences, computer engineering, electrical/electronics/communications engineering, elementary education, engineering management, English, English education, finance, fine arts, food science and nutrition, geography, geology, health education, history, home economics, home economics education, human environment and housing, individual and family development, industrial arts education, industrial engineering, industrial technology, interior design, journalism, junior high education, management science, marketing management, mathematics, mathematics education, mechanical engineering, music, music education, natural gas engineering, ornamental horticulture, petroleum engineering, physical education, physics, plant sciences, political science and government, predentistry, prelaw, premedicine, prepharmacy, preveterinary, psychology, public administration, range management, real estate, secondary education, sociology, soil sciences, Spanish, speech/communication/theater education, textiles and clothing, visual and performing arts, wildlife management.

ACADEMIC PROGRAMS. Accelerated program, cooperative education, double major, dual enrollment of high school students, education specialist degree, independent study, internships, study abroad, teacher preparation. **Remedial services:** Learning center, reduced course load, remedial instruction, special counselor, tutoring. **ROTC:** Army. **Placement/credit:** AP, CLEP General and Subject, institutional tests.

ACADEMIC REQUIREMENTS. Freshmen must earn minimum GPA of 2.0 to continue in good standing. 60% of freshmen return for sophomore year. Students must declare major by end of second year. **Graduation requirements:** 124 hours for bachelor's. Most students required to take courses in arts/fine arts, English, history, mathematics, biological/physical sciences, social sciences.

FRESHMAN ADMISSIONS. Selection criteria: Open admissions. **High school preparation:** 16 units required. Required and recommended units include English 4, mathematics 2-3, social science 2-3 and science 2-3. Foreign language or 2 natural science also required. **Test requirements:** SAT or ACT; score report by August 15. **Additional information:** Unconditional admission for applicants in top quarter of graduating class. Those in lower three-fourths with ACT score of 21 or SAT score of 850, admission unconditional; conditional admission for those with lower test scores.

1992 FRESHMAN CLASS PROFILE. 1,510 men, 702 women enrolled. **Characteristics:** 95% from in state, 70% commute, 55% have minority backgrounds, 1% are foreign students, 5% join fraternities/sororities. Average age is 20.

FALL-TERM APPLICATIONS. No fee. No closing date; applicants notified on a rolling basis. Audition required for music applicants. Interview recommended. Deferred admission available.

STUDENT LIFE. Housing: Dormitories (men, women, coed); apartment, fraternity housing available. **Activities:** Student government, radio, student newspaper, yearbook, choral groups, concert band, dance, drama, jazz band, marching band, music ensembles, musical theater, Mariachi-Javelina (Spanish band), fraternities, sororities.

ATHLETICS. NCAA. **Intercollegiate:** Basketball, cross-country, football M, tennis, volleyball W. **Intramural:** Bowling, golf, horseback riding, racquetball, softball, volleyball.

STUDENT SERVICES. Aptitude testing, career counseling, employment service for undergraduates, freshman orientation, health services, on-campus day care, personal counseling, placement service for graduates, special adviser for adult students, veterans counselor, services/facilities for handicapped.

ANNUAL EXPENSES. Tuition and fees: $1,514, $4,080 additional for out-of-state students. **Room and board:** $2,816. **Books and supplies:** $484. **Other expenses:** $1,714.

FINANCIAL AID. 85% of freshmen, 60% of continuing students receive some form of aid. Grants, loans, jobs available. Academic, music/drama, art, athletic, leadership scholarships available. **Aid applications:** Closing date April 15; must reply within 2 weeks.

ADDRESS/TELEPHONE. Ruth Fletcher, Director of Admissions and Registrar, Texas A&I University, Campus Box 116, Kingsville, TX 78363-8201. (512) 595-3907. Fax: (512) 595-3108.

Texas A&M University
College Station, Texas CB code: 6003

Admissions: 71% of applicants accepted
Based on: ••• School record, test scores
•• Activities, special talents
• Essay, recommendations
Completion: 86% of freshmen end year in good standing
57% graduate, 6% of these enter graduate study

4-year public university, coed. Founded in 1876. **Accreditation:** Regional. **Undergraduate enrollment:** 17,291 men, 13,638 women full time; 1,546 men, 1,004 women part time. **Graduate enrollment:** 4,305 men, 1,937 women full time; 1,108 men, 881 women part time. **Faculty:** 2,426 total (2,004 full time), 2,117 with doctorates or other terminal degrees. **Location:** Suburban campus in small city; 100 miles from Houston. **Calendar:** Semester, extensive summer session. **Microcomputers:** 3,000 located in dormitories, libraries, classrooms, computer centers, campus-wide network. **Special facilities:** Reactor, cyclotron, observatory, extensive university farm property, art display areas, extensive theater facilities, 18-hole golf course, supercomputer center, oceanographic research vessel, Japanese campus, Italian study center. **Additional facts:** University operates the Santa Chiara Study Center in Castiglion, Fiorentino, Italy. Both Japanese and U. S. students are enrolled at Texas A + M University-Koriyama, Japan.

DEGREES OFFERED. BA, BS, MA, MS, MBA, MEd, PhD, EdD, MD, DVM. 6,896 bachelor's degrees awarded in 1992. 10% in agriculture, 6% architecture and environmental design, 21% business and management, 5% communications, 9% education, 17% engineering, 5% psychology, 9% social sciences. Graduate degrees offered in 101 major fields of study.

UNDERGRADUATE MAJORS. Accounting, adult and continuing education administration, aerospace/aeronautical/astronautical engineering, agribusiness, agricultural business and management, agricultural development, agricultural economics, agricultural education, agricultural engineering, agricultural journalism, agricultural mechanics, agricultural sciences, agronomy, animal sciences, anthropology, applied mathematics, atmospheric sciences and meteorology, basic clinical health sciences, biochemistry, bioengineering and biomedical engineering, biology, biomedical science, botany, business administration and management, business systems analysis, chemical engineering, chemistry, civil engineering, computer and information sciences, computer engineering, construction management, dairy, dramatic arts, earth sciences, economics, electrical/electronics/communications engineering, engineering and engineering-related technologies, engineering and other disciplines, English, entomology, environmental design, environmental science, finance, food science and nutrition, food sciences, foreign languages (multiple emphasis), forestry and related sciences, genetics, human and animal, geography, geology, geophysics and seismology, health education, history, horticultural science, industrial engineering, journalism, landscape architecture, marketing and distribution, marketing management, mathematics, mechanical engineering, microbiology, multi/interdisciplinary studies, nuclear engineering, ocean engineering, operations research, ornamental horticulture, parks and recreation management, petroleum engineering, philosophy, physical education, physics, plant sciences, political science and government, poultry, psychology, radiological health engineering, range management, sociology, soil sciences, speech, technical education, wildlife management, zoology.

ACADEMIC PROGRAMS. Cooperative education, double major, dual enrollment of high school students, honors program, independent study, internships, semester at sea, study abroad, teacher preparation, visiting/exchange student program, cross-registration, exchange program in architecture with Instituto Tecnologico y de Estudios Superiores de Monterrey, exchange programs with Kings College-London, University of Lancaster (England), Denmark's International Study Program; combined bachelor's/graduate program in business administration, medicine. **Remedial services:** Learning center, reduced course load, remedial instruction, tutoring, reading and writing laboratories. **ROTC:** Air Force, Army, Naval. **Placement/credit:** AP, CLEP Subject, IB, institutional tests.

ACADEMIC REQUIREMENTS. Freshmen must earn minimum GPA of 2.0 to continue in good standing. 83% of freshmen return for sophomore year. Students must declare major by end of second year. **Graduation requirements:** 128 hours for bachelor's (30 in major). Most students required to take courses in computer science, English, foreign languages, history, humanities, mathematics, biological/physical sciences, social sciences. **Postgraduate studies:** 3% enter law school, 3% enter medical school. **Additional information:** Core curriculum requirements in foreign language and computer science may be satified by selected high school courses.

FRESHMAN ADMISSIONS. Selection criteria: Texas applicants who apply by February 1 and are in top quarter of class and have SAT combined score of 1000 or ACT score of 24; in second quarter, 1100 or 27; in third quarter, 1200 or 29; in fourth quarter, 1200 or 29 are admitted, as are out-of-state applicants who must have SAT combined score of 1100 or ACT composite score of 27 and rank in top quarter of class. Applicants with SAT 800 or ACT 19 for top quarter of class, 950 or 22 for second quarter, and 1100 or 27 for bottom half are reviewed for admission in March. **High school preparation:** 16 units required. Required units include English 4, mathematics 3.5, social science 2.5 and science 2. Applicants with 3 mathematics are reviewed. 1 computer science and 2 units of same foriegn language recommended. **Test requirements:** SAT or ACT; score report by March 1. **Additional information:** 3 types of admission: priority based on academic credentials and test score; regular based on academics, activities, and leadership experience; and limited summer provisional admission.

1992 FRESHMAN CLASS PROFILE. 7,784 men applied, 5,385 accepted, 3,120 enrolled; 6,577 women applied, 4,766 accepted, 2,886 enrolled. 49% were in top tenth and 85% were in top quarter of graduating class. **Academic background:** Mid 50% of enrolled freshmen had SAT-V between 430-540, SAT-M between 520-640; ACT composite between 22-27. 93% submitted SAT scores, 46% submitted ACT scores. **Characteristics:** 90% from in state, 80% live in college housing, 18% have minority backgrounds, 1% are foreign students, 10% join fraternities/sororities. Average age is 18.

FALL-TERM APPLICATIONS. $25 fee, may be waived for applicants with need. Closing date March 1; priority given to applications received by February 1; applicants notified on or about April 1; must reply by May 1. Early admission available. Institutional early decision plan.

STUDENT LIFE. Housing: Dormitories (men, women, coed); apartment, fraternity, sorority housing available. Campus housing guaranteed to members of Corps of Cadets and holders of certain competitive academic scholarships. **Activities:** Student government, film, magazine, radio, student newspaper, television, yearbook, choral groups, concert band, dance, drama, jazz band, marching band, music ensembles, musical theater, symphony orchestra, fraternities, sororities, Black Awareness Committee, Committee for the Awareness of Mexican American Culture, Student Y Association, Student Conference on National Affairs, social service organizations. **Additional information:** Student leadership opportunities on campus exceptionally numerous.

ATHLETICS. NCAA. **Intercollegiate:** Baseball M, basketball, cross-country, football M, golf, rifle, soccer W, softball W, swimming, tennis, track and field, volleyball W. **Intramural:** Archery, badminton, basketball, bowling, boxing M, cross-country, fencing, field hockey W, golf, gymnastics, handball, lacrosse, racquetball, rugby, sailing, soccer, softball, swimming, table tennis, tennis, track and field, volleyball, water polo, wrestling M. **Clubs:** Rodeo, polo.

STUDENT SERVICES. Aptitude testing, career counseling, employment service for undergraduates, freshman orientation, health services, personal counseling, placement service for graduates, veterans counselor, legal counseling, services/facilities for handicapped.

ANNUAL EXPENSES. Tuition and fees: $1,526, $4,080 additional for out-of-state students. **Room and board:** $4,062. **Books and supplies:** $560. **Other expenses:** $1,224.

FINANCIAL AID. 47% of freshmen, 59% of continuing students receive some form of aid. 53% of grants, 81% of loans, 2% of jobs based on need. 1,655 enrolled freshmen were judged to have need, 1,545 were offered aid. Academic, state/district residency, leadership, minority scholarships available. **Aid applications:** No closing date; priority given to applications received by April 15; applicants notified on a rolling basis beginning on or about April 15; must reply within 2 weeks. **Additional information:** Short-term loans available. Out-of-state students awarded academic scholarships of $500 or more are eligible for waiver of out-of-state tuition.

ADDRESS/TELEPHONE. Gary R. Engelgaw, Exec Dir Admissions/Records, Texas A&M University, College Station, TX 77843-0100. (409) 845-1031. Fax: (409) 845-0727.

Texas A&M University at Galveston

Galveston, Texas CB code: 6835

Admissions: 86% of applicants accepted
Based on: ••• School record, test scores
Completion: 88% of freshmen end year in good standing
43% graduate

4-year public university, coed. Founded in 1962. **Accreditation:** Regional. **Undergraduate enrollment:** 661 men, 499 women full time; 60 men, 58 women part time. **Faculty:** 99 total (56 full time), 57 with doctorates or other terminal degrees. **Location:** Suburban campus in small city; 50 miles from Houston. **Calendar:** Semester, limited summer session. **Microcomputers:** 80 located in dormitories, libraries, classrooms, computer centers. **Special facilities:** Boat basin, extensive fleet, including Texas Clipper (534-foot training ship), Roamin' Empire and Northern Star (smaller research boats). **Additional facts:** Location near open ocean, estuarine systems, and bays facilitates marine science/biology studies.

DEGREES OFFERED. BS. 125 bachelor's degrees awarded in 1992. 29% in business and management, 13% engineering, 48% life sciences, 10% physical sciences.

UNDERGRADUATE MAJORS. Business and management, fishing and fisheries, marine biology, marine fisheries, marine transportation, maritime administration, maritime systems engineering, naval architecture and marine engineering, transportation management.

ACADEMIC PROGRAMS. Double major, dual enrollment of high school students, semester at sea. **Remedial services:** Remedial instruction, tutoring. **ROTC:** Naval. **Placement/credit:** AP, CLEP Subject, institutional tests.

ACADEMIC REQUIREMENTS. Freshmen must earn minimum GPA of 2.0 to continue in good standing. 64% of freshmen return for sophomore year. Students must declare major by end of second year. **Graduation requirements:** 141 hours for bachelor's. Most students required to take courses in computer science, English, foreign languages, history, humanities, mathematics, biological/physical sciences, social sciences. **Additional information:** Ship's officer's license may be earned through license option program.

FRESHMAN ADMISSIONS. Selection criteria: School achievement record and test scores. **High school preparation:** 16 units required. Required and recommended units include English 4, foreign language 2, mathematics 3.5-4, social science 2.5 and science 2-3. One unit computer literacy, 2 science courses must be selected from biology, chemistry, or physics. **Test requirements:** SAT or ACT; score report by September 1.

1992 FRESHMAN CLASS PROFILE. 325 men applied, 280 accepted, 156 enrolled; 299 women applied, 257 accepted, 126 enrolled. **Characteristics:** 71% from in state, 85% live in college housing, 4% have minority backgrounds, 1% are foreign students. Average age is 18.

FALL-TERM APPLICATIONS. $25 fee. Closing date September 1; priority given to applications received by June 1; applicants notified on a rolling basis. Deferred and early admission available.

STUDENT LIFE. Housing: Dormitories (coed). **Activities:** Student government, student newspaper, yearbook, literary publication, drama, propeller club, American Society of Mechanical Engineers, caving club, student association of maritime administrators, hydrographic society.

ATHLETICS. Intercollegiate: Lacrosse M, rowing (crew), sailing. **Intramural:** Baseball, basketball, diving, lacrosse M, rowing (crew), sailing, skin diving, soccer, softball, swimming, tennis, volleyball. **Clubs:** Sailing, diving, surfing.

STUDENT SERVICES. Career counseling, employment service for undergraduates, freshman orientation, health services, personal counseling, placement service for graduates, services/facilities for handicapped.

ANNUAL EXPENSES. Tuition and fees: $1,300, $4,080 additional for out-of-state students. **Room and board:** $3,384. **Books and supplies:** $680. **Other expenses:** $800.

FINANCIAL AID. 48% of freshmen, 43% of continuing students receive some form of aid. 77% of grants, 54% of loans, 7% of jobs based on need. 152 enrolled freshmen were judged to have need, all were offered aid. Academic, leadership, minority scholarships available. **Aid applications:** No closing date; priority given to applications received by April 1; applicants notified on a rolling basis beginning on or about June 1; must reply within 2 weeks.

ADDRESS/TELEPHONE. Su-Zan Harper, Admissions and Records Officer, Texas A&M University at Galveston, PO Box 1675, Galveston, TX 77553-1675. (409) 740-4422. Fax: (409) 740-4407.

Texas Christian University

Fort Worth, Texas CB code: 6820

Admissions: 79% of applicants accepted
Based on: ••• School record
•• Activities, essay, interview, recommendations, test scores
• Special talents
Completion: 100% of freshmen end year in good standing
62% graduate, 61% of these enter graduate study

4-year private university, coed, affiliated with Christian Church (Disciples of Christ). Founded in 1873. **Accreditation:** Regional. **Undergraduate enrollment:** 2,078 men, 2,963 women full time; 266 men, 385 women part time. **Graduate enrollment:** 275 men, 220 women full time; 280 men, 261 women part time. **Faculty:** 329 total, 301 with doctorates or other terminal degrees. **Location:** Suburban campus in large city; 5 miles from downtown, 29 miles from Dallas. **Calendar:** Semester, limited summer session. **Microcomputers:** 323 located in dormitories, libraries, classrooms, computer centers, campus-wide network. **Special facilities:** Geological center for remote sensing, nuclear magnetic resonance facility, observatory, art gallery.

DEGREES OFFERED. BA, BS, BFA, MA, MS, MBA, MFA, MEd, PhD, M.Div. 1,064 bachelor's degrees awarded in 1992. 22% in business and management, 16% communications, 7% education, 5% health sciences, 6% home economics, 5% letters/literature, 8% psychology, 11% social sciences, 6% visual and performing arts. Graduate degrees offered in 32 major fields of study.

UNDERGRADUATE MAJORS. Accounting, advertising, art education, art history, astrophysics, biochemistry, biology, business administration and management, business and management, business education, chemistry, clothing and textiles management/production/services, communications, computer and information sciences, criminal justice studies, dance, dramatic arts, early childhood education, economics, education of the deaf and hearing impaired, elementary education, engineering, English, English education, environmental science, fashion design, fashion merchandising, finance, fitness promotion, food management, food science and nutrition, foreign languages education, French, geology, graphic design, health education, history, interior merchandising, journalism, Latin American studies, liberal/general studies, marketing management, mathematics, mathematics education, medical laboratory technologies, music, music education, music history and appreciation, music performance, music theory and composition, neurosciences, nursing, philosophy, physical education, physics, political science and government, psychology, radio/television broadcasting, reading education, religion, science education, secondary education, social science education, social studies education, social work, sociology, Spanish, special education, speech pathology/audiology, speech/communication/theater education, sports/recreation leadership, studio art, urban studies.

ACADEMIC PROGRAMS. Accelerated program, double major, dual enrollment of high school students, education specialist degree, honors program, independent study, internships, semester at sea, student-designed major, study abroad, teacher preparation, Washington semester; liberal arts/career combination in health sciences; combined bachelor's/graduate program in business administration. **Remedial services:** Tutoring, writing center. **ROTC:** Air Force, Army. **Placement/credit:** AP, CLEP General and Subject, IB, institutional tests.

ACADEMIC REQUIREMENTS. Freshmen must earn minimum GPA of 1.75 to continue in good standing. 76% of freshmen return for sophomore year. Students must declare major by end of second year. **Graduation requirements:** 124 hours for bachelor's (45 in major). Most students required to take courses in arts/fine arts, computer science, English, foreign languages, history, humanities, mathematics, philosophy/religion, biological/physical sciences, social sciences. **Postgraduate studies:** 17% enter law school, 17% enter medical school, 11% enter MBA programs, 16% enter other graduate study. **Additional information:** Interdisciplinary studies and specialized research in chosen major honors program.

FRESHMAN ADMISSIONS. Selection criteria: School achievement record of primary importance. Test scores, school and community activities, recommendations, essay, and other supportive documents considered. **High school preparation:** 17 units recommended. Recommended units include biological science 1, English 4, foreign language 2, mathematics 3, physical science 2 and social science 3. 2 academic electives in fine arts or computer science recommended. **Test requirements:** SAT or ACT (SAT preferred); score report by March 1.

1992 FRESHMAN CLASS PROFILE. 1,599 men applied, 1,263 accepted, 516 enrolled; 2,218 women applied, 1,734 accepted, 746 enrolled. 33% were in top tenth and 61% were in top quarter of graduating class. **Academic background:** Mid 50% of enrolled freshmen had SAT-V between 420-530, SAT-M between 470-590; ACT composite between 21-27. 90% submitted SAT scores, 10% submitted ACT scores. **Characteristics:** 63% from in state, 93% live in college housing, 12% have minority backgrounds, 2% are foreign students, 41% join fraternities/sororities. Average age is 18.

FALL-TERM APPLICATIONS. $30 fee, may be waived for applicants with need. Closing date February 15; priority given to applications received by November 15; applicants notified on or about April 1; must reply by

May 1. Essay required. Interview recommended. CRDA. Deferred and early admission available. Institutional early decision plan. Early consideration deadline November 15 for January 1 notification.

STUDENT LIFE. Housing: Dormitories (men, women, coed); fraternity, sorority housing available. Limited housing for divinity students. **Activities:** Student government, film, magazine, radio, student newspaper, television, yearbook, choral groups, concert band, dance, drama, jazz band, marching band, music ensembles, musical theater, opera, symphony orchestra, fraternities, sororities, over 120 social, religious, service, academic, and preprofessional organizations.

ATHLETICS. NCAA. **Intercollegiate:** Baseball M, basketball, cross-country, diving, football M, golf, rifle W, soccer, swimming, tennis, track and field. **Intramural:** Basketball, golf, racquetball, soccer, softball, table tennis, tennis, volleyball, wrestling M.

STUDENT SERVICES. Aptitude testing, career counseling, employment service for undergraduates, freshman orientation, health services, personal counseling, placement service for graduates, special adviser for adult students, veterans counselor, services/facilities for handicapped.

ANNUAL EXPENSES. Tuition and fees: $8,970. **Room and board:** $3,210. **Books and supplies:** $596. **Other expenses:** $1,850.

FINANCIAL AID. 57% of grants, 66% of loans, 11% of jobs based on need. Academic, music/drama, art, athletic, religious affiliation scholarships available. **Aid applications:** No closing date; priority given to applications received by May 1; applicants notified on a rolling basis beginning on or about April 2; must reply by May 1 or within 2 weeks if notified thereafter.

ADDRESS/TELEPHONE. Leo Munson, Dean of Admissions, Texas Christian University, 2800 South University Drive, Fort Worth, TX 76129. (817) 921-7490. (800) 828-3764. Fax: (817) 921-7333.

Texas College
Tyler, Texas — CB code: 6821

4-year private liberal arts college, coed, affiliated with Christian Methodist Episcopal Church. Founded in 1894. **Accreditation:** Regional. **Undergraduate enrollment:** 366 men and women. **Faculty:** 40 total (28 full time), 17 with doctorates or other terminal degrees. **Location:** Urban campus in small city; 90 miles from Dallas, 90 miles from Shreveport, Louisiana. **Calendar:** Semester, limited summer session. **Microcomputers:** Located in computer centers.

DEGREES OFFERED. BA, BS. 44 bachelor's degrees awarded in 1992.

UNDERGRADUATE MAJORS. Art education, biology, business administration and management, business and office, business education, computer and information sciences, early childhood education, elementary education, English, English education, history, mathematics, mathematics education, music, music education, office supervision and management, physical education, political science and government, social science education, social sciences, social studies education, social work, sociology, studio art.

ACADEMIC PROGRAMS. Double major. **Remedial services:** Learning center, reduced course load, remedial instruction, tutoring. **Placement/credit:** Institutional tests.

ACADEMIC REQUIREMENTS. Freshmen must earn minimum GPA of 1.5 to continue in good standing. Students must declare major by end of second year. **Graduation requirements:** 124 hours for bachelor's (24 in major). Most students required to take courses in arts/fine arts, computer science, English, foreign languages, history, humanities, mathematics, philosophy/religion, biological/physical sciences, social sciences. **Postgraduate studies:** 12% enter MBA programs, 10% enter other graduate study.

FRESHMAN ADMISSIONS. Selection criteria: Open admissions. **High school preparation:** 16 units required. Required units include biological science 2, English 4 and mathematics 2. 2 units history, 6 units electives. **Test requirements:** SAT or ACT for placement and counseling only; score report by August 15.

1992 FRESHMAN CLASS PROFILE. 128 men and women enrolled. **Characteristics:** 48% from in state, 75% commute, 99% have minority backgrounds, 23% are foreign students. Average age is 18.

FALL-TERM APPLICATIONS. $5 fee, may be waived for applicants with need. Closing date August 15; applicants notified on a rolling basis. Audition recommended for music applicants. Deferred and early admission available.

STUDENT LIFE. Housing: Dormitories (men, women); apartment housing available. **Activities:** Student government, student newspaper, yearbook, choral groups, concert band, drama, jazz band, music ensembles, pep band, fraternities, sororities, Alpha Kappa Mu Omega Minister's Alliance, international students organization. **Additional information:** Students encouraged to participate in religious activities on campus.

ATHLETICS. NAIA. **Intercollegiate:** Baseball M, basketball, softball W, track and field, volleyball W. **Intramural:** Archery M, badminton M, baseball M, basketball, cross-country, soccer M, softball M, tennis, track and field M, volleyball.

STUDENT SERVICES. Aptitude testing, career counseling, employment service for undergraduates, freshman orientation, health services, on-campus day care, personal counseling, placement service for graduates, services/facilities for handicapped.

ANNUAL EXPENSES. Tuition and fees: $3,605. **Room and board:** $2,430. **Books and supplies:** $400. **Other expenses:** $1,095.

FINANCIAL AID. 90% of freshmen, 90% of continuing students receive some form of aid. All aid based on need. 590 enrolled freshmen were judged to have need, all were offered aid. Academic, music/drama, art, athletic, religious affiliation scholarships available. **Aid applications:** No closing date; applicants notified on a rolling basis beginning on or about June 15.

ADDRESS/TELEPHONE. Sandra L. Smith, Director of Admissions, Texas College, 2404 North Grand Avenue, Tyler, TX 75702-2404. (903) 593-8311 ext. 236.

Texas Lutheran College
Seguin, Texas — CB code: 6823

Admissions: 87% of applicants accepted
Based on: ••• School record, test scores
• Activities, essay, interview, recommendations
Completion: 87% of freshmen end year in good standing
40% graduate, 14% of these enter graduate study

4-year private liberal arts college, coed, affiliated with Evangelical Lutheran Church in America. Founded in 1891. **Accreditation:** Regional. **Undergraduate enrollment:** 376 men, 509 women full time; 230 men, 242 women part time. **Faculty:** 90 total (64 full time), 49 with doctorates or other terminal degrees. **Location:** Suburban campus in large town; 39 miles from San Antonio. **Calendar:** Two semester 4-4 with optional summer terms. Saturday classes. **Microcomputers:** 50 located in libraries, computer centers. **Special facilities:** Biology field station at Lake McQueeney, Fiedler Memorial Museum, Jackson Auditorium. **Additional facts:** Associate degree offered at Randolph campus.

DEGREES OFFERED. AS, BA, BS. 7 associate degrees awarded in 1992. 90% in business and management, 10% computer sciences. 185 bachelor's degrees awarded. 30% in business and management, 5% communications, 15% teacher education, 10% life sciences, 6% psychology, 15% social sciences, 7% visual and performing arts.

UNDERGRADUATE MAJORS. Associate: Business administration and management, computer and information sciences, marketing and distribution. **Bachelor's:** Art education, biology, business administration and management, chemistry, communications, computer and information sciences, early childhood education, economics, elementary education, English, fine arts, German, history, junior high education, marketing and distribution, mathematics, music, music education, philosophy, physical education, political science and government, predentistry, prelaw, premedicine, prepharmacy, preveterinary, psychology, secondary education, sociology, Spanish, theological studies, visual and performing arts.

ACADEMIC PROGRAMS. Double major, dual enrollment of high school students, honors program, independent study, internships, student-designed major, study abroad, teacher preparation, visiting/exchange student program, Washington semester. **Remedial services:** Tutoring, study skills program, writing center, supplemental instruction. **Placement/credit:** AP, CLEP Subject, institutional tests; 30 credit hours maximum for bachelor's degree.

ACADEMIC REQUIREMENTS. Freshmen must earn minimum GPA of 2.0 to continue in good standing. 74% of freshmen return for sophomore year. Students must declare major by end of second year. **Graduation requirements:** 64 hours for associate (21 in major), 124 hours for bachelor's (51 in major). Most students required to take courses in arts/fine arts, computer science, English, history, humanities, mathematics, philosophy/religion, biological/physical sciences, social sciences. **Postgraduate studies:** 2% enter law school, 3% enter medical school, 4% enter MBA programs, 5% enter other graduate study.

FRESHMAN ADMISSIONS. Selection criteria: Quality of academic curriculum pursued and class rank most important. Academic record and test scores also important. **High school preparation:** 13 units recommended. Recommended units include English 4, foreign language 2, mathematics 2, social science 3 and science 2. **Test requirements:** SAT or ACT; score report by August 1.

1992 FRESHMAN CLASS PROFILE. 220 men applied, 182 accepted, 99 enrolled; 356 women applied, 319 accepted, 147 enrolled. 27% were in top tenth and 57% were in top quarter of graduating class. **Academic background:** Mid 50% of enrolled freshmen had SAT-V between 350-480, SAT-M between 450-600; ACT composite between 20-25. 84% submitted SAT scores, 62% submitted ACT scores. **Characteristics:** 89% from in state, 78% live in college housing, 20% have minority backgrounds, 3% are foreign students. Average age is 18.

FALL-TERM APPLICATIONS. $20 fee, may be waived for applicants with need. Closing date August 1; priority given to applications received by May 1; applicants notified on a rolling basis; August 15. Interview recommended. CRDA. Deferred admission available.

STUDENT LIFE. Housing: Dormitories (men, women); apartment housing available. **Activities:** Student government, magazine, student newspaper, yearbook, choral groups, concert band, drama, music ensembles, pep band, fraternities, sororities, Black Student Union, Mexican American Student Association, Young Democrats, College Republicans, campus ministry, Fellowship of Christian Athletes, Students Organized Against Worldwide Injustice, Amnesty International.

ATHLETICS. NAIA. **Intercollegiate:** Baseball M, basketball, golf M, soccer, softball W, tennis, volleyball W. **Intramural:** Basketball, bowling, handball, racquetball, rifle, softball, swimming, table tennis, tennis, volleyball.

STUDENT SERVICES. Aptitude testing, career counseling, employment service for undergraduates, freshman orientation, health services, personal counseling, placement service for graduates, veterans counselor, campus pastor, strong advising program, resident assistants, services/facilities for handicapped.

ANNUAL EXPENSES. Tuition and fees (1992-93): $6,790. **Room and board:** $3,120. **Books and supplies:** $450. **Other expenses:** $950.

FINANCIAL AID. 85% of freshmen, 87% of continuing students receive some form of aid. 38% of grants, 63% of loans, all jobs based on need. 113 enrolled freshmen were judged to have need, all were offered aid. Academic, music/drama, art, athletic, leadership, alumni affiliation, religious affiliation, minority scholarships available. **Aid applications:** No closing date; priority given to applications received by May 1; applicants notified on a rolling basis beginning on or about March 1; must reply within 2 weeks.

ADDRESS/TELEPHONE. Jennifer Ehlers, Director of Admissions, Texas Lutheran College, 1000 West Court Street, Seguin, TX 78155. (512) 372-8050. (800) 880-1107. Fax: (512) 372-8096.

Texas Southern University
Houston, Texas CB code: 6824

4-year public university, coed. Founded in 1947. **Accreditation:** Regional. **Undergraduate enrollment:** 1,975 men, 3,699 women full time; 1,114 men, 2,044 women part time. **Graduate enrollment:** 331 men, 238 women full time; 271 men, 843 women part time. **Faculty:** 519 total (391 full time), 272 with doctorates or other terminal degrees. **Location:** Urban campus in very large city; 2 miles from downtown Houston. **Calendar:** Semester, extensive summer session. Saturday and extensive evening/early morning classes. **Microcomputers:** Located in libraries, computer centers.

DEGREES OFFERED. BA, BS, MA, MS, MBA, MEd, EdD, Pharm D, JD. 560 bachelor's degrees awarded in 1992. 15% in business and management, 10% business/office and marketing/distribution, 5% communications, 20% education, 10% engineering technologies, 11% law, 10% life sciences, 5% mathematics, 5% psychology, 9% social sciences. Graduate degrees offered in 31 major fields of study.

UNDERGRADUATE MAJORS. Accounting, biology, business administration and management, business and management, business economics, chemistry, communications, community services, computer and information sciences, criminal justice studies, economics, elementary education, engineering and engineering-related technologies, English, finance, food science and nutrition, French, health care administration, history, home economics, human environment and housing, individual and family development, journalism, law , mathematics, medical records administration, music, pharmacy, photography, physics, political science and government, psychology, public administration, radio/television broadcasting, radio/television technology, secondary education, secretarial and related programs, social work, sociology, Spanish, special education, speech, speech correction, textiles and clothing, transportation studies.

ACADEMIC PROGRAMS. Cooperative education, double major, honors program, internships, teacher preparation, cross-registration; combined bachelor's/graduate program in business administration, law. **Remedial services:** Remedial instruction, tutoring. **Placement/credit:** Institutional tests.

ACADEMIC REQUIREMENTS. Freshmen must earn minimum GPA of 2.0 to continue in good standing. 1.5 GPA required for first 30 semester hours, 1.75 for 31-60 hours, and 2.0 for 61 or more hours. 65% of freshmen return for sophomore year. Students must declare major by end of second year. **Graduation requirements:** 124 hours for bachelor's (36 in major). Most students required to take courses in English, mathematics, biological/physical sciences, social sciences. **Postgraduate studies:** 15% enter law school, 2% enter medical school, 10% enter MBA programs, 20% enter other graduate study.

FRESHMAN ADMISSIONS. Selection criteria: Open admissions. Selective admissions to some programs. High school achievement, personal interview, essay very important. High school activities, test scores, individual talents, skills, abilities, alumni relations considered. **High school preparation:** 18 units recommended. Recommended units include English 4, mathematics 4, physical science 2, social science 4 and science 2. **Test requirements:** SAT or ACT for placement and counseling only; score report by August 31.

1992 FRESHMAN CLASS PROFILE. 956 men applied, 956 accepted, 648 enrolled; 1,489 women applied, 1,489 accepted, 1,091 enrolled. **Characteristics:** 82% from in state, 90% commute, 90% have minority backgrounds, 12% are foreign students, 50% join fraternities/sororities. Average age is 19.

FALL-TERM APPLICATIONS. $10 fee. $50 fee for international applicants. Closing date August 15; priority given to applications received by July 31; applicants notified on a rolling basis.

STUDENT LIFE. Housing: Dormitories (men, women); apartment housing available. **Activities:** Student government, film, radio, student newspaper, television, yearbook, choral groups, concert band, drama, jazz band, marching band, music ensembles, musical theater, fraternities, sororities, united ministries.

ATHLETICS. NAIA, NCAA. **Intercollegiate:** Baseball M, basketball, cross-country, football M, golf M, soccer M, tennis, track and field, volleyball W. **Intramural:** Bowling, gymnastics, swimming, tennis, track and field, volleyball.

STUDENT SERVICES. Aptitude testing, career counseling, employment service for undergraduates, health services, personal counseling, placement service for graduates, veterans counselor, services/facilities for handicapped.

ANNUAL EXPENSES. Tuition and fees: $1,230, $4,080 additional for out-of-state students. **Room and board:** $3,320. **Books and supplies:** $500. **Other expenses:** $1,700.

FINANCIAL AID. 80% of freshmen, 75% of continuing students receive some form of aid. Grants, loans, jobs available. **Aid applications:** No closing date; priority given to applications received by May 1; applicants notified on a rolling basis beginning on or about June 1.

ADDRESS/TELEPHONE. Audrey Pearsall, Director of Admissions, Recruitment, and Academic Advisement, Texas Southern University, 3100 Cleburne Street, Houston, TX 77004. (713) 527-7420. Fax: (713) 527-4317.

Texas Southmost College
Brownsville, Texas CB code: 6825

2-year public community college, coed. Founded in 1926. **Accreditation:** Regional. **Undergraduate enrollment:** 7,092 men and women. **Location:** Urban campus in small city; 160 miles from Corpus Christi. **Calendar:** Semester.

FRESHMAN ADMISSIONS. Selection criteria: Open admissions. Selective admissions to some allied health programs.

ANNUAL EXPENSES. Tuition and fees (1992-93): $824, $300 additional for out-of-district students, $2,400 additional for out-of-state students. **Books and supplies:** $400. **Other expenses:** $412.

ADDRESS/TELEPHONE. Alfonso Gutierrez, Director of Admissions, Registrar, Texas Southmost College, 80 Fort Brown, Brownsville, TX 78520. (512) 544-8200.

Texas State Technical College: Amarillo
Amarillo, Texas CB code: 0363

2-year public technical college, coed. Founded in 1969. **Accreditation:** Regional. **Undergraduate enrollment:** 285 men, 70 women full time; 167 men, 38 women part time. **Faculty:** 60 total. **Location:** Suburban campus in small city; 10 miles from Amarillo. **Calendar:** 4 quarters for academic year required. **Microcomputers:** 50 located in libraries, classrooms.

DEGREES OFFERED. AAS. 48 associate degrees awarded in 1992. 8% in business/office and marketing/distribution, 14% computer sciences, 54% engineering technologies, 16% trade and industry.

UNDERGRADUATE MAJORS. Air conditioning/heating/refrigeration mechanics, aircraft mechanics, business data entry equipment operation, business data programming, chemical manufacturing technology, commercial art, computer and information sciences, computer programming, computer servicing technology, drafting, drafting and design technology, electromechanical technology, electronic technology, graphic arts technology, information sciences and systems, instrumentation technology, interior design, laser electro-optic technology, machine tool operation/machine shop, mechanical design technology, quality control technology, secretarial and related programs, telecommunications, word processing.

ACADEMIC PROGRAMS. Cooperative education, dual enrollment of high school students. **Remedial services:** Learning center, reduced course load, remedial instruction, special counselor, tutoring. **Placement/credit:** CLEP General and Subject, institutional tests.

ACADEMIC REQUIREMENTS. Freshmen must earn minimum GPA of 2.0 to continue in good standing. Students must declare major on application. **Graduation requirements:** 90 hours for associate. Most students required to take courses in computer science, English, mathematics, social sciences.

FRESHMAN ADMISSIONS. Selection criteria: Open admissions. **Test requirements:** Pre-TASP test required.

1992 FRESHMAN CLASS PROFILE. 158 men applied, 158 accepted, 109 enrolled; 55 women applied, 55 accepted, 29 enrolled. **Characteristics:** 98% from in state, 64% commute, 23% have minority backgrounds.

FALL-TERM APPLICATIONS. No fee. No closing date; applicants notified on a rolling basis.

STUDENT LIFE. Housing: Apartment housing available. Married students can apply for campus housing. **Activities:** Student government.

ATHLETICS. Intramural: Baseball, basketball, bowling, golf, handball, racquetball, softball, table tennis, volleyball.

STUDENT SERVICES. Aptitude testing, employment service for undergraduates, freshman orientation, health services, personal counseling, placement service for graduates, veterans counselor, services/facilities for handicapped.

ANNUAL EXPENSES. Tuition and fees (1992-93): $1,086, $2,970 additional for out-of-state students. **Room and board:** $2,820. **Books and supplies:** $900. **Other expenses:** $4,524.

FINANCIAL AID. 51% of freshmen, 61% of continuing students receive some form of aid. All grants, 90% of loans, 47% of jobs based on need. **Aid applications:** No closing date; priority given to applications received by July 1; applicants notified on a rolling basis; must reply within 2 weeks.

ADDRESS/TELEPHONE. Sharon Harrison, Director of Admissions and Records, Texas State Technical College: Amarillo, PO Box 11197, Amarillo, TX 79111. (806) 335-2316.

Texas State Technical College: Harlingen

Harlingen, Texas CB code: 6843

2-year public technical college, coed. Founded in 1969. **Accreditation:** Regional. **Undergraduate enrollment:** 1,191 men, 792 women full time; 586 men, 659 women part time. **Faculty:** 195 total (162 full time), 7 with doctorates or other terminal degrees. **Location:** Suburban campus in large town; 25 miles from Brownsville, 30 miles from South Padre Island. **Calendar:** Quarter. Saturday classes. **Microcomputers:** 85 located in libraries, computer centers.

DEGREES OFFERED. AAS. 223 associate degrees awarded in 1992. 5% in business/office and marketing/distribution, 14% computer sciences, 63% engineering technologies, 11% allied health.

UNDERGRADUATE MAJORS. Agricultural business and management, air conditioning/heating/refrigeration mechanics, biomedical equipment technology, chemical manufacturing technology, computer programming, computer servicing technology, computer technology, construction, dental laboratory technology, drafting and design technology, electronic technology, food production/management/services, instrumentation technology, legal secretary, manufacturing technology, medical records technology, robotics, secretarial and related programs, welding technology.

ACADEMIC PROGRAMS. Cooperative education, dual enrollment of high school students, independent study, internships, weekend college. **Remedial services:** Learning center, remedial instruction, tutoring. **Placement/credit:** Institutional tests.

ACADEMIC REQUIREMENTS. Freshmen must earn minimum GPA of 2.0 to continue in good standing. Students must declare major on application. **Graduation requirements:** 90 hours for associate. Most students required to take courses in English, mathematics.

FRESHMAN ADMISSIONS. Selection criteria: Open admissions. **Test requirements:** SAT or ACT for placement. **Additional information:** Associate degree canidates required to take state-mandated TASP, (Texas Academic Skills Program).

1992 FRESHMAN CLASS PROFILE. 822 men applied, 811 accepted, 750 enrolled; 805 women applied, 792 accepted, 678 enrolled. 50% had high school GPA of 3.0 or higher, 6% between 2.0 and 2.99. **Characteristics:** 95% from in state, 80% commute, 91% have minority backgrounds, 1% are foreign students. Average age is 19.

FALL-TERM APPLICATIONS. No fee. No closing date; applicants notified on a rolling basis.

STUDENT LIFE. Housing: Dormitories (coed); apartment housing available. **Activities:** Student government, student newspaper, yearbook, Baptist Student Union.

ATHLETICS. Intramural: Baseball, basketball M, bowling, soccer M, softball, table tennis, volleyball.

STUDENT SERVICES. Aptitude testing, career counseling, employment service for undergraduates, freshman orientation, health services, personal counseling, placement service for graduates, veterans counselor, services/facilities for handicapped.

ANNUAL EXPENSES. Tuition and fees (1992-93): $1,086, $2,970 additional for out-of-state students. **Room and board:** $2,520. **Books and supplies:** $836. **Other expenses:** $1,260.

FINANCIAL AID. 80% of freshmen, 80% of continuing students receive some form of aid. Grants, loans, jobs available. **Aid applications:** Closing date June 15; priority given to applications received by May 5; applicants notified on a rolling basis; must reply by June 30.

ADDRESS/TELEPHONE. Agustin V. Rangel, Director of Admissions and Records, Texas State Technical College: Harlingen, 2424 Boxwood, Harlingen, TX 78550-3697. (210) 425-0600. (800) 852-TSTI. Fax: (210) 425-0796.

Texas State Technical College: Sweetwater

Sweetwater, Texas CB code: 3137

2-year public technical college, coed. Founded in 1970. **Accreditation:** Regional. **Undergraduate enrollment:** 329 men, 225 women full time; 123 men, 119 women part time. **Faculty:** 66 total (56 full time). **Location:** Rural campus in large town; 46 miles from Abilene, 70 miles from San Angelo, 121 miles from Lubbock. **Calendar:** Quarter, limited summer session. **Microcomputers:** 122 located in libraries, classrooms. **Additional facts:** Extension sites at Abilene, Breckenridge and Brownwood.

DEGREES OFFERED. AAS. 106 associate degrees awarded in 1992. 11% in business and management, 9% business/office and marketing/distribution, 10% communications, 30% computer sciences, 40% engineering technologies.

UNDERGRADUATE MAJORS. Accounting, business data processing and related programs, computer programming, computer servicing technology, data processing, drafting and design technology, electronic technology, emergency medical technologies, information sciences and systems, manufacturing technology, office supervision and management, robotics, secretarial and related programs, telecommunications.

ACADEMIC PROGRAMS. Cooperative education, double major, independent study, internships. **Remedial services:** Learning center, reduced course load, remedial instruction, tutoring. **Placement/credit:** Institutional tests.

ACADEMIC REQUIREMENTS. Freshmen must earn minimum GPA of 2.0 to continue in good standing. 42% of freshmen return for sophomore year. Students must declare major on enrollment. **Graduation requirements:** 103 hours for associate. Most students required to take courses in computer science, English, mathematics, biological/physical sciences.

FRESHMAN ADMISSIONS. Selection criteria: Open admissions. Nursing admission determined by structured interview and base score on DAT test.

1992 FRESHMAN CLASS PROFILE. 271 men, 170 women enrolled. **Characteristics:** 100% from in state, 79% commute, 27% have minority backgrounds.

FALL-TERM APPLICATIONS. No fee. No closing date; applicants notified on a rolling basis; must reply by registration. Early admission available.

STUDENT LIFE. Housing: Dormitories (men); apartment, handicapped housing available. **Activities:** Student government, student newspaper, yearbook, Mexican American Club, Baptist Student Union, Technical Students Association.

ATHLETICS. Intramural: Basketball, bowling, golf, horseback riding, softball, swimming, table tennis, tennis, volleyball.

STUDENT SERVICES. Aptitude testing, career counseling, employment service for undergraduates, freshman orientation, health services, on-campus day care, personal counseling, placement service for graduates, veterans counselor, services/facilities for handicapped.

ANNUAL EXPENSES. Tuition and fees (1992-93): $1,086, $2,970 additional for out-of-state students. **Room and board:** $2,760. **Books and supplies:** $800. **Other expenses:** $585.

FINANCIAL AID. 60% of freshmen, 60% of continuing students receive some form of aid. All grants, 89% of loans, all jobs based on need. 274 enrolled freshmen were judged to have need, all were offered aid. **Aid applications:** No closing date; priority given to applications received by July 15; applicants notified on a rolling basis.

ADDRESS/TELEPHONE. Linda L. Graham, Director of Admissions and Records, Texas State Technical College: Sweetwater, 300 College Drive, Sweetwater, TX 79556. (915) 235-7300.

Texas State Technical College: Waco

Waco, Texas CB code: 6328

2-year public technical college, coed. Founded in 1965. **Accreditation:** Regional. **Undergraduate enrollment:** 2,345 men, 452 women full time; 408 men, 103 women part time. **Faculty:** 361 total (326 full time), 30 with doctorates or other terminal degrees. **Location:** Suburban campus in small city; 90 miles from Dallas and Fort Worth. **Calendar:** Quarter. **Microcomputers:** 1,100 located in dormitories, libraries, classrooms, computer centers. **Special facilities:** Advanced manufacturing center; 8600-foot runway at TSTI-Waco airport (largest airport in the United States operated by a public educational institution).

DEGREES OFFERED. AAS. 738 associate degrees awarded in 1992. 12% in agriculture, 78% trade and industry.

UNDERGRADUATE MAJORS. Aeronautical technology, air conditioning/heating/refrigeration mechanics, air conditioning/heating/refrigeration technology, aircraft mechanics, airline piloting and navigation, automotive mechanics, automotive technology, aviation computer technology, biomedical equipment technology, chemistry, commercial art, computer and information sciences, computer servicing technology, data processing, drafting, drafting and design technology, electrical and electronics equipment repair, electrical technology, electronic technology, engineering and engineering-related technologies, food production/management/services, graphic and printing production, graphic arts technology, horticulture, industrial equipment maintenance and repair, instrumentation technology, laser electro-optic technology, machine tool operation/machine shop, mechanical design technology, nuclear technologies, occupational safety and health technology, power plant operation and maintenance, quality control technology, welding technology.

ACADEMIC PROGRAMS. Cooperative education, dual enrollment of high school students, cross-registration. **Remedial services:** Learning center, remedial instruction, tutoring. **Placement/credit:** CLEP General and Subject, institutional tests.

ACADEMIC REQUIREMENTS. Freshmen must earn minimum GPA of 2.0 to continue in good standing. 75% of freshmen return for sophomore year. **Graduation requirements:** 105 hours for associate (85 in major). Most students required to take courses in computer science, English, mathematics, social sciences.

FRESHMAN ADMISSIONS. Selection criteria: Open admissions. **Test requirements:** CPT and TASP tests required of all students for placement.

1992 FRESHMAN CLASS PROFILE. 1,944 men, 555 women enrolled. **Characteristics:** 98% from in state, 58% commute, 18% have minority backgrounds, 1% are foreign students. Average age is 23.

FALL-TERM APPLICATIONS. No fee. No closing date; applicants notified on a rolling basis. Interview recommended. Deferred and early admission available.

STUDENT LIFE. Housing: Dormitories (men, women, coed); apartment, handicapped housing available. Duplexes and houses available to married students or students with families. **Activities:** Student government, student newspaper, yearbook.

ATHLETICS. Intramural: Basketball, field hockey M, softball, volleyball.

STUDENT SERVICES. Aptitude testing, career counseling, employment service for undergraduates, freshman orientation, on-campus day care, personal counseling, placement service for graduates, special adviser for adult students, veterans counselor, services/facilities for handicapped.

ANNUAL EXPENSES. Tuition and fees (1992-93): $1,086, $2,970 additional for out-of-state students. **Room and board:** $2,895. **Books and supplies:** $650. **Other expenses:** $1,200.

FINANCIAL AID. 52% of freshmen, 72% of continuing students receive some form of aid. 96% of grants, 82% of loans, 49% of jobs based on need. Academic, state/district residency, minority scholarships available. **Aid applications:** No closing date; priority given to applications received by May 31; applicants notified on a rolling basis beginning on or about June 15; must reply within 2 weeks. **Additional information:** Tuition for Texas veterans provided by state.

ADDRESS/TELEPHONE. Dr. Lance Hayes, Director of Registration and Records, Texas State Technical Institute: Waco, 3801 Campus Drive, Waco, TX 76705. (817) 799-3611 ext. 2250. Fax: (817) 867-1700.

Texas Tech University

Lubbock, Texas — CB code: 6827

Admissions: 70% of applicants accepted
Based on: ••• School record, test scores
Completion: 74% of freshmen end year in good standing
33% graduate

4-year public university, coed. Founded in 1923. **Accreditation:** Regional. **Undergraduate enrollment:** 9,133 men, 7,796 women full time; 1,374 men, 1,308 women part time. **Graduate enrollment:** 1,788 men, 1,094 women full time; 779 men, 943 women part time. **Faculty:** 944 total (826 full time), 807 with doctorates or other terminal degrees. **Location:** Urban campus in small city; 320 miles from Dallas. **Calendar:** Semester, extensive summer session. Extensive evening/early morning classes. **Microcomputers:** 800 located in libraries. **Special facilities:** Museum, ranching heritage center, Lubbock Lake Landwork (archaeological dig/state park).

DEGREES OFFERED. BA, BS, BFA, BArch, MA, MS, MBA, MFA, MEd, PhD, EdD, MD, JD. 3,104 bachelor's degrees awarded in 1992. 6% in agriculture, 19% business and management, 7% communications, 8% education, 7% engineering, 15% home economics, 6% social sciences. Graduate degrees offered in 95 major fields of study.

UNDERGRADUATE MAJORS. Accounting, advertising, agricultural economics, agricultural engineering, agricultural mechanics, agricultural sciences, agronomy, animal sciences, anthropology, architectural technologies, architecture, art history, biochemistry, biology, botany, business and management, cell biology, chemical engineering, chemistry, child development/care/guidance, city/community/regional planning, civil engineering, clothing and textiles management/production/services, curriculum and instruction, dance, dietetic aide/assistant, dramatic arts, economics, education of the deaf and hearing impaired, electrical technology, electrical/electronics/communications engineering, engineering, engineering physics, English, entomology, family and community services, family/consumer resource management, fashion design, fashion merchandising, finance, fine arts, food production/management/services, food science and nutrition, food sciences, French, geography, geology, geophysics and seismology, German, history, history of architecture, home economics, horticultural science, horticulture, hotel/motel and restaurant management, human environment and housing, humanities, individual and family development, industrial engineering, interior design, international business management, journalism, landscape architecture, Latin, Latin American studies, liberal/general studies, management information systems, marketing management, mathematics, mechanical design technology, mechanical engineering, microbiology, molecular biology, music, music history and appreciation, music performance, music theory and composition, parks and recreation management, petroleum engineering, philosophy, photocommunications, physics, political science and government, psychology, public administration, public relations, radio/television broadcasting, radio/television technology, range management, Russian, secretarial and related programs, social work, sociology, Spanish, speech pathology/audiology, structures, studio art, textile engineering, textiles and clothing, urban design, wildlife management, zoology.

ACADEMIC PROGRAMS. Double major, dual enrollment of high school students, honors program, independent study, internships, student-designed major, study abroad, teacher preparation, telecourses; combined bachelor's/graduate program in business administration. **Remedial services:** Learning center, preadmission summer program, reduced course load, remedial instruction, special counselor, tutoring. **ROTC:** Air Force, Army, Naval. **Placement/credit:** AP, CLEP General and Subject, institutional tests; 12 credit hours maximum for bachelor's degree.

ACADEMIC REQUIREMENTS. Freshmen must earn minimum GPA of 2.0 to continue in good standing. 75% of freshmen return for sophomore year. Students must declare major by end of second year. **Graduation requirements:** 134 hours for bachelor's (30 in major). Most students required to take courses in arts/fine arts, English, history, humanities, mathematics, biological/physical sciences, social sciences.

FRESHMAN ADMISSIONS. Selection criteria: Students in top 10% of graduating class unconditionally admitted. Next 15%, unconditional requirements: SAT 900 or ACT 22. 2nd quartile, unconditional: SAT 1100 or ACT 27. Lower half, unconditional: SAT 1200 or ACT 29. Applicants not meeting assured criteria may have records reviewed, admitted as space allows. **High school preparation:** 15 units required. Required units include English 4, foreign language 2, mathematics 3, social science 2.5 and science 2. Algebra 2 required of business and engineering majors. Geometry, trigonometry, chemistry, and physics required of engineering majors. Algebra I and II, geometry, trigonometry, physics, or chemistry required of architecture majors. **Test requirements:** SAT or ACT; score report by August 15.

1992 FRESHMAN CLASS PROFILE. 3,403 men applied, 2,371 accepted, 1,355 enrolled; 3,412 women applied, 2,411 accepted, 1,391 enrolled. 23% were in top tenth and 52% were in top quarter of graduating class. **Characteristics:** 93% from in state, 50% commute, 17% have minority backgrounds, 1% are foreign students. Average age is 19.

FALL-TERM APPLICATIONS. $25 fee. $50 fee for foreign applicants. Closing date August 1; applicants notified on a rolling basis.

STUDENT LIFE. Housing: Dormitories (men, women, coed); apartment housing available. **Activities:** Student government, magazine, radio, student newspaper, television, yearbook, choral groups, concert band, dance, drama, jazz band, marching band, music ensembles, musical theater, opera, pep band, symphony orchestra, fraternities, sororities, honorary and service organizations, Young Democrats, Young Republicans, Wesley Foundation, Baptist Student Center, Campus Crusade for Christ.

ATHLETICS. NCAA. **Intercollegiate:** Baseball M, basketball, cross-country, diving W, football M, golf, tennis, track and field, volleyball W, wrestling M. **Intramural:** Archery, badminton, basketball, bowling, boxing M, cross-country, fencing M, golf, handball, racquetball, rugby M, skiing, soccer, softball, table tennis, tennis, volleyball, water polo.

STUDENT SERVICES. Aptitude testing, career counseling, employment service for undergraduates, freshman orientation, health services, on-campus day care, personal counseling, placement service for graduates, special adviser for adult students, veterans counselor, services/facilities for handicapped.

ANNUAL EXPENSES. Tuition and fees: $1,411, $4,080 additional for out-of-state students. **Room and board:** $4,000. **Books and supplies:** $600. **Other expenses:** $1,480.

FINANCIAL AID. 30% of freshmen, 25% of continuing students receive some form of aid. 76% of grants, 91% of loans, 33% of jobs based on need. 1,284 enrolled freshmen were judged to have need, 963 were offered aid. Academic, music/drama, art, athletic, minority scholarships available. **Aid applications:** No closing date; priority given to applications received by April 1; applicants notified on a rolling basis beginning on or about May 1; must reply within 3 weeks.

ADDRESS/TELEPHONE. Dr. Gene Medley, Dean of Admissions and Records, Texas Tech University, PO Box 45005, Lubbock, TX 79409-5005. (806) 742-1480.

Texas Wesleyan University

Fort Worth, Texas CB code: 6828

Admissions: 88% of applicants accepted
Based on: ••• School record, test scores
•• Activities
• Essay, interview, recommendations, special talents
Completion: 90% of freshmen end year in good standing
34% graduate, 17% of these enter graduate study

4-year private university, coed, affiliated with United Methodist Church. Founded in 1890. **Accreditation:** Regional. **Undergraduate enrollment:** 440 men, 612 women full time; 180 men, 261 women part time. **Graduate enrollment:** 31 men, 33 women full time; 36 men, 179 women part time. **Faculty:** 93 total (68 full time), 52 with doctorates or other terminal degrees. **Location:** Urban campus in large city; 7 miles from Ft. Worth. **Calendar:** Semester, limited summer session. Saturday and extensive evening/early morning classes. **Microcomputers:** 75 located in libraries, classrooms, computer centers. **Special facilities:** Library with computer access to reference books and other materials.

DEGREES OFFERED. BA, BS, MA, MS, JD. 234 bachelor's degrees awarded in 1992. 45% in business and management, 15% business/office and marketing/distribution, 10% communications, 5% computer sciences, 10% education, 5% teacher education. Graduate degrees offered in 5 major fields of study.

UNDERGRADUATE MAJORS. Accounting, advertising, art education, bilingual/bicultural education, biology, business administration and management, business and management, business economics, chemistry, clinical laboratory science, communications, computer and information sciences, counseling psychology, criminal justice studies, dramatic arts, drawing, early childhood education, education, elementary education, English, English education, environmental science, finance, fine arts, foreign languages education, history, humanities and social sciences, information sciences and systems, international business management, journalism, junior high education, management information systems, marketing and distribution, marketing management, mathematics, mathematics education, music, music education, musical theater, philosophy, physical education, political science and government, predentistry, premedicine, prepharmacy, psychology, radio/television broadcasting, reading education, religion, science education, secondary education, social sciences, social studies education, Spanish, speech, sports management, theological studies.

ACADEMIC PROGRAMS. Accelerated program, double major, dual enrollment of high school students, independent study, internships, study abroad, teacher preparation, visiting/exchange student program; liberal arts/career combination in engineering; combined bachelor's/graduate program in law. **Remedial services:** Learning center, preadmission summer program, reduced course load, remedial instruction, special counselor, tutoring. **ROTC:** Air Force, Army. **Placement/credit:** AP, CLEP General and Subject; 30 credit hours maximum for bachelor's degree.

ACADEMIC REQUIREMENTS. Freshmen must earn minimum GPA of 1.7 to continue in good standing. 65% of freshmen return for sophomore year. Students must declare major by end of second year. **Graduation requirements:** 128 hours for bachelor's. Most students required to take courses in arts/fine arts, English, history, humanities, mathematics, philosophy/religion, biological/physical sciences, social sciences. **Postgraduate studies:** 1% enter law school, 2% enter medical school, 8% enter MBA programs, 6% enter other graduate study.

FRESHMAN ADMISSIONS. Selection criteria: Class rank, course selection, combined SAT score of 800 or ACT, 19. Students in top half of class given priority. **High school preparation:** 17 units required. Required and recommended units include English 4, mathematics 2, social science 2 and science 2. Foreign language 2 recommended. **Test requirements:** SAT or ACT; score report by August 1. 2 ACH required of applicants seeking advanced credit. Score report by June 1.

1992 FRESHMAN CLASS PROFILE. 480 men and women applied, 420 accepted; 257 enrolled. 69% had high school GPA of 3.0 or higher, 31% between 2.0 and 2.99. 14% were in top tenth and 40% were in top quarter of graduating class. **Academic background:** Mid 50% of enrolled freshmen had SAT-V between 500-550, SAT-M between 450-500; ACT composite between 17-22. 76% submitted SAT scores, 44% submitted ACT scores. **Characteristics:** 86% from in state, 66% commute, 25% have minority backgrounds, 1% are foreign students, 8% join fraternities/sororities. Average age is 18.

FALL-TERM APPLICATIONS. $20 fee, may be waived for applicants with need. Closing date August 1; priority given to applications received by April 1; applicants notified on a rolling basis; must reply by May 1 or within 4 weeks if notified thereafter. Audition required for music, theater applicants. Portfolio required for art applicants. Interview recommended. Essay recommended. Interview required for applicants in bottom half of high school class. CRDA. Deferred admission available.

STUDENT LIFE. Housing: Dormitories (men, women, coed); apartment, fraternity housing available. Honors apartments for junior and senior women. All campus housing fills early. **Activities:** Student government, magazine, student newspaper, yearbook, choral groups, concert band, drama, jazz band, music ensembles, musical theater, opera, fraternities, sororities, Methodist and Baptist student unions, Student Foundation, Alpha Phi Omega, Gamma Sigma Sigma, Chi Rho.

ATHLETICS. NAIA. **Intercollegiate:** Baseball M, basketball, golf M, soccer M, softball W, tennis, volleyball W. **Intramural:** Archery, badminton, basketball, bowling, diving, golf M, racquetball, skin diving, soccer, softball, swimming, table tennis, tennis W, volleyball.

STUDENT SERVICES. Aptitude testing, career counseling, employment service for undergraduates, freshman orientation, health services, personal counseling, placement service for graduates, special adviser for adult students, veterans counselor, services/facilities for handicapped.

ANNUAL EXPENSES. Tuition and fees: $6,150. **Room and board:** $3,230. **Books and supplies:** $428. **Other expenses:** $1,138.

FINANCIAL AID. 93% of freshmen, 83% of continuing students receive some form of aid. 43% of grants, 71% of loans, 53% of jobs based on need. 226 enrolled freshmen were judged to have need, all were offered aid. Academic, music/drama, art, athletic, leadership, religious affiliation, minority scholarships available. **Aid applications:** No closing date; priority given to applications received by April 15; applicants notified on a rolling basis beginning on or about April 15; must reply within 2 weeks.

ADDRESS/TELEPHONE. Dave Voskuil, Enrollment Mgmt, Texas Wesleyan University, 1201 Wesleyan, Fort Worth, TX 76105-1536. (817) 531-4422. (800) 580-8980. Fax: (817) 531-4204. (800) 580-8980.

Texas Woman's University

Denton, Texas CB code: 6826

4-year public university, coed. Founded in 1901. **Accreditation:** Regional. **Undergraduate enrollment:** 155 men, 3,541 women full time; 98 men, 1,816 women part time. **Graduate enrollment:** 147 men, 1,129 women full time; 367 men, 2,530 women part time. **Faculty:** 555 total (364 full time). **Location:** Suburban campus in small city; 35 miles from Dallas and Fort Worth. **Calendar:** Semester, extensive summer session. **Microcomputers:** 150 located in dormitories, libraries, classrooms, computer centers. **Special facilities:** 2 art galleries, history of Texas women collection, DAR museum, historical collection, women's collection, university gardens. **Additional facts:** Men may apply for admission to undergraduate level of Institute of Health Science and all areas of graduate school.

DEGREES OFFERED. BA, BS, BFA, MA, MS, MBA, MFA, PhD, EdD. 1,094 bachelor's degrees awarded in 1992. 10% in teacher education, 48% health sciences, 7% parks/recreation, protective services, public affairs, 9% social sciences, 5% visual and performing arts. Graduate degrees offered in 63 major fields of study.

UNDERGRADUATE MAJORS. Accounting, advertising, art history, biology, business administration and management, ceramics, chemistry, child development/care/guidance, community health work, computer and information sciences, criminal justice studies, dance, dental hygiene, dramatic arts, drawing, economics, elementary bilingual education, English, family/consumer resource management, fashion design, fashion merchandising, fiber/textiles/weaving, food production/management/services, food science and nutrition, history, illustration design, institutional/home management/supporting programs, interdisciplinary studies, journalism, legal assistant/paralegal, library science, marketing management, mathematics, medical illustrating, metal/jewelry, music, music performance, music therapy, nursing, nutritional sciences, occupational therapy, office supervision and management, painting, photography, political science and government, printmaking, psychology, radio/television broadcasting, recreation and community services technologies, sculpture, secretarial and related programs, social work, sociology, Spanish, special education, speech pathology/audiology, studio art, textiles and clothing.

ACADEMIC PROGRAMS. Cooperative education, double major, dual enrollment of high school students, honors program, internships, teacher preparation, visiting/exchange student program, cross-registration. **Remedial services:** Learning center, preadmission summer program, reduced course load, remedial instruction, special counselor, tutoring. **ROTC:** Air Force, Army. **Placement/credit:** AP, CLEP General and Subject, institutional tests; 30 credit hours maximum for bachelor's degree.

ACADEMIC REQUIREMENTS. Freshmen must earn minimum GPA of 1.4 to continue in good standing. 64% of freshmen return for sophomore year. Students must declare major on application. **Graduation requirements:** 124 hours for bachelor's (30 in major). Most students required to take courses in English, history.

FRESHMAN ADMISSIONS. Selection criteria: School achievement record, and test scores: TASP, SAT (630) or ACT (14). **High school preparation:** 15 units required. Required units include English 3, mathematics 2, social science 2 and science 2. **Test requirements:** SAT or ACT; score report by August 23.

1992 FRESHMAN CLASS PROFILE. 16 men, 429 women enrolled. **Academic background:** Mid 50% of enrolled freshmen had SAT-V between 320-450, SAT-M between 340-470; ACT composite between 16-20. 52% submitted SAT scores, 66% submitted ACT scores. **Characteristics:** 93%

from in state, 50% commute, 39% have minority backgrounds, 2% are foreign students. Average age is 24.

FALL-TERM APPLICATIONS. $25 fee. Closing date July 15; priority given to applications received by February 1; applicants notified on a rolling basis beginning on or about March 1; must reply by May 1. Audition required for music, drama applicants. Portfolio recommended for art applicants. Deferred and early admission available.

STUDENT LIFE. Housing: Dormitories (men, women, coed); apartment housing available. Family housing available. **Activities:** Student government, student newspaper, television, choral groups, dance, drama, jazz band, music ensembles, musical theater, sororities.

ATHLETICS. NCAA. **Intercollegiate:** Basketball W, gymnastics W, tennis W, volleyball W. **Intramural:** Archery W, basketball W, bowling W, fencing W, softball W, tennis W, volleyball W.

STUDENT SERVICES. Aptitude testing, career counseling, employment service for undergraduates, freshman orientation, health services, on-campus day care, personal counseling, placement service for graduates, veterans counselor, Advising Center, services/facilities for handicapped.

ANNUAL EXPENSES. Tuition and fees: $1,498, $4,080 additional for out-of-state students. **Room and board:** $3,049. **Books and supplies:** $450. **Other expenses:** $1,156.

FINANCIAL AID. 58% of freshmen, 53% of continuing students receive some form of aid. 77% of grants, 66% of loans, 31% of jobs based on need. Academic, music/drama, art, athletic, alumni affiliation, minority scholarships available. **Aid applications:** No closing date; priority given to applications received by April 1; applicants notified on a rolling basis beginning on or about April 1; must reply within 2 weeks.

ADDRESS/TELEPHONE. Dr. Paul Travis, Dean of Enrollment Management, Texas Woman's University, PO Box 22909, TWU Station, Denton, TX 76204-0909. (817) 898-3000. Fax: (817) 898-3198.

Trinity University
San Antonio, Texas — CB code: 6831

Admissions: 75% of applicants accepted
Based on: ••• School record, test scores
•• Activities, essay, interview, recommendations, special talents
Completion: 98% of freshmen end year in good standing
75% graduate, 67% of these enter graduate study

4-year private liberal arts college, coed, affiliated with Presbyterian Church (USA). Founded in 1869. **Accreditation:** Regional. **Undergraduate enrollment:** 1,031 men, 1,137 women full time; 47 men, 66 women part time. **Graduate enrollment:** 44 men, 72 women full time; 62 men, 59 women part time. **Faculty:** 261 total (231 full time), 237 with doctorates or other terminal degrees. **Location:** Urban campus in very large city; 4 miles from downtown. **Calendar:** Semester, limited summer session. **Microcomputers:** 200 located in classrooms, computer centers. **Additional facts:** Undergraduates encouraged to pursue original research. Many students published in scholarly journals, leading to opportunities at some of the country's most selective graduate schools.

DEGREES OFFERED. BA, BS, MA, MS, MEd. 507 bachelor's degrees awarded in 1992. 20% in business and management, 8% communications, 5% letters/literature, 8% life sciences, 5% philosophy, religion, theology, 6% psychology, 30% social sciences. Graduate degrees offered in 6 major fields of study.

UNDERGRADUATE MAJORS. Anthropology, art history, Asian studies, biochemistry, biology, business administration and management, business and management, business economics, chemistry, classics, communications, computer and information sciences, dramatic arts, earth sciences, economics, engineering, English, European studies, fine arts, French, geology, German, history, journalism, Latin American studies, mathematics, music, music performance, music theory and composition, philosophy, physics, political science and government, psychology, religion, Russian, sociology, Spanish, speech, urban studies.

ACADEMIC PROGRAMS. Double major, dual enrollment of high school students, independent study, internships, study abroad, teacher preparation, Washington semester, cross-registration. **Placement/credit:** AP, institutional tests; 36 credit hours maximum for bachelor's degree.

ACADEMIC REQUIREMENTS. Freshmen must earn minimum GPA of 1.8 to continue in good standing. 90% of freshmen return for sophomore year. Students must declare major by end of second year. **Graduation requirements:** 124 hours for bachelor's (36 in major). Most students required to take courses in arts/fine arts, computer science, English, foreign languages, history, humanities, mathematics, philosophy/religion, biological/physical sciences, social sciences. **Postgraduate studies:** 10% enter law school, 7% enter medical school, 5% enter MBA programs, 45% enter other graduate study.

FRESHMAN ADMISSIONS. Selection criteria: GPA, high school rank, test scores, essay, interview, recommendations, extracurricular involvement and achievement important. **High school preparation:** 13 units required. Required units include English 4, foreign language 2, mathematics 3, social science 2 and science 2. **Test requirements:** SAT or ACT (SAT preferred); score report by February 15.

1992 FRESHMAN CLASS PROFILE. 1,069 men applied, 782 accepted, 286 enrolled; 1,161 women applied, 889 accepted, 286 enrolled. 95% had high school GPA of 3.0 or higher, 5% between 2.0 and 2.99. 62% were in top tenth and 85% were in top quarter of graduating class. **Academic background:** Mid 50% of enrolled freshmen had SAT-V between 520-620, SAT-M between 580-670; ACT composite between 24-30. 95% submitted SAT scores, 45% submitted ACT scores. **Characteristics:** 61% from in state, 100% live in college housing, 16% have minority backgrounds, 2% are foreign students. Average age is 18.

FALL-TERM APPLICATIONS. $25 fee, may be waived for applicants with need. Closing date February 1; applicants notified on or about April 1; must reply by May 1. Essay required. Interview recommended. Audition recommended for music applicants. CRDA. Deferred admission available. EDP-S.

STUDENT LIFE. Housing: Dormitories (men, women, coed). **Activities:** Student government, magazine, radio, student newspaper, yearbook, choral groups, concert band, dance, drama, jazz band, music ensembles, musical theater, pep band, symphony orchestra, fraternities, sororities, volunteer social action organization, honor society, Hispanic and black students organizations, Young Democrats and Young Republicans.

ATHLETICS. NCAA. **Intercollegiate:** Baseball M, basketball, cross-country, diving, football M, golf M, rifle, soccer, softball W, swimming, tennis, track and field, volleyball W. **Intramural:** Badminton, basketball, cross-country, fencing, golf, handball, lacrosse W, racquetball, rifle, soccer, softball, swimming, table tennis, tennis, track and field, volleyball, water polo, wrestling M.

STUDENT SERVICES. Aptitude testing, career counseling, employment service for undergraduates, freshman orientation, health services, personal counseling, placement service for graduates, veterans counselor, personal development programs, services/facilities for handicapped.

ANNUAL EXPENSES. Tuition and fees: $11,720. **Room and board:** $4,950. **Books and supplies:** $500. **Other expenses:** $490.

FINANCIAL AID. 80% of freshmen, 73% of continuing students receive some form of aid. 55% of grants, 96% of loans, all jobs based on need. Academic, music/drama, art, state/district residency, leadership, religious affiliation, minority scholarships available. **Aid applications:** Closing date February 1; applicants notified on or about April 1; must reply by May 1. **Additional information:** Full financial need met for all admitted students. FAF and institutional form required for all students.

ADDRESS/TELEPHONE. Beth Allen, Director of Admissions, Trinity University, 715 Stadium Drive, San Antonio, TX 78212-7200. (512) 736-7207. (800) TRINITY. Fax: (210) 736-8164.

Trinity Valley Community College
Athens, Texas — CB code: 6271

2-year public community college, coed. Founded in 1946. **Accreditation:** Regional. **Undergraduate enrollment:** 748 men, 1,000 women full time; 1,249 men, 1,603 women part time. **Faculty:** 197 total (115 full time), 14 with doctorates or other terminal degrees. **Location:** Rural campus in large town; 70 miles from Dallas. **Calendar:** Semester, limited summer session. Extensive evening/early morning classes. **Microcomputers:** Located in libraries, classrooms, computer centers. **Special facilities:** 2 operating ranches with more than 500 acres. **Additional facts:** 3 extension centers in state.

DEGREES OFFERED. AA, AS, AAS. 375 associate degrees awarded in 1992.

UNDERGRADUATE MAJORS. Accounting, agricultural sciences, air conditioning/heating/refrigeration mechanics, air conditioning/heating/refrigeration technology, biology, business and management, business and office, business data entry equipment operation, business data processing and related programs, chemistry, computer and information sciences, drafting, drafting and design technology, education, elementary education, English, fashion merchandising, finance, fine arts, horticulture, journalism, law enforcement and corrections technologies, liberal/general studies, marketing and distribution, mathematics, music, nursing, ornamental horticulture, personal services, physical education, physics, practical nursing, psychology, range management, real estate, secondary education, secretarial and related programs, social sciences, Spanish, speech.

ACADEMIC PROGRAMS. 2-year transfer program, dual enrollment of high school students, honors program, internships, telecourses, weekend college. **Remedial services:** Learning center, preadmission summer program, remedial instruction, special counselor, tutoring. **Placement/credit:** CLEP Subject, institutional tests; 18 credit hours maximum for associate degree.

ACADEMIC REQUIREMENTS. Freshmen must earn minimum GPA of 2.0 to continue in good standing. 50% of freshmen return for sophomore year. Students must declare major on enrollment. **Graduation requirements:** 65 hours for associate. Most students required to take courses in English, history, mathematics, biological/physical sciences, social sciences.

FRESHMAN ADMISSIONS. Selection criteria: Open admissions.

1992 FRESHMAN CLASS PROFILE. 696 men, 773 women enrolled.

Characteristics: 97% from in state, 90% commute, 15% have minority backgrounds, 2% are foreign students. Average age is 27.

FALL-TERM APPLICATIONS. No fee. No closing date; applicants notified on a rolling basis. Early admission available.

STUDENT LIFE. Housing: Dormitories (men, women). **Activities:** Student government, student newspaper, choral groups, concert band, dance, drama, jazz band, marching band, music ensembles, Baptist Student Union, United Campus Ministry.

ATHLETICS. NJCAA. **Intercollegiate:** Basketball, football M. **Intramural:** Basketball, bowling, handball M, racquetball, soccer M, softball, table tennis, tennis, volleyball.

STUDENT SERVICES. Aptitude testing, career counseling, employment service for undergraduates, freshman orientation, on-campus day care, personal counseling, placement service for graduates, veterans counselor, services/facilities for handicapped.

ANNUAL EXPENSES. Tuition and fees: $420, $300 additional for out-of-district students, $1,560 additional for out-of-state students. **Room and board:** $2,420. **Books and supplies:** $400. **Other expenses:** $850.

FINANCIAL AID. 65% of freshmen, 50% of continuing students receive some form of aid. 83% of grants, 91% of loans, 15% of jobs based on need. 940 enrolled freshmen were judged to have need, all were offered aid. Academic, music/drama, art, athletic, leadership scholarships available. **Aid applications:** No closing date; priority given to applications received by July 1; applicants notified on a rolling basis beginning on or about July 1; must reply within 2 weeks.

ADDRESS/TELEPHONE. Darlene Birdsong, Director of Admissions/School Relations, Trinity Valley Community College, 500 South Prairieville, Athens, TX 75751. (903) 675-6217. Fax: (903) 675-6316.

Tyler Junior College
Tyler, Texas — CB code: 6833

2-year public community college, coed. Founded in 1926. **Accreditation:** Regional. **Undergraduate enrollment:** 8,259 men and women. **Faculty:** 340 total (195 full time), 27 with doctorates or other terminal degrees. **Location:** Urban campus in small city; 85 miles from Dallas, 85 miles from Shreveport, Louisiana. **Calendar:** Semester, limited summer session. **Microcomputers:** 75 located in libraries, classrooms. **Special facilities:** Planetarium, conservatory, art museum.

DEGREES OFFERED. AA, AAS. 635 associate degrees awarded in 1992. 25% in business/office and marketing/distribution, 25% education, 5% allied health, 30% trade and industry.

UNDERGRADUATE MAJORS. Agricultural sciences, air conditioning/heating/refrigeration mechanics, air conditioning/heating/refrigeration technology, biology, business administration and management, business and management, business and office, business computer/console/peripheral equipment operation, business data entry equipment operation, business data programming, chemistry, child development/care/guidance, clinical laboratory science, computer and information sciences, criminal justice technology, dental hygiene, drafting, drafting and design technology, education, electrical and electronics equipment repair, elementary education, emergency medical technologies, engineering, English, fashion merchandising, finance, fine arts, fire control and safety technology, foreign languages (multiple emphasis), geology, graphic and printing production, graphic arts technology, home economics, horticulture, journalism, law enforcement and corrections technologies, liberal/general studies, marketing and distribution, mathematics, medical laboratory technologies, music, nursing, ophthalmic services, ornamental horticulture, photographic technology, physical education, physics, practical nursing, precision metal work, predentistry, prelaw, premedicine, prepharmacy, preveterinary, psychology, radiograph medical technology, real estate, recreation and community services technologies, respiratory therapy technology, secondary education, secretarial and related programs, social sciences, special education, visual and performing arts.

ACADEMIC PROGRAMS. 2-year transfer program, dual enrollment of high school students, honors program, independent study, telecourses, weekend college, cross-registration. **Remedial services:** Learning center, remedial instruction, special counselor, tutoring. **Placement/credit:** AP, CLEP General and Subject, institutional tests; 15 credit hours maximum for associate degree.

ACADEMIC REQUIREMENTS. Freshmen must earn minimum GPA of 2.0 to continue in good standing. 37% of freshmen return for sophomore year. Students must declare major by end of first year. **Graduation requirements:** 64 hours for associate. Most students required to take courses in computer science, English, history, mathematics, biological/physical sciences, social sciences.

FRESHMAN ADMISSIONS. Selection criteria: Open admissions. Selective admissions to allied health programs based on test scores. **Test requirements:** SAT or ACT for placement and counseling only; score report by August 20.

1992 FRESHMAN CLASS PROFILE. 5,558 men and women enrolled. **Characteristics:** 85% from in state, 80% commute, 16% have minority backgrounds, 1% are foreign students, 10% join fraternities/sororities. Average age is 19.

FALL-TERM APPLICATIONS. No fee. No closing date; applicants notified on a rolling basis. Interview required for some allied health programs; recommended for others. TASP-(State Requirement).

STUDENT LIFE. Housing: Dormitories (men, women). **Activities:** Student government, student newspaper, choral groups, concert band, dance, drama, jazz band, marching band, music ensembles, musical theater, symphony orchestra, fraternities, sororities, student senate, Bible chairs, international student association.

ATHLETICS. NJCAA. **Intercollegiate:** Baseball M, basketball, football M, golf M, soccer M, tennis. **Intramural:** Badminton, basketball, handball, racquetball, softball, table tennis, tennis, volleyball.

STUDENT SERVICES. Career counseling, employment service for undergraduates, freshman orientation, health services, personal counseling, placement service for graduates, special adviser for adult students, veterans counselor, special services counselor, services/facilities for handicapped.

ANNUAL EXPENSES. Tuition and fees: $610, $300 additional for out-of-district students, $600 additional for out-of-state students. **Room and board:** $2,300. **Books and supplies:** $500. **Other expenses:** $556.

FINANCIAL AID. Grants, loans, jobs available. Academic, music/drama, art, athletic, state/district residency, leadership, alumni affiliation, minority scholarships available. **Aid applications:** No closing date; priority given to applications received by July 1; applicants notified on a rolling basis.

ADDRESS/TELEPHONE. Kenneth Lewis, Dean of Admissions, Tyler Junior College, PO Box 9020, Tyler, TX 75711-9020. (903) 510-2200. Fax: (903)510-2634.

University of Central Texas
Killeen, Texas — CB code: 6756

2-year upper-division private university, coed. Founded in 1973. **Accreditation:** Regional. **Undergraduate enrollment:** 102 men, 74 women full time; 163 men, 134 women part time. **Graduate enrollment:** 52 men, 65 women full time; 134 men, 116 women part time. **Location:** Suburban campus in small city; 60 miles from Austin, 70 miles from Waco. **Calendar:** Semester. Saturday and extensive evening/early morning classes. **Additional facts:** Share campus with a community college.

ANNUAL EXPENSES. Tuition and fees: $3,750. **Room and board:** $3,028. **Books and supplies:** $783. **Other expenses:** $1,102.

ADDRESS/TELEPHONE. Nanci Olds, Admissions Adviser, University of Central Texas, PO Box 1416, Highway 190 West, Killeen, TX 76540-1416. (817) 526-8262. (800) 826-6308.

University of Dallas
Irving, Texas — CB code: 6868

Admissions:	89% of applicants accepted
Based on:	••• Essay, school record
	•• Interview, recommendations, test scores
	• Activities, special talents
Completion:	96% of freshmen end year in good standing
	61% graduate, 55% of these enter graduate study

4-year private business, liberal arts college, coed, affiliated with Roman Catholic Church. Founded in 1956. **Accreditation:** Regional. **Undergraduate enrollment:** 478 men, 554 women full time; 37 men, 47 women part time. **Graduate enrollment:** 285 men, 172 women full time; 823 men, 473 women part time. **Faculty:** 225 total (101 full time), 211 with doctorates or other terminal degrees. **Location:** Suburban campus in small city; 5 miles from Dallas. **Calendar:** Semester, limited summer session. **Microcomputers:** 50 located in computer centers. **Special facilities:** Observatory, art galleries.

DEGREES OFFERED. BA, BS, MA, MBA, MFA, PhD. 203 bachelor's degrees awarded in 1992. 16% in letters/literature, 15% life sciences, 8% philosophy, religion, theology, 9% psychology, 33% social sciences, 8% visual and performing arts. Graduate degrees offered in 20 major fields of study.

UNDERGRADUATE MAJORS. Art education, art history, biochemistry, biology, ceramics, chemistry, dramatic arts, economics, education, elementary education, English literature, foreign languages (multiple emphasis), French, German, Greek (classical), history, Latin, mathematics, painting, philosophy, physics, political science and government, predentistry, prelaw, premedicine, prepharmacy, preveterinary, printmaking, psychology, sculpture, secondary education, Spanish, theological studies.

ACADEMIC PROGRAMS. Double major, internships, student-designed major, study abroad, teacher preparation, telecourses, intensive honors chemistry summer program for freshmen; combined bachelor's/graduate program in business administration. **Remedial services:** Learning center, preadmission summer program, reduced course load, tutoring. **ROTC:** Air Force, Army. **Placement/credit:** AP, CLEP Subject, institutional tests; 30 credit hours maximum for bachelor's degree.

ACADEMIC REQUIREMENTS. Freshmen must earn minimum GPA of 1.0 to continue in good standing. 82% of freshmen return for sophomore

year. Students must declare major by end of second year. **Graduation requirements:** 120 hours for bachelor's. Most students required to take courses in arts/fine arts, English, foreign languages, history, mathematics, philosophy/religion, biological/physical sciences, social sciences. **Additional information:** 85% of undergraduates spend 1 semester of sophomore year at university's campus in Rome, Italy. Optional credit-bearing intersession.

FRESHMAN ADMISSIONS. Selection criteria: Class rank, high school curriculum, essay, and test scores most important. Interview and recommendation also important. **High school preparation:** 16 units required. Required and recommended units include English 4, foreign language 2-4, mathematics 3-4 and social science 2-3. Science 4 recommended. **Test requirements:** SAT or ACT; score report by June 1.

1992 FRESHMAN CLASS PROFILE. 263 men applied, 230 accepted, 119 enrolled; 355 women applied, 320 accepted, 137 enrolled. 40% were in top tenth and 64% were in top quarter of graduating class. **Academic background:** Mid 50% of enrolled freshmen had SAT-V between 470-610, SAT-M between 520-640; ACT composite between 23-28. 85% submitted SAT scores, 54% submitted ACT scores. **Characteristics:** 63% from in state, 81% live in college housing, 27% have minority backgrounds, 3% are foreign students. Average age is 19.

FALL-TERM APPLICATIONS. $30 fee, may be waived for applicants with need. Closing date February 1; priority given to applications received by December 1; applicants notified on a rolling basis; must reply by May 1. Essay required. Interview recommended for academically marginal applicants. Portfolio recommended for art applicants. CRDA. Deferred and early admission available.

STUDENT LIFE. Housing: Dormitories (men, women, coed); apartment housing available. **Activities:** Student government, magazine, student newspaper, yearbook, choral groups, dance, drama, music ensembles, musical theater, social and religious service organizations, ethnic organizations.

ATHLETICS. NAIA. **Intercollegiate:** Basketball, cross-country, golf M, tennis, volleyball W. **Intramural:** Badminton, basketball, fencing, rugby M, sailing, soccer, softball, table tennis, tennis, volleyball, water polo.

STUDENT SERVICES. Career counseling, employment service for undergraduates, freshman orientation, health services, personal counseling, placement service for graduates, services/facilities for handicapped.

ANNUAL EXPENSES. Tuition and fees: $10,180. **Room and board:** $4,650. **Books and supplies:** $500. **Other expenses:** $600.

FINANCIAL AID. 92% of freshmen, 82% of continuing students receive some form of aid. 49% of grants, 86% of loans, 81% of jobs based on need. 173 enrolled freshmen were judged to have need, all were offered aid. Academic, music/drama, art, leadership scholarships available. **Aid applications:** No closing date; priority given to applications received by March 1; applicants notified on a rolling basis beginning on or about March 20; must reply by May 1 or within 4 weeks if notified thereafter. **Additional information:** Aid available for Rome semester.

ADDRESS/TELEPHONE. Christopher Lydon, Director of Admissions/Financial Aid, University of Dallas, 1845 East Northgate, Irving, TX 75062-4799. (214) 721-5266. Fax: (214) 721-5017.

University of Houston
Houston, Texas CB code: 6870

4-year public university, coed. Founded in 1927. **Accreditation:** Regional. **Undergraduate enrollment:** 22,386 men and women. **Graduate enrollment:** 6,196 men and women. **Faculty:** 2,280 total (907 full time). **Location:** Urban campus in very large city; 3 miles from central business district. **Calendar:** Semester, extensive summer session. **Microcomputers:** Located in dormitories, libraries, classrooms, computer centers. **Special facilities:** Art gallery, theater complex, hotel, observatory.

DEGREES OFFERED. BA, BS, MA, MS, MBA, MFA, MEd, MSW, PhD, EdD, OD, B. Pharm. 3,131 bachelor's degrees awarded in 1992. Graduate degrees offered in 108 major fields of study.

UNDERGRADUATE MAJORS. Accounting, anthropology, applied mathematics, architecture, art history, bilingual/bicultural education, biochemical and biophysical sciences, biology, business administration and management, business economics, business education, business statistics, ceramics, chemical engineering, chemistry, civil engineering, classics, communication disorders, computer and information sciences, computer graphics, computer technology, control systems construction management technology, creative writing, drafting and design technology, dramatic arts, early childhood education, economics, education computer information systems, education of the mentally handicapped, electrical technology, electrical/electronics/communications engineering, electronic technology, English, English education, environmental design, fashion merchandising, finance, fine arts, food science and nutrition, foreign languages education, French, geology, geophysics and seismology, German, graphic and printing production, graphic design, health education, history, home economics, home economics education, hotel/motel and restaurant management, human performance education, human resources development, individual and family development, industrial arts education, industrial engineering, industrial technology, information sciences and systems, journalism, journalism education, management information systems, management science, manufacturing technology, marketing and distributive education, marketing management, mathematics, mathematics education, mechanical engineering, medical laboratory technologies, metal/jewelry, music, music education, music history and appreciation, music performance, music theory and composition, nuclear medical technology, nursing, operations research, optometry, organizational behavior, painting, pharmacy, philosophy, photography, physical education, physics, political science and government, predentistry, prelaw, premedicine, prepharmacy, preveterinary, printmaking, psychology, psychology education, radio/television broadcasting, reading education, science education, sculpture, social science education, social studies education, sociology, Spanish, special education, speech, speech pathology/audiology, speech/communication/theater education, statistics, studio art interior design, survey and mapping technology, systems analysis, technical education, trade and industrial education, trade and industrial supervision and management, training and development.

ACADEMIC PROGRAMS. Cooperative education, double major, dual enrollment of high school students, honors program, independent study, internships, study abroad, teacher preparation, cross-registration; combined bachelor's/graduate program in business administration, law. **Remedial services:** Learning center, reduced course load, remedial instruction, special counselor, tutoring. **ROTC:** Army, Naval. **Placement/credit:** AP, CLEP General and Subject, institutional tests.

ACADEMIC REQUIREMENTS. Freshmen must earn minimum GPA of 2.0 to continue in good standing. Students must declare major by end of second year. **Graduation requirements:** 122 hours for bachelor's (36 in major). Most students required to take courses in English, history, humanities, mathematics, biological/physical sciences, social sciences. **Additional information:** College of Technology offers job-oriented degrees in 10 fields.

FRESHMAN ADMISSIONS. Selection criteria: Class rank, SAT verbal score of 400, completion of high school core curriculum, and 2.0 GPA important factors. **High school preparation:** 12 units required. Required and recommended units include English 4, mathematics 3, social science 3 and science 2. Foreign language 2 recommended. Chemistry, physics 1, mathematics 4 required, mechanical drawing 1 recommended for engineering and science applicants. **Test requirements:** SAT or ACT; score report by June 14.

1992 FRESHMAN CLASS PROFILE. 4,717 men and women enrolled. **Characteristics:** Average age is 19.

FALL-TERM APPLICATIONS. $25 fee, may be waived for applicants with need. $50 fee for foreign applicants. Closing date June 14; priority given to applications received by April 15; applicants notified on a rolling basis. Audition required for music applicants. Essay recommended for honors program applicants. Deferred and early admission available.

STUDENT LIFE. Housing: Dormitories (coed); apartment, fraternity, sorority, handicapped housing available. High-rise dormitories and housing for handicapped available. **Activities:** Student government, film, magazine, radio, student newspaper, television, yearbook, choral groups, concert band, dance, drama, jazz band, marching band, music ensembles, musical theater, opera, symphony orchestra, mime, fraternities, sororities, numerous ethnic, social service, political, and religious organizations.

ATHLETICS. NAIA, NCAA. **Intercollegiate:** Baseball M, basketball, cross-country, diving W, football M, golf M, swimming W, tennis W, track and field, volleyball W. **Intramural:** Archery, badminton, baseball M, basketball, bowling, cross-country, diving, football, golf, handball, racquetball, rugby M, soccer, softball, swimming, table tennis, tennis, track and field, volleyball, water polo.

STUDENT SERVICES. Aptitude testing, career counseling, employment service for undergraduates, freshman orientation, health services, on-campus day care, personal counseling, placement service for graduates, special adviser for adult students, veterans counselor, Handicapped Student Services, Learning Support Services, services/facilities for handicapped.

ANNUAL EXPENSES. Tuition and fees: $1,462, $4,080 additional for out-of-state students. **Room and board:** $4,191. **Books and supplies:** $470. **Other expenses:** $1,568.

FINANCIAL AID. 35% of freshmen, 39% of continuing students receive some form of aid. 68% of grants, 78% of loans, 29% of jobs based on need. Academic, music/drama, art, athletic, leadership, minority scholarships available. **Aid applications:** No closing date; priority given to applications received by April 1; applicants notified on a rolling basis beginning on or about May 1; must reply within 4 weeks. **Additional information:** 45-day and 90-day institutional loans available.

ADDRESS/TELEPHONE. Dr. Wayne Sigler, Dean of Admissions, University of Houston, 4800 Calhoun Street, Houston, TX 77204-2161. (713) 743-1010.

University of Houston: Clear Lake
Houston, Texas CB code: 6916

2-year upper-division public university, coed. Founded in 1971. **Accreditation:** Regional. **Undergraduate enrollment:** 509 men, 987 women full time; 912 men, 1,148 women part time. **Graduate enrollment:** 361 men, 519 women full time; 1,264 men, 1,581 women part time. **Faculty:** 360 total (197 full time), 280 with doctorates or other terminal degrees. **Location:**

Suburban campus in very large city; 21 miles from downtown. **Calendar:** Semester, limited summer session. **Microcomputers:** Located in libraries, computer centers.

DEGREES OFFERED. BA, BS, MA, MS, MBA. 357 bachelor's degrees awarded in 1992. 36% in business and management, 9% computer sciences, 18% teacher education, 6% multi/interdisciplinary studies, 6% psychology. Graduate degrees offered in 24 major fields of study.

UNDERGRADUATE MAJORS. Accounting, allied health, anthropology, behavioral sciences, biology, business administration and management, business and management, chemistry, clinical laboratory science, comparative literature, computer and information sciences, dance, dramatic arts, elementary education, finance, fine arts, health care administration, history, humanities, humanities and social sciences, industrial hygiene and safety, laser electro-optic technology, management science, marketing management, mathematics, medical laboratory technologies, physical sciences, political science and government, prelaw, premedicine, psychology, public administration, sociology.

ACADEMIC PROGRAMS. Cooperative education, independent study, internships, student-designed major, study abroad, teacher preparation, weekend college; liberal arts/career combination in engineering. **Remedial services:** Reduced course load. **ROTC:** Army. **Placement/credit:** CLEP Subject; 18 credit hours maximum for bachelor's degree.

ACADEMIC REQUIREMENTS. Students must declare major by end of third year. **Graduation requirements:** 123 hours for bachelor's (30 in major). Most students required to take courses in English, history, humanities, mathematics, biological/physical sciences, social sciences.

STUDENT LIFE. Housing: Limited apartments on campus. **Activities:** Student government, magazine, student newspaper, dance, drama, musical theater, Baptist Student Union, Catholic Campus Ministries, Chinese Student Association, Bilingual Education Student Association, Phi Theta Kappa, Omicron Delta Kappa, Hispanics United for Education, international student organization, Ebony Society. **Additional information:** University draws adult commuter student population.

ATHLETICS. Intramural: Baseball, racquetball, soccer M, softball, table tennis, tennis, volleyball.

STUDENT SERVICES. Career counseling, employment service for undergraduates, health services, personal counseling, placement service for graduates, veterans counselor, services/facilities for handicapped.

ANNUAL EXPENSES. Tuition and fees: $1,451, $4,080 additional for out-of-state students. **Books and supplies:** $600. **Other expenses:** $1,669.

FINANCIAL AID. 20% of continuing students receive some form of aid. 88% of grants, 23% of loans, all jobs based on need. Academic, leadership, minority scholarships available. **Aid applications:** No closing date; priority given to applications received by May 1; applicants notified on a rolling basis; must reply within 4 weeks.

ADDRESS/TELEPHONE. Mike Henry, Director of Admissions, University of Houston: Clear Lake, 2700 Bay Area Boulevard, Houston, TX 77058-1080. (713) 283-2500. Fax: (713) 283-2530.

University of Houston: Downtown

Houston, Texas — CB code: 6922

4-year public university, coed. Founded in 1974. **Accreditation:** Regional. **Undergraduate enrollment:** 1,680 men, 1,622 women full time; 1,921 men, 1,938 women part time. **Faculty:** 361 total (166 full time). **Location:** Urban campus in very large city. **Calendar:** Semester, limited summer session. **Microcomputers:** Located in computer centers. **Special facilities:** Art gallery.

DEGREES OFFERED. BA, BS. 477 bachelor's degrees awarded in 1992. 41% in business and management, 5% business/office and marketing/distribution, 16% computer sciences, 6% engineering technologies, 5% mathematics, 13% multi/interdisciplinary studies, 11% social sciences.

UNDERGRADUATE MAJORS. Accounting, applied mathematics, applied microbiology, biology, business administration and management, business and management, business data processing and related programs, computer and information sciences, creative writing, criminal justice studies, data processing, drafting and design technology, electrical technology, electronic technology, finance, industrial chemistry, liberal/general studies, management information systems, microbiology, office supervision and management, operations research, petroleum land management, professional writing, real estate, secretarial and related programs, structural design and analysis, technical and business writing, word processing.

ACADEMIC PROGRAMS. Cooperative education, dual enrollment of high school students, independent study, internships, student-designed major, visiting/exchange student program. **Remedial services:** Learning center, reduced course load, remedial instruction, special counselor, tutoring. **ROTC:** Army, Naval. **Placement/credit:** CLEP General and Subject, institutional tests.

ACADEMIC REQUIREMENTS. Freshmen must earn minimum GPA of 2.0 to continue in good standing. 66% of freshmen return for sophomore year. Students must declare major by end of first year. **Graduation requirements:** 126 hours for bachelor's. Most students required to take courses in arts/fine arts, English, history, mathematics, biological/physical sciences, social sciences.

FRESHMAN ADMISSIONS. Selection criteria: Open admissions. **Test requirements:** SAT or ACT for placement.

1992 FRESHMAN CLASS PROFILE. 1,432 men and women enrolled. **Characteristics:** 86% from in state, 100% commute, 66% have minority backgrounds, 2% are foreign students. Average age is 20.

FALL-TERM APPLICATIONS. $10 fee, may be waived for applicants with need. Closing date August 2; applicants notified on a rolling basis. Interview recommended. Deferred and early admission available.

STUDENT LIFE. Activities: Student government, magazine, student newspaper, choral groups, drama, musical theater, sororities, international student organization.

ATHLETICS. Intramural: Baseball, basketball, bowling, cross-country, football, golf M, handball M, soccer, softball, swimming, table tennis, track and field, volleyball.

STUDENT SERVICES. Aptitude testing, career counseling, employment service for undergraduates, freshman orientation, health services, personal counseling, placement service for graduates, veterans counselor, services/facilities for handicapped.

ANNUAL EXPENSES. Tuition and fees: $1,474, $4,080 additional for out-of-state students. **Books and supplies:** $300. **Other expenses:** $703.

FINANCIAL AID. 70% of freshmen, 27% of continuing students receive some form of aid. 93% of grants, 61% of loans, all jobs based on need. 790 enrolled freshmen were judged to have need, all were offered aid. Academic, art, state/district residency, leadership, minority scholarships available. **Aid applications:** No closing date; priority given to applications received by June 1; applicants notified on a rolling basis beginning on or about June 1.

ADDRESS/TELEPHONE. Anne McDonald, Director of Enrollment Services, University of Houston: Downtown, 1 Main, Houston, TX 77002. (713) 221-8533. Fax: (713) 221-8157.

University of Houston: Victoria

Victoria, Texas — CB code: 6917

2-year upper-division public university, coed. Founded in 1973. **Accreditation:** Regional. **Undergraduate enrollment:** 87 men, 216 women full time; 107 men, 269 women part time. **Graduate enrollment:** 18 men, 28 women full time; 115 men, 383 women part time. **Faculty:** 60 total (30 full time), 27 with doctorates or other terminal degrees. **Location:** Urban campus in small city; 120 miles from Houston, Austin, and San Antonio. **Calendar:** Semester, limited summer session. **Microcomputers:** 59 located in classrooms, computer centers, campus-wide network.

DEGREES OFFERED. BA, BS, MA, MBA, MEd. 144 bachelor's degrees awarded in 1992. 46% in business and management, 31% teacher education, 8% letters/literature, 8% social sciences. Graduate degrees offered in 7 major fields of study.

UNDERGRADUATE MAJORS. Accounting, business administration and management, business education, computer and information sciences, elementary education, English, English education, history, humanities and social sciences, mathematics, mathematics education, psychology, secondary education, speech/communication/theater education.

ACADEMIC PROGRAMS. Teacher preparation. **Remedial services:** Tutoring.

ACADEMIC REQUIREMENTS. Students must declare major on application. **Graduation requirements:** 122 hours for bachelor's. Most students required to take courses in English, history, mathematics, biological/physical sciences, social sciences. **Additional information:** Degree program in liberal arts for graduates of 2-year vocational programs.

STUDENT LIFE. Activities: Student government.

STUDENT SERVICES. Career counseling, employment service for undergraduates, personal counseling, placement service for graduates, veterans counselor, services/facilities for handicapped.

ANNUAL EXPENSES. Tuition and fees: $1,452, $4,080 additional for out-of-state students. **Books and supplies:** $431. **Other expenses:** $1,468.

FINANCIAL AID. 28% of continuing students receive some form of aid. 80% of grants, 92% of loans, all jobs based on need. Academic scholarships available. **Aid applications:** No closing date; priority given to applications received by April 15; applicants notified on a rolling basis beginning on or about July 15; must reply within 2 weeks. **Additional information:** Short-term loans available at registration.

ADDRESS/TELEPHONE. Claude F. Gilson, Director of Admissions and Records, University of Houston: Victoria, 2506 East Red River, Victoria, TX 77901-4450. (512) 576-3151 ext. 222.

University of Mary Hardin-Baylor

Belton, Texas — CB code: 6396

4-year private university, coed, affiliated with Southern Baptist Convention. Founded in 1845. **Accreditation:** Regional. **Undergraduate enrollment:** 1,689 men and women. **Graduate enrollment:** 215 men and women. **Faculty:** 92

total (74 full time), 51 with doctorates or other terminal degrees. **Location:** Suburban campus in large town; 60 miles from Austin. **Calendar:** Semester, limited summer session. Extensive evening/early morning classes. **Microcomputers:** 20 located in computer centers. **Special facilities:** Child development center for daycare and research.

DEGREES OFFERED. BA, BS, BFA, MA, MBA, MEd. 322 bachelor's degrees awarded in 1992. 27% in business and management, 12% education, 7% teacher education, 19% health sciences, 13% social sciences. Graduate degrees offered in 11 major fields of study.

UNDERGRADUATE MAJORS. Accounting, administration of special education, applied mathematics, art education, behavioral sciences, biology, business administration and management, business and management, business data processing and related programs, business economics, business education, business home economics, chemistry, clinical laboratory science, clothing and textiles management/production/services, communications, computer and information sciences, driver and safety education, early childhood education, economics, education, education administration, education of the gifted and talented, education of the mentally handicapped, elementary education, English, English education, family and community services, family/consumer resource management, fashion design, fashion merchandising, finance, fine arts, food production/management/services, food science and nutrition, foreign languages education, health education, health sciences, history, home economics, home economics education, home furnishings and equipment management/production/services, individual and family development, information sciences and systems, institutional/home management/supporting programs, junior high education, liberal/general studies, management information systems, marketing and distribution, mathematics, mathematics education, medical laboratory technologies, music, music education, music performance, nursing, nutritional education, physical education, political science and government, predentistry, prelaw, premedicine, prepharmacy, psychology, reading education, recreation and community services technologies, religion, religious music, remedial education, science education, secondary education, social science education, social studies education, social work, sociology, Spanish, special education, speech, speech/communication/theater education, textiles and clothing, theological studies, visual and performing arts.

ACADEMIC PROGRAMS. Accelerated program, double major, dual enrollment of high school students, honors program, independent study, internships, study abroad, teacher preparation; liberal arts/career combination in health sciences. **Remedial services:** Preadmission summer program, reduced course load, remedial instruction, special counselor, tutoring, English as a foreign language. **ROTC:** Air Force. **Placement/credit:** AP, CLEP General and Subject, institutional tests; 31 credit hours maximum for bachelor's degree.

ACADEMIC REQUIREMENTS. Freshmen must earn minimum GPA of 1.5 to continue in good standing. 80% of freshmen return for sophomore year. Students must declare major by end of second year. **Graduation requirements:** 124 hours for bachelor's (36 in major). Most students required to take courses in arts/fine arts, computer science, English, foreign languages, history, humanities, mathematics, philosophy/religion, biological/physical sciences, social sciences. **Postgraduate studies:** 3% enter medical school, 5% enter MBA programs, 12% enter other graduate study.

FRESHMAN ADMISSIONS. Selection criteria: School achievement record and test scores important. Student must be in top half of graduating class, or score 18 on ACT or 700 on SAT. Academically deficient students may be accepted on individual basis by approval of admissions committee. **High school preparation:** 15 units required. Required units include English 3, mathematics 2 and social science 2. **Test requirements:** SAT or ACT (ACT preferred); score report by August 15.

1992 FRESHMAN CLASS PROFILE. 259 men and women enrolled. **Characteristics:** 95% from in state, 70% commute, 15% have minority backgrounds, 3% are foreign students. Average age is 19.

FALL-TERM APPLICATIONS. $35 fee. No closing date; priority given to applications received by July 31; applicants notified on a rolling basis. Interview recommended for academically marginal applicants. Audition recommended for music applicants. CRDA. Deferred and early admission available. EDP-F.

STUDENT LIFE. Housing: Dormitories (men, women). **Activities:** Student government, film, magazine, radio, student newspaper, television, yearbook, alumni publication, choral groups, concert band, drama, music ensembles, musical theater, opera, pep band, sororities, honor societies, religious organizations, Crusaders for Christ, Baptist Student Union, International Club, Commuter Club.

ATHLETICS. NAIA. **Intercollegiate:** Baseball M, basketball, golf M, soccer M, softball W, tennis, volleyball W. **Intramural:** Basketball, boxing M, diving, golf, gymnastics, soccer, softball, swimming, table tennis, tennis, track and field, volleyball, water polo.

STUDENT SERVICES. Aptitude testing, career counseling, employment service for undergraduates, health services, on-campus day care, personal counseling, placement service for graduates, special adviser for adult students, veterans counselor, services/facilities for handicapped.

ANNUAL EXPENSES. Tuition and fees: $5,250. **Room and board:** $3,106. **Books and supplies:** $600. **Other expenses:** $1,200.

FINANCIAL AID. 80% of freshmen, 75% of continuing students receive some form of aid. 60% of grants, 86% of loans, 58% of jobs based on need. 175 enrolled freshmen were judged to have need, all were offered aid. Academic, music/drama, athletic, leadership, alumni affiliation, religious affiliation, minority scholarships available. **Aid applications:** No closing date; priority given to applications received by May 1; applicants notified on a rolling basis beginning on or about May 1; must reply within 2 weeks.

ADDRESS/TELEPHONE. Bobby Johnson, Director of Admissions, University of Mary Hardin-Baylor, Belton, TX 76513. (817) 939-4508. (800) 727-8642.

University of North Texas
Denton, Texas — CB code: 6481

4-year public university, coed. Founded in 1890. **Accreditation:** Regional. **Undergraduate enrollment:** 7,016 men, 7,556 women full time; 2,576 men, 2,485 women part time. **Graduate enrollment:** 1,360 men, 1,350 women full time; 1,674 men, 2,416 women part time. **Faculty:** 1,088 total (782 full time), 677 with doctorates or other terminal degrees. **Location:** Suburban campus in small city; 35 miles from Dallas-Fort Worth. **Calendar:** Semester, extensive summer session. **Microcomputers:** 388 located in libraries, classrooms, computer centers. **Special facilities:** Art gallery, laser, observatory, accelerators.

DEGREES OFFERED. BA, BS, BFA, MA, MS, MBA, MFA, MEd, PhD, EdD. 3,132 bachelor's degrees awarded in 1992. 23% in business and management, 11% business/office and marketing/distribution, 8% communications, 9% teacher education, 5% home economics, 5% multi/interdisciplinary studies, 5% parks/recreation, protective services, public affairs, 5% social sciences, 11% visual and performing arts. Graduate degrees offered in 78 major fields of study.

UNDERGRADUATE MAJORS. Accounting, accounting control systems, advertising art, anthropology, applied arts and sciences, art education, art history, biochemistry, biology, business administration and management, business and management, business economics, chemistry, child development/care/guidance, commercial art, communications, computer and information sciences, counseling associate studies, crafts, criminal justice studies, cytotechnology, dance, dramatic arts, drawing, early childhood education, economics, elementary education, emergency/disaster science, English, entrepreneurial business, fashion design, finance, fine arts, French, geography, German, gerontology, graphic design, health education, history, hotel/motel and restaurant management, human environment and housing, human resources development, industrial technology, information sciences and systems, insurance and risk management, interior design, jazz, journalism, kinesiology, labor/industrial relations, liberal/general studies, library science, management information systems, marketing and distribution, mathematics, medical laboratory technologies, merchandising and fabric analytics, music, music history and appreciation, music performance, music theory and composition, office skills education, painting, personnel management, philosophy, photography, physical education, physics, piano pedagogy, political science and government, printmaking, production and operation management, psychology, radio/television broadcasting, real estate, recreation and community services technologies, sculpture, social sciences, social work, sociology, Spanish, speech pathology/audiology, textiles and clothing.

ACADEMIC PROGRAMS. Cooperative education, double major, dual enrollment of high school students, honors program, internships, student-designed major, study abroad, teacher preparation; combined bachelor's/graduate program in business administration. **Remedial services:** Remedial instruction, tutoring, study skills courses. **ROTC:** Air Force. **Placement/credit:** AP, CLEP General and Subject, institutional tests; 24 credit hours maximum for bachelor's degree.

ACADEMIC REQUIREMENTS. Freshmen must earn minimum GPA of 1.8 to continue in good standing. 68% of freshmen return for sophomore year. **Graduation requirements:** 124 hours for bachelor's (24 in major). Most students required to take courses in English, history, biological/physical sciences, social sciences.

FRESHMAN ADMISSIONS. Selection criteria: School achievement record most important. Class rank in top 10%, no minimum scores required, but must submit scores. Remainder of top quarter, minimum 800 SAT or 19 ACT; 2nd quarter, minimum 900 SAT or 21 ACT; 3rd quarter, minimum 1000 SAT or 24 ACT; 4th quarter, minimum 1100 SAT or 27 ACT. Recommended units include English 4, mathematics 3, social science 2.5 and science 2. Recommended units in economics, health education, computer sciences, and foreign language. **Test requirements:** SAT or ACT; score report by June 15.

1992 FRESHMAN CLASS PROFILE. 1,575 men, 1,753 women enrolled. 16% were in top tenth and 47% were in top quarter of graduating class. **Characteristics:** 53% live in college housing, 16% have minority backgrounds, 4% are foreign students.

FALL-TERM APPLICATIONS. $25 fee, may be waived for applicants with need. Closing date June 15; applicants notified on a rolling basis. Audition required for music applicants. Early admission available. Students seeking early admission must be in top quarter of class with strong B average, complete 3 units of English and 2 each of mathematics, social science, natural science; present minimum SAT score of 1100 or ACT 27, submit letters from principal or high school counselor and from parents or guardian, arrange interview with admissions office.

STUDENT LIFE. Housing: Dormitories (men, women, coed); apartment, fraternity housing available. **Activities:** Student government, film, radio, student newspaper, television, yearbook, choral groups, concert band, dance, drama, jazz band, marching band, music ensembles, musical theater, opera, pep band, symphony orchestra, fraternities, sororities, honorary societies, religious, ethnic, and social service organizations.

ATHLETICS. NCAA. **Intercollegiate:** Basketball, cross-country, football M, golf, soccer M, tennis, track and field, volleyball W. **Intramural:** Badminton, basketball, football M, golf, racquetball, soccer, softball, tennis, track and field, volleyball, water polo.

STUDENT SERVICES. Aptitude testing, career counseling, employment service for undergraduates, freshman orientation, health services, on-campus day care, personal counseling, placement service for graduates, special adviser for adult students, veterans counselor, services/facilities for handicapped.

ANNUAL EXPENSES. Tuition and fees: $1,500, $4,100 additional for out-of-state students. **Room and board:** $3,508. **Books and supplies:** $450. **Other expenses:** $1,100.

FINANCIAL AID. 27% of freshmen, 27% of continuing students receive some form of aid. All grants, 74% of loans, all jobs based on need. Academic, music/drama, art, athletic, state/district residency scholarships available. **Aid applications:** No closing date; priority given to applications received by June 1; applicants notified on a rolling basis beginning on or about June 1; must reply within 3 weeks.

ADDRESS/TELEPHONE. Don Palermo, Director of Admissions, University of North Texas, PO Box 13797, Denton, TX 76203-3797. (817) 565-2681. Fax: (817) 565-4913.

University of St. Thomas
Houston, Texas — CB code: 6880

4-year private university, coed, affiliated with Roman Catholic Church. Founded in 1947. **Accreditation:** Regional. **Undergraduate enrollment:** 1,310 men and women. **Graduate enrollment:** 769 men and women. **Faculty:** 148 total (87 full time), 69 with doctorates or other terminal degrees. **Location:** Urban campus in very large city; 3 miles from downtown. **Calendar:** Semester, limited summer session. Saturday and extensive evening/early morning classes. **Microcomputers:** 61 located in dormitories, libraries, computer centers. **Special facilities:** English department writing lab.

DEGREES OFFERED. BA, BS, MA, MBA, MEd, PhD, M.Div. 107 bachelor's degrees awarded in 1992. 25% in business and management, 8% communications, 15% education, 6% life sciences, 7% multi/interdisciplinary studies, 7% psychology, 12% social sciences. Graduate degrees offered in 9 major fields of study.

UNDERGRADUATE MAJORS. Accounting, bilingual/bicultural education, biology, business administration and management, business economics, chemistry, communications, computer and information sciences, dramatic arts, economics, education, elementary education, English, fine arts, French, history, international relations, international studies, junior high education, legal assistant/paralegal, liberal/general studies, management information systems, marketing management, mathematics, music, philosophy, political science and government, predentistry, prelaw, premedicine, preveterinary, psychology, religious education, secondary education, social sciences, sociology, Spanish, special education, theological studies.

ACADEMIC PROGRAMS. Cooperative education, double major, dual enrollment of high school students, honors program, independent study, internships, study abroad, teacher preparation, visiting/exchange student program, cross-registration; liberal arts/career combination in engineering, health sciences. **Remedial services:** Learning center, preadmission summer program, reduced course load, remedial instruction, tutoring. **ROTC:** Army, Naval. **Placement/credit:** AP, CLEP General and Subject, institutional tests; 30 credit hours maximum for bachelor's degree.

ACADEMIC REQUIREMENTS. Freshmen must earn minimum GPA of 1.55 to continue in good standing. Students in computer science and education must maintain GPA of 2.5 to continue in good academic standing. 69% of freshmen return for sophomore year. Students must declare major by end of second year. **Graduation requirements:** 126 hours for bachelor's (36 in major). Most students required to take courses in English, foreign languages, history, mathematics, philosophy/religion, biological/physical sciences, social sciences.

FRESHMAN ADMISSIONS. Selection criteria: School achievement record and test scores most important. Interview and letters of recommendation considered. **High school preparation:** 16 units required. Required units include biological science 1, English 4, foreign language 2, mathematics 3, social science 2 and science 2. **Test requirements:** SAT or ACT; score report by August 1.

1992 FRESHMAN CLASS PROFILE. 178 men and women enrolled. **Characteristics:** 90% from in state, 84% commute, 44% have minority backgrounds, 5% are foreign students. Average age is 19.

FALL-TERM APPLICATIONS. $15 fee, may be waived for applicants with need. Closing date August 1; priority given to applications received by March 1; applicants notified on a rolling basis; must reply by August 1 or within 30 days if notified thereafter. Audition required for applied music, voice, drama applicants. Portfolio required for art applicants. Essay required. Interview recommended. Deferred and early admission available.

STUDENT LIFE. Housing: Dormitories (coed); apartment housing available. **Activities:** Student government, magazine, student newspaper, yearbook, choral groups, concert band, drama, jazz band, music ensembles, Campus Ministry, Young Republicans, black union, Aquinas leadership and service honors association, office of volunteer opportunities.

ATHLETICS. Intramural: Basketball, bowling, football, golf, handball, racquetball, rugby, soccer, softball, tennis, volleyball.

STUDENT SERVICES. Career counseling, employment service for undergraduates, freshman orientation, health services, personal counseling, placement service for graduates, veterans counselor, services/facilities for handicapped.

ANNUAL EXPENSES. Tuition and fees: $8,162. **Room and board:** $3,870. **Books and supplies:** $425. **Other expenses:** $1,050.

FINANCIAL AID. 50% of freshmen, 50% of continuing students receive some form of aid. 63% of grants, 76% of loans, 82% of jobs based on need. Academic, music/drama, state/district residency, leadership, religious affiliation, minority scholarships available. **Aid applications:** No closing date; priority given to applications received by March 1; applicants notified on a rolling basis beginning on or about May 1; must reply within 4 weeks.

ADDRESS/TELEPHONE. Elsie P. Biron, Director of Admissions, University of St. Thomas, 3800 Montrose Boulevard, Houston, TX 77006-4696. (713) 525-3500. Fax: (713) 522-9920.

University of Texas at Arlington
Arlington, Texas — CB code: 6013

Admissions:	73% of applicants accepted
Based on:	••• School record, test scores
	• Activities, interview, recommendations
Completion:	85% of freshmen end year in good standing
	25% enter graduate study

4-year public university, coed. Founded in 1895. **Accreditation:** Regional. **Undergraduate enrollment:** 6,095 men, 5,412 women full time; 4,532 men, 4,365 women part time. **Graduate enrollment:** 1,222 men, 759 women full time; 1,354 men, 988 women part time. **Faculty:** 881 total (555 full time). **Location:** Suburban campus in large city; 15 miles from Dallas and Fort Worth. **Calendar:** Semester, extensive summer session. **Microcomputers:** Located in classrooms, computer centers. **Special facilities:** Art gallery, library special collections, robotics center, observatory.

DEGREES OFFERED. BA, BS, BFA, BArch, MA, MS, MBA, MSW, PhD. 2,778 bachelor's degrees awarded in 1992. 32% in business and management, 8% communications, 11% engineering, 9% health sciences, 9% social sciences. Graduate degrees offered in 41 major fields of study.

UNDERGRADUATE MAJORS. Accounting, aerospace/aeronautical/astronautical engineering, anthropology, architecture, art history, biochemistry, biology, business and management, business economics, chemistry, civil engineering, classics, clinical laboratory science, computer and information sciences, computer engineering, criminal justice studies, criminology, dramatic arts, education, electrical/electronics/communications engineering, English, finance, fine arts, French, geology, German, history, industrial engineering, interior design, journalism, landscape architecture, liberal/general studies, management information systems, management science, marketing management, mathematics, mechanical engineering, medical laboratory technologies, microbiology, music, nursing, philosophy, physical education, physics, political science and government, prelaw, psychology, radio/television broadcasting, real estate, Russian, social work, sociology, Spanish, speech.

ACADEMIC PROGRAMS. Cooperative education, dual enrollment of high school students, honors program, student-designed major, study abroad, teacher preparation, telecourses, cross-registration. **Remedial services:** Preadmission summer program, reduced course load, remedial instruction, special counselor, tutoring. **ROTC:** Army. **Placement/credit:** AP, CLEP Subject, institutional tests; 30 credit hours maximum for bachelor's degree.

ACADEMIC REQUIREMENTS. Freshmen must earn minimum GPA of 2.0 to continue in good standing. 66% of freshmen return for sophomore year. Students must declare major by end of second year. **Graduation requirements:** 128 hours for bachelor's (30 in major). Most students required to take courses in arts/fine arts, English, foreign languages, history, mathematics, biological/physical sciences, social sciences.

FRESHMAN ADMISSIONS. Selection criteria: Class rank and test scores very important. **High school preparation:** 20 units required. Required units include English 4, mathematics 2, social science 3 and science 2. 2 units of foreign languages or 2 units of additional mathematics and/or sciences also required. 2 algebra or 1 algebra and 1 geometry required. **Test requirements:** SAT or ACT; score report by August 15.

1992 FRESHMAN CLASS PROFILE. 3,562 men and women applied, 2,609 accepted; 872 men enrolled, 808 women enrolled. 70% had high school GPA of 3.0 or higher, 28% between 2.0 and 2.99. **Academic background:** Mid 50% of enrolled freshmen had SAT-V between 370-500, SAT-

M between 430-560; ACT composite between 17-24. 75% submitted SAT scores, 25% submitted ACT scores. **Characteristics:** 97% from in state, 90% commute, 31% have minority backgrounds, 2% are foreign students, 10% join fraternities/sororities. Average age is 19.

FALL-TERM APPLICATIONS. No fee. Closing date August 1; priority given to applications received by July 1; applicants notified on a rolling basis beginning on or about March 15. Interview recommended for handicapped, academically weak applicants. Audition recommended for music applicants. Portfolio recommended for architecture, art applicants. Deferred admission available.

STUDENT LIFE. Housing: Dormitories (men, women, coed); apartment, fraternity, sorority housing available. **Activities:** Student government, student newspaper, television, choral groups, concert band, dance, drama, jazz band, marching band, music ensembles, musical theater, fraternities, sororities, religious organizations, Black and Mexican American organizations, service organizations, foreign student groups, political groups.

ATHLETICS. NCAA. **Intercollegiate:** Baseball M, basketball, cross-country, golf, softball W, tennis, track and field, volleyball W. **Intramural:** Baseball M, basketball, bowling, gymnastics, racquetball W, rifle M, soccer M, softball, swimming, tennis, track and field, volleyball.

STUDENT SERVICES. Aptitude testing, career counseling, employment service for undergraduates, freshman orientation, health services, on-campus day care, personal counseling, placement service for graduates, veterans counselor, services/facilities for handicapped.

ANNUAL EXPENSES. Tuition and fees: $1,248, $4,080 additional for out-of-state students. **Room and board:** $2,780. **Books and supplies:** $420. **Other expenses:** $1,000.

FINANCIAL AID. 27% of freshmen, 62% of continuing students receive some form of aid. 83% of grants, 76% of loans, all jobs based on need. Academic, music/drama, art, athletic, minority scholarships available. **Aid applications:** No closing date; priority given to applications received by June 1; applicants notified on a rolling basis beginning on or about April 15.

ADDRESS/TELEPHONE. Zack Prince, Registrar and Director of Admissions, University of Texas at Arlington, PO Box 19088, Arlington, TX 76019-0088. (817) 273-2119.

University of Texas at Austin

Austin, Texas CB code: 6882

Admissions: 65% of applicants accepted
Based on: ••• School record, test scores
•• Activities, essay, recommendations, special talents
Completion: 94% of freshmen end year in good standing
56% graduate

4-year public university, coed. Founded in 1883. **Accreditation:** Regional. **Undergraduate enrollment:** 16,238 men, 14,533 women full time; 2,677 men, 2,163 women part time. **Graduate enrollment:** 6,976 men, 4,777 women full time; 682 men, 904 women part time. **Faculty:** 2,308 total (2,169 full time), 2,044 with doctorates or other terminal degrees. **Location:** Urban campus in large city; 70 miles from San Antonio. **Calendar:** Semester, extensive summer session. **Microcomputers:** 10,000 located in dormitories, libraries, classrooms, computer centers. **Special facilities:** Lyndon Baines Johnson Library and Museum, art galleries, major humanities and scientific research centers, observatory, fusion reactor.

DEGREES OFFERED. BA, BS, BFA, BArch, MA, MS, MBA, MFA, MEd, PhD, EdD, Pharm D, JD. 7,475 bachelor's degrees awarded in 1992. 20% in business and management, 11% communications, 9% engineering, 6% letters/literature, 6% life sciences, 7% psychology, 16% social sciences. Graduate degrees offered in 85 major fields of study.

UNDERGRADUATE MAJORS. Accounting, advertising, aerospace/aeronautical/astronautical engineering, Afro-American (black) studies, American studies, anthropology, applied learning and development, applied music, archeology, architectural engineering, architectural studies, architecture, art history, Asian studies, astronomy, biochemistry, biology, botany, business administration and management, business and management, chemical engineering, chemistry, civil engineering, classics, communication sciences and disorders, computer and information sciences, Czechoslovakian, dance, drama production and theatre studies, dramatic arts, economics, electrical/electronics/communications engineering, engineering management, English, fashion merchandising, finance, food science and nutrition, French, geography, geology, geophysics and seismology, German, Greek (classical), health promotion and fitness, Hebrew, history, home economics, humanities, individual and family development, interior design, international business management, Italian, journalism, kinesiology, Latin, Latin American studies, linguistics, management information systems, management science, marine biology, marketing management, mathematics, mechanical engineering, medical laboratory technologies, Mexican American studies, microbiology, Middle Eastern studies, molecular biology, music, music literature, music theory and composition, nursing, Oriental/African languages/literatures, petroleum engineering, pharmacy, philosophy, physics, political science and government, Portuguese, psychology, radio/television broadcasting, Russian, Scandinavian languages, social work, sociology, Soviet and East European studies, Spanish, speech, studio art, textiles and clothing, theater design, visual and performing arts, youth and community studies, zoology.

ACADEMIC PROGRAMS. Cooperative education, double major, dual enrollment of high school students, honors program, independent study, internships, student-designed major, study abroad, teacher preparation, telecourses, visiting/exchange student program, weekend college, cross-registration; liberal arts/career combination in engineering, business. **Remedial services:** Learning center, preadmission summer program, remedial instruction, tutoring. **ROTC:** Air Force, Army, Naval. **Placement/credit:** AP, CLEP Subject, institutional tests.

ACADEMIC REQUIREMENTS. Freshmen must earn minimum GPA of 2.0 to continue in good standing. 85% of freshmen return for sophomore year. Students must declare major by end of second year. **Graduation requirements:** 120 hours for bachelor's (24 in major). Most students required to take courses in arts/fine arts, English, foreign languages, history, humanities, mathematics, biological/physical sciences, social sciences.

FRESHMAN ADMISSIONS. Selection criteria: Class rank, test scores, and required high school units very important. Minimum test scores for admission depend on high school class rank. Recommendations from mathematics and English teachers may be requested. **High school preparation:** 15.5 units required. Required and recommended units include English 4, foreign language 2, mathematics 3-4, social science 3 and science 2-3. Foreign language must be same language; 1.5 units electives, of which .5 fine arts strongly recommended. **Test requirements:** SAT or ACT. Mathematics Level I or II and English Composition ACH required for enrolling students with no previous college work. Score report by August 15. **Additional information:** ACH required of all applicants for placement purposes. ACH also required of students who plan to register for courses for which prerequisite tests are required and who do not present high enough AP test scores and for those graduating from nonaccredited high schools.

1992 FRESHMAN CLASS PROFILE. 7,540 men applied, 4,961 accepted, 2,755 enrolled; 6,695 women applied, 4,358 accepted, 2,402 enrolled. 48% were in top tenth and 84% were in top quarter of graduating class. **Academic background:** Mid 50% of enrolled freshmen had ACT composite between 23-27. 33% submitted ACT scores. **Characteristics:** 92% from in state, 55% commute, 31% have minority backgrounds, 2% are foreign students, 10% join fraternities/sororities. Average age is 18.

FALL-TERM APPLICATIONS. $35 fee, may be waived for applicants with need. $75 fee for foreign applicants. Closing date February 1; applicants notified on a rolling basis. Audition required for music applicants. Essay required for honors program applicants. Interview recommended for Plan II (Liberal Arts Honors Program), art applicants. CRDA. January 20 closing for Plan II Liberal Arts Honors Program applications. Some other programs fill early.

STUDENT LIFE. Housing: Dormitories (men, women, coed); apartment, fraternity, sorority, cooperative housing available. Special housing for handicapped students available on one floor in four dormitories. **Activities:** Student government, film, magazine, radio, student newspaper, television, yearbook, choral groups, concert band, dance, drama, jazz band, marching band, music ensembles, musical theater, opera, pep band, symphony orchestra, fraternities, sororities, wide variety of religious, political, ethnic, and social service organizations.

ATHLETICS. NCAA. **Intercollegiate:** Baseball M, basketball, cross-country, diving, football M, golf, swimming, tennis, track and field, volleyball W. **Intramural:** Archery, badminton, basketball, bowling, cross-country, fencing, football, golf, gymnastics, handball, horseback riding, lacrosse M, racquetball, rifle, rowing (crew), rugby M, sailing, skiing, soccer, softball, squash, swimming, table tennis, tennis, track and field, volleyball, water polo, wrestling M.

STUDENT SERVICES. Aptitude testing, career counseling, employment service for undergraduates, freshman orientation, health services, on-campus day care, personal counseling, placement service for graduates, special adviser for adult students, veterans counselor, services/facilities for handicapped.

ANNUAL EXPENSES. Tuition and fees: $1,394, $4,080 additional for out-of-state students. **Room and board:** $4,100. **Books and supplies:** $650. **Other expenses:** $1,600.

FINANCIAL AID. 46% of freshmen, 47% of continuing students receive some form of aid. 57% of grants, 93% of loans, 17% of jobs based on need. 1,350 enrolled freshmen were judged to have need, all were offered aid. Academic, music/drama, art, athletic, state/district residency, leadership, minority scholarships available. **Aid applications:** No closing date; priority given to applications received by April 1; applicants notified on a rolling basis beginning on or about April 1; must reply within 3 weeks.

ADDRESS/TELEPHONE. Shirley F. Binder, MEd, Associate Vice President for Student Affairs and Director of Admissions, University of Texas at Austin, Austin, TX 78712-1159. (512) 471-7601. Fax: (512) 471-3529.

University of Texas at Brownsville
Brownsville, Texas CB code: 2054

2-year upper-division public branch campus college. Founded in 1977. **Accreditation:** Regional. **Undergraduate enrollment:** 7,822 men and women. **Graduate enrollment:** 299 men and women. **Faculty:** 200 total. **Location:** Very large city. **Microcomputers:** Located in libraries, classrooms, computer centers. **Additional facts:** Campus has both lower and upper division students.

DEGREES OFFERED. BA, MA, MS, MBA, MEd. 317 associate degrees awarded in 1992. 235 bachelor's degrees awarded. Graduate degrees offered in 12 major fields of study.

UNDERGRADUATE MAJORS. Associate: Clinical laboratory science, drafting, early childhood education, emergency medical technologies, human services, legal secretary, practical nursing, radiograph medical technology, respiratory therapy technology. **Bachelor's:** Accounting, aviation management, biology, biology education, business and management, criminal justice studies, English education, marketing management, mathematics, mathematics education, physical education, Spanish, spanish education.

ACADEMIC PROGRAMS. Cooperative education, double major, dual enrollment of high school students, honors program, independent study, internships. **Remedial services:** Learning center, preadmission summer program, reduced course load, remedial instruction, special counselor, tutoring.

ACADEMIC REQUIREMENTS. Graduation requirements: 124 hours for bachelor's (36 in major). Most students required to take courses in humanities, mathematics, biological/physical sciences, social sciences.

STUDENT LIFE. 1992 freshman class profile: 100% commute. Average age is 24. **Activities:** Student government, student newspaper, yearbook, music ensembles.

ATHLETICS. NJCAA.

STUDENT SERVICES. Career counseling, health services, on-campus day care, personal counseling, placement service for graduates, veterans counselor, services/facilities for handicapped.

ANNUAL EXPENSES. Tuition and fees:

ADDRESS/TELEPHONE. Ernesto Garcia, Director of Enrollment, University of Texas at Brownsville, 80 Fort Brown, Brownsville, TX 78520. (512) 544-8254. (512) 544-8832.

University of Texas at Dallas
Richardson, Texas CB code: 6897

4-year public university, coed. Founded in 1961. **Accreditation:** Regional. **Undergraduate enrollment:** 945 men, 936 women full time; 1,382 men, 1,578 women part time. **Graduate enrollment:** 381 men, 313 women full time; 2,061 men, 1,397 women part time. **Faculty:** 291 total (219 full time), 267 with doctorates or other terminal degrees. **Location:** Suburban campus in very large city; 18 miles from downtown Dallas. **Calendar:** Semester, extensive summer session. Saturday and extensive evening/early morning classes. **Microcomputers:** 224 located in libraries, classrooms, computer centers, campus-wide network. **Special facilities:** Geological Information Library, world's most comprehensive collection of petroleum well logs and associated geological data, Callier Center for Communications Disorders offering assessment, education, and clinical services to communicatively handicapped. **Additional facts:** First freshman class admitted in fall 1990.

DEGREES OFFERED. BA, BS, MA, MS, MBA, PhD. 1,266 bachelor's degrees awarded in 1992. 38% in business and management, 7% computer sciences, 5% letters/literature, 13% multi/interdisciplinary studies, 9% psychology, 16% social sciences. Graduate degrees offered in 27 major fields of study.

UNDERGRADUATE MAJORS. Accounting, American studies, applied mathematics, biology, business and management, chemistry, Cognitive Science, comparative literature, computer and information sciences, computer engineering, economics, electrical/electronics/communications engineering, geology, history, humanities, liberal/general studies, mathematics, physics, political science and government, psychology, public administration, sociology, speech pathology/audiology, statistics, visual and performing arts.

ACADEMIC PROGRAMS. Accelerated program, double major, dual enrollment of high school students, independent study, internships, student-designed major, teacher preparation, cross-registration, 3-2 engineering and 2-2 transfer programs. **Remedial services:** Learning center, reduced course load, remedial instruction, special counselor, tutoring, learning resource center. **ROTC:** Air Force, Army. **Placement/credit:** AP, CLEP Subject, institutional tests.

ACADEMIC REQUIREMENTS. Freshmen must earn minimum GPA of 2.0 to continue in good standing. 65% of freshmen return for sophomore year. Students must declare major by end of second year. **Graduation requirements:** 120 hours for bachelor's (36 in major). Most students required to take courses in English, history, humanities, mathematics, biological/physical sciences, social sciences.

FRESHMAN ADMISSIONS. Selection criteria: Applicants with 1100 SAT/26 ACT and in top 25% of high school graduating class admitted on space-available basis. All others will be reviewed for admission. **High school preparation:** 17.5 units required; 24.5 recommended. Required and recommended units include English 4-4, foreign language 2-3, mathematics 3.5-4, social science 3-4 and science 3-3. Additional requirements include: .5 fine arts and 1.5 electives, 2 units same foreign language (unless native language is not English), 3.5 units mathematics (algebra I or higher including trigonometry); 3 units laboratory science (beyond physical science), 4 units language arts (including 1 unit of writing skills). Additional recommendations include: .5 unit health, .5 unit fine arts, 1.5 units physical instruction, 1 unit computer science, and 1 unit general education. **Test requirements:** SAT or ACT (SAT preferred); score report by March 1. Mathematics Level II (taken during freshman orientation). Score report by August 15.

1992 FRESHMAN CLASS PROFILE. 201 men applied, 105 accepted, 63 enrolled; 205 women applied, 103 accepted, 34 enrolled. 100% had high school GPA of 3.0 or higher. 47% were in top tenth and 80% were in top quarter of graduating class. **Academic background:** Mid 50% of enrolled freshmen had SAT-V between 440-570, SAT-M between 560-660; ACT composite between 24-29. 97% submitted SAT scores, 27% submitted ACT scores. **Characteristics:** 97% from in state, 41% have minority backgrounds, 2% are foreign students. Average age is 18.

FALL-TERM APPLICATIONS. No fee. $75 fee for international applicants. No closing date; priority given to applications received by January 1; must reply by registration. Deferred admission available. Institutional early decision plan. Texas Academic Skills Program (TASP) required. High school studies may enroll on part-time basic while attending high school.

STUDENT LIFE. Housing: Apartment housing available. A 400-unit, privately-owned and managed complex of 1 and 2 bedroom apartments located on campus; students given priority consideration for occupancy. **Activities:** Student government, student newspaper, literary magazine, drama, fraternities, sororities, Baptist Student Union, Alpha Kappa Psi, Petitioning Group, College Republicans, Campus Hispanic Association., African American Student Alliance, Friendship Association. of Chinese Students and Visting Scholars, Indian Students Association, Multi-Cultural Association.

ATHLETICS. Intramural: Baseball, basketball M, racquetball, softball, table tennis, tennis, volleyball.

STUDENT SERVICES. Aptitude testing, career counseling, employment service for undergraduates, freshman orientation, health services, personal counseling, placement service for graduates, veterans counselor, minority adviser, foreign student adviser, test preparation, on-campus evening childcare, services/facilities for handicapped.

ANNUAL EXPENSES. Tuition and fees: $1,390, $4,080 additional for out-of-state students. **Books and supplies:** $626. **Other expenses:** $1,358.

FINANCIAL AID. 36% of freshmen, 28% of continuing students receive some form of aid. 93% of grants, 87% of loans, 39% of jobs based on need. 54 enrolled freshmen were judged to have need, all were offered aid. Academic scholarships available. **Aid applications:** Closing date November 1; priority given to applications received by May 1; applicants notified on a rolling basis beginning on or about July 15.

ADDRESS/TELEPHONE. Barry Samsula, Director of Admissions, University of Texas at Dallas, PO Box 830688, Richardson, TX 75083-0688. (214) 690-2296. Fax: (214) 690-2599.

University of Texas at El Paso
El Paso, Texas CB code: 6829

Admissions:	86% of applicants accepted
Based on:	••• School record, test scores
	• Recommendations
Completion:	67% of freshmen end year in good standing
	25% graduate

4-year public university, coed. Founded in 1913. **Accreditation:** Regional. **Undergraduate enrollment:** 4,577 men, 5,081 women full time; 2,280 men, 2,671 women part time. **Graduate enrollment:** 525 men, 311 women full time; 720 men, 1,058 women part time. **Faculty:** 748 total (384 full time), 398 with doctorates or other terminal degrees. **Location:** Urban campus in very large city; 1 mile from downtown. **Calendar:** Semester, extensive summer session. **Microcomputers:** 600 located in libraries, classrooms, computer centers. **Special facilities:** Museum, solar energy facility. **Additional facts:** Bilingual community, programs, and student body. Located within 100 yards of Mexico, within half hour of New Mexico.

DEGREES OFFERED. BA, BS, BFA, MA, MS, MBA, MEd, PhD. 1,421 bachelor's degrees awarded in 1992. 25% in business and management, 21% education, 11% engineering, 8% health sciences, 9% parks/recreation, protective services, public affairs, 5% social sciences. Graduate degrees offered in 55 major fields of study.

UNDERGRADUATE MAJORS. Accounting, American literature, anthropology, applied mathematics, biology, botany, business and management, business economics, ceramics, chemistry, Chicano studies, civil engineering, communications, computer and information sciences, computer engineering, creative writing, criminal justice studies, dramatic arts, drawing, education, interdisciplinary studies, electrical/electronics/communications engineering, English, English literature, finance, fine arts, French, geology, geophysics and seismology, German, graphic design, health care administration, health sciences, history, industrial engineering, information sciences and systems, journalism, Latin American studies, linguistics, marketing management, mathematics, mechanical engineering, medical laboratory technologies, metal/jewelry, metallurgical engineering, microbiology, music performance, music theory and composition, nursing, painting, philosophy, physics, political science and government, printmaking, psychology, radio/television broadcasting, real estate, sculpture, social work, sociology, Spanish, speech, speech pathology/audiology, studio art, zoology.

ACADEMIC PROGRAMS. Accelerated program, cooperative education, double major, dual enrollment of high school students, honors program, independent study, internships, study abroad, teacher preparation. **Remedial services:** Reduced course load, remedial instruction, special counselor, tutoring. **ROTC:** Air Force, Army. **Placement/credit:** AP, CLEP General and Subject, institutional tests.

ACADEMIC REQUIREMENTS. Freshmen must earn minimum GPA of 2.0 to continue in good standing. 65% of freshmen return for sophomore year. Students must declare major by end of second year. **Graduation requirements:** 123 hours for bachelor's (30 in major). Most students required to take courses in English, history, mathematics, biological/physical sciences, social sciences. **Additional information:** Bilingual inter-American science and humanities program.

FRESHMAN ADMISSIONS. Selection criteria: Minimum GED score of 45, or top half of high school class with composite ACT score of 15 or combined SAT score of 700, or bottom half of class with ACT composite of 18 or SAT combined score of 800. Provisional admission for in-state residents not meeting these criteria. For students in top quarter of high school class, any score acceptable. **High school preparation:** 15 units recommended. Recommended units include English 4, foreign language 2, mathematics 3, social science 3 and science 3. **Test requirements:** SAT or ACT; score report by July 1. Prueba de Aptitud Academica for Spanish speaking applicants.

1992 FRESHMAN CLASS PROFILE. 3,441 men and women applied, 2,946 accepted; 1,088 men enrolled, 1,253 women enrolled. 10% were in top tenth and 40% were in top quarter of graduating class. **Characteristics:** 98% commute. Average age is 19.

FALL-TERM APPLICATIONS. No fee. Closing date July 1; applicants notified on a rolling basis beginning on or about April 1. Deferred and early admission available.

STUDENT LIFE. Housing: Dormitories (coed); apartment, fraternity housing available. **Activities:** Student government, student newspaper, literary magazine, choral groups, concert band, dance, drama, jazz band, marching band, music ensembles, musical theater, opera, pep band, symphony orchestra, fraternities, sororities, Movimiento Estudiantil Chicano de Aztlan, National Chicano Health Organization, honorary fraternities, political party and religious groups.

ATHLETICS. NCAA. **Intercollegiate:** Basketball, cross-country, football M, golf, rifle, tennis, track and field, volleyball W. **Intramural:** Badminton, baseball, basketball, bowling, fencing, football M, golf, gymnastics, handball, racquetball, skiing, soccer, softball, squash, swimming, table tennis, tennis, track and field, volleyball, water polo, wrestling.

STUDENT SERVICES. Aptitude testing, career counseling, employment service for undergraduates, freshman orientation, health services, on-campus day care, personal counseling, placement service for graduates, veterans counselor, services/facilities for handicapped.

ANNUAL EXPENSES. Tuition and fees: $1,408, $4,080 additional for out-of-state students. Mexican citizens who show need may qualify for in-state tuition. **Room and board:** $3,550. **Books and supplies:** $374. **Other expenses:** $1,142.

FINANCIAL AID. 55% of freshmen, 53% of continuing students receive some form of aid. All grants, 95% of loans, all jobs based on need. 866 enrolled freshmen were judged to have need, 745 were offered aid. Academic, music/drama, athletic, state/district residency scholarships available. **Aid applications:** No closing date; priority given to applications received by March 15; applicants notified on a rolling basis beginning on or about June 1; must reply within 2 weeks. **Additional information:** Emergency loans available.

ADDRESS/TELEPHONE. Diana Guerrero, Director of Admissions, University of Texas at El Paso, 500 West University Avenue, El Paso, TX 79968. (915) 747-5576.

University of Texas Health Science Center at Houston

Houston, Texas — CB code: 6888

2-year upper-division public university and health science college, coed. Founded in 1972. **Accreditation:** Regional. **Undergraduate enrollment:** 74 men, 307 women full time; 43 men, 158 women part time. **Graduate enrollment:** 988 men, 865 women full time; 227 men, 537 women part time. **Faculty:** 984 total (817 full time). **Location:** Urban campus in very large city; 5 miles from downtown. **Calendar:** Semester, limited summer session. **Microcomputers:** Located in classrooms, computer centers. **Additional facts:** Located in medical center.

DEGREES OFFERED. BS, MS, PhD, DMD, MD. 288 bachelor's degrees awarded in 1992. 79% in health sciences, 11% allied health, 10% life sciences. Graduate degrees offered in 28 major fields of study.

UNDERGRADUATE MAJORS. Medical records technology, nursing, practical nursing, radiobiology, respiratory therapy, respiratory therapy technology.

ACADEMIC PROGRAMS. Accelerated program, double major, independent study, internships, study abroad, visiting/exchange student program, cross-registration, master of nursing program with University of Texas-Pan American; army nurse anesthesia program at Fort Sam Houston in San Antonio; master of public health with University of Texas at El Paso; combined bachelor's/graduate program in medicine. **Remedial services:** Learning center. **Placement/credit:** CLEP General and Subject.

ACADEMIC REQUIREMENTS. Students must declare major on application. **Graduation requirements:** 125 hours for bachelor's (65 in major). Most students required to take courses in English, history, mathematics, philosophy/religion, biological/physical sciences, social sciences.

STUDENT LIFE. 1992 freshman class profile: 100% commute. Average age is 30. **Housing:** Apartment housing available. University operates apartment complex as only student housing available. Complex located approximately 1 mile from campus. **Activities:** Student government, student newspaper.

ATHLETICS. Intramural: Basketball, racquetball, softball, tennis, volleyball.

STUDENT SERVICES. Health services, personal counseling, special adviser for adult students, veterans counselor, off-campus daycare, services/facilities for handicapped.

ANNUAL EXPENSES. Tuition and fees: $990, $4,080 additional for out-of-state students. Additional fee charge of $13 per semester for nursing students. **Books and supplies:** $450. **Other expenses:** $168.

FINANCIAL AID. 50% of continuing students receive some form of aid. All grants, 71% of loans based on need. Academic scholarships available. **Aid applications:** Closing date December 31; priority given to applications received by March 1; applicants notified on a rolling basis beginning on or about May 1; must reply within 10 days.

ADDRESS/TELEPHONE. Office of the Registrar, University of Texas Health Science Center at Houston, PO Box 20036, 7000 Fannin #2250, Houston, TX 77030. (713) 792-7444. Fax: (713) 794-5701.

University of Texas Health Science Center at San Antonio

San Antonio, Texas — CB code: 6908

2-year upper-division public university, coed. Founded in 1969. **Accreditation:** Regional. **Undergraduate enrollment:** 135 men, 532 women full time; 56 men, 131 women part time. **Graduate enrollment:** 879 men, 572 women full time; 57 men, 192 women part time. **Faculty:** 1,136 total (843 full time). **Location:** Urban campus in very large city; 10 miles from downtown San Antonio. **Calendar:** Semester, limited summer session. **Microcomputers:** 50 located in libraries. **Additional facts:** Located in South Texas Medical Center.

DEGREES OFFERED. BS, MS, PhD, DMD, MD, B. Pharm. 256 bachelor's degrees awarded in 1992. 72% in health sciences, 28% allied health. Graduate degrees offered in 12 major fields of study.

UNDERGRADUATE MAJORS. Clinical laboratory science, nursing, occupational therapy, physical therapy.

ACADEMIC PROGRAMS. Internships, cross-registration, pharmacy program with University of Texas-Austin; joint degree program with University of Texas-San Antonia allied health sciences; joint PhD nursing program with Texas Technical University. **Remedial services:** Tutoring. **Placement/credit:** Institutional tests.

ACADEMIC REQUIREMENTS. Students must declare major on application. **Graduation requirements:** 120 hours for bachelor's (60 in major). Most students required to take courses in English, mathematics, biological/physical sciences. **Postgraduate studies:** 1% enter other graduate study.

STUDENT LIFE. 1992 freshman class profile: 100% commute. **Activities:** Student newspaper, Texas Association of Mexican-American Medical Students, Latin-American Nursing Student Association, Diversified Dental Students.

ATHLETICS. Intramural: Baseball, basketball, tennis, volleyball.

STUDENT SERVICES. Health services, personal counseling, services/facilities for handicapped.

ANNUAL EXPENSES. Tuition and fees: $905, $4,080 additional for out-of-state students. **Books and supplies:** $792. **Other expenses:** $1,022.

FINANCIAL AID. 59% of continuing students receive some form of aid. 90% of grants, 87% of loans based on need. 46 enrolled freshmen were judged to have need, all were offered aid. Academic, state/district residency, minority scholarships available. **Aid applications:** No closing date; priority given to applications received by March 12; applicants notified on a rolling basis; within 90 days registration. **Additional information:** Strongly recommend students provide parental information on the need analysis form regardless of dependency status.

ADDRESS/TELEPHONE. James Peak, Registrar, University of Texas Health Science Center at San Antonio, 7703 Floyd Curl Drive, San Antonio, TX 78284-7702. (512) 567-2621. Fax: (512) 567-2685.

University of Texas Medical Branch at Galveston
Galveston, Texas CB code: 6887

2-year upper-division public health science, nursing college, coed. Founded in 1881. **Accreditation:** Regional. **Undergraduate enrollment:** 131 men, 350 women full time; 62 men, 383 women part time. **Graduate enrollment:** 632 men, 371 women full time; 64 men, 129 women part time. **Faculty:** 172 total (149 full time). **Location:** Suburban campus in small city; 50 miles from Houston. **Calendar:** Semester, limited summer session. **Microcomputers:** Located in libraries, classrooms, computer centers. **Special facilities:** Truman G. Blocker, Jr. History of Medicine collections. **Additional facts:** Coursework associated with clinical experience in one of 7 hospitals on campus.

DEGREES OFFERED. BS, MA, MS. 283 bachelor's degrees awarded in 1992. 100% in allied health. Graduate degrees offered in 9 major fields of study.

UNDERGRADUATE MAJORS. Health care administration, medical laboratory technologies, medical records administration, nursing, occupational therapy, physician's assistant.

ACADEMIC PROGRAMS. Internships. **Remedial services:** Learning center, preadmission summer program, reduced course load, remedial instruction, special counselor, tutoring. **Placement/credit:** CLEP General and Subject, institutional tests; 30 credit hours maximum for bachelor's degree.

ACADEMIC REQUIREMENTS. Students must declare major on application. **Graduation requirements:** 120 hours for bachelor's (40 in major). Most students required to take courses in English, humanities, mathematics, biological/physical sciences, social sciences. **Additional information:** Institution located in a medical complex. Curriculum provides clinical experience in 7 hospitals, 85 clinics, Shrines Burn Institute, nearby geriatric hospital and school for cerebral palsied children.

STUDENT LIFE. Housing: Dormitories (coed); apartment, fraternity housing available. **Activities:** Student government, television, yearbook, newsletter, annual talent show, concert series, fraternities, Baptist Student Union, Student/Faculty Minority Council, Wesley Foundation Newman Center, sports clubs, numerous religious, ethnic, health, and social organizations.

ATHLETICS. Intramural: Basketball, golf, softball, swimming, volleyball.

STUDENT SERVICES. Aptitude testing, career counseling, employment service for undergraduates, health services, on-campus day care, personal counseling, veterans counselor, job fairs, services/facilities for handicapped.

ANNUAL EXPENSES. Tuition and fees: $951, $4,080 additional for out-of-state students. **Room and board:** $4,586. **Books and supplies:** $800. **Other expenses:** $3,190.

FINANCIAL AID. 34% of continuing students receive some form of aid. All grants, 86% of loans, all jobs based on need. **Aid applications:** No closing date; priority given to applications received by March 15; applicants notified on a rolling basis beginning on or about April 15; must reply within 4 weeks.

ADDRESS/TELEPHONE. Curtis C. Coonrod, Director of University Admissions, University of Texas Medical Branch at Galveston, 1.212 Ashbel Smith, Galveston, TX 77555-1305. (409) 772-1215. Fax: (409) 772-5056.

University of Texas: Pan American
Edinburg, Texas CB code: 6570

4-year public liberal arts college, coed. Founded in 1927. **Accreditation:** Regional. **Undergraduate enrollment:** 12,473 men and women. **Location:** Rural campus in large town; 225 miles from San Antonio. **Calendar:** Semester, extensive summer session.

DEGREES OFFERED. AA, BA, BS, BFA, MA, MS. 13 associate degrees awarded in 1992. 964 bachelor's degrees awarded. Graduate degrees offered in 13 major fields of study.

UNDERGRADUATE MAJORS. Associate: Business data programming, law enforcement and corrections technologies, nursing, recreation and community services technologies. **Bachelor's:** Accounting, biology, business administration and management, business and management, business economics, chemistry, clinical laboratory science, communications, elementary education, English, finance, health sciences, history, information sciences and systems, Latin American studies, law enforcement and corrections, mathematics, Mexican American studies, military science (Army), music, nursing, physics, political science and government, psychology, secondary education, secretarial and related programs, social work, sociology, Spanish, special education, speech correction, speech pathology/audiology.

ACADEMIC PROGRAMS. Cooperative education, double major, honors program, internships. **Remedial services:** Learning center, remedial instruction, special counselor, tutoring. **ROTC:** Army. **Placement/credit:** 45 credit hours maximum for bachelor's degree.

ACADEMIC REQUIREMENTS. Freshmen must earn minimum GPA of 2.0 to continue in good standing. 50% of freshmen return for sophomore year.

FRESHMAN ADMISSIONS. Selection criteria: Open admissions. **Test requirements:** SAT or ACT (ACT preferred) for placement and counseling only; score report by August 9.

1992 FRESHMAN CLASS PROFILE. 1,873 men and women enrolled. **Characteristics:** 95% from in state, 93% commute, 78% have minority backgrounds, 2% are foreign students. Average age is 18.

FALL-TERM APPLICATIONS. No fee. Closing date July 17; priority given to applications received by May 1; applicants notified on a rolling basis.

STUDENT LIFE. Housing: Dormitories (men, women); fraternity housing available. **Activities:** Student government, student newspaper, yearbook, choral groups, dance, drama, jazz band, music ensembles, musical theater, pep band, symphony orchestra, fraternities, sororities.

ATHLETICS. NCAA.

STUDENT SERVICES. Aptitude testing, career counseling, employment service for undergraduates, health services, personal counseling, placement service for graduates.

ANNUAL EXPENSES. Tuition and fees: $1,410, $4,080 additional for out-of-state students. Mexican citizens may attend at in-state tuition rates. **Room and board:** $4,101. **Books and supplies:** $478. **Other expenses:** $2,252.

FINANCIAL AID. 77% of freshmen, 60% of continuing students receive some form of aid. 93% of grants, 96% of loans, all jobs based on need. 1,156 enrolled freshmen were judged to have need, 1,136 were offered aid. Academic, music/drama, art, athletic, leadership, alumni affiliation, minority scholarships available. **Aid applications:** Closing date April 15; applicants notified on or about June 30; must reply within 10 days.

ADDRESS/TELEPHONE. David Zuniga, Director of Admissions and Registrar, University of Texas: Pan American, 1201 West University Drive, Edinburg, TX 78539. (512) 381-2206.

University of Texas of the Permian Basin
Odessa, Texas CB code: 0448

4-year public university, coed. Founded in 1969. **Accreditation:** Regional. **Undergraduate enrollment:** 269 men, 550 women full time; 279 men, 470 women part time. **Graduate enrollment:** 61 men, 71 women full time; 209 men, 375 women part time. **Faculty:** 119 total (76 full time), 75 with doctorates or other terminal degrees. **Location:** Urban campus in small city; 125 miles from Lubbock, 300 miles from Dallas, and 285 miles from El Paso. **Calendar:** Semester, extensive summer session. Extensive evening/early morning classes. **Microcomputers:** 50 located in classrooms, computer centers.

DEGREES OFFERED. BA, BS, MA, MS, MBA. 339 bachelor's degrees awarded in 1992. 34% in business and management, 5% letters/literature, 5% psychology, 33% social sciences. Graduate degrees offered in 16 major fields of study.

UNDERGRADUATE MAJORS. Accounting, American literature, anthropology, biology, business administration and management, business economics, chemistry, communications, computer and information sciences, control engineering, criminal justice studies, earth sciences, English literature, finance, geology, history, humanities and social sciences, marketing management, mathematics, music, physical education, political science and government, psychology, sociology, Spanish, speech, studio art.

ACADEMIC PROGRAMS. Double major, independent study, internships, teacher preparation. **Remedial services:** Reduced course load, remedial instruction. **Placement/credit:** 28 credit hours maximum for bachelor's degree.

ACADEMIC REQUIREMENTS. Students must declare major on application. **Graduation requirements:** 120 hours for bachelor's (30 in major). Most students required to take courses in arts/fine arts, English, history, mathematics, biological/physical sciences, social sciences.

FALL-TERM APPLICATIONS. No fee.

STUDENT LIFE. Housing: Dormitories (men, women); apartment housing available. Mobile home units available on first-come, first-served basis. **Activities:** Student government, magazine, student newspaper, Baptist Student Union, Hispanic Club.

ATHLETICS. Intramural: Badminton, baseball, basketball, bowling, golf, handball, racquetball, softball, table tennis, tennis, volleyball.

STUDENT SERVICES. Career counseling, employment service for undergraduates, personal counseling, placement service for graduates, veterans counselor, Off-campus day care, services/facilities for handicapped.

ANNUAL EXPENSES. Tuition and fees: $1,432, $4,080 additional for out-of-state students. **Room and board:** $1,800 room only. **Books and supplies:** $555. **Other expenses:** $1,375.

FINANCIAL AID. 82% of loans, all jobs based on need. Academic scholarships available. **Aid applications:** No closing date; priority given to applications received by May 1; applicants notified on a rolling basis beginning on or about May 15; must reply within 2 weeks.

ADDRESS/TELEPHONE. Vickie Gomez, Dir Admissions, University of Texas of the Permian Basin, 4901 East University, Odessa, TX 79762. (915) 367-2210. Fax: (915) 367-2115.

University of Texas at San Antonio

San Antonio, Texas CB code: 6919

Admissions: 78% of applicants accepted
Based on: ••• School record, test scores
Completion: 60% of freshmen end year in good standing
20% graduate, 19% of these enter graduate study

4-year public university, coed. Founded in 1969. **Accreditation:** Regional. **Undergraduate enrollment:** 4,347 men, 4,676 women full time; 2,511 men, 3,129 women part time. **Graduate enrollment:** 293 men, 207 women full time; 683 men, 921 women part time. **Faculty:** 712 total (298 full time), 296 with doctorates or other terminal degrees. **Location:** Suburban campus in very large city; 15 miles from downtown. **Calendar:** Semester, limited summer session. **Microcomputers:** 200 located in dormitories, libraries, classrooms, computer centers.

DEGREES OFFERED. BA, BS, BFA, MA, MS, MBA, MFA, PhD. 1,633 bachelor's degrees awarded in 1992. 26% in business and management, 14% teacher education, 6% engineering, 6% letters/literature, 10% life sciences, 5% parks/recreation, protective services, public affairs, 8% psychology, 13% social sciences. Graduate degrees offered in 38 major fields of study.

UNDERGRADUATE MAJORS. Accounting, American studies, anthropology, biology, business administration and management, business economics, chemistry, civil engineering, clinical laboratory science, computer and information sciences, criminal justice studies, economics, electrical/electronics/communications engineering, English, finance, fine arts, French, geography, geology, German, history, human resources development, humanities, interdisciplinary studies, interior design, management information systems, management science, marketing management, mathematics, mechanical engineering, music, music business management, music performance, music theory and composition, occupational therapy, personnel management, physical education, physical therapy, physics, political science and government, psychology, sociology, Spanish, statistics.

ACADEMIC PROGRAMS. Accelerated program, double major, dual enrollment of high school students, honors program, independent study, internships, study abroad, teacher preparation, 2+2 programs with Alamo Community CollegeDistrict, Southwest Texas Junior College, Texas State Technological Institute-Harlengen, Laredo Junior College, Victoria College, and Delmar College. **Remedial services:** Learning center, remedial instruction, special counselor, tutoring. **ROTC:** Air Force, Army. **Placement/credit:** AP, CLEP General and Subject, institutional tests.

ACADEMIC REQUIREMENTS. Freshmen must earn minimum GPA of 2.0 to continue in good standing. 55% of freshmen return for sophomore year. Students must declare major on enrollment. **Graduation requirements:** 120 hours for bachelor's (30 in major). Most students required to take courses in arts/fine arts, computer science, English, foreign languages, history, humanities, mathematics, biological/physical sciences, social sciences.

FRESHMAN ADMISSIONS. Selection criteria: SAT 700 or ACT 18 required of students in top quarter of high school rank but not those in top 10%. Higher cutoffs used for lower class rank. **High school preparation:** 14 units recommended. Recommended units include English 4, foreign language 2, mathematics 3, social science 2 and science 2. One fine arts also recommended. **Test requirements:** SAT or ACT; score report by July 1.

1992 FRESHMAN CLASS PROFILE. 1,569 men applied, 1,285 accepted, 999 enrolled; 2,078 women applied, 1,571 accepted, 1,214 enrolled. 18% were in top tenth and 47% were in top quarter of graduating class. **Academic background:** Mid 50% of enrolled freshmen had SAT-V between 370-420, SAT-M between 420-520. 80% submitted SAT scores. **Characteristics:** 97% from in state, 97% commute, 43% have minority backgrounds, 1% are foreign students, 2% join fraternities/sororities. Average age is 25.

FALL-TERM APPLICATIONS. $20 fee, may be waived for applicants with need. Closing date July 1; applicants notified on a rolling basis beginning on or about November 1.

STUDENT LIFE. Housing: Dormitories (coed); apartment housing available. **Activities:** Student government, student newspaper, yearbook, choral groups, concert band, jazz band, music ensembles, fraternities, sororities.

ATHLETICS. NCAA. **Intercollegiate:** Baseball M, basketball, cross-country, golf, softball W, tennis, track and field, volleyball. **Intramural:** Badminton, basketball, cross-country, soccer, softball, table tennis, tennis, volleyball.

STUDENT SERVICES. Aptitude testing, career counseling, employment service for undergraduates, freshman orientation, health services, personal counseling, placement service for graduates, veterans counselor, services/facilities for handicapped.

ANNUAL EXPENSES. Tuition and fees: $1,579, $4,080 additional for out-of-state students. **Room and board:** $2,250 room only. **Books and supplies:** $500. **Other expenses:** $1,439.

FINANCIAL AID. 76% of freshmen, 44% of continuing students receive some form of aid. 94% of grants, 81% of loans, all jobs based on need. Academic, athletic scholarships available. **Aid applications:** No closing date; priority given to applications received by March 31; applicants notified on a rolling basis beginning on or about May 5; must reply within 3 weeks.

ADDRESS/TELEPHONE. Dr. John H. Brown, Director of Admissions and Registrar, University of Texas at San Antonio, 6900 North Loop 1604 West, San Antonio, TX 78285. (210) 691-4530. (800) 669-0919. Fax: (210) 691-4655.

University of Texas Southwestern Medical Center at Dallas Southwestern Allied Health Sciences School

Dallas, Texas CB code: 0273

2-year upper-division public health science college, coed. Founded in 1943. **Accreditation:** Regional. **Undergraduate enrollment:** 79 men, 169 women full time; 31 men, 100 women part time. **Graduate enrollment:** 757 men, 470 women full time; 22 men, 6 women part time. **Faculty:** 1,058 total (899 full time). **Location:** Urban campus in very large city; 3 miles from downtown. **Calendar:** Semester, limited summer session. **Microcomputers:** Located in libraries, classrooms, computer centers.

DEGREES OFFERED. BS, MA, MS, PhD, MD. 161 bachelor's degrees awarded in 1992. 100% in allied health. Graduate degrees offered in 15 major fields of study.

UNDERGRADUATE MAJORS. Clinical laboratory science, food science and nutrition, gerontology, health care administration, medical laboratory technologies, nutritional sciences, physical therapy, physician's assistant, prosthetics and orthotics, rehabilitation counseling/services.

ACADEMIC PROGRAMS. Double major, independent study, internships, cross-registration. **Remedial services:** Learning center. **Placement/credit:** CLEP General and Subject; 3 credit hours maximum for bachelor's degree.

ACADEMIC REQUIREMENTS. Students must declare major on enrollment. **Graduation requirements:** 120 hours for bachelor's (30 in major). Most students required to take courses in English, history, philosophy/religion, biological/physical sciences, social sciences. **Additional information:** Post-bachelor's program in blood bank technology.

STUDENT LIFE. Activities: Student government, film, yearbook, Student Dietetic Association, student membership in American Physical Therapy Association, American Academy of Physician Assistants, American Dietetic Association, American Society for Medical Technology, National Rehabilitation Association, American Society of Allied Health Professions.

ATHLETICS. Intramural: Baseball, basketball, fencing, golf, softball, table tennis, tennis, volleyball.

STUDENT SERVICES. Career counseling, health services, personal counseling, placement service for graduates, services/facilities for handicapped.

ANNUAL EXPENSES. Tuition and fees: $998, $4,080 additional for out-of-state students. **Books and supplies:** $610. **Other expenses:** $4,336.

FINANCIAL AID. 52% of continuing students receive some form of aid. 99% of grants, 77% of loans, all jobs based on need. Academic scholarships available. **Aid applications:** No closing date; applicants notified on a rolling basis beginning on or about May 1; must reply within 3 weeks.

ADDRESS/TELEPHONE. Charles Kettlewell, Registrar and Director of Financial Aid, University of Texas Southwestern Medical Center at Dallas Southwestern Allied Health Sciences School, 5323 Harry Hines Boulevard, Dallas, TX 75235-9096. (214) 688-3606.

University of Texas at Tyler

Tyler, Texas CB code: 0389

2-year upper-division public university, coed. Founded in 1971. **Accreditation:** Regional. **Undergraduate enrollment:** 368 men, 803 women full time; 437 men, 699 women part time. **Graduate enrollment:** 128 men, 163 women full time; 378 men, 814 women part time. **Faculty:** 207 total (136 full time), 117 with doctorates or other terminal degrees. **Location:** Urban campus in small city; 80 miles from Dallas. **Calendar:** Semester, limited summer session. **Microcomputers:** Located in classrooms, computer centers. **Special facilities:** Hypercube computer, access to CRAY computer linked to the University of Texas at Austin, electron microscope, access to research facility at UT Health Center-Tyler. **Additional facts:** Regular off-campus sites at Longview, Kilgore, and Waco; and as needed basis off-campus sites at Palestine and Athens, Texas.

DEGREES OFFERED. BA, BS, BFA, MA, MS, MBA, MEd. 717 bachelor's degrees awarded in 1992. 19% in business and management, 6% computer sciences, 33% teacher education, 6% health sciences, 6% psychology, 8% social sciences, 6% visual and performing arts. Graduate degrees offered in 20 major fields of study.

UNDERGRADUATE MAJORS. Accounting, allied health, biology, business administration and management, business and management, business economics, chemistry, computer and information sciences, criminal justice studies, dramatic arts, English, finance, fine arts, health education, history, humanities and social sciences, industrial arts education, industrial technology, journalism, liberal/general studies, management science, marketing management, mathematics, medical laboratory technologies, music, nursing, physical education, political science and government, psychology, sociology, Spanish, special education, speech, speech/communication/theater education, technical education.

ACADEMIC PROGRAMS. Double major, honors program, independent study, internships, student-designed major, study abroad, teacher preparation. **Remedial services:** Learning center, reduced course load, remedial instruction, special counselor.

ACADEMIC REQUIREMENTS. Students must declare major on enrollment. **Graduation requirements:** 124 hours for bachelor's (36 in major). Most students required to take courses in arts/fine arts, computer science, English, history, humanities, mathematics, biological/physical sciences, social sciences.

STUDENT LIFE. 1992 freshman class profile: 100% commute. **Activities:** Student government, student newspaper, electronic message board; weekly memogram, choral groups, music ensembles, Campus Bible study fellowship, Baptist Student Union, Catholic Students Organization, Minority Student Union, University Democrats, University Republicans, Chi Alpha, Criminal Justice Club, Highest Praise Gospel Choir, Pi Sigma Alpha.

ATHLETICS. NAIA. **Intercollegiate:** Tennis. **Intramural:** Basketball, racquetball, tennis, volleyball.

STUDENT SERVICES. Career counseling, employment service for undergraduates, personal counseling, placement service for graduates, veterans counselor, services/facilities for handicapped.

ANNUAL EXPENSES. Tuition and fees: $1,616, $4,080 additional for out-of-state students. **Books and supplies:** $400. **Other expenses:** $934.

FINANCIAL AID. 66% of continuing students receive some form of aid. 76% of grants, 87% of loans, 80% of jobs based on need. Academic, music/drama, art, leadership, alumni affiliation, minority scholarships available. **Aid applications:** Closing date July 1; priority given to applications received by June 1; applicants notified on a rolling basis beginning on or about June 1; must reply by August 1. **Additional information:** Apply early for all programs.

ADDRESS/TELEPHONE. Martha D. Wheat, Director of Admissions/Student Records, University of Texas at Tyler, 3900 University Boulevard, Tyler, TX 75701-6699. (903) 566-7000. (800) 888-9537. Fax: (903) 566-8368.

Vernon Regional Junior College

Vernon, Texas · CB code: 6913

2-year public community, junior college, coed. Founded in 1970. **Accreditation:** Regional. **Undergraduate enrollment:** 247 men, 334 women full time; 488 men, 712 women part time. **Faculty:** 115 total (50 full time), 23 with doctorates or other terminal degrees. **Location:** Rural campus in large town; 50 miles from Wichita Falls, Texas. **Calendar:** Semester, limited summer session. **Microcomputers:** 60 located in classrooms, computer centers. **Special facilities:** Museum.

DEGREES OFFERED. AA, AS, AAS. 293 associate degrees awarded in 1992. 10% in business and management, 10% computer sciences, 40% multi/interdisciplinary studies, 35% trade and industry.

UNDERGRADUATE MAJORS. Accounting, agricultural sciences, automotive mechanics, biological and physical sciences, business administration and management, business and office, business data processing and related programs, computer graphics, dramatic arts, electronic technology, fine arts, humanities and social sciences, law enforcement and corrections technologies, liberal/general studies, marketing and distribution, nursing, secretarial and related programs, social sciences.

ACADEMIC PROGRAMS. 2-year transfer program, dual enrollment of high school students, internships. **Remedial services:** Learning center, reduced course load, remedial instruction, tutoring, personalized instruction. **Placement/credit:** AP, CLEP General and Subject, institutional tests; 45 credit hours maximum for associate degree.

ACADEMIC REQUIREMENTS. Freshmen must earn minimum GPA of 2.0 to continue in good standing. 60% of freshmen return for sophomore year. Students must declare major on application. **Graduation requirements:** 62 hours for associate. Most students required to take courses in computer science, English, history, mathematics, biological/physical sciences, social sciences.

FRESHMAN ADMISSIONS. Selection criteria: Open admissions.

1992 FRESHMAN CLASS PROFILE. 503 men, 670 women enrolled. **Characteristics:** 95% from in state, 87% commute, 18% have minority backgrounds. Average age is 19.

FALL-TERM APPLICATIONS. No fee. No closing date; applicants notified on a rolling basis beginning on or about July 1.

STUDENT LIFE. Housing: Dormitories (coed). **Activities:** Student government, choral groups, drama, music ensembles, musical theater. **Additional information:** Rodeo scholarships available for men and women.

ATHLETICS. NJCAA. **Intercollegiate:** Baseball M, volleyball W. **Intramural:** Archery, badminton, baseball, basketball, golf, handball, racquetball, softball, swimming, table tennis, tennis, track and field, volleyball. **Clubs:** Rodeo.

STUDENT SERVICES. Aptitude testing, career counseling, employment service for undergraduates, health services, personal counseling, placement service for graduates, veterans counselor, services/facilities for handicapped.

ANNUAL EXPENSES. Tuition and fees (1992-93): $680, $20 additional for out-of-district students, $150 additional for out-of-state students. **Room and board:** $1,860. **Books and supplies:** $600. **Other expenses:** $3,000.

FINANCIAL AID. 35% of freshmen, 48% of continuing students receive some form of aid. 93% of grants, all jobs based on need. 240 enrolled freshmen were judged to have need, all were offered aid. Academic, music/drama, art, athletic scholarships available. **Aid applications:** No closing date; priority given to applications received by July 15; applicants notified on a rolling basis beginning on or about May 1; must reply within 2 weeks. **Additional information:** Rodeo scholarships available for men and women.

ADDRESS/TELEPHONE. Joe W. Hite, Director of Admissions/Registrar, Vernon Regional Junior College, 4400 College Drive, Vernon, TX 76384-4092. (817) 552-6291. Fax: (817) 553-1753.

Victoria College

Victoria, Texas · CB code: 6915

2-year public community college, coed. Founded in 1925. **Accreditation:** Regional. **Undergraduate enrollment:** 529 men, 809 women full time; 706 men, 1,367 women part time. **Faculty:** 129 total (90 full time), 15 with doctorates or other terminal degrees. **Location:** Urban campus in small city; 125 miles from Houston, San Antonio, and Austin. **Calendar:** Semester, limited summer session. **Microcomputers:** Located in classrooms.

DEGREES OFFERED. AA, AS, AAS. 259 associate degrees awarded in 1992.

UNDERGRADUATE MAJORS. Accounting, air conditioning/heating/refrigeration mechanics, biology, business and management, business and office, business data processing and related programs, business data programming, communications, computer and information sciences, computer programming, data processing, drafting, education, electrical/electronics/communications engineering, elementary education, engineering, finance, foreign languages (multiple emphasis), health care administration, health sciences, information sciences and systems, instrumentation technology, investments and securities, labor/industrial relations, law enforcement and corrections technologies, liberal/general studies, management science, marketing and distribution, medical laboratory technologies, nursing, practical nursing, respiratory therapy, respiratory therapy technology, secondary education, secretarial and related programs, tourism.

ACADEMIC PROGRAMS. 2-year transfer program, dual enrollment of high school students. **Remedial services:** Learning center, remedial instruction, tutoring.

ACADEMIC REQUIREMENTS. Freshmen must earn minimum GPA of 2.0 to continue in good standing. 60% of freshmen return for sophomore year. **Graduation requirements:** 62 hours for associate. Most students required to take courses in English, history, social sciences.

FRESHMAN ADMISSIONS. Selection criteria: Open admissions. **Test requirements:** TASP required.

1992 FRESHMAN CLASS PROFILE. 757 men, 1,261 women enrolled. **Characteristics:** 99% from in state, 100% commute, 28% have minority backgrounds.

FALL-TERM APPLICATIONS. No fee. No closing date; applicants notified on a rolling basis beginning on or about July 1. Interview required for allied health applicants.

STUDENT LIFE. Activities: Student government, magazine, student newspaper, choral groups, concert band, drama, jazz band, music ensembles.

ATHLETICS. Intramural: Badminton, baseball, basketball, bowling, golf, racquetball, softball, swimming, tennis, volleyball.

STUDENT SERVICES. Aptitude testing, career counseling, employment service for undergraduates, freshman orientation, personal counseling, veterans counselor, services/facilities for handicapped.

ANNUAL EXPENSES. Tuition and fees: $668, $2,010 additional for out-of-state students. **Books and supplies:** $405. **Other expenses:** $1,105.

FINANCIAL AID. 25% of freshmen, 35% of continuing students receive some form of aid. 82% of grants, all jobs based on need. Academic, music/drama scholarships available. **Aid applications:** No closing date; priority given to applications received by July 31; applicants notified on a rolling basis.

ADDRESS/TELEPHONE. Martha Watts, Registrar, Victoria College, 2200 East Red River, Victoria, TX 77901. (512) 573-3291 ext. 400. Fax: (512) 572-3850.

Wayland Baptist University

Plainview, Texas · CB code: 6930

4-year private university and liberal arts college, coed, affiliated with Southern Baptist Convention. Founded in 1908. **Accreditation:** Regional. **Undergraduate enrollment:** 245 men, 389 women full time; 93 men, 153 women part time. **Graduate enrollment:** 1 man, 3 women full time; 9 men, 26 women part time. **Faculty:** 77 total (57 full time), 28 with doctorates or other terminal degrees. **Location:** Urban campus in large town; 50 miles from Lubbock, 70 miles from Amarillo. **Calendar:** 4-1-4, limited summer session. **Microcomputers:** 32 located in libraries, computer centers. **Special facilities:** Museum. **Additional facts:** Off-campus sites in Amarillo, Lubbock, San Antonio, and in Alaska, Arizona, Hawaii, and Kansas.

DEGREES OFFERED. AA, AAS, BA, BS, MBA, MEd. 30 associate degrees awarded in 1992. 100% in business/office and marketing/distribution. 125 bachelor's degrees awarded. 27% in business and management, 31% education, 7% life sciences, 6% mathematics, 5% philosophy, religion, theology, 14% social sciences. Graduate degrees offered in 2 major fields of study.

UNDERGRADUATE MAJORS. Office technology. **Bachelor's:** Art education, biology, business administration and management, business education, ceramics, chemistry, communications, early childhood education, education, elementary education, English, English education, fine arts, history, law enforcement and corrections, mathematics, mathematics education, music, music education, philosophy, physical education, political science and government, psychology, reading education, religion, religious education, religious music, science education, secondary education, social science education, social sciences, social studies education, speech, speech/communication/theater education, theological studies.

ACADEMIC PROGRAMS. Accelerated program, double major, dual enrollment of high school students, external degree, honors program, internships, teacher preparation; liberal arts/career combination in engineering, health sciences. **Remedial services:** Learning center, reduced course load, remedial instruction, tutoring. **Placement/credit:** AP, CLEP General and Subject; 30 credit hours maximum for bachelor's degree.

ACADEMIC REQUIREMENTS. Freshmen must earn minimum GPA of 2.0 to continue in good standing. 67% of freshmen return for sophomore year. Students must declare major by end of second year. **Graduation requirements:** 62 hours for associate, 124 hours for bachelor's (30 in major). Most students required to take courses in arts/fine arts, computer science, English, history, mathematics, philosophy/religion, biological/physical sciences, social sciences.

FRESHMAN ADMISSIONS. Selection criteria: Open admissions. **High school preparation:** 15 units recommended. Recommended units include English 3, mathematics 2 and science 2. Maximum of 4 vocational units accepted. **Test requirements:** SAT or ACT (ACT preferred) for placement and counseling only; score report by September 1.

1992 FRESHMAN CLASS PROFILE. 74 men, 122 women enrolled. **Characteristics:** 87% from in state, 80% live in college housing, 15% have minority backgrounds, 1% are foreign students.

FALL-TERM APPLICATIONS. $35 fee. Closing date September 1; priority given to applications received by August 1; applicants notified on a rolling basis beginning on or about March 1. Interview recommended. Audition recommended. Deferred admission available.

STUDENT LIFE. Housing: Dormitories (men, women); apartment housing available. **Activities:** Student government, magazine, radio, student newspaper, television, yearbook, choral groups, concert band, drama, marching band, music ensembles, musical theater, pep band, fraternities, sororities, religious, service, and special interest organizations.

ATHLETICS. NAIA. **Intercollegiate:** Baseball M, basketball, cross-country, track and field, volleyball W. **Intramural:** Basketball, golf, volleyball.

STUDENT SERVICES. Career counseling, employment service for undergraduates, freshman orientation, health services, on-campus day care, personal counseling, placement service for graduates, special adviser for adult students, veterans counselor, services/facilities for handicapped.

ANNUAL EXPENSES. Tuition and fees: $4,766. **Room and board:** $3,121. **Books and supplies:** $482. **Other expenses:** $1,000.

FINANCIAL AID. 65% of continuing students receive some form of aid. Grants, loans, jobs available. **Aid applications:** No closing date; applicants notified on a rolling basis; must reply within 10 days.

ADDRESS/TELEPHONE. Claude Lusk, Director of Admissions, Wayland Baptist University, 1900 West Seventh Street, Plainview, TX 79072-6998. (806) 296-4709. (800) 588-1WBU. Fax: (806) 296-4580.

Weatherford College
Weatherford, Texas — CB code: 6931

2-year public community college, coed. Founded in 1869. **Accreditation:** Regional. **Undergraduate enrollment:** 529 men, 616 women full time; 418 men, 714 women part time. **Faculty:** 94 total (42 full time), 4 with doctorates or other terminal degrees. **Location:** Suburban campus in large town; 25 miles from Fort Worth. **Calendar:** 4-1-4, extensive summer session. Extensive evening/early morning classes. **Microcomputers:** 70 located in libraries, classrooms, computer centers. **Additional facts:** Off-campus courses held at education center in Mineral Wells and high schools in Aledo, Bridgeport, Granbury, Decatur, Jacksboro, and Springtown.

DEGREES OFFERED. AA, AAS. 110 associate degrees awarded in 1992.

UNDERGRADUATE MAJORS. Agribusiness, agricultural sciences, business and management, business and office, business data processing and related programs, computer and information sciences, computer programming, criminal justice studies, drafting, electronic technology, emergency medical technologies, law enforcement and corrections, liberal/general studies, marketing management, personnel management, precision metal work, preengineering, secretarial and related programs, welding technology.

ACADEMIC PROGRAMS. 2-year transfer program, dual enrollment of high school students, honors program, internships. **Remedial services:** Learning center, remedial instruction, tutoring. **ROTC:** Air Force. **Placement/credit:** CLEP Subject, institutional tests; 30 credit hours maximum for associate degree.

ACADEMIC REQUIREMENTS. Freshmen must earn minimum GPA of 2.0 to continue in good standing. 45% of freshmen return for sophomore year. Students must declare major on enrollment. **Graduation requirements:** 62 hours for associate. Most students required to take courses in arts/fine arts, computer science, English, history, mathematics, biological/physical sciences, social sciences.

FRESHMAN ADMISSIONS. Selection criteria: Open admissions. Nursing school requires entrance examination. **Additional information:** Texas Academic Skills Program (TASP) test required for placement and counseling.

1992 FRESHMAN CLASS PROFILE. 447 men, 586 women enrolled. **Characteristics:** 99% from in state, 91% commute, 8% have minority backgrounds, 1% are foreign students. Average age is 19.

FALL-TERM APPLICATIONS. No fee. No closing date; applicants notified on a rolling basis. Early admission available.

STUDENT LIFE. Housing: Dormitories (coed). **Activities:** Student newspaper, choral groups, drama, jazz band, music ensembles.

ATHLETICS. NJCAA. **Intercollegiate:** Basketball, golf M, tennis M. **Intramural:** Basketball, tennis, volleyball.

STUDENT SERVICES. Aptitude testing, career counseling, employment service for undergraduates, freshman orientation, personal counseling, placement service for graduates, veterans counselor, services/facilities for handicapped.

ANNUAL EXPENSES. Tuition and fees (1992-93): $620, $210 additional for out-of-district students, $1,980 additional for out-of-state students. **Room and board:** $2,632. **Books and supplies:** $300. **Other expenses:** $1,000.

FINANCIAL AID. 20% of freshmen, 20% of continuing students receive some form of aid. 84% of grants, 75% of loans, all jobs based on need. 250 enrolled freshmen were judged to have need, 200 were offered aid. Academic, music/drama, athletic scholarships available. **Aid applications:** Closing date June 1; applicants notified on or about August 15; must reply by September 1.

ADDRESS/TELEPHONE. Dr. Dennie K. Richardson, Director of Admissions, Weatherford College, 308 East Park Avenue, Weatherford, TX 76086. (817) 594-5471 ext. 240. Fax: (817) 594-0627.

West Texas A & M University
Canyon, Texas — CB code: 6938

Admissions: 78% of applicants accepted
Based on:
- ••• School record
- •• Special talents, test scores
- • Interview, recommendations

Completion: 90% of freshmen end year in good standing
35% graduate

4-year public university, coed. Founded in 1909. **Accreditation:** Regional. **Undergraduate enrollment:** 1,967 men, 2,342 women full time; 243 men, 316 women part time. **Graduate enrollment:** 144 men, 190 women full time; 335 men, 519 women part time. **Faculty:** 320 total (185 full time), 135 with doctorates or other terminal degrees. **Location:** Suburban campus in large town; 17 miles from Amarillo. **Calendar:** Semester, limited summer session. Extensive evening/early morning classes. **Microcomputers:** 250 located in dormitories, classrooms, computer centers. **Special facilities:** 24,000-acre farm and ranch, alternative energy institute, Panhandle Plains Historical Museum.

DEGREES OFFERED. BA, BS, BFA, MA, MS, MBA, MFA, MEd. 710 bachelor's degrees awarded in 1992. Graduate degrees offered in 48 major fields of study.

UNDERGRADUATE MAJORS. Accounting, agribusiness, agricultural economics, agricultural sciences, agronomy, animal sciences, applied mathematics, art education, basic clinical health sciences, bilingual/bicultural education, biological and physical sciences, biology, business administration and management, business and management, business economics, business education, chemistry, clinical laboratory science, communications, computer and information sciences, criminal justice studies, dance, dramatic arts, driver and safety education, economics, education of the emotionally handicapped, education of the mentally handicapped, education of the physically handicapped, elementary education, engineering and engineering-related technologies, English, English education, finance, fishing and fisheries, foreign languages education, geography, geology, history, humanities and social sciences, industrial arts education, industrial engineering, journalism, law enforcement and corrections, liberal/general studies, marketing and distribution, mathematics, mathematics education, music, music business management, music education, music performance, music therapy, nursing, parks and recreation management, physical education, physics, plant sciences, political science and government, predentistry, prelaw, premedicine, prepharmacy, preveterinary, psychology, public administration, public relations, radio/television broadcasting, recreation and community services technologies, science education, secondary education, social sciences, social studies education, social work, sociology, Spanish, specific learning disabilities, speech, speech correction, speech pathology/audiology, speech/communication/theater education, systems analysis, teaching English as a second language/foreign language, wildlife management.

ACADEMIC PROGRAMS. Cooperative education, double major, dual enrollment of high school students, honors program, independent study, internships, student-designed major, teacher preparation. **Remedial services:** Remedial instruction, special counselor, tutoring. **Placement/credit:** AP, CLEP Subject, institutional tests; 30 credit hours maximum for bachelor's degree.

ACADEMIC REQUIREMENTS. Freshmen must earn minimum GPA of 2.0 to continue in good standing. 67% of freshmen return for sophomore year. Students must declare major by end of second year. **Graduation requirements:** 130 hours for bachelor's (85 in major). Most students required to take courses in arts/fine arts, computer science, English, history, humanities, mathematics, biological/physical sciences, social sciences.

FRESHMAN ADMISSIONS. Selection criteria: Freshmen applicants must be in top half of graduating class, meet minimum 800 SAT or 21 ACT scores, or obtain individual approval through recommendation and interview. Recommended units include biological science 2, English 4, mathematics 4 and social science 2. **Test requirements:** SAT or ACT; score report by August 24.

1992 FRESHMAN CLASS PROFILE. 1,824 men and women applied, 1,414 accepted; 437 men enrolled, 447 women enrolled. **Characteristics:** 88% from in state, 73% live in college housing, 14% have minority backgrounds, 1% are foreign students. Average age is 18.

FALL-TERM APPLICATIONS. No fee. No closing date; priority given to applications received by February 1; applicants notified on a rolling basis beginning on or about February 1. Audition required for music applicants. Portfolio recommended. Deferred and early admission available.

STUDENT LIFE. Housing: Dormitories (men, women, coed); fraternity housing available. **Activities:** Student government, magazine, radio, student newspaper, choral groups, concert band, dance, drama, jazz band, marching band, music ensembles, musical theater, opera, pep band, symphony orchestra, fraternities, sororities.

ATHLETICS. NCAA. **Intercollegiate:** Baseball M, basketball, bowling, football M, rifle, soccer M, tennis, volleyball W. **Intramural:** Basketball, bowling, cross-country, golf M, gymnastics, handball, horseback riding, racquetball, soccer M, softball, swimming, table tennis, tennis, track and field, volleyball, wrestling M.

STUDENT SERVICES. Aptitude testing, career counseling, employment service for undergraduates, freshman orientation, health services, on-campus day care, personal counseling, placement service for graduates, veterans counselor, services/facilities for handicapped.

ANNUAL EXPENSES. Tuition and fees: $1,466, $4,080 additional for out-of-state students. **Room and board:** $2,588. **Books and supplies:** $500. **Other expenses:** $1,040.

FINANCIAL AID. 55% of freshmen, 35% of continuing students receive some form of aid. Grants, jobs available. Academic, music/drama, art, athletic, minority scholarships available. **Aid applications:** No closing date; priority given to applications received by July 15; applicants notified on a rolling basis beginning on or about April 15; must reply within 2 weeks.

ADDRESS/TELEPHONE. Lila Vars, Director of Admissions, West Texas A & M University, PO WT Box 907, Canyon, TX 79016. (806) 656-2020. (800) 99-WTAMU. Fax: (806) 656-2071.

Western Texas College
Snyder, Texas CB code: 6951

2-year public community college, coed. Founded in 1969. **Accreditation:** Regional. **Undergraduate enrollment:** 1,147 men and women. **Location:** Rural campus in large town; 80 miles from Lubbock and Abilene. **Calendar:** Semester. Extensive evening/early morning classes.

FRESHMAN ADMISSIONS. Selection criteria: Open admissions. Selective admissions to nursing and cosmetology programs.

ANNUAL EXPENSES. Tuition and fees (1992-93): $540, $150 additional for out-of-district students, $300 additional for out-of-state students. **Room and board:** $2,090. **Books and supplies:** $350. **Other expenses:** $720.

ADDRESS/TELEPHONE. Duane Hood, Dean of Student Services, Western Texas College, 6200 S. College Avenue, Snyder, TX 79549. (915) 573-8511. Fax: (915) 573-8511 ext. 330.

Wharton County Junior College
Wharton, Texas CB code: 6939

2-year public junior college, coed. Founded in 1946. **Accreditation:** Regional. **Undergraduate enrollment:** 735 men, 1,004 women full time; 575 men, 1,047 women part time. **Faculty:** 174 total (100 full time), 18 with doctorates or other terminal degrees. **Location:** Rural campus in small town; 60 miles from Houston. **Calendar:** Semester, limited summer session. **Microcomputers:** 330 located in computer centers. **Special facilities:** Experimental farm.

DEGREES OFFERED. AA, AAS. 275 associate degrees awarded in 1992. 14% in business and management, 7% business/office and marketing/distribution, 9% education, 8% engineering technologies, 37% allied health, 8% multi/interdisciplinary studies.

UNDERGRADUATE MAJORS. Agricultural business and management, agricultural sciences, biology, business and management, business and office, business computer/console/peripheral equipment operation, business data entry equipment operation, business data processing and related programs, chemistry, communications, computer and information sciences, criminal justice studies, criminology, dental hygiene, drafting, drafting and design technology, dramatic arts, economics, education, electronic technology, engineering, English, fine arts, history, liberal/general studies, mathematics, medical laboratory technologies, medical records technology, music, nuclear technologies, nursing, physical therapy assistant, physics, political science and government, psychology, radiograph medical technology, sociology.

ACADEMIC PROGRAMS. 2-year transfer program. **Remedial services:** Learning center, remedial instruction. **Placement/credit:** AP, CLEP Subject, institutional tests; 16 credit hours maximum for associate degree.

ACADEMIC REQUIREMENTS. Freshmen must earn minimum GPA of 2.0 to continue in good standing. 43% of freshmen return for sophomore year. **Graduation requirements:** 62 hours for associate. Most students required to take courses in English, history, humanities, mathematics, biological/physical sciences, social sciences.

FRESHMAN ADMISSIONS. Selection criteria: Open admissions. Selective admissions for nursing and dental hygiene programs. Recommended units include biological science 1, English 4, foreign language 2, mathematics 3 and physical science 2. **Test requirements:** SAT or ACT (ACT preferred) for placement and counseling only; score report by July 15.

1992 FRESHMAN CLASS PROFILE. 930 men, 1,403 women enrolled. **Characteristics:** 97% from in state, 93% commute, 29% have minority backgrounds. Average age is 20.

FALL-TERM APPLICATIONS. No fee. Closing date August 15; priority given to applications received by July 1; applicants notified on a rolling basis beginning on or about February 1. Interview required for dental hygiene, nursing applicants. Audition required for music applicants.

STUDENT LIFE. Housing: Dormitories (men, women). **Activities:** Student government, choral groups, dance, drama, marching band, music ensembles, musical theater.

ATHLETICS. NJCAA. **Intercollegiate:** Tennis, volleyball W.

STUDENT SERVICES. Aptitude testing, career counseling, freshman orientation, personal counseling, placement service for graduates, services/facilities for handicapped.

ANNUAL EXPENSES. Tuition and fees: $720, $570 additional for out-of-district students, $1,740 additional for out-of-state students. **Room and board:** $2,050. **Books and supplies:** $575. **Other expenses:** $1,090.

FINANCIAL AID. 30% of continuing students receive some form of aid. 70% of grants, 77% of loans, all jobs based on need. Academic, music/drama, athletic, leadership, minority scholarships available. **Aid applications:** No closing date; priority given to applications received by June 1; applicants notified on a rolling basis beginning on or about August 1.

ADDRESS/TELEPHONE. Albert Barnes, Director of Admissions/Registrar, Wharton County Junior College, 911 Boling Highway, Wharton, TX 77488-0080. (409) 532-4560 ext. 229.

Wiley College
Marshall, Texas CB code: 6940

4-year private liberal arts college, coed, affiliated with United Methodist Church. Founded in 1873. **Accreditation:** Regional. **Undergraduate enrollment:** 195 men, 312 women full time; 8 men, 19 women part time. **Faculty:** 36 total (28 full time), 16 with doctorates or other terminal degrees. **Location:** Urban campus in large town; 40 miles from Shreveport, Louisiana, and 150 from Dallas. **Calendar:** Semester, extensive summer session. **Microcomputers:** 60 located in libraries, computer centers.

DEGREES OFFERED. AA, BA, BS. 27 bachelor's degrees awarded. 48% in business and management, 6% business/office and marketing/distribution, 6% communications, 6% computer sciences, 5% life sciences, 17% social sciences.

UNDERGRADUATE MAJORS. Associate: Business data processing and related programs, computer programming, secretarial and related programs. **Bachelor's:** Biology, business and management, business and office, business education, chemistry, communications, computer and information sciences, elementary education, English, English education, history, hotel/motel and restaurant management, liberal/general studies, mathematics, mathematics education, music, music education, music performance, philosophy, physical education, physics, religion, secondary education, social science education, social sciences, sociology, special education.

ACADEMIC PROGRAMS. Honors program, internships. **Remedial services:** Learning center, reduced course load, remedial instruction, special counselor, tutoring. **Placement/credit:** Institutional tests.

ACADEMIC REQUIREMENTS. Freshmen must earn minimum GPA of 2.0 to continue in good standing. 55% of freshmen return for sophomore year. Students must declare major on enrollment. **Graduation requirements:** 65 hours for associate (50 in major), 124 hours for bachelor's (30 in major). Most students required to take courses in computer science, English, history, humanities, mathematics, philosophy/religion, biological/physical sciences, social sciences. **Postgraduate studies:** 1% enter law school, 2% enter medical school, 1% enter MBA programs, 8% enter other graduate study.

FRESHMAN ADMISSIONS. Selection criteria: Open admissions. **Test requirements:** SAT or ACT for placement; score report by August 20.

1992 FRESHMAN CLASS PROFILE. 75 men, 97 women enrolled. 24% had high school GPA of 3.0 or higher, 72% between 2.0 and 2.99. **Characteristics:** 50% from in state, 93% live in college housing, 100% have minority backgrounds, 3% are foreign students. Average age is 20.

FALL-TERM APPLICATIONS. $10 fee. No closing date; priority given to applications received by September 15; applicants notified on a rolling basis; must reply by May 1 or within 2 weeks if notified thereafter. Audition required for music applicants. Deferred and early admission available.

STUDENT LIFE. Housing: Dormitories (men, women). **Activities:** Student government, radio, student newspaper, yearbook, choral groups, drama, music ensembles, fraternities, sororities, national service fraternity, Interdenominational Student Movement, religion majors club.

ATHLETICS. NAIA, NCAA. **Intercollegiate:** Baseball M, basketball, softball W, track and field, volleyball W. **Intramural:** Baseball M, basketball, softball, table tennis, tennis, track and field, volleyball.

STUDENT SERVICES. Aptitude testing, career counseling, employment service for undergraduates, freshman orientation, health services, personal counseling, placement service for graduates, veterans counselor, services/facilities for handicapped.

ANNUAL EXPENSES. Tuition and fees (1992-93): $3,946. Cost of books included in tuition and fees. **Room and board:** $2,544. **Books and supplies:** $200. **Other expenses:** $900.

FINANCIAL AID. 55% of freshmen, 45% of continuing students receive some form of aid. 91% of grants, 94% of loans, 86% of jobs based on need. 102 enrolled freshmen were judged to have need, all were offered aid. Academic, music/drama, athletic, state/district residency, leadership, religious affiliation scholarships available. **Aid applications:** No closing date; priority given to applications received by June 1; applicants notified on a rolling basis beginning on or about June 15; must reply within 10 days.

ADDRESS/TELEPHONE. Lee Marcus Roberts, Director of Admissions and Recruitment, Wiley College, 711 Wiley Avenue, Marshall, TX 75670. (903) 938-8341.

Utah

Brigham Young University

Provo, Utah CB code: 4019

Admissions: 73% of applicants accepted
Based on: ••• Interview, school record, test scores
•• Recommendations, religious affiliation/commitment, special talents
• Activities, essay
Completion: 24% enter graduate study

4-year private university, coed, affiliated with Church of Jesus Christ of Latter-day Saints. Founded in 1875. **Accreditation:** Regional. **Undergraduate enrollment:** 13,445 men, 13,638 women full time; 990 men, 1,142 women part time. **Graduate enrollment:** 1,210 men, 597 women full time; 704 men, 633 women part time. **Faculty:** 1,652 total (1,335 full time), 1,062 with doctorates or other terminal degrees. **Location:** Suburban campus in small city; 45 miles from Salt Lake City. **Calendar:** 4-4-2-2. Extensive evening/early morning classes. **Microcomputers:** 1,800 located in dormitories, libraries, classrooms, computer centers. **Special facilities:** Underground laboratories for nuclear, plasma, and solid state physics, aquatic ecology laboratory, dairy, poultry, agricultural farms, science and anthropological museums, veterinary pathology laboratory, fine arts museum. **Additional facts:** Educational center in Salt Lake City.

DEGREES OFFERED. AA, AS, BA, BS, BFA, MA, MS, MBA, MFA, MEd, MSW, PhD, EdD, MD, OD, B. Pharm, DPM, DVM, JD. 31 associate degrees awarded in 1992. 48% in letters/literature, 52% multi/interdisciplinary studies. 5,390 bachelor's degrees awarded. 12% in business and management, 6% communications, 9% education, 9% engineering, 6% languages, 7% letters/literature, 12% library science, 6% life sciences, 6% psychology, 16% social sciences, 6% visual and performing arts. Graduate degrees offered in 96 major fields of study.

UNDERGRADUATE MAJORS. **Associate:** English, liberal/general studies. **Bachelor's:** Accounting, advertising, agricultural business and management, agricultural economics, agricultural production, agronomy, American studies, animal sciences, anthropology, art education, art history, Asian studies, biochemistry, biology, biotechnology, botany, business and management, business education, ceramics, chemical engineering, chemistry, Chinese, cinematography/film, civil engineering, classics, communications, comparative literature, computer and information sciences, conservation biology, construction, dance, design, dramatic arts, economics, electrical/electronics/communications engineering, electronic technology, elementary education, English, English education, entomology, European studies, exercise science, family/consumer resource management, fashion design, fashion merchandising, fine arts, food science and nutrition, food sciences, foreign languages education, French, genealogy, geography, geological engineering, geology, German, graphic design, health education, health sciences, history, home economics education, horticultural science, human biology, humanities, illustration design, industrial arts education, industrial design, industrial engineering, interior design, international relations, Italian, Japanese, journalism, Korean, Latin American studies, linguistics, manufacturing technology, mathematics, mathematics education, mechanical engineering, microbiology, Middle Eastern studies, molecular biology, motion picture technology, music, music education, music performance, musical theater, nursing, painting, parks and recreation management, philosophy, photography, physical education, physics, planning and research management, political science and government, Portuguese, printmaking, psychology, public policy studies, public relations, radio/television broadcasting, range management, Russian, sculpture, secondary education, social science education, social work, sociology, Spanish, Spanish translation, speech pathology/audiology, speech/communication/theater education, statistics, studio art, textiles and clothing, trade and industrial education, wildlife management, zoology.

ACADEMIC PROGRAMS. Accelerated program, cooperative education, double major, dual enrollment of high school students, education specialist degree, external degree, honors program, independent study, internships, student-designed major, study abroad, teacher preparation, Washington semester, combined master's degree program in accounting/engineering. **Remedial services:** Learning center, reduced course load, remedial instruction, special counselor, tutoring, special program for Native Americans. **ROTC:** Air Force, Army. **Placement/credit:** AP, CLEP General, institutional tests.

ACADEMIC REQUIREMENTS. Freshmen must earn minimum GPA of 2.0 to continue in good standing. 80% of freshmen return for sophomore year. Students must declare major by end of second year. **Graduation requirements:** 64 hours for associate, 128 hours for bachelor's. Most students required to take courses in arts/fine arts, English, history, humanities, mathematics, philosophy/religion, biological/physical sciences, social sciences. **Postgraduate studies:** 35% from 2-year programs enter 4-year programs.

FRESHMAN ADMISSIONS. **Selection criteria:** School achievement record, test scores, personal interview most important. **High school preparation:** 16 units recommended. Recommended units include biological science 2, English 4, foreign language 3, mathematics 2, physical science 2 and social science 2. At least 50% of high school program in college-preparatory courses recommended. **Test requirements:** ACT; score report by April 15.

1992 FRESHMAN CLASS PROFILE. 3,259 men applied, 2,367 accepted, 1,984 enrolled; 4,106 women applied, 3,035 accepted, 2,631 enrolled. 97% had high school GPA of 3.0 or higher, 3% between 2.0 and 2.99. 46% were in top tenth and 76% were in top quarter of graduating class. **Academic background:** Mid 50% of enrolled freshmen had ACT composite between 23-29. 90% submitted ACT scores. **Characteristics:** 31% from in state, 75% live in college housing, 5% have minority backgrounds, 3% are foreign students. Average age is 19.

FALL-TERM APPLICATIONS. $25 fee. Closing date February 15; applicants notified on a rolling basis. Interview required. Essay required. Early admission available. Students who submitted SATs must take ACT test on university campus.

STUDENT LIFE. **Housing:** Dormitories (men, women); apartment housing available. Language houses available. **Activities:** Student government, film, magazine, radio, student newspaper, television, yearbook, choral groups, concert band, dance, drama, jazz band, marching band, music ensembles, musical theater, opera, pep band, symphony orchestra, College Republicans/Democrats, African-American Club, Black Student Union, Latin-American Student Association, International Student Association, Intercollegiate Knights, Catholic Newman Club, Circle K International, Southeast Asian Club.

ATHLETICS. NCAA. **Intercollegiate:** Baseball M, basketball, cross-country, diving, football M, golf, gymnastics, skiing, swimming, tennis, track and field, volleyball, wrestling M. **Intramural:** Archery, badminton, basketball, bowling, cross-country, fencing, field hockey W, golf, handball, lacrosse, racquetball, rugby M, skiing, soccer, softball, table tennis, tennis, volleyball, water polo M, wrestling M.

STUDENT SERVICES. Aptitude testing, career counseling, employment service for undergraduates, freshman orientation, health services, personal counseling, placement service for graduates, services/facilities for handicapped.

ANNUAL EXPENSES. **Tuition and fees:** $2,200. Undergraduate tuition is $1,100 additional and graduate tuition $1,290 additional for nonmembers of Church of Jesus Christ of Latter-day Saints. **Room and board:** $3,450. **Books and supplies:** $630. **Other expenses:** $1,110.

FINANCIAL AID. Academic, music/drama, art, athletic, leadership scholarships available. **Aid applications:** No closing date; priority given to applications received by March 1; applicants notified on a rolling basis.

ADDRESS/TELEPHONE. Jeffery M. Tanner, Director of Admissions, Brigham Young University, A-172 ASB, Provo, UT 84602. (801) 378-2507. Fax: (801) 378-4264.

College of Eastern Utah

Price, Utah CB code: 4040

2-year public junior college, coed. Founded in 1937. **Accreditation:** Regional. **Undergraduate enrollment:** 647 men, 787 women full time; 778 men, 534 women part time. **Faculty:** 96 total (76 full time), 16 with doctorates or other terminal degrees. **Location:** Rural campus in small town; 65 miles from Provo. **Calendar:** Quarter, limited summer session. Extensive evening/early morning classes. **Microcomputers:** 150 located in classrooms, computer centers. **Special facilities:** Art gallery, observatory, prehistoric museum.

DEGREES OFFERED. AA, AS, AAS. 270 associate degrees awarded in 1992.

UNDERGRADUATE MAJORS. Automotive mechanics, business administration and management, carpentry, child development/care/guidance, construction, cosmetology, diesel engine mechanics, early childhood education, liberal/general studies, machine tool operation/machine shop, mining and petroleum technologies, nursing, secretarial and related programs, welding technology.

ACADEMIC PROGRAMS. 2-year transfer program, cooperative education, double major, dual enrollment of high school students. **Remedial services:** Learning center, remedial instruction, tutoring. **Placement/credit:** AP, CLEP General, institutional tests; 48 credit hours maximum for associate degree.

ACADEMIC REQUIREMENTS. Freshmen must earn minimum GPA of 2.0 to continue in good standing. 30% of freshmen return for sophomore year. Students must declare major on application. **Graduation requirements:** 93 hours for associate. Most students required to take courses in arts/fine arts, computer science, English, foreign languages, history, humanities, mathematics, biological/physical sciences, social sciences.

FRESHMAN ADMISSIONS. **Selection criteria:** Open admissions. Selective admission to nursing program based on test scores and prerequisites. **Test requirements:** SAT or ACT for placement and counseling only; score report by September 20. Institutional tests required for typing, teaching, emergency medical technology and nursing applicants for admission.

1992 FRESHMAN CLASS PROFILE. 746 men, 528 women enrolled. 25% had high school GPA of 3.0 or higher, 73% between 2.0 and 2.99.

Characteristics: 97% from in state, 90% commute, 11% have minority backgrounds. Average age is 19.

FALL-TERM APPLICATIONS. $15 fee. No closing date; applicants notified on a rolling basis. Early admission available.

STUDENT LIFE. Housing: Dormitories (men, women, coed); apartment housing available. **Activities:** Student government, student newspaper, choral groups, concert band, dance, drama, jazz band, music ensembles, musical theater, pep band, girls' drill team, Sigma Gamma Chi, Lambda Delta Sigma (religious clubs).

ATHLETICS. NJCAA. **Intercollegiate:** Baseball M, basketball, softball W, volleyball W. **Intramural:** Basketball M, racquetball, tennis.

STUDENT SERVICES. Aptitude testing, career counseling, employment service for undergraduates, freshman orientation, personal counseling, placement service for graduates, special adviser for adult students, veterans counselor, Women's Resource Center, services/facilities for handicapped.

ANNUAL EXPENSES. Tuition and fees: $1,128, $2,390 additional for out-of-state students. **Room and board:** $3,862. **Books and supplies:** $562. **Other expenses:** $1,106.

FINANCIAL AID. 63% of grants, 95% of loans, all jobs based on need. Academic, music/drama, art, athletic, state/district residency, leadership, alumni affiliation, religious affiliation, minority scholarships available. **Aid applications:** No closing date; priority given to applications received by May 1; applicants notified on a rolling basis beginning on or about July 1; must reply within 3 weeks.

ADDRESS/TELEPHONE. Jan Young, Director of Admissions and Records, College of Eastern Utah, 451 East 400 North, Price, UT 84501. (801) 637-2120 ext. 226. Fax: (801) 637-4102.

Dixie College
St. George, Utah — CB code: 4283

2-year public community college, coed. Founded in 1911. **Accreditation:** Regional. **Undergraduate enrollment:** 954 men, 1,023 women full time; 417 men, 474 women part time. **Faculty:** 167 total (77 full time), 32 with doctorates or other terminal degrees. **Location:** Rural campus in large town; 120 miles from Las Vegas, Nevada, 50 miles from Cedar City. **Calendar:** Quarter, extensive summer session. Extensive evening/early morning classes. **Microcomputers:** 60 located in libraries, classrooms, computer centers. **Special facilities:** 3 national parks within 100 miles. **Additional facts:** Bachelor's and master's degree course work from Utah's 4-year universities presented over distance-learning media.

DEGREES OFFERED. AA, AS, AAS. 514 associate degrees awarded in 1992. 9% in business and management, 10% business/office and marketing/distribution, 10% teacher education, 33% multi/interdisciplinary studies, 9% trade and industry.

UNDERGRADUATE MAJORS. Accounting, agricultural sciences, agronomy, aircraft mechanics, airline piloting and navigation, architecture, art history, automotive mechanics, automotive technology, biology, botany, business administration and management, business and management, business and office, carpentry, chemistry, child development/care/guidance, chiropractic, communications, computer and information sciences, construction, criminal justice studies, dance, dental assistant, drafting, drafting and design technology, early childhood education, economics, electrical installation, elementary education, engineering, engineering and engineering-related technologies, English, family/consumer resource management, fashion design, fashion merchandising, flight attendants, food production/management/services, food science and nutrition, forestry and related sciences, French, geology, German, graphic arts technology, history, home economics, horticultural science, humanities and social sciences, interior design, journalism, liberal/general studies, marketing and distribution, mathematics, mechanical design technology, medical laboratory technologies, music, nursing, philosophy, physical education, physics, plumbing/pipefitting/steamfitting, political science and government, power plant operation and maintenance, predentistry, premedicine, prepharmacy, preveterinary, psychology, radiograph medical technology, range management, Russian, secondary education, sociology, solar heating and cooling technology, Spanish, textiles and clothing, tourism, transportation and travel marketing, visual and performing arts, wildlife management, zoology.

ACADEMIC PROGRAMS. 2-year transfer program, cooperative education, dual enrollment of high school students, honors program, internships, teacher preparation, telecourses. **Remedial services:** Learning center, remedial instruction, special counselor, tutoring. **Placement/credit:** AP, CLEP General and Subject, institutional tests; 46 credit hours maximum for associate degree.

ACADEMIC REQUIREMENTS. Freshmen must earn minimum GPA of 2.0 to continue in good standing. 30% of freshmen return for sophomore year. Students must declare major by end of first year. **Graduation requirements:** 96 hours for associate (38 in major). Most students required to take courses in arts/fine arts, computer science, English, history, humanities, mathematics, biological/physical sciences, social sciences.

FRESHMAN ADMISSIONS. Selection criteria: Open admissions. **High school preparation:** 15 units recommended. Recommended units include English 4, mathematics 3, social science 1 and science 2. One typewriting skills/computer literacy recommended. **Test requirements:** SAT or ACT (ACT preferred) for placement and counseling only; score report by September 15. Institutional test may be substituted for SAT/ACT.

1992 FRESHMAN CLASS PROFILE. 410 men, 480 women enrolled. **Academic background:** Mid 50% of enrolled freshmen had SAT-V between 310-470, SAT-M between 300-440; ACT composite between 17-20. 1% submitted SAT scores, 89% submitted ACT scores. **Characteristics:** 86% from in state, 85% commute, 8% have minority backgrounds, 1% are foreign students.

FALL-TERM APPLICATIONS. $20 fee. Closing date October 1; priority given to applications received by September 22; applicants notified on a rolling basis; must reply by registration. Early admission available.

STUDENT LIFE. Housing: Dormitories (men, coed); cooperative housing available. **Activities:** Student government, radio, student newspaper, yearbook, choral groups, concert band, drama, jazz band, music ensembles, musical theater, pep band, symphony orchestra, Church of Jesus Christ of Latter-day Saints Institute of Religion, international club, other Religions Groups.

ATHLETICS. NJCAA. **Intercollegiate:** Baseball M, basketball, football M, softball W, volleyball W. **Intramural:** Baseball M, basketball, football M, golf, racquetball, softball, tennis, volleyball.

STUDENT SERVICES. Aptitude testing, career counseling, employment service for undergraduates, freshman orientation, health services, personal counseling, placement service for graduates, special adviser for adult students, veterans counselor, services/facilities for handicapped.

ANNUAL EXPENSES. Tuition and fees: $1,282, $2,913 additional for out-of-state students. **Room and board:** $2,460. **Books and supplies:** $525. **Other expenses:** $900.

FINANCIAL AID. 45% of freshmen, 45% of continuing students receive some form of aid. 96% of loans based on need. Academic, music/drama, art, athletic, leadership scholarships available. **Aid applications:** No closing date; priority given to applications received by June 1; applicants notified on a rolling basis; must reply within 2 weeks.

ADDRESS/TELEPHONE. Dell R. Taylor, Director of Admissions and Records, Dixie College, 225 South 700 East, St. George, UT 84770. (801) 673-4811 ext. 275. Fax: (801) 673-8552.

ITT Technical Institute: Salt Lake City
Murray, Utah — CB code: 3601

2-year proprietary technical college, coed. **Undergraduate enrollment:** 540 men, 76 women full time. **Faculty:** 25 total (24 full time). **Location:** Urban campus in small city; 10 miles from Salt Lake City. **Calendar:** Quarter. Extensive evening/early morning classes.

DEGREES OFFERED. AAS. 190 associate degrees awarded in 1992. 100% in engineering technologies.

UNDERGRADUATE MAJORS. Computer-aided drafting, electronic technology.

ACADEMIC PROGRAMS. Remedial services: Learning center, remedial instruction, tutoring.

ACADEMIC REQUIREMENTS. Freshmen must earn minimum GPA of 2.0 to continue in good standing. Students must declare major on application.

FRESHMAN ADMISSIONS. Selection criteria: Satisfactory scores on English and mathematics tests.

1992 FRESHMAN CLASS PROFILE. 165 men, 25 women enrolled. **Characteristics:** 100% commute, 14% have minority backgrounds.

FALL-TERM APPLICATIONS. $100 fee. Application fee refunded if student not accepted. No closing date; applicants notified on a rolling basis. Interview required.

STUDENT SERVICES. Employment service for undergraduates, freshman orientation, placement service for graduates, services/facilities for handicapped.

ANNUAL EXPENSES. Tuition and fees (1992-93): Tuition for 18-month computer-aided drafting program $12,817; books, supplies, and tools, $1,250. Tuition for 2-year electronics program $14,405; books and supplies, $1,500. Laboratory fees $50 per quarter. **Other expenses:** $1,143.

FINANCIAL AID. Aid applications: No closing date; applicants notified on a rolling basis.

ADDRESS/TELEPHONE. John Drinkall, Director of Recruitment, ITT Technical Institute: Salt Lake City, 920 West LeVoy Drive, Murray, UT 84123. (801) 263-3313. (800) 365-2136. Fax: (801) 263-3497.

LDS Business College
Salt Lake City, Utah — CB code: 4412

2-year private business, junior college, coed, affiliated with Church of Jesus Christ of Latter-day Saints. Founded in 1886. **Accreditation:** Regional. **Undergraduate enrollment:** 844 men and women. **Faculty:** 68 total (18 full time), 5 with doctorates or other terminal degrees. **Location:** Urban campus in small city. **Calendar:** Quarter, limited summer session. Extensive evening/early morning classes. **Microcomputers:** 140 located in libraries, classrooms, computer centers.

DEGREES OFFERED. AS, AAS. 130 associate degrees awarded in 1992. 8% in business and management, 83% business/office and marketing/distribution, 6% computer sciences, 5% health sciences, 6% multi/interdisciplinary studies.

UNDERGRADUATE MAJORS. Accounting, business administration and management, business and management, business and office, business data processing and related programs, business data programming, computer programming, data processing, fashion merchandising, interior design, legal secretary, liberal/general studies, marketing and distribution, marketing management, medical assistant, medical secretary, office supervision and management, secretarial and related programs.

ACADEMIC PROGRAMS. 2-year transfer program, accelerated program, cooperative education, double major, dual enrollment of high school students, internships. **Remedial services:** Reduced course load, remedial instruction, special counselor, tutoring. **Placement/credit:** AP, CLEP General and Subject, institutional tests; 50 credit hours maximum for associate degree.

ACADEMIC REQUIREMENTS. Freshmen must earn minimum GPA of 2.0 to continue in good standing. 50% of freshmen return for sophomore year. Students must declare major by end of first year. **Graduation requirements:** 110 hours for associate (45 in major). Most students required to take courses in computer science, English, humanities, mathematics, philosophy/religion, social sciences.

FRESHMAN ADMISSIONS. Selection criteria: Open admissions. **Additional information:** Students must sign commitment to conform to dress and conduct standards.

1992 FRESHMAN CLASS PROFILE. 358 men and women enrolled. 62% had high school GPA of 3.0 or higher, 33% between 2.0 and 2.99. **Academic background:** Mid 50% of enrolled freshmen had ACT composite between 10-21. 47% submitted ACT scores. **Characteristics:** 61% from in state, 62% commute, 5% have minority backgrounds, 15% are foreign students, 8% join fraternities/sororities. Average age is 18.

FALL-TERM APPLICATIONS. $25 fee. No closing date; applicants notified on a rolling basis. Deferred and early admission available. ACT test recommended for counseling.

STUDENT LIFE. Housing: Dormitories (women). All on-campus housing facilities include kitchens. **Activities:** Student government, student newspaper, choral groups, sororities, Latter-day Saint Student Association (LDSSA). **Additional information:** Religious observance required.

ATHLETICS. Intramural: Basketball, volleyball.

STUDENT SERVICES. Career counseling, employment service for undergraduates, freshman orientation, health services, personal counseling, placement service for graduates, special adviser for adult students, veterans counselor, services/facilities for handicapped.

ANNUAL EXPENSES. Tuition and fees: $1,810. **Room and board:** $1,265 room only. **Books and supplies:** $600. **Other expenses:** $932.

FINANCIAL AID. 50% of freshmen, 45% of continuing students receive some form of aid. 83% of grants, 89% of loans based on need. Academic, leadership scholarships available. **Aid applications:** No closing date; applicants notified on a rolling basis; must reply within 6 weeks.

ADDRESS/TELEPHONE. Ross Derbidge, Director of Admissions, LDS Business College, 411 East South Temple, Salt Lake City, UT 84111-1392. (801) 363-2765. (800) 999-5767. Fax: (801) 359-1304.

Phillips Junior College: Salt Lake City Campus
Salt Lake City, Utah — CB code: 5341

2-year proprietary business, junior college, coed. **Undergraduate enrollment:** 175 men, 500 women full time. **Faculty:** 37 total (8 full time), 5 with doctorates or other terminal degrees. **Location:** Suburban campus in small city; 8 miles from Salt Lake City. **Calendar:** Quarter. Extensive evening/early morning classes. **Microcomputers:** 50 located in libraries, classrooms, computer centers.

DEGREES OFFERED. AA, AS. 145 associate degrees awarded in 1992. 31% in business and management, 30% business/office and marketing/distribution, 10% computer sciences, 29% law.

UNDERGRADUATE MAJORS. Accounting, business and management, business and office, business computer/console/peripheral equipment operation, business data programming, computer and information sciences, computer programming, legal assistant/paralegal, legal secretary, medical secretary, secretarial and related programs, tourism.

ACADEMIC PROGRAMS. Accelerated program, double major, internships. **Remedial services:** Learning center, reduced course load, remedial instruction, tutoring. **Placement/credit:** CLEP General and Subject, institutional tests; 16 credit hours maximum for associate degree.

ACADEMIC REQUIREMENTS. Freshmen must earn minimum GPA of 1.67 to continue in good standing. 70% of freshmen return for sophomore year. Students must declare major on application. **Graduation requirements:** 90 hours for associate (48 in major). Most students required to take courses in computer science, English, history, humanities, mathematics, philosophy/religion, biological/physical sciences.

FRESHMAN ADMISSIONS. Selection criteria: CPAT test required for all applicants. Levels for each program have been set for acceptance. General passing ACT scores also accepted.

1992 FRESHMAN CLASS PROFILE. 50 men, 200 women enrolled. **Characteristics:** 99% from in state, 100% commute, 17% have minority backgrounds, 1% are foreign students. Average age is 23.

FALL-TERM APPLICATIONS. $25 fee, may be waived for applicants with need. No closing date; applicants notified on a rolling basis. Interview required.

STUDENT LIFE. Activities: Student government, student newspaper, data processing mangement association, Legal Assistant of Utah, tutoring club.

STUDENT SERVICES. Aptitude testing, career counseling, employment service for undergraduates, freshman orientation, placement service for graduates, special adviser for adult students, veterans counselor, services/facilities for handicapped.

ANNUAL EXPENSES. Tuition and fees (1992-93): $5,000. Books included in tuition.

FINANCIAL AID. 90% of freshmen, 88% of continuing students receive some form of aid. 99% of grants, 73% of loans, all jobs based on need. Academic scholarships available. **Aid applications:** No closing date.

ADDRESS/TELEPHONE. Rod Hadean, Admissions Director, Phillips Junior College: Salt Lake City Campus, 3098 Highland Drive, Salt Lake City, UT 84106. (801) 485-0221. Fax: (801) 485-0057.

Salt Lake Community College
Salt Lake City, Utah — CB code: 4864

2-year public community, technical college, coed. Founded in 1948. **Accreditation:** Regional. **Undergraduate enrollment:** 3,480 men, 3,210 women full time; 5,159 men, 5,180 women part time. **Faculty:** 884 total (259 full time), 29 with doctorates or other terminal degrees. **Location:** Urban campus in small city; 5 miles from downtown. **Calendar:** Quarter, extensive summer session. Saturday and extensive evening/early morning classes. **Microcomputers:** 275 located in libraries, classrooms, computer centers, campus-wide network. **Additional facts:** Two campus locations, 3 teaching centers, and 4 satellite locations.

DEGREES OFFERED. AA, AS, AAS. 1,014 associate degrees awarded in 1992. 22% in business and management, 20% education, 8% engineering technologies, 11% allied health, 25% trade and industry.

UNDERGRADUATE MAJORS. Accounting, air conditioning/heating/refrigeration mechanics, air conditioning/heating/refrigeration technology, aircraft mechanics, architectural technologies, architecture, automotive mechanics, aviation maintenance, biological and physical sciences, biology, business administration and management, business and management, business and office, business computer/console/peripheral equipment operation, business data processing and related programs, child development/care/guidance, commercial art, communications, computer and information sciences, construction, criminal justice studies, data processing, diesel engine mechanics, drafting, drafting and design technology, early childhood education, education, electrical and electronics equipment repair, electrical installation, electrical technology, electronic technology, elementary education, engineering and engineering-related technologies, engineering and other disciplines, finance, graphic and printing production, graphic design, interpreter for the deaf, legal assistant/paralegal, liberal/general studies, management information systems, manufacturing technology, marketing and distribution, marketing management, medical assistant, mental health/human services, nursing, occupational therapy assistant, office supervision and management, physical sciences, physical therapy assistant, preengineering, radiograph medical technology, secretarial and related programs, surgical technology, survey and mapping technology, transportation management, welding technology, word processing.

ACADEMIC PROGRAMS. 2-year transfer program, cooperative education, double major, dual enrollment of high school students, internships, study abroad, telecourses. **Remedial services:** Learning center, preadmission summer program, reduced course load, remedial instruction, special counselor, tutoring. **ROTC:** Air Force, Army. **Placement/credit:** AP, CLEP General and Subject, institutional tests; 50 credit hours maximum for associate degree.

ACADEMIC REQUIREMENTS. Freshmen must earn minimum GPA of 2.0 to continue in good standing. 33% of freshmen return for sophomore year. Students must declare major on application. **Graduation requirements:** 101 hours for associate (72 in major). Most students required to take courses in computer science, English, history, humanities, mathematics, biological/physical sciences, social sciences.

FRESHMAN ADMISSIONS. Selection criteria: Open admissions. Selective admissions for health science and aircraft maintenance programs based on testing, and for health sciences recommendations and school records. Biological science recommended for nursing and surgical technician programs. Algebra recommended for preengineering and electronics. **Test requirements:** Institutional placement test required of aviation maintenance applicants.

1992 FRESHMAN CLASS PROFILE. 2,145 men, 2,051 women enrolled. **Characteristics:** 97% from in state, 100% commute, 8% have minority backgrounds.

FALL-TERM APPLICATIONS. $20 fee. No closing date; applicants notified on a rolling basis. Deferred and early admission available. CPT/ACT recommended for placement scores and should be submitted by September 26.

STUDENT LIFE. Activities: Student government, student newspaper, television, choral groups, concert band, dance, drama, jazz band, musical theater, pep band, Circle-K, Latter Day Saints Student Association, PBL, DEX, and 25 additional clubs.

ATHLETICS. NJCAA. **Intercollegiate:** Basketball. **Intramural:** Archery, baseball, basketball, bowling, cross-country, golf, racquetball, skiing, soccer, softball, table tennis, tennis, track and field.

STUDENT SERVICES. Aptitude testing, career counseling, employment service for undergraduates, freshman orientation, health services, on-campus day care, personal counseling, placement service for graduates, veterans counselor, services/facilities for handicapped.

ANNUAL EXPENSES. Tuition and fees: $1,359, $2,679 additional for out-of-state students. **Books and supplies:** $630. **Other expenses:** $1,020.

FINANCIAL AID. 44% of freshmen, 44% of continuing students receive some form of aid. 93% of loans based on need. Academic, art, athletic, leadership, minority scholarships available. **Aid applications:** No closing date; priority given to applications received by April 1; applicants notified on a rolling basis.

ADDRESS/TELEPHONE. Jane Townsend, Director of Admissions, Salt Lake Community College, PO Box 30808, Salt Lake City, UT 84130-0808. (801) 967-4297.

Snow College
Ephraim, Utah

CB code: 4727

2-year public community college, coed. Founded in 1888. **Accreditation:** Regional. **Undergraduate enrollment:** 2,032 men and women full time; 312 men and women part time. **Faculty:** 103 total (79 full time), 18 with doctorates or other terminal degrees. **Location:** Rural campus in small town; 120 miles from Salt Lake City, 70 miles from Provo. **Calendar:** Quarter, limited summer session. **Microcomputers:** 235 located in dormitories, libraries, classrooms, computer centers.

DEGREES OFFERED. 403 associate degrees awarded in 1992.

UNDERGRADUATE MAJORS. Accounting, agricultural business and management, agricultural economics, agricultural sciences, American literature, animal sciences, anthropology, automotive mechanics, automotive technology, biological and physical sciences, biology, botany, business administration and management, business and management, business and office, business computer/console/peripheral equipment operation, business data entry equipment operation, business data processing and related programs, business data programming, carpentry, chemistry, child development/care/guidance, communications, computer and information sciences, computer programming, drafting, economics, education, electronic technology, engineering, engineering and other disciplines, English, French, geography, history, home economics, humanities and social sciences, individual and family development, liberal/general studies, marketing management, mathematics, nursing, philosophy, physical sciences, physics, political science and government, precision metal work, predentistry, premedicine, prepharmacy, preveterinary, psychology, public affairs, secretarial and related programs, social sciences, sociology, visual and performing arts, wildlife management, zoology.

ACADEMIC PROGRAMS. 2-year transfer program, cooperative education, honors program, independent study, study abroad, teacher preparation, cross-registration. **Remedial services:** Learning center, reduced course load, remedial instruction, special counselor, tutoring. **Placement/credit:** AP, CLEP General, institutional tests; 48 credit hours maximum for associate degree.

ACADEMIC REQUIREMENTS. Freshmen must earn minimum GPA of 2.0 to continue in good standing. 37% of freshmen return for sophomore year. Students must declare major on application. **Graduation requirements:** 96 hours for associate. Most students required to take courses in arts/fine arts, English, history, mathematics, biological/physical sciences, social sciences.

FRESHMAN ADMISSIONS. Selection criteria: Open admissions. Recommended units include biological science 2, English 4, mathematics 2 and physical science 2. **Test requirements:** ACT for placement and counseling only; score report by September 1.

1992 FRESHMAN CLASS PROFILE. 780 men, 974 women enrolled. **Characteristics:** 87% from in state, 50% commute, 10% have minority backgrounds, 1% are foreign students. Average age is 19.

FALL-TERM APPLICATIONS. $15 fee. No closing date; priority given to applications received by May 15; applicants notified on a rolling basis beginning on or about December 1. Deferred and early admission available. Applications received after May 15 will be on a space available basis.

STUDENT LIFE. Housing: Dormitories (men, women, coed); apartment housing available. **Activities:** Student government, magazine, student newspaper, yearbook, choral groups, concert band, dance, drama, jazz band, marching band, music ensembles, musical theater, pep band, symphony orchestra, fraternities, sororities, Latter-day Saints Student Association.

ATHLETICS. NJCAA. **Intercollegiate:** Baseball M, basketball, softball W, tennis M, volleyball W. **Intramural:** Badminton, basketball, bowling, golf, handball, racquetball, soccer, softball, table tennis, tennis, volleyball.

STUDENT SERVICES. Aptitude testing, career counseling, employment service for undergraduates, health services, on-campus day care, personal counseling, placement service for graduates, veterans counselor, services/facilities for handicapped.

ANNUAL EXPENSES. Tuition and fees: $1,125, $3,555 additional for out-of-state students. **Room and board:** $2,505. **Books and supplies:** $530. **Other expenses:** $900.

FINANCIAL AID. 42% of freshmen, 38% of continuing students receive some form of aid. Grants, loans, jobs available. Academic, music/drama, art, athletic, leadership scholarships available. **Aid applications:** Closing date July 15; applicants notified on a rolling basis beginning on or about August 1; must reply within 1 week.

ADDRESS/TELEPHONE. Gerhard Bolli, Director of Admissions and Records, Snow College, 150 East College Avenue, Ephraim, UT 84627. (801) 283-4021. Fax: (801) 283-6879.

Southern Utah University
Cedar City, Utah

CB code: 4092

4-year public university, coed. Founded in 1897. **Accreditation:** Regional. **Undergraduate enrollment:** 1,605 men, 1,830 women full time; 171 men, 326 women part time. **Graduate enrollment:** 19 men, 12 women full time. **Faculty:** 200 total (150 full time), 98 with doctorates or other terminal degrees. **Location:** Rural campus in large town; 265 miles from Salt Lake City, 180 miles from Las Vegas, Nevada. **Calendar:** Quarter, extensive summer session. Extensive evening/early morning classes. **Microcomputers:** 350 located in dormitories, libraries, classrooms, computer centers, campus-wide network. **Special facilities:** Natural life museum, art gallery, observatory, Shakespearean theater.

DEGREES OFFERED. AA, AS, AAS, BA, BS, MEd. 66 associate degrees awarded in 1992. 585 bachelor's degrees awarded. Graduate degrees offered in 2 major fields of study.

UNDERGRADUATE MAJORS. Associate: Agricultural sciences, agronomy, animal sciences, automotive technology, business computer/console/peripheral equipment operation, business data programming, chemical engineering, data processing, drafting, engineering, forestry and related sciences, law enforcement and corrections technologies, marketing and distribution, mechanical design technology, mechanical engineering, nursing, office supervision and management, practical nursing, precision metal work, real estate, secretarial and related programs, teacher aide, wildlife management. **Bachelor's:** Accounting, advertising, agribusiness, agricultural economics, agronomy, archeology, behavioral sciences, biology, botany, business administration and management, business education, chemistry, clothing and textiles management/production/services, communications, computer and information sciences, dramatic arts, education, elementary education, English, English education, English literature, foreign languages (multiple emphasis), foreign languages education, forest products processing technology, French, geology, German, history, home economics, individual and family development, industrial arts education, journalism, junior high education, library science, mathematics, mathematics education, music, music education, philosophy, physical sciences, political science and government, prelaw, psychology, public relations, small business management and ownership, social sciences, social work, sociology, soil sciences, Spanish, specific learning disabilities, speech, telecommunications, wildlife management, zoology.

ACADEMIC PROGRAMS. 2-year transfer program, double major, dual enrollment of high school students, honors program, internships, teacher preparation, cross-registration. **Remedial services:** Learning center, preadmission summer program, reduced course load, remedial instruction, special counselor, tutoring. **Placement/credit:** AP, CLEP General.

ACADEMIC REQUIREMENTS. Freshmen must earn minimum GPA of 2.0 to continue in good standing. 70% of freshmen return for sophomore year. **Graduation requirements:** 93 hours for associate (50 in major), 183 hours for bachelor's (77 in major). Most students required to take courses in computer science, English, history, mathematics, biological/physical sciences, social sciences.

FRESHMAN ADMISSIONS. Selection criteria: Test scores and high school academic record most important. Recommended units include biological science 2, English 4, mathematics 3 and social science 2. **Test requirements:** SAT or ACT (ACT preferred); score report by June 1.

1992 FRESHMAN CLASS PROFILE. 426 men, 547 women enrolled. **Characteristics:** 77% from in state, 80% commute, 3% have minority backgrounds, 1% are foreign students. Average age is 19.

FALL-TERM APPLICATIONS. $25 fee. Closing date July 1; applicants notified on a rolling basis. Deferred and early admission available.

STUDENT LIFE. Housing: Dormitories (men, women); apartment, fraternity housing available. **Activities:** Student government, magazine, radio, student newspaper, television, yearbook, choral groups, concert band, dance, drama, jazz band, marching band, music ensembles, musical theater, opera, pep band, symphony orchestra, fraternities, sororities, Intercultural Club.

ATHLETICS. NAIA, NCAA. **Intercollegiate:** Baseball M, basketball, football M, golf, gymnastics, soccer M, softball W, track and field, volleyball W.

STUDENT SERVICES. Career counseling, employment service for undergraduates, freshman orientation, health services, personal counseling, placement service for graduates, veterans counselor.

ANNUAL EXPENSES. Tuition and fees: $1,599, $3,161 additional for out-of-state students. **Room and board:** $960 room only. **Books and supplies:** $700.

FINANCIAL AID. 55% of freshmen, 53% of continuing students receive some form of aid. 67% of grants, 96% of loans, 58% of jobs based on need. 365 enrolled freshmen were judged to have need, 348 were offered aid. Academic, music/drama, state/district residency, leadership scholarships available. **Aid applications:** No closing date; applicants notified on a rolling basis beginning on or about May 1; must reply within 2 weeks.

ADDRESS/TELEPHONE. Dale S. Orton, Director of Admissions, Southern Utah University, 351 West Center Street, Cedar City, UT 84720. (801) 586-7740. Fax: (801) 586-5475.

Stevens-Henager College of Business
Provo, Utah — CB code: 4751

2-year proprietary business college, coed. Founded in 1891. **Undergraduate enrollment:** 240 men and women. **Faculty:** 18 total (8 full time), 1 with doctorate or other terminal degree. **Location:** Urban campus in small city; 45 miles from Salt Lake City. **Calendar:** 10-month plus 4-month session for associate degree. Extensive evening/early morning classes. **Microcomputers:** 26 located in libraries, computer centers.

DEGREES OFFERED. 135 associate degrees awarded in 1992. 100% in business and management.

UNDERGRADUATE MAJORS. Accounting, business and office, business computer/console/peripheral equipment operation, business data processing and related programs, legal secretary, medical assistant, medical records technology, medical secretary, secretarial and related programs, word processing.

ACADEMIC PROGRAMS. Accelerated program. **Remedial services:** Reduced course load, special counselor, tutoring. **Placement/credit:** Institutional tests.

ACADEMIC REQUIREMENTS. Freshmen must earn minimum GPA of 2.0 to continue in good standing. 76% of freshmen return for sophomore year. Students must declare major on application. **Graduation requirements:** 90 hours for associate. Most students required to take courses in English. **Additional information:** Individualized program of studies.

FRESHMAN ADMISSIONS. Selection criteria: Interview, test scores very important. Previous academic record and recoommendations considered.

1992 FRESHMAN CLASS PROFILE. 240 men and women enrolled. 90% had high school GPA between 2.0 and 2.99. **Characteristics:** 90% from in state, 84% commute, 5% have minority backgrounds. Average age is 20.

FALL-TERM APPLICATIONS. $50 fee. No closing date; applicants notified on a rolling basis; must reply as soon as possible. Interview required. Deferred and early admission available.

STUDENT LIFE. Housing: Dormitories (women); cooperative housing available. **Activities:** Student government, student newsletter, Future Business Leaders Association, Latter-day Saints Student Association.

STUDENT SERVICES. Career counseling, employment service for undergraduates, personal counseling, placement service for graduates.

ANNUAL EXPENSES. Tuition and fees (projected): $11,133. Tuition and fees for 14-month associate degree program. **Room and board:** $2,600 room only. **Books and supplies:** $1,000.

FINANCIAL AID. 95% of freshmen, 95% of continuing students receive some form of aid. Grants, loans, jobs available. Academic scholarships available. **Aid applications:** No closing date; applicants notified on a rolling basis beginning on or about September 10; must reply within 3 weeks.

ADDRESS/TELEPHONE. Robert Fox, Executive Director, Stevens-Henager College of Business, 25 East 1700 Street, Provo, UT 84606-6157. (801) 375-5455.

University of Utah
Salt Lake City, Utah — CB code: 4853

Admissions:	92% of applicants accepted
Based on:	••• School record, test scores
	• Activities, interview, recommendations
Completion:	80% of freshmen end year in good standing
	26% graduate, 22% of these enter graduate study

4-year public university, coed. Founded in 1850. **Accreditation:** Regional. **Undergraduate enrollment:** 7,999 men, 6,150 women full time; 3,758 men, 3,228 women part time. **Graduate enrollment:** 2,300 men, 1,292 women full time; 572 men, 569 women part time. **Faculty:** 3,422 total. **Location:** Urban campus in small city; 14 blocks from downtown. **Calendar:** Quarter, extensive summer session. Extensive evening/early morning classes. **Microcomputers:** 800 located in dormitories, libraries, classrooms, computer centers, campus-wide network. **Special facilities:** State Arboretum, Utah Museums of Fine Arts and Natural History.

DEGREES OFFERED. BA, BS, BFA, BArch, MA, MS, MBA, MFA, MEd, MSW, PhD, EdD, MD, B. Pharm, Pharm D, JD. 2,999 bachelor's degrees awarded in 1992. 16% in business and management, 9% communications, 8% engineering, 7% psychology, 24% social sciences, 5% visual and performing arts. Graduate degrees offered in 83 major fields of study.

UNDERGRADUATE MAJORS. Accounting, anthropology, architecture, art history, Asian studies, atmospheric sciences and meteorology, biology, business administration and management, business economics, chemical engineering, chemistry, civil engineering, classics, communications, computer and information sciences, computer engineering, dance, dramatic arts, economics, electrical/electronics/communications engineering, elementary education, English, family/consumer resource management, finance, fine arts, food science and nutrition, French, geography, geological engineering, geology, geophysics and seismology, German, health education, health sciences, history, home economics education, individual and family development, industrial engineering, journalism, liberal/general studies, linguistics, marketing management, materials engineering, mathematics, mechanical engineering, medical laboratory technologies, metallurgical engineering, Middle Eastern studies, mining and mineral engineering, music, nursing, parks and recreation management, petroleum engineering, pharmacy, philosophy, physical education, physical therapy, physics, political science and government, psychology, Russian, secondary education, social sciences, sociology, Spanish, special education, speech pathology/audiology, urban studies.

ACADEMIC PROGRAMS. Accelerated program, double major, dual enrollment of high school students, honors program, independent study, internships, semester at sea, student-designed major, study abroad, teacher preparation, telecourses, visiting/exchange student program, New York semester, Washington semester, cross-registration. **Remedial services:** Learning center, preadmission summer program, reduced course load, remedial instruction, special counselor, tutoring. **ROTC:** Air Force, Army, Naval. **Placement/credit:** AP, CLEP General and Subject, IB, institutional tests; 96 credit hours maximum for bachelor's degree.

ACADEMIC REQUIREMENTS. Freshmen must earn minimum GPA of 2.0 to continue in good standing. 62% of freshmen return for sophomore year. Students must declare major by end of second year. **Graduation requirements:** 183 hours for bachelor's. Most students required to take courses in arts/fine arts, English, history, humanities, mathematics, biological/physical sciences, social sciences.

FRESHMAN ADMISSIONS. Selection criteria: High school course requirements, admissions index using high school GPA and test scores important. Recommendation, extracurricular activities considered. **High school preparation:** 15 units required. Required units include English 4, foreign language 2, mathematics 2, social science 1 and science 2. **Test requirements:** SAT or ACT (ACT preferred); score report by July 1.

1992 FRESHMAN CLASS PROFILE. 2,452 men applied, 2,236 accepted, 1,267 enrolled; 2,315 women applied, 2,156 accepted, 1,175 enrolled. 75% had high school GPA of 3.0 or higher, 24% between 2.0 and 2.99. **Academic background:** Mid 50% of enrolled freshmen had SAT-V between 370-560, SAT-M between 450-620; ACT composite between 19-27. 21% submitted SAT scores, 95% submitted ACT scores. **Characteristics:** 87% from in state, 90% commute, 7% have minority backgrounds, 3% are foreign students, 16% join fraternities/sororities. Average age is 19.

FALL-TERM APPLICATIONS. $30 fee, may be waived for applicants with need. Closing date July 1; applicants notified on a rolling basis. Audition required for music, dance, drama applicants. Portfolio required for art applicants. Deferred and early admission available.

STUDENT LIFE. Housing: Dormitories (men, women, coed); apartment, fraternity, sorority housing available. **Activities:** Student government, film, magazine, radio, student newspaper, television, choral groups, concert band, dance, drama, jazz band, marching band, music ensembles, musical theater, opera, pep band, symphony orchestra, fraternities, sororities, political and religious groups, ethnic clubs, outdoor clubs, community service organization.

ATHLETICS. NCAA. **Intercollegiate:** Baseball M, basketball, cross-country, diving, football M, golf M, gymnastics W, skiing, softball W, swimming, tennis, track and field, volleyball W. **Intramural:** Badminton, basketball, bowling, cross-country, golf, handball, ice hockey M, racquetball, rifle, rugby M, skiing, soccer, softball, squash, swimming, table tennis, tennis, volleyball, water polo M, wrestling M. **Clubs:** Several sports clubs.

STUDENT SERVICES. Aptitude testing, career counseling, employment service for undergraduates, freshman orientation, health services, personal counseling, placement service for graduates, special adviser for adult students, veterans counselor, ethnic student adviser, services/facilities for handicapped.

ANNUAL EXPENSES. Tuition and fees (projected): $2,244, $4,497 additional for out-of-state students. Room and board figure is projected. **Room and board:** $5,175. **Books and supplies:** $700. **Other expenses:** $2,178.

FINANCIAL AID. 70% of freshmen, 65% of continuing students receive some form of aid. 83% of grants, 96% of loans, 28% of jobs based on need. 1,700 enrolled freshmen were judged to have need, 1,650 were offered aid. Academic, music/drama, art, athletic, state/district residency, leadership, alumni affiliation, minority scholarships available. **Aid applications:** No closing date; priority given to applications received by March 1; applicants notified on a rolling basis beginning on or about May 15; must reply within 3 weeks.

ADDRESS/TELEPHONE. J. Stayner Landward, Director of Admissions, University of Utah, 200 South University Street, Salt Lake City, UT 84112. (800) 581-8761. (800) 444-UofU. Fax: (801) 585-3034.

Utah State University
Logan, Utah CB code: 4857

4-year public university, coed. Founded in 1888. **Accreditation:** Regional. **Undergraduate enrollment:** 4,793 men, 4,629 women full time; 1,779 men, 1,653 women part time. **Graduate enrollment:** 518 men, 272 women full time; 1,011 men, 770 women part time. **Faculty:** 784 total (754 full time). **Location:** Rural campus in large town; 80 miles from Salt Lake City. **Calendar:** Quarter, extensive summer session. Extensive evening/early morning classes. **Microcomputers:** 900 located in dormitories, libraries, classrooms, computer centers. **Special facilities:** Art gallery, agricultural experiment stations, water research laboratory, space shuttle experiments, CAD/CAM facility.

DEGREES OFFERED. AAS, BA, BS, BFA, MA, MS, MBA, MFA, MEd, PhD, EdD. 55 associate degrees awarded in 1992. 7% in agriculture, 78% business/office and marketing/distribution, 15% trade and industry. 1,653 bachelor's degrees awarded. 6% in agriculture, 17% business and management, 22% teacher education, 7% engineering, 6% social sciences. Graduate degrees offered in 62 major fields of study.

UNDERGRADUATE MAJORS. Associate: Aeronautical technology, agricultural mechanics, aircraft mechanics, drafting and design technology, ornamental horticulture, secretarial and related programs. **Bachelor's:** Accounting, aeronautical technology, agribusiness, agricultural business and management, agricultural economics, agricultural education, agricultural engineering, agronomy, American studies, animal sciences, biology, business administration and management, business and management, business and office, business economics, business education, chemistry, clinical laboratory science, computer and information sciences, dairy, dance, dramatic arts, early childhood education, economics, electrical and electronics equipment repair, electrical/electronics/communications engineering, elementary education, English, environmental health engineering, family/consumer resource management, fashion merchandising, finance, fine arts, fishing and fisheries, food science and nutrition, food sciences, forestry and related sciences, French, geography, geology, German, health education, history, home economics, home economics education, horticulture, human resources development, individual and family development, industrial arts education, international agriculture, journalism, landscape architecture, liberal/general studies, management information systems, marketing and distribution, marketing and distributive education, mathematics, mathematics education, mechanical engineering, music, music therapy, operations research, parks and recreation management, personal services, personnel management, philosophy, physical education, physics, plant sciences, political science and government, predentistry, prelaw, premedicine, preveterinary, psychology, public health laboratory science, range management, renewable natural resources, secondary education, social work, sociology, soil sciences, Spanish, special education, speech, speech pathology/audiology, statistics, textiles and clothing.

ACADEMIC PROGRAMS. Accelerated program, cooperative education, double major, dual enrollment of high school students, education specialist degree, external degree, honors program, independent study, internships, student-designed major, study abroad, teacher preparation, telecourses, visiting/exchange student program, weekend college, cross-registration. **Remedial services:** Learning center, reduced course load, remedial instruction, special counselor, tutoring. **ROTC:** Air Force, Army. **Placement/credit:** AP, CLEP General and Subject, IB, institutional tests; 60 credit hours maximum for bachelor's degree.

ACADEMIC REQUIREMENTS. Freshmen must earn minimum GPA of 2.0 to continue in good standing. 58% of freshmen return for sophomore year. Students must declare major by end of second year. **Graduation requirements:** 96 hours for associate, 186 hours for bachelor's (60 in major). Most students required to take courses in arts/fine arts, computer science, English, history, humanities, mathematics, biological/physical sciences, social sciences. **Postgraduate studies:** 2% enter law school, 1% enter medical school, 5% enter MBA programs, 18% enter other graduate study.

FRESHMAN ADMISSIONS. Selection criteria: High school record, test scores most important. **High school preparation:** 15 units required. Required and recommended units include English 4, mathematics 3, social science 3 and science 2. Foreign language 2 recommended. 1.5 fine arts, 2 physical education/health recommended. **Test requirements:** SAT or ACT (ACT preferred); score report by July 1.

1992 FRESHMAN CLASS PROFILE. 884 men, 1,157 women enrolled. 84% had high school GPA of 3.0 or higher, 15% between 2.0 and 2.99. **Academic background:** Mid 50% of enrolled freshmen had ACT composite between 17-26. 91% submitted ACT scores. **Characteristics:** 78% from in state, 82% commute, 5% have minority backgrounds, 1% are foreign students, 3% join fraternities/sororities. Average age is 19.

FALL-TERM APPLICATIONS. $25 fee. Closing date July 1; applicants notified on a rolling basis; must reply by September 1. Audition required. Portfolio required. CRDA. Deferred and early admission available.

STUDENT LIFE. Housing: Dormitories (men, women); apartment, fraternity, sorority, cooperative housing available. Honor student dormitory available. **Activities:** Student government, magazine, radio, student newspaper, television, choral groups, concert band, dance, drama, jazz band, marching band, music ensembles, musical theater, opera, pep band, symphony orchestra, fraternities, sororities, Latter-day Saints, Catholic, Lutheran, Baptist organizations, Crusade for Christ, Christian Fellowship, black and Indian organizations.

ATHLETICS. NCAA. **Intercollegiate:** Basketball M, cross-country, football M, golf M, gymnastics W, softball W, tennis, track and field, volleyball W. **Intramural:** Badminton, basketball, bowling, cross-country, fencing, golf, handball, racquetball, soccer, softball, squash, table tennis, tennis, volleyball, water polo, wrestling M.

STUDENT SERVICES. Aptitude testing, career counseling, employment service for undergraduates, freshman orientation, health services, on-campus day care, personal counseling, placement service for graduates, special adviser for adult students, veterans counselor, services/facilities for handicapped.

ANNUAL EXPENSES. Tuition and fees: $1,878, $3,645 additional for out-of-state students. **Room and board:** $3,990. **Books and supplies:** $660. **Other expenses:** $1,380.

FINANCIAL AID. 75% of grants, 95% of loans, 12% of jobs based on need. Academic, music/drama, art, athletic, state/district residency, leadership, minority scholarships available. **Aid applications:** Closing date May 15; priority given to applications received by March 15; applicants notified on a rolling basis beginning on or about May 15; must reply within 3 weeks.

ADDRESS/TELEPHONE. Lynn J. Poulsen, Director of Admissions and Records, Utah State University, UMC 1600, Logan, UT 84322-1600. (801) 750-1107.

Utah Valley Community College
Orem, Utah CB code: 4870

2-year public community college, coed. Founded in 1941. **Accreditation:** Regional. **Undergraduate enrollment:** 3,358 men, 2,949 women full time; 1,822 men, 1,494 women part time. **Faculty:** 519 total (203 full time), 37 with doctorates or other terminal degrees. **Location:** Suburban campus in small city; 45 miles from Salt Lake City. **Calendar:** Semester, limited summer session. Extensive evening/early morning classes. **Microcomputers:** Located in computer centers. **Additional facts:** Access to libraries at Brigham Young University.

DEGREES OFFERED. AA, AS, AAS. 730 associate degrees awarded in 1992. 18% in business and management, 15% business/office and marketing/distribution, 17% engineering technologies, 11% law, 6% parks/recreation, protective services, public affairs, 27% trade and industry.

UNDERGRADUATE MAJORS. Accounting, air conditioning/heating/refrigeration mechanics, air conditioning/heating/refrigeration technology, automotive mechanics, business administration and management, carpentry, child development/care/guidance, computer and information sciences, construction, diesel engine mechanics, drafting, electromechanical technology, electronic technology, fashion merchandising, finance, fire control and safety technology, graphic and printing production, hotel/motel and restaurant management, legal assistant/paralegal, legal secretary, liberal/general studies, machine tool operation/machine shop, marketing and distribution, medical secretary, mental health/human services, nursing, office supervision and management, precision metal work, radiograph medical technology, secretarial and related programs, water and wastewater technology, woodworking, word processing.

ACADEMIC PROGRAMS. 2-year transfer program, cooperative education, double major, dual enrollment of high school students, honors program, internships. **Remedial services:** Learning center, reduced course load, remedial instruction, tutoring. **ROTC:** Air Force, Army. **Placement/credit:** AP, CLEP General and Subject, institutional tests.

ACADEMIC REQUIREMENTS. Freshmen must earn minimum GPA of 2.0 to continue in good standing. Students must declare major on application. **Graduation requirements:** 96 hours for associate. Most students required to take courses in English, history, mathematics, philosophy/religion, biological/physical sciences, social sciences.

FRESHMAN ADMISSIONS. Selection criteria: Open admissions.

1992 FRESHMAN CLASS PROFILE. 2,475 men and women enrolled. 46% had high school GPA of 3.0 or higher, 53% between 2.0 and 2.99. **Academic background:** Mid 50% of enrolled freshmen had ACT composite between 16-18. 100% submitted ACT scores. **Characteristics:** 91% from in state, 100% commute, 4% have minority backgrounds.

FALL-TERM APPLICATIONS. $15 fee. No closing date; applicants notified on a rolling basis. Early admission available. ACT or basic skills exam used for assessment.

STUDENT LIFE. Activities: Student government, student newspaper, choral groups, drama, musical theater, pep band, Latter-day Saints fraternity and sorority. **Additional information:** Intercollegiate rodeo scholarships available.

ATHLETICS. NJCAA. **Intercollegiate:** Baseball M, basketball, softball W, tennis M, volleyball W. **Intramural:** Basketball, bowling, golf, racquetball, softball, tennis, volleyball.

STUDENT SERVICES. Aptitude testing, career counseling, employment service for undergraduates, on-campus day care, personal counseling, placement service for graduates, veterans counselor, services/facilities for handicapped.

ANNUAL EXPENSES. Tuition and fees: $1,366, $2,643 additional for out-of-state students. **Books and supplies:** $670. **Other expenses:** $650.

FINANCIAL AID. 65% of freshmen, 60% of continuing students receive some form of aid. Grants, loans, jobs available. Academic, state/district residency, leadership scholarships available. **Aid applications:** No closing date; priority given to applications received by July 1; applicants notified on a rolling basis beginning on or about July 1; must reply within 2 weeks.

ADDRESS/TELEPHONE. Grant Cook, Dean of Academic Support Services, Utah Valley Community College, 800 West 1200 South, Orem, UT 84058. (801) 222-8000. Fax: (801) 226-5207.

Weber State University
Ogden, Utah

CB code: 4941

4-year public university, coed. Founded in 1889. **Accreditation:** Regional. **Undergraduate enrollment:** 4,237 men, 4,553 women full time; 2,694 men, 3,155 women part time. **Graduate enrollment:** 42 men, 29 women full time; 35 men, 50 women part time. **Faculty:** 457 total (444 full time), 276 with doctorates or other terminal degrees. **Location:** Urban campus in small city; 35 miles from Salt Lake City. **Calendar:** Quarter, extensive summer session. Saturday and extensive evening/early morning classes. **Microcomputers:** 558 located in libraries, classrooms, computer centers, campus-wide network. **Special facilities:** Science museum, observatory, planetarium, art gallery, working crime laboratory.

DEGREES OFFERED. AA, AS, AAS, BA, BS, MEd. 1,022 associate degrees awarded in 1992. 5% in business and management, 39% allied health, 45% multi/interdisciplinary studies, 5% trade and industry. 1,153 bachelor's degrees awarded. 17% in business and management, 6% computer sciences, 15% education, 10% engineering technologies, 9% allied health, 5% multi/interdisciplinary studies, 6% parks/recreation, protective services, public affairs, 9% social sciences. Graduate degrees offered in 5 major fields of study.

UNDERGRADUATE MAJORS. Associate: Aerospace science (Air Force), archeology, architectural technologies, automotive mechanics, automotive technology, biological laboratory technology, biotechnology, business computer/console/peripheral equipment operation, business data processing and related programs, business data programming, child development/care/guidance, clinical laboratory science, computer and information sciences, computer technology, criminal justice studies, dental hygiene, drafting, drafting and design technology, electrical technology, electromechanical technology, electronic technology, emergency medical technologies, engineering and engineering-related technologies, fashion merchandising, geology, graphic design, interior design, law enforcement and corrections, law enforcement and corrections technologies, liberal/general studies, machine tool operation/machine shop, manufacturing technology, mechanical design technology, medical laboratory technologies, medical records administration, medical records technology, military science (Army), nursing, precision metal work, radiograph medical technology, respiratory therapy, respiratory therapy technology, retailing, secretarial and related programs, transportation management. **Bachelor's:** Accounting, allied health, applied mathematics, art education, automotive technology, bilingual/bicultural education, biological and physical sciences, botany, business administration and management, business and management, business economics, business education, chemistry, child development/care/guidance, clinical laboratory science, communications, computer and information sciences, computer programming, computer technology, criminal justice studies, data processing, dramatic arts, early childhood education, earth sciences, economics, electrical technology, electronic technology, elementary education, engineering and engineering-related technologies, English, English and theater arts, English education, English literature, family/consumer resource management, finance, fine arts, foreign languages education, French, geography, geology, German, health care administration, health education, health sciences, history, human resources development, humanities and social sciences, individual and family development, information sciences and systems, journalism, junior high education, law enforcement and corrections, law enforcement and corrections technologies, liberal/general studies, logistics, management science, manufacturing technology, marketing and distribution, marketing management, mathematics, mathematics education, mechanical engineering technology/computer integrated manufacturing, mechanical engineering technology/industrial engineering technology, microbiology, music, music education, music history and appreciation, music performance, music theory and composition, musical theater, nuclear medical technology, nursing, philosophy, photography, physical education, physical sciences, physics, political science and government, predentistry, prelaw, premedicine, prepharmacy, preveterinary, psychology, public relations, radio/television broadcasting, radiograph medical technology, retailing, science education, secondary education, secretarial and related programs, social science education, social sciences, social studies education, social work, sociology, Spanish, speech, speech/communication/theater education, telecommunications, ultrasound technology, visual and performing arts, zoology.

ACADEMIC PROGRAMS. 2-year transfer program, accelerated program, cooperative education, double major, dual enrollment of high school students, honors program, independent study, internships, student-designed major, study abroad, teacher preparation, telecourses, weekend college, United Nations semester, Washington semester, cross-registration. **Remedial services:** Learning center, preadmission summer program, reduced course load, remedial instruction, special counselor, tutoring. **ROTC:** Air Force, Army, Naval. **Placement/credit:** AP, CLEP General and Subject, IB, institutional tests; 45 credit hours maximum for bachelor's degree.

ACADEMIC REQUIREMENTS. Freshmen must earn minimum GPA of 2.0 to continue in good standing. Students must declare major by end of second year. **Graduation requirements:** 93 hours for associate (28 in major), 183 hours for bachelor's (45 in major). Most students required to take courses in English, history, humanities, mathematics, biological/physical sciences, social sciences.

FRESHMAN ADMISSIONS. Selection criteria: High school GPA and test scores important. Additional requirements for nursing, dental hygiene, and health professions programs. **Test requirements:** SAT or ACT (ACT preferred); score report by July 1. General Aptitude Test Battery required for nursing, dental health, and health professions programs.

1992 FRESHMAN CLASS PROFILE. 984 men, 1,115 women enrolled. **Characteristics:** 93% from in state, 90% commute, 6% have minority backgrounds, 2% are foreign students, 1% join fraternities/sororities. Average age is 20.

FALL-TERM APPLICATIONS. $20 fee. Closing date July 1; priority given to applications received by February 1; applicants notified on a rolling basis. Interview required for allied health applicants. Deferred and early admission available.

STUDENT LIFE. Housing: Dormitories (men, women, coed); apartment housing available. **Activities:** Student government, film, magazine, radio, student newspaper, television, choral groups, concert band, dance, drama, jazz band, marching band, music ensembles, musical theater, opera, pep band, symphony orchestra, fraternities, sororities, Latter-day Saint Student Association, Newman Center, Black Scholars United, International Student Association, Physically Challenged Student Association.

ATHLETICS. NCAA. **Intercollegiate:** Basketball, cross-country, football M, golf, tennis, track and field, volleyball W. **Intramural:** Archery, badminton, basketball, bowling, fencing, racquetball, skiing, soccer, softball, swimming, tennis, track and field, volleyball.

STUDENT SERVICES. Aptitude testing, career counseling, employment service for undergraduates, freshman orientation, health services, on-campus day care, personal counseling, placement service for graduates, special adviser for adult students, veterans counselor, services/facilities for handicapped.

ANNUAL EXPENSES. Tuition and fees: $1,638, $3,228 additional for out-of-state students. **Room and board:** $3,345. **Books and supplies:** $504. **Other expenses:** $1,059.

FINANCIAL AID. 50% of continuing students receive some form of aid. Grants, loans, jobs available. Academic, music/drama, art, athletic, leadership scholarships available. **Aid applications:** No closing date; priority given to applications received by May 1; applicants notified on a rolling basis beginning on or about July 1; must reply within 2 weeks.

ADDRESS/TELEPHONE. Winslow Hurst, Director of Admissions/Registration, Weber State University, 3750 Harrison Boulevard, Ogden, UT 84408-1015. (801) 626-6050. Fax: (801) 626-6747.

Westminster College of Salt Lake City
Salt Lake City, Utah

CB code: 4948

Admissions:	80% of applicants accepted
Based on:	••• School record
	•• Test scores
	• Interview, recommendations
Completion:	85% of freshmen end year in good standing
	14% enter graduate study

4-year private liberal arts college, coed, affiliated with Presbyterian Church (USA) and United Church of Christ. Founded in 1875. **Accreditation:** Regional. **Undergraduate enrollment:** 344 men, 632 women full time; 282 men, 453 women part time. **Graduate enrollment:** 62 men, 49 women full time; 173 men, 146 women part time. **Faculty:** 201 total (82 full time), 49 with doctorates or other terminal degrees. **Location:** Suburban campus in small city; 3 miles from downtown. **Calendar:** 4-4-1, limited summer session. Saturday classes. **Microcomputers:** 48 located in computer centers.

DEGREES OFFERED. BA, BS, MBA, MEd. 283 bachelor's degrees awarded in 1992. Graduate degrees offered in 4 major fields of study.

UNDERGRADUATE MAJORS. Accounting, aviation management, behavioral sciences, biological and physical sciences, biology, business administration and management, business and management, business economics, chemistry, communications, computer and information sciences, dramatic arts, early childhood education, education, elementary education, English, finance, history, human resources development, humanities and social sciences, junior high education, liberal/general studies, marketing and distribution, mathematics, nursing, philosophy, physical sciences, physics, political science and government, prelaw, psychology, religion, secondary education, social sciences, sociology, theological studies, visual and performing arts.

ACADEMIC PROGRAMS. Accelerated program, cooperative education, double major, dual enrollment of high school students, honors program, independent study, internships, semester at sea, student-designed major, study abroad, teacher preparation, cross-registration. **Remedial services:** Learning center, reduced course load, remedial instruction, special counselor, tutoring. **ROTC:** Air Force, Army, Naval. **Placement/credit:** AP, CLEP General and Subject, institutional tests; 40 credit hours maximum for bachelor's degree.

ACADEMIC REQUIREMENTS. Freshmen must earn minimum GPA of 2.0 to continue in good standing. 60% of freshmen return for sophomore year. Students must declare major by end of second year. **Graduation requirements:** 124 hours for bachelor's (40 in major). Most students required to take courses in arts/fine arts, computer science, English, foreign languages, history, humanities, mathematics, philosophy/religion, biological/physical sciences, social sciences. **Postgraduate studies:** 3% enter law school, 1% enter medical school, 8% enter MBA programs, 2% enter other graduate study.

FRESHMAN ADMISSIONS. Selection criteria: Minimum 2.0 GPA, counselor's recommendation, and test scores required. Equivalent of 3.0 GPA for foreign students required. **Test requirements:** SAT or ACT (ACT preferred); score report by August 30.

1992 FRESHMAN CLASS PROFILE. 362 men applied, 276 accepted, 85 enrolled; 590 women applied, 490 accepted, 152 enrolled. 80% had high school GPA of 3.0 or higher, 20% between 2.0 and 2.99. **Characteristics:** 80% from in state, 79% commute, 10% have minority backgrounds, 1% are foreign students. Average age is 26.

FALL-TERM APPLICATIONS. No fee. No closing date; applicants notified on a rolling basis. Interview recommended. Portfolio recommended for art applicants. CRDA. Deferred and early admission available. EDP-F.

STUDENT LIFE. Housing: Dormitories (coed). **Activities:** Student government, magazine, student newspaper, yearbook, choral groups, drama, symphony orchestra, honorary fraternities, clubs, religious activities.

ATHLETICS. NAIA. **Intercollegiate:** Soccer M. **Intramural:** Basketball, golf, racquetball, skiing, softball, tennis, volleyball.

STUDENT SERVICES. Aptitude testing, career counseling, employment service for undergraduates, freshman orientation, personal counseling, placement service for graduates, special adviser for adult students, veterans counselor, services/facilities for handicapped.

ANNUAL EXPENSES. Tuition and fees: $8,220. **Room and board:** $3,880. **Books and supplies:** $600. **Other expenses:** $1,650.

FINANCIAL AID. 80% of freshmen, 70% of continuing students receive some form of aid. 35% of grants, 74% of loans, 92% of jobs based on need. Academic, music/drama, art, alumni affiliation, minority scholarships available. **Aid applications:** No closing date; priority given to applications received by May 31; applicants notified on a rolling basis beginning on or about May 1; must reply within 3 weeks.

ADDRESS/TELEPHONE. Craig Green, Vice President of Enrollment Management, Westminster College of Salt Lake City, 1840 South 1300 East, Salt Lake City, UT 84105. (801) 488-4200. (800) 748-4753. Fax: (801) 466-6916.

Vermont

Bennington College

Bennington, Vermont CB code: 3080

Admissions: 72% of applicants accepted
Based on: ••• Essay, recommendations, school record
•• Activities, interview, special talents
• Test scores
Completion: 85% of freshmen end year in good standing
65% graduate, 40% of these enter graduate study

4-year private liberal arts college, coed. Founded in 1925. **Accreditation:** Regional. **Undergraduate enrollment:** 201 men, 308 women full time. **Graduate enrollment:** 12 men, 9 women full time. **Faculty:** 77 total (53 full time), 40 with doctorates or other terminal degrees. **Location:** Rural campus in large town; 50 miles from Albany, New York, 150 miles from Boston, Massachusetts. **Calendar:** Semester. **Microcomputers:** 18 located in computer centers. **Special facilities:** Jennings Mansion, Carriage Barn, Center for the Visual and Performing Arts, Early Childhood Center, Usdan Gallery (art), dance archives, script library, music library. **Additional facts:** Located on 550 acres at foot of Green Mountains. Campus was once a farm, and some of the buildings housing studios and classrooms were originally barns and stables. With permission of Dean of Studies, students may enroll in courses at Williams College.

DEGREES OFFERED. BA, MFA. 126 bachelor's degrees awarded in 1992. 15% in letters/literature, 31% multi/interdisciplinary studies, 9% social sciences, 42% visual and performing arts. Graduate degrees offered in 6 major fields of study.

UNDERGRADUATE MAJORS. American literature, anthropology, architecture, astronomy, biochemistry, biological and physical sciences, biology, cell biology, ceramics, chemistry, Chinese, classics, comparative literature, creative writing, dance, developmental psychology, dramatic arts, drawing, early childhood education, economics, elementary education, English, English literature, environmental science, experimental psychology, fine arts, folklore and mythology, French, German, history, humanities, humanities and social sciences, inorganic chemistry, international relations, international studies, jazz, junior high education, language interpretation and translation, liberal/general studies, mathematics, microbiology, molecular biology, music, music performance, music theory and composition, organic chemistry, painting, philosophy, photography, physical chemistry, physical sciences, physics, political science and government, printmaking, psychobiology, psychology, sculpture, social psychology, social sciences, Spanish, studio art, theater design, visual and performing arts, women's studies.

ACADEMIC PROGRAMS. Double major, independent study, internships, student-designed major, study abroad, BA/MS program with Bank Street College of Education (NY); post-baccalaureate plan of study for those preparing to apply to medical or allied health sciences graduate schools. **Remedial services:** Remedial instruction, tutoring. **Placement/credit:** Institutional tests.

ACADEMIC REQUIREMENTS. No policy requiring minimum GPA; records of students having academic difficulty are reviewed individually. 80% of freshmen return for sophomore year. Students must declare major by end of second year. **Graduation requirements:** 128 hours for bachelor's (64 in major). **Additional information:** 8-week required nonresident midwinter term during which students hold off-campus jobs (secured with help from college) that relate to their course of study or career interests. Many faculty/student designed tutorials allow students to expand curriculum to meet specific interests in advanced levels of study.

FRESHMAN ADMISSIONS. Selection criteria: Essay and recommendations important part of application. Equally important is evidence of challenge to student in classroom. Close attention paid to high school course selection and performance. Committee looks for self-motivated students, encourages applicants to submit samples of their work, analytical and creative. **High school preparation:** 16 units recommended. Recommended units include English 4, foreign language 3, mathematics 3, social science 3 and science 3. Recommend demanding and rigorous course schedule. **Test requirements:** SAT or ACT; score report by January 15. **Additional information:** Grades, class rank, test scores interpreted within context of whole application rather than in isolation. Case candidate makes in writing is critical. Purpose of application process is to ensure student's success in college.

1992 FRESHMAN CLASS PROFILE. 202 men applied, 118 accepted, 49 enrolled; 344 women applied, 274 accepted, 98 enrolled. 11% were in top tenth and 27% were in top quarter of graduating class. **Academic background:** Mid 50% of enrolled freshmen had SAT-V between 490-610, SAT-M between 450-590; ACT composite between 23-26. 90% submitted SAT scores, 5% submitted ACT scores. **Characteristics:** 6% from in state, 100% live in college housing, 11% have minority backgrounds, 8% are foreign students. Average age is 17.

FALL-TERM APPLICATIONS. $40 fee, may be waived for applicants with need. Closing date January 1; applicants notified on or about March 25; must reply by May 1. Interview required. Essay required. CRDA. Deferred and early admission available. EDP-F. Applicants who visit college interviewed by student as well as by admissions staff person and invited to attend classes when in session.

STUDENT LIFE. Housing: Dormitories (coed). 15 student houses located on campus with livingrooms with working fireplaces and small kitchens. **Activities:** Student government, magazine, student newspaper, choral groups, dance, drama, music ensembles, symphony orchestra, Film Society, weekly Coffee House, student performances, Amnesty (minority concerns group), women's studies group, recycling club, community service groups, housechairs (resident assistants), Student Educational Policy Committee.

ATHLETICS. Intercollegiate: Soccer. **Intramural:** Soccer, softball, tennis, volleyball.

STUDENT SERVICES. Career counseling, employment service for undergraduates, freshman orientation, health services, personal counseling, placement service for graduates, services/facilities for handicapped.

ANNUAL EXPENSES. Tuition and fees: Comprehensive fee: $24,850. **Books and supplies:** $400. **Other expenses:** $600.

FINANCIAL AID. 73% of freshmen, 67% of continuing students receive some form of aid. 99% of grants, 95% of loans, all jobs based on need. 109 enrolled freshmen were judged to have need, all were offered aid. Academic, state/district residency scholarships available. **Aid applications:** Closing date March 1; applicants notified on or about April 1; must reply by May 1 or within 2 weeks if notified thereafter.

ADDRESS/TELEPHONE. Karen Kristof, Director of Admissions, Bennington College, Bennington, VT 05201. (802) 442-6349. (800) 833-6845. Fax: (802) 442-6164.

Burlington College

Burlington, Vermont CB code: 1119

4-year private liberal arts college, coed. Founded in 1972. **Accreditation:** Regional. **Undergraduate enrollment:** 31 men, 38 women full time; 42 men, 73 women part time. **Faculty:** 60 total, 15 with doctorates or other terminal degrees. **Location:** Urban campus in small city; 100 miles from Montreal, Canada, 200 miles from of Boston. **Calendar:** Semester, limited summer session. Saturday and extensive evening/early morning classes. **Microcomputers:** 10 located in libraries, computer centers. **Additional facts:** Offers a flexible, supportive liberal arts education for adult learners.

DEGREES OFFERED. AA, BA. 4 associate degrees awarded in 1992. 100% in multi/interdisciplinary studies. 32 bachelor's degrees awarded. 6% in education, 47% multi/interdisciplinary studies, 41% psychology.

UNDERGRADUATE MAJORS. Associate: Liberal/general studies. **Bachelor's:** Education, fine arts, humanities, liberal/general studies, psychology, sociology, transpersonal psychology, women's studies.

ACADEMIC PROGRAMS. 2-year transfer program, accelerated program, double major, external degree, independent study, internships, student-designed major, teacher preparation, weekend college, cross-registration. **Remedial services:** Learning center, reduced course load, remedial instruction, special counselor, tutoring. **Placement/credit:** AP, CLEP General and Subject, institutional tests; 30 credit hours maximum for associate degree; 30 credit hours maximum for bachelor's degree.

ACADEMIC REQUIREMENTS. Students must complete 75% of courses attempted to remain in good academic standing. 59% of freshmen return for sophomore year. Students must declare major by end of second year. **Graduation requirements:** 60 hours for associate (9 in major), 120 hours for bachelor's (36 in major). Most students required to take courses in English, humanities, mathematics, biological/physical sciences, social sciences. **Postgraduate studies:** 70% from 2-year programs enter 4-year programs.

FRESHMAN ADMISSIONS. Selection criteria: Open admissions.

1992 FRESHMAN CLASS PROFILE. 16 men applied, 15 accepted, 13 enrolled; 22 women applied, 20 accepted, 19 enrolled. **Characteristics:** 87% from in state, 100% commute, 13% have minority backgrounds, 2% are foreign students.

FALL-TERM APPLICATIONS. $30 fee. Closing date August 20; priority given to applications received by July 1; applicants notified on a rolling basis. Interview required. Deferred and early admission available. Application fee may be deferred until enrollment for qualified financial aid applicants.

STUDENT LIFE. Activities: Student government, dance, drama, music ensembles, VPIRG chapter, single parent support group. **Additional information:** With 5 other colleges in the area, students are offered many social, cultural, and outdoor recreational opportunities year-round.

STUDENT SERVICES. Aptitude testing, career counseling, freshman orientation, personal counseling, services/facilities for handicapped.

ANNUAL EXPENSES. Tuition and fees (1992-93): $7,330. **Books and supplies:** $600. **Other expenses:** $2,160.

FINANCIAL AID. 80% of freshmen, 80% of continuing students receive some form of aid. All grants, 82% of loans, all jobs based on need. **Aid applications:** No closing date; priority given to applications received by June 1; applicants notified on a rolling basis; must reply within 4 weeks. **Addi-**

tional information: Average award per student on aid was $5,550 in 1990-91.

ADDRESS/TELEPHONE. Larry Lewack, Director of Admissions, Burlington College, 95 North Avenue, Burlington, VT 05401. (802) 862-9616.

Castleton State College
Castleton, Vermont CB code: 3765

Admissions: 77% of applicants accepted
Based on:
- ••• School record
- •• Essay, interview, recommendations, test scores
- • Activities, special talents

Completion: 90% of freshmen end year in good standing
42% graduate

4-year public liberal arts college, coed. Founded in 1787. **Accreditation:** Regional. **Undergraduate enrollment:** 687 men, 801 women full time; 42 men, 130 women part time. **Graduate enrollment:** 4 men, 9 women full time; 32 men, 58 women part time. **Faculty:** 115 total (88 full time), 72 with doctorates or other terminal degrees. **Location:** Rural campus in small town; 12 miles from Rutland, 7 miles from New York border. **Calendar:** Semester, limited summer session. **Microcomputers:** 180 located in dormitories, libraries, classrooms, computer centers. **Special facilities:** Observatory, primate laboratory.

DEGREES OFFERED. AA, AS, BA, BS, MEd. 67 associate degrees awarded in 1992. 22% in business and management, 7% communications, 6% education, 30% health sciences, 16% multi/interdisciplinary studies, 12% parks/recreation, protective services, public affairs. 265 bachelor's degrees awarded. 15% in business and management, 5% business/office and marketing/distribution, 11% communications, 26% education, 6% health sciences, 8% parks/recreation, protective services, public affairs, 5% psychology, 11% social sciences. Graduate degrees offered in 3 major fields of study.

UNDERGRADUATE MAJORS. Associate: Accounting, business administration and management, business and office, communications, computer programming, criminal justice studies, geology, liberal/general studies, marketing research, nursing. **Bachelor's:** Accounting, American literature, art education, athletic training, biochemistry, biological and physical sciences, biology, business administration and management, business education, chemistry, children's literature, communications, comparative literature, corporate communications, criminal justice studies, dramatic arts, drawing, early childhood education, elementary education, English, English education, English literature, finance, fine arts, foreign languages education, geology, history, information sciences and systems, journalism, marketing and distribution, marketing research, mathematics, mathematics education, music, music education, painting, physical education, psychology, radio/television broadcasting, reading education, science education, secondary education, social science education, social sciences, social studies education, social work, sociology, Spanish, special education, sports medicine, studio art.

ACADEMIC PROGRAMS. Cooperative education, double major, honors program, independent study, internships, student-designed major, study abroad, teacher preparation, 2-3 pharmacy program with Albany College of Pharmacy (NY); liberal arts/career combination in engineering; combined bachelor's/graduate program in business administration. **Remedial services:** Reduced course load, remedial instruction, special counselor, tutoring. **Placement/credit:** AP, CLEP General and Subject, institutional tests; 30 credit hours maximum for associate degree; 60 credit hours maximum for bachelor's degree.

ACADEMIC REQUIREMENTS. Freshmen must earn minimum GPA of 1.5 to continue in good standing. 72% of freshmen return for sophomore year. Students must declare major by end of second year. **Graduation requirements:** 64 hours for associate (40 in major), 128 hours for bachelor's (82 in major). Most students required to take courses in computer science, English, history, humanities, mathematics, biological/physical sciences, social sciences.

FRESHMAN ADMISSIONS. Selection criteria: School achievement record (class rank, if available), test scores, recommendations considered. **High school preparation:** 16 units recommended. Recommended units include English 4, foreign language 2, mathematics 3, social science 3 and science 2. **Test requirements:** SAT or ACT (SAT preferred); score report by April 1.

1992 FRESHMAN CLASS PROFILE. 561 men applied, 408 accepted, 146 enrolled; 647 women applied, 525 accepted, 192 enrolled. **Academic background:** Mid 50% of enrolled freshmen had SAT-V between 380-480, SAT-M between 390-530. 93% submitted SAT scores. **Characteristics:** 53% from in state, 70% live in college housing, 1% have minority backgrounds, 1% are foreign students. Average age is 19.

FALL-TERM APPLICATIONS. $40 fee, may be waived for applicants with need. Closing date May 1; priority given to applications received by April 1; applicants notified on a rolling basis; must reply by May 1 or within 2 weeks if notified thereafter. Essay required. Interview recommended. Audition recommended for music applicants. CRDA. Deferred and early admission available.

STUDENT LIFE. Housing: Dormitories (coed). Honors dormitory available. **Activities:** Student government, magazine, radio, student newspaper, television, yearbook, choral groups, dance, drama, jazz band, music ensembles, musical theater, pep band, social and cultural committees, Christian fellowships, political discussion group, international club, Volunteer Income Tax Assistance.

ATHLETICS. NAIA. **Intercollegiate:** Baseball M, basketball, cross-country, lacrosse, soccer, softball W, tennis. **Intramural:** Badminton, basketball, racquetball, softball, swimming, table tennis, volleyball.

STUDENT SERVICES. Aptitude testing, career counseling, employment service for undergraduates, freshman orientation, health services, on-campus day care, personal counseling, placement service for graduates, services/facilities for handicapped.

ANNUAL EXPENSES. Tuition and fees (projected): $3,748, $4,152 additional for out-of-state students. **Room and board:** $4,640. **Books and supplies:** $400. **Other expenses:** $600.

FINANCIAL AID. 80% of freshmen, 60% of continuing students receive some form of aid. 93% of grants, 83% of loans, 76% of jobs based on need. 224 enrolled freshmen were judged to have need, all were offered aid. Academic, music/drama, state/district residency, leadership scholarships available. **Aid applications:** No closing date; priority given to applications received by March 15; applicants notified on a rolling basis beginning on or about April 15; must reply by May 1 or within 2 weeks if notified thereafter.

ADDRESS/TELEPHONE. Gary Fallis, Director of Admissions, Castleton State College, Castleton, VT 05735-9987. (802) 468-5611 ext. 213. Fax: (802) 468-5237.

Champlain College
Burlington, Vermont CB code: 3291

Admissions: 87% of applicants accepted
Based on:
- ••• School record
- •• Interview, recommendations
- • Activities, essay, special talents, test scores

Completion: 70% of freshmen end year in good standing
66% graduate, 19% of these enter 4-year programs

2-year private business, junior college, coed. Founded in 1878. **Accreditation:** Regional. **Undergraduate enrollment:** 489 men, 776 women full time; 301 men, 400 women part time. **Faculty:** 137 total (61 full time), 18 with doctorates or other terminal degrees. **Location:** Suburban campus in large town; 200 miles from Boston, 90 miles from Montreal, Canada. **Calendar:** Semester, limited summer session. Extensive evening/early morning classes. **Microcomputers:** 100 located in dormitories, libraries, classrooms, computer centers, campus-wide network. **Special facilities:** Hauke Family Campus Center, video production studio, preschool for 3-5 year olds. **Additional facts:** Technology-related courses on site at IBM, Vermont Insurance Institute housed at the college.

DEGREES OFFERED. AS. 550 associate degrees awarded in 1992. 37% in business and management, 14% business/office and marketing/distribution, 17% computer sciences, 5% teacher education, 9% multi/interdisciplinary studies, 7% parks/recreation, protective services, public affairs.

UNDERGRADUATE MAJORS. Accounting, advertising, apparel and accessories marketing, business administration and management, business and management, business and office, business computer/console/peripheral equipment operation, business data processing and related programs, business data programming, business systems analysis, communications, community services, computer and information sciences, computer programming, criminal justice studies, criminology, data processing, early childhood education, education, electronic technology, elementary education, engineering and engineering-related technologies, fashion merchandising, hospitality and recreation marketing, hotel/motel and restaurant management, information sciences and systems, law enforcement and corrections, legal assistant/paralegal, legal secretary, liberal/general studies, marketing and distribution, marketing management, medical secretary, office supervision and management, public relations, radiograph medical technology, respiratory therapy, respiratory therapy technology, retailing, secretarial and related programs, small business management and ownership, social work, teacher aide, tourism, transportation and travel marketing, word processing. accounting, business administration and management, business and management.

ACADEMIC PROGRAMS. 2-year transfer program, accelerated program, double major, dual enrollment of high school students, independent study, internships, telecourses, cross-registration, clinical internships at Medical Center Hospital of Vermont, 2-2 baccalaureate in accounting and business management. **Remedial services:** Learning center, reduced course load, special counselor, tutoring. **ROTC:** Air Force, Army, Naval. **Placement/credit:** AP, CLEP General and Subject, institutional tests; 30 credit hours maximum for associate degree.

ACADEMIC REQUIREMENTS. Freshmen must earn minimum GPA of 2.0 to continue in good standing. 68% of freshmen return for sophomore

year. Students must declare major on application. **Graduation requirements:** 60 hours for associate (60 in major). Most students required to take courses in computer science, English, mathematics, social sciences. **Additional information:** 2 bachelor level programs available in accounting and business management.

FRESHMAN ADMISSIONS. Selection criteria: GPA, class rank, interview, counselor recommendations, test scores, extracurricular activities, job experience, and maturity all considered. **High school preparation:** 18 units recommended. Recommended units include biological science 2, English 4, foreign language 2, mathematics 2, physical science 2, social science 2 and science 2. Electronics engineering technology, accounting, radiography, respiratory therapy, computer programming, and paralegal programs have specific course requirements. **Test requirements:** SAT or ACT (SAT preferred); score report by August 20. SAT or ACT required of applicants to electronics technology program; score report by August 28.

1992 FRESHMAN CLASS PROFILE. 618 men applied, 562 accepted, 336 enrolled; 953 women applied, 803 accepted, 529 enrolled. 39% had high school GPA of 3.0 or higher, 60% between 2.0 and 2.99. 10% were in top tenth and 30% were in top quarter of graduating class. **Characteristics:** 75% from in state, 50% commute, 3% have minority backgrounds, 1% are foreign students. Average age is 19.

FALL-TERM APPLICATIONS. $25 fee, may be waived for applicants with need. No closing date; applicants notified on a rolling basis; must reply by May 1 or within 4 weeks if notified thereafter. Essay required. Interview recommended. CRDA. Deferred and early admission available.

STUDENT LIFE. Housing: Dormitories (men, women). Students may rent rooms in college-authorized private homes and take meals on campus. **Activities:** Student government, student newspaper, yearbook, drama, musical theater, Cultural Diversity Committee, Gender Equity Committee, Champlain Democrats, Champlain Republicans, residential hall programs, community service projects.

ATHLETICS. NJCAA. **Intercollegiate:** Basketball M, golf, skiing, soccer, softball W. **Intramural:** Basketball, bowling, golf, ice hockey M, racquetball, skiing, soccer, volleyball, water polo.

STUDENT SERVICES. Aptitude testing, career counseling, employment service for undergraduates, freshman orientation, health services, on-campus day care, personal counseling, placement service for graduates, special adviser for adult students, veterans counselor, services/facilities for handicapped.

ANNUAL EXPENSES. Tuition and fees: $7,840. Seniors pay graduation fee of $80. **Room and board:** $5,550. **Books and supplies:** $375. **Other expenses:** $600.

FINANCIAL AID. 74% of freshmen, 88% of continuing students receive some form of aid. 95% of grants, 82% of loans, all jobs based on need. 727 enrolled freshmen were judged to have need, all were offered aid. Athletic scholarships available. **Aid applications:** No closing date; priority given to applications received by May 1; applicants notified on a rolling basis beginning on or about April 1; must reply by May 1 or within 3 weeks if notified thereafter.

ADDRESS/TELEPHONE. Josephine Churchill, Director of Admissions, Champlain College, PO Box 670, 163 South Willard Street, Burlington, VT 05402. (802) 860-2727. Fax: (802) 860-2772.

College of St. Joseph in Vermont
Rutland, Vermont

CB code: 3297

Admissions: 83% of applicants accepted
Based on:
- ••• Essay, school record
- •• Activities, interview, recommendations, test scores
- • Special talents

Completion: 84% of freshmen end year in good standing
5% enter graduate study

4-year private business, liberal arts college, coed, affiliated with Roman Catholic Church. Founded in 1950. **Accreditation:** Regional. **Undergraduate enrollment:** 78 men, 129 women full time; 61 men, 119 women part time. **Graduate enrollment:** 1 woman full time; 22 men, 62 women part time. **Faculty:** 54 total (15 full time), 21 with doctorates or other terminal degrees. **Location:** Rural campus in large town; 70 miles from Burlington, 100 miles from Albany, New York. **Calendar:** Semester, extensive summer session. Extensive evening/early morning classes. **Microcomputers:** 35 located in libraries, computer centers. **Special facilities:** Photography and ceramics studios.

DEGREES OFFERED. AA, AS, BA, BS, MEd. 10 associate degrees awarded in 1992. 50% in business and management, 10% computer sciences, 40% multi/interdisciplinary studies. 60 bachelor's degrees awarded. 42% in business and management, 21% teacher education, 5% multi/interdisciplinary studies, 22% psychology, 10% social sciences. Graduate degrees offered in 6 major fields of study.

UNDERGRADUATE MAJORS. Associate: Accounting, business and management, computer and information sciences, liberal/general studies, special education. **Bachelor's:** Accounting, American studies, business and management, computer and information sciences, early childhood education, education of the mentally handicapped, elementary education, English, English education, history, liberal/general studies, mental health/human services, political science and government, prelaw, psychology, secondary education, social studies education, social work, special education.

ACADEMIC PROGRAMS. 2-year transfer program, double major, dual enrollment of high school students, independent study, internships, study abroad, teacher preparation. **Remedial services:** Learning center, preadmission summer program, reduced course load, remedial instruction, special counselor, tutoring. **Placement/credit:** AP, CLEP General, institutional tests.

ACADEMIC REQUIREMENTS. Freshmen must earn minimum GPA of 1.6 to continue in good standing. 63% of freshmen return for sophomore year. Students must declare major by end of second year. **Graduation requirements:** 60 hours for associate (30 in major), 127 hours for bachelor's (51 in major). Most students required to take courses in arts/fine arts, computer science, English, history, mathematics, philosophy/religion, biological/physical sciences, social sciences. **Postgraduate studies:** 50% from 2-year programs enter 4-year programs. 1% enter MBA programs, 4% enter other graduate study.

FRESHMAN ADMISSIONS. Selection criteria: High school record, 2.0 high school GPA in college preparatory coursework, essay, test scores, interview, and recommendations considered. **High school preparation:** 11 units required. Required and recommended units include English 4, mathematics 3, social science 2 and science 2. Foreign language 2 recommended. One science must be laboratory science. **Test requirements:** SAT or ACT (SAT preferred); score report by June 6.

1992 FRESHMAN CLASS PROFILE. 154 men and women applied, 128 accepted; 61 enrolled. 51% had high school GPA of 3.0 or higher, 49% between 2.0 and 2.99. 2% were in top tenth and 9% were in top quarter of graduating class. **Academic background:** Mid 50% of enrolled freshmen had SAT-V between 310-440, SAT-M between 320-450. 95% submitted SAT scores. **Characteristics:** 38% from in state, 75% live in college housing, 3% are foreign students. Average age is 19.

FALL-TERM APPLICATIONS. $25 fee, may be waived for applicants with need. No closing date; applicants notified on a rolling basis; must reply by May 1 if possible. Essay required. Interview recommended. CRDA. Deferred and early admission available.

STUDENT LIFE. Housing: Dormitories (women, coed). Some single rooms available. Most rooms double occupancy, in suites housing 8 students. **Activities:** Student government, student newspaper, yearbook, choral groups, dance, drama, special education club, Big Brother/Big Sister program, Women's Issue Club, Newman Club (campus ministry).

ATHLETICS. NAIA. **Intercollegiate:** Basketball, soccer, softball W. **Intramural:** Basketball, bowling, golf, skiing, soccer W, softball, tennis, volleyball.

STUDENT SERVICES. Career counseling, employment service for undergraduates, freshman orientation, personal counseling, special adviser for adult students, veterans counselor, services/facilities for handicapped.

ANNUAL EXPENSES. Tuition and fees: $8,000. **Room and board:** $4,650. **Books and supplies:** $600. **Other expenses:** $900.

FINANCIAL AID. 75% of freshmen, 71% of continuing students receive some form of aid. 83% of grants, 87% of loans, all jobs based on need. Academic, state/district residency, leadership, religious affiliation scholarships available. **Aid applications:** Closing date May 1; priority given to applications received by March 1; applicants notified on a rolling basis beginning on or about March 15; must reply within 2 weeks.

ADDRESS/TELEPHONE. Carl N. Tichenor, Dean of Admissions, College of St. Joseph in Vermont, Clement Road, Rutland, VT 05701-9945. (802) 773-5905. Fax: (802) 773-5900 ext. 258.

Community College of Vermont
Waterbury, Vermont

2-year public community college, coed. Founded in 1970. **Accreditation:** Regional. **Undergraduate enrollment:** 109 men, 239 women full time; 1,032 men, 3,347 women part time. **Faculty:** 591 total, 45 with doctorates or other terminal degrees. **Location:** Rural campus in small town. **Calendar:** Semester, limited summer session. Saturday and extensive evening/early morning classes. **Microcomputers:** 90 located in classrooms. **Additional facts:** Courses offered in 50 communities. All majors student designed with advisement.

DEGREES OFFERED. AA, AS, AAS. 191 associate degrees awarded in 1992. 42% in business and management, 10% education, 12% allied health, 31% multi/interdisciplinary studies, 5% trade and industry.

UNDERGRADUATE MAJORS. Allied health, business and management, education, liberal/general studies, mechanics and repairer, mental health/human services.

ACADEMIC PROGRAMS. 2-year transfer program, double major, dual enrollment of high school students, external degree, independent study, internships, student-designed major, telecourses, weekend college. **Remedial services:** Learning center, reduced course load, remedial instruction, special counselor, tutoring. **Placement/credit:** CLEP General and Subject; 50 credit hours maximum for associate degree.

ACADEMIC REQUIREMENTS. No policy requiring minimum GPA; records of students having academic difficulty are reviewed individually. Student must satisfactorily complete 50% of courses taken. 60% of freshmen return for sophomore year. Students must declare major by end of first year. **Graduation requirements:** 60 hours for associate (24 in major).

FRESHMAN ADMISSIONS. Selection criteria: Open admissions.

1992 FRESHMAN CLASS PROFILE. 112 men applied, 112 accepted, 112 enrolled; 448 women applied, 448 accepted, 448 enrolled. **Characteristics:** 98% from in state, 100% commute, 2% have minority backgrounds. Average age is 32.

FALL-TERM APPLICATIONS. No fee. No closing date; applicants notified on a rolling basis. Interview recommended for degree program applicants. Recommendation required if applicant has neither high school diploma nor GED.

STUDENT SERVICES. Career counseling, special adviser for adult students, services/facilities for handicapped.

ANNUAL EXPENSES. Tuition and fees (1992-93): $2,370, $2,310 additional for out-of-state students. New England residents pay $3,480 tuition. **Books and supplies:** $350.

FINANCIAL AID. 86% of freshmen, 86% of continuing students receive some form of aid. All grants, 95% of loans, all jobs based on need. Academic scholarships available. **Aid applications:** No closing date; applicants notified on a rolling basis beginning on or about September 1; must reply within 3 weeks.

ADDRESS/TELEPHONE. Registrar, Community College of Vermont, PO Box 120, Waterbury, VT 05676. (802) 241-3535.

Goddard College
Plainfield, Vermont — CB code: 3416

4-year private liberal arts college, coed. Founded in 1938. **Accreditation:** Regional. **Undergraduate enrollment:** 75 men, 145 women full time. **Graduate enrollment:** 59 men, 100 women full time. **Faculty:** 58 total (19 full time). **Location:** Rural campus in rural community; 10 miles from Montpelier. **Calendar:** Semester. **Microcomputers:** 15 located in libraries, computer centers.

DEGREES OFFERED. BA, MA, MFA. 65 bachelor's degrees awarded in 1992. Graduate degrees offered in 34 major fields of study.

UNDERGRADUATE MAJORS. Afro-American (black) studies, agricultural sciences, American Indian studies, American studies, art education, biology, botany, business and management, communications, community services, crafts, early childhood education, ecology, education, education administration, elementary education, English, English education, environmental science, European studies, experimental psychology, fine arts, health sciences, humanities, humanities and social sciences, Jewish studies, journalism, junior high education, Latin American studies, liberal/general studies, library science, marketing and distribution, mathematics, Mexican American studies, Middle Eastern studies, music, philosophy, physical sciences, psychology, public administration, radio/television broadcasting, radio/television technology, religion, renewable natural resources, secondary education, social sciences, social studies education, social work, visual and performing arts, women's studies, zoology.

ACADEMIC PROGRAMS. External degree, independent study, internships, student-designed major, study abroad, teacher preparation. **Placement/credit:** CLEP General; 30 credit hours maximum for bachelor's degree.

ACADEMIC REQUIREMENTS. No policy requiring minimum GPA; records of students having academic difficulty are reviewed individually. 75% of freshmen return for sophomore year. **Graduation requirements:** 120 hours for bachelor's. **Additional information:** Written evaluations replace grades. Individually designed majors at bachelor's and masters levels.

FRESHMAN ADMISSIONS. Selection criteria: Academic potential, maturity, ability to work independently, personal statement, and campus interview important.

1992 FRESHMAN CLASS PROFILE. 10 men, 17 women enrolled. **Characteristics:** 10% from in state, 95% live in college housing, 5% have minority backgrounds, 1% are foreign students. Average age is 19.

FALL-TERM APPLICATIONS. $25 fee, may be waived for applicants with need. No closing date; applicants notified on a rolling basis; must reply by May 1 or within 4 weeks if notified thereafter. Interview required. Essay required. CRDA. SAT or ACT scores optional.

STUDENT LIFE. Housing: Dormitories (women, coed); apartment, cooperative housing available. Special interest housing available. **Activities:** Student government, radio, student newspaper, occasional student publications, choral groups, dance, drama, jazz band, music ensembles, Social Justice Coalition, Vermont Public Interest Research Group, Women's Center, Gay Lesbian and Bisexual Alliance. **Additional information:** Students participate in administration of college. All students participate in work program 8 hours per week.

STUDENT SERVICES. Career counseling, employment service for undergraduates, freshman orientation, on-campus day care, personal counseling, placement service for graduates, special adviser for adult students, services/facilities for handicapped.

ANNUAL EXPENSES. Tuition and fees: $13,400. **Room and board:** $4,520. **Books and supplies:** $508. **Other expenses:** $911.

FINANCIAL AID. 55% of freshmen receive some form of aid. All grants, 96% of loans, all jobs based on need. 23 enrolled freshmen were judged to have need, all were offered aid. **Aid applications:** Closing date June 15; priority given to applications received by April 1; applicants notified on a rolling basis beginning on or about April 15; must reply within 4 weeks.

ADDRESS/TELEPHONE. Peter S. Burns, Director of Admissions, Goddard College, Plainfield, VT 05667. (802) 454-8311. (800) 468-4888. Fax: (802)454-8017.

Green Mountain College
Poultney, Vermont — CB code: 3418

Admissions: 75% of applicants accepted
Based on:
- ••• School record
- •• Essay, interview, recommendations, test scores
- • Activities, special talents

Completion: 75% of freshmen end year in good standing
60% graduate, 28% of these enter graduate study

4-year private liberal arts college, coed. Founded in 1834. **Accreditation:** Regional. **Undergraduate enrollment:** 291 men, 300 women full time; 11 men, 20 women part time. **Faculty:** 53 total (36 full time), 29 with doctorates or other terminal degrees. **Location:** Rural campus in small town; 20 miles from Rutland. **Calendar:** Semester. **Microcomputers:** 24 located in libraries, computer centers. **Special facilities:** Substantial collection of Welsh artifacts and literature, Ramsey collection of Early American Decoration, Vargas art collection, extensive rare books collection.

DEGREES OFFERED. BA, BS, BFA. 76 bachelor's degrees awarded in 1992. 39% in business and management, 13% education, 21% multi/interdisciplinary studies, 20% parks/recreation, protective services, public affairs, 10% social sciences, 5% visual and performing arts.

UNDERGRADUATE MAJORS. Behavioral sciences, business administration and management, business and management, elementary education, English, fine arts, humanities and social sciences, journalism, leisure resource management facilities, liberal/general studies, parks and recreation management, prelaw, public relations, recreation and community services technologies, recreation therapy, retailing, special education.

ACADEMIC PROGRAMS. Double major, independent study, internships, study abroad, teacher preparation. **Remedial services:** Learning center, reduced course load, remedial instruction, special counselor, tutoring. **Placement/credit:** AP, CLEP General and Subject, institutional tests; 90 credit hours maximum for bachelor's degree.

ACADEMIC REQUIREMENTS. Freshmen must earn minimum GPA of 1.8 to continue in good standing. 74% of freshmen return for sophomore year. Students must declare major by end of second year. **Graduation requirements:** 120 hours for bachelor's (65 in major). Most students required to take courses in arts/fine arts, English, history, humanities, mathematics, biological/physical sciences, social sciences. **Postgraduate studies:** 1% enter law school, 6% enter MBA programs, 21% enter other graduate study.

FRESHMAN ADMISSIONS. Selection criteria: Academic achievement, recommendations, interview, test scores, personal statement school and community activities considered. **High school preparation:** 16 units required. Required and recommended units include biological science 1, English 4, mathematics 2-3, physical science 1 and social science 2-3. Foreign language 2 and science 1 recommended. **Test requirements:** SAT or ACT; score report by August 1.

1992 FRESHMAN CLASS PROFILE. 430 men applied, 330 accepted, 123 enrolled; 420 women applied, 310 accepted, 90 enrolled. 11% had high school GPA of 3.0 or higher, 84% between 2.0 and 2.99. **Academic background:** Mid 50% of enrolled freshmen had SAT-V between 400-490, SAT-M between 400-510; ACT composite between 19-23. 93% submitted SAT scores, 6% submitted ACT scores. **Characteristics:** 8% from in state, 97% live in college housing, 1% have minority backgrounds, 3% are foreign students. Average age is 18.

FALL-TERM APPLICATIONS. $20 fee, may be waived for applicants with need. No closing date; priority given to applications received by April 1; applicants notified on a rolling basis; must reply by May 1 or within 4 weeks if notified thereafter. Essay required. Interview recommended. Portfolio recommended for art applicants. CRDA. Deferred and early admission available. EDP-F.

STUDENT LIFE. Housing: Dormitories (coed); cooperative housing available. All students, unless living with parents, required to live on campus until they are 21, have attained 2.5 GPA, and senior status. At that time, students may petition to move off campus. **Activities:** Student government, student newspaper, yearbook, choral groups, dance, drama, music ensembles, volunteer programs with Rutland Mental Health Association, after-school programs for children, services to senior citizens, GMC Cares organization for community outreach, special olympics/senior games. **Additional information:** Honors Residence (students selected by major and GPA).

ATHLETICS. NAIA. **Intercollegiate:** Basketball, lacrosse M, skiing, soccer, softball W, volleyball W. **Intramural:** Basketball, bowling, golf, horseback riding, soccer, softball, table tennis, tennis, volleyball, water polo.

STUDENT SERVICES. Aptitude testing, career counseling, employment service for undergraduates, freshman orientation, health services, personal counseling, placement service for graduates.

ANNUAL EXPENSES. Tuition and fees: $11,100. **Room and board:** $2,860. **Books and supplies:** $400. **Other expenses:** $340.

FINANCIAL AID. 63% of freshmen, 59% of continuing students receive some form of aid. 71% of grants, 97% of loans, 77% of jobs based on need. 85 enrolled freshmen were judged to have need, all were offered aid. Academic, art, athletic, leadership scholarships available. **Aid applications:** No closing date; priority given to applications received by February 15; applicants notified on a rolling basis beginning on or about March 1; must reply by May 1 or within 2 weeks if notified thereafter.

ADDRESS/TELEPHONE. Kevin M. R. Mayne, Vice President for External Affairs and Admissions, Green Mountain College, 16 College Street, Poultney, VT 05764. (802) 287-9313. (800) 776-6675. Fax: (802) 287-9313.

Johnson State College
Johnson, Vermont CB code: 3766

4-year public liberal arts college, coed. Founded in 1828. **Accreditation:** Regional. **Undergraduate enrollment:** 1,665 men and women. **Graduate enrollment:** 93 men and women. **Faculty:** 140 total (64 full time), 57 with doctorates or other terminal degrees. **Location:** Rural campus in rural community; 40 miles from Burlington, 90 miles from Montreal, Canada. **Calendar:** Semester, limited summer session. **Microcomputers:** 95 located in libraries, classrooms, computer centers. **Special facilities:** Art gallery, nature preserve, visual arts center. **Additional facts:** External Degree Program offers classes at 8 locations throughout the state.

DEGREES OFFERED. AA, AS, BA, BS, BFA, MA. 12 associate degrees awarded in 1992. 276 bachelor's degrees awarded. Graduate degrees offered in 11 major fields of study.

UNDERGRADUATE MAJORS. Associate: Accounting, business administration and management, computer and information sciences, early childhood education, liberal/general studies, management information systems, teacher aide. **Bachelor's:** Allied health, anthropology, art education, biology, business administration and management, creative writing, dramatic arts, early childhood education, ecology, education, education of the gifted and talented, elementary education, English, environmental science, health sciences, history, hotel/motel and restaurant management, journalism, junior high education, mathematics, mathematics education, music, music education, music performance, physical education, political science and government, psychology, science education, secondary education, social studies education, social work, sociology, speech/communication/theater education, sports medicine, studio art, visual and performing arts.

ACADEMIC PROGRAMS. Cooperative education, double major, education specialist degree, external degree, honors program, independent study, internships, study abroad, teacher preparation, weekend college; liberal arts/career combination in health sciences. **Remedial services:** Learning center, preadmission summer program, reduced course load, remedial instruction, special counselor, tutoring. **Placement/credit:** AP, CLEP General and Subject, institutional tests.

ACADEMIC REQUIREMENTS. Freshmen must earn minimum GPA of 1.75 to continue in good standing. 65% of freshmen return for sophomore year. Students must declare major by end of second year. **Graduation requirements:** 60 hours for associate (30 in major), 120 hours for bachelor's (60 in major). Most students required to take courses in arts/fine arts, English, humanities, mathematics, biological/physical sciences, social sciences. **Postgraduate studies:** 10% from 2-year programs enter 4-year programs.

FRESHMAN ADMISSIONS. Selection criteria: School achievement record, SAT or ACT scores, interview, and recommendations important. **High school preparation:** 16 units recommended. Recommended units include English 4, mathematics 3, social science 1 and science 2. Recommended mathematics must include algebra II. **Test requirements:** SAT or ACT (SAT preferred); score report by August 15. SAT or ACT requirement may be waived on appeal.

1992 FRESHMAN CLASS PROFILE. 265 men and women enrolled. **Characteristics:** 60% from in state, 85% live in college housing, 2% have minority backgrounds, 1% are foreign students. Average age is 18.

FALL-TERM APPLICATIONS. $40 fee, may be waived for applicants with need. No closing date; priority given to applications received by March 1; applicants notified on a rolling basis beginning on or about November 1; must reply by May 1 or within 2 weeks if notified thereafter. Essay required. Interview recommended. Audition recommended for theater, music applicants. Portfolio recommended for studio arts applicants. CRDA. Deferred admission available.

STUDENT LIFE. Housing: Dormitories (coed); apartment, cooperative housing available. **Activities:** Student government, film, magazine, radio, student newspaper, yearbook, Green Mountain Writer's Workshop, choral groups, dance, drama, jazz band, music ensembles, musical theater, madrigal ensemble, first aid team, peace studies group, art guild, photography club, Young Republicans, Behavioral Sciences Club, Christian Fellowship Club, Hotel/Hospitality Management Club.

ATHLETICS. NAIA, NCAA. **Intercollegiate:** Baseball M, basketball, cross-country, skiing, soccer, softball W, tennis. **Intramural:** Badminton, baseball, basketball, golf, lacrosse, racquetball, rugby, skiing, soccer, softball, swimming, table tennis, tennis, volleyball, wrestling M. **Clubs:** Outing, weightlifting.

STUDENT SERVICES. Aptitude testing, career counseling, employment service for undergraduates, freshman orientation, health services, on-campus day care, personal counseling, placement service for graduates, special adviser for adult students, veterans counselor, services/facilities for handicapped.

ANNUAL EXPENSES. Tuition and fees (projected): $3,748, $4,152 additional for out-of-state students. **Room and board:** $4,640. **Books and supplies:** $500. **Other expenses:** $624.

FINANCIAL AID. 65% of freshmen, 62% of continuing students receive some form of aid. 94% of grants, 79% of loans, 81% of jobs based on need. 209 enrolled freshmen were judged to have need, all were offered aid. Academic, music/drama, leadership scholarships available. **Aid applications:** No closing date; priority given to applications received by March 1; applicants notified on a rolling basis; must reply within 3 weeks.

ADDRESS/TELEPHONE. Jon Henry, Director of Admissions, Johnson State College, Stowe Road, Johnson, VT 05656. (802) 635-2356. (800) 635-2356. Fax: (802) 635-7615.

Landmark College
Putney, Vermont CB code: 0081

2-year private liberal arts college, coed. Founded in 1983. **Accreditation:** Regional. **Undergraduate enrollment:** 152 men, 40 women full time. **Faculty:** 75 total, 2 with doctorates or other terminal degrees. **Location:** Rural campus in rural community; 8 miles from Brattleboro, 23 miles from Keene. **Calendar:** Semester, limited summer session. **Microcomputers:** 20 located in dormitories, libraries, computer centers. **Special facilities:** Fine Arts Building, ropes course (series of obstacles and exercises designed to develop confidence, leadership). **Additional facts:** Nation's only accredited college exclusively for bright dyslexic students.

DEGREES OFFERED. AA. 5 associate degrees awarded in 1992. 100% in multi/interdisciplinary studies.

UNDERGRADUATE MAJORS. Liberal/general studies.

ACADEMIC PROGRAMS. 2-year transfer program. **Remedial services:** Preadmission summer program, reduced course load, remedial instruction, special counselor, tutoring, All courses specially designed for dyslexic students. **Placement/credit:** AP, institutional tests.

ACADEMIC REQUIREMENTS. Freshmen must earn minimum GPA of 2.0 to continue in good standing. 30% of freshmen return for sophomore year. **Graduation requirements:** 60 hours for associate. Most students required to take courses in computer science, English, humanities, mathematics, biological/physical sciences, social sciences.

FRESHMAN ADMISSIONS. Selection criteria: All applicants must have average to superior intellectual ability, diagnosis of dyslexia or specific learning disability, absence of primary emotional disturbance or behavioral disorders, and high motivation to undertake program. Applicants must have upper high school level reading, writing, and study skills and ability to understand and manipulate abstract concepts, as demonstrated on entrance examination.

1992 FRESHMAN CLASS PROFILE. 35 men and women enrolled. **Characteristics:** 100% live in college housing. Average age is 20.

FALL-TERM APPLICATIONS. $50 fee. No closing date; priority given to applications received by August 1; applicants notified on a rolling basis. Interview required. Essay required. Deferred admission available.

STUDENT LIFE. Housing: Dormitories (men, women, coed). All students required to live on campus except for married students. **Activities:** Student government, student newspaper, choral groups, dance, drama, student mentors, community service club.

ATHLETICS. Intercollegiate: Baseball M, basketball, cross-country, skiing, soccer, tennis, volleyball, wrestling M. **Intramural:** Archery, badminton, baseball, basketball, boxing M, cross-country, golf, horseback riding, ice hockey M, lacrosse M, skiing, soccer, softball, swimming, table tennis, tennis, volleyball.

STUDENT SERVICES. Career counseling, freshman orientation, health services, on-campus day care, personal counseling, placement service for graduates, services/facilities for handicapped.

ANNUAL EXPENSES. Tuition and fees: $22,550. **Room and board:** $5,200. **Books and supplies:** $500. **Other expenses:** $1,500.

FINANCIAL AID. 13% of freshmen, 24% of continuing students receive some form of aid. All grants, 58% of loans based on need. All jobs based on criteria other than need. 21 enrolled freshmen were judged to have need, all were offered aid. **Aid applications:** No closing date; applicants notified on a rolling basis. **Additional information:** Students encouraged to apply to their state departments of Vocational Rehabilitation for additional financial assistance.

ADDRESS/TELEPHONE. Carolyn Olivier, Director of Admissions, Landmark College, River Road, RR 1 Box 1000, Putney, VT 05346. (802) 387-4767. Fax: (802) 387-4779.

Lyndon State College
Lyndonville, Vermont — CB code: 3767

Admissions: 87% of applicants accepted
Based on:
••• Recommendations, school record
•• Activities, interview, test scores
• Essay, special talents
Completion: 85% of freshmen end year in good standing
40% graduate, 15% of these enter graduate study

4-year public liberal arts college, coed. Founded in 1911. **Accreditation:** Regional. **Undergraduate enrollment:** 544 men, 462 women full time; 53 men, 76 women part time. **Graduate enrollment:** 1 man full time; 16 men, 43 women part time. **Faculty:** 116 total (62 full time), 64 with doctorates or other terminal degrees. **Location:** Rural campus in rural community; 9 miles form St. Johnsbury. **Calendar:** Semester, limited summer session. **Microcomputers:** 50 located in classrooms, computer centers. **Special facilities:** Museum, gallery, electronic inter-library on-line catalog (access to over 3,000,000 titles).

DEGREES OFFERED. AA, AS, BA, BS, MEd. 41 associate degrees awarded in 1992. 39% in business and management, 32% communications, 27% multi/interdisciplinary studies. 208 bachelor's degrees awarded. 18% in business and management, 14% communications, 18% teacher education, 9% parks/recreation, protective services, public affairs, 11% physical sciences, 10% psychology, 7% visual and performing arts. Graduate degrees offered in 5 major fields of study.

UNDERGRADUATE MAJORS. Associate: Business administration and management, communications, computer programming, liberal/general studies, small business management and ownership. **Bachelor's:** Accounting, atmospheric sciences and meteorology, biology, business administration and management, communications, community services, community/commercial/resort recreation, computer programming, creative writing, early childhood education, elementary education, English education, English literature, environmental science, graphic design, humanities, humanities and social sciences, journalism, mathematics, parks and recreation management, physical education, physical sciences, psychology, radio/television broadcasting, radio/television technology, science education, secondary education, small business management and ownership, social science education, social sciences, special education, sports management.

ACADEMIC PROGRAMS. Cooperative education, double major, dual enrollment of high school students, independent study, internships, study abroad, teacher preparation. **Remedial services:** Learning center, preadmission summer program, reduced course load, remedial instruction, special counselor, tutoring. **ROTC:** Air Force. **Placement/credit:** AP, CLEP General and Subject; 60 credit hours maximum for bachelor's degree.

ACADEMIC REQUIREMENTS. Freshmen must earn minimum GPA of 1.6 to continue in good standing. 60% of freshmen return for sophomore year. Students must declare major by end of second year. **Graduation requirements:** 62 hours for associate, 122 hours for bachelor's. Most students required to take courses in arts/fine arts, English, humanities, mathematics, biological/physical sciences, social sciences. **Postgraduate studies:** 65% from 2-year programs enter 4-year programs.

FRESHMAN ADMISSIONS. Selection criteria: High school courses and grades most important, then class rank (top half preferred), recommendations, and test scores. **High school preparation:** 16 units recommended. Recommended units include English 4, foreign language 1, mathematics 2, social science 2 and science 2. Physics and advanced mathematics for meteorology and computer science. **Test requirements:** SAT; score report by April 1.

1992 FRESHMAN CLASS PROFILE. 476 men applied, 409 accepted, 142 enrolled; 406 women applied, 357 accepted, 100 enrolled. **Academic background:** Mid 50% of enrolled freshmen had SAT-V between 350-450, SAT-M between 350-450. 98% submitted SAT scores. **Characteristics:** 60% from in state, 75% live in college housing, 3% have minority backgrounds, 1% are foreign students. Average age is 18.

FALL-TERM APPLICATIONS. $37 fee, may be waived for applicants with need. No closing date; priority given to applications received by May 1; applicants notified on a rolling basis beginning on or about November 1; must reply by May 1 or within 3 weeks if notified thereafter. Essay required. Interview recommended. CRDA. Deferred admission available.

STUDENT LIFE. Housing: Dormitories (men, women, coed). All students under 23 years of age must live on campus unless residing with parents. **Activities:** Student government, radio, student newspaper, yearbook, choral groups, drama, jazz band, musical theater, fraternities, sororities, rescue squad, Student Association for Exceptional Children, American Meteorological society (student chapter), adult learners peer support group.

ATHLETICS. NAIA. **Intercollegiate:** Baseball M, basketball, cross-country, skiing M, soccer, softball W, tennis. **Intramural:** Badminton W, basketball, bowling, cross-country, golf, handball, ice hockey, racquetball, rugby, skiing, soccer, softball, squash, swimming, table tennis, tennis, track and field, volleyball, water polo, wrestling.

STUDENT SERVICES. Career counseling, employment service for undergraduates, freshman orientation, health services, personal counseling, placement service for graduates, veterans counselor, services/facilities for handicapped.

ANNUAL EXPENSES. Tuition and fees (1992-93): $3,551, $3,912 additional for out-of-state students. New England residents pay $4,464 tuition. **Room and board:** $4,462. **Books and supplies:** $400. **Other expenses:** $400.

FINANCIAL AID. 59% of freshmen, 82% of continuing students receive some form of aid. 69% of grants, 83% of loans, 49% of jobs based on need. Academic, state/district residency, leadership scholarships available. **Aid applications:** No closing date; priority given to applications received by March 15; applicants notified on a rolling basis beginning on or about April 20; must reply within 2 weeks.

ADDRESS/TELEPHONE. Russell S. Powden, Jr, Director of Admissions, Lyndon State College, Lyndonville, VT 05851. (802) 626-9371 ext. 113. (800) 225-1998. Fax: (802) 626-9770.

Marlboro College
Marlboro, Vermont — CB code: 3509

Admissions: 66% of applicants accepted
Based on:
••• Essay, interview, school record
•• Activities, recommendations, special talents
• Test scores
Completion: 21% enter graduate study

4-year private college of arts and sciences, coed. Founded in 1946. **Accreditation:** Regional. **Undergraduate enrollment:** 114 men, 146 women full time; 6 men, 5 women part time. **Faculty:** 44 total (34 full time), 28 with doctorates or other terminal degrees. **Location:** Rural campus in rural community; 120 miles from Boston, 12 miles from Brattleboro, VT. **Calendar:** Semester. **Microcomputers:** 15 located in computer centers. **Special facilities:** Art gallery, observatory, mountain-bike and cross-country ski paths, ceramics studio, theater in-the-round, 24-hour dark room. **Additional facts:** Small classes, one-on-one tutorials.

DEGREES OFFERED. BA, BS, MA. 50 bachelor's degrees awarded in 1992. 10% in area and ethnic studies, 6% languages, 8% letters/literature, 12% life sciences, 20% multi/interdisciplinary studies, 8% philosophy, religion, theology, 6% psychology, 10% social sciences, 12% visual and performing arts. Graduate degrees offered in 1 major field of study.

UNDERGRADUATE MAJORS. African studies, American Indian studies, American literature, American studies, analytical chemistry, anatomy, anthropology, art history, Asian studies, astronomy, astrophysics, atomic/molecular physics, biochemistry, biological and physical sciences, biology, botany, cell biology, ceramics, chemistry, classics, comparative literature, computer and information sciences, computer programming, creative writing, dance, developmental psychology, dramatic arts, drawing, earth sciences, East Asian studies, ecology, economics, English, English literature, entomology, environmental design, environmental science, European studies, experimental psychology, film arts, fine arts, folklore and mythology, foreign languages (multiple emphasis), forestry and related sciences, French, genetics, human and animal, geography, German, Greek (classical), Hispanic American studies, history, humanities, humanities and social sciences, inorganic chemistry, international development, international public service, international relations, international studies, Italian, language interpretation and translation, Latin, Latin American studies, liberal/general studies, linguistics, marine biology, mathematics, medieval studies, Middle Eastern studies, molecular biology, music, music history and appreciation, music performance, music theory and composition, nuclear physics, organic chemistry, painting, philosophy, physical sciences, physics, physiological psychology, physiology, human and animal, plant genetics, plant pathology, plant physiology, political science and government, Portuguese, premedicine, psychology, religion, rhetoric, Russian, Russian and Slavic studies, Scandinavian studies, sculpture, social sciences, sociology, South Asian studies, Southeast Asian studies, Spanish, statistics, studio art, video, visual and performing arts, Western European studies, women's studies, zoology.

ACADEMIC PROGRAMS. Double major, dual enrollment of high school students, independent study, internships, student-designed major, study abroad, visiting/exchange student program, cross-registration, world studies program. **Remedial services:** Reduced course load. **Placement/credit:** AP, CLEP General and Subject, IB, institutional tests; 16 credit hours maximum for bachelor's degree.

ACADEMIC REQUIREMENTS. Freshmen must earn minimum GPA of 2.0 to continue in good standing. Students must pass college's writing requirement during first year. Students who cannot pass the writing requirement are ask to leave. Students must declare major by end of second year. **Graduation requirements:** 120 hours for bachelor's (50 in major). **Postgraduate studies:** 1% enter law school, 1% enter medical school, 1% enter MBA programs, 18% enter other graduate study. **Additional information:** Students may choose any academic area, or combination of areas of traditional liberal arts curriculum to continue on to graduate study.

FRESHMAN ADMISSIONS. Selection criteria: School achievement record, test scores, samples of expository writing, personal interview, autobiographical statement, and 1 academic recommendation important. College looks for students who are self-motivated, independent self-starters. Recommended units include English 4, foreign language 3, mathematics 3, social science 3 and science 2. Advanced electives in area of interest and in arts also recommended. **Test requirements:** SAT or ACT; score report by August 15.

1992 FRESHMAN CLASS PROFILE. 95 men applied, 61 accepted, 25 enrolled; 143 women applied, 95 accepted, 32 enrolled. **Academic background:** Mid 50% of enrolled freshmen had SAT-V between 540-650, SAT-M between 530-600. 95% submitted SAT scores. **Characteristics:** 20% from in state, 100% live in college housing, 1% have minority backgrounds, 3% are foreign students. Average age is 19.

FALL-TERM APPLICATIONS. $30 fee, may be waived for applicants with need. No closing date; priority given to applications received by January 15; applicants notified on a rolling basis beginning on or about February 1; must reply by May 1 or within 10 days if notified after April 21. Interview required. Essay required. Audition recommended for music applicants. Portfolio recommended for art applicants. CRDA. Deferred and early admission available. EDP-S. Early Action Plan application deadline January 15, notification by February 1, reply date May 1. Early decision deadline December 1, notification December 15.

STUDENT LIFE. Housing: Dormitories (men, women, coed); apartment, cooperative housing available. cottages and cabins available. **Activities:** Student government, film, magazine, student newspaper, choral groups, dance, drama, music ensembles, musical theater, opera, chamber orchestra, Marlboro Volunteer Corps, fire brigade, volunteer placement service, numerous committees. **Additional information:** Marlboro is a self-govering community based on New-England style town meeting. Students, faculty, and staff all have equal votes. Elected community court enforces bylaws.

ATHLETICS. Intercollegiate: Skiing, soccer, volleyball. **Intramural:** Archery, badminton, basketball, cross-country, fencing, field hockey, skiing, softball, swimming, volleyball.

STUDENT SERVICES. Career counseling, employment service for undergraduates, freshman orientation, health services, on-campus day care, personal counseling, special adviser for adult students, veterans counselor, outdoor program, foreign student advising, committees for campus life, social activities, cultural field trips, lectures and concerts, services/facilities for handicapped.

ANNUAL EXPENSES. Tuition and fees: $17,615. **Room and board:** $5,680. **Books and supplies:** $400. **Other expenses:** $320.

FINANCIAL AID. 65% of freshmen, 70% of continuing students receive some form of aid. All grants, 91% of loans, all jobs based on need. **Aid applications:** Closing date May 1; priority given to applications received by March 1; applicants notified on or about April 15; must reply within 15 days.

ADDRESS/TELEPHONE. Wayne R. Wood, Director of Admissions, Marlboro College, Marlboro, Vermont 05344, Marlboro, VT 05344-0300. (802) 257-4333. (800) 343-0049. Fax: (802) 257-4154.

Middlebury College

Middlebury, Vermont — CB code: 3526

Admissions:	30% of applicants accepted
Based on:	••• School record, test scores
	• Activities, essay, interview, recommendations, special talents
Completion:	98% of freshmen end year in good standing
	92% graduate

4-year private liberal arts college, coed. Founded in 1800. **Accreditation:** Regional. **Undergraduate enrollment:** 980 men, 980 women full time. **Faculty:** 220 total (180 full time), 209 with doctorates or other terminal degrees. **Location:** Rural campus in small town; 200 miles from Boston, 250 miles from New York City. **Calendar:** 4-1-4, limited summer session. **Microcomputers:** 220 located in dormitories, libraries, classrooms, computer centers. **Special facilities:** Art gallery, observatory, new Fine Arts Center.

DEGREES OFFERED. BA. 437 bachelor's degrees awarded in 1992. 11% in languages, 19% letters/literature, 5% life sciences, 5% physical sciences, 39% social sciences, 5% visual and performing arts.

UNDERGRADUATE MAJORS. American literature, American studies, anthropology, biochemistry, biology, chemistry, Chinese, classics, computer and information sciences, dance, East Asian studies, economics, English, environmental science, film arts, fine arts, French, geography, geology, German, history, humanities and social sciences, international politics and economics, international studies, Italian, liberal/general studies, literary studies, mathematics, molecular biology, music, philosophy, physics, political science and government, psychology, religion, Russian, Russian and Slavic studies, sociology, Spanish, theater/dance and film, women's studies.

ACADEMIC PROGRAMS. Double major, honors program, independent study, internships, semester at sea, student-designed major, study abroad, teacher preparation, visiting/exchange student program, Washington semester, international major abroad, Williams College-Mystic Seaport Program in American Maritime Studies, Oxford University summer program, independent scholar program, exchange programs with Berea College and Swarthmore College; liberal arts/career combination in engineering, forestry, health sciences, business. **Remedial services:** Preadmission summer program, remedial instruction, tutoring. **Placement/credit:** AP.

ACADEMIC REQUIREMENTS. No policy requiring minimum GPA; records of students having academic difficulty are reviewed individually. 98% of freshmen return for sophomore year. Students must declare major by end of first year. **Graduation requirements:** 120 hours for bachelor's (34 in major). Most students required to take courses in English, foreign languages, humanities, social sciences.

FRESHMAN ADMISSIONS. Selection criteria: School record most important followed by standardized tests and activities. Recommended units include English 4, foreign language 4, mathematics 4, social science 3 and science 3. 1 fine arts also recommended. **Test requirements:** 3 test options: SAT and 3 ACH including English Composition, 5 ACH in 5 different areas of study including English Composition with or without essay, or ACT. Score reports by March 1.

1992 FRESHMAN CLASS PROFILE. 1,652 men applied, 521 accepted, 235 enrolled; 1,976 women applied, 574 accepted, 232 enrolled. 65% were in top tenth and 86% were in top quarter of graduating class. **Academic background:** Mid 50% of enrolled freshmen had SAT-V between 540-640, SAT-M between 590-690; ACT composite between 27-30. 97% submitted SAT scores, 23% submitted ACT scores. **Characteristics:** 5% from in state, 100% live in college housing, 13% have minority backgrounds, 9% are foreign students. Average age is 18.

FALL-TERM APPLICATIONS. $50 fee, may be waived for applicants with need. Closing date January 1; applicants notified on or about April 10; must reply by May 1. Essay required. Interview recommended. CRDA. Deferred and early admission available. EDP-F.

STUDENT LIFE. Housing: Dormitories (men, women, coed). Special interest housing available: Multicultural House, Environmental House, Foreign Language Houses. **Activities:** Student government, magazine, radio, student newspaper, yearbook, choral groups, dance, drama, jazz band, music ensembles, musical theater, symphony orchestra, over 75 student organizations and activites.

ATHLETICS. NCAA. **Intercollegiate:** Baseball M, basketball, cross-country, diving, field hockey W, football M, golf M, ice hockey M, lacrosse, skiing, soccer, squash W, swimming, tennis, track and field. **Intramural:** Badminton, baseball W, basketball, cross-country, diving, field hockey W, golf, ice hockey M, lacrosse, rugby, soccer, softball, swimming, tennis, volleyball. **Clubs:** Rugby.

STUDENT SERVICES. Career counseling, employment service for undergraduates, freshman orientation, health services, personal counseling, placement service for graduates, services/facilities for handicapped.

ANNUAL EXPENSES. Tuition and fees: Comprehensive fee: $24,570. **Books and supplies:** $530. **Other expenses:** $1,000.

FINANCIAL AID. 38% of freshmen, 35% of continuing students receive some form of aid. Grants, loans, jobs available. **Aid applications:** Closing date January 31; applicants notified on or about April 15; must reply by May 1. **Additional information:** Maintains a need-blind admissions policy which guarantees meeting the full demonstrated financial need of students who qualify for admission.

ADDRESS/TELEPHONE. Geoff Smith, Dean of Admissions, Middlebury College, The Emma Willard House, Middlebury, VT 05753-6002. (802) 388-3711 ext. 5153.

New England Culinary Institute

Montpelier, Vermont — CB code: 3405

2-year proprietary college of culinary arts, coed. Founded in 1980. **Undergraduate enrollment:** 278 men, 102 women full time. **Faculty:** 40 total (30 full time). **Location:** Rural campus in small town; 45 miles from Burlington. **Calendar:** Semester. **Microcomputers:** Located in classrooms, computer centers. **Special facilities:** Gourmet restaurant, bakeshop, cafeteria, catering business, American cuisine restaurant. **Additional facts:** Branch campus at the Inn at Essex, 7 miles north of Burlington. Same educational program offered at both campuses.

DEGREES OFFERED. 60 associate degrees awarded in 1992. 100% in home economics.

UNDERGRADUATE MAJORS. Food management, food production/management/services.

ACADEMIC PROGRAMS. Accelerated program, internships, study abroad. **Remedial services:** Tutoring.

ACADEMIC REQUIREMENTS. No policy requiring minimum GPA; records of students having academic difficulty are reviewed individually. 90% of freshmen return for sophomore year. Students must declare major on enrollment. **Graduation requirements:** 88 hours for associate (38 in major). Most students required to take courses in computer science, English, history, mathematics, biological/physical sciences.

FRESHMAN ADMISSIONS. Selection criteria: High school achievement record, essay or personal statement, and 3 letters of recommendation most important. **Additional information:** Sophmore standing is available to students through school testing.

1992 FRESHMAN CLASS PROFILE. 144 men, 72 women enrolled. **Characteristics:** Average age is 24.

FALL-TERM APPLICATIONS. $25 fee, may be waived for applicants with need. No closing date; applicants notified on a rolling basis; must reply within 30 days. Essay required. Interview recommended. Deferred admission available.

STUDENT LIFE. Housing: Dormitories (men, women, coed).

STUDENT SERVICES. Career counseling, employment service for undergraduates, freshman orientation, personal counseling, placement service for graduates.

ANNUAL EXPENSES. Tuition and fees: $14,460. **Room and board:** $2,530. **Books and supplies:** $500. **Other expenses:** $3,996.

FINANCIAL AID. 90% of freshmen, 90% of continuing students receive some form of aid. All grants, 47% of loans, all jobs based on need. **Aid applications:** No closing date; applicants notified on a rolling basis.

ADDRESS/TELEPHONE. Mary Beth Rowe, Associate Director of Admissions, New England Culinary Institute, 250 Main Street, Montpelier, VT 05602. (802) 223-6324. Fax: (802) 223-0634.

Norwich University
Northfield, Vermont — CB code: 3669

Admissions:	94% of applicants accepted
Based on:	••• School record
	•• Activities, test scores
	• Essay, interview, recommendations, special talents
Completion:	75% of freshmen end year in good standing
	60% graduate, 20% of these enter graduate study

4-year private university and military college, coed. Founded in 1819. **Accreditation:** Regional. **Undergraduate enrollment:** 1,267 men, 613 women full time; 43 men, 207 women part time. **Graduate enrollment:** 181 men, 296 women full time; 8 women part time. **Faculty:** 194 total (156 full time), 145 with doctorates or other terminal degrees. **Location:** Rural campus in small town; 50 miles from Burlington, 180 miles from Boston. **Calendar:** Semester, limited summer session. **Microcomputers:** 200 located in libraries, classrooms, computer centers, campus-wide network. **Additional facts:** 2 divisions: Military College of Vermont and Vermont College (nonmilitary, traditional campus of university). Students enroll in any major and study on campus of division they choose.

DEGREES OFFERED. AS, BA, BS, BArch, MA, MFA, MEd. 26 associate degrees awarded in 1992. 403 bachelor's degrees awarded. Graduate degrees offered in 5 major fields of study.

UNDERGRADUATE MAJORS. Associate: Nursing. **Bachelor's:** Accounting, architecture, biology, business administration and management, chemistry, civil engineering, communications, computer and information sciences, computer engineering, criminal justice studies, electrical/electronics/communications engineering, elementary education, English, environmental engineering technology, French, geology, German, history, international relations, marketing management, mathematics, mechanical engineering, medical laboratory technologies, nursing, peace studies, physical education, physics, physics education, political science and government, psychology, Russian, Spanish.

ACADEMIC PROGRAMS. Accelerated program, cooperative education, double major, external degree, honors program, independent study, internships, student-designed major, study abroad, teacher preparation, weekend college. **Remedial services:** Learning center, reduced course load, remedial instruction, special counselor, tutoring. **ROTC:** Air Force, Army, Naval. **Placement/credit:** AP, CLEP General and Subject, institutional tests; 12 credit hours maximum for bachelor's degree.

ACADEMIC REQUIREMENTS. Freshmen must earn minimum GPA of 1.25 to continue in good standing. 70% of freshmen return for sophomore year. Students must declare major by end of second year. **Graduation requirements:** 60 hours for associate, 114 hours for bachelor's (24 in major). Most students required to take courses in English, history, humanities, mathematics, biological/physical sciences. **Postgraduate studies:** 35% from 2-year programs enter 4-year programs. **Additional information:** ROTC required of all members of Corps of Cadets at Military College, but students without government contract not required to accept commission and have no military obligation. Students without contract may choose to participate in the university's first-in-the-nation Peace Corps Preparatory Program during junior and senior years.

FRESHMAN ADMISSIONS. Selection criteria: High school record, recommendations, activities, honors, awards, test scores important. Consideration given to class rank. **High school preparation:** 18 units recommended. Recommended units include English 4, foreign language 2, mathematics 3, social science 2 and science 1. Laboratory physics and chemistry, and trigonometry or pre-calculus required for engineering programs. **Test requirements:** SAT or ACT; score report by August 1. ACH required of foreign language majors. Score report by August 1.

1992 FRESHMAN CLASS PROFILE. 1,107 men applied, 1,049 accepted, 361 enrolled; 348 women applied, 322 accepted, 109 enrolled. 40% had high school GPA of 3.0 or higher, 60% between 2.0 and 2.99. 9% were in top tenth and 21% were in top quarter of graduating class. **Academic background:** Mid 50% of enrolled freshmen had SAT-V between 390-520, SAT-M between 420-560; ACT composite between 20-26. 80% submitted SAT scores, 20% submitted ACT scores. **Characteristics:** 10% from in state, 96% live in college housing, 11% have minority backgrounds, 4% are foreign students. Average age is 19.

FALL-TERM APPLICATIONS. $35 fee, may be waived for applicants with need. No closing date; priority given to applications received by May 1; applicants notified on a rolling basis; must reply by May 1 or within 3 weeks if notified thereafter. Interview recommended. Essay recommended. CRDA. Deferred admission available. EDP-F. ACH recommended in any language student has studied for 2 or more years and plans to continue.

STUDENT LIFE. Housing: Dormitories (coed). Military campus students must live in dormitories. **Activities:** Student government, magazine, radio, student newspaper, yearbook, choral groups, concert band, drama, jazz band, marching band, music ensembles, musical theater, pep band, symphony orchestra, Big Brothers, Big Sisters, Arnold Air Society, rescue squad, Mountain Rescue Team, National Ski Patrol, International Student Organization, Newman Club, political forum.

ATHLETICS. NCAA. **Intercollegiate:** Baseball M, basketball, cross-country, diving, football M, golf, ice hockey M, lacrosse M, rifle, rugby, soccer, softball W, swimming, tennis, track and field, wrestling M. **Intramural:** Baseball M, basketball, boxing M, cross-country, diving, fencing, football M, golf, ice hockey M, lacrosse M, racquetball, rifle, rugby, sailing, skiing, soccer, softball, swimming, tennis, track and field, volleyball, water polo.

STUDENT SERVICES. Aptitude testing, career counseling, employment service for undergraduates, freshman orientation, health services, personal counseling, placement service for graduates, special adviser for adult students, veterans counselor, services/facilities for handicapped.

ANNUAL EXPENSES. Tuition and fees (1992-93): $12,820. **Room and board:** $5,020. **Books and supplies:** $500. **Other expenses:** $800.

FINANCIAL AID. 84% of freshmen, 84% of continuing students receive some form of aid. Grants, loans, jobs available. 374 enrolled freshmen were judged to have need, 368 were offered aid. Academic, leadership scholarships available. **Aid applications:** No closing date; priority given to applications received by March 1; applicants notified on a rolling basis beginning on or about March 15. **Additional information:** Winners of ROTC scholarships receive full room and board scholarships. Scholarships renewable up to 4 years.

ADDRESS/TELEPHONE. Frank Griffis, Director of Admissions, Norwich University, Northfield, VT 05663. (802) 485-2002. (800) 468-6679. Fax: (802) 485-2580.

St. Michael's College
Colchester, Vermont — CB code: 3757

Admissions:	67% of applicants accepted
Based on:	••• School record
	•• Activities, essay, recommendations, test scores
	• Interview, special talents
Completion:	92% of freshmen end year in good standing
	75% graduate, 15% of these enter graduate study

4-year private liberal arts college, coed, affiliated with Roman Catholic Church. Founded in 1904. **Accreditation:** Regional. **Undergraduate enrollment:** 799 men, 873 women full time; 18 men, 24 women part time. **Graduate enrollment:** 41 men, 71 women full time; 209 men, 362 women part time. **Faculty:** 168 total (119 full time), 104 with doctorates or other terminal degrees. **Location:** Suburban campus in large town; 3 miles from Burlington. **Calendar:** Semester, limited summer session. **Microcomputers:** 290 located in libraries, classrooms, computer centers. **Special facilities:** Observatory.

DEGREES OFFERED. BA, BS, MA, MS, MEd. 414 bachelor's degrees awarded in 1992. 31% in business and management, 9% teacher education, 15% letters/literature, 8% psychology, 15% social sciences. Graduate degrees offered in 12 major fields of study.

UNDERGRADUATE MAJORS. Accounting, American studies, art education, biochemistry, biology, business administration and management, business and management, chemistry, classics, computer and information sciences, computer programming, dramatic arts, economics, elementary education, English, English education, English literature, environmental science, fine arts, foreign languages (multiple emphasis), foreign languages education, French, history, journalism, mathematics, mathematics education, music, music education, philosophy, physics, political science and government, pre-engineering, prelaw, psychology, religion, science education, secondary education, social science education, sociology, Spanish, studio art.

ACADEMIC PROGRAMS. Honors program, independent study, internships, student-designed major, study abroad, teacher preparation, visiting/exchange student program, Washington semester, cross-registration, exchange program with Xavier University of Louisiana; liberal arts/career combination in engineering; combined bachelor's/graduate program in business administration. **Remedial services:** Tutoring. **ROTC:** Air Force, Army. **Placement/credit:** AP, CLEP General and Subject, institutional tests; 30 credit hours maximum for bachelor's degree.

ACADEMIC REQUIREMENTS. Freshmen must earn minimum GPA of 1.6 to continue in good standing. 85% of freshmen return for sophomore year. Students must declare major by end of first year. **Graduation requirements:** 124 hours for bachelor's (30 in major). Most students required to take courses in arts/fine arts, English, history, humanities, mathematics, philosophy/religion, biological/physical sciences, social sciences.

FRESHMAN ADMISSIONS. Selection criteria: High school achievement, test scores, rank in top quarter of graduating class most important. Recommendations, extracurricular activities, interview also considered. Special consideration given to relatives of alumni, to minorities, and to those with significant social service activities. **High school preparation:** 16 units required. Required and recommended units include biological science 1, English 4, foreign language 2-3, mathematics 3-4, physical science 1 and social science 2-3. Physics, mathematics, chemistry, and biology emphasized for science applicants. **Test requirements:** SAT or ACT (SAT preferred); score report by March 1.

1992 FRESHMAN CLASS PROFILE. 913 men applied, 556 accepted, 198 enrolled; 912 women applied, 665 accepted, 211 enrolled. 18% were in top tenth and 52% were in top quarter of graduating class. **Academic background:** Mid 50% of enrolled freshmen had SAT-V between 450-540, SAT-M between 480-590. 93% submitted SAT scores. **Characteristics:** 21% from in state, 97% live in college housing, 3% have minority backgrounds, 1% are foreign students. Average age is 18.

FALL-TERM APPLICATIONS. $30 fee, may be waived for applicants with need. Closing date February 15; priority given to applications received by November 15; applicants notified on or about April 1; must reply by May 1. Essay required. Interview recommended. CRDA. Deferred and early admission available. Institutional early decision plan.

STUDENT LIFE. Housing: Dormitories (men, women, coed); apartment, handicapped housing available. Townhouse apartments available to seniors. **Activities:** Student government, magazine, radio, student newspaper, yearbook, choral groups, dance, drama, jazz band, music ensembles, musical theater, liturgical folk group, Knights of Columbus, Big Brother/Big Sister programs, fire and rescue squad, Arnold Air Society, Mobilization of Volunteer Efforts (MOVE)Martin Luther King Society, Diversity Coalition. **Additional information:** Outing club available to students.

ATHLETICS. NCAA. **Intercollegiate:** Baseball M, basketball, cross-country, diving, field hockey W, golf M, ice hockey M, lacrosse, skiing, soccer, softball W, swimming, tennis, volleyball W. **Intramural:** Basketball, cross-country, soccer, softball, swimming, table tennis, tennis, volleyball, water polo.

STUDENT SERVICES. Aptitude testing, career counseling, employment service for undergraduates, freshman orientation, health services, on-campus day care, personal counseling, placement service for graduates, special adviser for adult students, office of volunteer programs, services/facilities for handicapped.

ANNUAL EXPENSES. Tuition and fees: $12,430. **Room and board:** $5,600. **Books and supplies:** $350. **Other expenses:** $400.

FINANCIAL AID. 67% of freshmen, 48% of continuing students receive some form of aid. 81% of grants, 98% of loans, all jobs based on need. 346 enrolled freshmen were judged to have need, all were offered aid. Academic, athletic, alumni affiliation scholarships available. **Aid applications:** No closing date; priority given to applications received by March 15; applicants notified on a rolling basis beginning on or about April 1; must reply by May 1 or within 10 days if notified thereafter.

ADDRESS/TELEPHONE. Jerry E. Flanagan, Dean of Admissions, St. Michael's College, Winooski Park, Colchester, VT 05439. (802) 654-3000. (800) 762-8000. Fax: (802) 654-2591.

School for International Training
Brattleboro, Vermont CB code: 0974

2-year upper-division private college of languages and international studies, coed. Founded in 1964. **Accreditation:** Regional. **Undergraduate enrollment:** 31 men, 35 women full time. **Graduate enrollment:** 70 men, 171 women full time; 35 men, 71 women part time. **Faculty:** 35 total (30 full time), 23 with doctorates or other terminal degrees. **Location:** Rural campus in large town; 120 miles from Boston, 60 miles from Springfield, Massachusetts. **Calendar:** 20 to 35 weeks, followed by overseas internship. **Microcomputers:** 16 located in libraries, computer centers. **Special facilities:** International professional development resource center. **Additional facts:** Academic arm of World Learning Inc. Undergraduate and graduate students attend classes on Brattleboro campus and participate in overseas internships and independent work.

DEGREES OFFERED. B, MA. 21 bachelor's degrees awarded in 1992. 100% in multi/interdisciplinary studies. Graduate degrees offered in 5 major fields of study.

UNDERGRADUATE MAJORS. International studies.

ACADEMIC PROGRAMS. Double major, independent study, internships, study abroad, teacher preparation, Joint 4-year degree program in international studies with Marlboro College. **Remedial services:** Remedial instruction, special counselor, tutoring, language laboratory, research and writing skills. **Placement/credit:** CLEP General and Subject; 15 credit hours maximum for bachelor's degree.

ACADEMIC REQUIREMENTS. No policy requiring minimum GPA; records of students having academic difficulty are reviewed individually. Students must declare major by end of third year. **Graduation requirements:** 120 hours for bachelor's (12 in major). Most students required to take courses in foreign languages. **Additional information:** Flexible, individualized program emphasizing self-directed and cooperative group study during first term as preparation for independent internships.

ADMISSIONS. Essay and recommendations required. Social science background and international experience preferred. Arbitur (Germany), Baccalaureate (France), and A levels (Britain) accepted. GED considered in lieu of high school diploma.

FALL-TERM APPLICATIONS. $35 fee.

STUDENT LIFE. Housing: Dormitories (men, women, coed). **Activities:** Student government, film, campus newsletter for students and staff, choral groups, dance, Women and Gender Issues, Amnesty International.

ATHLETICS. Intramural: Basketball, bowling, skiing, soccer, softball, table tennis, volleyball.

STUDENT SERVICES. Career counseling, employment service for undergraduates, health services, personal counseling, placement service for graduates.

ANNUAL EXPENSES. Tuition and fees: $11,071. **Room and board:** $4,264. **Books and supplies:** $400. **Other expenses:** $960.

FINANCIAL AID. 60% of continuing students receive some form of aid. All grants, 74% of loans, all jobs based on need. Academic, leadership, minority scholarships available. **Aid applications:** Closing date August 15; priority given to applications received by June 1; applicants notified on a rolling basis beginning on or about April 30; must reply within 3 weeks. **Additional information:** Institutional aid limited. Short residence period limits employment opportunities, most students must secure loans.

ADDRESS/TELEPHONE. Tim McMains, Director of Enrollment Management, School for International Training, Kipling Road, Brattleboro, VT 05301. (802) 257-7751. (800) 451-4465. Fax: (802) 257-5576.

Southern Vermont College
Bennington, Vermont CB code: 3796

Admissions: 39% of applicants accepted
Based on: ••• Recommendations, school record
•• Essay, interview
• Activities, test scores
Completion: 84% of freshmen end year in good standing
45% graduate, 26% of these enter graduate study

4-year private college of liberal arts and management, coed. Founded in 1926. **Accreditation:** Regional. **Undergraduate enrollment:** 231 men, 194 women full time; 68 men, 250 women part time. **Faculty:** 69 total (29 full time), 6 with doctorates or other terminal degrees. **Location:** Rural campus in large town; 40 miles from Albany, New York, 100 miles from Springfield, Massachusetts. **Calendar:** Semester, limited summer session. Saturday classes. **Microcomputers:** 33 located in computer centers. **Special facilities:** Old Castle Theatre Group. **Additional facts:** Brattleboro branch campus offers degrees in nursing, accounting, human services, business, business management, gerontology, liberal arts management, and social work.

DEGREES OFFERED. AA, AS, BA, BS. 44 associate degrees awarded in 1992. 27% in business and management, 32% health sciences, 11% home economics, 7% multi/interdisciplinary studies, 20% parks/recreation, protective services, public affairs. 79 bachelor's degrees awarded. 48% in business and management, 8% communications, 13% multi/interdisciplinary studies, 28% parks/recreation, protective services, public affairs.

UNDERGRADUATE MAJORS. Associate: Accounting, business and management, child development/care/guidance, criminal justice studies, environmental science, gerontology, human services, liberal/general studies, nursing. **Bachelor's:** Accounting, business and management, child care management, communications, criminal justice studies, English, environmental science, gerontology, gerontology management, liberal arts management, liberal/general studies, nursing, protective services, social work.

ACADEMIC PROGRAMS. 2-year transfer program, accelerated program, double major, dual enrollment of high school students, honors program, independent study, internships, student-designed major, study abroad, weekend college, cross-registration. **Remedial services:** Learning center, reduced course load, remedial instruction, special counselor, tutoring. **Placement/credit:** AP, CLEP General and Subject, institutional tests; 45 credit hours maximum for associate degree; 90 credit hours maximum for bachelor's degree.

ACADEMIC REQUIREMENTS. Freshmen must earn minimum GPA of 1.75 to continue in good standing. 60% of freshmen return for sophomore year. Students must declare major by end of second year. **Graduation requirements:** 60 hours for associate (24 in major), 120 hours for bachelor's (30 in major). Most students required to take courses in arts/fine arts, computer science, English, history, humanities, mathematics, philosophy/religion, biological/physical sciences, social sciences. **Postgraduate studies:** 44% from 2-year programs enter 4-year programs. **Additional information:** Career-oriented programs offered, combining theoretical and practical experience.

FRESHMAN ADMISSIONS. Selection criteria: Potential for academic achievement most important. Test scores interview and personal references considered. Recommended units include English 4, mathematics 3, social science 3 and science 2. **Additional information:** Students who have not shown their full potential and/or students not eligible for financial need encouraged to apply.

1992 FRESHMAN CLASS PROFILE. 263 men applied, 83 accepted, 52 enrolled; 257 women applied, 121 accepted, 56 enrolled. 33% had high school GPA of 3.0 or higher, 57% between 2.0 and 2.99. **Characteristics:** 29% from in state, 65% live in college housing, 7% have minority backgrounds, 1% are foreign students. Average age is 18.

FALL-TERM APPLICATIONS. $25 fee, may be waived for applicants with need. No closing date; applicants notified on a rolling basis; must reply within 4 weeks. Essay required. Interview recommended. Deferred and early admission available.

STUDENT LIFE. Housing: Dormitories (coed). Quiet dormitory, summer residency on campus. **Activities:** Student government, student newspaper, yearbook, drama, MISA Minority and International Student Association, Drug Prevention Action Committee, Business Club, Criminal Justice Club, Residence Life Council, Environmental Association, Student Nurses Association.

ATHLETICS. NAIA. **Intercollegiate:** Baseball M, basketball, soccer, softball W. **Intramural:** Basketball, bowling, golf, ice hockey, skiing, soccer, softball, table tennis, tennis, volleyball. **Clubs:** Skiing, snowboarding, outing.

STUDENT SERVICES. Aptitude testing, career counseling, employment service for undergraduates, freshman orientation, on-campus day care, personal counseling, placement service for graduates, special adviser for adult students, veterans counselor, services/facilities for handicapped.

ANNUAL EXPENSES. Tuition and fees: $8,620. **Room and board:** $4,304. **Books and supplies:** $500. **Other expenses:** $550.

FINANCIAL AID. 92% of freshmen, 61% of continuing students receive some form of aid. 96% of grants, 91% of loans, 75% of jobs based on need. 73 enrolled freshmen were judged to have need, all were offered aid. State/district residency scholarships available. **Aid applications:** No closing date; priority given to applications received by May 1; applicants notified on a rolling basis beginning on or about April 15; must reply within 2 weeks.

ADDRESS/TELEPHONE. Mary Van Arsdale, Director of Admissions, Southern Vermont College, Monument Avenue Extension, Bennington, VT 05201. (802) 442-5427. Fax: (802) 442-5529.

Sterling College

Craftsbury Common, Vermont — CB code: 3752

Admissions: 75% of applicants accepted
Based on:
- ••• Essay, interview, recommendations
- •• Activities, school record
- • Special talents, test scores

Completion: 92% of freshmen end year in good standing
80% graduate, 70% of these enter 4-year programs

2-year private junior, liberal arts college, coed. Founded in 1958. **Accreditation:** Regional. **Undergraduate enrollment:** 52 men, 38 women full time. **Faculty:** 17 total (10 full time), 1 with doctorate or other terminal degree. **Location:** Rural campus in rural community; 40 miles from Montpelier, 70 miles from Burlington. **Calendar:** Quarter. **Microcomputers:** 10 located in libraries, computer centers. **Special facilities:** Demonstration farm, managed woodlots, extensive cross-country ski trails, back country recreation. **Additional facts:** Smallest fully-accredited, coeducational, degree-granting college in the United States.

DEGREES OFFERED. AA. 24 associate degrees awarded in 1992. 60% in agriculture, 40% life sciences.

UNDERGRADUATE MAJORS. Agricultural sciences, conservation and regulation, ecology, environmental science, forestry and related sciences, renewable natural resources, rural resource management, science technologies, wildlife management.

ACADEMIC PROGRAMS. 2-year transfer program, cooperative education, independent study, internships. **Remedial services:** Preadmission summer program.

ACADEMIC REQUIREMENTS. Freshmen must earn minimum GPA of 1.7 to continue in good standing. 85% of freshmen return for sophomore year. Students must declare major by end of first year. **Graduation requirements:** 60 hours for associate. Most students required to take courses in English, history, humanities, biological/physical sciences, social sciences. **Additional information:** All freshmen enroll in The Grassroots Year, a combination of traditional classroom, laboratory, and outdoor learning.

FRESHMAN ADMISSIONS. Selection criteria: Demonstrated interest in programs, motivation, interview, academic record, recommendations important, test scores considered.

1992 FRESHMAN CLASS PROFILE. 83 men applied, 56 accepted, 35 enrolled; 51 women applied, 45 accepted, 25 enrolled. **Academic background:** Mid 50% of enrolled freshmen had SAT-V between 430-590, SAT-M between 420-580. 54% submitted SAT scores. **Characteristics:** 7% from in state, 100% live in college housing, 12% have minority backgrounds, 2% are foreign students. Average age is 19.

FALL-TERM APPLICATIONS. $35 fee, may be waived for applicants with need. No closing date; priority given to applications received by December 15; applicants notified on a rolling basis; must reply within 6 weeks. Essay required. Interview recommended. CRDA. Deferred admission available.

STUDENT LIFE. Housing: Dormitories (men, women, coed); apartment housing available. **Activities:** Student government, yearbook.

ATHLETICS. Intramural: Basketball, skiing, tennis, volleyball.

STUDENT SERVICES. Career counseling, employment service for undergraduates, freshman orientation, health services, personal counseling, placement service for graduates.

ANNUAL EXPENSES. Tuition and fees: Comprehensive fee: $17,317. **Books and supplies:** $600. **Other expenses:** $350.

FINANCIAL AID. 65% of freshmen, 65% of continuing students receive some form of aid. All grants, 85% of loans, all jobs based on need. 45 enrolled freshmen were judged to have need, all were offered aid. **Aid applications:** No closing date; priority given to applications received by March 15; applicants notified on a rolling basis beginning on or about March 1; must reply within 4 weeks.

ADDRESS/TELEPHONE. Sarabelle Hitchner, Director of Admissions, Sterling College, Main Street, Craftsbury Common, VT 05827-0072. (802) 586-7711. (800) 648-3591.

Trinity College of Vermont

Burlington, Vermont — CB code: 3900

4-year private liberal arts college, women only, affiliated with Roman Catholic Church. Founded in 1925. **Accreditation:** Regional. **Undergraduate enrollment:** 24 men, 469 women full time; 124 men, 354 women part time. **Graduate enrollment:** 8 men, 48 women part time. **Faculty:** 103 total (48 full time), 47 with doctorates or other terminal degrees. **Location:** Urban campus in small city; 90 miles from Montreal, Canada. **Calendar:** Semester, limited summer session. Saturday and extensive evening/early morning classes. **Microcomputers:** 44 located in libraries, computer centers. **Special facilities:** Shelburne Museum, Child Care Center. **Additional facts:** Traditional program for young women out of high school less than four years. Non-traditional program provides motivated adults, women and men, opportunity to begin or resume college study.

DEGREES OFFERED. AA, AS, BA, BS, MEd. 24 associate degrees awarded in 1992. 83% in business and management, 13% computer sciences. 225 bachelor's degrees awarded. 31% in business and management, 8% communications, 22% teacher education, 9% letters/literature, 6% parks/recreation, protective services, public affairs, 10% psychology, 5% social sciences. Graduate degrees offered in 3 major fields of study.

UNDERGRADUATE MAJORS. Associate: Accounting, business administration and management, computer programming, computer science/business administration, liberal/general studies. **Bachelor's:** Accounting, biology, business administration and management, chemistry, clinical laboratory science, communications, comparative cultural studies, comparative cultural studies, criminal justice studies, cytotechnology, early childhood education, economics, elementary education, English, foreign languages (multiple emphasis), French, history, mathematics, mathematics education, medical laboratory technologies, mental health/human services, philosophy, psychology, science education, secondary education, social work, sociology, sociology/criminal justice, Spanish, special education.

ACADEMIC PROGRAMS. 2-year transfer program, double major, dual enrollment of high school students, education specialist degree, independent study, internships, student-designed major, study abroad, teacher preparation, weekend college, cross-registration; liberal arts/career combination in health sciences. **Remedial services:** Reduced course load, remedial instruction, tutoring, writing center, mathematics workshop. **ROTC:** Air Force. **Placement/credit:** AP, CLEP General and Subject, institutional tests; 90 credit hours maximum for bachelor's degree.

ACADEMIC REQUIREMENTS. Freshmen must earn minimum GPA of 1.8 to continue in good standing. 70% of freshmen return for sophomore year. Students must declare major by end of second year. **Graduation requirements:** 60 hours for associate, 120 hours for bachelor's. Most students required to take courses in arts/fine arts, computer science, English, foreign languages, history, humanities, mathematics, philosophy/religion, biological/physical sciences, social sciences. **Postgraduate studies:** 70% from 2-year programs enter 4-year programs. 10% enter other graduate study. **Additional information:** Adult degree education programs for men and women.

FRESHMAN ADMISSIONS. Selection criteria: High school achievement, test scores, class rank, principal or guidance counselor recommendation, interview considered. **High school preparation:** 16 units recommended. Recommended units include English 4, foreign language 2, mathematics 2, social science 2 and science 2. **Test requirements:** SAT or ACT (SAT preferred); score report by August 31.

1992 FRESHMAN CLASS PROFILE. 5 men, 97 women enrolled. 56% had high school GPA of 3.0 or higher, 44% between 2.0 and 2.99. **Academic background:** Mid 50% of enrolled freshmen had SAT-V between 370-470, SAT-M between 390-490. 98% submitted SAT scores. **Characteristics:** 60% from in state, 88% live in college housing, 1% have minority backgrounds. Average age is 18.

FALL-TERM APPLICATIONS. $25 fee, may be waived for applicants with need. No closing date; applicants notified on a rolling basis; must reply by May 1 or within 4 weeks if notified thereafter. Essay required. Interview recommended. CRDA. Deferred and early admission available.

STUDENT LIFE. Housing: Dormitories (women). **Activities:** Student government, student newspaper, yearbook, choral groups, drama, music ensembles, musical theater, campus ministry team, national biology honor society, community service learning program, Future Educators Club, psychology club, social work club, Peace and Justice Club, US/Canadian Multicultural Club. **Additional information:** New fitness center with cardiovascular and free weight equipment.

ATHLETICS. NSCAA. **Intercollegiate:** Basketball, soccer. **Intramural:** Basketball, bowling, cross-country, skiing, soccer, softball, tennis, volleyball.

STUDENT SERVICES. Aptitude testing, career counseling, employment service for undergraduates, freshman orientation, health services, on-campus day care, personal counseling, placement service for graduates, special adviser for adult students, services/facilities for handicapped.

ANNUAL EXPENSES. Tuition and fees: $10,722. **Room and board:** $5,070. **Books and supplies:** $550. **Other expenses:** $250.

FINANCIAL AID. 77% of freshmen, 70% of continuing students receive some form of aid. 95% of grants, 72% of loans, all jobs based on need. 84 enrolled freshmen were judged to have need, all were offered aid. Academic, leadership, alumni affiliation scholarships available. **Aid applications:** No closing date; priority given to applications received by March 1; applicants notified on a rolling basis beginning on or about April 10; must reply within 2 weeks.

ADDRESS/TELEPHONE. Michele Drabant, Director of Admissions, Trinity College of Vermont, 208 Colchester Avenue, Burlington, VT 05401. (802) 658-0337 ext. 218. Fax: (802) 658-5446.

University of Vermont
Burlington, Vermont

CB code: 3920

Admissions: 82% of applicants accepted
Based on:
- ••• School record
- •• Activities, essay, recommendations, special talents
- • Interview, test scores

Completion: 95% of freshmen end year in good standing
74% graduate, 21% of these enter graduate study

4-year public university, coed. Founded in 1791. **Accreditation:** Regional. **Undergraduate enrollment:** 3,558 men, 3,865 women full time; 209 men, 293 women part time. **Graduate enrollment:** 431 men, 422 women full time; 336 men, 418 women part time. **Faculty:** 1,014 total (864 full time), 811 with doctorates or other terminal degrees. **Location:** Suburban campus in large town; 200 miles from Boston, 90 miles from Montreal. **Calendar:** Semester, extensive summer session. **Microcomputers:** 396 located in dormitories, libraries, classrooms, computer centers. **Special facilities:** Art museum, nature preserve, Morgan horse farm.

DEGREES OFFERED. AS, BA, BS, MA, MS, MBA, MEd, PhD, EdD, MD, JD. 49 associate degrees awarded in 1992. 46% in health sciences, 54% allied health. 1,688 bachelor's degrees awarded. 7% in agriculture, 14% business and management, 8% education, 8% engineering, 6% health sciences, 8% letters/literature, 5% multi/interdisciplinary studies, 22% social sciences. Graduate degrees offered in 63 major fields of study.

UNDERGRADUATE MAJORS. Associate: Dental hygiene, nuclear medical technology, nursing, radiograph medical technology. **Bachelor's:** Accounting, agricultural economics, agricultural education, animal sciences, anthropology, art education, art history, Asian studies, biochemistry, biology, botany, business administration and management, business and management, chemistry, civil engineering, classics, clinical laboratory science, clothing and textiles management/production/services, computer and information sciences, dairy, dramatic arts, early childhood education, Eastern European studies, economics, education, electrical/electronics/communications engineering, elementary education, engineering management, English, English education, environmental science, European studies, family/consumer resource management, fashion design, finance, fishing and fisheries, food science and nutrition, food sciences, foreign languages education, forestry and related sciences, French, geography, geology, German, Greek (classical), health education, history, home economics, home economics education, horticultural science, human development education, humanities, individual and family development, industrial arts education, Latin, Latin American studies, liberal/general studies, mathematics, mathematics education, mechanical engineering, medical laboratory technologies, music, music education, music performance, music theory and composition, nursing, parks and recreation management, philosophy, physical education, physical therapy, physics, plant sciences, political science and government, psychology, reading education, religion, renewable natural resources, resource economics, Russian, Russian and Slavic studies, science education, secondary education, social science education, social work, sociology, soil sciences, Spanish, special education, speech correction, speech pathology/audiology, statistics, studio art, textiles and clothing, trade and industrial education, visual and performing arts, wildlife management, zoology.

ACADEMIC PROGRAMS. Cooperative education, double major, honors program, independent study, internships, student-designed major, study abroad, teacher preparation, visiting/exchange student program, Washington semester. **Remedial services:** Learning center, preadmission summer program, reduced course load, remedial instruction, special counselor, tutoring. **ROTC:** Air Force, Army. **Placement/credit:** AP, CLEP General and Subject, institutional tests.

ACADEMIC REQUIREMENTS. No policy requiring minimum GPA; records of students having academic difficulty are reviewed individually. 85% of freshmen return for sophomore year. Students must declare major by end of second year. **Graduation requirements:** 60 hours for associate, 122 hours for bachelor's. Most students required to take courses in English, humanities, mathematics, biological/physical sciences, social sciences. **Postgraduate studies:** 3% enter law school, 3% enter medical school, 3% enter MBA programs, 12% enter other graduate study.

FRESHMAN ADMISSIONS. Selection criteria: School achievement record of primary importance; test scores considered. Interview, or 2 letters of recommendation, essay, extracurricular activities also considered. Special consideration to children of alumni, minority students, foreign and in-state students. **High school preparation:** 16 units required. Required units include English 4, foreign language 2, mathematics 3, social science 3 and science 2. Additional mathematics and/or science units required in some programs. **Test requirements:** SAT or ACT (SAT preferred); score report by February 1.

1992 FRESHMAN CLASS PROFILE. 3,447 men applied, 2,736 accepted, 827 enrolled; 4,037 women applied, 3,375 accepted, 989 enrolled. 17% were in top tenth and 51% were in top quarter of graduating class. **Academic background:** Mid 50% of enrolled freshmen had SAT-V between 440-530, SAT-M between 500-610. 99% submitted SAT scores. **Characteristics:** 33% from in state, 87% live in college housing, 3% have minority backgrounds, 5% join fraternities/sororities. Average age is 18.

FALL-TERM APPLICATIONS. $30 fee, may be waived for applicants with need. $45 fee for out-of-state applicants. Closing date February 1; priority given to applications received by November 1; applicants notified on or about April 15; must reply by May 1. Audition required for music performance applicants. Essay required. Interview recommended. CRDA. Deferred and early admission available. EDP-F.

STUDENT LIFE. Housing: Dormitories (men, women, coed); apartment, fraternity, sorority, cooperative housing available. Living Learning Center enables students to combine academic and residential life. **Activities:** Student government, film, magazine, radio, student newspaper, television, yearbook, choral groups, concert band, dance, drama, jazz band, music ensembles, musical theater, pep band, symphony orchestra, fraternities, sororities, Catholic Center, Episcopal organization, Hillel, Council for Cooperative Ministry, social service programs, Black Student Union, Asian/American Student Union, New Alpha Baptist Church. **Additional information:** Students in College of Engineering and Mathematics and School of Business Administration must purchase microcomputers.

ATHLETICS. NCAA. **Intercollegiate:** Baseball M, basketball, cross-country, diving, field hockey W, golf M, gymnastics, ice hockey M, lacrosse, skiing, soccer, softball W, swimming, tennis, track and field, volleyball W. **Intramural:** Badminton, basketball, bowling, golf, handball M, ice hockey, racquetball, skiing, soccer, softball, squash, swimming, table tennis, tennis, track and field W, volleyball, water polo.

STUDENT SERVICES. Aptitude testing, career counseling, employment service for undergraduates, freshman orientation, health services, personal counseling, placement service for graduates, special adviser for adult students, veterans counselor, Office of multicultural affairs, services/facilities for handicapped.

ANNUAL EXPENSES. Tuition and fees (1992-93): $6,150, $8,600 additional for out-of-state students. **Room and board:** $4,266. **Books and supplies:** $475. **Other expenses:** $972.

FINANCIAL AID. 42% of freshmen, 38% of continuing students receive some form of aid. 90% of grants, 93% of loans, all jobs based on need. 789 enrolled freshmen were judged to have need, all were offered aid. Academic, music/drama, art, athletic scholarships available. **Aid applications:** No closing date; priority given to applications received by March 1; applicants notified on a rolling basis beginning on or about April 7; must reply by May 1 or within 3 weeks if notified thereafter.

ADDRESS/TELEPHONE. Carol Cotman Hogan, Director of Admissions, University of Vermont, 194 South Prospect Street, Burlington, VT 05401-3596. (802) 656-3370. Fax: (802) 656-8611.

Vermont Technical College
Randolph Center, Vermont — CB code: 3941

Admissions:	90% of applicants accepted
Based on:	••• School record
	•• Test scores
	• Activities, essay, interview, recommendations
Completion:	75% of freshmen end year in good standing
	65% graduate, 18% of these enter 4-year programs

2-year public technical college, coed. Founded in 1910. **Accreditation:** Regional. **Undergraduate enrollment:** 682 men, 190 women full time; 21 men, 21 women part time. **Faculty:** 84 total (59 full time), 14 with doctorates or other terminal degrees. **Location:** Rural campus in rural community; 20 miles from Montpelier, 160 miles from Boston. **Calendar:** Semester, limited summer session. **Microcomputers:** 325 located in libraries, classrooms, computer centers, campus-wide network. **Special facilities:** Computer-assisted design laboratories, robotics laboratory, veterinary technology laboratory.

DEGREES OFFERED. AAS. 238 associate degrees awarded in 1992. 7% in agriculture, 24% architecture and environmental design, 6% business/office and marketing/distribution, 58% engineering technologies, 5% allied health.

UNDERGRADUATE MAJORS. Agricultural business and management, architectural technologies, architecture, automotive technology, biomedical equipment technology, business and office, civil technology, computer servicing technology, computer technology, construction, dairy, electrical technology, electromechanical technology, electronic technology, engineering and engineering-related technologies, horticulture, landscape architecture, mechanical design technology, veterinarian's assistant.

ACADEMIC PROGRAMS. Double major, dual enrollment of high school students, independent study, internships, telecourses. **Remedial services:** Learning center, preadmission summer program, reduced course load, remedial instruction, special counselor, tutoring. **Placement/credit:** AP, CLEP General and Subject, institutional tests; 36 credit hours maximum for associate degree.

ACADEMIC REQUIREMENTS. Freshmen must earn minimum GPA of 1.6 to continue in good standing. 70% of freshmen return for sophomore year. Students must declare major on application. **Graduation requirements:** 72 hours for associate (57 in major). Most students required to take courses in computer science, English, humanities, mathematics, biological/physical sciences. **Additional information:** 50% of academic work is theory; 50% is hands-on.

FRESHMAN ADMISSIONS. Selection criteria: School achievement record most important, followed by SAT or ACT scores, recommendations, interview. **High school preparation:** 16 units required. Required units include English 4, mathematics 3, physical science 2 and social science 2. 2 laboratory science required. **Test requirements:** SAT or ACT (SAT preferred); score report by July 15. Basic skills placement examination required after acceptance.

1992 FRESHMAN CLASS PROFILE. 439 men applied, 398 accepted, 311 enrolled; 111 women applied, 98 accepted, 93 enrolled. 58% had high school GPA of 3.0 or higher, 40% between 2.0 and 2.99. **Academic background:** Mid 50% of enrolled freshmen had SAT-V between 350-450, SAT-M between 450-550; ACT composite between 18-28. 98% submitted SAT scores, 1% submitted ACT scores. **Characteristics:** 85% from in state, 95% live in college housing, 1% have minority backgrounds, 1% are foreign students. Average age is 18.

FALL-TERM APPLICATIONS. $40 fee, may be waived for applicants with need. No closing date; applicants notified on a rolling basis beginning on or about January 1; must reply by May 1 or within 4 weeks if notified thereafter. Essay required for some majors applicants. Interview recommended. CRDA. Deferred and early admission available.

STUDENT LIFE. Housing: Dormitories (men, women); handicapped housing available. **Activities:** Student government, film, radio, student newspaper, yearbook, national student chapters of: American Institute of Architects (AIA), American Society of Civil Engineers (ASCE), Future Farmers of America (FFA), Institute of Electrical and Electronic Engineers (IEEE), Society of Manufacturing Engineers (SME), Tau Alpha Pi, Society of Women Engineers.

ATHLETICS. NJCAA. **Intercollegiate:** Baseball M, basketball, skiing, soccer, softball W, volleyball. **Intramural:** Badminton, basketball, bowling, fencing, golf, ice hockey M, lacrosse M, racquetball, rifle, skiing, soccer, softball, swimming, table tennis, tennis, volleyball, water polo.

STUDENT SERVICES. Career counseling, employment service for undergraduates, freshman orientation, health services, personal counseling, placement service for graduates, student support services special counseling, services/facilities for handicapped.

ANNUAL EXPENSES. Tuition and fees (projected): $4,390, $1,920 additional for out-of-district students, $3,840 additional for out-of-state students. **Room and board:** $4,640. **Books and supplies:** $700. **Other expenses:** $650.

FINANCIAL AID. 70% of freshmen, 53% of continuing students receive some form of aid. 94% of grants, 81% of loans, 44% of jobs based on need. 274 enrolled freshmen were judged to have need, all were offered aid. Academic, state/district residency scholarships available. **Aid applications:** No closing date; priority given to applications received by March 1; applicants notified on a rolling basis beginning on or about June 1; must reply within 2 weeks.

ADDRESS/TELEPHONE. Stephen Waterman, III, Director of Admissions, Vermont Technical College, P.O. Box 500, Randolph Center, VT 05061. (802) 728-3391. (800) 442-8821. Fax: (802) 728-3321.

Virginia

Averett College

Danville, Virginia CB code: 5017

Admissions: 88% of applicants accepted
Based on: ••• School record, test scores
•• Recommendations
• Activities, essay, interview, special talents
Completion: 85% of freshmen end year in good standing
63% graduate, 23% of these enter graduate study

4-year private liberal arts college, coed, affiliated with Southern Baptist Convention. Founded in 1859. **Accreditation:** Regional. **Undergraduate enrollment:** 267 men, 337 women full time; 261 men, 269 women part time. **Graduate enrollment:** 367 men, 173 women part time. **Faculty:** 70 total (68 full time), 53 with doctorates or other terminal degrees. **Location:** Suburban campus in small city; 45 miles from Greensboro, North Carolina. **Calendar:** Semester, limited summer session. **Microcomputers:** 62 located in classrooms, computer centers. **Special facilities:** 65-acre equestrian center, air traffic control simulators. **Additional facts:** Aviation majors have use of facilities at Danville Regional Airport.

DEGREES OFFERED. AA, AS, BA, BS, MBA, MEd. 1 associate degree awarded in 1992. 100% in trade and industry. 235 bachelor's degrees awarded. 5% in agriculture, 50% business and management, 5% communications, 5% psychology, 9% social sciences. Graduate degrees offered in 5 major fields of study.

UNDERGRADUATE MAJORS. Associate: Air traffic control. **Bachelor's:** Accounting, airline piloting and navigation, anatomy, applied mathematics, art education, art history, aviation management, behavioral sciences, biochemistry, biology, botany, business administration and management, business and management, business statistics, chemistry, clinical laboratory science, clinical psychology, communications, comparative literature, computer and information sciences, computer mathematics, computer programming, counseling psychology, criminal justice studies, data processing, developmental psychology, dramatic arts, drawing, early childhood education, ecology, education, elementary education, embryology, English, English education, English literature, environmental science, equestrian science, experimental psychology, finance, fine arts, genetics, human and animal, health education, history, humanities, humanities and social sciences, industrial and organizational psychology, information sciences and systems, journalism, junior high education, labor/industrial relations, law enforcement and corrections, liberal/general studies, management science, marketing and distribution, marketing management, marketing research, mathematics, mathematics education, medical laboratory technologies, medical radiation dosimetry, music, music history and appreciation, music performance, music theory and composition, painting, parks and recreation management, personnel management, physical education, physiology, human and animal, predentistry, prelaw, premedicine, prepharmacy, preveterinary, psychology, public relations, pure mathematics, reading education, recreation and community services technologies, religion, religious education, religious music, retailing, science education, sculpture, secondary education, small business management and ownership, social psychology, social science education, social sciences, social studies education, sociology, sports management, sports medicine, studio art, systems analysis, theater design, theological studies, visual and performing arts, zoology.

ACADEMIC PROGRAMS. Accelerated program, double major, independent study, internships, student-designed major, study abroad; liberal arts/career combination in health sciences; combined bachelor's/graduate program in business administration. **Remedial services:** Reduced course load, remedial instruction, special counselor, tutoring. **Placement/credit:** AP, CLEP General and Subject, institutional tests.

ACADEMIC REQUIREMENTS. Freshmen must earn minimum GPA of 2.0 to continue in good standing. 75% of freshmen return for sophomore year. Students must declare major by end of second year. **Graduation requirements:** 63 hours for associate, 123 hours for bachelor's (45 in major). Most students required to take courses in arts/fine arts, English, history, mathematics, philosophy/religion, biological/physical sciences, social sciences. **Postgraduate studies:** 2% enter law school, 1% enter medical school, 12% enter MBA programs, 8% enter other graduate study.

FRESHMAN ADMISSIONS. Selection criteria: High school achievement record and test scores most important. **High school preparation:** 15 units required; 18 recommended. Required and recommended units include biological science 1-2, English 4, mathematics 2-3, social science 2 and science 1-2. Foreign language 2 and physical science 1 recommended. **Test requirements:** SAT or ACT (SAT preferred); score report by August 1.

1992 FRESHMAN CLASS PROFILE. 182 men applied, 153 accepted, 52 enrolled; 250 women applied, 228 accepted, 73 enrolled. 34% had high school GPA of 3.0 or higher, 64% between 2.0 and 2.99. **Academic background:** Mid 50% of enrolled freshmen had SAT-V between 430-550, SAT-M between 430-550; ACT composite between 20-25. 90% submitted SAT scores, 10% submitted ACT scores. **Characteristics:** 60% from in state, 85% live in college housing, 15% have minority backgrounds, 3% are foreign students, 15% join fraternities/sororities. Average age is 19.

FALL-TERM APPLICATIONS. $20 fee, may be waived for applicants with need. Closing date August 1; priority given to applications received by May 1; applicants notified on a rolling basis; must reply by May 1. Essay required. Interview recommended. Audition recommended for music applicants. Portfolio recommended for art applicants. Riding test required of equestrian studies applicants. CRDA. Deferred and early admission available.

STUDENT LIFE. Housing: Dormitories (men, women). One suite-style dormitory with 10 students per suite. Each suite contains 5 bedroom areas, living room/lounge area, and bath. **Activities:** Student government, magazine, student newspaper, choral groups, drama, musical theater, fraternities, sororities, Baptist Student Union, Jaycees, Young Republicans, campus service club, business majors club, Student Foundation, Fellowship of Christian Athletes.

ATHLETICS. NCAA. **Intercollegiate:** Basketball, golf M, horseback riding, soccer M, softball W, tennis, volleyball W. **Intramural:** Basketball, soccer, softball, table tennis, volleyball.

STUDENT SERVICES. Aptitude testing, career counseling, employment service for undergraduates, freshman orientation, personal counseling, placement service for graduates, special adviser for adult students, veterans counselor, services/facilities for handicapped.

ANNUAL EXPENSES. Tuition and fees (1992-93): $9,090. **Room and board:** $3,900. **Books and supplies:** $400. **Other expenses:** $600.

FINANCIAL AID. 82% of freshmen, 86% of continuing students receive some form of aid. 30% of grants, 71% of loans, 78% of jobs based on need. 101 enrolled freshmen were judged to have need, all were offered aid. Academic, state/district residency, leadership, religious affiliation scholarships available. **Aid applications:** No closing date; priority given to applications received by April 1; applicants notified on a rolling basis beginning on or about May 1; must reply within 2 weeks. **Additional information:** Virginia Baptist students may receive a $2000 Virginia Baptist Resident Student Scholarship.

ADDRESS/TELEPHONE. Admissions Office, Averett College, West Main Street, Danville, VA 24541. (804) 791-5660. Fax: (804) 791-5637.

Blue Ridge Community College

Weyers Cave, Virginia CB code: 5083

2-year public community college, coed. Founded in 1965. **Accreditation:** Regional. **Undergraduate enrollment:** 2,882 men and women. **Graduate enrollment:** 643 men and women. **Faculty:** 173 total (53 full time), 19 with doctorates or other terminal degrees. **Location:** Rural campus in rural community; 12 miles from Harrisonburg, 15 miles from Staunton. **Calendar:** Semester, limited summer session. **Microcomputers:** 195 located in libraries, classrooms, computer centers.

DEGREES OFFERED. AA, AAS. 168 associate degrees awarded in 1992.

UNDERGRADUATE MAJORS. Accounting, business and management, business and office, business data programming, electronic technology, finance, industrial technology, information sciences and systems, liberal/general studies, marketing and distribution, mechanical design technology, mental health/human services, nursing, secretarial and related programs, veterinarian's assistant.

ACADEMIC PROGRAMS. 2-year transfer program, accelerated program, dual enrollment of high school students, honors program, internships. **Remedial services:** Learning center, remedial instruction, special counselor, tutoring. **Placement/credit:** AP, CLEP General and Subject, institutional tests; 18 credit hours maximum for associate degree.

ACADEMIC REQUIREMENTS. Freshmen must earn minimum GPA of 2.0 to continue in good standing. 69% of freshmen return for sophomore year. Students must declare major on application. **Graduation requirements:** 65 hours for associate. Most students required to take courses in English, mathematics, social sciences.

FRESHMAN ADMISSIONS. Selection criteria: Open admissions. Selective admissions to veterinary assistant technology and nursing programs. Recommended units include English 4, mathematics 1 and science 1. High school diploma or GED recommended for all applicants, required for state license in nursing program.

1992 FRESHMAN CLASS PROFILE. 736 men and women enrolled. **Characteristics:** 98% from in state, 100% commute, 3% have minority backgrounds. Average age is 24.

FALL-TERM APPLICATIONS. No fee. No closing date; applicants notified on a rolling basis. Interview recommended for veterinary technology, nursing applicants. Portfolio recommended. Essay recommended. Early admission available. Closing date for veterinary assistant technology, nursing applications is March 1.

STUDENT LIFE. Activities: Student government, student newspaper, choral groups.

ATHLETICS. Intramural: Basketball M, softball, tennis, volleyball.

STUDENT SERVICES. Aptitude testing, career counseling, em-

ployment service for undergraduates, freshman orientation, personal counseling, placement service for graduates, veterans counselor, services/facilities for handicapped.

ANNUAL EXPENSES. Tuition and fees: $1,332, $3,030 additional for out-of-state students. **Books and supplies:** $600. **Other expenses:** $500.

FINANCIAL AID. 15% of freshmen, 15% of continuing students receive some form of aid. All grants, 78% of loans, all jobs based on need. **Aid applications:** No closing date; priority given to applications received by May 15; applicants notified on a rolling basis beginning on or about June 1; must reply within 2 weeks.

ADDRESS/TELEPHONE. Kathy Hahn, Director of Admissions and Records, Blue Ridge Community College, PO Box 80, Weyers Cave, VA 24486-9989. (703) 234-9261 ext. 251. Fax: (703) 234-9066.

Bluefield College
Bluefield, Virginia CB code: 5063

Admissions: 92% of applicants accepted
Based on: ••• School record
• Activities, essay, interview, recommendations, special talents, test scores
Completion: 85% of freshmen end year in good standing
45% graduate, 40% of these enter graduate study

4-year private liberal arts college, coed, affiliated with Southern Baptist Convention. Founded in 1920. **Accreditation:** Regional. **Undergraduate enrollment:** 278 men, 290 women full time; 28 men, 111 women part time. **Faculty:** 50 total (36 full time), 23 with doctorates or other terminal degrees. **Location:** Rural campus in large town; 95 miles from Roanoke, and from Charleston, West Virginia. **Calendar:** Semester, limited summer session. Saturday classes. **Microcomputers:** 50 located in libraries, classrooms, computer centers. **Special facilities:** Equine studies.

DEGREES OFFERED. AA, AS, BA, BS. 2 associate degrees awarded in 1992. 100% in multi/interdisciplinary studies. 90 bachelor's degrees awarded. 34% in business and management, 35% education, 15% psychology.

UNDERGRADUATE MAJORS. Associate: Allied health, business and management, business and office, business data programming, clinical laboratory science, engineering, fine arts, legal assistant/paralegal, legal secretary, liberal/general studies, medical secretary, premedicine, prepharmacy, preveterinary, secretarial and related programs, sports medicine. **Bachelor's:** Accounting, art education, biblical languages, biology, business administration and management, business and management, business computer/console/peripheral equipment operation, business data programming, business education, chemistry, communications, computer and information sciences, computer programming, criminal justice studies, education, elementary education, English, English education, equestrian science, fine arts, health education, history, human resources development, humanities, humanities and social sciences, information sciences and systems, junior high education, liberal/general studies, mathematics, mathematics education, music, music education, music performance, music theory and composition, philosophy, physical education, physical sciences, prelaw, psychology, recreation and community services technologies, religion, religious education, religious music, science education, secondary education, social sciences, social studies education, speech/communication/theater education, visual and performing arts.

ACADEMIC PROGRAMS. 2-year transfer program, accelerated program, double major, dual enrollment of high school students, honors program, independent study, internships, study abroad, teacher preparation; liberal arts/career combination in health sciences. **Remedial services:** Learning center, reduced course load, remedial instruction, special counselor, tutoring. **Placement/credit:** AP, CLEP General and Subject, institutional tests. Hours of credit by examination that may be counted toward degree varies.

ACADEMIC REQUIREMENTS. Freshmen must earn minimum GPA of 1.44 to continue in good standing. 62% of freshmen return for sophomore year. Students must declare major by end of second year. **Graduation requirements:** 64 hours for associate, 126 hours for bachelor's (33 in major). Most students required to take courses in arts/fine arts, computer science, English, foreign languages, history, humanities, mathematics, philosophy/religion, biological/physical sciences, social sciences. **Postgraduate studies:** 80% from 2-year programs enter 4-year programs. 2% enter law school, 1% enter medical school, 12% enter MBA programs, 25% enter other graduate study.

FRESHMAN ADMISSIONS. Selection criteria: School grades, class rank, and SAT or ACT score considered. **High school preparation:** 16 units recommended. Recommended units include English 4, mathematics 2, social science 2 and science 1. **Test requirements:** SAT or ACT; score report by August 15.

1992 FRESHMAN CLASS PROFILE. 183 men applied, 169 accepted, 80 enrolled; 201 women applied, 184 accepted, 91 enrolled. 10% had high school GPA of 3.0 or higher, 78% between 2.0 and 2.99. **Academic background:** Mid 50% of enrolled freshmen had SAT-V between 450-520, SAT-M between 450-500. 90% submitted SAT scores. **Characteristics:** 80% from in state, 70% live in college housing, 5% have minority backgrounds, 4% are foreign students. Average age is 19.

FALL-TERM APPLICATIONS. $15 fee, may be waived for applicants with need. No closing date; applicants notified on a rolling basis; must reply by May 1 or within 6 weeks if notified thereafter. Interview recommended. Audition recommended for music applicants. Deferred and early admission available.

STUDENT LIFE. Housing: Dormitories (men, women); apartment housing available. **Activities:** Student government, student newspaper, yearbook, choral groups, dance, drama, music ensembles, musical theater, pep band, fraternities, sororities, religious vocation organization, Baptist Student Union. **Additional information:** Religious observance required.

ATHLETICS. NAIA. **Intercollegiate:** Baseball M, basketball, golf M, soccer M, tennis, volleyball W. **Intramural:** Basketball, softball, tennis, volleyball.

STUDENT SERVICES. Career counseling, freshman orientation, personal counseling, placement service for graduates, services/facilities for handicapped.

ANNUAL EXPENSES. Tuition and fees: $6,500. **Room and board:** $4,100. **Books and supplies:** $400. **Other expenses:** $800.

FINANCIAL AID. 85% of freshmen, 90% of continuing students receive some form of aid. 26% of grants, 92% of loans, 58% of jobs based on need. 118 enrolled freshmen were judged to have need, all were offered aid. Academic, music/drama, art, athletic, state/district residency, religious affiliation, minority scholarships available. **Aid applications:** No closing date; priority given to applications received by March 13; applicants notified on a rolling basis; must reply within 10 days.

ADDRESS/TELEPHONE. Nina Wilburn, Director of Enrollment Management, Bluefield College, 3000 College Drive, Bluefield, VA 24605-1799. (703) 326-4213. (800) 872-0175. Fax: (703) 326-4288.

Bridgewater College
Bridgewater, Virginia CB code: 5069

Admissions: 85% of applicants accepted
Based on: ••• School record
•• Essay, interview, recommendations, test scores
• Activities
Completion: 92% of freshmen end year in good standing
60% graduate, 19% of these enter graduate study

4-year private liberal arts college, coed, affiliated with Church of the Brethren. Founded in 1880. **Accreditation:** Regional. **Undergraduate enrollment:** 399 men, 461 women full time; 22 men, 39 women part time. **Faculty:** 84 total (70 full time), 46 with doctorates or other terminal degrees. **Location:** Rural campus in small town; 8 miles from Harrisonburg. **Calendar:** Three 10-week terms and one 3-week interterm. **Microcomputers:** 52 located in classrooms, computer centers. **Special facilities:** Historical museum.

DEGREES OFFERED. BA, BS. 230 bachelor's degrees awarded in 1992. 26% in business and management, 20% teacher education, 6% home economics, 10% life sciences, 5% psychology, 17% social sciences, 7% visual and performing arts.

UNDERGRADUATE MAJORS. Accounting, biology, business administration and management, business and management, chemistry, clinical laboratory science, computer and information sciences, early childhood education, economics, elementary education, English, fine arts, French, German, health sciences, history, home economics, international relations, junior high education, liberal/general studies, mathematics, music, philosophy, physical sciences, physics, political science and government, preengineering, psychology, religion, secondary education, sociology, Spanish.

ACADEMIC PROGRAMS. Accelerated program, double major, honors program, independent study, internships, study abroad, teacher preparation, telecourses; liberal arts/career combination in engineering, forestry. **Remedial services:** Preadmission summer program, reduced course load, remedial instruction, special counselor, tutoring. **Placement/credit:** AP, institutional tests.

ACADEMIC REQUIREMENTS. Freshmen must earn minimum GPA of 1.6 to continue in good standing. 76% of freshmen return for sophomore year. Students must declare major by end of second year. **Graduation requirements:** 123 hours for bachelor's (30 in major). Most students required to take courses in arts/fine arts, English, foreign languages, history, mathematics, philosophy/religion, biological/physical sciences, social sciences. **Postgraduate studies:** 3% enter law school, 1% enter medical school, 2% enter MBA programs, 13% enter other graduate study.

FRESHMAN ADMISSIONS. Selection criteria: Class rank or high school GPA most important, followed by test scores and letters of recommendation. Prefer applicants in top half of high school class. Those in bottom half with strong compensating qualities considered. **High school preparation:** 16 units required; 19 recommended. Required and recommended units include English 4, foreign language 2-3, mathematics 2-4, social science 2-4 and science 2. Biological science 2 and physical science 2 recommended. **Test requirements:** SAT or ACT (SAT preferred); score report by August 15.

1992 FRESHMAN CLASS PROFILE. 390 men applied, 311 accepted,

122 enrolled; 389 women applied, 351 accepted, 133 enrolled. **Characteristics:** 71% from in state, 85% live in college housing, 4% have minority backgrounds, 1% are foreign students. Average age is 18.

FALL-TERM APPLICATIONS. $15 fee. Closing date August 1; applicants notified on a rolling basis; must reply within 4 weeks. Interview recommended. Deferred and early admission available.

STUDENT LIFE. Housing: Dormitories (men, women). Students may live off campus with their families. **Activities:** Student government, radio, student newspaper, yearbook, literary journal, choral groups, concert band, drama, jazz band, music ensembles, musical theater, pep band, Brethren Student Fellowship, Baptist Student Union, Student Committee on Religious Activities, College Republicans, Young Democrats, Omicron Delta Kappa, Campus Center Program Council, Alpha Chi, Lambda Society, academic societies.

ATHLETICS. NCAA. **Intercollegiate:** Baseball M, basketball, cross-country, field hockey W, football M, golf M, lacrosse W, soccer M, softball W, tennis, track and field M, volleyball W. **Intramural:** Badminton, basketball, diving, handball, racquetball, softball, table tennis, tennis, track and field, volleyball, water polo, wrestling M.

STUDENT SERVICES. Aptitude testing, career counseling, employment service for undergraduates, freshman orientation, health services, personal counseling, placement service for graduates, services/facilities for handicapped.

ANNUAL EXPENSES. Tuition and fees: $10,770. **Room and board:** $4,530. **Books and supplies:** $525. **Other expenses:** $875.

FINANCIAL AID. 97% of freshmen, 94% of continuing students receive some form of aid. 30% of grants, all loans, all jobs based on need. 184 enrolled freshmen were judged to have need, all were offered aid. Academic, music/drama, state/district residency, religious affiliation scholarships available. **Aid applications:** Closing date March 15; applicants notified on a rolling basis beginning on or about April 1; must reply within 2 weeks.

ADDRESS/TELEPHONE. Brian C. Hildebrand, Dean for Enrollment Management, Bridgewater College, East College Street, Bridgewater, VA 22812-1599. (703) 828-2501 ext. 400. Fax: (703) 828-2160.

Central Virginia Community College
Lynchburg, Virginia — CB code: 5141

2-year public community college, coed. Founded in 1966. **Accreditation:** Regional. **Undergraduate enrollment:** 438 men, 577 women full time; 1,907 men, 2,198 women part time. **Faculty:** 124 total (64 full time), 10 with doctorates or other terminal degrees. **Location:** Suburban campus in small city; 120 miles from Richmond. **Calendar:** Semester, limited summer session. Saturday and extensive evening/early morning classes. **Microcomputers:** 80 located in libraries, classrooms, computer centers.

DEGREES OFFERED. AA, AS, AAS. 286 associate degrees awarded in 1992. 23% in business and management, 13% business/office and marketing/distribution, 7% computer sciences, 16% education, 7% teacher education, 6% engineering technologies, 10% allied health, 7% life sciences, 6% parks/recreation, protective services, public affairs.

UNDERGRADUATE MAJORS. Accounting, architectural technologies, business administration and management, business and management, business and office, commercial art, computer and information sciences, drafting, drafting and design technology, education, electronic technology, engineering and engineering-related technologies, finance, fire control and safety technology, law enforcement and corrections technologies, liberal/general studies, mechanical design technology, medical laboratory technologies, microcomputer software, radiograph medical technology, Science, science technologies, secretarial and related programs.

ACADEMIC PROGRAMS. 2-year transfer program, cooperative education, dual enrollment of high school students, independent study, internships. **Remedial services:** Learning center, reduced course load, remedial instruction, tutoring. **Placement/credit:** AP, CLEP General and Subject, institutional tests; 49 credit hours maximum for associate degree.

ACADEMIC REQUIREMENTS. Freshmen must earn minimum GPA of 2.0 to continue in good standing. Students must declare major on enrollment. **Graduation requirements:** 65 hours for associate. Most students required to take courses in English, mathematics, social sciences. **Additional information:** GPA of 2.0 required to graduate.

FRESHMAN ADMISSIONS. Selection criteria: Open admissions. Allied Health programs have special admissions procedures. Student must have 2 interviews with program head and meet specific criteria before being accepted. Only 15 applicants a year accepted in each program.

1992 FRESHMAN CLASS PROFILE. 743 men and women enrolled. **Characteristics:** 97% from in state, 100% commute, 14% have minority backgrounds. Average age is 24.

FALL-TERM APPLICATIONS. No fee. No closing date; applicants notified on a rolling basis. Interview required for health program applicants. Early admission available. All students are required to take the Comparative Guidance and Placement Test for math and English, unless they have transfer credit in both areas.

STUDENT LIFE. Activities: Student government, student newspaper, Black Student Union, Inter-Varsity Christian Fellowship.

ATHLETICS. Intramural: Baseball M, basketball M, softball, volleyball.

STUDENT SERVICES. Aptitude testing, career counseling, employment service for undergraduates, freshman orientation, personal counseling, placement service for graduates, veterans counselor, services/facilities for handicapped.

ANNUAL EXPENSES. Tuition and fees: $1,340, $3,030 additional for out-of-state students. **Books and supplies:** $450. **Other expenses:** $3,000.

FINANCIAL AID. 20% of freshmen, 20% of continuing students receive some form of aid. 98% of grants, 83% of loans, all jobs based on need. Academic scholarships available. **Aid applications:** No closing date; priority given to applications received by May 15; applicants notified on a rolling basis beginning on or about June 1; must reply within 2 weeks. **Additional information:** 30-day emergency loans available.

ADDRESS/TELEPHONE. Robert L. Bashore, Dean of Student Services, Central Virginia Community College, 3506 Wards Road, Lynchburg, VA 24502. (804) 386-4500. Fax: (804) 386-4681.

Christendom College
Front Royal, Virginia — CB code: 5691

Admissions:	90% of applicants accepted
Based on:	•• Essay, recommendations, school record, test scores
	• Activities, interview, religious affiliation/commitment, special talents
Completion:	90% of freshmen end year in good standing

4-year private liberal arts college, coed, affiliated with Roman Catholic Church. Founded in 1976. **Accreditation:** Regional. **Undergraduate enrollment:** 57 men, 79 women full time; 1 man, 1 woman part time. **Faculty:** 18 total (13 full time), 11 with doctorates or other terminal degrees. **Location:** Rural campus in large town; 70 miles from Washington, D.C. **Calendar:** Semester. **Microcomputers:** Located in computer centers. **Additional facts:** Located on banks of Shenandoah River. Summer program in Rome, Italy.

DEGREES OFFERED. AA, BA. 6 associate degrees awarded in 1992. 100% in multi/interdisciplinary studies. 35 bachelor's degrees awarded. 6% in letters/literature, 49% philosophy, religion, theology, 40% social sciences.

UNDERGRADUATE MAJORS. Associate: Liberal/general studies. **Bachelor's:** English, history, philosophy, political science and government, theological studies.

ACADEMIC PROGRAMS. Honors program, internships, study abroad. **Placement/credit:** AP, institutional tests.

ACADEMIC REQUIREMENTS. Freshmen must earn minimum GPA of 2.0 to continue in good standing. 87% of freshmen return for sophomore year. Students must declare major by end of second year. **Graduation requirements:** 66 hours for associate, 120 hours for bachelor's (30 in major). Most students required to take courses in English, foreign languages, history, mathematics, philosophy/religion, social sciences.

FRESHMAN ADMISSIONS. Selection criteria: Student's verbal skills very important. **High school preparation:** 14 units required. Required units include biological science 1, English 4, foreign language 2, mathematics 2, physical science 1 and social science 4. **Test requirements:** SAT or ACT (SAT preferred); score report by June 1.

1992 FRESHMAN CLASS PROFILE. 28 men applied, 27 accepted, 8 enrolled; 44 women applied, 38 accepted, 17 enrolled. 72% had high school GPA of 3.0 or higher, 28% between 2.0 and 2.99. **Academic background:** Mid 50% of enrolled freshmen had SAT-V between 450-560, SAT-M between 460-570. 92% submitted SAT scores. **Characteristics:** 32% from in state, 100% live in college housing. Average age is 18.

FALL-TERM APPLICATIONS. $25 fee. Closing date June 1; priority given to applications received by April 1; applicants notified on a rolling basis beginning on or about January 15; must reply within 30 days. Essay required. Interview recommended. Deferred and early admission available.

STUDENT LIFE. Housing: Dormitories (men, women). **Activities:** Student government, yearbook, choral groups, drama.

ATHLETICS. Intercollegiate: Basketball, soccer M, volleyball W. **Intramural:** Football M, table tennis, volleyball.

STUDENT SERVICES. Career counseling, personal counseling.

ANNUAL EXPENSES. Tuition and fees (projected): $8,350. **Room and board:** $3,400. **Books and supplies:** $416. **Other expenses:** $312.

FINANCIAL AID. 64% of freshmen, 50% of continuing students receive some form of aid. 43% of grants based on need. 15 enrolled freshmen were judged to have need, all were offered aid. Academic scholarships available. **Aid applications:** Closing date June 1; priority given to applications received by April 15; applicants notified on a rolling basis beginning on or about March 15; must reply within 30 days.

ADDRESS/TELEPHONE. John F. Ciskanik, Dean of Admissions, Christendom College, 2101 Shenandoah Shores Road, Front Royal, VA 22630. (703) 636-2900. (800) 877-5456. Fax: (703) 636-1655.

Christopher Newport University
Newport News, Virginia CB code: 5128

Admissions: 86% of applicants accepted
Based on: ••• School record, test scores
•• Essay
• Activities, interview, recommendations
Completion: 37% graduate, 33% of these enter graduate study

4-year public university, coed. Founded in 1960. **Accreditation:** Regional. **Undergraduate enrollment:** 1,180 men, 1,753 women full time; 783 men, 1,072 women part time. **Graduate enrollment:** 1 man, 1 woman full time; 30 men, 60 women part time. **Faculty:** 205 total (198 full time), 130 with doctorates or other terminal degrees. **Location:** Suburban campus in small city; 20 miles from Norfolk, 60 miles from Richmond. **Calendar:** Semester, extensive summer session. Extensive evening/early morning classes. **Microcomputers:** 150 located in libraries, classrooms, computer centers. **Special facilities:** Falk Art Gallery, the Japanese Tea House in Virginia.

DEGREES OFFERED. BA, BS, MS. 654 bachelor's degrees awarded in 1992. 38% in business and management, 20% teacher education, 5% letters/literature, 9% parks/recreation, protective services, public affairs, 6% psychology, 6% social sciences. Graduate degrees offered in 1 major field of study.

UNDERGRADUATE MAJORS. Accounting, applied physics/microelectronics, biochemistry, biological and physical sciences, biology, business and management, business economics, cell biology, city/community/regional planning, communications, comparative literature, computer and information sciences, computer engineering, criminal justice studies, criminology, dramatic arts, economics, English, English literature, finance, fine arts, foreign languages (multiple emphasis), French, German, history, humanities and social sciences, industrial and organizational psychology, information sciences and systems, international business management, international public service, international relations, journalism, law enforcement and corrections, liberal/general studies, management information systems, marketing and distribution, mathematics, microbiology, music, music history and appreciation, music performance, music theory and composition, nursing, ornamental horticulture, parks and recreation management, philosophy, physics, political science and government, predentistry, prelaw, premedicine, prepharmacy, preveterinary, psychology, public administration, public policy studies, real estate, religion, renewable natural resources, social work, sociology, Spanish, urban studies, visual and performing arts, wildlife management.

ACADEMIC PROGRAMS. Accelerated program, double major, dual enrollment of high school students, honors program, independent study, internships, student-designed major, study abroad, teacher preparation, cross-registration. **Remedial services:** Preadmission summer program, reduced course load, remedial instruction, special counselor, tutoring. **ROTC:** Army. **Placement/credit:** AP, CLEP General and Subject, IB, institutional tests; 60 credit hours maximum for bachelor's degree.

ACADEMIC REQUIREMENTS. Freshmen must earn minimum GPA of 1.5 to continue in good standing. 71% of freshmen return for sophomore year. Students must declare major by end of second year. **Graduation requirements:** 120 hours for bachelor's (36 in major). Most students required to take courses in English, foreign languages, humanities, mathematics, biological/physical sciences, social sciences. **Additional information:** Advanced certificate programs available in ethnic studies, teacher education, gerontology. State-approved early childhood/elementary, middle, and secondary teacher education programs available in 21 areas.

FRESHMAN ADMISSIONS. Selection criteria: GPA, rank in top half of class, test scores, English grades, essay, recommendations, interview considered. **High school preparation:** 16 units recommended. Recommended units include English 4, foreign language 2, mathematics 3, social science 2 and science 2. College-preparatory program recommended. **Test requirements:** SAT or ACT (SAT preferred); score report by August 15.

1992 FRESHMAN CLASS PROFILE. 333 men applied, 267 accepted, 189 enrolled; 497 women applied, 448 accepted, 319 enrolled. 8% were in top tenth and 32% were in top quarter of graduating class. **Academic background:** Mid 50% of enrolled freshmen had SAT-V between 380-480, SAT-M between 380-500. 97% submitted SAT scores. **Characteristics:** 93% from in state, 100% commute, 19% have minority backgrounds, 1% are foreign students. Average age is 19.

FALL-TERM APPLICATIONS. $20 fee, may be waived for applicants with need. Closing date August 1; priority given to applications received by April 1; applicants notified on a rolling basis; must reply by May 1 or within 2 weeks if notified thereafter. Audition required for music applicants. Essay required. Interview recommended for marginal applicants. Portfolio recommended for art applicants. CRDA. Deferred and early admission available. EDP-F.

STUDENT LIFE. Housing: Univeristy housing available to students in fall 1994. **Activities:** Student government, magazine, student newspaper, yearbook, choral groups, concert band, dance, drama, jazz band, music ensembles, musical theater, opera, symphony orchestra, Performing Artists Associations, fraternities, sororities, Baptist Student Union, Intervarsity Christian Fellowship, International Students Association, Minority Students Association, United Nations Society.

ATHLETICS. NCAA. **Intercollegiate:** Baseball M, basketball, cross-country, golf M, sailing, soccer M, softball W, tennis, track and field, volleyball W. **Intramural:** Baseball, basketball, bowling, cross-country, golf, softball, tennis, volleyball.

STUDENT SERVICES. Aptitude testing, career counseling, employment service for undergraduates, freshman orientation, personal counseling, placement service for graduates, veterans counselor, services/facilities for handicapped.

ANNUAL EXPENSES. Tuition and fees (1992-93): $2,860, $3,992 additional for out-of-state students. **Books and supplies:** $510. **Other expenses:** $2,640.

FINANCIAL AID. 35% of freshmen, 26% of continuing students receive some form of aid. 84% of grants, 82% of loans, 15% of jobs based on need. 242 enrolled freshmen were judged to have need, 230 were offered aid. Academic, music/drama, state/district residency, minority scholarships available. **Aid applications:** No closing date; priority given to applications received by April 1; applicants notified on a rolling basis beginning on or about July 1; must reply within 2 weeks.

ADDRESS/TELEPHONE. Keith F. McLoughland, Dean of Enrollment Services, Christopher Newport University, 50 Shoe Lane, Newport News, VA 23606-2998. (804) 594-7015. Fax: (804) 594-7713.

Clinch Valley College of the University of Virginia
Wise, Virginia CB code: 5124

Admissions: 70% of applicants accepted
Based on: ••• School record
•• Recommendations, test scores
• Activities, essay, interview, special talents
Completion: 50% of freshmen end year in good standing
33% graduate, 11% of these enter graduate study

4-year public liberal arts college, coed. Founded in 1954. **Accreditation:** Regional. **Undergraduate enrollment:** 637 men, 577 women full time; 85 men, 155 women part time. **Faculty:** 113 total (57 full time), 39 with doctorates or other terminal degrees. **Location:** Rural campus in small town; 65 miles from Bristol. **Calendar:** Semester, limited summer session. **Microcomputers:** 60 located in computer centers. **Special facilities:** Observatory, writing laboratory, scanning electron microscope.

DEGREES OFFERED. BA, BS. 222 bachelor's degrees awarded in 1992. 33% in business and management, 24% teacher education, 6% life sciences, 24% social sciences.

UNDERGRADUATE MAJORS. Accounting, biology, business administration and management, chemistry, communications, comparative literature, economics, elementary education, environmental science, history, information sciences and systems, liberal/general studies, marketing management, mathematics, medical laboratory technologies, political science and government, psychology, social sciences, sociology.

ACADEMIC PROGRAMS. Cooperative education, double major, dual enrollment of high school students, honors program, independent study, internships, student-designed major, teacher preparation, telecourses. **Remedial services:** Preadmission summer program, reduced course load, remedial instruction, tutoring. **Placement/credit:** AP, institutional tests.

ACADEMIC REQUIREMENTS. Freshmen must earn minimum GPA of 2.0 to continue in good standing. 65% of freshmen return for sophomore year. Students must declare major by end of second year. **Graduation requirements:** 124 hours for bachelor's. Most students required to take courses in arts/fine arts, English, foreign languages, humanities, mathematics, biological/physical sciences, social sciences. **Postgraduate studies:** 8% from 2-year programs enter 4-year programs. 4% enter law school, 1% enter medical school, 2% enter MBA programs, 4% enter other graduate study.

FRESHMAN ADMISSIONS. Selection criteria: lass rank and school achievement record most important. Test scores considered if class rank in bottom half. **High school preparation:** 14 units required. Required units include biological science 1, English 4, mathematics 2, physical science 2, social science 2 and science 3. **Test requirements:** SAT or ACT (SAT preferred); score report by August 15.

1992 FRESHMAN CLASS PROFILE. 1,003 men and women applied, 700 accepted; 340 enrolled. **Academic background:** Mid 50% of enrolled freshmen had SAT-V between 300-500, SAT-M between 300-500. 97% submitted SAT scores. **Characteristics:** 91% from in state, 67% commute, 4% have minority backgrounds. Average age is 18.

FALL-TERM APPLICATIONS. $15 fee, may be waived for applicants with need. Closing date August 15; applicants notified on a rolling basis. Interview recommended for marginal applicants. Deferred admission available.

STUDENT LIFE. Housing: Dormitories (men, women, coed); apartment, fraternity housing available. **Activities:** Student government, film, magazine, student newspaper, yearbook, choral groups, dance, drama, music ensembles, musical theater, fraternities, sororities, religious organizations, Young Republicans, Young Democrats, international students organization.

ATHLETICS. NAIA. **Intercollegiate:** Baseball M, basketball, cross-country, football M, golf M, tennis, volleyball W. **Intramural:** Basketball, football, softball, tennis, volleyball.

STUDENT SERVICES. Career counseling, freshman orientation, health services, personal counseling, placement service for graduates, services/facilities for handicapped.

ANNUAL EXPENSES. Tuition and fees (1992-93): $2,650, $3,374 additional for out-of-state students. **Room and board:** $3,200. **Books and supplies:** $600. **Other expenses:** $750.

FINANCIAL AID. 62% of freshmen, 65% of continuing students receive some form of aid. 96% of grants, 96% of loans, 93% of jobs based on need. 239 enrolled freshmen were judged to have need, 191 were offered aid. Academic, athletic, state/district residency, alumni affiliation, minority scholarships available. **Aid applications:** No closing date; priority given to applications received by April 1; applicants notified on a rolling basis beginning on or about March 1; must reply within 2 weeks.

ADDRESS/TELEPHONE. Dr. Lana Low, Director of Admissions, Clinch Valley College of the University of Virginia, College Avenue, Wise, VA 24293. (703) 328-0116. (800) 468-3412. Fax: (703) 328-0115.

College of Health Sciences
Roanoke, Virginia CB code: 5099

2-year private health science, nursing college, coed. Founded in 1982. **Accreditation:** Regional. **Undergraduate enrollment:** 86 men, 176 women full time; 47 men, 226 women part time. **Faculty:** 47 total (17 full time), 7 with doctorates or other terminal degrees. **Location:** Urban campus in small city; located downtown. **Calendar:** Semester, limited summer session. **Microcomputers:** 38 located in libraries, computer centers. **Special facilities:** Alumni Association Museum, on-campus fitness center. **Additional facts:** Access to educational seminars broadcast live by American Hospital Association, Hospital Satellite network, and other networks. One of 50 demonstration centers nationwide for interactive video in nursing education.

DEGREES OFFERED. AS. 76 associate degrees awarded in 1992. 53% in health sciences, 47% allied health.

UNDERGRADUATE MAJORS. Emergency medical technologies, medical records technology, nursing, occupational therapy assistant, physical therapy assistant, respiratory therapy technology.

ACADEMIC PROGRAMS. Independent study, internships. **Placement/credit:** AP, CLEP General and Subject, institutional tests.

ACADEMIC REQUIREMENTS. Freshmen must earn minimum GPA of 2.0 to continue in good standing. 78% of freshmen return for sophomore year. Students must declare major on application. **Graduation requirements:** 70 hours for associate (35 in major). Most students required to take courses in computer science, English, humanities, biological/physical sciences, social sciences. **Additional information:** LPN mobility program provides opportunties for LPNs to become eligible for registered nurse licensure. Students who are uncertain about choice of health care profession and those who have limited or unsatisfactory academic background can enter PACE program (Planning A Career Entry).

FRESHMAN ADMISSIONS. Selection criteria: Applicants should rank in top half of class. Health care experience considered. **High school preparation:** 18 units required; 20 recommended. Required and recommended units include biological science 1-2, English 4, mathematics 2-3 and physical science 1-2. Minimum 2.0 in algebra, geometry, biology, chemistry, and English required. **Test requirements:** SAT or ACT (SAT preferred); score report by July 31. **Additional information:** Emergency health sciences program requires emergency medical technician ambulance certification prior to entering program.

1992 FRESHMAN CLASS PROFILE. 17 men and women enrolled. **Characteristics:** Average age is 21.

FALL-TERM APPLICATIONS. $15 fee. Closing date February 1; priority given to applications received by October 15; applicants notified on or about April 1. Essay required. Interview recommended. Institutional early decision plan.

STUDENT LIFE. Housing: Dormitories (coed). Student dormitory in same building as college. **Activities:** Student government, student newspaper, yearbook, Allied Health Education Against Drugs (AHEAD), Phi Theta Kappa.

STUDENT SERVICES. Aptitude testing, career counseling, employment service for undergraduates, freshman orientation, health services, personal counseling, placement service for graduates, special adviser for adult students, academic advising by faculty, information and referral service, services/facilities for handicapped.

ANNUAL EXPENSES. Tuition and fees: $2,880. **Room and board:** $1,200 room only. **Books and supplies:** $750. **Other expenses:** $4,500.

FINANCIAL AID. 59% of freshmen, 60% of continuing students receive some form of aid. 50% of grants, 89% of loans, all jobs based on need. Academic, state/district residency scholarships available. **Aid applications:** No closing date; priority given to applications received by July 1; applicants notified on a rolling basis beginning on or about July 15; must reply within 30 days.

ADDRESS/TELEPHONE. Ruth Robertson, Coordinator of Admissions and Records, College of Health Sciences, P.O. Box 13186, Roanoke, VA 24031-3186. (703) 985-8483. (800) 422-8482. Fax: (703) 985-9773.

College of William and Mary
Williamsburg, Virginia CB code: 5115

Admissions:	41% of applicants accepted
Based on:	••• School record
	•• Activities, essay, special talents, test scores
	• Recommendations
Completion:	95% of freshmen end year in good standing
	88% graduate, 27% of these enter graduate study

4-year public university, coed. Founded in 1693. **Accreditation:** Regional. **Undergraduate enrollment:** 2,398 men, 2,868 women full time; 36 men, 33 women part time. **Graduate enrollment:** 741 men, 660 women full time; 346 men, 563 women part time. **Faculty:** 856 total (699 full time), 469 with doctorates or other terminal degrees. **Location:** Rural campus in large town; 50 miles from Richmond, 50 miles from Norfolk. **Calendar:** Semester, limited summer session. **Microcomputers:** 500 located in dormitories, libraries, classrooms, computer centers. **Special facilities:** Art museum and gallery, observatory, continuous beam accelerator, 3 interdisciplinary centers in humanities, international studies, writing resources.

DEGREES OFFERED. BA, BS, MA, MS, MBA, MEd, PhD, EdD, JD. 1,253 bachelor's degrees awarded in 1992. 13% in business and management, 12% letters/literature, 13% life sciences, 9% multi/interdisciplinary studies, 8% psychology, 27% social sciences. Graduate degrees offered in 28 major fields of study.

UNDERGRADUATE MAJORS. Accounting, American studies, anthropology, biological and physical sciences, biology, business administration and management, chemistry, classics, computer and information sciences, economics, English, finance, fine arts, French, geology, German, history, humanities and social sciences, international relations, international studies, liberal/general studies, marketing management, mathematics, music, philosophy, physical education, physics, political science and government, psychology, religion, sociology, Spanish, visual and performing arts.

ACADEMIC PROGRAMS. Double major, dual enrollment of high school students, education specialist degree, honors program, independent study, internships, student-designed major, study abroad, teacher preparation, visiting/exchange student program; liberal arts/career combination in engineering, forestry. **Remedial services:** Preadmission summer program, tutoring. **ROTC:** Army. **Placement/credit:** AP, institutional tests.

ACADEMIC REQUIREMENTS. Freshmen must earn minimum GPA of 1.0 to continue in good standing. 95% of freshmen return for sophomore year. Students must declare major by end of second year. **Graduation requirements:** 120 hours for bachelor's (30 in major). Most students required to take courses in English, foreign languages, humanities, biological/physical sciences, social sciences. **Postgraduate studies:** 5% enter law school, 5% enter medical school, 1% enter MBA programs, 16% enter other graduate study.

FRESHMAN ADMISSIONS. Selection criteria: Academic preparation, with particular emphasis on course selection and grades, test scores, special talents and abilities as well as geographic and ethnic background. Special consideration given to children of alumni. Preference given to Virginia residents. **High school preparation:** 20 units recommended. Recommended units include English 4, foreign language 4, mathematics 4, social science 4 and science 4. Recommend most demanding high school course available. **Test requirements:** SAT or ACT; score report by February 15. **Additional information:** College seeks students with diverse backgrounds (ethnic, socioeconomic, geographic), special abilities and unique interests and experiences. Application evaluated on its own merits without specific course requirements. Most candidates present as strong a college preparatory program as possible. Advanced placement, honors, and accelerated courses strongly weighed in evaluation process.

1992 FRESHMAN CLASS PROFILE. 2,736 men applied, 1,309 accepted, 520 enrolled; 4,486 women applied, 1,688 accepted, 674 enrolled. 68% were in top tenth and 89% were in top quarter of graduating class. **Academic background:** Mid 50% of enrolled freshmen had SAT-V between 540-650, SAT-M between 600-700. 100% submitted SAT scores. **Characteristics:** 69% from in state, 93% live in college housing, 19% have minority backgrounds, 2% are foreign students. Average age is 18.

FALL-TERM APPLICATIONS. $40 fee, may be waived for applicants with need. Closing date January 15; applicants notified on or about April 1; must reply by May 1. Essay required. CRDA. Deferred admission available. EDP-F.

STUDENT LIFE. Housing: Dormitories (men, women, coed); apartment, fraternity, sorority housing available. Special interest housing (Italian, French, German, Asian, Russian, Spanish, Project Plus, International Studies) available. **Activities:** Student government, magazine, radio, student newspaper, television, yearbook, literary magazine, choral groups, concert band, dance, drama, jazz band, marching band, music ensembles, musical theater, opera, pep band, symphony orchestra, fraternities, sororities, Black

Student Organization, Circle-K, community tutorial service, Collegiate Civitan, campus ministries, debating society, international students club, College Republicans, Young Democrats, women's group.

ATHLETICS. NAIA, NCAA. **Intercollegiate:** Baseball M, basketball, cross-country, diving, fencing, field hockey W, football M, golf, gymnastics, lacrosse W, soccer, swimming, tennis, track and field, volleyball W, wrestling M. **Intramural:** Badminton, basketball, bowling, golf M, handball M, lacrosse M, soccer, softball, squash, tennis, volleyball.

STUDENT SERVICES. Aptitude testing, career counseling, employment service for undergraduates, freshman orientation, health services, on-campus day care, personal counseling, placement service for graduates, minority student affairs, services/facilities for handicapped.

ANNUAL EXPENSES. Tuition and fees (1992-93): $4,046, $7,380 additional for out-of-state students. **Room and board:** $3,902. **Books and supplies:** $600. **Other expenses:** $800.

FINANCIAL AID. 23% of freshmen, 46% of continuing students receive some form of aid. 96% of grants, 72% of loans, 25% of jobs based on need. 290 enrolled freshmen were judged to have need, all were offered aid. Academic, athletic scholarships available. **Aid applications:** No closing date; priority given to applications received by February 15; applicants notified on a rolling basis beginning on or about April 10; must reply within 4 weeks.

ADDRESS/TELEPHONE. Virginia Carey, Dean of Admissions, College of William and Mary, Williamsburg, VA 23187-8795. (804) 221-4223.

Commonwealth College
Virginia Beach, Virginia CB code: 3707

2-year proprietary business, junior college, coed. **Undergraduate enrollment:** 98 men, 324 women full time; 8 men, 28 women part time. **Location:** Suburban campus in large city. **Calendar:** Quarter. **Additional facts:** Central Library for Virginia Beach adjacent to college. Four branch campuses at Hampton, Norfolk, Portsmouth, Richmond.

FRESHMAN ADMISSIONS. Selection criteria: Test scores and essay most important.

ANNUAL EXPENSES. Tuition and fees (1992-93): $5,720. **Room and board:** $3,375. **Books and supplies:** $750. **Other expenses:** $300.

ADDRESS/TELEPHONE. Kathryn Lyle, Dean of Admissions, Commonwealth College, 4160 Virginia Beach Boulevard, Virginia Beach, VA 23452. (804) 340-0222. (800) 735-2421. Fax: (804) 486-7982.

Dabney S. Lancaster Community College
Clifton Forge, Virginia CB code: 5139

2-year public community college, coed. Founded in 1967. **Accreditation:** Regional. **Undergraduate enrollment:** 212 men, 327 women full time; 429 men, 671 women part time. **Faculty:** 35 total, 6 with doctorates or other terminal degrees. **Location:** Rural campus in small town; 55 miles from Roanoke. **Calendar:** Semester, extensive summer session. **Microcomputers:** 60 located in libraries, classrooms, computer centers. **Special facilities:** Obstacle courses, modern sawmill, art displays.

DEGREES OFFERED. AA, AS, AAS. 120 associate degrees awarded in 1992. 15% in agriculture, 12% business and management, 10% education, 7% engineering technologies, 30% health sciences, 15% multi/interdisciplinary studies, 5% parks/recreation, protective services, public affairs.

UNDERGRADUATE MAJORS. Business administration and management, business and office, business computer/console/peripheral equipment operation, business data processing and related programs, computer programming, criminal justice technology, data processing, drafting, drafting and design technology, education, electronic technology, engineering and engineering-related technologies, forest products processing technology, forestry and related sciences, law enforcement and corrections technologies, liberal/general studies, mechanical design technology, nursing, paper engineering, physical sciences, secretarial and related programs.

ACADEMIC PROGRAMS. 2-year transfer program, cooperative education, double major, dual enrollment of high school students, honors program, independent study, internships, telecourses. **Remedial services:** Learning center, preadmission summer program, reduced course load, remedial instruction, special counselor, tutoring. **Placement/credit:** CLEP Subject, institutional tests.

ACADEMIC REQUIREMENTS. Freshmen must earn minimum GPA of 2.0 to continue in good standing. 80% of freshmen return for sophomore year. Students must declare major on enrollment. **Graduation requirements:** 97 hours for associate (45 in major). Most students required to take courses in English, humanities, mathematics, social sciences.

FRESHMAN ADMISSIONS. Selection criteria: Open admissions. Selective admissions to specific curricula. Course recommendations vary according to planned curriculum.

1992 FRESHMAN CLASS PROFILE. 215 men, 299 women enrolled. **Characteristics:** 97% from in state, 100% commute, 4% have minority backgrounds. Average age is 24.

FALL-TERM APPLICATIONS. No fee. No closing date; priority given to applications received by April 15; applicants notified on a rolling basis beginning on or about February 1. Interview required for nursing applicants. Deferred and early admission available. High school diploma or GED required for applicants under 18. Counseling, guidance and placement test required of all incoming students.

STUDENT LIFE. Activities: Student government, choral groups, drama, various social, religious and service clubs on campus.

ATHLETICS. Intercollegiate: Basketball M. **Intramural:** Basketball, bowling, softball, table tennis, volleyball.

STUDENT SERVICES. Aptitude testing, career counseling, employment service for undergraduates, freshman orientation, personal counseling, placement service for graduates, veterans counselor, free tutorial service, services/facilities for handicapped.

ANNUAL EXPENSES. Tuition and fees: $1,342, $3,030 additional for out-of-state students. **Books and supplies:** $500. **Other expenses:** $1,500.

FINANCIAL AID. 50% of freshmen, 62% of continuing students receive some form of aid. 91% of grants, 73% of loans, all jobs based on need. 275 enrolled freshmen were judged to have need, all were offered aid. Academic scholarships available. **Aid applications:** No closing date; priority given to applications received by June 1; applicants notified on a rolling basis beginning on or about June 15; must reply within 3 weeks.

ADDRESS/TELEPHONE. Gary Keener, Director Continuing Education, Dabney S. Lancaster Community College, PO Box 1000, Clifton Forge, VA 24422-1000. (703) 862-4246. Fax: (703) 862-2398.

Danville Community College
Danville, Virginia CB code: 5163

2-year public community college, coed. Founded in 1967. **Accreditation:** Regional. **Undergraduate enrollment:** 502 men, 587 women full time; 1,205 men, 1,784 women part time. **Faculty:** 132 total (59 full time), 14 with doctorates or other terminal degrees. **Location:** Suburban campus in small city; 45 miles from Greensboro, North Carolina. **Calendar:** Semester, limited summer session. **Microcomputers:** 45 located in libraries, computer centers. **Special facilities:** Natural history museum.

DEGREES OFFERED. AA, AS, AAS. 120 associate degrees awarded in 1992.

UNDERGRADUATE MAJORS. Accounting, automotive technology, business administration and management, business and management, business and office, business data programming, computer programming, drafting, early childhood education, education, elementary education, engineering, engineering and engineering-related technologies, general science, graphic and printing production, junior high education, law enforcement and corrections technologies, liberal/general studies, marketing and distribution, mathematics, public administration, secondary education, secretarial and related programs, social work, teacher aide.

ACADEMIC PROGRAMS. 2-year transfer program, double major, dual enrollment of high school students, internships. **Remedial services:** Learning center, preadmission summer program, reduced course load, remedial instruction, tutoring. **Placement/credit:** AP, institutional tests.

ACADEMIC REQUIREMENTS. Freshmen must earn minimum GPA of 1.5 to continue in good standing. Students must declare major on enrollment. **Graduation requirements:** Most students required to take courses in English.

FRESHMAN ADMISSIONS. Selection criteria: Open admissions. Selective admissions to some programs.

1992 FRESHMAN CLASS PROFILE. Characteristics: 98% from in state, 100% commute, 22% have minority backgrounds, 1% are foreign students.

FALL-TERM APPLICATIONS. No fee. No closing date; priority given to applications received by August 23; applicants notified on a rolling basis beginning on or about January 15.

STUDENT LIFE. Activities: Student government, student newspaper, choral groups, fraternities, sororities.

ATHLETICS. Intramural: Basketball, bowling, softball, tennis, volleyball.

STUDENT SERVICES. Career counseling, employment service for undergraduates, freshman orientation, personal counseling, placement service for graduates, services/facilities for handicapped.

ANNUAL EXPENSES. Tuition and fees: $1,325, $3,030 additional for out-of-state students. **Books and supplies:** $500. **Other expenses:** $1,024.

FINANCIAL AID. All grants, all jobs based on need. **Aid applications:** No closing date; applicants notified on a rolling basis beginning on or about May 1; must reply within 10 days.

ADDRESS/TELEPHONE. Dr. Grady Tuck, Coordinator of Admissions and Records, Danville Community College, 1008 Bonner Avenue, Danville, VA 24541. (804) 797-3553.

Eastern Mennonite College

Harrisonburg, Virginia CB code: 5181

Admissions: 97% of applicants accepted
Based on: ••• Essay, school record, test scores
•• Interview, recommendations, religious affiliation/commitment
• Activities
Completion: 91% of freshmen end year in good standing
65% graduate, 20% of these enter graduate study

4-year private liberal arts, seminary college, coed, affiliated with Mennonite Church. Founded in 1917. **Accreditation:** Regional. **Undergraduate enrollment:** 370 men, 519 women full time; 30 men, 39 women part time. **Graduate enrollment:** 45 men, 11 women full time; 30 men, 24 women part time. **Faculty:** 91 total (70 full time), 31 with doctorates or other terminal degrees. **Location:** Rural campus in large town; 110 miles from Richmond and Washington, D.C. **Calendar:** Semester, limited summer session. **Microcomputers:** 72 located in libraries, classrooms, computer centers. **Special facilities:** Anabaptist historical library, planetarium, observatory, natural history museum. **Additional facts:** Located in Shenandoah Valley. Courses offered at campus in Lancaster, PA.

DEGREES OFFERED. AA, AS, AAS, BA, BS, M.Div. 4 associate degrees awarded in 1992. 50% in teacher education, 50% multi/interdisciplinary studies. 267 bachelor's degrees awarded. 16% in business and management, 22% teacher education, 9% health sciences, 6% life sciences, 15% multi/interdisciplinary studies, 9% parks/recreation, protective services, public affairs, 5% psychology. Graduate degrees offered in 1 major field of study.

UNDERGRADUATE MAJORS. Associate: Bible studies, business data processing and related programs, data processing, legal assistant/paralegal, liberal/general studies, teacher aide. **Bachelor's:** Accounting, Bible studies, biology, business administration and management, business and management, chemistry, computer and information sciences, early childhood education, education of the emotionally handicapped, education of the mentally handicapped, elementary education, English, English education, fine arts, food management, food science and nutrition, foreign languages education, French, German, history, international agriculture, junior high education, liberal/general studies, mathematics, mathematics education, medical laboratory technologies, music, music education, nursing, physical education, psychology, recreation and community services technologies, religion, science education, secondary education, social science education, social sciences, social studies education, social work, sociology, Spanish, specific learning disabilities, theological studies, youth ministry.

ACADEMIC PROGRAMS. Double major, dual enrollment of high school students, honors program, independent study, internships, study abroad, teacher preparation, Washington semester. **Remedial services:** Learning center, reduced course load, special counselor, tutoring. **Placement/credit:** AP, CLEP General and Subject, institutional tests.

ACADEMIC REQUIREMENTS. Freshmen must earn minimum GPA of 2.0 to continue in good standing. 78% of freshmen return for sophomore year. Students must declare major by end of first year. **Graduation requirements:** 64 hours for associate (30 in major), 128 hours for bachelor's (35 in major). Most students required to take courses in arts/fine arts, English, history, humanities, mathematics, philosophy/religion, biological/physical sciences, social sciences. **Postgraduate studies:** 6% from 2-year programs enter 4-year programs. 3% enter medical school, 6% enter MBA programs, 11% enter other graduate study. **Additional information:** Missions and peace studies programs available.

FRESHMAN ADMISSIONS. Selection criteria: Rank in top half of class recommended, personal statement also important. **High school preparation:** 18 units recommended. Recommended units include English 4, foreign language 2, mathematics 3, social science 3 and science 3. **Test requirements:** SAT or ACT; score report by August 1. **Additional information:** Conditional admission possible for motivated applicants who fail to reach minimum admissions requirements.

1992 FRESHMAN CLASS PROFILE. 168 men applied, 158 accepted, 105 enrolled; 215 women applied, 213 accepted, 131 enrolled. 55% had high school GPA of 3.0 or higher, 40% between 2.0 and 2.99. 17% were in top tenth and 41% were in top quarter of graduating class. **Academic background:** Mid 50% of enrolled freshmen had SAT-V between 370-530, SAT-M between 400-570; ACT composite between 21-27. 83% submitted SAT scores, 17% submitted ACT scores. **Characteristics:** 33% from in state, 87% live in college housing, 10% have minority backgrounds, 3% are foreign students. Average age is 19.

FALL-TERM APPLICATIONS. $15 fee, may be waived for applicants with need. Closing date August 1; applicants notified on a rolling basis. Essay required. Interview recommended for learning disabled applicants. Deferred and early admission available. Application by March 1 strongly encouraged.

STUDENT LIFE. Housing: Dormitories (men, women, coed); apartment, cooperative housing available. **Activities:** Student government, radio, student newspaper, yearbook, literary annual (The Phoenix), choral groups, drama, jazz band, music ensembles, musical theater, opera, symphony orchestra, Young People's Christian Association, peace club, Mission Fellowship, Hispanic Club, African-American Student Allience. **Additional information:** Alcohol and drug use by students prohibited. Assembly attendance expected two-thirds of time.

ATHLETICS. NCAA. **Intercollegiate:** Baseball M, basketball, cross-country, field hockey W, soccer M, softball W, tennis, track and field, volleyball. **Intramural:** Badminton, basketball, bowling, racquetball M, soccer, softball, table tennis M, tennis, track and field, volleyball.

STUDENT SERVICES. Aptitude testing, career counseling, employment service for undergraduates, freshman orientation, health services, personal counseling, placement service for graduates, services/facilities for handicapped.

ANNUAL EXPENSES. Tuition and fees: $9,100. **Room and board:** $3,600. **Books and supplies:** $600. **Other expenses:** $400.

FINANCIAL AID. 90% of freshmen, 90% of continuing students receive some form of aid. Grants, loans, jobs available. Academic, state/district residency, leadership, religious affiliation scholarships available. **Aid applications:** No closing date; priority given to applications received by May 1; applicants notified on a rolling basis; must reply within 30 days.

ADDRESS/TELEPHONE. Ellen B. Miller, Director of Admissions, Eastern Mennonite College, 1200 Park Road, Harrisonburg, VA 22801-9980. (703) 432-4118. (800) 368-2665. Fax: (703) 432-4444.

Eastern Shore Community College

Melfa, Virginia CB code: 5844

2-year public community college, coed. Founded in 1971. **Accreditation:** Regional. **Undergraduate enrollment:** 75 men, 141 women full time; 94 men, 312 women part time. **Faculty:** 46 total (27 full time), 2 with doctorates or other terminal degrees. **Location:** Rural campus in rural community; 70 miles from Norfolk. **Calendar:** Semester, limited summer session. **Microcomputers:** 33 located in libraries, computer centers.

DEGREES OFFERED. AAS. 42 associate degrees awarded in 1992. 15% in business and management, 15% business/office and marketing/distribution, 8% computer sciences, 5% education, 10% engineering technologies, 31% health sciences, 8% multi/interdisciplinary studies, 8% physical sciences.

UNDERGRADUATE MAJORS. Business and management, business and office, computer and information sciences, education, electronic technology, liberal/general studies, nursing, science technologies, secretarial and related programs.

ACADEMIC PROGRAMS. 2-year transfer program, dual enrollment of high school students, cross-registration. **Remedial services:** Learning center, reduced course load, remedial instruction, tutoring. **Placement/credit:** AP, CLEP General and Subject, institutional tests; 30 credit hours maximum for associate degree.

ACADEMIC REQUIREMENTS. Freshmen must earn minimum GPA of 1.5 to continue in good standing. 55% of freshmen return for sophomore year. Students must declare major by end of first year. **Graduation requirements:** 65 hours for associate. Most students required to take courses in computer science, English, history, mathematics, biological/physical sciences, social sciences.

FRESHMAN ADMISSIONS. Selection criteria: Open admissions. **High school preparation:** 18 units recommended. Recommended units include English 4, mathematics 3, social science 2 and science 2. **Additional information:** All students must demonstrate ability to benefit by achieving minimum scores on institutional placement tests. Those who do not achieve minimum scores admitted but must enroll in developmental courses.

1992 FRESHMAN CLASS PROFILE. 215 men and women enrolled. **Characteristics:** 100% commute. Average age is 28.

FALL-TERM APPLICATIONS. No fee. Closing date August 16; applicants notified on a rolling basis. Interview required for full-time status applicants. Early admission available.

STUDENT LIFE. Activities: Student government, Phi Theta Kappa, Phi Beta Lambda.

ATHLETICS. Intramural: Softball, volleyball.

STUDENT SERVICES. Aptitude testing, career counseling, employment service for undergraduates, freshman orientation, health services, personal counseling, placement service for graduates, veterans counselor, services/facilities for handicapped.

ANNUAL EXPENSES. Tuition and fees: $1,335, $3,030 additional for out-of-state students. **Books and supplies:** $450. **Other expenses:** $2,790.

FINANCIAL AID. 66% of freshmen, 25% of continuing students receive some form of aid. 94% of grants, 92% of jobs based on need. Academic, state/district residency, leadership, minority scholarships available. **Aid applications:** No closing date; priority given to applications received by June 1; applicants notified on a rolling basis beginning on or about June 15; must reply within 2 weeks.

ADDRESS/TELEPHONE. Richard E. Jenkins, Dean of Student Services, Eastern Shore Community College, Route 1, Box 6, Melfa, VA 23410-9755. (804) 787-5912. Fax: (804) 787-5919.

Emory and Henry College

Emory, Virginia CB code: 5185

Admissions: 76% of applicants accepted
Based on: ••• Essay, school record
•• Activities, recommendations, test scores
• Interview, special talents
Completion: 90% of freshmen end year in good standing
63% graduate, 20% of these enter graduate study

4-year private liberal arts college, coed, affiliated with United Methodist Church. Founded in 1836. **Accreditation:** Regional. **Undergraduate enrollment:** 380 men, 354 women full time; 11 men, 31 women part time. **Faculty:** 75 total (64 full time), 55 with doctorates or other terminal degrees. **Location:** Rural campus in rural community; 25 miles from Bristol. **Calendar:** Semester, limited summer session. **Microcomputers:** Located in libraries, classrooms, computer centers. **Special facilities:** Observatory.

DEGREES OFFERED. BA, BS. 227 bachelor's degrees awarded in 1992. 27% in business and management, 7% communications, 14% teacher education, 7% letters/literature, 7% psychology, 20% social sciences.

UNDERGRADUATE MAJORS. Accounting, applied mathematics, art education, bioengineering and biomedical engineering, biology, business administration and management, chemical engineering, chemistry, civil engineering, classics, clinical laboratory science, communications, computer and information sciences, computer mathematics, creative writing, dramatic arts, early childhood education, economics, electrical/electronics/communications engineering, elementary education, engineering, engineering and other disciplines, English, English education, English literature, foreign languages education, French, geography, German, history, journalism, junior high education, Latin, liberal/general studies, mathematics, mathematics education, mechanical engineering, music, music education, music history and appreciation, music performance, music theory and composition, philosophy, physical education, physics, political science and government, predentistry, prelaw, premedicine, preveterinary, psychology, pure mathematics, radio/television broadcasting, religion, religious music, science education, secondary education, social studies education, sociology, Spanish, studio art.

ACADEMIC PROGRAMS. Double major, dual enrollment of high school students, independent study, internships, student-designed major, study abroad, teacher preparation; liberal arts/career combination in engineering, forestry, health sciences. **Remedial services:** Learning center, preadmission summer program, reduced course load, special counselor, tutoring, preparatory mathematics and writing laboratories. **Placement/credit:** AP, CLEP Subject, institutional tests.

ACADEMIC REQUIREMENTS. Freshmen must earn minimum GPA of 1.8 to continue in good standing. 85% of freshmen return for sophomore year. Students must declare major by end of second year. **Graduation requirements:** 116 hours for bachelor's (30 in major). Most students required to take courses in English, history, humanities, mathematics, philosophy/religion, biological/physical sciences, social sciences.

FRESHMAN ADMISSIONS. Selection criteria: Essay or personal statement, school achievement record, test scores, school and community activities, recommendations, interview considered. **High school preparation:** 16 units required; 22 recommended. Required units include English 4, foreign language 2, mathematics 3, social science 2 and science 2. One unit fine arts recommended. **Test requirements:** SAT or ACT; score report by May 1.

1992 FRESHMAN CLASS PROFILE. 399 men applied, 281 accepted, 109 enrolled; 230 women applied, 196 accepted, 79 enrolled. 71% had high school GPA of 3.0 or higher, 29% between 2.0 and 2.99. 30% were in top tenth and 60% were in top quarter of graduating class. **Academic background:** Mid 50% of enrolled freshmen had SAT-V between 400-540, SAT-M between 440-570; ACT composite between 21-28. 90% submitted SAT scores, 10% submitted ACT scores. **Characteristics:** 82% from in state, 80% live in college housing, 3% have minority backgrounds, 1% are foreign students, 40% join fraternities/sororities. Average age is 18.

FALL-TERM APPLICATIONS. $20 fee, may be waived for applicants with need. No closing date; applicants notified on a rolling basis; must reply by May 1 or within 4 weeks if notified thereafter. Essay required. Interview recommended. CRDA. Deferred and early admission available.

STUDENT LIFE. Housing: Dormitories (men, women). **Activities:** Student government, magazine, radio, student newspaper, yearbook, choral groups, dance, drama, music ensembles, musical theater, opera, symphony orchestra, fraternities, sororities, Young Democrats, Young Republicans, Alpha Phi Omega, Fellowship of Christian Athletes, Kerygma, college church class, bible study group.

ATHLETICS. NCAA. **Intercollegiate:** Baseball M, basketball, cross-country, football M, tennis, track and field, volleyball W. **Intramural:** Badminton, basketball, bowling, football, golf, racquetball, rugby M, soccer M, softball, swimming, table tennis, tennis, track and field, volleyball, water polo.

STUDENT SERVICES. Career counseling, employment service for undergraduates, freshman orientation, health services, personal counseling, placement service for graduates.

ANNUAL EXPENSES. Tuition and fees: $8,546. **Room and board:** $4,230. **Books and supplies:** $700. **Other expenses:** $1,000.

FINANCIAL AID. 94% of freshmen, 89% of continuing students receive some form of aid. 35% of grants, 96% of loans, all jobs based on need. 130 enrolled freshmen were judged to have need, all were offered aid. Academic, state/district residency, leadership, religious affiliation scholarships available. **Aid applications:** Closing date April 1; applicants notified on or about April 15; must reply within 2 weeks. **Additional information:** Virginia residents eligible for in-state tuition grants.

ADDRESS/TELEPHONE. Jean R. Luce, Dean of Admissions, Emory and Henry College, Emory, VA 24327. (703) 944-4121. (800) 848-5493.

Ferrum College

Ferrum, Virginia CB code: 5213

Admissions: 78% of applicants accepted
Based on: ••• School record
•• Activities, interview, recommendations, test scores
• Essay, special talents
Completion: 83% of freshmen end year in good standing
25% graduate, 12% of these enter graduate study

4-year private liberal arts college, coed, affiliated with United Methodist Church. Founded in 1913. **Accreditation:** Regional. **Undergraduate enrollment:** 680 men, 451 women full time; 38 men, 65 women part time. **Faculty:** 112 total (87 full time), 51 with doctorates or other terminal degrees. **Location:** Rural campus in rural community; 35 miles from Roanoke. **Calendar:** Semester, limited summer session. **Microcomputers:** 100 located in dormitories, libraries, computer centers. **Special facilities:** Blue Ridge Institute and Farm Museum.

DEGREES OFFERED. BA, BS. 159 bachelor's degrees awarded in 1992. 6% in agriculture, 27% business and management, 11% life sciences, 8% multi/interdisciplinary studies, 14% psychology, 20% social sciences.

UNDERGRADUATE MAJORS. Accounting, agricultural education, agricultural sciences, biology, business administration and management, business and management, chemistry, computer and information sciences, decision support systems, dramatic arts, English, English education, environmental science, financial management, fine arts, foreign languages (multiple emphasis), foreign languages education, French, history, international relations, international studies, liberal/general studies, management science, marketing management, mathematics, mathematics education, medical laboratory technologies, music, parks and recreation management, philosophy, political science and government, preprofessional science, psychology, religion, Russian, science education, secondary education, small business management and ownership, social studies education, social work, Spanish.

ACADEMIC PROGRAMS. 2-year transfer program, double major, independent study, internships, study abroad, teacher preparation. **Remedial services:** Learning center, preadmission summer program, reduced course load, special counselor, tutoring. **Placement/credit:** AP, CLEP General and Subject, institutional tests; 32 credit hours maximum for bachelor's degree.

ACADEMIC REQUIREMENTS. Freshmen must earn minimum GPA of 1.4 to continue in good standing. 65% of freshmen return for sophomore year. Students must declare major by end of second year. **Graduation requirements:** 127 hours for bachelor's (54 in major). Most students required to take courses in arts/fine arts, English, history, humanities, mathematics, philosophy/religion, biological/physical sciences, social sciences.

FRESHMAN ADMISSIONS. Selection criteria: High school record most important, followed by test scores, counselor recommendations, areas of intended college study, and extracurricular activities. **High school preparation:** 16 units recommended. Recommended units include English 4, mathematics 3, social science 3 and science 1. **Test requirements:** SAT or ACT; score report by August 15.

1992 FRESHMAN CLASS PROFILE. 820 men applied, 642 accepted, 232 enrolled; 529 women applied, 414 accepted, 142 enrolled. 7% had high school GPA of 3.0 or higher, 59% between 2.0 and 2.99. 12% were in top tenth of graduating class. **Academic background:** Mid 50% of enrolled freshmen had SAT-V between 330-430, SAT-M between 360-470; ACT composite between 17-20. 98% submitted SAT scores, 2% submitted ACT scores. **Characteristics:** 9% from in state, 92% live in college housing, 12% have minority backgrounds, 1% are foreign students. Average age is 18.

FALL-TERM APPLICATIONS. $20 fee, may be waived for applicants with need. Closing date August 15; priority given to applications received by May 1; applicants notified on a rolling basis; must reply within 4 weeks. Interview recommended. Essay recommended. Deferred and early admission available.

STUDENT LIFE. Housing: Dormitories (men, women, coed); apartment housing available. **Activities:** Student government, magazine, radio, student newspaper, yearbook, choral groups, dance, drama, jazz band, music ensembles, musical theater, pep band.

ATHLETICS. NCAA. **Intercollegiate:** Baseball M, basketball, football M, golf M, horseback riding, lacrosse M, soccer, softball W, tennis, volleyball W. **Intramural:** Basketball, bowling, lacrosse M, softball, swimming, table tennis, tennis, volleyball, water polo M.

STUDENT SERVICES. Career counseling, employment service for undergraduates, freshman orientation, health services, personal counseling, placement service for graduates, veterans counselor, services/facilities for handicapped.

ANNUAL EXPENSES. Tuition and fees: $8,800. **Room and board:** $4,000. **Books and supplies:** $500. **Other expenses:** $1,200.

FINANCIAL AID. 62% of freshmen, 94% of continuing students receive some form of aid. 62% of grants, 97% of loans, 95% of jobs based on need. Academic, state/district residency, leadership, religious affiliation, minority scholarships available. **Aid applications:** No closing date; priority given to applications received by June 1; applicants notified on a rolling basis beginning on or about February 15; must reply within 2 weeks.

ADDRESS/TELEPHONE. Robert H. Bailey, Director of Admissions, Ferrum College, Ferrum, VA 24088. (703) 365-4290. (800) 868-9797. Fax: (703) 365-4203.

George Mason University

Fairfax, Virginia CB code: 5827

Admissions: 78% of applicants accepted
Based on: ••• School record, test scores
• Activities, essay, interview, recommendations, special talents
Completion: 41% graduate, 28% of these enter graduate study

4-year public university, coed. Founded in 1957. **Accreditation:** Regional. **Undergraduate enrollment:** 4,321 men, 5,205 women full time; 1,512 men, 2,061 women part time. **Graduate enrollment:** 617 men, 712 women full time; 2,686 men, 3,052 women part time. **Faculty:** 1,367 total (918 full time), 240 with doctorates or other terminal degrees. **Location:** Suburban campus in large town; 15 miles from Washington, D.C. **Calendar:** Semester, extensive summer session. Saturday and extensive evening/early morning classes. **Microcomputers:** 510 located in dormitories, libraries, classrooms, computer centers, campus-wide network. **Special facilities:** Library of Congress Federal Theater Project collection, Patriot Center, sports complex, center for arts. **Additional facts:** Resources of nation's capital.

DEGREES OFFERED. BA, BS, BFA, MA, MS, MBA, MFA, MEd, PhD, EdD, JD. 2,516 bachelor's degrees awarded in 1992. 17% in business and management, 5% communications, 8% education, 5% engineering, 7% health sciences, 7% letters/literature, 5% parks/recreation, protective services, public affairs, 22% social sciences. Graduate degrees offered in 46 major fields of study.

UNDERGRADUATE MAJORS. Accounting, American studies, anthropology, art history, biology, business administration and management, chemistry, classics, communications, computer and information sciences, computer engineering, dance, dramatic arts, economics, education, electrical/electronics/communications engineering, English, European studies, finance, foreign languages (multiple emphasis), geography, geology, health education, history, international relations, international studies, Latin American studies, law enforcement and corrections, liberal/general studies, management information systems, management science, marketing management, mathematics, music, music education, nursing, parks and recreation management, philosophy, physical education, physics, political science and government, psychology, public administration, Russian and Slavic studies, social work, sociology, studio art, systems engineering.

ACADEMIC PROGRAMS. Accelerated program, cooperative education, double major, dual enrollment of high school students, independent study, internships, student-designed major, study abroad, teacher preparation, cross-registration, alternative interdisciplinary core curriculum program. **Remedial services:** Learning center, preadmission summer program, tutoring, course in English composition for international students. **ROTC:** Air Force, Army. **Placement/credit:** AP, CLEP Subject, institutional tests; 30 credit hours maximum for bachelor's degree.

ACADEMIC REQUIREMENTS. Freshmen must earn minimum GPA of 2.0 to continue in good standing. 71% of freshmen return for sophomore year. Students must declare major by end of second year. **Graduation requirements:** 120 hours for bachelor's. Most students required to take courses in English, history, humanities, mathematics, biological/physical sciences, social sciences. **Postgraduate studies:** 28% enter other graduate study.

FRESHMAN ADMISSIONS. Selection criteria: Test scores, class rank, academic record with emphasis on courses taken, GPA, special talents and abilities, and counselor recommendations considered. **High school preparation:** 16 units required; 22 recommended. Required and recommended units include English 4, foreign language 2-4, mathematics 3-4, social science 3-4 and science 1-2. Additional mathematics and science for engineering, mathematics, and computer science applicants. **Test requirements:** SAT or ACT (SAT preferred); score report by February 1. ACH required of English and mathematics applicants. Score report by March 15.

1992 FRESHMAN CLASS PROFILE. 2,468 men applied, 1,853 accepted, 1,206 enrolled; 3,108 women applied, 2,513 accepted, 1,444 enrolled. **Characteristics:** Average age is 19.

FALL-TERM APPLICATIONS. $25 fee, may be waived for applicants with need. Closing date February 1; priority given to applications received by January 1; applicants notified on or about April 1; must reply by May 1. Audition required for music, dance applicants. Essay recommended. CRDA. Early admission available.

STUDENT LIFE. Housing: Dormitories (men, women, coed); apartment, fraternity, handicapped housing available. **Activities:** Student government, magazine, radio, student newspaper, television, yearbook, forensics team, debate team, choral groups, concert band, dance, drama, jazz band, music ensembles, musical theater, pep band, symphony orchestra, fraternities, sororities.

ATHLETICS. NCAA. **Intercollegiate:** Baseball M, basketball, cross-country, golf M, rifle, soccer, softball W, tennis, track and field, volleyball, wrestling M. **Intramural:** Basketball, lacrosse M, racquetball, soccer, softball, table tennis, volleyball.

STUDENT SERVICES. Aptitude testing, career counseling, employment service for undergraduates, freshman orientation, health services, personal counseling, placement service for graduates, veterans counselor, services/facilities for handicapped.

ANNUAL EXPENSES. Tuition and fees (projected): $3,840, $6,240 additional for out-of-state students. **Room and board:** $5,600. **Books and supplies:** $610. **Other expenses:** $1,100.

FINANCIAL AID. 38% of freshmen, 32% of continuing students receive some form of aid. 79% of grants, 79% of loans, 61% of jobs based on need. Academic, music/drama, athletic, state/district residency, leadership, minority scholarships available. **Aid applications:** No closing date; priority given to applications received by March 1; applicants notified on a rolling basis beginning on or about April 15; must reply by May 1 or within 3 weeks if notified thereafter.

ADDRESS/TELEPHONE. Dr. Patricia M. Riordan, Dean of Admissions, George Mason University, 4400 University Drive, Fairfax, VA 22030-4444. (703) 993-2400. Fax: (703) 993-2392.

Germanna Community College

Locust Grove, Virginia CB code: 5276

2-year public community college, coed. Founded in 1969. **Accreditation:** Regional. **Undergraduate enrollment:** 300 men, 500 women full time; 540 men, 1,200 women part time. **Location:** Rural campus in rural community; 18 miles from Fredericksburg, and 15 miles from Culpeper. **Calendar:** Semester.

FRESHMAN ADMISSIONS. Selection criteria: Open admissions. Selective admissions to nursing program with local applicants given preference. All new students must be assessed and possibly required to take placement tests in English and mathematics.

ANNUAL EXPENSES. Tuition and fees (1992-93): $1,239, $3,030 additional for out-of-state students. **Books and supplies:** $300. **Other expenses:** $1,274.

ADDRESS/TELEPHONE. Linda Crocker, Registrar, Germanna Community College, PO Box 339, Locust Grove, VA 22508. (703) 423-1333.

Hampden-Sydney College

Hampden-Sydney, Virginia CB code: 5291

Admissions: 75% of applicants accepted
Based on: ••• Essay, recommendations, school record, test scores
•• Activities
• Interview, special talents
Completion: 90% of freshmen end year in good standing
65% graduate, 25% of these enter graduate study

4-year private liberal arts college, men only, affiliated with Presbyterian Church (USA). Founded in 1776. **Accreditation:** Regional. **Undergraduate enrollment:** 945 men full time. **Faculty:** 90 total (66 full time), 70 with doctorates or other terminal degrees. **Location:** Rural campus in rural community; 70 miles from Richmond. **Calendar:** Semester, limited summer session. **Microcomputers:** 140 located in dormitories, libraries, classrooms, computer centers, campus-wide network. **Special facilities:** Museum, international communications center.

DEGREES OFFERED. BA, BS. 224 bachelor's degrees awarded in 1992. 22% in business and management, 11% letters/literature, 9% life sciences, 6% mathematics, 9% psychology, 33% social sciences.

UNDERGRADUATE MAJORS. Biochemistry, biological and physical sciences, biology, biophysics, business economics, chemistry, classics, computer mathematics, economics, English, French, German, Greek (classical), history, humanities, Latin, mathematics, philosophy, physical chemistry, physics, political science and government, psychology, religion, Spanish.

ACADEMIC PROGRAMS. Double major, honors program, independent study, internships, semester at sea, study abroad, Washington semester, cross-registration, Appalachian Semester, junior year exchange program with members of Virginia consortium; liberal arts/career combination in engineering. **Remedial services:** Reduced course load, tutoring, study skills program, writing laboratory. **ROTC:** Army. **Placement/credit:** AP, IB, institutional tests.

ACADEMIC REQUIREMENTS. Freshmen must earn minimum GPA of 1.5 to continue in good standing. 86% of freshmen return for sophomore year. Students must declare major by end of second year. **Graduation requirements:** 120 hours for bachelor's (30 in major). Most students required to take courses in arts/fine arts, English, foreign languages, history, humanities, mathematics, philosophy/religion, biological/physical sciences, social sciences. **Postgraduate studies:** 5% enter law school, 6% enter medical school, 8% enter MBA programs, 6% enter other graduate study.

FRESHMAN ADMISSIONS. Selection criteria: High school academic record most important, recommendations, test scores, school and community activities considered. **High school preparation:** 16 units required. Required units include English 4, foreign language 2, mathematics 3, social science 1 and science 2. Sciences must include 1 laboratory science. **Test requirements:** SAT or ACT; score report by March 1.

1992 FRESHMAN CLASS PROFILE. 850 men applied, 638 accepted, 265 enrolled. 17% were in top tenth and 40% were in top quarter of graduating class. **Academic background:** Mid 50% of enrolled freshmen had SAT-V between 450-560, SAT-M between 510-610. 95% submitted SAT scores. **Characteristics:** 51% from in state, 100% live in college housing, 5% have minority backgrounds, 1% are foreign students, 38% join fraternities/sororities. Average age is 18.

FALL-TERM APPLICATIONS. $30 fee, may be waived for applicants with need. Closing date March 1; applicants notified on a rolling basis beginning on or about March 1; must reply by May 1 or within 2 weeks if notified thereafter. Essay required. Interview recommended. CRDA. Early admission available. EDP-F.

STUDENT LIFE. Housing: Dormitories (men); apartment, fraternity housing available. **Activities:** Student government, magazine, radio, student newspaper, yearbook, choral groups, drama, music ensembles, pep band, fraternities, interreligious council, Circle-K, volunteer fire department, debate club, Republican Society, Good Men and Good Citizens (community services), The Outsiders Club,Student Environmental Action Coalition, Museum board.

ATHLETICS. NCAA. **Intercollegiate:** Baseball, basketball, cross-country, fencing, football, golf, lacrosse, rugby, soccer, tennis, volleyball, water polo. **Intramural:** Basketball, football, soccer, softball, volleyball, water polo, wrestling.

STUDENT SERVICES. Aptitude testing, career counseling, employment service for undergraduates, freshman orientation, health services, personal counseling, placement service for graduates, veterans counselor, services/facilities for handicapped.

ANNUAL EXPENSES. Tuition and fees: $12,974. **Room and board:** $4,398. **Books and supplies:** $600. **Other expenses:** $600.

FINANCIAL AID. 62% of freshmen, 70% of continuing students receive some form of aid. 86% of grants, 86% of loans, 44% of jobs based on need. Academic, state/district residency, leadership scholarships available. **Aid applications:** No closing date; priority given to applications received by March 1; applicants notified on a rolling basis beginning on or about March 16; must reply by May 1 or within 2 weeks if notified thereafter.

ADDRESS/TELEPHONE. Robert H. Jones, Dean of Admissions, Hampden-Sydney College, Hampden-Sydney, VA 23943. (804) 223-6120. (800) 755-0733. Fax: (804) 223-6346.

Hampton University
Hampton, Virginia — CB code: 5292

4-year private university and liberal arts college, coed. Founded in 1868. **Accreditation:** Regional. **Undergraduate enrollment:** 4,574 men and women. **Graduate enrollment:** 384 men and women. **Faculty:** 366 total (281 full time). **Location:** Urban campus in small city; 10 miles from Norfolk. **Calendar:** Semester, limited summer session. **Microcomputers:** Located in classrooms. **Special facilities:** Peabody Collection, University Archives, North American Indian, African, Oceanic, and Black American art collection.

DEGREES OFFERED. BA, BS, BArch, MA, MS, MBA, PhD. 843 bachelor's degrees awarded in 1992. Graduate degrees offered in 23 major fields of study.

UNDERGRADUATE MAJORS. Accounting, air traffic control, architecture, art history, aviation management, biology, business administration and management, business and management, chemical engineering, chemistry, commercial art, computer and information sciences, criminal justice studies, dramatic arts, early childhood education, economics, education, education of the deaf and hearing impaired, education of the emotionally handicapped, education of the mentally handicapped, electrical/electronics/communications engineering, elementary education, English, fashion design, fashion merchandising, finance, food science and nutrition, gerontology, history, home economics, individual and family development, journalism, junior high education, marine biology, mathematics, molecular biology, music, nursing, physical education, physics, political science and government, prelaw, premedicine, professional tennis management, psychology, public relations, radio/television broadcasting, recreation therapy, secondary education, secretarial and related programs, social work, sociology, special education, speech correction, speech pathology/audiology, sports management, sports medicine, textiles and clothing.

ACADEMIC PROGRAMS. Accelerated program, cooperative education, honors program, independent study, internships, study abroad, teacher preparation, cross-registration; liberal arts/career combination in engineering. **Remedial services:** Learning center, preadmission summer program, reduced course load, remedial instruction, special counselor, tutoring. **ROTC:** Army, Naval. **Placement/credit:** AP, CLEP Subject, institutional tests. Unlimited number of hours of credit by examination may be counted toward degree.

ACADEMIC REQUIREMENTS. Freshmen must earn minimum GPA of 2.0 to continue in good standing. Students must declare major by end of first year. **Graduation requirements:** 120 hours for bachelor's (83 in major). Most students required to take courses in English, foreign languages, history, humanities, mathematics, biological/physical sciences, social sciences.

FRESHMAN ADMISSIONS. Selection criteria: Academic record, rank in top half of graduating class, extracurricular activities, intended major, test scores are all considered. **High school preparation:** 17 units required. Required units include biological science 1, English 4, mathematics 3, physical science 1 and social science 2. One unit chemistry, 1 unit biology required. **Test requirements:** SAT or ACT; score report by June 30.

1992 FRESHMAN CLASS PROFILE. 1,139 men and women enrolled. **Characteristics:** 27% from in state, 70% live in college housing, 100% have minority backgrounds, 2% are foreign students. Average age is 18.

FALL-TERM APPLICATIONS. $15 fee. Closing date June 1; applicants notified on a rolling basis; must reply within 30 days. Audition required for music applicants. Deferred and early admission available.

STUDENT LIFE. Housing: Dormitories (men, women, coed). **Activities:** Student government, radio, student newspaper, television, yearbook, choral groups, concert band, dance, drama, jazz band, marching band, music ensembles, opera, pep band, symphony orchestra, fraternities, sororities, Student Christian Association.

ATHLETICS. NCAA. **Intercollegiate:** Basketball, cross-country, football M, golf M, rifle, softball W, tennis M, track and field, volleyball W, wrestling M. **Intramural:** Basketball, softball W.

STUDENT SERVICES. Aptitude testing, career counseling, employment service for undergraduates, freshman orientation, health services, personal counseling, placement service for graduates, veterans counselor, services/facilities for handicapped.

ANNUAL EXPENSES. Tuition and fees (1992-93): $7,006. **Room and board:** $3,120. **Books and supplies:** $600. **Other expenses:** $500.

FINANCIAL AID. 70% of freshmen, 64% of continuing students receive some form of aid. Grants, loans, jobs available. Academic, music/drama, athletic, state/district residency, minority scholarships available. **Aid applications:** Closing date June 1; priority given to applications received by March 31; applicants notified on a rolling basis beginning on or about March 1; must reply within 2 weeks.

ADDRESS/TELEPHONE. Dr. Ollie M. Bowman, Dean of Admissions, Hampton University, Hampton, VA 23668. (804) 727-5328. (800) 624-3328.

Hollins College
Roanoke, Virginia — CB code: 5294

Admissions: 81% of applicants accepted
Based on:
••• Recommendations, school record, test scores
•• Activities, essay, special talents
• Interview
Completion: 94% of freshmen end year in good standing
69% graduate, 34% of these enter graduate study

4-year private liberal arts college, women only. Founded in 1842. **Accreditation:** Regional. **Undergraduate enrollment:** 755 women full time; 71 women part time. **Graduate enrollment:** 18 men, 38 women full time; 21 men, 88 women part time. **Faculty:** 103 total (86 full time), 78 with doctorates or other terminal degrees. **Location:** Suburban campus in small city; 2 miles from downtown. **Calendar:** 4-1-4. **Microcomputers:** 165 located in libraries, classrooms, computer centers. Lease or purchase required**Special facilities:** Distinctive writing center, state-of-the-art science facilities, new athletic complex, art gallery, observatory, Communications Research Institute, electron microscope facilities. **Additional facts:** Graduate programs open to both men and women. Member of American Collegiate Consortium for East-West Cultural and Academic Exchange.

DEGREES OFFERED. BA, MA. 206 bachelor's degrees awarded in 1992. 11% in languages, 18% letters/literature, 6% life sciences, 13% psychology, 31% social sciences, 9% visual and performing arts. Graduate degrees offered in 6 major fields of study.

UNDERGRADUATE MAJORS. American studies, art history, biology, chemistry, classics, communications, computer and information sciences, creative writing, dramatic arts, economics, English, French, German, history, interdisciplinery studies, liberal/general studies, mathematics, music, philosophy, physics, political science and government, psychology, religion, sociology, Spanish, studio art.

ACADEMIC PROGRAMS. Accelerated program, double major, honors program, independent study, internships, student-designed major, study abroad, teacher preparation, United Nations semester, Washington semester, cross-registration, numerous college exchange programs; liberal arts/career combination in engineering, health sciences. **Remedial services:** Special counselor, tutoring. **Placement/credit:** AP, institutional tests.

ACADEMIC REQUIREMENTS. Freshmen must earn minimum GPA of 1.8 to continue in good standing. 81% of freshmen return for sophomore year. Students must declare major by end of second year. **Graduation requirements:** 144 hours for bachelor's (32 in major). Most students required to take courses in arts/fine arts, humanities, mathematics, biological/physical sciences, social sciences. **Postgraduate studies:** 3% enter law school, 1% enter medical school, 3% enter MBA programs, 27% enter other graduate study.

FRESHMAN ADMISSIONS. Selection criteria: School achievement record, school recommendation, test scores most important. Writing ability, interview, school and community activities, personal characteristics, leadership skills, talent, and special interests considered. **High school preparation:** 16 units recommended. Recommended units include biological science 1, English 4, foreign language 3, mathematics 3, physical science 2 and social science 3. **Test requirements:** SAT or ACT; score report by March 15. English Composition with 2 other ACH recommended. Score report by March 15.

1992 FRESHMAN CLASS PROFILE. 608 women applied, 490 accepted, 190 enrolled. 61% had high school GPA of 3.0 or higher, 39% between 2.0 and 2.99. 27% were in top tenth and 57% were in top quarter of graduating class. **Academic background:** Mid 50% of enrolled freshmen had SAT-V between 440-540, SAT-M between 460-550; ACT composite between 21-25. 96% submitted SAT scores, 32% submitted ACT scores. **Characteristics:** 32% from in state, 100% live in college housing, 9% have minority backgrounds, 2% are foreign students. Average age is 18.

FALL-TERM APPLICATIONS. $25 fee, may be waived for applicants with need. Closing date February 15; priority given to applications received by February 1; applicants notified on or about April 15; must reply by May 1. Essay required. Interview recommended. CRDA. Deferred and early admission available. EDP-F.

STUDENT LIFE. Housing: Dormitories (women); apartment housing available. Apartments available for upperclassmen, and special housing for fine arts and French majors. **Activities:** Student government, film, magazine, student newspaper, yearbook, choral groups, dance, drama, music ensembles, Religious Life Association, Amnesty International, Multicultural Club, Black Student Alliance, College Democrats, College Republicans, volunteer organizations. **Additional information:** Many opportunities to become involved in organizations, sports, volunteer work. Leaders on the Grow program develops leadership skills. 50% of students study abroad.

ATHLETICS. NCAA. **Intercollegiate:** Basketball, fencing, field hockey, horseback riding, lacrosse, soccer, swimming, tennis, volleyball.

STUDENT SERVICES. Aptitude testing, career counseling, employment service for undergraduates, freshman orientation, health services, on-campus day care, personal counseling, placement service for graduates, special adviser for adult students, services/facilities for handicapped.

ANNUAL EXPENSES. Tuition and fees: $13,170. **Room and board:** $5,300. **Books and supplies:** $500. **Other expenses:** $550.

FINANCIAL AID. 54% of freshmen, 57% of continuing students receive some form of aid. 83% of grants, 98% of loans, 89% of jobs based on need. Academic, music/drama, art, state/district residency, leadership scholarships available. **Aid applications:** Closing date March 31; priority given to applications received by February 15; applicants notified on a rolling basis beginning on or about March 1; must reply by May 1 or within 2 weeks if notified thereafter.

ADDRESS/TELEPHONE. Anne B. Parry, Dean of Admissions and Financial Aid, Hollins College, PO Box 9707, 7916 Williamson Road, N.W, Roanoke, VA 24020-1707. (703) 362-6401. (800) 456-9595. Fax: (703) 362-6642.

J. Sargeant Reynolds Community College
Richmond, Virginia CB code: 5676

2-year public community college, coed. Founded in 1972. **Accreditation:** Regional. **Undergraduate enrollment:** 1,232 men, 1,544 women full time; 3,255 men, 5,716 women part time. **Faculty:** 441 total (213 full time), 47 with doctorates or other terminal degrees. **Location:** Suburban campus in small city. **Calendar:** Semester, extensive summer session. **Microcomputers:** Located in libraries, classrooms, computer centers. **Additional facts:** Campuses in downtown and suburban Richmond and in rural Goochland.

DEGREES OFFERED. AA, AS, AAS. 477 associate degrees awarded in 1992.

UNDERGRADUATE MAJORS. Accounting, air conditioning/heating/refrigeration technology, biological and physical sciences, business administration and management, business and management, business data processing and related programs, business data programming, civil engineering, community services, computer and information sciences, computer technology, dental laboratory technology, drafting, education, electrical/electronics/communications engineering, engineering and engineering-related technologies, fashion merchandising, finance, fire control and safety technology, horticultural science, hotel/motel and restaurant management, law enforcement and corrections technologies, legal assistant/paralegal, legal secretary, liberal/general studies, marketing and distribution, medical assistant, medical laboratory technologies, medical secretary, nursing, occupational therapy assistant, ophthalmic services, secretarial and related programs.

ACADEMIC PROGRAMS. 2-year transfer program, cooperative education, double major, dual enrollment of high school students, independent study, internships, weekend college. **Remedial services:** Learning center, preadmission summer program, reduced course load, remedial instruction, special counselor, tutoring. **ROTC:** Army. **Placement/credit:** AP, CLEP General and Subject, institutional tests.

ACADEMIC REQUIREMENTS. Freshmen must earn minimum GPA of 2.0 to continue in good standing. 68% of freshmen return for sophomore year. **Graduation requirements:** 65 hours for associate (52 in major). Most students required to take courses in English, history, mathematics, social sciences.

FRESHMAN ADMISSIONS. Selection criteria: Open admissions.

1992 FRESHMAN CLASS PROFILE. 205 men and women enrolled. **Characteristics:** 99% from in state, 100% commute, 26% have minority backgrounds.

FALL-TERM APPLICATIONS. No fee. No closing date; applicants notified on a rolling basis. Interview required for medical, engineering, legal, public service applicants. Deferred and early admission available.

STUDENT LIFE. Activities: Student government, magazine, student newspaper, choral groups, Young Democrats, Circle-K, Phi Theta Kappa.

ATHLETICS. Intramural: Archery, badminton, basketball, bowling, cross-country, diving, golf, handball, racquetball, skin diving, soccer, softball, swimming, table tennis, tennis, track and field, volleyball, wrestling.

STUDENT SERVICES. Aptitude testing, career counseling, employment service for undergraduates, on-campus day care, personal counseling, placement service for graduates, veterans counselor, services/facilities for handicapped.

ANNUAL EXPENSES. Tuition and fees: $1,347, $3,030 additional for out-of-state students. **Books and supplies:** $600. **Other expenses:** $900.

FINANCIAL AID. 40% of freshmen, 30% of continuing students receive some form of aid. All grants, 63% of loans, all jobs based on need. **Aid applications:** No closing date; priority given to applications received by June 30; applicants notified on a rolling basis beginning on or about July 15; must reply within 2 weeks.

ADDRESS/TELEPHONE. Susan Marshall, Director of Admissions and Records, J. Sargeant Reynolds Community College, PO Box 85622, Richmond, VA 23285-5622. (804) 371-3270.

James Madison University
Harrisonburg, Virginia CB code: 5392

Admissions: 44% of applicants accepted
Based on: ••• School record
•• Test scores
• Activities, essay, recommendations, special talents
Completion: 90% of freshmen end year in good standing
79% graduate, 18% of these enter graduate study

4-year public university, coed. Founded in 1908. **Accreditation:** Regional. **Undergraduate enrollment:** 4,171 men, 5,220 women full time; 227 men, 169 women part time. **Graduate enrollment:** 163 men, 263 women full time; 142 men, 247 women part time. **Faculty:** 877 total (635 full time), 455 with doctorates or other terminal degrees. **Location:** Rural campus in large town; 120 miles from Washington, DC. **Calendar:** Semester, extensive summer session. Extensive evening/early morning classes. **Microcomputers:** 445 located in dormitories, libraries, classrooms, computer centers, campus-wide network. **Special facilities:** Planetarium, art gallery, life science museum.

DEGREES OFFERED. BA, BS, BFA, MA, MS, MBA, MFA, MEd. 2,297 bachelor's degrees awarded in 1992. 25% in business and management, 8% communications, 10% teacher education, 7% health sciences, 7% letters/literature, 7% psychology, 16% social sciences, 6% visual and performing arts. Graduate degrees offered in 22 major fields of study.

UNDERGRADUATE MAJORS. Accounting, anthropology, art education, art history, biology, business administration and management, business economics, chemistry, communications, computer and information sciences, dance, dramatic arts, early childhood education, economics, English, finance, fine arts, food science and nutrition, foreign languages (multiple emphasis), geography, geology, health education, history, home economics, hotel/motel and restaurant management, information sciences and systems, international business management, international relations, liberal/general studies, marketing and distributive education, marketing management, mathematics, medical laboratory technologies, music, music education, nursing, philosophy, physical education, physics, political science and government, production and operations management, psychology, public administration, public health laboratory science, religion, secretarial and related programs, social sciences, social work, sociology, speech pathology/audiology, trade and industrial education.

ACADEMIC PROGRAMS. Accelerated program, double major, education specialist degree, honors program, independent study, internships, study abroad, teacher preparation, 3-1 bachelor's degree in medical technology. **Remedial services:** Learning center, special counselor, tutoring. **ROTC:** Army. **Placement/credit:** AP, CLEP General and Subject, institutional tests; 30 credit hours maximum for bachelor's degree. CLEP credit awarded only to students seeking Bachelor of General Studies.

ACADEMIC REQUIREMENTS. Freshmen must earn minimum GPA of 2.0 to continue in good standing. 93% of freshmen return for sophomore year. Students must declare major by end of second year. **Graduation requirements:** 128 hours for bachelor's. Most students required to take courses in arts/fine arts, computer science, English, history, humanities, mathematics, philosophy/religion, biological/physical sciences, social sciences. **Postgraduate studies:** 2% enter law school, 1% enter medical school, 2% enter MBA programs, 13% enter other graduate study.

FRESHMAN ADMISSIONS. Selection criteria: Rigor of high school curriculum, as shown by the quantity and quality of courses, most important, followed by class rank, SAT scores, extracurricular activities, and special skills or talents. Recommendations considered. **High school preparation:** 22 units recommended. Recommended units include biological science 4, English 4, foreign language 4, mathematics 4, social science 3 and science 3. **Test requirements:** SAT; score report by January 15.

1992 FRESHMAN CLASS PROFILE. 11,832 men and women applied, 5,201 accepted; 871 men enrolled, 1,171 women enrolled. 32% were in top tenth and 71% were in top quarter of graduating class. **Academic background:** Mid 50% of enrolled freshmen had SAT-V between 460-570, SAT-M between 510-630. 100% submitted SAT scores. **Characteristics:** 70% from in state, 97% live in college housing, 14% have minority backgrounds, 1% are foreign students, 10% join fraternities/sororities. Average age is 18.

FALL-TERM APPLICATIONS. $25 fee, may be waived for applicants with need. Closing date January 15; priority given to applications received by December 1; applicants notified on or about April 1; must reply by May 1. Audition required for music, dance, theater applicants. Portfolio required for art applicants. Essay required. CRDA. Institutional early decision plan. Students who apply by December 1 are reviewed for early admissions. Applicants notified during the week of January 15th and have until May 1 to make deposit.

STUDENT LIFE. Housing: Dormitories (men, women, coed); fraternity, sorority housing available. **Activities:** Student government, film, magazine, radio, student newspaper, television, yearbook, debating club, choral groups, concert band, dance, drama, marching band, music ensembles, symphony orchestra, concert choir, stage band, fraternities, sororities, Young Republicans, Young Democrats, Black Student Alliance.

ATHLETICS. NCAA. **Intercollegiate:** Archery, baseball M, basketball, cross-country, diving, fencing W, field hockey W, football M, golf, gymnastics, lacrosse W, soccer, swimming, tennis, track and field, volleyball W, wrestling M. **Intramural:** Badminton, basketball, bowling, cross-country, diving, golf, racquetball, soccer, softball, swimming, table tennis, tennis, track and field, volleyball, wrestling M.

STUDENT SERVICES. Aptitude testing, career counseling, employment service for undergraduates, freshman orientation, health services, personal counseling, placement service for graduates, special adviser for adult students, services/facilities for handicapped.

ANNUAL EXPENSES. Tuition and fees (1992-93): $3,576, $3,664 additional for out-of-state students. **Room and board:** $4,284. **Books and supplies:** $500. **Other expenses:** $732.

FINANCIAL AID. 46% of freshmen, 47% of continuing students receive some form of aid. 48% of grants, 71% of loans, 9% of jobs based on need. 840 enrolled freshmen were judged to have need, all were offered aid. Academic, music/drama, art, athletic, state/district residency, leadership, alumni affiliation, minority scholarships available. **Aid applications:** Closing date March 19; priority given to applications received by February 15; applicants notified on or about April 15; must reply within 2 weeks. **Additional information:** Special state grants to minorities.

ADDRESS/TELEPHONE. Alan L. Cerveny, Director of Admissions, James Madison University, Harrisonburg, VA 22807. (703) 568-6147.

John Tyler Community College
Chester, Virginia — CB code: 5342

2-year public community college, coed. Founded in 1965. **Accreditation:** Regional. **Undergraduate enrollment:** 439 men, 574 women full time; 1,632 men, 2,917 women part time. **Faculty:** 247 total (77 full time), 16 with doctorates or other terminal degrees. **Location:** Suburban campus in large town; 16 miles from Richmond. **Calendar:** Semester, extensive summer session. Extensive evening/early morning classes. **Microcomputers:** 337 located in libraries, classrooms, computer centers. **Special facilities:** Business Industry and Government (BIGS) Center. **Additional facts:** Two campuses, 1 off-campus site.

DEGREES OFFERED. AA, AS, AAS. 204 associate degrees awarded in 1992. 9% in business and management, 12% business/office and marketing/distribution, 7% computer sciences, 17% engineering technologies, 29% allied health, 9% multi/interdisciplinary studies, 17% parks/recreation, protective services, public affairs.

UNDERGRADUATE MAJORS. Accounting, architectural technologies, automotive technology, business administration and management, child development/care/guidance, computer and information sciences, early childhood education, education, electronic technology, funeral services/mortuary science, instrumentation technology, law enforcement and corrections technologies, liberal/general studies, mechanical design technology, mental health/human services, nursing, physical sciences, physical therapy assistant, secretarial and related programs, word processing.

ACADEMIC PROGRAMS. 2-year transfer program, dual enrollment of high school students, independent study, internships, teacher preparation, telecourses, visiting/exchange student program. **Remedial services:** Learning center, remedial instruction, tutoring. **ROTC:** Army. **Placement/credit:** AP, CLEP General and Subject, institutional tests; 48 credit hours maximum for associate degree.

ACADEMIC REQUIREMENTS. Freshmen must earn minimum GPA of 2.0 to continue in good standing. 50% of freshmen return for sophomore year. Students must declare major on enrollment. **Graduation requirements:** 65 hours for associate (35 in major). Most students required to take courses in computer science, English, mathematics. **Additional information:** Students seeking associate degree must complete 20% of core courses at college.

FRESHMAN ADMISSIONS. Selection criteria: Open admissions. Applicants to nursing program require high school diploma. **Additional information:** Any person with a high school diploma, its equivalent, or aged 18 years and able to benefit from college program may be admitted. College may evaluate special cases.

1992 FRESHMAN CLASS PROFILE. 341 men and women enrolled. **Characteristics:** 98% from in state, 100% commute, 27% have minority backgrounds. Average age is 30.

FALL-TERM APPLICATIONS. No fee. No closing date; applicants notified on a rolling basis. Early admission available. Students without high school diploma or equivalent may attend college full time provided high school gives written approval.

STUDENT LIFE. Activities: Student government, magazine, student newspaper, Student Nurses Association, American Society of Certified Engineering Technicians, data processing club, human services organization, business honor society, funeral services student organization, veterans service club.

ATHLETICS. Intramural: Softball, tennis, volleyball.

STUDENT SERVICES. Aptitude testing, career counseling, freshman orientation, health services, personal counseling, veterans counselor, services/facilities for handicapped.

ANNUAL EXPENSES. Tuition and fees (1992-93): $1,244, $3,030 additional for out-of-state students. **Books and supplies:** $500. **Other expenses:** $800.

FINANCIAL AID. 10% of continuing students receive some form of aid. All aid based on need. Academic, minority scholarships available. **Aid applications:** No closing date; priority given to applications received by June 30; applicants notified on a rolling basis beginning on or about July 10; must reply within 2 weeks.

ADDRESS/TELEPHONE. Judy Wilhelm, Enrollment Services Coordinator, John Tyler Community College, 13101 Jefferson Davis Highway, Chester, VA 23831-5399. (804) 796-4150. Fax: (804) 796-4163.

Liberty University
Lynchburg, Virginia — CB code: 5385

4-year private university and seminary college, coed, evangelical Christian. Founded in 1971. **Accreditation:** Regional. **Undergraduate enrollment:** 3,350 men and women full time; 253 men and women part time. **Graduate enrollment:** 149 men and women full time; 82 men and women part time. **Faculty:** 216 total (194 full time), 112 with doctorates or other terminal degrees. **Location:** Suburban campus in small city; 180 miles from Washington, D.C. **Calendar:** Semester, limited summer session. **Microcomputers:** 140 located in computer centers. **Special facilities:** Museum of creation studies.

DEGREES OFFERED. AA, BA, BS, MA, MEd, D, M.Div. 8 associate degrees awarded in 1992. 100% in philosophy, religion, theology. 932 bachelor's degrees awarded. 25% in business and management, 6% communications, 19% teacher education, 7% health sciences, 6% multi/interdisciplinary studies, 9% philosophy, religion, theology, 16% psychology. Graduate degrees offered in 7 major fields of study.

UNDERGRADUATE MAJORS. Associate: Religion. **Bachelor's:** Accounting, Bible studies, biology, business administration and management, chemistry, communications, community health work, computer and information sciences, dramatic arts, economics, English, French, history, home economics, journalism, liberal/general studies, linguistics, mathematics, missionary studies, music, music performance, nursing, parks and recreation management, philosophy, political science and government, psychology, radio/television broadcasting, Spanish, speech, sports management, telecommunications, theological studies.

ACADEMIC PROGRAMS. Double major, dual enrollment of high school students, external degree, honors program, independent study, internships, student-designed major, study abroad, teacher preparation, Washington semester, associate school of the Institute of Holy Land Studies in Jerusalem. **Remedial services:** Learning center, reduced course load, remedial instruction, special counselor, tutoring. **ROTC:** Army. **Placement/credit:** AP, CLEP General and Subject, institutional tests; 30 credit hours maximum for bachelor's degree.

ACADEMIC REQUIREMENTS. Freshmen must earn minimum GPA of 1.5 to continue in good standing. **Graduation requirements:** 64 hours for associate (30 in major), 123 hours for bachelor's (64 in major). Most students required to take courses in arts/fine arts, English, history, humanities, mathematics, philosophy/religion, biological/physical sciences, social sciences. **Postgraduate studies:** 1% enter law school, 3% enter medical school, 3% enter MBA programs, 21% enter other graduate study.

FRESHMAN ADMISSIONS. Selection criteria: Personal relationship with Jesus Christ and essay considered. **High school preparation:** 12 units recommended. Recommended units include English 4, foreign language 1, mathematics 3, social science 2 and science 2. **Test requirements:** SAT or ACT (SAT preferred) for placement and counseling only; score report by June 1.

1992 FRESHMAN CLASS PROFILE. 2,814 men and women applied, 2,810 accepted; 769 enrolled. **Characteristics:** Average age is 19.

FALL-TERM APPLICATIONS. $35 fee, may be waived for applicants with need. Closing date August 1; priority given to applications received by May 1; applicants notified on a rolling basis; must reply within 2 weeks. Essay required. Deferred and early admission available.

STUDENT LIFE. Housing: Dormitories (men, women); handicapped housing available. Students required to live on campus except those living with parents or those over age 22. **Activities:** Student government, magazine, radio, student newspaper, television, yearbook, choral groups, concert band, drama, marching band, music ensembles, musical theater, pep band, symphony orchestra, Over 69 organizations including Circle K, Baptist Student Union, Youthquest, Light Ministries, political groups, Fellowship of Christian Athletes. **Additional information:** All students involved in Christian or community service. Religious observance required.

ATHLETICS. NCAA. **Intercollegiate:** Baseball M, basketball, cross-country, football M, golf M, soccer, tennis M, track and field, volleyball W, wrestling M. **Intramural:** Basketball, cross-country, ice hockey M, lacrosse W, soccer, softball, tennis, track and field, volleyball. **Clubs:** Ice hockey M, lacrosse M.

STUDENT SERVICES. Aptitude testing, career counseling, employment service for undergraduates, freshman orientation, health services, personal counseling, placement service for graduates, veterans counselor, services/facilities for handicapped.

ANNUAL EXPENSES. Tuition and fees: $6,600. **Room and board:** $4,380. **Books and supplies:** $550. **Other expenses:** $825.

FINANCIAL AID. 85% of freshmen, 85% of continuing students receive some form of aid. All loans, 50% of jobs based on need. 539 enrolled freshmen were judged to have need, all were offered aid. Academic, music/drama, athletic, state/district residency, leadership, minority scholarships available. **Aid applications:** No closing date; priority given to applications received by April 15; applicants notified on a rolling basis beginning on or about April 15; must reply within 3 weeks.

ADDRESS/TELEPHONE. T. Randall Scott, Director of Admission, Liberty University, P.O. Box 20,000, Lynchburg, VA 24506-8001. (804) 582-2158. (800) 522-6225. Fax: (804) 582-7401.

Longwood College

Farmville, Virginia — CB code: 5368

Admissions:	66% of applicants accepted
Based on:	••• School record, test scores
	•• Essay
	• Activities, interview, recommendations, special talents
Completion:	76% of freshmen end year in good standing
	56% graduate, 12% of these enter graduate study

4-year public schools of arts and sciences, business administration, and teacher ed, coed. Founded in 1839. **Accreditation:** Regional. **Undergraduate enrollment:** 931 men, 1,905 women full time; 29 men, 50 women part time. **Graduate enrollment:** 10 men, 21 women full time; 26 men, 175 women part time. **Faculty:** 283 total (220 full time), 131 with doctorates or other terminal degrees. **Location:** Suburban campus in small town; 60 miles from Richmond. **Calendar:** Semester, limited summer session. **Microcomputers:** 185 located in libraries, classrooms, computer centers, campus-wide network. **Special facilities:** Art gallery, science museum, telecommunication network, golf course, flora collection.

DEGREES OFFERED. BA, BS, BFA, MA, MS. 600 bachelor's degrees awarded in 1992. 30% in business and management, 23% teacher education, 8% life sciences, 8% psychology, 10% social sciences. Graduate degrees offered in 11 major fields of study.

UNDERGRADUATE MAJORS. Anthropology, applied mathematics, art history, biology, business administration and management, chemistry, clinical laboratory science, computer and information sciences, drama therapy, dramatic arts, earth sciences, education, English, fine arts, foreign languages (multiple emphasis), health education, history, mathematics, music, physical education, physics, political science and government, preengineering, prelaw, psychology, secondary education, social work, sociology, speech pathology/audiology, therapeutic recreation, visual and performing arts.

ACADEMIC PROGRAMS. Accelerated program, double major, dual enrollment of high school students, honors program, independent study, internships, study abroad, teacher preparation, cross-registration, summer field programs in archaeology, botany, speleology; liberal arts/career combination in engineering, health sciences. **Remedial services:** Learning center, preadmission summer program, reduced course load, remedial instruction, special counselor, tutoring. **ROTC:** Army. **Placement/credit:** AP, CLEP Subject, institutional tests.

ACADEMIC REQUIREMENTS. Freshmen must earn minimum GPA of 1.8 to continue in good standing. Scaled GPA requirement based on number of hours attempted. 76% of freshmen return for sophomore year. Students must declare major by end of second year. **Graduation requirements:** 126 hours for bachelor's (30 in major). Most students required to take courses in arts/fine arts, English, history, humanities, mathematics, biological/physical sciences, social sciences. **Postgraduate studies:** 1% enter law school, 1% enter medical school, 10% enter other graduate study.

FRESHMAN ADMISSIONS. Selection criteria: Rank in top half of class, combined SAT score of 860 and minimum GPA of 2.2 in college prep courses required. Extracurricular activities and recommendations are also considered. **High school preparation:** 18 units required. Required and recommended units include English 4, foreign language 2-3, mathematics 3-4, social science 3 and science 3. 2 units in physical education, 1 unit of fine or practical arts required. **Test requirements:** SAT or ACT (SAT preferred); score report by May 1. ACH required of foreign language majors.

1992 FRESHMAN CLASS PROFILE. 960 men applied, 532 accepted, 214 enrolled; 1,665 women applied, 1,195 accepted, 473 enrolled. 52% had high school GPA of 3.0 or higher, 48% between 2.0 and 2.99. 11% were in top tenth and 44% were in top quarter of graduating class. **Academic background:** Mid 50% of enrolled freshmen had SAT-V between 420-500, SAT-M between 460-540. 99% submitted SAT scores. **Characteristics:** 95% from in state, 95% live in college housing, 8% have minority backgrounds, 1% are foreign students, 22% join fraternities/sororities. Average age is 18.

FALL-TERM APPLICATIONS. $25 fee, may be waived for applicants with need. Closing date May 1; priority given to applications received by February 15; applicants notified on a rolling basis beginning on or about December 15; must reply by May 1 or within 2 weeks if notified thereafter. Audition required for music applicants. Essay required. Interview recommended for students with disabilities and adults (over age 25) applicants. Portfolio recommended for fine arts applicants. CRDA. Deferred and early admission available. Institutional early decision plan. For early admission school record through eleventh grade, and SAT scores considered. Applicants will be notified within 3 weeks after they apply.

STUDENT LIFE. Housing: Dormitories (women, coed); fraternity, sorority, handicapped housing available. Students required to live on campus for 4 years unless married or living with a relative. Exceptions for older students. **Activities:** Student government, magazine, radio, student newspaper, yearbook, literary magazine, choral groups, concert band, dance, drama, jazz band, music ensembles, musical theater, fraternities, sororities, 110 clubs and organizations including Black Student Alliance, Young Republicans, Young Democrats, church-affiliated organizations. **Additional information:** Comprehensive student development and student leadership development programs available.

ATHLETICS. NCAA. **Intercollegiate:** Baseball M, basketball, field hockey W, golf, lacrosse W, soccer M, softball W, tennis, wrestling M. **Intramural:** Badminton, basketball, bowling, racquetball, rugby M, soccer, softball, table tennis, volleyball, water polo.

STUDENT SERVICES. Aptitude testing, career counseling, employment service for undergraduates, freshman orientation, health services, personal counseling, placement service for graduates, special adviser for adult students, services/facilities for handicapped.

ANNUAL EXPENSES. Tuition and fees: $4,106, $5,084 additional for out-of-state students. **Room and board:** $3,842. **Books and supplies:** $550. **Other expenses:** $1,200.

FINANCIAL AID. 60% of freshmen, 60% of continuing students receive some form of aid. 81% of grants, 96% of loans, 55% of jobs based on need. 276 enrolled freshmen were judged to have need, 264 were offered aid. Academic, music/drama, art, athletic, leadership, minority scholarships available. **Aid applications:** No closing date; priority given to applications received by February 15; applicants notified on a rolling basis beginning on or about April 15; must reply within 2 weeks.

ADDRESS/TELEPHONE. Robert J. Chonko, Director of Admissions and Enrollment Management, Longwood College, 201 High Street, Farmville, VA 23909-1898. (804) 395-2060. Fax: (804) 395-4910.

Lord Fairfax Community College
Middletown, Virginia CB code: 5381

2-year public community college, coed. Founded in 1969. **Accreditation:** Regional. **Undergraduate enrollment:** 3,200 men and women part time. **Faculty:** 120 total (40 full time), 4 with doctorates or other terminal degrees. **Location:** Rural campus in rural community; 12 miles from Winchester, 70 miles from Washington, D.C. **Calendar:** Semester, limited summer session. **Microcomputers:** 80 located in libraries, classrooms, computer centers. **Additional facts:** Students can enroll at the Fauquier Center in Warrenton.

DEGREES OFFERED. AAS. 204 associate degrees awarded in 1992.

UNDERGRADUATE MAJORS. Accounting, agricultural business and management, agricultural production, American studies, biological and physical sciences, business administration and management, business and management, business data processing and related programs, civil technology, communications, computer and information sciences, education, electronic technology, engineering and engineering-related technologies, horticulture, liberal/general studies, mechanical design technology, secretarial and related programs, trade and industrial supervision and management.

ACADEMIC PROGRAMS. 2-year transfer program, cooperative education, double major, dual enrollment of high school students, honors program, independent study. **Remedial services:** Learning center, reduced course load, remedial instruction, tutoring. **Placement/credit:** AP, CLEP General and Subject, institutional tests; 32 credit hours maximum for associate degree. 50% of hours needed for degree may be earned by examination.

ACADEMIC REQUIREMENTS. Freshmen must earn minimum GPA of 1.5 to continue in good standing. Students must declare major on enrollment. **Graduation requirements:** 65 hours for associate. Most students required to take courses in computer science, English, mathematics, biological/physical sciences, social sciences.

FRESHMAN ADMISSIONS. Selection criteria: Open admissions.

1992 FRESHMAN CLASS PROFILE. 800 men and women enrolled. **Characteristics:** 99% from in state, 100% commute, 8% have minority backgrounds.

FALL-TERM APPLICATIONS. No fee. Closing date August 25; applicants notified on a rolling basis.

STUDENT LIFE. Activities: Student government, drama, special interest and program-related organizations, leadership organization, agriculture club, honor society, business fraternity, honors fraternity.

STUDENT SERVICES. Career counseling, employment service for undergraduates, freshman orientation, personal counseling, placement service for graduates, veterans counselor, services/facilities for handicapped.

ANNUAL EXPENSES. Tuition and fees (1992-93): $1,250, $3,030 additional for out-of-state students. **Books and supplies:** $450. **Other expenses:** $990.

FINANCIAL AID. 44% of freshmen, 23% of continuing students receive some form of aid. 94% of grants, all loans, all jobs based on need. 331 enrolled freshmen were judged to have need, 300 were offered aid. **Aid applications:** No closing date; priority given to applications received by May 1; applicants notified on a rolling basis beginning on or about May 1.

ADDRESS/TELEPHONE. C.T. Smith, Coordinator of Admissions and Records, Lord Fairfax Community College, PO Box 47, Middletown, VA 22645. (703) 869-1120. Fax: (703) 869-7881.

Lynchburg College
Lynchburg, Virginia CB code: 5372

Admissions: 86% of applicants accepted
Based on: ••• School record
•• Activities, essay, recommendations, test scores
• Interview, special talents
Completion: 84% of freshmen end year in good standing
61% graduate, 30% of these enter graduate study

4-year private liberal arts college, coed, affiliated with Christian Church (Disciples of Christ). Founded in 1903. **Accreditation:** Regional. **Undergraduate enrollment:** 619 men, 970 women full time; 105 men, 175 women part time. **Graduate enrollment:** 30 men, 90 women full time; 142 men, 248 women part time. **Faculty:** 186 total (134 full time), 98 with doctorates or other terminal degrees. **Location:** Suburban campus in small city; 180 miles from Washington, D.C., 60 miles from Roanoke. **Calendar:** Semester, extensive summer session. **Microcomputers:** 100 located in dormitories, libraries, classrooms, computer centers. **Special facilities:** Early iron industry collection, 17th, 18th and 19th century maps of North America and Virginia. **Additional facts:** College Consortium with Randolph-Macon Woman's College and Sweet Briar College.

DEGREES OFFERED. BA, BS, MBA, MEd. 479 bachelor's degrees awarded in 1992. 25% in business and management, 12% communications, 13% education, 7% health sciences, 5% psychology, 16% social sciences. Graduate degrees offered in 15 major fields of study.

UNDERGRADUATE MAJORS. Accounting, American studies, art history, biological and physical sciences, biology, business administration and management, chemistry, communications, community services, comparative literature, computer and information sciences, dramatic arts, economics, education, elementary education, English, environmental science, fine arts, French, German, health sciences, history, humanities, humanities and social sciences, international business management, international relations, international studies, marketing management, mathematics, medical laboratory technologies, music, nursing, philosophy, physics, political science and government, psychology, religion, social sciences, sociology, Spanish, special education, studio art, theater design, visual and performing arts.

ACADEMIC PROGRAMS. Accelerated program, double major, education specialist degree, honors program, independent study, internships, study abroad, teacher preparation, visiting/exchange student program, cross-registration; liberal arts/career combination in engineering, health sciences. **Remedial services:** Learning center, preadmission summer program, reduced course load, special counselor, tutoring, writing center, study skills workshops. **ROTC:** Army. **Placement/credit:** AP, CLEP Subject, institutional tests.

ACADEMIC REQUIREMENTS. Freshmen must earn minimum GPA of 1.7 to continue in good standing. 75% of freshmen return for sophomore year. Students must declare major by end of second year. **Graduation requirements:** 124 hours for bachelor's. Most students required to take courses in arts/fine arts, English, foreign languages, history, humanities, mathematics, philosophy/religion, biological/physical sciences, social sciences. **Postgraduate studies:** 2% enter law school, 2% enter medical school, 8% enter MBA programs, 18% enter other graduate study. **Additional information:** Honor code promoted and adhered to.

FRESHMAN ADMISSIONS. Selection criteria: School record, class rank, test scores, school and community involvement, recommendation, type of secondary school attended are all considered. Auditions and portfolios recommended for performing and fine arts applicants. **High school preparation:** 15 units required. Required and recommended units include English 4, mathematics 3, social science 2 and science 2. Foreign language 2 recommended. **Test requirements:** SAT or ACT (SAT preferred); score report by March 1. 3 ACH recommended. Score report by June 1.

1992 FRESHMAN CLASS PROFILE. 712 men applied, 573 accepted, 169 enrolled; 1,040 women applied, 929 accepted, 249 enrolled. 58% had high school GPA of 3.0 or higher, 42% between 2.0 and 2.99. 5% were in top tenth and 26% were in top quarter of graduating class. **Academic background:** Mid 50% of enrolled freshmen had SAT-V between 430-500, SAT-M between 430-500. 99% submitted SAT scores. **Characteristics:** 26% from in state, 90% live in college housing, 6% have minority backgrounds, 2% are foreign students, 10% join fraternities/sororities. Average age is 19.

FALL-TERM APPLICATIONS. $20 fee, may be waived for applicants with need. No closing date; priority given to applications received by May 1; applicants notified on a rolling basis; must reply within 2 weeks. Essay required. Interview recommended. Audition recommended for music and theatre arts applicants. Portfolio recommended for studio art applicants. Deferred and early admission available.

STUDENT LIFE. Housing: Dormitories (men, women, coed); apartment housing available. Students must live on campus for first 3 years unless living with family. 4 residential houses, French language house available for upperclassmen. Special section of dormitories available for honor students. **Activities:** Student government, film, magazine, student newspaper, yearbook, choral groups, concert band, dance, drama, jazz band, music ensembles, musical theater, symphony orchestra, madrigal singers, fraternities, sororities, Circle-K, Afro-American society, religious organizations, honor societies, political science, history clubs, service fraternities and sororities.

ATHLETICS. NCAA. **Intercollegiate:** Baseball M, basketball, cross-country, fencing, field hockey W, golf M, horseback riding, lacrosse, soccer, softball W, tennis, track and field, volleyball W, water polo M. **Intramural:** Badminton, basketball, bowling, field hockey W, football M, lacrosse M, racquetball, rugby M, skiing, soccer, softball, swimming, table tennis, tennis, volleyball.

STUDENT SERVICES. Aptitude testing, career counseling, employment service for undergraduates, freshman orientation, health services, personal counseling, placement service for graduates, special adviser for adult students, services/facilities for handicapped.

ANNUAL EXPENSES. Tuition and fees: $11,600. **Room and board:** $5,400. **Books and supplies:** $450. **Other expenses:** $440.

FINANCIAL AID. 80% of freshmen, 70% of continuing students receive some form of aid. 65% of grants, 90% of loans, 29% of jobs based on need. 216 enrolled freshmen were judged to have need, all were offered aid. Academic, music/drama, state/district residency, leadership, religious affiliation, minority scholarships available. **Aid applications:** No closing date; priority given to applications received by April 1; applicants notified on a rolling basis beginning on or about March 1; must reply within 3 weeks.

ADDRESS/TELEPHONE. Dee Hubble, Director of Admissions, Lynchburg College, 1501 Lakeside Drive, Lynchburg, VA 24501-9986. (804) 522-8300. (800) 426-8101. Fax: (804) 522-0653.

Mary Baldwin College
Staunton, Virginia CB code: 5397

Admissions: 86% of applicants accepted
Based on: ••• School record
•• Essay, test scores
• Activities, interview, recommendations, special talents
Completion: 80% of freshmen end year in good standing
60% graduate, 25% of these enter graduate study

4-year private liberal arts college, women only, affiliated with Presbyterian Church (USA). Founded in 1842. **Accreditation:** Regional. **Undergraduate enrollment:** 41 men, 801 women full time; 71 men, 268 women part time. **Graduate enrollment:** 6 men, 31 women full time; 2 men, 29 women part time. **Faculty:** 119 total (73 full time), 53 with doctorates or other terminal degrees. **Location:** Suburban campus in large town; 100 miles from Richmond, 150 miles from Washington, D.C. **Calendar:** 4-4-1. **Microcomputers:** 90 located in dormitories, libraries, classrooms, computer centers. **Special facilities:** Pearce Science Center with electrophoresis and chromatography equipment, electron microscope, art gallery. **Additional facts:** Men admitted to adult program and M.A.T program.

DEGREES OFFERED. BA. 316 bachelor's degrees awarded in 1992. 17% in business and management, 10% communications, 7% multi/interdisciplinary studies, 9% psychology, 22% social sciences, 12% visual and performing arts. Graduate degrees offered in 1 major field of study.

UNDERGRADUATE MAJORS. Art history, arts management, Asian studies, biological and physical sciences, biology, business administration and management, business and management, business economics, chemistry, communications, computer mathematics, dramatic arts, economics, education/psychology, English, fine arts, French, health care administration, history, humanities, humanities and social sciences, information sciences and systems, international relations, international studies, marketing communication, marketing management, mathematics, medical laboratory technologies, philosophy, political science and government, psychology, religion, sociology, Spanish, studio art, women's studies.

ACADEMIC PROGRAMS. Accelerated program, double major, dual enrollment of high school students, external degree, honors program, independent study, internships, semester at sea, student-designed major, study abroad, teacher preparation, visiting/exchange student program, cross-registration, summer exchange program with Doshisha Women's College in Kyoto, Japan. **Remedial services:** Learning center, reduced course load, remedial instruction, special counselor, tutoring, Learning Skills Center. **ROTC:** Army. **Placement/credit:** AP, institutional tests.

ACADEMIC REQUIREMENTS. Freshmen must earn minimum GPA of 1.65 to continue in good standing. 80% of freshmen return for sophomore year. Students must declare major by end of second year. **Graduation requirements:** 132 hours for bachelor's (33 in major). Most students required to take courses in arts/fine arts, English, humanities, mathematics, biological/physical sciences, social sciences. **Postgraduate studies:** 5% enter law school, 3% enter medical school, 4% enter MBA programs, 13% enter other graduate study. **Additional information:** Students complete requirements in experiential education, international education, women's studies. May term offers opportunity for individualized programming, externships, study abroad.

FRESHMAN ADMISSIONS. Selection criteria: Primarily school achievement record (3.0 GPA recommended). Recommendations, involvement in school or civic groups, and test scores also important. **High school preparation:** 16 units required. Required units include English 4, foreign language 2, mathematics 3, social science 3 and science 1. **Test requirements:** SAT or ACT; score report by April 1.

1992 FRESHMAN CLASS PROFILE. 8 men applied, 4 accepted, 2 enrolled; 511 women applied, 443 accepted, 197 enrolled. 45% were in top quarter of graduating class. **Characteristics:** 45% from in state, 95% live in college housing, 7% have minority backgrounds, 2% are foreign students. Average age is 18.

FALL-TERM APPLICATIONS. $25 fee, may be waived for applicants with need. Closing date March 15; applicants notified on a rolling basis beginning on or about January 1; must reply by May 1. Essay required. Interview recommended. Portfolio recommended for art applicants. CRDA. Deferred and early admission available. EDP-F.

STUDENT LIFE. Housing: Dormitories (women); apartment, cooperative housing available. Special interest houses include Japan, honors, leadership, and community service. **Activities:** Student government, film, magazine, radio, student newspaper, television, yearbook, choral groups, dance, drama, music ensembles, musical theater, Religious Life Council, Young Democrats, Young Republicans, Black Students Alliance, honor societies, Circle-K, Fine Arts Association. **Additional information:** Honor system. High degree of self-government.

ATHLETICS. NCAA. **Intercollegiate:** Basketball, fencing, field hockey, lacrosse, soccer, swimming, tennis, track and field, volleyball. **Intramural:** Basketball, cross-country, fencing, field hockey, horseback riding, racquetball, soccer, softball, swimming, table tennis, tennis, track and field, volleyball.

STUDENT SERVICES. Aptitude testing, career counseling, employment service for undergraduates, freshman orientation, health services, personal counseling, placement service for graduates, special adviser for adult students, services/facilities for handicapped.

ANNUAL EXPENSES. Tuition and fees: $10,654. **Room and board:** $7,046. **Books and supplies:** $600. **Other expenses:** $900.

FINANCIAL AID. 74% of freshmen, 70% of continuing students receive some form of aid. 78% of grants, 98% of loans, 66% of jobs based on need. 123 enrolled freshmen were judged to have need, all were offered aid. Academic, music/drama, art, state/district residency, leadership, religious affiliation, minority scholarships available. **Aid applications:** Closing date April 15; priority given to applications received by March 15; applicants notified on a rolling basis beginning on or about March 1; must reply by May 1 or within 2 weeks if notified thereafter.

ADDRESS/TELEPHONE. Douglas E. Clark, Executive Director of Enrollment, Mary Baldwin College, Staunton, VA 24401. (703) 887-7023. (800) 826-0154. Fax: (703) 886-5561.

Mary Washington College
Fredericksburg, Virginia CB code: 5398

Admissions: 46% of applicants accepted
Based on: ••• School record
•• Test scores
• Activities, essay, recommendations, special talents
Completion: 82% of freshmen end year in good standing
73% graduate, 28% of these enter graduate study

4-year public liberal arts college, coed. Founded in 1908. **Accreditation:** Regional. **Undergraduate enrollment:** 993 men, 1,944 women full time; 212 men, 488 women part time. **Graduate enrollment:** 16 men, 43 women part time. **Faculty:** 306 total (231 full time), 127 with doctorates or other terminal degrees. **Location:** Suburban campus in large town; 50 miles from Richmond, 50 miles from Washington, D.C. **Calendar:** Semester, limited summer session. **Microcomputers:** 110 located in libraries, classrooms, computer centers. **Special facilities:** Center for Historic Preservation, writing center, Computer Access Center for the Visually Impaired, Phyllis Ridderhof Martin Art Gallery.

DEGREES OFFERED. BA, BS, MA. 814 bachelor's degrees awarded in 1992. 17% in business and management, 9% letters/literature, 6% life sciences, 10% multi/interdisciplinary studies, 9% psychology, 21% social sciences, 8% visual and performing arts. Graduate degrees offered in 1 major field of study.

UNDERGRADUATE MAJORS. American studies, art history, biology, business administration and management, chemistry, classics, computer and information sciences, dance, dramatic arts, economics, English, environmental science, French, geography, geology, German, Greek (classical), historic preservation, history, international relations, Latin, liberal/general studies, mathematics, music, philosophy, physics, political science and government, psychology, religion, sociology, Spanish, studio art.

ACADEMIC PROGRAMS. Double major, independent study, internships, student-designed major, study abroad, teacher preparation. **Placement/credit:** AP, CLEP Subject, institutional tests.

ACADEMIC REQUIREMENTS. Freshmen must earn minimum GPA of 2.0 to continue in good standing. 92% of freshmen return for sophomore year. Students must declare major by end of second year. **Graduation requirements:** 122 hours for bachelor's (30 in major). Most students required to take courses in English, foreign languages, history, mathematics, biological/physical sciences, social sciences. **Postgraduate studies:** 4% enter law school, 2% enter medical school, 2% enter MBA programs, 20% enter other graduate study. **Additional information:** College provides grants for undergraduate research program enabling students to work individually with faculty members. Individualized program for older students leading to bachelor's or master's degree in liberal studies.

FRESHMAN ADMISSIONS. Selection criteria: High school record, test scores, teacher/counselor evaluation, extracurricular activities all considered. Minority applicants and out-of-state applicants encouraged. **High school preparation:** 16 units recommended. Recommended units include English 4, foreign language 3, mathematics 3, social science 3 and science 3. **Test requirements:** SAT; score report by February 1. English Composition and two other ACH recommended. Score report by February 1.

1992 FRESHMAN CLASS PROFILE. 1,292 men applied, 695 accepted, 221 enrolled; 3,259 women applied, 1,378 accepted, 479 enrolled. 95% had high school GPA of 3.0 or higher, 5% between 2.0 and 2.99. 39% were in top tenth and 76% were in top quarter of graduating class. **Academic background:** Mid 50% of enrolled freshmen had SAT-V between 480-560, SAT-M between 520-600. 100% submitted SAT scores. **Characteristics:** 69% from in state, 97% live in college housing, 12% have minority backgrounds, 1% are foreign students. Average age is 18.

FALL-TERM APPLICATIONS. $25 fee, may be waived for applicants with need. Closing date February 1; applicants notified on or about April 1;

must reply by May 1. Essay required. CRDA. Deferred and early admission available. EDP-F.

STUDENT LIFE. Housing: Dormitories (men, women, coed). Foreign language houses available for students studying French, Spanish, German. Additional houses available for upperclassmen with honors and students who need quiet environment. **Activities:** Student government, magazine, radio, student newspaper, yearbook, choral groups, concert band, dance, drama, jazz band, music ensembles, musical theater, symphony orchestra, Several religious, political, and social service organizations, Black Student Association, Asian Student Association, American Chemical Society, Community Outreach and Resources Center, Young Democrats, Young Republicans.

ATHLETICS. NCAA. **Intercollegiate:** Baseball M, basketball, cross-country, field hockey W, horseback riding, lacrosse, soccer, softball W, swimming, tennis, track and field, volleyball W. **Intramural:** Badminton, baseball M, basketball, handball, racquetball, rowing (crew), rugby, soccer, softball, swimming, table tennis, tennis, volleyball.

STUDENT SERVICES. Aptitude testing, career counseling, employment service for undergraduates, freshman orientation, health services, personal counseling, placement service for graduates, special adviser for adult students, veterans counselor, services/facilities for handicapped.

ANNUAL EXPENSES. Tuition and fees (1992-93): $2,896, $3,856 additional for out-of-state students. **Room and board:** $4,552. **Books and supplies:** $550. **Other expenses:** $1,048.

FINANCIAL AID. 35% of freshmen, 50% of continuing students receive some form of aid. Grants, loans, jobs available. 210 enrolled freshmen were judged to have need, 185 were offered aid. Academic, state/district residency, leadership, minority scholarships available. **Aid applications:** Closing date March 1; applicants notified on or about April 15; must reply by May 1 or within 2 weeks if notified thereafter.

ADDRESS/TELEPHONE. Dr. Martin A. Wilder, Jr, Vice President for Admissions and Financial Aid, Mary Washington College, 1301 College Avenue, Fredericksburg, VA 22401-5358. (703) 899-4681. (800) 468-5614.

Marymount University

Arlington, Virginia — CB code: 5405

Admissions: 70% of applicants accepted
Based on: ••• School record, test scores
•• Essay, recommendations
• Activities, interview, special talents
Completion: 80% of freshmen end year in good standing
42% graduate, 13% of these enter graduate study

4-year private university, coed, affiliated with Roman Catholic Church. Founded in 1950. **Accreditation:** Regional. **Undergraduate enrollment:** 332 men, 997 women full time; 189 men, 650 women part time. **Graduate enrollment:** 111 men, 265 women full time; 516 men, 757 women part time. **Faculty:** 328 total (112 full time), 147 with doctorates or other terminal degrees. **Location:** Suburban campus in small city; 3 miles from Washington, D.C. **Calendar:** Semester, extensive summer session. Extensive evening/early morning classes. **Microcomputers:** 135 located in dormitories, libraries, classrooms, computer centers. **Special facilities:** Barry Art Gallery, Gerard Majella Child Development Center. **Additional facts:** Classes available at several off-campus corporate and government sites including the Pentagon, Mitre Corporation, TRW, and U.S. Navy Annex.

DEGREES OFFERED. AA, AS, AAS, BA, BS, MA, MS, MBA, MEd. 107 associate degrees awarded in 1992. 95% in health sciences, 5% multi/interdisciplinary studies. 392 bachelor's degrees awarded. 10% in architecture and environmental design, 44% business and management, 6% business/office and marketing/distribution, 8% communications, 9% multi/interdisciplinary studies, 9% social sciences. Graduate degrees offered in 25 major fields of study.

UNDERGRADUATE MAJORS. Associate: Humanities, nursing. **Bachelor's:** Accounting, biological and physical sciences, biology, business administration and management, business and management, business economics, business law, communications, computer and information sciences, counseling psychology, developmental psychology, economics, English, fashion design, fashion merchandising, finance, graphic design, health care administration, industrial and organizational psychology, interior design, international business management, investments and securities, legal assistant/paralegal, liberal/general studies, management information systems, management science, marketing and distribution, marketing management, mathematics, mathematics education, military science (Army), nursing, personnel management, philosophy, physical sciences, political science and government, psychology, recreation and community services technologies, religion, retailing.

ACADEMIC PROGRAMS. Accelerated program, double major, honors program, independent study, internships, study abroad, teacher preparation, cross-registration. **Remedial services:** Learning center, reduced course load, tutoring. **ROTC:** Army. **Placement/credit:** AP, CLEP General and Subject, IB, institutional tests.

ACADEMIC REQUIREMENTS. Freshmen must earn minimum GPA of 2.0 to continue in good standing. 73% of freshmen return for sophomore year. Students must declare major by end of first year. **Graduation requirements:** 64 hours for associate (27 in major), 120 hours for bachelor's (45 in major). Most students required to take courses in computer science, English, history, humanities, mathematics, philosophy/religion, biological/physical sciences, social sciences. **Postgraduate studies:** 75% from 2-year programs enter 4-year programs. 3% enter law school, 1% enter medical school, 7% enter MBA programs, 2% enter other graduate study. **Additional information:** Senior year internships in major field required. London Program offers opportunity to juniors and seniors to secure credit-bearing internship in London.

FRESHMAN ADMISSIONS. Selection criteria: High school achievement, SAT or ACT scores important. Application writing sample considered. **High school preparation:** 16 units recommended. Recommended units include English 4, mathematics 2, social science 2 and science 2. **Test requirements:** SAT or ACT; score report by August 31. **Additional information:** Applicants to the freshman class are normally granted admission if they rank in the upper 50% of their high school class and have SAT scores above or within 100 points of our national average.

1992 FRESHMAN CLASS PROFILE. 326 men applied, 207 accepted, 62 enrolled; 856 women applied, 623 accepted, 158 enrolled. 31% had high school GPA of 3.0 or higher, 68% between 2.0 and 2.99. 7% were in top tenth and 25% were in top quarter of graduating class. **Academic background:** Mid 50% of enrolled freshmen had SAT-V between 360-470, SAT-M between 350-510. 82% submitted SAT scores. **Characteristics:** 32% from in state, 76% live in college housing, 26% have minority backgrounds, 15% are foreign students. Average age is 21.

FALL-TERM APPLICATIONS. $30 fee, may be waived for applicants with need. No closing date; applicants notified on a rolling basis; must reply by May 1 or within 2 weeks if notified thereafter. Essay required. Interview recommended. CRDA. Deferred admission available.

STUDENT LIFE. Housing: Dormitories (men, women, coed). **Activities:** Student government, magazine, student newspaper, yearbook, drama, campus ministry, Black Student Alliance, Circle K, student chapters of professional organizations for nurses, teachers, interior designers, S.E.A.R.C.H., Young Democrats, College Republicans, Best Buddies.

ATHLETICS. NCAA. **Intercollegiate:** Basketball, golf M, lacrosse M, soccer, swimming, tennis, volleyball W. **Intramural:** Basketball, golf M, soccer W, softball, volleyball, water polo M.

STUDENT SERVICES. Career counseling, employment service for undergraduates, freshman orientation, health services, personal counseling, placement service for graduates, veterans counselor, services/facilities for handicapped.

ANNUAL EXPENSES. Tuition and fees: $10,804. **Room and board:** $5,126. **Books and supplies:** $400. **Other expenses:** $600.

FINANCIAL AID. 48% of freshmen, 83% of continuing students receive some form of aid. 59% of grants, 63% of loans, 44% of jobs based on need. 136 enrolled freshmen were judged to have need, all were offered aid. Academic, state/district residency, leadership, alumni affiliation scholarships available. **Aid applications:** No closing date; priority given to applications received by March 1; applicants notified on a rolling basis beginning on or about March 15; must reply within 2 weeks.

ADDRESS/TELEPHONE. Charles D. Coe, Director of Admissions, Marymount University, 2807 North Glebe Road, Arlington, VA 22207-4299. (703) 284-1500. (800) 548-7638. Fax: (703) 522-0349.

Mountain Empire Community College

Big Stone Gap, Virginia — CB code: 5451

2-year public community college, coed. Founded in 1970. **Accreditation:** Regional. **Undergraduate enrollment:** 411 men, 805 women full time; 506 men, 919 women part time. **Faculty:** 135 total (60 full time), 22 with doctorates or other terminal degrees. **Location:** Rural campus in small town; 40 miles from Bristol. **Calendar:** Semester, limited summer session. Extensive evening/early morning classes. **Microcomputers:** 100 located in libraries, classrooms, computer centers.

DEGREES OFFERED. AA, AS, AAS. 140 associate degrees awarded in 1992. 10% in business and management, 24% business/office and marketing/distribution, 18% engineering technologies, 20% health sciences, 10% multi/interdisciplinary studies, 5% parks/recreation, protective services, public affairs, 7% trade and industry.

UNDERGRADUATE MAJORS. Accounting, architectural technologies, architecture, biology, business administration and management, business and management, business data processing and related programs, computer and information sciences, criminal justice studies, drafting, drafting and design technology, education, electrical and electronics equipment repair, electronic technology, elementary education, engineering, junior high education, law enforcement and corrections technologies, legal secretary, liberal/general studies, mathematics, medical secretary, mining and petroleum technologies, nursing, office supervision and management, predentistry, prelaw, premedicine, prepharmacy, psychology, respiratory therapy, secondary education, secretarial and related programs, social sciences, soil sciences, water and wastewater technology.

ACADEMIC PROGRAMS. 2-year transfer program, accelerated program, double major, dual enrollment of high school students, independent study, internships, student-designed major, teacher preparation, telecourses. **Remedial services:** Learning center, preadmission summer program, reduced course load, remedial instruction, special counselor, tutoring. **Placement/credit:** AP, CLEP General and Subject, institutional tests; 16 credit hours maximum for associate degree.

ACADEMIC REQUIREMENTS. Freshmen must earn minimum GPA of 2.0 to continue in good standing. 75% of freshmen return for sophomore year. Students must declare major on enrollment. **Graduation requirements:** 65 hours for associate (40 in major). Most students required to take courses in computer science, English, history, humanities, mathematics, biological/physical sciences, social sciences.

FRESHMAN ADMISSIONS. Selection criteria: Open admissions. High school diploma or GED required for nursing, respiratory care programs. Recommended units include English 4, mathematics 1 and social science 2. Algebra, biology, chemistry required for nursing; algebra, biology for respiratory care.

1992 FRESHMAN CLASS PROFILE. 550 men applied, 550 accepted, 500 enrolled; 1,100 women applied, 1,100 accepted, 1,000 enrolled. **Characteristics:** 96% from in state, 100% commute, 2% have minority backgrounds, 1% are foreign students. Average age is 25.

FALL-TERM APPLICATIONS. No fee. No closing date; applicants notified on a rolling basis beginning on or about January 1. Interview required for respiratory care applicants. Early admission available.

STUDENT LIFE. Activities: Student government, drama, service, business and nursing organizations.

ATHLETICS. Intramural: Archery, badminton, basketball, bowling, softball, table tennis, tennis, volleyball.

STUDENT SERVICES. Aptitude testing, career counseling, employment service for undergraduates, freshman orientation, personal counseling, placement service for graduates, veterans counselor, services/facilities for handicapped.

ANNUAL EXPENSES. Tuition and fees: $1,338, $3,030 additional for out-of-state students. **Books and supplies:** $500.

FINANCIAL AID. 75% of freshmen, 75% of continuing students receive some form of aid. 99% of grants, all jobs based on need. 560 enrolled freshmen were judged to have need, all were offered aid. Academic, minority scholarships available. **Aid applications:** No closing date; priority given to applications received by May 1; applicants notified on a rolling basis beginning on or about July 1; must reply by registration. **Additional information:** The college does not participate in loan programs. All financial aid is grant, scholarship, or work study.

ADDRESS/TELEPHONE. Perry Carroll, Director of Admissions, Records, and Financial Aid, Mountain Empire Community College, PO Drawer 700, Big Stone Gap, VA 24219. (703) 523-2400 ext. 209. Fax: (703) 523-2400 ext. 323.

National Business College
Roanoke, Virginia — CB code: 5502

4-year proprietary business, junior college, coed. Founded in 1886. **Undergraduate enrollment:** 1,319 men and women. **Faculty:** 171 total (14 full time), 9 with doctorates or other terminal degrees. **Location:** Suburban campus in small city; 233 miles from Washington DC, 168 miles from Richmond. **Calendar:** Quarter. Extensive evening/early morning classes. **Microcomputers:** Located in classrooms, computer centers. **Additional facts:** 8 campuses in Virginia: Bluefield, Charlottesville, Danville, Harrisonburg, Lynchburg, Martinsville, Roanoke, Bristol.

DEGREES OFFERED. AA, AS, BA. 304 associate degrees awarded in 1992. 20% in business and management, 33% business/office and marketing/distribution, 15% computer sciences, 15% allied health, 17% multi/interdisciplinary studies. 17 bachelor's degrees awarded. 100% in business and management.

UNDERGRADUATE MAJORS. Associate: Accounting, business administration and management, business and office, business data processing and related programs, business data programming, computer and information sciences, fashion merchandising, hotel/motel and restaurant management, legal secretary, liberal/general studies, marketing and distribution, medical assistant, medical records technology, medical secretary, office supervision and management, secretarial and related programs, tourism, transportation and travel marketing, word processing. **Bachelor's:** Accounting, business administration and management.

ACADEMIC PROGRAMS. Accelerated program, double major, internships. **Remedial services:** Tutoring. **Placement/credit:** Institutional tests.

ACADEMIC REQUIREMENTS. Freshmen must earn minimum GPA of 2.0 to continue in good standing. 72% of freshmen return for sophomore year. Students must declare major on enrollment. **Graduation requirements:** 108 hours for associate, 180 hours for bachelor's. Most students required to take courses in English, mathematics.

FRESHMAN ADMISSIONS. Selection criteria: Open admissions.

1992 FRESHMAN CLASS PROFILE. 35 men, 202 women enrolled. **Characteristics:** 98% from in state, 85% commute, 40% have minority backgrounds, 1% are foreign students. Average age is 20.

FALL-TERM APPLICATIONS. $20 fee. No closing date; applicants notified on a rolling basis. Interview recommended. Deferred admission available.

STUDENT LIFE. Housing: Dormitories (coed). **Activities:** Student government, student newspaper, fraternities, sororities.

STUDENT SERVICES. Career counseling, freshman orientation, personal counseling, placement service for graduates, services/facilities for handicapped.

ANNUAL EXPENSES. Tuition and fees (1992-93): $4,710. **Room and board:** $4,653. **Books and supplies:** $495. **Other expenses:** $500.

FINANCIAL AID. Grants, loans, jobs available. Academic, state/district residency scholarships available. **Aid applications:** No closing date; applicants notified on a rolling basis; must reply within 15 days.

ADDRESS/TELEPHONE. Larry W. Steele, Vice President of Admissions, National Business College, PO Box 6400, Roanoke, VA 24017-0400. (703) 986-1800. (800) 666-6221. Fax: (703) 986-1344.

New River Community College
Dublin, Virginia — CB code: 5513

2-year public community college, coed. Founded in 1966. **Accreditation:** Regional. **Undergraduate enrollment:** 761 men, 884 women full time; 806 men, 1,131 women part time. **Faculty:** 211 total (86 full time), 12 with doctorates or other terminal degrees. **Location:** Rural campus in rural community; 50 miles from Roanoke. **Calendar:** Semester, limited summer session. **Microcomputers:** Located in libraries, computer centers.

DEGREES OFFERED. AAS. 285 associate degrees awarded in 1992. 16% in business and management, 11% business/office and marketing/distribution, 5% computer sciences, 41% engineering technologies, 8% multi/interdisciplinary studies, 9% parks/recreation, protective services, public affairs, 8% trade and industry.

UNDERGRADUATE MAJORS. Accounting, architectural technologies, biological and physical sciences, business administration and management, business and management, child development/care/guidance, community services, data processing, drafting, drafting and design technology, education, electrical technology, electronic technology, fashion merchandising, forensic studies, industrial technology, instrumentation technology, liberal/general studies, machine tool operation/machine shop, marketing and distribution, secretarial and related programs, word processing.

ACADEMIC PROGRAMS. 2-year transfer program, cooperative education, dual enrollment of high school students, honors program, telecourses. **Remedial services:** Learning center, remedial instruction, special counselor, tutoring, developmental studies. **Placement/credit:** CLEP General and Subject, institutional tests.

ACADEMIC REQUIREMENTS. Freshmen must earn minimum GPA of 2.0 to continue in good standing. Students must declare major on enrollment. **Graduation requirements:** 65 hours for associate. Most students required to take courses in English, mathematics, social sciences.

FRESHMAN ADMISSIONS. Selection criteria: Open admissions.

1992 FRESHMAN CLASS PROFILE. 204 men, 230 women enrolled. **Characteristics:** 98% from in state, 100% commute, 5% have minority backgrounds. Average age is 26.

FALL-TERM APPLICATIONS. No fee. No closing date; applicants notified on a rolling basis. Interview required for nursing applicants. Early admission available.

STUDENT LIFE. Activities: Student government, student newspaper, choral groups, Black Student Union, Phi Beta Lambda, Phi Theta Kappa.

ATHLETICS. Intramural: Basketball, softball, volleyball.

STUDENT SERVICES. Aptitude testing, career counseling, employment service for undergraduates, freshman orientation, on-campus day care, personal counseling, placement service for graduates, veterans counselor, services/facilities for handicapped.

ANNUAL EXPENSES. Tuition and fees: $1,344, $3,030 additional for out-of-state students. **Books and supplies:** $250. **Other expenses:** $950.

FINANCIAL AID. 42% of freshmen, 50% of continuing students receive some form of aid. 98% of grants, 92% of loans, all jobs based on need. Academic, state/district residency scholarships available. **Aid applications:** No closing date; priority given to applications received by April 15; applicants notified on a rolling basis; must reply within 10 days.

ADDRESS/TELEPHONE. Margaret T. Chrisley, Coordinator of Admissions and Records, New River Community College, Drawer 1127, Dublin, VA 24084. (703) 674-3603. Fax: (703) 674-3642.

Norfolk State University
Norfolk, Virginia CB code: 5864

Admissions: 85% of applicants accepted
Based on: ••• Recommendations
•• Activities, school record, special talents
• Test scores
Completion: 80% of freshmen end year in good standing

4-year public university, coed. Founded in 1935. **Accreditation:** Regional. **Undergraduate enrollment:** 2,661 men, 4,090 women full time; 346 men, 544 women part time. **Graduate enrollment:** 60 men, 173 women full time; 119 men, 544 women part time. **Faculty:** 526 total (399 full time), 247 with doctorates or other terminal degrees. **Location:** Urban campus in large city; in metropolitan Tidewater area. **Calendar:** Semester, extensive summer session. **Special facilities:** Planetarium, art gallery.

DEGREES OFFERED. AS, BA, BS, MA, MS, MFA, MSW. 58 associate degrees awarded in 1992. 88% in health sciences, 9% trade and industry. 659 bachelor's degrees awarded. 16% in business and management, 9% communications, 19% education, 5% health sciences, 24% social sciences. Graduate degrees offered in 14 major fields of study.

UNDERGRADUATE MAJORS. Associate: Construction, drafting, electronic technology, library science, nursing, secretarial and related programs, textiles and clothing. **Bachelor's:** Accounting, biology, business and management, business education, chemistry, clinical laboratory science, computer and information sciences, construction, drafting and design technology, economics, electrical/electronics/communications engineering, elementary education, English, family/consumer resource management, fine arts, food science and nutrition, foreign languages education, health care administration, health education, history, home economics, home economics education, individual and family development, industrial arts education, institutional/home management/supporting programs, journalism, labor/industrial relations, liberal/general studies, mathematics, medical records administration, music, nursing, parks and recreation management, physical education, physics, political science and government, psychology, radio/television broadcasting, reading education, secretarial and related programs, social work, sociology, special education, speech pathology/audiology, urban studies.

ACADEMIC PROGRAMS. Accelerated program, cooperative education, double major, honors program, independent study, internships, teacher preparation, cross-registration. **Remedial services:** Learning center, reduced course load, remedial instruction, special counselor, tutoring. **ROTC:** Army, Naval. **Placement/credit:** AP, CLEP General and Subject, institutional tests; 30 credit hours maximum for bachelor's degree.

ACADEMIC REQUIREMENTS. Freshmen must earn minimum GPA of 1.6 to continue in good standing. 80% of freshmen return for sophomore year. Students must declare major by end of second year. **Graduation requirements:** 66 hours for associate, 126 hours for bachelor's. Most students required to take courses in English, mathematics, biological/physical sciences, social sciences.

FRESHMAN ADMISSIONS. Selection criteria: 2.0 GPA required for regular admission. Students with less than 2.0 may be admitted conditionally. 2 letters of recommendation required. **High school preparation:** 20 units recommended. Recommended units include English 4, mathematics 2, social science 3 and science 2. 2 science required for nursing applicants, 2 mathematics must include algebra II for computer science applicants. **Test requirements:** SAT or ACT (SAT preferred) for placement and counseling only; score report by September 1.

1992 FRESHMAN CLASS PROFILE. 1,706 men applied, 1,389 accepted, 614 enrolled; 2,585 women applied, 2,260 accepted, 920 enrolled. **Characteristics:** 60% from in state, 65% commute, 95% have minority backgrounds, 23% are foreign students.

FALL-TERM APPLICATIONS. $15 fee, may be waived for applicants with need. No closing date; priority given to applications received by June 1; applicants notified on a rolling basis beginning on or about February 1. Interview recommended for nursing, electronics, engineering applicants. Audition recommended for music applicants. Portfolio recommended for art applicants. Deferred and early admission available.

STUDENT LIFE. Housing: Dormitories (men, women). **Activities:** Student government, radio, student newspaper, yearbook, choral groups, concert band, dance, drama, jazz band, marching band, music ensembles, symphony orchestra, fraternities, sororities.

ATHLETICS. NCAA. **Intercollegiate:** Baseball M, basketball, cross-country, football M, softball W, track and field, volleyball W, wrestling M. **Intramural:** Badminton M, basketball, bowling, cross-country, rifle M, soccer M, softball, swimming, table tennis, tennis, track and field, volleyball, wrestling M.

STUDENT SERVICES. Aptitude testing, career counseling, employment service for undergraduates, health services, on-campus day care, personal counseling, placement service for graduates, veterans counselor, services/facilities for handicapped.

ANNUAL EXPENSES. Tuition and fees: $2,745, $3,280 additional for out-of-state students. **Room and board:** $3,600. **Books and supplies:** $500. **Other expenses:** $1,200.

FINANCIAL AID. 85% of freshmen, 75% of continuing students receive some form of aid. 99% of grants, 92% of loans, 67% of jobs based on need. Academic, leadership scholarships available. **Aid applications:** No closing date; priority given to applications received by April 15; applicants notified on a rolling basis beginning on or about May 15; must reply within 2 weeks.

ADDRESS/TELEPHONE. Dr. Frank W. Cool, Director of Admissions, Norfolk State University, 2401 Corprew Avenue, Norfolk, VA 23504. (804) 683-8396.

Northern Virginia Community College
Annandale, Virginia CB code: 5515

2-year public community college, coed. Founded in 1965. **Accreditation:** Regional. **Undergraduate enrollment:** 5,033 men, 4,380 women full time; 13,294 men, 16,543 women part time. **Faculty:** 1,449 total (619 full time). **Location:** Suburban campus in small city; 12 miles from Washington, D.C. **Calendar:** Semester, limited summer session. **Microcomputers:** Located in libraries, classrooms, computer centers. **Additional facts:** 5 campuses in Alexandria, Annandale, Loudoun County, Manassas, Woodbridge.

DEGREES OFFERED. AA, AS, AAS. 2,138 associate degrees awarded in 1992. 20% in business and management, 10% computer sciences, 6% health sciences, 5% allied health, 30% multi/interdisciplinary studies.

UNDERGRADUATE MAJORS. Accounting, aeronautical technology, air conditioning/heating/refrigeration mechanics, air conditioning/heating/refrigeration technology, airline piloting and navigation, animal sciences, architecture, art education, automotive mechanics, automotive technology, aviation management, biological and physical sciences, business administration and management, business and management, business and office, business data processing and related programs, child development/care/guidance, civil engineering, clinical laboratory science, commercial art, computer and information sciences, computer programming, contract management and procurement/purchasing, criminal justice studies, data processing, dental hygiene, electrical and electronics equipment repair, electrical/electronics/communications engineering, emergency medical technologies, engineering, engineering and engineering-related technologies, fashion merchandising, fine arts, fire control and safety technology, food management, food production/management/services, gerontology, horticulture, hotel/motel and restaurant management, institutional management, interior design, international studies, legal assistant/paralegal, liberal/general studies, marketing and distribution, mathematics, mechanical engineering, medical laboratory technologies, medical records administration, medical records technology, mental health/human services, microcomputer software, music, nursing, parks and recreation management, photographic technology, photography, physical therapy assistant, protective services, radiograph medical technology, real estate, respiratory therapy, respiratory therapy technology, secretarial and related programs, tourism, transportation and travel marketing, veterinarian's assistant, word processing.

ACADEMIC PROGRAMS. 2-year transfer program, cooperative education, double major, dual enrollment of high school students, honors program, independent study, internships, telecourses, weekend college. **Remedial services:** Learning center, reduced course load, remedial instruction, special counselor, tutoring. **Placement/credit:** AP, CLEP General and Subject, institutional tests.

ACADEMIC REQUIREMENTS. Freshmen must earn minimum GPA of 2.0 to continue in good standing. 31% of freshmen return for sophomore year. **Graduation requirements:** 65 hours for associate. Most students required to take courses in computer science, English, history, humanities, mathematics, biological/physical sciences, social sciences.

FRESHMAN ADMISSIONS. Selection criteria: Open admissions. Selective admissions to some programs. Developmental courses may be required for students who do not have certain basic academic skills.

1992 FRESHMAN CLASS PROFILE. 2,881 men, 2,772 women enrolled. **Characteristics:** 89% from in state, 100% commute, 35% have minority backgrounds, 1% are foreign students. Average age is 23.

FALL-TERM APPLICATIONS. No fee. No closing date; applicants notified on a rolling basis. Interview recommended for nursing, dental hygiene, animal science, allied health applicants. Deferred and early admission available.

STUDENT LIFE. Activities: Student government, student newspaper, literary journal, choral groups, concert band, dance, drama, jazz band, music ensembles, musical theater, symphony orchestra, Alpha Phi Omega, Alpha Sigma, Gamma Sigma Sigma, Phi Theta Kappa, black student organizations, religious groups, Korean and Vietnamese student organizations, Baptist Student Union, Newman student association.

STUDENT SERVICES. Aptitude testing, career counseling, freshman orientation, special adviser for adult students, veterans counselor, services/facilities for handicapped.

ANNUAL EXPENSES. Tuition and fees: $1,360, $3,030 additional for out-of-state students. **Books and supplies:** $526. **Other expenses:** $816.

FINANCIAL AID. 14% of freshmen, 10% of continuing students receive some form of aid. All aid based on need. Academic, state/district residency, leadership, minority scholarships available. **Aid applications:** No closing date; priority given to applications received by March 1; applicants notified on a rolling basis beginning on or about May 15; must reply within 2 weeks.

ADDRESS/TELEPHONE. Administrative Offices, Northern Virginia Community College, 4001 Wakefield Chapel Road, Annandale, VA 22003. (703) 323-3000.

Old Dominion University
Norfolk, Virginia CB code: 5126

4-year public university, coed. Founded in 1930. **Accreditation:** Regional. **Undergraduate enrollment:** 11,333 men and women. **Graduate enrollment:** 5,175 men and women. **Faculty:** 703 total, 465 with doctorates or other terminal degrees. **Location:** Suburban campus in large city; 2 miles from downtown. **Calendar:** Semester, extensive summer session. **Microcomputers:** 550 located in dormitories, libraries, classrooms, computer centers. **Special facilities:** Oceanographic research vessel, planetarium, student art gallery, pine barrens preserve, laser optics laboratory, robotics laboratory, subsonic and supersonic wind tunnels, wave motion laboratory. **Additional facts:** Graduate classes taught at multiple off-campus centers.

DEGREES OFFERED. BA, BS, MA, MS, MBA, MFA, PhD. 2,037 bachelor's degrees awarded in 1992. Graduate degrees offered in 57 major fields of study.

UNDERGRADUATE MAJORS. Accounting, anthropology, applied mathematics, art education, art history, biochemistry, biology, business administration and management, business economics, business education, chemistry, civil engineering, clinical laboratory science, computer and information sciences, computer engineering, criminal justice studies, criminology, dance, dental hygiene, dramatic arts, earth sciences, economics, education of exceptional children, education of the deaf and hearing impaired, education of the emotionally handicapped, education of the mentally handicapped, electrical/electronics/communications engineering, elementary education, engineering and engineering-related technologies, engineering and other disciplines, English, English education, environmental science, finance, fine arts, foreign languages education, French, geography, geology, German, health education, history, industrial arts education, information sciences and systems, international business management, international relations, journalism, junior high education, liberal/general studies, management information systems, management science, marketing and distributive education, marketing management, mathematics, mathematics education, mechanical engineering, medical laboratory technologies, music, music education, music history and appreciation, music performance, music theory and composition, nuclear medical technology, nursing, parks and recreation management, personnel management, philosophy, physical education, physics, political science and government, predentistry, premedicine, prepharmacy, preveterinary, psychology, public health laboratory science, religion, Russian, science education, secondary education, social science education, social studies education, social work, sociology, Spanish, special education, specific learning disabilities, speech, speech correction, speech pathology/audiology, sports medicine, statistics, visual and performing arts.

ACADEMIC PROGRAMS. Accelerated program, cooperative education, double major, dual enrollment of high school students, honors program, independent study, internships, student-designed major, study abroad, teacher preparation, telecourses, visiting/exchange student program, cross-registration; liberal arts/career combination in engineering; combined bachelor's/graduate program in business administration, medicine. **Remedial services:** Learning center, reduced course load, remedial instruction, tutoring, writing center. **ROTC:** Army, Naval. **Placement/credit:** AP, CLEP General and Subject, institutional tests; 45 credit hours maximum for bachelor's degree.

ACADEMIC REQUIREMENTS. Freshmen must earn minimum GPA of 2.0 to continue in good standing. 80% of freshmen return for sophomore year. Students must declare major by end of second year. **Graduation requirements:** 120 hours for bachelor's (35 in major). Most students required to take courses in arts/fine arts, computer science, English, foreign languages, history, mathematics, philosophy/religion, biological/physical sciences, social sciences.

FRESHMAN ADMISSIONS. Selection criteria: Rank in top half of class, GPA 2.5, and SAT combined score of 850 preferred. **High school preparation:** 16 units recommended. Recommended units include English 4, foreign language 3, mathematics 3, social science 3 and science 3. 3 units of mathematics required for engineering technology applicants, 4 units for engineering applicants. **Test requirements:** SAT or ACT (SAT preferred); score report by July 30.

1992 FRESHMAN CLASS PROFILE. 1,536 men and women enrolled. 33% had high school GPA of 3.0 or higher, 62% between 2.0 and 2.99. **Academic background:** Mid 50% of enrolled freshmen had SAT-V between 390-490, SAT-M between 430-550. 93% submitted SAT scores. **Characteristics:** 70% from in state, 60% live in college housing, 18% have minority backgrounds, 2% are foreign students, 7% join fraternities/sororities. Average age is 18.

FALL-TERM APPLICATIONS. $30 fee, may be waived for applicants with need. Closing date May 1; priority given to applications received by March 1; applicants notified on a rolling basis beginning on or about November 1. Audition required for music applicants. Portfolio required for art applicants. Essay recommended. CRDA. Deferred and early admission available.

STUDENT LIFE. Housing: Dormitories (men, women, coed); apartment, fraternity, sorority, cooperative housing available. **Activities:** Student government, magazine, radio, student newspaper, television, yearbook, choral groups, concert band, dance, drama, jazz band, music ensembles, musical theater, pep band, symphony orchestra, fraternities, sororities, nearly 200 student clubs and organizations.

ATHLETICS. NCAA. **Intercollegiate:** Baseball M, basketball, cross-country, diving, field hockey W, golf M, lacrosse W, sailing, soccer M, swimming, tennis, wrestling M. **Intramural:** Baseball M, basketball, fencing, ice hockey M, lacrosse M, racquetball, rowing (crew), rugby, soccer, softball, swimming, table tennis, tennis, volleyball.

STUDENT SERVICES. Aptitude testing, career counseling, employment service for undergraduates, freshman orientation, health services, personal counseling, placement service for graduates, veterans counselor, women's center, services/facilities for handicapped.

ANNUAL EXPENSES. Tuition and fees (projected): $3,788, $5,550 additional for out-of-state students. **Room and board:** $4,450. **Books and supplies:** $500. **Other expenses:** $1,170.

FINANCIAL AID. 63% of freshmen, 57% of continuing students receive some form of aid. 73% of grants, 89% of loans, all jobs based on need. Academic, music/drama, art, athletic, state/district residency, leadership, alumni affiliation, religious affiliation, minority scholarships available. **Aid applications:** No closing date; priority given to applications received by February 15; applicants notified on a rolling basis beginning on or about May 14; must reply within 2 weeks.

ADDRESS/TELEPHONE. Patricia Cavender, Director of Admissions, Old Dominion University, Hampton Boulevard, Norfolk, VA 23529-0050. (804) 683-3637. (800) 348-7926. Fax: (804) 683-5357.

Patrick Henry Community College
Martinsville, Virginia CB code: 5549

2-year public community college, coed. Founded in 1962. **Accreditation:** Regional. **Undergraduate enrollment:** 259 men, 416 women full time; 719 men, 1,176 women part time. **Faculty:** 119 total (43 full time), 7 with doctorates or other terminal degrees. **Location:** Rural campus in large town; 50 miles from Roanoke. **Calendar:** Semester, limited summer session. **Microcomputers:** 100 located in libraries, classrooms, computer centers. **Special facilities:** Southern history collection, Carter Collection of Literature, Fine Arts Theater.

DEGREES OFFERED. AAS. 137 associate degrees awarded in 1992. 30% in business and management, 14% computer sciences, 8% education, 22% health sciences, 15% multi/interdisciplinary studies, 5% physical sciences, 6% trade and industry.

UNDERGRADUATE MAJORS. Accounting, biological and physical sciences, business administration and management, business and management, business and office, business data processing and related programs, computer programming, education, electronic technology, engineering, engineering and engineering-related technologies, fine arts, information sciences and systems, liberal/general studies, marketing and distribution, nursing, science technologies, secretarial and related programs.

ACADEMIC PROGRAMS. 2-year transfer program, cooperative education, double major, dual enrollment of high school students, external degree, independent study, internships, teacher preparation, weekend college. **Remedial services:** Learning center, preadmission summer program, reduced course load, remedial instruction, special counselor, tutoring. **Placement/credit:** AP, institutional tests; 12 credit hours maximum for associate degree.

ACADEMIC REQUIREMENTS. Freshmen must earn minimum GPA of 1.5 to continue in good standing. Students must declare major on enrollment. **Graduation requirements:** 65 hours for associate (30 in major). Most students required to take courses in arts/fine arts, computer science, English, history, humanities, mathematics, social sciences.

FRESHMAN ADMISSIONS. Selection criteria: Open admissions. High school diploma or GED required for some programs.

1992 FRESHMAN CLASS PROFILE. 736 men and women enrolled. **Characteristics:** 99% from in state, 100% commute, 11% have minority backgrounds.

FALL-TERM APPLICATIONS. No fee. No closing date; priority given to applications received by August 1; applicants notified on a rolling basis beginning on or about February 1; must reply by registration. Interview recommended. Deferred and early admission available. Deadline for nursing applicants March 1.

STUDENT LIFE. Activities: Student government, student newspaper, drama, musical theater, Black Student Association, Phi Theta Kappa, Campus Awareness Network, Nurses Association.

ATHLETICS. Intercollegiate: Basketball M. **Intramural:** Basketball, softball, table tennis, tennis.

STUDENT SERVICES. Aptitude testing, career counseling, employment service for undergraduates, freshman orientation, personal counsel-

ing, placement service for graduates, special adviser for adult students, veterans counselor, services/facilities for handicapped.

ANNUAL EXPENSES. Tuition and fees: $1,330, $3,030 additional for out-of-state students. **Books and supplies:** $425. **Other expenses:** $840.

FINANCIAL AID. 45% of continuing students receive some form of aid. All grants, all jobs based on need. Academic, state/district residency, leadership scholarships available. **Aid applications:** No closing date; priority given to applications received by June 15; applicants notified on a rolling basis beginning on or about June 15.

ADDRESS/TELEPHONE. Graham Valentine, Admissions Counselor, Patrick Henry Community College, PO 5311, Martinsville, VA 24115-5311. (703) 638-8777. Fax: (703) 638-6469.

Paul D. Camp Community College
Franklin, Virginia CB code: 5557

2-year public community college, coed. Founded in 1970. **Accreditation:** Regional. **Undergraduate enrollment:** 111 men, 188 women full time; 443 men, 722 women part time. **Faculty:** 94 total (34 full time), 13 with doctorates or other terminal degrees. **Location:** Rural campus in small town; 50 miles from Norfolk. **Calendar:** Semester, extensive summer session. **Microcomputers:** 100 located in computer centers. **Additional facts:** Franklin and Suffolk campuses.

DEGREES OFFERED. AA, AS, AAS. 100 associate degrees awarded in 1992.

UNDERGRADUATE MAJORS. Biological and physical sciences, business administration and management, business and management, business and office, computer and information sciences, drafting and design technology, education, electrical and electronics equipment repair, electronic technology, law enforcement and corrections technologies, liberal/general studies, marketing and distribution, secretarial and related programs.

ACADEMIC PROGRAMS. 2-year transfer program, dual enrollment of high school students, honors program, independent study, internships, cross-registration. **Remedial services:** Learning center, preadmission summer program, reduced course load, remedial instruction, special counselor, tutoring. **Placement/credit:** AP, CLEP General and Subject, institutional tests; 52 credit hours maximum for associate degree.

ACADEMIC REQUIREMENTS. Freshmen must earn minimum GPA of 2.0 to continue in good standing. 45% of freshmen return for sophomore year. Students must declare major on enrollment. **Graduation requirements:** 65 hours for associate. Most students required to take courses in computer science, English, humanities, mathematics, social sciences.

FRESHMAN ADMISSIONS. Selection criteria: Open admissions.

1992 FRESHMAN CLASS PROFILE. 261 men, 521 women enrolled. **Characteristics:** 99% from in state, 100% commute, 17% have minority backgrounds, 1% are foreign students. Average age is 19.

FALL-TERM APPLICATIONS. No fee. No closing date; priority given to applications received by August 22; applicants notified on a rolling basis. Deferred admission available.

STUDENT LIFE. Activities: Student government, choral groups, fraternities, honor societies, circle k.

ATHLETICS. Intramural: Basketball, volleyball.

STUDENT SERVICES. Aptitude testing, career counseling, employment service for undergraduates, freshman orientation, personal counseling, placement service for graduates, veterans counselor, services/facilities for handicapped.

ANNUAL EXPENSES. Tuition and fees (1992-93): $1,230, $3,030 additional for out-of-state students. **Books and supplies:** $450. **Other expenses:** $900.

FINANCIAL AID. 48% of freshmen, 75% of continuing students receive some form of aid. 99% of grants, all jobs based on need. All loans based on criteria other than need. 300 enrolled freshmen were judged to have need, all were offered aid. Academic scholarships available. **Aid applications:** Closing date August 16; priority given to applications received by July 30; applicants notified on a rolling basis beginning on or about July 26; must reply within 2 weeks.

ADDRESS/TELEPHONE. Dr. Jerry Standahl, Director of Student Development, Paul D. Camp Community College, PO Box 737, 100 North College Drive, Franklin, VA 23851-0737. (804) 562-2171. (800) 777-5893. Fax: (804) 562-7430.

Piedmont Virginia Community College
Charlottesville, Virginia CB code: 5561

2-year public community college, coed. Founded in 1969. **Accreditation:** Regional. **Undergraduate enrollment:** 385 men, 458 women full time; 1,202 men, 2,280 women part time. **Faculty:** 209 total (59 full time), 55 with doctorates or other terminal degrees. **Location:** Suburban campus in large town; 70 miles from Richmond. **Calendar:** Semester, limited summer session. **Microcomputers:** 115 located in classrooms, computer centers.

DEGREES OFFERED. AA, AS, AAS. 168 associate degrees awarded in 1992. 25% in business and management, 7% computer sciences, 6% education, 30% health sciences, 19% multi/interdisciplinary studies, 5% visual and performing arts.

UNDERGRADUATE MAJORS. Accounting, biology, business administration and management, business and management, business and office, business data processing and related programs, business data programming, community services, computer and information sciences, drafting and design technology, education, electronic technology, engineering, finance, fine arts, insurance and risk management, law enforcement and corrections technologies, liberal/general studies, marketing and distribution, marketing management, mathematics, nursing, physical sciences, protective services, real estate, secretarial and related programs.

ACADEMIC PROGRAMS. 2-year transfer program, cooperative education, dual enrollment of high school students, honors program, independent study. **Remedial services:** Learning center, remedial instruction, tutoring. **ROTC:** Air Force, Army. **Placement/credit:** Institutional tests.

ACADEMIC REQUIREMENTS. Freshmen must earn minimum GPA of 1.5 to continue in good standing. 65% of freshmen return for sophomore year. Students must declare major on application. **Graduation requirements:** 65 hours for associate (48 in major). Most students required to take courses in computer science, English, humanities, mathematics, biological/physical sciences, social sciences.

FRESHMAN ADMISSIONS. Selection criteria: Open admissions.

1992 FRESHMAN CLASS PROFILE. 1,825 men and women enrolled. **Characteristics:** 98% from in state, 100% commute, 15% have minority backgrounds, 1% are foreign students. Average age is 26.

FALL-TERM APPLICATIONS. No fee. No closing date; applicants notified on a rolling basis. Interview required for nursing applicants. Early admission available. Accepted applicants to nursing program must reply within 10 days.

STUDENT LIFE. Activities: Student newspaper, yearbook, drama, Black Student Alliance, PEERS (tutoring), Phi Theta Kappa.

ATHLETICS. Intramural: Archery, basketball, bowling, football M, skiing, softball, tennis.

STUDENT SERVICES. Aptitude testing, career counseling, employment service for undergraduates, personal counseling, placement service for graduates, veterans counselor, services/facilities for handicapped.

ANNUAL EXPENSES. Tuition and fees: $1,336, $3,030 additional for out-of-state students. **Books and supplies:** $500. **Other expenses:** $1,200.

FINANCIAL AID. 15% of freshmen, 15% of continuing students receive some form of aid. All aid based on need. **Aid applications:** No closing date; priority given to applications received by April 15; applicants notified on a rolling basis beginning on or about June 15; must reply within 2 weeks.

ADDRESS/TELEPHONE. Joyce Knight, Student Services Specialist, Piedmont Virginia Community College, Route 6 Box 1A, Charlottesville, VA 22901-8714. (804) 977-3900.

Radford University
Radford, Virginia CB code: 5565

Admissions:	84% of applicants accepted
Based on:	••• School record, test scores
	• Activities, essay, interview, recommendations, special talents
Completion:	71% of freshmen end year in good standing
	45% graduate, 15% of these enter graduate study

4-year public university, coed. Founded in 1910. **Accreditation:** Regional. **Undergraduate enrollment:** 3,413 men, 4,697 women full time; 191 men, 226 women part time. **Graduate enrollment:** 118 men, 232 women full time; 158 men, 345 women part time. **Faculty:** 392 total, 297 with doctorates or other terminal degrees. **Location:** Rural campus in large town; 45 miles from Roanoke. **Calendar:** Semester, limited summer session. **Microcomputers:** 260 located in dormitories, libraries, classrooms, computer centers. **Special facilities:** Planetarium, greenhouse, art gallery, nature and recreational conservancy, radio/TV studios, speech and hearing clinic, brain research center, center for music technology.

DEGREES OFFERED. BA, BS, BFA, MA, MS, MBA, MFA. 1,780 bachelor's degrees awarded in 1992. 11% in business and management, 10% business/office and marketing/distribution, 18% teacher education, 9% health sciences, 7% mathematics, 5% parks/recreation, protective services, public affairs, 6% psychology, 11% social sciences. Graduate degrees offered in 39 major fields of study.

UNDERGRADUATE MAJORS. Accounting, art history, biology, business administration and management, business and management, business and office, business economics, chemistry, clinical laboratory science, communications, computer and information sciences, criminal justice studies, criminology, dance, dramatic arts, early childhood education, earth sciences, economics, education of the mentally handicapped, elementary education, English, fashion design, fashion merchandising, finance, fine arts, food management, food production/management/services, food science and nutrition, French, geography, geology, German, graphic design, history, human environment and housing, individual and family development, information sciences and systems, interior design, journalism, Latin, liberal/general studies, management information systems, marketing and distribution, mathematics, music, music business management, music performance, music therapy, nursing, office supervision and management, parks and recreation management, philosophy, physical sciences, political science and government, predentistry, prelaw, premedicine, psychology, public relations, radio/television broadcasting, radio/television technology, recreation therapy, religion, secondary education, small business management and ownership, social sciences, social work, sociology, Spanish, special education, speech, speech correction, speech pathology/audiology, sports management, sports medicine, statistics, studio art, textiles and clothing.

ACADEMIC PROGRAMS. Double major, dual enrollment of high school students, education specialist degree, external degree, honors program, independent study, internships, student-designed major, study abroad, teacher preparation, visiting/exchange student program. **Remedial services:** Learning center, tutoring. **ROTC:** Army. **Placement/credit:** AP, CLEP Subject, institutional tests; 30 credit hours maximum for bachelor's degree.

ACADEMIC REQUIREMENTS. Freshmen must earn minimum GPA of 1.5 to continue in good standing. 77% of freshmen return for sophomore year. Students must declare major by end of second year. **Graduation requirements:** 126 hours for bachelor's (75 in major). Most students required to take courses in arts/fine arts, computer science, English, history, humanities, mathematics, philosophy/religion, biological/physical sciences, social sciences.

FRESHMAN ADMISSIONS. Selection criteria: All aspects of academic record reviewed including SAT/ACT scores. **High school preparation:** 16 units required. Required and recommended units include English 4, mathematics 2-3, social science 2 and science 2. Foreign language 2 recommended. **Test requirements:** SAT or ACT (SAT preferred); score report by April 1.

1992 FRESHMAN CLASS PROFILE. 2,294 men applied, 1,823 accepted, 682 enrolled; 3,420 women applied, 2,951 accepted, 1,139 enrolled. 40% had high school GPA of 3.0 or higher, 60% between 2.0 and 2.99. **Characteristics:** 85% from in state, 94% live in college housing, 6% have minority backgrounds, 1% are foreign students, 8% join fraternities/sororities. Average age is 18.

FALL-TERM APPLICATIONS. $15 fee, may be waived for applicants with need. Closing date April 1; applicants notified on a rolling basis; must reply by May 1. Audition required for music, theater applicants. Portfolio required for art applicants. Interview recommended. Early admission available.

STUDENT LIFE. Housing: Dormitories (women, coed). Students may live on campus all 4 years. Almost all housing consists of suites with laundry and study facilities. **Activities:** Student government, magazine, radio, student newspaper, television, yearbook, choral groups, concert band, dance, drama, jazz band, music ensembles, musical theater, pep band, symphony orchestra, fraternities, sororities, Intervarsity Christy Fellowship, Circle-K International, African-American Heritage Associatiton, Amnesty International, College Republican, LaSociedad Hispanica, Diversity Promotion Council, International Club.

ATHLETICS. NCAA. **Intercollegiate:** Baseball M, basketball, cross-country, field hockey W, golf, gymnastics, lacrosse M, soccer, softball W, tennis, volleyball W. **Intramural:** Basketball, bowling, cross-country, diving, football, handball, horseback riding, racquetball, rugby M, soccer, softball, swimming, table tennis, tennis, volleyball, water polo.

STUDENT SERVICES. Aptitude testing, career counseling, employment service for undergraduates, freshman orientation, health services, on-campus day care, personal counseling, placement service for graduates, special adviser for adult students, veterans counselor, services/facilities for handicapped.

ANNUAL EXPENSES. Tuition and fees (1992-93): $2,746, $3,524 additional for out-of-state students. **Room and board:** $3,922. **Books and supplies:** $500. **Other expenses:** $750.

FINANCIAL AID. 47% of freshmen, 39% of continuing students receive some form of aid. 77% of grants, 71% of loans, 31% of jobs based on need. 547 enrolled freshmen were judged to have need, 531 were offered aid. Academic, music/drama, art, athletic, state/district residency, leadership, minority scholarships available. **Aid applications:** No closing date; priority given to applications received by March 1; applicants notified on a rolling basis beginning on or about April 15; must reply within 2 weeks.

ADDRESS/TELEPHONE. Vernon L. Beitzel, Director of Admissions, Radford University, PO Box 6903, Radford, VA 24142-6903. (703) 831-5371. Fax: (703) 831-5138.

Randolph-Macon College
Ashland, Virginia

CB code: 5566

Admissions:	75% of applicants accepted
Based on:	••• School record, test scores
	•• Recommendations
	• Activities, essay, interview, special talents
Completion:	95% of freshmen end year in good standing
	70% graduate, 29% of these enter graduate study

4-year private liberal arts college, coed, affiliated with United Methodist Church. Founded in 1830. **Accreditation:** Regional. **Undergraduate enrollment:** 527 men, 545 women full time; 18 men, 28 women part time. **Faculty:** 146 total (90 full time), 89 with doctorates or other terminal degrees. **Location:** Suburban campus in small town; 15 miles from Richmond, 90 miles from Washington, D.C. **Calendar:** 4-1-4, limited summer session. **Microcomputers:** 250 located in libraries, classrooms, computer centers. **Special facilities:** Observatory, 6 historic buildings. **Additional facts:** Proximity to Richmond and Washington, D.C. provides opportunities for internships, culture, and recreation.

DEGREES OFFERED. BA, BS. 252 bachelor's degrees awarded in 1992. 26% in business and management, 5% languages, 14% letters/literature, 7% life sciences, 17% psychology, 21% social sciences.

UNDERGRADUATE MAJORS. Art history, arts management, biology, business economics, chemistry, classics, computer and information sciences, dramatic arts, economics, English, environmental science, French, German, Greek (classical), history, international relations, international studies, Latin, mathematics, music, philosophy, physics, political science and government, psychology, religion, sociology, Spanish, studio art, women's studies.

ACADEMIC PROGRAMS. Accelerated program, double major, dual enrollment of high school students, honors program, independent study, internships, study abroad, teacher preparation, visiting/exchange student program, United Nations semester, Washington semester, cross-registration; liberal arts/career combination in engineering. **Remedial services:** Learning center, preadmission summer program, reduced course load, special counselor, tutoring, writing skills and reading centers. **ROTC:** Army. **Placement/credit:** AP, CLEP Subject, institutional tests; 30 credit hours maximum for bachelor's degree.

ACADEMIC REQUIREMENTS. Freshmen must earn minimum GPA of 1.6 to continue in good standing. 83% of freshmen return for sophomore year. Students must declare major by end of second year. **Graduation requirements:** 112 hours for bachelor's (30 in major). Most students required to take courses in arts/fine arts, computer science, English, foreign languages, history, mathematics, philosophy/religion, biological/physical sciences, social sciences. **Postgraduate studies:** 4% enter law school, 4% enter medical school, 3% enter MBA programs, 18% enter other graduate study. **Additional information:** Comprehensive liberal arts core curriculum, offered, computer literacy program, 4-1 program in accounting offered with Virginia Commonwealth University, forestry program with Duke University.

FRESHMAN ADMISSIONS. Selection criteria: School achievement record, class rank, and test scores most important. Personal recommendations, evidence of leadership and participation considered. **High school preparation:** 16 units required; 20 recommended. Required and recommended units include English 4, foreign language 3-4, mathematics 3-4, social science 3-4 and science 3-4. Selection of honors, advanced and A.P. courses enhances students' chances for admission. **Test requirements:** SAT or ACT (SAT preferred); score report by March 1.

1992 FRESHMAN CLASS PROFILE. 926 men applied, 637 accepted, 160 enrolled; 768 women applied, 629 accepted, 145 enrolled. 15% were in top tenth and 38% were in top quarter of graduating class. **Academic background:** Mid 50% of enrolled freshmen had SAT-V between 430-520, SAT-M between 480-570. 99% submitted SAT scores. **Characteristics:** 56% from in state, 95% live in college housing, 8% have minority backgrounds, 2% are foreign students. Average age is 18.

FALL-TERM APPLICATIONS. $30 fee, may be waived for applicants with need. No closing date; priority given to applications received by March 1; applicants notified on a rolling basis beginning on or about February 1; must reply by May 1 or within 2 weeks if notified thereafter. Essay required. Interview recommended. CRDA. Deferred and early admission available. EDP-F. Achievement tests in English, mathematics, and foreign language recommended.

STUDENT LIFE. Housing: Dormitories (men, women, coed); apartment, fraternity, sorority housing available. Several college owned houses available. **Activities:** Student government, magazine, radio, student newspaper, yearbook, choral groups, dance, drama, music ensembles, musical theater, debate, film series, fraternities, sororities, interdenominational groups and service organizations, Amnesty International, social and racial awareness groups, hunger task force, Waging Peace, Life Roles Awareness, Christian fellowship, weekly worship council, Volunteers in Action environmental group.

ATHLETICS. NCAA. **Intercollegiate:** Baseball M, basketball, cross-country, field hockey W, football M, golf M, lacrosse, soccer, tennis. **Intramural:** Basketball, lacrosse, soccer, softball, table tennis, tennis, volleyball.

STUDENT SERVICES. Career counseling, employment service for

undergraduates, freshman orientation, health services, personal counseling, placement service for graduates, special adviser for adult students, services/ facilities for handicapped.

ANNUAL EXPENSES. Tuition and fees (1992-93): $11,400. **Room and board:** $4,700. **Books and supplies:** $350. **Other expenses:** $550.

FINANCIAL AID. 68% of freshmen, 73% of continuing students receive some form of aid. 71% of grants, 99% of loans, 50% of jobs based on need. 130 enrolled freshmen were judged to have need, all were offered aid. Academic, state/district residency, religious affiliation, minority scholarships available. **Aid applications:** No closing date; priority given to applications received by March 1; applicants notified on a rolling basis beginning on or about March 15; must reply by May 1 or within 2 weeks if notified thereafter. **Additional information:** Scholorships and awards offered to outstanding students. Virginia residents eligible to receive the Virginia Tuition Assistance Grant (TAG): On-campus job opportunities and assistantships available through various academic departments and other college offices. Student referral service for part-time jobs with area employers within walking distance of college.

ADDRESS/TELEPHONE. John C. Conkright, Dean of Admissions and Financial Aid, Randolph-Macon College, Ashland, VA 23005-1697. (804) 752-7305. (800) 888-1762. Fax: (804) 752-4707.

Randolph-Macon Woman's College
Lynchburg, Virginia — CB code: 5567

Admissions: 87% of applicants accepted
Based on:
••• Recommendations, school record
•• Activities, essay, test scores
• Interview, special talents
Completion: 95% of freshmen end year in good standing
65% graduate, 28% of these enter graduate study

4-year private liberal arts college, women only, affiliated with United Methodist Church. Founded in 1891. **Accreditation:** Regional. **Undergraduate enrollment:** 2 men, 674 women full time; 4 men, 56 women part time. **Faculty:** 90 total (67 full time), 77 with doctorates or other terminal degrees. **Location:** Suburban campus in small city; 120 miles from Richmond, 200 miles from Washington, D.C. **Calendar:** Semester. **Microcomputers:** 80 located in dormitories, libraries, classrooms, computer centers. **Special facilities:** Maier Museum of Art, Winfree Observatory, learning resource center, 3 nature preserves, Ethyl science and mathematics resource center. **Additional facts:** Junior Year Program in England available at the University of Reading.

DEGREES OFFERED. BA. 175 bachelor's degrees awarded in 1992. 7% in communications, 11% letters/literature, 8% life sciences, 10% multi/ interdisciplinary studies, 9% psychology, 33% social sciences, 13% visual and performing arts.

UNDERGRADUATE MAJORS. Art history, biology, chemistry, classics, communications, dance, dramatic arts, economics, English, French, German, history, international relations, mathematics, Mathematics/Economics, music, philosophy, physics, Political economy, political science and government, psychology, religion, Russian and Slavic studies, Sociology/anthropology, Spanish, studio art.

ACADEMIC PROGRAMS. Accelerated program, double major, dual enrollment of high school students, honors program, independent study, internships, semester at sea, student-designed major, study abroad, teacher preparation, visiting/exchange student program, Washington semester, cross-registration, 7-college exchange with Washington and Lee University, Hollins College, Hampden-Sydney College, Mary Baldwin College, Sweet Briar College and Randolph-Macon College; liberal arts/career combination in engineering, health sciences. **Remedial services:** Learning center, special counselor, tutoring, writing center. **ROTC:** Army. **Placement/credit:** AP, CLEP Subject, institutional tests.

ACADEMIC REQUIREMENTS. Freshmen must earn minimum GPA of 2.0 to continue in good standing. 77% of freshmen return for sophomore year. Students must declare major by end of second year. **Graduation requirements:** 124 hours for bachelor's (24 in major). Most students required to take courses in arts/fine arts, English, foreign languages, history, mathematics, philosophy/religion, biological/physical sciences, social sciences. **Postgraduate studies:** 3% enter law school, 4% enter medical school, 1% enter MBA programs, 20% enter other graduate study. **Additional information:** Honor system includes self-scheduled, unproctored examinations. Curriculum offers options for independent study, self-designed majors, and academic internships.

FRESHMAN ADMISSIONS. Selection criteria: Rigor of and achievement in high school curriculum most important followed by teacher and counselor recommendations, test scores, activities, personal achievement. No single factor determines admission of candidate. **High school preparation:** 16 units recommended. Recommended units include biological science 1, English 4, foreign language 4, mathematics 3, physical science 1 and social science 2. **Test requirements:** SAT or ACT; score report by March 1.

1992 FRESHMAN CLASS PROFILE. 678 women applied, 592 accepted, 198 enrolled. 29% were in top tenth and 67% were in top quarter of graduating class. **Academic background:** Mid 50% of enrolled freshmen had SAT-V between 470-580, SAT-M between 460-580. 88% submitted SAT scores. **Characteristics:** 27% from in state, 98% live in college housing, 18% have minority backgrounds, 4% are foreign students. Average age is 18.

FALL-TERM APPLICATIONS. $25 fee, may be waived for applicants with need. No closing date; priority given to applications received by March 1; applicants notified on a rolling basis beginning on or about February 1; must reply by May 1 or within 2 weeks if notified thereafter. Essay required. Interview recommended. CRDA. Deferred and early admission available. EDP-F.

STUDENT LIFE. Housing: Dormitories (women). All students required to live in college housing unless living with family. **Activities:** Student government, film, magazine, radio, student newspaper, yearbook, choral groups, dance, drama, music ensembles, musical theater, international relations and current affairs clubs, Young Democrats, College Republicans, Black Students Association, women's organizations, Christian Fellowship, language clubs, volunteer service organizations. **Additional information:** R-MWC is located near many other colleges and universities in Virginia with over 28,000 college students within an hour's drive.

ATHLETICS. NCAA. **Intercollegiate:** Basketball, fencing, field hockey, horseback riding, lacrosse, soccer, softball, swimming, tennis, volleyball. **Intramural:** Basketball, horseback riding, soccer, softball, swimming, tennis, volleyball.

STUDENT SERVICES. Aptitude testing, career counseling, employment service for undergraduates, freshman orientation, health services, personal counseling, placement service for graduates, special adviser for adult students, services/facilities for handicapped.

ANNUAL EXPENSES. Tuition and fees: $13,440. **Room and board:** $5,780. **Books and supplies:** $350. **Other expenses:** $570.

FINANCIAL AID. 62% of freshmen, 51% of continuing students receive some form of aid. 83% of grants, 85% of loans, 78% of jobs based on need. 119 enrolled freshmen were judged to have need, all were offered aid. Academic, music/drama, state/district residency, leadership, minority scholarships available. **Aid applications:** No closing date; priority given to applications received by March 1; applicants notified on a rolling basis; must reply by May 1 or within 2 weeks if notified thereafter.

ADDRESS/TELEPHONE. James C. Kughn, Jr, Vice President for Admissions, Development, and Public Relations, Randolph-Macon Woman's College, 2500 Rivermont Avenue, Lynchburg, VA 24503. (804) 947-8100. (800) 745-7692. Fax: (804) 947-8138.

Rappahannock Community College
Glenns, Virginia — CB code: 5590

2-year public community college, coed. Founded in 1970. **Accreditation:** Regional. **Undergraduate enrollment:** 1,919 men and women. **Faculty:** 77 total (29 full time), 3 with doctorates or other terminal degrees. **Location:** Rural campus in rural community; 12 miles from West Point. **Calendar:** Semester, limited summer session. **Microcomputers:** Located in classrooms.

DEGREES OFFERED. AAS. 101 associate degrees awarded in 1992.

UNDERGRADUATE MAJORS. Accounting, automotive technology, business administration and management, business and office, drafting, drafting and design technology, education, electrical technology, electronic technology, liberal/general studies, nursing, secretarial and related programs.

ACADEMIC PROGRAMS. 2-year transfer program, dual enrollment of high school students, independent study, internships, weekend college, cross-registration. **Remedial services:** Learning center, reduced course load, remedial instruction, special counselor, tutoring, Student Support Services Program for culturally, economically, and educationally disadvantaged students. **Placement/credit:** AP, CLEP General and Subject, institutional tests; 77 credit hours maximum for associate degree.

ACADEMIC REQUIREMENTS. Freshmen must earn minimum GPA of 2.0 to continue in good standing. Students must declare major on application. **Graduation requirements:** 65 hours for associate (34 in major). Most students required to take courses in English, mathematics, social sciences.

FRESHMAN ADMISSIONS. Selection criteria: Open admissions.

1992 FRESHMAN CLASS PROFILE. 453 men and women enrolled. **Characteristics:** 99% from in state, 100% commute. Average age is 26.

FALL-TERM APPLICATIONS. No fee. Closing date August 28; applicants notified on a rolling basis. Interview recommended. Early admission available.

STUDENT LIFE. Activities: Student government, student newspaper.

ATHLETICS. Intramural: Baseball M, basketball, bowling, football M, softball, table tennis, tennis, volleyball.

STUDENT SERVICES. Career counseling, employment service for undergraduates, freshman orientation, personal counseling, placement service for graduates, special adviser for adult students, veterans counselor, Gender equity program, student support services program, services/facilities for handicapped.

ANNUAL EXPENSES. Tuition and fees (1992-93): $1,242, $3,030 additional for out-of-state students. **Books and supplies:** $500. **Other expenses:** $600.

FINANCIAL AID. 25% of freshmen, 30% of continuing students re-

ceive some form of aid. 99% of grants, 73% of loans, all jobs based on need. 60 enrolled freshmen were judged to have need, all were offered aid. Academic, state/district residency, leadership scholarships available. **Aid applications:** No closing date; priority given to applications received by June 1; applicants notified on a rolling basis beginning on or about July 1.

ADDRESS/TELEPHONE. Pamela Turner, Director of Student Personnel Services, Rappahannock Community College, PO Box 287, Glenns Campus, Glenns, VA 23149. (804) 758-5324 ext. 240. Fax: (804) 758-3852.

Richard Bland College

Petersburg, Virginia — CB code: 5574

Admissions: 91% of applicants accepted
Based on:
••• School record
•• Activities, interview
• Essay, recommendations, special talents, test scores
Completion: 86% of freshmen end year in good standing
45% graduate, 90% of these enter 4-year programs

2-year public junior, liberal arts college, coed. Founded in 1960. **Accreditation:** Regional. **Undergraduate enrollment:** 380 men, 449 women full time; 110 men, 325 women part time. **Faculty:** 63 total (41 full time), 13 with doctorates or other terminal degrees. **Location:** Suburban campus in large town; 25 miles from Richmond. **Calendar:** Semester, limited summer session. **Microcomputers:** 45 located in computer centers. **Special facilities:** Nature trail. **Additional facts:** Branch campus of College of William and Mary.

DEGREES OFFERED. AA, AS. 150 associate degrees awarded in 1992.

UNDERGRADUATE MAJORS. Biological and physical sciences, business and management, liberal/general studies, nursing.

ACADEMIC PROGRAMS. 2-year transfer program, accelerated program, dual enrollment of high school students, study abroad. **Remedial services:** Learning center, reduced course load, remedial instruction, special counselor, tutoring. **ROTC:** Army. **Placement/credit:** AP, CLEP General and Subject, institutional tests; 26 credit hours maximum for associate degree.

ACADEMIC REQUIREMENTS. Freshmen must earn minimum GPA of 1.5 to continue in good standing. 75% of freshmen return for sophomore year. Students must declare major on enrollment. **Graduation requirements:** 64 hours for associate. Most students required to take courses in arts/fine arts, English, history, humanities, mathematics, philosophy/religion, biological/physical sciences, social sciences.

FRESHMAN ADMISSIONS. Selection criteria: Academic record, extracurricular activities, recommendations, test scores considered. Recommended units include English 4, foreign language 2, mathematics 3 and science 2. 2 history also recommended. **Test requirements:** SAT or ACT; score report by August 15.

1992 FRESHMAN CLASS PROFILE. 256 men applied, 226 accepted, 179 enrolled; 346 women applied, 323 accepted, 252 enrolled. 21% had high school GPA of 3.0 or higher, 61% between 2.0 and 2.99. **Academic background:** Mid 50% of enrolled freshmen had SAT-V between 450-510, SAT-M between 470-510. 90% submitted SAT scores. **Characteristics:** 97% from in state, 100% commute, 20% have minority backgrounds, 1% are foreign students, 4% join fraternities/sororities. Average age is 18.

FALL-TERM APPLICATIONS. $10 fee, may be waived for applicants with need. Closing date August 15; applicants notified on a rolling basis beginning on or about January 15; must reply by August 23. Essay required. Interview recommended. CRDA. Deferred and early admission available.

STUDENT LIFE. Activities: Student government, magazine, radio, student newspaper, television, choral groups, concert band, dance, drama, music ensembles, fraternities, sororities, Rotaract Club (service organization), Circle K, and political groups.

ATHLETICS. NJCAA. **Intercollegiate:** Basketball M. **Intramural:** Basketball, bowling, golf, racquetball, soccer M, tennis, volleyball.

STUDENT SERVICES. Aptitude testing, career counseling, employment service for undergraduates, freshman orientation, personal counseling, special adviser for adult students, veterans counselor, services/facilities for handicapped.

ANNUAL EXPENSES. Tuition and fees (1992-93): $1,720, $3,230 additional for out-of-state students. **Books and supplies:** $500. **Other expenses:** $1,700.

FINANCIAL AID. 48% of freshmen, 35% of continuing students receive some form of aid. 92% of grants based on need. Academic scholarships available. **Aid applications:** Closing date June 1; priority given to applications received by April 1; applicants notified on or about July 1; must reply within 3 weeks.

ADDRESS/TELEPHONE. Roger Gill, Director of Enrollment Services, Richard Bland College, 11301 Johnson Road, Petersburg, VA 23805. (804) 862-6249. Fax: (804) 862-6189.

Roanoke College

Salem, Virginia — CB code: 5571

Admissions: 76% of applicants accepted
Based on:
••• School record, test scores
•• Interview
• Activities, essay, recommendations, special talents
Completion: 86% of freshmen end year in good standing
52% graduate

4-year private liberal arts college, coed, affiliated with Evangelical Lutheran Church in America. Founded in 1842. **Accreditation:** Regional. **Undergraduate enrollment:** 606 men, 854 women full time; 93 men, 124 women part time. **Faculty:** 146 total (101 full time), 97 with doctorates or other terminal degrees. **Location:** Suburban campus in large town; 7 miles from Roanoke. **Calendar:** Semester, limited summer session. **Microcomputers:** 113 located in libraries, classrooms, computer centers. **Special facilities:** Fine arts center with 3 galleries, media classroom, dance studio, full production theater, greenhouse, nuclear magnetic resonance equipment, center for community research, center for church and society.

DEGREES OFFERED. BA, BS. 367 bachelor's degrees awarded in 1992. 23% in business and management, 6% teacher education, 8% letters/literature, 8% psychology, 31% social sciences, 10% visual and performing arts.

UNDERGRADUATE MAJORS. Biology, business administration and management, business and management, chemistry, computer and information sciences, criminal justice studies, dramatic arts, economics, elementary education, English, fine arts, French, history, information sciences and systems, international relations, mathematics, medical laboratory technologies, music, physical education, physics, political science and government, psychology, religion/philosophy, sociology, Spanish, visual and performing arts.

ACADEMIC PROGRAMS. Accelerated program, double major, honors program, independent study, internships, study abroad, teacher preparation, Washington semester, cross-registration; liberal arts/career combination in engineering. **Remedial services:** Learning center, reduced course load, special counselor, tutoring. **Placement/credit:** AP, CLEP General and Subject, institutional tests; 27 credit hours maximum for bachelor's degree.

ACADEMIC REQUIREMENTS. Freshmen must earn minimum GPA of 1.5 to continue in good standing. 74% of freshmen return for sophomore year. Students must declare major by end of second year. **Graduation requirements:** 120 hours for bachelor's (36 in major). Most students required to take courses in arts/fine arts, English, foreign languages, history, humanities, mathematics, philosophy/religion, biological/physical sciences, social sciences.

FRESHMAN ADMISSIONS. Selection criteria: School achievement record and class rank most important. **High school preparation:** 16 units required. Required and recommended units include English 4, mathematics 3 and social science 3. Foreign language 2 and science 2 recommended. Mathematics must include algebra II. **Test requirements:** SAT or ACT (SAT preferred); score report by March 1.

1992 FRESHMAN CLASS PROFILE. 967 men applied, 665 accepted, 164 enrolled; 1,250 women applied, 1,012 accepted, 259 enrolled. 34% had high school GPA of 3.0 or higher, 59% between 2.0 and 2.99. 23% were in top tenth and 47% were in top quarter of graduating class. **Academic background:** Mid 50% of enrolled freshmen had SAT-V between 430-530, SAT-M between 470-570; ACT composite between 19-24. 87% submitted SAT scores, 12% submitted ACT scores. **Characteristics:** 42% from in state, 88% live in college housing, 6% have minority backgrounds, 1% are foreign students. Average age is 18.

FALL-TERM APPLICATIONS. $30 fee, may be waived for applicants with need. Closing date March 1; priority given to applications received by January 15; applicants notified on or about April 1; must reply by May 1. Interview recommended. Essay recommended. CRDA. Deferred and early admission available. EDP-F.

STUDENT LIFE. Housing: Dormitories (men, women, coed); fraternity, sorority housing available. Academic dormitories, freshman dormitories available. **Activities:** Student government, film, magazine, student newspaper, yearbook, choral groups, dance, drama, jazz band, music ensembles, musical theater, fraternities, sororities, political and social service organizations, 20 national honor societies, center for church and society, center for community research.

ATHLETICS. NCAA. **Intercollegiate:** Basketball, cross-country, field hockey W, golf M, lacrosse, soccer, tennis, track and field, volleyball W. **Intramural:** Badminton, baseball M, basketball, field hockey W, ice hockey M, racquetball, soccer, softball, table tennis, tennis, volleyball, water polo.

STUDENT SERVICES. Career counseling, employment service for undergraduates, freshman orientation, health services, personal counseling, placement service for graduates, special adviser for adult students, veterans counselor, services/facilities for handicapped.

ANNUAL EXPENSES. Tuition and fees: $12,625. **Room and board:** $4,350. **Books and supplies:** $450. **Other expenses:** $600.

FINANCIAL AID. 87% of freshmen, 78% of continuing students receive some form of aid. 49% of grants, 87% of loans, 25% of jobs based on

need. 200 enrolled freshmen were judged to have need, all were offered aid. Academic, music/drama, art, state/district residency, leadership, religious affiliation, minority scholarships available. **Aid applications:** No closing date; priority given to applications received by March 1; applicants notified on a rolling basis beginning on or about January 1; must reply by May 1 or within 2 weeks if notified thereafter.

ADDRESS/TELEPHONE. Michael C. Maxey, Vice President of Admissions Services, Roanoke College, 221 College Lane, Salem, VA 24153-3794. (703) 375-2270. (800) 388-2276.

St. Paul's College

Lawrenceville, Virginia CB code: 5604

Admissions: 84% of applicants accepted
Based on: ••• School record
•• Activities, recommendations, test scores
• Essay, interview, special talents
Completion: 75% of freshmen end year in good standing
35% graduate, 12% of these enter graduate study

4-year private liberal arts college, coed, affiliated with Episcopal Church. Founded in 1888. **Accreditation:** Regional. **Undergraduate enrollment:** 269 men, 388 women full time; 9 men, 35 women part time. **Faculty:** 64 total (46 full time), 27 with doctorates or other terminal degrees. **Location:** Rural campus in small town; 80 miles from Richmond. **Calendar:** Semester, limited summer session. Extensive evening/early morning classes. **Microcomputers:** Located in libraries, computer centers. **Special facilities:** Single Parent Support System. **Additional facts:** Organizational Management Program for adults 25 and older.

DEGREES OFFERED. BA, BS. 83 bachelor's degrees awarded in 1992. 46% in business and management, 15% education, 5% teacher education, 7% life sciences, 17% social sciences.

UNDERGRADUATE MAJORS. Biology, business administration and management, business and management, criminal justice studies, education, English, liberal/general studies, marketing and distribution, marketing management, mathematics, office supervision and management, physical sciences, political science and government, renewable natural resources, social sciences, sociology.

ACADEMIC PROGRAMS. Accelerated program, cooperative education, honors program, internships, teacher preparation. **Remedial services:** Learning center, preadmission summer program, reduced course load, remedial instruction, special counselor, tutoring. **ROTC:** Army. **Placement/credit:** AP, CLEP General and Subject, institutional tests; 24 credit hours maximum for bachelor's degree.

ACADEMIC REQUIREMENTS. Freshmen must earn minimum GPA of 1.4 to continue in good standing. 70% of freshmen return for sophomore year. Students must declare major by end of second year. **Graduation requirements:** 120 hours for bachelor's (30 in major). Most students required to take courses in arts/fine arts, computer science, English, history, humanities, mathematics, philosophy/religion, biological/physical sciences, social sciences. **Postgraduate studies:** 1% enter law school, 1% enter medical school, 1% enter MBA programs, 9% enter other graduate study.

FRESHMAN ADMISSIONS. Selection criteria: School achievement record most important. School recommendations considered. Rank in top half of class recommended. **High school preparation:** 20 units required; 21 recommended. Required and recommended units include English 4, mathematics 2-3, social science 2-3 and science 3. Biological science 3, foreign language 2 and physical science 2 recommended. **Test requirements:** SAT or ACT (SAT preferred) for placement and counseling only; score report by August 1.

1992 FRESHMAN CLASS PROFILE. 233 men applied, 196 accepted, 92 enrolled; 261 women applied, 219 accepted, 104 enrolled. 15% had high school GPA of 3.0 or higher, 80% between 2.0 and 2.99. 10% were in top tenth and 28% were in top quarter of graduating class. **Characteristics:** 70% from in state, 80% live in college housing, 92% have minority backgrounds, 1% are foreign students. Average age is 18.

FALL-TERM APPLICATIONS. $15 fee. No closing date; applicants notified on a rolling basis; must reply by May 1 or within 2 weeks if notified thereafter. Interview recommended. Essay recommended. CRDA. Deferred and early admission available. 3.0 GPA recommended.

STUDENT LIFE. Housing: Dormitories (men, women). **Activities:** Student government, student newspaper, yearbook, choral groups, dance, drama, pep band, fraternities, sororities, Altar Guild, veterans club, Canterbury Club, NAACP.

ATHLETICS. NCAA. **Intercollegiate:** Baseball M, basketball, cross-country, golf M, softball W, tennis, track and field, volleyball W. **Intramural:** Basketball, softball, volleyball.

STUDENT SERVICES. Career counseling, employment service for undergraduates, freshman orientation, health services, on-campus day care, personal counseling, placement service for graduates, special adviser for adult students, veterans counselor, services/facilities for handicapped.

ANNUAL EXPENSES. Tuition and fees: $5,521. **Room and board:** $3,650. **Books and supplies:** $486. **Other expenses:** $600.

FINANCIAL AID. 80% of freshmen, 90% of continuing students receive some form of aid. 90% of grants, 94% of loans, 91% of jobs based on need. Academic, state/district residency scholarships available. **Aid applications:** Closing date August 11; priority given to applications received by June 1; applicants notified on a rolling basis beginning on or about March 1; must reply by May 1 or within 2 weeks if notified thereafter.

ADDRESS/TELEPHONE. L.R. Parker, Director of Admissions and Recruitment, St. Paul's College, 406 Windsor Avenue, Lawrenceville, VA 23868. (804) 848-3984. (800) 678-7071. Fax: (804) 848-0403.

Shenandoah University

Winchester, Virginia CB code: 5613

Admissions: 98% of applicants accepted
Based on: ••• School record, special talents
•• Test scores
• Activities, interview, recommendations
Completion: 80% of freshmen end year in good standing
52% graduate, 30% of these enter graduate study

4-year private university, coed, affiliated with United Methodist Church. Founded in 1875. **Accreditation:** Regional. **Undergraduate enrollment:** 292 men, 523 women full time; 58 men, 166 women part time. **Graduate enrollment:** 78 men, 90 women full time; 107 men, 153 women part time. **Faculty:** 147 total (81 full time). **Location:** Suburban campus in large town; 75 miles from Washington, D.C. **Calendar:** Semester, limited summer session. **Microcomputers:** 50 located in libraries, computer centers. **Special facilities:** Arts and media centers, conservatory, recording studio.

DEGREES OFFERED. AS, BA, BS, BFA, MS, MBA. 72 associate degrees awarded in 1992. 95% in allied health, 5% visual and performing arts. 129 bachelor's degrees awarded. 25% in business and management, 19% teacher education, 8% allied health, 10% social sciences, 29% visual and performing arts. Graduate degrees offered in 7 major fields of study.

UNDERGRADUATE MAJORS. Associate: Nursing, respiratory therapy. **Bachelor's:** American studies, arts management, biology, business and management, chemistry, commercial music, communications, computer and information sciences, dance, dramatic arts, English, environmental science, health sciences, history, jazz, mathematics, music business management, music education, music pedagogy, music performance, music theory and composition, music therapy, musical theater, nursing, physical education, piano accompanying, psychology, religion, religious music, respiratory therapy, visual and performing arts.

ACADEMIC PROGRAMS. Accelerated program, double major, dual enrollment of high school students, honors program, independent study, internships, teacher preparation; liberal arts/career combination in health sciences, business. **Remedial services:** Reduced course load, remedial instruction, tutoring. **Placement/credit:** AP, CLEP Subject, institutional tests; 15 credit hours maximum for associate degree; 15 credit hours maximum for bachelor's degree.

ACADEMIC REQUIREMENTS. Freshmen must earn minimum GPA of 1.0 to continue in good standing. 70% of freshmen return for sophomore year. Students must declare major by end of second year. **Graduation requirements:** 69 hours for associate (37 in major), 120 hours for bachelor's (69 in major). Most students required to take courses in English, foreign languages, history, humanities, mathematics, philosophy/religion, biological/physical sciences, social sciences. **Postgraduate studies:** 50% from 2-year programs enter 4-year programs. 3% enter MBA programs, 27% enter other graduate study.

FRESHMAN ADMISSIONS. Selection criteria: Creative ability of music, theater or dance applicants is most important. **High school preparation:** 15 units required; 17 recommended. Recommended units include English 4, foreign language 2, mathematics 3, physical science 2, social science 2 and science 4. **Test requirements:** SAT or ACT; score report by July 1.

1992 FRESHMAN CLASS PROFILE. 191 men applied, 186 accepted, 83 enrolled; 318 women applied, 315 accepted, 149 enrolled. 30% had high school GPA of 3.0 or higher, 60% between 2.0 and 2.99. **Characteristics:** 59% from in state, 75% live in college housing, 9% have minority backgrounds, 3% are foreign students. Average age is 18.

FALL-TERM APPLICATIONS. $20 fee, may be waived for applicants with need. Closing date July 1; priority given to applications received by March 15; applicants notified on a rolling basis; must reply within 4 weeks. Audition required for music, dance, theater applicants. Interview recommended. CRDA. Deferred and early admission available. EDP-F.

STUDENT LIFE. Housing: Dormitories (women, coed). **Activities:** Student government, radio, choral groups, concert band, dance, drama, jazz band, music ensembles, musical theater, opera, pep band, symphony orchestra, more than 40 musical performing groups, fraternities, sororities, Youth Christian Fellowship, Circle-K.

ATHLETICS. NCAA. **Intercollegiate:** Baseball M, basketball, golf M, lacrosse M, soccer, softball W, tennis, volleyball W. **Intramural:** Basketball, bowling, softball, tennis, volleyball.

STUDENT SERVICES. Career counseling, employment service for undergraduates, freshman orientation, health services, personal counseling, placement service for graduates, veterans counselor, services/facilities for handicapped.

ANNUAL EXPENSES. Tuition and fees: $9,800. Tuition for physical and occupational therapy is $12,700. $1,050 additional for music programs. **Room and board:** $4,400. **Books and supplies:** $450. **Other expenses:** $900.

FINANCIAL AID. 80% of freshmen, 76% of continuing students receive some form of aid. 30% of grants, 84% of loans, 83% of jobs based on need. 143 enrolled freshmen were judged to have need, all were offered aid. Academic, music/drama, state/district residency, leadership, religious affiliation scholarships available. **Aid applications:** Closing date April 1; priority given to applications received by March 15; applicants notified on a rolling basis beginning on or about March 15; must reply within 4 weeks.

ADDRESS/TELEPHONE. Patricia Coyle, Director of Admissions, Shenandoah University, 1460 University Drive, Winchester, VA 22601-5195. (703) 665-4581. (800) 432-2266. Fax: (703) 665-4627.

Southern Virginia College for Women
Buena Vista, Virginia CB code: 5625

Admissions:	87% of applicants accepted
Based on:	•• Interview, school record
	• Activities, essay, recommendations, special talents, test scores
Completion:	75% of freshmen end year in good standing
	85% graduate, 85% of these enter 4-year programs

2-year private liberal arts college, women only. Founded in 1867. **Accreditation:** Regional. **Undergraduate enrollment:** 220 women full time; 5 women part time. **Faculty:** 36 total (17 full time), 7 with doctorates or other terminal degrees. **Location:** Rural campus in small town; 165 miles from Washington, D.C., 50 miles from Roanoke. **Calendar:** Semester, limited summer session. **Microcomputers:** 24 located in libraries, computer centers. **Special facilities:** Horsemanship center with state-of-the-art stable facility (69 stalls) and indoor riding arena.

DEGREES OFFERED. AA, AS. 85 associate degrees awarded in 1992. 22% in agriculture, 10% business and management, 56% multi/interdisciplinary studies.

UNDERGRADUATE MAJORS. Business and management, early childhood education, equestrian science, interior design, liberal/general studies.

ACADEMIC PROGRAMS. 2-year transfer program, double major, independent study, internships, student-designed major, study abroad, 3-year double major program, equine management degree program. **Remedial services:** Learning center, reduced course load, remedial instruction, special counselor, tutoring. **Placement/credit:** AP, CLEP General and Subject, institutional tests; 9 credit hours maximum for associate degree.

ACADEMIC REQUIREMENTS. Freshmen must earn minimum GPA of 1.5 to continue in good standing. 85% of freshmen return for sophomore year. Students must declare major by end of first year. **Graduation requirements:** 64 hours for associate (32 in major). Most students required to take courses in arts/fine arts, English, history, humanities, mathematics, philosophy/religion, biological/physical sciences, social sciences.

FRESHMAN ADMISSIONS. Selection criteria: High school GPA, transcript, interview, test scores, school community activities, and counselor recommendations considered. **High school preparation:** 16 units recommended. Recommended units include English 4, foreign language 2, mathematics 3, social science 3 and science 2. **Test requirements:** SAT or ACT (SAT preferred); score report by August 15.

1992 FRESHMAN CLASS PROFILE. 287 women applied, 250 accepted, 120 enrolled. 10% had high school GPA of 3.0 or higher, 60% between 2.0 and 2.99. **Academic background:** Mid 50% of enrolled freshmen had SAT-V between 320-450, SAT-M between 300-420; ACT composite between 13-19. 90% submitted SAT scores, 5% submitted ACT scores. **Characteristics:** 55% from in state, 90% live in college housing, 6% have minority backgrounds, 4% are foreign students. Average age is 18.

FALL-TERM APPLICATIONS. $35 fee, may be waived for applicants with need. Closing date August 15; applicants notified on a rolling basis; must reply by May 1 or within 4 weeks if notified thereafter. Essay required. Interview required for learning disabled applicants; recommended for late applicants. CRDA. Deferred and early admission available.

STUDENT LIFE. Housing: Dormitories (women). **Activities:** Student government, film, yearbook, choral groups, dance, drama, community service organizations. **Additional information:** Extensive social and cultural cooperation with nearby Washington and Lee University and Virginia Military Institute.

ATHLETICS. NJCAA. **Intercollegiate:** Horseback riding, soccer, softball, tennis, volleyball. **Intramural:** Horseback riding, soccer, softball. **Clubs:** Outing.

STUDENT SERVICES. Aptitude testing, career counseling, freshman orientation, health services, personal counseling, placement service for graduates, services/facilities for handicapped.

ANNUAL EXPENSES. Tuition and fees: $10,750. **Room and board:** $5,000. **Books and supplies:** $500. **Other expenses:** $1,030.

FINANCIAL AID. 100% of freshmen, 85% of continuing students receive some form of aid. Grants, loans, jobs available. Academic, state/district residency scholarships available. **Aid applications:** Closing date August 1; priority given to applications received by April 1; applicants notified on a rolling basis beginning on or about April 15; must reply within 2 weeks.

ADDRESS/TELEPHONE. Mark Camper, Assistant Director of Admissions, Southern Virginia College for Women, One College Hill Drive, Buena Vista, VA 24416-3097. (703) 261-8420. Fax: (703) 261-8451.

Southside Virginia Community College
Alberta, Virginia CB code: 5660

2-year public community college, coed. Founded in 1970. **Accreditation:** Regional. **Undergraduate enrollment:** 437 men, 620 women full time; 924 men, 1,241 women part time. **Faculty:** 206 total (70 full time), 20 with doctorates or other terminal degrees. **Location:** Rural campus in rural community; 70 miles from Richmond. **Calendar:** Semester, limited summer session. Extensive evening/early morning classes. **Microcomputers:** 60 located in libraries, classrooms. **Special facilities:** Nature trail, fitness trail. **Additional facts:** Additional campus at Keysville. Campus Without Walls at Emporia.

DEGREES OFFERED. AAS. 167 associate degrees awarded in 1992. 13% in business and management, 9% business/office and marketing/distribution, 16% engineering technologies, 38% multi/interdisciplinary studies, 20% parks/recreation, protective services, public affairs.

UNDERGRADUATE MAJORS. Biological and physical sciences, business administration and management, business and management, computer and information sciences, drafting and design technology, education, electronic technology, human resources development, law enforcement and corrections technologies, liberal/general studies, nursing, secretarial and related programs.

ACADEMIC PROGRAMS. 2-year transfer program, double major, dual enrollment of high school students, honors program, internships, visiting/exchange student program, cooperative programs in nursing with J. Sargeant Reynolds Community College, Danville Community College. **Remedial services:** Learning center, preadmission summer program, reduced course load, remedial instruction, special counselor, tutoring. **ROTC:** Army. **Placement/credit:** AP, CLEP General and Subject, institutional tests.

ACADEMIC REQUIREMENTS. Freshmen must earn minimum GPA of 1.5 to continue in good standing. 63% of freshmen return for sophomore year. Students must declare major on enrollment. **Graduation requirements:** 65 hours for associate. Most students required to take courses in computer science, English, mathematics, social sciences.

FRESHMAN ADMISSIONS. Selection criteria: Open admissions. Selective admissions to some programs. **Test requirements:** National League for Nursing Pre-Admissions Examination required for nursing applicants.

1992 FRESHMAN CLASS PROFILE. 285 men applied, 285 accepted, 203 enrolled; 299 women applied, 299 accepted, 244 enrolled. **Characteristics:** 99% from in state, 100% commute, 51% have minority backgrounds.

FALL-TERM APPLICATIONS. No fee. No closing date; applicants notified on a rolling basis. Interview required. Deferred and early admission available.

STUDENT LIFE. Activities: Student government, choral groups, drama, music ensembles, national honor society, numerous student clubs and organizations.

ATHLETICS. Intramural: Badminton, basketball, softball, table tennis, tennis, volleyball.

STUDENT SERVICES. Aptitude testing, career counseling, employment service for undergraduates, freshman orientation, personal counseling, placement service for graduates, veterans counselor, services/facilities for handicapped.

ANNUAL EXPENSES. Tuition and fees: $1,330, $3,030 additional for out-of-state students. **Books and supplies:** $523. **Other expenses:** $1,602.

FINANCIAL AID. 52% of freshmen, 51% of continuing students receive some form of aid. 98% of grants, 85% of jobs based on need. Academic, state/district residency, minority scholarships available. **Aid applications:** Closing date August 1; priority given to applications received by June 1; applicants notified on a rolling basis beginning on or about June 30; must reply within 10 days.

ADDRESS/TELEPHONE. Dr. John D. Sykes, Jr, Director of Admissions and Institutional Research, Southside Virginia Community College, Route 1, Box 60, Alberta, VA 23821. (804) 949-7111. Fax: (804) 947-7863.

Southwest Virginia Community College
Richlands, Virginia CB code: 5659

2-year public community college, coed. Founded in 1967. **Accreditation:** Regional. **Undergraduate enrollment:** 712 men, 1,189 women full time; 1,587 men, 1,388 women part time. **Faculty:** 300 total (90 full time), 21 with doctorates or other terminal degrees. **Location:** Rural campus in small town; 45 miles from Bluefield and Bristol. **Calendar:** Semester, extensive summer session. **Microcomputers:** 130 located in libraries, computer centers.

DEGREES OFFERED. AA, AS, AAS. 354 associate degrees awarded in 1992.

UNDERGRADUATE MAJORS. Accounting, biological and physical sciences, business administration and management, business and management, business data processing and related programs, computer and information sciences, drafting, drafting and design technology, education, electrical and electronics equipment repair, electrical technology, electronic technology, engineering, environmental science, land reclamation, law enforcement and corrections technologies, liberal/general studies, mining and petroleum technologies, music, nursing, radiograph medical technology, secretarial and related programs, social sciences.

ACADEMIC PROGRAMS. 2-year transfer program, accelerated program, cooperative education, double major, dual enrollment of high school students, honors program, independent study, internships, telecourses. **Remedial services:** Learning center, preadmission summer program, reduced course load, remedial instruction, special counselor, tutoring. **Placement/credit:** AP, CLEP General.

ACADEMIC REQUIREMENTS. Freshmen must earn minimum GPA of 2.0 to continue in good standing. Students must declare major on enrollment. **Graduation requirements:** 65 hours for associate (50 in major). Most students required to take courses in computer science, English, mathematics, social sciences.

FRESHMAN ADMISSIONS. Selection criteria: Open admissions. Selective admissions to engineering and health programs. Subject and unit requirements vary with degree programs. **Test requirements:** CGP required for full-time freshman applicants for counseling.

1992 FRESHMAN CLASS PROFILE. 1,638 men and women enrolled. **Characteristics:** 98% from in state, 100% commute, 2% have minority backgrounds.

FALL-TERM APPLICATIONS. No fee. No closing date; applicants notified on a rolling basis. Interview required for full-time applicants. Deferred and early admission available. Applicants for nursing and allied health programs must apply by January 15 and reply within 2 weeks of acceptance. No deferred admission for these programs.

STUDENT LIFE. Activities: Student government, student newspaper, yearbook, choral groups, drama, Intervoice Club, Black Student Union, Veteran's Club, Junior Chamber of Commerce groups, Young Democrats, Young Republicans.

ATHLETICS. Intercollegiate: Basketball M. **Intramural:** Basketball M, softball, tennis, volleyball.

STUDENT SERVICES. Aptitude testing, career counseling, employment service for undergraduates, freshman orientation, personal counseling, placement service for graduates, services/facilities for handicapped.

ANNUAL EXPENSES. Tuition and fees: $1,330, $3,030 additional for out-of-state students. **Books and supplies:** $500. **Other expenses:** $1,258.

FINANCIAL AID. 70% of continuing students receive some form of aid. 98% of grants, 48% of loans, all jobs based on need. Academic scholarships available. **Aid applications:** No closing date; priority given to applications received by May 30; applicants notified on a rolling basis beginning on or about July 1; must reply within 15 days.

ADDRESS/TELEPHONE. Mr. Roderick B. Moore, Coordinator, Admissions, Records and Financial Aid, Southwest Virginia Community College, Box 5UCC, Richlands, VA 24641-1510. (703) 964-2555. Fax: (703) 964-9307.

Sweet Briar College

Sweet Briar, Virginia CB code: 5634

Admissions: 90% of applicants accepted
Based on:
- ••• School record
- •• Essay, recommendations, test scores
- • Activities, interview, special talents

Completion: 92% of freshmen end year in good standing
60% graduate, 21% of these enter graduate study

4-year private liberal arts college, women only. Founded in 1901. **Accreditation:** Regional. **Undergraduate enrollment:** 1 man, 564 women full time; 2 men, 33 women part time. **Faculty:** 94 total (64 full time), 59 with doctorates or other terminal degrees. **Location:** Rural campus in rural community; 12 miles from Lynchburg, 160 miles from Washington, D.C. **Calendar:** 4-1-4. **Microcomputers:** 92 located in libraries, classrooms, computer centers. **Special facilities:** Art gallery, fine arts center, college museum, nursery school, language laboratories, indoor riding facility, nature sanctuary.

DEGREES OFFERED. BA, BS. 129 bachelor's degrees awarded in 1992. 12% in area and ethnic studies, 6% languages, 17% letters/literature, 5% life sciences, 5% multi/interdisciplinary studies, 6% psychology, 27% social sciences, 16% visual and performing arts.

UNDERGRADUATE MAJORS. American studies, anthropology, art history, biological and physical sciences, biology, chemistry, classics, creative writing, dance, dramatic arts, economics, economics/computer science, English, environmental science, foreign languages (multiple emphasis), French, German, Greek (classical), Hispanic American studies, history, international relations, Latin, mathematical physics, mathematics, mathematics/computer science, mathematics/economics, music, philosophy, physics, political economy, political science and government, preengineering, psychology, religion, sociology, Spanish, studio art, Western European studies.

ACADEMIC PROGRAMS. Accelerated program, double major, honors program, independent study, internships, student-designed major, study abroad, teacher preparation, visiting/exchange student program, Washington semester, cross-registration, environmental junior year at University of Washington, University of California: Santa Barbara, University of Wisconsin, University of Maine, Florida State University, or American University; 3-2 engineering with Washington University (MO), Columbia University (NY) and Georgia Institute of Technology (GA); liberal arts/career combination in engineering; combined bachelor's/graduate program in business administration. **Remedial services:** Learning center, tutoring. **Placement/credit:** AP, institutional tests.

ACADEMIC REQUIREMENTS. Freshmen must earn minimum GPA of 2.0 to continue in good standing. 80% of freshmen return for sophomore year. Students must declare major by end of second year. **Graduation requirements:** 120 hours for bachelor's (33 in major). Most students required to take courses in arts/fine arts, English, foreign languages, history, humanities, mathematics, philosophy/religion, biological/physical sciences, social sciences. **Postgraduate studies:** 3% enter law school, 3% enter medical school, 1% enter MBA programs, 14% enter other graduate study.

FRESHMAN ADMISSIONS. Selection criteria: High school curriculum and grades of primary importance, then school and teacher recommendations, followed by writing ability as demonstrated by essay or personal statement. Test scores, interview, extracurricular activities, and personal characteristics also considered. **High school preparation:** 16 units required; 20 recommended. Required and recommended units include English 4, foreign language 3-4, mathematics 3-4, social science 3-4 and science 2. Biological science 1 and physical science 1 recommended. Social science units must include 1 US history. Mathematics units must include 2 algebra and 1 plane geometry. Science units must include laboratory work. **Test requirements:** SAT or ACT; score report by February 15. 3 ACH required (including English Composition with essay). Score report by February 15.

1992 FRESHMAN CLASS PROFILE. 448 women applied, 403 accepted, 193 enrolled. **Academic background:** Mid 50% of enrolled freshmen had SAT-V between 450-550, SAT-M between 460-560; ACT composite between 21-26. 99% submitted SAT scores, 29% submitted ACT scores. **Characteristics:** 24% from in state, 96% live in college housing, 5% have minority backgrounds, 5% are foreign students. Average age is 18.

FALL-TERM APPLICATIONS. $25 fee, may be waived for applicants with need. Closing date February 15; applicants notified on or about April 1; must reply by May 1. Essay required. Interview recommended. Audition recommended for music applicants. Portfolio recommended for art applicants. CRDA. Deferred and early admission available. EDP-S.

STUDENT LIFE. Housing: Dormitories (women). Language house on campus. **Activities:** Student government, magazine, radio, student newspaper, yearbook, choral groups, dance, drama, music ensembles, musical theater, Young Republicans, Young Democrats, Challenge (tutoring local school children), Sweep (campus recycling group), Unity (racial awareness group), Interact (community work), Amnesty International, 10 Tap clubs. **Additional information:** Self-governing student body and honor system observed. Active participation in athletics and weekend outdoor programs encouraged.

ATHLETICS. NCAA. **Intercollegiate:** Basketball, diving, fencing, field hockey, horseback riding, lacrosse, soccer, softball, swimming, tennis, volleyball. **Intramural:** Cross-country, fencing, horseback riding, softball, tennis, volleyball.

STUDENT SERVICES. Aptitude testing, career counseling, employment service for undergraduates, freshman orientation, health services, personal counseling, placement service for graduates, special adviser for adult students.

ANNUAL EXPENSES. Tuition and fees: $14,015. **Room and board:** $5,755. **Books and supplies:** $500. **Other expenses:** $600.

FINANCIAL AID. 56% of freshmen, 66% of continuing students receive some form of aid. 81% of grants, 97% of loans, 84% of jobs based on need. 99 enrolled freshmen were judged to have need, all were offered aid. Academic, music/drama, state/district residency, leadership, alumni affiliation scholarships available. **Aid applications:** No closing date; priority given to applications received by March 1; applicants notified on a rolling basis beginning on or about March 1; must reply by May 1 or within 21 weeks if notified thereafter.

ADDRESS/TELEPHONE. Nancy E. Church, Executive Director of Admissions and Financial Aid, Sweet Briar College, Sweet Briar, VA 24595. (804) 381-6142. (800) 537-4300. Fax: (804) 381-6173.

Thomas Nelson Community College

Hampton, Virginia CB code: 5793

2-year public community college, coed. Founded in 1967. **Accreditation:** Regional. **Undergraduate enrollment:** 7,815 men and women. **Location:** Suburban campus in small city; 20 miles from Norfolk. **Calendar:** Semester.

FRESHMAN ADMISSIONS. Selection criteria: Open admissions.

ANNUAL EXPENSES. Tuition and fees (1992-93): $1,243, $3,030 additional for out-of-state students. **Books and supplies:** $400. **Other expenses:** $650.

ADDRESS/TELEPHONE. Judy B. McMillan, Coordinator of Admissions and Records, Thomas Nelson Community College, PO Box 9407, Briarfield Station, Hampton, VA 23670. (804) 825-2800. Fax: (804) 825-2870.

Tidewater Community College
Portsmouth, Virginia CB code: 5226

2-year public community college, coed. Founded in 1968. **Accreditation:** Regional. **Undergraduate enrollment:** 2,029 men, 2,441 women full time; 5,319 men, 7,154 women part time. **Faculty:** 787 total (326 full time), 98 with doctorates or other terminal degrees. **Location:** Suburban campus in small city. **Calendar:** Semester, extensive summer session. Saturday and extensive evening/early morning classes. **Microcomputers:** Located in classrooms, computer centers. **Additional facts:** Multilocation institution with campuses at Portsmouth, Virginia Beach, and Chesapeake. 60% of all students enrolled at Virgina Beach campus.

DEGREES OFFERED. AA, AS, AAS. 1,028 associate degrees awarded in 1992. 31% in business and management, 10% business/office and marketing/distribution, 8% computer sciences, 8% education, 14% allied health, 5% physical sciences, 7% trade and industry.

UNDERGRADUATE MAJORS. Accounting, advertising, automotive technology, biological and physical sciences, business administration and management, business and management, child development/care/guidance, civil engineering, contract management and procurement/purchasing, drafting and design technology, education, educational secretary, electrical/electronics/communications engineering, engineering, finance, fine arts, fire control and safety technology, graphic and printing production, horticulture, hotel/motel and restaurant management, information sciences and systems, interior design, legal secretary, liberal/general studies, marketing and distribution, medical records technology, nursing, physical sciences, physical therapy assistant, protective services, radiograph medical technology, real estate, recreation and community services technologies, respiratory therapy, secretarial and related programs, specific learning disabilities, telecommunications, trade and industrial supervision and management.

ACADEMIC PROGRAMS. 2-year transfer program, cooperative education, double major, dual enrollment of high school students, honors program, independent study, internships, telecourses, weekend college, cross-registration. **Remedial services:** Learning center, remedial instruction, tutoring. **ROTC:** Army. **Placement/credit:** AP, CLEP General and Subject, institutional tests.

ACADEMIC REQUIREMENTS. Freshmen must earn minimum GPA of 2.0 to continue in good standing. 44% of freshmen return for sophomore year. Students must declare major on enrollment. **Graduation requirements:** 65 hours for associate. Most students required to take courses in English, history, mathematics, biological/physical sciences, social sciences.

FRESHMAN ADMISSIONS. Selection criteria: Open admissions.

1992 FRESHMAN CLASS PROFILE. 2,767 men applied, 2,767 accepted, 1,465 enrolled; 3,122 women applied, 3,122 accepted, 1,486 enrolled. **Characteristics:** 89% from in state, 100% commute, 23% have minority backgrounds, 1% are foreign students. Average age is 24.

FALL-TERM APPLICATIONS. No fee. No closing date; applicants notified on a rolling basis. Interview required for medical technologies, other limited enrollment program applicants. Deferred and early admission available.

STUDENT LIFE. Activities: Student government, student newspaper, choral groups, drama, music ensembles, honorary societies, Black Student Alliance, Inter-Varsity Christian Fellowship, Student Nurses Association.

ATHLETICS. Intramural: Baseball, basketball, softball, volleyball.

STUDENT SERVICES. Aptitude testing, career counseling, employment service for undergraduates, freshman orientation, personal counseling, placement service for graduates, special adviser for adult students, veterans counselor, services/facilities for handicapped.

ANNUAL EXPENSES. Tuition and fees (1992-93): $1,305, $3,030 additional for out-of-state students. **Books and supplies:** $400. **Other expenses:** $810.

FINANCIAL AID. 13% of continuing students receive some form of aid. 94% of grants, 87% of loans, all jobs based on need. Academic scholarships available. **Aid applications:** No closing date; priority given to applications received by August 1; applicants notified on a rolling basis.

ADDRESS/TELEPHONE. Dr. Robert Grymes, Dean, Instructional and Student Services, Tidewater Community College, State Route 135, Portsmouth Campus, Portsmouth, VA 23703. (804) 484-2121.

University of Richmond
Richmond, Virginia CB code: 5569

Admissions:	47% of applicants accepted
Based on:	••• School record
	•• Special talents, test scores
	• Activities, essay, recommendations
Completion:	95% of freshmen end year in good standing
	83% graduate, 30% of these enter graduate study

4-year private university and liberal arts college, coed, affiliated with Baptist General Association of Virginia. Founded in 1830. **Accreditation:** Regional. **Undergraduate enrollment:** 1,468 men, 1,421 women full time; 243 men, 531 women part time. **Graduate enrollment:** 283 men, 250 women full time; 183 men, 194 women part time. **Faculty:** 384 total (260 full time), 300 with doctorates or other terminal degrees. **Location:** Suburban campus in small city; 6 miles from downtown. **Calendar:** Semester, limited summer session. **Microcomputers:** 400 located in dormitories, libraries, classrooms, computer centers. **Special facilities:** Greenhouse, electron microscope, radionuclide complex, art gallery, gem, rock, and mineral gallery. **Additional facts:** Certificate programs offered through evening school. University has 5 academic divisions: The School of Arts and Sciences, Robins School of Business and its Richard S. Reynolds Graduate Division, Jepson School of Leadership Studies, T.C. Williams School of Law, and University College. Undergraduate students become members of residential colleges: Richmond College (for men) and Westhampton College (for women). Classes and extracurricular activities coeducational, with separate student governments, honor/judicial councils, and deans.

DEGREES OFFERED. AAS, BA, BS, MA, MS, MBA, MEd. 13 associate degrees awarded in 1992. 38% in business and management, 15% computer sciences, 23% law, 23% multi/interdisciplinary studies. 702 bachelor's degrees awarded. 6% in area and ethnic studies, 26% business and management, 13% letters/literature, 5% life sciences, 5% psychology, 26% social sciences. Graduate degrees offered in 19 major fields of study.

UNDERGRADUATE MAJORS. Associate: Finance, humanities and social sciences, information sciences and systems, insurance and risk management, legal assistant/paralegal, personnel management, public administration, public affairs, public relations, real estate, transportation and physical distribution management, transportation management. **Bachelor's:** Accounting, American studies, art history, biology, business administration and management, business economics, chemistry, classics, computer and information sciences, criminal justice studies, dramatic arts, economics, education, elementary education, English, European studies, finance, French, German, Greek (classical), history, humanities and social sciences, information sciences and systems, international business management, international studies, journalism, junior high education, Latin, Latin American studies, leadership studies, marketing management, mathematics, music, music education, music history and appreciation, music performance, music theory and composition, personnel management, philosophy, physical education, physics, political science and government, psychology, religion, Russian and Slavic studies, secondary education, sociology, Spanish, speech, sports science, studio art, third world studies, urban studies, women's studies.

ACADEMIC PROGRAMS. Accelerated program, double major, dual enrollment of high school students, honors program, independent study, internships, semester at sea, student-designed major, study abroad, teacher preparation, visiting/exchange student program, Washington semester, cross-registration, exchange programs with Saga University in Japan, St. Mary's College and the University of Bath in England; liberal arts/career combination in forestry; combined bachelor's/graduate program in law. **Remedial services:** Tutoring. **ROTC:** Army. **Placement/credit:** AP, CLEP General and Subject, institutional tests; 30 credit hours maximum for bachelor's degree.

ACADEMIC REQUIREMENTS. Freshmen must earn minimum GPA of 1.5 to continue in good standing. 92% of freshmen return for sophomore year. Students must declare major by end of second year. **Graduation requirements:** 60 hours for associate (30 in major), 122 hours for bachelor's (30 in major). Most students required to take courses in arts/fine arts, English, foreign languages, history, humanities, mathematics, biological/physical sciences, social sciences. **Postgraduate studies:** 7% enter law school, 4% enter medical school, 2% enter MBA programs, 17% enter other graduate study.

FRESHMAN ADMISSIONS. Selection criteria: Half of admissions decision based on school transcript, half based on SAT and 3 ACH scores or ACT. Extracurricular activities, recommendations, and essay considered in some cases. **High school preparation:** 16 units required. Required and recommended units include English 4, mathematics 3-4, social science 1-2 and science 1-2. Biological science 1 and foreign language 3 recommended. **Test requirements:** SAT or ACT (SAT preferred); score report by March 1. 3 ACH required (including English Composition, Mathematics Level I or II, and 1 other, preferably foreign language) of those submitting SAT. Score report by March 1. **Additional information:** Campus visits recommended, interviews not considered.

1992 FRESHMAN CLASS PROFILE. 2,285 men applied, 1,305 accepted, 397 enrolled; 3,086 women applied, 1,203 accepted, 369 enrolled. 45% were in top tenth of graduating class. **Academic background:** Mid 50%

of enrolled freshmen had SAT-V between 510-620, SAT-M between 580-670; ACT composite between 26-30. 96% submitted SAT scores, 17% submitted ACT scores. **Characteristics:** 20% from in state, 95% live in college housing, 5% have minority backgrounds, 1% are foreign students, 45% join fraternities/sororities. Average age is 18.

FALL-TERM APPLICATIONS. $40 fee, may be waived for applicants with need. Closing date February 1; applicants notified on or about April 1; must reply by May 1. Audition required for music applicants. Essay required. CRDA. Deferred and early admission available. EDP-F. Early decision application deadline November 1.

STUDENT LIFE. Housing: Dormitories (men, women); apartment housing available. Housing guaranteed for freshman class size. University apartments available for foreign language students. International house available. **Activities:** Student government, magazine, radio, student newspaper, yearbook, choral groups, concert band, dance, drama, jazz band, music ensembles, musical theater, pep band, symphony orchestra, fraternities, sororities, religious organizations, Minority Student Union, Amnesty International, College Republicans, Young Democrats, debate team, Habitat for Humanity, Volunteer Action Council, Women Involved Living and Learning.

ATHLETICS. NCAA. **Intercollegiate:** Basketball, cross-country, diving, field hockey W, football M, golf M, lacrosse W, soccer M, swimming, tennis, track and field, water polo M. **Intramural:** Badminton, basketball, cross-country, golf, handball, lacrosse, racquetball, rowing (crew), rugby M, soccer, softball, squash, swimming, table tennis, tennis, track and field, volleyball, water polo M.

STUDENT SERVICES. Aptitude testing, career counseling, employment service for undergraduates, freshman orientation, health services, personal counseling, placement service for graduates, veterans counselor, services/facilities for handicapped.

ANNUAL EXPENSES. Tuition and fees: $13,540. **Room and board:** $3,160. **Books and supplies:** $600. **Other expenses:** $1,170.

FINANCIAL AID. 54% of freshmen, 54% of continuing students receive some form of aid. 33% of grants, 91% of loans, 27% of jobs based on need. 208 enrolled freshmen were judged to have need, all were offered aid. Academic, music/drama, athletic, state/district residency, leadership, religious affiliation, minority scholarships available. **Aid applications:** Closing date February 25; priority given to applications received by February 15; applicants notified on or about April 1; must reply by May 1 or within 2 weeks if notified thereafter. **Additional information:** Interview required for University, Oldham, Ethyl, CIGNA and Virginia Baptist Scholars. Undergraduate research grants available.

ADDRESS/TELEPHONE. Thomas N. Pollard, Dean of Admissions, University of Richmond, Sarah Brunet Hall, VA 23173. (804) 289-8640. Fax: (804) 287-6003.

University of Virginia
Charlottesville, Virginia — CB code: 5820

Admissions:	35% of applicants accepted
Based on:	••• School record, test scores
	•• Activities, essay, special talents
	• Recommendations
Completion:	99% of freshmen end year in good standing
	89% graduate, 64% of these enter graduate study

4-year public university, coed. Founded in 1819. **Accreditation:** Regional. **Undergraduate enrollment:** 5,492 men, 5,759 women full time; 45 men, 75 women part time. **Graduate enrollment:** 3,255 men, 2,382 women full time; 188 men, 408 women part time. **Faculty:** 2,395 total (2,168 full time), 1,517 with doctorates or other terminal degrees. **Location:** Suburban campus in small city; 110 miles from Washington, D.C., 70 miles from Richmond. **Calendar:** Semester, extensive summer session. **Microcomputers:** 820 located in dormitories, libraries, classrooms, computer centers, campus-wide network. **Special facilities:** Satellite dish receiving live television from former Soviet Union, nuclear reactor, art museum, observatory.

DEGREES OFFERED. BA, BS, BArch, MA, MS, MBA, MFA, MEd, PhD, EdD, MD, JD. 2,989 bachelor's degrees awarded in 1992. 10% in business and management, 10% engineering, 5% languages, 12% letters/literature, 5% physical sciences, 8% psychology, 27% social sciences. Graduate degrees offered in 70 major fields of study.

UNDERGRADUATE MAJORS. Aerospace/aeronautical/astronautical engineering, Afro-American (black) studies, anthropology, applied mathematics, architectural history, architecture, area studies, astronomy, biology, business and management, chemical engineering, chemistry, city/community/regional planning, civil engineering, classics, comparative literature, computer and information sciences, dramatic arts, economics, electrical/electronics/communications engineering, engineering science, English, environmental science, French, German, history, humanities and social sciences, international relations, Italian, mathematics, mechanical engineering, music, nuclear engineering, nursing, philosophy, physical education, physics, political science and government, psychology, religion, Slavic languages, sociology, Spanish, speech, speech pathology/audiology, studio art, systems engineering.

ACADEMIC PROGRAMS. Accelerated program, double major, education specialist degree, honors program, independent study, internships, student-designed major, study abroad, teacher preparation, telecourses, Echols and Rodman Scholar programs for highest achieving high school students. **Remedial services:** Learning center, preadmission summer program, special counselor, tutoring. **ROTC:** Air Force, Army, Naval. **Placement/credit:** Institutional tests.

ACADEMIC REQUIREMENTS. Freshmen must earn minimum GPA of 1.8 to continue in good standing. 97% of freshmen return for sophomore year. Students must declare major by end of second year. **Graduation requirements:** 120 hours for bachelor's (18 in major). Most students required to take courses in English, foreign languages, humanities, mathematics, biological/physical sciences, social sciences.

FRESHMAN ADMISSIONS. Selection criteria: School achievement record, class rank, test scores, extracurricular activities and interests, quality of writing, and school's recommendation are all considered. Preference given to state residents. Special consideration given to children of alumni and minorities. **High school preparation:** 16 units required. Required and recommended units include English 4, foreign language 2-5, mathematics 4-5, social science 1-3 and science 2-4. 2 laboratory science required from biology, chemistry, physics sequences. 1 chemistry, 1 physics required for engineering and applied science programs. **Test requirements:** SAT; score report by February 15. 3 ACH required (including English Composition, Mathematics Level I or II, and foreign language, natural sciences, American History, or European History). Score report by February 15. **Additional information:** Attendance at group admissions information sessions strongly encouraged.

1992 FRESHMAN CLASS PROFILE. 7,507 men applied, 2,493 accepted, 1,296 enrolled; 7,571 women applied, 2,789 accepted, 1,506 enrolled. 75% were in top tenth and 95% were in top quarter of graduating class. **Academic background:** Mid 50% of enrolled freshmen had SAT-V between 520-630, SAT-M between 590-700. 100% submitted SAT scores. **Characteristics:** 62% from in state, 100% live in college housing, 23% have minority backgrounds, 2% are foreign students, 30% join fraternities/sororities. Average age is 18.

FALL-TERM APPLICATIONS. $40 fee, may be waived for applicants with need. Closing date January 2; applicants notified on or about April 1; must reply by May 1. Essay required. CRDA. Early admission available. EDP-F. High school diploma not required but strongly recommended. Early admission appropriate only in exceptional cases.

STUDENT LIFE. Housing: Dormitories (coed); apartment, fraternity, sorority housing available. **Activities:** Student government, film, magazine, radio, student newspaper, television, yearbook, literary journal, science journal, choral groups, concert band, dance, drama, jazz band, music ensembles, musical theater, opera, pep band, symphony orchestra, fraternities, sororities, community service group, Black Student Alliance, general clubs and religious organizations, political organizations, service fraternities and sororities, debating union.

ATHLETICS. NCAA. **Intercollegiate:** Baseball M, basketball, cross-country, diving, field hockey W, football M, golf M, lacrosse, soccer, softball W, swimming, tennis, track and field, volleyball W, wrestling M. **Intramural:** Archery, badminton, basketball, bowling, boxing M, fencing, field hockey W, football M, golf, gymnastics, handball, horseback riding, lacrosse, racquetball, rifle, rowing (crew), rugby, skiing, skin diving, soccer, softball, squash, swimming, table tennis, tennis, track and field, volleyball, water polo.

STUDENT SERVICES. Aptitude testing, career counseling, employment service for undergraduates, freshman orientation, health services, on-campus day care, personal counseling, placement service for graduates, veterans counselor, services/facilities for handicapped.

ANNUAL EXPENSES. Tuition and fees: $4,350, $7,904 additional for out-of-state students. **Room and board:** $3,800. **Books and supplies:** $600. **Other expenses:** $1,000.

FINANCIAL AID. 40% of freshmen, 35% of continuing students receive some form of aid. 70% of grants, all loans, all jobs based on need. 950 enrolled freshmen were judged to have need, 780 were offered aid. Athletic, minority scholarships available. **Aid applications:** No closing date; priority given to applications received by March 1; applicants notified on a rolling basis beginning on or about April 9; must reply by May 15 or within 2 weeks if notified thereafter.

ADDRESS/TELEPHONE. John A. Blackburn, Dean of Admissions, University of Virginia, PO Box 9017, University Station, Charlottesville, VA 22903. (804) 982-3200.

Virginia Commonwealth University

Richmond, Virginia CB code: 5570

Admissions: 70% of applicants accepted
Based on: ••• School record
•• Test scores
• Activities, essay, interview, recommendations, special talents
Completion: 80% of freshmen end year in good standing
33% graduate

4-year public university, coed. Founded in 1838. **Accreditation:** Regional. **Undergraduate enrollment:** 4,410 men, 6,256 women full time; 2,181 men, 2,852 women part time. **Graduate enrollment:** 1,386 men, 1,753 women full time; 1,058 men, 2,043 women part time. **Faculty:** 2,190 total (1,598 full time), 1,367 with doctorates or other terminal degrees. **Location:** Urban campus in small city; 1.5 miles from downtown. **Calendar:** Semester, extensive summer session. **Microcomputers:** 200 located in libraries, classrooms, computer centers, campus-wide network. **Special facilities:** Art gallery. **Additional facts:** Medical College of Virginia, offering associate, upper-division, and graduate programs in health fields, is 1 of institution's 2 campuses in Richmond.

DEGREES OFFERED. AS, BA, BS, BFA, MA, MS, MBA, MFA, MEd, MSW, PhD, EdD, DMD, MD, B. Pharm. 11 associate degrees awarded in 1992. 100% in allied health. 2,335 bachelor's degrees awarded. 14% in business and management, 6% communications, 12% health sciences, 7% home economics, 7% parks/recreation, protective services, public affairs, 7% psychology, 6% social sciences, 14% visual and performing arts. Graduate degrees offered in 74 major fields of study.

UNDERGRADUATE MAJORS. Associate: Radiograph medical technology. **Bachelor's:** Accounting, anthropology, art education, art history, biological and physical sciences, biology, business administration and management, business and office, business economics, business education, chemistry, clinical laboratory science, communications arts and design, computer and information sciences, crafts, criminal justice studies, dance, dental hygiene, dramatic arts, economics, English, fashion design, fine arts, foreign languages (multiple emphasis), French, German, health education, history, information sciences and systems, interior design, journalism, law enforcement and corrections, liberal/general studies, marketing management, mathematics, medical radiation dosimetry, medical records technology, medical social work, mental health/human services, music, music education, music history and appreciation, music performance, music theory and composition, nursing, occupational therapy, office supervision and management, painting, parks and recreation management, pharmacy, philosophy, physical education, physics, political science and government, predentistry, prelaw, premedicine, prepharmacy, preveterinary, printmaking, psychology, religion, religious music, sculpture, social work, sociology, Spanish, speech/communication/theater education, theater design, urban studies.

ACADEMIC PROGRAMS. Accelerated program, cooperative education, double major, dual enrollment of high school students, honors program, independent study, internships, student-designed major, study abroad, teacher preparation, visiting/exchange student program; liberal arts/career combination in engineering; combined bachelor's/graduate program in business administration, medicine. **Remedial services:** Learning center, preadmission summer program, reduced course load, remedial instruction, special counselor, tutoring, Office of Academic Support. **ROTC:** Army. **Placement/credit:** AP, CLEP General and Subject, IB, institutional tests; 54 credit hours maximum for bachelor's degree.

ACADEMIC REQUIREMENTS. Freshmen must earn minimum GPA of 2.0 to continue in good standing. 78% of freshmen return for sophomore year. Students must declare major by end of second year. **Graduation requirements:** 126 hours for bachelor's. Most students required to take courses in English, foreign languages, history, mathematics, biological/physical sciences, social sciences. **Additional information:** Broad program in sciences with health field orientation.

FRESHMAN ADMISSIONS. Selection criteria: School achievement record most important, followed by test scores, community/school activities, recommendations. Limited number of low-income or minority students who have demonstrated academic promise with minimum SAT-verbal score of 350 are admitted under Educational Support Program. **High school preparation:** 20 units required. Required and recommended units include English 4, mathematics 3, social science 3 and science 2-3. Foreign language 3 recommended. School of the Arts flexible about unit distribution. **Test requirements:** SAT or ACT (SAT preferred); score report by March 1.

1992 FRESHMAN CLASS PROFILE. 1,857 men applied, 1,279 accepted, 618 enrolled; 2,810 women applied, 2,003 accepted, 910 enrolled. 48% had high school GPA of 3.0 or higher, 52% between 2.0 and 2.99. 20% were in top tenth and 49% were in top quarter of graduating class. **Academic background:** Mid 50% of enrolled freshmen had SAT-V between 430-520, SAT-M between 460-560. 98% submitted SAT scores. **Characteristics:** 92% from in state, 60% live in college housing, 34% have minority backgrounds, 2% are foreign students. Average age is 18.

FALL-TERM APPLICATIONS. $20 fee, may be waived for applicants with need. Closing date February 1; priority given to applications received by January 1; applicants notified on or about April 1; must reply by May 1. Audition required for music, theater, dance, choreography applicants. Portfolio required for visual arts applicants. Interview recommended for marginal applicants. Essay recommended. CRDA. Deferred and early admission available. EDP-F. Early decision deadline November 1, applicants notified December 1.

STUDENT LIFE. Housing: Dormitories (men, women, coed); apartment, cooperative housing available. Special honors program housing. Suites for upper class students. **Activities:** Student government, film, magazine, radio, student newspaper, choral groups, concert band, dance, drama, jazz band, music ensembles, musical theater, pep band, symphony orchestra, fraternities, sororities, Baptist Student Union, Catholic Campus Ministry, College Republicans, Young Democrats, NAACP, Black Student Alliance, International Student Union, Adult Organization, Activities Programming Board, Sexual Minority Student Alliance.

ATHLETICS. NAIA, NCAA. **Intercollegiate:** Baseball M, basketball, cross-country, field hockey W, golf M, soccer M, tennis, track and field, volleyball W. **Intramural:** Badminton, basketball, racquetball, soccer, softball, squash, swimming M, table tennis, tennis, volleyball.

STUDENT SERVICES. Aptitude testing, career counseling, employment service for undergraduates, freshman orientation, health services, on-campus day care, personal counseling, placement service for graduates, special adviser for adult students, veterans counselor, services/facilities for handicapped.

ANNUAL EXPENSES. Tuition and fees: $3,776, $6,520 additional for out-of-state students. **Room and board:** $4,053. **Books and supplies:** $500. **Other expenses:** $1,740.

FINANCIAL AID. 60% of freshmen, 62% of continuing students receive some form of aid. Grants, loans, jobs available. 900 enrolled freshmen were judged to have need, all were offered aid. Academic, music/drama, art, athletic scholarships available. **Aid applications:** Closing date November 1; priority given to applications received by March 15; applicants notified on or about June 10; must reply within 3 weeks.

ADDRESS/TELEPHONE. Horace W. Wooldridge, Jr, Director of Admissions, Virginia Commonwealth University, 821 West Franklin Street, Richmond, VA 23284-2526. (804) 367-1222. (800) 841-3638. Fax: (804) 367-1899.

Virginia Highlands Community College

Abingdon, Virginia CB code: 5927

2-year public community college, coed. Founded in 1967. **Accreditation:** Regional. **Undergraduate enrollment:** 2,112 men and women. **Location:** Rural campus in small town; 120 miles from Roanoke. **Calendar:** Semester.

FRESHMAN ADMISSIONS. Selection criteria: Open admissions.

ANNUAL EXPENSES. Tuition and fees (1992-93): $1,230, $3,030 additional for out-of-state students. **Books and supplies:** $420. **Other expenses:** $680.

ADDRESS/TELEPHONE. Edward A. Colley, Director of Admissions, Records and Financial Aid, Virginia Highlands Community College, PO Box 828, Abingdon, VA 24210-0828. (703) 628-6094 ext. 260. Fax: (703) 628-7576.

Virginia Intermont College

Bristol, Virginia CB code: 5857

Admissions: 71% of applicants accepted
Based on: ••• School record
•• Test scores
• Activities, essay, interview, recommendations, special talents
Completion: 90% of freshmen end year in good standing
40% graduate, 6% of these enter graduate study

4-year private liberal arts college, coed, affiliated with Baptist General Association of Virginia. Founded in 1884. **Accreditation:** Regional. **Undergraduate enrollment:** 179 men, 390 women full time; 20 men, 48 women part time. **Faculty:** 61 total (36 full time), 40 with doctorates or other terminal degrees. **Location:** Urban campus in large town; 120 miles from Roanoke and Asheville, North Carolina. **Calendar:** Semester. Saturday and extensive evening/early morning classes. **Microcomputers:** 25 located in libraries, computer centers. **Special facilities:** 129-acre riding center with 2 indoor riding arenas.

DEGREES OFFERED. AA, BA, BS, BFA. 7 associate degrees awarded in 1992. 14% in business/office and marketing/distribution, 43% allied health, 29% multi/interdisciplinary studies, 14% visual and performing arts. 109 bachelor's degrees awarded. 12% in agriculture, 12% business and management, 7% business/office and marketing/distribution, 6% teacher education, 12% law, 15% parks/recreation, protective services, public affairs, 16% visual and performing arts.

UNDERGRADUATE MAJORS. Associate: Allied health, graphic and printing production, graphic arts technology, graphic design, liberal/general studies, secretarial and related programs. **Bachelor's:** Art education, biological and physical sciences, biology, business and management, business education, clinical laboratory science, creative writing, dance, dramatic arts, English, English education, equestrian science, fashion merchandising, fine arts, history, history/political science, humanities and social sciences, legal assistant/paralegal, liberal/general studies, music education, musical theater, photography, political science and government, predentistry, prelaw, premedicine, prepharmacy, preveterinary, psychology, religion, science education, secretarial and related programs, social work, sports management, visual and performing arts.

ACADEMIC PROGRAMS. Double major, dual enrollment of high school students, honors program, independent study, internships, study abroad, teacher preparation, cross-registration. **Remedial services:** Learning center, reduced course load, remedial instruction, special counselor, tutoring. **Placement/credit:** AP, CLEP General and Subject, institutional tests.

ACADEMIC REQUIREMENTS. Freshmen must earn minimum GPA of 2.0 to continue in good standing. 60% of freshmen return for sophomore year. Students must declare major by end of second year. **Graduation requirements:** 64 hours for associate (32 in major), 124 hours for bachelor's (38 in major). Most students required to take courses in arts/fine arts, computer science, English, history, humanities, mathematics, philosophy/religion, biological/physical sciences, social sciences. **Postgraduate studies:** 50% from 2-year programs enter 4-year programs. 2% enter MBA programs, 4% enter other graduate study.

FRESHMAN ADMISSIONS. Selection criteria: School achievement record, SAT or ACT scores, school and community activities considered. **High school preparation:** 15 units required. Required units include English 4, mathematics 2, social science 4 and science 1. **Test requirements:** SAT or ACT; score report by August 20.

1992 FRESHMAN CLASS PROFILE. 103 men applied, 67 accepted, 39 enrolled; 278 women applied, 203 accepted, 91 enrolled. 29% had high school GPA of 3.0 or higher, 60% between 2.0 and 2.99. **Academic background:** Mid 50% of enrolled freshmen had SAT-V between 350-480, SAT-M between 370-480; ACT composite between 18-24. 90% submitted SAT scores, 10% submitted ACT scores. **Characteristics:** 58% from in state, 65% live in college housing, 2% have minority backgrounds, 3% are foreign students. Average age is 18.

FALL-TERM APPLICATIONS. $15 fee, may be waived for applicants with need. No closing date; applicants notified on a rolling basis; must reply by May 1 or immediately if notified thereafter. Interview recommended. Audition recommended for music, dance applicants. Portfolio recommended for art, photography applicants. Essay recommended. CRDA. Deferred and early admission available.

STUDENT LIFE. Housing: Dormitories (men, women). Students under 23 years of age not living with parents must live on campus. Students with senior status may live off campus. Special accommodations for the learning disabled. **Activities:** Student government, magazine, yearbook, choral groups, dance, drama, musical theater, Baptist Student Union, Cardinal Key, Social Work Action Group.

ATHLETICS. NAIA. **Intercollegiate:** Baseball M, basketball, horseback riding, tennis. **Intramural:** Basketball, bowling, horseback riding, skiing, swimming, table tennis, tennis, volleyball.

STUDENT SERVICES. Aptitude testing, career counseling, employment service for undergraduates, freshman orientation, personal counseling, placement service for graduates, special adviser for adult students, services/facilities for handicapped.

ANNUAL EXPENSES. Tuition and fees (1992-93): $7,320. **Room and board:** $3,980. **Books and supplies:** $500. **Other expenses:** $1,500.

FINANCIAL AID. 62% of freshmen, 47% of continuing students receive some form of aid. 32% of grants, 86% of loans, 68% of jobs based on need. 89 enrolled freshmen were judged to have need, all were offered aid. Academic, athletic, state/district residency, religious affiliation scholarships available. **Aid applications:** No closing date; priority given to applications received by March 1; applicants notified on a rolling basis beginning on or about March 15; must reply by May 1 or immediately if notified thereafter.

ADDRESS/TELEPHONE. R. Lawton Blandford, Jr, Dean of Admissions and Enrollment Management, Virginia Intermont College, 1013 Moore Street, Bristol, VA 24201-4298. (703) 669-6101. (800) 451-1842. Fax: (703) 669-5763.

Virginia Military Institute
Lexington, Virginia — CB code: 5858

Admissions: 78% of applicants accepted
Based on:
••• School record, test scores
•• Essay
• Activities, interview, recommendations, special talents
Completion: 70% of freshmen end year in good standing
8% enter graduate study

4-year public college of arts and sciences and military college, men only. Founded in 1839. **Accreditation:** Regional. **Undergraduate enrollment:** 1,265 men full time. **Faculty:** 111 total (94 full time), 80 with doctorates or other terminal degrees. **Location:** Rural campus in small town; approximately 55 miles from Roanoke, 140 miles from Richmond. **Calendar:** Semester, limited summer session. Saturday classes. **Microcomputers:** 150 located in libraries, classrooms, computer centers. **Special facilities:** Historical museums, research library, observatory. **Additional facts:** Mandatory ROTC classes and optional commissioning in the Army, Air Force, Navy, or Marines.

DEGREES OFFERED. BA, BS. 256 bachelor's degrees awarded in 1992. 25% in business and management, 35% engineering, 8% letters/literature, 24% social sciences.

UNDERGRADUATE MAJORS. Biology, business economics, chemistry, civil engineering, computer mathematics, economics, electrical/electronics/communications engineering, English, foreign languages (multiple emphasis), history, international studies, mathematics, mechanical engineering, physics.

ACADEMIC PROGRAMS. Double major, honors program, independent study, study abroad. **Remedial services:** Preadmission summer program, tutoring. **ROTC:** Air Force, Army, Naval. **Placement/credit:** AP, institutional tests.

ACADEMIC REQUIREMENTS. Freshmen must earn minimum GPA of 1.5 to continue in good standing. 80% of freshmen return for sophomore year. Students must declare major on enrollment. **Graduation requirements:** 140 hours for bachelor's. Most students required to take courses in computer science, English, history, mathematics, biological/physical sciences. **Postgraduate studies:** 2% enter law school, 1% enter medical school, 1% enter MBA programs, 4% enter other graduate study.

FRESHMAN ADMISSIONS. Selection criteria: High school academic record, class rank and GPA, SAT/ACT scores and extracurricular activities considered. All applicants must pass ROTC physical examination. **High school preparation:** 16 units required; 20 recommended. Required and recommended units include English 4 and mathematics 3-4. Foreign language 4, social science 3 and science 3 recommended. **Test requirements:** SAT or ACT; score report by March 1.

1992 FRESHMAN CLASS PROFILE. 961 men applied, 748 accepted, 406 enrolled. 39% had high school GPA of 3.0 or higher, 60% between 2.0 and 2.99. 14% were in top tenth and 34% were in top quarter of graduating class. **Academic background:** Mid 50% of enrolled freshmen had SAT-V between 430-540, SAT-M between 500-600; ACT composite between 20-24. 75% submitted SAT scores, 77% submitted ACT scores. **Characteristics:** 58% from in state, 100% live in college housing, 12% have minority backgrounds, 2% are foreign students. Average age is 18.

FALL-TERM APPLICATIONS. $25 fee, may be waived for applicants with need. Closing date March 1; applicants notified on a rolling basis; must reply by May 1 or within 2 weeks if notified thereafter. Essay required. Interview recommended. CRDA.

STUDENT LIFE. Housing: Dormitories (men). **Activities:** Student government, magazine, student newspaper, yearbook, choral groups, concert band, drama, jazz band, marching band, musical theater, pep band.

ATHLETICS. NCAA. **Intercollegiate:** Baseball, basketball, cross-country, diving, fencing, football, golf, lacrosse, rifle, soccer, swimming, tennis, track and field, wrestling. **Intramural:** Basketball, boxing, gymnastics, handball, racquetball.

STUDENT SERVICES. Aptitude testing, career counseling, employment service for undergraduates, freshman orientation, health services, personal counseling, placement service for graduates.

ANNUAL EXPENSES. Tuition and fees: $4,930, $5,820 additional for out-of-state students. **Room and board:** $3,690. **Books and supplies:** $600. **Other expenses:** $1,000.

FINANCIAL AID. 54% of freshmen, 62% of continuing students receive some form of aid. 53% of grants, 93% of loans, 26% of jobs based on need. 135 enrolled freshmen were judged to have need, 134 were offered aid. Academic, athletic, state/district residency, leadership scholarships available. **Aid applications:** No closing date; priority given to applications received by March 1; applicants notified on a rolling basis beginning on or about April 1; must reply by May 1 or within 2 weeks if notified thereafter.

ADDRESS/TELEPHONE. Daniel A. Troppoli, Director of Admissions, Virginia Military Institute, Lexington, VA 24450-9967. (703) 464-7211. Fax: (703) 464-7746.

Virginia Polytechnic Institute and State University
Blacksburg, Virginia — CB code: 5859

Admissions: 65% of applicants accepted
Based on:
••• School record
•• Test scores
• Activities, essay, recommendations, special talents
Completion: 93% of freshmen end year in good standing
67% graduate

4-year public university, coed. Founded in 1872. **Accreditation:** Regional. **Undergraduate enrollment:** 10,792 men, 7,474 women full time; 311 men, 242 women part time. **Graduate enrollment:** 2,324 men, 1,208 women full time; 572 men, 403 women part time. **Faculty:** 3,125 total (2,660 full time), 1,483 with doctorates or other terminal degrees. **Location:** Rural campus in large town; 38 miles from Roanoke. **Calendar:** Semester, extensive summer session. **Microcomputers:** Located in dormitories, libraries, classrooms, computer centers, campus-wide network. **Special facilities:** Natural history, geology and art museums; observatory, wind tunnels, art galleries, Black Cultural Center, digital music center, robotics laboratory. **Additional facts:** Honor system. Option of enrolling as nonmilitary or as military student and member of cadet corps.

DEGREES OFFERED. AS, BA, BS, BFA, BArch, MA, MS, MBA, MFA, MEd, PhD, EdD, DVM. 35 associate degrees awarded in 1992. 100% in agriculture. 4,066 bachelor's degrees awarded. 24% in business and management, 5% education, 23% engineering, 7% home economics, 7% social sciences. Graduate degrees offered in 101 major fields of study.

UNDERGRADUATE MAJORS. Associate: Agribusiness, animal sciences, plant sciences. **Bachelor's:** Accounting, aerospace/aeronautical/astronautical engineering, agricultural economics, agricultural education, agricultural engineering, agronomy, animal sciences, architecture, biochemistry, biochemistry and nutrition, biology, business and management, business economics, business education, chemical engineering, chemistry, civil engineering, communications, computer and information sciences, computer engineering, construction, dairy, dramatic arts, early childhood education, economics, electrical/electronics/communications engineering, elementary education, engineering mechanics, engineering science, English, English education, environmental science, family/consumer resource management, fashion design, finance, fine arts, food science and nutrition, food sciences, foreign languages education, forestry and related sciences, French, geography, geology, geophysics and seismology, German, health education, history, home economics education, horticulture, hotel/motel and restaurant management, human environment and housing, individual and family development, industrial arts education, industrial engineering, institutional management, interior design, international relations, international studies, junior high education, landscape architecture, liberal/general studies, management science, marketing and distributive education, marketing management, materials engineering, mathematics, mathematics education, mechanical engineering, mining and mineral engineering, music, music education, nutritional sciences, ocean engineering, philosophy, physical education, physics, political science and government, poultry, predentistry, premedicine, preveterinary, psychology, public administration, science education, secondary education, social studies education, sociology, Spanish, speech/communication/theater education, statistics, teaching English as a second language/foreign language, technical education, textiles and clothing, trade and industrial education, urban studies, wildlife management.

ACADEMIC PROGRAMS. Accelerated program, cooperative education, double major, dual enrollment of high school students, honors program, independent study, internships, student-designed major, study abroad, teacher preparation, telecourses, Washington semester, cross-registration, cadet corps. **ROTC:** Air Force, Army, Naval. **Placement/credit:** AP, IB, institutional tests; 38 credit hours maximum for bachelor's degree.

ACADEMIC REQUIREMENTS. Freshmen must earn minimum GPA of 1.5 to continue in good standing. 89% of freshmen return for sophomore year. Students must declare major by end of second year. **Graduation requirements:** 72 hours for associate, 126 hours for bachelor's (36 in major). Most students required to take courses in English, history, humanities, mathematics, biological/physical sciences, social sciences. **Additional information:** Freshman engineering, computer science, and statistics majors required to have departmentally-specified computers. Students in the college of business required to have access to computer by end of sophomore year.

FRESHMAN ADMISSIONS. Selection criteria: High school record, class rank, and SAT scores most important. In-state applicants receive preference in admissions process. **High school preparation:** 18 units required. Required and recommended units include English 4, mathematics 3-4, social science 2 and science 2-3. Foreign language 3 recommended. Preference given to applicants with mathematics beyond Algebra II. 4 mathematics required for science, engineering, computer science, mathematics, statistics, and building construction programs. 2 units of laboratory science required, 3 units including physics required for engineering and recommended for all science-related majors. **Test requirements:** SAT or ACT (SAT preferred); score report by February 1. 2 ACH required (English and Mathematics Level I or II). Score report by May 1. **Additional information:** Prospective students encouraged to pursue rigorous preparatory course of study.

1992 FRESHMAN CLASS PROFILE. 9,480 men applied, 5,938 accepted, 2,215 enrolled; 7,630 women applied, 5,172 accepted, 1,642 enrolled. **Academic background:** Mid 50% of enrolled freshmen had SAT-V between 450-550, SAT-M between 520-650. 99% submitted SAT scores. **Characteristics:** 75% from in state, 95% live in college housing, 7% have minority backgrounds, 2% join fraternities/sororities. Average age is 18.

FALL-TERM APPLICATIONS. $20 fee, may be waived for applicants with need. Closing date February 1; applicants notified on or about April 15; must reply by May 1. Audition required for music applicants. Portfolio required for studio art applicants. CRDA. Deferred and early admission available. EDP-F; institutional early decision plan. Application for early decision due November 1.

STUDENT LIFE. Housing: Dormitories (men, women, coed); fraternity, sorority housing available. Freshmen required to live on campus, unless living with parents or close relatives, married, veteran, or at least 21 years old. Cadets live in cadet residence halls. Foreign language hall and academic success hall available. **Activities:** Student government, film, magazine, radio, student newspaper, television, yearbook, choral groups, concert band, dance, drama, jazz band, marching band, music ensembles, musical theater, opera, pep band, symphony orchestra, fraternities, sororities, 400 clubs and organizations, many minority and international organizations.

ATHLETICS. NCAA. **Intercollegiate:** Baseball M, basketball, cross-country, football M, golf M, soccer, tennis, track and field, volleyball W, wrestling M. **Intramural:** Archery, badminton, basketball, bowling, cross-country, fencing, field hockey W, golf, gymnastics, handball, horseback riding, lacrosse, racquetball, rugby, skiing, soccer, softball, swimming, tennis, track and field, volleyball, water polo, wrestling M.

STUDENT SERVICES. Aptitude testing, career counseling, employment service for undergraduates, freshman orientation, health services, personal counseling, placement service for graduates, veterans counselor, academic success program for minorities, services/facilities for handicapped.

ANNUAL EXPENSES. Tuition and fees: $3,812, $5,868 additional for out-of-state students. Fees do not include required computer purchase for engineering and computer science majors. **Room and board:** $3,196. **Books and supplies:** $720. **Other expenses:** $1,600.

FINANCIAL AID. 55% of freshmen, 45% of continuing students receive some form of aid. 55% of grants, 68% of loans, 16% of jobs based on need. 2,366 enrolled freshmen were judged to have need, 1,869 were offered aid. Academic, music/drama, art, athletic, state/district residency, leadership, minority scholarships available. **Aid applications:** Closing date March 15; applicants notified on or about April 1; must reply by May 1.

ADDRESS/TELEPHONE. David R. Bousquet, Director of Enrollment Svcs and Office of Admissions, Virginia Polytechnic Institute and State University, 104 Burruss Hall, Blacksburg, VA 24061-0202. (703) 231-6267. Fax: (703) 231-3242.

Virginia State University
Petersburg, Virginia — CB code: 5860

4-year public university, coed. Founded in 1882. **Accreditation:** Regional. **Undergraduate enrollment:** 1,446 men, 1,984 women full time; 213 men, 206 women part time. **Graduate enrollment:** 20 men, 23 women full time; 167 men, 376 women part time. **Faculty:** 289 total (229 full time), 147 with doctorates or other terminal degrees. **Location:** Suburban campus in large town; 25 miles from Richmond. **Calendar:** Semester, extensive summer session. **Microcomputers:** 125 located in classrooms, computer centers.

DEGREES OFFERED. BA, BS, BFA, MA, MS, MEd. 423 bachelor's degrees awarded in 1992. 25% in business and management, 7% business/office and marketing/distribution, 6% education, 8% engineering technologies, 5% letters/literature, 6% mathematics, 5% multi/interdisciplinary studies, 6% physical sciences, 8% psychology, 9% social sciences. Graduate degrees offered in 16 major fields of study.

UNDERGRADUATE MAJORS. Accounting, agricultural sciences, art education, biology, business administration and management, business and office, business economics, business education, business home economics, chemistry, engineering and engineering-related technologies, English, English education, fine arts, foreign languages education, geology, history, hotel/motel and restaurant management, industrial technology education, information sciences and systems, international relations, international studies, management information systems, marketing management, mathematics, music, physical education, physics, political science and government, psychology, public administration, social work, sociology, special education, trade and industrial education.

ACADEMIC PROGRAMS. Cooperative education, double major, dual enrollment of high school students, honors program, internships, study abroad, teacher preparation. **Remedial services:** Reduced course load, remedial instruction, special counselor, tutoring. **ROTC:** Army. **Placement/credit:** CLEP General, institutional tests; 12 credit hours maximum for bachelor's degree.

ACADEMIC REQUIREMENTS. Freshmen must earn minimum GPA of 1.5 to continue in good standing. 60% of freshmen return for sophomore year. Students must declare major by end of first year. **Graduation requirements:** 120 hours for bachelor's (42 in major). Most students required to take courses in arts/fine arts, computer science, English, history, humanities, mathematics, biological/physical sciences, social sciences.

FRESHMAN ADMISSIONS. Selection criteria: School achievement record most important, recommendation required. **High school preparation:** 16 units required. Required and recommended units include biological science 2, English 4, foreign language 2, mathematics 2-3, physical science 2 and social science 2. **Test requirements:** SAT or ACT (SAT preferred); score report by June 1.

1992 FRESHMAN CLASS PROFILE. 1,303 men applied, 1,205 accepted, 404 enrolled; 1,797 women applied, 1,638 accepted, 493 enrolled. **Academic background:** Mid 50% of enrolled freshmen had SAT-V between 310-440, SAT-M between 320-470. 95% submitted SAT scores. **Characteris-**

tics: 53% from in state, 52% commute, 98% have minority backgrounds. Average age is 18.

FALL-TERM APPLICATIONS. $25 fee, may be waived for applicants with need. Closing date May 1; priority given to applications received by March 31; applicants notified on a rolling basis beginning on or about January 10; must reply by May 1 or within 2 weeks if notified thereafter. Audition required for music applicants. Essay recommended. CRDA. Deferred admission available.

STUDENT LIFE. Housing: Dormitories (men, women). **Activities:** Student government, film, magazine, radio, student newspaper, television, yearbook, choral groups, concert band, dance, drama, marching band, music ensembles, opera, symphony orchestra, fraternities, sororities, Student Christian Association.

ATHLETICS. NCAA. **Intercollegiate:** Baseball M, basketball, cross-country, football M, golf, softball W, tennis, track and field, wrestling M. **Intramural:** Archery, basketball M, softball, swimming, table tennis, tennis, volleyball W.

STUDENT SERVICES. Career counseling, employment service for undergraduates, freshman orientation, health services, personal counseling, placement service for graduates, veterans counselor, services/facilities for handicapped.

ANNUAL EXPENSES. Tuition and fees (1992-93): $2,913, $3,402 additional for out-of-state students. **Room and board:** $4,127. **Books and supplies:** $500. **Other expenses:** $500.

FINANCIAL AID. 85% of freshmen, 85% of continuing students receive some form of aid. 91% of grants, 96% of loans, 97% of jobs based on need. Academic, state/district residency, alumni affiliation, minority scholarships available. **Aid applications:** Closing date May 1; priority given to applications received by March 31; applicants notified on a rolling basis beginning on or about May 1; must reply by May 1 or within 2 weeks if notified thereafter. **Additional information:** We strongly recommend that students apply for scholarship assistance through federal, state, local and private agencies to assist them in defraying the costs.

ADDRESS/TELEPHONE. Karen R. Winston, Director of Admissions, Virginia State University, PO 9018, One Hayden Drive, Petersburg, VA 23806. (804) 524-5902. Fax: (804) 524-5055.

Virginia Union University
Richmond, Virginia — CB code: 5862

Admissions: 87% of applicants accepted
Based on: ••• Activities, school record, test scores
•• Essay, interview
• Recommendations, special talents
Completion: 70% of freshmen end year in good standing

4-year private university, coed, affiliated with American Baptist Churches in the USA. Founded in 1865. **Accreditation:** Regional. **Undergraduate enrollment:** 572 men, 709 women full time; 27 men, 53 women part time. **Graduate enrollment:** 107 men, 25 women full time; 14 men, 4 women part time. **Faculty:** 122 total (88 full time), 33 with doctorates or other terminal degrees. **Location:** Urban campus in small city; 90 miles from Norfolk, 100 miles from Washington, D.C. **Calendar:** Semester, limited summer session. **Microcomputers:** 233 located in libraries, classrooms, computer centers.

DEGREES OFFERED. BA, BS, M, D, M.Div. 125 bachelor's degrees awarded in 1992. 32% in business and management, 6% communications, 16% education, 8% life sciences, 7% mathematics, 5% psychology, 22% social sciences. Graduate degrees offered in 2 major fields of study.

UNDERGRADUATE MAJORS. Accounting, biology, business administration and management, chemistry, English, French, history, journalism, management information systems, mathematics, music, parks and recreation management, philosophy, political science and government, psychology, religion, school psychology, social work, sociology.

ACADEMIC PROGRAMS. Cooperative education, honors program, independent study, internships, teacher preparation; liberal arts/career combination in engineering. **Remedial services:** Reduced course load, remedial instruction, special counselor, tutoring. **ROTC:** Army. **Placement/credit:** Institutional tests; 18 credit hours maximum for bachelor's degree.

ACADEMIC REQUIREMENTS. Freshmen must earn minimum GPA of 1.8 to continue in good standing. 60% of freshmen return for sophomore year. Students must declare major by end of second year. **Graduation requirements:** 124 hours for bachelor's (36 in major). Most students required to take courses in English, history, humanities, mathematics, philosophy/religion, biological/physical sciences, social sciences.

FRESHMAN ADMISSIONS. Selection criteria: SAT or ACT scores and 2.0 GPA important. **High school preparation:** 16 units required. Required units include English 4, foreign language 2, mathematics 3, social science 2 and science 2. **Test requirements:** SAT or ACT; score report by June 1.

1992 FRESHMAN CLASS PROFILE. 821 men applied, 677 accepted, 214 enrolled; 1,026 women applied, 933 accepted, 239 enrolled. 13% had high school GPA of 3.0 or higher, 60% between 2.0 and 2.99. **Characteristics:** 39% from in state, 81% live in college housing, 99% have minority backgrounds, 1% are foreign students. Average age is 18.

FALL-TERM APPLICATIONS. $10 fee, may be waived for applicants with need. Closing date June 15; priority given to applications received by April 1; applicants notified on a rolling basis; must reply within 3 weeks. Audition required for music applicants. Interview recommended for academically weak applicants. Essay recommended. Deferred admission available.

STUDENT LIFE. Housing: Dormitories (men, women, coed). **Activities:** Student government, student newspaper, television, yearbook, choral groups, concert band, dance, drama, jazz band, marching band, pep band, fraternities, sororities, Students for Social Justice, Carisma Women's Fellowship. **Additional information:** Religious observance required.

ATHLETICS. NCAA. **Intercollegiate:** Basketball, football M, golf, tennis, track and field, volleyball W. **Intramural:** Basketball M, softball, table tennis, volleyball.

STUDENT SERVICES. Aptitude testing, career counseling, employment service for undergraduates, freshman orientation, health services, personal counseling, placement service for graduates.

ANNUAL EXPENSES. Tuition and fees: $7,061. **Room and board:** $3,494. **Books and supplies:** $500. **Other expenses:** $1,000.

FINANCIAL AID. 87% of freshmen, 94% of continuing students receive some form of aid. 53% of grants, 91% of loans, all jobs based on need. Academic, music/drama, athletic, state/district residency scholarships available. **Aid applications:** No closing date; priority given to applications received by May 15; applicants notified on a rolling basis beginning on or about May 1; must reply within 2 weeks.

ADDRESS/TELEPHONE. Gil Powell, Director of Admissions, Virginia Union University, 1500 North Lombardy Street, Richmond, VA 23220. (804) 257-5856. (800) 368-3227. Fax: (804) 257-5818.

Virginia Wesleyan College
Norfolk, Virginia — CB code: 5867

Admissions: 62% of applicants accepted
Based on: ••• School record, test scores
•• Activities, essay, interview
• Recommendations, special talents
Completion: 89% of freshmen end year in good standing
75% graduate, 35% of these enter graduate study

4-year private liberal arts college, coed, affiliated with United Methodist Church. Founded in 1961. **Accreditation:** Regional. **Undergraduate enrollment:** 584 men, 714 women full time; 86 men, 129 women part time. **Faculty:** 91 total (70 full time), 60 with doctorates or other terminal degrees. **Location:** Suburban campus in large city; 9 miles from Norfolk, 15 miles from Virginia Beach. **Calendar:** Semester, limited summer session. **Microcomputers:** 30 located in computer centers. **Special facilities:** Greenhouse (botanical laboratory), Vogan Music Room, Multi-Cultural Resource Center. **Additional facts:** 2-week January term offered. 2 such sessions required to complete degree.

DEGREES OFFERED. BA. 221 bachelor's degrees awarded in 1992. 30% in business and management, 9% communications, 12% teacher education, 7% letters/literature, 7% multi/interdisciplinary studies, 12% social sciences.

UNDERGRADUATE MAJORS. Accounting, American literature, American studies, anthropology, art education, art history, biochemistry, biological and physical sciences, biology, business administration and management, business and management, business economics, chemistry, clinical psychology, communications, community services, computer and information sciences, computer mathematics, computer programming, counseling psychology, creative writing, criminal justice studies, dramatic arts, drawing, early childhood education, elementary education, English, English education, English literature, environmental science, experimental psychology, fine arts, foreign languages education, French, German, history, humanities, humanities and social sciences, industrial and organizational psychology, international business management, international public service, international relations, international studies, journalism, junior high education, liberal/general studies, marketing management, mathematics, mathematics education, music, music education, music theory and composition, painting, parks and recreation management, personnel management, philosophy, physical sciences, physics, political science and government, predentistry, prelaw, premedicine, prepharmacy, preveterinary, psychology, public administration, public policy studies, public relations, pure mathematics, radio/television broadcasting, recreation therapy, religion, science education, secondary education, social psychology, social science education, social sciences, social studies education, social work, sociology, Spanish, studio art, visual and performing arts.

ACADEMIC PROGRAMS. Accelerated program, double major, dual enrollment of high school students, honors program, independent study, internships, student-designed major, study abroad, teacher preparation, visiting/exchange student program, cross-registration. **Remedial services:** Learning center, preadmission summer program, reduced course load, remedial instruction, special counselor, tutoring. **Placement/credit:** AP, CLEP General and Subject, IB, institutional tests; 30 credit hours maximum for bachelor's degree.

ACADEMIC REQUIREMENTS. Freshmen must earn minimum GPA of 2.0 to continue in good standing. 85% of freshmen return for sophomore year. Students must declare major by end of second year. **Graduation requirements:** 120 hours for bachelor's (40 in major). Most students required to take courses in arts/fine arts, English, foreign languages, history, humanities, mathematics, philosophy/religion, biological/physical sciences, social sciences. **Postgraduate studies:** 6% enter law school, 5% enter medical school, 2% enter MBA programs, 22% enter other graduate study. **Additional information:** English proficiency examination and 1 writing course per semester required.

FRESHMAN ADMISSIONS. Selection criteria: Above average grades in solid college-preparatory curriculum, SAT scores, campus interview, personal statement considered. **High school preparation:** 14 units recommended. Recommended units include biological science 1, English 4, foreign language 3, mathematics 3 and social science 3. **Test requirements:** SAT; score report by March 1.

1992 FRESHMAN CLASS PROFILE. 574 men applied, 398 accepted, 136 enrolled; 861 women applied, 487 accepted, 166 enrolled. 53% had high school GPA of 3.0 or higher, 46% between 2.0 and 2.99. 20% were in top tenth and 50% were in top quarter of graduating class. **Academic background:** Mid 50% of enrolled freshmen had SAT-V between 430-580, SAT-M between 450-590. 99% submitted SAT scores. **Characteristics:** 50% from in state, 70% live in college housing, 12% have minority backgrounds, 2% are foreign students, 10% join fraternities/sororities. Average age is 18.

FALL-TERM APPLICATIONS. $25 fee, may be waived for applicants with need. Closing date March 1; applicants notified on or about April 1; must reply by May 1. Essay required. Interview recommended. CRDA. Deferred and early admission available. EDP-F.

STUDENT LIFE. Housing: Dormitories (women, coed); apartment, fraternity, sorority housing available. Housing guaranteed for all 4 years. **Activities:** Student government, film, magazine, radio, student newspaper, television, yearbook, choral groups, drama, music ensembles, musical theater, fraternities, sororities, International Club, Political Science Association, Model United Nations, Amnesty International, Habitat for Humanity, Epsilon Sigma Alpha, African-American Society, Student Ecological Awareness League, Shalom, Campus Catholic Ministry.

ATHLETICS. NCAA. **Intercollegiate:** Baseball M, basketball, field hockey W, golf M, lacrosse M, soccer, softball W, tennis. **Intramural:** Basketball, bowling, cross-country, fencing, soccer, softball, table tennis, tennis, track and field, volleyball.

STUDENT SERVICES. Career counseling, employment service for undergraduates, freshman orientation, health services, personal counseling, placement service for graduates, special adviser for adult students, veterans counselor, services/facilities for handicapped.

ANNUAL EXPENSES. Tuition and fees: $10,275. **Room and board:** $4,800. **Books and supplies:** $600. **Other expenses:** $1,100.

FINANCIAL AID. 65% of freshmen, 70% of continuing students receive some form of aid. 26% of grants, 94% of loans, all jobs based on need. Academic scholarships available. **Aid applications:** No closing date; priority given to applications received by March 1; applicants notified on a rolling basis beginning on or about April 1; must reply by May 1 or within 2 weeks if notified thereafter.

ADDRESS/TELEPHONE. W. Steve Stocks, Vice President for Admission and Financial Aid, Virginia Wesleyan College, Wesleyan Drive, Norfolk, VA 23502-5599. (804) 455-3208. Fax: (804) 466-8526.

Virginia Western Community College
Roanoke, Virginia — CB code: 5868

2-year public community college, coed. Founded in 1966. **Accreditation:** Regional. **Undergraduate enrollment:** 6,904 men and women. **Faculty:** 325 total (100 full time). **Location:** Urban campus in small city; 3 miles from downtown. **Calendar:** Semester, extensive summer session. **Microcomputers:** Located in libraries, classrooms.

DEGREES OFFERED. AA, AS, AAS. 418 associate degrees awarded in 1992.

UNDERGRADUATE MAJORS. Accounting, architectural technologies, automotive mechanics, business administration and management, business and management, civil technology, commercial art, criminal justice technology, data processing, dental hygiene, education, electronic technology, engineering, fine arts, horticulture, mechanical design technology, mental health/human services, nursing, physical sciences, radio/television technology, radiograph medical technology, science technologies, secretarial and related programs, word processing.

ACADEMIC PROGRAMS. 2-year transfer program, cooperative education, dual enrollment of high school students, independent study, internships. **Remedial services:** Learning center, preadmission summer program, reduced course load, remedial instruction, special counselor, tutoring, mathematics laboratory, writing center. **Placement/credit:** AP, CLEP General and Subject, institutional tests; 80 credit hours maximum for associate degree.

ACADEMIC REQUIREMENTS. Freshmen must earn minimum GPA of 1.5 to continue in good standing. Students must declare major by end of first year. **Graduation requirements:** 65 hours for associate (30 in major). Most students required to take courses in English, mathematics, social sciences.

FRESHMAN ADMISSIONS. Selection criteria: Open admissions. Selective admissions to health programs.

1992 FRESHMAN CLASS PROFILE. 1,750 men and women enrolled. **Characteristics:** 99% from in state, 100% commute, 10% have minority backgrounds, 1% are foreign students. Average age is 24.

FALL-TERM APPLICATIONS. No fee. No closing date; applicants notified on a rolling basis. Interview required for health technologies applicants. Deferred admission available.

STUDENT LIFE. Activities: Student government, student newspaper, choral groups, drama, Circle-K, Baptist Student Union, Minority Student Alliance.

ATHLETICS. Intramural: Basketball M.

STUDENT SERVICES. Aptitude testing, career counseling, employment service for undergraduates, personal counseling, placement service for graduates, veterans counselor, services/facilities for handicapped.

ANNUAL EXPENSES. Tuition and fees: $1,324, $3,030 additional for out-of-state students. **Books and supplies:** $550. **Other expenses:** $1,200.

FINANCIAL AID. 20% of freshmen, 20% of continuing students receive some form of aid. 91% of grants, 84% of loans, 83% of jobs based on need. Academic, leadership scholarships available. **Aid applications:** No closing date; applicants notified on a rolling basis beginning on or about April 1; must reply within 10 days.

ADDRESS/TELEPHONE. F. Gordon Hancock, Coordinator of Admissions and Records, Virginia Western Community College, PO Box 14065, Roanoke, VA 24038. (703) 857-7319.

Washington and Lee University
Lexington, Virginia — CB code: 5887

Admissions:	29% of applicants accepted
Based on:	••• School record
	•• Activities, recommendations, test scores
	• Essay, interview, special talents
Completion:	98% of freshmen end year in good standing
	90% graduate, 24% of these enter graduate study

4-year private university and liberal arts college, coed. Founded in 1749. **Accreditation:** Regional. **Undergraduate enrollment:** 981 men, 613 women full time. **Graduate enrollment:** 221 men, 154 women full time. **Faculty:** 167 total, 160 with doctorates or other terminal degrees. **Location:** Rural campus in small town; 50 miles from Roanoke. **Calendar:** 2 12-week sessions followed by 6-week session. **Microcomputers:** 140 located in dormitories, libraries, classrooms, computer centers. **Special facilities:** Art museum, Robert E. Lee Chapel and tomb, Lenfest performing arts center.

DEGREES OFFERED. BA, BS, JD. 391 bachelor's degrees awarded in 1992. 12% in business and management, 9% communications, 9% languages, 7% letters/literature, 9% life sciences, 5% physical sciences, 5% psychology, 31% social sciences. Graduate degrees offered in 1 major field of study.

UNDERGRADUATE MAJORS. Accounting, anthropology, archeology, art history, biological and physical sciences, biology, business administration and management, chemical engineering, chemistry, classics, computer and information sciences, dramatic arts, East Asian studies, economics, engineering physics, English, foreign languages (multiple emphasis), forestry and related sciences, French, geology, geophysics and seismology, German, history, journalism, mathematics, music, philosophy, physics, political science and government, psychology, public policy studies, religion, Russian and Slavic studies, sociology, Spanish, studio art.

ACADEMIC PROGRAMS. Double major, honors program, independent study, internships, student-designed major, study abroad, teacher preparation, visiting/exchange student program, Washington semester, cross-registration, professional ethics seminars in business, law, medicine, journalism; liberal arts/career combination in engineering, forestry; combined bachelor's/graduate program in law. **Remedial services:** Tutoring. **Placement/credit:** AP, institutional tests.

ACADEMIC REQUIREMENTS. Freshmen must earn minimum GPA of 1.5 to continue in good standing. 96% of freshmen return for sophomore year. Students must declare major by end of second year. **Graduation requirements:** 121 hours for bachelor's (40 in major). Most students required to take courses in arts/fine arts, English, foreign languages, history, humanities, mathematics, philosophy/religion, biological/physical sciences, social sciences. **Postgraduate studies:** 10% enter law school, 4% enter medical school, 2% enter MBA programs, 8% enter other graduate study.

FRESHMAN ADMISSIONS. Selection criteria: School achievement record most important, followed closely by test scores, school and community activities, recommendations and personal interview. Special consideration given children of alumni and applicants from minorities and low-income families. **High school preparation:** 16 units required. Required and recommended units include English 4, foreign language 2-3, mathematics 3-4, social science 1-2 and science 1-3. One laboratory science required, 3 recommended. **Test requirements:** SAT or ACT; score report by March 1. 3 ACH required (including English Composition) except for those who submit ACT. Score report by March 1.

1992 FRESHMAN CLASS PROFILE. 1,911 men applied, 618 accepted, 277 enrolled; 1,522 women applied, 368 accepted, 158 enrolled. 69% were in top tenth of graduating class. **Academic background:** Mid 50% of enrolled freshmen had SAT-V between 560-640, SAT-M between 610-700. 89% submitted SAT scores. **Characteristics:** 12% from in state, 99% live in college housing, 4% have minority backgrounds, 80% join fraternities/sororities. Average age is 18.

FALL-TERM APPLICATIONS. $40 fee, may be waived for applicants with need. Closing date January 15; applicants notified on or about April 1; must reply by May 1. Essay required. Interview recommended. CRDA. Deferred admission available. EDP-S.

STUDENT LIFE. Housing: Dormitories (coed); apartment, fraternity housing available. Some students live in off-campus housing after their freshman year. **Activities:** Student government, film, magazine, radio, student newspaper, television, yearbook, literary magazine, choral groups, concert band, drama, jazz band, music ensembles, musical theater, symphony orchestra, community orchestra and chorus, fraternities, sororities, Young Democrats, College Republicans, Minority Student Association, Washington and Lee Christian Fellowship, Fellowship of Christian Athletes, University Federation, International Club, Lampost, honorary societies, Hillel. **Additional information:** Honor system observed.

ATHLETICS. NCAA. **Intercollegiate:** Baseball M, basketball M, cross-country, football M, golf M, lacrosse, soccer, swimming, tennis, track and field, volleyball W, water polo M, wrestling M. **Intramural:** Badminton, baseball, basketball, bowling M, cross-country, diving, fencing, football M, golf, handball M, horseback riding W, ice hockey, lacrosse, racquetball, rugby M, soccer, softball, squash, swimming, table tennis, tennis, track and field, volleyball, wrestling M.

STUDENT SERVICES. Aptitude testing, career counseling, employment service for undergraduates, freshman orientation, health services, personal counseling, placement service for graduates, services/facilities for handicapped.

ANNUAL EXPENSES. Tuition and fees (1992-93): $12,465. **Room and board:** $4,271. **Books and supplies:** $550. **Other expenses:** $955.

FINANCIAL AID. 32% of freshmen, 32% of continuing students receive some form of aid. 81% of grants, 97% of loans, 92% of jobs based on need. 109 enrolled freshmen were judged to have need, all were offered aid. Academic, state/district residency, leadership, minority scholarships available. **Aid applications:** No closing date; priority given to applications received by February 1; applicants notified on a rolling basis beginning on or about April 1; must reply by May 1 or within 4 weeks if notified thereafter.

ADDRESS/TELEPHONE. William M. Hartog, Dean of Admissions and Financial Aid, Washington and Lee University, Lexington, VA 24450. (703) 463-8710. Fax: (703) 463-8473.

Wytheville Community College
Wytheville, Virginia CB code: 5917

2-year public community college, coed. Founded in 1962. **Accreditation:** Regional. **Undergraduate enrollment:** 1,383 men and women. **Faculty:** 220 total (70 full time), 13 with doctorates or other terminal degrees. **Location:** Rural campus in small town; 74 miles from Roanoke. **Calendar:** Semester, limited summer session. **Microcomputers:** 133 located in libraries, classrooms, computer centers.

DEGREES OFFERED. AA, AS, AAS. 245 associate degrees awarded in 1992. 15% in business and management, 7% business/office and marketing/distribution, 9% engineering technologies, 21% health sciences, 21% allied health, 8% multi/interdisciplinary studies, 12% parks/recreation, protective services, public affairs.

UNDERGRADUATE MAJORS. Accounting, biological and physical sciences, business administration and management, civil technology, dental hygiene, drafting and design technology, education, electronic technology, information sciences and systems, law enforcement and corrections technologies, liberal/general studies, medical laboratory technologies, nursing, physical therapy assistant, precision metal work, radiograph medical technology, secretarial and related programs.

ACADEMIC PROGRAMS. 2-year transfer program, dual enrollment of high school students, honors program, independent study, internships, cooperative program in nursing with New River Community College. **Remedial services:** Remedial instruction, tutoring. **Placement/credit:** AP, CLEP General and Subject, institutional tests.

ACADEMIC REQUIREMENTS. Freshmen must earn minimum GPA of 2.0 to continue in good standing. Students must declare major on application. **Graduation requirements:** 72 hours for associate (57 in major). Most students required to take courses in English, mathematics, social sciences.

FRESHMAN ADMISSIONS. Selection criteria: Open admissions. Limited admissions to allied health programs.

1992 FRESHMAN CLASS PROFILE. 587 men and women enrolled. **Characteristics:** 98% from in state, 100% commute, 3% have minority backgrounds. Average age is 28.

FALL-TERM APPLICATIONS. No fee. No closing date; applicants notified on a rolling basis. Interview required for allied health, police science applicants. Deferred admission available.

STUDENT LIFE. Activities: Student government, student newspaper, choral groups, drama.

ATHLETICS. Intramural: Basketball, softball, table tennis, tennis, volleyball.

STUDENT SERVICES. Aptitude testing, career counseling, employment service for undergraduates, freshman orientation, personal counseling, placement service for graduates, veterans counselor, services/facilities for handicapped.

ANNUAL EXPENSES. Tuition and fees: $1,335, $3,130 additional for out-of-state students. **Books and supplies:** $525. **Other expenses:** $800.

FINANCIAL AID. 50% of freshmen, 50% of continuing students receive some form of aid. All grants, 91% of loans, all jobs based on need. 350 enrolled freshmen were judged to have need, 300 were offered aid. Academic scholarships available. **Aid applications:** No closing date; priority given to applications received by April 1; applicants notified on a rolling basis beginning on or about May 1; must reply within 2 weeks.

ADDRESS/TELEPHONE. Mrs. Sherry K. Dix, Registrar, Wytheville Community College, 1000 East Main Street, Wytheville, VA 24382. (703) 228-5541. Fax: (703) 228-6506.

Washington

Antioch University Seattle
Seattle, Washington CB code: 3070

2-year upper-division private liberal arts college, coed. Founded in 1852. **Accreditation:** Regional. **Undergraduate enrollment:** 147 men and women. **Graduate enrollment:** 503 men and women. **Faculty:** 75 total (26 full time), 37 with doctorates or other terminal degrees. **Location:** Suburban campus in large city; in downtown area. **Calendar:** Quarter, extensive summer session. Extensive evening/early morning classes. **Microcomputers:** 4 located in computer centers. **Additional facts:** Bachelor of arts completion program in liberal studies for working adults integrates work and life experience with college classroom experience.

DEGREES OFFERED. BA, MA. 44 bachelor's degrees awarded in 1992. 100% in multi/interdisciplinary studies. Graduate degrees offered in 3 major fields of study.

UNDERGRADUATE MAJORS. Liberal/general studies.

ACADEMIC PROGRAMS. Independent study, student-designed major, study abroad, cross-registration. **Placement/credit:** CLEP General and Subject.

ACADEMIC REQUIREMENTS. Students must declare major on enrollment. **Graduation requirements:** 180 hours for bachelor's (40 in major).

STUDENT LIFE. Activities: Student government, student newspaper.

STUDENT SERVICES. Career counseling, personal counseling, veterans counselor, services/facilities for handicapped.

ANNUAL EXPENSES. Tuition and fees (1992-93): $7,845. **Books and supplies:** $350.

FINANCIAL AID. 51% of continuing students receive some form of aid. All aid based on need. **Aid applications:** No closing date; applicants notified on a rolling basis; must reply within 4 weeks.

ADDRESS/TELEPHONE. Vicki Tolbert, Admissions Officer, Antioch University Seattle, 2607 Second Avenue, Seattle, WA 98121. (206) 441-5352. Fax: (206) 441-3307.

Art Institute of Seattle
Seattle, Washington CB code: 4805

2-year proprietary art, technical college, coed. Founded in 1982. **Undergraduate enrollment:** 828 men, 656 women full time; 33 men, 62 women part time. **Faculty:** 131 total (44 full time), 8 with doctorates or other terminal degrees. **Location:** Urban campus in very large city. **Calendar:** Quarter, extensive summer session. Extensive evening/early morning classes. **Microcomputers:** 107 located in classrooms, computer centers. **Special facilities:** Art gallery. **Additional facts:** Faculty members are working professionals.

DEGREES OFFERED. 419 associate degrees awarded in 1992. 14% in architecture and environmental design, 8% business/office and marketing/distribution, 78% visual and performing arts.

UNDERGRADUATE MAJORS. Apparel and accessories marketing, commercial art, fashion design, fashion merchandising, fiber/textiles/weaving, illustration design, industrial design, interior design, music business management, photography, tourism, transportation and travel marketing.

ACADEMIC PROGRAMS. Accelerated program, internships. **Remedial services:** Reduced course load, special counselor, tutoring.

ACADEMIC REQUIREMENTS. Freshmen must earn minimum GPA of 2.0 to continue in good standing. 65% of freshmen return for sophomore year. Students must declare major on application. **Graduation requirements:** 90 hours for associate (67 in major). Most students required to take courses in arts/fine arts, computer science, English, foreign languages, history, humanities, mathematics.

FRESHMAN ADMISSIONS. Selection criteria: Open admissions.

1992 FRESHMAN CLASS PROFILE. 300 men and women enrolled. 23% had high school GPA of 3.0 or higher, 55% between 2.0 and 2.99. **Characteristics:** 24% from in state, 90% commute, 12% have minority backgrounds, 10% are foreign students. Average age is 20.

FALL-TERM APPLICATIONS. $50 fee. No closing date; applicants notified on a rolling basis. Interview required. Portfolio required for advanced standing applicants. Deferred and early admission available.

STUDENT LIFE. Housing: Dormitories (coed); apartment housing available. **Activities:** Student government, student newspaper, television, yearbook.

STUDENT SERVICES. Career counseling, employment service for undergraduates, freshman orientation, personal counseling, placement service for graduates, veterans counselor, services/facilities for handicapped.

ANNUAL EXPENSES. Tuition and fees (projected): $8,215. **Room and board:** $4,686. **Books and supplies:** $937. **Other expenses:** $1,305.

FINANCIAL AID. 86% of freshmen, 86% of continuing students receive some form of aid. All grants, 59% of loans, all jobs based on need. **Aid applications:** No closing date; applicants notified on a rolling basis; must reply within 4 weeks. **Additional information:** Credit extension available.

ADDRESS/TELEPHONE. Doug Worsley, Director of Admissions, Art Institute of Seattle, 2323 Elliott Avenue, Seattle, WA 98121. (206) 448-6600. (800) 275-2471. Fax: (206) 448-2501.

Bastyr College
Seattle, Washington CB code: 0181

2-year upper-division private health science college, coed. Founded in 1978. **Accreditation:** Regional. **Undergraduate enrollment:** 49 men and women. **Graduate enrollment:** 234 men and women. **Faculty:** 100 total (16 full time), 67 with doctorates or other terminal degrees. **Location:** Urban campus in very large city. **Calendar:** Quarter, limited summer session. Extensive evening/early morning classes. **Microcomputers:** 3 located in libraries.

DEGREES OFFERED. BS, MA, MS. 6 bachelor's degrees awarded in 1992. 67% in health sciences, 33% life sciences. Graduate degrees offered in 3 major fields of study.

UNDERGRADUATE MAJORS. Acupuncture, nutritional sciences, organizational behavior.

ACADEMIC PROGRAMS. Double major, combined degree in oriental medicine and acupuncture.

ACADEMIC REQUIREMENTS. Students must declare major on application. **Graduation requirements:** 180 hours for bachelor's (45 in major). Most students required to take courses in English, humanities, mathematics, biological/physical sciences, social sciences. **Additional information:** Post-doctoral certificates in midwifery and professional doctoral degree in naturopathic medicine available.

STUDENT LIFE. Activities: Student government, student newspaper, Spiritual Development Group, Public Speaking Club, Outdoors Club, Power of Learning, Product Review Club, African-American Support Group, Vegetarian Task Force, Environment Sensitivities Group.

STUDENT SERVICES. Health services, personal counseling.

ANNUAL EXPENSES. Tuition and fees (projected): $6,000. **Books and supplies:** $750. **Other expenses:** $690.

FINANCIAL AID. 76% of continuing students receive some form of aid. 78% of grants, 79% of loans, all jobs based on need. Academic, state/district residency, leadership scholarships available. **Aid applications:** No closing date; priority given to applications received by April 15; applicants notified on a rolling basis beginning on or about June 1; must reply within 2 weeks.

ADDRESS/TELEPHONE. Ron Hobbs, Director of Admissions, Bastyr College, 144 Northeast 54th Street, Seattle, WA 98105. (206) 523-9585. Fax: (206) 527-4763.

Bellevue Community College
Bellevue, Washington CB code: 4029

2-year public community college, coed. Founded in 1965. **Accreditation:** Regional. **Undergraduate enrollment:** 2,344 men, 2,756 women full time; 1,577 men, 3,818 women part time. **Faculty:** 617 total (117 full time), 18 with doctorates or other terminal degrees. **Location:** Suburban campus in small city; 12 miles from Seattle. **Calendar:** Quarter, limited summer session. Extensive evening/early morning classes. **Microcomputers:** 50 located in computer centers. **Special facilities:** Planetarium.

DEGREES OFFERED. AA, AS, AAS. 1,040 associate degrees awarded in 1992.

UNDERGRADUATE MAJORS. Accounting, business and management, data processing, early childhood education, engineering and engineering-related technologies, fashion merchandising, fire control and safety technology, graphic arts technology, interior design, law enforcement and corrections technologies, liberal/general studies, marketing and distribution, marketing management, medical illustrating, nursing, radiograph medical technology, real estate, recreation and community services technologies, secretarial and related programs, ultrasound technology.

ACADEMIC PROGRAMS. 2-year transfer program, dual enrollment of high school students, cross-registration. **Remedial services:** Learning center, remedial instruction, special counselor, tutoring. **Placement/credit:** CLEP Subject, institutional tests; 15 credit hours maximum for associate degree.

ACADEMIC REQUIREMENTS. No policy requiring minimum GPA; records of students having academic difficulty are reviewed individually. 70% of freshmen return for sophomore year. Students must declare major by end of first year. **Graduation requirements:** 90 hours for associate. Most students required to take courses in English, humanities, mathematics, biological/physical sciences, social sciences.

FRESHMAN ADMISSIONS. Selection criteria: Open admissions. Selective admission to allied health programs. Allied health programs have special requirements.

1992 FRESHMAN CLASS PROFILE. 1,500 men and women enrolled. **Characteristics:** 96% from in state, 100% commute, 10% have minority backgrounds, 1% are foreign students. Average age is 27.

FALL-TERM APPLICATIONS. No fee. No closing date; applicants notified on a rolling basis. Interview required for radiologic technology, diagnostic ultrasound, radiation therapy applicants. Portfolio required for biomedical photography applicants. Early admission available.

STUDENT LIFE. Activities: Student government, magazine, radio, student newspaper, television, choral groups, dance, drama, jazz band, music ensembles, musical theater.

ATHLETICS. NAIA, NJCAA. **Intercollegiate:** Baseball M, basketball, cross-country, golf M, soccer M, tennis, track and field, volleyball W. **Intramural:** Badminton, basketball, racquetball, soccer W, softball W, table tennis, tennis, volleyball.

STUDENT SERVICES. Aptitude testing, career counseling, employment service for undergraduates, health services, on-campus day care, personal counseling, placement service for graduates, veterans counselor, women's center, services/facilities for handicapped.

ANNUAL EXPENSES. Tuition and fees: $1,170, $3,300 additional for out-of-state students. **Books and supplies:** $700. **Other expenses:** $700.

FINANCIAL AID. 26% of freshmen, 14% of continuing students receive some form of aid. All grants, 85% of loans, 84% of jobs based on need. 944 enrolled freshmen were judged to have need, all were offered aid. Academic, athletic, state/district residency, minority scholarships available. **Aid applications:** No closing date; priority given to applications received by April 1; applicants notified on a rolling basis beginning on or about August 1; must reply within 2 weeks.

ADDRESS/TELEPHONE. Tika Esler, Associate Dean of Enrollment Services, Bellevue Community College, 3000 Landerholm Circle Southeast, Bellevue, WA 98007-6484. (206) 641-2222. Fax: (206) 641-2230.

Big Bend Community College
Moses Lake, Washington — CB code: 4024

2-year public community college, coed. Founded in 1962. **Accreditation:** Regional. **Undergraduate enrollment:** 518 men, 420 women full time; 330 men, 599 women part time. **Faculty:** 147 total (48 full time), 2 with doctorates or other terminal degrees. **Location:** Rural campus in large town; 107 miles from Spokane, 170 miles from Seattle. **Calendar:** Quarter, limited summer session. Extensive evening/early morning classes. **Microcomputers:** 30 located in computer centers.

DEGREES OFFERED. AA, AS, AAS. 246 associate degrees awarded in 1992. 5% in business/office and marketing/distribution, 79% multi/interdisciplinary studies, 10% trade and industry.

UNDERGRADUATE MAJORS. Accounting, aircraft mechanics, airline piloting and navigation, automotive mechanics, business administration and management, business and management, business and office, business data processing and related programs, business data programming, civil technology, computer and information sciences, computer programming, data processing, drafting and design technology, engineering, legal secretary, liberal/general studies, marketing and distribution, medical secretary, microcomputer software, office supervision and management, practical nursing, secretarial and related programs, teacher aide, word processing.

ACADEMIC PROGRAMS. 2-year transfer program, dual enrollment of high school students. **Remedial services:** Learning center, reduced course load, remedial instruction. **Placement/credit:** AP, CLEP General and Subject, institutional tests; 45 credit hours maximum for associate degree.

ACADEMIC REQUIREMENTS. Freshmen must earn minimum GPA of 1.75 to continue in good standing. **Graduation requirements:** 90 hours for associate. Most students required to take courses in English, humanities, mathematics, biological/physical sciences, social sciences.

FRESHMAN ADMISSIONS. Selection criteria: Open admissions. Selective admission criteria for aviation and nursing programs.

1992 FRESHMAN CLASS PROFILE. 443 men, 356 women enrolled. **Characteristics:** 81% from in state, 81% commute, 10% have minority backgrounds, 3% are foreign students. Average age is 28.

FALL-TERM APPLICATIONS. $10 fee. No closing date; applicants notified on a rolling basis; must reply by registration. Deferred and early admission available.

STUDENT LIFE. Housing: Dormitories (coed). **Activities:** Student government, student newspaper, choral groups.

ATHLETICS. NJCAA. **Intercollegiate:** Baseball M, basketball, volleyball W, wrestling M. **Intramural:** Basketball, softball, volleyball.

STUDENT SERVICES. Career counseling, freshman orientation, personal counseling, veterans counselor, services/facilities for handicapped.

ANNUAL EXPENSES. Tuition and fees: $1,125, $3,300 additional for out-of-state students. **Room and board:** $3,300. **Books and supplies:** $550. **Other expenses:** $1,200.

FINANCIAL AID. 50% of freshmen, 50% of continuing students receive some form of aid. 92% of grants, 90% of loans, 76% of jobs based on need. Academic, music/drama, athletic, alumni affiliation scholarships available. **Aid applications:** No closing date; priority given to applications received by July 1; applicants notified on a rolling basis beginning on or about August 1; must reply within 2 weeks.

ADDRESS/TELEPHONE. Candy Lacher, Director of Admissions and Registrar, Big Bend Community College, 7662 Chanute Street, Moses Lake, WA 98837-3299. (509) 762-6226. Fax: (509) 762-6329.

Central Washington University
Ellensburg, Washington — CB code: 4044

Admissions: 72% of applicants accepted
Based on:
- ••• School record
- •• Test scores
- • Activities, essay, interview, recommendations, special talents

Completion: 36% graduate, 3% of these enter graduate study

4-year public university, coed. Founded in 1890. **Accreditation:** Regional. **Undergraduate enrollment:** 3,117 men, 3,008 women full time; 495 men, 547 women part time. **Graduate enrollment:** 85 men, 85 women full time; 35 men, 83 women part time. **Faculty:** 470 total (345 full time). **Location:** Rural campus in large town; 105 miles from Seattle. **Calendar:** Quarter, limited summer session. Extensive evening/early morning classes. **Microcomputers:** 325 located in dormitories, libraries, classrooms, computer centers.

DEGREES OFFERED. BA, BS, BFA, MA, MS. 1,669 bachelor's degrees awarded in 1992. 33% in business and management, 24% education, 6% parks/recreation, protective services, public affairs, 8% social sciences. Graduate degrees offered in 36 major fields of study.

UNDERGRADUATE MAJORS. Accounting, actuarial sciences, airline piloting and navigation, anthropology, art education, bilingual/bicultural education, biology, business administration and management, business and management, business and office, business economics, business education, carpentry, chemistry, clinical laboratory science, communications, community health work, community psychology, computer and information sciences, criminal justice studies, developmental psychology, dramatic arts, early childhood education, earth sciences, economics, education, electronic technology, elementary education, emergency medical technologies, English, English education, experimental psychology, family/consumer resource management, fashion design, fashion merchandising, finance, fine arts, food science and nutrition, foreign languages education, French, geography, geology, German, gerontology, graphic design, health education, history, home economics, home economics education, human resources development, individual and family development, industrial and organizational psychology, industrial arts education, industrial technology, information sciences and systems, journalism, junior high education, law enforcement and corrections, liberal/general studies, management information systems, management science, manufacturing technology, marketing and distribution, marketing and distributive education, marketing management, mathematics, mathematics education, mechanical design technology, medical laboratory technologies, microcomputer software, military science (Army), music, music education, music performance, music theory and composition, occupational safety and health technology, office supervision and management, operations research, organizational behavior, parks and recreation management, philosophy, physical education, physics, physiology, human and animal, political science and government, psychology, public health laboratory science, public relations, radio/television broadcasting, recreation and community services technologies, religion, science education, secondary education, social science education, social sciences, sociology, Spanish, special education, speech, speech/communication/theater education, systems analysis, textiles and clothing, trade and industrial education, trade and industrial supervision and management.

ACADEMIC PROGRAMS. Accelerated program, cooperative education, double major, dual enrollment of high school students, honors program, independent study, internships, student-designed major, study abroad, teacher preparation. **Remedial services:** Learning center, reduced course load, remedial instruction, special counselor, tutoring. **ROTC:** Air Force, Army. **Placement/credit:** AP, IB, institutional tests.

ACADEMIC REQUIREMENTS. Freshmen must earn minimum GPA of 2.0 to continue in good standing. 79% of freshmen return for sophomore year. Students must declare major by end of second year. **Graduation requirements:** 180 hours for bachelor's (60 in major). Most students required to take courses in English, foreign languages, humanities, biological/physical sciences, social sciences. **Additional information:** Extended degree programs at locations statewide.

FRESHMAN ADMISSIONS. Selection criteria: Admission based on weighted combination of standardized test scores and GPA. **High school preparation:** 15 units required. Required units include English 4, foreign language 2, mathematics 3, social science 3 and science 2. One performing or fine arts or any main subject area. **Test requirements:** SAT or ACT; score report by September 15.

1992 FRESHMAN CLASS PROFILE. 2,785 men and women applied, 2,011 accepted; 525 men enrolled, 458 women enrolled. 61% had high school GPA of 3.0 or higher, 39% between 2.0 and 2.99. **Academic background:** Mid 50% of enrolled freshmen had SAT-V between 370-470, SAT-M between 400-530. 94% submitted SAT scores. **Characteristics:** 96% from in state, 98% live in college housing, 10% have minority backgrounds, 1% are foreign students. Average age is 19.

FALL-TERM APPLICATIONS. $35 fee, may be waived for applicants with need. No closing date; priority given to applications received by March 1; applicants notified on a rolling basis beginning on or about December 1; must reply by May 1 or within 2 weeks if notified thereafter. Audition required for some music applicants. Interview recommended for marginal applicants. CRDA. Applications received after March accepted if space available.

STUDENT LIFE. Housing: Dormitories (men, women, coed); apartment housing available. **Activities:** Student government, radio, student newspaper, television, yearbook, student handbook and directory, choral groups, concert band, dance, drama, jazz band, marching band, music ensembles, musical theater, opera, pep band, symphony orchestra, religious, political, ethnic, minority student organizations, rodeo activities.

ATHLETICS. NAIA. **Intercollegiate:** Baseball M, basketball, cross-country, diving, football M, golf M, soccer, softball W, swimming, tennis, track and field, volleyball W, wrestling M. **Intramural:** Basketball, golf, soccer, softball, volleyball.

STUDENT SERVICES. Aptitude testing, career counseling, employment service for undergraduates, freshman orientation, health services, on-campus day care, personal counseling, placement service for graduates, special adviser for adult students, veterans counselor, Visitation program and Preview Week, services/facilities for handicapped.

ANNUAL EXPENSES. Tuition and fees: $1,971, $4,977 additional for out-of-state students. **Room and board:** $3,673. **Books and supplies:** $650. **Other expenses:** $1,368.

FINANCIAL AID. 66% of freshmen, 56% of continuing students receive some form of aid. 79% of grants, 83% of loans, 27% of jobs based on need. 409 enrolled freshmen were judged to have need, 368 were offered aid. Academic, music/drama, state/district residency, leadership, minority scholarships available. **Aid applications:** No closing date; priority given to applications received by March 15; applicants notified on a rolling basis beginning on or about May 31; must reply within 2 weeks.

ADDRESS/TELEPHONE. Dr. James G. Pappas, Dean of Admissions and Records, Central Washington University, Mitchell Hall, Ellensburg, WA 98926. (509) 963-1211.

Centralia College
Centralia, Washington — CB code: 4045

2-year public community college, coed. Founded in 1925. **Accreditation:** Regional. **Undergraduate enrollment:** 741 men, 890 women full time; 479 men, 894 women part time. **Faculty:** 166 total (63 full time), 8 with doctorates or other terminal degrees. **Location:** Suburban campus in large town; 90 miles from Seattle, 90 miles from Portland. **Calendar:** Quarter, limited summer session. Extensive evening/early morning classes. **Microcomputers:** Located in computer centers.

DEGREES OFFERED. AA, AS. 193 associate degrees awarded in 1992.

UNDERGRADUATE MAJORS. Accounting, agricultural sciences, biological and physical sciences, biology, botany, business administration and management, business and management, business and office, business data processing and related programs, business data programming, chemistry, civil technology, commercial art, communications, diesel engine mechanics, education, electrical and electronics equipment repair, electronic technology, engineering, engineering and engineering-related technologies, English, fine arts, foreign languages (multiple emphasis), forestry and related sciences, graphic arts technology, health sciences, humanities and social sciences, legal secretary, liberal/general studies, mathematics, medical secretary, music, nursing, office supervision and management, physical sciences, physics, practical nursing, predentistry, prelaw, premedicine, prepharmacy, preveterinary, psychology, radio/television broadcasting, secretarial and related programs, social sciences, social work, visual and performing arts, welding technology, wildlife management, word processing, zoology.

ACADEMIC PROGRAMS. 2-year transfer program, cooperative education, double major, honors program, independent study, internships, cross-registration. **Remedial services:** Learning center, reduced course load, remedial instruction, tutoring. **Placement/credit:** AP, CLEP General and Subject, institutional tests; 45 credit hours maximum for associate degree.

ACADEMIC REQUIREMENTS. Freshmen must earn minimum GPA of 2.0 to continue in good standing. **Graduation requirements:** 93 hours for associate. Most students required to take courses in English, humanities, mathematics, biological/physical sciences, social sciences.

FRESHMAN ADMISSIONS. Selection criteria: Open admissions. Selective admission to nursing program. **Test requirements:** SAT or ACT for placement; score report by September 1. ASSET may be submitted in place of SAT or ACT.

1992 FRESHMAN CLASS PROFILE. 1,300 men and women enrolled. **Characteristics:** 95% from in state, 100% commute, 2% have minority backgrounds, 1% are foreign students. Average age is 26.

FALL-TERM APPLICATIONS. No fee. No closing date; priority given to applications received by June 1; applicants notified on a rolling basis beginning on or about January 1. Deferred and early admission available.

STUDENT LIFE. Activities: Student government, radio, student newspaper, television, choral groups, concert band, drama, jazz band, music ensembles, single parents club, honors club, Parents With Children.

ATHLETICS. NJCAA. **Intercollegiate:** Baseball M, basketball, volleyball W.

STUDENT SERVICES. Aptitude testing, career counseling, employment service for undergraduates, freshman orientation, on-campus day care, personal counseling, placement service for graduates, veterans counselor, services/facilities for handicapped.

ANNUAL EXPENSES. Tuition and fees: $1,125, $3,300 additional for out-of-state students. **Books and supplies:** $600. **Other expenses:** $600.

FINANCIAL AID. 50% of freshmen, 50% of continuing students receive some form of aid. 95% of grants, 46% of loans, 71% of jobs based on need. 350 enrolled freshmen were judged to have need, all were offered aid. Academic, music/drama, athletic, state/district residency, leadership scholarships available. **Aid applications:** No closing date; priority given to applications received by April 15; applicants notified on a rolling basis beginning on or about June 15; must reply within 2 weeks. **Additional information:** College emergency loan/short-term loan program with up to $300 available.

ADDRESS/TELEPHONE. Neena Stoskopf, Director of Admissions and Records, Centralia College, 600 West Locust, Centralia, WA 98531. (206) 736-9391 ext.221. Fax: (206) 753-3404.

City University
Bellevue, Washington — CB code: 4042

2-year upper-division private university, coed. Founded in 1973. **Accreditation:** Regional. **Undergraduate enrollment:** 101 men, 104 women full time; 577 men, 660 women part time. **Graduate enrollment:** 208 men, 364 women full time; 812 men, 694 women part time. **Faculty:** 811 total (29 full time). **Location:** Urban campus in very large city; 12 miles from Seattle. **Calendar:** Quarter, extensive summer session. Saturday and extensive evening/early morning classes. **Microcomputers:** Located in computer centers. **Additional facts:** Associate degrees awarded to military personnel for military experience and 25 credits successfully completed through City University.

DEGREES OFFERED. BS, MA, MBA, MEd. 419 bachelor's degrees awarded. Graduate degrees offered in 12 major fields of study.

UNDERGRADUATE MAJORS. Associate: Legal assistant/paralegal, liberal/general studies. **Bachelor's:** Accounting, business administration and management, business and management, computer and information sciences, health care administration, legal administration, nursing.

ACADEMIC PROGRAMS. Accelerated program, double major, external degree, independent study, internships, teacher preparation, weekend college; combined bachelor's/graduate program in business administration. **Placement/credit:** CLEP General and Subject; 90 credit hours maximum for bachelor's degree.

ACADEMIC REQUIREMENTS. Students must declare major on application. **Graduation requirements:** 180 hours for bachelor's (30 in major). Most students required to take courses in English, humanities, mathematics, biological/physical sciences, social sciences. **Additional information:** Limited number of associate degree programs offered.

STUDENT LIFE. Activities: Student newspaper.

STUDENT SERVICES. Veterans counselor, services/facilities for handicapped.

ANNUAL EXPENSES. Tuition and fees (1992-93): $6,575. **Books and supplies:** $800. **Other expenses:** $1,200.

FINANCIAL AID. 22% of continuing students receive some form of aid. All grants, all jobs based on need. **Aid applications:** No closing date.

ADDRESS/TELEPHONE. Office of Admissions, City University, 14510 NE 20th Street, Suite D, Bellevue, WA 98007-3713. (206) 624-1688. (800) 422-4898. Fax: (206) 641-2017.

Clark College
Vancouver, Washington — CB code: 4055

2-year public community college, coed. Founded in 1933. **Accreditation:** Regional. **Undergraduate enrollment:** 1,700 men, 2,230 women full time; 1,910 men, 3,120 women part time. **Faculty:** 371 total (120 full time), 14 with doctorates or other terminal degrees. **Location:** Urban campus in small city; 8 miles from Portland, Oregon. **Calendar:** Quarter, limited summer session. Extensive evening/early morning classes. **Microcomputers:** 250 located in libraries, classrooms, computer centers. **Special facilities:** Art gallery.

DEGREES OFFERED. AA, AS, AAS. 812 associate degrees awarded in 1992.

UNDERGRADUATE MAJORS. Accounting, automotive mechanics, automotive technology, business administration and management, business and management, business and office, business computer/console/peripheral equipment operation, business data entry equipment operation, business data processing and related programs, business data programming, chemical manufacturing technology, chemistry, computer and information sciences, computer programming, criminal justice studies, dental hygiene, diesel engine mechanics, drafting, early childhood education, electromechanical technology, electronic technology, engineering, engineering and engineering-related technologies, fashion merchandising, food management, food production/management/services, graphic and printing production, graphic arts technology, horticulture, industrial technology, law enforcement and corrections technologies, legal assistant/paralegal, legal secretary, liberal/general studies, management information systems, marketing and distribution, mechanical design technology, medical records administration, medical records technology, medical secretary, nursing, plastic technology, practical nursing, precision metal work, radio/television broadcasting, real estate, secretarial and related programs, small business management and ownership, technical and business writing, trade and industrial supervision and management, welding technology, word processing.

ACADEMIC PROGRAMS. 2-year transfer program, cooperative education, dual enrollment of high school students, honors program, independent study, internships, study abroad, telecourses, cross-registration. **Remedial services:** Learning center, preadmission summer program, remedial instruction, special counselor, tutoring. **Placement/credit:** AP, CLEP General and Subject, institutional tests.

ACADEMIC REQUIREMENTS. Freshmen must earn minimum GPA of 2.0 to continue in good standing. 75% of freshmen return for sophomore year. Students must declare major on application. **Graduation requirements:** 90 hours for associate (60 in major). Most students required to take courses in English, humanities, mathematics, biological/physical sciences, social sciences.

FRESHMAN ADMISSIONS. Selection criteria: Open admissions. Selective admissions to health occupations, mechanical/industrial, and data processing/computer science programs. **Test requirements:** SAT or ACT for placement and counseling only; score report by September 15. ACT/ASSET required.

1992 FRESHMAN CLASS PROFILE. 3,500 men and women enrolled. 15% had high school GPA of 3.0 or higher, 65% between 2.0 and 2.99. **Characteristics:** 90% from in state, 100% commute, 3% have minority backgrounds, 3% are foreign students. Average age is 30.

FALL-TERM APPLICATIONS. No fee. No closing date; applicants notified on a rolling basis beginning on or about February 1. Interview required for dental hygiene, nursing applicants. Deferred admission available.

STUDENT LIFE. Activities: Student government, magazine, student newspaper, choral groups, concert band, dance, drama, jazz band, music ensembles, musical theater, pep band, symphony orchestra, Phi Theta Kappa.

ATHLETICS. Intercollegiate: Baseball M, basketball, cross-country M, track and field, volleyball W. **Intramural:** Baseball M, fencing, softball, table tennis M.

STUDENT SERVICES. Career counseling, employment service for undergraduates, freshman orientation, health services, on-campus day care, personal counseling, placement service for graduates, special adviser for adult students, veterans counselor, services/facilities for handicapped.

ANNUAL EXPENSES. Tuition and fees: $1,178, $3,300 additional for out-of-state students. **Books and supplies:** $500. **Other expenses:** $570.

FINANCIAL AID. 25% of freshmen, 25% of continuing students receive some form of aid. 93% of grants, 87% of loans, all jobs based on need. Academic, music/drama, athletic, leadership scholarships available. **Aid applications:** No closing date; priority given to applications received by May 1; applicants notified on a rolling basis beginning on or about June 15; must reply within 2 weeks.

ADDRESS/TELEPHONE. Linda Calvert, Coordinator of Admissions, Clark College, 1800 East McLoughlin Boulevard, Vancouver, WA 98663. (206) 699-0392.

Cogswell College North
Kirkland, Washington — CB code: 0584

4-year private engineering college, coed. Founded in 1979. **Accreditation:** Regional. **Undergraduate enrollment:** 7 men, 1 woman full time; 187 men, 19 women part time. **Faculty:** 50 total (10 full time), 19 with doctorates or other terminal degrees. **Location:** Suburban campus in very large city; 5 miles from Seattle. **Calendar:** Quarter. Extensive evening/early morning classes. **Microcomputers:** 30 located in libraries, computer centers. **Additional facts:** Evening and weekend college. 90% of students work full-time in engineering-related jobs.

DEGREES OFFERED. AS, BS. 5 associate degrees awarded in 1992. 100% in engineering technologies. 27 bachelor's degrees awarded. 30% in engineering, 70% engineering technologies.

UNDERGRADUATE MAJORS. Associate: Computer technology, electronic technology, mechanical design technology. **Bachelor's:** Computer engineering, computer technology, electrical/electronics/communications engineering, electronic technology, manufacturing technology, mechanical design technology.

ACADEMIC PROGRAMS. Double major. **Remedial services:** Tutoring. **Placement/credit:** AP, CLEP General and Subject, institutional tests; 24 credit hours maximum for bachelor's degree.

ACADEMIC REQUIREMENTS. Freshmen must earn minimum GPA of 2.0 to continue in good standing. 85% of freshmen return for sophomore year. Students must declare major on enrollment. **Graduation requirements:** 98 hours for associate (53 in major), 194 hours for bachelor's (104 in major). Most students required to take courses in computer science, English, humanities, mathematics, biological/physical sciences, social sciences. **Postgraduate studies:** 100% from 2-year programs enter 4-year programs.

FRESHMAN ADMISSIONS. Selection criteria: School achievement record most important. **High school preparation:** 7 units required. Required units include English 3, mathematics 2, social science 1 and science 1. **Test requirements:** Institutional tests in mathematics and English may be required for placement.

1992 FRESHMAN CLASS PROFILE. 41 men, 5 women enrolled. **Characteristics:** 100% from in state, 100% commute, 12% have minority backgrounds, 1% are foreign students. Average age is 31.

FALL-TERM APPLICATIONS. $50 fee. No closing date; applicants notified on a rolling basis.

STUDENT LIFE. Activities: Tau Alpha Pi, Institute of Electrical and Electronic Engineers (honorary societies).

STUDENT SERVICES. Career counseling, employment service for undergraduates, placement service for graduates, special adviser for adult students, veterans counselor, services/facilities for handicapped.

ANNUAL EXPENSES. Tuition and fees (1992-93): $7,200. **Books and supplies:** $550.

FINANCIAL AID. 8% of continuing students receive some form of aid. All grants, 50% of loans based on need. **Aid applications:** Closing date August 15; applicants notified on a rolling basis. **Additional information:** Most students qualify for tuition reimbursement from industry employers.

ADDRESS/TELEPHONE. Jacqueline B. Juras, Director of Admissions, Cogswell College North, 10626 Northeast 37th Circle, Kirkland, WA 98033. (206) 822-3137.

Columbia Basin College
Pasco, Washington — CB code: 4077

2-year public community college, coed. Founded in 1955. **Accreditation:** Regional. **Undergraduate enrollment:** 1,323 men, 1,503 women full time; 1,585 men, 2,025 women part time. **Faculty:** 334 total (96 full time), 8 with doctorates or other terminal degrees. **Location:** Suburban campus in large town; 130 miles from Spokane, 200 miles from Seattle. **Calendar:** Quarter, limited summer session. Extensive evening/early morning classes. **Microcomputers:** 210 located in libraries, classrooms, computer centers. **Special facilities:** Fred Esvelt Art Gallery. **Additional facts:** Branch campus in Richland serves Benton County residents.

DEGREES OFFERED. AA, AAS. 669 associate degrees awarded in 1992. 5% in agriculture, 16% business/office and marketing/distribution, 21% computer sciences, 10% engineering technologies, 15% health sciences, 5% allied health, 15% multi/interdisciplinary studies, 9% trade and industry.

UNDERGRADUATE MAJORS. Agribusiness, agricultural business and management, agricultural production, automotive mechanics, automotive technology, biological and physical sciences, business and office, business data programming, carpentry, child development/care/guidance, computer and information sciences, contract management and procurement/purchasing, drafting, electronic technology, engineering and engineering-related technologies, engineering and other disciplines, graphic arts technology, instrumentation technology, law enforcement and corrections technologies, liberal/general studies, machine tool operation/machine shop, marketing and distribution, nuclear technologies, nursing, practical nursing, real estate, visual and performing arts.

ACADEMIC PROGRAMS. 2-year transfer program, dual enrollment of high school students, internships, study abroad, telecourses, cross-registration. **Remedial services:** Learning center, reduced course load, remedial instruction, special counselor, tutoring. **Placement/credit:** AP, CLEP General and Subject, institutional tests; 30 credit hours maximum for associate degree.

ACADEMIC REQUIREMENTS. Freshmen must earn minimum GPA of 2.0 to continue in good standing. 75% of freshmen return for sophomore year. Students must declare major on enrollment. **Graduation requirements:** 93 hours for associate. Most students required to take courses in computer science, English, humanities, mathematics, biological/physical sciences, social sciences.

FRESHMAN ADMISSIONS. Selection criteria: Open admissions. **High school preparation:** 11 units recommended. Recommended units include biological science 1, English 3, foreign language 1, mathematics 2, physical science 1 and social science 3. **Test requirements:** Applicants who are not graduates of regional accredited high school or without GED must submit Washington Pre-College Test, SAT, or ACT scores.

1992 FRESHMAN CLASS PROFILE. 470 men, 535 women enrolled. **Characteristics:** 99% from in state, 100% commute, 10% have minority backgrounds.

FALL-TERM APPLICATIONS. No fee. No closing date; applicants notified on a rolling basis; must reply by registration. Deferred admission available.

STUDENT LIFE. Activities: Student government, student newspaper, choral groups, concert band, drama, jazz band, music ensembles, musical theater, pep band.

ATHLETICS. NJCAA. **Intercollegiate:** Baseball M, basketball, golf, tennis, volleyball W. **Intramural:** Basketball, bowling, softball, volleyball.

STUDENT SERVICES. Aptitude testing, career counseling, employment service for undergraduates, freshman orientation, personal counsel-

ing, placement service for graduates, veterans counselor, services/facilities for handicapped.

ANNUAL EXPENSES. Tuition and fees: $1,164, $3,300 additional for out-of-state students. **Books and supplies:** $654. **Other expenses:** $690.

FINANCIAL AID. 41% of freshmen, 9% of continuing students receive some form of aid. 92% of grants, 96% of loans, 17% of jobs based on need. 603 enrolled freshmen were judged to have need, 572 were offered aid. Academic, music/drama, art, athletic, leadership scholarships available. **Aid applications:** No closing date; priority given to applications received by April 1; applicants notified on a rolling basis beginning on or about June 15; must reply within 2 weeks.

ADDRESS/TELEPHONE. Dr. John Startzel, Associate Dean of Admissions/Registration, Columbia Basin College, 2600 North 20th Avenue, Pasco, WA 99301. (509) 547-0511. Fax: (509) 546-0401.

Cornish College of the Arts
Seattle, Washington — CB code: 0058

Admissions: 72% of applicants accepted
Based on: ••• Interview, special talents
•• Essay, school record
• Activities, recommendations, test scores
Completion: 80% of freshmen end year in good standing
25% graduate, 5% of these enter graduate study

4-year private college of visual and performing arts, coed. Founded in 1914. **Accreditation:** Regional. **Undergraduate enrollment:** 179 men, 243 women full time; 33 men, 95 women part time. **Faculty:** 128 total (27 full time), 8 with doctorates or other terminal degrees. **Location:** Urban campus in very large city; located in downtown Seattle. **Calendar:** Semester, limited summer session. Saturday classes. **Microcomputers:** 8 located in classrooms. **Special facilities:** 2 art galleries, 3 theaters. **Additional facts:** One of only 4 colleges in the United States preparing students for professional careers and awarding BFA's in visual and performing arts exclusively.

DEGREES OFFERED. BFA. 90 bachelor's degrees awarded in 1992. 100% in visual and performing arts.

UNDERGRADUATE MAJORS. Dance, dramatic arts, drawing, fine arts, graphic design, illustration design, interior design, jazz, music, music performance, music theory and composition, painting, performance production, photography, printmaking, sculpture, studio art, theater design.

ACADEMIC PROGRAMS. Dual enrollment of high school students, independent study, internships. **Remedial services:** Remedial instruction, special counselor, tutoring, pre-major first year/music. **Placement/credit:** AP, CLEP General and Subject, institutional tests; 8 credit hours maximum for bachelor's degree.

ACADEMIC REQUIREMENTS. Freshmen must earn minimum GPA of 2.0 to continue in good standing. 75% of freshmen return for sophomore year. Students must declare major on application. **Graduation requirements:** 130 hours for bachelor's (96 in major). Most students required to take courses in arts/fine arts, English, history, humanities, biological/physical sciences, social sciences. **Postgraduate studies:** 5% enter other graduate study.

FRESHMAN ADMISSIONS. Selection criteria: Artistic and/or dramatic arts ability and achievement, 2.0 high school GPA important. Applicants with lower averages but exceptional talent occassionally granted provisional acceptance for 2 semesters. **Test requirements:** SAT or ACT (SAT preferred); score report by August 15.

1992 FRESHMAN CLASS PROFILE. 473 men and women applied, 341 accepted; 82 men enrolled, 136 women enrolled. **Characteristics:** 79% from in state, 100% commute, 11% have minority backgrounds, 2% are foreign students. Average age is 24.

FALL-TERM APPLICATIONS. $30 fee, may be waived for applicants with need. Closing date August 15; priority given to applications received by March 31; applicants notified on a rolling basis beginning on or about January 15; must reply by May 1 or within 2 weeks if notified thereafter. Audition required for music, dance, theater, performance production applicants. Portfolio required for art, design applicants. Essay required. Interview recommended. Special audition and portfolio arrangements for distant applicants. CRDA. Deferred and early admission available. SAT or ACT recommended.

STUDENT LIFE. Housing: Coed facilities at Seattle University available. **Activities:** Student government, student newspaper, choral groups, dance, drama, jazz band, music ensembles, musical theater, opera, visual arts displays.

ATHLETICS. Intramural: Fencing.

STUDENT SERVICES. Career counseling, employment service for undergraduates, freshman orientation, personal counseling, placement service for graduates, services/facilities for handicapped.

ANNUAL EXPENSES. Tuition and fees (1992-93): $8,730. **Books and supplies:** $1,333. **Other expenses:** $600.

FINANCIAL AID. 75% of freshmen, 75% of continuing students receive some form of aid. 69% of grants, all jobs based on need. 86 enrolled freshmen were judged to have need, all were offered aid. Academic, music/drama, art, state/district residency, minority scholarships available. **Aid applications:** No closing date; priority given to applications received by February 28; applicants notified on a rolling basis.

ADDRESS/TELEPHONE. Jane Buckman, Director of Admissions and Financial Aid, Cornish College of the Arts, 710 East Roy Street, Seattle, WA 98102. (206) 323-1400. (800) 726-ARTS. Fax: (206) 323-1574 ext. 406.

Eastern Washington University
Cheney, Washington — CB code: 4301

Admissions: 86% of applicants accepted
Based on: ••• School record, test scores
• Activities, essay, interview, recommendations, special talents
Completion: 14% enter graduate study

4-year public university, coed. Founded in 1882. **Accreditation:** Regional. **Undergraduate enrollment:** 3,001 men, 3,774 women full time; 342 men, 474 women part time. **Graduate enrollment:** 179 men, 263 women full time; 125 men, 205 women part time. **Faculty:** 421 total (346 full time), 273 with doctorates or other terminal degrees. **Location:** Rural campus in small town; 16 miles from Spokane. **Calendar:** Quarter, extensive summer session. Saturday and extensive evening/early morning classes. **Microcomputers:** 300 located in libraries, classrooms, computer centers. **Special facilities:** Planetarium, wildlife refuge, 17,000-acre environmental studies laboratory, on-campus elementary school. **Additional facts:** Extensive course offerings available evenings in downtown Spokane.

DEGREES OFFERED. BA, BS, BFA, MA, MS, MBA, MFA, MEd, MSW. 1,661 bachelor's degrees awarded in 1992. 21% in business and management, 23% teacher education, 7% health sciences, 5% life sciences, 8% multi/interdisciplinary studies, 6% psychology, 10% social sciences. Graduate degrees offered in 55 major fields of study.

UNDERGRADUATE MAJORS. Accounting, anthropology, art education, art history, biochemistry, biological and physical sciences, biology, biophysics, biotechnology, botany, business administration and management, business and management, business economics, business education, business statistics, chemistry, city/community/regional planning, communications, computer and information sciences, construction, creative writing, criminal justice studies, dance, dental hygiene, drafting and design technology, dramatic arts, early childhood education, earth sciences, economics, education, education of the deaf and hearing impaired, education of the mentally handicapped, education of the physically handicapped, electronic technology, elementary education, English, English education, English literature, environmental science, finance, fine arts, foreign languages education, forestry and related sciences, French, geography, geology, German, health care administration, health education, health sciences, history, humanities, humanities and social sciences, industrial arts education, information sciences and systems, international public service, international relations, international studies, jazz, journalism, liberal/general studies, management information systems, management science, manufacturing technology, marketing and distribution, marketing and distributive education, marketing management, mathematics, mathematics education, medical laboratory technologies, microbiology, military science (Army), music, music education, music history and appreciation, music merchandising, music performance, music theory and composition, nursing, office supervision and management, operations research, parks and recreation management, personnel management, philosophy, photographic technology, photography, physical education, physical sciences, physical therapy, physics, political science and government, predentistry, prelaw, premedicine, prepharmacy, preveterinary, psychology, public administration, public relations, radio/television broadcasting, recreation therapy, remedial education, science education, secondary education, social science education, social sciences, social work, sociology, Spanish, special education, speech, speech correction, speech pathology/audiology, speech/communication/theater education, sports medicine, studio art, technical and business writing, technical education, urban design, urban studies, visual and performing arts, zoology.

ACADEMIC PROGRAMS. Cooperative education, double major, dual enrollment of high school students, education specialist degree, external degree, honors program, independent study, internships, student-designed major, study abroad, teacher preparation, telecourses, visiting/exchange student program, cross-registration, nursing consortium with Washington State University, Whitworth College; combined bachelor's/graduate program in business administration. **Remedial services:** Learning center, preadmission summer program, reduced course load, remedial instruction, special counselor, tutoring. **ROTC:** Army. **Placement/credit:** AP, institutional tests.

ACADEMIC REQUIREMENTS. Freshmen must earn minimum GPA of 2.0 to continue in good standing. 79% of freshmen return for sophomore year. Students must declare major by end of second year. **Graduation requirements:** 180 hours for bachelor's (45 in major). Most students required to take courses in arts/fine arts, English, foreign languages, history, humanities, mathematics, biological/physical sciences, social sciences.

FRESHMAN ADMISSIONS. Selection criteria: Admission based on index combining GPA and test scores. Essay and special talents considered for applicants who do not meet these standards. Limited number enrolled below index and core requirements. **High school preparation:** 15 units required; 16 recommended. Required and recommended units include English 4, foreign language 2, mathematics 3-4, social science 3 and science 2-3. Biological science 1 and physical science 1 recommended. Mathematics requirement inludes 1 algebra, and geometry or trigonometry or advanced algebra. Sciences include 1 laboratory science. 1 year fine arts or core elective required. **Test requirements:** SAT or ACT; score report by July 1. SAT or ACT required for academically weak applicants. Washington Pre-College Test may be submitted in place of SAT or ACT if taken before Spring 1989. **Additional information:** Mid-year application deadlines: Winter, Oct. 15; Spring, Feb. 1.

1992 FRESHMAN CLASS PROFILE. 2,149 men and women applied, 1,854 accepted; 302 men enrolled, 501 women enrolled. 61% had high school GPA of 3.0 or higher, 39% between 2.0 and 2.99. **Academic background:** Mid 50% of enrolled freshmen had SAT-V between 350-470, SAT-M between 390-520; ACT composite between 18-23. 84% submitted SAT scores, 24% submitted ACT scores. **Characteristics:** 92% from in state, 60% live in college housing, 11% have minority backgrounds, 5% are foreign students. Average age is 19.

FALL-TERM APPLICATIONS. $35 fee, may be waived for applicants with need. Closing date July 1; priority given to applications received by February 1; applicants notified on a rolling basis beginning on or about December 1; must reply by May 1. Essay recommended for academically weak applicants. Interview required for returning adult applicants, high school students with GPA below Washington admission index. CRDA. Early admission available.

STUDENT LIFE. Housing: Dormitories (coed); apartment, fraternity, sorority housing available. New 75-unit housing complex designed for single parents and family housing. **Activities:** Student government, film, magazine, radio, student newspaper, television, choral groups, concert band, dance, drama, jazz band, marching band, music ensembles, musical theater, opera, pep band, symphony orchestra, fraternities, sororities, Newman Club, Circle K, Native American Student Association, MECHA (Hispanic org.), Black Student Union, Model UN, Young Democrats, Habitat for Humanity. **Additional information:** Freshman year experience program provides extensive orientation and counseling/study skills resources for 1st year students.

ATHLETICS. NCAA. **Intercollegiate:** Basketball, cross-country, football M, golf, tennis, track and field, volleyball W. **Intramural:** Archery, baseball, basketball, bowling, cross-country, fencing, field hockey, football, golf, gymnastics, racquetball, sailing, soccer M, softball, squash, swimming, tennis, track and field, volleyball.

STUDENT SERVICES. Aptitude testing, career counseling, employment service for undergraduates, freshman orientation, health services, on-campus day care, personal counseling, placement service for graduates, special adviser for adult students, veterans counselor, services/facilities for handicapped.

ANNUAL EXPENSES. Tuition and fees: $1,971, $4,977 additional for out-of-state students. **Room and board:** $3,650. **Books and supplies:** $654. **Other expenses:** $1,368.

FINANCIAL AID. 50% of freshmen, 48% of continuing students receive some form of aid. 73% of grants, 94% of loans, 42% of jobs based on need. 449 enrolled freshmen were judged to have need, 419 were offered aid. Academic, music/drama, art, athletic, alumni affiliation scholarships available. **Aid applications:** No closing date; priority given to applications received by February 15; applicants notified on a rolling basis beginning on or about June 1; must reply within 3 weeks.

ADDRESS/TELEPHONE. Steve Neineisel, Director of Enrollment Management, Eastern Washington University, 117 Showalter Hall, MS-148, Cheney, WA 99004-2496. (509) 359-2397. Fax: (509) 359-6927.

Edmonds Community College
Lynnwood, Washington — CB code: 4307

2-year public community college, coed. Founded in 1967. **Accreditation:** Regional. **Undergraduate enrollment:** 1,639 men, 1,890 women full time; 1,795 men, 2,793 women part time. **Faculty:** 313 total (141 full time), 13 with doctorates or other terminal degrees. **Location:** Suburban campus in small city; 15 miles from Seattle. **Calendar:** Quarter, limited summer session. Extensive evening/early morning classes. **Microcomputers:** 200 located in libraries, classrooms, computer centers. **Special facilities:** Center for Business and Employment Development, Applied Technology Training Center, art gallery, golf course. **Additional facts:** Extensive international education program. College operates campus in Kobe Japan, for both Japanese and American students.

DEGREES OFFERED. AAS. 723 associate degrees awarded in 1992. 9% in business and management, 10% business/office and marketing/distribution, 6% engineering technologies, 33% law, 28% multi/interdisciplinary studies.

UNDERGRADUATE MAJORS. Accounting, business administration and management, business and office, business computer/console/peripheral equipment operation, business data processing and related programs, business data programming, child development/care/guidance, computer and information sciences, computer servicing technology, computer technology, construction, counseling/casework, court reporting, electrical and electronics equipment repair, electronic technology, fashion merchandising, fire protection, food management, gerontology, information sciences and systems, international business management, international studies, landscape architecture, legal assistant/paralegal, legal secretary, liberal/general studies, marketing and distribution, microcomputer software, office supervision and management, ornamental horticulture, retail nursery, retailing, secretarial and related programs, small business management and ownership, social work, tourism, trade and industrial supervision and management, word processing.

ACADEMIC PROGRAMS. 2-year transfer program, cooperative education, dual enrollment of high school students, honors program, independent study, internships, study abroad, telecourses, visiting/exchange student program, cross-registration. **Remedial services:** Learning center, remedial instruction, special counselor, tutoring. **Placement/credit:** AP, CLEP Subject, institutional tests.

ACADEMIC REQUIREMENTS. No policy requiring minimum GPA; records of students having academic difficulty are reviewed individually. Students must declare major on enrollment. **Graduation requirements:** 90 hours for associate. Most students required to take courses in computer science, English, humanities, mathematics, biological/physical sciences, social sciences.

FRESHMAN ADMISSIONS. Selection criteria: Open admissions. Selective admissions to international studies program for international students. Prospective students must be 18 years or older, or have earned a high school diploma or GED.

1992 FRESHMAN CLASS PROFILE. 2,546 men and women enrolled. **Characteristics:** 95% from in state, 100% commute, 12% have minority backgrounds, 1% are foreign students.

FALL-TERM APPLICATIONS. $12 fee, may be waived for applicants with need. No closing date; applicants notified on a rolling basis beginning on or about February 1; must reply by registration. Audition required for music performance applicants. Interview recommended for travel tourism, international studies applicants. Deferred and early admission available.

STUDENT LIFE. Housing: Host families available for international students. **Activities:** Student government, student newspaper, alumni newsletter, literary publication, choral groups, dance, drama, jazz band, music ensembles, musical theater, pep band, coffeehouse, vocal jazz ensembles, special interest and academic clubs.

ATHLETICS. Intercollegiate: Baseball M, basketball, golf, soccer M, softball W, volleyball W. **Intramural:** Badminton, basketball, bowling, golf, softball, table tennis, volleyball.

STUDENT SERVICES. Aptitude testing, career counseling, employment service for undergraduates, freshman orientation, on-campus day care, personal counseling, placement service for graduates, veterans counselor, multicultural services, women's programs, services/facilities for handicapped.

ANNUAL EXPENSES. Tuition and fees: $1,155, $3,300 additional for out-of-state students. **Books and supplies:** $654. **Other expenses:** $690.

FINANCIAL AID. 22% of freshmen, 15% of continuing students receive some form of aid. 95% of grants, 81% of loans, 28% of jobs based on need. 600 enrolled freshmen were judged to have need, 400 were offered aid. Academic, music/drama, art, athletic, state/district residency, minority scholarships available. **Aid applications:** No closing date; priority given to applications received by May 1; applicants notified on a rolling basis beginning on or about June 1; must reply within 4 weeks.

ADDRESS/TELEPHONE. Beth Rognlien, Admissions Office Manager, Edmonds Community College, 20000 68th Avenue West, Lynnwood, WA 98036. (206) 640-1372. Fax: (206) 771-3366.

Everett Community College
Everett, Washington — CB code: 4303

2-year public community college, coed. Founded in 1941. **Accreditation:** Regional. **Undergraduate enrollment:** 1,244 men, 1,760 women full time; 1,596 men, 2,798 women part time. **Faculty:** 252 total (107 full time), 14 with doctorates or other terminal degrees. **Location:** Suburban campus in small city; 30 miles from Seattle. **Calendar:** Quarter, limited summer session. Saturday and extensive evening/early morning classes. **Microcomputers:** 312 located in libraries, classrooms, computer centers. **Special facilities:** Northlight Art Gallery.

DEGREES OFFERED. AA, AAS. 501 associate degrees awarded in 1992. 13% in business and management, 5% engineering, 11% health sciences, 46% multi/interdisciplinary studies, 14% trade and industry.

UNDERGRADUATE MAJORS. Accounting, aeronautical technology, aircraft mechanics, American literature, anthropology, automotive mechanics, automotive technology, biological and physical sciences, biology, botany, business administration and management, business and management, business and office, business data processing and related programs, business data programming, chemistry, civil engineering, communications, comparative literature, computer and information sciences, computer programming, creative writing, criminal justice studies, criminal justice technology, dance, data processing, drafting, drafting and design technology, dramatic arts, economics, education, electronic technology, engineering, engineering and engineering-related technologies, engineering and other disciplines, English, English literature, entomology, environmental science, fashion merchandising, fine arts, fire control and safety technology, food production/management/services, French, geography, geology, German, health sciences, history, home economics, human resources development, humanities and social sciences, Japanese, journalism, liberal/general studies, marketing and distribution, mathematics, music, nursing, philosophy, photographic technology, photography, physical sciences, physics, political science and government, practical nursing, precision metal work, prelaw, psychology, quality control technology, real estate, recreation and community services technologies, secretarial and related programs, social sciences, sociology, Spanish, speech, visual and performing arts, zoology.

ACADEMIC PROGRAMS. 2-year transfer program, dual enrollment of high school students, independent study, internships, visiting/exchange student program, cross-registration. **Remedial services:** Learning center, reduced course load, remedial instruction, special counselor, tutoring. **Placement/credit:** AP, institutional tests; 45 credit hours maximum for associate degree.

ACADEMIC REQUIREMENTS. Freshmen must earn minimum GPA of 1.75 to continue in good standing. 46% of freshmen return for sophomore year. Students must declare major by end of first year. **Graduation requirements:** 90 hours for associate. Most students required to take courses in English, mathematics, biological/physical sciences, social sciences.

FRESHMAN ADMISSIONS. Selection criteria: Open admissions. Selective admissions to nursing program. Minimum 2.3 high school GPA required.

1992 FRESHMAN CLASS PROFILE. 564 men, 756 women enrolled. **Characteristics:** 98% from in state, 100% commute, 11% have minority backgrounds. Average age is 30.

FALL-TERM APPLICATIONS. $5 fee. No closing date; applicants notified on a rolling basis; must reply by registration. Interview recommended for nursing applicants. Deferred and early admission available.

STUDENT LIFE. Activities: Student government, magazine, student newspaper, television, choral groups, concert band, dance, drama, jazz band, music ensembles, musical theater, symphony orchestra, Phi Theta Kappa.

ATHLETICS. NCAA, NJCAA. **Intercollegiate:** Basketball, soccer M, volleyball W. **Intramural:** Basketball, racquetball, softball, tennis, volleyball.

STUDENT SERVICES. Aptitude testing, career counseling, employment service for undergraduates, freshman orientation, on-campus day care, personal counseling, placement service for graduates, special adviser for adult students, veterans counselor, services/facilities for handicapped.

ANNUAL EXPENSES. Tuition and fees: $1,125, $3,300 additional for out-of-state students. **Books and supplies:** $500. **Other expenses:** $1,000.

FINANCIAL AID. 20% of freshmen, 26% of continuing students receive some form of aid. 90% of grants, 97% of loans, all jobs based on need. 690 enrolled freshmen were judged to have need, 490 were offered aid. Academic, art, athletic, state/district residency, leadership scholarships available. **Aid applications:** No closing date; priority given to applications received by May 1; applicants notified on a rolling basis beginning on or about June 10; must reply within 2 weeks.

ADDRESS/TELEPHONE. Don Erickson, Dean of Enrollment Services, Everett Community College, 801 Wetmore, Everett, WA 98201. (206) 388-9222. Fax: (206) 339-9129.

Evergreen State College
Olympia, Washington — CB code: 4292

Admissions: 77% of applicants accepted
Based on: ••• School record, test scores
• Activities, essay
Completion: 16% enter graduate study

4-year public liberal arts college, coed. Founded in 1967. **Accreditation:** Regional. **Undergraduate enrollment:** 1,297 men, 1,589 women full time; 81 men, 106 women part time. **Graduate enrollment:** 50 men, 87 women full time; 63 men, 74 women part time. **Faculty:** 176 total (143 full time), 109 with doctorates or other terminal degrees. **Location:** Rural campus in large town; 6 miles from downtown, 60 miles from Seattle. **Calendar:** Quarter, limited summer session. Extensive evening/early morning classes. **Microcomputers:** 134 located in classrooms, computer centers. **Special facilities:** Organic farm, 3,000 feet of waterfront property on Puget Sound, 1,000 forested acres. **Additional facts:** Students enroll in interdisciplinary programs rather than individual courses.

DEGREES OFFERED. BA, BS, M. 820 bachelor's degrees awarded in 1992. 100% in multi/interdisciplinary studies. Graduate degrees offered in 5 major fields of study.

UNDERGRADUATE MAJORS. Agricultural business and management, agricultural sciences, American literature, American studies, anatomy, anthropology, art history, arts management, biochemistry, biological and physical sciences, biology, botany, business administration and management, business and management, cell biology, chemistry, cinematography/film, city/community/regional planning, classics, communications, community services, comparative literature, computer and information sciences, counseling psychology, creative writing, dramatic arts, drawing, earth sciences, ecology, economics, energy conservation and use technology, English, English literature, environmental design, environmental science, European studies, film animation, film arts, fine arts, folklore and mythology, food science and nutrition, foreign languages (multiple emphasis), French, geology, Greek (classical), health sciences, history, humanities, humanities and social sciences, industrial and organizational psychology, international studies, Japanese, labor/industrial relations, liberal/general studies, management information systems, marine biology, mathematics, microbiology, molecular biology, music, music history and appreciation, oceanography, organizational behavior, Pacific area studies, painting, parks and recreation management, peace studies, personnel management, philosophy, photography, physical sciences, physics, plant physiology, political science and government, prelaw, premedicine, preveterinary, printmaking, psychology, public administration, public health laboratory science, public policy studies, renewable natural resources, Russian, Russian and Slavic studies, science technologies, sculpture, social sciences, social work, sociology, Spanish, studio art, systems analysis, urban studies, video, visual and performing arts, women's studies.

ACADEMIC PROGRAMS. Independent study, internships, student-designed major, study abroad, teacher preparation. **Remedial services:** Learning center, preadmission summer program, reduced course load, special counselor, tutoring, programs for students from first generation families. **Placement/credit:** AP, CLEP General and Subject.

ACADEMIC REQUIREMENTS. No policy requiring minimum GPA; records of students having academic difficulty are reviewed individually. 75% of freshmen return for sophomore year. **Graduation requirements:** 180 hours for bachelor's. **Postgraduate studies:** 1% enter law school, 1% enter medical school, 14% enter other graduate study. **Additional information:** Students participate in fully integrated programs that are team taught by faculty, rather than taking separate courses.

FRESHMAN ADMISSIONS. Selection criteria: School achievement record, test scores, rank in top half of class or 60th percentile of GED, as well as individual's understanding of college's unique program of interdisciplinary study are all important. **High school preparation:** 15 units required. Required units include English 4, foreign language 2, mathematics 3, social science 3 and science 2. One fine or performing arts course required. **Test requirements:** SAT or ACT; score report by March 1.

1992 FRESHMAN CLASS PROFILE. 1,326 men and women applied, 1,021 accepted; 402 enrolled. 65% had high school GPA of 3.0 or higher, 35% between 2.0 and 2.99. **Academic background:** Mid 50% of enrolled freshmen had SAT-V between 450-590, SAT-M between 440-580. 85% submitted SAT scores. **Characteristics:** 60% from in state, 70% live in college housing, 12% have minority backgrounds, 1% are foreign students. Average age is 19.

FALL-TERM APPLICATIONS. $35 fee, may be waived for applicants with need. Closing date March 1; applicants notified on or about April 1; must reply by May 1. CRDA.

STUDENT LIFE. Housing: Dormitories (coed); apartment, cooperative housing available. **Activities:** Student government, film, radio, student newspaper, television, choral groups, dance, drama, jazz band, music ensembles, bluegrass band, poetry/literary readings, Asian Coalition, Native American Students Association, Environmental Resource Center, Self-Help Legal Aid, Movimiento Estudiantil Chicano de Aztlan, black student organization.

ATHLETICS. NAIA. **Intercollegiate:** Soccer, swimming. **Intramural:** Baseball, basketball, cross-country, fencing, handball, racquetball, rowing (crew), rugby, sailing, soccer, swimming, table tennis, tennis, volleyball.

STUDENT SERVICES. Career counseling, employment service for undergraduates, health services, on-campus day care, personal counseling, placement service for graduates, veterans counselor, men's and women's centers, women's clinic, services/facilities for handicapped.

ANNUAL EXPENSES. Tuition and fees: $1,971, $4,977 additional for out-of-state students. **Room and board:** $1,767 room only. **Books and supplies:** $600. **Other expenses:** $1,272.

FINANCIAL AID. 15% of freshmen, 50% of continuing students receive some form of aid. 89% of grants, 82% of loans, 39% of jobs based on need. Academic, music/drama, art, athletic, leadership, minority scholarships available. **Aid applications:** No closing date; priority given to applications received by March 15; applicants notified on a rolling basis beginning on or about April 15; must reply within 4 weeks. **Additional information:** Application deadline for merit and cultural diversity scholarships April 1; for other aid April 15. Emergency loans for resident or 50% of nonresident tuition available. Minority students may apply for tuition and fee waiver; amount of award equal to in-state tuition and fees.

ADDRESS/TELEPHONE. Doug Scrima, Assistant to the Dean of Enrollment Services, Evergreen State College, Olympia, WA 98505. (206) 866-6000.

Gonzaga University
Spokane, Washington — CB code: 4330

Admissions: 80% of applicants accepted
Based on: ••• School record
•• Essay, test scores
• Activities, interview, recommendations, special talents
Completion: 93% of freshmen end year in good standing
55% graduate, 16% of these enter graduate study

4-year private university, coed, affiliated with Roman Catholic Church. Founded in 1887. **Accreditation:** Regional. **Undergraduate enrollment:** 1,243 men, 1,372 women full time; 118 men, 205 women part time. **Graduate enrollment:** 779 men, 729 women full time; 199 men, 401 women part time. **Faculty:** 267 total (260 full time), 234 with doctorates or other terminal degrees. **Location:** Urban campus in small city; 300 miles from Seattle. **Calendar:** Semester, extensive summer session. Extensive evening/early morning classes. **Microcomputers:** 245 located in dormitories, libraries, classrooms, computer centers. **Special facilities:** 2 electron microscopes, Computer Aided Design Center, Foley Information and Technology Center. **Additional facts:** Institution in the Jesuit tradition.

DEGREES OFFERED. BA, BS, MA, MS, MBA, MEd, EdD, JD, M.Div. 532 bachelor's degrees awarded in 1992. 23% in business and management, 5% communications, 8% engineering, 6% life sciences, 5% parks/recreation, protective services, public affairs, 5% psychology, 24% social sciences. Graduate degrees offered in 15 major fields of study.

UNDERGRADUATE MAJORS. Accounting, biology, business administration and management, business economics, chemistry, civil engineering, classics, comparative literature, computer and information sciences, computer mathematics, criminology, dramatic arts, economics, electrical/electronics/communications engineering, English, European studies, finance, fine arts, French, German, Greek (classical), history, international business management, Italian, Italian studies, journalism, Latin, liberal/general studies, management science, marketing management, mathematics, mechanical engineering, music education, music performance, nursing, philosophy, physical education, physics, political science and government, psychology, public relations, radio/television broadcasting, religion, sociology, Spanish, special education, speech.

ACADEMIC PROGRAMS. Double major, dual enrollment of high school students, honors program, independent study, internships, student-designed major, study abroad, teacher preparation, visiting/exchange student program, cross-registration, master's in electrical engineering with Washington State University; combined bachelor's/graduate program in business administration, law. **Remedial services:** Reduced course load, special counselor, Limited special entry program for selected freshmen with high potential, but below admission grade point norm. **ROTC:** Army. **Placement/credit:** AP, CLEP Subject; 32 credit hours maximum for bachelor's degree.

ACADEMIC REQUIREMENTS. Freshmen must earn minimum GPA of 2.0 to continue in good standing. 82% of freshmen return for sophomore year. Students must declare major by end of second year. **Graduation requirements:** 128 hours for bachelor's (30 in major). Most students required to take courses in arts/fine arts, English, foreign languages, history, mathematics, philosophy/religion, biological/physical sciences, social sciences. **Postgraduate studies:** 5% enter law school, 1% enter medical school, 4% enter MBA programs, 6% enter other graduate study. **Additional information:** All undergraduates required to complete general core requirements including 11 credits of philosophy and 9 credits of religious studies.

FRESHMAN ADMISSIONS. Selection criteria: Academic achievement, scholastic aptitude, personal characteristics considered. GPA below 2.8 reevaluated to include only grades in academic subjects. Course content test scores important. **High school preparation:** 17 units required. Required units include English 4, foreign language 2, mathematics 3, social science 1 and science 1. Mathematics recommendations include 2 algebra. Algebra, geometry, trigonometry required of engineering applicants. Of 6 additional electives 4 must be from subjects mentioned and the arts. **Test requirements:** SAT or ACT; score report by May 15.

1992 FRESHMAN CLASS PROFILE. 884 men applied, 698 accepted, 311 enrolled; 967 women applied, 791 accepted, 327 enrolled. 84% had high school GPA of 3.0 or higher, 16% between 2.0 and 2.99. 33% were in top tenth and 83% were in top quarter of graduating class. **Academic background:** Mid 50% of enrolled freshmen had SAT-V between 430-560, SAT-M between 430-600; ACT composite between 22-28. 65% submitted SAT scores, 35% submitted ACT scores. **Characteristics:** 51% from in state, 92% live in college housing, 11% have minority backgrounds, 5% are foreign students. Average age is 18.

FALL-TERM APPLICATIONS. $30 fee, may be waived for applicants with need. Closing date April 1; applicants notified on a rolling basis beginning on or about December 1; must reply by May 1 or within 2 weeks if notified thereafter. Essay required for all applicants applicants. Interview recommended. Audition recommended for music, honors program applicants. CRDA. Deferred admission available.

STUDENT LIFE. Housing: Dormitories (men, women, coed); apartment housing available. Freshmen and sophomores under 21 must live on campus, unless living at home.International students must meet this requirement as well. **Activities:** Student government, magazine, radio, student newspaper, television, yearbook, literary publications, choral groups, concert band, dance, drama, jazz band, music ensembles, musical theater, pep band, symphony orchestra, over 40 student clubs and service organizations, international student club, Hawaii Club, Amnesty International, Cultural Awareness Association. **Additional information:** There is a cultural center and a mosque for international students.

ATHLETICS. NCAA. **Intercollegiate:** Baseball M, basketball, cross-country, golf M, rowing (crew), soccer, tennis, volleyball W. **Intramural:** Basketball, ice hockey M, lacrosse M, racquetball, rowing (crew), rugby, skiing, softball, volleyball.

STUDENT SERVICES. Aptitude testing, career counseling, employment service for undergraduates, freshman orientation, health services, personal counseling, placement service for graduates, special adviser for adult students, veterans counselor, foreign student advising, services/facilities for handicapped.

ANNUAL EXPENSES. Tuition and fees: $12,300. **Room and board:** $4,150. **Books and supplies:** $650. **Other expenses:** $1,450.

FINANCIAL AID. 83% of freshmen, 81% of continuing students receive some form of aid. 93% of grants, 95% of loans, 86% of jobs based on need. 414 enrolled freshmen were judged to have need, all were offered aid. Academic, music/drama, athletic, alumni affiliation, minority scholarships available. **Aid applications:** No closing date; priority given to applications received by February 10; applicants notified on a rolling basis beginning on or about April 1; must reply by May 1 or within 4 weeks if notified thereafter.

ADDRESS/TELEPHONE. Philip Ballinger, Dean of Admissions, Gonzaga University, East 502 Boone Avenue, Spokane, WA 99258-0001. (509) 484-6484. (800) 523-9712. Fax: (509) 484-2818.

Grays Harbor College
Aberdeen, Washington — CB code: 4332

2-year public community college, coed. Founded in 1930. **Accreditation:** Regional. **Undergraduate enrollment:** 1,382 men and women full time; 1,900 men and women part time. **Faculty:** 196 total (46 full time), 9 with doctorates or other terminal degrees. **Location:** Suburban campus in large town; 100 miles from Seattle. **Calendar:** Quarter, limited summer session. Extensive evening/early morning classes. **Microcomputers:** 50 located in libraries, classrooms, computer centers. **Special facilities:** 4-acre lake linked to Grays Harbor estuary and fish hatcheries.

DEGREES OFFERED. AA, AS, AAS. 235 associate degrees awarded in 1992.

UNDERGRADUATE MAJORS. Accounting, automotive mechanics, automotive technology, bacteriology, biological and physical sciences, biology, business and management, business data entry equipment operation, business data processing and related programs, carpentry, Chinese, communications, computer and information sciences, data processing, diesel engine mechanics, ecology, education, engineering, engineering and other disciplines, English, fishing and fisheries, health sciences, humanities and social sciences, industrial equipment maintenance and repair, Japanese, legal secretary, liberal/general studies, marine biology, marketing and distribution, mathematics, medical secretary, nursing, physical sciences, practical nursing, precision metal work, psychology, secretarial and related programs, social sciences, wildlife management, word processing, zoology.

ACADEMIC PROGRAMS. 2-year transfer program, cooperative education, independent study, study abroad. **Remedial services:** Learning center, remedial instruction, tutoring. **Placement/credit:** AP, CLEP General and Subject, institutional tests; 45 credit hours maximum for associate degree.

ACADEMIC REQUIREMENTS. Freshmen must earn minimum GPA of 2.0 to continue in good standing. 42% of freshmen return for sophomore year. Students must declare major by end of first year. **Graduation requirements:** 90 hours for associate (60 in major). Most students required to take courses in English, history, humanities, mathematics, biological/physical sciences, social sciences.

FRESHMAN ADMISSIONS. Selection criteria: Open admissions. **Test requirements:** All students required to take ASSET test for placement and counseling.

1992 FRESHMAN CLASS PROFILE. 950 men and women enrolled. **Characteristics:** 95% from in state, 100% commute, 7% have minority backgrounds. Average age is 26.

FALL-TERM APPLICATIONS. No fee. No closing date; applicants notified on a rolling basis beginning on or about February 4; must reply by registration. Interview required for vocational program applicants. Early admission available.

STUDENT LIFE. Activities: Student government, student newspaper, choral groups, concert band, dance, drama, jazz band, music ensembles, symphony orchestra, Phi Theta Kappa.

ATHLETICS. NJCAA. **Intercollegiate:** Basketball, cross-country, golf, softball W, track and field, volleyball W.

STUDENT SERVICES. Career counseling, employment service for

undergraduates, freshman orientation, on-campus day care, personal counseling, veterans counselor, services/facilities for handicapped.

ANNUAL EXPENSES. Tuition and fees: $1,125, $3,300 additional for out-of-state students. **Books and supplies:** $500. **Other expenses:** $570.

FINANCIAL AID. 66% of freshmen, 66% of continuing students receive some form of aid. Grants, loans, jobs available. Academic, music/drama, art, athletic, leadership, minority scholarships available. **Aid applications:** No closing date; priority given to applications received by May 15; applicants notified on a rolling basis beginning on or about August 15; must reply within 3 weeks.

ADDRESS/TELEPHONE. Thomas H. Sobottka, Assistant Dean for Student Services, Grays Harbor College, 1620 Edward P. Smith Drive, Aberdeen, WA 98520-7599. (206) 532-9020. Fax: (206) 532-6716.

Green River Community College
Auburn, Washington CB code: 4337

2-year public community college, coed. Founded in 1965. **Accreditation:** Regional. **Undergraduate enrollment:** 1,579 men, 1,570 women full time; 2,437 men and women part time. **Faculty:** 253 total (113 full time), 11 with doctorates or other terminal degrees. **Location:** Rural campus in large town; 30 miles from Seattle. **Calendar:** Quarter, limited summer session. Extensive evening/early morning classes. **Microcomputers:** Located in libraries, classrooms, computer centers.

DEGREES OFFERED. AA, AS, AAS. 696 associate degrees awarded in 1992. 7% in business and management, 6% business/office and marketing/distribution, 6% allied health, 66% multi/interdisciplinary studies, 11% trade and industry.

UNDERGRADUATE MAJORS. Accounting, aeronautical technology, air traffic control, airline piloting and navigation, automotive mechanics, business and office, carpentry, computer and information sciences, court reporting, drafting, early childhood education, electronic technology, forestry and related sciences, hazardous materials technology, law enforcement and corrections technologies, legal secretary, liberal/general studies, machine tool operation/machine shop, marketing and distribution, medical secretary, music performance, occupational therapy assistant, physical therapy assistant, radio/television broadcasting, real estate, secretarial and related programs, transportation management, water and wastewater technology, welding technology.

ACADEMIC PROGRAMS. 2-year transfer program, cooperative education, dual enrollment of high school students, independent study, study abroad, telecourses, cross-registration. **Remedial services:** Learning center, preadmission summer program, reduced course load, remedial instruction, special counselor, tutoring. **Placement/credit:** AP, CLEP General, institutional tests.

ACADEMIC REQUIREMENTS. No policy requiring minimum GPA; records of students having academic difficulty are reviewed individually. Students must declare major by end of first year. **Graduation requirements:** 90 hours for associate. Most students required to take courses in English, mathematics.

FRESHMAN ADMISSIONS. Selection criteria: Open admissions. Selective admissions to health occupation programs.

1992 FRESHMAN CLASS PROFILE. 2,372 men and women enrolled. **Characteristics:** 95% from in state, 100% commute, 12% have minority backgrounds, 1% are foreign students. Average age is 25.

FALL-TERM APPLICATIONS. No fee. No closing date; applicants notified on a rolling basis beginning on or about December 1; must reply by registration. Interview required for physical therapy, occupational therapy, practical nursing, water/wastewater technology applicants. Audition required for professional entertainment (second level) applicants. Early admission available. ASSET test recommended.

STUDENT LIFE. Activities: Student government, radio, student newspaper, choral groups, dance, drama, jazz band, music ensembles, multicultural clubs.

ATHLETICS. NJCAA. **Intercollegiate:** Baseball M, basketball, golf, soccer, softball W, tennis, volleyball W. **Intramural:** Badminton, baseball, basketball, bowling, cross-country, skiing, soccer, softball, tennis, volleyball.

STUDENT SERVICES. Aptitude testing, career counseling, employment service for undergraduates, freshman orientation, health services, on-campus day care, personal counseling, placement service for graduates, veterans counselor, special advisor for disabled students, services/facilities for handicapped.

ANNUAL EXPENSES. Tuition and fees: $1,140, $3,300 additional for out-of-state students. **Books and supplies:** $480. **Other expenses:** $600.

FINANCIAL AID. 17% of freshmen, 17% of continuing students receive some form of aid. 90% of grants, 86% of loans, 69% of jobs based on need. Academic, music/drama, art, athletic, leadership, minority scholarships available. **Aid applications:** No closing date; priority given to applications received by May 1; applicants notified on a rolling basis beginning on or about June 1; must reply within 2 weeks.

ADDRESS/TELEPHONE. Judy Burgeson, Director of Admissions, Green River Community College, 12401 Southeast 320th Street, Auburn, WA 98002-3699. (206) 833-9111 ext. 301. Fax: (206) 939-5135.

Heritage College
Toppenish, Washington CB code: 4344

4-year private liberal arts college, coed, interdenominational. Founded in 1982. **Accreditation:** Regional. **Undergraduate enrollment:** 88 men, 233 women full time; 47 men, 137 women part time. **Graduate enrollment:** 66 men, 169 women full time; 47 men, 139 women part time. **Faculty:** 179 total (34 full time), 74 with doctorates or other terminal degrees. **Location:** Rural campus in small town; 3 miles from downtown. **Calendar:** Semester, limited summer session. Extensive evening/early morning classes. **Microcomputers:** Located in libraries, computer centers. **Special facilities:** Wildlife preserve.

DEGREES OFFERED. AA, BA, BS, MEd. 11 associate degrees awarded in 1992. 9% in business and management, 18% health sciences, 73% multi/interdisciplinary studies. 55 bachelor's degrees awarded. 5% in business and management, 32% education, 56% multi/interdisciplinary studies, 5% social sciences. Graduate degrees offered in 5 major fields of study.

UNDERGRADUATE MAJORS. Associate: Biological and physical sciences, business and management, computer and information sciences, early childhood education, humanities, humanities and social sciences, liberal/general studies, nursing, psychology, renewable natural resources, social sciences. **Bachelor's:** Bilingual/bicultural education, biological and physical sciences, biology, business administration and management, business and management, chemistry, computer and information sciences, computer education, education, elementary education, English, English education, environmental science, foreign languages education, history, humanities and social sciences, junior high education, liberal/general studies, mathematics, mathematics education, political science and government, prelaw, psychology, science education, secondary education, social sciences, social studies education, Spanish.

ACADEMIC PROGRAMS. 2-year transfer program, double major, independent study, internships, student-designed major, teacher preparation. **Remedial services:** Learning center, reduced course load, remedial instruction, special counselor, tutoring. **Placement/credit:** AP, CLEP General and Subject, institutional tests; 14 credit hours maximum for associate degree; 30 credit hours maximum for bachelor's degree.

ACADEMIC REQUIREMENTS. Freshmen must earn minimum GPA of 2.0 to continue in good standing. Students must declare major by end of first year. **Graduation requirements:** 60 hours for associate (12 in major), 126 hours for bachelor's (44 in major). Most students required to take courses in arts/fine arts, computer science, English, foreign languages, history, humanities, mathematics, philosophy/religion, biological/physical sciences, social sciences. **Postgraduate studies:** 90% from 2-year programs enter 4-year programs.

FRESHMAN ADMISSIONS. Selection criteria: Open admissions. **High school preparation:** 13 units recommended. Recommended units include English 3, mathematics 2, social science 3 and science 1.

1992 FRESHMAN CLASS PROFILE. 4 men, 25 women enrolled. **Characteristics:** 100% from in state, 100% commute, 59% have minority backgrounds, 1% are foreign students. Average age is 30.

FALL-TERM APPLICATIONS. No fee. Closing date September 1; applicants notified on a rolling basis; must reply by September 5. Interview recommended. Deferred and early admission available.

STUDENT LIFE. Activities: Student government, magazine, student newspaper, literary publication, newsletter.

ATHLETICS. Intramural: Basketball, gymnastics, softball, volleyball.

STUDENT SERVICES. Career counseling, employment service for undergraduates, freshman orientation, personal counseling, placement service for graduates, special adviser for adult students, veterans counselor, services/facilities for handicapped.

ANNUAL EXPENSES. Tuition and fees (projected): $5,490. **Books and supplies:** $648. **Other expenses:** $690.

FINANCIAL AID. 63% of freshmen, 64% of continuing students receive some form of aid. 98% of grants, 95% of loans, all jobs based on need. Academic, leadership scholarships available. **Aid applications:** No closing date; priority given to applications received by March 10; applicants notified on a rolling basis; must reply within 4 weeks.

ADDRESS/TELEPHONE. Tangee Hyde, Director of Admissions, Heritage College, 3240 Fort Road, Toppenish, WA 98948-9599. (509) 865-2244. Fax: (509) 865-4469.

Highline Community College
Des Moines, Washington CB code: 4348

2-year public community college, coed. Founded in 1961. **Accreditation:** Regional. **Undergraduate enrollment:** 1,677 men, 2,465 women full time; 922 men, 2,122 women part time. **Faculty:** 376 total (131 full time), 18 with doctorates or other terminal degrees. **Location:** Suburban campus in small city; 18 miles from Seattle. **Calendar:** Quarter, limited summer session. Extensive evening/early morning classes. **Microcomputers:** Located in libraries, classrooms, computer centers. **Additional facts:** First 2 years in premedicine, prepharmacy, predentistry, preveterinary medicine transferable to 4-year college.

DEGREES OFFERED. AA, AAS. 821 associate degrees awarded in 1992.

UNDERGRADUATE MAJORS. Accounting, allied health, apparel and accessories marketing, automotive mechanics, automotive technology, business administration and management, business and management, business and office, business data processing and related programs, business data programming, clothing and textiles management/production/services, computer and information sciences, data processing, drafting, drafting and design technology, dramatic arts, drawing, early childhood education, education, engineering, fashion merchandising, graphic and printing production, graphic arts technology, home furnishings and equipment management/production/services, hospitality and recreation marketing, hotel/motel and restaurant management, illustration design, industrial technology, interior design, journalism, law enforcement and corrections, law enforcement and corrections technologies, legal assistant/paralegal, legal secretary, liberal/general studies, library assistant, management information systems, manufacturing technology, marketing and distribution, medical assistant, medical secretary, metal/jewelry, music, nursing, office supervision and management, painting, personal services, personnel management, precision metal work, radio/television broadcasting, real estate, respiratory therapy, respiratory therapy technology, secretarial and related programs, small business management and ownership, teacher aide, telecommunications, transportation and travel marketing, welding technology, word processing.

ACADEMIC PROGRAMS. 2-year transfer program, cooperative education, double major, dual enrollment of high school students, honors program, independent study, internships, cross-registration. **Remedial services:** Learning center, reduced course load, remedial instruction, special counselor, tutoring. **ROTC:** Air Force, Army. **Placement/credit:** AP, CLEP Subject, institutional tests; 30 credit hours maximum for associate degree.

ACADEMIC REQUIREMENTS. Freshmen must earn minimum GPA of 2.0 to continue in good standing. **Graduation requirements:** 90 hours for associate. Most students required to take courses in arts/fine arts, computer science, English, foreign languages, history, humanities, mathematics, philosophy/religion, biological/physical sciences, social sciences.

FRESHMAN ADMISSIONS. Selection criteria: Open admissions. School achievement record considered for health programs. College and work experience also considered for nursing. Health occupation programs require chemistry and algebra.

1992 FRESHMAN CLASS PROFILE. 800 men and women enrolled. **Characteristics:** 92% from in state, 100% commute, 10% have minority backgrounds, 1% are foreign students. Average age is 30.

FALL-TERM APPLICATIONS. No fee. No closing date; applicants notified on a rolling basis. Deferred admission available.

STUDENT LIFE. Activities: Student government, magazine, student newspaper, television, choral groups, concert band, dance, drama, jazz band, music ensembles, musical theater, black, Chicano, Indian, veterans, and international student clubs, political forum, paralegal and arts societies, computer club, academic honor society.

ATHLETICS. NJCAA. **Intercollegiate:** Basketball, cross-country, golf, soccer, softball W, swimming, tennis, track and field, volleyball W, wrestling M. **Intramural:** Archery, soccer.

STUDENT SERVICES. Aptitude testing, career counseling, employment service for undergraduates, freshman orientation, health services, on-campus day care, personal counseling, placement service for graduates, special adviser for adult students, veterans counselor, services for women and minority groups, services/facilities for handicapped.

ANNUAL EXPENSES. Tuition and fees: \$1,125, \$3,300 additional for out-of-state students. **Books and supplies:** \$560. **Other expenses:** \$630.

FINANCIAL AID. 28% of freshmen, 28% of continuing students receive some form of aid. 94% of grants, 86% of loans, 61% of jobs based on need. **Aid applications:** No closing date; priority given to applications received by April 1; applicants notified on a rolling basis beginning on or about June 1; must reply within 2 weeks.

ADDRESS/TELEPHONE. Michael Grubiak, Assistant Dean of Student Services, Highline Community College, PO Box 98000, Des Moines, WA 98198-9800. (206) 878-3710.

ITT Technical Institute: Seattle
Seattle, Washington — CB code: 3599

2-year proprietary technical/career training institute, coed. **Undergraduate enrollment:** 560 men and women. **Faculty:** 25 total (22 full time), 4 with doctorates or other terminal degrees. **Location:** Urban campus in very large city. **Calendar:** Quarter. Extensive evening/early morning classes. **Microcomputers:** Located in libraries, classrooms, computer centers.

DEGREES OFFERED. AAS. 160 associate degrees awarded in 1992.

UNDERGRADUATE MAJORS. Computer and information sciences, electrical and electronics equipment repair, electronic technology, information sciences and systems.

ACADEMIC PROGRAMS. Remedial services: Learning center, tutoring. **Placement/credit:** Institutional tests.

ACADEMIC REQUIREMENTS. Freshmen must earn minimum GPA of 2.0 to continue in good standing. 70% of freshmen return for sophomore year. Students must declare major on application. **Graduation requirements:** 121 hours for associate (121 in major). Most students required to take courses in computer science, mathematics, biological/physical sciences.

FRESHMAN ADMISSIONS. Selection criteria: Satisfactory scores on English and/or mathematics tests.

1992 FRESHMAN CLASS PROFILE. 170 men, 20 women enrolled. **Characteristics:** 99% from in state, 100% commute, 29% have minority backgrounds, 1% are foreign students. Average age is 22.

FALL-TERM APPLICATIONS. \$100 fee. Application fee refunded if student is not accepted. No closing date; applicants notified on a rolling basis. Interview required.

STUDENT LIFE. Activities: Student government.

STUDENT SERVICES. Employment service for undergraduates, freshman orientation, placement service for graduates, services/facilities for handicapped.

ANNUAL EXPENSES. Tuition and fees (1992-93): Tuition for 18-month computer-aided drafting program \$12,817; books, supplies, and tools, \$1,200. Tuition for 2-year electronics program \$14,405; books and supplies, \$1,700. Laboratory fees, \$50 per quarter.

FINANCIAL AID. Aid applications: No closing date; applicants notified on a rolling basis.

ADDRESS/TELEPHONE. Toby Stanley, Director of Recruitment, ITT Technical Institute: Seattle, 12720 Gateway Drive, Suite 100, Seattle, WA 98168-3333. (206) 244-3300. Fax: (206) 246-7635.

ITT Technical Institute: Spokane
Spokane, Washington — CB code: 7027

2-year proprietary technical college, coed. **Undergraduate enrollment:** 250 men and women. **Faculty:** 16 total (15 full time). **Location:** Suburban campus in small city; 5 miles from downtown Spokane. **Calendar:** Quarter. Extensive evening/early morning classes.

DEGREES OFFERED. AAS. 124 associate degrees awarded in 1992. 100% in engineering technologies.

UNDERGRADUATE MAJORS. Computer-aided drafting, drafting and design technology, electronic technology.

ACADEMIC PROGRAMS. Placement/credit: Institutional tests.

ACADEMIC REQUIREMENTS. Freshmen must earn minimum GPA of 2.0 to continue in good standing. Students must declare major on enrollment. **Graduation requirements:** Most students required to take courses in mathematics.

FRESHMAN ADMISSIONS. Selection criteria: Test score of reading and mathematical skills required. Spacial relations test required for computer-aided drafting.

1992 FRESHMAN CLASS PROFILE. 80 men and women enrolled. **Characteristics:** 50% from in state, 100% commute.

FALL-TERM APPLICATIONS. \$100 fee. Application fee refunded if student not accepted. No closing date; applicants notified on a rolling basis. Interview required.

ANNUAL EXPENSES. Tuition and fees (1992-93): Tuition for 18-month computer-aided drafting program \$12,817; books, supplies, and tools, \$1,300. Tuition for 2-year electronics program \$14,405; books and supplies, \$1,600. Laboratory fees, \$50 per quarter.

FINANCIAL AID. Aid applications: No closing date.

ADDRESS/TELEPHONE. Admissions Office, ITT Technical Institute: Spokane, North 1050 Argonne Road, Argonne Office Park, Spokane, WA 99212-2610. (509) 926-2900.

Lower Columbia College
Longview, Washington — CB code: 4402

2-year public community college, coed. Founded in 1934. **Accreditation:** Regional. **Undergraduate enrollment:** 897 men, 1,109 women full time; 859 men, 1,523 women part time. **Faculty:** 164 total (84 full time), 14 with doctorates or other terminal degrees. **Location:** Suburban campus in large town; 40 miles from Portland, Oregon, 100 miles from Seattle. **Calendar:** Quarter, limited summer session. Extensive evening/early morning classes. **Microcomputers:** 100 located in computer centers. **Special facilities:** Art gallery, theater.

DEGREES OFFERED. AA, AAS. 300 associate degrees awarded in 1992.

UNDERGRADUATE MAJORS. Accounting, anatomy, anthropology, astronomy, automotive mechanics, automotive technology, biological and physical sciences, biology, botany, business administration and management, business and management, business and office, business data processing and related programs, business data programming, chemical engineering, chemical manufacturing technology, chemistry, child development/care/guidance, communications, computer and information sciences, computer programming, data processing, diesel engine mechanics, drafting, drafting and design technology, dramatic arts, early childhood education, earth sciences, economics, education, electrical and electronics equipment repair, electrical/electronics/communications engineering, electronic technology, elementary education, engineering, engineering and engineering-related technologies, English, fine arts, geology, history, industrial equipment maintenance and repair, industrial technology, instrumentation technology, law enforcement and corrections technologies, legal secretary, liberal/general studies, mathematics, mechanical design technology, mechanical engineering, medical laboratory technologies, medical secretary, music, nursing, oceanography, office supervision and management, philosophy, physical sciences, physics, political science and government, practical nursing, precision metal work, predentistry, prelaw, premedicine, prepharmacy, preveterinary, psychology, science technologies, secondary education, secretarial and related programs, social sciences, sociology, welding technology, zoology.

ACADEMIC PROGRAMS. 2-year transfer program, cooperative education, dual enrollment of high school students, independent study, study abroad, telecourses, cross-registration. **Remedial services:** Learning center, remedial instruction, special counselor, tutoring, Educational Services Program. **Placement/credit:** AP, CLEP General and Subject, institutional tests.

ACADEMIC REQUIREMENTS. Freshmen must earn minimum GPA of 1.5 to continue in good standing. 60% of freshmen return for sophomore year. Students must declare major by end of first year. **Graduation requirements:** 90 hours for associate. Most students required to take courses in English, humanities, mathematics, biological/physical sciences, social sciences.

FRESHMAN ADMISSIONS. Selection criteria: Open admissions. Selective admissions to nursing program. **Test requirements:** ASSET test required of all applicants. **Additional information:** Early application advisable because of enrollment caps.

1992 FRESHMAN CLASS PROFILE. 700 men and women enrolled. **Characteristics:** 97% from in state, 100% commute, 9% have minority backgrounds, 1% are foreign students. Average age is 19.

FALL-TERM APPLICATIONS. No fee. No closing date; applicants notified on a rolling basis beginning on or about December 1. Early admission available.

STUDENT LIFE. Housing: Apartments normally available in local community. **Activities:** Student government, magazine, student newspaper, choral groups, concert band, dance, drama, jazz band, music ensembles, musical theater, pep band, muticultural students club.

ATHLETICS. NJCAA. **Intercollegiate:** Baseball M, basketball, cross-country, golf M, soccer M, softball W, tennis W, volleyball W, wrestling M. **Intramural:** Bowling, golf W.

STUDENT SERVICES. Aptitude testing, career counseling, employment service for undergraduates, freshman orientation, on-campus day care, personal counseling, placement service for graduates, special adviser for adult students, veterans counselor, services/facilities for handicapped.

ANNUAL EXPENSES. Tuition and fees: $1,152, $3,300 additional for out-of-state students. **Books and supplies:** $560. **Other expenses:** $610.

FINANCIAL AID. 35% of freshmen, 35% of continuing students receive some form of aid. 98% of grants, all loans, 85% of jobs based on need. Academic, music/drama, athletic, state/district residency, leadership, minority scholarships available. **Aid applications:** No closing date; priority given to applications received by July 1; applicants notified on a rolling basis; must reply within 3 weeks.

ADDRESS/TELEPHONE. Mary L. Harding, Associate Dean of Instruction, Lower Columbia College, PO Box 3010, Longview, WA 98632. (206) 577-2303. Fax: (206) 577-3400.

Lutheran Bible Institute of Seattle
Issaquah, Washington — CB code: 4408

4-year private Bible college, coed, affiliated with Lutheran churches. Founded in 1944. **Accreditation:** Regional. **Undergraduate enrollment:** 54 men, 59 women full time; 20 men, 23 women part time. **Faculty:** 20 total (10 full time), 8 with doctorates or other terminal degrees. **Location:** Suburban campus in large town; 15 miles from Seattle. **Calendar:** Quarter. Extensive evening/early morning classes. **Microcomputers:** 4 located in libraries. **Additional facts:** All students participate in off-campus ministry to provide community service.

DEGREES OFFERED. BA. 10 associate degrees awarded in 1992. 100% in philosophy, religion, theology. 30 bachelor's degrees awarded. 100% in philosophy, religion, theology.

UNDERGRADUATE MAJORS. Associate: Bible studies, religion. **Bachelor's:** Bible studies, geriatric services, missionary studies, religion, religious education, youth ministries.

ACADEMIC PROGRAMS. Accelerated program, independent study, internships. **Placement/credit:** AP, CLEP General and Subject, institutional tests; 15 credit hours maximum for associate degree; 15 credit hours maximum for bachelor's degree.

ACADEMIC REQUIREMENTS. Freshmen must earn minimum GPA of 2.0 to continue in good standing. Students must declare major by end of second year. **Graduation requirements:** 90 hours for associate (75 in major), 180 hours for bachelor's (50 in major). Most students required to take courses in arts/fine arts, English, history, humanities, mathematics, philosophy/religion, biological/physical sciences, social sciences.

FRESHMAN ADMISSIONS. Selection criteria: High school GPA, 2 recommendations, personal statement, and evidence of Christian commitment and church involvement important. Interview and test scores considered.

1992 FRESHMAN CLASS PROFILE. 20 men, 18 women enrolled. **Characteristics:** 65% from in state, 80% live in college housing, 5% have minority backgrounds, 1% are foreign students. Average age is 22.

FALL-TERM APPLICATIONS. $30 fee. Closing date August 15; applicants notified on a rolling basis; must reply by May 1 or within 2 weeks if notified thereafter. Essay required. Interview recommended for academically weak applicants. CRDA. Deferred and early admission available.

STUDENT LIFE. Housing: Dormitories (men, women); apartment housing available. Students given single rooms. Each dormitory floor has laundry facilities and lounge. **Activities:** Student government, yearbook, choral groups, drama, music ensembles, social service teams.

ATHLETICS. Intramural: Baseball, basketball, softball, volleyball.

STUDENT SERVICES. Career counseling, employment service for undergraduates, health services, placement service for graduates, services/facilities for handicapped.

ANNUAL EXPENSES. Tuition and fees: $2,840. **Room and board:** $3,600. **Books and supplies:** $500. **Other expenses:** $950.

FINANCIAL AID. 73% of freshmen, 75% of continuing students receive some form of aid. 97% of grants, 82% of loans, 87% of jobs based on need. Academic, music/drama, leadership, religious affiliation scholarships available. **Aid applications:** No closing date; priority given to applications received by May 1; applicants notified on a rolling basis beginning on or about May 15; must reply within 30 days.

ADDRESS/TELEPHONE. Dorothy Baumgartner, Director of Admissions, Lutheran Bible Institute of Seattle, 4221 228th Ave SE, Issaquah, WA 98027. (206) 392-0400. (800) 843-5659. Fax: (206) 392-0404.

North Seattle Community College
Seattle, Washington — CB code: 4554

2-year public community college, coed. Founded in 1970. **Accreditation:** Regional. **Undergraduate enrollment:** 1,551 men, 1,453 women full time; 2,253 men, 3,663 women part time. **Faculty:** 290 total (106 full time), 24 with doctorates or other terminal degrees. **Location:** Urban campus in very large city. **Calendar:** Quarter, limited summer session. Extensive evening/early morning classes. **Microcomputers:** 85 located in classrooms, computer centers. **Special facilities:** Art gallery.

DEGREES OFFERED. AA. 549 associate degrees awarded in 1992.

UNDERGRADUATE MAJORS. Accounting, air conditioning/heating/refrigeration mechanics, air conditioning/heating/refrigeration technology, allied health, biomedical equipment technology, business and office, business data entry equipment operation, business data processing and related programs, computer servicing technology, computer technology, data processing, drafting and design technology, early childhood education, electrical and electronics equipment repair, electromechanical technology, electronic technology, engineering and engineering-related technologies, fine arts, food production/management/services, liberal/general studies, medical assistant, practical nursing, preengineering, real estate, secretarial and related programs, teacher aide, word processing.

ACADEMIC PROGRAMS. 2-year transfer program, dual enrollment of high school students, cross-registration. **Remedial services:** Learning center, reduced course load, remedial instruction, special counselor, tutoring. **Placement/credit:** CLEP Subject, institutional tests; 45 credit hours maximum for associate degree.

ACADEMIC REQUIREMENTS. Freshmen must earn minimum GPA of 2.0 to continue in good standing. 60% of freshmen return for sophomore year. Students must declare major by end of first year. **Graduation requirements:** 90 hours for associate (60 in major). Most students required to take courses in English, humanities, mathematics, social sciences.

FRESHMAN ADMISSIONS. Selection criteria: Open admissions.

1992 FRESHMAN CLASS PROFILE. 950 men and women enrolled. **Characteristics:** 96% from in state, 100% commute, 15% have minority backgrounds, 2% are foreign students. Average age is 24.

FALL-TERM APPLICATIONS. No fee. Closing date September 24; priority given to applications received by August 27; applicants notified on a rolling basis beginning on or about February 1. Deferred admission available.

STUDENT LIFE. Activities: Student government, film, radio, student newspaper, television, choral groups, concert band, drama, jazz band, music ensembles, Phi Theta Kappa, paper recycling program, African American Club, Latino Americanos, TEAM (Telling Everyone About Messiah).

ATHLETICS. Intramural: Baseball, basketball, cross-country, racquetball, skiing, soccer, softball, tennis, volleyball.

STUDENT SERVICES. Aptitude testing, career counseling, employment service for undergraduates, freshman orientation, on-campus day care, personal counseling, placement service for graduates, special adviser for adult students, veterans counselor, services/facilities for handicapped.

ANNUAL EXPENSES. Tuition and fees: $1,125, $3,300 additional for out-of-state students. **Books and supplies:** $500. **Other expenses:** $1,000.

FINANCIAL AID. 30% of freshmen, 27% of continuing students receive some form of aid. 97% of grants, 92% of loans, all jobs based on need.

Academic, music/drama, art, state/district residency, minority scholarships available. **Aid applications:** Closing date August 31; priority given to applications received by June 1; applicants notified on a rolling basis beginning on or about July 15; must reply by September 16.

ADDRESS/TELEPHONE. Patrick H. Martin, Registrar and Director of Admissions, North Seattle Community College, 9600 College Way North, Seattle, WA 98103-3599. (206) 527-3668. Fax: (206) 527-3635.

Northwest College of the Assemblies of God
Kirkland, Washington CB code: 4541

4-year private Bible, liberal arts college, coed, affiliated with Assemblies of God. Founded in 1934. **Accreditation:** Regional. **Undergraduate enrollment:** 312 men, 285 women full time; 34 men, 56 women part time. **Faculty:** 59 total (32 full time), 16 with doctorates or other terminal degrees. **Location:** Suburban campus in large town; 10 miles from Seattle. **Calendar:** Semester, limited summer session. Extensive evening/early morning classes. **Microcomputers:** 18 located in computer centers.

DEGREES OFFERED. AA, BA. 35 associate degrees awarded in 1992. 100% in multi/interdisciplinary studies. 123 bachelor's degrees awarded. 13% in teacher education, 54% philosophy, religion, theology, 24% psychology, 6% visual and performing arts.

UNDERGRADUATE MAJORS. Associate: Business administration and management, business and office, health sciences, liberal/general studies, secretarial and related programs. **Bachelor's:** Behavioral sciences, Bible studies, business administration and management, elementary education, junior high education, liberal/general studies, missionary studies, music performance, philosophy, religion, religious education, religious music, theological studies.

ACADEMIC PROGRAMS. 2-year transfer program, cooperative education, double major, independent study, internships, student-designed major, study abroad, teacher preparation, Washington semester. **Remedial services:** Reduced course load, remedial instruction, special counselor. **Placement/credit:** AP, CLEP General and Subject; 30 credit hours maximum for associate degree; 30 credit hours maximum for bachelor's degree.

ACADEMIC REQUIREMENTS. Freshmen must earn minimum GPA of 1.7 to continue in good standing. 60% of freshmen return for sophomore year. Students must declare major by end of second year. **Graduation requirements:** 62 hours for associate, 124 hours for bachelor's (30 in major). Most students required to take courses in arts/fine arts, English, humanities, philosophy/religion, biological/physical sciences, social sciences. **Postgraduate studies:** 60% from 2-year programs enter 4-year programs.

FRESHMAN ADMISSIONS. Selection criteria: Essay and GPA of 2.0 required for students. Those with less than 2.0 admitted on probation. **High school preparation:** 16 units recommended. Recommended units include English 3, foreign language 1, mathematics 2, social science 1 and science 1. **Test requirements:** SAT or ACT for placement and counseling only; score report by August 1.

1992 FRESHMAN CLASS PROFILE. 52 men, 93 women enrolled. **Characteristics:** 68% from in state, 75% live in college housing, 12% have minority backgrounds, 4% are foreign students. Average age is 21.

FALL-TERM APPLICATIONS. $20 fee. No closing date; priority given to applications received by August 1; applicants notified on a rolling basis. Essay required. Audition recommended for music applicants. Deferred admission available. Institutional early decision plan.

STUDENT LIFE. Housing: Dormitories (men, women, coed); apartment housing available. **Activities:** Student government, radio, yearbook, choral groups, concert band, drama, music ensembles, pep band, community outreach groups. **Additional information:** Religious observance required.

ATHLETICS. Intercollegiate: Basketball, soccer M, volleyball W. **Intramural:** Basketball, football M, softball, tennis.

STUDENT SERVICES. Employment service for undergraduates, freshman orientation, health services, personal counseling, placement service for graduates, veterans counselor.

ANNUAL EXPENSES. Tuition and fees: $6,646. **Room and board:** $3,250. **Books and supplies:** $660. **Other expenses:** $1,370.

FINANCIAL AID. 96% of freshmen, 80% of continuing students receive some form of aid. 94% of grants, 79% of loans, 58% of jobs based on need. 110 enrolled freshmen were judged to have need, all were offered aid. Academic, music/drama, art, leadership, alumni affiliation, religious affiliation scholarships available. **Aid applications:** No closing date; priority given to applications received by March 1; applicants notified on a rolling basis beginning on or about April 15; must reply within 6 weeks.

ADDRESS/TELEPHONE. Dr. Calvin L. White, Director of Enrollment Services, Northwest College of the Assemblies of God, PO Box 579, Kirkland, WA 98083-0579. (206) 822-8266 ext. 231. (800) 6-NWEST-1. Fax: (206) 827-0148.

Northwest Indian College
Bellingham, Washington CB code: 5973

2-year private community college, coed, Tribally controlled. **Accreditation:** Regional candidate. **Undergraduate enrollment:** 1,281 men and women. **Location:** Rural campus in large town; 15 miles north of Bellingham. **Calendar:** Quarter. **Additional facts:** Branch campus with Pugallup tribe in Tacoma and teaching sites on reservations in the Pacific Northwest. Strong Native American focus.

FRESHMAN ADMISSIONS. Selection criteria: Open admissions.

ANNUAL EXPENSES. Tuition and fees: $1,605, $750 additional for out-of-state students. **Books and supplies:** $587. **Other expenses:** $1,072.

ADDRESS/TELEPHONE. Dr. Lucy Wood-Trast, Public Information Officer, Northwest Indian College, 2522 Kwina Road, Bellington, WA 98226. (206) 676-2772 ext. 107. Fax: (206) 738-0136.

Olympic College
Bremerton, Washington CB code: 4583

2-year public community college, coed. Founded in 1946. **Accreditation:** Regional. **Undergraduate enrollment:** 1,388 men, 1,637 women full time; 1,435 men, 2,125 women part time. **Faculty:** 415 total (97 full time), 27 with doctorates or other terminal degrees. **Location:** Suburban campus in large town; 20 miles across Puget Sound from Seattle. **Calendar:** Quarter, extensive summer session. Extensive evening/early morning classes. **Microcomputers:** 72 located in libraries, classrooms, computer centers.

DEGREES OFFERED. AA, AS. 566 associate degrees awarded in 1992. 7% in business and management, 28% business/office and marketing/distribution, 10% computer sciences, 18% engineering technologies, 21% health sciences, 6% home economics, 6% trade and industry.

UNDERGRADUATE MAJORS. Accounting, automotive mechanics, automotive technology, business administration and management, business and management, business and office, business data processing and related programs, business economics, child development/care/guidance, clothing and textiles management/production/services, drafting and design technology, electronic technology, engineering, engineering and engineering-related technologies, fashion merchandising, finance, fire control and safety technology, food management, food production/management/services, information sciences and systems, law enforcement and corrections technologies, legal secretary, liberal/general studies, medical assistant, mental health/human services, nursing, real estate, secretarial and related programs, welding technology, zoology.

ACADEMIC PROGRAMS. Cooperative education, dual enrollment of high school students, honors program, independent study, study abroad, weekend college, cross-registration. **Remedial services:** Learning center, remedial instruction, tutoring. **Placement/credit:** AP, institutional tests. Credit awarded for CLEP applies only to elective-credit category of Associate degree.

ACADEMIC REQUIREMENTS. No policy requiring minimum GPA; records of students having academic difficulty are reviewed individually. 51% of freshmen return for sophomore year. Students must declare major by end of first year. **Graduation requirements:** 90 hours for associate. Most students required to take courses in English, humanities, mathematics, biological/physical sciences, social sciences.

FRESHMAN ADMISSIONS. Selection criteria: Open admissions. Selective admissions to nursing program.

1992 FRESHMAN CLASS PROFILE. 2,000 men and women enrolled. **Characteristics:** 99% from in state, 100% commute, 12% have minority backgrounds. Average age is 30.

FALL-TERM APPLICATIONS. No fee. No closing date; applicants notified on a rolling basis; must reply by registration. Early admission available.

STUDENT LIFE. Activities: Student government, student newspaper, choral groups, concert band, drama, jazz band, musical theater, pep band, symphony orchestra.

ATHLETICS. Intercollegiate: Baseball M, basketball, softball W, volleyball W.

STUDENT SERVICES. Aptitude testing, career counseling, employment service for undergraduates, on-campus day care, personal counseling, placement service for graduates, veterans counselor, services/facilities for handicapped.

ANNUAL EXPENSES. Tuition and fees: $1,125, $3,300 additional for out-of-state students. **Books and supplies:** $653. **Other expenses:** $690.

FINANCIAL AID. 28% of freshmen, 28% of continuing students receive some form of aid. 99% of grants, 96% of loans, 57% of jobs based on need. 590 enrolled freshmen were judged to have need, all were offered aid. Academic, music/drama, art, athletic, state/district residency, minority scholarships available. **Aid applications:** No closing date; priority given to applications received by April 30; applicants notified on a rolling basis beginning on or about June 1; must reply within 2 weeks.

ADDRESS/TELEPHONE. Jack Stenhjem, Associate Dean of Students, Olympic College, 1600 Chester Avenue, Bremerton, WA 98310-1699. (206) 478-4504. Fax: (206) 478-7161.

Pacific Lutheran University
Tacoma, Washington CB code: 4597

4-year private university, coed, affiliated with Evangelical Lutheran Church in America. Founded in 1890. **Accreditation:** Regional. **Undergraduate enrollment:** 1,078 men, 1,586 women full time; 110 men, 190 women part time. **Graduate enrollment:** 69 men, 97 women full time; 117 men, 204 women part time. **Faculty:** 320 total (231 full time), 201 with doctorates or other terminal degrees. **Location:** Suburban campus in small city; 7 miles from downtown, 30 miles from Seattle. **Calendar:** 4-1-4, extensive summer session. Extensive evening/early morning classes. **Microcomputers:** 110 located in libraries, classrooms, computer centers. **Special facilities:** Herbarium, invertebrate and vertebrate museums, greenhouse, field station and boat equipped for studies of Puget Sound.

DEGREES OFFERED. BA, BS, BFA, MA, MS, MBA. 900 bachelor's degrees awarded in 1992. Graduate degrees offered in 19 major fields of study.

UNDERGRADUATE MAJORS. Accounting, advertising, anthropology, art education, artificial intelligence, biochemistry, biology, business administration and management, business and management, business education, chemistry, classics, clinical laboratory science, communications, comparative literature, computer and information sciences, computer engineering, computer programming, creative writing, data processing, dramatic arts, drawing, early childhood education, earth sciences, economics, education, electrical/electronics/communications engineering, elementary education, engineering physics, English, English education, English literature, finance, foreign languages education, French, geology, German, graphic design, health education, history, information sciences and systems, international business management, international relations, jazz, journalism, junior high education, labor/industrial relations, legal studies, management information systems, marketing and distribution, marketing management, mathematics, mathematics education, microcomputer software, music, music education, music performance, music theory and composition, nursing, painting, personnel management, philosophy, physical education, physics, political science and government, predentistry, prelaw, premedicine, prepharmacy, preveterinary, psychology, public relations, radio/television broadcasting, radio/television technology, reading education, religion, religious music, Scandinavian languages, Scandinavian studies, school psychology, science education, sculpture, secondary education, social science education, social studies education, social work, sociology, Spanish, special education, specific learning disabilities, speech, speech/communication/theater education, sports medicine, studio art, systems analysis, theater design, theological studies, 2-dimensional art, 3-dimensional art.

ACADEMIC PROGRAMS. Accelerated program, cooperative education, double major, dual enrollment of high school students, honors program, independent study, internships, student-designed major, study abroad, teacher preparation, visiting/exchange student program, cross-registration; liberal arts/career combination in engineering; combined bachelor's/graduate program in business administration. **Remedial services:** Preadmission summer program, reduced course load, special counselor, tutoring. **ROTC:** Army. **Placement/credit:** AP, CLEP General, institutional tests; 30 credit hours maximum for bachelor's degree.

ACADEMIC REQUIREMENTS. Freshmen must earn minimum GPA of 2.0 to continue in good standing. 79% of freshmen return for sophomore year. Students must declare major by end of second year. **Graduation requirements:** 128 hours for bachelor's (32 in major). Most students required to take courses in arts/fine arts, English, foreign languages, history, mathematics, philosophy/religion, biological/physical sciences, social sciences. **Additional information:** Core curriculum, called Integrated Studies Program, explores dynamics of change from variety of academic perspectives.

FRESHMAN ADMISSIONS. Selection criteria: School achievement record, rank in top half of class, pattern of grades, test scores, recommendations, and activity record considered. Commitment to social or community service, volunteerism, community involvement highly desirable. **High school preparation:** 4 units required. Required and recommended units include foreign language 2 and mathematics 2-3. English 4, social science 2 and science 2 recommended. Computer science, speech, debate, music also recommended. **Test requirements:** SAT or ACT; score report by May 1.

1992 FRESHMAN CLASS PROFILE. 209 men, 299 women enrolled. 81% had high school GPA of 3.0 or higher, 19% between 2.0 and 2.99. **Academic background:** Mid 50% of enrolled freshmen had SAT-V between 400-520, SAT-M between 450-580. 88% submitted SAT scores. **Characteristics:** 59% from in state, 73% live in college housing, 9% have minority backgrounds, 1% are foreign students. Average age is 19.

FALL-TERM APPLICATIONS. $35 fee. Closing date May 1; priority given to applications received by March 1; applicants notified on a rolling basis beginning on or about December 1; must reply by May 1 or within 2 weeks if notified thereafter. Audition required for music, forensics applicants. Essay required. Interview recommended for borderline, exceptional applicants. Portfolio recommended for art applicants. CRDA. Deferred and early admission available. EDP-F.

STUDENT LIFE. Housing: Dormitories (men, women, coed); apartment housing available. **Activities:** Student government, magazine, radio, student newspaper, television, yearbook, choral groups, concert band, dance, drama, jazz band, music ensembles, musical theater, opera, pep band, symphony orchestra, student congregation, Fellowship of Christian Athletes, BANTU (minority organization), Arete Society (liberal arts outstanding achievement), Spurs, University Students Social Action Committee.

ATHLETICS. NAIA. **Intercollegiate:** Baseball M, basketball, cross-country, football M, golf M, rowing (crew), skiing, soccer, softball W, swimming, tennis, track and field, volleyball W, wrestling M. **Intramural:** Badminton, basketball, bowling, golf, handball, racquetball, skiing, skin diving, soccer, softball, squash, swimming, table tennis, tennis, track and field, volleyball.

STUDENT SERVICES. Aptitude testing, career counseling, employment service for undergraduates, freshman orientation, health services, personal counseling, placement service for graduates, special adviser for adult students, veterans counselor, pastoral care, services/facilities for handicapped.

ANNUAL EXPENSES. Tuition and fees: $12,672. **Room and board:** $4,272. **Books and supplies:** $654. **Other expenses:** $1,368.

FINANCIAL AID. 79% of freshmen, 75% of continuing students receive some form of aid. 57% of grants, 83% of loans, 91% of jobs based on need. 375 enrolled freshmen were judged to have need, 350 were offered aid. Academic, music/drama, art, leadership, alumni affiliation, religious affiliation, minority scholarships available. **Aid applications:** Closing date May 1; priority given to applications received by March 1; applicants notified on a rolling basis beginning on or about April 1; must reply by May 1 or within 2 weeks if notified thereafter.

ADDRESS/TELEPHONE. David Hawsey, Dean of Admissions/Enrollment Mgmt, Pacific Lutheran University, Tacoma, WA 98447-0003. (206) 535-7151. (800) 274-6758. Fax: (206) 535-8320.

Peninsula College
Port Angeles, Washington CB code: 4615

2-year public community college, coed. Founded in 1961. **Accreditation:** Regional. **Undergraduate enrollment:** 490 men, 548 women full time; 916 men, 943 women part time. **Faculty:** 141 total (62 full time), 9 with doctorates or other terminal degrees. **Location:** Rural campus in large town; 75 miles from Seattle. **Calendar:** Quarter, limited summer session. **Microcomputers:** 55 located in classrooms, computer centers. **Special facilities:** Marine laboratory.

DEGREES OFFERED. AA, AAS. 185 associate degrees awarded in 1992.

UNDERGRADUATE MAJORS. Accounting, automotive mechanics, automotive technology, business and management, business data processing and related programs, child development/care/guidance, criminal justice technology, data processing, diesel engine mechanics, electronic technology, engineering and engineering-related technologies, fishing and fisheries, liberal/general studies, marketing and distribution, nursing, secretarial and related programs.

ACADEMIC PROGRAMS. 2-year transfer program, honors program, internships, study abroad. **Remedial services:** Learning center, reduced course load, remedial instruction, special counselor, tutoring. **Placement/credit:** AP.

ACADEMIC REQUIREMENTS. Freshmen must earn minimum GPA of 2.0 to continue in good standing. 50% of freshmen return for sophomore year. **Graduation requirements:** 90 hours for associate. Most students required to take courses in English, humanities, mathematics, biological/physical sciences, social sciences.

FRESHMAN ADMISSIONS. Selection criteria: Open admissions. **Test requirements:** CGP required for full-time applicants for placement. **Additional information:** Admission to the college does not guarantee admission to all courses or vocational education programs. Additional applications may be necessary.

1992 FRESHMAN CLASS PROFILE. 585 men and women enrolled. **Characteristics:** 99% from in state, 98% commute. Average age is 28.

FALL-TERM APPLICATIONS. No fee. No closing date; applicants notified on a rolling basis beginning on or about February 1; must reply by registration. Deferred admission available.

STUDENT LIFE. Housing: Dormitories (coed). Dormitory capacity for only 75 students. **Activities:** Student government, magazine, student newspaper, choral groups, drama, music ensembles, symphony orchestra.

ATHLETICS. Intramural: Archery, badminton, basketball, bowling, cross-country, sailing, softball, swimming, table tennis, tennis, volleyball.

STUDENT SERVICES. Career counseling, on-campus day care, personal counseling, veterans counselor, services/facilities for handicapped.

ANNUAL EXPENSES. Tuition and fees: $1,125, $3,300 additional for out-of-state students. **Room and board:** $3,600. **Books and supplies:** $600. **Other expenses:** $1,350.

FINANCIAL AID. 50% of freshmen, 40% of continuing students receive some form of aid. 90% of grants, all loans, 43% of jobs based on need. 300 enrolled freshmen were judged to have need, 290 were offered aid. Academic, music/drama, art, leadership scholarships available. **Aid applications:** No closing date; priority given to applications received by June 1;

applicants notified on a rolling basis beginning on or about July 1; must reply within 3 weeks.

ADDRESS/TELEPHONE. Steve Kelly, Registrar/Associate Dean of Instruction, Peninsula College, 1502 East Lauridsen Boulevard, Port Angeles, WA 98362. (206) 452-9277 ext. 208. Fax: (206) 457-8100.

Pierce College
Tacoma, Washington — CB code: 4103

2-year public community college, coed. Founded in 1967. **Accreditation:** Regional. **Undergraduate enrollment:** 2,600 men, 2,610 women full time; 2,140 men, 1,990 women part time. **Faculty:** 500 total (150 full time), 43 with doctorates or other terminal degrees. **Location:** Suburban campus in small city; 10 miles from downtown. **Calendar:** Quarter, limited summer session. Extensive evening/early morning classes. **Microcomputers:** 300 located in libraries, classrooms, computer centers. **Additional facts:** Campus in Puyallup and education centers at Fort Lewis, McChord, McNeil Island, Tacoma pre-release, Cedar Creek, Western State Hospital and Rainier School.

DEGREES OFFERED. AA, AS. 1,204 associate degrees awarded in 1992.

UNDERGRADUATE MAJORS. Accounting, agribusiness, agricultural products and processing, business and management, business and office, business data processing and related programs, business data programming, computer and information sciences, criminal justice studies, dental hygiene, early childhood education, education of the mentally handicapped, electrical/electronics/communications engineering, electromechanical technology, electronic technology, engineering, fashion merchandising, fire control and safety technology, food production/management/services, law enforcement and corrections technologies, legal assistant/paralegal, legal secretary, liberal/general studies, medical secretary, mental health/human services, music business management, office supervision and management, parks and recreation management, real estate, recreation and community services technologies, recreation therapy, rehabilitation counseling/services, secretarial and related programs, veterinarian's assistant, visual and performing arts, word processing.

ACADEMIC PROGRAMS. 2-year transfer program, cooperative education, double major, dual enrollment of high school students, honors program, independent study, internships, student-designed major, telecourses, weekend college, cross-registration. **Remedial services:** Learning center, preadmission summer program, reduced course load, remedial instruction, special counselor, tutoring. **ROTC:** Army. **Placement/credit:** AP, CLEP General and Subject, institutional tests.

ACADEMIC REQUIREMENTS. Freshmen must earn minimum GPA of 2.0 to continue in good standing. Students must declare major on enrollment. **Graduation requirements:** 90 hours for associate (60 in major). Most students required to take courses in English, humanities, mathematics, biological/physical sciences, social sciences.

FRESHMAN ADMISSIONS. Selection criteria: Open admissions. Selective admissions to dental hygiene and veterinary technology programs based on course work, high school GPA related work experience, and interviews. Running start students must test at college level prior to admission. Algebra, biology, and chemistry required of dental hygiene and veterinary technology applicants.

1992 FRESHMAN CLASS PROFILE. 1,870 men, 1,490 women enrolled. **Characteristics:** 98% from in state, 100% commute, 26% have minority backgrounds, 1% are foreign students. Average age is 26.

FALL-TERM APPLICATIONS. No fee. Application fee of $25 for dental hygiene and veterinary programs. No closing date; applicants notified on a rolling basis; must reply by registration. Interview required for dental hygiene, electronics, veterinary technology, running start applicants. Portfolio recommended for advanced art applicants. Deferred and early admission available. March 1 closing date for veterinary technology applications, February 1 for dental hygiene. High school students admitted early through Running Start Program. Must test at college level prior to admission.

STUDENT LIFE. Housing: 1500 off-campus apartment units nearby. **Activities:** Student government, student newspaper, posters, flyers, choral groups, concert band, drama, jazz band, music ensembles, musical theater, ethnic and foreign student associations, religious organizations, special interest clubs, Phi Theta Kappa, Phi Beta Lambda, and Barrier Breakers (handicapped students).

ATHLETICS. Intercollegiate: Baseball M, basketball, soccer M, softball W, volleyball W. **Intramural:** Tennis.

STUDENT SERVICES. Aptitude testing, career counseling, employment service for undergraduates, freshman orientation, health services, personal counseling, placement service for graduates, veterans counselor, special adviser for minority students, physical therapy facilities, services/facilities for handicapped.

ANNUAL EXPENSES. Tuition and fees: $1,156, $3,300 additional for out-of-state students. **Books and supplies:** $600. **Other expenses:** $660.

FINANCIAL AID. 18% of freshmen, 17% of continuing students receive some form of aid. 93% of grants, 49% of loans, all jobs based on need. 515 enrolled freshmen were judged to have need, all were offered aid. Academic, athletic scholarships available. **Aid applications:** No closing date; priority given to applications received by April 1; applicants notified on a rolling basis beginning on or about May 15; must reply within 2 weeks.

ADDRESS/TELEPHONE. Tana Hasart, Registrar, Pierce College, 9401 Farwest Drive Southwest, Tacoma, WA 98498-1999. (206) 964-6501. Fax: (206) 964-6764.

Puget Sound Christian College
Edmonds, Washington — CB code: 4618

Admissions:	84% of applicants accepted
Based on:	••• Recommendations, religious affiliation/commitment, school record
	•• Essay
	• Test scores
Completion:	92% of freshmen end year in good standing
	23% graduate, 18% of these enter graduate study

4-year private Bible college, coed, affiliated with Christian Church. Founded in 1950. **Undergraduate enrollment:** 41 men, 17 women full time; 9 men, 9 women part time. **Faculty:** 15 total (6 full time), 4 with doctorates or other terminal degrees. **Location:** Suburban campus in large town; 15 miles from Seattle. **Calendar:** Quarter, limited summer session. **Additional facts:** College educates men and women for church ministries.

DEGREES OFFERED. AA, BA. 9 bachelor's degrees awarded. 100% in philosophy, religion, theology.

UNDERGRADUATE MAJORS. Associate: Office supervision and management. **Bachelor's:** Bible studies, missionary studies, religious education, religious music, theological studies.

ACADEMIC PROGRAMS. Double major, internships. **Remedial services:** Reduced course load, remedial instruction, tutoring.

ACADEMIC REQUIREMENTS. Freshmen must earn minimum GPA of 1.75 to continue in good standing. 50% of freshmen return for sophomore year. Students must declare major by end of second year. **Graduation requirements:** 96 hours for associate (28 in major), 192 hours for bachelor's (64 in major). Most students required to take courses in English, foreign languages, history, humanities, philosophy/religion, biological/physical sciences, social sciences. **Additional information:** 60 credit hours of Bible required for bachelor's degree, 20 credit hours for associate's degree.

FRESHMAN ADMISSIONS. Selection criteria: 3 recommendations, 2.0 high school GPA, and test scores considered. Applicants who do not meet these standards will be evaluated individually. **High school preparation:** 15 units recommended. Recommended units include English 3, foreign language 2, mathematics 3, social science 1 and science 3. One speech, 3 history and/or literature also recommended. **Test requirements:** SAT or ACT for counseling; score report by September 15. Washington Pre-College Test may be submitted in place of SAT or ACT.

1992 FRESHMAN CLASS PROFILE. 16 men applied, 14 accepted, 11 enrolled; 15 women applied, 12 accepted, 8 enrolled. 31% had high school GPA of 3.0 or higher, 56% between 2.0 and 2.99. **Academic background:** Mid 50% of enrolled freshmen had SAT-V between 330-530, SAT-M between 360-540; ACT composite between 20-21. 66% submitted SAT scores, 16% submitted ACT scores. **Characteristics:** 58% from in state, 68% live in college housing, 21% have minority backgrounds, 5% are foreign students. Average age is 21.

FALL-TERM APPLICATIONS. $25 fee. Closing date September 15; priority given to applications received by May 1; applicants notified on a rolling basis. Essay required. Deferred and early admission available.

STUDENT LIFE. Housing: Apartment housing available. **Activities:** Student government, yearbook, choral groups, music ensembles, pep band. **Additional information:** Religious observance required.

ATHLETICS. Intercollegiate: Basketball. **Intramural:** Baseball, basketball, table tennis, tennis, volleyball.

STUDENT SERVICES. Career counseling, employment service for undergraduates, freshman orientation, health services, personal counseling, veterans counselor, services/facilities for handicapped.

ANNUAL EXPENSES. Tuition and fees (projected): $4,725. **Room and board:** $3,225. **Books and supplies:** $600. **Other expenses:** $1,305.

FINANCIAL AID. 93% of freshmen, 93% of continuing students receive some form of aid. 46% of grants, 82% of loans, 48% of jobs based on need. 18 enrolled freshmen were judged to have need, all were offered aid. Academic, music/drama, leadership, religious affiliation scholarships available. **Aid applications:** No closing date; priority given to applications received by May 1; applicants notified on a rolling basis beginning on or about May 15; must reply within 2 weeks.

ADDRESS/TELEPHONE. Delores A. Scarbrough, Admissions Officer, Puget Sound Christian College, 410 Fourth Avenue North, Edmonds, WA 98020-3171. (206) 775-8686.

Renton Technical College
Renton, Washington CB code: 0790

2-year public technical college, coed. **Accreditation:** Regional. **Undergraduate enrollment:** 756 men, 814 women full time; 2,716 men, 1,646 women part time. **Location:** Suburban campus in large town; 10 miles from Seattle. **Calendar:** Quarter. Saturday and extensive evening/early morning classes.

DEGREES OFFERED. AAS.

UNDERGRADUATE MAJORS. Accounting, air conditioning/heating/refrigeration mechanics, air conditioning/heating/refrigeration technology, automotive mechanics, business administration and management, business and office, business data programming, civil engineering, computer and information sciences, computer engineering, computer programming, computer servicing technology, electrical/electronics/communications engineering, food management, food production/management/services, machine tool operation/machine shop, music business management, office supervision and management, secretarial and related programs.

ACADEMIC PROGRAMS. Dual enrollment of high school students. **Remedial services:** Learning center, remedial instruction, tutoring.

ACADEMIC REQUIREMENTS. No policy requiring minimum GPA; records of students having academic difficulty are reviewed individually. Students must declare major on enrollment. **Graduation requirements:** 110 hours for associate (90 in major). Most students required to take courses in English, humanities, mathematics, social sciences.

FRESHMAN ADMISSIONS. Selection criteria: Open admissions.

1992 FRESHMAN CLASS PROFILE. Characteristics: 100% commute.

FALL-TERM APPLICATIONS. No fee. No closing date; applicants notified on a rolling basis.

ANNUAL EXPENSES. Tuition and fees (1992-93):

ADDRESS/TELEPHONE. Michael Crehan, College Admissions, Renton Technical College, 3000 Northeast 4th Street, Renton, WA 98056-4195. (206) 235-5840. Fax: (206) 235-7832.

St. Martin's College
Lacey, Washington CB code: 4674

Admissions:	89% of applicants accepted
Based on:	••• School record, test scores
	•• Activities, essay, recommendations
	• Interview, special talents
Completion:	84% of freshmen end year in good standing
	14% enter graduate study

4-year private college of arts and sciences, coed, affiliated with Roman Catholic Church. Founded in 1895. **Accreditation:** Regional. **Undergraduate enrollment:** 183 men, 289 women full time; 123 men, 291 women part time. **Graduate enrollment:** 110 men, 95 women part time. **Faculty:** 53 total (37 full time), 17 with doctorates or other terminal degrees. **Location:** Suburban campus in large town; 3 miles from Olympia, 60 miles from Seattle. **Calendar:** Semester, extensive summer session. **Microcomputers:** Located in computer centers. **Special facilities:** Educational computer software library, computerized retrieval systems, substantial collections in theology, children's literature, Northwest history.

DEGREES OFFERED. AA, AS, BA, BS, MA, MBA, MEd. 9 associate degrees awarded in 1992. 244 bachelor's degrees awarded. 28% in business and management, 5% computer sciences, 16% education, 7% engineering, 6% health sciences, 13% psychology, 14% social sciences. Graduate degrees offered in 12 major fields of study.

UNDERGRADUATE MAJORS. Associate: Aviation management, liberal/general studies. **Bachelor's:** Accounting, biological and physical sciences, biology, business administration and management, business and management, business economics, chemistry, civil engineering, community services, computer and information sciences, criminal justice studies, economics, education, elementary education, English, finance, history, humanities, humanities and social sciences, information sciences and systems, international business management, junior high education, liberal/general studies, marketing and distribution, mathematics, mechanical engineering, nursing, political science and government, psychology, religion, secondary education, special education.

ACADEMIC PROGRAMS. Accelerated program, double major, dual enrollment of high school students, education specialist degree, honors program, internships, teacher preparation, Washington semester. **Remedial services:** Learning center, reduced course load, remedial instruction, special counselor, tutoring, general studies for probationary students. **ROTC:** Army. **Placement/credit:** AP, CLEP General and Subject, institutional tests; 30 credit hours maximum for associate degree; 60 credit hours maximum for bachelor's degree.

ACADEMIC REQUIREMENTS. Freshmen must earn minimum GPA of 2.0 to continue in good standing. 70% of freshmen return for sophomore year. Students must declare major by end of second year. **Graduation requirements:** 64 hours for associate, 128 hours for bachelor's. Most students required to take courses in arts/fine arts, English, foreign languages, history, humanities, mathematics, philosophy/religion, biological/physical sciences, social sciences. **Postgraduate studies:** 80% from 2-year programs enter 4-year programs. 2% enter law school, 2% enter medical school, 2% enter MBA programs, 8% enter other graduate study.

FRESHMAN ADMISSIONS. Selection criteria: School achievement record most important. Test scores important. 2.5 GPA required for regular admittance. **High school preparation:** 17 units required; 20 recommended. Required and recommended units include English 4, mathematics 2-3, social science 2 and science 2. Foreign language 2 recommended. **Test requirements:** SAT or ACT; score report by August 1.

1992 FRESHMAN CLASS PROFILE. 67 men applied, 60 accepted, 40 enrolled; 95 women applied, 84 accepted, 49 enrolled. 65% had high school GPA of 3.0 or higher, 35% between 2.0 and 2.99. **Academic background:** Mid 50% of enrolled freshmen had SAT-V between 450-520, SAT-M between 410-490; ACT composite between 18-22. 90% submitted SAT scores, 10% submitted ACT scores. **Characteristics:** 72% from in state, 70% live in college housing, 8% have minority backgrounds, 3% are foreign students, 3% join fraternities/sororities. Average age is 18.

FALL-TERM APPLICATIONS. $25 fee, may be waived for applicants with need. Closing date August 1; priority given to applications received by March 1; applicants notified on a rolling basis beginning on or about December 1; must reply by May 1. Essay required. Interview recommended for academically weak applicants. CRDA. Deferred admission available.

STUDENT LIFE. Housing: Dormitories (coed). **Activities:** Student government, student newspaper, yearbook, drama, fraternities, sororities, campus ministry, international student club, Circle-K, Hawaiian club.

ATHLETICS. NAIA. **Intercollegiate:** Basketball, golf, softball W, volleyball W. **Intramural:** Basketball, bowling, rowing (crew), softball, table tennis, tennis, volleyball.

STUDENT SERVICES. Aptitude testing, career counseling, employment service for undergraduates, freshman orientation, personal counseling, placement service for graduates, special adviser for adult students, veterans counselor, services/facilities for handicapped.

ANNUAL EXPENSES. Tuition and fees: $10,870. **Room and board:** $4,060. **Books and supplies:** $654. **Other expenses:** $1,230.

FINANCIAL AID. 66% of freshmen, 65% of continuing students receive some form of aid. 76% of grants, 95% of loans, 82% of jobs based on need. 31 enrolled freshmen were judged to have need, all were offered aid. Academic, athletic, state/district residency, leadership, alumni affiliation, minority scholarships available. **Aid applications:** No closing date; priority given to applications received by March 1; applicants notified on a rolling basis beginning on or about April 1; must reply within 2 weeks.

ADDRESS/TELEPHONE. Rob Kvidt, Director of Admissions, St. Martin's College, 5300 Pacific Ave. SE, Lacey, WA 98503-1297. (206) 438-4311. (800) 368-8803. Fax: (206) 459-4124.

Seattle Central Community College
Seattle, Washington CB code: 4741

2-year public community college, coed. Founded in 1966. **Accreditation:** Regional. **Undergraduate enrollment:** 2,110 men, 2,808 women full time; 1,752 men, 3,047 women part time. **Faculty:** 388 total (139 full time). **Location:** Urban campus in very large city. **Calendar:** Quarter, limited summer session. Extensive evening/early morning classes. **Microcomputers:** 14 located in libraries, classrooms, computer centers. **Special facilities:** Art gallery.

DEGREES OFFERED. AA, AS, AAS. 380 associate degrees awarded in 1992.

UNDERGRADUATE MAJORS. Accounting, American literature, apparel and accessories marketing, biology, botany, business administration and management, business and office, business data processing and related programs, carpentry, chemical manufacturing technology, chemistry, commercial art, communications, computer and information sciences, creative writing, data processing, drafting, drafting and design technology, education of the deaf and hearing impaired, engineering, English, English literature, fashion design, fine arts, food production/management/services, foreign languages (multiple emphasis), French, geography, German, graphic and printing production, graphic arts technology, health sciences, humanities, humanities and social sciences, individual and family development, industrial technology, interpreter for the deaf, Japanese, Latin, liberal/general studies, library science, marine maintenance, marketing and distribution, mathematics, medieval studies, music, nursing, ophthalmic services, personal services, philosophy, photographic technology, photography, physical sciences, physics, psychology, recreation and community services technologies, rehabilitation counseling/services, respiratory therapy, respiratory therapy technology, secretarial and related programs, social sciences, sociology, Spanish, speech, surgical technology, telecommunications, textiles and clothing, video, visual and performing arts.

ACADEMIC PROGRAMS. 2-year transfer program, cooperative education, dual enrollment of high school students, independent study, internships, study abroad, telecourses. **Remedial services:** Learning center, remedial instruction, special counselor, tutoring. **Placement/credit:** CLEP Subject, institutional tests.

ACADEMIC REQUIREMENTS. No policy requiring minimum GPA; records of students having academic difficulty are reviewed individually. Students must declare major on application. **Graduation requirements:** 90 hours for associate. Most students required to take courses in English, humanities, mathematics, social sciences.

FRESHMAN ADMISSIONS. Selection criteria: Open admissions. Selective admissions to health sciences and vocational programs.

1992 FRESHMAN CLASS PROFILE. 2,130 men and women enrolled. **Characteristics:** 76% from in state, 100% commute, 31% have minority backgrounds, 2% are foreign students.

FALL-TERM APPLICATIONS. No fee. No closing date; applicants notified on a rolling basis; must reply by registration. Portfolio required for art, photography applicants. Interview recommended. Audition recommended for music applicants. Essay recommended. Deferred and early admission available.

STUDENT LIFE. Activities: Student government, student newspaper, choral groups, dance, drama, chamber music, ethnic minority student organizations.

ATHLETICS. Intramural: Baseball, basketball, soccer, volleyball.

STUDENT SERVICES. Aptitude testing, career counseling, employment service for undergraduates, freshman orientation, on-campus day care, personal counseling, veterans counselor, services/facilities for handicapped.

ANNUAL EXPENSES. Tuition and fees: $1,125, $3,300 additional for out-of-state students. **Books and supplies:** $594. **Other expenses:** $668.

FINANCIAL AID. 41% of freshmen receive some form of aid. 98% of grants, all loans, all jobs based on need. Academic, leadership, minority scholarships available. **Aid applications:** Closing date August 15; priority given to applications received by May 15; applicants notified on a rolling basis beginning on or about July 1; must reply within 2 weeks.

ADDRESS/TELEPHONE. Loris A. Blue, Director of Admissions, Seattle Central Community College, 1701 Broadway, Seattle, WA 98122. (206) 587-5450. Fax: (206) 587-3878.

Seattle Pacific University

Seattle, Washington CB code: 4694

Admissions: 89% of applicants accepted
Based on: •• Recommendations, religious affiliation/commitment, school record, test scores
• Activities, essay, interview, special talents
Completion: 88% of freshmen end year in good standing
35% graduate

4-year private university, coed, affiliated with Free Methodist Church of North America. Founded in 1891. **Accreditation:** Regional. **Undergraduate enrollment:** 626 men, 1,226 women full time; 149 men, 216 women part time. **Graduate enrollment:** 63 men, 130 women full time; 198 men, 346 women part time. **Faculty:** 176 total (164 full time), 119 with doctorates or other terminal degrees. **Location:** Urban campus in very large city; 3 miles from downtown. **Calendar:** Quarter, limited summer session. **Microcomputers:** 102 located in libraries, computer centers, campus-wide network. **Special facilities:** Art gallery, 2 island campuses used for biological studies.

DEGREES OFFERED. BA, BS, MA, MS, MBA, MEd. 449 bachelor's degrees awarded in 1992. 15% in business and management, 7% communications, 6% computer sciences, 13% teacher education, 9% health sciences, 5% letters/literature, 5% life sciences, 5% multi/interdisciplinary studies, 5% philosophy, religion, theology, 6% psychology, 9% social sciences. Graduate degrees offered in 12 major fields of study.

UNDERGRADUATE MAJORS. Accounting, anthropology, art education, Bible studies, biology, business administration and management, business economics, chemistry, Christian pedagogy, communications, computer and information sciences, cross-cultural ministries, dramatic arts, electrical/electronics/communications engineering, engineering science, English, English education, environmental science, European studies, exercise science, family/consumer resource management, fine arts, food science and nutrition, history, home economics education, interior design, leisure and recreation, liberal/general studies, linguistics, mathematics, mathematics education, mathematics-economics, music, music education, music performance, music theory and composition, nursing, philosophy, physical education, physics, political science and government, psychology, religion, religious education, science education, social science education, social work, sociology, special education, textiles and clothing, theological studies, visual and performing arts.

ACADEMIC PROGRAMS. Cooperative education, double major, honors program, independent study, internships, student-designed major, study abroad, teacher preparation, telecourses, visiting/exchange student program, weekend college, Washington semester, cross-registration, liaison program with Fashion Institute of Technology (NY) and Johnson & Wales University (RI). **Remedial services:** Learning center, reduced course load, remedial instruction, special counselor, tutoring. **ROTC:** Air Force, Army, Naval. **Placement/credit:** AP, CLEP General and Subject, IB, institutional tests; 45 credit hours maximum for bachelor's degree.

ACADEMIC REQUIREMENTS. Freshmen must earn minimum GPA of 2.0 to continue in good standing. 72% of freshmen return for sophomore year. Students must declare major by end of second year. **Graduation requirements:** 180 hours for bachelor's (90 in major). Most students required to take courses in arts/fine arts, English, foreign languages, history, humanities, mathematics, philosophy/religion, biological/physical sciences, social sciences.

FRESHMAN ADMISSIONS. Selection criteria: School grades, recommendations, test scores, leadership potential, church and community activities, special talents, personal traits. Recommended units include English 4, foreign language 3, mathematics 3, social science 2 and science 2. College-preparatory program recommended. **Test requirements:** SAT or ACT (SAT preferred); score report by September 1.

1992 FRESHMAN CLASS PROFILE. 359 men applied, 308 accepted, 130 enrolled; 638 women applied, 578 accepted, 258 enrolled. 76% had high school GPA of 3.0 or higher, 23% between 2.0 and 2.99. **Academic background:** Mid 50% of enrolled freshmen had SAT-V between 400-530, SAT-M between 430-580. 95% submitted SAT scores. **Characteristics:** 68% from in state, 92% live in college housing, 13% have minority backgrounds, 1% are foreign students. Average age is 19.

FALL-TERM APPLICATIONS. $35 fee, may be waived for applicants with need. Closing date September 1; priority given to applications received by February 1; applicants notified on a rolling basis; must reply by May 1 or within 4 weeks if notified thereafter. Audition required for music, and performing arts scholarship applicants. Portfolio required for fine arts scholarship applicants. Essay required. Interview recommended. CRDA. Deferred and early admission available. EDP-F.

STUDENT LIFE. Housing: Dormitories (women, coed); apartment housing available. All full-time students 22 years of age or younger required to live in residence hall on campus unless married or living with parents in area. **Activities:** Student government, film, magazine, student newspaper, yearbook, choral groups, concert band, drama, jazz band, music ensembles, musical theater, opera, pep band, symphony orchestra, multiethnic student affairs, international student affairs, student mission teams. **Additional information:** Religious observance required.

ATHLETICS. NAIA, NCAA. **Intercollegiate:** Basketball, cross-country, gymnastics W, rowing (crew), soccer M, tennis, track and field, volleyball W. **Intramural:** Badminton, basketball, bowling, cross-country, football, golf, racquetball, skiing, soccer, softball, swimming, table tennis, tennis, track and field, volleyball, wrestling M.

STUDENT SERVICES. Aptitude testing, career counseling, employment service for undergraduates, freshman orientation, health services, personal counseling, placement service for graduates, special adviser for adult students, veterans counselor, campus ministries, services/facilities for handicapped.

ANNUAL EXPENSES. Tuition and fees (1992-93): $11,301. **Room and board:** $4,263. **Books and supplies:** $525. **Other expenses:** $1,100.

FINANCIAL AID. 67% of continuing students receive some form of aid. 76% of grants, 94% of loans, 63% of jobs based on need. 335 enrolled freshmen were judged to have need, all were offered aid. Academic, music/drama, art, athletic, state/district residency, leadership, alumni affiliation, religious affiliation, minority scholarships available. **Aid applications:** No closing date; priority given to applications received by March 1; applicants notified on a rolling basis beginning on or about March 15; must reply by May 1 or within 2 weeks if notified thereafter.

ADDRESS/TELEPHONE. Marj Johnson, VP Enrollment Services, Seattle Pacific University, 3307 Third Avenue West, Seattle, WA 98119-1997. (206) 281-2021. (800) 366-3344. Fax: (206) 281-2500.

Seattle University

Seattle, Washington CB code: 4695

Admissions: 76% of applicants accepted
Based on: ••• School record
•• Activities, interview, recommendations, test scores
• Essay
Completion: 90% of freshmen end year in good standing
56% graduate, 23% of these enter graduate study

4-year private university, coed, affiliated with Roman Catholic Church. Founded in 1891. **Accreditation:** Regional. **Undergraduate enrollment:** 1,079 men, 1,329 women full time; 283 men, 304 women part time. **Graduate enrollment:** 123 men, 196 women full time; 712 men, 640 women part time. **Faculty:** 451 total (238 full time), 163 with doctorates or other terminal degrees. **Location:** Urban campus in very large city. **Calendar:** Quarter, extensive summer session. Saturday and extensive evening/early morning classes. **Microcomputers:** 250 located in libraries, classrooms, computer centers. **Special facilities:** University Design Center (where engineering students work with major companies in the area, one of only 2 such facilities in United States) and astronomy observatory. **Additional facts:** Affiliated with Jesuit order. Institute of Theological Studies has 7 programs. Courses also offered at Bellevue Campus. Extension evening college program offered.

DEGREES OFFERED. BA, BS, BFA, MA, MS, MBA, MEd, EdD, M.Div. 758 bachelor's degrees awarded in 1992. 29% in business and management, 14% engineering, 7% health sciences, 20% multi/interdisciplinary studies, 6% psychology. Graduate degrees offered in 22 major fields of study.

UNDERGRADUATE MAJORS. Accounting, allied health, biochemistry, biological and physical sciences, biology, business administration and management, business and management, business economics, chemistry, civil engineering, communications, comparative literature, computer and information sciences, computer programming, criminal justice studies, cytotechnology, dramatic arts, economics, electrical/electronics/communications engineering, English, English literature, environmental health engineering, finance, fine arts, French, German, health care administration, history, humanities, humanities and social sciences, international business management, international studies, Japanese, journalism, Latin, marine biology, marketing and distribution, marketing management, mathematics, mechanical engineering, medical laboratory technologies, medical records technology, military science (Army), nursing, pastoral studies, philosophy, physical sciences, physics, political science and government, psychology, public administration, religion, social sciences, sociology, Spanish, ultrasound technology, visual and performing arts, vocational rehabilitation.

ACADEMIC PROGRAMS. Accelerated program, double major, dual enrollment of high school students, education specialist degree, honors program, independent study, internships, semester at sea, student-designed major, study abroad, teacher preparation, visiting/exchange student program; combined bachelor's/graduate program in business administration. **Remedial services:** Learning center, preadmission summer program, reduced course load, remedial instruction, special counselor, tutoring. **ROTC:** Air Force, Army, Naval. **Placement/credit:** AP, CLEP Subject, IB, institutional tests; 45 credit hours maximum for bachelor's degree.

ACADEMIC REQUIREMENTS. Freshmen must earn minimum GPA of 2.0 to continue in good standing. 82% of freshmen return for sophomore year. Students must declare major by end of second year. **Graduation requirements:** 180 hours for bachelor's (65 in major). Most students required to take courses in arts/fine arts, computer science, English, foreign languages, history, humanities, mathematics, philosophy/religion, biological/physical sciences, social sciences.

FRESHMAN ADMISSIONS. Selection criteria: 2.5 GPA, class rank, and test scores most important; school and community activities, recommendations, and optional interview considered. Minorities and children of alumni given special consideration. **High school preparation:** 16 units required; 18 recommended. Required and recommended units include English 3-4, mathematics 2, physical science 1 and social science 1. Biological science 1 and foreign language 3 recommended. One algebra, 1 geometry, 1 laboratory science, 1 history also required. One additional mathematics and 1 laboratory science required of science/engineering and nursing applicants. **Test requirements:** SAT or ACT; score report by September 1.

1992 FRESHMAN CLASS PROFILE. 710 men applied, 544 accepted, 210 enrolled; 803 women applied, 611 accepted, 244 enrolled. 84% had high school GPA of 3.0 or higher, 16% between 2.0 and 2.99. 25% were in top tenth and 55% were in top quarter of graduating class. **Academic background:** Mid 50% of enrolled freshmen had SAT-V between 450-500, SAT-M between 480-540; ACT composite between 18-27. 85% submitted SAT scores, 20% submitted ACT scores. **Characteristics:** 58% from in state, 87% live in college housing, 38% have minority backgrounds, 8% are foreign students. Average age is 18.

FALL-TERM APPLICATIONS. $35 fee, may be waived for applicants with need. Closing date August 1; priority given to applications received by February 1; applicants notified on a rolling basis beginning on or about December 1; must reply by May 1 or within 4 weeks if notified thereafter. Interview recommended for marginal student applicants. Essay recommended. CRDA. Deferred and early admission available. EDP-F.

STUDENT LIFE. Housing: Dormitories (coed); handicapped housing available. **Activities:** Student government, film, magazine, student newspaper, yearbook, choral groups, dance, drama, jazz band, music ensembles, musical theater, pep band, symphony orchestra, chamber orchestra, 52 clubs, Alpha Sigma Nu, campus ministry, religious, honorary, and social service organizations.

ATHLETICS. NAIA, NCAA. **Intercollegiate:** Basketball, cross-country, rowing (crew), sailing, skiing, soccer, tennis, volleyball W. **Intramural:** Badminton, basketball, cross-country, fencing, field hockey, golf, handball, horseback riding, racquetball, rifle, rowing (crew), sailing, skiing, skin diving, soccer, softball, squash, swimming, table tennis, tennis, volleyball, water polo.

STUDENT SERVICES. Aptitude testing, career counseling, employment service for undergraduates, freshman orientation, health services, on-campus day care, personal counseling, placement service for graduates, special adviser for adult students, veterans counselor, services/facilities for handicapped.

ANNUAL EXPENSES. Tuition and fees: $12,150. Graduate per credit hour varies by program, education $270, business $350. **Room and board:** $4,680. **Books and supplies:** $654. **Other expenses:** $1,368.

FINANCIAL AID. 72% of freshmen, 60% of continuing students receive some form of aid. 63% of grants, 81% of loans, all jobs based on need. 290 enrolled freshmen were judged to have need, all were offered aid. Academic, music/drama, art, athletic, leadership, alumni affiliation, minority scholarships available. **Aid applications:** No closing date; priority given to applications received by March 1; applicants notified on a rolling basis beginning on or about February 15; must reply by May 1 or within 4 weeks if notified thereafter.

ADDRESS/TELEPHONE. Lee Gerig, Dean of Admission, Seattle University, 1200 East Columbia, Seattle, WA 98122. (206) 296-5900. (800) 426-7123. Fax: (206) 296-5656.

Shoreline Community College
Seattle, Washington — CB code: 4738

2-year public community college, coed. Founded in 1963. **Accreditation:** Regional. **Undergraduate enrollment:** 8,176 men and women. **Faculty:** 288 total (153 full time), 29 with doctorates or other terminal degrees. **Location:** Suburban campus in very large city; 10 miles from downtown. **Calendar:** Quarter, limited summer session. Extensive evening/early morning classes. **Microcomputers:** 270 located in libraries, computer centers. **Additional facts:** Courses available at Bothell campus.

DEGREES OFFERED. AA, AS. 751 associate degrees awarded in 1992. 15% in business and management, 5% engineering technologies, 8% health sciences, 55% multi/interdisciplinary studies, 10% trade and industry.

UNDERGRADUATE MAJORS. Accounting, automotive mechanics, automotive technology, biological laboratory technology, business administration and management, business and management, business and office, business data processing and related programs, chemical manufacturing technology, child development/care/guidance, civil technology, clinical laboratory science, clothing and textiles management/production/services, computer and information sciences, contract management and procurement/purchasing, counseling psychology, criminal justice studies, criminal justice technology, dental hygiene, dietetic aide/assistant, drafting, drafting and design technology, engineering, engineering and engineering-related technologies, environmental science, fashion design, fashion merchandising, food management, graphic and printing production, graphic arts technology, graphic design, hazardous materials management, histology, individual and family development, industrial technology, international business management, law enforcement and corrections, law enforcement and corrections technologies, legal secretary, liberal/general studies, machine tool operation/machine shop, management information systems, manufacturing technology, marine biology, marketing and distribution, mechanical design technology, medical laboratory technologies, medical records administration, medical records technology, medical secretary, music performance, nursing, oceanographic technologies, photography, precision metal work, retailing, secretarial and related programs, special education, teacher aide, video, word processing.

ACADEMIC PROGRAMS. 2-year transfer program, cooperative education, dual enrollment of high school students, independent study, internships, study abroad, telecourses, cross-registration. **Remedial services:** Learning center, remedial instruction, special counselor, tutoring. **Placement/credit:** AP, CLEP Subject.

ACADEMIC REQUIREMENTS. Freshmen must earn minimum GPA of 1.75 to continue in good standing. **Graduation requirements:** 93 hours for associate. Most students required to take courses in English, humanities, mathematics, biological/physical sciences, social sciences. **Additional information:** First 2 years of predentistry, premedicine, prepharmacy programs transferable to 4-year college.

FRESHMAN ADMISSIONS. Selection criteria: Open admissions. **Test requirements:** ASSET used for placement.

1992 FRESHMAN CLASS PROFILE. 800 men and women enrolled. **Characteristics:** 97% from in state, 100% commute, 9% have minority backgrounds, 2% are foreign students.

FALL-TERM APPLICATIONS. $10 fee. No closing date; applicants notified on a rolling basis beginning on or about February 1. CRDA. Early admission available.

STUDENT LIFE. Housing: Off-campus housing available nearby. **Activities:** Student government, magazine, student newspaper, choral groups, concert band, drama, jazz band, music ensembles, musical theater, opera, international club, Black Student Union,Arts & Entertainment Board, women's club, Cambodian Club, Vietnamese Club.

ATHLETICS. NJCAA. **Intercollegiate:** Baseball M, basketball, soccer M, softball W, tennis, volleyball W. **Intramural:** Archery, badminton, baseball M, basketball, bowling, cross-country, fencing, golf, handball, racquetball, soccer, softball, tennis, volleyball.

STUDENT SERVICES. Aptitude testing, career counseling, employment service for undergraduates, freshman orientation, on-campus day care, personal counseling, placement service for graduates, special adviser for adult students, veterans counselor, services/facilities for handicapped.

ANNUAL EXPENSES. Tuition and fees: $1,125, $3,300 additional for out-of-state students. **Books and supplies:** $654. **Other expenses:** $690.

FINANCIAL AID. 27% of continuing students receive some form of aid. All grants, 95% of loans, all jobs based on need. Academic, athletic scholarships available. **Aid applications:** No closing date; priority given to applications received by April 1; applicants notified on a rolling basis beginning on or about July 1; must reply within 3 weeks. **Additional information:** Tuition and/or fee waiver for students with need on space-available basis.

ADDRESS/TELEPHONE. William S. Ponder, Registrar/Director of Admissions, Shoreline Community College, 16101 Greenwood Avenue North, Seattle, WA 98133. (206) 546-4581. Fax: (206) 546-4599.

Skagit Valley College
Mount Vernon, Washington — CB code: 4699

2-year public community college, coed. Founded in 1926. **Accreditation:** Regional. **Undergraduate enrollment:** 1,309 men, 1,440 women full time; 1,318 men, 2,491 women part time. **Faculty:** 319 total (107 full time), 11 with doctorates or other terminal degrees. **Location:** Rural campus in large town; 60 miles from Seattle. **Calendar:** Quarter, limited summer session. Extensive evening/early morning classes. **Microcomputers:** 40 located in computer centers.

DEGREES OFFERED. AA. 474 associate degrees awarded in 1992. 9% in business/office and marketing/distribution, 5% engineering technologies, 71% multi/interdisciplinary studies, 6% trade and industry.

UNDERGRADUATE MAJORS. Accounting, agribusiness, agricultural business and management, agricultural sciences, automotive mechanics, automotive technology, biological and physical sciences, biology, botany, business and office, business data programming, chemistry, civil technology, communications, computer and information sciences, computer programming, computer servicing technology, computer technology, dairy, diesel engine mechanics, drafting, education, electronic technology, engineering, engineering and engineering-related technologies, engineering and other disciplines, English, fine arts, food production/management/services, graphic arts technology, home economics, hospitality and recreation marketing, humanities and social sciences, information sciences and systems, law enforcement and corrections technologies, liberal/general studies, marine maintenance, marketing and distribution, mathematics, mental health/human services, music, nursing, physical sciences, physics, practical nursing, psychology, robotics, science technologies, secretarial and related programs, small business management and ownership, social sciences, vehicle and equipment operation, visual and performing arts, zoology.

ACADEMIC PROGRAMS. 2-year transfer program, cooperative education, dual enrollment of high school students, external degree, honors program, independent study, internships, study abroad, cross-registration. **Remedial services:** Learning center, preadmission summer program, reduced course load, remedial instruction, special counselor, tutoring. **Placement/credit:** AP, CLEP General and Subject, institutional tests. Maximum of 15 quarter hours of credit by examination may be counted toward degree in college transfer program, 45 in general studies program.

ACADEMIC REQUIREMENTS. Freshmen must earn minimum GPA of 2.0 to continue in good standing. 70% of freshmen return for sophomore year. Students must declare major by end of first year. **Graduation requirements:** 90 hours for associate. Most students required to take courses in arts/fine arts, English, history, humanities, mathematics, biological/physical sciences, social sciences.

FRESHMAN ADMISSIONS. Selection criteria: Open admissions. **Test requirements:** Require ACT/ASSET test for placement and counseling.

1992 FRESHMAN CLASS PROFILE. 1,500 men and women enrolled. **Characteristics:** 95% from in state, 100% commute, 9% have minority backgrounds, 1% are foreign students. Average age is 22.

FALL-TERM APPLICATIONS. No fee. No closing date; applicants notified on a rolling basis beginning on or about December 1. Deferred and early admission available.

STUDENT LIFE. Activities: Student government, radio, student newspaper, choral groups, concert band, drama, jazz band, music ensembles, musical theater, pep band, symphony orchestra.

ATHLETICS. Intercollegiate: Baseball M, basketball, cross-country, soccer M, softball W, tennis, volleyball W. **Intramural:** Baseball, basketball, softball, tennis, volleyball.

STUDENT SERVICES. Aptitude testing, career counseling, employment service for undergraduates, freshman orientation, health services, on-campus day care, personal counseling, placement service for graduates, special adviser for adult students, veterans counselor, services/facilities for handicapped.

ANNUAL EXPENSES. Tuition and fees: $1,125, $3,300 additional for out-of-state students. **Books and supplies:** $690. **Other expenses:** $690.

FINANCIAL AID. 31% of freshmen, 49% of continuing students receive some form of aid. All grants, 92% of loans, 60% of jobs based on need. 470 enrolled freshmen were judged to have need, 440 were offered aid. Academic, music/drama, art, athletic, leadership scholarships available. **Aid applications:** No closing date; priority given to applications received by April 1; applicants notified on a rolling basis beginning on or about July 1; must reply within 2 weeks.

ADDRESS/TELEPHONE. Robin Thompson, Director of Admission, Skagit Valley College, 2405 College Way, Mount Vernon, WA 98273. (206) 428-1112.

South Puget Sound Community College
Olympia, Washington — CB code: 4578

2-year public community college, coed. Founded in 1962. **Accreditation:** Regional. **Undergraduate enrollment:** 820 men, 1,135 women full time; 662 men, 1,519 women part time. **Faculty:** 214 total (72 full time), 20 with doctorates or other terminal degrees. **Location:** Suburban campus in large town; 60 miles from Seattle. **Calendar:** Quarter, limited summer session. Extensive evening/early morning classes. **Microcomputers:** 210 located in classrooms, computer centers.

DEGREES OFFERED. AA. 330 associate degrees awarded in 1992. 13% in business and management, 7% computer sciences, 7% engineering technologies, 9% health sciences, 53% multi/interdisciplinary studies.

UNDERGRADUATE MAJORS. Accounting, automotive mechanics, business administration and management, data processing, dental assistant, drafting and design technology, electronic technology, fire control and safety technology, fire protection, food management, horticulture, information sciences and systems, interpreter for the deaf, legal assistant/paralegal, legal secretary, liberal/general studies, medical assistant, medical secretary, nursing, office supervision and management, precision metal work, preengineering, secretarial and related programs, welding technology.

ACADEMIC PROGRAMS. 2-year transfer program, cooperative education, dual enrollment of high school students, independent study, internships, study abroad, telecourses, cross-registration. **Remedial services:** Learning center, remedial instruction, special counselor, tutoring. **Placement/credit:** AP, CLEP General and Subject, institutional tests; 45 credit hours maximum for associate degree.

ACADEMIC REQUIREMENTS. Freshmen must earn minimum GPA of 2.0 to continue in good standing. 76% of freshmen return for sophomore year. Students must declare major on enrollment. **Graduation requirements:** 90 hours for associate (78 in major). Most students required to take courses in English, humanities, mathematics, biological/physical sciences, social sciences.

FRESHMAN ADMISSIONS. Selection criteria: Open admissions. Selective admissions for health occupation and vocational programs. **Test requirements:** SAT or ACT for placement and counseling only; score report by September 1. ASSET may be substituted for SAT or ACT.

1992 FRESHMAN CLASS PROFILE. 1,980 men and women enrolled. **Characteristics:** 95% from in state, 100% commute. Average age is 20.

FALL-TERM APPLICATIONS. No fee. No closing date; priority given to applications received by June 30; applicants notified on a rolling basis beginning on or about January 1. Deferred admission available.

STUDENT LIFE. Activities: Student government, student newspaper.

ATHLETICS. Intercollegiate: Basketball, soccer M, softball W. **Intramural:** Baseball, basketball, handball, racquetball, softball, volleyball.

STUDENT SERVICES. Aptitude testing, career counseling, employment service for undergraduates, on-campus day care, personal counseling, placement service for graduates, veterans counselor, veterans affairs office, services for the blind, services/facilities for handicapped.

ANNUAL EXPENSES. Tuition and fees: $1,125, $3,300 additional for out-of-state students. **Books and supplies:** $654. **Other expenses:** $690.

FINANCIAL AID. 45% of freshmen, 50% of continuing students receive some form of aid. 99% of grants, 96% of loans, 26% of jobs based on need. Academic, athletic scholarships available. **Aid applications:** No closing date; priority given to applications received by May 15; applicants notified on a rolling basis beginning on or about July 10; must reply within 2 weeks.

ADDRESS/TELEPHONE. Tom Woodnutt, Director of Admissions and Records, South Puget Sound Community College, 2011 Mottman Road, Olympia, WA 98512-6218. (206) 754-7711 ext. 241. Fax: (206) 586-6054.

South Seattle Community College
Seattle, Washington — CB code: 4759

2-year public community college, coed. Founded in 1969. **Accreditation:** Regional. **Undergraduate enrollment:** 1,685 men, 1,043 women full time; 2,263 men, 2,058 women part time. **Faculty:** 292 total (70 full time). **Location:** Urban campus in very large city. **Calendar:** Quarter, limited summer session. Saturday classes. **Microcomputers:** 150 located in libraries, classrooms, computer centers. **Additional facts:** Extensive vocational education programs.

DEGREES OFFERED. AA, AAS. 331 associate degrees awarded in 1992.

UNDERGRADUATE MAJORS. Accounting, aeronautical technology, automotive mechanics, automotive technology, business and management, business and office, civil technology, computer and information sciences, computer programming, computer technology, diesel engine mechanics, drafting, drafting and design technology, engineering and engineering-related technologies, food management, food production/management/services, industrial technology, information sciences and systems, landscape architecture, legal secretary, liberal/general studies, machine tool operation/machine shop, office supervision and management, ornamental horticulture, power plant operation and maintenance, robotics, secretarial and related programs, trade and industrial education, welding technology, word processing.

ACADEMIC PROGRAMS. 2-year transfer program, dual enrollment of high school students, independent study, study abroad, telecourses, concurrent enrollment agreements with other colleges in vicinity. **Remedial services:** Learning center, remedial instruction, special counselor, tutoring. **Placement/credit:** AP, CLEP General and Subject, institutional tests; 45 credit hours maximum for associate degree. Credit awarded for CLEP applies only to Electives category of Associate of Arts degree.

ACADEMIC REQUIREMENTS. Freshmen must earn minimum GPA of 2.0 to continue in good standing. Students must declare major by end of first year. **Graduation requirements:** 90 hours for associate. Most students required to take courses in English, foreign languages, history, humanities, mathematics, philosophy/religion, biological/physical sciences, social sciences.

FRESHMAN ADMISSIONS. Selection criteria: Open admissions.

1992 FRESHMAN CLASS PROFILE. 795 men, 464 women enrolled. **Characteristics:** 94% from in state, 100% commute, 27% have minority backgrounds, 2% are foreign students.

FALL-TERM APPLICATIONS. No fee. No closing date; applicants notified on a rolling basis.

STUDENT LIFE. Activities: Student government, student newspaper, choral groups, drama, jazz band, Veteran Student's Club, Vietnamese Student Club.

STUDENT SERVICES. Aptitude testing, career counseling, freshman orientation, on-campus day care, personal counseling, placement service for graduates, veterans counselor, services/facilities for handicapped.

ANNUAL EXPENSES. Tuition and fees: $1,125, $3,300 additional for out-of-state students. **Books and supplies:** $600. **Other expenses:** $675.

FINANCIAL AID. 27% of freshmen, 31% of continuing students receive some form of aid. All grants, all jobs based on need. Academic, music/drama, alumni affiliation scholarships available. **Aid applications:** No closing date; priority given to applications received by May 15; applicants notified on a rolling basis beginning on or about August 1.

ADDRESS/TELEPHONE. Karen M. Foss, Dean of Student Development, South Seattle Community College, 6000 16th Avenue Southwest, Seattle, WA 98106. (206) 764-5300. Fax: (206) 764-5393.

Spokane Community College
Spokane, Washington — CB code: 4739

2-year public community college, coed. Founded in 1963. **Accreditation:** Regional. **Undergraduate enrollment:** 2,043 men, 2,362 women full time; 531 men, 982 women part time. **Faculty:** 400 total (214 full time), 6 with doctorates or other terminal degrees. **Location:** Urban campus in small city; 300 miles from Seattle. **Calendar:** Quarter, limited summer session. **Microcomputers:** 100 located in classrooms, computer centers.

DEGREES OFFERED. AA, AAS. 1,349 associate degrees awarded in 1992.

UNDERGRADUATE MAJORS. Accounting, aeronautical technology, agribusiness, agricultural business and management, agricultural mechanics, agricultural production, agricultural sciences, agronomy, air conditioning/heating/refrigeration mechanics, air conditioning/heating/refrigeration technology, aircraft mechanics, animal sciences, anthropology, architectural technologies, auto body and fender repair, auto parts merchandising, automotive machinist, automotive mechanics, automotive technology, aviation management, biological and physical sciences, biology, biomedical equipment technology, business administration and management, business and management, business and office, business computer/console/peripheral equipment operation, business data processing and related programs, business data programming, business economics, carpentry, chemistry, civil technology, commercial baking, computer integrated manufacturing, computer servicing technology, cosmetology, data processing, dental assistant, dental hygiene, diesel engine mechanics, dietetic aide/assistant, drafting, drafting and design technology, economics, education, electrical and electronics equipment repair, electrical installation, electrical technology, electrodiagnostic technologies, electronic technology, English, farm operations technology, fire control and safety technology, fitness management technology, fluid power technology, forestry and related sciences, graphic and printing production, greenhouse/nursery, history, horticultural science, horticulture, hotel/motel and restaurant management, humanities and social sciences, invasive cardiovascular technology, journalism, landscape/turf, law enforcement and corrections, law enforcement and corrections technologies, legal assistant/paralegal, legal secretary, liberal/general studies, machine tool operation/machine shop, marketing and distribution, marketing management, mathematics, mechanical design technology, medical records technology, medical secretary, noninvasive cardiovascular technology, nursing, ophthalmic services, ornamental horticulture, parks and recreation management, philosophy, physical education, physics, plant protection, plant sciences, political science and government, precision metal work, psychology, renewable natural resources, respiratory therapy, respiratory therapy technology, robotics, salesmanship, secretarial and related programs, small engine repair, social sciences, sociology, soil sciences, speech, surgical technology, survey and mapping technology, water and wastewater technology, water resources, wildlife management, woodworking, word processing.

ACADEMIC PROGRAMS. 2-year transfer program, cooperative education, independent study, internships, telecourses, cross-registration. **Remedial services:** Learning center, remedial instruction, special counselor, tutoring. **ROTC:** Army. **Placement/credit:** AP, institutional tests; 60 credit hours maximum for associate degree.

ACADEMIC REQUIREMENTS. Freshmen must earn minimum GPA of 2.0 to continue in good standing. 75% of freshmen return for sophomore year. Students must declare major by end of first year. **Graduation requirements:** 90 hours for associate. Most students required to take courses in English.

FRESHMAN ADMISSIONS. Selection criteria: Open admissions. Selective admissions to health sciences programs.

1992 FRESHMAN CLASS PROFILE. 2,130 men and women enrolled. **Characteristics:** 90% from in state, 100% commute, 5% have minority backgrounds. Average age is 26.

FALL-TERM APPLICATIONS. No fee. No closing date; applicants notified on a rolling basis beginning on or about January 1. Interview recommended for health science applicants.

STUDENT LIFE. Activities: Student government, student newspaper, drama.

ATHLETICS. NJCAA. **Intercollegiate:** Baseball M, basketball, cross-country, golf M, soccer, softball W, tennis, track and field, volleyball W. **Intramural:** Basketball, soccer, softball, table tennis, volleyball.

STUDENT SERVICES. Aptitude testing, career counseling, employment service for undergraduates, on-campus day care, personal counseling, placement service for graduates, veterans counselor, Single Parent Counseling, services/facilities for handicapped.

ANNUAL EXPENSES. Tuition and fees: $1,125, $3,300 additional for out-of-state students. **Books and supplies:** $654. **Other expenses:** $510.

FINANCIAL AID. 70% of freshmen, 57% of continuing students receive some form of aid. 97% of grants, 97% of loans, 88% of jobs based on need. Athletic scholarships available. **Aid applications:** No closing date; priority given to applications received by March 15; applicants notified on a rolling basis beginning on or about June 1; must reply within 2 weeks.

ADDRESS/TELEPHONE. Georgiana Conrad, Assistant Dean of Student Personnel Services, Spokane Community College, North 1810 Greene Street, Spokane, WA 99207-5399. (509) 536-7001. Fax: (509) 536-7276.

Spokane Falls Community College
Spokane, Washington — CB code: 4752

2-year public community college, coed. Founded in 1967. **Accreditation:** Regional. **Undergraduate enrollment:** 1,612 men, 2,016 women full time; 1,437 men, 1,967 women part time. **Faculty:** 646 total (157 full time), 18 with doctorates or other terminal degrees. **Location:** Suburban campus in small city; 4 miles from downtown. **Calendar:** Quarter, limited summer session. **Microcomputers:** 200 located on campus. **Special facilities:** Art gallery.

DEGREES OFFERED. AA, AAS. 783 associate degrees awarded in 1992.

UNDERGRADUATE MAJORS. Accounting, anthropology, biology, business administration and management, business and management, business and office, business economics, chemistry, child development/care/guidance, Chinese, computer and information sciences, display merchandising, dramatic arts, early childhood education, economics, education, engineering, engineering mechanics, English, fashion merchandising, finance, fine arts, fitness management technician, French, German, gerontology, graphic design, history, home economics, humanities and social sciences, interior design, interpreter for the deaf, Japanese, journalism, liberal/general studies, library assistant, marketing and distribution, mathematics, microcomputer software, music, nursing, orthotic/prosthetic technology, philosophy, photographic technology, physical sciences, physics, political science and government, predentistry, prelaw, premedicine, prepharmacy, preveterinary, psychology, radio/television broadcasting, real estate, recreation and athletics, retailing, Russian, secretarial and related programs, small business management and ownership, social sciences, social work, sociology, software engineering technology, Spanish, special education, speech, substance abuse counseling, taxation, textiles and clothing, word processing.

ACADEMIC PROGRAMS. 2-year transfer program, independent study, cross-registration. **Remedial services:** Learning center, remedial instruction, tutoring. **ROTC:** Army. **Placement/credit:** AP, institutional tests; 60 credit hours maximum for associate degree.

ACADEMIC REQUIREMENTS. Freshmen must earn minimum GPA of 2.0 to continue in good standing. Students must declare major by end of first year. **Graduation requirements:** 96 hours for associate. Most students required to take courses in English, humanities, mathematics, biological/physical sciences, social sciences.

FRESHMAN ADMISSIONS. Selection criteria: Open admissions. Selective admissions to health science programs.

1992 FRESHMAN CLASS PROFILE. 2,303 men and women enrolled. **Characteristics:** 90% from in state, 100% commute, 8% have minority backgrounds. Average age is 26.

FALL-TERM APPLICATIONS. No fee. No closing date; applicants

notified on a rolling basis beginning on or about January 1. Interview recommended for academically weak, health science applicants. Deferred admission available.

STUDENT LIFE. Activities: Student government, radio, student newspaper, choral groups, concert band, drama, jazz band, music ensembles, opera, pep band, symphony orchestra.

ATHLETICS. NJCAA. **Intercollegiate:** Baseball M, basketball, cross-country, golf, gymnastics W, soccer, tennis, track and field, volleyball W. **Intramural:** Baseball, basketball, bowling, cross-country, soccer, softball, tennis, volleyball.

STUDENT SERVICES. Aptitude testing, career counseling, on-campus day care, personal counseling, veterans counselor, services/facilities for handicapped.

ANNUAL EXPENSES. Tuition and fees: $1,125, $3,300 additional for out-of-state students. **Books and supplies:** $540. **Other expenses:** $500.

FINANCIAL AID. 85% of freshmen, 52% of continuing students receive some form of aid. 76% of grants, 94% of loans, 92% of jobs based on need. 1,100 enrolled freshmen were judged to have need, all were offered aid. Athletic scholarships available. **Aid applications:** No closing date; priority given to applications received by April 1; applicants notified on a rolling basis beginning on or about May 15; must reply within 2 weeks.

ADDRESS/TELEPHONE. Larry Owens, Dean of Student Personnel Services, Spokane Falls Community College, West 3410 Fort George Wright Drive, Spokane, WA 99204-5288. (509) 533-3512. Fax: (509) 533-8052.

Tacoma Community College

Tacoma, Washington — CB code: 4826

2-year public community college, coed. Founded in 1965. **Accreditation:** Regional. **Undergraduate enrollment:** 1,131 men, 1,871 women full time; 608 men, 1,289 women part time. **Faculty:** 284 total (92 full time), 17 with doctorates or other terminal degrees. **Location:** Urban campus in small city; 5 miles from downtown. **Calendar:** Quarter, limited summer session. Saturday and extensive evening/early morning classes. **Microcomputers:** 185 located in classrooms, computer centers. **Additional facts:** Programs offered at several locations in Puget Sound area.

DEGREES OFFERED. AA, AS. 499 associate degrees awarded in 1992.

UNDERGRADUATE MAJORS. Accounting, allied health, American literature, anthropology, art history, biological and physical sciences, biology, botany, business administration and management, business and office, business data processing and related programs, business economics, chemistry, chiropractic, classics, comparative literature, computer and information sciences, creative writing, criminal justice studies, dramatic arts, drawing, economics, education, emergency medical technologies, engineering, English, English literature, fine arts, folklore and mythology, French, geology, history, humanities and social sciences, information sciences and systems, inorganic chemistry, Japanese, liberal/general studies, mathematics, medical records technology, medical secretary, mental health/human services, music, music history and appreciation, music performance, music theory and composition, nursing, oceanography, organic chemistry, painting, philosophy, physics, political science and government, predentistry, premedicine, preoccupational therapy, prepharmacy, preveterinary, psychology, radiograph medical technology, respiratory therapy technology, sculpture, secretarial and related programs, sociology, Spanish, statistics, studio art, teacher aide, technical and business writing, zoology.

ACADEMIC PROGRAMS. 2-year transfer program, internships, telecourses, concurrent enrollment with nearby community colleges. **Remedial services:** Learning center, reduced course load, remedial instruction, tutoring. **Placement/credit:** AP, CLEP General and Subject, institutional tests; 45 credit hours maximum for associate degree.

ACADEMIC REQUIREMENTS. Freshmen must earn minimum GPA of 2.0 to continue in good standing. **Graduation requirements:** 90 hours for associate. Most students required to take courses in English, humanities, mathematics, biological/physical sciences, social sciences.

FRESHMAN ADMISSIONS. Selection criteria: Open admissions. **Test requirements:** Community College Academic Placement Test required for placement. SAT scores also admissible.

1992 FRESHMAN CLASS PROFILE. 300 men and women enrolled. **Characteristics:** 99% from in state, 100% commute, 18% have minority backgrounds, 3% are foreign students. Average age is 26.

FALL-TERM APPLICATIONS. No fee. No closing date; applicants notified on a rolling basis; must reply by registration. Deferred admission available.

STUDENT LIFE. Housing: Homestay Program available for international students. **Activities:** Student government, student newspaper, choral groups, drama, music ensembles, musical theater, chamber orchestra.

ATHLETICS. Intercollegiate: Baseball M, basketball, golf, soccer M, tennis W, volleyball W. **Intramural:** Basketball M, golf, skiing, soccer M, softball M, tennis W, volleyball W.

STUDENT SERVICES. Aptitude testing, career counseling, employment service for undergraduates, freshman orientation, on-campus day care, personal counseling, veterans counselor, services/facilities for handicapped.

ANNUAL EXPENSES. Tuition and fees: $1,145, $3,300 additional for out-of-state students. **Books and supplies:** $594. **Other expenses:** $600.

FINANCIAL AID. 20% of freshmen, 17% of continuing students receive some form of aid. 91% of grants, 95% of loans, 44% of jobs based on need. Academic, music/drama, art, athletic, state/district residency, leadership, alumni affiliation, minority scholarships available. **Aid applications:** Closing date April 1; applicants notified on or about June 30; must reply by August 24.

ADDRESS/TELEPHONE. Julie Rudsit, Admissions Officer/High School Relations Coord, Tacoma Community College, 5900 South 12 Street, Tacoma, WA 98465-9971. (206) 566-5000. Fax: (206) 566-6011.

University of Puget Sound

Tacoma, Washington — CB code: 4067

Admissions:	71% of applicants accepted
Based on:	••• School record
	•• Activities, essay, recommendations, special talents, test scores
	• Interview
Completion:	94% of freshmen end year in good standing
	57% graduate, 38% of these enter graduate study

4-year private university and liberal arts college, coed, affiliated with United Methodist Church. Founded in 1888. **Accreditation:** Regional. **Undergraduate enrollment:** 1,143 men, 1,548 women full time; 44 men, 89 women part time. **Graduate enrollment:** 411 men, 470 women full time; 138 men, 211 women part time. **Faculty:** 230 total (201 full time), 180 with doctorates or other terminal degrees. **Location:** Suburban campus in small city; 35 miles from Seattle, 28 miles from Olympia. **Calendar:** Semester, extensive summer session. **Microcomputers:** 136 located in computer centers. **Special facilities:** Natural history museum, art gallery.

DEGREES OFFERED. BA, BS, MA, MEd, JD. 711 bachelor's degrees awarded in 1992. 25% in business and management, 5% communications, 5% allied health, 9% letters/literature, 7% life sciences, 6% psychology, 18% social sciences. Graduate degrees offered in 20 major fields of study.

UNDERGRADUATE MAJORS. Accounting, art history, Asian studies, biological and physical sciences, biology, business administration and management, business and management, chemical engineering, chemistry, civil engineering, communications, computer mathematics, computer science/business, dramatic arts, economics, electrical/electronics/communications engineering, engineering, English, English literature, foreign language and international affairs, French, geology, German, history, humanities and social sciences, liberal/general studies, mathematics, mechanical engineering, music, music business management, music education, music performance, occupational therapy, petroleum engineering, philosophy, physics, political science and government, psychology, public administration, religion, religious music, sociology, Spanish, studio art.

ACADEMIC PROGRAMS. Cooperative education, double major, dual enrollment of high school students, honors program, independent study, internships, study abroad, teacher preparation, 1 year of study in Asia, 3-2 engineering program, business leadership program; liberal arts/career combination in engineering. **Remedial services:** Learning center, reduced course load, tutoring. **Placement/credit:** AP, IB, institutional tests; 32 credit hours maximum for bachelor's degree.

ACADEMIC REQUIREMENTS. Freshmen must earn minimum GPA of 2.0 to continue in good standing. 83% of freshmen return for sophomore year. Students must declare major by end of second year. **Graduation requirements:** 128 hours for bachelor's (32 in major). Most students required to take courses in arts/fine arts, English, history, humanities, mathematics, philosophy/religion, biological/physical sciences, social sciences. **Postgraduate studies:** 3% enter law school, 2% enter medical school, 1% enter MBA programs, 32% enter other graduate study. **Additional information:** All students complete core curriculum including courses in written communication, oral communication or foreign language, mathematical reasoning, historical and humanistic perspectives, society, natural world, fine arts, comparative values, international studies, and science in context.

FRESHMAN ADMISSIONS. Selection criteria: High school record (including grades and course pattern), test scores most important. Extracurricular activities, recommendations, interview, and essays also considered. Recommended units include English 4, foreign language 2, mathematics 4, social science 3 and science 3. One fine, visual, and performing arts also recommended. **Test requirements:** SAT or ACT (SAT preferred); score report by March 1. **Additional information:** Portfolios in major or other field will be reviewed.

1992 FRESHMAN CLASS PROFILE. 1,532 men applied, 1,029 accepted, 279 enrolled; 2,063 women applied, 1,526 accepted, 446 enrolled. 89% had high school GPA of 3.0 or higher, 11% between 2.0 and 2.99. 47% were in top tenth and 79% were in top quarter of graduating class. **Academic background:** Mid 50% of enrolled freshmen had SAT-V between 450-570, SAT-M between 490-620; ACT composite between 22-28. 94% submitted

SAT scores, 43% submitted ACT scores. **Characteristics:** 31% from in state, 97% live in college housing, 16% have minority backgrounds, 1% are foreign students. Average age is 18.

FALL-TERM APPLICATIONS. $35 fee, may be waived for applicants with need. Closing date March 1; applicants notified on a rolling basis beginning on or about January 1; must reply by May 1. Audition required for music applicants. Essay required. Interview recommended. Portfolio recommended for art applicants. CRDA. Deferred and early admission available. EDP-F.

STUDENT LIFE. Housing: Dormitories (women, coed); fraternity, sorority housing available. Housing in university-owned homes adjacent to campus. **Activities:** Student government, magazine, radio, student newspaper, yearbook, choral groups, concert band, dance, drama, jazz band, music ensembles, musical theater, pep band, symphony orchestra, fraternities, sororities, religious fellowship groups, Black Student Union, Hawaiian Students Club, Model United Nations, Circle-K, Feminist Student Union, Lesbian/Gay/Bisexual Union, Latin America Awareness Group, Amnesty International.

ATHLETICS. NAIA. **Intercollegiate:** Baseball M, basketball, cross-country, football M, golf M, rowing (crew), skiing, soccer, softball W, swimming, tennis, track and field, volleyball W. **Intramural:** Basketball, bowling, golf, racquetball, soccer, softball, tennis, track and field, volleyball. **Clubs:** Lacrosse, sailing.

STUDENT SERVICES. Career counseling, employment service for undergraduates, freshman orientation, health services, personal counseling, placement service for graduates, services/facilities for handicapped.

ANNUAL EXPENSES. Tuition and fees: $15,220. **Room and board:** $4,300. **Books and supplies:** $600. **Other expenses:** $1,280.

FINANCIAL AID. 72% of freshmen, 74% of continuing students receive some form of aid. Grants, loans, jobs available. 424 enrolled freshmen were judged to have need, all were offered aid. Academic, music/drama, art, athletic, leadership scholarships available. **Aid applications:** No closing date; priority given to applications received by February 15; applicants notified on a rolling basis beginning on or about April 1; must reply by May 1 or within 2 weeks if notified thereafter. **Additional information:** Cooperative Education allows qualified upper-class students to alternate semesters of full-time study and full work.

ADDRESS/TELEPHONE. George Mills, Dean of Admission and Enrollment, University of Puget Sound, 1500 North Warner Street, Tacoma, WA 98416-0003. (206) 756-3211.

University of Washington

Seattle, Washington — CB code: 4854

Admissions: 56% of applicants accepted
Based on: ••• School record
•• Test scores
• Activities, special talents
Completion: 55% graduate

4-year public university, coed. Founded in 1861. **Accreditation:** Regional. **Undergraduate enrollment:** 10,377 men, 10,337 women full time; 2,164 men, 2,604 women part time. **Graduate enrollment:** 3,992 men, 3,352 women full time; 850 men, 922 women part time. **Faculty:** 3,999 total (3,756 full time), 3,398 with doctorates or other terminal degrees. **Location:** Urban campus in very large city; 5 miles from downtown area. **Calendar:** Quarter, extensive summer session. Extensive evening/early morning classes. **Microcomputers:** 1,500 located in dormitories, classrooms, computer centers. **Special facilities:** Arboretum, observatory, art gallery, anthropological museum, applied physics laboratory.

DEGREES OFFERED. BA, BS, BFA, MA, MS, MBA, MFA, MEd, MSW, PhD, EdD, DMD, MD, B. Pharm. 5,450 bachelor's degrees awarded in 1992. 14% in business and management, 11% engineering, 6% health sciences, 10% letters/literature, 5% life sciences, 7% psychology, 18% social sciences, 5% visual and performing arts. Graduate degrees offered in 125 major fields of study.

UNDERGRADUATE MAJORS. Accounting, aerospace/aeronautical/astronautical engineering, Afro-American (black) studies, American ethnic studies, American Indian studies, anthropology, Arabic, architecture, art history, Asian studies, astronomy, atmospheric sciences and meteorology, biochemistry, biological and physical sciences, botany, business administration and management, cell biology, ceramic engineering, ceramics, chemical engineering, chemistry, Chinese, civil engineering, classics, clinical laboratory science, communications, comparative literature, computer and information sciences, conservation and regulation, construction, creative writing, dance, dramatic arts, East Asian studies, Eastern European studies, economics, electrical/electronics/communications engineering, engineering, engineering and other disciplines, English, English education, enviromental health, environmental science, fiber/textiles/weaving, fishing and fisheries, foreign languages education, forest products processing technology, forestry and related sciences, French, geography, geology, German, graphic design, Greek (classical), Hebrew, Hispanic American studies, history, humanities and social sciences, Indic languages, industrial design, industrial engineering, international studies, Italian, Japanese, Jewish studies, landscape architecture, Latin, liberal/general studies, linguistics, mathematics, mathematics education, mechanical engineering, MEDEX/physician assistant, medical assistant, metal/jewelry, metallurgical engineering, microbiology, molecular biology, music, music education, music history and appreciation, music performance, music theory and composition, Near Eastern languages, nursing, occupational therapy, ocean engineering, oceanography, painting, paper engineering, peace studies, pharmacy, philosophy, photography, physical therapy, physics, political science and government, printmaking, prosthetics and orthotics, psychology, religion, Russian, Russian and Slavic studies, Scandinavian languages, science education, scientific and technical communication, sculpture, Slavic languages, social science education, social work, sociology, South Asian languages, South Asian studies, Spanish, speech, speech pathology/audiology, speech/communication/theater education, statistics, teaching English as a second language/foreign language, wildlife management, women's studies, zoology.

ACADEMIC PROGRAMS. Cooperative education, double major, dual enrollment of high school students, honors program, independent study, internships, student-designed major, study abroad, teacher preparation, telecourses, visiting/exchange student program, Washington semester, quarter at Friday Harbor Laboratories, San Juan Islands. **Remedial services:** Learning center, preadmission summer program, reduced course load, remedial instruction, special counselor, tutoring. **ROTC:** Air Force, Army, Naval. **Placement/credit:** AP, institutional tests; 90 credit hours maximum for bachelor's degree.

ACADEMIC REQUIREMENTS. Freshmen must earn minimum GPA of 2.0 to continue in good standing. 92% of freshmen return for sophomore year. **Graduation requirements:** 180 hours for bachelor's. Most students required to take courses in English, humanities, mathematics, biological/physical sciences, social sciences. **Additional information:** Students must declare major after completion of 105 quarter credits.

FRESHMAN ADMISSIONS. Selection criteria: Combined high school GPA and test scores most important. State residents and nonresident children of alumni given preference. **High school preparation:** 15 units required. Required units include English 4, foreign language 2, mathematics 3, social science 3 and science 2. One semester (.5) elective from required subjects list and .5 art course. **Test requirements:** SAT or ACT; score report by February 1. **Additional information:** Admission for most determined by GPA and test scores. Applicants whose admission index falls just below the minimum standards for Fall Quarter are reviewed more closely, with attention given to rigor of academic curriculum, number of honors/AP courses, improvement in GPA, and participation in leadership/school activities.

1992 FRESHMAN CLASS PROFILE. 12,516 men and women applied, 6,969 accepted; 1,794 men enrolled, 1,832 women enrolled. 95% had high school GPA of 3.0 or higher, 5% between 2.0 and 2.99. **Academic background:** Mid 50% of enrolled freshmen had SAT-V between 420-540, SAT-M between 500-630; ACT composite between 22-27. 95% submitted SAT scores, 19% submitted ACT scores. **Characteristics:** 87% from in state, 52% commute, 29% have minority backgrounds, 2% are foreign students, 35% join fraternities/sororities. Average age is 18.

FALL-TERM APPLICATIONS. $35 fee, may be waived for applicants with need. Closing date February 1; applicants notified on or about March 1; must reply by May 1. Audition required for performing arts applicants. Portfolio required for studio art applicants. CRDA. Early admission available. Applications accepted after February 1 on a space available basis.

STUDENT LIFE. Housing: Dormitories (coed); apartment, fraternity, sorority, handicapped housing available. Special interest houses in residence halls: frosh house, outdoor activities house, foreign language houses. **Activities:** Student government, magazine, radio, student newspaper, television, yearbook, departmental student magazines, choral groups, concert band, dance, drama, jazz band, marching band, music ensembles, musical theater, opera, pep band, symphony orchestra, fraternities, sororities, living groups, sports clubs, religious organizations, academic/professional groups, social/political action organizations, and international clubs.

ATHLETICS. NCAA. **Intercollegiate:** Baseball M, basketball, cross-country, diving, fencing W, football M, golf, gymnastics W, rowing (crew), soccer, softball W, swimming, tennis, track and field, volleyball W. **Intramural:** Basketball, bowling, fencing, handball, racquetball, soccer, softball, squash, tennis, volleyball.

STUDENT SERVICES. Aptitude testing, career counseling, employment service for undergraduates, freshman orientation, health services, personal counseling, placement service for graduates, veterans counselor, women's adviser and information center, services/facilities for handicapped.

ANNUAL EXPENSES. Tuition and fees: $2,532, $4,602 additional for out-of-state students. **Room and board:** $4,086. **Books and supplies:** $687. **Other expenses:** $1,725.

FINANCIAL AID. 30% of freshmen, 29% of continuing students receive some form of aid. All grants, 94% of loans, all jobs based on need. 1,302 enrolled freshmen were judged to have need, 1,164 were offered aid. Academic, athletic, state/district residency, alumni affiliation, minority scholarships available. **Aid applications:** No closing date; priority given to applications received by February 28; applicants notified on a rolling basis beginning on or about April 1; must reply by May 1 or within 3 weeks if notified thereafter. **Additional information:** Tuition not due until third week of term, emergency loans available.

ADDRESS/TELEPHONE. W.W. Washburn, Executive Director of Admissions and Records, University of Washington, 1400 Northeast Campus Parkway, Seattle, WA 98195. (206) 543-9686.

Walla Walla College
College Place, Washington CB code: 4940

4-year private college of arts and sciences, coed, affiliated with Seventh-day Adventists. Founded in 1892. **Accreditation:** Regional. **Undergraduate enrollment:** 791 men, 675 women full time; 77 men, 77 women part time. **Graduate enrollment:** 24 men, 57 women full time; 6 men, 27 women part time. **Faculty:** 181 total (123 full time), 72 with doctorates or other terminal degrees. **Location:** Rural campus in small town; 3 miles from Walla Walla. **Calendar:** Quarter, extensive summer session. Extensive evening/early morning classes. **Microcomputers:** 100 located in computer centers. **Additional facts:** Branch campus in Portland, Oregon for last 2 years of nursing program. Summer biology courses offered at Marine Station, Rosario Beach, Anacortes.

DEGREES OFFERED. AS, BA, BS, MA, MS, MEd. 21 associate degrees awarded in 1992. 29% in business and management, 14% business/office and marketing/distribution, 5% computer sciences, 14% engineering technologies, 19% home economics, 19% trade and industry. 238 bachelor's degrees awarded. 18% in business and management, 6% communications, 8% teacher education, 17% engineering, 5% engineering technologies, 13% health sciences, 5% social sciences. Graduate degrees offered in 7 major fields of study.

UNDERGRADUATE MAJORS. Associate: Airline piloting and navigation, automotive mechanics, automotive technology, business and management, business and office, business computer/console/peripheral equipment operation, business data processing and related programs, computer and information sciences, construction, electronic technology, graphic and printing production, graphic arts technology, information sciences and systems, power plant operation and maintenance. **Bachelor's:** Accounting, airline piloting and navigation, automotive mechanics, automotive technology, biblical languages, bioengineering and biomedical engineering, biological and physical sciences, biology, biomedical equipment technology, biophysics, business administration and management, business and management, business education, chemistry, civil engineering, communications, computer and information sciences, computer servicing technology, electrical/electronics/communications engineering, electronic technology, elementary education, engineering, English, fine arts, French, German, graphic and printing production, health sciences, history, humanities, industrial arts education, journalism, mathematics, mechanical engineering, music, music education, music performance, music theory and composition, nursing, physical education, physics, power plant operation and maintenance, psychology, religion, secondary education, social work, sociology, Spanish, speech, theological studies.

ACADEMIC PROGRAMS. Cooperative education, double major, dual enrollment of high school students, honors program, internships, study abroad, teacher preparation. **Remedial services:** Learning center, remedial instruction, special counselor, tutoring. **Placement/credit:** AP, CLEP Subject, institutional tests; 12 credit hours maximum for associate degree; 24 credit hours maximum for bachelor's degree.

ACADEMIC REQUIREMENTS. Freshmen must earn minimum GPA of 2.0 to continue in good standing. 63% of freshmen return for sophomore year. Students must declare major by end of second year. **Graduation requirements:** 96 hours for associate (50 in major), 192 hours for bachelor's (65 in major). Most students required to take courses in English, history, humanities, mathematics, philosophy/religion, biological/physical sciences, social sciences. **Postgraduate studies:** 25% from 2-year programs enter 4-year programs.

FRESHMAN ADMISSIONS. Selection criteria: 2.0 high school GPA, 3 recommendations preferred. **High school preparation:** 16 units required. Required and recommended units include English 4, mathematics 2-3, social science 2-3 and science 2-3. Foreign language 2 recommended. Mathematics units must be algebra and geometry. Science units must include 1 laboratory science. **Test requirements:** ACT for placement and counseling only; score report by September 1.

1992 FRESHMAN CLASS PROFILE. 145 men, 135 women enrolled. **Characteristics:** 38% from in state, 95% live in college housing, 15% have minority backgrounds, 8% are foreign students. Average age is 18.

FALL-TERM APPLICATIONS. $20 fee. No closing date; applicants notified on a rolling basis. Deferred admission available.

STUDENT LIFE. Housing: Dormitories (men, women); apartment, handicapped housing available. **Activities:** Student government, radio, student newspaper, yearbook, choral groups, concert band, drama, music ensembles, symphony orchestra, foreign student organizations.

ATHLETICS. Intramural: Badminton, basketball, racquetball, soccer, softball, volleyball.

STUDENT SERVICES. Aptitude testing, career counseling, employment service for undergraduates, freshman orientation, health services, on-campus day care, personal counseling, placement service for graduates, veterans counselor, services/facilities for handicapped.

ANNUAL EXPENSES. Tuition and fees (1992-93): $9,555. **Room and board:** $3,105. **Books and supplies:** $600. **Other expenses:** $450.

FINANCIAL AID. 54% of freshmen, 80% of continuing students receive some form of aid. 61% of grants, 94% of loans, all jobs based on need. 200 enrolled freshmen were judged to have need, all were offered aid. Academic, music/drama, art, leadership, alumni affiliation scholarships available. **Aid applications:** No closing date; priority given to applications received by April 1; applicants notified on a rolling basis beginning on or about April 1; must reply within 2 weeks.

ADDRESS/TELEPHONE. Gary Wisbey, Vice President for Admissions and Marketing, Walla Walla College, 204 South College Avenue, College Place, WA 99324-1198. (509) 527-2327. (800) 541-8900. Fax: (509) 527-2253.

Walla Walla Community College
Walla Walla, Washington CB code: 4963

2-year public community college, coed. Founded in 1967. **Accreditation:** Regional. **Undergraduate enrollment:** 1,115 men, 1,030 women full time; 1,207 men, 1,307 women part time. **Faculty:** 278 total (107 full time), 6 with doctorates or other terminal degrees. **Location:** Suburban campus in large town; 158 miles from Spokane, 262 miles from Seattle. **Calendar:** Quarter, limited summer session. Extensive evening/early morning classes. **Microcomputers:** 80 located in libraries, classrooms, computer centers.

DEGREES OFFERED. AA, AS. 325 associate degrees awarded in 1992.

UNDERGRADUATE MAJORS. Accounting, agribusiness, agricultural mechanics, agricultural production, air conditioning/heating/refrigeration mechanics, air conditioning/heating/refrigeration technology, automotive mechanics, automotive technology, business and management, business and office, carpentry, child development/care/guidance, civil technology, computer and information sciences, computer programming, data processing, diesel engine mechanics, engineering and engineering-related technologies, law enforcement and corrections technologies, legal secretary, liberal/general studies, machine tool operation/machine shop, marketing and distribution, medical secretary, nursing, recreation and community services technologies, respiratory therapy, respiratory therapy technology, retailing, secretarial and related programs.

ACADEMIC PROGRAMS. 2-year transfer program, cooperative education, dual enrollment of high school students, honors program, independent study, internships. **Remedial services:** Learning center, preadmission summer program, reduced course load, remedial instruction, special counselor, tutoring. **Placement/credit:** AP, CLEP General and Subject, institutional tests.

ACADEMIC REQUIREMENTS. Freshmen must earn minimum GPA of 2.0 to continue in good standing. 45% of freshmen return for sophomore year. **Graduation requirements:** 93 hours for associate. Most students required to take courses in English, humanities, mathematics, biological/physical sciences, social sciences.

FRESHMAN ADMISSIONS. Selection criteria: Open admissions. Special requirements for health science and vocational programs.

1992 FRESHMAN CLASS PROFILE. 500 men and women enrolled. **Characteristics:** 90% from in state, 100% commute, 20% have minority backgrounds, 1% are foreign students.

FALL-TERM APPLICATIONS. $20 fee. No closing date; applicants notified on a rolling basis; must reply within 15 days. Deferred and early admission available.

STUDENT LIFE. Activities: Student government, student newspaper, choral groups, dance, drama, jazz band, musical theater, pep band, International Student Organization.

ATHLETICS. NJCAA. **Intercollegiate:** Baseball M, basketball, football M, golf, tennis, volleyball W. **Intramural:** Basketball, golf, racquetball, softball, tennis, volleyball. **Clubs:** Rodeo.

STUDENT SERVICES. Aptitude testing, career counseling, employment service for undergraduates, freshman orientation, on-campus day care, personal counseling, placement service for graduates, veterans counselor, services/facilities for handicapped.

ANNUAL EXPENSES. Tuition and fees: $1,156, $3,300 additional for out-of-state students. **Books and supplies:** $510. **Other expenses:** $600.

FINANCIAL AID. 59% of continuing students receive some form of aid. 92% of grants, 87% of loans, 45% of jobs based on need. Academic, music/drama, athletic, leadership scholarships available. **Aid applications:** No closing date; priority given to applications received by June 1; applicants notified on a rolling basis beginning on or about July 15; must reply within 10 days. **Additional information:** Rodeo scholarships available for men and women.

ADDRESS/TELEPHONE. Joseph Frostad, Director of Admissions and Registrar, Walla Walla Community College, 500 Tausick Way, Walla Walla, WA 99362-9267. (509) 527-4283. Fax: (509) 527-4480.

Washington State University
Pullman, Washington CB code: 4705

Admissions: 91% of applicants accepted
Based on: ••• School record, test scores
• Activities, essay, recommendations, special talents
Completion: 83% of freshmen end year in good standing
50% graduate

4-year public university, coed. Founded in 1890. **Accreditation:** Regional. **Undergraduate enrollment:** 7,394 men, 6,286 women full time; 501 men, 709 women part time. **Graduate enrollment:** 1,091 men, 873 women full time; 588 men, 440 women part time. **Faculty:** 1,852 total (1,655 full time), 1,112 with doctorates or other terminal degrees. **Location:** Rural campus in large town; 80 miles from Spokane. **Calendar:** Semester, extensive summer session. **Microcomputers:** 5,000 located in dormitories, libraries, classrooms, computer centers. **Special facilities:** Museums, observatory, planetarium, nuclear radiation center, performing arts center, electron microscope, center for energy research, racehorse track, golf course.

DEGREES OFFERED. BA, BS, BFA, BArch, MA, MS, MBA, MFA, MEd, PhD, EdD, Pharm D, DVM. 3,044 bachelor's degrees awarded in 1992. 5% in agriculture, 21% business and management, 8% communications, 6% teacher education, 11% engineering, 8% health sciences, 5% letters/literature, 5% life sciences, 14% social sciences. Graduate degrees offered in 73 major fields of study.

UNDERGRADUATE MAJORS. Advertising, agribusiness, agricultural economics, agricultural education, agricultural engineering, agricultural mechanics, agricultural sciences, agronomy, American studies, animal sciences, anthropology, architecture, art education, Asian studies, biochemistry, biological and physical sciences, biology, business administration and management, chemical engineering, chemistry, civil engineering, communications, computer and information sciences, Correctional Administration, economics, electrical/electronics/communications engineering, elementary education, English, English education, entomology, environmental science, fashion design, finance, fine arts, food science and nutrition, foreign languages (multiple emphasis), foreign languages education, forestry and related sciences, geological engineering, geology, health education, history, home economics, home economics education, horticultural science, horticulture, hotel/motel and restaurant management, human environment and housing, human resources development, humanities, humanities and social sciences, insurance and risk management, interior design, international business management, journalism, landscape architecture, law enforcement and corrections, liberal/general studies, management information systems, marketing management, materials engineering, mathematics, mathematics education, mechanical engineering, microbiology, music, music education, nursing, parks and recreation management, personnel management, pharmacy, philosophy, physical education, physics, political science and government, prelaw, psychology, public relations, radio/television broadcasting, reading education, real estate, renewable natural resources, science education, secondary education, social sciences, social studies education, social work, sociology, soil sciences, speech pathology/audiology, speech/communication/theater education, textiles and clothing, wildlife management, zoology.

ACADEMIC PROGRAMS. Cooperative education, double major, external degree, honors program, independent study, internships, study abroad, teacher preparation, telecourses, visiting/exchange student program, cross-registration. **Remedial services:** Learning center, reduced course load, remedial instruction, special counselor, tutoring, reading center, speech and hearing clinic, precept tutorial services. **ROTC:** Air Force, Army, Naval. **Placement/credit:** AP, CLEP General and Subject, IB, institutional tests; 60 credit hours maximum for bachelor's degree.

ACADEMIC REQUIREMENTS. Freshmen must earn minimum GPA of 2.0 to continue in good standing. 82% of freshmen return for sophomore year. Students must declare major by end of second year. **Graduation requirements:** 120 hours for bachelor's (35 in major). Most students required to take courses in English, history, humanities, mathematics, biological/physical sciences, social sciences.

FRESHMAN ADMISSIONS. Selection criteria: Admission is based on a combination of high school GPA and SAT or ACT scores. Special circumstances, and community activities, recommendations, disabilities, and minority status considered in some cases. **High school preparation:** 15 units required. Required units include English 4, foreign language 2, mathematics 3, social science 3 and science 2. Mathematics units must include geometry and 2 years of algebra. Science units must include 1 laboratory science in biology, chemistry or physics. Foreign language must be 2 years of single language. 1 year of a fine arts or additional academic elective is also required. **Test requirements:** SAT or ACT; score report by May 1.

1992 FRESHMAN CLASS PROFILE. 5,727 men and women applied, 5,216 accepted; 1,193 men enrolled, 1,161 women enrolled. 68% had high school GPA of 3.0 or higher, 32% between 2.0 and 2.99. **Academic background:** Mid 50% of enrolled freshmen had SAT-V between 370-480, SAT-M between 410-540. 70% submitted SAT scores. **Characteristics:** 84% from in state, 90% live in college housing, 11% have minority backgrounds, 3% are foreign students, 11% join fraternities/sororities. Average age is 18.

FALL-TERM APPLICATIONS. $35 fee, may be waived for applicants with need. No closing date; priority given to applications received by May 1; applicants notified on a rolling basis; must reply by May 1 or within 2 weeks if notified thereafter. Audition required for music applicants. Portfolio required for art, architecture, landscape architecture applicants. Interview recommended for academically weak applicants. CRDA. Early admission available. $50 advance payment on tuition and fees required to finalize admission. Applicants accepted on first come first served basis until May 1 and later if space is still available.

STUDENT LIFE. Housing: Dormitories (men, women, coed); apartment, fraternity, sorority housing available. Single undergraduate freshmen under 20 required to live on campus. **Activities:** Student government, magazine, radio, student newspaper, television, yearbook, choral groups, concert band, dance, drama, jazz band, marching band, music ensembles, musical theater, opera, pep band, symphony orchestra, synchronized swimming, fraternities, sororities, over 200 clubs and special interest groups including YMCA, YWCA, Baptist Student Union, Jewish student organization, honor fraternities, Movimiento Estudiantil Chicano de Aztlan, Native American Student Association, Asian/Pacific American Students, Black Awareness, Association for Women Students.

ATHLETICS. NCAA. **Intercollegiate:** Baseball M, basketball, cross-country, diving W, football M, golf, rowing (crew) W, soccer W, swimming W, tennis, track and field, volleyball W. **Intramural:** Badminton, basketball, bowling, boxing M, cross-country, golf, handball, lacrosse M, racquetball, rifle, rowing (crew) M, rugby, skiing, soccer M, softball, swimming, table tennis, tennis, track and field, volleyball, water polo, wrestling M.

STUDENT SERVICES. Aptitude testing, career counseling, employment service for undergraduates, freshman orientation, health services, on-campus day care, personal counseling, placement service for graduates, special adviser for adult students, veterans counselor, services/facilities for handicapped.

ANNUAL EXPENSES. Tuition and fees: $2,532, $4,602 additional for out-of-state students. **Room and board:** $3,832. **Books and supplies:** $736. **Other expenses:** $1,208.

FINANCIAL AID. 35% of freshmen, 40% of continuing students receive some form of aid. 71% of grants, 89% of loans, 15% of jobs based on need. Academic, music/drama, art, athletic, leadership, alumni affiliation, minority scholarships available. **Aid applications:** No closing date; priority given to applications received by March 1; applicants notified on a rolling basis beginning on or about April 15; must reply by May 1 or within 2 weeks if notified thereafter. **Additional information:** Student budget counseling, short term loans, and computerized scholarship bank available.

ADDRESS/TELEPHONE. Terry Flynn, Director of Admissions, Washington State University, 342 French Administration Building, Pullman, WA 99164-1036. (509) 335-5586.

Wenatchee Valley College
Wenatchee, Washington CB code: 4942

2-year public community college, coed. Founded in 1939. **Accreditation:** Regional. **Undergraduate enrollment:** 695 men, 1,000 women full time; 279 men, 538 women part time. **Faculty:** 186 total (56 full time), 4 with doctorates or other terminal degrees. **Location:** Rural campus in large town; 145 miles from Seattle. **Calendar:** Quarter, limited summer session. Extensive evening/early morning classes. **Microcomputers:** 50 located in computer centers. **Special facilities:** Art gallery.

DEGREES OFFERED. AAS. 313 associate degrees awarded in 1992. 5% in agriculture, 21% business and management, 10% business/office and marketing/distribution, 15% teacher education, 11% health sciences, 5% physical sciences, 5% psychology, 5% social sciences, 15% trade and industry.

UNDERGRADUATE MAJORS. Accounting, agricultural business and management, agricultural sciences, air conditioning/heating/refrigeration mechanics, air conditioning/heating/refrigeration technology, automotive technology, biology, business and management, business and office, business computer/console/peripheral equipment operation, carpentry, chemistry, communications, community services, computer and information sciences, creative writing, drawing, early childhood education, education, engineering, English, fire control and safety technology, history, humanities and social sciences, legal secretary, liberal/general studies, marketing and distribution, mathematics, medical laboratory technologies, medical records technology, medical secretary, music, music performance, music theory and composition, nursing, painting, physical sciences, political science and government, predentistry, premedicine, prepharmacy, preveterinary, printmaking, psychology, radiograph medical technology, secretarial and related programs, social sciences, sociology, Spanish, speech, studio art, teacher aide, technical and business writing, visual and performing arts, welding technology.

ACADEMIC PROGRAMS. 2-year transfer program, accelerated program, cooperative education, double major, dual enrollment of high school students, honors program, independent study, internships, student-designed major. **Remedial services:** Learning center, reduced course load, remedial instruction, special counselor, tutoring. **Placement/credit:** AP, CLEP General and Subject.

ACADEMIC REQUIREMENTS. Freshmen must earn minimum GPA of 2.0 to continue in good standing. 55% of freshmen return for sophomore year. Students must declare major by end of first year. **Graduation requirements:** 94 hours for associate (30 in major). Most students required to take courses in arts/fine arts, English, humanities, mathematics, biological/physical sciences, social sciences.

FRESHMAN ADMISSIONS. Selection criteria: Open admissions.

1992 FRESHMAN CLASS PROFILE. 600 men and women enrolled. **Characteristics:** 95% from in state, 97% commute. Average age is 20.

FALL-TERM APPLICATIONS. No fee. No closing date; priority given to applications received by September 1; applicants notified on a rolling basis beginning on or about December 1. Deferred and early admission available.

STUDENT LIFE. Housing: Dormitories (coed). **Activities:** Student government, student newspaper, choral groups, music ensembles, Circle K Club, professional associations, Inter-Varsity Fellowship.

ATHLETICS. Intercollegiate: Basketball, softball W. **Intramural:** Basketball, skiing, soccer, softball, table tennis, tennis, volleyball.

STUDENT SERVICES. Career counseling, employment service for undergraduates, freshman orientation, personal counseling, special adviser for adult students, veterans counselor, services/facilities for handicapped.

ANNUAL EXPENSES. Tuition and fees: $1,125, $3,300 additional for out-of-state students. **Room and board:** $4,236. **Books and supplies:** $654. **Other expenses:** $1,368.

FINANCIAL AID. 35% of continuing students receive some form of aid. 96% of grants based on need. Academic, music/drama, art, athletic, state/district residency, leadership scholarships available. **Aid applications:** No closing date; priority given to applications received by April 1; applicants notified on a rolling basis beginning on or about June 15; must reply within 3 weeks.

ADDRESS/TELEPHONE. Marlene Slinko, Registrar/Associate Dean for Student Services, Wenatchee Valley College, 1300 Fifth Street, Wenatchee, WA 98801. (509) 662-1651.

Western Washington University
Bellingham, Washington

CB code: 4947

Admissions:	67% of applicants accepted
Based on:	••• School record
	•• Test scores
	• Essay, recommendations, special talents
Completion:	88% of freshmen end year in good standing
	41% graduate, 7% of these enter graduate study

4-year public university, coed. Founded in 1893. **Accreditation:** Regional. **Undergraduate enrollment:** 3,928 men, 4,863 women full time; 220 men, 263 women part time. **Graduate enrollment:** 145 men, 259 women full time; 88 men, 151 women part time. **Faculty:** 525 total (395 full time), 371 with doctorates or other terminal degrees. **Location:** Suburban campus in small city; 90 miles from of Seattle, 60 miles from of Vancouver, B.C., Canada. **Calendar:** Quarter, extensive summer session. Extensive evening/early morning classes. **Microcomputers:** 500 located in dormitories, libraries, classrooms, computer centers. **Special facilities:** Wind tunnel, electron microscope, neutron generator laboratory, planetarium, air pollution laboratory, motor vehicle research laboratory, electronic music studio, 11-acre recreational park on lake. **Additional facts:** Fairhaven College offers interdisciplinary, individualized liberal arts programs. Huxley College of Environmental Studies provides specialized education and research.

DEGREES OFFERED. BA, BS, BFA, MA, MS, MBA, MEd. 2,104 bachelor's degrees awarded in 1992. 17% in business and management, 5% communications, 10% teacher education, 5% engineering technologies, 5% life sciences, 5% multi/interdisciplinary studies, 11% parks/recreation, protective services, public affairs, 7% psychology, 14% social sciences, 6% visual and performing arts. Graduate degrees offered in 49 major fields of study.

UNDERGRADUATE MAJORS. Accounting, American literature, American studies, anthropology, art education, art history, astronomy, bilingual/bicultural education, biochemistry, biology, business administration and management, chemistry, classics, communications, community health work, comparative literature, computer and information sciences, creative writing, dramatic arts, early childhood education, earth sciences, East Asian studies, ecology, economics, education, educational media technology, electronic technology, elementary education, engineering and engineering-related technologies, English, English education, English literature, environmental design, environmental science, foreign languages education, French, fresh water studies, geography, geology, geophysics and seismology, German, health education, history, human resources development, humanities, industrial and organizational psychology, industrial arts education, industrial technology, information sciences and systems, interior design, international business management, jazz, journalism, junior high education, liberal/general studies, management information systems, management science, manufacturing technology, marine biology, marketing management, mathematics, mathematics education, mental health/human services, music, music education, music history and appreciation, music performance, music theory and composition, parks and recreation management, philosophy, physical education, physics, plastic technology, political science and government, psychology, Russian, science education, secondary education, Slavic languages, social studies education, sociology, Spanish, special education, speech, speech correction, speech pathology/audiology, speech/communication/theater education, studio art, visual and performing arts.

ACADEMIC PROGRAMS. Double major, honors program, independent study, internships, student-designed major, study abroad, teacher preparation, visiting/exchange student program; liberal arts/career combination in engineering, forestry. **Remedial services:** Learning center, special counselor, tutoring, basic writing course, basic mathematics workshop. **Placement/credit:** AP, CLEP Subject, IB, institutional tests; 45 credit hours maximum for bachelor's degree.

ACADEMIC REQUIREMENTS. Freshmen must earn minimum GPA of 2.5 to continue in good standing. 84% of freshmen return for sophomore year. Students must declare major by end of second year. **Graduation requirements:** 180 hours for bachelor's. Most students required to take courses in arts/fine arts, computer science, English, foreign languages, history, humanities, mathematics, philosophy/religion, biological/physical sciences, social sciences. **Postgraduate studies:** 7% enter MBA programs.

FRESHMAN ADMISSIONS. Selection criteria: School achievement record, 2.5 minimum school GPA, test scores, and speciifc course requirements considered, based on formula determined by higher education coordinating board of Washington state. **High school preparation:** 15 units required. Required units include English 4, foreign language 2, mathematics 3, social science 3 and science 2. Mathematics requirement includes 2 algebra. Sciences include 1 chemistry or physics. Foreign language should be in 1 language. .5 fine arts and .5 academic elective required. **Test requirements:** SAT or ACT; score report by March 1.

1992 FRESHMAN CLASS PROFILE. 5,167 men and women applied, 3,459 accepted; 1,456 enrolled. 94% had high school GPA of 3.0 or higher, 6% between 2.0 and 2.99. **Academic background:** Mid 50% of enrolled freshmen had SAT-V between 410-520, SAT-M between 460-580; ACT composite between 21-25. 96% submitted SAT scores, 4% submitted ACT scores. **Characteristics:** 95% from in state, 91% live in college housing, 14% have minority backgrounds, 2% are foreign students. Average age is 19.

FALL-TERM APPLICATIONS. $35 fee, may be waived for applicants with need. Closing date March 1; applicants notified on a rolling basis beginning on or about March 15; must reply by May 1 or within 2 weeks if notified thereafter. Audition required for music applicants. CRDA.

STUDENT LIFE. Housing: Dormitories (coed); apartment housing available. **Activities:** Student government, magazine, radio, student newspaper, television, forensics, choral groups, concert band, dance, drama, jazz band, music ensembles, musical theater, opera, symphony orchestra, ethnic student center, multicultural services center, women's center, Lesbian/Gay/Bisexual Alliance, STRATA (Students that return after time away), veteran's outreach center, volunteer services and resources, international student club, The Inn (nondenominational), Campus Christian Fellowship. **Additional information:** Office of Student Life helps connect students with university and community resources, including crisis intervention, student assistance service, and new student programs.

ATHLETICS. NAIA. **Intercollegiate:** Basketball, cross-country, football M, golf M, rowing (crew), soccer, softball W, tennis, track and field, volleyball W. **Intramural:** Badminton, baseball M, basketball, ice hockey M, lacrosse, racquetball, rugby, sailing, skiing M, soccer, softball, swimming, tennis, volleyball, wrestling M.

STUDENT SERVICES. Aptitude testing, career counseling, employment service for undergraduates, freshman orientation, health services, on-campus day care, personal counseling, placement service for graduates, special adviser for adult students, veterans counselor, services/facilities for handicapped.

ANNUAL EXPENSES. Tuition and fees: $1,971, $4,977 additional for out-of-state students. **Room and board:** $4,140. **Books and supplies:** $618. **Other expenses:** $1,350.

FINANCIAL AID. 66% of freshmen, 66% of continuing students receive some form of aid. 81% of grants, 93% of loans, 31% of jobs based on need. Academic, music/drama, art, athletic, state/district residency, leadership, minority scholarships available. **Aid applications:** No closing date; priority given to applications received by February 28; applicants notified on a rolling basis beginning on or about June 1; must reply within 2 weeks.

ADDRESS/TELEPHONE. Karen G. Copetas, Director of Admissions, Western Washington University, Old Main 200, Bellingham, WA 98225-9009. (206) 650-3440. Fax: (206) 650-7369.

Whatcom Community College
Bellingham, Washington

CB code: 1275

2-year public community college, coed. Founded in 1970. **Accreditation:** Regional. **Undergraduate enrollment:** 498 men, 627 women full time; 828 men, 1,125 women part time. **Faculty:** 157 total (32 full time), 5 with doctorates or other terminal degrees. **Location:** Rural campus in small city; 89 miles from Seattle. **Calendar:** Quarter, limited summer session. Extensive evening/early morning classes. **Microcomputers:** 60 located in libraries, classrooms.

DEGREES OFFERED. AS. 283 associate degrees awarded in 1992.

UNDERGRADUATE MAJORS. Accounting, business and management, business and office, business data processing and related programs, child development/care/guidance, criminal justice studies, legal assistant/paralegal, liberal/general studies, medical assistant, office supervision and management, physical therapy assistant, secretarial and related programs, teacher aide.

ACADEMIC PROGRAMS. 2-year transfer program, cooperative education, honors program, independent study, internships, student-designed major, study abroad, telecourses, cross-registration. **Remedial services:** Learning center, reduced course load, remedial instruction, special counselor, tutoring. **Placement/credit:** CLEP General and Subject, institutional tests.

ACADEMIC REQUIREMENTS. No policy requiring minimum GPA; records of students having academic difficulty are reviewed individually. Students must declare major on enrollment. **Graduation requirements:** 90 hours for associate. Most students required to take courses in English, humanities, mathematics, biological/physical sciences, social sciences.

FRESHMAN ADMISSIONS. Selection criteria: Open admissions.

1992 FRESHMAN CLASS PROFILE. Characteristics: 90% from in state, 100% commute.

FALL-TERM APPLICATIONS. No fee. No closing date; applicants notified on a rolling basis; must reply by registration.

STUDENT LIFE. Activities: Student government, student newspaper.

STUDENT SERVICES. Aptitude testing, career counseling, employment service for undergraduates, on-campus day care, personal counseling, special adviser for adult students, veterans counselor, services/facilities for handicapped.

ANNUAL EXPENSES. Tuition and fees: $1,125, $3,300 additional for out-of-state students. **Books and supplies:** $594. **Other expenses:** $669.

FINANCIAL AID. 10% of freshmen, 20% of continuing students receive some form of aid. 94% of grants, 58% of loans, all jobs based on need. 608 enrolled freshmen were judged to have need, 406 were offered aid. Academic, leadership scholarships available. **Aid applications:** No closing date; priority given to applications received by June 1; applicants notified on a rolling basis beginning on or about June 15; must reply within 3 weeks.

ADDRESS/TELEPHONE. Jan Hagan, Associate Dean of Admissions and Registration, Whatcom Community College, 237 West Kellogg Road, Bellingham, WA 98226. (206) 676-2170 ext. 214. Fax: (206) 676-2171 ext. 214.

Whitman College
Walla Walla, Washington — CB code: 4951

Admissions: 80% of applicants accepted
Based on:
••• Essay, school record
•• Activities, interview, recommendations, test scores
• Special talents
Completion: 97% of freshmen end year in good standing
75% graduate, 77% of these enter graduate study

4-year private liberal arts college, coed. Founded in 1859. **Accreditation:** Regional. **Undergraduate enrollment:** 574 men, 631 women full time; 3 men, 2 women part time. **Faculty:** 129 total (93 full time), 92 with doctorates or other terminal degrees. **Location:** Rural campus in large town; 150 miles from Spokane, 235 miles from Portland, Oregon. **Calendar:** Semester. **Microcomputers:** 75 located in libraries, classrooms, computer centers. **Special facilities:** Asian art collection, natural history museum, art gallery, planetarium, 2 electron microscopes, observatory. **Additional facts:** Foreign study opportunities in Europe, Mexico, Japan, Singapore, China, Costa Rica, Taiwan, and Australia. Exchange program in education with University of Exeter, England.

DEGREES OFFERED. BA. 273 bachelor's degrees awarded in 1992. 9% in letters/literature, 7% life sciences, 5% mathematics, 5% philosophy, religion, theology, 9% physical sciences, 8% psychology, 41% social sciences, 13% visual and performing arts.

UNDERGRADUATE MAJORS. Anthropology, art history, biology, chemistry, dramatic arts, economics, English, French, geology, German, history, mathematics, music, philosophy, physics, political science and government, psychology, sociology, Spanish, studio art.

ACADEMIC PROGRAMS. Double major, dual enrollment of high school students, honors program, independent study, internships, student-designed major, study abroad, teacher preparation, visiting/exchange student program, Washington semester, urban semester in Philadelphia, Chicago; liberal arts/career combination in engineering, forestry; combined bachelor's/graduate program in business administration, law. **Remedial services:** Learning center, reduced course load, special counselor, tutoring, writing laboratory. **Placement/credit:** AP, institutional tests; 30 credit hours maximum for bachelor's degree.

ACADEMIC REQUIREMENTS. Freshmen must earn minimum 1.7 GPA in first semester, 2.0 cumulative thereafter. 91% of freshmen return for sophomore year. Students must declare major by end of second year. **Graduation requirements:** 124 hours for bachelor's (34 in major). Most students required to take courses in arts/fine arts, English, foreign languages, history, mathematics, philosophy/religion, biological/physical sciences, social sciences. **Postgraduate studies:** 10% enter law school, 6% enter medical school, 14% enter MBA programs, 47% enter other graduate study.

FRESHMAN ADMISSIONS. Selection criteria: Scholastic record, test scores, letters of recommendation, interests, and goals are very important. Evidence of talent, motivation, imagination, creativity, responsibility, and maturity are also considered. **High school preparation:** 16 units recommended. Recommended units include English 4, foreign language 2, mathematics 4, social science 2 and science 2. **Test requirements:** SAT or ACT (SAT preferred); score report by February 15.

1992 FRESHMAN CLASS PROFILE. 621 men applied, 459 accepted, 171 enrolled; 657 women applied, 561 accepted, 173 enrolled. 89% had high school GPA of 3.0 or higher, 11% between 2.0 and 2.99. 42% were in top tenth and 73% were in top quarter of graduating class. **Academic background:** Mid 50% of enrolled freshmen had SAT-V between 480-600, SAT-M between 520-640. 86% submitted SAT scores. **Characteristics:** 42% from in state, 97% live in college housing, 13% have minority backgrounds, 7% are foreign students, 46% join fraternities/sororities. Average age is 18.

FALL-TERM APPLICATIONS. $35 fee, may be waived for applicants with need. Closing date February 15; applicants notified on or about April 1; must reply by May 1. Essay required. Interview recommended. CRDA. Deferred and early admission available. EDP-F. Early decision application deadline is December 1.

STUDENT LIFE. Housing: Dormitories (women, coed); apartment, fraternity, sorority housing available. German, French, Spanish, Japanese, and Chinese language houses, as well as multiethnic, environmental, fine arts, and global issues houses available. **Activities:** Student government, magazine, radio, student newspaper, yearbook, choral groups, concert band, dance, drama, jazz band, music ensembles, musical theater, symphony orchestra, fraternities, sororities, outing program, College Life, multiethnic cultural association. **Additional information:** Friendship Family Program and assistance for foreign students available.

ATHLETICS. NAIA. **Intercollegiate:** Baseball M, basketball, cross-country, golf M, skiing, soccer, swimming, tennis, track and field, volleyball W. **Intramural:** Basketball, fencing, lacrosse, racquetball, rugby, skiing, soccer, softball, squash, tennis, volleyball, water polo.

STUDENT SERVICES. Aptitude testing, career counseling, employment service for undergraduates, freshman orientation, health services, on-campus day care, personal counseling, placement service for graduates, veterans counselor, services/facilities for handicapped.

ANNUAL EXPENSES. Tuition and fees: $15,805. **Room and board:** $4,790. **Books and supplies:** $750. **Other expenses:** $500.

FINANCIAL AID. 79% of freshmen, 76% of continuing students receive some form of aid. 94% of grants, 95% of loans, 52% of jobs based on need. 210 enrolled freshmen were judged to have need, all were offered aid. Academic, music/drama, art, state/district residency, leadership scholarships available. **Aid applications:** Closing date February 15; applicants notified on or about April 1; must reply by May 1. **Additional information:** Parent loan program through affiliated lender.

ADDRESS/TELEPHONE. Madeleine R. Eagon, Director of Admission, Whitman College, 345 Boyer Street, Walla Walla, WA 99362-2085. (509) 527-5176. Fax: (509) 527-5859.

Whitworth College
Spokane, Washington — CB code: 4953

4-year private liberal arts college, coed, affiliated with Presbyterian Church (USA). Founded in 1890. **Accreditation:** Regional. **Undergraduate enrollment:** 468 men, 666 women full time; 71 men, 188 women part time. **Graduate enrollment:** 21 men, 37 women full time; 66 men, 218 women part time. **Faculty:** 92 total (78 full time), 62 with doctorates or other terminal degrees. **Location:** Suburban campus in small city; 6 miles from Spokane, 280 miles from Seattle. **Calendar:** 4-1-4, limited summer session. Extensive evening/early morning classes. **Microcomputers:** 90 located in libraries, classrooms, computer centers. **Special facilities:** Koehler Art Gallery, Whitworth Aquatic Center, Stage II (theater).

DEGREES OFFERED. BA, BS, MA, MEd. 281 bachelor's degrees awarded in 1992. 20% in business and management, 6% communications, 15% teacher education, 7% letters/literature, 6% philosophy, religion, theology, 6% psychology, 15% social sciences, 10% visual and performing arts. Graduate degrees offered in 10 major fields of study.

UNDERGRADUATE MAJORS. Accounting, American studies, art history, arts management, biology, business administration and management, business economics, chemistry, communications, computer and information sciences, creative writing, dramatic arts, economics, elementary education, English, English literature, French, history, international business management, international relations, international studies, international trade and politics, journalism, junior high education, labor/industrial relations, mathematics, military science (Army), music, music performance, nursing, peace studies, philosophy, physical education, physics, political science and government, psychology, public policy studies, religion, religious music, secondary education, sociology, Spanish, speech, sports medicine, studio art, theological studies.

ACADEMIC PROGRAMS. Cooperative education, double major, dual enrollment of high school students, independent study, internships, student-designed major, study abroad, teacher preparation, visiting/exchange student program, Washington semester, cross-registration. **Remedial services:** Learning center, reduced course load, remedial instruction, special counselor, tutoring, English as second language. **ROTC:** Army. **Placement/credit:** AP, CLEP General and Subject, institutional tests; 32 credit hours maximum for bachelor's degree.

ACADEMIC REQUIREMENTS. Freshmen must earn minimum GPA of 2.0 to continue in good standing. 75% of freshmen return for sophomore year. Students must declare major by end of second year. **Graduation requirements:** 130 hours for bachelor's (40 in major). Most students required to take courses in arts/fine arts, English, foreign languages, history, humanities, mathematics, philosophy/religion, biological/physical sciences, social sciences. **Postgraduate studies:** 4% enter law school, 5% enter medical school, 3% enter MBA programs, 28% enter other graduate study.

FRESHMAN ADMISSIONS. Selection criteria: School achievement record with minimum GPA of 2.7 and essay most important. Test scores (SAT or ACT), significant work in school and community activities also considered. **High school preparation:** 16 units recommended. Recommended units include English 4, foreign language 2, mathematics 3, social science 3 and science 3. **Test requirements:** SAT or ACT.

1992 FRESHMAN CLASS PROFILE. 134 men, 183 women enrolled. 78% had high school GPA of 3.0 or higher, 22% between 2.0 and 2.99. 27% were in top tenth and 62% were in top quarter of graduating class. **Academic background:** Mid 50% of enrolled freshmen had SAT-V between 410-540, SAT-M between 450-590; ACT composite between 20-27. 83% submitted SAT scores, 23% submitted ACT scores. **Characteristics:** 51% from in state, 95% live in college housing, 16% have minority backgrounds, 8% are foreign students. Average age is 19.

FALL-TERM APPLICATIONS. No fee. No closing date; priority given to applications received by March 1; applicants notified on a rolling basis beginning on or about April 1; must reply by May 1 or within 2 weeks if notified thereafter. Essay required. Interview recommended. CRDA. Deferred admission available. EDP-F.

STUDENT LIFE. Housing: Dormitories (men, women, coed); handicapped housing available. **Activities:** Student government, film, magazine, radio, student newspaper, yearbook, choral groups, concert band, dance, drama, jazz band, music ensembles, musical theater, Black Student Union, Fellowship of Christian Athletes, International Club, Hawaiian Club, Political Activist Club, Native American Club, Amnesty International, Habitat for Humanity, Asian American Club, Circle K International.

ATHLETICS. NAIA. **Intercollegiate:** Baseball M, basketball, cross-country, diving, football M, soccer, swimming, tennis, track and field, volleyball W. **Intramural:** Basketball, soccer, softball, table tennis, tennis, volleyball, water polo.

STUDENT SERVICES. Aptitude testing, career counseling, employment service for undergraduates, freshman orientation, health services, personal counseling, placement service for graduates, special adviser for adult students, veterans counselor, study skills/tutoring, services/facilities for handicapped.

ANNUAL EXPENSES. Tuition and fees: $11,965. **Room and board:** $4,300. **Books and supplies:** $500. **Other expenses:** $1,200.

FINANCIAL AID. 81% of freshmen, 82% of continuing students receive some form of aid. 91% of grants, 96% of loans based on need. 182 enrolled freshmen were judged to have need, all were offered aid. Academic, music/drama, art, leadership scholarships available. **Aid applications:** No closing date; priority given to applications received by February 15; applicants notified on a rolling basis beginning on or about April 1; must reply by May 1 or within 2 weeks if notified thereafter.

ADDRESS/TELEPHONE. Ken Moyer, Director of Admissions, Whitworth College, Spokane, WA 99251-0002. (509) 466-3212. (800) 533-4668. Fax: (509) 466-3773.

Yakima Valley Community College

Yakima, Washington — CB code: 4993

2-year public community college, coed. Founded in 1928. **Accreditation:** Regional. **Undergraduate enrollment:** 1,108 men, 1,747 women full time; 1,290 men, 2,016 women part time. **Faculty:** 410 total (110 full time), 12 with doctorates or other terminal degrees. **Location:** Rural campus in small city; 150 miles from Seattle. **Calendar:** Quarter, extensive summer session. Saturday classes. **Microcomputers:** 45 located in classrooms, computer centers. **Special facilities:** Art gallery.

DEGREES OFFERED. AA, AS. 538 associate degrees awarded in 1992. 8% in business/office and marketing/distribution, 9% health sciences, 9% allied health, 62% multi/interdisciplinary studies.

UNDERGRADUATE MAJORS. Accounting, agribusiness, agricultural mechanics, agricultural production, agricultural sciences, agronomy, animal sciences, automotive mechanics, automotive technology, business administration and management, business and management, business and office, business data processing and related programs, child development/care/guidance, civil engineering, community health work, computer and information sciences, computer servicing technology, criminal justice studies, dental hygiene, diesel engine mechanics, dietetic aide/assistant, engineering and engineering-related technologies, fire control and safety technology, food management, graphic design, hospitality and recreation marketing, hotel/motel and restaurant management, instrumentation technology, legal secretary, liberal/general studies, marketing management, medical secretary, nursing, occupational therapy assistant, radio/television broadcasting, radiograph medical technology, secretarial and related programs, tourism, wildlife management.

ACADEMIC PROGRAMS. 2-year transfer program, cooperative education, independent study. **Remedial services:** Learning center, remedial instruction, special counselor, tutoring. **ROTC:** Army. **Placement/credit:** AP, CLEP General and Subject, institutional tests; 35 credit hours maximum for associate degree.

ACADEMIC REQUIREMENTS. Freshmen with up to 17 credit hours must earn 1.5 minimum GPA to continue in good academic standing. Those with 18-23 credits must earn 1.75. 65% of freshmen return for sophomore year. Students must declare major on application. **Graduation requirements:** 90 hours for associate. Most students required to take courses in English, humanities, mathematics, social sciences.

FRESHMAN ADMISSIONS. Selection criteria: Open admissions. Selected admissions to allied health programs. **Test requirements:** ACT/ASSET required for mathmatics and English applicants for placement.

1992 FRESHMAN CLASS PROFILE. 1,925 men and women enrolled. **Characteristics:** 90% from in state, 98% commute, 22% have minority backgrounds, 1% are foreign students. Average age is 30.

FALL-TERM APPLICATIONS. No fee. Closing date August 30; priority given to applications received by June 1; applicants notified on a rolling basis; must reply by registration. Interview required for dental hygiene, radiologic technology applicants. Deferred admission available.

STUDENT LIFE. Housing: Dormitories (men, women, coed). **Activities:** Student government, choral groups, concert band, drama, jazz band, music ensembles, symphony orchestra.

ATHLETICS. Intercollegiate: Baseball M, basketball, softball W, tennis, track and field, volleyball W, wrestling M. **Intramural:** Archery, badminton, bowling, golf, skiing, swimming, tennis.

STUDENT SERVICES. Aptitude testing, career counseling, employment service for undergraduates, freshman orientation, health services, on-campus day care, personal counseling, placement service for graduates, veterans counselor, services/facilities for handicapped.

ANNUAL EXPENSES. Tuition and fees: $1,156, $3,300 additional for out-of-state students. **Room and board:** $3,570. **Books and supplies:** $550. **Other expenses:** $1,150.

FINANCIAL AID. 51% of freshmen, 43% of continuing students receive some form of aid. All grants, all loans, 73% of jobs based on need. **Aid applications:** No closing date; priority given to applications received by May 1; applicants notified on a rolling basis beginning on or about July 1; must reply within 2 weeks.

ADDRESS/TELEPHONE. Ellie Heffeman, Dean of Enrollment Services, Yakima Valley Community College, 16th Avenue and Nob Hill Boulevard, Yakima, WA 98907. (509) 575-2373. Fax: (509) 575-2461.

West Virginia

Alderson-Broaddus College
Philippi, West Virginia CB code: 5005

Admissions: 84% of applicants accepted
Based on: ••• School record
•• Interview, test scores
• Activities, essay, recommendations, religious affiliation/commitment, special talents
Completion: 90% of freshmen end year in good standing
50% graduate, 20% of these enter graduate study

4-year private liberal arts college, coed, affiliated with American Baptist Churches in the USA. Founded in 1871. **Accreditation:** Regional. **Undergraduate enrollment:** 319 men, 418 women full time; 25 men, 28 women part time. **Graduate enrollment:** 12 men, 7 women full time. **Faculty:** 77 total (60 full time), 34 with doctorates or other terminal degrees. **Location:** Rural campus in small town; 100 miles form Charleston, 125 miles from Pittsburgh, Pennsylvania. **Calendar:** Semester, limited summer session. **Microcomputers:** 60 located in libraries, classrooms, computer centers, campus-wide network. **Special facilities:** Hospital.

DEGREES OFFERED. AA, AS, BA, BS, MS. 6 associate degrees awarded in 1992. 50% in business and management, 50% multi/interdisciplinary studies. 130 bachelor's degrees awarded. 7% in business and management, 5% communications, 9% education, 58% health sciences, 5% physical sciences, 5% social sciences. Graduate degrees offered in 1 major field of study.

UNDERGRADUATE MAJORS. Associate: Engineering and other disciplines, preengineering. **Bachelor's:** Accounting, analytical chemistry, applied mathematics, biology, business administration and management, business and management, chemistry, clinical laboratory science, communications, computer and information sciences, creative writing, cytotechnology, dramatic arts, early childhood education, education, education of the gifted and talented, education of the mentally handicapped, elementary education, English literature, history, information sciences and systems, inorganic chemistry, junior high education, liberal/general studies, management information systems, mathematics, mathematics education, microbiology, music, music education, music performance, nursing, organic chemistry, physical chemistry, physical education, physician's assistant, political science and government, predentistry, prelaw, premedicine, prepharmacy, preveterinary, psychology, radio/television broadcasting, radiograph medical technology, recreation and community services technologies, religion, science education, secondary education, social studies education, sociology, special education, specific learning disabilities, speech, sports medicine, technical and business writing, zoology.

ACADEMIC PROGRAMS. Accelerated program, double major, dual enrollment of high school students, honors program, independent study, internships, study abroad, teacher preparation, visiting/exchange student program, cross-registration; liberal arts/career combination in health sciences. **Remedial services:** Learning center, reduced course load, remedial instruction, special counselor, tutoring. **Placement/credit:** AP, CLEP General and Subject, institutional tests; 40 credit hours maximum for associate degree; 60 credit hours maximum for bachelor's degree.

ACADEMIC REQUIREMENTS. Freshmen must earn minimum GPA of 1.6 to continue in good standing. 75% of freshmen return for sophomore year. Students must declare major by end of second year. **Graduation requirements:** 128 hours for bachelor's (45 in major). Most students required to take courses in English, history, humanities, mathematics, philosophy/religion, biological/physical sciences, social sciences.

FRESHMAN ADMISSIONS. Selection criteria: High school record, rank in top half of class, test scores, interview very important. Physician's assistant and nursing applicants should have strong background in science. **High school preparation:** 15 units recommended. Recommended units include biological science 2, English 4, mathematics 2, physical science 2 and social science 4. **Test requirements:** SAT or ACT (ACT preferred); score report by August 1.

1992 FRESHMAN CLASS PROFILE. 178 men applied, 151 accepted, 70 enrolled; 349 women applied, 291 accepted, 103 enrolled. 64% had high school GPA of 3.0 or higher, 32% between 2.0 and 2.99. **Academic background:** Mid 50% of enrolled freshmen had SAT-V between 400-550, SAT-M between 400-550; ACT composite between 18-24. 40% submitted SAT scores, 60% submitted ACT scores. **Characteristics:** 65% from in state, 75% live in college housing, 5% have minority backgrounds, 1% are foreign students, 1% join fraternities/sororities. Average age is 19.

FALL-TERM APPLICATIONS. $10 fee, may be waived for applicants with need. Closing date September 1; applicants notified on a rolling basis; must reply within 2 weeks. Interview required. Audition required for music applicants. Interview required for physician's assistant applicants; recommended for all others. Deferred and early admission available.

STUDENT LIFE. Housing: Dormitories (men, women); apartment housing available. **Activities:** Student government, film, magazine, radio, student newspaper, television, yearbook, debate, choral groups, concert band, dance, drama, jazz band, music ensembles, musical theater, opera, pep band, fraternities, sororities, professional, ethnic, political, academic, religious, and service clubs, 4-H. **Additional information:** Participation in campus activities stressed. Voluntary weekly chapel service offered.

ATHLETICS. NCAA. **Intercollegiate:** Baseball M, basketball, cross-country, golf W, soccer M, volleyball W. **Intramural:** Archery, badminton, basketball, bowling, golf, gymnastics, handball, racquetball, skiing, soccer, softball W, swimming, table tennis, tennis, volleyball, water polo.

STUDENT SERVICES. Career counseling, freshman orientation, health services, personal counseling, placement service for graduates, veterans counselor, pre-registration for freshman, services/facilities for handicapped.

ANNUAL EXPENSES. Tuition and fees: $9,838. **Room and board:** $3,180. **Books and supplies:** $630. **Other expenses:** $1,100.

FINANCIAL AID. 94% of freshmen, 94% of continuing students receive some form of aid. Grants, loans, jobs available. 169 enrolled freshmen were judged to have need, all were offered aid. Academic, music/drama, athletic, state/district residency, leadership, religious affiliation, minority scholarships available. **Aid applications:** No closing date; priority given to applications received by May 1; applicants notified on a rolling basis beginning on or about February 15; must reply by May 1 or within 3 weeks if notified thereafter.

ADDRESS/TELEPHONE. Craig Gould, Director of Admissions, Alderson-Broaddus College, Philippi, WV 26416. (304) 457-1700.

Appalachian Bible College
Bradley, West Virginia CB code: 7305

4-year private Bible college, coed, nondenominational. Founded in 1950. **Undergraduate enrollment:** 98 men, 73 women full time; 20 men, 37 women part time. **Faculty:** 20 total (16 full time), 5 with doctorates or other terminal degrees. **Location:** Rural campus in rural community; 5 miles from Beckley. **Calendar:** Semester.

DEGREES OFFERED. AA, BA. 2 associate degrees awarded in 1992. 100% in philosophy, religion, theology. 24 bachelor's degrees awarded. 100% in philosophy, religion, theology.

UNDERGRADUATE MAJORS. Associate: Bible studies. **Bachelor's:** Theological studies.

ACADEMIC PROGRAMS. Dual enrollment of high school students, internships. **Remedial services:** Reduced course load, remedial instruction. **Placement/credit:** AP, CLEP General and Subject, institutional tests; 29 credit hours maximum for bachelor's degree.

ACADEMIC REQUIREMENTS. Freshmen must earn minimum GPA of 1.25 to continue in good standing. 73% of freshmen return for sophomore year. **Graduation requirements:** 62 hours for associate (26 in major), 126 hours for bachelor's (42 in major). Most students required to take courses in English, history, philosophy/religion, biological/physical sciences, social sciences.

FRESHMAN ADMISSIONS. Selection criteria: Profession of Jesus Christ as Saviour, essential agreement with doctrinal statement of college, approved character. Minimum 2.0 GPA, test scores, achievement and potential in English and social sciences also considered. **Test requirements:** ACT; score report by August 20.

1992 FRESHMAN CLASS PROFILE. 39 men, 34 women enrolled. **Academic background:** Mid 50% of enrolled freshmen had ACT composite between 14-20. 95% submitted ACT scores.

FALL-TERM APPLICATIONS. $10 fee. No closing date; priority given to applications received by July 1; applicants notified on a rolling basis. Essay required. Interview recommended. CRDA. Deferred and early admission available.

STUDENT LIFE. Housing: Dormitories (men, women); apartment housing available. Trailers for sale on campus for married students. **Activities:** Student government, choral groups, drama, music ensembles, handbell choir, puppetry. **Additional information:** Chapel held three times a week. Annual Spiritual Life Conference, Distinguished Christian Lecture Series, Bible and missions conferences. Religious observance required.

ATHLETICS. Intercollegiate: Basketball M, soccer M, volleyball W. **Intramural:** Basketball, soccer M, softball, table tennis, tennis, volleyball.

STUDENT SERVICES. Aptitude testing, career counseling, freshman orientation, health services, personal counseling, placement service for graduates, veterans counselor, services/facilities for handicapped.

ANNUAL EXPENSES. Tuition and fees: $4,210. **Room and board:** $2,700. **Books and supplies:** $520. **Other expenses:** $720.

FINANCIAL AID. 91% of freshmen, 78% of continuing students receive some form of aid. All grants, all loans, 24% of jobs based on need. **Aid applications:** No closing date; priority given to applications received by June 1; applicants notified on a rolling basis beginning on or about June 1.

ADDRESS/TELEPHONE. Cathie Canary, Director of Admissions, Appalachian Bible College, Box ABC, Bradley, WV 25818-1353. (304) 877-6428. (800) 678-9222. Fax: (304) 877-6423.

Bethany College
Bethany, West Virginia CB code: 5060

Admissions: 81% of applicants accepted
Based on: ••• School record
•• Activities, interview, recommendations, test scores
• Essay, religious affiliation/commitment, special talents
Completion: 85% of freshmen end year in good standing
67% graduate, 35% of these enter graduate study

4-year private liberal arts college, coed, affiliated with Christian Church (Disciples of Christ). Founded in 1840. **Accreditation:** Regional. **Undergraduate enrollment:** 358 men, 381 women full time; 10 men, 12 women part time. **Faculty:** 73 total (58 full time), 47 with doctorates or other terminal degrees. **Location:** Rural campus in rural community; 40 miles from Pittsburgh, Pennsylvania, 14 miles from Wheeling. **Calendar:** 4-1-4, limited summer session. **Microcomputers:** 70 located in libraries, classrooms, computer centers. **Special facilities:** Milsop Center (conference and seminar facility), founder's residence, museum, 1300 acres of nature preserves. **Additional facts:** College is national historic site.

DEGREES OFFERED. BA, BS, BFA. 166 bachelor's degrees awarded in 1992. 14% in business and management, 20% communications, 6% computer sciences, 9% education, 6% letters/literature, 5% life sciences, 5% mathematics, 17% social sciences.

UNDERGRADUATE MAJORS. Accounting, advertising, American literature, applied mathematics, biochemistry, biological and physical sciences, biology, business administration and management, business and management, business economics, chemistry, communications, comparative literature, computer and information sciences, computer graphics, dramatic arts, drawing, economics, education, elementary education, engineering and other disciplines, English, English education, English literature, experimental psychology, finance, fine arts, foreign languages education, French, German, graphic design, history, humanities and social sciences, international business management, international studies, journalism, junior high education, liberal/general studies, marketing management, mathematics, mathematics education, painting, philosophy, physical education, physical sciences, physics, political science and government, predentistry, prelaw, premedicine, preveterinary, psychology, public administration, public policy studies, public relations, radio/television broadcasting, radio/television technology, religion, science education, sculpture, secondary education, social psychology, social science education, social sciences, social studies education, social work, Spanish, special education, specific learning disabilities, speech/communication/theater education, sports management, studio art, theological studies, visual and performing arts.

ACADEMIC PROGRAMS. Accelerated program, double major, honors program, independent study, internships, semester at sea, student-designed major, study abroad, teacher preparation, United Nations semester, Washington semester, 3-2 engineering programs with Columbia University(NY), Case Western Reserve University(OH), George Washington University(Washington, DC), Georgia Institute of Technology(GA); liberal arts/career combination in engineering. **Remedial services:** Learning center, preadmission summer program, reduced course load, special counselor, tutoring. **Placement/credit:** AP, CLEP General and Subject, institutional tests.

ACADEMIC REQUIREMENTS. Freshmen must earn minimum GPA of 2.0 to continue in good standing. 91% of freshmen return for sophomore year. Students must declare major by end of second year. **Graduation requirements:** 128 hours for bachelor's (34 in major). Most students required to take courses in English, humanities, mathematics, philosophy/religion, social sciences. **Postgraduate studies:** 10% enter law school, 6% enter medical school, 4% enter MBA programs, 15% enter other graduate study. **Additional information:** Students with learning disabilities must apply by Febuary 15 for priority consideration in learning disabled program. Space is limited.

FRESHMAN ADMISSIONS. Selection criteria: Rank in top half of graduating class, test scores, interview, activities, and recommendations important considerations. **High school preparation:** 15 units required. Required and recommended units include English 4, mathematics 3, physical science 2 and social science 4. Biological science 3, foreign language 2 and science 2 recommended. 2 laboratory science also required. **Test requirements:** SAT or ACT; score report by August 1.

1992 FRESHMAN CLASS PROFILE. 441 men applied, 336 accepted, 131 enrolled; 323 women applied, 285 accepted, 128 enrolled. 80% had high school GPA of 3.0 or higher, 20% between 2.0 and 2.99. **Academic background:** Mid 50% of enrolled freshmen had SAT-V between 420-530, SAT-M between 440-570; ACT composite between 22-27. 67% submitted SAT scores, 33% submitted ACT scores. **Characteristics:** 21% from in state, 99% live in college housing, 3% have minority backgrounds, 2% are foreign students, 65% join fraternities/sororities. Average age is 18.

FALL-TERM APPLICATIONS. $20 fee, may be waived for applicants with need. Closing date August 1; priority given to applications received by April 1; applicants notified on a rolling basis; must reply by May 1 or within 8 weeks if notified thereafter. Essay required. Interview recommended. CRDA. Deferred admission available.

STUDENT LIFE. Housing: Dormitories (men, women, coed); apartment, fraternity, sorority housing available. Guaranteed housing for all students. **Activities:** Student government, magazine, radio, student newspaper, television, yearbook, literary magazine, choral groups, dance, drama, music ensembles, musical theater, pep band, fraternities, sororities, community service organization, ecumenical religious organization, sports clubs, Association of International Students for Economic Cooperation, political science club, public relations club, advertising club.

ATHLETICS. NCAA. **Intercollegiate:** Baseball M, basketball, cross-country, football M, golf, soccer, softball W, swimming, track and field, volleyball W. **Intramural:** Basketball, cross-country, football, handball, horseback riding, ice hockey M, lacrosse, racquetball, rugby M, skiing, soccer, softball, swimming, table tennis, tennis, track and field, volleyball, water polo, wrestling M.

STUDENT SERVICES. Aptitude testing, career counseling, employment service for undergraduates, freshman orientation, health services, personal counseling, placement service for graduates, special adviser for adult students, veterans counselor, learning disabled program, services/facilities for handicapped.

ANNUAL EXPENSES. Tuition and fees (1992-93): $12,907. **Room and board:** $4,368. **Books and supplies:** $350. **Other expenses:** $775.

FINANCIAL AID. 75% of freshmen, 80% of continuing students receive some form of aid. 90% of grants, 97% of loans, 96% of jobs based on need. Academic, leadership, religious affiliation scholarships available. **Aid applications:** No closing date; priority given to applications received by April 1; applicants notified on a rolling basis; must reply by May 1 or within 2 weeks if notified thereafter.

ADDRESS/TELEPHONE. Gary R. Forney, VP Enrollment Management, Bethany College, Bethany, WV 26032. (304) 829-7611. (800) 922-7611. Fax: (304) 829-7108.

Bluefield State College
Bluefield, West Virginia CB code: 5064

4-year public college of arts and sciences and community college, coed. Founded in 1895. **Accreditation:** Regional. **Undergraduate enrollment:** 746 men, 789 women full time; 431 men, 965 women part time. **Faculty:** 183 total (94 full time), 33 with doctorates or other terminal degrees. **Location:** Suburban campus in large town; 100 miles from Charleston, West Virginia. **Calendar:** Semester, limited summer session. **Microcomputers:** 146 located in libraries, classrooms, computer centers. **Special facilities:** Instructional technology center. **Additional facts:** Off-campus locations at Lewisburg, Welch, and Beckley, West Virginia.

DEGREES OFFERED. AS, AAS, BA, BS. 221 associate degrees awarded in 1992. 19% in business and management, 7% computer sciences, 19% engineering technologies, 40% health sciences, 7% parks/recreation, protective services, public affairs. 276 bachelor's degrees awarded. 22% in business and management, 11% computer sciences, 20% teacher education, 14% engineering technologies, 7% health sciences, 9% allied health, 13% parks/recreation, protective services, public affairs, 6% social sciences.

UNDERGRADUATE MAJORS. Associate: Accounting, architectural technologies, business data programming, civil technology, computer programming, drafting, education, electrical technology, finance, law enforcement and corrections, legal secretary, liberal/general studies, marketing and distribution, marketing management, mechanical design technology, medical secretary, nursing, preengineering, radiograph medical technology, secretarial and related programs. **Bachelor's:** Accounting, architectural technologies, biology, business administration and management, chemistry, civil technology, computer programming, criminal justice studies, electrical technology, elementary education, English, English education, history, junior high education, law enforcement and corrections, mathematics, mathematics education, mining and petroleum technologies, nursing, office supervision and management, physical education, physics, science education, secondary education, social sciences, social studies education.

ACADEMIC PROGRAMS. 2-year transfer program, dual enrollment of high school students, independent study, internships, teacher preparation, telecourses, visiting/exchange student program, cross-registration; liberal arts/career combination in health sciences. **Remedial services:** Learning center, reduced course load, remedial instruction, special counselor, tutoring. **Placement/credit:** AP, CLEP General and Subject, institutional tests.

ACADEMIC REQUIREMENTS. Freshmen must earn minimum GPA of 1.8 to continue in good standing. 60% of freshmen return for sophomore year. Students must declare major on application. **Graduation requirements:** 64 hours for associate, 128 hours for bachelor's (36 in major). Most students required to take courses in computer science, English, humanities, mathematics, biological/physical sciences, social sciences. **Postgraduate studies:** 72% from 2-year programs enter 4-year programs. 2% enter law school, 2% enter medical school, 6% enter MBA programs, 5% enter other graduate study.

FRESHMAN ADMISSIONS. Selection criteria: Open admissions. Open admissions to associate degree programs except allied health. 2.0 GPA, ACT composite score of 17 or SAT combined score 690 for bachelor degree programs. **High school preparation:** 11 units required; 13 recommended. Required and recommended units include biological science 2, English 4, mathematics 2 and social science 3. Foreign language 2 recommended. Applicants without 11 units required for bachelor's degree program may start in associate degree program. **Test requirements:** SAT or ACT; score report by August 23.

1992 FRESHMAN CLASS PROFILE. 200 men, 254 women enrolled. 35% had high school GPA of 3.0 or higher, 65% between 2.0 and 2.99. 5% were in top tenth and 15% were in top quarter of graduating class. **Academic background:** Mid 50% of enrolled freshmen had ACT composite between 15-18. 98% submitted ACT scores. **Characteristics:** 95% from in state, 100% commute, 12% have minority backgrounds, 5% join fraternities/sororities. Average age is 23.

FALL-TERM APPLICATIONS. No fee. No closing date; applicants notified on a rolling basis beginning on or about December 1. Deferred and early admission available.

STUDENT LIFE. Activities: Student government, magazine, student newspaper, television, yearbook, choral groups, jazz band, pep band, fraternities, sororities.

ATHLETICS. NAIA. **Intercollegiate:** Baseball M, basketball, cross-country, golf, softball W, tennis. **Intramural:** Archery, badminton, basketball, bowling, cross-country, handball, skiing, soccer M, softball, swimming, table tennis, tennis, volleyball, water polo.

STUDENT SERVICES. Aptitude testing, career counseling, employment service for undergraduates, freshman orientation, health services, personal counseling, placement service for graduates, veterans counselor, minority counselor, services/facilities for handicapped.

ANNUAL EXPENSES. Tuition and fees (1992-93): $1,726, $2,270 additional for out-of-state students. **Books and supplies:** $800. **Other expenses:** $900.

FINANCIAL AID. 60% of freshmen, 44% of continuing students receive some form of aid. 96% of grants, 94% of loans, 57% of jobs based on need. Academic, athletic scholarships available. **Aid applications:** No closing date; priority given to applications received by March 1; applicants notified on or about July 15.

ADDRESS/TELEPHONE. John C. Cardwell, Director of Admissions, Bluefield State College, Rock Street, Bluefield, WV 24701. (304) 327-4065. (800) 654-7798. Fax: (304) 325-7747.

College of West Virginia
Beckley, West Virginia — CB code: 5054

4-year private liberal arts college, coed. Founded in 1933. **Accreditation:** Regional. **Undergraduate enrollment:** 350 men, 733 women full time; 217 men, 547 women part time. **Faculty:** 115 total (27 full time), 17 with doctorates or other terminal degrees. **Location:** Suburban campus in large town; 55 miles from Charleston. **Calendar:** Semester, limited summer session. Saturday and extensive evening/early morning classes. **Microcomputers:** 60 located in libraries, computer centers.

DEGREES OFFERED. AA, AS, BS. 163 associate degrees awarded in 1992. 15% in business/office and marketing/distribution, 48% education, 8% allied health, 25% multi/interdisciplinary studies.

UNDERGRADUATE MAJORS. Associate: Airline piloting and navigation, aviation management, business and office, computer programming, education, electronic technology, finance, information sciences and systems, legal assistant/paralegal, legal secretary, liberal/general studies, medical assistant, medical laboratory technologies, medical secretary, radio/television broadcasting, respiratory therapy technology, secretarial and related programs, social work, tourism. **Bachelor's:** Business administration and management, business and office, computer programming, health care administration, nursing.

ACADEMIC PROGRAMS. Dual enrollment of high school students, honors program, independent study, internships, 2-2 program with Bluefield State College in nursing, radiologic technology, and law enforcement. **Remedial services:** Remedial instruction, tutoring, basic skills laboratory. **Placement/credit:** CLEP General and Subject; 30 credit hours maximum for associate degree.

ACADEMIC REQUIREMENTS. Freshmen must earn minimum GPA of 2.0 to continue in good standing. 70% of freshmen return for sophomore year. Students must declare major by end of first year. **Graduation requirements:** 64 hours for associate, 128 hours for bachelor's. Most students required to take courses in arts/fine arts, computer science, English, history, humanities, mathematics, biological/physical sciences, social sciences. **Postgraduate studies:** 60% from 2-year programs enter 4-year programs.

FRESHMAN ADMISSIONS. Selection criteria: Open admissions. Selective admissions to health science programs. **Test requirements:** ACT for placement.

1992 FRESHMAN CLASS PROFILE. 27 men, 281 women enrolled. **Characteristics:** 99% from in state, 100% commute, 10% have minority backgrounds.

FALL-TERM APPLICATIONS. No fee. Closing date August 30; applicants notified on a rolling basis. Interview required. Deferred and early admission available.

STUDENT LIFE. Housing: Cooperative housing available. **Activities:** Student government, student newspaper.

ATHLETICS. Intramural: Basketball, bowling, racquetball, softball, swimming, table tennis, tennis, volleyball.

STUDENT SERVICES. Aptitude testing, career counseling, employment service for undergraduates, freshman orientation, health services, on-campus day care, personal counseling, placement service for graduates, special adviser for adult students, veterans counselor, services/facilities for handicapped.

ANNUAL EXPENSES. Tuition and fees (projected): $2,712. **Books and supplies:** $500. **Other expenses:** $1,000.

FINANCIAL AID. 20% of freshmen, 87% of continuing students receive some form of aid. 96% of grants, 89% of loans, 73% of jobs based on need. Academic scholarships available. **Aid applications:** No closing date; priority given to applications received by June 1; applicants notified on a rolling basis beginning on or about July 1; must reply within 2 weeks.

ADDRESS/TELEPHONE. Gloria Thompson, Registrar and Director of Admissions, College of West Virginia, PO Box AG, Beckley, WV 25802-2830. (304) 253-7351. (800) 766-6067. Fax: (304) 253-0789.

Concord College
Athens, West Virginia — CB code: 5120

Admissions: 98% of applicants accepted
Based on: ••• School record
•• Test scores
• Recommendations
Completion: 65% of freshmen end year in good standing
55% graduate, 20% of these enter graduate study

4-year public liberal arts college, coed. Founded in 1872. **Accreditation:** Regional. **Undergraduate enrollment:** 890 men, 1,236 women full time; 283 men, 551 women part time. **Faculty:** 145 total (95 full time), 48 with doctorates or other terminal degrees. **Location:** Rural campus in rural community; 5 miles from Princeton, 80 miles from Charleston. **Calendar:** Semester, limited summer session. Extensive evening/early morning classes. **Microcomputers:** 52 located in dormitories, classrooms, computer centers. **Special facilities:** Alexander Fine Arts Center.

DEGREES OFFERED. BA, BS. 362 bachelor's degrees awarded in 1992. 21% in business and management, 39% teacher education, 6% multi/interdisciplinary studies, 7% parks/recreation, protective services, public affairs, 15% social sciences.

UNDERGRADUATE MAJORS. Accounting, art education, biology, business and management, business education, chemistry, clinical laboratory science, communications, computer and information sciences, computer mathematics, early childhood education, education of the mentally handicapped, elementary education, English, English education, finance, geography, history, hospitality and recreation marketing, hotel/motel and restaurant management, journalism, junior high education, liberal/general studies, library science, marketing and distribution, marketing management, mathematics, mathematics education, music education, parks and recreation management, physical education, political science and government, predentistry, prelaw, premedicine, prepharmacy, preveterinary, psychology, public relations, pure mathematics, radio/television broadcasting, reading education, science education, secondary education, secretarial and related programs, social science education, social studies education, social work, sociology, special education, speech, studio art, tourism.

ACADEMIC PROGRAMS. Double major, dual enrollment of high school students, honors program, independent study, internships, student-designed major, study abroad, teacher preparation, last year in medical technology at Duke University. **Remedial services:** Learning center, reduced course load, remedial instruction, special counselor, tutoring. **Placement/credit:** AP, CLEP General and Subject, institutional tests; 96 credit hours maximum for bachelor's degree.

ACADEMIC REQUIREMENTS. Freshmen must earn minimum GPA of 1.5 to continue in good standing. 60% of freshmen return for sophomore year. Students must declare major by end of second year. **Graduation requirements:** 128 hours for bachelor's. Most students required to take courses in arts/fine arts, English, history, humanities, mathematics, biological/physical sciences, social sciences. **Postgraduate studies:** 2% enter law school, 3% enter medical school, 9% enter MBA programs, 6% enter other graduate study.

FRESHMAN ADMISSIONS. Selection criteria: 2.0 high school GPA and 680 SAT required. **High school preparation:** 20 units required; 22 recommended. Required and recommended units include English 4, mathematics 2, social science 3 and science 2. Foreign language 2 recommended. Mathematics courses must include algebra I and another higher level course. Require two science courses that must include laboratory. Social science requirement includes 1 US history. **Test requirements:** SAT or ACT; score report by August 15.

1992 FRESHMAN CLASS PROFILE. 726 men applied, 704 accepted, 395 enrolled; 945 women applied, 930 accepted, 562 enrolled. 28% had high school GPA of 3.0 or higher, 67% between 2.0 and 2.99. **Academic back-**

ground: Mid 50% of enrolled freshmen had ACT composite between 18-22. 90% submitted ACT scores. **Characteristics:** 85% from in state, 60% commute, 5% have minority backgrounds, 1% are foreign students, 20% join fraternities/sororities. Average age is 18.

FALL-TERM APPLICATIONS. No fee. No closing date; priority given to applications received by August 1; applicants notified on a rolling basis. Audition required for music education applicants. Portfolio recommended for art applicants. Early admission available.

STUDENT LIFE. Housing: Dormitories (men, women, coed); apartment, fraternity, sorority housing available. **Activities:** Student government, magazine, radio, student newspaper, television, yearbook, choral groups, concert band, drama, jazz band, marching band, music ensembles, pep band, fraternities, sororities, Black Student Union, social service club.

ATHLETICS. NAIA. **Intercollegiate:** Baseball M, basketball, football M, golf M, softball W, tennis, volleyball W. **Intramural:** Archery, badminton, basketball, bowling, cross-country, golf, handball, racquetball, soccer W, softball, swimming, tennis, track and field, volleyball, water polo.

STUDENT SERVICES. Aptitude testing, career counseling, employment service for undergraduates, freshman orientation, health services, on-campus day care, personal counseling, placement service for graduates, veterans counselor.

ANNUAL EXPENSES. Tuition and fees (1992-93): $1,736, $2,130 additional for out-of-state students. **Room and board:** $3,018. **Books and supplies:** $400. **Other expenses:** $1,008.

FINANCIAL AID. 64% of freshmen, 62% of continuing students receive some form of aid. 65% of grants, 71% of loans, 58% of jobs based on need. 392 enrolled freshmen were judged to have need, all were offered aid. Academic, music/drama, art, athletic scholarships available. **Aid applications:** No closing date; priority given to applications received by April 15; applicants notified on a rolling basis beginning on or about May 1; must reply within 2 weeks. **Additional information:** Room and board may be paid in 2 equal installments each semester.

ADDRESS/TELEPHONE. Dale Dickens, Director of Admissions, Concord College, Athens, WV 24712. (304) 384-5248. Fax: (304) 384-9044 ext. 5249.

Davis and Elkins College

Elkins, West Virginia CB code: 5151

Admissions: 90% of applicants accepted
Based on: ••• Recommendations, school record, test scores
•• Interview
• Activities, essay, special talents
Completion: 90% of freshmen end year in good standing

4-year private liberal arts college, coed, affiliated with Presbyterian Church (USA). Founded in 1904. **Accreditation:** Regional. **Undergraduate enrollment:** 330 men, 429 women full time; 85 men, 78 women part time. **Faculty:** 79 total (55 full time), 32 with doctorates or other terminal degrees. **Location:** Rural campus in small town; 130 miles from Pittsburgh, Pennsylvania, 200 miles from Washington, D.C. **Calendar:** Semester, extensive summer session. **Microcomputers:** 75 located in libraries, computer centers. **Special facilities:** Paull Art Gallery, planetarium.

DEGREES OFFERED. AA, AS, BA, BS. 43 associate degrees awarded in 1992. 14% in business and management, 63% health sciences, 14% multi/interdisciplinary studies, 7% psychology. 108 bachelor's degrees awarded. 40% in business and management, 7% business/office and marketing/distribution, 13% education, 5% life sciences, 6% parks/recreation, protective services, public affairs, 5% psychology, 10% social sciences.

UNDERGRADUATE MAJORS. Associate: Accounting, business administration and management, business and management, business data processing and related programs, business data programming, computer and information sciences, dramatic arts, fashion merchandising, health care administration, hospitality and recreation marketing, journalism, mental health/human services, nursing, office supervision and management, prepharmacy, psychology, real estate, secretarial and related programs, word processing. **Bachelor's:** Accounting, applied mathematics, art education, biology, business administration and management, business and management, business economics, business education, chemistry, communications, computer and information sciences, computer mathematics, computer programming, creative writing, dramatic arts, economics, education, elementary education, engineering, English, English education, English literature, environmental science, exercise science, fashion merchandising, finance, fine arts, foreign languages education, forestry and related sciences, French, health care administration, health education, history, hotel/motel and restaurant management, international business management, journalism, junior high education, marketing management, mathematics, mathematics education, medical laboratory technologies, music, music business management, music performance, nursing, occupational therapy, office supervision and management, painting, philosophy, physical education, political science and government, predentistry, preengineering, prelaw, premedicine, preveterinary, psychology, radio/television broadcasting, recreation and community services technologies, religion, religious education, science education, secondary education, secretarial and related programs, social studies education, sociology, Spanish, sports management, theater design, theological studies, tourism, transportation and travel marketing, word processing.

ACADEMIC PROGRAMS. Accelerated program, double major, honors program, independent study, internships, student-designed major, study abroad, teacher preparation, Washington semester, cross-registration. **Remedial services:** Learning center, reduced course load, remedial instruction, special counselor, tutoring. **Placement/credit:** AP, CLEP General and Subject, institutional tests.

ACADEMIC REQUIREMENTS. Freshmen must earn minimum GPA of 2.0 to continue in good standing. 65% of freshmen return for sophomore year. Students must declare major by end of second year. **Graduation requirements:** 62 hours for associate (30 in major), 124 hours for bachelor's (40 in major). Most students required to take courses in arts/fine arts, computer science, English, history, mathematics, philosophy/religion, biological/physical sciences, social sciences. **Postgraduate studies:** 75% from 2-year programs enter 4-year programs.

FRESHMAN ADMISSIONS. Selection criteria: School achievement record, interview, guidance counselor recommendation, school and community activities. **High school preparation:** 11 units required. Required and recommended units include English 4, mathematics 2, social science 3 and science 2. Foreign language 2 recommended. **Test requirements:** SAT or ACT; score report by June 1.

1992 FRESHMAN CLASS PROFILE. 332 men applied, 287 accepted, 94 enrolled; 335 women applied, 312 accepted, 115 enrolled. 22% had high school GPA of 3.0 or higher, 61% between 2.0 and 2.99. **Academic background:** Mid 50% of enrolled freshmen had SAT-V between 330-420, SAT-M between 340-490; ACT composite between 17-22. 43% submitted SAT scores, 38% submitted ACT scores. **Characteristics:** 50% from in state, 60% live in college housing, 9% have minority backgrounds, 4% are foreign students, 33% join fraternities/sororities. Average age is 18.

FALL-TERM APPLICATIONS. $25 fee, may be waived for applicants with need. No closing date; priority given to applications received by May 1; applicants notified on a rolling basis. Audition required for drama/music applicants. Portfolio required for art applicants. Interview recommended for academically weak applicants. Essay recommended. CRDA. Deferred and early admission available.

STUDENT LIFE. Housing: Dormitories (men, women, coed); fraternity, sorority housing available. **Activities:** Student government, magazine, radio, student newspaper, yearbook, literary magazine, choral groups, drama, jazz band, fraternities, sororities, student Christian group.

ATHLETICS. NAIA, NCAA. **Intercollegiate:** Baseball M, basketball, cross-country, field hockey W, golf M, soccer M, softball W, tennis. **Intramural:** Badminton, basketball, cross-country, soccer, softball, tennis, volleyball.

STUDENT SERVICES. Aptitude testing, career counseling, employment service for undergraduates, freshman orientation, health services, personal counseling, placement service for graduates, veterans counselor, services/facilities for handicapped.

ANNUAL EXPENSES. Tuition and fees (1992-93): $8,180. **Room and board:** $3,930. **Books and supplies:** $400.

FINANCIAL AID. 65% of freshmen, 65% of continuing students receive some form of aid. Grants, loans, jobs available. Academic, music/drama, art, athletic, state/district residency, leadership, religious affiliation scholarships available. **Aid applications:** No closing date; priority given to applications received by March 1; applicants notified on a rolling basis beginning on or about March 1; must reply by May 1 or within 2 weeks if notified thereafter.

ADDRESS/TELEPHONE. Kevin Chenoweth, Director of Admissions, Davis and Elkins College, 100 Campus Drive, Elkins, WV 26241. (304) 636-5850. (800) 624-3157. Fax: (304) 636-8624.

Fairmont State College

Fairmont, West Virginia CB code: 5211

4-year public college of arts and sciences and business, community, teachers, technical college, coed. Founded in 1865. **Accreditation:** Regional. **Undergraduate enrollment:** 2,133 men, 2,406 women full time; 976 men, 1,100 women part time. **Faculty:** 393 total (173 full time), 85 with doctorates or other terminal degrees. **Location:** Suburban campus in large town; 70 miles from Pittsburgh, Pennsylvania. **Calendar:** Semester, limited summer session. **Microcomputers:** 60 located in computer centers.

DEGREES OFFERED. AA, AS, AAS, BA, BS. 211 associate degrees awarded in 1992. 38% in business and management, 10% business/office and marketing/distribution, 5% computer sciences, 32% engineering technologies, 10% allied health, 5% trade and industry. 567 bachelor's degrees awarded. 25% in business and management, 5% business/office and marketing/distribution, 5% computer sciences, 27% teacher education, 25% engineering technologies, 10% social sciences.

UNDERGRADUATE MAJORS. Associate: Accounting, architectural technologies, business and office, business data processing and related programs, civil technology, clinical laboratory science, computer and information sciences, criminal justice studies, data processing, drafting, drafting and design technology, electronic technology, finance, food production/management/services, food science and nutrition, graphic and printing production, industrial technology, insurance and risk management, insurance marketing, law enforcement and corrections technologies, liberal/general studies, mechanical design technology, medical laboratory technologies, medical records technology, mining and petroleum technologies, nursing, real estate, retailing, secretarial and related programs, veterinarian's assistant. **Bachelor's:** Accounting, architectural technologies, art education, biology, business and management, business data processing and related programs, business economics, business education, chemistry, civil technology, community psychology, community services, computer and information sciences, criminal justice studies, early childhood education, education of the emotionally handicapped, education of the gifted and talented, education of the mentally handicapped, electronic technology, elementary education, English, English education, finance, foreign languages education, French, health sciences, history, home economics, home economics education, industrial and organizational psychology, industrial arts education, industrial technology, liberal/general studies, management science, marketing management, mathematics, mathematics education, mechanical design technology, mining and petroleum technologies, music education, nursing, occupational safety and health technology, physical education, political science and government, psychology, science education, secondary education, secretarial and related programs, social studies education, sociology, specific learning disabilities, speech/communication/theater education, technical education.

ACADEMIC PROGRAMS. Dual enrollment of high school students, teacher preparation. **Remedial services:** Learning center, remedial instruction, tutoring. **ROTC:** Army. **Placement/credit:** AP, CLEP General and Subject, institutional tests; 28 credit hours maximum for bachelor's degree.

ACADEMIC REQUIREMENTS. Freshmen must earn minimum GPA of 2.0 to continue in good standing. Students must declare major on enrollment. **Graduation requirements:** 64 hours for associate (38 in major), 128 hours for bachelor's (50 in major). Most students required to take courses in English, history, social sciences. **Postgraduate studies:** 30% from 2-year programs enter 4-year programs.

FRESHMAN ADMISSIONS. Selection criteria: 2.25 high school GPA or minimum ACT composite score of 19 or SAT combined score of 730 for bachelor's programs. Open admissions to associate degree programs except allied health. **High school preparation:** 11 units required. Required and recommended units include biological science 2, English 4, mathematics 2 and social science 3. Foreign language 2 recommended. Social science must include 1 US history. Mathematics must include algebra. 2 units laboratory science required in biology, chemistry, physics. **Test requirements:** SAT or ACT (ACT preferred); score report by August 20.

1992 FRESHMAN CLASS PROFILE. 920 men applied, 916 accepted, 699 enrolled; 1,077 women applied, 1,075 accepted, 838 enrolled. 30% had high school GPA of 3.0 or higher, 50% between 2.0 and 2.99. **Academic background:** Mid 50% of enrolled freshmen had ACT composite between 14-22. 85% submitted ACT scores. **Characteristics:** 95% from in state, 93% commute, 3% have minority backgrounds. Average age is 22.

FALL-TERM APPLICATIONS. No fee. Closing date June 15; applicants notified on a rolling basis. Deferred and early admission available.

STUDENT LIFE. Housing: Dormitories (men, women). **Activities:** Student government, student newspaper, yearbook, choral groups, concert band, drama, jazz band, marching band, music ensembles, opera, fraternities, sororities.

ATHLETICS. NAIA. **Intercollegiate:** Baseball M, basketball, cross-country, football M, golf M, swimming, tennis, volleyball W. **Intramural:** Archery, badminton W, basketball, bowling, cross-country, field hockey W, football M, golf, racquetball, softball, swimming, table tennis, tennis, track and field, volleyball, wrestling M.

STUDENT SERVICES. Aptitude testing, career counseling, employment service for undergraduates, freshman orientation, health services, personal counseling, placement service for graduates, special adviser for adult students, veterans counselor, services/facilities for handicapped.

ANNUAL EXPENSES. Tuition and fees (1992-93): $1,686, $2,320 additional for out-of-state students. **Room and board:** $3,040. **Books and supplies:** $500. **Other expenses:** $500.

FINANCIAL AID. 60% of freshmen, 60% of continuing students receive some form of aid. 86% of grants, 85% of loans, 41% of jobs based on need. 1,031 enrolled freshmen were judged to have need, all were offered aid. Academic, music/drama, athletic, leadership, alumni affiliation scholarships available. **Aid applications:** Closing date March 1; applicants notified on or about June 1; must reply within 10 days.

ADDRESS/TELEPHONE. John G. Conaway, EdD, Director of Admissions, Fairmont State College, Locust Avenue, Fairmont, WV 26554. (304) 367-4141.

Glenville State College
Glenville, West Virginia — CB code: 5254

Admissions:	98% of applicants accepted
Based on:	••• School record
	•• Test scores
	• Recommendations
Completion:	60% of freshmen end year in good standing
	52% graduate, 10% of these enter graduate study

4-year public liberal arts, teachers college, coed. Founded in 1872. **Accreditation:** Regional. **Undergraduate enrollment:** 886 men, 802 women full time; 260 men, 397 women part time. **Faculty:** 146 total (74 full-time), 50 with doctorates or other terminal degrees. **Location:** Rural campus in rural community; 90 miles from Charleston. **Calendar:** Semester, limited summer session. **Microcomputers:** 56 located in computer centers.

DEGREES OFFERED. AA, AS, BA, BS. 82 associate degrees awarded in 1992. 60% in business/office and marketing/distribution, 15% trade and industry, 22% visual and performing arts. 296 bachelor's degrees awarded. 20% in business and management, 47% education, 23% multi/interdisciplinary studies.

UNDERGRADUATE MAJORS. Associate: Arts management, business and office, business computer/console/peripheral equipment operation, business data processing and related programs, criminal justice technology, food management, forestry and related sciences, graphic arts technology, information sciences and systems, mining and petroleum technologies, music business management, recreation and community services technologies, secretarial and related programs, survey and mapping technology, surveying and mapping sciences, word processing. **Bachelor's:** Accounting, art education, biological and physical sciences, biology, business and management, business education, chemistry, computer and information sciences, driver and safety education, early childhood education, education, education of the mentally handicapped, elementary education, English, English education, finance, history, international business management, junior high education, liberal/general studies, marketing management, mathematics education, music education, nursing, physical education, predentistry, premedicine, prepharmacy, preveterinary, science education, secondary education, social science education, social studies education, special education, specific learning disabilities, speech/communication/theater education, sports management, sports medicine.

ACADEMIC PROGRAMS. Accelerated program, internships, student-designed major, teacher preparation, cross-registration; liberal arts/career combination in forestry. **Remedial services:** Remedial instruction. **Placement/credit:** AP, CLEP General and Subject, institutional tests. Unlimited number of hours of credit may be counted for degree.

ACADEMIC REQUIREMENTS. Freshmen must earn minimum GPA of 1.5 to continue in good standing. 66% of freshmen return for sophomore year. Students must declare major by end of second year. **Graduation requirements:** 64 hours for associate (56 in major), 128 hours for bachelor's (48 in major). Most students required to take courses in English, history, mathematics, biological/physical sciences, social sciences. **Postgraduate studies:** 15% from 2-year programs enter 4-year programs. **Additional information:** Credit for employment, military, and life experience awarded only in nontraditional bachelor of arts directors degree program.

FRESHMAN ADMISSIONS. Selection criteria: Applicants with high school GPA under 2.0 or ACT under 17 admitted on probation. Selective admissions to forest technology and land surveying programs based on school achievement record and counselor's recommendation. **High school preparation:** 21 units required. Required units include English 4, mathematics 2, social science 3 and science 2. 2 mathematics required of petroleum engineering technology applicants. **Test requirements:** SAT or ACT (ACT preferred); score report by August 22.

1992 FRESHMAN CLASS PROFILE. 842 men applied, 828 accepted, 358 enrolled; 759 women applied, 740 accepted, 420 enrolled. 32% had high school GPA of 3.0 or higher, 64% between 2.0 and 2.99. 5% were in top tenth and 16% were in top quarter of graduating class. **Academic background:** Mid 50% of enrolled freshmen had ACT composite between 22-34. 95% submitted ACT scores. **Characteristics:** 90% from in state, 60% live in college housing, 3% have minority backgrounds, 1% are foreign students, 1% join fraternities/sororities. Average age is 19.

FALL-TERM APPLICATIONS. No fee. No closing date; priority given to applications received by August 1; applicants notified on a rolling basis. Interview recommended for forest technology, land surveying, petroleum engineering technology, nursing applicants. Audition recommended for music education applicants. Portfolio recommended for art education applicants. Deferred and early admission available.

STUDENT LIFE. Housing: Dormitories (men, women); apartment, sorority housing available. Dormitories kept open for international students during vacations and holidays. **Activities:** Student government, student newspaper, yearbook, choral groups, concert band, drama, jazz band, marching band, music ensembles, musical theater, fraternities, sororities.

ATHLETICS. NAIA. **Intercollegiate:** Basketball, bowling M, football M, golf M. **Intramural:** Basketball, handball, softball, volleyball.

STUDENT SERVICES. Career counseling, employment service for

undergraduates, health services, personal counseling, placement service for graduates.

ANNUAL EXPENSES. Tuition and fees (1992-93): $1,606, $2,214 additional for out-of-state students. **Room and board:** $2,928. **Books and supplies:** $350. **Other expenses:** $1,000.

FINANCIAL AID. 73% of freshmen, 73% of continuing students receive some form of aid. 95% of grants, 90% of loans, 31% of jobs based on need. 327 enrolled freshmen were judged to have need, 290 were offered aid. Academic, music/drama, art, athletic, state/district residency scholarships available. **Aid applications:** Closing date March 1; applicants notified on a rolling basis beginning on or about April 1; must reply within 4 weeks.

ADDRESS/TELEPHONE. Mack K. Samples, Dean of Admissions and Records, Glenville State College, 200 High Street, Glenville, WV 26351-1292. (304) 462-7361. Fax: (304) 462-4407.

Huntington Junior College of Business
Huntington, West Virginia CB code: 7310

2-year proprietary business, junior college, coed. Founded in 1936. **Undergraduate enrollment:** 511 men and women. **Location:** Urban campus in small city; 45 miles from Charleston. **Calendar:** Quarter.

FRESHMAN ADMISSIONS. Selection criteria: Open admissions.

ANNUAL EXPENSES. Tuition and fees: $3,375. Costs noted include books.

ADDRESS/TELEPHONE. James Garrett, Director of Marketing and Education Services, Huntington Junior College of Business, 900 Fifth Avenue, Huntington, WV 25701. (304) 697-7550.

Marshall University
Huntington, West Virginia CB code: 5396

4-year public university, coed. Founded in 1837. **Accreditation:** Regional. **Undergraduate enrollment:** 3,642 men, 4,226 women full time; 1,178 men, 1,295 women part time. **Graduate enrollment:** 391 men, 426 women full time; 518 men, 1,417 women part time. **Faculty:** 762 total (523 full time), 425 with doctorates or other terminal degrees. **Location:** Urban campus in small city; 140 miles from Lexington, Kentucky, 160 miles from Columbus, Ohio. **Calendar:** Semester, limited summer session. Extensive evening/early morning classes. **Microcomputers:** 191 located in dormitories, libraries, computer centers. **Special facilities:** Art gallery.

DEGREES OFFERED. AAS, BA, BS, BFA, MA, MS, MBA, PhD, MD. 205 associate degrees awarded in 1992. 17% in business and management, 18% business/office and marketing/distribution, 13% engineering technologies, 17% allied health, 29% law, 6% multi/interdisciplinary studies. 1,212 bachelor's degrees awarded. 26% in business and management, 20% teacher education, 9% health sciences, 8% multi/interdisciplinary studies, 7% parks/recreation, protective services, public affairs, 5% psychology. Graduate degrees offered in 54 major fields of study.

UNDERGRADUATE MAJORS. Associate: Accounting, aeronautical technology, automotive technology, business and office, business data processing and related programs, business data programming, business management technology, computer technology, electronic technology, emergency medical technologies, engineering and engineering-related technologies, finance, fire control and safety technology, information sciences and systems, insurance and risk management, insurance marketing, legal assistant/paralegal, legal secretary, library assistant, marketing and distribution, medical laboratory technologies, medical records administration, medical records technology, medical secretary, office supervision and management, office technology, plastic technology, radiograph medical technology, real estate, retailing, science technologies, secretarial and related programs, trade and industrial supervision and management, word processing. **Bachelor's:** Accounting, adult fitness, anthropology, art history, biological and physical sciences, biology, business administration and management, business economics, chemistry, clinical laboratory science, commercial art, communications, computer and information sciences, computer programming, crafts, criminal justice studies, cytotechnology, dramatic arts, early childhood education, economics, education, education of the gifted and talented, education of the mentally handicapped, education of the physically handicapped, elementary education, English, fashion design, fashion merchandising, finance, fine arts, food science and nutrition, forestry and related sciences, French, geography, geology, German, graphic design, health care administration, history, home economics, humanities, humanities and social sciences, information sciences and systems, insurance and risk management, international relations, international studies, journalism, junior high education, Latin, law , law enforcement and corrections, legal assistant/paralegal, library science, marketing and distribution, mathematics, medical laboratory technologies, music, music history and appreciation, music performance, music theory and composition, nursing, painting, parks and recreation management, philosophy, photography, physical sciences, physics, political science and government, predentistry, prelaw, premedicine, prepharmacy, preveterinary, printmaking, psychology, public relations, radio/television broadcasting, rehabilitation counseling/services, religion, retailing, sculpture, secondary education, social sciences, social work, sociology, Spanish, special education, specific learning disabilities, speech, speech correction, speech pathology/audiology, sports management, sports medicine, systems analysis, theater design, transportation management, visual and performing arts, vocational/technical education.

ACADEMIC PROGRAMS. Accelerated program, cooperative education, double major, dual enrollment of high school students, honors program, independent study, internships, study abroad, teacher preparation, telecourses, 2-2 preengineering program, 3-2 program in forestry with Duke University. **Remedial services:** Learning center, preadmission summer program, reduced course load, remedial instruction, special counselor, tutoring. **ROTC:** Army. **Placement/credit:** AP, CLEP General and Subject, institutional tests; 18 credit hours maximum for bachelor's degree.

ACADEMIC REQUIREMENTS. Freshmen must earn minimum GPA of 2.0 to continue in good standing. 67% of freshmen return for sophomore year. Students must declare major by end of first year. **Graduation requirements:** 64 hours for associate (43 in major), 128 hours for bachelor's (35 in major). Most students required to take courses in arts/fine arts, English, foreign languages, history, humanities, mathematics, biological/physical sciences, social sciences. **Postgraduate studies:** 32% from 2-year programs enter 4-year programs.

FRESHMAN ADMISSIONS. Selection criteria: Minimum 2.0 high school GPA or 17 ACT composite or 700 SAT combined score. ACT composite score of 21 for admission to nursing program. **High school preparation:** 11 units required. Required and recommended units include English 4, mathematics 2, social science 3 and science 2. Foreign language 2 recommended. One biology, 1 chemistry with minimum 2.0 GPA, and 2 mathematics required of nursing applicants. **Test requirements:** SAT or ACT (ACT preferred); score report by August 15. **Additional information:** Those out of high school 4 years or more eligible for Regent's bachelor of arts program where credit is given for life experience.

1992 FRESHMAN CLASS PROFILE. 1,940 men applied, 1,929 accepted, 933 enrolled; 2,467 women applied, 2,463 accepted, 1,095 enrolled. 55% had high school GPA of 3.0 or higher, 42% between 2.0 and 2.99. **Academic background:** Mid 50% of enrolled freshmen had ACT composite between 14-22. 75% submitted ACT scores. **Characteristics:** 86% from in state, 60% commute, 5% have minority backgrounds, 1% are foreign students. Average age is 23.

FALL-TERM APPLICATIONS. $10 fee, may be waived for applicants with need. $25 application fee for out-of-state applicants. Closing date August 15; priority given to applications received by February 1; applicants notified on a rolling basis. Audition required for music applicants. Interview recommended for academically weak, learning disabled applicants. Portfolio recommended for art applicants. Deferred and early admission available.

STUDENT LIFE. Housing: Dormitories (men, women, coed); apartment, fraternity, sorority, handicapped housing available. Students permitted to build lofts, paint rooms at their own expense. For special consideration or priority on housing assignments, freshmen are encouraged to apply by December 15. **Activities:** Student government, film, magazine, radio, student newspaper, television, yearbook, choral groups, concert band, dance, drama, jazz band, marching band, music ensembles, musical theater, opera, pep band, symphony orchestra, fraternities, sororities, Campus Christian Center, Gamma Beta Phi (service honorary).

ATHLETICS. NCAA. **Intercollegiate:** Baseball M, basketball, cross-country, football M, golf M, soccer M, tennis W, track and field, volleyball W. **Intramural:** Badminton, baseball M, basketball, bowling, cross-country, diving, field hockey, football M, golf, handball, racquetball, soccer, softball, swimming, table tennis, tennis, track and field, volleyball, water polo, wrestling M.

STUDENT SERVICES. Aptitude testing, career counseling, employment service for undergraduates, freshman orientation, health services, on-campus day care, personal counseling, placement service for graduates, special adviser for adult students, services/facilities for handicapped.

ANNUAL EXPENSES. Tuition and fees (1992-93): $1,792, $1,344 additional for out-of-district students, $2,886 additional for out-of-state students. **Room and board:** $3,780. **Books and supplies:** $600. **Other expenses:** $1,000.

FINANCIAL AID. 44% of freshmen, 50% of continuing students receive some form of aid. 66% of grants, 93% of loans, 60% of jobs based on need. Academic, music/drama, art, athletic, state/district residency, leadership, minority scholarships available. **Aid applications:** No closing date; priority given to applications received by March 1; applicants notified on a rolling basis beginning on or about April 15; must reply within 2 weeks.

ADDRESS/TELEPHONE. Dr. James Harless, Director of Admissions, Marshall University, 125 Old Main, Huntington, WV 25755-2020. (304) 696-3160. Fax: (304) 696-3333.

National Education Center: National Institute of Technology Campus
Cross Lanes, West Virginia CB code: 1579

2-year proprietary technical college, coed. Founded in 1968. **Undergraduate** enrollment: 384 men and women. **Location:** Suburban campus in large town; 12 miles from Charleston. **Calendar:** Quarter.

FRESHMAN ADMISSIONS. Selection criteria: Applicants must have high school diploma or GED. School record, interview important.

ANNUAL EXPENSES. Tuition and fees (1992-93): $11,100. $8820 tuition and fees for 1-year medical program.

ADDRESS/TELEPHONE. Admissions Office, National Education Center: National Institute of Technology Campus, 5514 Big Tyler Road, Cross Lanes, WV 25313. (304) 776-6290. Fax: (304) 776-6262.

Ohio Valley College
Parkersburg, West Virginia CB code: 5519

4-year private liberal arts college, coed, affiliated with Church of Christ. Founded in 1960. **Accreditation:** Regional. **Undergraduate enrollment:** 117 men, 110 women full time; 9 men, 7 women part time. **Faculty:** 38 total (13 full time), 3 with doctorates or other terminal degrees. **Location:** Suburban campus in large town; 95 miles from Columbus, Ohio. **Calendar:** Semester, limited summer session. **Microcomputers:** 40 located in computer centers. **Additional facts:** Maymester program offers concentrated 2-week courses for credit immediately following spring semester. Consolidated with Northeastern Christian Junior College April 1, 1993.

DEGREES OFFERED. AA, AS, BA, BS. 45 associate degrees awarded in 1992. 8 bachelor's degrees awarded. 100% in philosophy, religion, theology.

UNDERGRADUATE MAJORS. Associate: Accounting, biology, business and management, communications, humanities and social sciences, liberal/general studies, radio/television broadcasting, science technologies, secretarial and related programs. **Bachelor's:** Theological studies.

ACADEMIC PROGRAMS. 2-year transfer program, honors program, independent study. **Remedial services:** Learning center, reduced course load, remedial instruction, tutoring. **ROTC:** Army. **Placement/credit:** AP, CLEP General and Subject; 30 credit hours maximum for associate degree.

ACADEMIC REQUIREMENTS. Freshmen must earn minimum GPA of 1.6 to continue in good standing. 63% of freshmen return for sophomore year. Students must declare major by end of second year. **Graduation requirements:** 64 hours for associate, 128 hours for bachelor's (60 in major). Most students required to take courses in English, history, mathematics, philosophy/religion, biological/physical sciences, social sciences. **Postgraduate studies:** 76% from 2-year programs enter 4-year programs. **Additional information:** Full-time students required to take Bible course each semester.

FRESHMAN ADMISSIONS. Selection criteria: School achievement record, test scores considered. **Test requirements:** SAT or ACT (ACT preferred); score report by August 20.

1992 FRESHMAN CLASS PROFILE. Academic background: Mid 50% of enrolled freshmen had ACT composite between 15-25. 95% submitted ACT scores. **Characteristics:** 42% from in state, 86% live in college housing, 83% join fraternities/sororities. Average age is 19.

FALL-TERM APPLICATIONS. $20 fee, may be waived for applicants with need. No closing date; applicants notified on a rolling basis. Interview recommended. Essay recommended. Deferred and early admission available.

STUDENT LIFE. Housing: Dormitories (men, women); apartment housing available. **Activities:** Student government, student newspaper, yearbook, choral groups, concert band, drama, music ensembles, musical theater, pep band, fraternities, sororities, prospective ministers, prospective missionaries clubs, women's club. **Additional information:** Religious observance required.

ATHLETICS. NJCAA. **Intercollegiate:** Baseball M, basketball, volleyball W. **Intramural:** Basketball, bowling, racquetball, softball, table tennis, track and field, volleyball.

STUDENT SERVICES. Career counseling, employment service for undergraduates, health services, personal counseling.

ANNUAL EXPENSES. Tuition and fees (projected): $5,384. **Room and board:** $3,110. **Books and supplies:** $425. **Other expenses:** $800.

FINANCIAL AID. 93% of freshmen, 92% of continuing students receive some form of aid. 61% of grants, 94% of loans, 89% of jobs based on need. Academic, music/drama, art, athletic, leadership scholarships available. **Aid applications:** No closing date; priority given to applications received by June 1; applicants notified on a rolling basis beginning on or about April 1; must reply within 4 weeks.

ADDRESS/TELEPHONE. Bob Crum, Director of Admissions, Ohio Valley College, College Parkway, Parkersburg, WV 26101-9975. (304) 485-7384. (800) 678-6780.

Potomac State College of West Virginia University
Keyser, West Virginia CB code: 5539

2-year public branch campus, junior college, coed. Founded in 1901. **Accreditation:** Regional. **Undergraduate enrollment:** 579 men, 343 women full time; 115 men, 168 women part time. **Faculty:** 84 total (39 full time), 14 with doctorates or other terminal degrees. **Location:** Rural campus in small town; 90 miles from Morgantown, 150 miles from Baltimore, Maryland, and Washington, D.C. **Calendar:** Semester, limited summer session. Extensive evening/early morning classes. **Microcomputers:** 100 located in libraries, classrooms, computer centers.

DEGREES OFFERED. AA, AAS. 115 associate degrees awarded in 1992. 8% in agriculture, 27% business and management, 11% business/office and marketing/distribution, 6% computer sciences, 6% engineering, 8% health sciences, 5% physical sciences, 8% social sciences.

UNDERGRADUATE MAJORS. Accounting, agricultural sciences, biology, business administration and management, business and management, business and office, business data processing and related programs, business data programming, business economics, chemistry, civil engineering, computer and information sciences, computer programming, data processing, economics, education, electrical/electronics/communications engineering, electronic technology, elementary education, engineering and engineering-related technologies, English, forestry and related sciences, French, geology, German, history, horticulture, journalism, liberal/general studies, marketing and distribution, mathematics, mechanical engineering, medical laboratory technologies, medical secretary, music, physical therapy, physics, political science and government, predentistry, prelaw, premedicine, prepharmacy, preveterinary, psychology, secondary education, secretarial and related programs, small business management and ownership, social work, sociology, Spanish.

ACADEMIC PROGRAMS. 2-year transfer program, accelerated program, computer delivered (on-line) credit-bearing course offerings, dual enrollment of high school students, honors program, cross-registration. **Remedial services:** Learning center, reduced course load, remedial instruction, special counselor, tutoring, writing laboratory, developmental reading and mathemetics. **Placement/credit:** AP, CLEP General and Subject, institutional tests; 30 credit hours maximum for associate degree.

ACADEMIC REQUIREMENTS. Freshmen must earn minimum GPA of 2.0 to continue in good standing. 48% of freshmen return for sophomore year. Students must declare major on enrollment. **Graduation requirements:** 64 hours for associate. Most students required to take courses in English, mathematics, biological/physical sciences, social sciences.

FRESHMAN ADMISSIONS. Selection criteria: Open admissions. Selective admissions to engineering, petroleum engineering, mining engineering, and computer science programs. Open admissions for West Virginia residents for all other programs. Moderately selective admissions for out-of-state residents. **Test requirements:** SAT or ACT (ACT preferred); score report by August 18.

1992 FRESHMAN CLASS PROFILE. 325 men, 167 women enrolled. 20% had high school GPA of 3.0 or higher, 54% between 2.0 and 2.99. **Academic background:** Mid 50% of enrolled freshmen had ACT composite between 16-21. 80% submitted ACT scores. **Characteristics:** 65% from in state, 67% commute, 9% have minority backgrounds. Average age is 19.

FALL-TERM APPLICATIONS. No fee. Closing date August 20; applicants notified on a rolling basis; must reply by August 20. Interview recommended. Audition recommended for music applicants. Deferred and early admission available.

STUDENT LIFE. Housing: Dormitories (men, women). **Activities:** Student government, student newspaper, choral groups, concert band, drama, jazz band, music ensembles, pep band, Christian Fellowship, Newman Club, Young Democrats, Young Republicans, Circle-K, Students Cooperating in the Public Effort, Black Unity Organization, agriculture club.

ATHLETICS. NJCAA. **Intercollegiate:** Baseball M, basketball, football M, horseback riding, volleyball W. **Intramural:** Archery, badminton, basketball, golf, softball, table tennis, tennis, volleyball.

STUDENT SERVICES. Aptitude testing, career counseling, employment service for undergraduates, freshman orientation, health services, personal counseling, placement service for graduates, special adviser for adult students, veterans counselor, services/facilities for handicapped.

ANNUAL EXPENSES. Tuition and fees (1992-93): $1,472, $2,806 additional for out-of-state students. **Room and board:** $3,200. **Books and supplies:** $450. **Other expenses:** $1,120.

FINANCIAL AID. 72% of continuing students receive some form of aid. 92% of grants, 74% of loans, 57% of jobs based on need. Academic scholarships available. **Aid applications:** No closing date; priority given to applications received by March 1; applicants notified on a rolling basis beginning on or about June 1; must reply within 2 weeks.

ADDRESS/TELEPHONE. Charles H. Via, Director of Admissions and Records, Potomac State College of West Virginia University, Fort Avenue, Keyser, WV 26726. (304) 788-6820. Fax: (304) 788-6940.

Salem-Teikyo University
Salem, West Virginia CB code: 5608

Admissions: 82% of applicants accepted
Based on: ••• School record
•• Interview, recommendations, test scores
• Essay
Completion: 74% of freshmen end year in good standing
21% enter graduate study

4-year private university, coed. Founded in 1888. **Accreditation:** Regional. **Undergraduate enrollment:** 472 men, 188 women full time; 1 man, 3 women part time. **Graduate enrollment:** 3 men, 1 woman full time; 16 men, 31 women part time. **Faculty:** 56 total (46 full time), 27 with doctorates or other terminal degrees. **Location:** Rural campus in small town; 12 miles from Clarksburg, 125 miles from Pittsburgh, Pennsylvania. **Calendar:** Four terms with full course offerings throughout year. **Microcomputers:** 22 located in computer centers. **Special facilities:** Equestrian center, Fort New Salem reconstructed 18th-century living museum. **Additional facts:** International student body comprised of half Japanese, half American and other foreign students.

DEGREES OFFERED. AA, AS, AAS, BA, BS, MA. 19 associate degrees awarded in 1992. 67 bachelor's degrees awarded. Graduate degrees offered in 8 major fields of study.

UNDERGRADUATE MAJORS. Associate: Accounting, aviation management, business administration and management, business and management, criminal justice studies, engineering and engineering-related technologies, equestrian science, liberal/general studies, marketing and distribution, marketing management, physical education, radio/television broadcasting, secretarial and related programs, telecommunications. **Bachelor's:** Accounting, airline piloting and navigation, aviation management, biological and physical sciences, biology, business administration and management, business and management, communications, computer and information sciences, criminal justice studies, driver and safety education, education, education of the mentally handicapped, elementary education, engineering and engineering-related technologies, environmental science, equestrian science, history, industrial arts education, industrial technology, Japanese, japanese studies, liberal/general studies, marketing and distribution, marketing management, mathematics, medical laboratory technologies, molecular biology, museum studies, outdoor science, physical education, prelaw, radio/television broadcasting, radio/television technology, radiograph medical technology, secondary education, special education, sports broadcasting, sports management, sports medicine, telecommunications, youth agency administration.

ACADEMIC PROGRAMS. Accelerated program, double major, independent study, internships, study abroad, teacher preparation, cross-registration; liberal arts/career combination in health sciences. **Remedial services:** Learning center, preadmission summer program, reduced course load, remedial instruction, special counselor, tutoring. **ROTC:** Air Force. **Placement/credit:** AP, CLEP Subject, institutional tests; 32 credit hours maximum for bachelor's degree.

ACADEMIC REQUIREMENTS. Freshmen must earn minimum GPA of 2.0 to continue in good standing. 80% of freshmen return for sophomore year. Students must declare major by end of second year. **Graduation requirements:** 64 hours for associate, 128 hours for bachelor's. Most students required to take courses in arts/fine arts, computer science, English, foreign languages, history, humanities, mathematics, philosophy/religion, biological/physical sciences, social sciences. **Postgraduate studies:** 35% from 2-year programs enter 4-year programs. 1% enter law school, 1% enter medical school, 2% enter MBA programs, 17% enter other graduate study.

FRESHMAN ADMISSIONS. Selection criteria: School achievement record, test scores, counselor recommendations considered. **High school preparation:** 16 units required; 22 recommended. Required and recommended units include English 4, mathematics 1-3, social science 1-3 and science 1-3. At least 11 of required units should be in academic areas; remaining 5 units can be in other areas such as business, foreign language, or health education. **Test requirements:** SAT or ACT; score report by August 30. **Additional information:** Applicants not meeting admissions standards are referred to committee which may or may not recommend their acceptance.

1992 FRESHMAN CLASS PROFILE. 289 men applied, 235 accepted, 187 enrolled; 189 women applied, 156 accepted, 69 enrolled. 100% had high school GPA between 2.0 and 2.99. **Characteristics:** 39% from in state, 85% live in college housing. Average age is 19.

FALL-TERM APPLICATIONS. $25 fee, may be waived for applicants with need. No closing date; applicants notified on a rolling basis; must reply within 4 weeks. Interview recommended for academically weak applicants. Essay recommended. Deferred and early admission available.

STUDENT LIFE. Housing: Dormitories (men, women, coed); fraternity, sorority housing available. Unless a local resident, freshmen and sophomores required to live on campus. On campus housing available for all students. Private rooms subject to availablity. **Activities:** Student government, radio, student newspaper, television, yearbook, drama, fraternities, sororities, Black Student Union, Rotoract, Gamma Beta Phi Honor Society, Humanic Student Association, chapel committee, Fort New Salem Association.

ATHLETICS. NAIA. **Intercollegiate:** Baseball M, basketball, golf M, soccer M, softball W, tennis, volleyball W. **Intramural:** Archery, badminton, basketball, football M, racquetball, rugby M, softball, swimming, table tennis, tennis, volleyball, water polo.

STUDENT SERVICES. Aptitude testing, career counseling, freshman orientation, health services, personal counseling, placement service for graduates, services/facilities for handicapped.

ANNUAL EXPENSES. Tuition and fees: $9,233. **Room and board:** $3,952. **Books and supplies:** $400. **Other expenses:** $300.

FINANCIAL AID. 62% of continuing students receive some form of aid. 42% of grants, 89% of loans, all jobs based on need. 151 enrolled freshmen were judged to have need, all were offered aid. Academic, athletic, state/district residency, leadership scholarships available. **Aid applications:** No closing date; priority given to applications received by April 15; applicants notified on a rolling basis beginning on or about February 15; must reply within 4 weeks.

ADDRESS/TELEPHONE. Director of Admissions, Salem-Teikyo University, Main Street, Salem, WV 26426. (304) 782-5336. (800) 283-4562. Fax: (304) 782-5395.

Shepherd College
Shepherdstown, West Virginia CB code: 5615

Admissions: 77% of applicants accepted
Based on: ••• School record, test scores
•• Essay, recommendations
• Activities, interview
Completion: 75% of freshmen end year in good standing
65% graduate, 47% of these enter graduate study

4-year public liberal arts college, coed. Founded in 1871. **Accreditation:** Regional. **Undergraduate enrollment:** 920 men, 1,435 women full time; 470 men, 734 women part time. **Faculty:** 261 total (129 full time), 135 with doctorates or other terminal degrees. **Location:** Rural campus in small town; 8 miles from Martinsburg, 70 miles from Washington, D.C. and Baltimore, Maryland. **Calendar:** Semester, extensive summer session. Extensive evening/early morning classes. **Microcomputers:** 178 located in libraries, classrooms, computer centers. **Special facilities:** Creative arts center with modern computer-controlled theater, recital hall, recording studio, nursery school for elementary education and home economics programs, 3 theaters, wellness/fitness center.

DEGREES OFFERED. AA, AS, AAS, BA, BS, BFA. 80 associate degrees awarded in 1992. 20% in business and management, 60% health sciences, 20% visual and performing arts. 500 bachelor's degrees awarded. 35% in business and management, 10% communications, 10% computer sciences, 10% teacher education, 5% letters/literature, 5% life sciences, 5% psychology, 5% visual and performing arts.

UNDERGRADUATE MAJORS. Associate: Accounting, business administration and management, business and management, business and office, business computer/console/peripheral equipment operation, business data processing and related programs, business data programming, commercial art, data processing, electrical and electronics equipment repair, electronic technology, engineering, engineering and engineering-related technologies, fashion merchandising, fire control and safety technology, food production/management/services, graphic design, hotel/motel and restaurant management, marketing and distribution, marketing management, nursing, photography, secretarial and related programs, word processing. **Bachelor's:** Accounting, American literature, American studies, anthropology, applied mathematics, art education, art history, biological and physical sciences, biology, botany, business administration and management, business and management, business and office, business data processing and related programs, business data programming, business economics, business education, business systems analysis, chemistry, commercial art, communications, comparative literature, computer and information sciences, computer mathematics, computer programming, creative writing, data processing, dramatic arts, early childhood education, earth sciences, economics, education, elementary education, English, English education, English literature, fashion merchandising, finance, fine arts, French, geography, graphic design, health education, history, home economics, home economics education, hospitality and recreation marketing, hotel/motel and restaurant management, information sciences and systems, junior high education, library science, marketing management, mathematics, mathematics education, music, music education, music history and appreciation, music performance, music theory and composition, musical theater, nursing, office supervision and management, painting, parks and recreation management, photography, physical education, physical sciences, political science and government, predentistry, prelaw, premedicine, prepharmacy, preveterinary, printmaking, psychology, pure mathematics, radio/television broadcasting, recreation therapy, science education, secondary education, secretarial and related programs, social science education, social sciences, social studies education, social work, sociology, speech, sports medicine, studio art, systems analysis, visual and performing arts, Western European studies, wildlife management, zoology.

ACADEMIC PROGRAMS. 2-year transfer program, cooperative educa-

tion, double major, dual enrollment of high school students, honors program, independent study, internships, teacher preparation, weekend college, Washington semester. **Remedial services:** Learning center, reduced course load, remedial instruction, tutoring, no services for learning disabled students. **ROTC:** Air Force. **Placement/credit:** AP, CLEP General and Subject, institutional tests; 32 credit hours maximum for associate degree; 32 credit hours maximum for bachelor's degree.

ACADEMIC REQUIREMENTS. Freshmen must earn minimum GPA of 2.0 to continue in good standing. 70% of freshmen return for sophomore year. Students must declare major by end of second year. **Graduation requirements:** 64 hours for associate (53 in major), 128 hours for bachelor's (30 in major). Most students required to take courses in arts/fine arts, computer science, English, history, humanities, mathematics, biological/physical sciences, social sciences. **Postgraduate studies:** 60% from 2-year programs enter 4-year programs. 4% enter law school, 3% enter medical school, 10% enter MBA programs, 30% enter other graduate study.

FRESHMAN ADMISSIONS. Selection criteria: Minimum 2.0 GPA for in-state and 2.5 for out-of-state applicants required. **High school preparation:** 21 units required. Required units include biological science 1, English 4, foreign language 2, mathematics 3, physical science 1, social science 3 and science 1. **Test requirements:** SAT or ACT; score report by February 1.

1992 FRESHMAN CLASS PROFILE. 606 men applied, 435 accepted, 232 enrolled; 771 women applied, 625 accepted, 290 enrolled. 60% had high school GPA of 3.0 or higher, 35% between 2.0 and 2.99. **Academic background:** Mid 50% of enrolled freshmen had ACT composite between 24-30. 60% submitted ACT scores. **Characteristics:** 67% from in state, 67% commute, 5% have minority backgrounds, 1% are foreign students, 20% join fraternities/sororities. Average age is 19.

FALL-TERM APPLICATIONS. $20 fee, may be waived for applicants with need. Closing date February 1; applicants notified on or about April 1; must reply by May 1. Audition required for music applicants. Portfolio required for art, photography, graphic design applicants. Essay required. Interview recommended. Interview required for nursing and engineering applicants; recommended for others. CRDA. Deferred and early admission available. Institutional early decision plan. Students applying before October 15 will be notified after December 15.

STUDENT LIFE. Housing: Dormitories (men, women, coed); fraternity housing available. **Activities:** Student government, magazine, radio, student newspaper, yearbook, choral groups, concert band, dance, drama, jazz band, marching band, music ensembles, musical theater, pep band, symphony orchestra, debate team, forensics team, fraternities, sororities, minority student organization, College Republicans, Young Democrats.

ATHLETICS. NAIA, NCAA. **Intercollegiate:** Baseball M, basketball, cross-country, diving, football M, golf, soccer M, softball W, tennis, volleyball. **Intramural:** Archery, badminton, baseball M, basketball, bowling, cross-country, diving, fencing, field hockey, football M, golf, gymnastics, handball, horseback riding, lacrosse M, racquetball, skiing, soccer M, softball, swimming, table tennis, tennis, track and field, volleyball, water polo, wrestling.

STUDENT SERVICES. Aptitude testing, career counseling, employment service for undergraduates, freshman orientation, health services, personal counseling, placement service for graduates, special adviser for adult students, veterans counselor, services/facilities for handicapped.

ANNUAL EXPENSES. Tuition and fees (1992-93): $1,954, $2,520 additional for out-of-state students. **Room and board:** $3,490. **Books and supplies:** $500. **Other expenses:** $900.

FINANCIAL AID. 22% of freshmen, 29% of continuing students receive some form of aid. 65% of grants, 78% of loans, 50% of jobs based on need. 117 enrolled freshmen were judged to have need, all were offered aid. Academic, music/drama, art, athletic, state/district residency, leadership, minority scholarships available. **Aid applications:** No closing date; priority given to applications received by March 1; applicants notified on a rolling basis beginning on or about May 15; must reply within 2 weeks.

ADDRESS/TELEPHONE. Karl L. Wolf, Director of Admissions, Shepherd College, Shepherdstown, WV 25443-1569. (304) 876-2511 ext. 212. (800) 344-5231. Fax: (304) 876-3101.

Southern West Virginia Community College
Logan, West Virginia CB code: 0770

2-year public community college, coed. Founded in 1971. **Accreditation:** Regional. **Undergraduate enrollment:** 530 men, 1,179 women full time; 436 men, 970 women part time. **Faculty:** 198 total (52 full time), 6 with doctorates or other terminal degrees. **Location:** Rural campus in small town; 60 miles from Charleston. **Calendar:** Semester, limited summer session. Saturday and extensive evening/early morning classes. **Microcomputers:** Located in libraries, classrooms. **Additional facts:** Additional campuses in Williamson, Saulsville and Madison.

DEGREES OFFERED. AA, AS, AAS. 396 associate degrees awarded in 1992. 14% in business and management, 5% health sciences, 65% multi/interdisciplinary studies.

UNDERGRADUATE MAJORS. Accounting, automotive mechanics, automotive technology, business and office, computer and information sciences, criminal justice technology, drafting and design technology, finance, liberal/general studies, medical laboratory technologies, nursing, precision metal work, radio/television technology, radiograph medical technology, secretarial and related programs, small business management and ownership.

ACADEMIC PROGRAMS. 2-year transfer program, dual enrollment of high school students, independent study, internships, teacher preparation, telecourses. **Remedial services:** Learning center, reduced course load, remedial instruction, special counselor, tutoring. **Placement/credit:** AP, CLEP General and Subject, institutional tests; 32 credit hours maximum for associate degree.

ACADEMIC REQUIREMENTS. Freshmen must earn minimum GPA of 2.0 to continue in good standing. 40% of freshmen return for sophomore year. Students must declare major on application. **Graduation requirements:** 63 hours for associate (30 in major). Most students required to take courses in English, history, mathematics, biological/physical sciences, social sciences.

FRESHMAN ADMISSIONS. Selection criteria: Open admissions. Nursing program applicants must have high school diploma or GED, minimum 21 ACT score, 12 credit hours of support courses with minimum 3.0 GPA, and completed chemistry and mathematics course with minimum grade of C. Medical laboratory program applicants require high school diploma or GED, minimum 21 ACT score, and completed mathematics and chemistry courses with minimum grade of C. **Test requirements:** Nursing and medical laboratory program applicants require minimum ACT score of 21.

1992 FRESHMAN CLASS PROFILE. 283 men, 630 women enrolled. **Characteristics:** 85% from in state, 100% commute, 6% have minority backgrounds. Average age is 24.

FALL-TERM APPLICATIONS. $10 fee. No closing date; applicants notified on a rolling basis. Interview recommended. Early admission available.

STUDENT LIFE. Activities: Student government, drama, musical theater, special interest clubs.

STUDENT SERVICES. Aptitude testing, career counseling, employment service for undergraduates, freshman orientation, on-campus day care, personal counseling, placement service for graduates, veterans counselor, services/facilities for handicapped.

ANNUAL EXPENSES. Tuition and fees (1992-93): $1,000, $1,850 additional for out-of-state students. **Books and supplies:** $450. **Other expenses:** $900.

FINANCIAL AID. 40% of freshmen, 40% of continuing students receive some form of aid. Grants, loans, jobs available. Academic, state/district residency scholarships available. **Aid applications:** No closing date; applicants notified on a rolling basis; must reply within 10 days.

ADDRESS/TELEPHONE. James P. Owens, Jr, Registrar/Enrollment Mgmt Dir, Southern West Virginia Community College, Box 2900 Dempsey Branch Road, Logan, WV 25601. (304) 792-4300 ext. 289. Fax: (304) 792-4399.

University of Charleston
Charleston, West Virginia CB code: 5419

Admissions: 73% of applicants accepted
Based on:
••• School record
•• Interview, recommendations, test scores
• Activities, essay
Completion: 67% of freshmen end year in good standing
55% graduate, 29% of these enter graduate study

4-year private university, coed. Founded in 1888. **Accreditation:** Regional. **Undergraduate enrollment:** 240 men, 521 women full time; 182 men, 468 women part time. **Graduate enrollment:** 2 women full time; 31 men, 35 women part time. **Faculty:** 232 total (74 full time), 44 with doctorates or other terminal degrees. **Location:** Urban campus in small city; 200 miles from Pittsburgh, Pennsylvania, Charlotte, North Carolina, Lexington, Kentucky, and Cleveland and Cincinnati, Ohio. **Calendar:** Semester, extensive summer session. Extensive evening/early morning classes. **Microcomputers:** 60 located in libraries, classrooms, computer centers. **Special facilities:** Art gallery, sports medicine clinic.

DEGREES OFFERED. AA, AS, BA, BS, MS, MBA. 135 associate degrees awarded in 1992. 8% in business and management, 68% health sciences, 8% law, 12% military sciences. 134 bachelor's degrees awarded. 17% in business and management, 12% teacher education, 23% health sciences, 5% letters/literature, 5% life sciences, 9% military sciences, 6% psychology, 7% social sciences, 5% visual and performing arts. Graduate degrees offered in 2 major fields of study.

UNDERGRADUATE MAJORS. Associate: Accounting, information sciences and systems, interior design, legal assistant/paralegal, liberal/general studies, marketing and distribution, military science (Army), nursing, radiograph medical technology, respiratory therapy, respiratory therapy technology. **Bachelor's:** Accounting, art education, arts management, biological and physical sciences, biology, business administration and management, business and management, chemistry, communications, elementary education, English, English education, environmental science, fine arts, health education, history, information sciences and systems, interior design, journalism, junior high education, marketing and distribution, marketing management, mathematics, mathematics education, military science (Army), music, music education, music performance, nursing, philosophy, physical education, political science and government, predentistry, prelaw, premedicine, preveterinary, psychology, radiograph medical technology, religion, respiratory therapy, respiratory therapy technology, science education, secondary education, social sciences, social studies education, sports medicine.

ACADEMIC PROGRAMS. Accelerated program, double major, dual enrollment of high school students, honors program, independent study, internships, student-designed major, teacher preparation, Washington semester. **Remedial services:** Learning center, reduced course load, remedial instruction, tutoring. **ROTC:** Army. **Placement/credit:** AP, CLEP Subject, institutional tests; 30 credit hours maximum for associate degree; 60 credit hours maximum for bachelor's degree.

ACADEMIC REQUIREMENTS. Freshmen must earn minimum GPA of 2.0 to continue in good standing. 80% of freshmen return for sophomore year. Students must declare major by end of second year. **Graduation requirements:** 60 hours for associate, 120 hours for bachelor's (48 in major). Most students required to take courses in arts/fine arts, computer science, English, history, humanities, mathematics, biological/physical sciences, social sciences. **Postgraduate studies:** 21% from 2-year programs enter 4-year programs. 1% enter law school, 1% enter medical school, 12% enter MBA programs, 15% enter other graduate study. **Additional information:** All full-time freshmen candidates for bachelor's degree are required to enroll in Freshman Seminar, a one-credit, first-semester course designed to acquaint students with college life.

FRESHMAN ADMISSIONS. Selection criteria: School achievement record and courses taken most important. Test scores, school recommendation, school and community activites, class rank, and interview also considered. High school GPA recomputed to reflect performance in academic subjects only. **High school preparation:** 16 units required. **Test requirements:** SAT or ACT.

1992 FRESHMAN CLASS PROFILE. 433 men applied, 236 accepted, 71 enrolled; 347 women applied, 337 accepted, 186 enrolled. 43% had high school GPA of 3.0 or higher, 54% between 2.0 and 2.99. 22% were in top tenth and 43% were in top quarter of graduating class. **Academic background:** Mid 50% of enrolled freshmen had SAT-V between 370-460, SAT-M between 420-540; ACT composite between 18-23. 44% submitted SAT scores, 68% submitted ACT scores. **Characteristics:** 86% from in state, 77% commute, 14% have minority backgrounds, 2% are foreign students, 4% join fraternities/sororities. Average age is 21.

FALL-TERM APPLICATIONS. $20 fee, may be waived for applicants with need. No closing date; priority given to applications received by May 1; applicants notified on a rolling basis; must reply by May 1 or within 2 weeks if notified thereafter. Audition required for music applicants. Interview recommended. Portfolio recommended. CRDA. Deferred and early admission available. EDP-F. For most health science programs, the application deadline is Dec. 31. Early decision is recommended for health science applicants.

STUDENT LIFE. Housing: Dormitories (coed). On-campus housing required for dependent freshmen not living with parents or legal guardian in local area. Some single rooms and suites available. **Activities:** Student government, student newspaper, yearbook, student activity board, student ambassadors, choral groups, drama, music ensembles, musical theater, show choir, fraternities, sororities, Honorary fraternities, International Student Association, interest groups, service organizations.

ATHLETICS. NAIA, NCAA. **Intercollegiate:** Baseball M, basketball, golf M, rowing (crew), soccer, softball W, tennis, volleyball W. **Intramural:** Basketball, bowling, cross-country, field hockey, handball, racquetball, soccer, softball, swimming, tennis, volleyball, water polo.

STUDENT SERVICES. Aptitude testing, career counseling, employment service for undergraduates, freshman orientation, personal counseling, placement service for graduates, veterans counselor, services/facilities for handicapped.

ANNUAL EXPENSES. Tuition and fees: $9,250. Graduate tuition shown is for MBA program and includes books. $265 per-credit-hour charge for master's in human resources management. **Room and board:** $3,540. **Books and supplies:** $400. **Other expenses:** $500.

FINANCIAL AID. 70% of freshmen, 70% of continuing students receive some form of aid. 65% of grants, 53% of loans, 88% of jobs based on need. 143 enrolled freshmen were judged to have need, 142 were offered aid. Academic, music/drama, athletic, leadership scholarships available. **Aid applications:** No closing date; priority given to applications received by March 1; applicants notified on a rolling basis beginning on or about March 15; must reply by May 1 or within 2 weeks if notified thereafter.

ADDRESS/TELEPHONE. Gloria Smith Kunik, Director of Admissions, University of Charleston, 2300 MacCorkle Avenue Southeast, Charleston, WV 25304-1099. (304) 357-4750. (800) 995-4682. Fax: (304) 357-4715.

West Liberty State College
West Liberty, West Virginia — CB code: 5901

Admissions: 91% of applicants accepted
Based on: ••• School record, test scores
Completion: 84% of freshmen end year in good standing
49% graduate, 18% of these enter graduate study

4-year public college of arts and sciences, coed. Founded in 1837. **Accreditation:** Regional. **Undergraduate enrollment:** 1,040 men, 1,105 women full time; 106 men, 126 women part time. **Faculty:** 153 total (131 full time), 35 with doctorates or other terminal degrees. **Location:** Rural campus in rural community; 10 miles from Wheeling. **Calendar:** Semester, limited summer session. Extensive evening/early morning classes. **Microcomputers:** 70 located in libraries, classrooms, computer centers. **Special facilities:** Rare book room. **Additional facts:** Selected course work available at West Liberty State College Elm Grove Center in Wheeling.

DEGREES OFFERED. AS, BA, BS. 26 associate degrees awarded in 1992. 100% in allied health. 379 bachelor's degrees awarded. 31% in business and management, 24% teacher education, 12% health sciences, 8% multi/interdisciplinary studies, 10% parks/recreation, protective services, public affairs.

UNDERGRADUATE MAJORS. Associate: Dental hygiene. **Bachelor's:** Accounting, art education, aviation science, biology, business administration and management, business economics, business education, chemistry, communications, criminal justice studies, dental hygiene, early childhood education, elementary education, English, English education, fashion merchandising, finance, foreign languages education, graphic design, health education, history, information sciences and systems, liberal/general studies, marketing and distribution, mathematics, mathematics education, medical laboratory technologies, music education, nursing, office supervision and management, physical education, political science and government, psychology, science education, science of exercise, secondary education, social science education, sociology, speech/communication/theater education, tourism.

ACADEMIC PROGRAMS. 2-year transfer program, accelerated program, double major, external degree, honors program, independent study, internships, student-designed major, teacher preparation, telecourses, cross-registration. **Remedial services:** Reduced course load, remedial instruction, special counselor, tutoring. **Placement/credit:** AP, CLEP General and Subject, institutional tests.

ACADEMIC REQUIREMENTS. No policy requiring minimum GPA; records of students having academic difficulty are reviewed individually. 71% of freshmen return for sophomore year. Students must declare major by end of first year. **Graduation requirements:** 72 hours for associate (57 in major), 128 hours for bachelor's (40 in major). Most students required to take courses in arts/fine arts, English, history, humanities, mathematics, philosophy/religion, biological/physical sciences, social sciences. **Postgraduate studies:** 95% from 2-year programs enter 4-year programs. 1% enter law school, 1% enter medical school, 6% enter MBA programs, 10% enter other graduate study.

FRESHMAN ADMISSIONS. Selection criteria: Minimum 2.0 high school GPA required or 17 on enhanced ACT or 680 on SAT. **High school preparation:** 11 units required; 13 recommended. Required and recommended units include English 4, mathematics 2, social science 3 and science 2. Foreign language 2 recommended. Sciences must be laboratory courses. Mathematics must be Algebra I and higher. 1 social science must be U.S. history. **Test requirements:** SAT or ACT (ACT preferred); score report by August 1.

1992 FRESHMAN CLASS PROFILE. 517 men applied, 458 accepted, 227 enrolled; 546 women applied, 512 accepted, 268 enrolled. 37% had high school GPA of 3.0 or higher, 58% between 2.0 and 2.99. 12% were in top tenth and 25% were in top quarter of graduating class. **Academic background:** Mid 50% of enrolled freshmen had ACT composite between 16-21. 85% submitted ACT scores. **Characteristics:** 65% from in state, 92% live in college housing, 3% have minority backgrounds, 1% are foreign students, 5% join fraternities/sororities. Average age is 18.

FALL-TERM APPLICATIONS. No fee. No closing date; applicants notified on a rolling basis. Audition required for music education applicants. Portfolio recommended for art applicants. Deferred admission available.

STUDENT LIFE. Housing: Dormitories (men, women); apartment housing available. **Activities:** Student government, radio, student newspaper, choral groups, concert band, drama, jazz band, music ensembles, musical theater, steel drum band, fraternities, sororities, Amnesty International, Hilltoppers, 4-H Club, Light on the Hill, Rescue Club, WLSC Students for Life, Students Against MS, Veterans Association.

ATHLETICS. NAIA, NCAA. **Intercollegiate:** Baseball M, basketball, cross-country M, football M, golf M, softball W, tennis, track and field M, volleyball W, wrestling M. **Intramural:** Basketball M, bowling, football M, handball M, racquetball, softball, swimming, table tennis, tennis.

STUDENT SERVICES. Aptitude testing, career counseling, employment service for undergraduates, freshman orientation, health services, personal counseling, placement service for graduates, veterans counselor, services/facilities for handicapped.

ANNUAL EXPENSES. Tuition and fees (1992-93): $1,590, $2,670

additional for out-of-state students. **Room and board:** $2,650. **Books and supplies:** $500. **Other expenses:** $900.

FINANCIAL AID. 60% of freshmen, 56% of continuing students receive some form of aid. 96% of grants, 82% of jobs based on need. 398 enrolled freshmen were judged to have need, all were offered aid. Academic, music/drama, art, athletic scholarships available. **Aid applications:** No closing date; priority given to applications received by March 1; applicants notified on a rolling basis beginning on or about March 15. **Additional information:** Non-need based student employment available at food service and college union.

ADDRESS/TELEPHONE. Paul B. Milam, Director of Admissions, West Liberty State College, West Liberty, WV 26074. (304) 336-8076. (800) 732-6204. Fax: (304) 336-8285.

West Virginia Institute of Technology
Montgomery, West Virginia CB code: 5902

Admissions: 99% of applicants accepted
Based on: ••• School record, test scores
Completion: 78% of freshmen end year in good standing
25% enter graduate study

4-year public engineering, technical college, coed. Founded in 1895. **Accreditation:** Regional. **Undergraduate enrollment:** 1,625 men, 786 women full time; 330 men, 286 women part time. **Graduate enrollment:** 21 men full time; 2 men, 1 woman part time. **Faculty:** 214 total (146 full time), 96 with doctorates or other terminal degrees. **Location:** Rural campus in small town; 30 miles from Charleston. **Calendar:** Semester, limited summer session. Extensive evening/early morning classes. **Microcomputers:** 625 located in dormitories, libraries, classrooms, computer centers. **Special facilities:** Art gallery, hiking trail.

DEGREES OFFERED. AA, AS, BA, BS, MS. 151 associate degrees awarded in 1992. 339 bachelor's degrees awarded.

UNDERGRADUATE MAJORS. Associate: Accounting, business administration and management, business and management, business and office, business data processing and related programs, business economics, civil technology, computer and information sciences, data processing, dental hygiene, drafting, drafting and design technology, electrical and electronics equipment repair, electrical technology, engineering and engineering-related technologies, graphic and printing production, legal secretary, liberal/general studies, mechanical design technology, medical secretary, nursing, office supervision and management, secretarial and related programs, survey and mapping technology. **Bachelor's:** Accounting, biology, business administration and management, business and management, business education, chemical engineering, chemistry, civil engineering, community services, computer and information sciences, drafting, drafting and design technology, driver and safety education, electrical and electronics equipment repair, electrical/electronics/communications engineering, electronic technology, engineering and engineering-related technologies, English education, finance, graphic and printing production, health care administration, health education, history, industrial arts education, industrial technology, junior high education, labor/industrial relations, management information systems, mathematics, mathematics education, mechanical design technology, mechanical engineering, music education, physical education, physics, public administration, science education, secondary education, social science education, social studies education, trade and industrial education.

ACADEMIC PROGRAMS. 2-year transfer program, cooperative education, double major, dual enrollment of high school students, internships, teacher preparation, telecourses, cooperative programs in engineering and business. **Remedial services:** Learning center, preadmission summer program, reduced course load, remedial instruction, special counselor, tutoring. **ROTC:** Army. **Placement/credit:** AP, CLEP General and Subject, institutional tests; 90 credit hours maximum for bachelor's degree.

ACADEMIC REQUIREMENTS. Freshmen must earn minimum GPA of 2.0 to continue in good standing. 70% of freshmen return for sophomore year. Students must declare major by end of second year. **Graduation requirements:** 64 hours for associate (40 in major), 128 hours for bachelor's (48 in major). Most students required to take courses in computer science, English, history, humanities, mathematics, biological/physical sciences, social sciences. **Postgraduate studies:** 20% from 2-year programs enter 4-year programs.

FRESHMAN ADMISSIONS. Selection criteria: Open admissions to all 2-year programs, except dental hygiene and nursing. School achievement record and test scores important for in-state applicants to 4-year program. Out-of-state applicants must rank in top three-quarters of class or have SAT combined score of 670 or ACT composite score of 14. Higher requirements for both in-state and out-of-state engineering applicants. Required and recommended units include English 4-4, mathematics 2-4, social science 3-3 and science 2-3. Biological science 1 and physical science 2 recommended. 17 academic units required of 4-year program applicants, including 4 English, 2 mathematics, 3 social sciences, 2 laboratory science. 2 algebra, 1 plane geometry, 1 advanced mathematics required of engineering majors. One algebra, 1 chemistry required of dental hygiene majors. 2 laboratory sciences one of which has to be chemistry, 2 higher mathematics for nursing. **Test requirements:** SAT or ACT (ACT preferred); score report by August 15.

1992 FRESHMAN CLASS PROFILE. 984 men applied, 963 accepted, 398 enrolled; 610 women applied, 609 accepted, 277 enrolled. 59% had high school GPA of 3.0 or higher, 36% between 2.0 and 2.99. **Academic background:** Mid 50% of enrolled freshmen had ACT composite between 16-24. 100% submitted ACT scores. **Characteristics:** 80% from in state, 60% commute, 8% have minority backgrounds, 4% are foreign students. Average age is 20.

FALL-TERM APPLICATIONS. No fee. Closing date August 1; applicants notified on a rolling basis; must reply within 2 weeks. Audition required for music education applicants. Deferred and early admission available.

STUDENT LIFE. Housing: Dormitories (men, women, coed); fraternity housing available. **Activities:** Student government, student newspaper, yearbook, choral groups, concert band, drama, jazz band, marching band, music ensembles, fraternities, sororities.

ATHLETICS. NAIA, NCAA. **Intercollegiate:** Baseball M, basketball, football M, softball W, tennis M, volleyball W. **Intramural:** Badminton, basketball, handball, racquetball, soccer, softball, swimming, table tennis, tennis, volleyball, water polo, wrestling M.

STUDENT SERVICES. Aptitude testing, career counseling, employment service for undergraduates, freshman orientation, health services, personal counseling, placement service for graduates, special adviser for adult students, veterans counselor, services/facilities for handicapped.

ANNUAL EXPENSES. Tuition and fees (1992-93): $1,784, $2,170 additional for out-of-state students. **Room and board:** $3,752. **Books and supplies:** $500. **Other expenses:** $700.

FINANCIAL AID. 40% of freshmen, 60% of continuing students receive some form of aid. 54% of grants, 93% of loans, 65% of jobs based on need. 334 enrolled freshmen were judged to have need, 294 were offered aid. Academic, music/drama, athletic scholarships available. **Aid applications:** Closing date April 1; priority given to applications received by January 31; applicants notified on or about May 1; must reply within 3 weeks. **Additional information:** Room and board may be deferred for up to 60 days. First 50% due in 30 days.

ADDRESS/TELEPHONE. Robert P. Scholl, Jr, Director of Admissions/Registrar, West Virginia Institute of Technology, Montgomery, WV 25136-2436. (304) 442-3167. Fax: (304) 442-3059.

West Virginia Northern Community College
Wheeling, West Virginia CB code: 0674

2-year public community college, coed. Founded in 1972. **Accreditation:** Regional. **Undergraduate enrollment:** 408 men, 713 women full time; 538 men, 1,332 women part time. **Faculty:** 147 total (64 full time), 10 with doctorates or other terminal degrees. **Location:** Urban campus in large town; 55 miles from Pittsburgh, Pennsylvania. **Calendar:** Semester, limited summer session. **Microcomputers:** 105 located in libraries, classrooms, computer centers. **Additional facts:** Multilocation institution.

DEGREES OFFERED. AA, AS, AAS. 272 associate degrees awarded in 1992. 18% in business and management, 12% business/office and marketing/distribution, 6% computer sciences, 32% health sciences, 13% allied health, 7% multi/interdisciplinary studies, 8% trade and industry.

UNDERGRADUATE MAJORS. Accounting, air conditioning/heating/refrigeration mechanics, air conditioning/heating/refrigeration technology, airline piloting and navigation, business administration and management, business and office, business computer/console/peripheral equipment operation, business data processing and related programs, business data programming, computer and information sciences, criminal justice technology, data processing, electrical and electronics equipment repair, electronic technology, finance, law enforcement and corrections technologies, liberal/general studies, medical laboratory technologies, nursing, respiratory therapy technology, secretarial and related programs, surgical technology.

ACADEMIC PROGRAMS. 2-year transfer program, accelerated program, double major, dual enrollment of high school students, independent study, internships. **Remedial services:** Learning center, preadmission summer program, reduced course load, remedial instruction, special counselor, tutoring. **Placement/credit:** AP, CLEP General and Subject, institutional tests; 45 credit hours maximum for associate degree.

ACADEMIC REQUIREMENTS. No policy requiring minimum GPA; records of students having academic difficulty are reviewed individually. **Graduation requirements:** 64 hours for associate. Most students required to take courses in English, history, mathematics, biological/physical sciences, social sciences.

FRESHMAN ADMISSIONS. Selection criteria: Open admissions. Selective admissions to health programs. **Test requirements:** SAT or ACT (ACT preferred) for counseling; score report by December 1. **Additional information:** Students born after January 1, 1957 must submit proof of immunization for Measles and Rubella. Freshmen must take the ASSET Tests for writing, reading, arithmetic and basic algebra and are placed in developmental courses if necessary.

1992 FRESHMAN CLASS PROFILE. 203 men, 401 women enrolled. **Characteristics:** 80% from in state, 100% commute. Average age is 28.

FALL-TERM APPLICATIONS. No fee. No closing date; applicants notified on a rolling basis; must reply within 3 weeks. Health science applicants are accepted by April 1, late applicants evaluated by June 30.

STUDENT LIFE. Activities: Student government, magazine, student newspaper.

ATHLETICS. Intramural: Basketball, bowling, golf, softball, table tennis, volleyball.

STUDENT SERVICES. Career counseling, employment service for undergraduates, freshman orientation, personal counseling, placement service for graduates, veterans counselor, services/facilities for handicapped.

ANNUAL EXPENSES. Tuition and fees (1992-93): $1,144, $1,992 additional for out-of-state students. **Books and supplies:** $450. **Other expenses:** $1,049.

FINANCIAL AID. 40% of freshmen, 25% of continuing students receive some form of aid. 98% of grants, 96% of loans, all jobs based on need. Academic, leadership scholarships available. **Aid applications:** No closing date; priority given to applications received by July 1; applicants notified on a rolling basis beginning on or about July 1; must reply within 2 weeks.

ADDRESS/TELEPHONE. Bonnie K. Ellis, Assistant Dean of Admissions, West Virginia Northern Community College, College Square, Wheeling, WV 26003. (304) 233-5900.

West Virginia State College

Institute, West Virginia — CB code: 5903

4-year public liberal arts college, coed. Founded in 1891. **Accreditation:** Regional. **Undergraduate enrollment:** 1,398 men, 1,439 women full time; 823 men, 1,236 women part time. **Faculty:** 233 total (139 full time), 57 with doctorates or other terminal degrees. **Location:** Suburban campus in small town; 8 miles from Charleston. **Calendar:** Semester, limited summer session. Saturday and extensive evening/early morning classes. **Microcomputers:** 48 located in dormitories, computer centers.

DEGREES OFFERED. AA, AS, AAS, BA, BS. 115 associate degrees awarded in 1992. 28% in business and management, 23% business/office and marketing/distribution, 6% communications, 12% computer sciences, 15% engineering technologies, 5% allied health, 5% parks/recreation, protective services, public affairs. 410 bachelor's degrees awarded. 22% in business and management, 6% communications, 23% teacher education, 22% multi/interdisciplinary studies, 9% parks/recreation, protective services, public affairs.

UNDERGRADUATE MAJORS. Associate: Accounting, advertising, architectural technologies, business administration and management, business and management, chemical manufacturing technology, chemical technology, communications, computer and information sciences, computer programming, criminal justice studies, dental laboratory technology, drafting, drafting and design technology, electrical technology, electrical/electronics/communications engineering, electronic technology, fashion merchandising, finance, fine arts, hotel/motel and restaurant management, legal secretary, liberal/general studies, marketing management, medical assistant, medical secretary, nuclear medical technology, nuclear technologies, radiograph medical technology, religious music, science technologies, secretarial and related programs, social work. **Bachelor's:** Accounting, applied mathematics, art education, biology, business administration and management, business and management, ceramics, chemistry, communications, construction, creative writing, criminal justice studies, drafting, drawing, early childhood education, economics, education, education of exceptional children, education of the mentally handicapped, elementary education, English, English education, fiber/textiles/weaving, finance, fine arts, graphic design, health education, history, industrial technology, junior high education, law enforcement and corrections, liberal/general studies, marketing and distribution, mathematics, mathematics education, music education, nuclear medical technology, painting, parks and recreation management, photography, physical education, physics, political science and government, printmaking, psychology, recreation therapy, science education, sculpture, secondary education, social studies education, social work, sociology, special education, technical and business writing.

ACADEMIC PROGRAMS. 2-year transfer program, cooperative education, double major, dual enrollment of high school students, external degree, honors program, internships, teacher preparation, telecourses, cross-registration, nontraditional life experience degree program. **Remedial services:** Learning center, reduced course load, remedial instruction, special counselor, tutoring, skills enhancement program for ROTC students. **ROTC:** Army. **Placement/credit:** AP, CLEP General and Subject, institutional tests.

ACADEMIC REQUIREMENTS. Freshmen must earn minimum GPA of 2.0 to continue in good standing. 68% of freshmen return for sophomore year. Students must declare major by end of second year. **Graduation requirements:** 60 hours for associate (24 in major), 121 hours for bachelor's (34 in major). Most students required to take courses in arts/fine arts, humanities, mathematics, biological/physical sciences, social sciences. **Postgraduate studies:** 45% from 2-year programs enter 4-year programs.

FRESHMAN ADMISSIONS. Selection criteria: School achievement record and test scores considered for 4-year programs. Open admission for community college component. **High school preparation:** 14 units required. Required units include English 4, foreign language 2, mathematics 2, social science 3 and science 2. One physical education required. **Test requirements:** SAT or ACT (ACT preferred); score report by August 27. **Additional information:** Fall classes begin third week of August; spring session starts third week of January.

1992 FRESHMAN CLASS PROFILE. 390 men, 417 women enrolled. 30% had high school GPA of 3.0 or higher, 60% between 2.0 and 2.99. **Academic background:** Mid 50% of enrolled freshmen had ACT composite between 10-18. 100% submitted ACT scores. **Characteristics:** 87% from in state, 85% commute, 12% have minority backgrounds, 1% are foreign students. Average age is 25.

FALL-TERM APPLICATIONS. No fee. No closing date; priority given to applications received by August 11; applicants notified on a rolling basis. Interview recommended for nuclear medicine technology, academically weak, regents bachelor of arts applicants. CRDA. Deferred and early admission available. New students encouraged to apply for admission several months before a semester begins.

STUDENT LIFE. Housing: Dormitories (men, women); apartment housing available. Apartments available for students with dependents. **Activities:** Student government, film, radio, student newspaper, television, yearbook, choral groups, concert band, drama, jazz band, music ensembles, fraternities, sororities, DNA Science Club, International Students, Pre-Alumni Club, College Students for Christ, Just Friends, Foreign Affairs Society, Kamawha Review, NAACP.

ATHLETICS. NAIA. **Intercollegiate:** Baseball M, basketball, football M, softball W, track and field. **Intramural:** Basketball, bowling, football M, softball, swimming, tennis, volleyball.

STUDENT SERVICES. Aptitude testing, career counseling, employment service for undergraduates, freshman orientation, health services, on-campus day care, personal counseling, placement service for graduates, veterans counselor, Peer Tutoring, services/facilities for handicapped.

ANNUAL EXPENSES. Tuition and fees (1992-93): $1,712, $2,290 additional for out-of-state students. **Room and board:** $3,050. **Books and supplies:** $500. **Other expenses:** $940.

FINANCIAL AID. 55% of freshmen, 45% of continuing students receive some form of aid. All grants, 87% of loans, 90% of jobs based on need. Academic, music/drama, art, athletic, state/district residency, leadership, religious affiliation, minority scholarships available. **Aid applications:** Closing date August 10; priority given to applications received by March 1; applicants notified on a rolling basis; must reply within 2 weeks.

ADDRESS/TELEPHONE. Robin Green, Assistant Director of Admissions, West Virginia State College, PO Box 197, Institute, WV 25112-0335. (304) 766-3221. Fax: (304) 766-9842.

West Virginia University

Morgantown, West Virginia — CB code: 5904

Admissions: 81% of applicants accepted
Based on: ••• School record, test scores
• Activities, special talents
Completion: 93% of freshmen end year in good standing
49% graduate, 26% of these enter graduate study

4-year public university, coed. Founded in 1867. **Accreditation:** Regional. **Undergraduate enrollment:** 8,169 men, 6,802 women full time; 439 men, 604 women part time. **Graduate enrollment:** 1,733 men, 1,368 women full time; 1,201 men, 2,396 women part time. **Faculty:** 1,543 total (1,359 full time), 1,189 with doctorates or other terminal degrees. **Location:** Suburban campus in large town; 70 miles from Pittsburgh, Pennsylvania, 200 miles from Baltimore, Maryland, and Washington, D.C. **Calendar:** Semester, extensive summer session. **Microcomputers:** 1,200 located in dormitories, libraries, classrooms, computer centers. **Special facilities:** Arboretum, planetarium, herbarium, pharmacy museum, 2 art galleries, experimental farms, forests, software development center, fluidization center, Concurrent Engineering Research Center, Appalachian Export Center for Hardwoods, National Research Center for Coal and Energy, Mineral and Energy Resources Museum. **Additional facts:** Off-campus graduate classes offered at Jackson's Mill, Keyser, Parkersburg, Shepherdstown and West Liberty. Health Sciences Center operates a division in Charleston; School of Medicine has a division in Wheeling.

DEGREES OFFERED. BA, BS, BFA, MA, MS, MBA, MFA, MSW, PhD, EdD, DDS, MD, B. Pharm, Pharm D, JD. 2,791 bachelor's degrees awarded in 1992. 19% in business and management, 7% communications, 8% teacher education, 10% engineering, 9% health sciences, 7% multi/interdisciplinary studies, 5% psychology, 9% social sciences. Graduate degrees offered in 88 major fields of study.

UNDERGRADUATE MAJORS. Accounting, advertising, aerospace/aeronautical/astronautical engineering, agricultural education, agronomy, animal sciences, anthropology, art education, athletic training, biology, business administration and management, business and foreign language, business economics, chemical engineering, chemistry, civil engineering, clinical laboratory science, communications, computer and information sciences, computer engineering, dental hygiene, dramatic arts, economics, electrical/electronics/communications engineering, elementary education, English, environmental science, family/consumer resource management, fashion merchandising, finance, fine arts, food science and nutrition, foreign languages (multiple emphasis), forest products processing technology, forestry production and processing, geography, geology, history, home economics education, horticultural science, individual and family development, industrial engineering, interior design, international studies, journalism, landscape architecture, liberal/general studies, management science, marketing management, mathematics, mechanical engineering, mining and mineral engineering, motion picture technology, music, nursing, parks and recreation management, petroleum engineering, pharmacy, philosophy, physical education, physical therapy, physics, plant sciences, political science and government, psychology, public relations, radio/television broadcasting, resource management, Russian and Slavic studies, secondary education, social work, sociology, speech pathology/audiology, sport studies, sports and exercise studies, sports medicine, statistics, textiles and clothing, wildlife management.

ACADEMIC PROGRAMS. Accelerated program, cooperative education, double major, dual enrollment of high school students, education specialist degree, honors program, independent study, internships, semester at sea, student-designed major, study abroad, teacher preparation, telecourses, visiting/exchange student program, weekend college, Washington semester, cross-registration; liberal arts/career combination in business. **Remedial services:** Learning center, reduced course load, remedial instruction, special counselor, tutoring, writing laboratory, mathematics learning center. **ROTC:** Air Force, Army. **Placement/credit:** AP, CLEP General and Subject, institutional tests.

ACADEMIC REQUIREMENTS. Freshmen must earn minimum GPA of 2.0 to continue in good standing. 77% of freshmen return for sophomore year. Students must declare major by end of second year. **Graduation requirements:** 128 hours for bachelor's. Most students required to take courses in arts/fine arts, computer science, English, humanities, mathematics, biological/physical sciences, social sciences.

FRESHMAN ADMISSIONS. Selection criteria: Minimum 2.0 high school GPA for state residents and minimum ACT of 19 or minimum SAT of 770; minimum 2.25 for out-of-state applicants and minimum ACT of 20 or minimum SAT of 820. **High school preparation:** 18 units recommended. Recommended units include English 4, foreign language 2, mathematics 3 and social science 3. 3.5 units mathematics, including .5 unit of trigonometry, required for mineral and energy resources, engineering, business and economics, and computer science applicants. 2 units algebra and 1 unit geometry required for applicants to programs requiring mathematics. 2 units laboratory science required. **Test requirements:** SAT or ACT; score report by August 1. **Additional information:** Applicants with high GPA, high test scores, or special talents in athletics or the arts who do not meet all admissions criteria, may be considered on an individual basis. Up to 5% of each incoming class may be accepted under this special policy.

1992 FRESHMAN CLASS PROFILE. 5,357 men applied, 4,257 accepted, 1,562 enrolled; 5,013 women applied, 4,129 accepted, 1,478 enrolled. 49% had high school GPA of 3.0 or higher, 50% between 2.0 and 2.99. **Academic background:** Mid 50% of enrolled freshmen had SAT-V between 380-470, SAT-M between 430-540; ACT composite between 20-25. 60% submitted SAT scores, 45% submitted ACT scores. **Characteristics:** 45% from in state, 7% have minority backgrounds, 1% are foreign students. Average age is 19.

FALL-TERM APPLICATIONS. $10 fee, may be waived for applicants with need. Nonresident application fee $25. No closing date; priority given to applications received by March 1; applicants notified on a rolling basis; must reply at least 4 weeks prior to registration. Interview required for dental hygiene applicants. Audition required for music applicants. Portfolio required. Deferred and early admission available. Applicants who require university housing must reply by May 1.

STUDENT LIFE. Housing: Dormitories (men, women, coed); apartment, fraternity, sorority, handicapped housing available. Honors and foreign language floors available. Apartments for single students with children available. **Activities:** Student government, radio, student newspaper, television, yearbook, American Advertising Federation; Public Relations Student Society of America; Radio and Television News Directors Association; Society of Professional Journalists, choral groups, concert band, dance, drama, jazz band, marching band, music ensembles, musical theater, opera, pep band, symphony orchestra, fraternities, sororities, over 200 student organizations. **Additional information:** The Center for Women's Studies facilitates teaching and research on women's and gender issues, and coordinates an interdisciplinary program leading to a certificate in women's studies. The Center for Black Culture and Research provides cultural, educational, and social events and coordinates an interdepartmental certificate program in African and African-American Studies.

ATHLETICS. NCAA. **Intercollegiate:** Baseball M, basketball, cross-country, football M, gymnastics W, rifle, soccer M, swimming, tennis, track and field, volleyball W, wrestling M. **Intramural:** Badminton, basketball, bowling, field hockey M, golf, racquetball, rifle, soccer, softball, swimming, table tennis, tennis, track and field, volleyball, wrestling M.

STUDENT SERVICES. Aptitude testing, career counseling, employment service for undergraduates, freshman orientation, health services, personal counseling, placement service for graduates, special adviser for adult students, veterans counselor, disability services, international student services, services/facilities for handicapped.

ANNUAL EXPENSES. Tuition and fees (1992-93): $1,928, $3,558 additional for out-of-state students. **Room and board:** $4,016. **Books and supplies:** $550. **Other expenses:** $1,155.

FINANCIAL AID. 57% of freshmen, 54% of continuing students receive some form of aid. 78% of grants, 96% of loans, 70% of jobs based on need. Academic, music/drama, art, athletic, state/district residency, leadership, alumni affiliation, minority scholarships available. **Aid applications:** No closing date; priority given to applications received by March 1; applicants notified on a rolling basis beginning on or about March 23; must reply within 3 weeks. **Additional information:** Closing date for freshman scholarships January 15. Comprehensive scholarship program supports as many as 550 students in each entering class. Awards range from full cost to one year awards of $250. Student may indicate interest in program on admissions application.

ADDRESS/TELEPHONE. Dr. Glenn G. Carter, Director of Admissions and Records, West Virginia University, PO Box 6009, PO Box 6009, Morgantown, WV 26506-6009. (304) 293-2121. (800) 344-WVU1. Fax: (304) 293-3080.

West Virginia University at Parkersburg
Parkersburg, West Virginia — CB code: 5932

2-year public community college, coed. Founded in 1971. **Accreditation:** Regional. **Undergraduate enrollment:** 3,961 men and women. **Faculty:** 160 total (70 full time), 10 with doctorates or other terminal degrees. **Location:** Suburban campus in large town; 4 miles from Parkersburg. **Calendar:** Semester, limited summer session. Extensive evening/early morning classes. **Additional facts:** Bachelor degree programs offered in elementary education and business administration. Students eligible to apply after completing sophomore year of associate degree program.

DEGREES OFFERED. AA, AS, AAS, BA, BS. 230 associate degrees awarded in 1992. 3 bachelor's degrees awarded.

UNDERGRADUATE MAJORS. Associate: Business administration and management, business and management, business data processing and related programs, criminal justice studies, electronic technology, engineering and engineering-related technologies, industrial technology, nursing, secretarial and related programs, social work, welding technology. **Bachelor's:** Business administration and management, elementary education.

ACADEMIC PROGRAMS. 2-year transfer program, cooperative education, dual enrollment of high school students, independent study, internships, teacher preparation, telecourses. **Remedial services:** Learning center, reduced course load, remedial instruction, tutoring. **Placement/credit:** AP, CLEP Subject, institutional tests.

ACADEMIC REQUIREMENTS. Freshmen must earn minimum GPA of 2.0 to continue in good standing. Students must declare major on application. **Graduation requirements:** 66 hours for associate. Most students required to take courses in computer science, English, humanities, mathematics, biological/physical sciences, social sciences.

FRESHMAN ADMISSIONS. Selection criteria: Open admissions. Selective admissions for nursing programs and bachelor's degree programs. **Test requirements:** SAT or ACT (ACT preferred); score report by December 31.

1992 FRESHMAN CLASS PROFILE. 1,750 men and women enrolled. **Characteristics:** 96% from in state, 100% commute, 1% have minority backgrounds. Average age is 25.

FALL-TERM APPLICATIONS. No fee. No closing date; applicants notified on a rolling basis beginning on or about June 1. Interview required for nursing applicants. Deferred admission available.

STUDENT LIFE. Activities: Student government, student newspaper, choral groups, drama.

ATHLETICS. Intramural: Baseball, basketball, bowling, softball, table tennis, tennis, volleyball.

STUDENT SERVICES. Aptitude testing, career counseling, employment service for undergraduates, freshman orientation, health services, on-campus day care, personal counseling, placement service for graduates, services/facilities for handicapped.

ANNUAL EXPENSES. Tuition and fees (1992-93): $864, $2,016 additional for out-of-state students. **Books and supplies:** $470. **Other expenses:** $1,270.

FINANCIAL AID. 40% of continuing students receive some form of aid. 82% of grants, 94% of loans, all jobs based on need. Academic, state/district residency, leadership scholarships available. **Aid applications:** No closing date; priority given to applications received by May 1; applicants notified on a rolling basis beginning on or about July 1.

ADDRESS/TELEPHONE. Ragina Copeland, Registrar/Director of Admissions, West Virginia University at Parkersburg, Route 5, Box 167-A, Parkersburg, WV 26101-9577. (304) 424-8220. Fax: (304) 424-8315.

West Virginia Wesleyan College

Buckhannon, West Virginia CB code: 5905

Admissions: 88% of applicants accepted
Based on: ••• School record
•• Activities, recommendations, test scores
• Essay, interview, special talents
Completion: 87% of freshmen end year in good standing
52% graduate, 21% of these enter graduate study

4-year private liberal arts college, coed, affiliated with United Methodist Church. Founded in 1890. **Accreditation:** Regional. **Undergraduate enrollment:** 730 men, 723 women full time; 31 men, 76 women part time. **Graduate enrollment:** 10 men, 3 women full time; 45 men, 37 women part time. **Faculty:** 126 total (83 full time), 53 with doctorates or other terminal degrees. **Location:** Rural campus in small town; 115 miles from Charleston, 135 miles from Pittsburgh, Pennsylvania. **Calendar:** 4-1-4, limited summer session. **Microcomputers:** 175 located in libraries, classrooms, computer centers. **Special facilities:** Planetarium, botany museum, Sleeth Gallery of Art, herbarium and greenhouse, Wesley Chapel, Rockefeller Physical Education Center.

DEGREES OFFERED. BA, BS, MBA. 264 bachelor's degrees awarded in 1992. 21% in business and management, 14% teacher education, 8% health sciences, 10% psychology, 14% social sciences, 5% visual and performing arts. Graduate degrees offered in 1 major field of study.

UNDERGRADUATE MAJORS. Accounting, art education, biology, business administration and management, business and management, chemistry, computer and information sciences, creative writing, dramatic arts, early and middle childhood education, early childhood education, economics, elementary education, engineering physics, English, English education, fashion merchandising, finance, food science and nutrition, forestry and related sciences, health education, history, home economics, home economics education, information sciences and systems, international studies, junior high education, management information systems, marketing and distribution, mathematics, mathematics education, music, music education, music performance, nursing, philosophy, physical education, physics, political science and government, predentistry, prelaw, premedicine, prepharmacy, preveterinary, psychology, public administration, public relations, rehabilitation counseling/services, religion, religious education, science education, secondary education, social sciences, social studies education, sociology, speech, sports medicine, studio art.

ACADEMIC PROGRAMS. Accelerated program, double major, dual enrollment of high school students, honors program, independent study, internships, student-designed major, study abroad, teacher preparation, visiting/exchange student program, Washington semester, Wesleyan Scholars Program. **Remedial services:** Learning center, reduced course load, remedial instruction, tutoring. **Placement/credit:** AP, CLEP General and Subject, institutional tests; 32 credit hours maximum for bachelor's degree.

ACADEMIC REQUIREMENTS. Freshmen must earn minimum GPA of 2.0 to continue in good standing. 75% of freshmen return for sophomore year. Students must declare major by end of first year. **Graduation requirements:** 128 hours for bachelor's (30 in major). Most students required to take courses in arts/fine arts, English, history, humanities, mathematics, philosophy/religion, biological/physical sciences, social sciences. **Postgraduate studies:** 3% enter law school, 2% enter medical school, 6% enter MBA programs, 10% enter other graduate study.

FRESHMAN ADMISSIONS. Selection criteria: School achievement record and test scores required. Interview recommended. **High school preparation:** 16 units required. Required and recommended units include English 4. Foreign language 2, mathematics 3, social science 3 and science 4 recommended. **Test requirements:** SAT or ACT; score report by August 20. **Additional information:** Applicants for the Special Support Services Program for students with a learning disability must complete all admission requirements by February 15. Required campus interview must be scheduled by December 1 or await invitation by college after initial application evaluation.

1992 FRESHMAN CLASS PROFILE. 766 men applied, 647 accepted, 245 enrolled; 633 women applied, 585 accepted, 230 enrolled. 57% had high school GPA of 3.0 or higher, 41% between 2.0 and 2.99. 28% were in top tenth and 54% were in top quarter of graduating class. **Academic background:** Mid 50% of enrolled freshmen had SAT-V between 370-500, SAT-M between 410-570; ACT composite between 19-26. 79% submitted SAT scores, 40% submitted ACT scores. **Characteristics:** 37% from in state, 85% live in college housing, 5% have minority backgrounds, 5% are foreign students, 29% join fraternities/sororities. Average age is 18.

FALL-TERM APPLICATIONS. $25 fee, may be waived for applicants with need. Closing date August 20; priority given to applications received by February 1; applicants notified on a rolling basis; must reply by August 30. Interview recommended. Essay recommended. Deferred and early admission available.

STUDENT LIFE. Housing: Dormitories (men, women); apartment, fraternity housing available. On campus housing guaranteed for all students. Full-time students required to live on campus unless married, living with parents, or have received written permission from the Housing Committee to live off campus. **Activities:** Student government, magazine, radio, student newspaper, television, yearbook, forensics team, choral groups, concert band, drama, jazz band, music ensembles, musical theater, pep band, lively arts cultural series, fraternities, sororities, Black Student Union, Christian Life Council, International Student Organization, Residence Hall Council, Campus Activities Board. **Additional information:** Emphasis placed on quality of living in residential community.

ATHLETICS. NAIA, NCAA. **Intercollegiate:** Baseball M, basketball, cross-country, diving, football M, golf M, soccer, softball W, swimming, tennis, track and field, volleyball W. **Intramural:** Badminton, basketball, bowling, racquetball, softball, table tennis, tennis, volleyball.

STUDENT SERVICES. Aptitude testing, career counseling, freshman orientation, health services, personal counseling, placement service for graduates, minority student adviser, study abroad advising, services/facilities for handicapped.

ANNUAL EXPENSES. Tuition and fees: $13,400. **Room and board:** $3,500. **Books and supplies:** $450. **Other expenses:** $1,100.

FINANCIAL AID. 94% of freshmen, 85% of continuing students receive some form of aid. 69% of grants, 91% of loans, 63% of jobs based on need. 411 enrolled freshmen were judged to have need, all were offered aid. Academic, music/drama, art, athletic, leadership, religious affiliation, minority scholarships available. **Aid applications:** No closing date; priority given to applications received by March 1; applicants notified on a rolling basis beginning on or about March 15; must reply within 3 weeks. **Additional information:** Both merit-based and need-based resources availible.

ADDRESS/TELEPHONE. Robert N. Skinner II, Director of Admission, West Virginia Wesleyan College, College Avenue, Buckhannon, WV 26201-2998. (304) 473-8479. (800) 722-9933. Fax: (304) 472-2571.

Wheeling Jesuit College

Wheeling, West Virginia CB code: 5906

Admissions: 86% of applicants accepted
Based on: ••• School record
•• Activities, interview, special talents, test scores
• Recommendations
Completion: 85% of freshmen end year in good standing
61% graduate, 25% of these enter graduate study

4-year private college of arts and sciences, coed, affiliated with Roman Catholic Church. Founded in 1954. **Accreditation:** Regional. **Undergraduate enrollment:** 405 men, 557 women full time; 69 men, 259 women part time. **Graduate enrollment:** 18 men, 5 women full time; 83 men, 42 women part time. **Faculty:** 93 total (68 full time), 48 with doctorates or other terminal degrees. **Location:** Suburban campus in small city; 55 miles from Pittsburgh, Pennsylvania, 125 miles from Columbus, Ohio. **Calendar:** Semester, limited summer session. Extensive evening/early morning classes. **Microcomputers:** 48 located in computer centers. **Special facilities:** NASA teacher resource center.

DEGREES OFFERED. BA, BS, MA, MBA. 232 bachelor's degrees awarded in 1992. 38% in business and management, 9% health sciences, 9% allied health, 6% multi/interdisciplinary studies, 9% psychology, 9% social sciences. Graduate degrees offered in 4 major fields of study.

UNDERGRADUATE MAJORS. Accounting, allied health, applied mathematics, biology, business administration and management, chemical engineering, chemistry, computer and information sciences, computer engineering, computer mathematics, criminal justice studies, English, English literature, French, history, human resources development, industrial engineering, international relations, international studies, liberal/general studies, marketing management, mathematics, nuclear medical technology, nursing, philosophy, physical sciences, physical therapy, physics, political and economic philosophy, political science and government, predentistry, prelaw, premedicine, preveterinary, professional writing, psychology, religion, respiratory therapy, respiratory therapy technology, romance languages, Spanish, technical and business writing, theological studies.

ACADEMIC PROGRAMS. Double major, honors program, independent study, internships, student-designed major, study abroad, teacher preparation, visiting/exchange student program, Washington semester, cross-registration; liberal arts/career combination in engineering, health sciences; combined bachelor's/graduate program in business administration. **Remedial services:** Learning center, preadmission summer program, reduced course load, remedial instruction, special counselor, tutoring. **Placement/credit:** AP, CLEP General, institutional tests; 30 credit hours maximum for bachelor's degree.

ACADEMIC REQUIREMENTS. Freshmen must earn minimum GPA of 2.0 to continue in good standing. 75% of freshmen return for sophomore year. Students must declare major by end of second year. **Graduation requirements:** 124 hours for bachelor's (60 in major). Most students required to take courses in English, foreign languages, history, mathematics, philosophy/religion, biological/physical sciences, social sciences. **Postgraduate studies:** 3% enter law school, 5% enter medical school, 5% enter MBA programs, 12% enter other graduate study. **Additional information:** To broaden their cocurricular experience, all students are required to complete Wellness Program credits by attending cultural, academic, athletic, and health events.

FRESHMAN ADMISSIONS. Selection criteria: High school GPA (minimum 2.5), class rank, and quality of courses taken most important. Test scores considered. Some exception made to minimum test scores and GPA when warranted by high school record. Personal recommendations and extracurricular activities important. In-state and out-of-state applicants treated equally. **High school preparation:** 15 units required. Required and recommended units include English 4, mathematics 2, social science 2 and science 2. Foreign language 2 recommended. One unit chemistry required of nursing applicants. One unit biology, 1 unit chemistry, 3 units mathematics for physical therapy applicants. **Test requirements:** SAT or ACT; score report by July 31.

1992 FRESHMAN CLASS PROFILE. 370 men applied, 335 accepted, 109 enrolled; 480 women applied, 397 accepted, 161 enrolled. 60% had high school GPA of 3.0 or higher, 38% between 2.0 and 2.99. 20% were in top tenth and 46% were in top quarter of graduating class. **Academic background:** Mid 50% of enrolled freshmen had SAT-V between 390-500, SAT-M between 410-540; ACT composite between 19-23. 51% submitted SAT scores, 71% submitted ACT scores. **Characteristics:** 47% from in state, 74% live in college housing, 5% have minority backgrounds, 3% are foreign students. Average age is 18.

FALL-TERM APPLICATIONS. $25 fee, may be waived for applicants with need. No closing date; priority given to applications received by April 1; applicants notified on a rolling basis; must reply by May 1 or within 2 weeks if notified thereafter. Interview recommended. CRDA. Deferred and early admission available.

STUDENT LIFE. Housing: Dormitories (men, women, coed). Housing available on campus for all undergraduate students. **Activities:** Student government, magazine, student newspaper, yearbook, choral groups, dance, drama, musical theater, pep band, special interest theater, social service outreach organization, student-operated Rathskellar, international student club, academic clubs, campus ministry groups. **Additional information:** Volunteer community service encouraged. Student activity budget controlled by students.

ATHLETICS. NAIA, NCAA. **Intercollegiate:** Basketball, cross-country, golf, soccer, volleyball W. **Intramural:** Basketball, ice hockey M, lacrosse M, rugby M, soccer, softball, tennis, volleyball. **Clubs:** Sports clubs.

STUDENT SERVICES. Aptitude testing, career counseling, employment service for undergraduates, freshman orientation, health services, personal counseling, placement service for graduates, special adviser for adult students, services/facilities for handicapped.

ANNUAL EXPENSES. Tuition and fees: $10,000. **Room and board:** $4,350. **Books and supplies:** $600. **Other expenses:** $600.

FINANCIAL AID. 89% of freshmen, 83% of continuing students receive some form of aid. 74% of grants, 90% of loans, 52% of jobs based on need. 212 enrolled freshmen were judged to have need, all were offered aid. Academic, music/drama, athletic, leadership scholarships available. **Aid applications:** No closing date; priority given to applications received by March 1; applicants notified on a rolling basis beginning on or about February 15; must reply by May 1 or within 2 weeks if notified thereafter.

ADDRESS/TELEPHONE. Lynne Henderson, Director of Admissions, Wheeling Jesuit College, 316 Washington Avenue, Wheeling, WV 26003. (304) 243-2359. (800) 624-6992. Fax: (304) 243-2243.

Wisconsin

Alverno College
Milwaukee, Wisconsin CB code: 1012

Admissions: 68% of applicants accepted
Based on: ••• School record
•• Test scores
• Activities, essay, interview, recommendations, special talents
Completion: 96% of freshmen end year in good standing
65% graduate, 7% of these enter graduate study

4-year private liberal arts college, women only, affiliated with Roman Catholic Church. Founded in 1887. **Accreditation:** Regional. **Undergraduate enrollment:** 1,285 women full time; 1,229 women part time. **Faculty:** 208 total (108 full time), 157 with doctorates or other terminal degrees. **Location:** Suburban campus in very large city; 10 miles from downtown. **Calendar:** Semester, limited summer session. Saturday classes. **Microcomputers:** 110 located in libraries, classrooms, computer centers. **Special facilities:** Art gallery, US Department of Natural Resources air monitoring site, research center on women, wellness center, theater.

DEGREES OFFERED. AA, BA, BS. 2 associate degrees awarded in 1992. 100% in multi/interdisciplinary studies. 346 bachelor's degrees awarded. 33% in business and management, 20% communications, 17% teacher education, 9% health sciences, 6% psychology, 6% visual and performing arts.

UNDERGRADUATE MAJORS. Associate: Liberal/general studies, religious music, teacher aide. **Bachelor's:** Art education, art therapy, biological and physical sciences, biology, business administration and management, business and management, chemistry, communications, early childhood education, elementary education, engineering and other disciplines, English, English education, health education, history, junior high education, mathematics, mathematics education, music, music education, music performance, music therapy, nuclear medical technology, nursing, philosophy, psychology, religion, religious music, science education, secondary education, social science education, social sciences, speech/communication/theater education, studio art.

ACADEMIC PROGRAMS. Double major, dual enrollment of high school students, internships, study abroad, teacher preparation, visiting/exchange student program, weekend college, cross-registration, art courses at Milwaukee Institute of Art and Design; liberal arts/career combination in engineering. **Remedial services:** Learning center, preadmission summer program, reduced course load, remedial instruction, special counselor, tutoring. **ROTC:** Army. **Placement/credit:** AP, CLEP General and Subject, institutional tests.

ACADEMIC REQUIREMENTS. No policy requiring minimum GPA; records of students having academic difficulty are reviewed individually. 90% of freshmen return for sophomore year. Students must declare major by end of second year. **Graduation requirements:** 64 hours for associate, 115 hours for bachelor's (30 in major). Most students required to take courses in arts/fine arts, computer science, English, history, humanities, mathematics, philosophy/religion, biological/physical sciences, social sciences. **Postgraduate studies:** 1% enter medical school, 2% enter MBA programs, 4% enter other graduate study. **Additional information:** Travelship program subsidizes out-of-town and overseas learning expenses for credit. Students acquire career orientation via off-campus internships and extensive career counseling.

FRESHMAN ADMISSIONS. Selection criteria: Program of study, high school GPA, test scores considered, and entrance assessment required of all new students. **High school preparation:** 16 units required. Required and recommended units include English 4. Mathematics 4, social science 4 and science 4 recommended. Science and mathematics course requirements vary according to intended program of study. **Test requirements:** ACT; score report by August 1. **Additional information:** Students not meeting minimum criteria may be admitted by showing academic readiness on entrance assessment.

1992 FRESHMAN CLASS PROFILE. 670 women applied, 458 accepted, 231 enrolled. 49% had high school GPA of 3.0 or higher, 48% between 2.0 and 2.99. 23% were in top tenth and 46% were in top quarter of graduating class. **Academic background:** Mid 50% of enrolled freshmen had ACT composite between 18-24. 43% submitted ACT scores. **Characteristics:** 86% from in state, 56% live in college housing, 26% have minority backgrounds, 1% are foreign students. Average age is 19.

FALL-TERM APPLICATIONS. $10 fee, may be waived for applicants with need. Closing date August 1; applicants notified on a rolling basis; must reply by May 1 or within 2 weeks if notified thereafter. Audition required for music applicants. Portfolio required for studio art applicants. Interview recommended for academically weak applicants. Essay recommended. CRDA. Deferred and early admission available. Early admission available on a case by case basis.

STUDENT LIFE. Housing: Dormitories (women). Semi-apartment living within residence halls available to older students, smoke free areas available. **Activities:** Magazine, student newspaper, student, faculty, staff newsletters, creative writing magazine, choral groups, dance, drama, music ensembles, musical theater, symphony orchestra, handbell choir, artourage, early music group, International cultures interest group, Women of Color, ministry committee, Guiding Lights (tour guides), Alverno College Enterpreneurs, Hispanic Women of Alverno, Voices for Liberal Legislation, College Republicans, Sisters Who Care, Student Life Committee.

ATHLETICS. Intramural: Basketball, table tennis, volleyball.

STUDENT SERVICES. Aptitude testing, career counseling, employment service for undergraduates, freshman orientation, health services, on-campus day care, personal counseling, placement service for graduates, special adviser for adult students, services/facilities for handicapped.

ANNUAL EXPENSES. Tuition and fees (1992-93): $7,332. **Room and board:** $3,250. **Books and supplies:** $550. **Other expenses:** $1,800.

FINANCIAL AID. 75% of freshmen, 63% of continuing students receive some form of aid. Grants, loans, jobs available. Academic, music/drama, art, state/district residency, leadership, alumni affiliation, minority scholarships available. **Aid applications:** No closing date; priority given to applications received by March 15; applicants notified on a rolling basis beginning on or about June 1; must reply by May 1 or within 2 weeks if notified thereafter. **Additional information:** To apply for institutional scholarships, students must take part in Scholarship Opportunity Day. Students participate in morning-long series of interviews and writing exercises in which students explain goals and motivations and demonstrate creativity and ability to work with others.

ADDRESS/TELEPHONE. Ellen Bartel, Dir Admissions, Alverno College, 3401 South 39th Street, Milwaukee, WI 53234-3922. (414) 382-6100. (800) 933-3401. Fax: (414) 382-6354.

Bellin College of Nursing
Green Bay, Wisconsin CB code: 1046

Admissions: 47% of applicants accepted
Based on: ••• Interview, school record, test scores
•• Recommendations
• Activities
Completion: 95% of freshmen end year in good standing

4-year private nursing college, coed. Founded in 1909. **Accreditation:** Regional. **Undergraduate enrollment:** 8 men, 182 women full time; 1 man, 23 women part time. **Faculty:** 25 total (21 full time). **Location:** Urban campus in small city; 120 miles from Milwaukee. **Calendar:** 4-1-4, limited summer session. **Microcomputers:** 10 located on campus.

DEGREES OFFERED. BS. 47 bachelor's degrees awarded in 1992. 100% in health sciences.

UNDERGRADUATE MAJORS. Nursing.

ACADEMIC PROGRAMS. Accelerated program, independent study, cross-registration. **Remedial services:** Learning center, preadmission summer program, remedial instruction, tutoring. **ROTC:** Army. **Placement/credit:** AP, CLEP General and Subject.

ACADEMIC REQUIREMENTS. Freshmen must earn minimum GPA of 2.0 to continue in good standing. 89% of freshmen return for sophomore year. Students must declare major on application. **Graduation requirements:** 132 hours for bachelor's (65 in major). Most students required to take courses in arts/fine arts, English, humanities, mathematics, philosophy/religion, biological/physical sciences, social sciences. **Additional information:** Students fulfill general education requirements at University of Wisconsin: Green Bay or another accredited college or university of their choice.

FRESHMAN ADMISSIONS. Selection criteria: Class rank in top third of high school graduating class and personal interview very important. 3 references required. ACT composite of 21 preferred. **High school preparation:** 12 units required. Required and recommended units include English 4, mathematics 2-3, social science 3 and science 3. Mathematics must include 1 algebra and 1 advanced mathematics. Sciences must include 1 chemistry, 1 biology, and 1 advanced science. **Test requirements:** ACT. ACT test scores used for admission of recent high school graduates only. ACT score report must be submitted with admissions application.

1992 FRESHMAN CLASS PROFILE. 185 men and women applied, 87 accepted; 2 men enrolled, 44 women enrolled. 49% had high school GPA of 3.0 or higher, 51% between 2.0 and 2.99. 28% were in top tenth and 60% were in top quarter of graduating class. **Characteristics:** 100% commute. Average age is 21.

FALL-TERM APPLICATIONS. $20 fee, may be waived for applicants with need. No closing date; priority given to applications received by December 1; applicants notified on a rolling basis; must reply within 3 weeks. Interview required for all applicants applicants. Limited freshman applications accepted. Application priority date January 1, closing date only if targeted number reached.

STUDENT LIFE. Housing: Students live on University of Wisconsin: Green Bay campus. **Activities:** Student government, student newspaper, yearbook, Student Nurses Association.

STUDENT SERVICES. Freshman orientation, health services, personal counseling, academic advisor.

ANNUAL EXPENSES. Tuition and fees (projected): $6,700. Out-of-state students must pay supplemental tuition of $4,478 for general education courses at University of Wisconsin: Green Bay. **Books and supplies:** $470. **Other expenses:** $666.

FINANCIAL AID. 83% of continuing students receive some form of aid. All grants, 87% of loans, 12% of jobs based on need. **Aid applications:** No closing date; priority given to applications received by March 1; must reply within 2 weeks. **Additional information:** Freshmen and sophomores receive aid through University of Wisconsin: Green Bay.

ADDRESS/TELEPHONE. Teresa Halcsik, Assistant Dean of Support Services, Bellin College of Nursing, PO PO Box 23400, 929 Cass Street, Green Bay, WI 54305-3400. (414) 433-3560. Fax: (414) 433-7416.

Beloit College
Beloit, Wisconsin CB code: 1059

Admissions: 77% of applicants accepted
Based on: ••• School record
•• Essay, recommendations, test scores
• Activities, interview, special talents
Completion: 88% of freshmen end year in good standing
66% graduate, 48% of these enter graduate study

4-year private liberal arts college, coed. Founded in 1846. **Accreditation:** Regional. **Undergraduate enrollment:** 466 men, 571 women full time; 41 men, 55 women part time. **Graduate enrollment:** 2 men, 1 woman full time; 1 woman part time. **Faculty:** 136 total (86 full time), 101 with doctorates or other terminal degrees. **Location:** Urban campus in large town; 50 miles from Madison, 75 miles from Milwaukee, 100 miles from Chicago. **Calendar:** Semester, limited summer session. **Microcomputers:** 115 located in dormitories, libraries, classrooms, computer centers. **Special facilities:** Art museum, anthropology museum, performing arts center, observatory, 2 nature preserves, social science research laboratory, limnology laboratory, 2 electron microscopes, superconducting NMR, ICAP spectrometer.

DEGREES OFFERED. BA, BS, M. 260 bachelor's degrees awarded in 1992. 9% in business and management, 7% languages, 15% letters/literature, 6% life sciences, 8% psychology, 32% social sciences, 9% visual and performing arts. Graduate degrees offered in 3 major fields of study.

UNDERGRADUATE MAJORS. American literature, anthropology, art education, art history, behavioral biology, biochemistry, biology, business administration and management, business and management, chemistry, classics, communications, comparative literature, computer and information sciences, creative writing, dramatic arts, economics, elementary education, English, English literature, environmental biology, environmental science, foreign languages (multiple emphasis), French, geology, geology/environmental studies, German, Greek (classical), history, international relations, Latin, mathematical biology, mathematics, mathematics and computer science, medical biology, medical laboratory technologies, molecular biology, music, music education, music performance, organismal biology, philosophy, physics, political science and government, psychology, religion, Russian, science education, secondary education, sociology, Spanish, studio art.

ACADEMIC PROGRAMS. Double major, dual enrollment of high school students, independent study, internships, student-designed major, study abroad, teacher preparation, visiting/exchange student program, Washington semester, cross-registration, 2-2 liberal arts and health professions combination with Rush University, early-entry MBA program and 3-2 social work program with University of Chicago, field schools in archeology and geology, the Center for Language Studies, intensive summer foreign language program, reserved admission to Medical College of Wisconsin, early-entry MBA program; liberal arts/career combination in engineering, forestry, health sciences, business; combined bachelor's/graduate program in business administration, medicine. **Remedial services:** Learning center, special counselor, tutoring, academic writing. **Placement/credit:** AP, CLEP Subject, institutional tests; 32 credit hours maximum for bachelor's degree.

ACADEMIC REQUIREMENTS. Freshmen must earn minimum GPA of 2.0 to continue in good standing. 92% of freshmen return for sophomore year. Students must declare major by end of second year. **Graduation requirements:** 124 hours for bachelor's (31 in major). Most students required to take courses in arts/fine arts, English, humanities, mathematics, biological/physical sciences, social sciences. **Postgraduate studies:** 5% enter law school, 5% enter medical school, 10% enter MBA programs, 28% enter other graduate study. **Additional information:** Students participate in field terms, internships, work-study experiences. First-Year Initiative combines orientation program with advising, academic course work, and volunteer service.

FRESHMAN ADMISSIONS. Selection criteria: In order of importance, rigor of high school curriculum and high school record, test scores, recommendations, essay, interview, and extracurricular activities. **High school preparation:** 16 units required. Required units include English 4, foreign language 2, mathematics 3, social science 3 and science 3. **Test requirements:** SAT or ACT; score report by May 15.

1992 FRESHMAN CLASS PROFILE. 596 men applied, 445 accepted, 151 enrolled; 665 women applied, 526 accepted, 160 enrolled. 77% had high school GPA of 3.0 or higher, 22% between 2.0 and 2.99. 31% were in top tenth and 65% were in top quarter of graduating class. **Academic background:** Mid 50% of enrolled freshmen had SAT-V between 460-580, SAT-M between 490-620; ACT composite between 22-28. 60% submitted SAT scores, 68% submitted ACT scores. **Characteristics:** 21% from in state, 99% live in college housing, 7% have minority backgrounds, 7% are foreign students, 8% join fraternities/sororities. Average age is 18.

FALL-TERM APPLICATIONS. $25 fee, may be waived for applicants with need. Closing date April 1; applicants notified on a rolling basis beginning on or about February 15; must reply by May 1 or within 2 weeks if notified thereafter. Essay required. Interview recommended. CRDA. Deferred and early admission available. EDP-F.

STUDENT LIFE. Housing: Dormitories (women, coed); fraternity, sorority, cooperative housing available. French house, Spanish house, German house, Russian house, arts co-op, women's center available as housing options. **Activities:** Student government, film, magazine, radio, student newspaper, television, yearbook, choral groups, dance, drama, jazz band, music ensembles, musical theater, pep band, symphony orchestra, debate, fraternities, sororities, Volunteer Community Tutoring Service, women's center program, International Club, various religious interest clubs, Students for Social Responsibility, Gay Alliance, Young Republicans, Young Democrats, Science Fiction and Fantasy Association, Outing-Environmental Club. **Additional information:** Residence hall system is student managed.

ATHLETICS. NCAA. **Intercollegiate:** Baseball M, basketball, cross-country, diving, football M, golf M, soccer, softball W, swimming, tennis, track and field, volleyball W. **Intramural:** Badminton, basketball, cross-country W, fencing, handball, ice hockey M, racquetball, rugby M, sailing, soccer, softball, swimming, table tennis, tennis, volleyball, water polo.

STUDENT SERVICES. Career counseling, employment service for undergraduates, freshman orientation, health services, on-campus day care, personal counseling, placement service for graduates, services/facilities for handicapped.

ANNUAL EXPENSES. Tuition and fees (1992-93): $14,250. **Room and board:** $3,420. **Books and supplies:** $350. **Other expenses:** $700.

FINANCIAL AID. 86% of freshmen, 82% of continuing students receive some form of aid. 97% of grants, 99% of loans, 90% of jobs based on need. 202 enrolled freshmen were judged to have need, all were offered aid. Academic, music/drama, state/district residency, leadership, minority scholarships available. **Aid applications:** No closing date; priority given to applications received by April 15; applicants notified on a rolling basis beginning on or about February 15; must reply by May 1 or within 4 weeks if notified thereafter. **Additional information:** Scholastic ability and financial need may qualify students for awards. Program designed to meet individual needs of all enrolled students. Tuition and/or fee reduction for adult students, family members enrolled simultaneously, and employees or families of employees.

ADDRESS/TELEPHONE. Alan G. McIvor, VP Enrollment Services, Beloit College, 700 College Street, Beloit, WI 53511-5595. (608) 363-2500. (800) 356-0751. Fax: (608) 363-2717.

Blackhawk Technical College
Janesville, Wisconsin CB code: 7319

2-year public technical college, coed. Founded in 1912. **Accreditation:** Regional. **Undergraduate enrollment:** 756 men, 726 women full time; 692 men, 665 women part time. **Faculty:** 167 total (122 full time). **Location:** Rural campus in small city; 75 miles from Milwaukee and Chicago. **Calendar:** Semester, limited summer session.

DEGREES OFFERED. AS. 192 associate degrees awarded in 1992.

UNDERGRADUATE MAJORS. Accounting, agribusiness, animal sciences, automotive mechanics, aviation computer technology, business and office, business data processing and related programs, data processing, drafting, electrical and electronics equipment repair, electrical/electronics/communications engineering, electromechanical technology, electronic technology, engineering and engineering-related technologies, fire control and safety technology, food production/management/services, food sciences, industrial engineering, law enforcement and corrections technologies, legal secretary, marketing and distribution, mechanical design technology, nursing, office supervision and management, physical therapy assistant, robotics, secretarial and related programs, trade and industrial supervision and management.

ACADEMIC PROGRAMS. Dual enrollment of high school students, independent study, internships, telecourses. **Remedial services:** Learning center, preadmission summer program, reduced course load, remedial instruction, special counselor, tutoring. **Placement/credit:** AP, CLEP General; 30 credit hours maximum for associate degree.

ACADEMIC REQUIREMENTS. Freshmen must earn minimum GPA of 2.0 to continue in good standing. 50% of freshmen return for sophomore year. Students must declare major on application. **Graduation requirements:** 66 hours for associate (40 in major). Most students required to take courses in English, social sciences.

FRESHMAN ADMISSIONS. Selection criteria: Open admissions. Applicants to nursing and physical therapist assistant programs must meet additional testing and interview requirements. **Test requirements:** National

League for Nursing Pre-Nursing and Guidance examination required for nursing applicants.

1992 FRESHMAN CLASS PROFILE. 356 men, 482 women enrolled. **Characteristics:** 99% from in state, 100% commute, 7% have minority backgrounds, 1% are foreign students. Average age is 28.

FALL-TERM APPLICATIONS. $10 fee. No closing date; priority given to applications received by December 1; applicants notified on a rolling basis beginning on or about February 15; must reply within 2 weeks. Early admission available.

STUDENT LIFE. Activities: Student government, student newspaper.

ATHLETICS. Intercollegiate: Bowling, volleyball. **Intramural:** Bowling, skiing.

STUDENT SERVICES. Aptitude testing, career counseling, employment service for undergraduates, freshman orientation, on-campus day care, personal counseling, placement service for graduates, veterans counselor, services/facilities for handicapped.

ANNUAL EXPENSES. Tuition and fees: $1,440, $8,760 additional for out-of-state students. **Books and supplies:** $425. **Other expenses:** $800.

FINANCIAL AID. 30% of freshmen, 45% of continuing students receive some form of aid. All grants, 98% of loans, all jobs based on need. 294 enrolled freshmen were judged to have need, 244 were offered aid. **Aid applications:** Closing date June 15; priority given to applications received by April 1; applicants notified on a rolling basis beginning on or about June 15; must reply within 15 days.

ADDRESS/TELEPHONE. Barbara Erlandson, Blackhawk Technical College, PO Box 5009, Janesville, WI 53547. (608) 757-7665.

Cardinal Stritch College
Milwaukee, Wisconsin CB code: 1100

Admissions: 76% of applicants accepted
Based on:
••• School record, test scores
•• Essay, recommendations
• Activities, interview, special talents
Completion: 95% of freshmen end year in good standing
55% graduate, 17% of these enter graduate study

4-year private liberal arts college, coed, affiliated with Roman Catholic Church. Founded in 1937. **Accreditation:** Regional. **Undergraduate enrollment:** 895 men, 1,385 women full time; 102 men, 285 women part time. **Graduate enrollment:** 317 men, 322 women full time; 384 men, 1,460 women part time. **Faculty:** 518 total (67 full time), 121 with doctorates or other terminal degrees. **Location:** Suburban campus in very large city; 7 miles from Milwaukee, 85 miles from Chicago. **Calendar:** Semester, limited summer session. Saturday and extensive evening/early morning classes. **Microcomputers:** 60 located in libraries, classrooms, computer centers. **Special facilities:** Art gallery, strong special education, business, and reading collections in library. **Additional facts:** College sponsored by Sisters of St. Francis of Assisi, operated by both religious and lay personnel.

DEGREES OFFERED. AA, AS, BA, BS, BFA, MA, MS, MBA, MEd. 146 associate degrees awarded in 1992. 59% in business and management, 39% health sciences. 474 bachelor's degrees awarded. 73% in business and management, 7% education. Graduate degrees offered in 9 major fields of study.

UNDERGRADUATE MAJORS. Associate: Business administration and management, business and management, computer and information sciences, graphic arts technology, liberal/general studies, nursing. **Bachelor's:** Accounting, art education, biology, business administration and management, business and management, business economics, chemistry, communications, computer and information sciences, computer mathematics, dramatic arts, early childhood education, education, elementary education, English, English education, fine arts, foreign languages education, French, history, international business management, junior high education, liberal/general studies, management science, mathematics, mathematics education, nursing, predentistry, prelaw, premedicine, preveterinary, psychology, public affairs, religion, religious education, science education, secondary education, social science education, social sciences, social studies education, sociology, Sociology of aging, Spanish, special education, speech/communication/theater education, studio art, visual and performing arts.

ACADEMIC PROGRAMS. 2-year transfer program, accelerated program, double major, dual enrollment of high school students, independent study, internships, study abroad, teacher preparation, telecourses. **Remedial services:** Learning center, reduced course load, remedial instruction, special counselor, tutoring. **Placement/credit:** AP, CLEP General and Subject, institutional tests; 30 credit hours maximum for associate degree; 60 credit hours maximum for bachelor's degree.

ACADEMIC REQUIREMENTS. Freshmen must earn minimum GPA of 2.0 to continue in good standing. 80% of freshmen return for sophomore year. Students must declare major by end of second year. **Graduation requirements:** 66 hours for associate (36 in major), 128 hours for bachelor's (34 in major). Most students required to take courses in arts/fine arts, English, foreign languages, history, humanities, mathematics, philosophy/religion, biological/physical sciences, social sciences. **Postgraduate studies:** 50% from 2-year programs enter 4-year programs. 1% enter law school, 1% enter medical school, 10% enter MBA programs, 5% enter other graduate study.

FRESHMAN ADMISSIONS. Selection criteria: High school GPA of 2.0, rank in top half of class, minimum ACT test score of 20. Interview, activities, recommendations considered. **High school preparation:** 16 units required. Required and recommended units include English 4, mathematics 2, social science 2 and science 2. Foreign language 2 recommended. **Test requirements:** SAT or ACT (ACT preferred); score report by August 15. Institutional tests used for admission of academically weak students.

1992 FRESHMAN CLASS PROFILE. 165 men applied, 86 accepted, 86 enrolled; 167 women applied, 167 accepted, 167 enrolled. 37% had high school GPA of 3.0 or higher, 52% between 2.0 and 2.99. 12% were in top tenth and 33% were in top quarter of graduating class. **Academic background:** Mid 50% of enrolled freshmen had ACT composite between 18-23. 92% submitted ACT scores. **Characteristics:** 80% from in state, 50% commute, 15% have minority backgrounds. Average age is 21.

FALL-TERM APPLICATIONS. $20 fee, may be waived for applicants with need. No closing date; priority given to applications received by April 1; applicants notified on a rolling basis; must reply one week before classes begin. Essay required. Interview recommended. Portfolio recommended for art applicants. CRDA. Deferred and early admission available. Institutional early decision plan.

STUDENT LIFE. Housing: Dormitories (coed). **Activities:** Student government, student newspaper, yearbook, newsletter, choral groups, drama, musical theater, social concerns committee, Students for Political Awareness, Organization for Afro-American Unity, Model United Nations, Organization for Minority Students.

ATHLETICS. NAIA. **Intercollegiate:** Baseball M, basketball, soccer M, softball W, volleyball W. **Intramural:** Basketball, bowling, golf M, softball, table tennis, volleyball, wrestling M.

STUDENT SERVICES. Aptitude testing, career counseling, employment service for undergraduates, freshman orientation, health services, on-campus day care, personal counseling, placement service for graduates, special adviser for adult students, veterans counselor, services/facilities for handicapped.

ANNUAL EXPENSES. Tuition and fees: $7,704. **Room and board:** $3,480. **Books and supplies:** $500. **Other expenses:** $1,200.

FINANCIAL AID. 82% of freshmen, 77% of continuing students receive some form of aid. 76% of grants, 61% of loans, 47% of jobs based on need. 82 enrolled freshmen were judged to have need, all were offered aid. Academic, music/drama, art, athletic, state/district residency, leadership scholarships available. **Aid applications:** No closing date; priority given to applications received by April 1; applicants notified on a rolling basis beginning on or about April 1; must reply by May 1 or within 3 weeks if notified thereafter.

ADDRESS/TELEPHONE. Dr. Alex Popovics, Vice President for Planning and Enrollment Management, Cardinal Stritch College, 6801 North Yates Road, Milwaukee, WI 53217-3985. (414) 351-7504. (800) 347-8822. Fax: (414) 351-7616.

Carroll College
Waukesha, Wisconsin CB code: 1101

Admissions: 89% of applicants accepted
Based on:
••• School record, test scores
•• Interview, recommendations, special talents
• Activities, essay
Completion: 82% of freshmen end year in good standing
59% graduate, 11% of these enter graduate study

4-year private liberal arts college, coed, affiliated with Presbyterian Church (USA). Founded in 1846. **Accreditation:** Regional. **Undergraduate enrollment:** 486 men, 850 women full time; 220 men, 487 women part time. **Graduate enrollment:** 13 men, 52 women part time. **Faculty:** 120 total (84 full time), 69 with doctorates or other terminal degrees. **Location:** Suburban campus in small city; 18 miles from Milwaukee. **Calendar:** 4-1-4, limited summer session. Saturday classes. **Microcomputers:** 225 located in dormitories, libraries, classrooms, computer centers. **Special facilities:** Greene scientific study and conservancy area: 40-acre laboratory with springs, ponds, and varied plant life. Genesee Creek Research station in 20-acre laboratory and watershed.

DEGREES OFFERED. BA, BS, MEd. 415 bachelor's degrees awarded in 1992. 16% in business and management, 14% communications, 6% computer sciences, 7% teacher education, 13% health sciences, 10% psychology, 10% social sciences, 8% visual and performing arts. Graduate degrees offered in 1 major field of study.

UNDERGRADUATE MAJORS. Accounting, art education, artificial intelligence, biology, business administration and management, business and management, business economics, business psychology, chemistry, city/community/regional planning, clinical laboratory science, clinical psychology, communication management, communications, computer and information sciences, counseling psychology, creative writing, criminal justice studies, dramatic arts, early childhood education, earth sciences, economics, education, elementary education, English, English education, environmental science, finance, fine arts, foreign languages education, French, geography, German, history, human resources development, illustration design, information sciences and systems, international relations, journalism, liberal/general studies, management information systems, marketing management, mathematics, mathematics education, medical laboratory technologies, museum studies, music, music business management, music education, music performance, music theory and composition, nursing, organizational behavior, personnel management, philosophy, physical education, physics, political science and government, predentistry, preengineering, prelaw, premedicine, prepharmacy, preveterinary, psychology, public campaigns, quantitative psychology, religion, science education, secondary education, social science education, social sciences, social studies education, social work, sociology, Spanish, speech/communication/theater education, visual and performing arts.

ACADEMIC PROGRAMS. Double major, dual enrollment of high school students, honors program, independent study, internships, student-designed major, study abroad, teacher preparation, visiting/exchange student program, United Nations semester, Washington semester, cross-registration; liberal arts/career combination in engineering, health sciences, business. **Remedial services:** Learning center, reduced course load, special counselor, tutoring. **Placement/credit:** AP, CLEP General and Subject, institutional tests; 48 credit hours maximum for bachelor's degree.

ACADEMIC REQUIREMENTS. Freshmen must earn minimum GPA of 2.0 to continue in good standing. 82% of freshmen return for sophomore year. Students must declare major by end of second year. **Graduation requirements:** 130 hours for bachelor's (40 in major). Most students required to take courses in arts/fine arts, computer science, English, foreign languages, history, humanities, mathematics, philosophy/religion, biological/physical sciences, social sciences. **Postgraduate studies:** 1% enter law school, 1% enter medical school, 3% enter MBA programs, 6% enter other graduate study. **Additional information:** Education majors must maintain 3.0 in major. Nursing students generally complete first 2 years at Carroll and last 2 years at Columbia College of Nursing.

FRESHMAN ADMISSIONS. Selection criteria: School achievement record most important, followed by test scores, recommendations, and school activities. **High school preparation:** 15 units recommended. Recommended units include English 4, foreign language 2, mathematics 3, social science 3 and science 2. **Test requirements:** SAT or ACT; score report by August 1.

1992 FRESHMAN CLASS PROFILE. 366 men applied, 287 accepted, 162 enrolled; 506 women applied, 486 accepted, 298 enrolled. 20% were in top tenth and 36% were in top quarter of graduating class. **Characteristics:** 92% from in state, 82% live in college housing, 6% have minority backgrounds, 1% are foreign students. Average age is 18.

FALL-TERM APPLICATIONS. No fee. No closing date; priority given to applications received by March 15; applicants notified on a rolling basis; must reply within 4 weeks. Interview recommended. Audition recommended for music applicants. Portfolio recommended for art applicants. Essay recommended. Deferred and early admission available.

STUDENT LIFE. Housing: Dormitories (women, coed); apartment, fraternity housing available. College-owned homes also provide housing. Wheelchair accessibility available in new campus buildings. Students may connect personal computers into school's mainframe system. **Activities:** Student government, magazine, radio, student newspaper, yearbook, choral groups, concert band, drama, jazz band, music ensembles, musical theater, pep band, symphony orchestra, fraternities, sororities, Fellowship of Christian Athletes, Inter-Varsity Christian Fellowship, black student organization, Amnesty International, International Student Organization, Latin student organization, Habitat for Humanity, College Republicans, Carroll Campus Democrats.

ATHLETICS. NCAA. **Intercollegiate:** Baseball M, basketball, cross-country, diving, football M, golf, soccer, softball W, swimming, tennis, track and field, volleyball W, wrestling M. **Intramural:** Badminton, basketball, bowling, golf, soccer, softball, swimming, table tennis, tennis, track and field M, volleyball.

STUDENT SERVICES. Aptitude testing, career counseling, employment service for undergraduates, freshman orientation, health services, personal counseling, placement service for graduates, veterans counselor, services/facilities for handicapped.

ANNUAL EXPENSES. Tuition and fees: $11,790. **Room and board:** $3,740. **Books and supplies:** $400. **Other expenses:** $900.

FINANCIAL AID. 90% of freshmen, 90% of continuing students receive some form of aid. 93% of grants, 90% of loans, 65% of jobs based on need. 258 enrolled freshmen were judged to have need, all were offered aid. Academic, music/drama, art, alumni affiliation, minority scholarships available. **Aid applications:** No closing date; priority given to applications received by April 15; applicants notified on a rolling basis beginning on or about May 1; must reply within 4 weeks.

ADDRESS/TELEPHONE. Debbie Morgan, Director of Admissions, Carroll College, 100 North East Avenue, Waukesha, WI 53186. (414) 524-7220. (800) 547-1233. Fax: (414) 524-7139.

Carthage College
Kenosha, Wisconsin

CB code: 1103

Admissions:	86% of applicants accepted
Based on:	••• School record
	•• Interview, special talents, test scores
	• Activities, essay, recommendations
Completion:	80% of freshmen end year in good standing
	55% graduate, 25% of these enter graduate study

4-year private liberal arts college, coed, affiliated with Evangelical Lutheran Church in America. Founded in 1847. **Accreditation:** Regional. **Undergraduate enrollment:** 564 men, 755 women full time; 200 men, 475 women part time. **Graduate enrollment:** 3 men, 7 women full time; 16 men, 77 women part time. **Faculty:** 151 total (97 full time), 86 with doctorates or other terminal degrees. **Location:** Suburban campus in small city; 60 miles from Chicago, 30 miles from Milwaukee on Lake Michigan. **Calendar:** 4-1-4, extensive summer session. Saturday and extensive evening/early morning classes. **Microcomputers:** 85 located in dormitories, libraries, computer centers, campus-wide network. **Special facilities:** Planetarium, Civil War museum, undergraduate science research laboratory, computer/mathematics research laboratory.

DEGREES OFFERED. BA, MEd. 289 bachelor's degrees awarded in 1992. 37% in business and management, 19% teacher education, 10% parks/recreation, protective services, public affairs, 5% psychology, 10% social sciences. Graduate degrees offered in 2 major fields of study.

UNDERGRADUATE MAJORS. Accounting, art education, art history, biological and physical sciences, biology, business administration and management, chemistry, clinical laboratory science, communications, criminal justice studies, dramatic arts, economics, education, education of the mentally handicapped, elementary education, engineering and other disciplines, English, English education, foreign languages education, French, geography, German, history, humanities and social sciences, international business management, junior high education, marketing management, mathematics, mathematics education, medical laboratory technologies, music, music education, occupational therapy, parks and recreation management, philosophy, physical education, physics, political science and government, predentistry, prelaw, premedicine, prepharmacy, preveterinary, psychology, public administration, religion, religious music, secondary education, social science education, social sciences, social studies education, social work, sociology, Spanish, special education, specific learning disabilities, speech, theological studies, visual and performing arts.

ACADEMIC PROGRAMS. Accelerated program, double major, dual enrollment of high school students, honors program, independent study, internships, student-designed major, study abroad, teacher preparation, visiting/exchange student program, weekend college, Washington semester, cross-registration; liberal arts/career combination in engineering, health sciences. **Remedial services:** Learning center, preadmission summer program, reduced course load, special counselor, tutoring, study skills and reading courses. **Placement/credit:** AP, CLEP General and Subject, IB, institutional tests; 32 credit hours maximum for bachelor's degree.

ACADEMIC REQUIREMENTS. Freshmen must earn minimum GPA of 2.0 to continue in good standing. 72% of freshmen return for sophomore year. Students must declare major by end of second year. **Graduation requirements:** 136 hours for bachelor's (60 in major). Most students required to take courses in arts/fine arts, English, foreign languages, history, humanities, mathematics, philosophy/religion, biological/physical sciences, social sciences. **Postgraduate studies:** 4% enter law school, 8% enter medical school, 4% enter MBA programs, 9% enter other graduate study. **Additional information:** Freshmen must take 4-course Heritage Seminar Series.

FRESHMAN ADMISSIONS. Selection criteria: High school GPA, rank in top half of class. Test scores of secondary importance. **High school preparation:** 16 units required. Required and recommended units include English 4, mathematics 2, social science 2 and science 2. Foreign language 2 recommended. **Test requirements:** SAT or ACT; score report by August 15.

1992 FRESHMAN CLASS PROFILE. 655 men applied, 522 accepted, 179 enrolled; 786 women applied, 715 accepted, 240 enrolled. 57% had high school GPA of 3.0 or higher, 39% between 2.0 and 2.99. 24% were in top tenth and 52% were in top quarter of graduating class. **Academic background:** Mid 50% of enrolled freshmen had SAT-V between 400-510, SAT-M between 450-600; ACT composite between 19-25. 19% submitted SAT scores, 81% submitted ACT scores. **Characteristics:** 60% from in state, 90% live in college housing, 8% have minority backgrounds, 2% are foreign students. Average age is 18.

FALL-TERM APPLICATIONS. $20 fee, may be waived for applicants with need. Closing date August 1; applicants notified on a rolling basis; must reply within 4 weeks. Interview recommended. Audition recommended for music applicants. Portfolio recommended. Essay recommended. CRDA. Deferred and early admission available. Students are encouraged to apply early in their senior year.

STUDENT LIFE. Housing: Dormitories (women, coed); fraternity, sorority housing available. **Activities:** Student government, student newspaper, yearbook, literary magazine, choral groups, concert band, drama, jazz band, music ensembles, musical theater, pep band, fraternities, sororities, Fellowship of Christian Athletes, Democratic Youth Caucus, Young Republicans, Black Student Union, International Students Association, Circle K, Gospel choir, United Women of Color. **Additional information:** Religious observance required.

ATHLETICS. NCAA. **Intercollegiate:** Baseball M, basketball, cross-country, football M, golf, soccer, softball W, swimming, tennis, track and field, volleyball W, wrestling M. **Intramural:** Basketball, cross-country, golf, ice hockey M, skiing, swimming, tennis, track and field, volleyball. **Clubs:** Ice hockey.

STUDENT SERVICES. Aptitude testing, career counseling, employment service for undergraduates, freshman orientation, health services, personal counseling, placement service for graduates, special adviser for adult students, veterans counselor, services/facilities for handicapped.

ANNUAL EXPENSES. Tuition and fees: $12,400. **Room and board:** $3,595. **Books and supplies:** $500. **Other expenses:** $1,000.

FINANCIAL AID. 89% of freshmen, 81% of continuing students receive some form of aid. 50% of grants, 96% of loans, 67% of jobs based on need. 307 enrolled freshmen were judged to have need, all were offered aid. Academic, music/drama, art, state/district residency, leadership, alumni affiliation, religious affiliation scholarships available. **Aid applications:** No closing date; priority given to applications received by February 15; applicants notified on a rolling basis beginning on or about March 1; must reply by May 1 or within 2 weeks if notified thereafter. **Additional information:** Fall 1993 merit/scholarship applicants notified beginning October 1992. Need-based applicants notified January 1993.

ADDRESS/TELEPHONE. Brenda A. Porter, Vice President for Enrollment, Carthage College, 2001 Alford Park Drive, Kenosha, WI 53140. (414) 551-6000. (800) 351-4058. Fax: (414) 551-6208.

Chippewa Valley Technical College
Eau Claire, Wisconsin CB code: 0786

2-year public technical college, coed. Founded in 1912. **Accreditation:** Regional. **Undergraduate enrollment:** 1,000 men, 1,100 women full time; 400 men, 900 women part time. **Faculty:** 194 total (165 full time), 10 with doctorates or other terminal degrees. **Location:** Urban campus in small city; 90 miles from Minneapolis-St. Paul, Minnesota. **Calendar:** Semester, limited summer session. Saturday and extensive evening/early morning classes. **Microcomputers:** 500 located in classrooms, computer centers.

DEGREES OFFERED. AAS. 500 associate degrees awarded in 1992. 40% in business/office and marketing/distribution, 9% computer sciences, 19% engineering technologies, 7% health sciences, 11% allied health, 13% trade and industry.

UNDERGRADUATE MAJORS. Accounting, agribusiness, agricultural production, air conditioning/heating/refrigeration mechanics, air conditioning/heating/refrigeration technology, alcohol and other drug abuse counseling, architectural technologies, architecture, automotive technology, business and management, business and office, business data entry equipment operation, business data processing and related programs, business data programming, civil technology, clinical laboratory science, dairy, data processing, diagnostic medical sonography, drafting, electrical and electronics equipment repair, electromechanical technology, electronic technology, fashion merchandising, food management, food sciences, histotechnology, hospitality and recreation marketing, hotel/motel and restaurant management, industrial technology, insurance and risk management, law enforcement and corrections technologies, legal assistant/paralegal, legal secretary, machine tool operation/machine shop, management information systems, marketing and distribution, marketing management, mechanical design technology, medical laboratory technologies, medical records administration, medical records technology, medical secretary, nursing, personal services, precision metal work, radiograph medical technology, real estate, rehabilitation counseling/services, robotics, secretarial and related programs, trade and industrial supervision and management, ultrasound technology, word processing.

ACADEMIC PROGRAMS. Double major, dual enrollment of high school students, independent study, internships, telecourses. **Remedial services:** Learning center, reduced course load, remedial instruction, special counselor, tutoring. **Placement/credit:** AP, CLEP General and Subject, institutional tests; 34 credit hours maximum for associate degree. 50% of semester hours needed for degree may be earned as credit by examination.

ACADEMIC REQUIREMENTS. Freshmen must earn minimum GPA of 1.5 to continue in good standing. 60% of freshmen return for sophomore year. Students must declare major on application. **Graduation requirements:** Most students required to take courses in computer science, English, history, mathematics, social sciences.

FRESHMAN ADMISSIONS. Selection criteria: Open admissions. Selective admissions to some degree programs. Algebra and science requirements for some degree programs. **Test requirements:** Entrance examination required for nursing applicants.

1992 FRESHMAN CLASS PROFILE. 1,000 men, 1,500 women enrolled. **Characteristics:** 99% from in state, 100% commute, 6% have minority backgrounds. Average age is 27.

FALL-TERM APPLICATIONS. $30 fee, may be waived for applicants with need. Closing date August 1; priority given to applications received by October 5; applicants notified on a rolling basis. Interview required for nursing, allied health, trade and industrial program, hospitality services applicants. Deferred admission available.

STUDENT LIFE. Activities: Student government, student newspaper, choral groups, drama.

ATHLETICS. Intercollegiate: Golf M, volleyball W. **Intramural:** Basketball, bowling, golf, skiing, softball, table tennis, tennis, volleyball.

STUDENT SERVICES. Aptitude testing, career counseling, employment service for undergraduates, freshman orientation, health services, on-campus day care, personal counseling, placement service for graduates, veterans counselor, services/facilities for handicapped.

ANNUAL EXPENSES. Tuition and fees: $1,440, $8,760 additional for out-of-state students. **Books and supplies:** $400. **Other expenses:** $800.

FINANCIAL AID. 76% of freshmen, 76% of continuing students receive some form of aid. 99% of grants, 89% of loans, all jobs based on need. 1,470 enrolled freshmen were judged to have need, 1,368 were offered aid. Academic, leadership scholarships available. **Aid applications:** No closing date; priority given to applications received by March 15; applicants notified on a rolling basis beginning on or about June 10; must reply within 10 days.

ADDRESS/TELEPHONE. Gene Hinrichsen, Admissions Coordinator, Chippewa Valley Technical College, 620 West Clairemont Avenue, Eau Claire, WI 54701. (715) 833-6244. Fax: (715) 833-6470.

Columbia College of Nursing
Milwaukee, Wisconsin CB code: 3409

4-year private nursing college, coed. Founded in 1901. **Accreditation:** Regional. **Undergraduate enrollment:** 12 men, 176 women full time; 11 men, 122 women part time. **Faculty:** 21 total (15 full time), 3 with doctorates or other terminal degrees. **Location:** Urban campus in very large city; 90 miles from Chicago. **Calendar:** 4-1-4, limited summer session. Extensive evening/early morning classes. **Microcomputers:** 6 located in computer centers. **Additional facts:** Joint bachelor's degree in nursing awarded with Carroll College, Waukesha.

DEGREES OFFERED. BS. 56 bachelor's degrees awarded in 1992. 100% in health sciences.

UNDERGRADUATE MAJORS. Nursing.

ACADEMIC PROGRAMS. Honors program, independent study, study abroad, cross-registration; liberal arts/career combination in health sciences. **Remedial services:** Learning center, preadmission summer program, reduced course load, remedial instruction, special counselor, tutoring. **Placement/credit:** AP, CLEP Subject, institutional tests; 48 credit hours maximum for bachelor's degree.

ACADEMIC REQUIREMENTS. Freshmen must earn minimum GPA of 2.0 to continue in good standing. 82% of freshmen return for sophomore year. Students must declare major on application. **Graduation requirements:** 130 hours for bachelor's (60 in major). Most students required to take courses in arts/fine arts, English, humanities, mathematics, philosophy/religion, biological/physical sciences, social sciences. **Postgraduate studies:** 4% enter other graduate study. **Additional information:** Students generally complete first 2 years on Carroll College campus and the last 2 years on Columbia Campus.

FRESHMAN ADMISSIONS. Selection criteria: Class rank, high school GPA and test scores important. Recommended units include biological science 2, English 4, foreign language 2, mathematics 2 and physical science 1. **Test requirements:** SAT or ACT; score report by July 1.

1992 FRESHMAN CLASS PROFILE. 3 men, 65 women enrolled. **Characteristics:** 90% live in college housing, 9% have minority backgrounds. Average age is 20.

FALL-TERM APPLICATIONS. No fee. No closing date; priority given to applications received by April 1; applicants notified on a rolling basis beginning on or about October 1. Interview recommended. Audition recommended. Portfolio recommended. Essay recommended. Deferred and early admission available. Students make application to Carroll College and must fulfill Carroll's requirements for admission.

STUDENT LIFE. Housing: Dormitories (women, coed). Fraternity housing for undergraduates available at Carroll Campus. **Activities:** Student government, student newspaper, yearbook, choral groups, concert band, dance, drama, music ensembles, musical theater, fraternities, sororities, student nursing organization, Nurse Club, student senate, black student organization, campus ministry, Amnesty International. **Additional information:** Most sports, activities, and general facilities available through Carroll College.

ATHLETICS. NCAA. **Intercollegiate:** Baseball M, basketball, cross-country, diving, football M, golf, softball W, swimming, tennis, track and field, volleyball W, wrestling M. **Intramural:** Badminton, basketball, bowling, golf, soccer, softball, swimming, table tennis, tennis, track and field M, volleyball.

STUDENT SERVICES. Career counseling, employment service for undergraduates, freshman orientation, health services, personal counseling, placement service for graduates, special adviser for adult students, NCLEX-RN Review Course, services/facilities for handicapped.

ANNUAL EXPENSES. Tuition and fees: $11,830. **Room and board:** $5,500. **Books and supplies:** $350. **Other expenses:** $850.

FINANCIAL AID. 88% of freshmen, 92% of continuing students receive some form of aid. 81% of grants, all loans, all jobs based on need. Academic, state/district residency, leadership, alumni affiliation, religious affiliation, minority scholarships available. **Aid applications:** No closing date; priority given to applications received by April 15; applicants notified on a rolling basis beginning on or about May 1; must reply within 4 weeks. **Additional information:** Students must apply to and meet financial aid requirements of Carroll College.

ADDRESS/TELEPHONE. Rebecca L. Sherrick, Vice President for Enrollment and Planning, Carroll College, 100 North East Avenue, Waukesha, WI 53186. (414) 524-7220. (800) 547-1233. Fax: (414) 961-8712.

Concordia University Wisconsin
Mequon, Wisconsin — CB code: 1139

Admissions:	87% of applicants accepted
Based on:	••• School record, test scores
	• Activities, essay, interview, recommendations, religious affiliation/commitment, special talents
Completion:	89% of freshmen end year in good standing
	75% graduate, 11% of these enter graduate study

4-year private university, coed, affiliated with Lutheran Church—Missouri Synod. Founded in 1881. **Accreditation:** Regional. **Undergraduate enrollment:** 833 men, 1,157 women full time; 125 men, 189 women part time. **Graduate enrollment:** 1 man full time; 45 men, 76 women part time. **Faculty:** 135 total (73 full time), 39 with doctorates or other terminal degrees. **Location:** Suburban campus in large town; 15 miles from downtown Milwaukee. **Calendar:** 4-1-4, limited summer session. **Microcomputers:** 90 located in libraries, classrooms, computer centers. **Special facilities:** Art gallery.

DEGREES OFFERED. AA, BA, BS, MS. 17 associate degrees awarded in 1992. 82% in business/office and marketing/distribution, 9% letters/literature, 9% philosophy, religion, theology. 368 bachelor's degrees awarded. 43% in business and management, 17% teacher education, 14% health sciences. Graduate degrees offered in 4 major fields of study.

UNDERGRADUATE MAJORS. Associate: Bible studies, court reporting, legal secretary, medical secretary, secretarial and related programs. **Bachelor's:** Accounting, airline piloting and navigation, biblical languages, biology, business administration and management, business and management, business and office, business education, civil engineering, communications, computer engineering, court reporting, criminology, early childhood education, education, electrical/electronics/communications engineering, elementary education, engineering, engineering and engineering-related technologies, English, English education, foreign languages (multiple emphasis), history, humanities and social sciences, industrial and organizational psychology, interior design, junior high education, legal assistant/paralegal, liberal/general studies, marketing management, mathematics, mathematics education, mechanical engineering, music, nursing, physical education, physical therapy, prelaw, premedicine, psychology, religion, religious education, religious music, science education, secondary education, social science education, social sciences, social studies education, social work, theological studies.

ACADEMIC PROGRAMS. Double major, independent study, internships, student-designed major, study abroad, teacher preparation, weekend college, cross-registration; liberal arts/career combination in engineering. **Remedial services:** Learning center, reduced course load, remedial instruction, special counselor, tutoring. **Placement/credit:** AP, CLEP General and Subject, institutional tests; 15 credit hours maximum for associate degree; 30 credit hours maximum for bachelor's degree.

ACADEMIC REQUIREMENTS. Freshmen must earn minimum GPA of 2.25 to continue in good standing. 93% of freshmen return for sophomore year. Students must declare major on enrollment. **Graduation requirements:** 67 hours for associate, 127 hours for bachelor's (35 in major). Most students required to take courses in arts/fine arts, computer science, English, history, humanities, mathematics, philosophy/religion, biological/physical sciences, social sciences. **Postgraduate studies:** 25% from 2-year programs enter 4-year programs. 1% enter law school, 3% enter MBA programs, 7% enter other graduate study.

FRESHMAN ADMISSIONS. Selection criteria: School achievement record and test scores important. Engineering and nursing applicants must have 3.0 high school GPA and demonstrated success in mathematics and science. All other applicants must have 2.25 minimum GPA. **High school preparation:** 16 units required. Required and recommended units include biological science 1, English 3-4, mathematics 2-3, physical science 1, social science 2 and science 2-3. Foreign language 1 recommended. **Test requirements:** SAT or ACT (ACT preferred); score report by August 15.

1992 FRESHMAN CLASS PROFILE. 286 men applied, 235 accepted, 130 enrolled; 295 women applied, 269 accepted, 165 enrolled. 47% had high school GPA of 3.0 or higher, 48% between 2.0 and 2.99. **Academic background:** Mid 50% of enrolled freshmen had ACT composite between 18-24. 96% submitted ACT scores. **Characteristics:** 70% from in state, 53% commute, 6% have minority backgrounds, 8% are foreign students. Average age is 19.

FALL-TERM APPLICATIONS. $25 fee, may be waived for applicants with need. Closing date August 15; priority given to applications received by March 15; applicants notified on a rolling basis beginning on or about October 15; must reply within 4 weeks. Interview recommended. Audition recommended for music applicants. CRDA.

STUDENT LIFE. Housing: Dormitories (men, women). Freshmen housing guaranteed. **Activities:** Student government, radio, student newspaper, yearbook, choral groups, concert band, drama, jazz band, music ensembles, musical theater, pep band, numerous student religious organizations. **Additional information:** Campus Lutheran church services available every Sunday. Chapel services held daily.

ATHLETICS. NAIA. **Intercollegiate:** Baseball M, basketball, cross-country, football M, golf, soccer M, softball W, tennis, track and field, volleyball W, wrestling M. **Intramural:** Archery, badminton, basketball, bowling, golf, skiing, soccer, softball, table tennis, tennis, volleyball.

STUDENT SERVICES. Aptitude testing, career counseling, employment service for undergraduates, freshman orientation, health services, on-campus day care, personal counseling, placement service for graduates, services/facilities for handicapped.

ANNUAL EXPENSES. Tuition and fees: $8,740. **Room and board:** $3,400. **Books and supplies:** $600. **Other expenses:** $1,260.

FINANCIAL AID. 90% of freshmen, 89% of continuing students receive some form of aid. 75% of grants, 78% of loans, 29% of jobs based on need. 240 enrolled freshmen were judged to have need, all were offered aid. Academic, music/drama, athletic, religious affiliation scholarships available. **Aid applications:** Closing date June 1; priority given to applications received by May 1; applicants notified on or about June 15; must reply within 4 weeks.

ADDRESS/TELEPHONE. William H. Ebel, VP Admissions, Concordia University Wisconsin, 12800 North Lake Shore Drive, Mequon, WI 53092-9650. (414) 243-5700 ext. 315. Fax: (414) 243-4351.

Edgewood College
Madison, Wisconsin — CB code: 1202

Admissions:	74% of applicants accepted
Based on:	••• School record, test scores
	•• Activities, interview, recommendations
	• Essay, special talents
Completion:	90% of freshmen end year in good standing
	42% graduate, 20% of these enter graduate study

4-year private liberal arts college, coed, affiliated with Roman Catholic Church. Founded in 1927. **Accreditation:** Regional. **Undergraduate enrollment:** 211 men, 496 women full time; 187 men, 424 women part time. **Graduate enrollment:** 2 men, 2 women full time; 160 men, 208 women part time. **Faculty:** 124 total (56 full time), 57 with doctorates or other terminal degrees. **Location:** Urban campus in small city; 82 miles from Milwaukee, 140 miles from Chicago. **Calendar:** 4-1-4, limited summer session. Saturday and extensive evening/early morning classes. **Microcomputers:** 43 located in libraries, computer centers. **Special facilities:** Theater, biological research station, nursery, art gallery.

DEGREES OFFERED. AA, BA, BS, MA, MBA, MEd. 135 bachelor's degrees awarded. 38% in business and management, 17% education, 11% allied health, 5% letters/literature, 7% psychology, 14% social sciences. Graduate degrees offered in 3 major fields of study.

UNDERGRADUATE MAJORS. Associate: Liberal/general studies. **Bachelor's:** Accounting, American studies, anthropology, art therapy, biological and physical sciences, biology, business administration and management, business and management, chemistry, clinical laboratory science, computer and information sciences, criminal justice studies, cytotechnology, early childhood education, economics, education, education of exceptional children, education of the emotionally handicapped, elementary education, English, environmental science, fine arts, French, history, humanities and social sciences, information sciences and systems, junior high education, liberal/general studies, mathematics, nursing, physical sciences, political science and government, premedicine, prepharmacy, preveterinary, psychology, public administration, religion, religious education, secondary education, social sciences, sociology, Spanish, special education, specific learning disabilities, theological studies, visual and performing arts.

ACADEMIC PROGRAMS. Double major, dual enrollment of high school students, honors program, independent study, internships, student-designed major, study abroad, teacher preparation, weekend college, cross-registration; liberal arts/career combination in health sciences. **Remedial services:** Learning center, reduced course load, remedial instruction, special counselor, tutoring, basic skills program. **Placement/credit:** AP, CLEP General and Subject, institutional tests.

ACADEMIC REQUIREMENTS. Freshmen must earn minimum GPA of 2.0 to continue in good standing. 76% of freshmen return for sophomore

year. Students must declare major by end of second year. **Graduation requirements:** 60 hours for associate (30 in major), 120 hours for bachelor's (40 in major). Most students required to take courses in arts/fine arts, computer science, English, foreign languages, history, humanities, mathematics, philosophy/religion, biological/physical sciences, social sciences.

FRESHMAN ADMISSIONS. Selection criteria: Scholastic standards of high school attended, scope and choice of courses taken, grades, test scores, class rank. **High school preparation:** 16 units required. Recommended units include English 4, foreign language 2, mathematics 3, social science 2 and science 2. 3 units of electives also recommended. **Test requirements:** SAT or ACT (ACT preferred); score report by August 15.

1992 FRESHMAN CLASS PROFILE. 379 men and women applied, 280 accepted; 46 men enrolled, 97 women enrolled. 46% had high school GPA of 3.0 or higher, 43% between 2.0 and 2.99. **Academic background:** Mid 50% of enrolled freshmen had ACT composite between 15-23. 96% submitted ACT scores. **Characteristics:** 78% from in state, 62% live in college housing, 2% have minority backgrounds, 1% are foreign students. Average age is 20.

FALL-TERM APPLICATIONS. $25 fee, may be waived for applicants with need. Closing date August 1; priority given to applications received by May 1; applicants notified on a rolling basis; must reply within 30 days. Interview recommended for academically weak applicants. Audition recommended. Portfolio recommended. Essay recommended. Deferred and early admission available. Institutional early decision plan.

STUDENT LIFE. Housing: Dormitories (women, coed); apartment housing available. **Activities:** Student government, student newspaper, yearbook, choral groups, drama, music ensembles, international student organization, Student Business Association, Student Nurse Association, Amnesty International, campus ministry, Habitat for Humanity.

ATHLETICS. NAIA. **Intercollegiate:** Baseball M, basketball, golf, soccer M, softball W, tennis, volleyball W. **Intramural:** Basketball, skiing, soccer, softball, swimming, table tennis, volleyball.

STUDENT SERVICES. Career counseling, employment service for undergraduates, freshman orientation, health services, personal counseling, placement service for graduates, veterans counselor, services/facilities for handicapped.

ANNUAL EXPENSES. Tuition and fees: $8,100. **Room and board:** $3,600. **Books and supplies:** $575. **Other expenses:** $1,250.

FINANCIAL AID. 85% of freshmen, 85% of continuing students receive some form of aid. 77% of grants, 73% of loans, 72% of jobs based on need. 72 enrolled freshmen were judged to have need, all were offered aid. Academic, music/drama, art, leadership scholarships available. **Aid applications:** No closing date; priority given to applications received by March 15; applicants notified on a rolling basis beginning on or about March 15; must reply by May 1 or within 3 weeks if notified thereafter. **Additional information:** Auditions, portfolios, or essays required of applicants for some scholarships and grants.

ADDRESS/TELEPHONE. Kevin Kucera, Director of Admissions and Financial Aid, Edgewood College, 855 Woodrow Street, Madison, WI 53711. (608) 257-4861. (800) 444-4861. Fax: (608) 257-1455.

Fox Valley Technical College
Appleton, Wisconsin — CB code: 0747

2-year public technical college, coed. Founded in 1967. **Accreditation:** Regional. **Undergraduate enrollment:** 1,369 men, 1,498 women full time; 3,523 men, 3,898 women part time. **Faculty:** 900 total (400 full time), 10 with doctorates or other terminal degrees. **Location:** Suburban campus in small city; 100 miles from Milwaukee. **Calendar:** Varies according to program of study. **Microcomputers:** 250 located in classrooms, computer centers.

DEGREES OFFERED. AAS. 594 associate degrees awarded in 1992.

UNDERGRADUATE MAJORS. Accounting, aeronautical technology, agribusiness, agricultural business and management, airline piloting and navigation, automated manufacturing systems, automotive technology, business and management, business computer/console/peripheral equipment operation, business data processing and related programs, business data programming, child development/care/guidance, criminal justice studies, data processing, diesel engine mechanics, drafting, electromechanical technology, electronic technology, engineering and engineering-related technologies, fashion merchandising, finance, fire control and safety technology, food management, food production/management/services, graphic and printing production, hospitality and recreation marketing, industrial engineering, insurance marketing, interior design, law enforcement and corrections technologies, legal secretary, marketing and distribution, mechanical design technology, nursing, occupational therapy assistant, precision metal work, recreation and community services technologies, renewable natural resources, secretarial and related programs.

ACADEMIC PROGRAMS. Double major, internships, telecourses. **Remedial services:** Reduced course load, remedial instruction, special counselor, tutoring. **Placement/credit:** Institutional tests; 45 credit hours maximum for associate degree.

ACADEMIC REQUIREMENTS. No policy requiring minimum GPA; records of students having academic difficulty are reviewed individually. Students must declare major on application. **Graduation requirements:** 68 hours for associate (60 in major). Most students required to take courses in English, history, mathematics, biological/physical sciences, social sciences.

FRESHMAN ADMISSIONS. Selection criteria: Open admissions. **Test requirements:** ACT for placement and counseling only; score report by August 15.

1992 FRESHMAN CLASS PROFILE. 1,902 men and women enrolled. **Characteristics:** 95% from in state, 100% commute, 2% have minority backgrounds. Average age is 23.

FALL-TERM APPLICATIONS. $20 fee. No closing date; applicants notified on a rolling basis. Interview required for nursing applicants. ACT or ASSET recommended.

STUDENT LIFE. Activities: Student government, student newspaper, 23 curriculum related clubs.

ATHLETICS. Intramural: Basketball, bowling, golf, soccer, softball, table tennis, tennis, volleyball.

STUDENT SERVICES. Aptitude testing, career counseling, employment service for undergraduates, health services, on-campus day care, personal counseling, placement service for graduates, veterans counselor, services/facilities for handicapped.

ANNUAL EXPENSES. Tuition and fees: $1,440, $8,760 additional for out-of-state students. Fees vary by program. **Books and supplies:** $500. **Other expenses:** $800.

FINANCIAL AID. 75% of freshmen, 75% of continuing students receive some form of aid. All grants, 89% of loans, all jobs based on need. Academic, state/district residency, leadership scholarships available. **Aid applications:** No closing date; applicants notified on a rolling basis; must reply within 15 days.

ADDRESS/TELEPHONE. Robert B. Burdick, Associate Dean of Students, Fox Valley Technical College, 1825 North Bluemound Drive, Appleton, WI 54913-2277. (414) 735-5727. Fax: (414) 735-2582.

Gateway Technical College
Kenosha, Wisconsin — CB code: 0761

2-year public technical college, coed. Founded in 1911. **Accreditation:** Regional. **Undergraduate enrollment:** 1,132 men, 2,212 women full time; 2,396 men, 3,154 women part time. **Faculty:** 755 total (236 full time), 8 with doctorates or other terminal degrees. **Location:** Urban campus in small city; 30 miles from Milwaukee, 60 miles from Chicago. **Calendar:** Semester, extensive summer session. Saturday and extensive evening/early morning classes. **Microcomputers:** 270 located in libraries, classrooms, computer centers. **Additional facts:** Multilocation institution with other campuses at Elkhorn and Racine.

DEGREES OFFERED. AAS. 390 associate degrees awarded in 1992. 16% in business and management, 27% business/office and marketing/distribution, 18% engineering technologies, 16% allied health, 5% parks/recreation, protective services, public affairs, 12% trade and industry.

UNDERGRADUATE MAJORS. Accounting, airline piloting and navigation, automotive mechanics, automotive technology, aviation management, business and management, business and office, business data processing and related programs, business data programming, child development/care/guidance, civil technology, computer servicing technology, computer technology, court reporting, drafting and design technology, electromechanical technology, electronic technology, fashion merchandising, finance, fire control and safety technology, food management, food production/management/services, horticulture, hotel/motel and restaurant management, human services, industrial technology, interior design, law enforcement and corrections technologies, legal secretary, manufacturing technology, marketing and distribution, mechanical design technology, nursing, radio/television technology, secretarial and related programs, social work, trade and industrial supervision and management, transportation and travel marketing, transportation management, word processing.

ACADEMIC PROGRAMS. Dual enrollment of high school students, independent study, internships, telecourses, cross-registration. **Remedial services:** Learning center, preadmission summer program, reduced course load, remedial instruction, special counselor, tutoring, developmental center. **Placement/credit:** CLEP General and Subject, institutional tests; 48 credit hours maximum for associate degree.

ACADEMIC REQUIREMENTS. Freshmen must earn minimum GPA of 2.0 to continue in good standing. 65% of freshmen return for sophomore year. Students must declare major on application. **Graduation requirements:** 64 hours for associate (32 in major). Most students required to take courses in English, mathematics, social sciences.

FRESHMAN ADMISSIONS. Selection criteria: Open admissions. GED or high school diploma required for some programs. Chemistry and biology required for applicants to nursing program. **Test requirements:** Institutional biology and chemistry test required for nursing applicants.

1992 FRESHMAN CLASS PROFILE. 419 women enrolled. **Characteristics:** 95% from in state, 100% commute, 18% have minority backgrounds, 1% are foreign students. Average age is 24.

FALL-TERM APPLICATIONS. No fee. No closing date; applicants

notified on a rolling basis; must reply within 2 weeks. Interview recommended. Deferred and early admission available.

STUDENT LIFE. Activities: Student government, radio, student newspaper. **Additional information:** Wide variety of occupationally-oriented and community-related organizations available.

STUDENT SERVICES. Aptitude testing, career counseling, employment service for undergraduates, health services, personal counseling, placement service for graduates, special adviser for adult students, veterans counselor, services/facilities for handicapped.

ANNUAL EXPENSES. Tuition and fees: $1,440, $8,760 additional for out-of-state students. **Books and supplies:** $538. **Other expenses:** $937.

FINANCIAL AID. 32% of continuing students receive some form of aid. All grants, 95% of loans, all jobs based on need. **Aid applications:** Closing date May 1; applicants notified on a rolling basis beginning on or about May 1; must reply by September 1.

ADDRESS/TELEPHONE. Dan Burrell, Vice President of Student Services, Gateway Technical College, 3520 30th Avenue, Kenosha, WI 53141-1582. (414) 656-6911. Fax: (414) 656-7209.

Lac Courte Oreilles Ojibwa Community College
Hayward, Wisconsin CB code: 7351

2-year public community college. **Accreditation:** Regional candidate. **Undergraduate enrollment:** 394 men and women. **Location:** Rural campus in small town. **Calendar:** Semester.

FRESHMAN ADMISSIONS. Selection criteria: Open admissions.

ANNUAL EXPENSES. Tuition and fees: $2,425.

ADDRESS/TELEPHONE. Lac Courte Oreilles Ojibwa Community College, Route 2, Box 2357, Hayward, WI 54843. (715) 634-4790.

Lakeland College
Sheboygan, Wisconsin CB code: 1393

4-year private liberal arts college, coed, affiliated with United Church of Christ. Founded in 1862. **Accreditation:** Regional. **Undergraduate enrollment:** 358 men, 426 women full time; 849 men, 998 women part time. **Graduate enrollment:** 1 man full time; 5 men, 20 women part time. **Faculty:** 165 total (43 full time), 65 with doctorates or other terminal degrees. **Location:** Rural campus in large town; 10 miles from city limits, 60 miles from Milwaukee, 60 miles from Green Bay. **Calendar:** 4-1-4, limited summer session. Saturday and extensive evening/early morning classes. **Microcomputers:** 40 located in libraries, computer centers. **Special facilities:** Museum, Art Gallery. **Additional facts:** Evening classes offered for nontraditional students at 10 in-state sites. Associate program available at Tokyo, Japan campus.

DEGREES OFFERED. BA, MEd. 320 bachelor's degrees awarded in 1992. 72% in business and management, 10% computer sciences, 6% teacher education. Graduate degrees offered in 1 major field of study.

UNDERGRADUATE MAJORS. Accounting, applied mathematics, behavioral sciences, biological and physical sciences, biology, business administration and management, business and management, business economics, chemistry, clinical laboratory science, computer and information sciences, computer mathematics, creative writing, dramatic arts, early childhood education, economics, education, elementary education, engineering, English, English education, English literature, fine arts, foreign languages education, German, history, hotel/motel and restaurant management, humanities and social sciences, international business management, journalism, junior high education, liberal/general studies, marketing and distribution, marketing management, marketing research, mathematics, mathematics education, music, music business management, music education, philosophy, physical fitness and health, predentistry, prelaw, premedicine, prepharmacy, preveterinary, psychology, public policy studies, religion, science education, secondary education, social science education, social sciences, social studies education, sociology, Spanish, speech/communication/theater education, theological studies, visual and performing arts.

ACADEMIC PROGRAMS. Double major, dual enrollment of high school students, honors program, independent study, internships, study abroad, teacher preparation, Washington semester, engineering program with University of Wisconsin: Madison; liberal arts/career combination in engineering. **Remedial services:** Reduced course load, remedial instruction, tutoring, developmental basic skills. **Placement/credit:** AP, CLEP General and Subject, institutional tests; 16 credit hours maximum for bachelor's degree.

ACADEMIC REQUIREMENTS. Freshmen must earn minimum GPA of 1.75 to continue in good standing. 65% of freshmen return for sophomore year. Students must declare major by end of second year. **Graduation requirements:** 136 hours for bachelor's (48 in major). Most students required to take courses in arts/fine arts, computer science, English, foreign languages, history, humanities, mathematics, philosophy/religion, biological/physical sciences, social sciences. **Postgraduate studies:** 2% enter law school, 2% enter medical school, 8% enter MBA programs, 2% enter other graduate study. **Additional information:** Applicants whose test scores reflect weakness in basic skills must take basic skills courses in freshman year.

FRESHMAN ADMISSIONS. Selection criteria: ACT test scores, rank in top half of class, minimum 2.0 high school GPA. Recommended units include biological science 1, English 4, foreign language 2, mathematics 2, physical science 1, social science 1 and science 2. **Test requirements:** SAT or ACT (ACT preferred); score report by August 15.

1992 FRESHMAN CLASS PROFILE. 310 men, 339 women enrolled. 34% had high school GPA of 3.0 or higher, 60% between 2.0 and 2.99. 13% were in top tenth and 26% were in top quarter of graduating class. **Academic background:** Mid 50% of enrolled freshmen had ACT composite between 18-22. 92% submitted ACT scores. **Characteristics:** 81% from in state, 66% live in college housing, 6% have minority backgrounds, 10% join fraternities/sororities. Average age is 18.

FALL-TERM APPLICATIONS. $20 fee. Closing date August 15; applicants notified on a rolling basis beginning on or about September 1. Interview recommended. Essay recommended. Deferred admission available.

STUDENT LIFE. Housing: Dormitories (men, women, coed). Honor suites and cultural suites available. **Activities:** Student government, radio, student newspaper, yearbook, choral groups, concert band, drama, jazz band, music ensembles, pep band, fraternities, sororities, chapel musicians, business fraternity, Inter-Greek Council, cultural club, education club, Circle-K, Habitat for Humanity.

ATHLETICS. NAIA. **Intercollegiate:** Baseball M, basketball, cross-country, football M, golf M, soccer, softball W, tennis, track and field, volleyball W, wrestling M. **Intramural:** Badminton, baseball, basketball, bowling, cross-country, field hockey, ice hockey, skiing, soccer, softball, table tennis, tennis, volleyball.

STUDENT SERVICES. Career counseling, employment service for undergraduates, freshman orientation, health services, on-campus day care, personal counseling, placement service for graduates, veterans counselor.

ANNUAL EXPENSES. Tuition and fees: $9,145. **Room and board:** $3,700. **Books and supplies:** $500. **Other expenses:** $750.

FINANCIAL AID. 95% of freshmen, 95% of continuing students receive some form of aid. All grants, 84% of loans, 80% of jobs based on need. Academic, religious affiliation scholarships available. **Aid applications:** Closing date August 1; priority given to applications received by May 1; applicants notified on a rolling basis beginning on or about March 1; must reply within 4 weeks. **Additional information:** Interest-Free Tuition Payment Plan (ITPP).

ADDRESS/TELEPHONE. Lyle Krueger, VP/ College Relations, Lakeland College, PO Box 359, Sheboygan, WI 53082-0359. (414) 565-1217. Fax: (414) 565-1206.

Lakeshore Technical College
Cleveland, Wisconsin CB code: 0618

2-year public technical college, coed. Founded in 1912. **Accreditation:** Regional. **Undergraduate enrollment:** 301 men, 522 women full time; 856 men, 1,253 women part time. **Faculty:** 915 total (265 full time), 9 with doctorates or other terminal degrees. **Location:** Rural campus in rural community; 15 miles from Sheboygan. **Calendar:** Semester, limited summer session. **Microcomputers:** Located in libraries, classrooms, computer centers.

DEGREES OFFERED. AS, AAS. 334 associate degrees awarded in 1992. 36% in business and management, 14% business/office and marketing/distribution, 18% engineering technologies, 9% health sciences, 5% allied health, 7% law, 5% physical sciences.

UNDERGRADUATE MAJORS. Accounting, business data entry equipment operation, chemical manufacturing technology, court reporting, data processing, electromechanical technology, electronic technology, engineering and engineering-related technologies, equestrian science, finance, fire control and safety technology, hazardous waste handling technician, law enforcement and corrections technologies, legal assistant/paralegal, legal secretary, marketing and distribution, mechanical design technology, medical laboratory technologies, medical secretary, nuclear technologies, nursing, ophthalmic services, plastic technology, radiation protection technician, real estate, secretarial and related programs.

ACADEMIC PROGRAMS. Double major, internships, cross-registration. **Remedial services:** Learning center, preadmission summer program, reduced course load, remedial instruction, tutoring. **Placement/credit:** Institutional tests.

ACADEMIC REQUIREMENTS. No policy requiring minimum GPA; records of students having academic difficulty are reviewed individually. 55% of freshmen return for sophomore year. Students must declare major on application. **Graduation requirements:** 64 hours for associate (50 in major). Most students required to take courses in English, mathematics, biological/physical sciences, social sciences.

FRESHMAN ADMISSIONS. Selection criteria: Open admissions. **Test requirements:** NLN Pre-Nursing and Guidance Examination required for nursing applicants. ASSET required for all students.

1992 FRESHMAN CLASS PROFILE. 345 men, 529 women enrolled. **Characteristics:** 99% from in state, 100% commute. Average age is 26.

FALL-TERM APPLICATIONS. $30 fee. No closing date; applicants notified on a rolling basis; must reply within 6 weeks. Interview required. Deferred and early admission available.

STUDENT LIFE. Activities: Student government, student newspaper.

ATHLETICS. Intercollegiate: Basketball M, golf, tennis. **Intramural:** Basketball M, golf, tennis.

STUDENT SERVICES. Aptitude testing, career counseling, employment service for undergraduates, health services, on-campus day care, personal counseling, placement service for graduates, services/facilities for handicapped.

ANNUAL EXPENSES. Tuition and fees: $1,440, $8,760 additional for out-of-state students. **Books and supplies:** $625. **Other expenses:** $1,100.

FINANCIAL AID. 70% of freshmen, 83% of continuing students receive some form of aid. 92% of loans, 80% of jobs based on need. 605 enrolled freshmen were judged to have need, 472 were offered aid. **Aid applications:** No closing date; applicants notified on a rolling basis beginning on or about May 25; must reply within 2 weeks.

ADDRESS/TELEPHONE. Dean Voskuil, Student Services Manager, Lakeshore Technical College, 1290 North Avenue, Cleveland, WI 53015-9761. (414) 458-4183. Fax: (414) 457-6211.

Lawrence University
Appleton, Wisconsin
CB code: 1398

Admissions: 75% of applicants accepted
Based on:
- ••• School record
- •• Essay, recommendations, special talents, test scores
- • Activities, interview

Completion: 90% of freshmen end year in good standing
74% graduate, 23% of these enter graduate study

4-year private college of arts and sciences and music college, coed. Founded in 1847. **Accreditation:** Regional. **Undergraduate enrollment:** 573 men, 599 women full time; 17 men, 22 women part time. **Faculty:** 138 total (127 full time), 108 with doctorates or other terminal degrees. **Location:** Urban campus in small city; 100 miles from Milwaukee. **Calendar:** Trimester. **Microcomputers:** 100 located in dormitories, libraries, classrooms, computer centers. **Special facilities:** Laser physics laboratory, 3 art galleries, 250 MHz nuclear magnetic resonance spectrometer, physics/computational graphics laboratory, hall of music.

DEGREES OFFERED. BA. 287 bachelor's degrees awarded in 1992. 10% in languages, 9% letters/literature, 9% life sciences, 8% philosophy, religion, theology, 7% physical sciences, 9% psychology, 27% social sciences, 14% visual and performing arts.

UNDERGRADUATE MAJORS. Anthropology, art education, art history, biochemistry, biological and physical sciences, biology, chemistry, classics, computer mathematics, dramatic arts, East Asian studies, economics, elementary education, English, English education, foreign languages education, French, geology, German, Greek (classical), history, humanities, humanities and social sciences, international studies, Latin, liberal/general studies, marine biology, mathematics, mathematics education, music, music education, music history and appreciation, music performance, music theory and composition, neurosciences, philosophy, physical sciences, physics, political science and government, predentistry, prelaw, premedicine, prepharmacy, preveterinary, psychology, religion, Russian, Russian and Slavic studies, science education, secondary education, social science education, Spanish, speech/communication/theater education, studio art, women's studies.

ACADEMIC PROGRAMS. Double major, honors program, independent study, internships, student-designed major, study abroad, teacher preparation, Washington semester, study abroad programs in 12 countries; marine biology term, marine geology term, Oak Ridge science semester; urban semester (in Chicago); Newberry Library Program in Humanities; liberal arts/career combination in engineering, forestry, health sciences. **Remedial services:** Learning center, tutoring, writing laboratory. **Placement/credit:** AP, IB, institutional tests; 30 credit hours maximum for bachelor's degree. Course credit awarded for scores of at least 5 on International Baccalaureate higher-level examinations. Sophomore status granted for completion of full IB diploma.

ACADEMIC REQUIREMENTS. Freshmen must earn minimum GPA of 1.8 to continue in good standing. 86% of freshmen return for sophomore year. Students must declare major by end of second year. **Graduation requirements:** 120 hours for bachelor's (30 in major). Most students required to take courses in arts/fine arts, English, foreign languages, history, humanities, mathematics, philosophy/religion, biological/physical sciences, social sciences. **Postgraduate studies:** 2% enter law school, 3% enter medical school, 1% enter MBA programs, 17% enter other graduate study. **Additional information:** As an adjunct to a major, students may pursue 1 of 7 interdisciplinary areas of study: biomedical ethics, environmental studies, gender studies, international studies, linguistics, neuroscience, or cognitive science.

FRESHMAN ADMISSIONS. Selection criteria: Strength of curriculum, school achievement record most important. Recommendations, out-of-class activities, test scores considered. Music applicants judged on musicianship, teacher's recommendations, and academic ability. **High school preparation:** 16 units required. Required and recommended units include English 4. Foreign language 3, mathematics 3, social science 3 and science 3 recommended. Strong preparation required of music applicants. **Test requirements:** SAT or ACT; score report by April 1. Institutional music theory/aptitude test required for music applicants.

1992 FRESHMAN CLASS PROFILE. 636 men applied, 427 accepted, 145 enrolled; 648 women applied, 530 accepted, 180 enrolled. 86% had high school GPA of 3.0 or higher, 14% between 2.0 and 2.99. 45% were in top tenth and 80% were in top quarter of graduating class. **Academic background:** Mid 50% of enrolled freshmen had SAT-V between 490-610, SAT-M between 540-660; ACT composite between 24-29. 74% submitted SAT scores, 70% submitted ACT scores. **Characteristics:** 40% from in state, 98% live in college housing, 12% have minority backgrounds, 11% are foreign students, 37% join fraternities/sororities. Average age is 18.

FALL-TERM APPLICATIONS. $25 fee, may be waived for applicants with need. Closing date February 15; applicants notified on or about April 1; must reply by May 1. Audition required for music applicants. Essay required. Interview recommended. Portfolio recommended for studio art applicants. CRDA. Deferred and early admission available. Early decision plan 1: deadline December 1, notification December 15, reply January 1. Plan 2: deadline January 15, notification February 1, reply February 15.

STUDENT LIFE. Housing: Dormitories (women, coed); apartment, fraternity, cooperative housing available. All single students, except those living with family, required to live in university residence halls for 12 terms. **Activities:** Student government, magazine, radio, student newspaper, yearbook, choral groups, concert band, dance, drama, jazz band, music ensembles, opera, pep band, symphony orchestra, fraternities, sororities, social service groups, religious organizations (Campus Crusade for Christ, Intervarsity Christian Fellowship, Chavurah), Black Organization of Students, international and political clubs, sports clubs, professional sororities and fraternities, academic clubs.

ATHLETICS. NCAA. **Intercollegiate:** Baseball M, basketball, cross-country, diving, fencing, football M, golf M, ice hockey M, lacrosse, rowing (crew), rugby W, soccer, softball W, swimming, tennis, track and field, volleyball W, wrestling M. **Intramural:** Badminton, basketball, bowling, cross-country, diving, fencing, golf, handball M, lacrosse, racquetball, rugby, sailing, skiing, softball, squash, swimming, table tennis, tennis, track and field, volleyball, water polo, wrestling M.

STUDENT SERVICES. Aptitude testing, career counseling, employment service for undergraduates, freshman orientation, health services, personal counseling, placement service for graduates, services/facilities for handicapped.

ANNUAL EXPENSES. Tuition and fees: $16,431. **Room and board:** $3,555. **Books and supplies:** $375. **Other expenses:** $660.

FINANCIAL AID. 83% of freshmen, 76% of continuing students receive some form of aid. 85% of grants, 89% of loans, 94% of jobs based on need. Academic, music/drama, state/district residency, minority scholarships available. **Aid applications:** No closing date; priority given to applications received by March 1; applicants notified on a rolling basis beginning on or about February 15; must reply by May 1 or within 2 weeks if notified thereafter.

ADDRESS/TELEPHONE. Steven T. Syverson, Dean of Admissions and Financial Aid, Lawrence University, PO Box 599, Appleton, WI 54912-0599. (414) 832-6500. (800) 227-0982. Fax: (414) 832-6782.

Madison Area Technical College
Madison, Wisconsin
CB code: 1536

2-year public community college, coed. Founded in 1912. **Accreditation:** Regional. **Undergraduate enrollment:** 2,410 men, 3,970 women full time; 2,473 men, 2,769 women part time. **Faculty:** 1,960 total (390 full time). **Location:** Urban campus in small city; 75 miles from Milwaukee. **Calendar:** Semester, limited summer session. **Microcomputers:** 470 located in libraries, classrooms, computer centers. **Special facilities:** Satellite downlink, theater.

DEGREES OFFERED. AA, AS, AAS. 1,052 associate degrees awarded in 1992.

UNDERGRADUATE MAJORS. Accounting, animal technician, architecture, automotive mechanics, automotive technology, business and office, business computer/console/peripheral equipment operation, business data processing and related programs, business data programming, clinical laboratory science, commercial art, community developmental disabilities, computer programming, data processing, dental assistant, dental hygiene, diesel engine mechanics, dietetic aide/assistant, drafting, electronic technology, engineering and engineering-related technologies, fashion merchandising, finance, fire control and safety technology, food production/management/services, graphic and printing production, graphic arts technology, hospitality and recreation marketing, hotel/motel and restaurant management, insurance and risk management, insurance marketing, interior design, laboratory animal technician, law enforcement and corrections, law enforcement and corrections technologies, liberal/general studies, marketing and distribution, mechanical design technology, medical assistant, medical laboratory technologies, nursing, occupational therapy assistant, ophthalmic services, photographic technology, practical nursing, precision metal work, real estate, recreation and community services technologies, respiratory therapy, respiratory therapy technology, secretarial and related programs, textiles and clothing, tourism, veterinarian's assistant, visual communication, word processing.

ACADEMIC PROGRAMS. 2-year transfer program, dual enrollment of high school students, internships, cross-registration. **Remedial services:** Learning center, reduced course load, remedial instruction, special counselor. **Placement/credit:** CLEP Subject, institutional tests; 32 credit hours maximum for associate degree.

ACADEMIC REQUIREMENTS. Freshmen must earn minimum GPA of 2.0 to continue in good standing. Students must declare major on application. **Graduation requirements:** 64 hours for associate (52 in major). Most students required to take courses in English, mathematics, biological/physical sciences, social sciences.

FRESHMAN ADMISSIONS. Selection criteria: Open admissions. School achievement record, class rank, test scores considered for some programs. High school academic subject requirements for health and technical programs. **Test requirements:** SAT or ACT (ACT preferred) required of health occupation applicants only; score report by August 1.

1992 FRESHMAN CLASS PROFILE. 2,620 men applied, 2,310 accepted, 1,309 enrolled; 2,900 women applied, 2,560 accepted, 1,447 enrolled. **Characteristics:** 98% from in state, 100% commute, 5% have minority backgrounds. Average age is 21.

FALL-TERM APPLICATIONS. No fee. Closing date August 1; applicants notified on a rolling basis; must reply within 2 weeks. Early admission available. Early application recommended for programs with limited enrollment.

STUDENT LIFE. Activities: Student government, student newspaper, television, choral groups, drama, jazz band, music ensembles.

ATHLETICS. NJCAA. **Intercollegiate:** Baseball M, basketball, bowling, cross-country M, golf M, softball W, volleyball W, wrestling M. **Intramural:** Basketball, racquetball, soccer, swimming, table tennis, tennis, volleyball.

STUDENT SERVICES. Aptitude testing, career counseling, employment service for undergraduates, freshman orientation, health services, on-campus day care, personal counseling, placement service for graduates, veterans counselor, services/facilities for handicapped.

ANNUAL EXPENSES. Tuition and fees: $1,440, $8,760 additional for out-of-state students. Fees vary by program. **Books and supplies:** $600. **Other expenses:** $950.

FINANCIAL AID. 60% of continuing students receive some form of aid. 98% of grants, 91% of loans, 34% of jobs based on need. Academic scholarships available. **Aid applications:** No closing date; priority given to applications received by June 1; applicants notified on a rolling basis beginning on or about June 1; must reply within 4 weeks.

ADDRESS/TELEPHONE. Peter Van Bramer, Admissions Administrator, Madison Area Technical College, 3350 Anderson St, Madison, WI 53704-2599. (608) 246-6205. Fax: (608) 258-2329.

Madison Junior College of Business
Madison, Wisconsin CB code: 0633

2-year private junior college, coed. Founded in 1856. **Undergraduate enrollment:** 49 men, 119 women full time; 15 men, 48 women part time. **Faculty:** 16 total (8 full time). **Location:** Suburban campus in small city; 77 miles from Milwaukee, 146 miles from Chicago. **Calendar:** Trimester, extensive summer session. **Microcomputers:** Located in classrooms. **Additional facts:** Morning classes only.

DEGREES OFFERED. AA. 107 associate degrees awarded in 1992. 34% in business and management, 66% business/office and marketing/distribution.

UNDERGRADUATE MAJORS. Accounting, accounting data processing, business and office, business data processing and related programs, legal secretary, marketing and distribution, medical secretary, secretarial and related programs.

ACADEMIC PROGRAMS. Accelerated program. **Remedial services:** Reduced course load.

ACADEMIC REQUIREMENTS. Freshmen must earn minimum GPA of 2.0 to continue in good standing. 75% of freshmen return for sophomore year. Students must declare major on application. **Graduation requirements:** 63 hours for associate. Most students required to take courses in English, mathematics, social sciences.

FRESHMAN ADMISSIONS. Selection criteria: Open admissions.

1992 FRESHMAN CLASS PROFILE. 78 men and women enrolled. **Characteristics:** 95% from in state, 100% commute, 2% have minority backgrounds, 1% are foreign students. Average age is 20.

FALL-TERM APPLICATIONS. $25 fee. No closing date; applicants notified on a rolling basis. Interview recommended. Deferred admission available.

STUDENT LIFE. Activities: Student government.

ATHLETICS. Intramural: Basketball, softball, volleyball.

STUDENT SERVICES. Placement service for graduates, services/facilities for handicapped.

ANNUAL EXPENSES. Tuition and fees (1992-93): $4,050. Books and supplies included in tuition. **Other expenses:** $906.

FINANCIAL AID. 48% of freshmen, 50% of continuing students receive some form of aid. Grants, loans, jobs available. Academic scholarships available. **Aid applications:** No closing date; applicants notified on a rolling basis beginning on or about August 1; must reply within 4 weeks.

ADDRESS/TELEPHONE. M. Jeanne Sears, Director of Admissions, Madison Junior College of Business, 1110 Spring Harbor Drive, Madison, WI 53705-1399. (608) 238-4266. Fax: (608) 238-9905.

Maranatha Baptist Bible College
Watertown, Wisconsin CB code: 2732

4-year private Bible college, coed, affiliated with Independent Baptist Church. Founded in 1968. **Accreditation:** Regional candidate. **Undergraduate enrollment:** 182 men, 222 women full time; 48 men, 25 women part time. **Graduate enrollment:** 10 men full time; 13 men part time. **Faculty:** 43 total (22 full time), 6 with doctorates or other terminal degrees. **Location:** Urban campus in large town; 45 miles from Milwaukee and 38 miles from Madison. **Calendar:** Semester, limited summer session. **Microcomputers:** 12 located in computer centers.

DEGREES OFFERED. AS, BA, BS, MA, MS. 5 associate degrees awarded in 1992. 100% in business/office and marketing/distribution. 63 bachelor's degrees awarded. 12% in business and management, 41% teacher education, 47% philosophy, religion, theology. Graduate degrees offered in 3 major fields of study.

UNDERGRADUATE MAJORS. Associate: Secretarial and related programs. **Bachelor's:** Bible studies, business and management, business education, elementary education, English education, fine arts, liberal/general studies, mathematics education, missionary studies, music, music education, nursing, physical education, religious music, secretarial and related programs, social studies education, speech/communication/theater education, theological studies.

ACADEMIC PROGRAMS. Double major, dual enrollment of high school students, independent study, internships. **Remedial services:** Reduced course load, remedial instruction. **Placement/credit:** Institutional tests.

ACADEMIC REQUIREMENTS. Freshmen must earn minimum GPA of 1.5 to continue in good standing. 68% of freshmen return for sophomore year. Students must declare major by end of second year. **Graduation requirements:** 64 hours for associate (30 in major), 128 hours for bachelor's (40 in major). Most students required to take courses in arts/fine arts, English, history, humanities, mathematics, philosophy/religion, biological/physical sciences, social sciences. **Postgraduate studies:** 11% from 2-year programs enter 4-year programs. **Additional information:** Hands on ministerial work available.

FRESHMAN ADMISSIONS. Selection criteria: Modified open admissions program used. At risk students placed on admissions probation, restricted to 13 hours and placed in remedial courses not applicable to graduation. Character qualifications extremely important. **High school preparation:** 16 units required. Required and recommended units include English 3-4, mathematics 2-3, social science 3 and science 2-3. Foreign language 2 recommended. 2 high school units of physical education recommended; 1 unit of keyboarding (typing or computer science) recommended. **Test requirements:** ACT for placement.

1992 FRESHMAN CLASS PROFILE. 107 men applied, 107 accepted, 76 enrolled; 103 women applied, 103 accepted, 76 enrolled. 55% had high school GPA of 3.0 or higher, 39% between 2.0 and 2.99. **Academic background:** Mid 50% of enrolled freshmen had ACT composite between 18-23. 80% submitted ACT scores. **Characteristics:** 40% from in state, 96% live in college housing. Average age is 18.

FALL-TERM APPLICATIONS. $25 fee. No closing date; applicants notified on a rolling basis. Audition required for fine arts applicants. Essay required. Deferred admission available. ACT recommended of freshman applicants for placement. Most recent scores used.

STUDENT LIFE. Housing: Dormitories (men, women). Assistance in locating off-campus housing available for undergraduate and graduate students. **Activities:** Student government, yearbook, choral groups, drama, music ensembles, musical theater, pep band, Societies for social and intramural activities, annual missionary conferences, evangelistic meetings, bible conferences, artist series, public speaking. **Additional information:** Religious observance required.

ATHLETICS. Intercollegiate: Baseball M, basketball, football M, golf M, soccer M, softball W, tennis M, volleyball W, wrestling M. **Intramural:** Basketball M, skiing, volleyball.

STUDENT SERVICES. Career counseling, freshman orientation, health services, personal counseling, placement service for graduates, veterans counselor.

ANNUAL EXPENSES. Tuition and fees: $4,820. **Room and board:** $2,700. **Books and supplies:** $460. **Other expenses:** $920.

FINANCIAL AID. 68% of freshmen, 73% of continuing students receive some form of aid. 70% of grants, 92% of loans, all jobs based on need. 130 enrolled freshmen were judged to have need, all were offered aid. Academic scholarships available. **Aid applications:** Closing date August 1; priority given to applications received by June 30; applicants notified on a rolling basis; must reply by May 1 or within 4 weeks if notified thereafter.

ADDRESS/TELEPHONE. Michael Shellman, Director of Admissions, Maranatha Baptist Bible College, 745 West Main Street, Watertown, WI 53094. (414) 261-9300 ext. 308. (800) 622-2947 ext. 308. Fax: (414) 261-9109.

Marian College of Fond du Lac
Fond du Lac, Wisconsin — CB code: 1443

Admissions: 82% of applicants accepted
Based on:
••• School record
•• Test scores
• Activities, essay, interview, recommendations, special talents
Completion: 90% of freshmen end year in good standing
63% graduate, 10% of these enter graduate study

4-year private liberal arts college, coed, affiliated with Roman Catholic Church. Founded in 1936. **Accreditation:** Regional. **Undergraduate enrollment:** 531 men, 831 women full time; 80 men, 179 women part time. **Graduate enrollment:** 10 men, 10 women full time; 216 men, 434 women part time. **Faculty:** 94 total (62 full time), 33 with doctorates or other terminal degrees. **Location:** Rural campus in large town; 60 miles from Milwaukee, 65 miles from Green Bay. **Calendar:** Semester, limited summer session. Extensive evening/early morning classes. **Microcomputers:** 50 located in libraries, computer centers. **Additional facts:** Cooperative education internship programs for all majors. Degree completion programs in nursing, business, quality management, radiologic technology and graduate studies offered throughout Wisconsin.

DEGREES OFFERED. BA, BS, MA, MS. 251 bachelor's degrees awarded in 1992. 50% in business and management, 15% teacher education, 35% health sciences. Graduate degrees offered in 2 major fields of study.

UNDERGRADUATE MAJORS. Accounting, art education, biochemistry, biology, business administration and management, business and management, business education, chemistry, clinical laboratory science, communications, criminal justice studies, cytotechnology, early childhood education, education, elementary education, English, English education, fine arts, foreign languages education, history, human relations, humanities and social sciences, junior high education, liberal/general studies, marketing and distributive education, marketing management, mathematics, mathematics education, medical laboratory technologies, music, music education, nursing, predentistry, prelaw, premedicine, prepharmacy, preveterinary, psychology, quality management, radiograph medical technology, secondary education, social studies education, social work, sports and leisure management.

ACADEMIC PROGRAMS. Accelerated program, cooperative education, double major, dual enrollment of high school students, independent study, internships, student-designed major, study abroad, teacher preparation, weekend college, accelerated programs for adults in business, nursing, quality and productivity management, and radiologic technology; liberal arts/career combination in health sciences. **Remedial services:** Reduced course load, remedial instruction, special counselor, tutoring. **ROTC:** Army. **Placement/credit:** AP, CLEP General and Subject, institutional tests; 30 credit hours maximum for bachelor's degree.

ACADEMIC REQUIREMENTS. Freshmen must earn minimum GPA of 2.0 to continue in good standing. 80% of freshmen return for sophomore year. Students must declare major by end of second year. **Graduation requirements:** 128 hours for bachelor's. Most students required to take courses in arts/fine arts, English, history, humanities, mathematics, philosophy/religion, biological/physical sciences, social sciences. **Additional information:** Most academic programs require field participation. Cooperative education program open to every major.

FRESHMAN ADMISSIONS. Selection criteria: School achievement record most important, followed by test scores. Applicants must meet 2 of following 3 criteria: minimum 2.0 high school GPA, top half of class, minimum ACT composite score of 18. Students judged on individual basis. Interview recommended. **High school preparation:** 16 units required. Required and recommended units include English 4, mathematics 2-3, social science 2 and science 1-2. Foreign language 2 recommended. One laboratory science and 1 history also required. Biology and chemistry prerequisite for nursing program. **Test requirements:** SAT or ACT (ACT preferred); score report by August 1. Institutional achievement test required for placement and counseling. **Additional information:** Special admissions procedures required for nursing and education divisions. High school sophomores, juniors and seniors may register for 1 freshman course per semester with principal's approval.

1992 FRESHMAN CLASS PROFILE. 741 men and women applied, 609 accepted; 350 enrolled. 36% had high school GPA of 3.0 or higher, 56% between 2.0 and 2.99. 15% were in top tenth and 23% were in top quarter of graduating class. **Characteristics:** 85% from in state, 60% live in college housing, 6% have minority backgrounds, 1% are foreign students. Average age is 19.

FALL-TERM APPLICATIONS. $15 fee, may be waived for applicants with need. Closing date August 1; priority given to applications received by April 1; applicants notified on a rolling basis; must reply by May 1 or within 4 weeks if notified thereafter. Interview recommended. Audition recommended. CRDA. Deferred and early admission available.

STUDENT LIFE. Housing: Dormitories (coed); apartment, handicapped housing available. Townhouses available. **Activities:** Student government, magazine, student newspaper, yearbook, literary magazine, choral groups, concert band, drama, jazz band, music ensembles, symphony orchestra, show choir, fraternities, Liturgy Committee, Retreat Committee, social service club, professional associations, minority student association. **Additional information:** Emphasis on community volunteer activity. A service transcript is available for graduates.

ATHLETICS. NAIA. **Intercollegiate:** Baseball M, basketball, cross-country, golf, ice hockey M, soccer, softball W, tennis, volleyball W. **Intramural:** Badminton, basketball, bowling, skiing, softball M, tennis, volleyball.

STUDENT SERVICES. Aptitude testing, career counseling, employment service for undergraduates, freshman orientation, health services, on-campus day care, personal counseling, placement service for graduates, special adviser for adult students, services/facilities for handicapped.

ANNUAL EXPENSES. Tuition and fees (1992-93): $8,100. **Room and board:** $3,500. **Books and supplies:** $350. **Other expenses:** $700.

FINANCIAL AID. 90% of freshmen, 82% of continuing students receive some form of aid. Grants, loans, jobs available. 100 enrolled freshmen were judged to have need, all were offered aid. Academic, music/drama, art, athletic, leadership, alumni affiliation, religious affiliation, minority scholarships available. **Aid applications:** No closing date; priority given to applications received by March 1; applicants notified on a rolling basis beginning on or about March 1; must reply within 4 weeks.

ADDRESS/TELEPHONE. Carol Reichenberger, Vice President of Enrollment Services, Marian College of Fond du Lac, 45 South National Avenue, Fond du Lac, WI 54935-4699. (414) 923-7650. (800) 2-MARIAN. Fax: (414) 923-7154.

Marquette University
Milwaukee, Wisconsin — CB code: 1448

Admissions: 83% of applicants accepted
Based on:
••• School record
•• Test scores
• Activities, essay, interview, recommendations
Completion: 73% graduate, 22% of these enter graduate study

4-year private university, coed, affiliated with Roman Catholic Church. Founded in 1881. **Accreditation:** Regional. **Undergraduate enrollment:** 3,553 men, 3,598 women full time; 494 men, 443 women part time. **Graduate enrollment:** 931 men, 618 women full time; 782 men, 598 women part time. **Faculty:** 984 total (554 full time), 448 with doctorates or other terminal degrees. **Location:** Urban campus in very large city; 70 miles from Chicago. **Calendar:** Semester, extensive summer session. **Microcomputers:** 500 located in dormitories, libraries, classrooms. **Special facilities:** Art museum, speech and hearing clinic, dental clinic, multi-recreation center, counseling center, student union, sports law center, designated by U.S. Department of Education as national resource center for International Studies. **Additional facts:** Jesuit institution.

DEGREES OFFERED. AA, BA, BS, MA, MS, MBA, MEd, PhD, EdD, DDS, JD. 1,916 bachelor's degrees awarded. 27% in business and management, 17% communications, 13% engineering, 6% letters/literature, 6% psychology, 6% social sciences. Graduate degrees offered in 56 major fields of study.

UNDERGRADUATE MAJORS. Associate: Criminal justice studies, criminology, law enforcement and corrections. **Bachelor's:** Accounting, advertising, anthropology, bilingual/bicultural education, biochemistry, bioengineering and biomedical engineering, biology, business administration and management, business and management, business economics, chemistry, civil engineering, communications, computer and information sciences, computer engineering, computer mathematics, creative writing, criminal justice studies, criminology, dental hygiene, dramatic arts, economics, electrical/electronics/communications engineering, elementary education, English, English education, finance, foreign languages education, French, German, history, humanities and social sciences, international business management, international studies, journalism, junior high education, Latin, law enforcement and corrections, management information systems, marketing management, mathematics, mathematics education, mechanical engineering, medical laboratory technologies, molecular biology, nursing, organizational behavior, personnel management, philosophy, physics, political science and government, predentistry, prelaw, premedicine, psychology, public relations, radio/television broadcasting, science education, secondary education, social science education, social sciences, social studies education, social work, sociology, Spanish, speech, speech pathology/audiology, speech/communication/theater education, technical and business writing, theological studies.

ACADEMIC PROGRAMS. Accelerated program, cooperative education, double major, honors program, independent study, internships, student-designed major, study abroad, teacher preparation, Washington semester, cross-registration, premedical scholars program, predental scholars program. **Remedial services:** Learning center, preadmission summer program, reduced course load, remedial instruction, tutoring, writing laboratory. **ROTC:** Air Force, Army, Naval. **Placement/credit:** AP, CLEP Subject, institutional tests; 30 credit hours maximum for bachelor's degree.

ACADEMIC REQUIREMENTS. No policy requiring minimum GPA; records of students having academic difficulty are reviewed individually. 88% of freshmen return for sophomore year. Students must declare major by end of second year. **Graduation requirements:** 65 hours for associate (30 in major), 128 hours for bachelor's (30 in major). Most students required to take courses in English, foreign languages, history, mathematics, philosophy/religion, biological/physical sciences, social sciences. **Postgraduate studies:** 6% enter law school, 1% enter medical school, 4% enter MBA programs, 11% enter other graduate study.

FRESHMAN ADMISSIONS. Selection criteria: School achievement record and test scores important and recommendations considered. **High school preparation:** 16 units recommended. Recommended units include English 4, foreign language 2, mathematics 3, social science 3 and science 2. Algebra, geometry and advanced algebra required for business administration, engineering and medical laboratory technology applicants. 4 year of math and science recommended for engineering applicants. Biology and chemistry required for dental hygiene, nursing and physical therapy applicants; 3 years of science recommended for physical therapy applicants. Chemistry required for medical laboratory technology applicants and 3 years of science recommended. **Test requirements:** SAT or ACT; score report by August 30. **Additional information:** Application closing date for physical therapy is December 15.

1992 FRESHMAN CLASS PROFILE. 2,707 men applied, 2,218 accepted, 806 enrolled; 2,824 women applied, 2,400 accepted, 852 enrolled. 28% were in top tenth and 63% were in top quarter of graduating class. **Academic background:** Mid 50% of enrolled freshmen had SAT-V between 430-540, SAT-M between 480-610; ACT composite between 22-27. 57% submitted SAT scores, 88% submitted ACT scores. **Characteristics:** 42% from in state, 88% live in college housing, 16% have minority backgrounds, 1% are foreign students. Average age is 18.

FALL-TERM APPLICATIONS. $25 fee, may be waived for applicants with need. No closing date; applicants notified on a rolling basis; must reply by May 1 or within 2 weeks if notified thereafter. Interview recommended. CRDA.

STUDENT LIFE. Housing: Dormitories (men, women, coed); apartment housing available. **Activities:** Student government, magazine, radio, student newspaper, television, yearbook, choral groups, concert band, drama, jazz band, music ensembles, musical theater, pep band, symphony orchestra, fraternities, sororities, 160 student organizations.

ATHLETICS. NCAA. **Intercollegiate:** Baseball M, basketball, cross-country, diving, golf M, ice hockey M, lacrosse M, rowing (crew), rugby M, sailing, soccer, softball W, swimming, tennis, track and field, volleyball, wrestling M. **Intramural:** Badminton, basketball, bowling, golf, racquetball, soccer, squash, tennis, volleyball, water polo.

STUDENT SERVICES. Aptitude testing, career counseling, employment service for undergraduates, freshman orientation, health services, on-campus day care, personal counseling, placement service for graduates, special adviser for adult students, veterans counselor, services/facilities for handicapped.

ANNUAL EXPENSES. Tuition and fees: $10,850. **Room and board:** $4,450. **Books and supplies:** $600. **Other expenses:** $1,350.

FINANCIAL AID. 93% of freshmen, 82% of continuing students receive some form of aid. 37% of jobs based on need. 1,071 enrolled freshmen were judged to have need, all were offered aid. Academic, music/drama, athletic, state/district residency, leadership scholarships available. **Aid applications:** No closing date; priority given to applications received by March 1; applicants notified on a rolling basis beginning on or about March 15; must reply by May 1 or within 2 weeks if notified thereafter.

ADDRESS/TELEPHONE. David Buckholdt, Enrollment Management, Marquette University, 517 N. 14th St, Milwaukee, WI 53233-9988. (414) 288-7302. (800) 222-6544.

Mid-State Technical College
Wisconsin Rapids, Wisconsin CB code: 0635

2-year public technical college, coed. Founded in 1967. **Accreditation:** Regional. **Undergraduate enrollment:** 456 men, 533 women full time; 664 men, 1,155 women part time. **Faculty:** 123 total (76 full time), 1 with doctorate or other terminal degree. **Location:** Rural campus in large town; 20 miles from Stevens Point, 115 miles from Madison. **Calendar:** Semester, limited summer session. **Microcomputers:** Located in classrooms, computer centers. **Additional facts:** Branch campuses at Marshfield and Stevens Point; outreach center at Adams.

DEGREES OFFERED. AS, AAS. 238 associate degrees awarded in 1992. 50% in business/office and marketing/distribution, 40% engineering technologies, 8% allied health.

UNDERGRADUATE MAJORS. Accounting, business and office, business data processing and related programs, civil technology, computer servicing technology, computer technology, criminal justice technology, data processing, electrical and electronics equipment repair, electronic technology, food production/management/services, hotel/motel and restaurant management, instrumentation technology, law enforcement and corrections technologies, manufacturing technology, marketing and distribution, marketing management, mechanical design technology, personnel management, power plant operation and maintenance, quality control technology, respiratory therapy, respiratory therapy technology, retailing, secretarial and related programs, trade and industrial supervision and management.

ACADEMIC PROGRAMS. Double major, dual enrollment of high school students, independent study, internships. **Remedial services:** Learning center, preadmission summer program, reduced course load, remedial instruction, special counselor, tutoring. **Placement/credit:** Institutional tests; 32 credit hours maximum for associate degree.

ACADEMIC REQUIREMENTS. Freshmen must earn minimum GPA of 1.5 to continue in good standing. 65% of freshmen return for sophomore year. Students must declare major on application. **Graduation requirements:** 64 hours for associate (46 in major). Most students required to take courses in English, mathematics, social sciences.

FRESHMAN ADMISSIONS. Selection criteria: High school record, test scores, and interview. Algebra recommended for applicants to electronic technology, computer technology, and business data processing programs. Algebra, chemistry, and physics required for respiratory therapist program. **Test requirements:** ASSET required of all applicants for counseling. SAT or ACT scores also considered for placement. Score report by August 20.

1992 FRESHMAN CLASS PROFILE. 830 men, 1,287 women enrolled. **Characteristics:** 99% from in state, 100% commute, 3% have minority backgrounds. Average age is 23.

FALL-TERM APPLICATIONS. $10 fee. Closing date August 29; priority given to applications received by August 1; applicants notified on a rolling basis. Interview required for health, home economics applicants. Deferred and early admission available.

STUDENT LIFE. Activities: Student government, student newspaper, Vocational Industrial Clubs of America, Office Education Association, Distributive Education Clubs of America, Health Occupations Club, veterans club.

ATHLETICS. NJCAA. **Intercollegiate:** Basketball M, bowling, golf M, tennis, volleyball W. **Intramural:** Basketball, bowling, golf, skiing, softball, tennis, volleyball.

STUDENT SERVICES. Aptitude testing, career counseling, employment service for undergraduates, freshman orientation, health services, on-campus day care, personal counseling, placement service for graduates, special needs services coordinator, services/facilities for handicapped.

ANNUAL EXPENSES. Tuition and fees: $1,440, $8,760 additional for out-of-state students. **Books and supplies:** $643. **Other expenses:** $464.

FINANCIAL AID. 65% of freshmen, 65% of continuing students receive some form of aid. 96% of grants, 97% of loans, all jobs based on need. Academic, leadership scholarships available. **Aid applications:** No closing date; priority given to applications received by May 1; applicants notified on a rolling basis beginning on or about June 1; must reply within 2 weeks.

ADDRESS/TELEPHONE. Thomas Liska, Administrative Student Services, Mid-State Technical College, 500 32nd Street North, Wisconsin Rapids, WI 54494. (715) 422-5500.

Milwaukee Area Technical College
Milwaukee, Wisconsin CB code: 1475

2-year public technical college, coed. Founded in 1912. **Accreditation:** Regional. **Undergraduate enrollment:** 33,000 men and women. **Location:** Urban campus in very large city. **Calendar:** Semester. **Additional facts:** Multi-location institution with campuses in suburban Oak Creek, Mequon, and West Allis.

FRESHMAN ADMISSIONS. Selection criteria: Satisfactory performance on ASSET test, or SAT test score of 850, or ACT test score of 20.

ANNUAL EXPENSES. Tuition and fees: $1,440, $8,760 additional for out-of-state students. Fees vary by program. **Books and supplies:** $600. **Other expenses:** $1,018.

ADDRESS/TELEPHONE. Dr. Diane Eddins, Director of Admissions, Milwaukee Area Technical College, 700 West State Street, Milwaukee, WI 53233. (414) 278-6220.

Milwaukee College of Business
Milwaukee, Wisconsin CB code: 1539

2-year private business college, coed. Founded in 1945. **Undergraduate enrollment:** 51 men, 308 women full time. **Faculty:** 25 total (1 full time). **Location:** Urban campus in very large city. **Calendar:** Quarter, extensive summer session. **Microcomputers:** 25 located in computer centers.

DEGREES OFFERED. AAS. 20 associate degrees awarded in 1992.

UNDERGRADUATE MAJORS. Accounting, business administration and management, business and management, fashion merchandising, interior design, legal secretary, medical secretary, secretarial and related programs, tourism, word processing.

ACADEMIC PROGRAMS. Internships. **Remedial services:** Tutoring.

ACADEMIC REQUIREMENTS. Freshmen must earn minimum GPA of 2.0 to continue in good standing. **Graduation requirements:** Most students required to take courses in English, mathematics.

FRESHMAN ADMISSIONS. Selection criteria: Open admissions. **Test requirements:** ASSET test used for placement only.

1992 FRESHMAN CLASS PROFILE. 140 men and women enrolled. **Characteristics:** 95% from in state, 100% commute, 60% have minority backgrounds, 10% join fraternities/sororities. Average age is 22.

FALL-TERM APPLICATIONS. No fee. Closing date September 15; applicants notified on a rolling basis; must reply by registration. Interview recommended. Deferred and early admission available.

STUDENT LIFE. Housing: Housing assistance, roommate assistance program. **Activities:** Student newspaper, social/cultural club.

STUDENT SERVICES. Career counseling, employment service for undergraduates, freshman orientation, personal counseling, placement service for graduates, services/facilities for handicapped.

ANNUAL EXPENSES. Tuition and fees (1992-93): $6,075. Books and materials included in tuition.

FINANCIAL AID. All grants, 78% of loans, all jobs based on need. **Aid applications:** No closing date; priority given to applications received by June 1; applicants notified on a rolling basis beginning on or about June 1; must reply immediately.

ADDRESS/TELEPHONE. Mary Jo Boyette, Vice President Administrative Services, Milwaukee College of Business, 161 West Wisconsin Avenue, Milwaukee, WI 53203. (414) 272-4736. (800) 767-7722. Fax: (414) 272-8322.

Milwaukee Institute of Art & Design
Milwaukee, Wisconsin CB code: 1506

Admissions:	57% of applicants accepted
Based on:	••• Interview, special talents
	•• Recommendations, school record
	• Activities, essay, test scores
Completion:	82% of freshmen end year in good standing
	55% graduate, 3% of these enter graduate study

4-year private art college, coed. Founded in 1974. **Accreditation:** Regional. **Undergraduate enrollment:** 256 men, 179 women full time; 39 men, 47 women part time. **Faculty:** 78 total (25 full time), 36 with doctorates or other terminal degrees. **Location:** Urban campus in very large city; 90 miles from Chicago. **Calendar:** Semester, limited summer session. **Microcomputers:** 20 located in classrooms, computer centers. **Special facilities:** Computer graphics center, Frederick Layton Art Gallery, Brooks Stevens Design Center.

DEGREES OFFERED. BFA. 81 bachelor's degrees awarded in 1992. 98% in visual and performing arts.

UNDERGRADUATE MAJORS. Drawing, graphic design, illustration design, industrial design, interior design, painting, photography, printmaking, sculpture.

ACADEMIC PROGRAMS. Cooperative education, double major, dual enrollment of high school students, independent study, internships, study abroad, visiting/exchange student program, New York semester, cross-registration. **Remedial services:** Reduced course load, remedial instruction, tutoring. **Placement/credit:** AP, institutional tests.

ACADEMIC REQUIREMENTS. Freshmen must earn minimum GPA of 2.0 to continue in good standing. 87% of freshmen return for sophomore year. Students must declare major by end of first year. **Graduation requirements:** 123 hours for bachelor's. Most students required to take courses in arts/fine arts, English, history, humanities, mathematics, philosophy/religion, biological/physical sciences, social sciences.

FRESHMAN ADMISSIONS. Selection criteria: Portfolio and interview most important. Must have 3.0 GPA in high school art class. 4 years high school art study recommended. **Additional information:** Conditional acceptance for applicants whose portfolios do not meet admission standards with approval of admissions director.

1992 FRESHMAN CLASS PROFILE. 206 men applied, 134 accepted, 88 enrolled; 157 women applied, 72 accepted, 54 enrolled. **Characteristics:** 80% from in state, 100% commute, 13% have minority backgrounds, 1% are foreign students. Average age is 19.

FALL-TERM APPLICATIONS. $25 fee, may be waived for applicants with need. No closing date; priority given to applications received by April 1; applicants notified on a rolling basis. Interview required. Portfolio required. Essay recommended. Interview required, may be waived for all applicants living at great distance. CRDA. Deferred admission available.

STUDENT LIFE. Housing: Dormitory facilities available nearby in apartments and at St. Catherine's Residence for Women. **Activities:** Student government, magazine, student newspaper, yearbook, Industrial Design Society of America, American Society of Interior Design Student Chapter.

STUDENT SERVICES. Career counseling, employment service for undergraduates, freshman orientation, personal counseling, placement service for graduates, veterans counselor, services/facilities for handicapped.

ANNUAL EXPENSES. Tuition and fees (1992-93): $8,410. **Books and supplies:** $1,000. **Other expenses:** $1,080.

FINANCIAL AID. 65% of freshmen, 67% of continuing students receive some form of aid. 90% of grants, 85% of loans, 53% of jobs based on need. 73 enrolled freshmen were judged to have need, all were offered aid. Art, minority scholarships available. **Aid applications:** No closing date; priority given to applications received by March 1; applicants notified on a rolling basis beginning on or about March 1; must reply within 3 weeks.

ADDRESS/TELEPHONE. Holly Grey, Director of Admissions, Milwaukee Institute of Art & Design, 273 East Erie Street, Milwaukee, WI 53202. (414) 276-7889. Fax: (414) 291-8077.

Milwaukee School of Engineering
Milwaukee, Wisconsin CB code: 1476

4-year private business, engineering college, coed. Founded in 1903. **Accreditation:** Regional. **Undergraduate enrollment:** 1,649 men, 274 women full time; 247 men, 101 women part time. **Graduate enrollment:** 351 men, 41 women part time. **Faculty:** 199 total (106 full time), 54 with doctorates or other terminal degrees. **Location:** Urban campus in very large city. **Calendar:** Quarter, extensive summer session. **Microcomputers:** Located in dormitories, libraries, classrooms, computer centers. **Special facilities:** Robotics laboratory, CAD/CAM system, fluid power applied technology and biomedical research facilities, energy systems laboratory, rapid prototyping laboratory, Micro UAX 3100 computer workstations.

DEGREES OFFERED. AAS, BA, BS, MS. 304 bachelor's degrees awarded. Graduate degrees offered in 1 major field of study.

UNDERGRADUATE MAJORS. Associate: Electrical technology, mechanical engineering. **Bachelor's:** Architectural engineering, bioengineering and biomedical engineering, business administration and management, computer engineering, electrical technology, electrical/electronics/communications engineering, industrial engineering, manufacturing technology, mechanical engineering, mechanical technology, technical communication, trade and industrial supervision and management.

ACADEMIC PROGRAMS. Double major, internships; liberal arts/career combination in engineering. **Remedial services:** Learning center, preadmission summer program, reduced course load, special counselor, tutoring. **ROTC:** Air Force, Army. **Placement/credit:** AP, CLEP Subject, institutional tests.

ACADEMIC REQUIREMENTS. Freshmen must earn minimum GPA of 2.0 to continue in good standing. 75% of freshmen return for sophomore year. Students must declare major on application. **Graduation requirements:** 203 hours for bachelor's (169 in major). Most students required to take courses in computer science, English, humanities, mathematics, biological/physical sciences, social sciences.

FRESHMAN ADMISSIONS. Selection criteria: Achievement record in mathematics, science, and English very important. Interview recommended. Interests and aptitudes as indicated by test scores also considered. **High school preparation:** 15 units required. Required and recommended units include English 4, mathematics 3-4, social science 1 and science 2-4. Foreign language 2 recommended. For business and technical communications, mathematics units should include 1 algebra, 1 geometry; for biomedical engineering, science units should include 1 biological science. **Test requirements:** SAT or ACT (ACT preferred); score report by September 6.

1992 FRESHMAN CLASS PROFILE. 93% had high school GPA of 3.0 or higher, 7% between 2.0 and 2.99. **Academic background:** Mid 50% of enrolled freshmen had SAT-V between 400-540, SAT-M between 500-640; ACT composite between 22-27. 21% submitted SAT scores, 92% submitted ACT scores. **Characteristics:** 80% from in state, 82% live in college housing, 6% have minority backgrounds, 2% are foreign students, 7% join fraternities/sororities. Average age is 18.

FALL-TERM APPLICATIONS. $15 fee, may be waived for applicants with need. No closing date; applicants notified on a rolling basis; must reply by May 1 or within 15 days if notified thereafter. Interview recommended. Deferred admission available.

STUDENT LIFE. Housing: Dormitories (coed); apartment, fraternity housing available. **Activities:** Student government, radio, student newspaper, yearbook, educational (FM) and amateur radio, drama, pep band, fraternities, sororities, Inter-Varsity Christian Fellowship, residence hall association, Circle-K, Society of International Students, Asian Student Organization, Campus Crusade for Christ, Society of Hispanic Professional Engineers, Society of Black Engineers.

ATHLETICS. NAIA. **Intercollegiate:** Baseball M, basketball, cross-country, golf M, ice hockey M, soccer M, softball W, volleyball W, wrestling M. **Intramural:** Basketball, fencing, ice hockey M, rowing (crew), sailing, skiing, softball, volleyball.

STUDENT SERVICES. Aptitude testing, career counseling, employment service for undergraduates, freshman orientation, health services, personal counseling, placement service for graduates, special adviser for adult students, veterans counselor, mentor program for 1st year students, services/facilities for handicapped.

ANNUAL EXPENSES. Tuition and fees: $10,800. **Room and board:** $3,480. **Books and supplies:** $1,000. **Other expenses:** $1,145.

FINANCIAL AID. 85% of freshmen, 80% of continuing students receive some form of aid. 44% of grants, 99% of loans, all jobs based on need. 375 enrolled freshmen were judged to have need, all were offered aid. Academic, leadership, alumni affiliation, minority scholarships available. **Aid applications:** No closing date; priority given to applications received by April 1; applicants notified on a rolling basis; must reply within 4 weeks.

ADDRESS/TELEPHONE. Owen Smith, Dean of Admissions, Milwaukee School of Engineering, 1025 North Milwaukee Street, Milwaukee, WI 53201-0644. (414) 277-7200. (800) 322-6763. Fax: (414) 277-7475.

Moraine Park Technical College

Fond du Lac, Wisconsin — CB code: 0667

2-year public technical college, coed. Founded in 1967. **Accreditation:** Regional. **Undergraduate enrollment:** 486 men, 693 women full time; 1,802 men, 2,855 women part time. **Faculty:** 139 total, 3 with doctorates or other terminal degrees. **Location:** Urban campus in large town; 60 miles from Milwaukee. **Calendar:** Semester, limited summer session. Saturday and extensive evening/early morning classes. **Microcomputers:** Located in classrooms, computer centers. **Additional facts:** Campuses at Beaver Dam and West Bend.

DEGREES OFFERED. AS, AAS. 500 associate degrees awarded in 1992. 6% in business and management, 36% business/office and marketing/distribution, 9% computer sciences, 27% engineering technologies, 10% health sciences, 8% parks/recreation, protective services, public affairs.

UNDERGRADUATE MAJORS. Accounting, air conditioning/heating/refrigeration technology, business data processing and related programs, business data programming, business systems analysis, child development/care/guidance, civil technology, computer programming, computer servicing technology, drafting, electrical and electronics equipment repair, electromechanical technology, engineering and engineering-related technologies, food production/management/services, food sciences, industrial technology, law enforcement and corrections technologies, legal secretary, manufacturing technology, marketing and distribution, mechanical design technology, medical records technology, medical secretary, nursing, office supervision and management, practical nursing, secretarial and related programs, trade and industrial supervision and management, water and wastewater technology, word processing.

ACADEMIC PROGRAMS. Double major, dual enrollment of high school students, independent study, internships. **Remedial services:** Learning center, preadmission summer program, reduced course load, remedial instruction, special counselor, tutoring. **Placement/credit:** CLEP General and Subject, institutional tests; 30 credit hours maximum for associate degree.

ACADEMIC REQUIREMENTS. Freshmen must earn minimum GPA of 2.0 to continue in good standing. Students must declare major on application. **Graduation requirements:** 64 hours for associate (36 in major). Most students required to take courses in English, social sciences.

FRESHMAN ADMISSIONS. Selection criteria: Open admissions. Selective admission to some programs. **High school preparation:** 16 units recommended. Recommended units include biological science 1, English 3, mathematics 2, physical science 1 and social science 2. **Test requirements:** ACT required of nursing applicants.

1992 FRESHMAN CLASS PROFILE. 368 men, 488 women enrolled. **Characteristics:** 100% from in state, 100% commute. Average age is 34.

FALL-TERM APPLICATIONS. $20 fee. Closing date August 25; priority given to applications received by May 1; applicants notified on a rolling basis. Interview required. Deferred and early admission available.

STUDENT LIFE. Activities: Student government.

ATHLETICS. Intercollegiate: Golf. **Intramural:** Basketball, bowling, softball, table tennis, volleyball.

STUDENT SERVICES. Aptitude testing, career counseling, employment service for undergraduates, freshman orientation, health services, on-campus day care, personal counseling, placement service for graduates, veterans counselor, services/facilities for handicapped.

ANNUAL EXPENSES. Tuition and fees: $1,440, $8,760 additional for out-of-state students. **Books and supplies:** $643. **Other expenses:** $1,091.

FINANCIAL AID. 40% of freshmen, 40% of continuing students receive some form of aid. 98% of grants, 93% of loans, 68% of jobs based on need. 600 enrolled freshmen were judged to have need, all were offered aid. Academic, leadership scholarships available. **Aid applications:** No closing date; priority given to applications received by May 1; applicants notified on a rolling basis beginning on or about June 15; must reply within 2 weeks.

ADDRESS/TELEPHONE. Larry Pasquini, Dean, Student Services, Moraine Park Technical College, 235 North National Avenue, Fond du Lac, WI 54935. (414) 922-8611. (800) 221-6430. Fax: (414) 929-2471.

Mount Mary College

Milwaukee, Wisconsin — CB code: 1490

Admissions: 90% of applicants accepted
Based on:
••• School record, test scores
•• Interview, recommendations
• Activities
Completion: 85% of freshmen end year in good standing
50% graduate, 6% of these enter graduate study

4-year private liberal arts college, women only, affiliated with Roman Catholic Church. Founded in 1913. **Accreditation:** Regional. **Undergraduate enrollment:** 909 women full time; 526 women part time. **Graduate enrollment:** 17 women full time; 74 women part time. **Faculty:** 155 total (78 full time), 47 with doctorates or other terminal degrees. **Location:** Suburban campus in very large city; 7 miles from Milwaukee. **Calendar:** Semester, limited summer session. **Microcomputers:** 52 located in classrooms, computer centers. **Special facilities:** Art gallery. **Additional facts:** Institution with Catholic tradition. Open to all faiths. Small number of men admitted as part-time students.

DEGREES OFFERED. BA, BS, MA, MS. 269 bachelor's degrees awarded in 1992. 26% in business and management, 15% teacher education, 18% allied health, 6% social sciences, 16% visual and performing arts. Graduate degrees offered in 3 major fields of study.

UNDERGRADUATE MAJORS. Accounting, art education, art therapy, behavioral sciences, bilingual/bicultural education, biological laboratory technology, biology, business administration and management, business and management, business education, chemistry, communications, computer and information sciences, early childhood education, elementary education, English, English education, fashion design, fashion merchandising, fine arts, food science and nutrition, foreign languages education, French, German, graphic design, history, home economics, home economics education, hotel/motel and restaurant management, interior design, junior high education, mathematics, mathematics education, music, music education, occupational therapy, philosophy, predentistry, prelaw, premedicine, preveterinary, public relations, religion, religious education, science education, secondary education, social studies education, social work, Spanish, theological studies.

ACADEMIC PROGRAMS. Accelerated program, double major, dual enrollment of high school students, honors program, independent study, internships, student-designed major, study abroad, teacher preparation, Washington semester. **Remedial services:** Learning center, reduced course load, remedial instruction, special counselor, tutoring, peer counseling. **Placement/credit:** AP, CLEP General and Subject, institutional tests; 16 credit hours maximum for bachelor's degree.

ACADEMIC REQUIREMENTS. Freshmen must earn minimum GPA of 2.0 to continue in good standing. 80% of freshmen return for sophomore year. Students must declare major by end of first year. **Graduation requirements:** 128 hours for bachelor's (24 in major). Most students required to take courses in arts/fine arts, computer science, English, history, mathematics, philosophy/religion, biological/physical sciences, social sciences. **Postgraduate studies:** 6% enter other graduate study.

FRESHMAN ADMISSIONS. Selection criteria: Rank in top half of class, school achievement record, test scores, interview, recommendations, and activities important. **High school preparation:** 15 units required. Required and recommended units include English 3-4, mathematics 2-3 and science 2. Foreign language 2 and social science 2 recommended. 4 units from history, science, or foreign language also required. **Test requirements:** SAT or ACT; score report by August 15.

1992 FRESHMAN CLASS PROFILE. 212 women applied, 190 accepted, 124 enrolled. 38% had high school GPA of 3.0 or higher, 52% between 2.0 and 2.99. **Academic background:** Mid 50% of enrolled freshmen had ACT composite between 17-22. 82% submitted ACT scores. **Characteristics:** 88% from in state, 60% commute, 12% have minority backgrounds, 1% are foreign students. Average age is 18.

FALL-TERM APPLICATIONS. $15 fee, may be waived for applicants with need. Closing date August 15; applicants notified on a rolling basis. Interview required for academically weak applicants. CRDA. Deferred and early admission available.

STUDENT LIFE. Housing: Dormitories (women). **Activities:** Student government, magazine, student newspaper, yearbook, choral groups, dance, drama, music ensembles, pep band, campus ministry, Women of Color Alliance.

ATHLETICS. Intercollegiate: Cross-country, tennis, volleyball. **Intramural:** Archery, badminton, basketball, bowling, skiing, soccer, softball, swimming, table tennis, tennis, volleyball.

STUDENT SERVICES. Career counseling, employment service for undergraduates, freshman orientation, health services, on-campus day care, personal counseling, special adviser for adult students, services/facilities for handicapped.

ANNUAL EXPENSES. Tuition and fees: $8,100. **Room and board:** $2,868. **Books and supplies:** $500. **Other expenses:** $1,125.

FINANCIAL AID. 93% of freshmen, 80% of continuing students receive some form of aid. 98% of grants, 84% of loans, 82% of jobs based on need. 72 enrolled freshmen were judged to have need, all were offered aid.

Academic, music/drama, art, leadership, alumni affiliation scholarships available. **Aid applications:** No closing date; priority given to applications received by March 15; applicants notified on a rolling basis beginning on or about March 1; must reply by June 1 or within 4 weeks if notified thereafter. **Additional information:** Individual budgeting and counseling service.

ADDRESS/TELEPHONE. Mary Jane Reilly, Director of Admissions, Mount Mary College, 2900 North Menomonee River Parkway, Milwaukee, WI 53222-4597. (414) 259-9220. (800) 351-6265. Fax: (414) 256-1205.

Mount Senario College
Ladysmith, Wisconsin — CB code: 1512

Admissions: 70% of applicants accepted
Based on:
••• Recommendations, school record, test scores
•• Activities, interview, special talents
• Essay
Completion: 58% of freshmen end year in good standing
15% enter graduate study

4-year private liberal arts college, coed. Founded in 1962. **Accreditation:** Regional. **Undergraduate enrollment:** 493 men and women full time; 506 men and women part time. **Faculty:** 61 total (30 full time), 23 with doctorates or other terminal degrees. **Location:** Rural campus in small town; 123 miles from Minneapolis-St. Paul, 60 miles from Eau Claire. **Calendar:** Semester, limited summer session. **Microcomputers:** 36 located in computer centers. **Special facilities:** Art gallery.

DEGREES OFFERED. AA, BA, BS, BFA. 33 associate degrees awarded in 1992. 123 bachelor's degrees awarded.

UNDERGRADUATE MAJORS. Associate: Law enforcement and corrections technologies. **Bachelor's:** Accounting, art education, biological and physical sciences, biology, business administration and management, business and management, business economics, criminal justice studies, criminology, early childhood education, education, elementary education, English, English education, fine arts, forestry and related sciences, graphic design, history, humanities, junior high education, law enforcement and corrections, liberal/general studies, mathematics, mathematics education, music, music education, prelaw, psychology, science education, secondary education, social science education, social sciences, social studies education, social work, studio art, visual and performing arts.

ACADEMIC PROGRAMS. 2-year transfer program, cooperative education, double major, external degree, honors program, independent study, internships, student-designed major, study abroad, weekend college; liberal arts/career combination in forestry. **Remedial services:** Learning center, reduced course load, remedial instruction, special counselor, tutoring. **Placement/credit:** AP, CLEP General and Subject, institutional tests.

ACADEMIC REQUIREMENTS. Freshmen must earn minimum GPA of 1.6 to continue in good standing. Students must declare major by end of second year. **Graduation requirements:** 64 hours for associate (20 in major), 128 hours for bachelor's (40 in major). Most students required to take courses in arts/fine arts, English, history, mathematics, philosophy/religion, biological/physical sciences, social sciences.

FRESHMAN ADMISSIONS. Selection criteria: Ability to profit from academic program and interest in contributing to college community important. **High school preparation:** 16 units recommended. Recommended units include English 4 and mathematics 2. **Test requirements:** SAT or ACT (ACT preferred); score report by August 30.

1992 FRESHMAN CLASS PROFILE. 425 men and women applied, 299 accepted; 182 enrolled. **Academic background:** Mid 50% of enrolled freshmen had ACT composite between 14-19. 76% submitted ACT scores. **Characteristics:** 76% from in state, 59% live in college housing, 27% have minority backgrounds, 3% are foreign students. Average age is 20.

FALL-TERM APPLICATIONS. $10 fee, may be waived for applicants with need. Closing date August 1; applicants notified on a rolling basis. Interview required for learning disabled applicants. Audition recommended for music applicants. Portfolio recommended for art applicants. CRDA. Deferred and early admission available.

STUDENT LIFE. Housing: Dormitories (coed). Freshmen and sophomores required to live in residence hall. **Activities:** Student government, student newspaper, yearbook, choral groups, dance, drama.

ATHLETICS. NSCAA. **Intercollegiate:** Baseball M, basketball, football M, softball W, volleyball W. **Intramural:** Baseball M, basketball, skiing, soccer M, softball, volleyball. **Clubs:** Several sports clubs.

STUDENT SERVICES. Aptitude testing, career counseling, employment service for undergraduates, freshman orientation, health services, personal counseling, placement service for graduates, services/facilities for handicapped.

ANNUAL EXPENSES. Tuition and fees: $7,720. **Room and board:** $3,250. **Books and supplies:** $600. **Other expenses:** $1,350.

FINANCIAL AID. 93% of freshmen, 92% of continuing students receive some form of aid. 92% of grants, 82% of loans, 95% of jobs based on need. 95 enrolled freshmen were judged to have need, 93 were offered aid. Academic, state/district residency, alumni affiliation scholarships available. **Aid applications:** No closing date; priority given to applications received by April 1; applicants notified on a rolling basis beginning on or about July 1; must reply by May 1 or within 3 weeks if notified thereafter.

ADDRESS/TELEPHONE. Dewey Floberg, Director of Admissions, Mount Senario College, College Avenue West, Ladysmith, WI 54848. (715) 532-5511 ext. 322. Fax: (715) 532-7690.

Nicolet Area Technical College
Rhinelander, Wisconsin — CB code: 0713

2-year public community, technical college, coed. Founded in 1967. **Accreditation:** Regional. **Undergraduate enrollment:** 242 men, 330 women full time; 327 men, 802 women part time. **Faculty:** 75 total (57 full time), 7 with doctorates or other terminal degrees. **Location:** Rural campus in small town; 240 miles from Milwaukee. **Calendar:** Semester, limited summer session. Extensive evening/early morning classes. **Microcomputers:** 80 located in libraries, classrooms, computer centers. **Special facilities:** Art gallery, hiking trails, weight room, theater. **Additional facts:** Lakeland Branch Campus located in Minocqua, Wisconsin.

DEGREES OFFERED. AA, AS. 75 associate degrees awarded in 1992. 19% in business and management, 37% business/office and marketing/distribution, 17% computer sciences, 8% engineering technologies, 19% multi/interdisciplinary studies.

UNDERGRADUATE MAJORS. Accounting, business and management, business data processing and related programs, business data programming, child development/care/guidance, data processing, hospitality and recreation marketing, hotel/motel and restaurant management, law enforcement and corrections technologies, legal secretary, liberal/general studies, marketing and distribution, medical secretary, nursing, secretarial and related programs, survey and mapping technology, surveying and mapping sciences, trade and industrial supervision and management, word processing.

ACADEMIC PROGRAMS. 2-year transfer program, dual enrollment of high school students, independent study, internships, student-designed major. **Remedial services:** Learning center, reduced course load, remedial instruction, tutoring. **Placement/credit:** AP, CLEP General and Subject, institutional tests; 44 credit hours maximum for associate degree.

ACADEMIC REQUIREMENTS. No policy requiring minimum GPA; records of students having academic difficulty are reviewed individually. 65% of freshmen return for sophomore year. Students must declare major on application. **Graduation requirements:** 64 hours for associate (43 in major). Most students required to take courses in English, history, humanities, mathematics, biological/physical sciences, social sciences.

FRESHMAN ADMISSIONS. Selection criteria: Open admissions. Selective admissions to some programs.

1992 FRESHMAN CLASS PROFILE. 282 men applied, 282 accepted, 282 enrolled; 384 women applied, 384 accepted, 384 enrolled. **Characteristics:** 99% from in state, 100% commute, 4% have minority backgrounds. Average age is 28.

FALL-TERM APPLICATIONS. No fee. No closing date; applicants notified on a rolling basis. Interview recommended.

STUDENT LIFE. Activities: Student government, student newspaper, choral groups, drama.

ATHLETICS. Intramural: Archery, basketball, bowling, golf, racquetball, skiing, softball, table tennis, tennis, volleyball.

STUDENT SERVICES. Aptitude testing, career counseling, employment service for undergraduates, freshman orientation, on-campus day care, personal counseling, placement service for graduates, veterans counselor, services/facilities for handicapped.

ANNUAL EXPENSES. Tuition and fees: $1,440, $8,760 additional for out-of-state students. **Books and supplies:** $660. **Other expenses:** $1,092.

FINANCIAL AID. 75% of freshmen, 75% of continuing students receive some form of aid. 98% of grants, 88% of loans, 93% of jobs based on need. Academic, state/district residency, leadership, minority scholarships available. **Aid applications:** No closing date; priority given to applications received by April 15; applicants notified on a rolling basis beginning on or about June 1; must reply within 2 weeks.

ADDRESS/TELEPHONE. Susan Kordula, Director of Admissions, Nicolet Area Technical College, PO Box 518, Rhinelander, WI 54501. (715) 365-4451. (800) 544-3039. Fax: (715) 365-4445.

Northcentral Technical College
Wausau, Wisconsin — CB code: 0735

2-year public technical college, coed. Founded in 1911. **Accreditation:** Regional. **Undergraduate enrollment:** 6,526 men and women. **Faculty:** 224 total (144 full time), 1 with doctorate or other terminal degree. **Location:** Suburban campus in large town; 200 miles from Milwaukee. **Calendar:** Semester, limited summer session. **Microcomputers:** 80 located in libraries, computer centers. **Special facilities:** Laser laboratory. **Additional facts:** Branch campuses located in Antigo, Medford, Phillips, and Wittenberg.

DEGREES OFFERED. AAS. 438 associate degrees awarded in 1992. 8% in architecture and environmental design, 12% business and management, 18% business/office and marketing/distribution, 5% computer sciences, 23% engineering technologies, 13% health sciences, 8% allied health, 6% parks/recreation, protective services, public affairs.

UNDERGRADUATE MAJORS. Accounting, agricultural mechanics, architecture, automotive technology, data processing, dental hygiene, electromechanical technology, engineering and engineering-related technologies, finance, industrial technology, insurance and risk management, insurance marketing, interpreter for the deaf, laser electro-optic technology, law enforcement and corrections technologies, legal secretary, marketing and distribution, mechanical design technology, medical secretary, nursing, radiograph medical technology, secretarial and related programs, small business management and ownership, surgical technology, trade and industrial supervision and management.

ACADEMIC PROGRAMS. Telecourses. **Remedial services:** Learning center, preadmission summer program, reduced course load, remedial instruction, special counselor, tutoring. **Placement/credit:** CLEP Subject, institutional tests; 24 credit hours maximum for associate degree.

ACADEMIC REQUIREMENTS. Freshmen must earn minimum GPA of 2.0 to continue in good standing. Students must declare major on application. **Graduation requirements:** 64 hours for associate (40 in major). Most students required to take courses in English, mathematics, social sciences.

FRESHMAN ADMISSIONS. Selection criteria: Open admissions. Selective admissions to specific programs with limited enrollment. Mathematics emphasis for technical programs, chemistry for nursing.

1992 FRESHMAN CLASS PROFILE. 1,700 men and women enrolled. **Characteristics:** 99% from in state, 70% commute, 4% have minority backgrounds. Average age is 22.

FALL-TERM APPLICATIONS. $20 fee. No closing date; applicants notified on a rolling basis beginning on or about October 15; must reply within 2 weeks. Interview required for health occupations applicants. Early admission available.

STUDENT LIFE. Housing: Dormitories (coed); apartment housing available. **Activities:** Student government, student newspaper, career clubs.

ATHLETICS. Intramural: Basketball, bowling, football, golf, racquetball, softball, table tennis, volleyball.

STUDENT SERVICES. Aptitude testing, career counseling, employment service for undergraduates, freshman orientation, health services, personal counseling, placement service for graduates, services/facilities for handicapped.

ANNUAL EXPENSES. Tuition and fees: $1,440, $8,760 additional for out-of-state students. **Room and board:** $3,500. **Books and supplies:** $600. **Other expenses:** $1,200.

FINANCIAL AID. 66% of freshmen, 66% of continuing students receive some form of aid. Grants, loans, jobs available. **Aid applications:** No closing date; priority given to applications received by April 1; applicants notified on a rolling basis beginning on or about June 15; must reply within 2 weeks.

ADDRESS/TELEPHONE. Thomas Goltz, Dean, Student Services, Northcentral Technical College, 1000 Campus Drive, Wausau, WI 54401. (715) 675-3331. Fax: (715)675-9776.

Northeast Wisconsin Technical College
Green Bay, Wisconsin — CB code: 4190

2-year public technical college, coed. Founded in 1913. **Accreditation:** Regional. **Undergraduate enrollment:** 1,115 men, 1,134 women full time; 2,832 men, 4,444 women part time. **Faculty:** 206 total. **Location:** Suburban campus in small city; 129 miles from Milwaukee, 150 miles from Madison. **Calendar:** Semester. **Microcomputers:** Located in libraries, classrooms, computer centers.

DEGREES OFFERED. AAS. 630 associate degrees awarded in 1992.

UNDERGRADUATE MAJORS. Accounting, agricultural business and management, air conditioning/heating/refrigeration technology, architectural industrial model building, architectural technologies, architecture, automotive mechanics, automotive technology, business administration and management, business and management, business data processing and related programs, civil engineering, data processing, dental hygiene, drafting, electromechanical technology, electronic technology, engineering management, fashion merchandising, finance, fire control and safety technology, food sciences, industrial equipment maintenance and repair, instrumentation technology, law enforcement and corrections technologies, legal assistant/paralegal, legal secretary, machine tool operation/machine shop, manufacturing technology, marketing and distribution, marketing communication, marketing management, mechanical design technology, medical records administration, medical secretary, microcomputer software, nursing, office supervision and management, physical therapy assistant, quality control technology, respiratory therapy, retailing, secretarial and related programs, transportation management.

ACADEMIC PROGRAMS. Double major, internships, telecourses. **Remedial services:** Learning center, reduced course load, remedial instruction, special counselor, tutoring. **Placement/credit:** Institutional tests; 48 credit hours maximum for associate degree.

ACADEMIC REQUIREMENTS. No policy requiring minimum GPA; records of students having academic difficulty are reviewed individually. Students must declare major on application. **Graduation requirements:** 64 hours for associate (64 in major). Most students required to take courses in English, mathematics, social sciences.

FRESHMAN ADMISSIONS. Selection criteria: Open admissions. Selective admissions for some programs. **Test requirements:** ACT required for health occupations programs.

1992 FRESHMAN CLASS PROFILE. 538 men, 516 women enrolled. **Characteristics:** 99% from in state, 100% commute, 2% have minority backgrounds. Average age is 19.

FALL-TERM APPLICATIONS. $10 fee. No closing date; applicants notified on a rolling basis; must reply within 2 weeks. Interview recommended.

STUDENT LIFE. Activities: Student government, student newspaper, television.

STUDENT SERVICES. Aptitude testing, career counseling, employment service for undergraduates, freshman orientation, health services, personal counseling, placement service for graduates, special adviser for adult students, veterans counselor, services/facilities for handicapped.

ANNUAL EXPENSES. Tuition and fees: $1,440, $8,760 additional for out-of-state students. **Books and supplies:** $645. **Other expenses:** $1,091.

FINANCIAL AID. 33% of continuing students receive some form of aid. 99% of grants, 89% of loans, all jobs based on need. Academic scholarships available. **Aid applications:** No closing date; applicants notified on a rolling basis beginning on or about June 1; must reply within 2 weeks.

ADDRESS/TELEPHONE. Henry Wallace, Jr, Dean of Student Services, Northeast Wisconsin Technical College, 2740 West Mason Street, Green Bay, WI 54307-9042. (414) 498-5600.

Northland College
Ashland, Wisconsin — CB code: 1561

Admissions:	89% of applicants accepted
Based on:	••• Recommendations, school record
	•• Test scores
	• Activities, essay, interview
Completion:	76% of freshmen end year in good standing
	42% graduate, 24% of these enter graduate study

4-year private liberal arts college, coed, affiliated with United Church of Christ. Founded in 1892. **Accreditation:** Regional. **Undergraduate enrollment:** 385 men, 351 women full time; 10 men, 27 women part time. **Faculty:** 52 total (42 full time), 29 with doctorates or other terminal degrees. **Location:** Rural campus in small town; 65 miles from Duluth, Minnesota. **Calendar:** 4-4-1, limited summer session. **Microcomputers:** 30 located in dormitories, libraries, classrooms, computer centers. **Special facilities:** Field stations for natural science courses, atmospheric environmental satellite links.

DEGREES OFFERED. BA, BS. 132 bachelor's degrees awarded in 1992. 20% in business and management, 6% teacher education, 27% life sciences, 9% parks/recreation, protective services, public affairs, 5% physical sciences, 14% social sciences, 5% visual and performing arts.

UNDERGRADUATE MAJORS. Accounting, American Indian studies, art education, atmospheric sciences and meteorology, biological and physical sciences, biology, business administration and management, business and management, business economics, business education, chemistry, city/community/regional planning, computer and information sciences, computer programming, creative writing, early childhood education, earth sciences, ecology, economics, education, elementary education, English, English education, English literature, environmental science, fishing and fisheries, forest products processing technology, forestry and related sciences, geology, history, humanities, humanities and social sciences, information sciences and systems, international business management, junior high education, liberal/general studies, marine biology, mathematics, mathematics education, music, music education, occupational therapy, parks and recreation management, peace studies, philosophy, physical sciences, political science and government, predentistry, prelaw, premedicine, prepharmacy, Preprofessional atmospheric sciences, preveterinary, psychology, public policy studies, religion, renewable natural resources, science education, secondary education, social science education, social sciences, social studies education, sociology, soil sciences, Spanish, wildlife management.

ACADEMIC PROGRAMS. Accelerated program, cooperative education, double major, dual enrollment of high school students, honors program, independent study, internships, student-designed major, study abroad, teacher preparation, cross-registration, 3-2 cooperative degree program in natural resources management with University of Michigan; liberal arts/career combination in engineering, forestry. **Remedial services:** Learning center, reduced course load, tutoring. **Placement/credit:** AP, CLEP General and Subject, institutional tests; 28 credit hours maximum for bachelor's degree.

ACADEMIC REQUIREMENTS. Freshmen must earn minimum GPA of 2.0 to continue in good standing. 68% of freshmen return for sophomore year. Students must declare major by end of second year. **Graduation requirements:** 124 hours for bachelor's (40 in major). Most students required

to take courses in arts/fine arts, English, history, humanities, mathematics, philosophy/religion, biological/physical sciences, social sciences. **Postgraduate studies:** 2% enter law school, 2% enter medical school, 2% enter MBA programs, 18% enter other graduate study.

FRESHMAN ADMISSIONS. Selection criteria: Class rank and high school counselor's recommendation most important, test scores secondary. Recommended units include biological science 1, English 4, foreign language 2, mathematics 3, physical science 1 and social science 4. **Test requirements:** SAT or ACT; score report by August 15.

1992 FRESHMAN CLASS PROFILE. 475 men applied, 425 accepted, 96 enrolled; 428 women applied, 380 accepted, 119 enrolled. **Academic background:** Mid 50% of enrolled freshmen had SAT-V between 440-550, SAT-M between 450-570; ACT composite between 21-26. 50% submitted SAT scores, 55% submitted ACT scores. **Characteristics:** 38% from in state, 80% live in college housing, 8% have minority backgrounds, 2% are foreign students, 8% join fraternities/sororities. Average age is 19.

FALL-TERM APPLICATIONS. No fee. Closing date August 15; priority given to applications received by June 1; applicants notified on or about December 15; must reply by May 1 or within 2 weeks if notified thereafter. Interview required for academically weak applicants. Essay required. Audition recommended. Portfolio recommended. CRDA. Deferred and early admission available. EDP-F.

STUDENT LIFE. Housing: Dormitories (men, women, coed); apartment, cooperative housing available. **Activities:** Student government, student newspaper, yearbook, literary magazine, choral groups, concert band, drama, jazz band, music ensembles, symphony orchestra, fraternities, sororities, Native American Council, veterans organization, environmental group, international students association.

ATHLETICS. NAIA, NSCAA. **Intercollegiate:** Baseball M, basketball, skiing, soccer M, softball W, volleyball W. **Intramural:** Archery, badminton, basketball, handball, ice hockey M, racquetball, skiing, soccer, softball, squash, tennis, volleyball, water polo.

STUDENT SERVICES. Aptitude testing, career counseling, employment service for undergraduates, freshman orientation, health services, on-campus day care, personal counseling, placement service for graduates, recreational specialist, services/facilities for handicapped.

ANNUAL EXPENSES. Tuition and fees (1992-93): $9,190. **Room and board:** $3,620. **Books and supplies:** $400. **Other expenses:** $1,000.

FINANCIAL AID. 80% of freshmen, 87% of continuing students receive some form of aid. 96% of grants, 90% of loans, 88% of jobs based on need. Academic, music/drama, athletic scholarships available. **Aid applications:** No closing date; priority given to applications received by May 1; applicants notified on a rolling basis beginning on or about March 1; must reply by May 1 or within 2 weeks if notified thereafter.

ADDRESS/TELEPHONE. James L. Miller, Dean of Student Development/Enrollment, Northland College, Ashland, WI 54806. (715) 682-1224. Fax: (715) 682-1308.

Northwestern College
Watertown, Wisconsin — CB code: 1563

Admissions: 87% of applicants accepted
Based on: ••• Religious affiliation/commitment, school record, test scores
•• Recommendations
• Activities, interview
Completion: 85% of freshmen end year in good standing
73% graduate, 90% of these enter graduate study

4-year private liberal arts, seminary college, men only, affiliated with Wisconsin Evangelical Lutheran Synod. Founded in 1865. **Accreditation:** Regional. **Undergraduate enrollment:** 203 men full time; 2 men part time. **Faculty:** 23 total. **Location:** Rural campus in large town; 45 miles from Milwaukee, 40 miles from Madison. **Calendar:** Semester. **Microcomputers:** 24 located in dormitories, libraries, computer centers.

DEGREES OFFERED. BA. 37 bachelor's degrees awarded in 1992. 100% in multi/interdisciplinary studies.

UNDERGRADUATE MAJORS. Liberal/general studies.

ACADEMIC PROGRAMS. Remedial services: Remedial instruction, tutoring. **Placement/credit:** AP, institutional tests.

ACADEMIC REQUIREMENTS. Freshmen must earn minimum GPA of 1.75 to continue in good standing. 77% of freshmen return for sophomore year. **Graduation requirements:** 134 hours for bachelor's. Most students required to take courses in English, foreign languages, history, mathematics, philosophy/religion, biological/physical sciences, social sciences.

FRESHMAN ADMISSIONS. Selection criteria: School achievement record, test scores, recommendations, and religious commitment most important. **High school preparation:** 22 units required. Required units include biological science 1, English 4, foreign language 5, mathematics 2, physical science 2 and social science 3. Religion and music also required. **Test requirements:** ACT; score report by August 1.

1992 FRESHMAN CLASS PROFILE. 53 men applied, 46 accepted, 42 enrolled. 68% had high school GPA of 3.0 or higher, 27% between 2.0 and 2.99. 19% were in top tenth and 45% were in top quarter of graduating class. **Academic background:** Mid 50% of enrolled freshmen had ACT composite between 22-28. 93% submitted ACT scores. **Characteristics:** 51% from in state, 91% live in college housing. Average age is 19.

FALL-TERM APPLICATIONS. $25 fee. Closing date August 15; priority given to applications received by June 1; applicants notified on a rolling basis.

STUDENT LIFE. Housing: Dormitories (men). **Activities:** Student government, magazine, yearbook, choral groups, concert band, drama, jazz band, music ensembles, pep band.

ATHLETICS. NCAA. **Intercollegiate:** Baseball, basketball, cross-country, football, golf, soccer, tennis, track and field, wrestling. **Intramural:** Basketball, bowling, softball, table tennis, tennis, volleyball.

STUDENT SERVICES. Employment service for undergraduates, freshman orientation, health services, personal counseling, special adviser for adult students.

ANNUAL EXPENSES. Tuition and fees: $3,455. **Room and board:** $1,790. **Books and supplies:** $255. **Other expenses:** $1,270.

FINANCIAL AID. 95% of freshmen, 93% of continuing students receive some form of aid. 80% of grants, all loans, 13% of jobs based on need. 36 enrolled freshmen were judged to have need, 33 were offered aid. Academic, leadership scholarships available. **Aid applications:** No closing date; priority given to applications received by May 1; applicants notified on a rolling basis beginning on or about June 30; must reply before receiving aid.

ADDRESS/TELEPHONE. John Braun, Admissions Officer, Northwestern College, 1300 Western Avenue, Watertown, WI 53094-4899. (414) 261-4352 ext. 20. Fax: (414) 261-8775.

Ripon College
Ripon, Wisconsin — CB code: 1664

Admissions: 84% of applicants accepted
Based on: ••• School record
•• Activities, recommendations, test scores
• Essay, interview, special talents
Completion: 94% of freshmen end year in good standing
75% graduate, 27% of these enter graduate study

4-year private liberal arts college, coed, affiliated with United Church of Christ. Founded in 1851. **Accreditation:** Regional. **Undergraduate enrollment:** 404 men, 400 women full time. **Faculty:** 104 total (75 full time), 82 with doctorates or other terminal degrees. **Location:** Rural campus in small town; 80 miles from Milwaukee, 80 miles from Madison. **Calendar:** Semester. **Microcomputers:** 139 located in dormitories, libraries, classrooms, computer centers. **Special facilities:** Art galleries, woodland preservation area. **Additional facts:** Domestic and international off-campus study programs.

DEGREES OFFERED. BA, BS. 170 bachelor's degrees awarded in 1992. 9% in business and management, 12% languages, 9% letters/literature, 7% life sciences, 8% physical sciences, 11% psychology, 29% social sciences, 8% visual and performing arts.

UNDERGRADUATE MAJORS. Allied health, anthropology, art history, biological and physical sciences, biology, business administration and management, chemistry, clinical laboratory science, communications, computer and information sciences, economics, education, engineering, English, foreign languages (multiple emphasis), forestry and related sciences, French, German, history, international business management, Latin American studies, mathematics, music, nursing, philosophy, physics, political science and government, predentistry, prelaw, premedicine, prepharmacy, preveterinary, psychobiology, psychology, religion, sociology, Spanish, speech, sports medicine, studio art, visual and performing arts.

ACADEMIC PROGRAMS. Accelerated program, double major, dual enrollment of high school students, independent study, internships, student-designed major, study abroad, teacher preparation, visiting/exchange student program, Washington semester; liberal arts/career combination in engineering, forestry, health sciences. **Remedial services:** Learning center, reduced course load, special counselor, tutoring. **ROTC:** Army. **Placement/credit:** AP, institutional tests.

ACADEMIC REQUIREMENTS. Freshmen must earn minimum GPA of 1.8 to continue in good standing. 91% of freshmen return for sophomore year. Students must declare major by end of second year. **Graduation requirements:** 124 hours for bachelor's. Most students required to take courses in arts/fine arts, English, foreign languages, history, humanities, mathematics, biological/physical sciences, social sciences. **Postgraduate studies:** 3% enter law school, 3% enter medical school, 2% enter MBA programs, 19% enter other graduate study.

FRESHMAN ADMISSIONS. Selection criteria: School achievement record, class rank, test scores, recommendations, extracurricular or community activities, interview important. **High school preparation:** 15 units required. Required and recommended units include English 4 and mathematics 2-3. Foreign language 2, social science 3 and science 3 recommended. Mathematics must include 1 algebra and geometry. **Test requirements:** SAT or ACT; score report by March 15.

1992 FRESHMAN CLASS PROFILE. 319 men applied, 245 accepted,

92 enrolled; 310 women applied, 284 accepted, 99 enrolled. 58% had high school GPA of 3.0 or higher, 42% between 2.0 and 2.99. 28% were in top tenth and 55% were in top quarter of graduating class. **Academic background:** Mid 50% of enrolled freshmen had SAT-V between 450-600, SAT-M between 510-630; ACT composite between 21-27. 30% submitted SAT scores, 70% submitted ACT scores. **Characteristics:** 55% from in state, 100% live in college housing, 11% have minority backgrounds, 5% are foreign students. Average age is 18.

FALL-TERM APPLICATIONS. $20 fee, may be waived for applicants with need. No closing date; priority given to applications received by March 15; applicants notified on a rolling basis; must reply by May 1 or within 2 weeks if notified thereafter. Essay required. Interview recommended. CRDA. Deferred and early admission available. EDP-F. Early decision application deadline is December 1; notification by December 15.

STUDENT LIFE. Housing: Dormitories (men, women, coed); fraternity, sorority housing available. **Activities:** Student government, magazine, radio, student newspaper, yearbook, literary journal, choral groups, concert band, dance, drama, jazz band, music ensembles, symphony orchestra, fraternities, sororities, Circle-K, International Club, Christian Fellowship, Women's Educational Support Organization, Big Brother/Big Sister, Multicultural Club, Romance Language Club, Student Faculty Unlimited, Math Modeling Club, environmental group.

ATHLETICS. NCAA. **Intercollegiate:** Baseball M, basketball, cross-country, diving, fencing, football M, golf M, ice hockey M, lacrosse, rifle, rugby M, skiing, soccer, softball W, swimming, tennis, track and field, volleyball W. **Intramural:** Archery, badminton, basketball, bowling, golf, handball, racquetball, soccer, softball, tennis, volleyball, water polo.

STUDENT SERVICES. Career counseling, employment service for undergraduates, freshman orientation, health services, personal counseling, placement service for graduates, tutoring services, academic counseling for learning disabled, services/facilities for handicapped.

ANNUAL EXPENSES. Tuition and fees: $14,520. **Room and board:** $3,810. **Books and supplies:** $350. **Other expenses:** $650.

FINANCIAL AID. 85% of freshmen, 84% of continuing students receive some form of aid. 81% of grants, 96% of loans, 83% of jobs based on need. 158 enrolled freshmen were judged to have need, all were offered aid. Academic, music/drama, state/district residency, leadership, alumni affiliation scholarships available. **Aid applications:** No closing date; priority given to applications received by March 1; applicants notified on a rolling basis beginning on or about April 1; must reply by May 1 or within 2 weeks if notified thereafter.

ADDRESS/TELEPHONE. Paul Weeks, Dean of Admission, Ripon College, PO Box 248, 300 Seward Street, Ripon, WI 54971. (414) 748-8102. (800) 94 RIPON. Fax: (414) 748-9262.

St. Norbert College
De Pere, Wisconsin CB code: 1706

Admissions:	96% of applicants accepted
Based on:	••• School record
	•• Essay, interview, recommendations, test scores
	• Activities, special talents
Completion:	92% of freshmen end year in good standing
	70% graduate, 19% of these enter graduate study

4-year private liberal arts college, coed, affiliated with Roman Catholic Church. Founded in 1898. **Accreditation:** Regional. **Undergraduate enrollment:** 818 men, 1,079 women full time; 24 men, 44 women part time. **Graduate enrollment:** 5 men, 11 women part time. **Faculty:** 143 total (118 full time), 96 with doctorates or other terminal degrees. **Location:** Suburban campus in large town; 5 miles from Green Bay. **Calendar:** Semester, limited summer session. **Microcomputers:** 90 located in libraries, computer centers, campus-wide network. **Special facilities:** Art gallery, electron microscope, nuclear magnetic resonance, Fouier Transform Infra-red Grass Instruments Physiograph. **Additional facts:** W. K. Kellogg Foundation, Center for Leadership Development, International Center with language laboratory, theaters, and computer center with mini/microcomputer laboratories.

DEGREES OFFERED. BA, BS, MA. 425 bachelor's degrees awarded in 1992. 20% in business and management, 15% communications, 8% education, 11% letters/literature, 9% life sciences, 8% multi/interdisciplinary studies, 5% psychology, 10% social sciences. Graduate degrees offered in 1 major field of study.

UNDERGRADUATE MAJORS. Accounting, art education, biological and physical sciences, biology, business administration and management, business and management, chemistry, clinical laboratory science, communications, computer and information sciences, computer mathematics, early childhood education, economics, education, elementary education, English, English education, environmental science, fine arts, foreign languages education, French, German, graphic design, history, humanities, humanities and social sciences, international business management, international relations, international studies, junior high education, management information systems, mathematics, mathematics education, medical laboratory technologies, music, music education, music performance, philosophy, physical sciences, physics, political science and government, predentistry, prelaw, premedicine, prepharmacy, preveterinary, psychology, religion, religious education, science education, secondary education, social science education, social sciences, social studies education, sociology, Spanish, speech/communication/theater education.

ACADEMIC PROGRAMS. Cooperative education, double major, dual enrollment of high school students, honors program, independent study, internships, student-designed major, study abroad, teacher preparation, visiting/exchange student program, Washington semester, 3-1 program in dentistry, 3-2 program in engineering. **Remedial services:** Learning center, preadmission summer program, reduced course load, remedial instruction, special counselor, tutoring. **ROTC:** Army. **Placement/credit:** AP, CLEP General and Subject, institutional tests; 64 credit hours maximum for bachelor's degree.

ACADEMIC REQUIREMENTS. Freshmen must earn minimum GPA of 1.75 to continue in good standing. Student must successfully complete 6 courses or 24 or more credit hours with 2.0 minimum GPA. 88% of freshmen return for sophomore year. Students must declare major by end of second year. **Graduation requirements:** 128 hours for bachelor's. Most students required to take courses in arts/fine arts, computer science, English, history, humanities, mathematics, philosophy/religion, biological/physical sciences, social sciences. **Postgraduate studies:** 2% enter law school, 2% enter medical school, 3% enter MBA programs, 12% enter other graduate study.

FRESHMAN ADMISSIONS. Selection criteria: High school record most important. Applicants with 2.75 high school GPA and/or in upper half of graduating class usually admitted. **High school preparation:** 16 units recommended. Recommended units include English 4, foreign language 3, mathematics 3, social science 3 and science 3. **Test requirements:** SAT or ACT; score report by August 1.

1992 FRESHMAN CLASS PROFILE. 1,276 men and women applied, 1,221 accepted; 236 men enrolled, 285 women enrolled. 69% had high school GPA of 3.0 or higher, 31% between 2.0 and 2.99. 32% were in top tenth and 58% were in top quarter of graduating class. **Academic background:** Mid 50% of enrolled freshmen had SAT-V between 440-540, SAT-M between 500-640; ACT composite between 21-26. 6% submitted SAT scores, 94% submitted ACT scores. **Characteristics:** 69% from in state, 90% live in college housing, 4% have minority backgrounds, 7% join fraternities/sororities. Average age is 18.

FALL-TERM APPLICATIONS. $25 fee, may be waived for applicants with need. No closing date; priority given to applications received by March 1; applicants notified on a rolling basis. Essay required. Interview recommended. Audition recommended for music applicants. Portfolio recommended for art, graphic communication applicants. CRDA. Deferred and early admission available.

STUDENT LIFE. Housing: Dormitories (women, coed); apartment housing available. International Culture House and living/learning dormitory experience for freshmen seminar students, college-owned houses near campus. Townhouse village to accommodate 100 students, limited services/facilities for visually and hearing impaired and those with speech or communications disorders. **Activities:** Student government, magazine, radio, student newspaper, television, yearbook, choral groups, concert band, dance, drama, jazz band, music ensembles, musical theater, pep band, fraternities, sororities, Parish Council, Knights of Columbus chapter, Student Democrats, Young Republicans, Amnesty International, Committee for Student Diversity, debate club, The Next Step, Circle K, INTERACT. **Additional information:** LEAD (Leadership Experience and Development) program for all students to improve leadership abilities through seminars, workshops, academic courses, internships, volunteer activities.

ATHLETICS. NCAA. **Intercollegiate:** Baseball M, basketball, cross-country, football M, golf, ice hockey M, soccer, softball W, tennis, track and field, volleyball W. **Intramural:** Basketball, racquetball, rowing (crew), soccer, softball, volleyball.

STUDENT SERVICES. Aptitude testing, career counseling, employment service for undergraduates, freshman orientation, health services, on-campus day care, personal counseling, placement service for graduates, special adviser for adult students, veterans counselor, services/facilities for handicapped.

ANNUAL EXPENSES. Tuition and fees: $11,465. **Room and board:** $4,245. **Books and supplies:** $425. **Other expenses:** $750.

FINANCIAL AID. 91% of freshmen, 90% of continuing students receive some form of aid. Grants, loans, jobs available. 354 enrolled freshmen were judged to have need, 353 were offered aid. Academic, music/drama, art, leadership, alumni affiliation, minority scholarships available. **Aid applications:** No closing date; priority given to applications received by March 1; applicants notified on a rolling basis beginning on or about March 1; must reply within 2 weeks.

ADDRESS/TELEPHONE. Craig S. Wesley, Dean of Admission, St. Norbert College, 100 Grant Street, De Pere, WI 54115-2099. (414) 337-3005. (800) 236-4878. Fax: (414) 337-4072.

Silver Lake College
Manitowoc, Wisconsin — CB code: 1300

Admissions: 83% of applicants accepted
Based on: ••• School record, test scores
•• Activities, recommendations
• Interview, special talents
Completion: 85% of freshmen end year in good standing
30% graduate, 9% of these enter graduate study

4-year private liberal arts college, coed, affiliated with Roman Catholic Church. Founded in 1935. **Accreditation:** Regional. **Undergraduate enrollment:** 112 men, 306 women full time; 153 men, 286 women part time. **Graduate enrollment:** 1 man, 1 woman full time; 22 men, 44 women part time. **Faculty:** 113 total (48 full time), 24 with doctorates or other terminal degrees. **Location:** Rural campus in large town; 80 miles from Milwaukee, 30 miles from Green Bay. **Calendar:** Semester, limited summer session. **Microcomputers:** 50 located in libraries, classrooms, computer centers. **Special facilities:** Vander Bloemen Bog nature preserve.

DEGREES OFFERED. AA, BA, BS, MA, MS. 5 associate degrees awarded in 1992. 10% in business and management, 10% letters/literature, 80% visual and performing arts. 143 bachelor's degrees awarded. 62% in business and management, 17% teacher education, 5% health sciences, 6% letters/literature. Graduate degrees offered in 2 major fields of study.

UNDERGRADUATE MAJORS. Associate: Graphic arts technology, liberal/general studies. **Bachelor's:** Accounting, art education, biology, business administration and management, education of the emotionally handicapped, education of the mentally handicapped, elementary education, English, history, human resources development, mathematics, Mathematics/computer science, music, music education, nursing, religion, social sciences, specific learning disabilities, studio art.

ACADEMIC PROGRAMS. 2-year transfer program, double major, dual enrollment of high school students, external degree, independent study, internships, student-designed major, study abroad, teacher preparation. **Remedial services:** Learning center, reduced course load, remedial instruction, special counselor. **Placement/credit:** CLEP General and Subject; 30 credit hours maximum for bachelor's degree.

ACADEMIC REQUIREMENTS. Freshmen must earn minimum GPA of 2.0 to continue in good standing. 58% of freshmen return for sophomore year. Students must declare major by end of second year. **Graduation requirements:** 60 hours for associate, 128 hours for bachelor's. Most students required to take courses in arts/fine arts, English, history, humanities, mathematics, philosophy/religion, biological/physical sciences. **Postgraduate studies:** 10% from 2-year programs enter 4-year programs. 5% enter law school, 4% enter other graduate study.

FRESHMAN ADMISSIONS. Selection criteria: Class rank (top two-thirds), high school GPA, test scores very important. **High school preparation:** 16 units required. Required and recommended units include English 3-4, mathematics 2-4, social science 2-3 and science 1-3. **Test requirements:** SAT or ACT (ACT preferred); score report by August 1.

1992 FRESHMAN CLASS PROFILE. 19 men applied, 13 accepted, 8 enrolled; 59 women applied, 52 accepted, 32 enrolled. 22% had high school GPA of 3.0 or higher, 68% between 2.0 and 2.99. 7% were in top tenth and 14% were in top quarter of graduating class. **Characteristics:** 100% from in state, 100% commute. Average age is 21.

FALL-TERM APPLICATIONS. $15 fee. No closing date; priority given to applications received by August 1; applicants notified on a rolling basis. Audition required for music applicants. Interview recommended for art, music applicants. Portfolio recommended for art applicants. Deferred and early admission available.

STUDENT LIFE. Housing: Men's and women's housing located off-campus. **Activities:** Student government, magazine, student newspaper, choral groups, concert band, drama, jazz band, music ensembles, symphony orchestra, campus ministry.

ATHLETICS. Intercollegiate: Basketball W, softball W, volleyball W. **Intramural:** Basketball, softball, volleyball.

STUDENT SERVICES. Career counseling, employment service for undergraduates, freshman orientation, personal counseling, placement service for graduates, services/facilities for handicapped.

ANNUAL EXPENSES. Tuition and fees: $8,280. $200 fee required of music students. **Room and board:** $3,414. **Books and supplies:** $500. **Other expenses:** $972.

FINANCIAL AID. 95% of freshmen, 61% of continuing students receive some form of aid. 81% of grants, 87% of loans, all jobs based on need. 31 enrolled freshmen were judged to have need, all were offered aid. Academic, music/drama, art, athletic, leadership, alumni affiliation, religious affiliation, minority scholarships available. **Aid applications:** No closing date; priority given to applications received by March 15; applicants notified on a rolling basis beginning on or about May 15; must reply within 4 weeks.

ADDRESS/TELEPHONE. Sandra Schwartz, Director of Admissions, Silver Lake College, 2406 South Alverno Road, Manitowoc, WI 54220-9391. (414) 684-5955. Fax: (414) 684-7082.

Southwest Wisconsin Technical College
Fennimore, Wisconsin — CB code: 0900

2-year public technical college, coed. Founded in 1967. **Accreditation:** Regional. **Undergraduate enrollment:** 272 men, 422 women full time; 779 men, 874 women part time. **Faculty:** 97 total (78 full time). **Location:** Rural campus in rural community; 75 miles from Madison and 38 miles from Dubuque, Iowa. **Calendar:** Semester, limited summer session. **Additional facts:** Courses for credit offered at 5 off-campus sites and by television.

DEGREES OFFERED. AS. 160 associate degrees awarded in 1992. 5% in agriculture, 45% business/office and marketing/distribution, 25% allied health, 15% home economics, 10% trade and industry.

UNDERGRADUATE MAJORS. Accounting, agribusiness, agricultural business and management, agricultural sciences, Bible studies, business data programming, child development/care/guidance, computer programming, electrical and electronics equipment repair, electromechanical technology, engineering and engineering-related technologies, fashion merchandising, finance, legal secretary, marketing and distribution, mechanical design, nursing, secretarial and related programs, teacher aide.

ACADEMIC PROGRAMS. Double major, dual enrollment of high school students, internships, telecourses. **Remedial services:** Learning center, preadmission summer program, reduced course load, remedial instruction, special counselor, tutoring. **Placement/credit:** Institutional tests.

ACADEMIC REQUIREMENTS. Freshmen must earn minimum GPA of 2.0 to continue in good standing. 80% of freshmen return for sophomore year. Students must declare major on application. **Graduation requirements:** Most students required to take courses in English, mathematics.

FRESHMAN ADMISSIONS. Selection criteria: Open admissions. Interview very important. **Test requirements:** National League for Nursing Pre-Admission Assessment for Practical Nursing required for LPN applicants, Psychological Bureau Profile of RN applicants.

1992 FRESHMAN CLASS PROFILE. 402 men and women enrolled. 44% had high school GPA of 3.0 or higher, 50% between 2.0 and 2.99. **Characteristics:** 98% from in state, 100% commute, 2% have minority backgrounds. Average age is 20.

FALL-TERM APPLICATIONS. $10 fee. No closing date; applicants notified on a rolling basis. Interview required. Deferred and early admission available. All applicants required to take Tests of Adult Basic Education.

STUDENT LIFE. Activities: Student government, student newspaper, yearbook, Marketing and Management Association, Business Professionals of America, Vocational and Industrial Clubs of America, Professional Food Preparers, Health Occupations Students of America.

ATHLETICS. Intramural: Basketball, bowling, softball, volleyball.

STUDENT SERVICES. Aptitude testing, career counseling, employment service for undergraduates, freshman orientation, health services, on-campus day care, personal counseling, placement service for graduates, displaced homemakers, services/facilities for handicapped.

ANNUAL EXPENSES. Tuition and fees: $1,440, $8,760 additional for out-of-state students. Required fees vary according to program. **Books and supplies:** $540. **Other expenses:** $700.

FINANCIAL AID. 80% of freshmen, 80% of continuing students receive some form of aid. 99% of grants, 86% of loans, all jobs based on need. **Aid applications:** No closing date; priority given to applications received by April 15; applicants notified on a rolling basis.

ADDRESS/TELEPHONE. Kathy Kruel, Admissions Specialist, Southwest Wisconsin Technical College, Highway 18 East, Fennimore, WI 53809. (608) 822-3262. Fax: (608) 822-6019.

Stratton College
Milwaukee, Wisconsin — CB code: 3617

2-year proprietary business, junior, technical college, coed. Founded in 1863. **Undergraduate enrollment:** 649 men and women. **Faculty:** 40 total (19 full time), 1 with doctorate or other terminal degree. **Location:** Urban campus in very large city. **Calendar:** Quarter, extensive summer session. Saturday classes. **Microcomputers:** 95 located in libraries, classrooms, computer centers.

DEGREES OFFERED. AA, AS. 146 associate degrees awarded in 1992. 26% in business and management, 49% business/office and marketing/distribution, 8% computer sciences, 16% allied health.

UNDERGRADUATE MAJORS. Accounting, business administration and management, business and management, business and office, business data entry equipment operation, business data processing and related programs, business data programming, computer and information sciences, computer programming, data processing, electrical and electronics equipment repair, electronic technology, hospitality and recreation marketing, hotel/motel and restaurant management, information sciences and systems, legal secretary, marketing and distribution, marketing management, medical assistant, medical secretary, office supervision and management, secretarial and related programs, tourism, transportation and travel marketing, word processing.

ACADEMIC PROGRAMS. 2-year transfer program, accelerated program, double major, internships. **Remedial services:** Reduced course load, special counselor, tutoring. **Placement/credit:** CLEP General and Subject, institutional tests; 46 credit hours maximum for associate degree.

ACADEMIC REQUIREMENTS. Freshmen must earn minimum GPA of 1.7 to continue in good standing. Students must declare major on application. **Graduation requirements:** 93 hours for associate (45 in major). Most students required to take courses in computer science, English, humanities, mathematics, social sciences.

FRESHMAN ADMISSIONS. Selection criteria: School achievement record, test scores, and interview considered.

1992 FRESHMAN CLASS PROFILE. 255 men and women enrolled. 13% had high school GPA of 3.0 or higher, 45% between 2.0 and 2.99. **Characteristics:** 95% from in state, 100% commute, 51% have minority backgrounds, 1% are foreign students. Average age is 20.

FALL-TERM APPLICATIONS. $30 fee. No closing date; applicants notified on a rolling basis. Interview recommended.

STUDENT LIFE. Housing: Nearby dormitories available through St. Catherine's Residence for Women, Petawa Residence, Plaza Hotel, and others. **Activities:** Student government, Administrative Management Society, Data Processing Management Association, Collegiate Secretaries International, National Travel Association, Medical Assisting Organization, Honor Society, Distributive Education Clubs of America, Future Electronic Technologists, Phi Beta Lambda, Student Board.

STUDENT SERVICES. Aptitude testing, career counseling, employment service for undergraduates, freshman orientation, personal counseling, placement service for graduates, veterans counselor, services/facilities for handicapped.

ANNUAL EXPENSES. Tuition and fees: $5,740. **Books and supplies:** $850. **Other expenses:** $1,542.

FINANCIAL AID. 76% of freshmen, 76% of continuing students receive some form of aid. 99% of grants, 69% of loans, all jobs based on need. 185 enrolled freshmen were judged to have need, all were offered aid. Academic, leadership scholarships available. **Aid applications:** No closing date; applicants notified on a rolling basis; must reply within 2 weeks.

ADDRESS/TELEPHONE. Jeffrey L. Jarmes, Dir. Admissions, Stratton College, 1300 North Jackson Street, Milwaukee, WI 53202-2608. (414) 276-5200. Fax: (414) 276-3930.

University of Wisconsin Center: Baraboo/Sauk County
Baraboo, Wisconsin — CB code: 1996

2-year public branch campus, liberal arts college, coed. Founded in 1968. **Accreditation:** Regional. **Undergraduate enrollment:** 135 men, 142 women full time; 56 men, 123 women part time. **Faculty:** 44 total (27 full time), 17 with doctorates or other terminal degrees. **Location:** Rural campus in small town; 46 miles from Madison. **Calendar:** Semester, limited summer session. **Microcomputers:** 19 located in libraries, computer centers, campus-wide network. **Special facilities:** International Crane Foundation, Ringling Circus World Museum. **Additional facts:** Library has computer ties to other University of Wisconsin system campus libraries. Upper division and graduate-level education courses provided by University of Wisconsin: La Crosse.

DEGREES OFFERED. 38 associate degrees awarded in 1992. 100% in multi/interdisciplinary studies.

UNDERGRADUATE MAJORS. Liberal/general studies.

ACADEMIC PROGRAMS. 2-year transfer program, computer delivered (on-line) credit-bearing course offerings, dual enrollment of high school students, independent study, telecourses, cross-registration. **Remedial services:** Reduced course load, remedial instruction, tutoring. **Placement/credit:** AP, CLEP General and Subject, institutional tests.

ACADEMIC REQUIREMENTS. Freshmen must earn minimum GPA of 2.0 to continue in good standing. 55% of freshmen return for sophomore year. **Graduation requirements:** 60 hours for associate. Most students required to take courses in arts/fine arts, English, humanities, mathematics, biological/physical sciences, social sciences.

FRESHMAN ADMISSIONS. Selection criteria: Applicants must have GED or be high school graduate with 16 college preparatory units. Rank in upper 75% of high school graduating class required with ACT. Students in bottom 25% of graduating class will be placed on waiting list. Students not admitted for specific semester applied for will be admitted at later date. **High school preparation:** 16 units required. Required units include English 4, mathematics 2, social science 3 and science 2. 3 additional units required from any of the above listed areas. 2 more required from above areas or fine arts, computer science, and other academic areas. **Test requirements:** ACT; score report by August 30.

1992 FRESHMAN CLASS PROFILE. 134 men, 179 women enrolled. **Characteristics:** 93% from in state, 100% commute, 9% have minority backgrounds, 1% are foreign students. Average age is 20.

FALL-TERM APPLICATIONS. $10 fee, may be waived for applicants with need. No closing date; priority given to applications received by May 31; applicants notified on a rolling basis. Interview required for borderline applicants. Deferred and early admission available.

STUDENT LIFE. Activities: Student government, student newspaper, choral groups, concert band, drama, jazz band, music ensembles, musical theater, Circle K, student association.

ATHLETICS. NJCAA. **Intercollegiate:** Cross-country, golf M, tennis. **Intramural:** Basketball, bowling, softball, table tennis, volleyball.

STUDENT SERVICES. Career counseling, employment service for undergraduates, freshman orientation, personal counseling, special adviser for adult students, veterans counselor, services/facilities for handicapped.

ANNUAL EXPENSES. Tuition and fees (projected): $1,485, $3,207 additional for out-of-state students. **Books and supplies:** $375. **Other expenses:** $700.

FINANCIAL AID. 48% of freshmen, 52% of continuing students receive some form of aid. Grants, loans, jobs available. 150 enrolled freshmen were judged to have need, all were offered aid. Academic, music/drama, art, leadership scholarships available. **Aid applications:** No closing date; priority given to applications received by April 15; applicants notified on a rolling basis; must reply within 3 weeks.

ADDRESS/TELEPHONE. Thomas Martin, Director of Student Services, University of Wisconsin Center: Baraboo/Sauk County, 1006 Connie Road, Baraboo, WI 53913-1098. (608) 356-8351. Fax: (608) 356-4074.

University of Wisconsin Center: Barron County
Rice Lake, Wisconsin — CB code: 1772

2-year public branch campus, junior college, coed. Founded in 1966. **Accreditation:** Regional. **Undergraduate enrollment:** 189 men, 212 women full time; 53 men, 101 women part time. **Faculty:** 29 total (20 full time), 9 with doctorates or other terminal degrees. **Location:** Rural campus in small town; 80 miles from Minneapolis-St. Paul. **Calendar:** Semester. **Microcomputers:** 24 located in computer centers, campus-wide network. **Special facilities:** Observatory, art gallery, amphitheater.

DEGREES OFFERED. 20 associate degrees awarded in 1992. 100% in multi/interdisciplinary studies.

UNDERGRADUATE MAJORS. Liberal/general studies.

ACADEMIC PROGRAMS. 2-year transfer program, dual enrollment of high school students, cross-registration. **Remedial services:** Learning center, preadmission summer program, reduced course load, remedial instruction, special counselor, tutoring. **Placement/credit:** AP, CLEP General and Subject, institutional tests.

ACADEMIC REQUIREMENTS. Freshmen must earn minimum GPA of 2.0 to continue in good standing. 65% of freshmen return for sophomore year. **Graduation requirements:** 60 hours for associate. Most students required to take courses in English, humanities, mathematics, biological/physical sciences, social sciences.

FRESHMAN ADMISSIONS. Selection criteria: Applicants must be high school graduates and have 16 college preparatory units. Rank in upper 75% of high school graduating class ensures admission. Students in bottom 25% of graduating class placed on waiting list. Students not admitted for specific semester applied for admitted at later date. **High school preparation:** 16 units required. Required units include English 4, mathematics 2, social science 3 and science 2. **Test requirements:** ACT; score report by September 1.

1992 FRESHMAN CLASS PROFILE. 84 men, 109 women enrolled. 6% were in top tenth and 23% were in top quarter of graduating class. **Characteristics:** 97% from in state, 100% commute, 2% have minority backgrounds, 1% are foreign students. Average age is 21.

FALL-TERM APPLICATIONS. $10 fee, may be waived for applicants with need. No closing date; priority given to applications received by July 1; applicants notified on a rolling basis. Early admission available.

STUDENT LIFE. Activities: Student government, student newspaper, choral groups, concert band, drama, jazz band, music ensembles, international club.

ATHLETICS. Intercollegiate: Baseball M, basketball, golf, soccer, volleyball W. **Intramural:** Basketball, table tennis, volleyball.

STUDENT SERVICES. Career counseling, employment service for undergraduates, freshman orientation, health services, personal counseling, veterans counselor, services/facilities for handicapped.

ANNUAL EXPENSES. Tuition and fees (projected): $1,784, $3,482 additional for out-of-state students. Required fees include textbook rental costs. **Books and supplies:** $450. **Other expenses:** $2,645.

FINANCIAL AID. 63% of continuing students receive some form of aid. Grants, loans, jobs available. Academic, music/drama, art, leadership scholarships available. **Aid applications:** No closing date; priority given to applications received by March 1; applicants notified on a rolling basis beginning on or about May 1; must reply within 3 weeks.

ADDRESS/TELEPHONE. Jennifer Gladden, Director of Student Services, University of Wisconsin Center: Barron County, 1800 College Drive, Rice Lake, WI 54868. (715) 234-8176. Fax: (715) 234-1975.

University of Wisconsin Center: Fond du Lac
Fond du Lac, Wisconsin — CB code: 1942

2-year public branch campus college, coed. Founded in 1968. **Accreditation:** Regional. **Undergraduate enrollment:** 770 men and women. **Location:** Suburban campus in large town; 70 miles from Milwaukee. **Calendar:** Semester. Saturday and extensive evening/early morning classes.

FRESHMAN ADMISSIONS. Selection criteria: Applicants must be high school graduates and have 16 college preparatory units. Rank in upper 75% of high school graduating class ensures admission. Students in bottom 25% of graduating class will be placed on waiting list. Student not admitted for specific semester applied for will be admitted at later date. Students withholding GED automatically placed on waiting list.

ANNUAL EXPENSES. Tuition and fees (projected): $1,620, $3,700 additional for out-of-state students. **Books and supplies:** $450. **Other expenses:** $800.

ADDRESS/TELEPHONE. Marilyn J. Krump, Director of Admissions and Financial Aids, University of Wisconsin Center: Fond du Lac, Campus Drive, Fond du Lac, WI 54935-2998. (414) 929-3606.

University of Wisconsin Center: Fox Valley
Menasha, Wisconsin CB code: 1889

2-year public branch campus, liberal arts college, coed. Founded in 1933. **Accreditation:** Regional. **Undergraduate enrollment:** 577 men, 802 women full time; 228 men, 414 women part time. **Faculty:** 62 total (35 full time), 25 with doctorates or other terminal degrees. **Location:** Urban campus in large town; 90 miles from Milwaukee. **Calendar:** Semester, limited summer session. Extensive evening/early morning classes. **Microcomputers:** Located in libraries, computer centers. **Special facilities:** Observatory, art gallery, planetarium.

DEGREES OFFERED. AAS. 107 associate degrees awarded in 1992. 100% in multi/interdisciplinary studies.

UNDERGRADUATE MAJORS. Liberal/general studies.

ACADEMIC PROGRAMS. 2-year transfer program, dual enrollment of high school students, honors program, independent study, internships. **Remedial services:** Learning center, reduced course load, remedial instruction, special counselor, tutoring. **Placement/credit:** AP, CLEP General and Subject, institutional tests.

ACADEMIC REQUIREMENTS. Freshmen must earn minimum GPA of 2.0 to continue in good standing. 50% of freshmen return for sophomore year. **Graduation requirements:** 60 hours for associate. Most students required to take courses in arts/fine arts, English, humanities, mathematics, biological/physical sciences, social sciences.

FRESHMAN ADMISSIONS. Selection criteria: Applicants must be high school graduates and have 16 college preparatory units. Rank in upper 75% of high school graduating class ensures admission. Students in bottom 25% of graduating class may be placed on waiting list. Students not admitted for specific semester applied for may be admitted later. **High school preparation:** 16 units required. Required units include English 4, mathematics 2, social science 3 and science 2. Mathematics units must be at algebra level and higher. 3 college preparatory electives; 2 other electives in above areas or fine arts and computer science. **Test requirements:** ACT.

1992 FRESHMAN CLASS PROFILE. 167 men, 227 women enrolled. 7% were in top tenth and 14% were in top quarter of graduating class. **Characteristics:** 99% from in state, 100% commute, 1% have minority backgrounds. Average age is 21.

FALL-TERM APPLICATIONS. $10 fee, may be waived for applicants with need. Closing date July 15; applicants notified on a rolling basis. Interview required of applicants in lower quarter of class and those who submit GED scores. CRDA. Early admission available.

STUDENT LIFE. Activities: Student government, film, radio, student newspaper, television, annual literary publication, choral groups, concert band, dance, drama, jazz band, music ensembles, musical theater, symphony orchestra.

ATHLETICS. NJCAA. **Intercollegiate:** Basketball M, golf M, soccer M, tennis, volleyball W. **Intramural:** Basketball M, softball, tennis, volleyball.

STUDENT SERVICES. Career counseling, freshman orientation, on-campus day care, special adviser for adult students, veterans counselor, services/facilities for handicapped.

ANNUAL EXPENSES. Tuition and fees (projected): $1,632, $3,700 additional for out-of-state students. **Books and supplies:** $300. **Other expenses:** $1,000.

FINANCIAL AID. 94% of grants, 94% of loans, 69% of jobs based on need. Academic, leadership scholarships available. **Aid applications:** No closing date; priority given to applications received by April 15; applicants notified on a rolling basis beginning on or about June 1; must reply within 3 weeks.

ADDRESS/TELEPHONE. Rhonda Uschan, Director of Student Services, University of Wisconsin Center: Fox Valley, 1478 Midway Road, P.O. Box 8002, Menasha, WI 54952-8002. (414) 832-2620.

University of Wisconsin Center: Manitowoc County
Manitowoc, Wisconsin CB code: 1890

2-year public branch campus, liberal arts college, coed. Founded in 1933. **Accreditation:** Regional. **Undergraduate enrollment:** 177 men, 175 women full time; 71 men, 75 women part time. **Faculty:** 32 total (20 full time), 16 with doctorates or other terminal degrees. **Location:** Urban campus in large town; 45 miles from Green Bay. **Calendar:** Semester, limited summer session. **Microcomputers:** Located in libraries, computer centers.

DEGREES OFFERED. 55 associate degrees awarded in 1992. 100% in multi/interdisciplinary studies.

UNDERGRADUATE MAJORS. Liberal/general studies.

ACADEMIC PROGRAMS. 2-year transfer program, dual enrollment of high school students, independent study, cross-registration. **Remedial services:** Reduced course load, remedial instruction, tutoring. **Placement/credit:** AP, CLEP General, institutional tests; 18 credit hours maximum for associate degree.

ACADEMIC REQUIREMENTS. Freshmen must earn minimum GPA of 2.0 to continue in good standing. 40% of freshmen return for sophomore year. **Graduation requirements:** 60 hours for associate. Most students required to take courses in English, humanities, mathematics, biological/physical sciences, social sciences.

FRESHMAN ADMISSIONS. Selection criteria: Rank in top 75% of high school class ensures admission. Students in bottom 25% placed on waiting list. Students not admitted for specific semester applied for will be admitted at later date. Students with GED placed on waiting list. **High school preparation:** 16 units required. Required units include English 4, mathematics 2, social science 3 and science 2. Additional 5 units required from above list; could include two college preparatory units. **Test requirements:** ACT; score report by August 15.

1992 FRESHMAN CLASS PROFILE. 87 men, 79 women enrolled. 40% had high school GPA of 3.0 or higher, 50% between 2.0 and 2.99. 10% were in top tenth and 25% were in top quarter of graduating class. **Academic background:** Mid 50% of enrolled freshmen had ACT composite between 16-23. 100% submitted ACT scores. **Characteristics:** 99% from in state, 100% commute, 3% have minority backgrounds. Average age is 19.

FALL-TERM APPLICATIONS. $10 fee, may be waived for applicants with need. No closing date; priority given to applications received by July 1; applicants notified on a rolling basis. Interview required for applicants in bottom quarter of class. Deferred admission available.

STUDENT LIFE. Activities: Student government, student newspaper, choral groups, concert band, drama, jazz band, symphony orchestra.

ATHLETICS. NAIA, NJCAA. **Intercollegiate:** Basketball, cross-country, golf M, tennis, volleyball W.

STUDENT SERVICES. Career counseling, freshman orientation, on-campus day care, personal counseling, services/facilities for handicapped.

ANNUAL EXPENSES. Tuition and fees (projected): $1,590, $3,600 additional for out-of-state students. **Books and supplies:** $400. **Other expenses:** $1,000.

FINANCIAL AID. 30% of freshmen, 30% of continuing students receive some form of aid. 98% of grants, all loans based on need. 100 enrolled freshmen were judged to have need, all were offered aid. Academic, state/district residency, leadership scholarships available. **Aid applications:** No closing date; priority given to applications received by March 1; applicants notified on a rolling basis beginning on or about May 1; must reply within 2 weeks.

ADDRESS/TELEPHONE. Susanne Skubal, Senior Program Manager, University of Wisconsin Center: Manitowoc County, 705 Viebahn Street, Manitowoc, WI 54220-6699. (414) 683-4707.

University of Wisconsin Center: Marathon County
Wausau, Wisconsin CB code: 1995

Admissions: 79% of applicants accepted
Based on:
••• School record
•• Test scores
• Activities, interview, recommendations, special talents
Completion: 82% of freshmen end year in good standing
10% graduate, 96% of these enter 4-year programs

2-year public branch campus college, coed. Founded in 1933. **Accreditation:** Regional. **Undergraduate enrollment:** 408 men, 416 women full time; 128 men, 265 women part time. **Faculty:** 63 total (46 full time), 50 with doctorates or other terminal degrees. **Location:** Urban campus in large town; 180 miles from Milwaukee, 180 miles from Minneapolis-St. Paul. **Calendar:** Semester, limited summer session. **Microcomputers:** 89 located in libraries, classrooms, computer centers, campus-wide network. **Special facilities:** Planetarium, hiking and cross-country ski trails, indoor skating and curling rinks.

DEGREES OFFERED. 100 associate degrees awarded in 1992. 100% in multi/interdisciplinary studies.

UNDERGRADUATE MAJORS. Liberal/general studies.

ACADEMIC PROGRAMS. 2-year transfer program, dual enrollment of high school students, honors program, independent study, internships, study abroad, cross-registration. **Remedial services:** Preadmission summer program, reduced course load, remedial instruction, tutoring. **Placement/credit:** AP,

CLEP General and Subject, IB, institutional tests; 18 credit hours maximum for associate degree.

ACADEMIC REQUIREMENTS. Freshmen must earn minimum GPA of 2.0 to continue in good standing. 76% of freshmen return for sophomore year. **Graduation requirements:** 60 hours for associate. Most students required to take courses in arts/fine arts, English, humanities, mathematics, biological/physical sciences, social sciences.

FRESHMAN ADMISSIONS. Selection criteria: Rank in upper 75% of high school graduating class ensures admission. Student in bottom 25% of graduating class placed on waiting list. Students not admitted for a specific semester may be admitted at later date. Students with GED automatically placed on waiting list. Effective fall 1995, applicants must have minimum 17 high school units (including 3 in mathematics and 3 in natural science). **High school preparation:** 16 units required. Required and recommended units include English 4, mathematics 2-4, social science 3 and science 2-4. Foreign language 4 recommended. Mathematics units must be algebra, geometry or other courses leading to calculus. **Test requirements:** ACT; score report by August 1.

1992 FRESHMAN CLASS PROFILE. 347 men applied, 273 accepted, 180 enrolled; 386 women applied, 303 accepted, 191 enrolled. 13% were in top tenth and 33% were in top quarter of graduating class. **Characteristics:** 96% from in state, 82% commute, 1% have minority backgrounds, 1% are foreign students. Average age is 19.

FALL-TERM APPLICATIONS. $10 fee, may be waived for applicants with need. Closing date August 1; priority given to applications received by June 1; applicants notified on a rolling basis. Interview required for those in lower 25% of class and those who submit GED scores. CRDA. Deferred and early admission available.

STUDENT LIFE. Housing: Dormitories (coed). **Activities:** Student government, magazine, student newspaper, choral groups, concert band, drama, jazz band, music ensembles, musical theater, pep band, symphony orchestra, Christian Fellowship, business club, computer club, drama club, international relations club.

ATHLETICS. NJCAA. **Intercollegiate:** Basketball, golf, soccer, tennis, volleyball W. **Intramural:** Archery, badminton, basketball, bowling, fencing, golf, handball, racquetball, skiing, skin diving, softball, swimming, table tennis, tennis, volleyball, water polo.

STUDENT SERVICES. Aptitude testing, career counseling, employment service for undergraduates, freshman orientation, personal counseling, special adviser for adult students, veterans counselor, services/facilities for handicapped.

ANNUAL EXPENSES. Tuition and fees (projected): $1,514, $3,482 additional for out-of-state students. **Room and board:** $2,348. **Books and supplies:** $320. **Other expenses:** $900.

FINANCIAL AID. 73% of freshmen, 65% of continuing students receive some form of aid. 81% of grants, 94% of loans, 83% of jobs based on need. 221 enrolled freshmen were judged to have need, all were offered aid. Academic, music/drama, art, leadership, minority scholarships available. **Aid applications:** No closing date; priority given to applications received by April 15; applicants notified on a rolling basis beginning on or about June 1; must reply within 3 weeks.

ADDRESS/TELEPHONE. John H. Runkel, Director of Admissions, University of Wisconsin Center: Marathon County, 518 South Seventh Avenue, Wausau, WI 54401-5396. (715) 845-9602. Fax: (715) 848-3568.

University of Wisconsin Center: Marinette County

Marinette, Wisconsin — CB code: 1891

2-year public 2-year liberal arts transfer college, coed. Founded in 1946. **Accreditation:** Regional. **Undergraduate enrollment:** 147 men, 158 women full time; 46 men, 138 women part time. **Faculty:** 21 total (16 full time), 7 with doctorates or other terminal degrees. **Location:** Rural campus in large town; 50 miles from Green Bay, 170 miles from Milwaukee. **Calendar:** Semester, limited summer session. **Microcomputers:** 50 located in libraries, computer centers.

DEGREES OFFERED. 39 associate degrees awarded in 1992. 100% in multi/interdisciplinary studies.

UNDERGRADUATE MAJORS. Liberal/general studies.

ACADEMIC PROGRAMS. 2-year transfer program, dual enrollment of high school students, independent study, telecourses, cross-registration. **Remedial services:** Reduced course load, remedial instruction, special counselor, tutoring. **Placement/credit:** AP, CLEP General and Subject, IB, institutional tests; 45 credit hours maximum for associate degree.

ACADEMIC REQUIREMENTS. Freshmen must earn minimum GPA of 2.0 to continue in good standing. **Graduation requirements:** 60 hours for associate. Most students required to take courses in arts/fine arts, English, humanities, mathematics, biological/physical sciences, social sciences.

FRESHMAN ADMISSIONS. Selection criteria: Applicants must be high school graduates and have 16 college preparatory units. Rank in upper 75% of high school graduating class ensures admission. Students in bottom 25% of graduating class placed on waiting list. Students not admitted for specific semester applied for will be admitted at later date. Students with GED automatically placed on waiting list. **High school preparation:** 16 units required. Required units include English 4, mathematics 2, social science 3 and science 2. 5 electives from above or computer science and fine arts. **Test requirements:** ACT; score report by August 31. **Additional information:** Applicants not meeting minimum standards may be accepted but required to take reduced course load and/or noncredit courses to remedy deficiencies.

1992 FRESHMAN CLASS PROFILE. 106 men, 116 women enrolled. 6% were in top tenth and 21% were in top quarter of graduating class. **Characteristics:** 66% from in state, 100% commute, 3% are foreign students.

FALL-TERM APPLICATIONS. $10 fee. No closing date; priority given to applications received by May 1; applicants notified on a rolling basis. Early admission available. Students may be conditionally admitted prior to receipt of ACT scores, but may not register for classes until scores received.

STUDENT LIFE. Housing: New four-unit, privately-owned, fully furnished student apartment complex which opened in January 1991 can accommodate 16 students. **Activities:** Student government, student newspaper, choral groups, drama, jazz band, music ensembles, musical theater.

ATHLETICS. NJCAA. **Intercollegiate:** Basketball M, golf W, tennis, volleyball W. **Intramural:** Basketball, bowling, skiing, table tennis, volleyball.

STUDENT SERVICES. Career counseling, freshman orientation, personal counseling, veterans counselor, services/facilities for handicapped.

ANNUAL EXPENSES. Tuition and fees (1992-93): $1,500, $3,482 additional for out-of-state students. **Books and supplies:** $380. **Other expenses:** $670.

FINANCIAL AID. 60% of freshmen, 60% of continuing students receive some form of aid. 95% of grants, 97% of loans, 83% of jobs based on need. Academic, leadership scholarships available. **Aid applications:** No closing date; priority given to applications received by March 1; applicants notified on a rolling basis beginning on or about June 1; must reply within 3 weeks.

ADDRESS/TELEPHONE. Stephen P. Richer, Director of Student Services, University of Wisconsin Center: Marinette County, Bay Shore, Marinette, WI 54143. (715) 735-7470.

University of Wisconsin Center: Marshfield/Wood County

Marshfield, Wisconsin — CB code: 1997

Admissions: 73% of applicants accepted
Based on: ••• School record
• Recommendations, test scores
Completion: 76% of freshmen end year in good standing

2-year public branch campus, junior college, coed. Founded in 1964. **Accreditation:** Regional. **Undergraduate enrollment:** 167 men, 224 women full time; 35 men, 96 women part time. **Faculty:** 32 total (20 full time), 4 with doctorates or other terminal degrees. **Location:** Suburban campus in large town; 138 miles from Madison. **Calendar:** Semester, limited summer session. **Microcomputers:** 15 located in libraries.

DEGREES OFFERED. 30 associate degrees awarded in 1992. 100% in multi/interdisciplinary studies.

UNDERGRADUATE MAJORS. Liberal/general studies.

ACADEMIC PROGRAMS. 2-year transfer program, dual enrollment of high school students, independent study, internships, cross-registration. **Remedial services:** Preadmission summer program, reduced course load, remedial instruction, special counselor, tutoring. **Placement/credit:** AP, CLEP General and Subject, institutional tests.

ACADEMIC REQUIREMENTS. Freshmen must earn minimum GPA of 2.0 to continue in good standing. 44% of freshmen return for sophomore year. **Graduation requirements:** 60 hours for associate. Most students required to take courses in arts/fine arts, English, humanities, mathematics, biological/physical sciences, social sciences.

FRESHMAN ADMISSIONS. Selection criteria: Rank in top 75% of high school class and 16 specified high school academic units ensure admission. Students in bottom 25% and or with missing units may be placed on waiting list. Students not admitted for specific semester applied for may be admitted later. Students with GED may be placed on waiting list. **High school preparation:** 16 units required. Required and recommended units include English 4, mathematics 2-4, social science 3 and science 2-4. 3 additional units from above areas; 2 more from other academic areas. **Test requirements:** ACT for counseling; score report by July 1.

1992 FRESHMAN CLASS PROFILE. 451 men and women applied, 330 accepted; 82 men enrolled, 207 women enrolled. **Characteristics:** 98% from in state, 100% commute, 2% have minority backgrounds, 1% are foreign students. Average age is 19.

FALL-TERM APPLICATIONS. $10 fee, may be waived for applicants with need. No closing date; priority given to applications received by July 1; applicants notified on a rolling basis. Deferred and early admission available.

STUDENT LIFE. Activities: Student government, student newspaper, creative writing annual, choral groups, concert band, drama, jazz band, music ensembles, musical theater, symphony orchestra, Inter-Varsity Christian Fellowship, business club, chess club, art club, nursing associaton, computer club, program board, honor fraternity.

ATHLETICS. Intercollegiate: Basketball, golf, soccer, tennis, volleyball W. **Intramural:** Basketball, bowling, football, skiing, soccer, softball, tennis, volleyball.

STUDENT SERVICES. Career counseling, freshman orientation, personal counseling, services/facilities for handicapped.

ANNUAL EXPENSES. Tuition and fees (projected): $1,514, $3,482 additional for out-of-state students. **Books and supplies:** $250. **Other expenses:** $800.

FINANCIAL AID. 46% of freshmen, 40% of continuing students receive some form of aid. 91% of grants, 70% of loans, all jobs based on need. Academic, leadership scholarships available. **Aid applications:** No closing date; priority given to applications received by April 15; applicants notified on a rolling basis beginning on or about May 15; must reply within 3 weeks.

ADDRESS/TELEPHONE. William C. Kuba, Director of Student Services, University of Wisconsin Center: Marshfield/Wood County, 2000 West Fifth Street, Marshfield, WI 54449. (715) 389-6530.

University of Wisconsin Center: Richland
Richland Center, Wisconsin CB code: 1662

Admissions:	99% of applicants accepted
Based on:	••• School record
	• Activities, essay, interview, recommendations, special talents, test scores
Completion:	73% of freshmen end year in good standing
	40% graduate, 80% of these enter 4-year programs

2-year public liberal arts college, coed. Founded in 1967. **Accreditation:** Regional. **Undergraduate enrollment:** 178 men, 169 women full time; 32 men, 54 women part time. **Faculty:** 36 total (18 full time), 14 with doctorates or other terminal degrees. **Location:** Rural campus in small town; 60 miles from Madison. **Calendar:** Semester, limited summer session. **Microcomputers:** 40 located in libraries, classrooms, computer centers. **Special facilities:** Fitness/wellness facilities.

DEGREES OFFERED. 60 associate degrees awarded in 1992. 100% in multi/interdisciplinary studies.

UNDERGRADUATE MAJORS. Liberal/general studies.

ACADEMIC PROGRAMS. 2-year transfer program, dual enrollment of high school students, independent study, teacher preparation, telecourses, cross-registration, Central American Scholarship Program through Georgetown University. **Remedial services:** Reduced course load, remedial instruction, special counselor, tutoring. **Placement/credit:** AP, CLEP General and Subject, institutional tests; 18 credit hours maximum for associate degree.

ACADEMIC REQUIREMENTS. Freshmen must earn minimum GPA of 2.0 to continue in good standing. 55% of freshmen return for sophomore year. **Graduation requirements:** 60 hours for associate. Most students required to take courses in arts/fine arts, English, history, humanities, mathematics, biological/physical sciences, social sciences. **Additional information:** Associate of arts and science degree accepted throughout University of Wisconsin system as transfer tool; satisfies general education requirements of any system campus.

FRESHMAN ADMISSIONS. Selection criteria: Applicants must be high school graduates and have 16 college preparatory units. Rank in upper 75% of high school graduating class ensures admission. Students in bottom 25% of graduating class may be admitted on a discretionary category basis. Students not admitted for specific semester applied for will be admitted at later date. Students with GED considered for admission. **High school preparation:** 16 units required. Required units include English 4, mathematics 2, social science 3 and science 2. 3 additional units may come from specified areas or foreign language; 2 additional may come from specified areas and/or fine arts, computer science and other areas. **Test requirements:** ACT; score report by June 20.

1992 FRESHMAN CLASS PROFILE. 118 men applied, 117 accepted, 103 enrolled; 134 women applied, 133 accepted, 104 enrolled. **Characteristics:** 99% from in state, 75% commute, 2% have minority backgrounds, 2% are foreign students. Average age is 19.

FALL-TERM APPLICATIONS. $10 fee. Closing date August 15; priority given to applications received by April 1; applicants notified on a rolling basis; must reply by July 1. Interview recommended. Interview required for applicants in bottom quarter of class. Early admission available.

STUDENT LIFE. Housing: Apartment housing available. **Activities:** Student government, student newspaper, literary magazine, choral groups, concert band, drama, music ensembles, musical theater, pep band, Campus Christian Fellowship. **Additional information:** A 5-km. hiking-cross country ski trail winds its way through rapidly growing arboretum.

ATHLETICS. NJCAA. **Intercollegiate:** Basketball, soccer M, volleyball W. **Intramural:** Badminton, basketball, handball, racquetball, softball, swimming, table tennis, tennis, water polo.

STUDENT SERVICES. Career counseling, employment service for undergraduates, freshman orientation, daycare financial assistance, services/facilities for handicapped.

ANNUAL EXPENSES. Tuition and fees (projected): $1,630, $3,482 additional for out-of-state students. Required fees include book rental costs. **Room and board:** $1,665 room only. **Books and supplies:** $450. **Other expenses:** $1,170.

FINANCIAL AID. 60% of freshmen, 61% of continuing students receive some form of aid. 89% of grants, 89% of loans, all jobs based on need. Academic, music/drama, art, leadership, minority scholarships available. **Aid applications:** Closing date August 1; priority given to applications received by April 15; applicants notified on a rolling basis beginning on or about June 1; must reply within 2 weeks.

ADDRESS/TELEPHONE. John Poole, Director of Student Services, University of Wisconsin Center: Richland, 1200 Highway 14 West, Richland Center, WI 53581. (608) 647-6186. Fax: (608) 647-6225.

University of Wisconsin Center: Rock County
Janesville, Wisconsin CB code: 1998

2-year public branch campus, liberal arts college, coed. Founded in 1966. **Accreditation:** Regional. **Undergraduate enrollment:** 201 men, 266 women full time; 199 men, 285 women part time. **Faculty:** 41 total (30 full time), 12 with doctorates or other terminal degrees. **Location:** Suburban campus in small city; 40 miles from Madison. **Calendar:** Semester, limited summer session. **Microcomputers:** Located in libraries, computer centers. **Special facilities:** Theodore Robinson Art Gallery.

DEGREES OFFERED. AA, AS. 120 associate degrees awarded in 1992. 100% in multi/interdisciplinary studies.

UNDERGRADUATE MAJORS. Liberal/general studies.

ACADEMIC PROGRAMS. 2-year transfer program, dual enrollment of high school students, independent study, weekend college. **Remedial services:** Learning center, reduced course load, remedial instruction, special counselor, tutoring. **Placement/credit:** AP, CLEP General and Subject, institutional tests.

ACADEMIC REQUIREMENTS. Freshmen must earn minimum GPA of 2.0 to continue in good standing. 40% of freshmen return for sophomore year. **Graduation requirements:** 60 hours for associate. Most students required to take courses in English, humanities, mathematics, biological/physical sciences, social sciences.

FRESHMAN ADMISSIONS. Selection criteria: Applicants must be high school graduates and have 16 college preparatory units. Rank in upper 75% of high school graduating class ensures admission. Students in bottom 25% of graduating class will be placed on waiting list. Students not admitted for specific semester applied for will be admitted at later date. Students with GED automatically placed on waiting list. **High school preparation:** 16 units recommended. Recommended units include English 4, mathematics 2, social science 3 and science 2. **Test requirements:** ACT for placement and counseling only.

1992 FRESHMAN CLASS PROFILE. 156 men, 209 women enrolled. **Characteristics:** 99% from in state, 100% commute, 3% have minority backgrounds. Average age is 22.

FALL-TERM APPLICATIONS. $10 fee, may be waived for applicants with need. No closing date; applicants notified on a rolling basis. Interview required of applicants in lower quarter of class. Deferred and early admission available.

STUDENT LIFE. Activities: Student government, student newspaper, choral groups, concert band, drama, jazz band, music ensembles.

ATHLETICS. NJCAA. **Intercollegiate:** Basketball M, soccer, volleyball W. **Intramural:** Badminton, basketball, soccer, volleyball.

STUDENT SERVICES. Career counseling, freshman orientation, personal counseling, adult support group, services/facilities for handicapped.

ANNUAL EXPENSES. Tuition and fees (projected): $1,508, $3,482 additional for out-of-state students. **Books and supplies:** $375. **Other expenses:** $640.

FINANCIAL AID. 50% of freshmen, 50% of continuing students receive some form of aid. 96% of grants, 78% of loans, all jobs based on need. Academic, music/drama, state/district residency, leadership, minority scholarships available. **Aid applications:** No closing date; priority given to applications received by April 15; applicants notified on a rolling basis beginning on or about June 1; must reply within 3 weeks.

ADDRESS/TELEPHONE. Terry Borg, Director of Student Services, University of Wisconsin Center: Rock County, 2909 Kellogg Avenue, Janesville, WI 53546-5699. (608) 758-6523.

University of Wisconsin Center: Sheboygan County
Sheboygan, Wisconsin CB code: 1994

2-year public junior college, coed. Founded in 1964. **Accreditation:** Regional. **Undergraduate enrollment:** 224 men, 187 women full time; 94 men, 177 women part time. **Faculty:** 33 total (24 full time), 11 with doctorates or other terminal degrees. **Location:** Suburban campus in large town; 60 miles from Milwaukee. **Calendar:** Semester, limited summer session. **Microcomputers:** 25 located in libraries, computer centers.

DEGREES OFFERED. 61 associate degrees awarded in 1992. 100% in multi/interdisciplinary studies.

UNDERGRADUATE MAJORS. Liberal/general studies.

ACADEMIC PROGRAMS. 2-year transfer program, dual enrollment of high school students, independent study. **Remedial services:** Reduced course load, remedial instruction, tutoring. **Placement/credit:** AP, CLEP General and Subject, institutional tests.

ACADEMIC REQUIREMENTS. Freshmen must earn minimum GPA of 2.0 to continue in good standing. **Graduation requirements:** 60 hours for associate. Most students required to take courses in English, humanities, mathematics, biological/physical sciences, social sciences.

FRESHMAN ADMISSIONS. Selection criteria: Applicants must be high school graduates and offer 16 college preparatory units. Rank in upper 75% of high school graduating class. **High school preparation:** 16 units required. Required units include English 4, mathematics 2, social science 3 and science 2. 5 electives required. **Test requirements:** ACT for placement and counseling only; score report by June 30.

1992 FRESHMAN CLASS PROFILE. 101 men, 92 women enrolled. **Characteristics:** 99% from in state, 100% commute. Average age is 19.

FALL-TERM APPLICATIONS. $10 fee, may be waived for applicants with need. No closing date; priority given to applications received by June 30; applicants notified on a rolling basis.

STUDENT LIFE. Activities: Student government, magazine, student newspaper, choral groups, concert band, drama, jazz band, musical theater.

ATHLETICS. NJCAA. **Intercollegiate:** Basketball, cross-country, golf, soccer M, tennis, volleyball W. **Intramural:** Basketball M, softball, volleyball.

STUDENT SERVICES. Career counseling, freshman orientation, personal counseling, services/facilities for handicapped.

ANNUAL EXPENSES. Tuition and fees (1992-93): $1,506, $3,482 additional for out-of-state students. **Books and supplies:** $380. **Other expenses:** $670.

FINANCIAL AID. 22% of freshmen, 22% of continuing students receive some form of aid. Grants, loans, jobs available. Academic, leadership scholarships available. **Aid applications:** No closing date; priority given to applications received by April 15; applicants notified on a rolling basis beginning on or about June 1; must reply within 2 weeks.

ADDRESS/TELEPHONE. Betsy L. West, Director of Student Services, University of Wisconsin Center: Sheboygan County, 1 University Drive, Sheboygan, WI 53081-4789. (414) 459-6633. Fax: (414) 459-6602.

University of Wisconsin Center: Washington County
West Bend, Wisconsin — CB code: 1993

Admissions: 97% of applicants accepted
Based on: ••• School record
•• Test scores
• Interview, recommendations
Completion: 90% enter 4-year programs

2-year public branch campus college, coed. Founded in 1968. **Accreditation:** Regional. **Undergraduate enrollment:** 247 men, 285 women full time; 90 men, 125 women part time. **Faculty:** 40 total (24 full time), 22 with doctorates or other terminal degrees. **Location:** Suburban campus in large town; 70 miles from Madison, 35 miles from Milwaukee. **Calendar:** Semester, limited summer session. **Microcomputers:** 50 located in computer centers. **Special facilities:** Observatory.

DEGREES OFFERED. 62 associate degrees awarded in 1992. 100% in multi/interdisciplinary studies.

UNDERGRADUATE MAJORS. Liberal/general studies.

ACADEMIC PROGRAMS. 2-year transfer program, dual enrollment of high school students, independent study, internships, study abroad, cross-registration. **Remedial services:** Preadmission summer program, reduced course load, remedial instruction, special counselor, tutoring. **Placement/credit:** AP, CLEP General and Subject, institutional tests.

ACADEMIC REQUIREMENTS. Freshmen must earn minimum GPA of 2.0 to continue in good standing. **Graduation requirements:** 60 hours for associate. Most students required to take courses in arts/fine arts, English, humanities, mathematics, biological/physical sciences, social sciences.

FRESHMAN ADMISSIONS. Selection criteria: Rank in top 75% of high school class ensures admission. Students in bottom 25% placed in discretionary category. Students not admitted for specific semester applied for will be admitted at later date. **High school preparation:** 16 units required. Required units include English 4, mathematics 2, social science 3 and science 2. **Test requirements:** ACT.

1992 FRESHMAN CLASS PROFILE. 382 men and women applied, 372 accepted; 124 men enrolled, 145 women enrolled. 6% were in top tenth and 17% were in top quarter of graduating class. **Characteristics:** 99% from in state, 100% commute, 1% have minority backgrounds. Average age is 18.

FALL-TERM APPLICATIONS. $10 fee, may be waived for applicants with need. No closing date; applicants notified on a rolling basis. Interview required for applicants with GED or those ranking in bottom 25% of high school class. Deferred and early admission available.

STUDENT LIFE. Activities: Student government, magazine, student newspaper, choral groups, concert band, drama, jazz band, music ensembles, musical theater, symphony orchestra, Phi Theta Kappa honorary, ACCESS, environmental club, Chi Alha religious club.

ATHLETICS. Intercollegiate: Basketball, golf, soccer, tennis, volleyball W. **Intramural:** Basketball, softball, volleyball.

STUDENT SERVICES. Aptitude testing, career counseling, freshman orientation, personal counseling, veterans counselor, services/facilities for handicapped.

ANNUAL EXPENSES. Tuition and fees (projected): $1,560, $3,482 additional for out-of-state students. **Books and supplies:** $450. **Other expenses:** $770.

FINANCIAL AID. 23% of freshmen, 22% of continuing students receive some form of aid. 80% of grants, 84% of loans, 35% of jobs based on need. Academic, music/drama scholarships available. **Aid applications:** No closing date; priority given to applications received by April 15; applicants notified on a rolling basis beginning on or about May 1; must reply within 3 weeks. **Additional information:** Campus jobs available. Work study recipients preferred but not required.

ADDRESS/TELEPHONE. Nancy Henderson, Director of Student Services, University of Wisconsin Center: Washington County, 400 University Drive, West Bend, WI 53095. (414) 335-5201. Fax: (414) 335-5220.

University of Wisconsin Center: Waukesha
Waukesha, Wisconsin — CB code: 1999

Admissions: 76% of applicants accepted
Based on: ••• School record
• Interview, recommendations, test scores
Completion: 70% of freshmen end year in good standing
25% graduate, 90% of these enter 4-year programs

2-year public branch campus, junior college, coed. Founded in 1966. **Accreditation:** Regional. **Undergraduate enrollment:** 580 men, 621 women full time; 351 men, 588 women part time. **Faculty:** 81 total (69 full time), 48 with doctorates or other terminal degrees. **Location:** Suburban campus in small city; 17 miles from Milwaukee. **Calendar:** Semester, limited summer session. Saturday and extensive evening/early morning classes. **Microcomputers:** 90 located in libraries, classrooms, computer centers. **Special facilities:** 98-acre environmental studies field station.

DEGREES OFFERED. AA, AS. 207 associate degrees awarded in 1992. 100% in multi/interdisciplinary studies.

UNDERGRADUATE MAJORS. Liberal/general studies.

ACADEMIC PROGRAMS. 2-year transfer program, dual enrollment of high school students, honors program, independent study, study abroad, cross-registration. **Remedial services:** Learning center, preadmission summer program, reduced course load, remedial instruction, special counselor, tutoring. **Placement/credit:** AP, CLEP General and Subject, institutional tests.

ACADEMIC REQUIREMENTS. Freshmen must earn minimum GPA of 2.0 to continue in good standing. 55% of freshmen return for sophomore year. **Graduation requirements:** 60 hours for associate. Most students required to take courses in arts/fine arts, English, humanities, mathematics, biological/physical sciences, social sciences.

FRESHMAN ADMISSIONS. Selection criteria: Rank in top 75% of high school class ensures admission. Students in bottom 25% placed on waiting list; if ACT score at 50th percentile nationally or higher, admission granted. Students not admitted for specific semester applied for will be admitted at later date. Students with GED score less than 300 placed on waiting list. Selective admission for foreign students. **High school preparation:** 16 units required; 19 recommended. Required and recommended units include English 4, mathematics 2-3, social science 3 and science 2. Foreign language 2 recommended. **Test requirements:** ACT; score report by August 1.

1992 FRESHMAN CLASS PROFILE. 1,064 men and women applied, 807 accepted; 308 men enrolled, 395 women enrolled. 33% had high school GPA of 3.0 or higher, 49% between 2.0 and 2.99. 5% were in top tenth and 18% were in top quarter of graduating class. **Academic background:** Mid 50% of enrolled freshmen had ACT composite between 14-20. 80% submitted ACT scores. **Characteristics:** 99% from in state, 100% commute, 2% have minority backgrounds. Average age is 20.

FALL-TERM APPLICATIONS. $10 fee. No closing date; priority given to applications received by May 31; applicants notified on a rolling basis. Interview required of applicants in bottom quarter of class or those submitting GED scores; recommended for applicants in bottom 35% of class. Deferred and early admission available. For English and mathematics enrollment, University of Wisconsin placement tests required.

STUDENT LIFE. Activities: Student government, magazine, radio, student newspaper, choral groups, concert band, drama, jazz band, music ensembles, musical theater, international student club, ecology club, philosophy club.

ATHLETICS. NJCAA. **Intercollegiate:** Basketball, cross-country, golf, soccer, tennis, volleyball W. **Intramural:** Basketball, fencing, skiing, softball, table tennis, track and field, volleyball.

STUDENT SERVICES. Career counseling, freshman orientation, personal counseling, special adviser for adult students, veterans counselor, services/facilities for handicapped.

ANNUAL EXPENSES. Tuition and fees (1992-93): $1,500, $3,482 additional for out-of-state students. **Books and supplies:** $375. **Other expenses:** $640.

FINANCIAL AID. 16% of freshmen, 16% of continuing students receive some form of aid. 93% of grants, 83% of loans, 39% of jobs based on need. Academic, music/drama, leadership, minority scholarships available. **Aid applications:** No closing date; priority given to applications received by March 1; applicants notified on a rolling basis beginning on or about May 1.

ADDRESS/TELEPHONE. Kurt Eisenmann, Assistant Director of Student Services, University of Wisconsin Center: Waukesha, 1500 University Drive, Waukesha, WI 53188-2799. (414) 521-5210. Fax: (414) 521-5116.

University of Wisconsin: Eau Claire

Eau Claire, Wisconsin CB code: 1913

Admissions: 79% of applicants accepted
Based on: ••• School record
•• Test scores
• Activities, recommendations, special talents
Completion: 82% of freshmen end year in good standing
40% graduate, 8% of these enter graduate study

4-year public university, coed. Founded in 1916. **Accreditation:** Regional. **Undergraduate enrollment:** 3,442 men, 5,225 women full time; 447 men, 777 women part time. **Graduate enrollment:** 50 men, 74 women full time; 90 men, 326 women part time. **Faculty:** 757 total (626 full time), 396 with doctorates or other terminal degrees. **Location:** Rural campus in small city; 90 miles from Minneapolis-St. Paul, Minnesota. **Calendar:** Semester, extensive summer session. Extensive evening/early morning classes. **Microcomputers:** 750 located in dormitories, libraries, classrooms, computer centers. **Special facilities:** Casey Observatory, Clark Bird Museum, Phillips Planetarium, Foster Art Gallery.

DEGREES OFFERED. AA, AS, BA, BS, BFA, MA, MS. 11 associate degrees awarded in 1992. 100% in multi/interdisciplinary studies. 1,690 bachelor's degrees awarded. 27% in business and management, 5% communications, 12% teacher education, 9% health sciences, 10% letters/literature, 6% parks/recreation, protective services, public affairs, 5% psychology, 6% social sciences. Graduate degrees offered in 21 major fields of study.

UNDERGRADUATE MAJORS. Associate: Liberal/general studies. **Bachelor's:** Accounting, advertising, art education, biochemistry, biology, botany, business administration and management, business and management, business and office, business economics, business education, ceramics, chemistry, clinical laboratory science, communications, computer and information sciences, criminal justice studies, dramatic arts, drawing, early childhood education, economics, education of the mentally handicapped, elementary education, English, English education, fiber/textiles/weaving, finance, fine arts, foreign languages education, French, geography, geology, German, health care administration, history, information sciences and systems, journalism, Latin American studies, management information systems, marketing and distribution, mathematics, mathematics education, medical laboratory technologies, metal/jewelry, music, music education, music theory and composition, music therapy, nursing, office supervision and management, painting, philosophy, photography, physical education, physical sciences, physics, political science and government, psychology, public health laboratory science, radio/television broadcasting, religion, science education, sculpture, secretarial and related programs, social science education, social sciences, social studies education, social work, sociology, Spanish, special education, specific learning disabilities, speech, speech correction, speech pathology/audiology, telecommunications, visual and performing arts, zoology.

ACADEMIC PROGRAMS. Cooperative education, double major, dual enrollment of high school students, education specialist degree, honors program, independent study, internships, study abroad, teacher preparation, visiting/exchange student program, program with University of Wisconsin: Stout in early childhood education; liberal arts/career combination in health sciences. **Remedial services:** Learning center, preadmission summer program, reduced course load, remedial instruction, special counselor, tutoring, study skills program. **Placement/credit:** AP, CLEP General and Subject, IB, institutional tests; 16 credit hours maximum for associate degree; 32 credit hours maximum for bachelor's degree.

ACADEMIC REQUIREMENTS. Freshmen must earn minimum GPA of 2.0 to continue in good standing. 82% of freshmen return for sophomore year. Students must declare major by end of second year. **Graduation requirements:** 64 hours for associate (18 in major), 128 hours for bachelor's (36 in major). Most students required to take courses in English, humanities, biological/physical sciences, social sciences. **Postgraduate studies:** 1% enter law school, 1% enter medical school, 3% enter MBA programs, 3% enter other graduate study.

FRESHMAN ADMISSIONS. Selection criteria: Applicants should be in top half of class. Special consideration to disadvantaged, veterans, and minority applicants. Applicants with ACT score of 22 or better given first priority. **High school preparation:** 16 units required. Required and recommended units include English 4-4, mathematics 3-4, social science 3-4 and science 3-3. Foreign language 2 recommended. One unit world or American history also required. 3 units English must be composition and/or literature. **Test requirements:** SAT or ACT (ACT preferred); score report by August 1. **Additional information:** Some applicants not admitted to the fall semester may be considered for admission to the following spring semester.

1992 FRESHMAN CLASS PROFILE. 5,119 men and women applied, 4,050 accepted; 717 men enrolled, 1,156 women enrolled. 23% were in top tenth and 57% were in top quarter of graduating class. **Academic background:** Mid 50% of enrolled freshmen had SAT-V between 420-530, SAT-M between 490-620; ACT composite between 21-25. 5% submitted SAT scores, 98% submitted ACT scores. **Characteristics:** 80% from in state, 74% live in college housing, 3% have minority backgrounds, 1% are foreign students. Average age is 19.

FALL-TERM APPLICATIONS. $10 fee, may be waived for applicants with need. No closing date; priority given to applications received by December 1; applicants notified on a rolling basis beginning on or about February 1. Audition required for music applicants. CRDA. Some programs close early. ACT required for Wisconsin residents. For out-of-state residents, SAT or ACT required, ACT preferred. Closing and priority dates vary; please contact admissions office for further details. Students must.

STUDENT LIFE. Housing: Dormitories (men, women, coed). Due to limited space, early applicants have best chance for on-campus housing. **Activities:** Student government, radio, student newspaper, television, yearbook, Creative Arts Quarterly, choral groups, concert band, dance, drama, jazz band, marching band, music ensembles, musical theater, opera, pep band, symphony orchestra, jazz ensembles, fraternities, sororities.

ATHLETICS. NAIA, NCAA. **Intercollegiate:** Baseball M, basketball, cross-country, diving, football M, golf M, gymnastics W, ice hockey M, soccer W, softball W, swimming, tennis, track and field, volleyball W, wrestling M. **Intramural:** Badminton, basketball, bowling, diving, golf, racquetball, skiing, soccer, softball, swimming, tennis, volleyball, water polo M.

STUDENT SERVICES. Aptitude testing, career counseling, employment service for undergraduates, freshman orientation, health services, on-campus day care, personal counseling, placement service for graduates, special adviser for adult students, veterans counselor, minority student adviser, services/facilities for handicapped.

ANNUAL EXPENSES. Tuition and fees (projected): $2,189, $4,454 additional for out-of-state students. Minnesota residents pay Minnesota State University tuition and Eau Claire's required fees. **Room and board:** $3,300. **Books and supplies:** $175. **Other expenses:** $1,235.

FINANCIAL AID. 74% of freshmen, 75% of continuing students receive some form of aid. 98% of grants, 73% of loans, 30% of jobs based on need. 820 enrolled freshmen were judged to have need, all were offered aid. Academic, music/drama, leadership scholarships available. **Aid applications:** Closing date April 15; priority given to applications received by February 28; applicants notified on a rolling basis beginning on or about June 15; must reply by July 15 or within 3 weeks if notified thereafter.

ADDRESS/TELEPHONE. Roger L. Groenewold, Director of Admissions, University of Wisconsin: Eau Claire, 112 Schofield Hall, Eau Claire, WI 54701. (715) 836-5415. Fax: (715) 836-2380.

University of Wisconsin: Green Bay

Green Bay, Wisconsin CB code: 1859

Admissions: 76% of applicants accepted
Based on: ••• School record
• Essay, interview, recommendations, special talents, test scores
Completion: 85% of freshmen end year in good standing
20% graduate, 14% of these enter graduate study

4-year public university, coed. Founded in 1965. **Accreditation:** Regional. **Undergraduate enrollment:** 1,467 men, 2,315 women full time; 267 men, 630 women part time. **Graduate enrollment:** 25 men, 8 women full time; 52 men, 37 women part time. **Faculty:** 241 total (186 full time), 217 with doctorates or other terminal degrees. **Location:** Rural campus in small city; 120 miles from Milwaukee. **Calendar:** 4-1-4, limited summer session. **Microcomputers:** 200 located in dormitories, libraries, computer centers. **Special facilities:** Natural history bird and egg collection, Lawton Art Gallery, Cofrin Aboretum.

DEGREES OFFERED. AA, BA, BS, MS. 15 associate degrees awarded in 1992. 750 bachelor's degrees awarded. 25% in business and management, 6% communications, 9% multi/interdisciplinary studies, 5% physical sciences, 20% psychology, 7% social sciences, 8% visual and performing arts. Graduate degrees offered in 4 major fields of study.

UNDERGRADUATE MAJORS. Associate: Liberal/general studies, women's studies. **Bachelor's:** Accounting, art education, art history, arts management, biological and physical sciences, biology, business administration and management, business and management, chemistry, city/community/regional planning, communications, computer and information sciences, criminal justice studies, dramatic arts, early childhood education, earth sciences, economics, education, elementary education, English, English education, environmental design, environmental science, finance, food science and nutrition, foreign languages education, French, geography, German, history, humanities, humanities and social sciences, information sciences and systems, junior high education, liberal/general studies, linguistics, mathematics, mathematics education, music, music education, music history and appreciation, music performance, nursing, nutritional sciences, personnel management, philosophy, photography, physical sciences, physics, physiology, human and animal, political science and government, predentistry, preengineering, prelaw, premedicine, prepharmacy, preveterinary, psychology, public administration, renewable natural resources, science education, secondary education, small business management and ownership, social science education, social sciences, social studies education, social work, sociology, Spanish, studio art, technical education, theater design, urban studies, visual and performing arts.

ACADEMIC PROGRAMS. 2-year transfer program, double major, dual enrollment of high school students, external degree, independent study, internships, student-designed major, study abroad, teacher preparation, visiting/exchange student program, cross-registration. **Remedial services:** Learning center, reduced course load, remedial instruction, special counselor, tutoring, Educational Opportunity Program. **ROTC:** Army. **Placement/credit:** AP, CLEP General and Subject, institutional tests; 47 credit hours maximum for associate degree; 93 credit hours maximum for bachelor's degree.

ACADEMIC REQUIREMENTS. Freshmen must earn minimum GPA of 2.0 to continue in good standing. 77% of freshmen return for sophomore year. Students must declare major by end of second year. **Graduation requirements:** 62 hours for associate (12 in major), 124 hours for bachelor's (30 in major). Most students required to take courses in arts/fine arts, English, humanities, mathematics, biological/physical sciences, social sciences. **Additional information:** Minimum credit hours required in major for bachelor's degree varies depending on field. Teacher certification available in conjunction with bachelor's degree.

FRESHMAN ADMISSIONS. Selection criteria: School achievement record and rank in top half of graduating class. Priority given to top 45% of class or combination of class rank and ACT of 23 or higher. **High school preparation:** 14 units required. Required and recommended units include English 4, mathematics 2, social science 3 and science 2. Foreign language 2 recommended. Mathematics must include algebra or more advanced course. 3 academic electives from English, mathematics, science, social studies, or foreign language. **Test requirements:** ACT for placement; score report by June 1.

1992 FRESHMAN CLASS PROFILE. 15% were in top tenth and 47% were in top quarter of graduating class. **Academic background:** Mid 50% of enrolled freshmen had ACT composite between 20-24. 98% submitted ACT scores. **Characteristics:** 96% from in state, 56% live in college housing, 5% have minority backgrounds. Average age is 19.

FALL-TERM APPLICATIONS. $10 fee, may be waived for applicants with need. Closing date February 1; priority given to applications received by December 30; applicants notified on a rolling basis. Interview recommended for academically weak applicants. CRDA.

STUDENT LIFE. Housing: Dormitories (coed); apartment, handicapped housing available. **Activities:** Student government, magazine, radio, student newspaper, television, choral groups, concert band, dance, drama, jazz band, music ensembles, musical theater, pep band, symphony orchestra, fraternities, sororities, Young Republicans, Young Democrats, Baha'i, campus activities group, environmental concern organizations, special interest clubs, ethnic clubs, ecumenical club.

ATHLETICS. NAIA, NCAA. **Intercollegiate:** Basketball, cross-country, diving, golf M, soccer, softball W, swimming, tennis, volleyball W. **Intramural:** Basketball, racquetball, soccer, softball, swimming, volleyball.

STUDENT SERVICES. Aptitude testing, career counseling, employment service for undergraduates, freshman orientation, health services, on-campus day care, personal counseling, placement service for graduates, special adviser for adult students, veterans counselor, women's center, intercultural center, services/facilities for handicapped.

ANNUAL EXPENSES. Tuition and fees (projected): $2,120, $4,478 additional for out-of-state students. Minnesota residents pay Minnesota State University tuition. **Room and board:** $2,807. **Books and supplies:** $470. **Other expenses:** $1,332.

FINANCIAL AID. 60% of freshmen, 65% of continuing students receive some form of aid. 86% of grants, 83% of loans, 25% of jobs based on need. Academic, music/drama, art, athletic, state/district residency, leadership scholarships available. **Aid applications:** No closing date; priority given to applications received by April 15; applicants notified on a rolling basis beginning on or about April 1; must reply within 3 weeks.

ADDRESS/TELEPHONE. Myron Van de Ven, Director of Admissions, University of Wisconsin: Green Bay, 2420 Nicolet Drive, Green Bay, WI 54311-7001. (414) 465-2111.

University of Wisconsin: La Crosse
La Crosse, Wisconsin CB code: 1914

Admissions: 86% of applicants accepted
Based on: ••• School record
•• Test scores
• Activities, recommendations, special talents
Completion: 80% of freshmen end year in good standing
6% enter graduate study

4-year public university, coed. Founded in 1909. **Accreditation:** Regional. **Undergraduate enrollment:** 3,118 men, 4,049 women full time; 287 men, 353 women part time. **Graduate enrollment:** 82 men, 118 women full time; 133 men, 222 women part time. **Faculty:** 490 total (430 full time), 352 with doctorates or other terminal degrees. **Location:** Urban campus in small city; 140 miles from Madison, 160 miles from Minneapolis, St Paul. **Calendar:** Semester, limited summer session. **Microcomputers:** 300 located in dormitories, classrooms, computer centers. **Special facilities:** Museum, art galleries, greenhouse, planetarium, Norskedalen arboretum, nuclear radiation laboratory.

DEGREES OFFERED. AA, AS, BA, BS, MS, MBA, MEd. 100% in letters/literature. 1,324 bachelor's degrees awarded. 26% in business and management, 5% communications, 19% teacher education, 12% health sciences, 7% allied health, 8% parks/recreation, protective services, public affairs, 6% psychology, 5% social sciences. Graduate degrees offered in 17 major fields of study.

UNDERGRADUATE MAJORS. Associate: Liberal/general studies. **Bachelor's:** Accounting, archeology, art education, biology, business administration and management, business economics, chemistry, communications, computer and information sciences, dramatic arts, early childhood education, economics, education, elementary education, English, English education, finance, fine arts, foreign languages education, French, geography, health education, history, junior high education, marketing management, mathematics, mathematics education, medical laboratory technologies, microbiology, music, music education, nuclear medical technology, parks and recreation management, philosophy, physical education, physical therapy, physics, political science and government, predentistry, premedicine, prepharmacy, preveterinary, psychology, public administration, recreation therapy, science education, secondary education, social science education, social studies education, social work, sociology, Spanish, speech, speech/communication/theater education.

ACADEMIC PROGRAMS. Cooperative education, double major, dual enrollment of high school students, honors program, independent study, internships, study abroad, teacher preparation, visiting/exchange student program, cross-registration. **Remedial services:** Learning center, preadmission summer program, remedial instruction, special counselor, tutoring. **ROTC:** Army. **Placement/credit:** AP, CLEP Subject, institutional tests; 32 credit hours maximum for bachelor's degree.

ACADEMIC REQUIREMENTS. Freshmen must earn minimum GPA of 1.8 to continue in good standing. 75% of freshmen return for sophomore year. Students must declare major by end of first year. **Graduation requirements:** 64 hours for associate, 128 hours for bachelor's. Most students required to take courses in English, history, humanities, mathematics, biological/physical sciences, social sciences.

FRESHMAN ADMISSIONS. Selection criteria: Applicants should rank in top 40% of class or have minimum ACT composite score of 22 and complete 16 specified academic units. Minority applicants should rank in top two-thirds of class or have minimum ACT composite score of 21 and complete 16 academic units. **High school preparation:** 16 units required; 17 recommended. Required and recommended units include biological science 2, English 4, mathematics 2-4 and social science 3. Foreign language 2 and science 4 recommended. 5 additional academic units required. **Test requirements:** ACT; score report by June 1. **Additional information:** Minority students in the 33rd to 49th percentile may be eligible for admissions under the Academic Summer Institute Program.

1992 FRESHMAN CLASS PROFILE. 1,409 men applied, 1,202 accepted, 623 enrolled; 2,336 women applied, 2,023 accepted, 969 enrolled. 16% were in top tenth and 35% were in top quarter of graduating class. **Academic background:** Mid 50% of enrolled freshmen had ACT composite between 19-24. 99% submitted ACT scores. **Characteristics:** 86% from in state, 80% live in college housing, 1% have minority backgrounds, 1% are foreign students. Average age is 18.

FALL-TERM APPLICATIONS. $10 fee, may be waived for applicants with need. No closing date; priority given to applications received by January 1; applicants notified on a rolling basis. Interview required for physical therapy applicants. Deferred and early admission available.

STUDENT LIFE. Housing: Dormitories (women, coed); handicapped housing available. Overnight housing available for campus visits. **Activities:** Student government, radio, student newspaper, television, choral groups, concert band, dance, drama, jazz band, marching band, music ensembles, musical theater, opera, pep band, symphony orchestra, fraternities, sororities, Black Students Unity, Native American Council, Hispanic Student Organization, Asian Association, Student Association, Amnesty International, United Campus Ministry, Newman Club, Hall Councils, Intervarsity Christian

Fellowship. **Additional information:** Campus served by mass transit bus system; airport 7 miles from campus, passenger rail service 5 miles from campus.

ATHLETICS. NAIA, NCAA. **Intercollegiate:** Baseball M, basketball, cross-country, diving, football M, gymnastics W, soccer W, softball W, swimming, tennis, track and field, volleyball W, wrestling M. **Intramural:** Badminton, basketball, bowling, football M, golf M, handball, lacrosse M, racquetball, rugby, skiing, soccer M, softball, swimming, tennis, volleyball.

STUDENT SERVICES. Aptitude testing, career counseling, employment service for undergraduates, freshman orientation, health services, on-campus day care, personal counseling, placement service for graduates, special adviser for adult students, veterans counselor, Academic Summer Institute, services/facilities for handicapped.

ANNUAL EXPENSES. **Tuition and fees (projected):** $2,200, $4,450 additional for out-of-state students. Minnesota residents pay Minnesota State University tuition. **Room and board:** $2,300. **Books and supplies:** $150. **Other expenses:** $1,630.

FINANCIAL AID. 45% of freshmen, 47% of continuing students receive some form of aid. 98% of grants, 95% of loans, 26% of jobs based on need. 900 enrolled freshmen were judged to have need, 800 were offered aid. Academic, music/drama, state/district residency, leadership, minority scholarships available. **Aid applications:** No closing date; priority given to applications received by March 15; applicants notified on a rolling basis beginning on or about May 15; must reply within 3 weeks. **Additional information:** Scholarship resource center and job location program.

ADDRESS/TELEPHONE. Tim Lewis, Associate Director of Admissions, University of Wisconsin: La Crosse, 1725 State Street, La Crosse, WI 54601. (608) 785-8067.

University of Wisconsin: Madison
Madison, Wisconsin — CB code: 1846

Admissions: 75% of applicants accepted
Based on: ••• School record, special talents, test scores
• Activities, essay, interview, recommendations
Completion: 85% of freshmen end year in good standing
77% graduate, 45% of these enter graduate study

4-year public university, coed. Founded in 1849. **Accreditation:** Regional. **Undergraduate enrollment:** 12,998 men, 13,309 women full time; 1,285 men, 1,316 women part time. **Graduate enrollment:** 5,239 men, 4,189 women full time; 1,393 men, 1,113 women part time. **Faculty:** 2,325 total (2,245 full time), 2,205 with doctorates or other terminal degrees. **Location:** Urban campus in small city; 70 miles from Milwaukee, 150 miles from Chicago. **Calendar:** Semester, extensive summer session. **Microcomputers:** 2,400 located in dormitories, libraries, classrooms, computer centers. **Special facilities:** Art museum, teaching nuclear reactor, biotron for simulating enviroments, 1260-acre nature preserve, radio/television station, observatory, planetarium.

DEGREES OFFERED. BA, BS, MA, MS, MBA, MFA, MSW, PhD, MD, B. Pharm, DVM. 5,882 bachelor's degrees awarded in 1992. 10% in business and management, 9% communications, 5% teacher education, 11% engineering, 5% health sciences, 5% letters/literature, 5% life sciences, 21% social sciences. Graduate degrees offered in 160 major fields of study.

UNDERGRADUATE MAJORS. Accounting, actuarial sciences, African languages, Afro-American (black) studies, agribusiness, agricultural business and management, agricultural economics, agricultural education, agricultural engineering, agronomy, animal sciences, anthropology, applied mathematics, art education, art history, Asian studies, astrophysics, atmospheric sciences and meteorology, bacteriology, biochemistry, botany, business administration and management, business and management, chemical engineering, chemistry, Chinese, civil engineering, classics, communications, comparative literature, computer and information sciences, computer engineering, dairy, dramatic arts, early childhood education, earth sciences, economics, electrical/electronics/communications engineering, elementary education, engineering mechanics, English, entomology, family/consumer resource management, finance, fine arts, food science and nutrition, food sciences, forestry and related sciences, French, genetics, human and animal, geography, geological engineering, geology, geophysics and seismology, German, Greek (classical), Hebrew, history, home economics, home economics education, horticultural science, horticulture, Indic languages, individual and family development, industrial engineering, information sciences and systems, insurance and risk management, interior design, international relations, investments and securities, Italian, Japanese, journalism, landscape architecture, Latin, Latin American studies, linguistics, management information systems, marketing management, mathematics, mathematics education, mechanical engineering, medical laboratory technologies, microbiology, mining and mineral engineering, molecular biology, music, music education, music performance, music theory and composition, naval science (Navy, Marines), nuclear engineering, nursing, nutritional sciences, occupational therapy, operations research, parks and recreation management, pharmacy, philosophy, physical education, physical therapy, physician's assistant, physics, plant pathology, political science and government, Portuguese, poultry, psychology, radio/television broadcasting, real estate, rural sociology, Russian, Scandinavian languages, Scandinavian studies, science education, Slavic languages, social science education, social work, sociology, soil sciences, South Asian studies, Spanish, specific learning disabilities, speech, speech correction, speech pathology/audiology, speech/communication/theater education, statistics, textiles and clothing, transportation management, wildlife management, women's studies, zoology.

ACADEMIC PROGRAMS. Accelerated program, cooperative education, double major, dual enrollment of high school students, honors program, independent study, internships, student-designed major, study abroad, teacher preparation, cross-registration; combined bachelor's/graduate program in medicine, law. **Remedial services:** Learning center, preadmission summer program, reduced course load, remedial instruction, special counselor, tutoring. **ROTC:** Air Force, Army, Naval. **Placement/credit:** AP, CLEP General and Subject, IB, institutional tests.

ACADEMIC REQUIREMENTS. Freshmen must earn minimum GPA of 2.0 to continue in good standing. 91% of freshmen return for sophomore year. Students must declare major by end of second year. **Graduation requirements:** 120 hours for bachelor's (30 in major). Most students required to take courses in English, foreign languages, humanities, mathematics, biological/physical sciences, social sciences.

FRESHMAN ADMISSIONS. **Selection criteria:** Admission selective and competitive. **High school preparation:** 16 units required; 21 recommended. Required and recommended units include English 4, foreign language 2-4, mathematics 3-4, social science 3-4 and science 2-4. Mathematics units must include 1 each algebra and geometry, plus one year advanced mathematics. Computer science or statistics will not fulfill mathematics requirement. Two-year language requirement must be in the same language. **Test requirements:** SAT or ACT; score report by March 1. Wisconsin residents must submit ACT test scores.

1992 FRESHMAN CLASS PROFILE. 6,796 men applied, 4,967 accepted, 2,157 enrolled; 7,099 women applied, 5,397 accepted, 2,259 enrolled. 74% had high school GPA of 3.0 or higher, 26% between 2.0 and 2.99. 34% were in top tenth and 76% were in top quarter of graduating class. **Academic background:** Mid 50% of enrolled freshmen had SAT-V between 450-580, SAT-M between 540-660; ACT composite between 24-28. 39% submitted SAT scores, 84% submitted ACT scores. **Characteristics:** 67% from in state, 82% live in college housing, 8% have minority backgrounds, 3% are foreign students, 12% join fraternities/sororities. Average age is 18.

FALL-TERM APPLICATIONS. $10 fee, may be waived for applicants with need. Closing date February 1; applicants notified on a rolling basis; must reply by May 1. Audition required for music applicants. Portfolio recommended for __ fine arts applicants. CRDA. Early admission available.

STUDENT LIFE. **Housing:** Dormitories (men, women, coed); apartment, fraternity, sorority, cooperative housing available. Housing guaranteed for all students. **Activities:** Student government, film, magazine, radio, student newspaper, television, yearbook, choral groups, concert band, dance, drama, jazz band, marching band, music ensembles, musical theater, opera, pep band, symphony orchestra, fraternities, sororities, Asian-American Student Union, Movimiento Estudiantil, Chicano de Aztlan, Union Puertorriquena, Wisconsin Black Student Union, Wunk-Sheek, Minority Coalition.

ATHLETICS. NCAA. **Intercollegiate:** Basketball, cross-country, diving, football M, golf, ice hockey M, rowing (crew), soccer, swimming, tennis, track and field, volleyball W, wrestling. **Intramural:** Archery, badminton, basketball, bowling, cross-country, golf, handball, horseback riding, ice hockey, lacrosse, racquetball, rugby M, sailing, skiing, skin diving, soccer, softball, squash, swimming, table tennis, tennis, track and field, volleyball, water polo M, wrestling M.

STUDENT SERVICES. Aptitude testing, career counseling, employment service for undergraduates, freshman orientation, health services, on-campus day care, personal counseling, placement service for graduates, special adviser for adult students, veterans counselor, adult career and educational counseling center, services/facilities for handicapped.

ANNUAL EXPENSES. **Tuition and fees (projected):** $2,550, $5,960 additional for out-of-state students. Minnesota residents pay Minnesota State University tuition. **Room and board:** $4,000. **Books and supplies:** $535. **Other expenses:** $1,200.

FINANCIAL AID. 39% of freshmen, 45% of continuing students receive some form of aid. 67% of grants, 94% of loans, 7% of jobs based on need. 1,772 enrolled freshmen were judged to have need, all were offered aid. Academic, music/drama, art, athletic, state/district residency, leadership, minority scholarships available. **Aid applications:** No closing date; priority given to applications received by March 1; applicants notified on a rolling basis beginning on or about April 15; must reply within 3 weeks.

ADDRESS/TELEPHONE. Millard Storey, Director of Admissions, University of Wisconsin: Madison, 750 University Avenue, Madison, WI 53706-1490. (608) 262-3961.

University of Wisconsin: Milwaukee
Milwaukee, Wisconsin CB code: 1473

4-year public university, coed. Founded in 1956. **Accreditation:** Regional. **Undergraduate enrollment:** 19,715 men and women. **Graduate enrollment:** 4,626 men and women. **Location:** Urban campus in very large city; 90 miles from Chicago. **Calendar:** Semester.

FRESHMAN ADMISSIONS. Selection criteria: High school academic record and class rank (top half) important. If applicant ranks in lower half of class, minimum enhanced ACT score of 21 required. Equivalent SAT score for out-of-state residents required. Additional requirements for architecture, engineering and fine arts applicants.

ANNUAL EXPENSES. Tuition and fees (projected): $2,392, $5,286 additional for out-of-state students. Minnesota residents pay Minnesota State University tuition. **Room and board:** $3,838. **Books and supplies:** $553. **Other expenses:** $3,838.

ADDRESS/TELEPHONE. Frederick Sperry, Executive Director of Enrollment Services and Registrar, University of Wisconsin: Milwaukee, PO Box 340, Milwaukee, WI 53201. (414) 229-1122. Fax: (414) 229-6967.

University of Wisconsin: Oshkosh
Oshkosh, Wisconsin CB code: 1916

Admissions:	77% of applicants accepted
Based on:	••• School record
	•• Test scores
	• Special talents
Completion:	70% of freshmen end year in good standing

4-year public university, coed. Founded in 1871. **Accreditation:** Regional. **Undergraduate enrollment:** 3,313 men, 4,489 women full time; 573 men, 833 women part time. **Graduate enrollment:** 46 men, 95 women full time; 495 men, 826 women part time. **Faculty:** 524 total (409 full time), 326 with doctorates or other terminal degrees. **Location:** Suburban campus in small city; 90 miles from Milwaukee. **Calendar:** Semester, extensive summer session. Extensive evening/early morning classes. **Microcomputers:** 500 located in dormitories, libraries, classrooms, computer centers. **Special facilities:** Student-run art gallery, Buckstaff Planetarium.

DEGREES OFFERED. AA, AS, BA, BS, BFA, MS, MBA, MEd. 40 associate degrees awarded in 1992. 1,468 bachelor's degrees awarded. 25% in business and management, 8% communications, 15% education, 9% health sciences, 5% letters/literature, 9% parks/recreation, protective services, public affairs, 11% social sciences. Graduate degrees offered in 22 major fields of study.

UNDERGRADUATE MAJORS. Associate: Liberal/general studies. **Bachelor's:** Accounting, advertising, anthropology, biology, business administration and management, business data processing and related programs, business data programming, business systems analysis, chemistry, chiropractic, cinematography/film, clinical laboratory science, communications, computer and information sciences, computer programming, criminal justice studies, data processing, dramatic arts, early childhood education, earth sciences, economics, education, education of the mentally handicapped, elementary education, English, English education, finance, fine arts, foreign languages education, French, geography, geology, German, history, human resources development, information sciences and systems, international business management, international relations, investments and securities, journalism, junior high education, law enforcement and corrections, management information systems, management science, marketing and distribution, marketing management, marketing research, mathematics, mathematics education, microbiology, military science (Army), motion picture technology, music, music business management, music education, music performance, music theory and composition, music therapy, nursing, operations research, optometry, personnel management, pharmacy, philosophy, photographic technology, physical education, physics, podiatry or podiatric medicine, political science and government, predentistry, prelaw, premedicine, prepharmacy, preveterinary, psychology, public administration, public affairs, public relations, radio/television broadcasting, radio/television technology, religion, science education, secondary education, small business management and ownership, social science education, social sciences, social studies education, social work, sociology, Spanish, special education, specific learning disabilities, speech, speech/communication/theater education, sports management, systems analysis, urban studies, visual and performing arts.

ACADEMIC PROGRAMS. Double major, dual enrollment of high school students, honors program, independent study, internships, student-designed major, study abroad, teacher preparation, weekend college. **Remedial services:** Learning center, preadmission summer program, reduced course load, special counselor, tutoring, basic skills program. **ROTC:** Army. **Placement/credit:** AP, CLEP General and Subject, institutional tests; 32 credit hours maximum for bachelor's degree.

ACADEMIC REQUIREMENTS. Freshmen must earn minimum GPA of 2.0 to continue in good standing. 73% of freshmen return for sophomore year. Students must declare major by end of second year. **Graduation requirements:** 64 hours for associate, 128 hours for bachelor's. Most students required to take courses in arts/fine arts, English, history, humanities, mathematics, biological/physical sciences, social sciences.

FRESHMAN ADMISSIONS. Selection criteria: Students must rank in top half of high school class or have ACT composite score of 23. **High school preparation:** 16 units required. Required units include English 4, mathematics 3, social science 3 and science 2. 4 academic electives. **Test requirements:** ACT.

1992 FRESHMAN CLASS PROFILE. 4,300 men and women applied, 3,300 accepted; 1,488 enrolled. 16% were in top tenth and 46% were in top quarter of graduating class. **Characteristics:** 96% from in state, 87% live in college housing. Average age is 18.

FALL-TERM APPLICATIONS. $10 fee, may be waived for applicants with need. No closing date; applicants notified on a rolling basis. Audition required for music applicants. Portfolio required for art applicants. Deferred and early admission available. ACT score must be submitted by registration.

STUDENT LIFE. Housing: Dormitories (women, coed); fraternity, sorority housing available. Select group of freshmen take part in residential college experience for more individualized instruction. **Activities:** Student government, film, magazine, radio, student newspaper, television, choral groups, concert band, dance, drama, jazz band, music ensembles, musical theater, pep band, symphony orchestra, debate, fraternities, sororities, multicultural center, campus ministry center.

ATHLETICS. NCAA. **Intercollegiate:** Baseball M, basketball, cross-country, football M, gymnastics, soccer M, softball W, swimming, tennis, track and field, volleyball W, wrestling M. **Intramural:** Badminton, basketball, bowling, sailing, skiing, softball, volleyball.

STUDENT SERVICES. Aptitude testing, career counseling, employment service for undergraduates, freshman orientation, health services, on-campus day care, personal counseling, placement service for graduates, special adviser for adult students, veterans counselor, services/facilities for handicapped.

ANNUAL EXPENSES. Tuition and fees (projected): $2,062, $4,356 additional for out-of-state students. Minnesota residents pay Minnesota State University tuition. **Room and board:** $2,400. **Books and supplies:** $494. **Other expenses:** $1,457.

FINANCIAL AID. 45% of freshmen, 45% of continuing students receive some form of aid. 96% of grants, 95% of loans, 40% of jobs based on need. 700 enrolled freshmen were judged to have need, all were offered aid. Academic, music/drama, art, state/district residency, leadership, minority scholarships available. **Aid applications:** No closing date; priority given to applications received by March 15; applicants notified on a rolling basis beginning on or about June 1; must reply within 2 weeks. **Additional information:** After 1 year of completed course work, foreign students may apply for out-of-state tuition waiver.

ADDRESS/TELEPHONE. August Helgerson, Director of Admissions, University of Wisconsin: Oshkosh, 800 Algoma Boulevard, Oshkosh, WI 54901. (414) 424-0202. (800) 624-1466. Fax: (414) 424-7317.

University of Wisconsin: Parkside
Kenosha, Wisconsin CB code: 1860

Admissions:	77% of applicants accepted
Based on:	••• School record
	•• Test scores
Completion:	63% of freshmen end year in good standing
	17% enter graduate study

4-year public university, coed. Founded in 1965. **Accreditation:** Regional. **Undergraduate enrollment:** 1,379 men, 1,710 women full time; 757 men, 1,042 women part time. **Graduate enrollment:** 3 men, 2 women full time; 48 men, 52 women part time. **Faculty:** 280 total (155 full time), 122 with doctorates or other terminal degrees. **Location:** Suburban campus in small city; 30 miles from downtown Milwaukee. **Calendar:** Semester, extensive summer session. **Microcomputers:** Located in libraries, computer centers.

DEGREES OFFERED. BA, BS, MS, MBA. 546 bachelor's degrees awarded in 1992. 25% in business and management, 9% communications, 8% letters/literature, 8% life sciences, 12% psychology, 20% social sciences. Graduate degrees offered in 2 major fields of study.

UNDERGRADUATE MAJORS. Biology, business and management, chemistry, communications, computer and information sciences, dramatic arts, economics, English, geography, geology, history, humanities and social sciences, international studies, labor/industrial relations, mathematics, music, philosophy, physics, political science and government, psychology, sociology, Spanish, visual and performing arts.

ACADEMIC PROGRAMS. Accelerated program, double major, honors program, independent study, internships, study abroad, teacher preparation, cross-registration, cooperative nursing program with University of Wisconsin: Milwaukee. **Remedial services:** Learning center, remedial instruction, special counselor, tutoring, basic skills program. **Placement/credit:** AP, CLEP General and Subject, institutional tests; 30 credit hours maximum for bachelor's degree.

ACADEMIC REQUIREMENTS. Freshmen must earn minimum GPA of 2.0 to continue in good standing. 81% of freshmen return for sophomore

year. Students must declare major by end of second year. **Graduation requirements:** 120 hours for bachelor's. Most students required to take courses in arts/fine arts, English, foreign languages, mathematics, biological/physical sciences, social sciences.

FRESHMAN ADMISSIONS. Selection criteria: Rank in top half of graduating class, specified distribution of high school units, or test scores important. **High school preparation:** 16 units required. Required units include English 4, mathematics 2, social science 3 and science 2. 5 units of fine arts and computer science. Mathematics must include algebra and geometry. **Test requirements:** ACT; score report by August 1. Out-of-state applicants may submit either SAT or ACT test scores.

1992 FRESHMAN CLASS PROFILE. 1,425 men and women applied, 1,101 accepted; 282 men enrolled, 464 women enrolled. 8% were in top tenth and 24% were in top quarter of graduating class. **Academic background:** Mid 50% of enrolled freshmen had ACT composite between 17-23. 81% submitted ACT scores. **Characteristics:** 95% from in state, 95% commute, 10% have minority backgrounds.

FALL-TERM APPLICATIONS. $10 fee, may be waived for applicants with need. Closing date August 1; applicants notified on a rolling basis.

STUDENT LIFE. Housing: Dormitories (coed). Residence halls offer apartment-style living. **Activities:** Student government, radio, student newspaper, choral groups, concert band, drama, jazz band, music ensembles, musical theater, pep band, symphony orchestra, Young Democrats, Newman Club, Christian fellowship, minority student union.

ATHLETICS. NAIA, NCAA. **Intercollegiate:** Baseball M, basketball, bowling, cross-country, fencing, golf M, soccer M, softball W, tennis, track and field, volleyball W, wrestling M. **Intramural:** Badminton, basketball, bowling, golf, handball, racquetball, skiing, softball, table tennis, volleyball.

STUDENT SERVICES. Career counseling, employment service for undergraduates, freshman orientation, health services, on-campus day care, personal counseling, placement service for graduates, special adviser for adult students, veterans counselor, services/facilities for handicapped.

ANNUAL EXPENSES. Tuition and fees (projected): $2,100, $4,500 additional for out-of-state students. Minnesota residents pay Minnesota State University tuition. **Room and board:** $3,650. **Books and supplies:** $500. **Other expenses:** $1,100.

FINANCIAL AID. 35% of freshmen, 30% of continuing students receive some form of aid. 83% of grants, 77% of loans, 19% of jobs based on need. Academic, music/drama, art, athletic, state/district residency, leadership, alumni affiliation, minority scholarships available. **Aid applications:** Closing date June 15; priority given to applications received by April 1; applicants notified on or about June 15; must reply within 2 weeks.

ADDRESS/TELEPHONE. Chuck Murphy, Director of Admissions, University of Wisconsin: Parkside, PO Box 2000, Kenosha, WI 53141-2000. (414) 595-2573.

University of Wisconsin: Platteville
Platteville, Wisconsin — CB code: 1917

4-year public university, coed. Founded in 1866. **Accreditation:** Regional. **Undergraduate enrollment:** 2,900 men, 1,481 women full time; 238 men, 199 women part time. **Graduate enrollment:** 36 men, 32 women full time; 59 men, 109 women part time. **Faculty:** 295 total (250 full time), 146 with doctorates or other terminal degrees. **Location:** Rural campus in small town; 70 miles from Madison, 25 miles from Dubuque, Iowa. **Calendar:** Semester, limited summer session. **Microcomputers:** Located in dormitories, libraries, classrooms, computer centers. **Special facilities:** Art gallery, center for the arts, pioneer prairie farm, hiking nature trail, prairie preserves.

DEGREES OFFERED. AA, BA, BS, MS. 1,100 bachelor's degrees awarded. 10% in agriculture, 70% engineering, 10% mathematics, 10% social sciences. Graduate degrees offered in 8 major fields of study.

UNDERGRADUATE MAJORS. Associate: Liberal/general studies. **Bachelor's:** Accounting, agribusiness, agricultural economics, agricultural education, agricultural engineering, agricultural sciences, agronomy, animal sciences, art education, biology, business administration and management, business and management, business economics, chemistry, civil engineering, communications, computer and information sciences, construction, criminal justice studies, early childhood education, economics, electrical/electronics/communications engineering, elementary education, English, English education, finance, foreign languages education, geography, German, graphic and printing production, graphic arts technology, graphic design, history, horticultural science, industrial arts education, industrial engineering, industrial technology, international studies, investments and securities, junior high education, library science, marketing management, mathematics, mathematics education, mechanical engineering, music, music education, occupational safety and health technology, personnel management, philosophy, photographic technology, physical education, physical sciences, physics, political science and government, psychology, public relations, radio/television broadcasting, radio/television technology, reading education, renewable natural resources, science education, secondary education, small business management and ownership, social science education, social sciences, social studies education, soil sciences, Spanish, speech, speech/communication/theater education, telecommunications, trade and industrial education.

ACADEMIC PROGRAMS. Cooperative education, double major, dual enrollment of high school students, external degree, honors program, independent study, internships, student-designed major, study abroad, visiting/exchange student program. **Remedial services:** Learning center, tutoring. **Placement/credit:** AP, CLEP Subject, institutional tests; 30 credit hours maximum for bachelor's degree.

ACADEMIC REQUIREMENTS. Freshmen must earn minimum GPA of 1.8 to continue in good standing. 65% of freshmen return for sophomore year. Students must declare major by end of first year. **Graduation requirements:** 64 hours for associate, 128 hours for bachelor's (36 in major). Most students required to take courses in arts/fine arts, English, foreign languages, history, humanities, mathematics, biological/physical sciences, social sciences. **Postgraduate studies:** 56% from 2-year programs enter 4-year programs.

FRESHMAN ADMISSIONS. Selection criteria: Rank in top 40% of graduating class or ACT composite score of 22 for standard admission. Applicants in top 65% of class or with ACT composit score of 20 may be put on waiting list. **High school preparation:** 14 units required. Required units include biological science 1, English 4, mathematics 2, physical science 1 and social science 3. 2 units natural science (1 from biology, chemistry, or physics), 2 units mathematics including algebra and geometry also required. 3 additional units to be chosen from English, mathematics, science, social science, and foreign language.

1992 FRESHMAN CLASS PROFILE. 575 men, 305 women enrolled. **Characteristics:** 85% from in state, 80% live in college housing, 3% have minority backgrounds, 1% are foreign students, 15% join fraternities/sororities. Average age is 18.

FALL-TERM APPLICATIONS. $10 fee. No closing date; priority given to applications received by February 1; applicants notified on a rolling basis. Audition required for music applicants. CRDA.

STUDENT LIFE. Housing: Dormitories (men, women, coed); handicapped housing available. **Activities:** Student government, magazine, radio, student newspaper, television, yearbook, choral groups, concert band, drama, jazz band, marching band, music ensembles, musical theater, pep band, symphony orchestra, fraternities, sororities.

ATHLETICS. NCAA. **Intercollegiate:** Baseball M, basketball, cross-country, football M, soccer, softball W, tennis W, track and field, volleyball W, wrestling M. **Intramural:** Baseball M, basketball, bowling, racquetball, soccer, softball, tennis, volleyball, water polo M.

STUDENT SERVICES. Aptitude testing, career counseling, employment service for undergraduates, freshman orientation, health services, on-campus day care, personal counseling, placement service for graduates, special adviser for adult students, veterans counselor, services/facilities for handicapped.

ANNUAL EXPENSES. Tuition and fees (projected): $2,200, $4,200 additional for out-of-state students. Minnesota residents pay Minnesota State University tuition. **Room and board:** $2,550. **Books and supplies:** $300. **Other expenses:** $1,100.

FINANCIAL AID. 75% of freshmen, 67% of continuing students receive some form of aid. All grants, 89% of loans, 32% of jobs based on need. 690 enrolled freshmen were judged to have need, 624 were offered aid. Academic, leadership scholarships available. **Aid applications:** No closing date; priority given to applications received by March 15; applicants notified on a rolling basis beginning on or about June 1; must reply within 2 weeks.

ADDRESS/TELEPHONE. Dr. Richard Schumacher, Dean of Admissions and Enrollment Managment, University of Wisconsin: Platteville, 1 University Plaza, Platteville, WI 53818. (608) 342-1125.

University of Wisconsin: River Falls
River Falls, Wisconsin — CB code: 1918

4-year public university, coed. Founded in 1874. **Accreditation:** Regional. **Undergraduate enrollment:** 2,064 men, 2,458 women full time; 209 men, 290 women part time. **Graduate enrollment:** 34 men, 100 women full time; 60 men, 225 women part time. **Faculty:** 246 total (241 full time). **Location:** Suburban campus in large town; 25 miles from Minneapolis-St. Paul. **Calendar:** Semester, limited summer session. **Microcomputers:** 250 located in dormitories, libraries, computer centers. **Special facilities:** 2 laboratory farms, 20-inch reflecting telescope, USDA-approved food science laboratory, computerized greenhouse, 42-foot rappelling and climbing wall, electron microscope, Education Technology Center.

DEGREES OFFERED. AA, BA, BS, BFA, MA, MS. 740 bachelor's degrees awarded. 26% in agriculture, 17% business and management, 9% education, 13% teacher education, 11% social sciences. Graduate degrees offered in 17 major fields of study.

UNDERGRADUATE MAJORS. Bachelor's: Accounting, agribusiness, agricultural business and management, agricultural economics, agricultural education, agricultural engineering, agricultural mechanics, agricultural sciences, agronomy, American studies, animal sciences, art education, biochemistry, biological and physical sciences, biology, biotechnology, business administration and management, business and management, chemistry, communications, computer and information sciences, conservation and regulation, dairy, dramatic arts, early childhood education, earth sciences, economics, education, elementary education, English, English education, equestrian science, food sciences, foreign languages education, French, geography, geology, German, history, horticultural science, horticulture, humanities and social sciences, journalism, junior high education, law enforcement and corrections, liberal/general studies, mathematics, mathematics education, music, music education, parks and recreation management, physical education, physical sciences, physics, plant sciences, political science and government, psychology, radio/television broadcasting, renewable natural resources, science education, secondary education, social science education, social sciences, social work, sociology, soil sciences, speech, speech correction, speech pathology/audiology, speech/communication/theater education, studio art, visual and performing arts.

ACADEMIC PROGRAMS. Accelerated program, cooperative education, double major, dual enrollment of high school students, external degree, honors program, independent study, internships, student-designed major, study abroad, teacher preparation, visiting/exchange student program. **Remedial services:** Learning center, reduced course load, tutoring. **Placement/credit:** AP, CLEP General, institutional tests; 33 credit hours maximum for bachelor's degree.

ACADEMIC REQUIREMENTS. Freshmen must earn minimum GPA of 2.0 to continue in good standing. 70% of freshmen return for sophomore year. Students must declare major by end of first year. **Graduation requirements:** 128 hours for bachelor's (34 in major). Most students required to take courses in English, humanities, mathematics, biological/physical sciences, social sciences. **Postgraduate studies:** 2% enter law school, 2% enter medical school, 1% enter MBA programs, 6% enter other graduate study.

FRESHMAN ADMISSIONS. Selection criteria: High school rank in top 40% of class or minimum ACT composite score of 22. Minority student applications given special consideration. **High school preparation:** 16 units required. Required and recommended units include English 4, mathematics 2-4, social science 3-4 and science 2-4. Vocational agriculture units also recommended for applicants to College of Agriculture. Wisconsin residents who receive GED must also complete Wisconsin high school equivalency diploma. **Test requirements:** ACT; score report by August 15.

1992 FRESHMAN CLASS PROFILE. 476 men, 550 women enrolled. 13% were in top tenth and 41% were in top quarter of graduating class. **Academic background:** Mid 50% of enrolled freshmen had ACT composite between 19-24. 98% submitted ACT scores. **Characteristics:** 57% from in state, 83% live in college housing, 3% have minority backgrounds, 2% are foreign students, 5% join fraternities/sororities. Average age is 19.

FALL-TERM APPLICATIONS. $10 fee, may be waived for applicants with need. No closing date; priority given to applications received by January 1; applicants notified on a rolling basis. Interview recommended. Late applicants considered on individual basis through appeal procedure.

STUDENT LIFE. Housing: Dormitories (men, women, coed); fraternity housing available. State of Wisconsin requires freshmen and sophomores to live in residence halls unless they reside with parents nearby. **Activities:** Student government, magazine, radio, student newspaper, television, choral groups, concert band, dance, drama, jazz band, marching band, music ensembles, musical theater, pep band, symphony orchestra, fraternities, sororities, African American Alliance, Hispanic Student Coalition, Native American Council, Hmong Student Association.

ATHLETICS. NCAA. **Intercollegiate:** Baseball M, basketball, cross-country, diving, football M, golf M, gymnastics W, ice hockey, soccer W, softball W, swimming, tennis, track and field, volleyball W, wrestling M. **Intramural:** Badminton, basketball, bowling, cross-country, golf, handball, ice hockey, racquetball, skiing, soccer, softball, swimming, table tennis, tennis, volleyball, water polo, wrestling M.

STUDENT SERVICES. Aptitude testing, career counseling, employment service for undergraduates, freshman orientation, health services, on-campus day care, personal counseling, placement service for graduates, special adviser for adult students, veterans counselor, services/facilities for handicapped.

ANNUAL EXPENSES. Tuition and fees (1992-93): $1,958, $4,185 additional for out-of-state students. Minnesota residents pay Minnesota State University tuition. **Room and board:** $2,240. **Books and supplies:** $175. **Other expenses:** $1,100.

FINANCIAL AID. 72% of freshmen, 78% of continuing students receive some form of aid. Grants, loans, jobs available. Academic, music/drama, art, state/district residency, leadership, minority scholarships available. **Aid applications:** No closing date; priority given to applications received by March 18; must reply within 2 weeks.

ADDRESS/TELEPHONE. Alan Tuchtenhagen, Director of Admissions, University of Wisconsin: River Falls, 112 South Hall, River Falls, WI 54022. (715) 425-3500.

University of Wisconsin: Stevens Point
Stevens Point, Wisconsin — CB code: 1919

Admissions: 61% of applicants accepted
Based on: ••• School record, test scores
• Recommendations, special talents
Completion: 85% of freshmen end year in good standing
27% graduate, 15% of these enter graduate study

4-year public university, coed. Founded in 1894. **Accreditation:** Regional. **Undergraduate enrollment:** 3,598 men, 3,770 women full time; 306 men, 484 women part time. **Graduate enrollment:** 468 men and women. **Faculty:** 462 total (392 full time), 297 with doctorates or other terminal degrees. **Location:** Rural campus in large town; 110 miles from Madison, 240 miles from Chicago. **Calendar:** Semester, extensive summer session. Saturday and extensive evening/early morning classes. **Microcomputers:** 1,500 located in dormitories, libraries, computer centers. **Special facilities:** Natural history museum, art gallery, planetarium and observatory, nature preserve, Foucault pendulum, electron microscope, 1,000-acre natural resources summer camp, fire science center.

DEGREES OFFERED. BA, BS, BFA, MA, MS, MFA. 12 associate degrees awarded in 1992. 1,423 bachelor's degrees awarded. 12% in agriculture, 13% business and management, 9% communications, 13% teacher education, 11% life sciences, 13% social sciences. Graduate degrees offered in 11 major fields of study.

UNDERGRADUATE MAJORS. Associate: Liberal/general studies. **Bachelor's:** Accounting, anthropology, art education, arts management, biological and physical sciences, biology, business administration and management, business economics, chemistry, clinical laboratory science, communications, Communicative disorders, dance, dramatic arts, early childhood education, elementary education, English, English education, fashion merchandising, fine arts, food management, forestry and related sciences, French, geography, German, health education, history, home economics education, information sciences and systems, interior design, mathematics, mathematics education, music, music education, music literature, musical theater, paper engineering, philosophy, physical education, physics, political science and government, psychology, public administration, renewable natural resources, Resource management, science education, secondary education, social science education, social sciences, sociology, soil sciences, Spanish, speech pathology/audiology, textiles and clothing, visual and performing arts, water and wastewater technology, water resources, wildlife management.

ACADEMIC PROGRAMS. Cooperative education, double major, dual enrollment of high school students, honors program, independent study, internships, student-designed major, study abroad, teacher preparation, weekend college, cross-registration, cooperative program with University of Wisconsin: Eau Claire and St. Joseph's Hospital. **Remedial services:** Learning center, preadmission summer program, reduced course load, remedial instruction, special counselor, tutoring. **ROTC:** Army. **Placement/credit:** AP, CLEP General and Subject, institutional tests.

ACADEMIC REQUIREMENTS. Freshmen must earn minimum GPA of 2.0 to continue in good standing. 76% of freshmen return for sophomore year. Students must declare major by end of second year. **Graduation requirements:** 62 hours for associate, 124 hours for bachelor's (34 in major). Most students required to take courses in English, history, mathematics, biological/physical sciences, social sciences. **Postgraduate studies:** 1% enter law school, 1% enter medical school, 13% enter other graduate study.

FRESHMAN ADMISSIONS. Selection criteria: Rank in top half of class or minimum ACT composite score of 22. Others may qualify based on combination of class rank and ACT composite score. **High school preparation:** 16 units required. Required and recommended units include English 4, mathematics 2, social science 3 and science 2. Foreign language 2 recommended. Additional 3 units from English, mathematics, social sciences, sciences or foreign language; 2 units from above areas or fine arts, computer science and other academic areas. **Test requirements:** ACT.

1992 FRESHMAN CLASS PROFILE. 3,975 men and women applied, 2,440 accepted; 1,398 enrolled. **Academic background:** Mid 50% of enrolled freshmen had ACT composite between 17-24. 97% submitted ACT scores. **Characteristics:** 90% from in state, 89% live in college housing, 2% are foreign students, 2% join fraternities/sororities. Average age is 19.

FALL-TERM APPLICATIONS. $10 fee, may be waived for applicants with need. No closing date; applicants notified on a rolling basis.

STUDENT LIFE. Housing: Dormitories (men, women, coed). Foreign language dormitory wings, quiet wings available. **Activities:** Student government, film, radio, student newspaper, television, yearbook, choral groups, concert band, dance, drama, jazz band, marching band, music ensembles, musical theater, pep band, symphony orchestra, opera workshop, fraternities, sororities, Campus Crusade for Christ, American Indians Resisting Ostracism, Black Student Coalition, College Republicans, Young Democrats, Christian Science Organization, Lutheran Student Community, academic and sports clubs, Association for Community Tasks, Baha'i club, Campus Advance-Cornerstone Christian Ministry, campus Bible fellowship, Lutheran Collegians.

ATHLETICS. NAIA, NCAA. **Intercollegiate:** Baseball M, basketball, cross-country, diving, football M, golf M, ice hockey M, soccer W, softball W, swimming, tennis, track and field, volleyball W, wrestling M. **Intramural:** Archery, badminton, basketball, football, racquetball, rugby M, soccer M, softball, swimming, tennis, track and field, volleyball, wrestling M.

STUDENT SERVICES. Aptitude testing, career counseling, employment service for undergraduates, freshman orientation, health services, on-campus day care, personal counseling, placement service for graduates, special adviser for adult students, veterans counselor, services/facilities for handicapped.

ANNUAL EXPENSES. Tuition and fees (projected): $2,250, $4,520 additional for out-of-state students. Minnesota residents pay Minnesota State University tuition. **Room and board:** $3,030. **Books and supplies:** $300. **Other expenses:** $1,190.

FINANCIAL AID. 60% of freshmen, 69% of continuing students receive some form of aid. Grants, loans, jobs available. Academic, music/drama, art, minority scholarships available. **Aid applications:** Closing date July 15; priority given to applications received by March 15; applicants notified on a rolling basis beginning on or about May 1; must reply within 4 weeks.

ADDRESS/TELEPHONE. Dr. John A. Larsen, Director of Admissions, University of Wisconsin: Stevens Point, Student Services Center, Stevens Point, WI 54481. (715) 346-2441. Fax: (715) 346-3957.

University of Wisconsin: Stout
Menomonie, Wisconsin — CB code: 1740

Admissions: 75% of applicants accepted
Based on: ••• School record, test scores
Completion: 70% of freshmen end year in good standing
50% graduate

4-year public university, coed. Founded in 1891. **Accreditation:** Regional. **Undergraduate enrollment:** 3,203 men, 3,019 women full time; 289 men, 292 women part time. **Graduate enrollment:** 294 men and women full time; 246 men and women part time. **Faculty:** 603 total (523 full time), 240 with doctorates or other terminal degrees. **Location:** Rural campus in large town; 60 miles from Minneapolis-St. Paul, Minnesota. **Calendar:** Semester, extensive summer session. **Microcomputers:** 800 located in dormitories, libraries, classrooms, computer centers. **Special facilities:** Furlong Art Gallery, Stout Teleproduction Center.

DEGREES OFFERED. BA, BS, BFA, MS, MEd. 1,131 bachelor's degrees awarded in 1992. 34% in business and management, 10% business/office and marketing/distribution, 7% education, 25% engineering technologies, 8% home economics, 6% visual and performing arts. Graduate degrees offered in 13 major fields of study.

UNDERGRADUATE MAJORS. Applied mathematics, applied technology, art education, business administration and management, business home economics, child development/care/guidance, clothing and textiles management/production/services, construction, early childhood education, fashion merchandising, fine arts, food production/management/services, food science and nutrition, home economics, home economics education, hotel/motel and restaurant management, industrial arts education, industrial technology, marketing and distributive education, psychology, retailing, textiles and clothing, trade and industrial education, vocational rehabilitation.

ACADEMIC PROGRAMS. Cooperative education, double major, dual enrollment of high school students, education specialist degree, independent study, internships, study abroad. **Remedial services:** Learning center, preadmission summer program, reduced course load, remedial instruction, special counselor, tutoring. **Placement/credit:** AP, CLEP Subject, institutional tests.

ACADEMIC REQUIREMENTS. Freshmen must earn minimum GPA of 2.0 to continue in good standing. 70% of freshmen return for sophomore year. Students must declare major on application. **Graduation requirements:** 130 hours for bachelor's. Most students required to take courses in arts/fine arts, computer science, English, history, mathematics, biological/physical sciences, social sciences.

FRESHMAN ADMISSIONS. Selection criteria: Limited enrollment in all programs. Rank in top 50% of high school class; if below 50th percentile, ACT score of 21 or better. **High school preparation:** 16 units required. Required units include English 4, mathematics 2, social science 3 and science 2. 5 electives in English, mathematics, social sciences, and sciences. **Test requirements:** ACT. ACT required for applicants in lower quarter of high school class.

1992 FRESHMAN CLASS PROFILE. 2,416 men and women applied, 1,819 accepted; 463 men enrolled, 536 women enrolled. 9% were in top tenth and 30% were in top quarter of graduating class. **Characteristics:** 71% from in state, 88% live in college housing, 6% have minority backgrounds, 1% are foreign students. Average age is 20.

FALL-TERM APPLICATIONS. $10 fee, may be waived for applicants with need. No closing date; priority given to applications received by January 1; applicants notified on a rolling basis. Deferred and early admission available. Enrollment limited by UW system. Early application recommended.

STUDENT LIFE. Housing: Dormitories (coed); apartment, fraternity, sorority, handicapped housing available. Summer housing available for married graduate students. **Activities:** Student government, film, radio, student newspaper, television, choral groups, concert band, dance, drama, jazz band, marching band, music ensembles, musical theater, pep band, symphony orchestra, Dixieland band, dance band, fraternities, sororities.

ATHLETICS. NAIA, NCAA. **Intercollegiate:** Baseball M, basketball, cross-country, football M, golf M, gymnastics W, swimming, tennis, track and field, volleyball W, wrestling M. **Intramural:** Archery, badminton, basketball, bowling, cross-country, golf, ice hockey, racquetball, skiing, soccer, softball, table tennis, tennis, volleyball, wrestling M.

STUDENT SERVICES. Aptitude testing, career counseling, employment service for undergraduates, freshman orientation, health services, on-campus day care, personal counseling, placement service for graduates, veterans counselor, services/facilities for handicapped.

ANNUAL EXPENSES. Tuition and fees (1992-93): $1,974, $4,185 additional for out-of-state students. Minnesota residents pay Minnesota State University tuition. **Room and board:** $2,462. **Books and supplies:** $342. **Other expenses:** $1,340.

FINANCIAL AID. 59% of freshmen, 57% of continuing students receive some form of aid. Grants, loans, jobs available. 543 enrolled freshmen were judged to have need, 504 were offered aid. Academic, music/drama, art, state/district residency, leadership, minority scholarships available. **Aid applications:** No closing date; priority given to applications received by April 15; applicants notified on a rolling basis beginning on or about June 1; must reply within 2 weeks.

ADDRESS/TELEPHONE. Charles Kell, Director of Admissions, University of Wisconsin: Stout, Broadway and Main, Menomonie, WI 54751. (715) 232-1411. (800) HI-STOUT.

University of Wisconsin: Superior
Superior, Wisconsin — CB code: 1920

4-year public university, coed. Founded in 1893. **Accreditation:** Regional. **Undergraduate enrollment:** 932 men, 981 women full time; 108 men, 190 women part time. **Faculty:** 185 total (115 full time), 90 with doctorates or other terminal degrees. **Location:** Urban campus in large town; 2 miles from Duluth, Minnesota. **Calendar:** Semester, extensive summer session. **Microcomputers:** 200 located in dormitories, libraries, classrooms, computer centers, campus-wide network. **Special facilities:** Research station on Lake Superior, 3 research vessels, Kathryn Ohman Film and Video Theater, Kruk Galleries.

DEGREES OFFERED. AA, BA, BS, BFA, MA. 21 associate degrees awarded in 1992. 279 bachelor's degrees awarded. 28% in business/office and marketing/distribution, 6% communications, 23% teacher education, 6% life sciences, 8% social sciences, 10% visual and performing arts. Graduate degrees offered in 20 major fields of study.

UNDERGRADUATE MAJORS. Associate: Law enforcement and corrections technologies, liberal/general studies. **Bachelor's:** Accounting, art education, art history, art therapy, biological and physical sciences, biology, business administration and management, business and management, business data processing and related programs, business economics, business education, chemistry, clinical laboratory science, communications, computer and information sciences, criminal justice studies, dramatic arts, early childhood education, economics, elementary education, English, English education, history, information sciences and systems, journalism, junior high education, liberal/general studies, management information systems, marketing and distribution, marketing management, mathematics, mathematics education, medical laboratory technologies, music, music education, music performance, office supervision and management, personnel management, physical education, physical sciences, physics, political science and government, prelaw, psychology, radio/television broadcasting, radio/television technology, reading education, science education, secondary education, secretarial and related programs, social science education, social sciences, social work, sociology, speech, speech/communication/theater education, studio art, visual and performing arts.

ACADEMIC PROGRAMS. Double major, dual enrollment of high school students, education specialist degree, external degree, honors program, independent study, internships, student-designed major, study abroad, teacher preparation, visiting/exchange student program, cross-registration, maritime studies with Texas A+M-Galveston; liberal arts/career combination in engineering, forestry. **Remedial services:** Learning center, preadmission summer program, remedial instruction, special counselor, tutoring, remedial English, mathematics, and study skills. **ROTC:** Air Force. **Placement/credit:** AP, CLEP General and Subject, institutional tests; 32 credit hours maximum for associate degree; 32 credit hours maximum for bachelor's degree.

ACADEMIC REQUIREMENTS. Freshmen must earn minimum GPA of 1.8 to continue in good standing. 57% of freshmen return for sophomore year. Students must declare major on application. **Graduation requirements:** 64 hours for associate, 128 hours for bachelor's. Most students required to take courses in arts/fine arts, English, history, humanities, mathematics, biological/physical sciences, social sciences.

FRESHMAN ADMISSIONS. Selection criteria: Applicants in top half or ACT score of 20 of graduating class admitted unconditionally. Those in bottom half must have minimum ACT composite score of 20. **High school preparation:** 16 units required. Required units include biological science 2, English 4, foreign language 2, mathematics 2 and social science 4. Mathematics must include algebra and plane geometey. **Test requirements:** ACT; score report by June 1.

1992 FRESHMAN CLASS PROFILE. 312 men, 364 women enrolled. 57% had high school GPA of 3.0 or higher, 41% between 2.0 and 2.99. 12% were in top tenth and 36% were in top quarter of graduating class. **Characteristics:** 58% from in state, 75% commute, 3% have minority backgrounds, 2% are foreign students. Average age is 19.

FALL-TERM APPLICATIONS. $10 fee, may be waived for applicants with need. Closing date June 1; priority given to applications received by April 1; applicants notified on a rolling basis. Deferred and early admission available.

STUDENT LIFE. Housing: Dormitories (men, women, coed); handicapped housing available. Suites available in nontraditional dormitories for married students. Single parents have access to student dormitories. **Activities:** Student government, film, radio, student newspaper, television, choral groups, drama, jazz band, music ensembles, musical theater, symphony orchestra, Black Student Union, United Campus Ministry, Criminal Justice Association.

ATHLETICS. NCAA. **Intercollegiate:** Baseball M, basketball, cross-country, football M, gymnastics W, ice hockey M, soccer W, softball W, track and field W, volleyball W, wrestling M. **Intramural:** Badminton, basketball, bowling, cross-country, golf, ice hockey M, racquetball, skiing, soccer, softball, swimming, tennis, volleyball.

STUDENT SERVICES. Aptitude testing, career counseling, employment service for undergraduates, freshman orientation, health services, on-campus day care, personal counseling, placement service for graduates, special adviser for adult students, veterans counselor, services/facilities for handicapped.

ANNUAL EXPENSES. Tuition and fees (projected): $2,050, $4,478 additional for out-of-state students. Minnesota residents pay Minnesota State University tuition. **Room and board:** $2,470. **Books and supplies:** $525. **Other expenses:** $1,350.

FINANCIAL AID. 68% of freshmen, 68% of continuing students receive some form of aid. 96% of grants, 88% of loans, 35% of jobs based on need. 300 enrolled freshmen were judged to have need, all were offered aid. Academic, leadership scholarships available. **Aid applications:** Closing date May 1; priority given to applications received by April 15; applicants notified on a rolling basis beginning on or about June 1; must reply within 10 days.

ADDRESS/TELEPHONE. Mr. Jon Wojciechowski, Director of Admissions, University of Wisconsin: Superior, 1800 Grand Avenue, Superior, WI 54880. (715) 394-8230. Fax: (715) 394-8107.

University of Wisconsin: Whitewater
Whitewater, Wisconsin — CB code: 1921

4-year public university, coed. Founded in 1868. **Accreditation:** Regional. **Undergraduate enrollment:** 3,812 men, 4,349 women full time; 463 men, 598 women part time. **Graduate enrollment:** 121 men, 176 women full time; 342 men, 651 women part time. **Faculty:** 675 total (539 full time), 332 with doctorates or other terminal degrees. **Location:** Suburban campus in large town; 40 miles from Madison, 50 miles from Milwaukee. **Calendar:** Semester, extensive summer session. **Microcomputers:** 1,200 located in dormitories, libraries, computer centers. **Special facilities:** Observatory, nature preserve and recreation area.

DEGREES OFFERED. AA, BA, BS, BFA, MS, MBA. 17 associate degrees awarded in 1992. 1,557 bachelor's degrees awarded. 38% in business and management, 20% education, 13% letters/literature, 5% parks/recreation, protective services, public affairs, 8% social sciences. Graduate degrees offered in 12 major fields of study.

UNDERGRADUATE MAJORS. Associate: Liberal/general studies. **Bachelor's:** Accounting, art education, art history, biological and physical sciences, biology, business administration and management, business and management, business economics, business education, chemistry, computer and information sciences, computer programming, dramatic arts, driver and safety education, early childhood education, economics, education, education of the mentally handicapped, elementary education, English, English education, finance, fine arts, foreign languages education, French, geography, German, health education, history, humanities and social sciences, international relations, international studies, investments and securities, journalism, junior high education, liberal/general studies, management information systems, marketing and distribution, marketing and distributive education, marketing management, marketing research, mathematics, mathematics education, music, music education, music performance, office supervision and management, personnel management, physical education, physics, political science and government, prelaw, production and operations management, psychology, public administration, science education, secondary education, secretarial and related programs, social science education, social sciences, social studies education, social work, sociology, Spanish, special education, specific learning disabilities, speech, speech correction, speech pathology/audiology, speech/communication/theater education, visual and performing arts.

ACADEMIC PROGRAMS. Double major, external degree, honors program, independent study, internships, student-designed major, study abroad, teacher preparation. **Remedial services:** Learning center, preadmission summer program, reduced course load, remedial instruction, special counselor, tutoring. **ROTC:** Army. **Placement/credit:** AP, CLEP General and Subject, institutional tests; 60 credit hours maximum for bachelor's degree.

ACADEMIC REQUIREMENTS. Freshmen must earn minimum GPA of 2.0 to continue in good standing. 76% of freshmen return for sophomore year. Students must declare major by end of first year. **Graduation requirements:** 60 hours for associate, 120 hours for bachelor's (34 in major). Most students required to take courses in arts/fine arts, English, history, humanities, mathematics, biological/physical sciences, social sciences. **Additional information:** Departmental GPA requirements range from 2.25 to 2.80.

FRESHMAN ADMISSIONS. Selection criteria: Rank in top half of class. Others may qualify on basis of combined class rank and ACT/SAT percentile. Special consideration given to minority, disabled, and adult applicants. **High school preparation:** 16 units required. Required units include English 4, mathematics 2, social science 3 and science 2. **Test requirements:** SAT or ACT (ACT preferred); score report by June 1.

1992 FRESHMAN CLASS PROFILE. 12% were in top tenth and 37% were in top quarter of graduating class. **Characteristics:** 92% from in state, 90% live in college housing, 6% have minority backgrounds, 1% are foreign students. Average age is 18.

FALL-TERM APPLICATIONS. $10 fee, may be waived for applicants with need. No closing date; priority given to applications received by January 1; applicants notified on a rolling basis. Audition required for music applicants. Portfolio recommended for art applicants. CRDA. ACT required for Wisconsin freshmen applicants.

STUDENT LIFE. Housing: Dormitories (men, women, coed); fraternity, sorority, handicapped housing available. Accessible housing for physically disabled students available. **Activities:** Student government, radio, student newspaper, television, choral groups, concert band, dance, drama, jazz band, marching band, music ensembles, musical theater, opera, pep band, symphony orchestra, fraternities, sororities.

ATHLETICS. NCAA. **Intercollegiate:** Baseball M, basketball, cross-country, diving, football M, golf W, gymnastics W, soccer, softball W, swimming, tennis, track and field, volleyball W, wrestling M. **Intramural:** Archery, basketball, bowling, diving, field hockey W, skiing, soccer, softball, swimming, table tennis, tennis, track and field, volleyball.

STUDENT SERVICES. Aptitude testing, career counseling, employment service for undergraduates, freshman orientation, health services, on-campus day care, personal counseling, placement service for graduates, special adviser for adult students, services/facilities for handicapped.

ANNUAL EXPENSES. Tuition and fees (1992-93): $1,985, $4,185 additional for out-of-state students. Minnesota residents pay Minnesota State University tuition. **Room and board:** $2,252. **Books and supplies:** $450. **Other expenses:** $1,040.

FINANCIAL AID. 44% of continuing students receive some form of aid. 97% of grants, 62% of loans, 24% of jobs based on need. Academic, music/drama, state/district residency, leadership, minority scholarships available. **Aid applications:** No closing date; priority given to applications received by April 15; applicants notified on a rolling basis beginning on or about July 1; must reply within 2 weeks.

ADDRESS/TELEPHONE. I.A. Madsen, Executive Director of Admissions, University of Wisconsin: Whitewater, 800 West Main Street, Whitewater, WI 53190-1791. (414) 472-1440.

Viterbo College
La Crosse, Wisconsin — CB code: 1878

Admissions:	83% of applicants accepted
Based on:	••• School record
	•• Test scores
	• Activities, interview, recommendations, special talents
Completion:	65% of freshmen end year in good standing
	85% graduate, 10% of these enter graduate study

4-year private liberal arts college, coed, affiliated with Roman Catholic Church. Founded in 1890. **Accreditation:** Regional. **Undergraduate enrollment:** 244 men, 644 women full time; 96 men, 295 women part time. **Graduate enrollment:** 36 men, 77 women part time. **Faculty:** 114 total (79 full time), 44 with doctorates or other terminal degrees. **Location:** Urban campus in small city; 140 miles from both Minneapolis-St.Paul and Madison. **Calendar:** Semester, limited summer session. **Microcomputers:** 65 located in libraries, computer centers. **Special facilities:** Fine arts center.

DEGREES OFFERED. BA, BS, MA. 201 bachelor's degrees awarded in 1992. Graduate degrees offered in 2 major fields of study.

UNDERGRADUATE MAJORS. Accounting, arts management, biological and physical sciences, biology, business administration and management, chemistry, computer and information sciences, dramatic arts, early childhood education, elementary education, English, food science and nutrition, health care administration, human resources development, humanities and social sciences, industrial and organizational psychology, information sciences and systems, journalism, liberal/general studies, marketing and distribution, marketing management, mathematics, music, nursing, personnel management, predentistry, prelaw, premedicine, prepharmacy, preveterinary, psychology, religion, religious education, religious music, sociology.

ACADEMIC PROGRAMS. Accelerated program, cooperative education, double major, dual enrollment of high school students, honors program, independent study, internships, student-designed major, study abroad, teacher preparation, weekend college. **Remedial services:** Learning center, reduced course load, remedial instruction, special counselor, tutoring. **ROTC:** Army. **Placement/credit:** AP, CLEP Subject, institutional tests; 18 credit hours maximum for bachelor's degree.

ACADEMIC REQUIREMENTS. Freshmen must earn minimum GPA of 2.0 to continue in good standing. 60% of freshmen return for sophomore year. Students must declare major by end of second year. **Graduation requirements:** 128 hours for bachelor's. Most students required to take courses in arts/fine arts, English, history, humanities, philosophy/religion, biological/physical sciences, social sciences.

FRESHMAN ADMISSIONS. Selection criteria: High school record, rank in top half of class or acceptable ACT composite score important. **High school preparation:** 16 units recommended. Recommended units include biological science 2, English 4, foreign language 2, mathematics 2 and social science 2. Chemistry required of nursing and dietetics majors. **Test requirements:** SAT or ACT (ACT preferred); score report by August 1.

1992 FRESHMAN CLASS PROFILE. 206 men applied, 159 accepted, 71 enrolled; 417 women applied, 357 accepted, 176 enrolled. **Academic background:** Mid 50% of enrolled freshmen had ACT composite between 18-23. 94% submitted ACT scores. **Characteristics:** 80% from in state, 70% live in college housing, 3% have minority backgrounds, 2% are foreign students. Average age is 18.

FALL-TERM APPLICATIONS. $15 fee, may be waived for applicants with need. No closing date; priority given to applications received by August 1; applicants notified on a rolling basis; must reply within 3 weeks. Audition recommended for music, theater, art applicants. Portfolio recommended for art applicants.

STUDENT LIFE. Housing: Dormitories (men, women, coed); cooperative housing available. **Activities:** Student government, magazine, student newspaper, yearbook, choral groups, concert band, dance, drama, music ensembles, musical theater, opera, symphony orchestra, campus ministry, campus fellowship, social welfare club.

ATHLETICS. NAIA. **Intercollegiate:** Baseball M, basketball, soccer M, softball W, volleyball W. **Intramural:** Badminton, basketball, golf, racquetball, softball, tennis, volleyball.

STUDENT SERVICES. Career counseling, employment service for undergraduates, freshman orientation, health services, personal counseling, placement service for graduates, special adviser for adult students, services/facilities for handicapped.

ANNUAL EXPENSES. Tuition and fees: $8,770. Graduate students pay $395 per course. **Room and board:** $3,360. **Books and supplies:** $600. **Other expenses:** $1,500.

FINANCIAL AID. 88% of freshmen, 90% of continuing students receive some form of aid. 82% of loans, 82% of jobs based on need. 190 enrolled freshmen were judged to have need, all were offered aid. Academic, music/drama, art, state/district residency, leadership, alumni affiliation, religious affiliation scholarships available. **Aid applications:** No closing date; priority given to applications received by March 1; applicants notified on a rolling basis beginning on or about March 15; must reply within 2 weeks.

ADDRESS/TELEPHONE. Dr. Roland Nelson, Director of Admissions, Viterbo College, 815 South Ninth Street, La Crosse, WI 54601. (608) 791-0040. (800) 542-5652. Fax: (608) 791-0367.

Waukesha County Technical College
Pewaukee, Wisconsin — CB code: 0724

2-year public technical college, coed. Founded in 1923. **Accreditation:** Regional. **Undergraduate enrollment:** 680 men, 630 women full time; 1,610 men, 2,060 women part time. **Faculty:** 525 total (150 full time). **Location:** Suburban campus in large town; 25 miles from Milwaukee. **Calendar:** Semester, limited summer session. **Microcomputers:** Located in libraries, classrooms, computer centers.

DEGREES OFFERED. AAS. 760 associate degrees awarded in 1992.

UNDERGRADUATE MAJORS. Accounting, automotive technology, business computer/console/peripheral equipment operation, business data processing and related programs, business data programming, child development/care/guidance, computer and information sciences, data processing, diesel engine mechanics, electrical technology, electronic circuit-board design technician, engineering and engineering-related technologies, fashion merchandising, food production/management/services, home furnishings and equipment management/production/services, hotel/motel and restaurant management, industrial technology, international business management, law enforcement and corrections technologies, marketing and distribution, mechanical design technology, medical assistant, nursing, precision metal work, real estate, secretarial and related programs, surgical technology, taxation, telecommunications.

ACADEMIC PROGRAMS. Accelerated program, cooperative education, double major, dual enrollment of high school students, independent study. **Remedial services:** Learning center, reduced course load, remedial instruction, special counselor, tutoring. **Placement/credit:** Institutional tests.

ACADEMIC REQUIREMENTS. Freshmen must earn minimum GPA of 2.0 to continue in good standing. 65% of freshmen return for sophomore year. Students must declare major on application. **Graduation requirements:** 60 hours for associate. Most students required to take courses in English, humanities, mathematics, social sciences.

FRESHMAN ADMISSIONS. Selection criteria: Open admissions. Selective admissions to health occupations programs. High school diploma recommended. Applicants to electronics programs must have algebra and geometry. Applicants to nursing program must have algebra and chemistry.

1992 FRESHMAN CLASS PROFILE. 660 men, 660 women enrolled. **Characteristics:** 99% from in state, 100% commute.

FALL-TERM APPLICATIONS. $20 fee, may be waived for applicants with need. No closing date; applicants notified on a rolling basis.

STUDENT LIFE. Activities: Student government, student newspaper, yearbook.

ATHLETICS. NJCAA. **Intercollegiate:** Baseball, basketball, bowling, cross-country, golf, soccer, wrestling M. **Intramural:** Baseball, bowling, golf, racquetball, skiing.

STUDENT SERVICES. Aptitude testing, career counseling, employment service for undergraduates, health services, on-campus day care, personal counseling, placement service for graduates, special adviser for adult students, veterans counselor, services/facilities for handicapped.

ANNUAL EXPENSES. Tuition and fees: $1,440, $8,760 additional for out-of-state students. Fees vary by program. **Books and supplies:** $643. **Other expenses:** $1,091.

FINANCIAL AID. 15% of freshmen, 20% of continuing students receive some form of aid. 96% of grants, 90% of loans, 31% of jobs based on need. Academic, leadership, minority scholarships available. **Aid applications:** No closing date; applicants notified on a rolling basis; must reply by registration.

ADDRESS/TELEPHONE. Stanley Goran, Director of Admissions, Waukesha County Technical College, 800 Main Street, Pewaukee, WI 53072. (414) 691-5200.

Western Wisconsin Technical College
La Crosse, Wisconsin — CB code: 1087

2-year public technical college, coed. Founded in 1912. **Accreditation:** Regional. **Undergraduate enrollment:** 786 men, 897 women full time; 909 men, 1,414 women part time. **Faculty:** 248 total (240 full time), 10 with doctorates or other terminal degrees. **Location:** Urban campus in small city; 200 miles from Milwaukee, 150 miles from Minneapolis-St. Paul. **Calendar:** Semester, limited summer session. **Microcomputers:** 500 located in libraries, classrooms, computer centers.

DEGREES OFFERED. AAS. 578 associate degrees awarded in 1992. 22% in business and management, 21% business/office and marketing/distribution, 7% engineering technologies, 12% health sciences, 12% allied health, 6% parks/recreation, protective services, public affairs, 8% trade and industry.

UNDERGRADUATE MAJORS. Accounting, agribusiness, air conditioning/heating/refrigeration technology, biomedical equipment technology, business and management, business data processing and related programs, child development/care/guidance, commercial art, community developmental disabilities associate, electrodiagnostic technologies, electromechanical technology, electronic technology, engineering and engineering-related technologies, fashion merchandising, finance, food marketing, food production/management/services, graphic and printing production, industrial technology, interior design, legal assistant/paralegal, legal secretary, marketing and distribution, mechanical design technology, medical laboratory technologies, medical records technology, medical secretary, nursing, personnel management, physical therapy assistant, protective services, quality control technology, radio/television technology, radiograph medical technology, respiratory therapy technology, retailing, secretarial and related programs, trade and industrial supervision and management.

ACADEMIC PROGRAMS. Cooperative education, double major, independent study, internships. **Remedial services:** Learning center, reduced course load, remedial instruction, special counselor, tutoring. **Placement/credit:** Institutional tests.

ACADEMIC REQUIREMENTS. Freshmen must earn minimum GPA of 2.0 to continue in good standing. Students must declare major on application. **Graduation requirements:** 68 hours for associate. Most students required to take courses in English, social sciences.

FRESHMAN ADMISSIONS. Selection criteria: Open admissions. Selective admission to health programs. Recommended units include biological science 1, English 3, mathematics 2, physical science 1 and social science 3. **Test requirements:** ACT. ASSET test required.

1992 FRESHMAN CLASS PROFILE. 457 men, 516 women enrolled. **Characteristics:** 80% from in state, 95% commute, 5% have minority backgrounds. Average age is 25.

FALL-TERM APPLICATIONS. $15 fee. No closing date; applicants notified on a rolling basis beginning on or about March 1. Interview recommended for all programs applicants. Portfolio recommended for commercial art applicants. Deferred admission available. ASSET required of students unless they have ACT scores or acceptable post-secondary credits.

STUDENT LIFE. Housing: Dormitories (coed); cooperative housing available. **Activities:** Student government, film, magazine, student newspaper, television, international club, vets club, 21 vocational-technical clubs.

ATHLETICS. NJCAA. **Intercollegiate:** Baseball M, basketball, bowling, volleyball W. **Intramural:** Basketball, volleyball.

STUDENT SERVICES. Aptitude testing, career counseling, employment service for undergraduates, freshman orientation, health services, on-campus day care, personal counseling, placement service for graduates, veterans counselor, women's programs, services/facilities for handicapped.

ANNUAL EXPENSES. Tuition and fees: $1,440, $8,760 additional for out-of-state students. **Room and board:** $1,150 room only. **Books and supplies:** $600. **Other expenses:** $975.

FINANCIAL AID. 60% of freshmen, 60% of continuing students receive some form of aid. All grants, 82% of loans, all jobs based on need. **Aid applications:** No closing date; priority given to applications received by March 1; applicants notified on a rolling basis beginning on or about July 1; must reply within 2 weeks.

ADDRESS/TELEPHONE. Diane Rud, Admissions Manager, Western Wisconsin Technical College, 304 N. Sixth Street, La Crosse, WI 54602-0908. (608) 785-9476.

Wisconsin Indianhead Technical College
Shell Lake, Wisconsin CB code: 1580

2-year public technical college, coed. Founded in 1972. **Accreditation:** Regional. **Undergraduate enrollment:** 694 men, 824 women full time; 717 men, 1,106 women part time. **Faculty:** 1,187 total (162 full time), 2 with doctorates or other terminal degrees. **Location:** Rural campus in rural community; 4 campuses located 50 to 200 miles from Minneapolis-St. Paul, Minnesota. **Calendar:** Semester, limited summer session. **Microcomputers:** Located in libraries, classrooms, computer centers. **Additional facts:** Multicampus institution covering 11-county area.

DEGREES OFFERED. AAS. 328 associate degrees awarded in 1992.

UNDERGRADUATE MAJORS. Accounting, agribusiness, architecture, business computer/console/peripheral equipment operation, court reporting, data processing, fashion merchandising, finance, food management, hospitality and recreation marketing, industrial technology, management information systems, marketing and distribution, mechanical design technology, nursing, protective services, secretarial and related programs, telecommunications.

ACADEMIC PROGRAMS. Double major, internships. **Remedial services:** Learning center, preadmission summer program, reduced course load, remedial instruction, special counselor, tutoring. **Placement/credit:** Institutional tests; 48 credit hours maximum for associate degree.

ACADEMIC REQUIREMENTS. Freshmen must earn minimum GPA of 2.0 to continue in good standing. Students must declare major by end of first year. **Graduation requirements:** 66 hours for associate. Most students required to take courses in English, mathematics, social sciences.

FRESHMAN ADMISSIONS. Selection criteria: Open admissions.

1992 FRESHMAN CLASS PROFILE. 1,736 men and women enrolled. **Characteristics:** 95% from in state, 100% commute, 4% have minority backgrounds.

FALL-TERM APPLICATIONS. $25 fee. No closing date; applicants notified on a rolling basis.

STUDENT LIFE. Activities: Student government, student newspaper, yearbook, vocational student organizations.

ATHLETICS. Intramural: Basketball, bowling, boxing M, skiing, softball, volleyball.

STUDENT SERVICES. Aptitude testing, career counseling, employment service for undergraduates, freshman orientation, health services, on-campus day care, personal counseling, placement service for graduates, services/facilities for handicapped.

ANNUAL EXPENSES. Tuition and fees: $1,440, $8,760 additional for out-of-state students. **Books and supplies:** $535. **Other expenses:** $945.

FINANCIAL AID. 75% of freshmen, 75% of continuing students receive some form of aid. 98% of grants, 88% of loans, all jobs based on need. Academic, state/district residency, leadership, minority scholarships available. **Aid applications:** No closing date; applicants notified on a rolling basis.

ADDRESS/TELEPHONE. Mimi Crandall, Cultural Diversity Specialist, Wisconsin Indianhead Technical College, 505 Pine Ridge Drive, HCR 69 Box 10B, Shell Lake, WI 54871. (715) 468-2815.

Wisconsin Lutheran College
Milwaukee, Wisconsin CB code: 1513

Admissions: 94% of applicants accepted
Based on: ••• Recommendations, school record, test scores
•• Religious affiliation/commitment
• Activities, essay, interview
Completion: 84% of freshmen end year in good standing
52% graduate, 23% of these enter graduate study

4-year private liberal arts college, coed, affiliated with Wisconsin Evangelical Lutheran Synod. Founded in 1973. **Accreditation:** Regional. **Undergraduate enrollment:** 110 men, 171 women full time; 20 men, 21 women part time. **Faculty:** 51 total (28 full time), 12 with doctorates or other terminal degrees. **Location:** Suburban campus in very large city. **Calendar:** Semester, limited summer session. **Microcomputers:** 40 located in libraries, classrooms, computer centers. **Special facilities:** Recording studio. **Additional facts:** Strong emphasis on Christian teachings, values.

DEGREES OFFERED. BA, BS. 53 bachelor's degrees awarded in 1992. 28% in business and management, 19% communications, 6% mathematics, 20% psychology, 13% social sciences.

UNDERGRADUATE MAJORS. Business and management, chemistry, communications, elementary education, English, English education, history, junior high education, mathematics, mathematics education, music education, music theory and composition, psychology, science education, secondary education, speech/communication/theater education, theological studies.

ACADEMIC PROGRAMS. Double major, dual enrollment of high school students, independent study, internships, study abroad, teacher preparation, cross-registration. **Remedial services:** Learning center, reduced course load, remedial instruction, tutoring. **Placement/credit:** AP, CLEP Subject, institutional tests.

ACADEMIC REQUIREMENTS. Freshmen must earn minimum GPA of 2.0 to continue in good standing. 85% of freshmen return for sophomore year. Students must declare major by end of second year. **Graduation requirements:** 128 hours for bachelor's (36 in major). Most students required to take courses in arts/fine arts, computer science, English, foreign languages, history, humanities, mathematics, philosophy/religion, biological/physical sciences, social sciences. **Postgraduate studies:** 4% enter law school, 2% enter medical school, 4% enter MBA programs, 13% enter other graduate study. **Additional information:** Students must declare major before 75 credits earned.

FRESHMAN ADMISSIONS. Selection criteria: Test scores, class rank, GPA, letters of recommendation required. **High school preparation:** 16 units required. Required and recommended units include English 3-4, foreign language 2-3, mathematics 2-3, social science 2-3 and science 2. Mathematics required units must include 1 algebra, 1 geometry. **Test requirements:** SAT or ACT (ACT preferred); score report by August 15.

1992 FRESHMAN CLASS PROFILE. 43 men applied, 42 accepted, 30 enrolled; 83 women applied, 77 accepted, 45 enrolled. 54% had high school GPA of 3.0 or higher, 42% between 2.0 and 2.99. 13% were in top tenth and 35% were in top quarter of graduating class. **Academic background:** Mid 50% of enrolled freshmen had SAT-V between 410-640, SAT-M between 430-730; ACT composite between 20-25. 12% submitted SAT scores, 88% submitted ACT scores. **Characteristics:** 76% from in state, 84% live in college housing, 4% have minority backgrounds, 3% are foreign students. Average age is 19.

FALL-TERM APPLICATIONS. $15 fee, may be waived for applicants with need. No closing date; priority given to applications received by May 1; applicants notified on a rolling basis beginning on or about January 1. Interview recommended. Deferred and early admission available.

STUDENT LIFE. Housing: Dormitories (men, women); apartment, cooperative housing available. Traditional age students must live in college housing unless living with parents, guardian or relative. **Activities:** Student government, student newspaper, yearbook, choral groups, concert band, drama, music ensembles, musical theater, pep band, several religious organizations.

ATHLETICS. NAIA. **Intercollegiate:** Baseball M, basketball, fencing, golf M, soccer M, softball W, volleyball W. **Intramural:** Basketball, bowling, volleyball.

STUDENT SERVICES. Career counseling, freshman orientation, health services, personal counseling, placement service for graduates, special adviser for adult students, services/facilities for handicapped.

ANNUAL EXPENSES. Tuition and fees (1992-93): $8,280. **Room and board:** $3,350. **Books and supplies:** $500. **Other expenses:** $990.

FINANCIAL AID. 90% of freshmen, 88% of continuing students receive some form of aid. 71% of grants, 98% of loans, 49% of jobs based on need. 55 enrolled freshmen were judged to have need, all were offered aid. Academic, music/drama, art, athletic, leadership scholarships available. **Aid applications:** No closing date; priority given to applications received by April 1; applicants notified on a rolling basis beginning on or about April 15; must reply within 2 weeks. **Additional information:** Portfolios required for art scholarship applicants; auditions required for drama and talent scholarship applicants.

ADDRESS/TELEPHONE. Joel Mischke, Director of Admissions, Wisconsin Lutheran College, 8800 West Bluemound Road, Milwaukee, WI 53226. (414) 774-8620. Fax: (414) 774-9367.

Wisconsin School of Electronics
Madison, Wisconsin

CB code: 0388

2-year proprietary technical college, coed. Founded in 1948. **Undergraduate enrollment:** 430 men and women full time. **Location:** Suburban campus in small city. **Calendar:** Trimester.

FRESHMAN ADMISSIONS. Selection criteria: Score on institutionally administered test and interview considered.

ANNUAL EXPENSES. Tuition and fees (1992-93): $6,330. **Books and supplies:** $500.

ADDRESS/TELEPHONE. William Henry, Director of Admissions, Wisconsin School of Electronics, 1227 North Sherman Avenue, Madison, WI 53704. (608) 249-6611. (800) 582-1227. Fax: (608) 249-8593.

Wyoming

Casper College
Casper, Wyoming

CB code: 4043

2-year public community college, coed. Founded in 1945. **Accreditation:** Regional. **Undergraduate enrollment:** 2,400 men and women full time; 2,375 men and women part time. **Faculty:** 232 total (179 full time), 25 with doctorates or other terminal degrees. **Location:** Urban campus in small city; 280 miles from Denver, Colorado. **Calendar:** Semester, extensive summer session. **Microcomputers:** 150 located in libraries, classrooms, computer centers. **Special facilities:** Wildlife museum, mineralogical museum, fitness and wellness center.

DEGREES OFFERED. AA, AS, AAS. 400 associate degrees awarded in 1992. 14% in business and management, 9% business/office and marketing/distribution, 8% education, 5% engineering, 10% engineering technologies, 12% health sciences, 5% life sciences, 7% parks/recreation, protective services, public affairs, 7% trade and industry, 5% visual and performing arts.

UNDERGRADUATE MAJORS. Accounting, agribusiness, agricultural mechanics, agricultural sciences, animal science technology, animal sciences, anthropology, automotive mechanics, automotive technology, biology, business administration and management, business and management, business and office, business computer/console/peripheral equipment operation, business data entry equipment operation, business data processing and related programs, business data programming, business education, chemical manufacturing technology, chemistry, communications, computer and information sciences, computer servicing technology, construction, criminal justice studies, data processing, diesel engine mechanics, drafting, drafting and design technology, dramatic arts, early childhood education, economics, education, electrical and electronics equipment repair, electronic technology, elementary education, emergency medical technologies, engineering, English, environmental science, fine arts, fire control and safety technology, forest products processing technology, French, geology, German, graphic arts technology, history, home economics, Italian, journalism, law enforcement and corrections technologies, legal assistant/paralegal, liberal/general studies, machine tool operation/machine shop, marketing and distribution, mathematics, mining and petroleum technologies, music, music performance, nursing, occupational therapy assistant, office supervision and management, photographic technology, photography, physical education, physics, political science and government, precision metal work, predentistry, prelaw, premedicine, prepharmacy, preveterinary, psychology, radiograph medical technology, retailing, secretarial and related programs, social sciences, social work, sociology, Spanish, speech, visual and performing arts, water and wastewater technology, welding technology, wildlife management, women's studies, word processing.

ACADEMIC PROGRAMS. 2-year transfer program, internships, cross-registration. **Remedial services:** Learning center, remedial instruction, special counselor, tutoring, mathematics and English laboratories. **Placement/credit:** AP, CLEP General and Subject, institutional tests; 30 credit hours maximum for associate degree.

ACADEMIC REQUIREMENTS. Freshmen must earn minimum GPA of 2.0 to continue in good standing. 55% of freshmen return for sophomore year. Students must declare major on application. **Graduation requirements:** 64 hours for associate. Most students required to take courses in English, mathematics, biological/physical sciences, social sciences.

FRESHMAN ADMISSIONS. Selection criteria: Open admissions. 2.0 GPA required for out-of-state applicants. **Test requirements:** SAT or ACT for placement and counseling only; score report by August 15.

1992 FRESHMAN CLASS PROFILE. 690 men and women enrolled. 30% had high school GPA of 3.0 or higher, 55% between 2.0 and 2.99. **Characteristics:** 95% from in state, 65% commute, 5% have minority backgrounds, 1% are foreign students. Average age is 24.

FALL-TERM APPLICATIONS. No fee. No closing date; priority given to applications received by April 1; applicants notified on a rolling basis; must reply by registration. Audition recommended for music, theater applicants. Portfolio recommended for art applicants. Deferred admission available.

STUDENT LIFE. Housing: Dormitories (coed); apartment, handicapped housing available. **Activities:** Student government, magazine, student newspaper, literary yearbook, choral groups, concert band, dance, drama, jazz band, music ensembles, musical theater, pep band, symphony orchestra. **Additional information:** Intercollegiate rodeo and livestock judging offered as part of athletic program.

ATHLETICS. NJCAA. **Intercollegiate:** Basketball, volleyball W. **Intramural:** Badminton, basketball, bowling, golf, racquetball, soccer, softball, swimming, table tennis, tennis, volleyball, water polo, wrestling M.

STUDENT SERVICES. Aptitude testing, career counseling, employment service for undergraduates, freshman orientation, health services, on-campus day care, personal counseling, placement service for graduates, special adviser for adult students, veterans counselor, services/facilities for handicapped.

ANNUAL EXPENSES. Tuition and fees: $820, $1,400 additional for out-of-state students. Students from Western Undergraduate Exchange schools and Nebraska residents pay $350 additional tuition per year. **Room and board:** $2,330. **Books and supplies:** $500. **Other expenses:** $900.

FINANCIAL AID. 83% of grants, 66% of loans, 52% of jobs based on need. Academic, music/drama, art, athletic, state/district residency, leadership scholarships available. **Aid applications:** No closing date; priority given to applications received by April 1; applicants notified on a rolling basis beginning on or about June 1. **Additional information:** Athletic scholarships offered in rodeo and livestock judging.

ADDRESS/TELEPHONE. Linda King, Director of Admission Services, Casper College, 125 College Drive, Casper, WY 82601. (307) 268-2110 ext. 2491.

Central Wyoming College
Riverton, Wyoming

CB code: 4115

2-year public community college, coed. Founded in 1966. **Accreditation:** Regional. **Undergraduate enrollment:** 235 men, 315 women full time; 278 men, 706 women part time. **Faculty:** 151 total (46 full time), 9 with doctorates or other terminal degrees. **Location:** Rural campus in large town; 120 miles from Casper. **Calendar:** Semester, limited summer session. Saturday and extensive evening/early morning classes. **Microcomputers:** 65 located in libraries, classrooms, computer centers. **Special facilities:** Horse arena, fine art center. **Additional facts:** Courses offered at 8 outreach centers in Fremont, Hot Springs, Carbon, and Teton counties.

DEGREES OFFERED. AA, AS, AAS. 130 associate degrees awarded in 1992. 6% in business/office and marketing/distribution, 6% teacher education, 14% health sciences, 45% multi/interdisciplinary studies.

UNDERGRADUATE MAJORS. Accounting, agribusiness, agricultural business and management, agricultural sciences, American Indian studies, animal sciences, automotive mechanics, automotive technology, biological and physical sciences, biology, business administration and management, business and management, business and office, business data processing and related programs, business education, chemistry, computer and information sciences, computer programming, criminal justice studies, data processing, dramatic arts, education, elementary education, English, equestrian science, fine arts, humanities, humanities and social sciences, law enforcement and corrections technologies, liberal/general studies, management information systems, marketing and distribution, mathematics, mental health/human services, music, nursing, physical education, physical sciences, political science and government, prelaw, psychology, radio/television broadcasting, rehabilitation counseling/services, renewable natural resources, science technologies, secondary education, secretarial and related programs, social sciences, sociology, visual and performing arts, welding technology, word processing.

ACADEMIC PROGRAMS. 2-year transfer program, cooperative education, dual enrollment of high school students, honors program, independent study, student-designed major, telecourses. **Remedial services:** Learning center, remedial instruction, special counselor, tutoring. **Placement/credit:** AP, CLEP Subject, institutional tests; 12 credit hours maximum for associate degree.

ACADEMIC REQUIREMENTS. Freshmen must earn minimum GPA of 2.0 to continue in good standing. 26% of freshmen return for sophomore year. Students must declare major by end of first year. **Graduation requirements:** 64 hours for associate. Most students required to take courses in computer science, English, humanities, mathematics, biological/physical sciences, social sciences.

FRESHMAN ADMISSIONS. Selection criteria: Open admissions.

1992 FRESHMAN CLASS PROFILE. 123 women enrolled. **Characteristics:** 95% from in state, 96% commute, 22% have minority backgrounds, 6% are foreign students. Average age is 31.

FALL-TERM APPLICATIONS. No fee. No closing date; applicants notified on a rolling basis beginning on or about January 1; must reply by registration. Interview recommended for music, art, nursing applicants. Audition recommended for music, theater applicants. Deferred and early admission available.

STUDENT LIFE. Housing: Dormitories (coed); apartment housing available. **Activities:** Student government, radio, student newspaper, television, choral groups, dance, drama, jazz band, music ensembles, musical theater, United Tribes (Native American) Club, DECA, Rodeo Club, International Students Club, Christian Association.

ATHLETICS. NJCAA. **Intramural:** Badminton, baseball, bowling, golf, softball, table tennis, tennis.

STUDENT SERVICES. Aptitude testing, career counseling, employment service for undergraduates, freshman orientation, personal counseling, placement service for graduates, veterans counselor, services/facilities for handicapped.

ANNUAL EXPENSES. Tuition and fees (1992-93): $900, $1,248 additional for out-of-state students. Students from Western Undergraduate Exchange schools and Nebraska residents pay $312 additional tuition per year. **Room and board:** $3,375. **Books and supplies:** $500. **Other expenses:** $675.

FINANCIAL AID. 43% of freshmen, 63% of continuing students receive some form of aid. 82% of grants, 81% of loans, 57% of jobs based on

need. 115 enrolled freshmen were judged to have need, all were offered aid. Academic, music/drama, art, athletic, leadership, minority scholarships available. **Aid applications:** No closing date; priority given to applications received by April 15; applicants notified on a rolling basis beginning on or about July 1; must reply within 2 weeks.

ADDRESS/TELEPHONE. Mary Gores, Recruitment Officer, Central Wyoming College, 2660 Peck Avenue, Riverton, WY 82501. (307) 856-9291 ext. 231. Fax: (307) 856-2264.

Eastern Wyoming College
Torrington, Wyoming
CB code: 4700

2-year public community college, coed. Founded in 1948. **Accreditation:** Regional. **Undergraduate enrollment:** 225 men, 278 women full time; 436 men, 1,085 women part time. **Faculty:** 64 total (45 full time), 4 with doctorates or other terminal degrees. **Location:** Rural campus in small town; 190 miles from Denver, Colorado. **Calendar:** Semester, limited summer session. Extensive evening/early morning classes. **Microcomputers:** Located in classrooms, computer centers, campus-wide network. **Special facilities:** Western history library, wellness center.

DEGREES OFFERED. AA, AS, AAS. 98 associate degrees awarded in 1992.

UNDERGRADUATE MAJORS. Accounting, agribusiness, agricultural sciences, air conditioning/heating/refrigeration mechanics, art history, biological and physical sciences, biology, business administration and management, business and management, business and office, chemistry, child development/care/guidance, communications, computer and information sciences, criminal justice studies, criminal justice technology, dramatic arts, early childhood education, economics, education, elementary education, English, English literature, French, health sciences, history, humanities and social sciences, industrial equipment maintenance and repair, journalism, law enforcement and corrections technologies, legal secretary, liberal/general studies, mathematics, medical secretary, music, personal services, physical sciences, physics, political science and government, precision metal work, psychology, school psychology, secondary education, secretarial and related programs, social sciences, sociology, Spanish, special education, teacher aide, tourism, veterinarian's assistant, visual and performing arts, word processing.

ACADEMIC PROGRAMS. 2-year transfer program, dual enrollment of high school students, independent study, internships, telecourses. **Remedial services:** Learning center, remedial instruction, special counselor, tutoring. **Placement/credit:** AP, CLEP Subject, institutional tests; 30 credit hours maximum for associate degree.

ACADEMIC REQUIREMENTS. Freshmen must earn minimum GPA of 2.0 to continue in good standing. 50% of freshmen return for sophomore year. Students must declare major by end of first year. **Graduation requirements:** 64 hours for associate (21 in major). Most students required to take courses in English, humanities, mathematics, biological/physical sciences, social sciences.

FRESHMAN ADMISSIONS. Selection criteria: Open admissions.

1992 FRESHMAN CLASS PROFILE. 168 men, 352 women enrolled. **Characteristics:** 65% from in state, 70% commute, 6% have minority backgrounds. Average age is 19.

FALL-TERM APPLICATIONS. No fee. No closing date; priority given to applications received by September 1; applicants notified on a rolling basis; must reply by registration. Deferred admission available. EDP-F.

STUDENT LIFE. Housing: Dormitories (men, women, coed); apartment housing available. **Activities:** Student government, magazine, choral groups, drama, music ensembles, musical theater, pep band.

ATHLETICS. NJCAA. **Intercollegiate:** Basketball M, volleyball W. **Intramural:** Badminton, basketball, bowling, handball, horseback riding, racquetball, skiing, softball, table tennis, tennis, volleyball.

STUDENT SERVICES. Aptitude testing, career counseling, employment service for undergraduates, freshman orientation, health services, on-campus day care, personal counseling, placement service for graduates, special adviser for adult students, veterans counselor, services/facilities for handicapped.

ANNUAL EXPENSES. Tuition and fees (1992-93): $804, $1,248 additional for out-of-state students. Students from Western Undergraduate Exchange schools and Nebraska residents pay $312 additional tuition per year. **Room and board:** $2,400. **Books and supplies:** $450. **Other expenses:** $350.

FINANCIAL AID. 76% of freshmen, 55% of continuing students receive some form of aid. 73% of grants, 95% of loans, 59% of jobs based on need. 274 enrolled freshmen were judged to have need, all were offered aid. Academic, music/drama, art, athletic, state/district residency, leadership scholarships available. **Aid applications:** No closing date; priority given to applications received by April 1; applicants notified on a rolling basis beginning on or about May 1; must reply within 2 weeks. **Additional information:** Installment payment plan on room and board contracts offered.

ADDRESS/TELEPHONE. Diana Ford, Admissions Counselor, Eastern Wyoming College, 3200 West C Street, Torrington, WY 82240. (307) 532-8230. (800) 658-3195. Fax: (307) 532-8222.

Laramie County Community College
Cheyenne, Wyoming
CB code: 0360

2-year public community college, coed. Founded in 1968. **Accreditation:** Regional. **Undergraduate enrollment:** 520 men, 751 women full time; 1,280 men, 1,801 women part time. **Faculty:** 220 total (120 full time), 8 with doctorates or other terminal degrees. **Location:** Rural campus in small city; 4 miles from downtown. **Calendar:** Semester, limited summer session. **Microcomputers:** Located in libraries, classrooms, computer centers. **Special facilities:** Art gallery, Bureau of Land Management Park, indoor arena.

DEGREES OFFERED. AA, AS, AAS. 300 associate degrees awarded in 1992. 10% in agriculture, 9% business and management, 6% business/office and marketing/distribution, 7% teacher education, 13% health sciences, 5% allied health, 6% parks/recreation, protective services, public affairs, 20% trade and industry.

UNDERGRADUATE MAJORS. Accounting, agricultural business and management, agricultural sciences, anthropology, automotive mechanics, automotive technology, biological and physical sciences, biology, business administration and management, business and management, business and office, business data programming, chemical manufacturing technology, chemistry, dental hygiene, diesel engine mechanics, dramatic arts, economics, education, elementary education, engineering, engineering and engineering-related technologies, engineering and other disciplines, English, equestrian science, finance, fine arts, graphic arts technology, history, information sciences and systems, journalism, law enforcement and corrections technologies, legal assistant/paralegal, liberal/general studies, marketing and distribution, marketing and distributive education, mathematics, music, nursing, occupational safety and health technology, philosophy, physical education, physical sciences, political science and government, practical nursing, precision metal work, prelaw, psychology, radiograph medical technology, secondary education, secretarial and related programs, social sciences, sociology, speech, welding technology.

ACADEMIC PROGRAMS. 2-year transfer program, cooperative education, dual enrollment of high school students, internships, telecourses. **Remedial services:** Learning center, remedial instruction, tutoring. **Placement/credit:** CLEP Subject, institutional tests; 15 credit hours maximum for associate degree.

ACADEMIC REQUIREMENTS. Freshmen must earn minimum GPA of 1.75 to continue in good standing. Students must declare major on application. **Graduation requirements:** 64 hours for associate. Most students required to take courses in arts/fine arts, English, humanities, mathematics, biological/physical sciences, social sciences.

FRESHMAN ADMISSIONS. Selection criteria: Open admissions. Selective admissions to nursing, radiography, horse management, dental hygiene programs.

1992 FRESHMAN CLASS PROFILE. 352 men, 434 women enrolled. **Characteristics:** 92% from in state, 98% commute, 10% have minority backgrounds. Average age is 20.

FALL-TERM APPLICATIONS. $5 fee. No closing date; applicants notified on a rolling basis; must reply by registration. Interview required for radiology, horse management applicants. Early admission available. Nursing and radiology applications must be received by February 1.

STUDENT LIFE. Housing: Dormitories (coed). **Activities:** Student government, student newspaper, drama, musical theater.

ATHLETICS. NJCAA. **Intramural:** Archery, badminton, basketball, bowling, cross-country, diving, fencing, golf, gymnastics, handball, racquetball, rifle, skiing, soccer, softball, swimming, table tennis, tennis, volleyball, water polo, wrestling.

STUDENT SERVICES. Aptitude testing, career counseling, employment service for undergraduates, freshman orientation, on-campus day care, personal counseling, placement service for graduates, special adviser for adult students, veterans counselor, services/facilities for handicapped.

ANNUAL EXPENSES. Tuition and fees (1992-93): $792, $1,248 additional for out-of-state students. Students from Western Undergraduate Exchange schools and Nebraska residents pay $312 additional tuition per semester. **Room and board:** $3,236. **Books and supplies:** $400. **Other expenses:** $500.

FINANCIAL AID. 75% of freshmen, 62% of continuing students receive some form of aid. 81% of grants, 83% of loans, 21% of jobs based on need. Academic, music/drama, art, athletic scholarships available. **Aid applications:** No closing date; priority given to applications received by April 1; applicants notified on a rolling basis beginning on or about June 1; must reply within 2 weeks.

ADDRESS/TELEPHONE. Donald J. Von Seggern, Director of Admissions, Laramie County Community College, 1400 East College Drive, Cheyenne, WY 82007. (307) 778-1212. Fax: (307) 778-1350.

Northwest College
Powell, Wyoming
CB code: 4542

2-year public community college, coed. Founded in 1946. **Accreditation:** Regional. **Undergraduate enrollment:** 546 men, 648 women full time; 202 men, 482 women part time. **Faculty:** 236 total (86 full time), 28 with doctorates or other terminal degrees. **Location:** Rural campus in small town; 70 miles from Yellowstone National Park, 90 miles from Billings, Montana. **Calendar:** Semester, limited summer session. Extensive evening/early morning classes. **Microcomputers:** 100 located in dormitories, libraries, classrooms, computer centers. **Special facilities:** Retreat facility in nearby mountains, Yellowstone Park summer branch.

DEGREES OFFERED. AA, AS, AAS. 365 associate degrees awarded in 1992. 8% in agriculture, 15% business and management, 8% business/office and marketing/distribution, 7% computer sciences, 20% education, 7% engineering, 7% health sciences, 8% life sciences, 5% multi/interdisciplinary studies, 5% physical sciences, 6% social sciences.

UNDERGRADUATE MAJORS. Accounting, agribusiness, agricultural business and management, agricultural economics, agricultural education, agricultural production, agricultural sciences, agronomy, animal sciences, biological and physical sciences, biology, business administration and management, business and management, business and office, business data entry equipment operation, business data processing and related programs, business data programming, business economics, chemistry, commercial art, communications, computer and information sciences, computer programming, dramatic arts, education, elementary education, engineering, engineering and other disciplines, English, equestrian science, fine arts, foreign languages (multiple emphasis), forestry and related sciences, graphic and printing production, graphic arts technology, graphic design, health sciences, history, home economics, horticultural science, horticulture, humanities, humanities and social sciences, information sciences and systems, journalism, liberal/general studies, management information systems, marketing and distribution, mathematics, music, nursing, occupational therapy, office supervision and management, parks and recreation management, photographic technology, photography, physical sciences, physical therapy, physics, political science and government, precision metal work, predentistry, prelaw, premedicine, prepharmacy, preveterinary, psychology, public administration, radiograph medical technology, range management, secondary education, secretarial and related programs, small business management and ownership, social sciences, social work, soil sciences, special education, tourism, visual and performing arts, wildlife management.

ACADEMIC PROGRAMS. 2-year transfer program, accelerated program, cooperative education, double major, dual enrollment of high school students, honors program, independent study, internships, study abroad, teacher preparation. **Remedial services:** Learning center, reduced course load, remedial instruction, special counselor, tutoring. **Placement/credit:** AP, CLEP Subject, institutional tests; 15 credit hours maximum for associate degree.

ACADEMIC REQUIREMENTS. Freshmen must earn minimum GPA of 2.0 to continue in good standing. 65% of freshmen return for sophomore year. Students must declare major by end of first year. **Graduation requirements:** 64 hours for associate. Most students required to take courses in English, mathematics, biological/physical sciences, social sciences.

FRESHMAN ADMISSIONS. Selection criteria: Open admissions. Selective admissions for out-of-state applicants based on high school GPA and test scores. Nursing, photography, and equestrian training programs require extra applications and qualifications. Recommended units include English 4, mathematics 2, social science 2 and science 1. **Test requirements:** SAT or ACT required of out-of-state applicants for admissions, placement, and counseling and recommended for in-state applicants for placement and counseling only. Score report by August 5. Placement tests in mathematics and English required for all first-time freshmen.

1992 FRESHMAN CLASS PROFILE. 328 men, 344 women enrolled. 25% had high school GPA of 3.0 or higher, 50% between 2.0 and 2.99. **Academic background:** Mid 50% of enrolled freshmen had SAT-V between 350-500, SAT-M between 400-550; ACT composite between 15-25. 5% submitted SAT scores, 65% submitted ACT scores. **Characteristics:** 80% from in state, 74% live in college housing, 3% have minority backgrounds, 1% are foreign students. Average age is 20.

FALL-TERM APPLICATIONS. No fee. $10 fee for out-of-state applicants. Closing date August 15; applicants notified on a rolling basis; must reply within 30 days. Audition required. Portfolio required. Interview recommended. Essay recommended. Deferred and early admission available. EDP-F.

STUDENT LIFE. Housing: Dormitories (men, women, coed); apartment housing available. **Activities:** Student government, student newspaper, choral groups, concert band, dance, drama, jazz band, music ensembles, musical theater, pep band, symphony orchestra, Northwest Trail Blazers, civic service organization.

ATHLETICS. NJCAA. **Intercollegiate:** Basketball, volleyball W, wrestling M. **Intramural:** Archery, badminton, baseball, basketball, cross-country, field hockey, golf, handball, racquetball, rifle M, sailing, skiing, soccer, softball, squash, swimming, table tennis, tennis, volleyball.

STUDENT SERVICES. Aptitude testing, career counseling, employment service for undergraduates, freshman orientation, health services, on-campus day care, personal counseling, placement service for graduates, special adviser for adult students, veterans counselor, services/facilities for handicapped.

ANNUAL EXPENSES. Tuition and fees: $944, $1,400 additional for out-of-state students. Students from Western Undergraduate Exchange schools and Nebraska residents pay $350 additional tuition per year. **Room and board:** $2,690. **Books and supplies:** $500. **Other expenses:** $1,000.

FINANCIAL AID. 78% of freshmen, 75% of continuing students receive some form of aid. 69% of grants, 88% of loans, 28% of jobs based on need. Academic, music/drama, art, athletic scholarships available. **Aid applications:** No closing date; applicants notified on a rolling basis beginning on or about May 1; must reply within 2 weeks.

ADDRESS/TELEPHONE. Karl Bear, Director of Admissions, Northwest College, 231 West 6th Street, Powell, WY 82435. (307) 754-6111. Fax: (307) 754-6700.

Sheridan College
Sheridan, Wyoming

CB code: 4536

2-year public community college, coed. Founded in 1948. **Accreditation:** Regional. **Undergraduate enrollment:** 454 men, 609 women full time; 623 men, 962 women part time. **Faculty:** 156 total (81 full time), 6 with doctorates or other terminal degrees. **Location:** Rural campus in large town; 130 miles from Billings, Montana. **Calendar:** Semester, limited summer session. **Microcomputers:** 348 located in libraries, classrooms, computer centers. **Special facilities:** Observatory, federal depository for government publications, special collections.

DEGREES OFFERED. AA, AS, AAS. 169 associate degrees awarded in 1992. 5% in agriculture, 14% business and management, 5% teacher education, 20% health sciences, 7% allied health, 17% multi/interdisciplinary studies, 6% parks/recreation, protective services, public affairs, 8% social sciences.

UNDERGRADUATE MAJORS. Accounting, agribusiness, agricultural business and management, agricultural production, agricultural sciences, animal sciences, biology, business administration and management, business and management, business and office, business economics, chemistry, communications, computer and information sciences, dental hygiene, diesel engine mechanics, drafting, drafting and design technology, education, electrical technology, electromechanical technology, elementary education, emergency medical technologies, engineering, engineering and engineering-related technologies, English, finance, fine arts, fluid power, health sciences, information sciences and systems, journalism, liberal/general studies, marketing and distribution, mathematics, microbiology, mining and petroleum technologies, music, nursing, office supervision and management, plant sciences, political science and government, protective services, psychology, range management, secondary education, secretarial and related programs, social sciences, social work, sociology, Spanish, welding technology, zoology.

ACADEMIC PROGRAMS. 2-year transfer program, double major, dual enrollment of high school students, independent study, internships, telecourses. **Remedial services:** Learning center, reduced course load, remedial instruction, special counselor, tutoring, English as a Second Language. **Placement/credit:** AP, CLEP Subject, institutional tests; 18 credit hours maximum for associate degree.

ACADEMIC REQUIREMENTS. Freshmen must earn minimum GPA of 1.6 to continue in good standing. 50% of freshmen return for sophomore year. Students must declare major on application. **Graduation requirements:** 64 hours for associate. Most students required to take courses in English, mathematics.

FRESHMAN ADMISSIONS. Selection criteria: Open admissions. Selective admissions to dental hygiene and nursing programs. One chemistry required of dental hygiene applicants. **Test requirements:** Dental Hygiene Aptitude Test required for dental hygiene applicants, Nursing Aptitude Test required of nursing applicants.

1992 FRESHMAN CLASS PROFILE. 214 men, 217 women enrolled. 30% had high school GPA of 3.0 or higher, 60% between 2.0 and 2.99. **Characteristics:** 94% from in state, 90% commute, 7% have minority backgrounds, 1% are foreign students. Average age is 27.

FALL-TERM APPLICATIONS. No fee. No closing date; applicants notified on a rolling basis; must reply by registration. Interview required for nursing applicants. Deferred and early admission available.

STUDENT LIFE. Housing: Dormitories (men, women, coed); apartment, handicapped housing available. Apartments available for single parents. **Activities:** Student government, film, magazine, student newspaper, television, choral groups, drama, jazz band, music ensembles, pep band, student senate, veteran's club, general delivery choir, adult non-traditional students, art club, nursing clubs, rodeo club, pep band, dental auxiliary.

ATHLETICS. NJCAA. **Intercollegiate:** Basketball, volleyball W. **Intramural:** Basketball, bowling, softball, tennis, volleyball.

STUDENT SERVICES. Aptitude testing, career counseling, employment service for undergraduates, freshman orientation, health services, personal counseling, placement service for graduates, special adviser for adult students, services/facilities for handicapped.

ANNUAL EXPENSES. Tuition and fees: $844, $1,400 additional for out-of-state students. Students from Western Undergraduate Exchange schools pay $350 additional tuition per year. **Room and board:** $2,450. **Books and supplies:** $450. **Other expenses:** $800.

FINANCIAL AID. 38% of freshmen, 27% of continuing students receive some form of aid. 88% of grants, 83% of loans, 82% of jobs based on

need. 362 enrolled freshmen were judged to have need, all were offered aid. Academic, music/drama, art, athletic, state/district residency scholarships available. **Aid applications:** No closing date; priority given to applications received by March 1; applicants notified on a rolling basis beginning on or about June 15; must reply within 3 weeks.

ADDRESS/TELEPHONE. Zane Garstad, Admissions Counselor, Sheridan College, PO Box 1500, 3059 Coffeen Avenue, Sheridan, WY 82801-1500. (307) 674-6446. Fax: (307) 674-4293.

University of Wyoming
Laramie, Wyoming — CB code: 4855

Admissions: 82% of applicants accepted
Based on:
••• School record
•• Test scores
• Interview, recommendations, special talents
Completion: 74% of freshmen end year in good standing
34% graduate

4-year public university, coed. Founded in 1886. **Accreditation:** Regional. **Undergraduate enrollment:** 4,098 men, 3,793 women full time; 601 men, 801 women part time. **Graduate enrollment:** 676 men, 463 women full time; 621 men, 999 women part time. **Faculty:** 754 total (719 full time), 632 with doctorates or other terminal degrees. **Location:** Rural campus in large town; 128 miles from Denver, Colorado. **Calendar:** Semester, extensive summer session. **Microcomputers:** 477 located in dormitories, libraries, classrooms, computer centers, campus-wide network. **Special facilities:** Geology museum, 2 herbariums, American heritage center, observatory, national park research center, art museum, planetarium, state veterinary laboratory, environmental biology laboratory, anthropology museum, vertebrate museum. **Additional facts:** Undergraduate and graduate degree programs offered in Casper through Casper College Center. Extension class available in off-campus locations throughout the state.

DEGREES OFFERED. BA, BS, BFA, MA, MS, MBA, MFA, PhD, EdD, JD. 1,781 bachelor's degrees awarded in 1992. 5% in agriculture, 14% business and management, 26% education, 9% engineering, 8% health sciences, 5% life sciences, 6% parks/recreation, protective services, public affairs, 8% social sciences. Graduate degrees offered in 65 major fields of study.

UNDERGRADUATE MAJORS. Accounting, agribusiness, agricultural business and management, agricultural education, agricultural sciences, agriculture communication, American studies, animal sciences, anthropology, applied mathematics, architectural engineering, art education, astronomy, bioengineering and biomedical engineering, biology, botany, business administration and management, business and management, business economics, business education, chemical engineering, chemistry, civil engineering, communications, computer and information sciences, criminal justice studies, dance, dental hygiene, dramatic arts, economics, electrical/electronics/communications engineering, elementary education, English, English education, entomology, finance, fine arts, food sciences, foreign languages education, French, geography, geology, geophysics and seismology, German, health education, history, home economics, home economics education, humanities and fine arts, industrial arts education, information sciences and systems, international agriculture, international relations, journalism, junior high education, management science, marketing and distributive education, marketing management, mathematics, mathematics education, mechanical engineering, medical laboratory technologies, molecular biology, music, music education, music performance, music theory and composition, nursing, parks and recreation management, petroleum engineering, pharmacy, philosophy, physical education, physics, plant sciences, political science and government, psychology, radio/television broadcasting, range management, Russian, secondary education, secretarial and related programs, small business management and ownership, social sciences, social studies education, social work, sociology, soil sciences, Spanish, special education, speech pathology/audiology, statistics, trade and industrial education, vocational education, wildlife management, women's studies, zoology.

ACADEMIC PROGRAMS. Accelerated program, computer delivered (on-line) credit-bearing course offerings, cooperative education, double major, dual enrollment of high school students, education specialist degree, honors program, independent study, internships, student-designed major, study abroad, teacher preparation, telecourses, visiting/exchange student program, United Nations semester, Washington semester, cross-registration, geology, botany, zoology and wildlife summer camps. **Remedial services:** Learning center, reduced course load, remedial instruction, special counselor, tutoring. **ROTC:** Air Force, Army. **Placement/credit:** AP, CLEP Subject, institutional tests.

ACADEMIC REQUIREMENTS. Freshmen must earn minimum GPA of 1.7 to continue in good standing. 71% of freshmen return for sophomore year. Students must declare major by end of second year. **Graduation requirements:** 128 hours for bachelor's (35 in major). Most students required to take courses in arts/fine arts, computer science, English, history, humanities, mathematics, biological/physical sciences, social sciences.

FRESHMAN ADMISSIONS. Selection criteria: Selective admissions for out-of-state applicants and those submitting GED test scores. Stricter admissions standards for all beginning fall 1995, currently open admissions for in-state high school graduates. **High school preparation:** 18 units recommended. Recommended units include English 4, foreign language 2, mathematics 3, social science 3 and science 3. Fine arts, computer science, and speech recommended. English recommendation includes composition. **Test requirements:** SAT or ACT (ACT preferred); score report by August 10.

1992 FRESHMAN CLASS PROFILE. 1,103 men applied, 874 accepted, 662 enrolled; 982 women applied, 842 accepted, 647 enrolled. 68% had high school GPA of 3.0 or higher, 30% between 2.0 and 2.99. 23% were in top tenth and 47% were in top quarter of graduating class. **Academic background:** Mid 50% of enrolled freshmen had ACT composite between 20-26. 87% submitted ACT scores. **Characteristics:** 74% from in state, 55% commute, 9% have minority backgrounds, 1% are foreign students, 11% join fraternities/sororities. Average age is 20.

FALL-TERM APPLICATIONS. $25 fee. Closing date August 10; priority given to applications received by March 1; applicants notified on a rolling basis; must reply by registration. Interview recommended. Deferred admission available. Institutional early decision plan. Early application recommended for those wishing university housing due to limited space. Applications for financial aid must be on file by March 1.

STUDENT LIFE. Housing: Dormitories (coed); apartment, fraternity, sorority, handicapped housing available. Honors floors, French and Spanish language floors available. **Activities:** Student government, magazine, radio, student newspaper, television, choral groups, concert band, dance, drama, jazz band, marching band, music ensembles, musical theater, opera, pep band, symphony orchestra, fraternities, sororities, Association of Black Student Leaders, MECHA, Keepers of the Fire, local church organizations, rodeo.

ATHLETICS. NCAA. **Intercollegiate:** Baseball M, basketball, cross-country, football M, golf, rifle, swimming, track and field, volleyball W, wrestling M. **Intramural:** Badminton, basketball, bowling, fencing, golf, ice hockey M, lacrosse, racquetball, rugby, soccer, softball, tennis, track and field, volleyball, water polo, wrestling M.

STUDENT SERVICES. Aptitude testing, career counseling, employment service for undergraduates, freshman orientation, health services, on-campus day care, personal counseling, placement service for graduates, special adviser for adult students, veterans counselor, services/facilities for handicapped.

ANNUAL EXPENSES. Tuition and fees: $1,698, $3,534 additional for out-of-state students. **Room and board:** $3,344. **Books and supplies:** $560. **Other expenses:** $1,500.

FINANCIAL AID. 54% of freshmen, 70% of continuing students receive some form of aid. 45% of grants, 74% of loans, 21% of jobs based on need. 590 enrolled freshmen were judged to have need, 580 were offered aid. Academic, music/drama, art, athletic, state/district residency, leadership, alumni affiliation scholarships available. **Aid applications:** No closing date; priority given to applications received by March 1; applicants notified on a rolling basis beginning on or about June 1; must reply within 3 weeks.

ADDRESS/TELEPHONE. Dr. Richard A. Davis, Dir Admissions/Enrollment Mgmt, University of Wyoming, University Station, Box 3435, Laramie, WY 82071-3435. (307) 766-5160. Fax: (307) 766-4042. (800) DIAL-WYO (instate, bordering states).

Western Wyoming Community College
Rock Springs, Wyoming — CB code: 4957

2-year public community college, coed. Founded in 1959. **Accreditation:** Regional. **Undergraduate enrollment:** 399 men, 589 women full time; 467 men, 1,117 women part time. **Faculty:** 222 total (75 full time), 20 with doctorates or other terminal degrees. **Location:** Suburban campus in large town; 180 miles from Salt Lake City, Utah. **Calendar:** Semester, limited summer session. **Microcomputers:** 75 located in libraries, classrooms, computer centers. **Special facilities:** Art gallery, geology/anthropology museum.

DEGREES OFFERED. AA, AS, AAS. 202 associate degrees awarded in 1992. 25% in business and management, 5% communications, 14% education, 13% health sciences, 6% multi/interdisciplinary studies, 5% psychology, 13% trade and industry.

UNDERGRADUATE MAJORS. Accounting, agricultural business and management, anthropology, automotive mechanics, automotive technology, biological and physical sciences, biology, business administration and management, business and management, business and office, business computer/console/peripheral equipment operation, business data entry equipment operation, business data processing and related programs, business data programming, business economics, chemical manufacturing technology, chemistry, communications, dance, diesel engine mechanics, dramatic arts, drawing, early childhood education, education, electrical and electronics equipment repair, elementary education, engineering, engineering and engineering-related technologies, engineering and other disciplines, English, finance, fine arts, foreign languages (multiple emphasis), French, geology, German, health sciences, history, humanities, humanities and social sciences, industrial technology, journalism, liberal/general studies, machine tool operation/machine shop, marketing and distribution, marketing management, mathematics, medical assistant, mining and petroleum technologies, music, nursing, office supervision and management, painting, personnel management, photographic technology, photography, physical sciences, physics, political science and government, precision metal work, predentistry, prelaw, premedicine, prepharmacy, preveterinary, psychology, radiograph medical technology, respiratory therapy technology, science technologies, secondary education, secretarial and related programs, social sciences, sociology, Spanish, speech, visual and performing arts, word processing.

ACADEMIC PROGRAMS. 2-year transfer program, cooperative education, dual enrollment of high school students, independent study, internships. **Remedial services:** Learning center, reduced course load, remedial instruction, tutoring. **Placement/credit:** AP, CLEP General and Subject, institutional tests; 40 credit hours maximum for associate degree.

ACADEMIC REQUIREMENTS. No policy requiring minimum GPA; records of students having academic difficulty are reviewed individually. 60% of freshmen return for sophomore year. Students must declare major on application. **Graduation requirements:** 64 hours for associate (24 in major). Most students required to take courses in English, history, mathematics, biological/physical sciences, social sciences.

FRESHMAN ADMISSIONS. Selection criteria: Open admissions. Selective admissions to health programs based on academic performance.

1992 FRESHMAN CLASS PROFILE. 516 men, 558 women enrolled. 40% had high school GPA of 3.0 or higher, 53% between 2.0 and 2.99. **Characteristics:** 90% from in state, 80% commute, 6% have minority backgrounds. Average age is 27.

FALL-TERM APPLICATIONS. No fee. No closing date; applicants notified on a rolling basis; must reply by registration. Interview required for health program applicants. Deferred and early admission available.

STUDENT LIFE. Housing: Dormitories (coed); apartment housing available. **Activities:** Student government, student newspaper, choral groups, concert band, dance, drama, jazz band, music ensembles, musical theater, pep band.

ATHLETICS. NJCAA. **Intercollegiate:** Basketball, wrestling M. **Intramural:** Badminton, basketball, cross-country, gymnastics, racquetball, skiing, soccer, softball, swimming, table tennis, tennis, volleyball, water polo, wrestling.

STUDENT SERVICES. Aptitude testing, career counseling, employment service for undergraduates, freshman orientation, health services, on-campus day care, personal counseling, placement service for graduates, special adviser for adult students, veterans counselor, services/facilities for handicapped.

ANNUAL EXPENSES. Tuition and fees (1992-93): $756, $1,248 additional for out-of-state students. Students from Western Undergraduate Exchange schools and Nebraska residents pay $312 additional tuition per year. **Room and board:** $2,400. **Books and supplies:** $400. **Other expenses:** $950.

FINANCIAL AID. 49% of freshmen, 51% of continuing students receive some form of aid. 92% of grants, 87% of loans, 15% of jobs based on need. 196 enrolled freshmen were judged to have need, 81 were offered aid. Academic, music/drama, art, athletic, state/district residency scholarships available. **Aid applications:** No closing date; priority given to applications received by April 1; applicants notified on a rolling basis beginning on or about June 1; must reply within 2 weeks.

ADDRESS/TELEPHONE. Jackie Freeze, Assoc Dean Enrollment Services, Western Wyoming Community College, PO Box 428, Rock Springs, WY 82901. (307) 382-1600. Fax: (307) 382-1636.

American Samoa, Caroline Islands, Guam, Marianas, Virgin Islands

American Samoa Community College
Pago Pago, American Samoa CB code: 0020

2-year public community college, coed. Founded in 1970. **Accreditation:** Regional. **Undergraduate enrollment:** 203 men, 232 women full time; 290 men, 433 women part time. **Location:** Rural campus in large town; 9 miles from downtown. **Calendar:** Semester. **Additional facts:** Only institution of higher education in American Samoa. Students seeking 4-year degrees transfer to colleges in Hawaii or mainland United States.

FRESHMAN ADMISSIONS. Selection criteria: Open admissions.

ADDRESS/TELEPHONE. Sina Peau-Ward, Registrar, American Samoa Community College, Box 2609, Pago Pago, AS 96799. (684) 699-9155.

College of Micronesia-FSM
Ponape, Federated States of Micronesia CB code: 0115

2-year public community college, coed. Founded in 1963. **Accreditation:** Regional. **Undergraduate enrollment:** 269 men, 226 women full time; 115 men, 105 women part time. **Faculty:** 37 total (35 full time), 3 with doctorates or other terminal degrees. **Location:** Rural campus in small town; 3,210 miles from Honolulu and 2,580 miles from Tokyo. **Calendar:** Semester, extensive summer session. **Microcomputers:** 12 located in computer centers. **Additional facts:** Students from 9 different cultures speaking 9 major languages. All courses in English.

DEGREES OFFERED. AA, AS. 275 associate degrees awarded in 1992. 48% in business and management, 50% multi/interdisciplinary studies.

UNDERGRADUATE MAJORS. Accounting, agricultural sciences, allied health, business and management, elementary education, liberal/general studies, marine biology, nursing, special education, teacher aide.

ACADEMIC PROGRAMS. Teacher preparation, extension program in 3 states of the former Trust Territory of the Pacific Islands. **Remedial services:** Remedial instruction. **Placement/credit:** Institutional tests; 16 credit hours maximum for associate degree.

ACADEMIC REQUIREMENTS. Freshmen must earn minimum GPA of 2.0 to continue in good standing. 80% of freshmen complete year in good standing. 70% return for sophomore year. Students must declare major on enrollment. **Graduation requirements:** 70 hours for associate. Most students required to take courses in computer science, English, humanities, mathematics, biological/physical sciences, social sciences. **Postgraduate studies:** 20% enter 4-year programs.

FRESHMAN ADMISSIONS. Selection criteria: School achievement record, class rank, test scores important. **High school preparation:** 10 units recommended. **Test requirements:** Institutional tests required.

1992 FRESHMAN CLASS PROFILE. 219 men, 224 women enrolled. 30% had high school GPA of 3.0 or higher, 65% between 2.0 and 2.99. **Characteristics:** 100% from in state, 75% live in college housing, 100% have minority backgrounds. Average age is 19.

FALL-TERM APPLICATIONS. $10 fee. Closing date June 1; applicants notified on a rolling basis beginning on or about May 15; must reply by July 31. Deferred admission available. Admission competitive because of limited facilities.

STUDENT LIFE. Housing: Dormitories (coed). **Activities:** Student government, student newspaper, yearbook. **Additional information:** 100% of freshmen are residents of 3 nations formed from former Trust Territory of Pacific Islands.

ATHLETICS. Intramural: Baseball M, basketball, softball, volleyball.

STUDENT SERVICES. Health services, personal counseling.

ANNUAL EXPENSES. Tuition and fees (1992-93): $2,625. **Room and board:** $2,352. **Books and supplies:** $300. **Other expenses:** $1,000.

FINANCIAL AID. 100% of freshmen receive some form of aid. All grants, all jobs based on need. **Aid applications:** Closing date July 1.

ADDRESS/TELEPHONE. Hers Tesei, Admissions Chairman, College of Micronesia-FSM, PO Box 159, Kolonia, Ponape, FM 96941. 011-691-320-2480. Fax: 011-691-320-2479.

Guam Community College
Barrigada, Guam Mariana Islands CB code: 2302

2-year public community college, coed. Founded in 1977. **Accreditation:** Regional. **Undergraduate enrollment:** 93 men, 90 women full time; 862 men, 644 women part time. **Faculty:** 232 total (144 full time), 4 with doctorates or other terminal degrees. **Location:** Suburban campus in small city; 1,500 miles east of Manila, Philippines, 3,600 miles west southwest of Honolulu, Hawaii, 1,500 miles south of Tokyo, Japan. **Calendar:** Semester, extensive summer session. Saturday and extensive evening/early morning classes. **Microcomputers:** 220 located in libraries, classrooms, computer centers. **Special facilities:** The Pacific Collection, including 400 books (many rare and out of print) about Guam, Micronesia, and the Pacific.

DEGREES OFFERED. AS, AAS. 52 associate degrees awarded in 1992. 25% in business/office and marketing/distribution, 10% computer sciences, 20% engineering technologies, 45% parks/recreation, protective services, public affairs.

UNDERGRADUATE MAJORS. Accounting, architectural technologies, automotive technology, business and office, child development/care/guidance, civil technology, computer and information sciences, criminal justice technology, electronic technology, fire control and safety technology, food management, food production/management/services, horticulture, hospitality and recreation marketing, hotel/motel and restaurant management, law enforcement and corrections, law enforcement and corrections technologies, marketing and distribution, secretarial and related programs, tourism, trade and industrial supervision and management, transportation and travel marketing, water and wastewater technology.

ACADEMIC PROGRAMS. Cooperative education, dual enrollment of high school students, independent study, internships, cross-registration. **Remedial services:** Learning center, remedial instruction, tutoring. **ROTC:** Army. **Placement/credit:** CLEP General and Subject, institutional tests; 48 credit hours maximum for associate degree.

ACADEMIC REQUIREMENTS. Freshmen must earn minimum GPA of 2.0 to continue in good standing. 40% of freshmen return for sophomore year. Students must declare major on application. **Graduation requirements:** 60 hours for associate (30 in major). Most students required to take courses in computer science, English, mathematics, biological/physical sciences, social sciences.

FRESHMAN ADMISSIONS. Selection criteria: Open admissions. Recommended units include English 4, mathematics 3, social science 3 and science 2. **Test requirements:** TABE Test of Adult Basic Skills required for English and mathematics applicants.

1992 FRESHMAN CLASS PROFILE. 115 men, 116 women enrolled. **Characteristics:** 80% from in state, 100% commute, 90% have minority backgrounds, 16% are foreign students. Average age is 22.

FALL-TERM APPLICATIONS. No fee. Closing date July 15; applicants notified on or about August 15. Interview recommended. Deferred and early admission available.

STUDENT LIFE. Housing: Students may live at University of Guam dormitories on space-available basis. **Activities:** Student government, yearbook, various foreign student associations.

STUDENT SERVICES. Aptitude testing, career counseling, employment service for undergraduates, health services, on-campus day care, personal counseling, placement service for graduates, special adviser for adult students, veterans counselor, services/facilities for handicapped.

ANNUAL EXPENSES. Tuition and fees: $325. **Books and supplies:** $504. **Other expenses:** $1,447.

FINANCIAL AID. 6% of freshmen, 5% of continuing students receive some form of aid. All grants, all jobs based on need. 20 enrolled freshmen were judged to have need, 19 were offered aid. Academic, state/district residency scholarships available. **Aid applications:** No closing date; priority given to applications received by May 1; applicants notified on a rolling basis beginning on or about August 28; must reply within 2 weeks.

ADDRESS/TELEPHONE. Dr. David G. Watt, Coordinator of Admissions, Guam Community College, PO Box 23069 GMF, Barrigada, GU 96921. (671) 734-4311. Fax: (671) 734-5238.

Micronesian Occupational College
Koror, Palau CB code: 7329

2-year public branch campus college, coed. Founded in 1969. **Accreditation:** Regional. **Undergraduate enrollment:** 224 men, 126 women full time; 28 men, 67 women part time. **Faculty:** 40 total. **Location:** Suburban campus in large town. **Calendar:** Semester, limited summer session.

DEGREES OFFERED. AA, AS. 10 associate degrees awarded in 1992.

UNDERGRADUATE MAJORS. Agricultural sciences, air conditioning/heating/refrigeration mechanics, automotive mechanics, carpentry, construction, diesel engine mechanics, electrical and electronics equipment repair, home economics, law enforcement and corrections technologies, mechanical engineering, secretarial and related programs.

ACADEMIC PROGRAMS. 2-year transfer program, cooperative education, dual enrollment of high school students, internships. **Remedial services:** Learning center, remedial instruction, tutoring. **Placement/credit:** Institutional tests.

ACADEMIC REQUIREMENTS. Freshmen must earn minimum GPA of 2.0 to continue in good standing. 95% of freshmen return for sophomore year. Students must declare major on application. **Graduation requirements:** Most students required to take courses in English, humanities, mathematics, biological/physical sciences, social sciences.

FRESHMAN ADMISSIONS. Selection criteria: Open admissions.

1992 FRESHMAN CLASS PROFILE. 166 men and women enrolled. **Characteristics:** 56% commute, 100% have minority backgrounds. Average age is 18.

FALL-TERM APPLICATIONS. $5 fee. Closing date July 15; priority given to applications received by June 30; applicants notified on a rolling basis. Deferred admission available. Recommend applicants take TOEFL Test.

STUDENT LIFE. Housing: Dormitories (men, women). **Activities:** Student government, film, magazine, television, dance.

ATHLETICS. Intramural: Badminton, baseball, basketball M, softball, table tennis, volleyball.

STUDENT SERVICES. Career counseling, freshman orientation, health services, personal counseling, placement service for graduates.

ANNUAL EXPENSES. Tuition and fees (1992-93): $2,200. **Room and board:** $2,352. **Books and supplies:** $200. **Other expenses:** $300.

FINANCIAL AID. 98% of freshmen, 98% of continuing students receive some form of aid. All grants, 88% of jobs based on need. **Aid applications:** No closing date; priority given to applications received by June 1; applicants notified on a rolling basis; must reply within 20 days.

ADDRESS/TELEPHONE. Valeria Toribiong, Director of Admissions, Micronesian Occupational College, P.O. Box 9, Koror, PW 96940-9999. 011-691-KOROR 488-2471 ext. 03. Fax: (680) 488-2447 ext. 01.

Northern Marianas College
Saipan, Commonwealth of the Northern Marianas — CB code: 0781

2-year public community college, coed. Founded in 1981. **Accreditation:** Regional. **Undergraduate enrollment:** 136 men, 158 women full time; 189 men, 338 women part time. **Location:** Rural campus in large town; 150 miles from Guam; 3000 miles from Hawaii. **Calendar:** Semester.

FRESHMAN ADMISSIONS. Selection criteria: Open admissions.

ANNUAL EXPENSES. Tuition and fees: $1,550, $1,500 additional for out-of-state students. **Books and supplies:** $350. **Other expenses:** $1,200.

ADDRESS/TELEPHONE. Rose L. Igitol, Director of Admissions, Northern Marianas College, Box 1250, Saipan, CM 96950. (670) 234-6128 ext. 37. Fax: (670) 234-0759.

University of Guam
Mangilao, Guam, Mariana Islands — CB code: 0959

4-year public university, coed. Founded in 1952. **Accreditation:** Regional. **Undergraduate enrollment:** 765 men, 1,148 women full time; 301 men, 461 women part time. **Graduate enrollment:** 38 men, 40 women full time; 85 men, 148 women part time. **Location:** Suburban campus in small town; 4,100 miles from Honolulu, Hawaii. **Calendar:** Semester.

FRESHMAN ADMISSIONS. Selection criteria: Open admissions.

ADDRESS/TELEPHONE. Kathleen R. Owings, Director of Admissions and Records, University of Guam, UOG Station, Mangilao, Mariana Islands 96923. (671) 734-2921.

University of the Virgin Islands
Charlotte Amalie, Virgin Islands — CB code: 0879

4-year public liberal arts college, coed. Founded in 1962. **Accreditation:** Regional. **Undergraduate enrollment:** 295 men, 851 women full time; 407 men, 1,115 women part time. **Graduate enrollment:** 56 men, 200 women part time. **Faculty:** 250 total (111 full time), 106 with doctorates or other terminal degrees. **Location:** Suburban campus in large town; 80 air miles from San Juan, Puerto Rico. **Calendar:** Semester, limited summer session. Extensive evening/early morning classes. **Microcomputers:** Located in libraries, classrooms, computer centers. **Special facilities:** Outdoor amphitheater, Caribbean collection, African art collection. **Additional facts:** Additional campus on St. Croix. Housing available on St. Thomas.

DEGREES OFFERED. AA, AS, BA, BS, MA, MBA. 67 associate degrees awarded in 1992. 35% in business and management, 11% business/office and marketing/distribution, 13% computer sciences, 16% health sciences, 23% multi/interdisciplinary studies. 139 bachelor's degrees awarded. 48% in business and management, 23% teacher education, 5% mathematics. Graduate degrees offered in 5 major fields of study.

UNDERGRADUATE MAJORS. Associate: Accounting, agricultural sciences, business administration and management, data processing, finance, law enforcement and corrections technologies, nursing, physics, secretarial and related programs. **Bachelor's:** Accounting, biology, business administration and management, Caribbean studies, chemistry, elementary education, English, humanities, marine biology, mathematics, music education, nursing, psychology, social sciences, social work, Spanish, trade and industrial education.

ACADEMIC PROGRAMS. 2-year transfer program, dual enrollment of high school students, independent study, internships, visiting/exchange student program. **Remedial services:** Learning center, preadmission summer program, reduced course load, remedial instruction, special counselor, tutoring. **Placement/credit:** AP, CLEP Subject, institutional tests.

ACADEMIC REQUIREMENTS. Freshmen must earn minimum GPA of 1.7 to continue in good standing. 35% of freshmen return for sophomore year. Students must declare major on enrollment. **Graduation requirements:** 62 hours for associate (32 in major), 120 hours for bachelor's (66 in major). Most students required to take courses in arts/fine arts, English, foreign languages, history, humanities, mathematics, philosophy/religion, biological/physical sciences, social sciences. **Postgraduate studies:** 30% from 2-year programs enter 4-year programs.

FRESHMAN ADMISSIONS. Selection criteria: School achievement record, test scores, and counselor's recommendation important. **High school preparation:** 11 units recommended. Recommended units include English 4, foreign language 1, mathematics 2, social science 2 and science 2. **Test requirements:** SAT or ACT; score report by April 15. Nursing Aptitude Test required of nursing applicants.

1992 FRESHMAN CLASS PROFILE. 730 men and women enrolled. **Characteristics:** 75% from in state, 80% commute, 79% have minority backgrounds, 15% are foreign students.

FALL-TERM APPLICATIONS. $20 fee. Closing date April 15; applicants notified on a rolling basis; must reply immediately. Essay required. Interview recommended for local applicants. Early admission available.

STUDENT LIFE. Housing: Dormitories (men, women, coed). **Activities:** Student government, radio, student newspaper, yearbook, choral groups, concert band, dance, drama, jazz band, music ensembles, political clubs, President's club, Future Business Leaders of America, Explorer's Club, Virgin Islands Student Association.

ATHLETICS. Intercollegiate: Soccer M. **Intramural:** Archery, badminton, basketball, fencing, golf, gymnastics, racquetball, softball, swimming, table tennis, tennis, track and field, volleyball.

STUDENT SERVICES. Aptitude testing, career counseling, employment service for undergraduates, freshman orientation, health services, personal counseling, placement service for graduates.

ANNUAL EXPENSES. Tuition and fees (1992-93): $1,440, $2,700 additional for out-of-state students. **Room and board:** $4,300. **Books and supplies:** $425. **Other expenses:** $800.

FINANCIAL AID. 80% of freshmen, 80% of continuing students receive some form of aid. 89% of grants, all loans, all jobs based on need. Academic scholarships available. **Aid applications:** Closing date April 15; applicants notified on or about June 30; must reply within 2 weeks.

ADDRESS/TELEPHONE. Dr. Judith W. Edwin, Director of Admissions, University of the Virgin Islands, Charlotte Amalie, St. Thomas, VI 00802. (809) 776-9200. Fax: (809) 774-2399 ext. 1406.

Arab Republic of Egypt

American University in Cairo
Cairo, Arab Republic of Egypt CB code: 0903

Admissions: 40% of applicants accepted
Based on: ••• School record, test scores
•• Recommendations, special talents
• Activities, essay
Completion: 86% of freshmen end year in good standing
65% graduate

4-year private university, coed. Founded in 1919. **Accreditation:** Regional. **Undergraduate enrollment:** 1,656 men, 1,623 women full time; 130 men, 91 women part time. **Graduate enrollment:** 111 men, 123 women full time; 169 men, 240 women part time. **Faculty:** 716 total (316 full time), 269 with doctorates or other terminal degrees. **Location:** Urban campus in very large city; in the center of Cairo. **Calendar:** Semester, extensive summer session. **Microcomputers:** 840 located in dormitories, libraries, computer centers. **Special facilities:** Pharoic and Greco-Roman art and architecture. **Additional facts:** Language of instruction English. 75% of degree-seeking students must be of Egyptian nationality. Located near Cairo Museum with world's largest collection of Egyptian antiquities.

DEGREES OFFERED. BA, BS, MA, MS, MBA. 517 bachelor's degrees awarded in 1992. 13% in business and management, 18% communications, 11% computer sciences, 14% engineering, 35% social sciences. Graduate degrees offered in 16 major fields of study.

UNDERGRADUATE MAJORS. Anthropology, Arabic, Arabic studies, business administration and management, chemistry, comparative literature, computer and information sciences, construction engineering, dramatic arts, economics, Egyptology, English literature, journalism, mathematics, mechanical engineering, Middle Eastern history, Middle Eastern studies, physics, political science and government, psychology, sociology.

ACADEMIC PROGRAMS. Double major, independent study, study abroad, visiting/exchange student program; liberal arts/career combination in engineering, business. **Remedial services:** Tutoring, intensive English as a second language program. **Placement/credit:** AP, IB, institutional tests; 30 credit hours maximum for bachelor's degree.

ACADEMIC REQUIREMENTS. Freshmen must earn minimum GPA of 2.0 to continue in good standing. 81% of freshmen return for sophomore year. Students must declare major by end of first year. **Graduation requirements:** 120 hours for bachelor's (70 in major). Most students required to take courses in arts/fine arts, English, foreign languages, history, humanities, philosophy/religion, biological/physical sciences, social sciences.

FRESHMAN ADMISSIONS. Selection criteria: Undergraduate degree applicants from the United States expected to have completed college preparatory (academic) high school program and to have taken SAT; minimum combined score of 1000 required. Arab students must take Thanawiya 'Amma; minimum score of 65% required. GCE/GCSE/IGCSE certificates will also be considered for admission. **High school preparation:** 16 units required. Required and recommended units include English 4. Foreign language 3, mathematics 4, social science 3 and science 4 recommended. **Test requirements:** SAT; score report by May 31. **Additional information:** For North American students October 31 deadline for February admission, March 31 deadline for summer admission for non-degree programs.

1992 FRESHMAN CLASS PROFILE. 2,882 men and women applied, 1,140 accepted; 415 men enrolled, 357 women enrolled. **Characteristics:** 87% commute. Average age is 18.

FALL-TERM APPLICATIONS. $30 fee. Closing date May 31; applicants notified on a rolling basis.

STUDENT LIFE. Housing: Dormitories (men, women). 351 spaces available for foreign students. Preference given to female students. **Activities:** Student government, film, student newspaper, television, yearbook, choral groups, dance, drama, African Students Association, Community Service Society.

ATHLETICS. Intercollegiate: Basketball, diving W, fencing, gymnastics, rowing (crew), soccer M, squash, swimming, table tennis, tennis, track and field, volleyball, water polo M, wrestling M. **Intramural:** Basketball, soccer, table tennis, tennis, volleyball.

STUDENT SERVICES. Career counseling, employment service for undergraduates, freshman orientation, health services, personal counseling, placement service for graduates, special adviser for adult students.

ANNUAL EXPENSES. Tuition and fees: $8,045. **Room and board:** $2,280 room only. **Books and supplies:** $600. **Other expenses:** $1,200.

FINANCIAL AID. 80% of freshmen, 75% of continuing students receive some form of aid. 95% of grants, all jobs based on need. 166 enrolled freshmen were judged to have need, all were offered aid. Academic, music/drama, art, athletic, leadership, alumni affiliation scholarships available. **Additional information:** 15 fellowships awarded annually in teaching English as a foreign language. To facilitate attendance of year-abroad U.S. students from state universities, tuition equivalent to difference between university's tuition and out-of-state tuition automatically offered. Up to 20 graduate fellowships for qualified applicants from African countries. Most financial aid for undergraduate students limited to local Egyptian applicants, on-campus jobs paid at local (Egyptian) wage scale.

ADDRESS/TELEPHONE. Mary Davidson, Coordinator, Student Affairs, American University in Cairo, 866 United Nations Plaza, Suite 517, New York, NY 10017-1889. (212) 421-6320. Fax: (212) 688-5341.

Canada

McGill University
Montreal, Quebec, Canada CB code: 0935

4-year public university, coed. Founded in 1821. **Undergraduate enrollment:** 6,710 men, 8,362 women full time; 3,496 men, 4,807 women part time. **Graduate enrollment:** 3,082 men, 2,102 women full time; 1,019 men, 892 women part time. **Faculty:** 2,747 total (2,042 full time). **Location:** Urban campus in very large city. **Calendar:** Semester, limited summer session. Extensive evening/early morning classes. **Microcomputers:** 350 located in libraries, computer centers, campus-wide network. **Special facilities:** McCord Museum, Morgan Arboretum, Gault Estate, Redpath Museum, Lyman Entomological Museum, Science and Conservation Center. **Additional facts:** Macdonald College campus located in St. Anne de Bellevue.

DEGREES OFFERED. BA, BS, BArch, MA, MS, MBA, MEd, MSW, PhD, EdD, DDS, MD, B.Div, M.Div. 3,782 bachelor's degrees awarded in 1992. 13% in business and management, 8% teacher education, 10% engineering, 7% letters/literature, 11% life sciences, 7% psychology, 16% social sciences. Graduate degrees offered in 156 major fields of study.

UNDERGRADUATE MAJORS. Accounting, African studies, agricultural economics, agricultural engineering, agricultural sciences, agronomy, anatomy, animal sciences, anthropology, architecture, art education, art history, atmospheric sciences and meteorology, biochemistry, biological and physical sciences, biology, business administration and management, business and management, business economics, business education, business statistics, Caribbean studies, cell biology, chemical engineering, chemistry, civil engineering, classics, computer and information sciences, computer engineering, conservation and regulation, developmental psychology, earth sciences, East Asian studies, ecology, economics, education, electrical/electronics/communications engineering, elementary education, English, English education, English literature, entomology, entrepreneurship, experimental psychology, finance, food management, food science and nutrition, food sciences, foreign languages (multiple emphasis), foreign languages education, French, French Canadian studies, geography, geology, geophysics and seismology, German, history, horticulture, humanities, humanities and social sciences, international business management, Italian, Jewish studies, labor/industrial relations, Latin American studies, linguistics, management information systems, management science, marine biology, marketing management, mathematics, mathematics education, mechanical engineering, metallurgical engineering, metallurgy, microbiology, Middle Eastern studies, mining and mineral engineering, molecular biology, music, music history and appreciation, music performance, music theory and composition, North American studies, nursing, nutritional sciences, occupational therapy, operations research, organizational behavior, personnel management, philosophy, physical education, physical therapy, physics, physiological psychology, physiology, human and animal, plant pathology, plant protection, plant sciences, political science and government, psychology, real estate, religion, religious music, renewable natural resources, Russian, Russian and Slavic studies, science education, secondary education, social psychology, social studies education, social work, sociology, soil sciences, Spanish, statistics, teaching English as a second language/foreign language, theological studies, trade and industrial education, wildlife management, women's studies, zoology.

ACADEMIC PROGRAMS. Cooperative education, double major, honors program, internships, student-designed major, study abroad, teacher preparation, visiting/exchange student program, cross-registration; combined bachelor's/graduate program in business administration. **Remedial services:** Reduced course load, special counselor, tutoring, study skills workshops. **Placement/credit:** AP, IB, institutional tests; 30 credit hours maximum for bachelor's degree.

ACADEMIC REQUIREMENTS. Freshmen must earn minimum GPA of 2.0 to continue in good standing. Students must declare major by end of first year. **Graduation requirements:** 120 hours for bachelor's.

FRESHMAN ADMISSIONS. Selection criteria: School achievement record, class rank, test scores, most important. Recommendations also considered. High school requirements vary according to program. **Test requirements:** SAT or ACT (SAT preferred); score report by June 30. 3 ACH required. Score report by June 30.

1992 FRESHMAN CLASS PROFILE. 1,929 men, 2,558 women enrolled. 100% had high school GPA of 3.0 or higher.

FALL-TERM APPLICATIONS. $28 fee. Closing date January 15; applicants notified on or about March 30; must reply by May 1 or within 2 weeks if notified thereafter. Audition required for music applicants. Interview required of second language teaching applicants; dentistry and medicine applicants may be invited to interview. Deferred admission available.

STUDENT LIFE. Housing: Dormitories (women, coed); apartment, cooperative housing available. **Activities:** Student government, film, magazine, radio, student newspaper, television, yearbook, choral groups, concert band, dance, drama, jazz band, music ensembles, musical theater, opera, symphony orchestra, fraternities, sororities, full range of political, ethnic, and religious associations.

ATHLETICS. Intercollegiate: Badminton, basketball, cross-country, fencing, field hockey W, football M, ice hockey, rowing (crew), rugby, sailing, skiing, soccer, squash, swimming, track and field, volleyball. **Intramural:** Badminton, basketball, bowling, football, ice hockey, rowing (crew), soccer, softball, squash, table tennis, tennis, volleyball, water polo.

STUDENT SERVICES. Aptitude testing, career counseling, employment service for undergraduates, freshman orientation, health services, on-campus day care, personal counseling, placement service for graduates, special adviser for adult students, services/facilities for handicapped.

ANNUAL EXPENSES. Tuition and fees (projected): $1,950, $5,740 additional for out-of-state students. All annual expense figures quoted in Canadian dollars. International students required to pay annual health fee of $440. **Room and board:** $5,704. **Books and supplies:** $1,000. **Other expenses:** $1,500.

FINANCIAL AID. 35% of continuing students receive some form of aid. 88% of grants, 98% of loans, all jobs based on need. **Aid applications:** No closing date; applicants notified on a rolling basis.

ADDRESS/TELEPHONE. C. Abbott Conway, Dean of Admissions, McGill University, 845 Sherbrooke Street West, Montreal, Quebec, Canada H3A 2T5. (514) 398-3910. Fax: (514) 398-4193.

France

American University of Paris
Paris, France CB code: 0866

4-year private liberal arts college, coed. Founded in 1962. **Accreditation:** Regional. **Undergraduate enrollment:** 1,005 men and women. **Faculty:** 107 total (38 full time), 50 with doctorates or other terminal degrees. **Location:** Urban campus in very large city. **Calendar:** Semester, extensive summer session. **Microcomputers:** 40 located in computer centers.

DEGREES OFFERED. BA, BS. 175 bachelor's degrees awarded in 1992. 48% in business and management, 5% languages, 10% letters/literature, 21% social sciences, 13% visual and performing arts.

UNDERGRADUATE MAJORS. Applied economics, art history, comparative literature, computer and information sciences, economics, European studies, French, history, international business management, international relations.

ACADEMIC PROGRAMS. Independent study, internships, study abroad, visiting/exchange student program, cross-registration, exchange program in fine arts with Parsons School of Design (NY). **Remedial services:** Reduced course load, tutoring. **Placement/credit:** AP, CLEP General and Subject, institutional tests; 30 credit hours maximum for bachelor's degree.

ACADEMIC REQUIREMENTS. Freshmen must earn minimum GPA of 2.0 to continue in good standing. 60% of freshmen return for sophomore year. Students must declare major by end of second year. **Graduation requirements:** 120 hours for bachelor's (42 in major). Most students required to take courses in English, foreign languages, humanities, mathematics, biological/physical sciences, social sciences. **Additional information:** 4 semesters (or equivalent) of French required for all degrees.

FRESHMAN ADMISSIONS. Selection criteria: Academic background and evidence of ability to contribute to an international setting important. Essay, recommendations, extracurricular activities, and test scores considered. For non-native English speakers, TOEFL score of 600 required for regular program, 500 for ESL program. **High school preparation:** 18 units recommended. Recommended units include English 4, foreign language 3, mathematics 3, social science 3 and science 2. **Test requirements:** SAT or ACT (SAT preferred); score report by July 31. SAT or ACT required of applicants from US school systems only. National examinations accepted in place of SAT or ACT for students applying from non-American style secondary institutions.

1992 FRESHMAN CLASS PROFILE. 145 men and women enrolled. **Characteristics:** 100% commute, 69% are foreign students. Average age is 19.

FALL-TERM APPLICATIONS. $45 fee, may be waived for applicants with need. Closing date July 1; priority given to applications received by May 1; applicants notified on a rolling basis; must reply by May 1 or within 2 weeks if notified thereafter. Essay required. Interview recommended. Deferred and early admission available.

STUDENT LIFE. Housing: Housing office accepts responsibility of finding appropriate housing arrangements for all full-time students. **Activities:** Student government, magazine, student newspaper, yearbook, drama, music ensembles. **Additional information:** Office of Student Affairs provides guidance and information for orientation in university and Paris. Group student travel in Europe and elsewhere available through Cultural Program.

ATHLETICS. Intramural: Basketball M, field hockey M, horseback riding, skiing, soccer W, squash, tennis.

STUDENT SERVICES. Career counseling, employment service for undergraduates, freshman orientation, health services, personal counseling, placement service for graduates.

ANNUAL EXPENSES. Tuition and fees: $14,706. **Books and supplies:** $750. **Other expenses:** $1,000.

FINANCIAL AID. 20% of freshmen, 25% of continuing students receive some form of aid. 98% of grants, 64% of loans, all jobs based on need. 57 enrolled freshmen were judged to have need, all were offered aid. Academic scholarships available. **Aid applications:** Closing date May 1; priority given to applications received by March 1; applicants notified on a rolling basis beginning on or about May 1; must reply within 3 weeks. **Additional information:** Au pair situations may be available for qualified students.

ADDRESS/TELEPHONE. Christine Broening, Director of Admissions, American University of Paris, 31 Avenue Bosqnet, Paris, France. 011-331-44-55-91-73. Fax: (331) 47.05.34.32. All North American candidates should write or call: Thelma Bullock Director of the New York Office, American University of Paris, 80 East 11th Street, Suite 434, New York, NY 10003. Telephone: (212) 677-4870. FAX: (212) 475-5205.

Mexico

Sistema Instituto Tecnologico y de Estudios Superiores de Monterrey

Monterrey, Nuevo Leon, Mexico CB code: 0843

4-year private university, coed. Founded in 1943. **Accreditation:** Regional. **Undergraduate enrollment:** 20,250 men, 12,517 women full time; 1,395 men and women part time. **Graduate enrollment:** 3,696 men and women. **Faculty:** 4,449 total (1,658 full time), 2,282 with doctorates or other terminal degrees. **Location:** Urban campus in very large city. **Calendar:** Semester, extensive summer session. **Microcomputers:** Located in libraries, computer centers. **Additional facts:** 26 campuses grouped into 6 administrative divisions: Monterrey Campus, Eugenio Garza Sada Campus, Northern Zone, Central Zone, Southern Zone, Pacific Zone. Locations range from very large city to small city, and from urban to rural. Undergraduate enrollment at campuses: Monterrey: 12,957; Eugenio Garza Sada: Ciudad Juarez: 416; Ciudad Obregon: 301; Chihuahua: 1182; Guaymas: 219; Laguna: 780; Mazatlan: 209; Saltillo: 235; Sinaloa: 556; Sonora Norte: 663; Colima: 116; Irapuato: 152; Leon: 886; Queretaro: 2279; San Luis Potosi: 513; Tampico: 422; Toluca: 1062; Zacatecas: 256; Central de Veracruz: 287; Chiapas: 282; Estado de Mexico: 6123; Hidalgo: 208; Ciudad de Mexico: 2375; Guadalajara: 513; Morelos: 1190. Major fields of study and athletic offerings vary by campus.

DEGREES OFFERED. BA, BS, BFA, MA, MS, MBA, MEd, PhD. 3,725 bachelor's degrees awarded in 1992. Graduate degrees offered in 27 major fields of study.

UNDERGRADUATE MAJORS. Accounting, agricultural production, agricultural products and processing, animal sciences, architecture, biochemistry, Biochemistry and food processing administration, Biochemistry in aquatic resources, business administration and management, chemical engineering, chemistry, civil engineering, communications, computer and information sciences, computer engineering, economics, electrical/electronics/communications engineering, electromechanical technology, finance, health sciences, hotel/motel and restaurant management, industrial and organizational psychology, industrial engineering, Industrial physics engineering, information sciences and systems, international business management, international relations, international studies, law (X), management information systems, marketing and distribution, mechanical engineering and management, physics, Spanish.

ACADEMIC PROGRAMS. Double major, study abroad, visiting/exchange student program. **Remedial services:** Remedial instruction, tutoring, academic counseling program. **Placement/credit:** Institutional tests.

ACADEMIC REQUIREMENTS. No policy requiring minimum GPA; records of students having academic difficulty are reviewed individually. Students must declare major on application. **Graduation requirements:** 162 hours for bachelor's. Most students required to take courses in computer science, English, foreign languages, humanities, mathematics.

FRESHMAN ADMISSIONS. Selection criteria: Test scores and GPA important. **Test requirements:** SAT; score report by July 29. Prueba de Aptitud Academica for Spanish speaking applicants.

1992 FRESHMAN CLASS PROFILE. 10,047 men and women applied, 7,290 accepted; 3,400 men enrolled, 2,234 women enrolled. **Characteristics:** 70% from in state, 2% are foreign students.

FALL-TERM APPLICATIONS. No fee. Closing date July 29; applicants notified on a rolling basis. Interview required for health sciences applicants. Deferred admission available.

STUDENT LIFE. Housing: Dormitories (men, women). Dormitories available only on Monterrey campus. **Activities:** Student government, magazine, radio, student newspaper, television, yearbook, choral groups, concert band, dance, drama, music ensembles, musical theater, Entrepreneur Leader Association.

ATHLETICS. Intercollegiate: Baseball M, basketball, football M, gymnastics, soccer M, softball, swimming, tennis, track and field, volleyball, water polo M. **Intramural:** Basketball, football M, handball, soccer M, softball, swimming, tennis, volleyball, water polo.

STUDENT SERVICES. Career counseling, freshman orientation, health services, personal counseling, placement service for graduates.

ANNUAL EXPENSES. Tuition and fees (1992-93): $4,967. **Room and board:** $2,000 room only. **Books and supplies:** $500.

FINANCIAL AID. 24% of continuing students receive some form of aid. 90% of grants, all loans based on need. Academic scholarships available. **Aid applications:** Closing date April 30; applicants notified on or about July 15. **Additional information:** Financial aid available for Mexican students only.

ADDRESS/TELEPHONE. Vice Rectoria Academica, Sistema Inst Tec Estudios Superiores Monterrey, 2501 Eugenio Garza Sada, Monterrey, Nuevo Leon, Mexico 64849. 011-52-83-58-41-63. Fax: (011) (52) (83) 58-45-55.

Switzerland

American College of Switzerland
Leysin, Switzerland CB code: 0878

4-year proprietary liberal arts college, coed. Founded in 1963. **Undergraduate enrollment:** 70 men and women. **Faculty:** 20 total (7 full time), 5 with doctorates or other terminal degrees. **Location:** Rural campus in small town; 25 miles from Lausanne, 60 miles from Geneva. **Calendar:** Semester, extensive summer session. **Microcomputers:** 20 located on campus. **Special facilities:** Multipurpose sports complex. **Additional facts:** Campus of Schiller International University. Semester and year-abroad program for visiting students. Students from more than 45 countries. International emphasis in all undergraduate programs with speakers from international organizations from Geneva.

DEGREES OFFERED. AA, BA, BS, MBA. 5 associate degrees awarded in 1992. 100% in multi/interdisciplinary studies. 10 bachelor's degrees awarded. 70% in business and management, 7% multi/interdisciplinary studies, 23% social sciences. Graduate degrees offered in 1 major field of study.

UNDERGRADUATE MAJORS. Associate: Liberal/general studies. **Bachelor's:** Accounting, business administration and management, business and management, business economics, economics, English literature, European studies, finance, fine arts, French, humanities, humanities and social sciences, international business management, international relations, international studies, liberal/general studies, marketing and distribution, marketing management, Middle Eastern studies, political science and government, prelaw, social sciences.

ACADEMIC PROGRAMS. 2-year transfer program, accelerated program, double major, independent study, internships, student-designed major, study abroad, visiting/exchange student program, United Nations semester, intensive French language program (credit and noncredit). **Remedial services:** Preadmission summer program, reduced course load, tutoring, ESL-college skills program. **Placement/credit:** AP, CLEP General and Subject, IB, institutional tests.

ACADEMIC REQUIREMENTS. Freshmen must earn minimum GPA of 2.0 to continue in good standing. 65% of freshmen return for sophomore year. Students must declare major by end of second year. **Graduation requirements:** 62 hours for associate, 124 hours for bachelor's (60 in major). Most students required to take courses in arts/fine arts, computer science, English, foreign languages, history, humanities, mathematics, philosophy/religion, biological/physical sciences, social sciences. **Postgraduate studies:** 95% from 2-year programs enter 4-year programs. 4% enter law school, 15% enter MBA programs, 4% enter other graduate study. **Additional information:** Course-related travel in Europe and beyond, foreign language training, and internships at multinational, international organizations, and United Nations in Geneva.

FRESHMAN ADMISSIONS. Selection criteria: High school GPA most important. **High school preparation:** 16 units recommended. Recommended units include English 4, foreign language 2, mathematics 4, social science 2 and science 4. **Additional information:** Course flexibility exists and recommendations considered within the context of the national system from which student graduates.

1992 FRESHMAN CLASS PROFILE. 20 men and women enrolled. **Characteristics:** 99% live in college housing, 55% are foreign students. Average age is 18.

FALL-TERM APPLICATIONS. $50 fee, may be waived for applicants with need. No closing date; applicants notified on a rolling basis; No closing date for applicants reply. Deferred admission available.

STUDENT LIFE. Housing: Dormitories (coed). **Activities:** Student government, yearbook, international student organizations.

ATHLETICS. Intramural: Basketball, horseback riding, ice hockey, skiing, soccer, softball, squash, swimming, table tennis, tennis, volleyball.

STUDENT SERVICES. Career counseling, freshman orientation, health services, personal counseling.

ANNUAL EXPENSES. Tuition and fees (1992-93): $18,675. **Room and board:** $5,225. **Books and supplies:** $1,000. **Other expenses:** $3,600.

FINANCIAL AID. 33% of continuing students receive some form of aid. All grants based on need. **Aid applications:** No closing date; priority given to applications received by April 1; applicants notified on a rolling basis beginning on or about April 1; must reply within 3 weeks.

ADDRESS/TELEPHONE. Cheryl Cook-McCormick, Associate Director of Admissions, American College of Switzerland, 453 Edgewater Drive, Dunedin, FL 34698-4964. (813) 736-5082. Fax: (813) 736-6263. If outside the United States: American College of Switzerland, CH-1854, Leysin, Switzerland; telephone: 0041-25-342223 Fax number 0041-25-341346.

Franklin College: Switzerland
Lugano, Switzerland CB code: 0922

Admissions:	90% of applicants accepted
Based on:	••• Activities, recommendations, school record
	•• Essay, interview, special talents, test scores
Completion:	85% of freshmen end year in good standing
	60% graduate

4-year private liberal arts college, coed. Founded in 1969. **Accreditation:** Regional. **Undergraduate enrollment:** 87 men, 132 women full time; 1 man, 2 women part time. **Faculty:** 25 total (16 full time), 11 with doctorates or other terminal degrees. **Location:** Suburban campus in small city; 60 miles from Milan, Italy, 80 miles from Lucerne. **Calendar:** Semester, limited summer session. **Microcomputers:** 12 located in libraries, classrooms. **Additional facts:** International undergraduate degree programs accredited in United States. Language of instruction English. Students from 45 different nations.

DEGREES OFFERED. AA, BA. 18 associate degrees awarded in 1992. 100% in multi/interdisciplinary studies. 31 bachelor's degrees awarded. 5% in area and ethnic studies, 59% business and management, 5% languages, 5% multi/interdisciplinary studies, 17% social sciences, 9% visual and performing arts.

UNDERGRADUATE MAJORS. Associate: Art history, European studies, international relations, liberal/general studies. **Bachelor's:** Art history, European studies, French, humanities, international business management, international relations, Italian, modern languages.

ACADEMIC PROGRAMS. Double major, dual enrollment of high school students, independent study, internships, study abroad, visiting/exchange student program, sophomore and junior year programs with cooperating US colleges; combined bachelor's/graduate program in business administration. **Remedial services:** Reduced course load, tutoring. **Placement/credit:** AP, IB, institutional tests; 21 credit hours maximum for associate degree; 42 credit hours maximum for bachelor's degree.

ACADEMIC REQUIREMENTS. Freshmen must earn minimum GPA of 2.0 to continue in good standing. 70% of freshmen return for sophomore year. Students must declare major by end of second year. **Graduation requirements:** 60 hours for associate, 120 hours for bachelor's (60 in major). Most students required to take courses in arts/fine arts, English, foreign languages, history, humanities, mathematics, biological/physical sciences, social sciences. **Postgraduate studies:** 99% from 2-year programs enter 4-year programs. **Additional information:** Two week academic travel required each semester.

FRESHMAN ADMISSIONS. Selection criteria: High school academic record, recommendations, and extracurricular participation most important. Essay, test scores, and interview considered. **High school preparation:** 16 units recommended. Recommended units include English 4, foreign language 3, mathematics 2, social science 3 and science 2. **Test requirements:** SAT or ACT; score report by March 15.

1992 FRESHMAN CLASS PROFILE. 66 men applied, 58 accepted, 24 enrolled; 99 women applied, 90 accepted, 36 enrolled. 10% had high school GPA of 3.0 or higher, 87% between 2.0 and 2.99. 2% were in top tenth and 14% were in top quarter of graduating class. **Academic background:** Mid 50% of enrolled freshmen had SAT-V between 480-620, SAT-M between 510-640. 97% submitted SAT scores. **Characteristics:** 99% live in college housing, 19% have minority backgrounds, 30% are foreign students. Average age is 18.

FALL-TERM APPLICATIONS. $40 fee, may be waived for applicants with need. Closing date March 15; applicants notified on a rolling basis; must reply by May 1 or within 4 weeks if notified thereafter. Essay required. Interview recommended. CRDA. Deferred and early admission available. EDP-F.

STUDENT LIFE. Housing: Dormitories (coed); apartment housing available. College-leased apartments adjacent to campus and in Lugano, mandatory for freshmen and sophomores. **Activities:** Student government, film, magazine, student newspaper, yearbook, choral groups, dance, drama, music ensembles, international business club, debate club, language clubs, and numerous sports clubs. **Additional information:** All students live within Lugano community. 30% from United States.

ATHLETICS. Intercollegiate: Skiing, softball. **Intramural:** Basketball, bowling, golf, ice hockey M, sailing, soccer, softball, swimming, table tennis, tennis, track and field, volleyball, water polo M.

STUDENT SERVICES. Career counseling, employment service for undergraduates, freshman orientation, personal counseling, placement service for graduates.

ANNUAL EXPENSES. Tuition and fees (1992-93): $16,430. $2,000 academic travel fee. **Room and board:** $4,858 room only. **Books and supplies:** $400. **Other expenses:** $3,600.

FINANCIAL AID. 20% of continuing students receive some form of aid. 76% of loans based on need. 20 enrolled freshmen were judged to have need, all were offered aid. **Aid applications:** Closing date March 15; applicants notified on or about April 5; must reply by May 1 or within 3 weeks if notified thereafter.

ADDRESS/TELEPHONE. Rebecca Russell, Director of Admissions, Franklin College: Switzerland, 135 East 65th Street, New York, NY 10021. (212) 772-2090. Fax: (212) 772-2718. Campus phone: (41-91) 55.01.01 Campus Fax: (41-91) 54.41.17).

Alphabetical list of colleges

MAKE YOUR MAJOR DECISION A WISE ONE

THE COLLEGE BOARD GUIDE TO
150 POPULAR
COLLEGE MAJORS

• WHAT YOU'LL REALLY STUDY
• WHETHER IT'S RIGHT FOR YOU
• WHAT JOBS YOU'LL BE READY FOR

Authoritative descriptions written by leading professors in each field

COUNTING • MUSIC PERFORMANCE • SCIENCE EDUCATION • PHYSICAL EDUC
OOD SCIENCES • BIOTECHNOLOGY • ARCHITECTURE • PETROLEUM ENGINEE
ERMAN • SOCIAL STUDIES EDUCATION • MATHEMATICS • CREATIVE WRITING
ENTAL HYGIENE • COMPUTER SCIENCE • PUBLIC RELATIONS • REAL ESTATE
ICULTURAL SCIENCE • BIOCHEMISTRY • MANAGEMENT INFORMATION SYSTE
• COMMUNICATION • LABOR/INDUSTRIAL RELATIONS • CLASSICS • TEXTILE
ECH PATHOLOGY/AUDIOLOGY • ART HISTORY • AGRIBUSINESS • MARINE BI
HING AND FISHERIES • MUSIC EDUCATION • CIVIL ENGINEERING • MARKETIN
PMENT • MEDICAL RECORD ADMINISTRATION • HOME ECONOMICS EDUCATI
INGUISTICS • FASHION MERCHANDISING • GERONTOLOGY • STATISTICS • A
VIRONMENTAL STUDIES • OCEANOGRAPHY • ECONOMICS • MIDDLE EASTER
• PSYCHOLOGY • INTERNATIONAL RELATIONS • SPANISH • DAY CARE ADMI
MERICAN LITERATURE • FINANCE • RADIO/TELEVISION • ELECTRICAL ENGIN
PECIAL EDUCATION • INTERIOR DESIGN • ZOOLOGY • SOIL SCIENCES • DAN
USIC THERAPY • INTERNATIONAL BUSINESS MANAGEMENT • NURSING • EN
TRONOMY • JEWISH STUDIES • GEOPHYSICS • CRIMINAL JUSTICE STUDIES •
TION • JAPANESE • RISK MANAGEMENT AND INSURANCE • FORESTRY • BOT
OGRAPHY/FILM • ENTOMOLOGY • ELEMENTARY EDUCATION • AEROSPACE/A
ILY DEVELOPMENT • PHYSICAL THERAPY • FRENCH • PHILOSOPHY • WOMEN
LINICAL LABORATORY SCIENCE • CITY, COMMUNITY, AND REGIONAL PLANNIN
IOUS MUSIC • WILDLIFE MANAGEMENT • ADVERTISING • RUSSIAN • GEOGRA
PUBLIC ADMINISTRATION • ASIAN STUDIES • HEALTH ADMINISTRATION • F
ICROBIOLOGY • DRAMATIC ARTS/THEATER • ANIMAL SCIENCES • INDUSTRIA
CATION • HISTORY • PHARMACY • PHYSICS • BIBLE STUDIES • JOURNALISM

THE COLLEGE BOARD

"This is an easy-to-use guide and contains very useful information." —*Voice of Youth Advocates*

"This unique book offers [students] information they need to make sound choices about bachelor's degree majors at 4-year colleges."
—*The International Educator*

"...presents a multitude of college majors."
—*Booklist*

The College Board Guide to 150 Popular College Majors is a unique guide that will help students and their parents make informed choices concerning college majors. It contains detailed, up-to-the-minute descriptions of the most widely offered undergraduate majors, each written by a leading professor in the field.

Majors are grouped into 17 fields ranging from the arts, business, and engineering to health services and the physical sciences.

Each entry in ***The College Board Guide to 150 Popular College Majors***:

- describes the content of the major
- explains what a student will study
- lists related majors for a student to consider

In addition to an overview of the major, including new territory being explored, each description lists:

- interests and skills associated with success in the major
- recommended high school preparation
- typical courses in the major
- specializations within the major
- what the major is like
- careers the major may lead to
- where to get more information

The introduction provides authoritative advice on what a major is, how to choose a major, and the connection of majors to careers and further education. In an introductory chapter, college students tell how they chose their majors. 004000 ISBN: 0-87447-400-0, 1992, 328 pages, glossary, indexes, $16.00

Order Form

Mail order form to: College Board Publications, Department T28, Box 886, New York, New York 10101-0886

Qty.	Item No.	Title	Price	Amount
____	004000	**The College Board Guide to 150 Popular College Majors**	$ 16.00	$______
____	004795	**The College Handbook, 1994**	$ 20.00	$______
____	004809	**Index of Majors and Graduate Degrees, 1994**	$ 17.00	$______
____	004817	**College Costs and Financial Aid Handbook, 1994**	$ 16.00	$______
____	239369	**3-Book Set: College Handbook, Index of Majors/Graduate Degrees, College Costs and Financial Aid Handbook, 1994**	$ 36.00	$______
____	004825	**The College Handbook for Transfer Students, 1994**	$ 17.00	$______
____	004833	**The College Handbook Foreign Student Supplement, 1994**	$ 16.00	$______
____	004566	**Introducing the New SAT**	$ 12.00	$______
____	003667	**10 SATs. Fourth edition**	$ 11.95	$______
____	003942	**The College Board Achievement Tests (rev. edition)**	$ 12.95	$______
____	004558	**The Official Handbook for the CLEP Examinations**	$ 15.00	$______
____	004418	**Breaking the Science Barrier: How to Explore and Understand the Sciences**	$ 14.00	$______
____	003543	**The College Board Guide to Jobs and Career Planning**	$ 12.95	$______
____	003330	**Choosing a College: The Student's Step-by-Step Decision-Making Workbook**	$ 9.95	$______
____	004280	**Your College Application**	$ 9.95	$______
____	003276	**Your College Application video cassette**	$ 29.95	$______
____	004299	**Writing Your College Application Essay**	$ 9.95	$______
____	002601	**Campus Visits and College Interviews**	$ 9.95	$______
____	002261	**The College Admissions Organizer**	$ 16.95	$______
____	003047	**College Bound: Getting Ready, Moving In, and Succeeding on Campus**	$ 9.95	$______
____	003357	**Countdown to College: Getting the Most Out of High School**	$ 9.95	$______
____	003179	**Campus Health Guide**	$ 14.95	$______
____	003349	**Coping with Stress in College**	$ 9.95	$______
____	003837	**Inside College: New Freedom, New Responsibility**	$ 10.95	$______
____	003535	**The Student's Guide to Good Writing**	$ 9.95	$______
____	002598	**Succeed with Math: Every Student's Guide to Conquering Math Anxiety**	$ 12.95	$______
____	003977	**ABC's of Eligibility for College-Bound Student Athletes video cassette**	$ 49.95	$______
____	002075	**The College Board Guide to Going to College While Working**	$ 9.95	$______
____	003055	**How to Help Your Teenager Find the Right Career**	$ 12.95	$______
____	003160	**The College Guide for Parents**	$ 12.95	$______
____		**College Explorer, 1994** ____ 004647 (Apple II) ____ 004639 (MS-DOS)	$ 125.00	$______
____		**College Planner** ____ 003683 (Apple II) ____ 003705 (MS-DOS)	$ 35.00	$______
____		**College Explorer Plus, 1993** ____ 004760 (MS-DOS)	$ 295.00	$______

Payment must accompany all orders not submitted on an institutional purchase order or charged to a credit card. The College Board pays UPS regular ground postage to the 48 contiguous states on credit card and prepaid orders (orders to P.O. boxes, Alaska, and Hawaii ship via 4th class). Credit card and purchase orders must be for a minimum of $25. Postage is charged on all orders received on purchase orders or requesting faster shipment. Allow 7–10 working days from receipt of order for delivery.

CA residents, add 7.25% sales tax	
PA residents, add 6% sales tax	$______
Subtotal	$______
Handling Charge	$ 3.95
Total	$______

___ Enclosed is my check or money order made payable to the College Board
___ Enclosed is an institutional purchase order (orders for $25 or more), or
___ Please charge my ___ MasterCard ___ Visa. My credit card number is ___ ___ ___ ___/___ ___ ___ ___/___ ___ ___ ___/___ ___ ___ ___

Card expiration date: ___/___ (month/year) ______________________________ Card holder's signature

Credit card holders only can place orders by calling toll-free 1-800-323-7155 Monday through Thursday from 8am to12 midnight; Friday, 8am to 11pm EST. Please have your credit card number ready when you call and give operator the department number T28. For other information or assistance, call (212) 713-8165, Monday through Friday, 9am to 5pm EST, FAX (212) 713-8143.

Ship to:

Name ______________________________ City ______________________________

Street Address (**No P.O. Box numbers**) ______________________________ State ______________ Zip ______________

______________________________ Telephone ______________________________